MUNICIPAL YEAR BOOK

WWW.MUNICIPALYEARBOOK.CO.UK *2016 EDITION*

MYB
MUNICIPAL
YEAR BOOK

MYB
MUNICIPAL YEAR BOOK

EDITOR Dean Wanless
ASSISTANT EDITOR Ali O'Gorman
EDITORIAL DIRECTOR Michael Burton
MANAGING DIRECTOR Graham Bond
MARKETING Pauline Smith

PUBLISHED BY: Hemming Information Services
A DIVISION OF HEMMING GROUP LTD
32 Vauxhall Bridge Road
t +44 (0)20 7973 6400
f +44 (0)20 7973 4794
e myb@hgluk.com

ISBN 978-0-7079-7145-2

Hemming Information Services is a division of Hemming Group Ltd.

Founded in 1893 with the launch of The MJ magazine, Hemming Group Ltd is a family owned company, specialising in the provision of business to business information.

Hemming Information Services deliver several print and online titles in the local government marketplace including: The Municipal Year Book, LocalGov.co.uk, The MJ, Surveyor, the Surveyor Highway Maintenance Yearbook, LAPV and TEC. Hemming Information Services also publishes a selection of private sector directories and magazines including the Retail Directory, Bridge Design and Engineering and Lingerie Buyer.

Other divisions of the Hemming Group include Hemming Conferences, which specialises in organising public sector conferences, and Brintex, the organisers of leading trade fairs such as the LGA Annual Conference and The London International Wine Trade Fair.

The Municipal Year Book was founded in 1897 by Sir Robert Donald, GBE, LLD

A member of the Professional Publishers Association

Letter from the editor

It seems that every year when I sit down to write this letter I say that local government has changed beyond recongnition in the last twelve months.

This year is no exception.

The most exciting and wide ranging reforms to our system of local government, devolution, will be in effect by 2020. The biggest impact that will be felt is the ability to set business rates, revolutionising the way that councils are able to raise funds for the provision of services to their citizens.

The shared infrastructure that the northern powerhouses will have access to will drive the economies onwards to be able to better compete with the south-east of England and hopefully lead to a more secure and prosperous future for these areas, many of which have been badly impacted by the loss of manufacturing and heavy industry over the last 30 years.

The tool-box that public sector professionals are able to use has never been bigger. The central government's recent £1.8billion commitment to the provision of digital services is one that should be replicated by local government, but in a way that is joined-up and will allow us to enjoy the efficiency and cost savings that good digital leadership should always bring.

These revolutionary changes to the way that we provide services are reliant on working together. The Municipal Year Book has been helping councils to work together for over 100 years and will continue to do so, both online and in hard-copy, for many years to come.

The compilation of a reference book as big as The Municipal Year Book is a long and complicated process and would be impossible without the local government professionals that take the time to ensure that we have the most up-to-date information available. As ever, I must extend my thanks to them.

Thanks also to Ali O'Gorman who has worked tirelessly to finesse the data into our systems and has the unenviable job of proof reading the whole book once it's ready to go to press. Sylke Elder also does invaluable work once the AGMs have been held and the race begins to update councillor information.

Our website, www.municipalyearbook.co.uk, is kept in order by Barry Halper who also steps in to administer the database as required.

Pauline Smith makes the job of getting Municipal Year Book onto the desks of the right people in the sector look easy. I'm sure it isn't!

I trust that you will find The Municipal Year Book a useful resource and, as ever, we welcome any feedback that you may have.

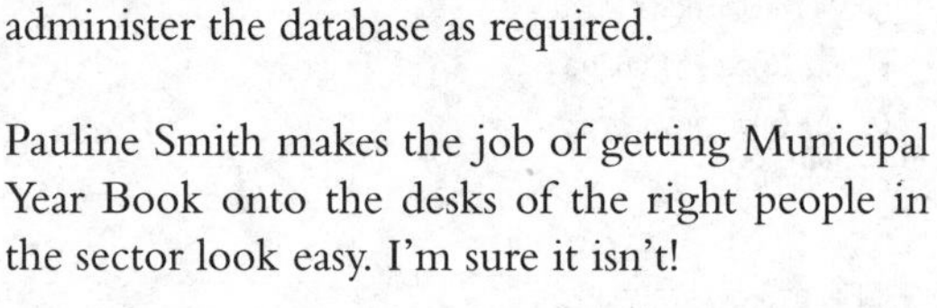

Dean Wanless
Managing Editor
d.wanless@hgluk.com

Foreword
By Rt Hon Greg Clark MP - Secretary of State for Communities and Local Government

I'm delighted to contribute this Foreword for the 2016 Municipal Year Book, because there has surely never been a more important time for leadership in our great local authorities.

No-one could pretend that the financial reality we inhabit makes that leadership straightforward. As a nation we have to deal with the deficit, and local government, which accounts for such a large proportion of public expenditure, has to play its part. Difficult choices about spending priorities have to be made; something local and central government have in common.

At the same time, there are more opportunities for local leadership to make a difference than at any time in living memory.

For decades, local authorities told central governments "Give us back our decision-making power." Well, this government has listened, and is putting a wide-ranging devolution framework in place. Deals that devolve powers to local authorities, and groups of local authorities, will be the one of the hallmarks of this Parliament.

The power to turn a locally-designed vision into reality, to drive growth by harnessing expert place-based knowledge, is no longer a theoretically desirable, but Whitehall-blocked, pipe dream.

During the last Parliament, Government agreed City Deals with 27 of our largest urban areas, and committed billions to place-based Growth Deals. Then in 2014 came the landmark Devolution Agreement with Greater Manchester.

And now devolution deals are in place for Cornwall – proving that devolution isn't an activity suitable only for areas of a largely urban nature – and the Sheffield City Region, the North East, Tees Valley, the West Midlands and Liverpool City Region.

But there's so much more to do. That's why I introduced the Cities and Local Government Bill, which will roll up all the currently available deal opportunities and extend them much further than anything seen before.
Government is playing its part, giving authorities the powers of competency required for a place-based revolution in public services and economic growth.

But that revolution will come only if council leaders and their chief executive officers exercise their new rights.

No matter where you are in this process – whether you've been working on a deal for some time, or if you're only just starting to consider one – it's important to understand that devolution is no longer an "if", but a "when and how". We are not going back to the Whitehall-template centralised model. Leaders should start working out how to build a deal to maximise the benefits available to their communities.

Don't be constrained in your thinking. If the boundary of your local authority doesn't cohere with the main transport routes or economic hubs of your wider community, then make use of the Municipal Year Book, reach out to your colleagues in neighbouring (or differently-tiered) authorities and LEPs, get together and start talking.

After all, those councils and LEPs which have been early adopters of the devolution mindset have not regretted it. Being in control of your place is a great platform from which to attract investment: both global and UK investors will take confidence from knowing that a deal has been agreed between authority and HM Government.

Devolved areas no longer require Westminster's permission to be entrepreneurial. You can be free to think of how to maximise the value that comes from your assets, particularly your land holdings. Those localities which can demonstrate plans for the entrepreneurial use of land to underpin economic growth stand to be rewarded through their devolution deal.

With your passion and these new powers, the great prize of our common endeavour will be reinvigorated communities the length and breadth of the country. Reinvigorated economically, of course, but reinvigorated also in terms of civic leadership and consequent community pride.

The Rt. Hon. Greg Clark MP

Contents

User Guide V

Local Government in Figures VII

Local Authorities A-Z 1

Index – Local Authorities by Type 1219

User Guide

MAIN COUNCIL CONTACT DETAILS

Under the council heading you will find the full council name followed by its main contact address. For Wales, Scotland and Northern Ireland the council's local language name is listed in brackets after the full council name.

The council type is indicated to the right of the council name.

ELECTION FREQUENCY

This shows the type and frequency of elections held by each local authority. If elections are "of whole council" this means elections are held every four years. If elections are "held by thirds" then one third of the seats are elected for each year for three years out of four.

MEMBERS OF THE COUNCIL

The Municipal Year Book asks local authorities to indicate the Leader and Deputy Leader of the council, the Chair / Mayor / Sheriff / Provost and their deputies and the Group Leaders of the political parties represented on their council.

A full political breakdown can be found in each council entry at the end of the "members of the council" section.

INDICES

An index for local authorities by type can be found at the end of the local authorities listings.

KEY TO POLITICAL PARTIES

ALL	Alliance Party
C	Conservative
CAP	Community Action Party
DUP	Democratic Unionist Party
GRN	Green
IND	Independent
INDNA	Independent (Non-Alligned)
INDU	Independent Unionists
LAB	Labour
LIB	Liberal
LD	Liberal Democrats
NILAB	Northern Ireland Labour Party
O	Other
OFF	Official Unionist
PC	Plaid Cymru
PUP	Progressive Unionist Party
R	Ratepayer or Residents Association
RSP	Respect the Unity Coalition
SD	Social Democrat Party
SF	Sinn Fein
SNP	Scottish National Party
UKIP	UK Independence Party
UU	Ulster Unionists
VCNY	Vacancy
WP	Workers Party

User Guide - Sample Entry

Below is an example of an entry from the Municipal Year Book. This page provides a brief explanation of all of the information contained within the local authority entry.

Council name and type (ie. Unitary, district etc)	**York, City of** U
Main Contact details for the local authority	City of York Council, West Offices, Station Rise, York YO1 6GA ☎ 01904 551550 🖷 01904 553560 💻 www.york.gov.uk
Useful information relating to the council	**FACTS AND FIGURES** **Parliamentary Constituencies:** York Central, York Outer **EU Constituencies:** Yorkshire and the Humber **Election Frequency:** Elections are of whole council
Details of decision making officers	**PRINCIPAL OFFICERS** **Chief Executive:** Mr Steve Stewart, Chief Executive, West Offices, Station Rise, York YO1 6GA ☎ 01904 552000 steve.stewart@york.gov.uk
Full list of council members	**COUNCILLORS** ***Leader of the Council*** **Steward**, Chris (CON - Rural West York) cllr.csteward@york.gov.uk
Overall political composition of the council	**POLITICAL COMPOSITION** LAB: 15, CON: 14, LD: 12, GRN: 4, IND: 2
Details of committee chairs.	**COMMITTEE CHAIRS** **Licensing:** Ms Helen Douglas

Local Government in Figures

Types of local authority

County	27	Unitary	55
District	201	Scottish Unitary	32
London	33	Welsh Unitary	22
Metropolitan	36	Northern Ireland	11
		TOTAL	**417**

Most populous authorities

Kent	1427.4	Hertfordshire	1107.5
Essex	1413	Birmingham City	1036.9
Hampshire	1296.8	Norfolk	862.3
Lancashire	1169.3	Staffordshire	831.3
Surrey	1127.3	West Sussex	799.7

Average population of local authorities by type ('000s) - 2011

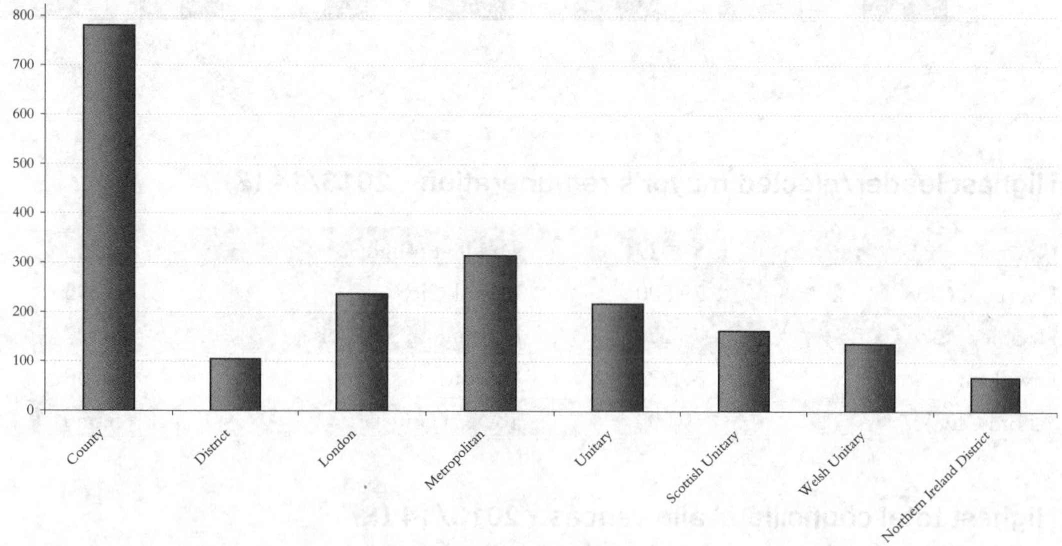

Highest gross budgets - 2013/14 (£'000s)

Birmingham City	3,327,500	Surrey	1,900,491
Glasgow, City of	2,221,136	Essex	1,879,704
Kent	2,174,873	Hampshire	1,833,188
Lancashire	2,012,400	Edinburgh, City of	1,758,888
Leeds City	1,969,007	Hertfordshire	1,538,782

Highest net budgets - 2013/14 (£'000s)

Glasgow, City of	1,450,890	Edinburgh, City of	953,729
Birmingham City	1,175,400	Hampshire	876,326
Surrey	1,048,754	Fife	840,388
Kent	992,008	Lancashire	789,200
Essex	956,871	North Lanarkshire	762,185

Average gross & net budgets by local authority type - 2013/14 (£'000s)

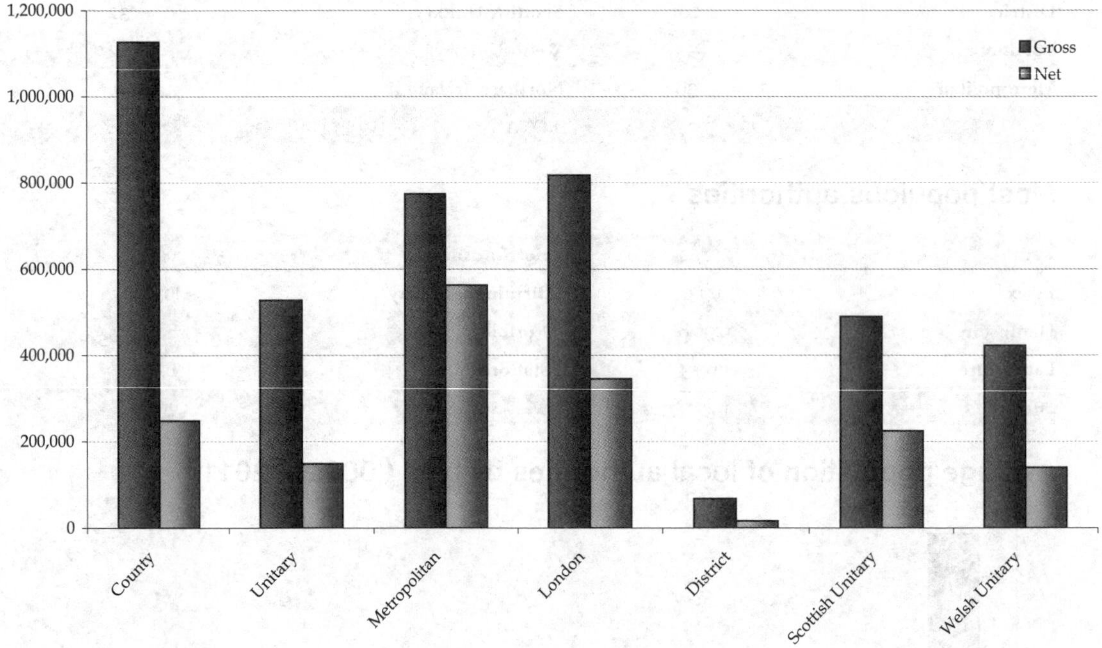

Highest leader/elected mayor's remuneration - 2013/14 (£)

Newham	81,029	Middlesbrough	67,430
Liverpool City	79,500	Bristol City	66,395
Hackney	78,290	Kensington & Chelsea	66,127
Lewisham	77,722	Watford	65,738
Salford City	69,000	Tower Hamlets	65,650

Highest total councillors' allowances - 2013/14 (£)

Birmingham City	2,800,000	Wiltshire Unitary	1,824,000
Durham	2,068,000	Highland	1,737,000
Bradford City	2,066,775	Kent	1,730,000
Cornwall	1,955,000	Glasgow, City of	1,700,000
Manchester City	1,948,000	Surrey	1,673,000

Highest chief executive salaries - 2013/14 (£)

West Sussex	370,779*	Hampshire	207,372
Wandsworth	215,696	Essex	205,972
Surrey	210,850	Manchester City	203,934
Buckinghamshire	209,070	Durham	200,000
City of London	208,000	Liverpool City	199,500

* includes compensation for loss of employment

Average chief executive salaries by local authority type - 2013/14 (£)

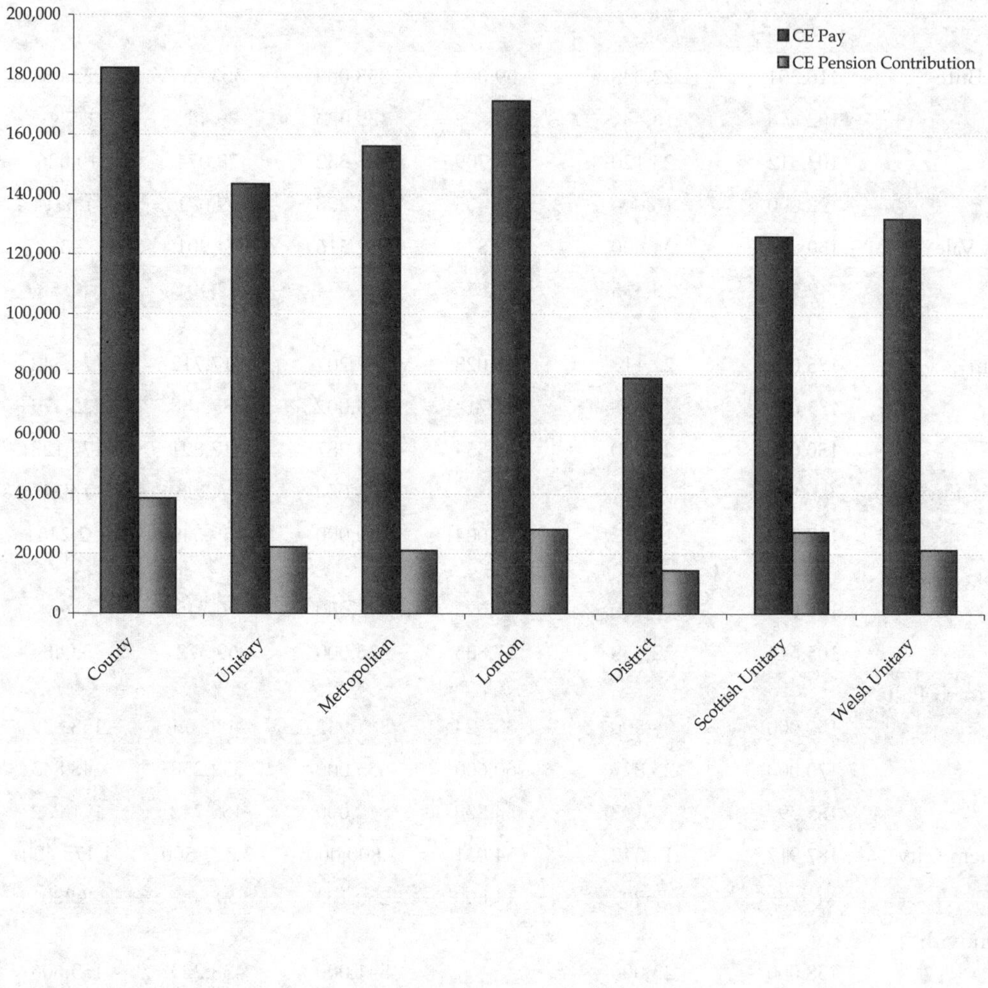

Remuneration & budget data - 2013/14

Council	Chief Executive Salary 2013/14 (£)	Chief Executive Pension 2013/14 (£)	Leaders' Allowance 2013/14 (£)	Total Members Allowances 2013/14 (£)	Gross Budget 2013/14 (£'000)	Net Budget 2013/14 (£'000)
Aberdeen City	143,253	27,648	38,259	522,675	676,312	437,456
Aberdeenshire	137,212	19,447	38,259	1,671,000	736,616	12,701
Adur	98,653	18,407	16,200	148,019	45,024	5,158
Allerdale	75,000	16,725	23,967	255,045	56,244	15,963
Amber Valley	68,000	8,000	15,036	233,973	53,730	13,122
Angus						
Argyll & Bute	116,351	22,038	59,000	858,000	303,654	233,684
Arun	102,968	18,431	18,872	439,423	89,483	8,786
Ashfield	103,512	23,120	24,709	383,352	78,074	10,026
Ashford	128,000	16,000	23,405	307,228	69,071	-14,814
Aylesbury Vale	139,000	34,000	18,844	452,516	94,901	32,381
Babergh	112,582	19,395	11,675	216,974	32,491	-8,158
Barking & Dagenham	185,000	22,117	45,028	762,207	817,712	174,342
Barnet	187,613	46,528	41,714	519,002	887,408	225,479
Barnsley	150,000	29,000	35,554	874,287	617,891	177,128
Barrow-in-Furness	93,000	8,000		123,000	48,223	7,832
Basildon	137,762	10,972	23,004	419,000	139,649	-2,246
Basingstoke & Deane	126,069	16,140	28,621	572,350	96,745	38,966
Bassetlaw	105,514	22,539	17,883	333,000	69,372	3,048
Bath & North East Somerset	150,000	28,500	38,324	804,942	409,971	158,839
Bedford	170,000	23,877	60,600	635,000	352,258	148,843
Bexley	185,397	38,192	35,809	862,000	465,742	191,232
Birmingham City	187,917	19,372	54,031	2,800,000	3,327,500	1,175,400
Blaby	96,642	17,202	14,600	230,123	30,600	8,220
Blackburn with Darwen	138,000	23,000		541,000	438,223	153,606
Blackpool	99,012	17,590	26,207	504,000	489,489	187,627
Blaenau Gwent	109,625	24,117	42,300	773,000	240,238	168,885
Bolsover	112,000	13,328	11,370	455,000	45,780	-2,412
Bolton	170,000	30,440	40,864	852,000	708,600	232,795
Boston	107,100		11,736	180,000	34,599	7,343
Bournemouth	125,000	24,000	36,518	768,000	439,020	170,481
Bracknell Forest	156,600	24,000	37,641	591,000	268,784	114,736

Council	Chief Executive Salary 2013/14 (£)	Chief Executive Pension 2013/14 (£)	Leaders' Allowance 2013/14 (£)	Total Members Allowances 2013/14 (£)	Gross Budget 2013/14 (£'000)	Net Budget 2013/14 (£'000)
Bradford City	178,476	26,771	49,187	2,066,775	1,357,464	506,899
Braintree	123,000	16,000	17,964	424,000	75,371	21,160
Breckland			22,921	460,000	62,594	14,239
Brent				297,000	1,095,847	242,157
Brentwood	102,000	12,266	19,037	283,000	38,293	-1,042
Bridgend	125,246	25,051	47,627	474,000	403,707	259,570
Brighton & Hove	150,000	27,000	40,221	853,000	774,069	236,812
Bristol City	137,364	26,178	66,395	1,100,000	1,151,393	379,212
Broadland	104,526	14,921	13,740	236,879	41,626	11,632
Bromley	178,056	25,337		1,094,000	647,097	49,264
Bromsgrove	127,500	13,388	17,304	259,000	38,514	12,599
Broxbourne			18,860	222,758	63,901	13,812
Broxtowe	105,757	24,205	17,229	310,000	59,208	10,011
Buckinghamshire	209,070	47,668	50,427	957,000	744,106	366,085
Burnley	112,635	14,079	13,500	180,897	77,703	17,983
Bury	149,300	26,621	30,912	581,943	498,705	170,452
Caerphilly	137,000	28,496	46,045	1,214,042	560,658	344,691
Calderdale	139,000	23,000	39,725		453,019	174,471
Cambridge City	117,859	21,922	13,632	240,236	110,320	9,652
Cambridgeshire	188,029	35,549	29,856	816,735	794,495	413,853
Camden	155,000	25,708	38,370	956,000	872,694	145,561
Cannock Chase	112,688	24,679	23,488	366,567	68,163	10,468
Canterbury City	110,000	16,000		377,921	116,854	13,654
Cardiff	136,957	32,733	53,000	1,287,408	1,183,940	737,045
Carlisle City	97,000	11,000	22,361	341,000	64,020	18,649
Carmarthenshire	180,889	0	47,500	1,283,669	584,608	365,350
Castle Point	124,000	0	15,975	253,000	43,143	3,265
Central Bedfordshire	181,300	43,331		1,224,000	473,033	179,107
Ceredigion	108,226	16,429	42,300	806,000	212,976	142,081
Charnwood	115,638	27,014	16,751	375,000	68,131	852
Chelmsford	130,625	8,727	27,009	502,000	131,999	1,083
Cheltenham	109,164	16,733	21,494	319,191	83,348	13,018
Cherwell	126,250	18,546	17,655	314,000	72,121	22,395
Cheshire East	107,500	22,300	39,200	1,057,000	694,318	308,046
Cheshire West & Chester	180,000	3,000	40,103	1,377,000	702,262	275,326

Council	Chief Executive Salary 2013/14 (£)	Chief Executive Pension 2013/14 (£)	Leaders' Allowance 2013/14 (£)	Total Members Allowances 2013/14 (£)	Gross Budget 2013/14 (£'000)	Net Budget 2013/14 (£'000)
Chesterfield	104,626	12,749	32,206	350,000	91,153	-9,237
Chichester	114,689	17,941	17,550	307,000	72,801	16,363
Chiltern	128,000	35,413	17,550	282,000	36,672	9,482
Chorley	108,000	22,000		295,000	52,590	17,615
Christchurch	72,283	14,822	14,252	154,000	30,849	7,939
City of London	208,000			10,100	284,700	125,500
Clackmannanshire	98,067	19,613	27,329	410,772	163,874	103,755
Colchester	120,145	14,161	19,719	545,338	148,975	29,172
Conwy	108,713	23,482	47,500	1,063,000	316,910	204,613
Copeland	110,000	22,110	25,534	256,000	41,694	14,834
Corby	91,000	27,000	17,872	170,000	53,930	4,748
Cornwall	119,962	19,197	31,386	1,955,000	1,191,896	513,677
Cotswold	116,691	16,865	16,000	268,750	45,162	12,187
Coventry City	175,000	28,788	34,795	974,000	783,427	306,941
Craven	95,000	11,798	11,700	160,000	22,574	5,759
Crawley	118,214	18,598	20,230	330,000	124,800	11,071
Croydon	180,000	23,580	53,223	1,590,000	1,160,735	341,563
Cumbria	148,391	15,778	29,691	1,059,000	801,807	410,620
Dacorum	132,843		19,804	377,000	116,786	-1,475
Darlington	153,720	28,438	30,960	645,456	242,591	82,865
Dartford	126,288	15,660	39,641	334,000	68,650	7,303
Daventry	115,457	13,278	15,022	255,375	33,161	9,373
Denbighshire	132,411	13,938	42,286	845,000	324,729	193,900
Derby City	160,000	31,658	39,152	815,000	666,907	247,743
Derbyshire	147,333	21,299	39,658	1,034,000	1,246,956	584,114
Derbyshire Dales	98,000	11,000	14,580	226,000	35,634	9,398
Derry City						
Devon	149,995	27,449	35,970	1,031,289	1,118,597	589,182
Doncaster	149,000	29,949	48,480	1,015,365	647,304	224,963
Dorset	143,000	28,000	38,596	725,000	716,206	262,767
Dover	122,000	13,000	18,812	269,000	77,000	1,187
Dudley	161,000	18,000		851,000	740,227	229,389
Dumfries & Galloway	134,999	28,831	25,426	988,000	439,969	345,227
Dundee City	134,067	72,000	39,795	607,000	552,345	365,536
Durham	200,000	15,283	49,875	2,068,000	1,290,215	466,227

Council	Chief Executive Salary 2013/14 (£)	Chief Executive Pension 2013/14 (£)	Leaders' Allowance 2013/14 (£)	Total Members Allowances 2013/14 (£)	Gross Budget 2013/14 (£'000)	Net Budget 2013/14 (£'000)
Ealing	170,631		41,503	960,730	1,083,643	268,851
East Ayrshire	121,680	6,267	32,470	23,484	403,311	276,617
East Cambridgeshire	125,850	24,541	12,739	213,298	36,169	10,841
East Devon	128,481	18,373	18,781	387,522	77,267	11,254
East Dorset	115,000	19,895	14,252	200,000	38,561	11,329
East Dunbartonshire	119,223	23,010	32,795	494,830	282,320	224,545
East Hampshire	91,910	12,042	16,176	307,000	44,440	10,545
East Hertfordshire	126,398	20,263	24,153	383,000	70,071	19,366
East Lindsey	112,875	25,305	19,427	372,000	80,124	18,689
East Lothian	110,551	23,401	27,329	451,677	288,003	212,026
East Northamptonshire	103,000	31,000	12,600	238,000	34,683	10,189
East Renfrewshire	109,521	21,137	20,497	384,793	295,895	227,027
East Riding of Yorkshire	170,000	15,000	46,741		675,089	248,605
East Staffordshire	119,947	21,720		259,218	52,763	14,876
East Sussex	182,909	36,765	33,938	871,000	829,470	387,017
Eastbourne	107,125	24,853	7,020	133,000	88,933	6,306
Eastleigh	108,473	10,046	19,761	384,000	78,098	19,669
Eden	65,664		14,245	234,000	22,637	8,709
Edinburgh, City of	160,207	34,110	49,191	1,288,618	1,758,888	953,729
Elmbridge	125,134	18,170	21,265	373,180	76,172	20,418
Enfield	188,955		27,275	1,000,000	1,186,700	336,400
Epping Forest	112,000	14,560	11,275	315,000	96,473	-14,987
Epsom & Ewell	105,000	16,000		157,000	46,311	11,679
Erewash	110,234	27,195	16,602	284,311	55,522	13,294
Essex	205,972	25,830	61,971	1,548,000	1,879,704	956,871
Exeter City	105,500	21,627	19,444	272,000	97,186	14,224
Falkirk	127,863	24,686	32,795	700,281	521,735	364,828
Fareham	118,257	14,469	26,122	415,000	48,241	9,128
Fenland	137,600	26,419	18,720	354,000	54,139	14,760
Fife	149,946	7,480	35,792	423,364	1,188,873	840,388
Flintshire	137,138	30,856	47,500	1,336,000	427,567	284,330
Forest Heath	65,600	12,923	14,889	215,000	31,513	9,940
Forest of Dean	84,229	12,045	14,090	291,524	39,095	9,831
Fylde	89,000	19,000	13,750	243,000	37,446	9,794
Gateshead	158,307	23,271	31,030	1,054,000	612,288	232,462

Council	Chief Executive Salary 2013/14 (£)	Chief Executive Pension 2013/14 (£)	Leaders' Allowance 2013/14 (£)	Total Members Allowances 2013/14 (£)	Gross Budget 2013/14 (£'000)	Net Budget 2013/14 (£'000)
Gedling	98,334	17,897	13,668	277,000	49,283	13,778
Glasgow, City of	193,800	25,194	49,047	1,700,000	2,221,136	1,450,890
Gloucester City	113,630	17,044	22,313	292,000	120,685	5,748
Gloucestershire	161,235	23,531	34,632	740,000	796,329	393,447
Gosport	93,051	11,930	19,062	236,000	59,904	776
Gravesham	114,155		23,707	219,075	74,635	-986
Great Yarmouth	97,782	15,103	12,943	221,194	82,803	7,217
Greenwich	190,000	35,150	62,668	941,852	784,182	114,708
Guildford	109,001	15,914	12,576	291,972	97,703	-593
Gwynedd	108,264	24,251	48,000	1,325,000	360,394	235,907
Hackney	177,956	29,127	78,290	1,437,000	1,078,822	185,086
Halton	167,500	34,000	28,931	725,429	370,133	141,566
Hambleton	107,100	22,226	20,412	263,743	39,126	12,174
Hammersmith & Fulham	158,620	16,655	44,703	819,000	477,586	-23,543
Hampshire	207,372	27,166	40,970	1,430,000	1,833,188	876,326
Harborough	100,449	20,090	17,326	295,000	39,615	11,380
Haringey	106,890	23,955	41,997	1,073,000	992,596	62,058
Harlow	141,279	17,377	11,907	184,000	133,746	26,425
Harrogate	112,318	14,545	11,786	369,000	94,509	17,257
Harrow	167,838	32,477	38,959	815,000	525,300	135,550
Hart	98,840	12,948	19,320	215,000	36,101	9,346
Hartlepool	140,833		22,173	277,116	269,764	98,027
Hastings	83,658	20,113	16,677	265,000	82,581	16,878
Havant	126,250	16,539	13,762	313,000	54,999	15,708
Havering	163,920		61,399	1,103,617	609,794	254,839
Herefordshire	143,887	32,625		643,000	344,378	148,149
Hertfordshire	170,000	35,651	47,940	1,339,000	1,538,782	719,487
Hertsmere	173,000	23,000	28,015	336,000	61,519	11,519
High Peak	93,748	10,687	12,907	185,433	52,490	1,434
Highland	141,513	10,613	38,259	1,737,000	756,992	519,670
Hillingdon	185,796	39,203	47,218	1,540,000	633,913	168,631
Hinckley & Bosworth	136,712	25,428	10,915	165,885	43,895	-7,614
Horsham	117,544	19,429	15,205	339,000	66,882	18,206
Hounslow	173,755	37,319	36,475	804,000	603,500	73,500
Huntingdonshire	98,026	17,367	18,245	410,000	87,234	28,722

Council	Chief Executive Salary 2013/14 (£)	Chief Executive Pension 2013/14 (£)	Leaders' Allowance 2013/14 (£)	Total Members Allowances 2013/14 (£)	Gross Budget 2013/14 (£'000)	Net Budget 2013/14 (£'000)
Hyndburn	116,560	32,805	24,796	284,804	49,046	10,925
Inverclyde	115,791	59,999	27,239	215,228	241,161	172,891
Ipswich	97,279	16,635	15,029	287,000	129,723	18,420
Isle of Anglesey	153,000	32,000	42,300	668,000	203,397	128,368
Isle of Wight	99,606		18,208	515,000	339,840	155,385
Islington	160,000	17,440	31,563	868,000	884,832	-162,579
Kensington & Chelsea	145,755		66,127	1,173,000	671,176	191,786
Kent			54,914	1,730,000	2,174,873	992,008
Kettering	131,000	17,000	18,401	307,000	57,307	7,849
King's Lynn & West Norfolk	124,881	17,461	19,899	441,000	84,226	19,114
Kingston upon Hull City	101,397	4,336	47,537	1,010,000	849,661	294,500
Kingston upon Thames	179,000	22,000	36,670	620,392	367,618	116,413
Kirklees	147,667	22,150	35,615		1,058,188	428,283
Knowsley	192,028	35,525	35,653	843,000	545,611	146,354
Lambeth	193,075	32,437	51,214	1,151,000	1,049,194	185,105
Lancashire	169,242	32,326	39,092	1,300,000	2,012,400	789,200
Lancaster City	107,000	22,000	14,360	282,000	126,059	34,976
Leeds City	176,367	25,573			1,969,007	658,795
Leicester City	137,560	21,353	49,303	964,079	978,581	297,515
Leicestershire	188,000	36,000	46,228	1,100,000	755,300	365,100
Lewes	103,000	22,000	16,093	196,000	58,935	664
Lewisham	115,432		77,722	1,083,000	1,033,793	271,492
Lichfield	93,714	17,676	15,157	272,000	48,460	15,084
Limavady						
Lincoln City	114,375	26,196	13,999	212,287	84,576	8,628
Lincolnshire	173,643	32,740	28,632	1,096,000	965,130	507,322
Liverpool City	199,500	24,446	79,500	1,341,000	1,360,701	475,185
Luton	177,300	24,000	22,500	447,000	558,015	179,880
Maidstone	112,000	15,000	27,992	386,569	105,375	23,379
Maldon	103,000	12,000	15,908	236,000	30,224	8,795
Malvern Hills	100,786	12,213	16,800	241,907	33,654	9,095
Manchester City	203,934	0	55,804	1,948,000	1,477,823	567,986
Mansfield	108,000	22,000	59,930	500,843	93,313	16,801

Council	Chief Executive Salary 2013/14 (£)	Chief Executive Pension 2013/14 (£)	Leaders' Allowance 2013/14 (£)	Total Members Allowances 2013/14 (£)	Gross Budget 2013/14 (£'000)	Net Budget 2013/14 (£'000)
Medway	146,640	28,730	28,879	776,000	574,541	213,261
Melton	82,906	15,641	16,537	181,000	27,119	5,327
Mendip	89,992	19,001	13,605	249,000	53,890	14,883
Merthyr Tydfil	111,100	15,247	41,275	714,000	183,075	124,004
Merton	185,000	26,085	43,106	766,000	488,413	178,223
Mid Devon	97,637	17,868	14,880	291,000	42,721	1,971
Mid Suffolk	146,394		7,432	235,000	38,848	1,499
Mid Sussex	110,000	17,417	24,647	368,704	58,051	15,427
Middlesbrough	142,006	17,272	67,430	577,000	412,087	148,690
Midlothian	109,027	21,835	22,974	190,983	339,532	258,945
Milton Keynes	153,957	19,604	39,195	724,000	523,186	118,719
Mole Valley	131,256		10,598	210,000	46,708	14,354
Monmouthshire	110,000	23,210	42,300	819,000	235,376	157,322
Moray	104,598	20,181	27,058	512,687	263,772	194,885
Neath Port Talbot	134,253	19,467	33,460	1,211,000	437,202	287,410
New Forest	130,374	16,870	24,736	476,818	86,552	-3,648
Newark & Sherwood	113,490	24,854	13,469	252,313	57,740	-2,759
Newcastle upon Tyne City	145,062	17,653	25,325	968,000	947,446	263,867
Newcastle-under-Lyme	103,168	24,705		328,545	62,388	20,532
Newham	195,000	44,655	81,029	1,211,000	1,134,154	203,747
Newport City	134,638	25,850	34,325	908,774	380,280	249,502
Norfolk	158,800	46,600		1,060,000	1,228,449	611,405
North Ayrshire	127,863	24,433	32,795	279,682	459,588	319,284
North Devon	99,150	19,136	20,565	302,598	59,739	6,311
North Dorset	91,871	15,618	14,370	227,000	28,216	7,617
North East Derbyshire	112,000	13,328	22,454	398,000	73,346	5,913
North East Lincolnshire	114,516	24,132	29,000	510,000	315,117	146,849
North Hertfordshire	112,051	16,748	17,100	346,000	71,326	22,027
North Kesteven	109,598	22,411	17,539	304,000	51,214	7,151
North Lanarkshire	149,524	28,819	38,146	1,487,243	1,052,654	762,185
North Lincolnshire	129,699	28,923	23,673	556,000	339,797	162,286
North Norfolk	99,771	14,467	12,165	287,983	52,295	12,726

Council	Chief Executive Salary 2013/14 (£)	Chief Executive Pension 2013/14 (£)	Leaders' Allowance 2013/14 (£)	Total Members Allowances 2013/14 (£)	Gross Budget 2013/14 (£'000)	Net Budget 2013/14 (£'000)
North Somerset	91,315	18,583	34,045	755,129	406,506	158,884
North Tyneside	59,208	8,467	61,734	644,000	513,348	130,307
North Warwickshire	98,153	17,668		228,000	42,197	7,999
North West Leicestershire	120,651	23,406	18,900	219,434	50,138	-3,862
North Yorkshire	170,000	21,080	33,698	641,226	943,394	407,325
Northampton	138,000	18,000	23,736	474,000	160,939	13,331
Northamptonshire	172,000	22,000		950,000	915,254	406,407
Northumberland	119,683	17,713	37,056	1,443,000	754,759	297,909
Norwich City	129,911	18,806	16,000	334,053	1,115,456	-7,160
Nottingham City	160,000	28,800	35,091	1,061,000	828,688	244,665
Nottinghamshire	184,410		44,885	1,441,432	1,140,460	570,555
Nuneaton & Bedworth	98,842	17,559	17,480	267,000	82,980	11,312
Oadby & Wigston	95,000	21,000	11,270	175,559	23,369	4,747
Oldham	136,000	7,000	36,956	933,000	574,933	189,301
Orkney	99,936	34,286	27,329	435,000	110,663	87,415
Oxford City	139,860	28,251	23,570	334,000	162,805	-24,838
Oxfordshire	184,255	35,561	33,508	792,000	1,018,429	54,634
Pembrokeshire	193,136	0	48,000	1,100,431	369,877	231,572
Pendle	85,203	7,886	7,000	181,569	60,160	23,229
Perth & Kinross	122,898	22,122	32,795	767,245	408,631	304,708
Peterborough City	169,625	29,951	29,460	678,000	481,727	179,220
Plymouth City	150,000	21,511	40,578	917,000	590,687	232,904
Poole	127,577	34,979	31,774	542,000	330,029	131,242
Portsmouth City	148,885	19,504	28,846	600,000	552,812	143,667
Powys	133,000	31,000	33,736	1,180,000	408,213	247,021
Preston	114,000	20,000	12,812	281,000	92,370	28,059
Purbeck	82,000	10,000	12,852	152,000	24,799	1,672
Reading	144,624	21,195	15,225	446,846	424,820	128,564
Redbridge	158,849	31,452	45,563	1,010,000	822,913	211,966
Redcar & Cleveland	145,239	21,931	22,440	819,000	328,753	119,967
Redditch	127,500	13,388	11,684	140,000	63,642	4,192
Reigate & Banstead	141,000	21,000	18,015	394,382	85,798	21,703
Renfrewshire	134,068	25,896	28,469	800,346	596,119	371,134
Rhondda Cynon Taff	139,000	29,000	52,700	1,320,000	710,857	492,040

Council	Chief Executive Salary 2013/14 (£)	Chief Executive Pension 2013/14 (£)	Leaders' Allowance 2013/14 (£)	Total Members Allowances 2013/14 (£)	Gross Budget 2013/14 (£'000)	Net Budget 2013/14 (£'000)
Ribble Valley	105,857	12,168	16,670	205,801	20,252	6,712
Richmond upon Thames	176,214	42,996	35,650	755,000	403,223	160,062
Rochdale	130,000	22,000	11,210	700,000	656,353	307,845
Rochford	88,471	10,784	25,500	287,443	35,273	11,776
Rossendale	95,410	12,785	16,710	213,000	37,553	9,255
Rother	84,000	20,000	16,613	228,000	55,521	19,244
Rotherham	157,000	0	37,757	1,200,000	646,427	201,693
Rugby	84,850	15,100	23,957	344,730	61,498	3,372
Runnymede	117,052	0	10,408	195,000	28,449	-20,299
Rushcliffe	112,522	14,448	16,682	318,000	38,559	14,275
Rushmoor	114,807	22,730	17,650	282,186	64,787	16,992
Rutland	117,609	20,463	15,190	178,000	59,089	31,784
Ryedale	104,460	13,684	11,540	129,000	25,258	8,457
Salford City	109,335	18,181	69,000	978,000	773,830	281,632
Sandwell	139,000	25,159	34,278	1,338,000	870,167	228,860
Scarborough	113,889	14,350	19,808	257,000	87,437	22,020
Scottish Borders	117,060	21,071	32,795	737,000	321,033	252,303
Sedgemoor	104,877	14,220	23,435	347,000	77,177	14,273
Sefton	135,059	29,627	34,421	757,000	639,781	231,013
Selby	84,000	10,000	14,404	255,000	36,803	2,979
Sevenoaks	135,709	19,262	20,602	359,000	51,587	14,850
Sheffield City	184,588	35,072	29,910	1,248,000	1,348,631	488,555
Shepway	112,696	13,917	25,537	338,000	71,719	2,996
Shetland	101,069	10,000	23,316	488,000	165,494	115,409
Shropshire Unitary	99,486	11,640	34,542	1,214,000	589,675	231,788
Slough	157,479	11,575	25,503	452,000	382,684	117,906
Solihull	128,971	22,209	26,888	543,000	454,251	154,203
Somerset	140,000	18,900	39,520	843,000	726,933	351,819
South Ayrshire	124,102	23,952	32,804	608,551	352,865	238,084
South Bucks	128,000	35,413	14,637	217,000	30,315	9,716
South Cambridgeshire	121,200	26,300	15,076	369,759	62,535	-2,210
South Derbyshire	120,103	26,723	24,294	335,000	43,306	7,034
South Gloucestershire	156,058	26,940	31,421	1,016,000	602,668	226,260
South Hams			17,372	273,000	63,103	1,799

Council	Chief Executive Salary 2013/14 (£)	Chief Executive Pension 2013/14 (£)	Leaders' Allowance 2013/14 (£)	Total Members Allowances 2013/14 (£)	Gross Budget 2013/14 (£'000)	Net Budget 2013/14 (£'000)
South Holland District Council			24,279	360,000	62,369	-2,387
South Kesteven	112,000	24,000	18,981	370,351	74,377	7,009
South Lakeland	102,888	25,722	16,000	280,339	45,053	13,333
South Lanarkshire	147,437	68,000	38,259	413,137	1,014,419	714,406
South Norfolk	127,224	18,816	14,317	317,119	55,775	15,418
South Northamptonshire	128,250	18,546	42,921	309,000	33,098	14,823
South Oxfordshire	131,674	17,513	12,900	211,000	57,367	16,754
South Ribble	104,985	22,362	16,756	172,000	42,362	14,442
South Somerset	61,000	12,000	20,506	512,000	81,032	22,249
South Staffordshire	94,731	18,097	15,000	303,363	42,280	11,271
South Tyneside	152,685	21,769	33,722	835,000	512,874	183,807
Southampton City	145,720	19,089	32,098	701,000	640,910	197,962
Southend-on-Sea	150,290	18,786	38,187	634,000	437,756	100,885
Southwark	173,944	24,351	60,634	1,232,732	1,073,259	237,010
Spelthorne	112,422	18,098	12,975	214,000	56,457	14,716
St. Albans City	100,000	28,400	19,110	423,000	68,048	-3,717
St. Edmundsbury	108,133	21,302	15,708	329,000	64,897	2,978
St. Helens	97,000	0	39,786	567,000	418,520	141,947
Stafford	103,660	18,722	11,115	313,184	58,161	17,070
Staffordshire	194,550	36,268	43,933	1,000,000	1,272,400	539,900
Staffordshire Moorlands	157,775	26,191	12,467	258,076	34,790	13,183
Stevenage	114,732	30,421	27,997	433,039	75,501	-19,514
Stirling	109,723	50,000	27,238	418,000	286,848	202,548
Stockport	170,000	0	38,661	931,000	642,558	234,828
Stockton-on-Tees	165,191	26,805	36,100	765,000	466,606	174,918
Stoke-on-Trent City	195,516	34,125	47,505	762,000	760,811	290,940
Stratford-upon-Avon	111,108	18,636	47,505	327,000	54,373	18,541
Stroud	110,569	25,197	14,907	337,000	135,521	79,470
Suffolk	156,313	34,875	35,964	1,137,000	1,068,198	527,252
Suffolk Coastal	128,061	19,487	16,254	337,000	57,736	15,301
Sunderland	198,726	25,356	46,036	1,198,000	705,817	282,624
Surrey	210,850	31,206	42,291	1,673,000	1,900,491	1,048,754
Surrey Heath	109,000	18,000	18,144	278,000	39,767	13,464

Council	Chief Executive Salary 2013/14 (£)	Chief Executive Pension 2013/14 (£)	Leaders' Allowance 2013/14 (£)	Total Members Allowances 2013/14 (£)	Gross Budget 2013/14 (£'000)	Net Budget 2013/14 (£'000)
Sutton	129,669	22,538	50,364	909,000	466,365	181,178
Swale	146,020	43,076	22,937	365,000	86,157	18,226
Swansea, City of	140,000	20,907	53,295	1,256,000	739,836	425,394
Swindon	161,003	24,795	27,140	626,000	479,313	181,848
Tameside	166,929	30,548	36,036	1,201,000	504,156	180,012
Tamworth	106,615	20,597	16,464	229,000	57,330	9,595
Tandridge	109,369	18,046	9,418	214,000	57,682	9,561
Taunton Deane	113,090	0		325,000	77,506	7,061
Teignbridge	105,506	19,308	22,363	335,325	68,261	17,031
Telford & Wrekin	137,000	22,331	31,638	619,000	431,121	114,193
Tendring	121,606	15,635	23,053	439,256	98,953	9,930
Test Valley	127,000	14,000	14,494	429,000	60,672	18,911
Tewkesbury	110,000	16,170	15,137	334,881	32,921	8,042
Thanet	116,500	15,123	22,652	370,000	130,430	20,802
Three Rivers	118,582	18,892	13,743	309,150	45,673	14,154
Thurrock	185,000	21,350	37,223	644,000	335,427	110,550
Tonbridge & Malling	106,000	15,000	22,968	425,000	62,609	16,053
Torbay	120,000	10,000	34,286	440,000	301,800	135,100
Torfaen	111,411	25,178	42,300	961,000	290,935	179,465
Torridge	81,838	14,976		232,000	33,962	9,118
Tower Hamlets	160,915	25,004	65,650	959,000	1,267,080	271,217
Trafford	147,436	23,691	33,078	707,000	407,775	157,703
Tunbridge Wells	15,068	13,938	24,250	366,000	61,365	10,809
Uttlesford	102,151	13,280	13,750	304,000	45,332	5,459
Vale of Glamorgan	146,412	0	47,500	841,000	351,376	216,545
Vale of White Horse	131,674	17,513	21,779	284,000	50,316	13,280
Wakefield City	175,190	26,103	44,949	1,051,000	686,213	276,718
Walsall	194,271	22,175	37,705	753,000	609,913	255,503
Waltham Forest	180,000	0	50,000	1,070,000	685,825	70,745
Wandsworth	215,696	45,059	51,267	1,082,316	1,559	1,105
Warrington	123,300	0	27,926	677,000	440,926	162,307
Warwick	110,006	17,683	10,454	299,000	59,568	-12,071
Warwickshire	172,866	26,794	31,451	799,000	838,200	447,900
Watford	136,456	21,696	65,738	447,539	73,198	22,233
Waveney	85,886	12,597	12,373	253,000	63,041	-8,527

Council	Chief Executive Salary 2013/14 (£)	Chief Executive Pension 2013/14 (£)	Leaders' Allowance 2013/14 (£)	Total Members Allowances 2013/14 (£)	Gross Budget 2013/14 (£'000)	Net Budget 2013/14 (£'000)
Waverley	104,111	11,073	17,722	365,000	66,052	-7,591
Wealden	124,281	23,983	16,880	334,000	60,506	6,878
Wellingborough	108,084	15,024	9,397	183,000	38,864	11,799
Welwyn Hatfield	122,000	37,000	14,417	340,000	100,360	-306
West Berkshire	138,418	20,546	22,545		329,484	158,539
West Devon	115,000	21,045	12,277	23,000	29,635	8,245
West Dorset	110,000	14,850	16,360	379,000	52,000	11,990
West Dunbartonshire	118,105	22,782	32,821	456,972	351,246	226,066
West Lancashire	88,482	18,510	16,947	335,000	83,481	19,231
West Lindsey	105,000	27,695	15,676	263,000	42,538	15,491
West Lothian	129,102	26,336	24,596	697,000	500,211	387,163
West Oxfordshire	101,691	16,865	23,925	325,248	48,252	14,113
West Somerset	62,381	8,093	10,192	155,000	23,147	6,091
West Sussex	370,779	25,364	41,774	1,229,000	1,386,497	719,731
Western Isles	99,936	17,988	27,329	661,104	131,134	105,518
Westminster City	151,787	0	44,000	887,000	853,950	153,685
Weymouth & Portland	110,000	14,850	20,187	246,778	55,505	13,571
Wigan	169,582	29,202	52,625	1,105,199	795,059	247,093
Wiltshire Unitary	139,096	20,864	59,646	1,824,000	885,669	406,066
Winchester City	96,000	12,000	22,314	445,763	45,023	-21,576
Windsor & Maidenhead	129,000	16,770	25,776	605,000	286,973	102,654
Wirral	134,804	0	31,639	769,000	743,792	275,876
Woking	119,700	17,718	20,665	255,761	61,565	-6,498
Wokingham	125,000	21,500	27,360	608,000	313,577	120,965
Wolverhampton	153,833	30,217	34,300	991,000	815,400	271
Worcester City	105,784	24,118	13,965	207,724	57,056	12,053
Worcestershire	180,320	37,034	40,094	800,000	811,700	356,900
Worthing	98,653	18,407	11,362	238,862	80,142	26,232
Wrexham	113,000	27,244	47,500	908,000	379,425	217,413
Wychavon	107,004	11,770	16,800	294,376		11,947
Wycombe	140,487	27,454	14,040	425,636	95,270	33,279
Wyre	95,793	22,590	23,025	304,604	55,055	14,245
Wyre Forest	106,500	12,993	17,150	297,465	55,164	14,006
York, City of	137,000	27,000	30,716	561,000	428,750	151,875

Aberdeen City S

Aberdeen City Council, 5th Floor, St Nicholas House, Broad Street, Aberdeen AB10 1BX
☎ 0845 608 0910 🖷 01224 636181 shfindlay@aberdeencity.gov.uk
www.aberdeencity.gov.uk

FACTS AND FIGURES

Parliamentary Constituencies: Aberdeen North, Aberdeen South, Gordon
EU Constituencies: Scotland
Election Frequency: Elections are of whole council

PRINCIPAL OFFICERS

Chief Executive: Mrs Angela Scott Chief Executive, Business Hub 12, Level 2 West, Marischal College, Broad Street, Aberdeen AB10 1AB ☎ 01224 522500 🖷 01224 346012 ascott@aberdeencity.gov.uk

Deputy Chief Executive: Mr Euan Couperwhite Head of Policy, Performance & Resources, Business Hub 13, 2nd Floor North, Marischal College, Broad Street, Aberdeen AB10 1AB ☎ 01224 522073 ecouperwhite@aberdeencity.gov.uk

Senior Management: Ms Gayle Gorman Director - Education & Children's Services, Business Hub 12, 2nd Floor West, Marischal College, Broad Street, Aberdeen AB10 1AB ☎ 01224 523458 🖷 01224 346012 ggorman@aberdeencity.gov.uk

Senior Management: Mr Pete Leonard, Director - Communities, Housing & Infrastructure, Business Hub 12, 2nd Floor West, Marischal College, Broad Street, Aberdeen AB10 1AB ☎ 01224 523899 🖷 01224 346012 pleonard@aberdeencity.gov.uk

Architect, Building / Property Services: Mr Hugh Murdoch, Transportation Manager, Business Hub 4, Ground Floor North, Marischal College, Broad Street, Aberdeen AB10 1AB ☎ 01224 523965 🖷 01224 523315 hughm@aberdeencity.gov.uk

Architect, Building / Property Services: Mr William Watson Principal Architect, Crown House, 27 - 29 Crown Street, Aberdeen AB11 6HA ☎ 01224 439215 🖷 01224 439216 williamwatson@aberdeencity.gov.uk

Best Value: Mr Ciaran Monaghan, Head of Service, Business Hub 12, 2nd Floor West, Marischal College, Broad Street, Aberdeen AB10 1AB ☎ 01224 522293 🖷 01224 644346 cmonaghan@aberdeencity.gov.uk

Building Control: Dr Margaret Bochel, Head of Planning & Sustainable Development, Business Hub 4, Ground Floor North, Marischal College, Broad Street, Aberdeen AB10 1AB ☎ 01224 523133 🖷 01224 523180 mbochel@aberdeencity.gov.uk

Building Control: Mr Gordon Spence, Building Standards Manager, Business Hub 4, Ground Floor North, Marischal College, Broad Street, Aberdeen AB10 1AB ☎ 01224 522436 🖷 01224 523180 gspence@aberdeencity.gov.uk

Catering Services: Mr John Landragon Catering Manager, Business Hub 10, 2nd Floor South, Marischal College, Broad Street, Aberdeen AB10 1AB ☎ 07801 129544 jlandragon@aberdeencity.gov.uk

Children / Youth Services: Mr Euan Couperwhite Head of Policy, Performance & Resources, Business Hub 13, 2nd Floor North, Marischal College, Broad Street, Aberdeen AB10 1AB ☎ 01224 522073 ecouperwhite@aberdeencity.gov.uk

Children / Youth Services: Ms Bernadette Oxley Head of Children's Social Work, Business Hub 13, 2nd Floor North, Marischal College, Broad Street, Aberdeen AB10 1AB ☎ 01224 522110 boxley@aberdeencity.gov.uk

Children / Youth Services: Mr Charlie Penman Head of Education Services, Business Hub 13, 2nd Floor North, Marischal College, Broad Street, Aberdeen AB10 1AB ☎ 01224 522375 🖷 01224 522022 cpenman@aberdeencity.gov.uk

Children / Youth Services: Ms Helen Shanks Head of Inclusion, Business Hub 13, 2nd Floor North, Marischal College, Broad Street, Aberdeen AB10 1AB ☎ 01224 522473 hshanks@aberdeencity.gov.uk

Civil Registration: Ms Carol Mair Senior Registrar, Business Hub 3, Ground Floor South, Marischal College, Broad Street, Aberdeen AB10 1AB ☎ 01224 523369 camair@aberdeencity.gov.uk

Civil Registration: Ms Marion Philip Senior Registrar, Business Hub 3, Ground Floor South, Marischal College, Broad Street, Aberdeen AB10 1AB ☎ 01224 522331 mphilip@aberdeencity.gov.uk

PR / Communications: Ms Dawn Schultz City Promotions Manager, Business Hub 4, Ground Floor North, Marischal College, Broad Street, Aberdeen AB10 1AB ☎ 01224 522767 🖷 01224 523315 dschultz@aberdeencity.gov.uk

Community Planning: Mr Donald Urquhart Head of Communities & Housing, Business Hub 11, 2nd Floor West, Marischal College, Broad Street, Aberdeen AB10 1AB ☎ 01224 522119 🖷 01224 523764 dourquhart@aberdeencity.gov.uk

Community Safety: Ms Nicola Murray Anti-Social Behaviour Officer, Community Safety Hub, 1st Floor, Frederick Street Centre, Frederick Street, Aberdeen AB24 5HY ☎ 01224 219453 nmurray@aberdeencity.gov.uk

Community Safety: Mr Rob Simpson Communities & Housing Citywide Manager, Business Hub 11, 2nd Floor West, Marischal College, Broad Street, Aberdeen AB10 1AB ☎ 01224 522540 robsimpson@aberdeencity.gov.uk

Community Safety: Mr Donald Urquhart Head of Communities & Housing, Business Hub 11, 2nd Floor West, Marischal College, Broad Street, Aberdeen AB10 1AB ☎ 01224 522119 🖷 01224 523764 dourquhart@aberdeencity.gov.uk

Computer Management: Mr Paul Alexander IT & Customer Services Manager, Business Hub 17, 3rd Floor North, Marischal College, Broad Street, Aberdeen AB10 1AB ☎ 01224 522343 paalexander@aberdeencity.gov.uk

Computer Management: Mr Simon Haston Head of IT & Transformation, Business Hub 17, 3rd Floor West, Marischal College, Broad Street, Aberdeen AB10 1AB ☎ 01224 523366 shaston@aberdeencity.gov.uk

ABERDEEN CITY

Computer Management: Ms Sandra Massey IT Manager, Business Hub 17, 3rd Floor North, Marischal College, Broad Street, Aberdeen AB10 1AB ☎ 01224 522778 ✉ smassey@aberdeencity.gov.uk

Consumer Protection and Trading Standards: Ms Carole Jackson, Protective Services Manager, Business Hub 15, 3rd Floor South, Marischal College, Broad Street, Aberdeen AB10 1AB ☎ 01224 522057 🖷 01224 523887 ✉ cjackson@aberdeencity.gov.uk

Contracts: Mr Craig Innes, Head of Commercial & Procurement Services, ☎ 01224 665650 ✉ cinnes@aberdeencity.gov.uk

Corporate Services: Ms Gayle Gorman Director - Education & Children's Services, Business Hub 12, 2nd Floor West, Marischal College, Broad Street, Aberdeen AB10 1AB ☎ 01224 523458 🖷 01224 346012 ✉ ggorman@aberdeencity.gov.uk

Corporate Services: Mr Pete Leonard, Director - Communities, Housing & Infrastructure, Business Hub 12, 2nd Floor West, Marischal College, Broad Street, Aberdeen AB10 1AB ☎ 01224 523899 🖷 01224 346012 ✉ pleonard@aberdeencity.gov.uk

Corporate Services: Mrs Angela Scott Chief Executive, Business Hub 12, Level 2 West, Marischal College, Broad Street, Aberdeen AB10 1AB ☎ 01224 522500 🖷 01224 346012 ✉ ascott@aberdeencity.gov.uk

Customer Service: Mr Ewan Sutherland, Head of HR, Business Hub 18, 4th Floor West, Marischal College, Broad Street, Aberdeen AB10 1AB ☎ 01224 522192 ✉ esutherland@aberdeencity.gov.uk

Economic Development: Ms Rita Stephen ACSEF Development Manager, Archibald Simpson House, 27 - 29 King Street, Aberdeen AB24 5AA ☎ 01224 627679 ✉ rstephen@aberdeencity.gov.uk

Education: Mr Charlie Penman Head of Education Services, Business Hub 13, 2nd Floor North, Marischal College, Broad Street, Aberdeen AB10 1AB ☎ 01224 522375 🖷 01224 522022 ✉ cpenman@aberdeencity.gov.uk

E-Government: Mr Ian Watt, E-Government Manager, Business Hub 17, 3rd Floor North, Marischal College, Broad Street, Aberdeen AB10 1AB ☎ 01224 522830 🖷 01224 522771 ✉ ianw@aberdeencity.gov.uk

Electoral Registration: Mr Ian Milton Assessor & Electoral Registration Officer, Grampian Valuation Joint Board, Woodhill House, Westburn Road, Aberdeen AB16 5GA ☎ 01224 664360 🖷 01224 664361 ✉ assessor@grampian-vjb.gov.uk

Emergency Planning: Mr David McIntosh, Emergency Planning Manager, Business Hub 15, 3rd Floor South, Marischal College, Broad Street, Aberdeen AB10 1AB ☎ 01224 522261 🖷 01224 645647 ✉ dmcintosh@aberdeencity.gov.uk

Energy Management: Ms Mai Muhammad Energy Manager, Business Hub 10, 2nd Floor South, Marischal College, Broad Street, Aberdeen AB10 1AB ☎ 01224 522383 ✉ mmuhammad@aberdeencity.gov.uk

Environmental / Technical Services: Mr Mark Reilly Head of Public Infrastructure & Environment, Kittybrewster Depot, 38 Powis Terrace, Aberdeen AB25 3RF ☎ 01224 523096 🖷 01224 487807 ✉ mareilly@aberdeencity.gov.uk

Environmental Health: Ms Carole Jackson, Protective Services Manager, Business Hub 15, 3rd Floor South, Marischal College, Broad Street, Aberdeen AB10 1AB ☎ 01224 522057 🖷 01224 523887 ✉ cjackson@aberdeencity.gov.uk

Estates, Property & Valuation: Mr Stephen Booth Property Estates Manager, Business Hub 10, 2nd Floor South, Marischal College, Broad Street, Aberdeen AB10 1AB ☎ 01224 522675 🖷 01224 813315 ✉ stbooth@aberdeencity.gov.uk

European Liaison: Mr Yasa Ratnayeke Senior Partnership, Performance & Funding Officer, Business Hub 4, Ground Floor North, Marischal College, Broad Street, Aberdeen AB10 1AB ☎ 01224 523807 🖷 01224 523807 ✉ yratnayeke@aberdeencity.gov.uk

Events Manager: Ms Dawn Schultz City Promotions Manager, Business Hub 4, Ground Floor North, Marischal College, Broad Street, Aberdeen AB10 1AB ☎ 01224 522767 🖷 01224 523315 ✉ dschultz@aberdeencity.gov.uk

Facilities: Mr Kiemon Stewart Building & Facilities Manager, Business Hub 10, 2nd Floor South, Marischal College, Broad Street, Aberdeen AB10 1AB ☎ 01224 489365 ✉ kiestewart@aberdeencity.gov.uk

Finance: Mr Steven Whyte Head of Finance, Business Hub 7, 1st Floor West, Marischal College, Broad Street, Aberdeen AB10 1AB ☎ 01224 523566 ✉ swhyte@aberdeencity.gov.uk

Pensions: Ms Laura Collis Principal Pensions Officer - Accounting & Investments, Business Hub 16, 3rd Floor West, Marischal College, Broad Street, Aberdeen AB10 1AB ☎ 01224 264160 ✉ lcollis@nespf.org.uk

Pensions: Mr Kenneth Lyon Principal Pensions Officer, Business Hub 16, 3rd Floor West, Marischal College, Broad Street, Aberdeen AB10 1AB ☎ 01224 814958 ✉ kelyon@nespf.org.uk

Pensions: Ms Caroline Mann Pensions Officer - Investments, Business Hub 16, 3rd Floor West, Marischal College, Broad Street, Aberdeen AB10 1AB ☎ 01224 264168 ✉ camann@nespf.org.uk

Pensions: Mr Michael Scroggie Senior Pensions Officer - Accounting & Investments, Business Hub 16, 3rd Floor West, Marischal College, Broad Street, Aberdeen AB10 1AB ☎ 01224 264178 ✉ mscroggie@nespf.org.uk

Fleet Management: Mr Nigel Buchan Fleet Manager, Kittybrewster Depot, Powis Terrace, Aberdeen AB25 3RF ☎ 01224 489317 🖷 01224 277728 ✉ nbuchan@aberdeencity.gov.uk

Grounds Maintenance: Mr Steven Shaw Environmental Manager, Kittybrewster Depot, Powis Terrace, Aberdeen AB25 3RF ☎ 01224 489273 🖷 01224 489270 ✉ stevens@aberdeencity.gov.uk

Health and Safety: Mrs Mary Agnew Health, Safety & Wellbeing Manager, Business Hub 18, 4th Floor West, Marischal College, Broad Street, Aberdeen AB10 1AB ☎ 01224 523088 🖷 01224 522257 ✉ magnew@aberdeencity.gov.uk

Highways: Mr Richard Blain Roads Operations Manager, West Tullos Roads Depot, Craigshaw Drive, Aberdeen AB12 3AL ☎ 01224 241525 ✉ rblain@aberdeencity.gov.uk

Housing: Ms Wendy Carle Housing Manager, Tillydrone Housing Office, Formartin Road, Aberdeen AB24 2UY ☎ 01224 489526 ✉ wcarle@aberdeencity.gov.uk

Housing: Mr John Quinn Head of Land & Property Assets, Business Hub 10, 2nd Floor South, Marischal College, Broad Street, Aberdeen AB10 1AB ☎ 01224 523363 ✉ jquinn@aberdeencity.gov.uk

Housing: Mr Martin Smith Housing Manager, Mastrick Customer Access Point, Spey Road, Aberdeen AB16 6SH ☎ 01224 788538 🖷 01224 663277 ✉ martinsmith@aberdeencity.gov.uk

Housing: Mr Graham Souter Housing Manager, Business Hub 1, Lower Ground Floor West, Marischal College, Broad Street, Aberdeen AB10 1AB ☎ 01224 522135 🖷 01224 523728 ✉ gsouter@aberdeencity.gov.uk

Housing: Mr Donald Urquhart Head of Communities & Housing, Business Hub 11, 2nd Floor West, Marischal College, Broad Street, Aberdeen AB10 1AB ☎ 01224 522119 🖷 01224 523764 ✉ dourquhart@aberdeencity.gov.uk

Housing Maintenance: Mr Donald MacLean Property Manager, Ground Floor, Kittybrewster Depot, Powis Place, Aberdeen AB25 3RF ☎ 01224 489432 ✉ dmcl@aberdeencity.gov.uk

Legal: Mr Fraser Bell Head of Legal & Democratic Services, Business Hub 6, 1St Floor South, Marischal College, Broad Street, Aberdeen AB10 1AB ☎ 01224 522084 ✉ frbell@aberdeencity.gov.uk

Leisure and Cultural Services: Mr Neil Bruce Service Manager - Culture, Business Hub 13, 2nd Floor North, Marischal College, Broad Street, Aberdeen AB10 1AB ☎ 01224 523144 🖷 01224 522022 ✉ neilbr@aberdeencity.gov.uk

Licensing: Mr Fraser Bell Head of Legal & Democratic Services, Business Hub 6, 1St Floor South, Marischal College, Broad Street, Aberdeen AB10 1AB ☎ 01224 522084 ✉ frbell@aberdeencity.gov.uk

Lifelong Learning: Ms Gail Woodcock Service Manager - Communities & Sport, Business Hub 13, 2nd Floor North, Marischal College, Broad Street, Aberdeen AB10 1AB ☎ 01224 522732 ✉ gwoodcock@aberdeencity.gov.uk

Lighting: Mr Richard Blain Roads Operations Manager, West Tullos Roads Depot, Craigshaw Drive, Aberdeen AB12 3AL ☎ 01224 241525 ✉ rblain@aberdeencity.gov.uk

Member Services: Mr Roderick MacBeath Head of Democratic Services, 1st Floor, Town House, Broad Street, Aberdeen AB10 1AQ ☎ 01224 523054 🖷 01224 523768 ✉ rmacbeath@aberdeencity.gov.uk

Parking: Mr Robin Donald City Warden Officer, Community Safety Hub, 1st Floor, Frederick Street Centre, Frederick Street, Aberdeen AB24 5HY ☎ 01224 219454 ✉ rdonald@aberdeencity.gov.uk

Parking: Mr Doug Ritchie Team Leader - Traffic Management, Business Hub 10, 2nd Floor South, Marischal College, Broad Street, Aberdeen AB10 1AB ☎ 01244 522325 ✉ dritchie@aberdeencity.gov.uk

Partnerships: Mr Yasa Ratnayeke Senior Partnership, Performance & Funding Officer, Business Hub 4, Ground Floor North, Marischal College, Broad Street, Aberdeen AB10 1AB ☎ 01224 523807 🖷 01224 523807 ✉ yratnayeke@aberdeencity.gov.uk

Personnel / HR: Mr Ewan Sutherland, Head of HR, Business Hub 18, 4th Floor West, Marischal College, Broad Street, Aberdeen AB10 1AB ☎ 01224 522192 ✉ esutherland@aberdeencity.gov.uk

Planning: Dr Margaret Bochel, Head of Planning & Sustainable Development, Business Hub 4, Ground Floor North, Marischal College, Broad Street, Aberdeen AB10 1AB ☎ 01224 523133 🖷 01224 523180 ✉ mbochel@aberdeencity.gov.uk

Procurement: Mr Craig Innes, Head of Commercial & Procurement Services, Woodhill House, Ashgrove Road, Aberdeen AB16 5GA ☎ 01224 665650 ✉ cinnes@aberdeencity.gov.uk

Public Libraries: Mr Neil Bruce Service Manager - Culture, Business Hub 13, 2nd Floor North, Marischal College, Broad Street, Aberdeen AB10 1AB ☎ 01224 523144 🖷 01224 522022 ✉ neilbr@aberdeencity.gov.uk

Recycling & Waste Minimisation: Mr Peter Lawrence Waste & Recycling Manager, Kittybrewster Depot, 38 Powis Terrace, Aberdeen AB25 3RF ☎ 01224 489331 🖷 01224 489270 ✉ plawrence@aberdeencity.gov.uk

Regeneration: Mr John Quinn Head of Land & Property Assets, Business Hub 10, 2nd Floor South, Marischal College, Broad Street, Aberdeen AB10 1AB ☎ 01224 523363 ✉ jquinn@aberdeencity.gov.uk

Road Safety: Mr Doug Ritchie Team Leader - Traffic Management, Business Hub 10, 2nd Floor South, Marischal College, Broad Street, Aberdeen AB10 1AB ☎ 01244 522325 ✉ dritchie@aberdeencity.gov.uk

Social Services: Ms Anne Donaldson Lead Service Manager (Services), Business Hub 8, 1st Floor North, Marischal College, Broad Street, Aberdeen AB10 1AB ☎ 01224 523019 ✉ adonaldson@aberdeencity.gov.uk

Social Services: Mr Martin Kasprowicz Lead Service Manager (Older Adults), Business Hub 8, 1st Floor North, Marischal College, Broad Street, Aberdeen AB10 1AB ☎ 01224 523283 ✉ mkasprowicz@aberdeencity.gov.uk

Social Services: Ms Judith Proctor Chief Officer, Business Hub 8, 1st Floor North, Marischal College, Broad Street, Aberdeen AB10 1AB ☎ 01224 558714 ✉ judith.proctor@aberdeencity.gov.uk

ABERDEEN CITY

Social Services: Mr Graeme Simpson Lead Service Manager (Practice), Business Hub 8, 1st Floor North, Marischal College, Broad Street, Aberdeen AB10 1AB ☎ 01224 523496 ✉ gsimpson@aberdeencity.gov.uk

Social Services: Ms Sally Wilkins Lead Service Manager (Younger Adults & Criminal Justice), Business Hub 8, 1st Floor North, Marischal College, Broad Street, Aberdeen AB10 1AB ☎ 01224 522860 ✉ sawilkins@aberdeencity.gov.uk

Social Services (Adult): Mr Tom Cowan Head of Joint Operations, Business Hub 8, 1st Floor North, Marischal College, Broad Street, Aberdeen AB10 1AB ☎ 01224 558415 🖷 01224 523195 ✉ tcowan@aberdencity.gov.uk

Social Services (Children): Ms Bernadette Oxley Head of Children's Social Work, Business Hub 13, 2nd Floor North, Marischal College, Broad Street, Aberdeen AB10 1AB ☎ 01224 522110 ✉ boxley@aberdeencity.gov.uk

Staff Training: Mr Ewan Sutherland, Head of HR, Business Hub 18, 4th Floor West, Marischal College, Broad Street, Aberdeen AB10 1AB ☎ 01224 522192 ✉ esutherland@aberdeencity.gov.uk

Street Scene: Mr Steven Shaw Environmental Manager, Kittybrewster Depot, Powis Terrace, Aberdeen AB25 2RF ☎ 01224 489273 🖷 01224 489270 ✉ stevens@aberdeencity.gov.uk

Sustainable Development: Dr Margaret Bochel, Head of Planning & Sustainable Development, Business Hub 4, Ground Floor, Marischal College, Broad Street, Aberdeen AB10 1AB ☎ 01224 523133 🖷 01224 523180 ✉ mbochel@aberdeencity.gov.uk

Tourism: Ms Dawn Schultz City Promotions Manager, Business Hub 4, Ground Floor North, Marischal College, Broad Street, Aberdeen AB10 1AB ☎ 01224 522767 🖷 01224 523315 ✉ dschultz@aberdeencity.gov.uk

Town Centre: Mr Andrew Win City Development Programme Manager, Business Hub 4, Ground Floor North, Marischal College, Broad Street, Aberdeen AB10 1AB ☎ 01224 523060 ✉ andrewwin@aberdeencity.gov.uk

Traffic Management: Mr Doug Ritchie Team Leader - Traffic Management, Business Hub 10, 2nd Floor South, Marischal College, Broad Street, Aberdeen AB10 1AB ☎ 01244 522325 ✉ dritchie@aberdeencity.gov.uk

Transport: Dr Margaret Bochel, Head of Planning & Sustainable Development, Business Hub 4, Ground Floor North, Marischal College, Broad Street, Aberdeen AB10 1AB ☎ 01224 523133 🖷 01224 523180 ✉ mbochel@aberdeencity.gov.uk

Transport Planner: Dr Margaret Bochel, Head of Planning & Sustainable Development, Business Hub 4, Ground Floor North, Marischal College, Broad Street, Aberdeen AB10 1AB ☎ 01224 523133 🖷 01224 523180 ✉ mbochel@aberdeencity.gov.uk

Waste Collection and Disposal: Mr Peter Lawrence Waste & Recycling Manager, 1st Floor, Kittybrewster Depot, Powis Terrace, Aberdeen AB25 3RF ☎ 01224 489331 🖷 01224 489270 ✉ plawrence@aberdeencity.gov.uk

Children's Play Areas: Mr Steven Shaw Environmental Manager, Kittybrewster Depot, Powis Terrace, Aberdeen AB25 3RF ☎ 01224 489273 🖷 01224 489270 ✉ stevens@aberdeencity.gov.uk

COUNCILLORS

***Provost* Adam**, George (LAB - Hilton / Woodside / Stockethill)
gadam@aberdeencity.gov.uk

***Deputy Provost* Reynolds**, John (IND - Bridge of Don)
jreynolds@aberdeencity.gov.uk

***Leader of the Council* Laing**, Jenny (LAB - Midstocket / Rosemount)
jelaing@aberdeencity.gov.uk

***Deputy Leader of the Council* Boulton**, Marie (IND - Lower Deeside)
mboulton@aberdeencity.gov.uk

Allan, Yvonne (LAB - Torry / Ferryhill)
yallan@aberdeencity.gov.uk

Cameron, David (SNP - Kingswell / Sheddocksley / Summerhill)
dacameron@aberdeencity.gov.uk

Carle, Scott (LAB - Northfield / Mastrick North)
sccarle@aberdeencity.gov.uk

Cooney, Neil (LAB - Kincorth / Nigg / Cove)
ncooney@aberdeencity.gov.uk

Corall, John (SNP - Hazlehead / Ashley / Queens Cross)
jcorall@aberdeencity.gov.uk

Cormie, Bill (SNP - Midstocket / Rosemount)
bcormie@aberdeencity.gov.uk

Crockett, Barney (LAB - Dyce / Bucksburn / Danestone)
bcrockett@aberdeencity.gov.uk

Delaney, Steve (LD - Kingswell / Sheddocksley / Summerhill)
sdelaney@aberdeencity.gov.uk

Dickson, Graham (SNP - Torry / Ferryhill)
gdickson@aberdeencity.gov.uk

Donelly, Alan (CON - Torry / Ferryhill)
adonnelly@aberdeencity.gov.uk

Dunbar, Jackie (SNP - Northfield / Mastrick North)
jdunbar@aberdeencity.gov.uk

Dunbar, Lesley (LAB - Hilton / Woodside / Stockethill)
lesdunbar@aberdeencity.gov.uk

Finlayson, Andrew (IND - Kincorth / Nigg / Cove)
afinlayson@aberdeencity.gov.uk

Forsyth, Fraser (INDNA - Midstocket / Rosemount)
fforsyth@aberdeencity.gov.uk

Graham, Gordon (LAB - Northfield / Mastrick North)
ggraham@aberdeencity.gov.uk

Grant, Ross (LAB - Tillydrone / Seaton / Old Aberdeen)
rossgrant@aberdeencity.gov.uk

Greig, Martin (LD - Hazlehead / Ashley / Queens Cross)
mgreig@aberdeencity.gov.uk

Ironside, Len (LAB - Kingswell / Sheddocksley / Summerhill)
lironside@aberdeencity.gov.uk

Jaffrey, Muriel (SNP - Bridge of Don)
mjaffrey@aberdeencity.gov.uk

Kiddie, James (SNP - Torry / Ferryhill)
jkiddie@aberdeencity.gov.uk

Lawrence, Graeme (LAB - Dyce / Bucksburn / Danestone)
glawrence@aberdeencity.gov.uk

MacGregor, Neil (SNP - Dyce / Bucksburn / Danestone)
nmacgregor@aberdeencity.gov.uk

Malik, M. Tauqeer (LAB - Lower Deeside)
mmalik@aberdeencity.gov.uk

Malone, Aileen (LD - Lower Deeside)
amalone@aberdeencity.gov.uk

May, Andrew (SNP - George Street / Harbour)
andrewmay@aberdeencity.gov.uk

Milne, Ramsay (LAB - Tillydrone / Seaton / Old Aberdeen)
rmilne@aberdeencity.gov.uk

Morrison, Nathan (LAB - George Street / Harbour)
namorrison@aberdeencity.gov.uk

Morrison, Jean (LAB - George Street / Harbour)
jemorrison@aberdeencity.gov.uk

Noble, Jim (SNP - Tillydrone / Seaton / Old Aberdeen)
jimnoble@aberdeencity.gov.uk

Samarai, Gill (SNP - Dyce / Bucksburn / Danestone)
gsamarai@aberdeencity.gov.uk

Stewart, Jennifer (LD - Hazlehead / Ashley / Queens Cross)
jastewart@aberdeencity.gov.uk

Stuart, Sandy (SNP - Bridge of Don)
sandystuart@aberdeencity.gov.uk

Taylor, Angela (LAB - Airyhall / Broomhill / Garthdee)
angelataylor@aberdeencity.gov.uk

Thomson, Ross (O - Hazlehead / Ashley / Queens Cross)
rossthomson@aberdeencity.gov.uk

Townson, Gordon (SNP - Airyhall / Broomhill / Garthdee)
gtownson@aberdeencity.gov.uk

Young, Willie (LAB - Bridge of Don)
wyoung@aberdeencity.gov.uk

Yuill, Ian (LD - Airyhall / Broomhill / Garthdee)
iyuill@aberdeencity.gov.uk

POLITICAL COMPOSITION
LAB: 17, SNP: 13, LD: 5, IND: 3, INDNA: 1, O: 1, CON: 1

COMMITTEE CHAIRS
Education & Children's Services: Ms Angela Taylor

Licensing: Mr Scott Carle

Pensions: Mr Barney Crockett

Planning: Mr Ramsay Milne

Aberdeenshire S

Aberdeenshire Council, Woodhill House, Westburn Road, Aberdeen AB16 5GB
☎ 0845 608 1207 🖳 www.aberdeenshire.gov.uk

FACTS AND FIGURES
Parliamentary Constituencies: Aberdeenshire West and Kincardine, Banff and Buchan, Gordon

EU Constituencies: Scotland
Election Frequency: Elections are of whole council

PRINCIPAL OFFICERS
Chief Executive: Mr Jim Savege Chief Executive, Woodhill House, Westburn Road, Aberdeen AB16 5GB ☎ 01224 665400 ✉ jim.savege@aberdeenshire.gov.uk; chief.executive@aberdeenshire.gov.uk

Senior Management: Mr Stephen Archer Director - Infrastructure Services, Woodhill House, Westburn Road, Aberdeen AB16 5GB
☎ 01224 664520 ✉ stephen.archer@aberdeenshire.gov.uk

Senior Management: Mr Ritchie Johnson, Director - Communities, Woodhill House, Westburn Road, Aberdeen AB16 5GB ☎ 01224 665444 🖷 01224 664992
✉ ritchie.johnson@aberdeenshire.gov.uk

Senior Management: Ms Maria Walker Director - Education & Children's Services, Woodhill House, Westburn Road, Aberdeen AB16 5GB ☎ 01224 665420 ✉ maria.walker@aberdeenshire.gov.uk

Architect, Building / Property Services: Mr Allan Whyte, Head of Property & Facilities Management, Woodhill House, Westburn Road, Aberdeen AB16 5GB ☎ 01224 664500 🖷 01224 664470
✉ allan.whyte@aberdeenshire.gov.uk

Building Control: Mr Robert Gray Head of Planning & Building Standards, Woodhill House, Westburn Road, Aberdeen AB16 5GB
☎ 01224 664728 ✉ robert.gray@aberdeenshire.gov.uk

Catering Services: Mr Allan Doig Catering Services Manager, Harlaw Road Depot, Harlaw Road, Inverurie AB51 4TE ☎ 01467 627500 ✉ allan.doig@aberdeenshire.gov.uk

Civil Registration: Ms Karen Wiles Head of Legal & Governance, Woodhill House, Westburn Road, Aberdeen AB16 5GB ☎ 01224 665430 ✉ karen.wiles@aberdeenshire.gov.uk

PR / Communications: Ms Kate Bond, Head of Customer Communication & Improvements, Woodhill House, Westburn Road, Aberdeen AB16 5GB ☎ 01224 664405 🖷 01224 665204
✉ kate.bond@aberdeenshire.gov.uk

Community Planning: Ms Elaine Brown Area Manager - Formantine, Formantine Area Office, 29 Bridge Street, , Ellon AB41 9AA ☎ 01358 726402 ✉ elaine.brown@aberdeenshire.gov.uk

Community Planning: Ms Janelle Clark Are Manager - Marr, Marr Area Office, School Road, , Alford AB33 8TY ☎ 01975 564800
✉ janelle.clark@aberdeenshire.gov.uk

Community Planning: Mr Alexander MacLeod Housing Manager - Strategy, Gordon House, Blackhall Road, Inverurie AB51 3WA
☎ 01467 628445 ✉ alexander.macleod@aberdeenshire.gov.uk

Community Planning: Mr Douglas Milne Area Manager - Garioch, Garioch Area Office, Gordon House, Blackhall Road, Inverurie AB51 3WA ☎ 01467 628222 ✉ douglas.milne@aberdeenshire.gov.uk

ABERDEENSHIRE

Community Planning: Mr William Munro, Area Manager - Kincardine & Mearns, Viewmount, Arduthie Road, Stonehaven AB3 2DQ ☎ 01569 768200 🖷 01569 767972 🖱 william.munro@aberdeenshire.gov.uk

Community Planning: Mr Chris White Area Manager - Buchan, Buchan House, 51 Peter Street, Peterhead AB42 1QF ☎ 01779 483200 🖱 chris.white@aberdeenshire.gov.uk

Computer Management: Ms Nicola Graham Head of ICT, Woodhill House, Westburn Road, Aberdeen AB16 5GB ☎ 01224 664287 🖷 01224 664001 🖱 nicola.graham@aberdeenshire.gov.uk

Contracts: Mr Craig Innes, Head of Central Procurement Services, Woodhill House, Westburn Road, Aberdeen AB16 5GB ☎ 01224 665650 🖱 craig.innes@aberdeenshire.gov.uk

Corporate Services: Mr Allan Wood Director - Business Services, Woodhill House, Westburn Road, Aberdeen AB16 5GB ☎ 01224 664202 🖱 allan.wood@aberdeenshire.gov.uk

Customer Service: Ms Morag Esson Customer Services Manager, Woodhill House, Westburn Road, Aberdeen AB16 5GB ☎ 01224 664583 🖷 01224 664022 🖱 morag.esson@aberdeenshire.gov.uk

Economic Development: Ms Belinda Miller Head of Economic Development, Woodhill House, Westburn Road, Aberdeen AB16 5GB ☎ 01224 664568 🖷 01224 664713 🖱 belinda.miller@aberdeenshire.gov.uk

Education: Mr Vincent Docherty Head of Service - Inclusion & Integration, Woodhill House, Westburn Road, Aberdeen AB16 5GB ☎ 01224 664397 🖱 vincent.docherty@aberdeenshire.gov.uk

Education: Mr Andrew Griffiths Head of Service - Education & Staff Development, Woodhill House, Westburn Road, Aberdeen AB16 5GB ☎ 01224 664142 🖱 andrew.griffiths@aberdeenshire.gov.uk

Education: Ms Maria Walker Director - Education & Children's Services, Woodhill House, Westburn Road, Aberdeen AB16 5GB ☎ 01224 665420 🖱 maria.walker@aberdeenshire.gov.uk

E-Government: Ms Nicola Graham Head of ICT, Woodhill House, Westburn Road, Aberdeen AB16 5GB ☎ 01224 664287 🖷 01224 664001 🖱 nicola.graham@aberdeenshire.gov.uk

Electoral Registration: Mr Allan Bell, Senior Committee Officer/ Elections Organiser, Woodhill House, Westburn Road, Aberdeen AB16 5GB ☎ 01224 665119 🖷 01224 664019 🖱 allan.bell@aberdeenshire.gov.uk

Emergency Planning: Mr David McIntosh, Emergency Planning Manager, 1 Queen's Gardens, Aberdeen AB15 4YD ☎ 01224 633030 🖷 01224 645647 🖱 david@grampian.epu.co.uk

Energy Management: Mr Brian Smith Engineering Services Manager, Woodhill House, Westburn Road, Aberdeen AB16 5GB ☎ 01224 664510 🖷 01224 664470 🖱 brian.smith@aberdeenshire.gov.uk

Environmental / Technical Services: Mr David Cooper, Environmental Health Officer, Gordon House, Blackhall Road, Inverurie AB51 3WA ☎ 01467 628159 🖱 david.cooper@aberdeenshire.gov.uk

Environmental Health: Mr David Cooper, Environmental Health Officer, Gordon House, Blackhall Road, Inverurie AB51 3WA ☎ 01467 628159 🖱 david.cooper@aberdeenshire.gov.uk

Estates, Property & Valuation: Mr John Gahagan Estates Manager, Woodhill House, Westburn Road, Aberdeen AB16 5GB ☎ 01224 664778 🖷 01224 664470 🖱 john.gahagan@aberdeenshire.gov.uk

European Liaison: Mr Martin Brebner European Programmes Executive, Woodhill House, Westburn Road, Aberdeen AB16 5GB ☎ 01224 665225 🖷 01224 664713 🖱 martin.brebner@aberdeenshire.gov.uk

Facilities: Mr Tom Buchan Facilities Manager, Woodhill House, Westburn Road, Aberdeen AB16 5GB ☎ 01224 664496 🖷 01224 664470 🖱 tom.buchan@aberdeenshire.gov.uk

Finance: Mr Alex Stephen Head of Service - Finance, Woodhill House, Westburn Road, Aberdeen AB16 5GB ☎ 01224 664202 🖱 allan.wood@aberdeenshire.gov.uk

Fleet Management: Mr Ian Paisley, Fleet Manager, Inverurie Repair Depot, Harlaw Way, Inverurie AB51 4TE ☎ 01467 627530 🖷 01467 624256 🖱 ian.paisley@aberdeenshire.gov.uk

Grounds Maintenance: Mr Philip McKay Head of Roads & Landscape Services, T & I Operations, Harlaw Way, Inverurie AB51 4SG ☎ 01467 627644 🖷 01467 624827 🖱 philip.mckay@aberdeenshire.gov.uk

Health and Safety: Ms Pamela Bruce Principal Health & Safety Adviser, Woodhill House, Westburn Road, Aberdeen AB16 5GB ☎ 01224 664067 🖷 01224 665122 🖱 pamela.bruce@aberdeenshire.gov.uk

Highways: Mr Philip McKay Head of Roads & Landscape Services, Harlaw Way, Inverurie AB51 4SG ☎ 01467 627644 🖷 01467 624827 🖱 philip.mckay@aberdeenshire.gov.uk

Housing: Mr Douglas Edwardson, Head of Housing, Woodhill House, Westburn Road, Aberdeen AB16 5GB ☎ 01224 664900 🖷 01224 664992 🖱 douglas.edwardson@aberdeenshire.gov.uk

Legal: Ms Karen Wiles Head of Legal & Governance, Woodhill House, Westburn Road, Aberdeen AB16 5GB ☎ 01224 665430 🖱 karen.wiles@aberdeenshire.gov.uk

Leisure and Cultural Services: Mr John Harding Head of Service - Lifelong Learning & Leisure, Woodhill House, Westburn Road, Aberdeen AB16 5GB ☎ 01224 664653 🖱 john.harding@aberdeenshire.gov.uk

Licensing: Ms Karen Wiles Head of Legal & Governance, Woodhill House, Westburn Road, Aberdeen AB16 5GB ☎ 01224 665430 🖱 karen.wiles@aberdeenshire.gov.uk

Lifelong Learning: Mr John Harding Head of Service - Lifelong Learning & Leisure, Woodhill House, Westburn Road, Aberdeen AB16 5GB ☎ 01224 664653 ✉ john.harding@aberdeenshire.gov.uk

Lighting: Mr Keith Melvin Strategy/Lighting Engineer, Gordon House, Blackhall Road, Inverurie AB51 3WA ☎ 01467 628014 🖷 01467 624558 ✉ brian.strachan@aberdeenshire.gov.uk

Lottery Funding, Charity and Voluntary: Mr Walter Taylor, Grants & Adventure Activities Officer, Woodhill House, Westburn Road, Aberdeen AB16 5GB ☎ 01224 664237 🖷 01224 664615 ✉ walter.taylor@aberdeenshire.gov.uk

Parking: Mr Mark Skilling Strategy Manager, Woodhill House, Westburn Road, Aberdeen AB16 5GB ☎ 01224 664809 🖷 01224 662005 ✉ mark.skilling@aberdeenshire.gov.uk

Personnel / HR: Ms Laura Simpson Head of HR & OD, Woodhill House, Westburn Road, Aberdeen AB16 5GB ☎ 01224 664021 ✉ laura.simpson@aberdeenshire.gov.uk

Planning: Mr Robert Gray Head of Planning & Building Standards, Woodhill House, Westburn Road, Aberdeen AB16 5GB ☎ 01224 664728 ✉ robert.gray@aberdeenshire.gov.uk

Procurement: Mr Craig Innes, Head of Central Procurement Services, Woodhill House, Westburn Road, Aberdeen AB16 5GB ☎ 01224 665650 ✉ craig.innes@aberdeenshire.gov.uk

Public Libraries: Ms Sharon Jamieson Library & Information Services Manager, Meldrum Meg Way, Olmeldron, Inverurie AB51 0GN ☎ 01651 871210 ✉ sharon.jamieson@aberdeenshire.gov.uk

Recycling & Waste Minimisation: Mrs Sue Horrobin Waste Manager, Unit 7, Harlaw Industrial Estate, Harlaw Way, Inverurie AB51 4SG ☎ 🖷 01467 625706 ✉ pam.walker@aberdeenshire.gov.uk

Regeneration: Ms Christine Webster Regeneration & Town Centre Manager, Banff Town House, Low Street, Banff AB45 1AU ☎ 07785 730652 ✉ christine.webster@aberdeenshire.gov.uk

Road Safety: Mr Mark Skilling Strategy Manager, Woodhill House, Westburn Road, Aberdeen AB16 5GB ☎ 01224 664809 🖷 01224 662005 ✉ mark.skilling@aberdeenshire.gov.uk

Social Services (Adult): Mr Philip English Head of Adult & Criminal Justice Services, Woodhill House, Westburn Road, Aberdeen AB16 5GB ☎ 01224 664940 🖷 01224 664992 ✉ philip.english@aberdeenshire.gov.uk

Social Services (Children): Mr Robert Driscoll Head of Child Services, Woodhill House, Westburn Road, Aberdeen AB16 5GB ☎ 01224 664803 ✉ robert.driscoll@aberdeenshire.gov.uk

Staff Training: Ms Laura Simpson Head of HR & OD, Woodhill House, Westburn Road, Aberdeen AB16 5GB ☎ 01224 664021 ✉ laura.simpson@aberdeenshire.gov.uk

Street Scene: Mr Philip McKay Head of Roads & Landscape Services, Harlaw Way, Inverurie AB51 4SG ☎ 01467 627644 🖷 01467 624827 ✉ philip.mckay@aberdeenshire.gov.uk

Sustainable Development: Mr Barry Simons Sustainability & Climate Change Co-ordinator, Woodhill House, Westburn Road, Aberdeen AB16 5GB ☎ 01224 664719 🖷 01224 664615 ✉ barry.simons@aberdeenshire.gov.uk

Tourism: Mr David Wright Industry Support Executive - Tourism, Woodhill House, Westburn Road, Aberdeen AB16 5GB ☎ 01224 664574 🖷 01224 664713 ✉ david.wright@aberdeenshire.gov.uk

Town Centre: Ms Audrey Michie Strategic Town Centres Executive, Woodhill House, Westburn Road, Aberdeen AB16 5GB ☎ 01467 628278 🖷 01224 664713 ✉ audrey.michie@aberdeenshire.gov.uk

Traffic Management: Mr Philip McKay Head of Roads & Landscape Services, Harlaw Way, Inverurie AB51 4SG ☎ 01467 627644 🖷 01467 624827 ✉ philip.mckay@aberdeenshire.gov.uk

Transport: Mr Richard McKenzie Public Transport Manager, Woodhill House, Westburn Road, Aberdeen AB16 5GB ☎ 01224 664580 🖷 01224 662005 ✉ richard.mckenzie@aberdeenshire.gov.uk

Transport Planner: Mr Richard McKenzie Public Transport Manager, Woodhill House, Westburn Road, Aberdeen AB16 5GB ☎ 01224 664580 🖷 01224 662005 ✉ richard.mckenzie@aberdeenshire.gov.uk

Total Place: Mr Alexander MacLeod Housing Manager - Strategy, Gordon House, Blackhall Road, Inverurie AB51 3WA ☎ 01467 628445 ✉ alexander.macleod@aberdeenshire.gov.uk

Waste Collection and Disposal: Mr Ian Robertson, Head of Service - Protective Services & Waste Management, Mercat Cross, 36 Low Street, Banff AB45 1AY ☎ 01261 813271 🖷 01261 818649 ✉ ian.robertson@aberdeenshire.gov.uk

Waste Management: Mr Ian Robertson, Head of Service - Protective Services & Waste Management, Mercat Cross, 36 Low Street, Banff AB45 1AY ☎ 01261 813271 🖷 01261 818649 ✉ ian.robertson@aberdeenshire.gov.uk

Children's Play Areas: Mr Philip McKay Head of Roads & Landscape Services, Harlaw Way, Inverurie AB51 4SG ☎ 01467 627644 🖷 01467 624827 ✉ philip.mckay@aberdeenshire.gov.uk

COUNCILLORS

***Leader of the Council* Kitts-Hayes**, Martine (LD - Inverurie & District)
cllr.m.kitts-hayes@aberdeenshire.gov.uk

***Leader of the Council* Thomson**, Richard (SNP - Ellon & District)
cllr.r.thomson@aberdeenshire.gov.uk

Agnew, Wendy (CON - Stonehaven & Lower Deeside)
cllr.w.agnew@aberdeenshire.gov.uk

Aitchison, David (SNP - Westhill & District)
cllr.d.aitchison@aberdeenshire.gov.uk

Allan, Anne (SNP - Peterhead North & Rattray)
cllr.a.m.allan@aberdeenshire.gov.uk

Allan, Amanda (SNP - Westhill & District)
cllr.a.j.allan@aberdeenshire.gov.uk

ABERDEENSHIRE

Argyle, Peter (LD - Aboyne, Upper Deeside & Donside)
cllr.p.argyle@aberdeenshire.gov.uk

Bellarby, Peter (LD - Stonehaven & Lower Deeside)
cllr.p.bellarby@aberdeenshire.gov.uk

Bews, Alistair (SNP - North Kincardine)
cllr.a.bews@aberdeenshire.gov.uk

Blackett, Geva (SNP - Aboyne, Upper Deeside & Donside)
cllr.g.blackett@aberdeenshire.gov.uk

Buchan, Charles (SNP - Fraserburgh & District)
cllr.c.buchan@aberdeenshire.gov.uk

Buchan, Alan (IND - Peterhead North & Rattray)
cllr.a.buchan@aberdeenshire.gov.uk

Carr, George (CON - Mearns)
cllr.g.carr@aberdeenshire.gov.uk

Cassie, Ross (SNP - Troup)
cllr.r.cassie@aberdeenshire.gov.uk

Chapman, Edie (CON - Central Buchan)
cllr.e.chapman@aberdeenshire.gov.uk

Christie, Raymond (LAB - Stonehaven & Lower Deeside)
cllr.r.christie@aberdeenshire.gov.uk

Clark, Graeme (SNP - Stonehaven & Lower Deeside)
cllr.g.clark@aberdeenshire.gov.uk

Clark, Karen (LD - Banchory & Mid-Deeside)
cllr.k.clark@aberdeenshire.gov.uk

Clark, Linda (SNP - Banchory & Mid-Deeside)
cllr.l.clark@aberdeenshire.gov.uk

Cowling, Richard (CON - Inverurie & District)
cllr.r.cowling@aberdeenshire.gov.uk

Cox, John (IND - Banff & District)
cllr.j.cox@aberdeenshire.gov.uk

Cullinane, Nan (LD - East Garioch)
cllr.n.cullinane@aberdeenshire.gov.uk

Davidson, Isobel (LD - Ellon & District)
cllr.i.davidson@aberdeenshire.gov.uk

Dick, Jean (SNP - Mearns)
cllr.j.dick@aberdeenshire.gov.uk

Duncan, Sandy (SNP - Turriff & District)
cllr.a.duncan@aberdeenshire.gov.uk

Evison, Alison (LAB - North Kincardine)
cllr.a.evison@aberdeenshire.gov.uk

Farquhar, Katrina (CON - Aboyne, Upper Deeside & Donside)
cllr.k.farquhar@aberdeenshire.gov.uk

Findlater, Mark (IND - Troup)
cllr.m.findlater@aberdeenshire.gov.uk

Ford, Martin (SGP - East Garioch)
cllr.m.ford@aberdeenshire.gov.uk

Gardiner, Alan (IND - Peterhead North & Rattray)
cllr.a.gardiner@aberdeenshire.gov.uk

Gifford, Jim (CON - Mid-Formartine)
cllr.j.gifford@aberdeenshire.gov.uk

Grant, Allison (SNP - West Garioch)
cllr.a.grant@aberdeenshire.gov.uk

Gray, Ian (SNP - Banff & District)
cllr.i.gray@aberdeenshire.gov.uk

Hendry, Allan (SNP - Mid-Formartine)
cllr.a.hendry@aberdeenshire.gov.uk

Hood, Fergus (SNP - East Garioch)
cllr.f.hood@aberdeenshire.gov.uk

Howatson, Bill (LD - Mearns)
cllr.w.howatson@aberdeenshire.gov.uk

Ingleby, Moira (CON - Huntly, Strathbogie & Howe of Alford)
cllr.m.ingleby@aberdeenshire.gov.uk

Ingram, Jim (SNP - Central Buchan)
cllr.j.ingram@aberdeenshire.gov.uk

Johnston, Paul (IND - Mid-Formartine)
cllr.p.johnston@aberdeenshire.gov.uk

Latham, John (IND - Huntly, Strathbogie & Howe of Alford)
cllr.j.latham@aberdeenshire.gov.uk

Lonchay, Sheena (LD - West Garioch)
cllr.s.lonchay@aberdeenshire.gov.uk

Malone, Tom (IND - Peterhead South & Cruden)
cllr.t.malone@aberdeenshire.gov.uk

McKail, Ron (CON - Westhill & District)
cllr.r.mckail@aberdeenshire.gov.uk

McRae, Fiona (SNP - Peterhead North & Rattray)
cllr.f.mcrae@aberdeenshire.gov.uk

Merson, Rob (SNP - Ellon & District)
cllr.r.merson@aberdeenshire.gov.uk

Mollison, Ian (LD - North Kincardine)
cllr.i.mollison@aberdeenshire.gov.uk

Nelson, Carl (CON - North Kincardine)
cllr.c.nelson@aberdeenshire.gov.uk

Norrie, Alisan (IND - Turriff & District)
cllr.a.norrie@aberdeenshire.gov.uk

Oddie, Patricia (CON - West Garioch)
cllr.p.oddie@aberdeenshire.gov.uk

Owen, Gillian (CON - Ellon & District)
cllr.g.owen@aberdeenshire.gov.uk

Partridge, Hamish (SNP - Troup)
cllr.h.partridge@aberdeenshire.gov.uk

Pirie, Lenny (SNP - Central Buchan)
cllr.l.pirie@aberdeenshire.gov.uk

Pratt, Stuart (SNP - Peterhead South & Cruden)
cllr.s.pratt@aberdeenshire.gov.uk

Robertson, Anne (LD - Turriff & District)
cllr.a.robertson@aberdeenshire.gov.uk

Ross, Alastair (LD - Huntly, Strathbogie & Howe of Alford)
cllr.a.ross@aberdeenshire.gov.uk

Roy, Mike (CON - Banff & District)
cllr.m.roy@aberdeenshire.gov.uk

Shand, Cryle (SNP - Mid-Formartine)
cllr.c.shand@aberdeenshire.gov.uk

Smith, Stephen (SNP - Peterhead South & Cruden)
cllr.s.smith@aberdeenshire.gov.uk

Smith, Norman (IND - Central Buchan)
cllr.n.smith@aberdeenshire.gov.uk

Stewart, Dave (IND - Mearns)
cllr.d.stewart@aberdeenshire.gov.uk

Strathdee, Joanna (SNP - Huntly, Strathbogie & Howe of Alford)
cllr.j.strathdee@aberdeenshire.gov.uk

Stuart, Bryan (SNP - Inverurie & District)
cllr.b.stuart@aberdeenshire.gov.uk

Tait, Ian (IND - Fraserburgh & District)
cllr.i.tait@aberdeenshire.gov.uk

Topping, Brian (SNP - Fraserburgh & District)
cllr.b.topping@aberdeenshire.gov.uk

Vernal, Hamish (SNP - Inverurie & District)
cllr.h.vernal@aberdeenshire.gov.uk

Walker, Iris (LD - Westhill & District)
cllr.i.walker@aberdeenshire.gov.uk

Watt, Michael (IND - Fraserburgh & District)
cllr.m.watt@aberdeenshire.gov.uk

Webster, Jill (CON - Banchory & Mid-Deeside)
cllr.j.webster@aberdeenshire.gov.uk

POLITICAL COMPOSITION

SNP: 28, CON: 13, IND: 12, LD: 12, LAB: 2, SGP: 1

COMMITTEE CHAIRS

Education, Learning & Leisure: Ms Alison Evison
Scrutiny & Audit: Ms Gillian Owen
Social Work & Housing: Ms Anne Allan

Adur D

Adur District Council, Civic Centre, Ham Road, Shoreham-by-Sea BN43 6PR
☎ 01273 263000 info@adur.gov.uk www.adur.gov.uk

FACTS AND FIGURES

EU Constituencies: South East
Election Frequency: Elections are biennial

PRINCIPAL OFFICERS

Chief Executive: Mr Alex Bailey Chief Executive, Civic Centre, Ham Road, Shoreham-by-Sea BN43 6PR ☎ 01903 221001 alex.bailey@adur-worthing.gov.uk

Senior Management: Mr Paul Brewer Director - Digital & Resources, Worthing Town Hall, Chapel Road, Worthing BN11 1HA ☎ 01903 221302 paul.brewer@adur-worthing.gov.uk

Senior Management: Ms Jane Eckford Director - Customer Service, Worthing Town Hall, Chapel Road, Worthing BN11 1HA ☎ 01903 221059 jane.eckford@adur-worthing.gov.uk

Senior Management: Mr John Mitchell, Director - Communities, Worthing Town Hall, Chapel Road, Worthing BN11 1HA ☎ 01903 221049 john.mitchell@adur-worthing.gov.uk

Senior Management: Mr Martin Randall Director - Economy, Civic Centre, Ham Road, Shoreham-by-Sea BN43 6PR ☎ 01903 221209 martin.randall@adur-worthing.gov.uk

Architect, Building / Property Services: Mr Steve Spinner, Head of Business & Technical Services, Portland House, Richmond Road, Worthing BN11 1LF ☎ 01903 221019 steve.spinner@adur-worthing.gov.uk

Building Control: Mr James Appleton Head of Growth, Portland House, Richmond Road, Worthing BN11 1HS ☎ 01903 221333 james.appleton@adur-worthing.gov.uk

PR / Communications: Mr Neil Hopkins Head of Communications, Worthing Town Hall, Chapel Road, Worthing BN11 1HA ☎ neil.hopkins@adur-worthing.gov.uk

Community Planning: Mr Paul Pennicott Strategic Projects Officer, Worthing Town Hall, Chapel Road, Worthing BN11 1HA ☎ 01903 221347 paul.pennicott@adur-worthing.gov.uk

Community Safety: Mrs Jacqui Cooke, Safer Communities Manager, Worthing Town Hall, Chapel Road, Worthing BN11 1HA ☎ 08456 070999 jacqui.cooke@adur-worthing.gov.uk

Computer Management: Mr Mark Gawley CenSus IT Operations Manager, Worthing Town Hall, Chapel Road, Worthing BN11 1HA ☎ 01903 221477; 01903 221197 mark.gawley@adur-worthing.gov.uk

Contracts: Mr Steve Spinner, Head of Business & Technical Services, Portland House, Richmond Road, Worthing BN11 1LF ☎ 01903 221019 steve.spinner@adur-worthing.gov.uk

Corporate Services: Mr Paul Brewer Director - Digital & Resources, Worthing Town Hall, Chapel Road, Worthing BN11 1HA ☎ 01903 221302 paul.brewer@adur-worthing.gov.uk

Customer Service: Ms Jane Eckford Director - Customer Service, Worthing Town Hall, Chapel Road, Worthing BN11 1HA ☎ 01903 221059 jane.eckford@adur-worthing.gov.uk

Direct Labour: Mr Paul Brewer Director - Digital & Resources, Worthing Town Hall, Chapel Road, Worthing BN11 1HA ☎ 01903 221302 paul.brewer@adur-worthing.gov.uk

Economic Development: Ms Tina Barker Economic Development Officer, Commerce Way, Lancing BN15 8TA ☎ 01273 263206 tina.barker@adur-worthing.gov.uk

E-Government: Mr Paul Brewer Director - Digital & Resources, Worthing Town Hall, Chapel Road, Worthing BN11 1HA ☎ 01903 221302 paul.brewer@adur-worthing.gov.uk

Electoral Registration: Ms Teresa Bryant, Electoral Services Manager, Worthing Town Hall, Chapel Road, Worthing BH11 1HA ☎ 01903 221474 teresa.bryant@adur-worthing.gov.uk

Emergency Planning: Mr Lloyd Harris Emergency Planning Officer, Worthing Town Hall, Chapel Road, Worthing BN11 1HA ☎ 01903 221025 lloyd.harris@adur-worthing.gov.uk

Energy Management: Mr Paul Brewer Director - Digital & Resources, Worthing Town Hall, Chapel Road, Worthing BN11 1HA ☎ 01903 221302 paul.brewer@adur-worthing.gov.uk

Environmental / Technical Services: Mr Paul Brewer Director - Digital & Resources, Worthing Town Hall, Chapel Road, Worthing BN11 1HA ☎ 01903 221302 ✉ paul.brewer@adur-worthing.gov.uk

Environmental Health: Mr James Elliot Senior Environmental Health Officer, Portland House, Richmond Road, Worthing BN11 1HS ☎ 01273 263032 ✉ james.elliot@adur-worthing.gov.uk

Estates, Property & Valuation: Mr Scott Marshall Director for the Economy, Worthing Town Hall, Chapel Road, Worthing BN11 1HA ☎ 01903 221209 ✉ scott.marshall@adur-worthing.gov.uk

Events Manager: Ms Jo Osborne Events Manager for Culture, Worthing Town Hall, , Worthing BN11 1HA ☎ 01903 231799 ✉ jo.osborne@adur-worthing.gov.uk

Facilities: Mr Steve Spinner, Head of Business & Technical Services, Portland House, Richmond Road, Worthing BN11 1LF ☎ 01903 221019 ✉ steve.spinner@adur-worthing.gov.uk

Finance: Mrs Sarah Gobey Executive Head of Financial Services, Worthing Town Hall, Chapel Road, Worthing BN11 1HA ☎ 01903 221221 ✉ sarah.gobey@adur-worthing.gov.uk

Fleet Management: Ms Jane Eckford Director - Customer Service, Worthing Town Hall, Chapel Road, Worthing BN11 1HA ☎ 01903 221059 ✉ jane.eckford@adur-worthing.gov.uk

Grounds Maintenance: Mr Andy Edwards Head of Environment, Commerce Way, Lancing BN15 8TA ☎ 01273 263137 ✉ andy.edwards@adur-worthing.gov.uk

Health and Safety: Mrs Lesley Dexter Senior Corporate Safety Officer, Portland House, Richmond Road, Worthing BN11 1LF ☎ 01273 263430 ✉ lesley.dexter@adur-worthing.gov.uk

Housing: Mr Paul Cooper Head of Housing, Portland House, Richmond Road, Worthing BN11 1LF ☎ 01903 221190 ✉ paul.cooper@adur-worthing.gov.uk

Housing Maintenance: Mr Paul Cooper Head of Housing, Portland House, Richmond Road, Worthing BN11 1LF ☎ 01903 221190 ✉ paul.cooper@adur-worthing.gov.uk

Legal: Ms Susan Sale Solicitor to the Council, Worthing Town Hall, Chapel Road, Worthing BN11 1HA ☎ 01903 221119 ✉ susan.sale@adur-worthing.gov.uk

Leisure and Cultural Services: Ms Amanda O'Reilly Head of Culture, Worthing Town Hall, Chapel Road, Worthing BN11 1HA ☎ 01903 221142 ✉ amanda.o'reilly@adur-worthing.gov.uk

Licensing: Ms Theresa Cuerva Licensing Officer, Commerce Way, Lancing BN15 8TA ☎ 01273 263193 ✉ theresa.cuerva@adur-worthing.gov.uk

Lottery Funding, Charity and Voluntary: Mr John Phelps External Funding Policy Manager, Worthing Town Hall, Chapel Road, Worthing BN11 1HA ☎ 01903 221283 ✉ john.phelps@adur-worthing.gov.uk

Member Services: Mrs Julia Smith, Democratic Services Manager, Worthing Town Hall, Chapel Road, Worthing BN11 1HA ☎ 01903 221150 ✉ julia.smith@adur-worthing.gov.uk

Parking: Mr Ashley Miles Technical Assistant, Worthing Town Hall, Chapel Road, Worthing BN11 1HA ☎ 01903 221022 ✉ ashley.miles@adur-worthing.gov.uk

Partnerships: Mr Alex Bailey Chief Executive, Civic Centre, Ham Road, Shoreham-by-Sea BN43 6PR ☎ 01903 221001 ✉ alex.bailey@adur-worthing.gov.uk

Personnel / HR: Mr Paul Brewer Director - Digital & Resources, Worthing Town Hall, Chapel Road, Worthing BN11 1HA ☎ 01903 221302 ✉ paul.brewer@adur-worthing.gov.uk

Personnel / HR: Mrs Tracy Darey Human Resources Manager, Worthing Town Hall, Chapel Road, Worthing BN11 1HA ☎ 01273 263063 ✉ tracy.darey@adur-worthing.gov.uk

Planning: Mr James Appleton Head of Growth, Portland House, Richmond Road, Worthing BN11 1HS ☎ 01903 221333 ✉ james.appleton@adur-worthing.gov.uk

Procurement: Mr Bill Williamson Procurement Officer, Worthing Town Hall, Chapel Road, Worthing BN11 1HA ☎ 01903 221056 ✉ bill.williamson@adur-worthing.gov.uk

Recycling & Waste Minimisation: Ms Jane Eckford Director - Customer Service, Worthing Town Hall, Chapel Road, Worthing BN11 1HA ☎ 01903 221059 ✉ jane.eckford@adur-worthing.gov.uk

Regeneration: Mr Scott Marshall Director for the Economy, Worthing Town Hall, Chapel Road, Worthing BN11 1HA ☎ 01903 221209 ✉ scott.marshall@adur-worthing.gov.uk

Staff Training: Ms Lois Ford Learning & Development Co-ordinator, Worthing Town Hall, Chapel Road, Worthing BN11 1HA ☎ 01903 221043 ✉ lois.ford@adur-worthing.gov.uk

Street Scene: Mr David Steadman Adur Town Centre & Street Scene Co-ordinator, Civic Centre, Ham Road, Shoreham-by-Sea BN43 6PR ☎ 01273 263152 ✉ david.steadman@adur-worthing.gov.uk

Sustainable Communities: Mr James Appleton Head of Growth, Portland House, Richmond Road, Worthing BN11 1HS ☎ 01903 221333 ✉ james.appleton@adur-worthing.gov.uk

Sustainable Development: Mr James Appleton Head of Growth, Portland House, Richmond Road, Worthing BN11 1HS ☎ 01903 221333 ✉ james.appleton@adur-worthing.gov.uk

Tourism: Ms Amanda O'Reilly Head of Culture, Worthing Town Hall, Chapel Road, Worthing BN11 1HA ☎ 01903 221142 ✉ amanda.o'reilly@adur-worthing.gov.uk

Town Centre: Mr David Steadman Adur Town Centre & Street Scene Co-ordinator, Civic Centre, Ham Road, Shoreham-by-Sea BN43 6PR ☎ 01273 263152 ✉ david.steadman@adur-worthing.gov.uk

Waste Collection and Disposal: Mr Paul Willis Waste Strategy Manager, Worthing Town Hall, Chapel Road, Worthing BN11 1HA
☎ 01903 223052 ✉ paul.willis@adur-worthing.gov.uk

Waste Management: Mr Paul Willis Waste Strategy Manager, Worthing Town Hall, Chapel Road, Worthing BN11 1HA
☎ 01903 223052 ✉ paul.willis@adur-worthing.gov.uk

COUNCILLORS

***Chair* Albury**, Carson (CON - Peverel)
carson.albury@adur.gov.uk

***Vice-Chair* Bridges**, Ann (CON - Widewater)
ann.bridges@adur.gov.uk

***Leader of the Council* Parkin**, Neil (CON - St Nicolas)
neil.parkin@adur.gov.uk

***Deputy Leader of the Council* Dunn**, Angus (CON - Hillside)
angus.dunn@adur.gov.uk

Albury, Carol (CON - Manor)
carol.albury@adur.gov.uk

Beresford, Pat (CON - Churchill)
pat.beresford@adur.gov.uk

Bishop, Ken (UKIP - Southlands)
ken.bishop@adur.gov.uk

Boggis, Brian (CON - Peverel)
brian.boggis@adur.gov.uk

Butcher, James (CON - Churchill)
james.butcher@adur.gov.uk

Chipp, Stephen (CON - St Mary's)
stephen.chipp@adur.gov.uk

Coomber, Brian (CON - St Nicolas)
brian.coomber@adur.gov.uk

Dollemore, Keith (CON - Manor)
keith.dollemore@adur.gov.uk

Donaldson, David (CON - Eastbrook)
david.donaldson@adur-worthing.gov.uk

Evans, Emma (CON - Buckingham)
emma.evans@adur.gov.uk

Funnell, Jim (CON - Eastbrook)
jim.funnell@adur.gov.uk

Graysmark, Paul (CON - Southlands)
paul.graysmark@adur.gov.uk

Haywood, Liz (UKIP - Mash Barn)
liz.haywood@adur.gov.uk

Hilditch, Emily (CON - Southwick Green)
emily.hilditch@adur.gov.uk

Hotton, Rod (CON - St Mary's)
rod.hotton@adur.gov.uk

Kennard, Debbie (CON - Buckingham)
debbie.kennard@adur.gov.uk

Lambourne, David (UKIP - Mash Barn)
david.lambourne@adur.gov.uk

Lewis, Fred (CON - Widewater)
fred.lewis@adur.gov.uk

McKinney, Liza (IND - Marine)
liza.mckinney@adur.gov.uk

Mear, Barry (LAB - Cokeham)
barry.mear@adur-worthing.gov.uk

Metcalfe, Peter (CON - Southwick Green)
peter.metcalfe@adur.gov.uk

Patmore, Geoff (UKIP - Widewater)
geoff.patmore@adur.gov.uk

Phillips, Lyn (UKIP - Cokeham)
lyn.phillips@adur.gov.uk

Simmons, David (CON - Hillside)
david.simmons@adur.gov.uk

Stride, Ben (IND - Marine)
ben.stride@adur.gov.uk

POLITICAL COMPOSITION

CON: 21, UKIP: 5, IND: 2, LAB: 1

COMMITTEE CHAIRS

Licensing: Mrs Emma Evans

Planning: Mr Brian Boggis

Allerdale D

Allerdale Borough Council, Allerdale House, Workington CA14 3YJ
☎ 01900 702702 🖷 01900 702507 💻 www.allerdale.gov.uk

FACTS AND FIGURES

Parliamentary Constituencies: Penrith and The Border, Workington
EU Constituencies: North West
Election Frequency: Elections are of whole council

PRINCIPAL OFFICERS

Chief Executive: Mr Ian Frost Chief Executive, Allerdale House, Workington CA14 3YJ ☎ 01900 702975 ✉ ian.frost@allerdale.gov.uk

Senior Management: Mr Andrew Seekings Corporate Director, Allerdale House, Workington CA14 3YJ ☎ 01900 702528
✉ andrew.seekings@allerdale.gov.uk

Architect, Building / Property Services: Mr David Bryden Construction Services Manager - Property Services, Allerdale House, Workington CA14 3YJ ☎ 01900 702753
✉ david.bryden@allerdale.gov.uk

Building Control: Mr Kevin Kerrigan Head of Development Services, Allerdale House, Workington CA14 3YJ ☎ 01900 702799
✉ kevin.kerrigan@allerdale.gov.uk

PR / Communications: Mr Andrew Gilbert Communications & Marketing Manager, Allerdale House, Workington CA14 3YJ
☎ 01900 702701 ✉ andrew.gilbert@allerdale.gov.uk

Community Safety: Mr Charles Holmes Head of Community Services, Allerdale House, Workington CA14 3YJ ☎ 01900 702959
✉ charles.holmes@allerdale.gov.uk

ALLERDALE

Computer Management: Mr Paul Wood Head of Organisational Development & Transformation, Allerdale House, Workington CA14 3YJ ☎ 01900 702889 🖱 paul.wood@allerdale.gov.uk

Customer Service: Ms Colette Symes Customer Services Team Leader, Allerdale House, Workington CA14 3YJ ☎ 01900 702702 🖱 colette.eymes@allerdale.gov.uk

Electoral Registration: Mr Andrew Seekings Corporate Director, Allerdale House, Workington CA14 3YJ ☎ 01900 702528 🖱 andrew.seekings@allerdale.gov.uk

Emergency Planning: Mr Graeme Wilson Head of Housing & Health, Allerdale House, Workington CA14 3YJ ☎ 01900 702661 🖱 graeme.wilson@allerdale.gov.uk

Environmental Health: Mr Graeme Wilson Head of Housing & Health, Allerdale House, Workington CA14 3YJ ☎ 01900 702661 🖱 graeme.wilson@allerdale.gov.uk

Estates, Property & Valuation: Ms Linda Doyle Valuation Officer, Allerdale House, Workington CA14 3YJ ☎ 01900 702762 🖱 linda.doyle@allerdale.gov.uk

Finance: Ms Catherine Nicholson Head of Finance, Allerdale House, Workington CA14 3YJ ☎ 01900 702503 🖱 catherine.nicholson@allerdale.gov.uk

Treasury: Mr John Kemp Treasurer, Allerdale House, Workington CA14 3YJ ☎ 01900 702702 🖱 john.kemp@allerdale.gov.uk

Health and Safety: Mr Barry Chambers Corporate Health & Safety Advisor, Allerdale House, Workington CA14 3YJ ☎ 01900 702599 🖱 barry.chambers@allerdale.gov.uk

Housing: Mr Graeme Wilson Head of Housing & Health, Allerdale House, Workington CA14 3YJ ☎ 01900 702661 🖱 graeme.wilson@allerdale.gov.uk

Legal: Ms Sharon Sewell Head of Governance, Allerdale House, Workington CA14 3YJ ☎ 01900 702887 🖱 sharon.sewell@allerdale.gov.uk

Leisure and Cultural Services: Ms Rebecca Stamper Sport Development Officer, Allerdale House, Workington CA14 3YJ ☎ 0190 702711 🖱 rebecca.stamper@allerdale.gov.uk

Licensing: Ms Gillian Collinson, Senior Land Charges & Licensing Officer, Allerdale House, Workington CA14 3YJ ☎ 01900 702692 🖷 01900 702698 🖱 gillian.collinson@allerdale.gov.uk

Member Services: Ms Gayle Roach Democratic Services Co-ordinator, Allerdale House, Workington CA14 3YJ ☎ 01900 702817 🖱 gayle.roach@allerdale.gov.uk

Parking: Mr Mike Rollo Parking Operations Manager, Allerdale House, Workington CA14 3YJ ☎ 01900 702859 🖱 mike.rollo@allerdale.gov.uk

Personnel / HR: Ms Zoe Pluckrose Head of People Resources, Allerdale House, Workington CA14 3YJ ☎ 01900 702725 🖱 zoe.pluckrose@allerdale.gov.uk

Planning: Mr Kevin Kerrigan Head of Development Services, Allerdale House, Workington CA14 3YJ ☎ 01900 702799 🖱 kevin.kerrigan@allerdale.gov.uk

Regeneration: Mr Nik Hardy Head of Economic Growth, Allerdale House, Workington CA14 3YJ ☎ 01900 702778 🖱 nik.hardy@allerdale.gov.uk

Street Scene: Mr Robert Henderson Locality Officer, Allerdale House, Workington CA14 3YJ ☎ 01900 702819 🖱 robert.henderson@allerdale.gov.uk

Town Centre: Mr Joe Broomfield Joint Town Centre Manager, Allerdale House, Workington CA14 3YJ ☎ 01900 702766 🖱 joe.broomfield@allerdale.gov.uk

Town Centre: Ms Toni Magean Town Centre Manager, Allerdale House, Workington CA14 3YJ ☎ 01900 702568 🖱 toni.magean@allerdale.gov.uk

Waste Management: Mr Charles Holmes Head of Community Services, Allerdale House, Workington CA14 3YJ ☎ 01900 702959 🖱 charles.holmes@allerdale.gov.uk

COUNCILLORS

***Mayor* Davies**, Len (LAB - All Saints Cockermouth)
len.davies@allerdale.gov.uk

***Leader of the Council* Smith**, Alan (LAB - All Saints Cockermouth)
alan.smith@allerdale.gov.uk

***Deputy Leader of the Council* Fryer**, Mark (LAB - Stainburn Workington)
mark.fryer@allerdale.gov.uk

***Group Leader* Finlay**, Bill (IND - Aspatria)
bill.finlay@allerdale.gov.uk

***Group Leader* Wilson**, David (UKIP - Aspatria)
david.wilson@allerdale.gov.uk

Annison, Tony (CON - Crummock)
anthony.annison@allerdale.gov.uk

Armstrong, Carole (LAB - Moss Bay Workington)
carole.armstrong@allerdale.gov.uk

Bacon, Bill (LAB - Moss Bay Workington)
bill.bacon@allerdale.gov.uk

Bainbridge, Mary (LAB - St Michaels Workington)
mary.bainbridge@allerdale.gov.uk

Bales, Peter (LAB - Moorclose Workington)
peter.bales@allerdale.gov.uk

Cannon, Barbara (LAB - Moss Bay Workington)
barbara.cannon@allerdale.gov.uk

Cockburn, Nicky (IND - Broughton St Bridgets)
nicky.cockburn@allerdale.gov.uk

Colhoun, John (LAB - Ellen)
john.colhoun@allerdale.gov.uk

Cook, John (CON - Silloth)
john.cook@allerdale.gov.uk

Cowell, Joseph (CON - Wigton)
joe.cowell@allerdale.gove uk

Crouch, John (LAB - Wigton)
john.crouch@allerdale.gov.uk

Davis-Johnston, Adrian (CON - Derwent Valley)
adrian.davis-johnston@allerdale.gov.uk

Fairbairn, Duncan (CON - Warnell)
duncan.fairbairn@allerdale.gov.uk

Farebrother, Janet (LAB - Broughton St Bridgets)
janet.farebrother@allerdale.gov.uk

Grainger, Malcolm (CON - Boltons)
malcolm.grainger@allerdale.gov.uk

Hansen, Konrad (LAB - St Johns Workington)
konrad.hansen@allerdale.gov.uk

Harrington, Hilary (IND - Harrington Workington)
hilary.harrington@allerdale.gov.uk

Heaslip, Michael (LAB - St Johns Workington)
michael.heaslip@allerdale.gov.uk

Hedworth, Alan (CON - Waver)
alan.hedworth@allerdale.gov.uk

Hodgson, Vaughan (CON - Marsh)
vaughan.hodgson@allerdale.gov.uk

Holliday, Joe (IND - St Johns Workington)
joe.holliday@allerdale.gov.uk

Jackson, Margaret (CON - Christchurch Cockermouth)
margaret.jackson@allerdale.gov.uk

Jefferson, William (IND - Silloth)
william.jefferson@allerdale.gov.uk

Jenkinson, Mark (UKIP - Seaton)
mark.jenkinson@allerdale.gov.uk

Kendall, Peter (LAB - Flimby)
peter.kendall@allerdale.gov.uk

Kendall, Angela (LAB - Netherhall Maryport)
angela.kendall@allerdale.gov.uk

Lister, Jim (CON - Solway)
jim.lister@allerdale.gov.uk

Lywood, Tony (LAB - Keswick)
tony.lywood@allerdale.gov.uk

Macdonald, Patricia (CON - Wampool)
patricia.macdonald@allerdale.gov.uk

Maguire, Lousie (LAB - Ellen)
louise.maguire@allerdale.gov.uk

Markley, Anthony (CON - Holme)
anthony.markley@allerdale.gov.uk

McCarron-Holmes, Carni (LAB - Ewanrigg Maryport)
carni.mccarron-holmes@allerdale.gov.uk

Miskelly, Billy (LAB - St Michaels Workington)
billy.miskelly@allerdale.gov.uk

Mounsey, Jacqueline (CON - Wharrels)
jacqueline.mounsey@allerdale.gov.uk

Munby, Ronald (CON - Keswick)
ron.munby@allerdale.gov.uk

Nicholson, Eric (CON - Christchurch Cockermouth)
eric.nicholson@allerdale.gov.uk

Osborn, Jim (LAB - Harrington Workington)
jim.osborn@allerdale.gove.uk

Pegram, Bill (LAB - Netherhall Maryport)
bill.pegram@allerdale.gov.uk

Pitcher, Alan (CON - Wigton)
alan.pitcher@allerdale.gov.uk

Pugmire, Martin (IND - Keswick)
martin.pugmire@allerdale.gov.uk

Robertson, Denis (IND - Moorclose Workington)
denis.robertson@allerdale.gov.uk

Sandwith, Joe (UKIP - Seaton)
joe.sandwith@allerdale.gov.uk

Scholfield, Neil (LAB - St Michaels Workington)
neil.scholfield@llerdale.gov.uk

Sharpe, Colin (CON - Dalton)
colin.sharpe@allerdale.gov.uk

Smith, Christine (LAB - All Saints Cockermouth)
christine.smith@allerdale.gov.uk

Stoddart, Stephen (IND - Moorclose Workington)
stephen.stoddart@allerdale.gov.uk

Tibble, Philip (LAB - Clifton)
philip.tibble@allerdale.gov.uk

Tibble, Celia (LAB - Seaton)
celia.tibble@allerdale.gov.uk

Williamson, Lee (LAB - Ewanrigg Maryport)
lee.williamson@allerdale.gov.uk

Wood, Janice (LAB - Ellenborough Maryport)
janice.wood@allerdale.gov.uk

Wood, Martin (LAB - Ellenborough Maryport)
martin.wood@allerdale.gov.uk

POLITICAL COMPOSITION
LAB: 28, CON: 17, IND: 8, UKIP: 3

COMMITTEE CHAIRS
Audit: Ms Mary Bainbridge

Development: Mr Peter Bales

Licensing: Mrs Angela Kendall

Amber Valley D

Amber Valley Borough Council, Po Box 17, Town Hall, Ripley DE5 3BT
☎ 01773 570222 🖷 01773 841616 ✉ enquiry@ambervalley.gov.uk
💻 www.ambervalley.gov.uk

FACTS AND FIGURES
Parliamentary Constituencies: Amber Valley
EU Constituencies: East Midlands
Election Frequency: Elections are by thirds

PRINCIPAL OFFICERS
Senior Management: Mr Julian Townsend, Executive Director - Operations, Town Hall, Market Place, Ripley DE5 3BT ☎ 01773 841316 ✉ julian.townsend@ambervalley.gov.uk

AMBER VALLEY

Architect, Building / Property Services: Mr Simon Gladwin Assistant Director - Landscape Services, Town Hall, Market Place, Ripley DE5 3BT ☎ 01773 841415 simon.gladwin@ambervalley.gov.uk

Best Value: Ms Sylvia Delahay, Executive Director - Resources, PO Box 1, Town Hall, Market Place, Ripley DE5 3BT ☎ 01773 841610 sylvia.delahay@ambervalley.gov.uk

Building Control: Mr Dave Chard, Building Control Manager, Town Hall, Market Place, Ripley DE5 3BT ☎ 01773 841513 dave.chard@ambervalley.gov.uk

Community Planning: Mr Derek Stafford, Assistant Director - Planning & Regeneration, Town Hall, Market Place, Ripley DE5 3BT ☎ 01773 841581 derek.stafford@ambervalley.gov.uk

Community Safety: Ms Sally Price Community Safety Officer, Town Hall, Market Place, Ripley DE5 3BT ☎ 01773 841652 sally.price@ambervalley.gov.uk

Computer Management: Mr Carl Marples IT Operations & Support Manager, PO Box 1, Town Hall, Market Place, Ripley DE5 3BT ☎ 01773 841347 carl.marples@ambervalley.gov.uk

Corporate Services: Ms Sylvia Delahay, Executive Director - Resources, PO Box 1, Town Hall, Market Place, Ripley DE5 3BT ☎ 01773 841610 sylvia.delahay@ambervalley.gov.uk

Customer Service: Ms Olive Green, Head of Customer Services & Exchequer, PO Box 1, Town Hall, Market Place, Ripley DE5 3BT ☎ 01773 841614 olive.green@ambervalley.gov.uk

Economic Development: Mr Stephen Jackson Regeneration Manager, Town Hall, Market Place, Ripley DE5 3BT ☎ 01773 841520 stephen.jackson@ambervalley.gov.uk

E-Government: Mr Andy Wilde, Information Development Manager, PO Box 1, Town Hall, Market Place, Ripley DE5 3BT ☎ 01773 570222 andy.wilde@ambervalley.gov.uk

Electoral Registration: Ms Jill Harris Democratic Services Officer - Elections, Po Box 17, Town Hall, Ripley DE5 3BT ☎ 01773 841634 jill.harris@ambervalley.gov.uk

Emergency Planning: Ms Helen Holmes Emergency Planning Officer, Town Hall, Market Place, Ripley DE5 3BT ☎ 01773 570222 helen.holmes@ambervalley.gov.uk

Energy Management: Mrs Sharon Hampson Facilities & Energy Co-ordinator, Town Hall, Market Place, Ripley DE5 3BT ☎ 01773 841563 sharon.hampson@ambervalley.gov.uk

Environmental / Technical Services: Mr Julian Townsend, Executive Director - Operations, Town Hall, Market Place, Ripley DE5 3BT ☎ 01773 841316 julian.townsend@ambervalley.gov.uk

Environmental Health: Mr Julian Townsend, Executive Director - Operations, Town Hall, Market Place, Ripley DE5 3BT ☎ 01773 841316 julian.townsend@ambervalley.gov.uk

Estates, Property & Valuation: Ms Marie Winter Legal Executive - Property & Contracts, Po Box 17, Town Hall, Ripley DE5 3BT ☎ 01773 841643 marie.winter@ambervalley.gov.uk

Events Manager: Mrs Joanne Bamford Town Centres Development Officer, Town Hall, Market Place, Ripley DE5 3BT ☎ 01773 841485 joanne.bamford@ambervalley.gov.uk

Facilities: Mrs Sharon Hampson Facilities & Energy Co-ordinator, Town Hall, Market Place, Ripley DE5 3BT ☎ 01773 841563 sharon.hampson@ambervalley.gov.uk

Finance: Ms Sylvia Delahay, Executive Director - Resources, PO Box 1, Town Hall, Market Place, Ripley DE5 3BT ☎ 01773 841610 sylvia.delahay@ambervalley.gov.uk

Treasury: Ms Sylvia Delahay, Executive Director - Resources, PO Box 1, Town Hall, Market Place, Ripley DE5 3BT ☎ 01773 841610 sylvia.delahay@ambervalley.gov.uk

Fleet Management: Mr Shane Staley Fleet & Depot Officer, Town Hall, Market Place, Ripley DE5 3BT ☎ 01773 841491 shane.staley@ambervalley.gov.uk

Grounds Maintenance: Mr Simon Gladwin Assistant Director - Landscape Services, Town Hall, Market Place, Ripley DE5 3BT ☎ 01773 841415 simon.gladwin@ambervalley.gov.uk

Health and Safety: Mr Brian Shore Safety & Resilience Advisor, Town Hall, Market Place, Ripley DE5 3BT ☎ 01773 841668 brian.shore@ambervalley.gov.uk

Home Energy Conservation: Ms Joanne Walker, Housing Officer, Town Hall, Market Place, Ripley DE5 3BT ☎ 01773 841332 joanne.walker@ambervalley.gov.uk

Housing: Mr David Arkle Housing Manager, Town Hall, Market Place, Ripley DE5 3BT ☎ 01773 841334 david.arkle@ambervalley.gov.uk

Legal: Mrs Anne Brown Assistant Director - Legal & Democratic Services, Po Box 17, Town Hall, Ripley DE5 3BT ☎ 01773 841397 anne.brown@ambervalley.gov.uk

Leisure and Cultural Services: Mr Kirk Monk Assistant Director - Wellbeing, Town Hall, Market Place, Ripley DE5 3BT ☎ 01773 841646 kirk.monk@ambervalley.gov.uk

Licensing: Ms Heather Adams Licensing Manager, Town Hall, Market Place, Ripley DE5 3BT ☎ 01773 841602 heather.adams@ambervalley.gov.uk

Lottery Funding, Charity and Voluntary: Mr Stephen Jackson Regeneration Manager, Town Hall, Market Place, Ripley DE5 3BT ☎ 01773 841520 stephen.jackson@ambervalley.gov.uk

Member Services: Mr Paul Benski Democratic Services Manager, Po Box 17, Town Hall, Ripley DE5 3BT ☎ 01773 841641 paul.benski@ambervalley.gov.uk

Parking: Ms Pam Leigh Central Operations Team Leader, Town Hall, Market Place, Ripley DE5 3BT ☎ 01773 841437 ✉ pam.leigh@ambervalley.gov.uk

Partnerships: Mr Julian Townsend, Executive Director - Operations, Town Hall, Market Place, Ripley DE5 3BT ☎ 01773 841316 ✉ julian.townsend@ambervalley.gov.uk

Personnel / HR: Ms Sylvia Delahay, Executive Director - Resources, PO Box 1, Town Hall, Market Place, Ripley DE5 3BT ☎ 01773 841610 ✉ sylvia.delahay@ambervalley.gov.uk

Planning: Mr Derek Stafford, Assistant Director - Planning & Regeneration, Town Hall, Market Place, Ripley DE5 3BT ☎ 01773 841581 ✉ derek.stafford@ambervalley.gov.uk

Procurement: Ms Sylvia Delahay, Executive Director - Resources, PO Box 1, Town Hall, Market Place, Ripley DE5 3BT ☎ 01773 841610 ✉ sylvia.delahay@ambervalley.gov.uk

Recycling & Waste Minimisation: Ms Theresa Barnes Principal Waste Performance & Recycling Officer, Town Hall, Market Place, Ripley DE5 3BT ☎ 01773 841323 ✉ theresa.barnes@ambervalley.gov.uk

Regeneration: Mr Stephen Jackson Regeneration Manager, Town Hall, Market Place, Ripley DE5 3BT ☎ 01773 841520 ✉ stephen.jackson@ambervalley.gov.uk

Street Scene: Mrs Sharon Sutton Landscape Development Manager, Town Hall, Market Place, Ripley DE5 3BT ☎ 01773 841570 ✉ sharon.sutton@ambervalley.gov.uk

Sustainable Communities: Mr Derek Stafford, Assistant Director - Planning & Regeneration, Town Hall, Market Place, Ripley DE5 3BT ☎ 01773 841581 ✉ derek.stafford@ambervalley.gov.uk

Sustainable Development: Mr Derek Stafford, Assistant Director - Planning & Regeneration, Town Hall, Market Place, Ripley DE5 3BT ☎ 01773 841581 ✉ derek.stafford@ambervalley.gov.uk

Tourism: Mrs Joanne Bamford Town Centres Development Officer, Town Hall, Market Place, Ripley DE5 3BT ☎ 01773 841485 ✉ joanne.bamford@ambervalley.gov.uk

Town Centre: Mr Simon Gladwin Assistant Director - Landscape Services, Town Hall, Market Place, Ripley DE5 3BT ☎ 01773 841415 ✉ simon.gladwin@ambervalley.gov.uk

Waste Collection and Disposal: Mr Ian Shaw, Environment Manager, Town Hall, Ripley DE5 3BT ☎ 01773 841324 ✉ ian.shaw@ambervalley.gov.uk

Waste Management: Mr Ian Shaw, Environment Manager, Town Hall, Ripley DE5 3BT ☎ 01773 841324 ✉ ian.shaw@ambervalley.gov.uk

Children's Play Areas: Mr Simon Gladwin Assistant Director - Landscape Services, Town Hall, Market Place, Ripley DE5 3BT ☎ 01773 841415 ✉ simon.gladwin@ambervalley.gov.uk

COUNCILLORS

***Mayor* Ainsworth**, Trevor (CON - Kilburn, Denby & Holbrook)
cllr.trevor.ainsworth@ambervalley.gov.uk

***Leader of the Council* Cox**, Alan (CON - Belper North)
cllr.alan.cox@ambervalley.gov.uk

***Deputy Leader of the Council* Wilson**, David (CON - Swanwick)
david.wilson@ambervalley.gov.uk

Ainstrop, Barrie (LAB - Heanor East)
cllr.barrie.aistrop@ambervalley.gov.uk

Ashton, Ron (CON - Ripley & Marehay)
ron.ashton@ambervalley.gov.uk

Bennett, Marlene (LAB - Alfreton)
cllr.marlene.bennett@ambervalley.gov.uk

Booth, Dan (CON - Belper Central)
daniel.booth@ambervalley.gov.uk

Booth, Joseph (CON - Belper North)
joseph.booth@ambervalley.gov.uk

Bull, Norman (CON - Kilburn, Denby & Holbrook)
cllr.norman.bull@ambervalley.gov.uk

Buttery, Kevin (CON - Kilburn, Denby & Holbrook)
cllr.kevin.buttery@ambervalley.gov.uk

Cox, Celia (LAB - Heanor West)
cllr.celia.cox@ambervalley.gov.uk

Cox, Jackie (CON - Belper East)
cllr.jackie.cox@ambervalley.gov.uk

Dolman, Gail (LAB - Alfreton)
cllr.gail.dolman@ambervalley.gov.uk

Emmas-Williams, Christopher (LAB - Codnor & Waingroves)
cllr.chris.emmas-williams@ambervalley.gov.uk

Emmas-Williams, Roland (LAB - Ripley)
cllr.roland.emmas-williams@ambervalley.gov.uk

Evanson, Steven (CON - Duffield)
steven.evanson@ambervalley.gov.uk

Gee, Gareth (CON - Crich)
cllr.gareth.gee@ambervalley.gov.uk

Gration, Brian (LAB - Langley Mill & Aldercar)
cllr.brian.gration@ambervalley.gov.uk

Hamilton, Eileen (LAB - Langley Mill & Aldercar)
cllr.eileen.hamilton@ambervalley.gov.uk

Harry, Isobel (LAB - Codnor & Waingroves)
cllr.isobel.harry@ambervalley.gov.uk

Hayes, Stephen (CON - Swanwick)
cllr.stephen.hayes@ambervalley.gov.uk

Hillier, Paul (CON - Belper South)
paul.hillier@ambervalley.gov.uk

Holmes, Tony (LAB - Ripley)
cllr.tony.holmes@ambervalley.gov.uk

Iliffe, Richard (CON - Shipley Park, Horsley & Horsley Woodhouse)
cllr.richard.iliffe@ambervalley.gov.uk

Johnsen, Erik (LAB - Belper South)
cllr.erik.johnsen@ambervalley.gov.uk

Jones, Paul (LAB - Heanor West)
cllr.paul.jones@ambervalley.gov.uk

Longden, Heather (LAB - Heanor & Loscoe)
cllr.heather.longden@ambervalley.gov.uk

AMBER VALLEY

Longdon, Alan (LAB - Heanor & Loscoe)
cllr.alan.longdon@ambervalley.gov.uk

Lyttle, Brian (LAB - Somercotes)
cllr.brian.lyttle@ambervalley.gov.uk

McCabe, John (LAB - Somercotes)
cllr.john.mccabe@ambervalley.gov.uk

Moss, Paul (CON - Ripley)
paul.moss@ambervalley.gov.uk

Nelson, John (CON - Belper Central)
cllr.john.nelson@ambervalley.gov.uk

Oakes, Sheila (LAB - Heanor East)
cllr.sheila.oakes@ambervalley.gov.uk

Orton, Jane (CON - South West Parishes)
cllr.jane.orton@ambervalley.gov.uk

Short, Christopher (CON - Duffield)
cllr.chris.short@ambervalley.gov.uk

Smith, Paul (LAB - Ironville & Riddings)
cllr.paul.smith@ambervalley.gov.uk

Stevenson, Alex (CON - Shipley Park, Horsley & Horsley Woodhouse)
cllr.alex.stevenson@ambervalley.gov.uk

Taylor, Valerie (CON - Heage & Ambergate)
valerie.taylor@ambervalley.gov.uk

Taylor, David (CON - Alport)
cllr.david.taylor@ambervalley.gov.uk

Thorpe, Valerie (CON - Wingfield)
cllr.valerie.thorpe@ambervalley.gov.uk

Tomlinson, Martin (CON - Belper East)
cllr.martin.tomlinson@ambervalley.gov.uk

Walker, John (LAB - Alfreton)
cllr.john.walker@ambervalley.gov.uk

Walker, Roy (LAB - Ironville & Riddings)
cllr.roy.walker@ambervalley.gov.uk

Ward, Angela (CON - Heage & Ambergate)
cllr.angela.ward@ambervalley.gov.uk

Wilson, Mick (LAB - Ripley & Marehay)
cllr.mick.wilson@ambervalley.gov.uk

POLITICAL COMPOSITION

CON: 24, LAB: 21

COMMITTEE CHAIRS

Audit: Mr Christopher Short

Licensing: Ms Jackie Cox

Planning: Mr Alan Cox

Angus S

Angus Council, Council Headquarters, The Cross, Forfar DD8 1BX
☎ 01307 461460 🖷 01307 461874 ✉ chiefexec@angus.gov.uk
💻 www.angus.gov.uk

FACTS AND FIGURES

Parliamentary Constituencies: Angus, Dundee West
EU Constituencies: Scotland
Election Frequency: Elections are of whole council

PRINCIPAL OFFICERS

Chief Executive: Mr Richard Stiff Chief Executive, Angus House, Orchardbank Business Park, Forfar DD8 1AX ☎ 01307 476101 🖷 01370 476140 ✉ chiefexec@angus.gov.uk

Deputy Chief Executive: Mr Mark Armstrong Strategic Director - Resources, Angus House, Orchardbank Business Park, Forfar DD8 1AX ☎ 01307 476469 🖷 01307 476140 ✉ armstrongm@angus.gov.uk

Senior Management: Mr Mark Armstrong Strategic Director - Resources, Angus House, Orchardbank Business Park, Forfar DD8 1AX ☎ 01307 476469 🖷 01307 476140 ✉ armstrongm@angus.gov.uk

Senior Management: Mr Alan McKeown, Strategic Director - Communities, Angus House, Orchardbank Business Park, Forfar DD8 1AX ☎ 01307 474711 🖷 01307 476140 ✉ mckeowna@angus.gov.uk

Senior Management: Mrs Margo Williamson Strategic Director - People, Angus House, Orchardbank Business Park, Forfar DD8 1AX ☎ 01307 476468 🖷 01307 476140 ✉ williamsonm@angus.gov.uk

Access Officer / Social Services (Disability): Ms Fiona Rennie Service Manager - People Directorate, Ravenswood, Forfar DD8 2ZG ☎ 01307 473130 ✉ rennief@angus.gov.uk

Architect, Building / Property Services: Mr Ken Brown Service Manager - Property & Communities Directorate, Bruce House, Wellgate, Arbroath DD11 3TP ☎ 01241 43500 ✉ brownka@angus.gov.uk

Building Control: Mr Iain Mitchell, Service Manager - Communities Directorate, County Buildings, Market Street, Forfar DD8 3LG ☎ 01307 473290 🖷 01307 461895 ✉ mitchelli@angus.gov.uk

Catering Services: Ms Fiona Dawson Catering Advisor, Angus House, Orchardbank Business Park, Forfar DD8 1AE ☎ 01307 461460 ✉ dawsonf@angus.gov.uk

Children / Youth Services: Mr Tim Armstrong Head of Children & Young People's Services, Ravenswood, New Road, Forfar DD8 2ZG ☎ 01307 462405 🖷 01307 461261 ✉ armstrongt@angus.gov.uk

Civil Registration: Ms Sandra Pattie Chief Registrar - Resources Directorate, 9 West High Street, Forfar DD8 1BD ☎ 01307 464973 ✉ patties@angus.gov.uk

PR / Communications: Ms Moira Naulty, Communications Manager, Angus House, Orchardbank Business Park, Forfar DD8 1AX ☎ 01307 476090 🖷 01307 476140 ✉ naultym@angus.gov.uk

Community Planning: Ms Vivien Smith, Head of Planning & Place - Communities Directorate, William Wallace House, Orchardbank Business Park, Forfar DD8 1WH ☎ 01307 476105 🖷 01307 476140 ✉ smithv@angus.gov.uk

Community Safety: Mr Bob Myles Service Manager - Community Safety, The Mart, 13 Market Street, Forfar DD8 3EY ☎ 01307 477470 🖷 01307 462590 ✉ mylesb@angus.gov.uk

Computer Management: Mr Steve Roud Service Manager - Resources, Angus House, Orchardbank Business Park, Forfar DD8 1AX ☎ 01307 476406 ✉ rouds@angus.gov.uk

Consumer Protection and Trading Standards: Mr Stewart Ball Service Manager - Regulatory & Protective Services, County Buildings, Market Street, Forfar DD8 3WR ☎ 01307 473213 ✉ ballsl@angus.gov.uk

Economic Development: Ms Alison Smith, Service Manager - Economic Development, County Buildings, Market Street, Forfar DD8 3WD ☎ 01307 473222 ✉ smithaj@angus.gov.uk

Education: Ms Pauline Stephen Head of Schools & Learning, Angus House, Orchardbank Business Park, Forfar DD8 1AX ☎ 01307 467347 ✉ stephenp@angus.gov.uk

Electoral Registration: Mrs Shona Cameron, Elections & Business Support Manager, Angus House, Orchardbank Business Park, Forfar DD8 1AN ☎ 01307 476226 🖷 01307 476299 ✉ cameronsd@angus.gov.uk

Emergency Planning: Ms Jacqui Semple, Resilience Manager, Angus House, Orchardbank Business Park, Forfar DD8 1AX ☎ 01307 476123 🖷 01307 476140 ✉ semplej@angus.gov.uk

Energy Management: Mr Ken Brown Service Manager - Property & Communities Directorate, Bruce House, Wellgate, Arbroath DD11 3TP ☎ 01241 43500 ✉ brownka@angus.gov.uk

Environmental Health: Mr Stewart Ball Service Manager - Regulatory & Protective Services, County Buildings, Market Street, Forfar DD8 3WR ☎ 01307 473213 ✉ ballsl@angus.gov.uk

Estates, Property & Valuation: Mr Neil MacKenzie Principal Estates Manager, Bruce House, Wellgate, Arbroath DD11 3TP ☎ 01307 435037 ✉ mackenzien@angus.gov.uk

European Liaison: Ms Shelley Hague Senior External Funding Officer, Angus House, Orchardbank Business Park, Forfar DD8 1AX ☎ 01307 473222 ✉ hagues@angus.gov.uk

Events Manager: Ms Jacqui Semple, Resilience Manager, Angus House, Orchardbank Business Park, Forfar DD8 1AX ☎ 01307 476123 🖷 01307 476140 ✉ semplej@angus.gov.uk

Finance: Mr Ian Lorimer, Head of Finance, Angus House, Orchardbank Business Park, Forfar DD8 1AF ☎ 01307 476222 🖷 01307 476216 ✉ lorimeri@angus.gov.uk

Fleet Management: Mr Graham Robertson Fleet Manager, Burgh Yard, Cairnie Loan, Arbroath DD11 4DS ☎ 01241 876736 ✉ robertsong@angus.gov.uk

Grounds Maintenance: Mr Kevin Robertson Service Manager - Parks & Burial Grounds, The Mart, 13 Market Street, Forfar DD8 3EY ☎ 01307 433193 ✉ robertsonk@angus.gov.uk

Health and Safety: Mrs Susan Bruce Safety Manager, Angus House, Orchardbank Business Park, Forfar DD8 1AP ☎ 01307 476120 ✉ bruces@angus.gov.uk

Highways: Mr Ian Cochrane Head of Technical & Property Services, County Buildings, Market Street, , Forfar DD8 1BX ☎ 01307 473278 ✉ cochraneia@angus.gov.uk

Home Energy Conservation: Mr Bob Berry, Service Manager (Technical), William Wallace House, Orchard Loan, Orchardbank Business Park, Forfar DD8 1WH ☎ 01307 474795 🖷 01307 474799 ✉ berrybh@angus.gov.uk

Housing: Mr John Morrow Service Manager - Housing, William Wallace House, Orchard Loan, Forfar DD8 1WH ☎ 01307 474786 ✉ morrowj@angus.gov.uk

Housing Maintenance: Mr Alan McKeown, Strategic Director - Communities, Angus House, Orchardbank Business Park, Forfar DD8 1AX ☎ 01307 474711 🖷 01307 476140 ✉ mckeowna@angus.gov.uk

Legal: Mrs Sheona Hunter, Head of Legal & Democratic Services, Angus House, Orchardbank Business Park, Forfar DD8 1AN ☎ 01307 476262 🖷 01307 476299 ✉ hunters@angus.gov.uk

Leisure and Cultural Services: Mr Alastair Wilson Interim Head of Services to Communities, The Yard, Queenswell Road, Forfar DD8 3JA ☎ 01307 475360 ✉ wilsona@angus.gov.uk

Licensing: Mrs Sheona Hunter, Head of Legal & Democratic Services, Angus House, Orchardbank Business Park, Forfar DD8 1AN ☎ 01307 476262 🖷 01307 476299 ✉ hunters@angus.gov.uk

Lifelong Learning: Mrs Margo Williamson Strategic Director - People, Angus House, Orchardbank Business Park, Forfar DD8 1AX ☎ 01307 476468 🖷 01307 476140 ✉ williamsonm@angus.gov.uk

Lighting: Mr John Shand Lighting Partnership Manager, Tayside Contracts Area Office, Kirriemuir Road, Forfar DD8 3TH ☎ 01307 473932 ✉ shandj@angus.gov.uk

Lottery Funding, Charity and Voluntary: Ms Shelley Hague Senior External Funding Officer, Angus House, Orchardbank Business Park, Forfar DD8 1AX ☎ 01307 473222 ✉ hagues@angus.gov.uk

Member Services: Mrs Elaine Whittet Manager - Executive Support, Angus House, Orchardbank Business Park, Forfar DD8 1AX ☎ 01307 476099 🖷 01307 476140 ✉ whittete@angus.gcsx.gov.uk

Parking: Mr Ian Cochrane Head of Technical & Property Services, County Buildings, Market Street, , Forfar DD8 1BX ☎ 01307 473278 ✉ cochraneia@angus.gov.uk

Personnel / HR: Mrs Sharon Faulkner Head of HR, IT & Organisational Development, Angus House, Orchardbank Business Park, Forfar DD8 1AP ☎ 01307 476091 ✉ personnel@angus.gov.uk

Planning: Mr Iain Mitchell, Service Manager - Communities Directorate, County Buildings, Market Street, Forfar DD8 3LG ☎ 01307 473290 🖷 01307 461895 ✉ mitchelli@angus.gov.uk

ANGUS

Procurement: Mr Mark Allan Procurement Manager, Angus House, Orchardbank Business Park, Forfar DD8 1AF ☎ 01307 476195 🖷 01307 476216 ✉ allanm@angus.gov.uk

Public Libraries: Mr Alastair Wilson Interim Head of Services to Communities, The Yard, Queenswell Road, Forfar DD8 3JA ☎ 01307 475360 ✉ wilsona@angus.gov.uk

Recycling & Waste Minimisation: Mr Graeme Dailly Service Manager - Environmental Management, Dewar House, Hill Terrace, Arbroath DD11 1AH ☎ 01241 435602 ✉ daillyg@angus.gov.uk

Regeneration: Ms Debbie Gowans Community Regeneration Officer, William Wallace House, Orchardbank Business Park, Forfar DD8 1WH ☎ 01307 474153 ✉ gowansd@angus.gov.uk

Road Safety: Mr Ian Cochrane Head of Technical & Property Services, County Buildings, Market Street, , Forfar DD8 1BX ☎ 01307 473278 ✉ cochraneia@angus.gov.uk

Social Services: Mrs Margo Williamson Strategic Director - People, Angus House, Orchardbank Business Park, Forfar DD8 1AX ☎ 01307 476468 🖷 01307 476140 ✉ williamsonm@angus.gov.uk

Social Services (Adult): Mr George Bowie Head of Adult Services, St Margaret's House, Orchardbank Business Park, Forfar DD8 1WS ☎ 01307 474840 ✉ bowiegs@angus.gov.uk

Social Services (Children): Mr Tim Armstrong Head of Children & Young People's Services, Ravenswood, New Road, Forfar DD8 2ZG ☎ 01307 462405 🖷 01307 461261 ✉ armstrongt@angus.gov.uk

Staff Training: Mr Ken Ritchie, Senior Service Manager - Human Resources, Angus House, Orchardbank Business Park, Forfar DD8 1AP ☎ 01307 476091 🖷 01307 476410 ✉ personnel@angus.gov.uk

Street Scene: Mr Ian Cochrane Head of Technical & Property Services, County Buildings, Market Street, , Forfar DD8 1BX ☎ 01307 473278 ✉ cochraneia@angus.gov.uk

Sustainable Development: Mr Iain Mitchell, Service Manager - Communities Directorate, County Buildings, Market Street, Forfar DD8 3LG ☎ 01307 473290 🖷 01307 461895 ✉ mitchelli@angus.gov.uk

Tourism: Ms Alison Smith, Service Manager - Economic Development, County Buildings, Market Street, Forfar DD8 3WD ☎ 01307 473222 🖷 01307 467357 ✉ smithaj@angus.gov.uk

Traffic Management: Mr Graham Harris Traffic Manager, County Buildings, Market Street, Forfar DD8 3WR ☎ 01307 473283 🖷 01307 473388

Transport: Mr Iain Mitchell, Service Manager - Communities Directorate, County Buildings, Market Street, Forfar DD8 3LG ☎ 01307 473290 🖷 01307 461895 ✉ mitchelli@angus.gov.uk

Transport Planner: Mr Iain Mitchell, Service Manager - Communities Directorate, County Buildings, Market Street, Forfar DD8 3LG ☎ 01307 473290 🖷 01307 461895 ✉ mitchelli@angus.gov.uk

Waste Collection and Disposal: Mr Graeme Dailly Service Manager - Environmental Management, Dewar House, Hill Terrace, Arbroath DD11 1AH ☎ 01241 435602 ✉ daillyg@angus.gov.uk

Waste Management: Mr Graeme Dailly Service Manager - Environmental Management, Dewar House, Hill Terrace, Arbroath DD11 1AH ☎ 01241 435602 ✉ daillyg@angus.gov.uk

COUNCILLORS

Leader of the Council **Gaul**, Iain (SNP - Kirriemuir & Dean)
cllrgaul@angus.gov.uk

Bowles, Bill (IND - Carnoustie & District)
cllrbowles@angus.gov.uk

Boyd, Brian (IND - Carnoustie & District)
cllrboyd@angus.gov.uk

Brown, Colin (IND - Forfar & District)
cllrbrown@angus.gov.uk

Devine, Lynne (SNP - Forfar & District)
cllrdevine@angus.gov.uk

Duff, Bill (SNP - Montrose & District)
cllrduff@anugs.gov.uk

Evans, Mairi (SNP - Brechin & Edzell)
cllrevans@angus.gov.uk

Fairweather, David (IND - Arbroath West & Letham)
cllrfairweather@angus.gov.uk

Fotheringham, Craig (CON - Monifieth & Sidlaw)
cllrfotheringham@angus.gov.uk

Gaul, Jeanette (SNP - Kirriemuir & Dean)
cllrgaulje@angus.gov.uk

Geddes, Martyn (CON - Arbroath East & Lunan)
cllrgeddes@angus.gov.uk

Hands, Sheila (SNP - Monifieth & Sidlaw)
cllrhands@angus.gov.uk

Houston, Jim (SNP - Brechin & Edzell)
cllrhouston@angus.gov.uk

King, Alex (SNP - Arbroath West & Letham)
cllrking@angus.gov.uk

Lumgair, David (CON - Arbroath West & Letham)
cllrlumgair@angus.gov.uk

May, David (LD - Montrose & District)
cllrmay@angus.gov.uk

McLaren, Ian (IND - Forfar & District)
cllrmclaren@angus.gov.uk

Middleton, Glennis (SNP - Forfar & District)
cllrmiddletong@angus.gov.uk

Morrison, Donald (SNP - Arbroath East & Lunan)
cllrmorrison@angus.gov.uk

Murray, Rob (SNP - Monifieth & Sidlaw)
cllrmurray@angus.gov.uk

Myles, Bob (IND - Brechin & Edzell)
cllrmyles@angus.gov.uk

Oswald, Helen (SNP - Carnoustie & District)
cllroswald@angus.gov.uk

Proctor, Ronnie (CON - Kirriemuir & Dean)
cllrproctor@angus.gov.uk

Salmond, Mark (IND - Montrose & District)
cllrsalmond@angus.gov.uk

Smith, Ewan (IND - Arbroath West & Letham)
cllrsmith@angus.gov.uk

Spink, Bob (IND - Arbroath East & Lunan)
cllrspink@angus.gov.uk

Thomson, Margaret (LAB - Monifieth & Sidlaw)
cllrthomson@angus.gov.uk

Valentine, Paul (SNP - Montrose & District)
cllrvalentine@angus.gov.uk

Welsh, Sheena (SNP - Arbroath East & Lunan)
cllrwelsh@angus.gov.uk

POLITICAL COMPOSITION

SNP: 14, IND: 9, CON: 4, LAB: 1, LD: 1

COMMITTEE CHAIRS

Children & Learning: Ms Sheena Welsh

Development: Mr David Lumgair

Licensing: Mr Alex King

Scrutiny & Audit: Mr Bob Spink

Social Work & Health: Mrs Glennis Middleton

Antrim & Newtownabbey N

Antrim & Newtownabbey, Antrim Civic Centre, 50 Stiles Way, Antrim BT41 2UB

PRINCIPAL OFFICERS

Chief Executive: Ms Jacqui Dixon Chief Executive, Interim Head Office, Antrim Civic Centre, 50 Stiles Way, Antrim BT41 2UB
✉ jacqui.dixon@antrimandnewtownabbey.gov.uk

Senior Management: Mr John Balmer Assistant Director - Finance, Antrim Civic Centre, 50 Stiles Way, Antrim BT41 2UB
☎ 028 9446 3113 ✉ john.balmer@antrim.gov.uk

Senior Management: Ms Diane Irwin Health, Safety & Wellbeing Advisor, Antrim Civic Centre, 50 Stiles Way, Antrim BT41 2UB
☎ 028 9446 3113 ✉ diane.irwin@antrim.gov.uk

Senior Management: Ms Liz Johnston Assistant Director - Administration, Antrim Civic Centre, 50 Stiles Way, Antrim BT41 2UB
☎ 028 9446 3113 ✉ liz.johnston@antrim.gov.uk

Senior Management: Ms Elaine Magee Assistant Director - HR, Antrim Civic Centre, 50 Stiles Way, Antrim BT41 2UB ☎ 028 9446 3113 ✉ elaine.magee@antrim.gov.uk

Senior Management: Ms Elish Martin Public Relations Manager, Antrim Civic Centre, 50 Stiles Way, Antrim BT41 2UB ☎ 028 9446 3113 ✉ elish.martin@antrim.gov.uk

Senior Management: Mr Alistair Mawhinney Management Accountant, Antrim Civic Centre, 50 Stiles Way, Antrim BT41 2UB
☎ 028 9446 3113 ✉ alistair.mawhinney@antrim.gov.uk

Senior Management: Ms Catherine McFarland Director of Corporate & Regulatory Services, Antrim Civic Centre, 50 Stiles Way, Antrim BT41 2UB ☎ 028 9446 3113
✉ catherine.mcfarland@antrim.gov.uk

Senior Management: Mr Stuart Wilson People Development Manager, Antrim Civic Centre, 50 Stiles Way, Antrim BT41 2UB
☎ 028 9446 3113 ✉ stuart.wilson@antrim.gov.uk

PR / Communications: Ms Elish Martin Public Relations Manager, Antrim Civic Centre, 50 Stiles Way, Antrim BT41 2UB
☎ 028 9446 3113 ✉ elish.martin@antrim.gov.uk

Corporate Services: Ms Catherine McFarland Director of Corporate & Regulatory Services, Antrim Civic Centre, 50 Stiles Way, Antrim BT41 2UB ☎ 028 9446 3113
✉ catherine.mcfarland@antrim.gov.uk

Finance: Mr John Balmer Assistant Director - Finance, Antrim Civic Centre, 50 Stiles Way, Antrim BT41 2UB ☎ 028 9446 3113
✉ john.balmer@antrim.gov.uk

Health and Safety: Ms Diane Irwin Health, Safety & Wellbeing Advisor, Antrim Civic Centre, 50 Stiles Way, Antrim BT41 2UB
☎ 028 9446 3113 ✉ diane.irwin@antrim.gov.uk

Personnel / HR: Ms Elaine Magee Assistant Director - HR, Antrim Civic Centre, 50 Stiles Way, Antrim BT41 2UB ☎ 028 9446 3113 ✉ elaine.magee@antrim.gov.uk

Staff Training: Mr Stuart Wilson People Development Manager, Antrim Civic Centre, 50 Stiles Way, Antrim BT41 2UB ☎ 028 9446 3113 ✉ stuart.wilson@antrim.gov.uk

COUNCILLORS

***Mayor* Hogg**, Thomas (DUP - Macedon)
thomas.hogg@antrimandnewtownabbey.gov.uk

***Deputy Mayor* Blair**, John (ALL - Glengormley Urban)
john.blair@antrimandnewtownabbey.gov.uk

***Alderman* Agnew**, Fraser (UUP - Threemilewater)
fraser.agnew@antrimandnewtownabbey.gov.uk

***Alderman* Ball**, William (DUP - Threemilewater)
william.ball@antrimandnewtownabbey.gov.uk

***Alderman* Barr**, Pamela (DUP - Threemilewater)
pamela.barr@antrimandnewtownabbey.gov.uk

***Alderman* Burns**, Thomas (SDLP - Airport)
thomas.burns@antrimandnewtownabbey.gov.uk

***Alderman* Campbell**, Tom (ALL - Threemilewater)
tom.campbell@antrimandnewtownabbey.gov.uk

***Alderman* Cochrane-Watson**, Adrian (UUP - Antrim)
adrian.watson@antrimandnewtownabbey.gov.uk

ANTRIM & NEWTOWNABBEY

***Alderman* Cosgrove**, Mark (UUP - Glengormley Urban)
mark.cosgrove@antrimandnewtownabbey.gov.uk

***Alderman* DeCourcy**, William (DUP - Macedon)
william.decourcy@antrimandnewtownabbey.gov.uk

***Alderman* Girvan**, Mandy (DUP - Ballyclare)
mandy.girvan@antrimandnewtownabbey.gov.uk

***Alderman* Smyth**, John (DUP - Antrim)
john.smyth@antrimandnewtownabbey.gov.uk

Arthurs, David (O - Ballyclare)
david.arthurs@antrimandnewtownabbey.gov.uk

Ball, Audrey (DUP - Glengormley Urban)
audrey.ball@antrimandnewtownabbey.gov.uk

Beatty, Trevor (DUP - Dunsilly)
trevor.beatty@antrimandnewtownabbey.gov.uk

Bingham, Jim (UUP - Ballyclare)
jim.bingham@antrimandnewtownabbey.gov.uk

Brett, Phillip (DUP - Glengormley Urban)
phillip.brett@antrimandnewtownabbey.gov.uk

Clarke, Linda (DUP - Dunsilly)
linda.clarke@antrimandnewtownabbey.gov.uk

Cushinan, Henry (SF - Dunsilly)
henry.cushinan@antrimandnewtownabbey.gov.uk

Duffin, Brian (SDLP - Dunsilly)
brian.duffin@antrimandnewtownabbey.gov.uk

Girvan, Tim (DUP - Ballyclare)
tim.girvan@antrimandnewtownabbey.gov.uk

Goodman, Michael (SF - Glengormley Urban)
michael.goodman@antrimandnewtownabbey.gov.uk

Hamill, Paul (DUP - Macedon)
paul.hamill@antrimandnewtownabbey.gov.uk

Hollis, David (O - Macedon)
david.hollis@antrimandnewtownabbey.gov.uk

Kells, Nigel (DUP - Antrim)
nigel.kells@antrimandnewtownabbey.gov.uk

Kelly, Neil (ALL - Antrim)
neil.kelly@antrimandnewtownabbey.gov.uk

Kelso, Ben (UUP - Threemilewater)
ben.kelso@antrimandnewtownabbey.gov.uk

Logue, Annemarie (SF - Airport)
annemarie.logue@antrimandnewtownabbey.gov.uk

Lynch, Roisin (SDLP - Antrim)
roisin.lynch@antrimandnewtownabbey.gov.uk

Magill, Matthew (DUP - Airport)
matthew.magill@antrimandnewtownabbey.gov.uk

Maguire, Michael (UUP - Glengormley Urban)
michael.maguire@antrimandnewtownabbey.gov.uk

McClelland, Noreen (SDLP - Glengormley Urban)
noreen.mcclelland@antrimandnewtownabbey.gov.uk

McWilliam, Vera (UUP - Ballyclare)
vera.mcwilliam@antrimandnewtownabbey.gov.uk

Michael, Paul (UUP - Airport)
paul.michael@antrimandnewtownabbey.gov.uk

Rea, Mervyn (UUP - Airport)
mervyn.rea@antrimandnewtownabbey.gov.uk

Ritchie, Drew (UUP - Antrim)
drew.ritchie@antrimandnewtownabbey.gov.uk

Ross, Stephen (DUP - Threemilewater)
stephen.ross@antrimandnewtownabbey.gov.uk

Scott, John (UUP - Macedon)
john.scott@antrimandnewtownabbey.gov.uk

Swann, Roderick (UUP - Dunsilly)
roderick.swann@antrimandnewtownabbey.gov.uk

Webb, William (ALL - Macedon)
billy.webb@antrimandnewtownabbey.gov.uk

POLITICAL COMPOSITION

DUP: 15, UUP: 12, SDLP: 4, ALL: 4, SF: 3, O: 2

Argyll & Bute S

Argyll & Bute Council, Kilmory, Lochgilphead PA31 8RT
☎ 01546 602127 🖷 01546 604138 ✉ enquiries@argyll-bute.gov.uk
💻 www.argyll-bute.gov.uk

FACTS AND FIGURES

Parliamentary Constituencies: Argyll and Bute
EU Constituencies: Scotland
Election Frequency: Elections are of whole council

PRINCIPAL OFFICERS

Chief Executive: Ms Sally Loudon Chief Executive, Kilmory, Lochgilphead PA31 8RT ☎ 01546 604350 🖷 01546 604349 ✉ sally.loudon@argyll-bute.gov.uk

Senior Management: Mr Steve Barrett Interim Head of Strategic Finance, Kilmory, Lochgilphead PA31 8RT ☎ 01546 604351 ✉ steve.barrett@argyll-bute.gov.uk

Senior Management: Mr Douglas Hendry Executive Director - Customer Services, Kilmory, Lochgilphead PA31 8RT ☎ 01546 604244 ✉ douglas.hendry@argyll-bute.gov.uk

Senior Management: Ms Pippa Milne Executive Director - Development & Infrastructure, Kilmory, Lochgilphead PA31 8RT ☎ 01546 604076 ✉ pippa.milne@argyll-bute.gov.uk

Senior Management: Mr Cleland Sneddon Executive Director - Community Services, Kilmory, Lochgilphead PA31 8RT ☎ 01546 604112 🖷 01546 604434 ✉ cleland.sneddon@argyll-bute.gov.uk

Architect, Building / Property Services: Mr Angus Gilmour, Head of Planning & Regulatory Services, Kilmory, Lochgilphead PA31 8RT ☎ 01546 604288 ✉ angus.gilmour@argyll-bute.gov.uk

Best Value: Ms Jane Fowler Head of Improvement & HR, Kilmory, Lochgilphead PA31 8RT ☎ 01546 604466 ✉ jane.fowler@argyll-bute.gov.uk

Building Control: Mr Martin Matheson Building Standards Manager, Blairbadach House, Helensburgh G84 8ND ☎ 01436 658881 ✉ martin.matheson@argyll-bute.gov.uk

Catering Services: Mr Malcolm MacFadyen Head of Facility Services, Kilmory, Lochgilphead PA31 8RT ☎ 01546 604412 🖷 01546 604434 ✉ malcolm.macfadyen@argyll-bute.gov.uk

Children / Youth Services: Ms Louise Long Head of Children & Families, Kilmory, Lochgilphead PA31 8RT ☎ 01546 604256 🖷 01546 604434 🖱 louise.long@argyll-bute.gov.uk

Civil Registration: Ms Shona Brechin Area Registrar, Dalriada House, Lochgilphead PA31 8ST ☎ 01546 604515 🖷 01546 604530 🖱 shona.brechin@argyll-bute.gov.uk

Community Planning: Ms Eileen Wilson, Community Planning Manager, 25 West King Street, Helensburgh G84 8UW ☎ 01436 658726 🖱 eileen.wilson@argyll-bute.gov.uk

Community Safety: Mr Charles Reppke, Head of Governance & Law, Kilmory, Lochgilphead PA31 8RT ☎ 01546 604192 🖷 01546 604434 🖱 charles.reppke@argyll-bute.gov.uk

Computer Management: Ms Judy Orr, Head of Support & Customer Services, Witchburn Road, Campbeltown PA28 6JX ☎ 01586 555280 🖷 01586 553050 🖱 judy.orr@argyll-bute.gov.uk

Consumer Protection and Trading Standards: Mr Angus Gilmour, Head of Planning & Regulatory Services, Kilmory Lochgilphead PA31 8RT ☎ 01546 604288 🖱 angus.gilmour@argyll-bute.gov.uk

Contracts: Ms Anne MacColl-Smith Service Commissioning Manager, Kilmory, Lochgilphead PA31 8RT ☎ 01546 604194 🖷 01546 604434 🖱 anne.maccoll-smith@argyll-bute.gov.uk

Customer Service: Mr Douglas Hendry Executive Director of Customer Services, Kilmory, Lochgilphead PA31 8RT ☎ 01546 604244 🖷 01546 604434 🖱 douglas.hendry@argyll-bute.gov.uk

Customer Service: Mrs Judy Orr Head of Customer & Support Services, Witchburn Road, Campbeltown PA28 6JU ☎ 01586 555280 🖱 judy.orr@argyll-bute.gov.uk

Economic Development: Mr Fergus Murray Head of Economic Development & Strategic Transport, Kilmory, Lochgilphead PA31 8RT ☎ 01546 604293 🖱 fergus.murray@argyll-bute.gov.uk

Education: Ms Ann Marie Knowles Head of Education, Kilmory, Lochgilphead PA31 8RT

E-Government: Ms Judy Orr, Head of Support & Customer Services, Witchburn Road, Campbeltown PA28 6JX ☎ 01586 555280 🖷 01586 553050 🖱 judy.orr@argyll-bute.gov.uk

Electoral Registration: Mr Charles Reppke, Head of Governance & Law, Kilmory, Lochgilphead PA31 8RT ☎ 01546 604192 🖷 01546 604434 🖱 charles.reppke@argyll-bute.gov.uk

Emergency Planning: Ms Carol Keeley, Emergency Planning Officer, 25 West King Street, Helensburgh G84 8UW ☎ 01436 677819 🖷 01436 672531 🖱 carol.keeley@argyll-bute.gov.uk

Energy Management: Mr Paul Gillies Energy Manager, Argyll House, Alexandra Parade, Dunoon PA23 8AJ ☎ 01369 708573 🖷 01369 708554 🖱 paul.gillies@argyll-bute.gov.uk

Environmental / Technical Services: Mr Angus Gilmour, Head of Planning & Regulatory Services, Kilmory Lochgilphead PA31 8RT ☎ 01546 604288 🖱 angus.gilmour@argyll-bute.gov.uk

Environmental Health: Mr Angus Gilmour, Head of Planning & Regulatory Services, Kilmory Lochgilphead PA31 8RT ☎ 01546 604288 🖱 angus.gilmour@argyll-bute.gov.uk

Estates, Property & Valuation: Mr Malcolm MacFadyen Head of Facility Services, Kilmory, Lochgilphead PA31 8RT ☎ 01546 604412 🖷 01546 604434 🖱 malcolm.macfadyen@argyll-bute.gov.uk

European Liaison: Mr Fergus Murray Head of Economic Development & Strategic Transport, Kilmory, Lochgilphead PA31 8RT ☎ 01546 604293 🖱 fergus.murray@argyll-bute.gov.uk

Facilities: Mr Malcolm MacFadyen Head of Facility Services, Kilmory, Lochgilphead PA31 8RT ☎ 01546 604412 🖷 01546 604434 🖱 malcolm.macfadyen@argyll-bute.gov.uk

Finance: Mr Steve Barrett Interim Head of Strategic Finance, Kilmory, Lochgilphead PA31 8RT ☎ 01546 604351 🖱 steve.barrett@argyll-bute.gov.uk

Fleet Management: Mr Walter MacArthur Fleet & Waste Manager, Manse Brae, Lochgilphead PA31 8RD ☎ 01546 604190 🖱 walter.macarthur@argyll-bute.gov.uk

Grounds Maintenance: Mr Tom Murphy Assistant Operations Manager - Roads & Grounds, Blairvedach House, Helensburgh G84 8ND ☎ 01436 658908 🖱 tom.murphy@argyll-bute.gov.uk

Health and Safety: Mr Andrew MacKrell Health & Safety Manager, Whitegate Offices, Lochgilphead PA31 8SY ☎ 01546 604133 🖱 andrew.mackrell@argyll-bute.gov.uk

Highways: Mr Jim Smith Head of Roads & Amenity Services, Kilmory, Lochgilphead PA31 8RT ☎ 01546 604324 🖱 jim.smith@argyll-bute.gov.uk

Housing: Mr Donald MacVicar, Head of Community & Culture, Kilmory, Lochgilphead PA31 8RT ☎ 01546 604364 🖷 01546 604434 🖱 donald.macvicar@argyll-bute.gov.uk

Housing Maintenance: Mr Donald MacVicar, Head of Community & Culture, Kilmory, Lochgilphead PA31 8RT ☎ 01546 604364 🖷 01546 604434 🖱 donald.macvicar@argyll-bute.gov.uk

Legal: Mr Charles Reppke, Head of Governance & Law, Kilmory, Lochgilphead PA31 8RT ☎ 01546 604192 🖷 01546 604434 🖱 charles.reppke@argyll-bute.gov.uk

Leisure and Cultural Services: Mr Donald MacVicar, Head of Community & Culture, Kilmory, Lochgilphead PA31 8RT ☎ 01546 604364 🖷 01546 604434 🖱 donald.macvicar@argyll-bute.gov.uk

Licensing: Mr Charles Reppke, Head of Governance & Law, Kilmory, Lochgilphead PA31 8RT ☎ 01546 604192 🖷 01546 604434 🖱 charles.reppke@argyll-bute.gov.uk

ARGYLL & BUTE

Lighting: Mr Ryan McGlynn, Technical Officer - Street Lighting, Manse Brae, Lochgilphead PA31 8RD ☎ 01546 604646 🖷 01546 606443 🖰 ryan.mcglynn@argyll-bute.gov.uk

Lottery Funding, Charity and Voluntary: Ms Arlene Cullum Funding Officer, 25 West King Street, Helensburgh G84 8UW ☎ 07979 214501 🖰 arlene.cullum@argyll-bute.gov.uk

Member Services: Mr Charles Reppke, Head of Governance & Law, Kilmory, Lochgilphead PA31 8RT ☎ 01546 604192 🖷 01546 604434 🖰 charles.reppke@argyll-bute.gov.uk

Partnerships: Ms Eileen Wilson, Community Planning Manager, 25 West King Street, Helensburgh G84 8UW ☎ 01436 658726 🖰 eileen.wilson@argyll-bute.gov.uk

Personnel / HR: Ms Jane Fowler Head of Improvement & HR, Kilmory, Lochgilphead PA31 8RT ☎ 01546 604466 🖰 jane.fowler@argyll-bute.gov.uk

Planning: Mr Angus Gilmour, Head of Planning & Regulatory Services, Kilmory Lochgilphead PA31 8RT ☎ 01546 604288 🖰 angus.gilmour@argyll-bute.gov.uk

Procurement: Ms Anne MacColl-Smith Service Commissioning Manager, Kilmory, Lochgilphead PA31 8RT ☎ 01546 604194 🖷 01546 604434 🖰 anne.maccoll-smith@argyll-bute.gov.uk

Public Libraries: Ms Pat McCann Culture & Libraries Manager, West King Street Library, West King Street, Helensburgh G84 8GB ☎ 01436 658811 🖰 pat.mccann@argyll-bute.gov.uk

Recycling & Waste Minimisation: Mr Alan Millar, Performance Manager - Waste Management, Manse Brae, Lochgilphead PA31 8RD ☎ 01546 604628 🖷 01546 606443 🖰 alan.millar@argyll-bute.gov.uk

Regeneration: Mr Donald MacVicar, Head of Community & Culture, Kilmory, Lochgilphead PA31 8RT ☎ 01546 604364 🖷 01546 604434 🖰 donald.macvicar@argyll-bute.gov.uk

Road Safety: Mrs June Graham Road Safety Officer, Kilmory, Lochgilphead PA31 8RT ☎ 01546 604182 🖷 01546 604386 🖰 june.graham@argyll-bute.gov.uk

Social Services: Mr Cleland Sneddon Executive Director - Community Services, Kilmory, Lochgilphead PA31 8RT ☎ 01546 604112 🖷 01546 604434 🖰 cleland.sneddon@argyll-bute.gov.uk

Social Services (Adult): Mr Jim Robb Head of Adult Services, Struan Lodge - Top Floor, Bencorrum Brae, Dunoon PA23 8HU ☎ 01369 708911 🖷 01369 708909 🖰 jim.robb@argyll-bute.gov.uk

Social Services (Children): Ms Louise Long Head of Children & Families, Kilmory, Lochgilphead PA31 8RT ☎ 01546 604256 🖷 01546 604434 🖰 louise.long@argyll-bute.gov.uk

Staff Training: Ms Jane Fowler Head of Improvement & HR, Kilmory, Lochgilphead PA31 8RT ☎ 01546 604466 🖰 jane.fowler@argyll-bute.gov.uk

Street Scene: Mr Tom Murphy Assistant Operations Manager - Roads & Grounds, Blairvedach House, Helensburgh G84 8ND ☎ 01436 658908 🖰 tom.murphy@argyll-bute.gov.uk

Sustainable Communities: Mr Fergus Murray Head of Economic Development & Strategic Transport, Kilmory, Lochgilphead PA31 8RT ☎ 01546 604293 🖰 fergus.murray@argyll-bute.gov.uk

Sustainable Development: Mr Angus Gilmour, Head of Planning & Regulatory Services, Kilmory Lochgilphead PA31 8RT ☎ 01546 604288 🖰 angus.gilmour@argyll-bute.gov.uk

Tourism: Mr Fergus Murray Head of Economic Development & Strategic Transport, Kilmory, Lochgilphead PA31 8RT ☎ 01546 604293 🖰 fergus.murray@argyll-bute.gov.uk

Town Centre: Mr Fergus Murray Head of Economic Development & Strategic Transport, Kilmory, Lochgilphead PA31 8RT ☎ 01546 604293 🖰 fergus.murray@argyll-bute.gov.uk

Traffic Management: Mr Jim Smith Head of Roads & Amenity Services, Kilmory, Lochgilphead PA31 8RT ☎ 01546 604324 🖰 jim.smith@argyll-bute.gov.uk

Transport: Ms Moya Ingram Strategic Transportation Manager, Whitegates Office, Whitegates Road, Lochgilphead PA31 8RD ☎ 01546 604190 🖷 01546 604386 🖰 moya.ingram@argyll-bute.gov.uk

Waste Collection and Disposal: Mr Tom Murphy Assistant Operations Manager - Roads & Grounds, Blairvedach House, Helensburgh G84 8ND ☎ 01436 658908 🖰 tom.murphy@argyll-bute.gov.uk

Waste Management: Mr Alan Millar, Performance Manager - Waste Management, Manse Brae, Lochgilphead PA31 8RD ☎ 01546 604628 🖷 01546 606443 🖰 alan.millar@argyll-bute.gov.uk

COUNCILLORS

***Provost* Scoullar**, Len (IND - Isle of Bute)
len.scoullar@argyll-bute.gov.uk

***Deputy Provost* Philand**, Douglas (IND - Mid Argyll)
dougie.philand@argyll-bute.gov.uk

***Leader of the Council* Walsh**, Dick (IND - Dunoon)
dick.walsh@argyll-bute.gov.uk

***Deputy Leader of the Council* Morton**, Ellen (LD - Helensburgh & Lomond South)
ellen.morton@argyll-bute.gov.uk

Armour, John (SNP - South Kintyre)
john.armour@argyll-bute.gov.uk

Blair, William Gordon (SNP - Cowal)
gordon.blair@argyll-bute.gov.uk

Breslin, Michael (INDNA - Dunoon)
michael.breslin@argyll-bute.gov.uk

Colville, Rory (LD - South Kintyre)
rory.colville@argyll-bute.gov.uk

Corry, Maurice (CON - Lomond North)
maurice.corry@argyll-bute.gov.uk

Currie, Robin (LD - Kintyre & the Islands)
robin.currie@argyll-bute.gov.uk

Dance, Vivien (INDNA - Helensburgh Central)
vivien.dance@argyll-bute.gov.uk

Devon, Mary-Jean (IND - Oban South & Isles)
mary-jean.devon@argyll-bute.gov.uk

Freeman, George (IND - Lomond North)
george.freeman@argyll-bute.gov.uk

Horn, Anne (SNP - Kintyre & the Islands)
anne.horn@argyll-bute.gov.uk

Kelly, Donald (IND - South Kintyre)
donald.kelly2@argyll-bute.gov.uk

Kinniburgh, David (CON - Helensburgh & Lomond South)
david.kinniburgh@argyll-bute.gov.uk

MacDonald, Iain Angus (IND - Oban North & Lorn)
iainangus.macdonald@argyll-bute.gov.uk

MacDougall, Alistair (IND - Oban South & Isles)
alistair.macdougall@argyll-bute.gov.uk

MacIntyre, Duncan (IND - Oban North & Lorn)
duncan.macintyre@argyll-bute.gov.uk

MacIntyre, Robert (IND - Lomond North)
robertgraham.macintyre@argyll-bute.gov.uk

MacIntyre, Robert (IND - Isle of Bute)
robert.macintyre@argyll-bute.gov.uk

MacIntyre, Neil (LAB - Oban South & Isles)
neil.macintyre@argyll-bute.gov.uk

MacLean, Iain Stewart (INDNA - Oban North & Lorn)
iainstewart.MacLean@argyll-bute.gov.uk

MacMillan, Donald (IND - Mid Argyll)
donald.macmillan@argyll-bute.gov.uk

Marshall, Bruce (IND - Cowal)
bruce.marshall@argyll-bute.gov.uk

McAlpine, John (IND - Kintyre & the Islands)
john.mcalpine@argyll-bute.gov.uk

McCuish, Roddy (IND - Oban South & Isles)
roderick.mccuish@argyll-bute.gov.uk

McNaughton, Alex (IND - Cowal)
alex.mcnaughton@argyll-bute.gov.uk

McQueen, James (IND - Dunoon)
james.mcqueen@argyll-bute.gov.uk

Morton, Aileen (LD - Helensburgh Central)
aileen.morton@argyll-bute.gov.uk

Mulvaney, Gary (CON - Helensburgh Central)
gary.mulvaney@argyll-bute.gov.uk

Robb, James (SNP - Helensburgh Central)
james.robb@argyll-bute.gov.uk

Robertson, Elaine (IND - Oban North & Lorn)
elaine.robertson@argyll-bute.gov.uk

Strong, Isobel (SNP - Isle of Bute)
isobel.strong@argyll-bute.gov.uk

Taylor, Sandy (SNP - Mid Argyll)
sandy.taylor@argyll-bute.gov.uk

Trail, Richard (SNP - Helensburgh & Lomond South)
richard.trail@argyll-bute.gov.uk

POLITICAL COMPOSITION

IND: 18, SNP: 7, LD: 4, CON: 3, INDNA: 3, LAB: 1

COMMITTEE CHAIRS

Community Services: Mr Robin Currie

Licensing: Mr Rory Colville

Planning, Protective Services & Licensing: Mr David Kinniburgh

Policy & Resources: Mr Dick Walsh

Armagh City, Banbridge & Craigavon District N

Armagh City, Banbridge & Craigavon District, Council Offices, The Palace Demesne, Armagh BT60 4EL

PRINCIPAL OFFICERS

Chief Executive: Mr Roger Wilson Chief Executive, Council Offices, The Palace Demesne, Armagh BT60 4EL

Senior Management: Ms Olga Murtagh Strategic Director - Place, Council Offices, The Palace Demesne, Armagh BT60 4EL
olga.murtagh@armaghbanbridgecraigavon.gov.uk

Senior Management: Ms Sharon O'Gorman Strategic Director - Position, Council Offices, The Palace Demesne, Armagh BT60 4EL
sharon.o'gorman@armaghbanbridgecraigavon.gov.uk

Senior Management: Mr Mike Reardon Interim Strategic Director - People, Council Offices, The Palace Demesne, Armagh BT60 4EL
mike.reardon@armaghbanbridgecraigavon.gov.uk

Finance: Mr Graham Coulter Head of Finance, For details see Armagh City, Banbridge & Craigavon District, Council Offices, The Palace Demesne, Armagh BT60 4EL

Personnel / HR: Ms Sharon Currans Head of HR, For details see Armagh City, Banbridge & Craigavon District, Council Offices, The Palace Demesne, Armagh BT60 4EL

COUNCILLORS

Barr, Glenn (UUP - Banbridge)

Baxter, Mark (DUP - Lagan River)

Beattie, Doug (UUP - Portadown)

Berry, Paul (O - Cusher)

Black, Carol (UUP - Lagan River)

Buckley, Jonathan (DUP - Portadown)

Burns, Ian (UUP - Banbridge)

Cairns, Maire (SF - Lurgan)

Campbell, Mealla (SDLP - Armagh)

Causby, Darryn (DUP - Portadown)

Curran, Brendan (SF - Banbridge)

Donnelly, Freda (DUP - Armagh)

Doyle, Seamus (SDLP - Banbridge)

Gamble, Hazel (DUP - Lagan River)

Greenfield, Paul (DUP - Banbridge)

Hatch, Arnold (UUP - Portadown)

Haughey, Sharon (SDLP - Cusher)

Haughian, Keith (SF - Lurgan)

Ingram, Elizabeth (UUP - Banbridge)

Jones, David (UKIP - Portadown)

Keating, Garath (SF - Armagh)

Kennedy, Gordon (UUP - Cusher)

Lennon, Fergal (SF - Craigavon)

Lockhart, Carla (DUP - Lurgan)

McAlinden, Declan (SDLP - Craigavon)

McCrum, Junior (DUP - Banbridge)

McCusker, Colin (UUP - Lurgan)

McKenna, Gemma (SF - Portadown)

McNally, Darren (SF - Armagh)

Moutray, Philip (UUP - Lurgan)

Nelson, Joe (SDLP - Lurgan)

Nicholson, Sam (UUP - Armagh)

O'Hanlon, Thomas (SDLP - Armagh)

Rankin, Paul (DUP - Lagan River)

Seeley, Catherine (SF - Lurgan)

Smith, Robert (DUP - Craigavon)

Speers, Jim (UUP - Cusher)

Tinsley, Margaret (DUP - Craigavon)

Twyble, Kenneth (UUP - Craigavon)

Wilson, Gareth (DUP - Cusher)

Woods, Marc (UUP - Lagan River)

POLITICAL COMPOSITION
UUP: 13, DUP: 12, SF: 8, SDLP: 6, UKIP: 1, O: 1

Arun D

Arun District Council, Arun Civic Centre, Maltravers Road, Littlehampton BN17 5LF
☎ 01903 737500 🖷 01903 730442 💻 www.arun.gov.uk

FACTS AND FIGURES
Parliamentary Constituencies: Arundel and South Downs, Bognor Regis and Littlehampton, Worthing West
EU Constituencies: South East
Election Frequency: Elections are of whole council

PRINCIPAL OFFICERS

Chief Executive: Mr Nigel Lynn Chief Executive, Arun Civic Centre, Maltravers Road, Littlehampton BN17 5LF ☎ 01903 737600 ✉ nigel.lynn@arun.gov.uk

Deputy Chief Executive: Mr Nigel Croad, Resources Director & Deputy Chief Executive, Arun Civic Centre, Maltravers Road, Littlehampton BN17 5LF ☎ 01903 737810 ✉ nigel.croad@arun.gov.uk

Senior Management: Mrs Philippa Dart, Director for Environmental Services, Town Hall, Clarence Road, Bognor Regis PO21 1LD ☎ 01903 737811 ✉ philippa.dart@arun.gov.uk

Senior Management: Mr Karl Roberts Director of Planning & Economic Regeneration, Arun Civic Centre, Maltravers Road, Littlehampton BN17 5LF ☎ 01903 737760 🖷 01903 716019 ✉ karl.roberts@arun.gov.uk

Senior Management: Mr Roger Spencer Engineering Services Manager, Arun Civic Centre, Maltravers Road, Littlehampton BN17 5LF ☎ 01903 737812 ✉ roger.spencer@arun.gov.uk

Senior Management: Mr Paul Warters Director of Customer Services, Arun Civic Centre, Maltravers Road, Littlehampton BN17 5LF ☎ 01903 737510 🖷 01903 730442 ✉ paul.warters@arun.gov.uk

Best Value: Mr Paul Askew Head of Policy & Partnerships, Arun Civic Centre, Maltravers Road, Littlehampton BN17 5LF ☎ 01903 737515 🖷 01903 730442 ✉ paul.askew@arun.gov.uk

Building Control: Mr James Henn, Building Control Manager, Arun Civic Centre, Maltravers Road, Littlehampton BN17 5LF ☎ 01903 737596 🖷 01903 716019 ✉ jim.henn@arun.gov.uk

PR / Communications: Ms Justine Vincent Communications Manager, Arun Civic Centre, Maltravers Road, Littlehampton BN17 5LF ☎ 01903 737606 🖷 01903 737707 ✉ justine.vincent@arun.gov.uk

Community Safety: Ms Georgina Bouette Community Safety Manager, Arun Civic Centre, Maltravers Road, Littlehampton BN17 5LF ☎ 01903 737605 ✉ georgina.bouette@arun.gov.uk

Computer Management: Mr Chris Lawrence ICT Manager, Arun Civic Centre, Maltravers Road, Littlehampton BN17 5LF ☎ 01903 737803 ✉ chris.lawrence@arun.gov.uk

Contracts: Mr Philip Pickard, Procurement Officer, Arun Civic Centre, Maltravers Road, Littlehampton BN17 5LF ☎ 01903 737677 🖷 01903 730442 ✉ philip.pickard@arun.gov.uk

Customer Service: Mrs Jackie Follis, Head of HR & Customer Services, Arun Civic Centre, Maltravers Road, Littlehampton BN17 5LF ☎ 01903 737580 🖷 01903 713606 ✉ jackie.follis@arun.gov.uk

Economic Development: Ms Denise Vine Head of Economic Regeneration, Arun Civic Centre, Maltravers Road, Littlehampton BN17 5LF ☎ 01903 737846 🖷 01903 737701 ✉ denise.vine@arun.gov.uk

Electoral Registration: Mrs Liz Futcher, Head of Democratic Services, Arun Civic Centre, Maltravers Road, Littlehampton BN17 5LF ☎ 01903 737610 🖷 01903 730442 ✉ liz.futcher@arun.gov.uk

Emergency Planning: Mr Guy Edwards Emergency Planning Officer, Town Hall, Clarence Road, Bognor Regis PO21 1LD ☎ 01903 737953 guy.edwards@arun.gov.uk

Energy Management: Ms Helen Cooper Energy Efficiency Officer, Arun Civic Centre, Maltravers Road, Littlehampton BN17 5LF ☎ 01903 737743 helen.cooper@arun.gov.uk

Environmental Health: Mr Nat Slade Environmental Health Manager, Arun Civic Centre, Maltravers Road, Littlehampton BN17 5LF ☎ 01903 737683 nat.slade@arun.gov.uk

Estates, Property & Valuation: Mr Alan Peach, Head of Finance & Property, Arun Civic Centre, Maltravers Road, Littlehampton BN17 5LF ☎ 01903 737558 🖷 01903 730747 alan.peach@arun.gov.uk

Events Manager: Ms Jasmine Ede Marketing & Events Assistant, Arun Civic Centre, Maltravers Road, Littlehampton BN17 5LF ☎ 01903 737920 jasmine.ede@arun.gov.uk

Facilities: Ms Kim Breden Facilities Team Leader, Arun Civic Centre, Maltravers Road, Littlehampton BN17 5LF ☎ 01903 737964 kim.breden@arun.gov.uk

Finance: Mr Nigel Croad, Resources Director & Deputy Chief Executive, Arun Civic Centre, Maltravers Road, Littlehampton BN17 5LF ☎ 01903 737810 nigel.croad@arun.gov.uk

Treasury: Ms Sian Southerton Senior Accountant / Treasury & Investment Officer, Arun Civic Centre, Maltravers Road, Littlehampton BN17 5LF ☎ 01903 737861 sian.southerton@arun.gov.uk

Grounds Maintenance: Mrs Philippa Dart, Director for Environmental Services, Town Hall, Clarence Road, Bognor Regis PO21 1LD ☎ 01903 737811 philippa.dart@arun.gov.uk

Health and Safety: Mr Colin Combes Corporate Health & Safety Officer, Arun Civic Centre, Maltravers Road, Littlehampton BN17 5LF ☎ 01903 737682 colin.combes@arun.gov.uk

Home Energy Conservation: Mr Brian Pople Head of Housing, Arun Civic Centre, Maltravers Road, Littlehampton BN17 5LF ☎ 01903 737718 brian.pople@arun.gov.uk

Housing: Mr Brian Pople Head of Housing, Arun Civic Centre, Maltravers Road, Littlehampton BN17 5LF ☎ 01903 737718 brian.pople@arun.gov.uk

Housing Maintenance: Ms Elaine Gray Housing Customer Services Manager, Arun Civic Centre, Maltravers Road, Littlehampton BN17 5LF ☎ 01903 737823 elaine.gray@arun.gov.uk

Legal: Mrs Wendy Ashenden-Bax, Head of Legal & Administration, Arun Civic Centre, Maltravers Road, Littlehampton BN17 5LF ☎ 01903 737589 🖷 01903 716019 wendy.ashenden-bax@arun.gov.uk

Leisure and Cultural Services: Mrs Philippa Dart, Director for Environmental Services, Town Hall, Clarence Road, Bognor Regis PO21 1LD ☎ 01903 737811 philippa.dart@arun.gov.uk

Licensing: Mrs Sarah Meeting Licensing Team Manager, Arun Civic Centre, Maltravers Road, Littlehampton BN17 5LF ☎ 01903 737681 sarah.meeting@arun.gov.uk

Member Services: Mrs Liz Futcher, Head of Democratic Services, Arun Civic Centre, Maltravers Road, Littlehampton BN17 5LF ☎ 01903 737610 🖷 01903 730442 liz.futcher@arun.gov.uk

Parking: Mr Calvin Baylis, Outdoor Services Manager, Arun Civic Centre, Maltravers Road, Littlehampton BN17 5LF ☎ 01903 737649 🖷 01903 716019 calvin.baylis@arun.gov.uk

Partnerships: Mr Roger Wood, Head of Neighbourhoods, Arun Civic Centre, Maltravers Road, Littlehampton BN17 5LF ☎ 01903 737671 🖷 01903 723936 roger.wood@arun.gov.uk

Personnel / HR: Mrs Jackie Follis, Head of HR & Customer Services, Arun Civic Centre, Maltravers Road, Littlehampton BN17 5LF ☎ 01903 737580 🖷 01903 713606 jackie.follis@arun.gov.uk

Planning: Mr Karl Roberts Director of Planning & Economic Regeneration, Arun Civic Centre, Maltravers Road, Littlehampton BN17 5LF ☎ 01903 737760 🖷 01903 716019 karl.roberts@arun.gov.uk

Procurement: Mr Philip Pickard, Procurement Officer, Arun Civic Centre, Maltravers Road, Littlehampton BN17 5LF ☎ 01903 737677 🖷 01903 730442 philip.pickard@arun.gov.uk

Recycling & Waste Minimisation: Mrs Philippa Dart, Director for Environmental Services, Town Hall, Clarence Road, Bognor Regis PO21 1LD ☎ 01903 737811 philippa.dart@arun.gov.uk

Regeneration: Mr Karl Roberts Director of Planning & Economic Regeneration, Arun Civic Centre, Maltravers Road, Littlehampton BN17 5LF ☎ 01903 737760 🖷 01903 716019 karl.roberts@arun.gov.uk

Regeneration: Ms Denise Vine Head of Economic Regeneration, Arun Civic Centre, Maltravers Road, Littlehampton BN17 5LF ☎ 01903 737846 🖷 01903 737701 denise.vine@arun.gov.uk

Staff Training: Mrs Jackie Follis, Head of HR & Customer Services, Arun Civic Centre, Maltravers Road, Littlehampton BN17 5LF ☎ 01903 737580 🖷 01903 713606 jackie.follis@arun.gov.uk

Sustainable Communities: Mr Karl Roberts Assistant Director of Planning & Housing Strategy, Arun Civic Centre, Maltravers Road, Littlehampton BN17 5LF ☎ 01903 737760 🖷 01903 716019 karl.roberts@arun.gov.uk

Sustainable Development: Mr Roger Wood, Head of Neighbourhoods, Arun Civic Centre, Maltravers Road, Littlehampton BN17 5LF ☎ 01903 737671 🖷 01903 723936 roger.wood@arun.gov.uk

Town Centre: Mr John Edgvet Littlehampton Town Centre Regeneration Officer, Arun Civic Centre, Maltravers Road, Littlehampton BN17 5LF ☎ 01903 737856 john.edgvet@arun.gov.uk

ARUN

Waste Collection and Disposal: Mr Gareth Rollings Cleansing Operations Manager, Arun Civic Centre, Maltravers Road, Littlehampton BN17 5LF ☎ 01903 737659
🖱 gareth.rollings@arun.gov.uk

Children's Play Areas: Mr Oliver Handson Greenspace Contract & Development Manager, Town Hall, Clarence Road, Bognor Regis PO21 1LD ☎ 01903 737955 🖱 oliver.handson@arun.gov.uk

COUNCILLORS

***Chair* Cooper**, Andy (CON - Angmering & Findon)
cllr.andy.cooper@arun.gov.uk

***Vice-Chair* Haymes**, Stephen (CON - Yapton)
cllr.stephen.haymes@arun.gov.uk

***Leader of the Council* Brown**, Gillian (CON - Aldwick East)
gillianannabrown@aol.com

***Deputy Leader of the Council* Wensley**, Dudley (CON - Angmering & Findon)
cllr.dudley.wensley@arun.gov.uk

Ambler, Derek (UKIP - Yapton)
cllr.derek.ambler@arun.gov.uk

Ayres, Marian (CON - Courtwick with Toddington)
cllr.marian.ayres@arun.gov.uk

Ballard, Keith (CON - Barnham)
cllr.keith.ballard@arun.gov.uk

Bence, Susan (CON - Bersted)
cllr.susan.bence@arun.gov.uk

Bence, Trevor (CON - Pevensey (Bognor Regis))
cllr.trevor.bence@arun.gov.uk

Bicknell, Paul (CON - Angmering & Findon)
paul@bicknells.f2s.com

Blampied, George (CON - River)
cllr.george.blampied@arun.gov.uk

Bower, Richard (CON - East Preston)
r.bower@btconnect.com

Bower, Philipa (CON - Rustington West)
philippa.bower@btconnect.com

Brooks, James (IND - Marine)
cllr.jim.brooks@arun.gov.uk

Brown, Leonard (CON - Orchard)

Buckland, Ian (LD - River)
cllr.ian.buckland@arun.gov.uk

Cates, Colin (UKIP - River)
cllr.colin.cates@arun.gov.uk

Chapman, Terence (CON - East Preston)
cllr.terence.chapman@arun.gov.uk

Charles, John (CON - Barnham)
cllr.john.charles@arun.gov.uk

Clayden, Mike (CON - East Preston)
cllr.mike.clayden@arun.gov.uk

Daniells, Sandra (CON - Pevensey)
cllr.sandra.daniells@arun.gov.uk

Dendle, Paul (CON - Arundel & Walberton)
cllr.paul.dendle@arun.gov.uk

Dillon, Pat (CON - Pevensey)
cllr.pat.dillon@arun.gov.uk

Dingemans, Norman (CON - Arundel & Walberton)
cllr.norman.dingemans@arun.gov.uk

Edwards, David (CON - Felpham East)
cllr.david.edwards@arun.gov.uk

Elkins, Roger (CON - Ferring)
cllr.roger.elkins@arun.gov.uk

English, Paul (CON - Felpham East)
cllr.paul.english@arun.gov.uk

Gammon, Alan (CON - Brookfield)
cllr.alan.gammon@arun.gov.uk

Hall, Dawn (CON - Pagham)
cllr.dawn.hall@arun.gov.uk

Harrison-Horn, Pauline (CON - Rustington West)
cllr.pauline.harrison-horn@arun.gov.uk

Hitchins, Phil (CON - Aldwick West)
cllr.phil.hitchins@arun.gov.uk

Hughes, Christopher (CON - Barnham)
cllr.christopher.hughes@arun.gov.uk

Maconachie, Dougal (CON - Marine)
cllr.dougal.maconachie@arun.gov.uk

Maconachie, Jacqui (CON - Aldwick West)

Madeley, Gill (CON - Felpham West)
cllr.gill.madeley@arun.gov.uk

Neno, Emma (CON - Rustington East)
cllr.emma.neno@arun.gov.uk

Northeast, Michael (LAB - Courtwick with Toddington)
cllr.mike.northeast@arun.gov.uk

Oakley, Barbara (CON - Middleton-on-Sea)
cllr.barbara.oakley@arun.gov.uk

Oliver-Redgate, Colin (CON - Ferring)
cllr.colin.oliver-redgate@arun.gov.uk

Oppler, Francis (LD - Orchard)
cllr.francis.oppler@arun.gov.uk

Patel, Ashvin (CON - Pagham)
ashvinpatel@hotmail.co.uk

Pendleton, Jacky (CON - Bersted)
cllr.jacky.pendleton@arun.gov.uk

Porter, Stella (CON - Rustington West)
cllr.stella.porter@arun.gov.uk

Purchese, Daniel (LD - Beach)
cllr.dan.purchese@arun.gov.uk

Rapnik, Ann (UKIP - Bersted)
cllr.ann.rapnik@arun.gov.uk

Reynolds, Stephen (CON - Hotham)
cllr.steve.reynolds@arun.gov.uk

Rhodes, Vicky (UKIP - Courtwick with Toddington)
cllr.vicky.rhodes@arun.gov.uk

Stainton, Elaine (CON - Felpham West)
cllr.elaine.stainton@arun.gov.uk

Tyler, Graham (CON - Rustington East)
cllr.graham.tyler@arun.gov.uk

Walsh, James (LD - Beach)
cllr.james.walsh@arun.gov.uk

Warren, Mick (CON - Brookfield)
cllr.mick.warren@arun.gov.uk

Wells, Paul (LD - Hotham)
cllr.paul.wells@arun.gov.uk

Wheal, Robert (CON - Arundel & Walberton)
cllr.robert.wheal@arun.gov.uk

Wotherspoon, Paul (CON - Middleton-on-Sea)
cllr.paul.wotherspoon@arun.gov.uk

POLITICAL COMPOSITION

CON: 43, LD: 5, UKIP: 4, IND: 1, LAB: 1

COMMITTEE CHAIRS

Audit & Governance: Mrs Barbara Oakley

Development Control: Mr Stephen Haymes

Licensing: Mr Trevor Bence

Ashfield D

Ashfield District Council, Council Offices, Urban Road, Kirkby-in-Ashfield NG17 8DA
☎ 01623 450000 🖷 01623 457585 💻 www.ashfield-dc.gov.uk

FACTS AND FIGURES

Parliamentary Constituencies: Ashfield, Newark
EU Constituencies: East Midlands
Election Frequency: Elections are of whole council

PRINCIPAL OFFICERS

Chief Executive: Mr Robert Mitchell Chief Executive, Council Offices, Urban Road, Kirkby-in-Ashfield NG17 8DA ☎ 01623 457251 🖱 r.mitchell@ashfield-dc.gov.uk

Deputy Chief Executive: Mr David Greenwood Deputy Chief Executive of Resources, Council Offices, Urban Road, Kirkby-in-Ashfield NG17 8DA ☎ 01623 457201 🖷 01623 457585 🖱 d.greenwood@ashfield-dc.gov.uk

Assistant Chief Executive: Mrs Ruth Dennis, Assistant Chief Executive of Governance, Council Offices, Urban Road, Kirkby-in-Ashfield NG17 8DA ☎ 01623 457009 🖱 r.dennis@ashfield-dc.gov.uk

Access Officer / Social Services (Disability): Ms Sharon Allman Equality & Diversity Research Officer, Mansfield District Council, Civic Centre, Chesterfield Road South, Mansfield NG19 7BH ☎ 01623 463042 🖱 sallman@mansfield.gov.uk

Architect, Building / Property Services: Ms Elaine Saxton, Asset Manager, Council Offices, Urban Road, Kirkby-in-Ashfield NG17 8DA ☎ 01623 457360 🖷 01623 457590 🖱 e.p.saxton@ashfield-dc.gov.uk

Best Value: Mrs Joanne Wright Corporate Performance & Improvement Manager, Council Offices, Urban Road, Kirkby-in-Ashfield NG17 8DA ☎ 01623 457328 🖱 j.wright@ashfield-dc.gov.uk

Building Control: Mr Richard Scott Building Control Manager, Council Offices, Urban Road, Kirkby-in-Ashfield NG17 8DA ☎ 01623 457387 🖱 r.j.scott@ashfield-dc.gov.uk

Catering Services: Ms Elaine Saxton, Asset Manager, Council Offices, Urban Road, Kirkby-in-Ashfield NG17 8DA ☎ 01623 457360 🖷 01623 457590 🖱 e.p.saxton@ashfield-dc.gov.uk

PR / Communications: Ms Carys Turner-Jones Corporate Communications Manager, Ashfield District Council, Urban Road, Kirkby-in-Ashfield NG17 8DA ☎ 01623 457004 🖱 c.turner-jones@ashfield-dc.gov.uk

Community Planning: Mr Stuart Wiltshire Interim Forward Planning Team Manager, Council Offices, Urban Road, Kirkby-in-Ashfield NG17 8DA ☎ 01623 457383 🖱 s.wiltshire@ashfield-dc.gov.uk

Community Safety: Mr Carl Holland Interim Community Protection Manager, Council Offices, Urban Road, Kirkby-in-Ashfield NG17 8DA ☎ 01623 457349 🖱 c.holland@ashfield-dc.gov.uk

Computer Management: Mr Andy Slate ICT Manager, Council Offices, Urban Road, Kirkby-in-Ashfield NG17 8DA ☎ 01623 457555 🖱 a.slate@ashfield-dc.gov.uk

Corporate Services: Mr Craig Bonar Service Director of Corporate Services, Council Offices, Urban Road, Kirkby-in-Ashfield NG17 8DA ☎ 01623 457203 🖱 c.bonar@ashfield-dc.gov.uk

Customer Service: Mr Craig Scott Revenues & Customer Services Manager, Council Offices, Urban Road, Kirkby-in-Ashfield NG17 8DA ☎ 01623 457263 🖱 c.scott@ashfield-dc.gov.uk

Economic Development: Mr Paul Thomas Regeneration Manager, Civic Centre, Chesterfield Road South, Mansfield NG19 7BH ☎ 01623 463369 🖱 pthomas@mansfield.gov.uk

Emergency Planning: Ms Jenni French Business Contingency & Sustainability Manager, Ashfield District Council, Urban Road, Kirkby-in-Ashfield NG17 8DA ☎ 01623 457370 🖱 j.french@ashfield-dc.gov.uk

Energy Management: Ms Jenni French Business Contingency & Sustainability Manager, Ashfield District Council, Urban Road, Kirkby-in-Ashfield NG17 8DA ☎ 01623 457370 🖱 j.french@ashfield-dc.gov.uk

Environmental Health: Mr Chris Booth Environmental Health Manager, Council Offices, Urban Road, Kirkby-in-Ashfield NG17 8DA ☎ 01623 457228 🖱 c.booth@ashfield-dc.gov.uk

Estates, Property & Valuation: Mr Matthew Kirk Estates Manager, Council Offices, Urban Road, Kirkby-in-Ashfield NG17 8DA ☎ 01623 457277 🖱 m.kirk@ashfield-dc.gov.uk

Facilities: Mr Neil Cotterill Facilities Manager, Council Offices, Urban Road, Kirkby-in-Ashfield NG17 8DA ☎ 01623 457257 🖱 n.cotterill@ashfield-dc.gov.uk

ASHFIELD

Finance: Mr David Greenwood Deputy Chief Executive of Resources, Council Offices, Urban Road, Kirkby-in-Ashfield NG17 8DA ☎ 01623 457201 🖷 01623 457585 🖰 d.greenwood@ashfield-dc.gov.uk

Fleet Management: Mr David White, Transport Services Manager, Northern Depot, Station Road, Sutton-in-Ashfield NG17 5HB ☎ 01623 457883 🖰 d.c.white@ashfield-dc.gov.uk

Grounds Maintenance: Mrs Sam Dennis Service Lead - Waste & Environment, Northern Depot, Station Road, Sutton-in-Ashfield NG17 5HB ☎ 01623 457873 🖰 s.dennis@ashfield-dc.gov.uk

Health and Safety: Mr Patrick Godsall Health & Safety Officer, Council Offices, Urban Road, Kirkby-in-Ashfield NG17 8DA ☎ 01623 457282 🖷 01623 457585 🖰 p.godsall@ashfield-dc.gov.uk

Home Energy Conservation: Mr Martin Trouse Energy Co-ordinator, Council Offices, Urban Road, Kirkby-in-Ashfield NG17 8DA ☎ 01623 457034 🖰 m.trouse@ashfield-dc.gov.uk

Housing: Mr Peter Kandola Strategic Housing & Development Manager, Council Offices, Urban Road, Kirkby-in-Ashfield NG17 8DA ☎ 01623 457351 🖰 p.kandola@ashfield-dc.gov.uk

Housing Maintenance: Mr Paul Bingham Director of Asset Management, Ashfield Homes Ltd, Broadway, Brook Street, Sutton-in-Ashfield NG17 1AL ☎ 01623 608877 🖰 p.bingham@ashfield-dc.gov.uk

Legal: Ms Beth Brown Principal Solicitor, Council Offices, Urban Road, Kirkby-in-Ashfield NG17 8DA ☎ 01623 457339 🖰 principalsolicitor@ashfield-dc.gov.uk

Leisure and Cultural Services: Mrs Theresa Hodgkinson, Locality & Community Empowerment Manager, Council Offices, Urban Road, Kirkby-in-Ashfield NG17 8DA ☎ 01623 457588 🖰 t.hodgkinson@ashfield-dc.gov.uk

Licensing: Mr Chris Booth Environmental Health Manager, Council Offices, Urban Road, Kirkby-in-Ashfield NG17 8DA ☎ 01623 457228 🖰 c.booth@ashfield-dc.gov.uk

Member Services: Mr David Dalby Democracy Manager, Council Offices, Urban Road, Kirkby-in-Ashfield NG17 8DA ☎ 01623 457314 🖰 d.dalby@ashfield-dc.gov.uk

Parking: Mr Neil Cotterill Facilities Manager, Council Offices, Urban Road, Kirkby-in-Ashfield NG17 8DA ☎ 01623 457257 🖰 n.cotterill@ashfield-dc.gov.uk

Personnel / HR: Mrs Mariam Amos HR Manager, Civic Centre, Chesterfield Road South, Mansfield NG19 7BH ☎ 01623 663032 🖰 mamos@mansfield.gov.uk

Planning: Mrs Christine Sarris Corporate Planning & Building Control Manager, Council Offices, Urban Road, Kirkby-in-Ashfield NG17 8DA ☎ 01623 457375 🖰 c.m.sarris@ashfield-dc.gov.uk

Procurement: Ms Sharon Lynch Corporate Finance Manager, Council Offices, Urban Road, Kirkby-in-Ashfield NG17 8DA ☎ 01623 457202 🖰 s.lynch@ashfield-dc.gov.uk

Recycling & Waste Minimisation: Mrs Sam Dennis Service Lead - Waste & Environment, Council Offices, Urban Road, Kirkby-in-Ashfield NG17 8DA ☎ 01623 457873 🖰 s.dennis@ashfield-dc.gov.uk

Regeneration: Mr Paul Thomas Regeneration Manager, Civic Centre, Chesterfield Road South, Mansfield NG19 7BH ☎ 01623 463369 🖰 pthomas@mansfield.gov.uk

Staff Training: Mrs Lorraine Powney Principal Learning & Development Adviser, Civic Centre, Chesterfield Road South, Mansfield NG19 7BH ☎ 01623 463250 🖷 01623 463900 🖰 lpowney@mansfield.gov.uk

Street Scene: Mr Carl Holland Interim Community Protection Manager, Council Offices, Urban Road, Kirkby-in-Ashfield NG17 8DA ☎ 01623 457349 🖰 c.holland@ashfield-dc.gov.uk

Sustainable Development: Ms Jenni French Business Contingency & Sustainability Manager, Ashfield District Council, Urban Road, Kirkby-in-Ashfield NG17 8DA ☎ 01623 457370 🖰 j.french@ashfield-dc.gov.uk

Town Centre: Mr Trevor Watson Service Director - Economy, Council Offices, Urban Road, Kirkby-in-Ashfield NG17 8DA ☎ 01623 457374 🖰 t.watson@ashfield-dc.gov.uk

Transport: Mr David White, Transport Services Manager, Northern Depot, Station Road, Sutton-in-Ashfield NG17 5HB ☎ 01623 457883 🖰 d.c.white@ashfield-dc.gov.uk

Waste Collection and Disposal: Mr Paul Rowbotham Waste Operations Officer, Northern Depot, Station Road, Sutton-in-Ashfield NG17 5HB ☎ 01623 457860 🖰 p.rowbotham@ashfield-dc.gov.uk

Waste Management: Mr Paul Rowbotham Waste Operations Officer, Northern Depot, Station Road, Sutton-in-Ashfield NG17 5HB ☎ 01623 457860 🖰 p.rowbotham@ashfield-dc.gov.uk

COUNCILLORS

***Chair* Maxwell**, Glenys (LAB - Huthwaite & Brierley)
cllr.g.c.maxwell@ashfield-dc.gov.uk

***Vice-Chair* Griffiths**, David (LAB - Leamington)
cllr.d.griffiths@ashfield-dc.gov.uk

***Leader of the Council* Butler**, Cheryl (LAB - Kirkby Cross & Portland)
cllr.c.butler@ashfield-dc.gov.uk

***Deputy Leader of the Council* Davis**, Don (LAB - Annesley & Kirkby Woodhouse)
cllr.d.davis@ashfield-dc.gov.uk

Anderson, Lee (LAB - Huthwaite & Brierley)
cllr.l.anderson@ashfield-dc.gov.uk

Aspinall, James (LAB - St Mary's)
cllr.j.aspinall@ashfield-dc.gov.uk

Baron, Christopher (LAB - Hucknall West)
cllr.c.baron@ashfield-dc.gov.uk

Bissett, Rachel (LAB - Hucknall North)
cllr.r.bissett@ashfield-dc.gov.uk

Bradley, Benjamin (CON - Hucknall North)
cllr.b.bradley@ashfield-dc.gov.uk

Brewer, Anthony (LD - Skegby)
cllr.a.brewer@ashfield-dc.gov.uk

Brown, Amanda (LAB - Central & New Cross)
cllr.a.brown@ashfield-dc.gov.uk

Brown, Tim (LAB - Central & New Cross)
cllr.t.brown@ashfield-dc.gov.uk

Carroll, Steven (LAB - Sutton Junction & Harlow Wood)
cllr.s.t.carroll@ashfield-dc.gov.uk

Chapman, Christian (LD - Jacksdale)
cllr.c.chapman@ashfield-dc.gov.uk

Donnelly, Joanne (LAB - Abbey Hill)
cllr.j.donnelly@ashfield-dc.gov.uk

Hollis, Helen (LAB - The Dales)
cllr.h.hollis@ashfield-dc.gov.uk

Hollis, Tom (LD - Ashfields)
cllr.t.j.hollis@ashfield-dc.gov.uk

James, Jacqueline (LAB - Summit)
cllr.j.james@ashfield-dc.gov.uk

Knight, John (LAB - Summit)
cllr.j.knight@ashfield-dc.gov.uk

Madden, Rachel (LD - Annesley & Kirkby Woodhouse)
cllr.r.e.madden@ashfield-dc.gov.uk

Mason, Catherine Ann (LAB - Carsic)
cllr.c.mason@ashfield-dc.gov.uk

Mitchell, Lauren (LAB - Hucknall South)
cllr.l.mitchell@ashfield-dc.gov.uk

Morrison, Keir (LAB - Hucknall South)
cllr.k.a.morrison@ashfield-dc.gov.uk

Morrison, Lachlan (LAB - Hucknall Central)
cllr.l.s.morrison@ashfield-dc.gov.uk

Murphy, Michael (CON - Hucknall North)
cllr.m.murphy@ashfield-dc.gov.uk

Ndiweni, Nicolle (LAB - Hucknall Central)
cllr.n.ndiweni@ashfield-dc.gov.uk

Roberts, Paul (LAB - Skegby)
cllr.p.roberts@ashfield-dc.gov.uk

Rostance, Philip (CON - Hucknall West)
cllr.p.rostance@ashfield-dc.gov.uk

Rostance, Kevin (CON - Hucknall West)
cllr.k.rostance@ashfield-dc.gov.uk

Sears-Piccavey, Robert (IND - Underwood)
cllr.sears-piccavey@ashfield-dc.gov.uk

Smith, Helen (LD - Stanton Hill & Teversal)
cllr.h.smith@ashfield-dc.gov.uk

Smith, Michael (LAB - Kingsway)
cllr.m.smith@ashfield-dc.gov.uk

Turner, Beverley (IND - Selston)
cllr.b.g.turner@ashfield-dc.gov.uk

Wilson, Samuel (IND - Selston)
cllr.s.wilson@ashfield-dc.gov.uk

Zadrozny, Jason (IND - Larwood)
cllr.j.zadrozny@ashfield-dc.gov.uk

POLITICAL COMPOSITION
LAB: 22, LD: 5, CON: 4, IND: 4

COMMITTEE CHAIRS
Audit: Mr Kevin Rostance

Planning: Mr John Knight

Ashford D

Ashford Borough Council, Civic Centre, Tannery Lane, Ashford TN23 1PL
☎ 01233 331111 🖷 01233 645654 💻 www.ashford.gov.uk

FACTS AND FIGURES
Parliamentary Constituencies: Ashford
EU Constituencies: South East
Election Frequency: Elections are of whole council

PRINCIPAL OFFICERS
Chief Executive: Mr John Bunnett Chief Executive, Civic Centre, Tannery Lane, Ashford TN23 1PL ☎ 01233 330201 ✉ john.bunnett@ashford.gov.uk

Deputy Chief Executive: Mr Paul Naylor Deputy Chief Executive, Civic Centre, Tannery Lane, Ashford TN23 1PL ☎ 01233 330436 ✉ paul.naylor@ashford.gov.uk

Architect, Building / Property Services: Mrs Tracey Kerly, Head of Community & Housing, Civic Centre, Tannery Lane, Ashford TN23 1PL ☎ 01233 330607 ✉ tracey.kerly@ashford.gov.uk

Building Control: Mr Tim Parrett, Head of Development Delivery, Civic Centre, Tannery Lane, Ashford TN23 1PL ☎ 01233 330275 ✉ tim.parrett@ashford.gov.uk

Children / Youth Services: Mrs Christina Fuller Cultural Projects Manager, Civic Centre, Tannery Lane, Ashford TN23 1PL ☎ 01233 330228 ✉ christina.fuller@ashford.gov.uk

PR / Communications: Mr Dean Spurrell Communications & Marketing Manager, Civic Centre, Tannery Lane, Ashford TN23 1PL ☎ 01233 330647 ✉ dean.spurrell@ashford.gov.uk

Community Safety: Mr James Hann Health, Parking & Community Safety Manager, Ashford Community Safety Unit, Tufton Street, Ashford TN23 1BT ☎ 01233 330608 ✉ james.hann@ashford.gov.uk

Computer Management: Mr Rob Neil, Head of Business Change & Technology, Civic Centre, Tannery Lane, Ashford TN23 1PL ☎ 01233 330850 ✉ rob.neil@ashford.gov.uk

Contracts: Mr Mark Carty, Head of Cultural & Project Services, Civic Centre, Tannery Lane, Ashford TN23 1PL ☎ 01233 330477 ✉ mark.carty@ashford.gov.uk

Customer Service: Mrs Julie Rogers, Head of Environmental & Customer Service, Civic Centre, Tannery Lane, Ashford TN23 1PL ☎ 01233 330856 ✉ julie.rogers@ashford.gov.uk

ASHFORD

Economic Development: Mr Andrew Osborne Economic Development Manager, Civic Centre, Tannery Lane, Ashford TN23 1PL ☎ 01233 330310 andrew.osborne@ashford.gov.uk

E-Government: Mr Rob Neil, Head of Business Change & Technology, Civic Centre, Tannery Lane, Ashford TN23 1PL ☎ 01233 330850 rob.neil@ashford.gov.uk

Electoral Registration: Mrs Valma Page Senior Electoral Services Officer, Civic Centre, Tannery Lane, Ashford TN23 1PL ☎ 01233 330462 valma.page@ashford.gov.uk

Emergency Planning: Ms Della Fackrell, Resilience Partnership Manager, Civic Centre, Tannery Lane, Ashford TN23 1PL ☎ 01233 330389 della.fackrell@ashford.gov.uk

Environmental Health: Mrs Sheila Davison Head of Health, Parking & Community Safety, Civic Centre, Tannery Lane, Ashford TN23 1PL ☎ 01233 330224 sheila.davison@ashford.gov.uk

Estates, Property & Valuation: Mrs Tracey Kerly, Head of Community & Housing, Civic Centre, Tannery Lane, Ashford TN23 1PL ☎ 01233 330607 tracey.kerly@ashford.gov.uk

Facilities: Mrs Tracey Kerly, Head of Community & Housing, Civic Centre, Tannery Lane, Ashford TN23 1PL ☎ 01233 330607 tracey.kerly@ashford.gov.uk

Finance: Mr Paul Naylor Deputy Chief Executive, Civic Centre, Tannery Lane, Ashford TN23 1PL ☎ 01233 330436 paul.naylor@ashford.gov.uk

Treasury: Mr Ben Lockwood Head of Finance, Civic Centre, Tannery Lane, Ashford TN23 1PL ☎ 01233 330540 ben.lockwood@ashford.gov.uk

Fleet Management: Ms Michelle Pecci, Head of Personnel & Development, Civic Centre, Tannery Lane, Ashford TN23 1PL ☎ 01233 330602 michelle.pecci@ashford.gov.uk

Grounds Maintenance: Mr Mark Carty, Head of Cultural & Project Services, Civic Centre, Tannery Lane, Ashford TN23 1PL ☎ 01233 330477 mark.carty@ashford.gov.uk

Health and Safety: Mrs Sheila Davison Head of Health, Parking & Community Safety, Civic Centre, Tannery Lane, Ashford TN23 1PL ☎ 01233 330224 sheila.davison@ashford.gov.uk

Housing: Mrs Tracey Kerly, Head of Community & Housing, Civic Centre, Tannery Lane, Ashford TN23 1PL ☎ 01233 330607 tracey.kerly@ashford.gov.uk

Housing Maintenance: Mr Chris Tillin, Planned Maintenance Manager, Civic Centre, Tannery Lane, Ashford TN23 1PL ☎ 01233 330483 chris.tillin@ashford.gov.uk

Legal: Mr Terry Mortimer, Head of Legal & Democratic Services, Civic Centre, Tannery Lane, Ashford TN23 1PL ☎ 01233 330210 terry.mortimer@ashford.gov.uk

Leisure and Cultural Services: Mr Mark Carty, Head of Cultural & Project Services, Civic Centre, Tannery Lane, Ashford TN23 1PL ☎ 01233 330477 mark.carty@ashford.gov.uk

Licensing: Mr Jack Godley Licensing Manager, Civic Centre, Tannery Lane, Ashford TN23 1PL ☎ 01233 330722 jack.godley@ashford.gov.uk

Lottery Funding, Charity and Voluntary: Ms Michelle Byrne, Funding & Partnerships Officer, Civic Centre, Tannery Lane, Ashford TN23 1PL ☎ 01233 330485 michelle.byrne@ashford.gov.uk

Member Services: Mr Keith Fearon, Member Services & Scrutiny Manager, Civic Centre, Tannery Lane, Ashford TN23 1PL ☎ 01233 330564 keith.fearon@ashford.gov.uk

Parking: Mrs Jo Fox Health, Parking & Community Safety Manager, Civic Centre, Tannery Lane, Ashford TN23 1PL ☎ 01233 330641 jo.fox@ashford.gov.uk

Personnel / HR: Ms Michelle Pecci, Head of Personnel & Development, Civic Centre, Tannery Lane, Ashford TN23 1PL ☎ 01233 330602 michelle.pecci@ashford.gov.uk

Planning: Mr Richard Alderton, Head of Planning & Development, Civic Centre, Tannery Lane, Ashford TN23 1PL ☎ 01233 330239 richard.alderton@ashford.gov.uk

Procurement: Miss Caroline Carney Procurement Officer, Civic Centre, Tannery Lane, Ashford TN23 1PL ☎ 01233 330605 caroline.carney@ashford.gov.uk

Recycling & Waste Minimisation: Mrs Julie Rogers, Head of Environmental & Customer Service, Civic Centre, Tannery Lane, Ashford TN23 1PL ☎ 01233 330856 julie.rogers@ashford.gov.uk

Regeneration: Ms Michelle Byrne, Funding & Partnerships Officer, Civic Centre, Tannery Lane, Ashford TN23 1PL ☎ 01233 330485 michelle.byrne@ashford.gov.uk

Staff Training: Ms Michelle Pecci, Head of Personnel & Development, Civic Centre, Tannery Lane, Ashford TN23 1PL ☎ 01233 330602 michelle.pecci@ashford.gov.uk

Street Scene: Mrs Julie Rogers, Head of Environmental & Customer Service, Civic Centre, Tannery Lane, Ashford TN23 1PL ☎ 01233 330856 julie.rogers@ashford.gov.uk

Sustainable Communities: Mr Richard Alderton, Head of Planning & Development, Civic Centre, Tannery Lane, Ashford TN23 1PL ☎ 01233 330239 richard.alderton@ashford.gov.uk

Sustainable Development: Mr Richard Alderton, Head of Planning & Development, Civic Centre, Tannery Lane, Ashford TN23 1PL ☎ 01233 330239 richard.alderton@ashford.gov.uk

Tourism: Miss Sarah Barber, Tourism & Nature Conservation Manager, Civic Centre, Tannery Lane, Ashford TN23 1PL ☎ 01233 330345 sarah.barber@ashford.gov.uk

Town Centre: Miss Jo Wynn-Carter Town Team Member, Civic Centre, Tannery Lane, Ashford TN23 1PL ☎ 01233 330612 ✉ jo.wynn-carter@ashford.gov.uk

Waste Collection and Disposal: Mrs Julie Rogers, Head of Environmental & Customer Service, Civic Centre, Tannery Lane, Ashford TN23 1PL ☎ 01233 330856 ✉ julie.rogers@ashford.gov.uk

Waste Management: Mrs Julie Rogers, Head of Environmental & Customer Service, Civic Centre, Tannery Lane, Ashford TN23 1PL ☎ 01233 330856 ✉ julie.rogers@ashford.gov.uk

COUNCILLORS

***Mayor* Link**, John (CON - St. Michaels)

***Deputy Mayor* Dyer**, Geraldine (CON - Weald North)
geraldine.dyer@ashford.gov.uk

***Leader of the Council* Clarkson**, Gerry (CON - Charing)
gerrydclarkson@aol.com

***Deputy Leader of the Council* Bell**, Clair (CON - Weald Central)
clairbell@solutionprovider.co.uk

***Group Leader* Chilton**, Brendan (LAB - Stanhope (Ashford))
brendan.chilton@ashford.gov.uk

***Group Leader* Ovenden**, Noel (IND - Wye with Hinxhill)
noel.ovenden@ashford.gov.uk

Adby, Jeremy (LD - North Willesborough (Ashford))
jeremy.adby@btinternet.com

Apps, Harold (CON - Victoria (Ashford))

Barrett, Bill (CON - Singleton South)
barrettwbarrett@aol.com

Bartlett, Paul (CON - Weald East)
paul.bartlett@ashford.gov.uk

Bell, Neil (CON - Biddenden)
neilbell@solutionprovider.co.uk

Bennett, Mike (CON - Rolvenden & Tenterden West)
mikebennettkm@tiscali.co.uk

Blanford, Jessamy (CON - Great Chart with Singleton North)
jessamy.blandford@ashford.gov.uk

Bradford, Brad (CON - Weald South)
brad.bradford@ashford.gov.uk

Britcher, Jill (LAB - Beaver (Ashford))
jill.britcher@ashford.gov.uk

Buchanan, Andrew (CON - Bybrook (Ashford))
andrewjohnbuchanan@hotmail.com

Burgess, Michael (CON - Isle of Oxney)
michael.burgess@ashford.gov.uk

Clokie, Paul (CON - Tenterden North)
paul.clokie@ashford.gov.uk

Dehnel, Stephen (CON - Downs North)
stephen.dehnel@ashford.gov.uk

Farrell, Dara (LAB - Victoria (Ashford))
dara.farrell@ashford.gov.uk

Feacey, Peter (CON - Godinton (Ashford))
peterfeacey@talktalk.net

Galpin, Graham (CON - Stour (Ashford))
graham.galpin@ashford.gov.uk

Heyes, Bernard (CON - Godinton (Ashford))
bernardjdheys@talktalk.net

Heyes, Tina (CON - Park Farm North)
tinaheyes@btinternet.com

Hicks, Aline (CON - Weald South)
aline.hicks@ashford.gov.uk

Hooker, Kate (LAB - Aylesford Green (Ashford))
katehooker12@yahoo.co.uk

Howard, William (CON - Saxon Shore)
william.howard@ashford.gov.uk

Knowles, Callum (CON - Tenterden)
callum@tenterden.co.uk

Koowaree, George (LD - North Willesborough (Ashford))

Krause, Larry (CON - Downs West)
larry.krause@btinternet.com

Martin, Jane (CON - Saxon Shore)
jane.martin@ashford.gov.uk

Martin, Marion (CON - Little Burton Farm (Ashford))
marionmartin06@btinternet.com

Michael, Winston (IND - Boughton Aluph & Eastwell)
winston.michael@ashford.gov.uk

Murphy, Beverley (UKIP - Beaver (Ashford))

Pickering, Alan (CON - Weald Central)
alan@ampickering.com

Powell, Luke (CON - Bockhanger (Ashford))
lukejpowell1@gmail.com

Shorter, Neil (CON - Washford)
njshorter@btinternet.com

Sims, Philip (IND - Kennington (Ashford))
philip.sims@ashford.gov.uk

Smith, David (IND - South Willesborough (Ashford))
david.smith@ashford.gov.uk

Waters, Chris (CON - Stour (Ashford))
chris.waters@ashford.gov.uk

Webb, Jenny (CON - Norman (Ashford))
jennywebb@live.co.uk

Wedgbury, Jim (CON - Park Farm South)
jimwedgbury@aol.com

White, Gerald (CON - Highfield (Ashford))
gerald.white@ashford.gov.uk

POLITICAL COMPOSITION

CON: 32, IND: 4, LAB: 4, LD: 2, UKIP: 1

Aylesbury Vale D

Aylesbury Vale District Council, Council Offices, The Gateway, Gatehouse Road, Aylesbury HP19 8FF
☎ 01296 585858 🖷 01296 336977
💻 www.aylesburyvaledc.gov.uk

FACTS AND FIGURES

Parliamentary Constituencies: Aylesbury, Buckingham
EU Constituencies: South East
Election Frequency: Elections are of whole council

AYLESBURY VALE

PRINCIPAL OFFICERS

Chief Executive: Mr Andrew Grant, Chief Executive, The Gateway, Gatehouse Road, Aylesbury HP19 8FF ☎ 01296 585001 agrant@aylesburyvaledc.gov.uk

Senior Management: Ms Tracey Aldworth Director, The Gateway, Gatehouse Road, Aylesbury HP19 8FF ☎ 01296 585003 taldworth@aylesburyvaledc.gov.uk

Senior Management: Mr Andrew Small Director, The Gateway, Gatehouse Road, Aylesbury HP19 8FF ☎ 01296 585507 asmall@aylesburyvaledc.gov.uk

Building Control: Mr Adam Heeley, Building Control & Access Manager, The Gateway, Gatehouse Road, Aylesbury HP19 8FF ☎ 01296 585459 aheely@aylesburyvaledc.gov.uk

PR / Communications: Miss Teresa Lane, Head of Communications, Marketing & Town Centre Management, The Gateway, Gatehouse Road, Aylesbury HP19 8FF ☎ 01296 585006 🖷 01296 336977 tlane@aylesburyvaledc.gov.uk

Community Safety: Ms Kay Aitken, Community Safety Officer, The Gateway, Gatehouse Road, Aylesbury HP19 8FF ☎ 01296 585005 kaitken@aylesburyvaledc.gov.uk

Computer Management: Mr Alan Evans, Head of IT Services, The Gateway, Gatehouse, Aylesbury HP19 8FF ☎ 01296 585767 aevans@aylesburyvaledc.gov.uk

Contracts: Ms Sarah Deyes, Procurement Strategy Officer, The Gateway, Gatehouse Road, Aylesbury HP19 8FF ☎ 01296 585871 sdeyes@aylesburyvaledc.gov.uk

Customer Service: Ms Janet Forsdike Service Improvement Manager, Council Offices, The Gateway, Gatehouse Road, Aylesbury HP19 8FF ☎ 01296 585083 jforsdike@aylesburyvaledc.gov.uk

Direct Labour: Mr Andy Wilkins Operations Manager, Pembroke Road, Aylesbury HP20 1DG ☎ 01296 585303 awilkins@aylesburyvaledc.gov.uk

Economic Development: Mr Steve McAteer Interim Economy Partnership Manager, Council Offices, The Gateway, Gatehouse Road, Aylesbury HP19 8FF ☎ 01296 585657 smcateer@aylesburyvaledc.gov.uk

E-Government: Mr Alan Evans, Head of IT Services, The Gateway, Gatehouse Road, Aylesbury HP19 8FF ☎ 01296 585767 aevans@aylesburyvaledc.gov.uk

Electoral Registration: Mr Chris Sheard, Electoral Registration Officer, The Gateway, Gatehouse Road, Aylesbury HP19 8FF ☎ 01296 585050

Emergency Planning: Mr David Thomas, Corporate Health & Safety Advisor, The Gateway, Gatehouse Road, Aylesbury HP19 8FF ☎ 01296 585158 dthomas@aylesburyvaledc.gov.uk

Energy Management: Mr Alan Asbury, Sustainability Team Leader, The Gateway, Gatehouse Road, Aylesbury HP19 8FF ☎ 01296 585112 aasbury@aylesburyvaledc.gov.uk

Environmental / Technical Services: Mr Robert Smart, Environment Officer, The Gateway, Gatehouse Road, Aylesbury HP19 8FF ☎ 01296 585147 rsmart@aylesburyvaledc.gov.uk

Environmental Health: Mr Richard Hiscock Environmental Support Manager, The Gateway, Gatehouse Road, Aylesbury HP19 8FF ☎ 01296 585156 rhiscock@aylesburyvaledc.gov.uk

Events Manager: Ms Sophia Fulchini Conference Centre Manager, The Gateway, Gatehouse Road, Aylesbury HP19 8FF ☎ 01296 585969 sfulchini@aylesburyvaledc.gov.uk

Facilities: Ms Jane Heywood Facilities Manager, The Gateway, Gatehouse Road, Aylesbury HP19 8FF ☎ 01296 585191 sfulchini@aylesburyvaledc.gov.uk

Finance: Mr Andrew Small Director, The Gateway, Gatehouse Road, Aylesbury HP19 8FF ☎ 01296 585507 asmall@aylesburyvaledc.gov.uk

Treasury: Mr Andrew Small Director, The Gateway, Gatehouse Road, Aylesbury HP19 8FF ☎ 01296 585507 asmall@aylesburyvaledc.gov.uk

Grounds Maintenance: Mr Gareth Bird Community Spaces Manager, Council Offices, The Gateway, Gatehouse Road, Aylesbury HP19 8FF ☎ 01296 585228 gbird@aylesburyvaledc.gov.uk

Health and Safety: Mr David Thomas, Corporate Health & Safety Advisor, The Gateway, Gatehouse Road, Aylesbury HP19 8FF ☎ 01296 585158 dthomas@aylesburyvaledc.gov.uk

Home Energy Conservation: Mr Robert Smart, Environment Officer, The Gateway, Gatehouse Road, Aylesbury HP19 8FF ☎ 01296 585147 rsmart@aylesburyvaledc.gov.uk

Housing: Mr Will Rysdale Housing Development & Strategy Manager, Council Offices, The Gateway, Gatehouse Road, Aylesbury HP19 8FF ☎ 01296 585561 housingneeds@aylesburyvaledc.gov.uk

Licensing: Mr Peter Seal, Licensing Officer, The Gateway, Gatehouse Road, Aylesbury HP19 8FF ☎ 01296 585083 pseal@aylesburyvaledc.gov.uk

Lottery Funding, Charity and Voluntary: Ms Sarah Rothwell Community Chest Grants Officer, Council Offices, The Gateway, Gatehouse Road, Aylesbury HP19 8FF ☎ 01296 585634 srothwell@aylesburyvaledc.gov.uk

Member Services: Mr Bill Ashton Democratic Services Manager, Council Offices, The Gateway, Gatehouse Road, Aylesbury HP19 8FF ☎ 01296 585040 🖷 01296 488887 washton@aylesburyvaledc.gov.uk

Parking: Mr Stephen Harding, Parking Manager, The Gateway, Gatehouse Road, Aylesbury HP19 8FF ☎ 01296 585381 sharding@aylesburyvaledc.gov.uk

Planning: Ms Susan Kitchen Manager - Development Management, Council Offices, The Gateway, Gatehouse Road, Aylesbury HP19 8FF ☎ 01296 585436 skitchen@aylesburyvaledc.gov.uk

Procurement: Ms Sarah Deyes, Procurement Strategy Officer, The Gateway, Gatehouse Road, Aylesbury HP19 8FF ☎ 01296 585871 sdeyes@aylesburyvaledc.gov.uk

Recycling & Waste Minimisation: Mr Alan Asbury, Sustainability Team Leader, The Gateway, Gatehouse Road, Aylesbury HP19 8FF ☎ 01296 585112 aasbury@aylesburyvaledc.gov.uk

Staff Training: Ms Sarah Rodda Training Administrator, Council Offices, The Gateway, Gatehouse Road, Aylesbury HP19 8FF ☎ 01296 585015 srodda@aylesburyvaledc.gov.uk

Sustainable Communities: Mrs Stephanie Moffat Community Engagement Manager, The Gateway, Gatehouse Road, Aylesbury HP19 8FF ☎ 01296 585295 smoffat@aylesburyvaledc.gov.uk

Town Centre: Ms Diana Fawcett Town Centre Manager, The Gateway, Gatehouse Road, Aylesbury HP19 8FF ☎ 01296 396370 dfawcett@aylesburyvaledc.gov.uk

Transport: Mr Barry Waters, Transport Manager, New Century House, 18 Pembroke Road, Stocklake Industrial Estate, Aylesbury HP20 1DG ☎ 01296 585514 Fax 01296 397325 bwaters@aylesburyvaledc.gov.uk

Waste Collection and Disposal: Mr Andy Wilkins Operations Manager, Pembroke Road, Aylesbury HP20 1DG ☎ 01296 585303 awilkins@aylesburyvaledc.gov.uk

Waste Management: Mr Pete Randall Refuse Manager, Pembroke Road, Aylesbury HP20 1DG ☎ 01296 585858

COUNCILLORS

Leader of the Council **Blake**, Neil (CON - Great Brickhill & Newton Longville)
nblake@aylesburyvaledc.gov.uk

Deputy Leader of the Council **Bowles**, Steve (CON - Wendover & Halton)
sbowles@aylesburyvaledc.gov.uk

Adams, Chris (UKIP - Riverside)
chris.adams@ukip.org

Adams, Brian (UKIP - Walton Court & Hawkslade)
badams@aylesburyvaledc.gov.uk

Agoro, Peter (LD - Southcourt)
pagoro9@gmail.com

Bateman, Mark (LAB - Southcourt)
mbateman@aylesburyvaledc.gov.uk

Blake, Janet (CON - Stewkley)
jblake@aylesburyvaledc.gov.uk

Bloom, Jenny (CON - Mandeville & Elm Farm)
jbloom@aylesburyvaledc.gov.uk

Bond, Ashley (CON - Watermead)
abond@aylesburyvaledc.gov.uk

Brandis, Judy (CON - Haddenham & Stone)
jbrandis@aylesburyvaledc.gov.uk

Cartwright, John (CON - Grendon Underwood & Brill)
jcartwright@aylesburyvaledc.gov.uk

Chapple, Sue (CON - Mandeville & Elm Farm)
schapple@aylesburyvaledc.gov.uk

Chapple, Bill (CON - Aston Clinton)
bchapple@aylesburyvaledc.gov.uk

Chilver, John (CON - Steeple Claydon)
jchilver@aylesburyvaledc.gov.uk

Christensen, Anders (LD - Gatehouse)
achristensen@aylesburyvaledc.gov.uk

Cole, Andrew (CON - Coldharbour)
acole@aylesburyvaledc.gov.uk

Cole, Simon (CON - Buckingham North)
scole@aylesburyvaledc.gov.uk

Collins, Michael (CON - Aston Clinton)
mcollins@aylesburyvaledc.gov.uk

Cooper, Peter (IND - Wingrave)
pcooper@aylesburyvaledc.gov.uk

Edmonds, Michael (CON - Haddenham & Stone)
medmonds@aylesburyvaledc.gov.uk

Everitt, Ben (CON - Great Brickhill & Newton Longville)
beveritt@aylesburyvaledc.gov.uk

Fealey, Patrick (CON - Tingewick)
pfealey@aylesburyvaledc.gov.uk

Foster, Brian (CON - Haddenham & Stone)
bfoster@aylesburyvaledc.gov.uk

Glover, Netta (CON - Wing)
nglover@aylesburyvaledc.gov.uk

Harrison, Allison (LD - Oakfield & Bierton)
aharrison@aylesburyvaledc.gov.uk

Hawkett, Mike (CON - Long Crendon)
mhawkett@aylesburyvaledc.gov.uk

Hetherington, Andy (UKIP - Elmhurst)
ahetherington@aylesburyvaledc.gov.uk

Hewson, Kevin (CON - Quainton)
khewson@aylesburyvaledc.gov.uk

Hunter-Watts, Tom (CON - Bedgrove)
tom.hunterwatts@gmail.com

Hussain, Tuffail (LD - Gatehouse)
thussain@aylesburyvaledc.gov.uk

Huxley, Andy (UKIP - Riverside)
ahuxley@aylesburyvaledc.gov.uk

Irwin, Paul (CON - Waddesdon)
pirwin@aylesburyvaledc.gov.uk

Jenkins, Sandra (CON - Pitstone & Cheddington)
sjenkins@aylesburyvaledc.gov.uk

Khan, Raj (LD - Elmhurst)
rkhan@buckscc.gov.uk

King, Roger (CON - Mandeville & Elm Farm)
rking@aylesburyvaledc.gov.uk

Lambert, Steven (LD - Coldharbour)
slambert@aylesburyvaledc.gov.uk

Lewis, Nick (CON - Riverside)
nelewis@aylesburyvaledc.gov.uk

AYLESBURY VALE

Macpherson, Angela (CON - Marsh Gibbon)
amacpherson@aylesburyvaledc.gov.uk

Mills, Timothy (CON - Buckingham North)
tmills@aylesburyvaledc.gov.uk

Monger, Llew (LD - Winslow)
lmonger@aylesburyvaledc.gov.uk

Moore, Graham (CON - Gatehouse)
gmoore@aylesburyvaledc.gov.uk

Mordue, Howard (CON - Buckingham South)
hmordue@aylesburyvaledc.gov.uk

Paternoster, Carole (CON - Aston Clinton)
cpaternoster@aylesburyvaledc.gov.uk

Poll, Chris (CON - Edlesborough)
cpoll@aylesburyvaledc.gov.uk

Powell, Gary (CON - Walton Court & Hawkslade)
gpowell@aylesburyvaledc.gov.uk

Rand, Michael (CON - Oakley)
mrand@aylesburyvaledc.gov.uk

Renshell, Susan (CON - Winslow)
srenshaell@aylesburyvaledc.gov.uk

Russel, Barbara (CON - Central & Walton)
brussel@aylesburyvaledc.gov.uk

Sims, Edward (CON - Central & Walton)

Smith, Mike (LD - Coldharbour)
msmith2@aylesburyvaledc.gov.uk

Southam, Andrew (CON - Wendover & Halton)
asoutham@aylesburyvaledc.gov.uk

Stamp, Mary (CON - Oakfield & Bierton)

Stanier Bt, Beville (CON - Great Horwood)
bstanier@aylesburyvaledc.gov.uk

Strachan, Peter (CON - Wendover & Halton)
pstrachan@aylesburyvaledc.gov.uk

Stuchbury, Robin (LAB - Buckingham South)
stuchbury@dsl.pipex.com

Town, Derek (CON - Pitstone & Cheddington)
dtown@aylesburyvaledc.gov.uk

Ward, Julie (LD - Oakfield & Bierton)
jward@aylesburyvaledc.gov.uk

Ward, Julie (LD - Bierton)
jward@aylesburyvaledc.gov.uk

Whyte, Warren (CON - Luffield Abbey)
wwhyte@aylesburyvaledc.gov.uk

Winn, Mark (CON - Bedgrove)
mwinn@aylesburyvaledc.gov.uk

POLITICAL COMPOSITION

CON: 43, LD: 10, UKIP: 4, LAB: 2, IND: 1

Babergh D

Babergh District Council, Council Offices,
Corks Lane, Hadleigh,
Ipswich IP7 6SJ
☎ 01473 822801 🖷 01473 825742 💻 www.babergh.gov.uk

FACTS AND FIGURES

EU Constituencies: Eastern
Election Frequency: Elections are of whole council

PRINCIPAL OFFICERS

Chief Executive: Mrs Charlie Adan Chief Executive, Council Offices, Corks Lane, Hadleigh, Ipswich IP7 6SJ ☎ 01473 825710 🖷 01473 825742 ✉ charlie.adan@baberghmidsuffolk.gov.uk

Senior Management: Ms Lindsay Barker Strategic Director - Place, Council Offices, Corks Lane, Hadleigh, Ipswich IP7 6SJ ☎ 01473 825844 🖷 01473 825742 ✉ lindsay.barker@midsuffolk.gov.uk; lindsay.barker@baberghmidsuffolk.gov.uk

Senior Management: Mr Mike Evans Strategic Director - People, Council Offices, Corks Lane, Hadleigh, Ipswich IP7 6SJ ☎ 01473 825746 🖷 01473 825742 ✉ michael.evans@misuffolk.gov.uk; michael.evans@baberghmidsuffolk.gov.uk

Senior Management: Mr Andrew Hunkin Strategic Director - Corporate, Council Offices, Corks Lane, Hadleigh, Ipswich IP7 6SJ ☎ 01473 825820 🖷 01473 825742 ✉ andrew.hunkin@baberghmidsuffolk.gov.uk

Architect, Building / Property Services: Mr Ben Hancock, Senior Surveyor - Building Services, Council Offices, Corks Lane, Hadleigh IP7 6SJ ☎ 01473 825785 🖷 01473 825770 ✉ ben.hancock@baberghmidsuffolk.gov.uk

Best Value: Mr Peter Quirk Head - Corporate Organisation, Council Offices, Corks Lane, Hadleigh, Ipswich IP7 6SJ ☎ 01473 825829 🖷 01473 825742 ✉ peter.quirk@baberghmidsuffolk.gov.uk

Building Control: Mr Gary Starling Corporate Manager - Building Control, Council Offices, Corks Lane, Hadleigh, Ipswich IP7 6SJ ☎ 01473 825856 🖷 01473 825708 ✉ gary.starling@baberghmidsuffolk.gov.uk

PR / Communications: Mr Paul Simon Corporate Manager - Communications, Council Offices, Corks Lane, Hadleigh IP7 6SJ ☎ 01473 826634 🖷 01473 825742 ✉ paul.simon@baberghmidsuffolk.gov.uk

Community Planning: Ms Sue Clements Corporate Manager - Strong Communities, Council Offices, Corks Lane, Hadleigh, Ipswich IP7 6SJ ☎ 01449 724657 🖷 01449 724655 ✉ sue.clemments@baberghmidsuffolk.gov.uk

Community Safety: Ms Peta Jones Corporate Manager - Safe Communities, Council Offices, 131 High Street, Needham Market IP6 8DL ☎ 01449 724642 🖷 01449 724655 ✉ peta.jones@baberghmidsuffolk.gov.uk

Computer Management: Mr Kevin Peck Technical Support Manager, Council Offices, Corks Lane, Hadleigh, Ipswich IP7 6SJ ☎ 01473 825824 🖷 01473 823594 ✉ kevin.peck@baberghmidsuffolk.gov.uk

Computer Management: Mr Carl Reeder Corporate Manager - Information Management & ICT, Council Offices, Corks Lane, Hadleigh, Ipswich IP7 6SJ ☎ 01473 825790 ✉ carl.reeder@baberghmidsuffolk.gov.uk

Contracts: Ms Tracey Farthing Senior Commissioning & Procurement Officer, Council Offices, Corks Lane, Hadleigh, Ipswich IP7 6SJ ☎ 01473 825715 🖷 01473 825770 ✉ tracey.farthing@baberghmidsuffolk.gov.uk

Contracts: Mrs Rachel Hodson-Gibbons Corporate Manager - Commissioning, Council Offices, 131 High Street, Needham Market IP6 8DL ☎ 01449 724587 ✉ rachel.hodson-gibbons@baberghmidsuffolk.gov.uk

Corporate Services: Ms Suki Binjal Monitoring Officer, Council Offices, Corks Lane, Hadleigh, Ipswich IP7 6SJ ☎ 01473 825729 ✉ suki.binjal@baberghmidsuffolk.gov.uk

Corporate Services: Mr Andrew Hunkin, Strategic Director - Corporate, Council Offices, Corks Lane, Hadleigh IP7 6SJ ☎ 01473 825820 🖷 01473 823742 ✉ andrew.hunkin@baberghmidsuffolk.gov.uk

Corporate Services: Mr Peter Quirk Head - Corporate Organisation, Council Offices, Corks Lane, Hadleigh, Ipswich IP7 6SJ ☎ 01473 825829 🖷 01473 825742 ✉ peter.quirk@baberghmidsuffolk.gov.uk

Corporate Services: Ms Katherine Steel Head - Corporate Resources, Council Offices, Corks Lane, Hadleigh, Ipswich IP7 6SJ ☎ 01473 826649 🖷 01473 825742 ✉ katherine.steel@baberghmidsuffolk.gov.uk

Customer Service: Mr David Cleary Corporate Manager - Customer Services, Council Offices, Corks Lane, Hadleigh, Ipswich IP7 6SJ ☎ 01473 825722 ✉ david.cleary@baberghmidsuffolk.gov.uk

Direct Labour: Mr Ryan Jones Corporate Manager - Asset Management Operations, Council Offices, Corks Lane, Hadleigh, Ipswich IP7 6SJ ☎ 01473 825787 🖷 01473 825770 ✉ ryan.jones@baberghmidsuffolk.gov.uk

Economic Development: Mr Tom Barker Corporate Manager - Strong Communities, Council Offices, Corks Lane, Hadleigh, Ipswich IP7 6SJ ☎ 01449 724647 🖷 01449 724655 ✉ tom.barker@midsuffolk.gov.uk

Economic Development: Mr David Benham, Corporate Manager - Economic Development & Tourism, Council Offices, 131 High Street, Needham Market IP6 8DL ☎ 01449 724649 🖷 01449 724655 ✉ david.benham@baberghmidsuffolk.gov.uk

Economic Development: Ms Lou Rawsthorne Head of Economy, Investment & Development, Council Offices, Corks Lane, Hadleigh, Ipswich IP7 6SJ ☎ 01449 724772 ✉ lou.rawsthorne@baberghmidsuffolk.gov.uk

E-Government: Mr Carl Reeder Corporate Manager - Information Management & ICT, Council Offices, Corks Lane, Hadleigh, Ipswich IP7 6SJ ☎ 01473 825790 ✉ carl.reeder@baberghmidsuffolk.gov.uk

Electoral Registration: Mrs Emily Yule Corporate Manager - Elections & Electoral Management, Council Offices, Corks Lane, Hadleigh, Ipswich IP7 6SJ ☎ 01473 825891 🖷 01473 825742 ✉ emily.yule@baberghmidsuffolk.gov.uk

Emergency Planning: Ms Sue Herne Emergency Planning Responsive Officer, Council Offices, 131 High Street, Needham Market, Ipswich IP6 8DL ☎ 01449 724851 🖷 01449 724655 ✉ sue.herne@baberghmidsuffolk.gov.uk

Energy Management: Mr Chris Fry Head - Environment, Council Offices, Corks Lane, Hadleigh, Ipswich IP7 6SJ ☎ 01473 826649 🖷 01473 825742 ✉ chris.fry@baberghmidsuffolk.gov.uk

Energy Management: Mr Ben Hancock, Senior Surveyor - Building Services, Council Offices, Corks Lane, Hadleigh IP7 6SJ ☎ 01473 825785 🖷 01473 825770 ✉ ben.hancock@baberghmidsuffolk.gov.uk

Environmental / Technical Services: Mr Ryan Jones Corporate Manager - Asset Management Operations, Council Offices, Corks Lane, Hadleigh, Ipswich IP7 6SJ ☎ 01473 825787 🖷 01473 825770 ✉ ryan.jones@baberghmidsuffolk.gov.uk

Environmental Health: Mr James Buckingham Corporate Manager - Environmental Protection, Council Offices, Corks Lane, Hadleigh, Ipswich IP7 6SJ ☎ 01473 825880 🖷 01473 825738 ✉ james.buckingham@midsuffolk.gov.uk; james.buckingham@baberghmidsuffolk.gov.uk

Environmental Health: Mr Chris Fry Head - Environment, Council Offices, Corks Lane, Hadleigh, Ipswich IP7 6SJ ☎ 01473 826649 🖷 01473 825742 ✉ chris.fry@baberghmidsuffolk.gov.uk

Estates, Property & Valuation: Mr Ryan Jones Corporate Manager - Asset Management Operations, Council Offices, Corks Lane, Hadleigh, Ipswich IP7 6SJ ☎ 01473 825787 🖷 01473 825770 ✉ ryan.jones@baberghmidsuffolk.gov.uk

European Liaison: Mrs Sue Dawes Economic Development Technical Officer, Council Offices, Corks Lane, Hadleigh, Ipswich IP7 6SJ ☎ 01473 825868 🖷 01473 825708 ✉ sue.dawes@baberghmidsuffolk.gov.uk

European Liaison: Mr Jonathan Free Head - Communities, Council Offices, Corks Lane, Hadleigh, Ipswich IP7 6SJ ☎ 01473 826649 🖷 01473 825742 ✉ jonathan.free@baberghmidsuffolk.gov.uk

Facilities: Mr Ryan Jones Corporate Manager - Asset Management Operations, Council Offices, Corks Lane, Hadleigh, Ipswich IP7 6SJ ☎ 01473 825787 🖷 01473 825770 ✉ ryan.jones@baberghmidsuffolk.gov.uk

Finance: Ms Katherine Steel Head - Corporate Resources, Council Offices, Corks Lane, Hadleigh, Ipswich IP7 6SJ ☎ 01473 826649 🖷 01473 825742 ✉ katherine.steel@baberghmidsuffolk.gov.uk

Treasury: Mr John Moyles Corporate Manager - Financial Services & Treasury, Council Offices, Corks Lane, Hadleigh, Ipswich IP7 6SJ ☎ 01473 825819 ✉ john.moyles@baberghmidsuffolk.gov.uk

Fleet Management: Mr Ryan Jones Corporate Manager - Asset Management Operations, Council Offices, 131 High Street, Needham Market IP6 8DL ☎ 01473 825787 🖷 01473 825770 ✉ ryan.jones@baberghmidsuffolk.gov.uk

BABERGH

Grounds Maintenance: Mr Peter Garrett Corporate Manager - Public Realm, Council Offices, Corks Lane, Hadleigh, Ipswich IP7 6SJ ☎ 01473 826615 🖷 01473 823594 🖰 ryan.jones@baberghmidsuffolk.gov.uk

Health and Safety: Mr Kevin Collins Joint Corporate Health & Safety Officer, Council Offices, 131 High Street, Needham Market IP6 8DL ☎ 01449 724704 🖰 kevin.collins@baberghmidsuffolk.gov.uk

Health and Safety: Mr John Graylings Corporate Manager - Food & Safety, Council Offices, 131 High Street, Needham Market, Ipswich IP6 8DL ☎ 01449 724722 🖰 john.grayling@baberghmidsuffolk.gov.uk

Home Energy Conservation: Mr James Buckingham Corporate Manager - Environmental Protection, Council Offices, Corks Lane, Hadleigh, Ipswich IP7 6SJ ☎ 01473 825880 🖷 01473 825738 🖰 james.buckingham@midsuffolk.gov.uk; james.buckingham@baberghmidsuffolk.gov.uk

Housing: Mr Martin King Head - Housing, Council Offices, 131 High Street, Needham Market IP6 8DL ☎ 01473 826649 🖷 01473 825742 🖰 martin.king@midsuffolk.gov.uk; martin.king@baberghmidsuffolk.gov.uk

Housing Maintenance: Mr Ryan Jones Corporate Manager - Asset Management Operations, Council Offices, 131 High Street, Needham Market IP6 8DL ☎ 01473 825787 🖷 01473 825770 🖰 ryan.jones@baberghmidsuffolk.gov.uk

Legal: Ms Suki Binjal Monitoring Officer, Council Offices, Corks Lane, Hadleigh, Ipswich IP7 6SJ ☎ 01473 825729 🖰 suki.binjal@baberghmidsuffolk.gov.uk

Leisure and Cultural Services: Mr Jonathan Free Head - Communities, Council Offices, Corks Lane, Hadleigh, Ipswich IP7 6SJ ☎ 01473 826649 🖷 01473 825742 🖰 jonathan.free@baberghmidsuffolk.gov.uk

Leisure and Cultural Services: Mr Jonathan Seed Corporate Manager - Healthy Communities, Council Offices, 131 High Street, Needham Market IP6 8DL ☎ 01449 724857 🖷 01449 724655 🖰 jonathan.seed@baberghmidsuffolk.gov.uk

Licensing: Mr Lee Carvell Corporate Manager - Licensing, Council Offices, Corks Lane, Hadleigh, Ipswich IP7 6SJ ☎ 01473 825719 🖰 lee.carvell@baberghmidsuffolk.gov.uk

Member Services: Mr Steve Ellwood, Democratic Services Manager, Council Offices, Corks Lane, Hadleigh IP7 6SJ ☎ 01473 825876 🖷 01473 825742 🖰 steve.ellwood@baberghmidsuffolk.gov.uk

Member Services: Mr Peter Quirk Head - Corporate Organisation, Council Offices, Corks Lane, Hadleigh, Ipswich IP7 6SJ ☎ 01473 825829 🖷 01473 825742 🖰 peter.quirk@baberghmidsuffolk.gov.uk

Parking: Mr Chris Fry Head - Environment, Council Offices, Corks Lane, Hadleigh, Ipswich IP7 6SJ ☎ 01473 826649 🖷 01473 825742 🖰 chris.fry@baberghmidsuffolk.gov.uk

Partnerships: Ms Sue Clements Corporate Manager - Strong Communities, Council Offices, Corks Lane, Hadleigh, Ipswich IP7 6SJ ☎ 01449 724657 🖷 01449 724655 🖰 sue.clemments@baberghmidsuffolk.gov.uk

Personnel / HR: Ms Carla Doyle Corporate Manager - Organisational Development, Council Offices, Corks Lane, Hadleigh, Ipswich IP7 6SJ ☎ 01473 825744 🖷 01473 825742 🖰 carla.doyle@baberghmidsuffolk.gov.uk

Planning: Mr Tom Barker Corporate Manager - Strong Communities, Council Offices, Corks Lane, Hadleigh, Ipswich IP7 6SJ ☎ 01449 724647 🖷 01449 724655 🖰 tom.barker@midsuffolk.gov.uk

Planning: Mr Peter Burrows Head - Economy, Council Offices, Corks Lane, Hadleigh, Ipswich IP7 6SJ ☎ 01449 724503 🖷 01449 724514 🖰 peter.burrows@baberghmidsuffolk.gov.uk

Planning: Ms Lou Rawsthorne Head of Economy, Investment & Development, Council Offices, Corks Lane, Hadleigh, Ipswich IP7 6SJ ☎ 01449 724772 🖰 lou.rawsthorne@baberghmidsuffolk.gov.uk

Procurement: Ms Tracey Farthing Senior Commissioning & Procurement Officer, Council Offices, Corks Lane, Hadleigh, Ipswich IP7 6SJ ☎ 01473 825715 🖷 01473 825770 🖰 tracey.farthing@baberghmidsuffolk.gov.uk

Procurement: Mrs Rachel Hodson-Gibbons Corporate Manager - Commissioning, Council Offices, 131 High Street, Needham Market IP6 8DL ☎ 01449 724587 🖰 rachel.hodson-gibbons@baberghmidsuffolk.gov.uk

Recycling & Waste Minimisation: Mr Oliver Faiers Corporate Manager - Waste, Council Offices, Corks Lane, Hadleigh, Ipswich IP7 6SJ ☎ 01449 778621 🖰 oliver.faiers@baberghmidsuffolk.gov.uk

Recycling & Waste Minimisation: Mr Chris Fry Head - Environment, Council Offices, Corks Lane, Hadleigh, Ipswich IP7 6SJ ☎ 01473 826649 🖷 01473 825742 🖰 chris.fry@baberghmidsuffolk.gov.uk

Regeneration: Mr David Benham, Corporate Manager - Economic Development & Tourism, Council Offices, 131 High Street, Needham Market IP6 8DL ☎ 01449 724649 🖷 01449 724655 🖰 david.benham@baberghmidsuffolk.gov.uk

Staff Training: Mrs Jo Knight OD & HR Advisor, Council Offices, Corks Lane, Hadleigh, Ipswich IP7 6SJ ☎ 01473 825804 🖷 01473 825742 🖰 jo.knight@baberghmidsuffolk.gov.uk

Sustainable Communities: Mr Jonathan Free Head - Communities, Council Offices, Corks Lane, Hadleigh, Ipswich IP7 6SJ ☎ 01473 826649 🖷 01473 825742 🖰 jonathan.free@baberghmidsuffolk.gov.uk

Sustainable Development: Mr Chris Fry Head - Environment, Council Offices, Corks Lane, Hadleigh, Ipswich IP7 6SJ ☎ 01473 826649 🖷 01473 825742 🖰 chris.fry@baberghmidsuffolk.gov.uk

Tourism: Mr David Benham, Corporate Manager - Economic Development & Tourism, Council Offices, 131 High Street, Needham Market IP6 8DL ☎ 01449 724649 🖷 01449 724655 🖰 david.benham@baberghmidsuffolk.gov.uk

Waste Collection and Disposal: Mr Oliver Faiers Corporate Manager - Waste, Council Offices, Corks Lane, Hadleigh, Ipswich IP7 6SJ ☎ 01449 778621 🖰 oliver.faiers@baberghmidsuffolk.gov.uk

Waste Collection and Disposal: Mr Chris Morton Joint Client Manager, Mid Suffolk District Council, 131 High Street, Needham Market, Ipswich IP6 8DL ☎ 01449 778645 🖰 chris.morton@baberghmidsuffolk.gov.uk

Waste Management: Mr Oliver Faiers Corporate Manager - Waste, Council Offices, Corks Lane, Hadleigh, Ipswich IP7 6SJ ☎ 01449 778621 🖰 oliver.faiers@baberghmidsuffolk.gov.uk

Waste Management: Mr Chris Fry Head - Environment, Council Offices, Corks Lane, Hadleigh, Ipswich IP7 6SJ ☎ 01473 826649 🖷 01473 825742 🖰 chris.fry@baberghmidsuffolk.gov.uk

Children's Play Areas: Mr Jonathan Free Head - Communities, Council Offices, Corks Lane, Hadleigh, Ipswich IP7 6SJ ☎ 01473 826649 🖷 01473 825742 🖰 jonathan.free@baberghmidsuffolk.gov.uk

COUNCILLORS

***Chair* Ridley**, Nick (CON - Brook)
nick.ridley@babergh.gov.uk

***Vice-Chair* Ward**, John (CON - Lower Brett)
john.ward@babergh.gov.uk

***Leader of the Council* Jenkins**, Jennifer (CON - Leavenheath)
jennifer.jenkins@babergh.gov.uk

***Group Leader* Carpendale**, Sue (LD - Mid Samford)
sue.carpendale@babergh.gov.uk

Arthey, Clive (O - North Cosford)
clive.arthey@babergh.gov.uk

Ayres, Sue (CON - Sudbury)
sue.ayres@babergh.gov.uk

Barrett, Melanie (CON - Nayland)
melanie.barrett@babergh.gov.uk

Barrett, Simon (CON - Sudbury South)
simon.barrett@babergh.gov.uk

Bavington, Tony (LAB - Great Cornard (North))
tony.bavington@babergh.gov.uk

Beer, Peter (CON - Great Cornard (South))
peter.beer@babergh.gov.uk

Burgoyne, Peter (CON - Pinewood)
peter.burgoyne@babergh.gov.uk

Burgoyne, Sue (CON - Hadleigh)
sue.burgoyne@babergh.gov.uk

Burrows, Tom (CON - Great Conrad)
tom.burrows@babergh.gov.uk

Busby, David (LD - Pinewood)
david.busby@babergh.gov.uk

Campbell, Tina (CON - Hadleigh (North))
tina.campbell@babergh.gov.uk

Creffield, Michael (CON - Brett Vale)
michael.creffield.gov.uk

Davis, Derek (IND - Berners)
derek.davis@babergh.gov.uk

Dawson, Sian (CON - Hadliegh (North))
sian.dawson@babergh.gov.uk

Ferguson, Alan (CON - South Cosford)
alan.ferguson@babergh.gov.uk

Gasper, Barry (CON - Brook)
barry.gasper@babergh.gov.uk

Grandon, Kathryn (CON - Hadleigh South)
kathryn.grandon@babergh.gov.uk

Hinton, John (CON - Dodnash)
john.hinton@babergh.gov.uk

Holland, David (CON - Sudbury (South))
david.holland@babergh.gov.uk

Holt, Michael (CON - Glemsford and Stanstead)
michael.holt@babergh.go.uk

Hurren, Bryn (LD - Boxford)
bryn.hurrren@babergh.gov.uk

Kemp, Richard (IND - Long Melford)
richard.kemp@babergh.gov.uk

Lawrenson, Frank (CON - Waldingfield)
frank.lawrenson@babergh.gov.uk

Long, James (IND - Chadacre)
james.long@babergh.gov.uk

Maybury, Margaret (CON - Waldingfield)
margaret.maybury@babergh.gov.uk

McCraw, Alistair (IND - Alton)
alastair.mccraw@babergh.gov.uk

Newman, Mark (CON - Great Cornard (South))
mark.newman@babergh.gov.uk

Nunn, John (IND - Long Melford)
john.nunn@babergh.gov.uk

Osborne, Adrian (CON - Sudbury (East))
adrian.osborne@babergh.gov.uk

Osborne, Jan (CON - Sudbury (East))
jan.osborne@babergh.gov.uk

Parker, Lee (CON - Bures St Mary)
lee.parker@babergh.gov.uk

Patrick, Peter (CON - Berners)
peter.patrick@babergh.gov.uk

Plumb, Stephen (IND - Glemsford and Stanstead)
stephen.plumb@babergh.gov.uk

Rose, David (IND - Holbrook)
david.rose@babergh.gov.uk

Shropshire, William (CON - Lavenham)
william.shropshire@babergh.gov.uk

Smith, Ray (CON - Sudbury (North))
ray.smith@babergh.gov.uk

Steer, Harriet (CON - Alton)
harriet.steet@babergh.gov.uk

Swan, Fenella (CON - Mid Samford)
fenella.swan@babergh.gov.uk

BABERGH

Williams, Stephen (CON - Dodnash)
stephen.williams@babergh.gov.uk

POLITICAL COMPOSITION

CON: 31, IND: 7, LD: 3, O: 1, LAB: 1

COMMITTEE CHAIRS

Audit: Mr William Shropshire

Planning: Mr Peter Beer

Barking & Dagenham L

Barking & Dagenham London Borough Council, Civic Centre, Dagenham RM10 7BN
☎ 020 8215 3000 🖷 020 8227 5184; 020 8227 2806 ✉ 3000direct@lbbd.gov.uk 💻 www.lbbd.gov.uk

FACTS AND FIGURES

Parliamentary Constituencies: Barking, Dagenham and Rainham
EU Constituencies: London
Election Frequency: Elections are of whole council

PRINCIPAL OFFICERS

Chief Executive: Mr Chris Naylor Chief Executive, Town Hall, Barking IG11 7LU ☎ 020 8227 2789 ✉ chris.naylor@lbbd.gov.uk

Senior Management: Ms Anne Bristow Corporate Director - Adult & Community Services, Town Hall, 1 Town Square, Barking IG11 7LU ☎ 020 8227 2300 ✉ anne.bristow@lbbd.gov.uk

Senior Management: Mr Matthew Cole Director - Public Health, Town Hall, Barking IG11 7LU ☎ 020 8227 3657 ✉ matthew.cole@lbbd.gov.uk

Senior Management: Mrs Helen Jenner Corporate Director - Children's Services, Town Hall, 1 Town Square, Barking IG11 7LU ☎ 020 8227 5800 ✉ helen.jenner@lbbd.gov.uk

Senior Management: Mr Steven Tucker Director - Housing, Town Hall, 1 Town Square, Barking IG11 7LU ☎ 020 8227 5700 ✉ steven.tucker@lbbd.gov.uk

Architect, Building / Property Services: Mr Richard Zurawik Land Data Manager, Civic Centre, Dagenham RM10 7BN ☎ 020 8227 3954 ✉ richard.zurawik@lbbd.gov.uk

Building Control: Mr Daniel Pope Group Manager - Development & Planning, Town Hall, 1 Town Square, Barking IG11 7LU ☎ 020 8227 3929 ✉ daniel.pope@lbbd.gov.uk

Catering Services: Ms Maureen Lowes, Catering Services Manager, Town Hall, 1 Town Square, Barking IG11 7LU ☎ 020 8227 5505 ✉ maureen.lowes@lbbd.gov.uk

Children / Youth Services: Ms Meena Kishinani Divisional Director - Strategic Commissioning & Safeguarding, Town Hall, 1 Town Square, Barking IG11 7LU ☎ 020 8227 3507 ✉ meena.kishinani@lbbd.gov.uk

Civil Registration: Ms Cheryl Davis Registration & Citizenship Manager, Arden House, 198 Long Bridge Road, Barking IG11 8SY ☎ 020 8270 4744 ✉ cheryl.davis@lbbd.gov.uk

PR / Communications: Ms Sal Asghar Interim Strategy & Performance Manager, Town Hall, Barking IG11 7LU ☎ 020 8227 3734 ✉ salauoddin.asghar@lbbd.gov.uk

Community Planning: Ms Sal Asghar Interim Strategy & Performance Manager, Town Hall, Barking IG11 7LU ☎ 020 8227 3734 ✉ salauoddin.asghar@lbbd.gov.uk

Community Safety: Ms Glynis Rogers Divisional Director - Community Safety & Public Protection, Town Hall, 1 Town Square, Barking IG11 7LU ☎ 020 8227 2827 ✉ glynis.rogers@lbbd.gov.uk

Consumer Protection and Trading Standards: Mr Robin Payne Divisional Director - Environment, Frizlands Municipal Offices, Dagenham RM10 7HX ☎ 020 8227 5660 ✉ robin.payne@lbbd.gov.uk

Economic Development: Mr David Harley Group Manager - Economic Development, Town Hall, 1 Town Square, Barking IG11 7LU ☎ 020 8227 5316 ✉ david.harley@lbbd.gov.uk

Education: Ms Jane Hargreaves Divisional Director - Education, Roycraft House, 15 Linton Road, Barking IG11 7LU ☎ 020 8227 2686 ✉ jane.hargreaves@lbbd.gov.uk

Education: Mrs Helen Jenner Corporate Director - Children's Services, Town Hall, 1 Town Square, Barking IG11 7LU ☎ 020 8227 5800 ✉ helen.jenner@lbbd.gov.uk

Electoral Registration: Mr John Dawe, Group Manager - Democratic Services, Civic Centre, Dagenham RM10 7BN ☎ 020 8227 2135 ✉ john.dawe@lbbd.gov.uk

Emergency Planning: Mr David McClory Civil Protection Manager, Town Hall, 1 Town Square, Barking IG11 7LU ☎ 020 8227 3588 ✉ david.mcclory@lbbd.gov.uk

Energy Management: Ms Sandra Joseph Manager - Energy, Town Hall, 1 Town Square, Barking IG11 7LU ☎ 020 8227 3385 ✉ sandra.joseph@lbbd.gov.uk

Environmental Health: Mr Robin Payne Divisional Director - Environment, Frizlands Municipal Offices, Dagenham RM10 7HX ☎ 020 8227 5660 ✉ robin.payne@lbbd.gov.uk

Estates, Property & Valuation: Mr Andy Bere Strategy Manager, Town Hall, , Barking IG11 7LU ☎ 020 8227 3047 ✉ andy.bere@lbbd.gov.uk

Facilities: Mr Clive Bennett Facilities Manager, Town Hall, , Barking IG11 7LU ☎ 020 8227 3669 ✉ clive.bennett@lbbd.gov.uk

Finance: Mr Jonathan Bunt Chief Finance Officer, Civic Centre, Dagenham RM10 7BN ☎ 020 8724 8427 ✉ jonathan.bunt@lbbd.gov.uk

Pensions: Mr David Dickinson Group Manager - Treasury & Pensions, Civic Centre, Dagenham RM10 7BN ☎ 020 8227 2722 ✉ david.dickinson@lbbd.gov.uk

Pensions: Ms Justine Springfield Pensions Manager, Civic Centre, Dagenham RM10 7BN ☎ 020 8227 2607 ✉ justine.spring@lbbd.gov.uk

Fleet Management: Mr Mark Fransener Group Manager - Transport & Asset Management, Frizland Depot, Frizlands Lane, Dagenham RM10 7HX ☎ 020 8724 2834 ✉ mark.fransener@lbbd.gov.uk

Grounds Maintenance: Mr Tony Ralph Group Manager - Direct Services, Frizland Depot, Frizlands Lane, Dagenham RM10 7HX ☎ 020 8227 2974 ✉ tony.ralph@lbbd.gov.uk

Health and Safety: Ms Gail Clark Group Manager - HR Strategy, Civic Centre, Dagenham RM10 7BN ☎ 020 8227 3543 ✉ gail.clark@lbbd.gov.uk

Highways: Mr Robert Curtis Service Manager - Networks & Street Enforcement, Frizlands Depot, Frizlands Lane, Dagenham RM10 7BN ☎ 020 8227 2122 ✉ robert.curtis@lbbd.gov.uk

Home Energy Conservation: Ms Sandra Joseph Manager - Energy, Town Hall, 1 Town Square, Barking IG11 7LU ☎ 020 8227 3385 ✉ sandra.joseph@lbbd.gov.uk

Housing: Mr Steven Tucker Director - Housing, Town Hall, 1 Town Square, Barking IG11 7LU ☎ 020 8227 5700 ✉ steven.tucker@lbbd.gov.uk

Housing Maintenance: Mr Rob Wood Head of Housing, Pondfield House, Wantz Road, Dagenham RM10 8PP ☎ 020 8724 8831 ✉ robert.wood@lbbd.gov.uk

Legal: Mr David Lawson Acting Head of Legal, c/o The Town Hall, Ingrave Road, Brentwood CM15 8AY ☎ 01277 312860 ✉ david.lawson@brentwood.gov.uk

Legal: Mrs Fiona Taylor Head of Legal Services, Civic Centre, Dagenham RM10 7BN ☎ 020 8227 2114 ✉ fiona.taylor@bdtlegal.org.uk

Leisure and Cultural Services: Mr Paul Hogan Divisional Director - Culture & Sport, Town Hall, 1 Town Square, Barking IG11 7LU ☎ 020 8227 3576 ✉ paul.hogan@lbbd.gov.uk

Licensing: Mr Theo Lamptey Team Leader - Trading Standards & Licensing Officer, Roycraft House, Linton Road, Barking IG11 8HE ☎ 020 8227 5655 ✉ theo.lamptey@lbbd.gov.uk

Lottery Funding, Charity and Voluntary: Ms Monica Needs Market Development Manager, Integration & Commissioning, Town Hall, Barking IG11 7LU ☎ 020 8227 2936 ✉ monica.needs@lbbd.gov.uk

Member Services: Ms Belinda Lee PA to the Leader, Town Hall, 1 Town Square, Barking IG11 7LU ☎ 020 8724 8448 ✉ belinda.lee@lbbd.gov.uk

Parking: Ms Sharon Harrington Group Manager - Parking, Town Hall, 1 Town Square, Barking IG11 7LU ☎ 020 8227 2952 ✉ sharon.harrington@lbbd.gov.uk

Personnel / HR: Mr Martin Rayson Divisional Director - Human Resources & OD, Town Hall, 1 Town Square, Barking IG11 7LU ☎ 020 8227 3113 ✉ martin.rayson@lbbd.gov.uk

Planning: Mr Jeremy Grint, Divisional Director - Regeneration, Barking Town Hall, Barking IG11 7LU ☎ 020 8227 2443 ✉ jeremy.grint@lbbd.gov.uk

Public Libraries: Mr Zoinul Abidin Group Manager - Libraries, Barking Town Hall, Barking RM10 7HX ☎ 020 8724 8533 ✉ zoinul.abidin@lbbd.gov.uk

Recycling & Waste Minimisation: Mr Tony Ralph Group Manager - Direct Services, Frizland Depot, Frizlands Lane, Dagenham RM10 7HX ☎ 020 8227 2974 ✉ tony.ralph@lbbd.gov.uk

Regeneration: Mr Jeremy Grint, Divisional Director - Regeneration, Barking Town Hall, 1 Town Square, Barking IG11 7LU ☎ 020 8227 2443 ✉ jeremy.grint@lbbd.gov.uk

Road Safety: Mr Daniel Connelly Highways Traffic & Parking Officer, Frizlands Depot, Frizlands Lane, Dagenham RM10 7HX ☎ 020 8227 2465 ✉ daniel.connelly@lbbd.gov.uk

Social Services (Adult): Mr Bruce Morris, Divisional Director - Adult Social Care, Town Hall, 1 Town Square, Barking IG11 7LU ☎ 020 8227 2749 ✉ bruce.morris@lbbd.gov.uk

Social Services (Children): Mrs Helen Jenner Corporate Director - Children's Services, Town Hall, 1 Town Square, Barking IG11 7LU ☎ 020 8227 5800 ✉ helen.jenner@lbbd.gov.uk

Safeguarding: Ms Meena Kishinani Divisional Director - Strategic Commissioning & Safeguarding, Town Hall, 1 Town Square, Barking IG11 7LU ☎ 020 8227 3507 ✉ meena.kishinani@lbbd.gov.uk

Childrens Social Care: Ms Ann Graham Divisional Director - Complex Needs & Social Care, Town Hall, 1 Town Square, Barking IG11 7LU ☎ 020 8227 2233 ✉ ann.graham@lbbd.gov.uk

Public Health: Mr Matthew Cole Director - Public Health, Civic Centre, Dagenham RM10 7BN ☎ 020 8227 3657 ✉ matthew.cole@lbbd.gov.uk

Staff Training: Ms Gail Clark Group Manager - HR Strategy, Civic Centre, Dagenham RM10 7BN ☎ 020 8227 3543 ✉ gail.clark@lbbd.gov.uk

Sustainable Communities: Mr Jeremy Grint, Divisional Director - Regeneration, Barking Town Hall, 1 Town Square, Barking IG11 7LU ☎ 020 8227 2443 ✉ jeremy.grint@lbbd.gov.uk

Sustainable Development: Mr Jeremy Grint, Divisional Director - Regeneration, Barking Town Hall, 1 Town Square, Barking IG11 7LU ☎ 020 8227 2443 ✉ jeremy.grint@lbbd.gov.uk

BARKING & DAGENHAM

Town Centre: Mr Ralph Cook, Manager - Market Contracts, Roycroft House, Linton Road, Barking IG11 8HE ☎ 020 8227 6015 ✉ ralph.cook@lbbd.gov.uk

Traffic Management: Mr Blane Parker Traffic Officer, Frizlands Depot, Frizlands Lane, Dagenham RM10 7HX ☎ 020 8227 3489 ✉ blane.parker@lbbd.gov.uk

Transport Planner: Mr Jeremy Grint, Divisional Director - Regeneration, Barking Town Hall, 1 Town Square, Barking IG11 7LU ☎ 020 8227 2443 ✉ jeremy.grint@lbbd.gov.uk

Waste Collection and Disposal: Mr Tony Ralph Group Manager - Direct Services, Frizland Depot, Frizlands Lane, Dagenham RM10 7HX ☎ 020 8227 2974 ✉ tony.ralph@lbbd.gov.uk

Waste Management: Mr Tony Ralph Group Manager - Direct Services, Frizland Depot, Frizlands Lane, Dagenham RM10 7HX ☎ 020 8227 2974 ✉ tony.ralph@lbbd.gov.uk

COUNCILLORS

***Mayor* Kangethe**, Elizabeth (LAB - Parsloes)
elizabeth.kangethe@lbbd.gov.uk

***Leader of the Council* Rodwell**, Darren (LAB - Alibon)
darren.rodwell@lbbd.gov.uk

***Deputy Leader of the Council* Ashraf**, Saima (LAB - Gascoigne)
saima.ashraf@lbbd.gov.uk

***Deputy Leader of the Council* Twomey**, Dominic (LAB - Gascoigne)
dominic.twomey@lbbd.gov.uk

Ahammad, Syed (LAB - Longbridge)
syed.ahammad@lbbd.gov.uk

Alasia, Sanchia (LAB - Alibon)
sanchia.alasia@lbbd.gov.uk

Alexander, Jeannette (LAB - Eastbury)
jeannette.alexander@lbbd.gov.uk

Bartlett, Melanie (LAB - Whalebone)
melanine.bartlett2@lbbd.gov.uk

Bremmer, Simon (LAB - Goresbrook)

Bright, Sade (LAB - Chadwell Heath)
sade.bright@lbbd.gov.uk

Butt, Laila (LAB - Abbey)
laila.butt@lbbd.gov.uk

Carpenter, Evelyn (LAB - Becontree)
evelyn.carpenter@lbbd.gov.uk

Chand, Peter (LAB - River)
peter.chand@lbbd.gov.uk

Channer, Josephine (LAB - Thames)
josephine.channer@lbbd.gov.uk

Choudhury, Faruk (LAB - Becontree)
faruk.choudhury@lbbd.gov.uk

Fergus, Edna (LAB - Eastbrook)
edna.fergus@lbbd.gov.uk

Freeborn, Irma (LAB - Goresbrook)
irma.freeborn@lbbd.gov.uk

Gafoor Aziz, Abdul (LAB - Gascoigne)
abdul.gafooraziz@lbbd.gov.uk

Geddes, Cameron (LAB - Thames)
cameron.geddes2@lbbd.gov.uk

Ghani, Syed (LAB - Valence)
syed.ghani@lbbd.gov.uk

Gill, Rocky (LAB - Longbridge)
rocky.gill@lbbd.gov.uk

Haroon, Kashif (LAB - Mayesbrook)
kashif.haroom@lbbd.gov.uk

Hughes, Chris (LAB - Alibon)
christopher.hughes@lbbd.gov.uk

Jamu, Amardeep (LAB - River)
amardeep.jamu@lbbd.gov.uk

Jones, Jane (LAB - Valence)
jane.jones@lbbd.gov.uk

Keller, Eileen (LAB - River)
eileen.keller2@lbbd.gov.uk

Lawrence, Danielle (LAB - Abbey)
danielle.lawrence@lbbd.gov.uk

McCarthy, Mick (LAB - Eastbrook)
mick.mccarthy@lbbd.gov.uk

Miah, Giasuddin (LAB - Abbey)
miah.giasuddin@lbbd.gov.uk

Miles, Dave (LAB - Heath)
dave.miles2@lbbd.gov.uk

Mullane, Margaret (LAB - Village)
margaret.mullane@lbbd.gov.uk

Ogungbose, James (LAB - Becontree)
james.ogungbose@lbbd.gov.uk

Oluwole, Adegboyega (LAB - Mayesbrook)
adeboyega.oluwole@lbbd.gov.uk

Quadri, Moin (LAB - Goresbrook)
moin.quadri@lbbd.gov.uk

Rai, Hardial (LAB - Eastbury)
hardialsingh.rai@lbbd.gov.uk

Ramsay, Tony (LAB - Eastbrook)
tony.ramsay@lbbd.gov.uk

Reason, Linda (LAB - Heath)
linda.reason2@lbbd.gov.uk

Rice, Chris (LAB - Parsloes)
chris.rice@lbbd.gov.uk

Rice, Lynda (LAB - Longbridge)
lynda.rice@lbbd.gov.uk

Shaukat, Faraaz (LAB - Eastbury)
faraaz.shaukut@lbbd.gov.uk

Smith, Liam (LAB - Whalebone)
liam.smith@lbbd.gov.uk

Smith, Danielle (LAB - Mayesbrook)
daniellej.smith@lbbd.gov.uk

Tarry, Sam (LAB - Chadwell Heath)
sam.tarry@lbbd.gov.uk

Turner, Bill (LAB - Thames)
bill.turner@lbbd.gov.uk

Wade, Jeff (LAB - Chadwell Heath)
jeff.wade@lbbd.gov.uk

Waker, Lee (LAB - Village)
lee.waker@lbbd.gov.uk

Waker, Philip (LAB - Village)
philip.waker@lbbd.gov.uk

White, John (LAB - Whalebone)
john.white@lbbd.gov.uk

Worby, Maureen (LAB - Valence)
maureen.worby@lbbd.gov.uk

Young, Dan (LAB - Heath)
daniel.young@lbbd.gov.uk

Zanitchkhah, Linda (LAB - Parsloes)
linda.zanitchkhah2@lbbd.gov.uk

POLITICAL COMPOSITION

LAB: 51

COMMITTEE CHAIRS

Audit: Mr Dave Miles

Children's Services: Mr John White

Development: Ms Sanchia Alasia

Health & Adult Services: Ms Eileen Keller

Health & Wellbeing: Ms Maureen Worby

Licensing: Ms Josephine Channer

Pensions: Mr Dominic Twomey

Barnet L

London Borough of Barnet, North London Business Park, Oakleigh Road South, New Southgate, London N11 1NP
☎ 020 8359 2000 🖷 0871 911 6188 ✉ first.contact@barnet.gov.uk
💻 www.barnet.gov.uk

FACTS AND FIGURES

Parliamentary Constituencies: Chipping Barnet, Finchley and Golders Green, Hendon
EU Constituencies: London
Election Frequency: Elections are of whole council

PRINCIPAL OFFICERS

Chief Executive: Mr Andrew Travers Chief Executive, Building 2, North London Business Park, Oakleigh Road South, New Southgate, London N11 1NP ☎ 020 8359 2000
✉ andrew.travers@barnet.gov.uk

Senior Management: Mrs Lynn Bishop Street Scene Director, Building 2, North London Business Park, Oakleigh Road South, New Southgate, London N11 1NP ☎ 020 8359 2000
✉ lynn.bishop@barnet.gov.uk

Senior Management: Mr Jamie Blake Commissioning Director - Environment, Building 2, North London Business Park, Oakleigh Road South, New Southgate, London N11 1NP ☎ 020 8359 2000
✉ jamie.blake@barnet.gov.uk

Senior Management: Mr Stephen Evans Director - Strategy, Building 2, North London Business Park, Oakleigh Road South, New Southgate, London N11 1NP ☎ 020 8359 2000
✉ stephen.evans@barnet.gov.uk

Senior Management: Ms Davina Fiore Director - Assurance, Building 2, North London Business Park, Oakleigh Road South, New Southgate, London N11 1NP ☎ 020 8359 2000
✉ maryellen.salter@barnet.gov.uk

Senior Management: Ms Nicola Francis Family Services Director, Building 2, North London Business Park, Oakleigh Road South, New Southgate, London N11 1NP ☎ ✉ nicola.francis@barnet.gov.uk

Senior Management: Dr Andrew Howe Director - Public Health, Building 2, North London Business Park, Oakleigh Road South, New Southgate, London N11 1NP ☎ 020 8359 3970
✉ andrew.howe@harrow.gov.uk

Senior Management: Mr Mathew Kendall Director - Adults & Communities, Building 2, North London Business Park, Oakleigh Road South, New Southgate, London N11 1NP ☎ 020 8359 2000
✉ mathew.kendall@barnet.gov.uk

Senior Management: Ms Kate Kennally, Strategic Director - Commissioning, Building 2, North London Business Park, Oakleigh Road South, New Southgate, London N11 1NP ☎ 020 8359 2000
✉ kate.kennally@barnet.gov.uk

Senior Management: Mr Chris Munday Commissioning Director - Children & Young People, Building 2, North London Business Park, Oakleigh Road South, New Southgate, London N11 1NP
☎ 020 8359 2000 ✉ chris.munday@barnet.gov.uk

Senior Management: Ms Cath Shaw Commissioning Director - Growth & Development, Building 2, North London Business Park, Oakleigh Road South, New Southgate, London N11 1NP
☎ 020 8539 2000 ✉ cath.shaw@barnet.gov.uk

Senior Management: Ms Claire Symonds Director - Commercial & Customer Services, Building 2, North London Business Park, Oakleigh Road South, New Southgate, London N11 1NP
☎ 020 8359 2000 ✉ claire.symonds@barnet.gov.uk

Senior Management: Ms Dawn Wakeling Director - Adults & Health, North London Business Park, Oakleigh Road South, New Southgate, London N11 1NP ☎ 020 8359 2000
✉ dawn.wakeling@barnet.gov.uk

Access Officer / Social Services (Disability): Mr Jon Dickinson Assistant Director - Adult Social Care, North London Business Park, Oakleigh Road South, New Southgate, London N11 1NP ☎ ✉ jon.dickinson@barnet.gov.uk

Architect, Building / Property Services: Mr Chris Smith Head of Estates Management, Building 2, North London Business Park, Oakleigh Road South, New Southgate, London N11 1NP
☎ 020 8359 2000 ✉ chris.smith@barnet.gov.uk

Building Control: Mr Nick Lennox Area Manager for Building Control, Building 2, North London Business Park, Oakleigh Road South, New Southgate, London N11 1NP ☎ 020 8359 2000
✉ nick.lennox@barnet.gov.uk

BARNET

Building Control: Mr Steve Snell Area Manager For Building Control, Building 2, North London Business Park, Oakleigh Road South, New Southgate, London N11 1NP ☎ 020 8359 2000 ✉ steve.snell@barnet.gov.uk

Catering Services: Ms Teresa Goodall, Catering Services Manager, Building 4, North London Business Patk, Oakleigh Road South, New Southgate, London N11 1NP ☎ 020 8359 2000 ✉ teresa.goodall@barnet.gov.uk

Children / Youth Services: Ms Flo Armstrong Head of Youth & Communities, North London Business Park, Oakleigh Road South, New Southgate, London N11 1NP ☎ 020 8359 2000 ✉ flo.armstrong@barnet.gov.uk

Children / Youth Services: Mr Ian Harrison Education & Skills Director, North London Business Park, Oakleigh Road South, New Southgate, London N11 1NP ☎ 020 8359 2000 ✉ ian.harrison@barnet.gov.uk

Children / Youth Services: Ms Jo Pymont Assistant Director - Children's Social Care, North London Business Park, Oakleigh Road South, New Southgate, London N11 1NP ☎ 020 8359 5734 ✉ jo.pymont@barnet.gov.uk

Children / Youth Services: Mr Duncan Tessier Early Intervention & Prevention Assistant Director, North London Business Park, Oakleigh Road South, New Southgate, London N11 1NP ☎ 020 8359 2000 ✉ duncan.tessier@barnet.gov.uk

Community Planning: Mr Joe Henry Assistant Director - Planning, North London Business Park, Oakleigh Road South, New Southgate, London N11 1NP ☎ 020 8359 2000 ✉ joe.henry@barnet.gov.uk

Community Safety: Ms Kiran Vagarwal Head of Community Safety, North London Business Park, Oakleigh Road South, New Southgate, London N11 1NP ☎ 020 8359 2000 ✉ kiran.vagarwal@barnet.gov.uk

Computer Management: Mr Andrew Gee Head of I.S. Service Delivery, North London Business Park, Oakleigh Road South, New Southgate, London N11 1NP ☎ 020 8359 2000 ✉ andrew.gee@barnet.gov.uk

Consumer Protection and Trading Standards: Ms Emma Phasey Trading Standards Licensing Manager, Building 4, North London Business Park, Oakleigh Road South, New Southgate, London N11 1NP ☎ 020 8359 2000 ✉ emma.phasey@barnet.gov.uk

Corporate Services: Mr Tom Pike Head of Programme & Resources, Building 2, North London Business Park, Oakleigh Road South, New Southgate, London N11 1NP ☎ 020 8359 2000 ✉ tom.pike@barnet.gov.uk

Corporate Services: Ms Claire Symonds Director - Commercial & Customer Services, North London Business Park, Oakleigh Road South, New Southgate, London N11 1NP ☎ 020 8359 2000 ✉ claire.symonds@barnet.gov.uk

Customer Service: Ms Kari Manovitch Head of Customer Strategy & Programmes, Building 2, North London Business Park, Oakleigh Road South, New Southgate, London N11 1NP ☎ 020 8359 2000 ✉ kari.manovitch@barnet.gov.uk

Education: Mr Ian Harrison Education & Skills Director, North London Business Park, Oakleigh Road South, New Southgate, London N11 1NP ☎ 020 8359 2000 ✉ ian.harrison@barnet.gov.uk

Electoral Registration: Ms Davina Fiore Director - Assurance, North London Business Park, Oakleigh Road South, New Southgate, London N11 1NP ☎ 020 8359 2000 ✉ maryellen.salter@barnet.gov.uk

Emergency Planning: Ms Kate Solomon Emergency Planning Manager, Building 2, North London Business Park, Oakleigh Road South, New Southgate, London N11 1NP ☎ 020 8359 2000 ✉ kate.solomon@barnet.gov.uk

Environmental Health: Mr Rick Mason Assistant Director for Environmental Health, North London Business Park, Oakleigh Road South, New Southgate, London N11 1NP ✉ rick.mason@barnet.gov.uk

Estates, Property & Valuation: Mr Chris Smith Head of Estates Management, Building 2, North London Business Park, Oakleigh Road South, New Southgate, London N11 1NP ☎ 020 8359 2000 ✉ chris.smith@barnet.gov.uk

Facilities: Ms Jenny Hastings Facilities Manager, Building 2, North London Business Park, Oakleigh Road South, New Southgate, London N11 1NP ☎ 020 8359 2000 ✉ jenny.hastings@barnet.gov.uk

Finance: Ms Anisa Darr Director - Finance, Building 2, North London Business Park, Oakleigh Road South, New Southgate, London N11 1NP ☎ 020 8359 2000 ✉ anisa.darr@barnet.gov.uk

Finance: Mr John Hooton Chief Operating Officer, Building 2, North London Business Park, Oakleigh Road South, New Southgate, London N11 1NP ☎ 020 8359 2000 ✉ john.hooton@barnet.gov.uk

Fleet Management: Mr Bernard McGreevy Environment Transport Service Manager, Building 2, North London Business Park, Oakleigh Road South, New Southgate, London N11 1NP ☎ 020 8359 2000 ✉ bernard.mcgreevy@barnet.gov.uk

Grounds Maintenance: Ms Jenny Warren Head of Parks, Street Cleansing & Grounds Maintenance, Building 2, North London Business Park, North London Business Park, Oakleigh, London N11 1NP ☎ 020 8359 2000 ✉ jenny.warren@barnet.gov.uk

Health and Safety: Mr Mike Koumi Head of Health, Safety & Wellbeing, Building 2, North London Business Park, Oakleigh Road South, New Southgate, London N11 1NP ☎ 020 8359 2000 ✉ mike.houmi@barnet.gov.uk

Highways: Mr Richard Chalmers Associate Director - Highways, Building 2, North London Business Park, Oakleigh Road South, New Southgate, London N11 1NP ☎ 020 8359 2000 ✉ richard.chalmers@capita.gov.uk

Highways: Mr Dean Cronk Assistant Director - Highways, Building 2, North London Business Park, Oakleigh Road South, New Southgate, London N11 1NP ☎ 020 8359 2000 ✉ dean.cronk@capita.gov.uk

Highways: Mr Michael Hitchings Regulation Services Manager - Highways, Building 2, North London Business Park, Oakleigh Road, New Southgate, London N11 1NP ☎ 020 8359 2000 ✉ michael.hitchings@capita.gov.uk

Housing: Ms Cath Shaw Commissioning Director - Growth & Development, Building 2, North London Business Park, Oakleigh Road South, New Southgate, London N11 1NP ☎ 020 8539 2000 ✉ cath.shaw@barnet.gov.uk

Housing: Mr Paul Shipway Head of Strategy & Performance, North London Business Park, Oakleigh Road South, New Southgate, London N11 1NP ☎ 020 8359 2000 ✉ paul.shipway@barnet.gov.uk

Legal: Ms Jennifer Farmer Head of Joint Legal Services, Building 2, North London Business Park, Oakleigh Road South, New Southgate, London N11 1NP ☎ 020 8359 2000 ✉ jennifer.farmer@barnet.gov.uk

Licensing: Ms Emma Phasey Trading Standards Licensing Manager, Building 4, North London Business Park, Oakleigh Road South, New Southgate, London N11 1NP ☎ 020 8359 2000 ✉ emma.phasey@barnet.gov.uk

Lighting: Mr Roger Gilbert Street Lighting Project Manager, Building 2, North London Business Park, Oakleigh Road South, New Southgate, London N11 1NP ☎ 020 8359 2000 ✉ roger.gilbert@barnet.gov.uk

Lottery Funding, Charity and Voluntary: Mr Ken Argent, Grants Manager, Building 4, North London Business Park, Oakleigh Road South, New Southgate, London N11 1NP ☎ 020 8359 2000 ✉ ken.argent@barnet.gov.uk

Member Services: Mr Andrew Charlwood Head of Governance, Building 2, North London Business Park, Oakleigh Road South, New Southgate, London N11 1NP ☎ 020 8359 2000 ✉ andrew.charlwood@barnet.gov.uk

Parking: Mr Paul Bragg Head of Parking, Building 2, North London Business Park, Oakleigh Road South, New Southgate, London N11 1NP ☎ 020 8359 2000 ✉ paul.bragg@barnet.gov.uk

Personnel / HR: Mr Graeme Lennon Human Resources Director, Building 2, North Business Park, Oakleigh Road South, New Southgate, London N11 1NP ☎ 020 8359 2000 ✉ graeme.lennon@barnet.gov.uk

Planning: Mr Joe Henry Assistant Director - Planning, North London Business Park, Oakleigh Road South, New Southgate, London N11 1NP ☎ 020 8359 2000 ✉ joe.henry@barnet.gov.uk

Procurement: Ms Elizabeth Stavreski Head of Procurement, Building 2, North London Business Park, Oakleigh Road South, New Southgate, London N11 1NP ☎ 020 8359 2000 ✉ elizabeth.stavreski@barnet.gov.uk

Recycling & Waste Minimisation: Mr Jason Armitage Head of Waste & Recycling, North London Business Park, Oakleigh Road South, New Southgate, London N11 1NP ✉ jason.armitage@barnet.gov.uk

Recycling & Waste Minimisation: Mrs Lynn Bishop Street Scene Director, North London Business Park, Oakleigh Road South, New Southgate, London N11 1NP ☎ 020 8359 2000 ✉ lynn.bishop@barnet.gov.uk

Regeneration: Ms Cath Shaw Commissioning Director - Growth & Development, North London Business Park, Oakleigh Road South, New Southgate, London N11 1NP ☎ 020 8539 2000 ✉ cath.shaw@barnet.gov.uk

Road Safety: Ms Lisa Wright Principal Engineer of Traffic Management & Schools, Building 4, North London Business Park, Oakleigh Road South, New Southgate, London N11 1NP ☎ 020 8359 2000 ✉ lisa.wright@barnet.gov.uk

Social Services: Ms Jo Pymont Assistant Director - Children's Social Care, North London Business Park, Oakleigh Road South, New Southgate, London N11 1NP ☎ 020 8359 5734 ✉ jo.pymont@barnet.gov.uk

Social Services (Adult): Mr Jon Dickinson Assistant Director - Adult Social Care, North London Business Park, Oakleigh Road South, New Southgate, London N11 1NP ✉ jon.dickinson@barnet.gov.uk

Social Services (Adult): Mr Mathew Kendall Director - Adults & Communities, Building 2, North London Business Park, Oakleigh Road South, New Southgate, London N11 1NP ☎ 020 8359 2000 ✉ mathew.kendall@barnet.gov.uk

Social Services (Adult): Ms Dawn Wakeling Director - Adults & Health, North London Business Park, Oakleigh Road South, New Southgate, London N11 1NP ☎ 020 8359 2000 ✉ dawn.wakeling@barnet.gov.uk

Safeguarding: Ms Jo Moses Head of Safeguarding, North London Business Park, Oakleigh Road South, New Southgate, London N11 1NP ☎ ✉ jo.moses@barnet.gov.uk

Families: Ms Nicola Francis Family Services Director, North London Business Park, Oakleigh Road South, New Southgate, London N11 1NP ☎ ✉ nicola.francis@barnet.gov.uk

Families: Mr Duncan Tessier Early Intervention & Prevention Assistant Director, North London Business Park, Oakleigh Road South, New Southgate, London N11 1NP ☎ 020 8359 2000 ✉ duncan.tessier@barnet.gov.uk

Looked after Children: Ms Carolyn Greenaway Head of Assesment & Children in Need, North London Business Park, Oakleigh Road South, New Southgate, London N11 1NP ☎ 020 8359 5734 ✉ carolyn.greenaway@barnet.gov.uk

Looked after Children: Ms Jo Pymont Assistant Director - Children's Social Care, North London Business Park, Oakleigh Road South, New Southgate, London N11 1NP ☎ 020 8359 5734 ✉ jo.pymont@barnet.gov.uk

Childrens Social Care: Ms Jo Pymont Assistant Director - Children's Social Care, North London Business Park, Oakleigh Road South, New Southgate, London N11 1NP ☎ 020 8359 5734 ✉ jo.pymont@barnet.gov.uk

BARNET

Public Health: Dr Andrew Howe Director - Public Health, North London Business Park, Oakleigh Road South, New Southgate, London N11 1NP ☎ 020 8359 3970 ✉ andrew.howe@harrow.gov.uk

Street Scene: Mrs Lynn Bishop Street Scene Director, North London Business Park, Oakleigh Road South, New Southgate, London N11 1NP ☎ 020 8359 2000 ✉ lynn.bishop@barnet.gov.uk

Sustainable Development: Mr Michael Lai, Waste Strategy Group Manager, Building 4, North London Business Park, Oakleigh Road South, New Southgate, London N11 1NP ☎ 020 8359 2000 ✉ michael.lai@barnet.gov.uk

Traffic Management: Mr Richard Chalmers Associate Director - Highways, Building 2, North London Business Park, Oakleigh Road South, New Southgate, London N11 1NP ☎ 020 8359 2000 ✉ richard.chalmers@capita.gov.uk

Transport: Mr Bernard McGreevy Environment Transport Service Manager, Building 2, North London Business Park, Oakleigh Road South, New Southgate, London N11 1NP ☎ 020 8359 2000 ✉ bernard.mcgreevy@barnet.gov.uk

Waste Collection and Disposal: Mr Jason Armitage Head of Waste & Recycling, North London Business Park, Oakleigh Road South, New Southgate, London N11 1NP ✉ jason.armitage@barnet.gov.uk

Waste Collection and Disposal: Mrs Lynn Bishop Street Scene Director, North London Business Park, Oakleigh Road South, New Southgate, London N11 1NP ☎ 020 8359 2000 ✉ lynn.bishop@barnet.gov.uk

Waste Management: Mrs Nicola Cross, Waste Strategy Manager, Building 4, North London Business Park, Oakleigh Road South, New Southgate, London N11 1NP ☎ 020 8359 2000 ✉ nicola.cross@barnet.gov.uk

COUNCILLORS

***Chair* Shooter**, Mark (CON - Hendon)
cllr.m.shooter@barnet.gov.uk

***Mayor* Cohen**, Melvin (CON - Golders Green)
cllr.m.cohen@barnet.gov.uk

***Leader of the Council* Cornelius**, Richard (CON - Totteridge)
cllr.r.cornelius@barnet.gov.uk

***Deputy Leader of the Council* Thomas**, Daniel (CON - Finchley Church End)
cllr.d.thomas@barnet.gov.uk

Braun, Maureen (CON - Hendon)
cllr.m.braun@barnet.gov.uk

Challice, Rebecca (LAB - East Barnet)
cllr.r.challice@barnet.gov.uk

Coakley Webb, Pauline (LAB - Coppetts)
cllr.p.coakleywebb@barnet.gov.uk

Cohen, Jack (LD - Childs Hill)
cllr.j.cohen@barnet.gov.uk

Cohen, Dean (CON - Golders Green)
cllr.d.cohen@barnet.gov.uk

Cohen, Philip (LAB - East Barnet)
cllr.p.cohen@barnet.gov.uk

Cooke, Geof (LAB - Woodhouse)
cllr.g.cooke@barnet.gov.uk

Cornelius, Alison (CON - Totteridge)
cllr.a.cornelius@barnet.gov.uk

Davey, Tom (CON - Hale)
cllr.t.davey@barnet.gov.uk

Duschinksy, Val (CON - Mill Hill)
cllr.v.duschinskly@barnet.gov.uk

Edwards, Paul (LAB - Underhill)
cllr.p.edwards@barnet.gov.uk

Farrier, Claire (LAB - Burnt Oak)
cllr.c.farrier@barnet.gov.uk

Finn, Anthony (CON - Hendon)
cllr.a.finn@barnet.gov.uk

Gordon, Brian (CON - Edgware)
cllr.b.gordon@barnet.gov.uk

Greenspan, Eva (CON - Finchley Church End)
cllr.e.greenspan@barnet.gov.uk

Grover, Rohit (CON - Gardem Sibirb)
cllr.R.Grover@barnet.gov.uk

Hart, Helena (CON - Edgware)
cllr.h.hart@barnet.gov.uk

Hart, John (CON - Mill Hill)
cllr.j.hart@barnet.gov.uk

Houston, Ross (LAB - West Finchley)
cllr.r.houston@barnet.gov.uk

Hutton, Anne (LAB - Woodhouse)
cllr.a.hutton@barnet.gov.uk

Ioannidis, Andreas (LAB - Brunswick Park)
cllr.a.ioannidis@barnet.gov.uk

Kay, Devra (LAB - West Hendon)
cllr.d.kay@barnet.gov.uk

Khatri, Sury (CON - Mill Hill)
cllr.s.khatri@barnet.gov.uk

Langleben, Adam (LAB - West Hendon)
cllr.a.langleben@barnet.gov.uk

Levine, Kathy (LAB - Brunswick Park)
cllr.k.levine@barnet.gov.uk

Longstaff, David (CON - High Barnet)
cllr.d.longstaff@barnet.gov.uk

Lyons, Kitty (LAB - Hale)

Marshall, John (CON - Garden Suburb)
cllr.j.marshall@barnet.gov.uk|

McGuirk, Kathy (LAB - West Finchley)
cllr.k.mcguirk@barnet.gov.uk

Mittra, Arjun (LAB - East Finchley)
cllr.a.mittra@barnet.gov.uk

Moore, Alison (LAB - East Finchley)
cllr.a.moore@barnet.gov.uk

Naqvi, Ammar (LAB - Burnt Oak)
cllr.A.Naqvi@Barnet.gov.uk

Narenthira, Nagus (LAB - Colindale)
cllr.n.narenthira@Barnet.gov.uk

Old, Graham (CON - Finchley Church End)
cllr.g.old@barnet.gov.uk

O-Macauley, Charlie (LAB - Burnt Oak)
cllr.c.omacauley@barnet.gov.uk

Or-Bach, Alon (LAB - East Finchley)

Patel, Reema (LAB - Coppetts)
cllr.r.patel@barnet.gov.uk

Perry, Bridget (CON - High Barnet)
cllr.b.perry@barnet.gov.uk

Prentice, Wendy (CON - High Barnet)
cllr.w.prentice@barnet.gov.uk

Rajput, Sachin (CON - Oakleigh)
cllr.s.rajput@barnet.gov.uk

Rawlings, Barry (LAB - Coppetts)
cllr.b.rawlings@barnet.gov.uk

Rayner, Hugh (CON - Hale)
cllr.h.rayner@barnet.gov.uk

Roberts, Tim (LAB - Underhill)
cllr.T.Roberts@barnet.gov.uk

Rozenberg, Gabriel (CON - Garden Suburb)
cllr.g.rozenberg@barnet.gov.uk

Rutter, Lisa (CON - Brunswick Park)
cllr.l.rutter@barnet.gov.uk

Ryde, Shimon (CON - Childs Hill)
cllr.s.ryde@barnet.gov.uk

Salinger, Brian (CON - Oakleigh)
cllr.b.salinger@barnet.gov.uk

Sargeant, Gill (LAB - Colindale)
cllr.g.sargeant@barnet.gov.uk

Scannell, Joan (CON - Edgware)
cllr.j.scannell@barnet.gov.uk

Schneiderman, Alan (LAB - Woodhouse)
cllr.a.schneiderman@barnet.gov.uk

Slocombe, Agnes (LAB - West Hendon)
cllr.a.slocombe@barnet.gov.uk

Sowerby, Stephen (CON - Oakleigh)
cllr.s.sowerby@barnet.gov.uk

Stock, Caroline (CON - Totteridge)
caroline.stock9@gmail.com

Thompstone, Reuben (CON - Golders Green)
cllr.r.thompstone@barnet.gov.uk

Tierney, Jim (LAB - West Finchley)
cllr.j.tierney@barnet.gov.uk

Trevethan, Amy (LAB - Underhill)
cllr.a.trevethan@barnet.gov.uk

Williams, Laurie (LAB - East Barnet)
cllr.l.williams@barnet.gov.uk

Zinkin, Peter (CON - Childs Hill)
cllr.p.zinkin@barnet.gov.uk

Zubairi, Zakia (LAB - Colindale)
cllr.z.zubairi@barnet.gov.uk

POLITICAL COMPOSITION

CON: 32, LAB: 30, LD: 1

COMMITTEE CHAIRS

Audit: Mr Brian Salinger

Enviroment: Mr Dean Cohen

Health & Wellbeing: Ms Alison Cornelius

Licensing: Mr John Hart

Pensions: Mr Mark Shooter

Barnsley M

Barnsley Metropolitan Borough Council, Town Hall, Church Street, Barnsley S70 2TA
☎ 01226 770770 🖷 01226 773099 ✉ townhall@barnsley.gov.uk
💻 www.barnsley.gov.uk

FACTS AND FIGURES

Parliamentary Constituencies: Barnsley Central, Barnsley East
EU Constituencies: Yorkshire and the Humber
Election Frequency: Elections are by thirds

PRINCIPAL OFFICERS

Chief Executive: Ms Diana Terris Chief Executive, Westgate Plaza One, PO Box 609, Barnsley S70 9FH ☎ 01226 773301 ✉ dianaterris@barnsley.gov.uk

Senior Management: Ms Julia Bell, Director - Human Resources, Performance & Communications, Westgate Plaza One, PO Box 634, Barnsley S70 9GG ☎ 01226 773304 ✉ juliabell@barnsley.gov.uk

Senior Management: Ms Julia Burrows Director - Public Health, Westgate Plaza One, PO Box 609, Barnsley S70 9FH ☎ 01226 773477 ✉ juliaburrows@barnsley.gov.uk

Senior Management: Ms Rachel Dickinson Executive Director - People, Westgate Plaza One, PO Box 609, Barnsley S70 9FH ☎ 01226 773602 ✉ judithharwood@barnsley.gov.uk

Senior Management: Ms Frances Foster Director - Finance, Assets & Information Services, Westgate Plaza One, PO Box 609, Barnsley S70 9FH ☎ 01226 773163 ✉ francesfoster@barnsley.gov.uk

Senior Management: Mr Andrew Frosdick, Director - Legal & Governance, Westgate Plaza One, PO Box 609, Barnsley S70 9FH ☎ 01226 773001 ✉ andrewfrosdick@barnsley.gov.uk

Senior Management: Mr Matt Gladstone Executive Director - Place, Westgate Plaza One, PO Box 602, Barnsley S70 9FB ☎ 01226 772001 ✉ mattgladstone@barnsley.gov.uk

Senior Management: Mrs Wendy Lowder Interim Executive Director - Communities, Gateway Plaza, Sackville Street, Barnsley S70 9JE ☎ ✉ wendylowder@barnsley.gov.uk

Architect, Building / Property Services: Mr Jeremy Sykes Service Director - Assets, Gateway Plaza, PO Box 634, Barnsley S70 9GG ☎ 01226 774607 ✉ jeremysykes@barnsley.gov.uk

Building Control: Mr Tim Cliffe Group Leader - Building Control, Westgate Plaza One, PO Box 609, Barnsley S70 9FH ☎ 01226 772660 ✉ timcliffe@barnsley.gov.uk

BARNSLEY

Children / Youth Services: Ms Margaret Libreri Service Director - Education, Early Start & Prevention, Gateway Plaza, Sackville Street, Barnsley S70 9JF ☎ 01226 773598 🖱 margaretlibreri@barnsley.gov.uk

Civil Registration: Ms Kathryn Green Head of Customer Service Operations, Gateway Plaza, PO Box 609, Barnsley S70 9FH ☎ 01226 773144 🖱 kathryngreen@barnsley.gov.uk

PR / Communications: Mrs Rachel King Head of Communications & Marketing, Westgate Plaza One, PO Box 634, Barnsley S70 9GG ☎ 01226 774586 🖱 rachelking@barnsley.gov.uk

Community Planning: Mrs Wendy Lowder Interim Executive Director - Communities, Gateway Plaza, Sackville Street, , Barnsley S70 9JE 🖱 wendylowder@barnsley.gov.uk

Community Safety: Mr Paul Brannan Head of Service - Safer Barnsley, Beevor Court 2, PO Box 609, Barnsley S71 1 ☎ 01226 770770 🖱 paulbrannan@barnsley.gov.uk

Computer Management: Mr Luke Sayers Service Director - Information Services, Gateway Plaza, PO Box 609, Barnsley S70 9FH ☎ 01226 775702 🖱 lukesayers@barnsley.gov.uk

Consumer Protection and Trading Standards: Mr Simon Frow Head of Service - Regulatory Services, Westgate Plaza One, PO Box 609, Barnsley S70 9FH ☎ 01226 772541 🖱 simonfrow@barnsley.gov.uk

Contracts: Ms Karen Temple Managing Director - NPS Barnsley Ltd, Gateway Plaza, Sackville Street, Barnsley S70 2RD ☎ 01226 774392 🖱 karen.temple@nps.co.uk

Customer Service: Ms Ann O'Flynn Service Director - Customer Services, Gateway Plaza, PO Box 634, Barnsley S70 9GG ☎ 01226 772080 🖱 annoflynn@barnsley.gov.uk

Economic Development: Mr David Shepherd Service Director - Economic Regeneration, Westgate Plaza One, PO Box 609, Barnsley S70 9FH ☎ 01226 772621 🖱 davidshepherd@barnsley.gov.uk

Education: Ms Margaret Libreri Service Director - Education, Early Start & Prevention, Gateway Plaza, Sackville Street, Barnsley S70 9JF ☎ 01226 773598 🖱 margaretlibreri@barnsley.gov.uk

E-Government: Mr Luke Sayers Service Director - Information Services, Gateway Plaza, PO Box 609, Barnsley S70 9FH ☎ 01226 775702 🖱 lukesayers@barnsley.gov.uk

Electoral Registration: Ms Debra Buckingham Elections & Local Land Charges Manager, Town Hall, Church Street, Barnsley S70 2TA ☎ 01226 772343 🖱 debrabuckingham@barnsley.gov.uk

Emergency Planning: Mr Simon Dobby Head of Health, Safety & Emergency Resilience, Westgate Plaza One, PO Box 634, Barnsley S70 9GG ☎ 01226 772289 🖱 simondobby@barnsley.gov.uk

Estates, Property & Valuation: Mr Tim Hartley Corporate Asset Management Manager, Westgate Plaza One, PO Box 609, Barnsley S70 9FH ☎ 01226 774615 🖱 timhartley@barnsley.gov.uk

Finance: Ms Frances Foster Director - Finance, Assets & Information Services, Westgate Plaza One, PO Box 609, Barnsley S70 9FH ☎ 01226 773163 🖱 francesfoster@barnsley.gov.uk

Health and Safety: Mr Simon Dobby Head of Health, Safety & Emergency Resilience, Westgate Plaza One, PO Box 634, Barnsley S70 9GG ☎ 01226 772289 🖱 simondobby@barnsley.gov.uk

Legal: Mr Andrew Frosdick, Director - Legal & Governance, Westgate Plaza One, PO Box 609, Barnsley S70 9FH ☎ 01226 773001 🖱 andrewfrosdick@barnsley.gov.uk

Licensing: Mr Simon Frow Head of Service - Regulatory Services, Westgate Plaza One, PO Box 609, Barnsley S70 9FH ☎ 01226 772541 🖱 simonfrow@barnsley.gov.uk

Lifelong Learning: Mr Tom Smith Head of Service - Employment & Skills, Gateway Plaza, PO Box 634, Barnsley S70 9GG ☎ 01226 773830 🖱 tomsmith@barnsley.gov.uk

Member Services: Mr Ian Turner Service Director - Governance & Member Support, Gateway Plaza, PO Box 634, Barnsley S70 9GG ☎ 01226 773421 🖱 ianturner@barnsley.gov.uk

Personnel / HR: Ms Julia Bell, Director - Human Resources, Performance & Communications, Westgate Plaza One, PO Box 634, Barnsley S70 9GG ☎ 01226 773304 🖱 juliabell@barnsley.gov.uk

Planning: Mr Joe Jenkinson Head of Service - Planning & Building Control, Westgate Plaza One, PO Box 609, Barnsley S70 9FH ☎ 01226 772588 🖱 joejenkinson@barnsley.gov.uk

Procurement: Ms Karen Temple Managing Director - NPS Barnsley Ltd, Gateway Plaza, Sackville Street, Barnsley S70 2RD ☎ 01226 774392 🖱 karen.temple@nps.co.uk

Public Libraries: Ms Kathryn Green Head of Customer Service Operations, Gateway Plaza, PO Box 609, Barnsley S70 9FH ☎ 01226 773144 🖱 kathryngreen@barnsley.gov.uk

Regeneration: Mr David Shepherd Service Director - Economic Regeneration, Westgate Plaza One, PO Box 609, Barnsley S70 9FH ☎ 01226 772621 🖱 davidshepherd@barnsley.gov.uk

Safeguarding: Ms Mel John-Ross Service Director - Children's Social Care & Safeguarding, Gateway Plaza, Sackville Street, Barnsley S70 9JF ☎ 01226 773665 🖱 melaniejohn-ross@barnsley.gov.uk

Childrens Social Care: Ms Mel John-Ross Service Director - Children's Social Care & Safeguarding, Gateway Plaza, Sackville Street, Barnsley S70 9JF ☎ 01226 773665 🖱 melaniejohn-ross@barnsley.gov.uk

Public Health: Ms Julia Burrows Director - Public Health, Westgate Plaza One, PO Box 609, Barnsley S70 9FH ☎ 01226 773477 🖱 juliaburrows@barnsley.gov.uk

Staff Training: Mr Michael Potter Service Director - Organisation & Workforce Improvement, Westgate Plaza One, PO Box 634, Barnsley S70 9GG ☎ 01226 774594 🖱 michaelpotter@barnsley.gov.uk

Transport: Mr Paul Castle Service Director - Environment & Transport, Westgate Plaze One, PO Box 609, Barnsley S70 9FH ☎ 01226 774369 ✉ paulcastle@barnsley.gov.uk

Transport Planner: Mr Paul Castle Service Director - Environment & Transport, Westgate Plaze One, PO Box 609, Barnsley S70 9FH ☎ 01226 774369 ✉ paulcastle@barnsley.gov.uk

COUNCILLORS

***Directly Elected Mayor* Burgess**, Linda (LAB - Darton West)
CllrLindaBurgess@barnsley.gov.uk

***Mayor* Mathers**, Brian (LAB - Stairfoot)
cllrbrianmathers@barnsley.gov.uk

***Deputy Mayor* Shepherd**, Tim (LAB - Hoyland Milton)
cllrtimshepherd@barnsley.gov.uk

***Leader of the Council* Houghton**, Stephen (LAB - Cudworth)
cllrstephenhoughton@barnsley.gov.uk

***Deputy Leader of the Council* Andrews**, Jim (LAB - Rockingham)
CllrJamesAndrews@barnsley.gov.uk

***Group Leader* Birkinshaw**, Phillip (IND - Dodworth)
CllrPhillipBirkinshaw@barnsley.gov.uk

***Group Leader* Wilson**, John (CON - Penistone East)
CllrJohnWilson@barnsley.gov.uk

Barnard, Robert (CON - Penistone East)
CllrRobertBarnard@barnsley.gov.uk

Birkinshaw, Doug (LAB - Central)
Cllrdougbirkinshaw@barnsley.gov.uk

Brook, Sharron (LAB - Dearne South)
CllrSharronBrook@barnsley.gov.uk

Bruff, Margaret (LAB - Central)
CllrMargaretBruff@barnsley.gov.uk

Carr, Gill (IND - Worsbrough)
CllrGillCarr@barnsley.gov.uk

Carr, Jack (IND - Dodworth)
CllrJackCarr@barnsley.gov.uk

Cave, Alice (LAB - Darton West)
CllrAliceCave@barnsley.gov.uk

Cheetham, Tim (LAB - Royston)
CllrTimCheetham@barnsley.gov.uk

Cherryholme, Anita (LAB - Old Town)
cllranitacherryholme@barnsley.gov.uk

Clarke, John (LAB - Worsbrough)
CllrJohnClarke@barnsley.gov.uk

Clements, Malcolm (LAB - Royston)
cllrmalcolmclements@barnsley.gov.uk

Coates, Dorothy (LAB - Darfield)
cllrdorothycoates@barnsley.gov.uk

Davies, Phil (LAB - Old Town)
cllrphildavies@barnsley.gov.uk

Duerden, Lesley (LAB - Darton East)
cllrlesleyduerden@barnsley.gov.uk

Dures, Emma (LAB - Rockingham)
cllremmadures@barnsley.gov.uk

Dyson, Martin (LAB - Central)
cllrmartindyson@barnsley.gov.uk

Dyson, Karen (LAB - Stairfoot)
CllrKarenDyson@barnsley.gov.uk

Ennis, Jeff (LAB - North East)
cllrjeffennis@barnsley.gov.uk

Franklin, Robin (LAB - Hoyland Milton)
CllrRobinFranklin@barnsley.gov.uk

Frost, Robert (LAB - Wombwell)
cllrrobertfrost@barnsley.gov.uk

Gardiner, Alan (LAB - Dearne North)
CllrAlanGardiner@barnsley.gov.uk

Gollick, Annette (LAB - Dearne North)
cllrannettegollick@barnsley.gov.uk

Green, Donna (LAB - Kingstone)
cllrdonnagreen@barnsley.gov.uk

Green, Steve (LAB - Monk Bretton)
cllrstevegreen@barnsley.gov.uk

Griffin, Dave (LAB - Penistone West)
Cllrdavidgriffin@barnsley.gov.uk

Grundy, Liz (IND - Old Town)
cllrlizgrundy@barnsley.gov.uk

Hampson, Allan (LAB - North East)
cllrallanhampson@barnsley.gov.uk

Hand-Davis, Paul (CON - Penistone East)
CllrPaulHand-Davis@barnsley.gov.uk

Hayward, Joseph (LAB - Cudworth)
cllrjoehayward@barnsley.gov.uk

Higginbottom, Dorothy (LAB - North East)
CllrDorothyHigginbottom@barnsley.gov.uk

Howard, Sharon (LAB - Darton West)
CllrSharonHoward@barnsley.gov.uk

Johnson, Wayne (LAB - Stairfoot)
cllrwaynejohnson@barnsley.gov.uk

Lamb, Chris (LAB - Rockingham)
cllrchrislamb@barnsley.gov.uk

Leech, David (LAB - St. Helen's)
cllrdavidleech@barnsley.gov.uk

Makinson, Caroline (LAB - Royston)
cllrcarolinemakinson@barnsley.gov.uk

Markham, Pauline (LAB - Darfield)
CllrPaulineMarkham@barnsley.gov.uk

Miller, Roy (LAB - Darton East)
CllrRoyMiller@barnsley.gov.uk

Millner, Andrew (CON - Penistone West)
cllrandrewmillner@barnsley.gov.uk

Mitchell, Kath (LAB - Kingstone)
CllrKathMitchell@barnsley.gov.uk

Morgan, Margaret (LAB - Wombwell)
cllrmargaretmorgan@barnsley.gov.uk

Noble, May (LAB - Dearne South)
CllrMayNoble@barnsley.gov.uk

Platts, Jenny (LAB - St. Helen's)
CllrJennyPlatts@barnsley.gov.uk

BARNSLEY

Pourali, Roya (LAB - Worsbrough)
cllrroyapourali@barnsley.gov.uk

Richardson, Kenneth (LAB - Monk Bretton)
cllrkenrichardson@barnsley.gov.uk

Riggs, Richard (LAB - Dodworth)
cllrrichardriggs@barnsley.gov.uk

Saunders, Caroline (LAB - Darfield)
cllrcarolinesaunders@barnsley.gov.uk

Sheard, Margaret (LAB - Monk Bretton)
CllrMargaretSheard@barnsley.gov.uk

Sixsmith, Ralph (LAB - Dearne South)
cllrralphsixsmith@barnsley.gov.uk

Spence, Harry (NP - Darton East)
CllrHarrySpence@barnsley.gov.uk

Stowe, Mick (LAB - Hoyland Milton)
cllrmickstowe@barnsely.gov.uk

Tattersall, Sarah (LAB - St Helen's)
CllrSarahJaneTattersall@barnsley.gov.uk

Unsworth, Joe (LAB - Penistone West)
cllrjoeunsworth@barnsley.gov.uk

Williams, Kevin (LAB - Kingstone)
cllrkevinwilliams@barnsley.gov.uk

Worton, Jennifer (LAB - Dearne North)
CllrJenniferWorton@barnsley.gov.uk

Wraith, Charlie (LAB - Cudworth)
CllrCharlesWraith@barnsley.gov.uk

Wraith, Richard (LAB - Wombwell)
CllrRichardWraith@barnsley.gov.uk

POLITICAL COMPOSITION

LAB: 54, CON: 4, IND: 4, NP: 1

COMMITTEE CHAIRS

Audit: Mr Kenneth Richardson

Licensing: Mr Charlie Wraith

Overview & Scrutiny: Mr Jeff Ennis

Planning: Mr Doug Birkinshaw

Barrow-in-Furness D

Barrow-in-Furness Borough Council, Town Hall, Duke Street Barrow-in-Furness LA14 2LD
☎ 01229 876300 🖶 01229 876317 💻 www.barrowbc.gov.uk

FACTS AND FIGURES

Parliamentary Constituencies: Barrow and Furness
EU Constituencies: North West
Election Frequency: Elections are by thirds

PRINCIPAL OFFICERS

Chief Executive: Mr Phil Huck Executive Director, Town Hall, Duke Street Barrow-in-Furness LA14 2LD ☎ 01229 876543 🖶 01229 876317 🖱 philhuck@barrowbc.gov.uk

Senior Management: Ms Susan Roberts Director - Resources, Town Hall, Duke Street Barrow-in-Furness LA14 2LD ☎ 01229 876543 🖶 01229 876317 🖱 smroberts@barrowbc.gov.uk

Access Officer / Social Services (Disability): Mr Kevin Morrison, Development Services Manager, Town Hall, Duke Street, Barrow-in-Furness LA14 2LD ☎ 01229 876543 🖶 01229 876317 🖱 kcmorrison@barrowbc.gov.uk

Architect, Building / Property Services: Mr Brian Vickers, Building Surveyor, Town Hall, Duke Street Barrow-in-Furness LA14 2LD ☎ 01229 876543 🖶 01229 876317 🖱 bvickers@barrowbc.gov.uk

Best Value: Mr John Penfold, Corporate Support Division, Town Hall, Duke Street, Barrow-in-Furness LA14 2LD ☎ 01229 876543 🖶 01229 876317 🖱 jpenfold@barrowbc.gov.uk

Building Control: Mr Kevin Morrison, Development Services Manager, Town Hall, Duke Street, Barrow-in-Furness LA14 2LD ☎ 01229 876543 🖶 01229 876317 🖱 kcmorrison@barrowbc.gov.uk

Community Planning: Mr Steve Solsby Assistant Director - Regeneration & Built Environment, Town Hall, Duke Street Barrow-in-Furness LA14 2LD ☎ 01229 876543 🖶 01229 876317 🖱 ssolsby@barrowbc.gov.uk

Community Safety: Mr Steve Robson Neighbourhood Manager, Town Hall, Duke Street Barrow-in-Furness LA14 2LD ☎ 01229 876543 🖱 srobson@barrowbc.gov.uk

Computer Management: Mr John Penfold, Corporate Support Division, Town Hall, Duke Street, Barrow-in-Furness LA14 2LD ☎ 01229 876543 🖶 01229 876317 🖱 jpenfold@barrowbc.gov.uk

Contracts: Mr Chris Jones Property Services Group Manager, Town Hall, Duke Street Barrow-in-Furness LA14 2LD ☎ 01229 876543 🖶 01229 876317 🖱 cwjones@barrowbc.gov.uk

Contracts: Mrs Margaret Wilson, Leisure Centre Manager, Parks Leisure Centre, Greengate Street, Barrow-in-Furness LA13 9DT ☎ 01229 871146 🖶 01229 430224 🖱 mwilson@barrowbc.gov.uk

Corporate Services: Mr John Penfold, Corporate Support Division, Town Hall, Duke Street, Barrow-in-Furness LA14 2LD ☎ 01229 876543 🖶 01229 876317 🖱 jpenfold@barrowbc.gov.uk

Customer Service: Ms Debbie Reid Customer Relations Supervisor, Town Hall, Duke Street Barrow-in-Furness LA14 2LD ☎ 01229 876543 🖶 01229 876446 🖱 dareid@barrowbc.gov.uk

Economic Development: Mr Steve Solsby Assistant Director - Regeneration & Built Environment, Town Hall, Duke Street Barrow-in-Furness LA14 2LD ☎ 01229 876543 🖶 01229 876317 🖱 ssolsby@barrowbc.gov.uk

Electoral Registration: Mr Jon Huck, Democratic Services Manager, Town Hall, Duke Street, Barrow-in-Furness LA14 2LD ☎ 01229 876543 🖶 01229 876317 🖱 jwhuck@barrowbc.gov.uk

Electoral Registration: Mrs Judith Swarbrick, Electoral Services Co-ordinator, Town Hall, Duke Street, Barrow-in-Furness LA14 2LD ☎ 01229 876543 🖶 01229 873617 🖱 jswarbrick@barrowbc.gov.uk

Emergency Planning: Mr Andy Buck, Health & Safety Advisor, Town Hall, Duke Street, Barrow-in-Furness LA14 2LD ☎ 01229 876543 🖷 01229 876317 🖰 abuck@barrowbc.gov.uk

Energy Management: Mr Chris Jones Property Services Group Manager, Town Hall, Duke Street Barrow-in-Furness LA14 2LD ☎ 01229 876543 🖷 01229 876317 🖰 cwjones@barrowbc.gov.uk

Environmental / Technical Services: Mr Alan Barker, Streetcare Manager, Town Hall, Duke Street Barrow-in-Furness LA14 2LD ☎ 01229 876543 🖷 01229 876317 🖰 abarker@barrowbc.gov.uk

Environmental Health: Mrs Anne Pearson Environmental Health Manager, Town Hall, Duke Street Barrow-in-Furness LA14 2LD ☎ 01229 876543 🖷 01229 876317 🖰 apearson@barrowbc.gov.uk

Estates, Property & Valuation: Mr David Joyce Commercial Estates Manager, Town Hall, Duke Street Barrow-in-Furness LA14 2LD ☎ 01229 876543 🖷 01229 876317 🖰 djjoyce@barrowbc.gov.uk

European Liaison: Mr Steve Solsby Assistant Director - Regeneration & Built Environment, Town Hall, Duke Street Barrow-in-Furness LA14 2LD ☎ 01229 876543 🖷 01229 876317 🖰 ssolsby@barrowbc.gov.uk

Events Manager: Mrs Sandra Baines Forum Venue Manager, The Forum, Duke Street, Barrow-in-Furness LA14 1HH ☎ 01229 876484 🖰 sbaines@barrowbc.gov.uk

Events Manager: Mrs Ann Taylforth, Town Centre & Festivals Manager, Town Hall, Duke Street Barrow-in-Furness LA14 2LD ☎ 01229 876543 🖷 01229 876317 🖰 ataylforth@barrowbc.gov.uk

Facilities: Mr Chris Jones Property Services Group Manager, Town Hall, Duke Street Barrow-in-Furness LA14 2LD ☎ 01229 876543 🖷 01229 876317 🖰 cwjones@barrowbc.gov.uk

Treasury: Ms Gill Punton Accountacny Services Manager, Town Hall, Duke Street Barrow-in-Furness LA14 2LD ☎ 01229 876543 🖷 01229 876317 🖰 smroberts@barrowbc.gov.uk

Grounds Maintenance: Mr Alan Barker, Streetcare Manager, Town Hall, Duke Street Barrow-in-Furness LA14 2LD ☎ 01229 876543 🖷 01229 876317 🖰 abarker@barrowbc.gov.uk

Health and Safety: Mr Andy Buck, Health & Safety Advisor, Town Hall, Duke Street, Barrow-in-Furness LA14 2LD ☎ 01229 876543 🖷 01229 876317 🖰 abuck@barrowbc.gov.uk

Home Energy Conservation: Mr Chris Jones Property Services Group Manager, Town Hall, Duke Street Barrow-in-Furness LA14 2LD ☎ 01229 876543 🖷 01229 876317 🖰 cwjones@barrowbc.gov.uk

Housing: Mr Colin Garnett, Assistant Director - Housing, Town Hall, Duke Street Barrow-in-Furness LA14 2LD ☎ 01229 876462 🖷 01229 813591 🖰 cgarnett@barrowbc.gov.uk

Housing Maintenance: Mr Les Davies Maintenance & Asset Manager, Housing Department, Cavendish House, 78 Duke Street, Barrow-in-Furness LA14 1RR ☎ 01229 876540 🖰 ldavies@barrowbc.gov.uk

Legal: Mrs Jane Holden, Acting Principal Legal Officer, Town Hall, Duke Street, Barrow-in-Furness LA14 2LD ☎ 01229 876543 🖷 01229 876317 🖰 jmholden@barrowbc.gov.uk

Leisure and Cultural Services: Mrs Sandra Baines Venue Manager, The Forum, Duke Street, Barrow-in-Furness LA14 1HH ☎ 01229 876482 🖰 sbaines@barrowbc.gov.uk

Leisure and Cultural Services: Mr Keith Johnson Assistant Director - Community Services, Town Hall, Duke Street Barrow-in-Furness LA14 2LD ☎ 01229 876543 🖷 01229 876317 🖰 kjohnson@barrowbc.gov.uk

Leisure and Cultural Services: Ms Sabine Skae, Collections & Exhibitions Manager, The Dock Museum, North Road, Barrow-in-Furness LA14 2PW ☎ 01229 876401 🖷 01229 811361 🖰 sskae@barrowbc.gov.uk

Leisure and Cultural Services: Mrs Ann Taylforth Town Centre & Festivals Manager, Town Hall, Duke Street Barrow-in-Furness LA14 2LD ☎ 01229 876543 🖷 01229 876317 🖰 ataylforth@barrowbc.gov.uk

Leisure and Cultural Services: Mrs Margaret Wilson, Leisure Centre Manager, Parks Leisure Centre, Greengate Street, Barrow-in-Furness LA13 9DT ☎ 01229 871146 🖷 01229 430224 🖰 mwilson@barrowbc.gov.uk

Licensing: Mrs Anne Pearson Environmental Health Manager, Town Hall, Duke Street Barrow-in-Furness LA14 2LD ☎ 01229 876543 🖷 01229 876317 🖰 apearson@barrowbc.gov.uk

Lottery Funding, Charity and Voluntary: Mr Keith Johnson Assistant Director - Community Services, Town Hall, Duke Street Barrow-in-Furness LA14 2LD ☎ 01229 876543 🖷 01229 876317 🖰 kjohnson@barrowbc.gov.uk

Member Services: Mr Jon Huck, Democratic Services Manager, Town Hall, Duke Street, Barrow-in-Furness LA14 2LD ☎ 01229 876543 🖷 01229 876317 🖰 jwhuck@barrowbc.gov.uk

Parking: Mr Mike Otto Car Parks & Admin Services Team Leader, Town Hall, Duke Street Barrow-in-Furness LA14 2LD ☎ 01229 876543 🖷 01229 876317 🖰 mwotto@barrowbc.gov.uk

Personnel / HR: Miss Cathy Noade HR Manager, Town Hall, Duke Street Barrow-in-Furness LA14 2LD ☎ 01229 876543 🖷 01229 876317 🖰 cnoade@barrowbc.gov.uk

Planning: Mr Jason Hipkiss Development Services Manager, Town Hall, Duke Street Barrow-in-Furness LA14 2LD ☎ 01229 876543 🖷 01229 876317 🖰 jhipkiss@barrowbc.gov.uk

Procurement: Mr Chris Jones Property Services Group Manager, Town Hall, Duke Street Barrow-in-Furness LA14 2LD ☎ 01229 876543 🖷 01229 876317 🖰 cwjones@barrowbc.gov.uk

Recycling & Waste Minimisation: Mr Peter Buckley Recycling Officer, Town Hall, Duke Street Barrow-in-Furness LA14 2LD ☎ 01229 876543 🖷 01229 876317 🖰 pbuckley@barrowbc.gov.uk

BARROW-IN-FURNESS

Regeneration: Mr Steve Solsby Assistant Director - Regeneration & Built Environment, Town Hall, Duke Street Barrow-in-Furness LA14 2LD ☎ 01229 876543 🖷 01229 876317 ✉ ssolsby@barrowbc.gov.uk

Staff Training: Miss Cathy Noade, HR Manager, Town Hall, Duke Street Barrow-in-Furness LA14 2LD ☎ 01229 876543 🖷 01229 876317 ✉ cnoade@barrowbc.gov.uk

Street Scene: Mr Alan Barker, Streetcare Manager, Town Hall, Duke Street Barrow-in-Furness LA14 2LD ☎ 01229 876543 🖷 01229 876317 ✉ abarker@barrowbc.gov.uk

Sustainable Communities: Mr Steve Solsby Assistant Director - Regeneration & Built Environment, Town Hall, Duke Street Barrow-in-Furness LA14 2LD ☎ 01229 876543 🖷 01229 876317 ✉ ssolsby@barrowbc.gov.uk

Sustainable Development: Mr Steve Solsby Assistant Director - Regeneration & Built Environment, Town Hall, Duke Street Barrow-in-Furness LA14 2LD ☎ 01229 876543 🖷 01229 876317 ✉ ssolsby@barrowbc.gov.uk

Tourism: Mrs Ann Taylforth, Town Centre & Festivals Manager, Town Hall, Duke Street, Barrow-in-Furness LA14 2LD ☎ 01229 876543 🖷 01229 876317 ✉ ataylforth@barrowbc.gov.uk

Town Centre: Mrs Ann Taylforth, Town Centre & Festivals Manager, Town Hall, Duke Street, Barrow-in-Furness LA14 2LD ☎ 01229 876543 🖷 01229 876317 ✉ ataylforth@barrowbc.gov.uk

Waste Collection and Disposal: Mr Alan Barker, Streetcare Manager, Town Hall, Duke Street Barrow-in-Furness LA14 2LD ☎ 01229 876543 🖷 01229 876317 ✉ abarker@barrowbc.gov.uk

Waste Management: Mr Alan Barker, Streetcare Manager, Town Hall, Duke Street Barrow-in-Furness LA14 2LD ☎ 01229 876543 🖷 01229 876317 ✉ abarker@barrowbc.gov.uk

Children's Play Areas: Mr Alan Barker, Streetcare Manager, Town Hall, Duke Street Barrow-in-Furness LA14 2LD ☎ 01229 876543 🖷 01229 876317 ✉ abarker@barrowbc.gov.uk

COUNCILLORS

***Mayor* Derbyshire**, Marie (LAB - Newbarns)
mderbyshire@barrowbc.gov.uk

***Deputy Mayor* Thomson**, Ann (LAB - Hindpool)
mathomson@barrowbc.gov.uk

***Leader of the Council* Pidduck**, David (LAB - Hindpool)
dpidduck@barrowbc.gov.uk

Barlow, Desmond (LAB - Walney North)
dbarlow@barrowbc.gov.uk

Biggins, Trevor (LAB - Central)
tabiggins@barrowbc.gov.uk

Bleasdale, (CON - Dalton South)
wbleasdale@barrowbc.gov.uk

Brook, (LAB - Ormsgill)
dbrook@barrowbc.gov.uk

Burns, A (LAB - Hindpool)
aburns@barrowbc.gov.uk

Callister, Anthony (LAB - Walney North)
acallister@barrowbc.gov.uk

Cassidy, F (LAB - Walney South)
fcassidy@barrowbc.gov.uk

Gawne, (CON - Roosecote)
dgawne@barrowbc.gov.uk

Gill, (CON - Hawcoat)
lgill@barrowbc.gov.uk

Graham, L (LAB - Risedale)
lmgraham@barrowbc.gov.uk

Hamilton, K (LAB - Risedale)
krhamilton@barrowbc.gov.uk

Harkin, (LAB - Dalton North)
sharkin@barrowbc.gov.uk

Heath, (CON - Dalton North)
jdheath@barrowbc.gov.uk

Husband, A G (LAB - Walney North)
aghusband@barrowbc.gov.uk

Johnston, A (LAB - Barrow Island)
ajohnston@barrowbc.gov.uk

Maddox, Wendy (LAB - Dalton South)
wemaddox@barrowbc.gov.uk

McClure, W (CON - Newbarns)
wmcclure@barrowbc.gov.uk

McClure, Rory (CON - Roosecote)
rmcclure@barrowbc.gov.uk

McEwan, (LAB - Ormsgill)
wmcewan@barrowbc.gov.uk

McLeavey, (CON - Roosecote)
mmcleavy@barrowbc.gov.uk

Murphy, John (LAB - Newbarns)
jdmurphey@barrowdc.gov.uk

Murray, F (LAB - Dalton South)
fgmurray@barrowbc.gov.uk

Opie, S (LAB - Parkside)
sopie@barrowdc.gov.uk

Pemberton, A (CON - Hawcoat)
aipemberton@barrowbc.gov.uk

Preston, (LAB - Risedale)
hpreston@barrowbc.gov.uk

Proffitt, (LAB - Central)
aproffitt@barrowbc.gov.uk

Roberts, David (CON - Hawcoat)
droberts@barrowbc.gov.uk

Seward, D (LAB - Parkside)
dmseward@barrowbc.gov.uk

Sweeney, M B (LAB - Parkside)
mbsweeney@barrowbc.gov.uk

Thomson, Colin (LAB - Walney South)
cthomson@barrowbc.gov.uk

Thurlow, A (LAB - Dalton North)
athurlow@barrowbc.gov.uk

Wall, H (LAB - Walney South)
hwall@barrowbc.gov.uk

Williams, (LAB - Ormsgill)
lwilliams@barrowbc.gov.uk

POLITICAL COMPOSITION
LAB: 27, CON: 9

COMMITTEE CHAIRS

Audit: Mrs A Burns

Executive: Mr David Pidduck

Licensing: Mr Anthony Callister

Overview & Scrutiny: Ms Heath

Planning: Ms Ann Thomson

Basildon D

Basildon Borough Council, The Basildon Centre, St. Martin's Square, Basildon SS14 1DL
☎ 01268 533333 🖷 01268 294350 🖳 www.basildon.gov.uk

FACTS AND FIGURES
Parliamentary Constituencies: Basildon and Billericay, Basildon South and Thurrock East
EU Constituencies: Eastern
Election Frequency: Elections are by thirds

PRINCIPAL OFFICERS

Chief Executive: Mr Bala Mahendran, Chief Executive, The Basildon Centre, St. Martins Square, Basildon SS14 1DL ☎ 01268 294560 🖷 01268 294747 🖱 bala.mahendran@basildon.gov.uk

Senior Management: Mr Kieran Carrigan, Commissioning Director - Resourcing & Place Shaping, The Basildon Centre, St. Martin's Square, Basildon SS14 1DL ☎ 01268 294614 🖷 01268 294662 🖱 kieran.carrigan@basildon.gov.uk

Senior Management: Miss Dawn French, Commissioning Director - Corporate Support, The Basildon Centre, St. Martin's Square, Basildon SS14 1DL ☎ 01268 294858 🖷 01268 294858 🖱 dawn.french@basildon.gov.uk

Senior Management: Mr Gerry Levelle, Head of Executive Support, The Basildon Centre, St. Martin's Square, Basildon SS14 1DL ☎ 01268 294617 🖷 01268 294662 🖱 gerry.levelle@basildon.gov.uk

Senior Management: Mr Scott Logan Commissioning Director - People & Place, The Basildon Centre, St. Martin's Square, Basildon SS14 1DL ☎ 01268 294777 🖷 01268 294662 🖱 scott.logan@basildon.gov.uk

Architect, Building / Property Services: Mr Phil Jones Manager - Building Control, The Basildon Centre, St. Martin's Square, Basildon SS14 1DL ☎ 01268 294178 🖷 01268 294181 🖱 phil.jones@basildon@gov.uk

Best Value: Mr Paul Burkinshaw Group Manager - Corporate Governance & Support, The Basildon Centre, St. Martin's Square, Basildon SS14 1DL ☎ 01268 294422 🖷 01268 294599 🖱 paul.burkinshaw@basildon.gov.uk

Building Control: Mr Diljeet Assi Team Manager - Building Services, The Basildon Centre, St. Martin's Square, Basildon SS14 1DL ☎ 01268 294175 🖷 01268 294181 🖱 diljeet.assi@basildon.gov.uk

Catering Services: Mr Paul Brace, Manager of Leisure, Open Space & Community Facilities, The Basildon Centre, St. Martin's Square, Basildon SS14 1DL ☎ 01268 295452 🖷 01268 289844 🖱 paul.brace@basildon.gov.uk

PR / Communications: Ms Nicola Bowen-Rees Interim Manager - Marketing & Communications, The Basildon Centre, St. Martin's Square, Basildon SS14 1DL ☎ 01268 294056 🖱 nicola.bowenrees@basildon.gov.uk

Community Safety: Ms Paula Mason Community Safety Manager, The Basildon Centre, St. Martin's Square, Basildon SS14 1DL ☎ 01268 294764 🖷 01268 294324 🖱 paula.mason@basildon.gov.uk

Computer Management: Mr Lee Hession, Manager of Information & Communication Technology, The Basildon Centre, St. Martin's Square, Basildon SS14 1DL ☎ 01268 294029 🖷 01268 289844 🖱 lee.hession@basildon.gov.uk

Contracts: Mrs Lorraine Browne Solicitor to the Council, The Basildon Centre, St. Martin's Square, Basildon SS14 1DL ☎ 01268 294461 🖷 01268 294451 🖱 lorraine.browne@basildon.gov.uk

Corporate Services: Miss Dawn French, Commissioning Director - Corporate Support, The Basildon Centre, St. Martin's Square, Basildon SS14 1DL ☎ 01268 294858 🖷 01268 294858 🖱 dawn.french@basildon.gov.uk

Customer Service: Mr Tom Walker Customer Delivery Manager, The Basildon Centre, St. Martin's Square, Basildon SS14 1DL ☎ 01268 294064 🖱 lee.washbrook@basildon.gov.uk

Economic Development: Ms Gunilla Edwards, Team Manager - Economic Development, The Basildon Centre, St. Martin's Square, Basildon SS14 1DL ☎ 01268 294230 🖷 01268 294318 🖱 gunilla.edwards@basildon.gov.uk

Electoral Registration: Mr Paul Burkinshaw Group Manager - Corporate Governance & Support, The Basildon Centre, St. Martin's Square, Basildon SS14 1DL ☎ 01268 294422 🖷 01268 294599 🖱 paul.burkinshaw@basildon.gov.uk

Emergency Planning: Mr Lee Hession, Manager of Information & Communication Technology, The Basildon Centre, St. Martin's Square, Basildon SS14 1DL ☎ 01268 294029 🖷 01268 289844 🖱 lee.hession@basildon.gov.uk

Emergency Planning: Mr Scott Logan Commissioning Director - People & Place, The Basildon Centre, St. Martin's Square, Basildon SS14 1DL ☎ 01268 294777 🖷 01268 294662 🖱 scott.logan@basildon.gov.uk

BASILDON

Environmental Health: Mr Phil Easteal Group Manager - Regulation, The Basildon Centre, St. Martin's Square, Basildon SS14 1DL ☎ 01268 294271 🖷 01268 294550 phil.easteal@basildon.gov.uk

Estates, Property & Valuation: Ms Elaine Parry Manager - Corporate Property, The Basildon Centre, St. Martin's Square, Basildon SS14 1DL ☎ 01268 294381 🖷 01268 294181 elaine.parry@basildon.gov.uk

European Liaison: Ms Gunilla Edwards, Team Manager - Economic Development, The Basildon Centre, St. Martin's Square, Basildon SS14 1DL ☎ 01268 294230 🖷 01268 294318 gunilla.edwards@basildon.gov.uk

Facilities: Ms Claire Hamilton Head of Regeneration & Economic Development, The Basildon Centre, St. Martin's Square, Basildon SS14 1DL ☎ 01268 294173 claire.hamilton@basildon.gov.uk

Finance: Mr Kieran Carrigan, Commissioning Director - Resourcing & Place Shaping, The Basildon Centre, St Martin's Square, Basildon SS14 1DL ☎ 01268 294614 🖷 01268 294662 kieran.carrigan@basildon.gov.uk

Pensions: Mr Stuart Brian Manager of Human Resources & Organisational Design, The Basildon Centre, St. Martin's Square, Basildon SS14 1DL ☎ 01268 294939 stuart.brian@basildon.gov.uk

Fleet Management: Mr Hugh Reynolds Manager of Street Scene & Technical Services, Central Depot, Barleylands Road, Billericay CM11 2UF ☎ 01268 294939 hugh.reynolds@basildon.gov.uk

Grounds Maintenance: Mr Hugh Reynolds Manager of Street Scene & Technical Services, Central Depot, Barleylands Road, Billericay CM11 2UF ☎ 01268 294939 hugh.reynolds@basildon.gov.uk

Health and Safety: Miss Dawn French, Commissioning Director - Corporate Support, The Basildon Centre, St. Martin's Square, Basildon SS14 1DL ☎ 01268 294858 🖷 01268 294858 dawn.french@basildon.gov.uk

Home Energy Conservation: Mr Phil Easteal Group Manager - Regulation, The Basildon Centre, St. Martin's Square, Basildon SS14 1DL ☎ 01268 294271 🖷 01268 294550 phil.easteal@basildon.gov.uk

Housing: Ms Mandi Skeat Head - Housing Services, The Basildon Centre, St. Martin's Square, Basildon SS14 1DL ☎ 01268 295129 🖷 01268 294518 mandi.skeat@basildon.gov.uk

Housing Maintenance: Mr James Henderson Property Services Business Manager, The Basildon Centre, St. Martin's Square, Basildon SS14 1DL ☎ 01268 465301 james.henderson@basildon.gov.uk

Legal: Mrs Lorraine Browne Solicitor to the Council, The Basildon Centre, St. Martin's Square, Basildon SS14 1DL ☎ 01268 294461 🖷 01268 294451 lorraine.browne@basildon.gov.uk

Leisure and Cultural Services: Mr Paul Brace Manager - Leisure, Open Space & Community Facilities, Towngate Theatre, St Martin's Square, Basildon SS14 1DL ☎ 01268 465452 🖷 01268 465457 paul.brace@basildon.gov.uk

Leisure and Cultural Services: Mr Gary Edwards, Head of Street Scene & Leisure Services, Central Depot, Barleylands Road, Billericay CM11 2UF ☎ 01268 294614 🖷 01268 294968 gary.edwards@basildon.gov.uk

Lottery Funding, Charity and Voluntary: Ms Leah Douglas Community Involvement Manager, The Basildon Centre, St. Martin's Square, Basildon SS14 1DL ☎ 01268 295081 🖷 01268 295206 leah.douglas@basildon.gov.uk

Member Services: Mr Paul Burkinshaw Group Manager - Corporate Governance & Support, The Basildon Centre, St. Martin's Square, Basildon SS14 1DL ☎ 01268 294422 🖷 01268 294599 paul.burkinshaw@basildon.gov.uk

Parking: Mr Hugh Reynolds Manager of Street Scene & Technical Services, Central Depot, Barleylands Road, Billericay CM11 2UF ☎ 01268 294939 hugh.reynolds@basildon.gov.uk

Partnerships: Mr Paul Burkinshaw Group Manager - Corporate Governance & Support, The Basildon Centre, St. Martin's Square, Basildon SS14 1DL ☎ 01268 294422 🖷 01268 294599 paul.burkinshaw@basildon.gov.uk

Personnel / HR: Mr Stuart Brian Manager of Human Resources & Organisational Design, The Basildon Centre, St. Martin's Square, Basildon SS14 1DL ☎ 01268 294939 stuart.brian@basildon.gov.uk

Planning: Mr Phil Easteal Group Manager - Regulation, The Basildon Centre, St. Martin's Square, Basildon SS14 1DL ☎ 01268 294271 🖷 01268 294550 phil.easteal@basildon.gov.uk

Procurement: Mr Chris Perry Group Manager - Commercial Services, The Basildon Centre, St. Martin's Square, Basildon SS14 1DL ☎ 01268 294377 🖷 01268 294451 chris.perry@basildon.gov.uk

Recycling & Waste Minimisation: Mr Gary Edwards, Head of Street Scene & Leisure Services, Central Depot, Barleylands Road, Billericay CM11 2UF ☎ 01268 294614 🖷 01268 294968 gary.edwards@basildon.gov.uk

Regeneration: Ms Claire Hamilton Head of Regeneration & Economic Development, The Basildon Centre, St. Martin's Square, Basildon SS14 1DL ☎ 01268 294173 claire.hamilton@basildon.gov.uk

Staff Training: Mr Stuart Brian Manager of Human Resources & Organisational Design, The Basildon Centre, St. Martin's Square, Basildon SS14 1DL ☎ 01268 294939 stuart.brian@basildon.gov.uk

Street Scene: Mr Hugh Reynolds Manager of Street Scene & Technical Services, Central Depot, Barleylands Road, Billericay CM11 2UF ☎ 01268 294939 hugh.reynolds@basildon.gov.uk

Sustainable Communities: Ms Leah Douglas Community Involvement Manager, The Basildon Centre, St. Martin's Square, Basildon SS14 1DL ☎ 01268 295081 🖷 01268 295206 leah.douglas@basildon.gov.uk

Sustainable Development: Ms Mandi Skeat Head - Housing Services, The Basildon Centre, St. Martin's Square, Basildon SS14 1DL ☎ 01268 295129 🖷 01268 294518 mandi.skeat@basildon.gov.uk

Transport: Mr Hugh Reynolds Manager of Street Scene & Technical Services, Central Depot, Barleylands Road, Billericay CM11 2UF ☎ 01268 294939 hugh.reynolds@basildon.gov.uk

Total Place: Mr Kieran Carrigan, Commissioning Director - Resourcing & Place Shaping, The Basildon Centre, St. Martin's Square, Basildon SS14 1DL ☎ 01268 294614 🖷 01268 294662 kieran.carrigan@basildon.gov.uk

Waste Collection and Disposal: Mr Gary Edwards, Head of Street Scene & Leisure Services, Central Depot, Barleylands Road, Billericay CM11 2UF ☎ 01268 294614 🖷 01268 294968 gary.edwards@basildon.gov.uk

Waste Management: Mr Gary Edwards, Head of Street Scene & Leisure Services, Central Depot, Barleylands Road, Billericay CM11 2UF ☎ 01268 294614 🖷 01268 294968 gary.edwards@basildon.gov.uk

Children's Play Areas: Mr Paul Brace Manager - Leisure, Open Space & Community Facilities, Towngate Theatre, St Martin's Square, Basildon SS14 1DL ☎ 01268 465452 🖷 01268 465457 paul.brace@basildon.gov.uk

COUNCILLORS

***Mayor* Morris**, Don (CON - Wickford Castledon)
don.morris@members.basildon.gov.uk

***Deputy Mayor* Lawrence**, Daniel (CON - Billericay West)
daniel.lawrence@members.basildon.gov.uk

***Leader of the Council* Turner**, Philip (CON - Billericay West)
phil.turner@members.basildon.gov.uk

***Deputy Leader of the Council* Blake**, Kevin (CON - Burstead)
kevin.blake@members.basildon.gov.uk

***Group Leader* Allport-Hodge**, Linda (UKIP - Langdon Hills)
linda.allport-hodge@members.basildon.gov.uk

***Group Leader* Callaghan**, Gavin (LAB - Pitsea North West)
gavin.callaghan@members.basildon.gov.uk

***Group Leader* Rackley**, Philip (LD - St Martin's)
phil.rackley1@btopenworld.com

***Group Leader* Smith**, Kerry (IND - Nethermayne)
kerry.smith@members.basildon.gov.uk

Allen, Stuart (CON - Crouch)
stuart.allen@members.basildon.gov.uk

Arnold, Amanda (CON - Pitsea South East)
amanda.arnold@members.basildon.gov.uk

Baggott, Andrew (CON - Burstead)
andrew.baggott@members.basildon.gov.uk

Ball, Alan (UKIP - Wickford Castledon)
alan.ball@members.basildon.gov.uk

Barnes, Andrew (CON - Laindon Park)
andrew.barnes@members.basildon.gov.uk

Bennett, Alan (LAB - Lee Chapel North)
alan.bennett@members.basildon.gov.uk

Brown, Adele (LAB - Fryerns)
adele.brown@members.basildon.gov.uk

Buxton, Andrew (LAB - St Martin's)
andrew.buxton@members.basildon.gov.uk

Canham, Gary (UKIP - Pitsea North West)
gary.canham@members.basildon.gov.uk

Clancy, Imelda (IND - Pitsea North West)
imelda.clancy@members.basildon.gov.uk

Dadds, David (CON - Billericay East)
david.dadds@members.basildon.gov.uk

Davies, Allan (LAB - Fryerns)
allan.davies@members.basildon.gov.uk

Ellis, Mark (UKIP - Laindon Park)
mark.ellis@members.basildon.gov.uk

Ferguson, Frank (UKIP - Lee Chapel North)
frank.ferguson@members.basildon.gov.uk

Harrison, David (UKIP - Wickford Park)
david.harrison@members.basildon.gov.uk

Hedley, Anthony (CON - Billericay West)
anthony.hedley@members.basildon.gov.uk

Hillier, Stephen (CON - Langdon Hills)
stephen.hillier@members.basildon.gov.uk

Hodge, Stephen (UKIP - Nethermayne)
stephen.hodge@members.basildon.gov.uk

Holliman, Peter (UKIP - Wickford North)
peter.holliman@members.basildon.gov.uk

Jackman, Christopher (CON - Wickford Park)
chris.jackman@members.basildon.gov.uk

Malsbury, Trevor (UKIP - Lee Chapel North)
trevor.malsbury@members.basildon.gov.uk

McGeorge, Melissa (LAB - Vange)
melissa.mcgeorge@members.basildon.gov.uk

McGurran, Aidan (LAB - Pitsea South East)
aidan.mcgurran@members.basildon.gov.uk

Moore, Richard (CON - Burstead)
richard.moore@members.basildon.gov.uk

Morris, Carole (CON - Wickford North)
carole.morris@members.basildon.gov.uk

Mowe, Michael (CON - Wickford North)
michael.mowe@members.basildon.gov.uk

Sargent, Terri (CON - Crouch)
terri.sargent@members.basildon.gov.uk

Scarola, John (LAB - Laindon Park)
john.scarola@members.basildon.gov.uk

Schrader, Andrew (CON - Billericay East)
andrew.schrader@members.basildon.gov.uk

Sheppard, David (UKIP - Fryerns)
david.sheppard@members.basildon.gov.uk

Sullivan, Stuart (CON - Billericay East)
stuart.sullivan@members.basildon.gov.uk

BASILDON

Taylor, Byron (LAB - Vange)
byron.taylor@members.basildon.gov.uk

Ward, Stephen (UKIP - Pitsea South East)
stephen.ward@members.basildon.gov.uk

Williams, Geoffrey (LD - Nethermayne)
geoff.williams@members.basildon.gov.uk

POLITICAL COMPOSITION
CON: 18, UKIP: 11, LAB: 9, LD: 2, IND: 2

COMMITTEE CHAIRS

Audit & Risk: Mr Kerry Smith

Licensing: Mr Stephen Hillier

Planning: Mrs Carole Morris

Basingstoke & Deane D

Basingstoke & Deane Borough Council, Civic Offices, London Road, Basingstoke RG21 4AH
☎ 01256 844844 🖷 01256 845200 🖳 www.basingstoke.gov.uk

FACTS AND FIGURES
Parliamentary Constituencies: Basingstoke, Hampshire North West
EU Constituencies: South East
Election Frequency: Elections are by thirds

PRINCIPAL OFFICERS

Chief Executive: Mr Melbourne Barrett Chief Executive, Civic Offices, London Road, Basingstoke RG21 4AH ☎ 01256 845788 ✉ melbourne.barrett@basingstoke.gov.uk

Senior Management: Mrs Karen Brimacombe, Director - Borough Council Services, Civic Offices, London Road, Basingstoke RG21 4AH ☎ 01256 845789 🖷 01256 845200 ✉ karen.brimacombe@basingstoke.gov.uk

Senior Management: Mrs Laura Taylor Director - Governance & Commissioning, Civic Offices, London Road, Basingstoke RG21 4AH ☎ 01256 845797 🖷 01256 845200 ✉ laura.taylor@basingstoke.gov.uk

Best Value: Mr Kevin Jaquest Head of Resources, Civic Offices, London Road, Basingstoke RG21 4AH ☎ 01256 845513 🖷 01256 845200 ✉ kevin.jaquest@basingstoke.gov.uk

Building Control: Ms Tracey Cole Head of Residents' Services, Civic Offices, London Road, Basingstoke RG21 4AH ☎ 01256 845759 🖷 01256 845200 ✉ tracey.cole@basingstoke.gov.uk

PR / Communications: Mrs Sara Shepherd Communications Manager, Civic Offices, London Road, Basingstoke RG21 4AH ☎ 01256 844844 ✉ sara.shepherd@basingstoke.gov.uk

Community Planning: Ms Sue Rayden Community Development Manager, Civic Offices, London Road, Basingstoke RG21 4AH ✉ sue.rayden@basingstoke.gov.uk

Community Safety: Mr Tim Boschi, Head of Community Services, Civic Offices, London Road, Basingstoke RG21 4AH ☎ 01256 845473 🖷 01256 845200 ✉ tim.boschi@basingstoke.gov.uk

Community Safety: Mr James Knight Community Safety Manager, Civic Offices, London Road, Basingstoke RG21 4AH ☎ 01256 844844 ✉ james.knight@basingstoke.gov.uk

Contracts: Mrs Laura Taylor Director - Governance & Commissioning, Civic Offices, London Road, Basingstoke RG21 4AH ☎ 01256 845797 🖷 01256 845200 ✉ laura.taylor@basingstoke.gov.uk

Corporate Services: Mrs Karen Brimacombe, Director - Borough Council Services, Civic Offices, London Road, Basingstoke RG21 4AH ☎ 01256 845789 🖷 01256 845200 ✉ karen.brimacombe@basingstoke.gov.uk

Customer Service: Mrs Katy Sallis Customer Services Manager, Civic Offices, London Road, Basingstoke RG21 4AH ☎ 01256 844844 ✉ katy.sallis@basingstoke.gov.uk

Economic Development: Ms Di Haywood Policy Manager for Economic & Community Strategy, Civic Offices, London Road, Basingstoke RG21 4AH ☎ 01256 844844 ✉ di.haywood@basingstoke.gov.uk

Electoral Registration: Mrs Karen Brimacombe, Director - Borough Council Services, Civic Offices, London Road, Basingstoke RG21 4AH ☎ 01256 845789 🖷 01256 845200 ✉ karen.brimacombe@basingstoke.gov.uk

Electoral Registration: Mr Wayne Dash Electoral Services Team Leader, Civic Offices, London Road, Basingstoke RG21 4AH ☎ 01256 844844; 01256 844844 ✉ wayne.dash@basingstoke.gov.uk; wayne.dash@basingstoke.gov.uk

Emergency Planning: Mrs Karen Brimacombe, Director - Borough Council Services, Civic Offices, London Road, Basingstoke RG21 4AH ☎ 01256 845789 🖷 01256 845200 ✉ karen.brimacombe@basingstoke.gov.uk

Environmental Health: Mr Tom Payne Environmental Health Officer, Civic Offices, London Road, Basingstoke RG21 4AH ☎ 01256 844844 🖷 01256 8452200 ✉ tom.payne@basingstoke.gov.uk

European Liaison: Mr Daniel Garnier Economic Development Manager, Civic Offices, London Road, Basingstoke RG21 4AH ☎ 01256 845720 🖷 01256 845200 ✉ daniel.garnier@basingstoke.gov.uk

Events Manager: Mr Andrew Grove, Events Officer, Civic Offices, London Road, Basingstoke RG21 4AH ☎ 01256 845455 🖷 01256 845200 ✉ andrew.grove@basingstoke.gov.uk

Facilities: Ms Sheila Smith Head of HR, Civic Offices, London Road, Basingstoke RG21 4AH ☎ 01256 844844 🖷 01256 845200 ✉ sheila.smith@basingstoke.gov.uk

Finance: Mr Kevin Jaquest Head of Resources, Civic Offices, London Road, Basingstoke RG21 4AH ☎ 01256 845513 🖷 01256 845200 ✉ kevin.jaquest@basingstoke.gov.uk

Finance: Mr Dean Pletts Director - Finance & Treasury, Civic Offices, London Road, Basingstoke RG21 4AH ☎ 01256 844844 ✉ dean.pletts@basingstoke.gov.uk

Treasury: Mr Dean Pletts Director - Finance & Treasury, Civic Offices, London Road, Basingstoke RG21 4AH ☎ 01256 844844 ✉ dean.pletts@basingstoke.gov.uk

Pensions: Ms Sarah Finch Pensions & Investments Manager, Civic Offices, London Road, Basingstoke RG21 4AH ☎ 01256 844844 ✉ sarah.finch@basingstoke.gov.uk

Grounds Maintenance: Mr Steve Featherstone, Environmental Care Operations Manager, Civic Offices, London Road, Basingstoke RG21 4AH ☎ 01256 845335 🖷 01256 845200 ✉ steve.featherstone@basingstoke.gov.uk

Health and Safety: Mr Paul Beaumont Corporate Health & Safety Advisor, Civic Offices, London Road, Basingstoke RG21 4AH ☎ 01256 844844 ✉ paulk.beaumont@basingstoke.gov.uk

Highways: Mr Tim Boschi, Head of Community Services, Civic Offices, London Road, Basingstoke RG21 4AH ☎ 01256 845473 🖷 01256 845200 ✉ tim.boschi@basingstoke.gov.uk

Home Energy Conservation: Ms Lucy Martins Climate Change Officer, Civic Offices, London Road, Basingstoke RG21 4AH ☎ 01256 844844 🖷 01256 845200 ✉ lucy.martins@basingstoke.gov.uk

Housing: Ms Tracey Cole Head of Residents' Services, Civic Offices, London Road, Basingstoke RG21 4AH ☎ 01256 845759 🖷 01256 845200 ✉ tracey.cole@basingstoke.gov.uk

Legal: Ms Lisa Kirkman Head of Legal, Democratic Services, Elections & Land Charges, Civic Offices, London Road, Basingstoke RG21 4AH ☎ 01256 845345 🖷 01256 845200 ✉ lisa.kirkman@basingstoke.gov.uk

Leisure and Cultural Services: Ms Di Haywood Policy Manager for Economic & Community Strategy, Civic Offices, London Road, Basingstoke RG21 4AH ☎ 01256 844844 ✉ di.haywood@basingstoke.gov.uk

Licensing: Mrs Linda Cannon Interim Head of Service, Civic Offices, London Road, Basingstoke RG21 4AH ☎ 01256 844844 🖷 01256 845200 ✉ linda.cannon@basingstoke.gov.uk

Lifelong Learning: Mr Tim Boschi, Head of Community Services, Civic Offices, London Road, Basingstoke RG21 4AH ☎ 01256 845473 🖷 01256 845200 ✉ tim.boschi@basingstoke.gov.uk

Lighting: Mr Tim Boschi, Head of Community Services, Civic Offices, London Road, Basingstoke RG21 4AH ☎ 01256 845473 🖷 01256 845200 ✉ tim.boschi@basingstoke.gov.uk

Lottery Funding, Charity and Voluntary: Mr Tim Boschi, Head of Community Services, Civic Offices, London Road, Basingstoke RG21 4AH ☎ 01256 845473 🖷 01256 845200 ✉ tim.boschi@basingstoke.gov.uk

Member Services: Ms Karen Widdowson Democratic Services Manager, Civic Offices, London Road, Basingstoke RG21 4AH ☎ 01256 844844 ✉ karen.widdowson@basingstoke.gov.uk

Parking: Mr Tim Boschi, Head of Community Services, Civic Offices, London Road, Basingstoke RG21 4AH ☎ 01256 845473 🖷 01256 845200 ✉ tim.boschi@basingstoke.gov.uk

Partnerships: Ms Di Haywood Policy Manager for Economic & Community Strategy, Civic Offices, London Road, Basingstoke RG21 4AH ☎ 01256 844844 ✉ di.haywood@basingstoke.gov.uk

Personnel / HR: Ms Sheila Smith Head of HR, Civic Offices, London Road, Basingstoke RG21 4AH ☎ 01256 844844 🖷 01256 845200 ✉ sheila.smith@basingstoke.gov.uk

Planning: Mr Mike Townsend Planning Manager, Civic Offices, London Road, Basingstoke RG21 4AH ☎ 01256 844844 ✉ mike.townsend@basingstoke.gov.uk

Procurement: Mr Kevin Jaquest Head of Resources, Civic Offices, London Road, Basingstoke RG21 4AH ☎ 01256 845513 🖷 01256 845200 ✉ kevin.jaquest@basingstoke.gov.uk

Recycling & Waste Minimisation: Mrs Sarah Robinson Waste & Recycling Manager, Civic Offices, London Road, Basingstoke RG21 4AH ☎ 01252 774426 🖷 01256 845200 ✉ sarah.robinson@hart.gov.uk

Regeneration: Mr Tim Boschi, Head of Community Services, Civic Offices, London Road, Basingstoke RG21 4AH ☎ 01256 845473 🖷 01256 845200 ✉ tim.boschi@basingstoke.gov.uk

Street Scene: Mr Steve Featherstone, Environmental Care Operations Manager, Civic Offices, London Road, Basingstoke RG21 4AH ☎ 01256 845335 🖷 01256 845200 ✉ steve.featherstone@basingstoke.gov.uk

Sustainable Communities: Mrs Karen Brimacombe, Director - Borough Council Services, Civic Offices, London Road, Basingstoke RG21 4AH ☎ 01256 845789 🖷 01256 845200 ✉ karen.brimacombe@basingstoke.gov.uk

Sustainable Development: Mrs Karen Brimacombe, Director - Borough Council Services, Civic Offices, London Road, Basingstoke RG21 4AH ☎ 01256 845789 🖷 01256 845200 ✉ karen.brimacombe@basingstoke.gov.uk

Traffic Management: Mr Tim Boschi, Head of Community Services, Civic Offices, London Road, Basingstoke RG21 4AH ☎ 01256 845473 🖷 01256 845200 ✉ tim.boschi@basingstoke.gov.uk

Transport: Mr Richard Wareham Community Design & Regeneration Manager, Civic Offices, London Road, Basingstoke RG21 4AH ☎ 01256 844844 ✉ richard.wareham@basingstoke.gov.uk

Waste Collection and Disposal: Mrs Sarah Robinson Waste & Recycling Manager, Civic Offices, London Road, Basingstoke RG21 4AH ☎ 01252 774426 🖷 01256 845200 ✉ sarah.robinson@hart.gov.uk

BASINGSTOKE & DEANE

Waste Management: Mrs Sarah Robinson Waste & Recycling Manager, Civic Offices, London Road, Basingstoke RG21 4AH
☎ 01252 774426 🖷 01256 845200 ✉ sarah.robinson@hart.gov.uk

COUNCILLORS

Leader of the Council **Sanders**, Clive (CON - East Woodhay)
cllr.clive.sanders@basingstoke.gov.uk

Deputy Leader of the Council **Reid**, Terri (CON - Hatch Warren & Beggarwood)
cllr.terri.reid@basingstoke.gov.uk

Bean, Rebecca (CON - Hatch Warren & Beggarwood)
cllr.rebecca.bean@basingstoke.gov.uk

Bound, Simon (CON - Rooksdown)
cllr.simon.bound@basingstoke.gov.uk

Bound, Michael (LD - Baughurst & Tadley North)
cllr.michael.bound@basingstoke.gov.uk

Bower, Joyce (CON - Chineham)
cllr.joyce.bower@basingstoke.gov.uk

Burgess, Rita (CON - Kempshott)
cllr.rita.burgess@basingstoke.gov.uk

Court, Anne (CON - Kempshott)
cllr.anne.court@basingstoke.gov.uk

Cousens, Jack (LAB - Brookvale & Kings Furlong)
cllr.jack.cousens@basingstoke.gov.uk

Cubit, Onnalee (IND - Basing)
cllr.onnalee.cubitt@basingstoke.gov.uk

Day, Stephen (LD - Grove)
cllr.stephen.day@basingstoke.gov.uk

Dunlop, Eric (LD - Whitchurch)
cllr.eric.dunlop@basingstoke.gov.uk

Eachus, Hayley (CON - Kempshott)
cllr.hayley.eachus@basingstoke.gov.uk

Edwards, Laura (CON - Winklebury)
cllr.laura.edwards@basingstoke.gov.uk

Ellery, Matt (UKIP - Brighton Hill South)
cllr.matthew.ellery@basingstoke.gov.uk

Falconer, Graham (CON - Burghclere, Highclere & St Mary Bourne)
cllr.graham.falconer@basingstoke.gov.uk

Frankum, Paul (LAB - Popley West)
cllr.paul.frankum@basingstoke.gov.uk

Frankum, Jane (LAB - Popley West)
cllr.jane.frankum@basingstoke.gov.uk

Frost, Stuart (CON - Oakley & North Waltham)
cllr.stuart.frost@basingstoke.gov.uk

Gardiner, Roger (CON - Pamber & Silchester)
cllr.roger.gardiner@basingstoke.gov.uk

Godesen, Sven (CON - Basing)
cllr.sven.godesen@basingstoke.gov.uk

Golding, Hannah (CON - Brighton Hill North)
cllr.hannah.golding@basingstoke.gov.uk

Golding, Rob (CON - Oakley & North Waltham)
cllr.rob.goulding@basingstoke.gov.uk

Harvey, Paul (LAB - Norden)
cllr.paul.harvey@basingstoke.gov.uk

Hood, George (LAB - Norden)
cllr.george.hood@basingstoke.gov.uk

Hussey, Ronald (LD - Grove)
cllr.ron.hussey@basingstoke.gov.uk

Izett, John (CON - Burghclere, Highclere & St Mary Bourne)
cllr.john.izett@basingstoke.gov.uk

James, Gavin (LD - Eastrop)
cllr.gavin.james@basingstoke.gov.uk

James, Laura (LAB - Norden)
cllr.laura.james@basingstoke.gov.uk

Jones, Tony (LAB - Buckskin)
cllr.tony.jones@basingstoke.gov.uk

Keating, Sean (LAB - South Ham)
cllr.sean.keating@basingstoke.gov.uk

Leek, John (CON - Sherborne St John)
cllr.john.leek@basingstoke.gov.uk

Leeks, David (CON - Tadley South)
cllr.david.leeks@basingstoke.gov.uk

Lonie, Pamela (LAB - Brighton Hill South)
cllr.pamela.lonie@basingstoke.gov.uk

Miller, Paul (CON - Chineham)
cllr.paul.miller@basingstoke.gov.uk

Musson, Robert (CON - Tadley South)
cllr.robert.musson@basingstoke.gov.uk

Osselton, Cathy (CON - Kingsclere)
cllr.cathy.osselton@basingstoke.gov.uk

Parker, Stuart (LD - Eastrop)
cllr.stuart.parker@basingstoke.gov.uk

Phillimore, Colin (LAB - Overton, Laverstoke & Steventon)
cllr.colin.phillimore@basingstoke.gov.uk

Pierce, Nigel (LAB - Buckskin)
cllr.nigel.pierce@basingstoke.gov.uk

Pinder, Clive (CON - Basing)
cllr.clive.pinder@basingstoke.gov.uk

Potter, David (LAB - Popley East)
cllr.david.potter@basingstoke.gov.uk

Putty, Dan (CON - Hatch Warren & Beggarwood)
cllr.dan.putty@basingstoke.gov.uk

Regan, Colin (LAB - South Ham)
cllr.colin.regan@basingstoke.gov.uk

Richards, Jonathan (CON - Tadley Central)
cllr.jonathan.richards@basingstoke.gov.uk

Robinson, Nicholas (CON - Bramley & Sherfield)
cllr.nick.robinson@basingstoke.gov.uk

Ruffell, Mark (CON - Upton Grey & The Candovers)
cllr.mark.ruffell@basingstoke.gov.uk

Sherlock, Donald (CON - Kingsclere)
cllr.donald.sherlock@basingstoke.gov.uk

Smith, Joseph (CON - Winklebury)
cllr.joe.smith@basingstoke.gov.uk

Still, Elaine (CON - Chineham)
cllr.elaine.still@basingstoke.gov.uk

Tate, Robert (CON - Baughurst & Tadley North)
cllr.robert.tate@basingstoke.gov.uk

Taylor, Diane (CON - Oakley & North Waltham)
cllr.diane.taylor@basingstoke.gov.uk

Taylor, Mark (LAB - Brighton Hill North)
cllr.mark.taylor@basingstoke.gov.uk

Tilbury, Ian (IND - Overton, Laverstoke & Steventon)
cllr.ian.tilbury@basingstoke.gov.uk

Tomblin, Chris (IND - Bramley & Sherfield)
cllr.chris.tomblin@basingstoke.gov.uk

Tucker, Marilyn (CON - Pamber & Silchester)
cllr.marilyn.tucker@basingstoke.gov.uk

Washbourne, Vivien (LAB - Popley East)
cllr.vivien.washbourne@basingstoke.gov.uk

Watts, Gary (LAB - South Ham)
cllr.gary.watts@basingstoke.gov.uk

Watts, Keith (LD - Whitchurch)
cllr.keith.watts@basingstoke.gov.uk

Westbrook, Michael (LAB - Brookvale & Kings Furlong)
cllr.michael.westbrook@basingstoke.gov.uk

POLITICAL COMPOSITION
CON: 32, LAB: 17, LD: 7, IND: 3, UKIP: 1

COMMITTEE CHAIRS
Audit & Accounts: Mr Roger Gardiner

Development Control: Mr Donald Sherlock

Economic Planning & Housing: Mr Paul Miller

Licensing: Ms Diane Taylor

Bassetlaw D

Bassetlaw District Council, Queen's Buildings, Potter Street, Worksop S80 2AH
☎ 01909 533533 🖷 01909 501758 💻 www.bassetlaw.gov.uk

FACTS AND FIGURES
Parliamentary Constituencies: Bassetlaw
EU Constituencies: East Midlands
Election Frequency: Elections are by thirds

PRINCIPAL OFFICERS
Chief Executive: Mr Neil Taylor Chief Executive, Queen's Buildings, Potter Street, Worksop S80 2AH ☎ 01909 533221 🖷 01909 535498 ✉ neil.taylor@bassetlaw.gov.uk

Senior Management: Mr David Armiger, Interim Director - Regeneration & Neighbourhoods, Queen's Buildings, Potter Street, Worksop S80 2AH ☎ 01909 533187 🖷 01909 533400 ✉ david.armiger@bassetlaw.gov.uk

Senior Management: Ms Ros Theakstone, Director - Corporate Resources, Queen's Buildings, Potter Street, Worksop S80 2AH ☎ 01909 533160 ✉ ros.theakstone@bassetlaw.gov.uk

Access Officer / Social Services (Disability): Mr Malcolm Robson, Access Officer, Queen's Buildings, Potter Street, Worksop S80 2AH ☎ 01909 533195 🖷 01909 533400 ✉ malcolm.robson@bassetlaw.gov.uk

Architect, Building / Property Services: Mr John Unstead Property Manager, Queen's Buildings, Worksop S80 2AH ☎ 01909 533706 🖷 01909 501246 ✉ john.unstead@bassetlaw.gov.uk

Building Control: Mrs Angela Edwards Building Control Manager, Queen's Buildings, Potter Street, Worksop S80 2AH ☎ 01909 533130 🖷 01909 533400 ✉ angela.edwards@bassetlaw.gov.uk

Building Control: Mr Robert Whatley, Principal Building Control Officer, Queen's Buildings, Potter Street, Worksop S80 2AH ☎ 01909 533130 🖷 01909 482622 ✉ bob.whatley@bassetlaw.gov.uk

PR / Communications: Mr Jonathan Brassington Communications Manager, Queen's Buildings, Potter Street, Worksop S80 2AH ☎ 01909 533726 🖷 01909 501758 ✉ jonathan.brassington@bassetlaw.gov.uk

Community Safety: Mr Gerald Connor Community Safety Co-ordinator, Queen's Buildings, Potter Street, Worksop S80 2AH ☎ 01909 533153 ✉ gerald.connor@bassetlaw.gov.uk

Computer Management: Mr Andrew Bramall Strategic ICT Manager, Queen's Buildings, Potter Street, Worksop S80 2AH ☎ 01909 533122 🖷 01909 535506 ✉ andrew.bramall@bassetlaw.gov.uk

Corporate Services: Ms Ros Theakstone, Director - Corporate Resources, Queen's Buildings, Potter Street, Worksop S80 2AH ☎ 01909 533160 ✉ ros.theakstone@bassetlaw.gov.uk

Customer Service: Mr Stephen Brown, Head of Corporate Services, Queen's Buildings, Potter Street, Worksop S80 2AH ☎ 01909 533767 🖷 01909 535498 ✉ steve.brown@bassetlaw.gov.uk

Economic Development: Mr Robert Wilkinson, Economic Development Team Manager, Queen's Buildings, Potter Street, Worksop S80 2AH ☎ 01909 533230 🖷 01909 501246 ✉ robert.wilkinson@bassetlaw.gov.uk

E-Government: Mr Stephen Brown, Head of Corporate Services, Queen's Buildings, Potter Street, Worksop S80 2AH ☎ 01909 533767 🖷 01909 535498 ✉ steve.brown@bassetlaw.gov.uk

Electoral Registration: Mrs Julie Briggs Election Officer, Queen's Buildings, Potter Street, Worksop S80 2AH ☎ 01909 533464 🖷 01909 501758 ✉ julie.briggs@bassetlaw.gov.uk

Emergency Planning: Mr Jim Moran Principal Safety Officer, Carlton Forest House, Hundred Acre Lane, Carlton Forest, Worksop S81 0TS ☎ 01909 534337 ✉ jim.moran@bassetlaw.gov.uk

Energy Management: Miss Kerri Ellis Sustainability Officer, Queen's Buildings, Potter Street, Worksop S80 2AH ☎ 01909 533211 🖷 01909 533486 ✉ kerri.ellis@bassetlaw.gov.uk

Environmental / Technical Services: Mr David Armiger, Interim Director - Regeneration & Neighbourhoods, Queen's Buildings, Potter Street, Worksop S80 2AH ☎ 01909 533187 🖷 01909 533400 ✉ david.armiger@bassetlaw.gov.uk

BASSETLAW

Environmental Health: Mrs Elizabeth Prime Head of Neighbourhoods, Queen's Buildings, Potter Street, Worksop S80 2AH ☎ 01909 533219 🖷 01909 533397 🖰 elizabeth.prime@bassetlaw.gov.uk

Environmental Health: Mr Julian Proudman Environmental Health Team Manager, Queen's Buildings, Potter Street, Worksop S80 2AH ☎ 01909 533219 🖷 01909 533397 🖰 julian.proudman@bassetlaw.gov.uk

Estates, Property & Valuation: Mr John Unstead Property Manager, Queen's Buildings, Worksop S80 2AH ☎ 01909 533706 🖷 01909 501246 🖰 john.unstead@bassetlaw.gov.uk

Finance: Mr Mike Hill Head - Finance & Property, Queen's Buildings, Potter Street, Worksop S80 2AH ☎ 01909 533174 🖷 01909 501246 🖰 mike.hill@bassetlaw.gov.uk

Fleet Management: Mr Peter Jones Operational Services Manager - Fleet & Admin Services, Hundred Acre Lane, Carlton Forest, Worksop S81 0TS ☎ 01909 534487 🖷 01909 730586 🖰 peter.jones@bassetlaw.gov.uk

Grounds Maintenance: Mr Keith Somers Operational Services Manager - Parks, Open Spaces & Cemeteries, West House, Hundred Acre Lane, Carlton Forest, Worksop S81 0TS ☎ 01919 534420 🖰 keith.somers@bassetlaw.gov.uk

Health and Safety: Mr Jim Moran Principal Safety Officer, Carlton Forest House, Hundred Acre Lane, Carlton Forest, Worksop S81 0TS ☎ 01909 534337 🖰 jim.moran@bassetlaw.gov.uk

Home Energy Conservation: Mrs Wendy Piggott Strategic Housing Development Manager, Queen's Buildings, Potter Street, Worksop S80 2AH ☎ 01909 533425 🖰 wendy.piggott@bassetlaw.gov.uk

Legal: Mr Stephen Brown, Head of Corporate Services, Queen's Buildings, Potter Street, Worksop S80 2AH ☎ 01909 533767 🖷 01909 535498 🖰 steve.brown@bassetlaw.gov.uk

Leisure and Cultural Services: Mr Peter Clark Leisure & Cultural Services Manager, 17b The Square, Retford DN22 6DB ☎ 01909 534507 🖷 01909 534529 🖰 peter.clark@bassetlaw.gov.uk

Licensing: Mr Stephen Wormald Senior Solicitor, Queen's Buildings, Potter Street, Worksop S80 2AH ☎ 01909 533456 🖷 01909 535498 🖰 stephen.wormald@bassetlaw.gov.uk

Lottery Funding, Charity and Voluntary: Mr Mike Hill Head - Finance & Property, Queen's Buildings, Potter Street, Worksop S80 2AH ☎ 01909 533174 🖷 01909 501246 🖰 mike.hill@bassetlaw.gov.uk

Member Services: Ms Ros Theakstone, Director - Corporate Resources, Queen's Buildings, Potter Street, Worksop S80 2AH ☎ 01909 533160 🖰 ros.theakstone@bassetlaw.gov.uk

Parking: Mr Richard Blagg Town Centre Manager - Operational, Queen's Buildings, Potter Street, Worksop S80 2AH ☎ 01909 535104 🖷 01909 501246 🖰 richard.blagg@bassetlaw.gov.uk

Partnerships: Ms Ros Theakstone, Director - Corporate Resources, Queen's Buildings, Potter Street, Worksop S80 2AH ☎ 01909 533160 🖰 ros.theakstone@bassetlaw.gov.uk

Personnel / HR: Mr Len Hull, Head - Human Resources, Queen's Buildings, Potter Street, Worksop S80 2AH ☎ 01909 534136 🖷 01909 533451 🖰 len.hull@bassetlaw.gov.uk

Planning: Mrs Beverley Alderton-Sambrook Head - Regeneration, Queen's Buildings, Potter Street, Worksop S80 2AH ☎ 01909 533187 🖰 beverley.alderton-sambrook@bassetlaw.gov.uk

Procurement: Mr Mike Hill Head - Finance & Property, Queen's Buildings, Potter Street, Worksop S80 2AH ☎ 01909 533174 🖷 01909 501246 🖰 mike.hill@bassetlaw.gov.uk

Recycling & Waste Minimisation: Mr Tim Andrew Operational Services Manager - Waste & Recyling, Hundred Acre Lane, Carlton Forest, Worksop S81 0TS ☎ 01909 534422 🖷 01909 730586 🖰 tim.andrew@bassetlaw.gov.uk

Recycling & Waste Minimisation: Mr David Armiger, Interim Director - Regeneration & Neighbourhoods, Queen's Buildings, Potter Street, Worksop S80 2AH ☎ 01909 533187 🖷 01909 533400 🖰 david.armiger@bassetlaw.gov.uk

Regeneration: Mr Robert Wilkinson, Economic Development Team Manager, Queen's Buildings, Potter Street, Worksop S80 2AH ☎ 01909 533230 🖷 01909 501246 🖰 robert.wilkinson@bassetlaw.gov.uk

Staff Training: Mrs Jenny Rodriguez HR Business Partner - Learning & Development, Queen's Buildings, Potter Street, Worksop S80 2AH ☎ 01909 534134 🖰 jenny.rodriguez@bassetlaw.gov.uk

Street Scene: Mr Tim Andrew Operational Services Manager - Waste & Recyling, Hundred Acre Lane, Carlton Forest, Worksop S81 0TS ☎ 01909 534422 🖷 01909 730586 🖰 tim.andrew@bassetlaw.gov.uk

Sustainable Communities: Mr David Armiger, Interim Director - Regeneration & Neighbourhoods, Queen's Buildings, Potter Street, Worksop S80 2AH ☎ 01909 533187 🖷 01909 533400 🖰 david.armiger@bassetlaw.gov.uk

Sustainable Communities: Ms Ros Theakstone, Director - Corporate Resources, Queen's Buildings, Potter Street, Worksop S80 2AH ☎ 01909 533160 🖰 ros.theakstone@bassetlaw.gov.uk

Sustainable Development: Mr David Armiger, Interim Director - Regeneration & Neighbourhoods, Queen's Buildings, Potter Street, Worksop S80 2AH ☎ 01909 533187 🖷 01909 533400 🖰 david.armiger@bassetlaw.gov.uk

Tourism: Ms Sandra Withington, Development & Marketing Officer, Queen's Buildings, Potter Street, Worksop S80 2AH ☎ 01909 533533 🖷 01909 501246 🖰 sandra.withington@bassetlaw.gov.uk

Town Centre: Mr Richard Blagg Town Centre Manager - Operational, Queen's Buildings, Potter Street, Worksop S80 2AH ☎ 01909 535104 🖷 01909 501246 🖰 richard.blagg@bassetlaw.gov.uk

Transport: Mr Peter Jones Operational Services Manager - Fleet & Admin Services, Hundred Acre Lane, Carlton Forest, Worksop S81 0TS ☎ 01909 534487 🖷 01909 730586 🖰 peter.jones@bassetlaw.gov.uk

Waste Collection and Disposal: Mr Tim Andrew Operational Services Manager - Waste & Recyling, Hundred Acre Lane, Carlton Forest, Worksop S81 0TS ☎ 01909 534422 🖷 01909 730586 🖰 tim.andrew@bassetlaw.gov.uk

Waste Collection and Disposal: Mr Mark Ladyman Director - Regeneration & Neighbourhood Services, Queen's Buildings, Potter Street, Worksop S80 2AH ☎ 01909 533160 🖷 01909 535498 🖰 mark.ladyman@bassetlaw.gov.uk

Waste Management: Mr Tim Andrew Operational Services Manager - Waste & Recyling, Hundred Acre Lane, Carlton Forest, Worksop S81 0TS ☎ 01909 534422 🖷 01909 730586 🖰 tim.andrew@bassetlaw.gov.uk

Waste Management: Mr David Armiger, Interim Director - Regeneration & Neighbourhoods, Queen's Buildings, Potter Street, Worksop S80 2AH ☎ 01909 533187 🖷 01909 533400 🖰 david.armiger@bassetlaw.gov.uk

Children's Play Areas: Mr Peter Clark Leisure & Cultural Services Manager, 17b The Square, Retford DN22 6DB ☎ 01909 534507 🖷 01909 534529 🖰 peter.clark@bassetlaw.gov.uk

COUNCILLORS

***Chair* Jones**, Gwynneth (LAB - Worksop North)
gwynneth.jones@bassetlaw.gov.uk

***Vice-Chair* Freeman**, Gillian (LAB - Langold)
gillian.freeman@bassetlaw.gov.uk

***Leader of the Council* Greaves**, Simon (LAB - Worksop North East)
simon.greaves@bassetlaw.gov.uk

***Deputy Leader of the Council* White**, Jo (LAB - Worksop East)
jo.white@bassetlaw.gov.uk

Anderson, James (LAB - East Retford West)
jim.anderson@bassetlaw.gov.uk

Bowles, Barry (CON - Blyth)
barry.bowles@bassetlaw.gov.uk

Brand, Hazel (IND - Misterton)
hazel.brand@bassetlaw.gov.uk

Brett, Dean (LAB - Worksop North West)
dean.brett@bassetlaw.gov.uk

Burton, Hugh (IND - Sturton)
hugh.burton@bassetlaw.gov.uk

Carrington-Wilde, Robin Brian (LAB - Carlton)
robin.carrington-wilde@bassetlaw.gov.uk

Challinor, David (LAB - Harworth)
david.challinor@bassetlaw.gov.uk

Chambers, Alan (LAB - East Retford West)
alan.chambers@bassetlaw.gov.uk

Clarkson, Garry (LAB - East Retford North)
garry.clarkson@bassestlaw/gov.uk

Critchley, Marie Francis Teresa (CON - Rampton)
teresa.critchley@bassetlaw.gov.uk

Dukes, Kevin (LAB - Welbeck)
kevin.dukes@bassetlaw.gov.uk

Entwistle, Clifford (LAB - Worksop East)
cliff.entwistle@bassetlaw.gov.uk

Evans, June (LAB - harworth)
june.evans@bassetlaw.gov.uk

Farncombe, Sarah (LAB - Worksop North)
sarah.farncombe@bassetlaw.gov.uk

Fielding, Sybil (LAB - Worksop North West)
sybil.fielding@bassetlaw.gov.uk

Foley, Deidre (LAB - Worksop South East)
deidre.foley@bassetlaw.gov.uk

Gray, Michael (CON - Ranskill)
michael.gray@bassetlaw.gov.uk

Greaves, Kevin (LAB - Worksop South)
kevin.greaves@bassetlaw.gov.uk

Hare, Dianne (CON - Worksop South)
dianne.hare@bassetlaw.gov.uk

Isard, Keith (CON - Tuxford & Trent)
keith.isard@bassetlaw.gov.uk

Isard, Shirley (CON - Tuxford & Trent)
shirley.isard@bassetlaw.gov.uk

Leigh, Julie (LAB - Worksop South)
julie.leigh@bassetlaw.gov.uk

Merryweather, Deborah (LAB - Worksop East)
deborah.merryweather@bassetlaw.gov.uk

Ogle, John (CON - East Markham)
john.ogle@bassetlaw.gov.uk

Oxby, Graham (LAB - East Retford North)
graham.oxby@bassetlaw.gov.uk

Pidwell, David George (LAB - Carlton)
david.pidwell@bassetlaw.gov.uk

Potts, David (LAB - Worksop North)
david.potts@bassetlaw.gov.uk

Potts, Josie (LAB - Worksop South East)
josie.potts@bassetlaw.gov.uk

Pressley, David (LAB - Worksop North West)
david.pressley@bassetlaw.gov.uk

Quigley, Michael (CON - East Retford East)
michael.quigley@bassetlaw.gov.uk

Rhodes, Alan (LAB - Worksop North East)
alan.rhodes@bassetlaw.gov.uk

Richards, Helen (LAB - East Retford South)
helen.richards@bassetlaw.gov.uk

Richardson, Madelaine (LAB - Worksop North East)
madelaine.richardson@bassetlaw.gov.uk

Sanger, Joan (IND - Beckingham)
joan.sanger@bassetlaw.gov.uk

Scottorne, Steve (LAB - Carlton)
steve.scotthorne@bassetlaw.gov.uk

Shaw, Susan (LAB - East Retford East)
susan.shaw@basssetlaw.gov.uk

Shephard, John (LAB - Worksop South East)
john.shephard@bassetlaw.gov.uk

Simpson, Annette (CON - Everton)
annette.simpson@bassetlaw.gov.uk

Smith, Anita (LAB - Harworth)
anita.smith@bassetlaw.gov.uk

Storey, Michael (LAB - East Retford East)
michael.storey@bassetlaw.gov.uk

Sutton, Kathleen (CON - Clayworth)
kath.sutton@bassetlaw.gov.uk

Taylor, Tracey (CON - Sutton)
traceuy.taylor@bassellaw.gov.uk

Tromans, Anthony (CON - East Retford North)
anthony.tromans@bassetlaw.gov.uk

Troop, Carolyn (LAB - East Retford South)
carolyn.troop@bassetlaw.gov.uk

POLITICAL COMPOSITION

LAB: 33, CON: 12, IND: 3

Bath & North East Somerset U

Bath & North East Somerset Council, Guildhall, High Street, Bath BA1 5AW
☎ 01225 477000 🖷 01225 477499
council_connect@bathnes.gov.uk www.bathnes.gov.uk

FACTS AND FIGURES

Parliamentary Constituencies: Bath
EU Constituencies: South West
Election Frequency: Elections are of whole council

PRINCIPAL OFFICERS

Chief Executive: Dr Jo Farrar Chief Executive, Guildhall, High Street, Bath BA1 5AW ☎ 01225 477400 🖷 01225 477062 jo_farrar@bathnes.gov.uk

Senior Management: Mr Ashley Ayre, Strategic Director - People & Communities, Guildhall, High Street, Bath BA1 1LA ☎ 01225 394200 🖷 01225 394011 ashley_ayre@bathnes.gov.uk

Senior Management: Ms Louise Fradd Strategic Director - Place, Guildhall, High Street, Bath BA1 5AW ☎ 01225 394567 louise_fradd@bathnes.gov.uk

Senior Management: Dr Bruce Lawrence Director - Public Health, Guildhall, High Street, Bath BA1 5AW bruce_lawrence@bathnes.gov.uk

Senior Management: Mr Andrew Pate Strategic Director - Resources, Guildhall, High Street, Bath BA1 5AW ☎ 01225 477300 🖷 01225 477377 andrew_pate@bathnes.gov.uk

Architect, Building / Property Services: Mr Derek Quilter Divisional Director - Project Delivery, 10 Palace Mews, Bath BA1 2NH ☎ 01225 477739 derek_quilter@bathnes.gov.uk

Building Control: Mr David Trigwell, Divisional Director - Planning & Transport Development, Riverside, Temple Street, Keynsham BS31 1LA ☎ 01225 477702 🖷 01225 394199 david_trigwell@bathnes.gov.uk

Catering Services: Mr Derek Quilter Divisional Director - Project Delivery, 10 Palace Mews, Bath BA1 2NH ☎ 01225 477739 derek_quilter@bathnes.gov.uk

Children / Youth Services: Mr Richard Baldwin Divisional Director - CYP Specialist Services, Guildhall, High Street, Bath BA1 5AW ☎ 01225 396289 richard_baldwin@bathnes.gov.uk

Civil Registration: Ms Maria Lucas Monitoring Officer, Riverside, Temple Street, Keynsham, Bristol BS31 1LA ☎ 01225 395171 maria_lucas@bathnes.gov.uk

PR / Communications: Mr David Thompson, Divisional Director - Organisational Development, Guildhall, High Street, Bath BA1 5AW ☎ 01225 394368 🖷 01225 394298 dave_thompson@bathnes.gov.uk

Community Planning: Mr David Trethewey Divisional Director - Strategy & Performance, Guildhall, High Street, Bath BA1 5AW ☎ 01225 477300 🖷 01225 396353 david_trethewey@bathnes.gov.uk

Community Safety: Mr David Trethewey Divisional Director - Strategy & Performance, Guildhall, High Street, Bath BA1 5AW ☎ 01225 477300 🖷 01225 396353 david_trethewey@bathnes.gov.uk

Computer Management: Mrs Angela Parratt Head - Transformation, Guildhall, High Street, Bath BA1 5AW ☎ 01225 476576 🖷 01225 477377 angela_parratt@bathnes.gov.uk

Consumer Protection and Trading Standards: Mr Matthew Smith, Divisional Director - Environmental Services, Royal Victoria Park Nursery, Marlborough Lane, Bath BA1 2LZ ☎ 01225 396888 🖷 01225 480072 matthew_smith@bathnes.gov.uk

Contracts: Mr Jeff Wring Head - Audit West, Guildhall, High Street, Bath BA1 5AW ☎ 01225 477323 jeff_wring@bathnes.gov.uk

Corporate Services: Mr Tim Richens Divisional Director - Business Support, Guildhall, High Street, Bath BA1 5AW ☎ 01225 477468 🖷 01225 477377 tim_richens@bathnes.gov.uk

Customer Service: Mr Ian Savigar Divisional Director - Customer Services, Lewis House, Manvers Street, Bath BA1 1JG ☎ 01225 477327 ian_savigar@bathnes.gov.uk

Direct Labour: Mr Matthew Smith, Divisional Director - Environmental Services, Royal Victoria Park Nursery, Marlborough Lane, Bath BA1 2LZ ☎ 01225 396888 🖷 01225 480072 matthew_smith@bathnes.gov.uk

Economic Development: Mr John Wilkinson Divisional Director - Community Regeneration, 10 Palace Mews, Bath BA1 2NH ☎ 01225 396593 john_Wilkinson@bathnes.gov.uk

Education: Mr Richard Baldwin Divisional Director - CYP Specialist Services, Guildhall, High Street, Bath BA1 5AW ☎ 01225 396289 🖱 richard_baldwin@bathnes.gov.uk

Electoral Registration: Ms Maria Lucas Monitoring Officer, Riverside, Temple Street, Keynsham, Bristol BS31 1LA ☎ 01225 395171 🖱 maria_lucas@bathnes.gov.uk

Emergency Planning: Mr Jeff Wring Head - Audit West, Guildhall, High Street, Bath BA1 5AW ☎ 01225 477323 🖱 jeff_wring@bathnes.gov.uk

Energy Management: Mr Derek Quilter Divisional Director - Project Delivery, 10 Palace Mews, Bath BA1 2NH ☎ 01225 477739 🖱 derek_quilter@bathnes.gov.uk

Environmental / Technical Services: Mr Matthew Smith, Divisional Director - Environmental Services, Royal Victoria Park Nursery, Marlborough Lane, Bath BA1 2LZ ☎ 01225 396888 🖷 01225 480072 🖱 matthew_smith@bathnes.gov.uk

Environmental Health: Mr Matthew Smith, Divisional Director - Environmental Services, Royal Victoria Park Nursery, Marlborough Lane, Bath BA1 2LZ ☎ 01225 396888 🖷 01225 480072 🖱 matthew_smith@bathnes.gov.uk

Estates, Property & Valuation: Mr Derek Quilter Divisional Director - Project Delivery, 10 Palace Mews, Bath BA1 2NH ☎ 01225 477739 🖱 derek_quilter@bathnes.gov.uk

Events Manager: Mr Mike Butler, Interim Divisional Director - Tourism, Leisure & Culture, Guildhall, High Street, Bath BA1 5AW ☎ 01225 395385 🖱 michael_butler@bathnes.gov.uk

Facilities: Mr Derek Quilter Divisional Director - Project Delivery, 10 Palace Mews, Bath BA1 2NH ☎ 01225 477739 🖱 derek_quilter@bathnes.gov.uk

Finance: Mr Tim Richens Divisional Director - Business Support, Guildhall, High Street, Bath BA1 5AW ☎ 01225 477468 🖷 01225 477377 🖱 tim_richens@bathnes.gov.uk

Pensions: Ms Liz Woodyard Pensions Investments Manager, Riverside, Temple Street, Keynsham BS31 1LA ☎ 01225 395306 🖱 liz_woodyard@bathnes.gov.uk

Fleet Management: Mr Matthew Smith, Divisional Director - Environmental Services, Royal Victoria Park Nursery, Marlborough Lane, Bath BA1 2LZ ☎ 01225 396888 🖷 01225 480072 🖱 matthew_smith@bathnes.gov.uk

Grounds Maintenance: Mr Matthew Smith, Divisional Director - Environmental Services, Royal Victoria Park Nursery, Marlborough Lane, Bath BA1 2LZ ☎ 01225 396888 🖷 01225 480072 🖱 matthew_smith@bathnes.gov.uk

Health and Safety: Mr William Harding, Head - Human Resources, Riverside, Temple Street, Keynsham, Bristol BS31 1LA ☎ 01225 477203 🖷 01225 477423 🖱 william_harding@bathnes.gov.uk

Highways: Mr David Trigwell, Divisional Director - Planning & Transport Development, Lewis House, PO BOX 5006, Bath BA1 1`JG ☎ 01225 477702 🖷 01225 394199 🖱 david_trigwell@bathnes.gov.uk

Home Energy Conservation: Mrs Jane Shayler, Divisional Director - Adult Care, Health & Housing Strategy & Commissioning, St Martin's Hospital, Clara Cross Lane, Midford Road, Bath BA2 5RP ☎ 01225 396120 🖷 01225 396268 🖱 jane_shayler@bathnes.gov.uk

Housing: Mrs Jane Shayler, Divisional Director - Adult Care, Health & Housing Strategy & Commissioning, St Martin's Hospital, Clara Cross Lane, Midford Road, Bath BA2 5RP ☎ 01225 396120 🖷 01225 396268 🖱 jane_shayler@bathnes.gov.uk

Local Area Agreement: Mr David Tretheway Divisional Director - Strategy & Performance, Lewis House, Manvers Street, Bath BA11 1JG ☎ 01225 396353 🖱 david_trethewey@bathnes.gov.uk

Legal: Ms Maria Lucas Monitoring Officer, Riverside, Temple Street, Keynsham, Bristol BS31 1LA ☎ 01225 395171 🖱 maria_lucas@bathnes.gov.uk

Leisure and Cultural Services: Mr Mike Butler, Interim Divisional Director - Tourism, Leisure & Culture, Guildhall, High Street, Bath BA1 5AW ☎ 01225 395385 🖱 michael_butler@bathnes.gov.uk

Licensing: Mr Matthew Smith, Divisional Director - Environmental Services, Royal Victoria Park Nursery, Marlborough Lane, Bath BA1 2LZ ☎ 01225 396888 🖷 01225 480072 🖱 matthew_smith@bathnes.gov.uk

Lifelong Learning: Mr Jeremy Smalley, Divisional Director - Development & Regeneration, Riverside, Temple Street, Keynsham, Bristol BS31 1LA ☎ 01225 477822 🖱 jeremy_smalley@bathnes.gov.uk

Lighting: Mr Matthew Smith, Divisional Director - Environmental Services, Royal Victoria Park Nursery, Marlborough Lane, Bath BA1 2LZ ☎ 01225 396888 🖷 01225 480072 🖱 matthew_smith@bathnes.gov.uk

Lottery Funding, Charity and Voluntary: Mr David Tretheway Divisional Director - Strategy & Performance, Lewis House, Manvers Street, Bath BA11 1JG ☎ 01225 396353 🖱 david_trethewey@bathnes.gov.uk

Member Services: Ms Maria Lucas Monitoring Officer, Riverside, Temple Street, Keynsham, Bristol BS31 1LA ☎ 01225 395171 🖱 maria_lucas@bathnes.gov.uk

Parking: Mr Matthew Smith, Divisional Director - Environmental Services, Royal Victoria Park Nursery, Marlborough Lane, Bath BA1 2LZ ☎ 01225 396888 🖷 01225 480072 🖱 matthew_smith@bathnes.gov.uk

Partnerships: Mr David Tretheway Divisional Director - Strategy & Performance, Lewis House, Manvers Street, Bath BA11 1JG ☎ 01225 396353 🖱 david_trethewey@bathnes.gov.uk

BATH & NORTH EAST SOMERSET

Personnel / HR: Mr William Harding, Head - Human Resources, Riverside, Temple Street, Keynsham, Bristol BS31 1LA ☎ 01225 477203 🖷 01225 477423 🖱 william_harding@bathnes.gov.uk

Planning: Ms Lisa Bartlett Divisional Director - Development, Guildhall, High Street, Bath BA1 5AW 🖱 lisa_bartlett@bathnes.gov.uk

Procurement: Mr Jeff Wring Head - Audit West, Guildhall, High Street, Bath BA1 5AW ☎ 01225 477323 🖱 jeff_wring@bathnes.gov.uk

Public Libraries: Mr Mike Butler, Interim Divisional Director - Tourism, Leisure & Culture, Guildhall, High Street, Bath BA1 5AW ☎ 01225 395385 🖱 michael_butler@bathnes.gov.uk

Recycling & Waste Minimisation: Mr Matthew Smith, Divisional Director - Environmental Services, Royal Victoria Park Nursery, Marlborough Lane, Bath BA1 2LZ ☎ 01225 396888 🖷 01225 480072 🖱 matthew_smith@bathnes.gov.uk

Regeneration: Mr Derek Quilter Divisional Director - Project Delivery, 10 Palace Mews, Bath BA1 2NH ☎ 01225 477739 🖱 derek_quilter@bathnes.gov.uk

Road Safety: Mr David Trigwell, Divisional Director - Planning & Transport Development, Riverside, Temple Street, Keynsham BS31 1LA ☎ 01225 477702 🖷 01225 394199 🖱 david_trigwell@bathnes.gov.uk

Social Services: Mr Richard Baldwin Divisional Director - CYP Specialist Services, Guildhall, High Street, Bath BA1 5AW ☎ 01225 396289 🖱 richard_baldwin@bathnes.gov.uk

Social Services (Adult): Mrs Jane Shayler, Divisional Director - Adult Care, Health & Housing Strategy & Commissioning, St Martin's Hospital, Clara Cross Lane, Midford Road, Bath BA2 5RP ☎ 01225 396120 🖷 01225 396268 🖱 jane_shayler@bathnes.gov.uk

Social Services (Children): Mr Maurice Lindsay, Divisional Director - Children, YP & Family Support Services, Riverside, Temple Street, Keynsham, Bristol BS31 1LA ☎ 01225 396289 🖷 01225 396115 🖱 maurice_lindsay@bathnes.gov.uk

Fostering & Adoption: Mr Richard Baldwin Divisional Director - CYP Specialist Services, Guildhall, High Street, Bath BA1 5AW ☎ 01225 396289 🖱 richard_baldwin@bathnes.gov.uk

Safeguarding: Mr Mike Bowden CYP Strategy & Commissioning, Guildhall, High Street, Bath BA1 5AW ☎ 01225 396289 🖱 mike_bowden@bathnes.gov.uk

Families: Mr Richard Baldwin Divisional Director - CYP Specialist Services, Guildhall, High Street, Bath BA1 5AW ☎ 01225 396289 🖱 richard_baldwin@bathnes.gov.uk

Childrens Social Care: Mr Richard Baldwin Divisional Director - CYP Specialist Services, Guildhall, High Street, Bath BA1 5AW ☎ 01225 396289 🖱 richard_baldwin@bathnes.gov.uk

Public Health: Dr Bruce Lawrence Director - Public Health, Guildhall, High Street, Bath BA1 5AW 🖱 bruce_lawrence@bathnes.gov.uk

Staff Training: Mr William Harding, Head - Human Resources, Riverside, Temple Street, Keynsham, Bristol BS31 1LA ☎ 01225 477203 🖷 01225 477423 🖱 william_harding@bathnes.gov.uk

Street Scene: Mr Matthew Smith, Divisional Director - Environmental Services, Royal Victoria Park Nursery, Marlborough Lane, Bath BA1 2LZ ☎ 01225 396888 🖷 01225 480072 🖱 matthew_smith@bathnes.gov.uk

Sustainable Communities: Mr David Tretheway Divisional Director - Strategy & Performance, Lewis House, Manvers Street, Bath BA11 1JG ☎ 01225 396353 🖱 david_trethewey@bathnes.gov.uk

Sustainable Development: Mr David Tretheway Divisional Director - Strategy & Performance, Lewis House, Manvers Street, Bath BA11 1JG ☎ 01225 396353 🖱 david_trethewey@bathnes.gov.uk

Tourism: Mr Mike Butler, Interim Divisional Director - Tourism, Leisure & Culture, Guildhall, High Street, Bath BA1 5AW ☎ 01225 395385 🖱 michael_butler@bathnes.gov.uk

Town Centre: Mr Matthew Smith, Divisional Director - Environmental Services, Royal Victoria Park Nursery, Marlborough Lane, Bath BA1 2LZ ☎ 01225 396888 🖷 01225 480072 🖱 matthew_smith@bathnes.gov.uk

Traffic Management: Mr David Trigwell, Divisional Director - Planning & Transport Development, Trimbridge House, Trim Street, Bath BA1 2DP ☎ 01225 477702 🖷 01225 394199 🖱 david_trigwell@bathnes.gov.uk

Transport: Mr David Trigwell, Divisional Director - Planning & Transport Development, Trimbridge House, Trim Street, Bath BA1 2DP ☎ 01225 477702 🖷 01225 394199 🖱 david_trigwell@bathnes.gov.uk

Transport Planner: Mr David Trigwell, Divisional Director - Planning & Transport Development, Trimbridge House, Trim Street, Bath BA1 2DP ☎ 01225 477702 🖷 01225 394199 🖱 david_trigwell@bathnes.gov.uk

Total Place: Mr David Tretheway Divisional Director - Strategy & Performance, Lewis House, Manvers Street, Bath BA11 1JG ☎ 01225 396353 🖱 david_trethewey@bathnes.gov.uk

Waste Collection and Disposal: Mr Matthew Smith, Divisional Director - Environmental Services, Royal Victoria Park Nursery, Marlborough Lane, Bath BA1 2LZ ☎ 01225 396888 🖷 01225 480072 🖱 matthew_smith@bathnes.gov.uk

Waste Management: Mr Matthew Smith, Divisional Director - Environmental Services, Royal Victoria Park Nursery, Marlborough Lane, Bath BA1 2LZ ☎ 01225 396888 🖷 01225 480072 🖱 matthew_smith@bathnes.gov.uk

Children's Play Areas: Mr Matthew Smith, Divisional Director - Environmental Services, Royal Victoria Park Nursery, Marlborough Lane, Bath BA1 2LZ ☎ 01225 396888 🖷 01225 480072 🖱 matthew_smith@bathnes.gov.uk

COUNCILLORS

***Chair* Gilchrist**, Ian (LD - Widcombe)
ian_gilchrist@bathnes.gov.uk

***Vice-Chair* Hale**, Alan (CON - Keynsham South)
alan_hale@bathnes.gov.uk

***Leader of the Council* Warren**, Tim (CON - Mendip)
tim@warrenequestrian.co.uk

***Group Leader* Carr**, Jonathan (GRN - Abbey)
jonathan.carr@bathnesgreens.org.uk

***Group Leader* Moss**, Robin (LAB - Westfield)
robin_moss@bathnes.gov.uk

***Group Leader* Romero**, Dine (LD - Southdown)
dine_romero@bathnes.gov.uk

Anketell-Jones, Patrick (CON - Lansdown)
patrick_aneketell-jones@bathnes.gov.uk

Appleyard, Rob (LD - Lambridge)
rob_appleyard@bathnes.gov.uk

Ball, Timothy (LD - Twerton)
tim_ball@bathnes.gov.uk

Barrett, Colin (CON - Weston)
barrettsofbath@yahoo.co.uk

Beath, Cherry (LD - Combe Down)
cherry_beath@bathnes.gov.uk

Becker, Jasper (CON - Widcombe)
jasper_becker@bathnes.gov.uk

Bevan, Sarah (IND - Peasedown)
sarah_bevan@bathnes.gov.uk

Blackburn, Colin (IND - Westmoreland)
colin_blackburn@bathnes.gov.uk

Brett, Lisa (LD - Walcot)
lisa_brett@bathnes.gov.uk

Bull, John (LAB - Paulton)
john_bull@bathnes.gov.uk

Butters, Neil (LD - Bathavon South)
cllrneilbutters@aol.com

Clarke, Anthony (CON - Lansdown)
anthony_clarke@bathnes.gov.uk

Cochrane, Matt (CON - Bathwick)
matt_cochrane@bathnes.gov.uk

Crossley, Paul (LD - Southdown)
paul_crossley@bathnes.gov.uk

Dando, Chris (LAB - Radstock)
christopher_dando@bathnes.gov.uk

Darey, Fiona (CON - Walcot)
fiona_darey@bathnes.gov.uk

Davies, Matthew (CON - Weston)
matthew_davies@bathnes.gov.uk

Davis, Sally (CON - Farmborough)
sally_davis@bathnes.gov.uk

Deacon, Douglas (IND - Timsbury)
douglas_deacon@bathnes.gov.uk

Dixon, Emma (CON - Saltford)
emma_dixon@bathnes.gov.uk

Evans, Michael (CON - Midsomer Norton North)
michael_evans@bathnes.gov.uk

Furse, Andrew (LD - Kingsmead)
andrew_furse@bathnes.gov.uk

Gerrish, Charles (CON - Keynsham North)
charles_gerrish@bathnes.gov.uk

Goodman, Bob (CON - Combe Down)
bob_goodman@bathnes.gov.uk

Haeberling, Francine (CON - Saltford)
francine_haeberling@bathnes.gov.uk

Hardman, Liz (LAB - Paulton)
liz_hardman@bathnes.gov.uk

Hassett, Donal (CON - Newbridge)
donal_hassett@bathnes.gov.uk

Hedges, Stephen (LD - Odd Down)
steve_hedges@bathnes.gov.uk

Horstmann, Deirdre (CON - Radstock)
deirdre_horstmann@bathnes.gov.uk

Jackson, Eleanor (LAB - Westfield)
eleanor_jackson@bathnes.gov.uk

Jeffries, Steve (CON - Bathwick)
steve_jeffries@bathnes.gov.uk

Kew, Les (CON - High Littleton)
les_kew@bathnes.gov.uk

Longstaff, Marie (CON - Keynsham East)
marie_brewer@bathnes.gov.uk

Macrae, Barry (CON - Midsomer Norton North)
barry_macrae@bathnes.gov.uk

May, Paul (CON - Publow & Whitchurch)
paul_may@bathnes.gov.uk

McGill, Shaun (LD - Oldfield)
shaun_mcgall@bathnes.gov.uk

Millar, Alison (LD - Bathavon North)
alison_millar@bathnes.gov.uk

Myers, Paul (CON - Midsomer Norton Redfield)
paul_myers@bathnes.gov.uk

Norton, Michael (CON - Lyncombe)
michael_norton@bathnes.gov.uk

O'Brien, Lisa (CON - Keynsham South)
lisa_o'brien@bathnes.gov.uk

Organ, Bryan (CON - Keynsham East)
bryan_organ@bathnes.gov.uk

Patterson, Lin (GRN - Lambridge)
lin_patterson@bathnes.gov.uk

Pearce, Christopher (CON - Kingsmead)
chris_pearce@bathnes.gov.uk

Player, June (IND - Westmoreland)
june_player@bathnes.gov.uk

Pritchard, Victor (CON - Chew Valley South)
vic_pritchard@bathnes.gov.uk

Rayment, Joe (LAB - Twerton)
joe_rayment@bathnes.gov.uk

Richardson, Liz (CON - Chew Valley North)
liz_richardson@bathnes.gov.uk

Roberts, Nigel (LD - Odd Down)
nigelroberts@clara.co.uk

Roberts, Caroline (LD - Newbridge)
cmroberts@clara.co.uk

Sandry, Will (LD - Oldfield)
willsandry@blueyonder.co.uk

Shelford, Mark (CON - Lyncombe)
mark_shelford@bathnes.gov.uk

Simmons, Brian (CON - Keynsham North)
brian_simmons@bathnes.gov.uk

Turner, Peter (CON - Abbey)
peter_turner@bathnes.gov.uk

Veal, Martin (CON - Bathavon North)
martin_veal@bathnes.gov.uk

Veale, David (CON - Bathavon West)
david_veale@bathnes.gov.uk

Walker, Karen (IND - Peasedown)
karen_walker@bathnes.gov.uk

Ward, Geoff (CON - Bathavon North)
geoff_ward@bathnes.gov.uk

Warrington, Karen (CON - Clutton)
karen_warrington@bathnes.gov.uk

Watt, Christopher (CON - Midsomer Norton Redfield)
chris.watt@cognisantresearch.com

POLITICAL COMPOSITION
CON: 37, LD: 15, LAB: 6, IND: 5, GRN: 2

COMMITTEE CHAIRS
Audit: Mr Brian Simmons

Development Management: Ms Sally Davis

Health & Wellbeing: Mrs Francine Haeberling

Licensing: Mr Paul Myers

Pensions: Mr David Veale

Planning, Housing & Economic Development: Mr Rob Appleyard

Bedford U

Bedford Borough Council, Borough Hall, Cauldwell Street, Bedford MK42 9AP
☎ 01234 267422 🖷 01234 221606 ✉ enquiries@bedford.gov.uk
💻 www.bedford.gov.uk

FACTS AND FIGURES
Parliamentary Constituencies: Bedford
EU Constituencies: Eastern
Election Frequency: Elections are by thirds

PRINCIPAL OFFICERS
Chief Executive: Mr Philip Simpkins Chief Executive, Borough Hall, Cauldwell Street, Bedford MK42 9AP ☎ 01234 718202 🖷 01234 718201 ✉ philip.simpkins@bedford.gov.uk

Senior Management: Mr Kevin Crompton Director of Children's & Adults' Services, Borough Hall, Cauldwell Street, Bedford MK42 9AP ☎ 01234 228620 ✉ kevin.crompton@bedford.gov.uk

Senior Management: Mr Mark Minion Head of Corporate Policy & Programme Management, Borough Hall, Cauldwell Street, Bedford MK42 9AP ☎ 01234 228078 ✉ mark.minion@bedford.gov.uk

Senior Management: Ms Muriel Scott Director - Public Health, Borough Hall, Cauldwell Street, Bedford MK42 9AP ☎ 0300 300 5616 ✉ muriel.scott@centralbedfordshire.gov.uk

Access Officer / Social Services (Disability): Mr Stuart O'Dell Access Officer, Borough Hall, Cauldwell Street, Bedford MK42 9AP ☎ 01234 221762 🖷 01234 325671 ✉ stuart.odell@bedford.gov.uk

Architect, Building / Property Services: Mr Malcolm Parker Business Manager (Consultancy), Borough Hall, Cauldwell Street, Bedford MK42 9AP ☎ 01234 718662 🖷 01234 221716 ✉ malcolm.parker@bedford.gov.uk

Best Value: Mr Jashpal Mann Corporate Performance & Policy Manager, Borough Hall, Cauldwell Street, Bedford MK42 9AP ☎ 01234 228380 ✉ jashpal.mann@bedford.gov.uk

Building Control: Mr Steven Eyre Building Control Manager, Borough Hall, Cauldwell Street, Bedford MK42 9AP ☎ 01234 221759 ✉ steven.eyre@bedford.gov.uk

Catering Services: Mr Adrian Piper Head of Property Services, Borough Hall, Cauldwell Street, Bedford MK42 9AP ☎ 01234 718248 ✉ adrian.piper@bedford.gov.uk

Children / Youth Services: Mr Kevin Crompton Director of Children's & Adults' Services, Borough Hall, Cauldwell Street, Bedford MK42 9AP ☎ 01234 228620 ✉ kevin.crompton@bedford.gov.uk

Civil Registration: Mr Keith Simmons, Head of Member & Election Services, Borough Hall, Cauldwell Street, Bedford MK42 9AP ☎ 01234 221676 🖷 01234 221837 ✉ keith.simmons@bedford.gov.uk

PR / Communications: Mr Keiron Fletcher, Senior Communications Officer, Borough Hall, Cauldwell Street, Bedford MK42 9AP ☎ 01234 276277 ✉ keiron.fletcher@bedford.gov.uk

Community Planning: Mr Stewart Briggs Executive Director of Environment & Sustainable Communities, Borough Hall, Cauldwell Street, Bedford MK42 9AP ☎ 01234 228283 ✉ stewart.briggs@bedford.gov.uk

Community Safety: Mr Craig Austin Assistant Director of Regulatory Services, Borough Hall, Cauldwell Street, Bedford MK42 9AP ☎ 01234 276774 ✉ craig.austin@bedford.gov.uk

Computer Management: Mr Lawrence McArdle, Head of IT Services, Borough Hall, Cauldwell Street, Bedford MK42 9AP ☎ 01234 276221 🖷 01234 227406 ✉ lawrence.mcardle@bedford.gov.uk

Consumer Protection and Trading Standards: Mr Craig Austin Assistant Director of Regulatory Services, Borough Hall, Cauldwell Street, Bedford MK42 9AP ☎ 01234 276774 🖰 craig.austin@bedford.gov.uk

Contracts: Mr Mark Stephens Procurement & Review Manager, Borough Hall, Cauldwell Street, Bedford MK42 9AP ☎ 01234 228150 🖰 mark.stephens@bedford.gov.uk

Corporate Services: Mr Andy Watkins Assistant Chief Executive & Chief Finance Officer, Borough Hall, Cauldwell Street, Bedford MK42 9AP ☎ 01234 718208 🖰 andy.watkins@bedford.gov.uk

Customer Service: Mr Lee Phanco Assistant Chief Financial Officer & Head of Revenues & Benefits, Borough Hall, Cauldwell Street, , Bedford MK40 1SJ ☎ 01234 718358 🖰 lee.phanco@bedford.gov.uk

Economic Development: Mr Mark Oakley Head of Economic Development, Borough Hall, Cauldwell Street, Bedford MK42 9AP ☎ 01234 221730 🖰 mark.oakley@bedford.gov.uk

E-Government: Mr Lawrence McArdle, Head of IT Services, Borough Hall, Cauldwell Street, Bedford MK42 9AP ☎ 01234 276221 🖷 01234 227406 🖰 lawrence.mcardle@bedford.gov.uk

Electoral Registration: Mr Keith Simmons, Head of Member & Election Services, Borough Hall, Cauldwell Street, Bedford MK42 9AP ☎ 01234 221676 🖷 01234 221837 🖰 keith.simmons@bedford.gov.uk

Emergency Planning: Mr Craig Austin Assistant Director of Regulatory Services, Borough Hall, Cauldwell Street, Bedford MK42 9AP ☎ 01234 276774 🖰 craig.austin@bedford.gov.uk

Energy Management: Mr Craig Austin Assistant Director of Regulatory Services, Borough Hall, Cauldwell Street, Bedford MK42 9AP ☎ 01234 276774 🖰 craig.austin@bedford.gov.uk

Environmental / Technical Services: Mr Craig Austin Assistant Director of Regulatory Services, Borough Hall, Cauldwell Street, Bedford MK42 9AP ☎ 01234 276774 🖰 craig.austin@bedford.gov.uk

Environmental Health: Mr Craig Austin Assistant Director of Regulatory Services, Borough Hall, Cauldwell Street, Bedford MK42 9AP ☎ 01234 276774 🖰 craig.austin@bedford.gov.uk

Estates, Property & Valuation: Mr Adrian Piper Head of Property Services, Borough Hall, Cauldwell Street, Bedford MK42 9AP ☎ 01234 718248 🖰 adrian.piper@bedford.gov.uk

Events Manager: Mr Andy Pidgen, Events & Marketing Manager, Corn Exchange, St Paul's Square, Bedford MK40 1SL ☎ 01234 227392 🖰 andy.pidgen@bedford.gov.uk

Facilities: Mr Adrian Piper Head of Property Services, Borough Hall, Cauldwell Street, Bedford MK42 9AP ☎ 01234 718248 🖰 adrian.piper@bedford.gov.uk

Finance: Mr Andy Watkins Assistant Chief Executive & Chief Finance Officer, Borough Hall, Cauldwell Street, Bedford MK42 9AP ☎ 01234 718208 🖰 andy.watkins@bedford.gov.uk

Treasury: Mr Geoff Reader Head of Pensions & Treasury, Borough Hall, Cauldwell Street, Bedford MK42 9AP ☎ 01234 228562 🖰 geoff.reader@bedford.gov.uk

Pensions: Mr Geoff Reader Head of Pensions & Treasury, Borough Hall, Cauldwell Street, Bedford MK42 9AP ☎ 01234 228562 🖰 geoff.reader@bedford.gov.uk

Fleet Management: Mr Chris Pettifer Head of Transport Operations, Borough Hall, Cauldwell Street, Bedford MK42 9AP ☎ 01234 228881 🖰 chris.pettifer@bedford.gov.uk

Grounds Maintenance: Mr Craig Austin Assistant Director of Regulatory Services, Borough Hall, Cauldwell Street, Bedford MK42 9AP ☎ 01234 276774 🖰 craig.austin@bedford.gov.uk

Health and Safety: Mr Craig Austin Assistant Director of Regulatory Services, Borough Hall, Cauldwell Street, Bedford MK42 9AP ☎ 01234 276774 🖰 craig.austin@bedford.gov.uk

Highways: Mr Glenn Barcham Assistant Director of Highways & Transport, Borough Hall, Cauldwell Street, Bedford MK42 9AP ☎ 01234 228075 🖰 glenn.barcham@bedford.gov.uk

Highways: Mr Brian Hayward Head of Highways, Borough Hall, Cauldwell Street, Bedford MK42 9AP ☎ 01234 228012 🖰 brian.hayward@bedford.gov.uk

Home Energy Conservation: Mr James Shearman Corporate Carbon & Energy Manager, Borough Hall, Cauldwell Street, Bedford MK42 9AP ☎ 01234 718286 🖰 james.shearman@bedford.gov.uk

Housing: Mr Paul Rowland Assistant Director of Planning, Borough Hall, Cauldwell Street, Bedford MK42 9AP ☎ 01234 221720 🖰 paul.rowland@bedford.gov.uk

Housing: Mr Simon White Assistant Director of Commissioning & Business Support, Borough Hall, Cauldwell Street, Bedford MK42 9AP ☎ 01234 276097 🖰 simon.white@bedford.gov.uk

Local Area Agreement: Mr Mark Minion Head of Corporate Policy & Programme Management, Borough Hall, Cauldwell Street, Bedford MK42 9AP ☎ 01234 228078 🖰 mark.minion@bedford.gov.uk

Legal: Mr Michael Gough, Assistant Chief Executive (Governance), Borough Hall, Cauldwell Street, Bedford MK42 9AP ☎ 01234 718206 🖷 01234 718666 🖰 michael.gough@bedford.gov.uk

Leisure and Cultural Services: Mr Craig Austin Assistant Director of Regulatory Services, Borough Hall, Cauldwell Street, Bedford MK42 9AP ☎ 01234 276774 🖰 craig.austin@bedford.gov.uk

Licensing: Mr Keith Simmons, Head of Member & Election Services, Borough Hall, Cauldwell Street, Bedford MK42 9AP ☎ 01234 221676 🖷 01234 221837 🖰 keith.simmons@bedford.gov.uk

Lifelong Learning: Mr Kevin Crompton Director of Children's & Adults' Services, Borough Hall, Cauldwell Street, Bedford MK42 9AP ☎ 01234 228620 🖰 kevin.crompton@bedford.gov.uk

Lighting: Mr Darryl Hall Project Engineer (Electrical), Borough Hall, Cauldwell Street, Bedford MK42 9AP ☎ 01234 221702 darryl.hall@bedford.gov.uk

Lottery Funding, Charity and Voluntary: Mr Lee Phanco Assistant Chief Financial Officer & Head of Revenues & Benefits, Borough Hall, Cauldwell Street, , Bedford MK40 1SJ ☎ 01234 718358 lee.phanco@bedford.gov.uk

Member Services: Mr Keith Simmons, Head of Member & Election Services, Borough Hall, Cauldwell Street, Bedford MK42 9AP ☎ 01234 221676 🖷 01234 221837 keith.simmons@bedford.gov.uk

Parking: Mr Stewart Briggs Executive Director of Environment & Sustainable Communities, Borough Hall, Cauldwell Street, Bedford MK42 9AP ☎ 01234 228283 stewart.briggs@bedford.gov.uk

Partnerships: Mr Mark Minion Head of Corporate Policy & Programme Management, Borough Hall, Cauldwell Street, Bedford MK42 9AP ☎ 01234 228078 mark.minion@bedford.gov.uk

Personnel / HR: Mrs Barbara Morris Assistant Chief Executive - CG & HR, Borough Hall, Cauldwell Street, Bedford MK42 9AP ☎ 01234 228434 barbara.morris@bedford.gov.uk

Planning: Mr Paul Rowland Assistant Director of Planning, Borough Hall, Cauldwell Street, Bedford MK42 9AP ☎ 01234 221720 paul.rowland@bedford.gov.uk

Procurement: Mr Mark Stephens Procurement & Review Manager, Borough Hall, Cauldwell Street, Bedford MK42 9AP ☎ 01234 228150 mark.stephens@bedford.gov.uk

Public Libraries: Mrs Jenny Poad Head of Libraries, Bedford Central Library, Harpur Street, Bedford MK40 1PG ☎ 01234 718158 jenny.poad@bedford.gov.uk

Recycling & Waste Minimisation: Mr Stewart Briggs Executive Director of Environment & Sustainable Communities, Borough Hall, Cauldwell Street, Bedford MK42 9AP ☎ 01234 228283 stewart.briggs@bedford.gov.uk

Regeneration: Mr Mark Oakley Head of Economic Development, Borough Hall, Cauldwell Street, Bedford MK42 9AP ☎ 01234 221730 mark.oakley@bedford.gov.uk

Road Safety: Mr Glenn Barcham Assistant Director of Highways & Transport, Borough Hall, Cauldwell Street, Bedford MK42 9AP ☎ 01234 228075 glenn.barcham@bedford.gov.uk

Social Services (Adult): Mr Kevin Crompton Director of Children's & Adults' Services, Borough Hall, Cauldwell Street, Bedford MK42 9AP ☎ 01234 228620 kevin.crompton@bedford.gov.uk

Public Health: Ms Muriel Scott Director - Public Health, Borough Hall, Cauldwell Street, Bedford MK42 9AP ☎ 0300 300 5616 muriel.scott@centralbedfordshire.gov.uk

Staff Training: Mr John McCann Head of Learning & Development, Borough Hall, Cauldwell Street, Bedford MK42 9AP ☎ 01234 228358 john.mccann@bedford.gov.uk

Street Scene: Mr Stewart Briggs Executive Director of Environment & Sustainable Communities, Borough Hall, Cauldwell Street, Bedford MK42 9AP ☎ 01234 228283 stewart.briggs@bedford.gov.uk

Sustainable Development: Mr Craig Austin Assistant Director of Regulatory Services, Borough Hall, Cauldwell Street, Bedford MK42 9AP ☎ 01234 276774 craig.austin@bedford.gov.uk

Tourism: Mr Mark Oakley Head of Economic Development, Borough Hall, Cauldwell Street, Bedford MK42 9AP ☎ 01234 221730 mark.oakley@bedford.gov.uk

Town Centre: Mr Mark Oakley Head of Economic Development, Borough Hall, Cauldwell Street, Bedford MK42 9AP ☎ 01234 221730 mark.oakley@bedford.gov.uk

Traffic Management: Mr Glenn Barcham Assistant Director of Highways & Transport, Borough Hall, Cauldwell Street, Bedford MK42 9AP ☎ 01234 228075 glenn.barcham@bedford.gov.uk

Traffic Management: Mr Brian Hayward Head of Highways, Borough Hall, Cauldwell Street, Bedford MK42 9AP ☎ 01234 228012 brian.hayward@bedford.gov.uk

Transport: Mr Glenn Barcham Assistant Director of Highways & Transport, Borough Hall, Cauldwell Street, Bedford MK42 9AP ☎ 01234 228075 glenn.barcham@bedford.gov.uk

Transport: Mr Chris Pettifer Head of Transport Operations, Borough Hall, Cauldwell Street, Bedford MK42 9AP ☎ 01234 228881 chris.pettifer@bedford.gov.uk

Transport Planner: Mr Glenn Barcham Assistant Director of Highways & Transport, Borough Hall, Cauldwell Street, Bedford MK42 9AP ☎ 01234 228075 glenn.barcham@bedford.gov.uk

Waste Collection and Disposal: Mr Stewart Briggs Executive Director of Environment & Sustainable Communities, Borough Hall, Cauldwell Street, Bedford MK42 9AP ☎ 01234 228283 stewart.briggs@bedford.gov.uk

Waste Management: Mr Stewart Briggs Executive Director of Environment & Sustainable Communities, Borough Hall, Cauldwell Street, Bedford MK42 9AP ☎ 01234 228283 stewart.briggs@bedford.gov.uk

Children's Play Areas: Mr Stewart Briggs Executive Director of Environment & Sustainable Communities, Borough Hall, Cauldwell Street, Bedford MK42 9AP ☎ 01234 228283 stewart.briggs@bedford.gov.uk

COUNCILLORS

***Mayor* Hodgson**, Dave (LD - No Ward)
dave.hodgson@bedford.gov.uk

***Deputy Mayor* Royden**, Charles (LD - Brickhill)
CharlesRoyden@gmail.com

***Group Leader* Gerard**, Anita (LD - Kingsbrook)
anitagerard.kb@gmail.com

***Group Leader* Moon**, Stephen (CON - Great Barford)
shmoon@tiscali.co.uk

***Group Leader* Oliver**, Susan (LAB - Cauldwell)
s.j.oliver@ntlworld.com

***Group Leader* Olney**, Patricia (IND - Oakley)
pat.olney@btopenworld.com

***Group Leader* Rider**, Wendy (LD - Brickhill)
wendyrider41@gmail.com

Atkins, Colleen (LAB - Harpur)
colleenatkins@ntlworld.com

Bootiman, Rosemary (LD - Putnoe)

Boutall, Anthony (CON - Kempston Central & East)
anthony.boutall@bedford.gov.uk

Carofano, Giovanni (CON - Newnham)
giovanni.carofano@bedford.gov.uk

Charles, Randolph (LAB - Cauldwell)
randolph.charles@bedford.gov.uk

Coombes, Graeme (CON - Wilshamstead)
wilhamstead.ward@yahoo.co.uk

Corp, Sheryl (CON - Great Barford)
sheryl.corp@bedford.gov.uk

Fletcher, David (CON - Castle)
david.fletcher@bedford.gv.uk

Forth, Anthony (LAB - Goldington)
anthony.forth@bedford@bedofrd.gov.uk

Foster, Alison (CON - Harrold)
afield_foster@btinternet.com

Gam, Jon (CON - Bromham & Biddenham)
jonathan.gam@btinternet.com

Headley, Michael (LD - Putnoe)
michael.mheadley.co.uk

Hill, Tim (LD - Elstow & Stewartby)
tim.hill@bedford.gov.uk

Holland, Sarah-Jayne (LD - Eastcotts)
sarahjayne.holland@bedford.gov.uk

Hunt, Shan (LAB - Kempston North)
shanhunt@ntlworld.com

Hunt, Will (LAB - Kempston West)
willhunt@ntlworld.com

Jackson, Louise (LAB - Harpur)
louise.king@bedford.gov.uk

Masud, Mohammed (LAB - Queens Park)
mohammed.masud@bedford.gov.uk

McMurdo, Doug (IND - Sharnbrook)
doug.mcmurdo@bedford.gov.uk

Meader, Carl (LAB - Kempston South)
carl.meader@bedford.gov.uk

Mingay, John (CON - Newnham)
john.mingay@bedford.gov.uk

Nawaz, Mohammed (LAB - Kempston Central & East)
mohammed.nawaz@bedford.gov.uk

Reale, Luigi (LAB - Castle)
luigi.reale@bedford.gov.uk

Rigby, Roger (CON - Bromham & Biddenham)
roger.rigby110@googlemail.com

Saunders, James (LAB - Kingsbrook)
james.saunders@bedford.gov.uk

Sawyer, David (LD - De Parys)
sawyerbedford@hotmail.com

Smith, Mark (CON - Kempston Rural)
mark.smith792@googlemail.com

Towler, Martin (CON - Riseley)
martin.towler@bedford.gov.uk

Uko, Jade (LAB - Goldington)
jadeluko@bedford.gov.uk

Vann, Henry (LD - De Parys)
henry.vann@bedford.gov.uk

Walker, Jane (CON - Clapham)
Jane@Janewalker.co.uk

Wooton, John (CON - Wooton)
joh.wheeler@bedford.gov.uk

Wootton, Tom (CON - Wyboston)
tom.wootton@bedford.gov.uk

Yasin, Mohammad (LAB - Queens Park)
mohammad.yasin@bedford.gov.uk

POLITICAL COMPOSITION

CON: 15, LAB: 14, LD: 10, IND: 2

COMMITTEE CHAIRS

Adult Services: Mr John Mingay

Belfast City N

Belfast City, Belfast City Hall, Belfast BT1 5GS
☎ 028 9032 0202

PRINCIPAL OFFICERS

Chief Executive: Ms Suzanne Wylie Chief Executive, Belfast City Hall, Belfast BT1 5GS ☎ 028 9027 0201 ✉ wylies@belfastcity.gov.uk

Deputy Chief Executive: Mr Rogan Cregan Deputy Chief Executive & Director of Finance & Resources, Belfast City Hall, Belfast BT1 5GS ☎ 028 9050 0532 ✉ creganr@belfastcity.gov.uk

Senior Management: Mr John Walsh Interim Town Solicitor, Belfast City Hall, Belfast BT1 5GS ☎ 028 9027 0239 ✉ walshj@belfastcity.gov.uk

Architect, Building / Property Services: Mr George Wright Head - Facilities Management, Duncrue Complex, Duncrue Road, Belfast BT3 9BP ☎ 028 9037 3034 ✉ wrightg@belfastcity.gov.uk

Building Control: Mr Trevor Martin Head - Building Control, 5th Floor, 9 Lanyon Place, Belfast BT1 3LP ☎ 028 9027 0283 ✉ martint@belfastcity.gov.uk

Catering Services: Ms Gail Maguire Restaurant & Catering Manager, Cecil Ward Building, 4 - 10 Linenhall Street, , Belfast BT2 8BP ☎ 028 9027 0326 maguireg@belfastcity.gov.uk

Civil Registration: Ms Vivienne Fullerton Registrar, Belfast City Hall, Belfast BT1 5GS ☎ 028 9027 0274 fullertonv@belfastcity.gov.uk

Civil Registration: Miss Aileen Tyney Registrar, Belfast City Hall, Belfast BT1 5GS ☎ 028 9027 0274 tyneya@belfast.gov.uk

PR / Communications: Mr Eamon Deeny Head - Corporate Communications, Belfast City Hall, Belfast BT1 5GS ☎ 028 9027 0664 deenye@belfastcity.gov.uk

Community Planning: Mr David Cuthbert Community Planning Project Officer, Belfast City Hall, Belfast BT1 5GS ☎ 028 9032 0202 Ext 3320 cuthebertd@belfastcity.gov.uk

Community Planning: Ms Kim Walsh Community Planning Project Officer, Belfast City Hall, Belfast BT1 5GS ☎ 028 9032 0202 Ext 3640 walshk@belfastcity.gov.uk

Community Safety: Ms Alison Allen Safer City Manager, Cecil Ward Building, 4 - 10 Linenhall Street, , Belfast BT2 8BP ☎ 028 9032 0202 Ext 3780 allena@belfastcity.gov.uk

Computer Management: Mr Paul Gribben Head - Digital Services, 22 - 38 Gloucester Street, Belfast BT1 4LS ☎ 028 9024 4832 gribbenp@belfastcity.gov.uk

Consumer Protection and Trading Standards: Mrs Siobhan Toland Head - Environmental Health Service, Cecil Ward Building, 4 - 10 Linenhall Street, , Belfast BT2 8BP ☎ 028 9027 0304 tolands@belfastcity.gov.uk

Contracts: Mr Donal Rogan Head of Contracts, 24 - 26 Adelaide Street, Belfast BT2 8GD ☎ 028 9027 0289 rogand@belfastcity.gov.uk

Corporate Services: Mr Andrew Harrison Head - Audit, Governance & Risk, 24 - 26 Adelaide Street, Belfast BT2 8GD ☎ 028 9027 0513 harrisona@belfastcity.gov.uk

Economic Development: Ms Lisa Toland Head - Economic & International Development, Cecil Ward Building, 4 - 10 Linenhall Street, , Belfast BT2 8BP ☎ 028 9027 0529 tolandl@belfastcity.gov.uk

E-Government: Mr Paul Gribben Head - Digital Services, 22 - 38 Gloucester Street, Belfast BT1 4LS ☎ 028 9024 4832 gribbenp@belfastcity.gov.uk

Emergency Planning: Mr David Neill Emergency Co-ordination Officer, Cecil Ward Building, 4 - 10 Linenhall Street, Belfast BT2 8BP ☎ 028 9027 0734 neilld@belfastcity.gov.uk

Energy Management: Mr Ciaran McGrath Energy Manager, Duncrue Complex, Duncrue Road, Belfast BT3 9BP ☎ 028 9027 0383 mcgrathc@belfastcity.gov.uk

Environmental / Technical Services: Mrs Siobhan Toland Head - Environmental Health Service, Cecil Ward Building, 4 - 10 Linenhall Street, Belfast BT2 8BP ☎ 028 9027 0304 tolands@belfastcity.gov.uk

Environmental Health: Mrs Siobhan Toland Head - Environmental Health Service, Cecil Ward Building, 4 - 10 Linenhall Street, , Belfast BT2 8BP ☎ 028 9027 0304 tolands@belfastcity.gov.uk

Estates, Property & Valuation: Ms Cathy Reynolds Estates Manager, Adelaide Exchange, 24 - 26 Adelaide Street, Belfast BT2 8GD ☎ 028 9027 0386 reynoldsc@belfastcity.gov.uk

European Liaison: Ms Laura Leonard European Manager, Cecil Ward Building, 4 - 10 Linenhall Street, Belfast BT2 8BP ☎ 028 9027 0317 leonardl@belfastcity.gov.uk

Events Manager: Mr Gerry Copeland City Events Manager, Cecil Ward Building, 4 - 10 Linenhall Street, Belfast BT2 8BP ☎ 028 9027 0341 copelandg@belfastcity.gov.uk

Facilities: Mr George Wright Head - Facilities Management, Duncrue Complex, Duncrue Road, Belfast BT3 9BP ☎ 028 9037 3034 wrightg@belfastcity.gov.uk

Finance: Mr Rogan Cregan Deputy Chief Executive & Director of Finance & Resources, Belfast City Hall, Belfast BT1 5GS ☎ 028 9050 0532 creganr@belfastcity.gov.uk

Grounds Maintenance: Ms Rose Crozier Assistant Director - Parks & Leisure Services, Adelaide Exchange, 24 - 26 Adelaide Street, Belfast BT2 8GD ☎ 028 9032 0202 Ext 3460 crozierr@belfastcity.gov.uk

Health and Safety: Ms Emma Eaton Corporate Health & Safety Manager, Adelaide Exchange, 24 - 26 Adelaide Street, Belfast BT2 8GD ☎ 028 9027 0581 eatone@belfastcity.gov.uk

Legal: Mr John Walsh Interim Town Solicitor, Belfast City Hall, Belfast BT1 5GS ☎ 028 9027 0239 walshj@belfastcity.gov.uk

Licensing: Mr Stephen Hewitt Building Control Manager, 9 Lanyon Place, Belfast BT1 3LP ☎ 028 9027 0287 hewitts@belfastcity.gov.uk

Member Services: Mr Stephen McCrory Democratic Services Manager, Belfast City Hall, Belfast BT1 5GS ☎ 028 9027 0382 mccrorys@belfastcity.gov.uk

Personnel / HR: Ms Jill Minne Director of HR & Organisational Development, Belfast City Hall, Belfast BT1 5GS ☎ 028 9027 0395 minnej@belfastcity.gov.uk

Planning: Mr Phil Williams Director of Planning & Place, Cecil Ward Building, 4 - 10 Linenhall Street, Belfast BT2 8BP williamsp@belfastcity.gov.uk

Procurement: Mr Donal Rogan Head of Contracts, 24 - 26 Adelaide Street, Belfast BT2 8GD ☎ 028 9027 0289 rogand@belfastcity.gov.uk

Recycling & Waste Minimisation: Mr Tim Walker Head - Waste Management Service, Cecil Ward Building, 4 - 10 Linenhall Street, , Belfast BT2 8BP ☎ 028 9032 0202 walkert@belfastcity.gov.uk

Regeneration: Ms Lisa Toland Head - Economic & International Development, Cecil Ward Building, 4 - 10 Linenhall Street, , Belfast BT2 8BP ☎ 028 9027 0529 ✉ tolandl@belfastcity.gov.uk

Staff Training: Ms Catherine Christy Human Resources Manager, 21 Linenhall Street, Belfast BT2 8AB ☎ 028 9037 3021 ✉ christyc@belfastcity.gov.uk

Street Scene: Mr Sam Skimin Head - Cleansing Services, 5th Floor, 9 Lanyon Place, Belfast BT7 3LP ☎ 028 9037 3021 ✉ skimins@belfastcity.gov.uk

Sustainable Development: Ms Clare McKeown Sustainable Development Manager, Cecil Ward Building, 4 - 10 Linenhall Street, , Belfast BT2 8BP ☎ 028 9027 0492 ✉ mckeownc@belfastcity.gov.uk

Tourism: Mr Brian Johnston Tourism, Culture & Arts Manager, Cecil Ward Building, 4 - 10 Linenhall Street, , Belfast BT2 8BP ☎ 028 9027 0228 ✉ johnstonbrian@belfastcity.gov.uk

Waste Collection and Disposal: Mr Jim Ferguson Operations Manager, 5th Floor, 9 Lanyon Place, Belfast BT1 3LP ☎ 028 9032 0202 ✉ fergusonj@belfastcity.gov.uk

Waste Management: Mr Tim Walker Head - Waste Management Service, Cecil Ward Building, 4 - 10 Linenhall Street, , Belfast BT2 8BP ☎ 028 9032 0202 ✉ walkert@belfastcity.gov.uk

COUNCILLORS

***The Lord Mayor* Carson**, Arder (SF - Black Mountain)
ardercarson@yahoo.co.uk

***Deputy Lord Mayor* Spence**, Guy (DUP - Castle)
speceg@belfastcity.gov.uk

***High Sheriff* McKee**, Gareth (DUP - Oldpark)
gareth@dup-belfast.co.uk

***Alderman* Browne**, David (UUP - Castle)
d.browne@ntlworld.com

***Alderman* Convery**, Patrick (SDLP - Castle)
converyp@belfastcity.gov.uk

***Alderman* Kingston**, Brian (DUP - Court)
kingstonb@belfastcity.gov.uk

***Alderman* McCoubrey**, Frank (DUP - Court)
frankmccoubrey1@hotmail.co.uk

***Alderman* McGimpsey**, Chris (UUP - Lisnasharragh)
drcdmcgimpsey@live.co.uk

***Alderman* Patterson**, Lydia (DUP - Castle)
lydia@dup-belfast.co.uk

***Alderman* Patterson**, Ruth (DUP - Botanic)
dup_patterson@yahoo.co.uk

***Alderman* Rodgers**, Jim (UUP - Ormiston)
rodgersj@belfastcity.gov.uk

***Alderman* Stalford**, Christopher (DUP - Balmoral)
stalfordc@belfastcity.gov.uk

Armitage, David (ALL - Titanic)
armitaged@belfastcity.gov.uk

Attwood, Tim (SDLP - Black Mountain)
attwoodt@belfastcity.gov.uk

Austin, Janice (SF - Black Mountain)

Beattie, Ciaran (SF - Black Mountain)
ciaranbeattie@aol.com

Bell, David (SF - Collin)
daithi2@hotmail.com

Boyle, Declan (SDLP - Botanic)
declan.boyle@belfastcity.gov.uk

Bradshaw, Paula (ALL - Balmoral)
paula.bradshaw@belfastcity.gov.uk

Brown, Ross (GRN - Ormiston)
brownr@belfastcity.gov.uk

Bunting, Jolene (O - Court)
jolene.bunting@belfastcity.gov.uk

Campbell, Mary Ellen (SF - Castle)
maryellencampbell@hotmail.com

Carroll, Gerry (O - Black Mountain)
carrollg@belfastcity.gov.uk

Clarke, Mary (SF - Oldpark)
maryclarke111@hotmail.com

Copeland, Sonia (UUP - Titanic)
sonia.copeland@belfastcity.gov.uk

Corr, Steven (SF - Black Mountain)
steviecorr@gmail.com

Corr Johnston, Julie-Anne (O - Oldpark)
julieacorr@pupni.co.uk

Craig, Graham (UUP - Botanic)
craiggraham@belfastcity.gov.uk

Dudgeon, Jeffrey (UUP - Balmoral)
jeffreydudgeon@hotmail.com

Garrett, Matt (SF - Collin)
garrettm@belfastcity.gov.uk

Graham, Aileen (DUP - Lisnasharragh)
aileen.graham@belfastcity.gov.uk

Groves, Bill (SF - Collin)
bill.groves@belfastcity.gov.uk

Groves, Emma (SF - Black Mountain)
empgroves@msn.com

Haire, Tom (DUP - Ormiston)
hairet@belfastcity.gov.uk

Hanna, Claire (SDLP - Balmoral)
hannac@belfastcity.gov.uk

Hargey, Deirdre (SF - Botanic)
deirdrehargey@hotmail.com

Heading, Brian (SDLP - Collin)
headingb@belfastcity.gov.uk

Howard, Carole (ALL - Lisnasharragh)
carole.howard@belfastcity.gov.uk

Hussey, John (DUP - Ormiston)
john.hussey@belfastcity.gov.uk

Hutchinson, Billy (O - Court)
hutchinsonb@belfastcity.gov.uk

BELFAST CITY

Johnston, Peter (UUP - Ormiston)
peter.johnston@belfastcity.gov.uk

Jones, Mervyn (ALL - Ormiston)
mervynjones54@yahoo.co.uk

Kennedy, Brian (DUP - Titanic)
kennedyb@belfastcity.gov.uk

Kyle, John (O - Titanic)
kylej@belfastcity.gov.uk

Long, Michael (ALL - Lisnasharragh)
long_m_a@hotmail.com

Magee, JJ (SF - Oldpark)
jj@sinnfein.ie

Magennis, Stephen (SF - Collin)
magennis@belfastcity.gov.uk

Mallon, Nichola (SDLP - Oldpark)
mallonn@belfastcity.gov.uk

McAllister, Nuala (ALL - Castle)
nuala.mcallister@belfastcity.gov.uk

McAteer, Geraldine (SF - Balmoral)
mcateer@belfastcity.gov.uk

McCabe, Gerry (SF - Oldpark)
mccabeg@belfastcity.gov.uk

McConville, Mary (SF - Court)
mcconville@belfastcity.gov.uk

McDonough-Brown, Emmet (ALL - Botanic)
mcdonough-brown@belfastcity.gov.uk

McNamee, Laura (ALL - Ormiston)

McVeigh, Jim (SF - Court)
mcveighjames@belfastcity.gov.uk

Mullan, Kate (SDLP - Lisnasharragh)
mullankate@belfastcity.gov.uk

Newton, Adam (DUP - Titanic)
adam.newton@live.co.uk

Ó Donnghaile, Niall (SF - Titanic)
niallodonnghaile@gmail.com

O'Hara, Charlene (SF - Collin)
charlene.ohara@belfastcity.gov.uk

Sandford, Tommy (DUP - Lisnasharragh)
tommy.sandford@belfastcity.gov.uk

POLITICAL COMPOSITION

SF: 19, DUP: 13, ALL: 8, UUP: 7, SDLP: 7, O: 5, GRN: 1

COMMITTEE CHAIRS

Licensing: Mr John Hussey

People & Communities: Ms Julie-Anne Corr Johnston

Planning: Mr Matt Garrett

Bexley L

London Borough of Bexley, Bexley Civic Offices, 2 Watling Street, Bexleyheath DA6 7AT
☎ 020 8303 7777 🖷 020 8301 2661
✉ customer.services@bexley.gov.uk 🖳 www.bexley.gov.uk

FACTS AND FIGURES

Parliamentary Constituencies: Bexleyheath & Crayford, Erith and Thamesmead, Old Bexley and Sidcup
EU Constituencies: South East
Election Frequency: Elections are of whole council

PRINCIPAL OFFICERS

Chief Executive: Mr Paul Moore Interim Chief Executive (Director of Regeneration, Communities & Customer Services), Bexley Civic Offices, 2 Watling Street, Bexleyheath DA6 7AT ☎ 020 3045 4901 ✉ paul.moore@bexley.gov.uk

Senior Management: Ms Alison Griffin Director of Finance & Resources, Bexley Civic Offices, 2 Watling Street, Bexleyheath DA6 7AT ☎ 020 3045 4955 ✉ alison.griffin@bexley.gov.uk

Senior Management: Dr Nada Lemic Director - Public Health, Bexley Civic Offices, 2 Watling Street, Bexleyheath DA6 7AT ☎ 020 8303 7777 ✉ nada.lemic@bromley.gov.uk

Senior Management: Mr Paul Moore Interim Chief Executive (Director of Regeneration, Communities & Customer Services), Bexley Civic Offices, 2 Watling Street, Bexleyheath DA6 7AT ☎ 020 3045 4901 ✉ paul.moore@bexley.gov.uk

Senior Management: Ms Jackie Tiotto Director of Children's Services, Bexley Civic Offices, 2 Watling Street, Bexleyheath DA6 7AT ☎ 020 3045 4090 ✉ jackie.tiotto@bexley.gov.uk

Access Officer / Social Services (Disability): Prof Vinod Kumar Khanna, Chief Executive Inspire Community Trust, 20 Whitehall Lane, Erith DA8 2DH ☎ 020 3045 5312 ✉ vinod.kumar@bexley.gov.uk

Best Value: Mr Trevor Wentworth Surveying Services Manager, Bexley Civic Offices, 2 Watling Street, Bexleyheath DA6 7AT ☎ 020 3045 5757 ✉ trevor.wentworth@bexley.gov.uk

Catering Services: Ms Helen Sellick Facilities Senior Contract Officer, Bexley Civic Offices, 2 Watling Street, Bexleyheath DA6 7AT ☎ ; 020 3045 3639 ✉ helen.sellick@bexley.gov.uk

Children / Youth Services: Ms Jackie Tiotto Director of Children's Services, Bexley Civic Offices, 2 Watling Street, Bexleyheath DA6 7AT ☎ 020 3045 4090 ✉ jackie.tiotto@bexley.gov.uk

PR / Communications: Mr John Ferry, Head of Communications, Bexley Civic Offices, 2 Watling Street, Bexleyheath DA6 7AT ☎ 020 3045 4867 ✉ john.ferry@bexley.gov.uk

Community Safety: Mr Mark Usher Project Officer, Bexley Civic Offices, 2 Watling Street, Bexleyheath DA6 7AT ☎ 020 3045 3580 ✉ mark.usher@bexley.gov.uk

Computer Management: Mr James Scott Head of ICT (Systems & Security), Bexley Civic Offices, 2 Watling Street, Bexleyheath DA6 7AT ☎ 020 3045 4350 ✉ james.scott@bexley.gov.uk

Consumer Protection and Trading Standards: Mr David Bryce-Smith, Deputy Director - Development, Housing & Community, Bexley Civic Offices, 2 Watling Street, Bexleyheath DA6 7AT ☎ 020 3045 5718 ✉ david.brycesmith@bexley.gov.uk

Corporate Services: Mr Steve Hobdell Development Control Admin & Systems Manager, Bexley Civic Offices, 2 Watling Street, Bexleyheath DA6 7AT ☎ 020 3045 5740 steve.hobdell@bexley.gov.uk

Customer Service: Mr Graham Ward, Deputy Director (Customer Relations & Corporate Services), Bexley Civic Offices, 2 Watling Street, Bexleyheath DA6 7AT ☎ 020 3045 4622 graham.ward@bexley.gov.uk

Electoral Registration: Mr David Easton Head of Electoral & Members' Services, Bexley Civic Offices, 2 Watling Street, Bexleyheath DA6 7AT ☎ 020 3045 3675 david.easton@bexley.gov.uk

Emergency Planning: Mr Tony Plowright, Emergency Planning & Business Continuity Manager, Bexley Civic Offices, 2 Watling Street, Bexleyheath DA6 7AT ☎ 020 3045 4623 tony.plowright@bexley.gov.uk

Energy Management: Mr Kevin Murphy, Head of Housing Services, Bexley Civic Offices, 2 Watling Street, Bexleyheath DA6 7AT ☎ 020 3045 5623 kevin.murphy@bexley.gov.uk

Environmental Health: Mr David Bryce-Smith, Deputy Director - Development, Housing & Community, Bexley Civic Offices, 2 Watling Street, Bexleyheath DA6 7AT ☎ 020 3045 5718 david.brycesmith@bexley.gov.uk

Estates, Property & Valuation: Ms Suzanne Jackson Head of Regeneration & Assets, Bexley Civic Offices, 2 Watling Street, Bexleyheath DA6 7AT ☎ 020 3045 4830 suzanne.jackson@bexley.gov.uk

Finance: Ms Alison Griffin Director of Finance & Resources, Bexley Civic Offices, 2 Watling Street, Bexleyheath DA6 7AT ☎ 020 3045 4955 alison.griffin@bexley.gov.uk

Finance: Mr John Peters, Deputy Director of Finance, Bexley Civic Offices, 2 Watling Street, Bexleyheath DA6 7AT ☎ 020 3045 4954 john.peters@bexley.gov.uk

Home Energy Conservation: Mr Kevin Murphy, Head of Housing Services, Bexley Civic Offices, 2 Watling Street, Bexleyheath DA6 7AT ☎ 020 3045 5623 kevin.murphy@bexley.gov.uk

Legal: Mr Akin Alabi Head of Legal Services & Monitoring Officer, Bexley Civic Offices, 2 Watling Street, Bexleyheath DA6 7AT ☎ 020 3045 3922 akin.alabi@bexley.gov.uk

Leisure and Cultural Services: Ms Toni Ainge, Deputy Director - Communities, Libraries, Leisure & Parks, Bexley Civic Offices, 2 Watling Street, Bexleyheath DA6 7AT ☎ 020 3045 4879 antonia.ainge@bexley.gov.uk

Licensing: Mr David Bryce-Smith, Deputy Director - Development, Housing & Community, Bexley Civic Offices, 2 Watling Street, Bexleyheath DA6 7AT ☎ 020 3045 5718 david.brycesmith@bexley.gov.uk

Parking: Mr Benjamin Stephens Head of Parking Shared Services, Bexley Civic Offices, 2 Watling Street, Bexleyheath DA6 7AT ☎ 020 8313 4514 benjamin.stephens@bexley.gov.uk

Personnel / HR: Mr Nick Hollier, Deputy Director - HR & Corporate Support, Bexley Civic Offices, 2 Watling Street, Bexleyheath DA6 7AT ☎ 020 3045 4091 nick.hollier@bexley.gov.uk

Public Libraries: Ms Judith Mitlin, Head of Libraries, Heritage & Archives, Footscray Offices, Maidstone road, Sidcup DA14 5HS ☎ 020 3045 4531 judith.mitlin@bexley.gov.uk

Regeneration: Mr Paul Moore Interim Chief Executive (Director of Regeneration, Communities & Customer Services), Bexley Civic Offices, 2 Watling Street, Bexleyheath DA6 7AT ☎ 020 3045 4901 paul.moore@bexley.gov.uk

Road Safety: Mr Mark Bunting Team Leader - Road Safety, Bexley Civic Offices, 2 Watling Street, Bexleyheath DA6 7AT ☎ 020 3045 5875 mark.bunting@bexley.gov.uk

Social Services (Adult): Mr Tom Brown Deputy Director of Adult Care, Bexley Civic Offices, 2 Watling Street, Bexleyheath DA6 7AT ☎ 020 3045 4318 tom.brown@bexley.gov.uk

Social Services (Children): Ms Sheila Murphy, Deputy Director - Social Care, Safeguarding & SEN, Bexley Civic Offices, 2 Watling Street, Bexleyheath DA6 7AT ☎ 020 3045 4128 sheila.murphy@bexley.gov.uk

Public Health: Dr Nada Lemic Director - Public Health, Bexley Civic Offices, 2 Watling Street, Bexleyheath DA6 7AT ☎ 020 8303 7777 nada.lemic@bromley.gov.uk

Staff Training: Mr Nick Hollier, Deputy Director - HR & Corporate Support, Bexley Civic Offices, 2 Watling Street, Bexleyheath DA6 7AT ☎ 020 3045 4091 nick.hollier@bexley.gov.uk

Sustainable Communities: Ms Susan Clark Head of Development Control, Bexley Civic Offices, 2 Watling Street, Bexleyheath DA6 7AT ☎ 020 3045 5761 susan.clark@bexley.gov.uk

Tourism: Ms Toni Ainge, Deputy Director - Communities, Libraries, Leisure & Parks, Bexley Civic Offices, 2 Watling Street, Bexleyheath DA6 7AT ☎ 020 3045 4879 antonia.ainge@bexley.gov.uk

Children's Play Areas: Mr Colin Rowland Head of Parks & Open Spaces, Bexley Civic Offices, 2 Watling Street, Bexleyheath DA6 7AT ☎ 020 3045 3686 colin.rowland@bexley.gov.uk

COUNCILLORS

***Mayor* Camsey**, Sybil (CON - Brampton)
councillor.sybil.camsey@bexley.gov.uk

***Deputy Mayor* Hurt**, David (CON - Barnehurst)
councillor.david.hurt@bexley.gov.uk

***Leader of the Council* O'Neill**, Teresa (CON - Brampton)
councillor.teresa.o'neill@bexley.gov.uk

***Deputy Leader of the Council* Bacon**, Gareth (CON - Longlands)
councillor.gareth.bacon@bexley.gov.uk

***Deputy Leader of the Council* Sawyer**, Alex (CON - St Mary's)
councillor.alex.sawyer@bexley.gov.uk

BEXLEY

Amaning, Esther (LAB - Lesnes Abbey)
esther.amaning@bexley.gov.uk

Ashmole, Roy (CON - Christchurch)
councillor.roy.ashmole@bexley.gov.uk

Bacon, Cheryl (CON - Cray Meadows)
councillor.cheryl.bacon@bexley.gov.uk

Bailey, Linda (CON - Danson Park)
councillor.linda.bailey@bexley.gov.uk

Beazley, Chris (UKIP - St Michael's)
chris.beazley@bexley.gov.uk

Beckwith, Aileen (CON - Sidcup)
councillor.aileen.beckwith@bexley.gov.uk

Beckwith, Brian (CON - Blackfen & Lamorbey)
councillor.brian.beckwith@bexley.gov.uk

Begho, Derry (LAB - Thamesmead East)
derry.begho@bexley.gov.uk

Betts, Nigel (CON - Falconwood & Welling)
councillor.nigel.betts@bexley.gov.uk

Bishop, Christine (CON - Crayford)
christine.bishop@bexley.gov.uk

Bishop, Brian (CON - Colyers)
councillor.brian.bishop@bexley.gov.uk

Boateng, Edward (LAB - Erith)
councillor.edward.boateng@bexley.gov.uk

Borella, Stefano (LAB - North End)
councillor.stefano.borella@bexley.gov.uk

Catterall, Christine (CON - East Wickham)
christine.catterall@bexley.gov.uk

Clark, Val (CON - Falconwood & Welling)
councillor.val.clark@bexley.gov.uk

Craske, Peter (CON - Blackfen & Lamorbey)
councillor.peter.craske@bexley.gov.uk

D'Amiral, Graham (CON - Blendon & Penhill)
councillor.graham.d'amiral@bexley.gov.uk

Davey, John (CON - Crayford)
councillor.john.davey@bexley.gov.uk

Deadman, Alan (LAB - North End)
christina.ford@bexley.gov.uk

Dourmoush, Andy (CON - Longlands)
andy.dourmoush@bexley.gov.uk

Downing, Alan (CON - St Mary's)
councillor.alan.downing@bexley.gov.uk

Downing, Ross (CON - Cray Meadows)
councillor.ross.downing@bexley.gov.uk

Ezenwata, Endy (LAB - Thamesmead East)
endy.exenwata@bexley.gov.uk

Ferreira, Joe (LAB - Erith)
joe.ferreira@bexley.gov.uk

Fothergill, Maxine (CON - Colyers)
councillor.maxine.fothergill@bexley.gov.uk

Francis, Daniel (LAB - Belvedere)
daniel.francis@bexley.gov.uk

French, Louie (CON - Falconwood & Welling)
louie.french@bexley.gov.uk

Fuller, John (CON - Christchurch)
councillor.john.fuller@bexley.gov.uk

Hackett, Danny (LAB - Lesnes Abbey)
danny.hackett@bexley.gov.uk

Hall, Steven (CON - Blendon & Penhill)
councillor.steven.hall@bexley.gov.uk

Hunt, James (CON - East Wickham)
councillor.james.hunt@bexley.gov.uk

Husband, John (LAB - Lesnes Abbey)
john.husband@bexley.gov.uk

Langstead, Brenda (LAB - North End)
councillor.brenda.langstead@bexley.gov.uk

Leaf, David (CON - Longlands)
david.leaf@bexley.gov.uk

Leitch, Rob (CON - Sidcup)
rob.leitch@bexley.gov.uk

Lucia-Hennis, Geraldene (CON - Crayford)
councillor.geraldene.lucia-hennis@bexley.gov.uk

MacDonald, Gill (LAB - Belvedere)
councillor.gill.macdonald@bexley.gov.uk

Marriner, Howard (CON - Barnehurst)
councillor.howard.marriner@bexley.gov.uk

Massey, Sharon (CON - Danson Park)
councillor.sharon.massey@bexley.gov.uk

Massey, Donald (CON - Cray Meadows)
councillor.donald.massey@bexley.gov.uk

McGannon, Colin (UKIP - Colyers)
mac.mcgannon@bexley.gov.uk

Munur, Cafer (CON - East Wickham)
cafer@munur@bexley.gov.uk

Newman, Sean (LAB - Belvedere)
councillor.sean.newman@bexley.gov.uk

Newton, Caroline (CON - St Michael's)
councillor.caroline.newton@bexley.gov.uk

Ogundayo, Mabel (LAB - Thamesmead East)
mabel.ogundayo@bexley.gov.uk

O'Hare, Nick (CON - Blendon & Penhill)
councillor.nick.o'hare@bexley.gov.uk

Oppong-Asare, Abena (LAB - Erith)
abena.oppong-asare@bexley.gov.uk

Pallen, Eileen (CON - Barnehurst)
councillor.eileen.pallen@bexley.gov.uk

Pollard, Joseph (CON - St Michael's)
councillor.joseph.pollard@bexley.gov.uk

Read, Philip (CON - Northumberland Heath)
councillor.philip.read@bexley.gov.uk

Reader, Peter (CON - Northumberland Heath)
councillor.peter.reader@bexley.gov.uk

Seymour, Melvin (CON - Northumberland Heath)
councillor.melvin.seymour@bexlye.gov.uk

Slaughter, June (CON - Sidcup)
councillor.june.slaughter@bexley.gov.uk

Smith, Brad (CON - Christchurch)
councillor.brad.smith@bexley.gov.uk

Smith, Lynn (UKIP - Blackfen & Lamorbey)
lynn.smith@bexley.gov.uk

Tandy, Colin (CON - St Mary's)
councillor.colin.tandy@bexley.gov.uk

Waters, John (CON - Danson Park)
councillor.john.waters@bexley.gov.uk

Wilkinson, John (CON - Brampton)
john.wilkinson@bexley.gov.uk

POLITICAL COMPOSITION

CON: 45, LAB: 15, UKIP: 3

COMMITTEE CHAIRS

Audit: Mr Joseph Pollard

Licensing: Mr Brad Smith

Pensions: Mr John Waters

Planning: Mr Peter Reader

Birmingham City M

Birmingham City Council, The Council House, Victoria Square, Birmingham B1 1BB
☎ 0121 303 9944 contact@birmingham.gov.uk
www.birmingham.gov.uk

FACTS AND FIGURES

Parliamentary Constituencies: Birmingham, Edgbaston, Birmingham, Erdington, Birmingham, Hall Green, Birmingham, Hodge Hill, Birmingham, Ladywood, Birmingham, Northfield, Birmingham, Perry Bar, Birmingham, Selly Oak, Birmingham, Yardley, Sutton Coldfield
EU Constituencies: West Midlands
Election Frequency: Elections are by thirds

PRINCIPAL OFFICERS

Chief Executive: Mr Mark Rogers Chief Executive, The Council House, Victoria Square, Birmingham B1 1BB ☎ 0121 303 2000 mark.rogers@birmingham.gov.uk

Assistant Chief Executive: Ms Piali DasGupta Assistant Chief Executive, The Council House, Victoria Square, Birmingham B1 1BB ☎ 0121 303 2000 piala.dasgupta@birmingham.gov.uk

Senior Management: Mr Paul Dransfield Strategic Director - Major Projects, The Council House, Victoria Square, Birmingham B1 1BB ☎ 0121 303 3803 🖷 0121 464 9791 paul.dransfield@birmingham.gov.uk

Senior Management: Mr Peter Duxbury Strategic Director - Children, Young People & Families, Birmingham City Council, Margaret Street, Birmingham B3 3BU ☎ 0121 303 2550 🖷 0121 303 1712 peter.duxbury@birmingham.gov.uk

Senior Management: Mr Peter Hay Strategic Director - People, Louisa Ryland House, 44 Newhall Street, Birmingham B3 3PL ☎ 0121 303 2992 peter.hay@birmingham.gov.uk

Senior Management: Ms Jacqui Kennedy, Interim Strategic Director - Place (Service Director of Regulation & Enforcement), Louisa Ryland House, 44 Newhall Street, Birmingham B3 3PL ☎ 0121 303 6121 jacqui.kennedy@birmingham.gov.uk

Senior Management: Dr Adrian Phillips Director - Public Health, The Council House, Victoria Square, Birmingham B1 1BB ☎ 0121 303 4909 adrian.x.phillips@birmingham.gov.uk

Senior Management: Ms Angela Probert Strategic Director - Change & Corporate Services, The Council House, Victoria Square, Birmingham B1 1BB ☎ angela.probert@birmingham.gov.uk

Access Officer / Social Services (Disability): Mr Chris Bush Head of Disabled Children's Social Care, The Council House, Victoria Square, Birmingham B1 1BB ☎ 0121 675 0463 chris.bush@birmingham.gov.uk

Access Officer / Social Services (Disability): Ms Jill Crosbie Head of Access to Education, The Council House, Victoria Square, Birmingham B1 1BB ☎ 0121 303 1795 jill.crosbie@birmingham.gov.uk

Access Officer / Social Services (Disability): Ms Diana Morgan Strategic Delivery Manager - Specialist Care Services, The Council House, Victoria Square, Birmingham B1 1BB ☎ 0121 303 4061 diana.morgan@birmingham.gov.uk

Access Officer / Social Services (Disability): Mr Steve Wise Service Director of Specialist Care Services, The Council House, Victoria Square, Birmingham B1 1BB ☎ 0121 303 2367 steve.wise@birmingham.gov.uk

Architect, Building / Property Services: Mr Phil Andrews Head of Asset Management, The Council House, Victoria Square, Birmingham B1 1BB ☎ 0121 303 3696 phil.andrews@birmingham.gov.uk

Architect, Building / Property Services: Mr Mark Bieganski Head of Property Strategy & Information, Birmingham City Council, PO Box 16255, Birmingham B2 2WT ☎ 0121 303 3645 mark.bieganski@birmingham.gov.uk

Architect, Building / Property Services: Mr David Fletcher Head of Corporate Landlord, The Council House, Victoria Square, Birmingham B1 1BB ☎ 0121 303 2007 david.fletcher@birmingham.gov.uk

Architect, Building / Property Services: Mr Peter Jones Director of Property, Birmingham City Council, PO Box 16255, Birmingham B2 2WT ☎ 0121 303 3844 peter.jones@birmingham.gov.uk

Architect, Building / Property Services: Mr Azmat Mir Head of Property Consultancy, The Council House, Victoria Square, Birmingham B1 1BB ☎ 0121 303 3298 azmat.mir@birmingham.gov.uk

Catering Services: Muir Wilson Head of Civic Catering, The Council House, Victoria Square, Birmingham B1 1BB ☎ 0121 303 4987 muir.wilson@brimingham.gov.uk

BIRMINGHAM CITY

Children / Youth Services: Mr Trevor Brown Acting Head of Service - Youth Offending, The Council House, Victoria Square, Birmingham B1 1BB ☎ 0121 464 0600
✉ trevor.brown@birmingham.gov.uk

Children / Youth Services: Mr Ian Burgess Head of Children's Services & Education, The Council House, Victoria Square, Birmingham B1 1BB ☎ 0121 303 4643
✉ ian.burgess@birmingham.gov.uk

Children / Youth Services: Mr Alastair Gibbons Executive Director - Children's Services, The Council House, Victoria Square, Birmingham B1 1BB ☎ 0121 675 7743
✉ alastair.gibbons@birmingham.gov.uk

Children / Youth Services: Mr Sukhwinder Singh Head of Children's Services (Safeguarding), The Council House, Victoria Square, Birmingham B1 1BB ☎ 0121 303 7812
✉ sukhwinder.singh@birmingham.gov.uk

Civil Registration: Ms Andrea Haines Registrar (South), The Council House, Victoria Square, Birmingham B1 1BB
☎ 0121 303 0200 ✉ andrea.haines@birmingham.gov.uk

Civil Registration: Ms Alison Harwood Head of Operations - Bereavement Services, Coroners & Mortuary and Registration Services, The Council House, Victoria Square, Birmingham B1 1BB
☎ 0121 303 0201 ✉ alison.harwood@birmingham.gov.uk

Civil Registration: Ms Bev Nash Registrar (North), The Council House, Victoria Square, Birmingham B1 1BB ☎ 0121 303 0138
✉ bev.nash@birmingham.gov.uk

PR / Communications: Mr David Potts Head of Learning Resources - Library of Birmingham, The Council House, Victoria Square, Birmingham B1 1BB ☎ 0121 303 6883
✉ david.potts@birmingham.gov.uk

PR / Communications: Ms Janet Priestley Head of Press, PR & Communications, The Council House, Victoria Square, Birmingham B1 1BB ☎ 0121 303 3531 ✉ janet.priestley@birmingham.gov.uk

PR / Communications: Ms Dawn Wise Head of Corporate Communications, The Council House, Victoria Square, Birmingham B1 1BB ☎ 0121 303 4302 ✉ dawn.wise@birmingham.gov.uk

Community Safety: Jagveen Bagary Professional Lead in Safer Communities, 1 Lancaster Circus, 2nd Floor, Queensway, Birmingham B4 7DQ ☎ 0121 464 3525
✉ jagveen.bagary@birmingham.gov.uk

Community Safety: Ms Jan Kimber Head of Community Safety Partnership, 1 Lancaster Circus, 2nd Floor, Queensway, Birmingham B4 7DQ ☎ 0121 303 9202 🖷 0121 464 6220
✉ jan.kimber@birmingham.gov.uk

Consumer Protection and Trading Standards: Ms Donna Bensley Operations Manager - Trading Standards, The Council House, Victoria Square, Birmingham B1 1BB ☎ 0121 303 9339
✉ donna.bensley@birmingham.gov.uk

Corporate Services: Ms Helen Burnett Business Development Manager, The Council House, Victoria Square, Birmingham B1 1BB
☎ 0121 303 2095 🖷 0121 303 1311
✉ helen.burnett@birmingham.gov.uk

Corporate Services: Mr Paul Dransfield Strategic Director - Major Projects, The Council House, Victoria Square, Birmingham B1 1BB
☎ 0121 303 3803 🖷 0121 464 9791
✉ paul.dransfield@birmingham.gov.uk

Corporate Services: Mr Steve Glaze Head of Intelligent Client Function, 1 Lancaster Circus, Birmingham B4 7AB ☎ 0121 303 4605
✉ steve.glaze@birmingham.gov.uk

Corporate Services: Mr Kevin Hubery Head of Strategic Policy, The Council House, Victoria Square, Birmingham B1 1BB
☎ 0121 303 4821 🖷 0121 303 1318
✉ kevin.hubery@birmingham.gov.uk

Corporate Services: Mr Richard Kenny Head of Strategic Development, The Council House, Victoria Square, Birmingham B1 1BB

Corporate Services: Mr Jason Lowther Head of Corporate Strategy, The Council House, Victoria Square, Birmingham B1 1BB
☎ 0121 303 4960 🖷 0121 303 1318
✉ jason.lowther@birmingham.gov.uk

Corporate Services: Ms Wendy Terry Head of Performance Management, 1 Lancaster Circus, Birmingham B4 7AB
☎ 0121 675 5617 ✉ wendy.terry@birmingham.gov.uk

Corporate Services: Mr Malkiat Thiarai Head of Corporate Management Information, 1 Lancaster Circus, Birmingham B4 7AB
☎ 0121 303 1909 ✉ malkiat.thiarai@birmingham.gov.uk

Customer Service: Mr Paul Buckley Assistant Director - Customer Services, The Council House, Victoria Square, Birmingham B1 1BB ☎ 0121 464 8298
✉ paul.buckley@birmingham.gov.uk

Customer Service: Mr Chris Gibbs Service Director - Customer Services, The Council House, Victoria Square, Birmingham B1 1BB
☎ 0121 464 6387 ✉ chris.gibbs@birmingham.gov.uk

Customer Service: Mr Martin O'Neill Head of Benefits, The Council House, Victoria Square, Birmingham B1 1BB ☎ 0121 464 1450 ✉ martin.o'neill@birmingham.gov.uk

Economic Development: Mr Paul Dransfield Strategic Director - Major Projects, The Council House, Victoria Square, Birmingham B1 1BB ☎ 0121 303 3803 🖷 0121 464 9791
✉ paul.dransfield@birmingham.gov.uk

Economic Development: Ms Sue Jones Revenues Director, The Council House, Victoria Square, Birmingham B1 1BB ☎ 07808 585389 ✉ sue.jones@birmingham.gov.uk

Education: Mr Ian Burgess Head of Children's Services & Education, The Council House, Victoria Square, Birmingham B1 1BB
☎ 0121 303 4643 ✉ ian.burgess@birmingham.gov.uk

Education: Mr Colin Diamond Interim Executive Director - Education, The Council House, Victoria Square, Birmingham B1 1BB ☎ 0121 675 8995 ✉ colin.diamond@birmingham.gov.uk

Education: Ms Julie New Head of School Admissions & Pupil Placements, The Council House, Victoria Square, Birmingham B1 1BB ☎ 0121 303 2268 ✉ julie.new@birmingham.gov.uk

Environmental / Technical Services: Mr Rob James Assistant Director of Environment & Culture, Birmingham City Council, House of Sport, 300 Broad Street, Birmingham B1 2DR ☎ 0121 464 9819 🖷 0121 303 2418 ✉ rob.james@birmingham.gov.uk

Environmental / Technical Services: Mr Darren Share, Head of Parks, The Council House, Victoria Square, Birmingham B1 1BB ☎ 0121 303 4103 ✉ darren.share@birmingham.gov.uk

Environmental Health: Mr Mark Croxford Head of Environmental Health & Markets Service, The Council House, Victoria Square, Birmingham B1 1BB ☎ 0121 303 6350 ✉ mark.croxford@birmingham.gov.uk

Estates, Property & Valuation: Mr John Jamieson Head of Asset Management, Louisa Ryland House, 44 Newhall Street, Birmingham B3 3PL ☎ 0121 303 9420 ✉ john.jamieson@birmingham.gov.uk

European Liaison: Mr Lloyd Broad Head of European & International Affairs, The Council House, Victoria Square, Birmingham B1 1BB ☎ 0121 303 2377 ✉ lloyd.broad@birmingham.gov.uk

Events Manager: Ms Joan Durose Head of Events, The Council House, Victoria Square, Birmingham B1 1BB ☎ 0121 303 4469 ✉ joan.durose@birmingham.gov.uk

Facilities: Ms Ann Brookes, Head of Performance & Support, Louisa Ryland House, 44 Newhall Street, Birmingham B3 3PL ☎ 0121 303 2516 ✉ ann.brookes@birmingham.gov.uk

Finance: Ms Sarah Dunlavey Assistant Director - Financial Services, The Council House, Victoria Square, Birmingham B1 1BB ☎ 0121 675 8714 ✉ sarah.dunlavey@birmingham.gov.uk

Finance: Ms Kay Reid Assistant Director - Audit & Risk, The Council House, Victoria Square, Birmingham B1 1BB ☎ 0121 464 3396 ✉ kay.reid@birmingham.gov.uk

Finance: Mr Jon Warlow, Director of Finance & S151 Officer, Birmingham City Coucil, PO Box 16306, Woodstock Street, Aston, Birmingham B7 4BL ☎ 0121 303 2950 🖷 0121 303 1356 ✉ jon.warlow@birmingham.gov.uk

Pensions: Ms Sally Plant Pensions Manager, The Council House, Victoria Square, Birmingham B1 1BB ☎ 0121 303 2388 ✉ sally.plant@birmingham.gov.uk

Fleet Management: Mr Tommy Wallace Director - Fleet & Waste Management, The Council House, Victoria Square, Birmingham B1 1BB ☎ 0121 303 6171 ✉ tommy.wallace@birmingham.gov.uk

Grounds Maintenance: Mr Bob Chum Acting Head - Landscape & Contract Developments, The Council House, Victoria Square, Birmingham B1 1BB ☎ 0121 303 3536 ✉ bob.chum@birmingham.gov.uk

Grounds Maintenance: Mr Darren Share Head of Parks, The Council House, Victoria Square, Birmingham B1 1BB ☎ 0121 303 4477 ✉ darren.share@birmingham.gov.uk

Health and Safety: Mr Alan Lotinga Service Director - Health & Wellbeing, The Council House, Victoria Square, Birmingham B1 1BB ☎ 0121 303 6694 ✉ alan.lotinga@birmingham.gov.uk

Highways: Mr John Blakemore Director of Highways & Resilience, Birmingham City Council, 1 Lancaster Circus, Birmingham B4 7DQ ☎ 0121 303 7329 🖷 0121 303 6599 ✉ john.blakemore@birmingham.gov.uk

Highways: Mr Alistair Campbell Head of Resilience & Local Engineering, Birmingham City Council, 1 Lancaster Circus, Birmingham B4 7DQ ☎ 0121 303 7305 🖷 0121 303 6599 ✉ alistair.campbell@birmingham.gov.uk

Highways: Mr Paul O'Day Street Services Manager, Birmingham City Council, 1 Lancaster Circus, Birmingham B4 7DQ ☎ 0121 303 7412 🖷 0121 303 1318 ✉ paul.o'day@birmingham.gov.uk

Housing: Mr Pete Hobbs Service Head - Tenant Engagement & Private Rented Sector, The Council House, Victoria Square, Birmingham B1 1BB ☎ 0121 675 7936 ✉ pete.hobbs@birmingham.gov.uk

Housing: Mr Robert James Service Director - Housing Transformation, The Council House, Victoria Square, Birmingham B1 1BB ☎ 0121 464 7699 ✉ robert.james@birmingham.gov.uk

Housing: Ms Tracey Radford Service Head - Landlord Services, The Council House, Victoria Square, Birmingham B1 1BB ☎ 0121 303 3334 ✉ tracey.radford@birmingham.gov.uk

Legal: Ms Kate Charlton Head of Employment Law, The Council House, Victoria Square, Birmingham B1 1BB ☎ 0121 464 1173 ✉ kate_charlton@birmingham.gov.uk

Legal: Mr Stuart Evans Head of Law (Economy), The Council House, Victoria Square, Birmingham B1 1BB ☎ 0121 303 4868 ✉ stuart_j_evans@birmingham.gov.uk

Legal: Ms Lisa Morgan Head of Law (Place), The Council House, Victoria Square, Birmingham B1 1BB ☎ 0121 303 4938 ✉ lisa_morgan@birmingham.gov.uk

Legal: Ms Charmaine Murray Head of Adult Services & Human Rights Law, The Council House, Victoria Square, Birmingham B1 1BB ☎ 0121 303 2857 ✉ charmaine_murray@birmingham.gov.uk

Legal: Mr David Tatlow Director of Legal & Democratic Services, Birmingham City Council, PO Box 15992, Birmingham B2 2UQ ☎ 0121 303 2151 ✉ david.tatlow@brimingham.gov.uk

BIRMINGHAM CITY

Leisure and Cultural Services: Ms Val Birchall Assistant Director - Culture & Visitor Economy, The Council House, Victoria Square, Birmingham B1 1BB ☎ 0121 303 2919
🖱 val.birchall@birmingham.gov.uk

Leisure and Cultural Services: Mr Symon Easton Head of Cultural Commissioning, The Council House, Victoria Square, Birmingham B1 1BB ☎ 0121 303 1301
🖱 symon.easton@birmingham.gov.uk

Leisure and Cultural Services: Mr Steve Hollingworth Assistant Director - Sport, Events & Parks, The Council House, Victoria Square, Birmingham B1 1BB ☎ 0121 464 2024
🖱 steve.hollingworth@birmingham.gov.uk

Licensing: Mr Chris Neville Head of Licensing, The Council House, Victoria Square, Birmingham B1 1BB ☎ 0121303 6103
🖱 chris.neville@birmingham.gov.uk

Member Services: Ms Janet Lescott PA to the Director of Legal & Democratic Services, Birmingham City Council, PO Box 15992, Birmingham B2 2UQ ☎ 0121 303 2151
🖱 janet_lescott@brimingham.gov.uk

Member Services: Mr Prakash Patel Head of Committee & Member Services, The Council House, Victoria Square, Birmingham B1 1BB ☎ 0121 303 2018 🖱 prakash.patel@birmingham.gov.uk

Member Services: Mr David Tatlow Director of Legal & Democratic Services, Birmingham City Council, PO Box 15992, Birmingham B2 2UQ ☎ 0121 303 2151
🖱 david.tatlow@brimingham.gov.uk

Partnerships: Mr David Bull Director of Sustainability, Transportation & Partnerships, Birmingham City Council, 1 Lancaster Circus, PO Box 14439, Birmingham B2 2JE ☎ 0121 303 6467 🖷 0121 303 3679 🖱 david.bull@birmingham.gov.uk

Personnel / HR: Mr Tarik Chawdry Assistant Director of Human Resources, The Council House, Victoria Square, Birmingham B1 1BB ☎ 0121 303 2120 🖷 0121 303 1311
🖱 tarik.chawdry@birmingham.gov.uk

Personnel / HR: Mr Seamus Cooney Payroll Manager, The Council House, Victoria Square, Birmingham B1 1BB
🖱 seamus.cooney@birmingham.gov.uk

Planning: Mr Ghaz Hussain Area Planning & Regeneration Manager, The Council House, Victoria Square, Birmingham B1 1BB ☎ 0121 464 7738 🖱 ghaz.hussain@birmingham.gov.uk

Planning: Waheed Nazir Director of Planning & Regeneration, Birmingham City Council, 1 Lancaster Circus, PO Box 28, Birmingham B1 1TU ☎ 0121 464 7735
🖱 waheed.nazir@birmingham.gov.uk

Planning: Ms Louise Robinson Area Planning Manager (City Centre), The Council House, Victoria Square, Birmingham B1 1BB ☎ 0121 303 5929 🖱 louise.robinson@birmingham.gov.uk

Planning: Mr Andrew Round Assistant Director of Planning & Development, Birmingham City Council, 1 Lancaster Circus, PO Box 28, Birmingham B1 1TU ☎ 0121 303 2676
🖱 andrew.round@birmingham.gov.uk

Planning: Mr Peter Wright Area Planning & Regeneration Manager (East & South), The Council House, Victoria Square, Birmingham B1 1BB ☎ 0121 303 3170
🖱 peter.wright@birmingham.gov.uk

Procurement: Mr Rob Barker Head of Service Delivery & Procurement, The Council House, Victoria Square, Birmingham B1 1BB ☎ 0121 303 3870 🖱 rob_barker@birmingham.gov.uk

Procurement: Mr Haydn Brown Category Head - Procurement Strategy & Development, Birmingham City Council, PO Box 10680, 10 Woodstock Street, Birmingham B7 4BG ☎ 0121 303 0016
🖱 haydn.brown@birmingham.gov.uk

Procurement: Mr Neil Hopkins Head of Strategy & Performance, Birmingham City Council, PO Box 10680, 10 Woodstock Street, Birmingham B7 4BG ☎ 0121 303 0071
🖱 neil.hopkins@birmingham.gov.uk

Procurement: Ms Debbie Husler Head of Procurement, Birmingham City Council, PO Box 10680, 10 Woodstock Street, Birmingham B7 4BG ☎ 0121 303 0017
🖱 debbie.husler@birmingham.gov.uk

Procurement: Mr Richard Tibbatts Head of Category - Corporate Procurement, Birmingham City Council, PO Box 10680, 10 Woodstock Street, Birmingham B7 4BG ☎ 0121 303 0015
🖱 richard.tibbatts@birmingham.gov.uk

Public Libraries: Ms Dawn Beaumont Head of Customer Experience - Library of Birmingham, The Council House, Victoria Square, Birmingham B1 1BB ☎ 0121 303 6884
🖱 dawn.beaumont@birmingham.gov.uk

Public Libraries: Mr Kevin Duffy Service Manager - Community Libraries Service, The Council House, Victoria Square, Birmingham B1 1BB ☎ 0121 303 0454 🖱 kevin.duffy@birmingham.gov.uk

Regeneration: Ms Sharon Freedman Assistant Director of Regeneration, Birmingham City Council, 1 Lancaster Circus, PO Box 28, Birmingham B1 1TU ☎ 0121 464 9835
🖱 sharon.freedman@birmingham.gov.uk

Regeneration: Mr Jack Glonek Assistant Director - Investment, Enterprise & Employment, Baskerville House, Centenary Square, Broad Street, Birmingham B1 2ND ☎ 0121 464 5518
🖱 jack.glonek@birmingham.gov.uk

Regeneration: Mr Ghaz Hussain Area Planning & Regeneration Manager, The Council House, Victoria Square, Birmingham B1 1BB ☎ 0121 464 7738 🖱 ghaz.hussain@birmingham.gov.uk

Regeneration: Waheed Nazir Director of Planning & Regeneration, Birmingham City Council, Baskerville House, Broad Street, Birmingham B1 2ND ☎ 0121 464 7735
🖱 waheed.nazir@birmingham.gov.uk

Regeneration: Mr Andrew Round Assistant Director of Planning & Development, 1 Lancaster Circus, PO Box 28, Birmingham B1 1TU ☎ 0121 303 2676 andrew.round@birmingham.gov.uk

Regeneration: Mr Peter Wright Area Planning & Regeneration Manager (East & South), The Council House, Victoria Square, Birmingham B1 1BB ☎ 0121 303 3170 peter.wright@birmingham.gov.uk

Social Services: Ms Jacqui Jensen Service Director of Integrated Services & Care, Birmingham City Council, Margaret Street, Birmingham B3 3BU ☎ 0121 375 7743 🖷 0121 303 1318 jacqui.jensen@birmingham.gov.uk

Social Services: Mr Chris Jordan Head of Service Integration, Louisa Ryland House, 44 Newhall Street, Birmingham B3 3PL ☎ 0121 303 9387 chris.jordan@birmingham.gov.uk

Social Services: Mr Alan Lotinga Service Director of Assessment & Support Planning / Health & Wellbeing, The Council House, Victoria Square, Birmingham B1 1BB ☎ 0121 303 6694 alan.lotinga@birmingham.gov.uk

Social Services: Mr Steve Wise Service Director of Specialist Care Services, The Council House, Victoria Square, Birmingham B1 1BB ☎ 0121 303 2367 steve.wise@birmingham.gov.uk

Social Services (Adult): Mr Peter Hay Strategic Director - People, Louisa Ryland House, 44 Newhall Street, Birmingham B3 3PL ☎ 0121 303 2992 peter.hay@birmingham.gov.uk

Social Services (Adult): Ms Charmaine Murray Head of Adult Services & Human Rights Law, The Council House, Victoria Square, Birmingham B1 1BB ☎ 0121 303 2857 charmaine_murray@birmingham.gov.uk

Social Services (Children): Ms Nicky Hale Interim Head of Service - Fostering & Adoption, The Council House, Victoria Square, Birmingham B1 1BB ☎ 0121 303 3726 nicky.hale@birmingham.gov.uk

Social Services (Children): Mr Andy Pepper Assistant Director - Children & Care Provider Services, The Council House, Victoria Square, Birmingham B1 1BB ☎ 0121 675 5762 andy.pepper@birmingham.gov.uk

Social Services (Children): Mr Sukhwinder Singh Head of Children's Services (Safeguarding), The Council House, Victoria Square, Birmingham B1 1BB ☎ 0121 303 7812 sukhwinder.singh@birmingham.gov.uk

Fostering & Adoption: Ms Nicky Hale Interim Head of Service - Fostering & Adoption, The Council House, Victoria Square, Birmingham B1 1BB ☎ 0121 303 3726 nicky.hale@birmingham.gov.uk

Public Health: Dr Adrian Phillips Director - Public Health, The Council House, Victoria Square, Birmingham B1 1BB ☎ 0121 303 4909 adrian.x.phillips@birmingham.gov.uk

Staff Training: Ms Jan Marr Head of Learning & Workforce Development, The Council House, Victoria Square, Birmingham B1 1BB ☎ 0121 303 2278 jan.marr@birmingham.gov.uk

Street Scene: Mr Paul O'Day Street Services Manager, Birmingham City Council, 1 Lancaster Circus, Birmingham B4 7DQ ☎ 0121 303 7412 🖷 0121 303 1318 paul.o'day@birmingham.gov.uk

Sustainable Development: Mr Nick Grayson Climate Change & Sustainability Officer, The Council House, Victoria Square, Birmingham B1 1BB ☎ 0121 464 1045 nick.grayson@birmingham.gov.uk

Tourism: Ms Caroline Alexander Corporate Support Manager - Culture & Visitor Economy, The Council House, Victoria Square, Birmingham B1 1BB ☎ 020 303 3899 caroline.alexander@birmingham.gov.uk

Town Centre: Mr Mick Taylor Principal Officer of Retail Markets & Street Trading, The Council House, Victoria Square, Birmingham B1 1BB ☎ 0121 303 0258 mick.taylor@birmingam.gov.uk

Traffic Management: Mr Kevin Hicks Traffic Manager, Birmingham City Council, 1 Lancaster Circus, Birmingham B4 7DQ ☎ 0121 303 7693 🖷 0121 303 6599 kevin.hicks@birmingham.gov.uk

Transport: Dr Chloe Taylor Transportation Programmes & Partnerships Manager, The Council House, Victoria Square, Birmingham B1 1BB

Transport Planner: Mr Phil Edwards Head of Growth & Transportation, The Council House, Victoria Square, Birmingham B1 1BB ☎ 0121 303 7409 phil.edwards@birmingham.gov.uk

Transport Planner: Ms Anne Shaw Head of Transportation Services, The Council House, Victoria Square, Birmingham B1 1BB ☎ 0121 303 6467 anne.shaw@birmingham.gov.uk

Waste Collection and Disposal: Ms Chloe Tringham Contract & Waste Disposal Manager, The Council House, Victoria Square, Birmingham B1 1BB ☎ 0121 303 3595 chloe.tringham@birmingham.gov.uk

Waste Management: Mr Matt Kelly Assistant Director of Fleet & Waste Management, Birmingham City Council, House of Sport, 300 Broad Street, Birmingham B1 2DR ☎ 0121 303 6171 matt.kelly@birmingham.gov.uk

Waste Management: Mr Kevin Mitchell Assistant Director of Fleet & Waste Management, Birmingham City Council, House of Sport, 300 Broad Street, Birmingham B1 2DR ☎ 0121 675 0648 keivn.mitchell@birmingham.gov.uk

Waste Management: Ms Chloe Tringham Contract & Waste Disposal Manager, The Council House, Victoria Square, Birmingham B1 1BB ☎ 0121 303 3595 chloe.tringham@birmingham.gov.uk

Waste Management: Mr Tommy Wallace Director of Fleet & Waste Management, Birmingham City Council, House of Sport, 300 Broad Street, Birmingham B1 2DR ☎ 0121 303 6171 tommy.wallace@birmingham.gov.uk

Children's Play Areas: Mr Nigel Cartwright Playground Services Manager, The Council House, Victoria Square, Birmingham B1 1BB ☎ 0121 464 0425 nigel.cartwright@birmingham.gov.uk

BIRMINGHAM CITY

COUNCILLORS

***The Lord Mayor* Hassall**, Ray (LD - Perry Barr)
ray.hassall@birmingham.gov.uk

***Deputy Lord Mayor* Shah**, Shafique (LAB - Bordesley Green)
shafique.shah@birmingham.gov.uk

***Leader of the Council* Bore**, Albert (LAB - Ladywood)
albert.bore@birmingham.gov.uk

***Deputy Leader of the Council* Ward**, Ian (LAB - Shard End)
ian.ward@birmingham.gov.uk

***Group Leader* Alden**, Robert (CON - Erdington)
robert.alden@birmingham.gov.uk

***Group Leader* Tilsley**, Paul (LD - Sheldon)
paul.tilsley@birmingham.gov.uk

Afzal, Muhammad (LAB - Aston)
muhammad.afzal@birmingham.gov.uk

Ahmed, Uzma (LAB - Bordesley Green)
uzma.ahmed@birmingham.gov.uk

Aikhlaq, Mohammed (LAB - Bordesley Green)
mohammed.aikhlaq@birmingham.gov.uk

Alden, John (CON - Harborne)
john.alden@birmingham.gov.uk

Alden, Deirdre (CON - Edgbaston)
deirdre.alden@birmingham.gov.uk

Ali, Tahir (LAB - Nechells)
tahir.ali@birmingham.gov.uk

Ali, Nawaz (LAB - South Yardley)
nawaz.ali@birmingham.gov.uk

Anderson, Sue (LD - Sheldon)
sue.anderson@birmingham.gov.uk

Atwal, Gurdial Singh (LAB - Handsworth Wood)
gurdialsingh.atwal@birmingham.gov.uk

Azim, Mohammed (LAB - Sparkbrook)
mohammed.azim@birmingham.gov.uk

Badley, Caroline (LAB - Quinton)
caroline.badley@birmingham.gov.uk

Barnett, Susan (LAB - Billesley)
susan.barnett@birmingham.gov.uk

Barrie, David (CON - Sutton New Hall)
david.barrie@birmingham.gov.uk

Barton, Vivienne (CON - Bartley Green)
vivienne.barton@birmingham.gov.uk

Beauchamp, Bob (CON - Erdington)
bob.beauchamp@birmingham.gov.uk

Bennett, Matt (CON - Edgbaston)
matt.s.bennett@birmingham.gov.uk

Booton, Steve (LAB - Weoley)
Steve.Booton@birmingham.gov.uk

Bowles, Barry (LAB - Hall Green)
barry.bowles@birmingham.gov.uk

Brew, Randal (CON - Northfield)
randal.brew@birmingham.gov.uk

Bridle, Marje (LAB - Shard End)
marje.bridle@birmingham.gov.uk

Brown, Mick (LAB - Tyburn)
mick.brown@birmingham.gov.uk

Buchanan, Alex (LAB - Billesley)
alex.buchanan@birmingham.gov.uk

Burden, Sam (LAB - Hall Green)
samburden1@gmail.com

Cartwright, Andy (LAB - Longbridge)
andy.cartwright@birmingham.gov.uk

Chatfield, Tristan (LAB - Oscott)
tristan.chatfield@birmingham.gov.uk

Choudhry, Zaker (LD - South Yardley)
zaker.choudhry@birmingham.gov.uk

Clancy, John (LAB - Quinton)
john.clancy@birmingham.gov.uk

Clancy, Debbie (CON - Northfield)
Debbie.Clancy@birmingham.gov.uk

Clinton, Lynda (LAB - Tyburn)
lynda.clinton@birmingham.gov.uk

Collin, Lyn (CON - Sutton Vesey)
lyn.collin@birmingham.gov.uk

Cornish, Maureen (CON - Sutton Four Oaks)
maureen.cornish@birmingham.gov.uk

Cotton, John (LAB - Shard End)
john.cotton@birmingham.gov.uk

Cruise, Ian (LAB - Longbridge)
ian.cruise@birmingham.gov.uk

Dad, Basharat (LAB - Stechford & Yardley North)
basharat.dad@birmingham.gov.uk

Davis, Philip (LAB - Billesley)
phil.davis@birmingham.gov.uk

Douglas Osborn, Peter (CON - Weoley)
peter.douglasosborn@birmingham.gov.uk

Dring, Barbara (LAB - Oscott)
barbara.dring@birmingham.gov.uk

Eustace, Neil (LD - Stechford & Yardley North)
neil.eustace@birmingham.gov.uk

Evans, Jerry (LD - Springfield)
jerry.evans@birmingham.gov.uk

Fazal, Mohammed (LAB - Springfield)
mohammed.fazal@birmingham.gov.uk

Finnegan, Mick (LAB - Stockland Green)
mick.finnegan@birmingham.gov.uk

Freeman, Eddie (CON - Weoley)
eddie.freeman@birmingham.gov.uk

Gregson, Matthew (LAB - Quinton)
matthew.gregson@birmingham.gov.uk

Griffiths, Peter (LAB - Kings Norton)
peter.griffiths@birmingham.gov.uk

Hamilton, Paulette (LAB - Handsworth Wood)
paulette.hamilton@birmingham.gov.uk

Hardie, Andrew (CON - Sutton Vesey)
andrew.hardie@birmingham.gov.uk

Harmer, Roger (LD - Acocks Green)
roger.harmer@birmingham.gov.uk

Hartley, Kath (LAB - Ladywood)
kath.hartley@birmingham.gov.uk

Henley, Barry (LAB - Brandwood)
barry.henley@birmingham.gov.uk

Holbrook, Penny (LAB - Stockland Green)
penny.holbrook@birmingham.gov.uk

Hughes, Des (LAB - Kingstanding)
Des.S.Hughes@birmingham.gov.uk

Hunt, Jon (LD - Perry Barr)
jon.hunt@birmingham.gov.uk

Hussain, Mahmood (LAB - Lozells & East Handsworth)
mahmood.hussain@birmingham.gov.uk

Huxtable, Timothy (CON - Bournville)
timothy.huxtable@birmingham.gov.uk

Idrees, Mohammed (LAB - Washwood Heath)
mohammed.idrees@birmingham.gov.uk

Iqbal, Zafar (LAB - South Yardley)
zafar@southyardley.co.uk

Islam, Ziaul (LAB - Aston)
ziaul.islam@birmingham.gov.uk

Jenkins, Meirion (CON - Sutton Four Oaks)
m.jenkins@rapidcomputing.co.uk

Jenkins, Kerry (LAB - Hall Green)
kerry.jenkins@birmingham.gov.uk

Jevon, Simon (CON - Kings Norton)
simon.jevon@conservatives.com

Jones, Carol (LD - Stechford & Yardley North)
carol.jones@birmingham.gov.uk

Jones, Josh (LAB - Stockland Green)
josh.jones@birmingham.gov.uk

Jones, Brigid (LAB - Selly Oak)
brigid.jones@birmingham.gov.uk

Kauser, Nagina (LAB - Aston)
nagina.kauser@birmingham.gov.uk

Kennedy, Tony (LAB - Sparkbrook)
tony.kennedy@birmingham.gov.uk

Khan, Mariam (LAB - Washwood Heath)
mariam.khan@birmingham.gov.uk

Khan, Ansar Ali (LAB - Washwood Heath)
ansar.ali.khan@birmingham.gov.uk

Khan, Changese (LAB - Selly Oak)
changese.khan@birmingham.gov.uk

Kooner, Narinder Kaur (LAB - Handsworth Wood)
narinderkaur.kooner@birmingham.gov.uk

Lal, Chaman (LAB - Soho)
chaman.lal@birmingham.gov.uk

Leddy, Mike (LAB - Brandwood)
mike.leddy@birmingham.gov.uk

Lines, John (CON - Bartley Green)
john.lines@birmingham.gov.uk

Lines, Bruce (CON - Bartley Green)
bruce.lines@birmingham.gov.uk

Linnecor, Keith (LAB - Oscott)
keith.linnecor@birmingham.gov.uk

Mackey, Ewan (CON - Sutton Trinity)
ewan.mackey@suttontrinityconservatives.co.uk126

Mahmood, Majid (LAB - Hodge Hill)
majid.mahmood@birmingham.gov.uk

McCarthy, Karen (LAB - Selly Oak)
karen.mccarthy@birmingham.gov.uk

McKay, James (LAB - Harborne)
james.mckay@birmingham.gov.uk

Moore, Gareth (CON - Erdington)
gareth.moore@birmingham.gov.uk

Mosquito, Yvonne (LAB - Nechells)
yvonne.mosquito@birmingham.gov.uk

O'Reilly, Brett (LAB - Northfield)
brett.o'reilly@birmingham.gov.uk

O'Shea, John (LAB - Acocks Green)
john.o'shea@birmingham.gov.uk

Pears, David (CON - Sutton Trinity)
david.pears@birmingham.gov.uk

Phillips, Eva (LAB - Brandwood)
eva.phillips@birmingham.gov.uk

Phillips, Jess (LAB - Longbridge)
jess.phillips@birmingham.gov.uk

Pocock, Rob (LAB - Sutton Vesey)
rob.pocock@birmingham.gov.uk

Quinn, Victoria (LAB - Sparkbrook)
victoria.quinn@birmingham.gov.uk

Quinnen, Hendrina (LAB - Lozells & East Handsworth)
hendrina.quinnen@birmingham.gov.uk

Rashid, Chauhdry (LAB - Nechells)
chauhdry.rashid@birmingham.gov.uk

Rehman, Habib (LAB - Springfield)
habib.ul.rehman@birmingham.gov.uk

Rice, Carl (LAB - Ladywood)
carl.rice@birmingham.gov.uk

Robinson, Fergus (CON - Edgbaston)
fergus.robinson@birmingham.gov.uk

Sambrook, Gary (CON - Kingstanding)
gary.sambrook@birmingham.gov.uk

Seabright, Valerie (LAB - Kings Norton)
valerie.seabright@birmingham.gov.uk

Sealey, Rob (CON - Bournville)
robert.sealey@birmingham.gov.uk

Sharpe, Mike (LAB - Tyburn)
mike.sharpe@birmingham.gov.uk

Spence, Sybil (LAB - Soho)
sybil.spence@birmingham.gov.uk

Spencer, Claire (LAB - Moseley & Kings Heath)
claire.spencer@birmingham.gov.uk

Stacey, Stewart (LAB - Acocks Green)
stewart.stacey@birmingham.gov.uk

Storer, Ron (CON - Kingstanding)
ron.storer@birmingham.gov.uk

Straker-Welds, Martin (LAB - Moseley & Kings Heath)
martin.straker.welds@birmingham.gov.uk

Thompson, Sharon (LAB - Soho)
sharon.thompson@birmingham.gov.uk

Trench, Karen (LD - Perry Barr)
karen.trench@birmingham.gov.uk

Trickett, Lisa (LAB - Moseley & Kings Heath)
lisa.trickett@birmingham.gov.uk

Underwood, Anne (CON - Sutton Four Oaks)
anne.underwood@birmingham.gov.uk

Waddington, Margaret (CON - Sutton Trinity)
margaret.waddington@birmingham.gov.uk

Walkling, Phil (LAB - Bournville)
phil.walkling@birmingham.gov.uk

Ward, Mike (LD - Sheldon)
mike.ward@birmingham.gov.uk

Ward, Anita (LAB - Hodge Hill)
anita.ward@birmingham.gov.uk

Williams, Fiona (LAB - Hodge Hill)
fiona.williams@birmingham.gov.uk

Williams, Elaine (LAB - Harborne)
elaine.v.williams@birmingham.gov.uk

Wood, Ken (CON - Sutton New Hall)
ken.wood@birmingham.gov.uk

Yip, Alex (CON - Sutton New Hall)
Alex.Yip@birmingham.gov.uk

Zaffar, Waseem (LAB - Lozells & East Handsworth)
waseem.zaffar@birmingham.gov.uk

POLITICAL COMPOSITION
LAB: 79, CON: 30, LD: 11

COMMITTEE CHAIRS
Audit: Mr Sam Burden

Education & Vulnerable Children: Ms Susan Barnett

Health & Social Care: Mr Majid Mahmood

Licensing & Public Protection: Ms Barbara Dring

Planning: Mr Mike Sharpe

Blaby D

Blaby District Council, Council Offices, Desford Road, Narborough LE19 2EP
☎ 0116 275 0555 🖷 0116 275 0368 ✉ customer.services@blaby.gov.uk
💻 www.blaby.gov.uk

FACTS AND FIGURES
Parliamentary Constituencies: Charnwood, Leicestershire South
EU Constituencies: East Midlands
Election Frequency: Elections are of whole council

PRINCIPAL OFFICERS
Chief Executive: Mrs Sandra Whiles, Chief Executive, Council Offices, Desford Road, Narborough LE19 2EP ☎ 0116 272 7501 🖷 0116 272 7600 ✉ chief.executive@blaby.gov.uk

Deputy Chief Executive: Mrs Jane Toman, Director of People, Council Offices, Desford Road, Narborough LE19 2EP ☎ 0116 272 7576 🖷 0116 272 7600 ✉ jane.toman@blaby.gov.uk

Senior Management: Mr Mark Alflat Director of Place, Council Offices, Desford Road, Narborough LE19 2EP ☎ 0116 272 7504 🖷 0116 272 7504 ✉ mark.alflat@blaby.gov.uk

Best Value: Mrs Alison Moran, Performance & Audit Manager, Council Offices, Desford Road, Narborough LE19 2EP ☎ 0116 272 7732 🖷 0116 272 7600 ✉ alison.moran@blaby.gov.uk

Building Control: Mr Jon Wells Regulatory & Leisure Services Group Manager, Council Offices, Desford Road, Narborough LE19 2EP ☎ 0116 272 7545 🖷 0116 275 0368 ✉ jon.wells@blaby.gov.uk

PR / Communications: Ms Julie Hutchinson, Communications Manager, Council Offices, Desford Road, Narborough LE19 2EP ☎ 0116 272 7648 🖷 0116 275 0368 ✉ julie.hutchinson@blaby.gov.uk

Community Safety: Ms Quin Quinney Community Services Group Manager, Council Offices, Desford Road, Narborough LE19 2EP ☎ 0116 272 7595 🖷 0116 275 0368 ✉ quin.quinney@blaby.gov.uk

Computer Management: Mr Colin Jones Corporate Services Group Manager, Council Offices, Desford Road, Narborough LE19 2EP ☎ 0116 272 7569 🖷 0116 275 0368 ✉ colin.jones@blaby.gov.uk

Contracts: Mr Colin Jones Corporate Services Group Manager, Council Offices, Desford Road, Narborough LE19 2EP ☎ 0116 272 7569 🖷 0116 275 0368 ✉ colin.jones@blaby.gov.uk

Corporate Services: Mr Colin Jones Corporate Services Group Manager, Council Offices, Desford Road, Narborough LE19 2EP ☎ 0116 272 7569 🖷 0116 275 0368 ✉ colin.jones@blaby.gov.uk

Customer Service: Mr Colin Jones Corporate Services Group Manager, Council Offices, Desford Road, Narborough LE19 2EP ☎ 0116 272 7569 🖷 0116 275 0368 ✉ colin.jones@blaby.gov.uk

Economic Development: Ms Catherine Hartley Planning & Economic Development Group Manager, Council Offices, Desford Road, Narborough LE19 2EP ☎ 0116 272 7727 ✉ catherine.hartley@blaby.gov.uk

E-Government: Ms Julie Hutchinson, Communications Manager, Council Offices, Desford Road, Narborough LE19 2EP ☎ 0116 272 7648 🖷 0116 275 0368 ✉ julie.hutchinson@blaby.gov.uk

Electoral Registration: Mr Neil Briggs Customer Services & Electoral Services Manager, Council Offices, Desford Road, Narborough LE19 2EP ☎ 0116 272 7667 🖷 0116 275 0638 ✉ neil.briggs@blaby.gov.uk

Emergency Planning: Mr Jon Wells Regulatory & Leisure Services Group Manager, Council Offices, Desford Road, Narborough LE19 2EP ☎ 0116 272 7545 🖷 0116 275 0368 ✉ jon.wells@blaby.gov.uk

Energy Management: Mr Jon Wells Regulatory & Leisure Services Group Manager, Council Offices, Desford Road, Narborough LE19 2EP ☎ 0116 272 7545 🖷 0116 275 0368 ✉ jon.wells@blaby.gov.uk

Environmental / Technical Services: Mr Kevin Pegg Neighbourhood Services Group Manager, Council Offices, Desford Road, Narborough LE19 2EP ☎ 0116 272 7615 🖷 0116 275 0368 🖱 kevin.pegg@blaby.gov.uk

Environmental Health: Mr Jon Wells Regulatory & Leisure Services Group Manager, Council Offices, Desford Road, Narborough LE19 2EP ☎ 0116 272 7545 🖷 0116 275 0368 🖱 jon.wells@blaby.gov.uk

Estates, Property & Valuation: Ms Sarah Pennelli Financial Services Group Manager, Council Offices, Desford Road, Narborough LE19 2EP ☎ 0116 272 7650 🖷 0116 275 0368 🖱 sarah.pennelli@blaby.gov.uk

Finance: Ms Sarah Pennelli Financial Services Group Manager, Council Offices, Desford Road, Narborough LE19 2EP ☎ 0116 272 7650 🖷 0116 275 0368 🖱 sarah.pennelli@blaby.gov.uk

Fleet Management: Mr Kevin Pegg, Neighbourhood Services Group Manager, Council Offices, Desford Road, Narborough LE19 2EP ☎ 0161 272 7615 🖷 0116 275 0368 🖱 kevin.pegg@blaby.gov.uk

Grounds Maintenance: Mr Kevin Pegg, Neighbourhood Services Group Manager, Council Offices, Desford Road, Narborough LE19 2EP ☎ 0161 272 7615 🖷 0116 275 0368 🖱 kevin.pegg@blaby.gov.uk

Health and Safety: Mr Jon Thorpe, Corporate Health & Safety Advisor, Council Offices, Desford Road, Narborough LE19 2EP ☎ 0116 272 7571 🖷 0116 275 0368 🖱 jon.thorpe@blaby.gov.uk

Home Energy Conservation: Ms Quin Quinney Community Services Group Manager, Council Offices, Desford Road, Narborough LE19 2EP ☎ 0116 272 7595 🖷 0116 275 0368 🖱 quin.quinney@blaby.gov.uk

Housing: Ms Quin Quinney Community Services Group Manager, Council Offices, Desford Road, Narborough LE19 2EP ☎ 0116 272 7595 🖷 0116 275 0368 🖱 quin.quinney@blaby.gov.uk

Legal: Mr Colin Jones Corporate Services Group Manager, Council Offices, Desford Road, Narborough LE19 2EP ☎ 0116 272 7569 🖷 0116 275 0368 🖱 colin.jones@blaby.gov.uk

Leisure and Cultural Services: Mr Jon Wells Regulatory & Leisure Services Group Manager, Council Offices, Desford Road, Narborough LE19 2EP ☎ 0116 272 7545 🖷 0116 275 0368 🖱 jon.wells@blaby.gov.uk

Licensing: Mr Jon Wells Regulatory & Leisure Services Group Manager, Council Offices, Desford Road, Narborough LE19 2EP ☎ 0116 272 7545 🖷 0116 275 0368 🖱 jon.wells@blaby.gov.uk

Lottery Funding, Charity and Voluntary: Ms Jill Stevenson Domestic Violence Co-ordinator Outreach, Council Offices, Desford Road, Narborough LE19 2EP ☎ 0116 272 7582 🖷 0116 275 0368 🖱 jill.stevenson@blaby.gov.uk

Member Services: Mrs Sandeep Tiensa Democratic Services Officer, Council Offices, Desford Road, Narborough LE19 2EP ☎ 0116 272 7640 🖷 0116 272 0368 🖱 sandeep.tiensa@blaby.gov.uk

Parking: Mr Jon Wells Regulatory & Leisure Services Group Manager, Council Offices, Desford Road, Narborough LE19 2EP ☎ 0116 272 7545 🖷 0116 275 0368 🖱 jon.wells@blaby.gov.uk

Partnerships: Ms Jill Stevenson Domestic Violence Co-ordinator Outreach, Council Offices, Desford Road, Narborough LE19 2EP ☎ 0116 272 7582 🖷 0116 275 0368 🖱 jill.stevenson@blaby.gov.uk

Personnel / HR: Mr Mark Foote Strategic Manager - People & Performance, Council Offices, Desford Road, Narborough LE19 2EP ☎ 0116 272 7570 🖱 mark.foote@blaby.gov.uk

Planning: Ms Catherine Hartley Planning & Economic Development Group Manager, Council Offices, Desford Road, Narborough LE19 2EP ☎ 0116 272 7727 🖱 catherine.hartley@blaby.gov.uk

Procurement: Ms Sarah Pennelli Financial Services Group Manager, Council Offices, Desford Road, Narborough LE19 2EP ☎ 0116 272 7650 🖷 0116 275 0368 🖱 sarah.pennelli@blaby.gov.uk

Recycling & Waste Minimisation: Mr Kevin Pegg, Neighbourhood Services Group Manager, Council Offices, Desford Road, Narborough LE19 2EP ☎ 0161 272 7615 🖷 0116 275 0368 🖱 kevin.pegg@blaby.gov.uk

Sustainable Communities: Mrs Jane Toman, Director of People, Council Offices, Desford Road, Narborough LE19 2EP ☎ 0116 272 7576 🖷 0116 272 7600 🖱 jane.toman@blaby.gov.uk

Sustainable Development: Ms Catherine Hartley Planning & Economic Development Group Manager, Council Offices, Desford Road, Narborough LE19 2EP ☎ 0116 272 7727 🖱 catherine.hartley@blaby.gov.uk

Town Centre: Mr Jon Wells Regulatory & Leisure Services Group Manager, Council Offices, Desford Road, Narborough LE19 2EP ☎ 0116 272 7545 🖷 0116 275 0368 🖱 jon.wells@blaby.gov.uk

Waste Collection and Disposal: Mr Kevin Pegg, Neighbourhood Services Group Manager, Council Offices, Desford Road, Narborough LE19 2EP ☎ 0161 272 7615 🖷 0116 275 0368 🖱 kevin.pegg@blaby.gov.uk

Waste Management: Mr Kevin Pegg, Neighbourhood Services Group Manager, Council Offices, Desford Road, Narborough LE19 2EP ☎ 0161 272 7615 🖷 0116 275 0368 🖱 kevin.pegg@blaby.gov.uk

Children's Play Areas: Mr Jon Wells Regulatory & Leisure Services Group Manager, Council Offices, Desford Road, Narborough LE19 2EP ☎ 0116 272 7545 🖷 0116 275 0368 🖱 jon.wells@blaby.gov.uk

COUNCILLORS

***Chair* Broomhead**, M G (CON - Blaby South) cllr.broomhead@blaby.gov.uk

***Vice-Chair* Merrill**, Christine (LD - Saxondale) cllr.chris.merrill@blaby.gov.uk

***Leader of the Council* Richardson**, Terry (CON - Pastures) cllr.terry.richardson@blaby.gov.uk

BLABY

Deputy Leader of the Council **Wright**, M A (CON - Normanton)
cllr.maggie.wright@blaby.gov.uk

Aslam, Shabbir (LAB - Ravenhurst & Fosse)
cllr.shabbir.aslam@blaby.gov.uk

Breckon, Lee (CON - Fairstone)
cllr.olee.breckon@blaby.gov.uk

Breckon, Scarlet (CON - Ellis)
cllr.scarlet.breckon@blaby.gov.uk

Cashmore, Cheryl (CON - Enderby & St John's)
cllr.cheryl.cashmore@blaby.gov.uk

Clements, D R (CON - Forest)
cllr.clements@blaby.gov.uk

Clifford, Adrian (CON - Countesthorpe)

Coar, Stuart (CON - Forest)
cllr.stuart.coar@blaby.gov.uk

Coe, Sharon (CON - North Whetstone)
cllr.sharon.coe@blaby.gov.uk

Denney, Roy (CON - Fairstone)
cllr.roy.denney@blaby.goiv.uk

DeWinter, Alex (LAB - Winstanley)
cllr.alex.dewinter@blaby.gov.uk

Dracup, Lindsay (CON - Forest)
cllr.lindsay.dracup@blaby.gov.uk

Findlay, D J (CON - Countesthorpe)
ccllr.david.findley@blaby.gov.uk

Freer, D (CON - Croft Hill)
cllr.freer@blaby.gov.uk

Frost, Chris (CON - Muxloe)
cllr.chris.frost@blaby.gov.uk

Garner, B (CON - Narborough & Littlethorpe)
cllr.garner@blaby.gov.uk

Greenwood, Tony (CON - Muxloe)
cllr.tony.greenwood@blaby.gov.uk

Hewson, Iain (CON - Stanton & Flamville)
cllr.iain.hewson@blaby.gov.uk

Huss, Graham (CON - Ellis)
cllr.graham.huss@blaby.gov.uk

Jackson, Mark (CON - North Whestone)
cllr.mark.jackson@blaby.gov.uk

Jackson, Guy (CON - Pastures)
cllr.guy.jackson@blaby.gov.uk

Jennings, D (CON - Countesthorpe)
cllr.jennings@blaby.gov.uk

Matthews, Trevor (CON - Narborough & Littlethorpe)
cllr.trevor.matthews@blaby.gov.uk

Maxwell, S J (LAB - Ravenhurst & Fosse)
cllr.sam.maxwell@blaby.gov.uk

Moitt, P L (LAB - Ravenhurst & Fosse)
cllr.moitt@blaby.gov.uk

Moseley, A (LD - Blaby South)
cllr.moseley@blaby.gov.uk

Phillimore, Les (CON - Cosby with South Whetstone)
cllt.les.phillimore@blaby.gov.uk

Riachardson, Louise (CON - Enderby & St John's)
cllr.louis.richardson@blaby.gov.uk

Sanders, Gary (LAB - Winstanley)
cllr.sanders@blaby.gov.uk

Scott, Sheila (CON - Stanton & Flamville)
cllr.sheila.scott@blaby.gov.uk

Tanner, A C (CON - Cosby with South Whetstone)
cllr.tanner@blaby.gov.uk

Taylor, Ben (CON - Winstanley)
cllr.ben.taylor@blaby.gov.uk

Welsh, Bev (LD - Saxondale)
cllr.bev.welsh@blaby.gov.uk

Welsh, Geoff (LD - Saxondale)
cllr.chris.welsh@blaby.gov.uk

Woods, Deanne (DUP - Stanton & Flamville)
cllr.deanne.woods@blaby.gov.uk

Wright, Bill (LAB - Millfield)
cllr.bill.wright@blaby.gov.uk

POLITICAL COMPOSITION

CON: 28, LAB: 6, LD: 4, DUP: 1

COMMITTEE CHAIRS

Audit: Ms Sharon Coe

Blackburn with Darwen U

Blackburn with Darwen Borough Council, Town Hall, Blackburn BB1 7DY
☎ 01254 585585 🖷 01254 682201 ✉ blackburnwithdarwen@blackburn.gov.uk 💻 www.blackburn.gov.uk

FACTS AND FIGURES

Parliamentary Constituencies: Blackburn, Rossendale and Darwen
EU Constituencies: North West
Election Frequency: Elections are by thirds

PRINCIPAL OFFICERS

Chief Executive: Mr Harry Catherall, Chief Executive, Town Hall, Blackburn BB1 7DY ☎ 01254 585370 🖷 01254 697223 ✉ harry.catherall@blackburn.gov.uk

Deputy Chief Executive: Ms Denise Park, Executive Director - Resources, Town Hall, Blackburn BB1 7DY ☎ 01254 585655 🖷 01254 697223 ✉ denise.park@blackburn.gov.uk

Senior Management: Mr Tom Flanagan Executive Director - Place, Town Hall, Blackburn BB1 7DY ☎ 01254 585504 🖷 01254 697223 ✉ tom.flanagan@blackburn.gov.uk

Senior Management: Mr Dominic Harrison Director of Public Health, 10 Duke Street, Blackburn BB2 1DH ☎ 01254 666933 ✉ dominic.harrison@blackburn.gov.uk

Senior Management: Ms Sally McIvor Executive Director - People, Town Hall, Blackburn BB1 7DY ☎ 01254 585299 🖷 01254 697223 ✉ sally.mcivor@blackburn.gov.uk

Architect, Building / Property Services: Mr Stuart Davey Building Services Manager, Capita Symonds, Castleway House, 17 Preston New Road, Blackburn BB2 1AU ☎ 01254 273342 🖷 01254 273429 🖰 stuart.davey@capita.co.uk

Building Control: Mr Brian Bailey Director - Growth & Prosperity, Town Hall, Blackburn BB1 7DY ☎ 01254 585360 🖰 brian.bailey@blackburn.gov.uk

Catering Services: Mr Neil Dagnall Bar & Catering Manager, King Georges Hall, Northgate, Blackburn BB2 1AA ☎ 01254 582579 🖰 neil.dagnall@blackburn.gov.uk

Children / Youth Services: Ms Linda Clegg Director of Children's Services, 10 Duke Street, Blackburn BB2 1DH ☎ 01254 666762 🖰 linda.clegg@blackburn.gov.uk

PR / Communications: Mr Marc Schmid Head of Corporate Services, Town Hall, Blackburn BB1 7DY ☎ 01254 585480 🖰 marc.schmid@blackburn.gov.uk

Community Safety: Mr Mark Aspin Community Safety Manager, Town Hall, Blackburn BB1 7DY ☎ 01254 585512 🖰 mark.aspin@blackburn.gov.uk

Computer Management: Mr Shane Agnew Head of IT, Strategy & Operations, Town Hall, Blackburn BB1 7DY ☎ 01254 588808 🖰 shane.agnew@blackburn.gov.uk

Consumer Protection and Trading Standards: Mr Tony Watson Head of Environment & Public Protection Services, Davyfield Road, Davyfield, Blackburn BB1 2QY ☎ 01254 266362 🖰 tony.watson@blackburn.gov.uk

Corporate Services: Mr Marc Schmid Head of Corporate Services, Town Hall, Blackburn BB1 7DY ☎ 01254 585480 🖰 marc.schmid@blackburn.gov.uk

Customer Service: Mr Andy Ormerod Head of Revenues, Benefits & Customer Services, Town Hall, Blackburn BB1 7DY ☎ 01254 585773 🖰 andy.ormerod@blackburn.gov.uk

Economic Development: Mr Brian Bailey Director - Growth & Prosperity, Town Hall, Blackburn BB1 7DY ☎ 01254 585360 🖰 brian.bailey@blackburn.gov.uk

Education: Mr Mebz Bobat Head of Education, Partnership Services, 10 Duke Street, , Blackburn BB2 1DH ☎ 01254 666510 🖰 mebz.bobat@blackburn.gov.uk

E-Government: Ms Denise Park, Executive Director - Resources, Town Hall, Blackburn BB1 7DY ☎ 01254 585655 🖷 01254 697223 🖰 denise.park@blackburn.gov.uk

Electoral Registration: Mr Ben Aspinall Scrutiny Elections & School Appeals Manager, Town Hall, Blackburn BB1 7DY ☎ 01254 585191 🖰 ben.aspinall@blackburn.gov.uk

Emergency Planning: Ms Rachel Hutchinson Civil Contingencies Manager, Town Hall, Blackburn BB1 7DY 🖰 rachel.hutchinson@blackburn.gov.uk

Energy Management: Ms Gwen Kinloch Environmental Strategy & Projects Manager, Town Hall, Blackburn BB1 7DY 🖰 gwen.kinloch@blackburn.gov.uk

Environmental / Technical Services: Mr Martin Eden Director - Environment & Leisure, Town Hall, Blackburn BB1 7DY ☎ 01254 585102 🖰 martin.eden@blackburn.gov.uk

Environmental Health: Mr Gary Johnston Service Manager - Environmental Health, Town Hall, Blackburn BB1 7DY ☎ 01254 266375 🖰 gary.johnston@blackburn.gov.uk

European Liaison: Mr Sayyed Osman Director - Housing & Localities, Town Hall, Blackburn BB1 7DY ☎ 01254 585340 🖰 sayyed.osman@blackburn.gov.uk

Events Manager: Mr Steve Burch Events & Promotion Manager, King George's Hall, Northgate, Blackburn BB2 1AA ☎ 01254 582579 🖰 steve.burch@blackburn.gov.uk

Facilities: Mr Steve Cox, Facilities Manager, C Floor, Tower Block, Town Hall, Blackburn BB1 7DY ☎ 01254 585497 🖷 01254 585101 🖰 steve.cox@blackburn.gov.uk

Finance: Ms Louise Mattinson Director - Finance & IT, Town Hall, Blackburn BB1 7DY ☎ 01254 585600 🖷 01254 663416 🖰 louise.mattinson@blackburn.gov.uk

Fleet Management: Mr Neil Bolton Head of Fleet Management, Davyfield Road, Davyfield, Blackburn BB1 2QY ☎ 01254 585095 🖰 neil.bolton@blackburn.gov.uk

Grounds Maintenance: Mr Gary Blackshaw Assistant Manager - Green Spaces, Town Hall, Blackburn BB1 7DY ☎ 01254 666350 🖰 garry.blackshaw@blackburn.gov.uk

Health and Safety: Mr David Almond Health & Safety & Wellbeing Manager, Town Hall, Blackburn BB1 7DY ☎ 01254 585873 🖷 01254 585101 🖰 david.almond@blackburn.gov.uk

Highways: Mr Brian Bailey Director - Growth & Prosperity, Town Hall, Blackburn BB1 7DY ☎ 01254 585360 🖰 brian.bailey@blackburn.gov.uk

Home Energy Conservation: Mr Stuart Pye, Home Improvement & Energy Solutions Manager, Town Hall, Blackburn BB1 7DY ☎ 01254 588890 🖷 01254 588889 🖰 stuart.pye@blackburn.gov.uk

Housing: Mr Stephen Richards Housing Needs & Support Manager, Town Hall, Blackburn BB1 7DY ☎ 01254 585132 🖰 stephen.richards@blackburn.gov.uk

Local Area Agreement: Ms Philippa Cross Policy & Performance Manager, Town Hall, Blackburn BB1 7DY ☎ 01254 585245 🖰 philippa.cross@blackburn.gov.uk

Legal: Ms Sian Roxborough Head of Legal / Council Solicitor, Town Hall, Blackburn BB1 7DY ☎ 01254 585252 🖰 sian.roxborough@blackburn.gov.uk

BLACKBURN WITH DARWEN

Leisure and Cultural Services: Mr Martin Eden Director - Environment & Leisure, Town Hall, Blackburn BB1 7DY ☎ 01254 585102 ✉ martin.eden@blackburn.gov.uk

Leisure and Cultural Services: Ms Claire Ramwell Head of Service, Town Hall, Blackburn BB1 7DY ☎ 01254 585201 ✉ claire.ramwell@blackburn.gov.uk

Licensing: Ms Janet White Senior Public Protection Officer, Town Hall, Blackburn BB1 7DY ☎ 01254 585007 ✉ janet.white@blackburn.gov.uk

Member Services: Mr Phil Llewllyn Executive & Councillor Support Manager, Town Hall, Blackburn BB1 7DY ☎ 01254 585369 ✉ phil.llewellyn@blackburn.gov.uk

Parking: Mr George Bell Associate Director - Highways & Transportation, Capita, Castleway House, 17 Preston New Road, Blackburn BB2 1AU ☎ 01254 273454

Personnel / HR: Ms Mandy Singh Head of HR, Town Hall, Blackburn BB1 7DY ☎ 01254 585612 ✉ mandy.singh@blackburn.gov.uk

Planning: Mr David Proctor Head of Regeneration (Planning & Transport), Town Hall, Blackburn BB1 7DY ☎ 01254 585521 ✉ david.proctor@blackburn.gov.uk

Procurement: Mr Chris Bradley Strategic Procurement Manager, Town Hall, Blackburn BB1 7DY ☎ 01254 585296 ✉ christopher.bradley@blackburn.gov.uk

Public Libraries: Ms Kath Sutton Service Manager, Blackburn Library, Blackburn BB2 1AG ☎ 01254 587907 ✉ kath.sutton@blackburn.gov.uk

Recycling & Waste Minimisation: Mr Stuart Hammond, Environmental Sustainability & Enforcement Manager, Davyfield Road, Blackburn BB1 2LX ☎ 01254 585863 📠 01254 585803 ✉ stuart.hammond@blackburn.gov.uk

Regeneration: Mr Brian Bailey Director - Growth & Prosperity, Town Hall, Blackburn BB1 7DY ☎ 01254 585360 ✉ brian.bailey@blackburn.gov.uk

Road Safety: Ms Lisa Heywood Road Safety Officer, Capita, Castleway House, 17 Preston New Road, Blackburn BB2 1AU ☎ 01254 273223 ✉ lisa.heywood@capita.gov.uk

Social Services: Mr Steve Tingle Director - Adult Services (DASS), 10 Duke Street, Blackburn BB2 1DH ☎ 01254 585349 ✉ stephen.tingle@blackburn.gov.uk

Social Services (Adult): Mr Steve Tingle Director - Adult Services (DASS), 10 Duke Street, Blackburn BB2 1DH ☎ 01254 585349 ✉ stephen.tingle@blackburn.gov.uk

Social Services (Children): Ms Linda Clegg Director of Children's Services, 10 Duke Street, Blackburn BB2 1DH ☎ 01254 666762 ✉ linda.clegg@blackburn.gov.uk

Childrens Social Care: Ms Linda Clegg Director of Children's Services, 10 Duke Street, Blackburn BB2 1DH ☎ 01254 666762 ✉ linda.clegg@blackburn.gov.uk

Street Scene: Mr Brian Bailey Director - Growth & Prosperity, Town Hall, Blackburn BB1 7DY ☎ 01254 585360 ✉ brian.bailey@blackburn.gov.uk

Tourism: Ms Susan Walmsley Visitor Services Manager, Town Hall, Blackburn BB1 7DY ☎ 01254 588923 ✉ susan.walmsley@blackburn.gov.uk

Town Centre: Ms Julia Simpson Town Centre Projects Manager, Town Hall, Blackburn BB1 7DY ☎ 01254 588958 ✉ julie.simpson@blackburn.gov.uk

Transport: Mr Mike Cliffe Strategic Transport Manager, Town Hall, Blackburn BB1 7DY ☎ 01254 585310 ✉ mike.cliffe@blackburn.gov.uk

Waste Collection and Disposal: Mr Tony Watson Head of Environment & Public Protection Services, Davyfield Road, Davyfield, Blackburn BB1 2QY ☎ 01254 266362 ✉ tony.watson@blackburn.gov.uk

Waste Management: Mr Tony Watson Head of Environment & Public Protection Services, Davyfield Road, Davyfield, Blackburn BB1 2QY ☎ 01254 266362 ✉ tony.watson@blackburn.gov.uk

COUNCILLORS

***Mayor* Hussain**, Faryad (LAB - Queen's Park)
faryad.hussain@blackburn.gov.uk

***Deputy Mayor* Akhtar**, Hussain (LAB - Shear Brow)
hussain.akhtar@blackburn.gov.uk

***Leader of the Council* Khan**, Mohammed (LAB - Wensley Fold)
mohammed.khan@blackburn.gov.uk

***Deputy Leader of the Council* Riley**, Phil (LAB - Roe Lee)
phil.riley@blackburn.gov.uk

***Group Leader* Foster**, David (LD - Whitehall)
david.foster@blackburn.gov.uk

***Group Leader* Lee**, Michael (CON - Beardwood with Lammack)
michael.lee@blackburn.gov.uk

Akhtar, Parwaiz (LAB - Bastwell)
parwaiz.akhtar@blackburn.gov.uk

Ali, Imtiaz (CON - Beardwood with Lammack)
imitaz.ali@blackburn.gov.uk

Bateson, Maureen (LAB - Ewood)
maureen.bateson@blackburn.gov.uk

Brookfield, Stephanie (LAB - Earcroft)
stephanie.brookfield@blackburn.gov.uk

Browne, Paul (LD - Sudell)
paul.browne@blackburn.gov.uk

Casey, Jim (LAB - Ewood)
jim.casey@blackburn.gov.uk

Connor, Kevin (CON - Marsh House)
kevin.connor@blackburn.gov.uk

Cottam, Alan (CON - Livesey with Pleasington)
alan.cottam@blackburn.gov.uk

Daley, Julie (CON - Beardwood with Lammack)
julie.daley@blackburn.gov.uk

Desai, Mustafa (LAB - Queen's Park)
mustafa.desai@blackburn.gov.uk

Entwistle, Eileen (LAB - Sudell)
eileen.entwhistle@blackburn.gov.uk

Evans, Tom (LAB - Marsh House)
tom.evans@blackburn.gov.uk

Foster, Karimeh (LD - Whitehall)
karimeh.foster@blackburn.gov.uk

Gee, Denise (CON - Fernhurst)
denise.gee@blackburn.gov.uk

Groves, Jamie (LAB - Ewood)
jamie.groves@blackburn.gov.uk

Gunn, Julie (LAB - Meadowhead)
julie.gunn@gov.uk

Hardman, Derek (CON - Livesey with Pleasington)
derek.hardman@blackburn.gov.uk

Harling, Dave (LAB - Wensley Fold)
dave.harling@blackburn.gov.uk

Hollings, Pete (LAB - Sunnyhurst)
peter.hollings@blackburn.gov.uk

Humphrys, Tony (LAB - Shadsworth with Whitebirk)
anthony.humphrys@blackburn.gov.uk

Hussain, Iftakhar (LAB - Bastwell)
iftakhar.hussain@blackburn.gov.uk

Hussain, Shaukat (LAB - Bastwell)
shaukat.hussain@blackburn.gov.uk

Jan-Virmani, Yusuf (LAB - No Ward)
yusuf.jan-virmani@blackburn.gov.uk

Johnson, Mike (LAB - Higher Croft)
m.johnson@blackburn.gov.uk

Kay, Andy (LAB - Higher Croft)
andy.kay@blackburn.gov.uk

Khan, Zamir (LAB - Audley)
zamir.khan@blackburn.gov.uk

Khonat, Suleman (LAB - Shear Brow)
suleman.khonat@blackburn.gov.uk

Liddle, Sylvia (LAB - Roe Lee)
sylvia.liddle@blackburn.gov.uk

Mahmood, Quesir (LAB - Wensley Fold)
quesir.mahmood@blackburn.gov.uk

Mahmood, Arshid (LAB - Corporation Park)
arshid.mahmood@blackburn.gov.uk

Maxfield, Trevor (LAB - Earcroft)
trevor.maxfield@blackburn.gov.uk

McFall, Pat (LAB - Little Harwood)
pat.mcfall@blackburn.gov.uk

McKinlay, Don (LAB - Higher Croft)
don.mckinlay@blackburn.gov.uk

Mulla, Salim (LAB - Queen's Park)
salim.mulla@blackburn.gov.uk

O' Keeffe, Ronald (LAB - Shadsworth with Whitebirk)
ronald.okeeffe@blackburn.gov.uk

Oates, Jane Margaret (LAB - Sudell)
jane.oates@blackburn.gov.uk

Patel, Abdul (LAB - Little Harwood)
abdul.patel@blackburn.gov.uk

Pearson, John (CON - Livesey with Pleasington)
john.pearson@blackburn.gov.uk

Rehman, Abdul (LAB - Corporation Park)
abdul.rehman@blackburn.gov.uk

Rigby, Jean (CON - North Turton with Tockholes)
jean.rigby@blackburn.gov.uk

Rigby, Colin (CON - North Turton with Tockholes)
colin.rigby@blackburn.gov.uk

Roberts, John (LAB - Marsh House)
john.roberts@blackburn.gov.uk

Shorrock, James (LAB - Shadsworth with Whitebirk)
james.shorrock@blackburn.gov.uk

Sidat, Salim (LAB - Audley)
salim.sidat@blackburn.gov.uk

Slater, Julie (CON - East Rural)
julie.slater@blackburn.gov.uk

Slater, Jacqueline (CON - Fernhurst)
jacqueline.slater@blackburn.gov.uk

Slater, John (CON - Fernhurst)
john.slater@blackburn.gov.uk

Smith, Jim (LAB - Mill Hill)
jim.smith@blackburn.gov.uk

Smith, Dave (LAB - Sunnyhurst)
david.smith@blackburn.gov.uk

Surve, Naushad (LAB - Little Harwood)
naushad.surve@blackburn.gov.uk

Talbot, Damian (LAB - Mill Hill)
damian.talbot@blackburn.gov.uk

Tapp, Konrad (CON - Meadowhead)
konrad.tapp@blackburn.gov.uk

Taylor, Brian (LAB - Sunnyhurst)
brian.taylor@blackburn.gov.uk

Vali, Shiraj Adam (LAB - Shear Brow)
shiraj.vali@blackburn.gov.uk

Whalley, Ashley (LAB - Meadowhead)
ashley.whalley@blackburn.gov.uk

Whittle, Ron (LAB - Roe Lee)
ron.whittle@blackburn.gov.uk

Wright, John (LAB - Corporation Park)
john.wright@blackburn.gov.uk

POLITICAL COMPOSITION

LAB: 46, CON: 14, LD: 3

COMMITTEE CHAIRS

Audit: Mr Salim Sidat

Children & Young People: Ms Sylvia Liddle

Finance: Mr Faryad Hussain

Health & Adults: Mr Ronald O' Keeffe

Licensing: Mr John Wright

Planning & Highways: Mr Dave Smith

Standards: Mr Abdul Rehman

Blackpool U

Blackpool Borough Council, Number One Bickerstaffe Square, Talbot Road, Blackpool FY1 3AH
☎ 01253 477477 🖷 01253 477101 webmaster@blackpool.gov.uk
www.blackpool.gov.uk

FACTS AND FIGURES

Parliamentary Constituencies: Blackpool North and Cleveleys, Blackpool South
EU Constituencies: North West
Election Frequency: Elections are of whole council

PRINCIPAL OFFICERS

Chief Executive: Mr Neil Jack, Chief Executive, Number One Bickerstaffe Square, Talbot Road, Blackpool FY1 3AH ☎ 01253 477000 🖷 01253 477003 chief.executive@blackpool.gov.uk

Deputy Chief Executive: Ms Carmel McKeogh Deputy Chief Executive, Number One Bickerstaffe Square, Talbot Road, Blackpool FY1 3AH ☎ 01253 477247 carmel.mckeogh@blackpool.gov.uk

Senior Management: Mr Carl Baker Deputy Director of People - Children's Services, Number One Bickerstaffe Square, Talbot Road, Blackpool FY1 3AH ☎ 01253 478972 carl.baker@blackpool.gov.uk

Senior Management: Mr John Blackledge Director - Community & Environmental Services, Number One Bickerstaffe Square, Talbot Road, Blackpool FY1 3AH ☎ 01253 478400 john.blackledge@blackpool.gov.uk

Senior Management: Mr Alan Cavill Director - Place, Number One Bickerstaffe Square, Talbot Road, Blackpool FY1 3AH ☎ 01253 477006 alan.cavill@blackpool.gov.uk

Senior Management: Ms Delyth Curtis Director - People (Statutory Director - Children's Services), Number One Bickerstaffe Square, Talbot Road, Blackpool FY1 3AH ☎ 01253 476558 delyth.curtis@blackpool.gov.uk

Senior Management: Dr Arif Rajpura Director - Public Health, Number One Bickerstaffe Square, Talbot Road, Blackpool FY1 3AH ☎ 01253 476367 arif.rajpura@blackpool.gov.uk

Senior Management: Ms Karen Smith Deputy Director of People - (Statutory Director - Adult Services), Number One Bickerstaffe Square, Talbot Road, Blackpool FY1 3AH ☎ 01253 477502 karen.smith@blackpool.gov.uk

Senior Management: Mr Steve Thompson Director - Resources, Number One Bickerstaffe Square, Talbot Road, Blackpool FY1 3AH ☎ 01253 478505 steve.thompson@blackpool.gov.uk

Senior Management: Mr Mark Towers Director - Governance & Regulatory Services, Number One Bickerstaffe Square, Talbot Road, Blackpool FY1 3AH ☎ 01253 477007 mark.towers@blackpool.gov.uk

Architect, Building / Property Services: Mr Stephen Waterfield, Head of Property & Asset Management, Number One Bickerstaffe Square, Talbot Road, Blackpool FY1 3AH ☎ 01253 476069 stephen.waterfield@blackpool.gov.uk

Building Control: Mr Steve Matthews Head of Housing, Planning & Transport, The Enterprise Centre, Lytham Road, , Blackpool FY1 6DU ☎ 01253 476122 steve.matthews@blackpool.gov.uk

Children / Youth Services: Mr Carl Baker Deputy Director of People - Children's Services, Number One Bickerstaffe Square, Talbot Road, Blackpool FY1 3AH ☎ 01253 478972 carl.baker@blackpool.gov.uk

Children / Youth Services: Ms Delyth Curtis Director - People (Statutory Director - Children's Services), Number One Bickerstaffe Square, Talbot Road, Blackpool FY1 3AH ☎ 01253 476558 delyth.curtis@blackpool.gov.uk

Civil Registration: Ms Joceline Greenaway Head of Registration & Bereavement Services, Number One Bickerstaffe Square, Talbot Road, Blackpool FY1 3AH ☎ 01253 477173 joceline.greenaway@blackpool.gov.uk

PR / Communications: Ms Sally Shaw Head of Development, Engagement & Communication, Number One Bickerstaffe Square, Talbot Road, Blackpool FY1 3AH ☎ 07747 648216 sally.shaw@blackpool.gov.uk

Computer Management: Mr Tony Doyle Head of ICT Services, Number One Bickerstaffe Square, Talbot Road, Blackpool FY1 3AH ☎ 01253 478834 tony.doyle@blackpool.gov.uk

Corporate Services: Mr Trevor Rayner Head of Corporate Procurement & Development, Number One Bickerstaffe Square, Talbot Road, Blackpool FY1 3AH ☎ 01253 478531 trevor.bayliss@blackpool.gov.uk

Customer Service: Ms Marie McRoberts Assistant Treasurer, Revenues, Benefits & Customer Services, Number One Bickerstaffe Square, Talbot Road, Blackpool FY1 3AH ☎ 01253 478910 marie.mcroberts@blackpool.gov.uk

Economic Development: Mr Peter Legg Head of Economic Development, FYCreatives, 154-158 Church Street, Blackpool FY1 3PS ☎ 01253 477320 peter.legg@blackpool.gov.uk

Environmental Health: Mr Tim Coglan Service Manager - Public Protection, Number One Bickerstaffe Square, Talbot Road, Blackpool FY1 3AH ☎ 01253 478367 tim.coglen@blackpool.gov.uk

Estates, Property & Valuation: Mr Stephen Waterfield, Head of Property & Asset Management, Number One Bickerstaffe Square, Talbot Road, Blackpool FY1 3AH ☎ 01253 476069 stephen.waterfield@blackpool.gov.uk

Treasury: Ms Marie McRoberts Assistant Treasurer, Revenues, Benefits & Customer Services, Number One Bickerstaffe Square, Talbot Road, Blackpool FY1 3AH ☎ 01253 478910 ✉ marie.mcroberts@blackpool.gov.uk

Grounds Maintenance: Mr John Hawkin Head of Leisure, Catering Services & Illuminations, Number One Bickerstaffe Square, Talbot Road, Blackpool FY1 3AH ☎ 01253 478169 ✉ john.hawkin@blackpool.gov.uk

Health and Safety: Mr Terry Hall Health & Safety Manager, Number One Bickerstaffe Square, Talbot Road, Blackpool FY1 3AH ☎ 01253 477264 ✉ terry.hall@blackpool.gov.uk

Housing: Mr Steve Matthews Head of Housing, Planning & Transport, Number One Bickerstaffe Square, Talbot Road, Blackpool FY1 3AH ☎ 01253 476200 ✉ steve.matthews@blackpool.gov.uk

Legal: Mrs Carmel White Chief Corporate Solicitor, Number One Bickerstaffe Square, Talbot Road, Blackpool FY1 3AH ☎ 01253 477477 ✉ carmel.white@blackpool.gov.uk

Leisure and Cultural Services: Ms Polly Hamilton Head of Cultural Services, Number One Bickerstaffe Square, Talbot Road, Blackpool FY1 3AH ☎ 01253 476155 ✉ polly.hamilton@blackpool.gov.uk

Licensing: Ms Sharon Davies Head of Licensing Services, Number One Bickerstaffe Square, Talbot Road, Blackpool FY1 3AH ☎ 01253 478518 ✉ sharon.davies@blackpool.gov.uk

Member Services: Ms Lorraine Hurst Head of Democratic Governance (Deputy Monitoring Officer), Number One Bickerstaffe Square, Talbot Road, Blackpool FY1 3AH ☎ 01253 477127 ✉ lorraine.hurst@blackpool.gov.uk

Personnel / HR: Mr Andy Divall Pay, Equality & Policy Manager, Number One Bickerstaffe Square, Talbot Road, Blackpool FY1 3AH ☎ 07789 617085 ✉ andy.divall@blackpool.gov.uk

Personnel / HR: Ms Linda Dutton Head of Human Resources, Organisation & Workplace Development, Number One Bickerstaffe Square, Talbot Road, Blackpool FY1 3AH ☎ 07584 606831 ✉ linda.dutton@blackpool.gov.uk

Planning: Mr Steve Matthews Head of Housing, Planning & Transport, Number One Bickerstaffe Square, Talbot Road, Blackpool FY1 3AH ☎ 01253 476200 ✉ steve.matthews@blackpool.gov.uk

Procurement: Mr Trevor Rayner Head of Corporate Procurement & Development, Number One Bickerstaffe Square, Talbot Road, Blackpool FY1 3AH ☎ 01253 478531 ✉ trevor.bayliss@blackpool.gov.uk

Regeneration: Mr Peter Legg Head of Economic Development, Number One Bickerstaffe Square, Talbot Road, Blackpool FY1 3AH ☎ 01253 477320 ✉ peter.legg@blackpool.gov.uk

Social Services (Adult): Ms Lynn Gornall Principal Social Worker & Head of Safeguarding (Adults), Number One Bickerstaffe Square, Talbot Road, Blackpool FY1 3AH ☎ 01253 477477 ✉ lynn.gornell@blackpool.gov.uk

Social Services (Adult): Mr Les Marshall Head of Adult Social Care, Number One Bickerstaffe Square, Talbot Road, Blackpool FY1 3AH ☎ 01253 476782 ✉ les.marshall@blackpool.gov.uk

Social Services (Adult): Ms Karen Smith Deputy Director of People - (Statutory Director - Adult Services), Number One Bickerstaffe Square, Talbot Road, Blackpool FY1 3AH ☎ 01253 477502 ✉ karen.smith@blackpool.gov.uk

Social Services (Children): Ms Dominic Tumelty Head of Children's Social Care, Number One Bickerstaffe Square, Talbot Road, Blackpool FY1 3AH ☎ 01253 477477 ✉ dominic.tumelty@blackpool.gov.uk

Fostering & Adoption: Ms Dominic Tumelty Head of Children's Social Care, Number One Bickerstaffe Square, Talbot Road, Blackpool FY1 3AH ☎ 01253 477477 ✉ dominic.tumelty@blackpool.gov.uk

Safeguarding: Ms Linda Evans Principal Social Worker, Number One Bickerstaffe Square, Talbot Road, Blackpool FY1 3AH ☎ 01253 476827 ✉ linda.evans@blackpool.gov.uk

Families: Ms Merle Davies Head of Early Help for Children & Families, Number One Bickerstaffe Square, Talbot Road, Blackpool FY1 3AH ☎ 01253 476168 ✉ merle.davies@blackpool.gov.uk

Public Health: Dr Arif Rajpura Director - Public Health, Number One Bickerstaffe Square, Talbot Road, Blackpool FY1 3AH ☎ 01253 476367 ✉ arif.rajpura@blackpool.gov.uk

Tourism: Mr Philip Welsh Head of Visitor Economy, Number One Bickerstaff Square, Talbot Road, Blackpool FY1 3AH ☎ 01253 477312 ✉ philip.welsh@blackpool.gov.uk

COUNCILLORS

Leader of the Council **Blackburn**, Simon (LAB - Brunswick)
cllr.simon.blackburn@blackpool.gov.uk

Deputy Leader of the Council **Campbell**, Gillian (LAB - Park)
cllr.gillian.campbell@blackpool.gov.uk

Benson, Kath (LAB - Layton)
cllr.kathryn.benson@blackpool.gov.uk

Brown, Tony (CON - Warbreck)
cllr.tony.brown@blackpool.gov.uk

Cain, Graham (LAB - Bloomfield)
cllr.graham.cain@blackpool.gov.uk

Callow, Maxine (CON - Norbreck)
cllr.maxine.callow@blackpool.gov.uk

Callow, Peter (CON - Norbreck)
cllr.peter.callow@blackpool.gov.uk

Clapham, Donald (CON - Bispham)
cllr.don.clapham@blackpool.gov.uk

Coleman, Debbie (CON - Hawes Side)
cllr.debbie.coleman@blackpool.gov.uk

BLACKPOOL

Coleman, Ian (LAB - Talbot)
cllr.ian.coleman@blackpool.gov.uk

Coleman, Gary (LAB - Brunswick)
cllr.gary.coleman@blackpool.gov.uk

Collett, Eddie (LAB - Tyldesley)
cllr.eddie.collett@blackpool.gov.uk

Cox, Christian (CON - Squires Gate)
cllr.christian.cox@blackpool.gov.uk

Critchley, Kim (LAB - Hawes Side)
cllt.kim.critchley@blackpool.gov.uk

Cross, Amy (LAB - Ingthorpe)
cllr.amy.cross@blackpool.gov.uk

Elmes, Jim (LAB - Marton)
cllr.jim.elmes@blackpool.gov.uk

Galley, Paul (CON - Anchorsholme)
cllr.paul.galley@blackpool.gov.uk

Henderson, Lily (CON - Highfield)
cllr.lily.henderson@blackpool.gov.uk

Humphreys, Alistair (LAB - Squires Gate)
cllr.alistaire.humphreys@blackpool.gov.uk

Hunter, Peter (LAB - Highfield)
cllr.peter.hunter@blackpool.gov.uk

Hutton, Adrian (LAB - Clifton)
cllr.adrian.hutton@blackpool.gov.uk

Jackson, Fred (LAB - Victoria)
cllr.fred.jackson@blackpool.gov.uk

Jones, John (LAB - Bloomfield)
cllr.john.jones@blackpool.gov.uk

Kirkwood, Maria (LAB - Park)
cllr.maria.kirkwood@blackpool.gov.uk

Matthews, Allan (LAB - Tyldesley)
cllr.allan.matthews@blackpool.gov.uk

Maycock, Colin (CON - Bispham)
cllr.colinlmaycock@blackpool.gov.uk

Mitchell, Martin (LAB - Layton)
cllr.martin.mitchell@blackpool.gov.uk

O'Hara, David (LAB - Waterloo)
cllr.david.ohara@blackpool.gov.uk

Owen, David (LAB - Victoria)
cllr.david.owen@blackpool.gov.uk

Roberts, Jason (CON - Stanley)
cllr.jason.roberts@blackpool.gov.uk

Robertson, Derek (CON - Waterloo)
cllr.derek.robertson@blackpool.gov.uk

Rowson, Kath (LAB - Ingthorpe)
cllr.kath.rowson@blackpool.gov.uk

Ryan, Chris (LAB - Greenlands)
cllr.chris.ryan@blackpool.gov.uk

Scott, Danny (CON - Warbreck)
cllr.danny.scott@blackpool.gov.uk

Singleton, Vikki (LAB - Marton)
cllr.vikki.singleton@blackpool.gov.uk

Smith, Mark (LAB - Talbot)
cllr.mark.smith@blackpool.gov.uk

Stansfield, Andrew (CON - Stanley)
cllr.andrew.stansfield@blackpool.gov.uk

Taylor, Ivan (LAB - Claremont)
cllr.ivan.taylor@blackpool.gov.uk

Taylor, Luke (LAB - Clifton)
cllr.luke.taylor@blackpool.gov.uk

Williams, Lynn (LAB - Claremont)
cllr.lynn.williams@blackpool.gov.uk

Williams, Tony (CON - Anchorsholme)
cllr.tony.williams@blackpool.gov.uk

Wright, Christine (LAB - Greenlands)
cllr.christine.wright@blackpool.gov.uk

POLITICAL COMPOSITION
LAB: 28, CON: 14

COMMITTEE CHAIRS
Licensing: Mr Adrian Hutton

Blaenau Gwent W

Blaenau Gwent County Borough Council, Municipal Offices, Civic Centre, Ebbw Vale NP23 6XB
☎ 01495 350555 🖷 01495 301255 🖱 💻 www.blaenau-gwent.gov.uk

FACTS AND FIGURES
Parliamentary Constituencies: Blaenau Gwent
EU Constituencies: Wales
Election Frequency: Elections are of whole council

PRINCIPAL OFFICERS
Chief Executive: Mr David Waggett, Chief Executive, Municipal Offices, Civic Centre, Ebbw Vale NP23 6XB ☎ 01495 355001 🖱 david.waggett@blaenau-gwent.gov.uk

Senior Management: Mr Richard Crook Corporate Director of Environment & Regeneration, Municipal Offices, Civic Centre, Ebbw Vale NP23 6XB ☎ 01495 355530 🖱 richard.crook@blaenau-gwent.gov.uk

Senior Management: Ms Liz Majer, Corporate Director of Social Services, Anvil Court, Church Street, Abertillery NP13 1DB ☎ 01495 355261 🖷 01495 355285 🖱 liz.majer@blaenau-gwent.gov.uk

Senior Management: Mr Dave McAuliffe Chief Finance Officer, Municipal Offices, Civic Centre, Ebbw Vale NP23 6XB ☎ 01495 355005 🖷 01495 355788 🖱 dave.mcauliffe@blaenau-gwent.gov.uk

Access Officer / Social Services (Disability): Mr Huw Lewis Equalities Officer, Municipal Offices, Civic Centre, Ebbw Vale NP23 6XB ☎ 01495 355108 🖱 huw.lewis@blaenau-gwent.gov.uk

Architect, Building / Property Services: Mr Clive Rogers Head of Technical Services, Baldwin House, Victoria Park, Ebbw Vale NP23 6ED ☎ 01495 355384

Best Value: Mrs Bernadette Elias, Head of Policy & Performance, Municipal Offices, Civic Centre, Ebbw Vale NP23 6XB ☎ 01495 355016 🖱 bernadette.elias@blaenau-gwent.gov.uk

Building Control: Mr Steve Smith, Service Manager - Development, Blaina District Office, High Street, Blaina, Blaenau NP13 3XD ☎ 01495 355510 🖷 01495 355598 🖰 steve.smith@blaenau-gwent.gov.uk

Catering Services: Mr Matthew Perry Service Manager - Community Services, Central Depot, Barleyfield Industrial Estate, Brynmawr NP23 4YF ☎ 01495 355955 🖷 01495 312357 🖰 matthew.perry@blaenau-gwent.gov.uk

Children / Youth Services: Mrs Joanne Sims Youth Services Manager, Ebbw Vale Institute, Ebbw Vale, Blaenau NP23 6BE ☎ 01495 357866 🖰 joanne.sims@blaenau-gwent.gov.uk

Civil Registration: Mrs Sue Mitchell, Superintendent Registrar, Blaenau Gwent Register Office, Registration Suite, Bedwellty House, Morgan Street, Tredegar NP22 3XN ☎ 01495 353370 🖰 sue.mitchell@blaenau-gwent.gov.uk

PR / Communications: Mr Sean Scannell Corporate Communications, Marketing & Customer Access Manager, Municipal Offices, Civic Centre, Ebbw Vale NP23 6XB ☎ 01495 355113 🖰 sean.scannell@blaenau-gwent.gov.uk

Community Planning: Mrs Bernadette Elias, Head of Policy & Performance, Municipal Offices, Civic Centre, Ebbw Vale NP23 6XB ☎ 01495 355016 🖰 bernadette.elias@blaenau-gwent.gov.uk

Community Safety: Mrs Helena Hunt Policy Team Leader, Municipal Offices, Civic Centre, Ebbw Vale NP23 6XB ☎ 01495 356145 🖰 helena.hunt@blaenau-gwent.co.uk

Computer Management: Mrs Linda Squire Assistant Director Revenues, Benefits & ICT, Municipal Offices, Civic Centre, Ebbw Vale NP23 6XB ☎ 01495 355176 🖷 01495 355789 🖰 linda.squire@blaenau-gwent.gov.uk

Consumer Protection and Trading Standards: Mr Dave Thompson Service Manager - Public Protection, Anvil Court, Abertillery NP13 1DB ☎ 01495 355067 🖷 01495 355834 🖰 dave.thompson@blaenau-gwent.gov.uk

Contracts: Mr John Parsons, Corporate Director of Environment & Regeneration, Municipal Offices, Civic Centre, Ebbw Vale NP23 6XB ☎ 01495 356088 🖷 01495 357770 🖰 john.parsons@blaenau-gwent.gov.uk

Corporate Services: Mrs Angela O'Leary, Corporate Support Manager, Municipal Offices, Civic Centre, Ebbw Vale NP23 6XB ☎ 01495 355090 🖷 01495 357789 🖰 angela.oleary@blaenau-gwent.gov.uk

Customer Service: Mr Sean Scannell Corporate Communications, Marketing & Customer Access Manager, Municipal Offices, Civic Centre, Ebbw Vale NP23 6XB ☎ 01495 355113 🖰 sean.scannell@blaenau-gwent.gov.uk

Direct Labour: Mr John Parsons, Corporate Director of Environment & Regeneration, Municipal Offices, Civic Centre, Ebbw Vale NP23 6XB ☎ 01495 356088 🖷 01495 357770 🖰 john.parsons@blaenau-gwent.gov.uk

Economic Development: Mrs Frances Williams Service Manager - Regeneration, Central Depot, Barleyfield Industrial Estate, Brynmawr NP23 4YF ☎ 01495 355616 🖷 01495 312357 🖰 frances.williams@blaenau-gwent.gov.uk

Education: Mr Trevor Guy Interim Corporate Director of Education, Anvil Court, Church Street, Abertillery NP13 1DB

Education: Mr Byron Jones Learning Services Manager, Leisure Services & School Transformation, Anvil Court, Church Street, Abertillery NP13 1DB ☎ 01495 355608 🖷 01495 355900 🖰 byron.jones@blaenau-gwent.gov.uk

Electoral Registration: Mrs Angela O'Leary, Corporate Support Manager, Municipal Offices, Civic Centre, Ebbw Vale NP23 6XB ☎ 01495 355090 🖷 01495 357789 🖰 angela.oleary@blaenau-gwent.gov.uk

Emergency Planning: Mrs Deanne Griffiths Principal Civil Contingencies Officer, Municipal Offices, Civic Centre, Ebbw Vale NP23 6XB ☎ 01495 355568 🖷 01495 312357 🖰 deanne.griffiths@blaenau-gwent.gov.uk

Energy Management: Mr Peter Morgan Senior Energy Officer, Baldwin House, Victoria Park, Abertillery NP23 8ED ☎ 01495 355562 🖰 peter.morgan@blaenau-gwent.gov.uk

Environmental / Technical Services: Mr Alan Reed, Head of Public Services, Business Resource Centre, Tafarnaubach Industrial Estate, Tredegar NP22 3AA ☎ 01495 355612 🖷 01495 312357 🖰 alan.reed@blaenau-gwent.gov.uk

Environmental Health: Mr Dave Thompson Service Manager - Public Protection, Municipal Offices, Civic Centre, Ebbw Vale NP23 6XB ☎ 01495 355067 🖷 01495 355834 🖰 dave.thompson@blaenau-gwent.gov.uk

Estates, Property & Valuation: Mr Paul Miles, Valuation & Estates Officer, Municipal Offices, Civic Centre, Ebbw Vale NP23 6XB ☎ 01495 355030 🖷 01495 301255 🖰 paul.miles@blaenau-gwent.gov.uk

European Liaison: Mrs Frances Williams Service Manager - Regeneration, Central Depot, Barleyfield Industrial Estate, Brynmawr NP23 4YF ☎ 01495 355616 🖷 01495 312357 🖰 frances.williams@blaenau-gwent.gov.uk

Events Manager: Mr Peter Henry Venues & Events Officer, Beaufort Theatre, Beaufort Hill, Ebbw Vale NP23 5QQ ☎ 01495 354766 🖰 peter.henry@blaenau-gwent.gov.uk

Facilities: Mr Karl Hale Sports Facilities Manager, Leisure Services & School Transformation, Anvil Court, Church Street, Abertillery NP13 1DB ☎ 01495 355322 🖷 01495 355900 🖰 karl.hale@blaenau-gwent.gov.uk

Facilities: Mr John Parsons, Corporate Director of Environment & Regeneration, Municipal Offices, Civic Centre, Ebbw Vale NP23 6XB ☎ 01495 356088 🖷 01495 357770 🖰 john.parsons@blaenau-gwent.gov.uk

BLAENAU GWENT

Finance: Mr Dave McAuliffe Chief Finance Officer, Municipal Offices, Civic Centre, Ebbw Vale NP23 6XB ☎ 01495 355005 🖷 01495 355788 ✉ dave.mcauliffe@blaenau-gwent.gov.uk

Fleet Management: Mr Neil Hughes, Transport & Highways Principal Officer, Central Depot, Barleyfield Industrial Estate, Brynmawr NP23 4YF ☎ 01495 355629 🖷 01495 355699 ✉ neil.hughes@blaenau-gwent.gov.uk

Grounds Maintenance: Mr Karl Hale Sports Facilities Manager, Leisure Services & School Transformation, Anvil Court, Church Street, Abertillery NP13 1DB ☎ 01495 355322 🖷 01495 355900 ✉ karl.hale@blaenau-gwent.gov.uk

Health and Safety: Mr Jim Thomas Health & Safety Manager, Municipal Offices, Civic Centre, Ebbw Vale NP23 6XB ☎ 01495 355035 🖷 01495 355245 ✉ jim.thomas@blaenau-gwent.gov.uk

Highways: Mr Alan Reed, Head of Public Services, Business Resource Centre, Tafarnaubach Industrial Estate, Tredegar NP22 3AA ☎ 01495 355612 🖷 01495 312357 ✉ alan.reed@blaenau-gwent.gov.uk

Home Energy Conservation: Mr John Parsons, Corporate Director of Environment & Regeneration, Municipal Offices, Civic Centre, Ebbw Vale NP23 6XB ☎ 01495 356088 🖷 01495 357770 ✉ john.parsons@blaenau-gwent.gov.uk

Housing: Mr Dave Thompson Service Manager - Public Protection, Anvil Court, Abertillery NP13 1DB ☎ 01495 355067 🖷 01495 355834 ✉ dave.thompson@blaenau-gwent.gov.uk

Legal: Mrs Andrea Jones Head of Legal & Corp Compliance, Municipal Offices, Civic Centre, Ebbw Vale NP23 6XB ☎ 01495 355024 🖷 01495 301255 ✉ andrea.jones@blaenau-gwent.gov.uk

Leisure and Cultural Services: Mr Lynn Phillips, Assistant Director - Leisure Services & School Transformation, Leisure Services & School Transformation, Anvil Court, Church Street, Abertillery NP13 1DB ☎ 01495 355603 🖷 01495 355900 ✉ lynn.phillips@blaenau-gwent.gov.uk

Licensing: Mr Dave Thompson Service Manager - Public Protection, Municipal Offices, Civic Centre, Ebbw Vale NP23 6XB ☎ 01495 355067 🖷 01495 355834 ✉ dave.thompson@blaenau-gwent.gov.uk

Lifelong Learning: Ms Sylvia Lindoe Director of Education & Leisure, Central Depot, Barleyfield Industrial Estate, Brynmawr NP23 4YF ☎ 01495 355334 🖷 01495 355468 ✉ sylvia.lindoe@blaenau-gwent.gov.uk

Member Services: Mrs Ceri Edwards Brown Member Development Co-ordinator/Member Services, Municipal Offices, Civic Centre, Ebbw Vale NP23 6XB ☎ 01495 356139 ✉ ceri.edwardsbrown@blaenau-gwent.gov.uk

Partnerships: Ms Sharn Annett, Assistant Director - Department Business Management & Support (S.M.S.), Catering & Partnerships, Heart of the Valleys Children's Centre, High Street, Blaenau NP13 3BN ☎ 01495 354719 🖷 01495 291813 ✉ sharn.annett@blaenau-gwent.gov.uk

Personnel / HR: Ms Andrea Prosser Head of Organisational Development, Municipal Offices, Civic Centre, Ebbw Vale NP23 6XB ☎ 01495 355041 ✉ andrea.prosser@blaenau-gwent.gov.uk

Planning: Mr Steve Smith, Service Manager - Development, Blaina District Office, High Street, Blaina, Blaenau NP13 3XD ☎ 01495 355510 🖷 01495 355598 ✉ steve.smith@blaenau-gwent.gov.uk

Procurement: Mr Lee Williams, Corporate Procurement Manager, Municipal Offices, Civic Centre, Ebbw Vale NP23 6XB ☎ 01495 355686 🖷 01495 301255 ✉ lee.williams@blaenau-gwent.gov.uk

Public Libraries: Mr Lynn Phillips, Assistant Director - Leisure Services & School Transformation, Leisure Services & School Transformation, Anvil Court, Church Street, Abertillery NP13 1DB ☎ 01495 355603 🖷 01495 355900 ✉ lynn.phillips@blaenau-gwent.gov.uk

Recycling & Waste Minimisation: Mr Matthew Perry Service Manager - Community Services, Central Depot, Barleyfield Industrial Estate, Brynmawr NP23 4YF ☎ 01495 355955 🖷 01495 312357 ✉ matthew.perry@blaenau-gwent.gov.uk

Regeneration: Mr Alan Reed, Head of Public Services, Business Resource Centre, Tafarnaubach Industrial Estate, Tredegar NP22 3AA ☎ 01495 355612 🖷 01495 312357 ✉ alan.reed@blaenau-gwent.gov.uk

Social Services: Ms Liz Majer, Corporate Director of Social Services, Anvil Court, Church Street, Abertillery NP13 1DB ☎ 01495 355261 🖷 01495 355285 ✉ liz.majer@blaenau-gwent.gov.uk

Social Services (Adult): Mr Damien McCann Head of Adult Services, Anvil Court, Church Street, Abertillery NP13 1DB ☎ 01495 355383 🖷 01495 355285 ✉ damien.mccann@blaenau-gwent.gov.uk

Social Services (Children): Mrs Tanya Evans Head of Children's Services, Anvil Court, Church Street, Abertillery NP13 1DB ☎ 01495 356067 🖷 01495 355285 ✉ tanya.evans@blaenau-gwent.gov.uk

Staff Training: Mr Simon Green, Organisational Development Officer, Municipal Offices, Civic Centre, Ebbw Vale NP23 6XB ☎ 01495 355040 🖷 01495 355787 ✉ simon.green@blaenau-gwent.gov.uk

Street Scene: Mr Matthew Perry Service Manager - Community Services, Central Depot, Barleyfield Industrial Estate, Brynmawr NP23 4YF ☎ 01495 355955 🖷 01495 312357 ✉ matthew.perry@blaenau-gwent.gov.uk

Tourism: Mr Lynn Phillips, Assistant Director - Leisure Services & School Transformation, Leisure Services & School Transformation, Anvil Court, Church Street, Abertillery NP13 1DB ☎ 01495 355603 🖷 01495 355900 ✉ lynn.phillips@blaenau-gwent.gov.uk

Town Centre: Ms Beth Cartwright Town Centre Manager, Municipal Offices, Civic Centre, Ebbw Vale NP23 6XB ☎ 01495 355539

Transport: Mr John Parsons, Corporate Director of Environment & Regeneration, Central Depot, Barleyfield Industrial Estate, Brynmawr NP23 4YF ☎ 01495 356088 🖷 01495 357770 ✉ john.parsons@blaenau-gwent.gov.uk

Transport Planner: Ms Sharn Annett, Assistant Director - Department Business Management & Support (S.M.S.), Catering & Partnerships, Heart of the Valleys Children's Centre, High Street, Blaenau NP13 3BN ☎ 01495 354719 🖷 01495 291813 ✉ sharn.annett@blaenau-gwent.gov.uk

Waste Collection and Disposal: Mr Matthew Perry Service Manager - Community Services, Central Depot, Barleyfield Industrial Estate, Brynmawr NP23 4YF ☎ 01495 355955 🖷 01495 312357 ✉ matthew.perry@blaenau-gwent.gov.uk

Waste Management: Mr Matthew Perry Service Manager - Community Services, Central Depot, Barleyfield Industrial Estate, Brynmawr NP23 4YF ☎ 01495 355955 🖷 01495 312357 ✉ matthew.perry@blaenau-gwent.gov.uk

Children's Play Areas: Mr Alun Watkins Team Leader - Grounds Maintenance & Bereavement Services, Central Depot, Barleyfield Industrial Estate, Brynmawr NP23 4YF ☎ 01495 355603 🖷 01495 355675 ✉ alun.watkins@blaenau-gwent.gov.uk

COUNCILLORS

***Mayor* Bevan**, Derrick (LAB - Cwm)
derrick.bevan@blaenau-gwent.gov.uk

***Deputy Mayor* Willis**, Bernard (LAB - Tredegar Central & West)
bernard.willis@blaenau-gwent.gov.uk

Baldwin, Peter (LAB - Nantyglo)
peter.baldwin@blaenau-gwent.gov.uk

Bartlett, Graham (LAB - Cwmtillery)
graham.bartlett@blaenau-gwent.gov.uk

Bartlett, Mike (LAB - Llanhilleth)
mike.bartlett@blaenau-gwent.gov.uk

Bender, Keren (LAB - Cwm)
keren.bender@blaenau-gwent.gov.uk

Brown, Kevin (IND - Brynmawr)
kevin.brown@blaenau-gwent.gov.uk

Chaplin, Keith (LAB - Abertillery)
keith.haplin@blaenau-gwent.gov.uk

Clements, Brian (LAB - Ebbw Vale South)
brian.clements@blaenau-gwent.gov.uk

Collier, Garth (IND - Blaina)
garth.collier@blaenau-gwent.gov.uk

Coughlin, Derek (LAB - Ebbw Vale North)
derek.coughlin@blaenau-gwent.gov.uk

Cross, Malcolm (LAB - Sirhowy)
malcolm.cross@blaenau-gwent.gov.uk

Dally, Malcolm (LAB - Nantyglo)
malcolmdally1@blaenau-gwent.gov.uk

Daniels, Nigel (INDNA - Abertillery)
nigel.daniels@blaenau-gwent.gov.uk

Hancock, Denzil (IND - Six Bells)
denzil.hancock@blaenau-gwent.gov.uk

Hayden, Keith (LAB - Georgetown)
keith.hayden@blaenau-gwent.gov.uk

Hobbs, Anita (LAB - Tredegar Central & West)
nita.hobbs@blaenau-gwent.gov.uk

Holland, Mark (LAB - Six Bells)
mark.holland@blaenau-gwent.gov.uk

Hopkins, John (IND - Brynmawr)
john.hopkins@blaenau-gwent.gov.uk

Jones, Richard (LAB - Abertillery)
richard.jones@blaenau-gwent.gov.uk

Lewis, Ann (LAB - Ebbw Vale North)
ann.lewis@blaenau-gwent.gov.uk

Lewis, Mostyn (LAB - Ebbw Vale South)
mostyn.lewis@blaenau-gwent.gov.uk

Mason, John (IND - Nantyglo)
john.mason@blaenau-gwent.gov.uk

McCarthy, Hedley (LAB - Llanhilleth)
hedley.mccarthy@blaenau-gwent.gov.uk

McLlwee, Jim (LAB - Llanhilleth)
jim.mcillwee@blaenau-gwent.gov.uk

Meredith, Clive (IND - Badminton)
clive.meredith@blaenau-gwent.gov.uk

Morgan, Jennifer (LAB - Ebbw Vale North)
jennifer.morgan@blaenau-gwent.gov.uk

Morgan, John (LAB - Georgetown)
john.morgan@blaenau-gwent.gov.uk

Owens, Dennis (LAB - Sirhowy)
dennis.owens@blaenau-gwent.gov.uk

Pagett, Bob (LAB - Blaina)
bob.pagett@blaenau-gwent.gov.uk

Rowberry, Diane (LAB - Sirhowy)
diane.rowberry@blaenau-gwent.gov.uk

Scully, Brian (LAB - Badminton)
brian.scully@blaenau-gwent.gov.uk

Sharrem, Tim (LAB - Cwntillery)
tim.sharrem@blaenau-gwent.gov.uk

Sutton, Barrie (LAB - Brynmawr)
barrie.sutton@blaenau-gwent.gov.uk

Thomas, Stephen (LAB - Tredegar Central & West)
stephen.thomas@blaenau-gwent.gov.uk

Thomas, Godfrey (IND - Beaufort)
godfrey.thomas@blaenua-gwent.gov.uk

Tidey, Christine (LAB - Cwmtillery)
christine.tidey@blaenau-gwent.gov.uk

Trollope, Haydn (LAB - Tredegar Central & West)
hayden.trollope@blaenau-gwent.gov.uk

White, David (IND - Beaufort)
david.wilkshire@blaenau-gwent.gov.uk

Wilkshire, David (LAB - Rassau)
david.wilkshire@blaenau-gwent.gov.uk

Williams, John (IND - Rassau)
john.williams@blaenau-gwent.gov.uk

Winnett, Lisa (LAB - Blaina)
lisa.winnett@blaenau-gwent.gov.uk

BLAENAU GWENT

POLITICAL COMPOSITION
LAB: 32, IND: 9, INDNA: 1

Bolsover D

Bolsover District Council, The Arc, High Street, Clowne, Staveley S43 4JY
☎ 01246 242424 🖷 01246 242423 🖱 enquiries@bolsover.gov.uk
🖳 www.bolsover.gov.uk

FACTS AND FIGURES
Parliamentary Constituencies: Bolsover
EU Constituencies: East Midlands
Election Frequency: Elections are of whole council

PRINCIPAL OFFICERS

Chief Executive: Mr Wes Lumley, Joint Chief Executive Officer, The Arc, High Street, Clowne, Staveley S43 4JY ☎ 01246 217155 🖱 wes.lumley@bolsover.gov.uk

Senior Management: Mr Paul Hackett Joint Executive Director - Transformation, The Arc, High Street, Clowne, Staveley S43 4JY ☎ 01246 217543 🖱 paul.hackett@ne-derbyshire.gov.uk

Senior Management: Mr Bryan Mason Joint Executive Director - Operations, The Arc, High Street, Clowne, Staveley S43 4JY ☎ 01246 242431 🖱 bryan.mason@ne-derbyshire.gov.uk

Architect, Building / Property Services: Mr Grant Galloway, Assistant Director of Property & Estates, The Arc, High Street, Clowne, Staveley S43 4JY ☎ 01246 242284 🖷 01246 242423 🖱 grant.galloway@bolsover.gov.uk

Architect, Building / Property Services: Mr Tim Robinson, Principal Building Surveyor, The Arc, High Street, Clowne, Staveley S43 4JY ☎ 01246 242239 🖷 01246 242423 🖱 tim.robinson@bolsover.gov.uk

Building Control: Mr Malcolm Clinton Business Manager, Unit 2, Dunston Technology Park, Millennium Way, Dunston Road, Chesterfield S41 8ND ☎ 01246 345817; 01246 354900 🖱 malcolm.clinton@ne-derbyshire.gov.uk; malcolm.clinton@bcnconsultancy.co.uk

PR / Communications: Mr Scott Chambers, Communications, Marketing & Design Manager, The Arc, High Street, Clowne, Staveley S43 4JY ☎ 01246 242323 🖷 01246 242423 🖱 scott.chambers@bolsover.gov.uk

Community Planning: Mrs Pam Brown, Partnership Co-ordinator, The Arc, High Street, Clowne, Staveley S43 4JY ☎ 01246 242499 🖷 01246 242423 🖱 pam.brown@bolsover.gov.uk

Community Planning: Mr Wes Lumley, Joint Chief Executive Officer, The Arc, High Street, Clowne, Staveley S43 4JY ☎ 01246 217155 🖱 wes.lumley@bolsover.gov.uk

Community Safety: Mr Peter Campbell, Assistant Director of Community Safety & Head of Housing, The Arc, High Street, Clowne, Staveley S43 4JY ☎ 01246 593038 🖷 01246 242423 🖱 peter.campbell@bolsover.gov.uk

Computer Management: Mr Nick Blaney Joint IT Services Manager, The Arc, High Street, Clowne, Staveley S43 4JY ☎ 01246 217103; 01246 217103; 01246 717097 🖱 nick.blaney@ne-derbyshire.gov.uk

Customer Service: Mrs Jane Foley, Joint Assistant Director - Customer Service & Improvement, The Arc, High Street, Clowne, Staveley S43 4JY ☎ 01246 242343; 01246 217029 🖷 01246 242423; 01246 217442 🖱 jane.foley@bolsover.gov.uk

Economic Development: Mrs Allison Westray-Chapman Joint Assistant Director - Economic Growth, The Arc, High Street, Clowne, Staveley S43 4JY ☎ 01246 217199 🖱 allison.westray-chapman@ne-derbyshire.gov.uk

Electoral Registration: Miss Kath Whittingham Head of Elections, The Arc, High Street, Clowne, Staveley S43 4JY ☎ 🖱 kath.whittingham@ne-derbyshire.gov.uk; kath.whittingham@bolsover.gov.uk

Emergency Planning: Mr Paul Hackett Joint Executive Director - Transformation, The Arc, High Street, Clowne, Staveley S43 4JY ☎ 01246 217543 🖱 paul.hackett@ne-derbyshire.gov.uk

Energy Management: Mr Edward Owen Energy Officer, The Arc, High Street, Clowne, Staveley S43 4JY ☎ 01246 217847 🖱 edward.owen@ne-derbyshire.gov.uk

Environmental / Technical Services: Mr James Arnold Joint Assistant Director - Planning & Environmental Health, The Arc, High Street, Clowne, Staveley S43 4JY ☎ 01246 217436 🖱 james.arnold@bolsover.gov.uk

Environmental Health: Ms Sharon Gillott Environmental Health Commercial Manager, District Council Offices, 2013 Mill Lane, Wingerworth, Chesterfield S42 6NG ☎ 01246 237848 🖷 01246 242423 🖱 sharon.gillott@bolsover.gov.uk; sharon.gillott@ne-derbyshire.gov.uk

Estates, Property & Valuation: Mr Grant Galloway, Assistant Director of Property & Estates, The Arc, High Street, Clowne, Staveley S43 4JY ☎ 01246 242284 🖷 01246 242423 🖱 grant.galloway@bolsover.gov.uk

European Liaison: Mr Wes Lumley, Joint Chief Executive Officer, The Arc, High Street, Clowne, Staveley S43 4JY ☎ 01246 217155 🖱 wes.lumley@bolsover.gov.uk

Facilities: Mr Tim Robinson, Principal Building Surveyor, The Arc, High Street, Clowne, Staveley S43 4JY ☎ 01246 242239 🖷 01246 242423 🖱 tim.robinson@bolsover.gov.uk

Finance: Ms Dawn Clarke Joint Assistant Director - Finance, Revenues & Benefits, The Arc, High Street, Clowne, Staveley S43 4JY ☎ 01246 217658 🖱 dawn.clarke@ne-derbyshire.gov.uk

Fleet Management: Ms Pam Burrows Joint Fleet & Transport Manager, Riverside Depot, Doe Lea, Bolsover S44 5NY ☎ 01246 593043 🖱 pam.burrows@bolsover.gov.uk

Grounds Maintenance: Mr Steve Jowett Joint Street Services Manager, Riverside Depot, Doe Lea, Bolsover S44 5NY ☎ 01246 593044 🖷 01246 242423 ✉ steve.jowett@ne-derbyshire.gov.uk

Health and Safety: Mr Mark Spotswood Health & Safety Officer, Riverside Depot, Doe Lea, Bolsover S44 5NY ☎ 01246 242403 ✉ mark.spotswood@bolsover.gov.uk

Housing: Mr Peter Campbell, Assistant Director of Community Safety & Head of Housing, The Arc, High Street, Clowne, Staveley S43 4JY ☎ 01246 593038 🖷 01246 242423 ✉ peter.campbell@bolsover.gov.uk

Housing Maintenance: Mr Peter Campbell, Assistant Director of Community Safety & Head of Housing, The Arc, High Street, Clowne, Staveley S43 4JY ☎ 01246 593038 🖷 01246 242423 ✉ peter.campbell@bolsover.gov.uk

Legal: Mrs Sarah Sternberg Joint Assistant Director - Governance, The Arc, High Street, Clowne, Staveley S43 4JY ☎ 01246 242414 🖷 01246 242423 ✉ sarah.sternberg@bolsover.gov.uk

Leisure and Cultural Services: Mr Lee Hickin Joint Assistant Director - Leisure, The Arc, High Street, Clowne, Staveley S43 4JY ☎ 01246 217218 ✉ lee.hickin@bolsover.gov.uk

Licensing: Mr John Chambers, Licensing Co-ordinator, 2013 Mill Lane, Wingerworth, , Chesterfield S42 6NG ☎ 01246 217216 🖷 01246 217447 ✉ john.chambers@ne-derbyshire.gov.uk

Member Services: Mr Matthew Kane, Democratic Services Manager, The Arc, High Street, Clowne, Staveley S43 4JY ☎ 01246 242505 🖷 01246 242423 ✉ matthew.kane@ne-derbyshire.gov.uk

Partnerships: Mrs Pam Brown, Partnership Co-ordinator, The Arc, High Street, Clowne, Staveley S43 4JY ☎ 01246 242499 🖷 01246 242423 ✉ pam.brown@bolsover.gov.uk

Planning: Mr James Arnold Joint Assistant Director - Planning & Environmental Health, The Arc, High Street, Clowne, Staveley S43 4JY ☎ 01246 217436 ✉ james.arnold@bolsover.gov.uk

Recycling & Waste Minimisation: Mr Steve Brunt Joint Assistant Director - Street Scene, Riverside Depot, Doe Lea, Bolsover S44 5NY ☎ 01246 593044 🖷 01246 242423 ✉ steve.brunt@bolsover.gov.uk

Street Scene: Mr Steve Brunt Joint Assistant Director - Street Scene, Riverside Depot, Doe Lea, Bolsover S44 5NY ☎ 01246 593044 🖷 01246 242423 ✉ steve.brunt@bolsover.gov.uk

Waste Collection and Disposal: Mr Steve Brunt Joint Assistant Director - Street Scene, Riverside Depot, Doe Lea, Bolsover S44 5NY ☎ 01246 593044 🖷 01246 242423 ✉ steve.brunt@bolsover.gov.uk

Waste Management: Mr Steve Brunt Joint Assistant Director - Street Scene, Riverside Depot, Doe Lea, Bolsover S44 5NY ☎ 01246 593044 🖷 01246 242423 ✉ steve.brunt@bolsover.gov.uk

COUNCILLORS

***Chair* Walker**, Kenneth (LAB - Shirebrook Langwith)
ken.walker@bolsover.gov.uk

***Vice-Chair* Turner**, Rita (LAB - Elmton with Creswell)
rita.turner@bolsover.gov.uk

***Leader of the Council* Syrett**, Ann (LAB - Pleasley)
ann.syrett@bolsover.gov.uk

***Deputy Leader of the Council* Dooley**, Mary (LAB - Pinxton)
mary.dooley@bolsover.gov.uk

Alexander, Tom (LAB - Pinxton)
tom.alexander@bolsover.gov.uk

Anderson, Andrew (LAB - Shirebrook South East)
andrew@shirebrooktowncouncil.co.uk

Barnes, Paul (LAB - South Normanton West)
paul.barnes@bolsover.gov.uk

Bennett, Toni (LAB - Bolsover South)
toni.bennet@bolsover.gov.uk

Bowler, Rosemary (LAB - Bolsover West)
rose.bowler@bolsover.gov.uk

Bowmer, Pauline (LAB - Pleasley)
pauline.bowmer@bolsover.gov.uk

Bulolock, Dextor (IND - Blackwell)
dexter.bullock@bolsover.gov.uk

Buxton, Gwyneth (LAB - Clowne North)
gwyneth.buston@bolsover.gov.uk

Cannon, Tracey (LAB - South Normanton East)
tracey.cannon@bolsover.gov.uk

Clifton, James (IND - Elmton with Creswell)
jim.clifton@bolsover.gov.uk

Connerton, Terry (LAB - Clowne North)
terry.connerton@bolsover.gov.uk

Cooper, Paul (LAB - Bolsover North West)
paul.cooper@bolsover.gov.uk

Crane, Malcolm (LAB - Scarcliffe)
malc.crane@bolsover.gov.uk

Dixey, Mark (LAB - Bolsover West)
mark.dixey@bolsover.gov.uk

Fritchley, Stephen (LAB - Shirebrook North West)
steve.fritchley@bolsover.gov.uk

Gilmour, Hilary (LAB - Barlborough)
hilary.gilmour@bolsover.gov.uk

Hall, Eric (LAB - Bolsover South)
eric.hall@bolsover.gov.uk

Heffer, Ray (IND - Tibshelf)
ray.heffer@bolsover.gov.uk

Joesbury, Andrew (IND - South Normanton East)
andrew.joesbury@bolsover.gov.uk

McGregor, Duncan (LAB - Elmton with Creswell)
duncan.mcgregor@bolsover.gov.uk

Moesby, Clive (LAB - Blackwell)
clive-moesby@bolsover.gov.uk

Munro, Tom (LAB - Whitwell)
tom.munro@bolsover.gov.uk

Murray-Carr, Brian (LAB - Shirebrook East)
brian.murray-carr@bolsover.gov.uk

BOLSOVER

Peake, Sandra (LAB - Shirebrook South West)
sandra.peake@bolsover.gov.uk

Reid, Karl (LAB - Clowne South)
karl.reid@bolsover.gov.uk

Smith, Jim (LAB - Clowne South)
jim.smith@bolsover.gov.ukl

Smith, Paul (LAB - South Normanton West)
phil.smith@bolsover.gov.uk

Statter, Sue (LAB - Bolsover North West)
sue.statter@bolsover.gov.uk

Stevenson, Emma (LAB - South Normanton West)
emma.stevenson@bolsover.gov.uk

Watson, Deborah (IND - Tibshelf)
deborah.watson@bolsover.gov.uk

Watson, Brian (LAB - Barlborough)
brian.watson@bolsover.gov.uk

Wilson, Jen (LAB - Scarcliffe)
jennifer.wilson@bolsover.gov.uk

POLITICAL COMPOSITION
LAB: 31, IND: 5

COMMITTEE CHAIRS
Licensing: Mr Kenneth Walker

Bolton M

Bolton Metropolitan Borough Council, Town Hall, Bolton BL1 1RU
☎ 01204 333333 🖷 01204 331042 ✉ firstname.surname@bolton.gov.uk
💻 www.bolton.gov.uk

FACTS AND FIGURES
Parliamentary Constituencies: Bolton North East, Bolton South East, Bolton West
EU Constituencies: North West
Election Frequency: Elections are by thirds

PRINCIPAL OFFICERS
Chief Executive: Mr Paul Najsarek Chief Executive, Town Hall, Bolton BL1 1RU ✉ paul.najsarek@bolton.gov.uk

Deputy Chief Executive: Mrs Margaret Asquith, Deputy Chief Executive, Town Hall, Bolton BL1 1RU ☎ 01204 332010 🖷 01204 332228 ✉ margaret.asquith@bolton.gov.uk

Senior Management: Mr Malcolm Cox, Director - Environmental Services, 3rd Floor, Town Hall, Bolton BL1 1RU ☎ 01204 336711 ✉ malcolm.cox@bolton.gov.uk

Senior Management: Mr Keith Davies, Director - Development & Regeneration, 3rd Floor, Town Hall, Bolton BL1 1RU ☎ 01204 334002 🖷 ; 01204 362018 ✉ keith.davies@bolton.gov.uk

Senior Management: Ms Wendy Meredith Director - Public Health, 1st Floor, Town Hall, Bolton BL1 1RU ✉ wendy.meredith@bolton.gov.uk

Architect, Building / Property Services: Mr Stephen Young Assistant Director - Development & Regeneration Services, 3rd Floor, Town Hall, Bolton BL1 1RU ☎ 01204 336490 🖷 01204 336709 ✉ stephen.young@bolton.gov.uk

Best Value: Ms Lynne Ridsdale Assistant Director - People, Policy & Transformation, 2nd Floor, Town Hall, Bolton BL1 1RU ☎ 01204 331201 ✉ lynne.ridsdale@bolton.gov.uk

Building Control: Mr Keith Davies, Director - Development & Regeneration, 3rd Floor, Town Hall, Bolton BL1 1RU ☎ 01204 334002 🖷 ; 01204 362018 ✉ keith.davies@bolton.gov.uk

Catering Services: Ms Donna Ball Assistant Director - Environmental Services, 3rd Floor, Town Hall, Bolton BL1 1RU ☎ 01204 336713 🖷 01204 336889 ✉ donna.ball@bolton.gov.uk

Children / Youth Services: Mr John Liversey Acting Director - Children & Adult Services, 1st Floor, Town Hall, Bolton BL1 1RU ☎ 01204 332010 ✉ john.liversey@bolton.gov.uk

Civil Registration: Mrs Helen Gorman Borough Solicitor, 2nd Floor, Town Hall, Bolton BL1 1RU ☎ 01204 331314 ✉ helen.gorman@bolton.gov.uk

PR / Communications: Ms Lynne Ridsdale Assistant Director - People, Policy & Transformation, 2nd Floor, Town Hall, Bolton BL1 1RU ☎ 01204 331201 ✉ lynne.ridsdale@bolton.gov.uk

Community Safety: Ms Sarah Schofield Assistant Director - Neighbourhood & Regulatory Services, 3rd Floor, Town Hall, Bolton BL1 1RU ☎ 01204 336718 ✉ sarah.schofield@bolton.gov.uk

Computer Management: Ms Sue Johnson Assistant Director - Financial Services & Corporate ICT, 2nd Floor, Town Hall, Bolton BL1 1RU ☎ 01204 331504 ✉ sue.johnson@bolton.gov.uk

Consumer Protection and Trading Standards: Ms Sarah Schofield Assistant Director - Neighbourhood & Regulatory Services, 3rd Floor, Town Hall, Bolton BL1 1RU ☎ 01204 336718 ✉ sarah.schofield@bolton.gov.uk

Direct Labour: Ms Donna Ball Assistant Director - Environmental Services, 3rd Floor, Town Hall, Bolton BL1 1RU ☎ 01204 336713 🖷 01204 336889 ✉ donna.ball@bolton.gov.uk

Economic Development: Mr Keith Davies, Director - Development & Regeneration, 3rd Floor, Town Hall, Bolton BL1 1RU ☎ 01204 334002 🖷 ; 01204 362018 ✉ keith.davies@bolton.gov.uk

Education: Mr John Liversey Acting Director - Children & Adult Services, 1st Floor, Town Hall, Bolton BL1 1RU ☎ 01204 332010 ✉ john.liversey@bolton.gov.uk

E-Government: Mrs Helen Gorman Borough Solicitor, 2nd Floor, Town Hall, Bolton BL1 1RU ☎ 01204 331314 ✉ helen.gorman@bolton.gov.uk

Electoral Registration: Mrs Helen Gorman Borough Solicitor, Town Hall, Bolton BL1 1RU ☎ 01204 331314 ✉ helen.gorman@bolton.gov.uk

Emergency Planning: Mr Malcolm Cox, Director - Environmental Services, 3rd Floor, Town Hall, Bolton BL1 1RU ☎ 01204 336711 ✉ malcolm.cox@bolton.gov.uk

Energy Management: Ms Mandy Lee Interim Assistant Director - Corporate Policy, 3rd Floor, Town Hall, Bolton BL1 1RU ✉ mandy.lee@bolton.gov.uk

Environmental / Technical Services: Mr Malcolm Cox, Director - Environmental Services, 3rd Floor, Town Hall, Bolton BL1 1RU ☎ 01204 336711 ✉ malcolm.cox@bolton.gov.uk

Environmental Health: Ms Sarah Schofield Assistant Director - Neighbourhood & Regulatory Services, 3rd Floor, Town Hall, Bolton BL1 1RU ☎ 01204 336718 ✉ sarah.schofield@bolton.gov.uk

Estates, Property & Valuation: Ms Mandy Lee Interim Assistant Director - Corporate Policy, 3rd Floor, Town Hall, Bolton BL1 1RU ✉ mandy.lee@bolton.gov.uk

Events Manager: Mrs Nicola Littlewood Marketing Manager, 2nd Floor, Town Hall, Bolton BL1 1RU ☎ 01204 334072 ✉ nicola.littlewood@bolton.gov.uk

Facilities: Ms Mandy Lee Interim Assistant Director - Corporate Policy, 3rd Floor, Town Hall, Bolton BL1 1RU ✉ mandy.lee@bolton.gov.uk

Finance: Ms Sue Johnson Assistant Director - Financial Services & Corporate ICT, 2nd Floor, Town Hall, Bolton BL1 1RU ☎ 01204 331504 ✉ sue.johnson@bolton.gov.uk

Fleet Management: Ms Donna Ball Assistant Director - Environmental Services, 3rd Floor, Town Hall, Bolton BL1 1RU ☎ 01204 336713 🖷 01204 336889 ✉ donna.ball@bolton.gov.uk

Grounds Maintenance: Ms Sarah Schofield Assistant Director - Neighbourhood & Regulatory Services, 3rd Floor, Town Hall, Bolton BL1 1RU ☎ 01204 336718 ✉ sarah.schofield@bolton.gov.uk

Health and Safety: Mr Shaun Wheeler Head of Human Resources, 2nd Floor, Town Hall, Bolton BL1 1RU ☎ 01204 331209 ✉ shaun.wheeler@bolton.gov.uk

Highways: Mr Stephen Young Assistant Director - Development & Regeneration Services, 3rd Floor, Town Hall, Bolton BL1 1RU ☎ 01204 336490 🖷 01204 336709 ✉ stephen.young@bolton.gov.uk

Housing: Mr Keith Davies, Director - Development & Regeneration, 3rd Floor, Town Hall, Bolton BL1 1RU ☎ 01204 334002 🖷 ; 01204 362018 ✉ keith.davies@bolton.gov.uk

Legal: Mrs Helen Gorman Borough Solicitor, 2nd Floor, Town Hall, Bolton BL1 1RU ☎ 01204 331314 ✉ helen.gorman@bolton.gov.uk

Leisure and Cultural Services: Mr Keith Davies, Director - Development & Regeneration, 3rd Floor, Town Hall, Bolton BL1 1RU ☎ 01204 334002 🖷 01204 362018 ✉ keith.davies@bolton.gov.uk

Licensing: Ms Sarah Schofield Assistant Director - Neighbourhood & Regulatory Services, 3rd Floor, Town Hall, Bolton BL1 1RU ☎ 01204 336718 ✉ sarah.schofield@bolton.gov.uk

Lifelong Learning: Mr Phil Green Head of Economic Strategy, 3rd Floor, Town Hall, Bolton BL1 1RU ☎ 01204 334187 ✉ phil.green@bolton.gov.uk

Lighting: Mr Stephen Young Assistant Director - Development & Regeneration Services, 3rd Floor, Town Hall, Bolton BL1 1RU ☎ 01204 336490 🖷 01204 336709 ✉ stephen.young@bolton.gov.uk

Lottery Funding, Charity and Voluntary: Ms Lynne Ridsdale Assistant Director - People, Policy & Transformation, 2nd Floor, Town Hall, Bolton BL1 1RU ☎ 01204 331201 ✉ lynne.ridsdale@bolton.gov.uk

Member Services: Mrs Helen Gorman Borough Solicitor, 2nd Floor, Town Hall, Bolton BL1 1RU ☎ 01204 331314 ✉ helen.gorman@bolton.gov.uk

Parking: Mr Stephen Young Assistant Director - Development & Regeneration Services, 3rd Floor, Town Hall, Bolton BL1 1RU ☎ 01204 336490 🖷 01204 336709 ✉ stephen.young@bolton.gov.uk

Partnerships: Ms Lynne Ridsdale Assistant Director - People, Policy & Transformation, 2nd Floor, Town Hall, Bolton BL1 1RU ☎ 01204 331201 ✉ lynne.ridsdale@bolton.gov.uk

Personnel / HR: Ms Lynne Ridsdale Assistant Director - People, Policy & Transformation, 2nd Floor, Town Hall, Bolton BL1 1RU ☎ 01204 331201 ✉ lynne.ridsdale@bolton.gov.uk

Planning: Mr John Berry Head of Development Management, 3rd Floor, Town Hall, Bolton BL1 1RU ☎ 01204 336004 ✉ john.berry@bolton.gov.uk

Procurement: Ms Sue Johnson Assistant Director - Financial Services & Corporate ICT, 2nd Floor, Town Hall, Bolton BL1 1RU ☎ 01204 331504 ✉ sue.johnson@bolton.gov.uk

Public Libraries: Mrs Julie Spencer, Head of Libraries, Museums & Archives, Central Library, Le Mans Crescent, Bolton BL1 1SA ☎ 01204 332276 ✉ julie.spencer@bolton.gov.uk

Recycling & Waste Minimisation: Ms Donna Ball Assistant Director - Environmental Services, 3rd Floor, Town Hall, Bolton BL1 1RU ☎ 01204 336713 🖷 01204 336889 ✉ donna.ball@bolton.gov.uk

Regeneration: Mr Keith Davies, Director - Development & Regeneration, 3rd Floor, Town Hall, Bolton BL1 1RU ☎ 01204 334002 🖷 ; 01204 362018 ✉ keith.davies@bolton.gov.uk

Road Safety: Mr Stephen Young Assistant Director - Development & Regeneration Services, 3rd Floor, Town Hall, Bolton BL1 1RU ☎ 01204 336490 🖷 01204 336709 ✉ stephen.young@bolton.gov.uk

Social Services: Mr John Liversey Acting Director - Children & Adult Services, 1st Floor, Town Hall, Bolton BL1 1RU ☎ 01204 332010 ✉ john.liversey@bolton.gov.uk

Social Services (Children): Mr John Daly Assistant Director - Staying Safe, Town Hall, Bolton BL1 1RU ☎ 01204 332130 🖷 01204 337288 ✉ john.daly@bolton.gov.uk

BOLTON

Public Health: Ms Wendy Meredith Director - Public Health, Town Hall, Bolton BL1 1RU 🖱 wendy.meredith@bolton.gov.uk

Staff Training: Ms Lynne Ridsdale Assistant Director - People, Policy & Transformation, 2nd Floor, Town Hall, Bolton BL1 1RU ☎ 01204 331201 🖱 lynne.ridsdale@bolton.gov.uk

Street Scene: Ms Sarah Schofield Assistant Director - Neighbourhood & Regulatory Services, 3rd Floor, Town Hall, Bolton BL1 1RU ☎ 01204 336718 🖱 sarah.schofield@bolton.gov.uk

Sustainable Communities: Ms Lynne Ridsdale Assistant Director - People, Policy & Transformation, 2nd Floor, Town Hall, Bolton BL1 1RU ☎ 01204 331201 🖱 lynne.ridsdale@bolton.gov.uk

Sustainable Development: Mr Stephen Young Assistant Director - Development & Regeneration Services, 3rd Floor, Town Hall, Bolton BL1 1RU ☎ 01204 336490 🖷 01204 336709 🖱 stephen.young@bolton.gov.uk

Tourism: Mr Keith Davies, Director - Development & Regeneration, 3rd Floor, Town Hall, Bolton BL1 1RU ☎ 01204 334002 🖷 01204 362018 🖱 keith.davies@bolton.gov.uk

Town Centre: Ms Kathryn Carr Head of Strategic Development, 3rd Floor, Town Hall, Bolton BL1 1RU ☎ 01204 336236 🖷 01204 336236 🖱 kathryn.carr@bolton.gov.uk

Traffic Management: Mr Stephen Young Assistant Director - Development & Regeneration Services, The Wellsprings, Civic Centre, Bolton BL1 1US ☎ 01204 336490 🖷 01204 336709 🖱 stephen.young@bolton.gov.uk

Transport Planner: Mr Stephen Young Assistant Director - Development & Regeneration Services, 3rd Floor, Town Hall, Bolton BL1 1RU ☎ 01204 336490 🖷 01204 336709 🖱 stephen.young@bolton.gov.uk

Total Place: Mr Paul Najsarek Chief Executive, Town Hall, Bolton BL1 1RU 🖱 paul.najsarek@bolton.gov.uk

Waste Collection and Disposal: Ms Donna Ball Assistant Director - Environmental Services, 3rd Floor, Town Hall, Bolton BL1 1RU ☎ 01204 336713 🖷 01204 336889 🖱 donna.ball@bolton.gov.uk

Waste Management: Ms Donna Ball Assistant Director - Environmental Services, 3rd Floor, Town Hall, Bolton BL1 1RU ☎ 01204 336713 🖷 01204 336889 🖱 donna.ball@bolton.gov.uk

Children's Play Areas: Ms Sarah Schofield Assistant Director - Neighbourhood & Regulatory Services, 3rd Floor, Town Hall, Bolton BL1 1RU ☎ 01204 336718 🖱 sarah.schofield@bolton.gov.uk

COUNCILLORS

***Mayor* Swarbrick**, Carole (LD - Smithills)
carole.swarbrick@bolton.gov.uk

***Deputy Mayor* Donaghy**, Martin (LAB - Tonge with the Haulgh)
martin.donaghy@bolton.gov.uk

***Leader of the Council* Morris**, Cliff (LAB - Halliwell)
cliff.morris@bolton.gov.uk

***Deputy Leader of the Council* Thomas**, Linda (LAB - Halliwell)
linda.thomas@bolton.gov.uk

***Group Leader* Greenhalgh**, David (CON - Bromley Cross)
david.greenhalgh@bolton.gov.uk

***Group Leader* Hayes**, Roger (LD - Smithills)
roger.hayes@bolton.gov.uk

***Group Leader* Parkinson**, Diane (UKIP - Hulton)
diane.parkinson@bolton.gov.uk

Adia, Ebrahim (LAB - Rumworth)
ebrahim.adia@bolton.gov.uk

Allen, Robert (CON - Heaton & Lostock)
robert.allen@bolton.gov.uk

Ayub, Mohammed (LAB - Great Lever)
mohammed.ayub@bolton.gov.uk

Bashir-Ismail, Sufrana (LAB - Crompton)
sufrana.bashir-ismail@bolton.gov.uk

Burrows, Derek (LAB - Kearsley)
derek.burrows@bolton.gov.uk

Burrows, Carol (LAB - Kearsley)
carol.burrows@bolton.gov.uk

Bury, Alan (LAB - Horwich & Blackrod)
alan.bury@bolton.gov.uk

Byrne, Lynda (LAB - Breightmet)
lynda.byrne@bolton.gov.uk

Byrne, John (LAB - Breightmet)
john.bynre@bolton.gov.uk

Chadwick, David (LAB - Westhoughton South)
david.chadwick@bolton.gov.uk

Cox, Martyn (CON - Westhoughton North & Chew Moor)
martyn.cox@bolton.gov.uk

Critchley, Norman (CON - Bromley Cross)
norman.critchley@bolton.gov.uk

Cunliffe, Ann (LAB - Horwich & Blackrod)
ann.cuncliffe@bolton.gov.uk

Darvesh, Hanif (LAB - Crompton)
hanif.darvesh@bolton.gov.uk

Dean, Mudasir (CON - Bradshaw)
mudasir.dean@bolton.gov.uk

Evans, David (LAB - Little Lever & Darcy Lever)
david.evans@bolton.gov.uk

Fairclough, Hilary (CON - Astley Bridge)
hilary.fairclough@bolton.gov.uk

Francis, Mike (LAB - Harper Green)
michael.francis@bolton.gov.uk

Gillies, Jean (LAB - Farnworth)
jean.gillies@bolton.gov.uk

Graham, Anne (LAB - Westhoughton North & Chew Moor)
anne.graham@bolton.gov.uk

Hall, Walter (CON - Bradshaw)
walter.hall@bolton.gov.uk

Harkin, Guy (LAB - Crompton)
guy.harkin@bolton.gov.uk

Haslam, Stuart (CON - Bradshaw)
stuart.haslam@bolton.gov.uk

Haworth, Susan (LAB - Harper Green)
susan.haworth@bolton.gov.uk

Hornby, Sean (UKIP - Little Lever & Darcy Lever)
sean.hornby@bolton.gov.uk

Ibrahim, Ismail (LAB - Rumworth)
ismail.ibrahim@bolton.gov.uk

Ibrahim, Asif (LAB - Farnworth)
asif.ibrahim@bolton.gov.uk

Iqbal, Mohammed (LAB - Great Lever)
mohammed.iqbal@botlon.gov.uk

Irving, Liam (LAB - Kearsley)
liam.irving@bolton.gov.uk

Jones, Kevan (LAB - Westhoughton South)
kevan.jones@bolton.gov.uk

Kay, Rosa (LAB - Rumworth)
rosa.kay@bolton.gov.uk

Kellett, Joyce (LAB - Horwich North East)
joyce.kellett@bolton.gov.uk

Kirk-Robinson, Zoe (CON - Westhoughton North & Chew Moor)
zoe.kirk-robinson@bolton.gov.uk

Lewis, Kate (LAB - Breightmet)
kate.lewis@bolton.gov.uk

Martin, Andrew (LD - Smithills)
andrew.martin@bolton.gov.uk

McKeon, Kevin (LAB - Horwich North East)
kevin.mckeon@bolton.gov.uk

Mistry, Champak (LAB - Harper Green)
champak.mistry@bolton.gov.uk

Morgan, Andrew (CON - Heaton & Lostock)
andrew.morgan@bolton.gov.uk

Murray, Madeline (LAB - Great Lever)
madeline.murray@bolton.gov.uk

Peel, Nicholas (LAB - Tonge with the Haulgh)
nicholas.peel@bolton.gov.uk

Pickup, Stephen (LAB - Horwich & Blackrod)
stephen.pickup@bolton.gov.uk

Richardson, Paul (UKIP - Little Lever & Darcy Lever)
paul.richardson@bolton.gov.uk

Shaikh, Shafaqat (LAB - Hulton)
shafaqat.shaikh@bolton.gov.uk

Shaw, Colin (CON - Heaton & Lostock)
colin.shaw@bolton.gov.uk

Sherrington, Elaine (LAB - Tonge with the Haulgh)
elaine.sherrington@bolton.gov.uk

Silvester, Richard (LAB - Horwich North East)
richard.silvester@bolton.gov.uk

Spencer, Noel (LAB - Farnworth)
noel.spencer@bolton.gov.uk

Walsh, John (CON - Astley Bridge)
john.walsh@bolton.gov.uk

Walsh, Alan (CON - Hulton)
alan.walsh@bolton.gov.uk

Watters, Anna-Marie (LAB - Westhoughton South)
anna-marie.watters@bolton.gov.uk

Wild, Paul (CON - Astley Bridge)
paul.wild@bolton.gov.uk

Wilkinson, Alan (CON - Bromley Cross)
alan.wilkinson@bolton.gov.uk

Zaman, Akhtar (LAB - Halliwell)
akhtar.zaman@bolton.gov.uk

POLITICAL COMPOSITION

LAB: 39, CON: 15, LD: 3, UKIP: 3

COMMITTEE CHAIRS

Audit: Mr David Greenhalgh

Health & Wellbeing: Mrs Linda Thomas

Licensing & Environmental Regulation: Mr Martin Donaghy

Planning: Mr Hanif Darvesh

Boston — D

Boston Borough Council, Municipal Buildings, West Street, Boston PE21 8QR
☎ 01205 314200 🖷 01205 364604 ✉ info@boston.gov.uk
🖳 www.boston.gov.uk

FACTS AND FIGURES

Parliamentary Constituencies: Boston and Skegness
EU Constituencies: East Midlands
Election Frequency: Elections are of whole council

PRINCIPAL OFFICERS

Chief Executive: Mr Phil Drury, Chief Executive, Municipal Buildings, West Street, Boston PE21 8QR ☎ 01205 314200 🖷 01205 364604 ✉ phil.drury@boston.gov.uk

Senior Management: Mr Robert Barlow Deputy Chief Executive & Strategic Director - Resources & S151 Officer, Municipal Buildings, West Street, Boston PE21 8QR ☎ 01205 314200; 01507 613411 🖷 01205 364604; 01507 329486 ✉ robert.barlow@boston.gov.uk

Architect, Building / Property Services: Mr Steve Lumb Head of Built Environment & Development, Municipal Buildings, West Street, Boston PE21 8QR ☎ 01205 314200 🖷 01205 364604 ✉ steve.lumb@boston.gov.uk

Architect, Building / Property Services: Mr Gary Sargeant, Corporate Asset Manager, Tedder Hall, Manby Park, Louth LN11 8UP ☎ 01507 613020 ✉ gary.sargeant@e-lindsey.gov.uk

Building Control: Mr Steve Lumb Head of Built Environment & Development, Municipal Buildings, West Street, Boston PE21 8QR ☎ 01205 314200 🖷 01205 364604 ✉ steve.lumb@boston.gov.uk

PR / Communications: Mr Andrew Malkin Communications Manager, Municipal Buildings, West Street, Boston PE21 8QR ☎ 01205 314308 🖷 01205 364604 ✉ andrew.malkin@boston.gov.uk

Community Safety: Mr Andy Fisher, Head of Housing, Health & Communities, Municipal Buildings, West Street, Boston PE21 8QR ☎ 01205 314200 🖷 01205 364604 ✉ andy.fisher@boston.gov.uk

BOSTON

Customer Service: Ms Michelle Sacks Head of Customer & Democratic Services, Municipal Buildings, West Street, Boston PE21 8QR ✉ michelle.sacks@boston.gov.uk

Direct Labour: Mr George Bernard, Head of Operations, Fen Road, Frampton Fen, Boston PE20 1RZ ☎ 01205 311112 ✉ george.bernard@boston.gov.uk

Economic Development: Mr Steve Lumb Head of Built Environment & Development, Municipal Buildings, West Street, Boston PE21 8QR ☎ 01205 314200 🖷 01205 364604 ✉ steve.lumb@boston.gov.uk

Electoral Registration: Mrs Lorraine Bush, Democratic Services Manager, Municipal Buildings, West Street, Boston PE21 8QR ☎ 01205 314224 🖷 01205 364604 ✉ lorraine.bush@boston.gov.uk

Emergency Planning: Mr Andy Fisher, Head of Housing, Health & Communities, Municipal Buildings, West Street, Boston PE21 8QR ☎ 01205 314200 🖷 01205 364604 ✉ andy.fisher@boston.gov.uk

Energy Management: Mr Ian Farmer, Partnerships & Sustainability Manager, Municipal Buildings, West Street, Boston PE21 8QR ☎ 01205 314200 🖷 01205 364604 ✉ ian.farmer@boston.gov.uk

Environmental Health: Mr Andy Fisher, Head of Housing, Health & Communities, Municipal Buildings, West Street, Boston PE21 8QR ☎ 01205 314200 🖷 01205 364604 ✉ andy.fisher@boston.gov.uk

Estates, Property & Valuation: Mr Andy Fisher, Head of Housing, Health & Communities, Municipal Buildings, West Street, Boston PE21 8QR ☎ 01205 314200 🖷 01205 364604 ✉ andy.fisher@boston.gov.uk

Finance: Mr Robert Barlow Deputy Chief Executive & Strategic Director - Resources & S151 Officer, Municipal Buildings, West Street, Boston PE21 8QR ☎ 01205 314200; 01507 613411 🖷 01205 364604; 01507 329486 ✉ robert.barlow@boston.gov.uk

Finance: Mr Paul Julian Head of Finance, Municipal Buildings, West Street, Boston PE21 8QR ☎ ✉ paul.julian@boston.gov.uk

Grounds Maintenance: Mr George Bernard, Head of Operations, Fen Road, Frampton Fen, Boston PE20 1RZ ☎ 01205 311112 ✉ george.bernard@boston.gov.uk

Health and Safety: Ms Katharine Nundy, Head of HR & Transformation, Municipal Buildings, West Street, Boston PE21 8QR ☎ 01205 314274 🖷 01205 364604 ✉ katharine.nundy@boston.gov.uk

Housing: Mr Andy Fisher, Head of Housing, Health & Communities, Municipal Buildings, West Street, Boston PE21 8QR ☎ 01205 314200 🖷 01205 364604 ✉ andy.fisher@boston.gov.uk

Legal: Ms Eleanor Hoggart, Assistant Director of Legal Services Lincolnshire, Municipal Buildings, West Street, Boston PE21 8QR ☎ 01205 314200 🖷 01205 364604 ✉ eleanor.hoggart@lincolnshire.gov.uk

Leisure and Cultural Services: Mr Phil Drury, Chief Executive, Municipal Buildings, West Street, Boston PE21 8QR ☎ 01205 314200 🖷 01205 364604 ✉ phil.drury@boston.gov.uk

Licensing: Ms Fiona White, Principal Licensing & Land Charges Officer, Municipal Buildings, West Street, Boston PE21 8QR ☎ 01205 314242 ✉ fiona.white@boston.gov.uk

Lottery Funding, Charity and Voluntary: Mr Andy Fisher, Head of Housing, Health & Communities, Municipal Buildings, West Street, Boston PE21 8QR ☎ 01205 314200 🖷 01205 364604 ✉ andy.fisher@boston.gov.uk

Member Services: Mrs Lorraine Bush, Democratic Services Manager, Municipal Buildings, West Street, Boston PE21 8QR ☎ 01205 314224 🖷 01205 364604 ✉ lorraine.bush@boston.gov.uk

Parking: Mr Steve Lumb Head of Built Environment & Development, Municipal Buildings, West Street, Boston PE21 8QR ☎ 01205 314200 🖷 01205 364604 ✉ steve.lumb@boston.gov.uk

Partnerships: Mr Steve Lumb Head of Built Environment & Development, Municipal Buildings, West Street, Boston PE21 8QR ☎ 01205 314200 🖷 01205 364604 ✉ steve.lumb@boston.gov.uk

Personnel / HR: Ms Katharine Nundy, Head of HR & Transformation, Municipal Buildings, West Street, Boston PE21 8QR ☎ 01205 314274 🖷 01205 364604 ✉ katharine.nundy@boston.gov.uk

Planning: Mr Steve Lumb Head of Built Environment & Development, Municipal Buildings, West Street, Boston PE21 8QR ☎ 01205 314200 🖷 01205 364604 ✉ steve.lumb@boston.gov.uk

Recycling & Waste Minimisation: Mr George Bernard, Head of Operations, Fen Road, Frampton Fen, Boston PE20 1RZ ☎ 01205 311112 ✉ george.bernard@boston.gov.uk

Staff Training: Ms Katharine Nundy, Head of HR & Transformation, Municipal Buildings, West Street, Boston PE21 8QR ☎ 01205 314274 🖷 01205 364604 ✉ katharine.nundy@boston.gov.uk

Sustainable Communities: Mr Andy Fisher, Head of Housing, Health & Communities, Municipal Buildings, West Street, Boston PE21 8QR ☎ 01205 314200 🖷 01205 364604 ✉ andy.fisher@boston.gov.uk

Sustainable Development: Mr Steve Lumb Head of Built Environment & Development, Municipal Buildings, West Street, Boston PE21 8QR ☎ 01205 314200 🖷 01205 364604 ✉ steve.lumb@boston.gov.uk

Tourism: Mr Phil Drury, Chief Executive, Municipal Buildings, West Street, Boston PE21 8QR ☎ 01205 314200 🖷 01205 364604 ✉ phil.drury@boston.gov.uk

Town Centre: Mr Steve Lumb Head of Built Environment & Development, Municipal Buildings, West Street, Boston PE21 8QR ☎ 01205 314200 🖷 01205 364604 ✉ steve.lumb@boston.gov.uk

Waste Collection and Disposal: Mr George Bernard, Head of Operations, Fen Road, Frampton Fen, Boston PE20 1RZ ☎ 01205 311112 ✉ george.bernard@boston.gov.uk

Waste Management: Mr George Bernard, Head of Operations, Fen Road, Frampton Fen, Boston PE20 1RZ ☎ 01205 311112 ✉ george.bernard@boston.gov.uk

COUNCILLORS

***Mayor* Austin**, Richard (IND - Wyberton)
richard.austin@boston.gov.uk

***Deputy Mayor* Brotherton**, Colin (CON - Kirton & Frampton)
colin.brotherton@boston.gov.uk

***Leader of the Council* Bedford**, Peter (CON - Coastal)
peter.bedford@boston.gov.uk

***Deputy Leader of the Council* Brookes**, Michael (CON - Swineshead & Holland Fen)
michael.brookes@boston.gov.uk

***Group Leader* Austin**, Alison (IND - South)
alison.austin@boston.gov.uk

***Group Leader* Gleeson**, Paul (LAB - Skirbeck)
paul.gleeson@boston.gov.uk

***Group Leader* Ransome**, Sue (UKIP - Station)
sue.ransome@boston.gov.uk

Ball, Stephen (UKIP - Skirbeck)
stephen.ball@boston.gov.uk

Brown, David (UKIP - Wyberton)
david.brown@boston.gov.uk

Cooper, Mike (CON - Five Villages)
michael.cooper@boston.gov.uk

Dani, Anton (UKIP - Fenside)
anton.dani@boston.gov.uk

Dennis, Maureen (CON - Old Leake & Wrangle)
maureen.dennis@boston.gov.uk

Edge, Viven (UKIP - Witham)
viven.edge@boston.gov.uk

Edwards, James (UKIP - Kirton & Frampton)
james.edwards@boston.gov.uk

Evans, Ben (CON - Staniland)
ben.evans@boston.gov.uk

Gregory, Gordon (CON - Trinity)
gordon.gregory@boston.gov.uk

Griggs, Martin (CON - Skirbeck)
martin.griggs@boston.gov.uk

Noble, Jonathan (UKIP - Fishtoft)
jonathan.noble@boston.gov.uk

Pierpoint, Barrie (INDNA - Old Leake & Wrangle)
barrie.pierpoint@boston.gov.uk

Ransome, Elizabeth (UKIP - Swineshead & Holland Fen)
elizabeth.ransome@boston.gov.uk

Ransome, Felicity (UKIP - Costal)
felicity.ransome@boston.gov.uk

Raven, Stephen (UKIP - Witham)
stephen.raven@boston.gov.uk

Rush, Brian (UKIP - Staniland)
brian.rush@boston.gov.uk

Rylott, Claire (CON - Kirton & Frampton)
claire.rylott@boston.gov.uk

Skinner, Paul (CON - Fishtoft)
paul.skinner@boston.gov.uk

Skinner, Judith Ann (CON - Fishtoft)
judith.skinner@boston.gov.uk

Spencer, Aaron (CON - Five Villages)
aaron.spencer@boston.gov.uk

Stevens, Yvonne (UKIP - Trinity)
yvonne.stevens@boston.gov.uk

Welton, Nigel (LAB - Fenside)
nigel.welton@boston.gov.uk

Woodliffe, Stephen (CON - West)
stephen.woodliffe@boston.gov.uk

POLITICAL COMPOSITION

CON: 13, UKIP: 12, LAB: 2, IND: 2, INDNA: 1

COMMITTEE CHAIRS

Audit & Governance: Mr Gordon Gregory

Licensing & Regulatory: Mr Colin Brotherton

Planning: Mrs Alison Austin

Bournemouth U

Bournemouth Council, Town Hall, Bourne Avenue, Bournemouth BH2 6DY
☎ 01202 451451 🖷 01202 451000
✉ firstname.surname@bournemouth.gov.uk 💻 www.bournemouth.gov.uk

FACTS AND FIGURES

Parliamentary Constituencies: Bournemouth East, Bournemouth West
EU Constituencies: South West
Election Frequency: Elections are of whole council

PRINCIPAL OFFICERS

Chief Executive: Mr Tony Williams Chief Executive, Town Hall, Bourne Avenue, Bournemouth BH2 6DY ☎ 01202 451130 🖷 01202 451000 ✉ tony.williams@bournemouth.gov.uk

Deputy Chief Executive: Ms Jane Portman Deputy Chief Executive & Executive Director - Adult & Children, Town Hall, Bourne Avenue, Bournemouth BH2 6DY ☎ 01202 456104 🖷 01202 451000 ✉ jane.portman@bournemouth.gov.uk

Senior Management: Mrs Carole Aspden Service Director - Children & Young People's Services, Town Hall, Bourne Avenue, Bournemouth BH2 6DY ☎ 01202 456118 🖷 01202 456105 ✉ carole.aspden@bournemouth.gov.uk

Senior Management: Mr Roger Ball Service Director - Technical Services, Town Hall Annexe, St. Stephen's Road, Bournemouth BH2 6EA ☎ 01202 451340 🖷 01202 451006 ✉ roger.ball@bournemouth.gov.uk

BOURNEMOUTH

Senior Management: Ms Sue Bickler Head of Community Regeneration, Town Hall, Bourne Avenue, Bournemouth BH2 6DY ☎ 01202 454966 🖷 01202 451000 sue.bickler@bournemouth.gov.uk

Senior Management: Ms Ivor Cawthorn Strategic Commissioning Manager, Town Hall, Bourne Avenue, Bournemouth BH2 6DY ☎ 01202 458703 🖷 01202 451000 ivor.cawthorn@bournemouth.gov.uk

Senior Management: Ms Tanya Coulter Service Director - Legal & Democratic Services, Town Hall, Bourne Avenue, Bournemouth BH2 6DY ☎ 01202 451172 🖷 01202 451000 tanya.coulter@bournemouth.gov.uk

Senior Management: Mr Neil Goddard Service Director - Community Learning & Commissioning, Town Hall, Bourne Avenue, Bournemouth BH2 6DY ☎ 01202 456136 🖷 01202 456105 neil.goddard@bournemouth.gov.uk

Senior Management: Mr Mike Holmes Service Director - Planning, Transport & Regulation, Town Hall Annexe, St. Stephen's Road, Bournemouth BH2 6EA ☎ 01202 451315 🖷 01202 451005 mike.holmes@bournemouth.gov.uk

Senior Management: Mr Ian Milner Service Director - Corporate & Commercial, Town Hall, Bourne Avenue, Bournemouth BH2 6DY ☎ 01202 451129 maria.o'reilly@bournemouth.gov.uk

Senior Management: Dr David Phillips Director - Public Health, Civic Centre, Poole BH15 2RU ☎ 01202 451828 d.phillips@poole.gov.uk

Senior Management: Mr Mark Smith Interim Executive Director - Finance & S151 Officer, Visitor Information Bureau, Westover Road, Bournemouth BH1 2BU ☎ 01202 451706 🖷 01202 451743 mark.smith@bournemouth.gov.uk

Architect, Building / Property Services: Mr Roger Ball Service Director - Technical Services, Town Hall Annexe, St. Stephen's Road, Bournemouth BH2 6EA ☎ 01202 451340 🖷 01202 451006 roger.ball@bournemouth.gov.uk

Best Value: Ms Clare Matthews Policy, Strategy & Performance Officer, Town Hall, Bourne Avenue, Bournemouth BH2 6DY ☎ 01202 454958 🖷 01202 451000 clare.matthews@bournemouth.gov.uk

Building Control: Mr Roger Ball Service Director - Technical Services, Town Hall Annexe, St. Stephen's Road, Bournemouth BH2 6EA ☎ 01202 451340 🖷 01202 451006 roger.ball@bournemouth.gov.uk

Catering Services: Mr Graham Twigg Facilities Management Service Delivery Manager, Town Hall, Bourne Avenue, Bournemouth BH2 6DY ☎ graham.twigg@bournemouth.gov.uk

Children / Youth Services: Mrs Carole Aspden Service Director - Children & Young People's Services, Town Hall, Bourne Avenue, Bournemouth BH2 6DY ☎ 01202 456118 🖷 01202 456105 carole.aspden@bournemouth.gov.uk

Civil Registration: Ms Helen Rigg, Registration & Coroners Services Manager, Town Hall, Bourne Avenue, Bournemouth BH2 6DY ☎ 01202 454629 helen.rigg@bournemouth.gov.uk

PR / Communications: Ms Georgia Turner, Corporate Communications Manager, Town Hall, Bournemouth BH2 6DY ☎ 01202 451039 🖷 01202 451000 georgia.turner@bournemouth.gov.uk

Community Planning: Mr Lee Green, Environmental Strategy & Sustainability Manager, Town Hall, Bourne Avenue, Bournemouth BH2 6DY ☎ 01202 451144 🖷 01202 451000 lee.green@bournemouth.gov.uk

Community Safety: Mr Andrew Williams Team Manager - Safer & Stronger Communities, Town Hall, Bourne Avenue, Bournemouth BH2 6DY ☎ 01202 458240 🖷 01202 451000 andrew.williams@bournemouth.gov.uk

Computer Management: Mr Nick Palmer Head of Strategic ICT, Town Hall, Bourne Avenue, Bournemouth BH2 6DY ☎ 01202 451312 🖷 01202 451000 nick.palmer@bournemouth.gov.uk

Consumer Protection and Trading Standards: Mr Andy Sherriff Principal Trading Standards Officer, Town Hall, Bourne Avenue, Bournemouth BH2 6DY ☎ 01202 541440 🖷 01202 451011 andy.sherriff@bournemouth.gov.uk

Contracts: Mr Jeremy Richardson Head of Strategic Procurement & Commissioning, Town Hall, Bourne Avenue, Bournemouth BH2 6DY ☎ 01202 458233 jeremy.richardson@bournemouth.gov.uk

Customer Service: Ms Maria O'Reilly, Head of Customer Services, Town Hall, Bourne Avenue, Bournemouth BH2 6DY ☎ 01202 454953 maria.o'reilly@bournemouth.gov.uk

Customer Service: Mr Stuart Walters, Customer Services Manager, Town Hall, Bourne Avenue, Bournemouth BH2 6DY ☎ 01202 454711 stuart.walters@bournemouth.gov.uk

Economic Development: Mr Christopher Kelu Business Support Officer, Town Hall, Bourne Avenue, Bournemouth BH2 6DY ☎ 01202 545630 christopher.kelu@bournemouth.gov.uk

Education: Ms Jane Portman Deputy Chief Executive & Executive Director - Adult & Children, Town Hall, Bourne Avenue, Bournemouth BH2 6DY ☎ 01202 456104 🖷 01202 451000 jane.portman@bournemouth.gov.uk

Electoral Registration: Mr Matt Pitcher, Electoral Services Officer, Room 40, Town Hall, Bourne Avenue, Bournemouth BH2 6DY ☎ 01202 451122 🖷 01202 451003 matt.pitcher@bournemouth.gov.uk

Emergency Planning: Ms Alyson Whitley Resilience & Safety Manager, Town Hall, Bourne Avenue, Bournemouth BH2 6DY ☎ 01202 451281 🖷 01202 451000 alyson.whitley@bournemouth.gov.uk

Energy Management: Mr Roger Ball Service Director - Technical Services, Town Hall Annexe, St. Stephen's Road, Bournemouth BH2 6EA ☎ 01202 451340 🖷 01202 451006 ✉ roger.ball@bournemouth.gov.uk

Environmental / Technical Services: Mr Roger Ball Service Director - Technical Services, Town Hall Annexe, St. Stephen's Road, Bournemouth BH2 6EA ☎ 01202 451340 🖷 01202 451006 ✉ roger.ball@bournemouth.gov.uk

Environmental Health: Mr Roger Ball Service Director - Technical Services, Town Hall Annexe, St. Stephen's Road, Bournemouth BH2 6EA ☎ 01202 451340 🖷 01202 451006 ✉ roger.ball@bournemouth.gov.uk

Estates, Property & Valuation: Mr Gary Platt Property Services Manager, Town Hall Annexe, St. Stephen's Road, Bournemouth BH2 6EA ☎ 01202 451477 ✉ gary.platt@bournemouth.gov.uk

European Liaison: Mr Christopher Kelu Business Support Officer, Town Hall, Bourne Avenue, Bournemouth BH2 6DY ☎ 01202 545630 ✉ christopher.kelu@bournemouth.gov.uk

Events Manager: Mr Jon Weaver, Marketing & Events Manager, Visitor Information Bureau, Westover Road, Bournemouth BH1 2BU ☎ 01202 451737 ✉ jon.weaver@bournemouth.gov.uk

Facilities: Mr Graham Twigg Facilities Management Service Delivery Manager, Town Hall, Bourne Avenue, Bournemouth BH2 6DY ✉ graham.twigg@bournemouth.gov.uk

Finance: Mr Ian Milner Service Director - Corporate & Commercial, Town Hall, Bourne Avenue, Bournemouth BH2 6DY ☎ 01202 451129 ✉ maria.o'reilly@bournemouth.gov.uk

Fleet Management: Mr Mike Holmes Service Director - Planning, Transport & Regulation, Town Hall Annexe, St. Stephen's Road, Bournemouth BH2 6EA ☎ 01202 451315 🖷 01202 451005 ✉ mike.holmes@bournemouth.gov.uk

Grounds Maintenance: Mr Michael Rowland, Green Spaces Project Officer, Queens Park Pavilion, Queens Park West Drive, Bournemouth BH8 9BY ☎ 01202 451632 ✉ michael.rowlands@bournemouth.gov.uk

Health and Safety: Mr John Towner Corporate Health & Safety Officer, Town Hall, Bourne Avenue, Bournemouth BH2 6DY ☎ 01202 451484 ✉ john.towner@bournemouth.gov.uk

Highways: Mr Ken Hobbs Principal Traffic Engineer, Town Hall Annexe, St. Stephen's Road, Bournemouth BH2 6EA ☎ 01202 451388 🖷 01202 451005 ✉ ken.hobbs@bournemouth.gov.uk

Home Energy Conservation: Mr Roger Ball Service Director - Technical Services, Town Hall Annexe, St. Stephen's Road, Bournemouth BH2 6EA ☎ 01202 451340 🖷 01202 451006 ✉ roger.ball@bournemouth.gov.uk

Housing: Ms Lorraine Mealings Strategic Housing Services Manager, Town Hall, Bourne Avenue, Bournemouth BH2 6DY ☎ 01202 458226 ✉ lorraine.mealings@bournemouth.gov.uk

Housing Maintenance: Mr Gary Josey, Service Director - Housing, Parks & Bereavement Services, Housing Technical Services, Unit 4, Dalling Road, Poole BH12 6DJ ☎ 01202 458301 ✉ gary.josey@bournemouth.gov.uk

Legal: Ms Sian Ballingall Legal & Democratic Services Manager, Town Hall, Bourne Avenue, Bournemouth BH2 6DY ☎ 01202 454648 ✉ sian.ballingall@bournemouth.gov.uk

Leisure and Cultural Services: Mr Neil Goddard Service Director - Community Learning & Commissioning, Town Hall, Bourne Avenue, Bournemouth BH2 6DY ☎ 01202 456136 🖷 01202 456105 ✉ neil.goddard@bournemouth.gov.uk

Licensing: Mr Roger Ball Service Director - Technical Services, Town Hall Annexe, St. Stephen's Road, Bournemouth BH2 6EA ☎ 01202 451340 🖷 01202 451006 ✉ roger.ball@bournemouth.gov.uk

Lighting: Mr Roger Ball Service Director - Technical Services, Technical Services, Town Hall Annexe, St Stephen's Road, Bournemouth BH2 6EA ☎ 01202 451340 🖷 01202 451006 ✉ roger.ball@bournemouth.gov.uk

Lottery Funding, Charity and Voluntary: Mr Gary Bentham, Community Liaison Officer, Town Hall, Bourne Avenue, Bournemouth BH2 6DY ☎ 01202 451165 🖷 01202 451000 ✉ gary.bentham@bournemouth.gov.uk

Member Services: Mrs Karen Tompkins Democratic & Member Support Services Manager, Town Hall, Bourne Avenue, Bournemouth BH2 6DY ☎ 01202 454689 ✉ karen.tompkins@bournemouth.gov.uk

Parking: Mr Gary Powell Enforcement & Parking Manager, Enforcement & Parking Centre, Town Hall Annexe, St Stephen's Road, Bournemouth BH2 6DY ☎ 01202 451456 🖷 01202 451492 ✉ gary.powell@bournemouth.gov.uk

Personnel / HR: Ms Saskia DeVries Interim Head of Strategic PR, Town Hall, Bourne Avenue, Bournemouth BH2 6DY ☎ 01202 451134 ✉ saskia.devries@bournemouth.gov.uk

Planning: Mr Mike Holmes Service Director - Planning, Transport & Regulation, Town Hall Annexe, St. Stephen's Road, Bournemouth BH2 6EA ☎ 01202 451315 🖷 01202 451005 ✉ mike.holmes@bournemouth.gov.uk

Procurement: Mr Jeremy Richardson Head of Strategic Procurement & Commissioning, Town Hall, Bourne Avenue, Bournemouth BH2 6DY ☎ 01202 458233 ✉ jeremy.richardson@bournemouth.gov.uk

Public Libraries: Mr Neil Goddard Service Director - Community Learning & Commissioning, Town Hall, Bourne Avenue, Bournemouth BH2 6DY ☎ 01202 456136 🖷 01202 456105 ✉ neil.goddard@bournemouth.gov.uk

Recycling & Waste Minimisation: Mr Roger Ball Service Director - Technical Services, Town Hall Annexe, St. Stephen's Road, Bournemouth BH2 6EA ☎ 01202 451340 🖷 01202 451006 ✉ roger.ball@bournemouth.gov.uk

BOURNEMOUTH

Recycling & Waste Minimisation: Mr Reg Hutton, Head of Operations - Technical Services, Technical Services Division, Southcote Road Depot, Southcote Road, Bournemouth BH1 3SW ☎ 01202 451643 🖷 01202 451084 ✉ reg.hutton@bournemouth.gov.uk

Road Safety: Mr John Satchwell Road Safety Manager, Town Hall Annexe, St. Stephen's Road, Bournemouth BH2 6EA ☎ 01202 451461 ✉ john.satchwell@bournemouth.gov.uk

Social Services: Ms Kim Drake Service Director - Children's Social Care, Town Hall, Bourne Avenue, Bournemouth BH2 6DY ☎ 01202 458721 🖷 01202 456105 ✉ kim.drake@bournemouth.gov.uk

Social Services (Adult): Mr Andy Sharp Service Director - Adult Social Care, Town Hall, Bourne Avenue, Bournemouth BH2 6DY ✉ andy.sharp@bournemouth.gov.uk

Social Services (Children): Ms Kim Drake Service Director - Children's Social Care, Town Hall, Bourne Avenue, Bournemouth BH2 6DY ☎ 01202 458721 🖷 01202 456105 ✉ kim.drake@bournemouth.gov.uk

Public Health: Dr David Phillips Director - Public Health, Civic Centre, Poole BH15 2RU ☎ 01202 451828 ✉ d.phillips@poole.gov.uk

Street Scene: Mr Larry Austin Street Services Manager, Southcote Road Depot, 103 Southcote Road, Bournemouth BH1 3SW ☎ 01202 451690 ✉ larry.austin@bournemouth.gov.uk

Sustainable Development: Mr Bill Cotton Executive Director - Environment & Economy, Town Hall, Bourne Avenue, Bournemouth BH2 6DY ☎ 01202 458702 🖷 01202 451000 ✉ bill.cotton@bournemouth.gov.uk

Tourism: Mr Mark Smith Interim Executive Director - Finance & S151 Officer, Visitor Information Bureau, Westover Road, Bournemouth BH1 2BU ☎ 01202 451706 🖷 01202 451743 ✉ mark.smith@bournemouth.gov.uk

Traffic Management: Mr Ken Hobbs Principal Traffic Engineer, Town Hall Annexe, St. Stephen's Road, Bournemouth BH2 6EA ☎ 01202 451388 🖷 01202 451005 ✉ ken.hobbs@bournemouth.gov.uk

Transport: Mr Mike Holmes Service Director - Planning, Transport & Regulation, Town Hall Annexe, St. Stephen's Road, Bournemouth BH2 6EA ☎ 01202 451315 🖷 01202 451005 ✉ mike.holmes@bournemouth.gov.uk

Transport Planner: Mr Ian Kalra Transportation Services Manager, Town Hall, Bourne Avenue, Bournemouth BH2 6DY ☎ 01202 451447 ✉ ian.kalra@bournemouth.gov.uk

Waste Collection and Disposal: Mr Reg Hutton, Head of Operations - Technical Services, Technical Services Division, Southcote Road Depot, Southcote Road, Bournemouth BH1 3SW ☎ 01202 451643 🖷 01202 451084 ✉ reg.hutton@bournemouth.gov.uk

Waste Management: Mr Roger Ball Service Director - Technical Services, Town Hall Annexe, St. Stephen's Road, Bournemouth BH2 6EA ☎ 01202 451340 🖷 01202 451006 ✉ roger.ball@bournemouth.gov.uk

Children's Play Areas: Mr Andy McDonald Parks Manager - Operations, Town Hall, Bourne Avenue, Bournemouth BH2 6DY ☎ 01202 451695 ✉ andy.mcdonald@bournemouth.gov.uk

COUNCILLORS

***Mayor* Adams**, John (CON - Strouden Park)
john.adams@bournemouth.gov.uk

***Deputy Mayor* Mayne**, Chris (CON - West Southbourne)
chris.mayne@bournemouth.gov.uk

***Leader of the Council* Beesley**, John (CON - Westbourne & West Cliff)
john.beesley@bournemouth.gov.uk

***Deputy Leader of the Council* Greene**, Nicola (CON - Wallisdown & Winton West)
nicola.greene@bournemouth.gov.uk

Anderson, Sue (CON - Moordown)
sue.anderson@bournemouth.gov.uk

Anderson, Mark (CON - Queens Park)
mark.anderson@bournemouth.gov.uk

Angiolini, Amedeo (CON - Kinson North)
amedeo.angiolini@bournemouth.gov.uk

Bartlett, Stephen (CON - Redhill & Northbourne)
stephen.bartlett@bournmouth.gov.uk

Battistini, Mark (CON - Kinson North)
mark.battistini@bournemouth.gov.uk

Borthwick, Derek (CON - Throop & Muscliff)
derek.borthwich@bournemouth.gov.uk

Broadhead, Philip (CON - Talbot & Branksome Woods)
philip.boradhead@bournemouth.gov.uk

Bull, Simon (GRN - Winton East)
simon.bull@bournemouth.gov.uk

Chapman, Robert (CON - Central)
robert.chapman@bournemouth.gov.uk

Clark, Ian (CON - Throop & Muscliff)
ian.clark@bournemouth.gov.uk

Coope, Eddie (CON - East Southbourne & Tuckton)
eddie.coope@bournemouth.gov.uk

Crawford, Blair (CON - West Southbourne)
blair.crawford@bouremouth.gov.uk

Davies, Malcolm (CON - East Southbourne & Tuckton)
malcolm.davies@bournemouth.gov.uk

Decent, Norman (CON - Kinson South)
norman.decent@bournmout.gov.uk

D'Orton-Gibson, David (CON - Redhill & Northbourne)
david.dorton-gibson@bournemouth.gov.uk

Dove, Bobbie (CON - Litteldown & Ilford)
bobbi.dove@bournemouth.gov.k

Dunlop, Beverley (CON - Moordown)
beverley.dunlop@bournemouth.gov.uk

Edwards, Jackie (CON - Redhill & Northbuorne)
jacki.edwards@bournmouth.gov.uk

Fear, Laurence (UKIP - Kinson South)
laurence.fear@bournmouth.gov.uk

Filer, Anne (CON - East Cliff & Springbourne)
anne.filer@bournemouth.gov.uk

Filer, Michael (CON - East Cliff & Springbourne)
michael.filer@bournemouth.gov.uk

Greene, Mike (CON - Central)
mike.greene@bournemouth.gov.uk

Hedges, Nigel (CON - Wallisdown & Winton West)
nigel.hedges@bournemouth.gov.uk

Johnson, Cheryl (CON - Queens Park)
cheryl.johnson@bournemouth.gov.uk

Jones, Andy (CON - Boscombe East)
andy.jones@bournmouth@gov.uk

Kelly, Jane (CON - Boscombe West)
jane.kelly@bournemouth.gov.uk

Kelsey, David (CON - East Cliff & Springbourne)
david.kelsey@bournemouth.gov.uk

Lancashire, Ian (CON - Moordown)
ian.lancashire@bournemouth.gov.uk

Lawton, Robert (CON - East Southbourne & Tuckton)

Marley, Roger (CON - Kinson South)
roger.marley@bournemouth.gov.uk

McQueen, Donald (CON - Winton East)
donald.mcqueen@bournemouth.gov.uk

Morgan, Andrew (CON - Talbot & Branksome Woods)
andrew.morgan@bournemouth.gov.uk

Oakley, Patrick (CON - Winton East)
patrick.oakley@bournemouth.gov.uk

Pacifico-Mackin, Gina (CON - Boscombe East)
gina.pacificomakin@bournmouth.gov.uk

Phillips, Susan (CON - Wallisdown & Winton West)
susan.phillips@bournemouth.gov.uk

Price, Lynda (CON - Talbot & Branksome Woods)
lynda.price@bournemouth.gov.uk

Rey, Anne (IND - Throop & Muscliff)
anne.rey@bournemouth.gov.uk

Rochester, Christopher (CON - Boscombe East)
christopher.rochester@bournemouth.gov.uk

Ross, Nick (CON - Westbourne & West Cliff)
ncik.ross@bournemouth.gov.uk

Russell, Allister (CON - West Southbourne)
allister.russell@bournemouth.gov.uk

Seymour, Gill (CON - Littledown & Iford)
gill.seymour@bournemouth.gov.uk

Smith, David (CON - Central)
david.smith@bournemouth.gov.uk

Stanley-Watts, Philip (CON - Boscombe West)
philip.stanley-watts@bournemouth.gov.uk

Stollard, Rae (CON - Westbourne & West Cliff)
rae.stollard@bournemouth.gov.uk

Trickett, John (CON - Strouden Park)
john.trickett@bournemouth.gov.uk

Turtle, David (CON - Kinson North)
david.turtle@bournemouth.gov.uk

Wakefield, Christopher (CON - Boscombe West)
christopher.wakefield@bournemouth.gov.uk

Weinhonig, Michael (CON - Strouden Park)
michael.weinhonig@bournemouth.gov.uk

Williams, Lawrence (CON - Littledown & Iford)
lawrence.williams@bournemouth.gov.uk

POLITICAL COMPOSITION
CON: 50, IND: 1, GRN: 1, UKIP: 1

Bracknell Forest U

Bracknell Forest Borough Council, Easthampstead House, Town Square, Bracknell RG12 1AQ
☎ 01344 352000 🖷 01344 411875 🖳 www.bracknell-forest.gov.uk

FACTS AND FIGURES
Parliamentary Constituencies: Bracknell
EU Constituencies: South East
Election Frequency: Elections are of whole council

PRINCIPAL OFFICERS

Chief Executive: Mr Timothy Wheadon, Chief Executive, Easthampstead House, Town Square, Bracknell RG12 1AQ ☎ 01344 352000 ✉ timothy.wheadon@bracknell-forest.gov.uk

Deputy Chief Executive: Mrs Alison Sanders, Director - Corporate Services, Easthampstead House, Town Square, Bracknell RG12 1AQ ☎ 01344 352000 ✉ alison.sanders@bracknell-forest.gov.uk

Assistant Chief Executive: Mr Victor Nicholls, Assistant Chief Executive, Easthampstead House, Town Square, Bracknell RG12 1AQ ☎ 01344 352000 ✉ victor.nicholls@bracknell-forest.gov.uk

Senior Management: Dr Janette Karklins Director - Children, Young People & Learning, Time Square, Market Street, Bracknell RG12 1JD ☎ 01344 352000 ✉ janette.karklins@bracknell-forest.gov.uk

Senior Management: Dr Lise Llewellyn Director - Public Health, Easthampstead House, Town Square, Bracknell RG12 1AQ ✉ lise.llewellyn@bracknell-forest.gov.uk

Senior Management: Mr John Nawrockyi Interim Director - Adult Social Care, Health & Housing, Time Square, Market Street, Bracknell RG12 1JD ☎ 01344 352000 🖷 01344 351441 ✉ john.nawrockyi@bracknell-forest.gov.uk

Senior Management: Mr Vincent Paliczka, Director - Environment, Culture & Communities, Time Square, 4th Floor Time Square South, Market Street, Bracknell RG12 1AU ☎ 01344 352000 ✉ vincent.paliczka@bracknell-forest.gov.uk

Senior Management: Mrs Alison Sanders, Director - Corporate Services, Easthampstead House, Town Square, Bracknell RG12 1AQ ☎ 01344 352000 ✉ alison.sanders@bracknell-forest.gov.uk

Access Officer / Social Services (Disability): Mrs Ann Groves, Urban Design Officer, Time Square, Market Street, Bracknell RG12 1JD ☎ 01344 352000 ✉ ann.groves@bracknell-forest.gov.uk

Architect, Building / Property Services: Mr Steven Caplan Chief Officer - Property, Easthampstead House, Town Square, Bracknell RG12 1AQ ☎ 01344 352000 ✉ steven.caplan@bracknell-forest.gov.uk

BRACKNELL FOREST

Best Value: Mr Richard Beaumont, Head - Overview & Scrutiny, Easthampstead House, Town Square, Bracknell RG12 1AQ ☎ 01344 352000 ✉ richard.beaumont@bracknell-forest.gov.uk

Building Control: Mr David Constable Senior Building Control Surveyor, Time Square, Market Street, Bracknell RG12 1JD ☎ 01344 352000 ✉ david.constable@bracknell-forest.gov.uk

Catering Services: Mr David Eagle, Contracts Monitoring Officer, Time Square, Market Street, Bracknell RG12 1JD ☎ 01344 352000 ✉ david.eagle@bracknell-forest.gov.uk

Children / Youth Services: Mrs Lorna Hunt Chief Officer - Children's Social Care, Time Square, Market Street, Bracknell RG12 1JD ☎ 01344 352000 ✉ lorna.hunt@bracknell-forest.gov.uk

Children / Youth Services: Dr Janette Karklins Director - Children, Young People & Learning, Time Square, Market Street, Bracknell RG12 1JD ☎ 01344 352000 ✉ janette.karklins@bracknell-forest.gov.uk

Civil Registration: Mrs Ann Moore Head - Democratic & Registration Services, Easthampstead House, Town Square, Bracknell RG12 1AQ ☎ 01344 352000 ✉ ann.moore@bracknell-forest.gov.uk

PR / Communications: Ms Melinda Brown Head - Communications & Marketing, Easthampstead House, Town Square, Bracknell RG12 1AQ ☎ 01344 352000 ✉ melinda.brown@bracknell-forest.gov.uk

Community Planning: Mr Victor Nicholls, Assistant Chief Executive, Easthampstead House, Town Square, Bracknell RG12 1AQ ☎ 01344 352000 ✉ victor.nicholls@bracknell-forest.gov.uk

Community Safety: Mr Ian Boswell, Safer Communities Manager, Easthampstead House, Town Square, Bracknell RG12 1AQ ☎ 01344 352000 ✉ ian.boswell@bracknell-forest.gov.uk

Computer Management: Mr Pat Keane, Chief Officer - Information Services, Easthampstead House, Town Square, Bracknell RG12 1AQ ☎ 01344 352000 🖷 01344 352277 ✉ pat.keane@bracknell-forest.gov.uk

Consumer Protection and Trading Standards: Mr Robert Sexton, Trading Standards & Services Manager, Time Square, Market Street, Bracknell RG12 1JD ☎ 01344 352000 🖷 01344 353122 ✉ robert.sexton@bracknell-forest.gov.uk

Contracts: Mr Timothy Wheadon, Chief Executive, Easthampstead House, Town Square, Bracknell RG12 1AQ ☎ 01344 352000 ✉ timothy.wheadon@bracknell-forest.gov.uk

Corporate Services: Mrs Alison Sanders, Director - Corporate Services, Easthampstead House, Town Square, Bracknell RG12 1AQ ☎ 01344 352000 ✉ alison.sanders@bracknell-forest.gov.uk

Customer Service: Mrs Bobby Mulheir Chief Officer - Customer Services, Time Square, Market Street, Bracknell RG12 1JD ☎ 01344 352000 ✉ bobby.mulheir@bracknell-forest.gov.uk

Economic Development: Mr Victor Nicholls, Assistant Chief Executive, Easthampstead House, Town Square, Bracknell RG12 1AQ ☎ 01344 352000 ✉ victor.nicholls@bracknell-forest.gov.uk

Education: Dr Janette Karklins Director - Children, Young People & Learning, Time Square, Market Street, Bracknell RG12 1JD ☎ 01344 352000 ✉ janette.karklins@bracknell-forest.gov.uk

E-Government: Mr Pat Keane, Chief Officer - Information Services, Easthampstead House, Town Square, Bracknell RG12 1AQ ☎ 01344 352000 🖷 01344 352277 ✉ pat.keane@bracknell-forest.gov.uk

Electoral Registration: Ms Glenda Favor-Anderson Registration Services Manager, Easthampstead House, Town Square, Bracknell RG12 1AQ ☎ 01344 352000 ✉ glenda.favor-anderson@bracknell-forest.gov.uk

Emergency Planning: Mrs Louise Osborn, Emergency Planning Officer, The Central Depot, Old Bracknell Lane West, Bracknell Forest Borough Council, Bracknell RG12 7QT ☎ 01344 352000 ✉ louise.osborn@bracknell-forest.gov.uk

Energy Management: Mr Steven Milne, Energy Manager, Time Square, Market Street, Bracknell RG12 1JD ☎ 01344 352000 ✉ steven.milne@bracknell-forest.gov.uk

Environmental / Technical Services: Mr Vincent Paliczka, Director - Environment, Culture & Communities, Time Square, Market Street, Bracknell RG12 1JD ☎ 01344 352000 ✉ vincent.paliczka@bracknell-forest.gov.uk

Environmental Health: Mr Steve Loudoun, Chief Officer - Environment & Public Protection, Time Square, Market Street, Bracknell RG12 1JD ☎ 01344 352000 🖷 01344 353122 ✉ steve.loudoun@bracknell-forest.gov.uk

Estates, Property & Valuation: Mr Steven Caplan Chief Officer - Property, Easthampstead House, Town Square, Bracknell RG12 1AQ ☎ 01344 352000 ✉ steven.caplan@bracknell-forest.gov.uk

Facilities: Mr Steve Bull Head of Property & Facilities, Easthampstead House, Town Square, Bracknell RG12 1AQ ☎ 01344 352000 ✉ steve.booth@bracknell-forest.gov.uk

Finance: Mr Alan Nash Borough Treasurer, Easthampstead House, Town Square, Bracknell RG12 1AQ ☎ 01344 352000 🖷 01344352255 ✉ alan.nash@bracknell-forest.gov.uk

Fleet Management: Mr Damian James Head - Transport Provision, The Central Depot, Old Bracknell Lane West, Bracknell Forest Borough Council, Bracknell RG12 7QT ☎ 01344 352000 ✉ damian.james@bracknell-forest.gov.uk

Health and Safety: Mr Andy Anderson Senior Health & Safety Advisor, Easthampstead House, Town Square, Bracknell RG12 1AQ ☎ 01344 352000 🖷 01344 353122 ✉ andy.anderson@bracknell-forest.gov.uk

Highways: Mr Steve Loudoun, Chief Officer - Environment & Public Protection, Time Square, Market Street, Bracknell RG12 1JD ☎ 01344 352000 🖷 01344 353122 ✉ steve.loudoun@bracknell-forest.gov.uk

Home Energy Conservation: Mrs Hazel Hill, Sustainable Energy Officer, Time Square, Market Street, Bracknell RG12 1JD ☎ 01344 352000 ✉ hazel.hill@bracknell-forest.gov.uk

Housing: Mr Simon Hendey Chief Officer - Housing, Time Square, Market Street, Bracknell RG12 1JD ☎ 01344 352000 ✉ simon.hendey@bracknell-forest.gov.uk

Local Area Agreement: Mr Victor Nicholls, Assistant Chief Executive, Easthampstead House, Town Square, Bracknell RG12 1AQ ☎ 01344 352000 ✉ victor.nicholls@bracknell-forest.gov.uk

Legal: Mr Sanjay Prashar Borough Solicitor, Easthampstead House, Town Square, Bracknell RG12 1AQ ☎ 01344 352000 🖷 01344 352236 ✉ sanjay.prashar@bracknall-forest.gov.uk

Leisure and Cultural Services: Mr Vincent Paliczka, Director - Environment, Culture & Communities, Time Square, Market Street, Bracknell RG12 1JD ☎ 01344 352000 ✉ vincent.paliczka@bracknell-forest.gov.uk

Licensing: Ms Laura Driscoll Licensing Team Leader, Easthampstead House, Town Square, Bracknell RG12 1AQ ☎ 01344 352517 ✉ laura.driscoll@bracknell-forest.gov.uk

Lighting: Mr Steve Loudoun, Chief Officer - Environment & Public Protection, Time Square, Market Street, Bracknell RG12 1JD ☎ 01344 352000 🖷 01344 353122 ✉ steve.loudoun@bracknell-forest.gov.uk

Lottery Funding, Charity and Voluntary: Mr Victor Nicholls, Assistant Chief Executive, Easthampstead House, Town Square, Bracknell RG12 1AQ ☎ 01344 352000 ✉ victor.nicholls@bracknell-forest.gov.uk

Member Services: Mrs Kirsty Hunt Senior Democratic Services Officer, Easthampstead House, Town Square, Bracknell RG12 1AQ ☎ 01344 352000 ✉ kirsty.hunt@bracknell-forest.gov.uk

Parking: Mr Andrew Hunter Chief Officer - Planning & Transport, Time Square, Market Street, Bracknell RG12 1JD ☎ 01344 352000 ✉ andrew.hunter@bracknell-forest.gov.uk

Partnerships: Mrs Genny Webb Head - Performance & Partnerships, Easthampstead House, Town Square, Bracknell RG12 1AQ ☎ 01344 352000 ✉ genny.webb@bracknell-forest.gov.uk

Personnel / HR: Mr Tony Madden, Chief Officer - Human Resources, Easthampstead House, Town Square, Bracknell RG12 1AQ ☎ 01344 352000 🖷 01344 352029 ✉ tony.madden@bracknell-forest.gov.uk

Planning: Mr Vincent Haines, Head - Planning & Building Control, Time Square, Market Street, Bracknell RG12 1JD ☎ 01344 352000 ✉ vincent.haines@bracknell-forest.gov.uk

Procurement: Mr Geoff Reynolds Head - Procurement, Easthampstead House, Town Square, Bracknell RG12 1AQ ☎ 01344 352000 ✉ geoff.reynolds@bracknell-forest.gov.uk

Public Libraries: Ms Ruth Burgess, Head - Libraries, Time Square, Market Street, Bracknell RG12 1JD ☎ 01344 352000 🖷 01344 354100 ✉ ruth.burgess@bracknell-forest.gov.uk

Recycling & Waste Minimisation: Mrs Janet Dowlman, Waste & Recycling Manager, Time Square, Market Street, Bracknell RG12 1JD ☎ 01344 352000 🖷 01344 353122 ✉ janet.dowlman@bracknell-forest.gov.uk

Regeneration: Mr Victor Nicholls, Assistant Chief Executive, Easthampstead House, Town Square, Bracknell RG12 1AQ ☎ 01344 352000 ✉ victor.nicholls@bracknell-forest.gov.uk

Social Services: Mr John Nawrockyi Interim Director - Adult Social Care, Health & Housing, Time Square, Market Street, Bracknell RG12 1JD ☎ 01344 352000 🖷 01344 351441 ✉ john.nawrockyi@bracknell-forest.gov.uk

Social Services (Adult): Mr John Nawrockyi Interim Director - Adult Social Care, Health & Housing, Time Square, Market Street, Bracknell RG12 1JD ☎ 01344 352000 🖷 01344 351441 ✉ john.nawrockyi@bracknell-forest.gov.uk

Social Services (Children): Mrs Lorna Hunt Chief Officer - Children's Social Care, Time Square, Market Street, Bracknell RG12 1JD ☎ 01344 352000 ✉ lorna.hunt@bracknell-forest.gov.uk

Childrens Social Care: Mrs Lorna Hunt Chief Officer - Children's Social Care, Time Square, Market Street, Bracknell RG12 1JD ☎ 01344 352000 ✉ lorna.hunt@bracknell-forest.gov.uk

Public Health: Dr Lise Llewellyn Director - Public Health, Easthampstead House, Town Square, Bracknell RG12 1AQ ✉ lise.llewellyn@bracknell-forest.gov.uk

Staff Training: Mr Tony Madden, Chief Officer - Human Resources, Easthampstead House, Town Square, Bracknell RG12 1AQ ☎ 01344 352000 🖷 01344 352029 ✉ tony.madden@bracknell-forest.gov.uk

Street Scene: Mr Steve Loudoun, Chief Officer - Environment & Public Protection, Time Square, Market Street, Bracknell RG12 1JD ☎ 01344 352000 🖷 01344 353122 ✉ steve.loudoun@bracknell-forest.gov.uk

Sustainable Communities: Mr Simon Hendey Chief Officer - Housing, Time Square, Market Street, Bracknell RG12 1JD ☎ 01344 352000 ✉ simon.hendey@bracknell-forest.gov.uk

Tourism: Mr Vincent Paliczka, Director - Environment, Culture & Communities, Time Square, Market Street, Bracknell RG12 1JD ☎ 01344 352000 ✉ vincent.paliczka@bracknell-forest.gov.uk

Waste Collection and Disposal: Mrs Janet Dowlman, Waste & Recycling Manager, Time Square, Market Street, Bracknell RG12 1JD ☎ 01344 352000 🖷 01344 353122 ✉ janet.dowlman@bracknell-forest.gov.uk

Waste Collection and Disposal: Mr Vincent Paliczka, Director - Environment, Culture & Communities, Time Square, Market Street, Bracknell RG12 1JD ☎ 01344 352000 ✉ vincent.paliczka@bracknell-forest.gov.uk

BRACKNELL FOREST

Waste Management: Mr Vincent Paliczka, Director - Environment, Culture & Communities, Time Square, Market Street, Bracknell RG12 1JD ☎ 01344 352000
vincent.paliczka@bracknell-forest.gov.uk

COUNCILLORS

***Mayor* Hamilton**, Dee (CON - Wildridings & Central)
dee.hamilton@bracknell-forest.gov.uk

***Deputy Mayor* Virgo**, Tony (CON - Ascot)
tony.virgo@bracknell-forest.gov.uk

***Leader of the Council* Bettison**, Paul (CON - Little Sandhurst & Wellington)
paul.bettison@bracknell-forest.gov.uk

***Deputy Leader of the Council* Birch**, Dale (CON - Little Sandhurst & Wellington)
dale.birch@bracknell-forest.gov.uk

Allen, Nick (CON - College Town)
nick.allen@bracknell-forest.gov.uk

Angell, Bob (CON - Bullbrook)
robert.angell@bracknell-forest.gov.uk

Angell, Jan (CON - Great Hollands South)
jan.angell@bracknell-forest.gov.uk

Barnard, Gareth (CON - Warfield Harvest Ride)
gareth.barnard@bracknell-forest.gov.uk

Birch, Gill (CON - Hanworth)
gill.birch@bracknell-forest.gov.uk

Birch, Graham (CON - Priestwood and Garth)
graham.birch@bracknell-forest.gov.uk

Brossard, Michael (CON - Central Sandhurst)
michael.brossard@bracknell-forest.gov.uk

Brunel-Walker, Marc (CON - Crown Wood)
marc.brunel-walker@bracknell-forest.gov.uk

Dudley, Colin (CON - Crown Wood)
colin.dudley@bracknell-forest.gov.uk

Finch, Alvin (CON - Priestwood & Garth)
alvin.finch@bracknell-forest.gov.uk

Finnie, Jim (CON - Crowthorne)
jim.finnie@bracknell-forest.gov.uk

Gaw, Moira (CON - Winkfield & Cranbourne)
moira.gaw@bracknell-forest.gov.uk

Harrison, John (CON - Binfield with Warfield)
john.harrison@bracknell-forest.gov.uk

Hayes, Suki (CON - Crown Wood)
suki.hayes@bracknell-forest.gov.uk

Hayes, Dorothy (CON - Ascot)
dorothy.hayes@bracknell-forest.gov.uk

Heydon, Peter (CON - Old Bracknell)
peter.heydon@bracknell-forest.gov.uk

Hill, Peter (CON - Great Hollands North)
peter.hill@bracknell-Forest.gov.uk

Ingham, Sandrea (CON - Hanworth)
sandra.ingham@bracknell-froest.gov.uk

King, Phillip (CON - Central Sandhurst)
phillip.king@bracknell.gov.uk

Leake, Ian (CON - Binfield with Warfield)
ian.leake@bracknell-forest.gov.uk

Mattick, Isabel (CON - Harmans Water)
isabel.mattick@bracknell-forest@gov.uk

McCracken, Jennifer (CON - Great Hollands South)
jennie.mccracken@bracknell-forest.gov.uk

McCracken, Iain (CON - Old Bracknell)
iain.mccracken@bracknell-forest.gov.uk

McKenzie, Pauline (CON - College Town)
pauline.mckenzie@bracknell-forest.gov.uk

McKenzie-Boyle, Tina (CON - Priestwood and Garth)
tina.mckenzie-boyle@bracknell-forest.gov.uk

McLean, Robert (CON - Warfield Harvest Ride)
robert.mclean@bracknell-forest.gov.uk

Merry, Ash (CON - Harmans Water)
ash.merry@bracknell-forest.gov.uk

Miller, Kirsten (CON - Bullbrook)
kirsten.miller@bracknell-forest.gov.uk

Peacey, Sarah (CON - Binfield with Warfield)
sara.peacey@bracknell-forest.gov.uk

Phillips, Susie (CON - Winkfield & Cranbourne)
susie.phillips@bracknell-forest.gov.uk

Porter, John (CON - Owlsmoor)
john.porter@bracknell-forest.gov.uk

Skinner, Michael (CON - Wildridings & Central)
michael.skinner@bracknell-forest.gov.uk

Temperton, Mary (LAB - Great Hollands North)
mary.temperton@bracknell-forest.gov.uk

Thompson, Clifton (CON - Warfield Harvest Ride)
cliff.thompson@bracknell-forest.gov.uk

Tullett, Malcolm (CON - Hanwell)
malcolm.tullett@bracknell-forest.gov.uk

Turrell, Chris (CON - Harmans Water)
chris.turrell@bracknell-forest.gov.uk

Wade, Bob (CON - Crowthorne)
bob.wade@bracknell-forest.gov.uk

Worrall, David (CON - Owlsmoor)
david.worrall@bracknell-forest.gov.uk

POLITICAL COMPOSITION

CON: 41, LAB: 1

COMMITTEE CHAIRS

Planning: Mr Colin Dudley

Bradford City M

Bradford City Council, City Hall, Channing Way, Bradford BD1 1HY
☎ 01274 431000 www.bradford.gov.uk

FACTS AND FIGURES

Parliamentary Constituencies: Bradford East, Bradford South, Bradford West, Keighley, Shipley
EU Constituencies: Yorkshire and the Humber
Election Frequency: Elections are by thirds

PRINCIPAL OFFICERS

Chief Executive: Ms Kersten England Chief Executive, City Hall, Channing Way, Bradford BD1 1HY kirsten.england@bradford.gov.uk

Senior Management: Mr Mike Cowlam, Strategic Director - Regeneration & Culture, Olicana House, 35 Chapel Street, Little Germany Bradford BD1 5RE ☎ 01274 433761 🖷 01274 432516 mike.cowlam@bradford.gov.uk

Senior Management: Ms Sue Dunkley Director of Human Resources, City Hall, Channing Way, Bradford BD1 1HY sue.dunkley@bradford.gov.uk

Senior Management: Mr Steve Hartley Strategic Director - Environment & Sport, City Hall, Channing Way, Bradford BD1 1HY ☎ 01274 434748 steve.hartley@bradford.gov.uk

Senior Management: Ms Suzan Hemingway Acting Chief Executive (City Solicitor), City Hall, Channing Way, Bradford BD1 1HY ☎ 01274 432496 🖷 01274 730337 suzan.hemingway@bradford.gov.uk

Senior Management: Mr Michael Jameson Strategic Director - Children's Services, City Hall, Channing Way, Bradford BD1 1HY michael.jameson@bradford.gov.uk

Senior Management: Mr Bernard Lanigan Interim Strategic Director - Adult & Community Services, City Hall, Channing Way, Bradford BD1 1HY ☎ 01274 432900 bernard.lanigan@bradford.gov.uk

Senior Management: Mr Stuart McKinnon-Evans Director - Finance, City Hall, Channing Way, Bradford BD1 1HY stuart.mckinnon-evans@bradford.gov.uk

Senior Management: Ms Anita Parkin Director - Public Health, City Hall, Channing Way, Bradford BD1 1HY anita.parkin@bradford.gov.uk

Access Officer / Social Services (Disability): Ms Linda Mason Interim Assistant Director - Access & Inclusion, City Hall, Channing Way, Bradford BD1 1HY linda.mason@bradford.gov.uk

Building Control: Mr Chris Eaton Head - Building Control, City Hall, Channing Way, Bradford BD1 1HY ☎ 01274 431000 chris.eaton@bradford.gov.uk

Children / Youth Services: Mr Michael Jameson Strategic Director - Children's Services, City Hall, Channing Way, Bradford BD1 1HY michael.jameson@bradford.gov.uk

Children / Youth Services: Ms Cindy Peek Deputy Director - Children's Services, City Hall, Channing Way, Bradford BD1 1HY cindy.peek@bradford.gov.uk

Civil Registration: Ms Christina Smith Superintendent Registrar, City Hall, Channing Way, Bradford BD1 1HY ☎ 01274 432151 christina.smith@bradford.gov.uk

PR / Communications: Ms Alison Milner Assistant Director - Communications, City Hall, Channing Way, Bradford BD1 1HY ☎ 01274 432131 🖷 01274 432321 alison.milner@bradford.gov.uk

Computer Management: Mr James Drury Assistant Director - Council Change Program, City Hall, Channing Way, Bradford BD1 1HY ☎ 01274 432850 james.drury@bradford.gov.uk

Corporate Services: Mr Stuart McKinnon-Evans Director - Finance, City Hall, Channing Way, Bradford BD1 1HY stuart.mckinnon-evans@bradford.gov.uk

Economic Development: Mr Mike Cowlam, Strategic Director - Regeneration & Culture, Jacob's Well, Nelson Street, Bradford BD1 5RW ☎ 01274 433761 🖷 01274 432516 mike.cowlam@bradford.gov.uk

Education: Mr Michael Jameson Strategic Director - Children's Services, City Hall, Channing Way, Bradford BD1 1HY michael.jameson@bradford.gov.uk

E-Government: Mr Stuart McKinnon-Evans Director - Finance, City Hall, Channing Way, Bradford BD1 1HY stuart.mckinnon-evans@bradford.gov.uk

Electoral Registration: Ms Susan Saunders, Electoral Services Manager, Ground Floor, City Hall, Channing Way, Bradford BD1 1HY ☎ 01274 432285 🖷 01274 432799 susan.saunders@bradford.gov.uk

Emergency Planning: Mr Mike Powell, Emergency Planning Manager, City Hall, Channing Way, Bradford BD1 1HY ☎ 01274 432011 🖷 01274 434910 mike.powell@bradford.gov.uk

Energy Management: Mr Steve Hartley Strategic Director - Environment & Sport, City Hall, Channing Way, Bradford BD1 1HY ☎ 01274 434748 steve.hartley@bradford.gov.uk

Environmental / Technical Services: Mr Steve Hartley Strategic Director - Environment & Sport, City Hall, Channing Way, Bradford BD1 1HY ☎ 01274 434748 steve.hartley@bradford.gov.uk

Environmental Health: Mr Steve Hartley Strategic Director - Environment & Sport, City Hall, Channing Way, Bradford BD1 1HY ☎ 01274 434748 steve.hartley@bradford.gov.uk

Estates, Property & Valuation: Mr Mike Cowlam, Strategic Director - Regeneration & Culture, Olicana House, 35 Chapel Street, Little Germany Bradford BD1 5RE ☎ 01274 433761 🖷 01274 432516 mike.cowlam@bradford.gov.uk

Events Manager: Ms Vanessa Mitchell, Manager - Major Programmes, Jacobs Well, Bradford BD1 5RW ☎ 01274 434783 🖷 01274 434676 vanessa.mitchell@bradford.gov.uk

Finance: Mr Stuart McKinnon-Evans Director - Finance, City Hall, Channing Way, Bradford BD1 1HY stuart.mckinnon-evans@bradford.gov.uk

BRADFORD CITY

Pensions: Mr Rodney Barton Pensions Manager, City Hall, Channing Way, Bradford BD1 1HY ☎ 01274 434999 🖱 rodney.barton@bradford.gov.uk

Health and Safety: Ms Susan Ingham Senior Occupational Safety Officer, City Hall, Channing Way, Bradford BD1 1HY ☎ 01274 434246 🖱 susan.ingham@bradford.gov.uk

Highways: Mr Julian Jackson Assistant Director - Planning, Transportation & Highways, City Hall, Channing Way, Bradford BD1 1HY ☎ 01274 437419 🖱 julian.jackson@bradford.gov.uk

Housing: Ms Sheila O'Neill Interim Assitant Director - Housing, Employment & Skills, City Hall, Channing Way, Bradford BD1 1HY 🖱 shelia.o'neill@bradford.gov.uk

Local Area Agreement: Ms Roz Hall Assistant Director - Strategic Support, Argus Chambers, Britannia House, Bradford BD1 1HX ☎ 01274 431000 🖱 roz.hall@bradford.gov.uk

Legal: Ms Suzan Hemingway Acting Chief Executive (City Solicitor), City Hall, Channing Way, Bradford BD1 1HY ☎ 01274 432496 🖶 01274 730337 🖱 suzan.hemingway@bradford.gov.uk

Leisure and Cultural Services: Mr Mike Cowlam, Strategic Director - Regeneration & Culture, Olicana House, 35 Chapel Street, Little Germany Bradford BD1 5RE ☎ 01274 433761 🖶 01274 432516 🖱 mike.cowlam@bradford.gov.uk

Licensing: Ms Tracy McLuckie, Manager - Local Land Charges & Licensing, City Hall, Channing Way, Bradford BD1 1HY ☎ 01274 432209 🖱 tracy.mcluckie@bradford.gov.uk

Lifelong Learning: Mr Michael Jameson Strategic Director - Children's Services, City Hall, Channing Way, Bradford BD1 1HY 🖱 michael.jameson@bradford.gov.uk

Lighting: Mr Allun Preece, Principal Engineer, Flockton House Flockton Road Bradford BD4 7RY ☎ 01274 434019 🖶 01274 737722 🖱 allun.preece@bradford.gov.uk

Member Services: Ms Suzan Hemingway Acting Chief Executive (City Solicitor), City Hall, Channing Way, Bradford BD1 1HY ☎ 01274 432496 🖶 01274 730337 🖱 suzan.hemingway@bradford.gov.uk

Parking: Mr Paul Ratcliffe Parking Services Manager, City Hall, Channing Way, Bradford BD1 1HY 🖱 paul.ratcliffe@bradford.gov.uk

Personnel / HR: Mr Matt Burghardt Assistant Director - Human Resources, City Exchange, 61 Hall Ings, Bradford BD1 5SG ☎ 01274 436135 🖶 01274 730337 🖱 matt.burghardt@bradford.gov.uk; rushna.ullah@bradford.gov.uk

Procurement: Ms Jill Cambell Assistant Director, Procurement, City Hall, Channing Way, Bradford BD1 1HY ☎ 01274 431000 🖱 jill.cambell@bradford.gov.uk

Procurement: Mr Shahid Nazir Interim Assistant Director - Commissioning & Procurement, City Hall, Channing Way, Bradford BD1 1HY 🖱 shahid.nazir@bradford.gov.uk

Public Libraries: Ms Christine Dyson Principal Head of Libraries, Archives & Information Service, City Hall, Channing Way, Bradford BD1 1HY ☎ 01274 431000 🖱 christine.dyson@bradford.gov.uk

Public Libraries: Ms Jackie Kitwood Principal Head - Libraries, Archives & Information Service, City Hall, Channing Way, Bradford BD1 1HY ☎ 01274 431000 🖱 jackie.knitwood@bradford.gov.uk

Recycling & Waste Minimisation: Ms Edith Grooby Recycling Officer & Waste Minimisation, City Hall, Channing Way, Bradford BD1 1HY ☎ 01274 432854 🖱 edith.grooby@bradford.gov.uk

Regeneration: Mr Mike Cowlam, Strategic Director - Regeneration & Culture, Olicana House, 35 Chapel Street, Little Germany Bradford BD1 5RE ☎ 01274 433761 🖶 01274 432516 🖱 mike.cowlam@bradford.gov.uk

Social Services (Adult): Mr Bernard Lanigan Interim Strategic Director - Adult & Community Services, City Hall, Channing Way, Bradford BD1 1HY ☎ 01274 432900 🖱 bernard.lanigan@bradford.gov.uk

Social Services (Children): Mr Michael Jameson Strategic Director - Children's Services, City Hall, Channing Way, Bradford BD1 1HY ☎ 🖱 michael.jameson@bradford.gov.uk

Safeguarding: Mr George McQueen Assistant Director - Access & Inclusion, City Hall, Channing Way, Bradford BD1 1HY 🖱 george.mcqueen@bradford.gov.uk

Childrens Social Care: Ms Julie Jenkins Assistant Director - Children's Specialist Services, City Hall, Channing Way, Bradford BD1 1HY 🖱 julie.jenkins@bradford.gov.uk

Public Health: Ms Anita Parkin Director - Public Health, City Hall, Channing Way, Bradford BD1 1HY 🖱 anita.parkin@bradford.gov.uk

Street Scene: Mr Steve Hartley Strategic Director - Environment & Sport, City Hall, Channing Way, Bradford BD1 1HY ☎ 01274 434748 🖱 steve.hartley@bradford.gov.uk

Tourism: Ms Jackie Bennett Senior Marketing Officer - Tourism, City Hall, Channing Way, Bradford BD1 1HY ☎ 01274 431847 🖶 01274 434857 🖱 jackie.bennett@bradford.gov.uk

Town Centre: Ms Yvonne Crossley, Town Centre Manager, Shipley Town Hall, Shipley BD18 3EJ ☎ 01274 437136 🖶 01274 433763 🖱 yvonne.crossley@bradford.gov.uk

Traffic Management: Mr Julian Jackson Assistant Director - Planning, Transportation & Highways, City Hall, Channing Way, Bradford BD1 1HY ☎ 01274 437419 🖱 julian.jackson@bradford.gov.uk

Transport: Mr Julian Jackson Assistant Director - Planning, Transportation & Highways, City Hall, Channing Way, Bradford BD1 1HY ☎ 01274 437419 🖱 julian.jackson@bradford.gov.uk

Transport Planner: Mr Julian Jackson Assistant Director - Planning, Transportation & Highways, City Hall, Channing Way, Bradford BD1 1HY ☎ 01274 433766 🖱 julian.jackson@bradford.gov.uk

Total Place: Mr Stuart McKinnon-Evans Director - Finance, City Hall, Channing Way, Bradford BD1 1HY
stuart.mckinnon-evans@bradford.gov.uk

Waste Collection and Disposal: Mr Steve Hartley Strategic Director - Environment & Sport, City Hall, Channing Way, Bradford BD1 1HY ☎ 01274 434748 steve.hartley@bradford.gov.uk

Waste Management: Mr Steve Hartley Strategic Director - Environment & Sport, City Hall, Channing Way, Bradford BD1 1HY
☎ 01274 434748 steve.hartley@bradford.gov.uk

COUNCILLORS

***The Lord Mayor* Dodds**, Joanne (LAB - Great Horton)
joanne.dodds@bradford.gov.uk

***Deputy Lord Mayor* Hussain**, Abid (LAB - Keighley Central)
cllr.abidhussain@bradford.gov.uk

***Leader of the Council* Green**, David (LAB - Wibsey)
david.green@bradford.gov.uk

***Deputy Leader of the Council* Slater**, Val (LAB - Royds)
val.slater@bradford.gov.uk

Ahmed, Ishtiaq (IND - Manningham)
ishtiaq.ahmed@bradford.gov.uk

Akhtar, Sameena (LAB - Manningham)
sameena.akhtar@bradford.gov.uk

Ali, Zafar (CON - Keighley Central)
zafar.ali@bradford.gov.uk

Amran, Mohammed (LAB - Heaton)
mohammed.amran@bradford.gov.uk

Azam, Nazam (LAB - City)
nazam.azam@bradford.gov.uk

Bacon, Cath (LAB - Keighley West)
cath.bacon@bradford.gov.uk

Barker, Gerry (CON - Wharfedale)
gerry.barker@bradford.gov.uk

Berry, Ralph (LAB - Wibsey)
ralph.berry@bradford.gov.uk

Brown, Russell (CON - Worth Valley)
russell.brown@bradford.gov.uk

Carmody, Lisa (CON - Queensbury)
lisa.carmody@bradford.gov.uk

Collector, Rugayyah (RSP - City)
rugayyah.collector@bradford.gov.uk

Cooke, Simon (CON - Bingley Rural)
simon.cooke@bradford.gov.uk

Cromie, Paul (IND - Queensbury)
paul.cromie@bradford.gov.uk

Davies, Debbie (CON - Baildon)
debbie.davies@bradford.gov.uk

Duffy, Sue (LAB - Thornton & Allerton)
sue.duffy@bradford.gov.uk

Dunbar, Richard (LAB - Thornton & Allerton)
richard.dunbar@bradford.gov.uk

Eaton, Margaret (CON - Bingley Rural)
margaret.eaton@bradford.gov.uk

Ellis, Michael (CON - Bingley Rural)
michael.ellis@bradford.gov.uk

Engel, Sinead (LAB - Clayton & Fairweather Green)
sinead.engel@bradford.gov.uk

Farley, Adrian (LAB - Keighley West)
adrian.farley@bradford.gov.uk

Fear, Dominic (LD - Idle & Thackley)
dominic.fear@bradford.gov.uk

Ferriby, Sarah (LAB - Wyke)
sarah.ferriby@bradford.gov.uk

Gibbons, Mike (CON - Ilkley)
mike.gibbons@bradford.gov.uk

Greenwood, Vanda (LAB - Windhill & Wrose)
vanda.greenwood@bradford.gov.uk

Griffiths, Alun (LD - Idle & Thackley)
alun.griffiths@bradford.gov.uk

Hawkesworth, Anne (IND - Ilkley)
anne.hawkesworth@bradford.gov.uk

Heseltine, David (CON - Bingley)
david.heseltine@bradford.gov.uk

Hinchcliffe, Susan (LAB - Windhill & Wrose)
susan.hinchcliffe@bradford.gov.uk

Hussain, Shabir (LAB - Manningham)
shabir.hussain@bradford.gov.uk

Hussain, Hawarun (GRN - Shipley)
hawarun.hussain@bradford.gov.uk

Hussain, Arshad (LAB - Toller)
arshad.hussain@bradford.gov.uk

Hussain, Tariq (LAB - Great Horton)
cllr.tariqhussain@bradford.gov.uk

Hussain, Imran (LAB - Toller)
cllr.imranhussain@bradford.gov.uk

Hussain, Khadim (LAB - Keighley Central)
khadim.hussain@bradford.gov.uk

Ikram, Naveeda (LAB - Little Horton)
naveeda.ikram@bradford.gov.uk

Iqbal, Zafar (LAB - Bradford Moor)
zafar.iqbal@bradford.gov.uk

Jabar, Abdul (LAB - Great Horton)
abdul.jabar@bradford.gov.uk

Jamil, Rizwana (LAB - Bowling & Barkerend)
rizwana.jamil@bradford.gov.uk

Johnson, Michael (LAB - Tong)
michael.johnson@bradford.gov.uk

Karmani, Alyas (IND - Little Horton)
alyas.karmani@bradford.gov.uk

Khan, Hassan (LAB - Bowling & Barkerend)
hassan.khan@bradford.gov.uk

Khan, Faisal (IND - Bradford Moor)
cllr.faisalkhan@bradford.gov.uk

Khan, Imran (LAB - Bowling & Barkerend)
cllr.imrankhan@bradford.gov.uk

Lal, Shakeela (LAB - City)
shakeela.lal@bradfod.gov.uk

BRADFORD CITY

Lee, Doreen (LAB - Keighley East)
doreen.lee@bradford.gov.uk

Leeming, Tracey (LD - Bolton & Undercliffe)
tracey.leeming@bradford.gov.uk

Love, Martin (GRN - Shipley)
martin.love@bradford.gov.uk

Mallinson, Andrew (CON - Craven)
andrew.mallinson@bradford.gov.uk

Miller, Glen (CON - Worth Valley)
glen.miller@bradford.gov.uk

Mohammed, Nussrat (LAB - Heaton)
nussrat.mohammed@bradford.gov.uk

Morries, Brian (UKIP - Keighley West)
brian.morris@bradford.gov.uk

Naylor, Adrian (IND - Craven)
adrian.naylor@bradford.gov.uk

Peart, Tess (LAB - Tong)
tess.peart@bradford.gov.uk

Pennington, John (CON - Bingley)
john.pennington@bradford.gov.uk

Pollard, Nicola (LD - Eccleshill)
nicola.pollard@bradford.gov.uk

Pollard, Mike (CON - Balidon)
mike.pollard@bradford.gov.uk

Poulsen, Rebecca (CON - Worth Valley)
rebecca.poulsen@bradford.gov.uk

Pullen, Steve (LAB - Keighley East)
steve.pullen@bradford.gov.uk

Reid, Geoff (LD - Eccleshill)
geoff.reid@bradford.gov.uk

Rickard, Jack (CON - Craven)
jack.rickard@bradford.gov.uk

Robinson, David (IND - Wyke)
cllr.davidrobinson@bradford.gov.uk

Ross-Shaw, Alexander (LAB - Windhill & Wrose)
alex.ross-shaw@bradford.gov.uk

Salam, Taj (LAB - Little Horton)
taj.salam@bradford.gov.uk

Shabbir, Mohammad (IND - Heaton)
mohammad.shabbir@bradford.gov.uk

Shafiq, Mohammed (LAB - Bradford Moor)
mohammed.shafiq@bradford.gov.uk

Shaheen, Fozia (LAB - Toller)
fozia.shaheen@bradford.gov.uk

Shaw, Mark (CON - Bingley)
mark.shaw@bradford.gov.uk

Slater, Malcolm (LAB - Keighley East)
malcolm.slater@bradford.gov.uk

Smith, Brian (CON - Ilkley)
martin.smith@bradford.gov.uk

Smith, Dale (CON - Wharfedale)
dale.smith@bradford.gov.uk

Smith, Lynne (LAB - Wibsey)
lynne.smith@bradford.gov.uk

Stelling, Michael (LD - Bolton & Undercliffe)
michael.stelling@bradford.gov.uk

Sunderland, Jeanette (LD - Idle & Thackley)
jeanette.sunderland@bradford.gov.uk

Sunderland, Rachel (LD - Bolton & Undercliffe)
rachel.sunderland@bradford.gov.uk

Swallow, Michelle (LAB - Clayton & Fairweather Green)
michelle.swallow@bradford.gov.uk

Sykes, Malcolm (CON - Thornton & Allerton)
malcolm.sykes@bradford.gov.uk

Tait, Angela (LAB - Royds)
angela.tait@bradford.gov.uk

Thirkill, Carol (LAB - Clayton & Fairweather Green)
carol.thirkill@bradford.gov.uk

Thornton, Andrew (LAB - Royds)
andrew.thornton@bradford.gov.uk

Townend, Valerie (CON - Balidon)
val.townend@bradford.gov.uk

Wainwright, Alan (LAB - Tong)
alan.wainwright@bradford.gov.uk

Wallace, Dorothy (LD - Eccleshill)
ann.wallace@bradford.gov.uk

Walls, Michael (CON - Queensbury)
michael.walls@bradford.gov.uk

Warburton, David (LAB - Wyke)
david.warburton@bradford.gov.uk

Warnes, Kevin (GRN - Shipley)
kevin.warnes@bradford.gov.uk

Whiteley, Jackie (CON - Wharfedale)
jackie.whiteley@bradford.gov.uk

POLITICAL COMPOSITION

LAB: 45, CON: 23, LD: 9, IND: 8, GRN: 3, UKIP: 1, RSP: 1

COMMITTEE CHAIRS

Children's Services: Mr Malcolm Sykes

Environment & Waste Management: Mr Martin Love

Governance & Audit: Ms Lynne Smith

Health & Wellbeing: Mr David Green

Licensing: Mr Malcolm Slater

Regeneration & Economy: Mr Adrian Farley

Braintree D

Braintree District Council, Causeway House, Braintree CM7 9HB

☎ 01376 552525 🖷 01376 552626 💻 www.braintree.gov.uk

FACTS AND FIGURES

Parliamentary Constituencies: Braintree, Witham
EU Constituencies: Eastern
Election Frequency: Elections are of whole council

PRINCIPAL OFFICERS

Chief Executive: Ms Nicola Beach Chief Executive, Causeway House, Braintree CM7 9HB 01376 552525 nicola.beach@braintree.gov.uk

Senior Management: Mr Chris Fleetham, Corporate Director, Causeway House, Bocking End, Braintree CM7 9HB 01376 552525 chris.fleetham@braintree.gov.uk

Senior Management: Mr Jon Hayden, Corporate Director, Causeway House, Braintree CM7 9HB 01376 552525 jon.hayden@braintree.gov.uk

Senior Management: Mr Ian Hunt Head of Governance, Causeway House, Braintree CM7 9HB 01376 552525 ian.hunt@braintree.gov.uk

Senior Management: Mr Andy Wright Corporate Director, Causeway House, Braintree CM7 9HB 01376 552525 andy.wright@braintree.gov.uk

Architect, Building / Property Services: Mr Trevor Wilson Head of Finance, Causeway House, Braintree CM7 9HB 01376 552525 trevor.wilson@braintree.gov.uk

Building Control: Mr Lee Crabb, Head of Environment, Causeway House, Braintree CM7 9HB 01376 552525 lee.crabb@braintree.gov.uk

PR / Communications: Ms Tania Roberge Marketing & Communications Manager, Causeway House, Braintree CM7 9HB 01376 552525 tania.roberge@braintree.gov.uk

Community Safety: Ms Joanne Albini Head of Housing & Community, Causeway House, Braintree CM7 9HB 01376 557753 joanne.albini@braintree.gov.uk

Computer Management: Ms Cherie Root, Head of Business Solutions, Causeway House, Bocking End, Braintree CM7 9HB 01376 552525 cherie.root@braintree.gov.uk

Corporate Services: Mr Ian Hunt Head of Governance, Causeway House, Braintree CM7 9HB 01376 552525 ian.hunt@braintree.gov.uk

Customer Service: Ms Cherie Root, Head of Business Solutions, Causeway House, Bocking End, Braintree CM7 9HB 01376 552525 cherie.root@braintree.gov.uk

Economic Development: Mr Peter Smith Head of Economic Development, Causeway House, Braintree CM7 9HB 01376 552525 peter.smith@braintree.gov.uk

Electoral Registration: Mr Steve Daynes Electoral Registration Manager, Causeway House, Braintree CM7 9HB 01376 552525 steve.daynes@braintree.gov.uk

Emergency Planning: Ms Kathy Brown, Health, Safety & Emergency Manager, Causeway House, Bocking End, Braintree CM7 9BR 01376 557753 kathy.brown@braintree.gov.uk

Energy Management: Mr Mark Wilson Climate Change Manager, Causeway House, Braintree CM7 9HB 01376 552525 mark.wilson@braintree.gov.uk

Environmental Health: Mr Lee Crabb, Head of Environment, Causeway House, Braintree CM7 9HB 01376 552525 lee.crabb@braintree.gov.uk

Estates, Property & Valuation: Mr Andrew Epsom, Asset & Property Manager, Causeway House, Bocking End, Braintree CM7 9HB 01376 552525 andrew.epsom@braintree.gov.uk

Facilities: Mr Andrew Epsom, Asset & Property Manager, Causeway House, Bocking End, Braintree CM7 9HB 01376 552525 andrew.epsom@braintree.gov.uk

Finance: Mr Chris Fleetham, Corporate Director, Causeway House, Bocking End, Braintree CM7 9HB 01376 552525 chris.fleetham@braintree.gov.uk

Fleet Management: Ms Hayley Goodard Waste & Transport Manager, Unit 4, Lakes Industrial Park, Lower Chapel Hill, Braintree CM7 3RU 01376 332300 hayley.goodard@braintree.gov.uk

Grounds Maintenance: Mr Paul Partridge, Head of Operations, Causeway House, Bocking End, Braintree CM7 9HB 01376 552525 paul.partridge@braintree.gov.uk

Health and Safety: Ms Kathy Brown, Health, Safety & Emergency Manager, Causeway House, Bocking End, Braintree CM7 9BR 01376 557753 kathy.brown@braintree.gov.uk

Home Energy Conservation: Mr Mark Wilson Climate Change Manager, Causeway House, Braintree CM7 9HB 01376 552525 mark.wilson@braintree.gov.uk

Housing: Ms Joanne Albini Head of Housing & Community, Causeway House, Braintree CM7 9HB 01376 557753 joanne.albini@braintree.gov.uk

Legal: Ms Sarah Stockings, Property Law Solicitor, Causeway House, Braintree CM7 9HB 01376 552525 sara.stockings@braintree.gov.uk

Leisure and Cultural Services: Mr Robert Rose Museum Services Manager, Town Hall Centre, Market Place, Braintree CM7 3YG 01376 325266 robert.rose@braintree.gov.uk

Licensing: Mr Lee Crabb, Head of Environment, Causeway House, Braintree CM7 9HB 01376 552525 lee.crabb@braintree.gov.uk

Lifelong Learning: Ms Sam Jenkins Learning & Development Consultant, Causeway House, Bocking End, Braintree CM7 9HB 01376 552525 sam.jenkins@braintree.gov.uk

Lottery Funding, Charity and Voluntary: Mrs Angela Verghese, External Funding & Voluntary Sector Development Manager, Causeway House, Braintree CM7 9HB 01376 552525 angela.verghese@braintree.gov.uk

BRAINTREE

Member Services: Ms Emma Wisbey Member Services Manager, Causeway House, Braintree CM7 9HB ☎ 01376 552525 ✉ emma.wisbey@braintree.gov.uk

Parking: Mr Paul Partridge, Head of Operations, Causeway House, Bocking End, Braintree CM7 9HB ☎ 01376 552525 ✉ paul.partridge@braintree.gov.uk

Personnel / HR: Ms Helen Krischock, HR Manager, Causeway House, Braintree CM7 9HB ☎ 01376 552525 ✉ helen.krischock@braintree.gov.uk

Planning: Mr Jon Hayden, Corporate Director, Causeway House, Braintree CM7 9HB ☎ 01376 552525 ✉ jon.hayden@braintree.gov.uk

Planning: Ms Tessa Lambert Development Control Manager, Causeway House, , Braintree CM7 9HB ☎ 01376 552525 ✉ tessa.lambert@braintree.gov.uk

Procurement: Mr Dominic Warren Procurement Manager, Causeway House, Braintree CM7 9HB ☎ 01376 552525 ✉ dominic.warren@braintree.gov.uk

Recycling & Waste Minimisation: Mr Nick Drake Waste & Transport Manager, Unit 4, Lakes Industrial Park, Lower Chapel Hill, Braintree CM7 3RU ☎ 01376 332300 ✉ nick.drake@braintree.gov.uk

Regeneration: Mr Peter Smith Head of Economic Development, Causeway House, Braintree CM7 9HB ☎ 01376 552525 ✉ peter.smith@braintree.gov.uk

Staff Training: Ms Sam Jenkins Learning & Development Consultant, Causeway House, Bocking End, Braintree CM7 9HB ☎ 01376 552525 ✉ sam.jenkins@braintree.gov,uk

Street Scene: Mr Paul Partridge, Head of Operations, Causeway House, Bocking End, Braintree CM7 9HB ☎ 01376 552525 ✉ paul.partridge@braintree.gov.uk

Sustainable Communities: Mr Jon Hayden, Corporate Director, Causeway House, Braintree CM7 9HB ☎ 01376 552525 ✉ jon.hayden@braintree.gov.uk

Sustainable Development: Mr Peter Smith Head of Economic Development, Causeway House, Braintree CM7 9HB ☎ 01376 552525 ✉ peter.smith@braintree.gov.uk

Tourism: Mr Peter Smith Head of Economic Development, Causeway House, Braintree CM7 9HB ☎ 01376 552525 ✉ peter.smith@braintree.gov.uk

Town Centre: Mr Jon Hayden, Corporate Director, Causeway House, Braintree CM7 9HB ☎ 01376 552525 ✉ jon.hayden@braintree.gov.uk

Transport: Mr Jon Hayden, Corporate Director, Causeway House, Braintree CM7 9HB ☎ 01376 552525 ✉ jon.hayden@braintree.gov.uk

Transport Planner: Mr Jon Hayden, Corporate Director, Causeway House, Braintree CM7 9HB ☎ 01376 552525 ✉ jon.hayden@braintree.gov.uk

Waste Collection and Disposal: Ms Hayley Goodard Waste & Transport Manager, Unit 4, Lakes Industrial Park, Lower Chapel Hill, Braintree CM7 3RU ☎ 01376 332300 ✉ hayley.goodard@braintree.gov.uk

Waste Management: Mr Paul Partridge, Head of Operations, Causeway House, Bocking End, Braintree CM7 9HB ☎ 01376 552525 ✉ paul.partridge@braintree.gov.uk

Children's Play Areas: Mr Paul Partridge, Head of Operations, Causeway House, Bocking End, Braintree CM7 9HB ☎ 01376 552525 ✉ paul.partridge@braintree.gov.uk

COUNCILLORS

***Leader of the Council* Butland**, Graham (CON - Great Notley & Black Notley)
cllr.gbutland@braintree.gov.uk

***Deputy Leader of the Council* Schmidt**, Wendy (CON - Bocking Blackwater)
cllr.wschmidt@braintree.gov.uk

Abbott, James (GRN - Silver End & Cressing)
cllr.jabbott@braintree.gov.uk

Allen, Julia (CON - Halstead Trinity)
cllr.jallen@braintree.gov.uk

Bailey, Christopher (CON - Witham North)
cllr.cbailey@braintree.gov.uk

Banthorpe, Michael (CON - Rayne)
cllr.mbanthorpe@braintree.gov.uk

Baugh, John (CON - Bocking South)
cllr.jbaugh@braintree.gov.uk

Beavis, Joanne (CON - Hedingham)
cllr.jbeavis@braintree.gov.uk

Bebb, David (CON - Hatfield Peverel & Terling)
cllr.dbebb@braintree.gov.uk

Bolton, Robert (CON - Bumpstead)
cllr.rbolton@braintree.gov.uk

Bowers, Kevin (CON - Silver End & Cressing)
cllr.kbowers@braintree.gov.uk

Bowers-Flint, Lynette (CON - Coggeshall)
cllr.lflint@braintree.gov.uk

Canning, Stephen (CON - Bocking Blackwater)
cllr.scanning@braintree.gov.uk

Cunningham, John (CON - Braintree Central & Beckers Green)
cllr.jcunningham@braintree.gov.uk

Cunningham, Mary (CON - Braintree Central & Beckers Green)
cllr.mcunningham@braintree.gov.uk

Cunningham, Tom (CON - Great Notley & Black Notley)
cllr.tcunningham@braintree.gov.uk

Dunn, Malcolm (CON - Braintree South)
cllr.mdunn@braintree.gov.uk

Elliott, John (CON - Kelvedon & Feering)
cllr.jelliott@braintree.gov.uk

Goodman, John (CON - Witham North)
cllr.jgoodman@braintree.gov.uk

Hensman, Andrew (CON - Braintree Central & Beckers Green)
cllr.ahensman@braintree.gov.uk

Horner, Patrick (CON - Witham West)
cllr.phorner@braintree.gov.uk

Hufton-Rees, Daryn (CON - Hatfield Peverel & Terling)
cllr.dhufton-rees@braintree.gov.uk

Hume, David (R - Halstead St Andrews)
cllr.dhume@braintree.gov.uk

Johnson, Hylton (CON - Hedingham)
cllr.hjohnson@braintree.gov.uk

Kilmartin, Angela (CON - Witham Central)
cllr.akilmartin@braintree.gov.uk

Kirby, Stephen (CON - Halstead St Andrews)
cllr.skirby@braintree.gov.uk

Mann, David (LAB - Bocking North)
cllr.dmann@braintree.gov.uk

McKee, John (CON - Braintree West)
cllr.jmckee@braintree.gov.uk

Mitchell, Robert (CON - Kelvedon & Feering)
cllr.rmitchell@braintree.gov.uk

Money, Janet (CON - Witham South)
cllr.jmoney@braintree.gov.uk

Newton, Patricia (CON - Coggeshall)
cllr.ladynewton@braintree.gov.uk

O'Reilly-Cicconi, John (CON - Gosfield & Greenstead Green)
cllr.jo'reilly-cicconi@braintree.gov.uk

Parker, Iona (CON - Stour Valley North)
cllr.iparker@braintree.gov.uk

Paul, Stephanie (CON - Bocking North)
cllr.spaul@braintree.gov.uk

Pell, Jacqueline (R - Halstead Trinity)
cllr.jpell@braintree.gov.uk

Ramage, Ron (CON - Braintree West)
cllr.rramage@braintree.gov.uk

Ricci, Frankie (CON - Great Notley & Black Notley)
cllr.fricci@braintree.gov.uk

Rose, Bill (CON - Witham West)
cllr.wrose@braintree.gov.uk

Santomauro, Vanessa (CON - Braintree South)
cllr.vsantomauro@braintree.gov.uk

Scattergood, Wendy (CON - Stour Valley South)
cllr.wscattergood@braintree.gov.uk

Schwier, Peter (CON - Three Fields)
cllr.pschwier@braintree.gov.uk

Siddall, Chris (CON - The Colnes)
cllr.csiddall@braintree.gov.uk

Spray, Gabrielle (CON - The Colnes)
cllr.gspray@braintree.gov.uk

Tattersley, Peter (CON - Three Fields)
cllr.ptattersley@braintree.gov.uk

Thompson, Corinne (CON - Witham South)
cllr.cthompson@braintree.gov.uk

Thorogood, Moia (LAB - Bocking South)
cllr.mthorogood@braintree.gov.uk

van Dulken, Richard (CON - Yeldham)
cllr.rvandulken@braintree.gov.uk

Walters, Lyn (CON - Bocking Blackwater)
cllr.lwaters@braintree.gov.uk

Wilson, Sue (CON - Witham Central)
cllr.swilson@braintree.gov.uk

POLITICAL COMPOSITION

CON: 44, LAB: 2, R: 2, GRN: 1

Breckland D

Breckland District Council, Elizabeth House, Walpole Loke, Dereham NR19 1EE
☎ 01362 656870 💻 www.breckland.gov.uk

FACTS AND FIGURES

EU Constituencies: Eastern
Election Frequency: Elections are of whole council

PRINCIPAL OFFICERS

Chief Executive: Ms Anna Graves Chief Executive, Elizabeth House, Walpole Loke, Dereham NR19 1EE ☎ 07833 503139 ✉ chief.executive@breckland-sholland.go.uk

Senior Management: Mr Mark Finch, Finance Manager, Elizabeth House, Walpole Loke, Dereham NR19 1EE ☎ 07917 587078 ✉ mark.finch@breckland-sholland.gov.uk

Senior Management: Mr Duncan Hall Housing Manager, Elizabeth House, Walpole Loke, Dereham NR19 1EE ☎ 07500 915488 ✉ duncan.hall@west-norfolk.gov.uk

Senior Management: Ms Julie Kennealy Executive Director - Place, Elizabeth House, Walpole Loke, Dereham NR19 1EE ☎ 07467 339021 ✉ julie.kennealy@breckland-sholland.gov.uk

Senior Management: Mrs Maxine O'Mahony Executive Director - Commissioning & Governance, Elizabeth House, Walpole Loke, Dereham NR19 1EE ☎ 07787 573444 ✉ maxine.omahony@breckland-sholland.gov.uk

Senior Management: Mrs Vicky Thomson Democratic Services & Legal Manager, Elizabeth House, Walpole Loke, Dereham NR19 1EE ☎ 07827 843173 ✉ vicky.thomson@breckland-sholland.gov.uk

Senior Management: Mr Robert Walker Assistant Director - Community, Elizabeth House, Walpole Loke, Dereham NR19 1EE ☎ 07867 988826 ✉ robert.walker@breckland-sholland.gov.uk

Architect, Building / Property Services: Mr Stephen Udberg Asset & Property Manager, Elizabeth House, Walpole Loke, Dereham NR19 1EE ☎ 07827 843157 ✉ steve.udberg@breckland-sholland.gov.uk

Building Control: Mr Phil Adams Public Protection Manager, Elizabeth House, Walpole Loke, Dereham NR19 1EE ☎ 07713 003330 ✉ phillip.adams@breckland-sholland.gov.uk

BRECKLAND

PR / Communications: Mr Rob Leigh Head of Information & Customer Access, Elizabeth House, Walpole Loke, Dereham NR19 1EE ☎ 07880 842190 ✉ rob.leigh@breckland-sholland.gov.uk

Community Safety: Ms Riana Rudland Community Development & Health Manager, Elizabeth House, Walpole Loke, Dereham NR19 1EE ☎ 07823 553988 ✉ riana.rutland@breckland-sholland.gov.uk

Computer Management: Mr Rob Leigh Head of Information & Customer Access, Elizabeth House, Walpole Loke, Dereham NR19 1EE ☎ 07880 842190 ✉ rob.leigh@breckland-sholland.gov.uk

Contracts: Mr Greg Pearson Corporate Improvement & Performance Manager, Elizabeth House, Walpole Loke, Dereham NR19 1EE ☎ 07500 030900 ✉ greg.pearson@breckland-sholland.gov.uk

Customer Service: Mr Rob Leigh Head of Information & Customer Access, Elizabeth House, Walpole Loke, Dereham NR19 1EE ☎ 07880 842190 ✉ rob.leigh@breckland-sholland.gov.uk

Economic Development: Mr Mark Stanton, Economic Development Manager, Elizabeth House, Walpole Loke, Dereham NR19 1EE ☎ 07748 116933 🖷 01362 656360 ✉ mark.stanton@breckland-sholland.gov.uk

E-Government: Mr Rob Leigh Head of Information & Customer Access, Elizabeth House, Walpole Loke, Dereham NR19 1EE ☎ 07880 842190 ✉ rob.leigh@breckland-sholland.gov.uk

Electoral Registration: Mr Rory Ringer Member Services Manager, Elizabeth House, Walpole Loke, Dereham NR19 1EE ☎ 01362 656870 ✉ rory.ringer@breckland.gov.uk

Emergency Planning: Mr David Rimmer Emergency Planning Officer, Elizabeth House, Walpole Loke, Dereham NR19 1EE ☎ 01362 656870 🖷 01362 693733 ✉ david.rimmer@breckland.gov.uk

Environmental Health: Mr Phil Adams Public Protection Manager, Elizabeth House, Walpole Loke, Dereham NR19 1EE ☎ 07713 003330 ✉ phillip.adams@breckland-sholland.gov.uk

Estates, Property & Valuation: Ms Zoe Footer Commercial Property Manager, Elizabeth House, Walpole Loke, Dereham NR19 1EE ☎ 01362 656870 ✉ zoe.footer@breckland.gov.uk

European Liaison: Mr Mark Stanton, Economic Development Manager, Elizabeth House, Walpole Loke, Dereham NR19 1EE ☎ 07748 116933 🖷 01362 656360 ✉ mark.stanton@breckland-sholland.gov.uk

Finance: Mr Mark Finch, Finance Manager, Elizabeth House, Walpole Loke, Dereham NR19 1EE ☎ 07917 587078 ✉ mark.finch@breckland-sholland.gov.uk

Treasury: Mr Mark Finch, Finance Manager, Elizabeth House, Walpole Loke, Dereham NR19 1EE ☎ 07917 587078 ✉ mark.finch@breckland-sholland.gov.uk

Health and Safety: Mr Nick Kendrick Health & Safety Officer, CPBS, South Holland District Council, Priory Road, Spalding PE11 2XE ☎ 07584 466665 ✉ nkendrick@sholland.gov.uk

Home Energy Conservation: Mr Gordon Partridge, Environmental Health Manager - Housing, Elizabeth House, Walpole Loke, Dereham NR19 1EE ☎ 01362 656275 🖷 01362 656353 ✉ gordon.partridge@breckland.gov.uk

Housing: Mr Duncan Hall Housing Manager, Elizabeth House, Walpole Loke, Dereham NR19 1EE ☎ 07500 915488 ✉ duncan.hall@west-norfolk.gov.uk

Legal: Mr Michael Horn, Solicitor to the Council, Elizabeth House, Walpole Loke, Dereham NR19 1EE ☎ 01362 656870 🖷 01362 690821 ✉ mike.horn@breckland.gov.uk

Leisure and Cultural Services: Ms Riana Rudland Community Development & Health Manager, Elizabeth House, Walpole Loke, Dereham NR19 1EE ☎ 07823 553988 ✉ riana.rutland@breckland-sholland.gov.uk

Licensing: Ms Fiona Inston Licensing Manager, Elizabeth House, Walpole Loke, Dereham NR19 1EE ☎ 01362 656870 ✉ fiona.inston@breckland-sholland.gov.uk

Member Services: Mrs Vicky Thomson Democratic Services & Legal Manager, Elizabeth House, Walpole Loke, Dereham NR19 1EE ☎ 07827 843173 ✉ vicky.thomson@breckland-sholland.gov.uk

Planning: Mr Paul Jackson Planning Manager, Elizabeth House, Walpole Loke, Dereham NR19 1EE ☎ 07949 494836 ✉ paul.jackson@breckland-sholland.gov.uk

Procurement: Mr Greg Pearson Corporate Improvement & Performance Manager, Elizabeth House, Walpole Loke, Dereham NR19 1EE ☎ 07500 030900 ✉ greg.pearson@breckland-sholland.gov.uk

Recycling & Waste Minimisation: Ms Emily Spicer Environmental Services Manager, Elizabeth House, Walpole Loke, Dereham NR19 1EE ☎ 07900 168280 ✉ emily.spicer@breckland-sholland.gov.uk

Regeneration: Mr Mark Stanton, Economic Development Manager, Elizabeth House, Walpole Loke, Dereham NR19 1EE ☎ 07748 116933 🖷 01362 656360 ✉ mark.stanton@breckland-sholland.gov.uk

Staff Training: Ms Julia Thaxton Training & Development Manager, Elizabeth House, Walpole Loke, Dereham NR19 1EE ☎ 01362 656896 ✉ julia.thaxton@breckland. gov.uk

Street Scene: Ms Emily Spicer Environmental Services Manager, Elizabeth House, Walpole Loke, Dereham NR19 1EE ☎ 07900 168280 ✉ emily.spicer@breckland-sholland.gov.uk

Sustainable Communities: Ms Riana Rudland Community Development & Health Manager, Elizabeth House, Walpole Loke, Dereham NR19 1EE ☎ 07823 553988 ✉ riana.rutland@breckland-sholland.gov.uk

Waste Collection and Disposal: Ms Emily Spicer Environmental Services Manager, Elizabeth House, Walpole Loke, Dereham NR19 1EE ☎ 07900 168280 ✉ emily.spicer@breckland-sholland.gov.uk

Waste Management: Ms Emily Spicer Environmental Services Manager, Elizabeth House, Walpole Loke, Dereham NR19 1EE
☎ 07900 168280 ✉ emily.spicer@breckland-sholland.gov.uk

COUNCILLORS

***Chair* Bambridge**, Gordon (CON - Upper Wensum)
gordon.bambridge@breckland.gov.uk

***Vice-Chair* Borrett**, Bill (CON - Upper Wensum)
bill.borrett@breckland.gov.uk

***Leader of the Council* Wassell**, Michael (CON - Watton)
michael.wassell@breckland.gov.uk

***Deputy Leader of the Council* Turner**, Lynda (CON - Shipdham with Scarning)
lynda.turner@breckland.gov.uk

***Group Leader* Jermy**, Terry (LAB - Thetford Burrell)
terry.jermy@breckland.gov.uk

Ashby, Tristan (CON - Attleborough Queens & Besthorpe)
tristan.ashby@breckland.gov.uk

Bishop, Jane (CON - Thetford Priory)
jane.bishop@breckland.gov.uk

Bowes, Claire (CON - Watton)
claire.bowes@breckland.gov.uk

Brame, Roy (CON - Thetford Castle)
roy.brame@breckland.gov.uk

Carter, Trevor (CON - Hermitage)
trevor.carter@breckland.gov.uk

Carter, Charles (CON - Saham Toney)
charles.carter@breckland.gov.uk

Chapman-Allen, Marion (CON - Guiltcross)
marion.chapman-allen@breckland.gov.uk

Chapman-Allen, Sam (CON - Forest)
sam.chapman-allen@breckland.gov.uk

Clarke, Harry (LAB - Dereham Withburga)
harry.clarke@breckland.gov.uk

Claussen, Paul (CON - Mattishall)
paul.claussen@breckland.gov.uk

Cowen, Phillip (CON - All Saints & Wayland)
phillip.cowen@breckland.gov.uk

Crawford, Denis (UKIP - Thetford Burrell)
denis.crawford@breckland.gov.uk

Darby, Paul (CON - Swaffham)
paul.darby@breckland.gov.uk

Dimoglou, Pablo (CON - Mattishall)
pablo.dimoglou@breckland.gov.uk

Duffield, Richard (CON - Lincoln)
richard.duffield@breckland.gov.uk

Duigan, Phillip (CON - Dereham Toftwood)
phillip.duigan@breckland.gov.uk

Gilbert, Keith (IND - Watton)
keith.gilbert@breckland.gov.uk

Gould, Elizabeth (CON - Launditch)
elizabeth.gould@breckland.gov.uk

Hewett, Paul (CON - Shipdham with Scarning)
paul.hewett@breckland.gov.uk

Hollis, Jennifer (UKIP - Thetford Boudica)
jennifer.hollis@breckland.gov.uk

Joel, Adrian (CON - The Buckenhams & Banham)
adrian.joel@breckland.gov.uk

Jolly, Ellen (CON - Harling & Heathlands)
ellen.jolly@breckland.gov.uk

Martin, Keith (CON - Attleborough Burgh & Haverscroft)
keith.martin@breckland.gov.uk

Matthews, Shirley (CON - Swaffham)
shirley.matthews@breckland.gov.uk

Millbank, Kate (CON - Dereham Toftwood)
kate.millbank@breckland.gov.uk

Monument, Linda (CON - Dereham Neatherd)
linda.monument@breckland.gov.uk

Monument, Thomas (CON - Dereham Withburga)
thomas.monument@breckland.gov.uk

Nairn, Mike (CON - Bedingfield)
mike.nairn@breckland.gov.uk

Newton, John (UKIP - Thetford Castle)
john.newton@breckland.gov.uk

Nunn, William (CON - Forest)
william.nunn@breckland.gov.uk

Oliver, Rhodri (CON - Attleborough Queens & Besthorpe)
rhodri.oliver@breckland.gov.uk

Pettitt, Karen (CON - Attleborough Queens & Besthorpe)
karen.pettitt@breckland.gov.uk

Richmond, William (CON - Dereham Neatherd)
william.richmond@breckland.gov.uk

Richmond, Robert (CON - Lincoln)
robert.richmond@breckland.gov.uk

Robinson, Mark (CON - Thetford Boudica)
mark.robinson@breckland.gov.uk

Rogers, John (CON - Saham Toney)
john.rogers@breckland.gov.uk

Sharpe, Frank (CON - Ashill)
frank.sharpe@breckland.gov.uk

Sherwood, Ian (CON - Swaffham)
ian.sherwood@breckland.gov.uk

Smith, William (CON - All Saints & Wayland)
william.smith@breckland.gov.uk

Stasiak, Adrian (CON - Attleborough Burgh & Haverscroft)
adrian.stasiak@breckland.gov.uk

Taylor, Mark (UKIP - Thetford Priory)
mark.taylor@breckland.gov.uk

Webb, Alison (CON - Dereham Neatherd)
alison.webb@breckland.gov.uk

Wilkin, Nigel (CON - Necton)
nigel.wilkin@breckland.gov.uk

Wilkinson, Peter (CON - Nar Valley)
peter.wilkinson@breckland.gov.uk

POLITICAL COMPOSITION

CON: 42, UKIP: 4, LAB: 2, IND: 1

BRECKLAND

COMMITTEE CHAIRS

Audit: Mr Bill Borrett

Licensing: Mr Gordon Bambridge

Planning: Mr Nigel Wilkin

Brent L

Brent London Borough Council, Brent Civic Centre, Engineers Way, Wembley HA9 0FJ
☎ 020 8937 1234 customer.services@brent.gov.uk
www.brent.gov.uk

FACTS AND FIGURES

Parliamentary Constituencies: Brent Central, Brent North, Hampstead and Kilburn
EU Constituencies: London
Election Frequency: Elections are of whole council

PRINCIPAL OFFICERS

Chief Executive: Ms Carolyn Downs Chief Executive, Brent Civic Centre, Engineers Way, Wembley HA9 0FJ ☎ 020 8937 1007 carolyn.downs@brent.gov.uk

Assistant Chief Executive: Mr Ben Spinks Assistant Chief Executive, Brent Civic Centre, Engineers Way, Wembley HA9 0FJ ben.spinks@brent.gov.uk

Senior Management: Mr Andrew Donald, Strategic Director - Regeneration & Growth, Brent Civic Centre, Engineers Way, Wembley HA9 0FJ ☎ 020 8937 1049 andrew.donald@brent.gov.uk

Senior Management: Ms Lorraine Langham Chief Operations Officer, Brent Civic Centre, Engineers Way, Wembley HA9 0FJ lorraine.langham@brent.gov.uk

Senior Management: Mr Philip Porter Strategic Director - Adult Social Care, Brent Civic Centre, Engineers Way, Wembley HA9 0FJ ☎ 020 8937 5937 phil.porter@brent.gov.uk

Senior Management: Ms Gail Tolley Strategic Director - Children & Young People, Brent Civic Centre, Engineers Way, Wembley HA9 0FJ ☎ 020 8937 6422 gail.tolley@brent.gov.uk

Access Officer / Social Services (Disability): Mr David Dunkley Director- Rehabilitation, 15 Brondesbury Road, Kilburn, London NW6 6BX ☎ 020 8937 4297 d.dunkley@nhs.net

Architect, Building / Property Services: Mr Richard Barrett, Operational Director - Property & Projects, Brent Civic Centre, Engineers Way, Wembley HA9 0FJ ☎ 020 8937 1330 richard.barrett@brent.gov.uk

Building Control: Mr John Humphries Head of Building Control, Brent Civic Centre, Engineers Way, Wembley HA9 0FJ ☎ 020 8937 5477 john.humphries@brent.gov.uk

Children / Youth Services: Ms Angela Chiswell Head of Youth Support Services, Brent Civic Centre, Engineers Way, Wembley HA9 0FJ ☎ 020 8937 3667 angela.chiswell@brent.go.uk

Children / Youth Services: Ms Sara Williams Director - Early Help & Education, Brent Civic Centre, Engineers Way, Wembley HA9 0FJ ☎ 020 8937 3510 sara.williams@brent.gov.uk

Civil Registration: Mr Mark Rimmer, Head - Registration & Nationality Service, Brent Civic Centre, Engineers Way, Wembley HA9 0FJ ☎ 020 8937 1011 mark.rimmer@brent.gov.uk

PR / Communications: Mr Robert Mansfield Head of Communications, Brent Civic Centre, Engineers Way, Wembley HA9 0FJ ☎ 020 8937 4229 robert.mansfield@brent.gov.uk

Community Safety: Mr Chris Williams Head of Community Safety & Emergency Planning, Brent Civic Centre, Engineers Way, Wembley HA9 0FJ ☎ 020 8937 3301 chris.williams@brent.gov.uk

Computer Management: Mr Prod Sarigianis Head of Digital Services (Acting), Brent Civic Centre, Engineers Way, Wembley HA9 0FJ ☎ 020 8937 6080 prod.sarigianis@brent.gov.uk

Consumer Protection and Trading Standards: Mr David Thrale, Head - Regulatory Services, Brent Civic Centre, Engineers Way, Wembley HA9 0FJ ☎ 020 8937 5454 david.thrale@brent.gov.uk

Contracts: Mr Jonathan Treherne Senior Contract Lawyer, Brent Civic Centre, Engineers Way, Wembley HA9 0FJ ☎ 020 8937 1542 jonathan.treherne@brent.gov.uk

Customer Service: Ms Margaret Read Director - Customer Services, Brent Civic Centre, Engineers Way, Wembley HA9 0FJ ☎ 020 8937 1521 margaret.read@brent.gov.uk

Education: Ms Carmen Coffey Head - Pupil Parent Services, Brent Civic Centre, Engineers Way, Wembley HA9 0FJ ☎ 020 8937 3033 carmen.coffey@brent.gov.uk

Electoral Registration: Mr Sean O'Sullivan, Electoral Services Manager, Brent Civic Centre, Engineers Way, Wembley HA9 0FJ ☎ 020 8937 1370 s.osullivan@brent.gov.uk

Emergency Planning: Mr Chris Williams Head of Community Safety & Emergency Planning, Brent Civic Centre, Engineers Way, Wembley HA9 0FJ ☎ 020 8937 3301 chris.williams@brent.gov.uk

Environmental Health: Mr David Thrale, Head - Regulatory Services, Brent Civic Centre, Engineers Way, Wembley HA9 0FJ ☎ 020 8937 5454 david.thrale@brent.gov.uk

Events Manager: Ms Kat Parker Head - Conference & Event Sales, Brent Civic Centre, Engineers Way, Wembley HA9 0FJ ☎ 020 8937 4344 kat.parker@brent.gov.uk

Finance: Mr Conrad Hall Chief Finance Officer, Brent Civic Centre, Engineers Way, Wembley HA9 0FJ ☎ 020 8937 6528 conrad.hall@brent.gov.uk

Pensions: Ms Anna McCormack Principal Consultant, Brent Civic Centre, Engineers Way, Wembley HA9 0FJ ☎ 020 8937 3936 anna.mccormack@brent.gov.uk

Pensions: Mr Julian Pendock Investments & Pensions Manager, Brent Civic Centre, Engineers Way, Wembley HA9 0FJ ☎ 020 8937 1234 ✉ julian.pendock@brent.gov.uk

Fleet Management: Mr Dave Shelley Head - Passenger Transport, Hirst Hall, Tower Lane, GEC Estate, East Lane, Wembley HA9 7NB ☎ 020 8937 6731 ✉ david.shelley@brent.gov.uk

Health and Safety: Mr David Thrale, Head - Regulatory Services, Brent Civic Centre, Engineers Way, Wembley HA9 0FJ ☎ 020 8937 5454 ✉ david.thrale@brent.gov.uk

Highways: Mr Tony Kennedy Head of Transportation, Brent Civic Centre, Engineers Way, Wembley HA9 0FJ ☎ 020 8937 5151 ✉ tony.kennedy@brent.gov.uk

Housing: Mr Jon Lloyd-Owen Operational Director - Housing & Employment, Brent Civic Centre, Engineers Way, Wembley HA9 0FJ ☎ 020 8937 5199 ✉ jon.lloyd-owen@brent.gov.uk

Housing Maintenance: Mr Tom Bremner Chief Executive - BHP, Brent Civic Centre, Engineers Way, Wembley HA9 0FJ ☎ 020 8937 2200 ✉ tom.bremner@bhphousing.co.uk

Legal: Ms Fiona Alderman Chief Legal Officer, Brent Civic Centre, Engineers Way, Wembley HA9 0FJ ☎ 020 8937 1292 ✉ fiona.alderman@brent.gov.uk

Licensing: Mr David Thrale, Head - Regulatory Services, Brent Civic Centre, Engineers Way, Wembley HA9 0FJ ☎ 020 8937 5454 ✉ david.thrale@brent.gov.uk

Lifelong Learning: Ms Rashmi Agarwal Head of Culture, Brent Civic Centre, Engineers Way, Wembley HA9 0FJ ☎ 020 8937 3143 ✉ rashmi.agarwal@brent.gov.uk

Lighting: Mr Gavin Moore Head of Parking & Lighting, Brent Civic Centre, Engineers Way, Wembley HA9 0FJ ☎ 020 8937 2979 ✉ gavin.f.moore@brent.gov.uk

Member Services: Mr Thomas Cattermole Head - Executive & Member Services, Brent Civic Centre, Engineers Way, Wembley HA9 0FJ ☎ 020 8937 5446 ✉ thomas.cattermole@brent.gov.uk

Parking: Mr Gavin Moore Head of Parking & Lighting, Brent Civic Centre, Engineers Way, Wembley HA9 0FJ ☎ 020 8937 2979 ✉ gavin.f.moore@brent.gov.uk

Personnel / HR: Ms Cara Davani Director - HR & Administration, Brent Civic Centre, Engineers Way, Wembley HA9 0FJ ☎ 020 8937 1909 ✉ cara.davani@brent.gov.uk

Planning: Mr Stephen Weeks Head of Planning, Brent Civic Centre, Engineers Way, Wembley HA9 0FJ ☎ 020 8937 5238 ✉ stephen.weeks@brent.gov.uk

Procurement: Mr Gary Salterpicco Procurement Manager, Brent Civic Centre, Engineers Way, Wembley HA9 0FJ ☎ 020 8937 1625 ✉ gary.salterpicco@brent.gov.uk

Public Libraries: Ms Rashmi Agarwal Head of Culture, Brent Civic Centre, Engineers Way, Wembley HA9 0FJ ☎ 020 8937 3143 ✉ rashmi.agarwal@brent.gov.uk

Road Safety: Ms Debbie Huckle Safety & Travel Planning, Brent Civic Centre, Engineers Way, Wembley HA9 0FJ ☎ 020 8903 5570 ✉ debbie.fowler@brent.gov.uk

Social Services: Mr Graham Genoni Operational Director - Children's Social Care, Brent Civic Centre, Engineers Way, Wembley HA9 0FJ ☎ 020 8937 4091 ✉ graham.genoni@brent.gov.uk

Social Services (Adult): Mr Philip Porter Strategic Director - Adult Social Care, Brent Civic Centre, Engineers Way, Wembley HA9 0FJ ☎ 020 8937 5937 ✉ phil.porter@brent.gov.uk

Public Health: Dr Melanie Smith Director - Public Health, Brent Civic Centre, Engineers Way, Wembley HA9 0FJ ☎ 020 8937 6227 ✉ melanie.smith@brent.gov.uk

Staff Training: Mr Sanmi Akinlab HR Manager, Brent Civic Centre, Engineers Way, Wembley HA9 0FJ ☎ 020 8937 3245 ✉ sanmi.akinlab@brent.gov.uk

Staff Training: Mr Afzal Ghany HR Manager, Brent Civic Centre, Engineers Way, Wembley HA9 0FJ ☎ 020 8937 1082 ✉ afzal.ghany@brent.gov.uk

Traffic Management: Mr Tony Kennedy Head of Transportation, Brent Civic Centre, Engineers Way, Wembley HA9 0FJ ☎ 020 8937 5151 ✉ tony.kennedy@brent.gov.uk

COUNCILLORS

***Mayor* Jones**, Lesley (LAB - Willesden Green)
cllr.lesley.jones@brent.gov.uk

***Deputy Mayor* Ahmed**, Parvez (LAB - Dollis Hill)
cllr.parvez.ahmed@brent.gov.uk

***Leader of the Council* Butt**, Muhammed (LAB - Tokyngton)
cllr.muhammed.butt@brent.gov.uk

***Deputy Leader of the Council* Pavey**, Michael (LAB - Barnhill)
cllr.michael.pavey@brent.gov.uk

Aden, Abdi (LAB - Sudbury)
cllr.abdifatah.aden@brent.gov.uk

Agha, Amer (LAB - Welsh Harp)
cllr.amer.agha@brent.gov.uk

Allie, James (LAB - Alperton)
cllr.james.allie@brent.gov.uk

Bradley, Matt (LAB - Preston)
cllr.matthew.bradley@brent.gov.uk

Carr, Helen (LD - Mapesbury)
cllr.helen.carr@brent.gov.uk

Chohan, Bhagwanji (LAB - Alperton)
cllr.bhagwanji.chohan@brent.gov.uk

Choudhary, Shafique (LAB - Barnhill)
cllr.shafique.choudhary@brent.gov.uk

Choudry, Aslam (LAB - Dudden Hill)
cllr.aslam.choudry@brent.gov.uk

BRENT

Colacicco, Lia (LAB - Mapesbury)
cllr.lia.colacicco@brent.gov.uk

Collier, Bernard (LAB - Willesden Green)
cllr.bernard.collier@brent.gov.uk

Colwill, Reg (CON - Kenton)
cllr.reg.colwill@brent.gov.uk

Conneely, Rita (LAB - Kilburn)
cllr.rita.conneely@brent.gov.uk

Crane, George (LAB - Fryent)
cllr.george.crane@brent.gov.uk

Daly, Mary (LAB - Sudbury)
cllr.mary.daly@brent.gov.uk

Davidson, Joel (CON - Brondesbury Park)
cllr.joel.davidson@brent.gov.uk

Denselow, James (LAB - Queen's Park)
cllr.james.denselow@brent.gov.uk

Dixon, Liz (LAB - Dollis Hill)
cllr.liz.dixon@brent.gov.uk

Duffy, John (LAB - Kilburn)
cllr.john.duffy@brent.gov.uk

Eniola, Aisha (LAB - Harlesden)
cllr.aisha.eniola@brent.gov.uk

Ezeajughi, Ernest (LAB - Stonebridge)
cllr.ernest.ezeajughi@brent.gov.uk

Farah, Harbi (LAB - Welsh Harp)
cllr.harbi.farah@brent.gov.uk

Filson, Dan (LAB - Kensal Green)
cllr.dan.filson@brent.gov.uk

Harrison, Patricia (LAB - Preston)
cllr.patricia.harrison@brent.gov.uk

Hector, Claudia (LAB - Kensal Green)
cllr.claudia.hector@brent.gov.uk

Hirani, Krupesh (LAB - Dudden Hill)
cllr.krupesh.hirani@brent.gov.uk

Hoda-Benn, Aisha (LAB - Sudbury)
cllr.aisha.hoda-benn@brent.gov.uk

Hossain, Jean (LAB - Preston)
cllr.jean.hossain@brent.gov.uk

Hylton, Orleen (LAB - Tokyngton)
cllr.orleen.hylton@brent.gov.uk

Kabir, Sandra (LAB - Queensbury)
cllr.sandra.kabir@brent.gov.uk

Kansagra, Suresh (CON - Kenton)
cllr.suresh.kansagra@brent.gov.uk

Kelcher, Matt (LAB - Kensal Green)
cllr.matt.kelcher@brent.gov.uk

Khan, Sabina (LAB - Stonebridge)
cllr.sabina.khan@brent.gov.uk

Long, Janice (LAB - Dudden Hill)
cllr.janice.long@brent.gov.uk

Mahmood, Arshad (LAB - Dollis Hill)
cllr.arshad.mahmood@brent.gov.uk

Marquis, Sarah (LAB - Barnhill)
cllr.sarah.marquis@brent.gov.uk

Mashari, Roxanne (LAB - Welsh Harp)
cllr.roxanne.mashari@brent.gov.uk

Maurice, Michael (CON - Kenton)
cllr.michael.maurice@brent.gov.uk

McLeish, Lloyd (LAB - Harlesden)
cllr.lloyd.mcleish@brent.gov.uk

McLennan, Margaret (LAB - Northwick Park)
cllr.margaret.mclennan@brent.gov.uk

Miller, Tom (LAB - Willesden Green)
cllr.tom.miller@brent.gov.uk

Mitchell Murray, Wilhelmina (LAB - Wembley Central)
cllr.wilhelmina.mitchellmurray@brent.gov.uk

Mitchell Murray, Joshua (LAB - Northwick Park)
cllr.joshua.murray@brent.gov.uk

Moher, Ruth (LAB - Fryent)
cllr.ruth.moher@brent.gov.uk

Naheerathan, Kana (LAB - Queensbury)
cllr.kana.naheerathan@brent.gov.uk

Nerva, Neil (LAB - Queen's Park)
cllr.neil.nerva@brent.gov.uk

Oladapo, Tayo (LAB - Kilburn)
cllr.tayo.oladapo@brent.gov.uk

Patel, Ramesh (LAB - Queensbury)
cllr.ramesh.patel@brent.gov.uk

Patel, Mili (LAB - Alperton)
cllr.mili.patel@brent.gov.uk

Perrin, Keith (LAB - Northwick Park)
cllr.keith.perrin@brent.gov.uk

Shahzad, Ahmad (LAB - Mapesbury)
cllr.ahmad.shahzad@brent.gov.uk

Shaw, Carol (LD - Brondesbury Park)
cllr.carol.shaw@brent.gov.uk

Sheth, Ketan (LAB - Tokyngton)
cllr.ketan.sheth@brent.gov.uk

Sheth, Krupa (LAB - Wembley Central)
cllr.krupa.sheth@brent.gov.uk

Southwood, Eleanor (LAB - Queen's Park)
cllr.eleanor.southwood@brent.gov.uk

Stopp, Sam (LAB - Wembley Central)
cllr.sam.stopp@brent.gov.uk

Tatler, Shama (LAB - Fryent)
cllr.shama.tatler@brent.gov.uk

Thomas, Bobby (LAB - Harlesden)
cllr.bobby.thomas@brent.gov.uk

Van Kalwala, Zaffar (LAB - Stonebridge)
cllr.zaffar.vankalwala@brent.gov.uk

Warren, John (CON - Brondesbury Park)
cllr.john.warren@brent.gov.uk

POLITICAL COMPOSITION
LAB: 56, CON: 5, LD: 2

COMMITTEE CHAIRS
Health & Wellbeing: Mr Muhammed Butt

Brentwood D

Brentwood Borough Council, c/o The Town Hall, Ingrave Road, Brentwood CM15 8AY
☎ 01277 312500 🖷 01277 312743 ✉ enquiries@brentwood.gov.uk
💻 www.brentwood.gov.uk

FACTS AND FIGURES

Parliamentary Constituencies: Brentwood and Ongar
EU Constituencies: Eastern
Election Frequency: Elections are by thirds

PRINCIPAL OFFICERS

Chief Executive: Mr Philip Ruck Head of Paid Service, c/o The Town Hall, Ingrave Road, Brentwood CM15 8AY ☎ 01277 312712 ✉ philip.ruck@brentwood.gov.uk

Senior Management: Mr Roy Ormsby Head of Streetscene & Environment, c/o The Town Hall, Ingrave Road, Brentwood CM15 8AY ☎ 01277 312554 🖷 01277 312743 ✉ roy.ormsby@brentwood.gov.uk

Building Control: Mr Gary Price Building Control Team Leader, c/o The Town Hall, Ingrave Road, Brentwood CM15 8AY ☎ 01277 312534 🖷 ; 01277 312743 ✉ gary.price@brentwood.gov.uk

Children / Youth Services: Ms Kim Anderson Partnerships, Leisure & Funding Manager, c/o The Town Hall, Ingrave Road, Brentwood CM15 8AY ☎ 01277 312634 🖷 01277 312743 ✉ kim.anderson@brentwood.gov.uk

PR / Communications: Mrs Leona Murray-Green Senior Communications Officer, c/o The Town Hall, Ingrave Road, Brentwood CM15 8AY ☎ 01277 312630 🖷 01277 312743 ✉ leona.murraygreen@brentwood.gov.uk

Community Planning: Mr Philip Drane Planning Policy Team Leader, c/o The Town Hall, Ingrave Road, Brentwood CM15 8AY ☎ 01277 312609 🖷 01277 312743 ✉ philipdrane@brentwood.gov.uk

Community Safety: Ms Tracey Lilley Anti-Social Behaviour Co-ordinator, c/o The Town Hall, Ingrave Road, Brentwood CM15 8AY ☎ 01277 312644 🖷 01277 312743 ✉ tracey.lilley@brentwood.gov.uk

Computer Management: Mr Tim Huggins, ICT Manager, Town Hall, Ingrave Road, Brentwood CM15 8AY ☎ 01277 312719 🖷 01277 312743 ✉ tim.huggins@brentwood.gov.uk

Corporate Services: Ms Laura Needham Executive Support Officer, c/o The Town Hall, Ingrave Road, Brentwood CM15 8AY ☎ 01277 312632 ✉ laura.needham@brentwood.gov.uk

Customer Service: Mr Rob Manser Revenues & Benefits Manager, c/o The Town Hall, Ingrave Road, Brentwood CM15 8AY ☎ 01277 312855 ✉ rob.manser@brentwood.gov.uk

Direct Labour: Mr Darren Laver Waste & Grounds Manager, c/o The Town Hall, Ingrave Road, Brentwood CM15 8AY ☎ 01277 312779 🖷 01277 312743 ✉ darren.laver@brentwood.gov.uk

Economic Development: Ms Anne Knight Economic Development Officer, c/o The Town Hall, Ingrave Road, Brentwood CM15 8AY ☎ 01277 312607 🖷 01277 312743 ✉ anne.knight@brentwood.gov.uk

E-Government: Mr Tim Huggins, ICT Manager, Town Hall, Ingrave Road, Brentwood CM15 8AY ☎ 01277 312719 🖷 01277 312743 ✉ tim.huggins@brentwood.gov.uk

Electoral Registration: Mrs Carole Tatton-Bennett Electoral Services Manager, c/o The Town Hall, Ingrave Road, Brentwood CM15 8AY ☎ 01277 312709 🖷 01277 312743 ✉ carole.tatton-bennett@brentwood.gov.uk

Emergency Planning: Ms Sue White Emergency Planning Officer, c/o The Town Hall, Ingrave Road, Brentwood CM15 8AY ☎ 01277 312821 🖷 01277 312743 ✉ sue.white@brentwood.gov.uk

Environmental Health: Mr Ashley Culverwell Head of Borough Health - Safety & Localism, c/o The Town Hall, Ingrave Road, Brentwood CM15 8AY ☎ 01277 312504 🖷 01277 312526 ✉ ashley.culverwell@brentwood.gov.uk

Estates, Property & Valuation: Mr Chris Gill Strategic Asset Manager, c/o The Town Hall, Ingrave Road, Brentwood CM15 8AY ☎ 01277 312690 ✉ chris.gill@brentwood.gov.uk

Events Manager: Ms Kim Anderson Partnerships, Leisure & Funding Manager, c/o The Town Hall, Ingrave Road, Brentwood CM15 8AY ☎ 01277 312634 🖷 01277 312743 ✉ kim.anderson@brentwood.gov.uk

Finance: Mr Chris Leslie Finance Director & S151 Officer, c/o The Town Hall, Ingrave Road, Brentwood CM15 8AY ☎ 01277 312542 ✉ chris.leslie@brentwood.gov.uk

Grounds Maintenance: Mr Stuart Anderson Open Space Strategy Co-ordinator, c/o The Town Hall, Ingrave Road, Brentwood CM15 8AY ☎ 01277 312654 🖷 01277 312743 ✉ stuart.anderson@brentwood.gov.uk

Health and Safety: Mr Mark Stanbury Senior Environmental Health Officer, c/o The Town Hall, Ingrave Road, Brentwood CM15 8AY ☎ 01277 312510 🖷 01277 312743 ✉ mark.stanbury@brentwood.gov.uk

Housing: Ms Helen Gregory Interim Head of Housing, c/o The Town Hall, Ingrave Road, Brentwood CM15 8AY ☎ 01277 312586 🖷 01277 312643 ✉ helen.gregory@brentwood.gov.uk

Housing Maintenance: Ms Helen Gregory Interim Head of Housing, c/o The Town Hall, Ingrave Road, Brentwood CM15 8AY ☎ 01277 312586 🖷 01277 312643 ✉ helen.gregory@brentwood.gov.uk

Legal: Mr David Lawson Acting Head of Legal, c/o The Town Hall, Ingrave Road, Brentwood CM15 8AY ☎ 01277 312860 ✉ david.lawson@brentwood.gov.uk

Leisure and Cultural Services: Ms Kim Anderson Partnerships, Leisure & Funding Manager, c/o The Town Hall, Ingrave Road, Brentwood CM15 8AY ☎ 01277 312634 🖷 01277 312743 ✉ kim.anderson@brentwood.gov.uk

Licensing: Mr Gary O'Shea Principal Licensing Officer, c/o The Town Hall, Ingrave Road, Brentwood CM15 8AY ☎ 01277 312503 🖷 01277 312643 ✉ garyo'shea@brentwood.gov.uk

BRENTWOOD

Member Services: Mr Christopher Potter Monitoring Officer & Head of Support Services, c/o The Town Hall, Ingrave Road, Brentwood CM15 8AY ☎ 01277 312860
✉ christopher.potter@brentwood.gov.uk

Parking: Ms Carol Tomlin Parking Manager, c/o The Town Hall, Ingrave Road, Brentwood CM15 8AY ☎ 01277 312583
📠 01277 312643 ✉ carol.tomlin@brentwood.gov.uk

Planning: Mr Gordon Glenday Head of Planning, c/o The Town Hall, Ingrave Road, Brentwood CM15 8AY ☎ 01277 312512
✉ gordon.glenday@brentwood.gov.uk

Procurement: Ms Jane Mitchell Payments & Procurement Officer, c/o The Town Hall, Ingrave Road, Brentwood CM15 8AY ☎ 01277 312853 📠 01277 312743 ✉ jane.mitchell@brentwood.gov.uk

Recycling & Waste Minimisation: Mr Darren Laver Waste & Grounds Manager, c/o The Town Hall, Ingrave Road, Brentwood CM15 8AY ☎ 01277 312779 📠 01277 312743
✉ darren.laver@brentwood.gov.uk

Street Scene: Mr Roy Ormsby Head of Streetscene & Environment, c/o The Town Hall, Ingrave Road, Brentwood CM15 8AY
☎ 01277 312554 📠 01277 312743 ✉ roy.ormsby@brentwood.gov.uk

Town Centre: Ms Elaine Richardson Interim Town Centre & Marketing Manager, c/o The Town Hall, Ingrave Road, Brentwood CM15 8AY ☎ 01277 312515 📠 01277 312743
✉ elaine.richardson@brentwood.gov.uk

Waste Collection and Disposal: Mr Darren Laver Waste & Grounds Manager, c/o The Town Hall, Ingrave Road, Brentwood CM15 8AY ☎ 01277 312779 📠 01277 312743
✉ darren.laver@brentwood.gov.uk

Waste Management: Mr Darren Laver Waste & Grounds Manager, c/o The Town Hall, Ingrave Road, Brentwood CM15 8AY
☎ 01277 312779 📠 01277 312743 ✉ darren.laver@brentwood.gov.uk

Children's Play Areas: Mr Stuart Anderson Open Space Strategy Co-ordinator, c/o The Town Hall, Ingrave Road, Brentwood CM15 8AY ☎ 01277 312654 📠 01277 312743
✉ stuart.anderson@brentwood.gov.uk

COUNCILLORS

***Mayor* Reed**, Mark (CON - Hutton South)
mark.reed@brentwood.gov.uk

***Deputy Mayor* Hones**, Noelle (CON - Ingatestone, Fryerning & Mountnessing)
noelle.hones@brentwood.gov.uk

***Leader of the Council* McKinlay**, Louise (CON - Hutton North)
louise.mckinlay@brentwood.gov.uk

***Deputy Leader of the Council* Hirst**, Roger (CON - Hutton South)
roger.hirst@brentwood.gov.uk

Aspinell, Barry (LD - Pilgrims Hatch)
barry.aspinell@brentwood.gov.uk

Barrell, Paul (CON - Warley)
paul.barrell@brentwood.gov.uk

Barrett, Gareth (LAB - Brentwood South)
gareth.barrett@brentwood.gov.uk

Carter, Ross (LD - Brentwood North)
ross.carter@brentwood.gov.uk

Chilvers, Karen (LD - Brentwood West)
karen.chilvers@brentwood.gov.uk

Clark, Graeme (LD - Shenfield)
graeme.clark@brentwood.gov.uk

Cloke, Jon (CON - Ingatestone, Fryerning & Mountnessing)
jon.cloke@brentwood.gov.uk

Coe, Ann (CON - South Weald)
ann.coe@brentwood.gov.uk

Cohen, Liz (LD - Shenfield)
liz.cohen@brentwood.gov.uk

Davies, Vicky (LD - Pilgrims Hatch)
vicky.davies@brentwood.gov.uk

Faragher, Paul (CON - Hutton Central)
paul.faragher@brentwood.gov.uk

Henwood, Madeline (CON - Tipps Cross)
madeline.henwood@brentwood.gov.uk

Hossack, Chris (CON - Hutton East)
chris.hossack@brentwood.gov.uk

Hubbard, Jill (LD - Warley)
jill.hubbard@brentwood.gov.uk

Keeble, Roger (IND - Tipps Cross)
roger.keeble@brentwood.gov.uk

Kendall, David (LD - Pilgrims Hatch)
david.kendall@brentwood.gov.uk

Kerslake, John (CON - Hutton Central)
john.kerslake@brentwood.gov.uk

McCheyne, Roger (CON - Brizes & Doddinghurst)
roger.mccheyne@brentwood.gov.uk

Morrissey, Julie (LAB - Brentwood South)
julie.morrissey@brentwood.gov.uk

Murphy, Sheila (CON - Herongate, Ingrave & West Horndon)
sheilah.murphy@brentwood.gov.uk

Mynott, Philip (LD - Brentwood North)
philip.mynott@brentwood.gov.uk

Newberry, John (LD - Brentwood West)
john.newberry@brentwood.gov.uk

Parker, Keith (CON - Brizes & Doddinghurst)
keith.parker@brentwood.gov.uk

Poppy, Cliff (CON - Brizes & Doddinghurst)
cliff.poppy@breentwood.gov.uk

Rowlands, Louise (CON - Shenfield)
louise.rowlland@brenford.gov.uk

Russell, Will (CON - Brentwood West)
will.russell@brentwood.gov.uk

Salde, Melissa (CON - Brentwood North)
melissa.slade@brentwood.gov.uk

Sanders, Olivia (CON - Hutton East)
olivia.sanders@brentwood.gov.uk

Sleep, Tony (CON - Ingatestone, Fryerning & Mountnessing)
tony.sleep@brentwood.gov.uk

Squirrell, Jo (LD - Herongate, Ingrave & West Hordon)
joanne.squirrell@brentwood.gov.uk

Tee, David (CON - Warley)
david.tee@brentwood.gov.uk

Trump, William (CON - Hutton North)
william.trump@brentwood.gov.uk

Wiles, Andrew (CON - Brentwood South)
andrew.wiles@brentwood.gov.uk

POLITICAL COMPOSITION

CON: 23, LD: 11, LAB: 2, IND: 1

COMMITTEE CHAIRS

Audit: Mr John Kerslake

Finance: Mrs Louise McKinlay

Licensing: Mr Roger McCheyne

Planning: Mr Roger McCheyne

Bridgend W

Bridgend County Borough Council, Civic Offices, Angel Street, Bridgend CF31 4WB
☎ 01656 643643 🖷 01656 668126 ✉ talktous@bridgend.gov.uk
🖳 www.bridgend.gov.uk

FACTS AND FIGURES

Parliamentary Constituencies: Bridgend, Ogmore
EU Constituencies: Wales
Election Frequency: Elections are of whole council

PRINCIPAL OFFICERS

Chief Executive: Mr Darren Mepham, Chief Executive, Civic Offices, Angel Street, Bridgend CF31 4WB ☎ 01656 643227 🖷 01656 643215 ✉ darren.mepham@bridgend.gov.uk

Assistant Chief Executive: Mr Andrew Jolley, Assistant Chief Executive, Civic Offices, Angel Street, Bridgend CF31 4WB ☎ 01656 643106 ✉ andrew.jolley@bridgend.gov.uk

Senior Management: Mrs Susan Cooper, Corporate Director - Social Services & Wellbeing, Civic Offices, Angel Street, Bridgend CF31 4WB ☎ 01656 642251 🖷 01656 766162 ✉ susan.cooper@bridgend.gov.uk

Senior Management: Ms Deborah McMillan Corporate Director - Education & Transformation, Civic Offices, Angel Street, Bridgend CF31 4WB ☎ 01656 642617 ✉ deborah.mcmillan@bridgend.gov.uk

Senior Management: Mr Mark Shephard, Corporate Director - Communities, Civic Offices, Angel Street, Bridgend CF31 4WB ☎ 01656 643227 ✉ mark.shephard@bridgend.gov.uk

Senior Management: Ms Ness Young Corporate Director - Resources, Civic Offices, Angel Street, Bridgend CF31 4WB ☎ 01656 643307 ✉ ness.young@bridgend.gov.uk

Architect, Building / Property Services: Mr Mark Evans Group Manager - Built Environment, Waterton Lane Depot, Bridgend CF31 3YP ☎ 01656 642827 ✉ mark.evans@bridgend.gov.uk

Best Value: Ms Yuan Shen, Corporate Improvement Manager & Integrated Partnerships Manager, Civic Offices, Angel Street, Bridgend CF31 4WB ☎ 01656 643224 ✉ yuan.shen@bridgend.gov.uk

Best Value: Ms Ness Young Corporate Director - Resources, Civic Offices, Angel Street, Bridgend CF31 4WB ☎ 01656 643307 ✉ ness.young@bridgend.gov.uk

Building Control: Mr Mark Evans Group Manager - Built Environment, Waterton Lane Depot, Bridgend CF31 3YP ☎ 01656 642827 ✉ mark.evans@bridgend.gov.uk

Catering Services: Ms Louise Kerton, Team Manager - Catering Services, Supplies Building, Waterton, Bridgend CF31 7YR ☎ 01656 664527 ✉ louise.kerton@bridgend.gov.uk

Children / Youth Services: Ms Nicola Echanis Head of Strategy Partnerships & Commissioning, Civic Offices, Angel Street, Bridgend CF31 4WB ☎ 01656 642611 ✉ nicola.echanis@bridgend.gov.uk

Children / Youth Services: Ms Laura Kinsey Head of Safeguarding & Family Support, Civic Offices, Angel Street, Bridgend CF31 4WB ☎ 0166 642314 ✉ laura.kinsey@bridgend.gov.uk

Civil Registration: Ms Lucy Bratcher, Superintendent Registrar, Register Office, Ty'r Ardd, Sunnyside, Bridgend CF31 4AR ☎ 01656 642391 🖷 01656 667529 ✉ lucy.bratcher@bridgend.gov.uk

Community Safety: Mr John Davies, Community Safety Team Leader, Bridgend Police Station, Brackla Street, Bridgend CF31 1BZ ☎ 01656 815918 ✉ john.davies@bridgend.gov.uk

Computer Management: Mr Martin Morgans Group Manager - ICT Services, Sunnyside House, Sunnyside, Bridgend CF31 4AR ☎ 01656 642110 ✉ martin.morgans@bridgend.gov.uk

Consumer Protection and Trading Standards: Mr Lee Jones, Head of Regulatory, Partnerships & Transformation, Civic Offices, Angel Street, Bridgend CF31 4WB ☎ 01656 643259 ✉ lee.jones@bridgend.gov.uk

Customer Service: Ms Beverley Davies Customer Service Manager, Civic Offices, Angel Street, Bridgend CF31 4WB ☎ 01656 643333 ✉ beverley.davies@bridgend.gov.uk

Economic Development: Ms Satwant Pryce Head of Regeneration & Development, Civic Offices, Angel Street, Bridgend CF31 4WB ☎ 01656 643151 🖷 01656 643190 ✉ satwant.pryce@bridgend.gov.uk

Education: Ms Deborah McMillan Corporate Director - Education & Transformation, Civic Offices, Angel Street, Bridgend CF31 4WB ☎ 01656 642617 ✉ deborah.mcmillan@bridgend.gov.uk

E-Government: Mr Martin Morgans Group Manager - ICT Services, Sunnyside House, Sunnyside, Bridgend CF31 4AR ☎ 01656 642110 ✉ martin.morgans@bridgend.gov.uk

Electoral Registration: Mr Gary Ennis Electoral Services Manager, Civic Offices, Angel Street, Bridgend CF31 4WB ☎ 01656 643609 ✉ gary.ennis@bridgend.gov.uk

BRIDGEND

Emergency Planning: Mrs Julie Cooper, Principal Emergency Planning Officer, Civic Offices, Angel Street, Bridgend CF31 4WB ☎ 01656 643300 🖷 01656 643215 🖰 julie.cooper@bridgend.gov.uk

Energy Management: Ms Satwant Pryce Head of Regeneration & Development, Civic Offices, Angel Street, Bridgend CF31 4WB ☎ 01656 643151 🖷 01656 643190 🖰 satwant.pryce@bridgend.gov.uk

Environmental / Technical Services: Mr Zak Shell Head of Neighbourhood Services, Civic Offices, Angel Street, Bridgend CF31 4WB ☎ 01656 643151 🖰 zak.shell@bridgend.gov.uk

Environmental Health: Mr Philip Stanton, Service Manager - Environmental Health, Raven's Court, Brewery Lane, Bridgend CF31 4AP ☎ 01656 643141 🖰 philip.stanton@bridgend.gov.uk

Estates, Property & Valuation: Ms Fiona Blick Group Manager - Property Services, Raven's Court, Brewery Lane, Bridgend CF31 4AP ☎ 01656 642702 🖷 01656 660137 🖰 fiona.blick@bridgend.gov.uk

European Liaison: Mr Mark Halliwell, Manager - Regeneration Funding, Innovation Centre, Bridgend Science Park, Bridgend CF31 3NA ☎ 01656 815329 🖷 01656 768098 🖰 mark.halliwell@bridgend.gov.uk

Events Manager: Ms Emma Blandon Marketing & Engagement Manager, Raven's Court, Brewery Lane, Bridgend CF31 4AP ☎ 01656 642047 🖰 emma.blandon@bridgend.gov.uk

Facilities: Mr Paul Thomas Principal Surveyor - Property & Facilities Management, Raven's Court, Brewery Lane, Bridgend CF31 4AP ☎ 01656 642704 🖰 paul.thomas@bridgend.gov.uk

Finance: Ms Ness Young Corporate Director - Resources, Civic Offices, Angel Street, Bridgend CF31 4WB ☎ 01656 643307 🖰 ness.young@bridgend.gov.uk

Fleet Management: Mr Trevor Lloyd, Joint Fleet Services Manager, Ty Thomas JVM, Newlands Avenue, Brackla Industrial Estate, Bridgend CF31 4WB ☎ 01656 642874 🖰 trevor.lloyd@bridgend.gov.uk

Grounds Maintenance: Mr Gareth Evans, Parks & Playing Fields Manager, Civic Offices, Angel Street, Bridgend CF31 4WB ☎ 01656 642720 🖷 01656 662150 🖰 gareth.evans@bridgend.gov.uk

Health and Safety: Ms Claire Howells Heath & Safety Manager, Waterton Lane Depot, Bridgend CF31 3YP ☎ 01656 642872 🖰 claire.howells@bridgend.gov.uk

Highways: Mr Kevin Mulcahy Group Manager - Highways Services, Civic Offices, Angel Street, Bridgend CF31 4WB ☎ 01656 642535 🖰 kevin.mulcahy@bridgend.gov.uk

Home Energy Conservation: Mr Mark Shephard, Corporate Director - Communities, Civic Offices, Angel Street, Bridgend CF31 4WB ☎ 01656 643227 🖰 mark.shephard@bridgend.gov.uk

Housing: Ms Satwant Pryce Head of Regeneration & Development, Civic Offices, Angel Street, Bridgend CF31 4WB ☎ 01656 643151 🖷 01656 643190 🖰 satwant.pryce@bridgend.gov.uk

Legal: Mr Andrew Jolley, Assistant Chief Executive, Civic Offices, Angel Street, Bridgend CF31 4WB ☎ 01656 643106 🖰 andrew.jolley@bridgend.gov.uk

Licensing: Ms Yvonne Witchell, Licensing & Registration Officer, Civic Offices, Angel Street, Bridgend CF31 4WB ☎ 01656 643105 🖷 01656 657899 🖰 yvonne.witchell@bridgend.gov.uk

Member Services: Mr Gary Jones, Head of Democratic Services, Civic Offices, Angel Street, Bridgend CF31 4WB ☎ 01656 643385 🖰 gary.jones@bridgend.gov.uk

Parking: Mr John Duddridge, Collaboration Manager, Morien House, Bennett Street, Bridgend Industrial Estate, Bridgend CF31 4WB ☎ 01656 642535 🖰 john.duddridge@bridgend.gov.uk

Partnerships: Mr Lee Jones, Head of Regulatory, Partnerships & Transformation, Civic Offices, Angel Street, Bridgend CF31 4WB ☎ 01656 643259 🖰 lee.jones@bridgend.gov.uk

Partnerships: Ms Yuan Shen, Corporate Improvement Manager & Integrated Partnerships Manager, Civic Offices, Angel Street, Bridgend CF31 4WB ☎ 01656 643224 🖰 yuan.shen@bridgend.gov.uk

Personnel / HR: Ms Sarah Kingsbury, Head of Human Resources & Organisational Development, Raven's Court, Brewery Lane, Bridgend CF31 4AP ☎ 01656 643209 🖷 01656 646966 🖰 sarah.kingsbury@bridgend.gov.uk

Planning: Ms Satwant Pryce Head of Regeneration & Development, Civic Offices, Angel Street, Bridgend CF31 4WB ☎ 01656 643151 🖷 01656 643190 🖰 satwant.pryce@bridgend.gov.uk

Recycling & Waste Minimisation: Mr Andrew Hobbs, Group Manager - Street Works, Civic Offices, Angel Street, Bridgend CF31 4WB ☎ 01656 643416 🖷 01656 646972 🖰 andrew.hobbs@bridgend.gov.ukj

Regeneration: Ms Satwant Pryce Head of Regeneration & Development, Civic Offices, Angel Street, Bridgend CF31 4WB ☎ 01656 643151 🖷 01656 643190 🖰 satwant.pryce@bridgend.gov.uk

Regeneration: Mr Mark Shephard, Corporate Director - Communities, Civic Offices, Angel Street, Bridgend CF31 4WB ☎ 01656 643227 🖰 mark.shephard@bridgend.gov.uk

Road Safety: Mr Zak Shell Head of Neighbourhood Services, Civic Offices, Angel Street, Bridgend CF31 4WB ☎ 01656 643151 🖰 zak.shell@bridgend.gov.uk

Social Services: Mrs Susan Cooper, Corporate Director - Social Services & Wellbeing, Civic Offices, Angel Street, Bridgend CF31 4WB ☎ 01656 642251 🖷 01656 766162 🖰 susan.cooper@bridgend.gov.uk

Social Services (Adult): Ms Jackie Davies Head of Adult Social Care, Civic Offices, Angel Street, Bridgend CF31 4WB ☎ 01656 642121 🖰 jacqueline.davies@bridgend.gov.uk

Social Services (Children): Ms Laura Kinsey Head of Safeguarding & Family Support, Civic Offices, Angel Street, Bridgend CF31 4WB ☎ 0166 642314 🖰 laura.kinsey@bridgend.gov.uk

Street Scene: Mr Zak Shell Head of Neighbourhood Services, Civic Offices, Angel Street, Bridgend CF31 4WB ☎ 01656 643151 ✉ zak.shell@bridgend.gov.uk

Sustainable Communities: Mr Michael Jenkins, Principal Sustainable Development Officer, Civic Offices, Angel Street, Bridgend CF31 4WB ☎ 01656 643179 🖷 01656 643669 ✉ michael.jenkins@bridgend.gov.uk

Sustainable Development: Mr Michael Jenkins, Principal Sustainable Development Officer, Civic Offices, Angel Street, Bridgend CF31 4WB ☎ 01656 643179 🖷 01656 643669 ✉ michael.jenkins@bridgend.gov.uk

Tourism: Ms Satwant Pryce Head of Regeneration & Development, Civic Offices, Angel Street, Bridgend CF31 4WB ☎ 01656 643151 🖷 01656 643190 ✉ satwant.pryce@bridgend.gov.uk

Town Centre: Ms Rhiannon Kingsley Town Centre Manager, Civic Offices, Angel Street, Bridgend CF31 4WB ☎ 01656 815225 ✉ rhiannon.kingsley@bridgend.gov.uk

Traffic Management: Mr Anthony Godsall Traffic & Transportation Manager, Civic Offices, Angel Street, Bridgend CF31 4WB ☎ 01656 642523 ✉ Tony.Godsall@bridgend.gov.uk

Transport: Mr John Duddridge, Collaboration Manager, Civic Offices, Angel Street, Bridgend CF31 4WB ☎ 01656 642535 ✉ john.duddridge@bridgend.gov.uk

Transport: Mr Anthony Godsall Traffic & Transportation Manager, Civic Offices, Angel Street, Bridgend CF31 4WB ☎ 01656 642523 ✉ Tony.Godsall@bridgend.gov.uk

Waste Collection and Disposal: Mr Andrew Hobbs, Group Manager - Street Works, Civic Offices, Angel Street, Bridgend CF31 4WB ☎ 01656 643416 🖷 01656 646972 ✉ andrew.hobbs@bridgend.gov.ukj

Waste Management: Mr Andrew Hobbs, Group Manager - Street Works, Civic Offices, Angel Street, Bridgend CF31 4WB ☎ 01656 643416 🖷 01656 646972 ✉ andrew.hobbs@bridgend.gov.uk

COUNCILLORS

***Mayor* Young**, Richard (LAB - Pendre)
cllr.richard.young@bridgend.gov.uk

***Deputy Mayor* Jenkins**, Reg (LAB - Pontycymer)
cllr.reg.jenkins@bridgend.gov.uk

***Leader of the Council* Nott**, Melvyn (LAB - Sarn)
Cllr.MEJ.Nott@bridgend.gov.uk

***Deputy Leader of the Council* David**, Huw (LAB - Cefn Cribwr)
Cllr.Huw.David@bridgend.gov.uk

Aspey, Sean (IND - Porthcawl West Central)
cllr.sean.aspey@bridgend.gov.uk

Butcher, Megan (IND - Cornelly)
Cllr.Megan.Butcher@bridgend.gov.uk

Clarke, Norah (LD - Nottage)
Cllr.Norah.Clarke@bridgend.gov.uk

Davies, Pamela (LAB - Bryntirion, Laleston & Merthyr Mawr)
cllr.pam.davies@bridgend.gov.uk

Davies, Gerald (LD - Rest Bay)
Cllr.Gerald.Davies@bridgend.gov.uk

Davies, Wyn (CON - Caerau)
cllr.wyn.davies@Bridgend.gov.uk

Dodd, Ella (IND - Coity)
Cllr.Ella.Dodd@bridgend.gv.uk

Edwards, Keith (LAB - Maesteg East)
Cllr.Keith.Edwards@bridgend.gov.uk

Ellis, Luke (LAB - Pyle)
cllr.luke.ellis@bridgend.gov.uk

Farr, Neelo (LAB - Newcastle)
cllr.neelo.farr@Bridgend.gov.uk

Foley, Peter (IND - Morfa)
cllr.peter.foley@bridgend.gov.uk

Green, Cheryl (LD - Bryntirion, Laleston & Merthyr Mawr)
cllr.cheryl.green@bridgend.gov.uk

Gregory, Michael (LAB - Felindre)
Cllr.Mike.Gregory@bridgend.gov.uk

Hughes, Edith (LAB - Oldcastle)
Cllr.Edith.M.Hughes@bridgend.gov.uk

Hughes, Della (IND - Ogmore Vale)
cllr.della.hughes@bridgend.gov.uk

James, Pauline (LAB - Pyle)
cllr.pauline.james@bridgend.gov.uk

James, Malcolm (PC - Llangynwyd)
Cllr.Malcolm.James@bridgend.gov.uk

James, Clive (LAB - Pyle)
cllr.clive.james@bridgend.gov.uk

John, Phil (LAB - Caerau)
cllr.phil.john@bridgend.gov.uk

Jones, Cherie (LAB - Litchard)
cllr.cherie.jones@bridgend.gov.uk

Jones, Craig (LAB - Brackla)
cllr.craig.l.jones@bridgend.gov.uk

Jones, Martyn (LAB - Bettws)
cllr.martyn.jones@bridgend.gov.uk

Jones, Brian (IND - Porthcawl East Central)
cllr.brian.jones@bridgend.gov.uk

Lewis, Janice (LAB - Bryncoch)
Cllr.janice.lewis@bridgend.gov.uk

Lewis, David (LAB - Pen-Y-Fai)
cllr.david.lewis@bridgend.gov.uk

McCarthy, John (LAB - Hendre)
cllr.john.mccarthy@bridgend.gov.uk

Morgan, Haydn (LAB - Morfa)
cllr.haydn.morgan@bridgend.gov.uk

Morgan, Lyn (LAB - Ynysawdre)
Cllr.Lyn.Morgan@bridgend.gov.uk

Owen, David (IND - Nant-y-Moel)
cllr.david.owen@bridgend.gov.uk

Owen, Alexander (LAB - Penprysg)
cllr.alex.owen@bridgend.gov.uk

BRIDGEND

Phillips, Gareth (LAB - Oldcastle)
cllr.gareth.phillips@bridgend.gov.uk

Pugh, David (LAB - Blaengarw)
membersbcbc@bridgend.gov.uk

Reeves, Mal (LAB - Maesteg East)
Cllr.Mal.Reeves@bridgend.gov.uk

Reeves, Ceri (LAB - Maesteg West)
cllr.ceri.reeves@bridgend.gov.uk

Sage, David (LAB - Brackla)
Cllr.David.Sage@bridgend.gov.uk

Smith, Charles E (LAB - Llangewydd & Brynhyfryd)
cllr.charles.smith@bridgend.gov.uk

Spanswick, John (LAB - Brackla)
Cllr.John.Spanswick@bridgend.gov.uk

Thomas, Marlene (LAB - Llangeinor)
Cllr.Marlene.Thomas@bridgend.gov.uk

Thomas, Gary (LAB - Bryncethin)
Cllr.Gary.Thomas@bridgend.gov.uk

Thomas, Ross (LAB - Maesteg West)
cllr.ross.thomas@bridgend.gov.uk

Tildesley, Jeff (IND - Cornelly)
Cllr.Jeff.Tildesley@bridgend.gov.uk

Townsend, Hailey (LAB - Brackla)
cllr.hailey.j.townsend@bridgend.gov.uk

Venables, Elaine (IND - Coychurch Lower)
cllr.elaine.venables@bridgend.gov.uk

Watts, Kenneth (CON - Newton)
cllr.ken.watts@bridgend.gov.uk

Westwood, Cleone (LAB - Cefn Glas)
Cllr.Cleone.Westwood@bridgend.gov.uk

White, David (LAB - Newcastle)
cllr.david.white@bridgend.gov.uk

White, Phillip (LAB - Caerau)
Cllr.Phil.White@bridgend.gov.uk

Williams, Richard (LAB - Hendre)
Cllr.Richard.Williams@bridgend.gov.uk

Williams, Hywel (LAB - Blackmill)
Cllr.Hywel.Williams@bridgend.gov.uk

Winter, Mel (IND - Aberkenfig)
membersbcbc@bridgend.gov.uk

POLITICAL COMPOSITION

LAB: 38, IND: 10, LD: 3, CON: 2, PC: 1

COMMITTEE CHAIRS

Audit: Ms Ella Dodd

Children & young People: Mr Peter Foley

Health & Wellbeing: Mr David Sage

Licensing: Mr Richard Williams

Brighton & Hove U

Brighton & Hove City Council, Kings House, Grand Avenue, Hove BN3 2LS
☎ 01273 290000 🖳 www.brighton-hove.gov.uk

FACTS AND FIGURES

Parliamentary Constituencies: Brighton, Kemptown, Brighton, Pavilion, Hove
EU Constituencies: South East
Election Frequency: Elections are of whole council

PRINCIPAL OFFICERS

Chief Executive: Mr Geoff Raw Chief Executive, Kings House, Grand Avenue, Hove BN3 2LS ☎ 01273 290453
🖰 geoff.raw@brighton-hove.gov.uk

Assistant Chief Executive: Ms Paula Murray Assistant Chief Executive, Kings House, Grand Avenue, Hove BN3 2LS ☎ 01273 292534 🖷 01273 292614 🖰 paula.murray@brighton-hove.gov.uk

Senior Management: Ms Denise D'Souza, Executive Director - Adult Services, Kings House, Grand Avenue, Hove BN3 2LS
☎ 01273 295048 🖷 01273 698312
🖰 denise.d'souza@brighton-hove.gov.uk

Senior Management: Mr Pinaki Ghoshal Executive Director - Children's Services, Kings House, Grand Avenue, Hove BN3 2LS
☎ 🖰 pinaki.ghoshal@brighton-hove.gov.uk

Senior Management: Ms Rachel Musson Executive Director - Finance & Resources, Kings House, Grand Avenue, Hove BN3 2LS
☎ 01273 291333 🖷 01273 292131
🖰 rachel.musson@brighton-hove.gov.uk

Senior Management: Dr Tom Scanlon Director - Public Health, Kings House, Grand Avenue, Hove BN3 2LS ☎ 01273 291480
🖰 tom.scanlon@brighton-hove.gov.uk

Access Officer / Social Services (Disability): Ms Denise D'Souza, Executive Director - Adult Services, Kings House, Grand Avenue, Hove BN3 2LS ☎ 01273 295048 🖷 01273 698312
🖰 denise.d'souza@brighton-hove.gov.uk

Architect, Building / Property Services: Mrs Angela Dymott, Head of Property Services, King's House, Grand Avenue, Hove BN3 2LS ☎ 01273 291450 🖷 01273 291467
🖰 angela.dymott@brighton-hove.gov.uk

Building Control: Mr Mike Sansom, Head of Building Control, Hove Town Hall, Norton Road, Hove BN3 3BE ☎ 01273 292188
🖷 01273 292075 🖰 mike.sansom@brighton-hove.gov.uk

Catering Services: Mrs Angela Dymott, Head of Property Services, King's House, Grand Avenue, Hove BN3 2LS ☎ 01273 291450 🖷 01273 291467 🖰 angela.dymott@brighton-hove.gov.uk

Children / Youth Services: Mr Pinaki Ghoshal Executive Director - Children's Services, Kings House, Grand Avenue, Hove BN3 2LS ☎ 🖰 pinaki.ghoshal@brighton-hove.gov.uk

Civil Registration: Ms Valerie Pearce, Head of City Services, 2nd Floor, Priory House, Bartholemew Square, Brighton BN1 1JR
☎ 01273 291850 🖷 01273 291862
🖰 valerie.pearce@brighton-hove.gov.uk

PR / Communications: Ms Ali Rigby Acting Head of Communications, Kings House, Grand Avenue, Hove BN3 2LS ☎ 01273 291031 🖷 01273 292855 ✉ ali.rigby@brighton-hove.gov.uk

Community Planning: Mr Rob Dumbrill Parks Development Manager, Kings House, Grand Avenue, Hove BN3 2LS ☎ 01273 292929 ✉ rob.dumbrill@brighton-hove.gov.uk

Community Planning: Mr Rob Fraser Head of Planning & Public Protection, Kings House, Grand Avenue, Hove BN3 2LS ☎ 01273 292257 🖷 01273 293330 ✉ rob.fraser@brighton-hove.gov.uk

Community Safety: Ms Linda Beanlands, Commissoner Community Safety, 162 North Street, Brighton BN1 2LS ☎ 01273 291115 🖷 01273 292808 ✉ linda.beanlands@brighton-hove.gov.uk

Computer Management: Mr Mark Watson Interim Head of ICT, Kings House, Grand Avenue, Hove BN3 2LS ☎ 01273 290283 ✉ mark.watson@brighton-hove.gov.uk

Consumer Protection and Trading Standards: Mr John Peerless-Mountford Principal Trading Standards Officer, 2nd Floor, Bartholemew House, Bartholemew Square, Brighton BN1 1JA ☎ 01273 292486 ✉ john.peerless@brighton-hove.gov.uk

Contracts: Ms Rachel Musson Executive Director - Finance & Resources, Kings House, Grand Avenue, Hove BN3 2LS ☎ 01273 291333 🖷 01273 292131 ✉ rachel.musson@brighton-hove.gov.uk

Corporate Services: Mr Richard Tuset Head of Policy & Performance, Kings House, Grand Avenue, Hove BN3 2LS ☎ 01273 295514 ✉ richard.tuset@brighton-hove.gov.uk

Corporate Services: Mr Ian Withers Head of Audit & Business Risk, Kings House, Grand Avenue, Hove BN3 2LS ☎ 01273 291323 ✉ ian.withers@brighton-hove.gov.uk

Customer Service: Ms Valerie Pearce, Head of City Services, 4th Floor, Priory House, Bartholomew Square, Brighton BN1 1JR ☎ 01273 291850 🖷 01273 291862 ✉ valerie.pearce@brighton-hove.gov.uk

Economic Development: Ms Cheryl Finella Economic Development Manager, Kings House, Grand Avenue, Hove BN3 2LS ☎ 01273 291095 ✉ cheryl.finella@brighton-hove.gov.uk

Economic Development: Mr Nick Hibberd Head of City Regeneration, Kings House, Grand Avenue, Hove BN3 2LS ☎ 01273 293020 🖷 01273 293709 ✉ nick.hibberd@brighton-hove.gov.uk

Education: Ms Jo Lyons Lead Commissoner of Schools, Skills & Learning, Kings House, Grand Avenue, Hove BN3 2LS ☎ 01273 293514 ✉ jo.lyons@brighton-hove.gov.uk

E-Government: Mr Mark Watson Interim Head of ICT, Kings House, Grand Avenue, Hove BN3 2LS ☎ 01273 290283 ✉ mark.watson@brighton-hove.gov.uk

Electoral Registration: Mr Paul Holloway Head of Life Events & ES, Town Hall, Bartholomew Square, Brighton BN1 1JA ☎ 01273 292005 🖷 01273 291222 ✉ paul.holloway@brighton-hove.gov.uk

Emergency Planning: Mr Robin Humphries Civil Contingencies Manager, Kings House, Grand Avenue, Hove BN3 2LS ☎ 01273 291313 🖷 01273 292362 ✉ robin.humphries@brighton-hove.gov.uk

Energy Management: Mrs Angela Dymott, Head of Property Services, King's House, Grand Avenue, Hove BN3 2LS ☎ 01273 291450 🖷 01273 291467 ✉ angela.dymott@brighton-hove.gov.uk

Environmental / Technical Services: Mr Geoff Raw Chief Executive, Kings House, Grand Avenue, Hove BN3 2LS ☎ 01273 290453 ✉ geoff.raw@brighton-hove.gov.uk

Environmental Health: Mr Tim Nichols, Head of Regulatory Services, Bartholemew House, Bartholemew Square, Brighton BN1 1JA ☎ 01273 292163 🖷 01273 292196 ✉ tim.nichols@brighton-hove.gov.uk

Estates, Property & Valuation: Mrs Angela Dymott, Head of Property Services, King's House, Grand Avenue, Hove BN3 2LS ☎ 01273 291450 🖷 01273 291467 ✉ angela.dymott@brighton-hove.gov.uk

Events Manager: Mr Ian Shurrock Commissioner - Sports & Leisure, Kings House, Grand Avenue, Hove BN3 2LS ☎ 01273 292084 🖷 01273 292360 ✉ ian.shurrock@brighton-hove.gov.uk

Facilities: Mrs Angela Dymott, Head of Property Services, King's House, Grand Avenue, Hove BN3 2LS ☎ 01273 291450 🖷 01273 291467 ✉ angela.dymott@brighton-hove.gov.uk

Finance: Mr Nigel Manvell Head of Financial Services, Kings House, Grand Avenue, Hove BN3 2LS ☎ 01273 291240 🖷 01273 292558 ✉ nigel.manvell@brighton-hove.gov.uk

Finance: Ms Rachel Musson Executive Director - Finance & Resources, Kings House, Grand Avenue, Hove BN3 2LS ☎ 01273 291333 🖷 01273 292131 ✉ rachel.musson@brighton-hove.gov.uk

Fleet Management: Mr Richard Bradley Head of City Infrastructure, Kings House, Grand Avenue, Hove BN3 2LS ☎ 01273 274701 🖷 01273 274666 ✉ richard.bradley@brighton-hove.gov.uk

Grounds Maintenance: Mr Richard Bradley Head of City Infrastructure, Kings House, Grand Avenue, Hove BN3 2LS ☎ 01273 274701 🖷 01273 274666 ✉ richard.bradley@brighton-hove.gov.uk

Health and Safety: Ms Hilary Ellis, Head of Health & Safety, King's House, Grand Avenue, Hove BN3 2LS ☎ 01273 291305 ✉ hilary.ellis@brighton-hove.gov.uk

Highways: Mr Jeff Elliott Highway & Traffic Manager, Kings House, Grand Avenue, Hove BN3 2LS ☎ 01273 292468 ✉ jeff.elliott@brighton-hove.gov.uk

Highways: Mr Mark Prior, Head of Transport, Kings House, Grand Avenue, Hove BN3 2LS ☎ 01273 292095 ✉ mark.prior@brighton-hove.gov.uk

BRIGHTON & HOVE

Home Energy Conservation: Mr Geoff Raw Chief Executive, Kings House, Grand Avenue, Hove BN3 2LS ☎ 01273 290453 geoff.raw@brighton-hove.gov.uk

Local Area Agreement: Mr Richard Tuset Head of Policy & Performance, Kings House, Grand Avenue, Hove BN3 2LS ☎ 01273 295514 richard.tuset@brighton-hove.gov.uk

Legal: Mr Abraham Ghebre-Ghiorghis, Head of Legal & Democratic Services, Kings House, Grand Avenue, Hove BN3 2LS ☎ 01273 291500 🖷 01273 291454 abraham.ghebre-ghiorghis@brighton-hove.gov.uk

Leisure and Cultural Services: Mr Toby Kingsbury Sports Facilities Manager, Kings House, Grand Avenue, Hove BN3 2LS ☎ 01273 292701 toby.kingsbury@brighton-hove.gov.uk

Leisure and Cultural Services: Mr Geoff Raw Chief Executive, Kings House, Grand Avenue, Hove BN3 2LS ☎ 01273 290453 geoff.raw@brighton-hove.gov.uk

Leisure and Cultural Services: Mr Ian Shurrock Commissioner - Sports & Leisure, Kings House, Grand Avenue, Hove BN3 2LS ☎ 01273 292084 🖷 01273 292360 ian.shurrock@brighton-hove.gov.uk

Licensing: Mr Tim Nichols, Head of Regulatory Services, Bartholemew House, Bartholemew Square, Brighton BN1 1JA ☎ 01273 292163 🖷 01273 292196 tim.nichols@brighton-hove.gov.uk

Lifelong Learning: Ms Jo Lyons Lead Commissoner of Schools, Skills & Learning, Kings House, Grand Avenue, Hove BN3 2LS ☎ 01273 293514 jo.lyons@brighton-hove.gov.uk

Lighting: Mr Geoff Raw Chief Executive, Kings House, Grand Avenue, Hove BN3 2LS ☎ 01273 290453 geoff.raw@brighton-hove.gov.uk

Member Services: Mr Mark Wall, Head of Democratic Services, King's House, Grand Avenue, Hove BN3 2LS ☎ 01273 291006 🖷 01273 291003 mark.wall@brighton-hove.gov.uk

Parking: Mr Mark Prior, Head of Transport, Kings House, Grand Avenue, Hove BN3 2LS ☎ 01273 292095 mark.prior@brighton-hove.gov.uk

Partnerships: Mr Simon Newell Head of Partnerships & External Relationships, Kings House, Grand Avenue, Hove BN3 2LS ☎ 01273 291128 simon.newell@brighton-hove.gov.uk

Partnerships: Mr Richard Tuset Head of Policy & Performance, Kings House, Grand Avenue, Hove BN3 2LS ☎ 01273 295514 richard.tuset@brighton-hove.gov.uk

Personnel / HR: Ms Sue Moorman Head of Resources & Organisational Development, Kings House, Grand Avenue, Hove BN3 2LS ☎ 01273 293629 sue.moorman@brighton-hove.gov.uk

Planning: Mr Rob Fraser Head of Planning & Public Protection, Kings House, Grand Avenue, Hove BN3 2LS ☎ 01273 292257 🖷 01273 293330 rob.fraser@brighton-hove.gov.uk

Procurement: Mr Nigel Manvell Head of Financial Services, Kings House, Grand Avenue, Hove BN3 2LS ☎ 01273 291240 🖷 01273 292558 nigel.manvell@brighton-hove.gov.uk

Public Libraries: Ms Sally McMahon, Head of Libraries & Information Services, Jubilee Library, Jubilee Street, Brighton BN1 1GE ☎ 01273 296933 🖷 01273 292871 sally.mcmahon@brighton-hove.gov.uk

Recycling & Waste Minimisation: Ms Gillian Marston, Head of City Infrastructure, Hollingdean Depot, Upper Hollingdean Road, Brighton BN1 7GA ☎ 01273 274701 🖷 01273 274666 gillian.marston@brighton-hove.gov.uk

Regeneration: Ms Gillian Marston, Head of City Infrastructure, Hollingdean Depot, Upper Hollingdean Road, Brighton BN1 7GA ☎ 01273 274701 🖷 01273 274666 gillian.marston@brighton-hove.gov.uk

Road Safety: Mr Dave Parker Head of Transport Planning, Hove Town Hall, Hove BN3 4AH ☎ 01273 292474 david.parker@brighton-hove.gov.uk

Social Services: Ms Denise D'Souza, Executive Director - Adult Services, Kings House, Grand Avenue, Hove BN3 2LS ☎ 01273 295048 🖷 01273 698312 denise.d'souza@brighton-hove.gov.uk

Social Services (Adult): Ms Denise D'Souza, Executive Director - Adult Services, Kings House, Grand Avenue, Hove BN3 2LS ☎ 01273 295048 🖷 01273 698312 denise.d'souza@brighton-hove.gov.uk

Social Services (Children): Mr Steve Barton Lead Commissioner - Integrated Families, Kings House, Grand Avenue, Hove BN3 2LS ☎ 01273 296105 steve.barton@brighton-hove.gov.uk

Social Services (Children): Ms Jo Lyons Lead Commissoner of Schools, Skills & Learning, Kings House, Grand Avenue, Hove BN3 2LS ☎ 01273 293514 jo.lyons@brighton-hove.gov.uk

Families: Mr Steve Barton Lead Commissioner - Integrated Families, Kings House, Grand Avenue, Hove BN3 2LS ☎ 01273 296105 steve.barton@brighton-hove.gov.uk

Childrens Social Care: Mr James Dougan Head of Children & Families, Kings House, Grand Avenue, Hove BN3 2LS james.dougan@brighton-hove.gov.uk

Public Health: Dr Tom Scanlon Director - Public Health, Kings House, Grand Avenue, Hove BN3 2LS ☎ 01273 291480 tom.scanlon@brighton-hove.gov.uk

Sustainable Communities: Mr Thurstan Crockett, Head of Sustainability & Environmental Policy, King's House, Grand Avenue, Hove BN3 2LS ☎ 01273 292503 🖷 01273 293330 thurstan.crockett@brighton-hove.gov.uk

Sustainable Development: Mr Martin Randall Head of Planning & Public Protection, Kings House, Grand Avenue, Hove BN3 2LS ☎ 01273 292257 🖷 01273 293330 martin.randall@brighton-hove.gov.uk

Tourism: Mr Adam Bates, Head of Tourism & Leisure, Brighton Town Hall, Brighton BN1 1JR ☎ 01273 292633 🖷 01273 292614 adam.bates@brighton-hove.gov.uk

Traffic Management: Mr Mark Prior, Head of Transport, Kings House, Grand Avenue, Hove BN3 2LS ☎ 01273 292095 mark.prior@brighton-hove.gov.uk

Transport Planner: Mr Austen Hunter Head of Transport Operations, 6a Pavilion Buildings, Brighton BN1 1EE ☎ 01273 292245 austen.hunter@brighton-hove.gov.uk

Waste Collection and Disposal: Ms Gillian Marston, Head of City Infrastructure, Hollingdean Depot, Upper Hollingdean Road, Brighton BN1 7GA ☎ 01273 274701 🖷 01273 274666 gillian.marston@brighton-hove.gov.uk

Waste Management: Ms Gillian Marston, Head of City Infrastructure, Hollingdean Depot, Upper Hollingdean Road, Brighton BN1 7GA ☎ 01273 274701 🖷 01273 274666 gillian.marston@brighton-hove.gov.uk

COUNCILLORS

***Mayor* Hyde**, Lynda (CON - Rottingdean Coastal)
lynda.hyde@brighton-hove.gcsx.gov.uk

***Deputy Mayor* West**, Pete (GRN - St. Peter's & North Laine)
pete.west@brighton-hove.gcsx.gov.uk

***Leader of the Council* Morgan**, Warren (LAB - East Brighton)
warren.morgan@brighton-hove.gcsx.gov.uk

***Group Leader* MacCafferty**, Phelim (GRN - Brunswick & Adelaide)
phelim.maccafferty@brighton-hove.gcsx.gov.uk

***Group Leader* Theobald**, Geoffrey (CON - Patcham)
geoffrey.theobald@brighton-hove.gcsx.gov.uk

Allen, Kevin (LAB - Preston Park)
kevin.allen@brighton-hove.gov.uk

Atkinson, Peter (LAB - North Portslade)
peter.atkinson@brighton-hove.gov.uk

Barford, Karen (LAB - Queen's Park)
karen.barford@brighton-hove.gov.uk

Barnett, Dawn (CON - Hangleton & Knoll)
dawn.barnett@brighton-hove.gcsx.gov.uk

Barradell, Maggie (LAB - East Brighton)
maggie.barradell@brighton-hove.gov.uk

Bell, Steve (CON - Woodingdean)
steve.bell@brighton-hove.gov.uk

Bennett, Jayne (CON - Hove Park)
jayne.bennett@brighton-hove.gcsx.gov.uk

Bewick, Tom (LAB - Westbourne)
tom.bewick@brighton-hove.gov.uk

Brown, Vanessa (CON - Hove Park)
vanessa.brown@brighton-hove.gcsx.gov.uk

Cattell, Julie (LAB - Preston Park)
julie.cattell@brighton-hove.gov.uk

Chapman, Daniel (LAB - Queen's Park)
daniel.chapman@brighton-hove.gov.uk

Cobb, Denise (CON - Westbourne)
denise.cobb@brighton-hove.gcsx.gov.uk

Daniel, Emma (LAB - Hanover & Elm Grove)
emma.daniel@brighton-hove.gcsx.gov.uk

Deane, Lizzie (GRN - St. Peter's & North Laine)
lizzie.deane@brighton-hove.gcsx.gov.uk

Druitt, Tom (GRN - Regency)
tom.druitt@brighton-hove.gov.uk

Gibson, David (GRN - Hanover & Elm Grove)
david.gibson@brighton-hove.gov.uk

Gilbey, Penny (LAB - North Portslade)
penny.gilbey@brighton-hove.gcsx.gov.uk

Greenbaum, Louisa (GRN - St. Peter's & North Laine)
louisa.greenbaum@brighton-hove.gov.uk

Hamilton, Les (LAB - South Portslade)
leslie.hamilton@brighton-hove.gcsx.gov.uk

Hill, Tracey (LAB - Hollingbury & Stanmer)
tracey.hill@brighton-hove.gov.uk

Horan, Saoirse (LAB - Goldsmid)
saoirse.horan@brighton-hove.gov.uk

Inkpin-Leissner, Michael (LAB - Hollingbury & Stanmer)
michael.inkpin-leissner@brighton-hove.gov.uk

Janio, Tony (CON - Hangleton & Knoll)
tony.janio@brighton-hove.gcsx.gov.uk

Knight, Amanda (GRN - Goldsmid)
amanda.knight@brighton-hove.gov.uk

Lewry, Nick (CON - Hangleton & Knoll)
nick.lewry@brighton-hove.gov.uk

Littman, Leo (GRN - Preston Park)
leo.littman@brighton-hove.gcsx.gov.uk

Marsh, Mo (LAB - Moulsecoomb & Bevendean)
mo.marsh@brighton-hove.gcsx.gov.uk

Meadows, Anne (LAB - Moulsecoomb & Bevendean)
anne.meadows@brighton-hove.gcsx.gov.uk

Mears, Mary (CON - Rottingdean Coastal)
mary.mears@brighton-hove.gov.uk

Miller, Joe (CON - Rottingdean Coastal)
joe.miller@brighton-hove.gov.uk

Mitchell, Gill (LAB - East Brighton)
gill.mitchell@brighton-hove.gcsx.gov.uk

Moonan, Clare (LAB - Central Hove)
clare.moonan@brighton-hove.gov.uk

Morris, Adrian (LAB - Queen's Park)
adrian.morris@brighton-hove.gov.uk

Nemeth, Robert (CON - Wish)
robert.nemeth@brighton-hove.gov.uk

Norman, Ken (CON - Withdean)
ken.norman@brighton-hove.gcsx.gov.uk

Norman, Ann (CON - Withdean)
ann.norman@brighton-hove.gcsx.gov.uk

O'Quinn, Jackie (LAB - Goldsmid)
Jackie.o'quinn@brighton-hove.gov.uk

Page, Dick (GRN - Hanover & Elm Grove)
dick.page@brighton-hove.gov.uk

BRIGHTON & HOVE

Peltzer Dunn, Garry (CON - Wish)
garry.peltzerdunn@brighton-hove.gcsx.gov.uk

Penn, Caroline (LAB - Hollingbury & Stanmer)
caroline.penn@brighton-hove.gov.uk

Phillips, Alex (GRN - Regency)
alex.phillips@brighton-hove.gov.uk

Robins, Alan (LAB - South Portslade)
alan.robins@brighton-hove.gcsx.gov.uk

Simson, Dee (CON - Woodingdean)
dee.simson@brighton-hove.gcsx.gov.uk

Sykes, Ollie (GRN - Brunswick & Adelaide)
ollie.sykes@brighton-hove.gcsx.gov.uk

Taylor, Nick (CON - Withdean)
nick.taylor@brighton-hove.gov.uk

Theobald, Carol (CON - Patcham)
carol.theobald@brighton-hove.gcsx.gov.uk

Wares, Lee (CON - Patcham)
lee.wares@brighton-hove.gov.uk

Wealls, Andrew (CON - Central Hove)
andrew.wealls@brighton-hove.gov.uk

Yates, Daniel (LAB - Moulsecoomb & Bevendean)
daniel.yates@brighton-hove.gov.uk

POLITICAL COMPOSITION
LAB: 23, CON: 20, GRN: 11

COMMITTEE CHAIRS
Audit & Standards: Mrs Ann Norman

Children, Young People & Skills: Mr Tom Bewick

Economic Development & Culture: Mr Warren Morgan

Health & Wellbeing: Mr Daniel Yates

Licensing: Ms Mo Marsh

Planning: Ms Julie Cattell

Policy & Rescources: Mr Warren Morgan

Bristol City U

Bristol City Council, City Hall, College Green, Bristol BS1 5TR
☎ 0117 922 2000 🖷 0117 922 2024 💻 www.bristol.gov.uk

FACTS AND FIGURES
Parliamentary Constituencies: Bristol East, Bristol North West, Bristol South, Bristol West
EU Constituencies: South West
Election Frequency: Elections are by thirds

PRINCIPAL OFFICERS
Chief Executive: Ms Nicola Yates City Director, SLT Management Suite, 100 Temple Street, PO Box 3176, Bristol BS3 9FS ☎ 0117 922 2341 nicola.yates@bristol.gov.uk

Senior Management: Ms Alison Comley Strategic Director - Neighbourhoods, SLT Management Suite, 100 Temple Street, PO Box 3176, Bristol BS3 9FS ☎ 0117 903 7860 alison.comley@bristol.gov.uk

Senior Management: Mr John Readman Strategic Director - People, SLT Management Suite, 100 Temple Street, PO Box 3176, Bristol BS3 9FS ☎ 0117 903 7960 john.readman@bristol.gov.uk

Senior Management: Mr Barra Mac Ruairi Strategic Director - Place, SLT Management Suite, 100 Temple Street, PO Box 3176, Bristol BS3 9FS ☎ 0117 352 5558 barra@bristol.gov.uk

Senior Management: Mr Max Wide Strategic Director - Business Change, SLT Management Suite, 100 Temple Street, PO Box 3176, Bristol BS3 9FS ☎ 0117 357 4451 max.wide@bristol.gov.uk

Access Officer / Social Services (Disability): Mr Tom Gilchrist Service Manager - Private Housing & Accessible Homes, 100 Temple Street, PO Box 3176, Bristol BS3 9FS ☎ 0117 352 1975 tom.gilchrist@bristol.gov.uk

Architect, Building / Property Services: Mr Robert Orrett Service Director - Property, 100 Temple Street, PO Box 3176, Bristol BS3 9FS ☎ 0117 922 4086 robert.orrett@bristol.gov.uk

Best Value: Ms Netta Meadow Service Director - Strategic Commissioning & Procurement, Parkview Office Campus, PO Box 3716, Bristol BS3 9FS ☎ 0117 923 7744 netta.meadow@bristol.gov.uk

Building Control: Mr Steve Pearce Group Manager, Brunel House, St George's Road, Bristol BS1 5TR ☎ 0117 922 3770 steve.pearce@bristol.gov.uk

Catering Services: Mr Andrew Dalley Catering Business Manager, Ashton Court Mansion, Bristol BS41 9JN ☎ 0117 963 3438 andrew.dalley@bristol.gov.uk

Civil Registration: Ms Yvonne Dawes, Statutory Services Manager, B Bond Floor 5, Smeaton Road, Bristol BS1 6XN ☎ 0117 922 3488 yvonne.dawes@bristol.gov.uk

PR / Communications: Mr Tim Borrett Service Manager - Public Relations, 100 Temple Street, PO Box 3176, Bristol BS3 9FS ☎ 0117 922 3332 tim.borrett@bristol.gov.uk

PR / Communications: Ms Zoe Willcox Service Director - Planning & Sustainable Development, 1st Floor, Brunel House, St George's Road, Bristol BS1 5UY ☎ 0117 922 2942 zoe.willcox@bristol.gov.uk

Community Planning: Ms Di Robinson Service Director - Neighbourhoods, 3rd Floor, Brunel House, St George's Road, Bristol BS1 5UY ☎ 0117 352 1036 di.robinson@bristol.gov.uk

Community Safety: Mr Peter Anderson Service Manager - Crime & Substance Misuse, St Anne's House, St Anne's Road, Bristol BS4 4AB ☎ 0117 922 2309 peter.anderson@bristol.gov.uk

Community Safety: Mr Nick Hooper Service Director - Housing Solutions & Crime Reduction, 100 Temple Street, PO Box 3176, Bristol BS3 9FS ☎ 0117 922 4681 nick.hooper@bristol.gov.uk

Computer Management: Mr Paul Arrigoni Service Director - Business Change & ICT, 100 Temple Street, PO Box 3176, Bristol BS3 9FS ☎ 0117 922 2081 paul.arrigoni@bristol.gov.uk

Consumer Protection and Trading Standards: Mr Jonathan Martin Regulatory Compliance Manager, 100 Temple Street, PO Box 3176, Bristol BS3 9FS ☎ 07710 397039 ✉ jonathan.martin@bristol.gov.uk

Corporate Services: Ms Michele Farmer Service Director - Policy, Strategy & Communications, 100 Temple Street, PO Box 3176, Bristol BS3 9FS ☎ 0117 922 2647 ✉ michele.farmer@bristol.gov.uk

Customer Service: Ms Patsy Mellor Service Director - Citizen Services, 100 Temple Street, PO Box 3176, Bristol BS3 9FS ☎ 0117 352 6218 ✉ patsy.mellor@bristol.gov.uk

Economic Development: Mr Alistair Reid Service Director - Economy, Management Suite, Brunel House, Bristol BS1 5UY ☎ 0117 903 7481 ✉ alistair.reid@bristol.gov.uk

Education: Mr Paul Jacobs Service Director - Education & Skills, SLT Management Suite, 100 Temple Street, PO Box 3176, Bristol BS3 9FS ☎ 0117 922 4836 ✉ paul.jacobs@bristol.gov.uk

Electoral Registration: Mr Gareth Cook Electoral Services Manager, c/o 9 Willway Street, Bedminster, Bristol BS3 4SP ☎ 0117 922 3451 ✉ gareth.cook@bristol.gov.uk

Electoral Registration: Ms Yvonne Dawes, Statutory Services Manager, B Bond Floor 5, Smeaton Road, Bristol BS1 6XN ☎ 0117 922 3488 ✉ yvonne.dawes@bristol.gov.uk

Emergency Planning: Mr Simon Creed Civil Protection Manager, The Create Centre, Smeaton Road, Bristol BS1 6XN ☎ 0117 922 3233 ✉ simon.creed@bristol.gov.uk

Energy Management: Mr Bill Edrich Service Director - Energy, 100 Temple Street, PO Box 3176, Bristol BS3 9FS ☎ 0117 922 4991 ✉ bill.edrich@bristol.gov.uk

Environmental / Technical Services: Ms Tracey Morgan Service Director - Environment & Leisure, Brunel House, St George Road, Bristol BS1 5UY ☎ 0117 922 3183 ✉ tracey.morgan@bristol.gov.uk

Estates, Property & Valuation: Mr Robert Orrett Service Director - Property, 100 Temple Street, PO Box 3176, Bristol BS3 9FS ☎ 0117 922 4086 ✉ robert.orrett@bristol.gov.uk

European Liaison: Ms Shelley Nania Interim Service Manager - European & International, Engine Shed, Station Approach, Temple Meads, Bristol BS1 6QH ☎ 0117 922 3229 ✉ shelley.nania@bristol.gov.uk

Events Manager: Ms Melissa Inman Head of City Art Programme, 3rd Floor, Brunel House, St George's Road, Bristol BS1 5UY ☎ 0117 922 2653 ✉ melissa.inman@bristol.gov.uk

Finance: Mr Peter Gillet Service Director - Finance, Parkview Office Campus, PO Box 3176, Bristol BS3 9FS ☎ 0117 922 2419 ✉ peter.gillet@bristol.gov.uk

Fleet Management: Mr Nick Gingell Team Manager - Fleet, Brislington Depot, Sandy Park, Bristol BS4 3NZ ☎ 0117 352 5611 ✉ nick.gingell@bristol.gov.uk

Grounds Maintenance: Mr Philip Thomas Service Manager - Environment & Leisure, 2nd Floor, Bazaar Wing, BCC, PO Box 3176, Bristol BS3 9FG ☎ 0117 925 6368 ✉ philip.thomas@bristol.gov.uk

Highways: Mr Gareth Vaugh-Williams Service Manager - Highways, Wilder House, Wilder Street, , Bristol BS2 8HP ☎ 0117 903 6833 ✉ gareth.vaughn-williams@bristol.gov.uk

Housing: Mr Steve Barrett Service Director - Housing, 1st Floor St Anne's House, St Anne's Road, Bristol BS4 4AB ☎ 0117 922 4082 ✉ steve.barrett@bristol.gov.uk

Housing: Mr Nick Hooper Service Director - Housing Solutions & Crime Reduction, 100 Temple Street, PO Box 3176, Bristol BS3 9FS ☎ 0117 922 4681 ✉ nick.hooper@bristol.gov.uk

Housing: Ms Mary Ryan Service Director - Landlord, 1st Floor St Anne's House, St Anne's Road, Bristol BS4 4AB ☎ 0117 922 4589 ✉ mary.ryan@bristol.gov.uk

Housing Maintenance: Ms Zara Naylor Service Manager - Responsive Repairs, The A Shed, Sandy Park Depot, Bristol BS4 3NZ ☎ 0117 922 4129 ✉ zara.naylor@bristol.gov.uk

Legal: Ms Shahzia Daya Interim Service Manager - Legal, 2nd Floor, Parkview Office Campus, PO Box 3176, Bristol BS3 9FS ☎ 0117 922 2413 ✉ shahzia.daya@bristol.gov.uk

Leisure and Cultural Services: Ms Tracey Morgan Service Director - Environment & Leisure, Brunel House, St George Road, Bristol BS1 5UY ☎ 0117 922 3183 ✉ tracey.morgan@bristol.gov.uk

Licensing: Mr Jonathan Martin Trading Standards & Licensing Manager, 100 Temple Street, PO Box 3176, Bristol BS3 9FS ☎ 07710 397039 ✉ jonathan.martin@bristol.gov.uk

Lifelong Learning: Ms Jane Taylor, Service Manager of Communities & Adult Skills, The Park, Daventry Road, Knowle, Bristol BS3 9FS ☎ 0117 922 4570 ✉ jane.taylor@bristol.gov.uk

Lighting: Mr Adam Crowther Traffic Signals & Lighting Manager, Wilder House, Wilder Street, Bristol BS2 8PH ☎ 0117 903 6854 ✉ adam.crowther@bristol.gov.uk

Member Services: Ms Shana Johnson Service Manager - Democratic, 4th Floor, Brunel House, PO Box 3176, Bristol BS3 9FS ☎ 0117 922 2908 ✉ shana.johnson@bristol.gov.uk

Parking: Mr David Bunting Service Manager - Traffic, Wilder House, Wilder Street, Bristol BS2 8PH ☎ 0117 922 3085 ✉ david.bunting@bristol.gov.uk

Partnerships: Mr Stephen Wray Partnerships Director - Creative Economy, 100 Temple Street, PO Box 3176, Bristol BS3 9FS ☎ 0117 922 3360 ✉ stephen.wray@bristol.gov.uk

Personnel / HR: Mr Richard Billingham Service Director - Human Resources, 100 Temple Street, PO Box 3176, Bristol BS3 9FS ☎ 0117 922 2670 ✉ richard.billingham@bristol.gov.uk

BRISTOL CITY

Planning: Ms Zoe Willcox Service Director - Planning & Sustainable Development, 1st Floor, Brunel House, St George's Road, Bristol BS1 5UY ☎ 0117 922 2942 ✉ zoe.willcox@bristol.gov.uk

Public Libraries: Ms Kate Murray, Head of Libraries, Bristol Central Library, College Green, Bristol BS1 5TL ☎ 0117 352 1264 ✉ k.murray@bristol.gov.uk

Recycling & Waste Minimisation: Ms Pam Jones Service Manager - Environment & Leisure Operations, Brunel House, St. Georges Road, , Bristol BS1 5UY ☎ 0117 922 3240 ✉ pam.jones@bristol.gov.uk

Regeneration: Mr Alistair Reid Service Director - Economy, Management Suite, Brunel House, Bristol BS1 5UY ☎ 0117 903 7481 ✉ alistair.reid@bristol.gov.uk

Road Safety: Mr Ed Plowden Service Manager - Sustainable Transport, Brunel House, St George Road, Bristol BS1 5UY ☎ 0117 922 2357 ✉ ed.plowden@bristol.gov.uk

Social Services: Mr John Readman Strategic Director - People, SLT Management Suite, 100 Temple Street, PO Box 3176, Bristol BS1 5UY ☎ 0117 903 7960 ✉ john.readman@bristol.gov.uk

Social Services (Adult): Mr Mike Hennessey Service Director - Care & Support (Adults), Parkview Campus, Whitchurch Lane, Bristol BS14 0DD ☎ 0117 903 7951 ✉ mike.hennessey@bristol.gov.uk

Public Health: Ms Becky Pollard Director - Public Health, Avon Quay, Cumberland Basin Road, Bristol BS1 6XL ☎ 0117 922 2874 ✉ becky.pollard@bristol.gov.uk

Street Scene: Ms Pam Jones Service Manager - Environment & Leisure Operations, Brunel House, St. Georges Road, , Bristol BS1 5UY ☎ 0117 922 3240 ✉ pam.jones@bristol.gov.uk

Sustainable Communities: Ms Zoe Willcox Service Director - Planning & Sustainable Development, 1st Floor Brunel House, St George Road, Bristol BS1 5UY ☎ 0117 922 2942 ✉ zoe.willcox@bristol.gov.uk

Sustainable Development: Ms Zoe Willcox Service Director - Planning & Sustainable Development, 1st Floor Brunel House, St George Road, Bristol BS1 5UY ☎ 0117 922 2942 ✉ zoe.willcox@bristol.gov.uk

Tourism: Mr John Hirst Chief Executive - Destination Bristol, E Shed, 1 Canons Road, Bristol BS1 5XT ☎ 0117 925 7053 ✉ john.hirst@bristol.gov.uk

Town Centre: Ms Jo Hawkins Broadmead BID Manager, E Shed, 1 Canons Road, Bristol BS1 5XT ☎ 0117 925 7053 ✉ jo.hawkins@destinationbristol.co.uk

Town Centre: Ms Eva Steutzenberger City Centre BID Development Manager, E Shed, 1 Canons Road, Bristol BS1 5XT ☎ 0117 929 0484 ✉ eva.steutzenberger@destinationbristol.co.uk

Traffic Management: Mr David Bunting Service Manager - Traffic, Wilder House, Wilder Street, Bristol BS2 8PH ☎ 0117 922 3085 ✉ david.bunting@bristol.gov.uk

Transport: Mr Peter Mann Service Director - Transport, 1st Floor, Brunel House, St George's Road, Bristol BS1 5UY ☎ 0117 922 2943 ✉ peter.mann@bristol.gov.uk

Transport Planner: Ms Tracey Dow Interim Service Manager - Strategic Planning, 3rd Floor, Brunel House, St George's Road, Bristol BS1 5UY ☎ 0117 922 2357 ✉ tracey.dow@bristol.gov.uk

Total Place: Mr Barra Mac Ruairi Strategic Director - Place, SLT Management Suite, 100 Temple Street, PO Box 3176, Bristol BS3 9FS ☎ 0117 352 5558 ✉ barra@bristol.gov.uk

Waste Collection and Disposal: Ms Tracey Morgan Service Director - Environment & Leisure, Brunel House, St George Road, Bristol BS1 5UY ☎ 0117 922 3183 ✉ tracey.morgan@bristol.gov.uk

Waste Management: Ms Tracey Morgan Service Director - Environment & Leisure, Brunel House, St George's Road, Bristol BS1 5UY ☎ 0117 922 3183 ✉ tracey.morgan@bristol.gov.uk

COUNCILLORS

***The Lord Mayor* Campion-Smith**, Clare (LD - Henleaze)
clare.campion-smith@bristol.gov.uk

***Deputy Lord Mayor* Watson**, Alastair (CON - Westbury-on-Trym)
alastair.watson@bristol.gov.uk

***Deputy Mayor* Gollop**, Geoffrey (CON - Westbury-on-Trym)
geoffrey.gollop@bristol.gov.uk

***Group Leader* Holland**, Helen (LAB - Whitchurch Park)
helen.holland@bristol.gov.uk

***Group Leader* Hopkins**, Gary (LD - Knowle)
gary.hopkins@bristol.gov.uk

***Group Leader* Telford**, Rob (GRN - Ashley)
rob.telford@bristol.gov.uk

***Group Leader* Weston**, Mark (CON - Henbury)
mark.weston@bristol.gov.uk

Abraham, Peter (CON - Stoke Bishop)
peter.abraham@bristol.gov.uk

Alexander, Lesley (CON - Frome Vale)
lesley.alexander@bristol.gov.uk

Bolton, Charlie (GRN - Southville)
charlie.bolton@bristol.gov.uk

Bradshaw, Mark (LAB - Bedminster)
mark.bradshaw@bristol.gov.uk

Brain, Mark (LAB - Hartcliffe)
mark.brain@bristol.gov.uk

Breckels, Fabian (LAB - St. George East)
fabian.breckels@bristol.gov.uk

Budd, Jason (IND - Kingsweston)
jason.budd@bristol.gov.uk

Cheney, Craig (LAB - Hillfields)
craig.cheney@bristol.gov.uk

Clark, Barry (LAB - Hengrove)
barry.clark@bristol.gov.uk

Clarke, Stephen (GRN - Southville)
stephen.clarke@bristol.gov.uk

Cook, Simon (LD - Clifton East)
simon.cook@bristol.gov.uk

Daniels, Noreen (LAB - Hillfields)
noreen.daniels@bristol.gov.uk

Davies, Christopher (LD - Knowle)
christopher.davies@bristol.gov.uk

Denyer, Carla (GRN - Clifton East)
carla.denyer@bristol.gov.uk

Eddy, Richard (CON - Bishopsworth)
richard.eddy@bristol.gov.uk

Fodor, Martin (GRN - Redland)
martin.fodor@bristol.gov.uk

Frost, Michael (UKIP - Hengrove)
michael.frost@bristol.gov.uk

Glazzard, Dani (GRN - Cotham)
dani.glazzard@bristol.gov.uk

Goulandris, John (CON - Stoke Bishop)
john.goulandris@bristol.gov.uk

Greaves, Rhian (LAB - Brislington West)
rhian.greaves@bristol.gov.uk

Hance, Fi (LD - Redland)
fi.hance@bristol.gov.uk

Harvey, Wayne (CON - Avonmouth)
wayne.harvey@bristol.gov.uk

Hickman, Margaret (LAB - Lawrence Hill)
margaret.hickman@bristol.gov.uk

Hiscott, Claire (CON - Horfield)
claire.hiscott@bristol.gov.uk

Hoyt, Gus (GRN - Ashley)
gus.hoyt@bristol.gov.uk

Jackson, Christopher (LAB - Filwood)
christopher.jackson@bristol.gov.uk

Jama, Hibaq (LAB - Lawrence Hill)
hibaq.jama@bristol.gov.uk

Joffe, Deborah (GRN - Windmill Hill)
deborah-mila.joffe@bristol.gov.uk

Kent, Tim (LD - Whitchurch Park)
tim.kent@bristol.gov.uk

Khan, Mahmadur (LAB - Eastville)
mahmadur.khan@bristol.gov.uk

Kirk, Gill (LAB - Lockleaze)
gill.kirk@bristol.gov.uk

Langley, Mike (LAB - Brislington East)
mike.langley@bristol.gov.uk

Leaman, Tim (LD - Kingsweston)
tim.leaman@bristol.gov.uk

Lovell, Jeff (LAB - Filwood)
jeff.lovell@bristol.gov.uk

Lucas, Charles (CON - Clifton)
charles.lucas@bristol.gov.uk

Malnick, Tim (GRN - Bishopston)
tim.malnick@bristol.gov.uk

Massey, Brenda (LAB - Southmead)
brenda.massey@bristol.gov.uk

McMullen, Anna (GRN - Easton)
anna.mcmullen@bristol.gov.uk

Mead, Olly (LAB - Horfield)
olly.mead@bristol.gov.uk

Means, Eileen (LAB - Brislington West)
eileen.means@bristol.gov.uk

Melias, Matthew (CON - Avonmouth)
matthew.melias@bristol.gov.uk

Milestone, Susan (LAB - St. George West)
sue.milestone@bristol.gov.uk

Mongon, Sam (LAB - Windmill Hill)
sam.mongon@bristol.gov.uk

Morgan, Glenise (LD - Henleaze)
glenise.morgan@bristol.gov.uk

Morris, Graham (CON - Stockwood)
graham.morris@bristol.gov.uk

Morris, David (CON - Stockwood)
david.morris@bristol.gov.uk

Negus, Anthony (LD - Cotham)
anthony.negus@bristol.gov.uk

Payne, Bill (LAB - Frome Vale)
bill.payne@bristol.gov.uk

Pearce, Steve (LAB - St. George East)
s.pearce@bristol.gov.uk

Phipps, Celia (LAB - Bedminster)
celia.phipps@bristol.gov.uk

Quartley, Kevin (CON - Bishopsworth)
kevin.quartley@bristol.gov.uk

Radice, Daniella (GRN - Bishopston)
daniella.radice@bristol.gov.uk

Rylatt, Naomi (LAB - Hartcliffe)
naomi.rylatt@bristol.gov.uk

Shah, Afzal (LAB - Easton)
afzal.shah@bristol.gov.uk

Smith, Jenny (LAB - Southmead)
jenny.m.smith@dsl.pipex.com

Stafford-Townsend, Ani (GRN - Cabot)
ani.stafford-townsend@bristol.gov.uk

Stone, Ron (LAB - St. George West)
ron.stone@bristol.gov.uk

Thomas, Jerome (GRN - Clifton)
jerome.thomas@bristol.gov.uk

Threlfall, Mhairi (LAB - Eastville)
mhairi.threlfall@bristol.gov.uk

Tincknell, Estella (LAB - Lockleaze)
estela.tincknell@bristol.gov.uk

Windows, Chris (CON - Henbury)
chris.windows@bristol.gov.uk

Wollacott, Mike (LAB - Brislington East)
mike.wollacott@bristol.gov.uk

Wright, Mark (LD - Cabot) mark.wright@bristol.gov.uk

POLITICAL COMPOSITION

LAB: 30, CON: 15, GRN: 13, LD: 10, IND: 1, UKIP: 1

BRISTOL CITY

COMMITTEE CHAIRS

Audit: Mr Mark Brain

Licensing: Ms Hibaq Jama

Broadland D

Broadland District Council, Thorpe Lodge, 1 Yarmouth Road, Thorpe St. Andrew, Norwich NR7 0DU
☎ 01603 431133 🖷 01603 300087 🖰 reception@broadland.gov.uk
💻 www.broadland.gov.uk

FACTS AND FIGURES

Parliamentary Constituencies: Norwich North
EU Constituencies: Eastern
Election Frequency: Elections are of whole council

PRINCIPAL OFFICERS

Chief Executive: Mr Phil Kirby, Chief Executive, Thorpe Lodge, 1 Yarmouth Road, Thorpe St. Andrew, Norwich NR7 0DU ☎ 01603 430521 🖷 01603 430565 🖰 phil.kirby@broadland.gov.uk

Deputy Chief Executive: Mr Matthew Cross, Deputy Chief Executive, Thorpe Lodge, 1 Yarmouth Road, Thorpe St. Andrew, Norwich NR7 0DU ☎ 01603 430588 🖷 01603 430565 🖰 matthew.cross@broadland.gov.uk

Access Officer / Social Services (Disability): Mr Kevin Philcox Divisional Environmental Health Officer for Housing, Thorpe Lodge, 1 Yarmouth Road, Thorpe St. Andrew, Norwich NR7 0DU ☎ 01603 430552 🖷 01603 430578 🖰 kevin.philcox@broadland.gov.uk

Architect, Building / Property Services: Mr John Frary Facilities Manager, Thorpe Lodge, 1 Yarmouth Road, Thorpe St. Andrew, Norwich NR7 0DU ☎ 01603 430416 🖷 01603 430614 🖰 john.frary@broadland.gov.uk

Building Control: Mr Alan Osborne Director of CNC Building Control Services, South Norfolk Council, Swan Lane, Long Stratton NR15 2XE ☎ 01508 533633

PR / Communications: Mr James Dunne Marketing & Communications Manager, Thorpe Lodge, 1 Yarmouth Road, Thorpe St. Andrew, Norwich NR7 0DU ☎ 01603 430523 🖷 01603 430614 🖰 james.dunne@broadland.gov.uk

Computer Management: Mr Stephen Fennell, Head of Corporate Resources, Thorpe Lodge, 1 Yarmouth Road, Thorpe St. Andrew, Norwich NR7 0DU ☎ 01603 430524 🖷 01603 430614 🖰 stephen.fennell@broadland.gov.uk

Corporate Services: Mr Martin Thrower Head of Democratic Services, Thorpe Lodge, 1 Yarmouth Road, Thorpe St. Andrew, Norwich NR7 0DU ☎ 01603 430546 🖷 01603 430591 🖰 martin.thrower@broadland.gov.uk

Customer Service: Ms Dee Young Personnel & Customer Services Manager, Thorpe Lodge, 1 Yarmouth Road, Thorpe St. Andrew, Norwich NR7 0DU ☎ 01603 430526 🖰 dee.young@broadland.gov.uk

Economic Development: Mr Hamish Melville, Business Development Manager, Thorpe Lodge, 1 Yarmouth Road, Thorpe St. Andrew, Norwich NR7 0DU ☎ 01603 430611 🖷 01603 430614 🖰 hamish.melville@broadland.gov.uk

Economic Development: Mr Kevin Philcox Divisional Environmental Health Officer for Housing, Thorpe Lodge, 1 Yarmouth Road, Thorpe St. Andrew, Norwich NR7 0DU ☎ 01603 430552 🖷 01603 430578 🖰 kevin.philcox@broadland.gov.uk

E-Government: Mr Matthew Cross, Deputy Chief Executive, Thorpe Lodge, 1 Yarmouth Road, Thorpe St. Andrew, Norwich NR7 0DU ☎ 01603 430588 🖷 01603 430565 🖰 matthew.cross@broadland.gov.uk

Electoral Registration: Mrs Linda Mockford Electoral Services Manager, Thorpe Lodge, 1 Yarmouth Road, Thorpe St. Andrew, Norwich NR7 0DU ☎ 01603 430424 🖷 01603 430591 🖰 linda.mockford@broadland.gov.uk

Emergency Planning: Mr Simon Faraday Drake Emergency Planning Manager, Thorpe Lodge, 1 Yarmouth Road, Thorpe St. Andrew, Norwich NR7 0DU ☎ 01603 430643 🖰 simon.faraday.drake@broadland.gov.uk

Energy Management: Ms Deborah Baillie-Murden Climate Change Officer, Thorpe Lodge, 1 Yarmouth Road, Thorpe St. Andrew, Norwich NR7 0DU ☎ 01603 430629 🖰 debra.baillie-murden@broadland.gov.uk

Environmental / Technical Services: Mr Richard Block Head of Environmental Services, Thorpe Lodge, 1 Yarmouth Road, Thorpe St. Andrew, Norwich NR7 0DU ☎ 01603 430535 🖷 01603 430616 🖰 richard.block@broadland.gov.uk

Environmental Health: Mr Richard Block Head of Environmental Services, Thorpe Lodge, 1 Yarmouth Road, Thorpe St. Andrew, Norwich NR7 0DU ☎ 01603 430535 🖷 01603 430616 🖰 richard.block@broadland.gov.uk

Facilities: Mr John Frary Facilities Manager, Thorpe Lodge, 1 Yarmouth Road, Thorpe St. Andrew, Norwich NR7 0DU ☎ 01603 430416 🖷 01603 430614 🖰 john.frary@broadland.gov.uk

Finance: Mrs Jill Penn Head of Finance, Revenues Services & S151 Officer, Thorpe Lodge, 1 Yarmouth Road, Thorpe St. Andrew, Norwich NR7 0DU ☎ 01603 430589 🖷 01603 430537 🖰 jill.penn@broadland.gov.uk

Treasury: Mrs Jill Penn Head of Finance, Revenues Services & S151 Officer, Thorpe Lodge, 1 Yarmouth Road, Thorpe St. Andrew, Norwich NR7 0DU ☎ 01603 430589 🖷 01603 430537 🖰 jill.penn@broadland.gov.uk

Health and Safety: Mr John Frary Facilities Manager, Thorpe Lodge, 1 Yarmouth Road, Thorpe St. Andrew, Norwich NR7 0DU ☎ 01603 430416 🖷 01603 430614 🖰 john.frary@broadland.gov.uk

Housing: Mrs Leigh Booth Strategic Housing Manager, Thorpe Lodge, 1 Yarmouth Road, Thorpe St. Andrew, Norwich NR7 0DU ☎ 01603 430566 🖷 01603 430565 🖰 leigh.booth@broadland.gov.uk

Legal: Mr Martin Thrower Head of Democratic Services, Thorpe Lodge, 1 Yarmouth Road, Thorpe St. Andrew, Norwich NR7 0DU ☎ 01603 430546 🖷 01603 430591 ✉ martin.thrower@broadland.gov.uk

Licensing: Mr Paul Hemnell, Environmental Enforcement Manager, Thorpe Lodge, 1 Yarmouth Road, Thorpe St. Andrew, Norwich NR7 0DU ☎ 01603 430577 🖷 01603 701859 ✉ paul.hemnell@broadland.gov.uk

Lifelong Learning: Mrs Sharon Tapp Economic Development Training Manager, 9 Hellesdon Park Road, Norwich NR6 5DR ☎ 01603 788950 🖷 01603 484102 ✉ sharon.tapp@broadland.gov.uk

Lighting: Mr Richard Block Head of Environmental Services, Thorpe Lodge, 1 Yarmouth Road, Thorpe St. Andrew, Norwich NR7 0DU ☎ 01603 430535 🖷 01603 430616 ✉ richard.block@broadland.gov.uk

Lottery Funding, Charity and Voluntary: Ms Sally Hoare, Partnership & Funding Officer, Thorpe Lodge, 1 Yarmouth Road, Thorpe St. Andrew, Norwich NR7 0DU ☎ 01603 430620 🖷 01603 430592 ✉ sally.hoare@broadland.gov.uk

Member Services: Mr Martin Thrower Head of Democratic Services, Thorpe Lodge, 1 Yarmouth Road, Thorpe St. Andrew, Norwich NR7 0DU ☎ 01603 430546 🖷 01603 430591 ✉ martin.thrower@broadland.gov.uk

Personnel / HR: Mr Stephen Fennell, Head of Corporate Resources, Thorpe Lodge, 1 Yarmouth Road, Thorpe St. Andrew, Norwich NR7 0DU ☎ 01603 430524 🖷 01603 430614 ✉ stephen.fennell@broadland.gov.uk

Planning: Mr Phil Courtier Head of Development Management & Conservation, Thorpe Lodge, 1 Yarmouth Road, Thorpe St. Andrew, Norwich NR7 0DU ☎ 01603 430566 🖷 01603 430565 ✉ phil.courtier@broadland.gov.uk

Procurement: Mr Stephen Fennell, Head of Corporate Resources, Thorpe Lodge, 1 Yarmouth Road, Thorpe St. Andrew, Norwich NR7 0DU ☎ 01603 430524 🖷 01603 430614 ✉ stephen.fennell@broadland.gov.uk

Recycling & Waste Minimisation: Mr Richard Block Head of Environmental Services, Thorpe Lodge, 1 Yarmouth Road, Thorpe St. Andrew, Norwich NR7 0DU ☎ 01603 430535 🖷 01603 430616 ✉ richard.block@broadland.gov.uk

Staff Training: Ms Dee Young Personnel & Customer Services Manager, Thorpe Lodge, 1 Yarmouth Road, Thorpe St. Andrew, Norwich NR7 0DU ☎ 01603 430526 ✉ dee.young@broadland.gov.uk

Street Scene: Mr Peter Leggett, Street Scene Officer, Thorpe Lodge, 1 Yarmouth Road, Thorpe St. Andrew, Norwich NR7 0DU ☎ 01603 431133 ✉ peter.leggett@broadland.gov.uk

Sustainable Communities: Mr Phil Courtier Head of Development Management & Conservation, Thorpe Lodge, 1 Yarmouth Road, Thorpe St. Andrew, Norwich NR7 0DU ☎ 01603 430566 🖷 01603 430565 ✉ phil.courtier@broadland.gov.uk

Sustainable Communities: Mr Phil Kirby, Chief Executive, Thorpe Lodge, 1 Yarmouth Road, Thorpe St. Andrew, Norwich NR7 0DU ☎ 01603 430521 🖷 01603 430565 ✉ phil.kirby@broadland.gov.uk

Tourism: Ms Kirstin Hughes, Economic Development Manager, Thorpe Lodge, 1 Yarmouth Road, Thorpe St. Andrew, Norwich NR7 0DU ☎ 01603 430563 ✉ kirstin.hughes@broadland.gov.uk

Waste Collection and Disposal: Mr Richard Block Head of Environmental Services, Thorpe Lodge, 1 Yarmouth Road, Thorpe St. Andrew, Norwich NR7 0DU ☎ 01603 430535 🖷 01603 430616 ✉ richard.block@broadland.gov.uk

Waste Management: Mr Richard Block Head of Environmental Services, Thorpe Lodge, 1 Yarmouth Road, Thorpe St. Andrew, Norwich NR7 0DU ☎ 01603 430535 🖷 01603 430616 ✉ richard.block@broadland.gov.uk

COUNCILLORS

***Chair* Leggett**, Kenneth (CON - Old Catton & Sprowston West)
cllr.ken.leggett@broadland.gov.uk

***Vice-Chair* Ward**, John (CON - Sprowston East)
cllr.john.ward@broadland.gov.uk

***Leader of the Council* Proctor**, Andrew (CON - Brundall)
cllr.andrew.proctor@broadland.gov.uk

***Deputy Leader of the Council* Clancy**, Stuart (CON - Taverham South)
cllr.stuart.clancy@broadland.gov.uk

***Group Leader* Harrison**, David (LD - Aylsham)
cllr.david.harrison@broadland.gov.uk

***Group Leader* Roper**, Dan (LD - Spixworth with St Faiths)
cllr.dan.roper@broadland.gov.uk

Adams, Tony (CON - Hellesdon South East)
cllr.tony.adams@broadland.gov.uk

Bannock, Claudette (CON - Taverham South)
cllr.claudette.bannock@broadland.gov.uk

Buck, Danny (CON - Hellesdon North West)
cllr.danny.buck@broadland.gov.uk

Carrick, Paul (CON - Hevingham)
cllr.paul.carrick@broadland.gov.uk

Cottingham, Jo (CON - Aylsham)
cllr.jo.cottingham@broadland.gov.uk

Dunn, Stuart (CON - Old Catton & Sprowston West)
cllr.stuart.dunn@broadland.gov.uk

Emsell, Jonathan (CON - Thorpe St Andrew South East)
cllr.jonathan.emsell@broadland.gov.uk

Everett, Graham (CON - Reepham)
cllr.graham.everett@broadland.gov.uk

Fisher, John (CON - Thorpe St Andrew North West)
cllr.john.fisher@broadland.gov.uk

Foulger, Roger (CON - Drayton South)
cllr.roger.foulger@broadland.gov.uk

Grady, Richard (CON - Hellesdon South East)
cllr.richard.grady@broadland.gov.uk

Graham, Ian (CON - Aylsham)
cllr.ian.graham@broadland.gov.uk

Gurney, Shelagh (CON - Hellesdon North West)
cllr.shelagh.gurney@broadland.gov.uk

Harrison, Chris (CON - Blofield with South Walsham)
cllr.chris.harrison@broadland.gov.uk

Hempsall, Lana (CON - Acle)
cllr.lana.hempsall@broadland.gov.uk

Keeler, Joanne (CON - Horsford & Felthorpe)
cllr.joanne.keeler@broadland.gov.uk

Knowles, Robin (CON - Sprowston Central)
cllr.robin.knowles@broadland.gov.uk

Kular, Balvinder (LD - Spixworth with St Faiths)
cllr.balvinder.kular@broadland.gov.uk

Landamore, Tony (CON - Sprowston Central)
cllr.tony.landamore@broadland.gov.uk

Lawn, Sue (CON - Thorpe St Andrew South East)
cllr.susan.lawn@broadland.gov.uk

Leggett, Judy (CON - Sprowston East)
cllr.judy.leggett@broadland.gov.uk

Lodge, Tamsin (CON - Horsford & Felthorpe)
cllr.tamsin.lodge@broadland.gov.uk

Mackie, Ian (CON - Thorpe St Andrew North West)
cllr.ian.mackie@broadland.gov.uk

Mallett, Andrew (CON - Taverham North)
cllr.andrew.mallett@broadland.gov.uk

Mallett, Alan (CON - Coltishall)
cllr.alan.mallett@broadland.gov.uk

Mancini-Boyle, Trudy (CON - Thorpe St Andrew South East)
cllr.trudy.mancini-boyle@broadland.gov.uk

Moncur, Ian (CON - Sprowston East)
cllr.ian.moncur@broadland.gov.uk

Nurden, Grant (CON - Marshes)
cllr.grant.nurden@broadland.gov.uk

O'Neill, Frank (CON - Blofield with South Walsham)
cllr.frank.oneill@broadland.gov.uk

Peck, Greg (CON - Eynesford)
cllr.greg.peck@broadland.gov.uk

Ray-Mortlock, Victor (CON - Drayton North)
cllr.victor.ray-mortlock@broadland.gov.uk

Rix, Barbara (LD - Buxton)
cllr.barbara.rix@broadland.gov.uk

Shaw, Nigel (CON - Thorpe St Andrew North West)
cllr.nigel.shaw@broadland.gov.uk

Snowling, Michael (CON - Brundall)
cllr.michael.snowling@broadland.gov.uk

Tapp, Vincent (CON - Wroxham)
cllr.vincent.tapp@broadland.gov.uk

Vincent, Shaun (CON - Plumstead)
cllr.shaun.vincent@broadland.gov.uk

Vincent, Karen (CON - Old Catton & Sprowston West)
cllr.karen.vincent@broadland.gov.uk

Ward, David (CON - Burlingham)
cllr.david.ward@broadland.gov.uk

Whymark, Fran (CON - Wroxham)
cllr.fran.whymark@broadland.gov.uk

Willmott, David (CON - Taverham North)
cllr.david.willmott@broadland.gov.uk

Woodbridge, Simon (CON - Great Witchingham)
cllr.simon.woodbridge@broadland.gov.uk

POLITICAL COMPOSITION
CON: 43, LD: 4

COMMITTEE CHAIRS
Audit: Mr Nigel Shaw

Licensing: Mr Stuart Dunn

Planning: Mr Michael Snowling

Standards: Mr Robin Knowles

Bromley L

Bromley London Borough Council, Civic Centre, Stockwell Close, Bromley BR1 3UH
☎ 020 8464 3333 🖳 www.bromley.gov.uk

FACTS AND FIGURES
Parliamentary Constituencies: Beckenham, Bromley and Chislehurst, Orpington
EU Constituencies: London
Election Frequency: Elections are of whole council

PRINCIPAL OFFICERS
Chief Executive: Mr Doug Patterson, Chief Executive, Civic Centre, Stockwell Close, Bromley BR1 3UH ☎ 020 8313 4354 🖷 020 8313 4444 ✉ doug.patterson@bromley.gov.uk

Senior Management: Mr Mark Bowen Director - Corporate Services, Civic Centre, Stockwell Close, Bromley BR1 3UH ☎ 020 8313 4355 🖷 020 8313 4444 ✉ mark.bowen@bromley.gov.uk

Senior Management: Mr Nigel Davies, Executive Director - Environment & Community Services, Civic Centre, Stockwell Close, Bromley BR1 3UH ☎ 020 8313 4443 🖷 020 8313 4460 ✉ nigel.davies@bromley.gov.uk

Senior Management: Mr Marc Hume Director - Regeneration & Transformation, Civic Centre, Stockwell Close, Bromley BR1 3UH ☎ 020 8461 7557 🖷 020 8313 4460 ✉ marc.hume@bromley.gov.uk

Senior Management: Dr Nada Lemic Director - Public Health, Bexley Civic Offices, 2 Watling Street, Bexleyheath DA6 7AT ☎ 020 8303 7777 ✉ nada.lemic@bromley.gov.uk

Senior Management: Mr Terry Parkin Executive Director - Education, Care & Health Services, Civic Centre, Stockwell Close, Bromley BR1 3UH ☎ 020 8313 4060 🖷 020 8313 4620 ✉ terry.parking@bromley.gov.uk

Senior Management: Mr Peter Turner Director - Finance, Civic Centre, Stockwell Close, Bromley BR1 3UH ☎ 020 8313 4338 🖷 020 8313 4335 ✉ peter.turner@bromley.gov.uk

Building Control: Mr Steve Moore, Head of Building Control, Building Control, Civic Centre, Stockwell Close, Bromley BR1 3UH ☎ 020 8313 4315 🖷 020 8313 4604 ✉ steve.moore@bromley.gov.uk

Civil Registration: Ms Carol Tyson Superintendent Registrar, Civic Centre, Stockwell Close, Bromley BR1 3UH ☎ 020 8313 7957 🖷 020 8313 4699 carol.tyson@bromley.gov.uk

PR / Communications: Ms Susie Clark Communications Analyst, Civic Centre, Stockwell Close, Bromley BR1 3UH ☎ 020 8461 7790 🖷 020 8313 4444 susie.clark@bromley.gov.uk

PR / Communications: Ms Amanda Day Communications Analyst, Civic Centre, Stockwell Close, Bromley BR1 3UH ☎ 020 8313 4390 🖷 020 8313 4444 amanda.day@bromley.gov.uk

Computer Management: Mr Stuart Elsey Acting Head of IT, Civic Centre, Stockwell Close, Bromley BR1 3UH 🖷 020 8313 4936 stuart.elsey@bromley.gov.uk

Consumer Protection and Trading Standards: Mr Rob Vale Head of Trading Standards & Community Protection, Civic Centre, Stockwell Close, Bromley BR1 3UH ☎ 020 8313 4785 🖷 020 8313 0095 robert.vale@bromley.gov.uk

Contracts: Mr Dave Starling, Head of Corporate Procurement, Civic Centre, Stockwell Close, Bromley BR1 3UH ☎ 020 8313 4639 🖷 020 8313 4746 dave.starling@bromley.gov.uk

Customer Service: Mr Duncan Bridgewater Head of Customer Services, Civic Centre, Stockwell Close, Bromley BR1 3UH ☎ 020 8313 7676 duncan.bridgewater@bromely.gov.uk

Education: Ms Jane Bailey Assistant Director - Education, Civic Centre, Stockwell Close, Bromley BR1 3UH ☎ 020 8313 4146 🖷 020 8313 4620 jane.bailey@bromley.gov.uk

Electoral Registration: Mrs Carol Ling, Electoral Services Manager, Civic Centre, Stockwell Close, Bromley BR1 3UH ☎ 020 8313 4367 🖷 020 8313 4995 carol.ling@bromley.gov.uk

Energy Management: Mr Gerry Kelly, Property Energy Manager, Civic Centre, Stockwell Close, Bromley BR1 3UH ☎ 020 8313 4570 🖷 020 8313 4504 gerry.kelly@bromley.gov.uk

Environmental Health: Mr Jim McGowan Head of Environmental Protection, Civic Centre, Stockwell Close, Bromley BR1 3UH ☎ 020 8313 4651 jim.mcgowan@bromley.gov.uk

Estates, Property & Valuation: Ms Heather Hosking Head of Strategic Property, Civic Centre, Stockwell Close, Bromley BR1 3UH ☎ 020 8313 4421 🖷 020 8313 4460 heather.hosking@bromley.gov.uk

Events Manager: Mr Toby Smith, Ranger Services Manager, Civic Centre, Stockwell Close, Bromley BR1 3UH ☎ 020 8658 1593 🖷 020 8650 9880 toby.smith@bromley.gov.uk

Facilities: Mr Andrew Champion, Facilities & Support Services Manager, Civic Centre, Stockwell Close, Bromley BR1 3UH ☎ 020 8313 4394 🖷 020 8290 0608 andrew.champion@bromley.gov.uk

Finance: Mr Peter Turner Director - Finance, Civic Centre, Stockwell Close, Bromley BR1 3UH ☎ 020 8313 4338 🖷 020 8313 4335 peter.turner@bromley.gov.uk

Pensions: Ms Janice Castle Pensions Manager, Civic Centre, Stockwell Close, Bromley BR1 3UH ☎ 020 8461 7503 🖷 020 8313 4600 janice.castle@bromley.gov.uk

Fleet Management: Mr Paul Chilton, Transport Operations Manager, Central Depot, Baths Road, Bromley BR2 9RB ☎ 020 8313 4849 🖷 020 8461 7689 paul.chilton@bromley.gov.uk

Grounds Maintenance: Mr Dan Jones Assistant Director - Streetscene & Greenspace, Civic Centre, Stockwell Close, Bromley BR1 3UH ☎ 020 8313 4211 dan.jones@bromley.gov.uk

Highways: Mr Paul Symonds Assistant Director - Transport & Highways, Civic Centre, Stockwell Close, Bromley BR1 3UH ☎ 020 8313 4540 🖷 020 8313 4478 paul.symonds@bromley.gov.uk

Housing: Ms Sara Bowrey Assistant Director - Housing Needs, Civic Centre, Stockwell Close, Bromley BR1 3UH ☎ 020 8313 4013 🖷 020 8313 4018 sara.bowrey@bromley.gov.uk

Leisure and Cultural Services: Mr Colin Brand, Assistant Director - Leisure & Culture, Civic Centre, Stockwell Close, Bromley BR1 3UH ☎ 020 8313 4107 🖷 020 8461 7890 colin.brand@bromley.gov.uk

Licensing: Mr Paul Lehane, Head of Food Safety & Licensing, Civic Centre, Stockwell Close, Bromley BR1 3UH ☎ 020 8313 4216 🖷 020 8313 4450 paul.lehane@bromley.gov.uk

Lighting: Mr Garry Warner, Head of Highways, Civic Centre, Stockwell Close, Bromley BR1 3UH ☎ 020 8313 4929 🖷 020 8313 4312 garry.warner@bromley.gov.uk

Member Services: Mr Graham Walton Democratic Services Manager, Civic Centre, Stockwell Close, Bromley BR1 3UH ☎ 020 8461 7743 🖷 020 8290 0608 graham.walton@bromley.gov.uk

Parking: Mr Benjamin Stephens Head of Parking Shared Services, Civic Centre, Stockwell Close, Bromley BR1 3UH ☎ 020 8313 4514 benjamin.stephens@bexley.gov.uk

Planning: Mr Jim Kehoe Chief Planner, Civic Centre, Stockwell Close, Bromley BR1 3UH ☎ 020 8313 4441 🖷 020 8313 0095 jim.kehoe@bromley.gov.uk

Public Libraries: Mr Tim Woolgar Library Operations & Commissioning Manager, Bromley Central Library, High Street, Bromley BR1 1EX ☎ 020 8461 7232 🖷 020 8461 7230 tim.woolgar@bromley.gov.uk

Recycling & Waste Minimisation: Mr John Woodruff, Head of Waste Services, Civic Centre, Stockwell Close, Bromley BR1 3UH ☎ 020 8313 4910 🖷 020 8313 4460 john.woodruff@bromley.gov.uk

Road Safety: Mr Angus Culverwell Head of Traffic & Road Safety, Civic Centre, Stockwell Close, Bromley BR1 3UH ☎ 020 8313 4959 🖷 020 8313 1948 angus.culverwell@bromley.gov.uk

Social Services (Adult): Mr Stephen John Assistant Director - Adult Social Care, Civic Centre, Stockwell Close, Bromley BR1 3UH ☎ 020 8313 4197 🖷 020 8313 4620 stephen.john@bromley.gov.uk

BROMLEY

Social Services (Children): Ms Kay Weiss Assistant Director - Children's Social Care, Civic Centre, Stockwell Close, Bromley BR1 3UH ☎ 020 8313 4062 🖷 020 8313 4122 ✉ kay.weiss@bromley.gov.uk

Public Health: Dr Nada Lemic Director - Public Health, Bexley Civic Offices, 2 Watling Street, Bexleyheath DA6 7AT ☎ 020 8303 7777 ✉ nada.lemic@bromley.gov.uk

Staff Training: Ms Antoinette Thorne Head of Workforce Development, Civic Centre, Stockwell Close, Bromley BR1 3UH ☎ 020 8313 4380 🖷 020 8313 4686 ✉ antoinette.thorne@bromley.gov.uk

Street Scene: Mr Peter McCready, Head of Area Management, Civic Centre, Stockwell Close, Bromley BR1 3UH ☎ 020 8313 4942 🖷 020 8313 4478 ✉ peter.mccready@bromley.gov.uk

Town Centre: Mr Martin Pinnell Head of Town Centre Management & Business Support, Civic Centre, Stockwell Close, Bromley BR1 3UH ☎ 020 8313 4457 🖷 020 8461 7890 ✉ martin.pinnell@bromley.gov.uk

Transport: Mr Paul Chilton, Transport Operations Manager, Central Depot, Baths Road, Bromley BR2 9RB ☎ 020 8313 4849 🖷 020 8461 7689 ✉ paul.chilton@bromley.gov.uk

COUNCILLORS

Leader of the Council **Carr**, Stephen (CON - Bromley Common & Keston)
stephen.carr@bromley.gov.uk

Deputy Leader of the Council **Smith**, Colin (CON - Bickley)
colin.smith@bromley.gov.uk

Allen, Vanessa (LAB - Clock House)
vanessa.allen2@bromley.gov.uk

Arthur, Graham (CON - Hayes & Coney Hall)
graham.arthur@bromley.gov.uk

Auld, Douglas (CON - Petts Wood & Knoll)
douglas.auld@bromley.gov.uk

Ball, Teresa (CON - Cray Valley East)
teresa.ball@bromley.gov.uk

Bance, Kathy (LAB - Penge & Cator)
katherine.bance@bromley.gov.uk

Benington, Julian (CON - Biggin Hill)
julian.benington@bromley.gov.uk

Bennett, Nicholas (CON - West Wickham)
md@kentrefurbishment.co.uk

Bennett, Ruth (CON - Bromley Common & Keston)
ruth.bennett@bromley.gov.uk

Bosshard, Eric (CON - Chislehurst)
eric.bosshard@bromley.gov.uk

Botting, Kim (CON - Orpington)
kim.botting@bromley.gov.uk

Boughey, Katy (CON - Chislehurst)
katy.boughey@bromley.gov.uk

Brooks, Kevin (LAB - Penge & Cator)
kevin.brooks@bromley.gov.uk

Buttinger, Lydia (CON - Chelsfield & Pratts Bottom)
lydia.buttinger@bromley.gov.uk

Cartwright, David (CON - Mottingham & Chislehurst North)
david.cartwright@bromley.gov.uk

Collins, Alan (CON - Kelsey & Eden Park)
alan.collins@bromley.gov.uk

Cooke, Mary (CON - Shortlands)
mary.cooke@bromley.gov.uk

Dean, Peter (CON - Kelsey & Eden Park)
peter.dean@bromley.gov.uk

Dunn, Ian (LAB - Clock House)
ian.dunn@bromley.gov.uk

Dykes, Nicky (CON - Bromley Town)
nicky.dykes@bromley.gov.uk

Ellis, Judi (CON - Cray Valley West)
judith.ellis@bromley.gov.uk

Evans, Robert (CON - Farnborough & Crofton)
robert.evans@bromley.gov.uk

Fawthrop, Simon (CON - Petts Wood & Knoll)
simon.fawthrop@bromley.gov.uk

Fookes, Peter (LAB - Penge & Cator)
peter.fookes@bromley.gov.uk

Fortune, Peter (CON - Hayes & Coney Hall)
peter.fortune@bromley.gov.uk

Gray, Hannah (CON - West Wickham)
hannah.gray@bromley.gov.uk

Harmer, Ellie (CON - Plaistow & Sundridge)
ellie.harmer@bromley.gov.uk

Harmer, Will (CON - Bromley Town)
will.harmer@bromley.gov.uk

Huntington-Thresher, William (CON - Orpington)
william.huntington-thresher@bromley.gov.uk

Huntington-Thresher, Samaris (CON - Chelsfield & Pratts Bottom)
samaris.huntington-thresher@bromley.gov.uk

Jeffreys, David (CON - Shortlands)
david.jeffreys@bromley.gov.uk

Joel, Charles (CON - Farnborough & Crofton)
charles.joel@bromley.gov.uk

Livett, David (UKIP - Cray Valley West)
david.livett@bromely.gov.uk

Lymer, Kate (CON - Bickley)
kate.lymer@bromley.gov.uk

Mellor, Russell (CON - Copers Cope)
russell.mellor@bromley.gov.uk

Michael, Alexa (CON - Bromley Common & Keston)
alexa.michael@bromley.gov.uk

Morgan, Peter (CON - Plaistow & Sundridge)
peter.morgan@bromley.gov.uk

Nathan, Terence (UKIP - Cray Valley West)
terence.nathan@bromley.gov.uk

Onslow, Keith (CON - Chelsfield & Pratts Bottom)
keith.onslow@bromley.gov.uk

Owen, Tony (CON - Petts Wood & Knoll)
tony.owen@bromley.gov.uk

Page, Angela (CON - Cray Valley East)
angela.page@bromley.gov.uk

Payne, Ian (CON - Chislehurst)
ian.payne@bromley.gov.uk

Phillips, Sarah (CON - Clock House)
sarah.phillips@bromley.gov.uk

Philpott, Tom (CON - West Wickham)
trphilpott@hotmail.com

Pierce, Chris (CON - Cray Valley East)
chris.pierce@bromley.gov.uk

Reddin, Neil (CON - Hayes & Coney Hall)
neil.reddin@bromley.gov.uk

Rideout, Charles (CON - Mottingham & Chislehurst North)
charles.rideout@bromley.gov.uk

Rideout, Catherine (CON - Bickley)
catherine.rideout@bromley.gov.uk

Rutherford, Michael (CON - Bromley Town)
michael.rutherford@bromley.gov.uk

Scoates, Richard (CON - Darwin)
richard.scoates@bromley.gov.uk

Smith, Diane (CON - Kelsey & Eden Park)
diane.smith@bromley.gov.uk

Stevens, Melanie (CON - Biggin Hill)
melanie.stevens@bromley.gov.uk

Stevens, Tim (CON - Farnborough & Crofton)
tim.stevens@bromley.gov.uk

Tickner, Michael (CON - Copers Cope)
michael.tickner@bromley.gov.uk

Tunnicliffe, Pauline (CON - Orpington)
pauline.tunnicliffe@bromley.gov.uk

Turner, Michael (CON - Plaistow & Sundridge)
michael.turner@bromley.gov.uk

Wells, Stephen (CON - Copers Cope)
stephen.wells@bromley.gov.uk

Wilkins, Angela (LAB - Crystal Palace)
angela.wilkins@bromley.gov.uk

Williams, Richard (LAB - Crystal Palace)
richard.williams@bromley.gov.uk

POLITICAL COMPOSITION

CON: 51, LAB: 7, UKIP: 2

COMMITTEE CHAIRS

Audit: Mr Neil Reddin

Development: Mr Peter Dean

Development: Mr Ian Payne

Pensions: Ms Teresa Ball

Bromsgrove D

Bromsgrove District Council, The Council House, Burcot Lane, Bromsgrove B60 1AA
☎ 01527 881288; 01527 881288 🖳 www.bromsgrove.gov.uk

FACTS AND FIGURES

Parliamentary Constituencies: Bromsgrove
EU Constituencies: West Midlands
Election Frequency: Elections are of whole council

PRINCIPAL OFFICERS

Chief Executive: Mr Kevin Dicks, Chief Executive, The Council House, Burcot Lane, Bromsgrove B60 1AA ☎ 01527 881400; 01527 64252 🖷 01527 881212; 01527 65216
🖰 k.dicks@bromsgroveandredditch.gov.uk

Deputy Chief Executive: Mrs Susan Hanley, Strategic Director & Deputy Chief Executive, The Council House, Burcot Lane, Bromsgrove B60 1AA ☎ 01527 64252 Extn 3601; 01527 881483 🖷 01527 65216 🖰 s.hanley@bromsgroveandredditch.gov.uk

Senior Management: Ms Jayne Pickering Strategic Director & S151 Officer, The Council House, Burcot Lane, Bromsgrove B60 1AA ☎ 01527 64252; 01527 881207 🖷 01527 65216
🖰 j.pickering@bromsgroveandredditch.gov.uk

Best Value: Ms Jayne Pickering Strategic Director & S151 Officer, Town Hall, Walter Stranz Square, Redditch B98 8AH ☎ 01527 64252; 01527 881207 🖷 01527 65216
🖰 j.pickering@bromsgroveandredditch.gov.uk

Building Control: Mr Adrian Wyre Principal Building Control Surveyor, The Council House, Burcot Lane, Bromsgrove B60 1AA ☎ 01562 732532 🖰 a.wyre@bromsgroveandredditch.gov.uk

PR / Communications: Mrs Anne-Marie Harley, Communications & Publicity Manager, The Council House, Burcot Lane, Bromsgrove B60 1AA ☎ 01527 881651; 01527 65252 🖷 01527 881212; 01527 65216 🖰 a.harley@bromsgroveandredditch.gov.uk

Community Planning: Ms Angie Heighway, Head of Community Services, The Council House, Burcot Lane, Bromsgrove B60 1AA ☎ 01527 64252; 01527 881747 🖷 01527 65216 🖰 a.heighway@bromsgroveandredditch.gov.uk

Community Safety: Ms Judy Willis Acting Head of Community Services, The Council House, Burcot Lane, Bromsgrove B60 1AA
🖰 j.willis@bromsgroveandredditch.gov.uk

Consumer Protection and Trading Standards: Mr Ivor Pumfrey, Acting Head of Regulatory Services, The Council House, Burcot Lane, Bromsgrove B60 1AA ☎ 01684 862296
🖰 ivor.pumfrey@malvernhills.gov.uk

Contracts: Ms Carmen Young Procurement Officer, The Council House, Burcot Lane, Bromsgrove B60 1AA

Customer Service: Ms Amanda de Warr Head of Customer Services, The Council House, Burcot Lane, Bromsgrove B60 1AA ☎ 01527 64252; 01527 881241 🖷 01527 65216
🖰 a.dewarr@bromsgroveandredditch.gov.uk

Direct Labour: Mr Guy Revans, Head of Environmental Services, The Council House, Burcot Lane, Bromsgrove B60 1AA ☎ 01527 64252; 01527 64252 ext. 3292 🖷 01527 65216
🖰 g.revans@bromsgroveandredditch.gov.uk

Economic Development: Mr Dean Piper Head of Economic Development & Regeneration - North Worcestershire, Wyre Forest House, Finepoint Way, Kidderminster DY11 7WF ☎ 01562 932192
🖰 dean.piper@wyreforestdc.gov.uk

BROMSGROVE

Economic Development: Mr Steve Singleton, Economic Development Manager - North Worcestershire, Wyre Forest House, Finepoint Way, Kidderminster DY11 7WF ☎ 01562 732168 🖰 steve.singleton@wyreforestdc.gov.uk

E-Government: Mrs Deb Poole Head of Business Transformation, Town Hall, Walter Stranz Square, Redditch B98 8AH ☎ 01527 64252 🖷 01527 65216 🖰 d.poole@bromsgroveandredditch.gov.uk

Electoral Registration: Mrs Claire Felton Head of Legal, Equalities & Democratic Services, Town Hall, Walter Stranz Square, Redditch B98 8AH ☎ 01572 64252; 01527 881429 🖷 01527 65216; 01527 881414 🖰 c.felton@bromsgroveandredditch.gov.uk

Emergency Planning: Mrs Susan Hanley, Strategic Director & Deputy Chief Executive, The Council House, Burcot Lane, Bromsgrove B60 1AA ☎ 01527 64252 Extn 3601; 01527 881483 🖷 01527 65216 🖰 s.hanley@bromsgroveandredditch.gov.uk

Emergency Planning: Ms Rebecca Pritchett North Worcestershire Civil Contingencies & Resilience Manager, Wyre Forest House, Finepoint Way, Kidderminster DY11 7WF 🖰 rebecca.pritchett@wyreforestdc.gov.uk

Energy Management: Ms Carmen Young Procurement Officer, The Council House, Burcot Lane, Bromsgrove B60 1AA

Environmental Health: Mr Ivor Pumfrey, Acting Head of Regulatory Services, The Council House, Burcot Lane, Bromsgrove B60 1AA ☎ 01684 862296 🖰 ivor.pumfrey@malvernhills.gov.uk

Estates, Property & Valuation: Mr Steve Martin, Facilities & Business Development Officer, The Council House, Burcot Lane, Bromsgrove B60 1AA ☎ 01527 881180 🖷 01527 881608 🖰 steve.martin@bromsgroveandredditch.gov.uk

Events Manager: Mr Jonathan Cochrane Arts & Events Manager, The Council House, Burcot Lane, Bromsgrove B60 1AA ☎ 01527 881381 🖰 jonathan.cochrane@bromsgroveandredditch.gov.uk

Facilities: Mr Steve Martin, Facilities & Business Development Officer, Central Depot, Aston Road, Aston Fields, Bromsgrove B60 3EX ☎ 01527 881180 🖷 01527 881608 🖰 steve.martin@bromsgroveandredditch.gov.uk

Finance: Ms Jayne Pickering Strategic Director & S151 Officer, Town Hall, Walter Stranz Square, Redditch B98 8AH ☎ 01527 64252; 01527 881207 🖷 01527 65216 🖰 j.pickering@bromsgroveandredditch.gov.uk

Treasury: Ms Jayne Pickering Strategic Director & S151 Officer, Town Hall, Walter Stranz Square, Redditch B98 8AH ☎ 01527 64252; 01527 881207 🖷 01527 65216 🖰 j.pickering@bromsgroveandredditch.gov.uk

Fleet Management: Mr Kevin Hirons Environmental Business Development Manager, The Council House, Burcot Lane, Bromsgrove B60 1AA ☎ 01527 881705 🖰 k.hirons@bromsgroveandredditch.gov.uk

Health and Safety: Ms Ruth Wooldridge Senior Advisor - Health, Safety & Wellbeing, The Council House, Burcot Lane, Bromsgrove B60 1AA ☎ 01527 991686 🖰 ruth.wooldridge@bromsgroveandredditch.gov.uk

Home Energy Conservation: Ms Kath Manning Climate Change Manager, The Council House, Burcot Lane, Bromsgrove B60 1AA ☎ 01527 64252 🖰 kath.manning@bromsgroveandredditch.gov.uk

Housing: Mr Derek Allen, Strategic Housing Manager, The Council House, Burcot Lane, Bromsgrove B60 1AA ☎ 01527 881278 🖷 01527 881414 🖰 d.allen@bromsgroveandredditch.gov.uk

Legal: Mrs Claire Felton Head of Legal, Equalities & Democratic Services, The Council House, Burcot Lane, Bromsgrove B60 1AA ☎ 01572 64252; 01527 881429 🖷 01527 65216; 01527 881414 🖰 c.felton@bromsgroveandredditch.gov.uk

Leisure and Cultural Services: Mr John Godwin Head of Leisure, The Council House, Burcot Lane, Bromsgrove B60 1AA ☎ 01527 64252; 01527 881762 🖷 01527 65216 🖰 j.godwin@bromsgroveandredditch.gov.uk

Licensing: Mrs Sue Garratt Senior Licensing Practitioner, Wyatt House, Farrier Street, Worcester WR1 3BH ☎ 01527 64252 ext. 3032 🖰 sue.garratt@worcsregservices.gov.uk

Lottery Funding, Charity and Voluntary: Ms Jayne Pickering Strategic Director & S151 Officer, The Council House, Burcot Lane, Bromsgrove B60 1AA ☎ 01527 64252; 01527 881207 🖷 01527 65216 🖰 j.pickering@bromsgroveandredditch.gov.uk

Member Services: Mrs Sheena Jones, Democratic Services Manager, The Council House, Burcot Lane, Bromsgrove B60 1AA ☎ 01527 01527 548240 🖷 01527 881414 🖰 s.jones@bromsgroveandredditch.gov.uk

Partnerships: Mrs Rebecca Dunn Policy Manager, Bromsgrove District Council, The Council House, Burcot Lane, Bromsgrove B66 1AA ☎ 01527 881616 🖰 r.dunn@bromsgroveandredditch.gov.uk

Personnel / HR: Mrs Deb Poole Head of Business Transformation, Town Hall, Walter Stranz Square, Redditch B98 8AH ☎ 01527 64252 🖷 01527 65216 🖰 d.poole@bromsgroveandredditch.gov.uk

Planning: Mr Dale Birch Development Control Manager, The Council House, Burcot Lane, Bromsgrove B60 1AA ☎ 01527 881341 🖷 01527 881313 🖰 d.birch@bromsgroveandredditch.gov.uk

Procurement: Ms Carmen Young Procurement Officer, The Council House, Burcot Lane, Bromsgrove B60 1AA

Recycling & Waste Minimisation: Mr Guy Revans, Head of Environmental Services, Central Depot, Aston Road, Aston Fields, Bromsgrove B60 3EX ☎ 01527 64252; 01527 64252 ext. 3292 🖷 01527 65216 🖰 g.revans@bromsgroveandredditch.gov.uk

Regeneration: Mr John Staniland Executive Director of Planning, Regeneration, Regulatory & Housing, The Council House, Burcot Lane, Bromsgrove B60 1AA ☎ 01527 64252 Extn 3702; 01527 881202; 01527 534002 🖷 01527 65216 🖰 j.staniland@bromsgroveandredditch.gov.uk

Road Safety: Ms Ruth Bamford Head of Planning & Regeneration Services, The Council House, Burcot Lane, Bromsgrove B60 1AA ☎ 01527 64252 Extn 3201; 01527 64252 ext. 3201 🖷 01527 65216 r.bamford@bromsgroveandredditch.gov.uk

Street Scene: Mr Guy Revans, Head of Environmental Services, Central Depot, Aston Road, Aston Fields, Bromsgrove B60 3EX ☎ 01527 64252; 01527 64252 ext. 3292 🖷 01527 65216 g.revans@bromsgroveandredditch.gov.uk

Tourism: Mr John Godwin Head of Leisure, The Council House, Burcot Lane, Bromsgrove B60 1AA ☎ 01527 64252; 01527 881762 🖷 01527 65216 j.godwin@bromsgroveandredditch.gov.uk

Waste Collection and Disposal: Mr Guy Revans, Head of Environmental Services, Central Depot, Aston Road, Aston Fields, Bromsgrove B60 3EX ☎ 01527 64252; 01527 64252 ext. 3292 🖷 01527 65216 g.revans@bromsgroveandredditch.gov.uk

Waste Management: Mr Guy Revans, Head of Environmental Services, Central Depot, Aston Road, Aston Fields, Bromsgrove B60 3EX ☎ 01527 64252; 01527 64252 ext. 3292 🖷 01527 65216 g.revans@bromsgroveandredditch.gov.uk

COUNCILLORS

***Chair* Spencer**, C J (CON - Slideslow)
c.spencer@bromsgrove.gov.uk

***Vice-Chair* Jones**, H (CON - Catshill North)
h.jones@bromsgrove.gov.uk

***Leader of the Council* Sherrey**, Margaret (CON - Belbroughton & Romsley)
m.sherry@bromsgrove.gov.uk

***Deputy Leader of the Council* Taylor**, C (CON - Lickey Hills)
k.taylor@bromsgrove.gov.uk

Allen-Jones, C (CON - Belbroughton & Romsley)
c.allen-jones@bromsgrove.gov.uk

Baxter, Sue (IND - Drakes Cross & Walkers Heath)
s.baxter@bromsgrove.gov.uk

Bloore, C (LAB - Sidemoor)
c.bloore@bromsgrove.gov.uk

Buxton, M T (LAB - Sanders Park)
m.buxton@bromsgrove.gov.uk

Colella, (IND - Hagley West)
s.colella@bromsgrove.gov.uk

Cooper, B T (CON - Marlbrock)
b.cooper@bromsgrove.gov.uk

Deeming, R J (CON - Cofton)
r.deeming@bromsgrove.gov.uk

Denaro, G N (CON - Wythall West)
g.denaro@bromsgrove.gov.uk

Dent, R L (CON - Bromsgrove Central)
r.dent@bromsgrove.gov.uk

Glass, (CON - Avoncroft)
m.glass@bromsgrove.gov.uk

Griffiths, J (CON - Alvechurch South)
j.griffiths@bromsgrove.gov.uk

Hotham, C A (IND - Barnt Green & Hopwood)
c.hotham@bromsgrove.gov.uk

Jenkins, (IND - Hagley East)
r.jenkins@bromsgrove.gov.uk

Laight, R J (CON - Lowes Hill)
r.laight@bromsgrove.gov.uk

Lammas, P (CON - Norton)
p.lammas@bromsgrove.gov.uk

Mallett, L (LAB - Hill Top)
l.mallett@bromsgrove.gov.uk

May, K J (CON - Perryfields)
k.may@bromsgrove.gov.uk

McDonald, P M (LAB - Rubery North)
p.mcdonald@bromsgrove.gov.uk

McDonald, C M (LAB - Rubery South)
c.mcdonald@bromsgrove.gov.uk

Peters, (IND - Hollywood)
s.peters@bromsgrove.gov.uk

Shannon, Sean (LAB - Charford)
s.shannon@bromsgrove.gov.uk

Smith, (CON - Alvechurch Village)
r.smith@bromsgrove.gov.uk

Thomas, (CON - Aston Fields)
p.thomas@bromsgrove.gov.uk

Thompson, M (LAB - Rock Hill)
m.thompson@bromsgrove.gov.uk

Turner, L J (IND - Wythall East)
l.turner@bromsgrove.gov.uk

Webb, (CON - Catshill South)
s.webb@bromsgrove.gov.uk

Whittaker, Peter (CON - Tardebigge)
p.whittaker@bromsgrove.gov.uk

POLITICAL COMPOSITION

CON: 18, LAB: 7, IND: 6

COMMITTEE CHAIRS

Planning: Mr R J Deeming

Broxbourne D

Broxbourne Borough Council, Borough Offices, Bishops' College, Churchgate, Cheshunt EN8 9XQ
☎ 01992 785555 🖷 01992 785578 enquiry@broxbourne.gov.uk
www.broxbourne.gov.uk

FACTS AND FIGURES

Parliamentary Constituencies: Broxbourne
EU Constituencies: Eastern
Election Frequency: Elections are by thirds

PRINCIPAL OFFICERS

Chief Executive: Mr Jeff Stack Chief Executive, Borough Offices, Bishops' College, Churchgate, Cheshunt EN8 9XQ ☎ 01992 785553 ceo@broxbourne.gov.uk

BROXBOURNE

Building Control: Mr Keith Loxley, Building Control Manager, Borough Offices, Bishop's College, Churchgate, Cheshunt EN8 9NF ☎ 01922 785555 buildingcontrol@broxbourne.gov.uk

PR / Communications: Ms Angela Fieldhouse, Communications Manager, Borough Offices, Bishops' College, Churchgate, Cheshunt EN8 9XQ ☎ 01992 785531 press@broxbourne.gov.uk

Community Safety: Mr Tony Cox, Community Safety & Town Centres Team Manager, Borough Offices, Bishops' College, Churchgate, Cheshunt EN8 9XQ ☎ 01992 785555 tony.cox@broxbourne.gov.uk

Computer Management: Mr Matt Hamilton Infrastructure Manager, Borough Offices, Bishops' College, Churchgate, Cheshunt EN8 9XQ ☎ 01992 785555 matt.hamilton@broxbourne.gov.uk

Corporate Services: Mrs Sandra Beck Group Manager - Corporate Services, Borough Offices, Bishops' College, Churchgate, Cheshunt EN8 9XQ ☎ 01992 785555 🖷 01992 626917 finance@broxbourne.gov.uk

Customer Service: Mr Clive Head Head of Business Management, Borough Offices, Bishops' College, Churchgate, Cheshunt EN8 9XQ ☎ clive.head@broxbourne.gov.uk

Direct Labour: Mr Peter Linkson, Group Manager - Environmental Services, Borough Offices, Bishops' College, Churchgate, Cheshunt EN8 9XQ ☎ 01992 785555 🖷 01992 642216 peter.linkson@broxbourne.gov.uk

Economic Development: Mr Greg Macdonald Group Manager - Economic Development, Borough Offices, Bishops' College, Churchgate, Cheshunt EN8 9XQ ☎ 01992 785555 🖷 01992 627183 greg.macdonald@broxbourne.gov.uk

Electoral Registration: Mr Stephen Billington, Head of Support Services, Borough Offices, Bishops' College, Churchgate, Cheshunt EN8 9XQ ☎ 01992 785534 stephen.billington@broxbourne.gov.uk

Emergency Planning: Mr Jeff Stack Chief Executive, Borough Offices, Bishops' College, Churchgate, Cheshunt EN8 9XQ ☎ 01992 785553 ceo@broxbourne.gov.uk

Environmental Health: Ms Barbara Goult Environmental Health Manager, Borough Offices, Bishops' College, Churchgate, Cheshunt EN8 9XQ ☎ 01992 785555 🖷 01992 350555 barbara.goult@broxbourne.gov.uk

Facilities: Mr Mick Mager Facilities Manager, Borough Offices, Bishops' College, Churchgate, Cheshunt EN8 9XQ ☎ 01992 785555 mick.mager@broxbourne.gov.uk

Treasury: Mrs Lesley Robinson Head of Revenues & Exchequer, Borough Offices, Bishops' College, Churchgate, Cheshunt EN8 9XQ ☎ 01992 785555 lesley.robinson@broxbourne.gov.uk

Health and Safety: Mr Peter Linkson, Group Manager - Environmental Services, Borough Offices, Bishops' College, Churchgate, Cheshunt EN8 9XQ ☎ 01992 785555 🖷 01992 642216 peter.linkson@broxbourne.gov.uk

Housing: Mr Stephen Tingley, Head of Housing & Benefits, Borough Offices, Bishops' College, Churchgate, Cheshunt EN8 9XQ ☎ 01992 785555 stephen.tingley@broxbourne.gov.uk

Legal: Mr Gavin Miles, Head of Legal Services, Borough Offices, Bishops' College, Churchgate, Cheshunt EN8 9NF ☎ 01992 785555 gavin.miles@broxbourne.gov.uk

Leisure and Cultural Services: Mr Steve Dupoy Head of Leisure & Culture, Borough Offices, Bishops' College, Churchgate, Cheshunt EN8 9XQ ☎ 01992 785555 steven.dupoy@broxbourne.gov.uk

Licensing: Mr Stephen Billington, Head of Support Services, Borough Offices, Bishops' College, Churchgate, Cheshunt EN8 9XQ ☎ 01992 785534 stephen.billington@broxbourne.gov.uk

Member Services: Mr Stephen Billington, Head of Support Services, Borough Offices, Bishops' College, Churchgate, Cheshunt EN8 9XQ ☎ 01992 785534 stephen.billington@broxbourne.gov.uk

Parking: Mr Tony Cox, Community Safety & Town Centres Team Manager, Borough Offices, Bishops' College, Churchgate, Cheshunt EN8 9XQ ☎ 01992 785555 tony.cox@broxbourne.gov.uk

Personnel / HR: Mr Richard Pennell, Head of Personnel & Payroll, Borough Offices, Bishops' College, Churchgate, Cheshunt EN8 9XG ☎ 01992 758809 richard.pennell@broxbourne.gov.uk

Planning: Mr Douglas Cooper Head of Planning & Development, Borough Offices, Bishops' College, Churchgate, Cheshunt EN8 9XQ ☎ 01992 785555 douglas.cooper@broxbourne.gov.uk

Procurement: Mr Clive Head Head of Business Management, Borough Offices, Bishops' College, Churchgate, Cheshunt EN8 9XQ ☎ clive.head@broxbourne.gov.uk

Recycling & Waste Minimisation: Mr Peter Linkson, Group Manager - Environmental Services, Borough Offices, Bishops' College, Churchgate, Cheshunt EN8 9XQ ☎ 01992 785555 🖷 01992 642216 peter.linkson@broxbourne.gov.uk

Staff Training: Mr Richard Pennell, Head of Personnel & Payroll, Borough Offices, Bishops' College, Churchgate, Cheshunt EN8 9XG ☎ 01992 758809 richard.pennell@broxbourne.gov.uk

Town Centre: Mr Tony Cox, Community Safety & Town Centres Team Manager, Borough Offices, Bishops' College, Churchgate, Cheshunt EN8 9XQ ☎ 01992 785555 tony.cox@broxbourne.gov.uk

Waste Collection and Disposal: Mr Peter Linkson, Group Manager - Environmental Services, Borough Offices, Bishops' College, Churchgate, Cheshunt EN8 9XQ ☎ 01992 785555 🖷 01992 642216 peter.linkson@broxbourne.gov.uk

Waste Management: Mr Peter Linkson, Group Manager - Environmental Services, Borough Offices, Bishops' College, Churchgate, Cheshunt EN8 9XQ ☎ 01992 785555 🖷 01992 642216 peter.linkson@broxbourne.gov.uk

COUNCILLORS

***Mayor* Greensmyth**, Martin (CON - Rosedale & Bury Green) m.greensmyth@ntlworld.com

***Deputy Mayor* Crump**, Carol (CON - Cheshunt South & Theobalds)
carolann.crump@sky.com

***Leader of the Council* Mills-Bishop**, Mark (CON - Goffs Oak)
cllr.m.mills-bishop@broxbourne.gov.uk

***Deputy Leader of the Council* Metcalf**, Jim (CON - Wormley & Turnford)
jmetcalf@btinternet.com

Aitken, Malcolm (LAB - Waltham Cross)
malcolm.aitken549@btinternet.com

Ayling, Ken (CON - Hoddesdon Town & Rye Park)
ken.ayling@ntlworld.com

Ball-Greenwood, Suzanne (CON - Flamstead End)

Bowman, Carol (LAB - Waltham Cross)
carol.bowman@sky.com

Brown, Keith (CON - Hoddesdon North)
keithbrown3@hotmail.com

Hannam, Ray (CON - Cheshunt North)
ray.hannam@btopenworld.com

Hart, Dee (CON - Flamstead End)
dee.hart@hertfordshire.gov.uk

Harvey, Neil (LAB - Waltham Cross)
neilandgillharvey@gmail.com

Hutchings, Tim (CON - Broxbourne & Hoddesdon South)
trhutchings59@gmail.com

Iszatt, Mike (CON - Cheshunt North)
iszatt@live.com

Jackson, Hazel (CON - Rosedale & Bury Green)
hazeljackson@talktalk.net

Macleod, Susie (CON - Broxbourne & Hoddesdon South)
susiemac4broxbourne@gmail.com

McCormick, Cody (CON - Cheshunt South & Theobalds)
cheshuntcody@gmail.com

Mobbs, Yvonne (CON - Rosedale & Bury Green)
yvonnemobbs@btinternet.com

Moule, Peter (CON - Goffs Oak)
peter@billmoule.co.uk

Nicholson, Gordon (CON - Wormley & Turnford)

Pearce, Jeremy (CON - Goffs Oak)
jeremy.n.pearce@gmail.com

Perryman, Bren (CON - Hoddesdon Town & Rye Park)
cllr.b.perryman@broxbourne.gov.uk

Platt, David (UKIP - Hoddesdon Town & Rye Park)
cllr.david.platt@gmail.com

Rowland, Eddy (CON - Broxbourne & Hoddesdon South)
cllr.e.rowland@broxbourne.gov.uk

Seeby, Paul (CON - Flamstead End)
cllr.p.seeby@broxbourne.gov.uk

Siracusa, Tony (CON - Cheshunt South & Theobalds)
cllr.t.siracusa@broxbourne.gov.uk

Soteris, Penny (CON - Cheshunt North)
p.soteris@hotmail.com

Taylor, David (CON - Wormley & Turnford)
davidwjtaylor@gmail.com

White, Lyn (CON - Hoddesdon North)
lyn.white@ntlworld.com

Wortley, Steve (CON - Hoddesdon North)
s.wortley@icloud.com

POLITICAL COMPOSITION

CON: 26, LAB: 3, UKIP: 1

COMMITTEE CHAIRS

Planning & Regulatory: Mr Tony Siracusa

Broxtowe D

Broxtowe Borough Council, Council Offices, Foster Avenue, Beeston NG9 1AB
☎ 0115 917 7777 🖷 0115 917 3030 💻 www.broxtowe.gov.uk

FACTS AND FIGURES

Parliamentary Constituencies: Ashfield, Broxtowe
EU Constituencies: East Midlands
Election Frequency: Elections are of whole council

PRINCIPAL OFFICERS

Chief Executive: Ms Ruth Hyde, Chief Executive, Town Hall, Foster Avenue, Beeston NG9 1AB ☎ 0115 917 3255 🖱 ceo@broxtowe.gov.uk

Deputy Chief Executive: Mr Shane Flynn Deputy Chief Executive & S151 Officer, Council Offices, Foster Avenue, Beeston NG9 1AB ☎ 0115 917 3232 🖷 0115 917 3131 🖱 shane.flynn@broxtowe.gov.uk

Senior Management: Mr Ted Czerniak, Director - Housing, Leisure & Property Services, Council Offices, Foster Avenue, Beeston NG9 1AB ☎ 0115 917 3419 🖷 0115 917 3508 🖱 ted.czerniak@broxtowe.gov.uk

Senior Management: Mr Phillip Horsfield Director - Legal & Planning Services, Council Offices, Foster Avenue, Beeston NG9 1AB ☎ 0115 917 3230 🖷 0115 917 3131 🖱 phillip.horsfield@broxtowe.gov.uk

Building Control: Mr Andy Limb, Chief Building Control Officer, Council Offices, Foster Avenue, Beeston NG9 1AB ☎ 0115 917 3470 🖷 0115 917 3377 🖱 andy.limb@broxtowe.gov.uk

PR / Communications: Miss Sarah Yates Corporate Communications Officer, Town Hall, Foster Avenue, Beeston NG9 1AB ☎ 0115 917 3825 🖱 sarah.yates@broxtowe.gov.uk

Community Planning: Mrs Marice Hawley Principal Community Development Officer, Council Offices, Foster Avenue, Beeston NG9 1AB ☎ 0115 917 3492 🖷 0115 917 3377 🖱 marice.hawley@broxtowe.gov.uk

Community Safety: Mr David Gell Head of Public Protection, Council Offices, Foster Avenue, Beeston NG9 1AB ☎ 0115 917 3504 🖷 0115 917 3377 🖱 david.gell@broxtowe.gov.uk

Computer Management: Mr Kevin Powell, CIO Officer, Town Hall, Foster Avenue, Beeston NG9 1AB ☎ 0115 917 3214 🖷 0115 917 3030 🖱 kevin.powell@broxtowe.gov.uk

BROXTOWE

Contracts: Mr Ted Czerniak, Director - Housing, Leisure & Property Services, Council Offices, Foster Avenue, Beeston NG9 1AB ☎ 0115 917 3419 🖷 0115 917 3508 🖱 ted.czerniak@broxtowe.gov.uk

Customer Service: Mr Robert Williams Customer Services Manager, Council Offices, Foster Avenue, Beeston NG9 1AB ☎ 0115 917 3940 🖱 robert.williams@broxtowe.gov.uk

Direct Labour: Mr John Delaney, Head of Built Environment, Council Offices, Foster Avenue, Beeston NG9 1AB ☎ 0115 917 3655 🖷 0115 917 3160 🖱 john.delaney@broxtowe.gov.uk

Economic Development: Mr Steffan Saunders Head of Neighbourhoods & Prosperity, Council Offices, Foster Avenue, Beeston NG9 1AB ☎ 0115 917 3482 🖷 0115 917 3377 🖱 steffan.saunders@broxtowe.gov.uk

E-Government: Mr Kevin Powell, CIO Officer, Town Hall, Foster Avenue, Beeston NG9 1AB ☎ 0115 917 3214 🖷 0115 917 3030 🖱 kevin.powell@broxtowe.gov.uk

Electoral Registration: Ms Ruth Hyde, Chief Executive, Town Hall, Foster Avenue, Beeston NG9 1AB ☎ 0115 917 3255 🖱 ceo@broxtowe.gov.uk

Emergency Planning: Mr Steve Newton, Health & Safety Officer, Council Offices, Foster Avenue, Beeston NG9 1AB ☎ 0115 917 3330 🖷 0115 917 3030 🖱 steve.newton@broxtowe.gov.uk

Environmental / Technical Services: Mr David Gell Head of Public Protection, Council Offices, Foster Avenue, Beeston NG9 1AB ☎ 0115 917 3504 🖷 0115 917 3377 🖱 david.gell@broxtowe.gov.uk

Environmental Health: Mr Rob Westwood Head of Revenues, Benefits & Customer Services, Council Offices, Foster Avenue, Beeston NG9 1AB ☎ 0115 917 3236 🖷 0115 917 3508 🖱 rob.westwood@broxtowe.gov.uk

Estates, Property & Valuation: Mr Steffan Saunders Head of Neighbourhoods & Prosperity, Council Offices, Foster Avenue, Beeston NG9 1AB ☎ 0115 917 3482 🖷 0115 917 3377 🖱 steffan.saunders@broxtowe.gov.uk

Finance: Mr Shane Flynn Deputy Chief Executive & S151 Officer, Council Offices, Foster Avenue, Beeston NG9 1AB ☎ 0115 917 3232 🖷 0115 917 3131 🖱 shane.flynn@broxtowe.gov.uk

Treasury: Mr Shane Flynn Deputy Chief Executive & S151 Officer, Council Offices, Foster Avenue, Beeston NG9 1AB ☎ 0115 917 3232 🖷 0115 917 3131 🖱 shane.flynn@broxtowe.gov.uk

Grounds Maintenance: Mr Tim Crawford, Parks & Environment Manager, Council Offices, Foster Avenue, Beeston NG9 1AB ☎ 0115 917 3643 🖷 0115 917 3600 🖱 tim.crawford@broxtowe.gov.uk

Health and Safety: Mr Steve Newton, Health & Safety Officer, Council Offices, Foster Avenue, Beeston NG9 1AB ☎ 0115 917 3330 🖷 0115 917 3030 🖱 steve.newton@broxtowe.gov.uk

Highways: Mr John Delaney, Head of Built Environment, Council Offices, Foster Avenue, Beeston NG9 1AB ☎ 0115 917 3655 🖷 0115 917 3160 🖱 john.delaney@broxtowe.gov.uk

Housing: Mr Ted Czerniak, Director - Housing, Leisure & Property Services, Council Offices, Foster Avenue, Beeston NG9 1AB ☎ 0115 917 3419 🖷 0115 917 3508 🖱 ted.czerniak@broxtowe.gov.uk

Housing Maintenance: Mr Gary Duckmanton, Building Maintenance Manager, Kimberley Depot, Eastwood Road, Kimberley, Nottingham NG16 2HX ☎ 0115 917 7777 🖷 0115 917 3106

Legal: Mr Phillip Horsfield Director - Legal & Planning Services, Council Offices, Foster Avenue, Beeston NG9 1AB ☎ 0115 917 3230 🖷 0115 917 3131 🖱 phillip.horsfield@broxtowe.gov.uk

Leisure and Cultural Services: Mr Ashley Marriott, Head of Leisure & Culture, Council Offices, Foster Avenue, Beeston NG9 1AB ☎ 0115 917 3626 🖷 0115 917 3394 🖱 ashley.marriott@broxtowe.gov.uk

Licensing: Mr David Gell Head of Public Protection, Council Offices, Foster Avenue, Beeston NG9 1AB ☎ 0115 917 3504 🖷 0115 917 3377 🖱 david.gell@broxtowe.gov.uk

Lighting: Mr John Delaney, Head of Built Environment, Council Offices, Foster Avenue, Beeston NG9 1AB ☎ 0115 917 3655 🖷 0115 917 3160 🖱 john.delaney@broxtowe.gov.uk

Lottery Funding, Charity and Voluntary: Mr Ashley Marriott, Head of Leisure & Culture, Council Offices, Foster Avenue, Beeston NG9 1AB ☎ 0115 917 3626 🖷 0115 917 3394 🖱 ashley.marriott@broxtowe.gov.uk

Member Services: Mrs Sue Rodden, Head of Administrative Services, Council Offices, Foster Avenue, Beeston NG9 1AB ☎ 0115 917 3295 🖷 0115 917 3131 🖱 sue.rodden@broxtowe.gov.uk

Parking: Mr John Delaney, Head of Built Environment, Council Offices, Foster Avenue, Beeston NG9 1AB ☎ 0115 917 3655 🖷 0115 917 3160 🖱 john.delaney@broxtowe.gov.uk

Partnerships: Ms Ruth Hyde, Chief Executive, Town Hall, Foster Avenue, Beeston NG9 1AB ☎ 0115 917 3255 🖱 ceo@broxtowe.gov.uk

Personnel / HR: Mrs Jane Lunn, Head of Human Resources, Town Hall, Foster Avenue, Beeston NG9 1AB ☎ 0115 917 3346 🖷 0115 917 3030 🖱 jane.lunn@broxtowe.gov.uk

Planning: Mr Phillip Horsfield Director - Legal & Planning Services, Council Offices, Foster Avenue, Beeston NG9 1AB ☎ 0115 917 3230 🖷 0115 917 3131 🖱 phillip.horsfield@broxtowe.gov.uk

Procurement: Mr Steve Cotterill, Procurement Officer, Council Offices, Foster Avenue, Beeston NG9 1AB ☎ 0115 917 3296 🖷 0115 917 3131 🖱 steve.cotterill@broxtowe.gov.uk

Recycling & Waste Minimisation: Mr Paul Wolverson, Waste & Recycling Officer, Kimberley Depot, Eastwood Road, Kimberley, Nottingham NG16 2HX ☎ 0115 917 3106 🖷 0115 917 3600 🖱 paul.wolverson@broxtowe.gov.uk

Regeneration: Mr Steffan Saunders Head of Neighbourhoods & Prosperity, Council Offices, Foster Avenue, Beeston NG9 1AB ☎ 0115 917 3482 🖷 0115 917 3377 🖱 steffan.saunders@broxtowe.gov.uk

Staff Training: Mrs Julie Fish, Training Officer, Town Hall, Foster Avenue, Beeston NG9 1AB ☎ 0115 917 3365 🖷 0115 917 3030 julie.fish@broxtowe.gov.uk

Sustainable Communities: Mrs Marice Hawley Principal Community Development Officer, Council Offices, Foster Avenue, Beeston NG9 1AB ☎ 0115 917 3492 🖷 0115 917 3377 marice.hawley@broxtowe.gov.uk

Sustainable Development: Mrs Marice Hawley Principal Community Development Officer, Council Offices, Foster Avenue, Beeston NG9 1AB ☎ 0115 917 3492 🖷 0115 917 3377 marice.hawley@broxtowe.gov.uk

Tourism: Ms Claire Bates Cultural Services Manager, DH Lawrence Heritage Centre, Mansfield Road, Eastwood NG16 3DZ ☎ 01773 717353 🖷 01773 713509 claire.bates@broxtowe.gov.uk

Waste Collection and Disposal: Mr Paul Syson, Refuse and Cleansing Manager, Kimberley Depot, Eastwood Road, Kimberley, Nottingham NG16 2HX ☎ 0115 9 17 3062 🖷 0115 927 3106 paul.syson@broxtowe.gov.uk

Waste Management: Mr Paul Wolverson, Waste & Recycling Officer, Kimberley Depot, Eastwood Road, Kimberley, Nottingham NG16 2HX ☎ 0115 917 3106 🖷 0115 917 3600 paul.wolverson@broxtowe.gov.uk

COUNCILLORS

***Mayor* Bagshaw**, Susan (LAB - Eastwood Hilltop)
susan.bagshaw@broxtowe.gov.uk

***Leader of the Council* Jackson**, Richard (CON - Attenborough & Chilwell East)
richard.jackson@broxtowe.gov.uk

***Deputy Leader of the Council* Owen**, Jill (CON - Watnall & Nuthall West)
jill.owen@broxtowe.gov.uk

Atherton, Eileen (CON - Chilwell West)
eileen.atherton@broxtowe.gov.uk

Bagshaw, David (LAB - Eastwood St Mary's)
david.bagshaw@broxtowe.gov.uk

Ball, Lydia (CON - Awsworth, Cossall & Trowell)
lydia.ball@broxtowe.gov.uk

Briggs, Joan (CON - Attenborough & Chilwell East)
joan.briggs@broxtowe.gov.uk

Brindley, Tim (CON - Chilwell West)
tim.brindley@broxtowe.gov.uk

Brown, Mick (CON - Greasley)
mick.brown@broxtowe.gov.uk

Burnett, Derek (CON - Watnall & Nuthall West)
derek.burnett@broxtowe.gov.uk

Carr, Barbara (LD - Beeston North)
Barbara.carr@broxtow.gov.uk

Carr, Stephen (LD - Beeston North)
steve.carr@broxtowe.gov.uk

Crow, Mel (CON - Kimberley)
Mel.crow@broxtowe.gov.uk

Cullen, Teresa (LAB - Beeston Rylands)
Teresa.cullen@broxtowe.gov.uk

Darby, Ray (LAB - Stapleford South West)
ray.darby@broxtowe.gov.uk

Doddy, John Anthony (CON - Bramcote)
John.doddy@broxtowe.gov.uk

Easom, Shane (CON - Kimberley)
Shane.easom@broxtowe.gov.uk

Elliott, Dawn (LAB - Beeston Rylands)
dawn.elliott@broxtowe.gov.uk

Goold, Jan (CON - Bramcote)
Jan.goold@broxtowe.gov.uk

Handley, Margaret (CON - Greasley)
margaret.handley@broxtowe.gov.uk

Handley, John William (CON - Brinsley)
john.handley@broxtowe.gov.uk

Harper, Tony (CON - Eastwood Hall)
Anthony.harper@broxtowe.gov.uk

Harvey, Graham (CON - Chilwell West)
graham.harvey@broxtowe.gov.uk

Harvey, Natalie (CON - Toton & Chilwell Meadows)
Natalie.harvey@broxtowe.gov.uk

Kee, Mia (CON - Toton & Chilwell Meadows)

Kerry, Eric (CON - Attenborough & Chilwell East)
eric.kerry@broxtowe.gov.uk

Khaled, Halimah (CON - Toton & Chilwell Meadows)
halimah.khaled@broxtowe.gov.uk

Lally, Patrick (LAB - Beeston Central)
pat.lally@broxtowe.gov.uk

Lally, Lynda (LAB - Beeston Central)
lynda.lally@broxtowe.gov.uk

Longdon, John (CON - Stapleford North)
John.longdon@broxtowe.gov.uk

Marshall, Greg (LAB - Beeston West)

Marsters, Josie (LD - Eastwood St Mary's)
Josie.marsters@broxtowe.gov.uk

McGrath, John (LAB - Stapleford South West)
john.mcgrath@broxtowe.gov.uk

McRae, Richard (IND - Stapleford North)
Richard.Mcrae@broxtowe.gov.uk

Owen, Philip (CON - Nuthall East & Strelley)
Philip.owen@broxtowe.gov.uk

Patrick, Janet (LAB - Beeston West)
janet.patrick@broxtowe.gov.uk

Plackett, Martin (CON - Bramcote)
Martin.plackett@broxtowe.gov.uk

Radulovic, Milan (LAB - Eastwood Hilltop)
milan.radulovic@broxtowe.gov.uk

Rice, Christopher (CON - Stapleford South East)
Christopher.rice@broxtowe.gov.uk

Rigby, Kenneth (LD - Awsworth, Cossall & Trowell)
ken.rigby@broxtowe.gov.uk

Robinson, Richard (LAB - Kimberley)
richard.robinson@broxtowe.gov.uk

BROXTOWE

Rowland, Stuart (CON - Greasley)
stuart.rowland@broxtowe.gov.uk

Simpson, Paul (CON - Nuthall East & Strelley)
paul.simpson@broxtowe.gov.uk

Stockwell, Adam (CON - Stapleford South East)
Adam.stockwell@broxtowe.gov.uk

POLITICAL COMPOSITION
CON: 27, LAB: 12, LD: 4, IND: 1

COMMITTEE CHAIRS

General Purposes & Audit: Mr Stuart Rowland

Licensing & Appeals: Mr Derek Burnett

Planning: Mrs Margaret Handley

Standards: Ms Eileen Atherton

Buckinghamshire C

Buckinghamshire County Council, County Hall, Walton Street, Aylesbury HP20 1YU
☎ 01296 395000 www.buckscc.gov.uk

FACTS AND FIGURES
EU Constituencies: South East
Election Frequency: Elections are of whole council

PRINCIPAL OFFICERS

Chief Executive: Mr Chris Williams, Chief Executive Officer, County Hall, Walton Street, Aylesbury HP20 1UY ☎ 01296 382201 cmwilliams@buckscc.gov.uk

Senior Management: Mr Trevor Boyd Strategic Director - Adults & Family Wellbeing, County Hall, Walton Street, Aylesbury HP20 1YU ☎ 01296 382074 tboyd@buckscc.gov.uk

Senior Management: Mr Neil Gibson, Strategic Director - Communities & Built Environment, County Hall, Walton Street, Aylesbury HP20 1YU ☎ 01296 383106 negibson@buckscc.gov.uk

Senior Management: Mr David Johnston MD of Children's Social Care & Learning, County Hall, Walton Street, Aylesbury HP20 1YU ☎ 01296 383104 djohnston@buckscc.gov.uk

Senior Management: Dr J O'Grady Director - Public Health, County Hall, Walton Street, Aylesbury HP20 1YU ☎ 01296 387623 jaogrady@buckscc.gov.uk

Senior Management: Mr Hugh Peart, Director - Legal & Governance Services, County Hall, Walton Street, Aylesbury HP20 1YU ☎ 020 8424 1272 hugh.peart@harrow.gov.uk

Senior Management: Mrs Gillian Quinton MD - Business Enterprise & Services, County Hall, Walton Street, Aylesbury HP20 1YU ☎ 01296 383127 gquinton@buckscc.gov.uk

Access Officer / Social Services (Disability): Ms Sarah Holding School Relationship Manager, County Hall, Walton Street, Aylesbury HP20 1YU ☎ 01296 383038 sholding@buckscc.gov.uk

Best Value: Ms Sarah Ashmead, Director - Strategy & Policy, County Hall, Walton Street, Aylesbury HP20 1YU ☎ 01296 383986 sashmead@buckscc.gov.uk

Best Value: Mrs Gillian Quinton MD - Business Enterprise & Services, County Hall, Walton Street, Aylesbury HP20 1YU ☎ 01296 383127 gquinton@buckscc.gov.uk

Children / Youth Services: Mr Chris Munday Service Director, County Hall, Walton Street, Aylesbury HP20 1YU ☎ 01296 387849 ccmunday@buckscc.gov.uk

Children / Youth Services: Ms Laura Nankin Head of Fair Access & Youth Provision, County Hall, Walton Street, Aylesbury HP20 1YU ☎ 01296 382078 lnankin@buckscc.gov.uk

PR / Communications: Ms Celia Logan Service Director - Customer Services & Communication, County Hall, Walton Street, Aylesbury HP20 1YU ☎ 01296 387416 clogan@buckscc.gov.uk

Computer Management: Mrs S Payne Head of Communications, County Hall, Walton Street, Aylesbury HP20 1YU ☎ 01296 382463 spayne@buckscc.gov.uk

Consumer Protection and Trading Standards: Mr Phil Dart, Service Director - Localities & Safer Communities, 5-7 Walton Street, Aylesbury HP20 1UY ☎ 01296 382398 pdart@buckscc.gov.uk

Contracts: Ms Tricia Hook, Senior Procurement Manager, County Hall, Walton Street, Aylesbury HP20 1YU ☎ 01296 383615 phook@buckscc.gov.uk

Education: Mr Trevor Boyd Strategic Director - Adults & Family Wellbeing, County Hall, Walton Street, Aylesbury HP20 1YU ☎ 01296 382074 tboyd@buckscc.gov.uk

Education: Ms Sarah Holding School Relationship Manager, County Hall, Walton Street, Aylesbury HP20 1YU ☎ 01296 383038 sholding@buckscc.gov.uk

E-Government: Mrs S Payne Head of Communications, County Hall, Walton Street, Aylesbury HP20 1YU ☎ 01296 382463 spayne@buckscc.gov.uk

Electoral Registration: Mr Clive Parker, Head of Civic & Ceremonial Services, Legal and Democratic Services, County Hall, Walton Street, Aylesbury HP20 1UA ☎ 01296 383685 cparker@buckscc.gov.uk

Emergency Planning: Mr Andrew Fyfe, Resilience Manager, County Hall, Walton Street, Aylesbury HP20 1YU ☎ 01296 382937 afyfe@buckscc.gov.uk

Environmental / Technical Services: Mr Neil Gibson, Strategic Director - Communities & Built Environment, County Hall, Walton Street, Aylesbury HP20 1YU ☎ 01296 383106 negibson@buckscc.gov.uk

Facilities: Mr Ian Boll Director - Infrastructure & Regeneration, County Hall, Walton Street, Aylesbury HP20 1YU ☎ 01296 382113 iboll@buckscc.gov.uk

Finance: Mr Richard Ambrose Service Director - Finance & Commercial Services, County Hall, Walton Street, Aylesbury HP20 1YU ☎ 01296 383120 rambrose@buckscc.gov.uk

Treasury: Mr Richard Ambrose Service Director - Finance, Treasury & Commercial Services, County Hall, Walton Street, Aylesbury HP20 1YU ☎ 01296 383120 rambrose@buckscc.gov.uk

Pensions: Ms Julie Edwards Pensions Manager, County Hall, Walton Street, Aylesbury HP20 1YU ☎ 01296 395000 jedwards@buckscc.gov.uk

Health and Safety: Ms Pat Beveridge Health & Safety Advisor, County Hall, Walton Street, Aylesbury HP20 1YU ☎ 01296 382954 pbeveridge@buckss.gov.uk

Highways: Mr Neil Gibson, Strategic Director - Communities & Built Environment, County Hall, Walton Street, Aylesbury HP20 1YU ☎ 01296 383106 negibson@buckscc.gov.uk

Local Area Agreement: Ms Sarah Ashmead, Director - Strategy & Policy, County Hall, Walton Street, Aylesbury HP20 1YU ☎ 01296 383986 sashmead@buckscc.gov.uk

Legal: Mr Hugh Peart, Director - Legal & Governance Services, Room 102 Labour Group Office, Civic Centre, Station Road, Harrow HA1 2UH ☎ 020 8424 1272 hugh.peart@harrow.gov.uk

Leisure and Cultural Services: Mr Phil Dart, Service Director - Localities & Safer Communities, 5-7 Walton Street, Aylesbury HP20 1UY ☎ 01296 382398 pdart@buckscc.gov.uk

Lifelong Learning: Mr Phil Dart, Service Director - Localities & Safer Communities, 5-7 Walton Street, Aylesbury HP20 1UY ☎ 01296 382398 pdart@buckscc.gov.uk

Member Services: Mr Clive Parker, Head of Civic & Ceremonial Services, Legal and Democratic Services, County Hall, Walton Street, Aylesbury HP20 1UA ☎ 01296 383685 cparker@buckscc.gov.uk

Personnel / HR: Mrs C Daltry Service Director - Human Resources, County Hall, Walton Street, Aylesbury HP20 1YU ☎ 01296 382528 cdaltry@buckscc.gov.uk

Planning: Mr David Sutherland, Resource Strategy Manager, County Hall, Walton Street, Aylesbury HP20 1UY ☎ 01296 383003 dsutherland@buckscc.gov.uk

Public Libraries: Ms Celia Logan Service Director - Customer Services & Communication, County Hall, Walton Street, Aylesbury HP20 1YU ☎ 01296 387416 clogan@buckscc.gov.uk

Recycling & Waste Minimisation: Mr David Sutherland, Resource Strategy Manager, County Hall, Walton Street, Aylesbury HP20 1UY ☎ 01296 383003 dsutherland@buckscc.gov.uk

Social Services (Adult): Mr Trevor Boyd Strategic Director - Adults & Family Wellbeing, County Hall, Walton Street, Aylesbury HP20 1YU ☎ 01296 382074 tboyd@buckscc.gov.uk

Social Services (Children): Mr David Johnston MD of Children's Social Care & Learning, County Hall, Walton Street, Aylesbury HP20 1YU ☎ 01296 383104 djohnston@buckscc.gov.uk

Families: Mr Trevor Boyd Strategic Director - Adults & Family Wellbeing, County Hall, Walton Street, Aylesbury HP20 1YU ☎ 01296 382074 tboyd@buckscc.gov.uk

Public Health: Dr J O'Grady Director - Public Health, County Hall, Walton Street, Aylesbury HP20 1YU ☎ 01296 387623 jaogrady@buckscc.gov.uk

Staff Training: Mrs Frances Mills Head of People & Organisational Development, County Hall, Walton Street, Aylesbury HP20 1YU ☎ 01296 382945 fmills@buckscc.gov.uk

Sustainable Communities: Ms Sarah Ashmead, Director - Strategy & Policy, County Hall, Walton Street, Aylesbury HP20 1YU ☎ 01296 383986 sashmead@buckscc.gov.uk

Sustainable Communities: Mr Neil Gibson, Strategic Director - Communities & Built Environment, County Hall, Walton Street, Aylesbury HP20 1YU ☎ 01296 383106 negibson@buckscc.gov.uk

Sustainable Development: Mrs Zoe Dixon, Senior Manager - Place Service, County Hall, Walton Street, Aylesbury HP20 1UZ ☎ 01296 382132 zdixon@buckscc.gov.uk

Traffic Management: Mr Neil Gibson, Strategic Director - Communities & Built Environment, County Hall, Walton Street, Aylesbury HP20 1YU ☎ 01296 383106 negibson@buckscc.gov.uk

Waste Management: Mr Gurbaksh Badhan Waste Business Manager, County Hall, Walton Street, Aylesbury HP20 1YU ☎ 01296 387678 gbadhan@buckscc.gov.uk

COUNCILLORS

***Chair* Chapple**, William (CON - Aston Clinton & Bierton)
bchapple@buckscc.gov.uk

***Vice-Chair* Letheren**, Valerie (CON - Terriers & Amersham Hill)
vletheren@buckscc.gov.uk

***Leader of the Council* Tett**, Martin (CON - Little Chalfont & Amersham Common)
mtett@buckscc.gov.uk

***Deputy Leader of the Council* Appleyard**, Mike (CON - The Wooburns, Bourne End & Hedsor)
mappleyard@buckscc.gov.uk

***Group Leader* Davies**, Avril (LD - Ivinghoe)
acdavies@buckscc.gov.uk

***Group Leader* Huxley**, Andy (UKIP - Aylesbury North West)
ahuxley@buckscc.gov.uk

Adams, Chris (UKIP - Wendover, Halton & Stoke Mandeville)
chadams@buckscc.gov.uk

Adams, Brian (UKIP - Aylesbury South West)
bradams@buckscc.gov.uk

Aston, Margaret (CON - Bernwood)
maston@buckscc.gov.uk

Bendyshe-Brown, Bill (CON - The Risboroughs)
bbendyshe-brown@buckscc.gov.uk

BUCKINGHAMSHIRE

Birchley, Patricia (CON - Chiltern Ridges)
pbirchley@buckscc.gov.uk

Blake, Janet (CON - Great Brickhill)
janetblake@buckscc.gov.uk

Brown, Noel (CON - Chess Valley)
nbrown@buckscc.gov.uk

Busby, Adrian (CON - Beaconsfield)
ajbusby@buckscc.gov.uk

Butcher, Timonthy (CON - Chalfont St Giles)
trbutcher@buckscc.gov.uk

Carroll, David (CON - Ridgeway East)
dcarroll@buckscc.gov.uk

Chilver, John (CON - Winslow)
jchilver@buckscc.gov.uk

Clarke, Lesley (CON - Abbey)
lmclarke@buckscc.gov.uk

Dhillon, Dev (CON - Cliveden)
ddhillon@buckscc.gov.uk

Ditta, Chaudhary (LD - Totteridge & Bowerdean)
cditta@buckscc.gov.uk

Egleton, Trevor (CON - Stoke Poges & Westham)
tegleton@buckscc.gov.uk

Etholen, Carl (CON - Ridgeway West)
cetholen@buckscc.gov.uk

Glover, Netta (CON - Wing)
nglover@buckscc.gov.uk

Gomm, Phil (IND - Aylesbury East)
pgomm@buckscc.gov.uk

Hardy, Peter (CON - Gerrards Cross)
phardy@buckscc.gov.uk

Hayday, Darren (IND - West Wycombe)
dhayday@buckscc.gov.uk

Hazell, Lin (CON - Farnham Common & Burnham Beeches)
lhazell@buckscc.gov.uk

Irwin, Paul (UKIP - Stone & Waddesdon)
pirwin@buckscc.gov.uk

Khan, Raj (LD - Aylesbury North)
rkhan@buckscc.gov.uk

Lambert, Steven (LD - Aylesbury West)
slambert@buckscc.gov.uk

Macpherson, Angela (CON - Grendon Underwood)
angmacpherson@buckscc.gov.uk

Mallen, Wendy (CON - Downley)
wmallen@buckscc.gov.uk

Martin, David (CON - Chalfont St Peter)
dmartin@buckscc.gov.uk

Mohammed, Zahir (CON - Booker Cressex & Castlefield)
zamohammed@buckscc.gov.uk

Phillips, Martin (CON - Amersham & Chesham Bois)
mphillips@buckscc.gov.uk

Reed, Roger (CON - Denham)
roreed@buckscc.gov.uk

Roberts, Brian (CON - Aylesbury South East)
broberts@buckscc.gov.uk

Schofield, David (CON - Penn Wood & Old Amersham)
dschofield@buckscc.gov.uk

Scott, Richard (CON - Marlow)
rjscott@buckscc.gov.uk

Shakespeare, David (CON - Tylers Green & Loudwater)
dshakespeare@buckscc.gov.uk

Shaw, Mark (CON - Chesham)
markshaw@buckscc.gov.uk

Stevens, Alan (UKIP - Great Missenden)
alstevens@buckscc.gov.uk

Stuchbury, Robin (LAB - Buckingham West)
rstuchbury@buckscc.gov.uk

Teesdale, Jean (CON - Chiltern Villages)
jteesdale@buckscc.gov.uk

Vigor-Hedderly, Ruth (CON - Iver)
rvhedderly@buckscc.gov.uk

Wassell, Julia (IND - Ryemead & Micklefield)
jwassell@buckscc.gov.uk

Watson, David (CON - Flackwell Heath, Little Marlow & Marlow South East)
dwatson@buckscc.gov.uk

Whyte, Warren (CON - Buckingham East)
wwhyte@buckscc.gov.uk

Wood, Katrina (CON - Hazelmere)
kwood@bucksc.gov.uk

POLITICAL COMPOSITION

CON: 36, UKIP: 5, LD: 4, IND: 3, LAB: 1

COMMITTEE CHAIRS

Children's Social Care & Learning: Ms Valerie Letheren

Development Control: Mr Roger Reed

Finance, Performance & Resources: Mr Brian Roberts

Health & Adult Social Care: Ms Angela Macpherson

Pensions: Mr John Chilver

Burnley D

Burnley Borough Council, Town Hall, Manchester Road, Burnley BB11 9SA
☎ 01282 425011 🖷 01282 450594 ✉ enquiries@burnley.gov.uk
💻 www.burnley.gov.uk

FACTS AND FIGURES

Parliamentary Constituencies: Burnley
EU Constituencies: North West
Election Frequency: Elections are by thirds

PRINCIPAL OFFICERS

Chief Executive: Ms Pam Smith Chief Executive, Town Hall, Manchester Road, Burnley BB11 9SA ☎ 01282 477101
✉ psmith@burnley.gov.uk

Senior Management: Mr Mick Cartledge, Director - Community Services, Town Hall, Manchester Road, Burnley BB11 9SA
☎ 01282 477280 ✉ mcartledge@burnley.gov.uk

Senior Management: Ms Helen Seechurn Director - Resources, Town Hall, Manchester Road, Burnley BB11 9SA ☎ 01282 425011 hseechurn@burnley.gov.uk

Architect, Building / Property Services: Mr Phil Moore Head of Finance & Property Management, Town Hall, Manchester Road, Burnley BB11 9SA ☎ 01282 425011 pmoore@burnley.gov.uk

Best Value: Mr Chris Gay, Performance & Committee Manager, Town Hall, Manchester Road, Burnley BB11 9SA ☎ 01282 425011 cgay@burnley.gov.uk

PR / Communications: Mr Mike Waite, Head of Corporate Engagement & Cohesion, Town Hall, Manchester Road, Burnley BB11 9SA ☎ 01282 425011 mwaite@burnley.gov.uk

Community Planning: Mr Mike Waite, Head of Corporate Engagement & Cohesion, Town Hall, Manchester Road, Burnley BB11 9SA ☎ 01282 425011 mwaite@burnley.gov.uk

Community Safety: Mr Sam McConnell Community Safety Manager, 18/20 Nicholas Street, Burnley BB11 2AP ☎ 01282 425011 smcconnell@burnley.gov.uk

Computer Management: Mrs Sharon Hargraves, IT & Customer Services Manager, Town Hall, Manchester Road, Burnley BB11 9SA ☎ 01282 425011 shargraves@burnley.gov.uk

Contracts: Mr Chris Gay, Performance & Committee Manager, Town Hall, Manchester Road, Burnley BB11 9SA ☎ 01282 425011 cgay@burnley.gov.uk

Corporate Services: Mr Rob Dobson Corporate Policy Officer, Town Hall, Manchester Road, Burnley BB11 9SA ☎ 01282 425011 rdobson@burnley.gov.uk

Customer Service: Mrs Sharon Hargraves, IT & Customer Services Manager, Town Hall, Manchester Road, Burnley BB11 9SA ☎ 01282 425011 shargraves@burnley.gov.uk

Economic Development: Ms Kate Ingram Head of Regeneration & Planning Policy, 1st Floor, Parker Lane Offices, Parker Lane, Burnley BB11 2DT ☎ 01282 477310 kingram@burnley.gov.uk

E-Government: Mrs Sharon Hargraves, IT & Customer Services Manager, Town Hall, Manchester Road, Burnley BB11 9SA ☎ 01282 425011 shargraves@burnley.gov.uk

Electoral Registration: Mrs Alison Morville, Elections Officer, Town Hall, Manchester Road, Burnley BB11 9SA ☎ 01282 425011 amorville@burnley.gov.uk

Emergency Planning: Mr Mick Cartledge, Director - Community Services, Town Hall, Manchester Road, Burnley BB11 9SA ☎ 01282 477280 mcartledge@burnley.gov.uk

Energy Management: Mr Phil Moore Head of Finance & Property Management, Town Hall, Manchester Road, Burnley BB11 9SA ☎ 01282 425011 pmoore@burnley.gov.uk

Environmental Health: Ms Karen Davies Environmental Health & Licensing Manager, Parker Lane Offices, Parker Lane, Burnley BB11 2DT ☎ 01282 425011 kdavies@burnley.gov.uk

Estates, Property & Valuation: Mr Phil Moore Head of Finance & Property Management, Town Hall, Manchester Road, Burnley BB11 9SA ☎ 01282 425011 pmoore@burnley.gov.uk

European Liaison: Ms Kate Ingram Head of Regeneration & Planning Policy, 1st Floor, Parker Lane Offices, Parker Lane, Burnley BB11 2DT ☎ 01282 477310 kingram@burnley.gov.uk

Events Manager: Mr Mike Waite, Head of Corporate Engagement & Cohesion, Town Hall, Manchester Road, Burnley BB11 9SA ☎ 01282 425011 mwaite@burnley.gov.uk

Facilities: Mr Phil Moore Head of Finance & Property Management, Town Hall, Manchester Road, Burnley BB11 9SA ☎ 01282 425011 pmoore@burnley.gov.uk

Finance: Ms Helen Seechurn Director - Resources, Town Hall, Manchester Road, Burnley BB11 9SA ☎ 01282 425011 hseechurn@burnley.gov.uk

Fleet Management: Mr Mark Rogers Operations Manager, 93 Rossendale Road, Burnley BB11 5DD ☎ 01282 425011 mrogers@burnley.gov.uk

Grounds Maintenance: Mr Simon Goff, Head of Greenspaces & Amenities, 93 Rossendale Road, Burnley BB11 5DD ☎ 01282 425011 sgoff@burnley.gov.uk

Health and Safety: Mr David Lawrence Strategic Health & Safety Consultant, Town Hall, Manchester Road, Burnley BB11 9SA ☎ 01282 425011 dlawrence@burnley.gov.uk

Home Energy Conservation: Mr Stephen Nutter Project Officer, Parker Lane Offices, Parker Lane, Burnley BB11 2DT ☎ 01282 425011 snutter@burnley.gov.uk

Housing: Mr Paul Gatrell Head of Housing & Development Control, Parker Lane Offices, Parker Lane, Burnley BB11 2DT ☎ 01282 425011 pgatrell@burnley.gov.uk

Legal: Mr Lukman Patel Head of Governance, Law & Regulation, Town Hall, Manchester Road, Burnley BB11 9SA ☎ 01282 425011 lpatel@burnley.gov.uk

Licensing: Ms Karen Davies Environmental Health & Licensing Manager, Parker Lane Offices, Parker Lane, Burnley BB11 2DT ☎ 01282 425011 kdavies@burnley.gov.uk

Member Services: Mr Chris Gay, Performance & Committee Manager, Town Hall, Manchester Road, Burnley BB11 9SA ☎ 01282 425011 cgay@burnley.gov.uk

Parking: Mrs Joanne Swift Head of Street Scene, 18/20 Nicholas Street, Burnley BB11 2AP ☎ 01282 425011 jswift@burnley.gov.uk

Partnerships: Mr Rob Dobson Corporate Policy Officer, Town Hall, Manchester Road, Burnley BB11 9SA ☎ 01282 425011 rdobson@burnley.gov.uk

BURNLEY

Personnel / HR: Ms Heather Brennan, Head of People & Development, Town Hall, Manchester Road, Burnley BB11 9SA ☎ 01282 425011 ✉ hbrennan@burnley.gov.uk

Planning: Mr Paul Gatrell Head of Housing & Development Control, Parker Lane Offices, Parker Lane, Burnley BB11 2DT ☎ 01282 425011 ✉ pgatrell@burnley.gov.uk

Procurement: Mr Chris Gay, Performance & Committee Manager, Town Hall, Manchester Road, Burnley BB11 9SA ☎ 01282 425011 ✉ cgay@burnley.gov.uk

Recycling & Waste Minimisation: Mrs Joanne Swift Head of Street Scene, 18/20 Nicholas Street, Burnley BB11 2AP ☎ 01282 425011 ✉ jswift@burnley.gov.uk

Regeneration: Ms Kate Ingram Head of Regeneration & Planning Policy, 1st Floor, Parker Lane Offices, Parker Lane, Burnley BB11 2DT ☎ 01282 477310 ✉ kingram@burnley.gov.uk

Staff Training: Ms Heather Brennan, Head of People & Development, Town Hall, Manchester Road, Burnley BB11 9SA ☎ 01282 425011 ✉ hbrennan@burnley.gov.uk

Street Scene: Mrs Joanne Swift Head of Street Scene, 18/20 Nicholas Street, Burnley BB11 2AP ☎ 01282 425011 ✉ jswift@burnley.gov.uk

Sustainable Communities: Ms Kate Ingram Head of Regeneration & Planning Policy, 1st Floor, Parker Lane Offices, Parker Lane, Burnley BB11 2DT ☎ 01282 477310 ✉ kingram@burnley.gov.uk

Sustainable Development: Ms Kate Ingram Head of Regeneration & Planning Policy, 1st Floor, Parker Lane Offices, Parker Lane, Burnley BB11 2DT ☎ 01282 477310 ✉ kingram@burnley.gov.uk

Tourism: Ms Kate Ingram Head of Regeneration & Planning Policy, 1st Floor, Parker Lane Offices, Parker Lane, Burnley BB11 2DT ☎ 01282 477310 ✉ kingram@burnley.gov.uk

Town Centre: Mr Phil Moore Head of Finance & Property Management, Town Hall, Manchester Road, Burnley BB11 9SA ☎ 01282 425011 ✉ pmoore@burnley.gov.uk

Waste Collection and Disposal: Mrs Joanne Swift Head of Street Scene, 18/20 Nicholas Street, Burnley BB11 2AP ☎ 01282 425011 ✉ jswift@burnley.gov.uk

Waste Management: Mrs Joanne Swift Head of Street Scene, 18/20 Nicholas Street, Burnley BB11 2AP ☎ 01282 425011 ✉ jswift@burnley.gov.uk

COUNCILLORS

***Mayor* Monk**, Elizabeth (LAB - Trinity)
emonk@burnley.gov.uk

***Deputy Mayor* Sumner**, Jeff (LD - Rosehill with Burnley Wood)
jsumner@burnley.gov.uk

***Leader of the Council* Townsend**, Mark (LAB - Brunshaw)
mtownsend@burnley.gov.uk

Baker, Howard (LAB - Trinity)
hbaker@burnley.gov.uk

Birtwistle, Gordon (LD - Coal Clough with Deerplay)
gordon.bitwistle.mp@parliament.uk

Briggs, Charlie (LD - Gannow)
cbriggs@burnley.gov.uk

Brindle, Margaret (LD - Coal Clough with Deerplay)
mbrindle@burnley.gov.uk

Bullas, Charles (LD - Coal Clough with Deerplay)
cbullas@burnley.gov.uk

Campbell, Paul (LAB - Rosehill with Burnley Wood)
pcampbell@burnley.gov.uk

Cant, Frank (LAB - Gawthorpe)
fcant@burnley.gov.uk

Carmichael, Ida (CON - Whittlefield with Ightenhill)
icarmichael@burnley.gov.uk

Chaudhary, Saeed (LAB - Daneshouse with Stoneyholme)
schauldhary@burnley.gov.uk

Cooper, Julie (LAB - Bank Hall)
jcooper@burnley.gov.uk

Cunningham, Jean (LAB - Hapton with Park)
jcunningham@burnley.gov.uk

Ellis, Trish (LAB - Lanehead)
tellis@burnley.gov.uk

Flemming, Danny (LAB - Rosehill with Burnley Wood)

Foster, Bea (LAB - Rosegrove with Lowerhouse)
bfoster@burnley.gov.uk

Frayling, Gary (LAB - Bank Hall)
gfrayling@burnley.gov.uk

Frost, Roger (LD - Briercliffe)
rfrost@burnley.gov.uk

Graham, Sue (LAB - Queensgate)
sgraham@burnley.gov.uk

Greenwood, Joanne (LAB - Hapton with Park)
joannegreenwood@burnley.gov.uk

Harbour, John (LAB - Gawthorpe)
jharbour@burnley.gov.uk

Harrison, Tony (LAB - Brunshaw)
tharrison@burnley.gov.uk

Heginbotham, David (CON - Cliviger with Worsthorne)
dheginbotham@burnley.gov.uk

Hosker, Alan (UKIP - Hampton with Park)

Hussain, Shah (LAB - Daneshouse with Stoneyholme)
shussain@burnley.gov.uk

Isherwood, Mathew (CON - Whittlefield with Ightenhill)
misherwood@burnley.gov.uk

Ishtiaq, Mohammed (LAB - Queensgate)
mishtiaq@burnley.gov.uk

Johnstone, Marcus (LAB - Rosegrove with Lowerhouse)
mjohnstone@burnley.gov.uk

Kelly, Anne (LD - Briercliffe)
annekelly@burnley.gov.uk

Khan, Wajid (LAB - Daneshouse with Stoneyholme)
wajidkhan@burnley.gov.uk

Khan, Arif (LAB - Queensgate)
arifkhan@burnley.gov.uk

Large, Stephen (LAB - Lanehead)
slarge@burnley.gov.uk

Lishman, Margaret (LD - Briercliffe)
mlishman@burnley.gov.uk

Malik, Sobia (LAB - Bank Hall)

Martin, Tony (LAB - Trinity)
tmartin@burnley.gov.uk

Mottershead, Neil (LD - Gannow)
nmottershead@burnley.gov.uk

Newhouse, Andrew (CON - Cliviger with Worsthorne)
anewhouse@burnley.gov.uk

Pate, Lian (LAB - Brunshaw)
lpate@burnley.gov.uk

Porter, Tom (LD - Whittlefield with Ightenhill)
tporter@burnley.gov.uk

Reynolds, Paul (LAB - Rosegrove with Lowerhouse)
preynolds@burnley.gov.uk

Royle, Ann (LAB - Lanehead)
aroyle@burnley.gov.uk

Stringer, Betsy (LAB - Gannow)
bstringer@burnley.gov.uk

Tatchell, Andrew (LAB - Gawthorpe)
atatchell@burnley.gov.uk

Towneley, Cosima (CON - Cliviger with Worsthorne)
mail@cositowneley.co.uk

POLITICAL COMPOSITION
LAB: 29, LD: 10, CON: 5, UKIP: 1

Bury M

Bury Metropolitan Borough Council, Town Hall, Knowsley Street, Bury BL9 0SW
☎ 0161 253 5000 🖷 0161 253 5119 ✉ info@bury.gov.uk
💻 www.bury.gov.uk

FACTS AND FIGURES
Parliamentary Constituencies: Bury North, Bury South
EU Constituencies: North West
Election Frequency: Elections are by thirds

PRINCIPAL OFFICERS
Chief Executive: Mr Michael Owen, Chief Executive, Town Hall, Knowsley Street, Bury BL9 0SW ☎ 0161 253 5000 🖷 0161 253 5070 ✉ m.a.owen@bury.gov.uk

Senior Management: Mr Mark Carriline Executive Director - Children, Young People & Culture, 3 Knowsley Place, Duke Street, Bury BL9 0EJ ☎ 0161 253 5603 ✉ m.carriline@bury.gov.uk

Senior Management: Mrs Pat Jones-Greenhalgh, Executive Director - Communities & Wellbeing, Town Hall, Knowsley Street, Bury BL9 0SW ☎ 0161 253 5405 🖷 0161 253 6961 ✉ p.jones-greenhalgh@bury.gov.uk

Architect, Building / Property Services: Mr Alex Holland Head - Property & Asset Management, Town Hall, Knowsley Street, Bury BL9 0SW ☎ 0161 253 5992 ✉ a.holland@bury.gov.uk

Architect, Building / Property Services: Mr Michael Owen, Chief Executive, Town Hall, Knowsley Street, Bury BL9 0SW ☎ 0161 253 5000 🖷 0161 253 5070 ✉ m.a.owen@bury.gov.uk

Best Value: Mr David Hipkiss Head - Risk Management, Town Hall, Knowsley Street, Bury BL9 0SW ☎ 0161 253 5084 ✉ d.hipkiss@bury.gov.uk

Building Control: Mr Rob Thorpe, Principal Building Control Officer, 3 Knowsley Place, Duke Street, Bury BL9 0EJ ☎ 0161 253 5289 🖷 0161 253 5290 ✉ r.c.thorpe@bury.gov.uk

Catering Services: Mr Charles Walton Head - Civics & Leisure Catering, Unit 3, Bradley Fold Trading Estate, Bradley Fold Road, Bolton BL2 6RF ☎ 0161 253 5709 ✉ c.k.walton@bury.gov.uk

Children / Youth Services: Ms Kate Allam IYSS Operational Manager, 3 Knowsley Place, Duke Street, Bury BL9 0EJ ☎ 0161 253 7921 ✉ k.allam@bury.gov.uk

Children / Youth Services: Mr Mark Carriline Executive Director - Children's Services, 3 Knowsley Place, Duke Street, Bury BL0 0EJ ☎ 0161 253 5603 🖷 0161 253 6093 ✉ m.carriline@bury.gov.uk

Civil Registration: Mr Haydn Keenan Head - Registration, Town Hall, Knowsley Street, Bury BL9 0SW ☎ 0161 253 6027 ✉ w.keenan@bury.gov.uk

Community Planning: Mr David Fowler, Assistant Director - Localities, Town Hall, Knowsley Street, Bury BL9 0SW ☎ 0161 253 5518 🖷 0161 253 5393 ✉ d.w.fowler@bury.gov.uk

Community Safety: Mr Harry Downie Assistant Director - Business Redesign & Development, Town Hall, Knowsley Street, Bury BL9 0SW ☎ 0161 253 7570 ✉ h.downie@bury.gov.uk

Computer Management: Mr Stephen Denton ICT Development & Programme Manager, Town Hall, Knowsley Street, Bury BL9 0SW ☎ 0161 253 6043 ✉ s.denton@bury.gov.uk

Corporate Services: Mr Michael Owen, Chief Executive, Town Hall, Knowsley Street, Bury BL9 0SW ☎ 0161 253 5000 🖷 0161 253 5070 ✉ m.a.owen@bury.gov.uk

Education: Mr Ian Chambers Assistant Director - Learning, 3 Knowsley Place, Duke Street, Bury BL9 0EJ ☎ 0161 253 5477 🖷 0161 253 6093 ✉ l.chambers@bury.gov.uk

E-Government: Mr Michael Owen, Chief Executive, Town Hall, Knowsley Street, Bury BL9 0SW ☎ 0161 253 5000 🖷 0161 253 5070 ✉ m.a.owen@bury.gov.uk

Electoral Registration: Mr Warren Rafferty, Elections & Land Charges Officer, Town Hall, Knowsley Street, Bury BL9 0SW ☎ 0161 253 6018 🖷 0161 253 5248 ✉ w.j.rafferty@bury.gov.uk

BURY

Emergency Planning: Mr Mike Moore Civil Contingency Co-ordinator, Town Hall, Knowsley Street, Bury BL9 0SW ☎ 0161 253 7732 ✉ m.moore@bury.gov.uk

Environmental / Technical Services: Mr Neil Long, Assistant Director - Operations, 3 Knowsley Place, Duke Street, Bury BL9 0EJ ☎ 0161 253 5735 ✉ n.s.long@bury.gov.uk

Environmental Health: Mr David Fowler, Assistant Director - Localities, 3 Knowsley Place, Duke Street, Bury BL9 0EJ ☎ 0161 253 5518 🖷 0161 253 5393 ✉ d.w.fowler@bury.gov.uk

Estates, Property & Valuation: Mr Alex Holland Head - Property & Asset Management, Town Hall, Knowsley Street, Bury BL9 0SW ☎ 0161 253 5992 ✉ a.holland@bury.gov.uk

European Liaison: Ms Tracey Flynn Principal Strategy & Resources Officer, 3 Knowsley Place, Duke Street, Bury BL9 0EJ ☎ 0161 253 6040 ✉ t.flynn@bury.gov.uk

Events Manager: Mr Neil Long, Assistant Director - Operations, 3 Knowsley Place, Duke Street, Bury BL9 0EJ ☎ 0161 253 5735 ✉ n.s.long@bury.gov.uk

Facilities: Mr Neil Long, Assistant Director - Operations, 3 Knowsley Place, Duke Street, Bury BL9 0EJ ☎ 0161 253 5735 ✉ n.s.long@bury.gov.uk

Fleet Management: Mr Stephen Fleming, Head - Transport Services & Workshop, Unit 34, Bradley Fold Trading Estate, Bradley Fold Road, Bolton BL2 6RF ☎ 0161 253 6624 🖷 0161 253 6130 ✉ s.j.fleming@bury.gov.uk

Grounds Maintenance: Mr Neil Long, Assistant Director - Operations, 3 Knowsley Place, Duke Street, Bury BL9 0EJ ☎ 0161 253 5735 ✉ n.s.long@bury.gov.uk

Health and Safety: Mr Alan Manchester Principal Occupational Health, Safety & Emergency Planning, Town Hall, Knowsley Street, Bury BL9 0SW ☎ 0161 253 5143 🖷 0161 253 5137 ✉ a.manchester@bury.gov.uk

Highways: Mr Neil Long, Assistant Director - Operations, 3 Knowsley Place, Duke Street, Bury BL9 0EJ ☎ 0161 253 5735 ✉ n.s.long@bury.gov.uk

Housing: Mrs Sharon McCambridge Chief Executive - Six Town Housing, 6 Knowsley Place, Angouleme Way, Bury BL9 0EL ☎ 0161 686 8000 🖷 0161 764 5078 ✉ s.mccambridge@sixtownhousing.org

Housing Maintenance: Mr Wayne Campbell Head - Repairs & Maintenance, 6 Knowsley Place, Angouleme Way, Bury BL9 0EL ☎ 0161 253 5000 ✉ w.campbell@bury.gov.uk

Legal: Mrs Jayne Hammond, Assistant Director - Legal & Democratic Services, Town Hall, Knowsley Street, Bury BL9 0SW ☎ ; 0161 253 5237 🖷 0161 253 6091 ✉ j.m.hammond@bury.gov.uk

Leisure and Cultural Services: Mr Neil Long, Assistant Director - Operations, 3 Knowsley Place, Duke Street, Bury BL9 0EJ ☎ 0161 253 5735 ✉ n.s.long@bury.gov.uk

Licensing: Mr David Fowler, Assistant Director - Localities, 3 Knowsley Place, Duke Street, Bury BL9 0EJ ☎ 0161 253 5518 🖷 0161 253 5393 ✉ d.w.fowler@bury.gov.uk

Licensing: Mr Andrew Johnson Head - Commercial & Lighting, 3 Knowsley Place, Duke Street, Bury BL9 0EJ ☎ 0161 253 5514 ✉ a.johnson@bury.gov.uk

Lighting: Mr Phil Hewitt, Principal Engineer - Street Lighting, Bradley Fold Depot, Bradley Fold Road, Bolton BL2 6RS ☎ 0161 253 5000 🖷 0161 763 6484 ✉ p.m.hewitt@bury.gov.uk

Member Services: Mr Leigh Webb Democratic Services Manager, Town Hall, Knowsley Street, Bury BL9 0SW ☎ 0161 253 5399 ✉ l.m.webb@bury.gov.uk

Parking: Mr John Foudy, Car Parking Manager, 3 Knowsley Place, Duke Street, Bury BL9 0EJ ☎ 0161 253 5445 ✉ j.foudy@bury.gov.uk

Partnerships: Mr David Fowler, Assistant Director - Localities, 3 Knowsley Place, Duke Street, Bury BL9 0EJ ☎ 0161 253 5518 🖷 0161 253 5393 ✉ d.w.fowler@bury.gov.uk

Personnel / HR: Ms Tracey Murphy Acting Assistant Director - Personnel, Town Hall, Knowsley Street, Bury BL9 0SW ☎ 0161 253 5151 ✉ t.e.murphy@bury.gov.uk

Procurement: Mrs Sarah Janusz, Corporate Procurement Manager, Town Hall, Knowsley Street, Bury BL9 0SW ☎ 0161 253 6147 🖷 0161 253 5779 ✉ s.e.janusz@bury.gov.uk

Public Libraries: Ms Julie Kenrick Adult Learning Officer - Social Inclusion, Bury Adult Education Centre, Market Street, Bury BL9 0AQ ☎ 0161 253 7457 ✉ j.a.kenrick@bury.gov.uk

Recycling & Waste Minimisation: Mr Glenn Stuart Head - Waste Management, Unit 3, Bradley Fold Trading Estate, Bradley Fold Road, Bolton BL2 6RF ☎ 0161 253 6621 🖷 0161 253 7473 ✉ g.stuart@bury.gov.uk

Road Safety: Ms Jan Brabin Principal Road Safety Officer, 3 Knowsley Place, Duke Street, Bury BL9 0EJ ☎ 0161 253 5787 ✉ j.brabin@bury.gov.uk

Social Services (Adult): Mrs Linda Jackson, Assistant Director - Operations, Town Hall, Knowsley Street, Bury BL9 0SW ☎ 0161 253 6033 🖷 0161 253 6961 ✉ l.a.jackson@bury.gov.uk

Social Services (Adult): Mrs Pat Jones-Greenhalgh, Executive Director - Communities & Wellbeing, Town Hall, Knowsley Street, Bury BL9 0SW ☎ 0161 253 5405 🖷 0161 253 6961 ✉ p.jones-greenhalgh@bury.gov.uk

Social Services (Children): Mr Mark Carriline Executive Director - Children, Young People & Culture, 3 Knowsley Place, Duke Street, Bury BL9 0EJ ☎ 0161 253 5603 ✉ m.carriline@bury.gov.uk

Safeguarding: Ms Jackie Gower Assistant Director - Social Care & Safeguarding, 3 Knowsley Place, Duke Street, Bury BL9 0EJ ☎ 0161 253 5603 ✉ j.gower@bury.gov.uk

Childrens Social Care: Ms Jackie Gower Assistant Director - Social Care & Safeguarding, 3 Knowsley Place, Duke Street, Bury BL9 0EJ ☎ 0161 253 5603 ✉ j.gower@bury.gov.uk

Public Health: Ms Lesley Jones Director - Public Health, 3 Knowsley Place, Duke Street, Bury BL9 0EJ ✉ l.jones@bury.gov.uk

Staff Training: Ms Tracey Murphy Acting Assistant Director - Personnel, Town Hall, Knowsley Street, Bury BL9 0SW ☎ 0161 253 5151 ✉ t.e.murphy@bury.gov.uk

Sustainable Communities: Mr David Fowler, Assistant Director - Localities, 3 Knowsley Place, Duke Street, Bury BL9 0EJ ☎ 0161 253 5518 🖷 0161 253 5393 ✉ d.w.fowler@bury.gov.uk

Tourism: Mr David Fowler, Assistant Director - Localities, 3 Knowsley Place, Duke Street, Bury BL9 0EJ ☎ 0161 253 5518 🖷 0161 253 5393 ✉ d.w.fowler@bury.gov.uk

Tourism: Ms Jill Youlton Tourism Development Officer, 3 Knowsley Place, Duke Street, Bury BL9 0EJ ☎ 0161 253 6075 ✉ j.youlton@bury.gov.uk

Traffic Management: Mr Ian Lord Manager - Traffic Management & Road Safety Services, 3 Knowsley Place, Duke Street, Bury BL9 0EJ ☎ 0161 253 5783 ✉ i.c.lord@bury.gov.uk

Transport: Mr Stephen Fleming, Head - Transport Services & Workshop, Unit 34, Bradley Fold Trading Estate, Bradley Fold Road, Bolton BL2 6RF ☎ 0161 253 6624 🖷 0161 253 6130 ✉ s.j.fleming@bury.gov.uk

Waste Collection and Disposal: Mr Glenn Stuart Head - Waste Management, Unit 3, Bradley Fold Trading Estate, Bradley Fold Road, Bolton BL2 6RF ☎ 0161 253 6621 🖷 0161 253 7473 ✉ g.stuart@bury.gov.uk

Waste Management: Mr Glenn Stuart Head - Waste Management, Unit 3, Bradley Fold Trading Estate, Bradley Fold Road, Bolton BL2 6RF ☎ 0161 253 6621 🖷 0161 253 7473 ✉ g.stuart@bury.gov.uk

COUNCILLORS

***Mayor* Wiseman**, Michelle (CON - Pilkington Park)
m.j.wiseman@bury.gov.uk

***Leader of the Council* Connolly**, Mike (LAB - East)
m.connolly@bury.gov.uk

***Deputy Leader of the Council* Shori**, Rishi (LAB - Radcliffe West)
r.shori@bury.gov.uk

***Group Leader* Gartside**, Iain (CON - Tottington)
i.b.gartside@bury.gov.uk

Adams, Paul (LAB - Unsworth)
p.adams@bury.gov.uk

Bailey, Daisy (LAB - Radcliffe East)
d.bailey@bury.gov.uk

Bayley, Noel (LAB - St Marys)
N.Bayley@bury.gov.uk

Bevan, Ian (CON - Ramsbottom)
i.bevan@bury.gov.uk

Black, Jane (LAB - St Marys)
j.black@bury.gov.uk

Briggs, Sharon (LAB - Radcliffe North)
s.briggs@bury.gov.uk

Carter, Simon (LAB - Tottington)
s.carter@bury.gov.uk

Caserta, Robert (CON - Pilkington Park)
r.caserta@bury.gov.uk

Cassidy, Dorothy (LAB - Moorside)
D.M.Cassidy@bury.gov.uk

D'Albert, Mary (LD - Holyrood)

Daly, James (CON - North Manor)
jdaly@cromptonhaliwell.co.uk

Fitzgerald, Elizabeth (LAB - Besses)
e.fitzgerald@bury.gov.uk

Fitzwalter, Luise (LAB - Ramsbottom)
l.fitzwalter@bury.gov.uk

Grimshaw, Joan (LAB - Unsworth)
j.grimshaw@bury.gov.uk

Gunther, Dorothy (CON - North Manor)
d.l.gunther@bury.gov.uk

Hankey, Michael (CON - Elton)
m.hankey@bury.gov.uk

Haroon, Shaheena (LAB - Redvales)
s.haroon@bury.gov.uk

Harris, Jackie (CON - Church)

Heneghan, Paddy (LAB - Holyrood)
p.heneghan@bury.gov.uk

Hodkinson, Robert (CON - Ramsbottom)

Holt, Trevor (LAB - East)
t.holt@bury.gov.uk

Hussain, Khalid (CON - North Manor)
K.Hussain@bury.gov.uk

Isherwood, Anthony (LAB - Radcliffe West)
a.isherwood@bury.gov.uk

James, Michael (LAB - Sedgley)
M.A.James@bury.gov.uk

Jones, David (LAB - Unsworth)
david.jones@bury.gov.uk

Kelly, Judith (LAB - Redvales)

Kerrison, Sarah (LAB - Elton)
s.kerrison@bury.gov.uk

Lewis, Jane (LAB - Radcliffe North)
j.lewis@bury.gov.uk

Mallon, John (LAB - Pilkington Park)
j.mallon@bury.gov.uk

Matthews, Alan (LAB - Besses)
a.k.matthews@bury.gov.uk

Nuttall, Susan (CON - Church)
sue.nuttall@bury.gov.uk

O'Brien, Eamonn (LAB - St Marys)
e.o'brien@bury.gov.uk

Parnell, Nick (LAB - Radcliffe East)
n.parnell@bury.gov.uk

Pickstone, Tim (LD - Holyrood)
t.d.pickstone@bury.gov.uk

Preston, Catherine (LAB - Radcliffe East)

Quinn, Alan (LD - Sedgley)
alan.quinn@bury.gov.uk

Simpson, Andrea (LAB - Sedgley)
a.simpson@bury.gov.uk

Skillen, Rachel (LAB - Radcliffe West)

Smith, Stella (LAB - East)
stella.smith@bury.gov.uk

Southworth, Susan (LAB - Elton)
s.southworth@bury.gov.uk

Southworth, Sarah (LAB - Moorside)

Tariq, Tamoor (LAB - Redvales)
t.tariq@bury.gov.uk

Walker, Jamie (LAB - Radcliffe North)

Walker, Roy (CON - Church)
roy@edwardwalker.freeserve.co.uk

Walmsley, Sandra (LAB - Moorside)
sandra.walmsley@gov.uk

Whitby, Mary (LAB - Besses)
m.whitby@bury.gov.uk

Wright, Yvonne (CON - Tottington)
y.s.wright@bury.gov.uk

POLITICAL COMPOSITION
LAB: 35, CON: 13, LD: 3

COMMITTEE CHAIRS

Audit: Ms Elizabeth Fitzgerald

Audit: Mr John Mallon

Licensing & Safety: Mr David Jones

Caerphilly W

Caerphilly County Borough Council, Penallta House, Tredomen Park, Ystrad Mynach, Hengoed CF82 7PG
☎ 01443 815588 🖷 01443 864443 🖱 info@caerphilly.gov.uk
💻 www.caerphilly.gov.uk

FACTS AND FIGURES
Parliamentary Constituencies: Caerphilly, Islwyn
EU Constituencies: Wales
Election Frequency: Elections are by thirds

PRINCIPAL OFFICERS

Chief Executive: Mr Chris Burns Interim Chief Executive, Penallta House, Tredomen Park, Ystrad Mynach, Hengoed CF82 7PG ☎ 01443 864410 🖱 chrisburns@caerphilly.gov.uk

Senior Management: Mrs Sandra Aspinall Corporate Director - Education & Lifelong Learning, Penallta House, Tredomen Park, Ystrad Mynach, Hengoed CF82 7PG ☎ 01443 864948 🖷 01443 864807 🖱 aspins@caerphilly.gov.uk

Access Officer / Social Services (Disability): Mr Simon Dixon Disabled Access Officer, Tredomen House, Tredomen Park, Ystrad Mynach, Hengoed CF82 7WF ☎ 01443 864085 🖷 01443 864141 🖱 dixons@caerphilly.gov.uk

Architect, Building / Property Services: Mr Colin Jones Head of Performance & Property, Penallta House, Tredomen Park, Ystrad Mynach, Hengoed CF82 7PG ☎ 01443 864382 🖷 01443 864235 🖱 jonesrc@caerphilly.gov.uk

Best Value: Mr Stephen Harris Acting Head of Corporate Finance, Penallta House, Tredomen Park, Ystrad Mynach, Hengoed CF82 7PG ☎ 01443 863022 🖷 01443 863347 🖱 harrisr@caerphilly.gov.uk

Building Control: Mr Jason Lear Team Leader - Building Control, Ty Pontllanfraith, Blackwood Road, Pontllanfraith, Blackwood NP12 2YW ☎ 01495 235091 🖷 01495 235013 🖱 learj@caerphilly.gov.uk

Catering Services: Ms Marcia Lewis Principal Catering Officer, Pontllanfraith House, Blackwood Road, Pontllanfraith, Blackwood NP12 2YW ☎ 01495 235212 🖷 01443 863303 🖱 lewism3@caerphilly.gov.uk

Children / Youth Services: Mr Tony Maher Assistant Director - Planning Strategy, Penallta House, Tredomen Park, Ystrad Mynach, Hengoed CF82 7PG ☎ 01443 864972 🖷 01443 864898 🖱 mahert@caerphilly.gov.uk

Civil Registration: Ms Della Mahony Superintendent Registrar, Penallta House, Tredomen Park, Ystrad Mynach, Hengoed CF82 7PG ☎ 01443 863074 🖷 01443 863385

PR / Communications: Mr Lynton Jones Acting Head of Information, Technology & Citizen Engagement, Penallta House, Tredomen Park, Ystrad Mynach, Hengoed CF82 7PG ☎ 01443 864005 🖷 01443 863488 🖱 joneslc@caerphilly.gov.uk

Community Planning: Ms Pauline Elliott Head of Planning & Regeneration, Council Offices, Pontllanfraith, Blackwood NP12 2YW ☎ 01495 235320 🖷 01495 235022 🖱 elliop@caerphilly.gov.uk

Community Safety: Mr Rob Hartshorn Head of Public Protection, Council Offices, Pontllanfraith, Blackwood NP12 2YW ☎ 01495 235315 🖷 01495 235018 🖱 hartsr@caerphilly.gov.uk

Computer Management: Mr Lynton Jones Acting Head of Information, Technology & Citizen Engagement, Penallta House, Tredomen Park, Ystrad Mynach, Hengoed CF82 7PG ☎ 01443 864005 🖷 01443 863488 🖱 joneslc@caerphilly.gov.uk

Consumer Protection and Trading Standards: Mr Rob Hartshorn Head of Public Protection, Council Offices, Pontllanfraith, Blackwood NP12 2YW ☎ 01495 235315 🖷 01495 235018 🖱 hartsr@caerphilly.gov.uk

Contracts: Mr Stephen Harris Acting Head of Corporate Finance, Penallta House, Tredomen Park, Ystrad Mynach, Hengoed CF82 7PG ☎ 01443 863022 🖷 01443 863347 🖱 harrisr@caerphilly.gov.uk

Corporate Services: Ms Nicole Scammel Acting Director - Corporate Services, Penallta House, Tredomen Park, Ystrad Mynach, Hengoed CF82 7PG ☎ 01443 864419 🖷 01443 863347 🖱 scammn@caerphilly.gov.uk

Customer Service: Mr David Titley, Customer Services Manager, Ty Duffryn, Duffryn Business Park, Ystrad Mynach, Hengoed CF82 7TW ☎ ; 01443 864548 🖷 01443 866501 🖱 titled@caerphilly.gov.uk

Direct Labour: Mr Shaun Couzens, Chief Housing Officer, Tir-y-berth Depot, New Road, Tir-y-berth, Hengoed CF82 8NR ☎ 01443 863282 🖷 01443 863401 🖱 couzes@caerphilly.gov.uk

Economic Development: Ms Pauline Elliott Head of Planning & Regeneration, Council Offices, Pontllanfraith, Blackwood NP12 2YW ☎ 01495 235320 🖷 01495 235022 🖱 elliop@caerphilly.gov.uk

Education: Ms Christina Harrhy Corporate Director - Education & Community Services, Penallta House, Tredomen Park, Ystrad Mynach, Hengoed CF82 7PG ☎ 01443 864948 🖷 01443 864807 🖱 harrhc@caerphilly.gov.uk

E-Government: Mr Lynton Jones Acting Head of Information, Technology & Citizen Engagement, Penallta House, Tredomen Park, Ystrad Mynach, Hengoed CF82 7PG ☎ 01443 864005 🖷 01443 863488 🖱 joneslc@caerphilly.gov.uk

Electoral Registration: Mr Dave Beecham Electoral Services Manager, Enterprise House, Tir y Berth Industrial Estate, New Road, Tir y Berth, Hengoed CF82 8AU ☎ 01443 864405 🖷 01443 864379 🖱 beechd@caerphilly.gov.uk

Emergency Planning: Ms Sheryl Andrews, Emergency Planning Manager, Pontllanfraith House, Blackwood Road, Pontllanfraith, Blackwood NP12 2YW ☎ 01495 235048 🖷 01443 864326 🖱 andres@caerphilly.gov.uk

Energy Management: Mr Colin Jones Head of Performance & Property, Penallta House, Tredomen Park, Ystrad Mynach, Hengoed CF82 7PG ☎ 01443 864382 🖷 01443 864235 🖱 jonesrc@caerphilly.gov.uk

Environmental / Technical Services: Mr Chris Burns Interim Chief Executive, Penallta House, Tredomen Park, Ystrad Mynach, Hengoed CF82 7PG ☎ 01443 864410 🖱 chrisburns@caerphilly.gov.uk

Environmental Health: Mr Rob Hartshorn Head of Public Protection, Council Offices, Pontllanfraith, Blackwood NP12 2YW ☎ 01495 235315 🖷 01495 235018 🖱 hartsr@caerphilly.gov.uk

Estates, Property & Valuation: Mr Colin Jones Head of Performance & Property, Penallta House, Tredomen Park, Ystrad Mynach, Hengoed CF82 7PG ☎ 01443 864382 🖷 01443 864235 🖱 jonesrc@caerphilly.gov.uk

Events Manager: Mr Paul Hudson Senior Events & Marketing Officer, Tredomen Business & Technology Centre, Tredomen Business Park, Ystrad Mynach, Hengoed CF82 7FN ☎ 01443 866228 🖷 01443 864446 🖱 hudsop@caerphilly.gov.uk

Facilities: Mr Mark Faulkner Senior Facilities Manager, Penallta House, Tredomen Park, Ystrad Mynach, Hengoed CF82 7PG ☎ 01443 864128 🖷 01443 866724 🖱 faulkm@caerphilly.gov.uk

Finance: Mr Stephen Harris Acting Head of Corporate Finance, Penallta House, Tredomen Park, Ystrad Mynach, Hengoed CF82 7PG ☎ 01443 863022 🖷 01443 863347 🖱 harrisr@caerphilly.gov.uk

Fleet Management: Ms Mary Powell Fleet Manager, Tir-y-berth Depot, New Road, Tir-y-berth, Hengoed CF82 8NR ☎ 01443 873720 🖷 01443 863446 🖱 powelem@caerphilly.gov.uk

Grounds Maintenance: Mr Derek Price, Principal Parks & Open Spaces Officer, Council Offices, Pontllanfraith, Blackwood NP12 2YW ☎ 01495 235470 🖷 01495 235471 🖱 priced@caerphilly.gov.uk

Health and Safety: Ms Emma Townsend, Corporate Health & Safety Manager, Nelson Road, Tredomen, Ystrad Mynach, Hengoed CF82 7SF ☎ 01443 864280 🖷 01443 864343 🖱 townsej@caerphilly.gov.uk

Highways: Mr Terry Shaw Head of Engineering Services, Pontllanfraith, Blackwood Road, Pontllanfraith, Blackwood NP12 2YW ☎ 01495 235319 🖷 01495 235012 🖱 shawt@caerphilly.gov.uk

Home Energy Conservation: Mr Steve Martin Energy Officer, Woodfieldside Business Park, Penmaen Road, Pontllanfriath, Blackwood NP12 2DG ☎ 01443 863215 🖱 martins@caerphilly.gov.uk

Housing: Mr Shaun Couzens, Chief Housing Officer, Tir y Berth Depot, New Road, Hengoed CF82 8NR ☎ 01443 863282 🖷 01443 863401 🖱 couzes@caerphilly.gov.uk

Housing Maintenance: Mr Shaun Couzens, Chief Housing Officer, Tir y Berth Depot, New Road, Hengoed CF82 8NR ☎ 01443 863282 🖷 01443 863401 🖱 couzes@caerphilly.gov.uk

Legal: Ms Gail Williams Interim Head of Legal Services & Monitoring Officer, Penallta House, Tredomen Park, Ystrad Mynach, Hengoed CF82 7PG ☎ 01443 863142 🖷 01443 861154 🖱 willige@caerphilly.gov.uk

Leisure and Cultural Services: Mr Mark Williams, Head of Community & Leisure Services, Pontllanfraith House, Pontllanfraith, Blackwood NP12 2YW ☎ 01495 235070 🖷 01495 235014 🖱 willims@caerphilly.gov.uk

Licensing: Ms Myra McSherry Licensing Manager, Penallta House, Tredomen Park, Ystrad Mynach, Hengoed CF82 7PG ☎ 01443 866750 🖱 mcshe@caerphilly.gov.uk

Lifelong Learning: Mr Tony Maher Assistant Director - Planning Strategy, Penallta House, Tredomen Park, Ystrad Mynach, Hengoed CF82 7PG ☎ 01443 864972 🖷 01443 864898 🖱 mahert@caerphilly.gov.uk

Lighting: Mr Terry Shaw Head of Engineering Services, Council Offices, Pontllanfraith, Blackwood NP12 2YW ☎ 01495 235319 🖷 01495 235012 🖱 shawt@caerphilly.gov.uk

Lottery Funding, Charity and Voluntary: Mr Colin Jones Head of Performance & Property, Penalta House, Tredomen Park, Ystrad Mynach, Hengoed CF82 7PG ☎ 01443 864382 🖷 01443 864235 🖱 jonesrc@caerphilly.gov.uk

Member Services: Ms Karen Green Cabinet Support Assistant, Penallta House, Tredomen Park, Ystrad Mynach, Hengoed CF82 7PG ☎ 01443 864369 🖷 01443 864240 🖱 greenk@caerphilly.gov.uk

CAERPHILLY

Parking: Mr Terry Shaw Head of Engineering Services, Council Offices, Pontllanfraith, Blackwood NP12 2YW ☎ 01495 235319 🖷 01495 235012 ✉ shawt@caerphilly.gov.uk

Partnerships: Mr Colin Jones Head of Performance & Property, Penallta House, Tredomen Park, Ystrad Mynach, Hengoed CF82 7PG ☎ 01443 864382 🖷 01443 864235 ✉ jonesrc@caerphilly.gov.uk

Personnel / HR: Mr Gareth Hardacre Head of People Management & Development, Penallta House, Tredomen Park, Ystrad Mynach, Hengoed CF82 7PG ☎ 01443 864309 🖷 01443 864389 ✉ hardag@caerphilly.gov.uk

Planning: Ms Pauline Elliott Head of Planning & Regeneration, Council Offices, Pontllanfraith, Blackwood NP12 2YW ☎ 01495 235320 🖷 01495 235022 ✉ elliop@caerphilly.gov.uk

Procurement: Mrs Elizabeth Lucas, Head of Procurement, Penallta House, Tredomen Park, Ystrad Mynach, Hengoed CF82 7PG ☎ 01443 863160 🖷 01443 863167 ✉ lucasej@caerphilly.gov.uk

Public Libraries: Mr Gareth Evans Senior Manager - Libraries, Penallta House, Tredomen Park, Ystrad Mynach, Hengoed CF82 7PG ☎ 01443 864033 ✉ evansg1@caerphilly.gov.uk

Recycling & Waste Minimisation: Mr Mark Williams, Head of Community & Leisure Services, Council Offices, Pontllanfraith, Blackwood NP12 2YW ☎ 01495 235070 🖷 01495 235014 ✉ willims@caerphilly.gov.uk

Regeneration: Ms Pauline Elliott Head of Planning & Regeneration, Council Offices, Pontllanfraith, Blackwood NP12 2YW ☎ 01495 235320 🖷 01495 235022 ✉ elliop@caerphilly.gov.uk

Road Safety: Mr Terry Shaw Head of Engineering Services, Council Offices, Pontllanfraith, Blackwood NP12 2YW ☎ 01495 235319 🖷 01495 235012 ✉ shawt@caerphilly.gov.uk

Social Services: Mr Dave Street Director of Social Services, Penallta House, Tredomen Park, Ystrad Mynach, Hengoed CF82 7PG ☎ 01443 864560 ✉ streed@caerphilly.gov.uk

Social Services (Adult): Ms Jo Williams Assistant Director - Adult Services, Penallta House, Tredomen Park, Ystrad Mynach, Hengoed CF82 7PG ☎ 01443 864776 🖷 01443 864513 ✉ willij6@caerphilly.gov.uk

Social Services (Children): Mr Gareth Jenkins Assistant Director - Children's Services, Penallta House, Tredomen Park, Ystrad Mynach, Hengoed CF82 7PG ☎ 01443 864512 ✉ jenkig2@caerphilly.gov.uk

Staff Training: Ms Jane Haile Interim Team Manager, Tredomen House, Nelson Road, Tredomen, Ystrad Mynach, Hengoed CF82 7WF ☎ 01443 863410 🖷 01443 863101 ✉ hailej@caerphilly.gov.uk

Sustainable Communities: Mrs Jan Bennett Group Manager - Advisory Services, Tredomen Business Centre, Nelson Road, Tredomen, Ystrad Mynach, Hengoed CF82 7FN ☎ 01443 866240 🖷 01443 864446 ✉ bennej@caerphilly.gov.uk

Sustainable Development: Ms Pauline Elliott Head of Planning & Regeneration, Council Offices, Pontllanfraith, Blackwood NP12 2YW ☎ 01495 235320 🖷 01495 235022 ✉ elliop@caerphilly.gov.uk

Tourism: Mr Paul Hudson Senior Events & Marketing Officer, Tredomen Business & Technology Centre, Tredomen Business Park, Ystrad Mynach, Hengoed CF82 7FN ☎ 01443 866228 🖷 01443 864446 ✉ hudsop@caerphilly.gov.uk

Town Centre: Mr Andrew Highway, Town Centre Development Manager, Tredomen Business and Technology Centre, Ystrad Mynach, Hengoed CF82 7FN ☎ 01443 866213 ✉ highwa@caerphilly.gov.uk

Traffic Management: Mr Terry Shaw Head of Engineering Services, Council Offices, Pontllanfraith, Blackwood NP12 2YW ☎ 01495 235319 🖷 01495 235012 ✉ shawt@caerphilly.gov.uk

Transport: Mr Clive Campbell Transportation Engineering Manager, Council Offices, Pontllanfraith, Blackwood NP12 2YW ☎ 01495 235339 🖷 01495 235045 ✉ campbc@caerphilly.gov.uk

Transport Planner: Mr Clive Campbell Transportation Engineering Manager, Council Offices, Pontllanfraith, Blackwood NP12 2YW ☎ 01495 235339 🖷 01495 235045 ✉ campbc@caerphilly.gov.uk

Waste Collection and Disposal: Mr Mark Williams, Head of Community & Leisure Services, Council Offices, Pontllanfraith, Blackwood NP12 2YW ☎ 01495 235070 🖷 01495 235014 ✉ willims@caerphilly.gov.uk

Waste Management: Mr Mark Williams, Head of Community & Leisure Services, Council Offices, Pontllanfraith, Blackwood NP12 2YW ☎ 01495 235070 🖷 01495 235014 ✉ willims@caerphilly.gov.uk

Children's Play Areas: Mr Derek Price, Principal Parks & Open Spaces Officer, Pontllanfraith House, Blackwood Road, Pontllanfraith, Blackwood NP12 2YW ☎ 01495 235470 🖷 01495 235471 ✉ priced@caerphilly.gov.uk

COUNCILLORS

***Mayor* Gardiner**, Leon (LAB - Argoed)
leongardiner@caerphilly.gov.uk

***Deputy Mayor* Price**, Dianne (LAB - Bargoed)
dianneprice@caerphilly.gov.uk

***Leader of the Council* Reynolds**, Keith (LAB - Aberbargoed)
keithreynolds@caerphilly.gov.uk

***Deputy Leader of the Council* Jones**, Barbara (LAB - St James)
barbarajones@caerphilly.gov.uk

***Group Leader* Mann**, Colin (PC - Llanbradach)
colinmann@caerphilly.gov.uk

***Group Leader* Rees**, Dave (IND - Risca West)
daverees@caerphilly.gov.uk

Ackerman, Lyn (PC - Newbridge)
lynackerman@caerphilly.gov.uk

Adams, Michael (LAB - Pontllanfraith)
michaeladams@caerphilly.gov.uk

Aldworth, Elizabeth (LAB - Bedwas, Trethomas & Machen)
lizaldworth@caerphilly.gov.uk

Andrews, Harry (LAB - Gilfach)
harryandrews@caerphilly.gov.uk

Angel, Alan (PC - Ystrad Mynach)
alanangel@caerphilly.gov.uk

Baker, Kath (PC - Newbridge)
kathbaker@caerphilly.gov.uk

Bevan, Gina (LAB - Moriah)
ginabevancaerphilly.gov.uk

Bevan, John (LAB - Moriah)
johnbevan@caerphilly.gov.uk

Bevan, Phil (PC - Morgan Jones)
philbevan@caerphilly.gov.uk

Binding, Lyndon (PC - Aber Valley)
lyndonbinding@caerphilly.gov.uk

Blackman, Anne (IND - Nelson)
anneblackman@caerphilly.gov.uk

Bolter, Dennis (PC - Hengoed)
dennisbolter@caerphilly.gov.uk

Carter, David (LAB - Bargoed)
davidcarter@caerphilly.gov.uk

Cook, Patrica (LAB - Blackwood)
patriciacook@caerphilly.gov.uk

Cuss, Carl (LAB - Twyn Carno)
carlcuss@caerphilly.gov.uk

David, Hefin (LAB - St Cattwg)
hefindavid@caerphilly.gov.uk

David, Wynne (LAB - St Cattwg)
wynnedavid@caerphilly.gov.uk

Davies, Tudor (LAB - Bargoed)
tudordavies@caerphilly.gov.uk

Davies, Huw (LAB - Penyrheol)
huwdavies@caerphilly.gov.uk

Dawson, Kevin (LAB - Pengam)
kevindawson@caerphilly.gov.uk

Dix, Nigel (LAB - Blackwood)
nigeldix@caerphilly.gov.uk

Durham, Colin (LAB - Ynysddu)
colindurham@caerphilly.gov.uk

Elsbury, Colin (PC - St Martins)
colinelsbury@caerphilly.gov.uk

Forehead, Christine (LAB - St James)
christineforehead@caerphilly.gov.uk

Forehead, Elaine (LAB - St James)
elaineforehead@caerphilly.gov.uk

Fussell, James (PC - St Martins)
jamesfussell@caerphilly.gov.uk

Gale, June (LAB - Bedwas, Trethomas & Machen)
junegalecaerphilly.gov.uk

George, Nigel (LAB - Risca East)
nigelgeorge@caerphilly.gov.uk

Gordon, Colin (LAB - Pontllanfraith)
colingordon@caerphilly.gov.uk

Gough, Rob (PC - Llanbradach)
robgough@caerphilly.gov.uk

Griffiths, Phyl (IND - Risca West)
phyllisgriffiths@caerphilly.gov.uk

Hardacre, David (LAB - Darren Valley)
davidhardacre@caerphilly.gov.uk

Havard, Derek (LAB - Bedwas, Trethomas & Machen)
derekhavard@caerphilly.gov.uk

Hawker, Chris (LAB - Cefn Fforest)
chrishawker@caerphilly.gov.uk

Higgs, Alan (LAB - Aberbargoed)
alanhiggs@caerphilly.gov.uk

Hughes, Graham (LAB - St Cattwg)
grahamhughes@caerphilly.gov.uk

James, Ken (LAB - Abercarn)
kenjames@caerphilly.gov.uk

James, Martyn (PC - Ystrad Mynach)
martynjames@caerphilly.gov.uk

Johnston, Gary (LAB - Newbridge)
garyjohnston@caerphilly.gov.uk

Jones, Janet (LAB - Ynysddu)
janetjones@caerphilly.gov.uk

Kent, Stephen (PC - St Martins)
stephenkent@caerphilly.gov.uk

Kirby, Gez (LAB - Pontllanfraith)
gezkirby@caerphilly.gov.uk

Leonard, Philippa (LAB - Risca East)
leonap@caerphilly.gov.uk

Lewis, Andrew (LAB - Crumlin)
andrewlewis@caerphilly.gov.uk

Lloyd, Keith (PC - Crumlin)
keithlloyd@caerphilly.gov.uk

Morgan, Sean (LAB - Nelson)
seanmorgan@caerphilly.gov.uk

Oliver, Gaynor (LAB - Pontlottyn)
gaynoroliver@caerphilly.gov.uk

Passmore, Rhianon (LAB - Risca East)

Poole, David (LAB - Pengam)
davidpoole@caerphilly.gov.uk

Preece, Denver (LAB - Abercarn)
denverpreece@caerphilly.gov.uk

Prew, Michael (PC - Morgan Jones)
michaelprew@caerphilly.gov.uk

Pritchard, James (LAB - Morgan Jones)
jamespritchard@caerphilly.gov.uk

Pritchard, Judith (PC - Hengoed)
judithpritchard@caerphilly.gov.uk

Rees, Allan (LAB - Blackwood)
reesa2@caerphilly.gov.uk

Roberts, John (PC - Aber Valley)
johnroberts@caerphilly.gov.uk

Saralis, Roy (LAB - Penmaen)
roysaralis@caerphilly.gov.uk

Sargent, Margaret (PC - Penyrheol)
margaretsargent@caerphilly.gov.uk

Skivens, Steve (PC - Penyrheol)
stevenskivens@caerphilly.gov.uk

Stenner, Eluned (LAB - New Tredegar)
elunedstenner@caerphilly.gov.uk

Summers, Jean (LAB - Penmaen)
jeansummers@caerphilly.gov.uk

Taylor, John (PC - Aber Valley)
johntaylor@caerphilly.gov.uk

Whittle, Lindsay (PC - Penyrheol)
lindsaywhittle@caerphilly.gov.uk

Williams, Tom (LAB - Cefn Fforest)
tomwilliams@caerphilly.gov.uk

Woodyatt, Robin (LAB - Maesycwmmer)
robinwoodyatt@caerphilly.gov.uk

POLITICAL COMPOSITION
LAB: 47, PC: 20, IND: 3

COMMITTEE CHAIRS
Audit: Mr Dave Rees

Health, Social Care & Wellbeing: Miss Lyn Ackerman

Licensing: Mr John Bevan

Pensions: Ms June Gale

Planning: Mr David Carter

Regeneration & Environment: Mr Tudor Davies

Calderdale M

Calderdale Metropolitan Borough Council, Northgate House, Halifax HX1 1UN
☎ 0845 245 6000 🖷 01422 393102 🖳 www.calderdale.gov.uk

FACTS AND FIGURES
Parliamentary Constituencies: Calder Valley, Halifax
EU Constituencies: Yorkshire and the Humber
Election Frequency: Elections are by thirds

PRINCIPAL OFFICERS
Chief Executive: Ms Merran McRae Chief Executive, Town Hall, Halifax HX1 1UJ ☎ 01422 393005 🖷 01422 393085 ✉ merran.mcrae@calderdale.gov.uk

Senior Management: Mr Paul Butcher Director - Public Health, Northgate House, Halifax HX1 1UJ ✉ paul.butcher@calderdale.gov.uk

Senior Management: Ms Bev Maybury Director - Adults, Health & Social Care, 1 Park Road, Halifax HX1 1UJ ☎ 01422 393800 🖷 01442 393815 ✉ bev.maybury@calderdale.gov.uk

Senior Management: Mr Stuart Smith Director - Children & Young People, Northgate House, Halifax HX1 1UJ ☎ 01422 392552 🖷 01422 392017 ✉ stuart.smith@calderdale.gov.uk

Senior Management: Mr Mark Thompson, Acting Director - Economy & Environment (Head of Housing, Environment & Renewal), Northgate House, Northgate, Halifax HX1 1UJ ☎ 01422 392435 ✉ mark.thompson@calderdale.gov.uk

Senior Management: Mr Robin Tuddenham Director - Communities & Service Support, Westgate House, Halifax HX1 1UJ ☎ 01422 393018 ✉ robin.tuddenham@calderdale.gov.uk

Access Officer / Social Services (Disability): Mr Iain Baines Head of Safeguarding & Quality, Northgate House, Halifax HX1 1UJ ☎ 01422 393809 🖷 01422 393815 ✉ iain.baines@calderdale.gov.uk

Access Officer / Social Services (Disability): Ms Pippa Corner Head of Partnerships & Personalisation, 1 Park Road, Halifax HX1 1UJ ☎ 01422 393864 ✉ pippa.corner@calderdale.gov.uk

Architect, Building / Property Services: Mr Stephen Hoyle Lead for Asset Management, Northgate House, Halifax HX1 1UJ ☎ 01422 392058 ✉ stephen.hoyle@calderdale.gov.uk

Architect, Building / Property Services: Ms Geraldine Rushton Disabilities Liaison Officer, Northgate House, Halifax HX1 1UJ ☎ 01422 393099 🖷 01422 393136 ✉ geraldine.rushton@calderdale.gov.uk

Building Control: Mr Mike Terry Building Control Manager, Westgate House, Halifax HX1 1UJ ☎ 01422 392221 🖷 01422 392203 ✉ mike.terry@calderdale.gov.uk

Catering Services: Mr Graham Dixon FM Operational Services Manager, Northgate House, Halifax HX1 1UJ ☎ 01422 392363 ✉ graham.dixon@calderdale.gov.uk

Children / Youth Services: Mr David Whalley Head of Learning, Northgate House, Halifax HX1 1UJ ☎ 01422 392716 🖷 01422 392017 ✉ david.whalley@calderdale.gov.uk

Civil Registration: Mrs Andrea Breen Acting Registration & Licensing Services, Northgate House, Halifax HX1 1UJ ☎ 01422 284470 🖷 01422 284472 ✉ andrea.breen@calderdale.gov.uk

PR / Communications: Mrs Lucy Bradwell PR & Public Information Officer, Westgate House, Westgate, Halifax HX1 1UJ ☎ 01422 393003 🖷 01422 393136 ✉ lucy.bradwell@calderdale.gov.uk

Community Safety: Mr Derek Benn Community Safety Partnership Manager, Hoover Building, 21 West Parade, Halifax HX1 1UJ ☎ 01422 393130 🖷 01422 393183 ✉ derek.benn@calderdale.gov.uk

Contracts: Ms Deborah Gaunt, Corporate Procurement Officer, Princess Buildings, Halifax HX1 1UJ ☎ 01422 393176 🖷 01422 393526 ✉ deborah.gaunt@calderdale.gov.uk

Contracts: Mrs Judith Wyllie Commissioning & Partnership Services, Northgate House, Halifax HX1 1UJ ☎ 01422 392527 🖷 01422 392017 ✉ judith.wyllie@calderdale.gov.uk

Customer Service: Ms Zohrah Zancudi Head of Customer Service, 2nd Floor, Westgate House, Halifax HX1 1UJ ☎ 01422 393201 🖷 01422 393220 ✉ zohrah.zancudi@calderdale.gov.uk

Economic Development: Mr Robert Campbell Business & Economy Manager, Northgate House, Halifax HX1 1UJ ☎ 01422 392235 ✉ robert.campbell@calderdale.gov.uk

Education: Ms Julie Jenkins Head of Early Intervention & Safeguarding, Northgate House, Halifax HX1 1UJ ☎ 01422 392722 ✉ julie.jenkins@calderdale.gov.uk

Electoral Registration: Ms Linda Clarkson Principal Electoral Services Officer, Westgate House, Westgate, Halifax HX1 1UJ ☎ 01422 393049 🖷 01422 393090 ✉ linda.clarkson@calderdale.gov.uk

Emergency Planning: Ms Amanda Webster Senior Emergency Planning Advisor, Westgate House, Halifax HX1 1UJ ☎ 01422 392870 🖷 01422 392879 ✉ amanda.webster@calderdale.gov.uk

Energy Management: Ms Helen Rhodes Head of Housing, Environment & Renewal, Northgate House, Halifax HX1 1UJ ☎ 01422 392485 ✉ helen.rhodes@calderdale.gov.uk

Environmental / Technical Services: Mr Peter Broadbent Environmental Health Manager, Northgate House, Halifax HX1 1UJ ☎ 01422 392345 ✉ peter.broadbent@calderdale.gov.uk

Environmental Health: Mr Peter Broadbent Environmental Health Manager, Northgate House, Halifax HX1 1UJ ☎ 01422 392345 ✉ peter.broadbent@calderdale.gov.uk

Estates, Property & Valuation: Mr Stephen Hoyle Lead for Asset Management, Northgate House, Halifax HX1 1UJ ☎ 01422 392058 🖷 01422 392059 ✉ stephen.hoyle@calderdale.gov.uk

Events Manager: Mr Peter Vardy, Recreation Officer - Licensing & Events, Ainley's Depot (Highway's Offices), c/o Highways & Engineering, Huddersfield Road, Elland HX5 9JR ☎ 01422 384796 ✉ peter.vardy@calderdale.gov.uk

Facilities: Ms Elaine Wynne Lead for Facilities Management, Northgate House, Halifax HX1 1UJ ☎ 01422 392066 ✉ elaine.wynne@calderdale.gov.uk

Finance: Mr Nigel Broadbent Head of Finance, Princess Buildings, Halifax HX1 1UJ ☎ 01422 393872 ✉ nigel.broadbent@calderdale.gov.uk

Fleet Management: Mr Paul Topham, Transport Manager, Economy & Environment, Battinson Road Depot, Queen's Road, Halifax HX1 1UJ ☎ 01422 264350 🖷 01422 264357 ✉ paul.topham@calderdale.gov.uk

Grounds Maintenance: Ms Amanda Firth Safer, Cleaner, Greener Manager, Spring Hall Mansion, Spring Hall, Halifax HX1 1UJ ☎ 01422 284441 🖷 01422 284421 ✉ amanda.firth@calderdale.gov.uk

Health and Safety: Mr Martin Allingham, Principal Health & Safety Adviser, Westgate House, Halifax HX1 1UJ ☎ 01422 393080 🖷 01422 353635 ✉ martin.allingham@calderdale.gov.uk

Highways: Ms Carolyn Walton Highways & Engineering Manager, Westgate House, Halifax HX1 1UJ ☎ 01422 392167 ✉ carolyn.walton@calderdale.gov.uk

Home Energy Conservation: Mr Richard Armitage Housing Projects Officer, Northgate House, Halifax HX1 1UJ ☎ 01422 392474 ✉ richard.armitage@calderdale.gov.uk

Housing: Ms Heidi Wilson Housing Access & Waste Management Manager, Northgate House, Halifax HX1 1UJ ☎ 01422 392406 🖷 01422 392399 ✉ heidi.wilson@calderdale.gov.uk

Housing Maintenance: Ms Helen Rhodes Head of Housing, Environment & Renewal, Northgate House, Halifax HX1 1UJ ☎ 01422 392485 ✉ helen.rhodes@calderdale.gov.uk

Local Area Agreement: Mr Alan Duncan LSP & Partnerships Manager, Town Hall, HHalifax HX1 1UJ ☎ 01422 392207 🖷 01422 393102 ✉ alan.duncan@calderdale.gov.uk

Legal: Mr Ian Hughes Policy & Partnership Manager, Westgate House, Westgate, Halifax HX1 1UJ ☎ 01422 393063 🖷 01422 393073 ✉ ian.hughes@calderdale.gov.uk

Licensing: Mrs Andrea Breen Acting Registration & Licensing Services, Spring Hall Mansion, Huddersfield Road, Halifax HX1 1UJ ☎ 01422 284470 🖷 01422 284472 ✉ andrea.breen@calderdale.gov.uk

Lifelong Learning: Mrs Anne Craven Service Manager - Commissioning Schools & Lifelong Learning, Northgate House, Halifax HX1 1UJ ☎ 01422 392806 🖷 01422 392017 ✉ anne.craven@calderdale.gov.uk

Lighting: Ms Carolyn Walton Highways & Engineering Manager, Westgate House, Halifax HX1 1UJ ☎ 01422 392167 ✉ carolyn.walton@calderdale.gov.uk

Lottery Funding, Charity and Voluntary: Ms Sarah Barker Commissioning & Monitoring Officer, 2nd Floor, Westgate House, Westgate, Halifax HX1 1UJ ☎ 01422 393218 ✉ sarahj.barker@calderdale.gov.uk

Member Services: Mr Peter Burton, Democratic Services Manager, Town Hall, Halifax HX1 1UJ ☎ 01422 393011 🖷 01422 393102 ✉ peter.burton@calderdale.gov.uk

Parking: Ms Debbie Harrison, Parking Operations Manager, Multure House, Halifax HX1 1UJ ☎ 01422 392185 🖷 01422 392191 ✉ debbie.harrison@calderdale.gov.uk

Partnerships: Mr Andrew Pitts Head of Neighbourhoods, Westgate House, Westgate, Halifax HX1 1UJ ☎ 01422 392600 ✉ andrew.pitts@calderdale.gov.uk

Personnel / HR: Ms Jackie Addison Corporate Lead for HR, 3rd Floor, Westgate, Westgate, Halifax HX1 1UJ ☎ 01422 288417 🖷 01422 288306 ✉ jackie.addison@calderdale.gov.uk

Planning: Mr Richard Seaman Development Manager, Westgate House, Halifax HX1 1UJ ☎ 01422 392241 🖷 01422 392205 ✉ richard.seaman@calderdale.gov.uk

Procurement: Ms Deborah Gaunt, Corporate Procurement Officer, Westgate House, Halifax HX1 1UJ ☎ 01422 393176 Halifax HX1 1UJ 🖷 01422 393526 ✉ deborah.gaunt@calderdale.gov.uk

CALDERDALE

Public Libraries: Ms Carole Knowles Library Services Manager, Central Library, Northgate, Halifax HX1 1UJ ☎ 01422 392623 carole.knowles@calderdale.gov.uk

Recycling & Waste Minimisation: Ms Heidi Wilson Housing Access & Waste Management Manager, Northgate House, Halifax HX1 1UJ ☎ 01422 392406 🖷 01422 392399 heidi.wilson@calderdale.gov.uk

Regeneration: Mr Robert Campbell Business & Economy Manager, Northgate House, Halifax HX1 1UJ ☎ 01422 392235 robert.campbell@calderdale.gov.uk

Road Safety: Ms Debbie Calcott Network Manager, Mulcture House, Halifax HX1 1UJ ☎ 01422 392185 debbie.calcott@calderdale.gov.uk

Social Services: Mr Iain Baines Head of Safeguarding & Quality, Northgate House, Halifax HX1 1UJ ☎ 01422 393809 🖷 01422 393815 iain.baines@calderdale.gov.uk

Social Services: Ms Beate Wagner Head of Early Intervention Safeguarding, Northgate House, Halifax HX1 1UJ ☎ 01422 392722 🖷 01422 392017 beate.wagner@calderdale.gov.uk

Social Services (Adult): Ms Pippa Corner Head of Partnerships & Personalisation, 1 Park Road, Halifax HX1 1UJ ☎ 01422 393864 pippa.corner@calderdale.gov.uk

Social Services (Children): Mr Stuart Smith Director - Children & Young People, Northgate House, Halifax HX1 1UJ ☎ 01422 392552 🖷 01422 392017 stuart.smith@calderdale.gov.uk

Fostering & Adoption: Mr Gary Pickles Service Manager - Children Looked After, Northgate House, Halifax HX1 1UJ ☎ 01422 392717 🖷 01422 392017 dean.howson@calderdale.gov.uk

Families: Ms Julie Killey Acting Strategic Commissioning - Children, Young People & Family, Northgate House, Halifax HX1 1UJ ☎ 01422 392816 🖷 01422 392017 julie.killey@calderdale.gov.uk

Childrens Social Care: Mr Sean Walsh Service Manager - Locality Teams, Northgate House, Halifax HX1 1UJ ☎ 01422 392805 🖷 01422 392017 lisa.handley@calderdale.gov.uk

Public Health: Mr Paul Butcher Director - Public Health, Northgate House, Halifax HX1 1UJ paul.butcher@calderdale.gov.uk

Public Health: Mrs Caron Walker Consultant in Public Health, Northgate House, Halifax HX1 1UJ ☎ 01422 266156 caron.walker@calderdale.gov.uk

Public Health: Mr Dean Wallace Consultant in Public Health, Northgate House, HHalifax HX1 1UJ ☎ 01422 266134 dean.wallace@calderdale.gov.uk

Staff Training: Ms Julie Comb Corporate Lead - Workforce Development, 3rd Floor, Westgate House, Westgate, Halifax HX1 1UJ ☎ 01422 288340 julie.comb@calderdale.gov.uk

Street Scene: Ms Amanda Firth Safer, Cleaner, Greener Manager, Spring Hall Mansion, Spring Hall, Halifax HX1 1UJ ☎ 01422 284441 🖷 01422 284421 amanda.firth@calderdale.gov.uk

Sustainable Communities: Mr Phil Ratcliffe Development Strategy Manager, Northgate House, Halifax HX1 1UJ ☎ 01422 392255 🖷 01422 392076 phil.ratcliffe@calderdale.gov.uk

Tourism: Ms Katie Kinsella Tourism Manager, Westgate House, Halifax HX1 1UJ ☎ 01422 392293 🖷 01422 393220 katie.kinsella@calderdale.gov.uk

Traffic Management: Ms Carolyn Walton Highways & Engineering Manager, Westgate House, Halifax HX1 1UJ ☎ 01422 392167 carolyn.walton@calderdale.gov.uk

Transport: Mr Paul Topham, Transport Manager, Economy & Environment, Battinson Road Depot, Queen's Road, Halifax HX1 1UJ ☎ 01422 264350 🖷 01422 264357 paul.topham@calderdale.gov.uk

Transport Planner: Mr Paul Topham, Transport Manager, Economy & Environment, Battinson Road Depot, Queen's Road, Halifax HX1 1UJ ☎ 01422 264350 🖷 01422 264357 paul.topham@calderdale.gov.uk

Waste Collection and Disposal: Ms Heidi Wilson Housing Access & Waste Management Manager, Northgate House, Halifax HX1 1UJ ☎ 01422 392406 🖷 01422 392399 heidi.wilson@calderdale.gov.uk

Waste Management: Ms Heidi Wilson Housing Access & Waste Management Manager, Northgate House, Halifax HX1 1UJ ☎ 01422 392406 🖷 01422 392399 heidi.wilson@calderdale.gov.uk

Children's Play Areas: Ms Amanda Firth Safer, Cleaner, Greener Manager, Spring Hall Mansion, Spring Hall, Halifax HX1 1UJ ☎ 01422 284441 🖷 01422 284421 amanda.firth@calderdale.gov.uk

COUNCILLORS

***Leader of the Council* Swift**, Tim (LAB - Town)
councillor.tswift@calderdale.gov.uk

***Deputy Leader of the Council* Collins**, Barry (LAB - Illingworth & Mixenden)
councillor.bcollins@calderdale.gov.uk

Ali, Ferman (LAB - Park)
councillor.fali@calderdale.gov.uk

Allen, Patricia (LD - Elland)
councillor.pallen@calderdale.gov.uk

Baines, Stephen (CON - Northowram & Shelf)
councillor.sbaines@calderdale.gov.uk

Baker, James (LD - Warley)
councillor.jbaker@calderdale.gov.uk

Battye, Janet (LD - Calder)
councillor.jbattye@calderdale.gov.uk

Beal, Christine (CON - Rastrick)
councillor.cbeal@calderdale.gov.uk

Benton, Scott (CON - Brighouse)
councillor.sbenton@calderdale.gov.uk

Blagbrough, Howard (CON - Brighouse)
councillor.hblagbrough@calderdale.gov.uk

Booth, Jayne (LAB - Todmorden)
councillor.jbooth@calderdale.gov.uk

Burton, Martin (LAB - Warley)
councillor.mburton@calderdale.gov.uk

Caffrey, Peter (CON - Northowram & Shelf)
councillor.pcaffrey@calderdale.gov.uk

Carter, Geraldine (CON - Ryburn)
councillor.gcarter@calderdale.gov.uk

Collins, Anne (LAB - Ovenden)
councillor.acollins@calderdale.gov.uk

Ford, John (CON - Elland)
councillor.jford@calderdale.gov.uk

Foster, Dot (LAB - Sowerby Bridge)
councillor.dfoster@calderdale.gov.uk

Foster, Michelle (LAB - Warley)
councillor.mfoster@calderdale.gov.uk

Gallagher, Angie (LAB - Elland)
councillor.agallagher@calderdale.gov.uk

Greenwood, Marilyn (LD - Greetland & Stainland)
councillor.mgreenwood@calderdale.gov.uk

Hall, Graham (CON - Hipperholme & Lightcliffe)
councillor.ghall@calderdale.gov.uk

Hardy, John (CON - Skircoat)
councillor.jhardy@calderdale.gov.uk

Holden, Robert (CON - Ryburn)
councillor.rholden@calderdale.gov.uk

James, Malcolm (LD - Greetland & Stainland)
councillor.mjames@calderdale.gov.uk

Jayne May, Nicola (CON - Luddendenfoot)
councillor.nmay@calcerdale.gov.uk

Kirton, David (CON - Hipperholme & Lightcliffe)
councillor.dkirton@calderdale.gov.uk

Lambert, Lisa (LAB - Illingworth & Mixenden)
councillor.llambert@calderdale.gov.uk

Lynn, Jenny (LAB - Park)
councillor.jlynn@calderdale.gov.uk

Martin, Ann (LAB - Brighouse)
councillor.amartin@calderdale.gov.uk

McAllister, Ann (CON - Rastrick)
councillor.amcallister@calderdale.gov.uk

Metcalfe, Bob (LAB - Town)
councillor.bmetcalfe@calderdale.gov.uk

Miles, Ali (LAB - Calder)
councillor.amiles@calderdale.gov.uk

Payne, Michael (CON - Sowerby Bridge)
councillor.mpayne@calderdale.gov.uk

Pearson, Chris (CON - Greetland & Stainland)
cpearson@calderdale.gov.uk

Pillai, Chris (CON - Rastrick)
councillor.cpillai@calderdale.gov.uk

Press, Susan (LAB - Todmorden)
councillor.spress@calderdale.gov.uk

Raistrick, Colin (IND - Hipperholme & Lightcliffe)
councillor.craistrick@calderdale.gov.uk

Rivron, Helen (LAB - Ovenden)
councillor.hrivron@calderdale.gov.uk

Shoukat, Faisal (LAB - Park)
councillor.fshoukat@calderdale.gov.uk

Smith, Bryan (LAB - Ovenden)
councillor.bsmith@calderdale.gov.uk

Smith-Moorhouse, Jill (CON - Luddendenfoot)
councillor.jsmith-moorhouse@calderdale.gov.uk

Sutherland, Daniel (LAB - Illingworth & Mixenden)
councillor.dsutherland@calderdale.gov.uk

Sweeney, Steve (LAB - Todmorden)
councillor.ssweeney@calderdale.gov.uk

Swift, Megan (LAB - Town)
councillor.mswift@calderdale.gov.uk

Tagg, Andrew (CON - Skircoat)
councillor.atagg@calderdale.gov.uk

Taylor, Roger (CON - Northowram & Shelf)
councillor.rtaylor@calderdale.gov.uk

Thompson, Marcus (CON - Skircoat)
councillor.mthompson@calderdale.gov.uk

Thornber, Robert (CON - Ryburn)
councillor.rthornber@calderdale.gov.uk

Wilkinson, Adam (LAB - Sowerby Bridge)
councillor.awilkinson@calderdale.gov.uk

Young, Dave (LAB - Calder)
councillor.dyoung@calderdale.gov.uk

Young, Simon (LAB - Luddendenfoot)
councillor.syoung@calderdale.gov.uk

POLITICAL COMPOSITION
LAB: 24, CON: 21, LD: 5, IND: 1

COMMITTEE CHAIRS
Audit: Mr Tim Swift

Health & Wellbeing: Ms Janet Battye

Cambridge City D

Cambridge City Council, Lion House, Lion Yard, Cambridge CB2 3NA
☎ 01223 457000 🖷 01223 457009 💻 www.cambridge.gov.uk

FACTS AND FIGURES
Parliamentary Constituencies: Cambridge, Cambridgeshire South
EU Constituencies: Eastern
Election Frequency: Elections are by thirds

PRINCIPAL OFFICERS
Chief Executive: Ms Antoinette Jackson, Chief Executive, The Guildhall, Cambridge CB2 3QJ ☎ 01223 457003
✉ antoinette.jackson@cambridge.gov.uk

CAMBRIDGE CITY

Senior Management: Ms Liz Bisset, Director of Customer & Community Services, Hobson House, 44 St. Andrew's Street, Cambridge CB2 3AS ☎ 01223 457801 ✉ liz.bisset@cambridge.gov.uk

Senior Management: Mr Simon Payne, Director of Environment, Mill Road Depot, Mill Road, Cambridge CB1 2AZ ☎ 01223 458517 🖷 01223 458249 ✉ simon.payne@cambridge.gov.uk

Senior Management: Mr Ray Ward Director of Business Transformation, Lion House, Lion Yard, Cambridge CB2 3NA ☎ 01223 457007 ✉ ray.ward@cambridge.gov.uk

Access Officer / Social Services (Disability): Mr Mark Taylor, Disability Access Officer, The Guildhall, Cambridge CB2 3QJ ☎ 01223 457075 🖷 01223 457379 ✉ mark.taylor@cambridge.gov.uk

Architect, Building / Property Services: Mr Will Barfield Asset Manager, Mill Road Depot, Mill Road, Cambridge CB1 2AZ ☎ 01223 457843 ✉ will.barfield@cambridge.gov.uk

Building Control: Mr Ian Boulton, Building Control Manager, The Guildhall, Cambridge CB2 3QJ ☎ 01223 457111 🖷 01223 457109 ✉ ian.boulton@cambridge.gov.uk

PR / Communications: Mr Ashley Perry, Corporate Marketing Manager, The Guildhall, Cambridge CB2 3QJ ☎ 01223 457064 🖷 01223 457009 ✉ ashley.perry@cambridge.gov.uk

Community Safety: Ms Lynda Kilkelly Community Safety Manager, Hobson House, 44 St. Andrew's Street, Cambridge CB2 3AS ☎ 01223 457045 ✉ lynda.kilkelly@cambridge.gov.uk

Computer Management: Mr James Nightingale, Head of ICT, The Guildhall, Cambridge CB2 3QJ ☎ 01223 457461 🖷 01223 558501 ✉ james.nightingale@cambridge.gov.uk

Corporate Services: Mr Steve Crabtree Head of Internal Audit, The Guildhall, Cambridge CB2 3QJ ☎ 01223 458181 ✉ steve.crabtree@cambridge.gov.uk

Corporate Services: Mr Andrew Limb Head of Corporate Strategy, The Guildhall, Cambridge CB2 3QJ ☎ 01223 457004 ✉ andrew.limb@cambridge.gov.uk

Customer Service: Mr Jonathan James Head of Customer Services, Mandela House, 4 Regent Street, Cambridge CB2 1BY ☎ 01223 458601 ✉ jonathan.james@cambridge.gov.uk

Electoral Registration: Ms Vicky Breading Electoral Services Manager, The Guildhall, Cambridge CB2 3QJ ☎ 01223 457057 🖷 01223 457079 ✉ vicky.breading@cambridge.gov.uk

Emergency Planning: Mr Paul Parry Corporate H&S and Emergency Planning Manager, The Guildhall, Cambridge CB2 3QJ ☎ 01223 458033 🖷 01223 458249 ✉ paul.parry@cambridge.gov.uk

Environmental Health: Mr Jas Lally Head of Refuse & Environment, Mill Road Depot, Mill Road, Cambridge CB1 2AZ ☎ 01223 458572 ✉ jas.lally@cambridge.gov.uk

Estates, Property & Valuation: Mr Dave Prinsep Head of Property Services, Lion House, Lion Yard, Cambridge CB2 3NA ☎ 01223 457318 ✉ dave.prinsep@cambridge.gov.uk

Finance: Ms Alison Cole Head of Revenues & Benefits, Mandela House, 4 Regent Street, Cambridge CB2 1BY ☎ 01223 457701 🖷 01233 457709 ✉ alison.cole@cambridge.gov.uk

Finance: Ms Caroline Ryba Head of Finance, The Guildhall, Cambridge CB2 3QJ ☎ 01223 458134 ✉ caroline.ryba@cambridge.gov.uk

Fleet Management: Mr David Cox Fleet Manager, Mill Road Depot, Mill Road, Cambridge CB1 2AZ ☎ 01223 458265 🖷 01223 458249 ✉ david.cox@cambridge.gov.uk

Grounds Maintenance: Mr Joel Carre Head of Streets & Open Spaces, Mill Road Depot, Mill Road, Cambridge CB1 2AZ ☎ 01223 458201 ✉ joel.carre@cambridge.gov.uk

Health and Safety: Mr Paul Parry Corporate H&S and Emergency Planning Manager, The Guildhall, Cambridge CB2 3QJ ☎ 01223 458033 🖷 01223 458249 ✉ paul.parry@cambridge.gov.uk

Home Energy Conservation: Mr Justin Smith Home Energy Officer, Mandela House, 4 Regent Street, Cambridge CB2 1BY ☎ 01223 457954 ✉ justin.smith@cambridge.gov.uk

Housing: Mr Alan Carter Head of Strategic Housing, Hobson House, 44 St. Andrew's Street, Cambridge CB4 2YG ☎ 01223 457948 ✉ alan.carter@cambridge.gov.uk

Housing: Mr Robert Hollingsworth Head of City Homes, City Homes North, 171 Arbury Road, Cambridge CB4 2YG ☎ 01223 458401 ✉ robert.hollingsworth@cambridge.gov.uk

Housing Maintenance: Mr Dave Prinsep Head of Property Services, The Guildhall, Cambridge CB2 3QJ ☎ 01223 457318 ✉ dave.prinsep@cambridge.gov.uk

Legal: Mr Simon Pugh, Head of Legal Services, The Guildhall, Cambridge CB2 3QJ ☎ 01223 457401 🖷 01223 457409 ✉ simon.pugh@cambridge.gov.uk

Leisure and Cultural Services: Ms Debbie Kaye Head of Communities, Arts & Recreation, Hobson House, 44 St Andrew's Street, Cambridge CB2 3AS ☎ 01223 458633 🖷 01223 457539 ✉ debbie.kaye@cambridge.gov.uk

Licensing: Mr Jas Lally Head of Refuse & Environment, Mill Road Depot, Mill Road, Cambridge CB1 2AZ ☎ 01223 457881 🖷 01223 457909 ✉ jas.lally@cambridge.gov.uk

Member Services: Mr Gary Clift Head of Democratic Services, The Guildhall, Cambridge CB2 3QJ ☎ 01223 457011 ✉ gary.clift@cambridge.gov.uk

Member Services: Ms Eleanor Reader-Moore EA to Leader & Members, The Guildhall, Cambridge CB2 3QJ ☎ 01223 457022 ✉ eleanor.reader-moore@cambridge.gov.uk

Parking: Mr Paul Necus, Head of Specialist Services, Mill Road Depot, Mill Road, Cambridge CB1 2AZ ☎ 01223 458510 ✉ paul.necus@cambridge.gov.uk

Personnel / HR: Ms Deborah Simpson Head of Human Resources, The Guildhall, Cambridge CB2 3QJ ☎ 01223 458101 🖷 01223 458109 ✉ deborah.simpson@cambridge.gov.uk

Planning: Ms Patsy Dell Head of Planning, The Guildhall, Cambridge CB2 3QJ ☎ 01223 457103 🖷 01223 457109 ✉ patsy.dell@cambridge.gov.uk

Procurement: Mr John Bridgwater Strategic Procurement Adviser, The Guildhall, Cambridge CB2 3QJ ☎ 01223 458178 ✉ john.bridgwater@cambridge.gov.uk

Recycling & Waste Minimisation: Ms Jen Robertson, Waste & Street Services Strategy Manager, Mill Road Depot, Mill Road, Cambridge CB1 2AZ ☎ 01223 458225 ✉ jen.robertson@cambridge.gov.uk

Staff Training: Ms Deborah Simpson Head of Human Resources, The Guildhall, Cambridge CB2 3QJ ☎ 01223 458101 🖷 01223 458109 ✉ deborah.simpson@cambridge.gov.uk

Street Scene: Mr Joel Carre Head of Streets & Open Spaces, Mill Road Depot, Mill Road, Cambridge CB1 2AZ ☎ 01223 458201 ✉ joel.carre@cambridge.gov.uk

Tourism: Mrs Emma Thornton, Head of Tourism & City Centre Management, The Guildhall, Cambridge CB2 3QJ ☎ 01223 457464 ✉ emma.thornton@cambridge.gov.uk

Town Centre: Mrs Emma Thornton, Head of Tourism & City Centre Management, The Guildhall, Cambridge CB2 3QJ ☎ 01223 457464 ✉ emma.thornton@cambridge.gov.uk

Waste Collection and Disposal: Mr Jas Lally Head of Refuse & Environment, Mill Road Depot, Mill Road, Cambridge CB1 2AZ ☎ 01223 458572 ✉ jas.lally@cambridge.gov.uk

Waste Management: Mr Jas Lally Head of Environmental Services, Mill Road Depot, Mill Road, Cambridge CB1 2AZ ☎ 01223 458572 ✉ jas.lally@cambridge.gov.uk

COUNCILLORS

***Mayor* Dryden**, Robert (LAB - Cherry Hinton)
robert.dryden@cambridge.gov.uk

***Deputy Mayor* Benstead**, Jeremy (LAB - Coleridge)
j_benstead@live.co.uk

***Leader of the Council* Herbert**, Lewis (LAB - Coleridge)
lewis.herbert@cambridge.gov.uk

***Deputy Leader of the Council* O'Reilly**, Carina (LAB - Arbury)
carinaoreilly@gmail.com

***Group Leader* Bick**, Tim (LD - Market)
tim.bick@btinternet.com

***Group Leader* Hipkin**, John (IND - Castle)
castleindependent@gmail.com

Abbott, Margery (LAB - East Chesterton)
margery.abbott.labour@hotmail.co.uk

Ashton, Mark (LAB - Cherry Hinton)
mark.ashton@cambridge.gov.uk

Austin, Ysanne (LD - West Chesterton)
ysanne.austin@cambridge.gov.uk

Avery, Nicholas (LD - Trumpington)
nick.avery@cambridge.gov.uk

Baigent, Dave (LAB - Romsey)
dave.baigent@cambridge.gov.uk

Bird, Gerri (LAB - East Chesterton)
gerribird@sky.com

Blencowe, Kevin (LAB - Petersfield)
kevin.blencowe@gmail.com

Cantrill, Rod (LD - Newnham)
rcantrill@millingtonadvisory.com

Gawthrope, Nigel (LAB - Kings Hedges)
nigel.gawthrope@cambridge.gov.uk

Gehring, Markus (LD - Newnham)
markus.gehring@cambridge.gov.uk

Gillespie, Oscar (GRN - Market)
oscar.gillespie@cambridge.gov.uk

Hart, Caroline (LAB - Abbey)
caroline.hart@cambridge.gov.uk

Holland, Marie-Louise (IND - Castle)
marie-louise.holland@cambridge.gov.uk

Holt, Valerie (LD - Castle)
valerie.holt@cambridge.gov.uk

Johnson, Richard (LAB - Abbey)
richard.johnston@cambridge.gov.uk

McPherson, Russell (LAB - Cherry Hinton)
russ.mcpherson@cambridge.gov.uk

Meftah, Shapour (CON - Trumpington)
shapour.meftah@cambridge.gov.uk

Moore, Tim (LD - Queen Edith's)
tim.moore@cambridge.gov.uk

O'Connell, Zoe (LD - Trumpington)
zoe.coconnell@cambridge.gov.uk

Owers, George (LAB - Coleridge)
george.owers@cambridge.gov.uk

Perry, Charlotte (LAB - Arbury)
charlotte.perry@cambridge.gov.uk

Pippas, George (LD - Queen Edith's)
george.pippas@cambridge.gov.uk

Pitt, Mike (LD - West Chesterton)
mike@einval.com

Price, Kevin (LAB - Kings Hedges)
kevin.price@cambridge.gov.uk

Ratcliffe, Dan (LAB - Market)
dan.ratcliffe@cambridge.gov.uk

Reid, Sian (LD - Newnham)
sianreid27@gmail.com

Roberts, Peter (LAB - Abbey)
peter.roberts@cambridge.gov.uk

Robertson, Richard (LAB - Petersfield)
richard.robertson@cambridge.gov.uk

Sanders, Viki (LD - Queen Edith's)
vikisanders@hotmail.com

Sarris, Peter (LAB - East Chesterton)
peter.sarris@cambridge.gov.uk

Sinnott, Ann (LAB - Petersfield)
ann.sinnott@cambridge.gov.uk

Smart, Martin (LAB - Kings Hedges)
martin.smart@cambridge.gov.uk

Smart, Catherine (LD - Romsey)
chlsmart@cix.co.uk

Smith, Anna (LAB - Romsey)
anna.smith@cambridge.gov.uk

Todd-Jones, Mike (LAB - Arbury)
mike.todd-jones@cambridge.gov.uk

Tunnacliffe, Damien (LD - West Chesterton)
damientunnacliffe@yahoo.gov.uk

POLITICAL COMPOSITION
LAB: 24, LD: 14, IND: 2, CON: 1, GRN: 1

COMMITTEE CHAIRS
Housing: Mr Mike Todd-Jones

Licensing: Mr Jeremy Benstead

Planning: Mr Robert Dryden

Cambridgeshire C

Cambridgeshire County Council, Box ET 1021, Shire Hall, Castle Hill, Cambridge CB3 0AP
☎ 0345 045 5200 🖷 01223 717201 ✉ info@cambridgeshire.gov.uk
🖳 www.cambridgeshire.gov.uk

FACTS AND FIGURES
Parliamentary Constituencies: Huntingdon
EU Constituencies: Eastern
Election Frequency: Elections are of whole council

PRINCIPAL OFFICERS
Chief Executive: Mrs Gillian Beasley, Chief Executive, Town Hall, Bridge Street, Peterborough PE1 1HL ☎ 01733 452390 🖷 01733 452694 ✉ gillian.beasley@peterborough.gov.uk

Senior Management: Ms Sue Grace Corporate Director - Customer Service & Transformation, Box SH1103, Shire Hall, Castle Hill, Cambridge CB3 0AP ☎ 01223 699248 ✉ sue.grace@cambridgeshire.gov.uk

Senior Management: Mr Graham Hughes Executive Director - Environment, Transport & Economy, Box CC1307, Shire Hall, Castle Hill, Cambridge CB3 0AP ☎ 01223 699246 ✉ graham.hughes@cambridgeshire.gov.uk

Senior Management: Mr Adrian Loades Executive Director - Children, Families & Adults, CC 1001, Shire Hall, Cambridge CB3 0AP ☎ 01223 727993 ✉ adrian.loades@cambridgeshire.gov.uk

Senior Management: Mr Chris Maylon Head of Finance, Box RES 1211, Shire Hall, Castle Hill, Cambridge CB3 0AP ☎ 01223 699796 ✉ chris.maylon@cambridgeshire.gov.uk

Senior Management: Dr Liz Robin Director - Public Health, Box ET 1021, Shire Hall, Castle Hill, Cambridge CB3 0AP ☎ 0345 045 5200 ✉ liz.robin@cambridgeshire.gov.uk

Best Value: Mr James Gemmell Data & Performance Manager, BH1107, Shire Hall, Castle Hill, Cambridge CB3 0AP ☎ 01223 699067 ✉ james.gemmell@cambridgeshire.gov.uk

Catering Services: Mr Richard Ware Head of Catering & Cleaning Services, CC 1105, Shire Hall, Castle Hill, Cambridge CB3 0AP ☎ 01223 703509 ✉ richard.ware@cambridgeshire.gov.uk

Children / Youth Services: Ms Sarah Ferguson Service Director - Children's Enhanced & Preventative Services, CC1001, Shire Hall, Cambridge CB3 0AP ☎ 01223 727990 ✉ sarah.ferguson@cambridgeshire.gov.uk

Children / Youth Services: Mr John Gregg Interim Director - Social Care, Children & Young People Services, CC 1001, Shire Hall, Cambridge CB3 0AP ☎ 01223 727989 🖷 01223 717307 ✉ john.gregg@cambridgeshire.gov.uk

Children / Youth Services: Mr Keith Grimwade Director - Learning, CC 1001, Shire Hall, Cambridge CB3 0AP ☎ 01223 727988 ✉ keith.grimwade@cambridgeshire.gov.uk

Children / Youth Services: Mr Adrian Loades Executive Director - Children, Families & Adults, CC 1001, Shire Hall, Cambridge CB3 0AP ☎ 01223 727993 ✉ adrian.loades@cambridgeshire.gov.uk

Civil Registration: Ms Louise Clover Support Manager - Registrations & Coroners, Lawrence Court, Princes Street, Huntingdon PE29 3PA ☎ 01223 715365 ✉ louise.clover@cambridgeshire.gov.uk

PR / Communications: Mr Simon Cobby Communications & Media Manager, Box Res 1101, Shire Hall, Castle Hill, Cambridge CB3 0AP ☎ 01223 699281 ✉ simon.cobby@cambridgeshire.gov.uk

Community Planning: Mr Joseph Whelan Head of Passenger Transport, CC 1212, Shire Hall, Castle Hill, Cambridge CB3 0AP ☎ 01223 715585 ✉ joseph.whelan@cambridgeshire.gov.uk

Community Safety: Dr Liz Robin, Director of Public Health, CC 1108, Shire Hall, Castle Hill, Cambridge CB3 0AP ☎ 01223 725401 ✉ liz.robin@cambridgeshire.gov.uk

Computer Management: Mr John Platten Channel Strategy Manager, SH 1001, Shire Hall, Castle Hill, Cambridge CB3 0AP ☎ 01223 699712 ✉ john.platten@cambridgeshire.gov.uk

Consumer Protection and Trading Standards: Ms Aileen Andrews Operations Manager - Supporting Business & Communities, Box ET 4000, Sackville House, Sackville Way, Great Cambourne, Cambridge CB3 0AP ☎ 01954 284659 ✉ aileen.andrews@cambridgeshire.gov.uk

Corporate Services: Ms Sue Grace Corporate Director - Customer Service & Transformation, Box SH1103, Shire Hall, Castle Hill, Cambridge CB3 0AP ☎ 01223 699248 ✉ sue.grace@cambridgeshire.gov.uk

Customer Service: Ms Sue Grace Corporate Director - Customer Service & Transformation, Box SH1103, Shire Hall, Castle Hill, Cambridge CB3 0AP ☎ 01223 699248 ✉ sue.grace@cambridgeshire.gov.uk

Customer Service: Ms Jo Tompkins Customer Services Manager, DA3 Contact Centre, St. Ives PE27 5JL ☎ 01480 373406 ✉ jo.tompkins@cambridgeshire.gov.uk

Economic Development: Mr Guy Mills, Enterprise & Economy Development Manager, SH1315, Shire Hall, Castle Hill, Cambridge CB3 0AP ☎ 01223 699929 ✉ guy.mills@cambridgeshire.gov.uk

Education: Mr Keith Grimwade Director - Learning, CC 1001, Shire Hall, Cambridge CB3 0AP ☎ 01223 727988 ✉ keith.grimwade@cambridgeshire.gov.uk

Emergency Planning: Mr Stewart Thomas Head of Emergency Planning, RES 1403, Shire Hall, Castle Hill, Cambridge CB3 0AP ☎ 01223 727944 ✉ stewart.thomas@cambridgeshire.gov.uk

Energy Management: Mr Roy Drayton Premises Engineering Manager, Box Res 1321, Shire Hall, Castle Hill, Cambridge CB3 0AP ☎ 01223 715507 ✉ roy.drayton@cambridgeshire.gov.uk

Estates, Property & Valuation: Ms Lesley Currie Capital Projects Manager, Box ET 1021, Shire Hall, Castle Hill, Cambridge CB3 0AP ☎ 01223 699711 ✉ lecurrie@northamptonshire.gov.uk

European Liaison: Mr David Arkell, Head of Innovation & Partnerships, CC1308, Castle Court, Shire Hall, Cambridge CB3 0AP ☎ 01223 715941 ✉ david.arkell@cambridgeshire.gov.uk

Facilities: Mr Jim Mowatt Service Facilities Manager, RES1010, Shire Hall, Castle Hill, Cambridge CB3 0AP ☎ 01223 699098 ✉ jim.mowatt@cambridgeshire.gov.uk

Finance: Ms Sarah Heywood Head of Finance & Performance (CFA), SH1395, Shire Hall, Castle Hill, Cambridge CB3 0AP ☎ 01223 699714 ✉ sarah.heywood@cambridgeshire.gov.uk

Finance: Mr Ian Smith Strategy Finance Manager, RES1303, Shire Hall, Castle Hill, Cambridge CB3 0AP ☎ 01223 699807 ✉ ian.smith@cambridgeshire.gov.uk

Treasury: Mr Mike Batty Principal Accountant, RES1211, Shire Hall, Castle Hill, Cambridge CB3 0AP ☎ 01223 699942 ✉ mike.batty@cambridgeshire.gov.uk

Pensions: Mr Steve Dainty Head of Pensions, Shire Hall, Shire Hall, Cambridge CB3 0AP ☎ 0345 045 5200 ✉ steve.dainty@cambridgeshire.gov.uk

Grounds Maintenance: Mr Richard Ware Head of Catering & Cleaning Services, CC 1105, Shire Hall, Castle Hill, Cambridge CB3 0AP ☎ 01223 703509 ✉ richard.ware@cambridgeshire.gov.uk

Health and Safety: Mr Chris Young Health & Safety Manager, RES 1413, Shire Hall, Castle Hill, Cambridge CB3 0AP ☎ 01223 699253 ✉ chris.young@cambridgeshire.gov.uk

Highways: Mr Richard Lumley Head of Local Infrastructure & Street Management, SH1204, Shire Hall, Castle Hill, Cambridge CB3 0AP ☎ 01223 703839 ✉ richard.lumley@cambridgeshire.gov.uk

Legal: Mr Quentin Baker Director of Legal Services, Shire Hall, Shire Hall, Cambridge CB3 0AP ☎ 01223 727961 ✉ quentin.baker@cambridgeshire.gov.uk

Lighting: Mr Richard Ling Signals & Systems Manager, Welbrook Court, Girton, Cambridge CB3 0NA ☎ 01223 715916 ✉ richard.ling@cambridgeshire.gov.uk

Lottery Funding, Charity and Voluntary: Mr Robert Sanderson, Senior Democratic Services Officer, Box ET 1021, Shire Hall, Castle Hill, Cambridge CB3 0AP ☎ 01223 699181 ✉ robert.sanderson@cambridgeshire.gov.uk

Member Services: Ms Karin Aston Member Services Officer, SH1102, Shire Hall, Castle Hill, Cambridge CB3 0AP ☎ 01223 699170 ✉ karin.astin@cambridgeshire.gov.uk

Parking: Mr Philip Hammer Parking Operations Manager, RES1416, Shire Hall, Castle Hill, Cambridge CB3 0AP ☎ 01223 727901 ✉ philip.hammer@cambridgeshire.gov.uk

Planning: Mr Bob Menzies Service Director - Strategy & Development, CC1307, Shire Hall, Castle Hill, Cambridge CB3 0AP ☎ 01223 715664 ✉ bob.menzies@cambridgeshire.gov.uk

Public Libraries: Ms Christine May Head of Libraries, Archives & Information, Box CC 1218, Shire Hall, Castle Hill, Cambridge CB3 0AP ☎ 01223 703521 ✉ christine.may@cambridgeshire.gov.uk

Recycling & Waste Minimisation: Mr Donald Haymes Waste Services Manager, Box CC 1215, Shire Hall, Castle Hill, Cambridge CB3 0AP ☎ 01223 728560 ✉ donald.haymes@cambridgeshire.gov.uk

Road Safety: Ms Amanda Mays Road Safety Manager, CC1309, Cambridgeshire Highways, Welbrooke Court, Girton, Cambridge CB3 0NA ☎ 01223 715923 ✉ amanda.mays@cambridgeshire.gov.uk

Social Services: Ms Jean Fletcher Head of Procurement (Social Care), Box CC 1006, Shire Hall, Castle Hill, Cambridge CB3 0AP ☎ 01223 729130 ✉ jean.fletcher@cambridgeshire.gov.uk

Social Services: Ms Sarah-Jane Smedmore Head of Safeguarding & Standards, CC1005, Shire Hall, Castle Hill, Cambridge CB3 0AP ☎ 01223 699920 ✉ sarah-jane.smedmore@cambridgeshire.gov.uk

Social Services (Adult): Ms Charlotte Black Director - Older People's Services & Mental Health, CC1323, Shire Hall, Castle Hill, Cambridge CB3 0AP ☎ 01223 727993 ✉ charlotte.black@cambridgeshire.gov.uk

CAMBRIDGESHIRE

Social Services (Adult): Ms Claire Bruin, Service Director of Adult Social Care, Box CC1315, Castle Court, Shire Hall, Castle Hill, Cambridge CB3 0AP ☎ 01223 715665 ✉ claire.bruin@cambridgeshire.gov.uk

Social Services (Adult): Mr Adrian Loades Executive Director - Children, Families & Adults, CC 1001, Shire Hall, Cambridge CB3 0AP ☎ 01223 727993 ✉ adrian.loades@cambridgeshire.gov.uk

Social Services (Children): Mr John Gregg Interim Director - Social Care, Children & Young People Services, CC 1001, Shire Hall, Cambridge CB3 0AP ☎ 01223 727989 🖷 01223 717307 ✉ john.gregg@cambridgeshire.gov.uk

Social Services (Children): Mr Adrian Loades Executive Director - Children, Families & Adults, Box CC 1001, Shire Hall, Castle Hill, Cambridge CB3 0AP ☎ 01223 727993 ✉ adrian.loades@cambridgeshire.gov.uk

Public Health: Dr Liz Robin Director - Public Health, Box ET 1021, Shire Hall, Castle Hill, Cambridge CB3 0AP ☎ 0345 045 5200 ✉ liz.robin@cambridgeshire.gov.uk

Staff Training: Mr Rob Parker Organisational & Workforce Development Advisor, RES 1227, Shire Hall, Castle Hill, Cambridge CB3 0AP ☎ 01223 706337 ✉ rob.parker@cambridgeshire.gov.uk

Transport: Mr Joseph Whelan Head of Passenger Transport, CC 1212, Shire Hall, Castle Hill, Cambridge CB3 0AP ☎ 01223 715585 ✉ joseph.whelan@cambridgeshire.gov.uk

Transport Planner: Ms Dearbhla Lawson Head of Service for Transport, Infrastructure Policy & Funding, Box 1301, Shire Hall, Castle Hill, Cambridge CB3 0AP ☎ 01223 714695 ✉ dearhbla.lawson@cambridgeshire.gov.uk

COUNCILLORS

***Leader of the Council* Count**, Steve (CON - March North)
steve.count@cambridgeshire.gov.uk

***Group Leader* Hipkin**, John (IND - Castle)
john.hipkin@cambridgeshire.gov.uk

***Group Leader* Nethsingha**, Lucy (LD - Newnham)
nethsingha@btinternet.com

Ashcroft, Peter (UKIP - Huntingdon)
peter.ashcroft@cambridgeshire.gov.uk

Ashwood, Barbara (LD - Trumpington)
barbara.ashwood@cambridgeshire.gov.uk

Bailey, Anna (CON - Ely South & West)
anna.bailey@cambridgeshire.gov.uk

Bates, Ian (CON - The Hemingfords & Fenstanton)
ian.bates@cambridgeshire.gov.uk

Boden, Chris (CON - Whittlesey North)
chris.boden@cambridgeshire.gov.uk

Brown, Peter (CON - Huntingdon)
sirpeter.brown@cambridgeshire.gov.uk

Brown, David (CON - Burwell)
david.brown@cambridgeshire.gov.uk

Bullen, Paul (UKIP - St Ives)
paul.bullen@cambridgeshire.gov.uk

Butcher, Ralph (CON - Whittlesey South)
butcher919@btinternet.com

Bywater, Simon (UKIP - Sawtry & Ellington)
simon.bywater@cambridgeshire.gov.uk

Cearns, Edward (LD - Market)
edward.cearns@cambridgeshire.gov.uk

Chapman, Barry (CON - Little Paxton & St Neots North)
barry.champan@cambridgeshire.gov.uk

Clapp, Paul (UKIP - Wisbech North)
paul.clapp@cambridgeshire.gov.uk

Clark, John (CON - March West)
johnclark786@btinternet.com

Connor, David (CON - Forty Foot)
david.connor@cambridgeshire.gov.uk

Crawford, Sandra (LAB - Cherry Hinton)
sandra.crawford@cambridgeshire.gov.uk

Criswell, Steve (CON - Somersham & Earith)
steve.criswell@cambridgeshire.gov.uk

Dent, Adrian (CON - Bassingbourn)
adrian.dent@cambridgeshire.gov.uk

Divine, Daniel (UKIP - Littleport)
daniel.divine@cambridgeshire.gov.uk

Downes, Peter (LD - Brampton & Kimbolton)
peter.downes@cambridgeshire.gov.uk

Frost, Stephen (CON - Hardwick)
stephen.frost@cambridgeshire.gov.uk

Giles, Derek (IND - St Neots Eaton Socon & Eynesbury)
derek.giles@cambridgeshire.gov.uk

Gillick, Gordon (UKIP - Waldersey)
gordon.gillick@cambridgeshire.gov.uk

Harford, Lynda (CON - Bar Hill)
lyndaharford@icloud.com

Harty, David (CON - Little Paxton & St Neots North)
david.harty@cambridgeshire.gov.uk

Henson, Roger (UKIP - Norman Cross)
roger.henson@cambridgeshire.gov.uk

Hickford, Roger (CON - Linton)
roger.hickford@cambridgeshire.gov.uk

Hoy, Samantha (CON - Wisbech South)
samantha.hoy@cambridgeshire.gov.uk

Hudson, Peter (CON - Willingham)
peter.hudson@cambridgeshire.gov.uk

Hunt, William (CON - Haddenham)
william.hunt@cambridgeshire.gov.uk

Jenkins, David (LD - Cottenham, Histon & Impington)
ccc@davidjenkins.org.uk

Kavanagh, Noel (LAB - Coleridge)
noel.kavanagh@cambridgeshire.gov.uk

Kenney, Gail (CON - Sawston)
gail.kenney@cambridgeshire.gov.uk

Kindersley, Sebastian (LD - Gamlingay)
skindersley@hotmail.com

Lay, Alan (UKIP - Roman Bank & Peckover)
alan.lay@cambridgeshire.gov.uk

Leeke, Maurice (LD - Waterbeach)
maurice.leeke@cambridgeshire.gov.uk

Loynes, Mervyn (CON - Bourn)
mervyn.loynes@cambridgeshire.gov.uk

Manning, Ian (LD - East Chesterton)
manning.ian@gmail.com

Mason, Mike (IND - Cottenham, Histon & Impington)
mike.mason@cambridgeshire.gov.uk

McGuire, Mac (CON - Norman Cross)
mac.mcguire@cambridgeshire.gov.uk

Moghadas, Zoe (LAB - Romsey)
zoe.moghadas@cambridgeshire.gov.uk

Onasanya, Fiona (LAB - King's Hedges)
fiona.onasanya@cambridgeshire.gov.uk

Orgee, Tony (CON - Sawston)
tony.orgee@cambridgeshire.gov.uk

Palmer, James (CON - Soham & Fordham Villages)
jpp@oakhouse@gmail.com

Read, Philip (CON - Sutton)
philip.read@eastcambs.gov.uk

Reeve, Peter (UKIP - Ramsey)
reeve@ukip.org

Reynolds, Kevin (CON - St Ives)
kevin.reynolds@cambridgeshire.gov.uk

Rouse, Michael (CON - Ely North & East)
michael.rouse@cambridgeshire.gov.uk

Rylance, Sandra (UKIP - Chatteris)
sandra.rylance@cambridgeshire.gov.uk

Sales, Paul (LAB - Arbury)
cccpaul.sales@gmail.com

Schumann, Joshua (CON - Soham & Fordham Villages)
joshua.schumann@cambridgeshire.gov.uk

Scutt, Jocelynne (LAB - West Chesterton)
jocelynne.scutt@cambridgeshire.gov.uk

Shellens, Michael (LD - Godmanchester & Huntingdon East)
shellens@waitrose.com

Shuter, Mathew (CON - Woodditton)
mshuter@btinternet.com

Smith, Mandy (CON - Papworth & Swavesey)
mandysmith310@btinternet.com

Taylor, Amanda (LD - Queen Edith's)
amanda.taylor@cambridgeshire.gov.uk

Tew, Michael (UKIP - Warboys & Upwood)
michael.tew@cambridgeshire.gov.uk

Topping, Peter (CON - Duxford)
peter.topping@cambridgeshire.gov.uk

Van de Kerkhove, Steven (IND - St Neots Eaton Socon & Eynesbury)
steven.vandekerkhove@cambridgeshire.gov.uk

van de Ven, Susan (LD - Melbourn)
susanvendeven@yahoo.co.uk

Walsh, Ashley (LAB - Petersfield)
ashley.walsh@cambridgeshire.gov.uk

Whitehead, Joan (LAB - Abbey)
joan.whitehead@cambridgeshire.gov.uk

Williams, John (LD - Fulbourn)
john.williams@cambridgeshire.gov.uk

Wilson, Graham (LD - Godmanchester & Huntingdon East)
graham.wilson@cambridgeshire.gov.uk

Wisson, Julie (CON - Buckden, Gransden & The Offords)
julie.wisson@cambridgeshire.gov.uk

Yeulett, Frederick (CON - March East)
fred.yeulett@cambridgeshire.gov.uk

POLITICAL COMPOSITION
CON: 33, LD: 13, UKIP: 11, LAB: 8, IND: 4

Camden L

Camden London Borough Council, Town Hall, Judd Street, London WC1H 9JE
☎ 020 7974 4444 🖳 www.camden.gov.uk

FACTS AND FIGURES
Parliamentary Constituencies: Hampstead and Kilburn, Holborn and St. Pancras
EU Constituencies: London
Election Frequency: Elections are of whole council

PRINCIPAL OFFICERS

Chief Executive: Mr Mike Cooke, Chief Executive, Town Hall, Judd Street, London WC1H 9JE ☎ 020 7974 5686 🖷 020 7974 5998 🖰 mike.cooke@camden.gov.uk

Deputy Chief Executive: Ms Rachel Stopard Deputy Chief Executive - Transformation & Policy, 5 St Pancras Square, London N1C 4AG ☎ 020 7974 5621 🖷 020 7974 5556 🖰 rachel.stopard@camden.gov.uk

Senior Management: Dr Julie Billett Director - Public Health, 5 St Pancras Square, London N1C 4AG ☎ 020 7527 1221 🖰 julie.billett@camden.gov.uk

Senior Management: Mr Mike O'Donnell, Director - Finance, 5 St Pancras Square, London N1C 4AG ☎ 020 7974 5933 🖰 mike.odonnell@camden.gov.uk

Senior Management: Mr Martin Pratt Director - Children, Schools & Families, 5 St Pancras Square, London N1C 4AG ☎ 020 7974 1505 🖰 martin.pratt@camden.gov.uk

Senior Management: Mr Ed Watson Director - Culture & Environment, 5 St Pancras Square, London N1C 4AG ☎ 020 7974 5622 🖰 ed.watson@camden.gov.uk

Senior Management: Ms Rosemary Westbrook Director - Housing & Adult Social Care, 5 St Pancras Square, London N1C 4AG ☎ 020 7974 5577 🖰 rosemary.westbrook@camden.gov.uk

Access Officer / Social Services (Disability): Ms Angela Neblett Head of Strategy & Comm/Mental Health/Subst Abuse, 5 St Pancras Square, London N1C 4AG ☎ 020 7974 6717 🖰 angela.neblett@camden.gov.uk

CAMDEN

Building Control: Mr Nasser Rad Head of Service - Building Control, 5 St Pancras Square, London N1C 4AG ☎ 020 7974 2387 🖱 nasser.rad@camden.gov.uk

Catering Services: Ms Jean Darko Assistant Facilities Management Contract & Performance Manager, 5 St Pancras Square, London N1C 4AG ☎ 020 7974 5072 🖱 jean.darko@camden.gov.uk

Children / Youth Services: Mr Martin Pratt Director - Children, Schools & Families, 5 St Pancras Square, London N1C 4AG ☎ 020 7974 1505 🖱 martin.pratt@camden.gov.uk

Civil Registration: Ms Jenni Grant, Registration Services Team Leader / Superintendent Registrar, Town Hall, Judd Street, London WC1H 9JE ☎ 020 7974 1057 🖷 020 7974 5792 🖱 jenni.grant@camden.gov.uk

PR / Communications: Ms Kathryn Myers Head of Communications, 5 St Pancras Square, London N1C 4AG ☎ 020 7974 6020 🖱 kathryn.myers@camden.gov.uk

Community Safety: Mr Tom Preest Head of Community Safety Services, 5 St Pancras Square, London N1C 4AG ☎ 020 7974 3461 🖱 tom.preest@camden.gov.uk

Computer Management: Mr John Jackson, Assistant Director - ICT, 5 St Pancras Square, London N1C 4AG ☎ 020 7974 1529 🖱 john.jackson@camden.gov.uk

Consumer Protection and Trading Standards: Mr Jim Foudy Head of Regulatory Services, 5 St Pancras Square, London N1C 4AG ☎ 020 7974 6962 🖷 020 7974 6940 🖱 jim.foudy@camden.gov.uk

Contracts: Mr Garry Griffiths Head of Joint Commissioning - Community Services, 5 St Pancras Square, London N1C 4AG ☎ 020 7974 2579 🖱 garry.griffiths@camden.gov.uk

Corporate Services: Ms Rachel Stopard Deputy Chief Executive - Transformation & Policy, 5 St Pancras Square, London N1C 4AG ☎ 020 7974 5621 🖷 020 7974 5556 🖱 rachel.stopard@camden.gov.uk

Customer Service: Ms Fiona Dean Assistant Director of Culture & Customers, 5 St Pancras Square, London N1C 4AG ☎ 020 7974 4172 🖱 fiona.dean@camden.gov.uk

Economic Development: Ms Karen Galey Head of Economic Development, 5 St Pancras Square, London N1C 4AG ☎ 020 7974 4059 🖱 karen.galey@camden.gov.uk

E-Government: Mr John Jackson, Assistant Director - ICT, 5 St Pancras Square, London N1C 4AG ☎ 020 7974 1529 🖱 john.jackson@camden.gov.uk

Electoral Registration: Ms Clare Oakley Elections Manager, Town Hall, Judd Street, London WC1H 9JE ☎ 020 7974 6372 🖱 clare.oakley@camden.gov.uk

Emergency Planning: Mr Trevor King Business Continuity Manager, 1st Floor, Borough Emergency Control Centre, Dennis Geffen Annexe, Camley Street, London NW1 0PS ☎ 020 7974 3495 🖷 020 7974 4904 🖱 trevor.king@camden.gov.uk

Emergency Planning: Mr Darren Wilsher Head of Emergency Management, Borough Emergency Control Centre, Dennis Geffen Annexe, Camley Street, London NW1 0PS ☎ 020 7974 2797 🖱 darren.wilsher@camden.gov.uk

Energy Management: Mr Harold Garner Energy & Sustainability Manager, 5 St Pancras Square, London N1C 4AG ☎ 020 7974 2701 🖱 harold.garner@camden.gov.uk

Environmental / Technical Services: Mr Ed Watson Director - Culture & Environment, 5 St Pancras Square, London N1C 4AG ☎ 020 7974 5622 🖱 ed.watson@camden.gov.uk

Environmental Health: Mr Andrew Woolmer Private Sector Housing Team Manager, 5 St Pancras Square, London N1C 4AG ☎ 020 7974 2159 🖷 020 7974 6955 🖱 andrew.woolmer@camden.gov.uk

Facilities: Mr Richard Spear Category Manager of FM & Capital, 5 St Pancras Square, London N1C 4AG ☎ 020 7974 4337 🖷 020 7974 1649 🖱 richard.spear@camden.gov.uk

Finance: Mr Mike O'Donnell, Director - Finance, 5 St Pancras Square, London N1C 4AG ☎ 020 7974 5933 🖱 mike.odonnell@camden.gov.uk

Finance: Mr Jon Rowney Deputy Director - Finance, 5 St Pancras Square, London N1C 4AG ☎ 020 7974 6960 🖱 jon.rowney@camden.gov.uk

Treasury: Mr Nigel Mascarenhas Head of Treasury & Financial Transactions, Crowndale Centre, 218 Eversholt Street, London NW1 1BD ☎ 020 7974 1904 🖱 nigel.mascarenhas@camden.gov.uk

Fleet Management: Mr Richard Clarke Fleet & Depot Manager, 7 York Way, London N1C 4BE ☎ 020 7974 5655 🖱 richard.clarke@camden.gov.uk

Grounds Maintenance: Mr Oliver Myers, Head of Sustainability & Green Space, 5 St Pancras Square, London N1C 4AG ☎ 020 7974 6370 🖱 oliver.myers@camden.gov.uk

Health and Safety: Ms Vivienne Broadhurst Head of Adult Social Care & Safeguarding, 5 St Pancras Square, London N1C 4AG ☎ 020 7974 6092 🖱 vivienne.broadhurst@camden.gov.uk

Health and Safety: Mr Darren Williams Health & Safety Manager, 5 St Pancras Square, London N1C 4AG ☎ 020 7974 2117 🖱 darren.williams@camden.gov.uk

Highways: Mr George Loureda Head of Engineering Service, 5 St Pancras Square, London N1C 4AG ☎ 020 7974 6949 🖱 george.loureda@camden.gov.uk

Home Energy Conservation: Mr Oliver Myers, Head of Sustainability & Green Space, 5 St Pancras Square, London N1C 4AG ☎ 020 7974 6370 🖱 oliver.myers@camden.gov.uk

Housing: Mr Tim Bishop Assistant Director - Adult Social Care & Joint Commissioning, 5 St Pancras Square, London N1C 4AG ☎ 020 7974 1441 🖱 tim.bishop@camden.gov.uk

Housing: Mr Stuart Dilley Assistant Director - Housing Repairs & Improvement, 5 St Pancras Square, London N1C 4AG ☎ 020 7974 2811 ✉ stuart.dilley@camden.gov.uk

Housing: Mr Rhys Makinson Assistant Director - Housing Needs & Resourcing, 5 St Pancras Square, London N1C 4AG ☎ 020 7974 3518 ✉ rhys.makinson@camden.gov.uk

Housing: Ms Mary McGowan Assistant Director - Housing Management, 5 St Pancras Square, London N1C 4AG ☎ 020 7974 5804 ✉ mary.mcgowan@camden.gov.uk

Housing: Ms Rosemary Westbrook Director - Housing & Adult Social Care, 5 St Pancras Square, London N1C 4AG ☎ 020 7974 5577 ✉ rosemary.westbrook@camden.gov.uk

Housing Maintenance: Mr Ross Barber Team Mananger - Major Repairs, Ground Floor, Holmes Road Depot, 79 Holmes Road, London NW5 3AP ☎ 020 7974 6763 ✉ ross.barber@camden.gov.uk

Housing Maintenance: Mr Kim Wells, Head of Camden Repairs, Holmes Road Depot, 79 Holmes Road, London NW5 3AP ☎ 020 7974 1746 🖷 020 7974 5371 ✉ kim.wells@camden.gov.uk

Legal: Mr Andrew Maughan Borough Solicitor, 5 St Pancras Square, London N1C 4AG ☎ 020 7974 5656 ✉ andrew.maughan@camden.gov.uk

Leisure and Cultural Services: Ms Fiona Dean Assistant Director of Culture & Customers, 5 St Pancras Square, London N1C 4AG ☎ 020 7974 4172 ✉ fiona.dean@camden.gov.uk

Leisure and Cultural Services: Ms Caroline Jenkinson, Head of Arts & Tourism, 5 St Pancras Square, London N1C 4AG ☎ 020 7974 1685 ✉ caroline.jenkinson@camden.gov.uk

Leisure and Cultural Services: Mr Nigel Robinson Head of Sport & Physical Activities, 5 St Pancras Square, London N1C 4AG ☎ 020 7974 1614 ✉ nigel.robinson@camden.gov.uk

Leisure and Cultural Services: Mr Ed Watson Director - Culture & Environment, 5 St Pancras Square, London N1C 4AG ☎ 020 7974 5622 ✉ ed.watson@camden.gov.uk

Licensing: Mr Jim Foudy Head of Regulatory Services, 5 St Pancras Square, London N1C 4AG ☎ 020 7974 6962 🖷 020 7974 6940 ✉ jim.foudy@camden.gov.uk

Lifelong Learning: Ms Helen Holden Acting Head of Adult Community Learning, 5 St Pancras Square, London N1C 4AG ☎ 020 7974 2162 ✉ helen.holden@camden.gov.uk

Lighting: Mr Martin Reading Implementation & Maintenance Manager, 5 St Pancras Square, London N1C 4AG ☎ 020 7974 2018 ✉ martin.reading@camden.gov.uk

Lottery Funding, Charity and Voluntary: Ms Fiona McKeith Head of Communities & Third Sector, 5 St Pancras Square, London N1C 4AG ☎ 020 7974 1547 ✉ fiona.mckeith@camden.gov.uk

Member Services: Ms Olivia Mensah Head of Member Support, Town Hall, Judd Street, London WC1H 9JE ☎ 020 7974 6409 ✉ olivia.mensah@camden.gov.uk

Member Services: Ms Asha Paul Head of Democratic Services, Town Hall, Judd Street, London WC1H 9JE ☎ 020 7974 5944 🖷 020 7974 5921 ✉ asha.paul@camden.gov.uk

Parking: Ms Nicolina Cooper Head of Parking Services, 5 St Pancras Square, London N1C 4AG ☎ 020 7974 4678 ✉ nicolina.cooper@camden.gov.uk

Partnerships: Ms Karen Swift Head of Strategy, Performance & Partnerships, 5 St Pancras Square, London N1C 4AG ☎ 020 7974 2195 ✉ karen.swift@camden.gov.uk

Personnel / HR: Ms Joanna Brown Assistant Director - HR, 5 St Pancras Square, London N1C 4AG ☎ 020 7974 6302 ✉ joanna.brown@camden.gov.uk

Planning: Mr Brian O'Donnell Strategic Planning & Information Manager, 5 St Pancras Square, London N1C 4AG ☎ 020 7974 5502 ✉ brian.o'donnell@camden.gov.uk

Procurement: Ms Lorraine Colledge Head of Strategic Procurement, 5 St Pancras Square, London N1C 4AG ☎ 020 7974 2827 ✉ lorraine.colledge@camden.gov.uk

Public Libraries: Mr Sam Eastop Head of Libraries & Registration Services, 5 St Pancras Square, London N1C 4AG ☎ 020 7974 6248 ✉ sam.eastop@camden.gov.uk

Recycling & Waste Minimisation: Mr Richard Bradbury Head of Environment Services, 211 Arlington Road, London NW1 7HD ☎ 020 7974 3725 ✉ richard.bradbury@camden.gov.uk

Regeneration: Ms Melissa Dillon Head of Regeneration & Development, 1st Floor, 33-35 Jamestown Road, London NW1 7DB ☎ 020 7974 3100 ✉ melissa.dillon@camden.gov.uk

Road Safety: Mr Robert Curtis Transport Policy Team Manager, 5 St Pancras Square, London N1C 4AG ☎ 020 7974 8904 ✉ robert.curtis@camden.gov.uk

Social Services (Adult): Mr Tim Bishop Assistant Director - Adult Social Care & Joint Commissioning, 5 St Pancras Square, London N1C 4AG ☎ 020 7974 1441 ✉ tim.bishop@camden.gov.uk

Social Services (Adult): Ms Vivienne Broadhurst Head of Adult Social Care & Safeguarding, 5 St Pancras Square, London N1C 4AG ☎ 020 7974 6092 ✉ vivienne.broadhurst@camden.gov.uk

Social Services (Children): Ms Anne Turner Assistant Director of Children, Schools & Families, 5 St Pancras Square, London N1C 4AG ☎ 020 7974 6641 ✉ anne.turner@camden.gov.uk

Childrens Social Care: Ms Anne Turner Assistant Director of Children, Schools & Families, 5 St Pancras Square, London N1C 4AG ☎ 020 7974 6641 ✉ anne.turner@camden.gov.uk

CAMDEN

Public Health: Dr Julie Billett Director - Public Health, 5 St Pancras Square, London N1C 4AG ☎ 020 7527 1221 ✉ julie.billett@camden.gov.uk

Staff Training: Ms Joanna Brown Assistant Director - HR, 5 St Pancras Square, London N1C 4AG ☎ 020 7974 6302 ✉ joanna.brown@camden.gov.uk

Sustainable Development: Mr Oliver Myers, Head of Sustainability & Green Space, 5 St Pancras Square, London N1C 4AG ☎ 020 7974 6370 ✉ oliver.myers@camden.gov.uk

Tourism: Ms Caroline Jenkinson, Head of Arts & Tourism, 5 St Pancras Square, London N1C 4AG ☎ 020 7974 1685 ✉ caroline.jenkinson@camden.gov.uk

Transport: Ms Louise McBride Head of Transport Strategy, 5 St Pancras Square, London N1C 4AG ☎ 020 7974 5543 ✉ louise.mcbride@camden.gov.uk

Transport Planner: Ms Josephine Allman Head of Camden Accessible Travel Solutions, York Way Depot, 7 York Way, London N1C 4BE ☎ 020 7974 5560 ✉ josephine.allman@camden.gov.uk

Waste Collection and Disposal: Mr Richard Bradbury Head of Environment Services, 211 Arlington Road, London NW1 7HD ☎ 020 7974 3725 ✉ richard.bradbury@camden.gov.uk

Waste Management: Mr David Beadle Managing Director of North London Waste Authority, c/o Unit 169, Lee Valley Technopark, Ashley Road, London N17 9LN ☎ 020 8489 5665 ✉ david.beadle@camden.gov.uk

COUNCILLORS

***Mayor* Revah**, Larraine (LAB - Gospel Oak)
larraine.revah@camden.gov.uk

***Deputy Mayor* Shah**, Nadia (LAB - Regent's Park)
nadia.shah@camden.gov.uk

***Leader of the Council* Hayward**, Sarah (LAB - King's Cross)
sarah.hayward@camden.gov.uk

***Deputy Leader of the Council* Callaghan**, Patricia (LAB - Camden Town with Primrose Hill)
patricia.callaghan@camden.gov.uk

Tomlinson, Paul (LAB - Sr Pancras & Somers Town)
paul.tomlinson@camden.gov.uk

Ali, Nasim (LAB - Regent's Park)
nasim.ali@camden.gov.uk

Apak, Meric (LAB - Kentish Town)
meric.apak@camden.gov.uk

Baillie, Siobhan (CON - Frognal & Fitzjohns)
siobhan.baillie@camden.gov.uk

Beales, Danny (LAB - Cantelowes)
danny.beales@camden.gov.uk

Beattie, Douglas (LAB - Kilburn)
douglas.beattie@camden.gov.uk

Berry, Sian (GRN - Highgate)
sian.berry@camden.gov.uk

Blackwell, Theo (LAB - Gospel Oak)
theo.blackwell@camden.gov.uk

Bucknell, Jonny (CON - Belsize)
jonny.bucknell@camden.gov.uk

Cooper, Olivar (CON - Hapstead Town)
oliver.cooper@camden.gov.uk

Cotton, Richard (LAB - Camden Town with Primrose Hill)
richard.cotton@camden.gov.uk

Currie, Tom (CON - Hampstead Town)
tom.currie@camden.gov.uk

Eslamdoust, Maryam (LAB - Kilburn)
maryam.eslamdoust@camden.gov.uk

Francis, Sabrina (LAB - Bloomsbury)
sabrina.francis@camden.gov.uk

Freeman, Roger (CON - Swiss Cottage)
roger.freeman@camden.gov.uk

Fulbrook, Julian (LAB - Holborn & Covent Garden)
julian.fulbrook@camden.gov.uk

Gardiner, Thomas (LAB - Kilburn)
thomas.gardiner@camden.gov.uk

Gimson, Sally (LAB - Highgate)
sally.gimson@camden.gov.uk

Gould, Georgia (LAB - Kentish Town)
georgia.gould@camden.gov.uk

Hai, Abdul (LAB - King's Cross)
abdul.hai@camden.gov.uk

Harrison, Adam (LAB - Bloomsbury)
adam.harrison@camden.gov.uk

Headlam-Wells, Jenny (LAB - Kentish Town)
jenny.headlam-wells@camden.gov.uk

Johnson, Heather (LAB - Regent's Park)
heather.johnson@camden.gov.uk

Jones, Phil (LAB - Cantelowes)
phil.jones@camden.gov.uk

Kelly, Alison (LAB - Haverstock)
alison.kelly@camden.gov.uk

Khatoon, Samata (LAB - St Pancras & Somers Town)
samata.khatoon@camden.gov.uk

Lewis, Oliver (LAB - Highgate)
oliver.lewis@camden.gov.uk

Leyland, Claire-Louise (CON - Belsize)
claire-louise.leyland@camden.gov.uk

Madlani, Rishi (LAB - Bloomsbury)
rishi.madlani@camden.gov.uk

Marshall, Andrew (CON - Swiss Cottage)
andrew.marshall@camden.gov.uk

Mason, Angela (LAB - Cantelowes)
angela.mason@camden.gov.uk

McCormack, Maeve (LAB - Gospel Oak)
maeve.mccormack@camden.gov.uk

Mennear, Andrew (CON - Frognal & Fitzjohns)
andrew.mennear@camden.gov.uk

Olad, Awale (LAB - Holborn & Covent Garden)
awale.olad@camden.gov.uk

Olszewski, Richard (LAB - Fortune Green)
richard.olszewski@camden.gov.uk

Pietragnoli, Lazzaro (LAB - Camden Town with Primrose Hill)
lazzaro.pietragnoli@camden.gov.uk

Pober, Angela (LAB - West Hampstead)
angela.pober@camden.gov.uk

Quadir, Abdul (LAB - Haverstock)
abdul.quadir@camden.gov.uk

Rea, Flick (LD - Fortune Green)
flick.rea@camden.gov.uk

Robinson, Roger (LAB - St Pancras & Somers Town)
roger.robinson@camden.gov.uk

Rosenberg, Phil (LAB - West Hampstead)
phil.rosenberg@camden.gov.uk

Roy, Leila (CON - Belsize)
leila.roy@camden.gov.uk

Russell, Lorna (LAB - Fortune Green)
lorna.russell@camden.gov.uk

Simpson, Jonathan (LAB - King's Cross)
jonathan.simpson@camden.gov.uk

Spinella, Gio (CON - Frognal & Fitzjohns)
gio.spinella@camden.gov.uk

Stark, Stephen (CON - Hampstead Town)
stephen.stark@camden.gov.uk

Vincent, Sue (LAB - Holborn & Covent Garden)
sue.vincent@camden.gov.uk

Williams, Don (CON - Swiss Cottage)
don.williams@camden.gov.uk

Wood, Abi (LAB - Haverstock)
abi.wood@camden.gov.uk

Yarde, James (LAB - West Hampstead)
james.yarde@camden.gov.uk

POLITICAL COMPOSITION

LAB: 40, CON: 12, LD: 1, GRN: 1

COMMITTEE CHAIRS

Audit: Ms Maeve McCormack

Children School & Families: Ms Jenny Headlam-Wells

Health & Adult Social Care: Ms Alison Kelly

Licensing: Ms Maryam Eslamdoust

Cannock Chase D

Cannock Chase District Council, Civic Centre, PO Box 28, Cannock WS11 1BG
☎ 01543 462621 🖷 01543 462317
customerservices@cannockchasedc.gov.uk
www.cannockchasedc.gov.uk

FACTS AND FIGURES

Parliamentary Constituencies: Cannock Chase
EU Constituencies: West Midlands
Election Frequency: Elections are by thirds

PRINCIPAL OFFICERS

Chief Executive: Mr Tony McGovern Managing Director, Civic Centre, Beecroft Road, Cannock WS11 1BG ☎ 01543 464438
tonymcgovern@cannockchasedc.gov.uk

Architect, Building / Property Services: Mr Michael Tichford Head of Economic Development, Civic Centre, PO Box 28, Cannock WS11 1BG ☎ 01543 464223
michaeltichford@cannockchasedc.gov.uk

Best Value: Mrs Judith Aupers, Head of Governance, Civic Centre, PO Box 28, Beecroft Road, Cannock WS11 1BG ☎ 01543 464411
judithaupers@cannockchasedc.gov.uk

Building Control: Mr Paul Beckley, Building Control Manager, Stafford Borough Council, Civic Centre, Riverside, Stafford ST16 3AQ ☎ 01785 619311 paulbeckley@cannockchasedc.gov.uk

PR / Communications: Miss Kerry Wright Partnerships & Communications Manager, Civic Centre, PO Box 28, Cannock WS11 1BG ☎ 01543 464368 kerrywright@cannockchasedc.gov.uk

Community Safety: Miss Kerry Wright Partnerships & Communications Manager, Civic Centre, PO Box 28, Cannock WS11 1BG ☎ 01543 464368 kerrywright@cannockchasedc.gov.uk

Computer Management: Mr Peter Kendrick Head of Technology, Stafford Borough Council, Civic Centre, Riverside, Stafford ST16 3AQ ☎ 01785 619274 pkendrick@stafford.gov.uk

Contracts: Mrs Judith Aupers, Head of Governance, Civic Centre, PO Box 28, Beecroft Road, Cannock WS11 1BG ☎ 01543 464411
judithaupers@cannockchasedc.gov.uk

Customer Service: Ms Amanda Wilkinson Customer Services & Central Control Manager, Civic Centre, PO Box 28, Cannock WS11 1BG ☎ 01543 464365 amandawilkinson@cannockchase.gov.uk

Economic Development: Mr Michael Tichford Head of Economic Development, Civic Centre, PO Box 28, Cannock WS11 1BG
☎ 01543 464223 michaeltichford@cannockchasedc.gov.uk

Electoral Registration: Mr Steve Partridge, Democratic Services Manager, Civic Centre, PO Box 28, Beecroft Road, Cannock WS11 1BG ☎ 01543 464588 🖷 01543 464321
stevepartridge@cannockchasedc.gov.uk

Emergency Planning: Mrs Judith Aupers, Head of Governance, Civic Centre, PO Box 28, Beecroft Road, Cannock WS11 1BG
☎ 01543 464411 judithaupers@cannockchasedc.gov.uk

Environmental Health: Mr Steve Shilvock, Head of Environmental Health, Civic Centre, Beecroft Road, Cannock WS11 1BG ☎ 01543 464597 🖷 01543 464213
steveshilvock@cannockchasedc.gov.uk

Estates, Property & Valuation: Mr Michael Tichford Head of Economic Development, Civic Centre, PO Box 28, Cannock WS11 1BG ☎ 01543 464223 michaeltichford@cannockchasedc.gov.uk

CANNOCK CHASE

European Liaison: Mr Glenn Watson, Economic Development Manager, Civic Centre, PO Box 28, Beecroft Road, Cannock WS11 1BG ☎ 01543 464529 🖷 01543 570475 ✉ glennwatson@cannockchasedc.gov.uk

Facilities: Mr Michael Tichford Head of Economic Development, Civic Centre, PO Box 28, Cannock WS11 1BG ☎ 01543 464223 ✉ michaeltichford@cannockchasedc.gov.uk

Finance: Mr Bob Kean, Head of Finance, Civic Centre, PO Box 28, Beecroft Road, Cannock WS11 1BG ☎ 01543 464334 ✉ bobkeane@cannockchasedc.gov.uk

Treasury: Mr Bob Kean, Head of Finance, Civic Centre, PO Box 28, Beecroft Road, Cannock WS11 1BG ☎ 01543 464334 ✉ bobkeane@cannockchasedc.gov.uk

Health and Safety: Mr Carl Morgan, Health & Safety Officer, Civic Centre, PO Box 28, Beecroft Road, Cannock WS11 1BG ☎ 01543 464227 🖷 01543 462317 ✉ carlmorgan@cannockchasedc.gov.uk

Legal: Mr Alistair Welch, Head of Law & Administration, Civic Centre, Riverside, Stafford ST16 3AQ ☎ 01785 619204 🖷 01785 619119 ✉ awelch@staffordbc.gov.uk

Leisure and Cultural Services: Mr Mike Edmonds, Head of Commissioning, Civic Centre, PO Box 28, Beecroft Road, Cannock WS11 1BG ☎ 01543 464416 🖷 01543 562317 ✉ mikeedmonds@cannockchasedc.gov.uk

Licensing: Mr Steve Shilvock, Head of Environmental Health, Civic Centre, Beecroft Road, Cannock WS11 1BG ☎ 01543 464597 🖷 01543 464213 ✉ steveshilvock@cannockchasedc.gov.uk

Member Services: Mr Steve Partridge, Democratic Services Manager, Civic Centre, PO Box 28, Beecroft Road, Cannock WS11 1BG ☎ 01543 464588 🖷 01543 464321 ✉ stevepartridge@cannockchasedc.gov.uk

Partnerships: Miss Kerry Wright Partnerships & Communications Manager, Civic Centre, PO Box 28, Cannock WS11 1BG ☎ 01543 464368 ✉ kerrywright@cannockchasedc.gov.uk

Personnel / HR: Mrs Anne Bird Human Resources Manager, Civic Centre, PO Box 28, Cannock WS11 1BG ☎ 01543 464426 🖷 01543 462317 ✉ annebird@cannockchasedc.gov.uk

Personnel / HR: Mr Neville Raby, Head of Human Resources, Civic Centre, Riverside, Stafford ST16 3AQ ☎ 01785 619205 🖷 01785 619450 ✉ nraby@staffordbc.gov.uk

Planning: Mr Michael Tichford Head of Economic Development, Civic Centre, PO Box 28, Cannock WS11 1BG ☎ 01543 464223 ✉ michaeltichford@cannockchasedc.gov.uk

Procurement: Mrs Judith Aupers, Head of Governance, Civic Centre, PO Box 28, Beecroft Road, Cannock WS11 1BG ☎ 01543 464411 ✉ judithaupers@cannockchasedc.gov.uk

Regeneration: Mr Michael Tichford Head of Economic Development, Civic Centre, PO Box 28, Cannock WS11 1BG ☎ 01543 464223 ✉ michaeltichford@cannockchasedc.gov.uk

Staff Training: Mrs Anne Bird Human Resources Manager, Civic Centre, PO Box 28, Cannock WS11 1BG ☎ 01543 464426 🖷 01543 462317 ✉ annebird@cannockchasedc.gov.uk

Tourism: Mrs Debbie Harris Economic Services Manager, Civic Centre, PO Box 28, Cannock WS11 1BG ☎ 01543 464490 ✉ debbie.harris@cannockchase.gov.uk

Town Centre: Mr Glenn Watson, Economic Development Manager, Civic Centre, PO Box 28, Beecroft Road, Cannock WS11 1BG ☎ 01543 464529 🖷 01543 570475 ✉ glennwatson@cannockchasedc.gov.uk

Waste Collection and Disposal: Mr Joss Pressland Waste & Engineering Services Manager, Civic Centre, PO Box 28, Cannock WS11 1BG ☎ 01543 456807 ✉ josspresland@cannockchasedc.gov.uk

Waste Management: Mr Joss Pressland Waste & Engineering Services Manager, Civic Centre, PO Box 28, Cannock WS11 1BG ☎ 01543 456807 ✉ josspresland@cannockchasedc.gov.uk

Children's Play Areas: Mr Tom Walsh Parks & Open Spaces Manager, Civic Centre, Beecroft Road, Cannock WS11 1BG ☎ 01543 434482 ✉ tomwalsh@cannockchasedc.gov.uk

COUNCILLORS

***Leader of the Council* Adamson**, George (LAB - Hednesford Green Heath)
georgeadamson@cannockchasedc.gov.uk

***Deputy Leader of the Council* Alcott**, Gordon (LAB - Cannock North)
gordonalcott@cannockchasedc.gov.uk

Allen, Frank (LAB - Cannock North)
frankallen@cannockchasedc.gov.uk

Alt, Anne (CON - Western Springs)
annealt@cannockchasedc.gov.uk

Anslow, Chris (CON - Cannock West)
chrisanslow@cannockchasedc.gov.uk

Bennett, Carl (LAB - Western Springs)
carlbennett@cannockchasedc.gov.uk

Bernard, Ann (UKIP - Hawks Green)
annbernard@cannockchasedc.gov.uk

Burnett, Graham (CON - Hednesford Green Heath)
grahamburnett@cannockchasedc.gov.uk

Buttery, Martyn (UKIP - Hawks Green)

Cartwright, Sheila (LAB - Hednesford North)
sheilacartwright@cannockchasedc.gov.uk

Christian, Joanne (CON - Hednesford South)
joannechristian@cannockchasedc.gov.uk

Cooper, Jessica (LAB - Cannock North)
jessicacooper@cannockchsedc.gov.uk

Davis, Muriel (LAB - Cannock East)
murieldavis@cannockchasedc.gov.uk

Dean, Alan (UKIP - Heath Hayes East & Wimblebury)
alandean@cannockchasedc.gov.uk

Dudson, Michelle (LAB - Hagley)
michellsdudson@cannockchasedc.gov.uk

Dudson, Alan (LAB - Brereton & Ravenhill)
alandudson@cannockchasedc.gov.uk

Foley, Darren (LAB - Brereton & Ravenhill)
darrenfoley@cannockchasedc.gov.uk

Freeman, Maureen (LAB - Cannock South)
maureenfreeman@cannockchasedc.gov.uk

Gamble, Brian (LAB - Hednesford South)
briangamble@cannockchasedc.gov.uk

Grice, Doris (LAB - Hednesford North)
d.grice316@btinternet.com

Grocott, Michael (IND - Western Springs)
michaelgrocott@cannockchasedc.gov.uk

Hardman, Bill (UKIP - Rawnsley)
billhardman@cannockchasedc.gov.uk

Heath, Jim (CON - Etching Hill and the Heath)
jamesbowater@cannockchasedc.gov.uk

Hoare, Mike (CON - Norton Canes)
michaelhoare@cannockchasedc.gov.uk

Johnson, Tony (LAB - Cannock East)
tonyjohnson@cannockchasedc.gov.uk

Johnson, Justin (CON - Etching Hill & the Heath)
justinjohnson@cannockchasedc.gov.uk

Kraujalis, John (LAB - Cannock South)
johnkraujalis@cannockchasedc.gov.uk

Lea, Colin (CON - Heath Hayes East & Wimblebury)
colinlea@cannockchasedc.gov.uk

Lovell, Andy (LAB - Hagley)
andylovell@cannockchasedc.gov.uk

Mitchell, Christine (LAB - Cannock East)
christinemitchell@cannockchasedc.gov.uk

Molineux, Gerald (LD - Brereton & Ravenhill)
geraldmolineux@cannockchasedc.gov.uk

Peake, Claire (CON - Rawnsley)
clairepeak@cannockchasedc.gov.uk

Pearson, Alan (LAB - Hednesford North)
alanpearson@cannockchasedc.gov.uk

Preece, John (LAB - Norton Canes)
jophnpreece@cannockchasaedc.gov.uk

Snape, Paul (CON - Cannock West)
paulsnape@cannockchasedc.gov.uk

Stretton, Zaphne (LAB - Norton Canes)
zaphnestretton@cannockchasedc.gov.uk

Sutherland, Mike (CON - Hawks Green)
michaelsutherland@cannockchasedc.gov.uk

Sutton, Hyra (CON - Cannock West)
hyrasutton@cannockchasedc.gov.uk

Todd, Diane (LAB - Heath Hayes East & Wimblebury)
dianetodd@cannockchasedc.gov.uk

Whitehouse, Stephanie (UKIP - Etching Hill & the Heath)
stephenaniewhitehouse@canonchasedc.gov.uk

Witton, Paul (LAB - Cannock South)
paulwitton@cannonchasedc.gov.uk

POLITICAL COMPOSITION

LAB: 22, CON: 12, UKIP: 5, IND: 1, LD: 1

COMMITTEE CHAIRS

Development: Ms Jessica Cooper

Development: Mr Alan Pearson

Health & Wellbeing: Ms Michellle Dudson

Canterbury City — D

Canterbury City Council, Council Offices, Military Road, Canterbury CT1 1YW
☎ 01227 862000 🖷 01227 862020 💻 www.canterbury.gov.uk

FACTS AND FIGURES

Parliamentary Constituencies: Canterbury
EU Constituencies: South East
Election Frequency: Elections are of whole council

PRINCIPAL OFFICERS

Chief Executive: Mr Colin Carmichael, Chief Executive, Council Offices, Military Road, Canterbury CT1 1YW ☎ 01227 862082 🖱 colin.carmichael@canterbury.gov.uk

Deputy Chief Executive: Ms Velia Coffey, Deputy Chief Executive, Council Offices, Military Road, Canterbury CT1 1YW ☎ 01227 862149 🖷 01227 862020 🖱 velia.coffey@canterbury.gov.uk

Senior Management: Ms Tricia Marshall Director - Resources, Council Offices, Military Road, Canterbury CT1 1YW ☎ 01227 862393 🖷 01227 862020 🖱 tricia.marshall@canterbury.gov.uk

Architect, Building / Property Services: Mr Martin Bovingdon Estates & Valuation Manager, Council Offices, Military Road, Canterbury CT1 1YW ☎ 01227 862088 🖷 01227 764955 🖱 martin.bovingdon@canterbury.gov.uk

Best Value: Mrs Lorna Ford Head of Strategy, Council Offices, Military Road, Canterbury CT1 1YW ☎ 01227 862068 🖷 01227 471635 🖱 lorna.ford@canterbury.gov.uk

Building Control: Mr Mark Webb Building Control Manager, Council Offices, Military Road, Canterbury CT1 1YW ☎ 01227 862502 🖷 01227 471635 🖱 mark.webb@canterbury.gov.uk

PR / Communications: Mrs Celia Glynn-Williams Head of Communications, Council Offices, Military Road, Canterbury CT1 1YW ☎ 01227 862065 🖱 celia.glynn-williams@canterbury.gov.uk

Community Planning: Mr Ian Brown Assistant Director - Planning & Regeneration, Council Offices, Military Road, Canterbury CT1 1YW ☎ 01227 862193 🖱 ian.brown@canterbury.gov.uk

Community Safety: Mr Doug Rattray Head of Safer Neighbourhoods, Council Offices, Military Road, Canterbury CT1 1YW ☎ 01227 862363 🖷 01227 471635 🖱 doug.rattray@canterbury.gov.uk

Computer Management: Mr Sean Hale Head of ICT, Council Offices, Military Road, Canterbury CT1 1YW ☎ 01227 862082 🖷 01227 862208 🖱 saen.hale@ekservices.org

Contracts: Mrs Janice McGuinness, Assistant Director - Commissioned Services, Council Offices, Military Road, Canterbury CT1 1YW ☎ 01227 862492 🖷 01227 470599 janice.mcguinness@canterbury.gov.uk

Corporate Services: Ms Tricia Marshall Director - Resources, Council Offices, Military Road, Canterbury CT1 1YW ☎ 01227 862393 🖷 01227 862020 tricia.marshall@canterbury.gov.uk

Customer Service: Mr Andrew Stevens Assistant Director - Customer Delivery, Council Offices, Military Road, Canterbury CT1 1YW ☎ 01227 862101 andrew.stevens@ekservices.org

Economic Development: Ms Caroline Hicks Head of Business & Regeneration, Council Offices, Military Road, Canterbury CT1 1YW ☎ 01227 862054 🖷 01227 470599 caroline.hicks@canterbury.gov.uk

E-Government: Mrs Roz Edridge, Business Systems Manager, East Kent Services, Council Offices, Cecil Street, Margate CT9 1XZ ☎ 01843 577033 roz.edridge@ekservices.org

Electoral Registration: Ms Lyn McDaid Elections Manager, Council Offices, Military Road, Canterbury CT1 1YW ☎ 01227 862006 🖷 01227 862020 lyn.mcdaid@canterbury.gov.uk

Emergency Planning: Mr Andy Jeffery Emergency Planning & Events Officer, Council Offices, Military Road, Canterbury CT1 1YW ☎ 01227 862012 andy.jeffery@canterbury.gov.uk

Energy Management: Mr Philip Kiss, Building Services Engineer (Mechanical) & Energy Officer, Council Offices, Military Road, Canterbury CT1 1YW ☎ 01227 862481 🖷 01227 471635 philip.kiss@canterbury.gov.uk

Environmental / Technical Services: Ms Larissa Reed Assistant Director - Direct Services, Council Offices, Military Road, Canterbury CT1 1YW ☎ 01227 862213 🖷 01227 471635 larissa.reed@canterbury.gov.uk

Environmental Health: Ms Larissa Reed Assistant Director - Direct Services, Council Offices, Military Road, Canterbury CT1 1YW ☎ 01227 862213 🖷 01227 471635 larissa.reed@canterbury.gov.uk

Estates, Property & Valuation: Mr Martin Bovingdon Estates & Valuation Manager, Council Offices, Military Road, Canterbury CT1 1YW ☎ 01227 862088 🖷 01227 764955 martin.bovingdon@canterbury.gov.uk

Events Manager: Mr Andy Jeffery Emergency Planning & Events Officer, Council Offices, Military Road, Canterbury CT1 1YW ☎ 01227 862012 andy.jeffery@canterbury.gov.uk

Facilities: Mrs Alexis Jobson, Central Services Manager, Council Offices, Military Road, Canterbury CT1 1YW ☎ 01227 862255 🖷 01227 862020 alexis.jobson@canterbury.gov.uk

Finance: Ms Lisa Fillery Assistant Director of Finance & Procurement, Council Offices, Military Road, Canterbury CT1 1YW ☎ 01227 862000 lisa.fillery@canterbury.gov.uk

Grounds Maintenance: Mrs Janice McGuinness, Assistant Director - Commissioned Services, Council Offices, Military Road, Canterbury CT1 1YW ☎ 01227 862492 🖷 01227 470599 janice.mcguinness@canterbury.gov.uk

Health and Safety: Mr Stephen Turner, Health & Safety Advisor, Council Offices, Military Road, Canterbury CT1 1YW stephen.turner@canterbury.gov.uk

Housing: Ms Larissa Reed Assistant Director - Direct Services, Council Offices, Military Road, Canterbury CT1 1YW ☎ 01227 862213 🖷 01227 471635 larissa.reed@canterbury.gov.uk

Housing Maintenance: Mr David Ashby, Head of Asset Management, East Kent Housing Ltd, 3 - 5 Shorncliffe Road, , Folkestone CT20 2SQ ☎ 01303 853749 david.ashby@eastkenthousing.org.uk

Legal: Ms Sarah Bowman Head of Legal, Council Offices, Military Road, Canterbury CT1 1YW ☎ 01227 862017 🖷 01227 862020 mark.ellender@canterbury.gov.uk

Leisure and Cultural Services: Mrs Janice McGuinness, Assistant Director - Commissioned Services, Council Offices, Military Road, Canterbury CT1 1YW ☎ 01227 862492 🖷 01227 470599 janice.mcguinness@canterbury.gov.uk

Licensing: Mr Doug Rattray Head of Safer Neighbourhoods, Council Offices, Military Road, Canterbury CT1 1YW ☎ 01227 862363 🖷 01227 471635 doug.rattray@canterbury.gov.uk

Lottery Funding, Charity and Voluntary: Ms Marie Royle Head of Community Services, Council Offices, Military Road, Canterbury CT1 1YW ☎ 01227 862517 marie.royle@canterbury.gov.uk

Member Services: Mr Mark Archer Head of Democratic Services, Council Offices, Military Road, Canterbury CT1 1YW ☎ 01227 862175 🖷 01227 862020 matthew.archer@canterbury.gov.uk

Parking: Mr Doug Rattray Head of Safer Neighbourhoods, Council Offices, Military Road, Canterbury CT1 1YW ☎ 01227 862363 🖷 01227 471635 doug.rattray@canterbury.gov.uk

Personnel / HR: Ms Juli Oliver-Smith Head of EK Human Resources, East Kent HR Partnership, Dover District Council, White Cliffs Business Park, Whitfield, Dover CT16 3PJ ☎ 07917 473616 hrpartnership@dover.gov.uk

Planning: Mr Ian Brown Assistant Director - Planning & Regeneration, Council Offices, Military Road, Canterbury CT1 1YW ☎ 01227 862193 ian.brown@canterbury.gov.uk

Recycling & Waste Minimisation: Mrs Janice McGuinness, Assistant Director - Commissioned Services, Council Offices, Military Road, Canterbury CT1 1YW ☎ 01227 862492 🖷 01227 470599 janice.mcguinness@canterbury.gov.uk

Regeneration: Mr Ian Brown Assistant Director - Planning & Regeneration, Council Offices, Military Road, Canterbury CT1 1YW ☎ 01227 862193 ian.brown@canterbury.gov.uk

Staff Training: Ms Paula Radcliffe Learning & Development Manager, Council Offices, Military Road, Canterbury CT1 1YW ☎ 01304 872799 ✉ paula.radcliffe@canterbury.gov.uk

Sustainable Communities: Ms Suzi Wakeham Assistant Director - Strategy & Democracy, Council Offices, Military Road, Canterbury CT1 1YW ☎ 01227 862057 ✉ suzi.wakeham@canterbury.gov.uk

Sustainable Development: Mr Ian Brown Assistant Director - Planning & Regeneration, Council Offices, Military Road, Canterbury CT1 1YW ☎ 01227 862193 ✉ ian.brown@canterbury.gov.uk

Tourism: Ms Caroline Hicks Head of Business & Regeneration, Council Offices, Military Road, Canterbury CT1 1YW ☎ 01227 862054 🖷 01227 470599 ✉ caroline.hicks@canterbury.gov.uk

Town Centre: Ms Caroline Hicks Head of Business & Regeneration, Council Offices, Military Road, Canterbury CT1 1YW ☎ 01227 862054 🖷 01227 470599 ✉ caroline.hicks@canterbury.gov.uk

Transport Planner: Mr Richard Moore Transport & Environment Manager, Council Offices, Military Road, Canterbury CT1 1YW ☎ 01227 862419 ✉ richard.moore@canterbury.gov.uk

Waste Collection and Disposal: Mrs Janice McGuinness, Assistant Director - Commissioned Services, Council Offices, Military Road, Canterbury CT1 1YW ☎ 01227 862492 🖷 01227 470599 ✉ janice.mcguinness@canterbury.gov.uk

COUNCILLORS

***The Lord Mayor* Waters**, Sally (CON - St Stephen's)
sally.waters@canterbury.gov.uk

***Leader of the Council* Cook**, Simon (CON - Nailbourne)
simon.cook@canterbury.gov.uk

***Deputy Leader of the Council* Todd**, Patt (CON - Chestfield)
pat.todd@canterbury.gov.uk

***Group Leader* Baldock**, Alan (LAB - Northgate)
alan.baldock@canterbury.gov.uk

***Group Leader* Hirst**, David (UKIP - Greenhill)
david.hirst@canterbury.gov.uk

Baker, Neil (CON - Tankerton)
neil.baker@canterbury.gov.uk

Baker, Amy (CON - Blean Forest)
amy.baker@canterbury.gov.uk

Baker, Brian (CON - Gorrell)
brian.baker@canterbury.gov.uk

Bartley, Stephen (CON - Seasalter)
stephen.bartley@canterbury.gov.uk

Brazier, John (CON - Westgate)
john.brazier@canterbury.gov.uk

Butcher, Jean (LAB - Northgate)
jean.butcher@canterbury.gov.uk

Clark, Ashley (CON - Gorrell)
ashley.clark@canterbury.gov.uk

Cook, Andrew (CON - Heron)
andrew.cook@canterbury.gov.uk

Dixey, Michael (LD - Westgate)
michael.dixey@canterbury.gov.uk

Doyle, Rosemary (CON - Chartham & Stone Street)
rosemary.doyle@canterbury.gov.uk

Eden-Green, Nick (LD - Wincheap)
nick.edengreen@canterbury.gov.uk

Fawcett, Oliver (CON - Barton)
oliver.fawcett@canterbury.gov.uk

Fisher, Bernadette (LAB - Gorrell)
bernadette.fisher@canterbury.gov.uk

Fitter, Ben (CON - Blean Forest)
ben.fitter@canterbury.gov.uk

Foster, Guy (CON - Reculver)
guy.foster@canterbury.gov.uk

Glover, Georgina (CON - Sturry)
georgina.glover@canterbury.gov.uk

Howes, Joe (CON - Heron)
joe.howes@canterbury.gov.uk

Jones, Robert (CON - Herne & Broomfield)
robert.jones@canterbury.gov.uk

Jones, Louise (CON - Barton)
louise.jones@canterbury.gov.uk

MacCaul, Charlotte (LD - Wincheap)
charlotte.maccaul@canterbury.gov.uk

Metcalfe, George (CON - Blean Forest)
george.metcalfe@canterbury.gov.uk

Samper, Jennifer (CON - Chestfield)
jenny.samper@canterbury.gov.uk

Sonnex, Sharron (CON - Herne & Broomfield)
sharron.sonnex@canterbury.gov.uk

Spooner, Colin (CON - Seasalter)
colin.spooner@canterbury.gov.uk

Stockley, Ian (CON - Beltinge)
ian.stockley@canterbury.gov.uk

Stockley, Jeanette (CON - Beltinge)
jeanette.stockley@canterbury.gov.uk

Taylor, Heather (CON - Sturry)
heather.taylor@canterbury.gov.uk

Thomas, Ian (CON - Swalecliffe)
ian.thomas@canterbury.gov.uk

Thomas, Robert (CON - Chartham & Stone Street)
robert.thomas@canterbury.gov.uk

Thomas, David (CON - Heron)
david.thomas@canterbury.gov.uk

Walker, Stuart (CON - Little Stour & Adisham)
stuart.walker@canterbury.gov.uk

Westgate, Terry (CON - St Stephen's)
terry.westgate@canterbury.gov.uk

Williams, Steven (CON - Barton)
steven.williams@canterbury.gov.uk

Wimble, Geoff (UKIP - West Bay)

POLITICAL COMPOSITION

CON: 31, LAB: 3, LD: 3, UKIP: 2

CANTERBURY CITY

COMMITTEE CHAIRS

Audit & Governance: Mr Robert Thomas

Planning: Ms Jennifer Samper

Cardiff W

Cardiff Council, County Hall, Atlantic Wharf, Cardiff CF10 4UW
☎ 029 2087 2087 🖷 029 2087 2086 ✉ c2c@cardiff.gov.uk
💻 www.cardiff.gov.uk

FACTS AND FIGURES

Parliamentary Constituencies: Cardiff Central, Cardiff North, Cardiff South and Penarth, Cardiff West, Pontypridd
EU Constituencies: Wales
Election Frequency: Elections are of whole council

PRINCIPAL OFFICERS

Chief Executive: Mr Paul Orders Chief Executive, County Hall, Atlantic Wharf, Cardiff CF10 4UW ☎ 029 2087 2401 🖷 029 2087 7081 ✉ paul.orders@cardiff.gov.uk

Senior Management: Mr Nick Batchelar Director - Education & Learning, County Hall, Atlantic Wharf, Cardiff CF10 4UW

Senior Management: Mr Andrew Gregory Director - City Operations, County Hall, Atlantic Wharf, Cardiff CF10 4UW ✉ a.gregory@cardiff.gov.uk

Senior Management: Ms Sarah McGill, Director - Communities, Housing & Customer Services, Wilcox House, Dunleavy Drive, Celtic Gateway, Cardiff CF11 0BA ☎ 029 2087 2900 ✉ s.mcgill@cardiff.gov.uk

Senior Management: Ms Marie Rosenthal Director - Governance & Legal Services, County Hall, Atlantic Wharf, Cardiff CF10 4UW ✉ m.rosenthal@cardiff.gov.uk

Senior Management: Ms Christine Salter, Corporate Director - Resources, County Hall, Atlantic Wharf, Cardiff CF10 4UW ☎ 029 2087 2300 🖷 029 2087 2206 ✉ c.salter@cardiff.gov.uk

Senior Management: Mr Tony Young Director - Social Services, County Hall, Atlantic Wharf, Cardiff CF10 4UW

Architect, Building / Property Services: Mr Philip Dee Project Design Development Manager, County Hall, Atlantic Wharf, Cardiff CF10 4UW ☎ 029 2233 0078 ✉ p.dee@cardiff.gov.uk

Catering Services: Mr Roberto Rossi Catering Manager, County Hall, Atlantic Wharf, Cardiff CF10 4UW ☎ 029 2087 2025 ✉ r.rossi@cardiff.gov.uk

Children / Youth Services: Mr Nick Batchelar Director - Education & Learning, County Hall, Atlantic Wharf, Cardiff CF10 4UW

Children / Youth Services: Mr Tony Young Director - Social Services, County Hall, Atlantic Wharf, Cardiff CF10 4UW

PR / Communications: Mr Tim Gordon Head of Corporate Communications & External Relations, County Hall, Atlantic Wharf, Cardiff CF10 4UW ✉ tgordon@cardiff.gov.uk

Consumer Protection and Trading Standards: Mr Dave Holland, Head of Service - Regulatory & Support Service, County Hall, Atlantic Wharf, Cardiff CF10 2TS ☎ 029 2087 2089 🖷 029 2087 2072 ✉ d.holland@cardiff.gov.uk

Corporate Services: Mr Jonathan Day Business Development Manager, County Hall, Atlantic Wharf, Cardiff CF10 4UW ☎ 029 2078 8573 ✉ j.day@cardiff.gov.uk

Corporate Services: Mr Alan Richards, Superintendent Registrar, Park Place, Cardiff CF10 4UW ☎ 029 2087 1680 🖷 029 2087 1691 ✉ a.richards@cardiff.gov.uk

Education: Mr Chris Jones, Chief Education Officer, County Hall, Atlantic Wharf, Cardiff CF10 4UW ☎ 029 2087 2700 🖷 029 2087 2705 ✉ chjones@cardiff.gov.uk

Emergency Planning: Mr Gavin Macho, Principal Emergency Management Officer, Strategic Planning & Environment, Emergency Planning Unit, City Hall, Cardiff CF10 3ND ☎ 029 2087 1831 🖷 029 2087 1836 ✉ gmacho@cardiff.gov.uk

European Liaison: Mr Jonathan Day Business Development Manager, County Hall, Atlantic Wharf, Cardiff CF10 4UW ☎ 029 2078 8573 ✉ j.day@cardiff.gov.uk

Finance: Ms Christine Salter, Corporate Director - Resources, County Hall, Atlantic Wharf, Cardiff CF10 4UW ☎ 029 2087 2300 🖷 029 2087 2206 ✉ c.salter@cardiff.gov.uk

Pensions: Mr Gareth Henson Manager of Pensions, County Hall, Atlantic Wharf, Cardiff CF10 4UW ☎ 029 2087 2975 ✉ g.henson@cardiff.gov.uk

Fleet Management: Mr Richard Jones Tactical Manager - Fleet & Procurement, County Hall, Atlantic Wharf, Cardiff CF10 4UW ☎ 029 2087 2087 ✉ RiJones@cardiff.gov.uk

Grounds Maintenance: Mr Jon Maidment Operational Manager for Parks & Sport, County Hall, Atlantic Wharf, Cardiff CF10 4UW ☎ 029 2087 2087 ✉ j.maidment@cardiff.gov.uk

Health and Safety: Miss Christina Lloyd, Operational Manager - Health & Safety, County Hall, Atlantic Wharf, Cardiff CF10 4UW ☎ 029 2087 2635 🖷 029 2087 2606 ✉ c.c.lloyd@cardiff.gov.uk

Highways: Mr Andrew Gregory Director - City Operations, County Hall, Atlantic Wharf, Cardiff CF10 4UW ✉ a.gregory@cardiff.gov.uk

Housing: Ms Sarah McGill, Director - Communities, Housing & Customer Services, Wilcox House, Dunleavy Drive, Celtic Gateway, Cardiff CF11 0BA ☎ 029 2087 2900 ✉ s.mcgill@cardiff.gov.uk

Housing Maintenance: Ms Sarah McGill, Director - Communities, Housing & Customer Services, Wilcox House, Dunleavy Drive, Celtic Gateway, Cardiff CF11 0BA ☎ 029 2087 2900 ✉ s.mcgill@cardiff.gov.uk

Legal: Ms Marie Rosenthal Director - Governance & Legal Services, County Hall, Atlantic Wharf, Cardiff CF10 4UW 🖱 m.rosenthal@cardiff.gov.uk

Licensing: Mr Andrew Gregory Director - City Operations, County Hall, Atlantic Wharf, Cardiff CF10 4UW 🖱 a.gregory@cardiff.gov.uk

Lighting: Mr Gary Brown Operational Manager - Highways Maintenance, County Hall, Atlantic Wharf, Cardiff CF10 4UW ☎ 029 2078 5280 🖱 gbrown@cardiff.gov.uk

Member Services: Ms Marie Rosenthal Director - Governance & Legal Services, County Hall, Atlantic Wharf, Cardiff CF10 4UW 🖱 m.rosenthal@cardiff.gov.uk

Parking: Mr Paul Carter, Head of Transportation & Network Management, County Hall, Atlantic Wharf, Cardiff CF10 4UW ☎ 029 2087 3243 🖶 029 2087 3108 🖱 p.carter@cardiff.gov.uk

Personnel / HR: Mr Laithe Bonni Specialist Support Manager, County Hall, Atlantic Wharf, Cardiff CF10 4UW ☎ 029 2087 2655 🖱 l.bonni@cardiff.gov.uk

Personnel / HR: Mr Philip Lenz Chief HR Officer, Room 470, County Hall, Atlantic Wharf, Cardiff CF10 4UW ☎ 029 2087 2000 🖱 plenz@cardiff.gov.uk

Planning: Mr James Clements Head of Planning, County Hall, Atlantic Wharf, Cardiff CF10 4UW ☎ 029 2233 0827 🖱 j.clements@cardiff.gov.uk

Planning: Mr Andrew Gregory Director - City Operations, County Hall, Atlantic Wharf, Cardiff CF10 4UW 🖱 a.gregory@cardiff.gov.uk

Procurement: Ms Christine Salter, Corporate Director - Resources, County Hall, Atlantic Wharf, Cardiff CF10 4UW ☎ 029 2087 2300 🖶 029 2087 2206 🖱 c.salter@cardiff.gov.uk

Public Libraries: Ms Nicola Richards Central Library Manager, County Hall, Atlantic Wharf, Cardiff CF10 4UW ☎ 029 2053 7027 🖱 n.richards@cardiff.gov.uk

Recycling & Waste Minimisation: Ms Tara King, Chief Officer Waste Management & City Services, Lamby Way, Cardiff CF3 2EQ ☎ 029 2087 2087 🖱 t.king@cardiff.gov.uk

Regeneration: Mr Gareth Harcombe Operational Manager - Regeneration, City Hall, Cathays Park, Cardiff CF10 3ND ☎ 029 2087 3489 🖱 gharcombe@cardiff.gov.uk

Road Safety: Ms Lisa Lewis Lead Officer - Road Safety & Training, County Hall, Atlantic Wharf, Cardiff CF10 4UW ☎ 029 2078 8521 🖱 l.lewis@cardiff.gov.uk

Tourism: Ms Sally Edwards Hart, Operational Manager - Venues & Tourism, County Hall, Atlantic Wharf, Cardiff CF10 4UW ☎ 029 2087 3360 🖶 029 2082 7161 🖱 sallyhart@cardiff.gov.uk

Tourism: Ms Kathryn Richards, Head of Marketing, Motorpoint Arena, Executive Suite 1, Mary Ann Street, Cardiff CF10 2EQ ☎ 029 2087 2452 🖶 029 2087 2499 🖱 k.richards@cardiff.gov.uk

Town Centre: Mr Paul Williams City Centre Manager, County Hall, Atlantic Wharf, Cardiff CF10 4UW ☎ 029 2066 2986 🖱 p.william@cardiff.gov.uk

Transport: Mr Paul Carter, Head of Transportation & Network Management, County Hall, Atlantic Wharf, Cardiff CF10 4UW ☎ 029 2087 3243 🖶 029 2087 3108 🖱 p.carter@cardiff.gov.uk

Transport Planner: Mr Paul Carter, Head of Transportation & Network Management, County Hall, Atlantic Wharf, Cardiff CF10 4UW ☎ 029 2087 3243 🖶 029 2087 3108 🖱 p.carter@cardiff.gov.uk

Waste Collection and Disposal: Ms Tara King, Chief Officer Waste Management & City Services, Lamby Way, Cardiff CF3 2EQ ☎ 029 2087 2087 🖱 t.king@cardiff.gov.uk

COUNCILLORS

***The Lord Mayor* Walker**, David (CON - Lisvane)
dwalker@cardiff.gov.uk

***Deputy Lord Mayor* Ali**, Dilwar (LAB - Llandaff North)
dilwar.ali@cardiff.gov.uk

***Leader of the Council* Bale**, Phil (LAB - Llanishen)
phil.bale@cardiff.gov.uk

***Deputy Leader of the Council* Lent**, Sue (LAB - Plasnewydd)
sue.lent@cardiff.gov.uk

***Group Leader* McEvoy**, Neil (PC - Fairwater)
nmcevoy@cardiff.gov.uk

***Group Leader* Sanders**, Eleanor (IND - Rhiwbina)
eleanor.sanders@cardiff.gov.uk

***Group Leader* Woodman**, Judith (LD - Pentwyn)
jwoodman@cardiff.gov.uk

Ahmed, Manzoor (LAB - Adamsdown)
manzoor.ahmed@cardiff.gov.uk

Ahmed, Ali (LAB - Butetown)
ali.ahmed@cardiff.gov.uk

Aubrey, Gareth (LD - Llandaff)
gaubrey@cardiff.gov.uk

Bowden, Fenella (IND - Heath)
fbowden@cardiff.gov.uk

Boyle, Joe (LD - Penylan)
joe.boyle@cardiff.gov.uk

Bradbury, Peter (LAB - Caerau)
peter.bradbury@cardiff.gov.uk

Bridges, Ed (LD - Gabalfa)
ebridges@cardiff.gov.uk

Burfoot, Tricia (LD - Penylan)
pburfoot@cardiff.gov.uk

Carter, Joseph (LD - Pentwyn)
jcarter@cardiff.gov.uk

Chaundy, Paul (LD - Pentwyn)
pchaundy@cardiff.gov.uk

Clark, Elizabeth (LD - Cathays)
eclark@cardiff.gov.uk

Cook, Richard (LAB - Canton)
ricook@cardiff.gov.uk

CARDIFF

Cook, Ralph (LAB - Trowbridge)
ralphcook@cardiff.gov.uk

Cowan, Jayne (CON - Rhiwbina)
j.cowan@cardiff.gov.uk

Davies-Warner, Kirsty (LD - Llandaff)
kirsty.davies-warner@cardiff.gov.uk

Davis, Chris (LAB - Whitchurch & Tongwynlais)
chris.davies@cardiff.gov.uk

De'Ath, Daniel (LAB - Plasnewydd)
daniel.de'ath@cardiff.gov.uk

Derbyshire, Bob (LAB - Rumney)
bob.derbyshire@cardiff.gov.uk

Elsmore, Susan (LAB - Canton)
susan.elsmore@cardiff.gov.uk

Evans, Jonathan (LAB - Whitchurch & Tongwynlais)
jonathan.evans@cardiff.gov.uk

Ford, Lisa (PC - Fairwater)
lisaford@cardiff.gov.uk

Goddard, Susan (LAB - Ely)
sgoddard@cardiff.gov.uk

Goodway, Russell (LAB - Ely)
r.v.goodway@cardiff.gov.uk

Gordon, Iona (LAB - Riverside)
iona.gordon@cardiff.gov.uk

Govier, Ashley (LAB - Grangetown)
ashley.govier@cardiff.gov.uk

Graham, Andrew (CON - Llanishen)
andrew.graham@cardiff.gov.uk

Groves, David (LAB - Whitchurch & Tongwynlais)
david.groves@cardiff.gov.uk

Hinchey, Graham (LAB - Heath)
graham.hinchey@cardiff.gov.uk

Holden, Gareth (IND - Gabalfa)
gareth.holden@cardiff.gov.uk

Howells, Nigel (LD - Adamsdown)
nhowells@cardiff.gov.uk

Hudson, Lyn (CON - Heath)
lhudson@cardiff.gov.uk

Hunt, Garry (LAB - Llanishen)
garry.hunt@cardiff.gov.uk

Hyde, Keith (LD - Pentwyn)
khyde@cardiff.gov.uk

Javed, Mohammad (LAB - Plasnewydd)
mohammad.javed@cardiff.gov.uk

Jones, Margaret (LD - Cyncoed)
mjones@cardiff.gov.uk

Jones, Keith (LAB - Llanrumney)
keith.jones@cardiff.gov.uk

Joyce, Heather (LAB - Llanrumney)
hjoyce@cardiff.gov.uk

Kelloway, Bill (LD - Penylan)
bkelloway@cardiff.gov.uk

Knight, Sam (LAB - Cathays)
sam.knight@cardiff.gov.uk

Lloyd, Kate (LD - Cyncoed)
klloyd@cardiff.gov.uk

Lomax, Chris (LAB - Grangetown)
chris.lomax@cardiff.gov.uk

Love, Cecelia (LAB - Riverside)
cecilia.love@cardiff.gov.uk

Magill, Julia (LAB - Llanishen)
julia.magill@cardiff.gov.uk

Marshall, Gretta (LAB - Splott)
gretta.marshall@cardiff.gov.uk

McGarry, Mary (LAB - Plasnewydd)
mary.mcgarry@cardiff.gov.uk

McKerlish, Roderick (CON - Radyr and Morganstown)
rmckerlich@cardiff.gov.uk

Merry, Sarah (LAB - Cathays)
sarah.merry@cardiff.gov.uk

Michael, Michael (LAB - Trowbridge)
michael.michael@cardiff.gov.uk

Mitchell, Paul (LAB - Fairwater)
paul.mitchell@cardiff.gov.uk

Morgan, Derek (LAB - Llanrumney)
derrickmorgan@cardiff.gov.uk

Murphy, Jim (LAB - Ely)
jim.murphy@cardiff.gov.uk

Parry, Jacqueline (LAB - Rumney)
JackieParry@cardiff.gov.uk

Patel, Ramesh (LAB - Canton)
rapatel@cardiff.gov.uk

Phillips, Georgina (LAB - Pontprennau & Old St. Mellons)
georgina.phillips@cardiff.gov.uk

Rees, Diane (CON - Pontprennau & Old St. Mellons)
direes@cardiff.gov.ukw

Rees, David (LD - Cyncoed)
davrees@cardiff.gov.uk

Robson, Adrian (CON - Rhiwbina)
arobson@cardiff.gov.uk

Simmons, Elaine (LAB - Caerau)
elaine.simmons@cardiff.gov.uk

Stubbs, Ed (LAB - Splott)
ed.stubbs@cardiff.gov.uk

Thomas, Huw (LAB - Splott)
huw.thomas@cardiff.gov.uk

Thomas, Graham (CON - Creigiau & St Fagans)
graham.thomas@cardiff.gov.uk

Thomas, Ben (LAB - Whitchurch & Tongwynlais)
ben.thomas@cardiff.gov.uk

Thorne, Lynda (LAB - Grangetown)
lynda.thorne@cardiff.gov.uk

Walsh, Monica (LAB - Trowbridge)
mowalsh@cardiff.gov.uk

Weaver, Chris (LAB - Cathays)
christopher.weaver@cardiff.gov.uk

White, Susan (LAB - Llandaff North)
susan.white@cardiff.gov.uk

Williams, Darren (LAB - Riverside)
darren.williams@cardiff.gov.uk

POLITICAL COMPOSITION

LAB: 46, LD: 15, CON: 8, IND: 3, PC: 2

COMMITTEE CHAIRS

Children & Young People: Mr Richard Cook

Economy & Culture: Mr Roderick McKerlish

Licensing: Ms Jacqueline Parry

Planning: Mr Michael Michael

Carlisle City D

Carlisle City Council, Civic Centre, Carlisle CA3 8QG
☎ 01228 817000 🖷 01228 817048 💻 www.carlisle.gov.uk

FACTS AND FIGURES

Parliamentary Constituencies: Carlisle, Penrith and The Border
EU Constituencies: North West
Election Frequency: Elections are by thirds

PRINCIPAL OFFICERS

Chief Executive: Dr Jason Gooding, Chief Executive, Civic Centre, Carlisle CA3 8QG ☎ 01228 817009 🖱 jason.gooding@carlisle.gov.uk

Deputy Chief Executive: Mr Darren Crossley Deputy Chief Executive, Civic Centre, Carlisle CA3 8QG ☎ 01228 817004 🖱 darren.crossley@carlisle.gov.uk

Senior Management: Ms Angela Culleton Director - Local Environment, Civic Centre, Carlisle CA3 8QG ☎ 01228 817325 🖱 angela.culleton@carlisle.gov.uk

Senior Management: Mr Mark Lambert Director - Governance, Civic Centre, Carlisle CA3 8QG ☎ 01228 817019 🖱 mark.lambert@carlisle.gov.uk

Senior Management: Mr Peter Mason Director - Resources, Civic Centre, Carlisle CA3 8QG ☎ 01228 817270 🖱 peter.mason@carlisle.gov.uk

Senior Management: Ms Jane Meek Director - Economic Development, Civic Centre, Carlisle CA3 8QG ☎ 01228 817190 🖱 jane.meek@carlisle.gov.uk

Access Officer / Social Services (Disability): Ms Karen Scrivener Access Officer, Civic Centre, Carlisle CA3 8QG ☎ 01228 817183 🖷 01228 817513 🖱 karen.scrivener@carlisle.gov.uk

Architect, Building / Property Services: Mr Raymond Simmons, Property Services Manager Civic Centre, Carlisle CA3 8QG ☎ 01228 817421 🖱 raymond.simmons@carlisle.gov.uk

Best Value: Mr Steven O'Keeffe Policy & Communications Manager, Civic Centre, Carlisle CA3 8QG ☎ 01228 817258 🖱 steven.o'keefe@carlisle.gov.uk

Building Control: Mr Mark Bowman Building Control Manager, Civic Centre, Carlisle CA3 8QG ☎ 01228 817189 🖱 mark.bowman@carlisle.gov.uk

PR / Communications: Mr Steven O'Keeffe Policy & Communications Manager, Civic Centre, Carlisle CA3 8QG ☎ 01228 817258 🖱 steven.o'keefe@carlisle.gov.uk

Community Planning: Ms Emma Dixon Partnership Manager, Civic Centre, Carlisle CA3 8QG ☎ 01228 817370 🖱 emma.dixon@carlisle.gov.uk

Community Safety: Ms Ruth Crane Communities & Family Development Officer, Civic Centre, Carlisle CA3 8QG ☎ 01228 817362 🖱 ruth.crane@carlisle.gov.uk

Computer Management: Mr Michael Scott DIS Manager, Civic Centre, Carlisle CA3 8QG ☎ 01228 817251 🖱 michael.scott@carlisle.gov.uk

Contracts: Mr Gavin Capstick Contracts & Community Services Manager, Civic Centre, Carlisle CA3 8QG ☎ 01228 817123 🖱 gavin.capstick@carlisle.gov.uk

Corporate Services: Mr Peter Mason Director - Resources, Civic Centre, Carlisle CA3 8QG ☎ 01228 817270 🖱 peter.mason@carlisle.gov.uk

Customer Service: Mrs Jillian Gillespie Customer Services Manager, Civic Centre, Carlisle CA3 8QG ☎ 01228 817461 🖱 jillian.gillespie@carlisle.gov.uk

Economic Development: Ms Jane Meek Director - Economic Development, Civic Centre, Carlisle CA3 8QG ☎ 01228 817190 🖱 jane.meek@carlisle.gov.uk

Electoral Registration: Mr Ian Dixon, Electoral Services Officer, Civic Centre, Carlisle CA3 8QG ☎ 01228 817555 🖱 ian.dixon@carlisle.gov.uk

Emergency Planning: Mr Steven O'Keeffe Emergency Planning Manager, Civic Centre, Carlisle CA3 8QG ☎ 01228 817258 🖱 steven.o'keefe@carlisle.gov.uk

Environmental / Technical Services: Ms Angela Culleton Director - Local Environment, Civic Centre, Carlisle CA3 8QG ☎ 01228 817325 🖱 angela.culleton@carlisle.gov.uk

Environmental Health: Mr Scott Burns Environmental Health Manager, Civic Centre, Carlisle CA3 8QG ☎ 01228 817328 🖱 scott.burns@carlisle.gov.uk

Estates, Property & Valuation: Mr Raymond Simmons, Property Services Manager Civic Centre, Carlisle CA3 8QG ☎ 01228 817421 🖱 raymond.simmons@carlisle.gov.uk

Facilities: Mr Mike Swindlehurst Building Projects Manager, Civic Centre, Carlisle CA3 8QG ☎ 01228 817292 🖱 mike.swindlehurst.gov.uk

CARLISLE CITY

Finance: Mr Peter Mason Director - Resources, Civic Centre, Carlisle CA3 8QG ☎ 01228 817270 ✉ peter.mason@carlisle.gov.uk

Grounds Maintenance: Ms Angela Culleton Director - Local Environment, Civic Centre, Carlisle CA3 8QG ☎ 01228 817325 ✉ angela.culleton@carlisle.gov.uk

Health and Safety: Mr Arup Majhi, Safety & Health Environmental Manager, Civic Centre, Carlisle CA3 8QG ☎ 01228 817507 ✉ arup.majhi@carlisle.gov.uk

Housing: Mrs Margaret Miller Communities, Housing & Health Manager, Civic Centre, Carlisle CA3 8QG ☎ 01228 817330 ✉ margaret.miller@carlisle.gov.uk

Legal: Mr Mark Lambert Director - Governance, Civic Centre, Carlisle CA3 8QG ☎ 01228 817019 ✉ mark.lambert@carlisle.gov.uk

Leisure and Cultural Services: Mr Gavin Capstick Contracts & Community Services Manager, Civic Centre, Carlisle CA3 8QG ☎ 01228 817123 ✉ gavin.capstick@carlisle.gov.uk

Licensing: Ms Susan Stashkiw Licensing Manager, Civic Centre, Carlisle CA3 8QG ☎ 01228 817029 ✉ susan.stashkiw@carlisle.gov.uk

Member Services: Mr Mark Lambert Director - Governance, Civic Centre, Carlisle CA3 8QG ☎ 01228 817019 ✉ mark.lambert@carlisle.gov.uk

Parking: Ms Sharon Jenkinson City Centre Manager, Civic Centre, Carlisle CA3 8QG ☎ 01228 817549 ✉ sharon.jenkinson@carlisle.gov.uk

Partnerships: Ms Emma Dixon Partnership Manager, Civic Centre, Carlisle CA3 8QG ☎ 01228 817370 ✉ emma.dixon@carlisle.gov.uk

Personnel / HR: Ms Julie Kemp HR Advisory Services Team Leader, Civic Centre, Carlisle CA3 8QG ☎ 01228 817081 ✉ julie.kemp@carlisle.gov.uk

Planning: Mr Christopher Hardman Planning Manager, Civic Centre, Carlisle CA3 8QG ☎ 01228 817502 ✉ chris.hardman@carlisle.gov.uk

Procurement: Ms Dawn Reid Assistant Procurement Officer, Civic Centre, Carlisle CA3 8QG ☎ 01228 817595 ✉ dawn.reid@carlisle.gov.uk

Recycling & Waste Minimisation: Ms Jan Boniface Neighbourhood Service Operations Manager, Civic Centre, Carlisle CA3 8QG ☎ 01228 817331 ✉ jan.boniface@carlisle.gov.uk

Staff Training: Ms Linda Mattinson, Learning & Development Co-ordinator, Civic Centre, Carlisle CA3 8QG ☎ 01228 817076 ✉ linda.mattinson@carlisle.gov.uk

Tourism: Ms Laura Thompson Tourist Information Officer, Civic Centre, Carlisle CA3 8QG ☎ 01228 598596 ✉ laura.thompson@carlisle.gov.uk

Waste Collection and Disposal: Ms Jan Boniface Neighbourhood Service Operations Manager, Civic Centre, Carlisle CA3 8QG ☎ 01228 817331 ✉ jan.boniface@carlisle.gov.uk

Waste Management: Ms Jan Boniface Neighbourhood Service Operations Manager, Civic Centre, Carlisle CA3 8QG ☎ 01228 817331 ✉ jan.boniface@carlisle.gov.uk

Children's Play Areas: Mr Phil Gray Greenspaces & Bereavement Services Manager, Civic Centre, Carlisle CA3 8QG ☎ 01228 817485 ✉ phil.gray@carlisle.gov.uk

COUNCILLORS

***Mayor* Layden**, Stephen (CON - Brampton)
stephen.layden@carlisle.gov.uk

***Deputy Mayor* Stothard**, Colin (LAB - Morton)
colin.stothard@carlisle.gov.uk

***Leader of the Council* Glover**, Colin (LAB - Currock)
colin.glover@carlisle.gov.uk

***Deputy Leader of the Council* Martlew**, Elsie (LAB - Castle)
elsie.martlew@carlisle.gov.uk

***Group Leader* Allison**, Trevor (LD - Dalston)
trevor.allison@carlisle.gov.uk

***Group Leader* Graham**, William (IND - Hayton)
bill.graham@carlisle.gov.uk

***Group Leader* Mallinson**, John (CON - Longtown & Rockcliffe)
john.mallinson@carlisle.gov.uk

Atkinson, Karen (LAB - Yewdale)
karen.atkinson@carlisle.gov.uk

Bainbridge, James (CON - Stanwix Rural)
james.bainbridge@carlisle.gov.uk

Bell, John (LAB - Morton)
john.bell@carlisle.gov.uk

Betton, Robert (IND - Botcherby)
robert.betton@carlisle.gov.uk

Bloxham, Raynor (CON - Longtown & Rockcliffe)
ray.bloxham@carlisle.gov.uk

Boaden, Michael (LAB - Botcherby)
michael.boaden@carlisle.gov.uk

Bowditch, Steven (LAB - Yewdale)
steven.bowditch@carlisle.gov.uk

Bowman, Cyril (CON - Irthing)
cyril.bowman@carlisle.gov.uk

Bowman, Marilyn (CON - Stanwix Rural)
marilyn.bowman@carlisle.gov.uk

Bradley, Heather (LAB - Currock)
heather.bradley@carlisle.gov.uk

Burns, Robert (LAB - Harraby)
rob.burns@carlisle.gov.uk

Caig, Gerald (LAB - Castle)
ged.caig@carlisle.gov.uk

Cape, Donald (LAB - Upperby)
donald.cape@carlisle.gov.uk

Christian, Nigel (CON - Dalston)
Nigel.christian@carlisle.gov.uk

Collier, John (CON - Burgh)
john.collier@carlisle.gov.uk

Dodd, Thomas (LAB - Yewdale)
tom.dodd@carlisle.gov.uk

Earp, Barry (CON - Wetheral)
barry.earp@carlisle.gov.uk

Ellis, Gareth (CON - Belah)
gareth.ellis@carlisle.gov.uk

Franklin, Jacqueline (LAB - Belle Vue)
jacqueline.franklin@carlisle.gov.uk

Harid, Abdul (LAB - Currock)
abdul.harid@carlisle.gov.uk

Higgs, Stephen (CON - Wetheral)
stephen.higgs@carlisle.gov.uk

Mallinson, Elizabeth (CON - Stanwix Urban)
liz.mallinson@carlisle.gov.uk

McDevitt, Hugh (LAB - Denton Holme)
hugh.mcdevitt@carlisle.gov.uk

McKerrell, Ann (CON - Dalston)
ann.mckerrell@carlisle.gov.uk

Mitchelson, Mike (CON - Brampton)
mike.mitchelson@carlisle.gov.uk

Morton, David (CON - Belah)
david.morton@carlisle.gov.uk

Nedved, Paul (CON - Stanwix Urban)
paul.nedved@carlisle.gov.uk

Osgood, Barrie (LAB - Castle)
barrie.osgood@carlisle.gov.uk

Parsons, Doreen (CON - Great Corby & Geltsdale)
doreen.parsons@carlisle.gov.uk

Patrick, Lucy (LAB - St Aidans)
lucy.patrick@carlisle.gov.uk

Quilter, Anne (LAB - St Aidans)
anne.quilter@carlisle.gov.uk

Riddle, Jessica (LAB - Belle Vue)
jessica.riddle@carlisle.gov.uk

Robson, Fiona (CON - Stanwix Urban)
fiona.robson@carlisle.gov.uk

Scarborough, Charles (LAB - Botcherby)
committeeservices@carlisle.gov.uk

Shepherd, David (CON - Lyne)
david.shepherd@carlisle.gov.uk

Sherriff, Lee (LAB - Harraby)
lee.sheriff@carlisle.gov.uk

Southward, Christopher (LAB - Denton Holme)
chris.southward@carlisle.gov.uk

Southward, Joan (LAB - Denton Holme)
joan.southward@carlisle.gov.uk

Stevenson, Elaine (LAB - Morton)
elaine.stevenson@carlisle.gov.uk

Tickner, Les (LAB - Belle Vue)
les.tickner@carlisle.gov.uk

Vasey, Patricia (CON - Belah)
trish.vasey@carlisle.gov.uk

Warwick, Ann (LAB - Upperby)
ann.warwick@carlisle.gov.uk

Watson, Reginald (LAB - St Aidans)
reg.watson@Carlisle.gov.uk

Williams, Jo (LAB - Harraby)
jo.williams@carlisle.gov.uk

Wilson, David (LAB - Upperby)
david.wilson@carlisle.gov.uk

POLITICAL COMPOSITION
LAB: 29, CON: 20, IND: 2, LD: 1

COMMITTEE CHAIRS
Environment & Economy: Mr Paul Nedved

Licensing: Mr John Bell

Carmarthenshire W

Carmarthenshire County Council, County Hall, Carmarthen SA31 1JP
☎ 01267 234567 🖷 01267 224911
🖱 information@carmarthenshire.gov.uk 💻 www.carmarthenshire.gov.uk

FACTS AND FIGURES
Parliamentary Constituencies: Carmarthen East and Dinefwr, Carmarthen West and South Pembrokeshire, Llanelli
EU Constituencies: Wales
Election Frequency: Elections are of whole council

PRINCIPAL OFFICERS
Chief Executive: Mr Mark James, Chief Executive, County Hall, Carmarthen SA31 1JP ☎ 01267 224110
🖱 mjames@carmarthenshire.gov.uk

Assistant Chief Executive: Mr Paul Thomas, Assistant Chief Executive - People Management & Performance, Parc Dewi Sant, Carmarthen SA31 3HB ☎ 01267 246123
🖱 prthomas@carmarthenshire.gov.uk

Assistant Chief Executive: Ms Wendy Walters Interim Assistant Chief Executive - Customer Focus & Policy, County Hall, Carmarthen SA31 1JP ☎ 01267 244112
🖱 wswalters@carmarthenshire.gov.uk

Senior Management: Mr Jake Morgan, Director - Communities, County Hall, Carmarthen SA31 1JP ☎ 01267 244698
🖷 01267 228908 🖱 jakemorgan@carmarthenshire.gov.uk

Access Officer / Social Services (Disability): Mr Richard Elms Civil Contingency Officer, Parc Myrddin, Wellfield Road, Carmarthen SA13 1DS ☎ 01267 228147
🖱 relms@carmarthenshire.gov.uk

Building Control: Mr Eifion Bowen, Head - Planning Services, 7/8 Spilman Street, Carmarthen SA31 1LQ ☎ 01267 228918
🖷 01267 237612 🖱 ebowen@carmarthenshire.gov.uk

Catering Services: Mrs Sandra Weigel Catering Services Manager, Parc Dewi Sant, Carmarthen SA31 3HB ☎ 01267 246484
🖱 sjweigel@carmarthenshire.gov.uk

CARMARTHENSHIRE

Children / Youth Services: Mr Stefan Smith, Head - Children's Services, Block 2, S David's Park, Jobswewl Road, Carmarthen SA31 3HB ☎ 01267 246530 🖷 01267 246746 ✉ sjsmith@carmarthenshire.gov.uk

Civil Registration: Mrs Andrea Rowlands Civil Registration, Parc Myrddin, Richmond Terrace, Carmarthen SA31 1HQ ☎ 01267 228375 ✉ akrowlands@carmarthenshire.gov.uk

PR / Communications: Ms Wendy Walters Interim Assistant Chief Executive - Customer Focus & Policy, County Hall, Carmarthen SA31 1JP ☎ 01267 244112 ✉ wswalters@carmarthenshire.gov.uk

Community Safety: Mrs Kate Carter, Community Safety Manager, County Hall, Carmarthen SA31 1JP ☎ 01267 224202 ✉ kcarter@carmarthenshire.gov.uk

Computer Management: Mr Phil Sexton, Head - Audit, Procurement & ICT, Parc Dewi Sant, Carmarthen SA31 3HB ☎ 01267 246217 ✉ psexton@carmarthenshire.gov.uk

Consumer Protection and Trading Standards: Mr Roger Edmunds Trading Standards Manager, Ty Elwyn, Llanelli SA15 3AP ☎ 01554 742280 ✉ redmunds@carmarthenshire.gov.uk

Customer Service: Mrs Penelope Graepel Customer Services Manager, County Hall, Carmarthen SA31 1JP ☎ 01558 825384 ✉ pgraepal@carmartenshire.gov.uk

Direct Labour: Mr Mario Cresci Head - Street Scene, Parc Myrddin, Carmarthen SA31 2HQ ☎ 01237 224502 ✉ mcresci@carmarthenshire.gov.uk

Economic Development: Mr Stuart Walters Regeneration Manager, Parc Ananwy, Business Resource Centre, Ammanford SA18 3EP ☎ 01269 590241 ✉ swalters@carmarthenshire.gov.uk

Education: Mr Robert Sully Director - Education & Children's Services, County Hall, Carmarthen SA31 1JP ☎ 01267 224888 ✉ rsully@carmarthenshire.gov.uk

E-Government: Mr Phil Sexton, Head - Audit, Procurement & ICT, Parc Dewi Sant, Carmarthen SA31 3HB ☎ 01267 246217 ✉ psexton@carmarthenshire.gov.uk

Electoral Registration: Ms Amanda Bebb Electoral Services Manager, Parc Myrddin, Richmond Terrace, Carmarthen SA31 1HQ ☎ 01267 228609 ✉ Abebb@carmarthenshire.gov.uk

Emergency Planning: Mr Richard Elms, Civil Contingency Manager, Parc Myrddin, Richmond Terrace, Carmarthen SA31 1HQ ☎ 01267 228195 🖷 01267 228193 ✉ relms@carmarthenshire.gov.uk

Environmental Health: Mr Robin Staines, Head - Public Protection & Housing, 3 Spilman Street, Carmarthen SA31 1LE ☎ 01267 228960 ✉ rstaines@carmarthenshire.gov.uk

Estates, Property & Valuation: Mr Jonathan Fearn, Head - Corporate Property, Parc Dewi, Carmarthen SA31 3HB ☎ 01267 246244 ✉ jfearn@carmarthenshire.gov.uk

European Liaison: Ms Helen Morgan Development Manager, Trinity College, , Carmarthen SA31 3EP ☎ 01267 224859 ✉ hlmorgan@carmarthenshire.gov.uk

Finance: Mr Christopher Moore Head - Financial Services, County Hall, Carmarthen SA31 1JP ☎ 01267 224160 ✉ cmoore@carmarthenshire.gov.uk

Pensions: Mr Kevin Gerard Pensions Manager, County Hall, Carmarthen SA31 1JP ☎ 01267 224157 ✉ kgerard@carmarthenshire.gov.uk

Pensions: Mr Anthony Parnell Treasurer, Pensions & Investment Manager, County Hall, Carmarthen SA31 1JP ☎ 01267 224180 ✉ aparnell@carmarthenshire.gov.uk

Fleet Management: Mr Steven Pilliner Head - Transport & Engineering, Parc Myrddin, Carmarthen SA31 2HQ ☎ 01267 228150 ✉ spilliner@carmarthenshire.gov.uk

Grounds Maintenance: Mr Mario Cresci Head - Street Scene, Parc Myrddin, Carmarthen SA31 2HQ ☎ 01237 224502 ✉ mcresci@carmarthenshire.gov.uk

Health and Safety: Mr Mark Millward Health & Safety Advisor, Parc Dewi Sant, Carmarthen SA31 3HB ☎ 01267 246131 ✉ mmilward@carmarthenshire.gov.uk

Highways: Mr Steven Pilliner Head - Transport & Engineering, Parc Myrddin, Carmarthen SA31 2HQ ☎ 01267 228150 ✉ spilliner@carmarthenshire.gov.uk

Home Energy Conservation: Mr Robin Staines, Head - Public Protection & Housing, 3 Spilman Street, Carmarthen SA31 1LE ☎ 01267 228960 ✉ rstaines@carmarthenshire.gov.uk

Housing: Mr Robin Staines, Head - Public Protection & Housing, 3 Spilmand Street, Carmarthen SA31 1LE ☎ 01267 228960 ✉ rstaines@carmarthenshire.gov.uk

Housing Maintenance: Mr Robin Staines, Head - Public Protection & Housing, 3 Spilman Street, Carmarthen SA31 1LE ☎ 01267 228960 ✉ rstaines@carmarthenshire.gov.uk

Legal: Mrs Linda Rees-Jones Head - Administration & Law, County Hall, Carmarthen SA31 1JP ☎ 01267 224012 ✉ LRJones@carmarthenshire.gov.uk

Leisure and Cultural Services: Mr Ian Jones, Head - Leisure, Parc Myrddin, Carmarthen SA13 1DS ☎ 01267 228309 ✉ ijones@carmarthenshire.gov.uk

Licensing: Mrs Sue Watts Public Health Services Manager, 3 Spilman Street, , Carmarthen SA31 1LE ☎ 01267 228929 ✉ sewatts@carmartenshire.gov.uk

Lifelong Learning: Mr Matt Morden Lifelong Skills Network Manager, County Hall, Carmarthen SA31 1JP ☎ 01267 246648 ✉ msmorden@carmarthenshire.gov.uk

Lighting: Mr Mario Cresci Head - Street Scene, Parc Myrddin, Carmarthen SA31 2HQ ☎ 01237 224502 mcresci@carmarthenshire.gov.uk

Member Services: Ms Gaynor Morgan Democratic Services Manager, County Hall, Carmarthen SA31 1JP ☎ 01267 224026 gmorgan@carmarthenshire.gov.uk

Parking: Mr John Mcevoy Road Safety & Traffic Manager, Parc Myrddin, Carmarthen SA31 2HQ ☎ 01267 228190 jmcevoy@carmarthenshire.gov.uk

Partnerships: Mrs Gwyneth Ayers Corporate Policy & Partnerships Manager, County Hall, Carmarthen SA31 1JP ☎ 01267 224112 gayers@carmarthenshire.gov.uk

Personnel / HR: Mr Paul Thomas, Assistant Chief Executive - People Management & Performance, Parc Dewi Sant, Carmarthen SA31 3HB ☎ 01267 246123 prthomas@carmarthenshire.gov.uk

Planning: Mr Eifion Bowen, Head - Planning Services, 7/8 Spilman Street, Carmarthen SA31 1LQ ☎ 01267 228918 🖷 01267 237612 ebowen@carmarthenshire.gov.uk

Procurement: Mr Phil Sexton, Head - Audit, Procurement & ICT, Parc Dewi Sant, Carmarthen SA31 3HB ☎ 01267 246217 psexton@carmarthenshire.gov.uk

Public Libraries: Mrs Jane Davies Senior Cultural Services Manager, County Hall, Carmarthen SA31 1JP ☎ 01554 742180 jdavies@carmarthenshire.gov.uk

Recycling & Waste Minimisation: Mr Mario Cresci Head - Street Scene, County Hall, Carmarthen SA31 1JP ☎ 01237 224502 mcresci@carmarthenshire.gov.uk

Regeneration: Mr Stuart Walters Regeneration Manager, Parc Ananwy, Business Resource Centre, Ammanford SA18 3EP ☎ 01269 590241 swalters@carmarthenshire.gov.uk

Road Safety: Mr John Mcevoy Road Safety & Traffic Manager, Parc Myrddin, Carmarthen SA31 2HQ ☎ 01267 228190 jmcevoy@carmarthenshire.gov.uk

Social Services: Mr Jake Morgan, Director - Communities, County Hall, Carmarthen SA31 1JP ☎ ; 01267 244698 🖷 01267 228908 jakemorgan@carmarthenshire.gov.uk

Social Services (Adult): Mr Anthony Maynard Head - Mental Health & Learning Disabilities, 3 Spliman Street, , Carmarthen SA31 1LE ☎ 01267 228849 🖷 01267 228908 amaynard@carmarthenshire.gov.uk

Social Services (Children): Mr Stefan Smith, Head - Children's Services, Block 2, S David's Park, Jobswewl Road, Carmarthen SA31 3HB ☎ 01267 246530 🖷 01267 246746 sjsmith@carmarthenshire.gov.uk

Street Scene: Mr Mario Cresci Head - Street Scene, Parc Myrddin, Carmarthen SA31 2HQ ☎ 01237 224502 mcresci@carmarthenshire.gov.uk

Sustainable Development: Mr Kendal Davies, Sustainable Development Manager, County Hall, Carmarthen SA31 1JP ☎ 01267 228351 🖷 01267 224652 jkdavies@carmarthenshire.gov.uk

Tourism: Mr Huw Parsons Marketing & Tourism Manager, Business Resource Centre, Parc Amanwy, New Road, Ammanford SA18 3EP ☎ ; 01267 234567 🖷 01269 590290 hlparsons@carmarthenshire.gov.uk

Traffic Management: Mr John Mcevoy Road Safety & Traffic Manager, Parc Myrddin, Carmarthen SA31 2HQ ☎ 01267 228190 jmcevoy@carmarthenshire.gov.uk

Transport: Mr Steven Pilliner Head - Transport & Engineering, Parc Myrddin, Carmarthen SA31 2HQ ☎ 01267 228150 spilliner@carmarthenshire.gov.uk

Transport Planner: Mr Steven Pilliner Head - Transport & Engineering, Parc Myrddin, Carmarthen SA31 2HQ ☎ 01267 228150 spilliner@carmarthenshire.gov.uk

Waste Collection and Disposal: Mr Mario Cresci Head - Street Scene, Parc Myrddin, Carmarthen SA31 2HQ ☎ 01237 224502 mcresci@carmarthenshire.gov.uk

Waste Management: Mr Mario Cresci Head - Street Scene, Parc Myrddin, Carmarthen SA31 2HQ ☎ 01237 224502 mcresci@carmarthenshire.gov.uk

COUNCILLORS

***Chair* Griffiths**, Peter (PC - Carmarthen Town North)
phughes-griffiths@carmarthenshire.gov.uk

***Vice-Chair* Morgan**, Eryl (LAB - Bigyn)
emorgan@carmarthenshire.gov.uk

***Leader of the Council* Dole**, Emlyn (PC - Llannon)
edole@carmarthenshire.gov.uk

***Deputy Leader of the Council* Palmer**, Pamela (IND - Abergwili)
papalmer@carmarthenshire.gov.uk

Deian (PC - Ammanford)
deharries@carmarthenshire.gov.uk

Allen, Susan (IND - Whitland)
smallen@carmarthenshire.gov.uk

Bartlett, John (LAB - Betws)
rbartlett@carmarthenshire.gov.uk

Bowen, Theressa (IND - Llwynhendy)
thbowen@carmarthenshire.gov.uk

Caiach, Sian (O - Hengoed)
smcaiach@carmarthenshire.gov.uk

Campbell, Cefin (PC - Llanfihangel Aberbythych)
cacampbell@carmarthenshire.gov.uk

Charles, John (PC - Llanegwad)
mcharles@carmarthenshire.gov.uk

Cooper, Peter (LAB - Saron)
apcooper@carmarthenshire.gov.uk

Cundy, Deryk (LAB - Bynea)
dcundy@carmarthenshire.gov.uk

CARMARTHENSHIRE

Davies, Terry (LAB - Gorslas)
tedavies@carmarthenshire.gov.uk

Davies, Keith (LAB - Kidwelly)
wkdavies@carmarthenshire.gov.uk

Davies, Alun (PC - Saron)
alundavies@carmarthenshire.gov.uk

Davies, Joseph (IND - Manordeib & Salem)
josdavies@carmarthenshire.gov.uk

Davies, Daff (IND - Llansteffan)
dbdavies@carmarthenshire.gov.uk

Davies, Ieuan (IND - Llanybydder)
iwdavies@carmarthenshire.gov.uk

Davies, Sharen (LAB - Llwynhendy)
sdavies@carmarthenshire.gov.uk

Davies, Glynog (PC - Quarter Bach)
gidavies@carmarthenshire.gov.uk

Davies, Anthony (IND - Llandybie)
antdavies@carmarthenshire.gov.uk

Davies Evans, Linda (PC - Llanfihangel-Ar-Arth)
ldaviesevans@carmarthenshire.gov.uk

Defis, Tom (PC - Carmarthen Town West)
tdefis@carmarthenshire.gov.uk

Devichand, Tegwen (LAB - Dafen)
tdevichand@carmarthenshire.gov.uk

Edmunds, Jeffrey (LAB - Bigyn)
jedmunds@carmarthenshire.gov.uk

Edwards, Penny (LAB - Hengoed)
PennyEdwards@carmarthenshire.gov.uk

Evans, Colin (LAB - Pontamman)
dcevans@carmarthenshire.gov.uk

Evans, Hazel (PC - Cenarth)
hazelevans@carmarthenshire.gov.uk

Evans, Wyn (IND - Llanddarog)
wjwevans@carmarthenshire.gov.uk

Evans, Tyssul (PC - Llangyndeyrn)
wtevans@carmarthenshire.gov.uk

Gravell, Meryl (IND - Trimsaran)
mgravell@carmarthenshire.gov.uk

Higgins, Calum (LAB - Tycroes)
chiggins@carmarthenshire.gov.uk

Hopkins, Gwyn (PC - Llangennech)
wghopkins@carmarthenshire.gov.uk

Howell, John (PC - Llangeler)
kenhowell@carmarthenshire.gov.uk

Hughes, Philip (IND - St Clears)
pmhughes@carmarthenshire.gov.uk

Jackson, Ivor (IND - Llandovery)
ijjackson@carmarthenshire.gov.uk

James, Andrew (IND - Llangadog)
andjames@carmarthenshire.gov.uk

James, John (LAB - Burry Port)
johnjames@carmarthenshire.gov.uk

Jenkins, David (PC - Glanamman)
dmjenkins@carmarthenshire.gov.uk

Jenkins, John (INDNA - Elli)
jpjenkins@carmarthenshire.gov.uk

Jones, Anthony (LAB - Llandybie)
awjones@carmarthenshire.gov.uk

Jones, Patricia (LAB - Burry Port)
pemjones@carmarthenshire.gov.uk

Jones, Irfon (IND - Cynwyl Elfed)
hijones@carmarthenshire.gov.uk

Jones, Jim (IND - Glyn)
tjjones@carmarthenshire.gov.uk

Jones, Gareth (PC - Carmarthen Town North)
gojones@carmarthenshire.gov.uk

Lemon, Winston (PC - Glanymor)
wjlemon@carmarthenshire.gov.uk

Lenny, Alun (PC - Carmarthen Town South)
alunlenny@carmarthenshire.gov.uk

Lewis, Jean (PC - Trelech)
JeanLewis@carmarthenshire.gov.uk

Llewellyn, Roy (PC - Llanboidy)
djrllewellyn@carmarthenshire.gov.uk

Madge, Kevin (LAB - Garnant)
kmadge@carmarthenshire.gov.uk

Matthews, Shirley (LAB - Pembrey)
smatthews@carmarthenshire.gov.uk

Morgan, Giles (IND - Swiss Valley)
agmorgan@carmarthenshire.gov.uk

Owen, Jeff (PC - Tyisha)
jeffowen@carmarthenshire.gov.uk

Price, Darren (PC - Gorslas)
daprice@carmarthenshire.gov.uk

Richards, Hugh (IND - Felinfoel)
dwhrichards@carmarthenshire.gov.uk

Roberts, Beatrice (LAB - Glanymor)
loroberts@carmarthenshire.gov.uk

Shepardson, Hugh (IND - Pembrey)
hbshepardson@carmarthenshire.gov.uk

Speake, Alan (PC - Carmarthen Town West)
adtspeake@carmarthenshire.gov.uk

Stephens, Mair (IND - St Ishmael)
lmstephens@carmarthenshire.gov.uk

Theophilus, Thomas (IND - Cilycwm)
ttheophilus@carmarthenshire.gov.uk

Thomas, Edward (IND - Llandeilo)
egthomas@carmarthenshire.gov.uk

Thomas, Gwyneth (PC - Llangennech)
gwythomas@carmarthenshire.gov.uk

Thomas, Siân (PC - Penygroes)
sethomas@sirgar.gov.uk

Thomas, Keri (LAB - Tyisha)
kpthomas@carmarthenshire.gov.uk

Thomas, Kim (LAB - Llannon)
mkthomas@carmarthenshire.gov.uk

Thomas, Bill (LAB - Lliedi)
bthomas@carmarthenshire.gov.uk

Thomas, Jeffrey (PC - Carmarthen Town South)
jeffthomas@carmarthenshire.gov.uk

Thomas, Gareth (PC - Hendy)
gbthomas@sirgar.gov.uk

Tremlett, Jane (IND - Laugharne Township)
jtremlett@carmarthenshire.gov.uk

Williams, Eirwyn (PC - Cynwyl Gaeo)
jewilliams@carmarthenshire.gov.uk

Williams, Janice (LAB - Lliedi)
janwilliams@carmarthenshire.gov.uk

Williams, Joy (PC - Pontyberem)
jswilliams@sirgar.gov.uk

Williams, Elwyn (PC - Llangunnor)
dewilliams@carmarthenshire.gov.uk

POLITICAL COMPOSITION

PC: 29, LAB: 22, IND: 21, INDNA: 1, O: 1

COMMITTEE CHAIRS

Audit: Mr Giles Morgan

Education & Children: Mr Eirwyn Williams

Licensing: Mr Thomas Theophilus

Planning: Mr Alun Lenny

Castle Point D

Castle Point Borough Council, Council Offices, Kiln Road, Thundersley, Benfleet SS7 1TF
☎ 01268 882200 🖷 01268 882455 ✉ enquiries@castlepoint.gov.uk
💻 www.castlepoint.gov.uk

FACTS AND FIGURES

Parliamentary Constituencies: Castle Point
EU Constituencies: Eastern
Election Frequency: Elections are by thirds

PRINCIPAL OFFICERS

Chief Executive: Mr David Marchant, Chief Executive, Council Offices, Kiln Road, Thundersley, Benfleet SS7 1TF ☎ 01268 882200 🖷 01268 882455 ✉ dmarchant@castlepoint.gov.uk

Deputy Chief Executive: Mrs Devinia Board Strategic Director - Transformation & Resources, Council Offices, Kiln Road, Thundersley, Benfleet SS7 1TF ☎ 01268 882363 🖷 01268 882455 ✉ dboard@castlepoint.gov.uk

Deputy Chief Executive: Mr Andrew Smith Strategic Director - Corporate Services & Monitoring Officer, Council Offices, Kiln Road, Thundersley, Benfleet SS7 1TF ☎ 01268 882433 🖷 01268 882455 ✉ asmith@castlepoint.gov.uk

Architect, Building / Property Services: Mr Jarl Jansen, Facilities & Asset Manager, Council Offices, Kiln Road, Thundersley, Benfleet SS7 1TF ☎ 01268 882408 🖷 01268 882455 ✉ jjansen@castlepoint.gov.uk

Best Value: Mr Craig Watts Head - Performance & Support Service, Council Offices, Kiln Road, Thundersley, Benfleet SS7 1TF ☎ 01268 882213 🖷 01268 755332 ✉ cwatts@castlepoint.gov.uk

Building Control: Mr Gary Martindill Principal Building Surveyor, Council Offices, Kiln Road, Thundersley, Benfleet SS7 1TF ☎ 01268 882288 ✉ gmartindill@castlepoint.gov.uk

PR / Communications: Miss Ann Horgan Head - Governance, Council Offices, Kiln Road, Thundersley, Benfleet SS7 1TF ☎ 01268 882413 ✉ ahorgan@castlepoint.gov.uk

Community Planning: Mr Stephen Rogers, Head - Regeneration & Neighbourhoods, Council Offices, Kiln Road, Thundersley, Benfleet SS7 1TF ☎ 01268 882200 🖷 01268 882382 ✉ srogers@castlepoint.gov.uk

Community Safety: Mrs Mel Harris, Head - Partnerships & Safer Places, Council Offices, Kiln Road, Thundersley, Benfleet SS7 1TF ☎ 01268 882369 ✉ mharris@castlepoint.gov.uk

Computer Management: Mr Barry Delf, ICT Service Manager, Council Offices, Kiln Road, Thundersley, Benfleet SS7 1TF ☎ 01268 882412 🖷 01268 755332 ✉ bdelf@castlepoint.gov.uk

Contracts: Ms Fiona Wilson, Head - Law & Deputy Monitoring Officer, Council Offices, Kiln Road, Thundersley, Benfleet SS7 1TF ☎ 01268 882436 🖷 01268 755332 ✉ fwilson@castlepoint.gov.uk

Corporate Services: Mr Andrew Smith Strategic Director - Corporate Services & Monitoring Officer, Council Offices, Kiln Road, Thundersley, Benfleet SS7 1TF ☎ 01268 882433 🖷 01268 882455 ✉ asmith@castlepoint.gov.uk

Customer Service: Ms Wendy Buck Head of Housing & Communities, Council Offices, Kiln Road, Thundersley, Benfleet SS7 1TF ☎ 01268 882245 ✉ wbuck@castlepoint.gov.uk

Economic Development: Mr Stephen Rogers, Head - Regeneration & Neighbourhoods, Council Offices, Kiln Road, Thundersley, Benfleet SS7 1TF ☎ 01268 882200 🖷 01268 882382 ✉ srogers@castlepoint.gov.uk

Electoral Registration: Mr John Riley, Cabinet & Electoral Services Manager, Council Offices, Kiln Road, Thundersley, Benfleet SS7 1TF ☎ 01268 882417 🖷 01268 755332 ✉ jriley@castlepoint.gov.uk

Emergency Planning: Mr Jarl Jansen, Facilities & Asset Manager, Council Offices, Kiln Road, Thundersley, Benfleet SS7 1TF ☎ 01268 882408 🖷 01268 882455 ✉ jjansen@castlepoint.gov.uk

Energy Management: Mr Rob Lawrence Property Technical Officer, Council Offices, Kiln Road, Thundersley, Benfleet SS7 1TF ☎ 01268 882200

Environmental / Technical Services: Mrs Trudie Bragg Head - Environment, Council Offices, Kiln Road, Thundersley, Benfleet SS7 1TF ☎ 01268 882476 ✉ tbragg@castlepoint.gov.uk

CASTLE POINT

Environmental Health: Mrs Trudie Bragg Head - Environment, Council Offices, Kiln Road, Thundersley, Benfleet SS7 1TF ☎ 01268 882476 ✉ tbragg@castlepoint.gov.uk

Events Manager: Mrs Mel Harris, Head - Partnerships & Safer Places, Council Offices, Kiln Road, Thundersley, Benfleet SS7 1TF ☎ 01268 882369 ✉ mharris@castlepoint.gov.uk

Facilities: Mr Jarl Jansen, Facilities & Asset Manager, Council Offices, Kiln Road, Thundersley, Benfleet SS7 1TF ☎ 01268 882408 🖷 01268 882455 ✉ jjansen@castlepoint.gov.uk

Finance: Ms Chris Mills, Head - Resources & S151 Officer, Council Offices, Kiln Road, Thundersley, Benfleet SS7 1TF ☎ 01268 882215 🖷 01268 882211 ✉ cmills@castlepoint.gov.uk

Treasury: Ms Chris Mills, Head - Resources & S151 Officer, Council Offices, Kiln Road, Thundersley, Benfleet SS7 1TF ☎ 01268 882215 🖷 01268 882211 ✉ cmills@castlepoint.gov.uk

Grounds Maintenance: Mr Ryan Lynch Operations Services Manager, Council Offices, Kiln Road, Thundersley, Benfleet SS7 1TF ☎ 01268 882377 🖷 01268 793137 ✉ rlynch@castlepoint.gov.uk

Health and Safety: Ms Chris Mills, Head - Resources & S151 Officer, Council Offices, Kiln Road, Thundersley, Benfleet SS7 1TF ☎ 01268 882215 🖷 01268 882211 ✉ cmills@castlepoint.gov.uk

Home Energy Conservation: Mr Simon Llewellyn Environmental Health Operational Manager, Council Offices, Kiln Road, Thundersley, Benfleet SS7 1TF ☎ 01268 882303 ✉ sllewellyn@castlepoint.gov.uk

Housing: Ms Wendy Buck Head of Housing & Communities, Council Offices, Kiln Road, Thundersley, Benfleet SS7 1TF ☎ 01268 882245 ✉ wbuck@castlepoint.gov.uk

Legal: Ms Fiona Wilson, Head - Law & Deputy Monitoring Officer, Council Offices, Kiln Road, Thundersley, Benfleet SS7 1TF ☎ 01268 882436 🖷 01268 755332 ✉ fwilson@castlepoint.gov.uk

Leisure and Cultural Services: Ms Diane Logue Community Services & Corporate Support Manager, Council Offices, Kiln Road, Thundersley, Benfleet SS7 1TF ☎ 01268 882669 ✉ dlogue@castlepoint.gov.uk

Member Services: Miss Ann Horgan, Head - Governance, Council Offices, Kiln Road, Thundersley, Benfleet SS7 1TF ☎ 01268 882413 🖷 01268 882455 ✉ ahorgan@castlepoint.gov.uk

Parking: Mr Ryan Lynch, Operational Services Manager, Council Offices, Kiln Road, Thundersley, Benfleet SS7 1TF ☎ 01268 882377 ✉ rlynch@castlepoint.gov.uk

Partnerships: Mrs Mel Harris, Head - Partnerships & Safer Places, Council Offices, Kiln Road, Thundersley, Benfleet SS7 1TF ☎ 01268 882369 ✉ mharris@castlepoint.gov.uk

Personnel / HR: Ms B Cree HR Manager, Council Offices, Kiln Road, Thundersley, Benfleet SS7 1TF ☎ 01268 882445 ✉ bcree@castlepoint.gov.uk

Personnel / HR: Ms Chris Mills, Head - Resources & S151 Officer, Council Offices, Kiln Road, Thundersley, Benfleet SS7 1TF ☎ 01268 882215 🖷 01268 882211 ✉ cmills@castlepoint.gov.uk

Planning: Mr Stephen Rogers, Head - Regeneration & Neighbourhoods, Council Offices, Kiln Road, Thundersley, Benfleet SS7 1TF ☎ 01268 882200 🖷 01268 882382 ✉ srogers@castlepoint.gov.uk

Procurement: Mr Jarl Jansen, Facilities & Asset Manager, Council Offices, Kiln Road, Thundersley, Benfleet SS7 1TF ☎ 01268 882408 🖷 01268 882455 ✉ jjansen@castlepoint.gov.uk

Recycling & Waste Minimisation: Mrs Trudie Bragg Head - Environment, Council Offices, Kiln Road, Thundersley, Benfleet SS7 1TF ☎ 01268 882476 ✉ tbragg@castlepoint.gov.uk

Regeneration: Mr Stephen Rogers, Head - Regeneration & Neighbourhoods, Council Offices, Kiln Road, Thundersley, Benfleet SS7 1TF ☎ 01268 882200 🖷 01268 882382 ✉ srogers@castlepoint.gov.uk

Staff Training: Ms Chris Mills, Head - Resources & S151 Officer, Council Offices, Kiln Road, Thundersley, Benfleet SS7 1TF ☎ 01268 882215 🖷 01268 882211 ✉ cmills@castlepoint.gov.uk

Street Scene: Mr Ryan Lynch, Operational Services Manager, Council Offices, Kiln Road, Thundersley, Benfleet SS7 1TF ☎ 01268 882377 ✉ rlynch@castlepoint.gov.uk

Sustainable Communities: Mr Stephen Rogers, Head - Regeneration & Neighbourhoods, Council Offices, Kiln Road, Thundersley, Benfleet SS7 1TF ☎ 01268 882200 🖷 01268 882382 ✉ srogers@castlepoint.gov.uk

Sustainable Development: Mr Rob Lawrence Property Technical Officer, Council Offices, Kiln Road, Thundersley, Benfleet SS7 1TF ☎ 01268 882200 ✉

Traffic Management: Mr Ryan Lynch, Operational Services Manager, Council Offices, Kiln Road, Thundersley, Benfleet SS7 1TF ☎ 01268 882377 ✉ rlynch@castlepoint.gov.uk

Waste Collection and Disposal: Mrs Trudie Bragg Head - Environment, Council Offices, Kiln Road, Thundersley, Benfleet SS7 1TF ☎ 01268 882476 ✉ tbragg@castlepoint.gov.uk

Waste Management: Mrs Trudie Bragg Head - Environment, Council Offices, Kiln Road, Thundersley, Benfleet SS7 1TF ☎ 01268 882476 ✉ tbragg@castlepoint.gov.uk

Children's Play Areas: Mr Ryan Lynch, Operational Services Manager, Council Offices, Kiln Road, Thundersley, Benfleet SS7 1TF ☎ 01268 882377 ✉ rlynch@castlepoint.gov.uk

COUNCILLORS

***Mayor* Sheldon**, Andrew (CON - St. Mary's)
cllr.asheldon@castlepoint.gov.uk

***Deputy Mayor* Cole**, Steven (CON - Canvey Island Winter Garden)
cllr.scole@catlepoint.gov.uk

***Leader of the Council* Riley**, Colin (CON - Victoria)
cllr.criley@castlepoint.gov.uk

***Deputy Leader of the Council* Stanley**, Jeffrey (CON - Boyce)
cllr.jstanley@castlepoint.gov.uk

Acott, Alan (IND - Canvey Island East)
cllr.aacott@castlepoint.gov.uk

Anderson, John (IND - Canvey Island Central)
cllr.janderson@castlepoint.gov.uk

Bayley, Alan (UKIP - Appleton)
cllr.abayley@castlepoint.gov.uk

Blackwell, Dave (IND - Canvey Island Central)
cllr.dblackwell@castlepoint.gov.uk

Campagna, Barry (IND - Canvey Island South)
cllr.bcampagna@castlepoint.gov.uk

Cross, David (CON - St. Mary's)
cllr.dcross@castlepoint.gov.uk

Dick, Bill (CON - St. Peter's)
cllr.wdick@castlepoint.gov.uk

Egan, Eoin (CON - Appleton)
cllr.eegan@castlepoint.gov.uk

Egan, Beverley (CON - St. Peter's)
cllr.began@castlepoint.gov.uk

Goodwin, Wendy (CON - Boyce)
cllr.wgoodwin@castlepoint.gov.uk

Govier, Jackie (CON - St. George's)
cllr.jgovier@castlepoint.gov.uk

Greig, Peter (IND - Canvey Island Winter Garden)
cllr.pgreig@castlepoint.gov.uk

Hart, Simon (CON - Victoria)
cllr.shart@castlepoint.gov.uk

Harvey, Nick (IND - Canvey Island North)
cllr.nharvey@castlepoint.gov.uk

Howard, Ray (CON - Canvey Island West)
cllr.rhoward@castlepoint.gov.uk

Hudson, John (UKIP - Cedar Hall)
cllr.jhudson@castlepoint.gov.uk

Hurrell, Ron (UKIP - St. Peter's)
cllr.rhurrell@castlepoint.gov.uk

Isaacs, Godfrey (CON - St. James')
cllr.gisaacs@castlepoint.gov.uk

King, Jane (IND - Canvey Island West)
cllr.jking@castlepoint.gov.uk

Ladzrie, Norman (CON - St. James')
cllr.nladzrie@castlepoint.gov.uk

Letchford, Colin (IND - Canvey Island East)
cllrletchofrd@castlepoint.gov.uk

Maclean, Colin (CON - Cedar Hall)
cllr.cmaclean@castlepoint.gov.uk

May, Peter (IND - Canvey Island Central)
cllr.pmay@castlepoint.gov.uk

Mumford, Charles (CON - Canvey Island East)
cllr.cmumford@castlepoint.gov.uk

Palmer, Barry (IND - Canvey Island South)
cllr.bpalmer@castlepoint.gov.uk

Partridge, Alf (CON - St. Mary's)
cllr.apartridge@castlepoint.gov.uk

Payne, Janice (IND - Canvey Island South)
cllr.jpayne@castlepoint.gov.uk

Sharp, Bill (CON - St. James')
cllr.wsharp@castlepoint.gov.uk

Skipp, Tom (CON - Appleton)
cllr.tskipp@castlepoint.gov.uk

Smith, Norman (CON - Boyce)
cllr.nsmith@castlepoint.gov.uk

Tucker, Martin (IND - Canvey Island North)
cllr.mtucker@castlepoint.gov.uk

Varker, Paul (UKIP - Victoria)
cllr.pvarker@castlepoint.gov.uk

Walter, Clive (CON - St. George's)
cllr.cwalter@castlepoint.gov.uk

Wass, Liz (CON - Cedar Hall)
cllr.lwass@castlepoint.gov.uk

Watson, Grace (IND - Canvey Island North)
cllr.gwatson@castlepoint.gov.uk

Watson, Neville (IND - Canvey Island Winter Garden)
cllr.nwatson@castlepoint.gov.uk

Wood, Brian (CON - St. George's)
cllr.bwood@castlepoint.gov.uk

POLITICAL COMPOSITION

CON: 23, IND: 14, UKIP: 4

COMMITTEE CHAIRS

Audit: Mr Norman Ladzrie

Development: Mr Simon Hart

Health & Wellbeing: Mrs Wendy Goodwin

Licensing: Mr Eoin Egan

Causeway Coast & Glens District Council N

Causeway Coast & Glens District Council, Statutory Transition Committee, Coleraine Borough Council, 66 Portstewart Road, Coleraine BT52 1EY
☎ 028 7034 7204 ✉ stephen.mcmaw@colerainebc.gov.uk
🖳 www.causewaycoastandglens.gov.uk

PRINCIPAL OFFICERS

Chief Executive: Mr David Jackson Chief Executive, Statutory Transition Committee, Coleraine Borough Council, 66 Portstewart Road, Coleraine BT52 1EY

Senior Management: Mr Stephen McMaw Head of Convergence, Statutory Transition Committee, Coleraine Borough Council, 66 Portstewart Road, Coleraine BT52 1EY

Senior Management: Mr Aiden McPeake Director of Environmental Services, Statutory Transition Committee, Coleraine Borough Council, 66 Portstewart Road, Coleraine BT52 1EY

CAUSEWAY COAST & GLENS DISTRICT COUNCIL

Senior Management: Ms Moira McQuinn Director of Performance, Statutory Transition Committee, Coleraine Borough Council, 66 Portstewart Road, Coleraine BT52 1EY

Senior Management: Mr D Wright Chief Finance Officer, Statutory Transition Committee, Coleraine Borough Council, 66 Portstewart Road, Coleraine BT52 1EY

Computer Management: Mr P McColgan Lead Officer - ICT, Statutory Transition Committee, Coleraine Borough Council, 66 Portstewart Road, Coleraine BT52 1EY

Economic Development: Ms Patricia O'Brien Economic Development Manager, Statutory Transition Committee, Coleraine Borough Council, 66 Portstewart Road, Coleraine BT52 1EY

Environmental / Technical Services: Mr Aiden McPeake Director of Environmental Services, Statutory Transition Committee, Coleraine Borough Council, 66 Portstewart Road, Coleraine BT52 1EY

Events Manager: Ms C McKee Events Officer, Statutory Transition Committee, Coleraine Borough Council, 66 Portstewart Road, Coleraine BT52 1EY

Finance: Mr D Wright Chief Finance Officer, Statutory Transition Committee, Coleraine Borough Council, 66 Portstewart Road, Coleraine BT52 1EY

Legal: Mr R Baker Lead Officer - Leisure & Development, Statutory Transition Committee, Coleraine Borough Council, 66 Portstewart Road, Coleraine BT52 1EY

Leisure and Cultural Services: Mr R Baker Lead Officer - Leisure & Development, Statutory Transition Committee, Coleraine Borough Council, 66 Portstewart Road, Coleraine BT52 1EY

Leisure and Cultural Services: Mr P Thompson Head of Tourism & Recreation, Statutory Transition Committee, Coleraine Borough Council, 66 Portstewart Road, Coleraine BT52 1EY

Member Services: Mrs C Toner Member Services Officer, Statutory Transition Committee, Coleraine Borough Council, 66 Portstewart Road, Coleraine BT52 1EY

Personnel / HR: Ms Sandra Kelly Lead Officer - Organisation Development, Statutory Transition Committee, Coleraine Borough Council, 66 Portstewart Road, Coleraine BT52 1EY

Planning: Mrs Denise Dickson Area Planning Manager, Statutory Transition Committee, Coleraine Borough Council, 66 Portstewart Road, Coleraine BT52 1EY

Regeneration: Mr Alan Jeffers Regeneration Manager, Statutory Transition Committee, Coleraine Borough Council, 66 Portstewart Road, Coleraine BT52 1EY

Public Health: Mr Bryan Edgar Head of Health & Built Environment, Statutory Transition Committee, Coleraine Borough Council, 66 Portstewart Road, Coleraine BT52 1EY

Tourism: Mr P Thompson Head of Tourism & Recreation, Statutory Transition Committee, Coleraine Borough Council, 66 Portstewart Road, Coleraine BT52 1EY

COUNCILLORS

Baird, Joan (UUP - The Glens)
cllr.jbaird@moyle-council.org

Beattie, Orla (SDLP - Benbradagh)
orlabeattie@hotmail.com

Blair, William (O - Ballymoney)
william.blair@ballymoney.gov.uk

Callan, Aaron (UUP - Limavady)
aaroncallan@live.co.uk

Chivers, Brenda (SF - Limavady)
bchivers5@aol.com

Clarke, Trevor (DUP - Coleraine)
trevor.clarke@colerainebc.gov.uk

Cole, Sam (DUP - Bann)
samuelcole@hotmail.co.uk

Douglas, Boyd (O - Benbradagh)
boyd.douglas@btinternet.com

Duddy, George (DUP - Coleraine)
william.duddy@colerainebc.gov.uk

Fielding, Mark (DUP - Causeway)
mark.fielding@colerainebc.gov.uk

Findlay, John (DUP - Ballymoney)
john.finlay@ballymoney.gov.uk

Fitzpatrick, Barney (ALL - Causeway)
bernard.fitzpatrick@colerainebc.gov.uk

Harding, David (UUP - Coleraine)
david.harding@colerainebc.gov.uk

Hickey, Maura (SDLP - Causeway)
maura.hickey@colerainebc.gov.uk

Hillis, Norman (UUP - Causeway)
norman.hills@colerainebc.gov.uk

Holmes, Richard (UUP - Bann)
richard.holmes@colerainebc.gov.uk

Hunter, Sandra (UUP - Causeway)
cllr.shunter@moyle-council.org

King, William (UUP - Bann)
william.king@colerainebc.gov.uk

Knight-McQuillan, Michelle (DUP - Bann)
michelle.knight-mcquillan@colerainebc.gov.uk

Loftus, Roisin (SD - Bann)
roisin.loftus@colerainebc.gov.uk

McCandless, William (UUP - Coleraine)
william.mccandless@colerainebc.gov.uk

McCaul, Tony (SF - Benbradagh)
tonymccaul1952@hotmail.com

McCorkell, James (DUP - Limavady)
jamesmccorkell@btinternet.com

McGlinchey, Sean (SF - Benbradagh)
carolinewhite65@hotmail.com

McGuigan, Philip (SF - Ballymoney)
philipmcguigan@hotmail.com

McKeown, Tom (UUP - Ballymoney)
thomas.mckeown@ballymoney.gov.uk

McKillop, Sharon (O - Causeway)
cllr.smckillop@moyle-council.org

McKillop, Margaret (SDLP - The Glens)
cllr.mamckillop@moyle-council.org

McLean, Alan (DUP - Ballymoney)
alan.mclean@causewaycoastandglens.gov.uk

McShane, Cara (SF - The Glens)
cllr.mcshane@moyle-council.org

McShane, Padraig (IND - The Glens)
cllr.pmcshane@moyle-council.org

Mulholland, Kieran (SF - The Glens)
kieranjmulholland@icloud.com

Mullan, Gerry (SDLP - Limavady)
gerry.mullan@causewaycoastandglens.gov.uk

Nicholl, Dermot (SF - Benbradagh)
dermot.nicholl@hotmail.com

Quigley, Stephanie (SDLP - Coleraine)
stephanie.quigley@colerainebc.gov.uk

Robinson, Alan (DUP - Limavady)
george.robinson14@btopenworld.com

Stevenson, Ian (DUP - Ballymoney)
ian.stevenson@ballymoney.gov.uk

Watton, Russell (PUP - Coleraine)
russellwatton@hotmail.co.uk

Wilson, Darryl (UUP - Ballymoney)
darrylwilson1979@gmail.com

POLITICAL COMPOSITION

DUP: 10, UUP: 10, SF: 7, SDLP: 5, O: 3, PUP: 1, IND: 1, ALL: 1, SD: 1

Central Bedfordshire U

Central Bedfordshire, Priory House, Monks Walk, Chicksands, Shefford SG17 5TQ
☎ 0300 300 8000 ⌂ customer.services@centralbedfordshire.gov.uk
www.centralbedfordshire.gov.uk

FACTS AND FIGURES

Parliamentary Constituencies: Bedfordshire Mid, Bedfordshire North East, Bedfordshire South West, Luton South, South West Bedfordshire

PRINCIPAL OFFICERS

Chief Executive: Mr Richard Carr Chief Executive, Priory House, Monks Walk, Chicksands, Shefford SG17 5TQ ☎ 0300 300 4004
richard.carr@centralbedfordshire.gov.uk

Assistant Chief Executive: Ms Deb Broadbent-Clarke Director of Improvement & Corporate Services, Priory House, Monks Walk, Chicksands, Shefford SG17 5TQ ☎ 0300 300 6651
deb.broadbent-clarke@centralbedfordshire.gov.uk

Senior Management: Mr Marcel Coiffait Director of Community Services, Priory House, Monks Walk, Chicksands, Shefford SG17 5TQ ☎ 0300 300 5637 marcel.coiffait@cenetralbedforshire.gov.uk

Senior Management: Ms Sue Harrison Director of Children's Services, Priory House, Monks Walk, Chicksands, Shefford SG17 5TQ ☎ 0300 300 4229 sue.harrison@centralbedfordshire.gov.uk

Senior Management: Mr Jason Longhurst Director of Regeneration & Business, Priory House, Monks Walk, Chicksands, Shefford SG17 5TQ ☎ 0300 300 4005
jason.longhurst@centralbedfordshire.gov.uk

Senior Management: Ms Karen Oellermann Assistant Director of Commissioning & Partnerships, Watling House, High Street North, Dunstable LU6 1LF ☎ 0300 300 5265
karen.oellermann@centralbedfordshire.gov.uk

Senior Management: Ms Julie Ogley Director of Social Care, Health & Housing, Priory House, Monks Walk, Chicksands, Shefford SG17 5TQ ☎ 0300 300 4221
julie.ogley@centralbedfordshire.gov.uk

Senior Management: Ms Muriel Scott Director - Public Health, 7 Hadleigh Close, Putnoe, Bedford MK41 8JW ☎ 0300 300 5616
muriel.scott@centralbedfordshire.gov.uk

Senior Management: Mr Charles Warboys Chief Finance Officer, Priory House, Monks Walk, Chicksands, Shefford SG17 5TQ
☎ 0300 300 6147 charles.warboys@centralbedfordshire.gov.uk

Architect, Building / Property Services: Mr David Cox Chief Assets Officer, Priory House, Monks Walk, Chicksands, Shefford SG17 5TQ ☎ 0300 3005474 david.cox@centralbedfordshire.gov.uk

Building Control: Mr Peter Keates Head of Building Control & Albion Archaeology, Priory House, Monks Walk, Chicksands SG17 5TQ ☎ 0300 300 4380 peter.keates@centralbedfordshire.gov.uk

Children / Youth Services: Mr Gerard Jones Assistant Director of Operations, Priory House, Monks Walk, Chicksands, Shefford SG17 5TQ ☎ 0300 300 4616 gerard.jones@wolverhampton.gov.uk

Children / Youth Services: Ms Karen Oellermann Assistant Director of Commissioning & Partnerships, Watling House, High Street North, , Dunstable LU6 1LF ☎ 0300 300 5265
karen.oellermann@centralbedfordshire.gov.uk

Children / Youth Services: Ms Helen Redding Assistant Director of Learning, Commissioning & Partnerships, Priory House, Monks Walk, Chicksands, Shefford SG17 5TQ ☎ 0300 300 6067
helen.redding@centralbedfordshire.gov.uk

Civil Registration: Mr Quentin Baker Interim Monitoring Officer, Priory House, Monks Walk, Chicksands, Shefford SG17 5TQ
☎ 0300 300 4204 quentin.baker@centralbedfordshire.gov.uk

PR / Communications: Ms Georgina Stanton Chief Communications Manager, Priory House, Monks Walk, Chicksands, Shefford SG17 5TQ ☎ 0300 300 4438
georgina.stanton@centralbedfordshire.gov.uk

Computer Management: Mr Stephan Conaway Chief Information Officer, Priory House, Monks Walk, Chicksands, Shefford SG17 5TQ ☎ 0300 300 5386 🖷 stephan.conaway@centralbedfordshire.gov.uk

Consumer Protection and Trading Standards: Ms Susan Childerhouse Head of Public Protection, Priory House, Monks Walk, Chicksands, Shefford SG17 5TQ ☎ 0300 300 4394 susan.childerhouse@centralbedfordshire.gov.uk

Customer Service: Ms Bernie McGill Head of Customer Relations & Services, Priory House, Monks Walk, Chicksands, Shefford SG17 5TQ ☎ 0300 300 5614 bernie.mcgill@centralbedfordshire.gov.uk

Economic Development: Ms Kate McFarlane Business Investment Group Manager, Priory House, Monks Walk, Chicksands, Shefford SG17 5TQ ☎ 0300 300 5858 kate.mcfarlane@centralbedfordshire.gov.uk

Education: Ms Sue Harrison Director of Children's Services, Priory House, Monks Walk, Chicksands, Shefford SG17 5TQ ☎ 0300 300 4229 sue.harrison@centralbedfordshire.gov.uk

Education: Ms Helen Redding Assistant Director of Learning, Commissioning & Partnerships, Priory House, Monks Walk, Chicksands, Shefford SG17 5TQ ☎ 0300 300 6067 helen.redding@centralbedfordshire.gov.uk

Electoral Registration: Mr Quentin Baker Interim Monitoring Officer, Priory House, Monks Walk, Chicksands, Shefford SG17 5TQ ☎ 0300 300 4204 quentin.baker@centralbedfordshire.gov.uk

Emergency Planning: Mr Iain Berry Acting Head of Public Protection, Priory House, Monks Walk, Chicksands, Shefford SG17 5TQ ☎ 0300 300 4475 iain.berry@centralbedfordshire.gov.uk

Energy Management: Mr Ben Finlayson Head of Capital Projects, Priory House, Monks Walk, Chicksands, Shefford SG17 5TQ ☎ 0300 300 6277 ben.finlayson@centralbedfordshire.gov.uk

Environmental / Technical Services: Mr Iain Berry Acting Head of Public Protection, Priory House, Monks Walk, Chicksands, Shefford SG17 5TQ ☎ 0300 300 4475 iain.berry@centralbedfordshire.gov.uk

Environmental Health: Ms Susan Childerhouse Head of Public Protection, Priory House, Monks Walk, Chicksands, Shefford SG17 5TQ ☎ 0300 300 4394 susan.childerhouse@centralbedfordshire.gov.uk

Estates, Property & Valuation: Mr David Cox Chief Assets Officer, Priory House, Monks Walk, Chicksands, Shefford SG17 5TQ ☎ 0300 3005474 david.cox@centralbedfordshire.gov.uk

Estates, Property & Valuation: Mr Andrew Gordon Head of Estates & Management, Priory House, Monks Walk, Chicksands, Shefford SG17 5TQ ☎ 0300 300 5882 andrew.gordon@centralbedfordshire.gov.uk

Facilities: Mr Steven Girling Head of Facilities Management & Maintenance, Priory House, Monks Walk, Chicksands, Shefford SG17 5TQ ☎ 0300 300 5246 steven.girling@centralbedfordshire.gov.uk

Finance: Mr Charles Warboys Chief Finance Officer, Priory House, Monks Walk, Chicksands, Shefford SG17 5TQ ☎ 0300 300 6147 charles.warboys@centralbedfordshire.gov.uk

Health and Safety: Mr Lee Butler Health, Safety & Wellbeing Manager, Priory House, Monks Walk, Chicksands, Shefford SG17 5TQ ☎ 0300 300 6793 lee.butler@centralbedfordshire.gov.uk

Highways: Mr Paul Mason Head of Highways & Transport, Priory House, Monks Walk, Chicksands, Shefford SG17 5TQ ☎ 0300 300 4708 paul.mason@centralbedfordshire.gov.uk

Housing: Mr Tony Keaveney Assistant Director of Housing, High Street North, , Dunstable LU6 1LF ☎ 0300 300 5210 tony.keaveney@centralbedfordshire.gov.uk

Legal: Mr Quentin Baker Interim Monitoring Officer, Priory House, Monks Walk, Chicksands, Shefford SG17 5TQ ☎ 0300 300 4204 quentin.baker@centralbedfordshire.gov.uk

Leisure and Cultural Services: Ms Jill Dickinson Head of Leisure & Libraries, Priory House, Monks Walk, Chicksands, Shefford SG17 5TQ ☎ 0300 300 4258 jill.dickinson@centralbedfordshire.gov.uk

Licensing: Ms Susan Childerhouse Head of Public Protection, Priory House, Monks Walk, Chicksands, Shefford SG17 5TQ ☎ 0300 300 4394 susan.childerhouse@centralbedfordshire.gov.uk

Member Services: Mr Quentin Baker Interim Monitoring Officer, Priory House, Monks Walk, Chicksands, Shefford SG17 5TQ ☎ 0300 300 4204 quentin.baker@centralbedfordshire.gov.uk

Personnel / HR: Ms Deb Broadbent-Clarke Director of Improvement & Corporate Services, Priory House, Monks Walk, Chicksands, Shefford SG17 5TQ ☎ 0300 300 6651 deb.broadbent-clarke@centralbedfordshire.gov.uk

Personnel / HR: Ms Catherine Jones Chief People Officer, Priory House, Monks Walk, Chicksands, Shefford SG17 5TQ ☎ 0300 300 6048 catherine.jones@centralbedfordshire.gov.uk

Planning: Mr Andrew Davie Development Infrastructure Group Manager, Priory House, Monks Walk, Chicksands, Shefford SG17 5TQ ☎ 0300 300 4426 andrew.davie@centralbedfordshire.gov.uk

Procurement: Mr Paul Meigh Chief Procurement Officer, Priory House, Monks Walk, Chicksands, Shefford SG17 5TQ ☎ 0300 300 6626 paul.meigh@centralbedfordshire.gov.uk

Public Libraries: Ms Jill Dickinson Head of Leisure & Libraries, Priory House, Monks Walk, Chicksands, Shefford SG17 5TQ ☎ 0300 300 4258 jill.dickinson@centralbedfordshire.gov.uk

Recycling & Waste Minimisation: Ms Tracey Harris Head of Waste Management, Priory House, Monks Walk, Chicksands, Shefford SG17 5TQ ☎ 0300 300 4646 tracey.harris@centralbedfordshire.gov.uk

Regeneration: Mr Jason Longhurst Director of Regeneration & Business, Priory House, Monks Walk, Chicksands, Shefford SG17 5TQ ☎ 0300 300 4005 jason.longhurst@centralbedfordshire.gov.uk

Social Services: Mr Stuart Mitchelmore Assistant Director of Adult Social Care, Houghton Lodge, Ampthill, Bedford MK45 2TB ☎ 0300 300 4796 ✉ stuart.mitchelmore@centralbedfordshire.gov.uk

Social Services (Adult): Mr Stuart Mitchelmore Assistant Director of Adult Social Care, Houghton Lodge, Ampthill, Bedford MK45 2TB ☎ 0300 300 4796 ✉ stuart.mitchelmore@centralbedfordshire.gov.uk

Social Services (Children): Mr Gerard Jones Assistant Director of Operations, Priory House, Monks Walk, Chicksands, Shefford SG17 5TQ ☎ 0300 300 4616 ✉ gerard.jones@wolverhampton.gov.uk

Public Health: Ms Muriel Scott Director - Public Health, 7 Hadleigh Close, Putnoe, Bedford MK41 8JW ☎ 0300 300 5616 ✉ muriel.scott@centralbedfordshire.gov.uk

Tourism: Ms Kate McFarlane Business Investment Group Manager, Priory House, Monks Walk, Chicksands, Shefford SG17 5TQ ☎ 0300 300 5858 ✉ kate.mcfarlane@centralbedfordshire.gov.uk

Traffic Management: Ms Jeanette Keyte Head of Community Safety, Priory House, Monks Walk, Chicksands, Shefford SG17 5TQ ☎ 0300 300 5252 ✉ jeanette.keyte@centralbedfordshire.gov.uk

Waste Collection and Disposal: Ms Tracey Harris Head of Waste Management, Technology House, 239 Ampthill Road, Bedford MK42 9BD ☎ 0300 300 4646 ✉ tracey.harris@centralbedfordshire.gov.uk

Waste Management: Ms Tracey Harris Head of Waste Management, Technology House, 239 Ampthill Road, Bedford MK42 9BD ☎ 0300 300 4646 ✉ tracey.harris@centralbedfordshire.gov.uk

COUNCILLORS

***Chair* Bowater**, David (CON - Leighton Buzzard South)
david.bowater@centralbedfordshire.gov.uk

***Vice-Chair* Chapman**, Fiona (CON - Flitwick)
fiona.chapman@centralbedfordshire.gov.uk

***Leader of the Council* Jamieson**, James (CON - Westoning, Flitton & Greenfield)
james.jamieson@centralbedfordshire.gov.uk

***Deputy Leader of the Council* Jones**, Maurice (CON - Biggleswade North)
maurice.jones@centralbedfordshire.gov.uk

Barker, Angela (CON - Houghton Conquest & Haynes)
angela.barker@centralbedfordshire.gov.uk

Berry, Raymond (CON - Leighton Buzzard South)
raymond.berry@centralbedfordshire.gov.uk

Birt, Lewis (CON - Shefford)
lewis.birt@centralbedfordshire.gov.uk

Blair, Michael (CON - Ampthill)
michael.blair@centralbedfordshire.gov.uk

Brown, Anthony (CON - Shefford)
anthony.brown@centralbedfordshire.gov.uk

Chatterley, John (CON - Dunstable Icknield)
john.chatterley@centralbedfordshire.gov.uk

Clark, Sue (CON - Cranfield & Marston Moretaine)
sue.clark@centralbedfordshire.gov.uk

Collins, Kevin (CON - Caddington)
kevin.collins@centralbedfordshire.gov.uk

Costin, Norman (CON - Toddington)
norman.costin@centralbedfordshire.gov.uk

Dalgarno, Ian (CON - Arlesey)
ian.dalgarno@centralbedfordshire.gov.uk

Dixon, Steven (CON - Stotfold & Langford)
steven.dixon@centralbedfordshire.gov.uk

Dodwell, Amanda (CON - Leighton Buzzard South)
amanda.dodwell@centralbedfordshire.gov.uk

Downing, Paul (CON - Ampthill)
paul.downing@centralbedfordshire.gov.uk

Duckett, Paul (CON - Ampthill)
paul.duckett@centralbedfordshire.gov.uk

Ferguson, Ken (CON - Leighton Buzzard North)
ken.ferguson@centralbedfordshire.gov.uk

Firth, Frank (CON - Northill)
frank.firth@centralbedfordshire.gov.uk

Freeman, Jeannette (CON - Dunstable Northfields)
jeannette.freeman@centralbedfordshire.gov.uk

Ghent, Eugene (CON - Dunstable Manshead)
eugene.ghent@centralbedfordshire.gov.uk

Gomm, Charles (CON - Flitwick)
charles.gomm@centralbedfordshire.gov.uk

Goodchild, Susan (LD - Houghton Hall)
susan.goodchild@centralbedfordshire.gov.uk

Graham, Alison (IND - Silsoe & Shillington)
alison.graham@centralbedfordshire.gov.uk

Gurney, Doreen (CON - Potton)
doreen.gurney@centralbedfordshire.gov.uk

Hegley, Carole (CON - Dunstable Central)
carole.hegley@centralbedfordshire.gov.uk

Hollick, Peter (CON - Dunstable Watling)
peter.hollick@centralbedfordshire.gov.uk

Janes, Ken (CON - Eaton Bray)
ken.janes@centralbedfordshire.gov.uk

Johnstone, Roy (CON - Leighton Buzzard North)
roy.johnstone@centralbedfordshire.gov.uk

Kane, John (CON - Houghton Hall)
john.kane@centralbedfordshire.gov.uk

Lawrence, David (CON - Biggleswade South)
david.lawrence@centralbedfordshire.gov.uk

Lawrence, Jane (CON - Biggleswade North)
jane.lawrence@centralbedfordshire.gov.uk

Matthews, Ken (CON - Cranfield & Marston Moretaine)
ken.matthews@centralbedfordshire.gov.uk

Maudlin, Caroline (CON - Sandy)
caroline.maudlin@centralbedfordshire.gov.uk

McVicar, David (CON - Dunstable Icknield)
david.mcvicar@centralbedfordshire.gov.uk

Morris, Robert (CON - Cranfield & Marston Moretaine)
robert.morris@centralbedfordshire.gov.uk

CENTRAL BEDFORDSHIRE

Nicols, Tom (CON - Toddington)
tom.nicols@centralbedfordshire.gov.uk

Perham, Gordon (CON - Linslade)
gordon.perham@centralbedfordshire.gov.uk

Ryan, Antonia (CON - Parkside)
antonia.ryan@centralbedfordshire.gov.uk

Saunders, John (CON - Stotfold & Langford)

Saunders, Brian (CON - Stotfold & Langford)
brian.saunders@centralbedfordshire.gov.uk

Shelvey, David (CON - Arlesey)
david.shelvey@centralbedfordshire.gov.uk

Shingler, Ian (IND - Barton-le-Clay)
ian.shingler@centralbedfordshire.gov.uk

Smith, Peter (CON - Sandy)
peter.smith3@centralbedfordshire.gov.uk

Spurr, Brian (CON - Leighton Buzzard North)
brian.spurr@centralbedfordshire.gov.uk

Stay, Richard (CON - Caddington)
richard.stay@centralbedfordshire.gov.uk

Stock, Tracey (CON - Sandy)
tracey.stock@centralbedfordshire.gov.uk

Swain, Tony (LAB - Tithe Farm)
tony.swain@centralbedfordshire.gov.uk

Tubb, Gary (CON - Linslade)
gary.tubb@centralbedfordshire.gov.uk

Turner, Andrew (CON - Flitwick)
andrewturner@flitwickfirst.com

Versallion, Mark (CON - Heath & Reach)
mark.versallion@centralbedfordshire.gov.uk

Walker, Ben (CON - Linslade)
ben.walker@centralbedfordshire.gov.uk

Warren, Nigel (CON - Dunstable Northfields)
nigel.warren@centralbedfordshire.gov.uk

Wells, Budge (CON - Aspley & Woburn)
budge.wells@centralbedfordshire.gov.uk

Wenham, Richard (CON - Arlesey)
richard.wenham@centralbedfordshire.gov.uk

Woodward, Tim (CON - Biggleswade South)
cllrtim.woodward@centralbedfordshire.gov.uk

Young, Nigel (CON - Dunstable Watling)
nigel.young@centralbedfordshire.gov.uk

Zerny, Adam (IND - Potton)
adam.zerny@centralbedforshire.gov.uk

POLITICAL COMPOSITION

CON: 54, IND: 3, LAB: 1, LD: 1

COMMITTEE CHAIRS

Audit: Mr Michael Blair

Children's Services: Mrs Angela Barker

Development Management: Mr Ken Matthews

Licensing: Mr Tom Nicols

Social Care, Health & Housing: Mr Peter Hollick

Ceredigion W

Ceredigion County Council, Neuadd Cygnor Ceredigion, Penmorfa, Aberaeron SA46 0PA
☎ 01545 570881 🖷 01545 572009 ✉ reception@ceredigion.gov.uk
💻 www.ceredigion.gov.uk

FACTS AND FIGURES

Parliamentary Constituencies: Ceredigion
EU Constituencies: Wales
Election Frequency: Elections are of whole council

PRINCIPAL OFFICERS

Chief Executive: Miss Bronwen Morgan, Chief Executive, Neuadd Cygnor Ceredigion, Penmorfa, Aberaeron SA46 0PA ☎ 01545 572004 🖷 01545 572029 ✉ chiefexecutive@ceredigion.ov.uk

Deputy Chief Executive: Mr Eifon Evans Deputy Chief Executive, Neuadd Cygnor Ceredigion, Penmorfa, Aberaeron SA46 0PA ☎ 01545 572021 ✉ eifion.evans@ceredigion.gov.uk

Senior Management: Mr Parry Davies, Strategic Director - Care, Protection & Lifestyle, Neuadd Cygnor Ceredigion, Penmorfa, Aberaeron SA46 0PA ☎ 01545 572601 🖷 01545 572619 ✉ parryd@ceredigion.gov.uk

Senior Management: Mr Huw Morgan, Strategic Director - Sustainable Communities, Neuadd Cygnor Ceredigion, Penmorfa, Aberaeron SA46 0PA ☎ 01545 572400 🖷 01545 571089 ✉ huwt.morgan@ceredigion.gov.uk

Access Officer / Social Services (Disability): Ms Donna Pritchard Team Manager - Disabilities, Min Areon, Rhiw Goch, Aberaeron SA46 0DY ☎ 01545 570881 ✉ donnap@ceredigion.gov.uk

Architect, Building / Property Services: Mr Huw Morgan, Strategic Director - Sustainable Communities, County Hall, Market Street, Aberaeron SA46 0AS ☎ 01545 572400 🖷 01545 571089 ✉ huwt.morgan@ceredigion.gov.uk

Best Value: Mr Russell Hughes-Pickering Head of Economic & Community Development Services, Neuadd Cygnor Ceredigion, Penmorfa, Aberaeron SA46 0PA
✉ russell.hughes-pickering@ceredigion.gov.uk

Building Control: Mr Huw Williams, Head of Lifestyle Services, Neuadd Cygnor Ceredigion, Penmorfa, Aberaeron SA46 0PA ☎ 01545 572151 🖷 01545 572117 ✉ huww@ceredigion.gov.uk

Catering Services: Ms Nia James Catering Services Manager, Canolfan Rheidol, Rhodfa Padarn, Llanbadarn Fawr, Aberystwyth SY23 3UE ☎ 01970 633364 ✉ nia.james@ceredigion.gov.uk

Children / Youth Services: Ms Ann Sweeting, Principal Youth Officer, Canolfan Rheidol, Rhodfa Padarn, Llanbadarn Fawr, Aberystwyth SY23 3UE ☎ 01970 633712 ✉ anns@ceredigion.gov.uk

Civil Registration: Ms Elin Prysor Monitoring Officer, Neuadd Cygnor Ceredigion, Penmorfa, Aberaeron SA46 0PA ☎ 01545 572120 ✉ elin.prysor@ceredigion.gov.uk

PR / Communications: Ms Siwan Davies Corporate Communications Officer, Neuadd Cygnor Ceredigion, Penmorfa, Aberaeron SA46 0PA ☎ 01545 572003 siwan.davies2@ceredigion.gov.uk

Community Planning: Mr Alun Williams Head of Policy Support, Neuadd Cyngor Ceredigion, Penmorfa, Aberaeron SA46 0PA ☎ 01545 574115 alun.williams2@ceredigion.gov.uk

Community Safety: Mr Alan Garrod, Manager - Community Safety, Neuadd Cyngor Ceredigion, Penmorfa, Aberaeron SA46 0PA ☎ 01545 570881 🖷 01545 572009 alang@ceredigion.gov.uk

Computer Management: Mr Arwyn Morris Head of Information, Communications Technology & Customer Services, Canolfan Rheidol, Rhodfa Padarn, Llanbadarn Fawr, Aberystwyth SY23 3UE ☎ 01970 633200 arwyn.morris@ceredigion.gov.uk

Consumer Protection and Trading Standards: Mr Huw Williams, Head of Lifestyle Services, Neuadd Cyngor Ceredigion, Penmorfa, Aberaeron SA46 0PA ☎ 01545 572151 🖷 01545 572117 huww@ceredigion.gov.uk

Contracts: Mr Huw Morgan, Strategic Director - Sustainable Communities, County Hall, Market Street, Aberaeron SA46 0AS ☎ 01545 572400 🖷 01545 571089 huwt.morgan@ceredigion.gov.uk

Customer Service: Mr Arwyn Morris Head of Information, Communications Technology & Customer Services, Canolfan Rheidol, Rhodfa Padarn, Llanbadarn Fawr, Aberystwyth SY23 3UE ☎ 01970 633200 arwyn.morris@ceredigion.gov.uk

Direct Labour: Mr Huw Morgan, Strategic Director - Sustainable Communities, County Hall, Market Street, Aberaeron SA46 0AS ☎ 01545 572400 🖷 01545 571089 huwt.morgan@ceredigion.gov.uk

Economic Development: Mr Russell Hughes-Pickering Head of Economic & Community Development Services, Neuadd Cyngor Ceredigion, Penmorfa, Aberaeron SA46 0PA russell.hughes-pickering@ceredigion.gov.uk

Education: Mr Eifon Evans Deputy Chief Executive, Canolfan Rheidol, Rhodfa Padarn, Llanbadarn Fawr, Aberystwyth SY23 3UE ☎ 01545 572021 eifion.evans@ceredigion.gov.uk

Education: Mr Barry Rees Head of Learning Services, Neuadd Cyngor Ceredigion, Penmorfa, Aberaeron SA46 0PA barryr@ceredigion.gov.uk

E-Government: Mr Arwyn Morris Head of Information, Communications Technology & Customer Services, Canolfan Rheidol, Rhodfa Padarn, Llanbadarn Fawr, Aberystwyth SY23 3UE ☎ 01970 633200 arwyn.morris@ceredigion.gov.uk

Electoral Registration: Miss Bronwen Morgan, Chief Executive, Neuadd Cyngor Ceredigion, Penmorfa, Aberaeron SA46 0PA ☎ 01545 572004 🖷 01545 572029 chiefexecutive@ceredigion.gov.uk

Emergency Planning: Mr Alan Garrod, Manager - Community Safety, Neuadd Cyngor Ceredigion, Penmorfa, Aberaeron SA46 0PA ☎ 01545 570881 🖷 01545 572009 alang@ceredigion.gov.uk

Energy Management: Mr Huw Morgan, Strategic Director - Sustainable Communities, County Hall, Market Street, Aberaeron SA46 0AS ☎ 01545 572400 🖷 01545 571089 huwt.morgan@ceredigion.gov.uk

Environmental / Technical Services: Mr Paul Arnold Head of Municipal & Environmental Services, Neuadd Cyngor Ceredigion, Penmorfa, Aberaeron SA46 0PA paula@ceredigion.gov.uk

Environmental / Technical Services: Mr Huw Williams, Head of Lifestyle Services, Neuadd Cyngor Ceredigion, Penmorfa, Aberaeron SA46 0PA ☎ 01545 572151 🖷 01545 572117 huww@ceredigion.gov.uk

Environmental Health: Mr Huw Williams, Head of Lifestyle Services, Neuadd Cyngor Ceredigion, Penmorfa, Aberaeron SA46 0PA ☎ 01545 572151 🖷 01545 572117 huww@ceredigion.gov.uk

Estates, Property & Valuation: Mr Jason Jones Group Manager - Development & Estates, Neuadd Cyngor Ceredigion, Penmorfa, Aberaeron SA46 0PA ☎ 01545 572070 jason.jones@ceredigion.gov.uk

European Liaison: Mr Mike Shaw, Group Manager - Community Regeneration & Europe, Neuadd Cyngor Ceredigion, Penmorfa, Aberaeron SA46 0PA ☎ 01545 572064 🖷 01545 572029 mikes@ceredigion.gov.uk

Finance: Mr Stephen Johnson Head of Financial Services, Neuadd Cyngor Ceredigion, Penmorfa, Aberaeron SA46 0PA ☎ 01970 633101 stephen.johnson@ceredigion.gov.uk

Fleet Management: Mr Huw Morgan, Strategic Director - Sustainable Communities, Neuadd Cyngor Ceredigion, Penmorfa, Aberaeron SA46 0PA ☎ 01545 572400 🖷 01545 571089 huwt.morgan@ceredigion.gov.uk

Grounds Maintenance: Mr Huw Morgan, Strategic Director - Sustainable Communities, Neuadd Cyngor Ceredigion, Penmorfa, Aberaeron SA46 0PA ☎ 01545 572400 🖷 01545 571089 huwt.morgan@ceredigion.gov.uk

Health and Safety: Mr Keith Holmes, Corporate Head - Health & Safety, Canolfan Rheidol, Rhodfa Padarn, Llanbadarn Fawr, Aberystwyth SY23 3UE ☎ 01970 627543 🖷 01970 627301 keithh@ceredigion.gov.uk

Highways: Mr Huw Morgan, Strategic Director - Sustainable Communities, Neuadd Cyngor Ceredigion, Penmorfa, Aberaeron SA46 0PA ☎ 01545 572400 🖷 01545 571089 huwt.morgan@ceredigion.gov.uk

Home Energy Conservation: Mr Huw Williams, Head of Lifestyle Services, Neuadd Cyngor Ceredigion, Penmorfa, Aberaeron SA46 0PA ☎ 01545 572151 🖷 01545 572117 huww@ceredigion.gov.uk

Housing: Mr Allan Jones Head of Strategic Commissioning (Care), Assurance & Housing Services, Neuadd Cyngor Ceredigion, Penmorfa, Aberaeron SA46 0PA ☎ allanj@ceredigion.gov.uk

CEREDIGION

Housing: Mr Huw Williams, Head of Lifestyle Services, Neuadd Cyngor Ceredigion, Penmorfa, Aberaeron SA46 0PA ☎ 01545 572151 🖷 01545 572117 ✉ huww@ceredigion.gov.uk

Housing Maintenance: Mr Huw Morgan, Strategic Director - Sustainable Communities, Neuadd Cyngor Ceredigion, Penmorfa, Aberaeron SA46 0PA ☎ 01545 572400 🖷 01545 571089 ✉ huwt.morgan@ceredigion.gov.uk

Legal: Mr Rhys Stephens Group Manager - Legal Services, Neuadd Cyngor Ceredigion, Penmorfa, Aberaeron SA46 0PA ☎ 01545 572055 ✉ rhys.stephens@ceredigion.gov.uk

Leisure and Cultural Services: Mr Darryl Evans, Recreation Manager, Canolfan Rheidol, Rhodfa Padarn, Llanbadarn Fawr, Aberystwyth SY23 3UE ☎ 01970 633587 🖷 01970 633663 ✉ darryle@ceredigion.gov.uk

Licensing: Mr Dafydd Roberts Consumer Services Manager, Neuadd Cyngor Ceredigion, Penmorfa, Aberaeron SA46 0PA ☎ 01545 572170 ✉ dafydd.roberts@ceredigion.gov.uk

Lifelong Learning: Mr Barry Rees Head of Learning Services, Neuadd Cyngor Ceredigion, Penmorfa, Aberaeron SA46 0PA ✉ barryr@ceredigion.gov.uk

Lighting: Mr Huw Morgan, Strategic Director - Sustainable Communities, Neuadd Cyngor Ceredigion, Penmorfa, Aberaeron SA46 0PA ☎ 01545 572400 🖷 01545 571089 ✉ huwt.morgan@ceredigion.gov.uk

Lottery Funding, Charity and Voluntary: Mr Gareth Rowlands, Manager - Community Regeneration, Neuadd Cyngor Ceredigion, Penmorfa, Aberaeron SA46 0PA ☎ 01545 572066 🖷 01545 572029

Member Services: Miss Lowri Edwards Manager - Community Regeneration, Neuadd Cyngor Ceredigion, Penmorfa, Aberaeron SA46 0PA ☎ 01545 572066

Parking: Mr Huw Morgan, Strategic Director - Sustainable Communities, Neuadd Cyngor Ceredigion, Penmorfa, Aberaeron SA46 0PA ☎ 01545 572400 🖷 01545 571089 ✉ huwt.morgan@ceredigion.gov.uk

Partnerships: Mr Alun Williams Head of Policy Support, Neuadd Cyngor Ceredigion, Penmorfa, Aberaeron SA46 0PA ☎ 01545 574115 ✉ alun.williams2@ceredigion.gov.uk

Personnel / HR: Mrs Caroline Lewis Head - Corporate Human Resources, Canolfan Rheidol, Rhodfa Padarn, Llanbadarn Fawr, Aberystwyth SY23 3UE ☎ 01970 633680 ✉ caroline.lewis@ceredigion.gov.uk

Planning: Mr Huw Williams, Head of Lifestyle Services, Neuadd Cyngor Ceredigion, Penmorfa, Aberaeron SA46 0PA ☎ 01545 572151 🖷 01545 572117 ✉ huww@ceredigion.gov.uk

Procurement: Mr Stephen Johnson Head of Financial Services, Neuadd Cyngor Ceredigion, Penmorfa, Aberaeron SA46 0PA ☎ 01970 633101 ✉ stephen.johnson@ceredigion.gov.uk

Public Libraries: Mr Arwyn Morris Head of Information, Communications Technology & Customer Services, Canolfan Rheidol, Rhodfa Padarn, Llanbadarn Fawr, Aberystwyth SY23 3UE ☎ 01970 633200 ✉ arwyn.morris@ceredigion.gov.uk

Recycling & Waste Minimisation: Mr Huw Morgan, Strategic Director - Sustainable Communities, Neuadd Cyngor Ceredigion, Penmorfa, Aberaeron SA46 0PA ☎ 01545 572400 🖷 01545 571089 ✉ huwt.morgan@ceredigion.gov.uk

Regeneration: Mr Russell Hughes-Pickering Head of Economic & Community Development Services, Neuadd Cyngor Ceredigion, Penmorfa, Aberaeron SA46 0PA ✉ russell.hughes-pickering@ceredigion.gov.uk

Road Safety: Mr Huw Morgan, Strategic Director - Sustainable Communities, Neuadd Cyngor Ceredigion, Penmorfa, Aberaeron SA46 0PA ☎ 01545 572400 🖷 01545 571089 ✉ huwt.morgan@ceredigion.gov.uk

Social Services: Mr Parry Davies, Strategic Director - Care, Protection & Lifestyle, Neuadd Cyngor Ceredigion, Penmorfa, Aberaeron SA46 0PA ☎ 01545 572601 🖷 01545 572619 ✉ parryd@ceredigion.gov.uk

Social Services (Adult): Ms Sue Darnbrook Head of Adult Social Care Services, Min Aeron, South Road, Aberaeron SA46 0DY ☎ 01545 572620 🖷 01545 572619 ✉ sue.darnbrook@ceredigion.gov.uk

Social Services (Children): Mr Elfed Hopkins Head of Families & Children's Services, Min Aeron, Rhiw Goch, Aberaeron SA46 0DY ☎ 01545 572694 ✉ elfed.hopkins@ceredigion.gov.uk

Staff Training: Ms Patricia Smith Training Manager, Canolfan Rheidol, Rhodfa Padarn, Llanbadarn Fawr, Aberystwyth SY23 3UE ☎ 01545 575009 ✉ patricia.smith@ceredigion.gov.uk

Street Scene: Mr Rhodri Llwyd Group Manager - Highways Services, County Hall, Market Street, Aberaeron SA46 0AS ☎ 01545 572434 ✉ rhodri.llwyd@ceredigion.gov.uk

Tourism: Mr A.E Jones Manager - Marketing & Tourism Service, Lisburn House, Terrace Road, Aberystwyth SY23 2AG ☎ 01970 633061

Town Centre: Mr Jason Jones Group Manager - Development & Estates, Neuadd Cyngor Ceredigion, Penmorfa, Aberaeron SA46 0PA ☎ 01545 572070 ✉ jason.jones@ceredigion.gov.uk

Traffic Management: Mr Huw Morgan, Strategic Director - Sustainable Communities, Neuadd Cyngor Ceredigion, Penmorfa, Aberaeron SA46 0PA ☎ 01545 572400 🖷 01545 571089 ✉ huwt.morgan@ceredigion.gov.uk

Transport: Mr Rhodri Llwyd Group Manager - Highways Services, County Hall, Market Street, Aberaeron SA46 0AS ☎ 01545 572434 ✉ rhodri.llwyd@ceredigion.gov.uk

Transport: Mr Huw Morgan, Strategic Director - Sustainable Communities, Neuadd Cyngor Ceredigion, Penmorfa, Aberaeron SA46 0PA ☎ 01545 572400 🖷 01545 571089 ✉ huwt.morgan@ceredigion.gov.uk

Waste Collection and Disposal: Mr Huw Morgan, Strategic Director - Sustainable Communities, Neuadd Cyngor Ceredigion, Penmorfa, Aberaeron SA46 0PA ☎ 01545 572400 🖷 01545 571089 huwt.morgan@ceredigion.gov.uk

Waste Management: Mr Huw Morgan, Strategic Director - Sustainable Communities, Neuadd Cyngor Ceredigion, Penmorfa, Aberaeron SA46 0PA ☎ 01545 572400 🖷 01545 571089 huwt.morgan@ceredigion.gov.uk

COUNCILLORS

***Chair* Adams-Lewis**, John (PC - Cardigan - Mwldan)
john.adams-lewis@ceredigion.gov.uk

***Vice-Chair* Hopley**, Sarah Gillian (IND - New Quay)
gill.hopley@ceredigion.gov.uk

***Leader of the Council* Ap Gwynn**, Ellen (PC - Ceulanamaesmawr)
ellen.apgwynn@ceredigion.gov.uk

***Deputy Leader of the Council* Quant**, Ray (IND - Borth)
ray.quant@ceredigion.gov.uk

Cole, John Mark (LD - Cardigan - Rhydyfuwch)
mark.cole@ceredigion.gov.uk

Davies, Euros (IND - Llanwenog)
euros.davies@ceredigion.gov.uk

Davies, Bryan (PC - Llanarth)
bryan.davies@ceredigion.gov.uk

Davies, John Aled (IND - Aberystwyth Rheidol)
aled.davis@ceredigion.gov.uk

Davies, Thomas Peter (IND - Capel Dewi)
peter.davies@ceredigion.gov.uk

Davies, Ifan (IND - Lledrod)
ifan.davies@ceredigion.gov.uk

Davies, John Odwyn (PC - Llangybi)
odwyn.davies@ceredigion.gov.uk

Davies, Ceredig (LD - Aberystwyth Central)
ceredig.davies@ceredigion.gov.uk

Davies, Steve (PC - Aberystwyth Penparcau)
steve.davies2@ceredigion.gov.uk

Davies, Gareth (PC - Llanbadarn Fawr - Padarn)
gareth.davies@ceredigion.gov.uk

Davies, Rhodri (PC - Melindwr)
rhodri.davies@ceredigion.gov.uk

Edwards, Dafydd (IND - Llansantffraid)
dafydd.edwards@live.co.uk

Evans, Elizabeth (LD - Aberaeron)
elizabeth.evans@ceredigion.gov.uk

Evans, Benjamin Towyn (PC - Llandyfriog)
towyn.evans@ceredigion.gov.uk

Evans, Peter (PC - Llandysul Town)
peter.evans3@ceredigion.gov.uk

Evans, David Rhodri (IND - Llangeitho)
rhodri.evans2@ceredigion.gov.uk

Harris, George (LAB - Lampeter)
hag.harries@ceredigion.gov.uk

Hinge, Paul (LD - Tirymynach)
paul.hinge@ceredigion.gov.uk

Hughes, Catherine (PC - Tregaron)
catherine.hughes@ceredigion.gov.uk

James, Gethin (INDNA - Aberporth)
gethin.james@ceredigion.gov.uk

James, Gwyn (IND - Penbryn)
gwyn.james@ceredigion.gov.uk

James, Paul (PC - Llanbadarn Fawr - Sulien)
paul.james@ceredigion.gov.uk

Jones, Rowland (LD - Ystwyth)
rowland.jones@ceredigion.gov.uk

Jones-Southgate, Lorrae (PC - Aberystwyth Penparcau)
lorrae.jones-southgate@ceredigion.gov.uk

Lewis, Thomas (IND - Penparc)
thomaslewis34@mypostoffice.co.uk

Lewis, Thomas Maldwyn (IND - Troedyraur)
maldwyn.lewis@ceredigion.gov.uk

Lloyd, Gareth (IND - Llandysiliogogo)
gareth.lloyd@ceredigion.gov.uk

Lloyd, Lyndon (PC - Beulah)

Lloyd Jones, Alun (PC - Llanfarian)
alun.lloydjones@ceredigion.gov.uk

Lumley, John (PC - Ciliau Aeron)
john.lumley@ceredigion.gov.uk

Mason, David (IND - Trefeurig)
dai.mason@ceredigion.gov.uk

Miles, Catrin (PC - Cardigan - Teifi)
catrin.miles@ceredigion.gov.uk

Rees-Evans, David Rowland (LD - Llanrhystud)
rowland.rees-evans@ceredigion.gov.uk

Roberts, John (LD - Faenor)
john.roberts@ceredigion.gov.uk

Strong, Mark (PC - Aberystwyth North)
mark.strong@ceredigion.gov.uk

Thomas, William Lynford (PC - Llanfihangel Ystrad)
lynford.thomas@ceredigion.gov.uk

Williams, Alun (PC - Aberystwyth Bronglais)
alun.williams@ceredigion.gov.uk

Williams, Ivor (IND - Lampeter)
ivor.williams@ceredigion.gov.uk

POLITICAL COMPOSITION

PC: 19, IND: 14, LD: 7, INDNA: 1, LAB: 1

COMMITTEE CHAIRS

Audit: Ms Elizabeth Evans

Development Control: Mr Rhodri Davies

Licensing: Mr Paul James

Charnwood D

Charnwood Borough Council, Southfields, Loughborough LE11 2TX
☎ 01509 263151 🖷 01509 263791 info@charnwood.gov.uk
www.charnwood.gov.uk

CHARNWOOD

FACTS AND FIGURES

Parliamentary Constituencies: Charnwood, Loughborough
EU Constituencies: East Midlands
Election Frequency: Elections are of whole council

PRINCIPAL OFFICERS

Chief Executive: Mr Geoff Parker, Chief Executive & Head of Paid Services, Southfields, Loughborough LE11 2TR ☎ 01509 634600 🖷 01509 263791 ✉ geoff.parker@charnwood.gov.uk

Senior Management: Mr Simon Jackson Strategic Director of Corporate Services, Southfields, Loughborough LE11 2TX ☎ 01509 634583 🖷 01509 263791 ✉ simon.jackson@charnwood.gov.uk

Senior Management: Ms Eileen Mallon, Strategic Director of Housing, Planning, Regulation & Regulatory Services, Southfields, Loughborough LE11 2TX ☎ 01509 634662 ✉ eileen.mallon@charnwood.gov.uk

Senior Management: Ms Christine Traill, Strategic Director of Neighbourhoods & Community Wellbeing, Southfields, Loughborough LE11 2TX ☎ 01509 634774 ✉ chris.traill@charnwood.gov.uk

Architect, Building / Property Services: Mr Richard Bennett Head of Planning & Regeneration, Southfields, Loughborough LE11 2TX ☎ 01509 634763 ✉ richard.bennett@charnwood.gov.uk

Architect, Building / Property Services: Mr John Casey Head of Finance & Property Services, Southfields, Loughborough LE11 2TX ☎ 01509 634583 ✉ john.casey@charnwood.gov.uk

Architect, Building / Property Services: Mr Dave Wall, Premises Manager, Southfields, Loughborough LE11 2TR ☎ 01509 634686 ✉ dave.wall@charnwood.gov.uk

Best Value: Mr Simon Jackson Strategic Director of Corporate Services, Southfields, Loughborough LE11 2TX ☎ 01509 634583 🖷 01509 263791 ✉ simon.jackson@charnwood.gov.uk

Best Value: Mr Adrian Ward Head of Strategic Support, Southfields, Loughborough LE11 2TX ☎ 01509 634573 ✉ adrian.ward@charnwood.gov.uk

Building Control: Mr Richard Bennett Head of Planning & Regeneration, Southfields, Loughborough LE11 2TX ☎ 01509 634763 ✉ richard.bennett@charnwood.gov.uk

Building Control: Ms Eileen Mallon, Strategic Director of Housing, Planning, Regulation & Regulatory Services, Southfields, Loughborough LE11 2TX ☎ 01509 634662 ✉ eileen.mallon@charnwood.gov.uk

Catering Services: Mr Dave Wall, Premises Manager, Southfields, Loughborough LE11 2TR ☎ ; 01509 634686 ✉ dave.wall@charnwood.gov.uk

Children / Youth Services: Ms Julie Robinson Head of Neighbourhoods & Communities, Southfields, Loughborough LE11 2TX ☎ 01509 634590 ✉ julie.robinson@charnwood.gov.uk

Children / Youth Services: Ms Christine Traill, Strategic Director of Neighbourhoods & Community Wellbeing, Southfields, Loughborough LE11 2TX ☎ 01509 634774 ✉ chris.traill@charnwood.gov.uk

PR / Communications: Mr Michael Roberts Communications Officer, Southfields, Loughborough LE11 2TX ☎ 01509 634517 ✉ mike.roberts@charnwood.gov.uk

PR / Communications: Mr Adrian Ward Head of Strategic Support, Southfields, Loughborough LE11 2TX ☎ 01509 634573 ✉ adrian.ward@charnwood.gov.uk

Community Planning: Ms Julie Robinson Head of Neighbourhoods & Communities, Southfields, Loughborough LE11 2TX ☎ 01509 634590 ✉ julie.robinson@charnwood.gov.uk

Community Safety: Ms Julie Robinson Head of Neighbourhoods & Communities, Southfields, Loughborough LE11 2TX ☎ 01509 634590 ✉ julie.robinson@charnwood.gov.uk

Computer Management: Mr Paul Bargewell Technical Service & Strategy Manager, Southfields, Loughborough LE11 2TX ☎ 01509 634777 ✉ paul.bargewell@charnwood.gov.uk

Computer Management: Mr David Platts Head of Revenue, Benefits & Customer Service, Southfields, Loughborough LE11 2TX ☎ 01509 634850 🖷 01509 263791 ✉ david.platts@charnwood.gov.uk

Corporate Services: Mr Simon Jackson Strategic Director of Corporate Services, Southfields, Loughborough LE11 2TX ☎ 01509 634583 🖷 01509 263791 ✉ simon.jackson@charnwood.gov.uk

Customer Service: Mr David Platts Head of Revenue, Benefits & Customer Service, Southfields, Loughborough LE11 2TX ☎ 01509 634850 🖷 01509 263791 ✉ david.platts@charnwood.gov.uk

Economic Development: Mr Richard Bennett Head of Planning & Regeneration, Southfields, Loughborough LE11 2TX ☎ 01509 634763 ✉ richard.bennett@charnwood.gov.uk

E-Government: Mr Paul Bargewell Technical Service & Strategy Manager, Southfields, Loughborough LE11 2TX ☎ 01509 634777 ✉ paul.bargewell@charnwood.gov.uk

E-Government: Mr David Platts Head of Revenue, Benefits & Customer Service, Southfields, Loughborough LE11 2TX ☎ 01509 634850 🖷 01509 263791 ✉ david.platts@charnwood.gov.uk

Electoral Registration: Mr Adrian Ward Head of Strategic Support, Southfields, Loughborough LE11 2TX ☎ 01509 634573 ✉ adrian.ward@charnwood.gov.uk

Emergency Planning: Mr Adrian Ward Head of Strategic Support, Southfields, Loughborough LE11 2TX ☎ 01509 634573 ✉ adrian.ward@charnwood.gov.uk

Energy Management: Mr Dave Wall, Premises Manager, Southfields, Loughborough LE11 2TR ☎ 01509 634686 ✉ dave.wall@charnwood.gov.uk

Environmental / Technical Services: Mr Neil Greenhalgh Head of Cleansing & Open Spaces, Southfields, Loughborough LE11 2TX ☎ 01509 634675 ✉ neil.greenhalgh@charnwood.gov.uk

Environmental Health: Ms Eileen Mallon, Strategic Director of Housing, Planning, Regulation & Regulatory Services, Southfields, Loughborough LE11 2TX ☎ 01509 634662 ✉ eileen.mallon@charnwood.gov.uk

Environmental Health: Mr Alan Twells Head of Regulatory Services, Southfields, Loughborough LE11 2TX ☎ 01509 634650 ✉ alan.twells@charnwood.gov.uk

Estates, Property & Valuation: Mr John Casey Head of Finance & Property Services, Southfields, Loughborough LE11 2TX ☎ 01509 634583 ✉ john.casey@charnwood.gov.uk

Events Manager: Ms Sylvia Wright Head of Leisure & Culture, Southfields, Loughborough LE11 2TX ☎ 01509 634658 ✉ sylvia.wright@charnwood.gov.uk

Facilities: Mr Dave Wall, Premises Manager, Southfields, Loughborough LE11 2TR ☎ 01509 634686 ✉ dave.wall@charnwood.gov.uk

Finance: Mr John Casey Head of Finance & Property Services, Southfields, Loughborough LE11 2TX ☎ 01509 634810 ✉ john.casey@charnwood.gov.uk

Finance: Mr Simon Jackson Strategic Director of Corporate Services, Southfields, Loughborough LE11 2TX ☎ 01509 634583 🖷 01509 263791 ✉ simon.jackson@charnwood.gov.uk

Fleet Management: Mr Dave Woolsey Engineering Manager, Southfields, Loughborough LE11 2TX ☎ 01509 634682 ✉ dave.woolsey@charnwood.gov.uk

Grounds Maintenance: Mr Neil Greenhalgh Head of Cleansing & Open Spaces, Southfields, Loughborough LE11 2TX ☎ 01509 634675 ✉ neil.greenhalgh@charnwood.gov.uk

Health and Safety: Mr David Hicks, Health & Safety Officer, Southfields, Loughborough LE11 3DH ☎ 01509 634637 🖷 01509 211703 ✉ david.hicks@charnwood.gov.uk

Health and Safety: Mr Adrian Ward Head of Strategic Support, Southfields, Loughborough LE11 2TX ☎ 01509 634573 ✉ adrian.ward@charnwood.gov.uk

Housing: Ms Christine Ansell Head of Landlord Services, Southfields, Loughborough LE11 2TX ☎ 01509 634592 ✉ christine.ansell@charnwood.gov.uk

Housing: Mrs Alison Simmons Head of Strategic & Private Sector Housing, Southfields, Loughborough LE11 2TX ☎ 01509 634780 ✉ alison.simmons@charnwood.gov.uk

Housing Maintenance: Ms Christine Ansell Head of Landlord Services, Southfields, Loughborough LE11 2TX ☎ 01509 634592 ✉ christine.ansell@charnwood.gov.uk

Legal: Mrs Sanjit Sull Legal Services Manager, Southfields, Loughborough LE11 2TX ☎ 01509 634611 🖷 01509 634718 ✉ sanjit.sull@charnwood.gov.uk

Legal: Mr Adrian Ward Head of Strategic Support, Southfield Road, Loughborough LE11 2TR ☎ 01509 634612 🖷 01509 634718 ✉ adrian.ward@charnwood.gov.uk

Leisure and Cultural Services: Ms Christine Traill, Strategic Director of Neighbourhoods & Community Wellbeing, Southfields, Loughborough LE11 2TX ☎ 01509 634774 ✉ chris.traill@charnwood.gov.uk

Leisure and Cultural Services: Ms Sylvia Wright Head of Leisure & Culture, Southfields, Loughborough LE11 2TX ☎ 01509 634658 ✉ sylvia.wright@charnwood.gov.uk

Licensing: Mr Alan Twells Head of Regulatory Services, Southfields, Loughborough LE11 2TX ☎ 01509 634650 ✉ alan.twells@charnwood.gov.uk

Lottery Funding, Charity and Voluntary: Ms Julie Robinson Head of Neighbourhoods & Communities, Southfields, Loughborough LE11 2TX ☎ 01509 634590 ✉ julie.robinson@charnwood.gov.uk

Member Services: Mr Adrian Ward Head of Strategic Support, Southfields, Loughborough LE11 2TX ☎ 01509 634573 ✉ adrian.ward@charnwood.gov.uk

Parking: Mr Alan Twells Head of Regulatory Services, Southfields, Loughborough LE11 2TX ☎ 01509 634650 ✉ alan.twells@charnwood.gov.uk

Partnerships: Ms Julie Robinson Head of Neighbourhoods & Communities, Southfields, Loughborough LE11 2TX ☎ 01509 634590 ✉ julie.robinson@charnwood.gov.uk

Personnel / HR: Mr Adrian Ward Head of Strategic Support, Southfields, Loughborough LE11 2TX ☎ 01509 634573 ✉ adrian.ward@charnwood.gov.uk

Planning: Mr Richard Bennett Head of Planning & Regeneration, Southfields, Loughborough LE11 2TX ☎ 01509 634763 ✉ richard.bennett@charnwood.gov.uk

Planning: Ms Eileen Mallon, Strategic Director of Housing, Planning, Regulation & Regulatory Services, Southfields, Loughborough LE11 2TX ☎ 01509 634662 ✉ eileen.mallon@charnwood.gov.uk

Procurement: Mr David Howkins Purchasing Manager, Southfields, Loughborough LE11 2TX ☎ 01509 634672 ✉ david.howkins@charnwood.gov.uk

Staff Training: Mr Kevin Brewin, Learning Co-ordinator, Southfields, Loughborough LE11 2TR ☎ 01509 634904 ✉ kevin.brewin@charnwood.gov.uk

Staff Training: Mr Adrian Ward Head of Strategic Support, Southfields, Loughborough LE11 2TX ☎ 01509 634573 ✉ adrian.ward@charnwood.gov.uk

CHARNWOOD

Street Scene: Mr Alan Twells Head of Regulatory Services, Southfields, Loughborough LE11 2TX ☎ 01509 634650 alan.twells@charnwood.gov.uk

Sustainable Communities: Ms Julie Robinson Head of Neighbourhoods & Communities, Southfields, Loughborough LE11 2TX ☎ 01509 634590 julie.robinson@charnwood.gov.uk

Tourism: Ms Christine Traill, Strategic Director of Neighbourhoods & Community Wellbeing, Southfields, Loughborough LE11 2TX ☎ 01509 634774 chris.traill@charnwood.gov.uk

Town Centre: Mr Michael Bird Markets & Fairs Manager, Southfields, Loughborough LE11 2TX ☎ 01509 634624 market.fairs@charnwood.gov.uk

Town Centre: Ms Sylvia Wright Head of Leisure & Culture, Southfields, Loughborough LE11 2TX ☎ 01509 634658 sylvia.wright@charnwood.gov.uk

Transport Planner: Mr Richard Bennett Head of Planning & Regeneration, Southfields, Loughborough LE11 2TX ☎ 01509 634763 richard.bennett@charnwood.gov.uk

Waste Collection and Disposal: Mr Neil Greenhalgh Head of Cleansing & Open Spaces, Southfields, Loughborough LE11 2TX ☎ 01509 634675 neil.greenhalgh@charnwood.gov.uk

Waste Management: Mr Neil Greenhalgh Head of Cleansing & Open Spaces, Southfields, Loughborough LE11 2TX ☎ 01509 634675 neil.greenhalgh@charnwood.gov.uk

COUNCILLORS

***Mayor* Capleton**, John (CON - Mountsorrel)
cllr.john.capleton@charnwood.gov.uk

***Deputy Mayor* Gaskell**, David (CON - Birstall Watermead)
cllr.david.gaskell@charnwood.gov.uk

***Leader of the Council* Slater**, David (CON - Quorn & Mountsorrel Castle)
cllr.david.slater@charnwood.gov.uk

***Deputy Leader of the Council* Morgan**, Jonathan (CON - Loughborough Outwoods)
cllr.jonathan.morgan@charnwood.gov.uk

Tillotson, Jenni (LAB - Loughborough Storer)
cllr.jenni.tillotson@charnwood.gov.uk

Barkley, Thomas (CON - Syston West)
cllr.thomas.barkley@charnwood.gov.uk

Bebbington, Liz (CON - Shepshed East)
cllr.liz.bebbington@charnwood.gov.uk

Bentley, Iain (CON - Birstall Watermead)
cllr.iain.bentley@charnwood.gov.uk

Bokor, Jenny (CON - The Wolds)
cllr.jenny.bokor@charnwood.gov.uk

Bradshaw, Julie (LAB - Loughborough Ashby)
cllr.julie.bradshaw@charnwood.gov.uk

Brookes, Matthew (CON - Thurmaston)
cllr.matthew.brookes@charnwood.gov.uk

Campsall, Roy (IND - Loughborough Garendon)
cllr.roy.campsall@charnwood.gov.uk

Cooper, Beatrice (CON - Loughborough Dishley & Hathern)
cllr.beatrice.cooper@charnwood.gov.uk

Forrest, Sandie (LAB - Loughborough Storer)
cllr.sandra.forrest@charnwood.gov.uk

Fryer, Hilary (CON - Barrow & Sileby West)
cllr.hilary.fryer@charnwood.gov.uk

Garrard, Sue (CON - East Gosgate)
cllr.sur.garrard@charnwood.gov.uk

Grimley, David (CON - Queniborough)
cllr.daniel.grimley@charnwood.gov.uk

Hachem, Harley (CON - Loughborough Ashby)
cllr.harley.hachem@charnwood.gov.uk

Hadji-Nikolaou, Leon (CON - Rothley & Thurcaston)
cllr.leon.hadji-nikolaou@charnwood.gov.uk

Hampson, Stephen (CON - Syston East)
cllr.stephen.hampson@charnwood.gov.uk

Harper-Davies, Leigh (CON - Mountsorrel)
cllr.leigh.harper-davies@charnwood.gov.uk

Harris, Christine (LAB - Loughborough Lemyngton)
cllr.christine.harris@charnwood.gov.uk

Harris, Keith (LAB - Loughborough Dishley & Hathern)
cllr.kieth.harris@charnwood.gov.uk

Hayes, David (CON - Loughborough Shelhorpe)
cllr.david.hayes@charnwood.gov.uk

Jones, Renata (CON - Birstall Wanlip)
cllr.renata.jones@charnwood.gov.uk

Jukes, Ron (CON - Loughborough Outwoods)
cllr.ron.jukes@charnwood.gov.uk

Lowe, Mark (CON - Thurmaston)
cllr.mark.lowe@charnwood.gov.uk

Maynard-Smith, Sarah (LAB - Loughborough Hastings)
cllr.sarah.maynard-smith@charnwood.gov.uk

Mercer, Paul (CON - Loughborough Southfields)
cllr.paul.mercer@charnwood.gov.uk

Miah, Jewel (LAB - Loughborough Lemyngton)
cllr.jewel.miah@charnwood.gov.uk

Murphy, Paul (CON - Sileby)
cllr.paul.murphy:charnwood.gov.uk

Pacey, Ken (CON - Syston East)
cllr.ken.pacey@charnwood.gov.uk

Page, Brian (CON - Rothley & Thurcaston)
cllr.brian.page@charnwood.gov.uk

Paling, Andy (CON - Sileby)
cllr.andrew.paling@charnwood.gov.uk

Parsons, Geoff (CON - Loughborough Nanpantan)
cllr.geoff.parsons@charnwood.gov.uk

Parton, Ted (CON - Loughborough Southfields)
cllr.ted.parton@charnwood.gov.uk

Poland, James (CON - Wreake Villages)
cllr.james.poland@charnwood.gov.uk

Radford, Christine (CON - Shepshed West)
cllr.christine.radford@charnwood.gov.uk

Ranson, Pauline (CON - Barrow & Sileby West)
cllr.pauline.ranson@charnwood.gov.uk

Savage, John (CON - Shepshed East)
cllr.john.savage@charnwood.gov.uk

Seaton, Brenda (CON - Thurmaston)
cllr.brenda.seaton@charnwood.gov.uk

Sharp, Robert (LAB - Loughborough Shelthorpe)
cllr.robert.sharp@charnwood.gov.uk

Shepherd, Richard (CON - Quorn & Mountsorrel Castle)
cllr.richard.shepherd@charnwood.gov.uk

Shergill, Serinda (CON - Birstall Wanlip)
cllr.serinda.shergill@charnwood.gov.uk

Smidowicz, Margaret (CON - Loughborough Nanpantan)
cllr.margaret.smidowicz@charnwood.gov.uk

Smith, Luke (CON - Loughborough Garendon)
cllr.luke.smith@charnwood.gov.uk

Snartt, David (CON - Forest Bradgate)
cllr.david.snartt@charnwood.gov.uk

Sutherington, John (LD - Anstey)
cllr.john.sutherington@charnwood.gov.uk

Tassell, Joan (CON - Shepshed West)
cllr.joan.tassell@charnwood.gov.uk

Taylor, Deborah (CON - Anstey)
cllr.deoborah.taylor@charnwood.gov.uk

Vardy, Eric (CON - Syston West)
cllr.eric.vardy@charnwood.gov.uk

Williams, Anne (LAB - Loughborough Hastings)
cllr.anne.williams@charnwood.gov.uk

POLITICAL COMPOSITION

CON: 41, LAB: 9, LD: 1, IND: 1

Chelmsford D

Chelmsford City Council, Civic Centre, Duke Street, Chelmsford CM1 1JE
☎ 01245 606606 🖷 01245 606310 ✉ mailbox@chelmsford.gov.uk
💻 www.chelmsford.gov.uk

FACTS AND FIGURES

Parliamentary Constituencies: Chelmsford
EU Constituencies: Eastern
Election Frequency: Elections are of whole council

PRINCIPAL OFFICERS

Chief Executive: Mr Steve Packham, Chief Executive, Civic Centre, Duke Street, Chelmsford CM1 1JE ☎ 01245 606901
✉ steve.packham@chelmsford.gov.uk

Senior Management: Mr Nick Eveleigh, Director - Financial Services, PO Box 457, Civic Centre, Duke Street, Chelmsford CM1 1JE ☎ 01245 606419 🖷 01245 606693
✉ nick.eveleigh@chelmsford.gov.uk

Senior Management: Ms Louise Goodwin, Director - Corporate Services, Civic Centre, Duke Street, Chelmsford CM1 1JE ☎ 01245 606802 🖷 01245 606657 ✉ louise.goodwin@chelmsford.gov.uk

Senior Management: Mr David Green, Director - Sustainable Communities, Civic Centre, Duke Street, Chelmsford CM1 1JE
☎ 01245 606503 🖷 01245 606642 ✉ david.green@chelmsford.gov.uk

Senior Management: Mr Keith Nicholson Director - Public Places, Civic Centre, Duke Street, Chelmsford CM1 1JE ☎ 01245 606606 🖷 01245 606681 ✉ keith.nicholson@chelmsford.gov.uk

Senior Management: Ms Averil Price, Director - Community Services, Civic Centre, Duke Street, Chelmsford CM1 1JE ☎ 01245 606473 ✉ averil.price@chelmsford.gov.uk

Access Officer / Social Services (Disability): Mr Paul Houghton, Access Officer, Civic Centre, Duke Street, Chelmsford CM1 1JE ☎ 01245 606328 🖷 01245 606288
✉ paul.houghton@chelmsford.gov.uk

Building Control: Mr Andrew Savage Director - Sustainable Communities, Civic Centre, Duke Street, Chelmsford CM1 1JE
☎ 01245 606541 🖷 01245 606642
✉ andrew.savage@chelmsford.gov.uk

PR / Communications: Ms Laura Ketley Senior Communications Officer, Civic Centre, Duke Street, Chelmsford CM1 1JE ☎ 01245 606795 🖷 01245 606657 ✉ laura.ketley@chelmsford.gov.uk

Community Planning: Mr David Green, Director - Sustainable Communities, Civic Centre, Duke Street, Chelmsford CM1 1JE
☎ 01245 606503 🖷 01245 606642 ✉ david.green@chelmsford.gov.uk

Community Safety: Mr Spencer Clarke Community Service & Play Manager, Civic Centre, Duke Street, Chelmsford CM1 1JE
☎ 01245 606477 ✉ spencer.clarke@chelmsford.gov.uk

Computer Management: Mr Tony Preston Corporate ICT Manager, Civic Centre, Duke Street, Chelmsford CM1 1JE ☎ 01245 606606 ✉ tony.preston@chelmsford.gov.uk

Corporate Services: Ms Louise Goodwin, Director - Corporate Services, Civic Centre, Duke Street, Chelmsford CM1 1JE ☎ 01245 606802 🖷 01245 606657 ✉ louise.goodwin@chelmsford.gov.uk

Customer Service: Mrs Elaine Peck Customer Services Manager, Civic Centre, Duke Street, Chelmsford CM1 1JE ☎ 01245 606406
🖷 01245 606657 ✉ elaine.peck@chelmsford.gov.uk

Economic Development: Mr Stuart Graham Inward Investment, Economy & Growth Manager, Civic Centre, Duke Street, Chelmsford CM1 1JE ☎ 01245 606364 ✉ stuart.graham@chelmsford.gov.uk

Electoral Registration: Ms Ann Coronel Legal & Democratic Services Manager, Civic Centre, Duke Street, Chelmsford CM1 1JE
☎ 01245 606560 🖷 01245 606245
✉ ann.coronel@chelmsford.gov.uk

Emergency Planning: Mr Gerry Richardson Emergency Planning Officer, Civic Centre, Duke Street, Chelmsford CM1 1JE
☎ 01245 606921 ✉ gerry.richardson@chelmsford.gov.uk

Energy Management: Ms Michelle Keene Energy Manager, Civic Centre, Duke Street, Chelmsford CM1 1JE ☎ 01245 606747
✉ michelle.keene@chelmsford.gov.uk

CHELMSFORD

Environmental / Technical Services: Mr Paul Brookes Public Health & Protection Services Manager, Civic Centre, Duke Street, Chelmsford CM1 1JE ☎ 01245 606436 🖱 paul.brookes@chelmsford.gov.uk

Environmental Health: Mr Paul Brookes Public Health & Protection Services Manager, Civic Centre, Duke Street, Chelmsford CM1 1JE ☎ 01245 606436 🖱 paul.brookes@chelmsford.gov.uk

Estates, Property & Valuation: Mr Andrew Larges Corporate Property Manager, Civic Centre, Duke Street, Chelmsford CM1 1JE ☎ 01245 606311 🖷 01245 606245 🖱 andrew.large@chelmsford.gov.uk

Events Manager: Mr Liam Rich Events Manager, Civic Centre, Duke Street, Chelmsford CM1 1JE ☎ 01245 606985 🖱 liam.rich@chelmsford.gov.uk

Facilities: Mr John Peacey Building Services Manager, Civic Centre, Duke Street, Chelmsford CM1 1JE ☎ 01245 606750 🖱 john.peacey@chelmsford.gov.uk

Finance: Mr Nick Eveleigh, Director - Financial Services, PO Box 457, Civic Centre, Duke Street, Chelmsford CM1 1JE ☎ 01245 606419 🖷 01245 606693 🖱 nick.eveleigh@chelmsford.gov.uk

Grounds Maintenance: Mr Richard Whiting Grounds Maintenance & Operations Manager, Civic Centre, Duke Street, Chelmsford CM1 1JE ☎ 01245 605560 🖷 01245 600803 🖱 richard.whiting@chelmsford.gov.uk

Housing: Mr David Green, Director - Sustainable Communities, Civic Centre, Duke Street, Chelmsford CM1 1JE ☎ 01245 606503 🖷 01245 606642 🖱 david.green@chelmsford.gov.uk

Legal: Ms Ann Coronel Legal & Democratic Services Manager, Civic Centre, Duke Street, Chelmsford CM1 1JE ☎ 01245 606560 🖷 01245 606245 🖱 ann.coronel@chelmsford.gov.uk

Leisure and Cultural Services: Ms Averil Price, Director - Community Services, Civic Centre, Duke Street, Chelmsford CM1 1JE ☎ 01245 606473 🖱 averil.price@chelmsford.gov.uk

Licensing: Mr Matthew Evans Licensing Lead Officer, Civic Centre, Duke Street, Chelmsford CM1 1JE ☎ 01245 606512 🖷 01245 606681 🖱 matthew.evans@chelmsford.gov.uk

Member Services: Ms Ann Coronel Legal & Democratic Services Manager, Civic Centre, Duke Street, Chelmsford CM1 1JE ☎ 01245 606560 🖷 01245 606245 🖱 ann.coronel@chelmsford.gov.uk

Parking: Ms Rosa Tanfield Parking & Highways Liaison Manager, Civic Centre, Duke Street, Chelmsford CM1 1JE ☎ 01245 606284 🖱 rosa.tanfield@chelmsford.gov.uk

Personnel / HR: Ms Florence Agyei Human Resources Manager, Civic Centre, Duke Street, Chelmsford CM1 1JE ☎ 01245 606582 🖷 01245 606657 🖱 florence.agyei@chelmsford.gov.uk

Planning: Mr David Green, Director - Sustainable Communities, Civic Centre, Duke Street, Chelmsford CM1 1JE ☎ 01245 606503 🖷 01245 606642 🖱 david.green@chelmsford.gov.uk

Procurement: Mr Chris Lay, Procurement Manager, Civic Centre, Duke Street, Chelmsford CM1 1JE ☎ 01245 606485 🖷 01245 606574 🖱 chris.lay@chelmsford.gov.uk

Recycling & Waste Minimisation: Mr Keith Nicholson Director - Public Places, Civic Centre, Duke Street, Chelmsford CM1 1JE ☎ 01245 606606 🖷 01245 606681 🖱 keith.nicholson@chelmsford.gov.uk

Regeneration: Mr Stuart Graham Inward Investment, Economy & Growth Manager, Civic Centre, Duke Street, Chelmsford CM1 1JE ☎ 01245 606364 🖱 stuart.graham@chelmsford.gov.uk

Staff Training: Ms Kerry Knowles HR Strategy & Development Manager, Civic Centre, Duke Street, Chelmsford CM1 1JE ☎ 01245 606592 🖱 kerry.knowles@chelmsford.gov.uk

Sustainable Communities: Mr David Green, Director - Sustainable Communities, Civic Centre, Duke Street, Chelmsford CM1 1JE ☎ 01245 606503 🖷 01245 606642 🖱 david.green@chelmsford.gov.uk

Sustainable Development: Mr David Green, Director - Sustainable Communities, Civic Centre, Duke Street, Chelmsford CM1 1JE ☎ 01245 606503 🖷 01245 606642 🖱 david.green@chelmsford.gov.uk

Town Centre: Mr Mike Wrays City Centre Manager, Civic Centre, Duke Street, Chelmsford CM1 1JE ☎ 01245 606253 🖷 01245 606657

Waste Collection and Disposal: Mr Keith Nicholson Director - Public Places, Civic Centre, Duke Street, Chelmsford CM1 1JE ☎ 01245 606606 🖷 01245 606681 🖱 keith.nicholson@chelmsford.gov.uk

Children's Play Areas: Mr Paul Van Damme Parks & Greens Spaces Manager, Civic Centre, Duke Street, Chelmsford CM1 1JE ☎ 01245 606477 🖱 spencer.clarke@chelmsford.gov.uk

COUNCILLORS

***Mayor* Hutchinson**, Paul (CON - Springfield North)
paul.hutchinson@chelmsford.gov.uk

***Deputy Mayor* Wilson**, Philip (CON - Boreham & the Leighs)
philip.wilson@chelmsford.gov.uk

***Leader of the Council* Whitehead**, Roy (CON - South Hanningfield - Stock & Margaretting)
r.whitehead@chelmsford.gov.uk

***Deputy Leader of the Council* Galley**, John (CON - Boreham & the Leighs)
j.galley@chelmsford.gov.uk

Ahmed, Liz (CON - Great Baddow East)
liz.ahmed@chelmsford.gov.uk

Alcock, Ron (CON - Chelmer Village & Beaulieu Park)
r.alcock@chelmsford.gov.uk

Ambor, Richard (CON - Little Baddow, Danbury & Sandon)
richard.ambor@chelmsford.gov.uk

Ashley, Lee (LD - St Andrews)
lee.ashley@chelmsford.gov.uk

Camp (nee Irwin), Victoria (CON - Moulsham & Central)
victoria.camp@chelmsford.gov.uk

Chambers, Nicolette (CON - Chelmsford Rural West)
n.chambers@chelmsford.gov.uk

Chambers, Alan (CON - Waterhouse Farm)
alan.chambers@chelmsford.gov.uk

Chandler, Jenny (CON - Great Baddow West)
jenny.chandler@chelmsford.gov.uk

Cook, Simon (CON - Moulsham Lodge)
simon.cook@chelmsford.gov.uk

Cousins, Peter (CON - St Andrews)
peter.cousins@chelmsford.gov.uk

de Vries, Jon (CON - Patching Hall)
jon.devries@chelmsford.gov.uk

Deakin, Jude (LD - Marconi)
jude.deakin@chelmsford.gov.uk

Denston, Bob (CON - South Woodham - Elmwood & Woodville)
r.denston@chelmsford.gov.uk

Denston, Linda (CON - South Woodham - Elmwood & Woodville)
linda.denston@chelmsford.gov.uk

Flack, Matt (CON - Bicknacre & East & West Hanningfield)
matt.flack@chelmsford.gov.uk

Fowell, Stephen Douglas (CON - St Andrews)
stephen.fowell@chelmsford.gov.uk

Garrett, Christine (CON - The Lawns)
christine.garrett@chelmsford.gov.uk

Grundy, Ian (CON - South Hanningfield - Stock & Margaretting)
i.grundy@chelmsford.gov.uk

Gulliver, Neil (CON - Chelmer Village & Beaulieu Park)
n.gulliver@chelmsford.gov.uk

Hindi, Sameh (CON - Moulsham & Central)
s.k.hindi@chelmsford.gov.uk

Holoway, Michael (CON - Patching Hall)
michael.holoway@chelmsford.gov.uk

Hughes, Patricia (CON - South Woodham - Elmwood & Woodville)
p.hughes@chelmsford.gov.uk

Jeapes, Julia (CON - The Lawns)
julia.jeapes@chelmsford.gov.uk

John, Ashley (CON - South Woodham - Chetwood & Collingwood)
ashley.john@chelmsford.gov.uk

Knight, Barry (CON - Broomfield & The Walthams)
gbr.knight@chelmsford.gov.uk

Lumley, Duncan (CON - Chelmer Village & Beaulieu Park)
d.lumley@chelmsford.gov.uk

Madden, Dick (CON - Moulsham & Central)
dick.madden@chelmsford.gov.uk

Massey, Bob (CON - South Woodham - Chetwood & Collingwood)
bob.massey@chelmsford.gov.uk

McQuiggan, Anthony (CON - Goat Hall)
anthony.mcquiggan@chelmsford.gov.uk

Millane, Lance (CON - Rettendon & Runwell)
lance.millane@chelmsford.gov.uk

Mountain, Freda (LD - Goat Hall)
f.mountain@chelmsford.gov.uk

Murray, Jean (CON - Trinity)
jean.murray@chelmsford.gov.uk

Pontin, Sandra (CON - Broomfield & The Walthams)
sandra.pontin@chelmsford.gov.uk

Potter, Janette (CON - Galleywood)
japotter@chelmsford.gov.uk

Poulter, Richard (CON - Bicknacre & East & West Hanningfield)
r.poulter@chelmsford.gov.uk

Raven, James (CON - Broomfield & The Walthams)
james.raven@chelmsford.gov.uk

Ride, Raymond (CON - Rettendon & Runwell)
r.ride@chelmsford.gov.uk

Robinson, Stephen (LD - Patching Hall)
stephen.robinson@chelmsford.gov.uk

Roper, Tim (CON - Writtle)
t.roper@chelmsford.gov.uk

Sach, Tony (CON - Writtle)
tony.sach@chelmsford.gov.uk

Scott, Stephanie (CON - Great Baddow East)
stephanie.scott@chelmsford.gov.uk

Seeley, Graham (CON - Trinity)
graham.seeley@chelmsford.gov.uk

Shepherd, Bob (CON - Little Baddow, Danbury & Sandon)
b.shepherd@chelmsford.gov.uk

Sismey, Malcolm (CON - South Woodham - Chetwood & Collingwood)
malcolm.sismey@chelmsford.gov.uk

Smith, Gillian (CON - Great Baddow East)
gillian.smith@chelmsford.gov.uk

Spence, Yvonne (CON - Marconi)
yvonne.spence@chelmsford.gov.uk

Springett, Mark (LD - Moulsham Lodge)
mark.springett@chelmsford.gov.uk

Stevenson, David (CON - Galleywood)
d.stevenson@chelmsford.gov.uk

Sullivan, Susan (CON - Springfield North)
susan.sullivan@chelmsford.gov.uk

Villa, Bob (CON - Great Baddow West)
bob.villa@chelmsford.gov.uk

Ward, Louis (CON - Springfield North)
louis.ward@chelmsford.gov.uk

Watson, Malcolm (CON - Waterhouse Farm)
malcolm.watson@chelmsford.gov.uk

Wright, Ian (CON - Little Baddow, Danbury & Sandon)
i.wright@chelmsford.gov.uk

POLITICAL COMPOSITION

CON: 52, LD: 5

COMMITTEE CHAIRS

Audit: Mr Alan Chambers

Licensing & Regulatory: Mr Lance Millane

Planning: Mr Ian Wright

CHELTENHAM

Cheltenham D

Cheltenham Borough Council, Municipal Offices, The Promenade, Cheltenham GL50 9SA
☎ 01242 262626 🖷 01242 227131 ✉ enquiries@cheltenham.gov.uk
💻 www.cheltenham.gov.uk

FACTS AND FIGURES

Parliamentary Constituencies: Cheltenham
EU Constituencies: South West
Election Frequency: Elections are biennial

PRINCIPAL OFFICERS

Chief Executive: Mr Andrew North, Chief Executive, Municipal Offices, The Promenade, Cheltenham GL50 9SA ☎ 01242 264100 🖷 01242 264360 ✉ andrew.north@cheltenham.gov.uk

Deputy Chief Executive: Mrs Pat Pratley, Deputy Chief Executive, Municipal Offices, Promenade, Cheltenham GL50 9SA ☎ 01242 775175 🖷 01242 775127 ✉ pat.pratley@cheltenham.gov.uk

Senior Management: Mr Mike Redman, Director - Environmental & Regulatory Services, Municipal Offices, The Promenade, Cheltenham GL50 9SA ☎ 01242 264160 🖷 01242 227323 ✉ mike.redman@cheltenham.gov.uk

Senior Management: Mr Mark Sheldon, Director - Corporate Resources, Municipal Offices, The Promenade, Cheltenham GL50 9SA ☎ 01242 264123 🖷 01242 264630 ✉ mark.sheldon@cheltenham.gov.uk

Architect, Building / Property Services: Mr David Roberts Head of Property & Asset Management, Municipal Offices, The Promenade, Cheltenham GL50 9SA ☎ 01242 264151 🖷 01242 264159 ✉ david.roberts@cheltenham.gov.uk

Building Control: Mr Iain Houston, Building Control Manager, Municipal Offices, The Promenade, Cheltenham GL50 9SA ☎ 01242 264293 🖷 01242 227323 ✉ iain.houston@cheltenham.gov.uk

Catering Services: Mr Gary Nejrup Entertainment & Business Manager, Town Hall, Imperial Square, Cheltenham GL50 1QA ☎ 01242 775853 🖷 01242 573902 ✉ gary.nejrup@cheltenham.gov.uk

PR / Communications: Mr Richard Gibson Strategy & Engagement Manager, Municipal Offices, The Promenade, Cheltenham GL50 9SA ☎ 01242 235354 🖷 01242 264360 ✉ richard.gibson@cheltenham.gov.uk

Community Planning: Mr Mike Redman, Director - Environmental & Regulatory Services, Municipal Offices, The Promenade, Cheltenham GL50 9SA ☎ 01242 264160 🖷 01242 227323 ✉ mike.redman@cheltenham.gov.uk

Community Safety: Mrs Barbara Exley, Head of Public Protection, Municipal Offices, Promenade, Cheltenham GL50 9SA ☎ 01242 264220 🖷 01242 264210 ✉ barbara.exley@cheltenham.gov.uk

Community Safety: Mrs Yvonne Hope Head of Public Protection, Municipal Offices, The Promenade, Cheltenham GL50 9SA ☎ 01242 775002 🖷 01242 264210 ✉ yvonne.hope@cheltenham.gov.uk

Computer Management: Mr Andy Barge, Group Manager - Customer Services, Council Offices, Coleford GL16 8HG ☎ 01594 812383 ✉ andy.barge@fdean.gov.uk

Contracts: Mrs Shirin Wotherspoon Principal Solicitor (Commercial), Tewkesbury Borough Council, Council Offices, Gloucester Road, Tewkesbury GL20 5TT ☎ 01684 272017 ✉ shirin.wotherspoon@tewkesbury.gov.uk

Corporate Services: Mr Mark Sheldon, Director - Corporate Resources, Municipal Offices, The Promenade, Cheltenham GL50 9SA ☎ 01242 264123 🖷 01242 264630 ✉ mark.sheldon@cheltenham.gov.uk

Customer Service: Mr Mark Sheldon, Director - Corporate Resources, Municipal Offices, The Promenade, Cheltenham GL50 9SA ☎ 01242 264123 🖷 01242 264630 ✉ mark.sheldon@cheltenham.gov.uk

Economic Development: Mr Mike Redman, Director - Environmental & Regulatory Services, Municipal Offices, The Promenade, Cheltenham GL50 9SA ☎ 01242 264160 🖷 01242 227323 ✉ mike.redman@cheltenham.gov.uk

Electoral Registration: Mrs Kim Smith Elections & Electoral Registration Manager, Municipal Offices, The Promenade, Cheltenham GL50 9SA ☎ 01242 264948 🖷 01242 264120 ✉ kim.smith@cheltenham.gov.uk

Emergency Planning: Mrs Sonia Phillips, DEPLO, Central Depot, Swindon Road, Cheltenham GL51 9JZ ☎ 01242 774973 🖷 01242 774989 ✉ sonia.phillips@cheltenham.gov.uk

Energy Management: Mr Garrie Dowling Senior Property Surveyor, Municipal Offices, The Promenade, Cheltenham GL50 9SA ☎ 01242 264394 🖷 01242 264159

Environmental Health: Mrs Barbara Exley, Head of Public Protection, Municipal Offices, Promenade, Cheltenham GL50 9SA ☎ 01242 264220 🖷 01242 264210 ✉ barbara.exley@cheltenham.gov.uk

Estates, Property & Valuation: Mr David Roberts Head of Property & Asset Management, Municipal Offices, The Promenade, Cheltenham GL50 9SA ☎ 01242 264151 🖷 01242 264159 ✉ david.roberts@cheltenham.gov.uk

Events Manager: Mr Gary Nejrup Entertainment & Business Manager, Town Hall, Imperial Square, Cheltenham GL50 1QA ☎ 01242 775853 🖷 01242 573902 ✉ gary.nejrup@cheltenham.gov.uk

Finance: Mr Mark Sheldon, Director - Corporate Resources, Municipal Offices, The Promenade, Cheltenham GL50 9SA ☎ 01242 264123 🖷 01242 264630 ✉ mark.sheldon@cheltenham.gov.uk

Treasury: Mr Mark Sheldon, Director - Corporate Resources, Municipal Offices, The Promenade, Cheltenham GL50 9SA ☎ 01242 264123 🖷 01242 264630 ✉ mark.sheldon@cheltenham.gov.uk

Fleet Management: Mr Mark Hulbert Fleet Services Manager, Central Depot, Swindon Road, Cheltenham GL51 9JZ ☎ 01242 264361 🖶 01242 265224 🖱 mark.hulbert@ubico.co.uk

Grounds Maintenance: Mr Adam Reynolds Green Space Development Manager, Central Depot, Swindon Road, Cheltenham GL51 9JZ ☎ 01242 774669 🖱 adam.reynolds@cheltenham.gov.uk

Health and Safety: Mrs Barbara Exley, Head of Public Protection, Municipal Offices, Promenade, Cheltenham GL50 9SA ☎ 01242 264220 🖶 01242 264210 🖱 barbara.exley@cheltenham.gov.uk

Home Energy Conservation: Mr Mark Nelson Enforcement Manager, Municipal Offices, The Promenade, Cheltenham GL50 9SA ☎ 01242 264165 🖶 01242 775119 🖱 mark.nelson@cheltenham.gov.uk

Housing: Mr Martin Stacy Lead Commissioner - Housing Services, Municipal Offices, The Promenade, Cheltenham GL50 9SA ☎ 01242 775214 🖶 01242 264397 🖱 martin.stacy@cheltenham.gov.uk

Housing Maintenance: Mr Paul Stephenson Chief Executive of Cheltenham Borough Homes, Cheltenham House, Clarence Street, Cheltenham GL50 3RD ☎ 01242 775319 🖱 paul.stephenson@cheltenham.gov.uk

Legal: Ms Sara Freckleton, Borough Solicitor & Monitoring Officer, Council Offices, Gloucester Road, Tewkesbury GL20 5TT ☎ 01684 272010 🖱 sara.freckleton@tewkesbury.gov.uk

Legal: Mr Peter Lewis Head of Legal Services, Council Offices, Gloucester Road, Tewkesbury GL20 5TT ☎ 01684 272012 🖱 peter.lewis@tewkesbury.gov.uk

Leisure and Cultural Services: Mrs Pat Pratley, Deputy Chief Executive, Municipal Offices, Promenade, Cheltenham GL50 9SA ☎ 01242 775175 🖶 01242 775127 🖱 pat.pratley@cheltenham.gov.uk

Licensing: Mrs Barbara Exley, Head of Public Protection, Municipal Offices, Promenade, Cheltenham GL50 9SA ☎ 01242 264220 🖶 01242 264210 🖱 barbara.exley@cheltenham.gov.uk

Lifelong Learning: Mrs Jane Lillystone Museum, Arts & Tourism Manager, Art Gallery & Museum, Clarence Street, Cheltenham GL50 3JT ☎ 01242 775706 🖱 jane.lillystone@cheltenham.gov.uk

Lottery Funding, Charity and Voluntary: Mr Richard Gibson Strategy & Engagement Manager, Municipal Offices, The Promenade, Cheltenham GL50 9SA ☎ 01242 235354 🖶 01242 264360 🖱 richard.gibson@cheltenham.gov.uk

Member Services: Mrs Rosalind Reeves, Democratic Services Manager, Municipal Offices, The Promenade, Cheltenham GL50 9SA ☎ 01242 774937 🖶 01242 227131 🖱 rosalind.reeves@cheltenham.gov.uk

Parking: Mr Mike Redman, Director - Environmental & Regulatory Services, Municipal Offices, The Promenade, Cheltenham GL50 9SA ☎ 01242 264160 🖶 01242 227323 🖱 mike.redman@cheltenham.gov.uk

Partnerships: Mr Richard Gibson Strategy & Engagement Manager, Municipal Offices, The Promenade, Cheltenham GL50 9SA ☎ 01242 235354 🖶 01242 264360 🖱 richard.gibson@cheltenham.gov.uk

Personnel / HR: Ms Deborah Bainbridge GO Shared Services Head of HR, Municipal Offices, The Promenade, Cheltenham GL50 9SA ☎ 01242 264186 🖱 deborah.bainbridge@cheltenham.gov.uk

Planning: Mr Mike Redman, Director - Environmental & Regulatory Services, Municipal Offices, The Promenade, Cheltenham GL50 9SA ☎ 01242 264160 🖶 01242 227323 🖱 mike.redman@cheltenham.gov.uk

Procurement: Mr David Baker Business Partner - Procurement, Municipal Offices, The Promenade, Cheltenham GL50 9SA ☎ 01242 775055 🖶 01242 227131 🖱 david.baker@cheltenham.gov.uk

Recycling & Waste Minimisation: Ms Beth Boughton Waste & Recycling Manager, Central Depot, Swindon Road, Cheltenham GL51 9JZ ☎ 01242 774644 🖶 01242 264338 🖱 beth.boughton@ubico.co.uk

Regeneration: Mr Mike Redman, Director - Environmental & Regulatory Services, Municipal Offices, The Promenade, Cheltenham GL50 9SA ☎ 01242 264160 🖶 01242 227323 🖱 mike.redman@cheltenham.gov.uk

Staff Training: Mrs Jan Bridges, Learning & Organisational Development Manager, Municipal Offices, Promenade, Cheltenham GL50 9SA ☎ 01242 775189 🖶 01242 264309 🖱 jan.bridges@cheltenham.gov.uk

Street Scene: Mr Wilf Tomaney Townscape Manager, Municipal Offices, The Promenade, Cheltenham GL50 9SA ☎ 01242 264145 🖱 wilf.tomaney@cheltenham.gov.uk

Sustainable Communities: Mrs Pat Pratley, Deputy Chief Executive, Municipal Offices, Promenade, Cheltenham GL50 9SA ☎ 01242 775175 🖶 01242 775127 🖱 pat.pratley@cheltenham.gov.uk

Sustainable Development: Ms Gill Morris Climate Change & Sustainability Officer, Municipal Offices, The Promenade, Cheltenham GL50 9SA ☎ 01242 264229 🖱 gill.morris@cheltenham.gov.uk

Tourism: Mrs Jane Lillystone Museum, Arts & Tourism Manager, Art Gallery & Museum, Clarence Street, Cheltenham GL50 3JT ☎ 01242 775706 🖱 jane.lillystone@cheltenham.gov.uk

Town Centre: Mr Kevan Blackadder Chelenham Business Partnership Manager, Cheltenham Business Partnership, 2 Trafalgar Square, , Cheltenham GL50 1UH ☎ 01242 252626 🖶 01242 541255 🖱 manager@cheltenhambp.org.uk

Waste Collection and Disposal: Mr Rob Bell, Managing Director of UBICO, Central Depot, Swindon Road, Cheltenham GL51 9JZ ☎ 01242 264181 🖱 rob.bell@ubico.co.uk

Waste Management: Mr Scott Williams Strategic Client Officer, Cotswold District Council, Trinity Road, Cirencester GL7 1PX ☎ 01285 623123 🖶 01285 623910 🖱 scott.williams@cotswold.gov.uk

CHELTENHAM

COUNCILLORS

***Mayor* Smith**, Duncan (CON - Charlton Park)
cllr.duncan.smith@cheltenham.gov.uk

***Deputy Mayor* Ryder**, Chris (CON - Warden Hill)
Christine.Ryer@cheltenham.gov.uk

***Leader of the Council* Jordan**, Stephen (LD - All Saints)
cllr.steve.jordan@cheltenham.gov.uk

***Deputy Leader of the Council* Rawson**, John (LD - St. Peter's)
cllr.john.rawson@cheltenham.gov.uk

Babbage, Matt (CON - Battledown)
cllr.matt.babbage@cheltenham.gov.uk

Baker, Paul (LD - Charlton Park)
cllr.paul.baker&cheltenham.gov.uk

Barnes, Garth (LD - College)
cllr.garth.barnes@cheltenham.gov.uk

Britter, Nigel (LD - Benhall & the Reddings)
cllr.nigel.britter@cheltenham.gov.uk

Chard, Andrew (CON - Leckhampton)
andrew4leckhampton@gmail.com

Clucas, Flor (LD - Swindon Village)

Coleman, Chris (LD - St. Mark's)
cllr.chris.coleman@cheltenham.gov.uk

Fisher, Bernard (LD - Swindon Village)
cllr.bernard.fisher@cheltenham.gov.uk

Fletcher, Jacky (CON - Benhall & the Reddings)
cllr.jacky.fletcher@cheltenham.gov.uk

Flynn, Wendy (LD - Hesters Way)
cllr.wendy.flynn@cheltenham.gov.uk

Harman, Tim (CON - Park)
cllr.tim.harman@cheltenham.gov.uk

Hay, Colin (LD - Oakley)

Hay, Rowena (LD - Oakley)
cllr.rowena.hay@cheltenham.gov.uk

Holliday, Sandra (LD - St. Mark's)
cllr.sandra.holliday@cheltenham.gov.uk

Jeffries, Peter (LD - Springbank)
cllr.peter.jeffries@cheltenham.gov.uk

Lansley, Andrew (IND - St. Pauls)
cllr.andrew.lansley@cheltenham.gov.uk

Lillywhite, Adam (O - Pittville)
cllr.adamlillywhite@cheltenham.gov.uk

Mason, Chris (CON - Lansdown)
cllr.chris.mason@cheltenham.gov.uk

McCloskey, Helena (LD - Charlton Kings)
cllr.helena.mccloskey@cheltenham.gov.uk

McKinlay, Andrew (LD - Up Hatherley)
cllr.andrew.mckinlay@cheltenham.gov.uk

Murch, Dan (LD - All Saints)
cllr.dan.murch@cheltenham.gov.uk

Nelson, Chris (CON - Leckhampton)
cllr.chris.nelson@cheltenham.gov.uk

Payne, John (O - Prestbury)
cllr.john.payne@cheltenham.gov.uk

Prince, David (O - Pittville)
david.prince@gloucestershire.gov.uk

Regan, Anne (CON - Warden Hill)
cllr.anne.regan@cheltenham.gov.uk

Reid, Rob (LD - Charlton Kings)
cllr.rob.reid@cheltenham.gov.uk

Savage, Louis (CON - Battledown)
cllr.louis.sagage@cheltenham.gov.uk

Seacome, Diggory (CON - Lansdown)
cllr.diggory.seacome@cheltenham.gov.uk

Stennett, Malcolm (O - Prestbury)
cllr.malcolm.stennett@cheltenham.gov.uk

Sudbury, Klara (LD - College)
cllr.klara.sudbury@cheltenham.gov.uk

Thornton, Pat (LD - St. Peter's)
cllr.pat.thornton@cheltenham.gov.uk

Walklett, Jon (LD - St. Pauls)
cllr.jon.walklett@cheltenham.gov.uk

Wheeler, Simon (LD - Hesters Way)
cllr.simon.wheeler@cheltenham.gov.uk

Whyborn, Roger (LD - Up Hatherley)
cllr.roger.whyborn@cheltenham.gov.uk

Wilkinson, Max (LD - Park)
cllr.max.wilkinson@cheltenham.gov.uk

Williams, Suzanne (LD - Springbank)
cllr.suzanne.williams@cheltenham.gov.uk

POLITICAL COMPOSITION

LD: 24, CON: 11, O: 4, IND: 1

COMMITTEE CHAIRS

Audit: Mr Colin Hay

Licensing: Mr Roger Whyborn

Planning: Mr Garth Barnes

Cherwell D

Cherwell District Council, Bodicote House, Bodicote, Banbury OX15 4AA
☎ 01295 252535 🖷 01295 270028 ✉ info@cherwell-dc.gov.uk
💻 www.cherwell-dc.gov.uk

FACTS AND FIGURES

Parliamentary Constituencies: Banbury
EU Constituencies: South East
Election Frequency: Elections are by thirds

PRINCIPAL OFFICERS

Chief Executive: Mrs Sue Smith Chief Executive, Bodicote House, Bodicote, Banbury OX15 4AA ☎ 0300 003 0100
✉ sue.smith@cherwellandsouthnorthants.gov.uk

Senior Management: Mr Calvin Bell, Director - Development, Council Offices, Springfields, Towcester NN12 6AE ☎ 0300 003 0103 🖷 01327 322310
✉ calvin.bell@cherwellandsouthnorthants.gov.uk

Senior Management: Mr Ian Davies, Director - Community & Environment, Bodicote House, Bodicote, Banbury OX15 4AA ☎ 01327 322302; 0300 003 0101 ✉ ian.davies@cherwellandsouthnorthants.gov.uk

Senior Management: Mr Martin Henry Director - Resources & S151 Officer, Bodicote House, Bodicote, Banbury OX15 4AA ☎ 0300 003 0102 ✉ martin.henry@cherwellandsouthnorthants.gov.uk

Access Officer / Social Services (Disability): Ms Caroline French Corporate Policy Officer, Bodicote House, Bodicote, Banbury OX15 4AA ☎ 01295 227928 ✉ caroline.french@cherwell-dc.gov.uk

Access Officer / Social Services (Disability): Mr Andy Kidd Joint Building Control Officer, The Forum, Moat Lane, Towcester NN12 6AD ✉ andy.kidd@southnorthants.gov.uk

Architect, Building / Property Services: Mr Chris Stratford Head of Regeneration & Housing, Bodicote House, Bodicote, Banbury OX15 4AA ☎ 01295 251871; 0300 003 0111 ✉ chris.stratford@cherwellandsouthnorthants.gov.uk

Building Control: Mr Andy Preston, Head of Development Management, The Forum, Moat Lane, Towcester NN12 6AD ☎ 0300 003 0109 ✉ andy.preston@cherwellandsouthnorthants.gov.uk

PR / Communications: Mrs Janet Ferris Communications Manager, Bodicote House, Bodicote, Banbury OX15 4AA ☎ 0300 003 0114 ✉ janet.ferris@cherwellandsouthnorthants.gov.uk

Community Planning: Ms Claire Taylor Performance Manager, Bodicote House, Bodicote, Banbury OX15 4AA ☎ 0300 003 0113 ✉ claire.taylor@cherwellandsouthnorthants.gov.uk

Community Safety: Mr Mike Grant Safer Communities Manager, Bodicote House, Bodicote, Banbury OX15 4AA ☎ 01295 227989 ✉ mike.grant@cherwell-dc.gov.uk

Computer Management: Ms Balvinder Heran, Head of Customer Access, Bodicote House, Bodicote, Banbury OX15 4AA ☎ 01295 227903 ✉ balvinder.heran@cherwellandsouthnorthants.gov.uk

Computer Management: Ms Jo Pitman Head of Transformation, The Forum, Moat Lane, Towcester NN12 6AD ☎ 0300 003 0108 ✉ jo.pitman@cherwellandsouthnorthants.gov.uk

Corporate Services: Mr Chris Rothwell Head of Community Services, Bodicote House, Bodicote, Banbury OX15 4AA ☎ 01295 251774; 0300 003 0104 ✉ chris.rothwell@cherwellandsouthnorthants.gov.uk

Customer Service: Ms Natasha Barnes Customer Service Manager, Bodicote House, Bodicote, Banbury OX15 4AA ☎ 01295 223301 ✉ natasha.barnes@cherwell-dc.gov.uk

Economic Development: Mr Adrian Colwell Head of Strategic Planning & the Economy, Bodicote House, Bodicote, Banbury OX15 4AA ☎ 0300 003 0110 ✉ adrian.colwell@cherwellandsouthnorthants.gov.uk

Economic Development: Mr Steven Newman Economic Development Officer, Bodicote House, Bodicote, Banbury OX15 4AA ☎ 01295 221860 ✉ steven.newman@cherwell-dc.gov.uk

Electoral Registration: Mr James Doble Democratic & Elections Manager, Bodicote House, Bodicote, Banbury OX15 4AA ☎ 01295 221587 ✉ james.doble@cherwellandsouthnorthants.gov.uk

Emergency Planning: Mr Jan Southgate Emergency Co-ordinator, Bodicote House, Bodicote, Banbury OX15 4AA ☎ 01295 227906 ✉ jan.southgate@cherwell-dc.gov.uk

Energy Management: Ms Eloise Attwood Team Leader - Service Development & Commercial, Bodicote House, Bodicote, Banbury OX15 4AA ☎ 01327 332095 ✉ eloise.attwood@cherwellandsouthnorthants.gov.uk

Environmental / Technical Services: Mr Ian Davies, Director - Community & Environment, Bodicote House, Bodicote, Banbury OX15 4AA ☎ 01327 322302; 0300 003 0101 ✉ ian.davies@cherwellandsouthnorthants.gov.uk

Environmental / Technical Services: Mr Ed Potter Head of Environmental Services, Thorpe Lane Depot, Banbury OX16 4UT ☎ 01295 227023; 0300 003 0105 ✉ ed.potter@cherwellandsouthnorthants.gov.uk

Estates, Property & Valuation: Mr Duncan Wigley, Estates Surveyor, Council Offices, Springfields, Towcester NN12 6AE ☎ 01327 322345 🖷 01327 322074 ✉ duncan.wigley@southnorthants.gov.uk

Facilities: Ms Linda Barlow Corporate Facilities Manager, Bodicote House, Bodicote, Banbury OX15 4AA ☎ 01295 221800 ✉ linda.barlow@cherwell-dc.gov.uk

Finance: Mr Paul Sutton Interim Head of Finance & Procurement, Bodicote House, Bodicote, Banbury OX15 4AA

Health and Safety: Mr David Bennett Corporate Health & Safety Adviser, Bodicote House, Bodicote, Banbury OX15 4AA ☎ 01295 221738 ✉ dave.bennett@cherwellandsouthnorthants.gov.uk

Health and Safety: Ms Jackie Fitzsimons Public Protection & Environmental Health Manager, The Forum, Moat Lane, Towcester NN12 6AD ☎ 01327 322283 ✉ jackie.fitzsimmons@southnorthants.gov.uk

Home Energy Conservation: Mr Tim Mills, Private Sector Housing Manager, Bodicote House, Bodicote, Banbury OX15 4AA ☎ 01295 221655 ✉ tim.mills@cherwell-dc.gov.uk

Housing: Mr Chris Stratford Head of Regeneration & Housing, Bodicote House, Bodicote, Banbury OX15 4AA ☎ 01295 251871; 0300 003 0111 ✉ chris.stratford@cherwellandsouthnorthants.gov.uk

Legal: Mr Nigel Bell Solicitor, Bodicote House, Bodicote, Banbury OX15 4AA ☎ 01295 221687 ✉ nigel.bell@cherwell-dc.gov.uk

Legal: Mr Kevin Lane, Head of Law & Governance, Council Offices, Springfields, Towcester NN12 6AE ☎ 0300 003 0107 ✉ kevin.lane@cherwellandsouthnorthants.gov.uk

CHERWELL

Leisure and Cultural Services: Mr Ian Davies, Director - Community & Environment, Bodicote House, Bodicote, Banbury OX15 4AA ☎ 01327 322302; 0300 003 0101 ✉ ian.davies@cherwellandsouthnorthants.gov.uk

Leisure and Cultural Services: Mr Chris Rothwell Head of Community Services, Bodicote House, Bodicote, Banbury OX15 4AA ☎ 01295 251774; 0300 003 0104 ✉ chris.rothwell@cherwellandsouthnorthants.gov.uk

Member Services: Ms Natasha Clark Democratic & Elections Team Leader, Bodicote House, Bodicote, Banbury OX15 4AA ☎ 01295 221589 ✉ natasha.clark@cherwellandsouthnorthants.gov.uk

Parking: Ms Jo Powell Vehicle, Parks & Town Team Leader, Bodicote House, Bodicote, Banbury OX15 4AA ☎ 01295 221766 ✉ jo.powell@cherwell-dc.gov.uk

Personnel / HR: Ms Paula Goodwin Shared HR & OD Manager, Bodicote House, Bodicote, Banbury OX15 4AA ☎ 01295 221735 ✉ paula.goodwin@cherwellandsouthnorthants.gov.uk

Planning: Mr Adrian Colwell Head of Strategic Planning & the Economy, Bodicote House, Bodicote, Banbury OX15 4AA ☎ 0300 003 0110 ✉ adrian.colwell@cherwellandsouthnorthants.gov.uk

Planning: Mr John Westerman Development Services Manager, 58 Appleby Close, Banbury OX16 0UX ☎ 01295 221821 ✉ john.westerman@cherwell-dc.gov.uk

Procurement: Ms Viv Hitchens Corporate Procurement Manager, Bodicote House, Bodicote, Banbury OX15 4AA ✉ viv.hitchens@cherwell-dc.gov.uk

Recycling & Waste Minimisation: Ms Eloise Attwood Team Leader - Service Development & Commercial, Bodicote House, Bodicote, Banbury OX15 4AA ☎ 01327 332095 ✉ eloise.attwood@cherwellandsouthnorthants.gov.uk

Street Scene: Mr Paul Almond Street & Landscape Services Manager, Bodicote House, Bodicote, Banbury OX15 4AA ☎ 01295 221705 ✉ paul.almond@cherwellandsouthnorthants.gov.uk

Sustainable Communities: Mr Chris Rothwell Head of Community Services, Bodicote House, Bodicote, Banbury OX15 4AA ☎ 01295 251774; 0300 003 0104 ✉ chris.rothwell@cherwellandsouthnorthants.gov.uk

Tourism: Ms Nicola Riley, Arts & Tourism Manager, Bodicote House, Bodicote, Banbury OX15 4AA ☎ 01295 221724 ✉ nicola.riley@cherwell-dc.gov.uk

Waste Collection and Disposal: Mr Ed Potter Head of Environmental Services, Thorpe Lane Depot, Banbury OX16 4UT ☎ 01295 227023 ✉ ed.potter@cherwellandsouthnorthants.gov.uk

COUNCILLORS

***Chair* Milne Home**, Alastair (CON - Banbury Calthorpe)
cllr.alastair.milnehome@cherwell-dc.gov.uk

***Deputy Chair* Heath**, Chris (CON - Bloxham & Bodicote)
cllr.chris.heath@cherwell-dc.gov.uk

***Leader of the Council* Wood**, Barry (CON - Fringford)
cllr.barry.wood@cherwell-dc.gov.uk

***Deputy Leader of the Council* Reynolds**, George (CON - Sibford)
cllr.george.reynolds@cherwell-dc.gov.uk

Atack, Ken (CON - Cropredy)
cllr.ken.atack@cherwell-dc.gov.uk

Beere, Andrew (LAB - Banbury Grimsbury & Castle)
cllr.andrew.beere@cherwell-dc.gov.uk

Bell, Claire (LAB - Banbury Grimsbury & Castle)
claire.bell@cherwell-dc.gov.uk

Billington, Maurice (CON - Kidlington South)
cllr.maurice.billington@cherwell-dc.gov.uk

Blackwell, Fred (CON - Banbury Easington)
cllr.fred.blackwell@cherwell-dc.gov.uk

Bolster, Norman (CON - Bicester West)
cllr.norman.bolster@cherwell-dc.gov.uk

Bonner, Ann (CON - Banbury Grimsbury & Castle)
cllr.ann.bonner@cherwell-dc.gov.uk

Cherry, Mark (LAB - Banbury Ruscote)
councillormark.cherry@cherwell-dc.gov.uk

Clarke, Colin (CON - Banbury Calthorpe)
cllr.colin.clarke@cherwell-dc.gov.uk

Corkin, Ian (CON - Caversfield)
ian.corkin@cherwell-dc.gov.uk

Dhesi, Surinder (LAB - Banbury Neithrop)
surinder.dhesi@cherwell-dc.gov.uk

Donaldson, John (CON - Banbury Hardwick)
cllr.john.donaldson@cherwell-dc.gov.uk

Gibbard, Michael (CON - Yarnton, Gosford & Water Eaton)
cllr.michael.gibbard@cherwell-dc.gov.uk

Griffiths, Carmen (CON - Kidlington South)
carmen.griffiths@cherwell-dc.gov.uk

Hallchurch, Timothy (CON - Otmoor)
cllr.timothy.hallchurch@cherwell-dc.gov.uk

Holland, Simon (CON - Kirtlington)
cllr.simon.holland@cherwell-dc.gov.uk

Hughes, David (CON - Launton)
cllr.david.hughes@cherwell-dc.gov.uk

Hurle, Russell (CON - Bicester West)
cllr.russell.hurle@cherwell-dc.gov.uk

Ilott, Anthony (CON - Banbury Hardwick)
cllr.tony.ilott@cherwell-dc.gov.uk

Jelf, Ray (CON - Hook Norton)
ray.jelf@cherwell-dc.gov.uk

Johnstone, Matt (LAB - Banbury Neithrop)
matt.johnstone@cherwell-dc.gov.uk

Kerford-Byrnes, Mike (CON - The Astons & Heyfords)
cllr.mike.kerfordbynes@cherwell-dc.gov.uk

MacNamara, James (CON - The Astons & Heyfords)
cllr.james.macnamara@cherwell-dc.gov.uk

Magee, Melanie (CON - Bicester North)
cllr.melanie.magee@cherwell-dc.gov.uk

Mallon, Kieron (CON - Banbury Easington)
cllr.kieron.mallon@cherwell-dc.gov.uk

Mawer, Nicholas (CON - Bicester North)
cllr.nicholas.mawer@cherwell-dc.gov.uk

Morris, Nigel (CON - Banbury Easington)
cllr.nigel.morris@cherwell-dc.gov.uk

Mould, Ridchard (CON - Bicester West)

Pickford, Debbie (CON - Bicester Town)
cllr.debbie.pickford@cherwell-dc.gov.uk

Porter, James (CON - Bicester South)
james.porter@cherwell-dc.gov.uk

Pratt, Lynn (CON - Ambrosden & Chesterton)
cllr.lynn.pratt@cherwell-dc.gov.uk

Prestidge, Neil (CON - Kidlington South)
cllr.neil.prestidge@cherwell-dc.gov.uk

Randall, Nigel (CON - Adderbury)
nigel.randall@cherwell-dc.gov.uk

Rhodes, Sandra (CON - Kidlington North)
sandra.rhodes@cherwell-dc.gov.uk

Richards, Barry (LAB - Banbury Ruscote)
barry.richards@cherwell-dc.gov.uk

Sames, Daniel (CON - Bicester South)
cllr.daniel.sames@cherwell-dc.gov.uk

Sibley, Leslie (LAB - Bicester West)
cllr.leslie.sibley@cherwell-dc.gov.uk

Stevens, Trevor (CON - Yarnton, Gosford & Water Eaton)
cllr.trevor.stevens@cherwell-dc.gov.uk

Stratford, Rose (CON - Bicester East)
cllr.rose.stratford@cherwell-dc.gov.uk

Stratford, Lawrence (CON - Bicester East)
cllr.lawrie.stratford@cherwell-dc.gov.uk

Thirzie Smart, Lynda (CON - Bloxham & Bodicote)
cllr.lynda.thirziesmart@cherwell-dc.gov.uk

Turner, Nicholas (CON - Banbury Hardwick)
cllr.nicholas.turner@cherwell-dc.gov.uk

Webb, Douglas (CON - Wroxton)
cllr.douglas.webb@cherwell-dc.gov.uk

Williams, Bryn (CON - Deddington)
bryn.williams@cherwell-dc.gov.uk

Williamson, Douglas (LD - Kidlington North)
cllr.douglas.williamson@cherwell-dc.gov.uk

Woodcock, Sean (LAB - Banbury Ruscote)
sean.woodcock@cherwell-dc.gov.uk

POLITICAL COMPOSITION

CON: 41, LAB: 8, LD: 1

COMMITTEE CHAIRS

Licensing: Mrs Rose Stratford

Planning: Mr Colin Clarke

Cheshire East — U

Cheshire East Council, Westfields, Middlewich Road, Sandbach CW11 1HZ
☎ 0300 123 5500 ✉ info@cheshireeast.gov.uk
💻 www.cheshireeast.gov.uk

FACTS AND FIGURES

Parliamentary Constituencies: Congleton, Crewe and Nantwich, Eddisbury, Macclesfield, Tatton
EU Constituencies: North West
Election Frequency: Elections are of whole council

PRINCIPAL OFFICERS

Chief Executive: Mr Mike Suarez Chief Executive, Westfields, Middlewich Road, Sandbach CW11 1HZ ☎ 01270 686018
✉ mike.suarez@cheshireeast.gov.uk

Deputy Chief Executive: Ms Kath O'Dwyer Director - Children's Services & Deputy Chief Executive, Westfields, Middlewich Road, Sandbach CW11 1HZ ☎ 01270 686018
✉ kath.odwyer@cheshireeast.gov.uk

Senior Management: Mr Peter Bates Chief Operating Manager, Westfields, Middlewich Road, Sandbach CW11 1HZ ☎ 01270 686013
✉ peter.bates@cheshireeast.gov.uk

Senior Management: Ms Anita Bradley Head of Legal Services (& Monitoring Officer), Westfields, Middlewich Road, Sandbach CW11 1HZ ☎ 01270 685850 ✉ anita.bradley@cheshireeast.gov.uk

Senior Management: Ms Lorraine Butcher Executive Director - Strategic Commissioning, Westfields, Middlewich Road, Sandbach CW11 1HZ ☎ 01270 686021 ✉ lorraine.butcher@cheshireeast.gov.uk

Senior Management: Ms Heather Grimbaldeston Director - Public Health, Westfields, Middlewich Road, Sandbach CW11 1HZ ☎ 01270 686242 ✉ heather.grimbaldeston@cheshireeast.gov.uk

Senior Management: Ms Kath O'Dwyer Director - Children's Services & Deputy Chief Executive, Westfields, Middlewich Road, Sandbach CW11 1HZ ☎ 01270 686018
✉ kath.odwyer@cheshireeast.gov.uk

Senior Management: Mr Brian Reed Head of Governance & Democratic Services, Westfields, Middlewich Road, Sandbach CW11 1HZ ☎ 01270 686670 ✉ brian.reed@cheshireeast.gov.uk

Senior Management: Ms Caroline Simpson Executive Director - Economic Growth & Prosperity, Westfields, Middlewich Road, Sandbach CW11 1HZ ☎ 01270 686640
✉ caroline.simpson@cheshireeast.gov.uk

Senior Management: Ms Brenda Smith Director - Adult Services, Social Care & Independent Living, Westfields, Middlewich Road, Sandbach CW11 1HZ ☎ 01270 685609
✉ brenda.smith@cheshireeast.gov.uk

Architect, Building / Property Services: Ms Denise Griffiths Facilities Manager, 2nd Floor, Delamere House, Delamere Street, Crewe CW1 2JZ ☎ 01270 686125
✉ denise.griffiths@cheshireeast.gov.uk

Catering Services: Ms Joanne Cooper Interim Catering Services Manager, Floor 1, Municipal Buildings, Earle Street, Crewe CW1 2BJ ☎ 01606 271565 ✉ joanne.cooper@cheshireeast.gov.uk

CHESHIRE EAST

Children / Youth Services: Mr Nigel Moorhouse Interim Director - Children's Services (Head of Early Intervention & Prevention), Dalton House, Dalton Way, Middlewich CW10 0HU ☎ 01606 271775 nigel.moorhouse@cheshireeast.gov.uk

Civil Registration: Ms Lindsey Parton Registration Service & Business Manager, Westfields, Middlewich Road, Sandbach CW11 1HZ ☎ 01270 686477 lindsey.parton@cheshireeast.gov.uk

Community Safety: Ms Stephanie Cordon Head of Communities, Westfields, Middlewich Road, Sandbach CW11 1HZ ☎ 01270 686401 steph.cordon@cheshireeast.gov.uk

Community Safety: Ms Kirstie Hercules Principal Manager - Local Area Working, Westfields, Middlewich Road, Sandbach CW11 1HZ ☎ 01270 686632 kirstie.hercules@cheshireeast.gov.uk

Computer Management: Mr Gareth Pawlett Corporate Manager ICT, 1st Floor, Delamere House, Delamere Street, Crewe CW1 2JZ ☎ 01270 686166

Consumer Protection and Trading Standards: Ms Tracey Bettaney Principal Manager - Regulatory & Health Protection, Municipal Buildings, Earle Street, Crewe CW1 2BJ ☎ 01270 686596 tracey.bettaney@cheshireeast.gov.uk

Customer Service: Mr Paul Bayley Principal Manager - Local Community Services, Macclesfield Town Hall, Market Place, Macclesfield SK10 1EA ☎ 01606 271567 paul.bayley@cheshireeast.gov.uk

Economic Development: Mr Julian Cobley Head of Investment, Westfields, Middlewich Road, Sandbach CW11 1HZ ☎ 01270 685906 julian.cobley@cheshireeast.gov.uk

Education: Mr Fintan Bradley Corporate Manager - Education Strategy, 2nd Floor, Westfields, Middlewich Road, Sandbach CW11 1HZ ☎ 01270 271504 fintan.bradley@cheshireeast.gov.uk

Electoral Registration: Ms Diane Todd Electoral Services Manager, Macclesfield Town Hall, Market Place, Macclesfield SK10 1EA ☎ 01270 686478 diane.todd@cheshireeast.gov.uk

Emergency Planning: Mr Norman Powell Lead Emergency Planning Officer, Ground Floor, Nicholas Street, Chester CM1 2NP ☎ 01244 973868

Energy Management: Mr Colin Farrelly Corporate Energy Manager, 2nd Floor, Delamere House, Delamere Street, Crewe CW1 2JZ ☎ 01270 686161 colin.farrelly@cheshireeast.gov.uk

Environmental Health: Ms Tracey Bettaney Principal Manager - Regulatory & Health Protection, Municipal Buildings, Earle Street, Crewe CW1 2BJ ☎ 01270 686596 tracey.bettaney@cheshireeast.gov.uk

Estates, Property & Valuation: Ms Heather McManus Interim Head of Assets, Delamere House Delamere Street Crewe CW1 2JZ ☎ 01270 686130 heather.mcmanus@cheshireeast.gov.uk

Events Manager: Mr Andrew Latham Events Manager, Oakley Building, Victoria Community Centre, West Street, Crewe CW1 2PZ ☎ 01270 686785 andrew.latham@cheshireeast.gov.uk

Facilities: Ms Denise Griffiths Facilities Manager, 2nd Floor, Delamere House, Delamere Street, Crewe CW1 2JZ ☎ 01270 686125 denise.griffiths@cheshireeast.gov.uk

Finance: Mr Peter Bates Chief Operating Manager, Westfields, Middlewich Road, Sandbach CW11 1HZ ☎ 01270 686013 peter.bates@cheshireeast.gov.uk

Finance: Ms Judith Tench Head of Corporate Resources & Stewardship, Westfields, Middlewich Road, Sandbach CW11 1HZ ☎ 01270 685859 judith.tench@cheshireeast.gov.uk

Health and Safety: Ms Bronwen MacArthur-Williams Corporate Health & Safety Manager, 5th Floor, Delamere House, Delamere Street, Crewe CW1 2JZ ☎ 01270 686331 bronwen.macarthur-williams@cheshireeast.gov.uk

Highways: Mr Paul Traynor Strategic Commissioning Manager - Highways, Floor 6, Delamere House, Delamere Street, Crewe CW1 2JZ ☎ 01260 371055 paul.traynor@cheshireeast.gov.uk

Housing: Ms Karen Carsberg Strategic Housing Manager, Westfields, Middlewich Road, Sandbach CW11 1HZ ☎ 01270 686654 karen.carsberg@cheshireeast.gov.uk

Legal: Ms Anita Bradley Head of Legal Services (& Monitoring Officer), Westfields, Middlewich Road, Sandbach CW11 1HZ ☎ 01270 685850 anita.bradley@cheshireeast.gov.uk

Leisure and Cultural Services: Mr Mark Wheelton Corporate Commissioning Manager - Leisure, Westfields, Middlewich Road, Sandbach CW11 1HZ ☎ 01270 686679 mark.wheelton@cheshireeast.gov.uk

Licensing: Ms Tracey Bettaney Principal Manager - Regulatory & Health Protection, Municipal Buildings, Earle Street, Crewe CW1 2BJ ☎ 01270 686596 tracey.bettaney@cheshireeast.gov.uk

Lifelong Learning: Mr Peter Cavanagh 14+ Skills Manager, Floor 7, Delamere House, Delamere Street, Crewe CW1 2JZ ☎ 01270 685992 peter.cavanagh@cheshireeast.gov.uk

Parking: Ms Carolyn Noonan Enforcement Notice Processing Supervisor, Macclesfield Town Hall, Market Place, Macclesfield SK10 1EA ☎ 01625 383760 carolyn.noonan@cheshireeast.gov.uk

Personnel / HR: Mr Phil Badley Interim Head of Human Resources & Organisational Development, Westfields, Middlewich Road, Sandbach CW11 1HZ ☎ 01270 686027 phil.badley@cheshireeast.gov.uk

Planning: Mr Adrian Fisher Head of Strategic & Economic Planning, Westfields, Middlewich Road, Sandbach CW11 1HZ ☎ 01270 686641 adrian.fisher@cheshireeast.gov.uk

Planning: Ms Caroline Simpson Executive Director - Economic Growth & Prosperity, Westfields, Middlewich Road, Sandbach CW11 1HZ ☎ 01270 686640 caroline.simpson@cheshireeast.gov.uk

Procurement: Ms Lianne Halliday Procurement Manager, Westfields, Middlewich Road, Sandbach CW11 1HZ ☎ 01270 685766 lianne.halliday@cheshireeast.gov.uk

Public Libraries: Mr Paul Bayley Principal Manager - Local Community Services, Macclesfield Town Hall, Market Place, Macclesfield SK10 1EA ☎ 01606 271567 paul.bayley@cheshireeast.gov.uk

Recycling & Waste Minimisation: Mr Ralph Kemp Manager - Commissioning Waste & Environment, Pyms Lane Depot, Pyms Lane, Crewe CW1 3PJ ☎ 01270 686683 ralph.kemp@cheshireeast.gov.uk

Regeneration: Mr Jez Goodman Regeneration Programme Manager, Westfields, Middlewich Road, Sandbach CW11 1HZ ☎ 01270 685906 jez.goodman@cheshireeast.gov.uk

Social Services: Mr Nigel Moorhouse Interim Director - Children's Services (Head of Early Intervention & Prevention), Dalton House, Dalton Way, Middlewich CW10 0HU ☎ 01606 271775 nigel.moorhouse@cheshireeast.gov.uk

Social Services (Adult): Ms Brenda Smith Director - Adult Services, Social Care & Independent Living, Westfields, Middlewich Road, Sandbach CW11 1HZ ☎ 01270 685609 brenda.smith@cheshireeast.gov.uk

Public Health: Ms Heather Grimbaldeston Director - Public Health, Westfields, Middlewich Road, Sandbach CW11 1HZ ☎ 01270 686242 heather.grimbaldeston@cheshireeast.gov.uk

Staff Training: Ms Lisa Burrows Senior Manager - Strategic Workforce Development, Westfields, Middlewich Road, Sandbach CW11 1HZ ☎ 01270 686093 lisa.burrow@cheshireeast.gov.uk

Tourism: Mr Brendan Flanagan Visitor Economy, Culture & Tatton Park Manager, Tatton Park, Tatton, , Knutsford WA16 6QN ☎ 01625 374415 brendan.flanagan@cheshireeast.gov.uk

Town Centre: Mr Julian Cobley Head of Investment, Westfields, Middlewich Road, Sandbach CW11 1HZ ☎ 01270 685906 julian.cobley@cheshireeast.gov.uk

COUNCILLORS

***Mayor* Gaddum**, Hilda (CON - Sutton)
hilda.gaddum@cheshireeast.gov.uk

***Deputy Mayor* Hunter**, Olivia (CON - High Legh)
olivia.hunter@cheshireeast.gov.uk

***Leader of the Council* Jones**, Michael (CON - Bunbury)
michael.e.jones@cheshireeast.gov.uk

***Deputy Leader of the Council* Brown**, David (CON - Congleton East)
david.brown@cheshireeast.gov.uk

***Group Leader* Fletcher**, Rod (LD - Alsager)
rod.fletcher@cheshireeast.gov.uk

***Group Leader* Moran**, Arthur (IND - Nantwich North and West)
arthur.moran@cheshireeast.gov.uk

***Group Leader* Newton**, David (LAB - Crewe East)
david.newton@cheshireeast.gov.uk

Andrew, Chris (CON - Macclesfield South)
chris.andrew@cheshireeast.gov.uk

Arnold, Ainsley (CON - Macclesfield Tytherington)
ainsley.arnold@cheshireeast.gov.uk

Bailey, Damian (LAB - Crewe St Barnabas)
damian.bailey@cheshireeast.gov.uk

Bailey, Rachel (CON - Audlem)
rachel.bailey@cheshireeast.gov.uk

Bailey, Rhoda (CON - Odd Rode)
rhoda.bailey@cheshireeast.gov.uk

Barton, Gary (CON - Wilmslow West and Chorley)
gary.barton@cheshireeast.gov.uk

Bates, Paul (CON - Congleton West)
paul.bates@cheshireeast.gov.uk

Baxendale, Gordon (CON - Congleton West)
gordon.baxendale@cheshireeast.gov.uk

Beanland, Michael (CON - Poynton West and Adlington)
michael.beanland@cheshireeast.gov.uk

Bebbington, Derek (CON - Leighton)
derek.bebbington@cheshireeast.gov.uk

Brookfield, Suzanne (LAB - Crewe East)
suzanne.brookfield@cheshireeast.gov.uk

Brooks, Ellie (CON - Wilmslow West and Chorley)
ellie.brooks@cheshireeast.gov.uk

Browne, Craig (O - Alderley Edge)
craig.browne@cheshireeast.gov.uk

Burkhill, Barry (R - Handforth)
barry.burkhill@cheshireeast.gov.uk

Butterill, Penny (IND - Nantwich North and West)
penny.butterill@cheshireeast.gov.uk

Carter, Steve (LAB - Macclesfield Hurdsfield)
stephen.carter@cheshireeast.gov.uk

Chapman, Clair (LAB - Crewe East)
clair.chapman@cheshireeast.gov.uk

Clowes, Janet (CON - Wybunbury)
janet.clowes@cheshireeast.gov.uk

Corcoran, Sam (LAB - Sandbach Heath and East)
sam.corcoran@cheshireeast.gov.uk

Davenport, Harold (CON - Disley)
harold.davenport@cheshireeast.gov.uk

Davies, Stan (CON - Wrenbury)
stanley.davies@cheshireeast.gov.uk

Deakin, Martin (CON - Alsager)
martin.deakin@cheshireeast.gov.uk

Dean, Tony (CON - Knutsford)
tony.dean@cheshireeast.gov.uk

Dooley, Beverley (CON - Macclesfield Central)
beverley.dooley@cheshireeast.gov.uk

Durham, Liz (CON - Broken Cross & Upton)
liz.durham@cheshireeast.gov.uk

Edgar, Steven (CON - Shavington)
steven.edgar@cheshireeast.gov.uk

Faseyi, Irene (LAB - Crewe Central)
irene.faseyi@cheshireeast.gov.uk

CHESHIRE EAST

Findlow, Paul (CON - Prestbury)
paul.findlow@cheshireeast.gov.uk

Flude, Dorothy (LAB - Crewe South)
dorothy.flude@cheshireeast.gov.uk

Fox, Toni (R - Wilmslow Dean Row)
toni.fox@cheshireeast.gov.uk

Gardiner, Stewart (CON - Knutsford)
stewart.gardiner@cheshireeast.gov.uk

Gardner, Sam (CON - Macclesfield Tytherington)
sam.gardner@cheshireeast.gov.uk

Gilbert, Les (CON - Dane Valley)
les.gilbert@cheshireeast.gov.uk

Grant, Mo (LAB - Crewe North)
mo.grant@cheshireeast.gov.uk

Groves, Peter (CON - Nantwich South and Stapeley)
peter.groves@cheshireeast.gov.uk

Hammond, John (CON - Haslington)
john.hammond@cheshireeast.gov.uk

Hardy, Martin (CON - Broken Cross & Upton)
martin.hardy@cheshireeast.gov.uk

Harewood, Alift (LAB - Macclesfield West and Ivy)
alift.harewood@cheshireeast.gov.uk

Hayes, George (CON - Congleton West)
george.hayes@cheshireeast.gov.uk

Hogben, Stephen (LAB - Crewe South)
steven.hogben@cheshireeast.gov.uk

Hough, Derek (LD - Alsager)
derek.hough@cheshireeast.gov.uk

Jackson, Janet (LAB - Macclesfield Central)
janet.jackson@cheshireeast.gov.uk

Jeuda, Laura (LAB - Macclesfield South)
laura.jeuda@cheshireeast.gov.uk

Kolker, Andrew (CON - Dane Valley)
andrew.kolker@cheshireeast.gov.uk

Macrae, Jamie (CON - Mobberley)
jamie.macrae@cheshireeast.gov.uk

Mahon, Dennis (R - Handforth)
dennis.mahon@cheshireeast.gov.uk

Mannion, Nick (LAB - Macclesfield West and Ivy)
nick.mannion@cheshireeast.gov.uk

Marren, David (CON - Haslington)
david.marren@cheshireeast.gov.uk

Martin, Andrew (CON - Nantwich South and Stapeley)
andrew.martin@cheshireeast.gov.uk

Mason, Peter (CON - Congleton East)
peter.mason@cheshireeast.gov.uk

McGrory, Simon (IND - Middlewich)
simon.mcgrory@cheshireeast.gov.uk

Menlove, Rod (CON - Wilmslow East)
rod.menlove@cheshireeast.gov.uk

Merry, Gill (CON - Sandbach Elworth)
gillian.merry@cheshireeast.gov.uk

Moran, Barry (CON - Sandbach Town)
barry.moran@cheshireeast.gov.uk

Murray, Howard (CON - Poynton East and Pott Shrigley)

Parsons, Michael (IND - Middlewich)
michael.parsons@cheshireeast.gov.uk

Pochin, Sarah (CON - Willaston and Rope)
sarah.pochin@cheshireeast.gov.uk

Rhodes, Jill (LAB - Crewe West)
jill.rhodes@cheshireeast.gov.uk

Roberts, Brian (LAB - Crewe West)
brian.roberts@cheshireeast.gov.uk

Saunders, Jos (CON - Poynton East and Pott Shrigley)
jos.saunders@cheshireeast.gov.uk

Simon, Margaret (CON - Wistaston)
margaret.simon@cheshireeast.gov.uk

Smetham, Lesley (CON - Gawsworth)
lesley.smetham@cheshireeast.gov.uk

Stewart, Mike (CON - Poynton West and Adlington)
mike.stewart@cheshireeast.gov.uk

Stockton, Don (CON - Wilmslow Lacey Green)
don.stockton@cheshireeast.gov.uk

Stott, Amanda (O - Bollington)
amanda.stott@cheshireeast.gov.uk

Wait, Gail (CON - Sandbach Ettiley Heath and Wheelock)
gail.wait@cheshireeast.gov.uk

Walmsley, Bernice (IND - Middlewich)
bernice.walmsley@cheshireeast.gov.uk

Walton, George (CON - Chelford)
george.walton@cheshireeast.gov.uk

Wardlaw, Liz (CON - Odd Rode)
liz.wardlaw@cheshireeast.gov.uk

Warren, Mick (IND - Macclesfield East)
mick.warren@cheshireeast.gov.uk

Weatherill, Jaqueline (CON - Wistaston)
jacquie.weatherill@cheshireeast.gov.uk

Wells-Bradshaw, Hayley (CON - Knutsford)
hayley.wells-bradshaw@cheshireeast.gov.uk

Weston, Jonathan (CON - Bollington)
jonathan.weston@cheshireeast.gov.uk

Williams, Glen (CON - Congleton East)
glen.williams@cheshireeast.gov.uk

Wray, John (CON - Brereton Rural)
john.wray@cheshireeast.gov.uk

POLITICAL COMPOSITION

CON: 53, LAB: 16, IND: 6, R: 3, LD: 2, O: 2

COMMITTEE CHAIRS

Audit & Governance: Ms Lesley Smetham

Children & Families: Ms Rhoda Bailey

Health & Adult Social Care: Ms Jos Saunders

Health & Wellbeing: Ms Janet Clowes

Licensing: Mr Stan Davies

Cheshire West & Chester U

Cheshire West & Chester, HQ, 58 Nicholas Street, Chester CH1 2NP
☎ 0300 123 8123 enquiries@cheshirewestandchester.gov.uk
www.cheshirewestandchester.gov.uk

FACTS AND FIGURES

Parliamentary Constituencies: Chester, City of, Eddisbury, Ellesmere Port and Neston, Tatton, Weaver Vale

PRINCIPAL OFFICERS

Chief Executive: Mr Steve Robinson Chief Executive, HQ, 58 Nicholas Street, Chester CH1 2NP ☎ 01244 977454
steve.robinson@cheshirewestandchester.gov.uk

Senior Management: Mr Gerald Meehan Strategic Director, HQ, 58 Nicholas Street, Chester CH1 2NP ☎ 01244 972033 gerald.meehan@cheshirewestandchester.gov.uk

Senior Management: Mr Mark Palethorpe Strategic Director, HQ, 58 Nicholas Street, Chester CH1 2NP ☎ 01244 976235
mark.palethorpe@cheshirewestandchester.gov.uk

Senior Management: Mr Charlie Seward Strategic Director, HQ, 58 Nicholas Street, Chester CH1 2NP ☎ 01244 972857
charlie.seward@cheshirewestandchester.gov.uk

Access Officer / Social Services (Disability): Mr Graham Garnett Senior Access Officer, HQ, 58 Nicholas Street, Chester CH1 2NP
☎ 01244 972609 graham.garnett@cheshirewestandchester.gov.uk

Architect, Building / Property Services: Mr Richard Green Principal Property & Information Manager, HQ, 58 Nicholas Street, Chester CH1 2NP ☎ 01244 977465
richard.green@cheshirewestandchester.gov.uk

Best Value: Mr Lawrence Ainsworth Head of Public Sector Reform, HQ, 58 Nicholas Street, Chester CH1 2NP ☎ 01244 977147
lawrence.ainsworth@cheshirewestandchester.gov.uk

Building Control: Mr John Adcock Building Control Consultancy Area Manager, HQ, 58 Nicholas Street, Chester CH1 2NP ☎ 01244 977797 john.adcock@cheshirewestandchester.gov.uk

Catering Services: Ms Tracy Moore Acting Senior Manager - Catering & Cleaning, HQ, 58 Nicholas Street, Chester CH1 2NP
☎ 01244 972715 tracy.moore@cheshirewestandchester.gov.uk

Children / Youth Services: Ms Helen Brackenbury Interim Head of Service - Early Support & Localities for Children, HQ, 58 Nicholas Street, Chester CH1 2NP
helen.brackenbury@cheshirewestandchester.gov.uk

Children / Youth Services: Mr Mark Parkinson Head of Achievement & Wellbeing, HQ, 58 Nicholas Street, Chester CH1 2NP
☎ 01244 975923 mark.parkinson@cheshirewestandchester.gov.uk

Children / Youth Services: Ms Emma Taylor Head of Children & Families, HQ, 58 Nicholas Street, Chester CH1 2NP ☎ 01244 973512 emma.taylor@cheshirewestandchester.gov.uk

PR / Communications: Ms Rachel Kerslake Senior Marketing Manager, HQ, 58 Nicholas Street, Chester CH1 2NP
☎ 01244 973111 rachel.kerslake@cheshirewestandchester.gov.uk

Community Safety: Ms Jane Makin Senior Manager - Chester Locality & Community Safety Management, HQ, 58 Nicholas Street, Chester CH1 2NP ☎ 01244 973464

Computer Management: Ms Simone Thomas Head of ICT Shared Services, HQ, 58 Nicholas Street, Chester CH1 2NP
☎ 01244 972347 simone.thomas@cheshirewestandchester.gov.uk

Consumer Protection and Trading Standards: Ms Vanessa Griffiths Head of Regulatory Services, HQ, 58 Nicholas Street, Chester CH1 2NP ☎ 01244 073987
vanessa.griffiths@cheshirewestandchester.gov.uk

Contracts: Mr Dave Thomas Contract Development Manager, HQ, 58 Nicholas Street, Chester CH1 2NP ☎ 01244 977410
david.b.thomas@cheshire.gov.uk

Customer Service: Ms Julie Bellis Senior Manager - Customer & Library Services, HQ, 58 Nicholas Street, Chester CH1 2NP
☎ 01244 976969 julie.bellis@cheshirewestandchester.gov.uk

Economic Development: Ms Alison Knight Head of Places Strategy, HQ, 58 Nicholas Street, Chester CH1 2NP ☎ 01244 976785 alison.knight@cheshirewestandchester.gov.uk

Education: Mr Mark Parkinson Head of Achievement & Wellbeing, HQ, 58 Nicholas Street, Chester CH1 2NP ☎ 01244 975923
mark.parkinson@cheshirewestandchester.gov.uk

Electoral Registration: Ms Mandy Ramsden Senior Manager - Democratic Services, HQ, 58 Nicholas Street, Chester CH1 2NP
☎ 01244 975985 mandy.ramsden@cheshirewestandchester.gov.uk

Emergency Planning: Mr Chris Samuel Emergency Planning Team Manager, HQ, 58 Nicholas Street, Chester CH1 2NP
☎ 01244 976720 chris.samuel@cheshirewestandchester.gov.uk

Energy Management: Mr Peter Bulmer Project Manager of Climate Change, HQ, 58 Nicholas Street, Chester CH1 2NP
☎ 01244 972427 peter.bulmer@cheshirewestandchester.gov.uk

Environmental / Technical Services: Ms Vanessa Griffiths Head of Regulatory Services, HQ, 58 Nicholas Street, Chester CH1 2NP ☎ 01244 073987
vanessa.griffiths@cheshirewestandchester.gov.uk

Environmental / Technical Services: Mr John Outram Head of Commissioning Places, HQ, 58 Nicholas Street, Chester CH1 2NP
☎ 01244 977539 john.outram@cheshirewestandchester.gov.uk

Estates, Property & Valuation: Mr Richard Green Principal Property & Information Manager, HQ, 58 Nicholas Street, Chester CH1 2NP ☎ 01244 977465
richard.green@cheshirewestandchester.gov.uk

Facilities: Ms Sam Brousas Head of Professional Services, HQ, 58 Nicholas Street, Chester CH1 2NP ☎ 01244 972739
samantha.brousas@cheshirewestandchester.gov.uk

CHESHIRE WEST & CHESTER

Finance: Mr Mark Wynn Head of Finance, HQ, 58 Nicholas Street, Chester CH1 2NP ☎ 01244 972537 ✉ mark.wynn@cheshirewestandchester.gov.uk

Treasury: Mr Mark Wynn Head of Finance, HQ, 58 Nicholas Street, Chester CH1 2NP ☎ 01244 972537 ✉ mark.wynn@cheshirewestandchester.gov.uk

Pensions: Mr Nick Jones Senior Financial Advisor (Pensions), HQ, 58 Nicholas Street, Chester CH1 2NP ☎ 01244 972652 ✉ nick.jones@cheshirewestandchester.gov.uk

Fleet Management: Ms Mary Jefferson Section Leader - Transport Commissioning Service, Rivacre Business Centre, Mill Lane, Ellesmere Port CH66 3TL ☎ 01244 973052 ✉ mary.jefferson@cheshirewestandchester.gov.uk

Health and Safety: Mr Eric Burt Health & Safety Manager, HQ, 58 Nicholas Street, Chester CH1 2NP ☎ 01244 972229 ✉ eric.burt@cheshirewestandchester.gov.uk

Highways: Mr Rob Brooks Senior Manager - Place Network & Environment Manager, HQ, 58 Nicholas Street, Chester CH1 2NP ☎ 01244 973621 ✉ rob.brooks@cheshirewestandchester.gov.uk

Legal: Ms Vanessa Whiting Head of Governance & Monitoring Officer, HQ, 58 Nicholas Street, Chester CH1 2NP ☎ 01244 977802 ✉ vanessa.whiting@cheshirewestandchester.gov.uk

Licensing: Ms Vanessa Whiting Head of Governance & Monitoring Officer, HQ, 58 Nicholas Street, Chester CH1 2NP ☎ 01244 977802 ✉ vanessa.whiting@cheshirewestandchester.gov.uk

Lifelong Learning: Ms Gemma Davies Senior Manager - Economic Growth, HQ, 58 Nicholas Street, Chester CH1 2NP ☎ 01244 976729 ✉ gemma.davies@cheshirewest.gov.uk

Lottery Funding, Charity and Voluntary: Ms Pam Bradley Head of Service, HQ, 58 Nicholas Street, Chester CH1 2NP ☎ 01244 976996 ✉ pam.bradley@cheshirewestandchester.gov.uk

Member Services: Ms Andrea Thwaite Team Leader - Civic & Member Support, HQ, 58 Nicholas Street, Chester CH1 2NP ☎ 01244 972283 ✉ andrea.thwaite@cheshirewestandchester.gov.uk

Parking: Ms Sarah Armstrong Manager - Lifetime Services & Car Parking, First Floor, The Forum, Chester CH1 2HS ☎ 01244 973774 ✉ sarah.armstrong@cheshirewestandchester.gov.uk

Partnerships: Mr Alistair Jeffs Head of Strategic Commissioning, HQ, 58 Nicholas Street, Chester CM1 2NP ☎ 01244 972228 ✉ alistair.jeffs@cheshirewestandchester.gov.uk

Personnel / HR: Ms Sam Brousas Head of Professional Services, HQ, 58 Nicholas Street, Chester CH1 2NP ☎ 01244 972739 ✉ samantha.brousas@cheshirewestandchester.gov.uk

Planning: Ms Fiona Hore Planning Manager, The Forum Offices, Chester CH1 2HS ☎ 01244 972859 ✉ fiona.hore@cheshirewestandchester.gov.uk

Procurement: Mr Julian Ablett Procurement Process & Planning Manager, HQ, 58 Nicholas Street, Chester CH1 2NP ☎ 01244 972952 ✉ julian.ablett@cheshirewestandchester.gov.uk

Public Libraries: Ms Rachel Foster Library Services Manager, HQ, 58 Nicholas Street, Chester CH1 2NP ☎ 01244 972612 ✉ rachel.foster@cheshirewestandchester.gov.uk

Recycling & Waste Minimisation: Mr Steve Bakewell Senior Manager - Waste Collection & Disposal, Phoenix House, Clough Road, Winsford CW7 4BD ☎ 01244 977847 ✉ steve.bakewell@cheshirewestandchester.gov.uk

Regeneration: Ms Alison Knight Head of Places Strategy, HQ, 58 Nicholas Street, Chester CH1 2NP ☎ 01244 976785 ✉ alison.knight@cheshirewestandchester.gov.uk

Road Safety: Ms Sarah Collins Senior Road Safety Officer, Rivacre Business Centre, Mill Lane, Ellesmere Port CH66 3TL ☎ 01244 976713 ✉ sarah.collins@cheshire.gov.uk

Social Services: Ms Emma Taylor Head of Children & Families, HQ, 58 Nicholas Street, Chester CH1 2NP ☎ 01244 973512 ✉ emma.taylor@cheshirewestandchester.gov.uk

Social Services (Adult): Ms Jill Broomhall Head of Prevention & Wellbeing, HQ, 58 Nicholas Street, Chester CH1 2NP ☎ 01244 972247 ✉ jill.broomhall@cheshirewestandchester.gov.uk

Social Services (Adult): Mr Alistair Jeffs Head of Strategic Commissioning, HQ, 58 Nicholas Street, Chester CM1 2NP ☎ 01244 972228 ✉ alistair.jeffs@cheshirewestandchester.gov.uk

Social Services (Adult): Mr Mark Palethorpe Strategic Director, HQ, 58 Nicholas Street, Chester CH1 2NP ☎ 01244 976235 ✉ mark.palethorpe@cheshirewestandchester.gov.uk

Social Services (Children): Ms Emma Taylor Head of Children & Families, HQ, 58 Nicholas Street, Chester CH1 2NP ☎ 01244 973512 ✉ emma.taylor@cheshirewestandchester.gov.uk

Families: Ms Helen Brackenbury Interim Head of Service - Early Support & Localities for Children, HQ, 58 Nicholas Street, Chester CH1 2NP ☎ ✉ helen.brackenbury@cheshirewestandchester.gov.uk

Public Health: Ms Fiona Reynolds Interim Director of Public Health, HQ, 58 Nicholas Street, Chester CH1 2NP ☎ 01244 977030 ✉ fiona.reynolds@cheshirewestandchester.gov.uk

Staff Training: Ms Monica Thornton Project Officer, HQ, 58 Nicholas Street, Chester CH1 2NP ☎ 01244 976096 ✉ monica.thornton@cheshirewestandchester.gov.uk

Street Scene: Mr Simon Lammond Senior Manager - Place Delivery, HQ, 58 Nicholas Street, Chester CH1 2NP ✉ simon.lammond@cheshirewestandchester.gov.uk

Sustainable Communities: Mr George Ablett Principal Sustainable Development Officer, HQ, 58 Nicholas Street, Chester CH1 2NP ☎ 01244 972419 ✉ george.ablett@cheshirewestandchester.gov.uk

Total Place: Ms Aleta Steele Senior Manager - Locality Working, HQ, 58 Nicholas Street, Chester CH1 2NP ☎ 01244 972143
aleta.steele@cheshirewestandchester.gov.uk

Waste Collection and Disposal: Mr Steve Bakewell Senior Manager - Waste Collection & Disposal, Phoenix House, Clough Road, Winsford CW7 4BD ☎ 01244 977847
steve.bakewell@cheshirewestandchester.gov.uk

Waste Management: Mr John Outram Head of Commissioning Places, HQ, 58 Nicholas Street, Chester CH1 2NP ☎ 01244 977539
john.outram@cheshirewestandchester.gov.uk

COUNCILLORS

***The Lord Mayor* Deynem**, Hugo (CON - Tarvin and Kelsall)
hugo.deynem@cheshirewestandchester.gov.uk

***Deputy Lord Mayor* Claydon**, Angela (LAB - St. Paul's)
angela.claydon@cheshirewestandchester.gov.uk

***Chair* Rudd**, Bob (LAB - Garden Quarter)
bob.rudd@cheshirewestandchester.gov.uk

***Sheriff* Black**, Alex (LAB - Hoole)
alex.black@cheshirewestandchester.gov.uk

***Leader of the Council* Dixon**, Samantha (LAB - Chester City)
samantha.dixon@cheshirewestandchester.gov.uk

***Deputy Leader of the Council* Gittins**, Louise (LAB - Little Neston and Burton)
louise.gittins@cheshirewestandchester.gov.uk

***Group Leader* Jones**, Mike (CON - Tattenhall)
mike.jones@cheshirewestandchester.gov.uk

Anderson, Gareth (CON - Ledsham and Manor)
gareth.anderson@cheshirewestandchester.gov.uk

Armstrong, Val (LAB - Witton and Rudheath)
val.armstrong@cheshirewestandchester.gov.uk

Armstrong, David (LAB - Winsford Swanlow and Dene)
david.armstrong@cheshirewestandchester.gov.uk

Barker, Martin (IND - Parkgate)
martin.barker@cheshirewestandchester.gov.uk

Baynham, Michael (CON - Winsford Over and Verdin)
michael.baynham@cheshirewestandchester.gov.uk

Beacham, Richard (LAB - Newton)
richard.beacham@cheshirewestandchester.gov.uk

Beckett, Don (LAB - Winsford Over and Verdin)
don.beckett@cheshirewestandchester.gov.uk

Bisset, Robert (LAB - St. Paul's)
robert.bisset@cheshirewestandchester.gov.uk

Blackmore, Tom (LAB - Winsford Over and Verdin)
tom.blackmore@cheshirewestandchester.gov.uk

Board, Keith (CON - Great Boughton)
keith.board@cheshirewestandchester.gov.uk

Booher, Pamela (LAB - Winsford Wharton)
pam.booher@cheshirewestandchester.gov.uk

Bryan, Matt (LAB - Upton)
matt.bryan@cheshirewestandchester.gov.uk

Burns, Stephen (LAB - Winsford Swanlow and Dene)
stephen.burns@cheshirewestandchester.gov.uk

Chidley, Angie (LAB - Hoole)
angie.chidley@cheshirewestandchester.gov.uk

Clare, Lynn (LAB - Ellesmere Port Town)
lynn.clare@cheshirewestandchester.gov.uk

Clarke, Brian (LAB - Winsford Wharton)
brian.clarke@cheshirewestandchester.gov.uk

Crook, Jess (LAB - Ellesmere Port Town)
jessica.crook@cheshirewestandchester.gov.uk

Crowe, Brian (CON - Saughall and Mollington)
brian.crowe@cheshirewestandchester.gov.uk

Daniels, Razia (CON - Handbridge Park)
razia.daniels@cheshirewestandchester.gov.uk

Dawson, Andrew (CON - Frodsham)
andrew.dawson@cheshirewestandchester.gov.uk

Delaney, Martyn (LAB - Boughton)
martyn.delaney@cheshirewestandchester.gov.uk

Dolan, Paul (LAB - Winnington and Castle)
paul.dolan@cheshirewestandchester.gov.uk

Donovan, Paul (LAB - Sutton)
paul.donovan@cheshirewestandchester.gov.uk

Fifield, Charles (CON - Weaver and Cuddington)
charles.fifield@cheshirewestandchester.gov.uk

Gahan, Carol (LAB - Blacon)
carol.gahan@cheshirewestandchester.gov.uk

Gibbon, Lynn (CON - Marbury)
lynn.gibbon@cheshirewestandchester.gov.uk

Greenwood, Howard (CON - Farndon)
howard.greenwood@cheshirewestandchester.gov.uk

Hall, Pamela (CON - Great Boughton)
pamela.hall@cheshirewestandchester.gov.uk

Hammond, Don (CON - Marbury)
don.hammond@cheshirewestandchester.gov.uk

Henesy, Mark (LAB - Strawberry)
mark.henesy@cheshirewestandchester.gov.uk

Hogg, Myles (CON - Willaston and Thornton)
myles.hogg@cheshirewestandchester.gov.uk

Houlbrook, Jill (CON - Upton)
jill.houlbrook@cheshirewestandchester.gov.uk

Johnson, Eleanor (CON - Gowy)
eleanor.johnson@cheshirewestandchester.gov.uk

Jones, Reggie (LAB - Blacon)
reggie.jones@cheshirewestandchester.gov.uk

Jones, Nige (CON - Little Neston and Burton)
nigel.jones@cheshirewestandchester.gov.uk

Jones, Brian (LAB - Whitby)
brian.jones@cheshirewestandchester.gov.uk

Kaur, Susan (CON - Hartford and Greenbank)
susan.kaur@cheshirewestandchester.gov.uk

Lawrenson, Tony (LAB - Witton and Rudheath)
tony.lawrenson@cheshirewestandchester.gov.uk

Leather, John (CON - Tarvin and Kelsall)
john.leather@cheshirewestandchester.gov.uk

McKie, Alan (CON - Helsby)
alan.mckie@cheshirewestandchester.gov.uk

CHESHIRE WEST & CHESTER

Meardon, Nicole (LAB - Sutton)
nicole.meardon@cheshirewestandchester.gov.uk

Mercer, Jane (LAB - Lache)
jane.mercer@cheshirewestandchester.gov.uk

Merrick, Pat (LAB - Rossmore)
pat.merrick@cheshirewestandchester.gov.uk

Moore, Eveleigh (CON - Tarporley)
eveleigh.mooredutton@cheshirewestandchester.gov.uk

Naylor, Sam (LAB - Winnington and Castle)
sam.naylor@cheshirewestandchester.gov.uk

Nelson, Marie (LAB - Blacon)
marie.nelson@cheshirewestandchester.gov.uk

Oultram, Ralph (CON - Kingsley)
ralph.oultram@cheshirewestandchester.gov.uk

Parker, Margaret (CON - Chester Villages)
margaret.parker@cheshirewestandchester.gov.uk

Parker, Stuart (CON - Chester Villages)
stuart.parker@cheshirewestandchester.gov.uk

Parkes, Patricia (CON - Hartford and Greenbank)
patricia.parkes@cheshirewestandchester.gov.uk

Pearson, James (CON - Davenham and Moulton)
james.pearson@cheshirewestandchester.gov.uk

Riley, Lynn (CON - Frodsham)
lynn.riley@cheshirewestandchester.gov.uk

Roberts, Diane (LAB - Netherpool)

Rooney, Peter (LAB - Ledsham and Manor)
peter.rooney@cheshirewestandchester.gov.uk

Sherlock, Tony (LAB - Grange)
tony.sherlock@cheshirewestandchester.gov.uk

Shore, Karen (LAB - Whitby)
karen.shore@cheshirewestandchester.gov.uk

Sinar, Gaynor (CON - Davenham and Moulton)
gaynor.sinar@cheshirewestandchester.gov.uk

Smith, Stephen (LAB - Elton)
ste.smith@cheshirewestandchester.gov.uk

Stocks, Mark (CON - Shakerley)
mark.stocks@cheshirewestandchester.gov.uk

Sullivan, Neil (CON - Handbridge Park)
neil.sullivan@cheshirewestandchester.gov.uk

Tonge, Harry (CON - Weaver and Cuddington)
harry.tonge@cheshirewestandchester.gov.uk

Watson, Gill (LAB - Newton)
gill.watson@cheshirewestandchester.gov.uk

Weltman, Helen (CON - Davenham and Moulton)
helen.weltman@cheshirewestandchester.gov.uk

Whitehurst, Chris (CON - Malpas)
chris.whitehurst@cheshirewestandchester.gov.uk

Williams, Andy (LAB - Neston)
andy.williams2@cheshirewestandchester.gov.uk

Williams, Mark (CON - Dodleston and Huntington)
mark.williams@cheshirewestandchester.gov.uk

Williams, Paul (CON - Weaver and Cuddington)
paul.williams2@cheshirewestandchester.gov.uk

Wright, Norman (CON - Marbury)
norman.wright@cheshirewestandchester.gov.uk

POLITICAL COMPOSITION
LAB: 38, CON: 36, IND: 1

COMMITTEE CHAIRS
Audit & Governance: Mr Stephen Burns

Health & Wellbeing: Ms Samantha Dixon

Licensing: Ms Lynn Clare

Planning: Mr Don Beckett

Chesterfield D

Chesterfield Borough Council, Town Hall, Rose Hill, Chesterfield S40 1LP
☎ 01246 345345 🖷 01246 345252 ✉ info@chesterfield.gov.uk
💻 www.chesterfield.gov.uk

FACTS AND FIGURES
Parliamentary Constituencies: Chesterfield
EU Constituencies: East Midlands
Election Frequency: Elections are of whole council

PRINCIPAL OFFICERS
Chief Executive: Mr Huw Bowen, Chief Executive, Town Hall, Rose Hill, Chesterfield S40 1LP ☎ 01246 345305 🖷 01246 345252 ✉ huw.bowen@chesterfield.gov.uk

Senior Management: Mr Barry Dawson Head of Finance, Town Hall, Rose Hill, Chesterfield S40 1LP ☎ 01246 345451 🖷 01246 345252 ✉ barry.dawson@chesterfield.gov.uk

Senior Management: Mr James Drury Executive Director, Town Hall, Rose Hill, Chesterfield S40 1LP ☎ 01246 345292 🖷 01246 345252 ✉ james.drury@chesterfield.gov.uk

Senior Management: Mr Michael Rich Executive Director, Town Hall, Rose Hill, Chesterfield S40 1LP ☎ 01246 345461 🖷 01246 345252 ✉ michael.rich@chesterfield.gov.uk

Architect, Building / Property Services: Mr Roger Farrand, Principal Architect, Town Hall, Rose Hill, Chesterfield S40 1LP ☎ 01246 345401 🖷 01246 345252 ✉ roger.farrand@chesterfield.gov.uk

Best Value: Miss Karen Brown Business Transformation Manager, Town Hall, Rose Hill, Chesterfield S40 1LP ☎ 01246 345293 ✉ karen.brown@chesterfield.gov.uk

Building Control: Mr Malcolm Clinton Business Manager, Town Hall, Rose Hill, Chesterfield S40 1LP ☎ 01246 345817; 01246 354900 ✉ malcolm.clinton@ne-derbyshire.gov.uk; malcolm.clinton@bcnconsultancy.co.uk

PR / Communications: Mr John Fern Communications & Marketing Manager, Town Hall, Rose Hill, Chesterfield S40 1LP ☎ 01246 345245 🖷 01246 345252 ✉ john.fern@chesterfield.gov.uk

Community Safety: Mr Joe Tomlinson Community Safety Officer, Town Hall, Rose Hill, Chesterfield S40 1LP ☎ 01246 345093 🖷 01246 345252 ✉ joe.tomlinson@chesterfield.gov.uk

Corporate Services: Mrs Jenny Williams Interim Head of Internal Audit, Town Hall, Rose Hill, Chesterfield S40 1LP ☎ 01246 345468 🖶 01246 345252 🖰 jenny.williams@chesterfield.gov.uk

Economic Development: Ms Lynda Sharp Joint Economic Development Manager, Town Hall, Rose Hill, Chesterfield S40 1LP ☎ 01246 345255 🖶 01246 345256 🖰 lynda.sharp@chesterfield.gov.uk

Economic Development: Ms Laurie Thomas, Joint Economic Development Manager, Town Hall, Rose Hill, Chesterfield S40 1LP ☎ 01246 345255 🖶 01246 345256 🖰 laurie.thomas@chesterfield.gov.uk

E-Government: Mr Jonathan Alsop ICT Projects Manager, Town Hall, Rose Hill, Chesterfield S40 1LP ☎ 01246 345249 🖰 jonathan.alsop@chesterfield.gov.uk

Electoral Registration: Mrs Sandra Essex, Democratic Services Manager, Town Hall, Rose Hill, Chesterfield S40 1LP ☎ 01246 345227 🖶 01246 345252 🖰 sandra.essex@chesterfield.gov.uk

Emergency Planning: Ms Sam Sherlock Emergency Planning Officer, Town Hall, Rose Hill, Chesterfield S40 1LP ☎ 01246 345407 🖶 01246 345252 🖰 sam.sherlock@chesterfield.gov.uk

Energy Management: Mr Jon Vaughan, Energy Manager, Town Hall, Rose Hill, Chesterfield S40 1LP ☎ 01246 345415 🖶 01246 345252 🖰 jon.vaughan@chesterfield.gov.uk

Environmental / Technical Services: Mr Russell Sinclair Environmental Health Manager, Town Hall, Rose Hill, Chesterfield S40 1LP ☎ 01246 345397 🖰 russell.sinclair@chesterfield.gov.uk

Environmental Health: Mr Russell Sinclair Environmental Health Manager, Town Hall, Rose Hill, Chesterfield S40 1LP ☎ 01246 345397 🖰 russell.sinclair@chesterfield.gov.uk

Estates, Property & Valuation: Mr Matthew Sorby Head of Asset Management, Town Hall, Rose Hill, Chesterfield S40 1LP ☎ 01246 345308 🖶 01246 345809 🖰 matthew.sorby@chesterfield.gov.uk

European Liaison: Ms Laurie Thomas, Joint Economic Development Manager, Town Hall, Rose Hill, Chesterfield S40 1LP ☎ 01246 345255 🖶 01246 345256 🖰 laurie.thomas@chesterfield.gov.uk

Finance: Mr Barry Dawson Head of Finance, Town Hall, Rose Hill, Chesterfield S40 1LP ☎ 01246 345451 🖶 01246 345252 🖰 barry.dawson@chesterfield.gov.uk

Finance: Ms Fran Rodway Customer Services & Revenues Manager, Town Hall, Rose Hill, Chesterfield S40 1LP ☎ 01246 345475 🖶 01246 345252 🖰 fran.rodway@chesterfield.gov.uk

Health and Safety: Miss Karen Brown Business Transformation Manager, Town Hall, Rose Hill, Chesterfield S40 1LP ☎ 01246 345293 🖰 karen.brown@chesterfield.gov.uk

Home Energy Conservation: Mr Paul Staniforth Development Management & Conservation Manager, Town Hall, Rose Hill, Chesterfield S40 1LP ☎ 01246 345781 🖰 paul.staniforth@chesterfield.gov.uk

Housing: Mrs Alison Craig Housing Service Manager, Town Hall, Rose Hill, Chesterfield S40 1LP ☎ 01246 345156 🖰 alison.craig@chesterfield.gov.uk

Housing: Ms Julie McGrogan Housing Service Manager, Town Hall, Rose Hill, Chesterfield S40 1LP ☎ 01246 345135 🖰 julie.mcgrogan@chesterfield.gov.uk

Housing Maintenance: Mr Martyn Bollands Operational Services Manager, Town Hall, Rose Hill, Chesterfield S40 1LP ☎ 01246 345020 🖶 01246 345252 🖰 martyn.bollands@chesterfield.gov.uk

Legal: Mr Gerard Rogers Local Government & Regulatory Law Manager, Town Hall, Rose Hill, Chesterfield S40 1LP ☎ 01246 345310 🖶 01246 345270 🖰 gerard.rogers@chesterfield.gov.uk

Leisure and Cultural Services: Ms Bernadette Wainwright, Cultural & Visitor Services Manager, Town Hall, Rose Hill, Chesterfield S40 1LP ☎ 01246 345779 🖶 01246 345252 🖰 bernadette.wainwright@chesterfield.gov.uk

Licensing: Mr Trevor Durham Licensing Manager, Town Hall, Rose Hill, Chesterfield S40 1LP ☎ 01246 345230 🖶 01246 345252 🖰 trevor.durham@chesterfield.gov.uk

Member Services: Mrs Sandra Essex, Democratic Services Manager, Town Hall, Rose Hill, Chesterfield S40 1LP ☎ 01246 345227 🖶 01246 345252 🖰 sandra.essex@chesterfield.gov.uk

Member Services: Mr Gerard Rogers Local Government & Regulatory Law Manager, Town Hall, Rose Hill, Chesterfield S40 1LP ☎ 01246 345310 🖶 01246 345270 🖰 gerard.rogers@chesterfield.gov.uk

Parking: Ms Bernadette Wainwright, Cultural & Visitor Services Manager, Tourist Information Centre, Rykneld Square, Chesterfield S40 1SB ☎ 01246 345779 🖶 01246 345252 🖰 bernadette.wainwright@chesterfield.gov.uk

Personnel / HR: Ms Jane Dackiewicz HR & Payroll Service Solution Lead, Town Hall, Rose Hill, Chesterfield S40 1LP ☎ 01246 345257 🖶 01246 345252 🖰 jane.dackiewicz@chesterfield.gov.uk

Planning: Mr Paul Staniforth Development Management & Conservation Manager, Town Hall, Rose Hill, Chesterfield S40 1LP ☎ 01246 345781 🖰 paul.staniforth@chesterfield.gov.uk

Procurement: Ms Leigh Pratt Procurement Officer, Town Hall, Rose Hill, Chesterfield S40 1LP ☎ 01246 345295 🖶 01246 345252 🖰 leigh.pratt@chesterfield.gov.uk

Recycling & Waste Minimisation: Mr David Bennett Waste & Street Cleaning Manager, Town Hall, Rose Hill, Chesterfield S40 1LP ☎ 01246 345399 🖶 01246 345760 🖰 dave.bennett@chesterfield.gov.uk

CHESTERFIELD

Regeneration: Mr Neil Johnson Development & Growth Manager, Town Hall, Rose Hill, Chesterfield S40 1LP ☎ 01246 345789 ✉ neil.johnson@chesterfield.gov.uk

Staff Training: Ms Jane Dackiewicz HR & Payroll Service Solution Lead, Town Hall, Rose Hill, Chesterfield S40 1LP ☎ 01246 345257 🖷 01246 345252 ✉ jane.dackiewicz@chesterfield.gov.uk

Street Scene: Mr Russell Sinclair Environmental Health Manager, Town Hall, Rose Hill, Chesterfield S40 1LP ☎ 01246 345397 ✉ russell.sinclair@chesterfield.gov.uk

Sustainable Communities: Mr Peter Corke Sustainability Officer, Town Hall, Rose Hill, Chesterfield S40 1LP ☎ 01246 345765 🖷 01246 345252 ✉ peter.corke@chesterfield.gov.uk

Sustainable Development: Mr Peter Corke Sustainability Officer, Town Hall, Rose Hill, Chesterfield S40 1LP ☎ 01246 345765 🖷 01246 345252 ✉ peter.corke@chesterfield.gov.uk

Tourism: Ms Bernadette Wainwright, Cultural & Visitor Services Manager, Town Hall, Rose Hill, Chesterfield S40 1LP ☎ 01246 345779 🖷 01246 345252 ✉ bernadette.wainwright@chesterfield.gov.uk

Town Centre: Ms Bernadette Wainwright, Cultural & Visitor Services Manager, Town Hall, Rose Hill, Chesterfield S40 1LP ☎ 01246 345779 🖷 01246 345252 ✉ bernadette.wainwright@chesterfield.gov.uk

Waste Collection and Disposal: Mr David Bennett Waste & Street Cleaning Manager, Town Hall, Rose Hill, Chesterfield S40 1LP ☎ 01246 345399 🖷 01246 345760 ✉ dave.bennett@chesterfield.gov.uk

Waste Management: Mr David Bennett Waste & Street Cleaning Manager, Town Hall, Rose Hill, Chesterfield S40 1LP ☎ 01246 345399 🖷 01246 345760 ✉ dave.bennett@chesterfield.gov.uk

COUNCILLORS

***Chair* Burrows**, John (LAB - Brimington North)
john.burrows@chesterfield.gov.uk

***Mayor* Bingham**, Barry (LD - Barrow Hill & New Whittington)
barry.bingham@chesterfield.gov.uk

***Deputy Mayor* Brunt**, Steve (LAB - Brockwell)
steve.brunt@chesterfield.gov.uk

Bagley, Helen (LAB - St Helens)
helen.bagley@chesterfield.gov.uk

Barr, Peter (LD - Linacre)
peter.barr@chesterfield.gov.uk

Barr, Jeannie (LD - Linacre)
jeannie.barr@chesterfield.gov.uk

Bellamy, Andy (LAB - Brimington South)
andy.bellamy@chesterfield.gov.uk

Bexton, Richard (UKIP - Barrow Hill and New Whittington)
richard.bexton@chesterfield.gov.uk

Blank, Sharon (LAB - St Leonards)
sharon.blank@chesterfield.gov.uk

Borrell, Howard (LD - West)
howard.borrell@chesterfield.gov.uk

Brady, Mick (LAB - Hasland)
mick.brady@chesterfield.gov.uk

Brittain, Stuart (LAB - Rother)
stuart.brittain@chesterfield.gov.uk

Brown, Keith (LAB - Moor)
keith.brown@chesterfield.gov.uk

Callan, Ian (LAB - Brimington South)
ian.callan@chesterfield.gov.uk

Catt, Ray (LAB - West)
raymong.catt@chesterfield.gov.uk

Caulfield, Kate (LAB - Moor)
kate.caulfield@chesterfield.gov.uk

Collins, Dean (LAB - Lowgates and Woodthorpe)
dean.collings@chesterfield.gov.uk

Collins, Lisa (LAB - Lowgates and Woodthorpe)
lisa.collings@chesterfield.gov.uk

Davenport, Maureen (LD - Brockwell)
maureen.davenport@chesterfield.gov.uk

Derbyshire, Lisa-Marie (LAB - Barrow Hill nad New Whittington)
lisa-marie.derbyshire@chesterfield.gov.uk

Dickinson, John (LAB - Brockwell)
john.dickinson@chesterfield.gov.uk

Diouf, Alexis (LD - Walton)
alexis.diouf@chesterfield.gov.uk

Diouf, Vicky-Anne (LD - Walton)
vickey.diouf@chesterfield.gov.uk

Dyke, Barry (LAB - Hollingwood & Inkersall)
barry.dyke@chesterfield.gov.uk

Elliott, Helen (LAB - Hollingwood & Inkersall)
helen.elliott@chesterfield.gov.uk

Flood, Jenny (LAB - Rother)
jenny.flood@chesterfield.gov.uk

Gilby, Tricia (LAB - Brimington South)
tricia.gilby@chesterfield.gov.uk

Gilby, Terry (LAB - Brimington North)
terry.gilby@chesterfield.gov.uk

Green, Mick (LAB - Loundsley Green)
mick.wall@chesterfield.gov.uk

Hill, Anthony (LAB - Hollingwood & Inkersall)
anthony.hill@chesterfield.gov.uk

Hitchin, Stephen (LAB - Holmebrook)
stephen.hitchin@chesterfield.gov.uk

Hollingworth, Sarah (LAB - Dunston)
sarah.hollingworth@chesterfield.gov.uk

Huckle, Ken (LAB - St Leonards)
ken.huckle@chesterfield.gov.uk

Innes, Jean (LAB - Old Whittington)
jean.innes@chesterfield.gov.uk

Innes, Peter (LAB - Old Whittington)
peter.innes@chesterfield.gov.uk

Ludlow, Chris (LAB - Middlecroft & Poolsbrook)
chris.ludlow@chesterfield.gov.uk

Miles, Keith (LAB - Rother)
keith.miles@chesterfield.gov.uk

Murphy, Avis (LAB - Loundsley Green)
avis.murphy@chesterfield.gov.uk

Murphy, Tom (LAB - St Helens)
tom.murphy@chesterfield.gov.uk

Niblock, Shirley (LD - West)
shirley.niblock@chesterfield.gov.uk

Parsons, Donald (LAB - Middlecroft & Poolsbrook)
donald.parsons@chesterfield.gov.uk

Perkins, Suzie (LAB - Holmebrook)
suzie.perkins@chesterfield.gov.uk

Rayner, Mark (LAB - Dunston)
mark.rayner@chesterfield.gov.uk

Redihough, Nicholas (LD - Walton)
nick.redihough@chesterfield.gov.uk

Sarvent, Kate (LAB - St. Leonards's)
kate.sarvent@chesterfield.gov.uk

Serjeant, Amanda (LAB - Hasland)
amanda.serjeant@chesterfield.gov.uk

Simmons, Gordon (LAB - Dunston)
gordon.simmons@chesterfield.gov.uk

Slack, Andy (LAB - Hasland)
andy.slack@chesterfield.gov.uk

POLITICAL COMPOSITION
LAB: 38, LD: 9, UKIP: 1

COMMITTEE CHAIRS
Licensing: Mr Andy Bellamy

Planning: Mr Stuart Brittain

Chichester D

Chichester District Council, Council Offices, East Pallant House, East Pallant, Chichester PO19 1TY
☎ 01243 785166 🖷 01243 776766 ✉ contact@chichester.gov.uk
🖳 www.chichester.gov.uk

FACTS AND FIGURES
Parliamentary Constituencies: Chichester
EU Constituencies: South East
Election Frequency: Elections are of whole council

PRINCIPAL OFFICERS
Chief Executive: Mrs Diane Shepherd, Chief Executive, Council Offices, East Pallant House, East Pallant, Chichester PO19 1TY ☎ 01243 534709 🖷 01243 776766 ✉ dshepherd@chichester.gov.uk

Senior Management: Mr Steve Carvell Executive Director - Environment, Council Offices, East Pallant House, East Pallant, Chichester PO19 1TJ ☎ 01243 534569 🖷 01243 776766 ✉ scarvell@chichester.gov.uk

Senior Management: Mr Paul Over, Executive Director - Support Services & Economy, Council Offices, East Pallant House, East Pallant, Chichester PO19 1TY ☎ 01243 534639 🖷 01243 534673 ✉ pover@chichester.gov.uk

Senior Management: Mr John Ward Head of Finance & Governance Services, Council Offices, East Pallant House, East Pallant, Chichester PO19 1TY ☎ 01243 534805 ✉ jward@chichester.gov.uk

Access Officer / Social Services (Disability): Mr John Bacon, Building & Facility Services Manager, Council Offices, East Pallant House, East Pallant, Chichester PO19 1TY ☎ 01243 534648 🖷 01243 776766 ✉ jbacon@chichester.gov.uk

Architect, Building / Property Services: Mr John Bacon, Building & Facility Services Manager, Council Offices, East Pallant House, East Pallant, Chichester PO19 1TY ☎ 01243 534648 🖷 01243 776766 ✉ jbacon@chichester.gov.uk

Best Value: Mr Joe Mildred Corporate Policy Advice Manager East Pallant House, East Pallant, Chichester PO19 1TY ☎ 01243 534728 🖷 01243 776766 ✉ jmildred@chichester.gov.uk

Building Control: Mr Russell Pugh Building Control Service Manager, East Pallant House, East Pallant, Chichester PO19 1TY ☎ 01243 534565 🖷 01243 776766 ✉ rpugh@chichester.gov.uk

Children / Youth Services: Mr Stephen Hansford, Head of Service - Community, Council Offices, East Pallant House, East Pallant, Chichester PO19 1TY ☎ 01243 534789 🖷 01243 776766 ✉ shansford@chichester.gov.uk

PR / Communications: Ms Sarah Parker, Public Relations Manager, Council Offices, East Pallant House, East Pallant, Chichester PO19 1TY ☎ 01243 534537 🖷 01243 776766 ✉ sparker@chichester.gov.uk

Community Planning: Mr Stephen Hansford, Head of Service - Community, Council Offices, East Pallant House, East Pallant, Chichester PO19 1TY ☎ 01243 534789 🖷 01243 776766 ✉ shansford@chichester.gov.uk

Community Safety: Mr Stephen Hansford, Head of Service - Community, Council Offices, East Pallant House, East Pallant, Chichester PO19 1TY ☎ 01243 534789 🖷 01243 776766 ✉ shansford@chichester.gov.uk

Computer Management: Mrs Jane Dodsworth Head of Service - Business Improvement, Council Offices, East Pallant House, East Pallant, Chichester PO19 1TY ☎ 01243 534729 🖷 01243 776766 ✉ jdodsworth@chichester.gov.uk

Contracts: Mr Bob Riley, Contracts Manager, Chichester Contract Services, Stane Street, Westhampnett, Chichester PO18 0NS ☎ 01243 534615 🖷 01243 532695 ✉ briley@chichester.gov.uk

Customer Service: Mrs Jane Dodsworth Head of Service - Business Improvement, Council Offices, East Pallant House, East Pallant, Chichester PO19 1TY ☎ 01243 534729 🖷 01243 776766 ✉ jdodsworth@chichester.gov.uk

Direct Labour: Mr Rod Darton, Head of Service - Contract Services, Chichester Contract Services, Stane Street, Westhampnett, Chichester PO18 0NS ☎ 01243 521177 🖷 01243 532695 ✉ rdarton@chichester.gov.uk

CHICHESTER

Economic Development: Mr Stephen Oates Economic Development Manager, Council Offices, East Pallant House, East Pallant, Chichester PO19 1TY ☎ 01243 534600 soates@chichester.gov.uk

E-Government: Mrs Jane Dodsworth Head of Service - Business Improvement, Council Offices, East Pallant House, East Pallant, Chichester PO19 1TY ☎ 01243 534729 🖶 01243 776766 jdodsworth@chichester.gov.uk

Electoral Registration: Ms Jo Timm Electoral Services Manager, Council Offices, East Pallant House, East Pallant, Chichester PO19 1TY ☎ 01243 534592 🖶 01243 776766 jtimm@chichester.gov.uk

Emergency Planning: Mrs Louise Rudziak Head of Service - Housing & Environment, East Pallant House, East Pallant, Chichester PO19 1TY ☎ 01243 785166 🖶 01243 776766 lrudziak@chichester.gov.uk

Energy Management: Mr John Bacon, Building & Facility Services Manager, Council Offices, East Pallant House, East Pallant, Chichester PO19 1TY ☎ 01243 534648 🖶 01243 776766 jbacon@chichester.gov.uk

Environmental / Technical Services: Mr John Bacon, Building & Facility Services Manager, Council Offices, East Pallant House, East Pallant, Chichester PO19 1TY ☎ 01243 534648 🖶 01243 776766 jbacon@chichester.gov.uk

Environmental / Technical Services: Mrs Louise Rudziak Head of Service - Housing & Environment, East Pallant House, East Pallant, Chichester PO19 1TY ☎ 01243 785166 🖶 01243 776766 lrudziak@chichester.gov.uk

Environmental Health: Mrs Louise Rudziak Head of Service - Housing & Environment, East Pallant House, East Pallant, Chichester PO19 1TY ☎ 01243 785166 🖶 01243 776766 lrudziak@chichester.gov.uk

Estates, Property & Valuation: Mr Peter LeGood Valuation & Estates Manager, East Pallant House, East Pallant, Chichester PO19 1TY ☎ 01243 534668 🖶 01243 776766 plegood@chichester.gov.uk

European Liaison: Mr Stephen Oates Economic Development Manager, Council Offices, East Pallant House, East Pallant, Chichester PO19 1TY ☎ 01243 534600 soates@chichester.gov.uk

Facilities: Mr John Bacon, Building & Facility Services Manager, Council Offices, East Pallant House, East Pallant, Chichester PO19 1TY ☎ 01243 534648 🖶 01243 776766 jbacon@chichester.gov.uk

Finance: Mr John Ward Head of Finance & Governance Services, Council Offices, East Pallant House, East Pallant, Chichester PO19 1TY ☎ 01243 534805 jward@chichester.gov.uk

Treasury: Mr John Ward Head of Finance & Governance Services, Council Offices, East Pallant House, East Pallant, Chichester PO19 1TY ☎ 01243 534805 jward@chichester.gov.uk

Fleet Management: Mr John Hoole Workshop Manager, Stane Street, Westhampnett, Chichester PO18 0NS ☎ 01243 521183 🖶 01243 532695 jhoole@chichester.gov.uk

Grounds Maintenance: Mr Rod Darton, Head of Service - Contract Services, Chichester Contract Services, Stane Street, Westhampnett, Chichester PO18 0NS ☎ 01243 521177 🖶 01243 532695 rdarton@chichester.gov.uk

Grounds Maintenance: Mr Andy Howard Green Spaces & Street Scene Manager, East Pallant House, East Pallant, Chichester PO19 1TY ☎ 01243 782747 ahoward@chichester.gov.uk

Health and Safety: Mr Warren Townsend, Health & Safety Manager, East Pallant House, East Pallant, Chichester PO19 1TY ☎ 01243 534605 🖶 01243 776766 wtownsend@chichester.gov.uk

Housing: Mrs Louise Rudziak Head of Service - Housing & Environment, East Pallant House, East Pallant, Chichester PO19 1TY ☎ 01243 785166 🖶 01243 776766 lrudziak@chichester.gov.uk

Legal: Mr David Stewart Legal Practice Manager, East Pallant House, East Pallant, Chichester PO19 1TY ☎ 01243 534663

Leisure and Cultural Services: Mrs Jane Hotchkiss Head of Service - Commercial, Council Offices, East Pallant House, East Pallant, Chichester PO19 1TY ☎ 01243 534790 🖶 01243 776766 jhotchkiss@chichester.gov.uk

Licensing: Mrs Louise Rudziak Head of Service - Housing & Environment, East Pallant House, East Pallant, Chichester PO19 1TY ☎ 01243 785166 🖶 01243 776766 lrudziak@chichester.gov.uk

Lifelong Learning: Mr Stephen Oates Economic Development Manager, Council Offices, East Pallant House, East Pallant, Chichester PO19 1TY ☎ 01243 534600 soates@chichester.gov.uk

Lottery Funding, Charity and Voluntary: Mrs Jane Hotchkiss Head of Service - Commercial, Council Offices, East Pallant House, East Pallant, Chichester PO19 1TY ☎ 01243 534790 🖶 01243 776766 jhotchkiss@chichester.gov.uk

Member Services: Mr Philip Coleman Member Services Manager, Council Offices, East Pallant House, East Pallant, Chichester PO19 1TY ☎ 01243 534655 🖶 01243 776766 pcoleman@chichester.gov.uk

Parking: Mrs Jane Hotchkiss Head of Service - Commercial, Council Offices, East Pallant House, East Pallant, Chichester PO19 1TY ☎ 01243 534790 🖶 01243 776766 jhotchkiss@chichester.gov.uk

Partnerships: Mr Stephen Hansford, Head of Service - Community, Council Offices, East Pallant House, East Pallant, Chichester PO19 1TY ☎ 01243 534789 🖶 01243 776766 shansford@chichester.gov.uk

Personnel / HR: Mrs Jane Dodsworth Head of Service - Business Improvement, Council Offices, East Pallant House, East Pallant, Chichester PO19 1TY ☎ 01243 534729 🖶 01243 776766 jdodsworth@chichester.gov.uk

Planning: Mr Andrew Frost Head of Planning Services, East Pallant House, East Pallant, Chichester PO19 1TY ☎ 01243 534892 🖷 01243 776766 ✉ afrost@chichester.gov.uk

Procurement: Mr Phil Pickard Procurement Officer, East Pallant House, East Pallant, Chichester PO19 1TY ☎ 01243 785166

Recycling & Waste Minimisation: Mr Bob Riley, Contracts Manager, Chichester Contract Services, Stane Street, Westhampnett, Chichester PO18 0NS ☎ 01243 534615 🖷 01243 532695 ✉ briley@chichester.gov.uk

Regeneration: Mr Stephen Oates Economic Development Manager, Council Offices, East Pallant House, East Pallant, Chichester PO19 1TY ☎ 01243 534600 ✉ soates@chichester.gov.uk

Staff Training: Mr Tim Radcliffe, Senior Personnel Manager, Council Offices, East Pallant House, East Pallant, Chichester PO19 1TY ☎ 01243 534528 🖷 01243 776766 ✉ tradcliffe@chichester.gov.uk

Sustainable Communities: Mr Andrew Frost Head of Planning Services, East Pallant House, East Pallant, Chichester PO19 1TY ☎ 01243 534892 🖷 01243 776766 ✉ afrost@chichester.gov.uk

Sustainable Development: Mrs Louise Rudziak Head of Service - Housing & Environment, East Pallant House, East Pallant, Chichester PO19 1TY ☎ 01243 785166 🖷 01243 776766 ✉ lrudziak@chichester.gov.uk

Tourism: Mrs Jane Hotchkiss Head of Service - Commercial, Council Offices, East Pallant House, East Pallant, Chichester PO19 1TY ☎ 01243 534790 🖷 01243 776766 ✉ jhotchkiss@chichester.gov.uk

Transport: Mr John Hoole Workshop Manager, Stane Street, Westhampnett, Chichester PO18 0NS ☎ 01243 521183 🖷 01243 532695 ✉ jhoole@chichester.gov.uk

Waste Collection and Disposal: Mr Bob Riley, Contracts Manager, Chichester Contract Services, Stane Street, Westhampnett, Chichester PO18 0NS ☎ 01243 534615 🖷 01243 532695 ✉ briley@chichester.gov.uk

Waste Management: Mr Bob Riley, Contracts Manager, Chichester Contract Services, Stane Street, Westhampnett, Chichester PO18 0NS ☎ 01243 534615 🖷 01243 532695 ✉ briley@chichester.gov.uk

Children's Play Areas: Mrs Sarah Peyman Sport & Leisure Development Manager East Pallant House, East Pallant, Chichester PO19 1TY ☎ 01243 534791 ✉ speyman@chichester.gov.uk

COUNCILLORS

***Chair* Thomas**, Nick (CON - Plaistow)
nthomas@chichester.gov.uk

***Vice-Chair* Hamilton**, Elizabeth (CON - West Wittering)
ehamilton@chichester.gov.uk

***Leader of the Council* Dignum**, Tony (CON - Chichester North)
pdignum@chichester.gov.uk

***Deputy Leader of the Council* Lintill**, Eileen (CON - Petworth)
elintill@chichester.gov.uk

Apel, C (LD - Chichester West)
capel@chichester.gov.uk

Barrett, Graeme (CON - West Wittering)
gbarrett@chichester.gov.uk

Barrow, Roger (CON - Selsey South)
rbarrow@chichester.gov.uk

Budge, Peter (CON - Chichester North)
pbudge@chichester.gov.uk

Connor, John (CON - Selsey North)
jconnor@chichester.gov.uk

Cullen, Miles (CON - Bosham)
mcullen@chichester.gov.uk

Curbishley, Ian (CON - East Wittering)
icurbishley@chichester.gov.uk

Dempster, Thomas (CON - Chichster East)
tdempster@chichster.gov.uk

Dignum, Pam (CON - Chichester South)
pdignum@chichester.gov.uk

Duncton, Janet (CON - Petworth)
janet@duncton.plus.com

Dunn, Mark (CON - Westbourne)
mdunn@chichester.gov.uk

Elliot, John (CON - Selsey South)
jelliot@chichester.gov.uk

Elliott, John (CON - Bury)
john.elliott811929@btopenworld.com

Finch, Bruce (CON - Southbourne)
bfinch@chichester.gov.uk

Galloway, Nigel (CON - Chichester South)
ngalloway@chichester.gov.uk

Graves, Norma (CON - Fernhurst)
ngraves@chichester.gov.uk

Hall, Mike (CON - Lavant)
mhall@chichester.gov.uk

Hardwick, Phillippa (CON - Fernhurst)
phardwick@chichester.gov.uk

Hayes, Robert (CON - Southbourne)
rhayes@chichester.gov.uk

Hicks, Graham (CON - Southbourne)
ghicks@chichester.gov.uk

Hixson, Les (CON - Chichster East)
ihixson@chichester.gov.uk

Hobbs, Francis (CON - Easebourne)
fhobbs@chichester.gov.uk

Jarvis, Paul (CON - North Mundham)
pjarvis@chichester.gov.uk

Keegan, Gillian (CON - Rogate)
gkeegan@chichester.gov.uk

Kilby, Jane (CON - Chichster East)
jkilby@chichester.gov.uk

Knightley, Denise (CON - Plaistow)
dknightley@chichester.gov.uk

CHICHESTER

Lloyd-Williams, Simon (CON - Chichester North)
slloyd-williams@chichester.gov.uk

Macey, Len (CON - Chichester South)

McAra, Gordon (IND - Midhurst)
gmcara@chichester.gov.uk

Morley, Steve (IND - Midhurst)
smorley@chichester.gov.uk

Neville, Caroline (CON - Stedman)
cneville@chichester.gov.uk

Oakley, Simon (CON - Tangmere)
soakley@chichester.gov.uk

Plant, Penny (CON - Bosham)
pplant@chichester.gov.uk

Ploughman, Richard (LD - Chichester West)
rploughman@chichester.gov.uk

Potter, Henry (CON - Boxgrove)
hpotter@chichester.gov.uk

Purnell, Carol (CON - Selsey North)
cpurnell@chichester.gov.uk

Ransley, Josef (CON - Wisborough Green)
jransley@chichester.gov.uk

Ridd, John (CON - Donnington)
jridd@chichester.gov.uk

Shaxson, Andrew (IND - Harting)
ashaxson@chichester.gov.uk

Tassell, Julie (CON - Funtington)
julie.tassell@virgin.net

Taylor, Susan (CON - East Wittering)
sttaylor@chichester.gov.uk

Tull, Tricia (CON - Sidlesham)
ttull@chichester.gov.uk

Wakeman, Darren (CON - Selsey North)
dwakeman@chichester.gov.uk

Westacott, Sandra (LD - Fishbourne)
sweatacott@chichester.gov.uk

POLITICAL COMPOSITION

CON: 42, IND: 3, LD: 3

COMMITTEE CHAIRS

Licensing: Mr John Ridd

Planning: Mr Robert Hayes

Chiltern D

Chiltern District Council, Council Offices, King George V Road, Amersham HP6 5AW
☎ 01494 729000 🖷 01494 586506 💻 www.chiltern.gov.uk

FACTS AND FIGURES

Parliamentary Constituencies: Aylesbury, Chesham and Amersham
EU Constituencies: South East
Election Frequency: Elections are of whole council

PRINCIPAL OFFICERS

Chief Executive: Mr Bob Smith, Interim Chief Executive (Director of Services), Council Offices, King George V Road, Amersham HP6 5AW ☎ 01895 837367; 01494 732178 🖷 01494 586506 ✉ bsmith@chiltern.gov.uk

Senior Management: Mr Jim Burness, Director of Resources, Council Offices, King George V Road, Amersham HP6 5AW ☎ 01895 837367; 01494 732905 ✉ jburness@chiltern.gov.uk

Senior Management: Mr Bob Smith, Interim Chief Executive (Director of Services), Council Offices, King George V Road, Amersham HP6 5AW ☎ 01895 837367; 01494 732178 🖷 01494 586506 ✉ bsmith@chiltern.gov.uk

Access Officer / Social Services (Disability): Mr Peter Beckford Head of Sustainable Development, Council Offices, King George V Road, Amersham HP6 5AW ☎ 01895 837208; 01494 732036 ✉ pbeckford@chiltern.gov.uk

Architect, Building / Property Services: Mr Chris Marchant Head of Environment, Council Offices, King George V Road, Amersham HP6 5AW ☎ 01895 837360; 01494 732250 ✉ cmarchant@chiltern.gov.uk

Building Control: Mr Peter Beckford Head of Sustainable Development, Council Offices, King George V Road, Amersham HP6 5AW ☎ 01895 837208; 01494 732036 ✉ pbeckford@chiltern.gov.uk

Children / Youth Services: Mr Paul Nanji Principal Leisure & Community Officer, Council Offices, King George V Road, Amersham HP6 5AW ☎ 01494 732110 🖷 01494 586504 ✉ pnanji@chiltern.gov.uk

PR / Communications: Mrs Rachel Prance Community & Partnerships Officer, Council Offices, King George V Road, Amersham HP6 5AW ☎ 01494 732903 🖷 01494 586506 ✉ rprance@chiltern.gov.uk

Community Planning: Mrs Rachel Prance Community & Partnerships Officer, Council Offices, King George V Road, Amersham HP6 5AW ☎ 01494 732903 🖷 01494 586506 ✉ rprance@chiltern.gov.uk

Community Safety: Mrs Katie Galvin, Senior Community Safety Officer, Council Offices, King George V Road, Amersham HP6 5AW ☎ 01494 732265 🖷 01494 586504 ✉ kgalvin@chiltern.gov.uk

Computer Management: Mrs Simonette Dixon, Head of Business Support, Council Offices, King George V Road, Amersham HP6 5AW ☎ 01494 732087 🖷 01494 586509 ✉ sdixon@chiltern.gov.uk

Customer Service: Mrs Nicola Ellis Head of Customer Services, Council Offices, King George V Road, Amersham HP6 5AW ☎ 01494 732231 ✉ nellis@chiltern.gov.uk

Economic Development: Mr Bob Smith, Interim Chief Executive (Director of Services), Council Offices, King George V Road, Amersham HP6 5AW ☎ 01895 837367; 01494 732178 🖷 01494 586506 ✉ bsmith@chiltern.gov.uk

E-Government: Mrs Simonette Dixon, Head of Business Support, Council Offices, King George V Road, Amersham HP6 5AW ☎ 01494 732087 🖷 01494 586509 ✉ sdixon@chiltern.gov.uk

Electoral Registration: Miss Lesley Blue Interim Democratic & Electoral Services Manager, Council Offices, King George V Road, Amersham HP6 5AW ☎ 01494 732010 🖷 01494 586506 ✉ lblue@chiltern.gov.uk

Emergency Planning: Mrs Glynis Chanell, Health & Safety Practitioner, Council Offices, King George V Road, Amersham HP6 5AW ☎ 01494 732062 🖷 01494 586504 ✉ gchanell@chiltern.gov.uk

Energy Management: Mr Ben Coakley Principal Environmental Protection Officer - Strategic, Council Offices, King George V Road, Amersham HP6 5AW ☎ 01494 732060 🖷 01494 586504 ✉ bcoakley@chiltern.gov.uk

Environmental / Technical Services: Mr Chris Marchant Head of Environment, Council Offices, King George V Road, Amersham HP6 5AW ☎ 01895 837360; 01494 732250 ✉ cmarchant@chiltern.gov.uk

Environmental Health: Mr Martin Holt, Head of Healthy Communities, Council Offices, King George V Road, Amersham HP6 5AW ☎ 01494 732055 🖷 01494 586504 ✉ mholt@chiltern.gov.uk

Estates, Property & Valuation: Mr Chris Marchant Head of Environment, Council Offices, King George V Road, Amersham HP6 5AW ☎ 01895 837360; 01494 732250 ✉ cmarchant@chiltern.gov.uk

European Liaison: Mr Bob Smith, Interim Chief Executive (Director of Services), Council Offices, King George V Road, Amersham HP6 5AW ☎ 01895 837367; 01494 732178 🖷 01494 586506 ✉ bsmith@chiltern.gov.uk

Facilities: Mr Simon Rycraft Administration Manager, Council Offices, King George V Road, Amersham HP6 5AW ☎ 01494 732073 ✉ srycraft@chiltern.gov.uk

Finance: Mr Rodney Fincham Head of Finance, Council Offices, King George V Road, Amersham HP6 5AW ☎ 01243 776766 ✉ rfincham.chiltern.gov.uk

Treasury: Mr Jim Burness, Director of Resources, Council Offices, King George V Road, Amersham HP6 5AW ☎ 01895 837367; 01494 732905 ✉ jburness@chiltern.gov.uk

Grounds Maintenance: Mr Chris Marchant Head of Environment, Council Offices, King George V Road, Amersham HP6 5AW ☎ 01895 837360; 01494 732250 ✉ cmarchant@chiltern.gov.uk

Health and Safety: Mrs Glynis Chanell, Health & Safety Practitioner, Council Offices, King George V Road, Amersham HP6 5AW ☎ 01494 732062 🖷 01494 586504 ✉ gchanell@chiltern.gov.uk

Home Energy Conservation: Mrs Louise Quinn Senior Private Sector Housing Officer, Council Offices, King George V Road, Amersham HP6 5AW ☎ 01494 732209 ✉ lquinn@chiltern.gov.uk

Housing: Mr Michael Veryard Principal Housing Officer, Council Offices, King George V Road, Amersham HP6 5AW ☎ 01494 732200 🖷 01494 586504 ✉ mveryard@chiltern.gov.uk

Legal: Mrs Joanna Swift, Head of Legal & Democratic Services, Council Offices, King George V Road, Amersham HP6 5AW ☎ 01895 837229; 01494 732761 ✉ jswift@chiltern.gov.uk

Leisure and Cultural Services: Mr Martin Holt, Head of Healthy Communities, Council Offices, King George V Road, Amersham HP6 5AW ☎ 01494 732055 🖷 01494 586504 ✉ mholt@chiltern.gov.uk

Licensing: Mr Nathan March Licensing Manager, Council Offices, King George V Road, Amersham HP6 5AW ☎ 01494 732056 ✉ nmarch@chiltern.gov.uk

Lottery Funding, Charity and Voluntary: Mr Martin Holt, Head of Healthy Communities, Council Offices, King George V Road, Amersham HP6 5AW ☎ 01494 732055 🖷 01494 586504 ✉ mholt@chiltern.gov.uk

Member Services: Miss Lesley Blue Interim Democratic & Electoral Services Manager, Council Offices, King George V Road, Amersham HP6 5AW ☎ 01494 732010 🖷 01494 586506 ✉ lblue@chiltern.gov.uk

Parking: Mr Oliver Asbury, Principal Engineer, Council Offices, King George V Road, Amersham HP6 5AW ☎ 01494 732066 ✉ oasbury@chiltern.gov.uk

Personnel / HR: Mrs Judy Benson Joint Principal Personnel Officer, Council Offices, King George V Road, Amersham HP6 5AW ☎ 01494 732015 ✉ jbenson@chiltern.gov.uk

Planning: Mr Peter Beckford Head of Sustainable Development, Council Offices, King George V Road, Amersham HP6 5AW ☎ 01895 837208; 01494 732036 ✉ pbeckford@chiltern.gov.uk

Procurement: Mr Jim Burness, Director of Resources, Council Offices, King George V Road, Amersham HP6 5AW ☎ 01895 837367; 01494 732905 ✉ jburness@chiltern.gov.uk

Recycling & Waste Minimisation: Ms Kitran Eastman Senior Officer - Waste, Council Offices, King George V Road, Amersham HP6 5AW ☎ 01494 732149 ✉ keastman@chiltern.gov.uk

Regeneration: Mr Bob Smith, Interim Chief Executive (Director of Services), Council Offices, King George V Road, Amersham HP6 5AW ☎ 01895 837367; 01494 732178 🖷 01494 586506 ✉ bsmith@chiltern.gov.uk

Staff Training: Mrs Judy Benson Joint Principal Personnel Officer, Council Offices, King George V Road, Amersham HP6 5AW ☎ 01494 732015 ✉ jbenson@chiltern.gov.uk

Sustainable Development: Mr Ben Coakley Principal Environmental Protection Officer - Strategic, Council Offices, King George V Road, Amersham HP6 5AW ☎ 01494 732060 🖷 01494 586504 ✉ bcoakley@chiltern.gov.uk

CHILTERN

Waste Collection and Disposal: Ms Kitran Eastman Senior Officer - Waste, Council Offices, King George V Road, Amersham HP6 5AW ☎ 01494 732149 ✉ keastman@chiltern.gov.uk

Waste Management: Mr Chris Marchant Head of Environment, Council Offices, King George V Road, Amersham HP6 5AW ☎ 01895 837360; 01494 732250 ✉ cmarchant@chiltern.gov.uk

COUNCILLORS

***Chair* Harker**, Mimi (CON - Chesham Bois & Weedon Hill)
mharker@chiltern.gov.uk

***Vice-Chair* Shepherd**, Nigel (CON - Amersham on the Hill)
nshepherd@chiltern.gov.uk

Allen, Davida (LD - Amersham Town)
dallen@chichester.gov.uk

Bacon, Alan (LD - Asheridge Vale & Lowndes)
abacon@chiltern.gov.uk

Berry, Seb (IND - Great Missenden)
sberry@chiltern.gov.uk

Bray, Des (CON - Chalfont St Giles)
dbray @chiltern.gov.uk

Burton, Julie (CON - Penn & Coleshill)
jburton@chiltern.gov.uk

Culverhouse, Emily (CON - Hilltop and Townsend)
eculverhouse@chiltern.gov.uk

Darby, Isobel (CON - Chalfont Common)
idarby@chiltern.gov.uk

Flys, Mark (CON - Amersham Town)
mflys@chiltern.gov.uk

Ford, Christopher (CON - Gold Hill)
cford@chiltern.gov.uk

Garth, Andrew (CON - Ashley Green, Latimer & Chenies)
agarth@chiltern.gov.uk

Gladwin, John (CON - Prestwood & Heath End)
jgladwin@chiltern.gov.uk

Hardie, Alan (CON - Penn & Coleshill)
ahardie@chiltern.gov.uk

Harris, Graham (CON - Chesham Bois and Weedon Hill)
gharris@chiltern.gov.uk

Harrold, Murrey (CON - Central)
mharrold@chiltern.gov.uk

Hudson, Peter (CON - St Mary's & Waterside)
phudson@chiltern.gov.uk

Jackson, Carl (CON - Chalfont St Giles)
cjackson@chiltern.gov.uk

Jones, Robert (CON - Prestwood & Heath End)
rjones@chiltern.gov.uk

Jones, Peter (LD - Ballinger, South Heath & Chartridge)
peter.m.jones@btinternet.com

Jones, Caroline (CON - Amersham Common)
cmjones@chiltern.gov.uk

Lacey, Derek (IND - Ridgeway)
dlacey@chiltern.gov.uk

MacBean, Jane (CON - Asheridge Vale & Lowndes)
jmacbean@chiltern.gov.uk

Martin, Peter (CON - Little Chalfont)
pmartin@chiltern.gov.uk

Patel, Siddharth (CON - Seer Green)
spatel@chiltern.gov.uk

Phillips, Don (CON - Little Chalfont)
dphillips@chiltern.gov.uk

Rose, Nick (CON - Cholesbury, The Lee & Bellingdon)
nrose@chiltern.gov.uk

Rouse, Caroline (CON - Chalfont St Giles)
crouse@chiltern.gov.uk

Rush, Jonathan (CON - Central)
jrush@chiltern.gov.uk

Shaw, Mark (CON - Newtown)
mshaw@chiltern.gov.uk

Smith, Linda (CON - Chalfont Common)
lsmith@chiltern.gov.uk

Smith, Michael (CON - Holmer Green)
msmith@chiltern.gov.uk

Stannard, Mike (CON - St Mary's & Waterside)
mstannard@chiltern.gov.uk

Titterington, Mark (CON - Holmer Green)
mtittering@chiltern.gov.uk

Varley, Diane (CON - Little Missenden)
dvarley@chiltern.gov.uk

Varley, Nick (CON - Vale)
nvarley@chiltern.gov.uk

Wallace, Heather (CON - Prestwood & Heath End)
hwallace@chiltern.gov.uk

Walsh, Liz (CON - Amersham on The Hill)
lwalsh@chiltern.gov.uk

Wertheim, John (CON - Austenwood)
jwertheim@chiltern.gov.uk

Wilson, Fred (CON - Hilltop & Townsend)
fwilson@chiltern.gov.uk

POLITICAL COMPOSITION

CON: 35, LD: 3, IND: 2

COMMITTEE CHAIRS

Audit: Mr John Gladwin

Licensing: Mr Jonathan Rush

Planning: Mr Don Phillips

Chorley D

Chorley Borough Council, Town Hall, Market Street, Chorley PR7 1DP
☎ 01257 515151 🖷 01257 515150 ✉ admin.townhall@chorley.gov.uk
🖳 www.chorley.gov.uk

FACTS AND FIGURES

Parliamentary Constituencies: Chorley
EU Constituencies: North West
Election Frequency: Elections are by thirds

PRINCIPAL OFFICERS

Chief Executive: Mr Gary Hall, Chief Executive, Town Hall, Market Street, Chorley PR7 1DP ☎ 01257 515151 🖷 01257 515150 🖱 gary.hall@chorley.gov.uk

Senior Management: Mr Jamie Carson, Director - Public Protection, Streetscene & Community, Civic Offices, Union Street, Chorley PR7 1AL ☎ 01257 515151 🖷 01257 515150 🖱 jamie.carson@chorley.gov.uk

Senior Management: Mrs Lesley-Ann Fenton, Director - Customer & Advice Services, Civic Offices, Union Street, Chorley PR7 1AL ☎ 01257 515151 🖷 01257 515150 🖱 lesley-ann.fenton@chorley.gov.uk

Architect, Building / Property Services: Mr Keith Davy Property Team Manager, Town Hall, Market Street, Chorley PR7 1DP ☎ 01257 515151 🖷 01257 515150 🖱 keith.davy@chorley.gov.uk

Best Value: Mrs Lesley-Ann Fenton, Director - Customer & Advice Services, Civic Offices, Union Street, Chorley PR7 1AL ☎ 01257 515151 🖷 01257 515150 🖱 lesley-ann.fenton@chorley.gov.uk

Building Control: Mr John Bethwaite, Building Control Team Leader, Civic Offices, Union Street, Chorley PR7 1AL ☎ 01257 515151 🖷 01257 515150 🖱 john.bethwaite@chorley.gov.uk

PR / Communications: Mr Andrew Daniels Communications Manager, Town Hall, Market Street, Chorley PR7 1DP ☎ 01257 515151 🖷 01257 515150 🖱 andrew.daniels@chorley.gov.uk

Community Safety: Mrs Louise Elo Neighbourhood Team Manager, Civic Offices, Union Street, Chorley PR7 1AL ☎ 01257 515151 🖷 01257 515150 🖱 louise.elo@chorley.gov.uk

Computer Management: Ms Debbie Wilson Digital Information Manager, Civic Offices, Union Street, Chorley PR7 1AL ☎ 01257 515151 🖷 01251 515150 🖱 debbie.wilson@chorley.gov.uk

Customer Service: Mr Asim Khan, Head of Customer, ICT & Transitional Services, Civic Offices, Union Street, Chorley PR7 1AL ☎ 01257 515151 🖷 01257 515150 🖱 asim.khan@chorley.gov.uk

Economic Development: Ms Cath Burns Head of Economic Development, Civic Offices, Union Street, Chorley PR7 1AL ☎ 01257 515151 🖷 01257 515150 🖱 cath.burns@chorley.gov.uk

E-Government: Ms Debbie Wilson Digital Information Manager, Civic Offices, Union Street, Chorley PR7 1AL ☎ 01257 515151 🖷 01251 515150 🖱 debbie.wilson@chorley.gov.uk

Electoral Registration: Mr Phil Davies, Electoral Services Manager, Town Hall, Market Street, Chorley PR7 1DP ☎ 01257 515151 🖷 01257 515150 🖱 phil.davies@chorley.gov.uk

Emergency Planning: Mr Simon Clark Head of Health, Environment & Neighbourhoods, Civic Offices, Union Street, Chorley PR7 1AL ☎ 01257 515151 🖷 01257 515150 🖱 simon.clark@chorley.gov.uk

Environmental / Technical Services: Mr Jamie Carson, Director - Public Protection, Streetscene & Community, Civic Offices, Union Street, Chorley PR7 1AL ☎ 01257 515151 🖷 01257 515150 🖱 jamie.carson@chorley.gov.uk

Environmental Health: Mr Simon Clark Head of Health, Environment & Neighbourhoods, Civic Offices, Union Street, Chorley PR7 1AL ☎ 01257 515151 🖷 01257 515150 🖱 simon.clark@chorley.gov.uk

European Liaison: Mrs Lesley-Ann Fenton, Director - Customer & Advice Services, Civic Offices, Union Street, Chorley PR7 1AL ☎ 01257 515151 🖷 01257 515150 🖱 lesley-ann.fenton@chorley.gov.uk

Events Manager: Mrs Louise Finch Campaigns & Engagement Manager (Events), Town Hall, Market Street, Chorley PR7 1DP ☎ 01257 515151 🖷 01257 515150 🖱 louise.finch@chorley.gov.uk

Finance: Ms Susan Guinness Head of Shared Financial Services, Town Hall, Market Street, Chorley PR7 1DP ☎ 01257 515151 🖷 01257 515150 🖱 susan.guinness@chorley.gov.uk

Grounds Maintenance: Mr Jamie Dixon Head of Streetscene & Leisure Contracts, Civic Offices, Union Street, Chorley PR7 1AL ☎ 01257 515151 🖷 01257 515150 🖱 jamie.dixon@chorley.gov.uk

Health and Safety: Mrs Denise Fisher Health & Safety Advisor, Town Hall, Market Street, Chorley PR7 1DP ☎ 01257 515151 🖷 01257 515150 🖱 denise.fisher@chorley.gov.uk

Housing: Mrs Zoe Whiteside Head of Housing, Union Street, Civic Offices, , Chorley PR7 1AL ☎ 01257 515151 🖷 01257 515150 🖱 zoe.whiteside@chorley.gov.uk

Legal: Mr Chris Moister Head of Governance, Town Hall, Market Street, Chorley PR7 1DP ☎ 01257 515151 🖷 01257 515150 🖱 chris.moister@chorley.gov.uk

Leisure and Cultural Services: Mr Jamie Carson, Director - Public Protection, Streetscene & Community, Civic Offices, Union Street, Chorley PR7 1AL ☎ 01257 515151 🖷 01257 515150 🖱 jamie.carson@chorley.gov.uk

Licensing: Mr Jamie Carson, Director - Public Protection, Streetscene & Community, Civic Offices, Union Street, Chorley PR7 1AL ☎ 01257 515151 🖷 01257 515150 🖱 jamie.carson@chorley.gov.uk

Lottery Funding, Charity and Voluntary: Ms Rebecca Huddleston Head of Policy & Communications, Town Hall, Market Street, Chorley PR7 1DP ☎ 01257 515151 🖷 01257 515150 🖱 rebecca.huddleston@chorley.gov.uk

Member Services: Ms Carol Russell Democratic Services Manager, Town Hall, Market Street, Chorley PR7 1DP ☎ 01257 515151 🖷 01257 515150 🖱 carol.russell@chorley.gov.uk

Parking: Ms Alison Wilding Customer Services Manager, Civic Offices, Union Street, Chorley PR7 1AL ☎ 01257 515151 🖷 01257 515150 🖱 alison.windling@chorley.gov.uk

CHORLEY

Partnerships: Ms Rebecca Huddleston Head of Policy & Communications, Town Hall, Market Street, Chorley PR7 1DP ☎ 01257 515151 🖷 01257 515150 ✉ rebecca.huddleston@chorley.gov.uk

Personnel / HR: Ms Camilla Oakes-Scofield Head of HR & OD, Town Hall, Market Street, Chorley PR7 1DP ☎ 01257 515151 🖷 01257 515150 ✉ camilla.scofield@chorley.gov.uk

Planning: Mr Jamie Carson, Director - Public Protection, Streetscene & Community, Civic Offices, Union Street, Chorley PR7 1AL ☎ 01257 515151 🖷 01257 515150 ✉ jamie.carson@chorley.gov.uk

Procurement: Mrs Janet Hinds, Principal Procurement Officer, Town Hall, Market Street, Chorley PR7 1DP ☎ 01257 515151 🖷 01257 515150 ✉ janet.hinds@chorley.gov.uk

Recycling & Waste Minimisation: Ms Jo Oliver Streetscene & Leisure Contracts Manager, Civic Offices, Union Street, Chorley PR7 1AL ☎ 01257 515151 ✉ jo.oliver@chorley.gov.uk

Regeneration: Mrs Lesley-Ann Fenton, Director - Customer & Advice Services, Civic Offices, Union Street, Chorley PR7 1AL ☎ 01257 515151 🖷 01257 515150 ✉ lesley-ann.fenton@chorley.gov.uk

Staff Training: Mr Graeme Walmsley Senior HR & OD Consultant, Town Hall, Market Street, Chorley PR7 1DP ☎ 01257 515151 🖷 01257 515150 ✉ graeme.walmsley@chorley.gov.uk

Street Scene: Mr Jamie Carson, Director - Public Protection, Streetscene & Community, Civic Offices, Union Street, Chorley PR7 1AL ☎ 01257 515151 🖷 01257 515150 ✉ jamie.carson@chorley.gov.uk

Sustainable Communities: Mrs Lesley-Ann Fenton, Director - Customer & Advice Services, Civic Offices, Union Street, Chorley PR7 1AL ☎ 01257 515151 🖷 01257 515150 ✉ lesley-ann.fenton@chorley.gov.uk

Sustainable Development: Mrs Lesley-Ann Fenton, Director - Customer & Advice Services, Civic Offices, Union Street, Chorley PR7 1AL ☎ 01257 515151 🖷 01257 515150 ✉ lesley-ann.fenton@chorley.gov.uk

Tourism: Ms Rebecca Huddleston Head of Policy & Communications, Town Hall, Market Street, Chorley PR7 1DP ☎ 01257 515151 🖷 01257 515150 ✉ rebecca.huddleston@chorley.gov.uk

Town Centre: Mr Gary Hall, Chief Executive, Town Hall, Market Street, Chorley PR7 1DP ☎ 01257 515151 🖷 01257 515150 ✉ gary.hall@chorley.gov.uk

Waste Collection and Disposal: Ms Jo Oliver Streetscene & Leisure Contracts Manager, Civic Offices, Union Street, Chorley PR7 1AL ☎ 01257 515151 ✉ jo.oliver@chorley.gov.uk

Waste Management: Ms Jo Oliver Streetscene & Leisure Contracts Manager, Civic Offices, Union Street, Chorley PR7 1AL ☎ 01257 515151 ✉ jo.oliver@chorley.gov.uk

COUNCILLORS

***Mayor* Lowe**, Marion (LAB - Chorley North East)
marion.lowe@chorley.gov.uk

***Deputy Mayor* Dickinson**, David (CON - Brindle & Hoghton)
david.dickinson@chorley.gov.uk

***Leader of the Council* Bradley**, Alistair (LAB - Chorley South East)
alistair.bradley@chorley.gov.uk

***Deputy Leader of the Council* Wilson**, Peter (LAB - Adlington & Anderton)
peter.wilson@chorley.gov.uk

Beaver, Aaron (LAB - Chorley North West)
aaron.beaver@chorley.gov.uk

Bell, Eric (CON - Clayton-le-Woods & Whittle-le-Woods)
eric.bell@chorley.gov.uk

Berry, Julia (LAB - Chorley East)
julia.berry@chorley.gov.uk

Boardman, Martin (CON - Eccleston & Mawdesley)
martin.boardman@chorley.gov.uk

Bromilow, Charlie (LAB - Clayton-le-Woods North)
charlie.bromilow@chorley.gov.uk

Brown, Terry (LAB - Chorley East)
terence.brown@chorley.gov.uk

Caunce, Henry (CON - Eccleston & Mawdesley)
henry.caunce@chorley.gov.uk

Clark, Paul (LAB - Coppull)
paul.clark@chorley.gov.uk

Cronshaw, Jean (LAB - Clayton-le-Woods North)
jean.cronshaw@chorley.gov.uk

Cullens, Alan (CON - Clayton-le-Woods West & Cuerden)
alan.cullens@chorley.gov.uk

Dalton, John (CON - Lostock)
john.dalton@chorley.gov.uk

Dickinson, Doreen (CON - Lostock)
doreen.dickinson@chorley.gov.uk

Dunn, Graham (LAB - Adlington & Anderton)
graham.dunn@chorley.gov.uk

Finnamore, Robert (LAB - Coppull)
robert.finnamore@chorley.gov.uk

France, Gordon (LAB - Pennine)
gordon.france@chorley.gov.uk

France, Christopher (LAB - Wheelton & Withnell)
chris.france@chorley.gov.uk

France, Margaret (LAB - Wheelton & Withnell)

Gee, Anthony (LAB - Chorley South West)
anthony.gee@chorley.gov.uk

Gee, Danny (LAB - Euxton North)
danny.gee@chorley.gov.uk

Handley, Mike (LAB - Euxton North)
mike.handley@chorley.gov.uk

Iddon, Keith (CON - Eccleston & Mawdesley)
keith.iddon@chorley.gov.uk

Jarnell, Mark (LAB - Euxton South)
mark.jarnell@chorley.gov.uk

Khan, Hasina (LAB - Chorley East)
hasina.khan@chorley.gov.uk

Leadbetter, Paul (CON - Chisnell)
paul.leadbetter@chorley.gov.uk

Lees, Roy (LAB - Chorley South West)
roy.lees@chorley.gov.uk

Lees, Margaret (LAB - Chorley South West)
margaret.lees@chorley gov.uk

Lowe, Adrian (LAB - Chorley North East)
adrian.lowe@chorley.gov.uk

Lynch, Matthew (LAB - Astley & Buckshaw)
matthew.lynch@chorley.gov.uk

Molyneaux, June (LAB - Adlington & Anderton)
june.molyneaux@chorley.gov.uk

Morgan, Greg (CON - Clayton-le-Woods & Whittle-le-Woods)
greg.morgan@chorley.gov.uk

Morwood, Alistair (LAB - Chorley North East)
alistair.morwood@chorley.gov.uk

Muncaster, Michael (CON - Clayton-le-Woods West & Cuerden)
mick.muncaster@chorley.gov.uk

Murfitt, Steve (LAB - Clayton-le-Woods North)
steve.murfitt@chorley.gov.uk

Murray, Beverley (LAB - Chorley South East)
beverley.murray@chorley.gov.uk

Perks, Mark (CON - Astley & Buckshaw)
mark.perks@chorley.gov.uk

Platt, Debra (CON - Euxton South)
debra.platt@chorley.gov.uk

Snape, Joyce (IND - Chorley North West)
joyce.snape@chorley.gov.uk

Snape, Ralph (IND - Chorley North West)
ralph.snape@chorley.gov.uk

Snape, Kim (LAB - Heath Charnock & Rivington)
kim.snape@chorley.gov.uk

Toon, Richard (LAB - Coppull)
richard.toon@chorley.gov.uk

Walker, John (CON - Clayton-le-Woods & Whittle-le-Woods)
john.walker@chorley.gov.uk

Walmsley, Paul (LAB - Chorley South East)
paul.walmsley@chorley.gov.uk

Whittaker, Alan (LAB - Chisnell)
alan.whittaker@chorleyl.gov.uk

POLITICAL COMPOSITION
LAB: 31, CON: 14, IND: 2

COMMITTEE CHAIRS
Licensing: Mr Roy Lees

Christchurch D

Christchurch Borough Council, Civic Offices, Bridge Street, Christchurch BH23 1AZ
☎ 01202 495000 🖷 01202 495234 💻 www.dorsetforyou.com

FACTS AND FIGURES
Parliamentary Constituencies: Christchurch County
EU Constituencies: South West
Election Frequency: Elections are of whole council

PRINCIPAL OFFICERS
Chief Executive: Mr David McIntosh Chief Executive, Civic Offices, Bridge Street, Christchurch BH23 1AZ ☎ 01202 886201 🖷 01202 639030; 01202 495001
dmcintosh@christchurchandeastdorset.gov.uk

Senior Management: Mr David Barnes, Strategic Director, Civic Offices, Bridge Street, Christchurch BH23 1AZ ☎ 01202 495077 🖷 01202 639030 dbarnes@christchurchandeastdorset.gov.uk

Senior Management: Mr Neil Farmer, Strategic Director, Civic Offices, Bridge Street, Christchurch BH23 1AZ
☎ 01202 795002 🖷 01202 639030; 01202 495107
nfarmer@christchurchandeastdorset.gov.uk

Architect, Building / Property Services: Mr Ashley Harman, Property & Engineering Services Manager, Civic Offices, Bridge Street, Christchurch BH23 1AZ ☎ 01202 795076 🖷 01202 795108
aharman@christchurchandeastdorset.gov.uk

Best Value: Mr David Barnes, Strategic Director, Civic Offices, Bridge Street, Christchurch BH23 1AZ ☎ 01202 495077
🖷 01202 639030 dbarnes@christchurchandeastdorset.gov.uk

Building Control: Mr Martin Thompson, Building Control Manager, Civic Offices, Bridge Street, Christchurch BH23 1AZ
☎ 01202 795033 🖷 01202 795105
mthompson@christchurchandeastdorset.gov.uk

Children / Youth Services: Ms Judith Plumley Head - Community & Economy, Civic Offices, Bridge Street, Christchurch BH23 1AZ ☎ 01202 886201; 01202 795043 🖷 01202 639030; 01202 795108 jplumpley@christchurchandeastdorset.gov.uk

PR / Communications: Mr Allan Wood, Communications Officer, Civic Offices, Bridge Street, Christchurch BH23 1AZ ☎ 01202 495133 🖷 01202 495107
awood@christchurchandeastdorset.gov.uk

Community Planning: Ms Judith Plumley Head - Community & Economy, Civic Offices, Bridge Street, Christchurch BH23 1AZ
☎ 01202 886201; 01202 795043 🖷 01202 639030; 01202 795108
jplumpley@christchurchandeastdorset.gov.uk

Community Planning: Mr Simon Trueick Community & Planning Policy Manager, Civic Offices, Bridge Street, Christchurch BH23 1AZ ☎ 01202 495038 🖷 01202 495107
strueick@christchurchandeastdorset.gov.uk

Community Safety: Ms Judith Plumley Head - Community & Economy, Civic Offices, Bridge Street, Christchurch BH23 1AZ
☎ 01202 886201; 01202 795043 🖷 01202 639030; 01202 795108
jplumpley@christchurchandeastdorset.gov.uk

Computer Management: Ms Fiona Hughes Partnership ICT Manager, Civic Offices, Bridge Street, Christchurch BH23 1AZ
fhughes@christchurchandeastdorset.gov.uk

CHRISTCHURCH

Computer Management: Mr Matti Raudsepp Head of Organisational Development, Civic Offices, Bridge Street, Christchurch BH23 1AZ ☎ 01202 795125 🖷 01202 639030 🖱 mraudsepp@christchurchandeastdorset.gov.uk

Corporate Services: Mr Matti Raudsepp Head of Organisational Development, Civic Offices, Bridge Street, Christchurch BH23 1AZ ☎ 01202 795125 🖷 01202 639030 🖱 mraudsepp@christchurchandeastdorset.gov.uk

Customer Service: Mrs Debbie Cliff Customer Services Manager, Civic Offices, Bridge Street, Christchurch BH23 1AZ ☎ 01202 579150 🖷 01202 795234 🖱 dcliff@christchurch.gov.uk

Customer Service: Mr Matti Raudsepp Head of Organisational Development, Civic Offices, Bridge Street, Christchurch BH23 1AZ ☎ 01202 795125 🖷 01202 639030 🖱 mraudsepp@christchurchandeastdorset.gov.uk

Economic Development: Mr James Hassett Head of Growth & Economy, Civic Offices, Bridge Street, Christchurch BH23 1AZ ☎ 🖱 jhassett@christchurchandeastdorset.gov.uk

E-Government: Mr David Barnes, Strategic Director, Civic Offices, Bridge Street, Christchurch BH23 1AZ ☎ 01202 495077 🖷 01202 639030 🖱 dbarnes@christchurchandeastdorset.gov.uk

E-Government: Ms Fiona Hughes Partnership ICT Manager, Civic Offices, Bridge Street, Christchurch BH23 1AZ 🖱 fhughes@christchurchandeastdorset.gov.uk

Electoral Registration: Mr Richard Jones Democratic Services & Elections Manager, Council Offices, Furzehill, Wimborne BH21 4HN ☎ 01202 795171 🖷 01202 639030 🖱 rjones@christchurchandeastdorset.gov.uk

Emergency Planning: Mr Gary Foyle, Senior Recreation Services Officer, Civic Offices, Bridge Street, Christchurch BH23 1AZ ☎ 01202 795070 🖷 01202 795110 🖱 gfoyle@christchurchandeastdorset.gov.uk

Energy Management: Ms Rachel Sharpe Sustainability Management Officer, Civic Offices, Bridge Street, Christchurch BH23 1AZ ☎ 01202 795047 🖷 01202 795108 🖱 rsharpe@christchurchandeastdorset.gov.uk

Environmental / Technical Services: Mr Lindsay Cass Head of Property & Engineering, Civic Offices, Bridge Street, Christchurch BH23 1AZ ☎ 01202 795003 🖷 01202 795110 🖱 lcass@christchurchandeastdorset.gov.uk

Environmental Health: Mr Steve Duckett, Head of Housing & Health, Civic Offices, Bridge Street, Christchurch BH23 1AZ ☎ 01202 795987 🖷 01202 795108 🖱 sduckett@christchurchandeastdorset.gov.uk

Estates, Property & Valuation: Mr Philip Marston, Estates Officer, Civic Offices, Bridge Street, Christchurch BH23 1AZ ☎ 01202 795187 🖷 01202 795108 🖱 pmarston@christchurchandeastdorset.gov.uk

Facilities: Mrs Debbie Cliff Customer Services Manager, Civic Offices, Bridge Street, Christchurch BH23 1AZ ☎ 01202 579150 🖷 01202 795234 🖱 dcliff@christchurch.gov.uk

Fleet Management: Mr Lindsay Cass Head of Property & Engineering, Civic Offices, Bridge Street, Christchurch BH23 1AZ ☎ 01202 795003 🖷 01202 795110 🖱 lcass@christchurchandeastdorset.gov.uk

Grounds Maintenance: Mr Clive Sinden, Countryside & Open Spaces Manager, Civic Offices, Bridge Street, Christchurch BH23 1AZ ☎ 01202 795072 🖷 01202 795110 🖱 csinden@christchurchandeastdorset.gov.uk

Health and Safety: Mr Steve Duckett, Head of Housing & Health, Civic Offices, Bridge Street, Christchurch BH23 1AZ ☎ 01202 795987 🖷 01202 795108 🖱 sduckett@christchurchandeastdorset.gov.uk

Health and Safety: Ms Pauline Miller-McIlravey Health & Safety Officer, Civic Offices, Bridge Street, Christchurch BH23 1AZ ☎ 01202 795198 🖱 pmiller-mcilraey@christchurchandeastdorset.gov.uk

Home Energy Conservation: Mr Steve Duckett, Head of Housing & Health, Civic Offices, Bridge Street, Christchurch BH23 1AZ ☎ 01202 795987 🖷 01202 795108 🖱 sduckett@christchurchandeastdorset.gov.uk

Housing: Ms Kathryn Blatchford, Strategic Housing Services Manager, Civic Offices, Bridge Street, Christchurch BH23 1AZ ☎ 01202 795158 🖱 kblatchford@christchurchandeastdorset.gov.uk

Legal: Mr Keith Mallett, Council Solicitor, Civic Offices, Bridge Street, Christchurch BH23 1AZ ☎ 01202 795989 🖷 01202 795107 🖱 kmallett@christchurchandeastdorset.gov.uk

Licensing: Mr Steve Ricketts Community Protection Team Leader, Civic Offices, Bridge Street, Christchurch BH23 1AZ ☎ 01202 886201 🖱 sricketts@christchurchandeastdorset.gov.uk

Member Services: Mr Richard Jones Democratic Services & Elections Manager, Council Offices, Furzehill, Wimborne BH21 4HN ☎ 01202 795171 🖷 01202 639030 🖱 rjones@christchurchandeastdorset.gov.uk

Parking: Mr Ashley Harman, Property & Engineering Services Manager, Civic Offices, Bridge Street, Christchurch BH23 1AZ ☎ 01202 795076 🖷 01202 795108 🖱 aharman@christchurchandeastdorset.gov.uk

Partnerships: Ms Judith Plumley Head - Community & Economy, Civic Offices, Bridge Street, Christchurch BH23 1AZ ☎ 01202 886201; 01202 795043 🖷 01202 639030; 01202 795108 🖱 jplumpley@christchurchandeastdorset.gov.uk

Personnel / HR: Mr Matti Raudsepp Head of Organisational Development, Civic Offices, Bridge Street, Christchurch BH23 1AZ ☎ 01202 795125 🖷 01202 639030 🖱 mraudsepp@christchurchandeastdorset.gov.uk

Personnel / HR: Ms Lynda Thomson Organisational Development, Civic Offices, Bridge Street, Christchurch BH23 1AZ ☎ 01202 795168 ✉ mharford@christchurchandeastdorset.gov.uk

Planning: Mr Steve Duckett, Head of Housing & Health, Civic Offices, Bridge Street, Christchurch BH23 1AZ ☎ 01202 795987 🖷 01202 795108 ✉ sduckett@christchurchandeastdorset.gov.uk

Planning: Mr James Hassett Head of Growth & Economy, Civic Offices, Bridge Street, Christchurch BH23 1AZ ✉ jhassett@christchurchandeastdorset.gov.uk

Recycling & Waste Minimisation: Mr Lindsay Cass Head of Property & Engineering, Civic Offices, Bridge Street, Christchurch BH23 1AZ ☎ 01202 795003 🖷 01202 795110 ✉ lcass@christchurchandeastdorset.gov.uk

Regeneration: Mr Neil Farmer, Strategic Director, Civic Offices, Bridge Street, Christchurch BH23 1AZ ☎ 01202 795002 🖷 01202 639030; 01202 495107 ✉ nfarmer@christchurchandeastdorset.gov.uk

Regeneration: Mr James Hassett Head of Growth & Economy, Civic Offices, Bridge Street, Christchurch BH23 1AZ ✉ jhassett@christchurchandeastdorset.gov.uk

Staff Training: Ms Lynda Thomson Organisational Development, Civic Offices, Bridge Street, Christchurch BH23 1AZ ☎ 01202 795168 ✉ mharford@christchurchandeastdorset.gov.uk

Sustainable Communities: Ms Rachel Sharpe Sustainability Management Officer, Civic Offices, Bridge Street, Christchurch BH23 1AZ ☎ 01202 495047 🖷 01202 495108 ✉ rsharpe@christchurchandeastdorset.gov.uk

Sustainable Development: Ms Judith Plumley Head - Community & Economy, Civic Offices, Bridge Street, Christchurch BH23 1AZ ☎ 01202 886201; 01202 795043 🖷 01202 639030; 01202 795108 ✉ jplumpley@christchurchandeastdorset.gov.uk

Tourism: Mr James Hassett Head of Growth & Economy, Civic Offices, Bridge Street, Christchurch BH23 1AZ ✉ jhassett@christchurchandeastdorset.gov.uk

Waste Collection and Disposal: Mr Lindsay Cass Head of Property & Engineering, Civic Offices, Bridge Street, Christchurch BH23 1AZ ☎ 01202 795003 🖷 01202 795110 ✉ lcass@christchurchandeastdorset.gov.uk

Waste Management: Mr Lindsay Cass Head of Property & Engineering, Civic Offices, Bridge Street, Christchurch BH23 1AZ ☎ 01202 795003 🖷 01202 795110 ✉ lcass@christchurchandeastdorset.gov.uk

COUNCILLORS

***Mayor* Neale**, Frederick (IND - Jumpers) cllr.fneale@christchurch.gov.uk

***Deputy Mayor* Jamieson**, Patricia (CON - West Highcliffe) cllr.tjamieson@christchurch.gov.uk

***Leader of the Council* Nottage**, Ray (CON - Purewell & Stanpit) cllr.rnottage@christchurch.gov.uk

***Deputy Leader of the Council* Jamieson**, Colin (CON - Burton & Winkton) cllr.cpjamieson@christchurch.gov.uk

Abbott, Janet (UKIP - Grange) cllr.jabbott@christchurch.gov.uk

Barfield, Andy (CON - Mudeford & Friars Cliff) cllr.abarfield@christchurch.gov.uk

Bath, Claire (CON - Mudeford & Friars Cliff) cllr.cbath@christchurch.gov.uk

Bungey, Colin (IND - Jumpers) cllr.cbungey@christchurch.gov.uk

Davis, Bernie (CON - Purewell & Stanpit) cllr.bdavis@christchurch.gov.uk

Dedman, Lesley (CON - West Highcliffe) cllr.ldedman@christchurch.gov.uk

Derham Wilkes, Sally (CON - North Highcliffe & Walkford) cllr.sjderhamwilkes@christchurch.gov.uk

Flagg, David (CON - Burton & Winkton) cllr.dflagg@christchurch.gov.uk

Fox, Tavis (CON - Portfield) cllr.tfox@christchurch.gov.uk

Geary, Nicholas (CON - North Highcliffe & Walkford) cllr.ngeary@christchurch.gov.uk

Grace, Wendy (CON - Town Centre) cllr.wgrace@christchurch.gov.uk

Hall, Peter (CON - Town Centre) cllr.phall@christchurch.gov.uk

Hallam, Vicki (CON - Highcliffe) cllr.vhallam@christchurch.gov.uk

Jones, Denise (CON - Grange) cllr.denisejones@christchurch.gov.uk

Jones, David (CON - West Highcliffe) cllr.djones@christchurch.gov.uk

Lofts, John (CON - Highcliffe) cllr.jlofts@christchurchanddorset.gov.uk

Phipps, Margaret (CON - St Catherine's and Hurn) cllr.mphipps@christchurch.gov.uk

Smith, Lisle (CON - Portfield) cllr.lsmith@christchurch.gov.uk

Spittle, Susan (CON - St. Catherine's & Hurn) cllr.sspittle@christchurch.gov.uk

Watts, Trevor (CON - Mudeford & Friars Cliff) cllr.trwatts@christchurch.gov.uk

POLITICAL COMPOSITION

CON: 21, IND: 2, UKIP: 1

COMMITTEE CHAIRS

Planning Control: Mr David Jones

City of London L

City of London, PO Box 270, Guildhall, London EC2P 2EJ
☎ 020 7332 1400; 020 7606 3030 🖷 020 7796 2621; 020 7332 1119
✉ pro@cityoflondon.gov.uk 🖳 www.cityoflondon.gov.uk

CITY OF LONDON

FACTS AND FIGURES

Parliamentary Constituencies: Cities of London and Westminster
EU Constituencies: London
Election Frequency: Common Councilmen- 4 years, Aldermen- 6 years

PRINCIPAL OFFICERS

Chief Executive: Mr John Barradell, Town Clerk & Chief Executive, PO Box 270, Guildhall, London EC2P 2EJ ☎ 020 7332 1400 🖷 020 7796 2621 ✉ townclerk@cityoflondon.gov.uk

Deputy Chief Executive: Ms Susan Attard, Deputy Town Clerk, PO Box 270, Guildhall, London EC2P 2EJ ☎ 020 7332 3724 🖷 020 7796 2621 ✉ susan.attard@cityoflondon.gov.uk

Assistant Chief Executive: Mr Peter Lisley, Assistant Town Clerk, PO Box 270, Guildhall, London EC2P 2EJ ☎ 020 7332 1438 🖷 020 7796 2621 ✉ peter.lisley@cityoflondon.gov.uk

Assistant Chief Executive: Mr Simon Murrells, Assistant Town Clerk, PO Box 270, Guildhall, London EC2P 2EJ ☎ 020 7332 1418 🖷 020 7796 2621 ✉ simon.murrells@cityoflondon.gov.uk

Senior Management: Mr Ade Adetosoye Director of Community & Children's Services, PO Box 270, Guildhall, London EC2P 2EJ ☎ 020 7332 1650 ✉ ade.adetosoye@cityoflondon.gov.uk

Senior Management: Mr Peter Bennett City Surveyor, PO Box 270, Guildhall, London EC2P 2EJ ☎ 020 7332 1502 🖷 020 7332 3031 ✉ peter.bennett@cityoflondon.gov.uk

Senior Management: Mr William Chapman Private Secretary & Chief of Staff to the Lord Mayor, PO Box 270, Guildhall, London EC2P 2EJ ☎ 020 7379 9302 ✉ william.chapman@cityoflondon.gov.uk

Senior Management: Mr Michael Cogher Comptroller & City Solicitor, PO Box 270, Guildhall, London EC2P 2EJ ☎ 020 7332 3699 ✉ michael.cogher@cityoflondon.gov.uk

Senior Management: Mr Paul Double Remembrancer, PO Box 270, Guildhall, London EC2P 2EJ ☎ 020 7332 1207 ✉ paul.double@cityoflondon.gov.uk

Senior Management: Mr Tony Halmos, Director of Public Relations, PO Box 270, Guildhall, London EC2P 2EJ ☎ 020 7332 1450 ✉ tony.halmos@cityoflondon.gov.uk

Senior Management: Mr Barry Ife Principale of the Guildhall School of Music & Drama, PO Box 270, Guildhall, London EC2P 2EJ ☎ 020 7628 2571 ✉ barry.ife@cityoflondon.gov.uk

Senior Management: Mrs Sue Ireland Director of Open Spaces, City of London Open Space Department, 1 Guildhall Yard, London EC2V 5AE ☎ 020 7332 3033 🖷 020 7332 3522 ✉ sue.ireland@cityoflondon.gov.uk

Senior Management: Mr Peter Kane Chamberlain, PO Box 270, Guildhall, London EC2P 2EJ ☎ 020 7332 1300 ✉ chamberlain@cityoflondon.gov.uk

Senior Management: Sir Nicholas Kenyon, Managing Director of the Barbican Centre, Barbican Centre, Silk Street, London EC2Y 8DS ☎ 020 7382 7001 🖷 020 7382 7245 ✉ nkenyon@barbican.org.uk

Senior Management: Ms Chrissie Morgan, Director of Human Resources, PO Box 270, Guildhall, London EC2P 2EJ ☎ 020 7332 1424 ✉ chrissie.morgan@cityoflondon.gov.uk

Senior Management: Mr Damian Nussbaum Director of the Economic Development, PO Box 270, Guildhall, London EC2P 2EJ ☎ 020 7332 3600 ✉ damian.nussbaum@cityoflondon.gov.uk

Senior Management: Mr David Pearson Director of Culture, Heritage & Libraries, PO Box 270, Guildhall, London EC2P 2EJ ☎ 020 7606 1850 ✉ david.pearson@cityoflondon.gov.uk

Senior Management: Mr David Smith Director of Markets & Consumer Protection, PO Box 270, Guildhall, London EC2P 2EJ ☎ 020 7332 3967 ✉ david.smith@cityoflondon.gov.uk

Civil Registration: Ms Andrea Streete, Registrar, St Bartholomew's Hospital, Pathology Block, Room 37, London EC1A 7BE ☎ 020 7600 4977 ✉ andrea.streete@cityoflondon.gov.uk

PR / Communications: Mr Tony Halmos, Director of Public Relations, PO Box 270, Guildhall, London EC2P 2EJ ☎ 020 7332 1450 ✉ tony.halmos@cityoflondon.gov.uk

Community Planning: Mr Alan Hughes Policy & Governance Officer, PO Box 270, Guildhall, London EC2P 2EJ ☎ 020 7332 1411 🖷 020 7796 2621 ✉ alan.hughes@cityoflondon.gov.uk

Computer Management: Mr Bill Limond Information Systems Director, 65 Basinghall Street, , London EC2V 5DZ ☎ 020 7332 1307 🖷 020 7332 3110 ✉ bill.limond@cityoflondon.gov.uk

Contracts: Mr Richard Jeffrey, Chief Legal Assistant, PO Box 270, Guildhall, London EC2P 2EJ ☎ 020 7332 1683 ✉ richard.jeffrey@cityoflondon.gov.uk

Customer Service: Ms Jill Bailey, Access to Services Programme Manager, PO Box 270, Guildhall, London EC2P 2EJ ☎ 020 7332 3422 ✉ jill.bailey@cityoflondon.gov.uk

Economic Development: Mr Damian Nussbaum Director of the Economic Development, PO Box 270, Guildhall, London EC2P 2EJ ☎ 020 7332 3600 ✉ damian.nussbaum@cityoflondon.gov.uk

Energy Management: Mr Paul Kennedy, Corporate Energy Manager, City Surveyor's Department, PO Box 270, Guildhall, London EC2P 2EJ ☎ 020 7332 1130 🖷 020 7332 3031 ✉ paul.kennedy@cityoflondon.gov.uk

European Liaison: Ms Audrey Nelson, Senior European Officer, PO Box 270, Guildhall, London EC2P 2EJ ☎ 020 7332 1054 🖷 020 7332 3616 ✉ audrey.nelson@cityoflondon.gov.uk

Events Manager: Ms Fiona Hoban, Assistant Remembrancer (Ceremonial), PO Box 270, Guildhall, London EC2P 2EJ ☎ 020 7332 1261 ✉ fiona.hoban@cityoflondon.gov.uk

Facilities: Ms Janet Woodvine Guildhall Facilities Manager, PO Box 270, Guildhall, London EC2P 2EJ ☎ 020 7606 1157

Finance: Mrs Carla-Maria Heath Head of Revenues, PO Box 270, Guildhall, London EC2P 2EJ ☎ 020 7332 1387 carla-maria.heath@cityoflondon.gov.uk

Finance: Mr Peter Kane Chamberlain, PO Box 270, Guildhall, London EC2P 2EJ ☎ 020 7332 1300 chamberlain@cityoflondon.gov.uk

Treasury: Mr Peter Kane Chamberlain, PO Box 270, Guildhall, London EC2P 2EJ ☎ 020 7332 1300 chamberlain@cityoflondon.gov.uk

Treasury: Ms Kate Limna Corporate Treasurer, PO Box 270, Guildhall, London EC2P 2EJ ☎ 020 7332 1309 kate.limna@cityoflondon.gov.uk

Pensions: Mr Charlie Partridge Pensions Manager, PO Box 270, Guildhall, London EC2P 2EJ ☎ 020 7332 1133 charlie.partridge@cityoflondon.gov.uk

Fleet Management: Mr Douglas Wilkinson Cleansing Services Assistant Director, Walbrook Wharf, Upper Thames Street, London EC4R 3TD ☎ 020 7332 4998 🖷 020 7236 6560 douglas.wilkinson@cityoflondon.gov.uk

Grounds Maintenance: Mr Martin Rodman, Superintendant of West Ham Park & City Gardens, PO Box 270, Guildhall, London EC2P 2EJ ☎ 020 7374 4152 🖷 020 7374 4116 martin.rodman@cityoflondon.gov.uk

Highways: Mr Paul Monaghan Assistant Director of Engineering, PO Box 270, Guildhall, London EC2P 2EJ paul.monaghan@cityoflondon.gov.uk

Highways: Mr Steve Presland Transportation & Public Realm Director, PO Box 270, Guildhall, London EC2P 2EJ ☎ 020 7332 4999 steve.presland@cityoflondon.gov.uk

Housing: Mr Ade Adetosoye Director of Community & Children's Services, PO Box 270, Guildhall, London EC2P 2EJ ☎ 020 7332 1650 ade.adetosoye@cityoflondon.gov.uk

Housing: Mr Stewart Crook Area Housing Manager, PO Box 270, Guildhall, London EC2P 2EJ ☎ 020 7332 3005 🖷 020 7332 1642 stewart.crook@cityoflondon.gov.uk

Housing: Mr Peter Snowdon Projects Director, PO Box 270, Guildhall, London EC2P 2EJ ☎ 020 7332 1802 peter.snowdon@cityoflondon.gov.uk

Housing Maintenance: Mr Edwin Stevens, Housing & Technical Services Director, 3 Lauderdale Place, Barbican, London EC2Y 8EN ☎ 020 7332 3015 edwin.stevens@cityoflondon.gov.uk

Local Area Agreement: Mr Alan Hughes Policy & Governance Officer, PO Box 270, Guildhall, London EC2P 2EJ ☎ 020 7332 1411 🖷 020 7796 2621 alan.hughes@cityoflondon.gov.uk

Legal: Mr Michael Cogher Comptroller & City Solicitor, PO Box 270, Guildhall, London EC2P 2EJ ☎ 020 7332 3699 michael.cogher@cityoflondon.gov.uk

Leisure and Cultural Services: Mrs Sue Ireland Director of Open Spaces, City of London Open Space Department, 1 Guildhall Yard, London EC2V 5AE ☎ 020 7332 3033 🖷 020 7332 3522 sue.ireland@cityoflondon.gov.uk

Leisure and Cultural Services: Sir Nicholas Kenyon, Managing Director of the Barbican Centre, Barbican Centre, Silk Street, London EC2Y 8DS ☎ 020 7382 7001 🖷 020 7382 7245 nkenyon@barbican.org.uk

Leisure and Cultural Services: Mr David Pearson Director of Culture, Heritage & Libraries, PO Box 270, Guildhall, London EC2P 2EJ ☎ 020 7606 1850 david.pearson@cityoflondon.gov.uk

Licensing: Mr Bryn Aldridge, Port Health & Veterinary Services Director, Walbrook Wharf, Upper Thames Street, London EC4R 3TD ☎ 020 7332 3405 bryn.aldridge@cityoflondon.gov.uk

Lighting: Mr John Burke, Mechanical & Electrical Services Manager, PO Box 270, Guildhall, London EC2P 2EJ ☎ 020 7332 1102 john.burke@cityoflondon.gov.uk

Lottery Funding, Charity and Voluntary: Mr David Farnsworth Chief Grants Officer, PO Box 270, Guildhall, London EC2P 2EJ ☎ 020 7332 3713 david.farnsworth@cityoflondon.gov.uk

Parking: Mr Ian Hughes, Assistant Highways Director, PO Box 270, Guildhall, London EC2P 2EJ ☎ 020 7332 1977 ian.hughes@cityoflondon.gov.uk

Personnel / HR: Ms Chrissie Morgan, Director of Human Resources, PO Box 270, Guildhall, London EC2P 2EJ ☎ 020 7332 1424 chrissie.morgan@cityoflondon.gov.uk

Planning: Ms Annie Hampson Chief Planning Officer, PO Box 270, Guildhall, London EC2P 2EJ ☎ 020 7332 1700 annie.hampson@cityoflondon.gov.uk

Procurement: Mr Gary Dowding, Head of Business Enablement, PO Box 270, Guildhall, London EC2P 2EJ ☎ 020 7332 1828 🖷 020 7332 1535 gary.dowding@cityoflondon.gov.uk

Public Libraries: Mr David Pearson Director of Culture, Heritage & Libraries, PO Box 270, Guildhall, London EC2P 2EJ ☎ 020 7606 1850 david.pearson@cityoflondon.gov.uk

Road Safety: Mr Matthew Collins, Road Safety Team Leader, PO Box 270, Guildhall, London EC2P 2EJ ☎ 020 7332 1546 🖷 020 7332 1806 matthew.collins@cityoflondon.gov.uk

Social Services (Adult): Mr Ade Adetosoye Director of Community and Children's Services, PO Box 270, Guildhall, London EC2P 2EJ ☎ 020 7332 1650

Social Services (Adult): Mr Dave Mason Interim Head of Adult Social Care, North Wing 2nd Floor, PO Box 270, Guildhall, London EC2P 2EJ ☎ 020 7332 1636 dave.mason@cityoflondon.gov.uk

CITY OF LONDON

Social Services (Children): Mr Ade Adetosoye Director of Community and Children's Services, PO Box 270, Guildhall, London EC2P 2EJ ☎ 020 7332 1650

Public Health: Dr Penny Bevan Director - Public Health, Town Hall, Mare Street, London E8 1EA
✉ penny.bevan@hackney.gov.uk

Street Scene: Mr Steve Presland Transportation & Public Realm Director, PO Box 270, Guildhall, London EC2P 2EJ
☎ 020 7332 4999 ✉ steve.presland@cityoflondon.gov.uk

Sustainable Communities: Mr Neal Hounsell, Assistant Director of Commissioning & Partnership, Department of Community and Children's Services, PO Box 270, Guildhall, London EC2P 2EJ
☎ 020 7332 1638 ✉ neal.hounsell@cityoflondon.gov.uk

Traffic Management: Mr Iain Simmons, Assitant Director (Local Transportation), PO Box 270, Guildhall, London EC2P 2EJ
☎ 020 7332 1151 🖷 020 7332 1806
✉ iain.simmons@cityoflondon.gov.uk

Waste Collection and Disposal: Mr Jim Graham Assistant Director of Operations/Cleansing, Walbrook Wharf, Upper Thames Street, London EC4R 3TD ☎ 020 7332 4972 🖷 020 7236 6560
✉ jim.graham@cityoflondon.gov.uk

Waste Collection and Disposal: Mr Steve Presland Transportation & Public Realm Director, PO Box 270, Guildhall, London EC2P 2EJ ☎ 020 7332 4999
✉ steve.presland@cityoflondon.gov.uk

Waste Management: Mr Lee Turner Senior Waste Disposal Officer, Walbrook Wharf, Upper Thames Street, London EC4R 3TD
☎ 020 7332 4976 🖷 020 7236 6560
✉ lee.turner@cityoflondon.gov.uk

COUNCILLORS

***The Lord Mayor* Yarrow**, Alan (NP - Bridge & Bridge Without)
alan.yarrow@dkib.com

***Alderman* Anstee**, Nick (IND - Aldersgate)
nick.anstee@sjberwin.com

***Alderman* Bear**, Michael (NP - Portsoken)
michael.bear@cityoflondon.gov.uk

***Alderman* Bowman**, Charles (NP - Lime Street)
charles.bowman@uk.pwc.com

***Alderman* Eskenzi**, Anthony (NP - Farringdon Within)
anthony.eskenzi@cityoflondon.gov.uk

***Alderman* Estlin**, Peter (NP - Coleman Street)
peter.estlin@barclays.com

***Alderman* Evans**, Jeffrey (NP - Cheap)
jeffrey.evans@cityoflondon.gov.uk

***Alderman* Garbutt**, John (NP - Walbrook)
john.garbutt@halbis.com

***Alderman* Gowman**, Alison (NP - Dowgate)
alison.gowman@dlapiper.com

***Alderman* Graves**, David (NP - Cripplegate)
david.graves@cityoflondon.gov.uk

***Alderman* Hailes**, Timothy (NP - Bassishaw)
tim.hailes@cityoflondon.gov.uk

***Alderman* Haines**, Gordon (NP - Queenhithe)
gordon.haines@cityoflondon.gov.uk

***Alderman* Hewitt**, Peter (NP - Aldgate)
peter.hewitt@aldgateward.com

***Alderman* Howard**, David (NP - Cornhill)
david.howard@charles-stanley.co.uk

***Alderman* Judge**, Paul (NP - Tower)
paul@paulrjudge.com

***Alderman* Keaveny**, Vincent (NP - Farringdon Within)
vincent.keaveny@cityoflondon.gov.uk

***Alderman* Luder**, Ian (NP - Castle Baynard)
ian.luder@cityoflondon.gov.uk

***Alderman* Mainelli**, Michael (NP - Broad Street)

***Alderman* Malins**, Julian (NP - Farringdon Without)
malins@btinternet.com

***Alderman* Parmley**, Andrew (NP - Vintry)
andrew.parmley@cityoflondon.gov.uk

***Alderman* Richardson**, Adam (NP - Farringdon Without)
adam@adamrichardson.co.uk

***Alderman* Richardson**, Matthew (NP - Billingsgate)

***Alderman* Russell**, William (NP - Bread Street)
thriplowbury@aol.com

***Alderman* Scotland of Asthal**, Patricia (IND - Bishopsgate)

***Alderman* Wootton**, David (NP - Langbourn)
david.wootton@cityoflondon.gov.uk

***Common Councilman* Abrahams**, George (NP - Farringdon Without)
georgea@georgeabrahams.co.uk

***Common Councilman* Absalom**, John (NP - Farringdon Without)
john.absalom@cityoflondon.gov.uk

***Common Councilman* Anderson**, Randall (IND - Aldersgate)
randall.anderson@cityoflondon.gov.uk

***Common Councilman* Bain-Stewart**, Alex (NP - Farringdon Within)
alex.bain-stewart@cityoflondon.gov.uk

***Common Councilman* Barker**, John (NP - Cripplegate)
john.barker@cityoflondon.gov.uk

***Common Councilman* Barrow**, Douglas (NP - Aldgate)

***Common Councilman* Bennett**, John (NP - Broad Street)
john.bennett@cityoflondon.gov.uk

***Common Councilman* Bensted-Smith**, Nicholas (NP - Cheap)

***Common Councilman* Boden**, Christopher (NP - Castle Baynard)
christopher.boden@cityoflondon.gov.uk

***Common Councilman* Boleat**, Mark (NP - Cordwainer)
mark.boleat@cityoflondon.gov.uk

***Common Councilman* Bradshaw**, David (NP - Cripplegate)
david.bradshaw@cityoflondon.gov.uk

***Common Councilman* Campbell-Taylor**, William Goodacre (LAB - Portsoken)
william.taylor@cityoflondon.gov.uk

***Common Councilman* Cassidy**, Michael (NP - Coleman Street)
michael.cassidy@dlapiper.com

***Common Councilman* Chadwick**, Roger (NP - Tower)
roger.chadwick@cityoflondon.gov.uk

***Common Councilman* Challis**, Nigel (NP - Castle Baynard)
nigel.challis@cityoflondon.gov.uk

***Common Councilman* Chapman**, John (NP - Langbourn)
johnc@jdconsultants.com

***Common Councilman* Clark**, Jamie (NP - Billingsgate)

***Common Councilman* Colthurst**, Henry (NP - Lime Street)

***Common Councilman* Cotgrove**, Dennis (NP - Lime Street)
dennis.cotgrove@cityoflondon.gov.uk

***Common Councilman* De Sausmarez**, James (IND - Candlewick)

***Common Councilman* Deane**, Alexander (NP - Farringdon Without)
alexanderdeane@ymail.com

***Common Councilman* D'Olier Duckworth**, Simon (NP - Bishopsgate)

***Common Councilman* Dostalova**, Karina (NP - Farringdon Within)

***Common Councilman* Dove**, William (NP - Bishopsgate)

***Common Councilman* Dudley**, Martin (IND - Aldersgate)
martin.dudley@cityoflondon.gov.uk

***Common Councilman* Dunphy**, Peter (NP - Cornhill)
petergdunphy@hotmail.com

***Common Councilman* Edhem**, Emma (NP - Castle Baynard)
emma_edhem@yahoo.co.uk

***Common Councilman* Everett**, Kevin (NP - Candlewick)
kevin.everett@cityoflondon.gov.uk

***Common Councilman* Fernandes**, Sophie (NP - Coleman Street)
sophieannefernandes@gmail.com

***Common Councilman* Fraser**, Bill (NP - Vintry)
william.fraser@cityoflondon.gov.uk

***Common Councilman* Fraser**, Stuart (NP - Coleman Street)
stuart.fraser@cityoflondon.gov.uk

***Common Councilman* Fredericks**, Marianne (NP - Tower)
marianne_fredericks@hotmail.com

***Common Councilman* Frew**, Lucy (NP - Walbrook)
lucy.frew@cityoflondon.gov.uk

***Common Councilman* Gillon**, George (NP - Cordwainer)
george.gillon@cityoflondon.gov.uk

***Common Councilman* Ginsburg**, Stanley (NP - Bishopsgate)
stanley.ginsburg@cityoflondon.gov.uk

***Common Councilman* Haines**, Stephen (NP - Cornhill)
stephen.haines@cityoflondon.gov.uk

***Common Councilman* Harris**, Brian (NP - Bridge & Bridge Without)
brian.harris@cityoflondon.gov.uk

***Common Councilman* Harrower**, George (IND - Bassishaw)

***Common Councilman* Hayward**, Christopher (NP - Broad Street)
chris@haywardinvestments.com

***Common Councilman* Hoffman**, Tom (NP - Vintry)
tom.hoffman@cityoflondon.gov.uk

***Common Councilman* Holmes**, Ann (NP - Farringdon Within)
ann.holmes@cityoflondon.gov.uk

***Common Councilman* Howard**, Robert (NP - Lime Street)
COL-EB-TC@cityoflondon.gov.uk

***Common Councilman* Hudson**, Michael (NP - Castle Baynard)
city@mhlaw.co.uk

***Common Councilman* Hyde**, Wendy (NP - Bishopsgate)
wendy.hyde@cityoflondon.gov.uk

***Common Councilman* James**, Clare (NP - Farringdon Within)
clare.james@puntersouthall.com

***Common Councilman* Jones**, Gregory (NP - Farringdon Without)

***Common Councilman* Jones**, Henry (NP - Portsoken)
henry.jones@cityoflondon.gov.uk

***Common Councilman* King**, Alastair (NP - Queenhithe)
alastair.king@cityoflondon.gov.uk

***Common Councilman* Lawrence**, Greg (NP - Farringdon Without)
gregory.lawrence@cityoflondon.gov.uk

***Common Councilman* Littlechild**, Vivienne (NP - Cripplegate)
vivienne.littlechild@cityoflondon.gov.uk

***Common Councilman* Lodge**, Oliver (NP - Bread Street)
oliver.lodge@cityoflondon.gov.uk

***Common Councilman* Lord**, Charles Edward (NP - Farringdon Without)
edward.lord@cityoflondon.gov.uk

***Common Councilman* Lumley**, John (IND - Aldersgate)

***Common Councilman* Martinelli**, Peter (NP - Farringdon Without)
peter.martinelli@cityoflondon.gov.uk

***Common Councilman* Mayhew**, Jeremy (IND - Aldersgate)
jeremymayhew@btinternet.com

***Common Councilman* McGuinness**, Catherine (NP - Castle Baynard)
catherine.mcguinness@cityoflondon.gov.uk

***Common Councilman* McMurtrie**, Andrew (NP - Coleman Street)
andrew.mcmurtrie@cityoflondon.gov.uk

***Common Councilman* Mead**, Wendy (NP - Farringdon Without)
wendy.mead@cityoflondon.gov.uk

***Common Councilman* Merrett**, Robert (NP - Bassishaw)
robert.merrett@jpmorgan.com

***Common Councilman* Mooney**, Brian (NP - Queenhithe)
brian.mooney@btinternet.com

***Common Councilman* Moore**, Gareth (NP - Cripplegate)
gareth.moore@cityoflondon.gov.uk

***Common Councilman* Morris**, Hugh (NP - Aldgate)

***Common Councilman* Moss**, Alastair (NP - Cheap)
alastair.moss@hotmail.com

***Common Councilman* Moys**, Sylvia (NP - Aldgate)
sylvia.moys@cityoflondon.gov.uk

***Common Councilman* Nash**, Joyce (IND - Aldersgate)
joyce.nash@cityoflondon.gov.uk

***Common Councilman* Newman**, Barbara (IND - Aldersgate)
barbara.newman@cityoflondon.gov.uk

***Common Councilman* Packham**, Graham (NP - Castle Baynard)

***Common Councilman* Patel**, Dhruv (NP - Aldgate)
dhruv.patel@cityoflondon.gov.uk

***Common Councilman* Pembroke**, Anne (NP - Cheap)
ann.pembroke@cityoflondon.gov.uk

***Common Councilman* Pleasance**, Judith (NP - Langbourn)

***Common Councilman* Pollard**, Henry (NP - Dowgate)
henry_pollard@invescoperpetual.co.uk

***Common Councilman* Price**, Emma (NP - Farringdon Without)

***Common Councilman* Priest**, Henrika (NP - Castle Baynard)
henrika.priest@cityoflondon.gov.uk

***Common Councilman* Pulman**, Gerald (NP - Tower)
geraldpulman@hotmail.com

***Common Councilman* Punter**, Christopher (NP - Cripplegate)
chris.punter@cityoflondon.gov.uk

***Common Councilman* Quilter**, Stephen (NP - Cripplegate)
vision@totalise.co.uk

***Common Councilman* Regan**, Richard (NP - Farringdon Within)
richard.regan@cityoflondon.gov.u

***Common Councilman* Regis**, Delis (NP - Portsoken)
delis.regis@cityoflondon.gov.uk

***Common Councilman* Rogula**, Elizabeth (NP - Lime Street)
er@btinternet.com

***Common Councilman* Rounding**, Virginia (NP - Farringdon Within)
virginia.rounding@cityoflondon.gov.uk

***Common Councilman* Scott**, John (NP - Broad Street)
john.scott@cityoflondon.gov.uk

***Common Councilman* Shilson**, Giles (NP - Bread Street)
giles.shilson@cityoflondon.gov.uk

***Common Councilman* Simons**, Jeremy (NP - Castle Baynard)
jeremy.simons@cityoflondon.gov.uk

***Common Councilman* Sleigh**, Tom (NP - Bishopsgate)
tom.sleigh@cityoflondon.gov.uk

***Common Councilman* Smith**, Graeme (NP - Farringdon Within)
graeme.smith@cityoflondon.gov.uk

***Common Councilman* Snyder**, Michael (NP - Cordwainer)
michael.snyder@cityoflondon.gov.uk

***Common Councilman* Starling**, Angela (NP - Cripplegate)
angela.starling@cityoflondon.gov.uk

***Common Councilman* Streeter**, Patrick (NP - Bishopsgate)

***Common Councilman* Thompson**, David (NP - Aldgate)

***Common Councilman* Thomson**, James (NP - Walbrook)
james.m.d.thomson@virgin.net

***Common Councilman* Tomlinson**, John (NP - Cripplegate)
john@johnandpaula.com

***Common Councilman* Tumbridge**, James (NP - Tower)
james.tumbridge@cityoflondon.gov.uk

***Common Councilman* Welbank**, Michael (NP - Billingsgate)
michael.welbank@cityoflondon.gov.uk

***Common Councilman* Wheatley**, Mark (NP - Dowgate)
markindowgate@gmail.com

***Common Councilman* Woodhouse**, Philip (NP - Langbourn)

Fletcher, John William (NP - Portsoken)

Gifford, Roger (NP - Cordwainer)
roger.gifford@seb.co.uk

Seaton, Ian (NP - Cornhill)

Woolf, Fiona (NP - Candlewick)
fiona.woolf@cms-cmck.com

POLITICAL COMPOSITION
NP: *, IND: 10, LAB: 1

Clackmannanshire S

Clackmannanshire Council, Kilncraigs, Alloa FK10 1EB
☎ 01259 450000 🖷 01259 452010 ✉ cutomerservice@clacks.gov.uk
💻 www.clacksweb.org.uk

FACTS AND FIGURES
Parliamentary Constituencies: Ochil and Perthshire South
EU Constituencies: Scotland
Election Frequency: Elections are of whole council

PRINCIPAL OFFICERS

Chief Executive: Ms Elaine McPherson, Chief Executive, Kilncraigs, Alloa FK10 1EB ☎ 01259 452002 ✉ emcpherson@clacks.gov.uk

Deputy Chief Executive: Mrs Nikki Bridle Depute Chief Executive, Kilncraigs, Alloa FK10 1EB ☎ 01259 452373 ✉ nbridle@clacks.gov.uk

Senior Management: Mr Stephen Coulter Head of Resources & Governance, Kilncraigs, Alloa FK10 1EB ☎ 01259 452373

Senior Management: Mr Stuart Crickmar Head of Strategy & Customer Services, Kilncraigs, , Alloa FK10 1EB ☎ 01259 452127 ✉ scrickmar@clacks.gov.uk

Senior Management: Mr Garry Dallas, Executive Director, Kilncraigs, Alloa FK10 1EB ☎ 01259 450002 ✉ gdallas@clacks.gov.uk

Senior Management: Ms Val de Souza Head of Social Services / Chief Social Worker, Kilncraigs, Alloa FK10 1EB ☎ 01259 225017 ✉ cdesouza@clacks.gov.uk

Senior Management: Mr Ahsan Khan Head of Housing & Community Safety, Kilncraigs, Alloa FK10 1EB ☎ 01259 452473 ✉ akhan@clacks.gov.uk

Senior Management: Mr David Leng Head of Education, Teith House, Kerse Road, Stirling FK7 7QA ☎ 01786 442669 ✉ dleng@clacks.gov.uk

Senior Management: Mr Gordon McNeil Head of Development & Environmental Services, Kilncraigs, Alloa FK10 1EB ☎ 01259 452533 ✉ gmcneil@clacks.gov.uk

Access Officer / Social Services (Disability): Mr Phillip Gillespie Assistant Head - Social Services (Adult Care), Kilncraigs, Alloa FK10 1EB ☎ 01259 455083 ✉ pgillespie2@clacks.gov.uk

Architect, Building / Property Services: Ms Eileen Turnbull Asset Manager, Kilncraigs, Greenside Street, , Alloa FK10 1EB ☎ 01259 452460 ✉ eturnbull2@clacks.gov.uk

Best Value: Mr Derek Barr, Procurement Manager, Greenfield, Alloa FK10 1EX ☎ 01259 452017 ✉ dbarr@clacks.gov.uk

Building Control: Mr Alistair Mackenzie, Team Leader - Building, Standards & Llicensing, Kilncraigs House, Greenside Street, Alloa FK10 1EB ☎ 01259 452554 ✉ amackenzie@clacks.gov.uk

Catering Services: Ms Diane MacKenzie Catering Manager, Class Cuisine, 21 Main Street, Sauchie, Alloa FK10 3JR ☎ 01259 452190 ✉ dmackenzie@clacks.gov.uk

Children / Youth Services: Mr Liam Purdie Assistant Head of Service - Child Care, Kilncraigs, Greenside Street, Alloa FK10 1EB ☎ 01259 452301 ✉ lpurdie@clacks.gov.uk

Civil Registration: Mr Brian Forbes, Customer Services Manager, Kilncraigs, Alloa FK10 1EB ☎ 01259 452187 ✉ bforbes@clacks.gov.uk

PR / Communications: Ms Karen Payton Communications & Marketing Team Leader, Kilncraigs, Alloa FK10 1EB ☎ 01259 452027 ✉ kpayton@clacks.gov.uk

Community Planning: Ms Cherie Jarvie Strategy & Performance Manager, Greenfield House, Alloa FK10 2AD ☎ 01259 452365 ✉ cjarvie@clacks.gov.uk

Community Safety: Mr Ahsan Khan Head of Housing & Community Safety, Kilncraigs, Alloa FK10 1EB ☎ 01259 452473 ✉ akhan@clacks.gov.uk

Computer Management: Mr John Munro, ICT Service Manager, Greenfield, Alloa FK10 2AD ☎ 01259 452510 ✉ jmunro@clacks.gov.uk

Consumer Protection and Trading Standards: Mr Ian Doctor, Service Manager - Environmental Health & Consumer Protection, Kilncraigs, Greenside Place, Alloa FK10 1EB ☎ 01259 452572 ✉ idoctor@clacks.gov.uk

Contracts: Mr Derek Barr, Procurement Manager, Greenfield, Alloa FK10 1EX ☎ 01259 452017 ✉ dbarr@clacks.gov.uk

Customer Service: Mr Brian Forbes, Customer Services Manager, Greenfield House, Alloa FK10 2AD ☎ 01259 452187 ✉ bforbes@clacks.gov.uk

Economic Development: Ms Julie Hamilton Development Services Manager, Kilncraigs, Greenside Place, Alloa FK10 1EB ☎ 01259 450000 ✉ jhamilton@clacks.gov.uk

Education: Ms Sharon Johnstone Senior Manager - Education, Children, Young People & Families, Teith House, Kerse Road, Stirling FK7 7QA ☎ 01786 233202 ✉ johnstones2@stirling.gov.uk

Education: Mr Kevin Kelman Senior Manager - Head of School Improvement, Viewforth, Stirling FK8 2ET ☎ 01786 233224 ✉ kelmank@stirling.gov.uk

Education: Mr Alan Milliken Head of Learning, Communities, Performance & Resources, Viewforth, Stirling FK8 2ET ☎ 01786 233225 ✉ millikina@stirling.gov.uk

Electoral Registration: Mr Andrew Hunter Senior Governance Officer, Kilncraigs, Alloa FK10 1EB ☎ 01259 452103 ✉ ahunter2@clackmannanshire.gov.uk

Emergency Planning: Mr David Johnstone Emergency Planning Officer, Kilncraigs, Alloa FK10 1EB ☎ 01259 452537 ✉ djohnstone@clacks.gov.uk

Energy Management: Mr Richard Scobbie, Energy Officer, Kilncraigs, Alloa FK10 1EB ☎ 01259 450000 ✉ rscobbie@clacks.gov.uk

Environmental / Technical Services: Mr Gordon McNeil Head of Development & Environmental Services, Kilncraigs, Alloa FK10 1EB ☎ 01259 452533 ✉ gmcneil@clacks.gov.uk

Environmental Health: Mr Andrew Crawford Environmental Health Team Leader, Kilncraigs, Greenside Street, , Alloa FK10 1EB ☎ 01259 452581 ✉ acrawford@clacks.gov.uk

Estates, Property & Valuation: Mr George Adamson, Team Leader - Estates, Kilncraigs, Alloa FK10 1EB ☎ 01259 452647

Facilities: Ms Eileen Turnbull Asset Manager, Kilncraigs, Greenside Street, , Alloa FK10 1EB ☎ 01259 452460 ✉ eturnbull2@clacks.gov.uk

Finance: Mr Lindsay Sim Chief Accountant, Kilncraigs, Alloa FK10 1EB ☎ 01259 452078 ✉ lsim@clacks.gov.uk

Fleet Management: Mr Donny Cameron Fleet Contract Manager, Kelliebank, Alloa FK10 1NT ☎ 01259 226936 ✉ dcameron@clacks.gov.uk

Grounds Maintenance: Mr Kenny Inglis Land Services Team Leader, Kilncraigs, Greenside Street, , Alloa FK10 1EB ☎ 01259 226933 ✉ kinglis@clacks.gov.uk

Health and Safety: Mrs Sarah Robertson, Health & Safety Adviser, Kilncraigs, Alloa FK10 1EB ☎ 01259 452174 ✉ hands@clacks.gov.uk

Housing: Mr Ahsan Khan Head of Housing & Community Safety, Kilncraigs, Alloa FK10 1EB ☎ 01259 452473 ✉ akhan@clacks.gov.uk

Housing Maintenance: Ms Jennifer Queripel, Service Manager Housing Operations, Kilncraigs, Alloa FK10 1EB ☎ 01259 452475

Legal: Mr Andrew Wyse Team Leader - Legal Services, Kilncraigs, Greenside Street, , Alloa FK10 1EB ☎ 01259 452088 ✉ awyse@clacks.gov.uk

Licensing: Ms June Andison, Administrator / Licensing, Kilncraigs, Alloa FK10 1EB ☎ 01259 452093 ✉ jandison@clacks.gov.uk

Lighting: Mr Malcolm West, Manager - Roads & Transportation, Kilncraigs, Alloa FK10 1EB ☎ 01259 452624 ✉ mwest@clacks.gov.uk

CLACKMANNANSHIRE

Member Services: Mrs Alison Bryce, Business Support Manager, Kilncraigs, Alloa FK10 1EB ☎ 01259 452003 ✉ abryce@clacks.gov.uk

Planning: Mr Grant Baxter Principal Planner, Kilncraigs, Alloa FK10 1EB ☎ 01259 450000 ✉ gbaxter@clacks.gov.uk

Procurement: Mr Derek Barr, Procurement Manager, Kilncraigs, Alloa FK10 1EB ☎ 01259 452017 ✉ dbarr@clacks.gov.uk

Public Libraries: Mr Brian Forbes, Customer Services Manager, Kilncraigs, Alloa FK10 1EB ☎ 01259 452187 ✉ bforbes@clacks.gov.uk

Recycling & Waste Minimisation: Mr Graeme Cunningham, Manager - Environment, Kilncraigs, Alloa FK10 1EB ☎ 01259 452548 ✉ wasteservices@clacks.gov.uk

Road Safety: Mr Malcolm West, Manager - Roads & Transportation, Kilncraigs House, Greenside Street, Alloa FK10 1EX ☎ 01259 452624 ✉ mwest@clacks.gov.uk

Social Services: Ms Val de Souza Head of Social Services / Chief Social Worker, Kilncraigs, Alloa FK10 1EB ☎ 01259 225017 ✉ cdesouza@clacks.gov.uk

Social Services (Adult): Mr Phillip Gillespie Assistant Head - Social Services (Adult Care), Kilncraigs, Alloa FK10 1EB ☎ 01259 455083 ✉ pgillespie2@clacks.gov.uk

Social Services (Children): Mr Liam Purdie Assistant Head of Service - Child Care, Kilncraigs, Greenside Street, , Alloa FK10 1EB ☎ 01259 452301 ✉ lpurdie@clacks.gov.uk

Staff Training: Ms Lorna Young Learning & Development Advisor, Kilncraigs, Alloa FK10 1EB ☎ 01259 450000 ✉ lorna.young@clacksweb.org.uk

Street Scene: Mr Charlie Norman, Team Leader of Road Services, Kilncraigs House, Greenside Street, Alloa FK10 1EB ☎ 01259 452590 ✉ cnorman@clacks.gov.uk

Traffic Management: Mr Malcolm West, Manager - Roads & Transportation, Kilncraigs House, Greenside Street, Alloa FK10 1EX ☎ 01259 452624 ✉ mwest@clacks.gov.uk

Transport: Mr Malcolm West, Manager - Roads & Transportation, Kilncraigs House, Greenside Street, Alloa FK10 1EX ☎ 01259 452624 ✉ mwest@clacks.gov.uk

Transport Planner: Mr Malcolm West, Manager - Roads & Transportation, Kilncraigs House, Greenside Street, Alloa FK10 1EX ☎ 01259 452624 ✉ mwest@clacks.gov.uk

Waste Collection and Disposal: Mr Graeme Cunningham, Environment Manager, Kilncraigs House, Greenside Street, Alloa FK10 1EB ☎ 01259 452548 ✉ gcunningham@clacks.gov.uk

Waste Management: Mr Graeme Cunningham, Environment Manager, Kilncraigs House, Greenside Street, Alloa FK10 1EB ☎ 01259 452548 ✉ gcunningham@clacks.gov.uk

COUNCILLORS

***Provost* Murphy**, Tina (SNP - Clackmannanshire West)
tmurphy@clacks.gov.uk

***Deputy Provost* Holden**, Craig (SNP - Clackmannanshire South)
cholden@clacks.gov.uk

***Leader of the Council* Sharp**, Les (SNP - Clackmannanshire West)
lsharp@clacks.gov.uk

Balsillie, Donald (SNP - Clackmannanshire North)
dbalsillie@clacks.gov.uk

Cadenhead, Janet (LAB - Clackmannanshire South)
jcadenhead@clacks.gov.uk

Campbell, Alastair (CON - Clackmannanshire East)
acampbell@clacks.gov.uk

Drummond, Archie (IND - Clackmannanshire North)
adrummond@clacks.gov.uk

Earle, Kenneth (LAB - Clackmannanshire South)
kearle@clacks.gov.uk

Forson, Ellen (SNP - Clackmannanshire South)
eforson@clacks.gov.uk

Hamilton, Irene (SNP - Clackmannanshire East)
ihamilton@clacks.gov.uk

Martin, Kathleen (LAB - Clackmannanshire East)
kmartin@clacks.gov.uk

Matchett, George (LAB - Clackmannanshire West)
gmatchett@clacks.gov.uk

McAdam, Walter (SNP - Clackmannanshire North)
wmcadam@clacks.gov.uk

McGill, Robert (LAB - Clackmannanshire North)
rmcgill@clacks.gov.uk

Stalker, Jim (LAB - Clackmannanshire West)
jstalker@clacks.gov.uk

Stewart, Derek (LAB - Clackmannanshire Central)
dstewart2@clacks.gov.uk

Watt, Graham (LAB - Clackmannanshire Central)
gwatt3@clacks.gov.uk

Womersley, Gary (SNP - Clackmannanshire Central)
gwomersley@clacks.gov.uk

POLITICAL COMPOSITION

LAB: 8, SNP: 8, CON: 1, IND: 1

COMMITTEE CHAIRS

Audit & Resources: Mr Jim Stalker

Audt & Resources: Mr Archie Drummond

Housing, Health & Care: Mr Les Sharp

Licensing: Mr Walter McAdam

Planning: Mr Alastair Campbell

Colchester D

Colchester Borough Council, Rowan House, 33 Sheepen Road, Colchester CO3 3WG
☎ 01206 282222 ✉ customerservicecentre@colchester.gov.uk
🖳 www.colchester.gov.uk

FACTS AND FIGURES

Parliamentary Constituencies: Colchester, Harwich and Essex North
EU Constituencies: Eastern
Election Frequency: Elections are by thirds

PRINCIPAL OFFICERS

Chief Executive: Mr Adrian Pritchard Chief Executive, Rowan House, 33 Sheepen Road, Colchester CO3 3WG ☎ 01206 282211 adrian.pritchard@colchester.gov.uk

Assistant Chief Executive: Mr Matthew Sterling Assistant Chief Executive, Rowan House, 33 Sheepen Road, Colchester CO3 3WG ☎ 01206 282577 matthew.sterling@colchester.gov.uk

Senior Management: Mrs Pam Donnelly Executive Director - Customer Operations & Partnerships, Rowan House, 33 Sheepen Road, Colchester CO3 3WG ☎ 01206 282212 pamela.donnelly@colchester.gov.uk

Senior Management: Mrs Ann Hedges Chief Operating Officer - Delivery & Performance, Rowan House, 33 Sheepen Road, Colchester CO3 3WG ☎ 01206 282212 ann.hedges@colchester.gov.uk

Senior Management: Mr Ian Vipond Strategic Director - Commerical & Place, Rowan House, 33 Sheepen Road, Colchester CO3 3WG ☎ 01206 282717 ian.vipond@colchester.gov.uk

Building Control: Mr Tony Tarran Building Control Manager, Rowan House, 33 Sheepen Road, Colchester CO3 3WG ☎ 01206 508646 tony.tarran@colchester.gov.uk

Children / Youth Services: Mrs Lucie Breadman Head - Community Services, Rowan House, 33 Sheepen Road, Colchester CO3 3WG ☎ 01206 282726 lucie.breadman@colchester.gov.uk

PR / Communications: Ms Joanne Partlett Communications Manager, Rowan House, 33 Sheepen Road, Colchester CO3 3WG ☎ 01206 282310 joanne.partlett@colchester.gov.uk

Community Planning: Mr Gareth Mitchell, Head - Commercial Services, Rowan House, 33 Sheepen Road, Colchester CO3 3WG ☎ 01206 282719 🖷 01206 507814 gareth.mitchell@colchester.gov.uk

Computer Management: Mr Kieran Johnston Strategic ICT & Communications Manager, Rowan House, 33 Sheepen Road, Colchester CO3 3WG ☎ 01206 507880 kieran.johnston@colchester.gov.uk

Contracts: Mr Julian Wilkins, Principal Lawyer, Rowan House, 33 Sheepen Road, Colchester CO3 3WG ☎ 01206 282257 julian.wilkins@colchester.gov.uk

Corporate Services: Mr Matthew Sterling Assistant Chief Executive, Rowan House, 33 Sheepen Road, Colchester CO3 3WG ☎ 01206 282577 matthew.sterling@colchester.gov.uk

Customer Service: Ms Leonie Rathbone, Head of Customer Services, Rowan House, 33 Sheepen Road, Colchester CO3 3WG ☎ 01206 507887 leonie.rathbone@colchester.gov.uk

Economic Development: Mr Nigel Myers Economic Development Manager, Rowan House, 33 Sheepen Road, Colchester CO3 3WG ☎ 01206 282878 nigel.myers@colchester.gov.uk

E-Government: Mr Kieran Johnston Strategic ICT & Communications Manager, Rowan House, 33 Sheepen Road, Colchester CO3 3WG ☎ 01206 507880 kieran.johnston@colchester.gov.uk

Electoral Registration: Mrs Sarah Cheek Electoral Services Manager, Rowan House, 33 Sheepen Road, Colchester CO3 3WG ☎ 01206 282271 sarah.cheek@colchester.gov.uk

Emergency Planning: Ms Hayley McGrath Corporate Governance Manager, Rowan House, 33 Sheepen Road, Colchester CO3 3WG ☎ 01206 508902 hayley.mcgrath@colchester.gov.uk

Environmental Health: Mr Rory Doyle Public Health & Enforcement Service Manager, Rowan House, 33 Sheepen Road, Colchester CO3 3WG ☎ 01206 507855 🖷 01206 282598 rory.doyle@colchester.gov.uk

Environmental Health: Mrs Beverley Jones Head of Professional Services, Rowan House, 33 Sheepen Road, Colchester CO3 3WG ☎ 01206 282593 beverley.jones@colchester.gov.uk

Estates, Property & Valuation: Ms Fiona Duhamel Economic Growth Manager, Rowan House, 33 Sheepen Road, Colchester CO3 3WG ☎ 01206 282252 fiona.duhamel@colchester.gov.uk

Events Manager: Mr Frank Turmel Events Manager, Charter Hall, Cowdray Avenue, Colchester CO1 1YH ☎ 01206 282946 frank.turmel@colchester.gov.uk

Facilities: Mr Lee Spalding Corporate Asset Manager, Rowan House, 33 Sheepen Road, Colchester CO3 3WG ☎ 01206 506905 lee.spalding@colchester.gov.uk

Finance: Mr Sean Plummer Finance Manager (Section 151 Officer), Rowan House, 33 Sheepen Road, Colchester CO3 3WG ☎ 01206 282347 🖷 01206 282538 sean.plummer@colchester.gov.uk

Fleet Management: Mr Chris Dowsing Group Manager - Recycling, Waste & Fleet, Rowan House, 33 Sheepen Road, Colchester CO3 3WG ☎ 01206 282752 chris.dowsing@colchester.gov.uk

Grounds Maintenance: Mr Bob Penny, Parks & Recreation Manager, Rowan House, 33 Sheepen Road, Colchester CO3 3WG ☎ 01206 282903 bob.penny@colchester.gov.uk

Health and Safety: Mrs Pam Donnelly Executive Director - Customer Operations & Partnerships, Rowan House, 33 Sheepen Road, Colchester CO3 3WG ☎ 01206 282212 pamela.donnelly@colchester.gov.uk

Health and Safety: Mr Rory Doyle Public Health & Enforcement Service Manager, Rowan House, 33 Sheepen Road, Colchester CO3 3WG ☎ 01206 507855 🖷 01206 282598 rory.doyle@colchester.gov.uk

COLCHESTER

Home Energy Conservation: Ms Melanie Rundle Community Welfare Co-ordinator, Rowan House, 33 Sheepen Road, Colchester CO3 3WG ☎ 01206 282541 ✉ melaine.rundle@colchester.gov.uk

Housing: Mr Nicorum Flaherty Housing Options Co-ordinator, Rowan House, 33 Sheepen Road, Colchester CO3 3WG ☎ 01206 282981 ✉ nicorum.flaherty@colchester.gov.uk

Legal: Mr Andrew Weavers, Legal Services Manager & Monitoring Officer, Rowan House, 33 Sheepen Road, Colchester CO3 3WG ☎ 01206 282213 ✉ andrew.weavers@colchester.gov.uk

Leisure and Cultural Services: Mr Tim Swallow Sport & Leisure Operations Manager, Rowan House, 33 Sheepen Road, Colchester CO3 3WG ☎ 01206 282106 ✉ tim.swallow@colchester.gov.uk

Licensing: Ms Sally Harrington Planning & Licensing Service Manager, Rowan House, 33 Sheepen Road, Colchester CO3 3WG ☎ 01206 506464 ✉ sally.harrington@colchester.gov.uk

Member Services: Ms Amanda Chidgey, Democratic Services Manager, Rowan House, 33 Sheepen Road, Colchester CO3 3WG ☎ 01206 282227 ✉ amanda.chidgey@colchester.gov.uk

Parking: Mr Richard Walker Parking Partnership Group Manager, Rowan House, 33 Sheepen Road, Colchester CO3 3WG ☎ 01206 282708 ✉ richard.walker@colchester.gov.uk

Personnel / HR: Ms Jessica Douglas Strategic People & Performance Manager, Rowan House, 33 Sheepen Road, Colchester CO3 3WG ☎ 01206 282239 ✉ jessica.douglas@colchester.gov.uk

Planning: Mrs Beverley Jones Head of Professional Services, Rowan House, 33 Sheepen Road, Colchester CO3 3WG ☎ 01206 282593 ✉ beverley.jones@colchester.gov.uk

Recycling & Waste Minimisation: Mr Chris Dowsing Group Manager - Recycling, Waste & Fleet, Rowan House, 33 Sheepen Road, Colchester CO3 3WG ☎ 01206 282752 ✉ chris.dowsing@colchester.gov.uk

Regeneration: Ms Fiona Duhamel Economic Growth Manager, Rowan House, 33 Sheepen Road, Colchester CO3 3WG ☎ 01206 282252 ✉ fiona.duhamel@colchester.gov.uk

Street Scene: Mr Matthew Young, Head - Operational Services, Rowan House, 33 Sheepen Road, Colchester CO3 3WG ☎ 01206 282902 ✉ matthew.young@colchester.gov.uk

Sustainable Communities: Mrs Lucie Breadman Head - Community Services, Rowan House, 33 Sheepen Road, Colchester CO3 3WG ☎ 01206 282726 ✉ lucie.breadman@colchester.gov.uk

Sustainable Development: Mr Gareth Mitchell, Head - Commercial Services, Rowan House, 33 Sheepen Road, Colchester CO3 3WG ☎ 01206 282719 🖷 01206 507814 ✉ gareth.mitchell@colchester.gov.uk

Tourism: Mr Gareth Mitchell, Head - Commercial Services, Rowan House, 33 Sheepen Road, Colchester CO3 3WG ☎ 01206 282719 🖷 01206 507814 ✉ gareth.mitchell@colchester.gov.uk

Tourism: Ms Karen Turnbull, Enterprise & Tourism Development Manager, Rowan House, 33 Sheepen Road, Colchester CO3 3WG ☎ 01206 282915 ✉ karen.turnbull@colchester.gov.uk

Town Centre: Mr Howard Davies Town Centre Project Manager, Rowan House, 33 Sheepen Road, Colchester CO3 3WG ☎ 01206 507885 🖷 01206 282711 ✉ howard.davies@colchester.gov.uk

Transport Planner: Mr Gareth Mitchell, Head - Commercial Services, Rowan House, 33 Sheepen Road, Colchester CO3 3WG ☎ 01206 282719 🖷 01206 507814 ✉ gareth.mitchell@colchester.gov.uk

Total Place: Mr Ian Vipond Strategic Director - Commerical & Place, Rowan House, 33 Sheepen Road, Colchester CO3 3WG ☎ 01206 282717 ✉ ian.vipond@colchester.gov.uk

Waste Collection and Disposal: Mr Chris Dowsing Group Manager - Recycling, Waste & Fleet, Rowan House, 33 Sheepen Road, Colchester CO3 3WG ☎ 01206 282752 ✉ chris.dowsing@colchester.gov.uk

Waste Management: Mr Chris Dowsing Group Manager - Recycling, Waste & Fleet, Rowan House, 33 Sheepen Road, Colchester CO3 3WG ☎ 01206 282752 ✉ chris.dowsing@colchester.gov.uk

Children's Play Areas: Mr Bob Penny, Parks & Recreation Manager, Rowan House, 33 Sheepen Road, Colchester CO3 3WG ☎ 01206 282903 ✉ bob.penny@colchester.gov.uk

COUNCILLORS

***Mayor* Higgins**, Theresa (LD - New Town)
cllr.theresa.higgins@colchester.gov.uk

***Deputy Mayor* Young**, Julie (LAB - St Andrew's)
cllr.julie.young@colchester.gov.uk

***Leader of the Council* Smith**, Paul (LD - St John's)
cllr.paul.smith@colchester.gov.uk

***Deputy Leader of the Council* Feltham**, Annie (LD - New Town)
cllr.Annie.Feltham@colchester.gov.uk

***Deputy Leader of the Council* Young**, Tim (LAB - St Andrew's)
cllr.tim.young@colchester.gov.uk

Arnold, Christopher (CON - Fordham & Stour)
cllr.christopher.arnold@colchester.gov.uk

Barton, Lyn (LD - Shrub End)
cllr.linda.barton@colchester.gov.uk

Bentley, Kevin (CON - Birch & Winstree)
cllr.kevin.bentley@colchester.gov.uk

Blundell, Elizabeth (CON - Marks Tey)
cllr.elizabeth.blundell@colchester.gov.uk

Bourne, Tina (LAB - St Andrew's)
cllr.tina.bourne@colchester.gov.uk

Buston, Roger (CON - Lexden)
cllr.roger.buston@colchester.gov.uk

Cable, Mark (CON - Dedham & Langham)
cllr.mark.cable@colchester.gov.uk

Chapman, Nigel (CON - Fordham & Stour)
cllr.nigel.chapman@colchester.gov.uk

Chillingworth, Peter (CON - Great Tey)
cllr.peter.chillingworth@colchester.gov.uk

Chuah, Helen (LD - St Anne's)
cllr.helen.chuah@colchester.gov.uk

Cook, Barrie (LD - St Anne's)
cllr.barrie.cook@colchester.gov.uk

Cope, Nick (LD - Christ Church)
cllr.nick.cope@colchester.gov.uk

Cory, Mark (LD - Wivenhoe Cross)
cllr.mark.cory@colchester.gov.uk

Davidson, Robert (CON - Pyefleet)
cllr.robert.davidson@colchester.gov.uk

Davies, Beverly (CON - Prettygate)
cllr.beverly.davies@colchester.gov.uk

Elliott, John (CON - Tiptree)
cllr.john.elliott@colchester.gov.uk

Ellis, Andrew (CON - Birch & Winstree)
cllr.andrew.ellis@colchester.gov.uk

Fairley-Crowe, Margaret (CON - Tiptree)
cllr.margaret.fairley-crowe@colchester.gov.uk

Frame, Bill (LD - Castle)
cllr.bill.frame@colchester.gov.uk

Gamble, Ray (LD - St John's)
cllr.ray.gamble@colchester.gov.uk

Goss, Martin (LD - Mile End)
cllr.martin.goss@colchester.gov.uk

Graham, Dominic (LD - Mile End)
cllr.dominic.graham@colchester.gov.uk

Hardy, Annesley (CON - Christ Church)
cllr.annesley.hardy@colchester.gov.uk

Harrington, Marcus (CON - West Bergholt & Eight Ash Green)
cllr.Marcus.Harrington@colchester.gov.uk

Harris, David (LAB - Berechurch)
cllr.david.harris@colchester.gov.uk

Havis, Julia (LD - Old Heath)
cllr.julia.havis@colchester.gov.uk

Hayes, Jo (LD - Castle)
cllr.jo.hayes@colchester.gov.uk

Hazell, Pauline (CON - Shrub End)
cllr.pauline.hazell@colchester.gov.uk

Higgins, Peter (LD - New Town)
cllr.peter.higgins@colchester.gov.uk

Hogg, Mike (LD - St Anne's)
cllr.mike.hogg@colchester.gov.uk

Jarvis, Brian (CON - Lexden)
cllr.brian.jarvis@colchester.gov.uk

Jowers, John (CON - West Mersea)
cllr.john.jowers@colchester.gov.uk

Knight, Justin (LD - Old Heath)
cllr.justin.knight@colchester.gov.uk

Laws, Darius (CON - Castle)
cllr.darius.laws@colchester.gov.uk

Liddy, Cyril (LAB - Wivenhoe Quay)
cllr.cyril.liddy@colchester.gov.uk

Lilley, Michael (LAB - East Donyland)
cllr.mike.lilley@colchester.gov.uk

Lissimore, Sue (CON - Prettygate)
cllr.sue.lissimore@colchester.gov.uk

Locker, Ben (CON - Mile End)

Maclean, Jackie (CON - Copford & West Stanway)
cllr.jackie.maclean@colchester.gov.uk

Maclean, Fiona (CON - Stanway)
cllr.fiona.maclean@colchester.gov.uk

Manning, Jon (LD - Wivenhoe Cross)
cllr.jon.manning@colchester.gov.uk

Martin, Richard (CON - Tiptree)
cllr.richard.martin@colchester.gov.uk

Moore, Patricia (CON - West Mersea)
cllr.patricia.moore@colchester.gov.uk

Naish, Kim (LAB - Berechurch)
cllr.kim.naish@colchester.gov.uk

Offen, Nigel (LD - Shrub End)
cllr.nigel.offen@colchester.gov.uk

Oxford, Beverley (IND - Highwoods)
cllr.beverley.oxford@colchester.gov.uk

Oxford, Gerard (IND - Highwoods)
cllr.gerard.oxford@colchester.gov.uk

Oxford, Philip (IND - Highwoods)
cllr.philip.oxford@colchester.gov.uk

Pearson, Chris (LAB - Berechurch)
cllr.chris.pearson@colchester.gov.uk

Quince, Will (CON - Prettygate)
cllr.Will.Quince@colchester.gov.uk

Scott, Rosalind (LAB - Wivenhoe Quay)
cllr.rosalind.scott@colchester.gov.uk

Scott-Boutell, Jessica (LD - Stanway)
cllr.jessica.scott-boutell@colchester.gov.uk

Sheane, Peter (CON - West Mersea)
cllr.peter.sheane@colchester.gov.uk

Sykes, Laura (IND - Stanway)
cllr.laura.sykes@colchester.gov.uk

Willetts, Dennis (CON - West Bergholt & Eight Ash Green)
cllr.dennis.willetts@colchester.gov.uk

POLITICAL COMPOSITION

CON: 27, LD: 20, LAB: 9, IND: 4

COMMITTEE CHAIRS

Licensing: Mr Michael Lilley

Planning: Mr Jon Manning

Conwy W

Conwy County Borough Council, Bodlondeb, Bangor Road, Conwy LL32 8DU
☎ 01492 574000 🖷 01492 592114 information@conwy.gov.uk
www.conwy.gov.uk

CONWY

FACTS AND FIGURES

Parliamentary Constituencies: Aberconwy, Clwyd West
EU Constituencies: Wales
Election Frequency: Elections are of whole council

PRINCIPAL OFFICERS

Chief Executive: Mr Iwan Davies, Chief Executive, Bodlondeb, Bangor Road, Conwy LL32 8DU ☎ 01492 576015 🖷 01492 576135 ✉ iwan.davies@conwy.gov.uk

Senior Management: Mrs Sasha Davies Strategic Director - Economy & Place, Bodlondeb, Bangor Road, Conwy LL32 8DU ☎ 01492 576001 ✉ sasha.davies@conwy.gov.uk

Senior Management: Mr Ken Finch, Strategic Director - Democracy & Environment, Bodlondeb, Bangor Road, Conwy LL32 8DU ☎ 01492 576200 🖷 01492 576203 ✉ ken.finch@conwy.gov.uk

Senior Management: Mr Andrew Kirkham, Strategic Director - Finance & Efficiencies, Bodlondeb, Bangor Road, Conwy LL32 8DU ☎ 01492 576170 ✉ andrew.kirkham@conwy.gov.uk

Senior Management: Ms Jenny Williams Strategic Director - Social Care & Education, Government Buildings, Dinerth Road, Rhos-on-Sea, Conwy LL28 4UL ☎ 01492 575687 🖷 01492 575687 ✉ jenny.williams@conwy.gov.uk

Access Officer / Social Services (Disability): Ms Claire Lister Head of Integrated Adult & Community Services, Government Buildings, Dinerth Road, Rhos-on-Sea, Conwy LL28 4UL ☎ 01492 575378 ✉ claire.lister@conwy.gov.uk

Architect, Building / Property Services: Mr Bleddyn Evans, County Valuer & Asset Manager, Bodlondeb, Bangor Road, Conwy LL32 8DU ☎ 01492 574283 🖷 01492 574040 ✉ bleddyn.evans@conwy.gov.uk

Building Control: Ms Paula Jones Development & Building Control Manager, Civic Offices, Colwyn Bay LL29 8AR ☎ 01492 575271 ✉ paula.jones@conwy.gov.uk

Catering Services: Mr Dafydd Williams Catering Manager, Government Buildings, Dinerth Road, Rhos-on-Sea, LL28 4UL ☎ 01492 575580 ✉ dafydd.aled.williams@conwy.gov.uk

Children / Youth Services: Ms Jane Williams Section Head - Conwy Youth Services, Bodlondeb, Bangor Road, Conwy LL32 8DU ☎ 01492 575051 ✉ jane.williams@conwy.gov.uk

Children / Youth Services: Ms Jenny Williams Strategic Director - Social Care & Education, Government Buildings, Dinerth Road, Rhos on Sea, Colwyn Bay LL28 4UL ☎ 01492 575687 🖷 01492 575687 ✉ jenny.williams@conwy.gov.uk

Civil Registration: Mrs Delyth Jones Head of Law & Governance, Bodlondeb, Bangor Road, Conwy LL32 8DU ☎ 01492 576075 ✉ delyth.e.jones@conwy.gov.uk

PR / Communications: Mrs Rachael Gill Marketing & Communications Manager, Bodlondeb, Bangor Road, Conwy LL32 8DU ☎ 01492 575941 ✉ rachael.gill@conwy.gov.uk

Community Planning: Ms Marianne Jackson Head of Community Development Services, Library Building, Mostyn Street, Llandudno LL30 2NG ☎ 01492 576314 ✉ marianne.jackson@conwy.gov.uk

Community Safety: Ms Sian Taylor Community Safety Manager, Civic Offices, Colwyn Bay LL29 8AR ☎ 01492 575190 ✉ sian.taylor@conwy.gov.uk

Computer Management: Mr Huw McKee Head of IT & Digital Transformation, Bodlondeb, Bangor Road, Conwy LL32 8DU ☎ 01492 576020 ✉ huw.mckee@conwy.gov.uk

Consumer Protection and Trading Standards: Mr John Donnelly Principal Licensing & Registration Officer, Civic Offices, Colwyn Bay LL29 8AR ☎ 01492 575197 ✉ john.donnelly@conwy.gov.uk

Contracts: Ms Diane Sandham Corporate Procurement & Contracts Manager, Bodlondeb, Bangor Road, Conwy LL32 8DU ☎ 01492 574117 ✉ diane.sandham@conwy.gov.uk

Economic Development: Mr Rob Dix Section Head: Business & Enterprise, 28 Wynnstay Road, Colwyn Bay LL29 8NB ☎ 01492 574506 ✉ rob.dix@conwy.gov.uk

Economic Development: Ms Marianne Jackson Head of Community Development Services, Library Building, Mostyn Street, Llandudno LL30 2NG ☎ 01492 576314 ✉ marianne.jackson@conwy.gov.uk

Education: Mr Richard Owen Head of Education Services, Government Buildings, Dinerth Road, Rhos on Sea, Colwyn Bay LL28 4UL ☎ 01492 575019 ✉ owen.richard@conwy.gov.uk

E-Government: Mrs Sarah Davies E-Government Manager, Bodlondeb, Bangor Road, Conwy LL32 8DU ☎ 01492 576290 ✉ sarah.davies@conwy.gov.uk

Electoral Registration: Mrs Sian Williams Democratic Services Manager, Bodlondeb, Bangor Road, Conwy LL32 8DU ☎ 01492 576062 ✉ sian.williams@conwy.gov.uk

Emergency Planning: Mr Jonathan Williams, Civil Contigencies Manager, Bodlondeb, Conwy LL32 8DU ☎ 01492 576099 ✉ jonathan.williams@conwy.gov.uk

Energy Management: Mr Neil Roberts Energy Manager, Mochdre Offices, Conwy Road, Mochdre, Colwyn Bay LL28 5AB ☎ 01492 574276 ✉ neil.derek.roberts@conwy.gov.uk

Environmental / Technical Services: Mr Geraint Edwards, Head of Environment, Roads & Facilities, Mochdre Offices, Conway Road, Mochdre, LL28 5AB ☎ 01492 575207 🖷 01492 575199 ✉ geraint.edwards@conwy.gov.uk

Environmental Health: Mr Nick Jones Environment Enforcement Manager, Civic Offices, Colwyn Bay LL29 8AR ☎ 01492 575281 ✉ nick.jones@conwy.gov.uk

Estates, Property & Valuation: Mr Bleddyn Evans, County Valuer & Asset Manager, Town Hall, Lloyd Street, Llandudno LL30 2UP ☎ 01492 574283 🖷 01492 574040 ✉ bleddyn.evans@conwy.gov.uk

European Liaison: Mrs Barbara Burchell Principal European Project Development Officer, Library Building, Mostyn Street, Llandudno LL30 2RP ☎ 01492 576011 ✉ barbara.burchell@conwy.gov.uk

European Liaison: Mr Rob Dix Section Head: Business & Enterprise, 28 Wynnstay Road, Colwyn Bay LL29 8NB ☎ 01492 574506 ✉ rob.dix@conwy.gov.uk

Events Manager: Mrs Rachael Gill Marketing & Communications Manager, Bodlondeb, Bangor Road, Conwy LL32 8DU ☎ 01492 575941 ✉ rachael.gill@conwy.gov.uk

Finance: Mr Andrew Kirkham, Strategic Director - Finance & Efficiencies, Bodlondeb, Conwy LL32 8DU ☎ 01492 576170 ✉ andrew.kirkham@conwy.gov.uk

Fleet Management: Mr Andrew Dawson Transport Manager, Mochdre Offices, Conway Road, Mochdre, Colwyn Bay LL28 5AB ☎ 01492 575966 ✉ andrew.dawson2@conwy.gov.uk

Grounds Maintenance: Mr Lyn Davies, Open Spaces Manager, Mochdre Offices, Conway Road, Mochdre, Colwyn Bay LL28 5AB ☎ 01492 575299 ✉ lyn.davies@conwy.gov.uk

Health and Safety: Mr Richard Evans Corporate Occupational Health & Safety Manager, Bron y Nant, Dinerth Road, Rhos on Sea, Colwyn Bay LL28 4YL ☎ 01492 576090 ✉ richard.h.evans@conwy.gov.uk

Highways: Mr Andrew Wilkinson Head of Neighbourhood Services, Mochdre Offices, Conway Road, Mochdre, Colwyn Bay LL28 5AB ☎ 01492 577619 ✉ andrew.j.wilkinson@conwy.gov.uk

Home Energy Conservation: Mrs Sam Parry Housing Services Manager, Civic Offices, Colwyn Bay LL29 8AR ☎ 01492 574224 ✉ sam.parry@conwy.gov.uk

Housing: Mrs Sam Parry Housing Services Manager, Civic Offices, Colwyn Bay LL29 8AR ☎ 01492 574224 ✉ sam.parry@conwy.gov.uk

Legal: Mrs Delyth Jones Head of Law & Governance, Bodlondeb, Bangor Road, Conwy LL32 8DU ☎ 01492 576075 ✉ delyth.e.jones@conwy.gov.uk

Leisure and Cultural Services: Ms Marianne Jackson Head of Community Development Services, Library Building, Mostyn Street, Llandudno LL30 2NG ☎ 01492 576314 ✉ marianne.jackson@conwy.gov.uk

Licensing: Mr John Donnelly Principal Licensing & Registration Officer, Civic Offices, Colwyn Bay LL29 8AR ☎ 01492 575197 ✉ john.donnelly@conwy.gov.uk

Lifelong Learning: Mr Richard Owen Head of Education Services, Government Buildings, Dinerth Road, Rhos on Sea, Colwyn Bay LL28 4UL ☎ 01492 575019 ✉ owen.richard@conwy.gov.uk

Lighting: Mr Victor Turner Traffic & Network Manager, The Heath, Penmaenmawr Road, Llanfairfechan, LL33 0PF ☎ 01492 575402 ✉ victor.turner@conwy.gov.uk

Member Services: Mrs Sian Williams Democratic Services Manager, Bodlondeb, Bangor Road, Conwy LL32 8DU ☎ 01492 576062 ✉ sian.williams@conwy.gov.uk

Parking: Mr Victor Turner Traffic & Network Manager, The Heath, Penmaenmawr Road, Llanfairfechan, LL33 0PF ☎ 01492 575402 ✉ victor.turner@conwy.gov.uk

Partnerships: Mrs Gill Hayes Corporate Partnerships Manager, Bodlondeb, Bangor Road, Conwy LL32 8DU ☎ 01492 576239 ✉ gill.hayes@conwy.gov.uk

Personnel / HR: Mr Phillip Davies, Head of Corporate Personnel Services, Bodlondeb, Bangor Road, Conwy LL32 8DU ☎ 01492 576124 🖷 01492 576135 ✉ phillip.davies@conwy.gov.uk

Planning: Ms Paula Jones Development & Building Control Manager, Civic Offices, Colwyn Bay LL29 8AR ☎ 01492 575271 ✉ paula.jones@conwy.gov.uk

Procurement: Mr Mike Halstead, Head of Audit & Procurement, Bodlondeb, Bangor Road, Conwy LL32 8DU ☎ 01492 574000 🖷 01492 592114 ✉ mike.halstead@conwy.gov.uk

Public Libraries: Ms Ann Lloyd Williams Section Head: Rural Community Development, Culture & Information, Library Building, Mostyn Street, Llandudno LL30 2NG ☎ 01492 575571 ✉ ann.lloyd.williams@conwy.gov.uk

Recycling & Waste Minimisation: Mr Jon Eastwood Waste Manager, Mochdre Offices, Conway Road, Mochdre, Colwyn Bay LL28 5AB ☎ 01492 575127 ✉ jon.eastwood@conwy.gov.uk

Recycling & Waste Minimisation: Mr Andrew Wilkinson Head of Neighbourhood Services, Mochdre Offices, Conway Road, Mochdre, Colwyn Bay LL28 5AB ☎ 01492 577619 ✉ andrew.j.wilkinson@conwy.gov.uk

Regeneration: Mr Rob Dix Section Head: Business & Enterprise, 28 Wynnstay Road, Colwyn Bay LL29 8NB ☎ 01492 574506 ✉ rob.dix@conwy.gov.uk

Regeneration: Ms Marianne Jackson Head of Community Development Services, Library Building, Mostyn Street, Llandudno LL30 2NG ☎ 01492 576314 ✉ marianne.jackson@conwy.gov.uk

Road Safety: Mr Victor Turner Traffic & Network Manager, The Heath, Penmaenmawr Road, Llanfairfechan, LL33 0PF ☎ 01492 575402 ✉ victor.turner@conwy.gov.uk

Social Services: Ms Jenny Williams Strategic Director - Social Care & Education, Government Buildings, Dinerth Road, Rhos on Sea, Colwyn Bay LL28 4UL ☎ 01492 575687 🖷 01492 575687 ✉ jenny.williams@conwy.gov.uk

CONWY

Social Services (Adult): Ms Claire Lister Head of Integrated Adult & Community Services, Government Buildings, Dinerth Road, Rhos-on-Sea, Conwy LL28 4UL ☎ 01492 575378 ✉ claire.lister@conwy.gov.uk

Social Services (Children): Ms Kate Devonport Head of Service - Children, Families & Safeguarding, Civic Offices, Annexe, , Colwyn Bay LL29 8AR ☎ 01492 575166 ✉ kate.devonport@conwy.gov.uk

Staff Training: Mr Phillip Davies, Head of Corporate Personnel Services, Bodlondeb, Bangor Road, Conwy LL32 8DU ☎ 01492 576124 🖷 01492 576135 ✉ phillip.davies@conwy.gov.uk

Street Scene: Mr Lyn Davies, Open Spaces Manager, Mochdre Offices, Conway Road, Mochdre, Colwyn Bay LL28 5AB ☎ 01492 575299 ✉ lyn.davies@conwy.gov.uk

Sustainable Communities: Ms Marianne Jackson Head of Community Development Services, Library Building, Mostyn Street, Llandudno LL30 2NG ☎ 01492 576314 ✉ marianne.jackson@conwy.gov.uk

Sustainable Development: Ms Marianne Jackson Head of Community Development Services, Library Building, Mostyn Street, Llandudno LL30 2NG ☎ 01492 576314 ✉ marianne.jackson@conwy.gov.uk

Tourism: Ms Marianne Jackson Head of Community Development Services, Library Building, Mostyn Street, Llandudno LL30 2NG ☎ 01492 576314 ✉ marianne.jackson@conwy.gov.uk

Town Centre: Ms Marianne Jackson Head of Community Development Services, Library Building, Mostyn Street, Llandudno LL30 2NG ☎ 01492 576314 ✉ marianne.jackson@conwy.gov.uk

Traffic Management: Mr Victor Turner Traffic & Network Manager, The Heath, Penmaenmawr Road, Llanfairfechan, LL33 0PF ☎ 01492 575402 ✉ victor.turner@conwy.gov.uk

Transport: Mr Andrew Dawson Transport Manager, Mochdre Offices, Conway Road, Mochdre, Colwyn Bay LL28 5AB ☎ 01492 575966 ✉ andrew.dawson2@conwy.gov.uk

Transport Planner: Mr Gethin George Integrated Transport (Policy) Officer, Library Building, Mostyn Street, Llandudno LL30 2NG ☎ 01492 575562 ✉ gethin.george@conwy.gov.uk

Waste Collection and Disposal: Mr Jon Eastwood Waste Manager, Mochdre Offices, Conway Road, Mochdre, Colwyn Bay LL28 5AB ☎ 01492 575127 ✉ jon.eastwood@conwy.gov.uk

Waste Collection and Disposal: Mr Andrew Wilkinson Head of Neighbourhood Services, Mochdre Offices, Conway Road, Mochdre, Colwyn Bay LL28 5AB ☎ 01492 577619 ✉ andrew.j.wilkinson@conwy.gov.uk

Waste Management: Mr Jon Eastwood Waste Manager, Mochdre Offices, Conway Road, Mochdre, Colwyn Bay LL28 5AB ☎ 01492 575127 ✉ jon.eastwood@conwy.gov.uk

Waste Management: Mr Andrew Wilkinson Head of Neighbourhood Services, Mochdre Offices, Conway Road, Mochdre, Colwyn Bay LL28 5AB ☎ 01492 577619 ✉ andrew.j.wilkinson@conwy.gov.uk

Children's Play Areas: Mr Lyn Davies, Open Spaces Manager, Mochdre Offices, Conway Road, Mochdre, Colwyn Bay LL28 5AB ☎ 01492 575299 ✉ lyn.davies@conwy.gov.uk

COUNCILLORS

***Chair* Roberts**, Elizabeth (PC - Betws Y Coed)
cllr.liz.roberts@conwy.gov.uk

***Vice-Chair* Cossey**, Brian (LD - Colwyn)
cllr.brian.cossey@conwy.gov.uk

***Leader of the Council* Roberts**, Dilwyn (PC - Llangernyw)
cllr.dilwyn.roberts@conwy.gov.uk

***Deputy Leader of the Council* Hughes**, Ronnie (LAB - Tudno)
cllr.ronnie.hughes@conwy.gov.uk

Allardice, Sarah Louise (LAB - Conwy)
cllr.sara.allardice@conwy.gov.uk

Anderson, Stuart (IND - Bae Cinmel / Kinmel Bay)
cllr.dr.stuart.anderson@conwy.gov.uk

Bradfield, Frank (CON - Craig Y Don)
cllr.frank.bradfield@conwy.gov.uk

Carlisle, Cheryl (CON - Colwyn)
cllr.cheryl.carlisle@conwy.gov.uk

Cater, Christopher (IND - Penrhyn)
cllr.christopher.cater@conwy.gov.uk

Cotton, Samantha (CON - Deganwy)
cllr.samantha.cotton@conwy.gov.uk

Cowans, Dave (IND - Eirias)
cllr.dave.cowans@conwy.gov.uk

Darwin, William (IND - Bae Cinmel / Kinmel Bay)
cllr.bill.darwin@conwy.gov.uk

Doyle, Mary (CON - Rhiw)
cllr.mary.doyle@conwy.gov.uk

Edwards, Goronwy (IND - Caerhun)
cllr.goronwy.edwards@conwy.gov.uk

Edwards, Philip (PC - Llandrillo-yn-Rhos)
cllr.phil.edwards@conwy.gov.uk

Eeles, Keith (IND - Llanddulas)
cllr.keith.eeles@conwy.gov.uk

Evans, Philip (IND - Tudno)
cllr.philip.evans@conwy.gov.uk

Fallon, Julie (CON - Deganwy)
cllr.julie.fallon@conwy.gov.uk

Groom, Linda (IND - Penrhyn)
cllr.linda.groom@conwy.gov.uk

Haworth, Janet (CON - Gogarth)
cllr.janet.haworth@conwy.gov.uk

Hinchliff, Andrew (LAB - Bryn)
cllr.andrew.hinchliff@conwy.gov.uk

Hold, Jobi (LAB - Mostyn)
cllr.jobi.hold@conwy.gov.uk

Hughes, Meirion (PC - Pensarn)
cllr.meirion.hughes@conwy.gov.uk

Hughes, Chris (LAB - Glyn)
cllr.chris.hughes@conwy.gov.uk

Jenkins, Ian (PC - Gower)
cllr.ian.jenkins@conwy.gov.uk

Jones, Gareth (PC - Craig Y Don)
cllr.gareth.jones@conwy.gov.uk

Jones, Wyn Ellis (PC - Uwch Conwy)
cyng.wyn.ellis.jones@conwy.gov.uk

Jones, Ray (LAB - Pandy)
cllr.ray.jones@conwy.gov.uk

Khan, Abdul (PC - Glyn)
cllr.abdul.khan@conwy.gov.uk

Knightly, Laura (CON - Tywyn)
cllr.laura.knightly@conwy.gov.uk

Lewis, Peter (IND - Uwchaled)
cllr.peter.lewis@conwy.gov.uk

Lloyd, Ifor (IND - Betws-Yn-Rhos)
cllr.ifor.glyn.lloyd@conwy.gov.uk

Lloyd-Williams, Susan (PC - Llansannan)
cllr.sue.lloyd-williams@conwy.gov.uk

Lyon, Margaret (IND - Gogarth)
cllr.margaret.lyon@conwy.gov.uk

MacLennan, John (CON - Pentre Mawr)
cllr.john.maclennan@conwy.gov.uk

MacRae, Delyth (PC - Gele)
cllr.delyth.macrae@conwy.gov.uk

McCaffrey, Anne (IND - Capelulo)
cllr.anne.mccaffrey@conwy.gov.uk

Miles, Dewi (IND - Mostyn)
cllr.dewi.miles@conwy.gov.uk

Milne, Donald (CON - Llandrillo-yn-Rhos)
cllr.donald.milne@conwy.gov.uk

Parry, Edgar (IND - Crwst)
cllr.edgar.parry@conwy.gov.uk

Parry, Roger (CON - Llandrillo-yn-Rhos)
cllr.roger.parry@conwy.gov.uk

Priestley, Michael (LD - Marl)
cllr.michael.priestley@conwy.gov.uk

Rayner, Mike (PC - Eglwysbach)
cllr.mike.rayner@conwy.gov.uk

Rees, Graham (IND - Llansanffraid)
cllr.graham.rees@conwy.gov.uk

Roberts, Dave (CON - Llandrillo-yn-Rhos)
cllr.david.m.roberts@conwy.gov.uk

Roberts, John (LD - Rhiw)
cllr.john.roberts@conwy.gov.uk

Rogers-Jones, Hilary (PC - Trefriw)
cllr.hilary.rogers-jones@conwy.gov.uk

Rowlands, Samuel (CON - Pentre Mawr)
cllr.sam.rowlands@conwy.gov.uk

Rowlands, Tim (CON - Gele)
cllr.tim.rowlands@conwy.gov.uk

Shotter, Susan (LD - Marl)
cllr.susan.shotter@conwy.gov.uk

Smith, Deion (LAB - Llysfaen)
cllr.deion.smith@conwy.gov.uk

Smith, Nigel (IND - Bae Cinmel / Kinmel Bay)
cllr.nigel.smith@conwy.gov.uk

Squire, Bob (IND - Eirias)
cllr.bob.squire@conwy.gov.uk

Stevens, Ken (LAB - Pant Yr Afon / Penmaenan)
cllr.ken.stevens@conwy.gov.uk

Stott, Trevor (LD - Rhiw)
cllr.trevor.stott@conwy.gov.uk

Stubbs, Rick (LAB - Abergele Pensarn)
cllr.rick.stubbs@conwy.gov.uk

Tansley, Adrian (LAB - Mochdre)
cllr.adrian.tansley@conwy.gov.uk

Vaughan, Joan (IND - Conwy)
cllr.joan.vaughan@conwy.gov.uk

Wood, Andrew (IND - Gele)
cllr.andrew.wood@conwy.gov.uk

POLITICAL COMPOSITION

IND: 19, CON: 13, PC: 12, LAB: 10, LD: 5

COMMITTEE CHAIRS

Audit: Mr Samuel Rowlands

Licensing: Mr Ken Stevens

Planning: Mr Christopher Cater

Copeland D

Copeland Borough Council, The Copeland Centre, Catherine Street, Whitehaven CA28 7SJ
☎ 0845 054 8600 ✉ info@copelandbc.gov.uk
🖳 www.copelandbc.gov.uk

FACTS AND FIGURES

Parliamentary Constituencies: Copeland
EU Constituencies: North West
Election Frequency: Elections are of whole council

PRINCIPAL OFFICERS

Chief Executive: Mr Paul Walker Chief Executive, The Copeland Centre, Catherine Street, Whitehaven CA28 7SJ ☎ 01946 598324 ✉ paul.walker@copeland.gov.uk

Senior Management: Mrs Pat Graham Director of Economic Growth, The Copeland Centre, Catherine Street, Whitehaven CA28 7SJ ☎ 01946 598440 ✉ pat.graham@copeland.gov.uk

Senior Management: Mr Steve Smith Interim Project Manager, The Copeland Centre, Catherine Street, Whitehaven CA28 7SJ ☎ 01946 598471 ✉ steve.smith@copeland.gov.uk

Building Control: Mrs Pat Graham Director of Economic Growth, The Copeland Centre, Catherine Street, Whitehaven CA28 7SJ ☎ 01946 598440 ✉ pat.graham@copeland.gov.uk

COPELAND

Building Control: Mr John Groves, Head of Nuclear, Energy & Planning, The Copeland Centre, Catherine Street, Whitehaven CA28 7SJ ☎ 01946 598416 ✉ john.groves@copeland.gov.uk

Building Control: Mr Mark Key Building Control Manager, The Copeland Centre, Catherine Street, Whitehaven CA28 7SJ ☎ 01946 598407 ✉ mark.key@copeland.gov.uk

Computer Management: Mr Martin Stroud ICT Manager, The Copeland Centre, Catherine Street, Whitehaven CA28 7SJ ☎ 01946 598481 ✉ martin.stroud@copeland.gov.uk

Consumer Protection and Trading Standards: Ms Jackie O'Reilly Environmental Health Manager, The Copeland Centre, Catherine Street, Whitehaven CA28 7SJ ☎ 01946 598335 🖷 01946 598304 ✉ jackie.oreilly@copeland.gov.uk

Contracts: Mr Martyn Morton Property Programmes Manager, The Copeland Centre, Catherine Street, Whitehaven CA28 7SJ ☎ 01946 598495

Corporate Services: Mrs Fiona Rooney Interim Director of Resources & Strategic Commissioning, The Copeland Centre, Catherine Street, Whitehaven CA28 7SJ ☎ 01946 598457 ✉ fiona.rooney@copeland.gov.uk

Customer Service: Mrs Julie Betteridge Director of Customer & Community Services, The Copeland Centre, Catherine Street, Whitehaven CA28 7SJ ☎ 01946 598415 ✉ julie.betteridge@copeland.gov.uk

Economic Development: Mrs Pat Graham Director of Economic Growth, The Copeland Centre, Catherine Street, Whitehaven CA28 7SJ ☎ 01946 598440 ✉ pat.graham@copeland.gov.uk

Economic Development: Mrs Sarah Mitchell Economic & Community Regeneration Manager, The Copeland Centre, Catherine Street, Whitehaven CA28 7SJ ☎ 01946 598438

Electoral Registration: Miss Stephanie Shaw, Elections Manager, The Copeland Centre, Catherine Street, Whitehaven CA28 7SJ ☎ 01946 598533 🖷 01946 598311 ✉ stephanie.shaw@copeland.gov.uk

Emergency Planning: Ms Jackie O'Reilly Environmental Health Manager, The Copeland Centre, Catherine Street, Whitehaven CA28 7SJ ☎ 01946 598335 🖷 01946 598304 ✉ jackie.oreilly@copeland.gov.uk

Energy Management: Mr John Groves, Head of Nuclear, Energy & Planning, The Copeland Centre, Catherine Street, Whitehaven CA28 7SJ ☎ 01946 598416 ✉ john.groves@copeland.gov.uk

Environmental Health: Mrs Janice Carrol Interim Head of Copeland Services, Whitehaven Commerical Park, Moresby Parks, Whitehaven CA28 8YD ☎ 01946 593024

Environmental Health: Mrs Pat Graham Director of Economic Growth, The Copeland Centre, Catherine Street, Whitehaven CA28 7SJ ☎ 01946 598440 ✉ pat.graham@copeland.gov.uk

Environmental Health: Ms Jackie O'Reilly Environmental Health Manager, The Copeland Centre, Catherine Street, Whitehaven CA28 7SJ ☎ 01946 598335 🖷 01946 598304 ✉ joreilly@copelandbc.gov.uk

Finance: Ms Angela Brown Interim Finance Manager & S151 Officer, The Copeland Centre, Catherine Street, Whitehaven CA28 7SJ ☎ 01946 598452 ✉ angela.brown@copeland.gov.uk

Fleet Management: Mrs Janice Carrol Interim Head of Copeland Services, Whitehaven Commerical Park, Moresby Parks, Whitehaven CA28 8YD ☎ 01946 593024

Grounds Maintenance: Mr John Davis Parks Manager, Whitehaven Commercial Park, Moresby Parks, Whitehaven CA28 8YD ☎ 02946 593022 ✉ john.davis@copeland.gov.uk

Housing: Mrs Julie Betteridge Director of Customer & Community Services, The Copeland Centre, Catherine Street, Whitehaven CA28 7SJ ☎ 01946 598415 ✉ julie.betteridge@copeland.gov.uk

Housing: Mrs Debbie Cochrane Housing Services Manager, The Copeland Centre, Catherine Street, Whitehaven CA28 7SJ ☎ 01946 598427 ✉

Local Area Agreement: Mrs Julie Betteridge Director of Customer & Community Services, The Copeland Centre, Catherine Street, Whitehaven CA28 7SJ ☎ 01946 598415 ✉ julie.betteridge@copeland.gov.uk

Legal: Mr Clinton Boyce Legal Services Manager, The Copeland Centre, Catherine Street, Whitehaven CA28 7SJ ☎ 01946 598516 ✉ clinton.boyce@copeland.gov.uk

Member Services: Mrs Lindsay Tomlinson Democratic Services Manager, The Copeland Centre, Catherine Street, Whitehaven CA28 7SJ ☎ 01946 598526 ✉ lindsay.tomlinson@copeland.gov.uk

Parking: Mrs Janice Carrol Interim Head of Copeland Services, Whitehaven Commerical Park, Moresby Parks, Whitehaven CA28 8YD ☎ 01946 593024

Partnerships: Mrs Julie Betteridge Director of Customer & Community Services, The Copeland Centre, Catherine Street, Whitehaven CA28 7SJ ☎ 01946 598415 ✉ julie.betteridge@copeland.gov.uk

Planning: Mrs Pat Graham Director of Economic Growth, The Copeland Centre, Catherine Street, Whitehaven CA28 7SJ ☎ 01946 598440 ✉ pat.graham@copeland.gov.uk

Planning: Mr John Groves, Head of Nuclear, Energy & Planning, The Copeland Centre, Catherine Street, Whitehaven CA28 7SJ ☎ 01946 598416 ✉ john.groves@copeland.gov.uk

Planning: Mr Nick Hayhurst Senior Planner - Development Manager, The Copeland Centre, Catherine Street, Whitehaven CA28 7SJ ☎ 01946 598331 ✉ nick.hayhurst@copeland.gov.uk

Planning: Mr Chris Hoban Senior Planner - Planning Policy, The Copeland Centre, Catherine Street, Whitehaven CA28 7SJ ☎ 01946 598439 ✉ chris.hoban@copeland.gov.uk

Recycling & Waste Minimisation: Ms Janice Carrol, Waste Services Manager, Whitehaven Commercial Park, Moresby Parks, Whitehaven CA28 8YD ☎ 01946 852915 🖷 01946 852965 jcarrol@copelandbc.gov.uk

Regeneration: Mrs Julie Betteridge Director of Customer & Community Services, The Copeland Centre, Catherine Street, Whitehaven CA28 7SJ ☎ 01946 598415 julie.betteridge@copeland.gov.uk

Regeneration: Mrs Sarah Mitchell Economic & Community Regeneration Manager, The Copeland Centre, Catherine Street, Whitehaven CA28 7SJ ☎ 01946 598438

Sustainable Communities: Mrs Julie Betteridge Director of Customer & Community Services, The Copeland Centre, Catherine Street, Whitehaven CA28 7SJ ☎ 01946 598415 julie.betteridge@copeland.gov.uk

Sustainable Development: Mrs Pat Graham Director of Economic Growth, The Copeland Centre, Catherine Street, Whitehaven CA28 7SJ ☎ 01946 598440 pat.graham@copeland.gov.uk

Waste Collection and Disposal: Ms Janice Carrol, Waste Services Manager, Whitehaven Commercial Park, Moresby Parks, Whitehaven CA28 8YD ☎ 01946 852915 🖷 01946 852965 jcarrol@copelandbc.gov.uk

Waste Management: Mrs Janice Carrol Interim Head of Copeland Services, Whitehaven Commerical Park, Moresby Parks, Whitehaven CA28 8YD ☎ 01946 593024

COUNCILLORS

***Mayor* Starkie**, Mike (IND - No Ward)
elected.mayor@copeland.gov.uk

***Deputy Chair* Hogg**, Lena (LAB - Egremont South)
lena.hogg@copeland.gov.uk

Arrighi, Carla (IND - Harbour)
carla.arrighi@copeland.gov.uk

Banks, David (LAB - Cleator Moor South)
david.banks@copeland.gov.uk

Barbour, Martin (CON - Moresby)

Bowman, Jackie (LAB - Distington)
jackie.bowman@copeland.gov.uk

Bowman, John (LAB - Distington)
john.bowman@copeland.gov.uk

Bradshaw, Anne (LAB - Bransty)
ann.bradshaw@copland.gov.uk

Branney, Hugh (LAB - Cleator Moor North)
hugh.branney@copeland.gov.uk

Burness, Denise (LAB - Holburn Hill)

Burns, John (LAB - Egremont North)
john.burns@copeland.gov.uk

Clarkson, Yvonne (CON - Beckermet)
yvonne.clarkson@copeland.gov.uk

Cole, Raymond (CON - Newtown)

Connolly, Peter (LAB - Frizington)
peter.connnolly@copeland.gov.uk

Dirom, John (CON - Ennerdale)
john.dirom@copeland.gov.uk

Everett, Gwynneth (LAB - Frizington)
gwynneth.everett@copeland.gov.uk

Ferguson, Neil (LAB - Egremont South)
neil.ferguson@copeland.gov.uk

Forster, Allan (LAB - Hensingham)
norman.williams@copeland.gov.uk

Forster, Jeanette (LAB - Hensingham)
jeanette.forster@copeland.gov.uk

Gill, Ray (LAB - Hensingham)
ray.gill@copeland.gov.uk

Gleaves, Frederick (CON - Holborn Hill)
fred.gleaves@copeland.gov.uk

Guest, Michael (IND - Kells)
michael.guest@copeland.gov.uk

Hill, Ian (CON - St Bees)
ian.hill@copeland.gov.uk

Hitchen, Keith (CON - Bootle)
keith.hitchen@copeland.gov.uk

Holliday, Allan (LAB - Kells)
allan.holliday@copeland.gov.uk

Holliday, Allan (LAB - Mirehouse)
allan.holliday@copeland.gov.uk

Hully, Joan (LAB - Cleator Moor North)
membersservices@copeland.gov.uk

Jacob, Alan (CON - Gosforth)
alan.jacob@copeland.gov.uk

Jones-Bulman, Linda (LAB - Cleator Moor North)
linda.jones-bulman@copland.gov.uk

Kane, John (LAB - Hillcrest)
john.kane@copeland.gov.uk

Kelly, Bob (LAB - Newtown)
bob.kelly@copeland.gov.uk

Kirkbride, William (LAB - Harbour)

Lewthwaite, Jean (CON - Egremont North)
jean.lewthwaite@copeland.gov.uk

Maulding, Charles (IND - Harbour)
charles.maulding@copeland.gov.uk

McVeigh, Michael (LAB - Egremont South)
micheal.mcveigh@copeland.gov.uk

Meteer, Sam (IND - Beckermet)
simon.meteer@copeland.gov.uk

Moore, David (CON - Seascale)
david.moore@copeland.gov.uk

Norwood, Alistair (CON - Hillcrest)
alistair.norwood@copeland.gov.uk

O'Kane, Brian (CON - Bransty)
brian.okane@copland.gov.uk

Pollen, Sam (LAB - Egremont North)
sam.pollen@copeland.gov.uk

Pratt, Andy (CON - Seascale)
andy.pratt@copeland.gov.uk

COPELAND

Reay, Christopher (LAB - Mirehouse)
christopher.reay@copeland.gov.uk

Riley, David (LAB - Cleator Moor South)
david.riley@copeland.gov.uk

Roberts, Graham (CON - Bransty)
graham.roberts@copeland.gov.uk

Scurrah, Gilbert (CON - Millom Without)
membersservices@copeland.gov.uk

Stephenson, Peter (LAB - Sandwith)
peter.stephenson@copeland.gov.uk

Sunderland, Graham (IND - Arlecdon)
graham.sunderland@copeland.gov.uk

Troughton, Gillian (LAB - Distington)
gillian.troughton@copeland.gov.uk

Tyson, Peter (LAB - Sandwith)
peter.tyson@copeland.gov.uk

Whalley, Paul (LAB - Mirehouse)
paul.whalley@copeland.gov.uk

Wilson, Douglas (CON - Haverigg)
douglas.wilson@copeland.gov.uk

Wilson, Fee (CON - Newtown)
felicity.wilson@copeland.gov.uk

POLITICAL COMPOSITION
LAB: 29, CON: 17, IND: 6

COMMITTEE CHAIRS

Planning: Mr Michael McVeigh

Training & Development: Mr Keith Hitchen

Corby D

Corby Borough Council, Grosvenor House, George Street, Corby NN17 1QB
☎ 01536 464000 🖷 01536 400200 🖳 www.corby.gov.uk

FACTS AND FIGURES
Parliamentary Constituencies: Corby
EU Constituencies: East Midlands
Election Frequency: Every 4 years

PRINCIPAL OFFICERS

Chief Executive: Mr Norman Stronach, Chief Executive, The Cube, Parkland Gateway, George Street, Corby NN17 1QG ☎ 01536 464156 ✉ norman.stronach@corby.gov.uk

Assistant Chief Executive: Mrs Angela Warburton, Assistant Chief Executive, Deene House, New Post Office Square, Corby NN17 1GD ☎ 01536 464003 ✉ angela.warburton@corby.gov.uk

Senior Management: Mr Adrian Sibley Director of Corporate Services, Deene House, New Post Office Square, Corby NN17 1GD ☎ 01536 464125 ✉ adrian.sibley@corby.gov.uk

Senior Management: Mr Iain Smith, Head of Service Planning & Environmental Quality, Deene House, New Post Office Square, Corby NN17 1GD ☎ 01536 464061 ✉ iain.smith@corby.gov.uk

Senior Management: Mr Chris Stephenson, Head of Service for Culture & Leisure, Deene House, New Post Office Square, Corby NN17 1GD ☎ 01536 464041 ✉ chris.stephenson@corby.gov.uk

Senior Management: Mr Jonathan Waterworth Interim Head of Service CB Property Services, Deene House, New Post Office Square, Corby NN17 1GD ☎ 01536 464686 ✉ jonathan.waterworth@corby.gov.uk

Access Officer / Social Services (Disability): Mr Colin Cox Principal Building Control Officer, Deene House, New Post Office Square, Corby NN17 1GD ☎ 01536 464172 ✉ colin.cox@corby.gov.uk

Architect, Building / Property Services: Mr Jonathan Waterworth Interim Head of Service CB Property Services, Deene House, New Post Office Square, Corby NN17 1GD ☎ 01536 464686 ✉ jonathan.waterworth@corby.gov.uk

Building Control: Mr Colin Cox Principal Building Control Officer, Deene House, New Post Office Square, Corby NN17 1GD ☎ 01536 464172 ✉ colin.cox@corby.gov.uk

PR / Communications: Ms Kimberley Buzzard Communications Officer, The Cube, Parklands Gateway, George Street, Corby NN17 1QG ☎ 01536 464020 ✉ kimberley.buzzard@corby.gov.uk

Community Safety: Ms Antonia Malpas Principal Community Safety Officer, Deene House, New Post Office Square, Corby NN17 1GD ☎ 01536 464647 ✉ antonia.malpas@corby.gov.uk

Community Safety: Mr Tom Todkill Head of CCTV Control Room, Grosvenor House, George Street, Corby NN17 1QB ☎ 01536 464000 ✉ thomas.todkill@corby.gov.uk

Computer Management: Mr Will McAlindon ICT Manager, Deene House, New Post Office Square, Corby NN17 1GD ☎ 01536 464089 ✉ will.mcalindon@corby.gov.uk

Contracts: Mr Chris Everett Procurement Officer, Deene House, New Post Office Square, Corby NN17 1GD ☎ 01536 464685 ✉ chris.everett@corby.gov.uk

Corporate Services: Mr Adrian Sibley Director of Corporate Services, Deene House, New Post Office Square, Corby NN17 1GD ☎ 01536 464125 ✉ adrian.sibley@corby.gov.uk

Corporate Services: Mr Norman Stronach, Chief Executive, The Cube, Parklands Gateway, George Street, Corby NN17 1QG ☎ 01536 464156 ✉ norman.stronach@corby.gov.uk

Customer Service: Mr Adrian Sibley Director of Corporate Services, Deene House, New Post Office Square, Corby NN17 1GD ☎ 01536 464125 ✉ adrian.sibley@corby.gov.uk

Direct Labour: Mr Iain Smith, Head of Service Planning & Environmental Quality, Deene House, New Post Office Square, Corby NN17 1GD ☎ 01536 464061 ✉ iain.smith@corby.gov.uk

Electoral Registration: Mr Aaron O'Sullivan Electoral Services Officer, The Cube, Parkland Gateway, George Street, Corby NN17 1QG ☎ 01536 464012 ✉ aaron.o'sullivan@corby.gov.uk

Environmental / Technical Services: Mr Iain Smith, Head of Service Planning & Environmental Quality, Deene House, New Post Office Square, Corby NN17 1GD ☎ 01536 464061 ✉ iain.smith@corby.gov.uk

Environmental Health: Mr Iain Smith, Head of Service Planning & Environmental Quality, Deene House, New Post Office Square, Corby NN17 1GD ☎ 01536 464061 ✉ iain.smith@corby.gov.uk

Estates, Property & Valuation: Mr Jonathan Waterworth Interim Head of Service CB Property Services, The Cube, Parklands Gateway, George Street, Corby NN17 1QG ☎ 01536 464686 ✉ jonathan.waterworth@corby.gov.uk

Facilities: Mr Jonathan Waterworth Interim Head of Service CB Property Services, The Cube, Parklands Gateway, George Street, Corby NN17 1QG ☎ 01536 464686 ✉ jonathan.waterworth@corby.gov.uk

Finance: Ms Claire Edwards Financial Services Manager, Deene House, New Post Office Square, Corby NN17 1GD ☎ 01536 464101 ✉ claire.edwards@corby.gov.uk

Health and Safety: Mr Iain Smith, Head of Service Planning & Environmental Quality, Deene House, New Post Office Square, Corby NN17 1GD ☎ 01536 464061 ✉ iain.smith@corby.gov.uk

Housing: Mrs Angela Warburton, Assistant Chief Executive, Deene House, New Post Office Square, Corby NN17 1GD ☎ 01536 464003 ✉ angela.warburton@corby.gov.uk

Housing Maintenance: Mr Iain Smith, Head of Service Planning & Environmental Quality, Deene House, New Post Office Square, Corby NN17 1GD ☎ 01536 464061 ✉ iain.smith@corby.gov.uk

Legal: Mr Nigel Channer Legal Services Manager, Deene House, New Post Office Square, Corby NN17 1GD ☎ 01536 464679 ✉ nigel.channer@corby.gov.uk

Leisure and Cultural Services: Mr Chris Stephenson, Head of Service for Culture & Leisure, Deene House, New Post Office Square, Corby NN17 1GD ☎ 01536 464041 ✉ chris.stephenson@corby.gov.uk

Licensing: Mr Iain Smith, Head of Service Planning & Environmental Quality, Deene House, New Post Office Square, Corby NN17 1GD ☎ 01536 464061 ✉ iain.smith@corby.gov.uk

Lottery Funding, Charity and Voluntary: Mr Chris Stephenson, Head of Service for Culture & Leisure, Deene House, New Post Office Square, Corby NN17 1GD ☎ 01536 464041 ✉ chris.stephenson@corby.gov.uk

Member Services: Mr Paul Goult, Democratic Services Manager & Monitoring Officer, The Cube, Parkland Gateway, George Street, Corby NN17 1QG ☎ 01536 464013 ✉ paul.goult@corby.gov.uk

Personnel / HR: Mrs Stella Jinks Human Resources Manager, Deene House, New Post Office Square, Corby NN17 1GD ☎ 01536 464032 ✉ stella.jinks@corby.gov.uk

Planning: Mr Rob Temperley Principal Planning Officer, Deene House, New Post Office Square, Corby NN17 1GD ☎ 01536 464161 ✉ rob.temperley@corby.gov.uk

Procurement: Mr Chris Everett Procurement Officer, Deene House, New Post Office Square, Corby NN17 1GD ☎ 01536 464685 ✉ chris.everett@corby.gov.uk

Regeneration: Mr Norman Stronach, Chief Executive, The Cube, Parklands Gateway, Corby NN17 1QB ☎ 01536 464156 ✉ norman.stronach@corby.gov.uk

Staff Training: Mrs Stella Jinks Human Resources Manager, Deene House, New Post Office Square, Corby NN17 1GD ☎ 01536 464032 ✉ stella.jinks@corby.gov.uk

Street Scene: Mr Iain Smith, Head of Service Planning & Environmental Quality, Deene House, New Post Office Square, Corby NN17 1GD ☎ 01536 464061 ✉ iain.smith@corby.gov.uk

Sustainable Communities: Mr Norman Stronach, Chief Executive, The Cube, Parklands Gateway, Corby NN17 1GD ☎ 01536 464156 ✉ norman.stronach@corby.gov.uk

Sustainable Development: Ms Sara Earl Sustainability Officer, Deene House, New Post Office Square, Corby NN17 1GD ☎ 01536 464685 ✉ sara.earl@corby.gov.uk

Waste Collection and Disposal: Mr Iain Smith, Head of Service Planning & Environmental Quality, Deene House, New Post Office Square, Corby NN17 1GD ☎ 01536 464061 ✉ iain.smith@corby.gov.uk

Waste Management: Mr Iain Smith, Head of Service Planning & Environmental Quality, Deene House, New Post Office Square, Corby NN17 1GD ☎ 01536 464061 ✉ iain.smith@corby.gov.uk

Children's Play Areas: Mr Lloyd Baines-Davies Community Recreation & Events Officer, Deene House, New Post Office Square, Corby NN17 1GD ☎ 01536 464674 ✉ lloyd.bainesdavies@corby.gov.uk

COUNCILLORS

***Mayor* McEwan**, Peter (LAB - Oakley North)
peter.mcewan@corby.gov.uk

***Deputy Mayor* Riley**, Julie (LAB - Stanion & Corby Village)
julie.riley@corby.gov.uk

***Leader of the Council* Beattie**, Tom (LAB - Lodge Park)
tom.beattie@corby.gov.uk

***Deputy Leader of the Council* Addison**, Jean (LAB - Rowlett)
jean.addison@corby.gov.uk

***Group Leader* McKellar**, Robert (CON - Weldon & Gretton)
robert.mckellar@corby.gov.uk

Beattie, Paul (LAB - Beanfield)
paul.beattie@corby.gov.uk

Beeby, Raymond (LAB - Oakley North)
ray.beeby@corby.gov.uk

Brown, Ann (LAB - Beanfield)
ann.brown@corby.gov.uk

CORBY

Butcher, Mary (LAB - Beanfield)
mary.butcher@corby.gov.uk

Caine, Judy (LAB - Oakley South)
judy.caine@corby.gov.uk

Carratt, Kenneth (LAB - Kingswood & Hazel Leys)
kenneth.carratt@corby.gov.uk

Cassidy, Colleen (LAB - Danesholme)
colleen.cassidy@corby.gov.uk

Colquhoun, William (LAB - Stanion & Corby Village)
william.colquhoun@corby.gov.uk

Dady, Anthony (LAB - Central)
anthony.dady@corby.gov.uk

Elliston, Elise (LAB - Kingswood & Hazel Leys)
elise.elliston@corby.gov.uk

Eyles, Bob (LAB - Lodge Park)
bob.eyles@corby.gov.uk

Ferguson, Lawrence (LAB - Central)
lawrence.ferguson@corby.gov.uk

Goult, Lucy (LAB - Lloyds)
Lucy.goult@corby.gov.uk

Keane, Matt (LAB - Lodge Park)
matt.keane@corby.gov.uk

Latta, Willie (LAB - Rowlett)
william.latta@corby.gov.uk

McGhee, John (LAB - Kingswood & Hazel Leys)
jmcghee@northamptonshire.gov.uk

Pengelly, Mark (LAB - Lloyds)
mark.pengelly@corby.gov.uk

Petch, Peter (LAB - Danesholme)
peter.petch@corby.gov.uk

Rahman, Mohammed (LAB - Oakley South)
Mohammed.rahman@corby.gov.uk

Reay, Matt (LAB - Lloyds)
matt.reay@corby.gov.uk

Rutt, Robert (CON - Rural West)
robert.rutt@corby.gov.uk

Sims, David (CON - Oakley South)
dsimonsonline.gmail.com

Watt, Kevin (CON - Weldon & Gretton) kevin.watt@corby.gov.uk

Watts, Bridget (CON - Weldon & Gretton)
bridget.watts@corby.gov.uk

POLITICAL COMPOSITION

LAB: 24, CON: 5

COMMITTEE CHAIRS

Audit & Governance: Mr Bob Eyles

Development Control: Mr Willie Latta

Cornwall U

Cornwall, County Hall, Treyew Road, Truro TR1 3AY
☎ 0300 1234 100 customerservices@cornwall.gov.uk
www.cornwall.gov.uk

FACTS AND FIGURES

Parliamentary Constituencies: Camborne and Redruth, St. Austell and Newquay, St. Ives, Truro and Falmouth

PRINCIPAL OFFICERS

Chief Executive: Mr Paul Masters Interim Head of Paid Service (Corporate Director for Communities & Organisational Development), County Hall, Treyew Road, Truro TR1 3AY
☎ 01872 322121 pmasters@cornwall.gov.uk

Senior Management: Ms Dawn Aunger Head of People Management, Development & Wellbeing, County Hall, Treyew Road, Truro TR1 3AY ☎ 01872 323119 daunger@cornwall.gov.uk

Senior Management: Mr S Bourne Acting Director - Public Health, Room 1E, New County Hall, Treyew Road, Truro TR1 3AY
☎ 01872 327890 sbourne@cornwall.gov.uk

Senior Management: Mr Michael Crich Corporate Director for Economy, Enterprise & Environment, County Hall, Treyew Road, Truro TR1 3AY ☎ 01872 323262 🖷 01872 322580
mcrich@cornwall.gov.uk

Senior Management: Mr Trevor Doughty Corporate Director for Education, Health & Social Care, County Hall, Treyew Road, Truro TR1 3AY ☎ 01872 322403 tdoughty@cornwall.gov.uk

Senior Management: Mr Paul Masters Interim Head of Paid Service (Corporate Director for Communities & Organisational Development), County Hall, Treyew Road, Truro TR1 3AY
☎ 01872 322121 pmasters@cornwall.gov.uk

Senior Management: Mr Mark Read Head of Customers & Communities, Room 204, Central 2 Office, 39 Penwinnick Road, St. Austell PL25 5DR ☎ 01726 223316 mark.read@cornwall.gov.uk

Senior Management: Ms Cath Robinson Head of Business, Planning & Development, County Hall, Treyew Road, Truro TR1 3AY
☎ 01872 324449 crobinson@cornwall.gov.uk

Senior Management: Mr Richard Williams Head of Governance & Information, County Hall, Treyew Road, Truro TR1 3AY
☎ 01872 322120 rawilliams@cornwall.gov.uk

Architect, Building / Property Services: Mr Adam Birchall Property Forward Planning Manager, Pydar House, 4th Floor, Pydar Street, Truro TR1 1EA ☎ 01872 323083 abirchall@cornwall.gov.uk

Building Control: Mr Phil Mason Head of Planning & Regeneration, Room 209, Restormel Offices, 39 Penwinnick Road, St. Austell PL25 5DR ☎ 01726 223452
phil.mason@cornwall.gov.uk

Children / Youth Services: Mr Trevor Doughty Corporate Director for Education, Health & Social Care, County Hall, Treyew Road, Truro TR1 3AY ☎ 01872 322403 tdoughty@cornwall.gov.uk

Civil Registration: Ms Anne McSeveney Assistant Head of Customers & Communities (Face to Face), Dalvenie House, Country Hall, Treyew Road, Truro TR1 3AY ☎ 01872 224300
amcseveney@cornwall.gov.uk

PR / Communications: Ms Patricia Hewitt Corporate Communications Manager, Room 3S, New County Hall, Treyew Road, Truro TR1 3AY ☎ 01872 322186 phewitt@cornwall.gov.uk

Community Safety: Mr Paul Walker Chief Fire Officer & Head of Community Safety, 4th Floor, New County Hall, Treyew Road, Truro TR1 3AY ☎ 01872 323739 pwalker@fire.cornwall.gov.uk

Computer Management: Mr David Picknett Head of Information Technology, County Hall, Truro TR1 3AY ☎ 0300 1234 100 dpicknett@cornwall.gov.uk

Consumer Protection and Trading Standards: Mr Allan Hampshire Head of Public Health & Protection, County Hall, Treyew Road, Truro TR1 3AY ☎ 01872 224409 allan.hampshire@cornwall.gov.uk

Corporate Services: Mr Paul Masters Interim Head of Paid Service (Corporate Director for Communities & Organisational Development), County Hall, Treyew Road, Truro TR1 3AY ☎ 01872 322121 pmasters@cornwall.gov.uk

Customer Service: Mr Mark Read Head of Customers & Communities, Room 204, Central 2 Office, 39 Penwinnick Road, St. Austell PL25 5DR ☎ 01726 223316 mark.read@cornwall.gov.uk

Education: Mr Trevor Doughty Corporate Director for Education, Health & Social Care, County Hall, Treyew Road, Truro TR1 3AY ☎ 01872 322403 tdoughty@cornwall.gov.uk

Electoral Registration: Mr Richard Williams Head of Legal & Democratic Services, Room 470, New County Hall, Treyew Road, Truro TR1 3AY ☎ 01872 322120 🖷 01872 323833 rawilliams@cornwall.gov.uk

Emergency Planning: Mr Richard Fedorowicz Head of Emergency Management, County Hall, Treyew Road, Truro TR1 3AY ☎ 01872 323121 rfedorowicz@cornwall.gov.uk

Energy Management: Mr Adam Birchall Property Forward Planning Manager, Pydar House, 4th Floor, Pydar Street, Truro TR1 1EA ☎ 01872 323083 abirchall@cornwall.gov.uk

Environmental / Technical Services: Mr Nigel Blackler Head of Strategy, Economy, Enterprise & Environment, County Hall, Treyew Road, Truro TR1 3AY ☎ ; 01872 324124 nblackler@cornwall.gov.uk

Environmental Health: Mr Allan Hampshire Head of Public Health & Protection, County Hall, Treyew Road, Truro TR1 3AY ☎ 01872 224409 allan.hampshire@cornwall.gov.uk

Estates, Property & Valuation: Mr Adam Birchall Property Forward Planning Manager, Pydar House, 4th Floor, Pydar Street, Truro TR1 1EA ☎ 01872 323083 abirchall@cornwall.gov.uk

European Liaison: Ms Sandra Rothwell CEO - Cornwall & Isles of Scilly Local Environment Partnership, 3rd Floor, New County Hall, Treyew Road, Truro TR1 3AY ☎ 01872 224385 srothwell@cornwall.gov.uk

Finance: Ms Cath Robinson Head of Business, Planning & Development, County Hall, Treyew Road, Truro TR1 3AY ☎ 01872 324449 crobinson@cornwall.gov.uk

Treasury: Mr Clive Sturthridge Treasury Officer, County Hall, Treyew Road, Truro TR1 3AY ☎ 01872 322228 csturthridge@cornwall.gov.uk

Pensions: Mr Matthew Trebilcock Pensions Investment Manager, New County Hall, Treyew Road, , Truro TR1 3AY ☎ 01872 322322 mtrebilcock@cornwall.gov.uk

Fleet Management: Mr Arthur Hooper Managing Director of CORMAC Solutions Ltd, North Building, Central GP Centre, Castle Canyke Road, Bodmin PL31 1DZ ☎ 01872 324559 ahooper@cornwall.gov.uk

Health and Safety: Mr Sean Oates Health, Safety & Wellbeing Manager, Fowey Building, New County Hall, Treyew Road, Truro TR1 3AY ☎ 01872 322182 soates1@cornwall.gov.uk

Highways: Mr Arthur Hooper Managing Director of CORMAC Solutions Ltd, County Hall, Treyew Road, Truro TR1 3AY ☎ 01872 324559 ahooper@cornwall.gov.uk

Housing: Ms Jane Barlow Managing Director of Cornwall Housing, Council Offices, 2nd Floor, Dolcoath Avenue, Camborne TR14 8SX ☎ 01209 614322 jane.barlow@cornwall.gov.uk

Housing Maintenance: Ms Jane Barlow Managing Director of Cornwall Housing, Council Offices, 2nd Floor, Dolcoath Avenue, Camborne TR14 8SX ☎ 01209 614322 jane.barlow@cornwall.gov.uk

Legal: Mr Richard Williams Head of Legal & Democratic Services, Room 470, New County Hall, Treyew Road, Truro TR1 3AY ☎ 01872 322120 🖷 01872 323833 rawilliams@cornwall.gov.uk

Leisure and Cultural Services: Mr Simon Blamey Managing Director of Carrick Leisure Ltd, Windwhistle House, Cooksland Road, Bodmin PL31 2RH ☎ 01208 262805 sblamey@tempusleisure.org.uk

Licensing: Mr Allan Hampshire Head of Public Health & Protection, Room C3.11, Carrick House, Pydar Street, Truro TR1 1EB ☎ 01872 224409 allan.hampshire@cornwall.gov.uk

Member Services: Mr Richard Williams Head of Legal & Democratic Services, Room 470, New County Hall, Treyew Road, Truro TR1 3AY ☎ 01872 322120 🖷 01872 323833 rawilliams@cornwall.gov.uk

Parking: Mr Jon Haskins Parking Manager, Room E2:20, Carrick House, Truro TR1 1EB ☎ 01872 224264 jhaskins@cornwall.gov.uk

Partnerships: Ms Rachael Bice Partnerships & Rural Policy Lead, Pydar House, 4th Floor, Pydar Street, Truro TR1 1EA ☎ 01872 224314 rbice@cornwall.gov.uk

CORNWALL

Personnel / HR: Ms Dawn Aunger Head of People Management, Development & Wellbeing, County Hall, Treyew Road, Truro TR1 3AY ☎ 01872 323119 🖰 daunger@cornwall.gov.uk

Planning: Mr Phil Mason Head of Planning & Regeneration, County Hall, Treyew Road, Truro TR1 3AY ☎ 01726 223452 🖰 phil.mason@cornwall.gov.uk

Procurement: Mr Ray Hughes Assistant Head of Business Planning & Development (Commercial Services), Room 2W, New County Hall, Truro TR1 3AY ☎ 01872 326510 🖰 rhughes@cornwall.gov.uk

Public Libraries: Mr Mark Read Head of Customers & Communities, Room 204, Central 2 Office, 39 Penwinnick Road, St. Austell PL25 5DR ☎ 01726 223316 🖰 mark.read@cornwall.gov.uk

Recycling & Waste Minimisation: Mr Peter Marsh Head of Commissioning & Contracts, The Exchange, New County Hall, Treyew Road, Truro TR1 3AY ☎ 01872 326932 🖰 pmarsh@cornwall.gov.uk

Regeneration: Mr Phil Mason Head of Planning & Regeneration, County Hall, Treyew Road, Truro TR1 3AY ☎ 01726 223452 🖰 phil.mason@cornwall.gov.uk

Road Safety: Mr Paul Walker Chief Fire Officer & Head of Community Safety, 4th Floor, New County Hall, Treyew Road, Truro TR1 3AY ☎ 01872 323739 🖰 pwalker@fire.cornwall.gov.uk

Social Services: Mr Trevor Doughty Corporate Director for Education, Health & Social Care, County Hall, Treyew Road, Truro TR1 3AY ☎ 01872 322403 🖰 tdoughty@cornwall.gov.uk

Social Services (Adult): Mr Trevor Doughty Corporate Director for Education, Health & Social Care, County Hall, Treyew Road, Truro TR1 3AY ☎ 01872 322403 🖰 tdoughty@cornwall.gov.uk

Social Services (Children): Mr Jack Cordery Head of Service for Social Work, Room 424, New County Hall, Treyew Road, Truro TR1 3AY ☎ 01872 323637 🖰 jcordery@cornwall.gov.uk

Childrens Social Care: Ms Marion Russell Principal Child & Family Social Worker, County Hall, Treyew Road, Truro TR1 3AY ☎ 0300 1234 100 🖰 marion.russell@cornwall.gov.uk

Public Health: Mr S Bourne Acting Director - Public Health, Room 1E, New County Hall, Treyew Road, Truro TR1 3AY ☎ 01872 327890 🖰 sbourne@cornwall.gov.uk

Staff Training: Ms Dawn Aunger Head of People Management, Development & Wellbeing, County Hall, Treyew Road, Truro TR1 3AY ☎ 01872 323119 🖰 daunger@cornwall.gov.uk

Tourism: Mr Malcom Bell Head of Tourism, Pydar House, Pydar Street, Truro TR1 1EA ☎ 01872 322820 🖰 malcolm.bell@cornwallenterprise.co.uk

Town Centre: Mr Rob Andrew Assistant Head of Service for Communities & Devolution, County Hall, Treyew Road, Truro TR1 3AY ☎ 01872 224239 🖰 randrew@cornwall.gov.uk

Traffic Management: Mr Arthur Hooper Managing Director of CORMAC Solutions Ltd, North Building, Central GP Centre, Castle Canyke Road, Bodmin PL31 1DZ ☎ 01872 324559 🖰 ahooper@cornwall.gov.uk

Transport: Mr Nigel Blackler Head of Strategy, Economy, Enterprise & Environment, County Hall, Treyew Road, Truro TR1 3AY ☎ ; 01872 324124 🖰 nblackler@cornwall.gov.uk

Transport Planner: Mr Nigel Blackler Head of Strategy, Economy, Enterprise & Environment, County Hall, Treyew Road, Truro TR1 3AY ☎ ; 01872 324124 🖰 nblackler@cornwall.gov.uk

Waste Collection and Disposal: Mr Peter Marsh Head of Commissioning & Contracts, The Exchange, New County Hall, Treyew Road, Truro TR1 3AY ☎ 01872 326932 🖰 pmarsh@cornwall.gov.uk

Waste Management: Mr Peter Marsh Head of Commissioning & Contracts, The Exchange, New County Hall, Treyew Road, Truro TR1 3AY ☎ 01872 326932 🖰 pmarsh@cornwall.gov.uk

Children's Play Areas: Mr Jon James Natural Environment Manager, Room 102, Scorrier Depot, Radnor Road, Scorrier, Redruth TR16 5EH ☎ 01209 614387 🖰 jjames@cornwall.gov.uk

COUNCILLORS

***Chair* Kerridge**, Ann (LD - Bodmin St Mary's)
akerridge@cornwall.gov.uk

***Vice-Chair* May**, Mary (IND - Penryn West)
mamay@cornwall.gov.uk

***Leader of the Council* Pollard**, John (IND - Hayle North)
jpollard1@cornwall.gov.uk

***Deputy Leader of the Council* Paynter**, Adam (LD - Launceston North & North Petherwin)
apaynter@cornwall.gov.uk

***Group Leader* Cole**, Dick (O - St Enoder)
ricole@cornwall.gov.uk

***Group Leader* Dwelly**, Tim (LAB - Penzance East)
tdwelly@cornwall.gov.uk

***Group Leader* Ferguson**, Fiona (CON - Truro Trehaverne)
fiferguson@cornwall.gov.uk

***Group Leader* McWilliam**, Stephanie (UKIP - Lynher)
smcwilliam@cornwall.gov.uk

***Group Leader* Mitchell**, Andrew (IND - St Ives West)
amitchell1@cornwall.gov.uk

Andrewes, Tim (INDNA - St Ives East)
tandrewes@cornwall.gov.uk

Atherton, Candy (LAB - Falmouth Smithick)
catherton@cornwall.gov.uk

Austin, Bob (LD - Saltash West)
baustin@cornwall.gov.uk

Bastin, John (CON - Constantine, Mawnan & Budock)
jbastin@cornwall.gov.uk

Batters, Chris (LD - Lanivet & Blisland)
cbatters@cornwall.gov.uk

Bay, Benedicte (CON - Lostwithiel)
bbay@cornwall.gov.uk

Biscoe, Bert (IND - Truro Boscawen)
bertbiscoe@btinternet.com

Brown, Glenton (LD - Tintagel)
gbrown@cornwall.gov.uk

Brown, Malcolm (LD - St Austell Bethel)
mbrown3@cornwall.gov.uk

Brown, Geoff (LD - Newquay Central)
geoff.brown@cornwall.gov.uk

Bull, Jackie (LD - St Austell Poltair)
jbull@cornwall.gov.uk

Burden, Neil (IND - Stokeclimsland)
nburden@cornwall.gov.uk

Buscombe, Richard (LD - Padstow)
rbuscombe@cornwall.gov.uk

Callan, Michael (IND - Perranporth)
mcallan@cornwall.gov.uk

Candy, Jim (LD - Trelawny)
jcandy@cornwall.gov.uk

Chamberlain, Steve (CON - Feock & Playing Place)
schamberlain1@cornwall.gov.uk

Chopak, Nicky (LD - Poundstock)
nchopal@cornwall.gov.uk

Coombe, John (IND - Hayle South)
jcoombe@cornwall.gov.uk

Curnow, Des (IND - St Stephen-In-Brannel)
descurrow@cornwall.gov.uk

Deeble, Tim (IND - Threemilestone & Gloweth)
tdeeble@cornwall.gov.uk

Dolley, Lisa (IND - Redruth North)
ldolley@cornwall.gov.uk

Dolphin, Paula (LD - Grenville & Stratton)
pdolphin@cornwall.gov.uk

Duffin, Joyce (LD - Mount Hawke & Portreath)
jmduffin@cornwall.gov.uk

Dyer, John (CON - Chacewater, Kenwyn & Baldhu)
fjdyer@cornwall.gov.uk

Eathorne-Gibbons, Mike (IND - Ladock, St Clement & St Erme)
meathornegibbons@cornwall.gov.uk

Eddowes, Mike (CON - Redruth Central)
meddowes@cornwall.gov.uk

Egerton, Bob (INDNA - Probus, Tregony & Grampound)
begerton@cornwall.gov.uk

Ekinsmyth, David (LD - Illogan)
dekinsmyth@cornwall.gov.uk

Elliott, Derek (UKIP - Four Lanes)
delliott@cornwall.gov.uk

Ellis, Bernie (CON - Menheniot)
bellis2@cornwall.gov.uk

Ellison, Joe (IND - Saltash North)
jellison1@cornwall.gov.uk

Evans, Geoffrey (CON - Falmouth Arwenack)
gfevans@cornwall.gov.uk

Farrington, Jade (LD - Launceston South)
jfarrington@cornwall.gov.uk

Fitter, John (CON - St Mawgan & Colan)
jfitter@cornwall.gov.uk

Flashman, Jim (CON - St Dominick, Harrowbarrow & Kelly Bray)
jflashman@cornwall.gov.uk

Folkes, Alex (INDNA - Launceston Central)
alexfolkes@cornwall.gov.uk

Fonk, Mario (LD - Gulval & Heamoor)
mfonk@cornwall.gov.uk

Frank, Hilary (LD - Saltash South)
hfrank@cornwall.gov.uk

French, Tom (CON - St Austell Bay)
tfrench@cornwall.gov.uk

George, Michael (LD - Liskeard West & Dobwalls)
mgeorge1@cornwall.gov.uk

German, Julian (IND - Roseland)
jgerman@cornwall.gov.uk

Greenslade, Fred (IND - St Dennis & Nanpean)
fred.greenslade@cornwall.gov.uk

Hall, Vivian (CON - Altarnun)
vhall@cornwall.gov.uk

Hannaford, Edwina (LD - Looe West, Lansallos & Lanteglos)
ehannaford@cornwall.gov.uk

Harding, Roger (CON - Newlyn & Mousehole)
rharding@cornwall.gov.uk

Harris, Malcolm (IND - St Mewan)
mharris2@cornwall.gov.uk

Harvey, Pat (IND - St Columb Major)
pharvey@cornwall.gov.uk

Hawken, Sally (IND - Liskeard East)
shawken@cornwall.gov.uk

Haycock, Judith (IND - Helston South)
jhaycock@cornwall.gov.uk

Herd, John (CON - Camborne Pendarves)
jherd@cornwall.gov.uk

Heyward, Sandra (IND - St Austell Gover)
sheyward@cornwall.gov.uk

Hicks, Mark (UKIP - Newquay Treviglas)
mhicks1@cornwall.gov.uk

Hobbs, Brian (LD - Torpoint East)
bhobbs@cornwall.gov.uk

Holley, Derek (IND - Saltash East)
dholley@cornwall.gov.uk

Holmes, Roger (IND - Liskeard North)
rholmes@cornwall.gov.uk

Hughes, David (LD - Fowey & Tywardreath)
dhughes@cornwall.gov.uk

James, Sue (LD - St Just In Penwith)
sjames@cornwall.gov.uk

Jenkin, Loveday (O - Crowan & Wendron)
letjenkin@cornwall.gov.uk

Jewell, Alan (CON - Falmouth Boslowick)
ajewell@cornwall.gov.uk

Kaczmarek, Mark (IND - Carharrack, Gwennap & St Day)
mkaczmarek@cornwall.gov.uk

CORNWALL

Keeling, John (CON - Breage, Germoe & Sithney)
jkeeling@cornwall.gov.uk

Kenny, Joanna (LD - Newquay Pentire)
jkenny@cornwall.gov.uk

King, Gary (IND - Mount Charles)
gking@cornwall.gov.uk

Kirk, Dorothy (LAB - Gunnislake & Calstock)
dkirk@cornwall.gov.uk

Knightley, Steve (LD - Wadebridge East)
sknightley@cornwall.gov.uk

Lambshead, Patrick (CON - Newquay Tretherras)
plambshead@cornwall.gov.uk

Long, Andrew (O - Callington)
ajlong@cornwall.gov.uk

Lugg, John (IND - St Teath & St Breward)
jlugg@cornwall.gov.uk

Luke, Matthew (O - Penwithick & Boscoppa)
mluke1@cornwall.gov.uk

Maddern, Bill (CON - St Buryan)
william.maddern@cornwall.gov.uk

Mann, Roy (CON - Ludgvan)
rmann@cornwall.gov.uk

Mann, Scott (CON - Wadebridge West)
smann@cornwall.gov.uk

Martin, Phil (IND - Helston North)
pmartin@cornwall.gov.uk

Martin, Tony (CON - Penryn East & Mylor)
tomartin@cornwall.gov.uk

McKenna, Jim (IND - Penzance Promenade)
jmckenna@cornwall.gov.uk

Mitchell, Pete (LD - St Agnes)
pmitchell1@cornwall.gov.uk

Moyle, Malcolm (LAB - Pool & Tehidy)
mmoyle@cornwall.gov.uk

Mustoe, James (CON - Mevagissey)
jmustoe@cornwall.gov.uk

Nicholas, Sue (CON - Marazion & Perranuthoe)
sunicholas@cornwall.gov.uk

Nolan, Rob (LD - Truro Redanick)
rnolan@cornwall.gov.uk

Olivier, Cornelius (LAB - Penzance Central)
colivier@cornwall.gov.uk

Parsons, David (LD - Bude)
dparsons@cornwall.gov.uk

Pascoe, Lionel (CON - Gwinear-Gwithian & St Erth)
lpascoe1@cornwall.gov.uk

Pearce, Nigel (LD - Bude)
nigelpearce33@hotmail.com

Pearn, Mike (CON - Torpoint West)
mpearn@cornwall.gov.uk

Penhaligon, Liz (CON - Lelant & Carbis Bay)
epenhaligon@cornwall.gov.uk

Penny, Andy (IND - St Minver & St Endellion)
apenny@cornwall.gov.uk

Pugh, Daniel (CON - St Germans & Landulph)
dpugh@cornwall.gov.uk

Rich, Loic (IND - Truro Tregolls)
lrich@cornwall.gov.uk

Rix, Simon (LD - Bugle)
srix@cornwall.gov.uk

Robinson, Jude (LAB - Camborne Treswithian)

Rogerson, Steve (LD - Bodmin St Petroc)
srogerson@cornwall.gov.uk

Rogerson, Pat (LD - Bodmin St Leonard)
progerson@cornwall.gov.uk

Rotchell, Rob (LD - Camelford)
rrotchell@cornwall.gov.uk

Rowe, Jeremy (LD - St Issey & St Tudy)
jerowe@cornwall.gov.uk

Rule, Carolyn (IND - Mullion & Grade-Ruan)
carorule@cornwall.gov.uk

Sanger, Walter (CON - St Keverne & Meneage)
wsanger@cornwall.gov.uk

Saunby, David (IND - Falmouth Trescobeas)

Scrafton, Douglas (LD - Par & St Blazey Gate)
dscrafton@cornwall.gov.uk

Shuttlewood, Lisa (CON - Newlyn & Goonhavern)
lshuttlewood@cornwall.gov.u

Sleeman, Dave (LD - Newquay Treloggan)
dsleeman@cornwall.gov.uk

Stoneman, Jon (CON - Camborne Trelowarren)
jstoneman@cornwall.gov.uk

Taylor, Roy (LD - St Blazey)
roytaylor@cornwall.gov.uk

Thomas, John (IND - Lanner & Stithians)
john.thomas@cornwall.gov.uk

Thomas, Ian (IND - Redruth South)
ithomas@cornwall.gov.uk

Toms, Hanna (LAB - Falmouth Penwerris)
htoms@cornwall.gov.uk

Toms, Armand (IND - Looe East)
atoms@cornwall.gov.uk

Trubody, George (IND - Rame Peninsular)
gtrubody@conrwall.gov.uk

Wallis, Andrew (IND - Porthleven & Helston West)
awallis@cornwall.gov.uk

Watson, Derris (LD - St Cleer)
dwatson@cornwall.gov.uk

Webber, Robert (LAB - Camborne Treslothan)
rwebber@cornwall.gov.uk

White, Paul (CON - Camborne Roskear)
pwhite@cornwall.gov.uk

Williams, Peter (CON - Mabe, Perranarworthal & St Gluvias)
prgwilliams@cornwall.gov.uk

Wood, John (IND - Roche) johnwood@cornwall.gov.uk

POLITICAL COMPOSITION

LD: 37, IND: 36, CON: 32, LAB: 8, O: 4, UKIP: 3, INDNA: 3

COMMITTEE CHAIRS

Audit: Ms Joanna Kenny

Health & Social Care: Mr Mike Eathorne-Gibbons

Licensing: Mr Malcolm Brown

Pensions: Mr Derek Holley

Planning: Mr Rob Nolan

Cotswold D

Cotswold District Council, Council Offices, Trinity Road, Cirencester GL7 1PX
☎ 01285 623000 🖷 01285 623900 ✉ cdc@cotswold.gov.uk
💻 www.cotswold.gov.uk

FACTS AND FIGURES

Parliamentary Constituencies: Cotswold
EU Constituencies: South West
Election Frequency: Elections are of whole council

PRINCIPAL OFFICERS

Chief Executive: Mr David Neudegg Chief Executive, Council Offices, Trinity Road, Cirencester GL7 1PX ☎ 01285 623100 ✉ david.neudegg@cotswold.gov.uk

Senior Management: Ms Christine Gore Strategic Director - Communities & Planning, Council Offices, Trinity Road, Cirencester GL7 1PX ☎ 01285 623500 ✉ christine.gore@cotswold.gov.uk

Senior Management: Mr Frank Wilson Shared Strategic Director - Resources, Council Offices, Trinity Road, Cirencester GL7 1PX ☎ 01993 861291 ✉ frank.wilson@westoxon.gov.uk

Senior Management: Mr Ralph Young, Strategic Director - Environment, Council Offices, Trinity Road, Cirencester GL7 1PX ☎ 01285 623600 🖷 01285 623906 ✉ ralph.young@cotswold.gov.uk

Architect, Building / Property Services: Mrs Bhavna Patel, Head of Legal & Property Services, Council Offices, Trinity Road, Cirencester GL7 1PX ☎ 01285 623219 🖷 01285 623900 ✉ bhavna.patel@cotswold.gov.uk

Best Value: Ms Kath Hoare, Business Improvement Manager, Council Offices, Trinity Road, Cirencester GL7 1PX ☎ 01285 623573 🖷 01285 623900 ✉ kath.hoare@cotswold.gov.uk

Building Control: Mr Andrew Jones Building Control Manager, Council Offices, Trinity Road, Cirencester GL7 1PX ☎ 01285 623633 🖷 01285 623905 ✉ andrew.jones@cotswold.gov.uk

PR / Communications: Mr Bob McNally Press & Media Liaison Officer, Council Offices, Trinity Road, Cirencester GL7 1PX ☎ 01285 623120 🖷 01285 623900 ✉ bob.mcnally@cotswold.gov.uk

Computer Management: Mr John Chorlton ICT Operations Manager, Council Offices, Trinity Road, Cirencester GL7 1PX ☎ 01285 623000 🖷 01285 623900 ✉ john.chorlton@cotswold.gov.uk

E-Government: Mr Dave Pennington Web Developer, Council Offices, Trinity Road, Cirencester GL7 1PX ☎ 01285 623000 🖷 01285 623900 ✉ dave.pennington@cotswold.gov.uk

Electoral Registration: Mr Nigel Adams, Head of Democratic Services, Council Offices, Trinity Road, Cirencester GL7 1PX ☎ 01285 623202 🖷 01285 623900 ✉ nigel.adams@cotswold.gov.uk

Emergency Planning: Mrs Claire Locke Head of Environmental Services, Council Offices, Trinity Road, Cirencester GL7 1PX ☎ 01285 623427 🖷 01285 623000 ✉ claire.locke@cotswold.gov.uk

Energy Management: Mr Gary Packer, Sustainable Energy Officer, Council Offices, Trinity Road, Cirencester GL7 1PX ☎ 01285 623428 🖷 01285 623900 ✉ gary.packer@cotswold.gov.uk

Environmental / Technical Services: Mrs Claire Locke Head of Environmental Services, Council Offices, Trinity Road, Cirencester GL7 1PX ☎ 01285 623427 🖷 01285 623000 ✉ claire.locke@cotswold.gov.uk

Environmental Health: Ms Amanda Morgan Interim Head of Public Protection, Council Offices, Trinity Road, Cirencester GL7 1PX ☎ 01285 623442 ✉ amanda.morgan@cotswold.gov.uk

Estates, Property & Valuation: Mrs Bhavna Patel, Head of Legal & Property Services, Council Offices, Trinity Road, Cirencester GL7 1PX ☎ 01285 623219 🖷 01285 623900 ✉ bhavna.patel@cotswold.gov.uk

Finance: Ms Jenny Poole, Shared Services Head of Finance & Audit, Council Offices, Trinity Road, Cirencester GL7 1PX ☎ 01285 623313 🖷 01285 623900 ✉ jenny.poole@cotswold.gov.uk

Health and Safety: Mr Iain Wilkie Health & Safety Officer, Council Offices, Trinity Road, Cirencester GL7 1PX ☎ 01285 623111 ✉ iain.wilkie@cotswold.gov.uk

Home Energy Conservation: Mr Gary Packer, Sustainable Energy Officer, Council Offices, Trinity Road, Cirencester GL7 1PX ☎ 01285 623428 🖷 01285 623900 ✉ gary.packer@cotswold.gov.uk

Legal: Mrs Bhavna Patel, Head of Legal & Property Services, Council Offices, Trinity Road, Cirencester GL7 1PX ☎ 01285 623219 🖷 01285 623900 ✉ bhavna.patel@cotswold.gov.uk

Leisure and Cultural Services: Ms Diane Shelton, Head of Leisure & Communities, Council Offices, Woodgreen, Witney OX28 1NB ☎ 01993 861551 🖷 01993 861450 ✉ diane.shelton@westoxon.gov.uk

Licensing: Ms Amanda Morgan Interim Head of Public Protection, Council Offices, Trinity Road, Cirencester GL7 1PX ☎ 01285 623442 ✉ amanda.morgan@cotswold.gov.uk

Member Services: Mr Nigel Adams, Head of Democratic Services, Council Offices, Trinity Road, Cirencester GL7 1PX ☎ 01285 623202 🖷 01285 623900 ✉ nigel.adams@cotswold.gov.uk

Parking: Ms Maria Wheatley, Parking Services Manager, Council Offices, Trinity Road, Cirencester GL7 1PX ☎ 01285 623228 🖷 01285 623900 ✉ maria.wheatley@cotswold.gov.uk

Personnel / HR: Ms Jenny Poole, Shared Services Head of Finance & Audit, Council Offices, Trinity Road, Cirencester GL7 1PX ☎ 01285 623313 🖷 01285 623900 ✉ jenny.poole@cotswold.gov.uk

COTSWOLD

Planning: Ms Philippa Lowe Head of Planning & Strategic Housing, Council Offices, Trinity Road, Cirencester GL7 1PX ☎ 01285 623515 🖷 01285 623900 ✉ philippa.field@cotswold.gov.uk

Procurement: Ms Kath Hoare, Business Improvement Manager, Council Offices, Trinity Road, Cirencester GL7 1PX ☎ 01285 623573 🖷 01285 623900 ✉ kath.hoare@cotswold.gov.uk

Procurement: Ms Sarah Turner, Business Solutions Manager, Municipal Offices, The Promenade, Cheltenham GL50 9SA ✉ sarah.turner@cotswold.gov.uk

Recycling & Waste Minimisation: Mr Scott Williams, Waste Manager, Council Offices, Trinity Road, Cirencester GL7 1PX ☎ 01285 623096 🖷 01285 623900 ✉ scott.williams@cotswold.gov.uk

Staff Training: Mrs Jan Bridges, Learning & Organisational Development Manager, Municipal Offices, Promenade, Cheltenham GL50 9SA ☎ 01242 775189 🖷 01242 264309 ✉ jan.bridges@cheltenham.gov.uk

Staff Training: Ms Jenny Poole, Shared Services Head of Finance & Audit, Council Offices, Trinity Road, Cirencester GL7 1PX ☎ 01285 623313 🖷 01285 623900 ✉ jenny.poole@cotswold.gov.uk

Tourism: Ms Sally Graff Tourism Manager, Council Offices, Trinity Road, Cirencester GL7 1PX ☎ 01608 650881 🖷 01285 623900 ✉ sally.graff@cotswold.gov.uk

Waste Collection & Disposal: Mrs Claire Locke Head of Environmental Services, Council Offices, Trinity Road, Cirencester GL7 1PX ☎ 01285 623427 🖷 01285 623000 ✉ claire.locke@cotswold.gov.uk

Waste Management: Mrs Claire Locke Head of Environmental Services, Council Offices, Trinity Road, Cirencester GL7 1PX ☎ 01285 623427 🖷 01285 623000 ✉ claire.locke@cotswold.gov.uk

COUNCILLORS

***Chair* Annett**, Mark (CON - Campden & Vale)
mark.annett@cotswold.gov.uk

***Vice-Chair* Beale**, Julian (CON - Fosseridge)
julian.beale@cotswold.gov.uk

***Leader of the Council* Stowe**, Lynden (CON - Campden & Vale)
lynden.stowe@cotswold.gov.uk

***Deputy Leader of the Council* Parsons**, Nicholas (CON - Ermin)
nicholas.parsons@cotswold.gov.uk

***Group Leader* Harris**, Joseph (LD - St Michael's)
joe.harris@cotswold.gov.uk

Andrews, Stephen (CON - Lechdale, Kempsford & Fairford South)
stephen.andrews@cotswold.gov.uk

Beccle, Abagail (CON - Fairford North)
abagail.beccle@cotswold.gov.uk

Berry, Tony (CON - Kemble)
tony.berry@cotswold.gov.uk

Brassington, Ray (LD - Four Acres)
ray.brassington@cotswold.gov.uk

Cheung, Tatyan (LD - New Mills)
tatyan.cheung@cotswold.gov.uk

Coakley, Sue (CON - Lechdale, Kempsford & Fairford South)
sue.coakley@cotswold.gov.uk

Coggins, Alison (CON - Moreton West)
alison.coggins@cotswold.gov.uk

Coleman, Patrick (LD - Stratton)
patrick.coleman@cotswold.gov.uk

Dare, Barry (CON - Stow)
barry.dare@cotswold.gov.uk

Dutton, Robert (CON - Moreton East)
robert.dutton@cotswold.gov.uk

Forde, Jenny (LD - Chedworth & Churn Valley)
jenny.forde@cotswold.gov.uk

Fowles, David (CON - The Ampneys & Hampton)
david.fowles@cotswold.gov.uk

Hancock, Christopher (CON - Northleach)
christopher.hancock@cotswold.gov.uk

Harris, Mark (LD - Abbey)
mark.harris@cotswold.gov.uk

Heaven, Maggie (CON - Tetbury & East Rural)
maggie.heaven@cotswold.gov.uk

Hicks, Jenny (LD - Watermoor)
jenny.hicks@cotswold.gov.uk

Hirst, Stephen (CON - Tetbury Town)
stephen.hirst@cotswold.gov.uk

Hughes, Roly (LD - Chesterton)
roly.hughes@cotswold.gov.uk

Hughes, Robin (CON - Sandywell)
robin.hughes@cotswold.gov.uk

Jepson, Sue (CON - Blockley)
sue.jepson@cotswold.gov.uk

Keeling, Richard (CON - Bourton Vale)
richard.keeling@cotswold.gov.uk

Layton, Juliet (LD - South Cerney Village)
juliet.layton@cotswold.gov.uk

MacKenzie-Charrington, Mark (CON - The Rissingtons)
mark.mackenzie-charrington@cotswold.gov.uk

Parsons, Shaun (CON - Siddington & Cerney Rural)
shaun.parsons@cotswold.gov.uk

Parsons, Jim (CON - Grumsbolds Ash with Avening)
jim.parsons@cotswold.gov.uk

Robbins, Nigel (LD - The Beeches)
nigel.robbins@cotswold.gov.uk

Stevenson, Tina (CON - Tetbury with Upton)
tina.stevenson@cotswold.gov.uk

Theodoulou, Raymond (CON - Coln Valley)
raymond.theodoulou@cotswold.gov.uk

Wilkins, Len (CON - Bourton Village)
len.wilkins@cotswold.gov.uk

POLITICAL COMPOSITION

CON: 24, LD: 10

COMMITTEE CHAIRS

Audit: Mr Barry Dare

Planning & Licensing: Mr Robin Hughes

Coventry City M

Coventry City Council, The Council House, Earl Street, Coventry CV1 5RR
☎ 024 7683 3333 🖷 024 7683 3680 ✉ coventrydirect@coventry.gov.uk
💻 www.coventry.gov.uk

FACTS AND FIGURES

Parliamentary Constituencies: Coventry North East, Coventry North West, Coventry South
EU Constituencies: West Midlands
Election Frequency: Elections are by thirds

PRINCIPAL OFFICERS

Chief Executive: Mr Martin Reeves Chief Executive, The Council House, Earl Street, Coventry CV1 5RR ☎ 024 7683 1100 🖷 024 7683 3680 ✉ martin.reeves@coventry.gov.uk

Senior Management: Dr Jane Moore Director - Public Health, The Council House, Earl Street, Coventry CV1 5RR ☎ 024 7683 2884 ✉ jane.moore@coventry.gov.uk

Senior Management: Ms Gail Quinton Executive Director - People, Civic Centre, 1 Little Park Street, Coventry CV1 5RS ☎ 024 7683 3405 🖷 024 7683 3494 ✉ gail.quinton@coventry.gov.uk

Senior Management: Mr Chris West Executive Director - Resources, The Council House, Earl Street, Coventry CV1 5RR ☎ 024 7683 3700 🖷 024 7683 3770 ✉ chris.west@coventry.gov.uk

Senior Management: Mr Martin Yardley Executive Director - Place, Floor 13, Civic Centre 4, Much Park Street, Coventry CV1 2PY ☎ 024 7683 1200 ✉ martin.yardley@coventry.gov.uk

Architect, Building / Property Services: Mr Nigel Clews Assistant Director for Property Asset Management, Civic Centre 4, Much Park Street, Coventry CV1 2PY ☎ 024 7683 4001 ✉ nigel.clews@coventry.gov.uk

Building Control: Mr Stuart Claridge Team Manager - Building Control, Civic Centre 4, Much Park Street, Coventry CV1 2PY ☎ 024 7683 2057 ✉ stuart.claridge@coventry.gov.uk

Catering Services: Mr Marcus Lynch Manager of St. Mary's Guildhall, St. Mary's Guildhall, Bayley Lane, Coventry CV1 5RN ☎ 024 7683 3327 ✉ marcus.lynch@coventry.gov.uk

Children / Youth Services: Ms Yolanda Corden Interim Assistant Director - Children's Social Care & Early Intervention Services, 2nd Floor, Civic Centre 1, Little Park Street, Coventry CV1 5RS ☎ 024 7689 1901 ✉ yolanda.corden@coventry.gov.uk

Children / Youth Services: Mr John Gregg Director of Children's Services, Civic Centre 1, Coventry CV1 5RS ☎ 024 7683 3621 ✉ john.gregg@coventry.gov.uk

Children / Youth Services: Mrs Isabel Merrifield Assistant Director for Strategy Commissioning and Policy, The Council House, Earl Street, Coventry CV1 5RR ☎ 024 7683 3403 ✉ isabel.merrifield@coventry.gov.uk

Children / Youth Services: Ms Kirston Nelson Director of Adult Education & Libraries, Civic Centre 1, Coventry CV1 5RS ☎ 024 7683 3621 🖷 024 7683 1505 ✉ kirtson.nelson@coventry.gov.uk

Civil Registration: Ms Bernadette Pennington Superintendent Registrar, The Register Office, Chelesmore Manor House, Manor House Drive, Coventry CV1 2ND ☎ 024 7683 3138 ✉ bernadette.pennington@coventry.gov.uk

PR / Communications: Ms Fran Collingham, Assistant Director of Communications, Council House, Earl Street, Coventry CV1 5RS ☎ 024 7683 1088 🖷 024 7683 1132 ✉ fran.collingham@coventry.gov.uk

Community Planning: Mr Simon Brake Director of Primary Care, Sustainability & Integration, Civic Centre 1, Little Park Street, Coventry CV1 5RS ☎ 024 7683 1652 ✉ simon.brake@coventry.gov.uk

Community Planning: Mr Peter Fahy Director of Adult Services, The Council House, Earl Street, Coventry CV1 5RR ☎ 024 7683 3555 ✉ peter.fahy@coventry.gov.uk

Community Planning: Ms Gail Quinton Executive Director - People, Civic Centre, 1 Little Park Street, Coventry CV1 5RS ☎ 024 7683 3405 🖷 024 7683 3494 ✉ gail.quinton@coventry.gov.uk

Community Safety: Mr Liam Nagle Offender Management Strategic Officer, Ground Floor, Christchurch House, Coventry CV1 2QL ☎ 024 7683 2063 ✉ liam.nagle@coventry.gov.uk

Computer Management: Mr Mark Chester Infrastructure Operations Manager, The Council House, Earl Street, Coventry CV1 5RR ☎ 024 7678 7970 ✉ mark.chester@coventry.gov.uk

Computer Management: Ms Lisa Commane Assistant Director of ICT, Transformation & Customer Services, The Council House, Earl Street, Coventry CV1 5RR ☎ 024 7683 3990 ✉ lisa.commane@coventry.gov.uk

Consumer Protection and Trading Standards: Mr Hamish Simmonds Head of Regulatory Services, 5th Floor, Broadgate House, Broadgate, Coventry CV1 5RS ☎ 024 7683 1871 🖷 024 7683 2128 ✉ hamish.simmonds@coventry.gov.uk

Contracts: Mr Mick Burn, Head of Procurement & Commissioning, Spire House, Floor 5, Coventry CV1 2PW ☎ 024 7683 3767 🖷 024 7683 3780 ✉ mick.burn@coventry.gov.uk

Customer Service: Mr Shokat Lal Assistant Director - HR & Workforce Services, The Council House, Earl Street, Coventry CV1 5RR ☎ 024 7683 3200 ✉ shokat.lal@coventry.gov.uk

Economic Development: Mr Richard Moon Senior Development Executive, Civic Centre 4, Much Park Street, Coventry CV1 2PY ☎ 024 7683 2350 ✉ richard.moon@coventry.gov.uk

Economic Development: Mr Martin Yardley Executive Director - Place, Floor 13, Civic Centre 4, Much Park Street, Coventry CV1 2PY ☎ 024 7683 1200 ✉ martin.yardley@coventry.gov.uk

Education: Ms Kirston Nelson Director of Adult Education & Libraries, Civic Centre 1, Coventry CV1 5RS ☎ 024 7683 3621 🖷 024 7683 1505 ✉ kirtson.nelson@coventry.gov.uk

COVENTRY CITY

Electoral Registration: Ms Liz Read Electoral Services Manager, The Council House, Earl Street, Coventry CV1 5RR ☎ 024 7683 3177 ✉ liz.read2@coventry.gov.uk

Emergency Planning: Mr Michael Enderby Head of CSW Resillience, The Council House, Earl Street, Coventry CV1 5RR ☎ 0121 704 8179 ✉ michael.enderby@coventry.gov.uk

Energy Management: Mr Kevin Palmer Energy Manager, City Development, Tower Block, Much Park Street, Coventry CV1 2QE ☎ 024 7683 2713 🖷 024 7683 3670 ✉ kevin.palmer@coventry.gov.uk

Environmental / Technical Services: Mr Craig Hickin Head of Environmental Services, 315 Broadgate House, Broadgate, Coventry CV1 1NH ☎ 024 7683 2585 ✉ craig.hackin@coventry.gov.uk

Environmental Health: Mr Craig Hickin Head of Environmental Services, 315 Broadgate House, Broadgate, Coventry CV1 1NH ☎ 024 7683 2585 ✉ craig.hackin@coventry.gov.uk

Estates, Property & Valuation: Mr Nigel Clews Assistant Director for Property Asset Management, Civic Centre 4, Much Park Street, Coventry CV1 2PY ☎ 024 7683 4001 ✉ nigel.clews@coventry.gov.uk

Events Manager: Ms Lee House, Senior Event Officer, Floor 2, West Orchard House, Corporation Street, Coventry CV1 1GF ☎ 024 7683 2351 ✉ lee.house@coventry.gov.uk

Facilities: Mr Ian Johnson Corporate Property Services Manager, Civic Centre 4, Much Park Street, Coventry CV1 2PY ☎ 024 7683 3054 🖷 024 7683 1294 ✉ ian.johnson@coventry.gov.uk

Finance: Mr Barry Hastie Assistant Director - Finance, The Council House, Earl Street, Coventry CV1 5RR ☎ 024 7683 3710 ✉ barry.hastie@coventry.gov.uk

Finance: Mr Chris West Executive Director - Resources, The Council House, Earl Street, Coventry CV1 5RR ☎ 024 7683 3700 🖷 024 7683 3770 ✉ chris.west@coventry.gov.uk

Fleet Management: Ms Sarah Elliott Head of Fleet & Waste Services, Whitley Depot, London Road, Coventry CV3 4AR ☎ 024 7683 3024 ✉ sarah.elliott@coventry.gov.uk

Grounds Maintenance: Mr Andrew Walster Assistant Director of Streetscene & Greenspace, Civic Centre 4, Much Park Street, Coventry CV1 2PY ☎ 024 7683 2621 ✉ andrew.walster@coventry.gov.uk

Health and Safety: Ms Angela White Occupational Health & Safety Manager, Christchurch Annexe, Greyfriars Lane, Coventry CV1 2PY ☎ 024 7683 3285 ✉ angela.white@coventry.gov.uk

Highways: Mr Colin Knight Assistant Director of Planning, Transport & Highways, Tower Block, Much Park Street, Coventry CV1 2PY ☎ 024 7683 2322 ✉ colin.knight@coventry.gov.uk

Highways: Ms Karen Seager Group Manager Highways, The Council House, Earl Street, Coventry CV1 5RR ☎ 024 7683 4014 ✉ karen.seager@coventry.gov.uk

Home Energy Conservation: Mr Michael Checkley Sustainability & Low Carbon Manager, Civic Centre 4, Much Park Street, Coventry CV1 2PY ☎ 024 7683 2155 ✉ michael.checkley@coventry.gov.uk

Housing: Mr Ayaz Maqsood Head of Housing, Spire House, New Union Street, , Coventry CV1 2PW ☎ 024 7683 1958 ✉ ayaz.magsood@coventry.gov.uk

Legal: Ms Helen Lynch Legal Services Manager, Christchurch House, Greyfriars Lane, Coventry CV1 2QL ☎ 028 7683 3011 ✉ helen.lynch@coventry.gov.uk

Legal: Ms Julie Newman People Manager - Legal Services, Christchurch House, Greyfriars Lane, Coventry CV1 2QL ☎ 024 7683 3544 ✉ julie.newman@coventry.gov.uk

Licensing: Ms Davina Blackburn Licensing Manager, Broadgate House, Coventry CV1 1NH ☎ 024 7683 1874 ✉ davina.blackburn@coventry.gov.uk

Lottery Funding, Charity and Voluntary: Mr Andy Williams Resources & New Projects Manager, Civic Centre 4, Much Park Street, Coventry CV1 2PY ☎ 024 7683 3731 ✉ andy.willliams@coventry.gov.uk

Member Services: Mr Adrian West Members & Elections Team Leader, The Council House, Earl Street, Coventry CV1 5RR ☎ 024 7683 2286 ✉ adrian.west@coventry.gov.uk

Parking: Mr Paul Bowman Team Manager for Parking Services, Civic Centre 4, Much Park Street, Coventry CV1 2PY ☎ 024 7683 4243 ✉ paul.bowman@coventry.gov.uk

Partnerships: Ms Dawn Ford Coventry Partnership & Communities Manager, Civic Centre 4, Much Park Street, Coventry CV1 2PY ☎ 024 7683 4356 ✉ dawn.ford@coventry.gov.uk

Personnel / HR: Mr Shokat Lal Assistant Director - HR & Workforce Services, The Council House, Earl Street, Coventry CV1 5RR ☎ 024 7683 3200 ✉ shokat.lal@coventry.gov.uk

Planning: Ms Tracy Miller Head of Planning, Civic Centre 4, Much Park Street, Coventry CV1 2PY ☎ 024 7683 1240 ✉ tracy.miller@coventry.gov.uk

Procurement: Mr Mick Burn, Head of Procurement & Commissioning, Spire House, Floor 5, Coventry CV1 2PW ☎ 024 7683 3767 🖷 024 7683 3780 ✉ mick.burn@coventry.gov.uk

Public Libraries: Mr Peter Barnett Head of Libraries, Advice, Health & Information Services, Civic Centre 1, Little Park Street, Coventry CV1 1RS ☎ 024 7683 1579 ✉ peter.barnett@coventry.gov.uk

Recycling & Waste Minimisation: Mr Anthony Campbell Waste & Recyling Manager, Whitley Depot, London Road, Coventry CV3 4AR ☎ 024 7683 4309 ✉ anthony.campbell@coventry.gov.uk

Regeneration: Ms Lucy Hobbs Community Regeneration Manager, Civic Centre 4, Much Park Street, Coventry CV1 2PY ☎ 024 7683 2642 ✉ lucy.hobbs@coventry.gov.uk

Road Safety: Ms Caron Archer Senior Engineer - Traffic Management, Civic Centre 4, Much Park Street, Coventry CV1 2PY ☎ 024 7683 2062 caron.archer@coventry.gov.uk

Social Services (Adult): Mr Peter Fahy Director of Adult Services, The Council House, Earl Street, Coventry CV1 5RR ☎ 024 7683 3555 peter.fahy@coventry.gov.uk

Social Services (Children): Ms Yolanda Corden Interim Assistant Director - Children's Social Care & Early Intervention Services, 2nd Floor, Civic Centre 1, Little Park Street, Coventry CV1 5RS ☎ 024 7689 1901 yolanda.corden@coventry.gov.uk

Safeguarding: Ms Jivan Sembi Head of Children's Regulatory Services, Civic Centre 1, Coventry CV1 5RS ☎ 024 7683 3443 🖷 024 7683 2490 jivan.sembi@coventry.gov.uk

Public Health: Dr Jane Moore Director - Public Health, The Council House, Earl Street, Coventry CV1 5RR ☎ 024 7683 2884 jane.moore@coventry.gov.uk

Street Scene: Mr Andrew Walster Assistant Director of Streetscene & Greenspace, Whitley Depot, London Road, Coventry CV3 4AR ☎ 024 7683 2621 andrew.walster@coventry.gov.uk

Sustainable Communities: Mr Andrew Walster Assistant Director of Streetscene & Greenspace, Whitley Depot, London Road, Coventry CV3 4AR ☎ 024 7683 2621 andrew.walster@coventry.gov.uk

Sustainable Development: Mr Michael Checkley Sustainability & Low Carbon Manager, Civic Centre 4, Much Park Street, Coventry CV1 2PY ☎ 024 7683 2155 michael.checkley@coventry.gov.uk

Tourism: Mr David Cockcroft Assistant Director of City Centre & Development Services, Tower Block, Much Park Street, Coventry CV1 2PY ☎ 024 7660 3964 david.cockcroft@discover.co.uk

Town Centre: Mr David Cockcroft Assistant Director of City Centre & Development Services, Tower Block, Much Park Street, Coventry CV1 2PY ☎ 024 7660 3964 david.cockcroft@discover.co.uk

Traffic Management: Mr Colin Knight Assistant Director of Planning, Transport & Highways, Tower Block, Much Park Street, Coventry CV1 2PY ☎ 024 7683 2322 colin.knight@coventry.gov.uk

Transport: Mr Colin Knight Assistant Director of Planning, Transport & Highways, Tower Block, Much Park Street, Coventry CV1 2PY ☎ 024 7683 2322 colin.knight@coventry.gov.uk

COUNCILLORS

***Chair* Hammon**, Michael (CON - Earlsdon)
michael.hammon@coventry.gov.uk

***Deputy Chair* Townshend**, Phil (LAB - Lower Stoke)
phil.townshend@coventry.gov.uk

***Leader of the Council* Lucas**, Ann (LAB - Holbrook)
ann.lucas@coventry.gov.uk

***Deputy Leader of the Council* Clifford**, Joe (LAB - Holbrook)
joseph.clifford@coventry.gov.uk

Abbott, Faye (LAB - Wyken)
faye.abbott@coventry.gov.uk

Akhtar, Perez (LAB - Whoberley)
perez.aktar@coventry.gov.uk

Akhtar, Naeem (LAB - St Michaels)
naeem.akhtar@coventry.gov.uk

Ali, Maya (LAB - Westwood)
maya.ali@coventry.gov.uk

Andrews, Allan (CON - Earlsdon)
allan.andrews@coventry.gov.uk

Auluck, Malkiat (LAB - Foleshill)
malkiat.auluck@coventry.gov.uk

Auluck, Randhir (LAB - Upper Stoke)

Bailey, Roger (CON - Cheylesmore)
roger.bailey@ceventry.gov.uk

Bains, Sucha (LAB - Upper Stoke)
sucha.bains@coventry.gov.uk

Bigham, Linda (LAB - Longford)
linda.bigham@coventry.gov.uk

Birdi, Jaswant (CON - Bablake)
jaswant.birdi@coventry.gov.uk

Blundell, John (CON - Wainbody)
john.blundell@coventry.gov.uk

Brown, Richard (LAB - Cheylesmore)
richard.brown@ceoventry.gov.uk

Caan, Kamram (LAB - Upper Stoke)
kamran.caan@coventry.gov.uk

Chater, Dave (LAB - Binley & Willenhall)
dave.chater@coventry.gov.uk

Crookes, Gary (CON - Wainbody)
gary.crookes@coventry.gov.uk

Duggins, George (LAB - Longford)
george.duggins@coventry.gov.uk

Galliers, David (LAB - Bablake)
david.galliers@coventry.gov.uk

Gannon, Damian (LAB - Sherbourne)
damian.gannon@coventry.gov.uk

Gingell, Alison (LAB - Sherbourne)
alison.gingell@coventry.gov.uk

Harvard, Lindsley (LAB - Longford)
lindsley@harvard.freeserve.co.uk

Innes, Jayne (LAB - Whoberley)
jayne.innes@coventry.gov.uk

Kershaw, David (LAB - Bablake)
david.kershaw@coventry.gov.uk

Khan, Tariq (LAB - Foleshill)
tariq.khan@coventry.gov.uk

Khan, Abdul (LAB - Foleshill)
abdul.khan@coventry.gov.uk

Lakha, Ram (LAB - Binley & Willenhall)
ram.lakha@coventry.gov.uk

Lancaster, Rachel (LAB - Holbrook)
rachel.lancaster@coventry.gov.uk

Lapsa, Marcus (CON - Westwood)
marcus.lapsa@coventry.gov.uk

COVENTRY CITY

Lepoidevin, Julia (CON - Woodlands)
julia.lepoidevin@coventry.gov.uk

Male, Peter (CON - Woodlands)
peter.male@coventr .gov.uk

Maton, Kevin (LAB - Henley)
kevin.maton@coventry.gov.uk

McNicholas, John (LAB - Lower Stoke)
john.mcnicholas@coventry.gov.uk

Miks, Catherine (LAB - Lower Stoke)
catherine.miks@coventry.gov.uk

Mullhall, Keiran (LAB - Radford)
keiran.mulhall@coventry.gov.uk

Mutton, Mal (LAB - Radford)
mal.mutton@coventry.gov.uk

Mutton, John (LAB - Binley & Willenhall)
john.mutton@coventry.gov.uk

Noonan, Hazel (CON - Cheylesmore)
hazel.noonan@coventry.gov.uk

O'Boyle, Jim (LAB - St Michaels)
jim.o'boyle@coventry.gov.uk

Ruane, Ed (LAB - Henley)
ed.ruane@coventry.gov.uk

Sawdon, Tim (CON - Wainbody)
tim.sawdon@coventry.gov.uk

Seaman, Patricia (LAB - Henley)
patricia.seaman@coventry.gov.uk

Singh, Bally (LAB - Whoberley)
bally.singh@coventry.gov.uk

Skinner, David (CON - Westwood)
david.skinner@coventry.gov.uk

Skipper, Tony (LAB - Radford)
tony.skipper@coventry.gov.uk

Sweet, Hazel (LAB - Wyken)
hazel.sweet@coventry.gov.uk

Taylor, Ken (CON - Earlsdon)
ken.taylor@coventry.gov.uk

Thay, Robert (LAB - Wyken)
robert.thay@coventry.gov.uk

Thomas, Steven (LAB - Woodlands)
steven.thomas@coventry.gov.uk

Walsh, Seamus (LAB - Sherbourne)
seamus.walsh@coventry.gov.uk

Welsh, David (LAB - St. Michaels)
david.welsh@coventry.gov.uk

POLITICAL COMPOSITION

LAB: 41, CON: 13

COMMITTEE CHAIRS

Audit: Mr Tony Skipper

Licensing: Mr David Galliers

Planning: Mrs Hazel Sweet

Craven D

Craven District Council, 1 Belle Vue Square, Broughton Road, Skipton BD23 1FJ
☎ 01756 700600 🖷 01756 700658 💻 www.cravendc.gov.uk

FACTS AND FIGURES

Parliamentary Constituencies: Skipton and Ripon
EU Constituencies: Yorkshire and the Humber
Election Frequency: Elections are by thirds

PRINCIPAL OFFICERS

Chief Executive: Mr Paul Shevlin Chief Executive, 1 Belle Vue Square, Broughton Road, Skipton BD23 1FJ ☎ 01756 706201 🖷 01756 706219 🖱 pshevlin@cravendc.gov.uk

Senior Management: Mr Paul Ellis Director of Services, 1 Belle Vue Square, Broughton Road, , Skipton BD23 1FJ ☎ 01756 706413 🖱 pellis@cravendc.gov.uk

Senior Management: Ms Samia Hussain, Corporate Head of Business Support, 1 Belle Vue Square, Broughton Road, , Skipton BD23 1FJ ☎ 01756 706207 🖷 01756 706218 🖱 shussain@cravendc.gov.uk

Senior Management: Mr David Smurthwaite, Strategic Manager of Planning & Regeneration, 1 Belle Vue Square, Broughton Road, Skipton BD23 1FJ ☎ 01756 706409 🖷 01756 700658 🖱 dsmurthwaite@cravendc.gov.uk

Best Value: Mrs Claire Hudson Corporate Performance & Improvement Manager, 1 Belle Vue Square, Broughton Road, , Skipton BD23 1FJ ☎ 01756 706493 🖱 chudson@cravendc.gov.uk

Building Control: Mr Ian Swain Development Control Manager, 1 Belle Vue Square, Broughton Road, Skipton BD23 1FJ ☎ 01756 706465 🖷 01756 700658 🖱 wgudger@cravendc.gov.uk

PR / Communications: Mrs Sharon Hudson, Communications Manager, 1 Belle Vue Square, Broughton Road, , Skipton BD23 1FJ ☎ 01756 706246 🖷 01756 700658 🖱 shudson@cravendc.gov.uk

Community Safety: Ms Stacey Reffin Community Safety Community Co-ordinator, 1 Belle Vue Square, Broughton Road, Skipton BD23 1FJ ☎ 01756 700600 🖱 sreffin@cravendc.gov.uk

Computer Management: Mr Chris Firth ICT Shared Services Interim Manager, 1 Belle Vue Square, Broughton Road, Skipton BD23 1FJ ☎ 🖱 cfirth@cravendc.gov.uk

Corporate Services: Ms Samia Hussain, Corporate Head of Business Support, 1 Belle Vue Square, Broughton Road, , Skipton BD23 1FJ ☎ 01756 706207 🖷 01756 706218 🖱 shussain@cravendc.gov.uk

Economic Development: Mr David Smurthwaite, Strategic Manager of Planning & Regeneration, 1 Belle Vue Square, Broughton Road, Skipton BD23 1FJ ☎ 01756 706409 🖷 01756 700658 🖱 dsmurthwaite@cravendc.gov.uk

E-Government: Mr Chris Firth ICT Shared Services Interim Manager, 1 Belle Vue Square, Broughton Road, Skipton BD23 1FJ ✉ cfirth@cravendc.gov.uk

Electoral Registration: Mr Andrew Mather Member Services Manager, 1 Belle Vue Square, Broughton Road, Skipton BD23 1FJ ☎ 01756 701126 ✉ amather@cravendc.gov.uk

Emergency Planning: Mr Paul Shevlin Chief Executive, 1 Belle Vue Square, Broughton Road, Skipton BD23 1FJ ☎ 01756 706201 🖷 01756 706219 ✉ pshevlin@cravendc.gov.uk

Environmental Health: Mr Wyn Ashton, Principal Housing Services Manager, 1 Belle Vue Square, Broughton Road, , Skipton BD23 1FJ ☎ 01756 706338 🖷 01756 700658 ✉ washton@cravendc.gov.uk

Estates, Property & Valuation: Ms Hazel Smith Assets & Project Manager, 1 Belle Vue Square, Broughton Road, Skipton BD23 1FJ ☎ 01756 706310 ✉ hsmith@cravendc.gov.uk

Finance: Ms Nicola Chick Strategic Manager - Financial Services, 1 Belle Vue Square, Broughton Road, Skipton BD23 1FJ ☎ 01756 706418 ✉ nchick@cravendc.gov.uk

Fleet Management: Mr Paul Florentine Waste & Recycling Manager, 1 Belle Vue Square, Broughton Road, , Skipton BD23 1FJ ☎ 01756 706429 🖷 01756 700658 ✉ pflorentine@cravendc.gov.uk

Grounds Maintenance: Ms Hazel Smith Assets & Projects Manager, 1 Belle Vue Square, Broughton Road, Skipton BD23 1FJ ☎ 01756 706310 🖷 01756 706219 ✉ hsmith@cravendc.gov.uk

Health and Safety: Ms Samia Hussain, Corporate Head of Business Support, 1 Belle Vue Square, Broughton Road, , Skipton BD23 1FJ ☎ 01756 706207 🖷 01756 706218 ✉ shussain@cravendc.gov.uk

Housing: Mr Wyn Ashton, Principal Housing Services Manager, 1 Belle Vue Square, Broughton Road, , Skipton BD23 1FJ ☎ 01756 706338 🖷 01756 700658 ✉ washton@cravendc.gov.uk

Legal: Ms Annette Moppett Solicitor to the Council & Monitoring Officer, 1 Belle Vue Square, Broughton Road, Skipton BD23 1FJ ☎ 01756 706325 🖷 01756 706257 ✉ amoppett@cravendc.gov.uk

Leisure and Cultural Services: Mr David Smurthwaite, Strategic Manager of Planning & Regeneration, 1 Belle Vue Square, Broughton Road, Skipton BD23 1FJ ☎ 01756 706409 🖷 01756 700658 ✉ dsmurthwaite@cravendc.gov.uk

Licensing: Ms Samia Hussain, Corporate Head of Business Support, 1 Belle Vue Square, Broughton Road, , Skipton BD23 1FJ ☎ 01756 706207 🖷 01756 706218 ✉ shussain@cravendc.gov.uk

Member Services: Mr Andrew Mather Member Services Manager, 1 Belle Vue Square, Broughton Road, Skipton BD23 1FJ ☎ 01756 701126 ✉ amather@cravendc.gov.uk

Parking: Ms Hazel Smith Assets & Project Manager, 1 Belle Vue Square, Broughton Road, Skipton BD23 1FJ ☎ 01756 706310 ✉ hsmith@cravendc.gov.uk

Partnerships: Ms Kate Senior Partnerships Manager, 1 Belle Vue Square, Broughton Road, Skipton BD23 1FJ ☎ 01756 706414 🖷 01756 700658 ✉ ksenior@cravendc.gov.uk

Personnel / HR: Ms Samia Hussain, Corporate Head of Business Support, 1 Belle Vue Square, Broughton Road, , Skipton BD23 1FJ ☎ 01756 706207 🖷 01756 706218 ✉ shussain@cravendc.gov.uk

Planning: Mr Ian Swain Development Control Manager, 1 Belle Vue Square, Broughton Road, Skipton BD23 1FJ ☎ 01756 706465 🖷 01756 700658 ✉ wgudger@cravendc.gov.uk

Procurement: Ms Carol Lee Procurement, Payments & Risk Manager, 1 Belle Vue Square, Broughton Road, Skipton BD23 1FJ ☎ 01756 706271 ✉ clee@cravendc.gov.uk

Recycling & Waste Minimisation: Mr Paul Florentine Waste & Recycling Manager, 1 Belle Vue Square, Broughton Road, , Skipton BD23 1FJ ☎ 01756 706429 🖷 01756 700658 ✉ pflorentine@cravendc.gov.uk

Regeneration: Mr David Smurthwaite, Strategic Manager of Planning & Regeneration, 1 Belle Vue Square, Broughton Road, Skipton BD23 1FJ ☎ 01756 706409 🖷 01756 700658 ✉ dsmurthwaite@cravendc.gov.uk

Tourism: Mr David Smurthwaite, Strategic Manager of Planning & Regeneration, 1 Belle Vue Square, Broughton Road, Skipton BD23 1FJ ☎ 01756 706409 🖷 01756 700658 ✉ dsmurthwaite@cravendc.gov.uk

Waste Management: Mr Paul Florentine Waste & Recycling Manager, 1 Belle Vue Square, Broughton Road, , Skipton BD23 1FJ ☎ 01756 706429 🖷 01756 700658 ✉ pflorentine@cravendc.gov.uk

COUNCILLORS

***Leader of the Council* Foster**, Richard (CON - Grassington) cllr.rfoster@cravendc.gov.uk

***Deputy Leader of the Council* Mulligan**, Patrick (CON - Aire Valley-with-Lothersdale) cllr.pmulligan@cravendc.gov.uk

***Group Leader* Barrett**, Philip (IND - Glusburn) cllr.philip.barrett@northyorks.gov.uk

***Group Leader* English**, Paul (LD - Skipton West) cllr.paulenglish@cravendc.gov.uk

Baxandall, Roger (UKIP - Glusburn) cllr.rbaxandall@cravendc.gov.uk

Brockbank, Linda (CON - Bentham) ccprod@uwclub.net

Clark, Christopher (CON - Upper Wharfedale) cllr.cclark@cravendc.gov.uk

Dawson, John (CON - Skipton North) cllr.jdawson@cravendc.gov.uk

Fairbank, Patricia (CON - Aire Valley with Lothersdale)

Green, Adrian (CON - Cowling) cllr.agreen@cravendc.gov.uk

Harbron, Christopher (CON - Skipton East) cllr.charbron@cravendc.gov.uk

CRAVEN

Heseltine, Robert (IND - Skipton South)
cllr.rheseltine@cravendc.gov.uk

Hull, Wendy (CON - Settle & Ribble Banks)
cllr.whull@cravendc.gov.uk

Ireton, David (IND - Ingleton & Clapham)
cllr.direton@cravendc.gov.uk

Jaquin, Eric (LD - Skipton East)
cllr.ejaquin@cravendc.gov.uk

Kerwin-Davey, John (IND - Skipton North)
cllr.jkerwin-davey@cravendc.gov.uk

Lis, Carl (CON - Ingleton & Clapham)
cllr.clis@cravendc.gov.uk

Madeley, Peter (LAB - Skipton West)
cllr.pmadeley@cravendc.gov.uk

Mason, Robert (IND - West Craven)
cllr.rmason@cravendc.gov.uk

Moorby, Robert (IND - Hellifield & Long Preston)
cllr.cmoorby@cravendc.gov.uk

Morrell, Stephen (IND - Sutton-in-Craven)
cllr.smorrell@cravendc.gov.uk

Myers, Simon (CON - Gargrave & Malhamdale)
cllr.smyers@cravendc.gov.uk

Place, Stephen (IND - Sutton-in-Craven)
cllr.splace@cravendc.gov.uk

Quinn, John (CON - Embsay-with-Eastby)
cllr.aquinn@cravendc.gov.uk

Quinn, Gillian (CON - Barden Fell)
cllr.gquinn@cravendc.gov.uk

Solloway, Andrew (IND - Skipton South)
cllr.asolloway@cravendc.gov.uk

Staveley, David (CON - Settle & Ribblebanks)
cllr.dstaveley@cravendc.gov.uk

Sutcliffe, Alan (CON - Gargrave & Malhamdale)
cllr.asutcliffe@cravendc.gov.uk

Thompson, Ian (CON - Bentham)
cllr.ithompson@cravendc.gov.uk

Welch, Richard (CON - Penyghent)
cllr.rwelch@cravendc.gov.uk

POLITICAL COMPOSITION

CON: 17, IND: 9, LD: 2, UKIP: 1, LAB: 1

COMMITTEE CHAIRS

Audit & Governance: Mr Christopher Harbron

Planning: Mr Richard Welch

Crawley D

Crawley Borough Council, Town Hall, The Boulevard, Crawley RH10 1UZ
☎ 01293 438000 🖷 01293 511803 ✉ crawleybc@crawley.gov.uk
💻 www.crawley.gov.uk

FACTS AND FIGURES

Parliamentary Constituencies: Crawley
EU Constituencies: South East
Election Frequency: Elections are by thirds

PRINCIPAL OFFICERS

Chief Executive: Mr Lee Harris Chief Executive, Town Hall, The Boulevard, Crawley RH10 1UZ ☎ 01293 438626 🖷 01293 438723 ✉ lee.harris@crawley.gov.uk

Deputy Chief Executive: Mr Peter Browning, Deputy Chief Executive, Town Hall, The Boulevard, Crawley RH10 1UZ ☎ 01293 438754 🖷 01293 438606 ✉ peter.browning@crawley.gov.uk

Senior Management: Mr Clem Smith Head of Economic & Environmental Services, Town Hall, The Boulevard, Crawley RH10 1UZ ☎ 01293 438567 ✉ clem.smith@crawley.gov.uk

Access Officer / Social Services (Disability): Mr Damian Brewer Access Officer of Horsham District Council, Town Hall, The Boulevard, Crawley RH10 1UZ ☎ 01403 215648 🖷 01403 215599 ✉ damian.brewer@crawley.gov.uk

Building Control: Ms Vanessa Good Building Development & Marketing Manager, Town Hall, The Boulevard, Crawley RH10 1UZ ☎ 01403 215157 ✉ vanessa.good@horsham.gov.uk

PR / Communications: Mr Allan Hambly Communications Manager, Town Hall, The Boulevard, Crawley RH10 1UZ ☎ 01293 438781 🖷 01293 438602 ✉ allan.hambly@crawley.gov.uk

Community Planning: Ms Carrie Burton, Transformation Manager, Town Hall, The Boulevard, Crawley RH10 1UZ ☎ 01293 438473 🖷 01293 438718 ✉ carrie.burton@crawley.gov.uk

Community Safety: Mrs Nora Davies Community Engagement Officer, Town Hall, The Boulevard, Crawley RH10 1UZ ☎ 01293 439225 ✉ nora.davies@crawley.gov.uk

Computer Management: Mrs Lucasta Grayson, Head of People & Technology, Town Hall, The Boulevard, Crawley RH10 1UZ ☎ 01293 438213 ✉ lucasta.grayson@crawley.gov.uk

Contracts: Ms Jo Newton-Smith Procurement Manager, Town Hall, The Boulevard, Crawley RH10 1UZ ☎ 01403 215299 ✉ jo.newton-smith@crawley.gov.uk

Customer Service: Mrs Lucasta Grayson, Head of People & Technology, Town Hall, The Boulevard, Crawley RH10 1UZ ☎ 01293 438213 ✉ lucasta.grayson@crawley.gov.uk

Direct Labour: Mr Peter Browning, Deputy Chief Executive, Town Hall, The Boulevard, Crawley RH10 1UZ ☎ 01293 438754 🖷 01293 438606 ✉ peter.browning@crawley.gov.uk

Economic Development: Mr Clem Smith Head of Economic & Environmental Services, Town Hall, The Boulevard, Crawley RH10 1UZ ☎ 01293 438567 ✉ clem.smith@crawley.gov.uk

Economic Development: Miss Lise Sorensen Economic Development Officer, Town Hall, The Boulevard, Crawley RH10 1UZ ☎ 01293 438519 ✉ lise.sorensen@crawley.gov.uk

E-Government: Mrs Lucasta Grayson, Head of People & Technology, Town Hall, The Boulevard, Crawley RH10 1UZ ☎ 01293 438213 ✉ lucasta.grayson@crawley.gov.uk

Electoral Registration: Ms Ann-Maria Brown, Head of Legal & Democratic Services, Town Hall, The Boulevard, Crawley RH10 1UZ ☎ 01293 438292 🖷 01293 511803 ✉ ann-maria.brown@crawley.gov.uk

Electoral Registration: Mr Andrew Oakley, Electoral Services Manager, Town Hall, The Boulevard, Crawley RH10 1UZ ☎ 01293 438346 🖷 01293 511803 ✉ andrew.oakley@crawley.gov.uk

Emergency Planning: Mr Andrew Gaffney Emergency Planning Officer, Town Hall, The Boulevard, Crawley RH10 1UZ ☎ 01293 468454 ✉ andy.gaffney@crawley.gov.uk

Energy Management: Mr Brett Hagen Environment Manager, Town Hall, The Boulevard, Crawley RH10 1UZ ☎ 01293 438543 🖷 01293 438604 ✉ brett.hagen@crawley.gov.uk

Environmental / Technical Services: Mr Peter Browning, Deputy Chief Executive, Town Hall, The Boulevard, Crawley RH10 1UZ ☎ 01293 438754 🖷 01293 438606 ✉ peter.browning@crawley.gov.uk

Environmental / Technical Services: Mr Clem Smith Head of Economic & Environmental Services, Town Hall, The Boulevard, Crawley RH10 1UZ ☎ 01293 438567 ✉ clem.smith@crawley.gov.uk

Environmental Health: Mr Clem Smith Head of Economic & Environmental Services, Town Hall, The Boulevard, Crawley RH10 1UZ ☎ 01293 438567 ✉ clem.smith@crawley.gov.uk

European Liaison: Mr Lee Harris Chief Executive, Town Hall, The Boulevard, Crawley RH10 1UZ ☎ 01293 438626 🖷 01293 438723 ✉ lee.harris@crawley.gov.uk

Facilities: Mr Mike Pidgeon, Facilities Manager, Town Hall, The Boulevard, Crawley RH10 1UZ ☎ 01293 438291 🖷 01293 438602 ✉ mike.pidgeon@crawley.gov.uk

Finance: Mrs Karen Hayes Head of Finance, Revenues & Benefits, Town Hall, The Boulevard, Crawley RH10 1UZ ☎ 01293 438263 ✉ karen.hayes@crawley.gov.uk

Grounds Maintenance: Mrs Karen Rham Parks & Green Spaces Officer, Town Hall, The Boulevard, Crawley RH10 1UZ ☎ 01293 535624 ✉ karen.rham@crawley.gov.uk

Health and Safety: Mr Andrew Gaffney Emergency Planning Officer, Town Hall, The Boulevard, Crawley RH10 1UZ ☎ 01293 468454 ✉ andy.gaffney@crawley.gov.uk

Home Energy Conservation: Mr Brett Hagen Environment Manager, Town Hall, The Boulevard, Crawley RH10 1UZ ☎ 01293 438543 🖷 01293 438604 ✉ brett.hagen@crawley.gov.uk

Housing: Mrs Karen Dodds Head of Crawley Homes, Town Hall, The Boulevard, Crawley RH10 1UZ ☎ 01293 438256 ✉ karen.dodds@crawley.gov.uk

Housing: Ms Diana Maughan Head of Strategic Planning & Housing, Town Hall, The Boulevard, Crawley RH10 1UZ ☎ 01293 438234 ✉ diana.maughan@crawley.gov.uk

Housing Maintenance: Mr Tim Honess Maintenance Operations Manager, Town Hall, The Boulevard, Crawley RH10 1UZ ☎ 01293 438253 ✉ tim.honess@crawley.gov.uk

Legal: Ms Ann-Maria Brown, Head of Legal & Democratic Services, Town Hall, The Boulevard, Crawley RH10 1UZ ☎ 01293 438292 🖷 01293 511803 ✉ ann-maria.brown@crawley.gov.uk

Leisure and Cultural Services: Mr Christian Harris Head of Community Services, Town Hall, The Boulevard, Crawley RH10 1UZ ☎ 01293 438420 ✉ christian.harris@crawley.gov.uk

Licensing: Mr Tony Baldock Environmental Health Manager, Town Hall, The Boulevard, Crawley RH10 1UZ ☎ 01293 438220 ✉ tony.baldock@crawley.gov.uk

Lottery Funding, Charity and Voluntary: Mr Nigel Sheehan Head of Partnership Services, Town Hall, The Boulevard, Crawley RH10 1UZ ☎ 01293 438728 ✉ nigel.sheehan@crawley.gov.uk

Member Services: Ms Ann-Maria Brown, Head of Legal & Democratic Services, Town Hall, The Boulevard, Crawley RH10 1UZ ☎ 01293 438292 🖷 01293 511803 ✉ ann-maria.brown@crawley.gov.uk

Parking: Mr Steve Kirby Enforcement & Technical Services Manager, Town Hall, The Boulevard, Crawley RH10 1UZ ☎ 01293 438961 ✉ steve.kirby@crawley.gov.uk

Personnel / HR: Mrs Lucasta Grayson, Head of People & Technology, Town Hall, The Boulevard, Crawley RH10 1UZ ☎ 01293 438213 ✉ lucasta.grayson@crawley.gov.uk

Planning: Mrs Jean McPherson Development Control Manager, Town Hall, The Boulevard, Crawley RH10 1UZ ☎ 01293 438577 🖷 01293 438495 ✉ jean.mcpherson@crawley.gov.uk

Procurement: Ms Jo Newton-Smith Procurement Manager, Town Hall, The Boulevard, Crawley RH10 1UZ ☎ 01293 438363 ✉ jo.newton-smith@crawley.gov.uk

Recycling & Waste Minimisation: Mr Nigel Sheehan Head of Partnership Services, Town Hall, The Boulevard, Crawley RH10 1UZ ☎ 01293 438728 ✉ nigel.sheehan@crawley.gov.uk

Staff Training: Ms Jo Gaywood HR & Development Manager, Town Hall, The Boulevard, Crawley RH10 1UZ ☎ 01293 438095 ✉ jo.gaywood@crawley.gov.uk

Street Scene: Mr Graham Rowe, Street Scene Services & Cleansing Manager, Town Hall, The Boulevard, Crawley RH10 1UZ ☎ 01293 438460 🖷 01293 438606 ✉ graham.rowe@crawley.gov.uk

Sustainable Communities: Mr Peter Browning, Deputy Chief Executive, Town Hall, The Boulevard, Crawley RH10 1UZ ☎ 01293 438754 🖷 01293 438606 ✉ peter.browning@crawley.gov.uk

Sustainable Development: Mr Brett Hagen Environment Manager, Town Hall, The Boulevard, Crawley RH10 1UZ ☎ 01293 438543 🖷 01293 438604 ✉ brett.hagen@crawley.gov.uk

Town Centre: Mr Alfredo Mendes Town Centre Co-ordinator, Town Hall, The Boulevard, Crawley RH10 1UZ ☎ 01293 438237 ✉ alfredo.mendes@crawley.gov.uk

Transport: Mr Graham Rowe, Street Scene Services & Cleansing Manager, Town Hall, The Boulevard, Crawley RH10 1UZ ☎ 01293 438460 🖷 01293 438606 ✉ graham.rowe@crawley.gov.uk

Waste Collection and Disposal: Mr Nigel Sheehan Head of Partnership Services, Town Hall, The Boulevard, Crawley RH10 1UZ ☎ 01293 438728 ✉ nigel.sheehan@crawley.gov.uk

COUNCILLORS

***Leader of the Council* Lamb**, Peter (LAB - Northgate)
peter.lamb@crawley.gov.uk

Ayling, Marion (LAB - Bewbush)
marion.ayling@crawley.gov.uk

Bloom, Howard (CON - Pound Hill South & Worth)

Brockwell, Keith (CON - Pound Hill North)
keith.brockwell@crawley.gov.uk

Burgess, Brenda (CON - Three Bridges)
brenda.burgess@crawley.gov.uk

Burgess, Bob (CON - Three Bridges)
bob.burgess@crawley.gov.uk

Burrett, Richard (CON - Pound Hill North)
richard.burrett@crawley.gov.uk

Cheshire, Chris (LAB - Bewbush)
chris.cheshire@crawley.gov.uk

Crow, Duncan (CON - Furnace Green)
duncan.crow@crawley.gov.uk

Eade, Carol (CON - Furnace Green)
carol.eade@crawley.gov.uk

Guidera, Francis (CON - Tilgate)

Irvine, Ian (LAB - Broadfield North)
ian.irvine@crawley.gov.uk

Jaggard, Kim (CON - Maidenbower)

Jones, Michael (LAB - Bewbush)
michael.jones@crawley.gov.uk

Joyce, Stephen (LAB - Langley Green)
stephen.joyce@crawley.gov.uk

Lanzer, Bob (CON - Pound Hill South & Worth)
bob.lanzer@crawley.gov.uk

Lloyd, Colin (LAB - Tilgate)
colin.lloyd@crawley.gov.uk

Lunnon, Timothy (LAB - Broadfield South)
hayley.thorne@crawley.gov.uk

Marshall-Ascough, Liam (CON - Southgate)
liam.marshall-ascough@crawley.gov.uk

McCarthy, Kevan (CON - Pound Hill)

Mecrow, Beryl (CON - Pound Hill South & Worth)

Moffatt, Colin (LAB - Broadfield South)
colin.moffatt@crawley.gov.uk

Mullins, Chris (LAB - Gossops Green)
chris.mullins@crawley.gov.uk

Peck, Duncan (CON - Maidenbower)
duncan.peck@crawley.gov.uk

Quinn, Brian (LAB - Broadfield North)
brian.quinn@crawley.gov.uk

Sharma, Raj (LAB - Southgate)

Skudder, Andrew (LAB - Langley Green)

Smith, Peter (LAB - Ifield)
peter.smith@crawley.gov.uk

Smith, Brenda (LAB - Langley Green)
brenda.smith@crawley.gov.uk

Stanley, John (LAB - Ifield)
hayley.thorne@crawley.gov.uk

Stone, Martin (CON - Ifield)

Sudan, Karen (LAB - West Green)

Tarrant, Jan (CON - Southgate)

Thomas, Geraint (LAB - Northgate)
geraint.thomas@crawley.gov.uk

Trussell, Ken (CON - Maidenbower)
ken.trussell@crawley.gov.uk

Vitler, Lisa (CON - Gossops Green)

Ward, Bill (LAB - West Green)
bill.ward@crawley.gov.uk

POLITICAL COMPOSITION

LAB: 19, CON: 18

COMMITTEE CHAIRS

Audit: Mr Bill Ward

Development Control: Mr Ian Irvine

Licensing: Mr Brian Quinn

Croydon L

Croydon London Borough Council, The Town Hall, Katherine Street, Croydon CR0 1NX
☎ 020 8726 6000 🖷 020 8760 5657 🖳 www.croydon.gov.uk

FACTS AND FIGURES

Parliamentary Constituencies: Croydon Central, Croydon North, Croydon South
EU Constituencies: London
Election Frequency: Elections are of whole council

PRINCIPAL OFFICERS

Chief Executive: Mr Nathan Elvery, Chief Executive, 9th Floor, Zone B, Bernard Weatherill House, 8 Mint Walk, Croydon CR0 1EA ☎ 020 8726 6000 Extn 62416 🖷 020 8686 7405 ✉ nathan.elvery@croydon.gov.uk

Senior Management: Mrs Julie Belvir Director of Democratic & Legal Services, 4th Floor, Zone G, Bernard Weatherill House, 8 Mint Walk, Croydon CR0 1EA ☎ 020 8726 6000 Extn 64985 ✉ julie.belvir@croydon.gov.uk

Senior Management: Ms Heather Daley Director of Human Resources, The Town Hall, Katherine Street, Croydon CR0 1NX ☎ 020 8760 6561 🖷 020 8760 5611 ✉ heather.daley@croydon.gov.uk

Senior Management: Mr Paul Greenhalgh Executive Director - People, 9th Floor Zone B, Bernard Weatherill House, 8 Mint Walk, Croydon CR0 1EA ☎ 020 8726 6000 Ext 65787 ✉ paul.greenhalgh@croydon.gov.uk

Senior Management: Ms Jo Negrini Executive Director - Place, 9th Floor, Zone B, Bernard Weatherill House, 8 Mint Walk, Croydon CR0 1EA ☎ 020 8726 6000 ✉ jo.negrini@croydon.gov.uk

Senior Management: Dr Mike Robinson Director - Public Health, The Town Hall, Katherine Street, Croydon CR0 1NX ✉ mike.robinson@croydon.gov.uk

Senior Management: Mr Richard Simpson Director of Finance & Assets, The Town Hall, Katherine Street, Croydon CR0 1NX

Architect, Building / Property Services: Mr Stephen Wingrave Head of Asset Management & Estates, The Town Hall, Katherine Street, Croydon CR0 1NX ☎ 020 8726 6000 Extn 61512 🖷 020 8760 5728 ✉ stephen.wingrave@croydon.gov.uk

Building Control: Mr Mike Kiely Director - Planning, The Town Hall, Katherine Street, Croydon CR0 1NX ☎ 020 8760 5599 ✉ mike.kiely@croydon.gov.uk

Catering Services: Ms Allyson Lloyd, Corporate Catering Manager, The Town Hall, Katherine Street, Croydon CR0 1NX ☎ 020 8760 5467 ✉ allyson.lloyd@croydon.gov.uk

Children / Youth Services: Mr Paul Greenhalgh Executive Director - People, 9th Floor, Zone B, Bernard Weatherill House, 8 Mint Walk, Croydon CR0 1EA ☎ 020 8726 6000 Ext 65787 ✉ paul.greenhalgh@croydon.gov.uk

PR / Communications: Ms Hayley Lewis Head of Communications & Engagement, The Town Hall, Katherine Street, Croydon CR0 1NX

Community Safety: Mr Andy Opie Director - Safety, The Town Hall, Katherine Street, Croydon CR0 1NX ☎ 020 8726 6000 Extn 65686 ✉ andy.opie@croydon.gov.uk

Computer Management: Mr Nathan Elvery, Chief Executive, 9th Floor, Zone B, Bernard Weatherill House, 8 Mint Walk, Croydon CR0 1EA ☎ 020 8726 6000 Extn 62416 🖷 020 8686 7405 ✉ nathan.elvery@croydon.gov.uk

Consumer Protection and Trading Standards: Mr Paul Foster, Head of Regulatory Services, The Town Hall, Katherine Street, Croydon CR0 1NX ☎ 020 8726 6000 Extn 65475 🖷 020 8760 5786 ✉ paul.foster@croydon.gov.uk

Contracts: Ms Sarah Ireland Director of Strategy Commissioning Procurement & Performance, The Town Hall, Katherine Street, Croydon CR0 1NX ☎ 020 8726 6000 Extn 62070 ✉ sarah.ireland@croydon.gov.uk

Customer Service: Mr Graham Cadle Director - Transformation & Communications Services, The Town Hall, Katherine Street, Croydon CR0 1NX ☎ 020 8726 6000 Extn 63295 ✉ graham.cadle@croydon.gov.uk

Economic Development: Ms Lisa McCance Head of Economic Development, The Town Hall, Katherine Street, Croydon CR0 1NX ☎ 020 8760 5655 ✉ lisa.mccance@croydon.gov.uk

E-Government: Mr Nathan Elvery, Chief Executive, 9th Floor, Zone B, Bernard Weatherill House, 8 Mint Walk, Croydon CR0 1EA ☎ 020 8726 6000 Extn 62416 🖷 020 8686 7405 ✉ nathan.elvery@croydon.gov.uk

Electoral Registration: Mr Lea Goddard, Head of Registration Services & Electoral, Town Hall, Katherine Street, Croydon CR9 1DE ☎ 020 8726 6000 Extn 65730 🖷 020 8407 1308 ✉ lea.goddard@croydon.gov.uk

Emergency Planning: Mr Maurice Egan, Corporate Security Manager, The Town Hall, Katherine Street, Croydon CR0 1NX ☎ 020 8760 5678 🖷 020 8760 5630 ✉ mo.egan@croydon.gov.uk

Environmental / Technical Services: Ms Jo Negrini Executive Director - Place, The Town Hall, Katherine Street, Croydon CR0 1NX ☎ 020 8726 6000 ✉ jo.negrini@croydon.gov.uk

Estates, Property & Valuation: Mr Stephen Wingrave Head of Asset Management & Estates, The Town Hall, Katherine Street, Croydon CR0 1NX ☎ 020 8726 6000 Extn 61512 🖷 020 8760 5728 ✉ stephen.wingrave@croydon.gov.uk

Finance: Mr Nigel Cook Head of Pensions & Treasury, The Town Hall, Katherine Street, Croydon CR0 1NX ☎ 020 8726 6000 ✉ nigel.cook@croydon.gov.uk

Finance: Mr Nathan Elvery, Chief Executive, The Town Hall, Katherine Street, Croydon CR0 1NX ☎ 020 8726 6000 Extn 62416 🖷 020 8686 7405 ✉ nathan.elvery@croydon.gov.uk

Treasury: Mr Nigel Cook Head - Treasury & Pensions, The Town Hall, Katherine Street, Croydon CR0 1NX ☎ 020 8726 6000 ✉ nigel.cook@croydon.gov.uk

Treasury: Mr Derek Fernandes Treasury Manager, The Town Hall, Katherine Street, Croydon CR0 1NX ☎ 020 8726 6000 Extn 62526 ✉ derek.fernandes@croydon.gov.uk

Pensions: Mr Nigel Cook Head of Pensions & Treasury, The Town Hall, Katherine Street, Croydon CR0 1NX ☎ 020 8726 6000 ✉ nigel.cook@croydon.gov.uk

Health and Safety: Ms Liz Johnston, Health & Safety Senior Consultant, The Town Hall, Katherine Street, Croydon CR0 1NX ☎ 020 8726 6000 Extn 62001 🖷 020 8760 5749 ✉ elizabeth.johnston@croydon.gov.uk

CROYDON

Highways: Mr Steve Iles Director - Streets, The Town Hall, Katherine Street, Croydon CR0 1NX ☎ 020 8726 6000 Ext 52821 steve.iles@croydon.gov.uk

Housing: Mr Peter Brown Director of Housing Needs & Renewal, The Town Hall, Katherine Street, Croydon CR0 1NX ☎ 020 8726 6100 peter.brown@croydon.gov.uk

Housing: Mr Mark Meehan Director - Housing Need, The Town Hall, Katherine Street, Croydon CR0 1NX ☎ 020 8726 6000 mark.meehan@croydon.gov.uk

Housing: Ms Hannah Miller Executive Director, The Town Hall, Katherine Street, Croydon CR0 1NX ☎ 020 8726 6000 Extn 64590 hannah.miller@croydon.gov.uk

Housing: Mr Stephen Tate , The Town Hall, Katherine Street, Croydon CR0 1NX ☎ 020 8726 6000 stephen.tate@croydon.gov.uk

Housing Maintenance: Mr Dave Sutherland, Divisional Director of Housing Management Services, The Town Hall, Katherine Street, Croydon CR0 1NX ☎ 020 8726 6000 Extn 4957 🖷 020 8760 5745 dave.sutherland@croydon.gov.uk

Housing Maintenance: Mr Stephen Tate , The Town Hall, Katherine Street, Croydon CR0 1NX ☎ 020 8726 6000 stephen.tate@croydon.gov.uk

Legal: Mrs Julie Belvir Director of Democratic & Legal Services, The Town Hall, Katherine Street, Croydon CR0 1NX ☎ 020 8726 6000 Extn 64985 julie.belvir@croydon.gov.uk

Leisure and Cultural Services: Mr Malcolm Kendall Head of Environmental & Leisure Services, The Town Hall, Katherine Street, Croydon CR0 1NX ☎ 020 8726 6000 malcolm.kendall@croydon.gov.uk

Licensing: Mr Michael Goddard, Licensing Team Leader, The Town Hall, Katherine Street, Croydon CR0 1NX ☎ 020 8726 6000 michael.goddard@croydon.gov.uk

Lottery Funding, Charity and Voluntary: Mr David Freeman, Policy Manager, The Town Hall, Katherine Street, Croydon CR0 1NX ☎ 020 8726 6000 🖷 020 8760 5463 david.freeman@croydon.gov.uk

Member Services: Mr Solomon Agutu Head of Democratic Services & Scrutiny, The Town Hall, Katherine Street, Croydon CR0 1NX ☎ 020 8726 6000 extn 62920 soloman.agutu@croydon.gov.uk

Personnel / HR: Ms Heather Daley Director of Human Resources, The Town Hall, Katherine Street, Croydon CR0 1NX ☎ 020 8760 6561 🖷 020 8760 5611 heather.daley@croydon.gov.uk

Planning: Mr Mike Kiely Director - Planning, The Town Hall, Katherine Street, Croydon CR0 1NX ☎ 020 8760 5599 mike.kiely@croydon.gov.uk

Planning: Mr Rory Macleod Head of Planning Control, The Town Hall, Katherine Street, Croydon CR0 1NX ☎ 020 8726 6000 Ext 65578 rory.macleod@croydon.gov.uk

Procurement: Ms Sarah Ireland Director of Strategy Commissioning Procurement & Performance, The Town Hall, Katherine Street, Croydon CR0 1NX ☎ 020 8726 6000 Extn 62070 sarah.ireland@croydon.gov.uk

Public Libraries: Ms Aileen Cahill Head of Libraries, Central Library, Katharine Street, Croydon CR9 1ET ☎ 020 8726 6000 Extn 1123 aileen.cahill@croydon.gov.uk

Recycling & Waste Minimisation: Mr Malcolm Kendall Head of Environmental & Leisure Services, Stubbs Mead Depot, Factory Lane, Croydon CR0 3RL ☎ 020 8726 6000 malcolm.kendall@croydon.gov.uk

Regeneration: Ms Jo Negrini Executive Director - Place, The Town Hall, Katherine Street, Croydon CR0 1NX ☎ 020 8726 6000 jo.negrini@croydon.gov.uk

Regeneration: Mr Stephen Tate , The Town Hall, Katherine Street, Croydon CR0 1NX ☎ 020 8726 6000 stephen.tate@croydon.gov.uk

Road Safety: Mr Mike Barton Strategic Technical Manager, The Town Hall, Katherine Street, Croydon CR0 1NX ☎ 020 8760 6197 mike.barton@croydon.gov.uk

Social Services: Mr Mark Fowler , The Town Hall, Katherine Street, Croydon CR0 1NX ☎ 020 8726 6000 mark.fowler@croydon.gov.uk

Social Services: Mrs Hannah Miller, Executive Director of Housing & Social Services, The Town Hall, Katherine Street, Croydon CR0 1NX ☎ 020 8760 5490 🖷 020 8686 1251 hannah.miller@croydon.gov.uk

Social Services (Adult): Mr Mark Fowler , The Town Hall, Katherine Street, Croydon CR0 1NX ☎ 020 8726 6000 mark.fowler@croydon.gov.uk

Social Services (Adult): Ms Pratima Solanki Director - Adult Care & 0-65 Disability Services, The Town Hall, Katherine Street, Croydon CR0 1NX ☎ 020 8760 5727 pratima.solanki@croydon.gov.uk

Public Health: Dr Mike Robinson Director - Public Health, The Town Hall, Katherine Street, Croydon CR0 1NX mike.robinson@croydon.gov.uk

Staff Training: Ms Sarah Garner Head of Learning, Organisational Change & Cultural Development, The Town Hall, Katherine Street, Croydon CR0 1NX ☎ 020 86047207 sarah.garner@croydon.gov.uk

Street Scene: Mr Andy Opie Director - Safety, The Town Hall, Katherine Street, Croydon CR0 1NX ☎ 020 8726 6000 Extn 65686 andy.opie@croydon.gov.uk

Traffic Management: Mr Dave Tomlinson Traffic Manager, The Town Hall, Katherine Street, Croydon CR0 1NX ☎ 020 8760 5425 dave.tomlinson@croydon.gov.uk

Transport: Mr Ian Plowright Head of Strategic Transport, The Town Hall, Katherine Street, Croydon CR0 1NX ☎ 020 8726 6000 Extn 62927 ian.plowright@croydon.gov.uk

Waste Collection and Disposal: Mr Malcolm Kendall Head of Environmental & Leisure Services, Stubbs Mead Depot, Factory Lane, Croydon CR0 3RL ☎ 020 8726 6000 ✉ malcolm.kendall@croydon.gov.uk

Waste Management: Mr Malcolm Kendall Head of Environmental & Leisure Services, Stubbs Mead Depot, Factory Lane, Croydon CR0 3RL ☎ 020 8726 6000 ✉ malcolm.kendall@croydon.gov.uk

COUNCILLORS

***Mayor* Hay-Justice**, Patricia (LAB - Addiscombe)
patricia.hay-justice@croydon.gov.uk

***Deputy Mayor* Lawlor**, Wayne (LAB - South Norwood)
wayne.lawlor@croydon.gov.uk

***Leader of the Council* Newman**, Tony (LAB - Woodside)
tony.newman@croydon.gov.uk

***Deputy Leader of the Council* Butler**, Alison (LAB - Bensham Manor)
alison.butler@croydon.gov.uk

Ali, Hamida (LAB - Woodside)
hamida.ali@croydon.gov.uk

Audsley, Jamie (LAB - Bensham Manor)
jamie.audsley@croydon.gov.uk

Avis, Jane (LAB - South Norwood)
jane.avis@croydon.gov.uk

Bains, Jeet (CON - Coulsdon West)
jeet.bains@croydon.gov.uk

Bashford, Sara (CON - Selsdon & Ballards)
sara.bashford@croydon.gov.uk

Bee, Kathy (LAB - South Norwood)
kathy.bee@croydon.gov.uk

Benn, Emily (LAB - West Thornton)
emily.benn@croydon.gov.uk

Bennett, Sue (CON - Shirley)
sue.bennett@croydon.gov.uk

Bird, Margaret (CON - Coulsdon East)
margaret.bird@croydon.gov.uk

Bonner, Carole (LAB - Fieldway)
carole.bonner@croydon.gov.uk

Brew, Simon (CON - Purley)
simon.brew@croydon.gov.uk

Buttinger, Jan (CON - Kenley)
jan.buttinger@croydon.gov.uk

Canning, Robert (LAB - Waddon)
robert.canning@croydon.gov.uk

Chatterjee, Richard (CON - Shirley)
richard.chatterjee@croydon.gov.uk

Chowdhury, Sherwan (LAB - Norbury)
sherwan.chowdhury@croydon.gov.uk

Clancy, Luke (CON - Coulsdon West)
luke.clancy@croydon.gov.uk

Clouder, Pat (LAB - Thornton Heath)
pat.clouder@croydon.gov.uk

Collins, Stuart (LAB - Broad Green)
stuart.collins@croydon.gov.uk

Creatura, Mario (CON - Coulsdon West)
mario.creatura@croydon.gov.uk

Cummings, Jason (CON - Heathfield)
jason.cummings@croydon.gov.uk

Fisher, Mike (CON - Shirley)
mike.fisher@croydon.gov.uk

Fitzsimons, Sean (LAB - Addiscombe)
sean.fitzsimons@croydon.gov.uk

Flemming, Alisa (LAB - Upper Norwood)
alisa.flemming@croydon.gov.uk

Gatland, Maria (CON - Croham)
maria.gatland@croydon.gov.uk

Godfrey, Timothy (LAB - Selhurst)
timothy.godfrey@croydon.gov.uk

Hale, Lynne (CON - Sanderstead)
lynne.hale@croydon.gov.uk

Hall, Simon (LAB - Fieldway)
simon.hall@croydon.gov.uk

Henson, Maddie (LAB - Ashburton)
maddie.henson@croydon.gov.uk

Hollands, Steve (CON - Kenley)
steven.hollands@croydon.gov.uk

Hopley, Yvette (CON - Sanderstead)
yvette.hopley@croydon.gov.uk

Jewitt, Karen (LAB - Thornton Heath)
karen.jewitt@croydon.gov.uk

Kabir, Humayun (LAB - Bensham Manor)
humayun.kabir@croydon.gov.uk

Khan, Shafi (LAB - Norbury)
shafi.khan@croydon.gov.uk

Khan, Bernadette (LAB - West Thornton)
bernadette.khan@croydon.gov.uk

King, Stuart (LAB - West Thornton)
stuart.king@croydon.gov.uk

Kyeremeh, Matthew (LAB - Thornton Heath)
matthew.kyeremeh@croydon.gov.uk

Letts, Toni (LAB - Selhurst)
toni.letts@croydon.gov.uk

Lewis, Oliver (LAB - New Addington)
oliver.lewis@croydon.gov.uk

Mann, Stephen (LAB - Ashburton)
stephen.mann@croydon.gov.uk

Mansell, Maggie (LAB - Norbury)
maggie.mansell@croydon.gov.uk

Mead, Dudley (CON - Selsdon & Ballards)
dudley.mead@croydon.gov.uk

Mead, Margaret (CON - Heathfield)
margaret.mead@croydon.gov.uk

Mohan, Vidhi (CON - Fairfield)
vidhi.mohan@croydon.gov.uk

Neal, Michael (CON - Croham)
michael.neal@croydon.gov.uk

O'Connell, Steve (CON - Kenley)
steve.o'connell@croydon.gov.uk

Pelling, Andrew (LAB - Waddon)
andrew.pelling@croydon.gov.uk

Perry, Jason (CON - Croham)
jason.perry@croydon.gov.uk

Pollard, Tim (CON - Sanderstead)
councillor@timpollard.co.uk

Pollard, Helen (CON - Fairfield)
helen.pollard@croydon.gov.uk

Prince, Joy (LAB - Waddon)
joy.prince@croydon.gov.uk

Quadir, Badsha (CON - Purley)
badsha.quadia@croydon.gov.uk

Rendle, Andrew (LAB - Ashburton)
andrew.rendle@croydon.gov.uk

Ryan, Pat (LAB - Upper Norwood)
pat.ryan@croydon.gov.uk

Scott, Paul (LAB - Woodside)
paul.scott@croydon.gov.uk

Selva, Mike (LAB - Broad Green)
mike.selva@croydon.gov.uk

Shahul-Hameed, Manju (LAB - Broad Green)
the.mayor@croydon.gov.uk

Speakman, Donald (CON - Purley)
donaldspeakman@croydon.gov.uk

Stranack, Andy (CON - Heathfield)
andy.stranack@croydon.gov.uk

Thomas, Phil (CON - Selsdon & Ballards)
phil.thomas@croydon.gov.uk

Thompson, James (CON - Coulsdon East)
james.thompson@croydon.gov.uk

Watson, Mark (LAB - Addiscombe)
mark.watson@croydon.gov.uk

Wentworth, John (LAB - Upper Norwood)
john.wentworth@croydon.gov.uk

Winborn, Sue (CON - Fairfield)
susan.winborn@croydon.gov.uk

Wood, David (LAB - Selhurst)
david.wood@croydon.gov.uk

Woodley, Louisa (LAB - New Addington)
louisa.woodley@croydon.gov.uk

Wright, Chris (CON - Coulsdon East)
chris.wright@croydon.gov.uk

POLITICAL COMPOSITION
LAB: 40, CON: 30

COMMITTEE CHAIRS

Licensing: Ms Jane Avis

Pensions: Mr John Wentworth

Planning: Mr Paul Scott

Cumbria — C

Cumbria County Council, The Courts, English Street, Carlisle CA3 8NA

☎ 01228 606060 🖷 01228 606327 ✉ information@cumbriacc.gov.uk
🖳 www.cumbria.gov.uk

FACTS AND FIGURES
EU Constituencies: North West
Election Frequency: Elections are of whole council

PRINCIPAL OFFICERS

Chief Executive: Mrs Diane Wood Chief Executive, The Courts, English Street, Carlisle CA3 8NA ☎ 01228 226301
✉ diane.wood@cumbria.gov.uk

Senior Management: Ms Sally Burton Interim Corporate Director - Health & Care Services, The Courts, English Street, Carlisle CA3 8NA ☎ 01228 227110 ✉ sally.burton@cumbria.gov.uk

Senior Management: Mr Colin Cox Director - Public Health, The Courts, English Street, Carlisle CA3 8NA
✉ colin.cox@cumbria.gov.uk

Senior Management: Mr Dominic Donnini Corporate Director - Environment & Community Services, The Courts, English Street, Carlisle CA3 8NA ☎ 01228 226260
✉ dominic.donnini@cumbria.gov.uk

Senior Management: Mr John Macilwraith Corporate Director - Children's Services, The Courts, English Street, Carlisle CA3 8NA
☎ 01228 226868 ✉ john.macilwraith@cumbria.gov.uk

Senior Management: Mr Jim Onions Chief Fire Officer, The Courts, English Street, Carlisle CA3 8NA ☎ 01768 812565
✉ jim.onions@cumbria.gov.uk

Architect, Building / Property Services: Mr Mike Smith Assistant Director - Capital Programmes & Property, Parkhouse Building, Baron Way, Carlisle CA6 4SJ ☎ 07717 003727
🖷 01228 226016 ✉ mike.smith@cumbria.gov.uk

Best Value: Mr Duncan McQueen, Senior Manager - Performance & Intelligence, The Courts, Carlisle CA3 8NA ☎ 01228 226293
🖷 01228 226331 ✉ duncan.mcqueen@cumbria.gov.uk

Building Control: Mr Mike Smith Assistant Director - Capital Programmes & Property, Parkhouse Building, Baron Way, Carlisle CA6 4SJ ☎ 07717 003727 🖷 01228 226016
✉ mike.smith@cumbria.gov.uk

Children / Youth Services: Ms Lyn Burns Assistant Director - Children & Families, The Courts, English Street, Carlisle CA3 8NA
☎ 01228 226859 ✉ lyn.burns@cumbria.gov.uk

Children / Youth Services: Mr John Macilwraith Corporate Director - Children's Services, The Courts, English Street, Carlisle CA3 8NA ☎ 01228 226868 ✉ john.macilwraith@cumbria.gov.uk

PR / Communications: Ms Sara Turnbull Communications Manager, The Courts, English Street, Carlisle CA3 8NA
☎ 01228 226614 ✉ sara.turnbull@cumbria.gov.uk

Community Safety: Mr Jim Onions Chief Fire Officer, The Courts, English Street, Carlisle CA3 8NA ☎ 01768 812565
✉ jim.onions@cumbria.gov.uk

Computer Management: Mr Ian Williamson Senior Manager - ICT Delivery, English Gate Plaza, Botchergate, Carlisle CA1 1RP ☎ 01228 223410 ✉ ian.williamson@cumbria.gov.uk

Consumer Protection and Trading Standards: Ms Angela Jones Assistant Director - Environment & Community Services, South Lakeland House, Lowther Street, Kendal LA9 4DQ ☎ 07920 814141 🖷 01539 773580 ✉ angela.jones@cumbria.gov.uk

Contracts: Mr Conway Stewart Senior Manager - Corporate Procurement & CM, The Courts, English Street, Carlisle CA3 8NA ☎ 01228 221744 🖷 01228 607605 ✉ conway.stewart@cumbria.gov.uk

Corporate Services: Mr Alan Ratcliffe Assistant Director - Business Services, The Courts, English Street, Carlisle CA3 8NA ☎ 01228 221013 ✉ alan.ratcliffe@cumbria.gov.uk

Customer Service: Mr Jim Grisenthwaite Assistant Director - Community Services, The Courts, English Street, Carlisle CA3 8NA ☎ 01228 221540 ✉ jim.grisenthwaite@cumbria.gov.uk

Education: Mr John Macilwraith Corporate Director - Children's Services, The Courts, English Street, Carlisle CA3 8NA ☎ 01228 226868 ✉ john.macilwraith@cumbria.gov.uk

Emergency Planning: Ms Angela Jones Assistant Director - Environment & Community Services, South Lakeland House, Lowther Street, Kendal LA9 4DQ ☎ 07920 814141 🖷 01539 773580 ✉ angela.jones@cumbria.gov.uk

Energy Management: Ms Angela Jones Assistant Director - Environment & Community Services, South Lakeland House, Lowther Street, Kendal LA9 4DQ ☎ 07920 814141 🖷 01539 773580 ✉ angela.jones@cumbria.gov.uk

Estates, Property & Valuation: Mr Mike Smith Assistant Director - Capital Programmes & Property, Parkhouse Building, Baron Way, Carlisle CA6 4SJ ☎ 07717 003727 🖷 01228 226016 ✉ mike.smith@cumbria.gov.uk

Facilities: Mr Mike Smith Assistant Director - Capital Programmes & Property, Parkhouse Building, Baron Way, Carlisle CA6 4SJ ☎ 07717 003727 🖷 01228 226016 ✉ mike.smith@cumbria.gov.uk

Finance: Mr Dominic Donnini Corporate Director - Environment & Community Services, The Courts, English Street, Carlisle CA3 8NA ☎ 01228 226260 ✉ dominic.donnini@cumbria.gov.uk

Treasury: Ms Julie Crellin Assistant Director - Finance & S151 Officer, The Courts, English Street, Carlisle CA3 8NA ☎ 01228 227291 ✉ julie.crellin@cumbria.gov.uk

Pensions: Mrs Fiona Miller Senior Manager - Pensions & Finance, The Courts, English Street, Carlisle CA3 8NA ☎ 01228 226280 ✉ fiona.miller@cumbria.gov.uk

Fleet Management: Mr David Jenkinson Interim Fleet & ITT Manager, Mintsfeet Depot, Mintsfeet Road North, Kendal LA9 6LZ ☎ 01539 713103 ✉ david.jenkins@cumbria.gov.uk

Grounds Maintenance: Mr Mike Smith Assistant Director - Capital Programmes & Property, Parkhouse Building, Baron Way, Carlisle CA6 4SJ ☎ 07717 003727 🖷 01228 226016 ✉ mike.smith@cumbria.gov.uk

Health and Safety: Mr Julian Stainton Senior Manager - Health, Safety & Wellbeing, Carlisle Fire Station East, Eastern Way, Carlisle CA1 3RA ☎ 07500227793 ✉ julian.stainton@cumbria.gov.uk

Highways: Mr Andrew Moss Assistant Director - Highways & Transport, Parkhouse Building, Baron Way, Carlisle CA6 4SJ ☎ 01228 221388 🖷 01228 607605 ✉ andrew.moss@cumbria.gov.uk

Local Area Agreement: Ms Clare Killeen Strategic Policy Advisor, The Courts, English Street, Carlisle CA3 8NA ☎ 01228 226514 ✉ clare.killeen@cumbria.gov.uk

Legal: Ms Caroline Elwood Interim Monitoring Officer, The Courts, English Street, Carlisle CA3 8NA ☎ 01228 227350 🖷 01228 607376 ✉ caroline.elwood@cumbria.gov.uk

Leisure and Cultural Services: Mr Jim Grisenthwaite Assistant Director - Community Services, The Courts, English Street, Carlisle CA3 8NA ☎ 01228 221540 ✉ jim.grisenthwaite@cumbria.gov.uk

Lighting: Mr Andrew Moss Assistant Director - Highways & Transport, Parkhouse Building, Baron Way, Carlisle CA6 4SJ ☎ 01228 221388 🖷 01228 607605 ✉ andrew.moss@cumbria.gov.uk

Parking: Mr Andrew Moss Assistant Director - Highways & Transport, The Courts, English Street, Carlisle CA3 8NA ☎ 01228 221388 🖷 01228 607605 ✉ andrew.moss@cumbria.gov.uk

Partnerships: Mrs Helen Blake Senior Manager - Policy, Planning & Communities, The Courts, English Street, Carlisle CA3 8NA ☎ 01228 226687 ✉ helen.blake@cumbria.gov.uk

Procurement: Mr Conway Stewart Senior Manager - Corporate Procurement & CM, The Courts, English Street, Carlisle CA3 8NA ☎ 01228 221744 🖷 01228 607605 ✉ conway.stewart@cumbria.gov.uk

Public Libraries: Mr Jim Grisenthwaite Assistant Director - Community Services, The Courts, English Street, Carlisle CA3 8NA ☎ 01228 221540 ✉ jim.grisenthwaite@cumbria.gov.uk

Recycling & Waste Minimisation: Mr Ian Stephenson Waste Services Manager, Parkhouse Building, Baron Way, Carlisle CA6 4SJ ☎ 07825 723046 ✉ ian.stephenson@cumbria.gov.uk

Road Safety: Mr Chris Broadbent Road Safety Co-ordinator, Parkhouse Building, Baron Way, Carlisle CA6 4SJ ☎ 07826 874354 ✉ chris.broadbent@cumbria.gov.uk

Social Services: Ms Sally Burton Interim Corporate Director - Health & Care Services, The Courts, English Street, Carlisle CA3 8NA ☎ 01228 227110 ✉ sally.burton@cumbria.gov.uk

Social Services (Adult): Ms Lyn Burns Assistant Director - Children & Families, The Courts, English Street, Carlisle CA3 8NA ☎ 01228 226859 ✉ lyn.burns@cumbria.gov.uk

CUMBRIA

Social Services (Adult): Ms Amanda Evans Assistant Director - Adult Social Care, The Courts, English Street, Carlisle CA3 8NA ☎ 01228 227116 ✉ amanda.evans@cumbria.gov.uk

Social Services (Children): Mr John Macilwraith Corporate Director - Children's Services, The Courts, English Street, Carlisle CA3 8NA ☎ 01228 226868 ✉ john.macilwraith@cumbria.gov.uk

Childrens Social Care: Mr John Macilwraith Corporate Director - Children's Services, The Courts, English Street, Carlisle CA3 8NA ☎ 01228 226868 ✉ john.macilwraith@cumbria.gov.uk

Public Health: Mr Colin Cox Director - Public Health, The Courts, English Street, Carlisle CA3 8NA ✉ colin.cox@cumbria.gov.uk

Sustainable Communities: Mrs Helen Blake Senior Manager - Policy, Planning & Communities, The Courts, English Street, Carlisle CA3 8NA ☎ 01228 226687 ✉ helen.blake@cumbria.gov.uk

Sustainable Communities: Mr Jim Grisenthwaite Assistant Director - Community Services, The Courts, English Street, Carlisle CA3 8NA ☎ 01228 221540 ✉ jim.grisenthwaite@cumbria.gov.uk

Sustainable Communities: Mr Jim Onions Chief Fire Officer, The Courts, English Street, Carlisle CA3 8NA ☎ 01768 812565 ✉ jim.onions@cumbria.gov.uk

Traffic Management: Mr Andrew Moss Assistant Director - Highways & Transport, Parkhouse Building, Baron Way, Carlisle CA6 4SJ ☎ 01228 221388 🖷 01228 607605 ✉ andrew.moss@cumbria.gov.uk

Transport: Mr Andrew Moss Assistant Director - Highways & Transport, Parkhouse Building, Baron Way, Carlisle CA6 4SJ ☎ 01228 221388 🖷 01228 607605 ✉ andrew.moss@cumbria.gov.uk

Transport Planner: Mr Andrew Moss Assistant Director - Highways & Transport, Parkhouse Building, Baron Way, Carlisle CA6 4SJ ☎ 01228 221388 🖷 01228 607605 ✉ andrew.moss@cumbria.gov.uk

Waste Collection and Disposal: Mr Ian Stephenson Waste Services Manager, Parkhouse Building, Baron Way, Carlisle CA6 4SJ ☎ 07825 723046 ✉ ian.stephenson@cumbria.gov.uk

Waste Management: Mr Ian Stephenson Waste Services Manager, Parkhouse Building, Baron Way, Carlisle CA6 4SJ ☎ 07825 723046 ✉ ian.stephenson@cumbria.gov.uk

COUNCILLORS

***Chair* Worth**, Melvyn (LAB - Walney North)
melvyn.worth@cumbria.gov.uk

***Vice-Chair* Cook**, Geoffrey (LD - Kendal Highgate)
geoffrey.cook@cumbriacc.gov.uk

***Leader of the Council* Young**, Stewart (LAB - Upperby)
stewart.young@cumbria.gov.uk

***Deputy Leader of the Council* Bell**, Patricia (LD - Penrith East)
patricia.bell@cumbriacc.gov.uk

***Group Leader* Airey**, James (CON - Ulverston West)
james.airey@cumbria.gov.uk

***Group Leader* Holliday**, Joseph (IND - St John's & Great Clifton)
joe.holliday@cumbria.gov.uk

Allison, Trevor (INDNA - Dalston & Burgh)
trevor.allison@cumbria.gov.uk

Barry, Alan (LAB - St Michaels)
alan.barry@cumbria.gov.uk

Bateman, Olivia (CON - Kirkby Stephen)
libby.bateman@cumbria.gov.uk

Bell, John (LAB - Morton)
john.bell@cumbria.gov.uk

Betton, Robert (INDNA - Botcherby)
robert.betton@cumbria.gov.uk

Bingham, Roger (CON - Lower Kentdale)
roger.bingham@cumbria.gov.uk

Bland, James (CON - Lyth Valley)
james.bland@cumbria.gov.uk

Bowditch, Christine (LAB - Belle Vue)

Bowness, Joseph (CON - Bothel & Wharrels)
alan.bowness@cumbria.gov.uk

Burns, Anne (LAB - Hindpool)
anne.burns@cumbriacc.gov.uk

Carrick, Hilary (CON - Penrith North)
hilary.carrick@cumbria.gov.uk

Cassidy, Frank (LAB - Walney South)

Clark, Alan (LAB - Dearham & Broughton)
alan.clarck@cumbria.gov.uk

Clarkson, Norman (CON - Gosforth)
norman.clarkson@cumbriacc.gov.uk

Collins, Stan (LD - Upper Kent)
stan.collins@cumbriacc.gov.uk

Cotton, Nicholas (LD - Sedbergh & Kirkby Lonsdale)
nicholas.cotton@cumbria.gov.uk

Crawford, Brian (CON - Millom)
brian.crawford@cumbria.gov.uk

Doughty, Barry (LAB - Dalton North)
barry.doughty@cumbria.gov.uk

Earl, Deborah (LAB - Harraby South)
deborah.earl@cumbria.gov.uk

Evans, Shirley (LD - Kendal Nether)
shirley.evans@cumbria.gov.uk

Fairbairn, Duncan (CON - Thursby)
duncan.fairbairn@cumbria.gov.uk

Fearon, Helen (CON - Penrith West)
helen.fearon@cumbria.gov.uk

Feeney-Johnson, Clare (LD - Kendal Castle)
clare.feeney-johnson@cumbria.gov.uk

Fisher, Lawrence (CON - Brampton)
lawrence.fisher@cumbriacc.gov.uk

Fletcher, David (LD - High Furness)
david.fletcher@cumbria.gov.uk

Furneaux, Beth (LAB - Yewdale)
beth.furneaux@cumbria.gov.uk

Graham, William (INDNA - Corby & Hayton)
william.graham@cumbria.gov.uk

Gray, Brenda (LD - Kendal South)
brenda.gray@cumbria.gov.uk

Halliday, Heidi (LD - Lakes)
heidi.halliday@cumbria.gov.uk

Hamilton, Kevin (LAB - Risedale)
kevin.hamilton@cumbria.gov.uk

Hawkins, Michael (LAB - Mirehouse)
mike.hawkins@cumbria.gov.uk

Hayman, Susan (LAB - Howgate)
susan.hayman@cumbria.gov.uk

Hitchen, Keith (CON - Millom Without)
keith.hitchen@cumbria.gov.uk

Hughes, Neil (LD - Eden Lakes)
neil.hughes@cumbria.gov.uk

Humes, Gerald (LAB - Moss Bay & Moorclose)
gerald.humes@cumbria.gov.uk

Jones, Colin (LD - Windermere)
colin.jones@cumbria.gov.uk

Kennon, Alan (CON - Cockermouth South)
alan.kennon@cumbria.gov.uk

Knowles, Timothy (LAB - Cleator Moor East & Frizington)
timothy.knowles@cumbriacc.gov.uk

Liddle, Roger (LAB - Wigton)
roger.liddle@cumbria.gov.uk

Lister, Jim (CON - Aspatria)
jim.lister@cumbria.gov.uk

Little, Keith (LAB - Maryport South)
keith.little@cumbria.gov.uk

Lysser, Andrew (INDNA - Keswick)
andrew.lysser@cumbria.gov.uk

Mallinson, Elizabeth (CON - Stanwix Urban)
elizabeth.mallinson@cumbria.gov.uk

Mallinson, John (CON - Houghton & Irthington)
john.mallinson@cumbria.gov.uk

Markley, Anthony (CON - Solway Coast)
anthony.markley@cumbria.gov.uk

Marriner, Nicholas (CON - Wetheral)
nick.marriner@cumbria.gov.uk

McCarron-Holmes, Carni (LAB - Maryport North)
carni.mccarron-holmes@cumbria.gov.uk

McCreesh, John (LD - Kendal Strickland & Fell)
john.mccreesh@cumbria.gov.uk

McDevitt, Hugh (LAB - Denton Holme)
hugh.mcdevitt@cumbria.gov.uk

McEwan, William (LAB - Ormsgill)
william.mcewan@cumbria.gov.uk

McGuckin, Alan (LAB - Castle)
alan.mcguckin@cumbria.gov.uk

Morgan, Frank (LAB - Cleator Moor West)
frank.morgan@cumbriacc.gov.uk

Murphy, Jane (LAB - Newbarns & Parkside)
jane.murphy@cumbria.gov.uk

Murphy, John (LAB - Old Barrow)
john.murphy1@cumbria.gov.uk

Nicholson, Eric (CON - Cockermouth North)
eric.nicholson@cumbriacc.gov.uk

Rae, Marjorie (IND - Harrington)
marjorie.rae@cumbria.gov.uk

Roberts, David (CON - Hawcoat)
david.roberts@cumbria.gov.uk

Robinson, Mary (INDNA - Alston & East Fellside)
mary.robinson@cumbria.gov.uk

Sanderson, Sue (LD - Cartmel)

Skillicorn, Wendy (LAB - Kells & Sandwith)
wendy.skillicorn@cumbria.gov.uk

Southward, David (LAB - Egremont)
david.southward@cumbria.gov.uk

Stephenson, Martin (CON - Appleby)
martin.stephenson@cumbria.gov.uk

Stewart, Ian (LD - Kent Estuary)
ian.stewart@cumbria.gov.uk

Strong, Gary (CON - Penrith Rural)
gary.b.strong@cumbria.gov.uk

Tarbitt, Val (CON - Longtown)
val.tarbitt@cumbria.gov.uk

Tibble, Celia (LAB - Seaton)

Toole, Alan (CON - Belah)
alan.toole@cumbria.gov.uk

Wall, Helen (LAB - Roosecote)
helen.wall@cumbria.gov.uk

Watson, Reg (LAB - Currock)
reg.watson@cumbria.gov.uk

Wearing, Bill (CON - Grange)
bill.wearing@cumbria.gov.uk

Weber, Cyril (LAB - Harraby North)
cyril.weber@cumbria.gov.uk

Weir, Eileen (LAB - Bransty)
eileen.weir@cumbria.gov.uk

Wentworth Waites, Tom (CON - Greystoke & Hesket)
tom.wentworth-waites@cumbria.gov.uk

Wharrier, Christine (LAB - Hillcrest & Hensingham)
christine.wharrier@cumbria.gov.uk

Willis, Janet (LD - Low Furness)
janet.willis@cumbria.gov.uk

Wilson, Ernie (LAB - Dalton South)
ernie.wilson~cumbria.gov.uk

Wilson, Mark (LAB - Ulverston East)
mark.wilson2@cumbria.gov.uk

Wormstrup, Henry (LAB - Egremont North & St Bees)
henry.wormstrup@cumbria.gov.uk

POLITICAL COMPOSITION

LAB: 36, CON: 26, LD: 15, INDNA: 5, IND: 2

COMMITTEE CHAIRS

Audit & Assurance: Mr Timothy Knowles

Development Control: Mr Alan Clark

Health & Wellbeing: Mr Stewart Young

Pensions: Mr Melvyn Worth

DACORUM

Dacorum Borough Council, Civic Centre, Marlowes, Hemel Hempstead HP1 1HH
☎ 01442 228000 🖷 01442 228995
✉ communications@dacorum.gov.uk 💻 www.dacorum.gov.uk

FACTS AND FIGURES

Parliamentary Constituencies: Hemel Hempstead
EU Constituencies: Eastern
Election Frequency: Elections are of whole council

PRINCIPAL OFFICERS

Chief Executive: Mrs Sally Marshall Chief Executive, Civic Centre, Marlowes, Hemel Hempstead HP1 1HH ☎ 01442 228213 ✉ sally.marshall@dacorum.gov.uk

Senior Management: Mr James Deane Corporate Director - Finance & Operations (Section 151 Officer), Civic Centre, Marlowes, Hemel Hempstead HP1 1HH ✉ james.deane@dacorum.gov.uk

Senior Management: Mr Mark Gaynor Corporate Director - Housing & Regeneration, Civic Centre, Marlowes, Hemel Hempstead HP1 1HH ☎ 01442 228500 ✉ mark.gaynor@dacorum.gov.uk

Children / Youth Services: Ms Julie Still Group Manager - Resident Services, Civic Centre, Marlowes, Hemel Hempstead HP1 1HH ☎ 01442 228453 ✉ julie.still@dacorum.gov.uk

Community Safety: Ms Julie Still Group Manager - Resident Services, Civic Centre, Marlowes, Hemel Hempstead HP1 1HH ☎ 01442 228453 ✉ julie.still@dacorum.gov.uk

Computer Management: Mr Ben Trueman Group Manager - Information, Communication & Technology, Civic Centre, Marlowes, Hemel Hempstead HP1 1HH ☎ 01442 228171 ✉ ben.trueman@dacorum.gov.uk

Corporate Services: Ms Lesley Crisp Strategic Planning & Regeneration Officer, Civic Centre, Marlowes, Hemel Hempstead HP1 1HH ☎ 01756 700600 ✉ lesley.crisp@dacorum.gov.uk

Corporate Services: Mr Jim Doyle Group Manager of Democratic Services, Civic Centre, Marlowes, Hemel Hempstead HP1 1HH ☎ 01442 228222 🖷 01442 228264 ✉ jim.doyle@dacorum.gov.uk

Economic Development: Ms Lesley Crisp Strategic Planning & Regeneration Officer, Civic Centre, Marlowes, Hemel Hempstead HP1 1HH ☎ 01756 700600 ✉ lesley.crisp@dacorum.gov.uk

Economic Development: Mrs Chris Taylor, Group Manager of Strategic Planning & Regeneration, Civic Centre, Marlowes, Hemel Hempstead HP1 1HH ☎ 01442 867805 🖷 01442 266056 ✉ chris.taylor@dacorum.gov.uk

E-Government: Mr Ben Trueman Group Manager - Information, Communication & Technology, Civic Centre, Marlowes, Hemel Hempstead HP1 1HH ☎ 01442 228171 ✉ ben.trueman@dacorum.gov.uk

Electoral Registration: Mr Jim Doyle Group Manager of Democratic Services, Civic Centre, Marlowes, Hemel Hempstead HP1 1HH ☎ 01442 228222 🖷 01442 228264 ✉ jim.doyle@dacorum.gov.uk

Emergency Planning: Mr Chris Troy Group Manager - Regulatory Services, Civic Centre, Marlowes, Hemel Hempstead HP1 1HH ☎ 01442 228473 ✉ chris.troy@dacorum.gov.uk

Environmental Health: Mr Chris Troy Group Manager - Regulatory Services, Civic Centre, Marlowes, Hemel Hempstead HP1 1HH ☎ 01442 228473 ✉ chris.troy@dacorum.gov.uk

Estates, Property & Valuation: Ms Adriana Livingstone Team Leader of Estates & Valuation, Civic Centre, Marlowes, Hemel Hempstead HP1 1HH ☎ 01442 228776 ✉ adriana.livingstone@dacroum.gov.uk

Finance: Mr James Deane Corporate Director - Finance & Operations (Section 151 Officer), Civic Centre, Marlowes, Hemel Hempstead HP1 1HH ✉ james.deane@dacorum.gov.uk

Grounds Maintenance: Mr Simon Coultas Assistant Operations Manager, Civic Centre, Marlowes, Hemel Hempstead HP1 1HH ☎ 01442 228032 🖷 01442 228884 ✉ simon.coultas@dacorum.gov.uk

Health and Safety: Mr Chris Troy Group Manager - Regulatory Services, Civic Centre, Marlowes, Hemel Hempstead HP1 1HH ☎ 01442 228473 ✉ chris.troy@dacorum.gov.uk

Housing Maintenance: Mr Neil Brown Programme & Procurement Team Leader, Civic Centre, Marlowes, Hemel Hempstead HP1 1HH ☎ 01442 228639

Legal: Mr Steven Baker, Assistant Director - Chief Executive's Department, Civic Centre, Marlowes, Hemel Hempstead HP1 1HH ☎ 01442 228229 ✉ steve.baker@dacorum.gov.uk

Member Services: Mr Jim Doyle Group Manager of Democratic Services, Civic Centre, Marlowes, Hemel Hempstead HP1 1HH ☎ 01442 228222 🖷 01442 228264 ✉ jim.doyle@dacorum.gov.uk

Parking: Mr Steve Barnes, Parking Services Team Leader, Civic Centre, Marlowes, Hemel Hempstead HP1 1HH ☎ 01442 249484 ✉ steve.barnes@dacorum.gov.uk

Personnel / HR: Mr Matthew Rawdon Group Manager - People, Civic Centre, Marlowes, Hemel Hempstead HP1 1HH ☎ 01442 228513 ✉ matthew.rawdon@dacorum.gov.uk

Planning: Mr James Doe Assistant Director of Planning, Development & Regeneration, Civic Centre, Marlowes, Hemel Hempstead HP1 1HH ☎ 01442 228000 ✉ james.doe@dacorum.gov.uk

Procurement: Mr Ben Hosier Group Manager of Commissioning, Procurement & Compliance, Civic Centre, Marlowes, Hemel Hempstead HP1 1HH ☎ 01442 228215 🖷 01442 228995 ✉ ben.hosier@dacorum.gov.uk

Recycling & Waste Minimisation: Mr Craig Thorpe Group Manager of Enviromental Services, Civic Centre, Marlowes, Hemel Hempstead HP1 1HH ☎ 01442 228030 ✉ craig.thorpe@dacorum.gov.uk

Regeneration: Mr Mark Gaynor Corporate Director - Housing & Regeneration, Civic Centre, Marlowes, Hemel Hempstead HP1 1HH ☎ 01442 228500 ✉ mark.gaynor@dacorum.gov.uk

Staff Training: Mr Bill Haylock Organisational Development & Training Team Leader, Civic Centre, Marlowes, Hemel Hempstead HP1 1HH ☎ 01442 228029 ✉ bill.haylock@dacorum.gov.uk

Street Scene: Mr David Austin Assistant Director of Neighbourhood Delivery, Civic Centre, Marlowes, Hemel Hempstead HP1 1HH ☎ 01442 228355 ✉ david.austin@dacorum.gov.uk

Town Centre: Mr James Doe Assistant Director of Planning, Development & Regeneration, Civic Centre, Marlowes, Hemel Hempstead HP1 1HH ☎ 01442 228000 ✉ james.doe@dacorum.gov.uk

Transport Planner: Mr James Doe Assistant Director of Planning, Development & Regeneration, Civic Centre, Marlowes, Hemel Hempstead HP1 1HH ☎ 01442 228000 ✉ james.doe@dacorum.gov.uk

Waste Collection and Disposal: Mr Craig Thorpe Group Manager of Enviromental Services, Civic Centre, Marlowes, Hemel Hempstead HP1 1HH ☎ 01442 228030 ✉ craig.thorpe@dacorum.gov.uk

Waste Management: Mr Craig Thorpe Group Manager of Enviromental Services, Civic Centre, Marlowes, Hemel Hempstead HP1 1HH ☎ 01442 228030 ✉ craig.thorpe@dacorum.gov.uk

COUNCILLORS

***Mayor* Adeleke**, Gbola (CON - Bovingdon, Flaunden & Chipperfield)
gbola.adeleke@dacorum.gov.uk

***Leader of the Council* Williams**, Andrew (CON - Boxmoor)
andrew.williams@dacorum.gov.uk

***Deputy Leader of the Council* Griffiths**, Margaret (CON - Leverstock Green)
margaret.griffiths@dacorum.gov.uk

Adshead, Sharon (CON - Adeyfield West)
sharon.adshead@dacorum.gov.uk

Anderson, Alan (CON - Kings Langley)
alan.anderson@dacorum.gov.uk

Ashburn, Julian (CON - Berkhamsted West)
julian.ashburn@dacorum.gov.uk

Ashead, Graham (CON - Adeyfield East)
grham.ashead.gov.uk

Banks, Julie (CON - Govehill)
julie.banks@dacorum.gov.uk

Barnes, Adam (CON - Bovingdon, Flaunden & Chipperfiled)
adam.barnes@dacorum.gov.uk

Bassadone, Hazel (CON - Leverstock Green)
hazel.bassadone@dacorum.gov.uk

Bateman, Stephen (CON - Berkhamsted East)
stephen.bateman@dacorum.gov.uk

Bhinder, Alexander (CON - Grovehill)
alexander.bhinder@dacorum.gov.uk

Birnie, John (CON - Bennetts End)
joh.birnie@dacorum.gov.uk

Brown, Christine (CON - Hemel Hempstead Town)
christine.brown@dacorum.gov.uk

Chapman, Herbert (CON - Watling)
herbert.chapman@dacorum.gov.uk

Clark, Michael (CON - Apsley & Corner Hall)
michael.clark@dacorum.gov.uk

Collins, David (CON - Berkhamsted Castle)
david.collins@dacorum.gov.uk

Collins, Elaine (CON - Berkhamsted East)
elaine.collins@dacorum.gov.uk

Conway, Olive (CON - Tring West & Rural)
olive.conway@dacorum.gov.uk

Douris, Terry (CON - Ashridge)
terry.douris@dacorum.gov.uk

Elliot, Graeme (CON - Chaulden & Warners End)
graeme.elliott@dacorum.gov.uk

Fantham, Alan (CON - Northchurch)
alan.fantham@dacorum.gov.uk

Fethney, Tony (LAB - Highfield)
tony.fethney@dacorum.gov.uk

Fisher, Anne (LAB - Hemel Hempstead Town)
anne.fisher@dacorum.gov.uk

Guest, Fiona (CON - Chaulden & Warners End)
fiona@dandfguest.eclipse.co.uk

Harden, Neil (CON - Boxmoor)
neil.harden@dacorum.gov.uk

Hearn, Penelope (CON - Tring East)
penny.hearn@dacorum.gov.uk

Hearne, Stephen (CON - Tring Central)
stephen.hearne@dacorum.gov.uk

Hicks, Mike (CON - Tring West & Rural)
mike.hicks@dacorum.gov.uk

Howard, Tina (CON - Apsley and Corner Hall)
tina.howard@dacorum.gov.uk

Imarni, Isy (CON - Gadbridge)
isy.imarni@dacorum.gov.uk

Link, Brenda (LD - Highfield)
brenda.link@dacorum.gov.uk

Maddern, Jan (CON - Nash Mills)
jan.maddern@dacorum.gov.uk

Mahmood, Suqlain (CON - Bennetts End)
suglain.mahmood@dacorum.gov.uk

Marshall, Janice (CON - Boxmoor)
janice.marshall@dacorum.gov.uk

Matthews, Peter (CON - Berkhamsted West)
peter.matthews@dacorum.gov.uk

McLean, Bob (CON - Kings Langley)
bob.mclean@dacorum.gov.uk

Mills, Stan (CON - Aldbury and Wigginton)
stan.mills@dacorum.gov.uk

Peter, Colin (CON - Apsley & Corner Hall)
colin.peter@dacorum.gov.uk

Ransley, Roxanne (LD - Tring Central)
roxanne.ransley@dacorum.gov.uk

Riddick, Stewart (CON - Bovingdon, Faluden & Chipperfield)
stewart.riddick@dacorum.gov.uk

Ritchie, Tom (CON - Berkhamsted Castle)
tom.ritchie@dacorum.gov.uk

Silwal, Goverdhan (CON - Grovehill)
goverdhan.silwal@dacorum.gov.uk

Sutton, Rosie (CON - Woodhall Farm)
rosie.sutton@dacorum.gov.uk

Sutton, Graham (CON - Leverstock Green)
graham.sutton@dacorum.gov.uk

Taylor, Roger (CON - Gadebridge)
roger.taylor@dacorum.gov.uk

Timmis, Jane (CON - Watling)
jane.timmis@dacorum.gov.uk

Tindall, Ron (LD - Adeyfield West)
ron.tindall@dacorum.go.uk

Whitman, John (CON - Chaulden & Warners End)
john.whitman@dacorum.gov.uk

Wyatt-Lowe, William (CON - Adeyfield East)
william.wyatt-lowe@dacorum.gov.uk

Wyatt-Lowe, Colette (CON - Woodhall Farm)
colette.wyatt-lowe@dacorum.gov.uk

POLITICAL COMPOSITION

CON: 46, LD: 3, LAB: 2

COMMITTEE CHAIRS

Audit: Mr Roger Taylor

Development: Mr David Collins

Finance: Mr Herbert Chapman

Licensing: Ms Penelope Hearn

Darlington U

Darlington Borough Council, Town Hall, Feethams, Darlington DL1 5QT
☎ 01325 380651 🖷 01325 382032 ✉ enquiries@darlington.gov.uk
💻 www.darlington.gov.uk

FACTS AND FIGURES

Parliamentary Constituencies: Darlington
EU Constituencies: North East
Election Frequency: Elections are of whole council

PRINCIPAL OFFICERS

Chief Executive: Ms Ada Burns Chief Executive, Town Hall, Feethams, Darlington DL1 5QT ☎ 01325 405813 ✉ ada.burns@darlington.gov.uk

Senior Management: Ms Jenni Cooke Service Director - Children's Services, Town Hall, Feethams, Darlington DL1 5QT ☎ 01325 405852 ✉ jenni.cooke@darlington.gov.uk

Senior Management: Ms Miriam Davidson Director - Public Health, Town Hall, Feethams, Darlington DL1 5QT ☎ 01325 406203 ✉ miriam.davidson@darlington.gov.uk

Senior Management: Mr Murray Rose Director - Commissioning, Town Hall, Feethams, Darlington DL1 5QT ☎ 01325 405824 ✉ murray.rose@darlington.gov.uk

Senior Management: Mr Paul Wildsmith Director - Neighbourhood Services & Resources, Town Hall, Feethams, Darlington DL1 5QT ☎ 01325 405829 ✉ paul.wildsmith@darlington.gov.uk

Senior Management: Mr Ian Williams Director - Economic Growth, Town Hall, Feethams, Darlington DL1 5QT ☎ 01325 406379 ✉ ian.williams@darlington.gov.uk

Architect, Building / Property Services: Mr Brian Robson Head of Capital Projects, Yarm Road Business Park, 17 Allington Way, Darlington DL1 4QB ☎ 01325 406608 ✉ brian.robson@darlington.gov.uk

Building Control: Mr Richard Collinson Building Control Manager, Town Hall, Feethams, Darlington DL1 5QT ☎ 01325 406213 ✉ richard.collinson@darlington.gov.uk

Catering Services: Mr Graham Carey, Catering Manager, Dolphin Centre, Horsemarket, Darlington DL1 5RP ☎ 01325 406970 ✉ graham.carey@darlington.gov.uk

Children / Youth Services: Mr David Mason Head of Social Care & YOS, Town Hall, Feethams, Darlington DL1 5QT ☎ 01325 405884 ✉ david.mason@darlington.gov.uk

Civil Registration: Mr Anthony Hall Superintendent Registrar, The Registrar Office, Backhouse Hall, Bull Wynd, Darlington DL1 5RG ☎ 01325 406400 ✉ anthony.hall@darlington.gov.uk

PR / Communications: Mr Neil Bowerbank Engagement Manager, Town Hall, Feethams, Darlington DL1 5QT ☎ 01325 406052 ✉ neil.bowerbank@darlington.gov.uk

Computer Management: Mr Ian Miles Head of ICT Services (Transaction & Operations), Town Hall, Feethams, Darlington DL1 5QT ☎ 01642 527012 ✉ ian.miles@xentrall.org.uk

Consumer Protection and Trading Standards: Mr Nigel Green, Principal Trading Standards Officer, Town Hall, Feethams, Darlington DL1 5QT ☎ 01325 406030 ✉ nigel.green@darlington.gov.uk

Customer Service: Mrs Linda Todd, Head of Democratic & Customer Services, Town Hall, Feethams, Darlington DL1 5QT ☎ 01325 405807 ✉ linda.todd@darlington.gov.uk

Economic Development: Mr Owen Wilson, Economy Manager, The Beehive, Lingfield Point, Darlington DL1 1YN ☎ 01325 406305 ✉ owen.wilson@darlington.gov.uk

Education: Ms Rachel Kershaw Head of School & Pupil Support Services, Town Hall, Feethams, Darlington DL1 5QT ☎ 01325 405885 ✉ rachel.kershaw@darlington.gov.uk

E-Government: Mr Ian Miles Head of ICT Services (Transaction & Operations), Town Hall, Feethams, Darlington DL1 5QT ☎ 01642 527012 ✉ ian.miles@xentrall.org.uk

Electoral Registration: Ms Lynne Wood Elections Manager, Town Hall, Feethams, Darlington DL1 5QT ☎ 01325 388287 ✉ lynne.wood@darlington.gov.uk

Emergency Planning: Mr Bill Westland, Head of Regulatory Services, Town Hall, Feethams, Darlington DL1 5QT ☎ 01325 406303 ✉ bill.westland@darlington.gov.uk

Energy Management: Mr Guy Metcalfe Head of Property Asset Management, Town Hall, Feethams, Darlington DL1 5QT ☎ 01325 406725 ✉ guy.metcalfe@darlington.gov.uk

Environmental / Technical Services: Mr Brian Graham Head of Environmental Services, Yarm Road Business Park, 17 Allington Way, Darlington DL1 4QB ☎ 01325 406607 ✉ brian.graham@darlington.gov.uk

Environmental Health: Mr Barry Pearson, Environmental Health Manager, Town Hall, Feethams, Darlington DL1 5QT ☎ 01325 406426 ✉ barry.pearson@darlington.gov.uk

Estates, Property & Valuation: Mr Guy Metcalfe Head of Property Asset Management, Town Hall, Feethams, Darlington DL1 5QT ☎ 01325 406725 ✉ guy.metcalfe@darlington.gov.uk

Events Manager: Mrs Marion Ogle Events Manager, Dolphin Centre, Horsemarket, Darlington DL1 5RP ☎ 01325 406990 ✉ marion.ogle@darlington.gov.uk

Finance: Mr Paul Wildsmith Director - Neighbourhood Services & Resources, Town Hall, Feethams, Darlington DL1 5QT ☎ 01325 405829 ✉ paul.wildsmith@darlington.gov.uk

Grounds Maintenance: Mr Brian Graham Head of Environmental Services, Yarm Road Business Park, 17 Allington Way, Darlington DL1 4QB ☎ 01325 406607 ✉ brian.graham@darlington.gov.uk

Health and Safety: Ms Joanne Skelton Health & Safety Manager, Town Hall, Feethams, Darlington DL1 5QT ☎ 01325 406256 ✉ joanne.skelton@darlington.gov.uk

Highways: Mr Steve Brannan Head of Highway Asset Management, Yarm Road Business Park, 17 Allington Way, Darlington DL1 4QB ☎ 01325 406663 ✉ steve.brannan@darlington.gov.uk

Highways: Mr Dave Winstanley Assistant Director - Transport & Capital Projects, Yarm Road Business Park, 17 Allington Way, Darlington DL1 4QB ☎ 01325 406618 ✉ david.winstanley@darlington.gov.uk

Housing: Mrs Pauline Mitchell Assistant Director - Housing & Building Services, Town Hall, Feethams, Darlington DL1 5QT ☎ 01325 405831 ✉ pauline.mitchell@darlington.gov.uk

Housing Maintenance: Ms Hazel Neasham, Head of Housing, Town Hall, Feethams, Darlington DL1 5QT ☎ 01325 405933 ✉ hazel.neasham@darlington.gov.uk

Legal: Mr Luke Swinhoe Head of Legal Services, Town Hall, Feethams, Darlington DL1 5QT ☎ 01325 405490 ✉ luke.swinhoe@darlington.gov.uk

Leisure and Cultural Services: Mr Mike Crawshaw Head of Culture, Dolphin Centre, Horsemarket, Darlington DL1 5RP ☎ 01325 406980 ✉ mike.crawshaw@darlington.gov.uk

Licensing: Ms Pam Ross Licensing, Parking & Trading Standards Manager, Town Hall, Feethams, Darlington DL1 5QT ☎ 01325 405988 ✉ pam.ross@darlington.gov.uk

Lifelong Learning: Mr Mike Crawshaw Head of Culture, Dolphin Centre, Horsemarket, Darlington DL1 5RP ☎ 01325 406980 ✉ mike.crawshaw@darlington.gov.uk

Lighting: Mr Paul Brownbridge Assistant Street Lighting Officer, Yarm Road Business Park, 17 Allington Way, Darlington DL1 4QB ☎ 01325 406652 ✉ paul.brownbridge@darlington.gov.uk

Member Services: Mrs Linda Todd, Head of Democratic & Customer Services, Town Hall, Feethams, Darlington DL1 5QT ☎ 01325 405807 ✉ linda.todd@darlington.gov.uk

Parking: Ms Pam Ross Licensing, Parking & Trading Standards Manager, Town Hall, Feethams, Darlington DL1 5QT ☎ 01325 405988 ✉ pam.ross@darlington.gov.uk

Partnerships: Mr Seth Pearson Executive Director - Darlington Partnership, Town Hall, Feethams, Darlington DL1 5QT ☎ 01325 406090 ✉ seth.pearson@darlington.gov.uk

Personnel / HR: Mrs Elizabeth Davison Assistant Director - Human Resources Management, Town Hall, Feethams, Darlington DL1 5QT ☎ 01325 405830 ✉ elizabeth.davison@darlington.gov.uk

Planning: Mr John Anderson Assistant Director - Economic Initiative, Town Hall, Feethams, Darlington DL1 5QT ☎ 01325 406322 ✉ john.anderson@darlington.gov.uk

Planning: Mr Roy Merrett Development Manager, Town Hall, Feethams, Darlington DL1 5QT ☎ 01325 406477 ✉ roy.merrett@darlington.gov.uk

Procurement: Ms Sarah Hutchinson Principal Lawyer (Commercial), Town Hall, Feethams, Darlington DL1 5QT ☎ 01325 405489 ✉ sarah.hutchinson@darlington.gov.uk

Public Libraries: Mr Mike Crawshaw Head of Culture, Dolphin Centre, Horsemarket, Darlington DL1 5RP ☎ 01325 406980 ✉ mike.crawshaw@darlington.gov.uk

Recycling & Waste Minimisation: Ms Phillippa Scrafton Waste Minimisation & Recycling Officer, Yarm Road Business Park, 17 Allington Way, Darlington DL1 4QB ☎ 01325 406648 ✉ phillippa.scrafton@darlington.gov.uk

Regeneration: Mr John Anderson Assistant Director - Economic Initiative, Town Hall, Feethams, Darlington DL1 5QT ☎ 01325 406322 ✉ john.anderson@darlington.gov.uk

DARLINGTON

Road Safety: Mr Andrew Casey Head of Highway Network Management, Yarm Road Business Park, 17 Allington Way, Darlington DL1 4QB ☎ 01325 406701 ✉ andrew.casey@darlington.gov.uk

Social Services: Mr Murray Rose Director - Commissioning, Town Hall, Feethams, Darlington DL1 5QT ☎ 01325 405824 ✉ murray.rose@darlington.gov.uk

Social Services (Adult): Mr Kevin Kelly Acting Assistant Director - Adult Social Care, Town Hall, Feethams, Darlington DL1 5QT ☎ 01325 406126 ✉ kevin.kelly@darlington.gov.uk

Social Services (Children): Ms Jenni Cooke Service Director - Children's Services, Town Hall, Feethams, Darlington DL1 5QT ☎ 01325 405852 ✉ jenni.cooke@darlington.gov.uk

Families: Ms Yvonne Coates Head of First Contact & Locality Services, Town Hall, Feethams, Darlington DL1 5QT ☎ 01325 405864 ✉ yvonne.coates@darlington.gov.uk

Families: Ms Jenni Cooke Service Director - Children's Services, Town Hall, Feethams, Darlington DL1 5QT ☎ 01325 405852 ✉ jenni.cooke@darlington.gov.uk

Childrens Social Care: Mr David Mason Head of Social Care & YOS, Town Hall, Feethams, Darlington DL1 5QT ☎ 01325 405884 ✉ david.mason@darlington.gov.uk

Public Health: Ms Miriam Davidson Director - Public Health, Town Hall, Feethams, Darlington DL1 5QT ☎ 01325 406203 ✉ miriam.davidson@darlington.gov.uk

Street Scene: Mr Brian Graham Head of Environmental Services, Yarm Road Business Park, 17 Allington Way, Darlington DL1 4QB ☎ 01325 406607 ✉ brian.graham@darlington.gov.uk

Sustainable Development: Ms Elizabeth Goodchild Green Economy Officer, Town Hall, Feethams, Darlington DL1 5QT ☎ 01325 406316 ✉ elizabeth.goodchild@darlington.gov.uk

Town Centre: Mr Owen Wilson, Economy Manager, Town Hall, Feethams, Darlington DL1 5QT ☎ 01325 406305 ✉ owen.wilson@darlington.gov.uk

Traffic Management: Mr Andrew Casey Head of Highway Network Management, Yarm Road Business Park, 17 Allington Way, Darlington DL1 4QB ☎ 01325 406701 ✉ andrew.casey@darlington.gov.uk

Transport: Ms Melanie Stainthorpe Admissions & Transport Team Leader, Yarm Road Business Park, 17 Allington Way, Darlington DL1 4QB ☎ 01325 405908 ✉ melanie.stainthorpe@darlington.gov.uk

Transport Planner: Mr Owen Wilson, Economy Manager, Yarm Road Business Park, 17 Allington Way, Darlington DL1 4QB ☎ 01325 406305 ✉ owen.wilson@darlington.gov.uk

Waste Collection and Disposal: Mr Brian Graham Head of Environmental Services, Yarm Road Business Park, 17 Allington Way, Darlington DL1 4QB ☎ 01325 406607 ✉ brian.graham@darlington.gov.uk

Waste Management: Mr Brian Graham Head of Environmental Services, Yarm Road Business Park, 17 Allington Way, Darlington DL1 4QB ☎ 01325 406607 ✉ brian.graham@darlington.gov.uk

Children's Play Areas: Mr Brian Graham Head of Environmental Services, Yarm Road Business Park, 17 Allington Way, Darlington DL1 4QB ☎ 01325 406607 ✉ brian.graham@darlington.gov.uk

COUNCILLORS

***Leader of the Council* Dixon**, Bill (LAB - Eastbourne)
bill.dixon@darlington.gov.uk

***Deputy Leader of the Council* Harker**, Stephen (LAB - Pierremont)
stephen.harker@darlington.gov.uk

Baldwin, Paul (LAB - Cockerton East)
paul.baldwin@darlington.gov.uk

Carson, Bob (LAB - Pierremont)
bob.carson@darlington.gov.uk

Cartwright, Gill (CON - Harrowgate Hill)
gill.cartwright@darlington.gov.uk

Copeland, Veronica (LAB - Banktop)
veronica.copeland@darlington.gov.uk

Cossins, Jan (LAB - Cockerton West)
jan.cossins@darlingon.gov.uk

Coultas, Alan (CON - Hummersknott)
alan.coultas@darlington.gov.uk

Crichlow, Roderick (LAB - Eastbourne)
roderick.crichlow@darlington.gov.uk

Crudass, Paul (CON - Heighington & Coniscliffe)
paul.crudass@darlington.gov.uk

Crumbie, Helen (LAB - Lascelles)
helen.crumbie@darlington.gov.uk

Culley, Pauline (CON - Mowden)
pauline.culley@darlington.gov.uk

Curry, Anne-Marie (LD - North Road)
annemarie.curry@darlington.gov.uk

Donoghue, Bob (CON - Park West)
bob.donoghue@darlington.gov.uk

Galletley, Ian (CON - College)
ian.galletley@darlington.gov.uk

Grundy, Richard (CON - Faverdale)
richard.grundy@darlington.gov.uk

Haszeldine, Ian (LAB - Lingfield)
ian.haszeldine@darlington.gov.uk

Haszeldine, Lynne (LAB - Lingfield)
lynne.haszeldine@darlington.gov.uk

Hughes, Cyndi (LAB - Park East)
cyndi.hughes@darlington.gov.uk

Hughes, Linda (LAB - Pierremont)
linda.hughes@darlington.gov.uk

Hutchinson, Beverley (LAB - Haughton North)
bev.hutchinson@darlington.gov.uk

Johnson, Charles (CON - Hummersknott)
charles.johnson@darlington.gov.uk

Jones, Doris (CON - Middleton St George)
doris.jones@darlington.gov.uk

Jones, Brian (CON - Sadberge & Whessoe)
brian.jones@darlington.gov.uk

Kane, Sonia (LAB - Northgate)
sonia.kane@darlington.gov.uk

Kelly, Katie (LAB - Stephenson)
katie.kelly@darlington.gov.uk

Kelly, Joe (LD - Hurworth)
joe.kelley@darlington.gov.uk

Knowles, Marjory (LAB - Harrowgate Hill)
marjory.knowles@darlington.gov.uk

Lawton, Fred (LD - North Road)
fred.lawton@darlington.gov.uk

Lee, Gerald (CON - Heighington & Coniscliffe)
gerald.lee@darlington.gov.uk

Lister, Eleanor (LAB - Northgate)
eleanor.lister@darlington.gov.uk

Lyonette, David (LAB - Haughton West)
david.lyonette@darlington.gov.uk

McEwan, Chris (LAB - Haughton East)
chris.mcewan@darlington.gov.uk

Mills, Rachel (CON - Brinkburn & Faverdale)
rachel.mills@darlington.gov.uk

Newall, Wendy (LAB - Lascelles)
wendy.newall@darlington.gov.uk

Nicholson, Kevin (IND - Eastbourne)
kevin.nicholson@darlington.gov.uk

Nicholson, Michael (LAB - Park East)
michael.nicholson@darlington.gov.uk

Nutt, Thomas (LAB - Haughton North)
thomas.nutt@darlington.gov.uk

Regan, David (LAB - Cockerton West)
david.regan@darlington.gov.uk

Richmond, Sue (LAB - Cockerton East)
sue.richmond@darlington.gov.uk

Richmond, Tony (CON - College)

Scott, Andrew (LAB - Haughton West)
andrew.scott@darlington.gov.uk

Scott, Heather (CON - Park West)
heather.scott@darlington.gov.uk

Stenson, Bill (CON - Mowden)
bill.stenson@darlington.gov.uk

Storr, Dawn (LAB - North Road)
dawn.storr@darlington.gov.uk

Taylor, Jan (LAB - Central)
jan.taylor@darlington.gov.uk

Taylor, Chris (LAB - Banktop)
chris.taylor@darlington.gov.uk

Tostevin, Lorraine (CON - Hurworth)
lorraine.tostevin@darlington.gov.uk

Wallis, Nick (LAB - Haughton West)
nick.wallis@darlington.gov.uk

Wright, Malcolm (LAB - Central)
malcolm.wright@darlington.gov.uk

York, Steve (CON - Middleton St George)
steve.york@darlington.gov.uk

POLITICAL COMPOSITION

LAB: 30, CON: 17, LD: 3, IND: 1

Dartford D

Dartford Borough Council, Civic Centre, Home Gardens, Dartford DA1 1DR
☎ 01322 343434 🖷 01322 343422 💻 www.dartford.gov.uk

FACTS AND FIGURES

Parliamentary Constituencies: Dartford
EU Constituencies: South East
Election Frequency: Elections are of whole council

PRINCIPAL OFFICERS

Chief Executive: Mr Graham Harris, Managing Director, Civic Centre, Home Gardens, Dartford DA1 1DR ☎ 01322 343434 🖷 01322 343422 ✉ graham.harris@dartford.gov.uk

Senior Management: Mrs Sheri Green, Strategic Director - External Services, Civic Centre, Home Gardens, Dartford DA1 1DR ☎ 01322 343434 🖷 01322 343045 ✉ sheri.green@dartford.gov.uk

Senior Management: Ms Sarah Martin Strategic Director - Internal Services, Civic Centre, Home Gardens, Dartford DA1 1DR ☎ 01322 343434 🖷 01322 343045 ✉ sarah.martin@dartford.gov.uk

Building Control: Mr Andrew Nichols, Building & Control Manager, Civic Centre, Home Gardens, Dartford DA1 1DR ☎ 01322 343434 🖷 01322 343422 ✉ andrew.nichols@dartford.gov.uk

PR / Communications: Ms Helen Clark Press & Design Officer, Civic Centre, Home Gardens, Dartford DA1 1DR ☎ 01322 343069 ✉ helen.clark@dartford.gov.uk

Community Planning: Ms Teresa Ryszkowska Head of Regeneration, Civic Centre, Home Gardens, Dartford DA1 1DR ☎ 01322 343631 🖷 01322 343422 ✉ teresa.ryszkowska@dartford.gov.uk

Community Safety: Mrs Sheri Green, Strategic Director - External Services, Civic Centre, Home Gardens, Dartford DA1 1DR ☎ 01322 343434 🖷 01322 343045 ✉ sheri.green@dartford.gov.uk

Computer Management: Mrs Sheri Green, Strategic Director - External Services, Civic Centre, Home Gardens, Dartford DA1 1DR ☎ 01322 343434 🖷 01322 343045 ✉ sheri.green@dartford.gov.uk

Corporate Services: Mr Andrew Hall Corporate Building Surveyor, Civic Centre, Home Gardens, Dartford DA1 1DR ☎ 01322 343489 🖷 01322 343422 ✉ andrew.hall@dartford.gov.uk

Customer Service: Mrs Carol Russell Customer Services Manager, Civic Centre, Home Gardens, Dartford DA1 1DR ☎ 01322 343030 🖷 01322 343422 ✉ carol.russell@dartford.gov.uk

DARTFORD

E-Government: Mrs Sheri Green, Strategic Director - External Services, Civic Centre, Home Gardens, Dartford DA1 1DR ☎ 01322 343434 🖷 01322 343045 🖱 sheri.green@dartford.gov.uk

Electoral Registration: Mr Graham Harris, Managing Director, Civic Centre, Home Gardens, Dartford DA1 1DR ☎ 01322 343434 🖷 01322 343422 🖱 graham.harris@dartford.gov.uk

Emergency Planning: Mr Andrew Nichols, Building & Control Manager, Civic Centre, Home Gardens, Dartford DA1 1DR ☎ 01322 343434 🖷 01322 343422 🖱 andrew.nichols@dartford.gov.uk

Environmental Health: Mrs Annie Sargent, Environmental Health Manager, Dartford Borough Council, Civic Centre, Home Gardens, Dartford DA1 1DR ☎ 01322 343434 🖷 01322 343422 🖱 annie.sargent@dartford.gov.uk

Estates, Property & Valuation: Mr Andrew Hall Corporate Building Surveyor, Civic Centre, Home Gardens, Dartford DA1 1DR ☎ 01322 343489 🖷 01322 343422 🖱 andrew.hall@dartford.gov.uk

Finance: Mr Tim Sams Financial Services Manager, Civic Centre, Home Gardens, Dartford DA1 1DR ☎ 01322 343434 🖷 01322 343422 🖱 tim.sams@dartford.gov.uk

Fleet Management: Ms Lynn Stewart, Senior Finance Assistant, Civic Centre, Home Gardens, Dartford DA1 1DR ☎ 01322 343434 🖷 01322 343422 🖱 lynn.stewart@dartford.gov.uk

Grounds Maintenance: Mr Dave Thomas, Waste & Recycling Manager, Civic Centre, Home Gardens, Dartford DA1 1DR ☎ 01322 343434 🖷 01322 343422 🖱 dave.thomas@dartford.gov.uk

Health and Safety: Mrs Annie Sargent, Environmental Health Manager, Dartford Borough Council, Civic Centre, Home Gardens, Dartford DA1 1DR ☎ 01322 343434 🖷 01322 343422 🖱 annie.sargent@dartford.gov.uk

Home Energy Conservation: Ms Sandra Woodfall, Environmental Promotions Officer, Civic Centre, Home Gardens, Dartford DA1 1DR ☎ 01322 343434 🖷 01322 343422 🖱 sandra.woodfall@dartford.gov.uk

Housing: Mr Peter Dosad, Head of Housing, Civic Centre, Home Gardens, Dartford DA1 1DR ☎ 01322 343434 🖷 01322 343422 🖱 peter.dosad@dartford.gov.uk

Legal: Ms Marie Kelly-Stone, Head of Legal Services, Civic Centre, Home Gardens, Dartford DA1 1DR ☎ 01322 343434 🖷 01322 343422 🖱 marie.kelly-stone@dartford.gov.uk

Leisure and Cultural Services: Mr Adrian Gowan Policy & Corporate Support Manager, Civic Centre, Home Gardens, Dartford DA1 1DR ☎ 01322 343434 🖱 adrian.gowan@dartford.gov.uk

Licensing: Mr Mark Salisbury Senior Licensing Officer, Civic Centre, Home Gardens, Dartford DA1 1DR ☎ 01322 343434 🖱 mark.salisbury@dartford.gov.uk

Member Services: Mr Alan Twyman Member Services Manager, Civic Centre, Home Gardens, Dartford DA1 1DR ☎ 01322 343434 🖷 01322 343422 🖱 alan.twyman@dartford.gov.uk

Parking: Mr Lewis Boudville Parking Services Manager, Civic Centre, Home Gardens, Dartford DA1 1DR ☎ 01322 434434 🖷 01322 343422 🖱 lewis.boudville@dartford.gov.uk

Planning: Ms Teresa Ryszkowska Head of Regeneration, Civic Centre, Home Gardens, Dartford DA1 1DR ☎ 01322 343631 🖷 01322 343422 🖱 teresa.ryszkowska@dartford.gov.uk

Procurement: Mr Bami Cole, Audit, Risk & Anti-Fraud Manager, Dartford Borough Council, Civic Centre, Home Gardens, Dartford DA1 1DR ☎ ; 01322 343023 🖱 ; bami.cole@dartford.gov.uk

Recycling & Waste Minimisation: Mr Dave Thomas, Waste & Parks Manager, Civic Centre, Home Gardens, Dartford DA1 1DR ☎ 01322 343334 🖷 01322 343422 🖱 dave.thomas@dartford.gov.uk

Regeneration: Ms Teresa Ryszkowska Head of Regeneration, Civic Centre, Home Gardens, Dartford DA1 1DR ☎ 01322 343631 🖷 01322 343422 🖱 teresa.ryszkowska@dartford.gov.uk

Sustainable Development: Ms Sandra Woodfall, Environmental Promotions Officer, Civic Centre, Home Gardens, Dartford DA1 1DR ☎ 01322 343434 🖷 01322 343422 🖱 sandra.woodfall@dartford.gov.uk

Town Centre: Mr Lewis Kirnon, Town Centre Liaison Officer, Civic Centre, Home Gardens, Dartford DA1 1DR ☎ 01322 343434 🖷 01322 343422 🖱 lewis.kirnon@dartford.gov.uk

Waste Collection and Disposal: Mr Dave Thomas, Waste & Recycling Manager, Civic Centre, Home Gardens, Dartford DA1 1DR ☎ 01322 343434 🖷 01322 343422 🖱 dave.thomas@dartford.gov.uk

Waste Management: Mr Dave Thomas, Waste & Recycling Manager, Civic Centre, Home Gardens, Dartford DA1 1DR ☎ 01322 343434 🖷 01322 343422 🖱 dave.thomas@dartford.gov.uk

COUNCILLORS

***Mayor* Armitt**, Ian (CON - Bean & Darenth)
ian.armitt@dartford.gov.uk

***Deputy Mayor* Burrell**, John (CON - Stone)
john.burrell@dartford.gov.uk

***Leader of the Council* Kite**, Jeremy (CON - Longfield, New Barn & Southfleet)
jeremy.kite@dartford.gov.uk

***Deputy Leader of the Council* Shippam**, Chris (CON - Town)
chris.shippam@dartford.gov.uk

Allen, Ann (CON - Joydens Wood)
ann.allen@dartford.gov.uk

Bardoe, Arron (CON - West Hill)
arron.bardoe@dartford.gov.uk

Brown, Steve (CON - Longfield, New Barn & Southfleet)
steve.brown@dartford.gov.uk

Canham, Lucy (CON - Stone)
Lucy.Canham@dartford.gov.uk

Coleman, Pat (CON - Sutton-at-Hone & Hawley)

Culter, Paul (CON - Castle)
paul.cutler@dartford.gov.uk

Currans, Rosanna (CON - Brent)
rossanna.currens@darford.gov.uk

Davis, Matthew (CON - Town)
matthew.davis@dartford.gov.uk

Garden, Brian (CON - Joydens Wood)
brian.garden@dartford.gov.uk

Hammock, David (CON - Bean & Darenth)
david.hammock@dartford.gov.uk

Hawkes, Jonathon (LAB - Stone)
jonathon.hawkes@dartford.gov.uk

Hayes, John (R - Swanscombe)
john.hayes@dartford.gov.uk

Hunnisett, Derek (CON - Wilmington)

Jarnell, Steven (CON - Newtown)
steven.jarnell@dartford.gov.uk

Jones, Joshua (LAB - Princes)
Joshua.Jones@dartford.gov.uk

Kaini, Bachchu (LAB - Joyce Green)
bachchu.kaini@dartford.gov.uk

Kelly, Maria (CON - Greenhithe)
maria.kelly@dartfordl.gov.uk

Kelly, Patrick (LAB - Princes)
patrick.kelly@dartford.gov.uk

Kelly, Keith (CON - Greenhithe)
keith.kelly@dartford.gov.uk

Lampkin, Eddy (CON - Wilmington)
eddy.lampkin@dartford.gov.uk

Lees, Richardq (O - Swanscombe)
Richard.Lees@dartford.gov.uk

Lloyd, Andy (CON - Heath)
andy.lloyd@dartford.gov.uk

Maddison, Mark (LAB - Joyce Green)
mark.maddison@dartford.gov.uk

Madison, Tom (LAB - Littlebrook)
tom.maddison@dartford.gov.uk

McLean, Calvin (CON - Newtown)
Calvin.McLean@dartford.gov.uk

Mote, David (CON - Greenhithe)
david.mote@dartford.gov.uk

Ozog, Jan (CON - West Hill)
jan.ozog@dartford.gov.uk

Ozog, Julie (CON - Newtown)
Julie.Ozog@dartford.gov.uk

Paige, Daisy (LAB - Littlebrook)
dais.paige@dartford.gov.uk

Perfitt, Roger (CON - Longfield, New Barn & Southfleet)

Peters, Marilyn (CON - Joydens Wood)
marilyn.peters@kcl.ac.uk

Read, Bryan (R - Swanscombe)
bryan.read@dartford.gov.uk

Reynolds, Lucas (CON - Sutton-at-Hone & Hawley)
Lucas.Reynolds@dartford.gov.uk

Reynolds, Denzil (CON - West Hill)
Denzil.Reynolds@dartford.gov.uk

Sandhu, Avtar (CON - Brent)
avtar.sandhu@dartford.gov.uk

Shanks, Rebecca (CON - Bean & Darenth)
rebecca.shanks@dartford.gov.uk

Storey, Rebecca (CON - Princes)

Swinerd, Drew (CON - Brent)
drew.swinerd@dartford.gov.uk

Thurlow, Patsy (CON - Heath)

Wells, Richard (CON - Heath)
richard.wells@dartford.gov.uk

POLITICAL COMPOSITION
CON: 34, LAB: 7, R: 2, O: 1

COMMITTEE CHAIRS
Licensing: Mr Arron Bardoe

Daventry D

Daventry District Council, Lodge Road, Daventry NN11 4FP
☎ 01327 871100 🖷 01327 300011 ✉ comments@daventrydc.gov.uk
💻 www.daventrydc.gov.uk

FACTS AND FIGURES
Parliamentary Constituencies: Daventry, Kettering
EU Constituencies: East Midlands
Election Frequency: Elections are by thirds

PRINCIPAL OFFICERS
Chief Executive: Mr Ian Vincent, Chief Executive & Returning Officer, Council Offices, Lodge Road, Daventry NN11 4FP ☎ 01327 871100 🖷 01327 300011 ✉ ivincent@daventrydc.gov.uk

Deputy Chief Executive: Mr Simon Bovey, Deputy Chief Executive & Monitoring Officer, Council Offices, Lodge Road, Daventry NN11 4FP ☎ 01327 871100 🖷 01327 300011 ✉ sbovey@daventrydc.gov.uk

Senior Management: Mr Simon Bowers Business Manager, Council Offices, Lodge Road, Daventry NN11 4FP ☎ 01327 302435 🖷 01327 300011 ✉ sbowers@daventrydc.gov.uk

Senior Management: Mr Tony Gillet, Resources Manager, Council Offices, Lodge Road, Daventry NN11 4FP ☎ 01327 302276 🖷 01327 300011 ✉ tgillet@daventrydc.gov.uk

Senior Management: Mrs Audra Statham Chief Financial Officer, Lodge Road, Daventry NN11 4FP ☎ 01327 302354 🖷 01327 300011 ✉ astatham@daventry.gov.uk

Senior Management: Mrs Maria Taylor Community Manager, Council Offices, Lodge Road, Daventry NN11 4FP ☎ 01327 302229 🖷 01327 300011 ✉ mtaylor@daventrydc.gov.uk

Architect, Building / Property Services: Mr Simon Bowers, Business Manager, Council Offices, Lodge Road, Daventry NN11 4FP ☎ 01327 302435 🖷 01327 300011 ✉ sbowers@daventrydc.gov.uk

Best Value: Ms Katie Jones Performance Manager, Lodge Road, Daventry NN11 4FP ☎ 01327 302417 🖷 01327 300011 ✉ kjones@daventrydc.gov.uk

PR / Communications: Mrs Becky Hutson Communications & Marketing Manager, Lodge Road, Daventry NN11 4FP ☎ 01327 302404 🖷 01327 300011 ✉ bhutson@daventrydc.gov.uk

Community Safety: Mr Kevin Fagan Community Partnership Team Manager, Lodge Road, Daventry NN11 4FP ☎ 01327 302424 🖷 01327 300011 ✉ kfagan@daventrydc.gov.uk

Computer Management: Mr Neil Smith Senior IT Officer, Lodge Road, Daventry NN11 4FP ☎ 01327 302331 🖷 01327 300011 ✉ nsmith@daventrydc.gov.uk

Economic Development: Mr Simon Bowers, Business Manager, Council Offices, Lodge Road, Daventry NN11 4FP ☎ 01327 302435 🖷 01327 300011 ✉ sbowers@daventrydc.gov.uk

Electoral Registration: Mrs Jane Lyons Principal Elections Officer, Lodge Road, Daventry NN11 4FP ☎ 01327 302321 🖷 01327 300011 ✉ jlyons@daventrydc.gov.uk

Emergency Planning: Mr Simon Bowers Business Manager, Council Offices, Lodge Road, Daventry NN11 4FP ☎ 01327 302435 🖷 01327 300011 ✉ sbowers@daventrydc.gov.uk

Environmental Health: Mrs Maria Taylor Community Manager, Council Offices, Lodge Road, Daventry NN11 4FP ☎ 01327 302229 🖷 01327 300011 ✉ mtaylor@daventrydc.gov.uk

Estates, Property & Valuation: Mr Simon Bowers, Business Manager, Council Offices, Lodge Road, Daventry NN11 4FP ☎ 01327 302435 🖷 01327 300011 ✉ sbowers@daventrydc.gov.uk

Facilities: Mr Simon Bowers Business Manager, Council Offices, Lodge Road, Daventry NN11 4FP ☎ 01327 302435 🖷 01327 300011 ✉ sbowers@daventrydc.gov.uk

Finance: Mrs Audra Statham Chief Financial Officer, Lodge Road, Daventry NN11 4FP ☎ 01327 302354 🖷 01327 300011 ✉ astatham@daventry.gov.uk

Treasury: Mrs Audra Statham Chief Financial Officer, Lodge Road, Daventry NN11 4FP ☎ 01327 302354 🖷 01327 300011 ✉ astatham@daventry.gov.uk

Health and Safety: Mrs Maria Taylor Community Manager, Council Offices, Lodge Road, Daventry NN11 4FP ☎ 01327 302229 🖷 01327 300011 ✉ mtaylor@daventrydc.gov.uk

Home Energy Conservation: Mrs Maria Taylor Community Manager, Council Offices, Lodge Road, Daventry NN11 4FP ☎ 01327 302229 🖷 01327 300011 ✉ mtaylor@daventrydc.gov.uk

Home Energy Conservation: Mrs Maria Taylor Corporate Manager - Community, Council Offices, Lodge Road, Daventry NN11 4FP ☎ 01327 302229 ✉ mtaylor@daventrydc.gov.uk

Housing: Mrs Maria Taylor Corporate Manager - Community, Council Offices, Lodge Road, Daventry NN11 4FP ☎ 01327 302229 ✉ mtaylor@daventrydc.gov.uk

Legal: Mr Tony Gillet, Resources Manager, Council Offices, Lodge Road, Daventry NN11 4FP ☎ 01327 302276 🖷 01327 300011 ✉ tgillet@daventrydc.gov.uk

Licensing: Mrs Maria Taylor Community Manager, Council Offices, Lodge Road, Daventry NN11 4FP ☎ 01327 302229 🖷 01327 300011 ✉ mtaylor@daventrydc.gov.uk

Member Services: Miss Fiona Rye PA to Deputy Chief Executive, Lodge Road, Daventry NN11 4FP ☎ 01327 302400 🖷 01327 300011 ✉ frye@daventrydc.gov.uk

Personnel / HR: Mr Tony Gillet, Resources Manager, Council Offices, Lodge Road, Daventry NN11 4FP ☎ 01327 302276 🖷 01327 300011 ✉ tgillet@daventrydc.gov.uk

Planning: Mrs Maria Taylor Community Manager, Council Offices, Lodge Road, Daventry NN11 4FP ☎ 01327 302229 🖷 01327 300011 ✉ mtaylor@daventrydc.gov.uk

Procurement: Mr Simon Bowers, Business Manager, Council Offices, Lodge Road, Daventry NN11 4FP ☎ 01327 302435 🖷 01327 300011 ✉ sbowers@daventrydc.gov.uk

Staff Training: Ms Rosemary Daniels Governance Manager, Lodge Road, Daventry NN11 4FP ☎ 01327 302412 🖷 01327 300011 ✉ rdaniel@daventrydc.gov.uk

Sustainable Communities: Mrs Maria Taylor Community Manager, Council Offices, Lodge Road, Daventry NN11 4FP ☎ 01327 302229 🖷 01327 300011 ✉ mtaylor@daventrydc.gov.uk

Town Centre: Mr Simon Bowers, Business Manager, Council Offices, Lodge Road, Daventry NN11 4FP ☎ 01327 302435 🖷 01327 300011 ✉ sbowers@daventrydc.gov.uk

COUNCILLORS

Leader of the Council **Millar**, Chris (CON - Long Buckby) cmillar@daventrydc.gov.uk

Deputy Leader of the Council **Griffin**, Elizabeth (CON - Woodford) egriffin@daventrydc.gov.uk

Aldridge, Bryn (CON - Ravensthorpe) baldridge@daventrydc.gov.uk

Amos, Johnnie (CON - Weedon) jamos@daventrydc.gov.uk

Auger, Richard (CON - Welford) rauger@daventrydc.gov.uk

Barratt, Ian (CON - Brixworth) ibarratt@daventrydc.gov.uk

Bunting, Nick (CON - Brixworth) nbunting@daventrydc.gov.uk

Campbell, Abigail (LAB - Braunston & Welton) acampbell@daventrydc.gov.uk

Carr, Nigel (UKIP - Abbey North)
ncarr@daventrydc.gov.uk

Carter, Ann (CON - Walgrave)
acarter@daventrydc.gov.uk

Chantler, Alan (CON - Yelvertoft)
aechantler@daventrydc.gov.uk

Connors, Sean (UKIP - Drayton)
sconnors@daventrydc.gov.uk

Cribbin, Daniel (CON - Moulton)
dcribbin@daventrydc.gov.uk

Eddon, Deanna (CON - Abbey South)
deddon@daventrydc.gov.uk

Frenchman, Barry (CON - Spratton)
bfrenchman@daventrydc.gov.uk

Gilford, Jo (CON - Woodford)
jmgilford@daventrydc.gov.uk

Hills, Alan (CON - Hill)
ahills@daventrydc.gov.uk

Howard, Wayne (CON - Hill)
whoward@daventrydc.gov.uk

Howard, Amy (CON - Drayton)
ahoward@daventrydc.gov.uk

Irving-Swift, Cecile (CON - Welford)
cirving-swift@daventrydc.gov.uk

James, David (CON - Abbey North)
djames@daventrydc.gov.uk

Lomax, Catherine (LD - Barby & Kilsby)
clomax@daventrydc.gov.uk

Long, Chris (CON - Abbey North)
clong@daventrydc.gov.uk

Morgan, Colin (CON - Abbey South)
cmorgan@daventrydc.gov.uk

Osborne, Diana (CON - Long Buckby)
dosborne@daventrydc.gov.uk

Osborne, Steve (CON - Long Buckby)
sosborne@daventrydc.gov.uk

Parker, Kevin (CON - Brixworth)
kparker@daventrydc.gov.uk

Patchett, Bob (CON - Woodford)
bpatchett@daventrydc.gov.uk

Perry, Kevin (CON - Weedon)
kperry@daventrydc.gov.uk

Poole, Colin (CON - Hill)
cpoole@daventrydc.gov.uk

Randall, Wendy (LAB - Drayton)
wrandall@daventrydc.gov.uk

Robertson, Ian (CON - Barby & Kilsby)
irobertson@daventrydc.gov.uk

Shephard, John (CON - Spratton)
jshephard@daventrydc.gov.uk

Smith, David (CON - Weedon)
dsmith1@daventrydc.gov.uk

Warren, Mike (CON - Moulton)
mwarren@daventrydc.gov.uk

Wesley, Mark (CON - Abbey South)
mwesley@daventrydc.gov.uk

POLITICAL COMPOSITION

CON: 31, LAB: 2, UKIP: 2, LD: 1

COMMITTEE CHAIRS

Planning: Mr Steve Osborne

Denbighshire W

Denbighshire County Council, County Hall, Wynnstay Road, Ruthin LL15 1YN
☎ 01824 706000 🖷 01824 707446 ✉ customerservicecentre@denbighshire.gov.uk / canolfangwasanaethcwsmer@sirddinbych.gov.uk
💻 www.denbighshire.gov.uk or www.sirddinbych.gov.uk

FACTS AND FIGURES

Parliamentary Constituencies: Clwyd South, Clwyd West, Vale of Clwyd
EU Constituencies: Wales
Election Frequency: Elections are of whole council

PRINCIPAL OFFICERS

Chief Executive: Dr Mohammed Mehmet Chief Executive, County Hall, Wynnstay Road, Ruthin LL15 1YN ☎ 01824 706128 🖷 01824 706045 ✉ mohammed.mehmet@denbighshire.gov.uk

Senior Management: Ms Rebecca Maxwell Corporate Director - Economic & Community Ambition, County Hall, Wynnstay Road, Ruthin LL15 1YN

Senior Management: Ms Nicola Stubbins Corporate Director - Social Services, County Hall, Wynnstay Road, Ruthin LL15 1YN ☎ 01824 706149 🖷 01824 406646 ✉ nicola.stubbins@denbighshire.gov.uk

Senior Management: Mr Gary Williams Head of Legal, HR & Democratic Services, County Hall, Wynnstay Road, Ruthin LL15 1YN ☎ 01824 712562 🖷 01824 706293 ✉ gary.williams@denbighshire.gov.uk

Senior Management: Mr Hywyn Williams Corporate Director - Customers, County Hall, Wynnstay Road, Ruthin LL15 1YN ☎ 01824 708224 ✉ hywyn.williams@denbighshire.gov.uk

Architect, Building / Property Services: Mr David Matthews Valuation & Estates Team Manager, County Hall, Wynnstay Road, Ruthin LL15 1YN ☎ 01824 706798 🖷 01824 708088 ✉ david.matthews@denbighshire.gov.uk

Building Control: Mr Robin Johnston, Building Control Officer, Caledfryn, Smithfield Road, Denbigh LL16 3RJ ☎ 01824 706714 🖷 01824 706953 ✉ robin.johnston@denbighshire.gov.uk

Catering Services: Ms Hayley Jones, Catering Manager, Kinmel Park Depot, Bodelwyddan, LL18 5UX ☎ 01824 712131 ✉ hayley.jones@denbighshire.gov.uk

Catering Services: Mr Ian Kemp, Catering Services Manager, Kinmel Park Depot, Bodelwyddan, LL18 5UX ☎ 01824 712125 🖷 01824 712131 ✉ ian.kemp@denbighshire.gov.uk

DENBIGHSHIRE

Children / Youth Services: Mr Jamie Groves Head of Communications, Marketing & Leisure, Caledfryn, Smithfield Road, Denbigh LL15 1YN ☎ 01824 712723 ✉ jamie.groves@denbighshire.gov.uk

Civil Registration: Mr Gary Williams Head of Legal, HR & Democratic Services, County Hall, Wynnstay Road, Ruthin LL15 1YN ☎ 01824 712562 🖷 01824 706293 ✉ gary.williams@denbighshire.gov.uk

PR / Communications: Mr Gareth Watson, Corporate Communications Manager County Hall, Wynnstay Road, Ruthin LL15 1YN ☎ 01824 706222 🖷 01824 707446 ✉ gareth.watson@denbighshire.gov.uk

Computer Management: Mr Barry Eaton ICT Manager, County Hall, Wynnstay Road, Ruthin LL15 1YN ☎ 01824 706211 ✉ barry.eaton@denbighshire.gov.uk

Consumer Protection and Trading Standards: Mr Graham Boase Head of Planning & Public Protection, County Hall, Wynnstay Road, Ruthin LL15 1YN ☎ 01824 706925 ✉ graham.boase@denbighshire.gov.uk

Contracts: Mr Steve Parker, Head of Highways & Environment, Kinmel Park Depot, Kinmel Park, Abergele Road, Bodelwyddan, Rhyl LL18 5UX ☎ 01824 706801 🖷 01824 706970 ✉ steve.parker@denbighshire.gov.uk

Customer Service: Ms Jackie Walley Head of Customers, County Hall, Wynnstay Road, Ruthin LL15 1YN ☎ 01824 712620 ✉ jackie.walley@denbighshire.gov.uk

Direct Labour: Mr Steve Parker, Head of Highways & Environment, Kinmel Park Depot, Kinmel Park, Abergele Road, Bodelwyddan, Rhyl LL18 5UX ☎ 01824 706801 🖷 01824 706970 ✉ steve.parker@denbighshire.gov.uk

Economic Development: Mr Mike Horrocks Economic Development Manager, County Hall, Wynnstay Road, Ruthin LL15 1YN ☎ 07824 509279 ✉ mike.horrocks@denbighshire.gov.uk

Education: Ms Karen Evans Head of School Improvement & Inclusion, County Hall, Wynnstay Road, Ruthin LL15 1YN ☎ 01824 708009 ✉ karen.evans@denbighshire.gov.uk

Education: Mr Hywyn Williams Corporate Director - Customers, County Hall, Wynnstay Road, Ruthin LL15 1YN ☎ 01824 708224 ✉ hywyn.williams@denbighshire.gov.uk

E-Government: Mr Barry Eaton ICT Manager, County Hall, Wynnstay Road, Ruthin LL15 1YN ☎ 01824 706211 ✉ barry.eaton@denbighshire.gov.uk

Electoral Registration: Mr Gareth Evans, County Electoral Services Administrator, County Hall, Wynnstay Road, Ruthin LL15 1YN ☎ 01824 706114 ✉ g.evans@denbighshire.gov.uk

Emergency Planning: Mr Philip Harrison Emergency Planning Co-ordinator, County Hall, , Mold CH7 6NJ ☎ 01352 752121 ✉ phillip.harrison@flintshire.gov.uk

Environmental Health: Mr Graham Boase Head of Planning & Public Protection, Caledfryn, Smithfield Road, Denbigh LL16 3RJ ☎ 01824 706925 ✉ graham.boase@denbighshire.gov.uk

Estates, Property & Valuation: Mr David Mathews Valuation & Estates Team Manager, Caledfryn, Smithfield Road, Denbigh LL16 3RJ ☎ 01824 706798 🖷 01824 708088 ✉ david.mathews@denbighshire.gov.uk

Events Manager: Ms Sian Davies Events Manager, Rhyl Pavillion Theatre, The Promenade, Rhyl LL18 3AQ ☎ 01745 332414

Fleet Management: Mr Chris Brown Transport Manager, Fleet Depot, Expressway Business Park, Bodelwyddan, Rhyl LL18 5SQ ☎ 01745 832231 ✉ chris.brown@denbighshire.gov.uk

Grounds Maintenance: Mr Steve Parker, Head of Highways & Environment, Kinmel Park Depot, Kinmel Park, Abergele Road, Bodelwyddan, Rhyl LL18 5UX ☎ 01824 706801 🖷 01824 706970 ✉ steve.parker@denbighshire.gov.uk

Health and Safety: Mr Gerry Lapington Corporate Health & Safety Manager, County Hall, Wynnstay Road, Ruthin LL15 1YN ☎ 01824 712582 ✉ gerry.lapington@denbighshire.gov.uk

Highways: Mr Steve Parker, Head of Highways & Environment, Kinmel Park Depot, Kinmel Park, Abergele Road, Bodelwyddan, Rhyl LL18 5UX ☎ 01824 706801 🖷 01824 706970 ✉ steve.parker@denbighshire.gov.uk

Home Energy Conservation: Mr Gareth Roberts, Housing & Renewal Officer, Ty Nant, 6/8 Nant Hall Road, Prestatyn LL19 9LL ☎ 01824 706679 🖷 01824 706575 ✉ gareth.roberts@denbighshire.gov.uk

Housing Maintenance: Mr Alan Jones Principal Housing Maintenance Officer, Kinmel Park Depot, Abergele Road, Bodelwyddan, Rhyl LL18 5UX ☎ 01824 712137 ✉ alan.jones@denbighshire.gov.uk

Legal: Mr Gary Williams Head of Legal, HR & Democratic Services, County Hall, Wynnstay Road, Ruthin LL15 1YN ☎ 01824 712562 🖷 01824 706293 ✉ gary.williams@denbighshire.gov.uk

Leisure and Cultural Services: Mr Jamie Groves Head of Communications, Marketing & Leisure, County Hall, Wynnstay Road, Ruthin LL15 1YN ☎ 01824 706476 🖷 01745 344516 ✉ jamie.groves@denbighshire.gov.uk

Leisure and Cultural Services: Mr Huw Rees Acting Head of Countryside Services, Yr Hen Garchar, Ruthin LL15 1QA ☎ 01824 708228 ✉ huw.rees@denbighshire.gov.uk

Lifelong Learning: Mr Hywyn Williams Corporate Director - Customers, County Hall, Wynnstay Road, Ruthin LL15 1YN ☎ 01824 708224 ✉ hywyn.williams@denbighshire.gov.uk

Lighting: Mr Andy Clark, Street Lighting Engineer, Kinmel Park Depot, Abergele Road, Bodelwyddan, LL18 5UX ☎ 01824 712140 ✉ andy.clark@denbighshire.gov.uk

Member Services: Mr Eleri Woodford Member Support & Development Manager, County Hall, Wynnstay Road, Ruthin LL15 1YN ☎ 01824 706196 🖷 01824 706293 ✉ eleri.woodford@denbighshire.gov.uk

Parking: Mr Steve Parker, Head of Highways & Environment, Kinmel Park Depot, Kinmel Park, Abergele Road, Bodelwyddan, Rhyl LL18 5UX ☎ 01824 706801 🖷 01824 706970 ✉ steve.parker@denbighshire.gov.uk

Partnerships: Mr Alan Smith Head of Business Planning & Performance, County Hall, Wynnstay Road, Ruthin LL15 1AT ☎ 01824 706246 🖷 01824 706045 ✉ alan.smith@denbighshire.gov.uk

Personnel / HR: Mr Gary Williams Head of Legal, HR & Democratic Services, County Hall, Wynnstay Road, Ruthin LL15 1YN ☎ 01824 712562 🖷 01824 706293 ✉ gary.williams@denbighshire.gov.uk

Planning: Mr Graham Boase Head of Planning & Public Protection, Caledfryn, Smithfield Road, Denbigh LL16 3RJ ☎ 01824 706925 ✉ graham.boase@denbighshire.gov.uk

Procurement: Mr Arwel Staples, Strategic Procurement Officer, County Hall, Wynnstay Road, Ruthin LL15 1YN ☎ 01824 706042 🖷 01824 706045 ✉ arwel.staples@denbighshire.gov.uk

Public Libraries: Mr Robert Arwyn Jones, Principal Librarian, County Hall, Wynnstay Road, Ruthin LL15 1YN ☎ 01824 708203 🖷 01824 708202 ✉ arwyn.jones@denbighshire.gov.uk

Recycling & Waste Minimisation: Mr Alan Roberts, Senior Waste Officer, Kinmel Park Depot, Engine Hill, LL18 5UX ☎ 01824 712408 🖷 01824 712125 ✉ alan.l.roberts@denbighshire.gov.uk

Regeneration: Mr Mike Horrocks Economic Development Manager, County Hall, Wynnstay Road, Ruthin LL15 1YN ☎ 07824 509279 ✉ mike.horrocks@denbighshire.gov.uk

Road Safety: Mr Alan Hinchcliffe, Road Safety Officer, Caledfryn, Smithfield Road, Denbigh LL16 3RJ ☎ 01824 706970 🖷 01824 706865 ✉ alan.hinchcliffe@denbighshire.gov.uk

Social Services: Mr Phil Gilroy Head of Adult Services (Community & Intermediate Care), County Hall, Wynnstay Road, Ruthin LL15 1YN ☎ 01824 706654 ✉ phil.gilroy@denbighshire.gov.uk

Social Services: Ms Nicola Stubbins Corporate Director - Social Services, County Hall, Wynnstay Road, Ruthin LL15 1YN ☎ 01824 706149 🖷 01824 706646 ✉ nicola.stubbins@denbighshire.gov.uk

Social Services (Children): Mr Leighton Rees Head of Children & Family Services, Ty Nant, Nant Hall Road, Prestatyn LL19 9LL ☎ 01824 706655 ✉ leighton.rees@denbighshire.gov.uk

Staff Training: Mr John Rees Principal Personnel Officer, Employee & Member Development, County Hall, Wynnstay Road, Ruthin LL15 1YN ☎ 01824 712537 🖷 01824 712526 ✉ john.rees@denbighshire.gov.uk

Tourism: Ms Sian Owen Lead Officer - Destination, Marketing & Communications, County Hall, Wynnstay Road, Ruthin LL15 1YN ☎ 01824 706125 ✉ sian.owen@denbighshire.gov.uk

Traffic Management: Mr Steve Parker, Head of Highways & Environment, Kinmel Park Depot, Kinmel Park, Abergele Road, Bodelwyddan, Rhyl LL18 5UX ☎ 01824 706801 🖷 01824 706970 ✉ steve.parker@denbighshire.gov.uk

Transport: Mr Steve Parker, Head of Highways & Environment, Kinmel Park Depot, Kinmel Park, Abergele Road, Bodelwyddan, Rhyl LL18 5UX ☎ 01824 706801 🖷 01824 706970 ✉ steve.parker@denbighshire.gov.uk

Transport Planner: Mr Steve Parker, Head of Highways & Environment, Kinmel Park Depot, Kinmel Park, Abergele Road, Bodelwyddan, Rhyl LL18 5UX ☎ 01824 706801 🖷 01824 706970 ✉ steve.parker@denbighshire.gov.uk

Waste Collection and Disposal: Mr Alan Roberts, Senior Waste Officer, Kinmel Park Depot, Engine Hill, LL18 5UX ☎ 01824 712408 🖷 01824 712125 ✉ alan.l.roberts@denbighshire.gov.uk

Waste Management: Mr Alan Roberts, Senior Waste Officer, Kinmel Park Depot, Engine Hill, LL18 5UX ☎ 01824 712408 🖷 01824 712125 ✉ alan.l.roberts@denbighshire.gov.uk

COUNCILLORS

***Chair* Kensler**, Gwyneth (PC - Denbigh Central)
gwyneth.kensler@denbighshire.gov.uk

***Vice-Chair* Davies**, Ann (CON - Rhuddlan)
j.ann.davies@denbighshire.gov.uk

***Leader of the Council* Evans**, Hugh (IND - Llanfair Dyffryn Clwyd / Gwyddelwern)
hugh.evans@denbighshire.gov.uk

***Deputy Leader of the Council* Williams**, Eryl (PC - Efenechtyd)
eryl.williams@denbighshire.gov.uk

***Group Leader* Butterfield**, Joan (LAB - Rhyl West)
joan.butterfield@denbighshire.gov.uk

***Group Leader* Holland**, Martyn (CON - Llanarmon-yn-Iâl/ Llandegla)
martyn.holland@denbighshire.gov.uk

***Group Leader* Roberts**, Arwel (PC - Rhuddlan)
arwel.roberts@denbighshire.gov.uk

***Group Leader* Welch**, Joe (IND - Llanrhaeadr-yng-Nghinmeirch)
joseph.welch@denbighshire.gov.uk

Armstrong, Ian (LAB - Rhyl West)
ian.armstrong@denbighshire.gov.uk

Bartley, Raymond (IND - Denbigh Lower)
ray.bartley@denbighshire.gov.uk

Blakeley, Brian (LAB - Rhyl South East)
brian.blakeley@denbighshire.gov.uk

Chamberlain Jones, Jeanette (LAB - Rhyl South)
jeanette.c.jones@denbighshire.gov.uk

Cowie, Bill (IND - St Asaph West)
bill.cowie@denbighshire.gov.uk

Davies, Meirick Lloyd (PC - Trefnant)
meirick.davies@denbighshire.gov.uk

DENBIGHSHIRE

Davies, Richard (IND - Denbigh Lower)
richard.lulu.davies@denbighshire.gov.uk

Davies, Stuart (IND - Llangollen)
stuart.a.davies@denbighshire.gov.uk

Duffy, Peter (LAB - Prestatyn Central)
peter.duffy@denbighshire.gov.uk

Evans, Peter (IND - Prestatyn Meliden)
peter.evans@denbighshire.gov.uk

Feeley, Bobby (IND - Ruthin)
bobby.feeley@denbighshire.gov.uk

Guy-Davies, Carys (LAB - Prestatyn North)
carys.guy-davies@denbighshire.gov.uk

Hilditch-Roberts, Huw (IND - Ruthin)
huw.hilditch-roberts@denbighshire.gov.uk

Hughes, Rhys (PC - Llangollen)
rhys.hughes@denbighshire.gov.uk

Hughes, Colin (LAB - Denbigh Upper & Henllan)
colin.hughes@denbighshire.gov.uk

Irving, Hugh (CON - Prestatyn Central)
hugh.irving@denbighshire.gov.uk

Jones, Pat (LAB - Rhyl South West)
pat.jones@denbighshire.gov.uk

Jones, Alice (PC - Bodelwyddan)
alice.jones@denbighshire.gov.uk

Jones, Huw (PC - Corwen)
huw.jones@denbighshire.gov.uk

Lloyd-Williams, Geraint (LAB - Denbigh Upper & Henllan)
geraint.lloyd-williams@denbighshire.gov.uk

McLellan, Jason (LAB - Prestatyn North)
jason.mcclellan@denbighshire.gov.uk

Mellor, Barry (LAB - Rhyl East)
barry.mellor@denbighshire.gov.uk

Mullen-James, Win (LAB - Rhyl South East)
win.mullen-james@denbighshire.gov.uk

Murray, Bob (LAB - Prestatyn South West)
bob.murray@denbighshire.gov.uk

Owen, Peter (CON - Dyserth)
peter.owen@denbighshire.gov.uk

Owens, Dewi (CON - St Asaph East)
dewi.owens@denbighshire.gov.uk

Parry, Merfyn (IND - Llandyrnog)
merfyn.parry@denbighshire.gov.uk

Penlington, Paul (LAB - Prestatyn North)
paul.penlington@denbighshire.gov.uk

Prendergast, Pete (LAB - Rhyl South West)
pete.prendergast@denbighshire.gov.uk

Sandilands, Gareth (LAB - Prestatyn South West)
gareth.sandilands@denbighshire.gov.uk

Simmons, David (LAB - Rhyl East)
david.simmons@denbighshire.gov.uk

Smith, Barbara (IND - Tremeirchion)
barbara.smith@denbighshire.gov.uk

Smith, David (IND - Ruthin)
david.smith@denbighshire.gov.uk

Tasker, Bill (LAB - Rhyl South East)
bill.tasker@denbighshire.gov.uk

Thompson-Hill, Julian (CON - Prestatyn East)
julian.thompson-hill@denbighshire.gov.uk

Williams, Cefyn (PC - Llandrillo)
cefyn.williams@denbighshire.gov.uk

Williams, Cheryl (LAB - Rhyl South)
cheryl.williams@denbighshire.gov.uk

Williams, Huw (CON - Llanbedr Dyffryn Clwyd/ Llangynhafal)
huw.o.williams@denbighshire.gov.uk

POLITICAL COMPOSITION
LAB: 19, IND: 12, PC: 8, CON: 7

COMMITTEE CHAIRS
Licensing: Mr Cefyn Williams

Planning: Mr Raymond Bartley

Derby City U

Derby City Council, 1st Floor, The Council House, Corporation Street, Derby DE1 2FS
☎ 01332 293111 🖷 01332 255500 💻 www.derby.gov.uk

FACTS AND FIGURES
Parliamentary Constituencies: Derby North, Derby South, Derbyshire Mid
EU Constituencies: East Midlands
Election Frequency: Elections are by thirds

PRINCIPAL OFFICERS
Chief Executive: Mr Paul Robinson Chief Executive, 1st Floor, The Council House, Corporation Street, Derby DE1 2FS
☎ 01332 643555 ✉ paul.robinson@derby.gov.uk

Senior Management: Dr Robyn Dewis Acting Director - Public Health, 1st Floor, The Council House, Corporation Street, Derby DE1 2FS ☎ 01332 643073 ✉ robyn.dewis@derby.gov.uk

Senior Management: Ms Christine Durrant, Acting Strategic Director - Neighbourhoods, 1st Floor, Council House, Corporation Street, Derby DE1 2FS ☎ 01332 642434
✉ christine.durrant@derby.gov.uk

Senior Management: Mr Perveez Sadiq Acting Strategic Director - Adults, Health & Housing, 1st Floor, Council House, Corporation Street, Derby DE1 2FS ☎ 01332 643550
✉ perveez.sadiq@derby.gov.uk

Senior Management: Mr Andy Smith Acting Strategic Director - Children & Young People, 1st Floor, Council House, Corporation Street, Derby DE1 2FS ☎ 01332 643557 ✉ andy.smith@derby.gov.uk

Best Value: Mr Gordon Stirling, Director - Strategic Services & Transformation, 1st Floor, Council House, Corporation Street, Derby DE1 2FS ☎ 01332 643430 ✉ gordon.stirling@derby.gov.uk

Building Control: Mr Paul Clarke Head of Planning, 1st Floor, Council House, Corporation Street, Derby DE1 2FS ☎ 01332 641642
✉ paul.clarke@derby.gov.uk

Building Control: Mr Mick Henman, Head of Building Consultancy & Emergency Planning, 1st Floor, Council House, Corporation Street, Derby DE1 2FS ☎ 01332 642096 ✉ mick.henman@derby.gov.uk

Catering Services: Mrs Sandra Cole Head of Facilities Management, 1st Floor, Council House, Corporation Street, Derby DE1 2FS ☎ 01332 642142 ✉ sandra.cole@derby.gov.uk

Children / Youth Services: Mr Andrew Kaiser Head of Service, 1st Floor, The Council House, Corporation Street, Derby DE1 2FS ☎ 01332 641340 ✉ kaiser.andrew@derby.gov.uk

Children / Youth Services: Ms Sally Penrose Specialist Services - Fostering & Adoption, Fostering and Adoption Centre, Perth Street, Derby DE21 6XX ☎ 01332 643817 ✉ sally.penrose@derby.gov.uk

Civil Registration: Mr James Clark Registration Services Manager, Royal Oak House, Market Place, Derby DE1 3AR ☎ 01332 642534 ✉ james.clark@derby.gov.uk

PR / Communications: Ms Yvonne Wilkinson Head of Communications, 1st Floor, Council House, Corporation Street, Derby DE1 2FS ☎ 01332 643501 ✉ yvonne.wilkinson@derby.gov.uk

Community Safety: Mr Tim Clegg Director - Partnerships & Streetpride, 15 Stores Road, Derby DE21 4BD ☎ 01332 641604 ✉ tim.clegg@derby.gov.uk

Computer Management: Mr Nick O'Reilly Director of ICT, 1st Floor, The Council House, Corporation Street, Derby DE1 2FS ☎ 01332 643254 ✉ nick.oreilly@derby.gov.uk

Consumer Protection and Trading Standards: Mr John Tomlinson, Director of Environmental & Regulatory Services, Ground Floor, Council House, Corporation Street, Derby DE1 2FS ☎ 01332 642435 ✉ john.tomlinson@derby.gov.uk

Corporate Services: Mr Richard Boneham Head of Governance & Assurance, 1st Floor, The Council House, Corporation Street, Derby DE1 2FS ☎ 01332 643280 ✉ richard.boneham@derby.gov.uk

Corporate Services: Mr Paul Clarke Head of Planning, 1st Floor, Council House, Corporation Street, Derby DE1 2FS ☎ 01332 641642 ✉ paul.clarke@derby.gov.uk

Corporate Services: Ms Lynda Innocent Head of Business Systems, 1st Floor, The Council House, Corporation Street, Derby DE1 2FS ☎ 01332 643235 ✉ lynda.innocent@derby.gov.uk

Customer Service: Mr Bernard Fenton Head of Customer Services, Ground Floor, The Council House, Corporation Street, Derby DE1 2FS ☎ 01332 643758 ✉ bernard.fenton@derby.gov.uk

Economic Development: Mr Richard Williams, Director - Regeneration, 2nd Floor, Council House, Corporation Street, Derby DE1 2FS ☎ 01332 642436 ✉ richard.williams@derby.gov.uk

Education: Mr Gurmail Nizzer Head of School Place Planning & Organisation, 1st Floor, Council House, Corporation Street, Derby DE1 2FS ☎ 01332 642720 ✉ gurmail.nizzer@derby.gov.uk

Education: Mr Andy Smith Acting Strategic Director - Children & Young People, 1st Floor, Council House, Corporation Street, Derby DE1 2FS ☎ 01332 643557 ✉ andy.smith@derby.gov.uk

Electoral Registration: Mr Mick Styne Electoral Services & Land Charges Manager, 1st Floor, Council House, Corporation Street, Derby DE1 2FS ☎ 01332 641663 ✉ mick.styne@derby.gov.uk

Emergency Planning: Mr Rob Ashton Senior Emergency Planning Officer, Ground Floor, Council House, Corporation Street, Derby DE1 2FS ☎ 01332 641867 ✉ rob.ashton@derby.gov.uk

Energy Management: Mr Richard Murrell Principal Home Energy Advisor, 1st Floor, Council House, Corporation Street, Derby DE1 2FS ☎ 01332 642016 ✉ richard.murrell@derby.gov.uk

Environmental Health: Mr Michael Kay Head of Environmental Health & Licensing, Ground Floor, Council House, Corporation Street, Derby DE1 2FS ☎ 01332 641940 ✉ michael.kay@derby.gov.uk

Estates, Property & Valuation: Mr Alistair Burg Interim Head - Strategic Asset Management, 2nd Floor, Council House, Corporation Street, Derby DE1 2FS ☎ 01332 643327 ✉ alistair.burg@derby.gov.uk

Facilities: Ms Sandra Cole Head of Facilities Management, 2nd Floor, Council House, Corporation Street, Derby DE1 2FS ☎ 01332 642142 ✉ sandra.cole@derby.gov.uk

Facilities: Mr Ian Shepherd Corporate Facilities Manager, 2nd Floor, Council House, Corporation Street, Derby DE1 2FS ☎ 01332 643338 ✉ ian.shepherd@derby.gov.uk

Finance: Mr Martyn Marples Director of Finance & Procurement, 1st Floor, Council House, Corporation Street, Derby DE1 2FS ☎ 01332 643377 ✉ martyn.marples@derby.gov.uk

Fleet Management: Mr Richard Kniveton Fleet & Depot Manager, 15 Stores Road, Derby DE21 4BD ☎ 01332 641514 🖷 01332 716469 ✉ richard.kniveton@derby.gov.uk

Grounds Maintenance: Mr Dave Bartram Head of Highways & Engineering, 15 Stores Road, Derby DE21 4BD ☎ 01332 641516 ✉ dave.bartram@derby.gov.uk

Highways: Mr Dave Bartram Head of Highways & Engineering, 15 Stores Road, Derby DE21 4BD ☎ 01332 641516 ✉ dave.bartram@derby.gov.uk

Home Energy Conservation: Mr Richard Murrell Principal Home Energy Advisor, 1st Floor, Council House, Corporation Street, Derby DE1 2FS ☎ 01332 642016 ✉ richard.murrell@derby.gov.uk

Housing: Ms Maria Murphy Director - Derby Homes, 839 London Road, Derby DE24 8UZ ☎ 01332 888522 ✉ maria.murphy@derbyhomes.org

Legal: Ms Janie Berry Director of Legal & Democratic Services & Interim Director - HR, 1st Floor, The Council House, Corporation Street, Derby DE1 2FS ☎ 01332 643616 ✉ janie.berry@derby.gov.uk

DERBY CITY

Leisure and Cultural Services: Mr Andrew Beddow Head of Service Facilities, Ground Floor, Council House, Corporation Street, Derby DE1 2FS ☎ 01332 641230 ✉ andrew.beddow@derby.gov.uk

Leisure and Cultural Services: Dr Peter Meakin Creative Producer, Assembly Rooms, Market Place, Derby DE1 3AH ☎ 01332 255806 ✉ peter.meakin@derby.gov.uk

Leisure and Cultural Services: Mr David Potton Head of Libraries, Ground Floor, Council House, Corporation Street, Derby DE1 2FS ☎ 01332 641719 ✉ david.potton@derby.gov.uk

Licensing: Mr John Tomlinson, Director of Environmental & Regulatory Services, Ground Floor, Council House, Corporation Street, Derby DE1 2FS ☎ 01332 642435 ✉ john.tomlinson@derby.gov.uk

Lifelong Learning: Ms Cath Harcula Head of Adult Learning, Allen Park Centre, Derby DE24 9DE ☎ 01332 642304 ✉ cath.harcula@derby.gov.uk

Member Services: Mr David Walsh Democratic Services Manager, 1st Floor, Council House, Corporation Street, Derby DE1 2FS ☎ 01332 643655 ✉ david.walsh@derby.gov.uk

Partnerships: Mr Tim Clegg Director - Partnerships & Streetpride, 15 Stores Road, Derby DE21 4BD ☎ 01332 641604 ✉ tim.clegg@derby.gov.uk

Personnel / HR: Ms Karen Jewell Director of HR & Business Support, 1st Floor, Council House, Corporation Street, Derby DE1 2FS ☎ 01332 643724 ✉ karen.jewell@derby.gov.uk

Planning: Mr Paul Clarke Head of Planning, 1st Floor, Council House, Corporation Street, Derby DE1 2FS ☎ 01332 641642 ✉ paul.clarke@derby.gov.uk

Procurement: Mr Martyn Marples Director of Finance & Procurement, 1st Floor, Council House, Corporation Street, Derby DE1 2FS ☎ 01332 643377 ✉ martyn.marples@derby.gov.uk

Procurement: Ms Linda Spiby Acting Head - Procurement, 1st Floor, Council House, Corporation Street, Derby DE1 2FS ☎ 01332 643274 ✉ linda.spiby@derby.gov.uk

Public Libraries: Mr David Potton Head of Libraries, Ground Floor, Council House, Corporation Street, Derby DE1 2FS ☎ 01332 641719 ✉ david.potton@derby.gov.uk

Public Libraries: Ms Jennie Preedy Libraries Support Manager, Ground Floor, Council House, Corporation Street, Derby DE1 2FS ☎ 01332 641723 ✉ jennie.preedy@derby.gov.uk

Recycling & Waste Minimisation: Mr Mick McLachlan, Head of Waste Management, 15 Stores Road, Derby DE21 4BE ☎ 01332 641503 ✉ mick.mclachlan@derby.gov.uk

Regeneration: Mr Richard Williams, Director - Regeneration, 2nd Floor, Council House, Corporation Street, Derby DE1 2FS ☎ 01332 642436 ✉ richard.williams@derby.gov.uk

Social Services (Children): Ms Hazel Lymbery Acting Director - Specialist Services, 2nd Floor, Council House, Corporation Street, Derby DE1 2FS ☎ 01332 642644 ✉ hazel.lymbery@derby.gov.uk

Social Services (Children): Mr Andy Smith Acting Strategic Director - Children & Young People, 1st Floor, Council House, Corporation Street, Derby DE1 2FS ☎ 01332 643557 ✉ andy.smith@derby.gov.uk

Safeguarding: Ms Maureen Darbon Acting Director - Early Intervention & Integrated Safeguarding, 1st Floor, The Council House, Corporation Street, Derby DE1 2FS ☎ 01332 256790 ✉ maureen.darbon@derby.gov.uk

Public Health: Dr Robyn Dewis Acting Director - Public Health, 1st Floor, The Council House, Corporation Street, Derby DE1 2FS ☎ 01332 643073 ✉ robyn.dewis@derby.gov.uk

Tourism: Mr Alan Smith Head of Economic Regeneration, 2nd Floor, Council House, Corporation Street, Derby DE1 2FS ☎ 01332 641624 ✉ alan.smith@derby.gov.uk

Tourism: Mr Richard Williams, Director - Regeneration, 2nd Floor, Council House, Corporation Road, Derby DE1 2FS ☎ 01332 642436 ✉ richard.williams@derby.gov.uk

Traffic Management: Mr David Gartside Head of Traffic & Transportation, Ground Floor, Council House, Corporation Street, Derby DE1 2FS ☎ 01332 641821 ✉ david.gartside@derby.gov.uk

Transport: Mr Tony Gascoigne Central & West Area Group Manager, Ground Floor, Council House, Corporation Street, Derby DE1 2FS ☎ 01332 641779 ✉ tony.gascoigne@derby.gov.uk

Waste Management: Mr Mick McLachlan, Head of Waste Management, 15 Stores Road, Derby DE21 4BE ☎ 01332 641503 ✉ mick.mclachlan@derby.gov.uk

COUNCILLORS

***Leader of the Council* Banwait**, Ranjit (LAB - Boulton)
ranjit.banwait@derby.gov.uk

Afzal, Asaf (LAB - Abbey)
asaf.afzal@derby.gov.uk

Ashburner, Eric (LD - Littleover)
eric.ashburner@derby.gov.uk

Barker, Mick (CON - Oakwood)
mick.barker@derby.gov.uk

Bayliss, Paul (LAB - Alvaston)
paul.bayliss@derby.gov.uk

Bolton, Sara (LAB - Chaddesden)
sara.bolton@derby.gov.uk

Care, Lucy (LD - Littleover)

Carr, Michael (LD - Littleover)
michael.carr@derby.gov.uk

Dhindsa, Hardyal (LAB - Normanton)
hardyal.dhindsa@derby.gov.uk

Eldret, Lisa (LAB - Darley)
lisa.eldret@derby.gov.uk

Froggatt, Diane (LAB - Mackworth)
diane.froggatt@derby.gov.uk

Graves, Alan (UKIP - Alvaston)

Grimadell, Alan (CON - Chellaston)
alan.grimadell@derby.gov.uk

Harwood, Frank (CON - Oakwood)
frank.harwood@derby.gov.uk

Hassall, Steve (CON - Allestree)
steve.hassall@derby.gov.uk

Hezelgrave, Paul (LAB - Abbey)

Hickson, Philip (CON - Allestree)
philip.hickson@derby.gov.uk

Holmes, Matthew (CON - Chellaston)
matthew.holmes@derby.gov.uk

Holmes, Alison (CON - Mickleover)
alison.holmes2@derby.gov.uk

Hussain, Fareed (LAB - Arboretum)
fareed.hussain@derby.gov.uk

Ingall, Philip John (CON - Chellaston)
philip.ingall@derby.gov.uk

Jackson, Barbara (LAB - Boulton)
barbara.jackson@derby.gov.uk

Jones, Hilary (LD - Mickleover)
hilary.jones@derby.gov.uk

Keith, John (CON - Mickleover)
john.keith@derby.gov.uk

Khan, Jangir (LAB - Normanton)
jangir.khan@derby.gov.uk

Khan, Shiraz (LD - Arboretum)
shiraz.khan@derby.gov.uk

MacDonald, Anne (LAB - Chaddesden)
anne.macdonald@derby.gov.uk

Martin, Alison (LAB - Boulton)
alison.martin@derby.gov.uk

Naitta, Joe (LD - Blagreaves)
joe.naitta@derby.gov.uk

Nawaz, Gulfraz (LAB - Arboretum)
gulfraz.nawaz@derby.gov.uk

Pegg, Paul (LAB - Mackworth)
paul.pegg@derby.gov.uk

Poulter, Christopher Paul (CON - Spondon)
christopher.poulter@derby.gov.uk

Raju, Amo (LAB - Blagreaves)
amo.raju@derby.gov.uk

Rawson, Martin (LAB - Derwent)
martin.rawson@derby.gov.uk

Redfern, Margaret (LAB - Derwent)
margaret.redfern@derby.gov.uk

Repton, Martin (LAB - Darley)
martin.repton@derby.gov.uk

Roulstone, Nicola (CON - Spondon)
nicola.roulstone@derby.gov.uk

Russell, Sarah (LAB - Abbey)
sarah.russell@derby.gov.uk

Sandhu, Balbir (LAB - Normanton)
balbir.sandhu@derby.gov.uk

Shanker, Baggy (LAB - Sinfin)
baggy.shankar@derby.gov.uk

Skelton, Ruth (LD - Blagreaves)
ruth.skelton@derby.gov.uk

Stanton, Jack (LAB - Darley)
jack.stanton@derby.gov.uk

Tittley, Mark (LAB - Alvaston)
mark.titley@derby.gov.uk

Turner, Robin (LAB - Sinfin)
robin.turner@derby.gov.uk

Webb, Roy (CON - Allestree)
roy.webb@derby.gov.uk

West, Joanna (LAB - Sinfin)
joanna.west@derby.gov.uk

Whitby, John (LAB - Mackworth)
john.whitby@derby.gov.uk

Williams, Evonne (CON - Spondon)
evonne.williams@derby.gov.uk

Winter, Linda (LAB - Chaddesden)
linda.winter@derby.gov.uk

Wood, Robin (CON - Oakwood)
robin.wood@derby.gov.uk

Wright, Bill (UKIP - Derwent)

POLITICAL COMPOSITION
LAB: 28, CON: 14, LD: 7, UKIP: 2

COMMITTEE CHAIRS
Audit & Accounts: Mr Paul Hezelgrave

Health & Wellbeing: Mr Martin Repton

Licensing: Mr Balbir Sandhu

Planning: Mr Shiraz Khan

Derbyshire C

Derbyshire County Council, County Hall, Matlock DE4 3AG
☎ 01629 580000 🖷 01629 585280 💻 www.derbyshire.gov.uk

FACTS AND FIGURES
EU Constituencies: East Midlands
Election Frequency: Elections are of whole council

PRINCIPAL OFFICERS
Chief Executive: Mr Ian Stephenson Chief Executive, County Hall, Matlock DE4 3AG ☎ 01629 538100
ian.stephenson@derbyshire.gov.uk

Assistant Chief Executive: Ms Mags Young Assistant Chief Executive, County Hall, Matlock DE4 3AG ☎ 01629 538501
mags.young@derbyshire.gov.uk

Senior Management: Mr Mike Ashworth, Strategic Director - Economy Transport & Environment, County Hall, Matlock DE4 3AG
☎ 01629 538544 mike.ashworth@derbyshire.gov.uk

DERBYSHIRE

Senior Management: Ms Judith Greenhalgh Strategic Director - Corporate Resources, County Hall, Matlock DE4 3AG ☎ 01629 538300 ✉ judith.greenhalgh@derbyshire.gov.uk

Senior Management: Ms Joy Hollister Strategic Director - Adult Care, County Hall, Matlock DE4 3AG ✉ joy.hollister@derbyshire.gov.uk

Senior Management: Mr Ian Johnson, Strategic Director - Children & Young Adults, County Hall, Matlock DE4 3AG ☎ 01629 532005 ✉ ian.johnson@derbyshire.gov.uk

Senior Management: Mr David Lowe, Strategic Director - Policy, Community Safety & Health, County Hall, Matlock DE4 3AG ☎ 01629 538340 ✉ david.lowe@derbyshire.gov.uk

Architect, Building / Property Services: Mr David Beard Design Manager, Chatsworth Hall, Chesterfield Road, Matlock DE4 3FW ☎ 01629 536337 ✉ david.beard@derbyshire.gov.uk

Architect, Building / Property Services: Mrs Sarah Morris Assistant Director of Property (Design), Corporate Resources Department, Chatsworth Hall, Chesterfield Road, Matlock DE4 3FW ☎ 01629 536260 ✉ sarah.morris@derbyshire.gov.uk

Best Value: Mrs Ester Croll, Policy Manager, County Hall, Matlock DE4 3AG ☎ 01629 538267 ✉ ester.croll@derbyshire.gov.uk

Best Value: Ms Veronica Weaver Acting Assistant Manager for Quality Assurance, County Hall, Matlock DE4 3AG ☎ 07881 694437 ✉ veronica.weaver@derbyshire.gov.uk

Building Control: Mr Kevin Firth Head of Development, County Hall, Matlock DE4 3AG ☎ 01629 536567 ✉ kevin.firth@derbyshire.gov.uk

Catering Services: Ms Sheila Murdoch Catering & Domestic Services Manager, County Hall, Matlock DE4 3AG ☎ 01629 532183 ✉ sheila.murdoch@derbyshire.gov.uk

Children / Youth Services: Ms Kathryn Boulton Assistant Director - Schools & Learning, County Hall, Matlock DE4 3AG ☎ 01629 532750 ✉ kathryn.boulton@derbyshire.gov.uk

Children / Youth Services: Mrs Isobel Fleming Assistant Director - Performance Quality & Commissioning, County Hall, Matlock DE4 3AG ☎ 01629 532211 ✉ isobel.fleming@derbyshire.gov.uk

Children / Youth Services: Mr Ian Johnson, Strategic Director - Children & Young Adults, County Hall, Matlock DE4 3AG ☎ 01629 532005 ✉ ian.johnson@derbyshire.gov.uk

Children / Youth Services: Ms Melanie Meggs Service Director - Safeguarding & Disability, County Hall, Matlock DE4 3AG ☎ 01629 532005 ✉ melanie.meggs@derbyshire.gov.uk

Civil Registration: Ms Gemma Duckworth Business Services Manager, County Hall, Matlock DE4 3AG ☎ 01629 538324 ✉ gemma.duckworth@derbyshire.gov.uk

PR / Communications: Ms Mags Young Assistant Chief Executive, County Hall, Matlock DE4 3AG ☎ 01629 538501 ✉ mags.young@derbyshire.gov.uk

Community Planning: Mrs Jude Wildgoose, Policy Manager, County Hall, Matlock DE4 3AG ☎ 01629 538439 ✉ jude.wildgoose@derbyshire.gov.uk

Community Safety: Mr David Lowe, Strategic Director - Policy, Community Safety & Health, County Hall, Matlock DE4 3AG ☎ 01629 538340 ✉ david.lowe@derbyshire.gov.uk

Computer Management: Mr Bob Busby Core Systems Programme Manager, County Hall, Matlock DE4 3AG ☎ 01629 536806 ✉ bob.busby@derbyshire.gov.uk

Consumer Protection and Trading Standards: Mr Rob Taylour, Head of Trading Standards, County Hall, Matlock DE4 3AG ☎ 01629 539830 ✉ rob.taylour@derbyshire.gov.uk

Contracts: Mr Simon West Deputy Director - Corporate Property, Chatsworth Hall, Chesterfield, Matlock DE4 3FW ☎ 01629 536686 ✉ simon.west@derbyshire.gov.uk

Corporate Services: Ms Judith Greenhalgh Strategic Director - Corporate Resources, County Hall, Matlock DE4 3AG ☎ 01629 538300 ✉ judith.greenhalgh@derbyshire.gov.uk

Direct Labour: Mr Simon West Deputy Director - Corporate Property, County Hall, Matlock DE4 3AG ☎ 01629 536686 ✉ simon.west@derbyshire.gov.uk

Economic Development: Mr Frank Horsley Head of Economic Regeneration, County Hall, Matlock DE4 3AG ☎ 01629 538348 ✉ frank.horsley@derbyshire.gov.uk

E-Government: Mr David Hickman, Director of Transformation, County Hall, Matlock DE4 3AG ☎ 01629 535801 ✉ david.hickman@derbyshire.gov.uk

Emergency Planning: Ms Elizabeth Partington Emergency Planning Manager, County Hall, Matlock DE4 3AG ✉ liz.partington@derbyshire.gov.uk

Energy Management: Ms Kathryn Warrington Carbon & Energy Manager, County Hall, Matlock DE4 3AG ☎ 01629 538440 ✉ kathryn.warrington@derbyshire.gov.uk

Environmental / Technical Services: Mrs Allison Thomas, Service Director - Environment & Transport, County Hall, Matlock DE4 3AG ☎ 01629 533300 ✉ allison.thomas@derbyshire.gov.uk

Estates, Property & Valuation: Mr Steve Dolby Group Manager of Estates, Chatsworth Hall, Chesterfield Road, Matlock DE4 3FW ☎ 01629 536333 ✉ steve.dolby@derbyshire.gov.uk

Estates, Property & Valuation: Mr Simon West Deputy Director - Corporate Property, County Hall, Matlock DE4 3AG ☎ 01629 536686 ✉ simon.west@derbyshire.gov.uk

European Liaison: Mr Frank Horsley Head of Economic Regeneration, County Hall, Matlock DE4 3AG ☎ 01629 538348 ✉ frank.horsley@derbyshire.gov.uk

Events Manager: Miss Stephanie Walsh, Economic Development Officer, County Hall, Matlock DE4 3AG ☎ 01629 538464 ✉ stephanie.walsh@derbyshire.gov.uk

Facilities: Mr Geoff Pickford Service Director - Highways, County Hall, Matlock DE4 3AG ☎ 01629 538194 ✉ geoff.pickford@derbyshire.gov.uk

Finance: Mr Peter Handford Director of Finance, County Hall, Matlock DE4 3AG ☎ 01629 538700 ✉ peter.handford@derbyshire.gov.uk

Treasury: Mr Peter Handford Director of Finance, County Hall, Matlock DE4 3AG ☎ 01629 538700 ✉ peter.handford@derbyshire.gov.uk

Pensions: Mr Nigel Dowey Pensions Manager, County Hall, Matlock DE4 3AG ☎ 01629 538827 ✉ nigel.dowey@derbyshire.gov.uk

Pensions: Ms Dawn Kinley Pension Investment Officer, County Hall, Matlock DE4 3AG ☎ 01629 538893 ✉ dawn.kinley@derbyshire.gov.uk

Fleet Management: Mr Brian Hattersley Principal Engineer, County Transport, Fleet Management, Ripley Road, Ambergate, Derby DE4 2ER ☎ 01629 532110 ✉ brian.hattersley@derbyshire.gov.uk

Grounds Maintenance: Mr Simon West Deputy Director - Corporate Property, Chatsworth Hall, , Matlock DE4 3FW ☎ 01629 536686 ✉ simon.west@derbyshire.gov.uk

Health and Safety: Mr John Davis, Corporate Health & Safety Advisor, County Hall, Matlock DE4 3AG ☎ 01629 536950 ✉ john.davis@derbyshire.gov.uk

Highways: Mr Geoff Pickford Service Director - Highways, County Hall, Matlock DE4 3AG ☎ 01629 538194 ✉ geoff.pickford@derbyshire.gov.uk

Legal: Mr John McEivaney Director of Legal Services, County Hall, Matlock DE4 3AG ☎ 01629 580000 ✉ john.mcelvaney@derbyshire.gov.uk

Leisure and Cultural Services: Mr David Lowe, Strategic Director - Policy, Community Safety & Health, County Hall, Matlock DE4 3AG ☎ 01629 538340 ✉ david.lowe@derbyshire.gov.uk

Licensing: Mr Rob Taylour, Head of Trading Standards, County Hall, Matlock DE4 3AG ☎ 01629 539830 ✉ rob.taylour@derbyshire.gov.uk

Lighting: Mr Geoff Pickford Service Director - Highways, County Hall, Matlock DE4 3AG ☎ 01629 538194 ✉ geoff.pickford@derbyshire.gov.uk

Lottery Funding, Charity and Voluntary: Ms Sarah Eaton, Head of Policy & Research, County Hall, Matlock DE4 3AG ☎ 01629 538268 ✉ sarah.eaton@derbyshire.gov.uk

Personnel / HR: Mr Toni Compai Director of HR, County Hall, Matlock DE4 3AG ☎ 01629 536927 ✉ toni.compai@derbyshire.gov.uk

Planning: Mrs Allison Thomas, Service Director - Environment & Transport, County Hall, Matlock DE4 3AG ☎ 01629 533300 ✉ allison.thomas@derbyshire.gov.uk

Procurement: Mrs Michelle Smith Corporate Procurement Manager, County Hall, Matlock DE4 3AG ☎ 01629 536870 ✉ michelle.smith@derbyshire.gov.uk

Public Libraries: Mr Don Gibbs Service Director - Libraries & Heritage, County Hall, Matlock DE4 3AG ☎ 01629 536572 ✉ don.gibbs@derbyshire.gov.uk

Recycling & Waste Minimisation: Ms Claire Brailsford Head of Waste Management, County Hall, Matlock DE4 3AG ☎ 01629 539775 ✉ claire.brailsford@derbyshire.gov.uk

Regeneration: Mr Frank Horsley Head of Economic Regeneration, County Hall, Matlock DE4 3AG ☎ 01629 538348 ✉ frank.horsley@derbyshire.gov.uk

Road Safety: Mr Geoff Pickford Service Director - Highways, County Hall, Matlock DE4 3AG ☎ 01629 538194 ✉ geoff.pickford@derbyshire.gov.uk

Social Services (Adult): Ms Joy Hollister Strategic Director - Adult Care, County Hall, Matlock DE4 3AG ✉ joy.hollister@derbyshire.gov.uk

Social Services (Adult): Ms Melanie Meggs Service Director - Safeguarding & Disability, County Hall, Matlock DE4 3AG ☎ 01629 532005 ✉ melanie.meggs@derbyshire.gov.uk

Social Services (Adult): Mr Roger Miller Assistant Director - Field Work, South, County Hall, Matlock DE4 3AG ☎ 01629 532002 ✉ roger.miller@derbyshire.gov.uk

Social Services (Adult): Mr Simon Stevens Assistant Director - Direct Care, County Hall, Matlock DE4 3AG ☎ 01629 532001 ✉ simon.stevens@derbyshire.gov.uk

Social Services (Adult): Ms Julie Voller Assistant Director - Strategy & Commissioning, County Hall, Matlock DE4 3AG ☎ 01629 532004 ✉ julie.voller@derbyshire.gov.uk

Social Services (Children): Mr Andrew Milroy, Assistant Director of Field Work - North, County Hall, Matlock DE4 3AG ☎ 01629 532177 ✉ andrew.milroy@derbyshire.gov.uk

Public Health: Ms Elaine Michel Director - Public Health, County Hall, Matlock DE4 3AG ☎ 01629 538437 ✉ elaine.michel@derbyshire.gov.uk

Staff Training: Mr Toni Compai Director of HR, County Hall, Matlock DE4 3AG ☎ 01629 536927 ✉ toni.compai@derbyshire.gov.uk

DERBYSHIRE

Tourism: Miss Stephanie Walsh, Economic Development Officer, County Hall, Matlock DE4 3AG ☎ 01629 538464 ✉ stephanie.walsh@derbyshire.gov.uk

Traffic Management: Mr Geoff Pickford Service Director - Highways, County Hall, Matlock DE4 3AG ☎ 01629 538194 ✉ geoff.pickford@derbyshire.gov.uk

Transport: Mr Brian Hattersley Principal Engineer, County Transport, Fleet Management, Ripley Road, Ambergate, Derby DE4 2ER ☎ 01629 532110 ✉ brian.hattersley@derbyshire.gov.uk

Waste Collection and Disposal: Ms Claire Brailsford Head of Waste Management, County Hall, Matlock DE4 3AG ☎ 01629 539775 ✉ claire.brailsford@derbyshire.gov.uk

Waste Management: Ms Claire Brailsford Head of Waste Management, County Hall, Matlock DE4 3AG ☎ 01629 539775 ✉ claire.brailsford@derbyshire.gov.uk

COUNCILLORS

***Leader of the Council* Western**, Anne (LAB - Barlborough & Clowne)
anne.western@derbyshire.gov.uk

***Deputy Leader of the Council* Smith**, Paul (LAB - Alfreton & Somercotes)
paul.smith@derbyshire.gov.uk

Allen, David (LAB - Birdholme)
dave.allen@derbyshire.gov.uk

Atkins, Elizabeth (LD - New Mills)
beth.atkins@derbyshire.gov.uk

Bambrick, Sean (LAB - Swadlincote North)
sean.bambrick@derbyshire.gov.uk

Birkin, Glennice (LAB - Ilkeston East)
glennice.birkin@derbyshire.gov.uk

Bisknell, Caitlin (LAB - Buxton North & East)
caitlin.bisknell@derbyshire.gov.uk

Blank, Sharon (LAB - Spire)
sharon.blank@derbyshire.gov.uk

Booth, Michelle (LAB - Ilkeston West)
michelle.booth@derbyshire.gov.uk

Botham, Andy (LAB - Matlock)
andy.botham@derbyshire.gov.uk

Bradford, Stuart (CON - Duffield & Belper South)
stuart.bradford@derbyshire.gov.uk

Brittain, Stuart (LAB - Loundsley Green & New**)**
stuart.brittain@derbyshire.gov.uk

Bull, Steve (CON - Ashbourne)
steve.bull@derbyshire.gov.uk

Buttery, Kevin (CON - Horsley)
kevin.buttery@derbyshire.gov.uk

Charles, Diane (LAB - Eckington & Killamarsh)
diane.charles@derbyshire.gov.uk

Chilton, Linda (CON - Melbourne)
linda.chilton@derbyshire.gov.uk

Collins, Dean (LAB - Staveley North & Whittington)
dean.collins@derbyshire.gov.uk

Cox, Celia (LAB - Heanor Central)
celia.cox@derbyshire.gov.uk

Coyle, Jim (LAB - Pinxton & South Normanton West)
jim.coyle@derbyshire.gov.uk

Davison, Robert (LAB - Aston)
rob.davison@derbyshire.gov.uk

Dixon, Joan (LAB - Bolsover South West & Scarcliffe)
joan.dixon@derbyshire.gov.uk

Dunn, Paul (LAB - Swadlincote Central)
paul.dunn@derbyshire.gov.uk

Ellis, Stuart (CON - Dronfield West & Walton)
stuart.ellis@derbyshire.gov.uk

Ford, Martyn (CON - Etwall & Repton)
martyn.ford@derbyshire.gov.uk

Freeborn, Steve (LAB - Ripley East & Codnor)
steve.freeborn@derbyshire.gov.uk

Frudd, John (LAB - Ilkeston South)
john.frudd@derbyshire.gov.uk

Gilby, Tricia (LAB - Brimington)

Gillott, Kevin (LAB - Clay Cross South)
kevin.gillott@derbyshire.gov.uk

Greenhalgh, Damien (LAB - Glossop & Charlesworth)
damien.greenhalgh@derbyshire.gov.uk

Hart, Carol (CON - Breadsall & West Hallam)
carol.hart@derbyshire.gov.uk

Hill, Janet (LAB - Dronfield East)
janet.hill2@derbyshire.gov.uk

Hill, Julie (LAB - Sutton)
julie.hill@derbsyshire.gov.uk

Hosker, Roland (LAB - Long Eaton)
roland.hosker@derbyshire.gov.uk

Innes, Jean (LAB - St Mary's)
jean.innes@derbyshire.gov.uk

Jones, Paul (LAB - Greater Heanor)
paul.jones@derbyshire.gov.uk

Kemp, Tony (CON - Buxton West)
tony.kemp@derbyshire.gov.uk

Lauro, Kath (LAB - Linton)
kath.lauro@derbyshire.gov.uk

Lewis, Barry (CON - Wingerworth & Shirland)
barry.lewis@derbyshire.gov.uk

Lomax, David (LD - Whaley Bridge)
david.lomax@derbyshire.gov.uk

Longden, Mike (CON - Derwent Valley)
michael.longden@derbyshire.gov.uk

Major, Wayne (CON - Sandicote)
wayne.major@derbyshire.gov.uk

Marshall-Clarke, Steve (LAB - Alfreton & Somercotes)
steve.marshall-clarke@derbyshire.gov.uk

McGregor, Duncan (LAB - Bolsolver North)
duncan.mcgregor@derbyshire.gov.uk

Mihaly, Ron (LAB - Boythorpe & Brampton South)
ron.mihaly@derbyshire.gov.uk

Moesby, Clive (LAB - Tibshelf)
clive.moesby@derbyshire.gov.uk

Morgan, Keith (LD - Walton & West)
keith.morgan@derbyshire.gov.uk

Neill, Clare (LAB - Petersham)
clare.neill@derbyshire.gov.uk

Owen, John (LAB - Belper)
john.owen@derbyshire.gov.uk

Parkinson, Robert (CON - Breaston)
robert.parkinson@derbyshire.gov.uk

Patten, Julie (CON - Hilton)
julie.patten@derbyshire.gov.uk

Ratcliffe, Irene (LAB - Wirksworth)
irene.ratcliffe@derbyshire.gov.uk

Ridgway, Brian (LAB - Eckington & Killamarsh)
brian.ridgway@derbyshire.gov.uk

Southerd, Trevor (LAB - Swadlincote South)
trevor.southerd@derbyshire.gov.uk

Spencer, Simon (CON - Dovedale)
simon.spencer@derbyshire.gov.uk

Stockdale, Marion (LAB - Shirebrook & Pleasley)
marian.stockdale@derbyshire.gov.uk

Street, Jocelyn (CON - Chapel & Hope Valley)
jocelyn.street@derbyshire.gov.uk

Taylor, David (CON - Alport & Derwent)
david.taylor@derbyshire.gov.uk

Twigg, Judith (CON - Bakewell)
judith.twigg@derbyshire.gov.uk

Walton, Daniel (CON - Sawley)
daniel.walton@derbyshire.gov.uk

Wilcox, Ellie (LAB - Glossop & Charlesworth)
ellie.wilcox@derbyshire.gov.uk

Wilcox, Dave (LAB - Etherow)
dave.wilcox@derbyshire.gov.uk

Williams, John (LAB - Staveley)
john.williams@derbyshire.gov.uk

Williams, Dave (LAB - Ripley West & Heage)
david.williams@derbyshire.gov.uk

Wright, Brian (LAB - Clay Cross North)
brian.wright@derbyshire.gov.uk

POLITICAL COMPOSITION

LAB: 43, CON: 18, LD: 3

Derbyshire Dales D

Derbyshire Dales District Council, Town Hall, Matlock DE4 3NN
☎ 01629 761100 🖷 01629 761148 💻 www.derbyshiredales.gov.uk

FACTS AND FIGURES

Parliamentary Constituencies: Derbyshire Dales, High Peak
EU Constituencies: East Midlands
Election Frequency: Elections are of whole council

PRINCIPAL OFFICERS

Chief Executive: Mrs Dorcas Bunton Chief Executive, Town Hall, Matlock DE4 3NN ☎ 01629 761126 🖷 01629 761149 🖰 dorcas.bunton@derbyshiredales.gov.uk

Deputy Chief Executive: Mr Paul Wilson Corporate Director & Deputy Chief Executive, Town Hall, Matlock DE4 3NN ☎ 01629 761324 🖷 01629 761163 🖰 paul.wilson@derbyshiredales.gov.uk

Architect, Building / Property Services: Mrs Karen Henriksen Head of Resources, Town Hall, Matlock DE4 3NN ☎ 01629 761203 🖰 karen.henriksen@derbyshiredales.gov.uk

Best Value: Dr Steve Capes Head of Regeneration & Policy, Town Hall, Matlock DE4 3NN ☎ 01629 761371 🖷 01629 761165 🖰 steve.capes@derbyshiredales.gov.uk

Building Control: Mr David Harris Building Control Manager, Town Hall, Matlock DE4 3NN ☎ 01629 761320 🖷 01629761163 🖰 david.harris@derbyshiredales.gov.uk

PR / Communications: Mr Jim Fearn Communications & Marketing Manager, Town Hall, Matlock DE4 3NN ☎ 01629 761195 🖷 01629 761165 🖰 jim.fearn@derbyshiredales.gov.uk

Community Planning: Mr Giles Dann Policy & Economic Development Manager, Town Hall, Matlock DE4 3NN ☎ 01629 761211 🖷 01629 761165 🖰 giles.dann@derbyshiredales.gov.uk

Community Safety: Mr Ashley Watts Head of Community Development, Town Hall, Matlock DE4 3NN ☎ 01629 761367 🖰 ashley.watts@derbyshiredales.gov.uk

Computer Management: Mr Nick Blaney Joint IT Services Manager, Town Hall, Matlock DE4 3NN ☎ 01246 217103; 01246 217103; 01246 717097 🖰 nick.blaney@ne-derbyshire.gov.uk

Corporate Services: Ms Sandra Lamb, Head of Corporate Services, Town Hall, Matlock DE4 3NN ☎ 01629 761281 🖷 01629 761307 🖰 sandra.lamb@derbyshiredales.gov.uk

Customer Service: Ms Sandra Lamb, Head of Corporate Services, Town Hall, Matlock DE4 3NN ☎ 01629 761281 🖷 01629 761307 🖰 sandra.lamb@derbyshiredales.gov.uk

Economic Development: Mr Giles Dann Policy & Economic Development Manager, Town Hall, Matlock DE4 3NN ☎ 01629 761211 🖷 01629 761165 🖰 giles.dann@derbyshiredales.gov.uk

E-Government: Mr Nick Blaney Joint IT Services Manager, Town Hall, Matlock DE4 3NN ☎ 01246 717097 🖰 nick.blaney@ne-derbyshire.gov.uk

Electoral Registration: Mrs Dorcas Bunton Chief Executive, Town Hall, Matlock DE4 3NN ☎ 01629 761126 🖷 01629 761149 🖰 dorcas.bunton@derbyshiredales.gov.uk

Emergency Planning: Mrs Dorcas Bunton Chief Executive, Town Hall, Matlock DE4 3NN ☎ 01629 761126 🖷 01629 761149 🖰 dorcas.bunton@derbyshiredales.gov.uk

Energy Management: Mr Mike Galsworthy Estates & Facilities Manager, Town Hall, Matlock DE4 3NN ☎ 01629 761362 🖷 01629 761146 🖰 mike.galsworthy@derbyshiredales.gov.uk

DERBYSHIRE DALES

Environmental / Technical Services: Mrs Heidi McDougall Head of Environmental Services, Town Hall, Matlock DE4 3NN ☎ 01629 761372 ✉ heidi.mcdougall@derbyshiredales.gov.uk

Environmental Health: Mr Tim Braund Head of Regulatory Services, Town Hall, Matlock DE4 3NN ☎ 01629 761118 ✉ tim.braund@derbyshiredales.gov.uk

Estates, Property & Valuation: Mr Mike Galsworthy Estates & Facilities Manager, Town Hall, Matlock DE4 3NN ☎ 01629 761362 🖷 01629 761146 ✉ mike.galsworthy@derbyshiredales.gov.uk

Events Manager: Ms Nicola Wildgoose, Events Manager Town Hall, Matlock DE4 3NN ☎ 01629 761390 ✉ nicola.wildgoose@derbyshiredales.gov.uk

Facilities: Mr Mike Galsworthy Estates & Facilities Manager, Town Hall, Matlock DE4 3NN ☎ 01629 761362 🖷 01629 761146 ✉ mike.galsworthy@derbyshiredales.gov.uk

Finance: Mrs Karen Henriksen Head of Resources, Town Hall, Matlock DE4 3NN ☎ 01629 761203 ✉ karen.henriksen@derbyshiredales.gov.uk

Fleet Management: Mr Mark Kiddier Street Scene & Works Transport Manager, Town Hall, Matlock DE4 3NN ☎ 01629 735497 🖷 01629 761165 ✉ mark.kiddier@derbyshiredales.gov.uk

Grounds Maintenance: Mrs Heidi McDougall Head of Environmental Services, Town Hall, Matlock DE4 3NN ☎ 01629 761372 ✉ heidi.mcdougall@derbyshiredales.gov.uk

Health and Safety: Mr Tim Braund Head of Regulatory Services, Town Hall, Matlock DE4 3NN ☎ 01629 761118 ✉ tim.braund@derbyshiredales.gov.uk

Home Energy Conservation: Mr Tim Braund Head of Regulatory Services, Town Hall, Matlock DE4 3NN ☎ 01629 761118 ✉ tim.braund@derbyshiredales.gov.uk

Housing: Mr Rob Cogings Head of Housing, Town Hall, Matlock DE4 3NN ☎ 01629 761354 ✉ robert.cogings@derbyshiredales.gov.uk

Legal: Miss Katie Hamill Solicitor, Town Hall, Matlock DE4 3NN ☎ 01629 761319 🖷 01629 761307 ✉ katie.hamill@derbyshiredales.gov.uk

Leisure and Cultural Services: Mr Ashley Watts Head of Community Development, Town Hall, Matlock DE4 3NN ☎ 01629 761367 ✉ ashley.watts@derbyshiredales.gov.uk

Licensing: Mr Tim Braund Head of Regulatory Services, Town Hall, Matlock DE4 3NN ☎ 01629 761118 ✉ tim.braund@derbyshiredales.gov.uk

Lottery Funding, Charity and Voluntary: Ms Sandra Lamb, Head of Corporate Services, Town Hall, Matlock DE4 3NN ☎ 01629 761281 🖷 01629 761307 ✉ sandra.lamb@derbyshiredales.gov.uk

Member Services: Ms Sandra Lamb, Head of Corporate Services, Town Hall, Matlock DE4 3NN ☎ 01629 761281 🖷 01629 761307 ✉ sandra.lamb@derbyshiredales.gov.uk

Parking: Mrs Heidi McDougall Head of Environmental Services, Town Hall, Matlock DE4 3NN ☎ 01629 761372 ✉ heidi.mcdougall@derbyshiredales.gov.uk

Partnerships: Dr Steve Capes Head of Regeneration & Policy, Town Hall, Matlock DE4 3NN ☎ 01629 761371 🖷 01629 761165 ✉ steve.capes@derbyshiredales.gov.uk

Personnel / HR: Mr Tim Furniss Personnel Assistant, Town Hall, Matlock DE4 3NN ☎ 01629 761155 ✉ tim.furniss@derbyshiredales.gov.uk

Personnel / HR: Mrs Deborah Unwin HR Manager, Town Hall, Matlock DE4 3NN ☎ 01629 761364 🖷 01629 761165 ✉ deborah.unwin@derbyshiredales.gov.uk

Planning: Mr Tim Braund Head of Regulatory Services, Town Hall, Matlock DE4 3NN ☎ 01629 761118 ✉ tim.braund@derbyshiredales.gov.uk

Recycling & Waste Minimisation: Mr Keith Hollinshead, Waste Management & Recycling Officer, Town Hall, Matlock DE4 3NN ☎ 01629 761112 🖷 01629 761165 ✉ keith.hollinshead@derbyshiredales.gov.uk

Recycling & Waste Minimisation: Mrs Heidi McDougall Head of Environmental Services, Town Hall, Matlock DE4 3NN ☎ 01629 761372 ✉ heidi.mcdougall@derbyshiredales.gov.uk

Regeneration: Dr Steve Capes Head of Regeneration & Policy, Town Hall, Matlock DE4 3NN ☎ 01629 761371 🖷 01629 761165 ✉ steve.capes@derbyshiredales.gov.uk

Staff Training: Mrs Deborah Unwin HR Manager, Town Hall, Matlock DE4 3NN ☎ 01629 761364 🖷 01629 761165 ✉ deborah.unwin@derbyshiredales.gov.uk

Street Scene: Mrs Heidi McDougall Head of Environmental Services, Town Hall, Matlock DE4 3NN ☎ 01629 761372 ✉ heidi.mcdougall@derbyshiredales.gov.uk

Sustainable Development: Mrs Dorcas Bunton Chief Executive, Town Hall, Matlock DE4 3NN ☎ 01629 761126 🖷 01629 761149 ✉ dorcas.bunton@derbyshiredales.gov.uk

Tourism: Ms Gill Chapman Tourism Officer, Town Hall, Matlock DE4 3NN ☎ 01629 761145 ✉ gill.chapman@derbyshiredales.gov.uk

Transport: Mr Mark Kiddier Street Scene & Works Transport Manager, Town Hall, Matlock DE4 3NN ☎ 01629 735497 🖷 01629 761165 ✉ mark.kiddier@derbyshiredales.gov.uk

Children's Play Areas: Mrs Heidi McDougall Head of Environmental Services, Town Hall, Matlock DE4 3NN ☎ 01629 761372 ✉ heidi.mcdougall@derbyshiredales.gov.uk

COUNCILLORS

***Chair* Walker**, Carol (CON - Bakewell)
carol.walker@derbyshiredales.gov.uk

***Vice-Chair* Catt**, Albert (CON - Doveridge & Sudbury)
albert.catt@derbyshiredales.gov.uk

***Leader of the Council* Rose**, Lewis (CON - Carsington Water)
lewis.rose@derbyshiredales.gov.uk

***Deputy Leader of the Council* Stevens**, Geoff (CON - Matlock All Saints)
geoff.stevens@derbyshiredales.gov.uk

Bevan, Jacqueline (CON - Hathersage & Eyam)
jacque.bevan@derbyshiredales.gov.uk

Bower, Jennifer (CON - Tideswell)
jennifer.bower@derbyshiredales.gov.uk

Bright, Richard (CON - Hulland)
richard.bright@derbyshiredales.gov.uk

Bull, Kenneth (CON - Norbury)
ken.bull@derbyshiredales.gov.uk

Bull, Stephen (CON - Ashbourne North)
stephen.bull@derbyshiredales.gov.uk

Burfoot, Susan (LD - Matlock All Saints)
sue.burfoot@derbyshiredales.gov.uk

Burton, David (LD - Darley Dale)
david.burton@derbyshiredales.gov.uk

Cartwright, Bob (LAB - Masson)
bob.cartwright@derbyshiredales.gov.uk

Chapman, David (CON - Hartington & Taddington)
david.chapman@derbyshiredales.gov.uk

Donnelly, Thomas (CON - Ashbourne South)
thomas.donnelly@derbyshiredales.gov.uk

Elliott, Ann (CON - Matlock All Saints)
ann.elliott@derbyshiredales.gov.uk

Fearn, David (LD - Darley Dale)
david.fearn@derbyshiredales.gov.uk

Fitzherbert, Richard (CON - Dovedale & Parwich)
richard.fitzherbert@derbyshiredales.gov.uk

Flitter, Steve (LD - Matlock St. Giles)
steve.flitter@derbyshiredales.gov.uk

Frederickson, David (IND - Lathkill & Bradford)
david.frederickson@derbyshiredales.gov.uk

Furness, Chris (CON - Bradwell)
chris.furness@derbyshiredales.gov.uk

Horton, Neil (CON - Litton & Longstone)
neil.horton@derbyshiredales.gov.uk

Hunt, Catherine (CON - Calver)
catherine.hunt@derbyshiredales.gov.uk

Jenkins, Angus (CON - Brailsford)
angus.jenkins@derbyshiredales.gov.uk

Lewer, Andrew (CON - Ashbourne South)
andrew.lewer@derbyshiredales.gov.uk

Longden, Michael (CON - Chatsworth)
mike.longden@derbyshiredales.gov.uk

Millward, Anthony (CON - Ashbourne North)
tony.millward@derbyshiredales.gov.uk

Monks, Jean (CON - Hathersage & Eyam)
jean.monks@derbyshiredales.gov.uk

Purdy, Garry (CON - Masson)
garry.purdy@derbyshiredales.gov.uk

Ratcliffe, Mike (LAB - Wirksworth)
mike.ratclife@derbyshiredales.gov.uk

Ratcliffe, Irene (LAB - Wirksworth)
irene.ratcliffe@derbyshiredales.gov.uk

Shirley, Andrew (CON - Clifton & Bradley)
andrew.shirley@derbyshiredales.gov.uk

Slack, Peter (LAB - Wirksworth)
peter.slack@derbyshiredales.gov.uk

Statham, Andrew (CON - Darley Dale)
andrew.statham@derbyshiredales.gov.uk

Stevens, Jacquie (CON - Matlock St. Giles)
jacquie.stevens@derbyshiredales.gov.uk

Swindell, Colin (LAB - Winster & South Darley)
colin.swindell@derbyshiredales.gov.uk

Tilbrook, Philippa (CON - Bakewell)
philippa.tilbrook@derbyshiredales.gov.uk

Tipping, Barrie (CON - Matlock St. Giles)
barrie.tipping@derbyshiredales.gov.uk

Twigg, Judith (CON - Bakewell)
judith.twigg@derbyshiredales.gov.uk

Wild, Joanne (CON - Stanton)
joanna.wild@derbyshiredales.gov.uk

POLITICAL COMPOSITION

CON: 29, LAB: 5, LD: 4, IND: 1

COMMITTEE CHAIRS

Community: Ms Jennifer Bower

Corporate: Mr Albert Catt

Licensing & Appeals: Mrs Jacqueline Bevan

Derry City & Strabane District Council N

Derry City & Strabane District Council, Derry City Council, 98 Strand Road, Derry BT48 7NN
☎ 028 7136 5151 info@derrycity.gov.uk

PRINCIPAL OFFICERS

Chief Executive: Mr John Kelpie Chief Executive, Derry City Council, 98 Strand Road, Derry BT48 7NN

COUNCILLORS

***Mayor* McCallion**, Elisha (SF - Ballyarnett)
elisha.mccallion@derrycityandstrabanedistrict.com

***Alderman* Bresland**, Allan (DUP - Sperrin)
allan.bresland@derrycityandstrabanedistrict.com

***Alderman* Devenney**, Maurice (DUP - Faughan)
maurice.devenney@derrycityandstrabanedistrict.com

***Alderman* Hamilton**, Mary (UUP - Waterside)
mary.hamilton@derrycityandstrabanedistrict.com

***Alderman* Hamilton**, Rhonda (DUP - Sperrin)
rhonda.hamilton@derrycityandstrabanedistrict.com

***Alderman* Hussey**, Derek (UUP - Derg)
derek.hussey@derrycityandstrabanedistrict.com

***Alderman* Kerrigan**, Thomas (DUP - Derg)
thomas.kerrigan@derrycityandstrabanedistrict.com

DERRY CITY & STRABANE DISTRICT COUNCIL

***Alderman* Warke**, Graham (DUP - Faughan)
graham.warke@derrycityandstrabanedistrict.com

Boyle, John (SDLP - Foyleside)
john.boyle@derrycityandstrabanedistrict.com

Campbell, Kevin (SF - The Moor)
kevin.campbell@derrycityandstrabanedistrict.com

Carlin, Karina (SF - Sperrin)
karina.carlin@derrycityandstrabanedistrict.com

Carr, Sean (SDLP - The Moor)
sean.carr@derrycityandstrabanedistrict.com

Cooper, Michael (SF - Foyleside)
michael.cooper@derrycityandstrabanedistrict.com

Cusack, Shauna (SDLP - Foyleside)
shauna.cusack@derrycityandstrabanedistrict.com

Diver, Gerard (SDLP - Waterside)
gerard.diver@derrycityandstrabanedistrict.com

Dobbins, Angela (SDLP - Ballyarnett)
angela.dobbins@derrycityandstrabanedistrict.com

Donnelly, Gary (IND - The Moor)
gary.donnelly@derrycityandstrabanedistrict.com

Duffy, Sandra (SF - Ballyarnett)
sandra.duffy@derrycityandstrabanedistrict.com

Fleming, Paul (SF - Faughan)
paul.fleming@derrycityandstrabanedistrict.com

Gallagher, Paul (IND - Sperrin)
paul.gallagher@derrycityandstrabanedistrict.com

Hassan, Tony (SF - Ballyarnett)
tony.hassan@derrycityandstrabanedistrict.com

Hastings, Hugh (Gus) (SDLP - Faughan)
gus.hastings@derrycityandstrabanedistrict.com

Kelly, Colly (SF - The Moor)
colly.kelly@derrycityandstrabanedistrict.com

Kelly, Dan (SF - Sperrin)
dan.kelly@derrycityandstrabanedistrict.com

Kelly, Patsy (SDLP - Sperrin)
patsy.kelly@derrycityandstrabanedistrict.com

Logue, Patricia (SF - The Moor)
patricia.logue@derrycityandstrabanedistrict.com

McGinley, Eric (SF - Foyleside)
eric.mcginley@derrycityandstrabanedistrict.com

McGuire, Kieran (SF - Derg)
kieran.mcguire@derrycityandstrabanedistrict.com

McHugh, Maolíosa (SF - Derg)
maoliosa.mchugh@derrycityandstrabanedistrict.com

McHugh, Ruairi (SF - Derg)
ruairi.mchugh@derrycityandstrabanedistrict.com

McKeever, Jim (SDLP - Faughan)
jim.mckeever@derrycityandstrabanedistrict.com

McMahon, Brian (SF - Sperrin)
brian.mcmahon@derrycityandstrabanedistrict.com

O'Reilly, Darren (IND - Foyleside)
darren.oreilly@derrycityandstrabanedistrict.com

Quigley, Dermot (IND - Ballyarnett)
dermot.quigley@derrycityandstrabanedistrict.com

Tierney, Brian (SDLP - Ballyarnett)
brian.tierney@derrycityandstrabanedistrict.com

POLITICAL COMPOSITION

SF: 15, SDLP: 9, DUP: 5, IND: 4, UUP: 2

COMMITTEE CHAIRS

Assurance, Audit & Risk: Ms Sandra Duffy

Environment & Regeneration: Mr Brian Tierney

Pensions: Mr Kieran McGuire

Devon C

Devon County Council, County Hall, Topsham Road, Exeter EX2 4QD
☎ 0845 155 1015 🖷 01392 382324 💻 www.devon.gov.uk

FACTS AND FIGURES

Parliamentary Constituencies: Devon Central, Devon East, Devon North, Devon South West, Devon West and Torridge, Exeter, Newton Abbot, Plymouth Moor View, Plymouth Sutton and Devonport, Tiverton and Honiton, Totnes
EU Constituencies: South West
Election Frequency: Elections are of whole council

PRINCIPAL OFFICERS

Chief Executive: Dr Phil Norrey, Chief Executive, County Hall, Topsham Road, Exeter EX2 4QD ☎ 01392 383201 🖷 01392 382286 🖱 phil.norrey@devon.gov.uk

Senior Management: Mr Heather Barnes Strategic Director - Place, County Hall, Topsham Road, Exeter EX2 4QD ☎ 01392 383274 🖷 01392 382684 🖱 heather.barnes@devon.gov.uk

Senior Management: Mr Mary Davis, County Treasurer, County Hall, Topsham Road, Exeter EX2 4QD ☎ 01392 383310 🖷 01392 382959 🖱 mary.davis@devon.gov.uk

Senior Management: Dr Virginia Pearson Director - Public Health, County Hall, Topsham Road, Exeter EX2 4QD ☎ 01392 386398 🖱 virginia.pearson@devon.gov.uk

Senior Management: Mr Jan Shadbolt, County Solicitor, County Hall, Topsham Road, Exeter EX2 4QD ☎ 01392 382285 🖷 01392 382286 🖱 jan.shadbolt@devon.gov.uk

Senior Management: Mrs Jennie Stephens, Strategic Director - People, County Hall, Topsham Road, Exeter EX2 4QR ☎ 01392 383299 🖷 01392 382684 🖱 jennie.stephens@devon.gov.uk

Access Officer / Social Services (Disability): Ms Carolyn Elliott Assistant Director - Community Service & Social Care, Bay House, Nicholson Road, Torquay TQ2 7TD ☎ 01803 210534 🖱 carolyn.elliott3@nhs.net

Architect, Building / Property Services: Mr Matthew Jones Corporate Asset Manager (Estates), County Hall, Topsham Road, Exeter EX2 4QD ☎ 01392 383000 🖱 matthew.jones@devon.gov.uk

Building Control: Mr Mike Deaton Planning Development Manager, Lucombe House, County Hall, Topsham Road, Exeter EX2 4QW ☎ 01392 382130 ✉ mike.deaton@devon.gov.uk

Catering Services: Ms Fran Perry Function & Food Procurement Manager, Capital Court, Sowton, Exeter EX2 7FW ☎ 01392 351157 ✉ fran.perry@ncsgrp.co.uk

Civil Registration: Ms Trish Harrogate Registration Services Manager, Larkbeare House, Topsham Road, Exeter EX2 4NG ☎ 01392 385618 🖷 01392 384232 ✉ trish.harrogate@devon.gov.uk

PR / Communications: Mr Peter Doyle Head of External Affairs, County Hall, Topsham Road, Exeter EX2 4QW ☎ 01392 383264 ✉ peter.doyle@devon.gov.uk

Community Safety: Mr John Smith Head of Services for Communities, County Hall, Topsham Road, Exeter EX2 4QD ☎ 01392 383021 🖷 01392 382286 ✉ john.smith@devon.gov.uk

Computer Management: Mr Rob Parkhouse, Head of Business Strategy & Support, County Hall, Topsham Road, Exeter EX2 4QJ ☎ 01392 382458 ✉ rob.parkhouse@devon.gov.uk

Consumer Protection and Trading Standards: Mr Paul Thomas, Head of Trading Standards & ACL, County Hall, Topsham Road, Exeter EX2 4QD ☎ 01392 382728 ✉ paul.thomas@devon.gov.uk

Contracts: Mr Justin Bennetts Strategic Procurement Manager, County Hall, Topsham Road, Exeter EX2 4QD ☎ 01392 383000 ✉ justin.bennetts@devon.gov.uk

Customer Service: Mr Roger Jenkins Customer Service Centre Manager, Customer Service Centre, 7 Millennium Place, Lowman Way, Tiverton EX16 6SB ☎ 01392 383000 ✉ roger.jenkins@devon.gov.uk

Economic Development: Ms Keri Denton, Head of Economy & Enterprise, County Hall, Topsham Road, Exeter EX2 4QD ☎ 01392 383684 ✉ keri.denton@devon.gov.uk

Education: Ms Sue Clarke Head of Education & Learning, County Hall, Topsham Road, Exeter EX2 4QD ☎ 01392 383212 ✉ sue.clarke@devon.gov.uk

Emergency Planning: Mr Simon Kitchen Head of Policy, Strategy & Organisation Change, County Hall, Topsham Road, Exeter EX2 4QD ☎ 01392 382699 ✉ simon.kitchen@devon.gov.uk

Energy Management: Mr Ian Bateman Climate Change Officer, County Hall, Topsham Road, Exeter EX2 4QD ☎ 01392 383390 ✉ ian.bateman@devon.gov.uk

Estates, Property & Valuation: Mr Matthew Jones Corporate Asset Manager (Estates), County Hall, Topsham Road, Exeter EX2 4QD ☎ 01392 383000 ✉ matthew.jones@devon.gov.uk

European Liaison: Ms Keri Denton, Head of Economy & Enterprise, County Hall, Topsham Road, Exeter EX2 4QD ☎ 01392 383684 ✉ keri.denton@devon.gov.uk

Events Manager: Ms Jenny Caldwell Marketing Account Manager, County Hall, Topsham Road, Exeter EX2 4QD ☎ 01392 382960 ✉ jenny.caldwell@devon.gov.uk

Facilities: Ms Linda Stevenson County Hall Facilities Manager, County Hall, Topsham Road, Exeter EX2 4QD ☎ 01392 383000 ✉ linda.stevenson@devon.gov.uk

Treasury: Ms Mary Davis County Treasurer, County Hall, Topsham Road, Exeter EX2 4QD ☎ 01392 383310 🖷 01392 382959 ✉ mary.davis@devon.gov.uk

Pensions: Ms Charlotte Thompson Head of Pension Services, County Hall, Topsham Road, Exeter EX2 4QD ☎ 01392 381933 ✉ charlotte.thompson@devon.gov.uk

Grounds Maintenance: Ms Linda Stevenson County Hall Facilities Manager, County Hall, Topsham Road, Exeter EX2 4QD ☎ 01392 383000 ✉ linda.stevenson@devon.gov.uk

Health and Safety: Ms Margaret Bullock County Health & Safety Wellbeing Manager, Great Moor House, Sowton, Exeter EX2 7NL ☎ 01392 382788 🖷 01392 382542 ✉ margaret.bullock@devon.gov.uk

Highways: Mr Dave Black Head of Planning Transport & Environment, County Hall, Topsham Road, Exeter EX2 4QD ☎ 01392 383247 ✉ dave.black@devon.gov.uk

Legal: Mr Jan Shadbolt, County Solicitor, County Hall, Topsham Road, Exeter EX2 4QD ☎ 01392 382285 🖷 01392 382286 ✉ jan.shadbolt@devon.gov.uk

Lighting: Mr Maurizio Dalesio Team Leader - Street Lighting, County Hall, Topsham Road, Exeter EX2 4QD ☎ 01392 382114 ✉ maurizio.dalesio@devon.gov.uk

Member Services: Mr Rob Hooper, Democratic Services & Scrutiny Manager, County Hall, Topsham Road, Exeter EX2 4QD ☎ 01392 382300 🖷 01392 382286 ✉ rob.hooper@devon.gov.uk

Member Services: Mrs Alison Howell Member Services Officer, County Hall, Topsham Road, Exeter EX2 4QD ☎ 01392 382888 🖷 01392 382324 ✉ alison.howell@devon.gov.uk

Member Services: Ms Karen Strahan Deputy Committee & Scrutiny Manager, County Hall, Topsham Road, Exeter EX2 4QD ☎ 01392 382264 🖷 01392 382324 ✉ karen.strahan@devon.gov.uk

Personnel / HR: Mr John Smith Head of Services for Communities, County Hall, Topsham Road, Exeter EX2 4QD ☎ 01392 383021 🖷 01392 382286 ✉ john.smith@devon.gov.uk

Planning: Mr Andy Bowman Principal Planning Officer, County Hall, Topsham Road, Exeter EX2 4QD ☎ 01392 382967 ✉ andy.bowman@devon.gov.uk

Procurement: Mr Justin Bennetts Strategic Procurement Manager, County Hall, Topsham Road, Exeter EX2 4QD ☎ 01392 383000 ✉ justin.bennetts@devon.gov.uk

DEVON

Public Libraries: Ms Ciara Eastell Head of Libraries, Great Moor House, Bittern Road, Sowton, Exeter EX2 7NL ☎ 01392 384315 ✉ ciara.eastell@devon.gov.uk

Recycling & Waste Minimisation: Ms Wendy Barratt County Waste Manager, County Hall, Topsham Road, Exeter EX2 4QD ☎ 01392 382901 ✉ wendy.barratt@devon.gov

Regeneration: Mr Andrew Lightfoot Head of Regeneration & Resources, Lucombe House, Topsham Road, Exeter EX2 4QD ☎ 01392 382889 ✉ andrew.lightfoot@devon.gov.uk

Road Safety: Mr Jeremy Phillips Sustainable & Safer Travel Team Manager, County Hall, Topsham Road, Exeter EX2 4QD ☎ 01392 383289 ✉ jeremy.phillips@devon.gov.uk

Social Services: Mr Tim Golby Head of Social Care Commissioning, County Hall, Topsham Road, Exeter EX2 4QD ☎ 01392 383527 ✉ tim.golby@devon.gov.uk

Social Services (Adult): Ms Sally Slade Adult Care Management, Room 137, County Hall, Topsham Road, Exeter EX2 4QD ☎ 01392 383000 ✉ sally.slade@devon.gov.uk

Fostering & Adoption: Ms Karen Cleave Professional & Governance Lead, County Hall, Topsham Road, Exeter EX2 4QD ☎ 01392 38 5635 ✉ karen.cleave@devon.gov.uk

Safeguarding: Ms Fiona Fitzpatrick Children's Social Work & Child Protection, County Hall, Topsham Road, Exeter EX2 4QD ☎ 01392 383000 ✉ fiona.fitzpatrick@devon.gov.uk

Safeguarding: Ms Nicky Scutt Senior Manager for Safeguarding and Specialist Services, County Hall, Topsham Road, Exeter EX2 4QD ☎ 01392 382741 ✉ nicky.scutt@devon.gov.uk

Families: Ms Karen Cleave Professional & Governance Lead, County Hall, Topsham Road, Exeter EX2 4QD ☎ 01392 38 5635 ✉ karen.cleave@devon.gov.uk

Childrens Social Care: Ms Karen Cleave Professional & Governance Lead, County Hall, Topsham Road, Exeter EX2 4QD ☎ 01392 38 5635 ✉ karen.cleave@devon.gov.uk

Public Health: Dr Virginia Pearson Director - Public Health, County Hall, Topsham Road, Exeter EX2 4QD ☎ 01392 386398 ✉ virginia.pearson@devon.gov.uk

Staff Training: Mr Bill Heasman HR Business Partner - Performance, Room 220, County Hall, Topsham Road, Exeter EX2 4QD ☎ 01392 382344 ✉ bill.heasman@devon.gov.uk

Sustainable Communities: Mr John Smith Head of Services for Communities, County Hall, Topsham Road, Exeter EX2 4QD ☎ 01392 383021 🖷 01392 382286 ✉ john.smith@devon.gov.uk

Tourism: Ms Keri Denton, Head of Economy & Enterprise, Lucombe House, County Hall, Topsham Road, Exeter EX2 4QD ☎ 01392 383684 ✉ keri.denton@devon.gov.uk

Traffic Management: Mr Mike Parnell Programme Delivery & Traffic Manager, Lucombe House, County Hall, Topsham Road, Exeter EX2 4QD ☎ 01392 383377 ✉ mike.parnell@devon.gov.uk

Transport: Mr Bruce Thompson Transport Co-ordination Services Manager, County Hall, Topsham Road, Exeter EX2 4QD ☎ 01392 383244 ✉ bruce.thompson@devon.gov.uk

Waste Collection and Disposal: Ms Wendy Barratt County Waste Manager, County Hall, Topsham Road, Exeter EX2 4QD ☎ 01392 382901 ✉ wendy.barratt@devon.gov

Waste Management: Mr David Whitton Head of Capital Development & Waste Management, County Hall, Topsham Road, Exeter EX2 4QD ☎ 01392 382701 ✉ david.whitton@devon.gov.uk

COUNCILLORS

***Chair* Channon**, Christine (CON - Budleigh)
christine.channon@devon.gov.uk

***Leader of the Council* Hart**, John (CON - Bickleigh & Wembury)
john.hart@devon.gov.uk

***Deputy Leader of the Council* Clatworthy**, John (CON - Dawlish)
john.clatworthy@devon.gov.uk

Ball, Kevin (CON - Okehampton Rural)
kevin.ball@devon.gov.uk

Barisic, Eve (CON - Newton Abbot North)
eve.barisic@devon.gov.uk

Barker, Stuart (CON - Ashburton & Buckfastleigh)
stuart.barker@devon.gov.uk

Berry, John (CON - Cullompton Rural)
john.berry@devon.gov.uk

Biederman, Frank (INDNA - Fremington Rural)
frank.biederman@devon.gov.uk

Bowden, Peter (CON - Broadclyst & Whimple)
peter.bowden@devon.gov.uk

Boyd, Andy (CON - Torrington Rural)
andy.boyd@devon.gov.uk

Brazil, Julian (LD - Kingsbridge & Stokenham)
julian.brazil@devon.gov.uk

Brook, Jerry (CON - Chudleigh Rural)
jerry.brook@devon.gov.uk

Chugg, Caroline (CON - Braunton Rural)
caroline.chugg@devon.gov.uk

Clarence, Chris (CON - Teign Estuary)
chris.clarence@devon.gov.uk

Colthorpe, Polly (CON - Tiverton West)
polly.colthorpe@devon.gov.uk

Connett, Alan (LD - Exminster & Kenton)
alan.connett@devon.gov.uk

Croad, Roger (CON - Ivybridge)
roger.croad@devon.gov.uk

Davis, Andrea (CON - Combe Martin Rural)
andrea.davis@devon.gov.uk

Dempster, Tony (UKIP - Kingsteignton)
tony.dempster@devon.gov.uk

Dewhirst, Alistair (LD - Teignbridge South)
alistair.dewhirst@devon.gov.uk

Dezart, Gaston (UKIP - Bideford East)
gaston.dezart@devon.gov.uk

Diviani, Paul (CON - Honiton St Paul's)
paul.diviani@devon.gov.uk

Eastman, Andrew (CON - Northam)
andrew.eastman@devon.gov.uk

Edgell, Richard (CON - Chulmleigh & Swimbridge)
richard.edgell@devon.gov.uk

Edmunds, Mike (IND - Ilfracombe)
mike.edmunds@devon.gov.uk

Foggin, Olwen (LAB - Heavitree & Whipton Barton)
olwen.foggin@devon.gov.uk

Gilbert, Rufus (CON - Thurlestone, Salcombe & Allington)
rufus.gilbert@devon.gov.uk

Greenslade, Brian (LD - Barnstaple North)
brian.greenslade@devon.gov.uk

Gribble, George (CON - Bovey Tracey Rural)
george.gribble@devon.gov.uk

Hannaford, Rob (LAB - Exwick & St Thomas)
rob.hannaford@devon.gov.uk

Hannan, Andy (LAB - Priory & St Leonard's)
andy.hannan@devon.gov.uk

Hannon, Des (LD - Tiverton East)
des.hannon@devon.gov.uk

Hawkins, Jonathan (CON - Dartmouth & Kingswear)
jonathan.hawkins@devon.gov.uk

Hill, Roy (LAB - Alphington & Cowick)
roy.hill@devon.gov.uk

Hone, John (UKIP - Exmouth Brixington & Withycombe)
john.hone@devon.gov.uk

Hook, Gordon (LD - Newton Abbot South)
gordon.hook@devon.gov.uk

Hosking, Richard (CON - Yealmpton)
richard.hosking@devon.gov.uk

Hughes, Stuart (CON - Sidmouth Sidford)
stuart.hughes@devon.gov.uk

Hughes, Bernard (CON - Exmouth Halsdon & Woodbury)
bernard.hughes@devon.gov.uk

Julian, Robin (UKIP - Bideford South & Hartland)
robin.julian@devon.gov.uk

Knight, Jim (CON - Seaton Coastal)
jim.knight@devon.gov.uk

Leadbetter, Andrew (CON - St Loyes & Topsham)
andrew.leadbetter@devon.gov.uk

Matthews, John (CON - Barnstaple South)
john.matthews@devon.gov.uk

McInnes, James (CON - Hatherleigh & Chagford)
james.mcinnes@devon.gov.uk

Morse, Emma (LAB - Pinhoe & Mincinglake)
emma.morse@devon.gov.uk

Moulding, Andrew (CON - Axminster)
andrew.moulding@devon.gov.uk

Owen, Jill (LAB - St David's & St James)
jill.owen@devon.gov.uk

Parsons, Barry (CON - Holsworthy Rural)
barry.parsons@devon.gov.uk

Prowse, Percy (CON - Duryard & Pennsylvania)
percy.prowse@devon.gov.uk

Radford, Ray (CON - Willand & Uffculme)
ray.radford@devon.gov.uk

Randall-Johnson, Sara (CON - Honiton St Michael's)
sara.randalljohnson@devon.gov.uk

Rowe, Rosemary (CON - South Brent & Dartington)
rose.rowe@devon.gov.uk

Sanders, Philip (CON - Yelverton Rural)
philip.sanders@devon.gov.uk

Sellis, Debo (CON - Tavistock)
debo.sellis@devon.gov.uk

Squires, Margaret (CON - Newton St Cyres & Sandford)
margaret.squires@devon.gov.uk

Vint, Robert (IND - Totnes Rural)
robert.vint@devon.gov.uk

Way, Nick (LD - Crediton Rural)
nick.way@devon.gov.uk

Westlake, Richard (LAB - Newtown & Polsloe)
richard.westlake@devon.gov.uk

Wragg, Eileen (LD - Exmouth Littleham & Town)
eileen.wragg@devon.gov.uk

Wright, Claire (IND - Ottery St Mary Rural)
claire.wright@devon.gov.uk

Yabsley, Jeremy (CON - South Molton Rural)
jeremy.yabsley@devon.gov.uk

Younger-Ross, Richard (LD - Teignmouth)
richard.younger-ross@devon.gov.uk

POLITICAL COMPOSITION

CON: 38, LD: 9, LAB: 7, UKIP: 4, IND: 3, INDNA: 1

Doncaster M

Doncaster Metropolitan Borough Council, Civic Office, Waterdale, Doncaster DN1 3BU
☎ 01302 736000 askus@doncaster.gov.uk www.doncaster.gov.uk

FACTS AND FIGURES

Parliamentary Constituencies: Don Valley, Doncaster Central, Doncaster North
EU Constituencies: Yorkshire and the Humber
Election Frequency: Elections are by thirds

PRINCIPAL OFFICERS

Chief Executive: Mrs Jo Miller Chief Executive, Civic Office, Waterdale, Doncaster DN1 3BU ☎ 01302 862230
jo.miller@doncaster.gov.uk

Senior Management: Mr Damian Allen Director - Learning & Opportunities: Children & Young People, Civic Office, Waterdale, Doncaster DN1 3BU ☎ 01302 737800
damian.allen@doncaster.gov.uk

DONCASTER

Senior Management: Mr Peter Dale, Director - Regeneration & Environment, Civic Office, Waterdale, Doncaster DN1 3BU ☎ 01302 862505 ✉ peter.dale@doncaster.gov.uk

Senior Management: Mr David Hamilton Director - Adults, Health & Wellbeing, Civic Office, Waterdale, Doncaster DN1 3BU ☎ 01302 737808 ✉ db.hamilton@doncaster.gov.uk

Senior Management: Dr Rupert Suckling Director - Public Health, Civic Office, Waterdale, Doncaster DN1 3BU ☎ 01302 566105 ✉ rupert.suckling@doncaster.gov.uk

Senior Management: Mr Simon Wiles Director - Finance & Corporate Services, Civic Office, Waterdale, Doncaster DN1 3BU ☎ 01302 736907 ✉ simon.wiles@doncater.gov.uk

Access Officer / Social Services (Disability): Mr Pat Higgs Assistant Director - Adult Social Care, Civic Office, Waterdale, Doncaster DN1 3BU ☎ 01302 737620 ✉ pat.higgs@doncaster.gov.uk

Architect, Building / Property Services: Mr Dave Wilkinson Assistant Director - Trading Services & Assets, Civic Office, Waterdale, Doncaster DN1 3BU ☎ 01302 737501 ✉ dave.wilkinson@doncaster.gov.uk

Building Control: Mr Richard Purcell Head of Planning, Civic Office, Waterdale, Doncaster DN1 3BU ☎ 01302 734862 ✉ richard.purcell@doncaster.gov.uk

Catering Services: Ms Andrea Swaby Catering Manager, Civic Office, Waterdale, Doncaster DN1 3BU ☎ 01302 862544 ✉ andrea.swaby@doncaster.gov.uk

Children / Youth Services: Mr Damian Allen Director - Learning & Opportunities: Children & Young People, Civic Office, Waterdale, Doncaster DN1 3BU ☎ 01302 737800 ✉ damian.allen@doncaster.gov.uk

Civil Registration: Ms Vivien Green Interim Superintendent Registrar, Register Office, Elmfield Park, South Parade, Doncaster DN1 2EB ☎ 01302 736432 ✉ vivien.green@doncaster.gov.uk

PR / Communications: Ms Steph Cunningham Head of Communications, Civic Office, Waterdale, Doncaster DN1 3BU ☎ 01302 737988 ✉ steph.cunningham@doncaster.gov.uk

Community Planning: Mr Scott Cardwell Assistant Director - Development (Regeneration), Civic Office, Waterdale, Doncaster DN1 3BU ☎ 01302 737655 ✉ scott.cardwell@doncaster.gov.uk

Community Safety: Ms Karen Johnson Assistant Director - Communities, Civic Office, Waterdale, Doncaster DN1 3BU ☎ 01302 862507 ✉ karen.johnson@doncaster.gov.uk

Computer Management: Ms Julie Grant Assistant Director - Customer Services & ICT, Civic Office, Waterdale, Doncaster DN1 3BU ☎ 01302 862496 ✉ julie.grant@doncaster.gov.uk

Consumer Protection and Trading Standards: Mr Dave McMurdo Trading Standards Manager, Civic Office, Waterdale, Doncaster DN1 3BU ☎ 01302 737522 ✉ dave.mcmurdo@doncaster.gov.uk

Contracts: Ms Denise Bann Head of Procurement, Civic Office, Waterdale, Doncaster DN1 3BU ☎ 01302 862222 ✉ denise.bann@doncaster.gov.uk

Corporate Services: Mr Simon Wiles Director - Finance & Corporate Services, Civic Office, Waterdale, Doncaster DN1 3BU ☎ 01302 736907 ✉ simon.wiles@doncater.gov.uk

Customer Service: Ms Julie Grant Assistant Director - Customer Services & ICT, Civic Office, Waterdale, Doncaster DN1 3BU ☎ 01302 862496 ✉ julie.grant@doncaster.gov.uk

Economic Development: Mr Scott Cardwell Assistant Director - Development (Regeneration), Civic Office, Waterdale, Doncaster DN1 3BU ☎ 01302 737655 ✉ scott.cardwell@doncaster.gov.uk

Education: Ms Jo Moxon Assistant Director - Learning & Achievement, Civic Office, Waterdale, Doncaster DN1 3BU ☎ 01302 737201 ✉ jo.moxon@doncaster.gov.uk

Electoral Registration: Mr Roger Harvey Assistant Director - Legal & Democratic Services, Civic Office, Waterdale, Doncaster DN1 3BU ☎ 01302 734646 🖷 ; 01302 736273 ✉ roger.harvey@doncaster.gov.uk

Emergency Planning: Ms Gill Gillies Assistant Director - Environment, Civic Office, Waterdale, Doncaster DN1 3BU ☎ 01302 736018 ✉ gill.gillies@doncaster.gov.uk

Energy Management: Mr Dave Wilkinson Assistant Director - Trading Services & Assets, Civic Office, Waterdale, Doncaster DN1 3BU ☎ 01302 737501 ✉ dave.wilkinson@doncaster.gov.uk

Environmental / Technical Services: Mr Dave Wilkinson Assistant Director - Trading Services & Assets, Civic Office, Waterdale, Doncaster DN1 3BU ☎ 01302 737501 ✉ dave.wilkinson@doncaster.gov.uk

Environmental Health: Ms Gill Gillies Assistant Director - Environment, Civic Office, Waterdale, Doncaster DN1 3BU ☎ 01302 736018 ✉ gill.gillies@doncaster.gov.uk

Estates, Property & Valuation: Ms Tracey Harwood Head of Asset Rationalisation & Client Function, Civic Office, Waterdale, Doncaster DN1 3BU ☎ 01302 862485 ✉ tracey.harwood@doncaster.gov.uk

European Liaison: Mr Christian Foster, Programmes Manager, Civic Office, Waterdale, Doncaster DN1 3BU ☎ 01302 736614 ✉ christian.foster@doncaster.gov.uk

Facilities: Mr Drew Oxley Head of Facilities Management, Civic Office, Waterdale, Doncaster DN1 3BU ☎ 01302 736857 ✉ drew.oxley@doncaster.gov.uk

Finance: Mr Simon Wiles Director - Finance & Corporate Services, Civic Office, Waterdale, Doncaster DN1 3BU ☎ 01302 736907 ✉ simon.wiles@doncater.gov.uk

Fleet Management: Mr Mick Hepple Head of Transport Services, North Bridge Depot, North Bridge Road, Doncaster DN5 9AN ☎ 01302 736810 ✉ mick.hepple@doncaster.gov.uk

Grounds Maintenance: Ms Gill Gillies Assistant Director - Environment, Civic Office, Waterdale, Doncaster DN1 3BU ☎ 01302 736018 ✉ gill.gillies@doncaster.gov.uk

Health and Safety: Mr Peter Harrison Corporate Health & Safety Manager, Civic Office, Waterdale, Doncaster DN1 3BU ☎ 01302 736095 ✉ peter.harrison@doncaster.gov.uk

Highways: Mr Lee Garrett Head of Service - Highways, Civic Office, Waterdale, Doncaster DN1 3BU ☎ 01302 734499 ✉ lee.garrett@doncaster.gov.uk

Home Energy Conservation: Mr Richard James Smith Energy Manager, Civic Office, Waterdale, Doncaster DN1 3BU ☎ 01302 862514 ✉ richardjames.smith@doncaster.gov.uk

Housing: Mr Scott Cardwell Assistant Director - Development (Regeneration), Civic Office, Waterdale, Doncaster DN1 3BU ☎ 01302 737655 ✉ scott.cardwell@doncaster.gov.uk

Housing Maintenance: Ms Susan Jordan Chief Executive St Leger Homes of Doncaster, St Leger Court, White Road Way, Doncaster DN4 5ND ☎ 01302 862700 ✉ susan.jordan@stlegerhomes.co.uk

Local Area Agreement: Mr Howard Monk Head of Corporate Policy & Performance, Civic Office, Waterdale, Doncaster DN1 3BU ☎ 01302 736911 ✉ howard.monk@doncaster.gov.uk

Legal: Mr Roger Harvey Assistant Director of Legal & Democratic Services, Civic Office, Waterdale, Doncaster DN1 3BU ☎ 01302 734646 ✉ roger.harvey@doncaster.gov.uk

Leisure and Cultural Services: Mr Nick Stopforth Head of Libraries & Culture, Civic Office, Waterdale, Doncaster DN1 3BU ☎ 01302 734298 ✉ nick.stopforth@doncaster.gov.uk

Licensing: Mr Paul Williams Business Safety & Licensing Manager, Civic Office, Waterdale, Doncaster DN1 3BU ☎ 01302 737837 ✉ pj.williams@doncaster.gov.uk

Lifelong Learning: Ms Ruth Brook, Adult, Family & Community Learning Manager, Civic Office, Waterdale, Doncaster DN1 3BU ☎ 01302 862688 ✉ ruth.brook@doncaster.gov.uk

Lighting: Mr Andy Rutherford Head of Service for Streetscene & Highways Operations, Civic Office, Waterdale, Doncaster DN1 3BU ☎ 01302 734494 ✉ andy.rutherford@doncaster.gov.uk

Lottery Funding, Charity and Voluntary: Mr Christian Foster, Programmes Manager, Civic Office, Waterdale, Doncaster DN1 3BU ☎ 01302 736614 ✉ christian.foster@doncaster.gov.uk

Member Services: Mr Andrew Sercombe Member Support & Scrutiny Manager, Civic Office, Waterdale, Doncaster DN1 3BU ☎ 01302 734354 ✉ andrew.sercombe@doncaster.gov.uk

Parking: Mr Tony Bidmead, Parking & Enforcement Manager, North Bridge Depot, North Bridge Road, Doncaster DN5 9AN ☎ 01302 736861 ✉ tony.bidmead@doncaster.gov.uk

Partnerships: Mr Christian Foster, Programmes Manager, Civic Office, Waterdale, Doncaster DN1 3BU ☎ 01302 736614 ✉ christian.foster@doncaster.gov.uk

Personnel / HR: Ms Jill Parker Assistant Director of HR and Communications, Civic Office, Waterdale, Doncaster DN1 3BU ☎ 01302 734444 ✉ jill.parker@doncaster.gov.uk

Planning: Mr Richard Purcell Head of Planning, Civic Office, Waterdale, Doncaster DN1 3BU ☎ 01302 734862 ✉ richard.purcell@doncaster.gov.uk

Procurement: Ms Denise Bann Head of Procurement, Civic Office, Waterdale, Doncaster DN1 3BU ☎ 01302 862222 ✉ denise.bann@doncaster.gov.uk

Public Libraries: Mr Nick Stopforth Head of Libraries & Culture, Civic Office, Waterdale, Doncaster DN1 3BU ☎ 01302 734298 ✉ nick.stopforth@doncaster.gov.uk

Recycling & Waste Minimisation: Ms Gill Gillies Assistant Director - Environment, Civic Office, Waterdale, Doncaster DN1 3BU ☎ 01302 736018 ✉ gill.gillies@doncaster.gov.uk

Regeneration: Mr Scott Cardwell Assistant Director - Development (Regeneration), Civic Office, Waterdale, Doncaster DN1 3BU ☎ 01302 737655 ✉ scott.cardwell@doncaster.gov.uk

Road Safety: Mr Lee Garrett Head of Service - Highways, Civic Office, Waterdale, Doncaster DN1 3BU ☎ 01302 734499 ✉ lee.garrett@doncaster.gov.uk

Social Services (Adult): Mr David Hamilton Director - Adults, Health & Wellbeing, Civic Office, Waterdale, Doncaster DN1 3BU ☎ 01302 737808 ✉ db.hamilton@doncaster.gov.uk

Social Services (Children): Mr Paul Moffat Chief Executive - Doncaster Children's Trust, The Blue Building, 38 - 40 High Street, Doncaster DN1 1DE ☎ 01302 735809 ✉ paul.moffat@dcstrust.co.uk

Fostering & Adoption: Mr Ian Walker Head of Service - CiC, The Blue Building, 38 - 40 High Street, Doncaster DN1 1DE ☎ 01302 736972 ✉ ian.walker@dcstrust.co.uk

Safeguarding: Mr Richard Fawcett Head of Service - Safeguarding & Standards, The Blue Building, 38 - 40 High Street, Doncaster DN1 1DE ☎ 01302 734523 ✉ richard.fawcett@dcstrust.co.uk

Families: Mr Mark Douglas Chief Operating Officer, The Blue Building, 38 - 40 High Street, Doncaster DN1 1DE ☎ 01302 734323 ✉ mark.douglas@dcstrust.co.uk

DONCASTER

Childrens Social Care: Mr Paul Moffat Chief Executive - Doncaster Children's Trust, The Blue Building, 38 - 40 High Street, Doncaster DN1 1DE ☎ 01302 735809 ✉ paul.moffat@dcstrust.co.uk

Public Health: Dr Rupert Suckling Director - Public Health, Civic Office, Waterdale, Doncaster DN1 3BU ☎ 01302 566105 ✉ rupert.suckling@doncaster.gov.uk

Public Health: Ms Jacqui Wiltschinsky Assistant Director - Public Health, Civic Office, Waterdale, Doncaster DN1 3BU ☎ 01302 734008 ✉ jacqui.wiltschinsky@doncaster.gov.uk

Staff Training: Ms Jill Parker Assistant Director of Human Resources & Communications, Civic Office, Waterdale, Doncaster DN1 3BU ☎ 01302 737004 ✉ jill.parker@doncaster.gov.uk

Street Scene: Mr Andy Rutherford Head of Service for Streetscene & Highways Operations, Civic Office, Waterdale, Doncaster DN1 3BU ☎ 01302 734494 ✉ andy.rutherford@doncaster.gov.uk

Sustainable Communities: Ms Gill Gillies Assistant Director - Environment, Civic Office, Waterdale, Doncaster DN1 3BU ☎ 01302 736018 ✉ gill.gillies@doncaster.gov.uk

Tourism: Mr Colin Joy Tourism & Visitor Economy Manager, Civic Office, Waterdale, Doncaster DN1 3BU ☎ 01302 737967 🖷 01302 736362 ✉ colin.joy@doncaster.gov.uk

Town Centre: Ms Tracey Harwood Head of Asset Rationalisation & Client Function, Civic Office, Waterdale, Doncaster DN1 3BU ☎ 01302 862485 ✉ tracey.harwood@doncaster.gov.uk

Traffic Management: Mr Lee Garrett Head of Service - Highways, Civic Office, Waterdale, Doncaster DN1 3BU ☎ 01302 734499 ✉ lee.garrett@doncaster.gov.uk

Transport: Mr Lee Garrett Head of Service - Highways, Civic Office, Waterdale, Doncaster DN1 3BU ☎ 01302 734499 ✉ lee.garrett@doncaster.gov.uk

Transport Planner: Mr Stephen King Principal Transport Planner, Civic Office, Waterdale, Doncaster DN1 3BU ☎ 01302 735122 🖷 01302 735028 ✉ stephen.king@doncaster.gov.uk

Waste Collection and Disposal: Ms Gill Gillies Assistant Director - Environment, Civic Office, Waterdale, Doncaster DN1 3BU ☎ 01302 736018 ✉ gill.gillies@doncaster.gov.uk

Waste Management: Ms Gill Gillies Assistant Director - Environment, Civic Office, Waterdale, Doncaster DN1 3BU ☎ 01302 736018 ✉ gill.gillies@doncaster.gov.uk

Children's Play Areas: Ms Gill Gillies Assistant Director - Environment, Civic Office, Waterdale, Doncaster DN1 3BU ☎ 01302 736018 ✉ gill.gillies@doncaster.gov.uk

COUNCILLORS

***Leader of the Council* Jones**, Ros (LAB - No Ward)
ros.jones@doncaster.gov.uk

***Deputy Leader of the Council* Jones**, Glyn (LAB - Hexthorpe & Balby North)
glyn.jones@doncaster.gov.uk

Allen, Nick (CON - Bessacarr)
nick.allen@doncaster.gov.uk

Ball, Nigel (LAB - Conisbrough)
nigel.ball@doncaster.gov.uk

Beech, Iris (LAB - Norton & Askern)
iris.beech@doncaster.gov.uk

Blackham, Joe (LAB - Thorne & Moorends)
joe.blackham@doncaster.gov.uk

Blake, Rachael (LAB - Rossington & Bawtry)
rachael.blake@doncaster.gov.uk

Butler, Elsie (LAB - Edlington & Warmsworth)
elsie.butler@doncaster.gov.uk

Chapman, Bev (O - Mexborough)
bev.chapman@doncaster.gov.uk

Cole, Phil (LAB - Edlington & Warmsworth)
phil.cole@doncaster.gov.uk

Cooke, John (IND - Rossington & Bawtry)
john.cooke@doncaster.gov.uk

Corden, Tony (LAB - Armthorpe)
tony.corden@doncaster.gov.uk

Cox, Jane (CON - Finningley)
jane.cox@doncaster.gov.uk

Cox, Steve (CON - Finningley)
steve.cox@doncaster.gov.uk

Credland, Jessie (UKIP - Hatfield)
jessie.credland@doncaster.gov.uk

Curran, Linda (LAB - Hatfield)
linda.curran@doncaster.gov.uk

Derx, George (LAB - Stainforth & Barnby Dun)
george.derx@doncaster.gov.uk

Durant, Susan (LAB - Thorne & Moorends)
susan.durant@doncaster.gov.uk

Fennelly, Nuala (LAB - Balby South)
nuala.fennelly@doncaster.gov.uk

Gethin, Neil (LAB - Bessacarr)
neil.gethin@doncaster.gov.uk

Gibbons, Sean (O - Mexborough)
sean.gibbons@doncaster.gov.uk

Haith, Pat (LAB - Roman Ridge)
pat.haith@doncaster.gov.uk

Hart, James (CON - Tickhill & Wadworth)
james.hart@doncaster.gov.uk

Healy, John (LAB - Balby South)
john.healy@doncaster.gov.uk

Hodson, Rachel (LAB - Adwick & Carcroft)
rachel.hodson@doncaster.gov.uk

Hogarth, Charlie (LAB - Bentley)
charlie.hogarth@doncaster.gov.uk

Holland, Sandra (LAB - Conisbrough)
sandra.holland@doncaster.gov.uk

Houlbrook, Mark (LAB - Thorne & Moorends)
mark.houlbrook@doncaster.gov.uk

Hughes, Eva (LAB - Wheatley Hills & Intake)
eva.hughes@doncaster.gov.uk

Jones, Alan (LAB - Norton & Askern)
a.jones@doncaster.gov.uk

Jones, Richard Allen (CON - Finningley)
richard.jones@doncaster.gov.uk

Keegan, Ken (LAB - Stainforth & Barnby Dun)
kenneth.keegan@doncaster.gov.uk

Khan, Majid (LAB - Bessacarr)
majid.khan@doncaster.gov.uk

Kidd, Jane (LAB - Wheatley Hills & Intake)
jane.kidd@doncaster.gov.uk

Kitchen, Ted (LAB - Adwick & Carcroft)
edwin.kitchen@doncaster.gov.uk

Knight, Pat (LAB - Hatfield)
pat.knight@doncaster.gov.uk

Knowles, Sue (LAB - Town)
s.knowles@doncaster.gov.uk

McGuinness, Chris (LAB - Armthorpe)
chris.mcguinness@doncaster.gov.uk

McGuinness, Sue (LAB - Armthorpe)
sue.mcguinness@doncaster.gov.uk

McHale, John (LAB - Town)
john.mchale@doncaster.gov.uk

Mordue, Bill (LAB - Bentley)
bill.mordue@doncaster.gov.uk

Mounsey, John (LAB - Adwick & Carcroft)
john.mounsey@doncaster.gov.uk

Nevett, David (LAB - Edenthorpe & Kirk Sandall)
david.nevett@doncaster.gov.uk

Nightingale, Jane (LAB - Bentley)
jane.nightingale@doncaster.gov.uk

Pickering, Andy (O - Mexborough)
andy.pickering@doncaster.gov.uk

Ransome, Cynthia (CON - Sprotbrough)
cynthia.ransome@doncaster.gov.uk

Revill, Tony (LAB - Edenthorpe & Kirk Sandall)
tony.revill@doncaster.gov.uk

Rodgers, Kevin (LAB - Roman Ridge)
kevin.rodgers@doncaster.gov.uk

Sahman, Craig (LAB - Conisbrough)
craig.sahman@doncaster.gov.uk

Shaw, Dave (LAB - Town)
dave.shaw@doncaster.gov.uk

Smith, Alan (CON - Tickhill & Wadworth)
alan.smith2@doncaster.gov.uk

Stone, Clive (UKIP - Rossington & Bawtry)
clive.stone@doncaster.gov.uk

White, Austen (LAB - Norton & Askern)
austen.white@doncaster.gov.uk

Wilkinson, Sue (LAB - Hexthorpe & Balby North)
sue.wilkinson@doncaster.gov.uk

Wood, Jonathan (CON - Sprotbrough)
jonathan.wood@doncaster.gov.uk

Wray, Paul (LAB - Wheatley Hills & Intake)
paul.wray@doncaster.gov.uk

POLITICAL COMPOSITION

LAB: 42, CON: 8, O: 3, UKIP: 2, IND: 1

COMMITTEE CHAIRS

Audit: Mr Austen White

Health & Wellbeing: Ms Pat Knight

Licensing: Mr Ken Keegan

Planning: Ms Iris Beech

Dorset C

Dorset County Council, County Hall, Colliton Park, Dorchester DT1 1XJ
☎ 01305 221000 🖷 01305 224839 ✉ dorsetdirect@dorsetcc.gov.uk
🖳 www.dorsetforyou.com; www.dorsetforyou.com

FACTS AND FIGURES

EU Constituencies: South West
Election Frequency: Elections are of whole council

PRINCIPAL OFFICERS

Chief Executive: Ms Debbie Ward Chief Executive, County Hall, Colliton Park, Dorchester DT1 1XJ ☎ 01305 224195 ✉ d.ward@dorsetcc.gov.uk

Assistant Chief Executive: Mr Patrick Ellis Assistant Chief Executive, County Hall, Colliton Park, Dorchester DT1 1XJ ☎ 01305 224116 ✉ p.ellis@dorsetcc.gov.uk

Senior Management: Dr Catherine Driscoll Director for Adult and Community Services, County hall, Dorchester DT1 1XJ ☎ 01305 224317 ✉ c.driscoll@dorsetcc.gov.uk

Senior Management: Mr Mike Harries, Director for Environment & The Economy, Princes House, Princes Street, Dorchester DT1 1TP ☎ 01305 224216 🖷 01305 225254 ✉ m.j.harries@dorsetcc.gov.uk

Senior Management: Mr Patrick Myers Head of Business Development, County Hall, Colliton Park, Dorchester DT1 1XJ ☎ 01305 224247 🖷 01305 224839 ✉ p.myers@dorsetcc.gov.uk

Senior Management: Dr David Phillips Director - Public Health, Town Hall, Bournemouth BH2 6EB ☎ 01202 451828 ✉ d.phillips@poole.gov.uk

Senior Management: Mrs Sarah Tough Director - Children's Services, County Hall, Colliton Park, Dorchester DT1 1XJ ☎ 01305 224166 ✉ s.tough@dorsetcc.gov.uk

Access Officer / Social Services (Disability): Mr Harry Capron Head of Adult Care, County Hall, Colliton Park, Dorchester DT1 1XJ ☎ 01305 224646 ✉ H.Capron@dorsetcc.gov.uk

Architect, Building / Property Services: Mr Mike Harries, Director for Environment & The Economy, Princes House, Princes Street, Dorchester DT1 1TP ☎ 01305 224216 🖷 01305 225254 ✉ m.j.harries@dorsetcc.gov.uk

DORSET

Best Value: Mr Martin Lockwood Senior Project Manager - Efficency & Change, County Hall, Colliton Park, Dorchester DT1 1XJ ☎ 01305 224653 ✉ m.lockwood@dorsetcc.gov.uk

Building Control: Mr Mike Harries, Director for Environment & The Economy, Princes House, Princes Street, Dorchester DT1 1TP ☎ 01305 224216 🖷 01305 225254 ✉ m.j.harries@dorsetcc.gov.uk

Catering Services: Ms Jackie Garland, Category Manager, County Hall, Colliton Park, Dorchester DT1 1XJ ☎ 01305 221267 🖷 01305 228567 ✉ j.a.garland@dorsetcc.gov.uk

Catering Services: Mrs Sue Hawkins Care Catering Services Manager, County Hall, Colliton Park, Dorchester DT1 1XJ ☎ 01305 225930 ✉ s.hawkins@dorsetcc.gov.uk

Civil Registration: Ms Jo Wenborne-Allen Registration Service Manager, Dorset History Centre, Bridport Road, Dorchester DT1 1RP ☎ 01305 228909 ✉ j.wenborne@dorsetcc.gov.uk

PR / Communications: Ms Sally Northeast Corporate Communications Manager, County Hall, Colliton Park, Dorchester DT1 1XJ ☎ 01305 228570 ✉ s.a.northeast@dorsetcc.gov.uk

Community Planning: Mr Don Gobbett, Head of Planning, County Hall, Colliton Park, Dorchester DT1 1XJ ☎ 01305 224490 🖷 01305 224914 ✉ d.gobbett@dorsetcc.gov.uk

Community Safety: Mr Andy Frost, Strategic Manager - Drug Addiction & Community Safety, County Hall, Colliton Park, Dorchester DT1 1XJ ☎ 01305 224331 ✉ a.frost@dorsetcc.gov.uk

Community Safety: Mrs Kay Wilson-White Head of Adult Services, County Hall, Colliton Park, Dorchester DT1 1XJ ☎ 01305 224768 ✉ k.wilson-white@dorsetcc.gov.uk

Computer Management: Mr Richard Pascoe, Head of ICT & Business Transformation, County Hall, Colliton Park, Dorchester DT1 1XJ ☎ 01305 224204 🖷 01305 224391 ✉ r.j.pascoe@dorsetcc.gov.uk

Consumer Protection and Trading Standards: Mr Ivan Hancock Trading Standards Service Manager, Colliton Annexe, Colliton Park, Dorchester DT1 1XJ ☎ 01305 224956 🖷 01305 224951 ✉ I.N.Hancock@dorsetcc.gov.uk

Contracts: Ms Karen Andrews Head Of Dorset Procurement, County Hall, Colliton Park, Dorchester DT1 1XJ ☎ 01305 221260 ✉ K.Andrews@dorsetcc.gov.uk

Customer Service: Mr Simon Bailey Customer Services Manager, County Hall, Colliton Park, Dorchester DT1 1XJ ☎ 01305 221762 ✉ Simon.Bailey@dorset.gov.uk

Economic Development: Mr Dave Walsh, Economy & Enterprise Team Leader, County Hall, Colliton Park, Dorchester DT1 1XJ ☎ 01305 224254 🖷 01305 224602 ✉ d.walsh@dorsetcc.gov.uk

Education: Mr Phillip Minns Head of Learning & Inclusion Services, County Hall, Colliton Park, Dorchester DT1 1XJ ☎ 01305 224770 ✉ p.minns@dorsetcc.gov.uk

Education: Mrs Sarah Tough Director - Children's Services, County Hall, Colliton Park, Dorchester DT1 1XJ ☎ 01305 224166 ✉ s.tough@dorsetcc.gov.uk

E-Government: Mr Richard Pascoe, Head of ICT & Business Transformation, County Hall, Colliton Park, Dorchester DT1 1XJ ☎ 01305 224204 🖷 01305 224391 ✉ r.j.pascoe@dorsetcc.gov.uk

Electoral Registration: Mr Lee Gallagher Democratic Services Manager, County Hall, Colliton Park, Dorchester DT1 1XJ ☎ 01305 224191 🖷 01305 224395 ✉ L.D.Gallagher@dorsetcc.gov.uk

Emergency Planning: Mr Simon Parker, County Emergency Planning Officer, County Hall, Colliton Park, Dorchester DT1 1XJ ☎ 01305 224510 🖷 01305 224108 ✉ s.parker@dorsetcc.gov.uk

Energy Management: Mr Mike Petitdemange, Sustainable Community Team Leader, Princes House, Princes Street, Dorchester DT1 1TP ☎ 01305 225279 🖷 01305 225222 ✉ m.j.petitdemange@dorsetcc.gov.uk

Environmental / Technical Services: Mr Peter Moore Head of Environment, County Hall, Colliton Park, Dorchester DT1 1XJ ✉ p.k.moore@dorsetcc.gov.uk

Environmental / Technical Services: Mr Matthew Piles, Head of Economy, County Hall, Colliton Park, Dorchester DT1 1XJ ☎ 01305 221336 🖷 01305 224498 ✉ m.d.piles@dorsetcc.gov.uk

Estates, Property & Valuation: Mr Peter Scarlett, Estates & Assets Service Manager, County Hall, Colliton Park, Dorchester DT1 1XJ ☎ 01305 221941 ✉ p.scarlett@dorsetcc.gov.uk

European Liaison: Mr Jon Bird European Policy & Funding Officer, County Hall, Colliton Park, Dorchester DT1 1XJ ☎ 01305 224602 ✉ j.bird@dorsetcc.gov.uk

Events Manager: Ms Sally Northeast Corporate Communications Manager, County Hall, Colliton Park, Dorchester DT1 1XJ ☎ 01305 228570 ✉ s.a.northeast@dorsetcc.gov.uk

Facilities: Mr Andrew Turner, Facilities Manager, County Hall, Colliton Park, Dorchester DT1 1XJ ☎ 01305 221943 🖷 01305 221957 ✉ a.p.turner@dorsetcc.gov.uk

Finance: Mr Richard Bates Head of Financial Services, County Hall, Colliton Park, Dorchester DT1 1XJ ☎ 01305 228548 ✉ r.bates@dorsetcc.gov.uk

Finance: Mr Jim McManus Chief Accountant, County Hall, Colliton Park, Dorchester DT1 1XJ ☎ 01305 221235 ✉ j.mcmanus@dorsetcc.gov.uk

Finance: Mr Andy Smith Group Finance Manager, County Hall, Colliton Park, Dorchester DT1 1XJ ☎ 01305 224031 ✉ a.g.smith@dorsetcc.gov.uk

Treasury: Mr Nick Buckland Chief Treasury & Pension Manager, County Hall, Colliton Park, Dorchester DT1 1XJ ☎ 01305 224763 ✉ n.j.buckland@dorsetcc.gov.uk

Pensions: Mr Nick Buckland Chief Treasury & Pension Manager, County Hall, Colliton Park, Dorchester DT1 1XJ ☎ 01305 224763 ✉ n.j.buckland@dorsetcc.gov.uk

Fleet Management: Mr Sean Adams, Fleet Services Manager, County Hall, Colliton Park, Dorchester DT1 1XJ ☎ 01305 221263 🖷 01305 228567 ✉ s.w.adams@dorsetcc.gov.uk

Fleet Management: Mr Andrew Martin, Head of Dorset Highways Operations, County Hall, Colliton Park, Dorchester DT1 1XJ ☎ 01305 228100 🖷 01305 228101 ✉ a.j.martin@dorsetcc.gov.uk

Grounds Maintenance: Ms Carmel Wilkinson Countryside Area Manager, County Hall, Colliton Park, Dorchester DT1 1XJ ☎ 01305 224191 ✉ c.wilkinson@dorsetcc.gov.uk

Health and Safety: Mr Ian Burke Health & Safety Manager, Charminster Depot, Wanchard Lane, Charminster, Dorchester DT2 9RP ☎ 01963 365923 ✉ i.s.burke@dorsetcc.gov.uk

Highways: Mr Andrew Martin, Head of Dorset Highways Operations, County Hall, Colliton Park, Dorchester DT1 1XJ ☎ 01305 228100 🖷 01305 228101 ✉ a.j.martin@dorsetcc.gov.uk

Legal: Mr Jonathan Mair, Head of Legal & Democratic Services, County Hall, Colliton Park, Dorchester DT1 1XJ ☎ 01305 224181 🖷 01305 224399 ✉ j.e.mair@dorsetcc.gov.uk

Leisure and Cultural Services: Mr Paul Leivers, Head of Community Services, Library Headquarters, Colliton Park, Dorchester DT1 1XJ ☎ 01305 224455 🖷 01305 224456 ✉ p.leivers@dorsetcc.gov.uk

Licensing: Mr Ivan Hancock Trading Standards Service Manager, Colliton Annexe, Colliton Park, Dorchester DT1 1XJ ☎ 01305 224956 🖷 01305 224951 ✉ I.N.Hancock@dorsetcc.gov.uk

Lifelong Learning: Mr Paul Leivers, Head of Community Services, Library Headquarters, Colliton Park, Dorchester DT1 1XJ ☎ 01305 224455 🖷 01305 224456 ✉ p.leivers@dorsetcc.gov.uk

Lighting: Mr Rod Mainstone, Streetlighting Team Leader, County Hall, Colliton Park, Dorchester DT1 1XJ ☎ 01305 225355 🖷 01305 225301 ✉ r.l.mainstone@dorsetcc.gov.uk

Lottery Funding, Charity and Voluntary: Mr Chris Scally, Joint Commissioning Manager, County Hall, Colliton Park, Dorchester DT1 1XJ ☎ 01305 228624 🖷 01305 224886 ✉ c.scally@dorsetcc.gov.uk

Member Services: Mr Lee Gallagher Democratic Services Manager, County Hall, Colliton Park, Dorchester DT1 1XJ ☎ 01305 224191 🖷 01305 224395 ✉ L.D.Gallagher@dorsetcc.gov.uk

Parking: Mr Simon Gledhill Network Management Services Manager, County Hall, Colliton Park, Dorchester DT1 1XJ ☎ 01305 228141 ✉ S.T.Gledhill@dorsetcc.gov.uk

Partnerships: Mrs Alison Waller Head of Partnerships & Performance, County Hall, Colliton Park, Dorchester DT1 1XJ ☎ 01305 224569 🖷 01305 224325 ✉ a.waller@dorsetcc.gov.uk

Personnel / HR: Miss Sheralyn Huntingford Head of Human Resources & Exchequer Services, County Hall, Colliton Park, Dorchester DT1 1XJ ☎ 01305 224090 🖷 01305 224620 ✉ s.huntingford@dorsetcc.gov.uk

Planning: Mr Don Gobbett, Head of Planning, County Hall, Colliton Park, Dorchester DT1 1XJ ☎ 01305 224490 🖷 01305 224914 ✉ d.gobbett@dorsetcc.gov.uk

Procurement: Ms Karen Andrews Head of Dorset Procurement, County Hall, Colliton Park, Dorchester DT1 1XJ ☎ 01305 221260 ✉ K.Andrews@dorsetcc.gov.uk

Public Libraries: Mr Paul Leivers, Head of Community Services, Library Headquarters, Colliton Park, Dorchester DT1 1XJ ☎ 01305 224455 🖷 01305 224456 ✉ p.leivers@dorsetcc.gov.uk

Recycling & Waste Minimisation: Mr Bill Davidson Head of Strategy & Commissioning, Grove House, Millers Close, Dorchester DT1 1SS ☎ 01305 225788 ✉ b.davidson@dorsetcc.gov.uk

Regeneration: Mr Dave Walsh, Economy & Enterprise Team Leader, County Hall, Colliton Park, Dorchester DT1 1XJ ☎ 01305 224254 🖷 01305 224602 ✉ d.walsh@dorsetcc.gov.uk

Road Safety: Mr Robert Smith, Road Safety Officer, County Hall, Colliton Park, Dorchester DT1 1XJ ☎ 01305 224680 🖷 01305 224835 ✉ r.smith@dorsetcc.gov.uk

Social Services (Adult): Mr Harry Capron Head of Adult Care, County Hall, Colliton Park, Dorchester DT1 1XJ ☎ 01305 224646 ✉ H.Capron@dorsetcc.gov.uk

Social Services (Adult): Ms Catherine Driscoll Director for Adult & Community Services, County hall, Dorchester DT1 1XJ ☎ 01305 224317 ✉ c.driscoll@dorsetcc.gov.uk

Social Services (Adult): Mrs Alison Waller Head of Partnerships & Performance, County Hall, Colliton Park, Dorchester DT1 1XJ ☎ 01305 224569 🖷 01305 224325 ✉ a.waller@dorsetcc.gov.uk

Social Services (Children): Mrs Anne Salter Head of Strategy, Partnerships & Performance, County Hall, Colliton Park, Dorchester DT1 1XJ ☎ 01305 224648 ✉ A.Salter@dorsetcc.gov.uk

Social Services (Children): Mrs Sarah Tough Director - Children's Services, County Hall, Colliton Park, Dorchester DT1 1XJ ☎ 01305 224166 ✉ s.tough@dorsetcc.gov.uk

Fostering & Adoption: Mr Jim Chamberlain Policy Manager - Adoption/Fostering & Adoption Panels, County Hall, Colliton Park, Dorchester DT1 1XJ ☎ 01305 251450 ✉ j.chamberlain@dorsetcc.gov.uk

Safeguarding: Mr Michael Hall Designated Safeguarding Manager, County Hall, Colliton Park, Dorchester DT1 1XJ ☎ 01305 228375 ✉ michael.hall@dorsetcc.gov.uk

Families: Mrs Vanessa Glenn Head of Family Support, County Hall, Colliton Park, Dorchester DT1 1XJ ☎ 01305 224328 ✉ v.glenn@dorsetcc.gov.uk

DORSET

Looked after Children: Mrs Vanessa Glenn Head of Family Support, County Hall, Colliton Park, Dorchester DT1 1XJ ☎ 01305 224328 ✉ v.glenn@dorsetcc.gov.uk

Childrens Social Care: Mrs Penny Lodwick Senior Manager - Family Support, Ferndown Local Officer, Penny's Walk, Ferndown BH22 9JY ☎ 01202 868222 ✉ p.lodwick@dorsetcc.gov.uk

Childrens Social Care: Mr Stuart Riddle Senior Manager - Family Support, Children's Services Directorate, County Hall, Colliton Street, Dorchester DT1 1XJ ☎ 01305 225089 ✉ s.riddle@dorsetcc.gcsx.gov.uk

Childrens Social Care: Mr Kevin Stenlake Senior Manager - Family Support, County Hall, Colliton Park, Dorchester DT1 1XJ ☎ 01258 475681 ✉ k.j.stenlake@dorsetcc.gov.uk

Public Health: Dr David Phillips Director - Public Health, Town Hall, Bournemouth BH2 6EB ☎ 01202 451828 ✉ d.phillips@poole.gov.uk

Staff Training: Mrs Helen Sotheran, Learning & Development Manager, County Hall, Colliton Park, Dorchester DT1 1XJ ☎ 01305 224088 🖷 01305 224620 ✉ h.l.sotheran@dorsetcc.gov.uk

Street Scene: Ms Karen Punchard Streetscene Manager, Grove House, Millers Close, Dorchester DT1 5SS ☎ 01305 225459 ✉ k.punchard@dorsetwastepartnership.gov.uk

Sustainable Communities: Mr Don Gobbett, Head of Planning, County Hall, Colliton Park, Dorchester DT1 1XJ ☎ 01305 224490 🖷 01305 224914 ✉ d.gobbett@dorsetcc.gov.uk

Sustainable Development: Ms Kate Hall, Community Energy Team Leader, County Hall, Colliton Park, Dorchester DT1 1XJ ☎ 01305 224774 🖷 01305 224602 ✉ k.m.hall@dorsetcc.gov.uk

Tourism: Mr Dave Walsh, Economy & Enterprise Team Leader, County Hall, Colliton Park, Dorchester DT1 1XJ ☎ 01305 224254 🖷 01305 224602 ✉ d.walsh@dorsetcc.gov.uk

Transport: Mr Chris Hook Travel Operations Manager, County Hall, Colliton Park, Dorchester DT1 1XJ ☎ 01305 225141 ✉ c.p.hook@dorsetcc.gov.uk

Transport Planner: Mr Matthew Piles, Head of Economy, County Hall, Colliton Park, Dorchester DT1 1XJ ☎ 01305 221336 🖷 01305 224498 ✉ m.d.piles@dorsetcc.gov.uk

Waste Collection and Disposal: Mr Steve Burdis, Director - Dorset Waste Partnership, Grove House, Millers Close, Dorchester DT1 5SS ☎ 01305 224691 🖷 01305 225002 ✉ steve.burdis@dorsetcc.gov.uk

Waste Management: Mr Steve Burdis, Director - Dorset Waste Partnership, Grove House, Millers Close, Dorchester DT1 5SS ☎ 01305 224691 🖷 01305 225002 ✉ steve.burdis@dorsetcc.gov.uk

COUNCILLORS

***Leader of the Council* Gould**, Robert (CON - Sherborne)
r.gould@dorsetcc.gov.uk

***Deputy Leader of the Council* Finney**, Peter (CON - West Moors & Holt)
p.finney@dorsetcc.gov.uk

***Group Leader* Dover**, Janet (LD - Colehill & Stapehill)
j.dover@dorsetcc.gov.uk

***Group Leader* Kimber**, Paul (LAB - Portland Tophill)
p.kimber@dorsetcc.gov.uk

Batstone, Pauline (CON - Blackmore Vale)
p.h.batstone@dorsetcc.gov.uk

Bevan, Michael (CON - Sherborne Rural)
m.bevan@dorsetcc.gov.uk

Biggs, Richard (LD - Dorchester)
r.m.biggs@dorsetcc.gov.uk

Brember, Dan (LAB - Rodwell)
d.brember@dorsetcc.gov.uk

Butler, Steve (CON - Cranborne Chase)
steve.butler@dorsetcc.gov.uk

Byatt, Mike (LAB - Weymouth Town)
m.byatt@dorsetcc.gov.uk

Canning, Andy (LD - Linden Lea)
a.canning@dorsetcc.gov.uk

Cattaway, Andrew (CON - Stour Vale)
a.r.cattaway@dorsetcc.gov.uk

Coatsworth, Ronald (CON - Bride Valley)
r.w.coatsworth@dorsetcc.gov.uk

Cook, Robin (CON - Minister)
r.cook@dorsetcc.gov.uk

Coombs, Toni (CON - Verwood & Three Legged Cross)
t.b.coombs@dorsetcc.gov.uk

Cooper, Barrie (LD - Blandford)
b.g.cooper@dorsetcc.gov.uk

Cox, Hilary (CON - Winterborne)
h.a.cox@dorsetcc.gov.uk

Croney, Deborah (CON - Hambledon)
d.croney@dorsetcc.gov.uk

Dedman, Lesley (CON - Mudeford & Highcliffe)
l.m.dedman@dorsetcc.gov.uk

Drane, Fred (LD - Lytchett)
f.h.drane@dorsetcc.gov.uk

Ezzard, Beryl (LD - Wareham)
b.r.ezzard@dorsetcc.gov.uk

Flower, Spencer (CON - Verwood & Three Legged Cross)
s.g.flower@dorsetcc.gov.uk

Gardner, Ian (CON - Chickerell & Chesil Bank)
i.gardner@dorsetcc.gov.uk

Hall, Peter (CON - Christchurch Central)
p.r.hall@dorsetcc.gov.uk

Harris, David (LD - Westham)
david.harris@dorsetcc.gov.uk

Haynes, Jill (CON - Three Valleys)
jill.haynes@dorsetcc.gov.uk

Jamieson, Colin (CON - Highcliffe & Walkford)
c.jamieson@dorsetcc.gov.uk

Jefferies, Susan (LD - Corfe Mullen)
s.jefferies@dorsetcc.gov.uk

Jeffery, Mervyn (LD - Shaftesbury)
m.jeffrey@dorsetcc.gov.uk

Jones, David (CON - Burton Grange)
david.jones@dorsetcc.gov.uk

Jones, Trevor (LD - Dorchester)
d.t.jones@dorsetcc.gov.uk

Kayes, Ros (LD - Bridport)
r.kayes@dorsetcc.gov.uk

Knox, Rebecca (CON - Beaminster)
r.knox@dorsetcc.gov.uk

Lovell, Mike (CON - Purbeck Hills)
m.v.lovell@dorsetcc.gov.uk

Mannings, David (LD - Lodmoor)
d.g.mannings@dorsetcc.gov.uk

Phipps, Margaret (CON - Commons)
m.phipps@dorsetcc.gov.uk

Richardson, Peter (CON - St Leonards & St Ives)
p.richardson@dorsetcc.gov.uk

Smith, Ian (UKIP - Ferndown)
i.m.smith@dorsetcc.gov.uk

Tewkesbury, Mark (LAB - Broadwey)
m.tewkesbury@dorsetcc.gov.uk

Trite, William (CON - Swanage)
w.trite@dorsetcc.gov.uk

Turner, Daryl (CON - Marshwood Vale)
d.w.turner@dorsetcc.gov.uk

Walsh, David (CON - Gillingham)
david.walsh@dorsetcc.gov.uk

Wharf, Peter (CON - Egdon Heath)
p.k.wharf@dorsetcc.gov.uk

Wheller, Kate (LAB - Portland Harbour)
k.wheller@dorsetcc.gov.uk

Wilson, John (CON - Ferndown)
j.l.wilson@dorsetcc.gov.uk

POLITICAL COMPOSITION

CON: 27, LD: 12, LAB: 5, UKIP: 1

Dover D

Dover District Council, Council Offices, White Cliffs Business Park, Dover CT16 3PJ
☎ 01304 821199 🖷 01304 872300 ✉ customerservices@dover.gov.uk
🖳 www.dover.gov.uk

FACTS AND FIGURES

Parliamentary Constituencies: Dover
EU Constituencies: South East
Election Frequency: Elections are of whole council

PRINCIPAL OFFICERS

Chief Executive: Mr Nadeem Aziz, Chief Executive, Council Offices, White Cliffs Business Park, Dover CT16 3PJ
☎ 01304 872400 🖷 01304 872004 ✉ nadeemaziz@dover.gov.uk

Senior Management: Mr Mike Davis, Director of Finance, Housing & Community, Council Offices, White Cliffs Business Park, Dover CT16 3PJ ☎ 01304 872107 🖷 01304 872104
✉ mikedavis@dover.gov.uk

Senior Management: Mr David Randall, Director of Governance, Council Offices, White Cliffs Business Park, Dover CT16 3PJ
☎ 01304 872141 🖷 01304 872300 ✉ davidrandall@dover.gov.uk

Senior Management: Mr Roger Walton, Director of Environment & Corporate Assets, Council Offices, White Cliffs Business Park, Dover CT16 3PJ ☎ 01304 872240 🖷 01304 872416
✉ rogerwalton@dover.gov.uk

Architect, Building / Property Services: Mr Roger Walton, Director of Environment & Corporate Assets, Council Offices, White Cliffs Business Park, Dover CT16 3PJ ☎ 01304 872240
🖷 01304 872416 ✉ rogerwalton@dover.gov.uk

Building Control: Mr Roger Walton, Director of Environment & Corporate Assets, Council Offices, White Cliffs Business Park, Dover CT16 3PJ ☎ 01304 872240 🖷 01304 872416
✉ rogerwalton@dover.gov.uk

PR / Communications: Mr Mike Davis, Director of Finance, Housing & Community, Council Offices, White Cliffs Business Park, Dover CT16 3PJ ☎ 01304 872107 🖷 01304 872104
✉ mikedavis@dover.gov.uk

Community Safety: Mr Roger Walton, Director of Environment & Corporate Assets, Council Offices, White Cliffs Business Park, Dover CT16 3PJ ☎ 01304 872240 🖷 01304 872416
✉ rogerwalton@dover.gov.uk

Computer Management: Mr Sean Hale Head of ICT, EK Services, Military Road, Canterbury CT1 1YW ☎ 01227 862341
✉ sean.hale@ekservices.org

Contracts: Mr Mike Davis, Director of Finance, Housing & Community, Council Offices, White Cliffs Business Park, Dover CT16 3PJ ☎ 01304 872107 🖷 01304 872104
✉ mikedavis@dover.gov.uk

Corporate Services: Mr David Randall, Director of Governance, Council Offices, White Cliffs Business Park, Dover CT16 3PJ
☎ 01304 872141 🖷 01304 872300 ✉ davidrandall@dover.gov.uk

Economic Development: Mr Nadeem Aziz, Chief Executive, Council Offices, White Cliffs Business Park, Dover CT16 3PJ
☎ 01304 872400 🖷 01304 872004 ✉ nadeemaziz@dover.gov.uk

E-Government: Mrs Roz Edridge, Business Systems Manager, East Kent Services, Council Offices, Cecil Street, Margate CT9 1XZ
☎ 01843 577033 ✉ roz.edridge@ekservices.org

Electoral Registration: Mr Nadeem Aziz, Chief Executive, Council Offices, White Cliffs Business Park, Dover CT16 3PJ
☎ 01304 872400 🖷 01304 872004 ✉ nadeemaziz@dover.gov.uk

Emergency Planning: Mr David Randall, Director of Governance, Council Offices, White Cliffs Business Park, Dover CT16 3PJ
☎ 01304 872141 🖷 01304 872300 ✉ davidrandall@dover.gov.uk

Energy Management: Mr Roger Walton, Director of Environment & Corporate Assets, Council Offices, White Cliffs Business Park, Dover CT16 3PJ ☎ 01304 872240 🖷 01304 872416 rogerwalton@dover.gov.uk

Environmental / Technical Services: Mr Roger Walton, Director of Environment & Corporate Assets, Council Offices, White Cliffs Business Park, Dover CT16 3PJ ☎ 01304 872240 🖷 01304 872416 rogerwalton@dover.gov.uk

Environmental Health: Mr David Randall, Director of Governance, Council Offices, White Cliffs Business Park, Dover CT16 3PJ ☎ 01304 872141 🖷 01304 872300 davidrandall@dover.gov.uk

Estates, Property & Valuation: Mr Roger Walton, Director of Environment & Corporate Assets, Council Offices, White Cliffs Business Park, Dover CT16 3PJ ☎ 01304 872240 🖷 01304 872416 rogerwalton@dover.gov.uk

Events Manager: Mr Mike Davis, Director of Finance, Housing & Community, Council Offices, White Cliffs Business Park, Dover CT16 3PJ ☎ 01304 872107 🖷 01304 872104 mikedavis@dover.gov.uk

Facilities: Mr Roger Walton, Director of Environment & Corporate Assets, Council Offices, White Cliffs Business Park, Dover CT16 3PJ ☎ 01304 872240 🖷 01304 872416 rogerwalton@dover.gov.uk

Finance: Mr Mike Davis, Director of Finance, Housing & Community, Council Offices, White Cliffs Business Park, Dover CT16 3PJ ☎ 01304 872107 🖷 01304 872104 mikedavis@dover.gov.uk

Treasury: Mr Mike Davis, Director of Finance, Housing & Community, Council Offices, White Cliffs Business Park, Dover CT16 3PJ ☎ 01304 872107 🖷 01304 872104 mikedavis@dover.gov.uk

Fleet Management: Mr Mike Davis, Director of Finance, Housing & Community, Council Offices, White Cliffs Business Park, Dover CT16 3PJ ☎ 01304 872107 🖷 01304 872104 mikedavis@dover.gov.uk

Grounds Maintenance: Mr Roger Walton, Director of Environment & Corporate Assets, Council Offices, White Cliffs Business Park, Dover CT16 3PJ ☎ 01304 872240 🖷 01304 872416 rogerwalton@dover.gov.uk

Health and Safety: Mr David Randall, Director of Governance, Council Offices, White Cliffs Business Park, Dover CT16 3PJ ☎ 01304 872141 🖷 01304 872300 davidrandall@dover.gov.uk

Home Energy Conservation: Mr Roger Walton, Director of Environment & Corporate Assets, Council Offices, White Cliffs Business Park, Dover CT16 3PJ ☎ 01304 872240 🖷 01304 872416 rogerwalton@dover.gov.uk

Housing: Mr Mike Davis, Director of Finance, Housing & Community, Council Offices, White Cliffs Business Park, Dover CT16 3PJ ☎ 01304 872107 🖷 01304 872104 mikedavis@dover.gov.uk

Housing Maintenance: Mr David Ashby, Head of Asset Management, East Kent Housing Ltd, 3 - 5 Shorncliffe Road, , Folkestone CT20 2SQ ☎ 01303 853749 david.ashby@eastkenthousing.org.uk

Legal: Mr Harvey Rudd, Solicitor to the Council, Council Offices, White Cliffs Business Park, Dover CT16 3PJ ☎ 01304 872321 🖷 01304 872300 harveyrudd@dover.gov.uk

Leisure and Cultural Services: Mr Roger Walton, Director of Environment & Corporate Assets, Council Offices, White Cliffs Business Park, Dover CT16 3PJ ☎ 01304 872240 🖷 01304 872416 rogerwalton@dover.gov.uk

Licensing: Mr David Randall, Director of Governance, Council Offices, White Cliffs Business Park, Dover CT16 3PJ ☎ 01304 872141 🖷 01304 872300 davidrandall@dover.gov.uk

Lighting: Mr Roger Walton, Director of Environment & Corporate Assets, Council Offices, White Cliffs Business Park, Dover CT16 3PJ ☎ 01304 872240 🖷 01304 872416 rogerwalton@dover.gov.uk

Lottery Funding, Charity and Voluntary: Mr Mike Davis, Director of Finance, Housing & Community, Council Offices, White Cliffs Business Park, Dover CT16 3PJ ☎ 01304 872107 🖷 01304 872104 mikedavis@dover.gov.uk

Member Services: Mr David Randall, Director of Governance, Council Offices, White Cliffs Business Park, Dover CT16 3PJ ☎ 01304 872141 🖷 01304 872300 davidrandall@dover.gov.uk

Parking: Mr Roger Walton, Director of Environment & Corporate Assets, Council Offices, White Cliffs Business Park, Dover CT16 3PJ ☎ 01304 872240 🖷 01304 872416 rogerwalton@dover.gov.uk

Partnerships: Mr Mike Davis, Director of Finance, Housing & Community, Council Offices, White Cliffs Business Park, Dover CT16 3PJ ☎ 01304 872107 🖷 01304 872104 mikedavis@dover.gov.uk

Personnel / HR: Ms Juli Oliver-Smith Head of EK Human Resources, East Kent HR Partnership, Dover District Council, White Cliffs Business Park, Whitfield, Dover CT16 3PJ ☎ 07917 473616 hrpartnership@dover.gov.uk

Planning: Mr Nadeem Aziz, Chief Executive, Council Offices, White Cliffs Business Park, Dover CT16 3PJ ☎ 01304 872400 🖷 01304 872004 nadeemaziz@dover.gov.uk

Procurement: Mr Mike Davis, Director of Finance, Housing & Community, Council Offices, White Cliffs Business Park, Dover CT16 3PJ ☎ 01304 872107 🖷 01304 872104 mikedavis@dover.gov.uk

Recycling & Waste Minimisation: Mr Roger Walton, Director of Environment & Corporate Assets, Council Offices, White Cliffs Business Park, Dover CT16 3PJ ☎ 01304 872240 🖷 01304 872416 rogerwalton@dover.gov.uk

Regeneration: Mr Tim Ingleton, Head of Inward Investment, Council Offices, White Cliffs Business Park, Dover CT16 3PJ ☎ 01304 872423 🖷 01304 872445 timingleton@dover.gov.uk

Staff Training: Mr David Randall, Director of Governance, Council Offices, White Cliffs Business Park, Dover CT16 3PJ ☎ 01304 872141 🖷 01304 872300 ✉ davidrandall@dover.gov.uk

Street Scene: Mr Roger Walton, Director of Environment & Corporate Assets, Council Offices, White Cliffs Business Park, Dover CT16 3PJ ☎ 01304 872240 🖷 01304 872416 ✉ rogerwalton@dover.gov.uk

Sustainable Communities: Mr Mike Davis, Director of Finance, Housing & Community, Council Offices, White Cliffs Business Park, Dover CT16 3PJ ☎ 01304 872107 🖷 01304 872104 ✉ mikedavis@dover.gov.uk

Tourism: Mr Roger Walton, Director of Environment & Corporate Assets, Council Offices, White Cliffs Business Park, Dover CT16 3PJ ☎ 01304 872240 🖷 01304 872416 ✉ rogerwalton@dover.gov.uk

Traffic Management: Mr Roger Walton, Director of Environment & Corporate Assets, Council Offices, White Cliffs Business Park, Dover CT16 3PJ ☎ 01304 872240 🖷 01304 872416 ✉ rogerwalton@dover.gov.uk

Waste Collection and Disposal: Mr Roger Walton, Director of Environment & Corporate Assets, Council Offices, White Cliffs Business Park, Dover CT16 3PJ ☎ 01304 872240 🖷 01304 872416 ✉ rogerwalton@dover.gov.uk

Waste Management: Mr Roger Walton, Director of Environment & Corporate Assets, Council Offices, White Cliffs Business Park, Dover CT16 3PJ ☎ 01304 872240 🖷 01304 872416 ✉ rogerwalton@dover.gov.uk

COUNCILLORS

Chair **Chandler**, Susan (CON - Little Stour & Ashstone)
cllrsusanchandler@dover.gov.uk

Vice-Chair **Hannent**, David (CON - Whitfield)
cllrdavid.hannent@dover.gov.uk

Leader of the Council **Watkins**, Paul (CON - St Margaret's-at-Cliffe)
cllrpaulwatkins@dover.gov.uk

Deputy Leader of the Council **Connolly**, Michael (CON - Little Stour & Ashstone)
cllrmichaelconolly@dover.gov.uk

Back, Jim (CON - Whitfield)
cllrjames.back@dover.gov.uk

Bannister, Simon (LAB - Buckland)
cllrsimon.bannister@dover.gov.uk

Bartlett, Trevor (CON - Little Stour & Ashstone)
cllrtrevorbartlett@dover.gov.uk

Beresford, Pauline (CON - River)
cllrpauline.beresford@dover.gov.uk

Bond, Trevor (CON - Middle Deal & Sholden)
cllrtrevorbond@dover.gov.uk

Brivio, Pamela (LAB - Tower Hamlets)
cllrpamela.brivio@dover.gov.uk

Butcher, Bernard (CON - Sandwich)
cllrbernardbutcher@dover.gov.uk

Carter, Paul (CON - Sandwich)
cllrpaul.carter@dover.gov.uk

Collor, Nigel (CON - Castle)
cllrnigelcollor@dover.gov.uk

Cosin, Margaret (LAB - Mill Hill)
cllrmargaret.cosin@dover.gov.uk

Cronk, David (LAB - Middle Deal & Sholden)
cllrdavid.cronk@dover.gov.uk

Dixon, Nicholas (CON - River)
cllrnicholas.dixon@dover.gov.uk

Eddy, Mike (LAB - Mill Hill)
cllrmichaeleddy@dover.gov.uk

Friend, Adrian (CON - North Deal)
cllradrian.friend@dover.gov.uk

Frost, Bob (CON - North Deal)
cllrbobfrost@dover.gov.uk

Gardner, Bill (LAB - North Deal)
billkimi@hotmail.co.uk

Glayzer, Ben (UKIP - Tower Hamlets)
cllrben.glayzer@dover.gov.uk

Hawkins, Pam (LAB - Middle Deal & Sholden)
cllrpamela.hawkins@dover.gov.uk

Heath, Patrick (CON - Walmer)
cllrpatrickheath@dover.gov.uk

Heron, John (LAB - Maxton, Elms Vale & Priory)
cllrjohn.heron@dover.gov.uk

Hill, Susan (LAB - Buckland)
cllr.susan.hill@dover.gov.uk

Holloway, Michael (CON - Sandwich)
cllrmichael.holloway@dover.gov.uk

Johnstone, Thomas (LAB - Aylesham)
cllr.thomas.johnstone@dover.gov.uk

Jones, Sue (LAB - St Radigunds)
cllrsue.jones@dover.gov.uk

Keen, Linda (LAB - Aylesham)
linda.keen@clara.co.uk

Kenton, Nicholas (CON - Eastry)
cllrnicholaskenton@dover.gov.uk

Le Chevalier, Sue (CON - Ringwould)
cllrsuzannelechevalier@dover.gov.uk

Le Chevalier, Paul (CON - Walmer)
cllrpaullechevalier@dover.gov.uk

Manion, Stephen (CON - Eastry)
cllrstephenmanion@dover.gov.uk

Mills, Kevin (LAB - St Radigunds)
cllrkevinmills@dover.gov.uk

Morris, Keith (CON - St Margaret's-at-Cliffe)
cllrkeith.morris@dover.gov.uk

Murphy, Derek (CON - Walmer)
cllrderek.murphy@dover.gov.uk

Ovenden, Marjorie (Mog) (CON - Eythorne & Shepherdswell)
cllrmogovenden@dover.gov.uk

Pollitt, Sid (LAB - Mill Hill)
cllrsid.pollitt@dover.gov.uk

Rapley, Georgette (UKIP - Town & Pier)
cllrgeorgette.rapley@dover.gov.uk

Richardson, Andrew (UKIP - Maxton, Elms Vale & Priory)
cllrandrew.richardon@dover.gov.uk

Rose, Mark (CON - Lydden and Temple Ewell)
cllrmark.rose@dover .gov.uk

Sargent, Daniel (LAB - Buckland)
cllrdaniel.sargent@dover.gov.uk

Scales, Frederick (CON - Capel-le-Ferne)
cllrfrederickscales@dover.gov.uk

Walker, Peter (LAB - Eythorne & Shepherdswell)
cllrpeterwalker@dover.gov.uk

Wallace, Peter (LAB - Maxton, Elms Vale & Priory)
cllrpeterwallace@dover.gov.uk

POLITICAL COMPOSITION

CON: 25, LAB: 17, UKIP: 3

COMMITTEE CHAIRS

Planning: Mr Frederick Scales

Dudley M

Dudley Metropolitan Borough Council, The Council House, Priory Road Dudley DY1 1HF
☎ 0300 555 2345 🖷 01384 815275 ✉ dudleycouncilplus@dudley.gov.uk
💻 www.dudley.gov.uk

FACTS AND FIGURES

Parliamentary Constituencies: Dudley North, Dudley South, Halesowen and Rowley Regis, Stourbridge
EU Constituencies: West Midlands
Election Frequency: Elections are by thirds

PRINCIPAL OFFICERS

Chief Executive: Ms Sarah Norman Chief Executive, The Council House, Priory Road Dudley DY1 1HF ☎ 01384 815201 🖷 01384 515275 ✉ sarah.norman@dudley.gov.uk

Senior Management: Dr Deborah Harkins Chief Officer - Health & Wellbeing, Falcon House, 8th Floor, The Minories, Dudley DY2 8PG ☎ 01384 816239 ✉ deborah.harkins@dudley.gov.uk

Senior Management: Mr Alan Lunt Strategic Director - Place, The Council House, Priory Road Dudley DY1 1HF ☎ 01384 814150 ✉ alan.lunt@dudley.gov.uk

Senior Management: Mr Tom Oakman Strategic Director - People, The Council House, Priory Road Dudley DY1 1HF ☎ 01384 815800 ✉ tony.oakman@dudley.gov.uk

Senior Management: Mr Philip Tart, Strategic Director - Resources & Transformation, The Council House, Priory Road Dudley DY1 1HF ☎ 01384 815300 🖷 01384 815379 ✉ philip.tart@dudley.gov.uk

Access Officer / Social Services (Disability): Mr Matt Bowsher Chief Officer - Adult Social Care, The Council House, Priory Road Dudley DY1 1HF ✉ matt.bowsher@dudley.gov.uk

Best Value: Mr Pete Sanford, Head of Equal Pay Project, The Council House, Priory Road Dudley DY1 1HF ☎ 01384 814717 ✉ pete.sanford@dudley.gov.uk

Building Control: Mr Phil Coyne Chief Officer - Planning & Economic Development, The Council House, Priory Road Dudley DY1 1HF ☎ 01384 814004 🖷 01384 814455 ✉ phil.coyne@dudley.gov.uk

Catering Services: Ms Penny Rushen General Manager, Westox House, Trinity Road, Dudley DY1 1JQ ☎ 01384 814320 ✉ penny.rushen@dudley.gov.uk

Civil Registration: Ms Jayne Catley Service Manager - Citizenship, Registration & Coroner Services, Priory Hall, Priory Road, Dudley DY1 4EU ☎ 01384 818349 ✉ jayne.catley@dudley.gov.uk

PR / Communications: Mr Phil Parker Head of Communication & Public Affairs, The Council House, Priory Road Dudley DY1 1HF ☎ 01384 818047 ✉ phil.parker@dudley.gov.uk

Community Safety: Ms Sue Haywood Head of Community Safety, Brierley Hill Police Station, Bank Street, Brierley Hill DY5 3DH ☎ 01384 815215 🖷 01384 818218 ✉ sue.haywood@dudley.gov.uk

Computer Management: Mrs Sandra Taylor Head of ICT Services, The Council House, Priory Road Dudley DY1 1HF ☎ 01384 815600 🖷 01384 815660 ✉ sandra.taylor@dudley.gov.uk

Consumer Protection and Trading Standards: Dr Deborah Harkins Chief Officer - Health & Wellbeing, Falcon House, 8th Floor, The Minories, Dudley DY2 8PG ☎ 01384 816239 ✉ deborah.harkins@dudley.gov.uk

Contracts: Mr Iain Newman Chief Officer - Finance & Legal Services, The Council House, Priory Road Dudley DY1 1HF ☎ 01384 814802 🖷 ; 01384 815379 ✉ iain.newman@dudley.gov.uk

Customer Service: Mr Sean Beckett Customer Services Manager, Dudley Council Plus, Castle Street, Dudley DY1 1JQ ☎ 01384 815281 ✉ sean.beckett@dudley.gov.uk

Economic Development: Mr Phil Coyne Chief Officer - Planning & Economic Development, 4 Ednam Road, Dudley DY1 1HL ☎ 01384 814004 🖷 01384 814455 ✉ phil.coyne@dudley.gov.uk

Education: Ms Nikki Hubbard Head of School Admissions, The Council House, Priory Road Dudley DY1 1HF ☎ 01384 814264 ✉ nikki.hubbard@dudley.gov.uk

Electoral Registration: Ms Alison Malkin Head of Electoral Services, The Council House, Priory Road Dudley DY1 1HF ☎ 01384 815274 🖷 01384 815299 ✉ alison.malkin@dudley.gov.uk

Emergency Planning: Mr John Hodt Prevent Co-ordinator for Dudley, The Council House, Priory Road Dudley DY1 1HF ☎ 01384 814736 ✉ john.hodt@dudley.gov.uk

Environmental / Technical Services: Mr Matt Williams, Chief Officer - Environmental Services, Lister Road Depot, Lister Road, Netherton, Dudley DY2 8JW ☎ 01384 814510 🖷 01384 814592 ✉ matt.williams@dudley.gov.uk

Environmental Health: Dr Deborah Harkins Chief Officer - Health & Wellbeing, Falcon House, 8th Floor, The Minories, Dudley DY2 8PG ☎ 01384 816239 deborah.harkins@dudley.gov.uk

Events Manager: Ms Sally Newell Himley Estate Manager, Himley Hall & Park, Himley Park, Dudley DY3 4DF ☎ 01384 817823 🖷 01384 814181 sally.newell@dudley.gov.uk

Finance: Mr Iain Newman Chief Officer - Finance & Legal Services, The Council House, Priory Road Dudley DY1 1HF ☎ 01384 814802 🖷 01384 815379 iain.newman@dudley.gov.uk

Fleet Management: Mr Matt Williams, Chief Officer - Environmental Services, Lister Road Depot, Lister Road, Netherton, Dudley DY2 8JT ☎ 01384 814510 🖷 01384 814592 matt.williams@dudley.gov.uk

Grounds Maintenance: Mr Matt Williams, Chief Officer - Environmental Services, Lister Road Depot, Lister Road, Netherton, Dudley DY2 8JT ☎ 01384 814510 🖷 01384 814592 matt.williams@dudley.gov.uk

Health and Safety: Mr Simon Reece Corporate Health & Safety Manager, The Council House, Priory Road Dudley DY1 1HF ☎ 01384 814722 🖷 01384 815979 simon.reece@dudley.gov.uk

Highways: Mr Matt Williams, Chief Officer - Environmental Services, Lister Road Depot, Lister Road, Netherton, Dudley DY2 8JT ☎ 01384 814510 🖷 01384 814592 matt.williams@dudley.gov.uk

Home Energy Conservation: Mr Andrew Leigh Head of Service - Housing Strategy, Harbour Buildings, Ground Floor, Waterfront West, Brierley Hill DY5 1LN ☎ 01384 815007 andrew.leigh@dudley.gov.uk

Housing: Mr Mark Rodgers Chief Officer - Housing, Harbour Buildings, 1st Floor, Waterfront West, Brierley Hill DY5 1LN ☎ 01384 815076 mark.rodgers@dudley.gov.uk

Legal: Mr Mohammed Farooq Head of Law & Governance, The Council House, Priory Road Dudley DY1 1HF ☎ 01384 815301 🖷 01384 815325 mohammed.farooq@dudley.gov.uk

Leisure and Cultural Services: Mr Stuart Connelly Head of Service, The Council House, Priory Road Dudley DY1 1HF ☎ 01384 813972 stuart.connelly@dudley.gov.uk

Leisure and Cultural Services: Mr Andy Webb Head of Service, The Council House, Priory Road Dudley DY1 1HF ☎ 01384 815579 andy.webb@dudley.gov.uk

Licensing: Mr Mohammed Farooq Head of Law & Governance, The Council House, Priory Road Dudley DY1 1HF ☎ 01384 815301 🖷 01384 815325 mohammed.farooq@dudley.gov.uk

Lighting: Mr Matt Williams, Chief Officer - Environmental Services, Lister Road Depot, Lister Road, Netherton, Dudley DY2 8JT ☎ 01384 814510 🖷 01384 814592 matt.williams@dudley.gov.uk

Member Services: Mr Steve Griffiths, Democratic Services Manager, The Council House, Priory Road Dudley DY1 1HF ☎ 01384 815235 🖷 01384 815202 steve.griffiths@dudley.gov.uk

Parking: Mr Garry Dean, Head of Service, Lister Road Depot, Lister Road, Netherton, Dudley DY2 8JW ☎ 01384 814506 🖷 01384 818393 garry.dean@dudley.gov.uk

Personnel / HR: Mrs Sharon Harthill Head of HR, 87 - 88 Regent House, King Street, Dudley DY2 8PR ☎ 01384 512125 sharon.harthill@dudley.gov.uk

Personnel / HR: Mrs Teresa Reilly, Temporary Lead for Corporate Transformation & Policy, 87 - 88 Regent House, King Street, Dudley DY2 8PR ☎ 01384 815330 🖷 01384 813391 teresa.reilly@dudley.gov.uk

Planning: Mrs Helen Martin Head of Planning, The Council House, Priory Road Dudley DY1 1HF ☎ 01384 814186 🖷 01384 814186 helen.martin@dudley.gov.uk

Procurement: Mr Christopher Morgan Procurement Manager, The Council House, Priory Road Dudley DY1 1HF ☎ 01384 814862 christopher.morgan@dudley.gov.uk

Recycling & Waste Minimisation: Mr Matt Williams, Chief Officer - Environmental Services, Lister Road Depot, Lister Road, Netherton, Dudley DY2 8JT ☎ 01384 814510 🖷 01384 814592 matt.williams@dudley.gov.uk

Regeneration: Mr Phil Coyne Chief Officer - Planning & Economic Development, The Council House, Priory Road Dudley DY1 1HF ☎ 01384 814004 🖷 01384 814455 phil.coyne@dudley.gov.uk

Road Safety: Mr Phil Coyne Chief Officer - Planning & Economic Development, The Council House, Priory Road Dudley DY1 1HF ☎ 01384 814004 🖷 01384 814455 phil.coyne@dudley.gov.uk

Social Services (Adult): Mr Matt Bowsher Chief Officer - Adult Social Care, The Council House, Priory Road Dudley DY1 1HF ☎ 01384 815805 matt.bowsher@dudley.gov.uk

Social Services (Children): Ms Merlin Joseph Chief Officer - Children's Services, The Council House, Priory Road Dudley DY1 1HF ☎ 01384 814200 merlin.joseph@dudley.gov.uk

Safeguarding: Ms Jassi Broadmeadow Divisional Lead - Safeguarding & Review, The Council House, Priory Road Dudley DY1 1HF ☎ 01384 814395 jassi.broadmeadow@dudley.gov.uk

Safeguarding: Ms Anne Harris Head of Adult Safeguarding, The Council House, Priory Road Dudley DY1 1HF ☎ 01384 815870 anne.harris@dudley.gov.uk

Public Health: Dr Deborah Harkins Chief Officer - Health & Wellbeing, Falcon House, 8th Floor, The Minories, Dudley DY2 8PG ☎ 01384 816239 deborah.harkins@dudley.gov.uk

Staff Training: Mrs Sarah Treneer Head of Learning & Organisational Development, 87 - 88 Regent House, King Street, Dudley DY2 8PR ☎ 01384 814727 🖷 01384 815204 sarah.treneer@dudley.gov.uk

DUDLEY

Street Scene: Mr Matt Williams, Chief Officer - Environmental Services, Lister Road Depot, Lister Road, Netherton, Dudley DY2 8JT ☎ 01384 814510 🖷 01384 814592 ✉ matt.williams@dudley.gov.uk

Sustainable Development: Mr Phil Coyne Chief Officer - Planning & Economic Development, The Council House, Priory Road Dudley DY1 1HF ☎ 01384 814004 🖷 01384 814455 ✉ phil.coyne@dudley.gov.uk

Tourism: Ms Nicola Beckley Tourism Development Assistant, The Council House, Priory Road Dudley DY1 1HF ☎ 01384 817611 ✉ nicola.beckley@dudley.gov.uk

Traffic Management: Mr Phil Coyne Chief Officer - Planning & Economic Development, The Council House, Priory Road Dudley DY1 1HF ☎ 01384 814004 🖷 01384 814455 ✉ phil.coyne@dudley.gov.uk

Transport: Mr Matt Williams, Chief Officer - Environmental Services, Lister Road Depot, Lister Road, Netherton, Dudley DY2 8JT ☎ 01384 814510 🖷 01384 814592 ✉ matt.williams@dudley.gov.uk

Waste Collection and Disposal: Mr Matt Williams, Chief Officer - Environmental Services, Lister Road Depot, Lister Road, Netherton, Dudley DY2 8JT ☎ 01384 814510 🖷 01384 814592 ✉ matt.williams@dudley.gov.uk

Waste Management: Mr Matt Williams, Chief Officer - Environmental Services, Lister Road Depot, Lister Road, Netherton, Dudley DY2 8JT ☎ 01384 814510 🖷 01384 814592 ✉ matt.williams@dudley.gov.uk

COUNCILLORS

***Leader of the Council* Lowe**, Peter (LAB - Lye & Stourbridge North)
cllr.peter.lowe@dudley.gov.uk

***Deputy Leader of the Council* Foster**, Judy (LAB - Brockmoor & Pensnett)
cllr.judy.foster@dudley.gov.uk

Ahmed, Asif (LAB - St James's)
cllr.asif.ahmed@dudley.gov.uk

Ahmed, Khurshid (LAB - St James's)
cllr.khurshid.ahmed@dudley.gov.uk

Ali, Shaukat (LAB - St Thomas's)
cllr.shaukat.ali@dudley.gov.uk

Aston, Margaret (LAB - Castle & Priory)

Aston, Adam (LAB - Upper Gornal & Woodsetton)
cllr.adam.aston@dudley.gov.uk

Attwood, Mike (CON - Norton)
cllr.mike.attwood@dudley.gov.uk

Barlow, Nicolas (CON - Wollaston & Stourbridge Town)
cllr.nicolas.barlow@dudley.gov.uk

Baugh, Clem (LAB - Coseley East)
cllr.clem.baugh@dudley.gov.uk

Bills, Hilary (LAB - Halesowen North)
cllr.hilary.bills@dudley.gov.uk

Blood, David (CON - Kingswinford South)
cllr.david.blood@dudley.gov.uk

Body, Richard (LAB - Cradley & Wollescote)
cllr.richard.body@dudley.gov.uk

Bradley, Paul (UKIP - Amblecote)
pwbradley69@googlemail.com

Branwood, Dave (LAB - Gornal)
cllr.dave.branwood@dudley.gov.uk

Brothwood, Paul (UKIP - Wordsley)
cllr.paul.brothwood@dudley.gov.uk

Casey, Keiran (LAB - Upper Gornal & Woodsetton)
cllr.keiran.casey@dudley.gov.uk

Clark, Steve (CON - Wollaston & Stourbridge Town)
cllr.steve.clark@dudley.gov.uk

Cooper, Ian (LAB - Belle Vale)
cllr.ian.cooper@dudley.gov.uk

Cotterill, Bryan (LAB - Quarry Bank & Dudley Wood)
cllr.bryan.cotterill@dudley.gov.uk

Cowell, Jackie (LAB - Quarry Bank & Dudley Wood)
cllr.jackie.cowell@dudley.gov.uk

Crumpton, Timothy (LAB - Cradley & Wollescote)
cllr.timothy.crumpton@dudley.gov.uk

Duckworth, Will (GRN - Netherton, Woodside & St Andrews)
cllr.will.duckworth@dudley.gov.uk

Elcock, Colin (CON - Norton)

Etheridge, Bill (UKIP - Sedgley)
cllr.bill.etheridge@dudley.gov.uk

Etheridge, Star (UKIP - Coseley East)
cllr.star.etheridge@dudley.gov.uk

Evans, Michael (CON - Sedgley)
cllr.michael.evans@dudley.gov.uk

Finch, Alan (LAB - Castle & Priory)
cllr.alan.finch@dudley.gov.uk

Finch, Ken (LAB - Castle & Priory)
cllr.ken.finch@dudley.gov.uk

Goddard, Andrea (CON - Hayley Green & Cradley South)
cllr.andrea.goddard@dudley.gov.uk

Gregory, Nick (CON - Halesowen South)
cllr.nick.gregory@dudley.gov.uk

Hale, Chris (LAB - Wollaston & Stourbridge Town)
cllr.chris.hale@dudley.gov.uk

Hanif, Mohammed (LAB - Lye & Stourbridge North)
cllr.mohammed.hanif@dudley.gov.uk

Harley, Patrick (CON - Kingswinford South)
cllr.patrick.harley@dudley.gov.uk

Harris, Rachel (LAB - Brierley Hill)
cllr.rachel.harris@dudley.gov.uk

Hemingsley, Derrick (LAB - Wordsley)
cllr.derrick.hemingsley@dudley.gov.uk

Henley, Stuart (UKIP - Halesowen North)
cllr.stuart.henley@dudley.gov.uk

Herbert, Tremaine (LAB - Lye & Stourbridge North)
cllr.tremaine.herbert@dudley.gov.uk

Hill, Jeff (CON - Hayley Green & Cradley South)
cllr.jeff.hill@Dudley.gov.uk

Islam, Zafar (LAB - Brierley Hill)
cllr.zafar.islam@dudley.gov.uk

Jones, Les (CON - Pedmore & Stourbridge East)
cllr.les.jones@dudley.gov.uk

Jordan, Karen (LAB - Brockmoor & Pensnett)
cllr.karen.jordan@dudley.gov.uk

Kettle, Ian (CON - Pedmore & Stourbridge East)
cllr.ian.kettle@dudley.gov.uk

Martin, John (LAB - Brockmoor & Pensnett)
cllr.john.martin@dudley.gov.uk

Miller, Peter (CON - Kingswinford South)
cllr.peter.miller@dudley.gov.uk

Millward, Anne (CON - Gornal)
cllr.anne.millward@dudley.gov.uk

Mottram, Melvyn (LAB - Coseley East)
cllr.melvyn.mottram@dudley.gov.uk

Neale, Natalie (CON - Kingswinford North & Wall Heath)
cllr.natalie.neale@dudley.gov.uk

Partridge, Gaye (LAB - Cradley & Wollescote)
cllr.gaye.partridge@dudley.gov.uk

Perks, Dean (UKIP - Upper Gornal & Woodsetton)
cllr.dean.perks@dudley.gov.uk

Perks, Christine (LAB - Amblecote)
cllr.christine.perks@dudley.gov.uk

Phipps, Simon (CON - Belle Vale)
cllr.simon.phipps@dudley.gov.uk

Richards, Nicola (CON - Kingswinford North & Wall Heath)
cllr.nicola.richards@dudley.gov.uk

Roberts, Mary (LAB - St James's)
cllr.mary.roberts@dudley.gov.uk

Rogers, Heather (CON - Norton)
cllr.heather.rogers@dudley.gov.uk

Russell, Donella (LAB - Belle Vale)
cllr.donella.russell@dudley.gov.uk

Scott-Dow, Roger (UKIP - Gornal)
cllr.roger.scott-dow@dudley.gov.uk

Shakespeare, Karen (CON - Halesowen North)
cllr.karen.shakespeare@dudley.gov.uk

Sparks, David (LAB - Quarry Bank & Dudley Wood)
cllr.david.sparks@dudley.gov.uk

Taylor, Alan (CON - Halesowen South)
cllr.alan.taylor@dudley.gov.uk

Taylor, Elaine (LAB - Netherton, Woodside & St Andrews)
cllr.elaine.taylor@dudley.gov.uk

Turner, Hazel (UKIP - Hayley Green & Cradley South)
cllr.hazel.turner@dudley.gov.uk

Tyler, Simon (CON - Ambercote)
cllr.simon.tyler@dudley.gov.uk

Tyler, Dave (LAB - Kingswinford North & Wall Heath)
cllr.dave.tyler@dudley.gov.uk

Vickers, David (CON - Halesowen South)
cllr.david.vickers@dudley.gov.uk

Waltho, Steve (LAB - St Thomas's)
cllr.steve.waltho@dudley.gov.uk

Westwood, Tina (CON - Sedgley)
cllr.tine.westwood@dudley.gov.uk

Wilson, Margaret (LAB - Brierley Hill)
cllr.margaret.wilson@dudley.gov.uk

Wood, Mike (CON - Pedmore & Stourbridge East)
cllr.mike.wood@dudley.gov.uk

Zada, Qadar (LAB - Netherton, Woodside & St Andrews)
cllr.qadar.zada@dudley.gov.uk

POLITICAL COMPOSITION

LAB: 37, CON: 24, UKIP: 8, GRN: 1

COMMITTEE CHAIRS

Development Control: Mr Qadar Zada

Health & Wellbeing: Ms Rachel Harris

Licensing: Ms Donella Russell

Dumfries & Galloway S

Dumfries & Galloway Council, Council Offices, English Street, Dumfries DG1 2DD
☎ 01387 260000 🖷 01387 260034 ✉ cis@dumgal.gov.uk
💻 www.dumgal.gov.uk

FACTS AND FIGURES

Parliamentary Constituencies: Dumfries and Galloway, Dumfriesshire, Clydesdale and Tweedale
EU Constituencies: Scotland
Election Frequency: Elections are of whole council

PRINCIPAL OFFICERS

Chief Executive: Mr Gavin Stevenson Chief Executive, Council Offices, English Street, Dumfries DG1 2DD ☎ 01387 260001 🖷 01387 260034 ✉ chief.executive@dumgal.gov.uk

Senior Management: Ms Lorna Meahan Director - Corporate Services, Council Offices, English Street, Dumfries DG1 2DD ☎ 01387 260003 ✉ lorna.meahan@dumgal.gov.uk

Civil Registration: Mrs Alison Quigley, Chief Registrar, 15 Ednam Street, Annan DG12 5EF ☎ 01461 204914 🖷 01461 206896 ✉ alisonq@dumgal.gov.uk

PR / Communications: Ms Claire Aitken Communications Manager, Council Offices, English Street, Dumfries DG1 2DD ☎ 01387 260058 🖷 01387 260334 ✉ claire.aitken@dumgal.gov.uk

Community Planning: Ms Liz Manson Operations Manager - Corporate & Community Planning, Council Offices, English Street, Dumfries DG1 2DD ☎ 01387 260074 ✉ liz.manson@dumgal.gov.uk

Community Safety: Mr David Gurney, Acting Emergency Planning & Community Safety Manager, Emergency Planning Unit, Carruthers House, English Street, Dumfries DG1 2HP ☎ 01387 260046 🖷 01387 265467

Consumer Protection and Trading Standards: Ms Sandra Harkness Service Manager - Trading Standards, 1 Newall Terrace, Dumfries DG1 1LN ☎ 03033 333000

Contracts: Mr Alistair Speedie, Director - Sustainable Development, Militia House, English Street, Dumfries DG1 2HR ☎ 01387 260376 ✉ alistair.speedie@dumgal.gov.uk

Economic Development: Mr Ewan Green Operations Manager - Economic Development, Council Offices, English Street, Dumfries DG1 2DD

Education: Mr Colin Grant Director - Education Services, Council Offices, English Street, Dumfries DG1 2DD ✉ cgrant@dumgal.gov.uk

Electoral Registration: Mr Keith Mossop Assessor & Electoral Registration Officer, Council Offices, English Street, Dumfries DG1 2DD ☎ 01387 260627 🖷 01387 260632 ✉ ero@dumgal.gov.uk

Emergency Planning: Mr David Gurney, Acting Emergency Planning & Community Safety Manager, Emergency Planning Unit, Carruthers House, English Street, Dumfries DG1 2HP ☎ 01387 260046 🖷 01387 265467

Energy Management: Mr John Currie, Service Leader - Energy, County House, 2 Great King Street, Dumfries DG1 1AE ☎ 01387 260718 🖷 01387 261661 ✉ johncu@dumgal.gov.uk

Finance: Mr Paul Garrett Operations Manager, Council Offices, English Street, Dumfries DG1 2DD

Treasury: Mr Kenneth Wright Treasurer & Principal Insurance Officer, Council Offices, English Street, Dumfries DG1 2DD ☎ 01387 260319 ✉ kenny.wright@dumgal.gov.uk

Pensions: Ms Islay Herrick Pensions Assistant, Monreith House, Bankend Road, Dumfries DG1 4ZE ☎ 01387 273853 ✉ islay.herrick@dumgal.gov.uk

Pensions: Mr Philip McGroggan Service Leader - Pension Investment Management, Marchmount House, , Dumfries DG1 1PY ☎ 01387 273824 ✉ philip.mcgroggan@dumgal.gov.uk

Highways: Mr Alistair Speedie, Director - Sustainable Development, Militia House, English Street, Dumfries DG1 2HR ☎ 01387 260376 ✉ alistair.speedie@dumgal.gov.uk

Housing: Mr John Lynch, Operations Manager - Strategic Housing & Commissioning, Carmont House, Bankend Road, Dumfries DG1 4ZJ ☎ 01387 245123 🖷 01387 245133 ✉ johnl@dumgal.gov.uk

Legal: Mr Willie Taylor Service Manager - Courts & Licensing, Council Offices, English Street, Dumfries DG1 2DD ☎ 01387 245913 🖷 01387 252978 ✉ willie.taylor@dumgal.gov.uk

Leisure and Cultural Services: Mr Richard Grieveson Head - Resource Planning & Community Services, Marchmount House, Dumfries DG1 1PY ☎ 01387 273875 ✉ richard.grieveson@dumgal.gov.uk

Licensing: Mr Willie Taylor Service Manager - Courts & Licensing, Council Offices, English Street, Dumfries DG1 2DD ☎ 01387 245913 🖷 01387 252978 ✉ willie.taylor@dumgal.gov.uk

Lighting: Mr Alistair Speedie, Director - Sustainable Development, Militia House, English Street, Dumfries DG1 2HR ☎ 01387 260376 ✉ alistair.speedie@dumgal.gov.uk

Lottery Funding, Charity and Voluntary: Ms Emma Berger Voluntary Sector Manager, Marchmount House, Dumfries DG1 1PY ☎ 01387 260000 ✉ emma.berger@dumgal.gov.uk

Parking: Mr Alistair Speedie, Director - Sustainable Development, Militia House, English Street, Dumfries DG1 2HR ☎ 01387 260376 ✉ alistair.speedie@dumgal.gov.uk

Personnel / HR: Mr Paul Clarkin Operations Manager - Human Resources, Council Offices, English Street, Dumfries DG1 2DD ☎ 01387 273842 ✉ paul.clarkin@dumgal.gov.uk

Planning: Mr Alistair Speedie, Director - Sustainable Development, Militia House, English Street, Dumfries DG1 2HR ☎ 01387 260376 ✉ alistair.speedie@dumgal.gov.uk

Procurement: Mrs Rhona Lewis Corporate Procurement Manager, Council Offices, English Street, Dumfries DG1 2DD ✉ rlewis@dumgal.gov.uk

Recycling & Waste Minimisation: Mr Alistair Speedie, Director - Sustainable Development, Militia House, English Street, Dumfries DG1 2HR ☎ 01387 260376 ✉ alistair.speedie@dumgal.gov.uk

Social Services: Mr Peter David Senior Social Work Manager, Council Offices, English Street, Dumfries DG1 2DD

Social Services: Mr Geoff Dean Senior Social Work Manager, Longacres Road, Kirkcudbright DG6 4AT ☎ 01557 339260

Social Services: Mr Allan Monteforte Senior Social Work Manager, 39 Lewis Street, Stranraer DG9 7AD ☎ 01776 706884

Fostering & Adoption: Ms Sandra Ritchie, Fostering & Adoption Manager, 122-124 Irish Street, , Dumfries DG1 2AW ☎ 01387 273700 ✉ sandra.ritchie@dumgal.gov.uk

Staff Training: Mr Paul Clarkin Operations Manager - Human Resources, Marchmount House, Dumfries DG1 1PY ☎ 01387 273842 ✉ paul.clarkin@dumgal.gov.uk

Sustainable Communities: Mr Bill Barker Operations Manager - Infrastructure & Commissioning, Cargen Towers, Garroch Business Park, Garroch Loaning, Dumfries DG2 8PN

Traffic Management: Mr Alistair Speedie, Director - Sustainable Development, Militia House, English Street, Dumfries DG1 2HR ☎ 01387 260376 ✉ alistair.speedie@dumgal.gov.uk

Waste Management: Mr Alistair Speedie, Director - Sustainable Development, Militia House, English Street, Dumfries DG1 2HR ☎ 01387 260376 ✉ alistair.speedie@dumgal.gov.uk

COUNCILLORS

***Leader of the Council* Nicholson**, Ronnie (LAB - North West Dumfries)
ronnie.nicholson@dumgal.gov.uk

***Deputy Leader of the Council* Thompson**, Ted (LAB - lochar)
ted.thompson@dumgal.gov.uk

***Group Leader* Ferguson**, Andy (SNP - North West Dumfries)
andy.ferguson@dumgal.gov.uk

***Group Leader* Maitland**, Jane (IND - Dee)
jane.maitland@dumgal.gov.uk

***Group Leader* Nicol**, Graham (CON - Mid Galloway)
graham.nicol@dumgal.gov.uk

Bell, Graham (CON - North West Dumfries)
john.bell2@dumgal.gov.uk

Blake, Ian (CON - Abbey)
ian.blake@dumgal.gov.uk

Brodie, Richard (IND - Annandale South)
richard.brodie@dumgal.gov.uk

Carruthers, Ian (CON - Annandale South)
ian.carruthers@dumgal.gov.uk

Carruthers, Karen (CON - Annandale East & Eskdale)
karen.carruthers3@dumgal.gov.uk

Carson, Finlay (CON - Castle Douglas & Glenkens)
finlay.carson@dumgal@gov.uk

Collins, Brian (SNP - Castle Douglas & Glenkens)
brian.collins@dumgal.gov.uk

Davidson, Rob (SNP - Abbey)
rob.davidson@dumgal.gov.uk

Dempster, James (LAB - Mid & Upper Nithsdale)
jim.dempster@dumgal.gov.uk

Dick, Iain (SNP - Stranraer & North Rhins)
iain.dick@dumgal.gov.uk

Diggle, Peter (CON - Annandale North)
peter.diggle@dumgal.gov.uk

Dryburgh, Archie (LAB - Annandale East & Eskdale)
archie.dryburgh@dumgal.gov.uk

Dykes, Gillian (CON - Mid & Upper Nithsdale)
gill.dykes@dumgal.gov.uk

Forster, Grahame (INDNA - Wigtown West)
grahame.forster@dumgal.gov.uk

Geddes, Alistair (SNP - Mid Galloway)

Gilroy, Patsy (CON - Dee)
patsy.gilroy@dumgal.gov.uk

Groom, Jack (CON - Nith)
jack.groom@dumgal.gov.uk

Hongmei Jin, Yen (SNP - Lochar)
yen.hongmeijin@dumgal.gov.uk

Hyslop, Ivor (CON - Lochar)
ivor.hyslop@dumgal.gov.uk

Leaver, Jeff (LAB - Lochar)
jeff.leaver@dumgal.gov.uk

MacGregor, Gail (CON - Annandale North)
gail.macgregor@dumgal.gov.uk

Male, Denis (CON - Annandale East & Eskdale)
denis.male@dumgal.gov.uk

Marshall, Sean (LAB - Annandale South)
sean.marshall@dumgal.gov.uk

Martin, John (LAB - Nith)
john.martin@dumgal.gov.uk

McAughtrie, Tom (LAB - Abbey)
tom.mcaughtrie@dumgal.gov.uk

McClung, Jim (SNP - Wigtown West)
jim.mcclung@dumgal.gov.uk

McColm, Jim (IND - Mid Galloway)
jim.mccolm@dumgal.gov.uk

McCutcheon, Marion (LAB - Stranraer & North Rhins)
marion.mccutcheon@dumgal.gov.uk

McKie, David (LAB - North West Dumfries)
david.mckie@dumgal.gov.uk

Oglivie, Ronald (LAB - Annandale South)
ronal.ogilvie@dumgal.gov.uk

Peacock, Craig (IND - Annandale East & Eskdale)
craig.peacock@dumgal.gov.uk

Prentice, George (IND - Castle Douglas & Glenkens)
george.prentice@dumgal.gov.uk

Scobie, William (NP - Stranraer & North Rhins)
william.scobie@dumgal.gov.uk

Smyth, Colin (LAB - Nith)
colin.smyth@dumgal.gov.uk

Stitt, David (LAB - Abbey)
davie.stitt@dumgal.gov.uk

Syme, John (LAB - Mid & Upper Nithsdale)
john.syme@dumgal.gov.uk

Tait, Graeme (CON - Annandale North)
graeme.tait2@dumgal.gov.uk

Thompson, Stephen (SNP - Annandale North)
stephen.thompson@dumgal.gov.uk

Tuckfield, Roberta (CON - Wigtown West)
roberta.tuckfield@dumgal.gov.uk

Witts, Alistair (SNP - Nith)
alistair.witts@dumgal.gov.uk

Wood, Andrew (SNP - Mid & Upper Nithsdale)
andrew.wood@dumgal.gov.uk

Wyper, Colin (INDNA - Dee)
colin.wyper@dumgal.gov.uk

POLITICAL COMPOSITION
CON: 15, LAB: 14, SNP: 10, IND: 5, INDNA: 2, NP: 1

COMMITTEE CHAIRS
Audit & Risk: Mrs Gillian Dykes
Economy, Environment & Infrastructure: Mr Colin Smyth
Planning: Mr John Martin

Dundee City S

Dundee City Council, 21 City Square, Dundee DD1 3BY
☎ 01382 434000 🖷 01382 434666 💻 www.dundeecity.gov.uk

FACTS AND FIGURES
Parliamentary Constituencies: Dundee East, Dundee West
EU Constituencies: Scotland

DUNDEE CITY

Election Frequency: Elections are of whole council

PRINCIPAL OFFICERS

Chief Executive: Mr David Martin, Chief Executive, 21 City Square, Dundee DD1 3BY ☎ 01382 434201 🖷 01382 434996 ✉ david.martin@dundeecity.gov.uk

Senior Management: Mr Stewart Murdoch, Director of Leisure & Communities, Central Library, Dundee DD1 2DB ☎ 01382 437460 🖷 01382 437487 ✉ stewart.murdoch@dundeecity.gov.uk

Access Officer / Social Services (Disability): Ms Dorothy Wilson Access Officer, Dundee House, 50 North Lindsay Street, Dundee DD1 1LS ☎ 01382 433865 🖷 01382 433034 ✉ dorothy.wilson@dundeecity.gov.uk

Architect, Building / Property Services: Mr Rob Pedersen, City Architectural Services Officer, Dundee House, 50 North Lindsay Street, Dundee DD1 1LS ☎ 01382 433640 🖷 01382 433034 ✉ rob.pedersen@dundeecity.gov.uk

Best Value: Mr Paul Carroll Performance & Improvement Manager, 21 City Square, Dundee DD1 3BY ☎ 01382 434452 🖷 01382 434996 ✉ paul.carroll@dundeecity.gov.uk

Building Control: Mr Kenneth Findlay Team Leader - Building Control, Dundee House, 50 North Lindsay Street, Dundee DD1 1LS ☎ 01382 433001 🖷 01382 433013 ✉ ken.findlay@dundeecity.gov.uk

Children / Youth Services: Ms Jane Martin Manager of Children's Services & Criminal Justice, Friarfield House, Barrack Street, Dundee DD1 1PQ ☎ 01382 435017 ✉ jane.martin@dundeecity.gov.uk

Civil Registration: Ms Jayne Allan Registrar, 21 City Square, Dundee DD1 3BY ☎ 01382 435225 ✉ jayne.allan@dundeecity.gov.uk

PR / Communications: Ms Merrill Smith Head of Corporate Communications, 21 City Square, Dundee DD1 3BY ☎ 01382 434500 🖷 01382 434834 ✉ merrill.smith@dundeecity.gov.uk

Community Planning: Mr Peter Allan Community Planning Manager, 21 City Square, Dundee DD1 3BY ☎ 01382 434465 🖷 01382 434996 ✉ peter.allan@dundeecity.gov.uk

Community Safety: Mr Neil Gunn, Head of Community Learning & Development, 21 City Square, Dundee DD1 3BY ☎ 01382 307464 🖷 01382 307487 ✉ neil.gunn@dundeecity.gov.uk

Computer Management: Ms Janet Robertson Head of HR & Business Support, Dundee House, 50 North Lindsay Street, Dundee DD1 1LS ☎ 01382 433335 ✉ janet.robertson@dundeecity.gov.uk

Consumer Protection and Trading Standards: Mr Ken Daly, Trading Standards Manager, Claverhouse West Industrial Park, Jack Martin Way, Dundee DD1 ☎ 01382 436263 ✉ ken.daly@dundeecity.gov.uk

Contracts: Mr Kenneth Laing Director of Environment, 3 City Square, Dundee DD1 3BA ☎ 01382 434729 🖷 01382 434777 ✉ ken.laing@dundeecity.gov.uk

Corporate Services: Ms Marjory Stewart Director of Corporate Services, Dundee House, 50 North Lindsay Street, Dundee DD1 1LS ☎ 01382 433555 🖷 01382 433045 ✉ marjory.stewart@dundeecity.gov.uk

Direct Labour: Mr Kenneth Laing Director of Environment, 3 City Square, Dundee DD1 3BA ☎ 01382 434729 🖷 01382 434777 ✉ ken.laing@dundeecity.gov.uk

Economic Development: Mr Mike Galloway, Director of City Development, Dundee House, 50 North Lindsay Street, Dundee DD1 1LS ☎ 01382 433610 🖷 01382 433013 ✉ mike.galloway@dundeecity.gov.uk

Education: Mr Michael Wood Director of Education, Dundee House, 50 North Lindsay Street, Dundee DD1 1LS ☎ 01382 433088 🖷 01382 433080 ✉ michael.wood@dundeecity.gov.uk

E-Government: Mr Paul Carroll Performance & Improvement Manager, 21 City Square, Dundee DD1 3BY ☎ 01382 434452 🖷 01382 434996 ✉ paul.carroll@dundeecity.gov.uk

Electoral Registration: Mr Roger Mennie Head of Legal & Democratic Services, 21 City Square, Dundee DD1 3BY ☎ 01382 434577 ✉ roger.mennie@dundeecity.gov.uk

Emergency Planning: Mr Graeme Mackenzie Risk & Business Continuity Manager, Dundee House, 50 North Lindsay Street, Dundee DD1 1NZ ☎ 01382 433301 🖷 01382 433045 ✉ graeme.mackenzie@dundeecity.gov.uk

Energy Management: Mr Alex Gibson Team Leader (Property Services), 3 City Square, , Dundee DD1 3BA ☎ 01382 434814 🖷 01382 434650 ✉ alex.gibson@dundeecity.gov.uk

Environmental Health: Mr Kenny Kerr Head of Environmental Protection, 34 Harefield Road, Dundee DD2 3JW ☎ 01382 436201 🖷 01382 436226 ✉ kenny.kerr@dundeecity.gov.uk

Estates, Property & Valuation: Mr Mike Galloway, Director of City Development, Dundee House, 50 North Lindsay Street, Dundee DD1 1LS ☎ 01382 433610 🖷 01382 433013 ✉ mike.galloway@dundeecity.gov.uk

European Liaison: Mr Gregor Hamilton Head of Planning & Economic Development, Dundee House, 50 Nirth Lindsay Street, , Dundee DD1 1LS ☎ 01382 433520 🖷 01382 433013 ✉ gregor.hamilton@dundeecity.gov.uk

Finance: Ms Marjory Stewart Director of Corporate Services, Dundee House, 50 North Lindsay Street, Dundee DD1 1NZ ☎ 01382 433555 🖷 01382 433045 ✉ marjory.stewart@dundeecity.gov.uk

Treasury: Ms Marjory Stewart Director of Corporate Services, Dundee House, 50 North Lindsay Street, Dundee DD1 1LS ☎ 01382 433555 🖷 01382 433045 ✉ marjory.stewart@dundeecity.gov.uk

Pensions: Ms Catherine Carruthers Depute Pensions Manager, Dundee House, 50 North Lindsay Street, Dundee DD1 1LS ☎ 01382 437925 ✉ catherine.carruthers@dundeecity.gov.uk

Grounds Maintenance: Mr Rod Houston Land Services Manager, 353 Clepington Road, Dundee DD3 8PL ☎ 01382 434747 🖷 01382 434777 ✉ rod.houston@dundeecity.gov.uk

Health and Safety: Mr Neil Doherty, Council Health & Safety Co-ordinator, 8 City Square, Dundee DD1 3BG ☎ 01382 434878 🖷 01382 434614 ✉ neil.doherty@dundeecity.gov.uk

Highways: Mr Fergus Wison City Engineer, Dundee House, 50 North Lindsay Street, Dundee DD1 1LS ☎ 01382 433711 🖷 01382 433313 ✉ fergus.wilson@dundeecity.gov.uk

Home Energy Conservation: Ms Heather McQuillan, HECA Officer, Housing Investment Unit, Dundee House, 50 North Lindsay Street, Dundee DD1 1NB ☎ 01382 434872 🖷 01382 434597 ✉ heather.mcquillan@dundeecity.gov.uk

Housing: Mrs Elaine Zwirlein, Director of Housing, 50 North Lindsay Street, Dundee DD1 1LS ☎ 01382 434538 🖷 01382 434942 ✉ elaine.zwirlein@dundeecity.gov.uk

Housing Maintenance: Mrs Elaine Zwirlein, Director of Housing, 50 North Lindsay Street, Dundee DD1 1LS ☎ 01382 434538 🖷 01382 434942 ✉ elaine.zwirlein@dundeecity.gov.uk

Legal: Mr Roger Mennie Head of Legal & Democratic Services, 21 City Square, Dundee DD1 3BY ☎ 01382 434577 ✉ roger.mennie@dundeecity.gov.uk

Leisure and Cultural Services: Mr Stewart Murdoch, Director of Leisure & Communities, Central Library, Dundee DD1 2DB ☎ 01382 437460 🖷 01382 437487 ✉ stewart.murdoch@dundeecity.gov.uk

Licensing: Mr Roger Mennie Head of Legal & Democratic Services, 21 City Square, Dundee DD1 3BY ☎ 01382 434577 ✉ roger.mennie@dundeecity.gov.uk

Lifelong Learning: Mr Stewart Murdoch, Director of Leisure & Communities, Central Library, Dundee DD1 2DB ☎ 01382 437460 🖷 01382 437487 ✉ stewart.murdoch@dundeecity.gov.uk

Lighting: Mr Lindsay McGregor, Team Leader (Street Lighting), Dundee House, 50 North Lindsay Street, Dundee DD1 1LS ☎ 01382 834132 🖷 01382 433013 ✉ lindsay.mcgregor@dundeecity.gov.uk

Lottery Funding, Charity and Voluntary: Ms Diane Milne Senior Policy Officer, Dundee House, 50 North Lindsay Street, Dundee DD1 1LS ☎ 01382 434653 🖷 01382 434650 ✉ diane.milne@dundeecity.gov.uk

Member Services: Mr Paul Carroll Performance & Improvement Manager, 21 City Square, Dundee DD1 3BY ☎ 01382 434452 🖷 01382 434996 ✉ paul.carroll@dundeecity.gov.uk

Parking: Mr Mike Galloway, Director of City Development, Dundee House, 50 North Lindsay Street, Dundee DD1 1LS ☎ 01382 433610 🖷 01382 433013 ✉ mike.galloway@dundeecity.gov.uk

Personnel / HR: Ms Janet Robertson Head of HR & Business Support, Dundee House, 50 North Lindsay Street, Dundee DD1 1LS ☎ 01382 433335 ✉ janet.robertson@dundeecity.gov.uk

Planning: Mr Mike Galloway, Director of City Development, Dundee House, 50 North Lindsay Street, Dundee DD1 1LS ☎ 01382 433610 🖷 01382 433013 ✉ mike.galloway@dundeecity.gov.uk

Public Libraries: Mr Stewart Murdoch, Director of Leisure & Communities, Central Library, Dundee DD1 2DB ☎ 01382 437460 🖷 01382 437487 ✉ stewart.murdoch@dundeecity.gov.uk

Recycling & Waste Minimisation: Mr Kenny Kerr Head of Environmental Protection, 34 Harefield Road, Dundee DD2 3JW ☎ 01382 436201 🖷 01382 436226 ✉ kenny.kerr@dundeecity.gov.uk

Road Safety: Mr Neil Gellatly Head of Transportation, Dundee House, 50 North Lindsay Street, Dundee DD1 1LS ☎ 01382 433116 🖷 01382 433313 ✉ neil.gellatly@dundeecity.gov.uk

Social Services: Ms Laura Bannerman Head of Strategy, Performance & Support, Dundee House, 50 North Lindsay Street, Dundee DD1 1LS ☎ 01382 433205 ✉ laura.bannerman@dundeecity.gov.uk

Social Services (Adult): Ms Diane McCulloch Community Care Manager, Claverhouse East Industrial Park, Jack Martin Way, Dundee DD4 9FF ☎ 01382 438302 🖷 01382 438360 ✉ diane.mcculloch@dundeecity.gov.uk

Social Services (Children): Ms Jane Martin Manager of Children's Services & Criminal Justice, Friarfield House, Barrack Street, Dundee DD1 1PQ ☎ 01382 435017 ✉ jane.martin@dundeecity.gov.uk

Staff Training: Ms Janet Robertson Head of HR & Business Support, Dundee House, 50 North Lindsay Street, Dundee DD1 1LS ☎ 01382 433335 ✉ janet.robertson@dundeecity.gov.uk

Town Centre: Mrs Sarah Craig City Centre Manager, 3 City Square, Dundee DD1 3BA ☎ 01382 434548 🖷 01382 434650 ✉ sarah.craig@dundeecity.gov.uk

Traffic Management: Mr Neil Gellatly Head of Transportation, Dundee House, 50 North Lindsay Street, Dundee DD1 1LS ☎ 01382 433116 🖷 01382 433313 ✉ neil.gellatly@dundeecity.gov.uk

Transport: Mr Mike Galloway, Director of City Development, Dundee House, 50 North Lindsay Street, Dundee DD1 1LS ☎ 01382 433610 🖷 01382 433013 ✉ mike.galloway@dundeecity.gov.uk

Transport Planner: Mr Mike Galloway, Director of City Development, Dundee House, 50 North Lindsay Street, Dundee DD1 1LS ☎ 01382 433610 🖷 01382 433013 ✉ mike.galloway@dundeecity.gov.uk

Waste Collection and Disposal: Mr Kenny Kerr Head of Environmental Protection, 34 Harefield Road, Dundee DD2 3JW ☎ 01382 436201 🖷 01382 436226 ✉ kenny.kerr@dundeecity.gov.uk

Waste Management: Mr Kenny Kerr Head of Environmental Protection, 34 Harefield Road, Dundee DD2 3JW ☎ 01382 436201 🖷 01382 436226 ✉ kenny.kerr@dundeecity.gov.uk

DUNDEE CITY

Children's Play Areas: Mr Gary Robertson Head of Environmental Management, 3 City Square, Dundee DD1 3BA ☎ 01382 436894 ✉ gary.robertson@dundeecity.gov.uk

COUNCILLORS

***Provost* Duncan**, Bob (SNP - Lochee)
bob.duncan@dundeecity.gov.uk

Alexander, John (SNP - Strathmartine)
john.alexander@dundeecity.gov.uk

Asif, Mohammed (LAB - Coldside)
mohammed.asif@dundeecity.gov.uk

Bidwell, Laurie (LAB - The Ferry)
laurie.bidwell@dundeecity.gov.uk

Black, Jimmy (SNP - Coldside)
jimmy.black@dundeecity.gov.uk

Borthwick, Ian (IND - Strathmartine)
ian.borthwick@dundeecity.gov.uk

Bowes, David (SNP - Coldside)
david.bowes@dundeecity.gov.uk

Brennan, Lesley (LAB - East End)
lesley.brennan@dundeecity.gov.uk

Campbell, Bill (SNP - West End)
bill.campbell@dundeecity.gov.uk

Cordell, Kevin (SNP - The Ferry)
kevin.cordell@dundeecity.gov.uk

Cruikshank, Georgia (LAB - Maryfield)
georgia.cruikshank@dundeecity.gov.uk

Dawson, Will (SNP - East End)
will.dawson@dundeecity.gov.uk

Ferguson, Tom (LAB - Lochee)
tom.ferguson@dundeecity.gov.uk

Gordon, Brian (LAB - North East)
brian.gordon@dundeecity.gov.uk

Guild, Kenneth (SNP - The Ferry)
ken.guild@dundeecity.gov.uk

Hunter, Stewart (SNP - Strathmartine)
stewart.hunter@dundeecity.gov.uk

Keenan, Kevin (LAB - Strathmartine)
kevin.keenan@dundeecity.gov.uk

Lynn, Ken (SNP - Maryfield)
ken.lynn@dundeecity.gov.uk

MacPherson, Fraser (LD - West End)
fraser.macpherson@dundeecity.gov.uk

McCready, Richard (LAB - West End)
richard.mccready@dundeecity.gov.uk

McDonald, Vari (SNP - West End)
vari.mcdonald@dundeecity.gov.uk

McGovern, Norma (LAB - Lochee)
Norma.mcgovern@dundeecity.gov.uk

Melville, Craig (SNP - Maryfield)
craig.melville@dundeecity.gov.uk

Murray, Gregor (SNP - North East)
gregor.murray@dundeecity.gov.uk

Roberts, Christina (SNP - East End)
christina.roberts@dundeecity.gov.uk

Ross, Alan (SNP - Lochee)
alan.ross@dundeecity.gov.uk

Sawers, Willie (SNP - North East)
willie.sawers@dundeecity.gov.uk

Scott, Derek (CON - The Ferry)
derek.scott@dundeecity.gov.uk

Wright, Helen (LAB - Coldside)
helen.wright@dundeecity.gov.uk

POLITICAL COMPOSITION

SNP: 16, LAB: 10, LD: 1, CON: 1, IND: 1

COMMITTEE CHAIRS

Education: Mr Stewart Hunter

Environment: Mr Craig Melville

Housing: Mr John Alexander

Licensing: Mr Stewart Hunter

Policy & Resources: Mr Kenneth Guild

Durham U

Durham, Durham County Council, County Hall, Durham DH1 5QF
☎ 0300 123 7070 🖷 0191 383 4500 💻 www.durham.gov.uk

FACTS AND FIGURES

Parliamentary Constituencies: Bishop Auckland, Durham North, Durham North West, Durham, City of Easington, Sedgefield
EU Constituencies:
Election Frequency:

PRINCIPAL OFFICERS

Chief Executive: Mr George Garlick Chief Executive, Durham County Council, County Hall, Durham DH1 5UF ☎ 03000 267331 ✉ george.garlick@durham.gov.uk

Assistant Chief Executive: Ms Lorraine O'Donnell Assistant Chief Executive, Durham County Council, County Hall, Durham DH1 5UF ☎ 03000 268060 ✉ lorraine.odonnell@durham.gov.uk

Senior Management: Mr Terry Collins Corporate Director - Neighbourhood Services, Durham County Council, County Hall, Durham DH1 5UQ ☎ 03000 268080 ✉ terry.collins@durham.gov.uk

Senior Management: Dr Anna Lynch Director - Public Health, Durham County Council, County Hall, Durham DH1 5QF ✉ anna.lynch@durham.gov.uk

Senior Management: Mr Don McLure Corporate Director - Resources, Durham County Council, County Hall, Durham DH1 5QF ☎ 03000 261945 ✉ don.mclure@durham.gov.uk

Senior Management: Ms Rachael Shimmin Corporate Director - Children & Adult Services, Durham County Council, County Hall, Durham DH1 5UG ☎ 03000 267353 ✉ rachael.shimmin@durham.gov.uk

Senior Management: Mr Ian Thompson Corporate Director - Regeneration & Economic Development, Durham County Council, County Hall, Durham DH1 5QF ☎ 03000 267330 ✉ ian_thompson@durham.gov.uk

Access Officer / Social Services (Disability): Ms Jeanette Stephenson Community Safety & Involvement Manager, Durham County Council, County Hall, Durham DH1 5QF ☎ 03000 267390 ✉ jeanette.stephenson@durham.gov.uk

Access Officer / Social Services (Disability): Ms Geraldine Waugh Operations Manager, Durham County Council, County Hall, Durham DH1 5QF ☎ 03000 268244 ✉ geraldine.waugh@durham.gov.uk

Architect, Building / Property Services: Mr David Taylor Property, Planning & Projects Manager, Durham County Council, County Hall, Durham DH1 5QF ☎ 03000 269727 ✉ david.taylor3@durham.gov.uk

Best Value: Mr Roger Goodes Head - Policy & Communications, Durham County Council, County Hall, Durham DH1 5UL ☎ 03000 268050 ✉ roger.goodes@durham.gov.uk

Building Control: Mr Paul Burr Building & Facilities Maintenance Manager, Durham County Council, County Hall, Durham DH1 5QF ☎ 03000 268263 ✉ paul.burr@durham.gov.uk

Children / Youth Services: Ms Gill Eshelby Strategic Manager - Co Durham Youth Offending Service, Durham County Council, County Hall, Durham DH1 5QF ☎ 03000 265989 ✉ gill.eshelby@durham.gov.uk

Children / Youth Services: Mr Paul Hebron Strategic Manager, Durham County Council, County Hall, Durham DH1 5QF ☎ 03000 268858 ✉ paul.hebron@durham.gov.uk

Children / Youth Services: Ms Carol Payne Head of Children's Services, Durham County Council, County Hall, Durham DH1 5QF ☎ 03000 268983 ✉ carole.payne@durham.gov.uk

Children / Youth Services: Ms Rachael Shimmin Corporate Director - Children & Adult Services, Durham County Council, County Hall, Durham DH1 5UG ☎ 03000 267353 ✉ rachael.shimmin@durham.gov.uk

PR / Communications: Mr Roger Goodes Head - Policy & Communications, Durham County Council, County Hall, Durham DH1 5QF ☎ 03000 268050 ✉ roger.goodes@durham.gov.uk

Community Planning: Ms Jenny Haworth Head - Planning & Performance, Durham County Council, County Hall, Durham DH1 5QF ☎ 03000 268071 ✉ jenny.haworth@durham.gov.uk

Computer Management: Mr Keith Forster Strategic Manager - Performance & Systems, Durham County Council, County Hall, Durham DH1 5QF ☎ 03000 267396 ✉ keith.forster@durham.gov.uk

Computer Management: Mr Phil Jackman Head - ICT Services, Durham County Council, County Hall, Durham DH1 5QF ☎ 03000 268372 ✉ phil.jackman@durham.gov.uk

Consumer Protection and Trading Standards: Mr Owen Cleugh Consumer Protection Manager, Durham County Council, County Hall, Durham DH1 5QF ☎ 03000 260925 ✉ owen.cleugh@durham.gov.uk

Consumer Protection and Trading Standards: Ms Joanne Waller Head - Environment, Health & Consumer Protection, Durham County Council, County Hall, Durham DH1 5UQ ☎ 03000 260924 ✉ joanne.waller@durham.gov.uk

Contracts: Ms Denise Elliot Strategic Commissioning Manager, Durham County Council, County Hall, Durham DH1 5QF ☎ 03000 267389 ✉ denise.elliot@durham.gov.uk

Contracts: Mr Dave Shipman Strategic Commissioning Manager, Durham County Council, County Hall, Durham DH1 5QF ☎ 03000 267391 ✉ dave.shipman@durham.gov.uk

Corporate Services: Mr Kevin Edworthy Corporate Policy & Planning Team Leader, Durham County Council, County Hall, Durham DH1 5QF ☎ 03000 268045 ✉ kevin.edworthy@durham.gov.uk

Corporate Services: Ms Vanessa Glover Corporate News Manager, Durham County Council, County Hall, Durham DH1 5QF ☎ 03000 268070 ✉ vanessa.glover@durham.gov.uk

Corporate Services: Mr Tom Gorman Corporate Improvement Manager, Durham County Council, County Hall, Durham DH1 5QF ☎ 03000 268027 ✉ tom.gorman@durham.gov.uk

Corporate Services: Ms Su Jordan CCU Programme Officer Manager, Durham County Council, County Hall, Durham DH1 5QF ☎ 03000 268055 ✉ su.jordan@durham.gov.uk

Customer Service: Mr Lawrence Serewicz Principal Information Manager, Durham County Council, County Hall, Durham DH1 5QF ☎ 03000 268038 ✉ lawrence.serewicz@durham.gov.uk

Customer Service: Mr Oliver Sherratt Head - Direct Services, Durham County Council, County Hall, Durham DH1 5QF ☎ 03000 269259 ✉ oliver.sherratt@durham.gov.uk

Economic Development: Ms Sarah Robson Head - Economic Development & Housing, Durham County Council, County Hall, Durham DH1 5QF ☎ 03000 267332 ✉ sarah_robson@durham.gov.uk

Economic Development: Mr Graham Wood Economic Development Manager, Durham County Council, County Hall, Durham DH1 5QF ☎ 03000 262002 ✉ graham.wood@durham.gov.uk

Education: Ms Jane le Sage Strategic Manager - SEN, Durham County Council, County Hall, Durham DH1 5QF ☎ 03000 267756 ✉ jane.le.sage@durham.gov.uk

Education: Ms Caroline O'Neill Head of Education, Durham County Council, County Hall, Durham DH1 5QF ☎ 03000 268982 ✉ caroline.oneill@durham.gov.uk

DURHAM

Electoral Registration: Ms Colette Longbottom Legal & Democratic Services, Durham County Council, County Hall, Durham DH1 5QF ☎ 03000 269732 colette.longbottom@durham.gov.uk

Environmental / Technical Services: Mr John Reed Head - Technical Services, Durham County Council, County Hall, Durham DH1 5QF ☎ 03000 267454 john.reed@durham.gov.uk

Environmental Health: Mr Gary Hutchinson Environment Protection Manager, Durham County Council, County Hall, Durham DH1 5QF ☎ 03000 261007 gary.hutchinson@durham.gov.uk

Environmental Health: Ms Joanne Waller Head - Environment, Health & Consumer Protection, Durham County Council, County Hall, Durham DH1 5UQ ☎ 03000 260924 joanne.waller@durham.gov.uk

Environmental Health: Mr Michael Yeadon Health Protection Manager, Durham County Council, County Hall, Durham DH1 5QF ☎ 03000 264655 michael.yeadon@durham.gov.uk

Estates, Property & Valuation: Mr Gerard Darby Asset Services Manager, Durham County Council, County Hall, Durham DH1 5QF ☎ 03000 267024 gerard.darby@durham.gov.uk

Events Manager: Ms Melanie Sensicle Chief Executive - Visit County Durham, Durham County Council, County Hall, Durham DH1 5QF ☎ 03000 261219 melanie.sensicle@durham.gov.uk

Finance: Ms Hilary Appleton Strategic Finance Manager - Corporate Finance, Durham County Council, County Hall, Durham DH1 5QF ☎ 03000 266239 hilary.appleton@durham.gov.uk

Finance: Mr Phillip Curran Finance Manager, Durham County Council, County Hall, Durham DH1 5QF ☎ 03000 261967 philip.curran@durham.gov.uk

Finance: Mr Paul Darby Head - Financial Services, Durham County Council, County Hall, Durham DH1 5QF ☎ 03000 261930 paul.darby@durham.gov.uk

Finance: Ms Susan Elliott Financial Services Manager, Durham County Council, County Hall, Durham DH1 5QF ☎ 03000 268211 susan.elliott@durham.gov.uk

Finance: Mr Jeff Garfoot Head - Corporate Finance, Durham County Council, County Hall, Durham DH1 5QF ☎ 03000 261946 jeff.garfoot@durham.gov.uk

Finance: Mr Andrew Gilmore Finance Manager, Durham County Council, County Hall, Durham DH1 5QF ☎ 03000 263497 andrew.gilmore@durham.gov.uk

Pensions: Mr Nick Orton Payroll, Pensions & Pension Investment Manager, Durham County Council, County Hall, Durham DH1 5QF ☎ 03000 269798 nick.orton@durham.gov.uk

Fleet Management: Mr Norman Ramsey County Fleet Manager, Durham County Council, County Hall, Durham DH1 5QF ☎ 03000 269262 norman.ramsey@durham.gov.uk

Health and Safety: Ms Kim Jobson Human Resources & Organisational Development Manager, Durham County Council, County Hall, Durham DH1 5QF ☎ 03000 267308 kim.jobson@durham.gov.uk

Highways: Mr Mark Readman Highways Services Manager, Durham County Council, County Hall, Durham DH1 5QF ☎ 03000 269261 mark.readman@durham.gov.uk

Housing: Ms Sarah Robson Head - Economic Development & Housing, Durham County Council, County Hall, Durham DH1 5QF ☎ 03000 267332 sarah_robson@durham.gov.uk

Housing Maintenance: Ms Kath Heathcote Housing Regeneration Manager, Durham County Council, County Hall, Durham DH1 5QF ☎ 03000 265264 kath.heathcote@durham.gov.uk

Legal: Ms Colette Longbottom Legal & Democratic Services, Durham County Council, County Hall, Durham DH1 5QF ☎ 03000 269732 colette.longbottom@durham.gov.uk

Legal: Mr Bryan Smith Litigation Manager, Durham County Council, County Hall, Durham DH1 5QF ☎ 03000 269732 bryan.smith@durham.gov.uk

Leisure and Cultural Services: Mr Neil Hillier Strategic Manager - Heritage & Culture, Durham County Council, County Hall, Durham DH1 5QF ☎ 03000 268179 neil.hillier@durham.gov.uk

Leisure and Cultural Services: Mr Stephen Howell Head - Sport & Leisure Services, Durham County Council, County Hall, Durham DH1 5UQ ☎ 03000 264550 stephen.howell@durham.gov.uk

Partnerships: Mr Gordon Elliott Head - Partnership & Community Engagement, Durham County Council, County Hall, Durham DH1 5UF ☎ 03000 263605 gordon.elliott@durham.gov.uk

Personnel / HR: Ms Lorraine Anderson Human Resources Manager - Operations & Projects, Durham County Council, County Hall, Durham DH1 5QF ☎ 03000 265857 lorraine.anderson@durham.gov.uk

Personnel / HR: Ms Kim Jobson Head - Human Resources & Organisational Development, Durham County Council, County Hall, Durham DH1 5UL ☎ 03000 267308 kim.jobson@durham.gov.uk

Personnel / HR: Ms Joanne Kemp Human Resources Manager - Policy & Organisational Development, Durham County Council, County Hall, Durham DH1 5QF ☎ 03000 265856 joanne.kemp@durham.gov.uk

Planning: Ms Jenny Haworth Head - Planning & Performance, Durham County Council, County Hall, Durham DH1 5QF ☎ 03000 268071 jenny.haworth@durham.gov.uk

Planning: Ms Andrea Petty Policy & Planning Manager, Durham County Council, County Hall, Durham DH1 5QF ☎ 03000 267312 andrea.petty@durham.gov.uk

Planning: Ms Beverley Stobbart Policy Performance & Planning Manager, Durham County Council, County Hall, Durham DH1 5QF ☎ 03000 268048 ✉ bev.stobbart@durham.gov.uk

Planning: Mr Stuart Timmiss Head - Planning & Assets, Durham County Council, County Hall, Durham DH1 5QF ☎ 03000 267334 ✉ stuart.timmiss@durham.gov.uk

Procurement: Mr Darren Knowd Corporate Procurement Manager, Durham County Council, County Hall, Durham DH1 5QF ☎ 03000 265416 ✉ darren.knowd@durham.gov.uk

Procurement: Ms Louise Lyons Commissioning Services Manager, Durham County Council, County Hall, Durham DH1 5QF ☎ 03000 268041 ✉ louise.lyons@durham.gov.uk

Public Libraries: Ms Anne Davison Strategic Manager - Libraries, Durham County Council, County Hall, Durham DH1 5QF ☎ 03000 268129 ✉ anne.davison@durham.gov.uk

Regeneration: Mr Peter Coe Regeneration & Development Manager, Durham County Council, County Hall, Durham DH1 5QF ☎ 03000 262042 ✉ peter.coe@durham.gov.uk

Social Services (Adult): Mr Lee Alexander Safeguarding & Practice Development Manager, Durham County Council, County Hall, Durham DH1 5QF ☎ 03000 268180 ✉ lee.alexander@durham.gov.uk

Social Services (Adult): Mr Philip Emberson Operations Manager - Provider Services, Durham County Council, County Hall, Durham DH1 5QF ☎ 03000 268245 ✉ philip.emberson@durham.gov.uk

Social Services (Adult): Mrs Lesley Jeavons Head - Adult Care, Durham County Council, County Hall, Durham DH1 5UG ☎ 03000 267354 ✉ lesley.jeavons@durham.gov.uk

Social Services (Adult): Ms Tracy Joisce Operations Manager, Durham County Council, County Hall, Durham DH1 5QF ☎ 03000 268243 ✉ tracy.joisce@durham.gov.uk

Social Services (Children): Mr Mark Gurney Strategic Manager, Durham County Council, County Hall, Durham DH1 5QF ☎ 03000 265758 ✉ mark.gurney@durham.gov.uk

Social Services (Children): Ms Carol Payne Head of Children's Services, Durham County Council, County Hall, Durham DH1 5QF ☎ 03000 268983 ✉ carole.payne@durham.gov.uk

Social Services (Children): Ms Karen Robb Strategic Manager, Durham County Council, County Hall, Durham DH1 5QF ☎ 03000 265759 ✉ karen.robb@durham.gov.uk

Public Health: Dr Anna Lynch Director - Public Health, Durham County Council, County Hall, Durham DH1 5QF ✉ anna.lynch@durham.gov.uk

Staff Training: Ms Kim Jobson Human Resources & Organisational Development Manager, Durham County Council, County Hall, Durham DH1 5QF ☎ 03000 267308 ✉ kim.jobson@durham.gov.uk

Street Scene: Mr Jimmy Bennett Streetscene Area Manager South, Durham County Council, County Hall, Durham DH1 5QF ☎ 03000 266047 ✉ james.bennett@durham.gov.uk

Street Scene: Mr Ian Hoult Streetscene Area Manager North, Durham County Council, County Hall, Durham DH1 5QF ☎ 03000 265571 ✉ ian.hoult@durham.gov.uk

Street Scene: Mr Keith Parkinson Streetscene Area Manager East, Durham County Council, County Hall, Durham DH1 5QF ☎ 03000 268371 ✉ keith.parkinson@durham.gov.uk

Sustainable Communities: Mr Peter Appleton Head - Planning & Service Strategy, Durham County Council, County Hall, Durham DH1 5QF ☎ 03000 267388 ✉ peter.appleton@durham.gov.uk

Transport: Mr Adrian White Head - Transport & Contract Services, Durham County Council, County Hall, Durham DH1 5UQ ☎ 03000 267455 ✉ adrian.white@durham.gov.uk

Transport Planner: Mr Andrew Leadbetter Sustainable Transport Manager, Durham County Council, County Hall, Durham DH1 5QF ☎ 03000 268512 ✉ andrew.leadbetter@durham.gov.uk

Total Place: Ms Jenny Haworth Head - Planning & Performance, Durham County Council, County Hall, Durham DH1 5QF ☎ 03000 268071 ✉ jenny.haworth@durham.gov.uk

Waste Management: Mr John Shannon Strategic Waste Manager, Durham County Council, County Hall, Durham DH1 5QF ☎ 03000 266098 ✉ john.shannon@durham.gov.uk

COUNCILLORS

***Leader of the Council* Henig**, Simon (LAB - Chester-le-Street West Central)
simon.henig@durham.gov.uk

Adam, Eddy (LAB - Aycliffe West)
eddy.adam@durham.gov.uk

Allen, Joy (LAB - Bishop Auckland Town)
joy.allen@durham.gov.uk

Alvey, Jimmy (LAB - Peterlee West)
jimmy.alvey@durham.gov.uk

Armstrong, Lawson (LAB - Chester-le-Street East)
lawson.armstrong@durham.gov.uk

Armstrong, Joseph (LAB - Esh & Witton Gilbert)
joseph.armstrong@durham.gov.uk

Armstrong, Barbara (LAB - Esh & Witton Gilbert)
barbara.armstrong@durham.gov.uk

Avery, Brian (IND - Ferryhill)
brian.avery@durham.gov.uk

Batey, Alison (LAB - Pelton)
alison.batey@durham.gov.uk

Bell, Alan (IND - Lumley)
alan.bell@durham.gov.uk

Bell, Edward (LAB - Deneside)
edward.bell@durham.gov.uk

Bell, Jennifer (LAB - Deneside)
jennifer.bell@durham.gov.uk

DURHAM

Bell, David (LAB - Deerness)
dbell@durham.gov.uk

Bell, Richard (CON - Barnard Castle West)
richard.bell@durham.gov.uk

Bennett, Harry (LAB - Peterlee East)
harry.bennett@durham.gov.uk

Blakey, Jan (LAB - Coxhoe)
jan.blakey@durham.gov.uk

Bleasdale, Gerry (LAB - Seaham)
gerry.bleasdale@durham.gov.uk

Bonner, Anne (LAB - Deerness)
anne.bonner@durham.gov.uk

Boyes, David (LAB - Easington)
david.boyes@durham.gov.uk

Brookes, Peter (LAB - Trimdon & Thornley)
peter.brookes@durham.gov.uk

Brown, Jane (LAB - Delves Lane)
jane.brown@durham.gov.uk

Carr, Joanne (LAB - Burnopfield & Dipton)
joanne.carr@durham.gov.uk

Carr, Colin (LAB - Pelton)
colin.carr@durham.gov.uk

Chaplow, Jean (LAB - Deerness)
jean.chaplow@durham.gov.uk

Charlton, Joyce (IND - Tanfield)
joyce.charlton@durham.gov.uk

Clare, John (LAB - Aycliffe North & Middridge)
john.clare@durham.gov.uk

Clark, June (LAB - Horden)
j.clark@durham.gov.uk

Conway, Patrick (LAB - Belmont)
patrick.conway@durham.gov.uk

Cordon, James (LAB - Pelton)
james.cordon@durham.gov.uk

Corrigan, Kate (LAB - Belmont)
katie.corrigan@durham.gov.uk

Crathorne, Pauline (LAB - Ferryhill)
pauline.crathorne@durham.gov.uk

Crute, Robert (LAB - Blackhalls)
rob.crute@durham.gov.uk

Davidson, Keith (LAB - Chester-le-Street South)
keith.davidson@durham.gov.uk

Davinson, Mark (LAB - Craghead & South Moor)
mark.davinson@durham.gov.uk

Dearden, Katherine (LAB - Stanley)
katherine.dearden@durham.gov.uk

Dixon, Mike (LAB - Aycliffe North & Middridge)
mike.dixon@durham.gov.uk

Forster, Sonia (LAB - Dawdon)
sonia.forster@durham.gov.uk

Foster, Neil (LAB - Tudhoe)
neil.foster@durham.gov.uk

Freeman, David (LD - Elvet & Gilesgate)
david.freeman@durham.gov.uk

Geldard, Ian (LAB - Spennymoor)
ian.geldard@durham.gov.uk

Glass, Bob (LAB - Delves Lane)
bob.glass@durham.gov.uk

Graham, Barbara (LAB - Tudhoe)
barbara.graham@durham.gov.uk

Gray, Joan (LAB - Aycliffe North & Middridge)
joan.gray@durham.gov.uk

Gunn, Olwyn (LAB - Willington & Hunwick)
olwyn.gunn@durham.gov.uk

Hall, David (LAB - Sherburn)
dhall@durham.gov.uk

Hampson, Carole (LAB - Craghead & South Moor)
carole.hampson@durham.gov.uk

Hart, John (LAB - Tow Law)
john.hart@durham.gov.uk

Henderson, Ted (CON - Barnard Castle West)
ted.henderson@durham.gov.uk

Henig, Katherine (LAB - Chester-le-Street South)
katherine.henig@durham.gov.uk

Hicks, Derek (IND - Consett South)
derek.hicks@durham.gov.uk

Hillary, Jed (LAB - Aycliffe East)
jed.hillary@durham.gov.uk

Hodgson, Michele (LAB - Annfield Plain)
michele.hodgson@durham.gov.uk

Holland, Grenville (LD - Nevilles Cross)
grenville.holland@durham.gov.uk

Hopgood, Amanda (LD - Framwellgate & Newton Hall)
amanda.hopgood@durham.gov.uk

Hopper, Kate (LAB - Aycliffe West)
kate.hopper@durham.gov.uk

Hovvells, Lucy (LAB - Trimdon & Thornley)
lucy.hovvels@durham.gov.uk

Huntington, Eunice (LAB - Shotton & South Hetton)
eunice.huntington@durham.gov.uk

Iveson, Sarah (LAB - Aycliffe East)
sarah.iveson@durham.gov.uk

Jewell, Ivan (LAB - Burnopfield & Dipton)
ivan.jewell@durham.gov.uk

Johnson, Ossie (LAB - Lanchester)
ossie.johnson@durham.gov.uk

Kay, Charlie (LAB - Coundon)
charlie.kay@durham.gov.uk

Kellett, Bill (LAB - Sherburn)
bill.kellett@durham.gov.uk

Laing, Audrey (LAB - Peterlee East)
audrey.laing@durham.gov.uk

Lawton, Pat (LAB - Spennymoor)
pat.lawton@durham.gov.uk

Lee, June (LAB - Woodhouse Close)
june.lee@durham.gov.uk

Lethbridge, John (LAB - Woodhouse Close)
john.lethbridge@durham.gov.uk

Liddle, Heather (LAB - Sacriston)
heather.liddle@durham.gov.uk

Lindsay, John (LAB - Ferryhill)
john.lindsay@durham.gov.uk

Lumsdon, Rachel (LAB - Sedgefield)
rachel.lumsdon@durham.gov.uk

Maitland, Joyce (LAB - Murton)
joyce.maitland@durham.gov.uk

Marshall, Linda (LAB - Chester-le-Street West Central)
linda.marshall@durham.gov.uk

Marshall, Carl (LAB - Stanley)
carl.marshall@durham.gov.uk

Martin, Nigel (LD - Nevilles Cross)
nigel.martin@durham.gov.uk

Maslin, Joan (IND - Passfield)
joan.maslin@durham.gov.uk

May, Peter (IND - North Lodge)
peter.may@durham.gov.uk

Measor, Jan (LAB - Peterlee West)
jan.measor@durham.gov.uk

Milburn, Olga (LAB - Tanfield)
olga.milburn@durham.gov.uk

Moir, Bill (LAB - Belmont)
bill.moir@durham.gov.uk

Morrison, Sue (LAB - Seaham)
sue.morrison@durham.gov.uk

Napier, Alan (LAB - Murton)
alan.napier@durham.gov.uk

Nearney, Thomas (LAB - Annfield Plain)
thomas.nearney@durham.gov.uk

Nicholls, Morris (LAB - Trimdon & Thornley)
morris.nicholls@durham.gov.uk

Nicholson, Henry (LAB - Shildon & Dene Valley)
henry.nicholson@durham.gov.uk

Oliver, Peter (IND - Benfieldside)
peter.oliver@durham.gov.uk

Ormerod, Richard (LD - Elvet & Gilesgate)
richard.ormerod@durham.gov.uk

Patterson, Andrea (LAB - Crook)
andrea.patterson@durham.gov.uk

Pemberton, Trish (LAB - Shildon & Dene Valley)
trish.pemberton@durham.gov.uk

Plews, Maria (LAB - Coxhoe)
maria.plews@durham.gov.uk

Potts, Christine (LAB - Chilton)
christine.potts@durham.gov.uk

Pounder, Lynn (LAB - Blackhalls)
lynn.pounder@durham.gov.uk

Richardson, George (CON - Barnard Castle East)
george.richardson@durham.gov.uk

Robinson, John (LAB - Sedgefield)
john.robinson@durham.gov.uk

Robinson, Stephen (IND - Benfieldside)
s.robinson@durham.gov.uk

Rowlandson, James (CON - Barnard Castle East)
james.rowlandson@durham.gov.uk

Savory, Anita (IND - Weardale)
anita.savory@durham.gov.uk

Shaw, Kevin (LAB - Dawdon)
kevin.shaw@durham.gov.uk

Shield, Alan (IND - Leadgate & Medomsley)
alan.shield@durham.gov.uk

Shuttleworth, John (IND - Weardale)
jshuttleworth@durham.gov.uk

Simmons, Mamie (LD - Framwellgate & Newton Hall)
mamie.simmons@durham.gov.uk

Simpson, Mick (LAB - Bishop Middleham & Cornforth)
m.simpson@durham

Smith, Tracie (LAB - Chester-le-Street North)
tracie.smith@durham.gov.uk

Smith, Heather (LAB - Evenwood)
heather.smith@durham.gov.uk

Stanton, Maureen (LAB - Crook)
maureen.stanton@durham.gov.uk

Stelling, Watts (IND - Leadgate & Medomsley)
watts.stelling@durham.gov.uk

Stephens, Brian (LAB - Shildon & Dene Valley)
brian.stephens@durham.gov.uk

Stoker, David (LD - Durham South)
david.stoker@durham.gov.uk

Stradling, Paul (LAB - Horden)
paul.stradling@durham.gov.uk

Surtees, Angela (LAB - Easington)
a.surtees@durham.gov.uk

Taylor, Leo (LAB - Wingate)
leo.taylor@durham.gov.uk

Taylor, Paul (LAB - Brandon)
paul.taylor@durham.gov.uk

Temple, Owen (LD - Consett North)
owen.temple@durham.gov.uk

Thompson, Kevin (IND - Spennymoor)
kevin.thompson@durham.gov.uk

Tinsley, Fraser (LAB - Willington & Hunwick)
fraser.tinsley@durham.gov.uk

Tomlinson, Eddie (LAB - Crook)
eddie.tomlinson@durham.gov.uk

Turnbull, John (LAB - Brandon)
john.turnbull@durham.gov.uk

Turner, Andy (LAB - Evenwood)
andy.turner@durham.gov.uk

Watson, Alex (IND - Consett North)
alex.watson@durham.gov.uk

Wilkes, Mark (LD - Framwellgate & Newton Hall)
mark.wilkes@durham.gov.uk

Williams, Mac (LAB - Coxhoe)
mac.williams@durham.gov.uk

Willis, Audrey (IND - Lumley)
audrey.willis@durham.gov.uk

Wilson, Simon (LAB - Sacriston)
swilson@durham.gov.uk

Wilson, Christine (LAB - West Auckland)
c.wilson@durham.gov.uk

Yorke, Robert (LAB - West Auckland)
robert.yorke@durham.gov.uk

Young, Richard (IND - Lanchester)
richie.young@durham.gov.uk

Zair, Samuel (IND - Bishop Auckland Town)
sam.zair@durham.gov.uk

POLITICAL COMPOSITION

LAB: 95, IND: 17, LD: 9, CON: 4

COMMITTEE CHAIRS

Audit: Mr Edward Bell

Children & Young People: Ms Christine Potts

Economy & Enterprise: Mr Robert Crute

Environment & Sustainable Communities: Mr David Bell

Environment & Sustainable Communities: Ms Barbara Graham

Health & Wellbeing: Ms Lucy Hovvells

Licensing: Mr Colin Carr

Pensions: Mr Andy Turner

Planning: Mr Keith Davidson

Safer & Stronger Communities: Mr David Boyes

Ealing L

Ealing London Borough Council, Perceval House, 14-16 Uxbridge Road, Ealing, London W5 2HL
☎ 020 8825 5000 🖷 020 8579 5224 ✉ webmaster@ealing.gov.uk
💻 www.ealing.gov.uk

FACTS AND FIGURES

Parliamentary Constituencies: Ealing Central and Acton, Ealing North, Ealing, Southall
EU Constituencies: London
Election Frequency: Elections are of whole council

PRINCIPAL OFFICERS

Chief Executive: Mr Martin Smith Chief Executive, Perceval House, 14-16 Uxbridge Road, London W5 2HL ☎ 020 8825 7089 🖷 020 8825 5500 ✉ chiefexecutive@ealing.gov.uk

Senior Management: Dr Jackie Chin Director - Public Health, Perceval House, 14-16 Uxbridge Road, Ealing, London W5 2HL ☎ 020 8825 6448 ✉ chinj@ealing.gov.uk

Senior Management: Ms Judith Finlay, Executive Director - Children, Adults & Public Health, Perceval House, 14-16 Uxbridge Road, Ealing, London W5 2HL ☎ 020 8825 7106 🖷 020 8825 6934 ✉ finlayj@ealing.gov.uk

Senior Management: Mr Pat Hayes, Executive Director - Regeneration & Housing, Perceval House, 14-16 Uxbridge Road, London W5 2HL ☎ 020 8825 7889 🖷 020 8825 5500 ✉ pat.hayes@ealing.gov.uk

Senior Management: Mr Ian O'Donnell Executive Director - Corporate Resources, Perceval House, 14-16 Uxbridge Road, London W5 2HL ☎ 020 8825 5269 🖷 020 8825 5500 ✉ odonnelli@ealing.gov.uk

Senior Management: Mr Keith Townsend, Executive Director - Environment & Customer Services, Perceval House, 14-16 Uxbridge Road, Ealing, London W5 2NL ☎ 020 8825 6306 🖷 020 8840 5500 ✉ keith.townsend@ealing.gov.uk

Architect, Building / Property Services: Mr Mark Newton Director of Business Services Group, Perceval House, 14-16 Uxbridge Road, London W5 2HL ☎ 020 8825 9645 🖷 020 8825 7476 ✉ mark.newton@ealing.gov.uk

Best Value: Mr Matthew Booth Director of Policy & Performance, Perceval House, 14-16 Uxbridge Road, Ealing, London W5 2HL ☎ 020 8825 8556 ✉ boothm@ealing.gov.uk

Building Control: Ms Aileen Jones Head of Planning Services, Perceval House, 14-16 Uxbridge Road, Ealing, London W5 2HL ☎ 020 8825 8371 🖷 020 8825 6610 ✉ jonesa@ealing.gov.uk

Building Control: Mr Noel Rutherford, Director of Built Environment, Perceval House, 14-16 Uxbridge Road, Ealing, London W5 2HL ☎ 020 8825 6639 🖷 020 8825 6610 ✉ rutherfn@ealing.gov.uk

Children / Youth Services: Ms Elaine Cunningham, Head of Youth & Connexions Service, Perceval House, 14-16 Uxbridge Road, Ealing, London W5 2HL ☎ 020 8825 7578 🖷 020 8825 5775 ✉ ecunningham@ealing.gov.uk

Children / Youth Services: Ms Judith Finlay, Executive Director - Children, Adults & Public Health, Perceval House, 14-16 Uxbridge Road, Ealing, London W5 2HL ☎ 020 8825 7106 🖷 020 8825 6934 ✉ finlayj@ealing.gov.uk

Civil Registration: Ms Franchene Allen Registration Services Manager, Ealing Town Hall, New Broadway, , London W5 2BY ☎ 020 8825 9277 🖷 020 8825 8560 ✉ fran.allen@ealing.gov.uk

Community Safety: Ms Susan Parsonage Director of Safer Communities, Perceval House, 14-16 Uxbridge Road, Ealing, London W5 2HL ☎ 020 8825 7398 🖷 020 8825 6661 ✉ parsonas@ealing.gov.uk

Computer Management: Mr Mark Newton Director of Business Services Group, Perceval House, 14-16 Uxbridge Road, London W5 2HL ☎ 020 8825 9645 🖷 020 8825 7476 ✉ mark.newton@ealing.gov.uk

Consumer Protection and Trading Standards: Mr Mark Wiltshire Head of Regulatory Services, Perceval House, 14-16 Uxbridge Road, Ealing, London W5 2HL ☎ 020 8825 8197 ✉ wiltshirema@ealing.gov.uk

Contracts: Mrs Kate Graefe Head of Strategic Procurement, Perceval House, 14-16 Uxbridge Road, Ealing, London W5 2HL ☎ 020 8825 9843 ✉ graefek@ealing.gov.uk

Customer Service: Ms Alison Reynolds Director of Customer Services, Perceval House, 14-16 Uxbridge Road, Ealing, London W5 2HL ☎ 020 8825 5329 ✉ reynolda@ealing.gov.uk

Economic Development: Ms Lucy Taylor Assistant Director of Regeneration & Planning Policy, Perceval House, 14-16 Uxbridge Road, Ealing, London W5 2HL ☎ 020 8825 9036 ✉ taylorl@ealing.gov.uk

Education: Ms Eileen Lustig Head of Admissions, Perceval House, 14-16 Uxbridge Road, Ealing, London W5 2HL ☎ 020 8825 5059 ✉ elustig@ealing.gov.uk

Electoral Registration: Mr Ross Jackson Head of Elections & Members' Services, Perceval House, 14-16 Uxbridge Road, Ealing, London W5 2HL ☎ 020 8825 6854 ✉ jacksonr@ealing.gov.uk

Emergency Planning: Ms Donna Wootton Interim Head of Civil Protection, Perceval House, 14-16 Uxbridge Road, Ealing, London W5 2HL ☎ 020 8825 9494 ✉ woottond@ealing.gov.uk

Environmental / Technical Services: Mr Darren Henaghan Interim Director of Environment, Perceval House, 14-16 Uxbridge Road, Ealing, London W5 2HL ☎ 020 8825 8576 ✉ henaghand@ealing.gov.uk

Environmental Health: Mr Mark Wiltshire Head of Regulatory Services, Perceval House, 14-16 Uxbridge Road, Ealing, London W5 2HL ☎ 020 8825 8197 ✉ wiltshirema@ealing.gov.uk

European Liaison: Mr Calum Murdoch External Funding Officer, Perceval House, 14-16 Uxbridge Road, Ealing, London W5 2HL ☎ 020 8825 7443 ✉ murdochc@ealing.gov.uk

Events Manager: Ms Jane Coughlan Head of Hospitality & Events, Perceval House, 14-16 Uxbridge Road, Ealing, London W5 2HL ☎ 020 8825 6700 ✉ coughlanj@ealing.gov.uk

Facilities: Miss Fiona Elliot Head of Hospitality & Events, Perceval House, 14-16 Uxbridge Road, Ealing, London W5 2HL ☎ 020 8825 6061 ✉ elliotf@ealing.gov.uk

Finance: Ms Maria Christolfi Finance Director, Perceval House, 14-16 Uxbridge Road, Ealing, London W5 2HL ☎ 020 8825 6193 ✉ mchristofi@ealing.gov.uk

Treasury: Mr Ian O'Donnell Executive Director - Corporate Resources, Perceval House, 14-16 Uxbridge Road, London W5 2HL ☎ 020 8825 5269 🖷 020 8825 5500 ✉ odonnelli@ealing.gov.uk

Pensions: Ms Bridget Uku Group Manager of Treasury & Investments, Perceval House, 14-16 Uxbridge Road, Ealing, London W5 2HL ☎ 020 8825 5981 ✉ ukub@ealing.gov.uk

Fleet Management: Mrs Kate Graefe Head of Strategic Procurement, Perceval House, 14-16 Uxbridge Road, Ealing, London W5 2HL ☎ 020 8825 9843 ✉ graefek@ealing.gov.uk

Grounds Maintenance: Mr Roger Jones Director of Environment & Leisure, Perceval House, 14-16 Uxbridge Road, Ealing, London W5 2HL ☎ 020 8825 8576 ✉ jonesrog@ealing.gov.uk

Health and Safety: Ms Sue Emery Interim Head of Health & Safety, Perceval House, 14-16 Uxbridge Road, Ealing, London W5 2HL ☎ 020 8825 6942 ✉ emerysu@ealing.gov.uk

Highways: Mr Shahid Iqbal, Assistant Director of Highways, Perceval House, 14-16 Uxbridge Road, Ealing, London W5 2HL ☎ 020 8825 7802 🖷 020 8825 5858 ✉ iqbalsp@ealing.gov.uk

Housing: Mr Mark Meehan Assistant Director of Housing Demand, Perceval House, 14-16 Uxbridge Road, Ealing, London W5 2HL ☎ 020 8825 9046 🖷 020 8825 6359 ✉ meehanm@ealing.gov.uk

Housing Maintenance: Mr Greg Birch Head of Repairs & Maintenance, Perceval House, 14-16 Uxbridge Road, Ealing, London W5 2HL ☎ 020 8825 8456 ✉ birchg@ealing.gov.uk

Local Area Agreement: Mr Jarvis Garrett Head of Improvement & Efficiency, Perceval House, 14-16 Uxbridge Road, Ealing, London W5 2HL ☎ 020 8825 7893 ✉ garrettj@ealing.gov.uk

Legal: Ms Helen Harris, Director of Legal & Democratic Services, Perceval House, 14-16 Uxbridge Road, Ealing, London W5 2HL ☎ 020 8825 8615 ✉ harrish@ealing.gov.uk

Leisure and Cultural Services: Mr Chris Bunting Assistant Director of Leisure, Perceval House, 14-16 Uxbridge Road, Ealing, London W5 2HL ☎ 020 8825 6429 ✉ buntingc@ealing.gov.uk

Leisure and Cultural Services: Ms Carole Stewart Assistant Director of Arts, Heritage & Libraries, Perceval House, 14-16 Uxbridge Road, Ealing, London W5 2HL ☎ 020 8825 7216 ✉ stewartc@ealing.gov.uk

Licensing: Ms Loraine Abbott Regulatory Services Officer, Perceval House, 14-16 Uxbridge Road, Ealing, London W5 2HL ☎ 020 8825 6298 ✉ abbottl@ealing.gov.uk

Lifelong Learning: Ms Sharon Thomas Adult Learning Manager, Perceval House, 14-16 Uxbridge Road, Ealing, London W5 2HL ☎ 020 8825 5279 ✉ thomassh@ealing.gov.uk

Lottery Funding, Charity and Voluntary: Mr Nigel Fogg, Grants Unit Manager, Perceval House, 14-16 Uxbridge Road, Ealing, London W5 2HL ☎ 020 8825 7589 ✉ foggn@ealing.gov.uk

Member Services: Ms Helen Harris, Director of Legal & Democratic Services, Perceval House, 14-16 Uxbridge Road, Ealing, London W5 2HL ☎ 020 8825 8615 ✉ harrish@ealing.gov.uk

Member Services: Mr Ross Jackson Head of Elections & Members' Services, Perceval House, 14-16 Uxbridge Road, Ealing, London W5 2HL ☎ 020 8825 6854 ✉ jacksonr@ealing.gov.uk

Parking: Mr Barry Francis Assistant Director of Parking, Perceval House, 14-16 Uxbridge Road, Ealing, London W5 2HL ☎ 020 8825 6252 ✉ francisb@ealing.gov.uk

EALING

Partnerships: Mr Matthew Booth Director of Policy & Performance, Perceval House, 14-16 Uxbridge Road, Ealing, London W5 2HL ☎ 020 8825 8556 ✉ boothm@ealing.gov.uk

Personnel / HR: Mr David Veale Assistant Director of HR & Organisational Development, Perceval House, 14-16 Uxbridge Road, Ealing, London W5 2HL ☎ 020 8825 7359 ✉ vealed@ealing.gov.uk

Planning: Ms Aileen Jones Head of Planning Services, Perceval House, 14-16 Uxbridge Road, Ealing, London W5 2HL ☎ 020 8825 8371 🖷 020 8825 6610 ✉ jonesa@ealing.gov.uk

Procurement: Mrs Kate Graefe Head of Strategic Procurement, Perceval House, 14-16 Uxbridge Road, Ealing, London W5 2HL ☎ 020 8825 9843 ✉ graefek@ealing.gov.uk

Public Libraries: Ms Carole Stewart Assistant Director of Arts, Heritage & Libraries, Perceval House, 14-16 Uxbridge Road, Ealing, London W5 2HL ☎ 020 8825 7216 ✉ stewartc@ealing.gov.uk

Recycling & Waste Minimisation: Mr Earl McKenzie, Assistant Director of Street Services, Perceval House, 14-16 Uxbridge Road, Ealing, London W5 2LX ☎ 020 8825 5194 ✉ mckenzie@ealing.gov.uk

Regeneration: Ms Lucy Taylor Assistant Director of Regeneration & Planning Policy, Perceval House, 14-16 Uxbridge Road, Ealing, London W5 2HL ☎ 020 8825 9036 ✉ taylorl@ealing.gov.uk

Road Safety: Mr Shahid Iqbal, Assistant Director of Highways, Perceval House, 14-16 Uxbridge Road, Ealing, London W5 2HL ☎ 020 8825 7802 🖷 020 8825 5858 ✉ iqbalsp@ealing.gov.uk

Social Services (Adult): Mr Stephen Day, Director of Adult Services, Perceval House, 14-16 Uxbridge Road, Ealing, London W5 2HL ☎ 020 8825 6286 ✉ days@ealing.gov.uk

Social Services (Children): Ms Judith Finlay, Executive Director - Children, Adults & Public Health, Perceval House, 14-16 Uxbridge Road, Ealing, London W5 2HL ☎ 020 8825 7106 🖷 020 8825 6934 ✉ finlayj@ealing.gov.uk

Safeguarding: Ms Finola Culbert Assistant Director - Safeguarding & Support, Perceval House, 14-16 Uxbridge Road, Ealing, London W5 2HL ☎ 020 8825 5177 ✉ culbertl@ealing.gov.uk

Looked after Children: Ms Bridie McDonagh Looked after Children, Perceval House, 14-16 Uxbridge Road, Ealing, London W5 2HL ☎ 020 8825 6648 ✉ bmcdonagh@ealing.gov.uk

Public Health: Dr Jackie Chin Director - Public Health, Perceval House, 14-16 Uxbridge Road, Ealing, London W5 2HL ☎ 020 8825 6448 ✉ chinj@ealing.gov.uk

Staff Training: Ms Liz Chiles HR Business Partner, Perceval House, 14-16 Uxbridge Road, Ealing, London W5 2HL ☎ 020 8825 9345 ✉ chilesl@ealing.gov.uk

Sustainable Communities: Ms Joanne Mortensen Programme Manager, Perceval House, 14-16 Uxbridge Road, Ealing, London W5 2HL ☎ 020 8825 9183 ✉ mortensenj@ealing.gov.uk

Sustainable Development: Ms Joanne Mortensen Programme Manager, Perceval House, 14-16 Uxbridge Road, Ealing, London W5 2HL ☎ 020 8825 9183 ✉ mortensenj@ealing.gov.uk

Town Centre: Ms Lucy Taylor Assistant Director of Regeneration & Planning Policy, Perceval House, 14-16 Uxbridge Road, Ealing, London W5 2HL ☎ 020 8825 9036 ✉ taylorl@ealing.gov.uk

Traffic Management: Mr Shahid Iqbal, Assistant Director of Highways, Perceval House, 14-16 Uxbridge Road, Ealing, London W5 2HL ☎ 020 8825 7802 🖷 020 8825 5858 ✉ iqbalsp@ealing.gov.uk

Transport: Mr Francis Torto Transport Development Manager, Perceval House, 14-16 Uxbridge Road, Ealing, London W5 2HL ☎ 020 8825 7382 ✉ tortof@ealing.gov.uk

Transport Planner: Mr Nick O'Donnell Assistant Director of Strategic Transport, Perceval House, 14-16 Uxbridge Road, Ealing, London W5 2HL ☎ 020 8825 8078 ✉ odonnelln@ealing.gov.uk

Waste Management: Mr Earl McKenzie, Assistant Director of Street Services, Perceval House, 14-16 Uxbridge Road, Ealing, London W5 2LX ☎ 020 8825 5194 ✉ mckenzie@ealing.gov.uk

Children's Play Areas: Mr Jeff Parkinson Children's Services Manager, Perceval House, 14-16 Uxbridge Road, Ealing, London W5 2HL ☎ 020 8825 8267 🖷 020 8825 9417 ✉ jeff.parkinson@ealing.gov.uk

COUNCILLORS

***Mayor* Bagha**, Tej (LAB - Dormers Wells)
tej.bagha@ealing.gov.uk

***Deputy Mayor* Kaur Dheer**, Harbhajan (LAB - Greenford Broadway)
harbhajan.kaur@ealing.gov.uk

***Leader of the Council* Bell**, Julian (LAB - Greenford Broadway)
julian.bell@ealing.gov.uk

***Deputy Leader of the Council* Dheer**, Ranjit (LAB - Dormers Wells)
ranjit.dheer@ealing.gov.uk

Ahmed, Munir (LAB - Perivale)
munir.ahmed@ealing.gov.uk

Ahmed-Shaikh, Natasha (LAB - Northolt Mandeville)
natasha.ahmeddhaikh@ealing.gov.uk

Anand, Jasbir (LAB - Southall Green)
jasbir.anand@ealing.gov.uk

Aslam, Mohammad (LAB - Norwood Green)
mohammad.aslam@ealing.gov.uk

Ball, Jon (LD - Ealing Common)
jon.ball@ealing.gov.uk

Blacker, Josh (LAB - South Acton)
josh.blacker@ealing.gov.uk

Busuttil, Gary (LD - Southfield)
gary.busuttil@ealing.gov.uk

Byrne, Theresa (LAB - North Greenford)
theresa.byrne@ealing.gov.uk

Camadoo, Joanna (LAB - Elthorne)
joanna.camadoo@ealing.gov.uk

Cogan, Patrick (LAB - North Greenford)
patrick.cogan@ealing.gov.uk

Conlan, Paul (LAB - Walpole)
paul.conlan@ealing.gov.uk

Conti, Fabio (CON - Northfield)

Crawford, Daniel (LAB - Acton Central)
daniel.crawford@ealing.gov.uk

Crawford, Kate (LAB - East Acton)
katherine.crawford@ealing.gov.uk

Dabrowska, Joanna (CON - Ealing Common)
joanna.dabrowska@ealing.gov.uk

Dhami, Tejinder (LAB - Dormers Wells)
tejinder.dhami@ealing.gov.uk

Dhindsa, Kamaljit (LAB - Southall Green)
kamaljit.dhindsa@ealing.gov.uk

Gavan, Kieron (LAB - East Acton)
kieron.gavan@ealing.gov.uk

Gordon, Yoel (LAB - Elthorne)
yoel.gordon@ealing.gov.uk

Gulaid, Abdullah (LAB - Acton Central)
abdullah.gulaid@ealing.gov.uk

Hynes, Steve (LAB - Northolt Mandeville)
steve.hynes@ealing.gov.uk

Johnson, Yvonne (LAB - South Acton)
yvonne.johnson@ealing.gov.uk

Jones, Penny (LAB - Hobbayne)
penny.jones@ealing.gov.uk

Kang, Swarn (LAB - Southall Green)
swarn.kang@ealing.gov.uk

Kelly, Anthony (LAB - Greenford Green)
anthony.kelly@ealing.gov.uk

Khan, Sarfraz (LAB - Southall Broadway)
sarfraz.khan@ealing.gov.uk

Kohli, Sanjai (LAB - Southall Broadway)
sanjai.kohli@ealing.gov.uk

Kumar, Seema (CON - Ealing Broadway)
seema.kumar@ealing.gov.uk

Mahfouz, Bassam (LAB - Northolt West End)
bassam.mahfouz@ealing.gov.uk

Mahmood, Tariq (LAB - Perivale)
tariq.mahmood@ealing.gov.uk

Malcolm, Gary (LD - Southfield)
gary.malcolm@ealing.gov.uk

Mann, Rajinder (LAB - Norwood Green)
rajinder.mann@ealing.gov.uk

Mann, Gurmit (LAB - Norwood Green)
gurmit.mann@ealing.gov.uk

Manro, Shital (LAB - North Greenford)
shital.manro@ealing.gov.uk

Martin, Dee (LAB - Northolt West End)
dee.martin@ealing.gov.uk

Mason, Peter (LAB - Elthorne)
peter.mason@ealing.gov.uk

McCartan, Ciaran (LAB - Hobbayne)
ciaran.mccartan@ealing.gov.uk

Midha, Mohinder (LAB - Lady Margaret)
mohinder.midha@ealing.gov.uk

Millican, David (CON - Northfield)
david.millican@ealing.gov.uk

Mohan, Karam (LAB - Lady Margaret)
karam.mohan@ealing.gov.uk

Morrissey, Joy (CON - Hanger Hill)
morrisseyj@ealing.gov.uk

Mullins, Theresa (CON - Northfield)
theresa.mullins@ealing.gov.uk

Murray, Lynne (LAB - Cleveland)
lynne.murray@ealing.gov.uk

Murtagh, Timothy (LAB - Greenford Broadway)
tim.murtagh@ealing.gov.uk

Nagpal, Kamaljit (LAB - Southall Broadway)
kamaljit.nagpal@ealing.gov.uk

Padda, Swaran (LAB - Lady Margaret)
swaran.padda@ealing.gov.uk

Proud, Ian (CON - Cleveland)
ian.proud@ealing.gov.uk

Rai, Binda (LAB - Walpole)
binda.rai@ealing.gov.uk

Raza, Aysha (LAB - Greenford Green)
aysha.raza@ealing.gov.uk

Reece, Roz (CON - Ealing Common)
roz.reece@ealing.gov.uk

Rodgers, David (LAB - Cleveland)
david.rodgers@ealing.gov.uk

Sabiers, Mik (LAB - South Acton)
mik.sabiers@ealing.gov.uk

Sharma, Charan (LAB - Perivale)
charan.sharma@ealing.gov.uk

Shaw, Gareth (LAB - Walpole)
gareth.shaw@ealing.gov.uk

Stafford, Gregory (CON - Hanger Hill)
gregory.stafford@ealing.gov.uk

Stafford, Alexander (CON - Ealing Broadway)
alex.stafford@ealing.gov.uk

Steed, Andrew (LD - Southfield)
andrew.steed@ealing.gov.uk

Summers, Chris (LAB - Northolt Mandeville)
chris.summers@ealing.gov.uk

Sumner, Nigel (CON - Hanger Hill)
nigel.sumner@ealing.gov.uk

Tailor, Hitesh (LAB - East Acton)
hitesh.tailor@ealing.gov.uk

Walker, Patricia (LAB - Acton Central)
patricia.walker@ealing.gov.uk

Wall, Lauren (LAB - Northolt West End)
lauren.wall@ealing.gov.uk

Wall, Ray (LAB - Hobbayne)
ray.wall@ealing.gov.uk

Woodroofe, Simon (LAB - Greenford Green)
simon.woodroofe@ealing.gov.uk

Young, Anthony (CON - Ealing Broadway)
anthony.young@ealing.gov.uk

POLITICAL COMPOSITION
LAB: 53, CON: 12, LD: 4

COMMITTEE CHAIRS
Audit: Mr Timothy Murtagh

Licensing: Ms Kate Crawford

Planning: Mr Karam Mohan

East Ayrshire S

East Ayrshire Council, Council Headquarters, London Road, Kilmarnock KA3 7BU
☎ 01563 576000 🖷 01563 576500 the.council@east-ayrshire.gov.uk
www.east-ayrshire.gov.uk

FACTS AND FIGURES
Parliamentary Constituencies: Ayr, Carrick and Cumnock, Kilmarnock and Loudoun
EU Constituencies: Scotland
Election Frequency: Elections are of whole council

PRINCIPAL OFFICERS
Chief Executive: Ms Fiona Lees, Chief Executive, Council Headquarters, London Road, Kilmarnock KA3 7BU ☎ 01563 576019 🖷 01563 576200 fiona.lees@east-ayrshire.gov.uk

Deputy Chief Executive: Mr Alex McPhee, Depute Chief Executive - Economy & Skills, Council Headquarters, London Road, Kilmarnock KA3 7BU ☎ 01563 576279 alex.mcphee@east-ayrshire.gov.uk

Assistant Chief Executive: Mr Chris McAleavey, Acting Depute Chief Executive - Safer Communities, Council Headquarters, London Road, Kilmarnock KA3 7BU ☎ 01563 576076 chris.mcaleavey@east-ayrshire.gov.uk

Architect, Building / Property Services: Mr Andrew Kennedy Head of Facilities & Property Management, Council Headquarters, London Road, Kilmarnock KA3 7BU ☎ 01563 576089 andrew.kennedy@east-ayrshire.gov.uk

Best Value: Ms Gwen Barker, Policy, Planning & Performance Manager, Council Headquarters, London Road, Kilmarnock KA3 7BU ☎ 01563 554602 gwen.barker@east-ayrshire.gov.uk

Building Control: Mr David McDowall, Building Standards & Development Manager, The Johnnie Walker Bond, 15 Strand Street, Kilmarnock KA1 1HU ☎ 01563 576767 david.mcdowall@east-ayrshire.gov.uk

Catering Services: Mr Andrew Kennedy Head of Facilities & Property Management, Council Headquarters, London Road, Kilmarnock KA3 7BU ☎ 01563 576089 andrew.kennedy@east-ayrshire.gov.uk

Children / Youth Services: Ms Kay Gilmour Head of Community Support, Council Headquarters, London Road, Kilmarnock KA3 7BU ☎ 01563 576104 kay.gilmour@east-ayrshire.gov.uk

Civil Registration: Ms Catherine Dunlop, Senior Registrar, Burns Monument Centre, Kay Park, Kilmarnock KA3 7RU ☎ 01563 576692 catherine.dunlop@east-ayrshire.gov.uk

PR / Communications: Ms Lynne Buchanan Communications Manager, Council Headquarters, London Road, Kilmarnock KA3 7BU ☎ 01563 576520 lynne.buchanan@east-ayrshire.gov.uk

Community Planning: Ms Gwen Barker, Policy, Planning & Performance Manager, Council Headquarters, London Road, Kilmarnock KA3 7BU ☎ 01563 554602 gwen.barker@east-ayrshire.gov.uk

Community Safety: Mr Gerry Darroch Acting Head of Housing & Communities, Council Headquarters, London Road, Kilmarnock KA3 7BU ☎ 01563 576291 gerry.darroch@east-ayrshire.gov.uk

Computer Management: Mr Craig McArthur Head of Finance Service, Council Headquarters, London Road, Kilmarnock KA3 7BU ☎ 01563 576513 craig.mcarthur@east-ayrshire.gov.uk

Consumer Protection and Trading Standards: Mr Paul Todd Regulatory Services Manager, Civic Centre South, John Dickie Street, Kilmarnock KA1 1HW ☎ 01563 576913 paul.todd@east-ayrshire.gov.uk

Contracts: Mr Stuart McCall Legal Services Manager, Council Headquarters, London Road, Kilmarnock KA3 7BU ☎ 01563 576085 stuart.mccall@east-ayrshire.gov.uk

Corporate Services: Mr Bill Walkinshaw Head of Democratic Services, Council Headquarters, London Road, Kilmarnock KA3 7BU ☎ 01563 576135 bill.walkinshaw@east-ayrshire.gov.uk

Direct Labour: Mr Derek Spence Housing Asset Services Manager, Burnside Street, Kilmarnock, KA1 4EX ☎ 01563 555501 derek.spence@east-ayrshire.gov.uk

Economic Development: Mr Michael Keane Head of Planning & Economic Development, The Johnnie Walker Bond, 15 Strand Street, Kilmarnock KA1 1HU ☎ 01563 576767 michael.keane@eastayrshire.gov.uk

Education: Mr Alan Ward Head of Education, Council Headquarters, London Road, Kilmarnock KA3 7BU ☎ 01563 576126 alan.ward@east-ayrshire.gov.uk

E-Government: Mr Roy Hair Systems & Performance Manager, Opera House, John Finnie Street, Kilmarnock KA1 1DD ☎ 01563 576817 roy.hair@east-ayrshire.gov.uk

E-Government: Mr Craig McArthur Head of Finance Service, Council Headquarters, London Road, Kilmarnock KA3 7BU ☎ 01563 576513 craig.mcarthur@east-ayrshire.gov.uk

Electoral Registration: Ms Julie McGarry Administration Manager, Council Headquarters, London Road, Kilmarnock KA3 7BU ☎ 01563 576147 ✉ julie.mcgarry@east-ayrshire.gov.uk

Emergency Planning: Ms Lesley Jeffrey Civil Contingencies Officer, Building 372, Alpha Freight Area, Robertson Road, Glasgow Prestwick International Airport, Prestwick KA9 2PL ☎ 01292 692185 ✉ acct@south-ayrshire.gov.uk

Energy Management: Mrs Sarah Farrell Energy Adviser, 2 The Cross, Kilmarnock KA1 1LR ☎ 01563 555224 ✉ sarah.farrell@east-ayrshire.gov.uk

Environmental / Technical Services: Mr Gerry Darroch Acting Head of Housing & Communities, Council Headquarters, London Road, Kilmarnock KA3 7BU ☎ 01563 576291 ✉ gerry.darroch@east-ayrshire.gov.uk

Environmental Health: Mr David Mitchell, Chief Governance Officer, Council Headquarters, London Road, Kilmarnock KA3 7BU ☎ 01563 576061 🖷 01563 576179 ✉ david.mitchell@east-ayrshire.gov.uk

Finance: Mr Alex McPhee, Depute Chief Executive - Economy & Skills, Council Headquarters, London Road, Kilmarnock KA3 7BU ☎ 01563 576279 ✉ alex.mcphee@east-ayrshire.gov.uk

Fleet Management: Mr George Fiddes Team Leader - Traffic & Transportation, Transport Unit, 34 Main Road, Crookedholm, Kilmarnock KA3 6JS ☎ 01563 576443 ✉ george.fiddes@ayrshireroadsalliance.org

Grounds Maintenance: Mr Robert McCulloch, Outdoor Amenities Manager, Outdoor Amenities, Western Road Depot, Kilmarnock KA3 1LL ☎ 01563 554066 ✉ robert.mcculloch@east-ayrshire.gov.uk

Health and Safety: Mr David Doran Health & Safety Manager, Council Headquarters, London Road, Kilmarnock KA3 7BU ☎ 01563 576095 ✉ david.doran@east-ayrshire.gov.uk

Highways: Mr Stewart Turner Head of Roads - Ayrshire Roads Alliance, The Johnnie Walker Bond, 15 Strand Street, Kilmarnock KA1 1HU ☎ 01563 503164 ✉ stewart.turner@ayrshireroadsalliance.org

Housing: Mr Gerry Darroch Acting Head of Housing & Communities, Council Headquarters, London Road, Kilmarnock KA3 7BU ☎ 01563 576291 ✉ gerry.darroch@east-ayrshire.gov.uk

Housing: Mr Chris McAleavey, Acting Depute Chief Executive - Safer Communities, Council Headquarters, London Road, Kilmarnock KA3 7BU ☎ 01563 576076 ✉ chris.mcaleavey@east-ayrshire.gov.uk

Housing Maintenance: Mr Gerry Darroch Acting Head of Housing & Communities, Council Headquarters, London Road, Kilmarnock KA3 7BU ☎ 01563 576291 ✉ gerry.darroch@east-ayrshire.gov.uk

Legal: Mr David Mitchell, Chief Governance Officer, Council Headquarters, London Road, Kilmarnock KA3 7BU ☎ 01563 576061 🖷 01563 576179 ✉ david.mitchell@east-ayrshire.gov.uk

Leisure and Cultural Services: Mr John Griffiths, Chief Executive - East Ayrshire Leisure, The Palace Theatre, 9 Green Street, Kilmarnock KA1 3BN ☎ 01563 554710 🖷 01563 554730 ✉ john.griffiths@east-ayrshire.gov.uk

Licensing: Mr David Mitchell, Chief Governance Officer, Council Headquarters, London Road, Kilmarnock KA3 7BU ☎ 01563 576061 🖷 01563 576179 ✉ david.mitchell@east-ayrshire.gov.uk

Lighting: Mr Stewart Turner Head of Roads - Ayrshire Roads Alliance, The Johnnie Walker Bond, 15 Strand Street, Kilmarnock KA1 1HU ☎ 01563 503164 ✉ stewart.turner@ayrshireroadsalliance.org

Member Services: Mr Bill Walkinshaw, Head of Democratic Services, Council Headquarters, London Road, Kilmarnock KA3 7BU ☎ 01563 576135 🖷 01563 576245 ✉ bill.walkinshaw@east-ayrshire.gov.uk

Parking: Mr Stewart Turner Head of Roads - Ayrshire Roads Alliance, The Johnnie Walker Bond, 15 Strand Street, Kilmarnock KA1 1HU ☎ 01563 503164 ✉ stewart.turner@ayrshireroadsalliance.org

Partnerships: Ms Gwen Barker, Policy, Planning & Performance Manager, Council Headquarters, London Road, Kilmarnock KA3 7BU ☎ 01563 554602 ✉ gwen.barker@east-ayrshire.gov.uk

Personnel / HR: Mr Chris McAleavey, Acting Depute Chief Executive - Safer Communities, Council Headq uarters, London Road, Kilmarnock KA3 7BU ☎ 01563 576076 ✉ chris.mcaleavey@east-ayrshire.gov.uk

Personnel / HR: Mr Martin Rose, Head of Human Resources, Council Headquarters, London Road, Kilmarnock KA3 7BU ☎ 01563 576092 ✉ martin.rose@east-ayrshire.gov.uk

Planning: Mr Michael Keane Head of Planning & Economic Development, The Johnnie Walker Bond, 15 Strand Street, Kilmarnock KA1 1HU ☎ 01563 576767 ✉ michael.keane@eastayrshire.gov.uk

Planning: Mr Alex McPhee, Depute Chief Executive - Economy & Skills, Council Headquarters, London Road, Kilmarnock KA3 7BU ☎ 01563 576279 ✉ alex.mcphee@east-ayrshire.gov.uk

Procurement: Ms Lesley McLean Procurement Manager, Council Headquarters, London Road, Kilmarnock KA3 7BU ☎ 01563 576186 ✉ lesley.mclean@east-ayrshire.gov.uk

Public Libraries: Mr John Griffiths, Chief Executive - East Ayrshire Leisure, The Palace Theatre, 9 Green Street, Kilmarnock KA1 3BN ☎ 01563 554710 🖷 01563 554730 ✉ john.griffiths@east-ayrshire.gov.uk

Recycling & Waste Minimisation: Mr Gerry Darroch Acting Head of Housing & Communities, Council Headquarters, London Road, Kilmarnock KA3 7BU ☎ 01563 576291 ✉ gerry.darroch@east-ayrshire.gov.uk

EAST AYRSHIRE

Regeneration: Mr Michael Keane Head of Planning & Economic Development, The Johnnie Walker Bond, 15 Strand Street, Kilmarnock KA1 1HU ☎ 01563 576767 ✉ michael.keane@eastayrshire.gov.uk

Road Safety: Mr Jim Melville Road Safety Officer, The Johnnie Walker Bond, 15 Strand Street, Kilmarnock KA3 1HU ☎ 01563 503132 ✉ jim.melville@east-ayrshire.gov.uk

Social Services: Mr Eddie Fraser Director of Health & Social Care Partnership, Council Headquarters, London Road, Kilmarnock KA3 7BU ☎ 01563 576546 ✉ eddie.fraser@east-ayrshire.gov.uk

Social Services: Ms Pamela Milliken Head of Primary Care & Out of Hours Community Response Services, Council Headquarters, London Road, Kilmarnock KA3 7BU ☎ 01563 576020 ✉ pamela.milliken@east-ayrshire.gov.uk

Social Services (Adult): Ms Annemargaret Black Head of Community Health & Care Services, Council Headquarters, London Road, Kilmarnock KA3 7BU ☎ 01563 576090 ✉ annemargaret.black@east-ayrshire.gov.uk

Social Services (Children): Ms Susan Taylor Head of Children's Health, Care & Justice, Council Headquarters, London Road, Kilmarnock KA3 7BU ☎ 01563 576920 ✉ susan.taylor@east-ayrshire.gov.uk

Staff Training: Ms Ailie Macpherson Organisational Development Manager, Greenholm Street, Kilmarnock KA1 4DJ ☎ 01563 503441 ✉ allie.macpherson@east-ayrshire.gov.uk

Street Scene: Mr Stewart Turner Head of Roads - Ayrshire Roads Alliance, The Johnnie Walker Bond, 15 Strand Street, Kilmarnock KA1 1HU ☎ 01563 503164 ✉ stewart.turner@ayrshireroadsalliance.org

Sustainable Development: Mr Michael Keane Head of Planning & Economic Development, The Johnnie Walker Bond, 15 Strand Street, Kilmarnock KA1 1HU ☎ 01563 576767 ✉ michael.keane@eastayrshire.gov.uk

Town Centre: Ms Fiona Nicolson Town Centre Manager - Kilmarnock & Cumnock, CARS Office, 34 John Finnie Street, Kilmarnock KA1 1DD ☎ 01563 503014 ✉ fiona.nicolson@east-ayrshire.gov.uk

Traffic Management: Mr Stewart Turner Head of Roads - Ayrshire Roads Alliance, The Johnnie Walker Bond, 15 Strand Street, Kilmarnock KA1 1HU ☎ 01563 503164 ✉ stewart.turner@ayrshireroadsalliance.org

Transport Planner: Mr Stewart Turner Head of Roads - Ayrshire Roads Alliance, The Johnnie Walker Bond, 15 Strand Street, Kilmarnock KA1 1HU ☎ 01563 503164 ✉ stewart.turner@ayrshireroadsalliance.org

Waste Collection and Disposal: Mr Gerry Darroch Acting Head of Housing & Communities, Council Headquarters, London Road, Kilmarnock KA3 7BU ☎ 01563 576291 ✉ gerry.darroch@east-ayrshire.gov.uk

Waste Management: Mr Gerry Darroch Acting Head of Housing & Communities, Council Headquarters, London Road, Kilmarnock KA3 7BU ☎ 01563 576291 ✉ gerry.darroch@east-ayrshire.gov.uk

COUNCILLORS

***Provost* Todd**, Jim (SNP - Kilmarnock South)
jim.todd@east-ayrshire.gov.uk

***Deputy Provost* Campbell**, John (SNP - Kilmarnock East & Hurlford)
john.campbell@east-ayrshire.gov.uk

***Leader of the Council* Reid**, Douglas (SNP - Kilmarnock West & Crosshouse)
douglas.reid@east-ayrshire.gov.uk

***Deputy Leader of the Council* Cook**, Tom (CON - Kilmarnock West & Crosshouse)
tom.cook@east-ayrshire.gov.uk

Bell, John (SNP - Doon Valley)
john.bell@east-ayrshire.gov.uk

Brown, Alan (SNP - Irvine Valley)
alan.brown@east-ayrshire.gov.uk

Buchanan, Jim (SNP - Kilmarnock East & Hurlford)
jim.buchanan@east-ayrshire.gov.uk

Coffey, Helen (SNP - Kilmarnock North)
helen.coffey@east-ayrshire.gov.uk

Cowan, Elaine (SNP - Kilmarnock North)
elaine.cowan@east-ayrshire.gov.uk

Crawford, William (LAB - Cumnock & New Cumnock)
william.crawford@east-ayrshire.gov.uk

Cree, Gordon (LAB - Kilmarnock East & Hurlford)
gordon.cree@east-ayrshire.gov.uk

Dinwoodie, Elaine (LAB - Doon Valley)
elaine.dinwoodie@east-ayrshire.gov.uk

Freel, Ellen (IND - Annick)
ellen.freel2@east-ayrshire.gov.uk

Jones, Lillian (LAB - Kilmarnock West & Crosshouse)
lillian.jones@east-ayrshire.gov.uk

Knapp, John (LAB - Kilmarnock South)
john.knapp@east-ayrshire.gov.uk

Linton, Iain (SNP - Kilmarnock West & Crosshouse)
iain.linton@east-ayrshire.gov.uk

MacColl, Eoghann (SNP - Annick)
eoghann.maccoll@east-ayrshire.gov.uk

Mair, George (LAB - Irvine Valley)
george.mair@east-ayrshire.gov.uk

McDill, Bobby (SNP - Irvine Valley)
robert.mcdill@east-ayrshire.gov.uk

McFadzean, John (CON - Irvine Valley)
john.mcfadzean@east-ayrshire.gov.uk

McGhee, John (LAB - Annick)
john.mcghee@east-ayrshire.gov.uk

McGhee, Neil (LAB - Ballochmyle)
neil.mcghee@east-ayrshire.gov.uk

McIntyre, Drew (LAB - Kilmarnock East & Hurlford)
andrew.mcintyre@east-ayrshire.gov.uk

McKay, Maureen (LAB - Kilmarnock North)
maureen.mckay@east-ayrshire.gov.uk

Menzies, William (LAB - Cumnock & New Cumnock)
william.menzies@east-ayrshire.gov.uk

Morrice, Kathy (SNP - Cumnock & New Cumnock)
kathy.morrice@east-ayrshire.gov.uk

Pirie, Moira (LAB - Doon Valley)
moira.pirie@east-ayrshire.gov.uk

Primrose, Stephanie (SNP - Ballochmyle)
stephanie.primrose@east-ayrshire.gov.uk

Roberts, Jim (SNP - Ballochmyle)
jim.roberts@east-ayrshire.gov.uk

Ross, Eric (LAB - Cumnock & New Cumnock)
eric.ross@east-ayrshire.gov.uk

Ross, Hugh (SNP - Kilmarnock South)
hugh.ross@east-ayrshire.gov.uk

Shaw, David (LAB - Ballochmyle)
david.shaw@east-ayrshire.gov.uk

POLITICAL COMPOSITION
SNP: 15, LAB: 14, CON: 2, IND: 1

COMMITTEE CHAIRS

Licensing: Mr Tom Cook

Planning: Mr Jim Roberts

East Cambridgeshire D

East Cambridgeshire District Council, The Grange, Nutholt Lane, Ely CB7 4EE
☎ 01353 665555 🖷 01353 665240 ✉ info@eastcambs.gov.uk
🖳 www.eastcambs.gov.uk

FACTS AND FIGURES
Parliamentary Constituencies: Cambridgeshire South East
EU Constituencies: Eastern
Election Frequency: Elections are of whole council

PRINCIPAL OFFICERS

Chief Executive: Mr John Hill, Chief Executive, The Grange, Nutholt Lane, Ely CB7 4EE ☎ 01353 616274 🖷 01353 616326 ✉ john.hill@eastcambs.gov.uk

Senior Management: Ms Jo Brooks Director - Regulatory Services, The Grange, Nutholt Lane, Ely CB7 4EE ☎ 01353 616498 ✉ jo.brooks@eastcambs.gov.uk

Senior Management: Mr Richard Quayle Director - Support Services, The Grange, Nutholt Lane, Ely CB7 4EE ☎ 01353 616303 ✉ richard.quayle@eastcambs.gov.uk

Access Officer / Social Services (Disability): Mr Rob Fysh Team Leader - Building Control, The Grange, Nutholt Lane, Ely CB7 4EE ✉ rob.fysh@eastcambs.gov.uk

Building Control: Mr Rob Fysh Team Leader - Building Control, The Grange, Nutholt Lane, Ely CB7 4EE ✉ rob.fysh@eastcambs.gov.uk

PR / Communications: Mr Tony Taylorson, Communications & Media Manager, The Grange, Nutholt Lane, Ely CB7 4EE ☎ 01353 665555 🖷 01353 665240 ✉ tony.taylorson@eastcambs.gov.uk

Community Planning: Ms Allison Conder Principal Community & Leisure Service Manager, The Grange, Nutholt Lane, Ely CB7 4EE ☎ 01353 616374 🖷 01353 665240 ✉ allison.conder@eastcambs.gov.uk

Community Safety: Ms Allison Conder Principal Community & Leisure Service Manager, The Grange, Nutholt Lane, Ely CB7 4EE ☎ 01353 616374 🖷 01353 665240 ✉ allison.conder@eastcambs.gov.uk

Computer Management: Mr Mark Chadwick Principal ICT Officer (Support & Information Security), The Grange, Nutholt Lane, Ely CB7 4EE ☎ 01353 616216 🖷 01353 665240 ✉ mark.chadwick@eastcambs.gov.uk

Customer Service: Mrs Annette Wade Customer Services Manager, The Grange, Nutholt Lane, Ely CB7 4EE ☎ 01353 616310 🖷 01353 665240 ✉ annette.wade@eastcambs.gov.uk

Direct Labour: Mr Spencer Clark Senior Open Spaces & Maintenance Officer, The Grange, Nutholt Lane, Ely CB7 4EE ☎ 01353 612553 🖷 01353 665240 ✉ spencer.clark@eastcambs.gov.uk

Economic Development: Mr Darren Hill Business Development Manager, The Grange, Nutholt Lane, Ely CB7 4EE ☎ 01353 616450 🖷 01353 665240 ✉ darren.hill@eastcambs.gov.uk

E-Government: Mr Mark Chadwick Principal ICT Officer (Support & Information Security), The Grange, Nutholt Lane, Ely CB7 4EE ☎ 01353 616216 🖷 01353 665240 ✉ mark.chadwick@eastcambs.gov.uk

Electoral Registration: Mrs Joan Cox Electoral Services Officer, The Grange, Nutholt Lane, Ely CB7 4EE ☎ 01353 616460 🖷 01353 665240 ✉ joan.cox@eastcambs.gov.uk

Emergency Planning: Mr John Hill, Chief Executive, The Grange, Nutholt Lane, Ely CB7 4EE ☎ 01353 616274 🖷 01353 616326 ✉ john.hill@eastcambs.gov.uk

Energy Management: Mrs Liz Knox, Environmental Services Manager, The Grange, Nutholt Lane, Ely CB7 4EE ☎ 01353 616313 ✉ liz.knox@eastcambs.gov.uk

Environmental Health: Mrs Liz Knox, Environmental Services Manager, The Grange, Nutholt Lane, Ely CB7 4EE ☎ 01353 616313 ✉ liz.knox@eastcambs.gov.uk

European Liaison: Mr Darren Hill Business Development Manager, The Grange, Nutholt Lane, Ely CB7 4EE ☎ 01353 616450 🖷 01353 665240 ✉ darren.hill@eastcambs.gov.uk

Events Manager: Mrs Tracey Harding, Team Leader - Tourism & Town Centre Services, The Grange, Nutholt Lane, Ely CB7 4EE ☎ 01363 665555 🖷 01353 665240 ✉ tracey.harding@eastcambs.gov.uk

EAST CAMBRIDGESHIRE

Facilities: Mrs Kathy Batey, HR & Facilities Services Manager, The Grange, Nutholt Lane, Ely CB7 4EE ☎ 01353 665555 🖷 01353 665240 🖱 kathy.batey@eastcambs.gov.uk

Finance: Mrs Linda Grinnell Financial Services Manager, The Grange, Nutholt Lane, Ely CB7 4EE ☎ 01353 665555 🖱 linda.grinnell@eastcambs.gov.uk

Grounds Maintenance: Mr Spencer Clark Senior Open Spaces & Maintenance Officer, The Grange, Nutholt Lane, Ely CB7 4EE ☎ 01353 612553 🖷 01353 665240 🖱 spencer.clark@eastcambs.gov.uk

Health and Safety: Mr David Vincent Health & Safety Officer, The Grange, Nutholt Lane, Ely CB7 4EE ☎ 01353 616239 🖱 david.vincent@eastcambs.gov.uk

Home Energy Conservation: Mrs Liz Knox, Environmental Services Manager, The Grange, Nutholt Lane, Ely CB7 4EE ☎ 01353 616313 🖱 liz.knox@eastcambs.gov.uk

Housing: Ms Jo Brooks Director - Regulatory Services, The Grange, Nutholt Lane, Ely CB7 4EE ☎ 01353 616498 🖱 jo.brooks@eastcambs.gov.uk

Legal: Ms Amanda Apcar Principal Solicitor, The Grange, Nutholt Lane, Ely CB7 4EE ☎ 01353 616347 🖷 01353 668803 🖱 amanda.apcar@eastcambs.gov.uk

Leisure and Cultural Services: Ms Allison Conder Principal Community & Leisure Service Manager, The Grange, Nutholt Lane, Ely CB7 4EE ☎ 01353 616374 🖷 01353 665240 🖱 allison.conder@eastcambs.gov.uk

Licensing: Mrs Liz Knox, Environmental Services Manager, The Grange, Nutholt Lane, Ely CB7 4EE ☎ 01353 616313 🖱 liz.knox@eastcambs.gov.uk

Member Services: Mrs Tracy Couper Principal Democratic Services Officer, The Grange, Nutholt Lane, Ely CB7 4EE ☎ 01353 616278 🖷 01353 665240 🖱 tracy.couper@eastcambs.gov.uk

Parking: Mrs Tracey Harding, Team Leader - Tourism & Town Centre Services, The Grange, Nutholt Lane, Ely CB7 4EE ☎ 01363 665555 🖷 01353 665240 🖱 tracey.harding@eastcambs.gov.uk

Personnel / HR: Mrs Kathy Batey, HR & Facilities Services Manager, The Grange, Nutholt Lane, Ely CB7 4EE ☎ 01353 665555 🖷 01353 665240 🖱 kathy.batey@eastcambs.gov.uk

Planning: Ms Sue Wheatley Planning Manager, The Grange, Nutholt Lane, Ely CB7 4EE ☎ 01353 665555 🖷 01353 665240 🖱 sue.wheatley@eastcambs.gov.uk

Recycling & Waste Minimisation: Mr Dave White Waste Strategy Team Leader, The Grange, Nutholt Lane, Ely CB7 4EE ☎ 01353 616232 🖱 dave.white@eastcambs.gov.uk

Staff Training: Mrs Kathy Batey, HR & Facilities Services Manager, The Grange, Nutholt Lane, Ely CB7 4EE ☎ 01353 665555 🖷 01353 665240 🖱 kathy.batey@eastcambs.gov.uk

Tourism: Mrs Tracey Harding, Team Leader - Tourism & Town Centre Services, The Grange, Nutholt Lane, Ely CB7 4EE ☎ 01363 665555 🖷 01353 665240 🖱 tracey.harding@eastcambs.gov.uk

Town Centre: Mrs Tracey Harding, Team Leader - Tourism & Town Centre Services, The Grange, Nutholt Lane, Ely CB7 4EE ☎ 01363 665555 🖷 01353 665240 🖱 tracey.harding@eastcambs.gov.uk

Waste Collection and Disposal: Mr Dave White Waste Strategy Team Leader, The Grange, Nutholt Lane, Ely CB7 4EE ☎ 01353 616232 🖱 dave.white@eastcambs.gov.uk

Waste Management: Mr Dave White Waste Strategy Team Leader, The Grange, Nutholt Lane, Ely CB7 4EE ☎ 01353 616232 🖱 dave.white@eastcambs.gov.uk

Children's Play Areas: Mr Spencer Clark Senior Open Spaces & Maintenance Officer, The Grange, Nutholt Lane, Ely CB7 4EE ☎ 01353 612553 🖷 01353 665240 🖱 spencer.clark@eastcambs.gov.uk

COUNCILLORS

***Chair* Allen**, Michael (CON - Burwell)
michael.allen@eastcambs.gov.uk

***Vice-Chair* Creesswell**, Peter (CON - Cheveley)
peter.cresswell@eastcambs.gov.uk

***Leader of the Council* Palmer**, James (CON - Soham North)

***Deputy Leader of the Council* Roberts**, Charles (CON - Stretham)
charles.roberts@eastcambs.gov.uk

Alderson, Allen (CON - Swaffhams)

Ambrose-Smith, Christine (CON - Littleport West)
christine.ambrose-smith@eastcambs.gov.uk

Ambrose-Smith, David (CON - Littleport East)
david.ambrose-smith@eastcambs.gov.uk

Austen, Sue (LD - Ely West)
sue.austen@eastcambs.gov.uk

Bailey, Anna (CON - Downham Villages)
anna.bailey@eastcambs.gov.uk

Beckett, Derrick (IND - Isleham)
derrick.beckett@eastcambs.gov.uk

Bovingdon, Ian (CON - Soham South)
ian.bovingdon@eastcambs.gov.uk

Bradley, Mike (CON - Downham Vilages)
mike.bradley@eastcambs.gov.uk

Brown, David (CON - Burwell)
david.brown@eastcambs.gov.uk

Campbell, Vince (CON - Bottisham)
vince.campbell@eastcambs.gov.uk

Chaplin, David (CON - Bottisham)
david.chaplin@eastcambs.gov.uk

Cheetham, Steve (CON - Haddenham)
steve.cheetham@eastcambs.gov.uk

Cox, Paul (CON - Littleport West)
paul.cox@eastcambs.gov.uk

Dupre, Lorna (LD - Sutton)

Edwards, Lavinia (CON - Burwell)
lavinia.edwards@eastcambs.gov.uk

Every, Lis (CAP - Ely East)

Green, Coralie (CON - Ely South)
coralie.green@eastcambs.gov.uk

Griffin-Singh, Elaine (CON - Ely North)
elaine.griffin-singh@eastcambs.gov.uk

Hitchin, Neil (CON - Ely West)
neil.hitchin@eastcambs.gov.uk

Hobbs, Richard (CON - Ely East)
richard.hobbs@eastcambs.gov.uk

Huffer, Julia (CON - Fordham Villages)
julia.huffer@eastcambs.gov.uk

Hugo, Mark (CON - Haddenham)
mark.hugo@eastcambs.gov.uk

Hunt, Bill (CON - Stretham)
bill.hunt@eastcambs.gov.uk

Hunt, Tom (CON - Ely South)
tom.hunt@eastcambs.gov.uk

Morris, Chris (CON - Dullingham Villages)
chris.morris@eastcambs.gov.uk

Pearson, Andrew (CON - Ely North)
andrew.pearson@eastcambs.gov.uk

Ross, Hamish (CON - Soham South)

Rouse, Mike (CON - Ely North)
mike.rouse@eastcambs.gov.uk

Schuman, Dan (CON - Soham South)
dan.shcuman@eastcambs.gov.uk

Schumann, Joshua (CON - Fordham Villages)
joshua.schumann@eastcambs.gov.uk

Sennitt, Carol (CON - SohaM North)
carol.sennitt@eastcambs.gov.uk

Shuter, Mathew (CON - Cheveley)
Mathew.shuter@eastcambs.gov.uk

Smith, Stuart (CON - Haddenham)
stuart.smith@eastcambs.gov.uk

Stubbs, Lisa (CON - Sutton)

Webber, Jo (CON - Littleport East)
jo.webber@eastcambs.gov.uk

POLITICAL COMPOSITION

CON: 35, LD: 2, CAP: 1, IND: 1

COMMITTEE CHAIRS

Development: Mr Bill Hunt

Licensing: Mrs Elaine Griffin-Singh

Planning: Mr Joshua Schumann

East Devon — D

East Devon District Council, Council Offices, Knowle, Sidmouth EX10 8HL
☎ 01395 516551 🖷 01395 517507 ✉ info@eastdevon.gov.uk
💻 www.eastdevon.gov.uk

FACTS AND FIGURES

EU Constituencies: South West

Election Frequency: Elections are of whole council

PRINCIPAL OFFICERS

Chief Executive: Mr Mark Williams Chief Executive, South Somerset & East Devon District Councils, Council Offices, Knowle, Sidmouth EX10 8HL ☎ 01395 571695 🖷 01395 517507 ✉ mwilliams@eastdevon.gov.uk

Deputy Chief Executive: Mr Richard Cohen Deputy Chief Executive of Development, Regeneration & Partnerships, Council Offices, Knowle, Sidmouth EX10 8HL ☎ 01395 571552 🖷 01395 517507 ✉ rcohen@eastdevon.gov.uk

Senior Management: Mr Simon Davey Strategic Lead - Finance, Council Offices, Knowle, Sidmouth EX10 8HL ☎ 01395 517490 ✉ sdavey@eastdevon.gov.uk

Senior Management: Mr John Golding, Strategic Lead - Housing & Environment, Council Offices, Knowle, Sidmouth EX10 8HL ☎ 01395 517567 🖷 01395 517508 ✉ jgolding@eastdevon.gov.uk

Senior Management: Mr Henry Gordon Lennox Strategic Lead - Legal, Democratic Services, Licensing & Monitoring Officer, Council Offices, Knowle, Sidmouth EX10 8HL ☎ 01395 517401 ✉ hgordonlennox@eastdevon.gov.uk

Senior Management: Ms Karen Jenkins, Strategic Lead - Organisational Development & Transformation, Council Offices, Knowle, Sidmouth EX10 8HL ☎ 01395 516551 🖷 01395 5175057 ✉ kjenkin@eastdevon.gov.uk

Architect, Building / Property Services: Mr Paul Seager Building Control Manager, Council Offices, Knowle, Sidmouth EX10 8HL ☎ 01395 517482 ✉ buildingcontrol@eastdevon.gov.uk

Building Control: Mr Paul Seager Building Control Manager, Council Offices, Knowle, Sidmouth EX10 8HL ☎ 01395 517482 ✉ buildingcontrol@eastdevon.gov.uk

PR / Communications: Mrs Richenda Oldham Communications Officer, Council Offices, Knowle, Sidmouth EX10 8HL ☎ 01395 517559 ✉ roldham@eastdevon.gov.uk

Community Safety: Mr G Moore, Community Safety Officer, Exmouth Police Station, North Street, Sidmouth EX8 1JZ ☎ 01395 273802 ✉ gmoore@eastdevon.gov.uk

Computer Management: Mr Chris Powell, Chief Operations Manager, Council Offices, Knowle, Sidmouth EX10 8HL ☎ 01395 517433 🖷 01395 517501 ✉ cpowell@eastdevon.gov.uk

Computer Management: Mr Chris Powell Chief Operations Officer, Civic Centre, Paris Street, Exeter EX1 1JN ☎ 01392 265600 🖷 01392 265268 ✉ cjpowell@eastdevon.gov.uk

Customer Service: Ms Cherise Foster Customer Service Manager, Council Offices, Knowle, Sidmouth EX10 8HL ☎ 01395 517535 🖷 01395 517504 ✉ cfoster@eastdevon.gov.uk

EAST DEVON

Economic Development: Mrs Alison Hayward Economy & Regeneration Manager, Council Offices, Knowle, Sidmouth EX10 8HL ☎ 01395 517406 ahayward@eastdevon.gov.uk

E-Government: Mr Chris Powell, Chief Operations Manager, Council Offices, Knowle, Sidmouth EX10 8HL ☎ 01395 517433 🖷 01395 517501 cpowell@eastdevon.gov.uk

Electoral Registration: Ms Jill Humphreys Electoral Services Manager, Council Offices, Knowle, Sidmouth EX10 8HL ☎ 01395 517550 🖷 01395 517507 jumphreys@eastdevon.gov.uk

Emergency Planning: Ms Pam Harvey, Emergency Planning Officer, Council Offices, Knowle, Sidmouth EX10 8HL ☎ 01935 462462 🖷 01935 462503 pharvey@eastdevon.gov.uk

Environmental Health: Mr Andrew Ennis Service Lead - Environmental Health & Car Parks, Council Offices, Knowle, Sidmouth EX10 8HL ☎ 01395 571583 aennis@eastdevon.gov.uk

Facilities: Mr Simon Allchurch Senior Building Surveyor, Council Offices, Knowle, Sidmouth EX10 8HL ☎ 01395 516551 sallchurch@eastdevon.gov.uk

Finance: Mr Simon Davey Strategic Lead - Finance, Council Offices, Knowle, Sidmouth EX10 8HL ☎ 01395 517490 sdavey@eastdevon.gov.uk

Pensions: Ms Charlotte Thompson Pensions Manager, Pension Service, Estuary House, Peninsula Park, Rydon Lane, Exeter EX2 7XB ☎ 01392 688210 charlotte.thompson@devon.gov.uk

Health and Safety: Mr S Cross, Safety Advisor, Council Offices, Knowle, Sidmouth EX10 8HL ☎ 01395 516551 🖷 01395 517508 scross@eastdevon.gov.uk

Housing: Mr John Golding, Strategic Lead - Housing & Environment, Council Offices, Knowle, Sidmouth EX10 8HL ☎ 01395 517567 🖷 01395 517508 jgolding@eastdevon.gov.uk

Legal: Mr Henry Gordon Lennox Strategic Lead - Legal, Democratic Services, Licensing & Monitoring Officer, Council Offices, Knowle, Sidmouth EX10 8HL ☎ 01395 517401 hgordonlennox@eastdevon.gov.uk

Licensing: Mr J Tippin, Licensing Manager, Council Offices, Knowle, Sidmouth EX10 8HL ☎ 01395 516551 🖷 01395 517507 jtippin@eastdevon.gov.uk

Lottery Funding, Charity and Voluntary: Miss Jamie Buckley Funding Officer, Council Offices, Knowle, Sidmouth EX10 8HL ☎ 01395 517569 🖷 01395 517507 jbuckley@eastdevon.gov.uk

Member Services: Mr Henry Gordon Lennox Strategic Lead - Legal, Democratic Services, Licensing & Monitoring Officer, Council Offices, Knowle, Sidmouth EX10 8HL ☎ 01395 517401 hgordonlennox@eastdevon.gov.uk

Personnel / HR: Ms Karen Jenkins, Strategic Lead - Organisational Development & Transformation, Council Offices, Knowle, Sidmouth EX10 8HL ☎ 01395 516551 🖷 01395 5175057 kjenkin@eastdevon.gov.uk

Planning: Mr Ed Freeman Service Lead - Planning Strategy & Development Management, Council Offices, Knowle, Sidmouth EX10 8HL efreeman@eastdevon.gov.uk

Procurement: Mr Colin Slater Procurement Officer, Council Offices, Knowle, Sidmouth EX10 8HL ☎ 01395 516551 🖷 01395 517509 procurement@eastdevon.gov.uk

Recycling & Waste Minimisation: Mr Paul McHenry Recycling & Waste Contract Manager, Council Offices, Knowle, Sidmouth EX10 8HL ☎ 01395 516551 pmchenry@eastdevon.gov.uk

Street Scene: Mr Andrew Hancock Service Lead - Street Scene, Council Offices, Knowle, Sidmouth EX10 8HL ahancock@eastdevon.gov.uk

Waste Collection and Disposal: Mr Paul McHenry Recycling & Waste Contract Manager, Council Offices, Knowle, Sidmouth EX10 8HL ☎ 01395 516551 pmchenry@eastdevon.gov.uk

Waste Management: Mr Paul McHenry Recycling & Waste Contract Manager, Council Offices, Knowle, Sidmouth EX10 8HL ☎ 01395 516551 pmchenry@eastdevon.gov.uk

COUNCILLORS

***Chair* Hughes**, Stuart (CON - Sidmouth Sidford)
shughes@eastdevon.gov.uk

***Vice-Chair* Parr**, Helen (CON - Coly Valley)
hparr@eastdevon.gov.uk

***Leader of the Council* Diviani**, Paul (CON - Yarty)
pdiviani@eastdevon.gov.uk

***Deputy Leader of the Council* Moulding**, Andrew (CON - Axminster Town)
amoulding@eastdevon.gov.uk

Allen, Mike (CON - Honiton St Michaels)
mallen@eastdevon.gov.uk

Armstrong, Megan (IND - Exmouth Halsdon)
marmstrong@eastdevon.gov.uk

Bailey, Brian (CON - Exmouth Withycombe Raleigh)
bbailey@eastdevon.gov.uk

Barratt, David (IND - Sidmouth Rural)
dbarratt@eastdevon.gov.uk

Barrow, Dean (CON - Honiton St Pauls)
dbarrow@eastdevon.gov.uk

Bond, Susie (IND - Feniton & Buckerell)
sbond@eastdevon.gov.uk

Booth, Matthew (IND - Sidmouth Town)
mbooth@@eastdevon.gov.uk

Bowden, Peter (CON - Whimple)
pbowden@eastdevon.gov.uk

Brown, Colin (CON - Dunkeswell)
cbrown@eastdevon.gov.uk

Burrows, Peter (LD - Seaton)
pburrows@eastdevon.gov.uk

Carter, Paul (CON - Ottery St Mary Rural)
pcarter@eastdevon.gov.uk

Chapman, David (CON - Exmouth Brixington)
dchapman@eastdevon.gov.uk

Chapman, Maddy (CON - Exmouth Brixington)
mchapman@eastdevonn.gov.uk

Chubb, Iain (CON - Newbridges)
ichubb@eastdevon.gov.uk

Cope, Trevor (IND - Exmouth Brixington)
tcope@eastdevon.gov.uk

Coppell, Matt (IND - Ottery St Mary Rural)
mcoppell@eastdevon.gov.uk

Dent, Alan (CON - Budleigh)
adent@eastdevon.gov.uk

Dyson, John (IND - Sidmouth Town)
jdyson@eastdevon.gov.uk

Elson, Jill (CON - Exmouth Halsdon)
jelson@eastdevon.gov.uk

Faithfull, Peter (IND - Ottery St Mary Town)
pfaithfull@eastdevon.gov.uk

Foster, David (CON - Honiton St Michaels)
dfoster@eastdevon.gov.uk

Gardner, Cathy (IND - Sidmouth Town)
cgardner@eastdevon.gov.uk

Gazzard, Steve (LD - Exmouth Town)
sgazzard@eastdevon.gov.uk

Giles, Roger (IND - Ottery St Mary Town)
rgiles@eastdevon.gov.uk

Godbeer, Graham (CON - Coly Valley)
ggodbeer@eastdevon.gov.uk

Graham, Pat (LD - Exmouth Town)
pgraham@eastdevon.gov.uk

Greenhalgh, Alison (CON - Exmouth Littleham)
agreenhalgh@eastdevon.gov.uk

Grundy, Simon (CON - Exe Valley)
sgrundy@eastdevon.gov.uk

Hale, Maria (CON - Broadclyst)
mhale@eastdevon.gov.uk

Hall, Steve (CON - Budleigh)
shall@eastdevon.gov.uk

Hall, Ian (CON - Axminster Rural)
ihall@eastdevon.gov.uk

Hartnell, Marcus (CON - Seaton)
mhartnell@eastdevon.gov.uk

Howe, Michael (CON - Clyst Valley)
mhowe@eastdevon.gov.uk

Hull, Douglas (LD - Axminster Town)
dhull@eastdevon.gov.uk

Humphreys, John (CON - Exmouth Littleham)
jhumphreys@eastdevon.gov.uk

Ingham, Ben (IND - Woodbury & Lympstone)
bingham@eastdevon.gov.uk

Jung, Geoff (IND - Raleigh)
gjung@eastdevon.gov.uk

Key, David (CON - Otterhead)
dkey@eastdevon.gov.uk

Knight, Jim (CON - Seaton)
jknight@eastdevon.gov.uk

Longhurst, Rob (IND - Woodbury & Lympstone)
rlonghurst@eastdevon.gov.uk

Manley, Dawn (IND - Sidmouth Sidford)
dmanley@eastdevon.gov.uk

Nash, Bill (CON - Exmouth Town)
bnash@eastdevon.gov.uk

Nicholas, Cherry (CON - Exmouth Brixington)
cnicholas@eastdevon.gov.uk

O'Leary, John (CON - Honiton St Pauls)
joleary@eastdevon.gov.uk

Pepper, Christopher (CON - Broadclyst)
cpepper@eastdevon.gov.uk

Pook, Geoff (IND - Beer & Branscome)
gpook@eastdevon.gov.uk

Ranger, Val (IND - Newton Poppleford & Harpford)
vranger@eastdevon.gov.uk

Rixson, Marianne (IND - Sidmouth Sidford)
mrixson@eastdevon.gov.uk

Skinner, Philip (CON - Tale Vale)
pskinner@eastdevon.gov.uk

Stott, Pauline (CON - Exmouth Halsdon)
pstott@eastdevon.gov.uk

Taylor, Brenda (LD - Exmouth Withycombe Raleigh)
btaylor@eastdevon.gov.uk

Thomas, Ian (CON - Trinity)
ithomas@eastdevon.gov.uk

Twiss, Phil (CON - Honiton St Michaels)
ptwiss@eastdevon.gov.uk

Williamson, Mark (CON - Exmouth Littleham)
mwilliamson@eastdevon.gov.uk

Wragg, Eileen (LD - Exmouth Town)
ewragg@eastdevon.gov.uk

Wright, Tom (CON - Budleigh)
twright@eastdevon.gov.uk

POLITICAL COMPOSITION
CON: 37, IND: 17, LD: 6

COMMITTEE CHAIRS
Audit & Governance: Mr Mark Williamson

Development Management: Mr David Key

Licensing & Enforcement: Mr Steve Hall

East Dorset D

East Dorset District Council, Council Offices, Furzehill, Wimborne BH21 4HN
☎ 01202 886201 🖷 01202 841390 💻 www.dorsetforyou.com

FACTS AND FIGURES
Parliamentary Constituencies: Christchurch County, Dorset Mid and Poole North
EU Constituencies: South West
Election Frequency: Elections are of whole council

EAST DORSET

PRINCIPAL OFFICERS

Chief Executive: Mr David McIntosh Chief Executive, Council Offices, Furzehill, Wimborne BH21 4HN ☎ 01202 886201 🖷 01202 639030; 01202 495001
✉ dmcintosh@christchurchandeastdorset.gov.uk

Senior Management: Mr David Barnes, Strategic Director, Council Offices, Furzehill, Wimborne BH21 4HN ☎ 01202 495077 🖷 01202 639030 ✉ dbarnes@christchurchandeastdorset.gov.uk

Senior Management: Mr Neil Farmer, Strategic Director, Council Offices, Furzehill, Wimborne BH21 4HN ☎ 01202 795002 🖷 01202 639030; 01202 495107 ✉ nfarmer@christchurchandeastdorset.gov.uk

Access Officer / Social Services (Disability): Mr David Gale, Building Control Partnership Manager, Council Offices, Furzehill, Wimborne BH21 4HN ☎ 01202 795058 🖷 01202 849182
✉ dgale@christchurchandeastdorset.gov.uk

Architect, Building / Property Services: Mr Ashley Harman Property & Estates Manager, Council Offices, Furzehill, Wimborne BH21 4HN ☎ 01202 795482 🖷 01202 639030
✉ aharman@christchurchandeastdorset.gov.uk

Building Control: Mr David Gale, Building Control Partnership Manager, Council Offices, Furzehill, Wimborne BH21 4HN ☎ 01202 795058 🖷 01202 849182 ✉ dgale@christchurchandeastdorset.gov.uk

Children / Youth Services: Ms Judith Plumley Head - Community & Economy, Council Offices, Furzehill, Wimborne BH21 4HN ☎ 01202 886201; 01202 795043 🖷 01202 639030; 01202 795108 ✉ jplumpley@christchurchandeastdorset.gov.uk

PR / Communications: Mr Allan Wood, Communications Officer, Council Offices, Furzehill, Wimborne BH21 4HN ☎ 01202 495133 🖷 01202 495107 ✉ awood@christchurchandeastdorset.gov.uk

Community Planning: Mr Neil Farmer, Strategic Director, Council Offices, Furzehill, Wimborne BH21 4HN ☎ 01202 795002 🖷 01202 639030; 01202 495107 ✉ nfarmer@christchurchandeastdorset.gov.uk

Community Safety: Ms Julia Howlett Community Safety Officer, Council Offices, Furzehill, Wimborne BH21 4HN ☎ 01202 795198
✉ jhowlett@christchurchandeastdorset.gov.uk

Computer Management: Mr Paul Downton Partnership ICT Manager, Civic Offices, Bridge Street, Christchurch BH23 1AZ
☎ 01202 795137 🖷 01202 495107
✉ pdownton@christchurchandeastdorset.gov.uk

Computer Management: Ms Fiona Hughes Partnership ICT Manager, Civic Offices, Bridge Street, Christchurch BH23 1AZ
✉ fhughes@christchurchandeastdorset.gov.uk

Customer Service: Ms Debbie Cliff Customer Services Team Leader, Civic Offices, Bridge Street, Christchurch BH23 1AZ
✉ dcliff@christchurchandeastdorset.gov.uk

Economic Development: Mr Nick James Manager - Economic Development, Council Offices, Furzehill, Wimborne BH21 4HN
☎ 01202 795328 🖷 01202 849182
✉ njames@christchurchandeastdorset.gov.uk

Electoral Registration: Mr Richard Jones Democratic Services & Elections Manager, Council Offices, Furzehill, Wimborne BH21 4HN
☎ 01202 795171 🖷 01202 639030
✉ rjones@christchurchandeastdorset.gov.uk

Emergency Planning: Mr Jonathan Ross Engineering & Parking Manager, Council Offices, Furzehill, Wimborne BH21 4HN ☎ 01202 795159 🖷 01202 639030 ✉ jross@christchurchandeastdorset.gov.uk

Energy Management: Mr Steve Duckett, Head of Housing & Health, Council Offices, Furzehill, Wimborne BH21 4HN ☎ 01202 795987 🖷 01202 795108
✉ sduckett@christchurchandeastdorset.gov.uk

Environmental / Technical Services: Mr Lindsay Cass Head of Property & Engineering, Council Offices, Furzehill, Wimborne BH21 4HN ☎ 01202 795003 🖷 01202 795110
✉ lcass@christchurchandeastdorset.gov.uk

Environmental Health: Mr Steve Duckett, Head of Housing & Health, Council Offices, Furzehill, Wimborne BH21 4HN ☎ 01202 795987 🖷 01202 795108
✉ sduckett@christchurchandeastdorset.gov.uk

European Liaison: Mr Nick James Manager - Economic Development, Council Offices, Furzehill, Wimborne BH21 4HN
☎ 01202 795328 🖷 01202 849182
✉ njames@christchurchandeastdorset.gov.uk

Facilities: Mr Ashley Harman Property & Estates Manager, Council Offices, Furzehill, Wimborne BH21 4HN ☎ 01202 795482 🖷 01202 639030 ✉ aharman@christchurchandeastdorset.gov.uk

Finance: Mr Ian Milner Head of Finance, Civic Offices, Bridge Street, Christchurch BH23 1AZ ☎ 01202 795176 🖷 01202 482200
✉ imilner@christchurchandeastdorset.gov.uk

Health and Safety: Mr Steve Duckett, Head of Housing & Health, Council Offices, Furzehill, Wimborne BH21 4HN ☎ 01202 795987 🖷 01202 795108 ✉ sduckett@christchurchandeastdorset.gov.uk

Housing: Ms Kathryn Blatchford, Strategic Housing Services Manager, Civic Offices, Bridge Street, Christchurch BH23 1AZ
☎ 01202 795158 ✉ kblatchford@christchurchandeastdorset.gov.uk

Legal: Mr Keith Mallett, Council Solicitor, Council Offices, Furzehill, Wimborne BH21 4HN ☎ 01202 795989 🖷 01202 795107
✉ kmallett@christchurchandeastdorset.gov.uk

Leisure and Cultural Services: Mr Matti Raudsepp Head of Organisational Development, Council Offices, Furzehill, Wimborne BH21 4HN ☎ 01202 795125 🖷 01202 639030
✉ mraudsepp@christchurchandeastdorset.gov.uk

Licensing: Mr Steve Ricketts Community Protection Team Leader, Council Offices, Furzehill, Wimborne BH21 4HN ☎ 01202 886201
✉ sricketts@christchurchandeastdorset.gov.uk

Lottery Funding, Charity and Voluntary: Mr Matti Raudsepp Head of Organisational Development, Council Offices, Furzehill, Wimborne BH21 4HN ☎ 01202 795125 🖷 01202 639030 ✉ mraudsepp@christchurchandeastdorset.gov.uk

Member Services: Mr Richard Jones Democratic Services & Elections Manager, Council Offices, Furzehill, Wimborne BH21 4HN ☎ 01202 795171 🖷 01202 639030 ✉ rjones@christchurchandeastdorset.gov.uk

Parking: Mr Jonathan Ross Engineering & Parking Manager, Council Offices, Furzehill, Wimborne BH21 4HN ☎ 01202 795159 🖷 01202 639030 ✉ jross@christchurchandeastdorset.gov.uk

Personnel / HR: Mrs Sue Weal, Personnel Manager, Council Offices, Furzehill, Wimborne BH21 4HN ☎ 01202 795420 🖷 01202 841390 ✉ sweal@christchurchandeastdorset.gov.uk

Planning: Mr Steve Duckett, Head of Housing & Health, Council Offices, Furzehill, Wimborne BH21 4HN ☎ 01202 795987 🖷 01202 795108 ✉ sduckett@christchurchandeastdorset.gov.uk

Recycling & Waste Minimisation: Mr Lindsay Cass Head of Property & Engineering, Council Offices, Furzehill, Wimborne BH21 4HN ☎ 01202 795003 🖷 01202 795110 ✉ lcass@christchurchandeastdorset.gov.uk

Staff Training: Mrs Sue Weal, Personnel Manager, Council Offices, Furzehill, Wimborne BH21 4HN ☎ 01202 795420 🖷 01202 841390 ✉ sweal@christchurchandeastdorset.gov.uk

Waste Management: Mr Lindsay Cass Head of Property & Engineering, Council Offices, Furzehill, Wimborne BH21 4HN ☎ 01202 795003 🖷 01202 795110 ✉ lcass@christchurchandeastdorset.gov.uk

COUNCILLORS

***Leader of the Council* Monks**, Ian (CON - Alderholt)
ijmonks@aol.com

***Deputy Leader of the Council* Tony**, Simon (CON - Handley Vale)
cllr.stong@eastdorsetdc.gov.uk

Bartlett, Shane (LD - Wimborne Minster)
cllr.sbartlett@eastdorsetdc.gov.uk

Bryan, Ray (CON - St Leonards)
cllr.rbryan@eastdorsetdc.gov.uk

Burns, Sarah (CON - Corfe Mullen)
cllr.sburns@eastdorsetdc.gov.uk

Burt, Derek (CON - Corfe Mullen)
cllr.dburt@eastdorsetdc.gov.uk

Butler, Steve (CON - Crane)
cllr.sbutler@eastdorsetdc.gov.uk

Clarke, Alex (CON - West Moors & Holt)
cllr.aclarke@eastdorsetdc.gov.uk

Cook, Robin (CON - Stour)
cllr.rcook@eastdorsetdc.gov.uk

Coombes, Toni (CON - Verwood West)
cllr.tcoombes@eastdorsetdc.gov.uk

Dover, Janet (LD - Colehill East)
cllr.jdover@eastdorset.gov.uk

Dyer, Mike (CON - St Leonards)
cllr.mdyer@eastdorsetdc.gov.uk

Flower, Spencer (IND - Verwood West)
cllr.sflower@eastdorsetdc.gov.uk

Gibson, Simon (CON - Verwood East)
cllr.sgibson@eastdorsetdc.gov.uk

Goringe, Barry (CON - St Leonards)
cllr.bgoringe@eastdorsetdc.gov.uk

Harrison, Paul (CON - Corfe Mullen)
cllr.pharrison@eastdorsetdc.gov.uk

Johnson, KD (CON - Colehill East)
cllr.kdjohnson@eastdorsetdc.gov.uk

Lugg, Cathy (CON - Ameysford)
cllr.clugg@eastdorsetdc.gov.uk

Lugg, Steven (CON - Ferndown Central)
cllr.slugg@eastdoresetdc.gov.uk

Manuel, Barbara (CON - Parley)
cllr.bmanuel@eastdorsetdc.gov.uk

Morgan, David (LD - Wimborne Minster)
cllr.dmorgan@eastdorsetdc.gov.uk

Mortimer, Boyd (CON - Verwood East)
cllr.bmortimer@eastdorsetdc.gov.uk

Ogglesby, Peter (CON - Ferndown Central)
cllr.pogglesby@eastdorsetdc.gov.uk

Packer, David (CON - Colehill West)
david.packer@btinternet.com

Robinson, Julie (CON - Ferndown Central)
cllr.jrobinson@eastdorsetdc.gov.uk

Russell, George (CON - Hampreston & Longham)
cllr.grussell@eastdorsetdc.gov.uk

Shortell, David (CON - West Moors & Holt)
cllr.dshortell@eastdorsetdc.gov.uk

Skeats, Andy (CON - West Moors & Holt)
cllr.askeats@eastdorsetdc.gov.uk

Wilson, John (CON - Parley) cllr.jwilson@eastdorsetdc.gov.uk

POLITICAL COMPOSITION

CON: 25, LD: 3, IND: 1

COMMITTEE CHAIRS

Planning: Mr Mike Dyer

East Dunbartonshire S

East Dunbartonshire Council, 12 Strathkelvin Place, Kirkintilloch, Glasgow G66 1TJ
☎ 0141 578 8000 🖷 0141 777 5576 ✉ general@eastdunbarton.gov.uk
🖳 www.eastdunbarton.gov.uk

FACTS AND FIGURES

Parliamentary Constituencies: Cumbernauld, Kilsyth and Kirkintilloch East
EU Constituencies: Scotland
Election Frequency: Elections are of whole council

EAST DUNBARTONSHIRE

PRINCIPAL OFFICERS

Chief Executive: Mr Gerry Cornes Chief Executive, 12 Strathkelvin Place, Kirkintilloch, Glasgow G66 1TJ ☎ 0141 578 8082; 0141 578 8082 ✉ gerry.cornes@eastdunbarton.gov.uk

Senior Management: Mr Ian Black Director - Finance & Shared Services, 12 Strathkelvin Place, Kirkintilloch, Glasgow G66 1TJ ☎ 0141 578 8212 ✉ ian.black@eastdunbarton.gov.uk

Senior Management: Mr Gordon Currie Director - Education & Children's Services, 12 Strathkelvin Place, Kirkintilloch, Glasgow G66 1TJ ☎ 0141 578 8720 ✉ gordon.curry@eastdunbarton.gov.uk

Senior Management: Ms Ann Davie Director - Customer Services & Transformation, 12 Strathkelvin Place, Kirkintilloch, , Glasgow G66 1TJ ☎ 0141 578 8025 ✉ ann.davie@eastdunbarton.gov.uk

Senior Management: Mr Thomas Glen Director - Development & Regeneration, 12 Strathkelvin Place, Kirkintilloch, Glasgow G66 1TJ ☎ 0141 578 8420 ✉ thomas.glen@eastdunbarton.gov.uk

Senior Management: Ms Grace Irvine Director - Neighbourhood Services, Broomhill Industrial Estate, Kilsyth Road, Kirkintilloch, Glasgow G66 1TF ☎ 0141 574 5502 ✉ grace.irvine@eastdunbarton.gov.uk

Senior Management: Mr John Simmons Director - Integrated Health & Social Care Transition, 12 Strathkelvin Place, Kirkintilloch, , Glasgow G66 1TJ ☎ 0300 123 4510 ✉ john.simmons@eastdunbarton.gov.uk

Catering Services: Ms Grace Irvine Director - Neighbourhood Services, Broomhill Industrial Estate, Kilsyth Road, Kirkintilloch, Glasgow G66 1TF ☎ 0141 574 5502 ✉ grace.irvine@eastdunbarton.gov.uk

Children / Youth Services: Mr Gordon Currie Director - Education & Children's Services, 12 Strathkelvin Place, Kirkintilloch, Glasgow G66 1TJ ☎ 0141 578 8720 ✉ gordon.curry@eastdunbarton.gov.uk

PR / Communications: Ms Angela Fegan Communications Manager, 12 Strathkelvin Place, Kirkintilloch, Glasgow G66 1TJ ☎ 0300 123 4510 ✉ angela.fegan@eastdunbarton.gov.uk

Computer Management: Mr Vince McNulty ICT Manager, 12 Strathkelvin Place, Kirkintilloch, Glasgow G66 1TJ ☎ 0300 123 4510 ✉ vince.mcnulty@eastdunbarton.gov.uk

Consumer Protection and Trading Standards: Ms Evonne Bauer Community Protection Manager, Southbank House, Environment Group, Kirkintilloch, Glasgow G66 1XH ☎ 0300 123 4510 ✉ evonne.bauer@eastdunbarton.gov.uk

Customer Service: Ms Ellen Beattie Customer Services Manager, Broomhill Industrial Estate, Kilsyth Road, Kirkintilloch, Glasgow G66 1QF ☎ 0300 123 4510 ✉ ellen.beattie@eastdunbarton.gov.uk

Economic Development: Mr Thomas Glen Director - Development & Regeneration, 12 Strathkelvin Place, Kirkintilloch, Glasgow G66 1TJ ☎ 0141 578 8420 ✉ thomas.glen@eastdunbarton.gov.uk

Education: Ms Jacqueline MacDonald Chief Education Officer, 12 Strathkelvin Place, Kirkintilloch, Glasgow G66 1TJ ☎ 0300 123 4510 ✉ jacqueline.macdonald@eastdunbarton.gov.uk

Electoral Registration: Mr Martin Cunningham Manager of Democratic Services, 12 Strathkelvin Place, Kirkintilloch, Glasgow G66 1TJ ☎ 0141 578 8000 ✉ martin.cunningham@eastdunbarton.gov.uk

Estates, Property & Valuation: Mr Alan Bauer Major Assets Manager, 12 Strathkelvin Place, Kirkintilloch, Glasgow G66 1TJ ☎ 0300 123 4510 ✉ alan.bauer@eastdunbarton.gov.uk

Facilities: Ms Grace Irvine Director - Neighbourhood Services, Broomhill Industrial Estate, Kilsyth Road, Kirkintilloch, Glasgow G66 1TF ☎ 0141 574 5502 ✉ grace.irvine@eastdunbarton.gov.uk

Finance: Mr Ian Black Director - Finance & Shared Services, 12 Strathkelvin Place, Kirkintilloch, Glasgow G66 1TJ ☎ 0141 578 8212 ✉ ian.black@eastdunbarton.gov.uk

Fleet Management: Mr Paul Curran Fleet Manager, Broomhill Industrial Estate, Kisyth Road, Kirkintilloch, Glasgow G66 1TF ☎ 0300 123 4510 ✉ paul.curran@eastdunbarton.gov.uk

Health and Safety: Mr Ian Black Director - Finance & Shared Services, 12 Strathkelvin Place, Kirkintilloch, Glasgow G66 1TJ ☎ 0141 578 8212 ✉ ian.black@eastdunbarton.gov.uk

Highways: Ms Grace Irvine Director - Neighbourhood Services, Broomhill Industrial Estate, Kilsyth Road, Kirkintilloch, Glasgow G66 1TF ☎ 0141 574 5502 ✉ grace.irvine@eastdunbarton.gov.uk

Housing: Mr Grant Macintosh Housing Services Manager, Broomhill Industrial Estate, Kilsyth Road, Kirkintilloch, Glasgow G66 1TF ☎ 0300 123 4510 ✉ grant.mackintosh@eastdunbarton.gov.uk

Leisure and Cultural Services: Mr Mark Grant East Dunbartonshire Leisure & Culture Trust General Manager, William Patrick Library, 2/3 West High Street, Kirkintilloch, Glasgow G66 1AD ☎ 0141 777 3143 ✉ mark.grant@eastdunbarton.gov.uk

Licensing: Mr Martin Cunningham Manager of Democratic Services, 12 Strathkelvin Place, Kirkintilloch, Glasgow G66 1TJ ☎ 0141 578 8000 ✉ martin.cunningham@eastdunbarton.gov.uk

Lighting: Ms Grace Irvine Director - Neighbourhood Services, Broomhill Industrial Estate, Kilsyth Road, Kirkintilloch, Glasgow G66 1TF ☎ 0141 574 5502 ✉ grace.irvine@eastdunbarton.gov.uk

Member Services: Mr Martin Cunningham Manager of Democratic Services, 12 Strathkelvin Place, Kirkintilloch, Glasgow G66 1TJ ☎ 0141 578 8000 ✉ martin.cunningham@eastdunbarton.gov.uk

Partnerships: Mr Thomas Glen Director - Development & Regeneration, 12 Strathkelvin Place, Kirkintilloch, Glasgow G66 1TJ ☎ 0141 578 8420 ✉ thomas.glen@eastdunbarton.gov.uk

Personnel / HR: Ms Ann Davie Director - Customer Services & Transformation, 12 Strathkelvin Place, Kirkintilloch, , Glasgow G66 1TJ ☎ 0141 578 8025 ✉ ann.davie@eastdunbarton.gov.uk

Planning: Mr Thomas Glen Director - Development & Regeneration, 12 Strathkelvin Place, Kirkintilloch, Glasgow G66 1TJ ☎ 0141 578 8420 ✉ thomas.glen@eastdunbarton.gov.uk

Procurement: Ms Kirsty Chisholm Procurement Manager, 12 Strathkelvin Place, Kirkintilloch, Glasgow G66 1TJ ☎ 0300 123 4510 ✉ kirsty.chisholm@eastdunbarton.gov.uk

Public Libraries: Mr Mark Grant East Dunbartonshire Leisure & Culture Trust General Manager, William Patrick Library, 2/3 West High Street, Kirkintilloch, Glasgow G66 1AD ☎ 0141 777 3143 ✉ mark.grant@eastdunbarton.gov.uk

Recycling & Waste Minimisation: Ms Grace Irvine Director - Neighbourhood Services, Broomhill Industrial Estate, Kilsyth Road, Kirkintilloch, Glasgow G66 1TF ☎ 0141 574 5502 ✉ grace.irvine@eastdunbarton.gov.uk

Road Safety: Ms Grace Irvine Director - Neighbourhood Services, Broomhill Industrial Estate, Kilsyth Road, Kirkintilloch, Glasgow G66 1TF ☎ 0141 574 5502 ✉ grace.irvine@eastdunbarton.gov.uk

Social Services: Ms Freda McShane Chief Social Worker, 12 Strathkelvin Place, Kirkintilloch, Glasgow G66 1TJ ☎ 0300 123 4510 ✉ freda.mcshane@eastdunbarton.gov.uk

Social Services (Adult): Ms Freda McShane Chief Social Worker, 12 Strathkelvin Place, Kirkintilloch, Glasgow G66 1TJ ☎ 0300 123 4510 ✉ freda.mcshane@eastdunbarton.gov.uk

Social Services (Children): Ms Freda McShane Chief Social Worker, 12 Strathkelvin Place, Kirkintilloch, Glasgow G66 1TJ ☎ 0300 123 4510 ✉ freda.mcshane@eastdunbarton.gov.uk

Staff Training: Ms Ceri Paterson Organisational Development Manager, 12 Strathkelvin Place, Kirkintilloch, Glasgow G66 1TJ ☎ 0300 123 4510 ✉ ceri.patterson@eastdunbarton.gov.uk

Traffic Management: Ms Grace Irvine Director - Neighbourhood Services, Broomhill Industrial Estate, Kilsyth Road, Kirkintilloch, Glasgow G66 1TF ☎ 0141 574 5502 ✉ grace.irvine@eastdunbarton.gov.uk

Transport Planner: Ms Grace Irvine Director - Neighbourhood Services, Broomhill Industrial Estate, Kilsyth Road, Kirkintilloch, Glasgow G66 1TF ☎ 0141 574 5502 ✉ grace.irvine@eastdunbarton.gov.uk

Waste Collection and Disposal: Ms Grace Irvine Director - Neighbourhood Services, Broomhill Industrial Estate, Kilsyth Road, Kirkintilloch, Glasgow G66 1TF ☎ 0141 574 5502 ✉ grace.irvine@eastdunbarton.gov.uk

Waste Management: Ms Grace Irvine Director - Neighbourhood Services, Broomhill Industrial Estate, Kilsyth Road, Kirkintilloch, Glasgow G66 1TF ☎ 0141 574 5502 ✉ grace.irvine@eastdunbarton.gov.uk

COUNCILLORS

***Provost* Walker**, Una (LAB - Bishopbriggs North & Torrance)
una.walker@eastdunbarton.gov.uk

***Leader of the Council* Geekie**, Rhondda (LAB - Lenzie & Kirkintilloch South)
rhondda.geekie@eastdunbarton.gov.uk

***Deputy Leader of the Council* Ghai**, Ashay (LD - Bearsden North)
ashay.ghai@eastdunbarton.gov.uk

***Group Leader* Hendry**, Billy (CON - Bishopbriggs North & Torrance)
billy.hendry@eastdunbarton.gov.uk

***Group Leader* Mackay**, Ian (SNP - Bearsden North)
ian.mackay@eastdunbarton.gov.uk

Cumming, Duncan (IND - Bearsden North)
duncan.cumming@eastdunbarton.gov.uk

Dempsey, John (LAB - Campsie & Kirkintilloch North)
john.dempsey@eastdunbarton.gov.uk

Gibbons, Jim (SNP - Milngavie)
jim.gibbons@eastdunbarton.gov.uk

Gotts, Eric (LD - Milngavie)
eric.gotts@eastdunbarton.gov.uk

Henry, Maureen (LAB - Milngavie)
maureen.henry@eastdunbarton.gov.uk

Jamieson, John (SNP - Kirkintilloch East & Twechar)
john.jamieson@eastdunbarton.gov.uk

Jarvis, Anne (CON - Lenzie & Kirkintilloch South)
anne.jarvis@eastdunbarton.gov.uk

Low, Gordon (SNP - Bishopbriggs South)
gordon.low@eastdunbarton.gov.uk

Macdonald, Stewart (LAB - Kirkintilloch East & Twechar)
stewart.macdonald@eastdunbarton.gov.uk

McNair, Anne (SNP - Bishopbriggs North & Torrance)
anne.mcnair@eastdunbarton.gov.uk

Moir, Alan (LAB - Bishopbriggs South)
alan.moir@eastdunbarton.gov.uk

Moody, Vaughan (LD - Bearsden South)
vaughan.moody@eastdunbarton.gov.uk

O'Donnell, Michael (LAB - Bishopbriggs South)
michael.o'donnell@eastdunbarton.gov.uk

Renwick, Gillian (SNP - Lenzie & Kirkintilloch South)
gillian.renwick@eastdunbarton.gov.uk

Ritchie, David (SNP - Campsie & Kirkintilloch North)
david.ritchie@eastdunbarton.gov.uk

Shergill, Manjinder (LAB - Bearsden South)
manjinder.shergill@eastdunbarton.gov.uk

Small, Keith (SNP - Bearsden South)
keith.small@eastdunbarton.gov.uk

Welsh, Gemma (LAB - Campsie & Kirkintilloch North)
gemma.welsh@eastdunbarton.gov.uk

Young, Jack (IND - Kirkintilloch East & Twechar)
jack.young@eastdunbarton.gov.uk

POLITICAL COMPOSITION

LAB: 9, SNP: 8, LD: 3, CON: 2, IND: 2

COMMITTEE CHAIRS

Education: Mr Eric Gotts

EAST DUNBARTONSHIRE

Licensing: Mr John Dempsey

Planning: Mr Billy Hendry

Policy & Resources: Ms Rhondda Geekie

East Hampshire D

East Hampshire District Council, Penns Place, Petersfield GU31 4EX
☎ 01730 266551 🖳 www.easthants.gov.uk

FACTS AND FIGURES

Parliamentary Constituencies: Hampshire East
EU Constituencies: South East
Election Frequency: Elections are of whole council

PRINCIPAL OFFICERS

Chief Executive: Ms Sandy Hopkins Joint Chief Executive, Penns Place, Petersfield GU31 4EX ☎ 023 9244 6150 🖷 023 9248 0263 ✉ sandy.hopkins@havant.gov.uk

Senior Management: Mr Tom Horwood, Executive Director, Penns Place, Petersfield GU31 4EX ☎ 01730 234025; 023 9244 6151 🖷 01730 267760; 023 9248 0263 ✉ tom.horwood@easthants.gov.uk

Senior Management: Ms Gill Kneller, Executive Director, Penns Place, Petersfield GU31 4EX ☎ 01730 234004; 023 9244 6151 🖷 01730 234012; 023 9248 0263 ✉ gill.kneller@easthants.gov.uk

Senior Management: Mr Steve Pearce Project Director, Penns Place, Petersfield GU31 4EX ☎ 01790 234005 ✉ steve.pearce@easthants.gov.uk

Senior Management: Mr Andrew Pritchard Executive Head of Marketing & Development, Penns Place, Petersfield GU31 4EX ☎ 01730 234326 ✉ andrew.pritchard@easthants.gov.uk

Architect, Building / Property Services: Mr Chris Fairhead, Land & Property Manager, Penns Place, Petersfield GU31 4EX ☎ 01730 234040 🖷 01730 234039 ✉ chris.fairhead@easthants.gov.uk

Building Control: Mrs Julia Potter Executive Head of Economy & Planning, Penns Place, Petersfield GU31 4EX ☎ 01730 234376; 023 9244 6520 🖷 01730 234385; 023 9244 6588 ✉ julia.potter@easthants.gov.uk

Children / Youth Services: Mr Tim Slater Executive Head of Communities, Penns Place, Petersfield GU31 4EX ☎ 01730 234613 ✉ tim.slater@havant.gov.uk

PR / Communications: Mrs Dawn Adey Service Manager of Marketing & Customer Relations, Penns Place, Petersfield GU31 4EX ☎ 023 9244 6392 🖷 023 9248 0263 ✉ dawn.adey@havant.gov.uk

Community Safety: Mr Ryan Gulliver Community Safety Manager, Penns Place, Petersfield GU31 4EX ☎ 01730 234167 ✉ ryan.gulliver@easthants.gov.uk

Computer Management: Mrs Sue Parker Service Manager - Business Improvement, Penns Place, Petersfield GU31 4EX ☎ 023 9244 6493 ✉ sue.parker@havant.gov.uk

Contracts: Mr Robert Heathcock Joint Environmental Services Manager, Penns Place, Petersfield GU31 4EX ☎ 01730 234383 ✉ rob.heathcock@easthants.gov.uk

Corporate Services: Mr Tom Horwood, Executive Director, Penns Place, Petersfield GU31 4EX ☎ 01730 234025; 023 9244 6151 🖷 01730 267760; 023 9248 0263 ✉ tom.horwood@easthants.gov.uk

Corporate Services: Ms Gill Kneller, Executive Director, Penns Place, Petersfield GU31 4EX ☎ 01730 234004; 023 9244 6151 🖷 01730 234012; 023 9248 0263 ✉ gill.kneller@easthants.gov.uk

Customer Service: Mrs Kathy Fowler Customer Services Manager, Penns Place, Petersfield GU31 4EX ☎ 01730 234026 ✉ kathy.fowler@easthants.gov.uk

Economic Development: Mrs Julia Potter Executive Head of Economy & Planning, Penns Place, Petersfield GU31 4EX ☎ 01730 234376; 023 9244 6520 🖷 01730 234385; 023 9244 6588 ✉ julia.potter@easthants.gov.uk

Electoral Registration: Mrs Lianne Richards Elections Manager, Penns Place, Petersfield GU31 4EX ☎ 01730 234370 ✉ eservices@easthants.gov.uk

Emergency Planning: Mr Stuart Pinkney, Safety & Emergency Planning Officer, Penns Place, Petersfield GU31 4EX ☎ 023 9244 6675 🖷 023 9244 6455 ✉ stuart.pinkney@havant.gov.uk

Energy Management: Ms Gill Kneller, Executive Director, Penns Place, Petersfield GU31 4EX ☎ 01730 234004; 023 9244 6151 🖷 01730 234012; 023 9248 0263 ✉ gill.kneller@easthants.gov.uk

Energy Management: Mr Jon Sanders Service Manager of Facilities, Penns Place, Petersfield GU31 4EX ☎ 023 9244 6566 ✉ jon.sanders@easthants.gov.uk

Environmental / Technical Services: Ms Gill Kneller, Executive Director, Penns Place, Petersfield GU31 4EX ☎ 01730 234004; 023 9244 6151 🖷 01730 234012; 023 9248 0263 ✉ gill.kneller@easthants.gov.uk

Environmental / Technical Services: Mr Steve Perkins Executive Head of Environmental Services, Penns Place, Petersfield GU31 4EX ☎ 023 9244 6520 ✉ steve.perkins@easthants.gov.uk

Environmental Health: Ms Gill Kneller, Executive Director, Penns Place, Petersfield GU31 4EX ☎ 01730 234004; 023 9244 6151 🖷 01730 234012; 023 9248 0263 ✉ gill.kneller@easthants.gov.uk

Environmental Health: Mr Andrew Pritchard Executive Head of Marketing & Development, Penns Place, Petersfield GU31 4EX ☎ 01730 234326 ✉ andrew.pritchard@easthants.gov.uk

Estates, Property & Valuation: Mr Chris Fairhead, Land & Property Manager, Penns Place, Petersfield GU31 4EX ☎ 01730 234040 🖷 01730 234039 ✉ chris.fairhead@easthants.gov.uk

Facilities: Mr Jon Sanders Service Manager of Facilities, Penns Place, Petersfield GU31 4EX ☎ 023 9244 6566 ✉ jon.sanders@easthants.gov.uk

Finance: Mr Mike Ball, Revenues & Benefits Service Manager, Penns Place, Petersfield GU31 4EX ☎ 01730 234171 🖷 01730 260645 ✉ mike.ball@easthants.gov.uk

Finance: Mrs Jane Eaton Executive Head of Governance & Logistics, Penns Place, Petersfield GU31 4EX ☎ 01730 234035 ✉ jane.eaton@easthants.gov.uk

Finance: Mr Simon Little Service Manager - Finance, Penns Place, Petersfield GU31 4EX ☎ 02392 446624 ✉ simon.little@havant.gov.uk

Health and Safety: Mr Jon Sanders Service Manager of Facilities, Penns Place, Petersfield GU31 4EX ☎ 023 9244 6566 ✉ jon.sanders@easthants.gov.uk

Housing: Ms Tracey Howard Service Manager of Housing, Public Service Plaza, Civic Centre Road, Havant PO9 2AX ☎ 023 9244 6626 🖷 023 9248 0263 ✉ tracey.howard@easthants.gov.uk

Housing: Mr Tim Slater Executive Head of Economy & Communities, Penns Place, Petersfield GU31 4EX ☎ 023 9244 6276 ✉ tim.slater@easthants.gov.uk

Legal: Mrs Jo Barden-Hernandez, Head of Legal Services, Penns Place, Petersfield GU31 4EX ☎ 01730 234068; 023 9244 6212 🖷 023 9248 0263 ✉ jo.barden-hernandez@easthants.gov.uk

Legal: Mrs Jane Eaton Executive Head of Governance, Logistics & S151 Officer, Penns Place, Petersfield GU31 4EX ☎ 01730 234035; 023 9244 6151 ✉ jane.eaton@havant.gov.uk

Leisure and Cultural Services: Mr Tim Slater Executive Head of Communities, Penns Place, Petersfield GU31 4EX ☎ 023 9244 6276 ✉ tim.slater@havant.gov.uk

Licensing: Mr Andrew Pritchard Executive Head of Marketing & Development, Penns Place, Petersfield GU31 4EX ☎ 01730 234326 ✉ andrew.pritchard@easthants.gov.uk

Member Services: Mrs Penny Milne Democratic Services Officer, Penns Place, Petersfield GU31 4EX ☎ 023 9244 6234 ✉ penny.milne@havant.gov.uk

Parking: Mrs Natalie Meagher Service Manager of Neigbourhood Quality, Penns Place, Petersfield GU31 4EX ☎ 023 9244 6561 ✉ natalie.meagher@easthants.gov.uk

Personnel / HR: Mrs Caroline Tickner Service Manager of HR, Penns Place, Petersfield GU31 4EX ☎ 023 9244 6139 ✉ caroline.tickner@havant.gov.uk

Planning: Mrs Julia Potter Executive Head of Economy & Planning, Penns Place, Petersfield GU31 4EX ☎ 01730 234376; 023 9244 6520 🖷 01730 234385; 023 9244 6588 ✉ julia.potter@easthants.gov.uk

Procurement: Mr Carl Mathias Strategic Procurement Manager, Penns Place, Petersfield GU31 4EX ☎ 01730 234351 ✉ carl.mathias@easthants.gov.uk

Recycling & Waste Minimisation: Mr Steve Perkins Executive Head of Environmental Services, Penns Place, Petersfield GU31 4EX ☎ 023 9244 6520 ✉ steve.perkins@easthants.gov.uk

Staff Training: Mrs Caroline Tickner Service Manager of HR, Penns Place, Petersfield GU31 4EX ☎ 023 9244 6139 ✉ caroline.tickner@havant.gov.uk

Town Centre: Mr Chris Fairhead, Land & Property Manager, Penns Place, Petersfield GU31 4EX ☎ 01730 234040 🖷 01730 234039 ✉ chris.fairhead@easthants.gov.uk

Waste Collection and Disposal: Mr Robert Heathcock Joint Environmental Services Manager, Penns Place, Petersfield GU31 4EX ☎ 01730 234383 ✉ rob.heathcock@easthants.gov.uk

Waste Management: Mr Steve Perkins Executive Head of Environmental Services, Penns Place, Petersfield GU31 4EX ☎ 023 9244 6520 ✉ steve.perkins@easthants.gov.uk

COUNCILLORS

***Chair* Muldoon**, Tony (LD - Whitehill (Deadwater)) tony.muldoon@easthants.gov.uk

***Vice-Chair* Ashcroft**, David (CON - Selborne) david.ashcroft@easthants.gov.uk

***Leader of the Council* Cowper**, Ferris (CON - Grayshott) ferris.cowper@easthants.gov.uk

***Deputy Leader of the Council* Millard**, Richard (CON - Headley) richard.millard@easthants.gov.uk

Abdey, James (CON - Petersfield (St Peters)) james.abdey@easthants.gov.uk

Ayer, Robert (IND - Petersfield (Rother)) bob.ayer@easthants.gov.uk

Bentley, Ben (CON - Petersfield (Causeway)) ben.bentley@easthants.gov.uk

Brandt, Edward (CON - Alton (Westbrooke)) edward.brandt@easthants.gov.uk

Butler, Julie (CON - Petersfield (Heath)) julie.butler@easthants.gov.uk

Carew, Adam (LD - Whitehill (Walldown)) adam.carew@easthants.gov.uk

Carter, Ken (CON - Binsted and Bentley) ken.carter@easthants.gov.uk

Costigan, Tony (CON - Downland) tonylcostigan@easthants.gov.uk

Denton, Tony (CON - Clanfield and Finchdean) ton.ydenton@easthants.gov.uk

Drew, Nick (CON - Froxfield and Steep) nick.drew@easthants.gov.uk

Evans, David (CON - Horndean (Kings)) david.evans@easthants.gov.uk

EAST HAMPSHIRE

Evans, Lynn (CON - Horndean (Murray))
lynn.evans@easthants.gov.uk

Glass, Angela (CON - Bramshott and Liphook)
angela.glass@easthants.gov.uk

Hill, Graham (CON - Alton (Whitedown))
graham.hill@easthants.gov.uk

Jackson, Deborah (CON - Four Marks and Medstead)
deborah.jackson@easthants.gov.uk

Joy, Andrew (CON - Alton (Ashdell))
andrew.joy@easthants.gov.uk

Kendall, Mike (CON - Liss)
mike.kendall@easthants.gov.uk

Louisson, Charles (CON - Ropely and Tisted)
charles.louisson@easthants.gov.uk

Mocatta, Robert (CON - East Meon)
robert.mocatta@easthants.gov.uk

Moon, Ken (CON - Clanfield and Finchdean)
ken.moon@easthants.gov.uk

Mouland, Bill (CON - Bramshott and Liphook)
bill.mouland@easthants.gov.uk

Noble, Nicky (CON - Petersfield (St Mary))
nicky.noble@esathants.gov.uk

Onslow, Judy (CON - The Hangers and Forest)
judyonslow@btinternet.com

Orme, David (CON - Alton (Wooteys))
david.orme@easthants.gov.uk

Parker-Smith, Yvonne (CON - Lindford)
yvonne.parker-smith@easthants.gov.uk

Phillips, Dean (CON - Alton (Eastbrooke))
dean.phillips@easthants.gov.uk

Pienaar, Laetitia (CON - Liss)
laetitia.pienaar@easthants.gov.uk

Pond, Sally (LD - Whitehill (Chase))
sally.pond@esathants.gov.uk

Saunders, Robert (CON - Alton (Amery))
robert.saunders@easthants.gov.uk

Schillemore, Sara (CON - Horndean (Catherington and Lovedean))
sara.schillemore@easthants.gov.uk

Shepherd, Guy (CON - Horndean (Downs))
guy.shepherd@easthants.gov.uk

Smith, Mervyn (CON - Whitehill (Hogmoor))
mervyn.smith@easthants.gov.uk

Spencer, Thomas (CON - Petersfield (Bell Hill))
thomas.spencer@easthants.gov.uk

Standish, Rebecca (CON - Bramshott and Liphook)
rebecca.standish@easthants.gov.uk

Thomas, Ingrid (CON - Four Marks and Medstead)
ingrid.thomas@easthants.gov.uk

Tickell, Elaine (CON - Horndean (Hazelton and Blendworth))
elaine.tickell@easthants.gov.uk

Waterhouse, Alan (LD - Whitehill (Pinewood))
alan.waterhouse@easthants.gov.uk

Watts, Glynis (CON - Holybourne and Froyle)
glynis.watts@easthants.gov.uk

Williams, Anthony (CON - Headley)
anthony.williams@easthants.gov.uk

POLITICAL COMPOSITION
CON: 38, LD: 4, IND: 1

COMMITTEE CHAIRS
Audit: Mr Anthony Williams

Licensing: Mr Robert Ayer

Planning: Mrs Ingrid Thomas

East Hertfordshire D

East Herts Council, The Causeway, Bishop's Stortford CM23 2EN
☎ 01279 655261 info@eastherts.gov.uk www.eastherts.gov.uk

FACTS AND FIGURES
Parliamentary Constituencies: Hertford and Stortford, Hertfordshire North East
EU Constituencies: Eastern
Election Frequency: Elections are of whole council

PRINCIPAL OFFICERS
Chief Executive: Ms Liz Watts Chief Executive, The Causeway, Bishop's Stortford CM23 2EN liz.watts@eastherts.gov.uk

Senior Management: Mr Simon Drinkwater, Interim Chief Executive (Director of Neighbourhood Services), Wallfields, Pegs Lane, Hertford SG13 8EQ ☎ 01279 501404 01279 757582 simon.drinkwater@eastherts.gov.uk

Senior Management: Ms Adele Taylor Director - Finance & Support Services, Wallfields, Pegs Lane, Hertford SG13 8EQ ☎ 01279 655261 adele.taylor@eastherts.gov.uk

Architect, Building / Property Services: Mr Steve Whinnett Principal Building Surveyor, Wallfields, Pegs Lane, Hertford SG13 8EQ ☎ 01992 531695 steve.whinnett@eastherts.gov.uk

Best Value: Ms Ceri Pettit, Corporate Planning & Performance Manager, Council Offices, The Causeway, Bishop's Stortford CM23 2EN ☎ 01279 502240 01279 502015 ceri.pettit@eastherts.gov.uk

Building Control: Mr Kevin Steptoe, Head of Planning & Building Control, East Herts Council, Wallfields, Pegs Lane, Hertford SG13 8EQ ☎ 01992 531407 kevin.steptoe@eastherts.gov.uk

PR / Communications: Ms Lorna Georgiou Communications Team Leader, Wallfields, Pegs Lane, Hertford SG13 8EQ ☎ 01992 532244 lorna.georgiou@eastherts.gov.uk

Community Safety: Mr Brian Simmonds Head of Community Safety & Health Services, Wallfields, Pegs Lane, Hertford SG13 8EQ ☎ 01992 531498 brian.simmonds@eastherts.gov.uk

Computer Management: Mr David Frewin Network & Systems Support Manager, Wallfields, Pegs Lane, Hertford SG13 8EQ ☎ 01279 502158 david.frewin@eastherts.gov.uk

Computer Management: Mr Henry Lewis, Head of Business & Technology Services, Daneshill House, Danestrete, Stevenage SG1 1HN ☎ 01438 242496 ✉ henry.lewis@stevenage.gov.uk

Contracts: Mr Cliff Cardoza, Head of Environmental Services, Wallfields, Pegs Lane, Hertford SG13 8EQ ☎ 01992 531698 ✉ cliff.cardoza@eastherts.gov.uk

Customer Service: Mr Neil Sloper, Head of Customer Services & Parking, Wallfields, Pegs Lane, Hertford SG13 8EQ ☎ 01992 531611 ✉ neil.sloper@eastherts.gov.uk

Economic Development: Mr Ben Wood Business Development Manager, Wallfields, Pegs Lane, Hertford SG13 8EQ ☎ 01992 531699 ✉ benjamin.wood@eastherts.gov.uk

Electoral Registration: Mr Jeff Hughes, Head of Democratic & Legal Services, Wallfields, Pegs Lane, Hertford SG13 8EQ ☎ 01279 502170 ✉ jeff.hughes@eastherts.gov.uk

Emergency Planning: Mr Brian Simmonds Head of Community Safety & Health Services, Wallfields, Pegs Lane, Hertford SG13 8EQ ☎ 01992 531498 ✉ brian.simmonds@eastherts.gov.uk

Environmental / Technical Services: Mr Cliff Cardoza, Head of Environmental Services, Wallfields, Pegs Lane, Hertford SG13 8EQ ☎ 01992 531698 ✉ cliff.cardoza@eastherts.gov.uk

Environmental Health: Mr Brian Simmonds Head of Community Safety & Health Services, Wallfields, Pegs Lane, Hertford SG13 8EQ ☎ 01992 531498 ✉ brian.simmonds@eastherts.gov.uk

Estates, Property & Valuation: Ms Anna Osbourne Assets & Estates Manager, Wallfields, Pegs Lane, Hertford SG13 8EQ ☎ 01992 531655 ✉ anna.osbourne@eastherts.gov.uk

European Liaison: Mr Paul Pullin, Economic Development Manager, Wallfields, Pegs Lane, Hertford SG13 8EQ ☎ 01992 531606 ✉ paul.pullin@eastherts.gov.uk

Facilities: Mr Roy Crow Facilities & Property Manager, Wallfields, Pegs Lane, Hertford SG13 8EQ ☎ 01992 531695 ✉ roy.crow@eastherts.gov.uk

Finance: Ms Adele Taylor Director - Finance & Support Services, Wallfields, Pegs Lane, Hertford SG13 8EQ ☎ 01279 655261 ✉ adele.taylor@eastherts.gov.uk

Grounds Maintenance: Mr Ian Sharratt, Environmental Manager - Open Spaces, Wallfields, Pegs Lane, Hertford SG13 8EQ ☎ 01992 531525 ✉ ian.sharratt@eastherts.gov.uk

Health and Safety: Mr Peter Dickinson, Health & Safety Officer, Wallfields, Pegs Lane, Hertford SG13 8EQ ☎ 01992 531636 ✉ peter.dickinson@eastherts.gov.uk

Home Energy Conservation: Mr David Thorogood, Environmental Co-ordinator, Wallfields, Pegs Lane, Hertford SG13 8EQ ☎ 01992 531621 ✉ david.thorogood@eastherts.gov.uk

Housing: Ms Claire Bennett Manager of Housing Services, Wallfields, Pegs Lane, Hertford SG13 8EQ ☎ 01992 531603 ✉ claire.bennet@eastherts.gov.uk

Leisure and Cultural Services: Mr Mark Kingsland Leisure Services Manager, Wallfields, Pegs Lane, Hertford SG13 8EQ ☎ 01279 655880 ✉ mark.kingsland@eastherts.gov.uk

Licensing: Mr Oliver Rawlings Senior Specialist Licensing Officer, Wallfields, Pegs Lane, Hertford SG13 8EQ ☎ 01992 531629 ✉ oliver.rawlings@eastherts.gov.uk

Lottery Funding, Charity and Voluntary: Ms Claire Pullen Engagement & Partnerships Officer of Grants, Wallfields, Pegs Lane, Hertford SG13 8EQ ☎ 01992 531593 ✉ claire.pullen@eastherts.gov.uk

Member Services: Mr Jeff Hughes, Head of Democratic & Legal Services, Wallfields, Pegs Lane, Hertford SG13 8EQ ☎ 01279 502170 ✉ jeff.hughes@eastherts.gov.uk

Parking: Mr Andrew Pulham, Parking Services Manager, Wallfields, Pegs Lane, Hertford SG13 8EG ☎ 01279 502030 ✉ andrew.pulham@eastherts.gov.uk

Partnerships: Ms Mekhola Ray Engagement & Partnerships Team Leader, Wallfields, Pegs Lane, Hertford SG13 8EQ ☎ 01992 531613 ✉ mekhola.ray@eastherts.gov.uk

Personnel / HR: Ms Emma Freeman Head of People, ICT & Property Services, Wallfields, Pegs Lane, Hertford SG13 8EQ ☎ 01992 531635 ✉ emma.freeman@eastherts.gov.uk

Planning: Mr Kevin Steptoe, Head of Planning & Building Control, Wallfields, Pegs Lane, Hertford SG13 8EQ ☎ 01992 531407 ✉ kevin.steptoe@eastherts.gov.uk

Procurement: Ms Tracey Sargent, Procurement Officer, Wallfields, Pegs Lane, Hertford SG13 8EQ ☎ 01992 532122 ✉ tracey.sargent@eastherts.gov.uk

Recycling & Waste Minimisation: Mr David Allen Waste Services Manager, Wallfields, Pegs Lane, Hertford SG13 8EQ ☎ 01992 531549 ✉ david.allen@eastherts.gov.uk

Sustainable Development: Mr David Thorogood, Environmental Co-ordinator, Wallfields, Pegs Lane, Hertford SG13 8EQ ☎ 01992 531621 ✉ david.thorogood@eastherts.gov.uk

Tourism: Ms Tilly Andrews, Economic & Tourism Development Officer, Wallfields, Pegs Lane, Hertford SG13 8EQ ☎ 01992 531506 ✉ tilly.andrews@eastherts.gov.uk

Town Centre: Mr Paul Pullin, Economic Development Manager, Wallfields, Pegs Lane, Hertford SG13 8EQ ☎ 01992 531606 ✉ paul.pullin@eastherts.gov.uk

Traffic Management: Mr Andrew Pulham, Parking Services Manager, Wallfields, Pegs Lane, Hertford SG13 8EQ ☎ 01279 502030 ✉ andrew.pulham@eastherts.gov.uk

EAST HERTFORDSHIRE

Waste Collection and Disposal: Mr Cliff Cardoza, Head of Environmental Services, Wallfields, Pegs Lane, Hertford SG13 8EQ ☎ 01992 531698 ✉ cliff.cardoza@eastherts.gov.uk

Waste Management: Mr Cliff Cardoza, Head of Environmental Services, Wallfields, Pegs Lane, Hertford SG13 8EQ ☎ 01992 531698 ✉ cliff.cardoza@eastherts.gov.uk

Children's Play Areas: Mrs Jackie Bruce Service Development Officer, Wallends, Pegs Lane, , Hertford SG13 8EQ ☎ 01992 531654 ✉ jackie.bruce@eastherts.gov.uk

COUNCILLORS

***Chair* Beeching**, Roger (CON - Sawbridgeworth)
roger.beeching@eastherts.gov.uk

***Vice-Chair* Moore**, Patricia (CON - Hertford (Sele))
patricia.moore@eastherts.gov.uk

***Leader of the Council* Jackson**, Tony (CON - Datchworth and Aston)
anthony.jackson@eastherts.gov.uk

***Deputy Leader of the Council* Alexander**, Malcolm (CON - Ware (Trinity))
malcolm.alexander@eastherts.gov.uk

Abbott, Daniel (CON - Bishop's Stortford (All Saints))
daniel.abbot@eastherts.gov.uk

Andrews, David (CON - Thundridge and Standon)
david.andrews@eastherts.gov.uk

Ashley, William (CON - Hertford Heath)
william.ashley@eastherts.gov.uk

Ballam, Phyllis (CON - Ware (Christchurch))
phyllis.ballam@eastherts.gov.uk

Bedford, Edward (CON - Ware (Christchurch))
edward.bedford@eastherts.gov.uk

Buckmaster, Eric (IND - Sawbridgeworth)

Bull, Stan (CON - Buntingford)
stan.bull@eastherts.gov.uk

Burlton, Allen (CON - Bishop's Stortford (South))
allen.burlton@eastherts.gov.uk

Carver, Mike (CON - Much Hadham)

Cheswright, Rose (CON - Braughing)
rosemary.cheswright@eastherts.gov.uk

Crofton, Ken (CON - Walkern)
henry.crofton@eastherts.gov.uk

Cutting, George (CON - Bishop's Stortford (Central))
george.cutting@eastherts.gov.uk

Dearman, Andrew (CON - Puckeridge)
andrew.dearman@eastherts.gov.uk

Haysey, Linda (CON - Hertford Rural South)
linda.haysey@eastherts.gov.uk

Herbert, Tim (CON - Bishop's Stortford (Meads))
tim.herbert@eastherts.gov.uk

Hollebon, Diane (CON - Bishop's Stortford (South))
diane.hollebon@eastherts.gov.uk

Hone, Dorothy (CON - Hertford (Castle))
dorothy.hone@eastherts.gov.uk

Jones, Gary (CON - Bishop's Stortford (Silverleys))
gary.jones@eastherts.gov.uk

Jones, Jeff (CON - Buntingford)
jeff.jones@eastherts.gov.uk

Lawrence, Graham (CON - Hertford (Bengeo))
graham.lawrence@eastherts.gov.uk

Mayes, Janet (CON - Great Amwell)
janet.mayes@eastherts.gov.uk

McAndrew, Graham (CON - Bishop's Stortford (Silverleys))
graham.mcandrew@eastherts.gov.uk

McMullen, Michael (CON - Hertford Rural North)
michael.mcmullen@eastherts.gov.uk

Mortimer, William (CON - Sawbridgeworth)
william.mortimer@eastherts.gov.uk

Newman, Michael (IND - Hunsdon)
michael.newman@eastherts.gov.uk

Page, Tim (CON - Bishop's Stortford (Central))
tim.page@eastherts.gov.uk

Phillips, Paul (CON - Hertford (Bengeo))
paul.phillips@eastherts.gov.uk

Pope, Mark (CON - Ware (Chadwell))
mark.pope@eastherts.gov.uk

Ranger, Jim (CON - The Mundens and Cottered)
jim.ranger@eastherts.gov.uk

Rowley, Charles (CON - Hertford (Sele))
charles.rowley@eastherts.gov.uk

Ruffles, Peter (CON - Hertford (Bengeo))
peter.ruffles@eastherts.gov.uk

Rutland-Barsby, Suzanne (CON - Hertford (Castle))
suzanne.rutland-barsby@eastherts.gov.uk

Sharma, Rik (CON - Watton-at-Stone)
rik.sharma@eastherts.gov.uk

Symonds, Norma (CON - Bishop's Stortford (Central))
norma.symonds@eastherts.gov.uk

Taylor, Jeanette (CON - Ware (St Mary's))

Thornton, Jim (IND - Hertford (Castle))
jim.thornton@eastherts.gov.uk

Tindale, Michael (CON - Little Hadham)
michael.tindale@eastherts.gov.uk

Warman, Alan (CON - Ware (St Mary's))
alan.warman@eastherts.gov.uk

Warnell, Keith (CON - Bishop's Stortford (Meads))
keith.warnell@eastherts.gov.uk

Williamson, Geoffrey (CON - Stanstead Abbotts)
geoffrey.williamson@eastherts.gov.uk

Wilson, Nicholas (CON - Hertford (Kingsmead))
nicholas.wilson@eastherts.gov.uk

Wing, John (LD - Ware (Trinity))
john.wing@easthearts.gov.uk

Wood, Mike (LD - Bishop's Stortford (All Saints))

Woodward, Colin (CON - Bishop's Stortford (All Saints))
colin.woodward@eastherts.gov.uk

Wrangles, Beryl (CON - Hertford (Kingsmead))
beryl.wrangles@eastherts.gov.uk

Wyllie, John (CON - Bishop's Stortford (South))
john.wyllie@eastherts.gov.uk

POLITICAL COMPOSITION

CON: 45, IND: 3, LD: 2

COMMITTEE CHAIRS

Audit: Mr Jim Ranger

Development Management: Mrs Rose Cheswright

Health & Wellbeing: Ms Norma Symonds

Licensing: Mr Roger Beeching

East Lindsey D

East Lindsey District Council, Tedder Hall, Manby Park, Louth LN11 8UP
☎ 01507 601111 🖷 01507 600206 🖰 customerservices@e-lindsey.gov.uk
💻 www.e-lindsey.gov.uk

FACTS AND FIGURES

Parliamentary Constituencies: Boston and Skegness, Louth and Horncastle
EU Constituencies: East Midlands
Election Frequency: Elections are of whole council

PRINCIPAL OFFICERS

Chief Executive: Mr Stuart Davy Chief Executive, Tedder Hall, Manby Park, Louth LN11 8UP ☎ 01507 613410 🖷 01507 329486 🖰 stuart.davy@e-lindsey.gov.uk

Deputy Chief Executive: Mr Robert Barlow Deputy Chief Executive & Strategic Director - Resources & S151 Officer, Tedder Hall, Manby Park, Louth LN11 8UP ☎ 01205 314200; 01507 613411 🖷 01205 364604; 01507 329486 🖰 robert.barlow@boston.gov.uk

Senior Management: Ms Victoria Burgess Strategic Development Manager, Tedder Hall, Manby Park, Louth LN11 8UP ☎ 01507 613214 🖰 victoria.burgess@e-lindsey.gov.uk

Senior Management: Ms Semantha Neal, Strategic Development Manager, Tedder Hall, Manby Park, Louth LN11 8UP ☎ 01507 613440 🖰 semantha.neal@e-lindsey.gov.uk

Senior Management: Ms Alison Penn Director, Tedder Hall, Manby Park, Louth LN11 8UP ☎ 01507 329411 🖰 alison.penn@e-lindsey.gov.uk

Senior Management: Ms Michelle Sacks Monitoring Officer, Tedder Hall, Manby Park, Louth LN11 8UP ☎ 01507 613203 🖰 michelle.sacks@e-lindsey.gov.uk

Senior Management: Mr Gary Sargeant, Corporate Asset Manager, Tedder Hall, Manby Park, Louth LN11 8UP ☎ 01507 613020 🖰 gary.sargeant@e-lindsey.gov.uk

Architect, Building / Property Services: Mr Gary Sargeant, Corporate Asset Manager, Tedder Hall, Manby Park, Louth LN11 8UP ☎ 01507 613020 🖰 gary.sargeant@e-lindsey.gov.uk

Building Control: Mr Paul Smith Building Control Team Leader, Tedder Hall, Manby Park, Louth LN11 8UP ☎ 01507 613189 🖷 01507 327069 🖰 paul.smith@e-lindsey.gov.uk

Children / Youth Services: Ms Semantha Neal, Strategic Development Manager, Tedder Hall, Manby Park, Louth LN11 8UP ☎ 01507 613440 🖰 semantha.neal@e-lindsey.gov.uk

PR / Communications: Mr James Gilbert Communications & Consultation Team Leader, Tedder Hall, Manby Park, Louth LN11 8UP ☎ 01507 613415 🖷 01507 329190 🖰 james.gilbert@e-lindsey.gov.uk

Community Safety: Mr Jonathan Challen Private Sector Housing Team Leader, Tedder Hall, Manby Park, Louth LN11 8UP ☎ 01507 613051 🖰 jonathan.challen@e-lindsey.gov.uk

Computer Management: Mr Gary Stephens ICT Director, Tedder Hall, Manby Park, Louth LN11 8UP ☎ 01507 613207 🖰 gary.stephens@cpbs.com

Economic Development: Mr James Makinson-Sanders Learning & Development Advisor, Tedder Hall, Manby Park, Louth LN11 8UP ☎ 🖰 james.makinson-sanders@e-lindsey.gov.uk

Electoral Registration: Mrs Sue Brewitt, Elections Officer, Tedder Hall, Manby Park, Louth LN11 8UP ☎ 01507 613430 🖰 sue.brewitt@e-lindsey.gov.uk

Emergency Planning: Mr Mike Harrison Environmental Health Team Leader, Tedder Hall, Manby Park, Louth LN11 8UP ☎ 01507 613470 🖷 01507 600206 🖰 mike.harrison@e-lindsey.gov.uk

Energy Management: Mr Gary Sargeant, Corporate Asset Manager, Tedder Hall, Manby Park, Louth LN11 8UP ☎ 01507 613020 🖰 gary.sargeant@e-lindsey.gov.uk

Environmental / Technical Services: Mr Mike Harrison Environmental Health Team Leader, Tedder Hall, Manby Park, Louth LN11 8UP ☎ 01507 613470 🖷 01507 600206 🖰 mike.harrison@e-lindsey.gov.uk

Environmental Health: Mr Mike Harrison Environmental Health Team Leader, Tedder Hall, Manby Park, Louth LN11 8UP ☎ 01507 613470 🖷 01507 600206 🖰 mike.harrison@e-lindsey.gov.uk

Estates, Property & Valuation: Mr Edward Cox Principal Valuer, Tedder Hall, Manby Park, Louth LN11 8UP ☎ 01507 613021 🖰 edward.cox@e-lindsey.gov.uk

Estates, Property & Valuation: Mr Gary Sargeant, Corporate Asset Manager, Tedder Hall, Manby Park, Louth LN11 8UP ☎ 01507 613020 🖰 gary.sargeant@e-lindsey.gov.uk

Events Manager: Mr James Brindle Culture Team Leader, Tedder Hall, Manby Park, Louth LN11 8UP ☎ 01507 613450 🖰 james.brindle@e-lindsey.gov.uk

Facilities: Mr Mark Humphreys, Strategic Development Manager, Tedder Hall, Manby Park, Louth LN11 8UP ☎ 01507 613441 🖰 mark.humphreys@e-lindsey.gov.uk

EAST LINDSEY

Finance: Mr Robert Barlow Deputy Chief Executive & Strategic Director - Resources & S151 Officer, Tedder Hall, Manby Park, Louth LN11 8UP ☎ 01205 314200; 01507 613411 🖷 01205 364604; 01507 329486 🖱 robert.barlow@boston.gov.uk

Treasury: Mr Robert Barlow Deputy Chief Executive & Strategic Director - Resources & S151 Officer, Tedder Hall, Manby Park, Louth LN11 8UP ☎ 01205 314200; 01507 613411 🖷 01205 364604; 01507 329486 🖱 robert.barlow@boston.gov.uk

Fleet Management: Mr Nick Davis Team Leader of Waste Services, Tedder Hall, Manby Park, Louth LN11 8UP ☎ 01507 613540 🖱 nick.davis@e-lindsey.gov.uk

Grounds Maintenance: Mr Danny Wilson Team Leader - Service Development, Tedder Hall, Manby Park, Louth LN11 8UP ☎ 01507 613541 🖱 danny.wilson@e-lindsey.gov.uk

Health and Safety: Mr Mike Gallagher Health & Safety Officer, Tedder Hall, Manby Park, Louth LN11 8UP ☎ 01507 613235 🖱 michael.gallagher@cpbs.com

Home Energy Conservation: Mr Jonathan Challen Private Sector Housing Team Leader, Tedder Hall, Manby Park, Louth LN11 8UP ☎ 01507 613051 🖱 jonathan.challen@e-lindsey.gov.uk

Housing: Mr Jason Oxby Housing Advice & Homelessness Team Leader, Tedder Hall, Manby Park, Louth LN11 8UP ☎ 01507 613120 🖱 jason.oxby@e-lindsey.gov.uk

Leisure and Cultural Services: Mr Mark Humphreys, Strategic Development Manager, Tedder Hall, Manby Park, Louth LN11 8UP ☎ 01507 613441 🖱 mark.humphreys@e-lindsey.gov.uk

Licensing: Mr Adrian Twiddy, Licensing Officer, Tedder Hall, Manby Park, Louth LN11 8UP ☎ 01507 613011 🖷 01507 600206 🖱 adrian.twiddy@e-lindsey.gov.uk

Lottery Funding, Charity and Voluntary: Mr James Ward Community Development Officer, Tedder Hall, Manby Park, Louth LN11 8UP ☎ 01507 613073 🖷 01507 600206 🖱 james.ward@e-lindsey .gov.uk

Member Services: Mrs Ann Good Senior Member Services Officer, Tedder Hall, Manby Park, Louth LN11 8UP ☎ 01507 613420 🖱 ann.good@e-lindsey@gov.uk

Parking: Mr Duncan Hollingworth Team Leader of Enforcement, Tedder Hall, Manby Park, Louth LN11 8UP ☎ 01507 613558 🖱 duncan.hollingworth@e-lindsey.gov.uk

Partnerships: Mr John Medler Team Leader of Performance, Commissioning & Governance, Tedder Hall, Manby Park, Louth LN11 8UP ☎ 01507 613072 🖱 john.medler@e-lindsey.gov.uk

Personnel / HR: Ms Wendy Cundy Head - HR, Tedder Hall, Manby Park, Louth LN11 8UP ☎ 01507 613230 🖱 wendy.cundy@cpbs.com

Planning: Mr Chris Panton Planning Team Leader, Tedder Hall, Manby Park, Louth LN11 8UP ☎ 01507 613158 🖱 chris.panton@e-lindsey.gov.uk

Recycling & Waste Minimisation: Mr Nick Davis Team Leader of Waste Services, Tedder Hall, Manby Park, Louth LN11 8UP ☎ 01507 613540 🖱 nick.davis@e-lindsey.gov.uk

Regeneration: Mr James Makinson-Sanders Learning & Development Advisor, Tedder Hall, Manby Park, Louth LN11 8UP ☎ 🖱 james.makinson-sanders@e-lindsey.gov.uk

Staff Training: Mr James Makinson-Sanders Learning & Development Advisor, Tedder Hall, Manby Park, Louth LN11 8UP ☎ 🖱 james.makinson-sanders@e-lindsey.gov.uk

Street Scene: Mr Danny Wilson Team Leader - Service Development, Tedder Hall, Manby Park, Louth LN11 8UP ☎ 01507 613541 🖱 danny.wilson@e-lindsey.gov.uk

Tourism: Ms Alison Macdonald Business Development Manager, Tedder Hall, Manby Park, Louth LN11 8UP ☎ 01507 613114 🖱 alison.macdonald@e-lindsey.gov.uk

Town Centre: Ms Alison Macdonald Business Development Manager, Tedder Hall, Manby Park, Louth LN11 8UP ☎ 01507 613114 🖱 alison.macdonald@e-lindsey.gov.uk

Town Centre: Mr James Makinson-Sanders Learning & Development Advisor, Tedder Hall, Manby Park, Louth LN11 8UP ☎ 🖱 james.makinson-sanders@e-lindsey.gov.uk

Waste Collection and Disposal: Mr Nick Davis Team Leader of Waste Services, Tedder Hall, Manby Park, Louth LN11 8UP ☎ 01507 613540 🖱 nick.davis@e-lindsey.gov.uk

Waste Management: Mr Nick Davis Team Leader of Waste Services, Tedder Hall, Manby Park, Louth LN11 8UP ☎ 01507 613540 🖱 nick.davis@e-lindsey.gov.uk

COUNCILLORS

***Leader of the Council* Leyland**, Craig (CON - Woodhall Spa) craig.leyland@e-lindsey.gov.uk

***Deputy Leader of the Council* Marsh**, Graham (CON - Alford) graham.marsh@e-lyndsey.gov.uk

Aldridge, Terrence (CON - Holton le Clay) terry.aldridge@e-lindsey.gov.uk

Anderson, Mark (LAB - Skegness St. Clements) mark.anderson@e-lindsey.gov.uk

Archer, Graham (LAB - Ingoldmells) graham.archer@e-lindsey.gov.uk

Avison, Richard (CON - Horncastle) richard.avison@e-lindsey.gov.uk

Avison, Stanley (CON - Coningsby / Mareham) stanley.avison@e-lindsey.gov.uk

Ayling, Victoria (UKIP - Stickney) victoria.ayling@e-lindsey.gov.uk

Blacklock, Clive (CON - Holton le Clay) clive.blacklock@e-lindsey.gov.uk

Bridges, Anthony (CON - Tetney) tony.bridges@e-lindsey.gov.uk

Byford, John (IND - Skegness Seacroft)
john.byford@e-lindsey.gov.uk

Campbell-Wardman, Sandra (LD - Horncastle)
sandra.campbell-wardman@e-lindsey.gov.uk

Cooper, Neil (CON - Burgh le Marsh)
neil.cooper@e-lindsey.gov.uk

Cooper, Pauline (CON - Croft)
pauline.cooper@e-lindsey.gov.uk

Cullen, Graham (LAB - Mablethorpe Central)
graham.cullen@e-lindsey.gov.uk

Dennis, Sidney (CON - Skegness St. Clements)
sidney.dennis@e-lindsey.gov.uk

Devereux, Sarah (IND - Alford)
sarah.devereux@e-lyndsey.gov.uk

Dodds, Sarah (LAB - Louth Priory)
sarah.dodds@e-lindsey.gov.uk

Edginton, Dick (CON - Skegness Seacroft)
david.edginton@e-lindsey.gov.uk

Flitcroft, Aimee (UKIP - Coningsby / Mareham)
aimee.flitcroft@e-lindsey.gov.uk

Foster, Martin (IND - Coningsby / Mareham)
martin.foster@e-lindsey.gov.uk

Fry, Richard (CON - Binbrook)
richard.fry@e-lindsey.gov.uk

Gray, William (CON - Roughton)
william.gray@e-lindsey.gov.uk

Grist, Adam (CON - Legbourne)
adam.grist@e-lindsey.gov.uk

Harness, Philip (CON - Woodhall Spa)
philip.harness@e-lindsey.gov.uk

Harrison, Sandra (CON - Skidbrooke with Saltfleet Haven)
sandra.harrison@e-lindsey.gov.uk

Harrison, Janet (IND - Mareham le Fen)
janet.harrison@e-lindsey.gov.uk

Harvey, Rick (IND - Sibsey)
rick.harvey@e-lindsey.gov.uk

Hibbert-Greaves, Paul (CON - Chapel St Leonards)
paul.hibbert-greaves@e.lindsey.gov.uk

Hopkins, James (CON - Hunleby)
james.hopkins@e-lindsey.gov.uk

Horton, George (LD - Louth St. Michaels)
george.horton@e-lindsey.gov.uk

Howard, Tony (LAB - Mablethorpe East)
tony.howard@e-lindsey.gov.uk

Jones, Neil (CON - Frithville)
neil.jones@e-lindsey.gov.uk

Kemp, Phillip (LAB - Skegness Scarbrough)
phillip.kemp@e-lindsey.gov.uk

Knowles, Terence (IND - Grimoldby)
terence.knowles@e-lindsey.gov.uk

Macey, Carl (CON - Skegness Winthorpe)
carl.macey@e-lindsey.gov.uk

Makinson-Sanders, Jill (IND - Louth St. Mary's)
jill.makinson-sanders@e-lindsey.gov.uk

Marfleet, Hugo (CON - Withern with Stain)
hugo.marfleet@e-lindsey.gov.uk

Marfleet, L-J (CON - Tetford)
l-j.marfleet@e-lindsey.gov.uk

Martin, Fiona (LD - Horncastle)
fiona.martin@e-lindsey.gov.uk

Milner, Kenneth (CON - Skegness Scarbrough)
kenneth.milner@e-lindsey.gov.uk

Mossop, Edward (IND - Marshchapel)
edward.mossop@e-lindsey.gov.uk

O'Dare, Steve (CON - Skegness Winthorpe)
steve.odare@e-lindsey.gov.uk

Palmer, Stephen (IND - Sutton on Sea North)
stephen.palmer@e-lindsey.gov.uk

Palmer, Robert (CON - North Somercotes)
robert.palmer@e-lindsey.gov.uk

Phillipson, Peter (IND - Wragby)

Preen, Michael (LAB - Louth Trinity)
michael.preen@e-lindsey.gov.uk

Prince, Paddy (LAB - Mablethorpe North)
paddy.prince@e-lindsey.gov.uk

Simpson, Daniel (IND - Ludford)
daniel.simpson@e-lindsey.gov.uk

Smith, Kevin (CON - Wainfleet/Friskney)
kevin.smith@e-lindsey.gov.uk

Smith, Angie (CON - Willoughby/Sloothby)
angie.smith@e-lindsey.gov.uk

Stephenson, Laura (LAB - Louth St. Margarets)
laura.stephenson@e-lindsey.gov.uk

Stephenson, Doreen (CON - North Thoresby)
doreen.stephenson@e-lindsey.gov.uk

Sturman, Philip (LAB - Louth North Holme)
philip.sturman@e-lindsey.gov.uk

Swanson, Jim (CON - Halton Holegate)
jim.swanson@e-lindsey.gov.uk

Turton-Leivers, Mel (CON - Chapel St Leonards)
mel.turton-l@e-lindsey.gov.uk

Upsall, John (CON - Wainfleet/Friskney)
john.upsall@e-lindsey.gov.uk

Veasey, Anne (IND - Sutton on Sea South)
anne.veasey@e-lindsey.gov.uk

Watson, Stuart (CON - Thusthorpe / Mablethorpe South)
stuart.watson@e-lindsey.gov.uk

Watson, Pauline (CON - Louth St James)
pauline.watson@e-lindsey.gov.uk

Williams, Roderick (CON - Spilsby)
roderick.williams@e-lindsey.gov.uk

POLITICAL COMPOSITION

CON: 34, IND: 12, LAB: 10, LD: 3, UKIP: 2

COMMITTEE CHAIRS

Planning: Mr Richard Fry

Planning: Mr Neil Cooper

EAST LOTHIAN

East Lothian S

East Lothian Council, John Muir House, Brewery Park, Haddington EH41 3HA
☎ 01620 827827 feedback@eastlothian.gov.uk
www.eastlothian.gov.uk

FACTS AND FIGURES

Parliamentary Constituencies: East Lothian
EU Constituencies: Scotland
Election Frequency: Elections are of whole council

PRINCIPAL OFFICERS

Chief Executive: Ms Angela Leitch Chief Executive, John Muir House, Brewery Park, Haddington EH41 3HA ☎ 01620 827588 🖷 01620 827410 aleitch@eastlothian.gov.uk

Deputy Chief Executive: Mr Alex McCrorie, Deputy Chief Executive (Resources & People Services), John Muir House, Haddington EH41 3HA ☎ 01620 827827 🖷 01620 827446 amccrorie@eastlothian.gov.uk

Senior Management: Mr Alex McCrorie, Deputy Chief Executive (Resources & People Services), John Muir House, Haddington EH41 3HA ☎ 01620 827827 🖷 01620 827446 amccrorie@eastlothian.gov.uk

Senior Management: Ms Monica Patterson Executive Director - Partnership & Community Services, John Muir House, Brewery Park, Haddington EH41 3HA ☎ 01620 827827 mpatterson@eastlothian.gov.uk

Architect, Building / Property Services: Ms Liz McLean, Principal Architect, Penston House, Macmerry Industrial Estate, Macmerry, EH33 1EX ☎ 01620 827353 🖷 01620 827454 lmclean@eastlothian.gov.uk

Best Value: Mr Jim Lamond, Head of Council Resources, John Muir House, Haddington EH41 3HA ☎ 01620 827278 jlamond@eastlothian.gov.uk

Building Control: Mr Frank Fairgrieve Principal Building Surveyor, John Muir House, Brewery Park, Haddington EH41 3HA ☎ 01620 827357 ffairfield@eastlothian.gov.uk

Civil Registration: Ms Diane Robertson Communications & Marketing Manager, John Muir House, Brewery Park, Haddington EH41 3HA ☎ 01875 824100 drobertson@eastlothian.gov.uk

PR / Communications: Mr David Russell Communications & Marketing Manager, John Muir House, Haddington EH41 3HA ☎ 01875 824100 drussell@eastlothian.gov.uk

PR / Communications: Mr Tom Shearer, Head of Communities & Partnerships, John Muir House, Brewery Park, Haddington EH41 3HA ☎ 01620 827413 🖷 01620 827291 tshearer@eastlothian.gov.uk

Community Planning: Mr Paolo Vestri Corporate Policy Manager, John Muir House, Haddington EH41 3HA ☎ 01620 827320 🖷 01620 827442 pvestri@eastlothian.gov.uk

Community Safety: Ms Claire Goodwin, Policy Officer, John Muir House, Haddington EH41 3HA ☎ 01620 827270 🖷 01620 827442 cgoodwin@eastlothian.gov.uk

Corporate Services: Mr Jim Lamond, Head of Council Resources, John Muir House, Brewery Park, Haddington EH41 3HA ☎ 01620 827278 jlamond@eastlothian.gov.uk

Customer Service: Ms Eileen Morrison, Customer Services Manager, John Muir House, Haddington EH33 1EX ☎ 01620 827211 🖷 01620 827253 emorrison@eastlothian.gov.uk

Customer Service: Mr Tom Shearer, Head of Communities & Partnerships, John Muir House, Brewery Park, Haddington EH41 3HA ☎ 01620 827413 🖷 01620 827291 tshearer@eastlothian.gov.uk

Economic Development: Mr Douglas Proudfoot Head of Development, John Muir House, Brewery Park, Haddington EH41 3HA ☎ 01620 827827 dproudfoot@eastlothian.gov.uk

Education: Mr Darrin Nightingale Head of Education, John Muir House, Brewery Park, Haddington EH41 3HA ☎ 01620 827633 dnightingale@eastlothian.gov.uk

Education: Mr Richard Parker Service Manager - Education, John Muir House, Brewery Park, Haddington EH41 3HA ☎ 01620 827494 rparker@eastlothian.gov.uk

Electoral Registration: Mr Jim Lamond, Head of Council Resources, John Muir House, Haddington EH41 3HA ☎ 01620 827278 jlamond@eastlothian.gov.uk

Emergency Planning: Mr Sandy Baptie Emergency Planning Officer, John Muir House, Brewery Park, Haddington EH41 3HA ☎ 01620 827779 🖷 01620 827438 sbaptie@eastlothian.gov.uk

Emergency Planning: Mr Paolo Vestri Corporate Policy Manager, John Muir House, Brewery Park, Haddington EH41 3HA ☎ 01620 827320 🖷 01620 827442 pvestri@eastlothian.gov.uk

European Liaison: Ms Susan Smith, Economic Development Manager, Carlyle House, Lodge Street, Haddington EH41 3DX ☎ 01620 827174 ssmith@eastlothian.gov.uk

Facilities: Mr Ray Montgomery, Head of Infrastructure, John Muir House, Brewery Park, Haddington EH41 3HA ☎ 01620 827658 🖷 01620 827923 rmontgomery@eastlothian.gov.uk

Finance: Ms Mala Garden Internal Audit Manager, John Muir House, Brewery Park, Haddington EH41 3HA ☎ 01620 827326 mgarden@eastlothian.gov.uk

Finance: Mr Jim Lamond, Head of Council Resources, John Muir House, Brewery Park, Haddington EH41 3HA ☎ 01620 827278 jlamond@eastlothian.gov.uk

Finance: Mr Alex McCrorie, Deputy Chief Executive (Resources & People Services), John Muir House, Haddington EH41 3HA ☎ 01620 827827 🖷 01620 827446 amccrorie@eastlothian.gov.uk

Fleet Management: Mr Ray Montgomery, Head of Infrastructure, John Muir House, Haddington EH41 3HA ☎ 01620 827658 🖷 01620 827923 rmontgomery@eastlothian.gov.uk

Grounds Maintenance: Mr Stuart Pryde Principal Amenities Officer - Landscape & Countryside, Block C, Brewery Park, Haddington EH41 3HA ☎ 01620 827430 spryde@eastlothian.gov.uk

Health and Safety: Mr Keith Flockhart Health & Safety Advisor, John Muir House, Brewery Park, Haddington EH41 3HA ☎ 01620 827639 clawson@eastlothian.gov.uk

Health and Safety: Mr Paolo Vestri Corporate Policy Manager, John Muir House, Brewery Park, Haddington EH41 3HA ☎ 01620 827320 🖷 01620 827442 pvestri@eastlothian.gov.uk

Highways: Mr Ray Montgomery, Head of Infrastructure, John Muir House, Haddington EH41 3HA ☎ 01620 827658 🖷 01620 827923 rmontgomery@eastlothian.gov.uk

Legal: Mr Jim Lamond, Head of Council Resources, John Muir House, Brewery Park, Haddington EH41 3HA ☎ 01620 827278 jlamond@eastlothian.gov.uk

Leisure and Cultural Services: Mr Tom Shearer, Head of Communities & Partnerships, John Muir House, Haddington EH41 3HA ☎ 01620 827413 🖷 01620 827291 tshearer@eastlothian.gov.uk

Lifelong Learning: Ms Myra Galloway, Service Manager - Community Partnerships, John Muir House, Haddington EH41 3HA ☎ 0131 653 4075 🖷 01620 827291 mgalloway@eastlothian.gov.uk

Lighting: Mr Glen Kane Senior Lighting Officer, John Muir House, Brewery Park, Haddington EH41 3HA ☎ 01620 827827 gkane@eastlothian.gov.uk

Lottery Funding, Charity and Voluntary: Ms Esther Wilson Service Manager, John Muir House, Brewery Park, Haddington EH41 3HA ☎ 01620 827361 🖷 01620 827482 ewilson@eastlothian.gov.uk

Member Services: Ms Lel Gillingwater Democratic Services Manager, John Muir House, Haddington EH41 3HA ☎ 01620 827225 lgillingwater@eastlothian.gov.uk

Member Services: Mr Jim Lamond, Head of Council Resources, John Muir House, Brewery Park, Haddington EH41 3HA ☎ 01620 827278 jlamond@eastlothian.gov.uk

Member Services: Ms Jill Totney Democratic Services Manager, John Muir House, Brewery Park, Haddington EH41 3HA ☎ 01620 827225 jtotney@eastlothian.gov.uk

Partnerships: Mr Tom Shearer, Head of Communities & Partnerships, John Muir House, Brewery Park, Haddington EH41 3HA ☎ 01620 827413 🖷 01620 827291 tshearer@eastlothian.gov.uk

Personnel / HR: Mr Jim Lamond, Head of Council Resources, John Muir House, Brewery Park, Haddington EH41 3HA ☎ 01620 827278 jlamond@eastlothian.gov.uk

Personnel / HR: Ms Sharon Saunders, Head of Children's Wellbeing, John Muir House, Haddington EH41 3HA ☎ 01620 827827 🖷 01620 827612 ssaunders@eastlothian.gov.uk

Procurement: Mr Jim Lamond, Head of Council Resources, John Muir House, Brewery Park, Haddington EH41 3HA ☎ 01620 827278 jlamond@eastlothian.gov.uk

Public Libraries: Ms Alison Hunter, Libraries Officer, Library Headquarters, Dunbar Road, Haddington EH41 3PJ ☎ 01620 828700 🖷 01620 828201 ahunter@eastlothian.gov.uk

Public Libraries: Mr Tom Shearer, Head of Communities & Partnerships, John Muir House, Brewery Park, Haddington EH41 3HA ☎ 01620 827413 🖷 01620 827291 tshearer@eastlothian.gov.uk

Recycling & Waste Minimisation: Mr Tom Reid Waste Services Manager, John Muir House, Brewery Park, Haddington EH41 3HA ☎ 01620 827830 treid@westlothian.gov.uk

Road Safety: Mr Colin Baird Senior Road Officer, John Muir House, Haddington EH41 3HA ☎ 01620 827739 🖷 01620 827710 cbaird@eastlothian.gov.uk

Social Services: Ms Monica Patterson Executive Director - Partnership & Community Services, John Muir House, Brewery Park, Haddington EH41 3HA ☎ 01620 827827 mpatterson@eastlothian.gov.uk

Social Services (Adult): Ms Trish Leddy Head of Adult Wellbeing, John Muir House, Brewery Park, Haddington EH41 3HA ☎ 01620 827827 tleddy@eastlothian.gov.uk

Social Services (Children): Ms Sharon Saunders, Head of Children's Wellbeing, John Muir House, Brewe ry Park, Haddington EH41 3HA ☎ 01620 827827 🖷 01620 827612 ssaunders@eastlothian.gov.uk

Staff Training: Mr Paolo Vestri Corporate Policy Manager, John Muir House, Brewery Park, Haddington EH41 3HA ☎ 01620 827320 🖷 01620 827442 pvestri@eastlothian.gov.uk

Sustainable Communities: Mr Paolo Vestri Corporate Policy Manager, John Muir House, Haddington EH41 3HA ☎ 01620 827320 🖷 01620 827442 pvestri@eastlothian.gov.uk

Tourism: Ms Claire Dutton, Tourism Officer, Carlyle House, Lodge Street, Haddington EH41 3DX ☎ 01620 827371 🖷 01620 827482 cdutton@eastlothian.gov.uk

Tourism: Mr Tom Shearer, Head of Communities & Partnerships, John Muir House, Brewery Park, Haddington EH41 3HA ☎ 01620 827413 🖷 01620 827291 tshearer@eastlothian.gov.uk

Traffic Management: Mr Ray Montgomery, Head of Infrastructure, John Muir House, Haddington EH41 3HA ☎ 01620 827658 🖷 01620 827923 rmontgomery@eastlothian.gov.uk

EAST LOTHIAN

Waste Collection and Disposal: Mr Tom Reid Waste Services Manager, John Muir House, Brewery Park, Haddington EH41 3HA ☎ 01620 827830 ✉ treid@westlothian.gov.uk

Waste Management: Mr Ray Montgomery, Head of Infrastructure, John Muir House, Brewery Park, Haddington EH41 3HA ☎ 01620 827658 🖷 01620 827923 ✉ rmontgomery@eastlothian.gov.uk

Waste Management: Mr Tom Reid Waste Services Manager, John Muir House, Brewery Park, Haddington EH41 3HA ☎ 01620 827830 ✉ treid@westlothian.gov.uk

COUNCILLORS

***Provost* Broun-Lindsay**, Ludovic (CON - Haddington and Lammermuir)
lbroun-linday@eastlothian.gov.uk

***Leader of the Council* Innes**, Willie (LAB - Preston/Seton/Gosford)
winnes@eastlothian.gov.uk

***Deputy Leader of the Council* Veitch**, Michael (CON - Dunbar and East Linton)
mveitch1@eastlothian.gov.uk

Akhtar, Shamin (LAB - Fa'side)
sakhtar@eastlothian.gov.uk

Berry, David (IND - North Berwick Coastal)
dberry@eastlothian.gov.uk

Brown, Steven (SNP - Preston/Seton/Gosford)
sbrown1@eastlothian.gov.uk

Caldwell, John (IND - Musselburgh East and Carberry)
jcaldwell1@eastlothian.gov.uk

Currie, Stuart (SNP - Musselburgh East and Carberry)
scurrie@eastlothian.gov.uk

Day, Tim (CON - North Berwick Coastal)
tday@eastlothian.gov.uk

Forrest, Andrew (LAB - Musselburgh East and Carberry)
aforrest2@eastlothian.gov.uk

Gillies, Jim (LAB - Fa'side)
jgillies@eastlothian.gov.uk

Goodfellow, Jim (LAB - North Berwick Coastal)
jgoodfellow@eastlothian.gov.uk

Grant, Donald (LAB - Fa'side)
dgrant@eastlothian.gov.uk

Hampshire, Norman (LAB - Dunbar and East Linton)
nhampshire@eastlothian.gov.uk

Libberton, Margaret (LAB - Preston/Seton/Gosford)
mlibberton1@eastlothian.gov.uk

MacKenzie, Peter (SNP - Preston/Seton/Gosford)
pmackenzie@eastlothian.gov.uk

McAllister, Fraser (SNP - Musselburgh West)
fmcallister@eastlothian.gov.uk

McLennan, Paul (SNP - Dunbar and East Linton)
pmclennan@eastlothian.gov.uk

McLeod, Kenny (SNP - Fa'side)
kmcleod1@eastlothian.gov.uk

McMillan, John (LAB - Haddington and Lammermuir)
jmcmillan@eastlothian.gov.uk

McNeil, John (LAB - Musselburgh West)
jmcneil@eastlothian.gov.uk

Trotter, Tom (SNP - Haddington and Lammermuir)
ttrotter@eastlothian.gov.uk

Williamson, John (SNP - Musselburgh West)
jwilliamson@eastlothian.gov.uk

POLITICAL COMPOSITION

LAB: 10, SNP: 8, CON: 3, IND: 2

COMMITTEE CHAIRS

Audit & Governance: Mr Kenny McLeod

Education: Cllr Shamin Akhtar

Planning: Mr Norman Hampshire

East Northamptonshire D

East Northamptonshire District Council, East Northamptonshire House, Cedar Drive, Thrapston NN14 4LZ
☎ 01832 742000 🖷 01832 734839
✉ info@east-northamptonshire.gov.uk
🖳 www.east-northamptonshire.gov.uk

FACTS AND FIGURES

Parliamentary Constituencies: Corby, Wellingborough
EU Constituencies: East Midlands
Election Frequency: Elections are of whole council

PRINCIPAL OFFICERS

Chief Executive: Mr David Oliver, Chief Executive, East Northamptonshire House, Cedar Drive, Thrapston NN14 4LZ
☎ 01832 742106 ✉ doliver@east-northamptonshire.gov.uk

Senior Management: Ms Sharn Matthews Executive Director & Monitoring Officer, East Northamptonshire House, Cedar Drive, Thrapston NN14 4LZ ☎ 01832 742108
✉ smatthews@east-northamptonshire.gov.uk

Children / Youth Services: Mr Mike Greenway Community Partnerships Manager, East Northamptonshire Council, Cedar Drive, Thrapston NN10 4LZ ☎ 01832 742244
✉ mgreenway@east-northamptonshire.gov.uk

PR / Communications: Mrs Louise Spolton Communications Manager, East Northamptonshire House, Cedar Drive, Thrapston NN14 4LZ ☎ 01832 742217
✉ lspolton@east-northamptonshire.gov.uk

Community Planning: Mr Mike Greenway Community Partnerships Manager, East Northamptonshire Council, Cedar Drive, Thrapston NN10 4LZ ☎ 01832 742244
✉ mgreenway@east-northamptonshire.gov.uk

Community Safety: Mr Mike Greenway Community Development Manager, East Northamptonshire Council, Cedar Drive, Thrapston NN10 4LZ ☎ 01832 742244
✉ mgreenway@east-northamptonshire.gov.uk

Computer Management: Mr Phil Grimley Head of ICT Services, East Northamptonshire Council, Cedar Drive, Thrapston NN14 4LZ ☎ 01832 742076 ✉ pgrimley@east_northamptonshire.gov.uk

Corporate Services: Mrs Katy Everitt, Head of Resources & Organisational Development, East Northamptonshire House, Cedar House, Thrapston NN14 4LZ ☎ 01832 742113 ✉ personnel@east-northamptonshire.gov.uk

Economic Development: Ms Sharn Matthews Executive Director & Monitoring Officer, East Northamptonshire House, Cedar Drive, Thrapston NN14 4LZ ☎ 01832 742108 ✉ smatthews@east-northamptonshire.gov.uk

E-Government: Ms Angela Hook Corporate Support Manager, East Northamptonshire House, Cedar Drive, Thrapston NN14 4LZ ☎ 01832 742203 ✉ ahook@east-northamptonshire.gov.uk

Electoral Registration: Mr James McLaughlin Democratic & Electoral Services Manager, Cedar Drive, Thrapston NN14 4LZ ☎ 01832 742113 ✉ jmclaughlin@east-northamptonshire.gov.uk

Environmental Health: Mr Mike Deacon, Head of Environmental Services, East Northamptonshire House, Cedar Drive, Thrapston NN14 4LZ ☎ 01832 742060 ✉ environmentalservices@east-northamptonshire.gov.uk

Facilities: Mr Richard Hankins, Amenities Manager, East Northamptonshire House, Cedar Drive, Thrapston NN14 4LZ ☎ 01832 742031 ✉ rhankins@east-northamptonshire.gov.uk

Finance: Mr Glenn Hammons Chief Finance Officer & Section 151 Officer, East Northamptonshire House, Cedar Drive, Thrapston NN14 4LZ ☎ 01832 742267 ✉ ghammons@east-northamptonshire.gov.uk

Grounds Maintenance: Mr Richard Hankins, Amenities Manager, East Northamptonshire House, Cedar Drive, Thrapston NN14 4LZ ☎ 01832 742031 ✉ rhankins@east-northamptonshire.gov.uk

Housing: Ms Carol Conway Housing Strategy & Delivery Manager, East Northamptonshire House, Cedar Drive, Thrapston NN14 4LZ ☎ 01832 742078 ✉ cconway@east-northamptonshire.gov.uk

Licensing: Mr Mike Deacon, Head of Environmental Services, East Northamptonshire House, Cedar Drive, Thrapston NN14 4LZ ☎ 01832 742060 ✉ environmentalservices@east-northamptonshire.gov.uk

Member Services: Mr James McLaughlin Democratic & Electoral Services Manager, Cedar Drive, Thrapston NN14 4LZ ☎ 01832 742113 ✉ jmclaughlin@east-northamptonshire.gov.uk

Partnerships: Mr Mike Greenway, Community Partnerships Manager, East Northamptonshire House, Cedar Drive, Thrapston NN14 4LZ ☎ 01832 742244 ✉ mgreenway@east-northamptonshire.gov.uk

Personnel / HR: Mrs Katy Everitt, Head of Resources & Organisational Development, East Northamptonshire House, Cedar House, Thrapston NN14 4LZ ☎ 01832 742113 ✉ personnel@east-northamptonshire.gov.uk

Planning: Mr David Reed Head of Planning Services, East Northamptonshire House, Cedar Drive, Thrapston NN14 4LZ ☎ 01832 742218 ✉ dreed@east-northamptonshire.gov.uk

Recycling & Waste Minimisation: Ms Charlotte Tompkins Waste Manager, East Northamptonshire House, Cedar Drive, Thrapston NN14 4LZ ☎ 01832 742208 ✉ waste@east-northamptonshire.gov.uk

Regeneration: Mr Mike Greenway, Community Partnerships Manager, East Northamptonshire House, Cedar Drive, Thrapston NN14 4LZ ☎ 01832 742244 ✉ mgreenway@east-northamptonshire.gov.uk

Staff Training: Mrs Katy Everitt, Head of Resources & Organisational Development, East Northamptonshire House, Cedar House, Thrapston NN14 4LZ ☎ 01832 742113 ✉ personnel@east-northamptonshire.gov.uk

Sustainable Communities: Mr Mike Greenway, Community Partnerships Manager, East Northamptonshire House, Cedar Drive, Thrapston NN14 4LZ ☎ 01832 742244 ✉ mgreenway@east-northamptonshire.gov.uk

Sustainable Development: Mr Mike Greenway Community Partnerships Manager, East Northamptonshire Council, Cedar Drive, Thrapston NN10 4LZ ☎ 01832 742244 ✉ mgreenway@east-northamptonshire.gov.uk

Tourism: Miss Karen Williams, Tourism Development & Promotion Officer, East Northamptonshire House, Cedar Drive, Thrapston NN14 4LZ ☎ 01832 742064 ✉ kwilliams@east-northamptonshire.gov.uk

Waste Collection and Disposal: Ms Charlotte Tompkins Waste Manager, East Northamptonshire House, Cedar Drive, Thrapston NN14 4LZ ☎ 01832 742208 ✉ waste@east-northamptonshire.gov.uk

Waste Management: Ms Charlotte Tompkins Waste Manager, East Northamptonshire House, Cedar Drive, Thrapston NN14 4LZ ☎ 01832 742208 ✉ waste@east-northamptonshire.gov.uk

COUNCILLORS

***Chair* Hillson**, Marika (CON - Irthlingborough Waterloo)
mhillson@east-northamptonshire.gov.uk

***Vice-Chair* Reichhold**, Rupert (CON - Oundle)

***Leader of the Council* North**, Steven (CON - Rushden Sartoris)
snorth@east-northamptonshire.gov.uk

***Deputy Leader of the Council* Harwood**, Glenn (CON - Higham Ferrers Lancaster)
gharwood@east-northamptonshire.gov.uk

Beattie, Rosalie (CON - Thrapston Market)
rbeattie@east-northamptonshire.gov.uk

Boto, Tony (CON - Raunds Saxon)
tboto@east-northamptonshire.gov.uk

Brackenbury, Wendy (CON - Thrapston Lakes)
wbrackenbury@east-northamptonshire.gov.uk

Brackenbury, David (CON - Lower Nene)
dbrackenbury@east-northamptonshire.gov.uk

EAST NORTHAMPTONSHIRE

Carter, Val (IND - Thrapston Lakes)
vcarter@east-northamtonshire.gov.uk

Farrar, John (LAB - Irthlingborough John Pyel)
jfarrar@east-northamptonshire.gov.uk

Gell, Richard (IND - Higham Ferrers Chichele)
rgell@east-northamptonshire.gov.uk

Glithero, Roger (CON - Kings Forest)
rglithero@east-northamptonshire.gov.uk

Greenwood-Smith, Glenvil (CON - Raunds Windmill)
glenvil@east-northamptonshire.gov.uk

Harrison, Helen (CON - Fineshade)
hharrison@east-northamptonshire.gov.uk

Hobbs, Sylvia (CON - Irthlingborough Waterloo)
shobbs@east-northamtponshire.gov.uk

Hollomon, Marian (CON - Rushden Hayden)
mhollomon@east-northamptonshire.gov.uk

Howell, Helen (DUP - Stanwick)
hhowell@east-northamptonshire.gov.uk

Hughes, Dudley (CON - Woodford)
dhughes@east-northamptonshire.gov.uk

Hughes, Sylvia (CON - Lyveden)
shughes@east-northamptonshire.gov.uk

Jenney, David (CON - Rushden Bates)
djenney@east-northamptonshire.gov.uk

Jenney, Barbara (CON - Rushden Hayden)
bjenney@east-northamptonshire.gov.uk

Jones, Lance (CON - Raunds Saxon)
ljones@east-hamptonshire.gov.uk

Lewis, Richard (CON - Rushden Hayden)
rlewis@east-northamptonshire.gov.uk

Maxwell, Dorothy (CON - Rushden Spencer)
dmaxwell@east-northamptonshire.gov.uk

Mercer, Andy (CON - Rushden Spencer)
amercer@east-northamptonshire.gov.uk

Mercer, Gill (CON - Rushden Pemberton)
gmercer@east-northamptonshire.gov.uk

Peacock, Sarah (CON - Rushden Spencer)
speacock@east-northamptonshire.gov.uk

Pinnock, Ron (CON - Rushden Sartoris)
rpinnock@east-northamptonshire.gov.uk

Pinnock, Janet (CON - Rushden Pemberton)
jpinnock@east-northamptonshire.gov.uk

Powell, Roger (CON - Irthlingborough John Pyel)
rpowell@east-northamptonshire.gov.uk

Raven-hill, Valerie (CON - Prebendal)
vraven@east-nothamptonshire.gov.uk

Saunston, Anna (CON - Higham Ferrers Chichele)
asaunton@east-northamptonshire.gov.uk

Shacklock, Geoff (CON - Barnwell)
gshacklock@east-northamptonshire.gov.uk

Smith, Alex (CON - Thrapston Market)
asmith@east-northamptonshire.gov.uk

Stearn, Phillip (CON - Oundle)
pstearn@east-northamptonshire.gov.uk

Underwood, Robin (CON - Rushden Bates)
runderwood@east-northamptonshire.gov.uk

Vowles, Jake (CON - Oundle)
jvowles@east-northamptonshire.gov.uk

Wathen, Peter (CON - Raunds Windmill)
pwathen@east-northamptonshire.gov.uk

Whiting, Pam (CON - Higham Ferrers Lancaster)
pwhiting@east-northamptonshire.gov.uk

Wright, Colin (CON - Rushden Pemberton)
cwright@east-northamptonshire.gov.uk

POLITICAL COMPOSITION

CON: 36, IND: 2, LAB: 1, DUP: 1

COMMITTEE CHAIRS

Audit: Mr Colin Wright

Licensing: Mr Glenvil Greenwood-Smith

Planning: Mr David Brackenbury

Planning: Mr Phillip Stearn

East Renfrewshire S

East Renfrewshire Council, Council Headquarters, Eastwood Park, Rouken Glen Road, Giffnock G46 6UG
☎ 0141 577 3000 🖷 0141 620 0884
🖱 customerservices@eastrenfrewshire.gov.uk
💻 www.eastrenfrewshire.gov.uk

FACTS AND FIGURES

Parliamentary Constituencies: Renfrewshire East
EU Constituencies: Scotland
Election Frequency: Elections are of whole council

PRINCIPAL OFFICERS

Chief Executive: Mrs Lorraine McMillan Chief Executive, Council Headquarters, Eastwood Park, Rouken Glen Road, Giffnock G46 6UG ☎ 0141 577 3009 🖷 0141 577 3017
🖱 lorraine.mcmillan@eastrenfrewshire.gov.uk

Deputy Chief Executive: Mrs Caroline Innes, Deputy Chief Executive, Council Headquarters, Eastwood Park, Rouken Glen Road, Giffnock G46 6UG ☎ 0141 577 3161 🖷 0141 577 3155
🖱 caroline.innes@eastrenfrewshire.gov.uk

Senior Management: Mr Andrew Cahill, Director - Environment, 2 Spiersbridge Way, Spiersbridge Business Park, Thornliebank G46 8NG ☎ 0141 577 3036 🖷 0141 577 3078
🖱 andrew.cahill@eastrenfrewshire.gov.uk

Senior Management: Mrs Julie Murray CHCP Director, Council Headquarters, Eastwood Park, Rouken Glen Road, Giffnock G46 6UG ☎ 0141 577 3840 🖷 0141 577 3846
🖱 julie.murray@eastrenfrewshire.gov.uk

Senior Management: Ms Mhairi Shaw Director - Education, Barrhead Council Offices, 211 Main Street, Barrhead G78 1SY
☎ 0141 577 3404 🖱 mhairi.shaw@eastrenfrewshire.gov.uk

Children / Youth Services: Mrs Julie Murray CHCP Director, Council Headquarters, Eastwood Park, Rouken Glen Road, Giffnock G46 6UG ☎ 0141 577 3840 🖷 0141 577 3846 ✉ julie.murray@eastrenfrewshire.gov.uk

Children / Youth Services: Ms Kate Rocks Head of Children's Services, 1 Burnfield Avenue, , Giffnock G46 7TT ☎ 0141 577 3841 ✉ kate.rocks@eastrenfrewshire.gov.uk

Civil Registration: Mr Jim Clarke Registrar, Council Headquarters, Eastwood Park, Rouken Glen Road, Giffnock G46 6UG ☎ ; 0141 577 3452 ✉ jim.clarke@eastrenfrewshire.gov.uk

PR / Communications: Ms Louisa Mahon Communications Manager, Council Headquarters, Eastwood Park, Rouken Glen Road, Giffnock G46 6UG ☎ 0141 577 3851 🖷 0141 577 3852 ✉ louisa.mahon@eastrenfrewshire.gov.uk

Community Planning: Mr Jamie Reid, Community Resources Manager, Council Headquarters, Eastwood Park, Rouken Glen Road, Giffnock G46 6UG ☎ 0141 577 8557 ✉ jamie.reid@eastrenfrewshire.gov.uk

Community Safety: Mr Jim Sneddon, Head of Democratic Services, Council Headquarters, Eastwood Park, Rouken Glen Road, Giffnock G46 6UG ☎ 0141 577 3744 ✉ jim.sneddon@eastrenfrewshire.gov.uk

Consumer Protection and Trading Standards: Mr Andrew Corry Head of Environmental Services, Council Headquarters, Eastwood Park, Rouken Glen Road, Giffnock G46 6UG ☎ 0141 577 3756 🖷 0141 577 3181 ✉ andrew.corry@eastrenfrewshire.gov.uk

Contracts: Ms Diane Pirie Chief Procurement Manager, Council Headquarters, Eastwood Park, Rouken Glen Road, Giffnock G46 6UG ☎ 0141 577 3676 ✉ diane.pirie@eastrenfrewshire.gov.uk

Customer Service: Mrs Louise Pringle Head of Customer & Business Change Services, Council Headquarters, Eastwood Park, Rouken Glen Road, Giffnock G46 6UG ☎ 0141 577 3000 ✉ louise.pringle@eastrenfrewshire.gov.uk

Economic Development: Mrs Gillian McNamara Regeneration & Economic Development Manager, 2 Spiersbridge Way, Spiersbridge Business Park, Thornliebank G46 8NG ☎ 0141 577 3753 ✉ gillian.mcnamara@eastrenfrewshire.gov.uk

Education: Ms Fiona Morrison Head of Education Services (Performance & Provision), Barrhead Council Offices, 211 Main Street, Barrhead G78 1SY ☎ 0141 577 3229 ✉ fiona.morrison@eastrenfrewshire.gov.uk

Education: Mr Mark Ratter Head of Education Services, Barrhead Council Offices, 211 Main Street, Barrhead G78 1SY ☎ 0141 577 3481 ✉ mark.ratter@eastrenfrewshire.gov.uk

Education: Ms Mhairi Shaw Director - Education, Barrhead Council Offices, 211 Main Street, Barrhead G78 1SY ☎ 0141 577 3404 ✉ mhairi.shaw@eastrenfrewshire.gov.uk

Environmental / Technical Services: Mr Andrew Cahill, Director - Environment, 2 Spiersbridge Way, Spiersbridge Business Park, Thornliebank G46 8NG ☎ 0141 577 3036 🖷 0141 577 3078 ✉ andrew.cahill@eastrenfrewshire.gov.uk

Environmental Health: Mr Andrew Corry Head of Environmental Services, 2 Spiersbridge Way, Spiersbridge Business Park, Thornliebank G46 8NG ☎ 0141 577 3756 🖷 0141 577 3181 ✉ andrew.corry@eastrenfrewshire.gov.uk

Events Manager: Mr Malcolm Wright Events Co-ordinator, Council Headquarters, Eastwood Park, Rouken Glen Road, Giffnock G46 6UG ☎ 0141 577 4854 ✉ malcolm.wright@eastrenfrewshire.gov.uk

Finance: Ms Margaret McCrossan Head of Accountancy Services, Council Headquarters, Eastwood Park, Rouken Glen Road, Giffnock G46 6UG ☎ 0141 577 3035 ✉ margaret.mccrossan@eastrenfrewshire.gov.uk

Health and Safety: Mr Steve Murray Principal Health & Safety Advisor, 2 Spiersbridge Way, Spiersbridge Business Park, Thornliebank G46 8NG ☎ 0141 577 3323 ✉ steve.murray@eastrenfrewshire.gov.uk

Housing: Mr Phil Dawes Housing of Environment, 2 Spiersbridge Way, Spiersbridge Business Park, Thornliebank G46 8NG ☎ 0141 577 3186 ✉ phil.dawes@eastrenfrewshire.gov.uk

Legal: Mr Gerry Mahon Chief Solicitor to the Council, Council Headquarters, Eastwood Park, Rouken Glen Road, Giffnock G46 6UG ☎ 0141 577 3024 ✉ gerry.mahon@eastrenfrewshire.gov.uk

Member Services: Ms Margaret Pettigrew, Member Services Officer, Council Headquarters, Eastwood Park, Rouken Glen Road, Giffnock G46 6UG ☎ 0141 577 3107 ✉ margaret.pettigrew@eastrenfrewshire.gov.uk

Partnerships: Mrs Julie Murray CHCP Director, Council Headquarters, Eastwood Park, Rouken Glen Road, Giffnock G46 6UG ☎ 0141 577 3840 🖷 0141 577 3846 ✉ julie.murray@eastrenfrewshire.gov.uk

Personnel / HR: Ms Sharon Beattie Human Resources Manager, Council Headquarters, Eastwood Park, Rouken Glen Road, Giffnock G46 6UG ☎ 0141 577 3161 🖷 0141 577 3155 ✉ sharon.beattie@eastrenfrewshire.gov.uk

Planning: Ms Gillian McCarney Planning & Building Standards Manager, 2 Spiersbridge Way, Spiersbridge Business Park, Thornliebank RG46 8NG ☎ 0141 577 3116 ✉ gillian.mccarney@eastrenfrewshire.gov.uk

Procurement: Ms Diane Pirie Chief Procurement Manager, Council Headquarters, Eastwood Park, Rouken Glen Road, Giffnock G46 6UG ☎ 0141 577 3676 ✉ diane.pirie@eastrenfrewshire.gov.uk

Recycling & Waste Minimisation: Mr Andrew Corry Head of Environmental Services, Council Headquarters, Eastwood Park, Rouken Glen Road, Giffnock G46 6UG ☎ 0141 577 3756 🖷 0141 577 3181 ✉ andrew.corry@eastrenfrewshire.gov.uk

EAST RENFREWSHIRE

Regeneration: Mrs Gillian McNamara Regeneration & Economic Development Manager, 2 Spiersbridge Way, Spiersbridge Business Park, Thornliebank G46 8NG ☎ 0141 577 3753
gillian.mcnamara@eastrenfrewshire.gov.uk

Social Services: Mrs Julie Murray CHCP Director, Council Headquarters, Eastwood Park, Rouken Glen Road, Giffnock G46 6UG ☎ 0141 577 3840 🖷 0141 577 3846
julie.murray@eastrenfrewshire.gov.uk

Social Services (Adult): Mrs Julie Murray CHCP Director, Council Headquarters, Eastwood Park, Rouken Glen Road, Giffnock G46 6UG ☎ 0141 577 3840 🖷 0141 577 3846
julie.murray@eastrenfrewshire.gov.uk

Social Services (Children): Mrs Julie Murray CHCP Director, Council Headquarters, Eastwood Park, Rouken Glen Road, Giffnock G46 6UG ☎ 0141 577 3840 🖷 0141 577 3846
julie.murray@eastrenfrewshire.gov.uk

Sustainable Development: Mr Andrew Cahill, Director - Environment, 2 Spiersbridge Way, Spiersbridge Business Park, Thornliebank G46 8NG ☎ 0141 577 3036 🖷 0141 577 3078
andrew.cahill@eastrenfrewshire.gov.uk

Waste Management: Mr Andrew Corry Head of Environmental Services, Council Headquarters, Eastwood Park, Rouken Glen Road, Giffnock G46 6UG ☎ 0141 577 3756 🖷 0141 577 3181
andrew.corry@eastrenfrewshire.gov.uk

COUNCILLORS

***Provost* Carmichael**, Alastair (SNP - Busby, Clarkston and Eaglesham)
alastair.carmichael@eastrenfrewshire.gov.uk

***Deputy Provost* Cunningham**, Betty (LAB - Barrhead)
betty.cunningham@eastrenfrewshire.gov.uk

***Leader of the Council* Fletcher**, Jim (LAB - Giffnock and Thornliebank)
jim.fletcher@eastrenfrewshire.gov.uk

***Deputy Leader of the Council* Buchanan**, Tony (SNP - Neilston, Uplawmoor and Newton Mearns North)
tony.buchanan@eastrenfrewshire.gov.uk

***Group Leader* Wallace**, Gordon (CON - Giffnock and Thornliebank)
gordon.wallace@eastrenfrewshire.gov.uk

Devlin, Danny (IND - Barrhead)
danny.devlin@eastrenfrewshire.gov.uk

Gilbert, Charlie (CON - Neilston, Uplawmoor and Newton Mearns North)
charlie.gilbert@eastrenfrewshire.gov.uk

Grant, Barbara (CON - Newton Mearns South)
barbara.grant@eastrenfrewshire.gov.uk

Green, Elaine (LAB - Neilston, Uplawmoor and Newton Mearns North)
elaine.green@eastrenfrewshire.gov.uk

Hay, Kenny (LAB - Barrhead)
kenny.hay@eastrenfrewshire.gov.uk

Lafferty, Alan (LAB - Busby, Clarkston and Eaglesham)
alan.lafferty@eastrenfrewshire.gov.uk

McAlpine, Ian (LAB - Newton Mearns South)
ian.mcalpine@eastrenfrewshire.gov.uk

McCaskill, Gordon (CON - Netherlee, Stamplerland and Williamwood)
gordon.mccaskil@eastrenfrewshire.gov.uk

Miller, Stewart (CON - Busy, Clarkston and Eaglesham)
stewart.miller@eastrenfrewshire.gov.uk

Montague, Mary (LAB - Netherlee, Stamplerland and Williamwood)
mary.montague@eastrenfrewshire.gov.uk

O'Kane, Paul (LAB - Neilston, Uplawmoor and Newton Mearns North)
paul.o'kane@eastrenfrewshire.gov.uk

Reilly, Tommy (SNP - Barrhead)
tommy.reilly@eastrenfrewshire.gov.uk

Robertson, Ralph (IND - Netherlee, Stamplerland and Williamwood)
ralph.robertson@eastrenfrewshire.gov.uk

Swift, Jim (CON - Newton Mearns South)
jim.swift@eastrenfrewshire.gov.uk

Waters, Vincent (SNP - Giffnock and Thornliebank)
vincent.waters@eastrenfrewshire.gov.uk

POLITICAL COMPOSITION

LAB: 8, CON: 6, SNP: 4, IND: 2

COMMITTEE CHAIRS

Appeals: Mr Ian McAlpine

Audit: Mr Gordon Wallace

Education: Ms Elaine Green

Licensing: Mr Tommy Reilly

Planning: Mr Kenny Hay

East Riding of Yorkshire U

East Riding of Yorkshire Council, County Hall, Beverley HU17 9BA
☎ 01482 887700 🖷 01482 884150 💻 www.eastriding.gov.uk

FACTS AND FIGURES

Parliamentary Constituencies: Beverley & Holderness, Haltemprice and Howden, Yorkshire East
EU Constituencies: Yorkshire and the Humber
Election Frequency: Elections are of whole council

PRINCIPAL OFFICERS

Chief Executive: Mr Nigel Pearson, Chief Executive, County Hall, Beverley HU17 9BA ☎ 01482 391000
nigel.pearson@eastriding.gov.uk

Senior Management: Mr Tim Allison Director - Public Health, County Hall, Beverley HU17 9BA ☎ 01482 391551; 01482 672068
tim.allison@eastriding.gov.uk; tim.allison@nhs.net

Senior Management: Mr Kevin Hall Director - Children, Families & Schools, County Hall, Beverley HU17 9BA ☎ 01482 392000
kevin.hall@eastriding.gov.uk

Senior Management: Mr Nigel Leighton Director - Environment & Neighbourhood Services, County Hall, Beverley HU17 9BA ☎ 01482 395000 ✉ nigel.leighton@eastriding.gov.uk

Senior Management: Mr Alan Menzies, Director - Planning & Economic Regeneration, County Hall, Beverley HU17 9BA ☎ 01482 391600 ✉ alan.menzies@eastriding.gov.uk

Senior Management: Mr Malcolm Sims Director - Corporate Resources, County Hall, Beverley HU17 9BA ☎ 01482 393000 ✉ malcolm.sims@eastriding.gov.uk

Senior Management: Mr John Skidmore, Director - Corporate Strategy & Commissioning, County Hall, Beverley HU17 9BA ☎ 01482 396000 ✉ john.skidmore@eastriding.gov.uk

Access Officer / Social Services (Disability): Miss Lianne Therkelson Area Manager, County Hall, Beverley HU17 9BA ☎ 01482 396416 ✉ lianne.therkelson@eastriding.gov.uk

Architect, Building / Property Services: Mr Dave Waudby Head of Infrastructure & Facilities, County Hall, Beverley HU17 9BA ☎ 01482 395800 ✉ dave.waudby@eastriding.gov.uk

Best Value: Mr Simon Laurie, VFM & Consultancy Manager, County Hall, Beverley HU17 9BA ☎ 01482 391480 ✉ simon.laurie@eastriding.gov.uk

Building Control: Mr Chris Ducker, Building Control Manager, County Hall, Beverley HU17 9BA ☎ 01482 393810 ✉ chris.ducker@eastriding.gov.uk

Catering Services: Mr Alan Woods, Catering Service Manager, County Hall, Beverley HU17 9BA ☎ 01482 395121 ✉ alan.woods@eastriding.gov.uk

Children / Youth Services: Mr Kevin Hall Director - Children, Families & Schools, County Hall, Beverley HU17 9BA ☎ 01482 392000 ✉ kevin.hall@eastriding.gov.uk

Civil Registration: Ms Patricia Mann, Superintendent Registrar, Walkergate House, Beverley HU17 9BP ☎ 01482 393601 ✉ patricia.mann@eastriding.gov.uk

PR / Communications: Mr Nick Procter Communications Manager, County Hall, Beverley HU17 9BA ☎ 01482 391440 ✉ nick.procter@eastriding.gov.uk

Community Planning: Mr Simon Lowe, Policy, Partnerships & Intelligence Manager, County Hall, Beverley HU17 9BA ☎ 01482 391422 ✉ simon.lowe@eastriding.gov.uk

Community Safety: Mr Max Hough, Crime & Disorder/Domestic Violence Services Manager, County Hall, Beverley HU17 9BA ☎ 01482 396421 ✉ max.hough@eastriding.gov.uk

Computer Management: Mr Kevin Woodcock ICT Business Solutions & Development Manager, County Hall, Beverley HU17 9BA ☎ 01482 394521 ✉ kevin.woodcock@eastriding.gov.uk

Consumer Protection and Trading Standards: Mr Colin Briggs Trading Standards Services Manager, Calibration Test Centre, Brudenell Way, Hull HU6 9DX ☎ 01482 396238 ✉ colin.briggs@eastriding.gov.uk

Corporate Services: Mr Malcolm Sims Director - Corporate Resources, County Hall, Beverley HU17 9BA ☎ 01482 393000 ✉ malcolm.sims@eastriding.gov.uk

Customer Service: Mr Dave Morley Head of Customer Services, County Hall, Beverley HU17 9BA ☎ 01482 395101 ✉ dave.morley@eastriding.gov.uk

Customer Service: Ms Amanda Wilde, Customer Service Strategy & Digital Services Manager, County Hall, Beverley HU17 9BA ☎ 01482 393360 ✉ amanda.wilde@eastriding.gov.uk

Economic Development: Mr Paul Bell Head of Economic Development, County Hall, Beverley HU17 9BA ☎ 01482 391610 ✉ paul.bell@eastriding.gov.uk

Education: Mr Mike Furbank Head of Children & Young People, Education & Schools, County Hall, Beverley HU17 9BA ☎ 01482 392400 ✉ mike.furbank@eastriding.gov.uk

E-Government: Mr Kevin Woodcock ICT Business Solutions & Development Manager, County Hall, Beverley HU17 9BA ☎ 01482 394521 ✉ kevin.woodcock@eastriding.gov.uk

Electoral Registration: Ms Helena Coates Democratic Services Manager, County Hall, Beverley HU17 9BA ☎ 01482 393210 ✉ helena.coates@eastriding.gov.uk

Emergency Planning: Mr Alan Bravey Emergency Planning Manager, County Hall, Beverley HU17 9BA ☎ 01482 393050 ✉ alan.bravey@eastriding.gov.uk

Energy Management: Ms Karen Williamson Strategic Investment & Development Manager, County Hall, Beverley HU17 9BA ☎ 01482 393907 ✉ karen.williamson@eastriding.gov.uk

Environmental / Technical Services: Mr Mike Featherby Head of Steetscene Services, County Hall, Beverley HU17 9BA ☎ 01482 395505 ✉ mike.featherby@eastriding.gov.uk

Estates, Property & Valuation: Mr John Read Valuation & Estates Manager, County Hall, Beverley HU17 9BA ☎ 01482 393930 ✉ john.read@eastriding.gov.uk

European Liaison: Miss Claire Watts External Funding & Policy Manager, County Hall, Beverley HU17 9BA ☎ 01482 391618 ✉ claire.watts@eastriding.gov.uk

Events Manager: Mr Will Hall Conference & Events Officer, County Hall, Beverley HU17 9BA ☎ 01482 391668 ✉ william.hall@eastriding.gov.uk

Facilities: Mr Darren Stevens Head of Culture & Information, County Hall, Beverley HU17 9BA ☎ 01482 392500 ✉ darren.stevens@eastriding.gov.uk

EAST RIDING OF YORKSHIRE

Finance: Mrs Caroline Lacey Head of Finance, County Hall, Beverley HU17 9BA ☎ 01482 394100 ✉ caroline.lacey@eastriding.gov.uk

Treasury: Mrs Caroline Lacey Head of Finance, County Hall, Beverley HU17 9BA ☎ 01482 394100 ✉ caroline.lacey@eastriding.gov.uk

Pensions: Mr Graham Ferry Pensions Manager, East Riding Pension Fund, PO Box 118, Council Offices, Church Street, Goole DN14 5BU ☎ 01482 394171 ✉ graham.ferry@eastriding.gov.uk

Fleet Management: Mr Carl Gillyon Fleet Services, Vehicle Maintenance Unit, Annie Reed Road, Beverley HU17 0LF ☎ 01482 395506 ✉ carl.gillyon@eastriding.gov.uk

Grounds Maintenance: Mr Andy Harper Operations Manager GMU Tech/Forestry, County Hall, Beverley HU17 9BA ☎ 01482 395863 ✉ andy.harper@eastriding.gov.uk

Health and Safety: Mr Garry Smith Safety Manager, County Hall, Beverley HU17 9BA ☎ 01482 391110 ✉ garry.smith@eastriding.gov.uk

Highways: Mr Mike White Group Manager Technical Services, County Hall, Beverley HU17 9BA ☎ 01482 395684 ✉ mike.white@eastriding.gov.uk

Home Energy Conservation: Mrs Jane Mears, Senior Environmental Health Officer, Town Hall, Quay Road, Bridlington YO16 4LT ☎ 01482 396278 ✉ jane.mears@eastriding.gov.uk

Housing: Mr Richard Ikin Housing & Safe Communities, County Hall, Beverley HU17 9BA ☎ 01482 396120 ✉ dick.ikin@eastriding.gov.uk

Housing Maintenance: Mr Danny Hill Housing Maintenance Unit Manager, 1st Floor, Beverley Depot, Annie Reed Road, , Beverley HU17 0LE ☎ 01482 395817 ✉ danny.hill@eastriding.gov.uk

Legal: Mr Mathew Buckley, Head of Legal & Democratic Services, County Hall, Beverley HU17 9BA ☎ 01482 393100 ✉ mathew.buckley@eastriding.gov.uk

Legal: Ms Lisa-Jane Nicholson Acting Litigation & Regulatory Services Manager, County Hall, Beverley HU17 9BA ☎ 01482 393143 ✉ lisajane.nicholson@eastriding.gov.uk

Leisure and Cultural Services: Mr Darren Stevens Head of Culture & Information, County Hall, Beverley HU17 9BA ☎ 01482 392500 ✉ darren.stevens@eastriding.gov.uk

Licensing: Ms Tina Holtby Licensing Manager, County Hall, Beverley HU17 9BA ☎ 01482 396291 ✉ tina.holtby@eastriding.gov.uk

Lifelong Learning: Mr Mike Furbank Head of Children & Young People, Education & Schools, County Hall, Beverley HU17 9BA ☎ 01482 392400 ✉ mike.furbank@eastriding.gov.uk

Lighting: Mr Iain Ferguson Lighting Engineer, County Hall, Beverley HU17 9BA ☎ 01482 395645 ✉ iain.ferguson@eastriding.gov.uk

Lottery Funding, Charity and Voluntary: Mr Simon Lowe, Policy, Partnerships & Intelligence Manager, County Hall, Beverley HU17 9BA ☎ 01482 391422 ✉ simon.lowe@eastriding.gov.uk

Member Services: Ms Helena Coates Democratic Services Manager, County Hall, Beverley HU17 9BA ☎ 01482 393210 ✉ helena.coates@eastriding.gov.uk

Parking: Mrs Paula Danby Service Manager, Mallard House, 6 Beck View Road, Beverley HU17 0JT ☎ 01482 395570 ✉ paula.danby@eastriding.gov.uk

Partnerships: Ms Gillian Barley Corporate Strategy & Performance Manager, County Hall, Beverley HU17 9BA ☎ 01482 391427 ✉ gillian.barley@eastriding.gov.uk

Personnel / HR: Mr David Smith, Head of Human Resources & Support Services, County Hall, Beverley HU17 9BA ☎ 01482 391100 ✉ david.smith@eastriding.gov.uk

Planning: Mr Stephen Hunt Interim Head of Planning & Development Management, County Hall, Beverley HU17 9BA ☎ 01482 391740 ✉ stephen.hunt@eastriding.gov.uk

Procurement: Mr Pete Arden Procurement Manager, County Hall, Beverley HU17 9BA ☎ 01482 395551 ✉ pete.arden@eastriding.gov.uk

Public Libraries: Ms Libby Herbert Libraries, Archives & Museums Service Manager, Council Offices, Main Road, Skirlaugh, Hull HU11 5HN ☎ 01482 392701 ✉ libby.herbert@eastriding.gov.uk

Recycling & Waste Minimisation: Mr Mike Featherby Head of Steetscene Services, County Hall, Beverley HU17 9BA ☎ 01482 395505 ✉ mike.featherby@eastriding.gov.uk

Regeneration: Ms Sue Lang Regeneration & Funding Group Manager, County Hall, Beverley HU17 9BA ☎ 01482 391617 ✉ sue.lang@eastriding.gov.uk

Road Safety: Mr Kevin Hall Director - Children, Families & Schools, County Hall, Beverley HU17 9BA ☎ 01482 392000 ✉ kevin.hall@eastriding.gov.uk

Social Services (Adult): Ms Rosy Pope Head of Adult Services, County Hall, Beverley HU17 9BA ☎ 01482 396400 ✉ rosy.pope@eastriding.gov.uk

Social Services (Children): Ms Pam Allen Head of Children & Young People's Support & Safeguarding Services, County Hall, Beverley HU17 9BA ☎ 01482 396404 ✉ pam.allen@eastriding.gov.uk

Staff Training: Mrs Tina Tate Learning & Development Manager, Council Offices, Main Road, Skirlaugh, Hull HU11 5HN ☎ 01482 391170 ✉ tina.tate@eastriding.gov.uk

Street Scene: Mr Mike Featherby Head of Steetscene Services, County Hall, Beverley HU17 9BA ☎ 01482 395505 ✉ mike.featherby@eastriding.gov.uk

Sustainable Communities: Mr Jeremy Pickles Principal Sustainable Communities & Coast Officer, County Hall, Beverley HU17 9BA ☎ 01482 391720 ✉ jeremy.pickles@eastriding.gov.uk

Sustainable Development: Mr Jeremy Pickles Principal Sustainable Communities & Coast Officer, County Hall, Beverley HU17 9BA ☎ 01482 391720 ✉ jeremy.pickles@eastriding.gov.uk

Tourism: Mr Andy Gray Tourism Manager, County Hall, Beverley HU17 9BA ☎ 01482 391526 ✉ andy.gray@eastriding.gov.uk

Town Centre: Ms Sue Lang Regeneration & Funding Group Manager, County Hall, Beverley HU17 9BA ☎ 01482 391617 ✉ sue.lang@eastriding.gov.uk

Traffic Management: Mr Mike White Group Manager - Technical Services, Beverley Depot, 2nd Floor, Beverley HU17 0JP ☎ 01482 395684 ✉ mike.white@eastriding.gov.uk

Transport: Ms Paula Danby, Service Manager, Mallard House, 6 Beck View Road, Beverley HU17 0JT ☎ 01482 395570 ✉ paula.danby@eastriding.gov.uk

Transport: Ms Claire Hoskins Interim Strategic Transport Planning Manager, County Hall, Beverley HU17 9BA ☎ 01482 391747 ✉ claire.hoskins@eastriding.gov.uk

Transport Planner: Ms Claire Hoskins Interim Strategic Transport Planning Manager, County Hall, Beverley HU17 9BA ☎ 01482 391747 ✉ claire.hoskins@eastriding.gov.uk

Waste Management: Ms Debbie Mansell Waste Contracts & Recycling Manager, Willerby Depot, Viking Close, Willerby, Hull HU10 6DZ ☎ 01482 392560 ✉ debbie.mansell@eastriding.gov.uk

Children's Play Areas: Ms Louise Adams Sport, Play & Arts Service Manager, County Hall, Beverley HU17 9BA ☎ 01482 392520 ✉ louise.adams@eastriding.gov.uk

COUNCILLORS

***Leader of the Council* Parnaby**, Stephen (CON - Beverley Rural)
councillor.parnaby@eastriding.gov.uk

***Deputy Leader of the Council* Owen**, Jonathan (CON - East Wolds and Coastal)
councillor.owen@eastriding.gov.uk

Abraham, Julie (CON - South Hunsley)
councillor.abraham@eastriding.gov.uk

Aird, Elaine (CON - St Marys)
councillor.aird@eastriding.gov.uk

Aitken, Victoria (CON - Howdenshire)
councillor.aitken@eastriding.gov.uk

Barrett, John (CON - Snaith Airmyn and Rawcliffe and Marshlands)
councillor.barrett@eastriding.gov.uk

Bayram, Linda (CON - Howdenshire)
councillor.bayram@eastriding.gov.uk

Bayram, Charlie (CON - Howden)
councillor.bayram@eastriding.gov.uk

Billinger, Iain (LAB - Hessle)
councillor.billinger@eastriding.gov.uk

Birmingham, Bradley (CON - Beverley Rural)
councillor.birmingham@eastriding.gov.uk

Boatman, Mally (LAB - Goole South)
councillor.boatman@eastriding.gov.uk

Bryan, Mike (CON - South West Holderness)
councillor.bryan@eastriding.gov.uk

Burton, Richard (CON - Bridlington Central and Old Town)
councillor.rburton@eastriding.gov.uk

Burton, Andy (CON - Wolds Weighton)
councillor.burton@eastriding.gov.uk

Chadwick, Margaret (CON - Bridlington South)
councillor.chadwick@eastriding.gov.uk

Chapman, Margaret (CON - East Wolds and Coastal)
councillor.chapman@eastriding.gov.uk

Charis, Irene (CON - St Marys)
councillor.charis@eastriding.gov.uk

Cracknell, Jackie (CON - South East Holderness)
councillor.cracknell@eastriding.gov.uk

Davison, Philip (LD - Hessle)
councillor.davison@eastriding.gov.uk

Dennis, John (CON - South West Holderness)
councillor.dennis@eastriding.gov.uk

Elvidge, David (CON - Minster and Woodmansey)
councillor.elvidge@eastriding.gov.uk

Evison, Jane (CON - East Wolds and Coastal)
councillor.evison@eastriding.gov.uk

Finlay, Shelagh (LAB - Bridlington South)
councillor.finlay@eastriding.gov.uk

Fox, Caroline (CON - Snaith Airmyn and Rawcliffe and Marshlands)
councillor.fox@eastriding.gov.uk

Fraser, Symon (CON - Driffield and Rural)
councillor.fraser@eastriding.gov.uk

Galbraith, Tony (CON - Dale)
councillor.gailbraith@eastriding.gov.uk

Green, Helen (CON - Cottingham South)
councillor.green@eastriding.gov.uk

Hall, Barbara (CON - Driffield and Rural)
councillor.hall@eastriding.gov.uk

Hardy, Mary-Rose (LD - Tranby)
councillor.hardy@eastriding.gov.uk

Harold, Kerri (CON - Minster and Woodmansey)
councillor.harold@eastriding.gov.uk

Harrap, Richard (CON - Bridlington North)
councillor.harrap@eastriding.gov.uk

Head, Josie (IND - Goole North)
councillor.head@eastriding.gov.uk

Healing, Lyn (CON - South East Holderness)
councillor.healing@eastriding.gov.uk

Hodgson, Arthur (CON - South East Holderness)
councillor.hodgson@eastriding.gov.uk

Hogan, Paul (LAB - Hessle)
councillor.hogan@eastriding.gov.uk

EAST RIDING OF YORKSHIRE

Holtby, John (CON - Mid Holderness)
councillor.holtby@eastriding.gov.uk

Horton, Shaun (CON - Willerby and Kirk Ella)
councillor.horton@eastriding.gov.uk

Jefferson, Barbara (IND - North Holderness)
councillor.jefferson@eastriding.gov.uk

Jump, Ros (IND - Cottingham North)
councillor.jump@eastriding.gov.uk

Kingston, Mary (CON - Tranby)
councillor.hardy@eastriding.gov.uk

Lane, Stephen (CON - Pocklington Provincial)
councillor.lane@eastriding.gov.uk

Mathieson, Geraldine (IND - Cottingham North)
cllr@mathieson1.karoo.co.uk

Matthews, Chris (CON - Bridlington North)
councillor.mathews@eastriding.gov.uk

McMaster, Gary (CON - Willerby and Kirk Ella)
councillor.mcmaster@eastriding.gov.uk

Medini, Mike (CON - Cottingham South)
councillor.medini@eastriding.gov.uk

Meredith, Richard (CON - Dale)
councillor.meredith@eastriding.gov.uk

Milns, Malcolm (UKIP - Bridlington Central and Old Town)
councillor.milns@eastriding.gov.uk

Milns, Thelma (UKIP - Bridlington North)
councillor.thelma@eastriding.gov.uk

Mole, Claude (CON - Pocklington Provincial)
councillor.mole@eastriding.gov.uk

Moore, Keith (LAB - Goole North)
councillor.moore@eastriding.gov.uk

O'Neil, Pat (LAB - Goole South)
councillor.o'neil@eastriding.gov.uk

Peacock, Dominic (CON - Minster and Woodmansey)
councillor.peacock@eastriding.gov.uk

Pearson, Bryan (CON - St Marys)
councillor.pearson@eastriding.gov.uk

Pollard, Phyllis (CON - Beverley Rural)
councillor.pollard@eastriding.gov.uk

Robinson, David (UKIP - Bridlington South)
councillor.robson@eastriding.gov.uk

Rudd, David (CON - Wolds Weighton)
councillor.rudd@eastriding .gov.uk

Sharpe, Dee (CON - Willerby and Kirk Ella)
coucillor.sharpe@eastriding.gov.uk

Skow, Brian (CON - Mid Holderness)
councillor.skow@eastriding.gov.uk

Smith, Pat (CON - Dale)
councillor.smith@eastriding.gov.uk

Stathers, Mike (CON - Wolds Weighton)
councillor.stathers@eastriding.gov.uk

Steel, Sue (CON - South West Holderness)
councillor.steel@eastriding.gov.uk

Temple, Felicity (CON - Driffield and Rural)
councillor.temple@eastriding.gov.uk

Turner, Peter (CON - Mid Holderness)
councillor.turner@eastriding.gov.uk

Walker, Vanessa (CON - South Hunsley)
councillor.walker@eastriding.gov.uk

West, Kay (CON - Pocklington Provincial)
councillor.west@eastriding.gov.uk

Whittle, John (IND - North Holderness)
councillor.whittle@eastriding.gov.uk

Wilkinson, Nigel (CON - Howdenshire)
councillor.nigel@eastriding.gov.uk

POLITICAL COMPOSITION

CON: 51, LAB: 6, IND: 5, UKIP: 3, LD: 2

East Staffordshire D

East Staffordshire Borough Council, Town Hall, Burton-on-Trent DE14 2EB
☎ 01283 508000 🖷 01283 535412 🖳 www.eaststaffsbc.gov.uk

FACTS AND FIGURES

Parliamentary Constituencies: Burton
EU Constituencies: West Midlands
Election Frequency: Elections are of whole council

PRINCIPAL OFFICERS

Chief Executive: Mr Andy O'Brien Chief Executive, The Maltsters, Wetmore Road, Burton-on-Trent DE14 1LS ☎ 01283 508300 🖷 01283 508388 ✉ andy.o'brien@eaststaffsbc.gov.uk

Senior Management: Mr Paul Costiff Head of Service, The Maltsters, Wetmore Road, Burton-on-Trent DE14 1LS ☎ 01283 505407 🖷 01283 508388 ✉ paul.costiff@eaststaffsbc.gov.uk

Senior Management: Mr Sal Khan Head of Service, The Maltsters, Wetmore Road, Burton-on-Trent DE14 1LS ☎ 01283 508674 🖷 01283 508388 ✉ sal.khan@eaststaffsbc.gov.uk

Senior Management: Mr Mark Rizk Head of Service, The Malsters, Wetmore Road, , Burton-on-Trent DE14 1LS ☎ 01283 508867 🖷 01283 508388 ✉ mark.rizk@eaststaffsbc.gov.uk

Building Control: Mr Paul Costiff Head of Service, The Maltsters, Wetmore Road, Burton-on-Trent DE14 1LS ☎ 01283 505407 🖷 01283 508388 ✉ paul.costiff@eaststaffsbc.gov.uk

PR / Communications: Mr Chris Ebberley Corporate & Commercial Manager, The Maltsters, Wetmore Road, Burton-on-Trent DE14 1LS ☎ 01283 508772 🖷 01283 508388 ✉ chris.ebberley@eaststaffsbc.gov.uk

Community Safety: Mr Mark Rizk Head of Service, The Malsters, Wetmore Road, , Burton-on-Trent DE14 1LS ☎ 01283 508867 🖷 01283 508388 ✉ mark.rizk@eaststaffsbc.gov.uk

Computer Management: Mr Guy Thornhill ICT Manager, The Maltsters, Wetmore Road, Burton-on-Trent DE14 1LS ☎ 01283 504351 🖷 01283 508388 ✉ guy.thornhill@eaststaffbc.gov.uk

Corporate Services: Mr Sal Khan Head of Service, The Maltsters, Wetmore Road, Burton-on-Trent DE14 1LS ☎ 01283 508674 🖷 01283 508388 ✉ sal.khan@eaststaffsbc.gov.uk

Customer Service: Mr Sal Khan Head of Service, The Maltsters, Wetmore Road, Burton-on-Trent DE14 1LS ☎ 01283 508674 🖷 01283 508388 ✉ sal.khan@eaststaffsbc.gov.uk

Economic Development: Mr Paul Costiff Head of Service, The Maltsters, Wetmore Road, Burton-on-Trent DE14 1LS ☎ 01283 505407 🖷 01283 508388 ✉ paul.costiff@eaststaffsbc.gov.uk

E-Government: Mr Sal Khan Head of Service, The Maltsters, Wetmore Road, Burton-on-Trent DE14 1LS ☎ 01283 508674 🖷 01283 508388 ✉ sal.khan@eaststaffsbc.gov.uk

Electoral Registration: Mr Chris Ebberley Corporate & Commercial Manager, The Maltsters, Wetmore Road, Burton-on-Trent DE14 1LS ☎ 01283 508772 🖷 01283 508388 ✉ chris.ebberley@eaststaffsbc.gov.uk

Emergency Planning: Mr Chris Ebberley Corporate & Commercial Manager, The Maltsters, Wetmore Road, Burton-on-Trent DE14 1LS ☎ 01283 508772 🖷 01283 508388 ✉ chris.ebberley@eaststaffsbc.gov.uk

Environmental Health: Mr Paul Costiff Head of Service, The Maltsters, Wetmore Road, Burton-on-Trent DE14 1LS ☎ 01283 505407 🖷 01283 508388 ✉ paul.costiff@eaststaffsbc.gov.uk

Estates, Property & Valuation: Mr Paul Costiff Head of Service, The Maltsters, Wetmore Road, Burton-on-Trent DE14 1LS ☎ 01283 505407 🖷 01283 508388 ✉ paul.costiff@eaststaffsbc.gov.uk

Events Manager: Mr Mark Rizk Head of Service, The Malsters, Wetmore Road, , Burton-on-Trent DE14 1LS ☎ 01283 508867 🖷 01283 508388 ✉ mark.rizk@eaststaffsbc.gov.uk

Facilities: Mr Mark Rizk Head of Service, The Malsters, Wetmore Road, , Burton-on-Trent DE14 1LS ☎ 01283 508867 🖷 01283 508388 ✉ mark.rizk@eaststaffsbc.gov.uk

Finance: Mr Sal Khan Head of Service, The Maltsters, Wetmore Road, Burton-on-Trent DE14 1LS ☎ 01283 508674 🖷 01283 508388 ✉ sal.khan@eaststaffsbc.gov.uk

Fleet Management: Mr Paul Farrer Environment Manager, The Maltsters, Wetmore Road, Burton-on-Trent DE14 1LS ☎ 01283 505899 🖷 01283 508388 ✉ paul.farrer@eaststaffsbc.gov.uk

Grounds Maintenance: Mr Michael Hovers Communities & Open Spaces Manager, The Maltsters, Wetmore Road, Burton-on-Trent DE14 1LS ☎ 01283 508776 🖷 01283 508388 ✉ paul.farrer@eaststaffsbc.gov.uk

Health and Safety: Mr Ian Boam Shared Services Centre Manager of H&S Facilities & Functions, The Maltsters, Wetmore Road, Burton-on-Trent DE14 1LS ☎ 01283 508653 🖷 01283 508388 ✉ ian.boam@eaststaffsbc.gov.uk

Home Energy Conservation: Mr Paul Costiff Head of Service, The Maltsters, Wetmore Road, Burton-on-Trent DE14 1LS ☎ 01283 505407 🖷 01283 508388 ✉ paul.costiff@eaststaffsbc.gov.uk

Housing: Mr Paul Costiff Head of Service, The Maltsters, Wetmore Road, Burton-on-Trent DE14 1LS ☎ 01283 505407 🖷 01283 508388 ✉ paul.costiff@eaststaffsbc.gov.uk

Legal: Mrs Angela Wakefield Monitoring Officer & Legal Services Manager, The Malsters, Wetmore Road, , Burton-on-Trent DE14 1LS ☎ 01283 508267 🖷 01283 535412 ✉ angela.wakefield@eaststaffsbc.gov.uk

Leisure and Cultural Services: Mr Mark Rizk Head of Service, The Malsters, Wetmore Road, , Burton-on-Trent DE14 1LS ☎ 01283 508867 🖷 01283 508388 ✉ mark.rizk@eaststaffsbc.gov.uk

Licensing: Mr Paul Costiff Head of Service, The Maltsters, Wetmore Road, Burton-on-Trent DE14 1LS ☎ 01283 505407 🖷 01283 508388 ✉ paul.costiff@eaststaffsbc.gov.uk

Member Services: Mr Chris Ebberley Corporate & Commercial Manager, The Maltsters, Wetmore Road, Burton-on-Trent DE14 1LS ☎ 01283 508772 🖷 01283 508388 ✉ chris.ebberley@eaststaffsbc.gov.uk

Parking: Mr Paul Costiff Head of Service, The Maltsters, Wetmore Road, Burton-on-Trent DE14 1LS ☎ 01283 505407 🖷 01283 508388 ✉ paul.costiff@eaststaffsbc.gov.uk

Partnerships: Mr Paul Costiff Head of Service, The Maltsters, Wetmore Road, Burton-on-Trent DE14 1LS ☎ 01283 505407 🖷 01283 508388 ✉ paul.costiff@eaststaffsbc.gov.uk

Personnel / HR: Mr Sal Khan Head of Service, The Maltsters, Wetmore Road, Burton-on-Trent DE14 1LS ☎ 01283 508674 🖷 01283 508388 ✉ sal.khan@eaststaffsbc.gov.uk

Planning: Mr Philip Somerfield Head of Regulatory Services, The Maltsters, Wetmore Road, Burton-on-Trent DE14 1LS ☎ 01283 508622 🖷 01283 508388 ✉ philip.somerfield@eaststaffbc.gov.uk

Procurement: Mr Chris Ebberley Corporate & Commercial Manager, The Maltsters, Wetmore Road, Burton-on-Trent DE14 1LS ☎ 01283 508772 🖷 01283 508388 ✉ chris.ebberley@eaststaffsbc.gov.uk

Recycling & Waste Minimisation: Mr Paul Farrer Environment Manager, Town Hall, Burton-on-Trent DE14 2EB ☎ 01283 505899 🖷 01283 508388 ✉ paul.farrer@eaststaffsbc.gov.uk

Regeneration: Mr Paul Costiff Head of Service, The Maltsters, Wetmore Road, Burton-on-Trent DE14 1LS ☎ 01283 505407 🖷 01283 508388 ✉ paul.costiff@eaststaffsbc.gov.uk

Staff Training: Mr Sal Khan Head of Service, The Maltsters, Wetmore Road, Burton-on-Trent DE14 1LS ☎ 01283 508674 🖷 01283 508388 ✉ sal.khan@eaststaffsbc.gov.uk

Street Scene: Mr Paul Farrer Environment Manager, Town Hall, Burton-on-Trent DE14 2EB ☎ 01283 505899 🖷 01283 508388 ✉ paul.farrer@eaststaffsbc.gov.uk

EAST STAFFORDSHIRE

Tourism: Mr Paul Costiff Head of Service, The Maltsters, Wetmore Road, Burton-on-Trent DE14 1LS ☎ 01283 505407 🖷 01283 508388 ✉ paul.costiff@eaststaffsbc.gov.uk

Waste Collection and Disposal: Mr Paul Farrer Environment Manager, Town Hall, Burton-on-Trent DE14 2EB ☎ 01283 505899 🖷 01283 508388 ✉ paul.farrer@eaststaffsbc.gov.uk

Waste Management: Mr Paul Farrer Environment Manager, Town Hall, Burton-on-Trent DE14 2EB ☎ 01283 505899 🖷 01283 508388 ✉ paul.farrer@eaststaffsbc.gov.uk

COUNCILLORS

***Mayor* Clarke**, Ron (LAB - Eton Park)
ron.clarke@eaststaffsbc.gov.uk

***Leader of the Council* Grosvenor**, Richard (CON - Branston)
richard.grosvenor@eaststaffsbc.gov.uk

Ackroyd, Patricia (CON - Branston)
patricia.ackroyd@eaststaffsbc.gov.uk

Allen, George (CON - Heath)
george.allen@eaststaffsbc.gov.uk

Andjelkovic, Sonia (LAB - Eton Park)
sonia.andjelkovic@eaststaffsbc.gov.uk

Barker, Edward (CON - Weaver)
edward.barker@eaststaffsbc.gov.uk

Bowering, Michael (CON - Branston)
michael.bowering@eaststaffsbc.gov.uk

Builth, Ken (LAB - Horninglow)
ken.builth@eaststaffsbc.gov.uk

Carlton, Rebecca (CON - Stretton)
rebecca.carlton@eaststaffsbc.gov.uk

Chaudhry, Ali (LAB - Anglesey)
ali.chaudhry@eaststaffsbc.gov.uk

Dyche, Steven (UKIP - Stapenhill)
steven.dyche@eaststaffsbc.gov.uk

Faulkner, Raymond (CON - Winshill)
raymond.faulkner@eaststaffsbc.gov.uk

Fitzpatrick, Michael (LAB - Stapenhill)
michael.fitzpatrick@eaststaffsbc.gov.uk

Fletcher, Dennis (LAB - Winshill)
dennis.fletcher@eaststaffsbc.gov.uk

Ganley, William (LAB - Shobnall)
william.ganley@eaststaffsbc.gov.uk

Gaskin, Simon (CON - Tutbury and Outwoods)
simon.gaskin@eaststaffsbc.gov.uk

Goodfellow, Duncan (CON - Tutbury and Outwoods)
duncan.goodfellow@eaststaffsbc.gov.uk

Haberfield, Karen (CON - Town)
karen.haberfield@eaststaffsbc.gov.uk

Hall, Greg (CON - Bagots)
greg.hall@eaststaffsbc.gov.uk

Hussain, Syed (LAB - Anglesey)
syed.hussain@eaststaffsbc.gov.uk

Jessel, Julia (CON - Needwood)
julia.jessel@eaststaffsbc.gov.uk

Johnson, Alan (CON - Yoxall)
alan.johnson@eaststaffsbc.gov.uk

Johnston, Bob (LAB - Horninglow)
robert.johnston@eaststaffsbc.gov.uk

Jones, Jacqui (CON - Needwood)
jacqui.jones@eaststaffsbc.gov.uk

Killoran, Julie (CON - Stretton)
julie.killoran@eaststaffsbc.gov.uk

Leese, David (CON - Winshill)
david.leese@eaststaffsbc.gov.uk

Legg, Alison (LAB - Stapenhill)
alison.legg@eaststaffsbc.gov.uk

McGarry, Susan (CON - Town)
susan.mcgarry@eaststaffsbc.gov.uk

McKiernan, Shelagh (LAB - Shobnall)
shelagh.mckiernan@eaststaffsbc.gov.uk

Milner, Len (CON - Stretton)
len.milner@eaststaffsbc.gov.uk

Mott, Julian (LAB - Horninglow)
julian.mott@eaststaffsbc.gov.uk

Peters, Bernard (CON - Brizlincote)
bernard.peters@eaststaffsbc.gov.uk

Rodgers, Michael (LD - Burton)
michael.rodgers@eaststaffsbc.gov.uk

Shelton, Lynne (CON - Heath)
lynne.shelton@eaststaffsbc.gov.uk

Smith, Stephen (CON - Crown)
stephen.smith@eaststaffsbc.gov.uk

Smith, Chris (CON - Churnett)
chris.smith@eaststaffsbc.gov.uk

Toon, Beryl (CON - Rolleston on Dove)
beryl.toon@eaststaffsbc.gov.uk

Whittaker, Colin (CON - Abbey)
colin.whittaker@eaststaffsbc.gov.uk

Wileman, Colin (CON - Brizlincote)
colin.wileman@eaststaffsbc.gov.uk

POLITICAL COMPOSITION

CON: 25, LAB: 12, LD: 1, UKIP: 1

COMMITTEE CHAIRS

Audit: Mr Len Milner

Licensing: Mr Bernard Peters

Planning: Mr Greg Hall

East Sussex C

East Sussex County Council, County Hall, St Anne's Crescent, Lewes BN7 1UE
☎ 0345 608 0190 🖳 www.eastsussex.gov.uk

FACTS AND FIGURES

Parliamentary Constituencies: Bexhill and Battle, Eastbourne, Hastings and Rye, Lewes, Wealden
EU Constituencies: South East
Election Frequency: Elections are of whole council

PRINCIPAL OFFICERS

Chief Executive: Ms Becky Shaw, Chief Executive, County Hall, St Anne's Crescent, Lewes BN7 1SW ☎ 01273 481950 🖷 01273 483317 ✉ becky.shaw@eastsussex.gov.uk

Assistant Chief Executive: Mr Philip Baker Assistant Chief Executive, County Hall, St Annes Crescent, Lewes BN7 1UN ☎ 01273 481564 ✉ philip.baker@eastsussex.gov.uk

Senior Management: Mr Rupert Clubb, Director - Communities, Economy & Transport, County Hall, St Anne's Crescent Lewes BN7 1SW ☎ 01273 482200 ✉ rupert.clubb@eastsussex.gov.uk

Senior Management: Mr Kevin Foster Chief Operating Officer, County Hall, St Anne's Crescent, Lewes BN7 1UE ☎ 01273 481412 ✉ kevin.foster@eastsussex.gov.uk

Senior Management: Mr Stuart Gallimore Director - Children's Services, County Hall, St Anne's Crescent, Lewes BN7 1UE ☎ 01273 481316 ✉ stuart.gallimore@eastsussex.gov.uk

Senior Management: Mr Keith Hinkley, Director - Adult Social Care & Health, County Hall, St Anne's Crescent, Lewes BN7 1UE ☎ 01273 481288 ✉ keith.hinkley@eastsussex.gov.uk

Senior Management: Ms Cynthia Lyons Acting Director of Public Health, County Hall, St Anne's Crescent, Lewes BN7 1UE ☎ 01273 336032 ✉ cynthia.lyons@eastsussex.gov.uk

Access Officer / Social Services (Disability): Mr Keith Hinkley, Director - Adult Social Care & Health, County Hall, St Anne's Crescent, Lewes BN7 1UE ☎ 01273 481288 ✉ keith.hinkley@eastsussex.gov.uk

Catering Services: Mr Andrew Little Senior Contracts Office - Catering, County Hall, St Anne's Crescent, Lewes BN7 1UE ☎ 01273 482402 ✉ andrew.little@eastsussex.gov.uk

Children / Youth Services: Mr Stuart Gallimore Director - Children's Services, County Hall, St Anne's Crescent, Lewes BN7 1UE ☎ 01273 481316 ✉ stuart.gallimore@eastsussex.gov.uk

Civil Registration: Mr Steve Quayle Team Manager - Registration Service Manager, West D, County Hall, St Anne's Crescent, Lewes BN7 1UE ☎ 01273 337148 ✉ steve.quayle@eastsussex.gov.uk

Community Planning: Mrs Sarah Feather Policy Manager of Equalities, County Hall, St Anne's Crescent, Lewes BN7 1UE ☎ 01273 335712 ✉ sarah.dyde@eastsussex.gov.uk

Computer Management: Mr Matt Scott Assistant Director - ICT, County Hall, St Anne's Crescent, Lewes BN7 1UE ☎ 01273 335677 ✉ matt.scott@eastsussex.gov.uk

Consumer Protection and Trading Standards: Ms Lucy Corrie Head of Communities, St Mary's House, 52 St. Leonard's Road, Eastbourne BN21 3UU ☎ 01323 463421 ✉ lucy.corrie@eastsussex.gov.uk

Contracts: Mr Mark Billington Contracts Manager, County Hall, St Anne's Crescent, Lewes BN7 1UE ☎ 07884 262583 ✉ mark.billington@eastsussex.gov.uk

Corporate Services: Mr Kevin Foster Chief Operating Officer, County Hall, St Anne's Crescent, Lewes BN7 1UE ☎ 01273 481412 ✉ kevin.foster@eastsussex.gov.uk

Customer Service: Ms Inga Smith Customer Services Manager, County Hall, St Anne's Crescent, Lewes BN7 1UE ☎ 01273 336039 ✉ frances.joseph@eastsussex.gov.uk

Economic Development: Mr James Harris Assistant Director of Economy, County Hall, St Anne's Crescent, Lewes BN7 1UE ☎ 01273 482158 ✉ james.harris@eastsussex.gov.uk

Education: Mr Stuart Gallimore Director - Children's Services, County Hall, St Anne's Crescent, Lewes BN7 1UE ☎ 01273 481316 ✉ stuart.gallimore@eastsussex.gov.uk

Emergency Planning: Mr David Broadley, Emergency Planning Manager, St Mary's House, 52 St Leonard's Road, Eastbourne BN21 3UU ☎ 01323 747085 ✉ david.broadley@eastsussex.gov.uk

Environmental / Technical Services: Mr Carl Valentine Head of Environment, County Hall, St Anne's Crescent, Lewes BN7 1UE ☎ 01273 336199 🖷 01273 486934 ✉ carl.valentine@eastsussexcc.gov.uk

Estates, Property & Valuation: Mr Richard Grass Interim Assistant Director, County Hall, St Anne's Crescent, Lewes BN7 1UE ☎ 01273 335819 ✉ richard.grass@eastsussexcc.gov.uk

European Liaison: Mr James Harris Assistant Director of Economy, County Hall, St Anne's Crescent, Lewes BN7 1UE ☎ 01273 482158 ✉ james.harris@eastsussex.gov.uk

Facilities: Mr Paul Barnard, Corporate Accommodation & Facilities Manager, County Hall, St. Anne's Crescent, Lewes BN7 1UE ☎ 01273 482120 ✉ paul.barnard@eastsussex.gov.uk

Finance: Mr Kevin Foster Chief Operating Officer, County Hall, St Anne's Crescent, Lewes BN7 1UE ☎ 01273 481412 ✉ kevin.foster@eastsussex.gov.uk

Pensions: Mr Ola Owalabi Head of Accounts & Pensions, County Hall, St Anne's Crescent, Lewes BN7 1UE ☎ 01273 482017 ✉ ola.owolabi@eastsussex.gov.uk

Fleet Management: Mr Richard Merrill, Fleet Management Officer, Ringmer Depot, The Broyle, Ringmer, BN8 5NP ☎ 01273 482933 ✉ richard.merrill@eastsussex.gov.uk

Health and Safety: Ms Judy Benoy Senior Health & Safety Adviser, County Hall, St Anne's Crescent, Lewes BN7 1UE ☎ 01273 481227 ✉ judy.benoy@eastsussex.gov.uk

Highways: Mr Rupert Clubb, Director - Communities, Economy & Transport, County Hall, St Anne's Crescent Lewes BN7 1SW ☎ 01273 482200 ✉ rupert.clubb@eastsussex.gov.uk

Local Area Agreement: Ms Becky Shaw, Chief Executive, County Hall, St Anne's Crescent, Lewes BN7 1SW ☎ 01273 481950 🖷 01273 483317 ✉ becky.shaw@eastsussex.gov.uk

EAST SUSSEX

Legal: Mr Philip Baker Assistant Chief Executive, County Hall, St Annes Crescent, Lewes BN7 1UN ☎ 01273 481564 🖰 philip.baker@eastsussex.gov.uk

Leisure and Cultural Services: Ms Sally Staples Cultural Strategy Manager, County Hall, St Anne's Crescent, Lewes BN7 1UE ☎ 01273 481871 🖰 arts@eastsussex.gov.uk

Lighting: Mr Simon Hall Team Manager - Street Lighting & Traffic Signals, Ringmer Depot, The Broyle, Ringmer, Lewes BN8 5NP ☎ 01273 482781 🖰 simon.hall@eastsussex.gov.uk

Member Services: Mr Paul Dean Member Services Manager, Room C3F County Hall, St. Anne's Crescent, Lewes BN7 1SW ☎ 01273 481751 🖷 01273 481208 🖰 paul.dean@eastsussex.gov.uk

Parking: Mr David Weeks Team Manager - Parking, County Hall, St Anne's Crescent, Lewes BN7 1UE ☎ 01323 466230 🖰 david.weeks@eastsussex.gov.uk

Personnel / HR: Mr Leatham Green Assistant Director of Personnel & Training, County Hall, St Anne's Crescent, Lewes BN7 1UE ☎ 01273 481415 🖰 leatham.green@eastsussex.gov.uk

Planning: Mr Tony Cook Head of Planning & Environment, C Floor, West Block, County Hall, Lewes BN7 1UE ☎ 01273 481653 🖰 tony.cook@eastsussex.gov.uk

Procurement: Ms Laura Langstaff Head of Procurement, County Hall, St Anne's Crescent, Lewes BN7 1UE ☎ 01273 335601 🖰 laura.langstaff@surreycc.gov.uk

Public Libraries: Mr Nick Skelton Assistant Director - Communities, County Hall, St Anne's Crescent, Lewes BN7 1UE ☎ 01273 482994 🖰 nick.skelton@eastsussex.gov.uk

Recycling & Waste Minimisation: Mr Ian Dudd Interim Team Manager - Waste, County Hall, St Anne's Crescent, Lewes BN7 1UE ☎ 01273 335804 🖰 ian.dudd@eastsussex.gov.uk

Regeneration: Mr James Harris Assistant Director of Economy, County Hall, St Anne's Crescent, Lewes BN7 1UE ☎ 01273 482158 🖰 james.harris@eastsussex.gov.uk

Road Safety: Mr Brian Banks Team Manager for Road Safety, County Hall, St Anne's Crescent, Lewes BN7 1UE ☎ 01424 724558 🖰 brian.banks@eastsussex.gov.uk

Social Services: Mr Keith Hinkley, Director - Adult Social Care & Health, County Hall, St Anne's Crescent, Lewes BN7 1UE ☎ 01273 481288 🖰 keith.hinkley@eastsussex.gov.uk

Social Services (Adult): Mr Mark Stainton, Assistant Director of Adult Social Care - Operations, County Hall, St Anne's Crescent, Lewes BN7 1UE ☎ 01273 481238 🖰 mark.stainton@eastsussex.gov.uk

Social Services (Children): Ms Liz Rugg, Assistant Director - Safeguarding LAC & Youth Justice, County Hall, St Anne's Crescent, Lewes BN7 1UE ☎ 01273 481274 🖰 liz.rugg@eastsussex.gov.uk

Social Services (Children): Mr Douglas Sinclair Head of Children's Safeguards & Quality Assurance, County Hall, St Anne's Crescent, Lewes BN7 1UE ☎ 01273 481289 🖰 douglas.sinclair@eastsussex.gov.uk

Public Health: Ms Cynthia Lyons Acting Director of Public Health, County Hall, St Anne's Crescent, Lewes BN7 1UE ☎ 01273 336032 🖰 cynthia.lyons@eastsussex.gov.uk

Staff Training: Mr Ed Howarth HR Manager, County Hall, St Anne's Crescent, Lewes BN7 1UE ☎ 01273 481527 🖰 ed.howarth@eastsussex.gov.uk

Sustainable Communities: Ms Becky Shaw, Chief Executive, County Hall, St Anne's Crescent, Lewes BN7 1SW ☎ 01273 481950 🖷 01273 483317 🖰 becky.shaw@eastsussex.gov.uk

Sustainable Development: Mr Rupert Clubb Director - Transport & Environment, County Hall, St Anne's Crescent, Lewes BN7 1UE ☎ 01273 4822000 🖷 01273 479536 🖰 rupert.clubb@eastsussex.gov.uk

Sustainable Development: Mr Carl Valentine Head of Environment, County Hall, St Anne's Crescent, Lewes BN7 1UE ☎ 01273 336199 🖷 01273 486934 🖰 carl.valentine@eastsussexcc.gov.uk

Traffic Management: Mr Rupert Clubb, Director - Communities, Economy & Transport, County Hall, St Anne's Crescent Lewes BN7 1SW ☎ 01273 482200 🖰 rupert.clubb@eastsussex.gov.uk

Transport: Mr Rupert Clubb, Director - Communities, Economy & Transport, County Hall, St Anne's Crescent Lewes BN7 1SW ☎ 01273 482200 🖰 rupert.clubb@eastsussex.gov.uk

Transport: Mr Roger Williams Head of Highways, County Hall, St Anne's Crescent, Lewes BN7 1UE ☎ 01273 481000 🖰 roger.williams@eastsussex.gov.uk

Waste Collection and Disposal: Mr Rupert Clubb, Director - Communities, Economy & Transport, County Hall, St Anne's Crescent Lewes BN7 1SW ☎ 01273 482200 🖰 rupert.clubb@eastsussex.gov.uk

Waste Management: Mr Rupert Clubb, Director - Communities, Economy & Transport, County Hall, St Anne's Crescent Lewes BN7 1SW ☎ 01273 482200 🖰 rupert.clubb@eastsussex.gov.uk

COUNCILLORS

***Chair* Belsey**, Colin (CON - Eastbourne - Ratton)
cllr.colin.belsey@eastsussex.gov.uk

***Vice-Chair* Ensor**, Michael (CON - Bexhill King Offa)
cllr.michael.ensor@eastsussex.gov.uk

***Leader of the Council* Glazier**, Keith (CON - Rye and Eastern Rother)
cllr.keith.glazier@eastsussex.gov.uk

***Deputy Leader of the Council* Elkin**, David (CON - Eastbourne - Sovereign)
cllr.david.elkin@eastsussex.gov.uk

Barnes, John (CON - Rother North West)
cll.john.barnes@eastsussex.gov.uk

Bennett, Nick (CON - Alfriston, East Hoathly & Hellingly)
cllr.nick.bennett@eastsussex.gov.uk

Bentley, Bill (CON - Hailsham and Herstmonceux)
cllr.bill.bentley@eastsussexcc.gov.uk

Birch, Jeremy (LAB - Hastings - Old Hastings & Tressell)
cllr.jeremy.birch@eastsussex.gov.uk

Blanch, Mike (LD - Eastbourne - Hampden Park)
Cllr.mike.blanch@eastsussex.gov.uk

Buchanan, Ian (UKIP - Peacehaven and Telscombe Towns)
cllr.ian.buchanan@eastsussex.gov.uk

Butler, Carla (LD - Newhaven and Ouse Valley West)
cllr.carla.butler@eastsussex.gov.uk

Carstairs, Frank (UKIP - Seaford Sutton)
cllr.frank.carstairs@eastsussex.gov.uk

Charlton, Peter (UKIP - Ouse Valley East)
cllr.peter.charlton@eastsussex.gov.uk

Clark, Charles (IND - Bexhill East)
cllr.charles.clark@eastsussex.gov.uk

Daniel, Godfrey (LAB - Hastings - Braybrooke & Castle)
cllr.godfrey.daniel@eastsussex.gov.uk

Davies, Angharad (CON - Northern Rother)
cllr.Angharad.Davies@eastsussex.gov.uk

Dowling, Chris (CON - Framfield and Horam)
cllr.chris.dowling@eastsussex.gov.uk

Dowling, Claire (CON - Uckfield)
cllr.claire.dowling@eastsussex.gov.uk

Earl, Stuart (IND - Bexhill West)
cllr.stuart.earl@eastsussex.gov.uk

Field, Kathryn (LD - Battle and Crowhurst)
kathryn.fied@btopenworld.com

Forward, Kim (LAB - Hastings - Maze Hill and West St Leonards)
cllr.kim.forward@eastsussex.gov.uk

Galley, Roy (CON - Buxted Maresfield)
cllr.roy.galley@eastsussex.gov.uk

Hodges, John (LAB - Hastings - St Helen's and Silverhill)
cllr.john.hodges@eastsussex.gov.uk

Howson, Phil (UKIP - Peacehaven and Telscombe Towns)
cllr.phillip.howson@eastsussexcc.gov.uk

Keeley, Laurence (UKIP - Hailsham and Hertsmonceux)
cllr.laurence.keeley@eastsussex.gov.uk

Lambert, Carolyn (LD - Seaford Blatchington)
cllr.carolyn.lambert@eastsussex.gov.uk

Maynard, Carl (CON - Brede Valley and Marsham)
cllr.carl.maynard@eastsussex.gov.uk

O'Keeffe, Ruth (IND - Lewes)
roklewes@gmail.com

Phillips, Michael (UKIP - Bexhill King Offa)
cllr.michael.phillips@eastsussex.govl.uk

Pragnell, Peter (CON - Hastings - Ashdown & Conquest)
cllr.peter.pragnell@eastsussex.gov.uk

Pursglove, Mike (UKIP - Pevensey & Westham)
cllr.michael.pursglov@eastsussex.gov.uk

Rodohan, Pat (LD - Eastbourne - Upperton)
cllr.Pat.Rodohan@eastsussex.gov.uk

Scott, Philip (LAB - Hastings - Holllington & Wishing Tree)
cllr.phil.scott@eastsussex.gov.uk

Sheppard, Jim (CON - Chailey)
cllr.jim.sheppard@eastsussex.gov.uk

Shing, Daniel (IND - Polegate, Willingdon & East Dean)
cllr.daniel.shing@eastsussex.gov.uk

Shing, Stephen (IND - Polegate, Willingdon & East Dean)
cllr.stephen.shing@eastsussex.gov.uk

Shuttleworth, Alan (LD - Eastbourne - Langney)
cllr.alan.shuttleworth@eastsussex.gov.uk

Simmons, Rupert (CON - Heathfield)
cllr.rupert.simmons@eastsussex.gov.uk

St Pierre, Rosalyn (LD - Ringmer and Lewes Bridge)
cllr.rosalyn.stpierre@eastsussexcc.gov.uk

Standley, Bob (CON - Wadhurst)
cllr.bob.standley@eastsussex.gov.uk

Stogdon, Richard (CON - Crowborough)
cllr.richard.stogdon@eastsussex.gov.uk

Taylor, Barry (CON - Eastbourne - Meads)
cllr.barry.taylor@eastsussex.gov.uk

Tidy, Sylvia (CON - Crowborough)
cllr.sylvia.tidy@eastsussex.gov.uk

Tutt, David (LD - Eastbourne - St Anthony's)
cllr.david.tutt@eastsussex.gov.uk

Ungar, John (LD - Eastbourne - Old Town)
cllr.john.ungar@eastsussex.gov.uk

Wallis, Steve (LD - Eastbourne - Devonshire)
cllr.steve.wallis@eastsussex.gov.uk

Webb, Trevor (LAB - Hastings - Central St Leonards & Gensing)
cllr.trevor.webb@eastsussex.gov.uk

Whetstone, Francis (CON - Forest Row)
cllr.francis.whetstone@eastsussex.gov.uk

Wincott, Michael (LAB - Hastings - Baird & Ore)
cllr.michael.wincott@eastsussex.gov.uk

POLITICAL COMPOSITION
CON: 20, LD: 10, UKIP: 7, LAB: 7, IND: 5

COMMITTEE CHAIRS
Audit: Mr Mike Blanch

Childrens Services: TBA

Pensions: Mr Richard Stogdon

Planning: Mr Godfrey Daniel

Eastbourne D

Eastbourne Borough Council, 1 Grove Road, Eastbourne BN21 4TW
☎ 01323 415000 🖷 01323 415130 ✉ enquiries@eastbourne.gov.uk
💻 www.eastbourne.gov.uk

FACTS AND FIGURES
Parliamentary Constituencies: Eastbourne

EASTBOURNE

EU Constituencies: South East
Election Frequency: Elections are of whole council

PRINCIPAL OFFICERS

Chief Executive: Mr Robert Cottrill, Chief Executive, 1 Grove Road, Eastbourne BN21 4TW ☎ 01323 415046 🖷 01323 430745 robert.cottrill@eastbourne.gov.uk

Deputy Chief Executive: Mr Alan Osborne Deputy Chief Executive, 1 Grove Road, Eastbourne BN21 4TW ☎ 01323 415149 alan.osborne@eastbourne.gov.uk

Best Value: Mr William Tompsett Senior Corporate Development Officer, 1 Grove Road, Eastbourne BN21 4TW ☎ 01323 415418 william.tompsett@eastbourne.gov.uk

Building Control: Mr Leigh Palmer Senior Specialist Advisor, 1 Grove Road, Eastbourne BN21 4TW ☎ 01323 410000 leigh.palmer@eastbourne.gov.uk

Catering Services: Mrs Annie Wills Head of Tourism & Enterprise, 1 Grove Road, Eastbourne BN21 4TW ☎ 01323 415410 annie.wills@eastbourne.gov.uk

PR / Communications: Mrs Annie Wills Head of Tourism & Enterprise, 1 Grove Road, Eastbourne BN21 4TW ☎ 01323 415410 annie.wills@eastbourne.gov.uk

Community Planning: Mr Ian Fitzpatrick Senior Head of Community, 1 Grove Road, Eastbourne BN21 4TW ☎ 01323 415935 ian.fitzpatrick@eastbourne.gov.uk

Community Safety: Mr Ian Fitzpatrick Senior Head of Community, 1 Grove Road, Eastbourne BN21 4TW ☎ 01323 415935 ian.fitzpatrick@eastbourne.gov.uk

Computer Management: Mr Henry Branson, Senior Head of Infrastructure, 1 Grove Road, Eastbourne BN21 4TW ☎ 01323 415155 henry.branson@eastbourne.gov.uk

Contracts: Ms Rachel Ayres Corporate Procurement Specialist, 1 Grove Road, Eastbourne BN21 4TW ☎ 01273 415989 rachel.ayres@eastbourne.gov.uk

Customer Service: Mr Ian Fitzpatrick Senior Head of Community, 1 Grove Road, Eastbourne BN21 4TW ☎ 01323 415935 ian.fitzpatrick@eastbourne.gov.uk

Economic Development: Mrs Kerry Barrett Specialist Advisor (Economic Development), 1 Grove Road, Eastbourne BN21 4TW ☎ 01323 415054 kerry.barrett@eastbourne.gov.uk

Economic Development: Ms Sara Taylor Specialist Advisor (Economic Development), 1 Grove Road, Eastbourne BN21 4TW ☎ 01323 415609 sara.taylor@eastbourne.gov.uk

E-Government: Mr Henry Branson, Senior Head of Infrastructure, 1 Grove Road, Eastbourne BN21 4TW ☎ 01323 415155 henry.branson@eastbourne.gov.uk

Electoral Registration: Mr Peter Finnis, Senior Head of Corporate Development & Governance, Town Hall, Grove Road, Eastbourne BN21 4UG ☎ 01323 415003 peter.finnis@eastbourne.gov.uk

Electoral Registration: Mrs Tracey Pannett, Electoral Services Manager, Town Hall, Grove Road, Eastbourne BN21 4UG ☎ 01323 415074 tracey.pannett@eastbourne.gov.uk

Emergency Planning: Mr Peter Finnis, Senior Head of Corporate Development & Governance, Town Hall, Grove Road, Eastbourne BN21 4UG ☎ 01323 415003 peter.finnis@eastbourne.gov.uk

Energy Management: Mr Nick Adlam, Specialist Advisor - Energy, 1 Grove Road, Eastbourne BN21 4TW ☎ 01323 415963 nick.adlam@eastbourne.gov.uk

Environmental Health: Mrs Sue Oliver, Manager - Specialist Advisor Team, 1 Grove Road, Eastbourne BN21 4TW ☎ 01323 415360 sue.oliver@eastbourne.gov.uk

Estates, Property & Valuation: Mr Paul Friend Corporate Property Manager, 1 Grove Road, Eastbourne BN21 4TW ☎ 01323 415261 paul.friend@eastbourne.gov.uk

Events Manager: Mr Mike Marchant, Events Development Manager, 1 Grove Road, Eastbourne BN21 4TW ☎ 01323 415407 mike.marchant@eastbourne.gov.uk

Facilities: Mr Lee Beckham Facilities Manager, Town Hall, Grove Road, Eastbourne BN21 4UG ☎ 01323 415038 lee.beckham@eastbourne.gov.uk

Finance: Mr Alan Osborne Deputy Chief Executive, 1 Grove Road, Eastbourne BN21 4TW ☎ 01323 415149 alan.osborne@eastbourne.gov.uk

Grounds Maintenance: Mr Gareth Williams, Senior Specialist Advisor, 1 Grove Road, Eastbourne BN21 4TW ☎ 01323 415281 gareth.williams@eastbourne.gov.uk

Health and Safety: Mrs Sue Oliver, Manager - Specialist Advisor Team, 1 Grove Road, Eastbourne BN21 4TW ☎ 01323 415360 sue.oliver@eastbourne.gov.uk

Health and Safety: Ms Caroline Wallis Environmental Health & Amenities Manager, 1 Grove Road, Eastbourne BN21 4TW ☎ 01323 415360 sue.oliver@eastbourne.gov.uk

Home Energy Conservation: Mr Nick Adlam, Specialist Advisor - Energy, 1 Grove Road, Eastbourne BN21 4TW ☎ 01323 415963 nick.adlam@eastbourne.gov.uk

Housing: Mr Ian Fitzpatrick Senior Head of Community, 1 Grove Road, Eastbourne BN21 4TW ☎ 01323 415935 ian.fitzpatrick@eastbourne.gov.uk

Legal: Ms Celia Cullen Director - Shared Legal Services Unit, Lewes House, 32 High Street, Lewes BN7 2LX ☎ 01273 471600 celia.cullen@lewes.gov.uk

Legal: Mr Peter Finnis, Senior Head of Corporate Development & Governance, Town Hall, Grove Road, Eastbourne BN21 4UG ☎ 01323 415003 ✉ peter.finnis@eastbourne.gov.uk

Leisure and Cultural Services: Mr Philip Evans Senior Head of Tourism & Enterprise, 1 Grove Road, Eastbourne BN21 4TW ☎ 01323 410000 ✉ philip.evans@eastbourne.gov.uk

Licensing: Mr Jay Virgo Senior Specialist Advisor, 1 Grove Road, Eastbourne BN21 4TW ☎ 01323 415933 ✉ jay.virgo@eastbourne.gov.uk

Member Services: Ms Katie Cullum Head of Local Democracy, 1 Grove Road, Eastbourne BN21 4TW ☎ 01323 415031 ✉ katie.cullum@eastbourne.gov.uk

Partnerships: Mr Ian Fitzpatrick Senior Head of Community, 1 Grove Road, Eastbourne BN21 4TW ☎ 01323 415935 ✉ ian.fitzpatrick@eastbourne.gov.uk

Personnel / HR: Ms Becky Cooke Strategic Organisational Development Manager, 1 Grove Road, Eastbourne BN21 4TW ☎ 01323 415106 ✉ becky.cooke@eastbourne.gov.uk

Planning: Mr Leigh Palmer Senior Specialist Advisor, 1 Grove Road, Eastbourne BN21 4TW ☎ 01323 410000 ✉ leigh.palmer@eastbourne.gov.uk

Procurement: Ms Rachel Ayres Corporate Procurement Specialist, 1 Grove Road, Eastbourne BN21 4TW ☎ 01273 415989 ✉ rachel.ayres@eastbourne.gov.uk

Recycling & Waste Minimisation: Mrs Sue Oliver, Manager - Specialist Advisor Team, 1 Grove Road, Eastbourne BN21 4TW ☎ 01323 415360 ✉ sue.oliver@eastbourne.gov.uk

Staff Training: Ms Elaine Wyatt, Resourcing & Development Manager, Town Hall, Grove Road, Eastbourne BN21 4UG ☎ 01323 415005 ✉ elaine.wyatt@eastbourne.gov.uk

Sustainable Communities: Mr Ian Fitzpatrick Senior Head of Community, 1 Grove Road, Eastbourne BN21 4TW ☎ 01323 415935 ✉ ian.fitzpatrick@eastbourne.gov.uk

Sustainable Development: Mrs Kerry Barrett Specialist Advisor (Economic Development), 1 Grove Road, Eastbourne BN21 4TW ☎ 01323 415054 ✉ kerry.barrett@eastbourne.gov.uk

Tourism: Mrs Annie Wills Head of Tourism & Enterprise, 1 Grove Road, Eastbourne BN21 4TW ☎ 01323 415410 ✉ annie.wills@eastbourne.gov.uk

COUNCILLORS

***Mayor* Coles**, Janet (LD - Old Town)
councillor.coles@eastbourne.gov.uk

***Deputy Mayor* Murray**, Jim (LD - Hampden Park)
councillor.murray@eastbourne.gov.uk

***Leader of the Council* Tutt**, David (LD - St Anthony's)
councillor.tutt@eastbourne.gov.uk

***Deputy Leader of the Council* Mattock**, Gill (LD - St Anthony's)
councillor.mattock@eastbourne.gov.uk

Bannister, Margaret (LD - Devonshire)
councillor.bannister@eastbourne.gov.uk

Belsey, Colin (CON - Ratton)
councillor.belsey@eastbourne.gov.uk

Blakebrouh, Raymond (CON - Sovereign)
councillor.blakebrough@eastbourne.gov.uk

Choudhury, Sammy (LD - Upperton)
councillor.choudhury@eastbourne.gov.uk

di Cara, Penny (CON - Sovereign)
councillor.dicara@eastbourne.gov.uk

Dow, Johnathan (LD - Old Town)
councillor.dow@eastbourne.gov.uk

Freebody, Tony (CON - Ratton)
cjouncillorfreebody@eastbourne.gov.uk

Hearn, Pat (LD - Hampden Park)
councillor.hearn@eastbourne.gov.uk

Holt, Steve (LD - Devonshire)
councillor.holt@eastbourne.gov.uk

Jenkins, Gordon (CON - Sovereign)
councillor.jenkins@eastbourne.gov.uk

Miah, Harun (LD - Langney)
councillor.miah@eastbourne.gov.uk

Murdoch, Colin (CON - Ratton)
councillor.murdoch@eastbourne.gov.uk

Rodohan, Pat (LD - Upperton)
councillor.rodohan@eastbourne.gov.uk

Sabri, Dean (LD - St Anthony's)
councillor.sabri@eastbourne.gov.uk

Salsbury, Margaret (LD - Upperton)
Councillor.salsbury@eastbourne.gov.uk

Shuttleworth, Alan (LD - Langney)
councillor.shuttleworth@eastbourne.gov.uk

Smart, Robert (CON - Meads)
councillor.smart@eastbourne.gov.uk

Smethers, Kathy (CON - Meads)
councillor.smethers@eastbourne.gov.uk

Swansborugh, Colin (LD - Hampdon Park)
councillor.swansborough@eastbourne.gov.uk

Taylor, Barry (CON - Meads)
councillor.taylor@eastbourne.gov.uk

Tester, Troy (LD - Langney)
councillor.tester@eastbourne.gov.uk

Ungar, John (LD - Old Town)
councillor.ungar@eastbourne.gov.uk

Wallis, Steven (LD - Devonshire)
councillor.wallis@eastbourne.gov.uk

POLITICAL COMPOSITION

LD: 18, CON: 9

COMMITTEE CHAIRS

Audit: Mr Colin Swansborough

Licensing: Mr Johnathan Dow

Planning: Mr Jim Murray

Eastleigh D

Eastleigh Borough Council, Civic Offices, Leigh Road, Eastleigh SO50 9YN
☎ 023 8068 8000 🖷 023 8064 3952
boroughcouncil@eastleigh.gov.uk www.eastleigh.gov.uk

FACTS AND FIGURES

Parliamentary Constituencies: Eastleigh
EU Constituencies: South East
Election Frequency: Elections are by thirds

PRINCIPAL OFFICERS

Chief Executive: Mr Nick Tustian, Chief Executive, Civic Offices, Leigh Road, Eastleigh SO50 9YN ☎ 023 8068 8101 🖷 023 8064 3952 nick.tustian@eastleigh.gov.uk

Senior Management: Mr Alex Parmley Corporate Director, Civic Offices, Leigh Road, Eastleigh SO50 9YN ☎ 023 8068 8305 🖷 023 8061 1528 alex.parmley@eastleigh.gov.uk

Senior Management: Ms Caroline Thomas Corporate Director, Civic Offices, Leigh Road, Eastleigh SO50 9YN ☎ 023 8068 8002 🖷 023 8064 3952 caroline.thomas@eastleigh.gov.uk

Architect, Building / Property Services: Mr Paul Ramshaw Head - Regeneration & Planning Policy, Civic Offices, Leigh Road, Eastleigh SO50 9YN ☎ 023 8068 8132 paul.ramshaw@eastleigh.gov.uk

Building Control: Mr Neil Ferris Head - Building Control, Civic Offices, Leigh Road, Eastleigh SO50 9YN ☎ 023 8068 8272 🖷 023 8064 3952 neil.ferris@eastleigh.gov.uk

PR / Communications: Mr Steve Collins Communications Officer, Civic Offices, Leigh Road, Eastleigh SO50 9YN ☎ 023 8068 8135 🖷 023 8061 1528 steve.collins@eastleigh.gov.uk

Community Planning: Ms Helen Coleman, Health & Community Team Manager, Civic Offices, Leigh Road, Eastleigh SO50 9YN ☎ 023 8068 8017 🖷 023 8068 8257 helen.coleman@eastleigh.gov.uk

Community Safety: Mr Melvin Hartley Head - Community Safety & Emergency Planning Officer, Civic Offices, Leigh Road, Eastleigh SO50 9YN ☎ 023 8068 8234 🖷 023 8064 3952 melvin.hartley@eastleigh.gov.uk

Computer Management: Mr Jim Nicholson Digital Solutions Manager, Civic Offices, Leigh Road, Eastleigh SO50 9YN ☎ 023 8068 8072 jim.nicholson@eastleigh.gov.uk

Customer Service: Ms Jessica Mendez Customer Services Manager, Civic Offices, Leigh Road, Eastleigh SO50 9YN ☎ 023 8068 8000 jessica.mendez@eastleigh.gov.uk

Direct Labour: Mr Andrew Trayer Head - Direct Services, Contract Services, Botley Road, Hedge End, Eastleigh SO30 2RA ☎ 023 8068 8370 🖷 01489 789146 andrew.trayer@eastleigh.gov.uk

Economic Development: Mrs Natalie Wigman Economic Development Manager, Civic Offices, Leigh Road, Eastleigh SO50 9YN ☎ 023 8068 8405 natalie.wigman@eastleigh.gov.uk

Electoral Registration: Mrs Samantha Jones Elections Officer, Civic Offices, Leigh Road, Eastleigh SO50 9YN ☎ 023 8068 8201 🖷 023 8064 3952 sam.jones@eastleigh.gov.uk

Emergency Planning: Mr Melvin Hartley Head - Community Safety & Emergency Planning Officer, Civic Offices, Leigh Road, Eastleigh SO50 9YN ☎ 023 8068 8234 🖷 023 8064 3952 melvin.hartley@eastleigh.gov.uk

Estates, Property & Valuation: Mr Paul Phillips Regeneration & Planning Policy Officer, Civic Offices, Leigh Road, Eastleigh SO50 9YN ☎ 023 8068 8000 paul.phillips@eastleigh.gov.uk

Facilities: Mrs Diane Hunter Facilities Manager, Civic Offices, Leigh Road, Eastleigh SO50 9YN ☎ 023 8068 8000 🖷 023 8064 3952 diana.hunter@eastleigh.gov.uk

Finance: Mrs Sarah King Chief Financial Officer, Civic Offices, Leigh Road, Eastleigh SO50 9YN ☎ 023 8068 8000 sarah.king@eastleigh.gov.uk

Finance: Mrs Loraine Radford Head - Revenue & Benefits, Civic Offices, Leigh Road, Eastleigh SO50 9YN ☎ 023 8068 8000 loraine.radford@eastleigh.gov.uk

Fleet Management: Mr Andrew Trayer Head - Direct Services, Contract Services, Botley Road, Hedge End, Eastleigh SO30 2RA ☎ 023 8068 8370 🖷 01489 789146 andrew.trayer@eastleigh.gov.uk

Grounds Maintenance: Mr Paul Naylor Streetscene Manager, Civic Offices, Leigh Road, Eastleigh SO50 9YN ☎ 023 8065 0970 paul.naylor@eastleigh.gov.uk

Health and Safety: Ms Phillippa Banner Corporate Health & Safety Officer, Civic Offices, Leigh Road, Eastleigh SO50 9YN ☎ 023 8068 8358 🖷 023 8064 3952 philippa.banner@eastleigh.gov.uk

Housing: Mr Nick James, Senior Housing Advisor, Civic Offices, Leigh Road, Eastleigh SO50 9YN ☎ 023 8068 8326 nick.james@oxford.gov.uk

Legal: Mr Richard Ward, Head - Legal & Democratic Services, Civic Offices, Leigh Road, Eastleigh SO50 9YN ☎ 023 8068 8103 🖷 023 8064 3952 richard.ward@eastleigh.gov.uk

Leisure and Cultural Services: Mr Andrew Thompson Sport & Active Lifestyles Manager, Civic Offices, Leigh Road, Eastleigh SO50 9YN ☎ 023 8068 8000 andy.thompson@eastleigh.gov.uk

Licensing: Mr Richard Ward, Head - Legal & Democratic Services, Civic Offices, Leigh Road, Eastleigh SO50 9YN ☎ 023 8068 8103 🖷 023 8064 3952 richard.ward@eastleigh.gov.uk

Lottery Funding, Charity and Voluntary: Mrs Cheryl Butler, Head - Culture, Civic Offices, Leigh Road, Eastleigh SO50 9YN ☎ 023 8068 8187 🖷 023 8064 3952 ✉ cheryl.butler@eastleigh.gov.uk

Member Services: Mr Jon Brown, Head - Democratic Services, Civic Offices, Leigh Road, Eastleigh SO50 9YN ☎ 023 8068 8000 🖷 023 8064 3952 ✉ jon.brown@eastleigh.gov.uk

Parking: Mr Wayne Bailey, Parking Services Manager, Civic Offices, Leigh Road, Eastleigh SO50 9YN ☎ 023 8068 8000 ✉ wayne.bailey@eastleigh.gov.uk

Personnel / HR: Mrs Melanie Swain Head - Human Resources, Civic Offices, Leigh Road, Eastleigh SO50 9YN ☎ 023 8068 8141 ✉ melanie.swain@eastleigh.gov.uk

Planning: Mrs Louise O'Driscoll Head - Development Control, Civic Offices, Leigh Road, Eastleigh SO50 9YN ☎ 023 8068 8248 🖷 023 8064 3952 ✉ louise.odriscoll@eastleigh.gov.uk

Regeneration: Mr Paul Ramshaw Head - Regeneration & Planning Policy, Civic Offices, Leigh Road, Eastleigh SO50 9YN ☎ 023 8068 8132 ✉ paul.ramshaw@eastleigh.gov.uk

Staff Training: Mrs Melanie Swain Head - Human Resources, Civic Offices, Leigh Road, Eastleigh SO50 9YN ☎ 023 8068 8141 ✉ melanie.swain@eastleigh.gov.uk

Street Scene: Mr Paul Naylor Streetscene Manager, Civic Offices, Leigh Road, Eastleigh SO50 9YN ☎ 023 8065 0970 ✉ paul.naylor@eastleigh.gov.uk

Traffic Management: Mr Stuart Robinson-Woledge, Traffic & Transport Sevices Manager, Civic Offices, Leigh Road, Eastleigh SO50 9YN ☎ 023 8068 8229 🖷 023 8068 3952 ✉ stuart.robinson-woledge@eastleigh.gov.uk

Transport: Mr Ed Vokes Head - Transportation & Engineering, Civic Offices, Leigh Road, Eastleigh SO50 9YN ☎ 023 8068 8234 🖷 023 8064 3952 ✉ ed.vokes@eastleigh.gov.uk

Waste Collection and Disposal: Mr Colin Ellis, Senior Inspector & Refuse Collection, Contract Services, Botley Road, Hedge End, Eastleigh SO30 2RA ☎ 023 8068 8000 🖷 01489 789146 ✉ colin.ellis@eastleigh.gov.uk

Waste Management: Mr Colin Ellis, Senior Inspector & Refuse Collection, Contract Services, Botley Road, Hedge End, Eastleigh SO30 2RA ☎ 023 8068 8000 🖷 01489 789146 ✉ colin.ellis@eastleigh.gov.uk

COUNCILLORS

***Mayor* Welsh**, Jane (LD - Hedge End St Johns)
jane.welsh@eastleigh.gov.uk

***Deputy Mayor* Scott**, Desmond (LD - Fair Oak and Horton Heath)
des.scott@eastleigh.gov.uk

***Leader of the Council* House**, Keith (LD - Hedge End Wildern)
keith.house@eastleigh.gov.uk

***Deputy Leader of the Council* Winstanley**, Anne (LD - Bishopstoke West)
anne.winstanley@eastleigh.gov.uk

Airey, David (LD - Netley Abbey)
david.airey@eastleigh.gov.uk

Allingham, Margaret (LD - Hedge End St Johns)

Atkinson, Margaret (CON - Hiltingbury East)
margaret.atkinson@eastleigh.gov.uk

Bain, Sarah (LD - Eastleigh North)
sarah.bain@eastleigh.gov.uk

Bancroft, Simon (LD - Eastleigh Central)
simon.bancroft@eastleigh.gov.uk

Bicknell, Paul (LD - Eastleigh South)
paul.bicknell@eastleigh.gov.uk

Bloom, Louise (LD - Hedge End Grange Park)
louis.bloom@eastleigh.gov.uk

Boulton, Carol (LD - West End South)
carol.boulton@eastleigh.gov.uk

Broadhurst, Haulwen (LD - Chandlers Ford East)
haulwen.broadhurst@eastleigh.gov.uk

Broadhurst, Alan (LD - Chandlers Ford West)
alan.broadhurst@eastleigh.gov.uk

Clarke, Daniel (LD - West End South)
daniel.clarke@eastleigh.gov.uk

Cossey, Andrew (LD - Fair Oak and Horton Heath)
andrew.cossey@eastleigh.gov.uk

Craig, Tonia (LD - Burlesden and Old Netley)
tonia.craig@eastleigh.gov.uk

Grajewski, Judith (CON - Hiltingbury West)
judith.grajewski@eastleigh.gov.uk

Hall, Jerry (CON - Hedge End St Johns)
jerry.hall@eastleigh.gov.uk

Hamel, Suzy (LD - Hamble-le-Rice and Butlocks Heath)
suzy.hamel@eastleigh.gov.uk

Holden-Brown, Pamela (LD - Chandlers Ford East)
pamela.holden-brown@eastleigh.gov.uk

Holes, Steve (LD - Burlesdon and Old Netley)
steve.holes@eastleigh.gov.uk

Hughes, Michael (CON - Hiltingbury West)
michael.hughes@eastleigh.gov.uk

Irish, Wayne (LD - Eastleigh Central)
wayne.irish@eastleigh.gov.uk

Kyrle, Rupert (LD - Botley)
rupert.kyrle@eastleigh.gov.uk

Lear, Elizabeth (CON - Hamble-le-Rice and Butlocks Heath)
elizabeth.lear@eastleigh.gov.uk

Mann, Darshan (LD - Eastleigh South)
darshan.mann@eastleigh.gov.uk

Mignot, Trevor (LD - Bishopstoke East)
trevor.mignot@eastleigh.gov.uk

Myerscough, Angel (LD - Botley)

Norman, Emma (LD - Hedge End Wildern)
emma.norman@eastleigh.gov.uk

Noyce, Tony (LD - West End North)
tony.noyce@eastleigh.gov.uk

Olson, Godfrey (CON - Hiltingbury East)
godfrey.olson@eastleigh.gov.uk

Parkinson-MacLachlan, Vickieye (NP - No Ward)

Pragnell, David (LD - Chandlers Ford West)
david.pragnell@eastleigh.gov.uk

Pretty, Derek (LD - Hedge End Grange Park)
derek.pretty@eastleigh.gov.uk

Rich, Jane (LD - Bursledon and Old Netley)
jane.rich@eastleigh.gov.uk

Roling, Angela (LD - Bishopstoke East)
angela.roling@eastleigh.gov.uk

Smith, Roger (LD - Fair Oak and Horton Heath)
roger.smith@eastleigh.gov.uk

Sollitt, Maureen (LD - Eastleigh North)
maureen.sollitt@eastleigh.gov.uk

Sollitt, Steve (LD - Eastleigh South)
steve.sollitt@eastleigh.gov.uk

Tennent, Bruce (LD - West End North)
bruce.tennent@eastleigh.gov.uk

Thomas, Chris (LD - Eastleigh North)
chris.thomas@eastleigh.gov.uk

Trenchard, Keith (LD - Eastleigh Central)
keithsmobile@gmx.com

van Niekerk, Lizette (LD - Netley Abbey)
lizette.vanniekerk@eastleigh.gov.uk

POLITICAL COMPOSITION

LD: 37, CON: 6, NP: 1

COMMITTEE CHAIRS

Audit: Mr Steve Holes

Licensing: Mr David Airey

Eden D

Eden District Council, Town Hall, Penrith CA11 7QF
☎ 01768 817817 🖷 01768 890470 ✉ customer.services@eden.gov.uk
💻 www.eden.gov.uk

FACTS AND FIGURES

Parliamentary Constituencies: Penrith and The Border, Westmorland and Lonsdale
EU Constituencies: North West
Election Frequency: Elections are of whole council

PRINCIPAL OFFICERS

Chief Executive: Mr Robin Hooper, Chief Executive, Town Hall, Penrith CA11 7QF ☎ 01768 212200 ✉ chief.exec@eden.gov.uk

Deputy Chief Executive: Mr Paul Foote, Director of Corporate & Legal Services, Town Hall, Penrith CA11 7QF ☎ 01768 212205 🖷 01768 890470 ✉ paul.foote@eden.gov.uk

Senior Management: Mrs Ruth Atkinson, Communities Director, Mansion House, Penrith CA11 7YG ☎ 01768 212202 🖷 01768 890732 ✉ ruth.atkinson@eden.gov.uk

Senior Management: Mr Paul Foote, Director of Corporate & Legal Services, Town Hall, Penrith CA11 7QF ☎ 01768 212205 🖷 01768 890470 ✉ paul.foote@eden.gov.uk

Senior Management: Mr David Rawsthorn, Director of Finance, Town Hall, Penrith CA11 7QF ☎ 01768 212211 🖷 01768 890470 ✉ david.rawsthorn@eden.gov.uk

Access Officer / Social Services (Disability): Ms Sally Hemsley Communities Officer, Town Hall, Penrith CA11 7QF ☎ 01768 212483 🖷 01768 890732 ✉ sallye.hemsley@eden.gov.uk

Architect, Building / Property Services: Mr Paul Foote, Director of Corporate & Legal Services, Town Hall, Penrith CA11 7QF ☎ 01768 212205 🖷 01768 890470 ✉ paul.foote@eden.gov.uk

Architect, Building / Property Services: Ms Jane Langston Property & Contracts Manager, Mansion House, Penrith CA11 7YG ☎ 01768 212448 ✉ jane.langston@eden.gov.uk

Best Value: Mrs Ruth Atkinson, Communities Director, Mansion House, Penrith CA11 7YG ☎ 01768 212202 🖷 01768 890732 ✉ ruth.atkinson@eden.gov.uk

Building Control: Mr Gwyn Clark, Head of Planning Services, Mansion House, Penrith CA11 7YG ☎ 01768 212388 🖷 01768 890732 ✉ gwyn.clark@eden.gov.uk

PR / Communications: Mr Barry Cooper, Communications Officer, Mansion House, Penrith CA11 7YG ☎ 01768 212137 🖷 01768 890470 ✉ barry.cooper@eden.gov.uk

PR / Communications: Mr Oliver Shimell Communities Manager, Mansion House, Penrith CA11 7YG ☎ 01768 212143 🖷 01768 890732 ✉ oliver.shimell@eden.gov.uk

Community Planning: Mrs Ruth Atkinson, Communities Director, Mansion House, Penrith CA11 7YG ☎ 01768 212202 🖷 01768 890732 ✉ ruth.atkinson@eden.gov.uk

Community Planning: Ms Deborah Garnett Senior Communities Officer, Mansion House, Penrith CA11 7YG ☎ 01768 212268 🖷 01768 890470 ✉ deborah.garnett@eden.gov.uk

Community Planning: Mr Oliver Shimell Communities Manager, Mansion House, Penrith CA11 7YG ☎ 01768 212143 🖷 01768 890732 ✉ oliver.shimell@eden.gov.uk

Community Safety: Mr Oliver Shimell Communities Manager, Mansion House, Penrith CA11 7YG ☎ 01768 212143 🖷 01768 890732 ✉ oliver.shimell@eden.gov.uk

Computer Management: Mr Ben Wright, Shared IT Manager, Town Hall, Penrith CA11 7QF ☎ 01539 733333 🖷 01539 740300 ✉ b.wright@southlakeland.gov.uk

Contracts: Ms Jane Langston Property & Contracts Manager, Mansion House, Penrith CA11 7YG ☎ 01768 212448 ✉ jane.langston@eden.gov.uk

Corporate Services: Mrs Linda Methven, Customer Services Manager, Town Hall, Penrith CA11 7QF ☎ 01768 212130 🖷 01768 890470 🖱 linda.methven@eden.gov.uk

Customer Service: Mrs Linda Methven, Customer Services Manager, Town Hall, Penrith CA11 7QF ☎ 01768 212130 🖷 01768 890470 🖱 linda.methven@eden.gov.uk

Economic Development: Mr Alan Houghton Economic Regeneration Officer, Mansion House, Penrith CA11 7YG ☎ 01768 212169 🖷 01768 890732 🖱 alan.houghton@eden.gov.uk

Economic Development: Mr Oliver Shimell Communities Manager, Town Hall, Penrith CA11 7QF ☎ 01768 212143 🖱 oliver.shimell@eden.gov.uk

E-Government: Mr Ben Wright, Shared IT Manager, Town Hall, Penrith CA11 7QF ☎ 01539 733333 🖷 01539 740300 🖱 b.wright@southlakeland.gov.uk

Electoral Registration: Mr Paul Foote, Director of Corporate & Legal Services, Town Hall, Penrith CA11 7QF ☎ 01768 212205 🖷 01768 890470 🖱 paul.foote@eden.gov.uk

Emergency Planning: Mr David Rawsthorn, Director of Finance, Town Hall, Penrith CA11 7QF ☎ 01768 212211 🖷 01768 890470 🖱 david.rawsthorn@eden.gov.uk

Environmental Health: Mrs Ruth Atkinson, Communities Director, Mansion House, Penrith CA11 7YG ☎ 01768 212202 🖷 01768 890732 🖱 ruth.atkinson@eden.gov.uk

Environmental Health: Miss Julie Monk Head of Environmental Services, Mansion House, Penrith CA11 7YG ☎ 01768 212328 🖷 01768 890732 🖱 julie.monk@eden.gov.uk

Estates, Property & Valuation: Mr Paul Foote, Director of Corporate & Legal Services, Town Hall, Penrith CA11 7QF ☎ 01768 212205 🖷 01768 890470 🖱 paul.foote@eden.gov.uk

Estates, Property & Valuation: Ms Jane Langston Property & Contracts Manager, Mansion House, Penrith CA11 7YG ☎ 01768 212448 🖱 jane.langston@eden.gov.uk

Events Manager: Mr Barry Cooper, Communications Officer, Mansion House, Penrith CA11 7YG ☎ 01768 212137 🖷 01768 890470 🖱 barry.cooper@eden.gov.uk

Facilities: Mr Paul Brunsdon Facilities Officer, Mansion House, Penrith CA11 7YG ☎ 01768 212371 🖷 01768 890732 🖱 paul.brundson@eden.gov.uk

Facilities: Ms Jane Langston Property & Contracts Manager, Mansion House, Penrith CA11 7YG ☎ 01768 212448 🖱 jane.langston@eden.gov.uk

Finance: Mr David Rawsthorn, Director of Finance, Town Hall, Penrith CA11 7QF ☎ 01768 212211 🖷 01768 890470 🖱 david.rawsthorn@eden.gov.uk

Grounds Maintenance: Mr Neil Buck Contracts Manager, Mansion House, Penrith CA11 7YG ☎ 01768 212337 🖷 01768 890732 🖱 neil.buck@eden.gov.uk

Grounds Maintenance: Ms Jane Langston Property & Contracts Manager, Mansion House, Penrith CA11 7YG ☎ 01768 212448 🖱 jane.langston@eden.gov.uk

Health and Safety: Mrs Tina Mason Contracts Officer, Mansion House, Penrith CA11 7YG ☎ 01768 212368 🖷 01768 890732 🖱 tina.mason@eden.gov.uk

Health and Safety: Mrs Bibian McRoy Human Resources Manager (Job Share), Town Hall, Penrith CA11 7QF ☎ 01768 212243 🖱 bibian.mcroy@eden.gov.uk

Housing: Miss Julie Monk Head of Environmental Services, Mansion House, Penrith CA11 7YG ☎ 01768 212328 🖷 01768 890732 🖱 julie.monk@eden.gov.uk

Housing: Mr Graham Tomlinson Principal EHO (Housing), Mansion House, Penrith CA11 7YG ☎ 01768 212364 🖷 01768 890732 🖱 graham.tomlinson@eden.gov.uk

Legal: Mr Paul Foote, Director of Corporate & Legal Services, Town Hall, Penrith CA11 7QF ☎ 01768 212205 🖷 01768 890470 🖱 paul.foote@eden.gov.uk

Legal: Mrs Lisa Tremble Senior Solicitor, Town Hall, Penrith CA11 7QF ☎ 01768 212249 🖷 01768 890470 🖱 lisa.tremble@eden.gov.uk

Leisure and Cultural Services: Mr Doug Huggon Leisure Services Manager, Mansion House, Penrith CA11 7YG ☎ 01768 212323 🖷 01768 890732 🖱 doug.huggon@eden.gov.uk

Leisure and Cultural Services: Mr Ian Parker Assistant Leisure Officer, Town Hall, Penrith CA11 7QF ☎ 01768 212473 🖷 01768 890732 🖱 ian.parker@eden.gov.uk

Licensing: Mr Paul Foote, Director of Corporate & Legal Services, Town Hall, Penrith CA11 7QF ☎ 01768 212205 🖷 01768 890470 🖱 paul.foote@eden.gov.uk

Licensing: Mrs Lisa Tremble Senior Solicitor, Town Hall, Penrith CA11 7QF ☎ 01768 212249 🖷 01768 890470 🖱 lisa.tremble@eden.gov.uk

Member Services: Mr Paul Foote, Director of Corporate & Legal Services, Town Hall, Penrith CA11 7QF ☎ 01768 212205 🖷 01768 890470 🖱 paul.foote@eden.gov.uk

Member Services: Miss Lauren Rushen Member Services Team Leader, Town Hall, Penrith CA11 7QF ☎ 01768 212142 🖷 01768 890470 🖱 lauren.rushen@eden.gov.uk

Parking: Mr Paul Foote, Director of Corporate & Legal Services, Town Hall, Penrith CA11 7QF ☎ 01768 212205 🖷 01768 890470 🖱 paul.foote@eden.gov.uk

Parking: Ms Jane Langston Property & Contracts Manager, Mansion House, Penrith CA11 7YG ☎ 01768 212448 ✉ jane.langston@eden.gov.uk

Partnerships: Mrs Ruth Atkinson, Communities Director, Mansion House, Penrith CA11 7YG ☎ 01768 212202 🖷 01768 890732 ✉ ruth.atkinson@eden.gov.uk

Partnerships: Mr Oliver Shimell Communities Manager, Mansion House, Penrith CA11 7YG ☎ 01768 212143 🖷 01768 890732 ✉ oliver.shimell@eden.gov.uk

Personnel / HR: Mrs Bibian McRoy Human Resources Manager (Job Share), Town Hall, Penrith CA11 7QF ☎ 01768 212243 ✉ bibian.mcroy@eden.gov.uk

Planning: Mr Gwyn Clark, Head of Planning Services, Mansion House, Penrith CA11 7YG ☎ 01768 212388 🖷 01768 890732 ✉ gwyn.clark@eden.gov.uk

Procurement: Mr Clive Howey Financial Services Manager, Town Hall, Penrith CA11 7QF ☎ 01768 212213 ✉ clive.howey@eden.gov.uk

Recycling & Waste Minimisation: Ms Jane Langston Property & Contracts Manager, Mansion House, Penrith CA11 7YG ☎ 01768 212448 ✉ jane.langston@eden.gov.uk

Regeneration: Mr Alan Houghton Economic Regeneration Officer, Mansion House, Penrith CA11 7YG ☎ 01768 212169 🖷 01768 890732 ✉ alan.houghton@eden.gov.uk

Staff Training: Mrs Bibian McRoy Human Resources Manager (Job Share), Town Hall, Penrith CA11 7QF ☎ 01768 212243 ✉ bibian.mcroy@eden.gov.uk

Street Scene: Mrs Ruth Atkinson, Communities Director, Mansion House, Penrith CA11 7YG ☎ 01768 212202 🖷 01768 890732 ✉ ruth.atkinson@eden.gov.uk

Street Scene: Mr Oliver Shimell Communities Manager, Town Hall, Penrith CA11 7QF ☎ 01768 212143 ✉ oliver.shimell@eden.gov.uk

Sustainable Communities: Ms Deborah Garnett Senior Communities Officer, Mansion House, Penrith CA11 7YG ☎ 01768 212268 🖷 01768 890470 ✉ deborah.garnett@eden.gov.uk

Sustainable Communities: Mr Oliver Shimell Communities Manager, Town Hall, Penrith CA11 7QF ☎ 01768 212143 ✉ oliver.shimell@eden.gov.uk

Sustainable Development: Mrs Ruth Atkinson, Communities Director, Mansion House, Penrith CA11 7YG ☎ 01768 212202 🖷 01768 890732 ✉ ruth.atkinson@eden.gov.uk

Tourism: Miss Jessica Goodfellow Tourism Manager (Job Share), Mansion House, Penrith CA11 7YG ☎ 01768 212165 🖷 01768 890732 ✉ jessica.goodfellow@eden.gov.uk

Tourism: Ms Sally Hemsley Communities Officer, Town Hall, Penrith CA11 7QF ☎ 01768 212483 🖷 01768 890732 ✉ sallye.hemsley@eden.gov.uk

Town Centre: Mrs Yvonne Burrows Town Centres Officer (Job Share), Mansion House, Penrith CA11 7YG ☎ 01768 212150 🖷 01768 890732 ✉ yvonne.burrows@eden.gov.uk

Town Centre: Mrs Carol Grey Town Centres Officer (Job Share), Mansion House, Penrith CA11 7YG ☎ 01768 212147 🖷 01768 890732 ✉ carol.grey@eden.gov.uk

Waste Collection and Disposal: Ms Jane Langston Property & Contracts Manager, Mansion House, Penrith CA11 7YG ☎ 01768 212448 ✉ jane.langston@eden.gov.uk

Waste Management: Ms Jane Langston Property & Contracts Manager, Mansion House, Penrith CA11 7YG ☎ 01768 212448 ✉ jane.langston@eden.gov.uk

Children's Play Areas: Mrs Yvonne Burrows Town Centres Officer (Job Share), Mansion House, Penrith CA11 7YG ☎ 01768 212150 🖷 01768 890732 ✉ yvonne.burrows@eden.gov.uk

Children's Play Areas: Mr Doug Huggon Leisure Services Manager, Mansion House, Penrith CA11 7YG ☎ 01768 212323 🖷 01768 890732 ✉ doug.huggon@eden.gov.uk

COUNCILLORS

***Chair* Tonkin**, Michael (O - Morland)
mike.tonkin@eden.gov.uk

***Vice-Chair* Raine**, Joan (CON - Crosby Ravensworth)
joan.raine@eden.gov.uk

***Leader of the Council* Beaty**, Kevin (CON - Skelton)
kevin.beaty@eden.gov.uk

***Deputy Leader of the Council* Grisedale**, Lesley (CON - Hesket)
lesley.grisedale@eden.gov.uk

***Group Leader* Howse**, Robin (LD - Penrith North)
robin.howse@eden.gov.uk

***Group Leader* Robinson**, Mary (O - Kirkoswald)
mary.robinson@eden.gov.uk

***Group Leader* Slee**, Michael (CON - Askham)
michael.slee@eden.gov.uk

***Common Councilman* Martin**, Elaine (CON - Hesket)
elaine.martin@eden.gov.uk

Armstrong, Allan (CON - Long Marton)
allan.armstrong@eden.gov.uk

Banks, Douglas (IND - Langwathby)
douglas.banks@eden gov.uk

Breen, Paula (CON - Penrith Carleton)
paula.breen@eden.gov.uk

Chambers, Ian (CON - Eamont)
ian.chambers@eden.gov.uk

Clark, Margaret (IND - Penrith South)

Connell, Andrew (LD - Appleby (Bongate))
andrew.connell@eden.gov.uk

Derbyshire, Judith (LD - Dacre)
judith.derbyshire@eden.gov.uk

Eyles, Michael (LD - Penrith East)
michael.eyles@eden.gov.uk

Godwin, Pat (O - Alston Moor)
patricia.godwin@eden.gov.uk

Hogg, Alistair (CON - Ullswater)

Holden, Deborah (LD - Penrith North)
deb.holden@eden.gov.uk

Hymers, David (CON - Alston Moor)
edencouncillor@davidhymers.com

Jackson, Scott (CON - Penrith North)
scott.jackson@eden.gov.uk

Kendall, Valerie (CON - Kirkby Stephen)

Ladhams, Trevor (IND - Kirkby Stephen)
trevor.ladhams@eden.gov.uk

Lynch, John (CON - Penrith East)

Meadowcroft, Angela (CON - Revenstonedale)

Morgan, Keith (IND - Appleby (Appleby))
keith.morgan@eden.gov.uk

Nicolson, Gordon (CON - Lazonby)
gordon.nicolson@eden.gov.uk

Orchard, Sheila (CON - Hartside)

Owen, John (CON - Shap)

Patterson, William (IND - Warcop)
william.patterson@eden.gov.uk

Sawrey-Cookson, Henry (O - Kirkby Thore)
henry.sawrey-cookson@eden.gov.uk

Sealby, Richard (CON - Greystoke)
richard.sealby@eden.gov.uk

Smith, Malcolm (O - Brough)
malcolm.smith@eden.gov.uk

Taylor, Virginia (LD - Penrith West)
virginia.taylor@eden.gov.uk

Temple, Malcolm (CON - Penrith South)
malcolm.temple@eden.gov.uk

Thompson, John (CON - Penrith West)
john.thompson@eden.gov.uk

Todd, Adrian (CON - Orton with Tebay)
adrian.todd@eden.gov.uk

Tompkins, John (LD - Penrith Pategill)
john.tompkins@eden.gov.uk

POLITICAL COMPOSITION

CON: 21, LD: 7, O: 5, IND: 5

COMMITTEE CHAIRS

Licensing: Mr Malcolm Temple

Planning: Mr William Patterson

Edinburgh, City of — S

City of Edinburgh Council, Waverley Court, 4 East Market Street, Edinburgh EH8 8BG
☎ 0131 200 2000 council.info@edinburgh.gov.uk
www.edinburgh.gov.uk

FACTS AND FIGURES

Parliamentary Constituencies: Edinburgh East, Edinburgh North and Leith, Edinburgh South, Edinburgh South West, Edinburgh West

EU Constituencies: Scotland

Election Frequency: Elections are of whole council

PRINCIPAL OFFICERS

Chief Executive: Mr Andrew Kerr Chief Executive, Waverley Court, 4 East Market Street, Edinburgh EH8 8BG ☎ 0131 469 3002 andrew.kerr@edinburgh.gov.uk

Senior Management: Mr Paul Lawrence Executive Director - Place, Waverley Court, 4 East Market Street, Edinburgh EH8 8BG ☎ 0131 529 3494 paul.lawrence@edinburgh.gov.uk

Senior Management: Mr Alistair Maclean Director - Corporate Governance, Waverley Court, Level 2.6, 4 East Market Street, Edinburgh EH8 8BG ☎ 0131 529 4136 alastair.maclean@edinburgh.gov.uk

Senior Management: Ms Michelle Miller Head of Service & Chief Social Work Officer, Waverley Court, Level 1.9, 4 East Market Street, Edinburgh EH8 8BG ☎ 0131 553 8520 michelle.miller@edinburgh.gov.uk

Senior Management: Ms Gillian Tee Director - Children & Families, Waverley Court, Level 2.6, 4 East Market Street, Edinburgh EH8 8BG ☎ 0131 529 3494 gillian.tee@edinburgh.gov.uk

Senior Management: Mr Greg Ward Director - Economic Development, Waverley Court, Level 1.9, 4 East Market Street, Edinburgh EH8 8BG ☎ 0131 529 4298 greg.ward@edinburgh.gov.uk

Architect, Building / Property Services: Mr Peter Watton Acting Head of Corporate Property, Waverley Court, Level 1.9, 4 East Market Street, Edinburgh EH8 8BG ☎ 0131 529 5962 peter.long@edinburgh.gov.uk

Building Control: Mr David Leslie Acting Head of Planning & Building Standards, Waverley Court, Level 1.9, 4 East Market Street, Edinburgh EH8 8BG ☎ 0131 529 3948 peter.long@edinburgh.gov.uk

Catering Services: Ms Helen Allan Acting Corporate Facilities Manager, Waverley Court, 4 East Market Street, Edinburgh EH8 8BG ☎ 0131529 6208 helen.allan@edinburgh.gov.uk

Children / Youth Services: Mr Alistair Gaw Head of Support to Children & Young People, Waverley Court, Level 1.9, 4 East Market Street, Edinburgh EH8 8BG ☎ 0131 469 3388 alistair.gaw@edinburgh.gov.uk

Civil Registration: Ms Liz Allan Chief Registrar, Lothian Chambers, Room 2a, 59-63 George IV Bridge, Edinburgh EH1 1RN ☎ 0131 529 2616 liz.allan@edinburgh@gov.uk

PR / Communications: Miss Lesley McPherson Chief Communications Officer, Waverley Court, Level 2.1, 4 East Market Street BC2.1, Edinburgh EH8 8BG ☎ 0131 529 4030 lesley.mcpherson@edinburgh.gov.uk

Community Safety: Ms Susan Mooney Head of Service, Community Safety & Libraries, Waverley Court, Level G.6, 4 East Market Street, Edinburgh EH8 8BG ☎ 0131 529 7587 susan.mooney@edinburgh.gov.uk

Computer Management: Mrs Claudette Jones Chief Information Officer, Waverley Court, Level C.4, East Market Street, Edinburgh EH8 8BG ☎ 0131 529 7847 claudette.jones@edinburgh.gov.uk

Consumer Protection and Trading Standards: Ms Susan Mooney Head of Service, Community Safety & Libraries, Waverley Court, Level G.6, 4 East Market Street, Edinburgh EH8 8BG ☎ 0131 529 7587 susan.mooney@edinburgh.gov.uk

Customer Service: Mr Danny Gallacher Head of Customer Services, Waverley Court, Level 1.9, 4 East Market Street, Edinburgh EH8 8BG ☎ 0131 469 5016 danny.gallacher@edinburgh.gov.uk

Economic Development: Mr Greg Ward Director - Economic Development, Waverley Court, Level 1.9, 4 East Market Street, Edinburgh EH8 8BG ☎ 0131 529 4298 greg.ward@edinburgh.gov.uk

Education: Mr Andy Gray Head of Schools & Community Services, Waverley Court, 4 East Market Street, Edinburgh EH8 8BG ☎ 0131 529 2217 andy.gray@edinburgh.gov.uk

E-Government: Mrs Claudette Jones Chief Information Officer, Waverley Court, Level C.4, East Market Street, Edinburgh EH8 8BG ☎ 0131 529 7847 claudette.jones@edinburgh.gov.uk

Emergency Planning: Ms Mary-Ellen Lang Council Corporate Resilience Manager, Level 2/1, Waverley Court, 4 East Market Street, Edinburgh EH8 8BG ☎ 0131 529 4684 mary-ellen.lang@edinburgh.gov.uk

Environmental Health: Ms Susan Mooney Head of Service, Community Safety & Libraries, Waverley Court, Level G.6, 4 East Market Street, Edinburgh EH8 8BG ☎ 0131 529 7587 susan.mooney@edinburgh.gov.uk

Estates, Property & Valuation: Mr Peter Watton Acting Head of Corporate Property, Waverley Court, Level 1.9, 4 East Market Street, Edinburgh EH8 8BG ☎ 0131 529 5962 peter.long@edinburgh.gov.uk

European Liaison: Ms Elaine Ballantyne Head of External Relations & Investor Support, Waverley Court, Level G.1, 4 East Market Street, Edinburgh EH8 8BG ☎ 0131 469 3854 elaine.ballantyne@edinburgh.gov.uk

Facilities: Ms Helen Allan Acting Corporate Facilities Manager, Waverley Court, 4 East Market Street, Edinburgh EH8 8BG ☎ 0131529 6208 helen.allan@edinburgh.gov.uk

Finance: Mr Hugh Dunn Head of Finance, Waverley Court, Level G.6, 4 East Market Street, Edinburgh EH8 8BG ☎ 0131 469 3150 hugh.dunn@edinburgh.gov.uk

Treasury: Ms Innes Edwards Principal Treasury & Banking Manager, Waverley Court, Level 2.5, 4 East Market Street, Edinburgh EH8 8BG ☎ 0131 469 6291 innes.edwards@edinburgh.gov.uk

Pensions: Ms Clare Scott Investments & Pensions Service Manager, Atria One, 144 Morrison Street, Edinburgh EH8 8BG ☎ 0131 469 3865 clare.scott@edinburgh.gov.uk

Fleet Management: Mr Jim Hunter Acting Head of Environment, Waverley Court, Level 1.9, 4 East Market Street, Edinburgh EH8 8BG ☎ 0131 469 5342 jim.hunter@edinburgh.gov.uk

Health and Safety: Ms Susan Tannahill Council Health & Safety Manager, Waverley Court, 4 East Market Street, Edinburgh EH8 8BG ☎ 0131 553 8336 susan.tannaill@edinburgh.gov.uk

Highways: Mr David Lyon Acting Head of Transport, Waverley Court, Level 1.9, 4 East Market Street, Edinburgh EH8 8BG ☎ 0131 529 7047 david.lyon@edinburgh.gov.uk

Housing: Ms Cathy King Head of Housing & Regeneration, Waverley Court, Level 1.9, 4 East Market Street, Edinburgh EH8 8BG ☎ 0131 529 7383 cathy.king@edinburgh.gov.uk

Housing Maintenance: Mr Alex Burns Edinburgh Building Services Manager, 33 Murrayburn Road, Edinburgh EH8 8BG ☎ 0131 529 5890 alexander.burns@edinburgh.gov.uk

Legal: Ms Carol Campbell Head of Legal, Risk & Compliance, Waverley Court, Level G.6, 4 East Market Street, Edinburgh EH8 8BG ☎ 0131 529 4822 carol.campbell@edinburgh.gov.uk

Leisure and Cultural Services: Ms Lynne Halfpenny, Head of Culture & Sport, Waverley Court, Level 1.9, 4 East Market Street, Edinburgh EH8 8BG ☎ 0131 529 3657 lynne.halfpenny@edinburgh.gov.uk

Licensing: Ms Susan Mooney Head of Service, Community Safety & Libraries, Waverley Court, Level G.6, 4 East Market Street, Edinburgh EH8 8BG ☎ 0131 529 7587 susan.mooney@edinburgh.gov.uk

Lighting: Mr David Lyon Acting Head of Transport, Waverley Court, Level 1.9, 4 East Market Street, Edinburgh EH8 8BG ☎ 0131 529 7047 david.lyon@edinburgh.gov.uk

Member Services: Mr Andy Nichol Head of Members' Services, Waverley Court, Level 2, 4 East Market Street, Edinburgh EH8 8BG ☎ 0131 529 4461 andy.nichol@edinburgh.gov.uk

Parking: Mr David Lyon Acting Head of Transport, Waverley Court, Level 1.9, 4 East Market Street, Edinburgh EH8 8BG ☎ 0131 529 7047 david.lyon@edinburgh.gov.uk

Personnel / HR: Ms Linda Holden Intermin Head of Organisational Development, Waverley Court, Level 2/3, 4 East Market Street, Edinburgh EH8 8BG ☎ 0131 469 3963 linda.holden@edinburgh.gov.uk

Planning: Mr David Leslie Acting Head of Planning & Building Standards, Waverley Court, Level 1.9, 4 East Market Street, Edinburgh EH8 8BG ☎ 0131 529 3948 peter.long@edinburgh.gov.uk

Procurement: Mr Nick Smith Commercial & Procurement Manager, Waverley Court, Level 3.3, 4 East Market Street, Edinburgh EH8 8BG ☎ 0131 529 4377 nick.smith@edinburgh.gov.uk

Public Libraries: Ms Susan Mooney Head of Service, Community Safety & Libraries, Waverley Court, Level G.6, 4 East Market Street, Edinburgh EH8 8BG ☎ 0131 529 7587 susan.mooney@edinburgh.gov.uk

Recycling & Waste Minimisation: Mr John Bury Acting Director - Services for Communities, Waverley Court, Level G.6, 4 East Market Street, Edinburgh EH8 8BG ☎ 0131 529 3494 john.bury@edinburgh.gov.uk

Regeneration: Ms Cathy King Head of Housing & Regeneration, Waverley Court, Level 1.9, 4 East Market Street, Edinburgh EH8 8BG ☎ 0131 529 7383 cathy.king@edinburgh.gov.uk

Road Safety: Mr David Lyon Acting Head of Transport, Waverley Court, Level 1.9, 4 East Market Street, Edinburgh EH8 8BG ☎ 0131 529 7047 david.lyon@edinburgh.gov.uk

Social Services: Ms Monica Boyle Head of Older People & Disability Services, Waverley Court, Level 1.9, 4 East Market Street, Edinburgh EH8 8BG ☎ 0131 553 8319 monica.boyle@edinburgh.gov.uk

Social Services: Ms Michelle Miller Head of Service & Chief Social Work Officer, Waverley Court, Level 1.9, 4 East Market Street, Edinburgh EH8 8BG ☎ 0131 553 8520 michelle.miller@edinburgh.gov.uk

Social Services (Children): Mr Alistair Gaw Head of Support to Children & Young People, Waverley Court, Level 1.9, 4 East Market Street, Edinburgh EH8 8BG ☎ 0131 469 3388 alistair.gaw@edinburgh.gov.uk

Fostering & Adoption: Mr Alistair Gaw Head of Support to Children & Young People, Waverley Court, Level 1.9, 4 East Market Street, Edinburgh EH8 8BG ☎ 0131 469 3388 alistair.gaw@edinburgh.gov.uk

Families: Mr Alistair Gaw Head of Support to Children & Young People, Waverley Court, Level 1.9, 4 East Market Street, Edinburgh EH8 8BG ☎ 0131 469 3388 alistair.gaw@edinburgh.gov.uk

Staff Training: Ms Linda Holden Intermin Head of Organisational Development, Waverley Court, Level 2/3, 4 East Market Street, Edinburgh EH8 8BG ☎ 0131 469 3963 linda.holden@edinburgh.gov.uk

Sustainable Development: Mr Nick Croft Corporate Policy & Strategy Manager, Waverley Court, 4 East Market Street, Edinburgh EH8 8BG ☎ 0131 469 3726 nick.croft@edinburgh.gov.uk

Town Centre: Mr Greg Ward Director - Economic Development, Waverley Court, Level 1.9, 4 East Market Street, Edinburgh EH8 8BG ☎ 0131 529 4298 greg.ward@edinburgh.gov.uk

Traffic Management: Mr David Lyon Acting Head of Transport, Waverley Court, Level 1.9, 4 East Market Street, Edinburgh EH8 8BG ☎ 0131 529 7047 david.lyon@edinburgh.gov.uk

Transport: Mr David Lyon Acting Head of Transport, Waverley Court, Level 1.9, 4 East Market Street, Edinburgh EH8 8BG ☎ 0131 529 7047 david.lyon@edinburgh.gov.uk

Waste Collection and Disposal: Mr Jim Hunter Acting Head of Environment, Waverley Court, Level 1.9, 4 East Market Street, Edinburgh EH8 8BG ☎ 0131 469 5342 jim.hunter@edinburgh.gov.uk

Waste Management: Mr Jim Hunter Acting Head of Environment, Waverley Court, Level 1.9, 4 East Market Street, Edinburgh EH8 8BG ☎ 0131 469 5342 jim.hunter@edinburgh.gov.uk

COUNCILLORS

Leader of the Council **Burns**, Andrew (LAB - Fountainbridge and Craiglockhart)
andrew.burns@edinburgh.gov.uk

Aitken, Elaine (CON - Colinton and Fairmilehead)
elaine.aitken@edinburgh.gov.uk

Aldridge, Robert (LD - Drum Brae and Gyle)
robert.aldridge@edinburgh.gov.uk

Bagshaw, Nigel (SGP - Inverleith)
nigel.bagshaw@edinburgh.gov.uk

Balfour, Jeremy (CON - Corstorphine and Murrayfield)
jeremy.balfour@edinburgh.gov.uk

Barrie, Gavin (SNP - Inverleith)
gavin.barrie@edinburgh.gov.uk

Blacklock, Angela (LAB - Leith Walk)
angela.blacklock@edinburgh.gov.uk

Booth, Chas (SGP - Leith)
chas.booth@edinburgh.gov.uk

Bridgman, Michael (SNP - Portobello and Craigmillar)
michael.bridgman@edinburgh.gov.uk

Burgess, Steve (GRN - Southside and Newington)
steve.burgess@edinburgh.gov.uk

Cairns, Ronald (SNP - Drum Brae and Gyle)
ronald.cairns@edinburgh.gov.uk

Cardownie, Stephen (SNP - Forth)
steve.cardownie@edinburgh.gov.uk

Chapman, Maggie (GRN - Leith Walk)
maggie.chapman@edinburgh.gov.uk

Child, Maureen (LAB - Portobello and Craigmillar)
maureen.child@edinburgh.gov.uk

Cook, Bill (LAB - Liberton and Gilmerton)
bill.cook@edinburgh.gov.uk

Cook, Nick (CON - Liberton and Gilmerton)
nick.cook@edinburgh.gov.uk

Corbett, Gavin (SGP - Fountainbridge and Craiglockhart)
gavin.corbett@edinburgh.gov.uk

Day, Cammy (LAB - Forth)
cammy.day@edinburgh.gov.uk

Dixon, Denis (SNP - Sighthill and Gorgie)
denis.dixon@edinburgh.gov.uk

Doran, Karen (LAB - City Centre)
karen.doran@edinburgh.gov.uk

Edie, Paul (LD - Corstorphine and Murrayfield)
paul.edie@edinburgh.gov.uk

EDINBURGH, CITY OF

Fullerton, Catherine (SNP - Sighthill and Gorgie)
cathy.fullerton@edinburgh.gov.uk

Gardner, Nick (LAB - Leith Walk)
nick.gardner@edinburgh.gov.uk

Godzik, Paul (LAB - Meadows and Morningside)
paul.godzik@edinburgh.gov.uk

Griffiths, Joan (LAB - Craigentinny and Duddingston)
joan.griffiths@edinburgh.gov.uk

Hart, Norma (LAB - Liberton and Gilberton)
norma.austinhart@edinburgh.gov.uk

Henderson, Ricky (LAB - Pentland Hills)
ricky.henderson@edinburgh.gov.uk

Henderson, Bill (SNP - Pentland Hills)
bill.rhenderson@edinburgh.gov.uk

Heslop, Dominic (CON - Pentland Hills)
dominic.heslop@edinburgh.gov.uk

Hinds, Lesley (LAB - Inverleith)
lesley.hinds@edinburgh.gov.uk

Howat, Sandy (SNP - Meadows and Morningside)
sandy.howat@edinburgh.gov.uk

Jackson, Allan (CON - Forth)
allan.jackson@edinburgh.gov.uk

Keil, Karen (LAB - Drum Brae and Gyle)
karen.keil@edinburgh.gov.uk

Key, David (SNP - Fountainbridge and Craiglockhart)
david.key@edinburgh.gov.uk

Lewis, Richard (SNP - Colinton and Fairmilehead)
richard.lewis@edinburgh.gov.uk

Lunn, Alex (LAB - Craigentinny and Duddingston)
alex.lunn@edinburgh.gov.uk

Main, Melanie (SGP - Meadows and Morningside)
melanie.main@edinburgh.gov.uk

McInnes, Mark (CON - Meadows and Morningside)
mark.mcinnes@edinburgh.gov.uk

McVey, Adam (SNP - Leith)
adam.mcvey@edinburgh.gov.uk

Milligan, Eric (LAB - Sighthill and Gorgie)
eric.milligan@edinburgh.gov.uk

Mowat, Joanna (CON - City Centre)
joanna.mowat@edinburgh

Munro, Gordon (LAB - Leith)
gordon.munro@edinburgh.gov.uk

Orr, Jim (SNP - Southside and Newington)
jim.orr@edinburgh.gov.uk

Paterson, Lindsay (CON - Almond)
linday.paterson@edinburgh.gov.uk

Perry, Ian (LAB - Southside and Newington)
ian.perry@edinburgh.gov.uk

Rankin, Alasdair (SNP - City Centre)
alasdair.rankin@edinburgh.gov.uk

Redpath, Vicki (LAB - Forth)
vicki.redpath@edinburgh.gov.uk

Robson, Keith (LAB - Liberton and Gilmerton)
keith.robson@edinburgh.gov.uk

Rose, Cameron (CON - Southside and Newington)
cameron.rose@edinburgh.gov.uk

Ross, Frank (SNP - Corstorphine and Murrayfield)
frank.ross@edinburgh.gov.uk

Rust, Jason (CON - Colinton and Fairmilehead)
jason.rust@edinburgh.gov.uk

Shields, Alastair (LD - Almond)
alastair.shields@edinburgh.gov.uk

Tymkewwycz, Stefan (SNP - Craigentinny and Duddingston)
stefan.tymkewycz@edinburgh.gov.uk

Walker, David (LAB - Portobello and Craigmillar)
david.walker1@edinburgh.gov.uk

Whyte, Iain (CON - Inverleith)
iain.whyte@edinburgh.gov.uk

Wilson, Donald (LAB - Sighthill and Gorgie)
donald.wilson@edinburgh.gov.uk

Work, Norman (SNP - Almond)
norman.work@edinburgh.gov.uk

POLITICAL COMPOSITION

LAB: 21, SNP: 16, CON: 11, SGP: 4, LD: 3, GRN: 2

COMMITTEE CHAIRS

Education, Children & Families: Mr Paul Godzik

Finance & Resources: Mr Alasdair Rankin

Health, Social Care & Housing: Mr Ricky Henderson

Pensions: Mr Alasdair Rankin

Planning: Mr Ian Perry

Transport & Environment: Ms Lesley Hinds

Elmbridge D

Elmbridge Borough Council, Civic Centre, High Street, Esher KT10 9SD
☎ 01372 474474 🖷 01372 474972 ✉ civiccentre@elmbridge.gov.uk
🖳 www.elmbridge.gov.uk

FACTS AND FIGURES

Parliamentary Constituencies: Esher and Walton
EU Constituencies: South East
Election Frequency: Elections are by thirds

PRINCIPAL OFFICERS

Chief Executive: Mr Robert Moran, Chief Executive, Civic Centre, High Street, Esher KT10 9SD ☎ 01372 474380 🖷 01372 474933 ✉ chiefexec@elmbridge.gov.uk

Deputy Chief Executive: Mrs Sarah Selvanathan Strategic Director, Civic Centre, High Street, Esher KT10 9SD ☎ 01372 474100 🖷 01372 474971 ✉ sdr@elmbridge.gov.uk

Senior Management: Mr Ray Lee Strategic Director, Civic Centre, High Street, Esher KT10 9SD ☎ 01372 474700 🖷 01372 474910 ✉ sds@elmbridge.gov.uk

Senior Management: Mrs Sarah Selvanathan Strategic Director, Civic Centre, High Street, Esher KT10 9SD ☎ 01372 474100 🖷 01372 474971 🖱 sdr@elmbridge.gov.uk

Architect, Building / Property Services: Mrs Alexandra Williams Head of Asset Management & Property Services, Civic Centre, High Street, Esher KT10 9SD ☎ 01372 474218 🖷 01372 474927 🖱 awilliams@elmbridge.gov.uk

Best Value: Mrs Natalie Anderson, Head of Organisational Development, Civic Centre, High Street, Esher KT10 9SD ☎ 01372 474111 🖷 01372 474932 🖱 corporatepolicy@elmbridge.gov.uk

Building Control: Mr Mark Webb Building Control Manager, Civic Centre, High Street, Esher KT10 9SD ☎ 01372 474801 🖷 01372 474912 🖱 bcon@elmbridge.gov.uk

PR / Communications: Mrs Natalie Anderson, Head of Organisational Development, Civic Centre, High Street, Esher KT10 9SD ☎ 01372 474111 🖷 01372 474932 🖱 corporatepolicy@elmbridge.gov.uk

Community Safety: Ms Annabel Crouch Community Safety Co-ordinator, Civic Centre, High Street, Esher KT10 9SD ☎ 01372 474398 🖷 01372 474932 🖱 communitysafety@elmbridge.gov.uk

Computer Management: Mr Mark Lumley Head of Information Systems, Civic Centre, High Street, Esher KT10 9SD 🖷 01372 474158 🖱 isd@elmbridge.gov.uk

Contracts: Mr Alan Harrison Head of Legal Services, Civic Centre, High Street, Esher KT10 9SD ☎ 01372 474192 🖷 01372 474973 🖱 legalservices@elmbridge.gov.uk

Corporate Services: Mrs Deanna Harris Head of Internal Audit Partnership, Civic Centre, High Street, Esher KT10 9SD ☎ 01372 474108 🖷 01372 474971 🖱 internalaudit@elmbridge.gov.uk

Corporate Services: Mrs Sarah Selvanathan Strategic Director, Civic Centre, High Street, Esher KT10 9SD ☎ 01372 474100 🖷 01372 474971 🖱 sdr@elmbridge.gov.uk

Customer Service: Ms Dawn Crewe Head of Customer Service, Civic Centre, High Street, Esher KT10 9SD ☎ 01372 474703 🖷 01372 474932 🖱 corporatepolicy@elmbridge.gov.uk

Economic Development: Mrs Natalie Anderson, Head of Organisational Development, Civic Centre, High Street, Esher KT10 9SD ☎ 01372 474111 🖷 01372 474932 🖱 corporatepolicy@elmbridge.gov.uk

Electoral Registration: Miss Alex Mammous Electoral Services Manager, Civic Centre, High Street, Esher KT10 9SD ☎ 01372 474182 🖷 01372 474981 🖱 electoral@elmbridge.gov.uk

Emergency Planning: Mrs Gill Marchbank Emergency Planning & Business Continuity Officer, Civic Centre, High Street, Esher KT10 9SD ☎ 01372 474208 🖷 01372 474208 🖱 gmarchbank@elmbridge.gov.uk

Environmental / Technical Services: Mr Anthony Jeziorski, Head of Environmental Care, Civic Centre, High Street, Esher KT10 9SD ☎ 01372 474762 🖷 01372 474929 🖱 envcare@elmbridge.gov.uk

Estates, Property & Valuation: Mrs Alexandra Williams Head of Asset Management & Property Services, Civic Centre, High Street, Esher KT10 9SD ☎ 01372 474218 🖷 01372 474927 🖱 awilliams@elmbridge.gov.uk

Facilities: Mrs Alexandra Williams Head of Asset Management & Property Services, Civic Centre, High Street, Esher KT10 9SD ☎ 01372 474218 🖷 01372 474927 🖱 awilliams@elmbridge.gov.uk

Finance: Mr Andrew Cooper Head of Finance & Treasury, Civic Centre, High Street, Esher KT10 9SD ☎ 01372 474123 🖱 acooper@elmbridge.gov.uk

Finance: Mrs Sarah Selvanathan Strategic Director, Civic Centre, High Street, Esher KT10 9SD ☎ 01372 474100 🖷 01372 474971 🖱 sdr@elmbridge.gov.uk

Treasury: Mr Andrew Cooper Head of Finance & Treasury, Civic Centre, High Street, Esher KT10 9SD ☎ 01372 474123 🖱 acooper@elmbridge.gov.uk

Grounds Maintenance: Mr Ian Burrows, Head of Leisure & Cultural Services, Civic Centre, High Street, Esher KT10 9SD ☎ 01372 474572 🖷 01372 474939 🖱 leisure@elmbridge.gov.uk

Health and Safety: Mr Richard Simms Health & Safety Advisor, Civic Centre, High Street, Esher KT10 9SD ☎ 01372 474215 🖷 01372 474979 🖱 rsimms@elmbridge.gov.uk

Housing: Ms Julie Cook, Head of Housing Services, Civic Centre, High Street, Esher KT10 9SD ☎ 01372 474640 🖷 01372 474934 🖱 jcook@elmbridge.gov.uk

Legal: Mr Alan Harrison Head of Legal Services, Civic Centre, High Street, Esher KT10 9SD ☎ 01372 474192 🖷 01372 474973 🖱 legalservices@elmbridge.gov.uk

Leisure and Cultural Services: Mr Ian Burrows, Head of Leisure & Cultural Services, Civic Centre, High Street, Esher KT10 9SD ☎ 01372 474572 🖷 01372 474939 🖱 leisure@elmbridge.gov.uk

Lottery Funding, Charity and Voluntary: Mrs Gail McKenzie, Preventative & Support Services Manager, Civic Centre, High Street, Esher KT10 9SD ☎ 01372 474549 🖷 01372 474937 🖱 commservices@elmbridge.gov.uk

Member Services: Ms Beverley Greenstein, Head of Executive & Member Services, Civic Centre, High Street, Esher KT10 9SD ☎ 01372 474173 🖷 ; 01372 474933 🖱 committee@elmbridge.gov.uk

Parking: Mr Anthony Jeziorski, Head of Environmental Care, Civic Centre, High Street, Esher KT10 9SD ☎ 01372 474762 🖷 01372 474929 🖱 envcare@elmbridge.gov.uk

Partnerships: Mrs Natalie Anderson, Head of Organisational Development, Civic Centre, High Street, Esher KT10 9SD ☎ 01372 474111 🖷 01372 474932 🖱 corporatepolicy@elmbridge.gov.uk

ELMBRIDGE

Personnel / HR: Mrs Natalie Anderson, Head of Organisational Development, Civic Centre, High Street, Esher KT10 9SD ☎ 01372 474111 🖷 01372 474932 🖰 corporatepolicy@elmbridge.gov.uk

Procurement: Mr Alan Harrison Head of Legal Services, Civic Centre, High Street, Esher KT10 9SD ☎ 01372 474192 🖷 01372 474973 🖰 legalservices@elmbridge.gov.uk

Recycling & Waste Minimisation: Mr Anthony Jeziorski, Head of Environmental Care, Civic Centre, High Street, Esher KT10 9SD ☎ 01372 474762 🖷 01372 474929 🖰 envcare@elmbridge.gov.uk

Regeneration: Mr Ray Lee Strategic Director, Civic Centre, High Street, Esher KT10 9SD ☎ 01372 474700 🖷 01372 474910 🖰 sds@elmbridge.gov.uk

Staff Training: Ms Becky Atwood Personnel Manager, Civic Centre, High Street, Esher KT10 9SD ☎ 01372 474214 🖰 personnel@elmbridge.gov.uk

Street Scene: Mr Anthony Jeziorski, Head of Environmental Care, Civic Centre, High Street, Esher KT10 9SD ☎ 01372 474762 🖷 01372 474929 🖰 envcare@elmbridge.gov.uk

Sustainable Development: Mr Mark Behrendt Planning Policy Manager, Civic Centre, High Street, Esher KT10 9SD ☎ 01372 474829

Waste Collection and Disposal: Mr Anthony Jeziorski, Head of Environmental Care, Civic Centre, High Street, Esher KT10 9SD ☎ 01372 474762 🖷 01372 474929 🖰 envcare@elmbridge.gov.uk

Waste Management: Mr Anthony Jeziorski, Head of Environmental Care, Civic Centre, High Street, Esher KT10 9SD ☎ 01372 474762 🖷 01372 474929 🖰 envcare@elmbridge.gov.uk

COUNCILLORS

***Leader of the Council* O'Reilly**, John (CON - Hersham South)
joreilly@elmbridge.gov.uk

***Deputy Leader of the Council* Oliver**, Tim (CON - Esher)
toliver@elmbridge.gov.uk

Ahmed, Ruby (R - Molesey South)
rahmed@elmbridge.gov.uk

Archer, David (CON - Esher)
darcher@elmbridge.gov.uk

Axton, Mike (R - Molesey South)
maxton@elmbridge.gov.uk

Bax, Steve (CON - Molesey East)
sbax@elmbridge.gov.uk

Bennison, Mike (CON - Cobham and Downside)
mbennison@elmbridge.gov.uk

Bland, Tricia (R - Thames Ditton)

Brown, Lewis (CON - Oatlands Park)
lbrown@elmbridge.gov.uk

Browne, James (CON - Cobham Fairmile)
jbrowne@elmbridge.gov.uk

Bruce, Ruth (R - Weston Green)
rbruce@elmbridge.gov.uk

Butcher, John (IND - Cobham and Downside)
jbutcher@elmbridge.gov.uk

Cheyne, Barry (CON - Oatlands Park)
bcheyne@elmbridge.gov.uk

Coomes, Alex (LD - Claygate)
acoomes@elmbridge.gov.uk

Cooper, Nigel (R - Molesey East)
ncooper@elmbridge.gov.uk

Cowin, Barbara (CON - Walton North)
bcowin@elmbridge.gov.uk

Cross, Kim (LD - Claygate)
kcross@elmbridge.gov.uk

Cross, Christine (CON - Walton North)
ccross@elmbridge.gov.uk

Davis, Andrew (LD - Weybridge North)
adavis@elmbridge.gov.uk

Dearlove, Glenn (CON - Weybridge South)
gdearlove@elmbridge.gov.uk

Donaldson, Ian (CON - Hersham North)
iandonaldson@elmsbridge.gov.uk

Dunweber, Elise (CON - Oxshott and Stoke D'Abernon)
edunweber@elmbridge.gov.uk

Eldridge, Victor (R - Molesey South)
veldridge@elmbridge.gov.uk

Elmer, Christine (CON - Walton South)
celmer@elmbridge.gov.uk

Elmer, Chris (CON - Walton South)
chriselmer@elmbridge.gov.uk

Fairbank, Barry (LD - Long Ditton)
bfairbank@elmbridge.gov.uk

Fairclough, Brian (IND - St. George's Hill)
bfairclough@elmbridge.gov.uk

Foale, Simon (CON - St George's Hill)
sfoale@elmbridge.gov.uk

Fuller, Jan (CON - Oxshott and Stoke D'Abernon)
jfuller@elmbridge.gov.uk

Gray, Ramon (CON - Weybridge North)
rgray@elmbridge.gov.uk

Green, Roy (O - Hersham North)
rgreen@elmbridge.gov.uk

Grey, Timothy (CON - Cobham Fairmile)
tgrey@elmbridge.gov.uk

Haig-Brown, Nigel (R - Hinchley Wood)
nhaigbrown@elmbridge.gov.uk

Hawkins, Stuart (CON - Walton South)
shawkins@embridge.gov.uk

Kapadia, Shetwa (LD - Long Ditton)
skapadia@elmbridge.gov.uk

Kelly, Andrew (CON - Walton Ambleside)
akelly@elmbridge.gov.uk

Knight, Richard (CON - Weybridge South)
rknight@elmbridge.gov.uk

Kopitko, Alan (CON - Walton Ambleside)
akopitko@elmbridge.gov.uk

Lake, Rachael (CON - Walton North)
rlake@elmbridge.gov.uk

Luxton, Neil (O - Walton Central)
nluxton@elmbridge.gov.uk

Lyon, Ruth (R - Thames Ditton)
rlyon@elmbridge.gov.uk

Manwinder, Toor (CON - St. George's Hill)
mtoor@elmbridge.gov.uk

Marshall, Mary (LD - Claygate)
mmarshall@elmbridge.gov.uk

Mitchell, Dorothy (CON - Cobham and Downside)
dmitchell@elmbridge.gov.uk

Mitchell, Ruth (CON - Hersham South)
rmitchell@elmbridge.gov.uk

Palmer, Alan (O - Walton Central)
apalmer@elmbridge.gov.uk

Randolph, Karen (R - Thames Ditton)
krandolph@elmbridge.gov.uk

Regan, Ivan (O - Molesey North)
iregan@elmbridge.gov.uk

Robertson, Liz (R - Molesey North)
lrobertson@elmbridge.gov.uk

Sadler, Chris (O - Walton Central)
csadler@elmbridge.gov.uk

Samuels, Lorraine (CON - Oatlands Park)
lsamuels@elmbridge.gov.uk

Selleck, Stuart (R - Molesey North)
sselleck@elmbridge.gov.uk

Sheldon, Mary (CON - Hersham North)
msheldon@elmbridge.gov.uk

Sheldon, John (CON - Hersham South)
jsheldon@elmbridge.gov.uk

Shipley, Tannia (R - Weston Green)
tshipley@elmbridge.gov.uk

Szanto, Peter (CON - Molesey East)
pszanto@elmbridge.gov.uk

Turner, Janet (R - Hinchley Wood)
jturner@elmbridge.gov.uk

Vickers, James (CON - Oxshott and Stoke D'Abernon)
javickers@elmbridge.gov.uk

Waugh, Simon (CON - Esher)
swaugh@elmbridge.gov.uk

POLITICAL COMPOSITION

CON: 33, R: 13, LD: 6, O: 5, IND: 2

COMMITTEE CHAIRS

Audit: Mr Simon Waugh

Licensing: Mr Ian Donaldson

Planning: Mr Barry Cheyne

Enfield L

Enfield London Borough Council, Civic Centre, Silver Street, Enfield EN1 3XA
☎ 020 8379 1000 🖷 020 8379 4453 🖳 www.enfield.gov.uk

FACTS AND FIGURES

Parliamentary Constituencies: Edmonton, Enfield North, Enfield, Southgate
EU Constituencies: London
Election Frequency: Elections are of whole council

PRINCIPAL OFFICERS

Chief Executive: Mr Rob Leak, Chief Executive, PO Box 61, Civic Centre, Silver Street, Enfield EN1 3XY ☎ 020 8379 3901 ✉ chief.executive@enfield.gov.uk

Senior Management: Dr Shahed Ahmad Director - Public Health, Civic Centre, Silver Street, Enfield EN1 3XA ☎ 020 8379 3211 ✉ shahed.ahmad@enfield.gov.uk

Senior Management: Mr Ian Davis Director of Regeneration & Environment, PO Box 52, Civic Centre, Silver Street, Enfield EN1 3XD ☎ 020 8379 3500 ✉ ian.davis@enfield.gov.uk

Senior Management: Mr Ray James, Director of Health, Housing & Adult Social Care, PO Box 59, Civic Centre, Silver Street, Enfield EN1 3XL ☎ 020 8379 4160 ✉ ray.james@enfield.gov.uk

Senior Management: Mr James Rolfe Director of Finance, Resources & Customer Services, PO Box 54, Civic Centre, Silver Street, Enfield EN1 3XF ☎ 020 8379 4600 ✉ james.rolfe@enfield.gov.uk

Senior Management: Mr Tony Theodoulou Acting Director of Schools & Children's Services, PO Box 56, Civic Centre, Silver Street, Enfield EN1 3XL ☎ 020 8379 4610 ✉ tony.theodoulou@enfield.gov.uk

Architect, Building / Property Services: Mr Keith Crocombe Assistant Director - Property Services, PO Box 51, Civic Centre, Silver Street, Enfield EN1 3XB ☎ 020 8379 4605 ✉ keith.crocombe@enfield.gov.uk

Best Value: Ms Alison Trew Head of Performance Management, Civic Centre, Silver Street, Enfield EN1 3XA ☎ 020 8379 3186 ✉ alison.trew@enfield.gov.uk

Building Control: Mr Bob Griffiths Assistant Director of Planning, Highways & Transformation, PO Box 52, Civic Centre, Silver Street, Enfield EN1 3XD ☎ 020 8379 3676 ✉ bob.griffiths@enfield.gov.uk

Catering Services: Ms Jenny Tosh Chief Education Officer, PO Box 56, Civic Centre, Silver Street, Enfield EN1 3XQ ☎ 020 8379 3350 ✉ jenny.tosh@enfield.gov.uk

Children / Youth Services: Mr Tony Theodoulou Acting Director of Schools & Children's Services, PO Box 56, Civic Centre, Silver Street, Enfield EN1 3XL ☎ 020 8379 4610 ✉ tony.theodoulou@enfield.gov.uk

Civil Registration: Mr Peter Stanyon, Head of Electoral, Registration & Governance Services, Civic Centre, Silver Street, Enfield EN1 3XA ☎ 020 8379 8580 ✉ peter.stanyon@enfield.gov.uk

PR / Communications: Mr David Greely Head of Communications, PO Box 61, Civic Centre, Silver Street, Enfield EN1 3XY ☎ 020 8379 5122 ✉ david.greely@enfield.gov.uk

Community Planning: Mr Shaun Rogan Head of Policy, Partnerships, Engagement & Consultation, Civic Centre, Silver Street, Enfield EN1 3XY ☎ 020 8379 3836 🖱 shaun.rogan@enfield.gov.uk

Community Safety: Ms Andrea Clemons Head of Community Safety, PO Box 52, Civic Centre, Silver Street, Enfield EN1 3XD ☎ 020 8379 4085 🖱 andrea.clemons@enfield.gov.uk

Computer Management: Mr James Rolfe Director of Finance, Resources & Customer Services, PO Box 54, Civic Centre, Silver Street, Enfield EN1 3XF ☎ 020 8379 4600 🖱 james.rolfe@enfield.gov.uk

Consumer Protection and Trading Standards: Ms Sue McDaid, Head of Trading Standards & Licensing, Civic Centre, Silver Street, Enfield EN1 3XA ☎ 020 8379 3680 🖱 sue.mcdaid@enfield.gov.uk

Contracts: Mr Bob Griffiths Assistant Director of Planning, Highways & Transformation, PO Box 52, Civic Centre, Silver Street, Enfield EN1 3XD ☎ 020 8379 3676 🖱 bob.griffiths@enfield.gov.uk

Corporate Services: Mr James Rolfe Director of Finance, Resources & Customer Services, PO Box 54, Civic Centre, Silver Street, Enfield EN1 3XF ☎ 020 8379 4600 🖱 james.rolfe@enfield.gov.uk

Customer Service: Ms Tracey Chamberlain Head of Assisted Service Delivery, Civic Centre, Silver Street, Enfield EN1 3XY ☎ 020 8379 6525 🖱 tracey.chamberlain@enfield.gov.uk

Direct Labour: Mr Bob Griffiths Assistant Director of Planning, Highways & Transformation, PO Box 52, Civic Centre, Silver Street, Enfield EN1 3XD ☎ 020 8379 3676 🖱 bob.griffiths@enfield.gov.uk

Economic Development: Mr Neil Issac Assistant Director of Business & Economic Development, PO Box 52, Civic Centre, Silver Street, Enfield EN1 3XD ☎ 020 8379 3760 🖱 neil.issac@enfield.gov.uk

Education: Ms Jenny Tosh Chief Education Officer, PO Box 56, Civic Centre, Silver Street, Enfield EN1 3XQ ☎ 020 8379 3350 🖱 jenny.tosh@enfield.gov.uk

Electoral Registration: Mr Peter Stanyon, Head of Electoral, Registration & Governance Services, Civic Centre, Silver Street, Enfield EN1 3XA ☎ 020 8379 8580 🖱 peter.stanyon@enfield.gov.uk

Emergency Planning: Ms Andrea Clemons Head of Community Safety, PO Box 52, Civic Centre, Silver Street, Enfield EN1 3XD ☎ 020 8379 4085 🖱 andrea.clemons@enfield.gov.uk

Energy Management: Mr Bob Griffiths Assistant Director of Planning, Highways & Transformation, PO Box 52, Civic Centre, Silver Street, Enfield EN1 3XD ☎ 020 8379 3676 🖱 bob.griffiths@enfield.gov.uk

Environmental / Technical Services: Mr Ian Davis Director of Regeneration & Environment, PO Box 52, Civic Centre, Silver Street, Enfield EN1 3XD ☎ 020 8379 3500 🖱 ian.davis@enfield.gov.uk

Environmental Health: Mr Ian Davis Director of Regeneration & Environment, PO Box 52, Civic Centre, Silver Street, Enfield EN1 3XD ☎ 020 8379 3500 🖱 ian.davis@enfield.gov.uk

Estates, Property & Valuation: Mr Keith Crocombe Assistant Director - Property Services, PO Box 51, Civic Centre, Silver Street, Enfield EN1 3XB ☎ 020 8379 4605 🖱 keith.crocombe@enfield.gov.uk

Facilities: Mr Stuart Simper Acting Head of Facilities Management, PO Box 54, Civic Centre, Silver Street, Enfield EN1 3XF ☎ 020 8379 3032 🖱 stuart.simper@enfield.gov.uk

Finance: Ms Isabel Brittain Assistant Director of Finance, PO Box 54, Civic Centre, Silver Street, Enfield EN1 3XF ☎ 020 8379 4744 🖱 isabel.brittain@enfield.gov.uk

Treasury: Mr Paul Reddaway Head of Finance, Treasury & Pensions, 4th Floor, Civic Centre, Silver Street, Enfield EN1 3XF ☎ 020 8379 4730 🖱 paul.reddaway@enfield.gov.uk

Pensions: Mr Paul Reddaway Head of Finance, Treasury & Pensions, 4th Floor, Civic Centre, Silver Street, Enfield EN1 3XF ☎ 020 8379 4730 🖱 paul.reddaway@enfield.gov.uk

Fleet Management: Mr Bob Griffiths Assistant Director of Planning, Highways & Transformation, PO Box 52, Civic Centre, Silver Street, Enfield EN1 3XD ☎ 020 8379 3676 🖱 bob.griffiths@enfield.gov.uk

Grounds Maintenance: Mr Bob Griffiths Assistant Director of Planning, Highways & Transformation, PO Box 52, Civic Centre, Silver Street, Enfield EN1 3XD ☎ 020 8379 3676 🖱 bob.griffiths@enfield.gov.uk

Health and Safety: Mr John Griffiths Corporate Safety Manager, PO Box 61, Civic Centre, Silver Street, Enfield EN1 3XY ☎ 020 8379 3696 🖱 john.griffiths@enfield.gov.uk

Highways: Mr Bob Griffiths Assistant Director of Planning, Highways & Transformation, PO Box 52, Civic Centre, Silver Street, Enfield EN1 3XD ☎ 020 8379 3676 🖱 bob.griffiths@enfield.gov.uk

Home Energy Conservation: Mr Peter George Programme Director - Neighbourhood & Regeneration, Civic Centre, Silver Street, Enfield EN1 3XA ☎ 020 8379 3318 🖱 peter.george@enfield.gov.uk

Housing: Ms Sally McTernan Assistant Director of Community Housing Services, Civic Centre, Silver Street, Enfield EN1 3XA ☎ 020 8379 4465 🖱 sally.mcternan@enfield.gov.uk

Housing Maintenance: Ms Sally McTernan Assistant Director of Community Housing Services, Civic Centre, Silver Street, Enfield EN1 3XA ☎ 020 8379 4465 🖱 sally.mcternan@enfield.gov.uk

Local Area Agreement: Ms Alison Trew Head of Performance Management, Civic Centre, Silver Street, Enfield EN1 3XA ☎ 020 8379 3186 🖱 alison.trew@enfield.gov.uk

Legal: Ms Asmat Hussain Assistant Director of Legal & Governance Services, PO Box 54, Civic Centre, Silver Street, Enfield EN1 3XF ☎ 020 8379 6438 ✉ asmat.hussain@enfield.gov.uk

Leisure and Cultural Services: Mr Simon Gardner Head of Leisure & Culture, PO Box 56, Civic Centre, Silver Street, Enfield EN1 3XQ ☎ 020 8379 3783 ✉ simon.gardner@enfield.gov.uk

Licensing: Ms Sue McDaid, Head of Trading Standards & Licensing, Civic Centre, Silver Street, Enfield EN1 3XA ☎ 020 8379 3680 ✉ sue.mcdaid@enfield.gov.uk

Lifelong Learning: Mr Tony Theodoulou Acting Director of Schools & Children's Services, PO Box 56, Civic Centre, Silver Street, Enfield EN1 3XL ☎ 020 8379 4610 ✉ tony.theodoulou@enfield.gov.uk

Lighting: Mr Bob Griffiths Assistant Director of Planning, Highways & Transformation, PO Box 52, Civic Centre, Silver Street, Enfield EN1 3XD ☎ 020 8379 3676 ✉ bob.griffiths@enfield.gov.uk

Lottery Funding, Charity and Voluntary: Mr Shaun Rogan Head of Policy, Partnerships, Engagement & Consultation, Civic Centre, Silver Street, Enfield EN1 3XY ☎ 020 8379 3836 ✉ shaun.rogan@enfield.gov.uk

Member Services: Ms Asmat Hussain Assistant Director of Legal & Governance Services, PO Box 54, Civic Centre, Silver Street, Enfield EN1 3XF ☎ 020 8379 6438 ✉ asmat.hussain@enfield.gov.uk

Parking: Mr David Morris Head of Parking, Civic Centre, Silver Street, Enfield EN1 3XA ☎ 020 8379 6556 ✉ david.morris@enfield.gov.uk

Partnerships: Mr Shaun Rogan Head of Policy, Partnerships, Engagement & Consultation, Civic Centre, Silver Street, Enfield EN1 3XY ☎ 020 8379 3836 ✉ shaun.rogan@enfield.gov.uk

Personnel / HR: Mr Tony Gilling Assistant Director - Human Resources, PO Box 61, Civic Centre, Silver Street, Enfield EN1 3XA ☎ 020 8379 4141 ✉ tony.gilling@enfield.gov.uk

Planning: Mr Bob Griffiths Assistant Director of Planning, Highways & Transformation, PO Box 52, Civic Centre, Silver Street, Enfield EN1 3XD ☎ 020 8379 3676 ✉ bob.griffiths@enfield.gov.uk

Procurement: Mr David Levy Assistant Director of Procurement & Commissioning, PO Box 54, Civic Centre, Silver Street, Enfield EN1 3XF ☎ 020 8496 3000 ✉ dave.levy@walthamforest.gov.uk

Public Libraries: Ms Julie Gibson Head of Libraries & Museums, Civic Centre, Silver Street, Enfield EN1 3XA ☎ 020 8379 3749 ✉ julie.gibson@enfield.gov.uk

Recycling & Waste Minimisation: Ms Nicky Fiedler Assistant Director of Public Realm, PO Box 52, Civic Centre, Silver Street, Enfield EN1 3XD ☎ 020 8379 2016 ✉ nicky.fiedler@enfield.gov.uk

Regeneration: Mr Peter George Programme Director - Neighbourhood & Regeneration, Civic Centre, Silver Street, Enfield EN1 3XA ☎ 020 8379 3318 ✉ peter.george@enfield.gov.uk

Road Safety: Mr David Taylor Head of Traffic & Transportation, PO Box 52, Civic Centre, Silver Street, Enfield EN1 3XD ☎ 020 8379 3576 ✉ david.b.taylor@enfield.gov.uk

Social Services: Mr Ray James, Director of Health, Housing & Adult Social Care, PO Box 59, Civic Centre, Silver Street, Enfield EN1 3XL ☎ 020 8379 4160 ✉ ray.james@enfield.gov.uk

Social Services (Adult): Mr Ray James, Director of Health, Housing & Adult Social Care, PO Box 59, Civic Centre, Silver Street, Enfield EN1 3XL ☎ 020 8379 4160 ✉ ray.james@enfield.gov.uk

Social Services (Children): Mr Tony Theodoulou Acting Director of Schools & Children's Services, PO Box 56, Civic Centre, Silver Street, Enfield EN1 3XL ☎ 020 8379 4610 ✉ tony.theodoulou@enfield.gov.uk

Public Health: Dr Shahed Ahmad Director - Public Health, Civic Centre, Silver Street, Enfield EN1 3XA ☎ 020 8379 3211 ✉ shahed.ahmad@enfield.gov.uk

Staff Training: Mr Tony Gilling Assistant Director - Human Resources, PO Box 61, Civic Centre, Silver Street, Enfield EN1 3XA ☎ 020 8379 4141 ✉ tony.gilling@enfield.gov.uk

Street Scene: Mr Ian Davis Director of Regeneration & Environment, PO Box 52, Civic Centre, Silver Street, Enfield EN1 3XD ☎ 020 8379 3500 ✉ ian.davis@enfield.gov.uk

Sustainable Communities: Mr Neil Issac Assistant Director of Business & Economic Development, PO Box 52, Civic Centre, Silver Street, Enfield EN1 3XD ☎ 020 8379 3760 ✉ neil.issac@enfield.gov.uk

Sustainable Development: Mr Peter George Programme Director - Neighbourhood & Regeneration, Civic Centre, Silver Street, Enfield EN1 3XA ☎ 020 8379 3318 ✉ peter.george@enfield.gov.uk

Tourism: Mr Simon Gardner Head of Leisure & Culture, PO Box 56, Civic Centre, Silver Street, Enfield EN1 3XQ ☎ 020 8379 3783 ✉ simon.gardner@enfield.gov.uk

Town Centre: Mr Bob Griffiths Assistant Director of Planning, Highways & Transformation, PO Box 52, Civic Centre, Silver Street, Enfield EN1 3XD ☎ 020 8379 3676 ✉ bob.griffiths@enfield.gov.uk

Traffic Management: Mr Bob Griffiths Assistant Director of Planning, Highways & Transformation, PO Box 52, Civic Centre, Silver Street, Enfield EN1 3XD ☎ 020 8379 3676 ✉ bob.griffiths@enfield.gov.uk

Transport: Mr Bob Griffiths Assistant Director of Planning, Highways & Transformation, PO Box 52, Civic Centre, Silver Street, Enfield EN1 3XD ☎ 020 8379 3676 ✉ bob.griffiths@enfield.gov.uk

Transport Planner: Mr Bob Griffiths Assistant Director of Planning, Highways & Transformation, PO Box 52, Civic Centre, Silver Street, Enfield EN1 3XD ☎ 020 8379 3676 ✉ bob.griffiths@enfield.gov.uk

ENFIELD

Waste Collection and Disposal: Ms Nicky Fiedler Assistant Director of Public Realm, PO Box 52, Civic Centre, Silver Street, Enfield EN1 3XD ☎ 020 8379 2016 ✉ nicky.fiedler@enfield.gov.uk

Waste Management: Ms Nicky Fiedler Assistant Director of Public Realm, PO Box 52, Civic Centre, Silver Street, Enfield EN1 3XD ☎ 020 8379 2016 ✉ nicky.fiedler@enfield.gov.uk

COUNCILLORS

***Mayor* Ekechi**, Patricia (LAB - Upper Edmonton)
cllr.patricia.ekechi@enfield.gov.uk

***Deputy Mayor* Lappage**, Bernie (LAB - Jubilee)
cllr.bernie.lappage@enfield.gov.uk

***Leader of the Council* Taylor**, Doug (LAB - Ponders End)
cllr.doug.taylor@enfield.gov.uk

***Deputy Leader of the Council* Georgiou**, Achilleas (LAB - Bowes)
cllr.achilleas.georgiou@enfield.gov.uk

***Group Leader* Hayward**, Elaine (CON - Winchmore Hill)
cllr.elaine.hayward@enfield.gov.uk

***Group Leader* Neville**, Terence (CON - Grange)
cllr.terence.neville@enfield.gov.uk

Abdullahi, Abdul (LAB - Edmonton Green)
cllr.abdul.abdullahi@enfield.gov.uk

Anderson, Daniel (LAB - Southgate Green)
cllr.daniel.anderson@enfield.gov.uk

Bakir, Ali (LAB - Upper Edmonton)
cllr.ali.bakir@enfield.gov.uk

Barry, Dinah (LAB - Winchmore Hill)
cllr.dinah.barry@enfield.gov.uk

Bond, Chris (LAB - Southbury)
cllr.chris.taylor@enfield.gov.uk

Brett, Yasemin (LAB - Bowes)
cllr.yasemin.brett@enfield.gov.uk

Cazimoglu, Alev (LAB - Jubilee)
cllr.alev.cazimoglu@enfield.gov.uk

Cazzimoglu, Nesil (LAB - Jubilee)

Celebi, Erin (CON - Bush Hill Park)
cllr.erin.celebi@enfield.gov.uk

Chamberlain, Lee (CON - Bush Hill Park)
cllr.lee.chamberlain@enfield.gov.uk

Charalambous, Jason (CON - Cockfosters)
cllr.jason.charalambous@enfield.gov.uk

Charalambous, Bambos (LAB - Palmers Green)
cllr.bambos.charalambous@enfield.gov.uk

Chibah, Katherine (LAB - Turkey Street)
cllr.katherine.chibah@enfield.gov.uk

David-Sanders, Lee (CON - Highlands)
cllr.lee.david-sanders@enfield.gov.uk

Delman, Dogan (CON - Highlands)
cllr.dogan.delman@enfield.gov.uk

Dines, Nick (CON - Chase)
cllr.nick.dines@enfield.gov.uk

Dogan, Guney (LAB - Lower Edmonton)
cllr.guney.dogan@enfield.gov.uk

Doyle, Sarah (LAB - Bush Hill Park)
cllr.sarah.doyle@enfield.gov.uk

During, Christina (LAB - Edmonton Green)
cllr.christina.during@enfield.gov.uk

Erbil, Nesimi (IND - Lower Edmonton)
cllr.nesimi.erbil@enfield.gov.uk

Esendagli, Turgut (LAB - Enfield Highway)
cllr.turgut.esendagli@enfield.gov.uk

Fallart, Peter (CON - Chase)
cllr.peter.fallart@enfield.gov.uk

Fonyonga, Krystle (LAB - Enfield Lock)
cllr.krystle.fonyonga@enfield.gov.uk

Georgiou, Alessandro (CON - Southgate Green)
cllr.alessandro.georgiou@enfield.gov.uk

Hamilton, Christine (LAB - Enfield Highway)
cllr.christine.hamilton@enfield.gov.uk

Hasan, Ahmet (LAB - Enfield Highway)
cllr.ahmet.hasan@enfield.gov.uk

Hayward, Robert (CON - Southgate)
cllr.robert.hayward@enfield.gov.uk

Hurer, Ertan (CON - Winchmore Hill)
cllr.ertan.hurer@enfield.gov.uk

Hurman, Suna (LAB - Haselbury)
cllr.suna.hurman@enfield.gov.uk

Jemal, Jansev (LAB - Southbury)
cllr.jansev.jemal@enfield.gov.uk

Jiagge, Doris (LAB - Upper Edmonton)
cllr.doris.jiagge@enfield.gov.uk

Jukes, Eric (CON - Grange)
cllr.eric.jukes@enfield.gov.uk

Keazor, Nneka (LAB - Enfield Lock)
cllr.nneka.keazor@enfield.gov.uk

Kepez, Adeline (LAB - Lower Edmonton)
cllr.adeline.kepez@enfield.gov.uk

Laban, Joanne (CON - Town)
cllr.joanne.laban@enfield.gov.uk

Lavender, Michael (CON - Cockfosters)
cllr.michael.lavender@enfield.gov.uk

Lemonides, Dino (LAB - Turkey Street)
cllr.dino.lemonides@enfield.gov.uk

Levy, Derek (LAB - Southbury)
cllr.derek.levy@enfield.gov.uk

Maguire, Mary (LAB - Palmers Green)
cllr.mary.maguire@enfield.gov.uk

McGowan, Donald (LAB - Ponders End)
cllr.donald.mcgowan@enfield.gov.uk

Milne, Andy (CON - Grange)
cllr.andy.milne@enfield.gov.uk

Orhan, Ayfer (LAB - Ponders End)
cllr.ayfer.orhan@enfield.gov.uk

Oykener, Ahmet (LAB - Palmers Green)
cllr.ahmet.oykener@enfield.gov.uk

Pearce, Daniel (CON - Southgate)
cllr.daniel.pearce@enfield.gov.uk

Pearce, Anne-Marie (CON - Cockfosters)
cllr.anne.pearce@enfield.gov.uk

Pite, Vicki (LAB - Chase)
cllr.vicki.pite@enfield.gov.uk

Rye, Michael (CON - Town)
cllr.michael.rye@enfield.gov.uk

Savva, George (LAB - Haselbury)
cllr.george.savva@enfield.gov.uk

Simon, Toby (LAB - Turkey Street)
cllr.toby.simon@enfield.gov.uk

Sitkin, Alan (LAB - Bowes)
cllr.alan.sitkin@enfield.gov.uk

Smith, Edward (CON - Southgate)
cllr.edward.smith@enfield.gov.uk

Stafford, Andrew (LAB - Edmonton Green)
cllr.andrew.stafford@enfield.gov.uk

Steven, Jim (CON - Town)
cllr.jim.steven@enfield.gov.uk

Stewart, Claire (LAB - Southgate Green)
cllr.claire.stewart@enfield.gov.uk

Ulus, Haydar (IND - Haselbury)
cllr.haydar.ulus@enfield.gov.uk

Uzoanya, Ozzie (LAB - Enfield Lock)
Cllr.Ozzie.Uzoanya@enfield.gov.uk

Vince, Glynis (CON - Highlands)
cllr.glynis.vince@enfield.gov.uk

POLITICAL COMPOSITION
LAB: 39, CON: 22, IND: 2

COMMITTEE CHAIRS
Audit: Mr Dino Lemonides

Licensing: Mr Chris Bond

Planning: Mr Toby Simon

Epping Forest D

Epping Forest District Council, Civic Offices, High Street, Epping CM16 4BZ
☎ 01992 564000 🖷 01992 578018 🖱 contactus@eppingforestdc.gov.uk
💻 www.eppingforestdc.gov.uk

FACTS AND FIGURES
Parliamentary Constituencies: Epping Forest
EU Constituencies: Eastern
Election Frequency: Elections are by thirds

PRINCIPAL OFFICERS
Chief Executive: Mr Glen Chipp Chief Executive, Civic Offices, High Street, Epping CM16 4BZ ☎ 01992 564080
🖱 gchipp@eppingforestdc.gov.uk

Deputy Chief Executive: Mr Derek McNab Director - Neighbourhoods & Deputy Chief Executive, Civic Offices, High Street, Epping CM16 4BZ ☎ 01992 564051
🖱 dmcnab@eppingforestdc.gov.uk

Senior Management: Mr Alan Hall, Director - Communities, Civic Offices, High Street, Epping CM16 4BZ ☎ 01992 564004
🖱 ahall@eppingforestdc.gov.uk

Senior Management: Ms Colleen O'Boyle Director - Governance; Solicitor to the Council, Civic Offices, High Street, Epping CM16 4BZ ☎ 01992 564475 🖱 coboyle@eppingforestdc.gov.uk

Senior Management: Mr Bob Palmer Director - Resources & S151 Chief Financial Officer, Civic Offices, High Street, Epping CM16 4BZ ☎ 01992 564279 🖱 bpalmer@eppingforestdc.gov.uk

PR / Communications: Mr Thomas Carne Public Relations & Marketing Officer, Civic Offices, High Street, Epping CM16 4BZ
☎ 01992 564039 🖱 tcarne@eppingforestdc.gov.uk

Community Planning: Ms Julie Chandler, Assistant Director - Community Services, Civic Offices, High Street, Epping CM16 4BZ
☎ 01992 564214 🖱 jchandler@eppingforestdc.gov.uk

Community Planning: Mr Derek McNab Director - Neighbourhoods & Deputy Chief Executive, Civic Offices, High Street, Epping CM16 4BZ ☎ 01992 564051
🖱 dmcnab@eppingforestdc.gov.uk

Community Planning: Mr James Nolan Assistant Director - Neighbourhood Services, Civic Offices, High Street, Epping CM16 4BZ ☎ 01992 564083 🖱 jnolan@eppingforestdc.gov.uk

Community Planning: Ms Kassandra Polyzoides Assistant Director - Forward Planning & Economic Development, Civic Offices, High Street, Epping CM16 4BZ ☎ 01992 564119
🖱 kpolyzoides@eppingforestdc.gov.uk

Community Planning: Ms Gill Wallis Community Development Officer, Civic Offices, High Street, Epping CM16 4BZ ☎ 01992 564557 🖱 gwallis@eppingforestdc.gov.uk

Community Planning: Mr Ian White Forward Planning Manager, Civic Offices, High Street, Epping CM16 4BZ ☎ 01992 564066
🖱 iwhite@eppingforestdc.gov.uk

Community Safety: Ms Caroline Wiggins Safer Communities Manager, Civic Offices, High Street, Epping CM16 4BZ
☎ 01992 564122 🖱 cwiggins@eppingforestdc.gov.uk

Computer Management: Mr David Newton Assistant Director - ICT & Facilities Management, Civic Offices, High Street, Epping CM16 4BZ ☎ 01992 564580 🖱 dnewton@eppingforestdc.gov.uk

Corporate Services: Mr Simon Hill Assistant Director - Governance & Performance Management, Civic Offices, High Street, Epping CM16 4BZ ☎ 01992 564249
🖱 shill@eppingforestdc.gov.uk

EPPING FOREST

Corporate Services: Mr Nigel Richardson Assistant Director - Development Management, Civic Offices, High Street, Epping CM16 4BZ ☎ 01992 564110 ✉ nrichardson@eppingforestdc.gov.uk

Customer Service: Ms Jenny Filby Complaints Officer, Civic Offices, High Street, Epping CM16 4BZ ☎ 01992 564512 ✉ jfilby@eppingforestdc.gov.uk

Economic Development: Ms Kassandra Polyzoides Assistant Director - Forward Planning & Economic Development, Civic Offices, High Street, Epping CM16 4BZ ☎ 01992 564119 ✉ kpolyzoides@eppingforestdc.gov.uk

Electoral Registration: Mr Glen Chipp Chief Executive, Civic Offices, High Street, Epping CM16 4BZ ☎ 01992 564080 ✉ gchipp@eppingforestdc.gov.uk

Environmental / Technical Services: Mr Qasim Durrani Assistant Director - Technical Services, Civic Offices, High Street, Epping CM16 4BZ ☎ 01992 564055 ✉ qdurrani@eppingforestdc.gov.uk

Facilities: Mr David Newton Assistant Director - ICT & Facilities Management, Civic Offices, High Street, Epping CM16 4BZ ☎ 01992 564580 ✉ dnewton@eppingforestdc.gov.uk

Finance: Mr Peter Maddock Assistant Director - Accountancy, Civic Offices, High Street, Epping CM16 4BZ ☎ 01992 564602 ✉ pmaddock@eppingforestdc.gov.uk

Finance: Mr Bob Palmer Director - Resources & S151 Chief Financial Officer, Civic Offices, High Street, Epping CM16 4BZ ☎ 01992 564279 ✉ bpalmer@eppingforestdc.gov.uk

Treasury: Mr Peter Maddock Assistant Director - Accountancy, Civic Offices, High Street, Epping CM16 4BZ ☎ 01992 564602 ✉ pmaddock@eppingforestdc.gov.uk

Housing: Mr James Nolan Assistant Director - Neighbourhood Services, Civic Offices, High Street, Epping CM16 4BZ ☎ 01992 564083 ✉ jnolan@eppingforestdc.gov.uk

Housing: Mr Paul Pledger Assistant Director - Housing Property, Civic Offices, High Street, Epping CM16 4BZ ☎ 01992 564248 ✉ ppledger@eppingforestdc.gov.uk

Housing: Ms Lyndsay Swan Assistant Director - Private Sector Housing & Community Support, Civic Offices, High Street, Epping CM16 4BZ ☎ 01992 564146 ✉ lswann@eppingforestdc.gov.uk

Housing: Mr Roger Wilson Assistant Director - Housing Operations, Civic Offices, High Street, Epping CM16 4BZ ☎ 01992 564419 ✉ rwilson@eppingforestdc.gov.uk

Housing Maintenance: Mr Roger Wilson Assistant Director - Housing Operations, Civic Offices, High Street, Epping CM16 4BZ ☎ 01992 564419 ✉ rwilson@eppingforestdc.gov.uk

Legal: Mr Simon Hill Assistant Director - Governance & Performance Management, Civic Offices, High Street, Epping CM16 4BZ ☎ 01992 564249 ✉ shill@eppingforestdc.gov.uk

Legal: Ms Alison Mitchell Assistant Director - Legal Services, Civic Offices, High Street, Epping CM16 4BZ ☎ 01992 564017 ✉ amitchell@eppingforestdc.gov.uk

Legal: Ms Colleen O'Boyle Director - Governance; Solicitor to the Council, Civic Offices, High Street, Epping CM16 4BZ ☎ 01992 564475 ✉ coboyle@eppingforestdc.gov.uk

Leisure and Cultural Services: Ms Jo Cowan Arts Officer, Civic Offices, High Street, Epping CM16 4BZ ☎ 01992 564553 ✉ jcowan@eppingforestdc.gov.uk

Leisure and Cultural Services: Mr James Warwick Sports Development Manager, Civic Offices, High Street, Epping CM16 4BZ ☎ 01992 564350 ✉ jwarwick@eppingforestdc.gov.uk

Member Services: Ms Wendy MacLeod Senior Electoral Services Manager, Civic Offices, High Street, Epping CM16 4BZ ☎ 01992 564023 ✉ wmacleod@eppingforestdc.gov.uk

Member Services: Mr Stephen Tautz Senior Democratic Services Officer, Civic Offices, High Street, Epping CM16 4BZ ☎ 01992 564180 ✉ stautz@eppingforestdc.gov.uk

Personnel / HR: Ms Paula Maginnis Assistant Director - Human Resources, Civic Offices, High Street, Epping CM16 4BZ ☎ 01992 564536 ✉ pmaginnis@eppingforestdc.gov.uk

Public Libraries: Mr Tony O'Connor Museum Officer, Civic Offices, High Street, Epping CM16 4BZ ☎ 01992 716882 ✉ toconnor@eppingforestdc.gov.uk

Staff Training: Ms Paula Maginnis Assistant Director - Human Resources, Civic Offices, High Street, Epping CM16 4BZ ☎ 01992 564536 ✉ pmaginnis@eppingforestdc.gov.uk

Tourism: Mr Tony O'Connor Museum Officer, Civic Offices, High Street, Epping CM16 4BZ ☎ 01992 716882 ✉ toconnor@eppingforestdc.gov.uk

COUNCILLORS

***Chair* Webster**, Elizabeth (CON - Waltham Abbey Paternoster)
cllr.elizabeth.webster@essexcc.gov.uk

***Deputy Chair* Lea**, Jeanne (CON - Waltham Abbey North East)

***Leader of the Council* Whitbread**, Chris (CON - Epping Lindsey and Thornwood Common)
cwhitbread@eppingforest.gov.uk

***Deputy Leader of the Council* Stavrou**, Syd (CON - Waltham Abbey High Beach)
sydstavrou@yahoo.com

Angold-Stephens, Kenneth (R - Loughton Roding)
ken@angold-stephens.co.uk

Avey, Nigel (CON - Epping Hemnell)
nigel.avey@btinternet.com

Bassett, Richard (CON - Lower Nazeing)
richard.d.bassett@ntlworld.com

Boyce, Tony (CON - Moreton and Fyfield)
tonyboyce@aol.com

Brady, Heather (CON - Passingford)
heatherbrady@hotmail.co.uk

Breare-Hall, Will (CON - Epping Lindsey and Thornwood Common)
wsbh@hotmail.co.uk

Butler, Rod (UKIP - Waltham Abbey Honey Lane)
rod.butler@btconnect.com

Chambers, Gavin (CON - Buckhurst Hill West)
gavin.chamberstraining@gmail.com

Chana, Kewel (CON - Grange Hill)
kewalchana@yahoo.co.uk

Church, Tony (CON - Epping Lindsey and Thornwood Common)

Dorrell, David (UKIP - Waltham Abbey Paternoster)
dave@cyprus.plus.com

Gadsby, Ricki (CON - Waltham Abbey South West)

Girling, Leon (R - Loughton Broadway)
leongirling@gmail.com

Gode, Peter (LAB - Shelley)

Grigg, Anne (CON - North Weald Bassett)

Hart, James (CON - Loughton Forest)
hartjmh@bloomberg.net

Hughes, Lynn (CON - Broadley Common, Epping Upland & Nazeing)
eppinglynn@live.com

Jennings, Bob (R - Loughton St Johns)
cllrrobertjennings@hotmail.com

Jones, Sue (CON - Theydon Bois)
sue.jones193@ntlworld.com

Kane, Helen (CON - Waltham Abbey South West)
helen@samkane.co.uk

Kauffmann, Howard (R - Loughton St Mary's)

Keska, Paul (CON - Chipping Ongar, Greensted and Marden Ash)
cllr.ps.keska@hotmail.co.uk

Knapman, John (CON - Chigwell Village)
jknapman@msn.com

Knight, Yolanda (CON - Lower Nazeing)
yogard@hotmail.co.uk

Lion, Alan (CON - Grange Hill)
al.lion@btinternet.com

Mann, Harvey (R - Loughton St Mary's)

McEwen, Maggie (CON - High Ongar, Willingale and The Rodings)
heath.lands@btinternet.com

Mead, Louise (R - Loughton Fairmead)
cllrlouisemead@hotmail.com

Mitchell, Ann (CON - Waltham Abbey North East)
lillianmitchell@sky.com

Mohindra, Gagan (CON - Grange Hill)
gaganmohindra1@gmail.com

Morgan, Richard (IND - Hastingwood, Matching and Sheering Village)

Murray, Stephen (IND - Loughton Roding)

Neville, Steven (GRN - Buckhurst Hill East)
cllrstevenjsneville@gmail.com

Patel, Aniket (CON - Buckhurst Will West)
patelaniket17@yahoo.co.uk

Philip, John (CON - Theydon Bois)
john.philip1@ntlworld.com

Pond, Chris (R - Loughton Broadway)
cllrccp@outlook.com

Pond, Caroline (R - Loughton St Johns)
caroline_pond@hotmail.com

Roberts, Chris (R - Loughton Alderton)
chrisroberts_lra@yahoo.gov.uk

Rolfe, Brian (CON - Lambourne)
cllrbrianrolfe@hotmail.co.uk

Sandler, Brian (CON - Chigwell Row)
bpsandler@aol.com

Sartin, Mary (CON - Roydon)
marysartin@yahoo.com

Shiell, Glynis (CON - Waltham Abbey Honey Lane)

Stallan, David (CON - North Weald Bassett)
dave.stallan@tesco.net

Surtees, Brian (LD - Chipping Ongar, Greensted and Marden Ash)
bsurtees@seetrus.com

Thomas, Tracey (R - Loughton Alderton)
traceythomas210@msn.com

Wagland, Lesley (CON - Chigwell Village)
lwebber@live.co.uk

Waller, Gary (CON - Lower Sheering)
gary.waller@which.net

Watson, Sylvia (CON - Buckhurst Hill West)
sylvia_watson@btconnect.com

Watts, Antony (CON - Waltham Abbey Honey Lane)

Weston, Sharon (R - Loughton Forest)
sharon.weston2@btinternet.com

Whitehouse, Jon (LD - Epping Hemnall)
jon@jonwhitehouse.org.uk

Whitehouse, Janet (LD - Epping Hemnall)
janet.whitehouse@eflibdems.org.uk

Wixley, David (R - Loughton Fairmead)
david.wixley@talktalk.net

Wright, Neville (CON - Buckhurst Hill East)
nevillewright64@hotmail.com

POLITICAL COMPOSITION

CON: 37, R: 12, LD: 3, UKIP: 2, IND: 2, LAB: 1, GRN: 1

COMMITTEE CHAIRS

District Development: Mr Brian Sandler

Epsom & Ewell D

Epsom & Ewell Borough Council, Town Hall, The Parade, Epsom KT18 5BY
☎ 01372 732000 🖷 01372 732020
contactus@epsom-ewell.gov.uk
www.epsom-ewell.gov.uk

FACTS AND FIGURES

Parliamentary Constituencies: Epsom and Ewell
EU Constituencies: South East
Election Frequency: Elections are of whole council

EPSOM & EWELL

PRINCIPAL OFFICERS

Chief Executive: Mrs Frances Rutter Chief Executive, Town Hall, The Parade, Epsom KT18 5BY ☎ 01372 732104 🖱 frutter@epsom-ewell.gov.uk

Senior Management: Ms Kathryn Beldon Director of Finance & Resources, Town Hall, The Parade, Epsom KT18 5BY ☎ 01372 732102 🖱 mbeldon@epsom-ewell.gov.uk

Building Control: Mr Mark Berry, Head of Place Development, Town Hall, The Parade, Epsom KT18 5BY ☎ 01372 732391 🖷 01372 732365 🖱 mberry@epsom-ewell.gov.uk

PR / Communications: Mr Mark Rouson Communications Officer, Town Hall, The Parade, Epsom KT18 5BY ☎ 01372 732080 🖱 mrouson@epson-ewell.gov.uk

Community Safety: Mr Kelvin Shooter Community Safety Officer, Town Hall, The Parade, Epsom KT18 5BY ☎ 01372 732133 🖱 kshooter@epsom-ewell.gov.uk

Computer Management: Mr Mark Lumley, Head of ICT, Town Hall, The Parade, Epsom KT18 5BY ☎ 01372 732174 🖱 mlumley@epsom-ewell.gov.uk

Customer Service: Mrs Joy Stevens, Head of Customer Services, Town Hall, The Parade, Epsom KT18 5BY ☎ 01372 732701 🖱 jstevens@epsom-ewell.gov.uk

Direct Labour: Mr Ian Dyer, Head of Operational Services, Longmead Depot, Blenheim Road, Epsom KT19 9AP ☎ 01372 732520 🖱 idyer@epsom-ewell.gov.uk

Electoral Registration: Ms Kerry Blundell, Electoral Registration Officer Town Hall, The Parade, Epsom KT18 5BY ☎ 01372 732152 🖱 kblundell@epsom-ewell.gov.uk

Emergency Planning: Mr Doug Earle, Head of Corporate Risk & Facilities, Town Hall, The Parade, Epsom KT18 5BY ☎ 01372 732211 🖱 dearle@epsom-ewell.gov.uk

Environmental Health: Mr Rod Brown Head - Housing & Environmental Services, Town Hall, The Parade, Epsom KT18 5BY ☎ 01372 732546 🖱 rbrown@epsom-ewell.gov.uk

Estates, Property & Valuation: Mr Chris Stone Estates Manager, Town Hall, The Parade, Epsom KT18 5BY ☎ 01372 732143 🖱 cstone@epsom-ewell.gov.uk

Facilities: Mr Andrew Lunt Head of Venues & Facilities, Town Hall, The Parade, Epsom KT18 5BY ☎ 01372 732302 🖱 alunt@epsom-ewell.gov.uk

Finance: Ms Judith Doney Head of Revenues & Benefits, Town Hall, The Parade, Epsom KT18 5BY ☎ 01372 732000 🖱 jdoney@epsom-ewell.gov.uk

Finance: Mr Lee Duffy Head of Financial Services, Town Hall, The Parade, Epsom KT18 5BY ☎ 01372 732210 🖱 lduffy@epsom-ewell.gov.uk

Health and Safety: Ms Pauline Baxter, Corporate Health & Safety Officer, Town Hall, The Parade, Epsom KT18 5BY ☎ 01372 732410 🖷 01372 732452 🖱 pbaxter@epsom-ewell.gov.uk

Housing: Ms Annette Snell Housing Manager, Town Hall, The Parade, Epsom KT18 5BY ☎ 01372 732436 🖷 01372 732440 🖱 asnell@epsom-ewell.gov.uk

Legal: Mr Simon Young Head of Legal & Democratic Services, Town Hall, The Parade, Epsom KT18 5BY ☎ 01372 732148 🖱 syoung@epsom-ewell.gov.uk

Leisure and Cultural Services: Dr Sam Beak Leisure Developments Manager, Town Hall, The Parade, Epsom KT18 5BY ☎ 01372 732460 🖷 01372 732452 🖱 sbeak@epsom-ewell.gov.uk

Licensing: Mrs Rachel Jackson, Licensing Officer, Town Hall, The Parade, Epsom KT18 5BY ☎ 01372 732449 🖷 01372 732365 🖱 rjackson@epsom-ewell.gov.uk

Member Services: Miss Fiona Cotter, Democratic Services Manager, Town Hall, The Parade, Epsom KT18 5BY ☎ 01372 732124 🖷 01372 732111 🖱 fcotter@epsom-ewell.gov.uk

Personnel / HR: Mrs Shona Mason Head of HR & OD, Town Hall, The Parade, Epsom KT18 5BY ☎ 01372 732127 🖱 smason@epsom-ewell.gov.uk

Planning: Mr Mark Berry, Head of Place Development, Town Hall, The Parade, Epsom KT18 5BY ☎ 01372 732391 🖷 01372 732365 🖱 mberry@epsom-ewell.gov.uk

Procurement: Mr Derek Smith Procurement Officer, Town Hall, The Parade, Epsom KT18 5BY ☎ 01372 732000 🖱 dsmith@epsom-ewell.gov.uk

Recycling & Waste Minimisation: Mr Ian Dyer, Head of Operational Services, Longmead Depot, Blenheim Road, Epsom KT19 9AP ☎ 01372 732520 🖱 idyer@epsom-ewell.gov.uk

Waste Collection and Disposal: Mr Ian Dyer, Head of Operational Services, Longmead Depot, Blenheim Road, Epsom KT19 9AP ☎ 01372 732520 🖱 idyer@epsom-ewell.gov.uk

Waste Management: Mr Ian Dyer, Head of Operational Services, Longmead Depot, Blenheim Road, Epsom KT19 9AP ☎ 01372 732520 🖱 idyer@epsom-ewell.gov.uk

COUNCILLORS

***Mayor* Frost**, Chris (R - Nonsuch)
cfrost@epsom-ewell.gov.uk

Arthur, Michael (R - Ewell)
marthur@epsom-ewell.gov.uk

Axelrod, Anthony (R - Town)
taxelrod@epsom-ewell.gov.uk

Baker, Richard (R - Stamford)
rbaker@epsom-ewell.gov.uk

Bansil, Rekha (R - Woodcote)
rbansil@epsom-ewell.gov.uk

Beckett, John (R - Auriol)
jbeckett@epsom-ewell.gov.uk

Bridger, Stephen (R - Stamford)
sbridger@epsom-ewell.gov.uk

Chin, Katherine (LAB - Court)
kchin@epsom-ewell.gov.uk

Clarke, Alexander (CON - College)
aclarke@epsom-ewell.gov.uk

Crawford, George (R - Cuddington)
gcrawford@epsom-ewell.gov.uk

Dallen, Neil (R - Town)
ndallen@epsom-ewell.gov.uk

Dallen, Lucie (R - Cuddington)
ldallen@epsom-ewell.gov.uk

Dalton, Hannah (R - Stoneleigh)
hdalton@epsom-ewell.gov.uk

Dudley, Graham (R - Nonsuch)
gdudley@epsom-ewell.gov.uk

Foote, Robert (R - Cuddington)

Frost, Liz (R - Woodcote)
lfrost@epsom-ewell.gov.uk

Geleit, Robert (LAB - Court)
rgeleit@epsom-ewell.gov.uk

Kington, Eber (R - Ewell Court)

Kokou-Tchri, Omer (CON - College)
okokou-tchri@epsom-ewell.gov.uk

Mason, Janet (R - Ruxley)

Mountain, Christina (R - Woodcote)
tmountain@epsom-ewell.gov.uk

Nash, Barry (R - West Ewell)
bnash@epsom-ewell.gov.uk

O'Donavan, Peter (R - Ewell Court)
po'donovan@epsom-ewell.gov.uk

Olney, Martin (R - Stamford)
molney@epsom-ewell.gov.uk

Partirdge, Keith (R - Ruxley)
kpartridge@epsom-ewell.gov.uk

Race, Jane (CON - College)
jrace@epsom-ewell.gov.uk

Reeve, David (R - Stoneleigh)
dreeve@epsom-ewell.gov.uk

Reynolds, Humphrey (R - Ewell)
hreynolds@epsom-ewell.gov.uk

Robbins, Guy (R - Ewell Court)
grobbins@epsom-ewell.gov.uk

Romagnuolo, Vincent (LAB - Court)
wromagnuolo@epsom-ewell.gov.uk

Smitherham, Clive (R - West Ewell)
csmitherham@epsom-ewell.gov.uk

Steer, Jean (R - West Ewell)
jsteer@epsom-ewell.gov.uk

Sursham, Alan (R - Ruxley)
asursham@epsom-ewell.gov.uk

Teasdale, Michael (R - Stoneleigh)
mteasdale@epsom-ewell.gov.uk

Webb, Peter (R - Auriol)
pwebb@epsom-ewell.gov.uk

Wood, David (R - Nonsuch)
dwood@epsom-ewell.gov.uk

Woodbridge, Clive (R - Ewell)
cwoodbridge@epsom-ewell.gov.uk

Wormington, Estelle (R - Town)
twormington@epsom-ewell.gov.uk

POLITICAL COMPOSITION

R: 32, CON: 3, LAB: 3

Erewash D

Erewash Borough Council, Town Hall, Wharncliffe Road, Ilkeston DE7 5RP
☎ 0845 907 2244 🖷 0115 907 1121 🖳 www.erewash.gov.uk

FACTS AND FIGURES

Parliamentary Constituencies: Erewash
EU Constituencies: Eastern
Election Frequency: Elections are of whole council

PRINCIPAL OFFICERS

Chief Executive: Mr Jeremy Jaroszek, Chief Executive, Town Hall, Ilkeston DE7 5RP ☎ 0115 907 1199 🖷 0115 944 3269 ✉ jeremy.jaroszek@erewash.gov.uk

Deputy Chief Executive: Mr Ian Sankey, Director of Resources & Deputy Chief Executive, Town Hall, Ilkeston DE7 5RP ☎ 0115 907 1157 🖷 0115 944 3269 ✉ ian.sankey@erewash.gov.uk

Assistant Chief Executive: Ms Lorraine Poyser, Director of Community Services / Assistant Chief Executive, Town Hall, Ilkeston DE7 5RP ☎ 0115 907 2244 🖷 0115 907 1121 ✉ lorraine.poyser@erewash.gov.uk

Senior Management: Mr Phillip Wright Director of Operational Services, Merlin House, Merlin Way, Ilkeston DE7 4RA ☎ 0115 907 2244 🖷 0115 931 6079 ✉ phillip.wright@erewash.gov.uk

Architect, Building / Property Services: Mr Tom Haddock Property & Estates Manager, Town Hall, , Long Eaton NG10 1HU ☎ 0115 907 2244 ✉ tom.haddock@erewash.gov.uk

Best Value: Mrs Rachel Fernandez Performance & Community Manager, Town Hall, , Ilkeston DE7 5RP ☎ 0115 907 2244 🖷 0115 907 1211 ✉ rachel.fernandez@erewash.gov.uk

Building Control: Mr Peter Baker, Building Control Manager, Town Hall, Long Eaton NG10 1HU ☎ 0115 907 2221 🖷 011 5907 2267 ✉ peter.baker@erewash.gov.uk

PR / Communications: Mr Stewart Millar Communications & Culture Manager, Town Hall, Ilkeston DE7 5RP ☎ 0115 907 1159 🖷 0115 907 1121 ✉ stewart.millar@erewash.gov.uk

EREWASH

Community Safety: Ms Lorraine Poyser, Director of Community Services / Assistant Chief Executive, Town Hall, Ilkeston DE7 5RP ☎ 0115 907 2244 🖷 0115 907 1121 lorraine.poyser@erewash.gov.uk

Computer Management: Mr Neil Webster ICT Manager, Town Hall, Long Eaton NG10 1HU ☎ 0115 907 2244 🖷 0115 931 6001 neil.webster@erewash.gov.uk

Corporate Services: Mr Ian Sankey, Director of Resources & Deputy Chief Executive, Town Hall, Ilkeston DE7 5RP ☎ 0115 907 1157 🖷 0115 944 3269 ian.sankey@erewash.gov.uk

Customer Service: Mrs Rachel Fernandez Performance & Community Manager, Town Hall, , Ilkeston DE7 5RP ☎ 0115 907 2244 🖷 0115 907 1211 rachel.fernandez@erewash.gov.uk

Economic Development: Mr Steve Birkinshaw Head of Planning & Regeneration, Town Hall, Long Easton NG10 1HU ☎ 0115 907 2244 🖷 011 5907 2237 steve.birkinshaw@erewash.gov.uk

Electoral Registration: Mrs Hayley Brailsford, Electoral Services Manager, Town Hall, Ilkeston DE7 5RP ☎ 0115 907 1112 🖷 0115 907 1121 hayley.brailsford@erewash.gov.uk

Emergency Planning: Mr David Bramwell Head of Green Space & Street Scene, Merlin House, Merlin Way, Ilkeston DE7 4RA ☎ 0115 907 2244 🖷 0115 931 6079 dave.bramwell@erewash.gov.uk

Environmental / Technical Services: Mr Phillip Wright Director of Operational Services, Merlin House, Merlin Way, Ilkeston DE7 4RA ☎ 0115 907 2244 🖷 0115 931 6079 phillip.wright@erewash.gov.uk

Environmental Health: Mr Nick Thurstan Head of Environment & Housing Services, Merlin House, Merlin Way, Ilkeston DE7 4RA ☎ 0115 931 6031 🖷 0115 931 6079 nick.thurstan@erewash.gov.uk

Estates, Property & Valuation: Mr Brendan Morris Head of Law & Corporate Governance, Town Hall, Ilkeston DE7 5RP ☎ 0115 907 1032 🖷 0115 907 1121 brendan.morris@erewash.gov.uk

Events Manager: Mr Stewart Millar Communications & Culture Manager, Town Hall, Ilkeston DE7 5RP ☎ 0115 907 1159 🖷 0115 907 1121 stewart.millar@erewash.gov.uk

Finance: Mr Ian Sankey, Director of Resources & Deputy Chief Executive, Town Hall, Ilkeston DE7 5RP ☎ 0115 907 1157 🖷 0115 944 3269 ian.sankey@erewash.gov.uk

Finance: Mr David Watson Head of Finance, Town Hall, Ilkeston DE7 5RP ☎ 0115 907 1032 🖷 0115 907 1018 david.watson@erewash.gov.uk

Treasury: Mrs Judy Fay Chief Accountant, Town Hall, Wharncliffe Road, Ilkeston DE7 5RP ☎ 0115 907 2244 judy.fay@erewash.gov.uk

Fleet Management: Mr Joe Kirby Area Supervisor (Waste / Fleet Manager), Merlin House, Merlin Way, Ilkeston DE7 4RA ☎ 0115 907 2244 joe.kirby@erewash.gov.uk

Grounds Maintenance: Mr David Bramwell Head of Green Space & Street Scene, Merlin House, Merlin Way, Ilkeston DE7 4RA ☎ 0115 907 2244 🖷 0115 931 6079 dave.bramwell@erewash.gov.uk

Health and Safety: Ms Liz Street Environmental Health Manager (Commercial), Merlin House, Merlin Way, Ilkeston DE7 4RA ☎ 0115 907 2244 🖷 0115 931 6079 elizabeth.street@erewash.gov.uk

Housing: Mr Nick Thurstan Head of Environment & Housing Services, Merlin House, Merlin Way, Ilkeston DE7 4RA ☎ 0115 931 6031 🖷 0115 931 6079 nick.thurstan@erewash.gov.uk

Legal: Mr Brendan Morris Head of Law & Corporate Governance, Town Hall, Ilkeston DE7 5RP ☎ 0115 907 1032 🖷 0115 907 1121 brendan.morris@erewash.gov.uk

Leisure and Cultural Services: Mr Tim Spencer Head of Leisure Services, Sandiacre Friesland Sports Centre, Nursery Avenue, Sandiacre NG10 5AE ☎ 0115 907 2244 🖷 0115 949 7062 tim.spencer@erewash.gov.uk

Licensing: Mr Phillip Wright Director of Operational Services, Merlin House, Merlin Way, Ilkeston DE7 4RA ☎ 0115 907 2244 🖷 0115 931 6079 phillip.wright@erewash.gov.uk

Member Services: Mr Brendan Morris Head of Law & Corporate Governance, Town Hall, Ilkeston DE7 5RP ☎ 0115 907 1032 🖷 0115 907 1121 brendan.morris@erewash.gov.uk

Parking: Mr Scott Cartledge Neighbourhood Warden Manager, Merlin House, Merlin Way, Ilkeston DE7 4RA ☎ 0115 907 2244 scott.cartledge@erewash.gov.uk

Partnerships: Ms Lorraine Poyser, Director of Community Services / Assistant Chief Executive, Town Hall, Ilkeston DE7 5RP ☎ 0115 907 2244 🖷 0115 907 1121 lorraine.poyser@erewash.gov.uk

Personnel / HR: Ms Jennifer Browne, Head of Personnel & ICT, Town Hall, Long Eaton NG10 1HU ☎ 0115 907 2244 🖷 0115 907 2266 jennifer.browne@erewash.gov.uk

Planning: Mr Steve Birkinshaw Head of Planning & Regeneration, Town Hall, Long Easton NG10 1HU ☎ 0115 907 2244 🖷 011 5907 2237 steve.birkinshaw@erewash.gov.uk

Procurement: Mr David Watson Head of Finance, Town Hall, Ilkeston DE7 5RP ☎ 0115 907 1032 🖷 0115 907 1018 david.watson@erewash.gov.uk

Recycling & Waste Minimisation: Mr David Bramwell Head of Green Space & Street Scene, Merlin House, Merlin Way, Ilkeston DE7 4RA ☎ 0115 907 2244 🖷 0115 931 6079 dave.bramwell@erewash.gov.uk

Regeneration: Mr Steve Birkinshaw Head of Planning & Regeneration, Town Hall, Long Easton NG10 1HU ☎ 0115 907 2244 🖷 011 5907 2237 steve.birkinshaw@erewash.gov.uk

Staff Training: Ms Joanna Till Personnel Manager, Town Hall, Long Eaton NG10 1HU ☎ 0115 907 2244 🖷 0115 907 2266 joanna.till@erewash.gov.uk

Street Scene: Mr David Bramwell Head of Green Space & Street Scene, Merlin House, Merlin Way, Ilkeston DE7 4RA ☎ 0115 907 2244 🖷 0115 931 6079 ✉ dave.bramwell@erewash.gov.uk

Sustainable Development: Mr Ian Sankey, Director of Resources & Deputy Chief Executive, Town Hall, Ilkeston DE7 5RP ☎ 0115 907 1157 🖷 0115 944 3269 ✉ ian.sankey@erewash.gov.uk

Tourism: Mr Tim Spencer Head of Leisure Services, Sandiacre Friesland Sports Centre, Nursery Avenue, Sandiacre NG10 5AE ☎ 0115 907 2244 🖷 0115 949 7062 ✉ tim.spencer@erewash.gov.uk

Waste Collection and Disposal: Mr David Bramwell Head of Green Space & Street Scene, Merlin House, Merlin Way, Ilkeston DE7 4RA ☎ 0115 907 2244 🖷 0115 931 6079 ✉ dave.bramwell@erewash.gov.uk

Waste Management: Mr David Bramwell Head of Green Space & Street Scene, Merlin House, Merlin Way, Ilkeston DE7 4RA ☎ 0115 907 2244 🖷 0115 931 6079 ✉ dave.bramwell@erewash.gov.uk

Children's Play Areas: Mr Richard Ashley Green Space & Street Scene Manager, Merlin House, Merlin Way, Ilkeston DE7 4RA ☎ 0115 907 2244 🖷 0115 931 6079 ✉ richard.ashley@erewash.gov.uk

COUNCILLORS

***Mayor* Custance**, Val (CON - Shipley View)
councillor.val.custance@erewash.gov.uk

***Deputy Mayor* Stevenson**, Abey (CON - Little Eaton and Stanley)
councillor.abey.stevenson@erewash.gov.uk

***Leader of the Council* Corbett**, Christopher (CON - Wilsthorpe)
councillor.chris.corbett@erewash.gov.uk

***Deputy Leader of the Council* Hart**, Carol (CON - West Hallam and Dale Abbey)
councillor.carol.hart@erewash.gov.uk

***Group Leader* Dawson**, James (LAB - Awsworth Road)
councillor.james.dawson@erewash.gov.uk

Athwal, Kewal (CON - Wilsthorpe)
councillor.kewal.athwal@erewash.gov.uk

Beardsley, Susan (CON - Little Hallam)
councillor.sue.beardsley@erewash.gov.uk

Bilbie, Leonie (CON - Sandiacre)
councillor.leonie.bilbie@erewash.gov.uk

Bilbie, Steve (CON - Sandiacre)
councillor.steve.bilbie@erewash.gov.uk

Birkin, Glennice (LAB - Awsworth Road)
councillor.glennice.birkin@erewash.gov.uk

Bonam, Joanne (CON - Sawley)
councillor.jo.bonam@erewash.gov.uk

Broughton, Bruce (CON - West Hallam and Dale Abbey)
councillor.bruce.broughton@erewash.gov.uk

Brown, Caroline (LAB - Long Eaton Central)
councillor.caroline.brown@erewash.gov.uk

Clare, Valerie (CON - Draycott and Risley)
councillor.val.clare@erewash.gov.uk

Doyle, David (LAB - Nottingham Road)
councillor.david.doyle@erewash.gov.uk

Frudd, John (LAB - Kirk Hallam and Stanton by Dale)
councillor.john.frudd@erewash.gov.uk

Green, Stephen (LAB - Kirk Hallam and Stanton by Dale)

Griffiths, Howard (LAB - Derby Road East)

Griffiths, Margaret (LAB - Derby Road East)

Harris, Richard (CON - Derby Road West)
councillor.richard.harris@erewash.gov.uk

Harrison, Barbara (CON - West Hallam and Dale Abbey)
councillor.barbara.harrison@erewash.gov.uk

Hickton, Garry (CON - Derby Road West)

Hickton, Gerri (CON - Derby Road West)
councillor.gerri.hickton@erewash.gov.uk

Holbrook, Terence (CON - Ockbrook and Borrowash)
councillor.terry.holbrook@erewash.gov.uk

Hopkinson, Mary (CON - Little Hallam)
councillor.mary.hopkinson@erewash.gov.uk

Hosker, Leah (LAB - Long Eaton Central)
councillor.leah.hosker@erewash.gov.uk

Major, Wayne (CON - Sandiacre)
councillor.wayne.major@erewash.gov.uk

McCandless, Andrew (CON - Draycott and Risley)
councillor.andrew.mccandless@erewash.gov.uk

McGraw, Linda (LAB - Kirk Hallam and Stanton by Dale)

Mellors, Denise (LAB - Nottingham Road)
councillor.denise.mellors@erewash.gov.uk

Miller, Kevin (CON - Breaston)
councillor.kevin.miller@erewash.gov.uk

Parkinson, Robert (CON - Breaston)
councillor.robert.parkinson@erewash.gov.uk

Pepios, Peter (CON - Long Eaton Central)
councillor.peter.pepios@erewash.gov.uk

Phillips, Alex (LAB - Hallam Fields)

Phillips, Frank (LAB - Larklands)
councillor.frank.phillips@erewash.gov.uk

Phillips, Pam (LAB - Larklands)
counciller.pam.phillips@erewash.gov.uk

Powell, Michael (CON - Wilsthorpe)
councillor.michael.powell@erewash.gov.uk

Sewell, John (CON - Sawley)
councillor.john.sewell@erewash.gov.uk

Shelton, Paul (CON - Shipley View)
councillor.paul.shelton@erewash.gov.uk

Summerfield, Alan (CON - Little Eaton and Stanley)
councillor.alan.summerfield@erewash.gov.uk

Tatham, Phillips (LAB - Larklands)

Treacy, Danny (LAB - Cotmanhay)
councillor.danny.treacy@erewash.gov.uk

Wallis, Michael (CON - Ockbrook and Borrowash)
councillor.michael.wallis@erewash.gov.uk

Walton, Daniel (CON - Sawley)
councillor.daniel.walton@erewash.gov.uk

White, Michael (CON - Ockbrook and Borrowash)
councillor.michael.white@erewash.gov.uk

EREWASH

Wilson, Jane (LAB - Cotmanhay)
councillor.jane.wilson@erewash.gov.uk

Wright, Jonathan (CON - Hallam Fields)
councillor.jon.wright@erewash.gov.uk

POLITICAL COMPOSITION
CON: 30, LAB: 17

COMMITTEE CHAIRS

Audit: Mr Alan Summerfield

Licensing: Mr Kewal Athwal

Planning: Mr Robert Parkinson

Essex C

Essex County Council, County Hall, Market Road, Chelmsford CM1 1LX
☎ 08457 430430 💻 www.essexcc.gov.uk

FACTS AND FIGURES
Parliamentary Constituencies: Maldon
EU Constituencies: Eastern
Election Frequency: Elections are of whole council

PRINCIPAL OFFICERS

Senior Management: Ms Sonia Davidson-Grant Executive Director - Place Commissioning, County Hall, Market Road, Chelmsford CM1 1LX 🖱 sonia.davidson-grant@essex.gov.uk

Senior Management: Dr Mike Gogarty Director - Public Health, County Hall, Market Road, Chelmsford CM1 1LX 🖱 mike.gogarty@essex.gov.uk

Senior Management: Mr Dave Hill Executive Director - People Commissioning, County Hall, Market Road, Chelmsford CM1 1LX ☎ 01245 431891 🖱 dave.hill@essex.gov.uk

Senior Management: Ms Margaret Lee Executive Director - Corporate Services & Customer Operations, County Hall, Market Road, Chelmsford CM1 1LX ☎ 08457 430430 🖷 01245 431960 🖱 margaret.lee@essex.gov.uk

Senior Management: Ms Helen Lincoln Executive Director - People Operations, County Hall, Market Road, Chelmsford CM1 1LX ☎ 01245 437157 🖱 helen.lincoln@essex.gov.uk

Senior Management: Mr Keir Lynch Executive Director - Strategy, Transformation & Commissioning Support, County Hall, Market Road, Chelmsford CM1 1LX ☎ 01245 431117 🖱 keir.lynch@essex.gov.uk

Senior Management: Mr David Wilde Executive Director - Place Operations & Chief Information Officer, County Hall, Market Road, Chelmsford CM1 1LX ☎ 01245 433172 🖱 david.wilde@essex.gov.uk

Access Officer / Social Services (Disability): Ms Liz Chidgey MD - Essex Cares Ltd, County Hall, Market Road, Chelmsford CM1 1LX ☎ 01245 434123 🖱 liz.chidgey@essex.gov.uk

Building Control: Mr Roy Leavitt Head - Development Control, County Hall, Market Road, Chelmsford CM1 1LX ☎ 01245 437522 🖱 roy.leavitt@essex.gov.uk

Children / Youth Services: Ms Stephanie Bishop Head - Fostering & Adoption, County Hall, Market Road, Chelmsford CM1 1LX ☎ 08457 430430 🖱 stephanie.bishop@essex.gov.uk

Children / Youth Services: Mr Tim Coulson Director - Education & Learning, County Hall, Market Road, Chelmsford CM1 1LX ☎ 01245 436031 🖱 tim.coulson@essex.gov.uk

Children / Youth Services: Ms Helen Lincoln Executive Director - People Operations, County Hall, Market Road, Chelmsford CM1 1LX ☎ 08457 430430 🖱 helen.lincoln@essex.gov.uk

Civil Registration: Mr Philip Thomson, Director - Essex Legal Services, New Bridge House, 60-68 New London Road, Chelmsford CM2 0PD ☎ 01245 506760 🖷 01245 357335 🖱 philip.thomson@essex.gov.uk

Computer Management: Mr David Wilde Executive Director - Place Operations & Chief Information Officer, County Hall, Market Road, Chelmsford CM1 1LX ☎ 01245 433172 🖱 david.wilde@essex.gov.uk

Contracts: Mr Mark Paget Corporate Lead - Supply Chain Management & Contract Management, County Hall, Market Road, Chelmsford CM1 1LX ☎ 01245 431846 🖱 mark.paget@essex.gov.uk

Corporate Services: Ms Katie Hadgraft Head - Employee Communications & Engagement, County Hall, Market Road, Chelmsford CM1 1LX ☎ 01245 434010 🖱 katie.hadgraft@essex.gov.uk

Corporate Services: Mr Mark Hobson Director - Corporate Operations, County Hall, Market Road, Chelmsford CM1 1LX ☎ 01245 431026 🖱 mark.hobson@essex.gov.uk

Corporate Services: Ms Denise Murray Head of Finance, County Hall, Market Road, Chelmsford CM1 1LX ☎ 01245 436721 🖱 denise.murray@essex.gov.uk

Education: Mr Tim Coulson Director - Education & Learning, County Hall, Market Road, Chelmsford CM1 1LX ☎ 01245 436031 🖱 tim.coulson@essex.gov.uk

Education: Mr Graham Ranby Lead Strategic Comissioner - Planning & Provision, County Hall, Market Road, Chelmsford CM1 1LX ☎ 01245 436704 🖱 graham.ranby@essex.gov.uk

Emergency Planning: Mr Adam Eckley Acting Chief Fire Officer & Head of Emergency Planning, County Hall, Market Road, Chelmsford CM1 1LX ☎ 01245 430366 🖱 adam.eckley@essex.gov.uk

European Liaison: Ms Lorraine George EU Funding Lead, County Hall, Market Road, Chelmsford CM1 1QH ☎ 01245 430472 🖱 lorraine.george@essex.gov.uk

Events Manager: Ms Sharon Collier, Events Management & Community Budgets, County Hall, Market Road, Chelmsford CM1 1QH ☎ 01245 436569 🖷 01245 430734 🖱 sharon.collier@essex.gov.uk

Finance: Ms Margaret Lee Executive Director - Corporate Services & Customer Operations, County Hall, Market Road, Chelmsford CM1 1LX ☎ 08457 430430 🖷 01245 431960 ✉ margaret.lee@essex.gov.uk

Finance: Mr Peter Tanton, Head - Internal Audit, County Hall, Market Road, Chelmsford CM1 1LX ☎ 01245 43110 ✉ peter.tanton@essex.gov.uk

Treasury: Mr Robin Paddock Treasurer & Deputy Chief Executive, 3 Hoffmanns Way, Chelmsford CM1 1GU ☎ 01245 291614 ✉ robin.paddock@essex.gov.uk

Pensions: Ms Anne-Marie Allen Investment Officer, County Hall, Market Road, Chelmsford CM1 1LX ☎ 01245 431733 ✉ annemarie.allen@essex.gov.uk

Pensions: Ms Jody Evans Pension Service Manager, County Hall, Market Road, Chelmsford CM1 1LX ☎ 01245 431700 ✉ jody.evans@essex.gov.uk

Pensions: Mr Kevin McDonald Director of Pensions & Investment, County Hall, Market Road, Chelmsford CM1 1LX ✉ kevin.mcdonald@essex.gov.uk

Fleet Management: Mr John Pope, Head - Passenger Transport, County Hall, Market Road, Chelmsford CM1 1QH ☎ 01245 437506 🖷 01245 496764 ✉ john.pope@essex.gov.uk

Grounds Maintenance: Mr Tim Dixon Head - Country Parks, County Hall, Market Road, Chelmsford CM1 1LX ☎ 08457 430430 ✉ tim.dixon@essex.gov.uk

Health and Safety: Ms Janet Ross Health, Safety & Risk Manager, County Hall, Market Road, Chelmsford CM1 1QH ☎ 08457 430430 🖷 01245 352710 ✉ janet.ross@essex.gov.uk

Highways: Mr Paul Bird, Director - Transport & Infrastructure, County Hall, Market Road, Chelmsford CM1 1QH ☎ 08457 430430 🖷 01245 251601 ✉ paul.bird@essex.gov.uk

Legal: Mr Philip Thomson, Director - Essex Legal Services, New Bridge House, 60-68 New London Road, Chelmsford CM2 0PD ☎ 01245 506760 🖷 01245 357335 ✉ philip.thomson@essex.gov.uk

Personnel / HR: Mr Keir Lynch Executive Director - Strategy, Transformation & Commissioning Support, County Hall, Market Road, Chelmsford CM1 1LX ☎ 01245 431117 ✉ keir.lynch@essex.gov.uk

Planning: Mr Paul Bird, Director - Transport & Infrastructure, County Hall, Market Road, Chelmsford CM1 1QH ☎ 08457 430430 🖷 01245 251601 ✉ paul.bird@essex.gov.uk

Recycling & Waste Minimisation: Mr Jason Searles, Head - Commissioning Sustainable Essex Integration & Waste, County Hall, Market Road, Chelmsford CM1 1QH ☎ 08457 430430 🖷 01245 437691 ✉ jason.searles@essex.gov.uk

Road Safety: Ms Katie Brimley Road Safety ETP Team Leader, County Hall, Market Road, Chelmsford CM1 1LX ☎ 01245 437781 🖷 01245 490705 ✉ katie.brimley@essex.gov.uk

Social Services (Children): Ms Helen Lincoln Executive Director - People Operations, County Hall, Market Road, Chelmsford CM1 1LX ☎ 01245 437157 ✉ helen.lincoln@essex.gov.uk

Public Health: Dr Mike Gogarty Director - Public Health, County Hall, Market Road, Chelmsford CM1 1LX ✉ mike.gogarty@essex.gov.uk

Staff Training: Mr Jeff Wren Head - Leadership & Development, County Hall, Market Road, Chelmsford CM1 1LX ☎ 01245 437806 ✉ jeff.wren@essex.gov.uk

Tourism: Ms Mary Tebje Tourism Manager, County Hall, Market Road, Chelmsford CM1 1LX ☎ 03330 134185 ✉ mary.tebje@essex.gov.uk

Traffic Management: Ms Nicola Foster Group Manager - Road Safety, County Hall, Market Road, Chelmsford CM1 1LX ☎ 01245 437004 ✉ nicola.foster@essex.gov.uk

Traffic Management: Mr John Pope, Head - Passenger Transport, County Hall, Market Road, Chelmsford CM1 1QH ☎ 01245 437506 🖷 01245 496764 ✉ john.pope@essex.gov.uk

Transport: Mr John Pope, Head - Passenger Transport, County Hall, Market Road, Chelmsford CM1 1QH ☎ 01245 437506 🖷 01245 496764 ✉ john.pope@essex.gov.uk

Transport Planner: Mr Christopher Stevenson Head - Commissioning: Integrated Transport, County Hall, Market Road, Chelmsford CM1 1LX ☎ 08457 430430 ✉ chris.stevenson@essex.gov.uk

Children's Play Areas: Mr Tim Dixon Head - Country Parks, County Hall, Market Road, Chelmsford CM1 1LX ☎ 08457 430430 ✉ tim.dixon@essex.gov.uk

COUNCILLORS

***Leader of the Council* Finch**, David (CON - Hedingham)
cllr.david.finch@essexcc.gov.uk

***Deputy Leader of the Council* Bentley**, Kevin (CON - Stanway and Pyefleet)
cllr.kevin.bentley@essex.gov.u

***Group Leader* Abbott**, James (GRN - Witham Northern)
cllr.james.abbott@essex.gov.uk

***Group Leader* Henderson**, Ivan (LAB - Harwich)
cllr.ivan.henderson@essex.gov.uk

***Group Leader* Huntman**, Jamie (UKIP - Thundersley)
cllr.jamie.huntman@essex.gov.uk

***Group Leader* Mackrory**, Michael (LD - Springfield)
cllr.mike.mackrory@essexcc.gov.uk

***Group Leader* Young**, Julie (LAB - Wivenhoe St Andrew)
cllr.julie.young@essex.gov.uk

Aldridge, John (CON - Broomfield and Writtle)
cllr.john.aldridge@essexcc.gov.uk

Archibald, William (LAB - Laindon Park and Fryerns)
cllr.bill.archibald@essex.gov.uk

ESSEX

Aspinell, Barry (LD - Brentwood North)
cllr.barry.aspinell@essex.gov.uk

Barker, Susan (CON - Dunmow)
cllr.susan.barker@essexcc.gov.uk

Bass, Rodney (CON - Heybridge and Tollesbury)
cllr.rodney.bass@essexcc.gov.uk

Bayley, Alan (UKIP - South Benfleet)
cllr.alan.bayley@essex.gov.uk

Blackwell, Dave (IND - Canvey Island East)
cllr.dave.blackwell@essex.gov.uk

Bobbin, Keith (LAB - Pitsea)
cllr.keith.bobbin@essex.gov.uk

Boyce, Bob (CON - Southminster)
cllr.bob.boyce@essexcc.gov.uk

Brown, Anne (CON - Constable)
cllr.anne.brown@essex.gov.uk

Buckley, Malcolm (CON - Wickford Crouch)
cllr.malcolm.buckley@essex.gov.uk

Butland, Graham (CON - Braintree Town)
cllr.graham.butland@essex.gov.uk

Canning, Stephen (CON - Bocking)
cllr.stephen.canning@essex.gov.uk

Chandler, Jenny (CON - Great Baddow)
cllr.jenny.chandler@essex.gov.uk

Channer, Penny (CON - Maldon)
cllr.penny.channer@essex.gov.uk

Clempner, Karen (LAB - Harlow West)
cllr.karen.clempner@essex.gov.uk

Cutmore, Terry (CON - Rochford North)
cllr.terry@cutmore@essex.gov.uk

Danvers, Michael (LAB - Harlow North)
cllr.michael.danvers@essex.gov.uk

Deakin, Judith (LD - Chelmsford West)
cllr.jude.deakin@essex.gov.uk

Donaldson, Magaret (LD - Abbey)
cllr.margaret.fisher@essex.gov.uk

Durcan, Anthony (LAB - Harlow West)
cllr.tony.durcan@essex.gov.uk

Ellis, Mark (UKIP - Laindon Park and Fryerns)
cllr.mark.ellis@essex.gov.uk

Erskine, Andrew (UKIP - Tendring Rural East)
cllr.andy.erskine@essex.gov.uk

Gadsby, Ricki (CON - Waltham Abbey)
cllr.ricki.gadsby@essex.gov.uk

Gibbs, Keith (UKIP - Rayleigh South)
cllr.keith.gibbs@essex.gov.uk

Goggin, Alan (CON - Brightlingsea)
alan.goggin@essex.gov.uk

Gooding, Raymond (CON - Stanstead)
cllr.ray.gooding@essexcc.gov.uk

Grundy, Ian (CON - Stock)
cllr.ian.grundy@essex.gov.uk

Guglielmi, Carlo (CON - Tendring Rural West)
cllr.carlo.gugleilmi@essex.gov.uk

Harris, Dave (LAB - Maypole)
cllr.dave.harris@essex.gov.uk

Hedley, Anthony (CON - Billericay and Burstead)
cllr.anthony.hedley@essexcc.gov.uk

Higgins, Theresa (LD - Parsons Heath and East Gates)
cllr.theresa.higgins@essex.gov.uk

Hirst, Roger (CON - Brentwood Hutton)
cllr.roger.hirst@essex.gov.uk

Honeywood, Paul (CON - Clacton West)
cllr.paul.honeywood@essex.gov.uk

Howard, Raymond (CON - Canvey Island West)
cllr.ray.howard@essexcc.gov.uk

Hoy, Michael (GRN - Rochford West)
cllr.michael.hoy@essex.gov.uk

Hume, Norman (CON - South Woodham Ferrers)
cllr.norman.hume@essex.gov.uk

Jackson, Anthony (CON - North Weald and Nazeing)
cllr.anthony.jackson@essex.gov.uk

Johnson, Edward (CON - Harlow South East)
cllr.edward.johnson@essexcc.gov.uk

Jowers, John (CON - Mersea and Tiptree)
cllr.john.jowers@essex.gov.uk

Kendall, David (LD - Brentwood South)
cllr.david.kendall@essex.gov.uk

Knapman, John (CON - Chigwell and Loughton Broadway)
cllr.john.knapman@essex.gov.uk

Le Gresley, Nigel (UKIP - Wickford Crouch)
cllr.nigel.legresley@essex.gov.uk

Lissimore, Sue (CAP - Drury)
cllr.sue.lissimore@essex.gov.uk

Lodge, John (INDNA - Saffron Walden)
cllr.john.lodge@essex.gov.uk

Louis, Derrick (CON - Witham Southern)
cllr.derrek.louis@essex.gov.uk

Madden, Dick (IND - Chelmsford Central)
cllr.dick.madden@essex.gov.uk

Maddocks, Malcolm (CON - Rayleigh North)
cllr.malcolm.maddocks@essex.gov.uk

McEwen, Maggie (CON - Ongar and Rural)
cllr.maggie.mcewen@essex.gov.uk

McGeorge, Melissa (LAB - Pitsea)
cllr.melissa.mcgeorge@essex.gov.uk

Metcalfe, Valerie (CON - Buckhurst Hill and Loughton South)
Cllr.valerie.metcalfe@essex.gov.uk

Naylor, Ann (CON - Brentwood Rural)
cllr.ann.naylor@essexcc.gov.uk

Newton, Patricia (CON - Braintree Eastern)
cllr.lady.newton@essex.gov.uk

Oxley, Pierre (O - Clacton East)
cllr.pierre.oxley@essex.gov.uk

Page, Michael (CON - Frinton and Walton)
cllr.mick.page@essexcc.gov.uk

Pike, Joe (CON - Halstead)
cllr.joe.pike@essex.gov.uk

Pond, Chris (R - Loughton Central)
cllr.chris.pond@essexcc.gov.uk

Reeves, Jillian (CON - Hadleigh)
cllr.jillian.reeves@essexcc.gov.uk

Robinson, Stephen (LD - Chelmsford North)
cllr.stephen.robinson@essex.gov.uk

Seagers, Colin (CON - Rochford South)
cllr.colin.seagers@essex.gov.uk

Smith, Kerry (UKIP - Basildon Westley Heights)
cllr.kerry.smith@essex.gov.uk

Spence, John (CON - Chelmer)
cllr.john.spence@essex.gov.uk

Turrell, Anne (LD - Mile End and Highwoods)
cllr.anne.turrell@essexcc.gov.uk

Twitchen, Kay (CON - Billericay and Burstead)
cllr.kay.twitchen@essexcc.gov.uk

Walsh, Simon (CON - Thaxted)
cllr.simon.walsh@essex.gov.uk

Walters, Roger (CON - Three Fields with Great Notley)
cllr.roger.walters@essex.gov.uk

Whitehouse, Jon (LD - Epping and Theydon Bois)
cllr.jon.whitehouse@essex.gov.uk

Wood, Andy (CON - Clacton North)
cllr.andy.wood@essex.gov.uk

POLITICAL COMPOSITION
CON: 41, LAB: 9, LD: 9, UKIP: 7, IND: 2, GRN: 2, CAP: 1, INDNA: 1, O: 1, R: 1

COMMITTEE CHAIRS
Audit: Mr Terry Cutmore

Development & Regulation: Mr Bob Boyce

Health & Wellbeing: Mr David Finch

Pensions: Mr Rodney Bass

People & Families: Mr Ian Grundy

Exeter City D

Exeter City Council, Civic Centre, Paris Street, Exeter EX1 1JN
☎ 01392 277888 🖷 01392 265265 ✉ exeter@exeter.gov.uk
💻 www.exeter.gov.uk

FACTS AND FIGURES
Parliamentary Constituencies: Exeter
EU Constituencies: South West
Election Frequency: Elections are by thirds

PRINCIPAL OFFICERS
Chief Executive: Mr Karime Hassan Chief Executive & Growth Director, Civic Centre, Paris Street, Exeter EX1 1JN ☎ 01392 265188 🖷 01392 265179 ✉ karime.hassan@exeter.gov.uk

Deputy Chief Executive: Mr Mark Parkinson Deputy Chief Executive, Civic Centre, Paris Street, Exeter EX1 1JN ☎ 01392 265105 🖷 01392 265268 ✉ mark.parkinson@exeter.gov.uk

Senior Management: Ms Bindu Arjoon, Assistant Director - Customer Access, Civic Centre, Paris Street, Exeter EX1 1JN ☎ 01392 265199 🖷 01392 265268 ✉ bindu.arjoon@exeter.gov.uk

Senior Management: Mr Richard Ball, Assistant Director - Economy, Civic Centre, Paris Street, Exeter EX1 1JN ☎ 01392 265140 🖷 01392 265625 ✉ richard.ball@exeter.gov.uk

Senior Management: Mr Roger Coombes, Assistant Director - Housing, Civic Centre, Paris Street, Exeter EX1 1JN ☎ 01392 265468 🖷 01392 265179 ✉ roger.coombes@exeter.gov.uk

Senior Management: Mr Bruce Luxton, Corporate Manager Policy - Communications & Community Engagement, Civic Centre, Paris Street, Exeter EX1 1JN ☎ 01392 265166 🖷 01392 265268 ✉ bruce.luxton@exeter.gov.uk

Senior Management: Mr Robert Norley, Assistant Director - Environment, Civic Centre, Paris Street, Exeter EX1 1RQ ☎ 01392 265170 🖷 01392 265852 ✉ robert.norley@exeter.gov.uk

Senior Management: Mr Richard Short, Assistant Director - City Development, Civic Centre, Paris Street, Exeter EX1 1JN ☎ 01392 265219 🖷 01392 265431 ✉ richard.short@exeter.gov.uk

Senior Management: Mrs Sarah Ward Assistant Director - Public Realm, Civic Centre, Paris Street, Exeter EX1 1JN ☎ 01392 265215 ✉ sarah.ward@exeter.gov.uk

PR / Communications: Mr Steve Upsher Policy, Communications & Community Engagement Officer, Civic Centre, Paris Street, Exeter EX1 1JN ☎ 01392 265103 🖷 01392 265265 ✉ steve.upsher@exeter.gov.uk

Computer Management: Mr Chris Powell Chief Operations Officer, Civic Centre, Paris Street, Exeter EX1 1JN ☎ 01392 265600 🖷 01392 265268 ✉ cjpowell@eastdevon.gov.uk

Contracts: Mr Michael Carson Corporate Manager - Property, Civic Centre, Paris Street, Exeter EX1 1JN ☎ 01392 265169 ✉ michael.carson@exeter.gov.uk

Corporate Services: Mr John Street, Corporate Manager of Democratic & Civic Support, Civic Centre, Paris Street, Exeter EX1 1JN ☎ 01392 265106 🖷 01392 265265 ✉ john.street@exeter.gov.uk

Customer Service: Ms Bindu Arjoon, Assistant Director - Customer Access, Civic Centre, Paris Street, Exeter EX1 1JN ☎ 01392 265199 🖷 01392 265268 ✉ bindu.arjoon@exeter.gov.uk

Customer Service: Mr John Street, Corporate Manager of Democratic & Civic Support, Civic Centre, Paris Street, Exeter EX1 1JN ☎ 01392 265106 🖷 01392 265265 ✉ john.street@exeter.gov.uk

Economic Development: Mr Richard Ball, Assistant Director - Economy, Civic Centre, Paris Street, Exeter EX1 1JN ☎ 01392 265140 🖷 01392 265625 ✉ richard.ball@exeter.gov.uk

E-Government: Mrs Christine Sheldon Web & IT Programme Manager, Civic Centre, Paris Street, Exeter EX1 1JN ☎ 01392 265719 🖷 01392 265217 ✉ christine.sheldon@exeter.gov.uk

EXETER CITY

Electoral Registration: Mr Jeff Chalk Electoral Services Manager, Civic Centre, Paris Street, Exeter EX1 1JN ☎ 01392 265640 🖷 01392 265752 ✉ jeff.chalk@exeter.gov.uk

Electoral Registration: Mr John Street, Corporate Manager of Democratic & Civic Support, Civic Centre, Paris Street, Exeter EX1 1JN ☎ 01392 265106 🖷 01392 265265 ✉ john.street@exeter.gov.uk

Emergency Planning: Mr Bruce Luxton, Corporate Manager Policy - Communications & Community Engagement, Civic Centre, Paris Street, Exeter EX1 1JN ☎ 01392 265166 🖷 01392 265268 ✉ bruce.luxton@exeter.gov.uk

Environmental / Technical Services: Mr Robert Norley, Assistant Director - Environment, Civic Centre, Paris Street, Exeter EX1 1RQ ☎ 01392 265170 🖷 01392 265852 ✉ robert.norley@exeter.gov.uk

Environmental Health: Mr Robert Norley, Assistant Director - Environment, Civic Centre, Paris Street, Exeter EX1 1RQ ☎ 01392 265170 🖷 01392 265852 ✉ robert.norley@exeter.gov.uk

Estates, Property & Valuation: Mr Michael Carson Corporate Manager - Property, Civic Centre, Paris Street, Exeter EX1 1JN ☎ 01392 265169 ✉ michael.carson@exeter.gov.uk

Events Manager: Ms Valerie Wilson Festivals & Events Manager, Civic Centre, Paris Street, Exeter EX1 1JN ☎ 01392 265205 🖷 01392 265268 ✉ val.wilson@exeter.gov.uk

Facilities: Mr John Street, Corporate Manager of Democratic & Civic Support, Civic Centre, Paris Street, Exeter EX1 1JN ☎ 01392 265106 🖷 01392 265265 ✉ john.street@exeter.gov.uk

Finance: Mr David Hodgson Assistant Director - Finance, Civic Centre, Paris Street, Exeter EX1 1JN ☎ 01392 265292 🖷 01392 265217 ✉ david.hodgson@exeter.gov.uk

Treasury: Mr David Hodgson Assistant Director - Finance, Civic Centre, Paris Street, Exeter EX1 1JN ☎ 01392 265292 🖷 01392 265217 ✉ david.hodgson@exeter.gov.uk

Grounds Maintenance: Mr Paul Faulkner, Parks & Open Spaces Manager, Belle Isle Nursery, Belle Isle Drive, Exeter EX2 4RY ☎ 01392 262638 🖷 01392 262631 ✉ paul.faulkner@exeter.gov.uk

Health and Safety: Mr Robert Norley, Assistant Director - Environment, Civic Centre, Paris Street, Exeter EX1 1RQ ☎ 01392 265170 🖷 01392 265852 ✉ robert.norley@exeter.gov.uk

Home Energy Conservation: Mr Keith Williams, Environmental Health Manager of Private Sector Housing, Civic Centre, Paris Street, Exeter EX1 1RQ ☎ 01392 265777 🖷 01392 265852 ✉ keith.williams@exeter.gov.uk

Housing: Mr Roger Coombes, Assistant Director - Housing, Civic Centre, Paris Street, Exeter EX1 1JN ☎ 01392 265468 🖷 01392 265179 ✉ roger.coombes@exeter.gov.uk

Legal: Miss Baan Al-Khafaji, Corporate Manager Legal, Civic Centre, Paris Street, Exeter EX1 1JN ☎ 01392 265874 🖷 01392 265265 ✉ bkhafaji@exeter.gov.uk

Licensing: Mr Robert Norley, Assistant Director - Environment, Civic Centre, Paris Street, Exeter EX1 1RQ ☎ 01392 265170 🖷 01392 265852 ✉ robert.norley@exeter.gov.uk

Member Services: Ms Sarah Selway Democratic Services Manager, Civic Centre, Paris Street, Exeter EX1 1JN ☎ 01392 265275 🖷 01392 265268 ✉ sarah.selway@exeter.gov.uk

Member Services: Mr John Street, Corporate Manager of Democratic & Civic Support, Civic Centre, Paris Street, Exeter EX1 1JN ☎ 01392 265106 🖷 01392 265265 ✉ john.street@exeter.gov.uk

Parking: Mrs Sarah Ward Assistant Director - Public Realm, Civic Centre, Paris Street, Exeter EX1 1JN ☎ 01392 265215 ✉ sarah.ward@exeter.gov.uk

Personnel / HR: Mr Mark Parkinson Deputy Chief Executive, Civic Centre, Paris Street, Exeter EX1 1JN ☎ 01392 265105 🖷 01392 265268 ✉ mark.parkinson@exeter.gov.uk

Planning: Mr Richard Short, Assistant Director - City Development, Civic Centre, Paris Street, Exeter EX1 1JN ☎ 01392 265219 🖷 01392 265431 ✉ richard.short@exeter.gov.uk

Recycling & Waste Minimisation: Mr Robert Norley, Assistant Director - Environment, Civic Centre, Paris Street, Exeter EX1 1RQ ☎ 01392 265170 🖷 01392 265852 ✉ robert.norley@exeter.gov.uk

Staff Training: Mrs June Callister Learning & Development Partner, Civic Centre, Paris Street, Exeter EX1 1JN ☎ 01392 265666 ✉ june.callister@exeter.gov.uk

Street Scene: Mrs Sarah Ward Assistant Director - Public Realm, Civic Centre, Paris Street, Exeter EX1 1JN ☎ 01392 265215 ✉ sarah.ward@exeter.gov.uk

Tourism: Mr Richard Ball, Assistant Director - Economy, Civic Centre, Paris Street, Exeter EX1 1JN ☎ 01392 265140 🖷 01392 265625 ✉ richard.ball@exeter.gov.uk

Tourism: Ms Victoria Hatfield, Tourism Development Manager, Civic Centre, Paris Street, Exeter EX1 1JJ ☎ 01392 265104 🖷 01392 265695 ✉ victoria.hatfield@exeter.gov.uk

Waste Management: Mr Robert Norley, Assistant Director - Environment, Civic Centre, Paris Street, Exeter EX1 1RQ ☎ 01392 265170 🖷 01392 265852 ✉ robert.norley@exeter.gov.uk

COUNCILLORS

***Mayor* Foggin**, Olwen (LAB - Heavitree)
cllr.olwen.foggin@exeter.gov.uk

***Deputy Mayor* Robson**, Lesley (LAB - Priory)
cllr.lesley.robson@exeter.gov.uk

***Group Leader* Edwards**, Peter (LAB - Whipton Barton)
cllr.peter.edwards@exeter.gov.uk

***Group Leader* Leadbetter**, Andrew (CON - St Loyes)
cllr.andrew.leadbetter@exter.gov.uk

Baldwin, Margaret (CON - Topsham)
cllr.margaret.baldwin@exeter.gov.uk

Bialyk, Philip (LAB - Exwick)
cllr.philip.bialyk@exeter.gov.uk

Bowkett, Simon (LAB - Pinhoe)
cllr.simon.bowkett@exeter.gov.uk

Branston, Richard (LAB - Newtown)
cllr.richard.branston@exeter.gov.uk

Brimble, Stephen (LAB - Mincinglake)
cllr.stephen.brimble@exeter.gov.uk

Brock, Stella (LD - St David's)
cllr.stella.brock@exeter.gov.uk

Bull, Paul (LAB - Cowick)
cllr.paul.bull@exeter.gov.uk

Buswell, Christine (LAB - St James)
cllr.christine.buswell@exeter.gov.uk

Choules, Marcel (LAB - Priory)
cllr.marcel.choules@exeter.gov.uk

Crew, Rob (LAB - Alphington)
cllr.rob.crew@exeter.gov.uk

Denham, Rosie (LAB - Whipton Barton)
cllr.rosie.denham@exeter.gov.uk

Donovan, Jake (CON - Pennsylvania)
cllr.jake.donovan@exeter.gov.uk

George, Suaad (LAB - Alphington)
cllr.suaad.george@exeter.gov.uk

Hannaford, Rob (LD - St Thomas)
cllr.rob.hannaford@exeter.co.uk

Hannan, Kate (LAB - Priory)
cllr.kate.hannan@exeter.gov.uk

Harvey, John (CON - Alphington)
cllr.john.harvey@exeter.gov.uk

Henson, David (CON - St Loyes)
cllr.david.henson@exeter.gov.uk

Holland, Peter (CON - Pennyslvania)
cllr.peter.holland@exeter.gov.uk

Laws, Sarah (LAB - St David's)
cllr.sarah.laws@exter.gov.uk

Lyons, Rachel (LAB - Polsloe)
cllr.rachel.lyons@exeter.gov.uk

Morris, Heather (LAB - Cowick)
cllr.heather.morris@exeter.gov.uk

Morse, Emma (LAB - Mincinglake)
cllr.emma.morse@exeter.gov.uk

Mottram, Lee (CON - Duryard)
cllr.lee.mottram@exeter.gov.uk

Newby, Rob (CON - Topsham)
cllr.rob.newby@exeter.gov.uk

Owen, Keith (LAB - St James)
cllr.keith.owen@exeter.gov.uk

Packham, Hannah (LAB - St Thomas)
cllr.hannah.packham@exeter.gov.uk

Pearson, Ollie (LAB - Exwick)
cllr.ollie.pearson@exeter.gov.uk

Prowse, Percy (CON - Duryard)
cllr.percy.prowse@exeter.gov.uk

Raybould, Christine (LAB - Polsloe)
cllr.christine.raybould@exeter.gov.uk

Sheldon, Greg (LAB - Heavitree)
cllr.greg.sheldon@exeter.gov.uk

Shiel, Norman (CON - St Leonard's)
cllr.norman.shiel@exeter.gov.uk

Spackman, Roger (LAB - Newtown)
cllr.roger.spackman@exeter.gov.uk

Sutton, Rachel (LAB - Exwick)
cllr.rachel.sutton@exeter.gov.uk

Vizard, Natalie (LAB - St Leonards)
cllr.natalie.vizard@exeter.gov.uk

Wardle, Tony (LAB - Whipton Barton)
cllr.tony.wardle@exeter.gov.uk

Williams, Megan (LAB - Pinhoe)
cllr.megan.williams@exeter.gov.uk

POLITICAL COMPOSITION
LAB: 28, CON: 10, LD: 2

COMMITTEE CHAIRS
Audit: Ms Natalie Vizard

Licensing: Mr Greg Sheldon

Planning: Mr Philip Bialyk

Falkirk S

Falkirk Council, Municipal Buildings, Falkirk FK1 5RS
☎ 01324 506070 🖷 01324 506071 ✉ info@falkirk.gov.uk
🖳 www.falkirk.gov.uk

FACTS AND FIGURES
Parliamentary Constituencies: Falkirk, Linlithgow and Falkirk East
EU Constituencies: Scotland
Election Frequency: Elections are of whole council

PRINCIPAL OFFICERS
Chief Executive: Mrs Mary Pitcaithly Chief Executive, Municipal Buildings, Falkirk FK1 5RS ☎ 01324 506002 🖷 01324 506001 ✉ mary.pitcaithly@falkirk.gov.uk

Senior Management: Ms Margaret Anderson, Director - Social Work Services, Social Work Headquarters, Denny Town House, 23 Glasgow Road, Denny FK6 5DL ☎ 01324 506400 🖷 01324 506401 ✉ margaret.anderson@falkirk.gov.uk

Senior Management: Ms Rhona Geisler, Director - Development Services, Abbotsford House, David's Loan, Falkirk FK2 7YZ ☎ 01324 504949 🖷 01324 504848 ✉ rhona.geisler@falkirk.gov.uk

Senior Management: Mr Robert Naylor Director - Education Services, Sealock House, 2 Inchyra House, Grangemouth FK3 9XB ☎ 01324 506213 ✉ robert.naylor@falkirk.gov.uk

Senior Management: Mr Stuart Ritchie, Director - Corporate & Neighbourhood Services, Municipal Buildings, Falkirk FK1 5RS ☎ 01324 506005 🖷 01324 506001 ✉ stuart.ritchie@falkirk.gov.uk

FALKIRK

Architect, Building / Property Services: Mr Robert McMaster, Head of Roads & Design Services, Abbotsford House, David's Loan, Falkirk FK2 7YZ ☎ 01324 504953 🖷 01324 504848 ✉ robert.mcmaster@falkirk.gov.uk

Best Value: Mr Stuart Ritchie, Director - Corporate & Neighbourhood Services, Municipal Buildings, Falkirk FK1 5RS ☎ 01324 506005 🖷 01324 506001 ✉ stuart.ritchie@falkirk.gov.uk

Building Control: Mr Russell Cartwright, Building Standards Manager, Falkirk Development Services, Abbotsford House, David's Loan, Falkirk FK2 7YZ ☎ 01324 504801 🖷 01324 504848 ✉ russell.cartwright@falkirk.gov.uk

Catering Services: Ms Judith Borg Catering Co-ordinator, Municipal Buildings, Falkirk FK1 5RS ☎ 01324 590461 ✉ judith.borg@falkirk.gov.uk

Civil Registration: Ms Gillian McIntyre, Customer & Development Manager, Municipal Buildings, Falkirk FK1 5RS ☎ 01324 506104 ✉ gillian.mcintyre@falkirk.gov.uk

PR / Communications: Ms Caroline Binnie, Communications Manager, Municipal Buildings, Falkirk FK1 5RS ☎ 01324 506051 🖷 01324 506061 ✉ caroline.binnie@falkirk.gov.uk

Community Planning: Ms Fiona Campbell, Head of Policy, Technology & Improvement, Municipal Buildings, Falkirk FK1 5RS ☎ 01324 506004 🖷 01324 506061 ✉ fiona.campbell@falkirk.gov.uk

Community Safety: Ms Fiona Campbell, Head of Policy, Technology & Improvement, Municipal Buildings, Falkirk FK1 5RS ☎ 01324 506004 🖷 01324 506061 ✉ fiona.campbell@falkirk.gov.uk

Computer Management: Ms Fiona Campbell, Head of Policy, Technology & Improvement, Municipal Buildings, Falkirk FK1 5RS ☎ 01324 506004 🖷 01324 506061 ✉ fiona.campbell@falkirk.gov.uk

Consumer Protection and Trading Standards: Mr Douglas Duff, Head of Economic Development & Environmental Services, Falkirk Council Development Services, Abbotsford House, David's Loan, Falkirk FK2 7YZ ☎ 01324 504952 🖷 01324 504848 ✉ douglas.duff@falkirk.gov.uk

Contracts: Mr David McGhee Head of Resources & Procurement, Suite 4, The Forum, Callendar Business Park, Falkirk FK1 1XR ☎ 01324 590788 🖷 01324 590781 ✉ david.mcghee@falkirk.gov.uk

Corporate Services: Mr Stuart Ritchie, Director - Corporate & Neighbourhood Services, Municipal Buildings, Falkirk FK1 5RS ☎ 01324 506005 🖷 01324 506001 ✉ stuart.ritchie@falkirk.gov.uk

Customer Service: Ms Karen Algie, Head of Human Resources & Customer First, Municipal Buildings, Falkirk FK1 5RS ☎ 01324 506223 🖷 01324 506220 ✉ karen.algie@falkirk.gov.uk

Direct Labour: Mr David McGhee Head of Resources & Procurement, Suite 4, The Forum, Callendar Business Park, Falkirk FK1 1XR ☎ 01324 590788 🖷 01324 590781 ✉ david.mcghee@falkirk.gov.uk

Economic Development: Mr Douglas Duff, Head of Economic Development & Environmental Services, Falkirk Council Development Services, Abbotsford House, David's Loan, Falkirk FK2 7YZ ☎ 01324 504952 🖷 01324 504848 ✉ douglas.duff@falkirk.gov.uk

Education: Mr Gary Greenhorn Head of Service, Sealock House, 2 Inchyra Road, Grangemouth FK3 9XB ☎ 01324 506683 ✉ gary.greenhorn@falkirk.gov.uk

Education: Mr Robert Naylor Director - Education Services, Sealock House, 2 Inchyra House, Grangemouth FK3 9XB ☎ 01324 506213 ✉ robert.naylor@falkirk.gov.uk

Education: Mrs Anne Pearson Head of Service, Sealock House, 2 Inchyra Road, Grangemouth FK3 9XB ☎ 01324 506686 ✉ anne.pearson@falkirk.gov.uk

E-Government: Ms Fiona Campbell, Head of Policy, Technology & Improvement, Municipal Buildings, Falkirk FK1 5RS ☎ 01324 506004 🖷 01324 506061 ✉ fiona.campbell@falkirk.gov.uk

Emergency Planning: Mr Malcolm Wilson Civil Contingencies Co-Ordinator, Development Services, Abbotsford House, David's Loan, Falkirk FK2 7YZ ☎ 01324 501000 🖷 01324 501001 ✉ m.wilson@falkirk.gov.uk

Energy Management: Mr Robert McMaster, Head of Roads & Design Services, Abbotsford House, David's Loan, Falkirk FK2 7YZ ☎ 01324 504953 🖷 01324 504848 ✉ robert.mcmaster@falkirk.gov.uk

Environmental / Technical Services: Ms Rhona Geisler, Director - Development Services, Abbotsford House, David's Loan, Falkirk FK2 7YZ ☎ 01324 504949 🖷 01324 504848 ✉ rhona.geisler@falkirk.gov.uk

Environmental Health: Mr Graeme Webster Environmental Health Co-ordinator, Abbotsford House, David's Loan, Falkirk FK2 7YZ ☎ 01324 504762 🖷 01324 504709 ✉ graeme.webster@falkirk.gov.uk

Estates, Property & Valuation: Mr Douglas Duff, Head of Economic Development & Environmental Services, Falkirk Council Development Services, Abbotsford House, David's Loan, Falkirk FK2 7YZ ☎ 01324 504952 🖷 01324 504848 ✉ douglas.duff@falkirk.gov.uk

European Liaison: Ms Fiona Campbell, Head of Policy, Technology & Improvement, Municipal Buildings, Falkirk FK1 5RS ☎ 01324 506004 🖷 01324 506061 ✉ fiona.campbell@falkirk.gov.uk

Finance: Mr Danny Cairney Acting Depute Chief Finance Officer, Municipal Buildings, Falkirk FK1 5RS ✉ danny.cairney@falkirk.gov.uk

Finance: Mrs Susan Mathers Depute Chief Finance Officer, Callendar Square, Falkirk FK1 1UJ ☎ 01324 506990 ✉ susan.mathers@falkirk.gov.uk

Finance: Mr Bryan Smail Chief Finance Officer, Municipal Buildings, Falkirk FK1 5RS ☎ 01324 506300 ✉ bryan.smail@falkirk.gov.uk

Finance: Mrs Amanda Templeman Acting Depute Chief Finance Officer, Municipal Buildings, Falkirk FK1 5RS ☎ 01324 506371 🖱 amanda.templeman@falkirk.gov.uk

Pensions: Mr Alistair McGirr Pensions Manager, Municipal Buildings, Falkirk FK1 5RS ☎ 01324 506304 🖱 alistair.mcgirr@falkirk.gov.uk

Fleet Management: Mr Carl Bullough Waste Manager, Dalgrain Depot, McCafferty Way, Grangemouth FK3 8EB ☎ 01324 590420 🖱 carl.bullough@falkirk.gov.uk

Grounds Maintenance: Mr David Crighton Estates Manager, Dalgrain Depot, McCafferty Way, Grangemouth FK3 8EB ☎ 01324 501107 🖱 david.crighton@falkirk.gov.uk

Health and Safety: Ms Karen Algie, Head of Human Resources & Customer First, Municipal Buildings, Falkirk FK1 5RS ☎ 01324 506223 🖷 01324 506220 🖱 karen.algie@falkirk.gov.uk

Highways: Mr Robert McMaster, Head of Roads & Design Services, Abbotsford House, David's Loan, Falkirk FK2 7YZ ☎ 01324 504953 🖷 01324 504848 🖱 robert.mcmaster@falkirk.gov.uk

Home Energy Conservation: Ms Lorna Fleming Private Sector Co-ordinator, Suite 5, The Forum, Callendar Business Park, Falkirk FK1 1XR ☎ 01324 590851 🖷 01324 590781 🖱 lorna.fleming@falkirk.gov.uk

Housing: Ms Jennifer Litts, Head of Housing Services, Suite 4, The Forum, Callendar Business Park, Falkirk FK1 1XR ☎ 01324 590789 🖷 01324 590781 🖱 jennifer.litts@falkirk.gov.uk

Housing Maintenance: Ms Jennifer Litts, Head of Housing Services, Suite 4, The Forum, Callendar Business Park, Falkirk FK1 1XR ☎ 01324 590789 🖷 01324 590781 🖱 jennifer.litts@falkirk.gov.uk

Legal: Ms Rose Mary Glackin, Chief Governance Officer, Municipal Buildings, Falkirk FK1 5RS ☎ 01324 506076 🖱 rosemary.glackin@falkirk.gov.uk

Licensing: Ms Alison Barr Consumer Protection Manager, Municipal Buildings, Falkirk FK1 5RS ☎ 01324 501265 🖷 01324 501588 🖱 alison.barr@falkirk.gov.uk

Lighting: Mr Graham Speirs Area Lighting Engineer, Falkirk Council Development Services, Abbotsford House, David's Loan, Falkirk FK2 7YZ ☎ 01324 504823 🖷 01324 504843 🖱 graham.speirs@falkirk.gov.uk

Lottery Funding, Charity and Voluntary: Ms Fiona Campbell, Head of Policy, Technology & Improvement, Municipal Buildings, Falkirk FK1 5RS ☎ 01324 506004 🖷 01324 506061 🖱 fiona.campbell@falkirk.gov.uk

Member Services: Mr Harry Forster, Member Services Administrator, Municipal Buildings, Falkirk FK1 5RS ☎ 01324 506152 🖷 01324 506151 🖱 harry.forster@falkirk.gov.uk

Parking: Mr Russell Steedman, Network Co-ordinator, Abbotsford House, David's Loan, Falkirk FK1 5RS ☎ 01324 504830 🖷 01324 504843 🖱 russell.steedman@falkirk.gov.uk

Personnel / HR: Ms Karen Algie, Head of Human Resources & Customer First, Municipal Buildings, Falkirk FK1 5RS ☎ 01324 506223 🖷 01324 506220 🖱 karen.algie@falkirk.gov.uk

Planning: Mr Ian Dryden Development Control Manager, Falkirk Council Development Services, Abbotsford House, David's Loan, Falkirk FK2 7HZ ☎ 01324 504756 🖷 01324 504747 🖱 ian.dryden@falkirk.gov.uk

Procurement: Mr David McGhee Head of Resources & Procurement, Suite 4, The Forum, Callendar Business Park, Falkirk FK1 1XR ☎ 01324 590788 🖷 01324 590781 🖱 david.mcghee@falkirk.gov.uk

Recycling & Waste Minimisation: Mr Robin Baird Waste Strategy Co-ordinator, Abbotsford House, David's Loan, Falkirk FK2 7YZ ☎ 01324 590437 🖷 01324 590421 🖱 robin.baird@falkirk.gov.uk

Regeneration: Ms Fiona Campbell, Head of Policy, Technology & Improvement, Municipal Buildings, Falkirk FK1 5RS ☎ 01324 506004 🖷 01324 506061 🖱 fiona.campbell@falkirk.gov.uk

Road Safety: Mr Greg Pender Engineering Design Manager, Falkirk Council Development Services, Abbotsford House, David's Loan, Falkirk FK2 7YZ ☎ 01324 504827 🖷 01324 804888 🖱 greg.pender@falkirk.gov.uk

Social Services (Adult): Ms Marion Reddie, Head of Community Care, Denny Town House, Glasgow Road, Denny FK6 5DL ☎ 01324 506400 🖷 01324 506401 🖱 marion.reddie@falkirk.gov.uk

Social Services (Children): Ms Kathy McCarroll Head of Children & Families & Criminal Justice, Social Work Headquarters, Denny Town House, 23 Glasgow Road, Denny FK6 5DL ☎ 01324 506400 🖷 01324 506401 🖱 kathy.mccarroll@falkirk.gov.uk

Staff Training: Ms Karen Algie, Head of Human Resources & Customer First, Municipal Buildings, Falkirk FK1 5RS ☎ 01324 506223 🖷 01324 506220 🖱 karen.algie@falkirk.gov.uk

Street Scene: Mr Raymond Smith Roads Manager, Development Services, Roads Unit, Earls Road, Grangemouth FK3 8XD ☎ 01324 504812 🖷 01324 504601 🖱 raymond.smith@falkirk.gov.uk

Sustainable Communities: Mr John Angell Head - Planning & Transportation, Municipal Buildings, Falkirk FK1 5RS ☎ 01324 504951 🖷 01324 504848 🖱 john.angell@falkirk.gov.uk

Sustainable Development: Mr John Angell Head - Planning & Transportation, Municipal Buildings, Falkirk FK1 5RS ☎ 01324 504951 🖷 01324 504848 🖱 john.angell@falkirk.gov.uk

Tourism: Mr Pete Reid Growth & Investment Manager, Falkirk Council Development Serivces, Abbotsford House, David's Loan, Falkirk FK2 7YZ ☎ 01324 590971 🖷 01324 590959 🖱 pete.reid@falkirk.gov.uk

Town Centre: Mr Alastair Mitchell, Town Centre Manager, Old Burgh Buildings, 12-14 Newmarket Street, Falkirk FK1 1JE ☎ 01324 611293 🖷 01324 632644 🖱 alastair.mitchell@btconnect.com

FALKIRK

Traffic Management: Mr Russell Steedman, Network Co-ordinator, Abbotsford House, David's Loan, Falkirk FK1 5RS ☎ 01324 504830 🖷 01324 504843 ✉ russell.steedman@falkirk.gov.uk

Transport: Mr Carl Bullough Waste Manager, Dalgrain Depot, McCafferty Way, Grangemouth FK3 8EB ☎ 01324 590420 ✉ carl.bullough@falkirk.gov.uk

Transport Planner: Mrs Julie Cole Acting Transport Planning Manager, Development Services, Abbotsford House, David's Loan, Falkirk FK2 7YZ ☎ 01324 404820 🖷 01324 504914 ✉ julie.cole@falkirk.gov.uk

Waste Collection and Disposal: Mr Carl Bullough Waste Manager, Dalgrain Depot, McCafferty Way, Grangemouth FK3 8EB ☎ 01324 590420 ✉ carl.bullough@falkirk.gov.uk

Waste Collection and Disposal: Mr Carl Bullough Waste Manager, Dalgrain Depot, McCafferty Way, Grangemouth FK3 8EB ☎ 01324 590420 ✉ carl.bullough@falkirk.gov.uk

Waste Management: Mr Carl Bullough Waste Manager, Dalgrain Depot, McCafferty Way, Grangemouth FK3 8EB ☎ 01324 590420 ✉ carl.bullough@falkirk.gov.uk

COUNCILLORS

Leader of the Council **Martin**, Craig (LAB - Carse Kinnaird and Tryst)
craig.martin@falkirk.gov.uk

Alexander, David (SNP - Falkirk North)
david.alexander@falkirk.gov.uk

Balfour, David (SNP - Grangemouth)
david.balfour@falkirk.gov.uk

Bird, Stephen (SNP - Carse Kinnaird and Tryst)
stephen.bird@falkirk.gov.uk

Black, Allyson (LAB - Grangemouth)
allyson.black@falkirk.gov.uk

Blackwood, Jim (LAB - Denny and Banknock)
jim.blackwood@falkirk.gov.uk

Buchanan, Billy (INDNA - Bonnybridge and Larbert)
william.buchanan@falkirk.gov.uk

Carleschi, Steven (SNP - Carse Kinnaird and Tryst)
steven.carleschi@falkirk.gov.uk

Chalmers, Colin (SNP - Falkirk South)
colin.chalmers@falkirk.gov.uk

Coleman, Tom (SNP - Bonnybridge and Larbert)
thomas.coleman@falkirk.gov.uk

Goldie, Gerry (LAB - Falkirk South)
gerry.goldie@falkirk.gov.uk

Goldie, Dennis (LAB - Falkirk South)
dennis.goldie@falkirk.gov.uk

Gow, Linda (LAB - Bonnybridge and Larbert)
linda.gow@falkirk.gov.uk

Hughes, Gordon (SNP - Upper Braes)
gordon.hughes@falkirk.gov.uk

Jackson, Steven (SNP - Lower Braes)
steven.jackson@falkirk.gov.uk

MacDonald, Charles (LAB - Carse Kinnaird and Tryst)
charles.macdonald@falkirk.gov.uk

Mahoney, Adrian (LAB - Bo'ness and Blackness)
adrian.mahoney@falkirk.gov.uk

Martin, Craig (LAB - Falkirk North)
craigr.martin@falkirk.gov.uk

McCabe, Brian (INDNA - Denny and Banknock)
brian.mccabe@falkirk.gov.uk

McLuckie, John (LAB - Upper Braes)
john.mcluckie@falkirk.gov.uk

McNally, John (SNP - Denny and Banknock)
john.mcnally@falkirk.gov.uk

Meiklejohn, Cecil (SNP - Falkirk North)
cecil.meiklejohn@falkirk.gov.uk

Murray, Roise (LAB - Upper Braes)
rosie.murray@falkirk.gov.uk

Nicol, Malcolm (CON - Lower Braes)
malcolm.nicol@falkirk.gov.uk

Nimmo, Alan (LAB - Lower Braes)
alan.nimmo@falkirk.gov.uk

Oliver, Martin (SNP - Denny and Banknock)
martin.oliver@falkirk.gov.uk

Paterson, Joan (LAB - Grangemouth)
joan.paterson@falkirk.gov.uk

Patrick, John (CON - Falkirk South)
john.patrick@falkirk.gov.uk

Reid, Pat (LAB - Falkirk North)
pat.reid@falkirk.gov.uk

Ritchie, Ann (SNP - Bo'ness and Blackness)
ann.ritchie@falkirk.gov.uk

Spears, Robert (INDNA - Grangemouth)
robert.spears@falkirk.gov.uk

Turner, Sandy (SNP - Bo'ness and Blackness)
sandy.turner@falkirk.gov.uk

POLITICAL COMPOSITION

LAB: 14, SNP: 13, INDNA: 3, CON: 2

Fareham D

Fareham Borough Council, Civic Offices, Civic Way, Fareham PO16 7AZ
☎ 01329 236100 🖷 01329 822732 ✉ cx@fareham.gov.uk
💻 www.fareham.gov.uk

FACTS AND FIGURES

Parliamentary Constituencies: Fareham
EU Constituencies: South East
Election Frequency: Elections are biennial

PRINCIPAL OFFICERS

Chief Executive: Mr Peter Grimwood, Chief Executive, Civic Offices, Civic Way, Fareham PO16 7AZ ☎ 01329 824300 ✉ cx@fareham.gov.uk

Access Officer / Social Services (Disability): Mr John Shaw, Head of Building Control, Civic Offices, Civic Way, Fareham PO16 7AZ ☎ 01329 824450 ✉ jshaw@fareham.gov.uk

Architect, Building / Property Services: Mr S Barnett Planned Maintenance Manager, Civic Offices, Civic Way, Fareham PO16 7AZ ☎ 01329 236100 ✉ sbarnett@fareham.gov.uk

Architect, Building / Property Services: Mr Graham Lloyd, Head of Estates, Civic Offices, Civic Way, Fareham PO16 7AZ ☎ 01329 824320 ✉ glloyd@fareham.gov.uk

Building Control: Mr John Shaw, Head of Building Control, Civic Offices, Civic Way, Fareham PO16 7AZ ☎ 01329 824450 ✉ jshaw@fareham.gov.uk

PR / Communications: Mrs Lindsey Ansell, Head of Corporate Services, Civic Offices, Civic Way, Fareham PO16 7AZ ☎ 01329 824567 🖷 01329 822732 ✉ lansell@fareham.gov.uk

Community Planning: Mr Richard Jolley, Director of Planning & Environment, Civic Offices, Civic Way, Fareham PO16 7AZ ☎ 01329 824388 ✉ rjolley@fareham.gov.uk

Community Safety: Ms Narinder Bains Community Safety Manager, Civic Offices, Civic Way, Fareham PO16 7AZ ☎ 01329 824496 ✉ nbains@fareham.gov.uk

Computer Management: Ms Sarah Robinson, Head of Personnel & ICT, Civic Offices, Civic Way, Fareham PO16 7AZ ☎ 01329 824564 ✉ srobinson@fareham.gov.uk

Corporate Services: Mrs Lindsey Ansell, Head of Corporate Services, Civic Offices, Civic Way, Fareham PO16 7AZ ☎ 01329 824567 🖷 01329 822732 ✉ lansell@fareham.gov.uk

Corporate Services: Ms Elaine Hammell Head of Audit & Assurance, Civic Offices, Civic Way, Fareham PO16 7AZ ☎ 01329 236100 ✉ ehammell@fareham.gov.uk

Customer Service: Mrs Lindsey Ansell, Head of Corporate Services, Civic Offices, Civic Way, Fareham PO16 7AZ ☎ 01329 824567 🖷 01329 822732 ✉ lansell@fareham.gov.uk

E-Government: Mr Peter Grimwood, Chief Executive, Civic Offices, Civic Way, Fareham PO16 7AZ ☎ 01329 824300 ✉ cx@fareham.gov.uk

Electoral Registration: Mrs Elaine Wildig Democratic Services Manager, Civic Offices, Civic Way, Fareham PO16 7AZ ☎ 01329 824587 🖷 01329 822732 ✉ electionservices@fareham.gov.uk

Emergency Planning: Mr Paul Doran Director of Environment, Civic Offices, Civic Way, Fareham PO16 7AZ ☎ 01329 824572 ✉ pdoran@fareham.gov.uk

Energy Management: Mr Robert Dunn, Facilities Services Officer, Civic Offices, Civic Way, Fareham PO16 7AZ ☎ 01329 824559 🖷 01329 821411 ✉ rdunn@fareham.gov.uk

Environmental / Technical Services: Mr Paul Doran Director of Environment, Civic Offices, Civic Way, Fareham PO16 7AZ ☎ 01329 824572 ✉ pdoran@fareham.gov.uk

Environmental Health: Mr Martyn George, Director of Community, Civic Offices, Civic Way, Fareham PO16 7AZ ☎ 01329 824400 ✉ mgeorge@fareham.gov.uk

Estates, Property & Valuation: Mr Graham Lloyd, Head of Estates, Civic Offices, Civic Way, Fareham PO16 7AZ ☎ 01329 824320 ✉ glloyd@fareham.gov.uk

Facilities: Mr Tony Hopkins Facilities Manager, Civic Offices, Civic Way, Fareham PO16 7AZ ☎ 01329 236100 ✉ thopkins@fareham.gov.uk

Finance: Mr Andy Wannell Director of Finance & Resources, Civic Offices, Civic Way, Fareham PO16 7AZ ☎ 01329 824620 🖷 01329 821541 ✉ awannell@fareham.gov.uk

Fleet Management: Ms Kitty Rose Refuse & Recycling Manager, Civic Offices, Civic Way, Fareham PO16 7AZ ☎ 01329 236100 ✉ krose@fareham.gov.uk

Grounds Maintenance: Mr Paul Doran Director of Environment, Civic Offices, Civic Way, Fareham PO16 7AZ ☎ 01329 824572 ✉ pdoran@fareham.gov.uk

Health and Safety: Mr Keith Perkins Health & Safety Officer, Civic Offices, Civic Way, Fareham PO16 7AZ ☎ 01329 236100 ✉ kperkins@fareham.gov.uk

Housing: Mr Martyn George, Director of Community, Civic Offices, Civic Way, Fareham PO16 7AZ ☎ 01329 824400 ✉ mgeorge@fareham.gov.uk

Legal: Mr Richard Ivory Acting Head of Legal & Democratic Services, Civic Offices, Civic Way, Fareham PO16 7AZ ☎ 02380 832794 ✉ richard.ivory@southampton.gov.uk

Leisure and Cultural Services: Mr Mark Bowler, Head of Leisure & Community, Civic Offices, Civic Way, Fareham PO16 7AZ ☎ 01329 824420 ✉ mbowler@fareham.gov.uk

Licensing: Ms Helen Spires Partnership Support Officer, Civic Offices, Civic Way, Fareham PO16 7AZ ☎ 01329 824411 ✉ hspires@fareham.gov.uk

Lottery Funding, Charity and Voluntary: Mr Mark Bowler, Head of Leisure & Community, Civic Offices, Civic Way, Fareham PO16 7AZ ☎ 01329 824420 ✉ mbowler@fareham.gov.uk

Member Services: Ms Leigh Usher, Head of Democratic Services, Civic Offices, Civic Way, Fareham PO16 7AZ ☎ 01329 236100 ✉ lusher@fareham.gov.uk

Parking: Mr K Wright Head of Community Safety & Enforcement, Civic Offices, Civic Way, Fareham PO16 7AZ ☎ 01329 236100 🖷 01329 824377 ✉ kwright@fareham.gov.uk

FAREHAM

Personnel / HR: Ms Sarah Robinson, Head of Personnel & ICT, Civic Offices, Civic Way, Fareham PO16 7AZ ☎ 01329 824564 ✉ srobinson@fareham.gov.uk

Planning: Mr Richard Jolley, Director of Planning & Environment, Civic Offices, Civic Way, Fareham PO16 7AZ ☎ 01329 824388 ✉ rjolley@fareham.gov.uk

Planning: Mr Lee Smith Head of Development Control, Civic Offices, Civic Way, Fareham PO16 7AZ ☎ 01329 236100 ✉ lsmith@fareham.gov.uk

Procurement: Mr Gary Jarvis, Procurement Officer, Civic Offices, Civic Way, Fareham PO16 7AZ ☎ 01329 824508 ✉ gjarvis@fareham.gov.uk

Recycling & Waste Minimisation: Mr Paul Doran Director of Environment, Civic Offices, Civic Way, Fareham PO16 7AZ ☎ 01329 824572 ✉ pdoran@fareham.gov.uk

Regeneration: Ms C Burnett Head of Planning Strategy & Regeneration, Civic Offices, Civic Way, Fareham PO16 7AZ ☎ 01329 236100 ✉ cburnett@fareham.gov.uk

Staff Training: Ms Sarah Robinson, Head of Personnel & ICT, Civic Offices, Civic Way, Fareham PO16 7AZ ☎ 01329 824564 ✉ srobinson@fareham.gov.uk

Street Scene: Mr Paul Doran Director of Environment, Civic Offices, Civic Way, Fareham PO16 7AZ ☎ 01329 824572 ✉ pdoran@fareham.gov.uk

Sustainable Communities: Mr Richard Jolley, Director of Planning & Environment, Civic Offices, Civic Way, Fareham PO16 7AZ ☎ 01329 824388 ✉ rjolley@fareham.gov.uk

Sustainable Development: Mr Richard Jolley, Director of Planning & Environment, Civic Offices, Civic Way, Fareham PO16 7AZ ☎ 01329 824388 ✉ rjolley@fareham.gov.uk

Town Centre: Mr Mark Bowler, Head of Leisure & Community, Civic Offices, Civic Way, Fareham PO16 7AZ ☎ 01329 824420 ✉ mbowler@fareham.gov.uk

Traffic Management: Mr C Oldham Traffic & Design Manager, Civic Offices, Civic Way, Fareham PO16 7AZ ☎ 01329 236100 ✉ coldham@fareham.gov.uk

Transport: Ms Kitty Rose Refuse & Recycling Manager, Civic Offices, Civic Way, Fareham PO16 7AZ ☎ 01329 236100 ✉ krose@fareham.gov.uk

Transport Planner: Mr Richard Burton Principal Transport Planner, Civic Offices, Civic Way, Fareham PO16 7AZ ☎ 01329 236100 ✉ rburton@fareham.gov.uk

Waste Collection and Disposal: Ms Kitty Rose Refuse & Recycling Manager, Civic Offices, Civic Way, Fareham PO16 7AZ ☎ 01329 236100 ✉ krose@fareham.gov.uk

Waste Management: Mr Paul Doran Director of Environment, Civic Offices, Civic Way, Fareham PO16 7AZ ☎ 01329 824572 ✉ pdoran@fareham.gov.uk

Children's Play Areas: Mrs S Woodbridge Public & Open Spaces Manager, Civic Offices, Civic Way, Fareham PO16 7AZ ☎ 01329 236100 ✉ swoodbridge@fareham.gov.uk

COUNCILLORS

***Mayor* Ford**, Michael (CON - Warsash)
mford@fareham.gov.uk

***Deputy Mayor* Hockley**, Connie (CON - Titchfield)
chockley@fareham.gov.uk

***Leader of the Council* Woodward**, Sean (CON - Sarisbury)
swoodward@fareham.gov.uk

***Deputy Leader of the Council* Cartwright**, Trevor (CON - Warsash)
tcartwright@fareham.gov.uk

Bayford, Susan (CON - Locks Heath)
sbayford@fareham.gov.uk

Bayford, Brian (CON - Park Gate)
bbayford@fareham.gov.uk

Bell, Susan (CON - Portchester West)
sbell@fareham.gov.uk

Bryant, John (CON - Fareham North)
jbryant@fareham.gov.uk

Bryant, Pamela (CON - Fareham North)
pbryant@fareham.gov.uk

Davies, Peter (CON - Fareham North West)
pdavies@fareham.gov.uk

Ellerton, Marian (CON - Park Gate)
mellerton@fareham.gov.uk

Englefield, Jack (IND - Titchfield Common)
jenglefield@fareham.gov.uk

Evans, Keith (CON - Locks Heath)
kevans@fareham.gov.uk

Fazackarley, Geoff (LD - Portchester East)
gfazackarley@fareham.gov.uk

Gregory, Nick (IND - Fareham West)
ngregory@fareham.gov.uk

Harper, Tiffany (CON - Titchfield)
tharper@fareham.gov.uk

Howard, Trevor (CON - Fareham South)
thoward@fareham.gov.uk

Keeble, Leslie (CON - Fareham West)
lkeeble@fareham.gov.uk

Knight, Tim (CON - Hill Head)
tknight@fareham.gov.uk

Mandry, Arthur (CON - Hill Head)
amandry@fareham.gov.uk

Mandry, Kay (CON - Stubbington)
kmandry@fareham.gov.uk

Norris, David (LD - Portchester East)
dnorris@fareham.gov.uk

Pankhurst, Sarah (CON - Titchfield Common)
spankhurt@fareham.gov.uk

Price, Roger (LD - Portchester East)
rprice@fareham.gov.uk

Steadman, Dennis (CON - Fareham South)
dsteadman@fareham.gov.uk

Swanbrow, David (CON - Sarisbury)
dswanbrow@fareham.gov.uk

Trott, Katrina (LD - Fareham East)
ktrott@fareham.gov.uk

Walker, Nick (CON - Portchester West)
nwalker@fareham.gov.uk

Whittingham, David (CON - Fareham North West)
dwhittingham@fareham.gov.uk

Whittle, Paul (LD - Fareham East)
pwhittle@fareham.gov.uk

Wood, Christopher (UKIP - Stubbington)
cwood@fareham.gov.uk

POLITICAL COMPOSITION
CON: 23, LD: 5, IND: 2, UKIP: 1

COMMITTEE CHAIRS
Audit & Governance: Mr Tim Knight

Licensing & Regulatory: Mrs Pamela Bryant

Planning: Mr Nick Walker

Fenland D

Fenland District Council, Fenland Hall, County Road, March PE15 8NQ
☎ 01354 654321 🖷 01354 622259 ✉ info@fenland.gov.uk
🖳 www.fenland.gov.uk

FACTS AND FIGURES
Parliamentary Constituencies: Cambridgeshire North East
EU Constituencies: Eastern
Election Frequency: Elections are of whole council

PRINCIPAL OFFICERS
Chief Executive: Mr Paul Medd, Chief Executive, Fenland Hall, County Road, March PE15 8NQ ☎ 01354 622303
✉ paulmedd@fenland.gov.uk

Architect, Building / Property Services: Mr Gary Garford, Corporate Director, Fenland Hall, County Road, March PE15 8NQ
☎ 01354 622373 ✉ garygarford@fenland.gov.uk

Best Value: Ms Carol Pilson Corporate Director, Fenland Hall, County Road, March PE15 8NQ ☎ 01354 622360
✉ cpilson@fenland.gov.uk

Building Control: Mr Rob Bridge Corporate Director, Fenland Hall, County Road, March PE15 8NQ ☎ 01354 622201
✉ robbridge@fenland.gov.uk

PR / Communications: Ms Carol Pilson Corporate Director, Fenland Hall, County Road, March PE15 8NQ ☎ 01354 622360
✉ cpilson@fenland.gov.uk

Community Planning: Mr Gary Garford, Corporate Director, Fenland Hall, County Road, March PE15 8NQ ☎ 01354 622373
✉ garygarford@fenland.gov.uk

Community Safety: Mr Richard Cassidy, Corporate Director, Fenland Hall, County Road, March PE15 8NQ ☎ 01354 622300
✉ richardcassidy@fenland.gov.uk

Computer Management: Mr Rob Bridge Corporate Director, Fenland Hall, County Road, March PE15 8NQ ☎ 01354 622201
✉ robbridge@fenland.gov.uk

Computer Management: Mr Geoff Kent, Head of Income & ICT, Fenland Hall, County Road, March PE15 8NQ ☎ 01354 654321
✉ gkent@fenland.gov.uk

Customer Service: Mr Rob Bridge Corporate Director, Fenland Hall, County Road, March PE15 8NQ ☎ 01354 622201
✉ robbridge@fenland.gov.uk

Economic Development: Mr Gary Garford, Corporate Director, Fenland Hall, County Road, March PE15 8NQ ☎ 01354 622373
✉ garygarford@fenland.gov.uk

E-Government: Mr Rob Bridge Corporate Director, Fenland Hall, County Road, March PE15 8NQ ☎ 01354 622201
✉ robbridge@fenland.gov.uk

Electoral Registration: Mr Paul Medd, Chief Executive, Fenland Hall, County Road, March PE15 8NQ ☎ 01354 622303
✉ paulmedd@fenland.gov.uk

Emergency Planning: Mr David Vincent Health, Safety & Emergency Planning Manager, Fenland Hall, County Road, March PE15 8NQ ☎ 01354 622353 ✉ dvincent@fenland.gov.uk

Energy Management: Mr Richard Cassidy, Corporate Director, Fenland Hall, County Road, March PE15 8NQ ☎ 01354 622300
✉ richardcassidy@fenland.gov.uk

Environmental / Technical Services: Mr Richard Cassidy, Corporate Director, Fenland Hall, County Road, March PE15 8NQ
☎ 01354 622300 ✉ richardcassidy@fenland.gov.uk

Environmental Health: Mr Richard Cassidy, Corporate Director, Fenland Hall, County Road, March PE15 8NQ ☎ 01354 622300
✉ richardcassidy@fenland.gov.uk

Estates, Property & Valuation: Mr Gary Garford, Corporate Director, Fenland Hall, County Road, March PE15 8NQ
☎ 01354 622373 ✉ garygarford@fenland.gov.uk

Facilities: Mr Gary Garford, Corporate Director, Fenland Hall, County Road, March PE15 8NQ ☎ 01354 622373
✉ garygarford@fenland.gov.uk

FENLAND

Finance: Mr Rob Bridge Corporate Director, Fenland Hall, County Road, March PE15 8NQ ☎ 01354 622201 ✉ robbridge@fenland.gov.uk

Fleet Management: Mr Richard Cassidy, Corporate Director, Fenland Hall, County Road, March PE15 8NQ ☎ 01354 622300 ✉ richardcassidy@fenland.gov.uk

Grounds Maintenance: Mr Richard Cassidy, Corporate Director, Fenland Hall, County Road, March PE15 8NQ ☎ 01354 622300 ✉ richardcassidy@fenland.gov.uk

Health and Safety: Mr Richard Cassidy, Corporate Director, Fenland Hall, County Road, March PE15 8NQ ☎ 01354 622300 ✉ richardcassidy@fenland.gov.uk

Home Energy Conservation: Mr Richard Cassidy, Corporate Director, Fenland Hall, County Road, March PE15 8NQ ☎ 01354 622300 ✉ richardcassidy@fenland.gov.uk

Housing: Mr Richard Cassidy, Corporate Director, Fenland Hall, County Road, March PE15 8NQ ☎ 01354 622300 ✉ richardcassidy@fenland.gov.uk

Local Area Agreement: Ms Carol Pilson Corporate Director, Fenland Hall, County Road, March PE15 8NQ ☎ 01354 622360 ✉ cpilson@fenland.gov.uk

Legal: Ms Anna Goodall Head of Governance & Legal, Fenland Hall, County Road, March PE15 8NQ ☎ 01354 622357 ✉ agoodall@fenland.gov.uk

Leisure and Cultural Services: Mr Richard Cassidy, Corporate Director, Fenland Hall, County Road, March PE15 8NQ ☎ 01354 622300 ✉ richardcassidy@fenland.gov.uk

Licensing: Mr Richard Cassidy, Corporate Director, Fenland Hall, County Road, March PE15 8NQ ☎ 01354 622300 ✉ richardcassidy@fenland.gov.uk

Lottery Funding, Charity and Voluntary: Mr Richard Cassidy, Corporate Director, Fenland Hall, County Road, March PE15 8NQ ☎ 01354 622300 ✉ richardcassidy@fenland.gov.uk

Member Services: Mr Paul Medd, Chief Executive, Fenland Hall, County Road, March PE15 8NQ ☎ 01354 622303 ✉ paulmedd@fenland.gov.uk

Parking: Mr Gary Garford, Corporate Director, Fenland Hall, County Road, March PE15 8NQ ☎ 01354 622373 ✉ garygarford@fenland.gov.uk

Partnerships: Mr Richard Cassidy, Corporate Director, Fenland Hall, County Road, March PE15 8NQ ☎ 01354 622300 ✉ richardcassidy@fenland.gov.uk

Personnel / HR: Mrs Sam Anthony Head of HR & OD, Fenland Hall, County Road, March PE15 8NQ ☎ 01354 654321 ✉ santhony@fenland.gov.uk

Planning: Mr Rob Bridge Corporate Director, Fenland Hall, County Road, March PE15 8NQ ☎ 01354 622201 ✉ robbridge@fenland.gov.uk

Procurement: Mr Rob Bridge Corporate Director, Fenland Hall, County Road, March PE15 8NQ ☎ 01354 622201 ✉ robbridge@fenland.gov.uk

Recycling & Waste Minimisation: Mr Richard Cassidy, Corporate Director, Fenland Hall, County Road, March PE15 8NQ ☎ 01354 622300 ✉ richardcassidy@fenland.gov.uk

Regeneration: Mr Gary Garford, Corporate Director, Fenland Hall, County Road, March PE15 8NQ ☎ 01354 622373 ✉ garygarford@fenland.gov.uk

Staff Training: Mrs Sam Anthony Head of HR & OD, Fenland Hall, County Road, March PE15 8NQ ☎ 01354 654321 ✉ santhony@fenland.gov.uk

Street Scene: Mr Richard Cassidy, Corporate Director, Fenland Hall, County Road, March PE15 8NQ ☎ 01354 622300 ✉ richardcassidy@fenland.gov.uk

Sustainable Communities: Mr Richard Cassidy, Corporate Director, Fenland Hall, County Road, March PE15 8NQ ☎ 01354 622300 ✉ richardcassidy@fenland.gov.uk

Tourism: Mr Richard Cassidy, Corporate Director, Fenland Hall, County Road, March PE15 8NQ ☎ 01354 622300 ✉ richardcassidy@fenland.gov.uk

Town Centre: Mr Gary Garford, Corporate Director, Fenland Hall, County Road, March PE15 8NQ ☎ 01354 622373 ✉ garygarford@fenland.gov.uk

Transport Planner: Mr Gary Garford, Corporate Director, Fenland Hall, County Road, March PE15 8NQ ☎ 01354 622373 ✉ garygarford@fenland.gov.uk

Waste Collection and Disposal: Mr Richard Cassidy, Corporate Director, Fenland Hall, County Road, March PE15 8NQ ☎ 01354 622300 ✉ richardcassidy@fenland.gov.uk

Waste Management: Mr Richard Cassidy, Corporate Director, Fenland Hall, County Road, March PE15 8NQ ☎ 01354 622300 ✉ richardcassidy@fenland.gov.uk

COUNCILLORS

***Vice-Chair* Cox**, Carol (CON - Clarkson - Wisbech)
ccox@fenland.gov.uk

***Leader of the Council* Clark**, John (CON - March East)
jclark@fenland.gov.uk

Bligh, Sarah (CON - Parson Drove and Wisbech St Mary)
sbligh@fenland.gov.uk

Boden, Chris (CON - Bassenhally - Whittlesey)
cboden@fenland.gov.uk

Booth, Gavin (O - Parson Drove and Wisbech St Mary)
gbooth@fenland.gov.uk

Bucknor, Michael (IND - Waterlees - Village)
mbucknor@fenland.gov.uk

Bucknor, Virginia (IND - Waterlees - Village)
vbucknor@fenland.gov.uk

Buckton, Mark (CON - Manea)
mbuckton@fenland.gov.uk

Butcher, Ralph (CON - Benwick, Coates and Estrea)
rbutcher@fenland.gov.uk

Clark, Sam (CON - Roman Bank - Wisbech)
samclark@fenland.gov.uk

Connor, David (CON - Doddington & Wimblington)
dconnor@fenland.gov.uk

Cornwell, Mike (CON - March North)
mcornwell@fenland.gov.uk

Count, Steve (CON - March North)
scount@fenland.gov.uk

Court, Stephen (CON - March North)
scourt@fenland.gov.uk

Davis, Maureen (CON - Doddington & Wimblington)
mdavis@fenland.gov.uk

French, Jan (CON - March West)
jfrench@fenland.gov.uk

Garratt, Steve (CON - Lattersey - Whittlesey)
sgarratt@fenland.gov.uk

Green, David (CON - Birch - Chatteris)
davidgreen@fenland.gov.uk

Hay, Anne (CON - The Mills - Chatteris)
ahay@fenland.gov.uk

Hodgson, David (CON - Staithe - Wisbech)
dhodgson@fenland.gov.uk

Hoy, Samantha (CON - Hill - Wisbech)
shoy@fenland.gov.uk

Humphrey, Michael (CON - Roman Bank - Wisbech)
mhumphrey@fenland.gov.uk

King, Simon (CON - Hill - Wisbech)
sking@fenland.gov.uk

Laws, Dee (CON - Stonald)
dlaws@fenland.gov.uk

Mason, David (CON - St Andrews - Whittlesey)
dmason@fenland.gov.uk

Mayor, Kay (CON - Bassenhally - Whittlesey)
kaymayor@fenland.gov.uk

Miscandlon, Alex (CON - Benwick, Coates and Eastrea)
amiscandlon@fenland.gov.uk

Murphy, Peter (CON - Wenneye - Chatteris)
pmurphy@fenland.gov.uk

Newell, Florence (CON - Slade Lode - Chatteris)
fnewell@fenland.gov.uk

Oliver, David (CON - Peckover - Wisbech)
doliver@fenland.gov.uk

Owen, Kit (CON - March West)
kowen@fenland.gov.uk

Pugh, Andrew (CON - March East)
apugh@fenland.gov.uk

Seaton, Christopher (CON - Roman Bank - Wisbech)
cseaton@fenland.gov.uk

Skoulding, Robert (IND - March West)
rskoulding@fenland.gov.uk

Sutton, Will (CON - Elm and Christchurch)
wsutton@fenland.gov.uk

Tanfield, Michelle (CON - Elm and Christchurch)
mtanfield@fenland.gov.uk

Tibbs, Garry (CON - Kirkgate - Wisbech)
gtibbs@fenland.gov.uk

Tierney, Steve (CON - Medworth - Wisbech)
stierney@fenland.gov.uk

Yeulett, Fred (CON - March East)
fyeulett@fenland.gov.uk

POLITICAL COMPOSITION

CON: 35, IND: 3, O: 1

COMMITTEE CHAIRS

Corporate Governance: Mr Kit Owen

Licensing: Mr Michael Humphrey

Planning: Mr Alex Miscandlon

Fermanagh & Omagh District Council N

Fermanagh & Omagh District Council, Fermanagh District Council, Townhall, 2 Townhall Street, Enniskillen BT74 7BA
☎ 028 6632 5050 fdc@fermanagh.gov.uk ww.fermanaghomagh.com

PRINCIPAL OFFICERS

Chief Executive: Mr Brendan Hegarty Chief Executive, Fermanagh District Council, Townhall, 2 Townhall Street, Enniskillen BT74 7BA brendan.hegarty@fermanaghomagh.com

Senior Management: Ms Thelma Browne Lead Officer for HR & OD, Fermanagh District Council, Townhall, 2 Townhall Street, Enniskillen BT74 7BA

Senior Management: Mr Robert Gibson Director of Community, Health & Leisure, Fermanagh District Council, Townhall, 2 Townhall Street, Enniskillen BT74 7BA
robert.gibson@fermanaghomagh.com

Senior Management: Ms Catherine Leonard Lead Officer for Finance & the Convergence of IT Systems, Fermanagh District Council, Townhall, 2 Townhall Street, Enniskillen BT74 7BA
catherine.leonard@fermanaghomagh.com

Senior Management: Ms Joan McCaffrey Director of Corporate Services & Governance, Fermanagh District Council, Townhall, 2 Townhall Street, Enniskillen BT74 7BA
joan.mccaffrey@fermanaghomagh.com

Senior Management: Ms Alison McCullagh Director of Regeneration & Planning, Fermanagh District Council, Townhall, 2 Townhall Street, Enniskillen BT74 7BA
alison.mccullagh@fermanaghomagh.com

Senior Management: Mr Kevin O'Gara Director of Environment & Place, Fermanagh District Council, Townhall, 2 Townhall Street, Enniskillen BT74 7BA kevin.ogara@fermanaghomagh.com

FERMANAGH & OMAGH DISTRICT COUNCIL

Community Planning: Mr Robert Gibson Director of Community, Health & Leisure, Fermanagh District Council, Townhall, 2 Townhall Street, Enniskillen BT74 7BA
robert.gibson@fermanaghomagh.com

Community Planning: Ms Sonya McAnulla Community Planning Project Officer, Fermanagh District Council, Townhall, 2 Townhall Street, Enniskillen BT74 7BA
sonya.mcanulla@fermanaghomagh.com

Computer Management: Mr Donal Cox ICT Project Manager, Fermanagh District Council, Townhall, 2 Townhall Street, Enniskillen BT74 7BA donal.cox@fermanaghomagh.com

Corporate Services: Ms Joan McCaffrey Director of Corporate Services & Governance, Fermanagh District Council, Townhall, 2 Townhall Street, Enniskillen BT74 7BA
joan.mccaffrey@fermanaghomagh.com

Environmental / Technical Services: Mr Kevin O'Gara Director of Environment & Place, Fermanagh District Council, Townhall, 2 Townhall Street, Enniskillen BT74 7BA
kevin.ogara@fermanaghomagh.com

Environmental Health: Mr Kevin O'Gara Director of Environment & Place, Fermanagh District Council, Townhall, 2 Townhall Street, Enniskillen BT74 7BA kevin.ogara@fermanaghomagh.com

Finance: Ms Catherine Leonard Lead Officer for Finance & the Convergence of IT Systems, Fermanagh District Council, Townhall, 2 Townhall Street, Enniskillen BT74 7BA
catherine.leonard@fermanaghomagh.com

Leisure and Cultural Services: Mr Robert Gibson Director of Community, Health & Leisure, Fermanagh District Council, Townhall, 2 Townhall Street, Enniskillen BT74 7BA
robert.gibson@fermanaghomagh.com

Personnel / HR: Ms Thelma Browne Lead Officer for HR & OD, Fermanagh District Council, Townhall, 2 Townhall Street, Enniskillen BT74 7BA

Planning: Ms Alison McCullagh Director of Regeneration & Planning, Fermanagh District Council, Townhall, 2 Townhall Street, Enniskillen BT74 7BA
alison.mccullagh@fermanaghomagh.com

Procurement: Ms Nuala Conlan Procurement Manager, Fermanagh District Council, Townhall, 2 Townhall Street, Enniskillen BT74 7BA nuala.conlan@fermanaghomagh.com

Regeneration: Ms Alison McCullagh Director of Regeneration & Planning, Fermanagh District Council, Townhall, 2 Townhall Street, Enniskillen BT74 7BA alison.mccullagh@fermanaghomagh.com

COUNCILLORS

***Chair* O'Reilly**, Thomas (SF - Erne East)
thomas.oreilly@fermanaghomagh.com

***Vice-Chair* Robinson**, Paul (DUP - Erne East)
paul.robinson@fermanaghomagh.com

Baird, Alex (UUP - Erne West)
alex.baird@fermanaghomagh.com

Barton, Rosemary (UUP - Erne North)
rosemary.barton@fermanaghomagh.com

Buchanan, Mark (DUP - West Tyrone)
mark.buchanan@fermanaghomagh.com

Campbell, Glenn (SF - West Tyrone)
glenn.campbell@fermanaghomagh.com

Clarke, Sean (SF - Mid Tyrone)
sean.clarke@fermanaghomagh.com

Coyle, John (SDLP - Erne North)
john.coyle@fermanaghomagh.com

Coyle, Debbie (SF - Enniskillen)
debbie.coyle@fermanaghomagh.com

Deehan, Josephine (SDLP - Omagh)
josephine.deehan@fermanaghomagh.com

Doherty, Barry (SF - Erne West)
barry.doherty@fermanaghomagh.com

Donnelly, Sean (SF - Mid Tyrone)
sean.donnelly@fermanaghomagh.com

Donnelly, Frankie (SF - West Tyrone)
frankie.donnelly@fermanaghomagh.com

Donnelly, Joanne (SDLP - Omagh)
joanne.donnelly@fermanaghomagh.com

Elliott, Keith (DUP - Enniskillen)
keith.elliott@fermanaghomagh.com

Farrell, Raymond (UUP - Erne North)
raymond.farrell@fermanghomagh.com

Feely, John (SF - Erne North)
john.feely@fermanaghomagh.com

Feely, Anthony (SF - Erne West)
anthony.feely@fermanaghomagh.com

Fitzgerald, Anne Marie (SF - Mid Tyrone)
annemarie.fitzgerald@fermanaghomagh.com

Gallagher, Brendan (SDLP - Erne West)
brendan.gallagher@fermanaghomagh.com

Garrity, Mary (SDLP - West Tyrone)
mary.garrity@fermanaghomagh.com

Greene, Sheamus (SF - Erne East)
sheamus.greene@fermanaghomagh.com

Irvine, Robert (UUP - Enniskillen)
robert.irvine@fermanaghomagh.com

Maguire, Tommy (SF - Enniskillen)
tommy.maguire@fermanaghomagh.com

Mahon, David (DUP - Erne North)
david.mahon@fermanaghomagh.com

McAnespy, Sorcha (SF - Omagh)
sorcha.mcanespy@fermanaghomagh.com

McCaffrey, Brian (SF - Erne East)
brian.mccaffrey@fermanaghomagh.com

McCann, Stephen (SF - West Tyrone)
stephen.mccann@fermanaghomagh.com

McColgan, Marty (SF - Omagh)
marty.mccolgan@fermanaghomagh.com

McNally, Barry (SF - Mid Tyrone)
bary.mcnally@fermanaghomagh.com

McPhillips, Richie (SDLP - Erne East)
richie.mcphillips@fermanaghomagh.com

Rainey, Allan (UUP - West Tyrone)
allan.rainey@fermanaghomagh.com

Rogers, Patricia (SDLP - Enniskillen)
patricia.rogers@fermanaghomagh.com

Shields, Rosemarie (SDLP - Mid Tyrone)
rosemarie.shields@fermanaghomagh.com

Smyth, Chris (UUP - Omagh)
chris.smyth@fermanaghomagh.com

Swift, Bernice (IND - Erne West)
bernice.swift@fermanaghomagh.com

Thompson, Errol (DUP - Omagh)
errol.thompson@fermanaghomagh.com

Thornton, Howard (UUP - Enniskillen)
howard.thornton@fermanaghomagh.com

Warrington, Victor (UUP - Erne East)
victor.warrington@fermanaghomagh.com

Wilson, Bert (UUP - Mid Tyrone)
bert.wilson@fermanaghomagh.com

POLITICAL COMPOSITION
SF: 17, UUP: 9, SDLP: 8, DUP: 5, IND: 1

Fife S

Fife Council, Fife House, North Street, Glenrothes KY7 5LT
☎ 0345 155 0000 ✉ fife.council@fife.gov.uk 🖳 www.fifedirect.org.uk

FACTS AND FIGURES
Parliamentary Constituencies: Dunfermline and West Fife, Fife North East, Glenrothes, Kirkcaldy and Cowdenbeath
EU Constituencies: Scotland
Election Frequency: Elections are of whole council

PRINCIPAL OFFICERS
Chief Executive: Mr Steve Grimmond, Chief Executive, Fife House, North Street, Glenrothes KY7 5LT ☎ 03451 555555 Ext 442332 ✉ steve.grimmond@fife.gov.uk

Senior Management: Mr David Heaney Divisional General Manager, Fife House, North Street, Glenrothes KY7 5LT

Senior Management: Ms Julie Paterson Divisional General Manager, Fife House, North Street, Glenrothes KY7 5LT

Senior Management: Ms Sandy Riddell Director of Health & Social Care, Fife House, North Street, Glenrothes KY7 5LT

Architect, Building / Property Services: Mr Alan Paul Senior Manager of Property Services, Bankhead Central, Bankhead Park, Glenrothes KY7 6GH ☎ 03451 555555 Ext 440464 ✉ alan.paul@fife.gov.uk

Best Value: Mr Michael Enston, Executive Director, Fife House, North Street, Glenrothes KY7 5LT ☎ 03451 555555 Ext 441198 ✉ michael.enston@fife.gov.uk

Building Control: Mr Robin Presswood Head of Economy, Planning & Employability Services, 3rd Floor, Kingdom House, Kingdom Avenue, Glenrothes KY7 5LY ☎ 03451 555555 Ext 442260 ✉ robin.presswood@fife.gov.uk

Catering Services: Mr Ken Gourlay Head of Assets, Transportation & Environment, Ground Floor, Bankhead Central, Bankhead Park, Glenrothes KY7 6GH ☎ 03451 555555 Ext 440473 ✉ ken.gourlay@fife.gov.uk

Community Planning: Mr Michael Enston, Executive Director, Fife House, North Street, Glenrothes KY7 5LT ☎ 03451 555555 Ext 441198 ✉ michael.enston@fife.gov.uk

Community Safety: Mr Michael Enston, Executive Director, Fife House, North Street, Glenrothes KY7 5LT ☎ 03451 555555 Ext 441198 ✉ michael.enston@fife.gov.uk

Computer Management: Mr Charlie Anderson Head of I.T. Services, 6th Floor, Fife House, North Street, Glenrothes KY7 5LT ☎ 03451 555555 Ext 440557 ✉ charlie.anderson@fife.gov.uk

Consumer Protection and Trading Standards: Mr Roy Stewart Senior Manager - Protective Services, Kingdom House, Kingdom Avenue, Glenrothes KY7 5LY ☎ 03451 555555 Ext 450466 ✉ roy.steward@fife.gov.uk

Contracts: Mr John Cosgrove Head of Procurement, Fife House, North Street, Glenrothes KY7 5LT ☎ 03451 555555 Ext 445926 ✉ John.Cosgrove@fife.gov.uk

Corporate Services: Mr Brian Livingston Executive Director of Finance & Resources including Treasury, Pensions & Pension Investments, Fife House, North Street, Glenrothes KY7 5LT ☎ 03451 555555 Ext 440972 ✉ Brian.Livingston@fife.gov.uk

Customer Service: Ms Lynne Harvie Head of Customer Service Improvement, Fife House, North Street, Glenrothes KY7 5LT ☎ 03451 555555 Ext 444263 ✉ lynne.harvie@fife.gov.uk

Direct Labour: Mr Bob McLellan, Head of Transportation & Environmental Services, First Floor, Bankhead Central, Bankhead Park, Glenrothes KY7 6GH ☎ 03451 555555 Ext 444424 ✉ bob.mclellan@fife.gov.uk

Economic Development: Mr Robin Presswood Head of Economy, Planning & Employability Services, 3rd Floor, Kingdom House, Kingdom Avenue, Glenrothes KY7 5LY ☎ 03451 555555 Ext 442260 ✉ robin.presswood@fife.gov.uk

Education: Mr Craig Munro Executive Director - Children's Services, 4th Floor, Fife House, North Street, Glenrothes KY7 5LT ☎ 03451 555555Ext 444219 ✉ craig.munro@fife.gov.uk

E-Government: Mr Charlie Anderson Head of I.T. Services, 6th Floor, Fife House, North Street, Glenrothes KY7 5LT ☎ 03451 555555 Ext 440557 ✉ charlie.anderson@fife.gov.uk

FIFE

Electoral Registration: Mr Lawrence Cooper Depute Electoral Registration Officer & Service Manager, Fife House, North Street, Glenrothes KY7 5TL 🖱 Lawrence.Cooper@fife.gov.uk

Emergency Planning: Mrs Lori Hutcheson Team Manager, 1st Floor, Fife House, North Street, Glenrothes KY7 5LT ☎ 03451 555555 Ext 442342 🖱 lori.hutcheson@fife.gov.uk

Energy Management: Mr Ken Gourlay Head of Asset & Facilities Management Services, Ground Floor, Bankhead Central, Bankhead Park, Glenrothes KY7 6GH ☎ 03451 555555 Ext 440473 🖱 ken.gourlay@fife.gov.uk

Environmental / Technical Services: Mr Roddy Mann Senior Manager - Environmental Operations, 1st Floor, Bankhead Central, Bankhead Park, Glenrothes KY7 6GH ☎ 03451 555555 Ext 493604 🖱 roddy.mann@fife.gov.uk

Environmental Health: Mr Roy Stewart Senior Manager - Protective Services, Kingdom House, Kingdom Avenue, Glenrothes KY7 5LY ☎ 03451 555555Ext 450466 🖱 roy.steward@fife.gov.uk

Estates, Property & Valuation: Mr Alan Paul Senior Manager of Property Services, Bankhead Central, Bankhead Park, Glenrothes KY7 6GH ☎ 03451 555555 Ext 440464 🖱 alan.paul@fife.gov.uk

European Liaison: Mr Michael Enston, Executive Director, Fife House, North Street, Glenrothes KY7 5LT ☎ 03451 555555 Ext 441198 🖱 michael.enston@fife.gov.uk

Events Manager: Linda Temple Cultural Partnership & Event Strategy Manager, Main Gate Lodge, Kirkcaldy KY2 5LZ ☎ 03451 555555 Ext 493296 🖱 linda.temple@fife.gov.uk

Facilities: Mr Ken Gourlay Head of Asset & Facilities Management Services, Bankhead Central, Bankhead Park, Glenrothes KY7 6GH ☎ 03451 555555 Ext 440473 🖱 ken.gourlay@fife.gov.uk

Finance: Mr Brian Livingston Executive Director of Finance & Resources including Treasury, Pensions & Pension Investments, Fife House, North Street, Glenrothes KY7 5LT ☎ 03451 555555 Ext 440972 🖱 Brian.Livingston@fife.gov.uk

Treasury: Mr Brian Livingston Executive Director of Finance & Resources including Treasury, Pensions & Pension Investments, Fife House, North Street, Glenrothes KY7 5LT ☎ 03451 555555 Ext 440972 🖱 Brian.Livingston@fife.gov.uk

Pensions: Mr Brian Livingston Executive Director of Finance & Resources including Treasury, Pensions & Pension Investments, Fife House, North Street, Glenrothes KY7 5LT ☎ 03451 555555 Ext 440972 🖱 Brian.Livingston@fife.gov.uk

Fleet Management: Mr Bob McLellan, Head of Transportation & Environmental Services, First Floor, Bankhead Central, Bankhead Park, Glenrothes KY7 6GH ☎ 03451 555555 Ext 444424 🖱 bob.mclellan@fife.gov.uk

Grounds Maintenance: Mr Grant Ward Head of Leisure & Cultural Services, Rothesay House, Rothesay Place, Glenrothes KY5 5PQ ☎ 03451 555555 Ext 444145 🖱 grant.ward@fife.gov.uk

Health and Safety: Mr Michael Enston, Executive Director, Fife House, North Street, Glenrothes KY7 5LT ☎ 03451 555555 Ext 441198 🖱 michael.enston@fife.gov.uk

Highways: Mr Bob McLellan, Head of Transportation & Environmental Services, First Floor, Bankhead Central, Bankhead Park, Glenrothes KY7 6GH ☎ 03451 555555 Ext 444424 🖱 bob.mclellan@fife.gov.uk

Home Energy Conservation: Mr John Mills Head of Housing Services, Rothesay House, North Street, Glenrothes KY5 5LT ☎ 03451 555555 Ext 480269 🖱 john.mills@fife.gov.uk

Housing: Mr John Mills Head of Housing Services, Rothesay House, North Street, Glenrothes KY5 5LT ☎ 03451 555555 Ext 480269 🖱 john.mills@fife.gov.uk

Housing Maintenance: Mr John Mills Head of Housing Services, Rothesay House, North Street, Glenrothes KY5 5LT ☎ 03451 555555 Ext 480269 🖱 john.mills@fife.gov.uk

Legal: Mr Brian Livingston Executive Director of Finance & Resources including Treasury, Pensions & Pension Investments, Fife House, North Street, Glenrothes KY7 5LT ☎ 03451 555555 Ext 440972 🖱 Brian.Livingston@fife.gov.uk

Licensing: Mr Brian Livingston Executive Director of Finance & Resources including Treasury, Pensions & Pension Investments, Fife House, North Street, Glenrothes KY7 5LT ☎ 03451 555555 Ext 440972 🖱 Brian.Livingston@fife.gov.uk

Lighting: Mr Bob McLellan, Head of Transportation & Environmental Services, First Floor, Bankhead Central, Bankhead Park, Glenrothes KY7 6GH ☎ 03451 555555 Ext 444424 🖱 bob.mclellan@fife.gov.uk

Member Services: Mr Brian Livingston Executive Director of Finance & Resources including Treasury, Pensions & Pension Investments, Fife House, North Street, Glenrothes KY7 5LT ☎ 03451 555555 Ext 440972 🖱 Brian.Livingston@fife.gov.uk

Parking: Mr Bob McLellan, Head of Transportation & Environmental Services, First Floor, Bankhead Central, Bankhead Park, Glenrothes KY7 6GH ☎ 03451 555555 Ext 444424 🖱 bob.mclellan@fife.gov.uk

Partnerships: Mr Michael Enston, Executive Director, Fife House, North Street, Glenrothes KY7 5LT ☎ 03451 555555 Ext 441198 🖱 michael.enston@fife.gov.uk

Personnel / HR: Ms Sharon McKenzie Head of Human Resources, Fife House, North Street, Glenrothes KY7 5LT ☎ 03451 555555 Ext 444265 🖱 sharon.mckenzie@fife.gov.uk

Planning: Mr Robin Presswood Head of Economy, Planning & Employability Services, 3rd Floor, Kingdom House, Kingdom Avenue, Glenrothes KY7 5LY ☎ 03451 555555 Ext 442260 🖱 robin.presswood@fife.gov.uk

Procurement: Mr John Cosgrove Head of Procurement, Fife House, North Street, Glenrothes KY7 5LT ☎ 03451 555555 Ext 445926 🖱 John.Cosgrove@fife.gov.uk

Public Libraries: Ms Heather Stuart Chief Executive Officer - Fife Cultural Trust, Libraries & Museums HQ, 16 East Fergus Place, Kirkcaldy KY1 1XR ☎ 03451 555555 Ext 472796 🖱 heather.stuart@fife.gov.uk

Recycling & Waste Minimisation: Mr Roddy Mann Senior Manager - Environmental Operations, 1st Floor, Bankhead Central, Bankhead Park, Glenrothes KY7 6GH ☎ 03451 555555 Ext 493604 🖱 roddy.mann@fife.gov.uk

Road Safety: Mr Bob McLellan, Head of Transportation & Environmental Services, First Floor, Bankhead Central, Bankhead Park, Glenrothes KY7 6GH ☎ 03451 555555 Ext 444424 🖱 bob.mclellan@fife.gov.uk

Social Services: Ms Sandy Riddell Director of Health & Social Care, Fife House, North Street, Glenrothes KY7 5LT

Social Services (Adult): Ms Sandy Riddell Director of Health & Social Care, Fife House, North Street, Glenrothes KY7 5LT

Social Services (Children): Ms Sandy Riddell Director of Health & Social Care, Fife House, North Street, Glenrothes KY7 5LT

Staff Training: Mr Brian Livingston Executive Director of Finance & Resources including Treasury, Pensions & Pension Investments, Fife House, North Street, Glenrothes KY7 5LT ☎ 03451 555555 Ext 440972 🖱 Brian.Livingston@fife.gov.uk

Sustainable Development: Mr Ken Gourlay Head of Assets, Transportation & Environment, Ground Floor, Bankhead Central, Bankhead Park, Glenrothes KY7 6GH ☎ 03451 555555 Ext 440473 🖱 ken.gourlay@fife.gov.uk

Traffic Management: Mr Bob McLellan, Head of Transportation & Environmental Services, First Floor, Bankhead Central, Bankhead Park, Glenrothes KY7 6GH ☎ 03451 555555 Ext 444424 🖱 bob.mclellan@fife.gov.uk

Transport: Mr Bob McLellan, Head of Transportation & Environmental Services, First Floor, Bankhead Central, Bankhead Park, Glenrothes KY7 6GH ☎ 03451 555555 Ext 444424 🖱 bob.mclellan@fife.gov.uk

Transport Planner: Mr Bob McLellan, Head of Transportation & Environmental Services, First Floor, Bankhead Central, Bankhead Park, Glenrothes KY7 6GH ☎ 03451 555555 Ext 444424 🖱 bob.mclellan@fife.gov.uk

Waste Collection and Disposal: Mr Roddy Mann Senior Manager - Environmental Operations, 1st Floor, Bankhead Central, Bankhead Park, Glenrothes KY7 6GH ☎ 03451 555555 Ext 493604 🖱 roddy.mann@fife.gov.uk

Waste Management: Mr Roddy Mann Senior Manager - Environmental Operations, 1st Floor, Bankhead Central, Bankhead Park, Glenrothes KY7 6GH ☎ 03451 555555 Ext 493604 🖱 roddy.mann@fife.gov.uk

COUNCILLORS

***Provost* Leishman**, Jim (LAB - Dunfermline Central)

***Deputy Provost* Morrison**, Kay (LAB - Glenrothes North, Leslie and Markinch)

***Leader of the Council* Ross**, David (LAB - Kirkcaldy North)

***Deputy Leader of the Council* Laird**, Lesley (LAB - Inverkeithing and Dalgety Bay)

***Group Leader* Dempsey**, Dave (CON - Inverkeithing and Dalgety Bay)

Adams, Tom (LAB - Leven, Kennoway and Largo)

Alexander, David (SNP - Leven, Kennoway and Largo)

Bain, Ann (SNP - The Lochs)

Bain, Alistair (SNP - Cowdenbeath)

Beare, John (SNP - Glenrothes North, Leslie and Markinch)

Brett, Tim (LD - Tay Bridgehead)

Brown, Bill (IND - Glenrothes West and Kinglassie)

Brown, Lawrence (LAB - Kirkcaldy East)

Callaghan, Pat (LAB - Rosyth)

Callaghan, Alice (LAB - West Fife and Coastal Villages)

Campbell, Alex (LAB - The Lochs)

Campbell, William (LAB - Dunfermline North)

Carrington, Kay (LAB - Kirkcaldy East)

Chapman, Douglas (SNP - Rosyth)

Chisholm, Ian (SNP - Lochgelly and Cardenden)

Clarke, William (IND - The Lochs)

Clelland, Bobby (LAB - West Fife and Coastal Villages)

Connor, Bill (SNP - Tay Bridgehead)

Craik, Altany (LAB - Glenrothes West and Kinglassie)

Crichton, Ian (LAB - Glenrothes Central and Thornton)

Crooks, Neil (LAB - Kirkcaldy North)

Docherty, John (SNP - East Neuk and Landward)

Erskine, Linda (LAB - Lochgelly and Cardenden)

Ferguson, William (IND - West Fife and Coastal Villages)

George, Peter (LAB - Burntisland, Kinghorn and Western Kirkcaldy)

Goodall, Brian (SNP - Dunfermline South)

Graham, David (LAB - Buckhaven, Methil and Wemyss)

Grant, Fiona (SNP - Glenrothes North, Leslie and Markinch)

Guichan, Gary (LAB - Cowdenbeath)

Haffey, Charles (LAB - Leven, Kennoway and Largo)

Hamilton, Judy (LAB - Kirkcaldy Central)

Hanvey, Neale (SNP - Dunfermline Central)

Heer, Andy (CON - Howe of Fife and Tay Coast)

Hood, Mark (LAB - Lochgelly and Cardenden)

Hunter, Alistair (SNP - Leven, Kennoway and Largo)

Kay, George (SNP - Burntisland, Kinghorn and Western Kirkcaldy)

Kennedy, Margaret (LD - Cupar)

Law, Helen (LAB - Dunfermline North)

Leslie, Susan (LD - Burntisland, Kinghorn and Western Kirkcaldy)

Lindsay, Carol (SNP - Kirkcaldy North)

Lockhart, Peter (LAB - Cowdenbeath)

Lothian, Donald (LD - Howe of Fife and Tay Coast)

MacDiarmid, David (SNP - Howe of Fife and Tay Coast)

MacGregor, Donald (LD - East Neuk and Landward)

MacPhail, Stuart (SNP - Kirkcaldy Central)

Marjoram, Karen (SNP - Cupar)

Martin, Tony (LD - Dunfermline South)

McCartney, Keith (SNP - St Andrews)

McGarry, Alice (SNP - Inverkeithing and Dalgety Bay)

Melville, Frances (LD - St Andrews)

Mogg, David (SNP - Dunfermline North)

Morrison, Dorothea (CON - St Andrews)

O'Brien, John (SNP - Buckhaven, Methil and Wemyss)

Penman, Marie (SNP - Kirkcaldy East)

Pollock, Billy (LAB - Dunfermline South)

Poole, Bryan (IND - Cupar)

Riches, Elizabeth (LD - East Neuk and Landward)

Rodger, Andrew (IND - Buckhaven, Methil and Wemyss)

Rosiejak, Joe (LD - Dunfermline Central)

Selbie, Kenny (LAB - Kirkcaldy Central)

Shirkie, Mike (LAB - Rosyth)

Sinclair, Fay (SNP - Dunfermline South)

Sloan, Ian (LAB - Glenrothes Central and Thornton)

Stewart, Kate (SNP - West Fife and Coastal Villages)

Taylor, Margaret (LD - Tay Bridgehead)

Thomson, Brian (LAB - St Andrews)

Vettraino, Ross (SNP - Glenrothes Central and Thornton)

Walker, Craig (SNP - Glenrothes West and Kinglassie)

Wincott, John (LAB - Glenrothes North, Leslie and Markinch)

Yates, Gavin (LAB - Inverkeithing and Dalgety Bay)

Young, Jim (LAB - Buckhaven, Methil and Wemyss)

Young, Bob (LAB - Dunfermline Central)

POLITICAL COMPOSITION

LAB: 33, SNP: 26, LD: 10, IND: 5, CON: 3

COMMITTEE CHAIRS

Standards & Audit: Mr John Beare

Flintshire W

Flintshire County Council, County Hall, Mold CH7 6NF
☎ 01352 752121 🖷 01352 758240 ✉ info@flintshire.gov.uk
💻 www.flintshire.gov.uk

FACTS AND FIGURES

Parliamentary Constituencies: Alyn and Deeside, Delyn
EU Constituencies: Wales
Election Frequency: Elections are by thirds

PRINCIPAL OFFICERS

Chief Executive: Mr Colin Everett, Chief Executive, County Hall, Mold CH7 6NB ☎ 01352 702100 ✉ chief.executive@flintshire.gov.uk

Senior Management: Mr Neil Ayling Chief Officer - Social Services, County Hall, Mold CH7 6NF ☎ 01352 702500 🖷 01352 70255 ✉ neil.j.ayling@flintshire.gov.uk

Senior Management: Mr Ian Bancroft Chief Officer - Organisational Change, County Hall, Mold CH7 6NF ☎ 01352 704180 ✉ ian.bancroft@flintshire.gov.uk

Senior Management: Mr Ian Budd Chief Officer - Education & Youth, County Hall, Mold CH7 6NF ☎ 01352 704010 🖷 01352 754202 ✉ ian.budd@flintshire.gov.uk

Senior Management: Ms Clare Budden Chief Officer - Community & Enterprise, County Offices, Chapel Street, Flint CH6 5BD ☎ 01352 703800 🖷 01352 762915 ✉ clare.budden@flintshire.gov.uk

Senior Management: Mr Neal Cockerton, Chief Officer - Organisational Change, County Hall, Mold CH7 6NF ☎ 01352 703169 🖷 01352 704550 ✉ neal.cockerton@flintshire.gov.uk

Senior Management: Mr Andy Farrow Chief Officer - Planning & Environment, County Hall, Mold CH7 6NB ☎ 01352 703201 🖷 01352 756444 ✉ andy.farrow@flintshire.gov.uk

Senior Management: Mr Steve Jones Chief Officer - Streetscene & Transportation, County Hall, Mold CH7 6NF ☎ 01352 704700 ✉ stephen.o.jones@flintshire.gov.uk

Senior Management: Mr Gareth Owens Chief Officer - Governance, County Hall, Mold CH7 6NF ☎ 01352 702344 🖷 01352 702494 ✉ gareth.legal@flintshire.gov.uk

Senior Management: Mrs Helen Stappleton Chief Officer - People & Resources, County Hall, Mold CH7 6NG ☎ 01352 702720 🖷 01352 700152 ✉ helen.stappleton@flintshire.gov.uk

Access Officer / Social Services (Disability): Ms Jo Taylor Disability, Progression & Recovery Service Manager, County Hall, Mold CH7 6NF ☎ 01352 701350 🖷 01352 702635 ✉ jo.taylor@flintshire.gov.uk

Architect, Building / Property Services: Mr Andy Smith Property & Design Consultancy Manager, County Offices, Chapel Street, Flint CH6 5BD ☎ 01352 703127 🖷 01352 762915 ✉ andy.smith@flintshire.gov.uk

Best Value: Mrs Karen Armstrong, Policy, Performance & Partnership Manager, County Hall, Mold CH7 6NT ☎ 01352 702740 🖷 01352 702807 ✉ karen.armstrong@flintshire.gov.uk

Building Control: Mr Glyn Jones Development Manager, County Hall, Mold CH7 6NF ☎ 01352 703248 ✉ glyn.p.jones@flintshire.gov.uk

Children / Youth Services: Miss Kim Brookes Interim Service Manager, County Hall, Mold CH7 6NF ☎ 01352 704025 ✉ kim.brookes@flintshire.gov.uk

Children / Youth Services: Mrs Ann Roberts Families First Lead & Youth Services Manager, County Hall, Mold CH7 6NF ☎ 01352 704112 ✉ ann.s.roberts@flintshire.gov.uk

Civil Registration: Mrs Denise Naylor, Customer Services Manager, County Hall, Mold CH7 6NT ☎ 01352 702421 🖷 01352 702807 ✉ denise.naylor@flintshire.gov.uk

PR / Communications: Ms Barbara Milne, Corporate Communications Manager, County Hall, Mold CH7 6NB ☎ 01352 702111 🖷 01352 704949 ✉ barbara.milne@flintshire.gov.uk

Community Planning: Mrs Karen Armstrong, Policy, Performance & Partnership Manager, County Hall, Mold CH7 6NT ☎ 01352 702740 🖷 01352 702807 ✉ karen.armstrong@flintshire.gov.uk

Community Safety: Mrs Sian Jones, Team Leader, County Hall, Mold CH7 6NT ☎ 01352 702132 🖷 01352 700152 ✉ sian.l.jones@flintshire.gov.uk

Computer Management: Mr Aled Griffith Network & IT Support Services Manager, County Hall, Mold CH7 6NF ☎ 01352 702801 🖷 01352 700149 ✉ aled.griffith@flintshire.gov.uk

Computer Management: Ms Mandy Humphreys IT Business Solutions Officer, County Hall, Mold CH7 6NF ☎ 01352 702821 ✉ mandy.humphreys@flintshire.gov.uk

Consumer Protection and Trading Standards: Mrs Sylvia Portbury Health Protection Manager, County Hall, Mold CH7 6NF ☎ 01352 703378 🖷 01352 703441 ✉ sylvia.portbury@flintshire.gov.uk

Corporate Services: Mr Gareth Owens Chief Officer - Governance, County Hall, Mold CH7 6NF ☎ 01352 702344 🖷 01352 702494 ✉ gareth.legal@flintshire.gov.uk

Customer Service: Mrs Denise Naylor, Customer Services Manager, County Hall, Mold CH7 6NT ☎ 01352 702421 🖷 01352 702807 ✉ denise.naylor@flintshire.gov.uk

E-Government: Mr Gareth Owens Chief Officer - Governance, County Hall, Mold CH7 6NF ☎ 01352 702344 🖷 01352 702494 ✉ gareth.legal@flintshire.gov.uk

Electoral Registration: Mrs Lyn Phillips Electoral Services Manager, County Hall, Mold CH7 6NF ☎ 01352 702329 🖷 01352 702494 ✉ lyn.phillips@flintshire.gov.uk

Emergency Planning: Mr Phil Harrison Regional Emergency Planning Manager, County Hall, Mold CH7 6NF ☎ 01352 702120 🖷 01352 754005 ✉ philip.harrison@flintshire.gov.uk

Energy Management: Mr Will Pierce, Energy Manager, County Offices, Chapel Street, Flint CH6 5BD ☎ 01352 703137 🖷 01352 703786 ✉ will.pierce@flintshire.gov.uk

Environmental Health: Mr Ian Vaughan-Evans Interim Head of Public Protection, County Hall, Mold CH7 6NF ☎ 01352 703413 🖷 01352 703441 ✉ ian.vaughan-evans@flintshire.gov.uk

Estates, Property & Valuation: Mr Tony Bamford, Corporate Valuer, County Offices, Chapel Street, Flint CH6 5BD ☎ 01352 703102 🖷 01352 703111 ✉ tony.bamford@flintshire.gov.uk

Events Manager: Mr Darell Jones Streetlighting Manager, Alltami Depot, Alltami, Mold CH7 6LG ☎ 01352 701290 🖷 01352 701270 ✉ darell.jones@flintshire.gov.uk

Facilities: Mr Steve Jones Facilities Services Manager, County Hall, Mold CH7 6NF ☎ 01352 704039 🖷 01352 754207 ✉ steve.w.jones@flintshire.gov.uk

Finance: Mr Gary Ferguson Corporate Finance Manager, County Hall, Mold CH7 6NF ☎ 01352 702271 ✉ gary.ferguson@flintshire.gov.uk

Pensions: Mr Philip Latham Pensions Manager, County Hall, Mold CH7 6NF ☎ 01352 702264 ✉ philip.latham@flintshire.gov.uk

Fleet Management: Mr Barry Wilkinson Fleet Services Operations Manager, Alltami Depot, Alltami, Mold CH7 6LG ☎ 01244 704656 🖷 01244 704660 ✉ barry.wilkinson@flintshire.gov.uk

Grounds Maintenance: Mr Derrick Charlton Interim Streetscene Manager, County Hall, Mold CH7 6NF ☎ 01352 701211 ✉ derrick.charlton@flintshire.gov.uk

Health and Safety: Ms Vanessa Johnson Corporate Health & Safety Manager, County Hall, Mold CH7 6NB ☎ 01352 702962 🖷 01352 703441 ✉ vanessa.johnson@flintshire.gov.uk

Highways: Mr Anthony Stanford Senior Engineer - Traffic, County Hall, Mold CH7 6NF ☎ 01352 704817 ✉ anthony.stanford@flintshire.gov.uk

Home Energy Conservation: Mr Will Pierce, Energy Manager, County Offices, Chapel Street, Flint CH6 5BD ☎ 01352 703137 🖷 01352 703786 ✉ will.pierce@flintshire.gov.uk

Housing: Mr Gavin Griffith Housing Regeneration & Strategy Manager, County Hall, Mold CH7 6NF ☎ 01352 703428 ✉ gavin.griffith@flintshire.gov.uk

Housing Maintenance: Ms Nikki Evans Senior Manager - Council Housing, County Hall, Mold CH7 6NF ☎ 01352 701658 ✉ nikki.evans@flintshire.gov.uk

Legal: Ms Sian Jones Acting Legal Services Manager, County Hall, Mold CH7 6NF ☎ 01352 702404 ✉ sian.jones@flintshire.gov.uk

Leisure and Cultural Services: Mr Mike Welch, Organisational Change, County Hall, Mold CH7 6NF ☎ 01352 702452 ✉ mike.welch@flintshire.gov.uk

FLINTSHIRE

Licensing: Mr Scott Rowley Interim Environmantal Protection Manager, County Hall, Mold CH7 6NF ☎ 01352 703272 ✉ scott.rowley@flintshire.gov.uk

Lifelong Learning: Mr Ian Budd Chief Officer - Education & Youth, County Hall, Mold CH7 6NF ☎ 01352 704010 🖷 01352 754202 ✉ ian.budd@flintshire.gov.uk

Lighting: Mr Darell Jones Streetlighting Manager, Alltami Depot, Alltami, Mold CH7 6LG ☎ 01352 701290 🖷 01352 701270 ✉ darell.jones@flintshire.gov.uk

Member Services: Mrs Karen Jones, Chairman's & Members' Assistant, County Hall, Mold CH7 6NF ☎ 01352 702151 🖷 01352 702150 ✉ karen.jones@flintshire.gov.uk

Member Services: Mrs Lesley Wood, Chairman's & Members' Assistant, County Hall, Mold CH7 6NR ☎ 01352 702151 🖷 01352 702150 ✉ lesley.wood@flintshire.gov.uk

Parking: Mrs Joanna Jones Parking Manager, County Hall, Mold CH7 6NF ☎ 01352 704637 ✉ joanna.l.jones@flintshire.gov.uk

Partnerships: Mrs Karen Armstrong, Policy, Performance & Partnership Manager, County Hall, Mold CH7 6NT ☎ 01352 702740 🖷 01352 702807 ✉ karen.armstrong@flintshire.gov.uk

Personnel / HR: Mrs Karen Carney Lead Business Partner, County Hall, Mold CH7 6NF ☎ 01352 702139 ✉ sharon.carney@flintshire.gov.uk

Planning: Mr Glyn Jones Development Manager, County Hall, Mold CH7 6NF ☎ 01352 703248 ✉ glyn.p.jones@flintshire.gov.uk

Procurement: Ms Arwel Staples Strategic Procurement Manager, County Hall, Mold CH7 6NF ☎ 01352 702267 ✉ arwel.staples@flintshire.gov.uk

Public Libraries: Ms Pennie Corbett Principal Librarian, County Hall, Mold CH7 6NF ☎ 01352 704402 🖷 01352 753662 ✉ pennie.corbett@flintshire.gov.uk

Recycling & Waste Minimisation: Mr Harvey Mitchell Business & Strategy Manager, Alltami Depot, Mold Road, Alltami, Mold CH7 6LG ☎ 01352 701710 🖷 01352 701270 ✉ harvey.mitchell@flintshire.gov.uk

Regeneration: Mr Niall Waller Economic Development Manager, County Hall, Mold CH7 6NF ☎ 01352 702137 ✉ niall.waller@flintshire.gov.uk

Road Safety: Mr Derrick Charlton Interim Streetscene Manager, County Hall, Mold CH7 6NF ☎ 01352 701211 ✉ derrick.charlton@flintshire.gov.uk

Social Services: Mr Neil Ayling Chief Officer - Social Services, County Hall, Mold CH7 6NF ☎ 01352 702500 🖷 01352 70255 ✉ neil.j.ayling@flintshire.gov.uk

Social Services (Adult): Mrs Christine Duffy Senior Manager - Adult First Contact & Localities Service, County Hall, Mold CH7 6NF ☎ 01352 702561 🖷 01352 702555 ✉ christine.duffy@flintshire.gov.uk

Social Services (Adult): Mrs Susie Lunt Senior Manager - Integrated Services, Lead Adults, County Hall, Mold CH7 6NF ☎ 01352 701407 🖷 01352 702555 ✉ susie.lunt@flintshire.gov.uk

Social Services (Children): Mr Ray Dickson Service Manager - Children's Fieldwork Services, County Hall, Mold CH7 6NF ☎ 01352 701003 ✉ ray.dickson@flintshire.gov.uk

Social Services (Children): Mr Peter Robson Children's Resources Service Manager, County Hall, Mold CH7 6NF ☎ 01352 701028 ✉ peter.robson@flintshire.gov.uk

Staff Training: Mrs Heather Johnson Corporate Training Officer, Northop Campus, Deeside College, Northop, Mold CH7 6AA ☎ 01352 841053 ✉ heather.johnson@flintshire.gov.uk

Street Scene: Mr Derrick Charlton Interim Streetscene Manager, County Hall, Mold CH7 6NF ☎ 01352 701211 ✉ derrick.charlton@flintshire.gov.uk

Tourism: Mr David Evans, Tourism Manager, County Hall, Mold CH7 6NB ☎ 01352 702468 🖷 01352 702050 ✉ david.p.evans@flintshire.gov.uk

Town Centre: Mr Niall Waller Economic Development Manager, County Hall, Mold CH7 6NF ☎ 01352 702137 ✉ niall.waller@flintshire.gov.uk

Transport: Mrs Kate Wilby Transportation Manager, County Hall, Mold CH7 6NF ☎ 01352 704530 🖷 01352 704550 ✉ katie.wilby@flintshire.gov.uk

Waste Collection and Disposal: Mr Kevin Edwards Operations Manager - Waste, Alltami Depot, Mold Road, Alltami, Mold CH7 6LG ☎ 01352 701718 🖷 01352 701270 ✉ kevin.edwards@flintshire.gov.uk

Waste Management: Mr Harvey Mitchell Business & Strategy Manager, County Hall, Mold CH7 6NB ☎ 01352 701710 🖷 01352 701270 ✉ harvey.mitchell@flintshire.gov.uk

Children's Play Areas: Mr Mike Welch, Organisational Change, County Hall, Mold CH7 6NF ☎ 01352 702452 ✉ mike.welch@flintshire.gov.uk

COUNCILLORS

***Chair* Hughes**, Raymond (IND - Leeswood)
raymond.hughes@flintshire.gov.uk

***Vice-Chair* Curtis**, Peter (LAB - Holywell Central)
peter.curtis@flintshire.gov.uk

***Leader of the Council* Shotton**, Aaron (LAB - Connah's Quay Central)
aaron.shotton@flintshire.gov.uk

***Deputy Leader of the Council* Attridge**, Bernie (LAB - Connah's Quay Central)
bernie.attridge@flintshire.gov.uk

***Group Leader* Carver**, Clive (CON - Hawarden)
clive.carver@flintshire.gov.uk

***Group Leader* Guest**, Robin (LD - Mold South)
robin.guest@flintshire.gov.uk

***Group Leader* Peers**, Mike (IND - Buckley Pentrobin)
mike.peers@flintshire.gov.uk

***Group Leader* Sharps**, Tony (IND - Northop Hall)
tony.sharps@flintshire.gov.uk

Aldridge, Alex (LAB - Flint Coleshill)
alex.aldridge@flintshire.gov.uk

Banks, Glyn (LAB - Ffynnongroyw)
glyn.banks@flintshire.gov.uk

Bateman, Haydn (IND - Mold Broncoed)
haydn.bateman@flintshire.gov.uk

Bateman, Marion (IND - Northop)
marion.bateman@flintshire.gov.uk

Bithell, Chris (LAB - Mold East)
christopher.bithell@flintshire.gov.uk

Bragg, Amanda (LD - New Brighton)
amanda.bragg@flintshire.gov.uk

Brown, Helen (IND - Aston)
helen.brown@flintshire.gov.uk

Butler, Derek (LAB - Broughton South)
derek.butler@flintshire.gov.uk

Cox, David (LAB - Flint Coleshill)
davidcox3b@gmail.com

Cunningham, Paul (LAB - Flint Trelawny)
paul.cunningham@flintshire.gov.uk

Davies, Ron (LAB - Shotton Higher)
rsdavi3s@aol.com

Davies-Cooke, Adele (CON - Gwernaffield)
adele.daviescooke@flintshire.gov.uk

Diskin, Glenys (LAB - Mancot)
glenys.diskin@flintshire.gov.uk

Diskin, Alan (LAB - Mancot)
alan.diskin@flintshire.gov.uk

Dolphin, Chris (LD - Whitford)
chris_dolphin@hotmail.co.uk

Dolphin, Rosetta (IND - Greenfield)
rosetta_dolphin@hotmail.co.uk

Dunbar, Ian (LAB - Connah's Quay South)
ian.dunbar@flintshire.gov.uk

Dunbobbin, Andy (LAB - Connah's Quay Golftyn)
andrew.dunbobbin@flintshire.gov.uk

Dunn, Brian (IND - Connah's Quay Wepre)
brian.dunn@flintshire.gov.uk

Ellis, Carol (IND - Buckley Mountain)
carol.ellis@flintshire.gov.uk

Evans, David (LAB - Shotton East)
david.evans@flintshire.gov.uk

Falshaw, Jim (CON - Caerwys)
jim.falshaw@flintshire.gov.uk

Gay, Veronica (IND - Saltney Stonebridge)
veronica.gay@flintshire.gov.uk

Halford, Alison (CON - Ewloe)
alison.halford@flintshire.gov.uk

Hampson, Ron (LAB - Buckley Bistre West)
ronald.hampson@flintshire.gov.uk

Hardcastle, George (IND - Aston)
george.hardcastle@flintshire.gov.uk

Healey, David (LAB - Caergwrle)
david.healey@flintshire.gov.uk

Hinds, Cindy (LAB - Pen-y-Ffordd)
cindy.r.dennis@gmail.com

Hutchinson, Dennis (IND - Buckley Pentrobin)
dennis.hutchinson@flintshire.gov.uk

Isherwood, Hilary (CON - Llanfynydd)
hilary.isherwood@flintshire.gov.uk

Johnson, Joe (LAB - Holywell East)
joe.johnson@flintshire.gov.uk

Johnson, Rita (IND - Flint Oakenholt)
rita.johnson@flintshire.gov.uk

Jones, Christine (LAB - Sealand)
christine.m.jones@flintshire.gov.uk

Jones, Kevin (LAB - Bagillt East)
kevin.jones@flintshire.gov.uk

Jones, Richard (IND - Buckley Bistre East)
richard.b.jones@flintshire.gov.uk

Legg, Colin (IND - Halkyn)
colin.legg@flintshire.gov.uk

Lightfoot, Phil (IND - Higher Kinnerton)
phil.lightfoot@flintshire.gov.uk

Lloyd, Brian (IND - Mold West)
brian.lloyd@flintshire.gov.uk

Lloyd, Richard (LAB - Saltney Mold Junction)
richard.lloyd@flintshire.gov.uk

Lowe, Mike (LAB - Broughton South)
mike.lowe@flintshire.gov.uk

Mackie, Dave (IND - Ewloe)
david.mackie@flintshire.gov.uk

Matthews, Nancy (LD - Gwernymyndd)
nancy.matthews@flintshire.gov.uk

McGuill, Hilary (LD - Argoed)
hilary.mcguill@flintshire.gov.uk

Minshull, Ann (LAB - Shotton West)
ann.minshull@flintshire.gov.uk

Mullin, Billy (LAB - Broughton North East)
billy.mullin@flintshire.gov.uk

Newhouse, Tim (IND - Hope)
tim@mucc.info

Perfect, Vicky (LAB - Flint Trelawny)
vicky.perfect@flintshire.gov.uk

Phillips, Neville (LD - Buckley Bistre West)
neville.phillips@flintshire.gov.uk

Reece, Mike (LAB - Bagillt West)
mikereece@talktalk.net

FLINTSHIRE

Roberts, Ian (LAB - Flint Castle)
ian.roberts@flintshire.gov.uk

Roberts, Gareth (PC - Holywell West)
h.gareth.roberts@flintshire.gov.uk

Roney, David (IND - Mostyn)
david.roney@flintshire.gov.uk

Shotton, Paul (LAB - Connah's Quay Golftyn)
paul.shotton@flintshire.gov.uk

Smith, Ian (LAB - Connah's Quay South)
ian.smith@flintshire.gov.uk

Steele-Mortimer, Nigel (CON - Trelawnyd and Gwaenysgor)
nigel.steele-mortimer@flintshire.gov.uk

Thomas, Owen (CON - Cilcain)
owen.thomas@flintshire.gov.uk

Thomas, Carolyn (IND - Treuddyn)
carolyn.thomas@flintshire.gov.uk

Williams, David (IND - Pen-y-Ffordd)
david.m.williams@flintshire.gov.uk

Williams, Sharon (LAB - Gronant)
sharon.williams@flintshire.gov.uk

Wisinger, David (LAB - Queensferry)
david.wisinger@flintshire.gov.uk

Woolley, Arnold (IND - Buckley Bistre East)
arnold.woolley@flintshire.gov.uk

Wright, Matt (CON - Brynford)
matt.wright@flintshire.gov.uk

POLITICAL COMPOSITION

LAB: 32, IND: 23, CON: 8, LD: 6, PC: 1

COMMITTEE CHAIRS

Audit: Mr Tim Newhouse

Licensing: Mr Tony Sharps

Planning & Development Control: Mr David Wisinger

Forest Heath D

Forest Heath District Council, District Offices, College Heath Road, Mildenhall IP28 7EY
☎ 01638 719000 🖷 01638 716493 ✉ info@forest-heath.gov.uk
💻 www.forest-heath.gov.uk

FACTS AND FIGURES

EU Constituencies: Eastern
Election Frequency: Elections are of whole council

PRINCIPAL OFFICERS

Chief Executive: Mr Ian Gallin Joint Chief Executive, District Offices, College Heath Road, Mildenhall IP28 7EY ☎ 01638 719324; 01284 757001 ✉ ian.gallin@forest-heath.gov.uk

Senior Management: Ms Davina Howes Head of Families & Communities, District Offices, College Heath Road, Mildenhall IP28 7EY ☎ 01284 757070 ✉ davina.howes@westsuffolk.gov.uk

Senior Management: Ms Rachael Mann Head of Resources & Performance, District Offices, College Heath Road, Mildenhall IP28 7EY ☎ 01638 719245 ✉ rachael.mann@westsuffolk.gov.uk

Senior Management: Mr Simon Phelan, Head of Housing, District Offices, College Heath Road, Mildenhall IP28 7EY ☎ 01638 719324 🖷 01638 716493 ✉ simon.phelan@forest-heath.gov.uk

Senior Management: Mrs Karen Points Head of HR, Legal & Democratic Services, District Offices, College Heath Road, Mildenhall IP28 7EY ☎ 01285 757015 ✉ karen.points@westsuffolk.gov.uk

Senior Management: Mr Mark Walsh Head of Operations, District Offices, College Heath Road, Mildenhall IP28 7EY ☎ 01284 757300 ✉ mark.walsh@westsuffolk.gov.uk

Senior Management: Mr Alex Wilson, Corporate Director, District Offices, College Heath Road, Mildenhall IP28 7EY ☎ 01284 757695 ✉ alex.wilson@westsuffolk.gov.uk

Senior Management: Mr Steven Wood Head of Planning & Growth, District Offices, College Heath Road, Mildenhall IP28 7EY ☎ 01284 757306 ✉ steven.wood@westsuffolk.gov.uk

Architect, Building / Property Services: Mr Mark Walsh, Head of Waste Management & Property Services, District Offices, College Heath Road, Mildenhall IP28 7EY ☎ 01284 757300 ✉ mark.walsh@westsuffolk.gov.uk

Best Value: Ms Davina Howes Head of Families & Communities, District Offices, College Heath Road, Mildenhall IP28 7EY ☎ 01284 757070 ✉ davina.howes@westsuffolk.gov.uk

Building Control: Mr Steven Wood Head of Planning & Growth, District Offices, College Heath Road, Mildenhall IP28 7EY ☎ 01284 757306 ✉ steven.wood@westsuffolk.gov.uk

PR / Communications: Ms Marianne Hulland, Communications Manager, District Offices, College Heath Road, Mildenhall IP28 7EY ☎ 01284 757034; 01638 719361 🖷 01638 716493 ✉ marianne.hulland@forest-heath.gov.uk

Community Planning: Ms Davina Howes Head of Families & Communities, District Offices, College Heath Road, Mildenhall IP28 7EY ☎ 01284 757070 ✉ davina.howes@westsuffolk.gov.uk

Community Safety: Ms Davina Howes Head of Families & Communities, District Offices, College Heath Road, Mildenhall IP28 7EY ☎ 01284 757070 ✉ davina.howes@westsuffolk.gov.uk

Computer Management: Ms Rachael Mann Head of Resources & Performance, District Offices, College Heath Road, Mildenhall IP28 7EY ☎ 01638 719245 ✉ rachael.mann@westsuffolk.gov.uk

Contracts: Ziaul Quader Procurement Manager, District Offices, College Heath Road, Mildenhall IP28 7EY ☎ 01284 757310 🖷 01284 757378 ✉ ziaul.quader@westsuffolk.gov.uk

Corporate Services: Ms Davina Howes Head of Families & Communities, District Offices, College Heath Road, Mildenhall IP28 7EY ☎ 01284 757070 ✉ davina.howes@westsuffolk.gov.uk

Customer Service: Ms Davina Howes Head of Families & Communities, District Offices, College Heath Road, Mildenhall IP28 7EY ☎ 01284 757070 ✉ davina.howes@westsuffolk.gov.uk

Economic Development: Mrs Andrea Mayley, Head of Economic Development & Growth, District Offices, College Heath Road, Mildenhall IP28 7EY ☎ 01284 757343 ✉ andrea.mayley@westsuffolk.gov.uk

Electoral Registration: Mrs Fiona Osman Electoral Services Manager, District Offices, College Heath Road, Mildenhall IP28 7EY ☎ 01285 757105 ✉ fiona.osman@westsuffolk.gov.uk

Emergency Planning: Mr Stephen Henthorn Emergency Planning Officer, District Offices, College Heath Road, Mildenhall IP28 7EY ☎ 01638 719321 🖷 01638 716493 ✉ stephen.henthorn@forest-heath.gov.uk

Energy Management: Mr Peter Gudde Environmental Manager, District Offices, College Heath Road, Mildenhall IP28 7EY ☎ 01284 757042 ✉ peter.gudde@westsuffolk.gov.uk

Environmental Health: Mr Tom Wright Business Regulation & Licensing Manager, District Offices, College Heath Road, Mildenhall IP28 7EY ☎ 01638 719223 ✉ tom.wright@westsuffolk.gov.uk

Estates, Property & Valuation: Mr Mark Walsh, Head of Waste Management & Property Services, District Offices, College Heath Road, Mildenhall IP28 7EY ☎ 01284 757300 ✉ mark.walsh@westsuffolk.gov.uk

European Liaison: Mr Ian Gallin Joint Chief Executive, District Offices, College Heath Road, Mildenhall IP28 7EY ☎ 01638 719324; 01284 757001 ✉ ian.gallin@forest-heath.gov.uk

Facilities: Mr Mark Walsh, Head of Waste Management & Property Services, District Offices, College Heath Road, Mildenhall IP28 7EY ☎ 01284 757300 ✉ mark.walsh@westsuffolk.gov.uk

Finance: Ms Rachael Mann Head of Resources & Performance, District Offices, College Heath Road, Mildenhall IP28 7EY ☎ 01638 719245 ✉ rachael.mann@westsuffolk.gov.uk

Treasury: Ms Rachael Mann Head of Resources & Performance, District Offices, College Heath Road, Mildenhall IP28 7EY ☎ 01638 719245 ✉ rachael.mann@westsuffolk.gov.uk

Fleet Management: Mr Mark Walsh, Head of Waste Management & Property Services, District Offices, College Heath Road, Mildenhall IP28 7EY ☎ 01284 757300 ✉ mark.walsh@westsuffolk.gov.uk

Grounds Maintenance: Mr Mark Walsh, Head of Waste Management & Property Services, District Offices, College Heath Road, Mildenhall IP28 7EY ☎ 01284 757300 ✉ mark.walsh@westsuffolk.gov.uk

Health and Safety: Mrs Karen Points Head of Human Resources, Legal & Democratic Services, District Offices, College Heath Road, Mildenhall IP28 7EY ☎ 01638 719793 ✉ karen.points@westsuffolk.gov.uk

Home Energy Conservation: Mr Peter Gudde Environmental Manager, District Offices, College Heath Road, Mildenhall IP28 7EY ☎ 01284 757042 ✉ peter.gudde@westsuffolk.gov.uk

Housing: Mr Simon Phelan Head of Housing, District Offices, College Heath Road, Mildenhall IP28 7EY ☎ 01638 719440 ✉ simon.phelan@westsuffolk.gov.uk

Legal: Miss Joy Bowes, Service Manager - Legal, District Offices, College Heath Road, Mildenhall IP28 7EY ☎ 01692 719308 🖷 01692 716493 ✉ joy.bowes@westsuffolk.gov.uk

Leisure and Cultural Services: Mr Damien Parker Leisure & Cultural Operations Manager, District Offices, College Heath Road, Mildenhall IP28 7EY ☎ 01284 757090 ✉ damien.parker@westsuffolk.gov.uk

Leisure and Cultural Services: Mr Mark Walsh Head of Operations, District Offices, College Heath Road, Mildenhall IP28 7EY ☎ 01284 757300 ✉ mark.walsh@westsuffolk.gov.uk

Licensing: Mr Tom Wright Business Regulation & Licensing Manager, District Offices, College Heath Road, Mildenhall IP28 7EY ☎ 01638 719223 ✉ tom.wright@westsuffolk.gov.uk

Member Services: Miss Joy Bowes, Service Manager - Legal, District Offices, College Heath Road, Mildenhall IP28 7EY ☎ 01692 719308 🖷 01692 716493 ✉ joy.bowes@westsuffolk.gov.uk

Parking: Mr Mark Walsh, Head of Waste Management & Property Services, District Offices, College Heath Road, Mildenhall IP28 7EY ☎ 01284 757300 ✉ mark.walsh@westsuffolk.gov.uk

Personnel / HR: Mrs Karen Points Head of Human Resources, Legal & Democratic Services, District Offices, College Heath Road, Mildenhall IP28 7EY ☎ 01638 719793 ✉ karen.points@westsuffolk.gov.uk

Planning: Mr Steven Wood Head of Planning & Growth, District Offices, College Heath Road, Mildenhall IP28 7EY ☎ 01284 757306 ✉ steven.wood@westsuffolk.gov.uk

Procurement: Ziaul Quader Procurement Manager, District Offices, College Heath Road, Mildenhall IP28 7EY ☎ 01284 757310 🖷 01284 757378 ✉ ziaul.quader@westsuffolk.gov.uk

Recycling & Waste Minimisation: Mr Mark Christie, Environmental Services Manager, District Offices, College Heath Road, Mildenhall IP28 7EY ☎ 01638 719220 🖷 01638 716493 ✉ mark.christie@westsuffolk.gov.uk

Regeneration: Mrs Andrea Mayley, Head of Economic Development & Growth, District Offices, College Heath Road, Mildenhall IP28 7EY ☎ 01284 757343 ✉ andrea.mayley@westsuffolk.gov.uk

Staff Training: Mrs Karen Points Head of Human Resources, Legal & Democratic Services, District Offices, College Heath Road, Mildenhall IP28 7EY ☎ 01638 719793 ✉ karen.points@westsuffolk.gov.uk

FOREST HEATH

Street Scene: Mr Mark Christie, Environmental Services Manager, District Offices, College Heath Road, Mildenhall IP28 7EY
☎ 01638 719220 🖷 01638 716493 ✉ mark.christie@westsuffolk.gov.uk

Sustainable Communities: Mr Mark Christie, Environmental Services Manager, District Offices, College Heath Road, Mildenhall IP28 7EY ☎ 01638 719220 🖷 01638 716493
✉ mark.christie@westsuffolk.gov.uk

Sustainable Development: Mr Mark Christie, Environmental Services Manager, District Offices, College Heath Road, Mildenhall IP28 7EY ☎ 01638 719220 🖷 01638 716493
✉ mark.christie@westsuffolk.gov.uk

Tourism: Mrs Andrea Mayley, Head of Economic Development & Growth, District Offices, College Heath Road, Mildenhall IP28 7EY
☎ 01284 757343 ✉ andrea.mayley@westsuffolk.gov.uk

Waste Collection and Disposal: Mr Mark Christie, Environmental Services Manager, District Offices, College Heath Road, Mildenhall IP28 7EY ☎ 01638 719220 🖷 01638 716493
✉ mark.christie@westsuffolk.gov.uk

Waste Management: Mr Mark Christie, Environmental Services Manager, District Offices, College Heath Road, Mildenhall IP28 7EY
☎ 01638 719220 🖷 01638 716493
✉ mark.christie@westsuffolk.gov.uk

COUNCILLORS

***Chair* Bimson**, David (CON - Brandon West)
david.bimson@forest-heath.gov.uk

***Vice-Chair* Lynch**, Carol (CON - Red Lodge)
carol.lynch@forest-heath.gov.uk

***Leader of the Council* Waters**, James (CON - Eriswell and The Rows)
james.waters@forest-heath.gov.uk

***Deputy Leader of the Council* Millar**, Robin (CON - All Saints)
robin.millar@forest-heath.gov.uk

Allen, Ruth (IND - Severals)
ruth.allen@forest-heath.gov.uk

Anderson, Michael (CON - Severals)
michael.anderson@forest-heath.gov.uk

Appleby, Andrew (IND - Severals)
andrew.appleby@forest-heath.gov.uk

Barker, Chris (CON - St Mary's)
chris.barker@forest-heath.gov.uk

Bloodworth, John (CON - Market)
john.bloodworth@forest-heath.gov.uk

Bowman, David (CON - Eriswell and The Rows)
david.bowman@forest-heath.gov.uk

Bowman, Ruth (CON - Market)
ruth.bowman@forest-heath.gov.uk

Burt, Rona (CON - Iceni)
rona.burt@forest-heath.gov.uk

Busuttil, Louis (CON - Great Heath)
louis.busuttil@forest-heath.gov.uk

Cole, Simon (IND - Exning)
simon.cole@forest-heath.gov.uk

Drummond, Andy (CON - St Mary's)
andy.drummond@forest-heath.gov.uk

Edwards, Stephen (CON - All Saints)
stephen.edwards@forest-heath.gov.uk

Harvey, Brian (CON - Manor)
brian.harvey@forest-heath.gov.uk

Lay, James (CON - South)

Marston, Louise (CON - Lakenheath)
louise.marston@forest-heath.gov.uk

Mason, Christine (CON - Brandon East)
christine.mason@forest-heath.gov.uk

Noble, Colin (CON - Lakenheath)
colin.noble@forest-heath.gov.uk

Palmer, David (IND - Brandon West)
david.palmer@forest-heath.gov.uk

Ridgwell, Peter (UKIP - Brandon East)
peter.ridgwell@forest-heath.gov.uk

Roman, Nigel (CON - Great Heath)
nigel.roman@forest-heath.gov.uk

Sadler, Bill (CON - St Mary's)
bill.sadler@forest-heath.gov.uk

Silvester, Reg (UKIP - Brandon East)
reg.silvester@forest-heath.gov.uk

Stanbury, Lance (CON - Red Lodge)
lance.stanbury@forest-heath.gov.uk

POLITICAL COMPOSITION

CON: 21, IND: 4, UKIP: 2

COMMITTEE CHAIRS

Development Control: Ms Rona Burt

Licensing: Mr Michael Anderson

Forest of Dean D

Forest of Dean District Council, Council Offices, High Street, Coleford GL16 8HG
☎ 01594 810000 🖷 01594 812590 ✉ council@fdean.gov.uk
🖳 www.fdean.gov.uk

FACTS AND FIGURES

Parliamentary Constituencies: Forest of Dean
EU Constituencies: South West
Election Frequency: Elections are of whole council

PRINCIPAL OFFICERS

Chief Executive: Ms Sue Pangbourne Head of Paid Service, Council Offices, High Street, Coleford GL16 8HG ☎ 01594 812501
✉ sue.pangborne@fdean.gov.uk

Senior Management: Mr Peter Hibberd Strategic Director, Council Offices, High Street, Coleford GL16 8HG ☎ 01594 812640
✉ peter.hibberd@fdean.gov.uk

Senior Management: Ms Sue Pangbourne Head of Paid Service, Council Offices, High Street, Coleford GL16 8HG ☎ 01594 812501
✉ sue.pangborne@fdean.gov.uk

Building Control: Mr Peter Williams, Group Manager - Planning & Housing, Council Offices, Coleford GL16 8HG ☎ 01594 812300 ✉ peter.williams@fdean.gov.uk

PR / Communications: Mrs Rachel Orchard Communications & Marketing Officer, Council Offices, High Street, Coleford GL16 8HG ☎ 01594 812622 ✉ rachel.orchard@fdean.gov.uk

Community Safety: Ms Nicola Mclean Community Engagement Officer, Council Offices, High Street, Coleford GL16 8HG ☎ 01594 812372 ✉ nicola.mclean@fdean.gov.uk

Computer Management: Mr Simon Walker ICT Manager, Council Offices, High Street, Coleford GL16 8HG ☎ 01594 812298 ✉ simon.walker@fdean.gov.uk

Corporate Services: Mrs Karen Rushworth Corporate Support Manager, Forest of Dean District Council, Council Offices, High Street, Coleford GL16 8HG ☎ 01594 812524 ✉ karen.rushworth@fdean.gov.uk

E-Government: Mr Simon Walker ICT Manager, Council Offices, High Street, Coleford GL16 8HG ☎ 01594 812298 ✉ simon.walker@fdean.gov.uk

Electoral Registration: Mrs Geraldine Randall-Wilce, Electoral Services Officer, Council Offices, Coleford GL16 8HG ☎ 01594 812626 🖷 01594 812470 ✉ geraldine.randall-wilce@fdean.gov.uk

Emergency Planning: Mrs Karen Rushworth Corporate Support Manager, Forest of Dean District Council, Council Offices, High Street, Coleford GL16 8HG ☎ 01594 812524 ✉ karen.rushworth@fdean.gov.uk

Environmental / Technical Services: Mr Roger Garbett, Group Manager - Environmental Services, Council Offices, High Street, Coleford GL16 8HG ☎ 01594 812431 ✉ roger.garbett@fdean.gov.uk

Environmental Health: Mr Roger Garbett, Group Manager - Environmental Services, Council Offices, High Street, Coleford GL16 8HG ☎ 01594 812431 ✉ roger.garbett@fdean.gov.uk

Estates, Property & Valuation: Mr Chris Johns Land & Property Manager, Council Offices, Gloucester Road, Tewkesbury GL20 5TT ☎ 01684 272274; 01594 810000 ✉ chris.johns@tewkesbury.gov.uk

Finance: Mr Paul Jones GOSS Head of Finance, Council Offices, High Street, Coleford GL16 8HG ☎ 01242 775154 ✉ paul.jones@cheltenham.gov.uk

Grounds Maintenance: Mr Chris Johns Land & Property Manager, Council Offices, Gloucester Road, Tewkesbury GL20 5TT ☎ 01684 272274; 01594 810000 ✉ chris.johns@tewkesbury.gov.uk

Health and Safety: Mr Roger Garbett, Group Manager - Environmental Services, Council Offices, High Street, Coleford GL16 8HG ☎ 01594 812431 ✉ roger.garbett@fdean.gov.uk

Housing: Mr Peter Williams, Group Manager - Planning & Housing, Council Offices, Coleford GL16 8HG ☎ 01594 812300 ✉ peter.williams@fdean.gov.uk

Legal: Ms Claire Hughes Legal Team Manager, Council Offices, High Street, Coleford GL16 8HG ☎ 01594 812515 ✉ claire.hughes@fdean.gov.uk

Leisure and Cultural Services: Mr Andy Barge, Group Manager - Customer Services, Council Offices, Coleford GL16 8HG ☎ 01594 812383 ✉ andy.barge@fdean.gov.uk

Licensing: Mr Roger Garbett, Group Manager - Environmental Services, Council Offices, High Street, Coleford GL16 8HG ☎ 01594 812431 ✉ roger.garbett@fdean.gov.uk

Member Services: Mrs Julie Jones Democratic Services Manager, Council Offices, High Street, Coleford GL16 8HG ☎ 01594 812623 ✉ julie.jones@fdean.gov.uk

Personnel / HR: Ms Deb Bainbridge GO Shared Services Head of HR, Council Offices, High Street, Coleford GL16 8HG ✉ deb.bainbridge@fdean.gov.uk

Planning: Mr Peter Williams, Group Manager - Planning & Housing, Council Offices, Coleford GL16 8HG ☎ 01594 812300 ✉ peter.williams@fdean.gov.uk

Procurement: Mr Dave Baker GO Shared Service, Council Offices, High Street, Coleford GL16 8HG ✉ dave.baker@fdean.gov.uk

Recycling & Waste Minimisation: Mr Roger Garbett, Group Manager - Environmental Services, Council Offices, High Street, Coleford GL16 8HG ☎ 01594 812431 ✉ roger.garbett@fdean.gov.uk

Staff Training: Mrs Jan Bridges, Learning & Organisational Development Manager, Municipal Offices, Promenade, Cheltenham GL50 9SA ☎ 01242 775189 🖷 01242 264309 ✉ jan.bridges@cheltenham.gov.uk

Street Scene: Mr Andy Barge, Group Manager - Customer Services, Council Offices, Coleford GL16 8HG ☎ 01594 812383 ✉ andy.barge@fdean.gov.uk

Sustainable Communities: Mr Alastair Chapman, Sustainability Team Leader, Council Offices, High Street, Coleford GL16 8HG ☎ 01594 812329 ✉ alastair.chapman@fdean.gov.uk

Sustainable Development: Mr Alastair Chapman, Sustainability Team Leader, Council Offices, High Street, Coleford GL16 8HG ☎ 01594 812329 ✉ alastair.chapman@fdean.gov.uk

Tourism: Ms Paula Burrows Manager - Commercial Services, Council Offices, High Street, Coleford GL16 8HG ☎ 01594 812389 ✉ paula.burrows@fdean.gov.uk

Waste Collection and Disposal: Mr Roger Garbett, Group Manager - Environmental Services, Council Offices, High Street, Coleford GL16 8HG ☎ 01594 812431 ✉ roger.garbett@fdean.gov.uk

Waste Management: Mr Roger Garbett, Group Manager - Environmental Services, Council Offices, High Street, Coleford GL16 8HG ☎ 01594 812431 ✉ roger.garbett@fdean.gov.uk

FOREST OF DEAN

COUNCILLORS

***Chair* Horne**, Jane (CON - Tibberton)
Jane.Horne@fdean.gov.uk

***Leader of the Council* Molyneux**, Patrick (CON - Hewelsfield and Woolaston)
Patrick.Molyneux@fdean.gov.uk

***Deputy Leader of the Council* Robinson**, Brian (CON - Mitcheldean and Drybrook)
Brian.Robinson@fdean.gov.uk

Allaway Martin, Carole (CON - Coleford Central)
Carole.Allawaymartin@fdean.gov.uk

Bevan, James (CON - Lydney East)
James.Bevan@fdean.gov.uk

Boyles, Richard (CON - Newnham and Westbury)
Richard.Boyles@fdean.gov.uk

Burford, Philip (IND - Hartpury)
Philip.Burford@fdean.gov.uk

Coborn, Max (LAB - Cinderford East)
Max.Coborn@fdean.gov.uk

Davies, Gethyn (CON - Tidenham)
Gethyn.Davies@fdean.gov.uk

East, David (IND - Blaisdon and Longhope)
David.East@fdean.gov.uk

Easton, David (CON - Coleford East)
David.Easton@fdean.gov.uk

Edwards, Diana (CON - Pillowell)
Diana.Edwards@fdean.gov.uk

Edwards, Maria (CON - Tidenham)
Maria.Edwards@fdean.gov.uk

Elsmore, Clive (IND - Coleford Central)
Clive.Elsmore@fdean.gov.uk

Evans, Frankie (CON - Alvington, Aylburton and West Lydney)
Frankie.Evans@fdean.gov.uk

Fraser, Jackie (LAB - Mitcheldean and Drybrook)
Jackie.Fraser@fdean.gov.uk

Gardiner, Andrew (INDNA - Lydbrook and Ruardean)
Andrew.Gardiner@fdean.gov.uk

Gooch, Julia (IND - Newent Central)
Julia.Gooch@fdean.gov.uk

Grant, Alan (UKIP - Pillowell)
Alan.Grant@fdean.gov.uk

Guyton, Colin (UKIP - Lydbrook and Ruardean)
Colin.Guyton@fdean.gov.uk

Gwilliam, Timothy (LAB - Berry Hill)
tim.gwilliam@fdean.gov.uk

Hale, Terry (CON - Newland and St Briavels)
Terry.Hale@fdean.gov.uk

Harris, Carol (UKIP - Lydney East)
Carol.Harris@fdean.gov.uk

Hawthorne, Dave (CON - Littledean and Ruspidge)
Dave.Hawthorne@fdean.gov.uk

Hiett, Paul (LAB - Bream)
Paul.Hiett@fdean.gov.uk

Hill, Martin (UKIP - Coleford East)
Martin.Hill@fdean.gov.uk

Hogan, Bruce (LAB - Lydbrook and Ruardean)
Bruce.Hogan@fdean.gov.uk

Hughes, Gareth (CON - Awre)
Gareth.Hughes@fdean.gov.uk

James, Roger (LAB - Coleford East)
Roger.James@fdean.gov.uk

Jones, Brian (CON - Churcham and Huntley)
Brian.Jones@fdean.gov.uk

Lawton, Craig (CON - Oxenhall and Newent North East)
Craig.Lawton@fdean.gov.uk

Lawton, Len (CON - Newent Central)
Len.Lawton@fdean.gov.uk

Leppington, Richard (UKIP - Bream)
Richard.Leppington@fdean.gov.uk

Martin, Di (LAB - Cinderford East)
Di.Martin@fdean.gov.uk

McFarling, Chris (INDNA - Newland and St. Briavels)
Chris.McFarling@fdean.gov.uk

Molyneux, Helen (CON - Tidenham)
Helen.Molyneux@fdean.gov.uk

Morgan, Graham (LAB - Cinderford West)
Graham.Morgan@fdean.gov.uk

O'Neill, Bernie (LAB - Littledean and Ruspidge)
Bernie.Oneill@fdean.gov.uk

Osborne, Bill (LAB - Lydney East)
Bill.Osborne@fdean.gov.uk

Phelps, Simon (IND - Newnham and Westbury)
simon.phelps@fdean.gov.uk

Preest, Alan (UKIP - Lydney North)
Alan.Preest@fdean.gov.uk

Scott, Douglas (LAB - Mitcheldean and Drybrook)
Douglas.Scott@fdean.gov.uk

Simpson, Jim (UKIP - Alvington, Aylburton and West Lydney)
jim.simpson@fdean.gov.uk

Smart, Marrilyn (CON - Christchurch and English Bicknor)
Marrilyn.Smart@fdean.gov.uk

Sterry, Lynn (LAB - Cinderford West)
Lynn.Sterry@fdean.gov.uk

Sterry, Roger (LAB - Cinderford West)
roger.sterry@fdean.gov.uk

Williams, Clayton (CON - Redmarley)
clayton.williams@fdean.gov.uk

Yeates, Roger (CON - Bromsberrow and Dymock)
Roger.Yeates@fdean.gov.uk

POLITICAL COMPOSITION

CON: 21, LAB: 13, UKIP: 7, IND: 5, INDNA: 2

COMMITTEE CHAIRS

Audit: Mr Brian Jones

Licensing: Mr Richard Leppington

Planning: Mr Philip Burford

Fylde D

Fylde Borough Council, Town Hall, St. Annes Road West, St. Annes-on-Sea FY8 1LW
☎ 01253 658658 🖷 01253 713113 ✉ listening@fylde.gov.uk
🖳 www.fylde.gov.uk

FACTS AND FIGURES

Parliamentary Constituencies: Fylde
EU Constituencies: North West
Election Frequency: Elections are of whole council

PRINCIPAL OFFICERS

Chief Executive: Mr Allan Oldfield, Chief Executive, Town Hall, St. Annes Road West, St. Annes-on-Sea FY8 1LW ☎ 01253 658500 ✉ allan.oldfield@fylde.gov.uk

Senior Management: Mr Mark Evans Head of Planning & Regeneration, Town Hall, St. Annes Road West, St. Annes-on-Sea FY8 1LW ☎ 01253 658460 ✉ mark.evans@fylde.gov.uk

Senior Management: Ms Tracy Morrison, Director - Resources & Council Monitoring Officer, Town Hall, St. Annes Road West, St. Annes-on-Sea FY8 1LW ☎ 01253 658521 ✉ tracy.morrison@fylde.gov.uk

Senior Management: Mr Paul O'Donoghue Chief Finance & S151 Officer, Town Hall, St. Annes Road West, St. Annes-on-Sea FY8 1LW ☎ 01253 658658 ✉ paul.o'donoghue@fylde.gov.uk

Senior Management: Mr Paul Walker Director - Development Services, Town Hall, St. Annes Road West, St. Annes-on-Sea FY8 1LW ☎ 01253 658658 ✉ paul.walker@fylde.gov.uk

Architect, Building / Property Services: Mr Andrew Dickson, Head - Technical Services, Town Hall, Lytham St. Annes FY8 1LW ☎ 01253 658675 ✉ andrew.dickson@fylde.gov.uk

Building Control: Mr Andrew Dickson, Head - Technical Services, Town Hall, Lytham St. Annes FY8 1LW ☎ 01253 658675 ✉ andrew.dickson@fylde.gov.uk

PR / Communications: Mr Neil Graham Communcations & Consultations Manager, Town Hall, St. Annes Road West, St. Annes-on-Sea FY8 1LW ☎ 01253 658499 ✉ neil.graham@fylde.gov.uk

Community Planning: Mr Mark Evans Head of Planning & Regeneration, Town Hall, St. Annes Road West, St. Annes-on-Sea FY8 1LW ☎ 01253 658460 ✉ mark.evans@fylde.gov.uk

Community Safety: Ms Tracy Morrison, Director - Resources & Council Monitoring Officer, Town Hall, St. Annes Road West, St. Annes-on-Sea FY8 1LW ☎ 01253 658521 ✉ tracy.morrison@fylde.gov.uk

Computer Management: Mr Andrew Cain Head of Customer & IT Services, Town Hall, St. Annes Road West, St. Annes-on-Sea FY8 1LW ☎ 01253 658450 ✉ andrew.cain@fylde.gov.uk

Customer Service: Mr Andrew Cain Head of Customer & IT Services, Town Hall, St. Annes Road West, St. Annes-on-Sea FY8 1LW ☎ 01253 658450 ✉ andrew.cain@fylde.gov.uk

Economic Development: Mr Stephen Smith Economic Development Officer, Town Hall, St. Annes Road West, St. Annes-on-Sea FY8 1LW ☎ 01253 658445 ✉ stephen.smith@fylde.gov.uk

E-Government: Mr Andrew Cain Head of Customer & IT Services, Town Hall, St. Annes Road West, St. Annes-on-Sea FY8 1LW ☎ 01253 658450 ✉ andrew.cain@fylde.gov.uk

Electoral Registration: Mrs Hazel McNicoll Electoral Services Manager, Town Hall, St. Annes Road West, St. Annes-on-Sea FY8 1LW ☎ 01253 658516 ✉ hazel.mcnicoll@fylde.gov.uk

Emergency Planning: Mr Andrew Wilsdon Risk & Emergency Planning Manager, Town Hall, Lytham St. Annes FY8 1LW ☎ 01253 658412 ✉ andrew.wilsdon@fylde.gov.uk

Energy Management: Mr Andrew Loynd Parking & Energy Officer, Town Hall, St. Annes Road West, St. Annes-on-Sea FY8 1LW ☎ 01253658527 ✉ andrew.loynd@fylde.gov.uk

Environmental / Technical Services: Mr Andrew Dickson, Head - Technical Services, Town Hall, Lytham St. Annes FY8 1LW ☎ 01253 658675 ✉ andrew.dickson@fylde.gov.uk

Environmental Health: Ms Sara Carrington Principal Officer Commercial, Town Hall, St. Annes Road West, St. Annes-on-Sea FY8 1LW ☎ 01253 658627 ✉ sara.carrington@fylde.gov.uk

Estates, Property & Valuation: Mr Gary Sams Principal Estates Surveyor, Town Hall, St. Annes Road West, St. Annes-on-Sea FY8 1LW ☎ 01253 658462 ✉ gary.sams@fylde.gov.uk

Finance: Mr Paul O'Donoghue Chief Finance & S151 Officer, Town Hall, St. Annes Road West, St. Annes-on-Sea FY8 1LW ☎ 01253 658658 ✉ paul.o'donoghue@fylde.gov.uk

Grounds Maintenance: Mr Peter Graveson, Grounds Maintenance Officer, Town Hall, Lytham St. Annes FY8 1LW ☎ 01253 658471 ✉ peterg@fylde.gov.uk

Health and Safety: Mr Andrew Wilsdon Risk & Emergency Planning Manager, Town Hall, Lytham St. Annes FY8 1LW ☎ 01253 658412 ✉ andrew.wilsdon@fylde.gov.uk

Legal: Mr Ian Curtis Head of Governance, Town Hall, St. Annes Road West, St. Annes-on-Sea FY8 1LW ☎ 01253 658506 ✉ ian.curtis@fylde.gov.uk

Leisure and Cultural Services: Mr Darren Bell Head of Leisure & Cultural Services, Town Hall, St. Annes Road West, St. Annes-on-Sea FY8 1LW ☎ 01253 658465 ✉ darren.bell@fylde.gov.uk

Licensing: Ms Chris Hambly Principal Licensing Officer, Town Hall, St. Annes Road West, St. Annes-on-Sea FY8 1LW ☎ 01253 658422 ✉ chris.hambly@fylde.gov.uk

FYLDE

Member Services: Mr Ian Curtis Head of Governance, Town Hall, St. Annes Road West, St. Annes-on-Sea FY8 1LW ☎ 01253 658506 ✉ ian.curtis@fylde.gov.uk

Parking: Mr Andrew Loynd Parking & Energy Officer, Town Hall, St. Annes Road West, St. Annes-on-Sea FY8 1LW ☎ 01253658527 ✉ andrew.loynd@fylde.gov.uk

Personnel / HR: Mr Allan Oldfield, Chief Executive, Town Hall, St. Annes Road West, St. Annes-on-Sea FY8 1LW ☎ 01253 658500 ✉ allan.oldfield@fylde.gov.uk

Planning: Mr Mark Evans Head of Planning & Regeneration, Town Hall, St. Annes Road West, St. Annes-on-Sea FY8 1LW ☎ 01253 658460 ✉ mark.evans@fylde.gov.uk

Recycling & Waste Minimisation: Ms Kathy Winstanley Waste & Fleet Services Manager, Town Hall, St. Annes Road West, St. Annes-on-Sea FY8 1LW ☎ 01253 658576 ✉ kathy.winstanley@fylde.gov.uk

Regeneration: Mr Paul Drinnan Regeneration Manager, Town Hall, St. Annes Road West, St. Annes-on-Sea FY8 1LW ☎ 01253 658434 ✉ paul.drinnan@fylde.gov.uk

Tourism: Mrs Vivien Wood, Tourism Officer, Town Hall, Lytham St. Annes FY8 1LW ☎ 01253 658436 ✉ viv.wood@fylde.gov.uk

Transport: Ms Kathy Winstanley Waste & Fleet Services Manager, Town Hall, St. Annes Road West, St. Annes-on-Sea FY8 1LW ☎ 01253 658576 ✉ kathy.winstanley@fylde.gov.uk

Waste Collection and Disposal: Ms Kathy Winstanley Waste & Fleet Services Manager, Town Hall, St. Annes Road West, St. Annes-on-Sea FY8 1LW ☎ 01253 658576 ✉ kathy.winstanley@fylde.gov.uk

Waste Management: Ms Kathy Winstanley Waste & Fleet Services Manager, Town Hall, St. Annes Road West, St. Annes-on-Sea FY8 1LW ☎ 01253 658576 ✉ kathy.winstanley@fylde.gov.uk

Children's Play Areas: Mr Mark Wilde Head of Parks & Greenspaces, Town Hall, St. Annes Road West, St. Annes-on-Sea FY8 1LW ☎ 01253 658475 ✉ mark.wilde@fylde.gov.uk

COUNCILLORS

***Mayor* Hardy**, Peter (IND - Kirkham South)
cllr.phardy@fylde.gov.uk

***Deputy Mayor* Speak**, Heather (IND - Newton and Treales)
cllr.hspeak@fylde.gov.uk

***Leader of the Council* Fazackerley**, Susan (CON - Central)
cllr.sfazackerley@fylde.gov.uk

***Deputy Leader of the Council* Buckley**, Karen (CON - St Leonards)
cllr.kbuckley@fylde.gov.uk

Aitken, Ben (CON - Ansdell)
cllr.baitken@fylde.gov.uk

Akeroyd, Christine (CON - Kilnhouse)
cllr.cakeroyd@fylde.gov.uk

Andrews, Frank (CON - Ribby-with-Wrea)
cllr.fandrews@fylde.gov.uk

Ashton, Timothy (CON - St Johns)
Tim.ashton@lancashire.gov.uk

Bamforth, Mark (R - St Johns)
cllr.mbamforth@fylde.gov.uk

Barker, Jan (LAB - Central)
cllr.jbarker@fylde.gov.uk

Beckett, Keith (IND - Kirkham North)
cllr.kbeckett@fylde.gov.uk

Blackshaw, Brenda (CON - Fairhaven)
cllr.bblackshaw@fylde.gov.uk

Brickles, Julie (IND - Warton and Westby)
cllr.jbrickles@fylde.gov.uk

Chew, Maxine (IND - Singleton and Greenhalgh)
cllr.mchew@fylde.gov.uk

Clayton, Alan (IND - Medlar-with-Wesham)
cllr.aclayton@fylde.gov.uk

Collins, Peter (IND - Newton and Treales)
petercollins4568@aol.com

Collins, Delma (CON - St Leonards)
cllr.dcollins@fylde.gov.uk

Cornah, Michael (CON - Warton and Westby)
cllr.mcornah@fylde.gov.uk

Davies, Leonard (CON - Clifton)
cllr.ldavies@fylde.gov.uk

Donaldson, David (CON - Fairhaven)
cllr.ddonaldson@fylde.gov.uk

Eaves, David (CON - Ansdell)
cllr.deaves@fylde.gov.uk

Fiddler, Trevor (CON - Freckleton West)
cllr.tfiddler@fylde.gov.uk

Ford, Tony (LD - Ashton)
cllr.tford@fylde.gov.uk

Fradley, Richard (CON - Clifton)
cllr.rfradley@flyde.gov.uk

Goodman, Gill (CON - Ashton)
cllr.ggoodman@fylde.gov.uk

Green, Shirley (CON - Park)
cllr.sgreen@fylde.gov.uk

Harvey, Neil (CON - Park)
cllr.nharvey@fylde.gov.uk

Hayhurst, Paul (INDNA - Elswick and Little Eccleston)
cllr.phayhurst@fylde.gov.uk

Henshaw, Karen (LD - Kilnhouse)
cllr.khenshaw@fylde.gov.uk

Hodgson, Paul (IND - Kirkham North)
cllr.phodgson@fylde.gov.uk

Jacques, Angela (CON - St Leonards)
cllr.ajacques@fylde.gov.uk

Little, Cheryl (CON - Fairhaven)
cllr.clittle@fylde.gov.uk

Lloyd, Roger (R - St Johns)
cllr.rlloyd@fylde.gov.uk

Mulholland, James (INDNA - Freckleton East)
kiranmul@dsl.pipex.com

Nash, Edward (CON - Central)
cllr.enash@fylde.gov.uk

Nash, Barbara Ann (CON - Heyhouses)
cllr.bnash@fylde.gov.uk

Neale, Graeme (CON - Ashton)
cllr.gneale@fylde.gov.uk

Nulty, Linda (IND - Medlar-with-Wesham)
cllr.lnulty@fylde.gov.uk

Oades, Elizabeth (IND - Kirkham South)
cllr.eoades@fylde.gov.uk

Pitman, Sandra (CON - Park)
cllr.spitman@fylde.gov.uk

Pounder, Albert (CON - Staining and Weeton)
cllr.apounder@fylde.gov.uk

Redcliffe, Richard (CON - Ansdell)
cllr.rredcliffe@fylde.gov.uk

Rigby, Louis (IND - Freckleton West)
cllr.lrigby@fylde.gov.uk

Settle, Vince (CON - Heyhouses)
cllr.vsettle@fylde.gov.uk

Silverwood, Elaine (IND - Kirkham North)
cllr.esilverwood@fylde.gov.uk

Singleton, John (CON - Staining and Weeton)
cllr.jsingleton@fylde.gov.uk

Small, Roger (CON - Kilnhouse)
cllr.rsmall@fylde.gov.uk

Taylor, Richard (CON - Warton and Westby)
cllr.rtaylor@fylde.gov.uk

Thomas, Raymond (CON - Clifton)
cllr.rthomas@fylde.gov.uk

Threlfall, Thomas (CON - Freckleton East)
cllr.tthrelfall@fylde.gov.uk

Willder, Vivienne (CON - Heyhouses)
cllr.vwillder@fylde.gov.uk

POLITICAL COMPOSITION

CON: 32, IND: 12, INDNA: 2, LD: 2, R: 2, LAB: 1

COMMITTEE CHAIRS

Audit: Mr John Singleton

Development Management: Mr Trevor Fiddler

Finance: Ms Karen Buckley

Gateshead M

Gateshead Council, Civic Centre, Regent Street, Gateshead NE8 1HH
☎ 0191 433 3000 ✉ enquiries@gateshead.gov.uk
🖳 www.gateshead.gov.uk

FACTS AND FIGURES

Parliamentary Constituencies: Blaydon, Gateshead, Jarrow, Tyne Bridge
EU Constituencies: North East
Election Frequency: Elections are by thirds

PRINCIPAL OFFICERS

Chief Executive: Mrs Jane Robinson, Chief Executive, Civic Centre, Regent Street, Gateshead NE8 1HH ☎ 0191 433 3000 🖷 0191 478 2755 ✉ janerobinson@gateshead.gov.uk

Assistant Chief Executive: Mrs Sheila Johnston Assistant Chief Executive, Civic Centre, Regent Street, Gateshead NE8 1HH ☎ 0191 433 3000 ✉ sheilajohnston@gateshead.gov.uk

Senior Management: Mr Mike Barker Strategic Director - Corporate Services & Governance, Civic Centre, Regent Street, Gateshead NE8 1HH ☎ 0191 433 2102 ✉ caroleshaw@gateshead.gov.uk

Senior Management: Mr David Bunce, Strategic Director - Care, Wellbeing & Learning, Civic Centre, Regent Street, Gateshead NE8 1HH ☎ 0191 433 3000 ✉ lyndacooper@gateshead.gov.uk

Senior Management: Mr Darren Collins, Strategic Director - Corporate Resources, Civic Centre, Regent Street, Gateshead NE8 1HH ☎ 0191 433 3581 ✉ carolsouter@gateshead.gov.uk

Senior Management: Mr Paul Dowling Strategic Director - Communities & Environment, Civic Centre, Regent Street, Gateshead NE8 1HH

Access Officer / Social Services (Disability): Mr Michael Laing Service Director - Social Care & Independent Living (including Housing), Civic Centre, Regent Street, Gateshead NE8 1HH ☎ 0191 433 2602 ✉ michaellaing@gateshead.gov.uk

Architect, Building / Property Services: Ms Victoria Beattie Service Director - Construction Services, Civic Centre, Regent Street, Gateshead NE8 1HH ☎ 0191 433 7311 ✉ victoriabeattie@gateshead.gov.uk

Architect, Building / Property Services: Mr Chris Tearney Highways & Purchasing Manager, Civic Centre, Regent Street, Gateshead NE8 1HH ☎ 0191 433 7201 ✉ christearney@gateshead.gov.uk

Architect, Building / Property Services: Mr Peter Udall Service Director - Property & Design, Civic Centre, Regent Street, Gateshead NE8 1HH ☎ 0191 433 2901 ✉ peterudall@gateshead.gov.uk

Best Value: Ms Marisa Jobling Service Director - Policy, Improvement & Communications, Civic Centre, Regent Street, Gateshead NE8 1HH ☎ 0191 433 3000 ✉ marisajobling@gateshead.gov.uk

Building Control: Mrs Anneliese Hutchinson Service Director - Development & Public Protection, Civic Centre, Regent Street, Gateshead NE8 1HH ☎ 0191 433 3881 ✉ anneliesehutchinson@gateshead.gov.uk

Building Control: Ms Emma Lucas Development Manager, Civic Centre, Regent Street, Gateshead NE8 1HH ☎ 0191 433 3000 ✉ emmalucas@gateshead.gov.uk

GATESHEAD

Catering Services: Mr Dale Robson, Service Director - Transport, Cleaning & Catering, Civic Centre, Regent Street, Gateshead NE8 1HH ☎ 0191 433 5510 ✉ dalerobson@gateshead.gov.uk

Children / Youth Services: Mr Martin Gray Service Director - Children's Commissioning, Civic Centre, Regent Street, Gateshead NE8 1HH

Children / Youth Services: Ms Debra Patterson Service Director - Social Work, Civic Centre, Regent Street, Gateshead NE8 1HH ☎ 0191 433 3000 ✉ debrapatterson@gateshead.gov.uk

Children / Youth Services: Ms Val Wilson Service Director - Children & Families Support, Civic Centre, Regent Street, Gateshead NE8 1HH ☎ 0191 433 3000 ✉ valwilson@gateshead.gov.uk

Civil Registration: Ms Deborah Hill, Service Director - Human Resources & Litigation, Civic Centre, Regent Street, Gateshead NE8 1HH ☎ 0191 433 2110 ✉ deborahhill@gateshead.gov.uk

PR / Communications: Ms Elaine Barclay Policy & Communications Team Leader, Civic Centre, Regent Street, Gateshead NE8 1HH ☎ 0191 433 3544 ✉ elainebarclay@gateshead.gov.uk

PR / Communications: Ms Marisa Jobling Service Director - Policy, Improvement & Communications, Civic Centre, Regent Street, Gateshead NE8 1HH ☎ 0191 433 3000 ✉ marisajobling@gateshead.gov.uk

Community Planning: Mrs Lindsay Murray Service Director - Communities, Neighbourhoods & Volunteering, Civic Centre, Regent Street, Gateshead NE8 1HH ☎ 0191 433 3000 ✉ lindsaymurray@gateshead.gov.uk

Community Safety: Ms Louise Rule Service Director - Commissioning & Business Development, Civic Centre, Regent Street, Gateshead NE8 1HH ☎ 0191 433 3000 ✉ louiserule@gateshead.gov.uk

Computer Management: Mr Joe Docherty IT Manager, Civic Centre, Regent Street, Gateshead NE8 1HH ☎ 0191 433 3000 ✉ joedocherty@gateshead.gov.uk

Computer Management: Mr Roy Sheehan Service Director - ICT, Civic Centre, Regent Street, Gateshead NE8 1HH ☎ 0191 433 3000 ✉ roysheehan@gateshead.gov.uk

Consumer Protection and Trading Standards: Mr Peter Wright Environmental Health & Trading Standards, Civic Centre, Regent Street, Gateshead NE8 1HH ☎ 0191 433 3910 ✉ peterwright@gateshead.gov.uk

Contracts: Mrs Andrea Tickner, Head of Corporate Procurement, Civic Centre, Regent Street, Gateshead NE8 1HH ☎ 0191 438 5995 ✉ andreatickner@gateshead.gov.uk

Corporate Services: Mr Martin Harrison Service Director - Development Law, Democratic Services & Corporate Procurement, Civic Centre, Regent Street, Gateshead NE8 1HH ☎ 0191 433 2101 ✉ martinharrison@gateshead.gov.uk

Customer Service: Mr John Jopling Service Director - Financial Services, Civic Centre, Regent Street, Gateshead NE8 1HH ☎ 0191 433 3000 ✉ johnjopling@gateshead.gov.uk

Economic Development: Mr Andrew Marshall Service Director - Economic & Housing Growth, Civic Centre, Regent Street, Gateshead NE8 1HH ☎ 0191 433 3000 ✉ andrewmarshall@gateshead.gov.uk

Education: Mr Steve Horne Service Director - Learning & Schools, Dryden Centre, Evistones Road, Low Fell, Gateshead NE9 5UR ☎ 0191 433 8612 ✉ stephenhorne@gateshead.gov.uk

E-Government: Mr Roy Sheehan Service Director - ICT, Civic Centre, Regent Street, Gateshead NE8 1HH ☎ 0191 433 3000 ✉ roysheehan@gateshead.gov.uk

Electoral Registration: Ms Christine Thomas Electoral Services Manager, Civic Centre, Regent Street, Gateshead NE8 1HH ☎ 0191 433 2152 ✉ christinethomas@gateshead.gov.uk

Emergency Planning: Ms Louise Rule Service Director - Commissioning & Business Development, Civic Centre, Regent Street, Gateshead NE8 1HH ☎ 0191 433 3000 ✉ louiserule@gateshead.gov.uk

Energy Management: Mr Jim Gillon Team Leader - Energy & Climate Change, Civic Centre, Regent Street, Gateshead NE8 1HH ☎ 0191 433 3000 ✉ jimgillon@gateshead.gov.uk

Environmental / Technical Services: Mr Anthony Alder Corporate Projects Director, Civic Centre, Regent Street, Gateshead NE8 1HH ☎ 0191 433 3000 ✉ anthonyalder@gateshead.gov.uk

Environmental Health: Mrs Anneliese Hutchinson Service Director - Development & Public Protection, Civic Centre, Regent Street, Gateshead NE8 1HH ☎ 0191 433 3881 ✉ anneliesehutchinson@gateshead.gov.uk

Estates, Property & Valuation: Mr Peter Udall Service Director - Property & Design, Civic Centre, Regent Street, Gateshead NE8 1HH ☎ 0191 433 2901 ✉ peterudall@gateshead.gov.uk

European Liaison: Ms Marisa Jobling Service Director - Policy, Improvement & Communications, Civic Centre, Regent Street, Gateshead NE8 1HH ☎ 0191 433 3000 ✉ marisajobling@gateshead.gov.uk

Events Manager: Ms Debbie Ross Service Manager - Events, Civic Centre, Regent Street, Gateshead NE8 1HH ☎ 0191 433 3000 ✉ debbieross@gateshead.gov.uk

Facilities: Mr Dale Robson, Service Director - Transport, Cleaning & Catering, Civic Centre, Regent Street, Gateshead NE8 1HH ☎ 0191 433 5510 ✉ dalerobson@gateshead.gov.uk

Finance: Mr Darren Collins, Strategic Director - Corporate Resources, Civic Centre, Regent Street, Gateshead NE8 1HH ☎ 0191 433 3581 ✉ carolsouter@gateshead.gov.uk

Finance: Mr John Jopling Service Director - Financial Services, Civic Centre, Regent Street, Gateshead NE8 1HH ☎ 0191 433 3000 ✉ johnjopling@gateshead.gov.uk

Finance: Mr Keith Purvis Service Director - Financial Management, Civic Centre, Regent Street, Gateshead NE8 1HH ☎ 0191 433 3000 ✉ keithpurvis@gateshead.gov.uk

Fleet Management: Mr Alasdair Tose Transport Services Manager, Civic Centre, Regent Street, Gateshead NE8 1HH ☎ 0191 533 7442 ✉ alasdairtose@gateshead.gov.uk

Grounds Maintenance: Mr Colin Huntington, Service Director - Waste Services & Grounds Maintenance, Civic Centre, Regent Street, Gateshead NE8 1HH ☎ 0191 433 7402 ✉ colinhuntington@gateshead.gov.uk

Health and Safety: Ms Susan Smith Occupational Health & Safety Manager, Civic Centre, Regent Street, Gateshead NE8 1HH ☎ 0191 433 3000

Highways: Mr Nick Clennett, Service Director - Transport Strategy, Civic Centre, Regent Street, Gateshead NE8 1HH ☎ 0191 433 2526 🖷 0191 478 8422 ✉ nickclennett@gateshead.gov.uk

Housing: Mr Andrew Marshall Service Director - Economic & Housing Growth, Civic Centre, Regent Street, Gateshead NE8 1HH ☎ 0191 433 3000 ✉ andrewmarshall@gateshead.gov.uk

Legal: Mr Mike Barker Strategic Director - Corporate Services & Governance, Civic Centre, Regent Street, Gateshead NE8 1HH ☎ 0191 433 2102 ✉ caroleshaw@gateshead.gov.uk

Legal: Ms Deborah Hill, Service Director - Human Resources & Litigation, Civic Centre, Regent Street, Gateshead NE8 1HH ☎ 0191 433 2110 ✉ deborahhill@gateshead.gov.uk

Leisure and Cultural Services: Mrs Lindsay Murray Service Director - Communities, Neighbourhoods & Volunteering, Civic Centre, Regent Street, Gateshead NE8 1HH ☎ 0191 433 3000 ✉ lindsaymurray@gateshead.gov.uk

Licensing: Ms Elaine Rudman Environmental Health, Licensing & Enforcement Manager, Civic Centre, Regent Street, Gateshead NE8 1HH ☎ 0191 433 3911 ✉ licensing@gateshead.gov.uk

Lifelong Learning: Mr Steve Horne Service Director - Learning & Schools, Dryden Centre, Evistones Road, Low Fell, Gateshead NE9 5UR ☎ 0191 433 8612 ✉ stephenhorne@gateshead.gov.uk

Lifelong Learning: Mr Kevin Pearson Principal Learning Skills Manager, Dryden Centre, Evistones Road, Low Fell, Gateshead NE9 5UR ☎ 0191 433 8652 ✉ kevinpearson@gateshead.gov.uk

Lighting: Ms Victoria Beattie Service Director - Construction Services, Civic Centre, Regent Street, Gateshead NE8 1HH ☎ 0191 433 7311 ✉ victoriabeattie@gateshead.gov.uk

Lottery Funding, Charity and Voluntary: Mrs Lindsay Murray Service Director - Communities, Neighbourhoods & Volunteering, Civic Centre, Regent Street, Gateshead NE8 1HH ☎ 0191 433 3000 ✉ lindsaymurray@gateshead.gov.uk

Member Services: Mr Martin Harrison Service Director - Development Law, Democratic Services & Corporate Procurement, Civic Centre, Regent Street, Gateshead NE8 1HH ☎ 0191 433 2101 ✉ martinharrison@gateshead.gov.uk

Parking: Mr Steve Donaldson Parking Services Manager, Civic Centre, Regent Street, Gateshead NE8 1HH ☎ 0191 433 3000

Partnerships: Ms Marisa Jobling Service Director - Policy, Improvement & Communications, Civic Centre, Regent Street, Gateshead NE8 1HH ☎ 0191 433 3000 ✉ marisajobling@gateshead.gov.uk

Personnel / HR: Ms Deborah Hill, Service Director - Human Resources & Litigation, Civic Centre, Regent Street, Gateshead NE8 1HH ☎ 0191 433 2110 ✉ deborahhill@gateshead.gov.uk

Planning: Ms Emma Lucas Development Manager, Civic Centre, Regent Street, Gateshead NE8 1HH ☎ 0191 433 3000 ✉ emmalucas@gateshead.gov.uk

Procurement: Mrs Andrea Tickner, Head of Corporate Procurement, Civic Centre, Regent Street, Gateshead NE8 1HH ☎ 0191 438 5995 ✉ andreatickner@gateshead.gov.uk

Public Libraries: Mrs Lindsay Murray Service Director - Communities, Neighbourhoods & Volunteering, Civic Centre, Regent Street, Gateshead NE8 1HH ☎ 0191 433 3000 ✉ lindsaymurray@gateshead.gov.uk

Public Libraries: Mr Stephen Walters Principal Library Manager, Civic Centre, Regent Street, Gateshead NE8 1HH ☎ 0191 433 8400 ✉ stephenwalters@gateshead.gov.uk

Recycling & Waste Minimisation: Mr Marc Morley Waste, Recycling & Contract Manager, Civic Centre, Regent Street, Gateshead NE8 1HH ☎ 0191 433 7420 🖷 0191 478 1138 ✉ marcmorley@gateshead.gov.uk

Regeneration: Mrs Sheila Johnston Assistant Chief Executive, Civic Centre, Regent Street, Gateshead NE8 1HH ☎ 0191 433 3000 ✉ sheilajohnston@gateshead.gov.uk

Regeneration: Mr Andrew Marshall Service Director - Economic & Housing Growth, Civic Centre, Regent Street, Gateshead NE8 1HH ☎ 0191 433 3000 ✉ andrewmarshall@gateshead.gov.uk

Road Safety: Mr Ian Gibson, Traffic Planning Manager, Civic Centre, Regent Street, Gateshead NE8 1HH ☎ 0191 433 3100 ✉ iangibson@gateshead.gov.uk

Social Services (Adult): Mr David Bunce, Strategic Director - Care, Wellbeing & Learning, Civic Centre, Regent Street, Gateshead NE8 1HH ☎ 0191 433 3000 ✉ lyndacooper@gateshead.gov.uk

Social Services (Adult): Mr Michael Laing Service Director - Social Care & Independent Living (including Housing), Civic Centre, Regent Street, Gateshead NE8 1HH ☎ 0191 433 2602 ✉ michaellaing@gateshead.gov.uk

GATESHEAD

Social Services (Children): Ms Frances Powell Service Director - Social Work, Civic Centre, Regent Street, Gateshead NE8 1HH ☎ 0191 433 3000 ✉ francespowell@gateshead.gov.uk

Public Health: Ms Carole Wood Director - Public Health, Civic Centre, Regent Street, Gateshead NE8 1HH ☎ 0191 433 3066 ✉ carolewood@gateshead.gov.uk

Street Scene: Mr Philip Hindmarsh Street Scene Manager, Civic Centre, Regent Street, Gateshead NE8 1HH ☎ 0191 433 7445 ✉ philiphindmarsh@gateshead.gov.uk

Sustainable Development: Mr Jim Gillon Team Leader - Energy & Climate Change, Civic Centre, Regent Street, Gateshead NE8 1HH ☎ 0191 433 3000 ✉ jimgillon@gateshead.gov.uk

Town Centre: Mr Andrew Marshall Service Director - Economic & Housing Growth, Civic Centre, Regent Street, Gateshead NE8 1HH ☎ 0191 433 3000 ✉ andrewmarshall@gateshead.gov.uk

Traffic Management: Mr Nick Clennett, Service Director - Transport Strategy, Civic Centre, Regent Street, Gateshead NE8 1HH ☎ 0191 433 2526 🖷 0191 478 8422 ✉ nickclennett@gateshead.gov.uk

Traffic Management: Mr Ian Gibson, Traffic Planning Manager, Civic Centre, Regent Street, Gateshead NE8 1HH ☎ 0191 433 3100 ✉ iangibson@gateshead.gov.uk

Transport: Mr Nick Clennett, Service Director - Transport Strategy, Civic Centre, Regent Street, Gateshead NE8 1HH ☎ 0191 433 2526 🖷 0191 478 8422 ✉ nickclennett@gateshead.gov.uk

Transport: Mr Andrew Haysey, Transport Planning Manager, Civic Centre, Regent Street, Gateshead NE8 1HH ☎ 0191 433 3124 ✉ andrewhaysey@gateshead.gov.uk

Transport: Mr Dale Robson, Service Director - Transport, Cleaning & Catering, Civic Centre, Regent Street, Gateshead NE8 1HH ☎ 0191 433 5510 ✉ dalerobson@gateshead.gov.uk

Waste Collection and Disposal: Mr Colin Huntington, Service Director - Waste Services & Grounds Maintenance, Civic Centre, Regent Street, Gateshead NE8 1HH ☎ 0191 433 7402 ✉ colinhuntington@gateshead.gov.uk

Waste Management: Mr Colin Huntington, Service Director - Waste Services & Grounds Maintenance, Civic Centre, Regent Street, Gateshead NE8 1HH ☎ 0191 433 7402 ✉ colinhuntington@gateshead.gov.uk

Waste Management: Mr Marc Morley Waste, Recycling & Contract Manager, Civic Centre, Regent Street, Gateshead NE8 1HH ☎ 0191 433 7420 🖷 0191 478 1138 ✉ marcmorley@gateshead.gov.uk

Children's Play Areas: Mr Colin Huntington, Service Director - Waste Services & Grounds Maintenance, Civic Centre, Regent Street, Gateshead NE8 1HH ☎ 0191 433 7402 ✉ colinhuntington@gateshead.gov.uk

COUNCILLORS

***Leader of the Council* Henry**, Mick (LAB - Saltwell)
cllr.m.henry@gateshead.gov.uk

***Deputy Leader of the Council* Gannon**, Martin (LAB - Deckham)
cllr.mgannon@gateshead.gov.uk

Adams, John (LAB - Saltwell)
cllr.jadams@gateshead.gov.uk

Beadle, Ron (LD - Low Fell)
cllr.rbeadle@gateshead.gov.uk

Bradley, Christine (LAB - Lamesley)
cllr.cbradley@gateshead.gov.uk

Brain, Malcolm (LAB - Blaydon)
cllr.mbrain@gateshead.gov.uk

Caffrey, Lynne (LAB - Chopwell and Rowlands Gill)
cllr.lcaffrey@gateshead.gov.uk

Charlton, Marilyn (LAB - Winlaton and High Spen)
cllr.mcharlton@gateshead.gov.uk

Clelland, Brenda (LAB - Dunston and Teams)
cllr.bclelland@gateshead.gov.uk

Coates, Brian (LAB - Deckham)
cllr.bcoates@gateshead.gov.uk

Craig, Peter (LD - Whickham North)
cllr.ptcraig@Gateshead.Gov.Uk

Craig, Susan (LD - Low Fell)
cllr.scraig@gateshead.gov.uk

Davidson, Doreen (LAB - High Fell)
cllr.ddavidson@gateshead.gov.uk

Dick, Bill (LAB - Felling)
cllr.wdick@gateshead.gov.uk

Dickie, Sonya (LAB - Felling)
cllr.sdickie@gateshead.gov.uk

Dillon, Pauline (LAB - Dunston and Teams)
cllr.pdillon@gateshead.gov.uk

Dodds, Kevin (LAB - Lobley Hill and Bensham)
cllr.k.dodds@gateshead.gov.uk

Donovan, Catherine (LAB - Lobley Hill and Bensham)
cllr.cdonovan@gateshead.gov.uk

Douglas, Angela (LAB - Bridges)
cllr.aarmstrong@gateshead.gov.uk

Eagle, John (LAB - Bridges)
cllr.jeagle@gateshead.gov.uk

Ferdinand, Kathryn (LAB - Blaydon)
cllr.k.ferdinand@gateshead.gov.uk

Foy, Mary (LAB - Lamesley)
cllr.mfoy@gateshead.gov.uk

Foy, Paul (LAB - Birtley)
cllr.pfoy@gateshead.gov.uk

Geddes, Alex (LAB - Ryton, Crookhill and Stella)
cllr.ageddes@gateshead.gov.uk

Goldsworthy, Bob (LAB - Bridges)
cllr.bgoldsworthy@gateshead.gov.uk

Goldsworthy, Maureen (LAB - Chowdene)
cllr.mgoldsworthy@gateshead.gov.uk

Graham, Malcolm (LAB - High Fell)
cllr.mgraham@gateshead.gov.uk

Graham, Jack (LAB - Crawcrook and Greenside)
cllr.jgraham@gateshead.gov.uk

Graham, Thomas (LAB - Windy Nook and Whitehills)
cllr.tgraham@gateshead.gov.uk

Green, Stuart (LAB - Wardley and Leam Lane)
cllr.sgreen@gateshead.gov.uk

Green, Jill (LAB - Pelaw and Heworth)
cllr.jgreen@gateshead.gov.uk

Green, Linda (LAB - Wardley and Leam Lane)
cllr.lgreen@gateshead.gov.uk

Haley, Gary (LAB - Dunston and Teams)
cllr.ghaley@gateshead.gov.uk

Hall, Maria (LAB - Winlaton and High Spen)
cllr.mhall@gateshead.gov.uk

Hamilton, John (LAB - Chopwell and Rowlands Gill)
cllr.jhamilton@gateshead.gov.uk

Hawkins, Sonya (LD - Whickham North)
cllr.shawkins@gateshead.gov.uk

Hindle, Frank (LD - Low Fell)
cllr.fhindle@gateshead.gov.uk

Holmes, Lee (LAB - Pelaw and Heworth)
cllr.lholmes@gateshead.gov.uk

Hood, Michael (LAB - Lamesley)
cllr.mhood@gateshead.gov.uk

Hughes, Helen (LAB - Crawcrook and Greenside)
cllr.hhughes@gateshead.gov.uk

Ilderton-Thompson, Allison (LAB - Dunston Hill and Whickham East)
cllr.achatto@gatesheadgov.uk

Lee, Jean (LAB - High Fell)
cllr.jlee@gateshead.gov.uk

Maughan, Peter (LD - Dunston Hill and Whickham East)
cllr.pmaughan@gateshead.gov.uk

McCartney, Kathleen (LAB - Crawcrook and Greenside)
cllr.kmccartney@gateshead.gov.uk

McClurey, John (LD - Whickham South and Sunniside)
cllr.jmcclurey@gateshead.gov.uk

McElroy, John (LAB - Chowdene)
cllr.jmcelroy@gateshead.gov.uk

McHatton, Christine (LD - Ryton, Crookhill and Stella)
cllr.cmchatton@gateshead.gov.uk

McHugh, Chris (LAB - Dunston Hll and Whickham East)
cllr.cmhugh@gateshead.gov.uk

McMaster, Eileen (LAB - Lobley Hill and Bensham)
cllr.emcmaster@gateshead.gov.uk

McNally, Paul (LAB - Felling)
cllr.pmcnally@gateshead.gov.uk

McNestry, Michael (LAB - Chopwell and Rowlands Gill)
cllr.mmcnestry@gateshead.gov.uk

Mole, Peter (LAB - Wardley and Leam Lane)
cllr.pmole@gateshead.gov.uk

Oliphant, Bernadette (LAB - Deckham)
cllr.boliphant@gateshead.gov.uk

Ord, Christopher (LD - Whickham North)
cllr.cord@gateshead.gov.uk

Ord, Marilynn (LD - Whickham South and Sunniside)
cllr.mord@gateshead.gov.uk

Robson, Denise (LAB - Saltwell)
cllr.drobson@gateshead.gov.uk

Ronan, Pat (LAB - Windy Nook and Whitehills)
cllr.pronan@gateshead.gov.uk

Ronchetti, Stephen (LAB - Blaydon)
cllr.sronchetti@gateshead.gov.uk

Simcox, Catherine (LAB - Birtley)
cllr.csimcox@gateshead.gov.uk

Simpson, Julie (LAB - Winlaton and High Spen)
cllr.jsimpson@gateshead.gov.uk

Turnbull, Jim (LAB - Windy Nook and Whitehills)
cllr.jturnbull@gateshead.gov.uk

Twist, Liz (LAB - Ryton, Crookhill and Stella)
cllr.ltwist@gateshead.gov.uk

Wallace, Jonathan (LD - Whickham South and Sunniside)
cllr.jwallace@gateshead.gov.uk

Weatherley, Neil (LAB - Birtley)
cllr.nweatherley@gateshead.gov.uk

Wheeler, Anne (LAB - Pelaw and Heworth)
cllr.awheeler@gateshead.gov.uk

Wood, Keith (LAB - Chowdene)
cllr.kwood@gateshead.gov.uk

POLITICAL COMPOSITION

LAB: 55, LD: 11

COMMITTEE CHAIRS

Audit: Mr Brian Coates

Planning: Mr John Hamilton

Gedling D

Gedling Borough Council, Civic Centre, Arnot Hill Park, Nottingham NG5 6LU
☎ 0115 901 3901 🖷 0115 901 3921 💻 www.gedling.gov.uk

FACTS AND FIGURES

Parliamentary Constituencies: Gedling, Sherwood
EU Constituencies: East Midlands
Election Frequency: Elections are of whole council

PRINCIPAL OFFICERS

Chief Executive: Mr John Robinson Chief Executive, Civic Centre, Arnot Hill Park, Nottingham NG5 6LU ☎ 0115 901 3915 ✉ john.robinson@gedling.gov.uk

Senior Management: Mr Stephen Bray, Corporate Director, Council Offices, Arnot Hill Park, Arnold, Nottingham NG5 6LU ☎ 0115 901 3808 ✉ stephen.bray@gedling.gov.uk

Senior Management: Mr Mark Kimberley, Corporate Director, Civic Centre, Arnot Hill Park, Nottingham NG5 6LU ☎ 0115 901 3990 ✉ mark.kimberley@gedling.gov.uk

GEDLING

Senior Management: Mr David Wakelin Corporate Director, Civic Centre, Arnot Hill Park, Nottingham NG5 6LU

Building Control: Mr Peter Baguley, Service Manager - Planning, Civic Centre, Arnot Hill Park, Nottingham NG5 6LU ☎ 0115 901 3751 ✉ peter.baguley@gedling.gov.uk

PR / Communications: Ms Caroline Newson Service Manager - Communications, Civic Centre, Arnot Hill Park, Nottingham NG5 6LU ☎ 0115 901 3801 ✉ caroline.newson@gedling.gov.uk

Computer Management: Mr Mark Lane Service Manager - Customer Services & IT, Civic Centre, Arnot Hill Park, Nottingham NG5 6LU ☎ 0115 901 3876 ✉ mark.lane@gedling.gov.uk

Corporate Services: Mr Mark Kimberley, Corporate Director, Civic Centre, Arnot Hill Park, Nottingham NG5 6LU ☎ 0115 901 3990 ✉ mark.kimberley@gedling.gov.uk

Customer Service: Mr Mark Lane Service Manager - Customer Services & IT, Civic Centre, Arnot Hill Park, Nottingham NG5 6LU ☎ 0115 901 3876 ✉ mark.lane@gedling.gov.uk

Economic Development: Mrs Louise Ashby Economic Development Officer, Civic Centre, Arnot Hill Park, Nottingham NG5 6LU ☎ 0115 901 3729 ✉ louise.ashby@gedling.gov.uk

E-Government: Mr Mark Lane Service Manager - Customer Services & IT, Civic Centre, Arnot Hill Park, Nottingham NG5 6LU ☎ 0115 901 3876 ✉ mark.lane@gedling.gov.uk

Emergency Planning: Mr John Evens Car Parks & Engineering Officer, Civic Centre, Arnot Hill Park, Nottingham NG5 6LU ☎ 0115 901 3767 ✉ john.evens@gedling.gov.uk

Energy Management: Mr Steve Wiseman, Architectural & Buildings Services Manager, Civic Centre, Arnot Hill Park, Arnold, Nottingham NG5 6LU ☎ 0115 901 3779 ✉ steve.wiseman@gedling.gov.uk

Environmental / Technical Services: Mr Andy Callingham, Service Manager - Public Protection, Civic Centre, Arnot Hill Park, Nottingham NG5 6LU ☎ 0115 901 3834 ✉ andy.callingham@gedling.gov.uk

Environmental Health: Mr Andy Callingham, Service Manager - Public Protection, Civic Centre, Arnot Hill Park, Nottingham NG5 6LU ☎ 0115 901 3834 ✉ andy.callingham@gedling.gov.uk

Estates, Property & Valuation: Mr Mark Kimberley Corporate Director, Civic Centre, Arnot Hill Park, Nottingham NG5 6LU ☎ 0115 901 3990 ✉ mark.kimberley@gedling.gov.uk

Events Manager: Ms Lorraine Brown Events & Play Officer, Civic Centre, Arnot Hill Park, Nottingham NG5 6LU ☎ 015 901 3602 ✉ lorraine.brown@gedling.gov.uk

Finance: Mr Mark Kimberley, Corporate Director, Civic Centre, Arnot Hill Park, Nottingham NG5 6LU ☎ 0115 901 3990 ✉ mark.kimberley@gedling.gov.uk

Treasury: Mr Mark Kimberley, Corporate Director, Civic Centre, Arnot Hill Park, Nottingham NG5 6LU ☎ 0115 901 3990 ✉ mark.kimberley@gedling.gov.uk

Fleet Management: Mr Mark Hurst Transport Services Manager, Civic Centre, Arnot Hill Park, Nottingham NG5 6LU ☎ 0115 901 3612 ✉ mark.hurst@gedling.gov.uk

Grounds Maintenance: Mr Melvyn Cryer Service Manager - Parks & Street Care, Civic Centre, Arnot Hill Park, Nottingham NG5 6LU ☎ 0115 901 3788 ✉ melvyn.cryer@gedling.gov.uk

Health and Safety: Mr Grant Illett, Safety Officer, Civic Centre, Arnot Hill Park, Arnold, Nottingham NG5 6LU ☎ 0115 901 3940 ✉ grant.illett@gedling.gov.uk

Housing: Ms Alison Bennett Service Manager - Housing & Localities, Civic Centre, Arnot Hill Park, Nottingham NG5 6LU ☎ 0115 901 3696 ✉ alison.bennett@gedling.gov.uk

Legal: Mrs Helen Barrington Council Solicitor & Monitoring Officer, Civic Centre, Arnot Hill Park, Nottingham NG5 6LU ☎ 0115 901 3896 ✉ helen.barrington@gedling.gov.uk

Leisure and Cultural Services: Mr Mark Kimberley, Corporate Director, Civic Centre, Arnot Hill Park, Nottingham NG5 6LU ☎ 0115 901 3990 ✉ mark.kimberley@gedling.gov.uk

Licensing: Mr Andy Callingham, Service Manager - Public Protection, Civic Centre, Arnot Hill Park, Nottingham NG5 6LU ☎ 0115 901 3834 ✉ andy.callingham@gedling.gov.uk

Member Services: Mr Alec Dubberley Service Manager - Elections & Member Services, Civic Centre, Arnot Hill Park, Nottingham NG5 6LU ☎ 0115 901 3906 ✉ alec.dubberley@gedling.gov.uk

Parking: Mr John Evens Car Parks & Engineering Officer, Civic Centre, Arnot Hill Park, Nottingham NG5 6LU ☎ 0115 901 3767 ✉ john.evens@gedling.gov.uk

Personnel / HR: Mr David Archer, Service Manager - Organisational Development, Civic Centre, Arnot Hill Park, Arnold, Nottingham NG5 6LU ☎ 0115 901 3937 ✉ david.archer@gedling.gov.uk

Planning: Mr Peter Baguley, Service Manager - Planning, Civic Centre, Arnot Hill Park, Nottingham NG5 6LU ☎ 0115 901 3751 ✉ peter.baguley@gedling.gov.uk

Procurement: Mr David Hayes Procurement Officer, Civic Centre, Arnot Hill Park, Nottingham NG5 6LU ☎ 0115 901 3911 ✉ david.hayes@gedling.gov.uk

Recycling & Waste Minimisation: Mrs Caroline McKenzie Service Manager - Waste Services, Civic Centre, Arnot Hill Park, Nottingham NG5 6LU ☎ 0115 901 3611 ✉ caroline.mckenzie@gedling.gov.uk

Staff Training: Mr Mike Calladine Training Officer, Civic Centre, Arnot Hill Park, Nottingham NG5 6LU ☎ 0115 901 3941 ✉ mike.calladine@gedling.gov.uk

Sustainable Communities: Mr Wayne Saruwaka Sustainability Officer, Civic Centre, Arnot Hill Park, Nottingham NG5 6LU ☎ 0115 901 3743 wayne.saruwaka@gedling.gov.uk

Sustainable Development: Mr Peter Baguley, Service Manager - Planning, Civic Centre, Arnot Hill Park, Nottingham NG5 6LU ☎ 0115 901 3751 peter.baguley@gedling.gov.uk

Tourism: Mr Andy Hardy Service Manager - Leisure & Culture, Civic Centre, Arnot Hill Park, Nottingham NG5 6LU ☎ 0115 901 3703 andy.hardy@gedling.gov.uk

Transport: Mr Mark Hurst Transport Services Manager, Civic Centre, Arnot Hill Park, Nottingham NG5 6LU ☎ 0115 901 3612 mark.hurst@gedling.gov.uk

Waste Collection and Disposal: Mrs Caroline McKenzie Service Manager - Waste Services, Civic Centre, Arnot Hill Park, Nottingham NG5 6LU ☎ 0115 901 3611 caroline.mckenzie@gedling.gov.uk

Waste Management: Mrs Caroline McKenzie Service Manager - Waste Services, Civic Centre, Arnot Hill Park, Nottingham NG5 6LU ☎ 0115 901 3611 caroline.mckenzie@gedling.gov.uk

Children's Play Areas: Mr Melvyn Cryer Service Manager - Parks & Street Care, Civic Centre, Arnot Hill Park, Nottingham NG5 6LU ☎ 0115 901 3788 melvyn.cryer@gedling.gov.uk

COUNCILLORS

***Leader of the Council* Clarke**, John (LAB - Netherfield and Colwick)
Cllr.John.Clarke@gedling.gov.uk

***Deputy Leader of the Council* Payne**, Michael (LAB - St Mary's)
Cllr.Michael.Payne@gedling.gov.uk

Ainley, Steve (LAB - Carlton)
cllr.steve.ainley@gedling.gov.uk

Allan, Roy (LAB - Bonington)
Cllr.Roy.Allan@gedling.gov.uk

Allan, Pauline (LAB - St Mary's)
Cllr.Pauline.Allan@gedling.gov.uk

Andrews, Bruce (CON - Ravenshead)
bruce@nodnol.org

Andrews, Patricia (CON - Newstead)
Cllr.Patricia.Andrews@gedling.gov.uk

Bailey, Emily (LAB - Calverton)
Cllr.Emily.Bailey@gedling.gov.uk

Barnes, Sandra (LAB - Daybrook)

Barnes, Peter (LAB - Daybrook)

Barnfather, Christopher (CON - Ravenshead)
Cllr.Chris.Barnfather@gedling.gov.uk

Beeston, Denis (LAB - Bestwood Village)
cllr.denis.beeston@gedling.gov.uk

Bexon, Alan (CON - Woodthorpe)
Cllr.Alan.Bexon@gedling.gov.uk

Blair, Krista (LAB - Gedling)
cllr.krista.blair@gedling.gov.uk

Boot, John (CON - Woodborough)
Cllr.John.Boot@gedling.gov.uk

Brooks, Nicki (LAB - Carlton)
Cllr.Nicki.Brooks@gedling.gov.uk

Clarke, Ged (CON - Mapperley Plains)
cllr.ged.clarke@gedling.gov.uk

Collis, Bob (LAB - Porchester)
cllr.bob.collis@gedling.gov.uk

Creamer, Jim (LAB - Carlton Hill)
Cllr.Seamus.Creamer@gedling.gov.uk

Ellis, David (LAB - Kingswell)
cllr.david.ellis@gedling.gov.uk

Ellis, Roxanne (LAB - Bonington)
Cllr.Roxanne.Ellis@gedling.gov.uk

Ellwood, Andrew (LD - Phoenix)
cllr.andrew.ellwood@gedling.gov.uk

Feeney, Paul (LAB - Carlton Hill)
Cllr.Paul.Feeney@gedling.gov.uk

Fox, Kathryn (LAB - St James)
Cllr.Kathryn.Fox@gedling.gov.uk

Gillam, Anthony (LD - St James)
Cllr.Anthony.Gillam@gedling.gov.uk

Glover, Mark (LAB - Carlton)
Cllr.Mark.Glover@gedling.gov.uk

Gregory, Gary (LAB - Valley)
Cllr.Gary.Gregory@gedling.gov.uk

Hewlett, Cheryl (LAB - Phoenix)
cherylhewlett44@hotmail.co.uk

Hewson, Sarah (CON - Kingswell)
sarah.hewson2@ntlworld.com

Hollingsworth, Jenny (LAB - Gedling)
Cllr.Jenny.Hollingsworth@gedling.gov.uk

Hope, Mike (LAB - Calverton)
Cllr.Mike.Hope@gedling.gov.uk

Hughes, Paul (LD - Valley)
paul.hughes@futuresnn.co.uk

Lawrence, Meredith (LAB - Netherfield and Colwick)
Cllr.Meredith.Lawrence@gedling.gov.uk

McCauley, Phil (LAB - Bonington)
philmccauley@yahoo.co.uk

Miller, Barbara (LAB - Netherfield and Colwick)
Cllr.Barbara.Miller@gedling.gov.uk

Nicholson, Richard (CON - Woodthorpe)

Paling, Marje (LAB - St Mary's)
Cllr.Marje.Paling@gedling.gov.uk

Parr, John (CON - Mapperley Plains)
Cllr.John.Parr@gedling.gov.uk

Pearson, Lynda (LAB - Gedling)
cllr.lynda.pearson@gedling.gov.uk

Pepper, Carol (CON - Mapperley Plains)
Cllr.Carol.Pepper@gedling.gov.uk

Poole, Stephen (CON - Burton Joyce and Stoke Bardolph)
Cllr.Stephen.Poole@gedling.gov.uk

Powell, Colin (CON - Ravenshead)
Cllr.Colin.Powell@gedling.gov.uk

Prew-Smith, Suzanne (CON - Woodthorpe)
Cllr.suzanne.prew-smith@gedling.gov.uk

Pulk, Darrell (LAB - Carlton Hill)
Cllr.Darrell.Pulk@gedling.gov.uk

Quilty, Nick (LAB - Calverton)
qcoach@googlemail.com

Spencer, Roland (CON - Lambley)
Cllr.Roland.Spencer@gedling.gov.uk

Tomlinson, Sarah (CON - Burton Joyce and Stoke Bardolph)
sarahj_tomlinson@hotmail.co.uk

Truscott, John (LAB - Porchester)
Cllr.John.Truscott@gedling.gov.uk

Weisz, Muriel (LAB - Porchester)
Cllr.Muriel.Weisz@gedling.gov.uk

Wheeler, Henry (LAB - Killisick)
Cllr.Henry.Wheeler@gedling.gov.uk

POLITICAL COMPOSITION
LAB: 32, CON: 15, LD: 3

Glasgow, City of S

Glasgow City Council, City Chambers, George Square, Glasgow G2 1DU
☎ 0141 287 2000 🖷 0141 287 5666 ✉ pr@glasgow.gov.uk
💻 www.glasgow.gov.uk

FACTS AND FIGURES
Parliamentary Constituencies: Glasgow Central, Glasgow East, Glasgow North, Glasgow North East, Glasgow North West, Glasgow South, Glasgow South West
EU Constituencies: Scotland
Election Frequency: Elections are of whole council

PRINCIPAL OFFICERS
Chief Executive: Ms Anne Marie O'Donnell Chief Executive, City Chambers, George Square, Glasgow G2 1DU ☎ 0141 287 4739 🖷 0141 287 3627 ✉ annemarie.o'donnell@ced.glasgow.gov.uk

Senior Management: Mr Richard Brown Executive Director - Financial Services, City Chambers, George Square, Glasgow G2 1DU ☎ 0141 287 3837 🖷 0141 287 3917 ✉ lynn.brown@fs.glasgow.gov.uk

Senior Management: Mr Brian Devlin Executive Director - Land & Environmental Services, Exchange House, 231 George Street, Glasgow G1 1RX ☎ 0141 287 9100 ✉ brian.devlin@glasgow.gov.uk

Senior Management: Mr Colin Edgar Head of Communication & Service Development, City Chambers, George Square, Glasgow G2 1DU

Senior Management: Ms Carole Forrest Acting Executive Director - Corporate Services, 40 John Street, Glasgow G1 1JT ☎ 0141 287 0467 🖷 0141 287 5589 ✉ carole.forrest@glasgow.gov.uk

Senior Management: Ms Maureen McKenna Executive Director - Education Services, City Chambers, George Square, Glasgow G2 1DU ☎ 0141 287 4551 🖷 0141 287 4895 ✉ maureen.mckenna@education.glasgow.gov.uk

Senior Management: Mr Hugh Munro City Assessor & Electoral Registration Officer, Richmond Square, 20 Cadogan Street, Glasgow G2 7AD ☎ 0141 287 7515 ✉ hugh.munro@fs.glasgow.gov.uk

Senior Management: Mr David Williams Executive Director - Social Work Services, City Chambers, George Square, Glasgow G2 1DU ☎ 0141 287 8853 ✉ david.williams@glasgow.gov.uk

Access Officer / Social Services (Disability): Ms Liz Oswald Policy Officer, City Chambers, George Square, Glasgow G2 1DU ☎ 0141 287 3840 🖷 0141 287 5997 ✉ liz.oswald@glasgow.gov.uk

Architect, Building / Property Services: Mr Richard Brown Executive Director - Financial Services, Exchange House, 231 George Street, Glasgow G1 1RX ☎ 0141 287 3837 🖷 0141 287 3917 ✉ lynn.brown@fs.glasgow.gov.uk

Architect, Building / Property Services: Mr Tom Turley Assistant Director of Development & Regeneration Services, Exchange House, 229 George Street, Glasgow G1 1QU ☎ 0141 287 8571 ✉ tom.turley@glasgow.gov.uk

Building Control: Mr Forbes Barron Head of Planning & Building Control, City Chambers, George Square, Glasgow G2 1DU ☎ 0141 287 6064 ✉ forbes.barron@glasgow.gov.uk

Children / Youth Services: Ms Jill Miller, Director of Cultural Services, Glasgow Life, 220 High Street, Glasgow G4 0QW ☎ 0141 287 8900 🖷 0141 287 8909 ✉ jill.miller@glasgow.gov.uk

Civil Registration: Ms Fiona Borland Chief Registrar, 1 Martha Street, Glasgow G1 1JJ ☎ 0141 287 7653 🖷 0141 287 7666 ✉ fiona.borland@glasgow.gov.uk

PR / Communications: Mr Chris Starrs PR Manager, City Chambers, George Square, Glasgow G2 1DU ☎ 0141 287 5742 🖷 0141 287 0925 ✉ chris.starrs@glasgow.gov.uk

Community Safety: Mr Phil Walker, Managing Director of Glasgow Community & Safety Services, Eastgate, 727 London Road, Glasgow G40 3AP ☎ 0141 276 7627 🖷 0141 276 7499 ✉ phil.walker@glasgow.gov.uk

Computer Management: Ms Angela Murphy, Head of Information Technology, 350 Darnick Street, Glasgow G21 4BA ☎ 0141 287 2381 🖷 0141 287 2238 ✉ angela.murphy@glasgow.gov.uk

Corporate Services: Mr Ian Hooper Director of Special Projects, Glasgow Life, 220 High Street, Glasgow G4 0QW ☎ 0141 287 0961 🖷 0141 287 5151 ✉ ian.hooper@glasgowlife.org.uk

Corporate Services: Ms Sharon Wearing Chief Officer - Finance & Resources, City Chambers, George Square, Glasgow G2 1DU ☎ 0141 287 8838 🖷 0141 287 8840 ✉ sharon.wearing@sw.glasgow.gov.uk

Corporate Services: Mr Jim Wilson Head of Quality Improvement, City Chambers, George Square, Glasgow G2 1DU ☎ 0141 287 4573 🖷 0141 287 4895 ✉ jim.wilson@education.glasgow.gov.uk

Customer Service: Ms Bernadette Cooklin, Corporate Customer Care Development Manager, Room 4, City Chambers, George Square, Glasgow G2 1DU ☎ 0141 276 1257 🖷 0141 287 4575 ✉ bernadette.cooklin@ced.glasgow.gov.uk

Economic Development: Mr David Coyne Head of City Deal, City Chambers, George Square, Glasgow G2 1DU ☎ 0141 287 6487 ✉ david.coyne@glasgow.gov.uk

Education: Ms Maureen McKenna Executive Director - Education Services, City Chambers, George Square, Glasgow G2 1DU ☎ 0141 287 4551 🖷 0141 287 4895 ✉ maureen.mckenna@education.glasgow.gov.uk

Electoral Registration: Mr Hugh Munro City Assessor & Electoral Registration Officer, Richmond Square, 20 Cadogan Street, Glasgow G2 7AD ☎ 0141 287 7515 ✉ hugh.munro@fs.glasgow.gov.uk

Events Manager: Mr Colin Hartley Head of Events, City Chambers, George Square, Glasgow G2 1DU ☎ 0141 287 2000 ✉ colin.hartley@glasgow.gov.uk

Events Manager: Mr Keith Russell Head of Sport, Glasgow Life, 220 High Street, Glasgow G4 0QW ☎ 0141 287 5975 🖷 0141 287 5151 ✉ keith.russell@glasgow.gov.uk

Finance: Ms Lynn Brown, Executive Director - Financial Services, City Chambers, George Square, Glasgow G2 1DU ☎ 0141 287 3837 🖷 0141 287 3917 ✉ lynn.brown@fs.glasgow.gov.uk

Treasury: Mr Paul Rooney, City Treasurer, City Chambers, George Square, Glasgow G2 1DU ☎ 0141 287 0234 ✉ paul.rooney@glasgow.gov.uk

Pensions: Ms Jacqueline Gillies Assistant Pension Investments Officer, PO Box 27001, Glasgow G2 9EW ☎ 0845 213 0202 ✉ spfo@glasgow.gov.uk

Pensions: Mr Richard Keery Pension Investments Manager, PO Box 27001, , Glasgow G2 9EW ☎ 0845 213 0202 ✉ spfo@glasgow.gov.uk

Pensions: Mr Richard McIndoe Pensions Manager, PO Box 27001, Glasgow G2 9EW ☎ 0845 213 0202 ✉ spdo@glasgow.gov.uk

Highways: Mr Brian Devlin Executive Director - Land & Environmental Services, Exchange House, 231 George Street, Glasgow G1 1RX ☎ 0141 287 9100 ✉ brian.devlin@glasgow.gov.uk

Housing: Mr Patrick Flynn Head of Housing Investment, City Chambers, George Square, Glasgow G2 1DU ☎ 0141 287 8467 ✉ patrick.flynn@glasgow.gov.uk

Housing Maintenance: Mr Graham Paterson Executive Director, 350 Darnick Street, Glasgow G21 4BA ☎ 0141 287 1786 🖷 0141 287 2159 ✉ graham.paterson@citybuildingglasgow.gov.uk

Legal: Ms Anne Marie O'Donnell Chief Executive, City Chambers, George Square, Glasgow G2 1DU ☎ 0141 287 4739 🖷 0141 287 3627 ✉ annemarie.o'donnell@ced.glasgow.gov.uk

Leisure and Cultural Services: Dr Bridget McConnell, Chief Executive - Glasgow Life, Glasgow Life, 220 High Street, Glasgow G4 0QW ☎ 0141 287 5058 🖷 0141 287 5151 ✉ bridget.mcconnell@csglasgow.org

Leisure and Cultural Services: Mr Mark O'Neill, Director of Policy & Research, Glasgow Life, 220 High Street, Glasgow G4 0QW ☎ 0141 287 0446 🖷 0141 287 5151 ✉ mark.o'neill@csglasgow.org

Leisure and Cultural Services: Mr Keith Russell Head of Sport, Glasgow Life, 220 High Street, Glasgow G4 0QW ☎ 0141 287 5975 🖷 0141 287 5151 ✉ keith.russell@glasgow.gov.uk

Lifelong Learning: Mrs Jane Edgar Head of Learning, Glasgow Life, 220 High Street, Glasgow G4 0QW ☎ 0141 287 8937 ✉ jane.edgar@glasgowlife.org.uk

Lighting: Mr George Gillespie, Assistant Director of Land & Environmental Services, 231 George Street, Glasgow G1 1RX ☎ 0141 287 9106 🖷 0141 287 9013 ✉ george.gillespie@glasgow.gov.uk

Lottery Funding, Charity and Voluntary: Ms Lynn Brown, Executive Director - Financial Services, City Chambers, George Square, Glasgow G2 1DU ☎ 0141 287 3837 🖷 0141 287 3917 ✉ lynn.brown@fs.glasgow.gov.uk

Member Services: Ms Carole Forrest Acting Executive Director - Corporate Services, 40 John Street, Glasgow G1 1JT ☎ 0141 287 0467 🖷 0141 287 5589 ✉ carole.forrest@glasgow.gov.uk

Parking: Mr Willie Taggart Managing Director - City Parking, Anderston Centre, 5 Cadogen Square, Glasgow G2 7PH ☎ 0141 276 1835 ✉ willie.taggart@cityparkingglasgow.co.uk

Personnel / HR: Mr Robert Anderson Executive HR Manager, City Chambers, George Square, Glasgow G2 1DU ✉ robert.anderson@glasgow.gov.uk

Planning: Mr Forbes Barron Head of Planning & Building Control, City Chambers, George Square, Glasgow G2 1DU ☎ 0141 287 6064 ✉ forbes.barron@glasgow.gov.uk

Planning: Mr Ian Manson, Chief Executive of Clyde Gateway, Clyde Gateway, 15 Bridgeton Cross, Glasgow G40 1BN ☎ 0141 276 1567 🖷 0141 276 1578 ✉ ian.manson@glasgow.gov.uk

Procurement: Ms Margaret McKechnie Head of Corporate Procurement, 235 Geroge Street, Glasgow G2 1DU ☎ 0141 287 2000 ✉ margaret.mckechnie@glasgow.gov.uk

Public Libraries: Mr Gordon Anderson Cultural Venues Manager, Glasgow Life, 220 High Street, Glasgow G4 0QW ☎ 0141 287 5114 ✉ gordon.anderson@glasgow.gov.uk

Recycling & Waste Minimisation: Mr Rolf Matthews, Waste Disposal Manager, Exchange House, 231 George Street, Glasgow G1 1RX ☎ 0141 287 2082 ✉ rolf.matthews@glasgow.gov.uk

GLASGOW, CITY OF

Regeneration: Mr Richard Brown Executive Director - Financial Services, Exchange House, 231 George Street, Glasgow G1 1RX ☎ 0141 287 3837 🖷 0141 287 3917 ✉ lynn.brown@fs.glasgow.gov.uk

Road Safety: Mr George Cairns Engineering Officer, Richmond Exchange, 20 Cadogan Street, Glasgow G2 7AD ☎ 0141 287 9043 🖷 0141 287 9041 ✉ george.cairns@land.glasgow.gov.uk

Social Services: Mr David Williams Executive Director - Social Work Services, City Chambers, George Square, Glasgow G2 1DU ☎ 0141 287 8853 ✉ david.williams@glasgow.gov.uk

Tourism: Mr Scott Taylor, Chief Executive of Glasgow City Marketing Bureau, 11 George Square, Glasgow G2 1DY ☎ 0141 566 0809 🖷 0141 566 4073 ✉ scott.taylor@seeglasgow.com

Waste Collection and Disposal: Mr Brian Devlin Executive Director - Land & Environmental Services, Exchange House, 231 George Street, Glasgow G1 1RX ☎ 0141 287 9100 ✉ brian.devlin@glasgow.gov.uk

COUNCILLORS

Leader of the Council **Matheson**, Gordon (LAB - Anderston/City)
gordon.matheson@councillors.glasgow.gov.uk

Adams, James (LAB - Govan)
james.adams2@councillors.glasgow.gov.uk

Aitken, Susan (SNP - Langside)
susan.aitken@councillors.glasgow.gov.uk

Andrew, Ken (SNP - Hillhead)
ken.andrew@councillors.glasgow.gov.uk

Baker, Nina (SGP - Anderston/City)
nina.baker@councillors.glasgow.gov.uk

Balfour, Malcolm (SNP - Drumchapel/Anniesland)
malcolm.balfour@councillors.glasgow.gov.uk

Bartos, Martin (SGP - Patrick West)
martin.bartos@councillors.glasgow.gov.uk

Bolander, Eva (SNP - Anderston/City)
eva.bolander@glasgow.gov.uk

Boyle, Gerry (SNP - North East)
gerry.boyle2@councillors.glasgow.gov.uk

Braat, Philip (LAB - Anderston/City)
philip.braat@councillors.glasgow.gov.uk

Burke, Maureen (LAB - North East)
maureen.burke@councillors.glasgow.gov.uk

Butler, Bill (LAB - Greater Pollok)
bill.butler@councillors.glasgow.gov.uk

Cameron, Liz (LAB - Garscadden/Scotstounhill)
liz.cameron@councillors.glasgow.gov.uk

Carey, Paul (LAB - Drumchapel/Anniesland)
paul.carey@councillors.glasgow.gov.uk

Clark, Margot (LD - Linn)
margot.clark@councillors.glasgow.gov.uk

Coleman, James (LAB - Baillieston)
james.coleman@councillors.glasgow.gov.uk

Colleran, Aileen (LAB - Patrick West)
aileen.colleran@councillors.glasgow.gov.uk

Cunning, Malcolm (LAB - Linn)
malcolm.cunning@councillors.glasgow.gov.uk

Curran, Stephen (LAB - Newlands/Auldburn)
stephen.curran@councillors.glasgow.gov.uk

Dalton, Feargal (SNP - Patrick West)
feargal.dalton@councillors.glasgow.gov.uk

Davidson, Gilbert (LAB - Springburn)
gilbert.davidson@councillors.glasgow.gov.uk

Docherty, Josephine (SNP - Newlands/Auldburn)
josephine.docherty@councillors.glasgow.gov.uk

Docherty, Sadie (LAB - Linn)
sadie.docherty@councillors.glasgow.gov.uk

Docherty, Frank (LAB - East Centre)
frank.docherty@councillors.glasgow.gov.uk

Dornan, Stephen (LAB - Govan)
stephen.dornan@councillors.glasgow.gov.uk

Dunn, Jennifer (SNP - East Centre)
jennifer.dunn@councilors.glasgow.gov.uk

Elder, Glenn (SNP - Linn)
glenn.elder@councillors.glasgow.gov.uk

Findlay, Jonathan (LAB - Drumchapel/Anniesland)
jonathan.findlay@councillors.glasgow.gov.uk

Fisher, Judith (LAB - Drumchapel/Anniesland)
judith.fisher@councillors.glasgow.gov.uk

Garrity, Marie (LAB - Baillieston)
marie.garrity@councillors.glasgow.gov.uk

Gillan, Emma (LAB - Newlands/Auldburn)
emma.gillan@councillors.glasgow.gov.uk

Graham, Archie (LAB - Langside)
archie.graham@councillors.glasgow.gov.uk

Greene, Phil (SNP - Springburn)
phil.greene@councillors.glasgow.gov.uk

Hanif, Jahangir (SNP - Southside Central)
jahangir.hanif@councillors.glasgow.gov.uk

Hendry, Graeme (SNP - Garscadden/Scotstounhill)
graeme.hendry@councillors.glasgow.gov.uk

Hepburn, Greg (SNP - Calton)
greg.hepburn@glasgow.gov.uk

Hunter, Mhairi (SNP - Southside Central)
mhairi.hunter@councillors.glasgow.gov.uk

Hussain, Rashid (LAB - Greater Pollok)
rashid.hussain@councillors.glasgow.gov.uk

Jaffri, Shabbar (SNP - Greater Pollok)
shabbar.jaffri@councillors.glasgow.gov.uk

Kane, John (LAB - Govan)
john.kane@councillors.glasgow.gov.ukj

Kelly, John (LAB - Garscadden/Scotstounhill)
john.kelly2@councillors.glasgow.gov.uk

Kelly, Chris (LAB - Canal)
chris.kelly@councillors.glasgow.gov.uk

Kerr, Matthew (LAB - Craigton)
matthew.kerr@councillors.glasgow.gov.uk

Kucuk, Yvonne (LAB - Calton)
yvonne.kucuk@councillors.glasgow.gov.uk

Leonard, Gerald (LAB - North East)
gerald.leonard@councillors.glasgow.gov.uk

Letford, John (SNP - Maryhill/Kelvin)
john.letford@councillors.glasgow.gov.uk

MacLeod, Norman (SNP - Pollokshields)
norman.macleod@councillors.glasgow.gov.uk

McAllister, Billy (SNP - Canal)
billy.mcallister@councillors.glasgow.gov.uk

McAveety, Frank (LAB - Shettleston)
frank.mcaveety@councillors.glasgow.gov.uk

McDonald, David (SNP - Greater Pollok)
david.mcdonald@councillors.glasgow.gov.uk

McDougall, Elaine (LAB - East Centre)
elaine.mcdougall@councillors.glasgow.gov.uk

McElroy, Martin (SNP - Hillhead)
martin.mcelroy@councillors.glasgow.gov.uk

McKeever, Pauline (LAB - Hillhead)
paulineann.mckeever@councillors.glasgow.gov.uk

McLaughlin, John (SNP - Shettleston)
john.mclaughlin@councillors.glasgow.gov.uk

McLean, Kenny (SNP - Patrick West)
kenny.mclean@councillors.glasgow.gov.uk

Meikle, David (CON - Pollokshields)
david.meikle@councillors.glasgow.gov.uk

Neill, Martin (LAB - Shettleston)
martin.neill@councillors.glasgow.gov.uk

Raja, Hanif (LAB - Pollokshields)
hanif.raja@councillors.glasgow.gov.uk

Razaq, Mohammed (LAB - Maryhill/Kelvin)
mohammed.razaq@councillors.glasgow.gov.uk

Redmond, George (LAB - Calton)
george.redmond@councillors.glasgow.gov.uk

Rhodes, Martin (LAB - Maryhill/Kelvin)
martin.rhodes@councillors.glasgow.gov.uk

Richardson, Anna (SNP - Langside)
anna.richardson@glasgow.gov.uk

Robertson, Russell (LAB - East Centre)
russell.robertson@councillors.glasgow.gov.uk

Rooney, Paul (LAB - Garscadden/Scotstounhill)
paul.rooney@councillors.glasgow.gov.uk

Scally, Franny (SNP - Maryhill/Kelvin)
franny.scally@councillors.glasgow.gov.uk

Scanlon, James (LAB - Southside Central)
james.scanlon@councillors.glasgow.gov.uk

Sheridan, Austin (SNP - Baillieston)
austin.sheridan@councillors.glasgow.gov.uk

Siddique, Soryia (LAB - Southside Central)
soryia.siddique@councillors.glasgow.gov.uk

Simpson, Anne (LAB - Shettleston)
anne.simpson@councillors.glasgow.gov.uk

Singh, Sohan (LAB - North East)
sohan.singh@councillors.glasgow.gov.uk

Stephen, Helen (LAB - Canal)
helen.stephen@councillors.glasgow.gov.uk

Stewart, Allan (LAB - Springburn)
allan.stewart@councillors.glasgow.gov.uk

Thomas, Fariha (LAB - Govan)
fariha.thomas@councillors.glasgow.gov.uk

Torrance, Jim (SNP - Craigton)
jim.torrance@councillors.glasgow.gov.uk

Turner, David (SNP - Baillieston)
david.turner@councillors.glasgow.gov.uk

Wardrop, Martha (SGP - Hillhead)
martha.wordrop@councillors.glasgow.gov.uk

Watson, Alistair (LAB - Craigton)
alistair.watson@councillors.glasgow.gov.uk

Wild, Kieran (GRN - Canal)
kieran.wild@councillors.glasgow.gov.uk

Wilson, Alex (SNP - Craigton)
alex.wilson@glasgow.gov.uk

POLITICAL COMPOSITION

LAB: 45, SNP: 28, SGP: 3, CON: 1, LD: 1, GRN: 1

COMMITTEE CHAIRS

Children & Families: Ms Soryia Siddique

Finance & Audit: Mr Kenny McLean

Health & Social Care: Mr Mohammed Razaq

Licensing: Mr Chris Kelly

Planning: Mr James Scanlon

Gloucester City D

Gloucester City Council, c/o Gloucester City Council, Herbert Warehouse, The Docks, Gloucester GL1 2EQ
☎ 01452 522232 🖷 01452 396140 ✉ thecouncil@gloucester.gov.uk
🖳 www.gloucester.gov.uk

FACTS AND FIGURES

Parliamentary Constituencies: Gloucester
EU Constituencies: South West
Election Frequency: Elections are by thirds

PRINCIPAL OFFICERS

Chief Executive: Mr John McGinty Managing Director (Gloucester City) & Director - Commissioning (Gloucestershire CC), c/o Gloucester City Council, Herbert Warehouse, The Docks, Gloucester GL1 2EQ ☎ ✉ john.mcginty@gloucester.gov.uk

Senior Management: Mr Ross Cook Corporate Director, Herbert Warehouse, The Docks, Gloucester GL1 2EQ ☎ 01452 396355 ✉ ross.cook@gloucester.gov.uk

Senior Management: Mr Martin Shields Corporate Director of Services & Neighbourhoods, Herbert Warehouse, The Docks, Gloucester GL1 2EQ ☎ 01452 396745 ✉ martin.shields@gloucester.gov.uk

GLOUCESTER CITY

Architect, Building / Property Services: Mr Mark Foyn Asset Manager, c/o Gloucester City Council, Herbert Warehouse, The Docks, Gloucester GL1 2EQ ☎ 01452 396271 ✉ mark.foyn@gloucester.gov.uk

Best Value: Mr Martin Shields Corporate Director of Services & Neighbourhoods, Herbert Warehouse, The Docks, Gloucester GL1 2EQ ☎ 01452 396745 ✉ martin.shields@gloucester.gov.uk

Building Control: Ms Ruth Silk Business Improvement Officer, Herbert Warehouse, The Docks, Gloucester GL1 2EQ ☎ 01452 396712 ✉ ruth.silk@gloucester.gov.uk

Catering Services: Mr David Baldwin Senior Custodian, Herbert Warehouse, The Docks, Gloucester GL1 2EQ ☎ 01452 396185 ✉ david.baldwin@gloucester.gov.uk

Community Safety: Mr Edward Pomfret Health & Safety Service Manager, Herbert Warehouse, The Docks, Gloucester GL1 2EQ ☎ 01452 396069 ✉ edward.pomfret@gloucester.gov.uk

Contracts: Ms Diana Mumford Procurement Officer, Herbert Warehouse, The Docks, Gloucester GL1 2EQ ☎ 01452 396419 ✉ diana.mumford@gloucester.gov.uk

Corporate Services: Mr Terry Rodway Group Manager of Audit & Assurance, Herbert Warehouse, The Docks, Gloucester GL1 2EQ ☎ 01452 396430 ✉ terry.rodway@gloucester.gov.uk

Customer Service: Ms Wendy Jones, Customer Service Manager, Herbert Warehouse, The Docks, Gloucester GL1 2EQ ☎ 01452 396101 ✉ wendy.jones@gloucester.gov.uk

Economic Development: Mr Anthony Hodge Head of Regeneration & Economic Development, Herbert Warehouse, The Docks, Gloucester GL1 2EQ ☎ 01452 396034 ✉ anthony.hodge@gloucester.gov.uk

Electoral Registration: Mrs Kirsty Cox Senior Electoral Services Officer, Legal and Democratic Services, Herbert Warehouse, The Docks, Gloucester GL1 2EP ☎ 01452 396203 ✉ kirsty.cox@gloucester.gov.uk

Emergency Planning: Ms Gill Ragon Head of Public Protection, Herbert Warehouse, The Docks, Gloucester GL1 2EP ☎ 01452 396321 🖷 01452 396140 ✉ gill.ragon@gloucester.gov.uk

Energy Management: Mr Stephen McDonnell, Environmental Co-ordinator, Herbert Warehouse, The Docks, Gloucester GL1 2EQ ☎ ; 01452 396209 🖷 01452 366899 ✉ stephen.mcdonnell@gloucester.gov.uk

Environmental / Technical Services: Ms Gill Ragon Head of Public Protection, Herbert Warehouse, The Docks, Gloucester GL1 2EP ☎ 01452 396321 🖷 01452 396140 ✉ gill.ragon@gloucester.gov.uk

Environmental Health: Ms Gill Ragon Head of Public Protection, Herbert Warehouse, The Docks, Gloucester GL1 2EP ☎ 01452 396321 🖷 01452 396140 ✉ gill.ragon@gloucester.gov.uk

Estates, Property & Valuation: Mr Mark Foyn Asset Manager, c/o Gloucester City Council, Herbert Warehouse, The Docks, Gloucester GL1 2EQ ☎ 01452 396271 ✉ mark.foyn@gloucester.gov.uk

Events Manager: Ms Sarah Gilbert Guildhall Manager, c/o Gloucester City Council, Herbert Warehouse, The Docks, Gloucester GL1 2EQ ☎ 01452 396372 ✉ sarah.gilbert@gloucester.gov.uk

Facilities: Mr Anthony Hodge Head of Regeneration & Economic Development, Herbert Warehouse, The Docks, Gloucester GL1 2EQ ☎ 01452 396034 ✉ anthony.hodge@gloucester.gov.uk

Finance: Mr Jon Topping Head of Finance, Herbert Warehouse, The Docks, Gloucester GL1 2EQ ☎ 01452 396242 ✉ jon.topping@gloucester.gov.uk

Health and Safety: Mr Edward Pomfret Health & Safety Service Manager, Herbert Warehouse, The Docks, Gloucester GL1 2EQ ☎ 01452 396069 ✉ edward.pomfret@gloucester.gov.uk

Home Energy Conservation: Mr Stephen McDonnell, Environmental Co-ordinator, Herbert Warehouse, The Docks, Gloucester GL1 2EQ ☎ ; 01452 396209 🖷 01452 366899 ✉ stephen.mcdonnell@gloucester.gov.uk

Housing: Ms Helen Chard Housing Strategy & Enabling Service Manager, Herbert Warehouse, The Docks, Gloucester GL1 2EQ ☎ 01452 396534 ✉ helen.chard@gloucester.gov.uk

Housing Maintenance: Mr Ashley Green, Chief Executive of Gloucester City Homes, Railway House, Bruton Way, Gloucester GL1 1DG ☎ 01452 396471 ✉ ashleyg@gloucester.gov.uk

Licensing: Ms Gill Ragon Head of Public Protection, Herbert Warehouse, The Docks, Gloucester GL1 2EP ☎ 01452 396321 🖷 01452 396140 ✉ gill.ragon@gloucester.gov.uk

Member Services: Mrs Tanya Davies Democratic & Electoral Services Manager, Herbert Warehouse, The Docks, Gloucester GL1 2EQ ☎ 01452 396127 ✉ tanya.davies@gloucester.gov.uk

Personnel / HR: Mr Ashley Gough HR Adviser, Herbert Warehouse, The Docks, Gloucester GL1 2EQ ☎ 01452 396043 ✉ ashley.gough@gloucester.gov.uk

Planning: Mr Jon Sutcliffe Development Control Service Manager, Herbert Warehouse, The Docks, Gloucester GL1 2EQ ☎ 01452 396783 ✉ jon.sutcliffe@gloucester.gov.uk

Procurement: Ms Diana Mumford Procurement Officer, Herbert Warehouse, The Docks, Gloucester GL1 2EQ ☎ 01452 396419 ✉ diana.mumford@gloucester.gov.uk

Recycling & Waste Minimisation: Mr Stephen McDonnell, Environmental Co-ordinator, Herbert Warehouse, The Docks, Gloucester GL1 2EQ ☎ ; 01452 396209 🖷 01452 366899 ✉ stephen.mcdonnell@gloucester.gov.uk

Regeneration: Mr Anthony Hodge Head of Regeneration & Economic Development, Herbert Warehouse, The Docks, Gloucester GL1 2EQ ☎ 01452 396034 ✉ anthony.hodge@gloucester.gov.uk

Street Scene: Mr Lloyd Griffiths Head of Neighbourhood Services, Herbert Warehouse, The Docks, Gloucester GL1 2EQ ☎ 01452 396355 ✉ lloyd.griffiths@gloucester.gov.uk

Sustainable Communities: Mr Stephen McDonnell, Environmental Co-ordinator, Herbert Warehouse, The Docks, Gloucester GL1 2EQ ☎ ; 01452 396209 🖷 01452 366899 ✉ stephen.mcdonnell@gloucester.gov.uk

Sustainable Development: Mr Stephen McDonnell, Environmental Co-ordinator, c/o Gloucester City Council, Herbert Warehouse, The Docks, Gloucester GL1 2EQ ☎ 01452 396209 🖷 01452 366899 ✉ stephen.mcdonnell@gloucester.gov.uk

Waste Collection and Disposal: Mr Lloyd Griffiths Head of Neighbourhood Services, Herbert Warehouse, The Docks, Gloucester GL1 2EQ ☎ 01452 396355 ✉ lloyd.griffiths@gloucester.gov.uk

COUNCILLORS

***Mayor* Field**, Sebastian (LD - Kingsholm and Wotton)
sebastian.field@gloucester.gov.uk

***Deputy Mayor* Beeley**, James (LD - Hucclecote)
james.beeley@gloucester.gov.uk

***Leader of the Council* James**, Paul (CON - Longlevens)

***Deputy Leader of the Council* Dallimore**, Jennie (CON - Podsmead)
jennie.dallimore@gloucester.gov.uk

***Group Leader* Haigh**, Katie (LAB - Matson and Robinswood)
kate.haigh@gloucester.gov.uk

***Group Leader* Hilton**, Jeremy (LD - Kingsholm and Wotton)
jeremy.hilton@gloucester.gov.uk

Bhaimia, Usman (LD - Barton and Tredworth)
usman.bhaimia@gloucester.gov.uk

Brown, David (LD - Hucclecote)
david.brown@gloucester.gov.uk

Chatterton, Chris (LAB - Grange)
chris.chatterton@gloucester.gov.uk

Dee, Gerald (CON - Tuffley)
gerald.dee@gloucester.gov.uk

Etheridge, Chris (CON - Hucclecote)
chris.etheridge@gloucester.gov.uk

Gravells, Andrew (CON - Abbey)
andrew.gravells@gloucester.gov.uk

Hampson, Neil (LAB - Moreland)
neil.hampsom@gloucester.gov.uj

Hanman, Nigel (CON - Grange)
nigel.hanman@gloucester.gov.uk

Hansdot, Said (LAB - Barton and Tredworth)
ahmed.hansdot@gloucester.gov.uk

Hobbs, Mark (LAB - Moreland)
mark.hobbs@gloucester.gov.uk

Lewis, Andrew (CON - Quedgeley Severn Vale)
anddrew.lewis@gloucester.gov.uk

Llewellyn, Debbie (CON - Quedgeley Fieldcourt)
debbie.llewellyn@gloucester.gov.uk

Lugg, Janet (LAB - Matson and Robinswood)
janet.lugg@gloucester.gov.uk

McLellan, Phil (LD - Barnwood)
philip.mclellan@gloucester.gov.uk

Noakes, Lise (CON - Barnwood)
lise.noakes@gloucester.gov.uk

Norman, David (CON - Quedgeley Fieldcourt)

Norman, Hannah (CON - Quedgeley Severn Vale)
hannah.norman@gloucester.gov.uk

Organ, Colin (CON - Tuffley)
colin.organ@gloucester.gov.uk

Patel, Sajid (CON - Barton and Tredworth)
sajid.patel@gloucester.gov.uk

Pearsall, Laura (CON - Abbey)
laura.pearsall@gloucester.gov.uk

Porter, Jim (CON - Longlevens)
kim.porter@gloucester.gov.uk

Pullen, Terry (LAB - Moreland)
terry.pullen@gloucester.gov.uk

Randle, Tarren (CON - Barnwood)
tarren.randle@gloucester.gov.uk

Smith, Mary (LAB - Matson and Robinswood)
mary.smith@gloucester.gov.uk

Taylor, Gordon (CON - Abbey)
gordon.taylor@gloucester.gov.uk

Toleman, Paul (CON - Westgate)
paul.toleman@gloucester.gov.uk

Tracey, Pam (CON - Westgate)
pam.tracey@gloucester.gov.uk

Williams, Kathy (CON - Longlevens)
kathy.williams@gloucester.gov.uk

Witts, Susan (LD - Elmbridge)
susan.witts@gloucester.gov.uk

Witts, Chris (LD - Elmbridge)
chris.witts@gloucester.gov.uk

POLITICAL COMPOSITION

CON: 20, LAB: 8, LD: 8

COMMITTEE CHAIRS

Licensing: Ms Tarren Randle

Planning: Mr Gordon Taylor

Gloucestershire C

Gloucestershire County Council, Shire Hall, Westgate Street, Gloucester GL1 2TG
☎ 01452 425000 🖷 01452 425850 💻 www.gloucestershire.gov.uk

GLOUCESTERSHIRE

FACTS AND FIGURES

EU Constituencies: South West
Election Frequency: Elections are of whole council

PRINCIPAL OFFICERS

Chief Executive: Mr Peter Bungard, Chief Executive, Shire Hall, Westgate Street, Gloucester GL1 2TG ☎ 01452 583444 🖶 01452 425875 🖱 peter.bungard@gloucestershire.gov.uk

Senior Management: Ms Jane Burns, Director - Strategy & Challenge, Shire Hall, Westgate Street, Gloucester GL1 2TG ☎ 01452 328472 🖶 01452 425876 🖱 jane.burns@gloucestershire.gov.uk

Senior Management: Mr Duncan Jordan Group Director - Chief Operating Officer, Shire Hall, Westgate Street, Gloucester GL1 2TG ☎ 01452 425523 🖱 duncan.jordan@gloucestershire.gov.uk

Senior Management: Mr John McGinty Managing Director (Gloucester City) & Director - Commissioning (Gloucestershire CC), c/o Gloucester City Council, Herbert Warehouse, The Docks, Gloucester GL1 2EQ 🖱 john.mcginty@gloucester.gov.uk

Senior Management: Mr Nigel Riglar Commissioning Director - Communities & Infrastructure, Shire Hall, Westgate Street, Gloucester GL1 2TG 🖱 nigel.riglar@gloucestershire.gov.uk

Senior Management: Ms Sarah Scott Interim Director - Public Health, Shire Hall, Westgate Street, Gloucester GL1 2TG ☎ 01452 328497 🖱 sarah.scott@gloucestershire.gov.uk

Senior Management: Ms Linda Uren Commissioning Director - Children, Shire Hall, Westgate Street, Gloucester GL1 2TG ☎ 01452 328471 🖱 linda.uren@gloucestershire.gov.uk

Senior Management: Ms Jo Walker Director - Strategic Finance, Shire Hall, Westgate Street, Gloucester GL1 2TG ☎ 01453 328469 🖱 jo.walker@gloucestershire.gov.uk

Senior Management: Ms Margaret Willcox, Commissioning Director - Adults, Shire Hall, Westgate Street, Gloucester GL1 2TG ☎ 01452 328468 🖱 margaret.willcox@gloucestershire.gov.uk

Senior Management: Mrs Dilys Wynn Director - People Services, Shire Hall, Westgate Street, Gloucester GL1 2TG ☎ 01452 583413 🖱 dilys.wynn@gloucestershire.gov.uk

Architect, Building / Property Services: Mr Neil Corbett Head of Corporate Property Services, Shire Hall, Westgate Street, Gloucester GL1 2TG ☎ 01452 328813 🖱 neil.corbett@gloucestershire.gov.uk

Best Value: Mr Rob Ayliffe, Head of Policy & Performance, Shire Hall, Westgate Street, Gloucester GL1 2TG ☎ 01452 426613 🖱 rob.ayliffe@gloucestershire.gov.uk

Building Control: Mr Neil Corbett Head of Corporate Property Services, Shire Hall, Westgate Street, Gloucester GL1 2TG ☎ 01452 328813 🖱 neil.corbett@gloucestershire.gov.uk

Building Control: Mr Stephen Hetenyi, Support Services Manager, Shire Hall, Gloucester GL1 2TG ☎ 01452 328827 🖱 stephen.hetenyi@gloucestershire.gov.uk

Children / Youth Services: Mr Tim Browne Head of Special Educational Needs, Shire Hall, Westgate Street, Gloucester GL1 2TG ☎ 01452 328693 🖱 tim.browne@gloucestershire.gov.uk

Children / Youth Services: Mr Ian Godfrey Children In Care Service Manager, Shire Hall, Westgate Street, Block 1, Gloucester GL2 5GH ☎ 01452 427650 🖱 ian.godfrey@gloucestershire.gov.uk

Children / Youth Services: Mr Duncan Jordan Chief Operating Officer (Group Director), Shire Hall, Gloucester GL1 2TG ☎ 01452 425523 🖱 duncan.jordan@gloucestershire.gov.uk

Children / Youth Services: Mr Eugene O'Kane Programme Manager, Shire Hall, Westgate Street, Gloucester GL1 2TG ☎ 01452 583591 🖱 eugene.okane@gloucestershire.gov.uk

Children / Youth Services: Ms Lynne Speak, Operations Manager, 92-96 Westgate Street, Gloucester GL1 2PF ☎ 01452 583791 🖱 lynne.speak@gloucestershire.gov.uk

Civil Registration: Ms Sally Bye, Registration & Coroner Services Manager, Hillfield House, Denmark Road, Gloucester GL1 3LD ☎ 01242 532451 🖱 sally.bye@gloucestershire.gov.uk

Computer Management: Mr Gareth Steer Strategic Lead for ICT, Shire Hall, Westgate Street, Gloucester GL1 2TG ☎ 01452 583598 🖱 gareth.steer@gloucestershire.gov.uk

Consumer Protection and Trading Standards: Mr Eddie Coventry, Head of Trading Standards, Registration & Coroners, Hillfield House, Denmark Road, Gloucester GL1 3LD ☎ 01452 426786 🖱 eddie.coventry@gloucestershire.gov.uk

Contracts: Mr Simon Bilous Head of Commissioning, Shire Hall, Westgate Street, Gloucester GL1 2TG ☎ 01452 328489 🖱 simon.bilous@gloucestershire.gov.uk

Corporate Services: Ms Jane Burns, Director - Strategy & Challenge, Shire Hall, Gloucester GL1 2TG ☎ 01452 328472 🖶 01452 425876 🖱 jane.burns@gloucestershire.gov.uk

Corporate Services: Mr Stewart King Head of Business Development, Shire Hall, Westgate Street, Gloucester GL1 2TG ☎ 01452 328488 🖱 stewart.king@gloucestershire.gov.uk

Corporate Services: Mrs Dilys Wynn Director - People Services, Shire Hall, Westgate Street, Gloucester GL1 2TG ☎ 01452 583413 🖱 dilys.wynn@gloucestershire.gov.uk

Customer Service: Ms Tricia Gallagher Customer Service Team Operations Manager, Shire Hall, Westgate Street, Gloucester GL1 2TG ☎ 01452 427339 🖱 tricia.gallagher@gloucestershire.gov.uk

Customer Service: Ms Margaret Willcox, Commissioning Director - Adults, Shire Hall, Westgate Street, Gloucester GL1 2TG ☎ 01452 328468 🖱 margaret.willcox@gloucestershire.gov.uk

Education: Ms Jo Grills, Operations Director - Education, Learning & Libraries, Shire Hall, Gloucester GL1 2TG ☎ 01452 583559 jo.grills@gloucestershire.gov.uk

Education: Mr Duncan Jordan Chief Operating Officer (Group Director), Shire Hall, Gloucester GL1 2TG ☎ 01452 425523 duncan.jordan@gloucestershire.gov.uk

Environmental / Technical Services: Ms Jo Walker Director - Strategic Finance, Shire Hall, Westgate Street, Gloucester GL1 2TG ☎ 01453 328469 jo.walker@gloucestershire.gov.uk

Environmental Health: Mr Paul Cobb Safety Health & Environment Manager, Shire Hall, Westgate Street, Gloucester GL1 2TG ☎ 01452 426762 paul.cobb@gloucestershire.gov.uk

Estates, Property & Valuation: Mr Neil Corbett Head of Corporate Property Services, Shire Hall, Westgate Street, Gloucester GL1 2TG ☎ 01452 328813 neil.corbett@gloucestershire.gov.uk

Facilities: Mr Neil Corbett Head of Corporate Property Services, Shire Hall, Westgate Street, Gloucester GL1 2TG ☎ 01452 328813 neil.corbett@gloucestershire.gov.uk

Facilities: Mr Stephen Hetenyi, Support Services Manager, Shire Hall, Gloucester GL1 2TG ☎ 01452 328827 stephen.hetenyi@gloucestershire.gov.uk

Finance: Mr Graham Burrow Head of Finance & Exchequer, Shire Hall, Westgate Street, Gloucester GL1 2TG ☎ 01452 328944 graham.burrow@gloucestershire.gov.uk

Finance: Mr Mark Spilsbury Head of Finance for Financial Management, Shire Hall, Westgate Street, Gloucester GL1 2TG ☎ 01452 328920 mark.spilsbury@gloucestershire.gov.uk

Pensions: Mr Alan Marshall Pensions Administration Manager, Shire Hall, Westgate Street, Gloucester GL1 2TG ☎ 01452 328866 alan.marshall@gloucestershire.gov.uk

Pensions: Ms Jenny Pitcher Investment Manager, Llanthony Warehouse, The Docks, Gloucester GL1 2EH ☎ 01452 328308 jenny.pitcher@gloucestershire.gov.uk

Health and Safety: Mr Paul Cobb Safety Health & Environment Manager, Shire Hall, Westgate Street, Gloucester GL1 2TG ☎ 01452 426762 paul.cobb@gloucestershire.gov.uk

Local Area Agreement: Mr Rob Ayliffe, Head of Performance & Need, Shire Hall, Westgate Street, Gloucester GL1 2TG ☎ 01452 328506 rob.ayliffe@gloucestershire.gov.uk

Local Area Agreement: Ms Jane Burns, Director - Strategy & Challenge, Shire Hall, Westgate Street, Gloucester GL1 2TG ☎ 01452 328472 🖷 01452 425876 jane.burns@gloucestershire.gov.uk

Legal: Ms Christine Wray Head of Legal Services, Shire Hall, Westgate Street, Gloucester GL1 2TG ☎ 01452 328730 christine.wray@gloucestershire.gov.uk

Leisure and Cultural Services: Mr Chris Dee, Marketing Manager, Llanthony Warehouse, The Docks, Gloucester GL1 2EH ☎ 01452 328302 🖷 01452 426363 chris.dee@gloucestershire.gov.uk

Lifelong Learning: Mr Jim Austin Head of Adult Education, Llanthony Warehouse, The Docks, Gloucester GL1 2EH ☎ 01452 583810 jim.austin@gloucestershire.gov.uk

Lottery Funding, Charity and Voluntary: Mrs Rachel Wright, Voluntary Sector Manager, Shire Hall, Westgate Street, Gloucester GL1 2TG ☎ 01452 427615 🖷 01452 328638 rachel.wright@gloucestershire.gov.uk

Member Services: Mr Simon Harper Lead Democratic Services Advisor, Shire Hall, Westgate Street, Gloucester GL1 2TG ☎ 01452 324202 simon.harper@gloucestershire.gov.uk

Member Services: Mr Nigel Roberts, Head of Legal Services, Quayside House, First Floor, Gloucester GL1 2TG ☎ 01452 425201 nigel.roberts@gloucestershire.gov.uk

Parking: Mr Jim Daniels Parking Manager, Shire Hall, Westgate Street, Gloucester GL1 2TG ☎ 01452 425610 jim.daniels@gloucestershire.gov.uk

Partnerships: Ms Jane Burns, Director - Strategy & Challenge, Shire Hall, Westgate Street, Gloucester GL1 2TG ☎ 01452 328472 🖷 01452 425876 jane.burns@gloucestershire.gov.uk

Partnerships: Ms Linda Uren Commissioning Director - Children, Shire Hall, Westgate Street, Gloucester GL1 2TG ☎ 01452 328471 linda.uren@gloucestershire.gov.uk

Personnel / HR: Ms Susan Scrivens, Change Management Advisor Shire Hall, Gloucester GL1 2TG ☎ 01452 427683 🖷 01452 427683 sue.scrivens@gloucestershire.gov.uk

Personnel / HR: Mrs Dilys Wynn Director - People Services, Shire Hall, Westgate Street, Gloucester GL1 2TG ☎ 01452 583413 dilys.wynn@gloucestershire.gov.uk

Procurement: Mr Graham Collins Procurement Consultant, Shire Hall, Westgate Street, Gloucester GL1 2TG ☎ 01452 328124 graham.collins@gloucestershire.gov.uk

Public Libraries: Ms Margaret Willcox, Commissioning Director - Adults, Shire Hall, Westgate Street, Gloucester GL1 2TG ☎ 01452 328468 margaret.willcox@gloucestershire.gov.uk

Social Services: Mr Ian Godfrey Children In Care Service Manager, Shire Hall, Westgate Street, Block 1, Gloucester GL2 5GH ☎ 01452 427650 ian.godfrey@gloucestershire.gov.uk

Social Services: Ms Tina Reid Operations Lead: Adult Social Care & Business Development, Shire Hall, Westgate Street, Gloucester GL1 2TG ☎ 01452 427300 tina.reid@gloucestershire.gov.uk

Social Services: Ms Margaret Willcox, Commissioning Director - Adults, Shire Hall, Westgate Street, Gloucester GL1 2TG ☎ 01452 328468 margaret.willcox@gloucestershire.gov.uk

GLOUCESTERSHIRE

Social Services (Adult): Ms Margaret Willcox, Commissioning Director - Adults, Shire Hall, Westgate Street, Gloucester GL1 2TG ☎ 01452 328468 ✉ margaret.willcox@gloucestershire.gov.uk

Public Health: Ms Sarah Scott Interim Director - Public Health, Shire Hall, Westgate Street, Gloucester GL1 2TG ☎ 01452 328497 ✉ sarah.scott@gloucestershire.gov.uk

Sustainable Communities: Mr Peter Wiggins, Outcome Manager, Environment Directorate, Shire Hall, Westgate Street, Gloucester GL1 2TG ☎ 01452 328536 🖷 01452 541305 ✉ peter.wiggins@gloucestershire.gov.uk

Tourism: Mr Chris Dee, Marketing Manager, Llanthony Warehouse, The Docks, Gloucester GL1 2EH ☎ 01452 328302 🖷 01452 426363 ✉ chris.dee@gloucestershire.gov.uk

Waste Collection and Disposal: Mr Tony Childs Waste Services & Sustainability Manager, Shire Hall, Westgate Street, Gloucester GL1 2TG ☎ 01452 425448 ✉ tony.childs@gloucestershire.gov.uk

Waste Management: Mr Tony Childs Waste Services & Sustainability Manager, Shire Hall, Westgate Street, Gloucester GL1 2TG ☎ 01452 425448 ✉ tony.childs@gloucestershire.gov.uk

Waste Management: Mr Ian Mawdsley, Project Lead of Residual Waste Management, Shire Hall, Gloucester GL1 2TH ☎ 01452 425835 🖷 01452 425126 ✉ ian.mawdsley@gloucestershire.gov.uk

COUNCILLORS

***Chair* Morgan**, Graham (LAB - Cinderford)
graham.morgan@gloucestershire.gov.uk

***Vice-Chair* Hay**, Colin (LD - All Saints & Oakley)
colin.hay@gloucestershire.gov.uk

***Leader of the Council* Hawthorne**, Mark (CON - Quedgeley)
mark.hawthorne@gloucestershire.gov.uk

***Deputy Leader of the Council* Theodoulou**, Raymond (CON - Fairford & Lechdale on Thames)
raymond.theodoulou@gloucestershire.gov.uk

***Group Leader* Hilton**, Jeremy (LD - Kingsholm & Wotton)
jeremy.hilton@gloucestershire.gov.uk

***Group Leader* Preest**, Alan (UKIP - Lydney)
alan.preest@gloucestershire.gov.uk

***Group Leader* Prince**, David (IND - Pittville & Prestbury)
david.prince@gloucestershire.gov.uk

***Group Leader* Williams**, Lesley (LAB - Stonehouse)
lesley.williams@gloucestershire.gov.uk

Awford, Phil (CON - Highnam)
philip.awford@gloucestershire.gov.uk

Binns, Dorcas (CON - Nailsworth)
dorcas.binns@gloucestershire.gov.uk

Bird, Robert (CON - Bishop's Cleeve)
robert.bird@gloucestershire.gov.uk

Blackburn, Anthony (CON - Hardwicke & Severn)
anthony.blackburn@gloucestershire.gov.uk

Brown, David (LD - Barnwood & Hucclecote)
cllrdavid.brown@gloucestershire.gov.uk

Bullingham, Jason (CON - Bisley & Painswick)
jason.bullingham@gloucestershire.gov.uk

Coleman, Christopher (LD - St Mark's & St Peter's)
christopher.coleman@gloucestershire.gov.uk

Cordwell, John (LD - Wotton-under-Edge)
john.cordwell@gloucestershire.gov.uk

Dobie, Iain (LD - Leckhampton & Warden Hill)
iain.dobie@gloucestershire.gov.uk

Fisher, Bernard (LD - St Paul's & Swindon)
bernard.fisher@gloucestershire.gov.uk

Gill, Jasminder (LAB - Barton and Tredworth)
jasminder.gill@gloucestershire.gov.uk

Gravells, Andrew (CON - Abbey)
andrew.gravells@gloucestershire.gov.uk

Guyton, Colin (UKIP - Drybrook & Lydbrook)
colin.guyton@gloucestershire.gov.uk

Harman, Tim (CON - Landsown & Park)
tim.harman@gloucestershire.gov.uk

Harris, Joe (LD - Cirencester Park)
joe.harris@gloucestershire.gov.uk

Hicks, Anthony (CON - Tetbury)
tony.hicks@gloucestershire.gov.uk

Hodgkinson, Paul (LD - Bourton-on-the-Water & Northleach)
paul.hodgkinson@gloucestershire.gov.uk

Kirby, Barry (LAB - Grange & Kingsway)
barry.kirby@gloucestershire.gov.uk

Leppington, Richard (UKIP - Blakeney & Bream)
richard.leppington@gloucestershire.gov.uk

Lunnon, Sarah (GRN - Stroud Central)
sarah.lunnon@gloucestershire.gov.uk

Lydon, Stephen (LAB - Dursley)
stephen.lydon@gloucestershire.gov.uk

McHale, Stephen (LAB - Coney Hill & Matson)
steve.mchale@gloucestershire.gov.uk

McLain, Paul (CON - Battledown & Carlton Kings)
paul.mclain@gloucestershire.gov.uk

McMahon, Paul (LAB - Coleford)
paul.mcmahon@gloucstershire.gov.uk

Millard, Tracy (LAB - Tuffley)
tracy.millard@gloucestershire.gov.uk

Molyneux, Patrick (CON - Sedbury)
patrick.molyneux@gloucestershire.gov.uk

Moor, Nigel (CON - Stow-on-the-Wold)
nigel.moor@gloucestershire.gov.uk

Oosthuysen, Brian (LAB - Rodborough)
brian.oosthuysen@gloucestershire.gov.uk

Parsons, Shaun (CON - South Cerney)
shaun.parsons@gloucestershire.gov.uk

Robbins, Nigel (LD - Cirencester Beeches)
nigel.robbins@gloucestershire.gov.uk

Robinson, Brian (CON - Mitcheldean)
brian.robinson@gloucestershire.gov.uk

Smith, Vernon (CON - Tewkesbury East)
vernon.smith@gloucestershire.gov.uk

Stowe, Lynden (CON - Campden-Vale)
lynden.stowe@gloucestershire.gov.uk

Sudbury, Klara (LD - Charlton Park & College)
klara.sudbury@gloucestershire.gov.uk

Sztymiak, Mike (IND - Tewkesbury)
mike.sztymiak@gloucestershire.gov.uk

Tipper, Brian (CON - Cam Valley)
brian.tipper@gloucestershire.gov.uk

Tracey, Pam (CON - Hempsted & Westgate)
pam.tracey@gloucestershire.gov.uk

Vines, Robert (CON - Brockworth)
robert.vines@gloucestershire.gov.uk

Waddington, Stan (CON - Minchinhampton)
stan.waddington@gloucestershire.gov.uk

Wheeler, Simon (LD - Benhall & Up Hatherley)
simon.wheeler@gloucestershire.gov.uk

Whelan, Bill (LD - Churchdown)
bill.whelan@gloucestershire.gov.uk

Williams, Suzanne (LD - Hesters Way & Springbank)
suzanne.williams@gloucestershire.gov.uk

Williams, Kathy (CON - Longlevens)
kathy.williams@gloucestershire.gov.uk

Wilson, Roger (CON - Winchcombe & Woodmancote)
roger.wilson@gloucestershire.gov.uk

Windsor-Clive, Will (CON - Newent)
will.windsor-clive@gloucestershire.gov.uk

POLITICAL COMPOSITION
CON: 24, LD: 14, LAB: 9, UKIP: 3, IND: 2, GRN: 1

COMMITTEE CHAIRS
Audit & Governance: Mr Nigel Robbins

Children & Families: Mr Tim Harman

Environment & Communities: Mr Robert Bird

Health & Wellbeing: Ms Dorcas Binns

Pensions: Mr Raymond Theodoulou

Planning: Mr Nigel Moor

Gosport D

Gosport Borough Council, Town Hall, High Street, Gosport PO12 1EB
☎ 023 9258 4242 🖷 023 9254 5587 ✉ enquiries@gosport.gov.uk
🖳 www.gosport.gov.uk

FACTS AND FIGURES
Parliamentary Constituencies: Gosport
EU Constituencies: South East
Election Frequency: Elections are biennial

PRINCIPAL OFFICERS
Chief Executive: Mr Ian Lycett, Chief Executive, Town Hall, High Street, Gosport PO12 1EB ☎ 023 9251 5201 🖷 023 9251 1279 ✉ ian.lycett@gosport.gov.uk

Deputy Chief Executive: Ms Linda Edwards, Deputy Chief Executive & Borough Solicitor, Town Hall, High Street, Gosport PO12 1EB ☎ 023 9254 5401 🖷 023 9254 5587 ✉ linda.edwards@gosport.gov.uk

Access Officer / Social Services (Disability): Mr John Shaw, Head of Building Control, Town Hall, High Street, Gosport PO12 1EB ☎ 01329 824450 ✉ jshaw@fareham.gov.uk

Architect, Building / Property Services: Mr Mark Johnson Head of Property Services, Town Hall, High Street, Gosport PO12 1EB ☎ 023 9254 5563 🖷 023 9254 5588 ✉ mark.johnson@gosport.gov.uk

Best Value: Mrs Julie Petty, Head of Corporate Policy & Performance, Town Hall, High Street, Gosport PO12 1EB ☎ 023 9254 5381 🖷 023 9254 5238 ✉ julie.petty@gosport.gov.uk

Building Control: Mr John Shaw, Head of Building Control, Town Hall, High Street, Gosport PO12 1EB ☎ 01329 824450 ✉ jshaw@fareham.gov.uk

PR / Communications: Mrs Brenda Brooker, Press Officer, Town Hall, High Street, Gosport PO12 1EB ☎ 023 9254 5255 🖷 023 9254 5229 ✉ brenda.brooker@gosport.gov.uk

Community Planning: Mrs Julie Petty, Head of Corporate Policy & Performance, Town Hall, High Street, Gosport PO12 1EB ☎ 023 9254 5381 🖷 023 9254 5238 ✉ julie.petty@gosport.gov.uk

Community Safety: Mrs Julie Petty, Head of Corporate Policy & Performance, Town Hall, High Street, Gosport PO12 1EB ☎ 023 9254 5381 🖷 023 9254 5238 ✉ julie.petty@gosport.gov.uk

Computer Management: Mr David Eland Head of IT, Town Hall, High Street, Gosport PO12 1EB ☎ 023 9254 5309 ✉ david.eland@gosport.gov.uk

Contracts: Mr Stevyn Ricketts, Head of Streetscene, Town Hall, High Street, Gosport PO12 1EB ☎ 023 9254 5282 🖷 023 9258 8053 ✉ stevyn.ricketts@gosport.gov.uk

Economic Development: Mrs Lynda Dine, Head of Economic Prosperity, Town Hall, High Street, Gosport PO12 1EB ☎ 023 9254 5231 🖷 023 9254 5238 ✉ lynda.dine@gosport.gov.uk

E-Government: Mr David Eland Head of IT, Town Hall, High Street, Gosport PO12 1EB ☎ 023 9254 5309 ✉ david.eland@gosport.gov.uk

Electoral Registration: Ms Linda Edwards, Deputy Chief Executive & Borough Solicitor, Town Hall, High Street, Gosport PO12 1EB ☎ 023 9254 5401 🖷 023 9254 5587 ✉ linda.edwards@gosport.gov.uk

Emergency Planning: Mr Graeme Jesty Emergency Planning Officer, Town Hall, High Street, Gosport PO12 1EB ☎ 023 9254 5271 🖷 023 9254 5253 ✉ graeme.jesty@gosport.gov.uk

Environmental Health: Mr Ian Rickman Head of Environmental Health, Town Hall, High Street, Gosport PO12 1EB ☎ 023 9258 5517 🖷 023 9254 5360 ✉ irickman@fareham.gov.uk

GOSPORT

Estates, Property & Valuation: Mr Mark Johnson Head of Property Services, Town Hall, High Street, Gosport PO12 1EB ☎ 023 9254 5563 🖷 023 9254 5588 ✉ mark.johnson@gosport.gov.uk

European Liaison: Mrs Lynda Dine, Head of Economic Prosperity, Town Hall, High Street, Gosport PO12 1EB ☎ 023 9254 5231 🖷 023 9254 5238 ✉ lynda.dine@gosport.gov.uk

Finance: Mr Julian Bowcher Borough Treasurer, Town Hall, High Street, Gosport PO12 1EB ☎ 023 9254 5301 🖷 023 9254 5341 ✉ julian.bowcher@gosport.gov.uk

Treasury: Mr Julian Bowcher Borough Treasurer, Town Hall, High Street, Gosport PO12 1EB ☎ 023 9254 5301 🖷 023 9254 5341 ✉ julian.bowcher@gosport.gov.uk

Grounds Maintenance: Ms Caroline Smith, Landscape Management Officer, Town Hall, High Street, Gosport PO12 1EB ☎ 023 9258 4566 🖷 023 9258 8053 ✉ caroline.smith@gosport.gov.uk

Health and Safety: Mr Keith Perkins Health & Safety Officer, Town Hall, High Street, Gosport PO12 1EB ☎ 023 9254 5547 🖷 023 9254 5360 ✉ keith.perkins@gosport.gov.uk

Housing: Ms Corrine Waterfield Housing Services Manager, Town Hall, High Street, Gosport PO12 1EB ☎ 023 9254 5327 ✉ corrine.waterfield@gosport.gov.uk

Housing Maintenance: Mr Charles Harman, Head of Operational Services, Town Hall, High Street, Gosport PO12 1EB ☎ 023 9254 5287 🖷 023 9254 5285 ✉ charles.harman@gosport.gov.uk

Legal: Ms Linda Edwards, Deputy Chief Executive & Borough Solicitor, Town Hall, High Street, Gosport PO12 1EB ☎ 023 9254 5401 🖷 023 9254 5587 ✉ linda.edwards@gosport.gov.uk

Licensing: Mr Ian Rickman Head of Environmental Health, Town Hall, High Street, Gosport PO12 1EB ☎ 023 9258 5517 🖷 023 9254 5360 ✉ irickman@fareham.gov.uk

Member Services: Mr Mark Simmonds Head of Legal Services, Town Hall, High Street, Gosport PO12 1EB ☎ 023 9254 5653 🖷 023 9254 5587 ✉ mark.simmonds@gosport.gov.uk

Parking: Mr Graeme Mudge Team Leader of Enforcement Officer, Town Hall, High Street, Gosport PO12 1EB ☎ 023 9254 5569 🖷 023 9258 8053 ✉ graeme.mudge@gosport.gov.uk

Personnel / HR: Mrs Kathy Inch, Head of Personnel, Town Hall, High Street, Gosport PO12 1EB ☎ 023 9251 5524 🖷 023 9254 5253 ✉ kathy.inch@gosport.gov.uk

Planning: Ms Linda Edwards, Deputy Chief Executive & Borough Solicitor, Town Hall, High Street, Gosport PO12 1EB ☎ 023 9254 5401 🖷 023 9254 5587 ✉ linda.edwards@gosport.gov.uk

Procurement: Mrs Maree Hall Senior Procurement Officer, Town Hall, High Street, Gosport PO12 1EB ☎ 023 9254 5379 🖷 023 9254 5253 ✉ maree.hall@gosport.gov.uk

Recycling & Waste Minimisation: Mrs Angela Benneworth, Principal Contracts Officer, Town Hall, High Street, Gosport PO12 1EB ☎ 023 9254 8053 🖷 023 9254 5395 ✉ angela.benneworth@gosport.gov.uk

Regeneration: Mrs Lynda Dine, Head of Economic Prosperity, Town Hall, High Street, Gosport PO12 1EB ☎ 023 9254 5231 🖷 023 9254 5238 ✉ lynda.dine@gosport.gov.uk

Road Safety: Mr David Duckett, Head of Traffic Management, Town Hall, High Street, Gosport PO12 1EB ☎ 023 9254 5424 🖷 023 9254 5588 ✉ david.duckett@gosport.gov.uk

Staff Training: Mrs Kathy Inch, Head of Personnel, Town Hall, High Street, Gosport PO12 1EB ☎ 023 9251 5524 🖷 023 9254 5253 ✉ kathy.inch@gosport.gov.uk

Street Scene: Mr Stevyn Ricketts, Head of Streetscene, Town Hall, High Street, Gosport PO12 1EB ☎ 023 9254 5282 🖷 023 9258 8053 ✉ stevyn.ricketts@gosport.gov.uk

Sustainable Communities: Mrs Julie Petty, Head of Corporate Policy & Performance, Town Hall, High Street, Gosport PO12 1EB ☎ 023 9254 5381 🖷 023 9254 5238 ✉ julie.petty@gosport.gov.uk

Traffic Management: Mr David Duckett, Head of Traffic Management, Town Hall, High Street, Gosport PO12 1EB ☎ 023 9254 5424 🖷 023 9254 5588 ✉ david.duckett@gosport.gov.uk

Transport: Mr David Duckett, Head of Traffic Management, Town Hall, High Street, Gosport PO12 1EB ☎ 023 9254 5424 🖷 023 9254 5588 ✉ david.duckett@gosport.gov.uk

Transport Planner: Mr David Duckett, Head of Traffic Management, Town Hall, High Street, Gosport PO12 1EB ☎ 023 9254 5424 🖷 023 9254 5588 ✉ david.duckett@gosport.gov.uk

Waste Collection and Disposal: Mr Stevyn Ricketts, Head of Streetscene, Town Hall, High Street, Gosport PO12 1EB ☎ 023 9254 5282 🖷 023 9258 8053 ✉ stevyn.ricketts@gosport.gov.uk

COUNCILLORS

***Mayor* Farr**, Keith (LAB - Forton)
keith.farr@gosport.gov.uk

***Deputy Mayor* Hook**, Lynn (CON - Peel Common)
lynn.hook@gosport.gov.uk

***Leader of the Council* Hook**, Mark (CON - Alverstoke)
mark.hook@gosport.gov.uk

***Deputy Leader of the Council* Burgess**, Graham (CON - Lee East)

Allen, Roger (CON - Hardway)
roger.allen@gosport.gov.uk

Ballard, Susan (LD - Elson)
susan.ballard@gosport.gov.uk

Bateman, Piers (CON - Lee East)
piers.bateman@gosport.gov.uk

Batty, Linda (LAB - Bridgemary South)
linda.batty@gosport.gov.uk

Beavis, John (CON - Lee West)
john.beavis@gosport.gov.uk

Bergin, Patrick (UKIP - Rowner and Holbrook)
patrick.bergin@gosport.gov.uk

Carter, Chris (CON - Lee West)
chris.carter@gosport.gov.uk

Chegwyn, Peter (LD - Leesland)
peter.chegwyn@gosport.gov.uk

Cully, June (LAB - Town)
june.cully@gosport.gov.uk

Dickson, Richard (CON - Christchurch)
richard.dickson@gosport.gov.uk

Diffey, Maria (LD - Leesland)
maria.diffey@gosport.gov.uk

Edgar, Peter (CON - Alverstoke)
peter.edgar@gosport.gov.uk

Forder, Ingeborg (CON - Privett)

Forder, Robert (O - Anglesey)
robert.forder@gosport.gov.uk

Foster-Reed, Clive (LD - Forton)
clive.foster-reed@gosport.gov.uk

Geddes, Michael (CON - Bridgemary South)
michael.geddes@gosport.gov.uk

Gill, Keith (CON - Privett)
keith.gill@gosport.gov.uk

Hazel, Craig (CON - Elson)
craig.hazel@gosport.gov.uk

Hicks, Austin (LD - Brockhurst)
austin.hicks@gosport.gov.uk

Hylands, Robert (LD - Brockhurst)
robert.hylands@gosport.gov.uk

Jessop, Tony (CON - Grange)
tony.jessop@gosport.gov.uk

Langdon, Peter (CON - Hardway)
peter.langdon@gosport.gov.uk

Morgan, Margaret (CON - Grange)
margaret.morgan@gosport.gov.uk

Murphy, Marcus (CON - Rowner and Holbrook)
marcus.murphy@gosport.gov.uk

Philpott, Stephen (CON - Peel Common)
stephen.philpott@gosport.gov.uk

Roynane, Wayne (CON - Christchurch)
wayne.roynane@gosport.gov.uk

Scard, Alan (CON - Anglesey)
alan.scard@gosport.gov.uk

Searle, Diane (LAB - Town)
diane.searle@gosport.gov.uk

Wright, Dennis (LAB - Bridgemary North)

Wright, Jill (LAB - Bridgemary North)
jill.wright@gosport.gov.uk

POLITICAL COMPOSITION

CON: 20, LAB: 6, LD: 6, O: 1, UKIP: 1

Gravesham D

Gravesham Borough Council, Civic Centre, Windmill Street, Gravesend DA12 1AU
☎ 01474 564422 🖷 01474 337453
forename.surname@gravesham.gov.uk 💻 www.gravesham.gov.uk

FACTS AND FIGURES

Parliamentary Constituencies: Gravesham
EU Constituencies: South East
Election Frequency: Elections are of whole council

PRINCIPAL OFFICERS

Chief Executive: Mr David Hughes Chief Executive, Civic Centre, Windmill Street, Gravesend DA12 1AU ☎ 01474 337380 david.hughes@gravesham.gov.uk

Senior Management: Mr Nick Brown, Director - Finance & Environment, Brookvale, Springhead Road, Northfleet DA11 8HW ☎ 01474 337229 nick.brown@gravesham.gov.uk

Senior Management: Mr Kevin Burbidge, Director - Housing & Regeneration, Civic Centre, Windmill Street, Gravesend DA12 1BQ ☎ 01474 337585 kevin.burbidge@gravesham.gov.uk

Senior Management: Mrs Melanie Norris, Director - Communities, Civic Centre, Windmill Street, Gravesend DA12 1AU ☎ 01474 337324 melanie.norris@gravesham.gov.uk

Architect, Building / Property Services: Mrs Elizabeth Thornton Estates & Valuation Manager, Civic Centre, Windmill Street, Gravesend DA12 1AU ☎ 01474 337522 elizabeth.thornton@gravesham.gov.uk

Best Value: Mr Stuart Bobby Assistant Director - Corporate Performance, Civic Centre, Windmill Street, Gravesend DA12 1AU ☎ 01474 337431 stuart.bobby@gravesham.gov.uk

PR / Communications: Mr Graham Cole Communications Manager, Civic Centre, Windmill Street, Gravesend DA12 1AU ☎ 01474 337304 graham.cole@gravesham.gov.uk

Community Safety: Mr Simon Hookway, Service Manager - Economic Development, Civic Centre, Windmill Street, Gravesend DA12 1BQ ☎ 01474 337238 simon.hookway@gravesham.gov.uk

Computer Management: Mr Darren Everden Service Manager of IT Services, Civic Centre, Windmill Street, Gravesend DA12 1AU ☎ 01474 337240 darren.everden@gravesham.gov.uk

Customer Service: Ms Anita Tysoe, Services Manager of Customer & Theatre Services, Civic Centre, Windmill Street, Gravesend DA12 1AU ☎ 01474 337360 anita.tysoe@gravesham.gov.uk

Direct Labour: Mr Nick Brown, Director - Finance & Environment, Brookvale, Springhead Road, Northfleet DA11 8HW ☎ 01474 337229 nick.brown@gravesham.gov.uk

Economic Development: Mr Simon Hookway, Service Manager - Economic Development, Civic Centre, Windmill Street, Gravesend DA12 1BQ ☎ 01474 337238 simon.hookway@gravesham.gov.uk

GRAVESHAM

E-Government: Mr Darren Everden Service Manager of IT Services, Civic Centre, Windmill Street, Gravesend DA12 1AU ☎ 01474 337240 ✉ darren.everden@gravesham.gov.uk

Electoral Registration: Mrs Susan Hill Committee & Elections Manager, Civic Centre, Windmill Street, Gravesend DA12 1AU ☎ 01474 337247 ✉ sue.hill@gravesham.gov.uk

Emergency Planning: Mr Nick Brown, Director - Finance & Environment, Brookvale, Springhead Road, Northfleet DA11 8HW ☎ 01474 337229 ✉ nick.brown@gravesham.gov.uk

Environmental / Technical Services: Mrs Sarah Kilkie, Assistant Director - Communities, Civic Centre, Windmill Street, Gravesend DA12 1BQ ☎ 01474 337235 ✉ sarah.kilkie@gravesham.gov.uk

Environmental Health: Mrs Sarah Kilkie, Assistant Director - Communities, Civic Centre, Windmill Street, Gravesend DA12 1BQ ☎ 01474 337235 ✉ sarah.kilkie@gravesham.gov.uk

Estates, Property & Valuation: Ms Elizabeth Thornton Estate & Valuation Manager, Civic Centre, Windmill Street, Gravesend DA12 1AU ☎ 01474 337552 ✉ elizabeth.thornton@gravesham.gov.uk

European Liaison: Mr Kevin Burbidge, Director - Housing & Regeneration, Civic Centre, Windmill Street, Gravesend DA12 1BQ ☎ 01474 337585 ✉ kevin.burbidge@gravesham.gov.uk

Events Manager: Mr Adrian Hickmott Sport & Recreation Manager, Civic Centre, Windmill Street, Gravesend DA12 1AU ☎ 01474 337322 ✉ adrian.hickmott@gravesham.gov.uk

Events Manager: Ms Lyndsey Thompson Arts Development Officer, Civic Centre, Windmill Street, Gravesend DA12 1AU ☎ 01474 337442 ✉ lyndsey.thompson@gravesham.gov.uk

Facilities: Mrs Melanie Norris, Director - Communities, Civic Centre, Windmill Street, Gravesend DA12 1AU ☎ 01474 337324 ✉ melanie.norris@gravesham.gov.uk

Finance: Mr Nick Brown, Director - Finance & Environment, Civic Centre, Windmill Street, Gravesend DA12 1AU ☎ 01474 337229 ✉ nick.brown@gravesham.gov.uk

Finance: Mrs Julie Gibbs Assistant Director - Finance, Civic Centre, Windmill Street, Gravesend DA12 1AU ☎ 01474 337202 ✉ julie.gibbs@gravesham.gov.uk

Treasury: Mrs Julie Gibbs Assistant Director - Finance, Civic Centre, Windmill Street, Gravesend DA12 1AU ☎ 01474 337202 ✉ julie.gibbs@gravesham.gov.uk

Fleet Management: Mr Nick Brown, Director - Finance & Environment, Brookvale, Springhead Road, Northfleet DA11 8HW ☎ 01474 337229 ✉ nick.brown@gravesham.gov.uk

Grounds Maintenance: Mr Nick Brown, Director - Finance & Environment, Brookvale, Springhead Road, Northfleet DA11 8HW ☎ 01474 337229 ✉ nick.brown@gravesham.gov.uk

Health and Safety: Mrs Sarah Kilkie, Assistant Director - Communities, Civic Centre, Windmill Street, Gravesend DA12 1BQ ☎ 01474 337235 ✉ sarah.kilkie@gravesham.gov.uk

Housing: Mr Wale Adetoro Assistant Director of Housing, Civic Centre, Windmill Street, Gravesend DA12 1AU ☎ 01474 337816 ✉ wale.adetoro@gravesham.gov.uk

Housing Maintenance: Mr Wale Adetoro Assistant Director of Housing, Civic Centre, Windmill Street, Gravesend DA12 1AU ☎ 01474 337816 ✉ wale.adetoro@gravesham.gov.uk

Legal: Mr Mike Hayley, Assistant Director of Governance & Law, Civic Centre, Windmill Street, Gravesend DA12 1AU ☎ 01474 337256 ✉ mike.hayley@gravesham.gov.uk

Leisure and Cultural Services: Mr Adrian Hickmott Sport & Recreation Manager, Civic Centre, Windmill Street, Gravesend DA12 1AU ☎ 01474 337322 ✉ adrian.hickmott@gravesham.gov.uk

Licensing: Mrs Sarah Kilkie, Assistant Director - Communities, Civic Centre, Windmill Street, Gravesend DA12 1BQ ☎ 01474 337235 ✉ sarah.kilkie@gravesham.gov.uk

Member Services: Mrs Susan Hill Committee & Elections Manager, Civic Centre, Windmill Street, Gravesend DA12 1AU ☎ 01474 337247 ✉ sue.hill@gravesham.gov.uk

Parking: Mr Daniel Killian Operations Manager (Parking & Amenities), Civic Centre, Windmill Street, Gravesend DA12 1AU ☎ 01474 337820 ✉ paul.gibbons@gravesham.gov.uk

Partnerships: Mr Nick Brown, Director - Finance & Environment, Brookvale, Springhead Road, Northfleet DA11 8HW ☎ 01474 337229 ✉ nick.brown@gravesham.gov.uk

Personnel / HR: Mrs Melanie Norris, Director - Communities, Civic Centre, Windmill Street, Gravesend DA12 1AU ☎ 01474 337324 ✉ melanie.norris@gravesham.gov.uk

Planning: Mr Kevin Burbidge, Director - Housing & Regeneration, Civic Centre, Windmill Street, Gravesend DA12 1BQ ☎ 01474 337585 ✉ kevin.burbidge@gravesham.gov.uk

Procurement: Mr David Hollands, Procurement Manager, Civic Centre, Windmill Street, Gravesend DA12 1AU ☎ 01474 337446 ✉ david.hollands@gravesham.gov.uk

Recycling & Waste Minimisation: Mr Nick Brown, Director - Finance & Environment, Brookvale, Springhead Road, Northfleet DA11 8HW ☎ 01474 337229 ✉ nick.brown@gravesham.gov.uk

Regeneration: Mr Kevin Burbidge, Director - Housing & Regeneration, Civic Centre, Windmill Street, Gravesend DA12 1BQ ☎ 01474 337585 ✉ kevin.burbidge@gravesham.gov.uk

Staff Training: Mrs Melanie Norris, Director - Communities, Civic Centre, Windmill Street, Gravesend DA12 1AU ☎ 01474 337324 ✉ melanie.norris@gravesham.gov.uk

Sustainable Communities: Mr David Hughes Chief Executive, Civic Centre, Windmill Street, Gravesend DA12 1AU ☎ 01474 337380 ✉ david.hughes@gravesham.gov.uk

Sustainable Development: Mrs Sarah Kilkie, Assistant Director - Communities, Civic Centre, Windmill Street, Gravesend DA12 1BQ ☎ 01474 337235 ✉ sarah.kilkie@gravesham.gov.uk

Tourism: Mr Simon Hookway, Service Manager - Economic Development, Civic Centre, Windmill Street, Gravesend DA12 1BQ ☎ 01474 337238 ✉ simon.hookway@gravesham.gov.uk

Town Centre: Mr Simon Hookway, Service Manager - Economic Development, Civic Centre, Windmill Street, Gravesend DA12 1BQ ☎ 01474 337238 ✉ simon.hookway@gravesham.gov.uk

Traffic Management: Mr Rob Bright Senior Engineer, Civic Centre, Windmill Street, Gravesend DA12 1AU ☎ 01474 337580 ✉ rob.bright@gravesham.gov.uk

Transport Planner: Mr Tony Chadwick, Principal Planning Officer, Civic Centre, Windmill Street, Gravesend DA12 1AU ☎ 01474 337404 ✉ tony.chadwick@gravesham.gov.uk

Waste Collection and Disposal: Mr Nick Brown, Director - Finance & Environment, Brookvale, Springhead Road, Northfleet DA11 8HW ☎ 01474 337229 ✉ nick.brown@gravesham.gov.uk

Waste Management: Mr Nick Brown, Director - Finance & Environment, Brookvale, Springhead Road, Northfleet DA11 8HW ☎ 01474 337229 ✉ nick.brown@gravesham.gov.uk

COUNCILLORS

***Mayor* Wenban**, Michael (CON - Woodlands)
michael.wenban@gravesham.gov.uk

***Deputy Mayor* Goatley**, Greta (CON - Central)
greta.goatley@gravesham.gov.uk

***Leader of the Council* Cubitt**, John (CON - Meopham North)
john.cubitt@gravesham.gov.uk

***Deputy Leader of the Council* Turner**, David (CON - Istead Rise)
david.turner@gravesham.gov.uk

***Group Leader* Burden**, John (LAB - Northfleet South)
john.burden@gravesham.gov.uk

Ashenden, Valerie (LAB - Westcourt)
valerie.ashenden@gravesham.gov.uk

Bains, Gurjit (CON - Whitehill)
gurjit.bains@gravesham.gov.uk

Boycott, Lesley (CON - Meopham South and Vigo)
lesley.boycott@gravesham.gov.uk

Bungar, Gurdip Ram (LAB - Central)
gurdip.bungar@gravesham.gov.uk

Burgoyne, Julia (CON - Meopham North)
julia.burgoyne@gravesham.gov.uk

Caller, Colin (LAB - Westcourt)
colin.caller@gravesham.gov.uk

Caller, John (LAB - Westcourt)
john.caller@gravesham.gov.uk

Craske, Harold (CON - Higham)
harold.craske@gravesham.gov.uk

Cribbon, Jane (LAB - Pelham)
jane.cribbon@gravesham.gov.uk

Croxton, Lee (LAB - Riverside)
lee.croxton@gravesham.gov.uk

Francis, Brian (LAB - Singlewell)
brian.francis@gravesham.gov.uk

Garside, Sandra (CON - Painters Ash)
sandra.garside@gravesham.gov.uk

Halpin, Rob (LAB - Singlewell)
robert.halpin@gravesham.gov.uk

Handley, Glen (CON - Whitehill)
glen.handley@gravesham.gov.uk

Hills, Leslie (CON - Chalk)
leslie.hills@gravesham.gov.uk

Howes, Susan (LAB - Coldharbour)
susan.howes@gravesham.gov.uk

Howes, Les (LAB - Painters Ash)
les.howes@gravesham.gov.uk

Hurley, David (CON - Riverview)
david.hurley@gravesham.gov.uk

Jassal, Samir (CON - Shorne, Cobham & Luddesdown)
samir.jassal@gravesham.gov.uk

Knight, John (CON - Istead Riase)
John.knight@gravesham.gov.uk

Lambert, William (CON - Riverview)
william.lambert@gravesham.gov.uk

Langdale, Sara (CON - Woodlands)
sara.langdale@gravesham.gov.uk

Loughlin, John (LAB - Northfleet South)
john.loughlin@gravesham.gov.uk

McGarrity, Bronwen (CON - Coldharbour)
bronwen.mcgarrity@gravesham.gov.uk

Meade, Jordan (CON - Singlewell)
jordan.meade@gravesham.gov.uk

Milner, Lyn (LAB - Riverside)
lyn.milner@gravesham.gov.uk

Pearton, Leslie (CON - Higham)
leslie.pearton@graveshem.gov.uk

Pritchard, Anthony (CON - Woodlands)
anthony.pritchard@gravesham.gov.uk

Rayner, Peter (LAB - Northfleet North)
peter.rayner@gravesham.gov.uk

Ridgers, Alan (CON - Painters Ash)
alan.ridgers@gravesham.gov.uk

Rolles, Lenny (LAB - Riverside)
lenny.rolles@gravesham.gov.uk

Sangha, Brian (LAB - Pelham)
brian.sangha@gravesham.gov.uk

Scollard, Peter (LAB - Northfleet North)
peter.scollard@gravesham.gov.uk

Shelbrooke, Derek (CON - Meopham South and Vigo)
derek.shelbrooke@gravesham.gov.uk

Singh, Makhan (LAB - Pelham)
makhan.singh@gravesham.gov.uk

Singh-Thandi, Narinderjit (LAB - Northfleet South)
narinderjit.singh.thandi@gravesham.gov.uk

Sullivan, Lauren (LAB - Northfleet North)
lauren.sullivan@gravesham.gov.uk

Theobald, Robin (CON - Shorne, Cobham and Luddesdown)
robin.theobald@gravesham.gov.uk

Thomas, Steve (LAB - Central)
steve.thomas@gravesham.gov.uk

POLITICAL COMPOSITION
CON: 23, LAB: 21

COMMITTEE CHAIRS

Audit: Mr Derek Shelbrooke

Finance: Mr Derek Shelbrooke

Licensing: Mr Harold Craske

Great Yarmouth D

Great Yarmouth Borough Council, Town Hall, Hall Plain, Great Yarmouth NR30 2QF
☎ 01493 856100 🖷 01493 846332 ✉ gy@great-yarmouth.gov.uk
💻 www.great-yarmouth.gov.uk

FACTS AND FIGURES
Parliamentary Constituencies: Great Yarmouth
EU Constituencies: Eastern
Election Frequency: Elections are by thirds

PRINCIPAL OFFICERS

Chief Executive: Mr Gordon Mitchell Interim Chief Executive, Town Hall, Hall Plain, Great Yarmouth NR30 2QF

Senior Management: Mrs Jane Beck Director - Customer Services, Town Hall, Hall Plain, Great Yarmouth NR30 2QF
☎ 01493 846418 ✉ jeb@great-yarmouth.gov.uk

Senior Management: Mr Robert Read Director - Housing & Neighbourhoods, Greyfriars House, Greyfriars Way, Great Yarmouth NR30 2QE ☎ 01493 846278 ✉ rr@great-yarmouth.gov.uk

Building Control: Mr Dean Minns Group Manager - Planning, Town Hall, Hall Plain, Great Yarmouth NR30 2QF ☎ 01493 856100

PR / Communications: Mr Alan Carr, Group Manager - Tourism & Communications, Maritime House, 25 Marine Parade, Great Yarmouth NR30 2EN ☎ 01493 846341
✉ aac@great-yarmouth.gov.uk

Community Planning: Mr Robert Gregory Group Manager - Neighbourhoods & Communities, Town Hall, Hall Plain, Great Yarmouth NR30 2QF

Computer Management: Mrs Miranda Lee Group Manager - Customer Services, Town Hall, Hall Plain, Great Yarmouth NR30 2QF ☎ 01493 846536 ✉ mvl@great-yarmouth.gov.uk

Customer Service: Mrs Miranda Lee Group Manager - Customer Services, Town Hall, Hall Plain, Great Yarmouth NR30 2QF
☎ 01493 846536 ✉ mvl@great-yarmouth.gov.uk

Economic Development: Mr David Glason Group Manager - Growth, Town Hall, Hall Plain, Great Yarmouth NR30 2QF
✉ dcg@great-yarmouth.gov.uk

Electoral Registration: Ms Denise Harvey Acting Group Manager - Licensing & Elections, Town Hall, Hall Plain, Great Yarmouth NR30 2QF ☎ 01493 846100
✉ dgh@great-yarmouth.gov.uk

Environmental Health: Mr Glenn Buck Group Manager - Environmental Services, Town Hall, Hall Plain, Great Yarmouth NR30 2QF ☎ 01493 856547 ✉ gb@great-yarmouth.gov.uk

Estates, Property & Valuation: Mr Andy Dyson Group Manager - Property & Construction, Town Hall, Hall Plain, Great Yarmouth NR30 2QF ☎ 01493 846440

Finance: Mr Andy Radford Finance Officer, Town Hall, Hall Plain, Great Yarmouth NR30 2QF ☎ 01493 846132
✉ aradford@great-yarmouth.gov.uk

Finance: Ms Donna Summers Group Manager - Resources, Town Hall, Hall Plain, Great Yarmouth NR30 2QF ☎ 01493 846339
✉ dsummers@great-yarmouth.gov.uk

Housing: Mr Robert Read Director - Housing & Neighbourhoods, Greyfriars House, Greyfriars Way, Great Yarmouth NR30 2QE
☎ 01493 846278 ✉ rr@great-yarmouth.gov.uk

Licensing: Ms Denise Harvey Acting Group Manager - Licensing & Elections, Town Hall, Hall Plain, Great Yarmouth NR30 2QF
☎ 01493 846100 ✉ dgh@great-yarmouth.gov.uk

Member Services: Mr Robin Hodds, Member Services Manager, Town Hall, Hall Plain, Great Yarmouth NR30 2QF ☎ 01493 856100
🖷 01493 846332 ✉ rh@great-yarmouth.gov.uk

Parking: Mrs Miranda Lee Group Manager - Customer Services, Town Hall, Hall Plain, Great Yarmouth NR30 2QF ☎ 01493 846536
✉ mvl@great-yarmouth.gov.uk

Personnel / HR: Ms Kate Watts Group Manager - Transformation, Town Hall, Hall Plain, Great Yarmouth NR30 2QF ☎ 01493 846547
✉ kaw@great-yarmouth.gov.uk

Planning: Mr Dean Minns Group Manager - Planning, Town Hall, Hall Plain, Great Yarmouth NR30 2QF ☎ 01493 856100

Staff Training: Ms Kate Watts Group Manager - Transformation, Town Hall, Hall Plain, Great Yarmouth NR30 2QF ☎ 01493 846547
✉ kaw@great-yarmouth.gov.uk

Street Scene: Mr Jonathan Newman, Town Centre Manager, Unit 5, Wilkinsons Yard, Marketgates, Great Yarmouth NR30 2AX
☎ 01493 745828 🖷 01493 335315

Tourism: Mr Alan Carr, Group Manager - Tourism & Communications, Maritime House, 25 Marine Parade, Great Yarmouth NR30 2EN ☎ 01493 846341 aac@great-yarmouth.gov.uk

Town Centre: Mr Jonathan Newman, Town Centre Manager, Unit 5, Wilkinsons Yard, Marketgates, Great Yarmouth NR30 2AX ☎ 01493 745828 🖷 01493 335315

Transport Planner: Mr Jonathan Newman, Town Centre Manager, Unit 5, Wilkinsons Yard, Marketgates, Great Yarmouth NR30 2AX ☎ 01493 745828 🖷 01493 335315

COUNCILLORS

***Mayor* Weymouth**, Shirley (CON - East Flegg)
cllr.shirley.weymouth@great-yarmouth.gov.uk

***Leader of the Council* Plant**, Graham (CON - Bradwell North)
cllr.graham.plant@great-yarmouth.gov.uk

Andrews, Tom (UKIP - Caister South)
cllr.tom.andrews@great-yarmouth.gov.uk

Annison, Carl (UKIP - Bradwell South and Hopton)
cllr.carl.annison@great-yarmouth.gov.uk

Bird, Malcolm (UKIP - Central and Northgate)
cllr.malcolm.bird@great-yarmouth.gov.uk

Blyth, Anthony (LAB - Claydon)
cllr.anthony.blyth@great-yarmouth.gov.uk

Carpenter, Penny (CON - Caister North)
cllr.penny.carpenter@great-yarmouth.gov.uk

Coleman, Mary (CON - West Flegg)
cllr.mary.coleman@great-yarmouth.gov.uk

Coleman, Barry (CON - West Flegg)
cllr.barry.coleman@great-yarmouth.gov.uk

Collins, Bert (CON - Gorleston)
cllr.bert.collins@great-yarmouth.gov.uk

Connell, Robert (UKIP - Southtown and Cobholm)
cllr.robert.connell@great-yarmouth.gov.uk

Cutting, Jack (UKIP - Caister North)
cllr.jack.cutting@great-yarmouth.gov.uk

Davis, Lea (LAB - Central & Northgate)
cllr.lea.davis@great-yarmouth.gov.uk

Fairhead, Marlene (LAB - St Andrews)
cllr.marlene.fairhead@great-yarmouth.gov.uk

Fox, Colin (LAB - Yarmouth North)
cllr.colin.fox@great-yarmouth.gov.uk

Grant, Andy (CON - Bradwell South and Hopton)
cllr.andy.grant@great-yartmouth.gov.uk

Grey, Kay (UKIP - Gorleston)
cllr.kay.grey@great-yarmouth.gov.uk

Hanton, Ronald (CON - Ormesby)
cllr.ronald.hanton@great-yarmouth.gov.uk

Jeal, Michael (LAB - Nelson)
cllr.michael.jeal@great-yarmouth.gov.uk

Jermany, George (CON - East Flegg)
cllr.george.jermany@great-yarmouth.gov.uk

Jones, Rachel (UKIP - Yarmouth North)
cllr.rachel.jones@great-yarmouth.gov.uk

Lawn, Brian (CON - Lothinghland)
cllr.brian.lawn@great-yarmouth.gov.uk

Linden, Penny (LAB - Southtown and Cobholm)
cllr.penny.linden@great-yarmouth.gov.uk

Mavroudis, Demetris (CON - Caister South)
cllr.demetris.mavroudis@great-yarmouth.gov.uk

Myers, Adrian (UKIP - Lothingland)
cllr.adrian.myers@great-yarmouth.gov.uk

Pratt, Sylvia (LAB - Magdalen)
cllr.sylvia.pratt@great-yarmouth.gov.uk

Reynolds, Charles (CON - Ormesby)
cllr.charles.reynolds@great-yarmouth.gov.uk

Robinson-Payne, Kerry (LAB - Nelson)
cllr.kelly.payne@great-yarmouth.gov.uk

Rodwell, Tabitha (UKIP - Claydon)
cllr.tabitha.rodwell@great-yarmouth.gov.uk

Smith, Jamie (LAB - Bradwell North)
cllr.jamie.smith@great-yarmouth.gov.uk

Smith, Carl (CON - Bradwell North)
cllr.carl.smith@great-yarmouth.gov.uk

Stenhouse, Katy (UKIP - Nelson)
cllr.katy.stenhouse@great-yarmouth.gov.uk

Sutton, Lee (LAB - Central and Northgate)
cllr.lee.sutton@great-yarmouth.gov.uk

Thirtle, Haydn (CON - Fleggburgh)
cllr.haydn.thirtle@great-yarmouth.gov.uk

Wainwright, Hilary (LAB - Bradwell South and Hopton)
cllr.hilary.wainwright@great-yarmouth.gov.uk

Wainwright, Trevor (LAB - Magdalen)
cllr.trevor.wainwright@great-yarmouth.gov.uk

Walker, Brian (LAB - Magdalen)
cllr.brian.walker@great-yarmouth.gov.uk

Williamson, Bernard (LAB - Claydon)
cllr.bernard.williamson@great-yarmouth.gov.uk

Wright, Barbara (LAB - St Andrews)
cllr.barbara.wright@great-yarmouth.gov.uk

POLITICAL COMPOSITION

LAB: 15, CON: 14, UKIP: 10

Greenwich L

Greenwich London Borough Council, The Woolwich Centre, 35 Wellington Street, Woolwich, London SE18 6HQ
☎ 020 8854 8888 🖷 020 8921 5074 🖳 www.greenwich.gov.uk

FACTS AND FIGURES

Parliamentary Constituencies: Eltham, Erith and Thamesmead, Greenwich and Woolwich
EU Constituencies: London
Election Frequency: Elections are of whole council

PRINCIPAL OFFICERS

Chief Executive: Mr John Comber, Chief Executive, The Woolwich Centre, 35 Wellington Street, Woolwich, London SE18 6HQ ☎ 020 8921 5000 john.comber@royalgreenwich.gov.uk

GREENWICH

Senior Management: Mr John Clark Director - Housing Services, The Woolwich Centre, 35 Wellington Street, Woolwich, London SE18 6HQ ☎ 020 8921 5635 ✉ john.clark@greenwich.gov.uk

Senior Management: Ms Katrina Delaney, Director - Culture, Sport & Media, The Woolwich Centre, 35 Wellington Street, Woolwich, London SE18 6HQ ☎ 020 8921 6101 🖷 020 8921 5252 ✉ katrina.delaney@greenwich.gov.uk

Senior Management: Ms Pippa Hack Director - Regeneration Enterprise & Skills, The Woolwich Centre, 35 Wellington Street, Woolwich, London SE18 6HQ ☎ 020 8921 5519 🖷 020 8921 5950 ✉ pippa.hack@royalgreenwich.gov.uk

Senior Management: Mr Matthew Norwell Director - Community Safety & Environment, The Woolwich Centre, 35 Wellington Street, Woolwich, London SE18 6HQ ☎ 020 8921 8291 🖷 020 8921 3112 ✉ matthew.norwell@royalgreenwich.gov.uk

Senior Management: Ms Gillian Palmer Director - Children's Services, The Woolwich Centre, 35 Wellington Street, Woolwich, London SE18 6HQ ☎ 020 8921 8230 🖷 020 8921 8097 ✉ gillian.palmer@royalgreenwich.gov.uk

Senior Management: Mr Simon Pearce Director - Health & Adult Social Care, The Woolwich Centre, 35 Wellington Street, Woolwich, London SE18 6HQ ☎ 020 8921 3000 ✉ simon.pearce@royalgreenwich.gov.uk

Senior Management: Ms Debbie Warren Director - Finance, The Woolwich Centre, 35 Wellington Street, Woolwich, London SE18 6HQ ☎ 020 8921 5201 ✉ debbie.warren@royalgreenwich.gov.uk

Senior Management: Mr Steve Whiteman Director - Public Health, The Woolwich Centre, 35 Wellington Street, Woolwich, London SE18 6HQ ☎ 020 8921 5514 ✉ steve.whiteman@royalgreenwich.gov.uk

Building Control: Mr Chris Stevens, Head - Building Control, The Woolwich Centre, 35 Wellington Street, Woolwich, London SE18 6HQ ☎ 020 8921 5414 🖷 020 8921 5544 ✉ chris.stevens@royalgreenwich.gov.uk

Children / Youth Services: Ms Jenny Kavanagh IYSS Manager - Health & Integrated Support, The Woolwich Centre, 35 Wellington Street, Woolwich, London SE18 6HQ ☎ 020 8921 8249 ✉ jenny.kavanagh@royalgreenwich.gov.uk

PR / Communications: Ms Katrina Delaney, Director - Culture, Sport & Media, The Woolwich Centre, 35 Wellington Street, Woolwich, London SE18 6HQ ☎ 020 8921 6101 🖷 020 8921 5252 ✉ katrina.delaney@greenwich.gov.uk

Community Planning: Mr Mike Hows, Assistant Director - Planning, The Woolwich Centre, 35 Wellington Street, Woolwich, London SE18 6HQ ☎ 020 8921 5363 🖷 020 8317 0806 ✉ mike.hows@royalgreenwich.gov.uk

Community Safety: Mr Matthew Norwell Director - Community Safety & Environment, The Woolwich Centre, 35 Wellington Street, Woolwich, London SE18 6HQ ☎ 020 8921 8291 🖷 020 8921 3112 ✉ matthew.norwell@royalgreenwich.gov.uk

Computer Management: Mr Kevin Gibbs Assistant Director - Customer Contact, The Woolwich Centre, 35 Wellington Street, Woolwich, London SE18 6HQ ☎ 020 8921 5244 🖷 020 8921 3112 ✉ kevin.gibbs@royalgreenwich.gov.uk

Consumer Protection and Trading Standards: Mr David Farrell Head of Environmental Health & Trading Standards, The Woolwich Centre, 35 Wellington Street, Woolwich, London SE18 6HQ ☎ 020 8921 8321 ✉ david.farrell@royalgreenwich.gov.uk

Contracts: Mr Ian Tasker Head - Financial Operations, The Woolwich Centre, 35 Wellington Street, Woolwich, London SE18 6HQ ☎ 020 8921 6189 ✉ ian.tasker@royalgreenwich.gov.uk

Customer Service: Mr Kevin Gibbs Assistant Director - Customer Contact, The Woolwich Centre, 35 Wellington Street, Woolwich, London SE18 6HQ ☎ 020 8921 5244 🖷 020 8921 3112 ✉ kevin.gibbs@royalgreenwich.gov.uk

Economic Development: Mr Trevor Dorling Assistant Director - Employment & Skills, The Woolwich Centre, 35 Wellington Street, Woolwich, London SE18 6HQ ☎ 020 8921 6147 🖷 020 8921 6283 ✉ trevor.dorling@royalgreenwich.gov.uk

Education: Ms Gillian Palmer Director - Children's Services, The Woolwich Centre, 35 Wellington Street, Woolwich, London SE18 6HQ ☎ 020 8921 8230 🖷 020 8921 8097 ✉ gillian.palmer@royalgreenwich.gov.uk

E-Government: Mr Kevin Gibbs Assistant Director - Customer Contact, The Woolwich Centre, 35 Wellington Street, Woolwich, London SE18 6HQ ☎ 020 8921 5244 🖷 020 8921 3112 ✉ kevin.gibbs@royalgreenwich.gov.uk

Electoral Registration: Mr Stephen O'Hare, Electoral Service Manager, The Woolwich Centre, 35 Wellington Street, Woolwich, London SE18 6HQ ☎ 020 8921 6130 🖷 020 8921 6338 ✉ stephen.ohare@royalgreenwich.gov.uk

Emergency Planning: Ms Lynette Russell, Head - Emergency Planning & Resilience, The Woolwich Centre, 35 Wellington Street, Woolwich, London SE18 6HQ ☎ 020 8921 6258 🖷 020 8921 6267 ✉ lynette.russell@royalgreenwich.gov.uk

Energy Management: Ms Pippa Hack Director - Regeneration Enterprise & Skills, The Woolwich Centre, 35 Wellington Street, Woolwich, London SE18 6HQ ☎ 020 8921 5519 🖷 020 8921 5950 ✉ pippa.hack@royalgreenwich.gov.uk

Environmental Health: Mr David Farrell Head of Environmental Health & Trading Standards, The Woolwich Centre, 35 Wellington Street, Woolwich, London SE18 6HQ ☎ 020 8921 8321 ✉ david.farrell@royalgreenwich.gov.uk

Estates, Property & Valuation: Ms Pippa Hack Director - Regeneration Enterprise & Skills, The Woolwich Centre, 35 Wellington Street, Woolwich, London SE18 6HQ ☎ 020 8921 5519 🖷 020 8921 5950 ✉ pippa.hack@royalgreenwich.gov.uk

Events Manager: Mr Bob Hills Principal Communications Officer, The Woolwich Centre, 35 Wellington Street, Woolwich, London SE18 6HQ ☎ 020 8921 5077 🖷 020 8921 5252 ✉ bob.hills@royalgreenwich.gov.uk

Finance: Ms Debbie Warren Director - Finance, The Woolwich Centre, 35 Wellington Street, Woolwich, London SE18 6HQ ☎ 020 8921 5201 ✉ debbie.warren@royalgreenwich.gov.uk

Treasury: Ms Debbie Warren Director - Finance, The Woolwich Centre, 35 Wellington Street, Woolwich, London SE18 6HQ ☎ 020 8921 5201 ✉ debbie.warren@royalgreenwich.gov.uk

Pensions: Ms Kelly Scotford Pensions & Operations Manager, The Woolwich Centre, 35 Wellington Street, Woolwich, London SE18 6HQ ☎ 020 8921 6949 ✉ kelly.scotford@royalgreenwich.gov.uk

Grounds Maintenance: Ms Dawn Squires Head of Parks & Open Spaces, The Woolwich Centre, 35 Wellington Street, Woolwich, London SE18 6HQ ☎ 020 8921 4133 ✉ dawn.squires@royalgreenwich.gov.uk

Health and Safety: Mr Al Parry, Manager - Health, Safety & Wellbeing, The Woolwich Centre, 35 Wellington Street, Woolwich, London SE18 6HQ ☎ 020 8921 5196 🖷 020 8921 6267 ✉ al.parry@royalgreenwich.gov.uk

Highways: Mr Tim Jackson Assistant Director - Strategic Transportation, The Woolwich Centre, 35 Wellington Street, Woolwich, London SE18 6HQ ☎ 020 8921 5453 ✉ tim.jackson@royalgreenwich.gov.uk

Home Energy Conservation: Ms Pippa Hack Director - Regeneration Enterprise & Skills, The Woolwich Centre, 35 Wellington Street, Woolwich, London SE18 6HQ ☎ 020 8921 5519 🖷 020 8921 5950 ✉ pippa.hack@royalgreenwich.gov.uk

Housing: Mr John Clark Director - Housing Services, The Woolwich Centre, 35 Wellington Street, Woolwich, London SE18 6HQ ☎ 020 8921 5635 ✉ john.clark@greenwich.gov.uk

Housing Maintenance: Mr Tim Derrik Project Manager - Technical Services, The Woolwich Centre, 35 Wellington Street, Woolwich, London SE18 6HQ ☎ 020 8921 4275 ✉ tim.derrik@royalgreenwich.gov.uk

Legal: Mr Russell Power, Head - Law & Governance, The Woolwich Centre, 35 Wellington Street, Woolwich, London SE18 6HQ ☎ 020 8921 5105 🖷 020 8921 5556 ✉ russell.power@royalgreenwich.gov.uk

Leisure and Cultural Services: Ms Katrina Delaney, Director - Culture, Sport & Media, The Woolwich Centre, 35 Wellington Street, Woolwich, London SE18 6HQ ☎ 020 8921 6101 🖷 020 8921 5252 ✉ katrina.delaney@royalgreenwich.gov.uk

Licensing: Mr Des Campbell, Manager - Trading Standards & Licensing, The Woolwich Centre, 35 Wellington Street, Woolwich, London SE18 6HQ ☎ 020 8921 8137 🖷 020 8921 8380 ✉ des.campbell@royalgreenwich.gov.uk

Member Services: Mr Russell Power, Head - Law & Governance, The Woolwich Centre, 35 Wellington Street, Woolwich, London SE18 6HQ ☎ 020 8921 5105 🖷 020 8921 5556 ✉ russell.power@royalgreenwich.gov.uk

Parking: Mr Ollie Miller Acting Head of Parking Services, The Woolwich Centre, 35 Wellington Street, Woolwich, London SE18 6HQ ☎ 020 8921 5877 ✉ ollie.miller@royalgreenwich.gov.uk

Partnerships: Mr John Clark Director - Housing Services, The Woolwich Centre, 35 Wellington Street, Woolwich, London SE18 6HQ ☎ 020 8921 5635 ✉ john.clark@greenwich.gov.uk

Planning: Mr Mike Hows, Assistant Director - Planning, The Woolwich Centre, 35 Wellington Street, Woolwich, London SE18 6HQ ☎ 020 8921 5363 🖷 020 8317 0806 ✉ mike.hows@royalgreenwich.gov.uk

Procurement: Mr Ian Tasker Head - Financial Operations, The Woolwich Centre, 35 Wellington Street, Woolwich, London SE18 6HQ ☎ 020 8921 6189 ✉ ian.tasker@royalgreenwich.gov.uk

Public Libraries: Mr Gareth Edmunson Head of Sport & Commissioning, The Woolwich Centre, 35 Wellington Street, Woolwich, London SE18 6HQ ☎ 020 8921 8006 ✉ gareth.edmunson@royalgreenwich.gov.uk

Recycling & Waste Minimisation: Mr Peter Dalley, Waste Services Operations Manager, The Woolwich Centre, 35 Wellington Street, Woolwich, London SE18 6HQ ☎ 020 8921 4641 🖷 020 8921 4636 ✉ peter.dalley@royalgreenwich.gov.uk

Regeneration: Mr John Comber, Chief Executive, The Woolwich Centre, 35 Wellington Street, Woolwich, London SE18 6HQ ☎ 020 8921 5000 ✉ john.comber@royalgreenwich.gov.uk

Road Safety: Ms Khair-un-nisa Simmonds, Safety Education Manager, The Woolwich Centre, 35 Wellington Street, Woolwich, London SE18 6HQ ☎ 020 8921 8075 🖷 020 8921 8080 ✉ khairunnisa.simmonds@royalgreenwich.gov.uk

Social Services (Adult): Mr Simon Pearce Director - Health & Adult Social Care, The Woolwich Centre, 35 Wellington Street, Woolwich, London SE18 6HQ ☎ 020 8921 3000 ✉ simon.pearce@royalgreenwich.gov.uk

Social Services (Children): Ms Gillian Palmer Director - Children's Services, The Woolwich Centre, 35 Wellington Street, Woolwich, London SE18 6HQ ☎ 020 8921 8230 🖷 020 8921 8097 ✉ gillian.palmer@royalgreenwich.gov.uk

Public Health: Mr Steve Whiteman Director - Public Health, The Woolwich Centre, 35 Wellington Street, Woolwich, London SE18 6HQ ☎ 020 8921 5514 ✉ steve.whiteman@royalgreenwich.gov.uk

Staff Training: Mr Lee Lucas Learning & Development Officer, The Woolwich Centre, 35 Wellington Street, Woolwich, London SE18 6HQ ☎ 020 8921 4981 ✉ lee.lucas@royalgreenwich.gov.uk

Sustainable Communities: Ms Pippa Hack Director - Regeneration Enterprise & Skills, The Woolwich Centre, 35 Wellington Street, Woolwich, London SE18 6HQ ☎ 020 8921 5519 🖷 020 8921 5950 ✉ pippa.hack@royalgreenwich.gov.uk

GREENWICH

Sustainable Development: Ms Pippa Hack Director - Regeneration Enterprise & Skills, The Woolwich Centre, 35 Wellington Street, Woolwich, London SE18 6HQ ☎ 020 8921 5519 🖷 020 8921 5950 🖱 pippa.hack@royalgreenwich.gov.uk

Tourism: Ms Katrina Delaney, Director - Culture, Sport & Media, The Woolwich Centre, 35 Wellington Street, Woolwich, London SE18 6HQ ☎ 020 8921 6101 🖷 020 8921 5252 🖱 katrina.delaney@royalgreenwich.gov.uk

Town Centre: Ms Pippa Hack Director - Regeneration Enterprise & Skills, The Woolwich Centre, 35 Wellington Street, Woolwich, London SE18 6HQ ☎ 020 8921 5519 🖷 020 8921 5950 🖱 pippa.hack@royalgreenwich.gov.uk

Traffic Management: Mr Tim Jackson Assistant Director - Strategic Transportation, The Woolwich Centre, 35 Wellington Street, Woolwich, London SE18 6HQ ☎ 020 8921 5453 🖱 tim.jackson@royalgreenwich.gov.uk

Transport Planner: Mr Tim Jackson Assistant Director - Strategic Transportation, The Woolwich Centre, 35 Wellington Street, Woolwich, London SE18 6HQ ☎ 020 8921 5453 🖱 tim.jackson@royalgreenwich.gov.uk

Waste Collection and Disposal: Mr Peter Dalley, Waste Services Operations Manager, The Woolwich Centre, 35 Wellington Street, Woolwich, London SE18 6HQ ☎ 020 8921 4641 🖷 020 8921 4636 🖱 peter.dalley@royalgreenwich.gov.uk

Waste Management: Mr Peter Dalley, Waste Services Operations Manager, The Woolwich Centre, 35 Wellington Street, Woolwich, London SE18 6HQ ☎ 020 8921 4641 🖷 020 8921 4636 🖱 peter.dalley@royalgreenwich.gov.uk

Children's Play Areas: Ms Dawn Squires Head of Parks & Open Spaces, The Woolwich Centre, 35 Wellington Street, Woolwich, London SE18 6HQ ☎ 020 8921 4133 🖱 dawn.squires@royalgreenwich.gov.uk

COUNCILLORS

***Mayor* Adams**, Norman (LAB - Kidbrooke and Hornfair)
norman.adams@royalgreenwich.gov.uk

***Deputy Mayor* Babatola**, Olu (LAB - Thamesmead Moorings)
olu.babatola@royalgreenwich.gov.uk

***Leader of the Council* Hyland**, Denise (LAB - Abbey Wood)
denise.hyland@royalgreenwich.gov.uk

***Deputy Leader of the Council* Fahy**, John (LAB - Woolwich Riverside)
john.fahy@royalgreenwich.gov.uk

***Group Leader* Hartley**, Matt (CON - Coldharbour and New Eltham)
matt.hartley@royalgreenwich.gov.uk

Austen, Don (LAB - Glyndon)
don.austen@royalgreenwich.gov.uk

Barwick, Barbara (LAB - Woolwich Riverside)
barbara.barwick@royalgreenwich.gov.uk

Bird, Linda (LAB - Eltham North)
linda.bird@royalgreenwich.gov.uk

Brain, Stephen (LAB - Peninsula)
stephen.brain@royalgreenwich.gov.uk

Brighty, Geoffrey (CON - Blackheath Westcombe)
geoffrey.brighty@royalgreenwich.gov.uk

Brinkhurst, Mandy (CON - Coldharbour and New Eltham)
mandy.brinkhurst@royalgreenwich.gov.uk

Brooks, Peter (LAB - Thamesmead Moorings)
peter.brooks@royalgreenwich.gov.uk

Clare, Matt (CON - Eltham South)
matt.clare@royalgreenwich.gov.uk

Cornforth, Angela (LAB - Plumstead)
angela.cornforth@royalgreenwich.gov.uk

Davies, Wynn (LAB - Eltham North)
wynn.davies@royalgreenwich.gov.uk

Drury, Spencer (CON - Eltham North)
spencer.drury@royalgreenwich.gov.uk

Elliott, Mark (CON - Eltham South)
mark.elliott@royalgreenwich.gov.uk

Freeman, Bill (LAB - Eltham West)
bill.freeman@royalgreenwich.gov.uk

Gardner, David (LAB - Woolwich Common)
david.gardner@royalgreenwich.gov.uk

Geary, Nuala (CON - Eltham South)
nuala.geary@royalgreenwich.gov.uk

Grice, Christine (LAB - Kidbrooke with Hornfair)
christine.grice@royalgreenwich.gov.uk

Hayes, Mick (LAB - Eltham West)
mick.hayes@royalgreenwich.gov.uk

Hills, John (CON - Coldharbour and New Eltham)
john.hills@royalgreenwich.gov.uk

Hisbani, Ambreen (LAB - Woolwich Common)
ambreen.hisbani@royalgreenwich.gov.uk

James, Swize (LAB - Thamesmead Moorings)
swize.james@royalgreenwich.gov.uk

James, Mark (LAB - Middle Park and Sutcliffe)
mark.james@royalgreenwich.gov.uk

Khan, Mehboob (LAB - Greenwich West)
mehboob.khan@royalgreenwich.gov.uk

Kirby, Chris (LAB - Shooters Hill)
chris.kirby@royalgreenwich.gov.uk

Lekau, Averil (LAB - Thameshead Moorings)
averil.lekau@royalgreenwich.gov.uk

Lloyd, Chris (LAB - Peninsula)
chris.lloyd@royalgreenwich.gov.uk

MacCarthy, Allan (LAB - Charlton)
allan.maccarthy@royalgreenwich.gov.uk

Mardner, Clive (LAB - Abbey Wood)
clive.mardner@royalgreenwich.gov.uk

May, Christine (LAB - Middle Park and Sutcliffe)
christine.may@royalgreenwich.gov.uk

Merrill, Sarah (LAB - Shooters Hill)
sarah.merrill@royalgreenwich.gov.uk

Morris, Clare (LAB - Middle Park and Sutcliffe)
clare.morris@royalgreenwich.gov.uk

Morrisey, Paul (LAB - Blackheat Westcombe)
paul.morrissey@royalgreenwich.gov.uk

Morrow, Matthew (LAB - Plumstead)
matthew.morrow@royalgreenwich.gov.uk

Offord, Steve (LAB - Abbey Wood)
steve.offord@royalgreenwich.gov.uk

O'Mara, Maureen (LAB - Greenwich West)
maureen.omara@royalgreenwich.gov.uk

Parker, Gary (LAB - Charlton)
gary.parker@royalgreenwich.gov.uk

Parker, Cherry (LAB - Blackheath Westcombe)
cherry.parker@royalgreenwich.gov.uk

Rabadia, Radhna (LAB - Glyndon)
radha.rabadia@royalgreenwich.gov.uk

Scott-McDonald, Denise (LAB - Peninsula)
denise.scott-mcdonald@royalgreenwich.gov.uk

Sehmar, Rajinder (LAB - Plumstead)
rajinder.sehmar@royalgreenwich.gov.uk

Singh, Harry (LAB - Woolwich Common)
harpinder.singh@royalgreenwich.gov.uk

Smith, Jackie (LAB - Thamesmead Moorings)
jackie.smith@royalgreenwich.gov.uk

Smith, Aidan (LAB - Greenwich West)
aidan.smith@royalgreenwich.gov.uk

Stanley, David (LAB - Kidbrooke with Hornfair)
david.stanley@royalgreenwich.gov.uk

Thorpe, Danny (LAB - Shooters Hill)
danny.thorpe@royalgreenwich.gov.uk

Walker, Ray (LAB - Eltham West)
ray.walker@royalgreenwich.gov.uk

Williams, Miranda (LAB - Peninsula)
miranda.williams@royalgreenwich.gov.uk

POLITICAL COMPOSITION
LAB: 43, CON: 8

COMMITTEE CHAIRS
Audit & Risk: Mr David Stanley

Children & Young People: Ms Barbara Barwick

Licensing: Ms Jackie Smith

Pensions: Mr Norman Adams

Planning: Mr Mark James

Safer & Stronger Communities: Mr Gary Parker

Guildford — D

Guildford Borough Council, Millmead House, Millmead, Guildford GU2 4BB
☎ 01483 505050 🖷 01483 444444 ✉ enquiries@guildford.gov.uk
💻 www.guildford.gov.uk

FACTS AND FIGURES
Parliamentary Constituencies: Guildford
EU Constituencies: South East
Election Frequency: Elections are of whole council

PRINCIPAL OFFICERS
Chief Executive: Ms Sue Sturgeon Managing Director, Millmead House, Millmead, Guildford GU2 4BB ☎ 01483 505050 ✉ sue.sturgeon@guildford.gov.uk

Senior Management: Mr Martyn Brake Executive Head of Organisational Development, Millmead House, Millmead, Guildford GU2 4BB ✉ martyn.brake@guildford.gov.uk

Senior Management: Mr Chris Mansfield Executive Head of Development, Millmead House, Millmead, Guildford GU2 4BB ☎ 01483 444550

Senior Management: Mr Satish Mistry Executive Head of Governance, Millmead House, Millmead, Guildford GU2 4BB ✉ satish.mistry@guildford.gov.uk

Senior Management: Mr Philip O'Dwyer, Executive Head of Housing & Health, Millmead House, Millmead, Guildford GU2 4BB ☎ 01483 444318

Senior Management: Mr Steve White, Executive Head of Financial Services, Millmead House, Millmead, Guildford GU2 4BB ☎ 01483 444920 🖷 01483 444874

Senior Management: Mr James Whiteman, Executive Head of Environment, Cleansing Department, Woking Road Depot, Woking Road, Guildford GU1 1QE ☎ 01483 445030 🖷 01483 445039 ✉ james.whiteman@guildford.gov.uk

Architect, Building / Property Services: Ms Marieke van der Reijden Asset Development Manager, Guildford Borough Council, Millmead House Millmead, Guildford GU2 4BB ☎ 01483 444995

Building Control: Ms Jacqui Barr, Building Control Manager, Millmead House, Millmead, Guildford GU2 4BB ☎ 01483 444680 🖷 01483 44451

Community Safety: Mr John Martin, Head of Health & Community Care Services, Millmead House, Millmead, Guildford GU2 4BB ☎ 01483 444350

Computer Management: Mr Jasvir Chohan Head of Business Systems, Millmead House, Millmead, Guildford GU2 4BB ☎ 01483 444900

Direct Labour: Mr James Whiteman, Executive Head of Environment, Cleansing Department, Woking Road Depot, Woking Road, Guildford GU1 1QE ☎ 01483 445030 🖷 01483 445039 ✉ james.whiteman@guildford.gov.uk

Economic Development: Mr Chris Mansfield Executive Head of Development, Millmead House, Millmead, Guildford GU2 4BB ☎ 01483 444550

E-Government: Ms Claire Morris Head of Financial Services, Millmead House, Millmead, Guildford GU2 4BB ☎ 01483 44827

Energy Management: Mr Kevin Handley, Facilities Manager,Millmead House, Millmead, Guildford GU2 5BB ☎ 01483 444447 🖷 01483 302221 ✉ kevin.handley@guildford.gov.uk

GUILDFORD

Environmental Health: Mr Chris Woodhatch Principal Environmental Health Officer, Millmead House, Millmead, Guildford GU2 4BB ☎ 01483 444370; 01483 444370 🖷 01483 444546; 01483 444546

Facilities: Mr Kevin Handley, Facilities Manager, Millmead House, Millmead, Guildford GU2 5BB ☎ 01483 444447 🖷 01483 302221 ✉ kevin.handley@guildford.gov.uk

Finance: Mr Steve White, Executive Head of Financial Services, Millmead House, Millmead, Guildford GU2 4BB ☎ 01483 444920 🖷 01483 444874

Fleet Management: Mr Paul Wells Waste & Fleet Operations Manager, Woking Road Depot, Woking Road, Guildford GU1 1QE ☎ 01483 445011

Health and Safety: Mr Paul Osborn Occupational Health & Safety Officer, Millmead House, Millmead, Guildford GU2 4BB ☎ 01483 444025

Housing: Ms Kim Rippett Head of Housing Advice, Millmead House, Millmead, Guildford GU2 4BB ☎ 01483 444240 ✉ kim.rippett@guildford.gov.uk

Housing Maintenance: Mr Philip O'Dwyer, Executive Head of Housing & Health, Millmead House, Millmead, Guildford GU2 4BB ☎ 01483 444318

Legal: Ms Glynis Mancini, Principal Solicitor, Millmead House, Millmead, Guildford GU2 4BB ☎ 01483 444060

Licensing: Mr David Curtis-Botting Licensing Services Manager, Millmead House, Millmead, Guildford GU2 4BB ☎ 01483 444387

Planning: Mr Barry Fagg Head of Planning Services, Millmead House, Millmead, Guildford GU2 4BB ☎ 01483 444620

Procurement: Mr Simon Gregory Procurement Officer, Millmead House, Millmead, Guildford GU2 4BB ☎ 01483 444421

Recycling & Waste Minimisation: Mr James Whiteman, Executive Head of Environment, Cleansing Department, Woking Road Depot, Woking Road, Guildford GU1 1QE ☎ 01483 445030 🖷 01483 445039 ✉ james.whiteman@guildford.gov.uk

Regeneration: Mr Chris Mansfield Executive Head of Development, Millmead House, Millmead, Guildford GU2 4BB ☎ 01483 444550

Social Services: Mr John Martin, Head of Health & Community Care Services, Millmead House, Millmead, Guildford GU2 4BB ☎ 01483 444350

Staff Training: Ms Hannah Cornick Training Officer, Millmead House, Millmead, Guildford GU2 4BB ☎ 01483 505050

Sustainable Development: Ms Carol Humphrey, Head of Planning Services, Millmead House, Millmead, Guildford GU2 4BB ☎ 01483 444620

Tourism: Mr Chris Mansfield Executive Head of Development, Millmead House, Millmead, Guildford GU2 4BB ☎ 01483 444550

Town Centre: Mr Chris Mansfield Executive Head of Development, Millmead House, Millmead, Guildford GU2 4BB ☎ 01483 444550

Transport: Mr Tim Pilsbury, Transportation Projects Manager, Millmead House, Millmead, Guildford GU2 4BB ☎ 01483 444521

Waste Collection and Disposal: Mr James Whiteman, Executive Head of Environment, Cleansing Department, Woking Road Depot, Woking Road, Guildford GU1 1QE ☎ 01483 445030 🖷 01483 445039 ✉ james.whiteman@guildford.gov.uk

Waste Management: Mr James Whiteman, Executive Head of Environment, Cleansing Department, Woking Road Depot, Woking Road, Guildford GU1 1QE ☎ 01483 445030 🖷 01483 445039 ✉ james.whiteman@guildford.gov.uk

COUNCILLORS

***Mayor* Nelson-Smith**, Nikki (CON - Christchurch)
nikki.nelson-smith@guildford.gov.uk

***Deputy Mayor* Jackson**, Gordon (CON - Pirbright)
gordon.jackson@guildford.gov.uk

***Leader of the Council* Mansbridge**, Stephen (CON - Ash South and Tongham)
Stephen.Mansbridge@guildford.gov.uk

***Deputy Leader of the Council* Manning**, Nigel (CON - Ash Vale)
Nigel.Manning@guildford.gov.uk

***Group Leader* Parker**, Susan (GRN - Send)
susan.parker@guildford.gov.uk

***Group Leader* Reeves**, Caroline (LD - Friary & St Nicolas)
Caroline.Reeves@guildford.gov.uk

Bilbe, David (CON - Normandy)
david.bilbe@guildford.gov.uk

Billington, Richard (CON - Tillingbourne)
richard.billington@guildford.gov.uk

Brooker, Philip (CON - Merrow)
philip.brooker@guildford.gov.uk

Chandler, Adrian (CON - Onslow)
adrian.chandler@guildford.gov.uk

Chesterfield, Alexandra (CON - Friary & St Nicolas)
alexanddra.chesterfield@guildford.gov.uk

Chesterfield, Will (CON - Stoke)
will.chesterfield.gov.uk

Christiansen, Nils (CON - Holy Trinity)
nils.christiansen@guildford.gov.uk

Cross, Colin (LD - Lovelace)
colin.cross@guilford.gov.uk

Davis, Geoff (CON - Holy Trinity)
geoff.davis@guildford.gov.uk

Ellwood, Graham (CON - Merrow)
graham.ellwood@guildford.gov.uk

Elms, David (CON - Worplesdon)
david.elms@guildford.gov.uk

Furniss, Matt (CON - Christchurch)
Matt.Furniss@guildford.gov.uk

Goodwin, Angela (LD - Friary & St Nocolas)
angela.goodwin@guildford.gov.uk

Goodwin, David (LD - Onlsow)
david.goodwin@guildford.gov.uk

Grubb Jnr, Murray (CON - Ash Wharf)
murray.grubb@guildford.gov.uk

Gunning, Angela (LAB - Stoke)
angela.gunning@guildford.gov.uk

Harwood, Gillian (LD - Stoughton)
Gillian.Harwood@guildford.gov.uk

Hogger, Liz (LD - Effingham)
Liz.Hogger@guildford.gov.uk

Holliday, Christian (CON - Burpham)
christian.holliday@guildford.gov.uk

Hooper, Liz (CON - Westborough)
liz.hooper@guildford.gov.uk

Hurdle, Mike (O - Send)
mike.hurdle@guildford.gov.uk

Illman, Michael (CON - Shalford)
michael.illman@guildford.gov.uk

Jordan, Jennifer (CON - Merrow)
Jennifer.Jordan@guildford.gov.uk

Kearse, Nigel (CON - Ash South and Tongham)
nigel.kearse@guildford.gov.uk

Kirkland, Sheila (CON - Westborough)
sheila.kirkland@guildford.gov.uk

McShame, Julia (LD - Westborough)
julia.mcshane@guildford.gov.uk

McShee, Bob (CON - Worplesdon)
bob.mcshee@guildford.gov.uk

Moseley, Marsha (CON - Ash Vale)
Marsha.Moseley@guildford.gov.uk

Parsons, Mike (CON - Shalford)
mike.parsons@guildford.gov.uk

Paul, Dennis (CON - Holy Trinity)
Dennis.oaul@guildford.gov.uk

Phillips, Tony (LD - Onslow)
Tony.Philips@guildford.gov.uk

Piper, Mike (CON - Burpham)
mike.piper@guildford@gov.uk

Quelch, David (CON - Stoughton)
david.quelch@guildford.gov.uk

Randall, Jo (CON - Ash Wharf)
jo.randall@guildford.gov.uk

Reeve, David (GRN - Clandon & Horsley)
david.reeve@guildford.gov.uk

Roche, Iseult (CON - Worplesdon)
iseult.roche@guildford.gov.uk

Rooth, Tony (CON - Pilgrims)
Tony.Rooth@guildford.gov.uk

Sarti, Matthew (CON - Clandon & Horsley)
mathew.sarti@guildford.gov.uk

Searle, Pauline (LD - Stoughton)
Pauline.Searle@guildford.gov.uk

Spooner, Paul (CON - Ash South and Tongham)
paul.spooner@guildford.gov.uk

Wicks, Jenny (CON - Clandon & Horsley)
Jenny.Wicks@guildford.gov.uk

Wright, David (CON - Tillingbourne)
David.Wright@guildford.gov.uk

POLITICAL COMPOSITION

CON: 35, LD: 9, GRN: 2, O: 1, LAB: 1

COMMITTEE CHAIRS

Licensing: Mr David Elms

Gwynedd W

Gwynedd Council, Swyddfa'r Cygnor, Stryd Y Jel, Caernarfon LL55 1SH
☎ 01286 672255 🖷 01286 673993 enquiries@gwynedd.gov.uk
www.gwynedd.gov.uk

FACTS AND FIGURES

Parliamentary Constituencies: Arfon, Dwyfor Meirionnydd
EU Constituencies: Wales
Election Frequency: Elections are of whole council

PRINCIPAL OFFICERS

Chief Executive: Mr Dilwyn Owen Williams Chief Executive, Swyddfa'r Cyngor, Stryd Y Jel, Caernarfon LL55 1SH ☎ 01286 679514 dilwynowenwilliams@gwynedd.gov.uk

Senior Management: Mrs Morwenna Edwards, Corporate Director, Swyddfa'r Cyngor, Stryd Y Jel, Caernarfon LL55 1SH ☎ 01286 679468 morwennaedwards@gwynedd.gov.uk

Senior Management: Mr Iwan Trefor Jones, Corporate Director, Swyddfa'r Cyngor, Stryd Y Jel, Caernarfon LL55 1SH ☎ 01286 679162 iwanj@gwynedd.gov.uk

Access Officer / Social Services (Disability): Mr Aled Davies, Head of Adults, Health & Wellbeing, Swyddfa'r Cyngor, Stryd Y Jel, Caernarfon LL55 1SH ☎ 01286 679371 aleddavies@gwynedd.gov.uk

Architect, Building / Property Services: Mr Huw Williams, Head of Gwynedd Consultancy, Swyddfa'r Cyngor, Stryd Y Jel, Caernarfon LL55 1SH ☎ 01286 679426 huwwilliams@gwynedd.gov.uk

Best Value: Mr Geraint Owen, Head of Corporate Support, Swyddfa'r Cyngor, Stryd Y Jel, Caernarfon LL55 1SH ☎ 01286 679084 geraintowen@gwynedd.gov.uk

Building Control: Mr Huw Williams, Head of Gwynedd Consultancy, Swyddfa'r Cyngor, Stryd Y Jel, Caernarfon LL55 1SH ☎ 01286 679426 huwwilliams@gwynedd.gov.uk

GWYNEDD

Catering Services: Mr Arwyn Thomas Head of Education, Swyddfa'r Cygnor, Stryd Y Jel, Caernarfon LL55 1SH ☎ 01286 679467 ✉ arwynthomas@gwynedd.gov.uk

Children / Youth Services: Mrs Marian Parry Hughes Head of Children & Supporting Families, Swyddfa'r Cygnor, Stryd Y Jel, Caernarfon LL55 1SH ☎ 01286 679228 ✉ marianhughes@gwynedd.gov.uk

Civil Registration: Mr Geraint Owen, Head of Corporate Support, Swyddfa'r Cygnor, Stryd Y Jel, Caernarfon LL55 1SH ☎ 01286 679084 ✉ geraintowen@gwynedd.gov.uk

PR / Communications: Mr Sion Gwynfryn Williams Communications Manager, Swyddfa'r Cygnor, Stryd Y Jel, Caernarfon LL55 1SH ☎ 01286 679310 ✉ siongwynfrynwilliams@gwynedd.gov.uk

Community Planning: Mrs Sioned Williams, Head of Economy & Community, Swyddfa'r Cygnor, Stryd Y Jel, Caernarfon LL55 1SH ☎ 01286 679547 ✉ sionedewilliams@gwynedd.gov.uk

Community Safety: Ms Catherine Roberts, Senior Community Safety Officer, Mona Building, Gwynedd Council, Caernarfon LL55 1SH ☎ ; 01286 679047 ✉ catherineeroberts@gwynedd.gov.uk

Computer Management: Mr Huw Ynyr Senior Manager - IT & Business Transformation, Swyddfa'r Cygnor, Stryd Y Jel, Caernarfon LL55 1SH ☎ 01286 679302 ✉ huwynyr@gwynedd.gov.uk

Consumer Protection and Trading Standards: Mr Dafydd Wyn Williams, Head of Regulatory, Swyddfa'r Cygnor, Stryd Y Jel, Caernarfon LL55 1SH ☎ 01286 679370 ✉ dafyddwynwilliams@gwynedd.gov.uk

Contracts: Mr Geraint Owen, Head of Corporate Support, Swyddfa'r Cygnor, Stryd Y Jel, Caernarfon LL55 1SH ☎ 01286 679084 ✉ geraintowen@gwynedd.gov.uk

Corporate Services: Mr Dilwyn Owen Williams Chief Executive, Swyddfa'r Cygnor, Stryd Y Jel, Caernarfon LL55 1SH ☎ 01286 679514 ✉ dilwynowenwilliams@gwynedd.gov.uk

Direct Labour: Mr Gwyn Morris Jones, Head of Highways & Municipal Services, Swyddfa'r Cygnor, Stryd Y Jel, Caernarfon LL55 1SH ☎ 01286 679402 ✉ gwynmorrisjones@gwynedd.gov.uk

Economic Development: Mrs Sioned Williams, Head of Economy & Community, Swyddfa'r Cygnor, Stryd Y Jel, Caernarfon LL55 1SH ☎ 01286 679547 ✉ sionedewilliams@gwynedd.gov.uk

Electoral Registration: Mr Iwan Evans Legal Service Manager, Swyddfa'r Cygnor, Stryd Y Jel, Caernarfon LL55 1SH ☎ 01286 679015 ✉ iwangdevans@gwynedd.gov.uk

Emergency Planning: Mrs Morwenna Edwards, Corporate Director, Swyddfa'r Cygnor, Stryd Y Jel, Caernarfon LL55 1SH ☎ 01286 679468 ✉ morwennaedwards@gwynedd.gov.uk

Energy Management: Mr David Mark Lewis Energy Conservation Manager, Swyddfa'r Cygnor, Stryd Y Jel, Caernarfon LL55 1SH ☎ 01286 679307 ✉ davidmarklewis@gwynedd.gov.uk

Environmental Health: Mr Dafydd Wyn Williams, Head of Regulatory, Swyddfa'r Cygnor, Stryd Y Jel, Caernarfon LL55 1SH ☎ 01286 679370 ✉ dafyddwynwilliams@gwynedd.gov.uk

Estates, Property & Valuation: Mr Dafydd Gibbard Corporate Property - Senior Manager, Swyddfa'r Cygnor, Stryd Y Jel, Caernarfon LL55 1SH ☎ 01286 679957 ✉ dafyddgibbard@gwynedd.gov.uk

European Liaison: Mrs Vivienne Pritchard European Officer, Swyddfa'r Cygnor, Stryd Y Jel, Caernarfon LL55 1SH ☎ 01286 679487 ✉ viviennepritchard@gwynedd.gov.uk

Events Manager: Mr Hugh Edwin Jones Events Manager, Swyddfa'r Cygnor, Stryd Y Jel, Caernarfon LL55 1SH ☎ 01286 679398 ✉ hughedwinjones@gwynedd.gov.uk

Finance: Mr Dafydd Edwards, Head of Finance, Finance Service, Penrallt, Caernarfon LL55 1BN ☎ 01286 682682 ✉ dafyddle@gwynedd.gov.uk

Treasury: Mr Dafydd Edwards, Head of Finance, Finance Service, Penrallt, Caernarfon LL55 1BN ☎ 01286 682682 ✉ dafyddle@gwynedd.gov.uk

Pensions: Mr Dafydd Edwards, Head of Finance, Finance Service, Penrallt, Caernarfon LL55 1BN ☎ 01286 682682 ✉ dafyddle@gwynedd.gov.uk

Fleet Management: Mr Gwyn Morris Jones, Head of Highways & Municipal Services, Swyddfa'r Cygnor, Stryd Y Jel, Caernarfon LL55 1SH ☎ 01286 679402 ✉ gwynmorrisjones@gwynedd.gov.uk

Grounds Maintenance: Mr Gwyn Morris Jones, Head of Highways & Municipal Services, Swyddfa'r Cygnor, Stryd Y Jel, Caernarfon LL55 1SH ☎ 01286 679402 ✉ gwynmorrisjones@gwynedd.gov.uk

Health and Safety: Mr Geraint Owen, Head of Corporate Support, Swyddfa'r Cygnor, Stryd Y Jel, Caernarfon LL55 1SH ☎ 01286 679084 ✉ geraintowen@gwynedd.gov.uk

Highways: Mr Gwyn Morris Jones, Head of Highways & Municipal Services, Swyddfa'r Cygnor, Stryd Y Jel, Caernarfon LL55 1SH ☎ 01286 679402 ✉ gwynmorrisjones@gwynedd.gov.uk

Housing: Mr Aled Davies, Head of Adults, Health & Wellbeing, Swyddfa'r Cygnor, Stryd Y Jel, Caernarfon LL55 1SH ☎ 01286 679371 ✉ aleddavies@gwynedd.gov.uk

Legal: Mr Iwan Evans Legal Service Manager, Swyddfa'r Cygnor, Stryd Y Jel, Caernarfon LL55 1SH ☎ 01286 679015 ✉ iwangdevans@gwynedd.gov.uk

Leisure and Cultural Services: Mrs Sioned Williams, Head of Economy & Community, Swyddfa'r Cygnor, Stryd Y Jel, Caernarfon LL55 1SH ☎ 01286 679547 ✉ sionedewilliams@gwynedd.gov.uk

Licensing: Mr Dafydd Wyn Williams, Head of Regulatory, Swyddfa'r Cyngor, Stryd Y Jel, Caernarfon LL55 1SH ☎ 01286 679370 ✉ dafyddwynwilliams@gwynedd.gov.uk

Lighting: Mr Gwyn Morris Jones, Head of Highways & Municipal Services, Swyddfa'r Cyngor, Stryd Y Jel, Caernarfon LL55 1SH ☎ 01286 679402 ✉ gwynmorrisjones@gwynedd.gov.uk

Lottery Funding, Charity and Voluntary: Ms Heather Wyn Williams Senior Gwynedd Cist Officer, Plas Llanwnda, Castle Street, Caernarfon LL55 1SH ☎ 01286 679153 ✉ heatherwilliams@gwynedd.gov.uk

Member Services: Mr Geraint Owen, Head of Corporate Support, Swyddfa'r Cyngor, Stryd Y Jel, Caernarfon LL55 1SH ☎ 01286 679084 ✉ geraintowen@gwynedd.gov.uk

Parking: Mr Dafydd Wyn Williams, Head of Regulatory, Swyddfa'r Cyngor, Stryd Y Jel, Caernarfon LL55 1SH ☎ 01286 679370 ✉ dafyddwynwilliams@gwynedd.gov.uk

Partnerships: Mr Geraint Owen, Head of Corporate Support, Swyddfa'r Cyngor, Stryd Y Jel, Caernarfon LL55 1SH ☎ 01286 679084 ✉ geraintowen@gwynedd.gov.uk

Personnel / HR: Mr Geraint Owen, Head of Corporate Support, Swyddfa'r Cyngor, Stryd Y Jel, Caernarfon LL55 1SH ☎ 01286 679084 ✉ geraintowen@gwynedd.gov.uk

Planning: Mr Dafydd Wyn Williams, Head of Regulatory, Swyddfa'r Cyngor, Stryd Y Jel, Caernarfon LL55 1SH ☎ 01286 679370 ✉ dafyddwynwilliams@gwynedd.gov.uk

Procurement: Mr Geraint Owen, Head of Corporate Support, Swyddfa'r Cyngor, Stryd Y Jel, Caernarfon LL55 1SH ☎ 01286 679084 ✉ geraintowen@gwynedd.gov.uk

Public Libraries: Mr Hywel James, Chief Librarian, Swyddfa'r Cyngor, Stryd Y Jel, Caernarfon LL55 1SH ☎ 01286 679463 ✉ hyweljames@gwynedd.gov.uk

Recycling & Waste Minimisation: Mr Gwyn Morris Jones, Head of Highways & Municipal Services, Swyddfa'r Cyngor, Stryd Y Jel, Caernarfon LL55 1SH ☎ 01286 679402 ✉ gwynmorrisjones@gwynedd.gov.uk

Regeneration: Mrs Sioned Williams, Head of Economy & Community, Swyddfa'r Cyngor, Stryd Y Jel, Caernarfon LL55 1SH ☎ 01286 679547 ✉ sionedewilliams@gwynedd.gov.uk

Road Safety: Mr Colin Jones Parking and Road Safety Manager, Swyddfa'r Cyngor, Stryd Y Jel, Caernarfon LL55 1SH ☎ 01286 679753 ✉ colinjones@gwynedd.gov.uk

Social Services: Mrs Morwenna Edwards, Corporate Director, Swyddfa'r Cyngor, Stryd Y Jel, Caernarfon LL55 1SH ☎ 01286 679468 ✉ morwennaedwards@gwynedd.gov.uk

Social Services (Adult): Mr Aled Davies, Head of Adults, Health & Wellbeing, Swyddfa'r Cyngor, Stryd Y Jel, Caernarfon LL55 1SH ☎ 01286 679371 ✉ aleddavies@gwynedd.gov.uk

Social Services (Children): Mrs Marian Parry Hughes Head of Children & Supporting Families, Swyddfa'r Cyngor, Stryd Y Jel, Caernarfon LL55 1SH ☎ 01286 679228 ✉ marianhughes@gwynedd.gov.uk

Staff Training: Mr Geraint Owen, Head of Corporate Support, Swyddfa'r Cyngor, Stryd Y Jel, Caernarfon LL55 1SH ☎ 01286 679084 ✉ geraintowen@gwynedd.gov.uk

Street Scene: Mr Dafydd Wyn Williams, Head of Regulatory, Swyddfa'r Cyngor, Stryd Y Jel, Caernarfon LL55 1SH ☎ 01286 679370 ✉ dafyddwynwilliams@gwynedd.gov.uk

Sustainable Communities: Mrs Sioned Williams, Head of Economy & Community, Swyddfa'r Cyngor, Stryd Y Jel, Caernarfon LL55 1SH ☎ 01286 679547 ✉ sionedewilliams@gwynedd.gov.uk

Sustainable Development: Mr Dafydd Wyn Williams, Head of Regulatory, Swyddfa'r Cyngor, Stryd Y Jel, Caernarfon LL55 1SH ☎ 01286 679370 ✉ dafyddwynwilliams@gwynedd.gov.uk

Tourism: Mrs Sian Jones, Tourism Marketing & Customer Care Service Manager, Swyddfa'r Cyngor, Stryd Y Jel, Caernarfon LL55 1SH ☎ 01286 679963 ✉ sianpjones@gwynedd.gov.uk

Town Centre: Mr Dafydd Wyn Williams, Head of Regulatory, Swyddfa'r Cyngor, Stryd Y Jel, Caernarfon LL55 1SH ☎ 01286 679370 ✉ dafyddwynwilliams@gwynedd.gov.uk

Traffic Management: Mr Dafydd Wyn Williams, Head of Regulatory, Swyddfa'r Cyngor, Stryd Y Jel, Caernarfon LL55 1SH ☎ 01286 679370 ✉ dafyddwynwilliams@gwynedd.gov.uk

Transport: Mr Dafydd Wyn Williams, Head of Regulatory, Swyddfa'r Cyngor, Stryd Y Jel, Caernarfon LL55 1SH ☎ 01286 679370 ✉ dafyddwynwilliams@gwynedd.gov.uk

Transport Planner: Mr Dafydd Wyn Williams, Head of Regulatory, Swyddfa'r Cyngor, Stryd Y Jel, Caernarfon LL55 1SH ☎ 01286 679370 ✉ dafyddwynwilliams@gwynedd.gov.uk

Total Place: Mr Iwan Trefor Jones, Corporate Director, Swyddfa'r Cyngor, Stryd Y Jel, Caernarfon LL55 1SH ☎ 01286 679162 ✉ iwanj@gwynedd.gov.uk

Waste Collection and Disposal: Mr Gwyn Morris Jones, Head of Highways & Municipal Services, Swyddfa'r Cyngor, Stryd Y Jel, Caernarfon LL55 1SH ☎ 01286 679402 ✉ gwynmorrisjones@gwynedd.gov.uk

Waste Management: Mr Gwyn Morris Jones, Head of Highways & Municipal Services, Swyddfa'r Cyngor, Stryd Y Jel, Caernarfon LL55 1SH ☎ 01286 679402 ✉ gwynmorrisjones@gwynedd.gov.uk

Children's Play Areas: Mr Gwyn Morris Jones, Head of Highways & Municipal Services, Swyddfa'r Cyngor, Stryd Y Jel, Caernarfon LL55 1SH ☎ 01286 679402 ✉ gwynmorrisjones@gwynedd.gov.uk

COUNCILLORS

***Chair* Morgan**, Dilwyn (PC - Y Bala)
Cynghordd.DilwynMorgan@gwynedd.gov.uk

GWYNEDD

***Vice-Chair* Jones**, Eric (IND - Groeslon)
cynghorydd.ericmerfynjones@gwynedd.gov.uk

***Leader of the Council* Edwards**, Dyfed (PC - Penygroes)
Cynghorydd.DyfedEdwards@gwynedd.gov.uk

***Deputy Leader of the Council* Siencyn**, Dyfrig (PC - Dolgellau (North))
Cynghorydd.DyfrigLewisSiencyn@gwynedd.gov.uk

Ab Iago, Craig (PC - Llanllyfni)
cynghorydd.craigabiago@gwynedd.gov.uk

Churchman, Stephen (LD - Dolbenmaen)
Cynghorydd.StephenChurchman@gwynedd.gov.uk

Cooke, Endaf (O - Seiont (1))
cynghorydd.endafcooke@gwynedd.gov.uk

Davies, Anwen (O - Efailnewydd/Buan)
Cynghorydd.AnwenJaneDavies@gwynedd.gov.uk

Day, Lesley (IND - Garth)
cynghorydd@gwynedd.gov.uk

Dogan, Edward (PC - Dewi)

Edwards, Huw (PC - Cadnant)

Edwards, Trefor (IND - Llanberis)

Edwards, Gwynfor (LAB - Deiniol)
cynghorryd.gwynforedwards@gwynedd.gov.uk

Edwards, Elwyn (PC - Llandderfel)
Cynghorydd.ElwynEdwards@gwynedd.gov.uk

Ellis, Thomas (IND - Trawsfynydd)
Cynghorydd.TomEllis@gwynedd.gov.uk

Evans, Alan (PC - Llanuwchllyn)
Cynghorydd.AlanJonesEvans@gwynedd.gov.uk

Evans, Aled (PC - Llanystumdwy)
Cynghorydd.AledEvans@gwynedd.gov.uk

Forsyth, Jean (IND - Hirael)
cynghorydd.jeanforsyth@gwynedd.gov.uk

Glyn, Simon (O - Tudweiliog)
Cynghorydd.SimonGlyn@gwynedd.gov.uk

Glyn, Gweno (O - Botwnnog)
Cynghorydd.GwenoGlyn@gwynedd.gov.uk

Griffith, Gwen (LAB - Tregarth and Mynydd Llandygai)
Cynghorydd.gwengriffith@gwynedd.gov.uk

Griffiths, Selwyn (PC - Porthmadog (West))
Cynghorydd.SelwynGriffiths@gwynedd.gov.uk

Gruffydd, Alwyn (O - Porthmadog/Tremadog)
Cynghorydd.AlwynGruffydd@gwynedd.gov.uk

Gwenllian, Sian (PC - Y Felinheli)
cynghorydd.siangwenllian.gov.uk

Hughes, Louise (O - Llangelynnin)
Cynghorydd.LouiseHughes@gwynedd.gov.uk

Hughes, Annwen (PC - Llanbedr)
Cynghorydd.AnwenHughes@gwynedd.gov.uk

Hughes, Christopher (PC - Bontnewydd)
cynghorydd.christopherhughes@gwynedd.gov.uk

Hughes, John (IND - Llanengan)
cynghorydd.JohnHughes@gwynedd.gov.uk

Humphreys, Jason (O - Porthmadog (East))
Cynghorydd.JasonHumphreys@gwynedd.gov.uk

Jenkins, Peredur (PC - Brithdir + Llanfachreth)
Cynghorydd.PeredurJenkins@gwynedd.gov.uk

Jones, Aeron (O - Llanwnda)
cynghorydd.aeronjones@gwynedd.gov.uk

Jones, Dyfrig (PC - Gerlan)
cynghorydd.dyfrigjones@gwynedd.gov.uk

Jones, John Wynn (PC - Hendre)
cynghorydd.johnwynnjones@gwynedd.gov.uk

Jones, Elin (PC - Glyder)
cynghorydd.elinwjones@gwynedd.gov.uk

Jones, Linda (PC - Teigl)
Cynghorydd.LindaAnnJones@gwynedd.gov.uk

Jones, Llywarch (O - Llanaelhaearn)
Cynghorydd.LlywarchBowenJones@gwynedd.gov.uk

Jones, Sion (LAB - Bethel)
cynghorydd.sionjones@gwynedd.gov.uk

Jones, Brian (LAB - Cwm y Glo)
Cynghorydd.BrianJones@gwynedd.gov.uk

Jones, Charles (O - Llanrug)
Cynghorydd.CharlesWynJones@gwynedd.gov.uk

Jones-Williams, Eryl (IND - Dyffryn Ardudwy)
cynghorydd.eryljoneswilliams@gwynedd.gov.uk

Lawton, Beth (IND - Bryncrug/Llanfihangel)
Cynhorydd.BethLawton@gwnedd.gov.uk

Lloyd, Ifor (O - Talysarn)
cynghorydd.dilwynlloyd@gwynedd.gov.uk

Lloyd-Jones, Anne (IND - Tywyn (1))
Cynghorydd.AnneLloyd-Jones@gwynedd.gov.uk

Marshall, June (LD - Menai (Bangor) (1))
cynghorydd.junemarshall@gwynedd.gov.uk

Meurig, Dafydd (PC - Arllechwedd)
cynghorydd.dafyddmeurig@gwynedd.gov.uk

Morgan, Linda (PC - Dolgellau (South))
cynghorydd.lindamorgan@gwynedd.gov.uk

O'Neal, Christopher (IND - Marchog (1))
cynghorydd.oneal@gwynedd.gov.uk

Owen, William Tudor (PC - Peblig)
cynghorydd.tudorowen@gwynedd.gov.uk

Owen, William (IND - Seoint (2))
cynghorydd.williamroyowen@gwynedd.gov.uk

Owen, Michael (PC - Pwllheli (North))
Cynghorydd.MichaelSolOwen@gwynedd.gov.uk

Owen, Dewi (IND - Aberdyfi)
Cynghorydd.DewiOwen@gwynedd.gov.uk

Pickavance, Nigel (IND - Marchog (2))
cynghorydd.nigelpickavance@gwynedd.gov.uk

Read, Peter (O - Abererch)
cynghorydd.peterread@gwynedd.gov.uk

Roberts, Liz (PC - Morfa Nefyn)
Cynghorydd.Liz.SavilleRoberts@gwynedd.gov.uk

Roberts, Gareth (PC - Aberdaron)
cynghorydd.garethroberts@gwynedd.gov.uk

Roberts, John (IND - Corris/ Mawddwy)
Cynghorydd.JohnPugheRoberts@gwynedd.gov.uk

Roberts, Caerwyn (PC - Harlech/Talsarnau)
Cynghorydd.CaerwynRoberts@gwynedd.gov.uk

Rowlands, Mair (PC - Menai (Bangor) (2))
cynghorydd.mairrowlands@gwymedd.gov.uk

Russell, Angela (IND - Llanbedrog)
Cynghorydd.AngelaRussell@gwynedd.gov.uk

Stevens, Mike (IND - Tywyn (2))
cynghorydd.mikestevens@gwynedd.gov.uk

Thomas, Gareth (PC - Penrhyndeudraeth)
Cynghorydd.GarethThomas@gwynedd.gov.uk

Thomas, Paul (PC - Bowydd + Rhiw)
Cynghorydd.PaulThomas@gwynedd.gov.uk

Thomas, Ioan (PC - Menai (Caernarfon))
Cynghorydd.IoanThomas@gwynedd.gov.uk

Williams, Gethin (PC - Abermaw)
cynghorydd.gethinglynwilliams@gwynedd.gov.uk

Williams, Elfed (IND - Deiniolen)
cynghorydd.elfedwilliams@gwynedd.gov.uk

Williams, Hywel (PC - Abersoch)
cynghorydd.RHywellWynWilliams@gwynedd.gov.uk

Williams, John (PC - Pentir)
cynghorydd.johnwynnwilliams@gwynedd.gov.uk

Williams, Gruffydd (O - Nefyn)
Cynghorydd.GruffyddWilliams@gwynedd.gov.uk

Williams, Owain (O - Clynnog Fawr)
Cynghorydd.OwainWilliams@gwynedd.gov.uk

Williams, Eirwyn (IND - Cricieth)
Cynghorydd.EirwynWilliams@gwynedd.gov.uk

Williams, Hefin (PC - Penisarwaun)
cynghorydd.hefinwilliams@gwynedd.gov.uk

Williams, Ann (PC - Ogwen)
cynghorydd.annwilliams@gwynedd.gov.uk

Williams-Davies, Mandy (PC - Diffwys + Maenofferen)
Cynghordd.MandyWDavies@gwynedd.gov.uk

Wright, Bob (O - Pwllheli (South))
Cynghorydd.BobWright@gwynedd.gov.uk

Wyn, Eurig (PC - Waunfawr)
cynghorydd.eurigwyn@gwynedd.gov.uk

POLITICAL COMPOSITION

PC: 36, IND: 18, O: 15, LAB: 4, LD: 2

Hackney L

Hackney London Borough Council, Town Hall, Mare Street, London E8 1EA
☎ 020 8356 5000 🖷 020 8356 2080 🖳 www.hackney.gov.uk

FACTS AND FIGURES

Parliamentary Constituencies: Hackney North and Stoke Newington, Hackney South and Shoreditch
EU Constituencies: London
Election Frequency: Elections are of whole council

PRINCIPAL OFFICERS

Chief Executive: Mr Tim Shields, Chief Executive, Town Hall, Mare Street, London E8 1EA ☎ 020 8356 3210 🖷 020 8356 3047 ✉ tim.shields@hackney.gov.uk

Senior Management: Dr Penny Bevan Director - Public Health, Town Hall, Mare Street, London E8 1EA ✉ penny.bevan@hackney.gov.uk

Senior Management: Ms Gifty Edila Corporate Director of Legal, HR & Regulatory Services, Town Hall, Mare Street, London E8 1EA ☎ 020 8356 3265 🖷 020 8536 3047 ✉ gifty.edila@hackney.gov.uk

Senior Management: Ms Charlotte Graves Corporate Director of Housing / Chief Executive of Hackney Homes, Christopher Addison House, 72 Wilton Way, London E8 1BJ ☎ 020 8356 3670 🖷 ; 020 8356 2242 ✉ charlotte.graves@hackney.gov.uk

Senior Management: Mr Ian Williams Corporate Director of Finance & Resources, Town Hall, Mare Street, London E8 1EA ☎ 020 8356 3003 ✉ ian.williams@hackney.gov.uk

Senior Management: Mr Alan Wood, Corporate Director of Children & Young People's Services, The Learning Trust, 1 Reading Lane, London E8 1GQ ☎ 020 8820 7515 ✉ alan.wood@hackney.gov.uk

Senior Management: Ms Kim Wright, Corporate Director of Health & Community Services, Town Hall, Mare Street, London E8 1EA ☎ 020 8356 7347 🖷 020 8356 7544 ✉ kim.wright@hackney.gov.uk

Access Officer / Social Services (Disability): Mr Rob Blackstone AD Adult Social Care, 1 Hillman Street, London E8 1DY ☎ 020 8356 4282

Architect, Building / Property Services: Mr Chris Pritchard Interim AD of Strategic Property Services, 1 Hillman Street, London E8 1DY ☎ 020 8356 3700 ✉ chris.pritchard@hackney.gov.uk

Building Control: Mr Jim Paterson, Assistant Director of Hackney Homes, 6-15 Florfield Street, London E8 1DT ☎ 020 8356 6899 🖷 020 8356 4740 ✉ jim.paterson@hackney.gov.uk

Children / Youth Services: Ms Pauline Adams Head of Young Hackney, 1 Hillman Street, London E8 1DY ☎ 020 8356 2709 ✉ pauline.adams@hackney.gov.uk

Civil Registration: Ms Christie Junor-Sheppard Head of Registrational Services, Town Hall, Mare Street, London E8 1EA ☎ 020 8356 4382 ✉ christie.sheppard@hackney.gov.uk

PR / Communications: Ms Polly Cziok Head of Communications & Consultation, Town Hall, Mare Street, London E8 1EA ☎ 020 8356 3323 ✉ polly.cziok@hackney.gov.uk

Community Safety: Mr Steve Bending Head of Safer Communities, Maurice Bishop House, 17 Reading Lane, London E8 1HH ☎ 020 8356 2070 ✉ steve.bending@hackney.gov.uk

HACKNEY

Computer Management: Ms Christine Peacock, Assistant Director of ICT, 6-15 Florfield Road, London E8 1DT ☎ 020 8356 2600 🖰 christine.peacock@hackney.gov.uk

Consumer Protection and Trading Standards: Mr Robin Jones Team Leader - Trading Standards, 2 Hillman Street, London E8 1DY ☎ 020 8356 4909 🖰 robin.jones@hackney.gov.uk

Contracts: Mr Michael Robson Head of Strategic Procurement, 3rd Floor Keltan House, 89 - 115 Mare Street, Hackney, London E8 4RU ☎ 0208 356 3821 🖰 michael.robson@hackney.gov.uk

Customer Service: Ms Lisa Cook Customer Services Operations Manager, 1 Hillman Street, London E8 1DY ☎ 020 8356 6501 🖰 lisa.cook@hackney.gov.uk

Education: Ms Anne Canning Director - Education, Town Hall, Mare Street, London E8 1EA ☎ 020 8820 7344 🖰 anne.canning@hackney.gov.uk

Electoral Registration: Mr Michael Summerville Head of Electoral & Member Services, Town Hall, Mare Street, London E8 1EA ☎ 020 8356 3115 🖰 michael.summerville@hackney.gov.uk

Emergency Planning: Mr Roy Hitching Head of Service of CCTV & Emergency Planning, Stoke Newington Municipal Offices, Stoke Newington Church Street, London N16 0JR ☎ 020 8356 2182 🖰 roy.hitching@hackney.gov.uk

Energy Management: Mr Kumar Zaman Head of Energy Management, 2 Hillman Street, London E8 1FB ☎ 020 8356 2764 🖰 kumar.zaman@hackney.gov.uk

Environmental / Technical Services: Mr Tom McCourt, Assistant Director of Public Realm, 2 Hillman Street, London E8 1FB ☎ 020 8356 8219 🖰 tom.mccourt@hackney.gov.uk

Environmental Health: Ms Aleyne Fontenelle Environmental Health Manager, Town Hall, Mare Street, London E8 1EA ☎ 020 8356 4918 🖷 020 8356 4740 🖰 aleyne.fontenelle@hackney.gov.uk

Estates, Property & Valuation: Mr Jonathan Angell Head of Commercial Estates, Keltan House, 89 - 115 Mare Street, Hackney, London E8 4RU ☎ 020 8536 4034 🖷 020 8536 8261 🖰 jonathan.angell@hackney.gov.uk

Events Manager: Mr Dan Cowdrill Strategic Sales & Marketing Manager for Venue Portfolio, 1st Floor, Maurice Bishop House, 17 Reading Lane, London E8 1HH ☎ 020 8356 2577

Facilities: Mr Gary Sherman Facilities Operations Manager, Hackney Service Centre, 1 Hillman Street, Hackney, London E8 1DY ☎ 020 8356 4647 🖰 gary.sherman@hackney.gov.uk

Finance: Ms Jill Davys Head of Financial Services, Keltan House, 89-155 Mare Street, Hackney, London E8 4RU ☎ 020 8356 2646 🖰 jill.davys@hackney.gov.uk

Finance: Mr Ian Williams Corporate Director of Finance & Resources, Town Hall, Mare Street, London E8 1EA ☎ 020 8356 3003 🖰 ian.williams@hackney.gov.uk

Pensions: Mr Gary Nash Pensions Liaison Officer, Keltan House, 89-115 Mare Street, London E8 4RU ☎ 020 8356 2745 🖰 gary.nash@hackney.gov.uk

Fleet Management: Mr Norman Harding Corporate Fleet Management, Keltan House, 89-115 Mare Street, London E8 4RU ☎ 020 8356 3613 🖰 norman.harding@hackney.gov.uk

Health and Safety: Ms Lynne Thornburn Health & Safety Adviser, 280 Mare Street, London E8 1EA ☎ 020 8356 4659 🖰 lynne.thornburn@hackney.gov.uk

Highways: Mr Mark Pinnock Group Engineer - Highways & Maintenance, Keltan House, 89 - 115 Mare Street, Hackney, London E8 4RU ☎ 020 8256 8312 🖷 020 8356 2863 🖰 mark.pinnock@hackney.gov.uk

Housing: Ms Charlotte Graves Corporate Director of Housing / Chief Executive of Hackney Homes, Christopher Addison House, 72 Wilton Way, London E8 1BJ ☎ 020 8356 3670 🖷 020 8356 2242 🖰 charlotte.graves@hackney.gov.uk

Local Area Agreement: Mr Bruce Devile Head of Corporate Performance, Town Hall, Mare Street, London E8 1EA ☎ 020 8356 3418 🖰 bruce.devile@hackney.gov.uk

Legal: Ms Gifty Edila Corporate Director of Legal, HR & Regulatory Services, Town Hall, Mare Street, London E8 1EA ☎ 020 8356 3265 🖷 020 8536 3047 🖰 gifty.edila@hackney.gov.uk

Legal: Mr Yinka Owa Assistant Director of Legal & Democratic Services, Town Hall, Mare Street, London E8 1EA ☎ 020 8356 6234 🖰 yinka.owa@hackney.gov.uk

Leisure and Cultural Services: Mr Ian Holland Head of Leisure & Open Spaces, Hackney Service Centre, 1 Hillman Street, Hackney, London E8 1DY ☎ 020 8356 3810 🖰 ian.holland@hackney.gov.uk

Licensing: Mr Mike Smith Senior Licensing Officer, 1 Hillman Street, London E8 1DY ☎ 020 8356 4973 🖰 mike.smith@hackney.gov.uk

Member Services: Ms Richa Kataria Deputy Head of Member Services, Town Hall, Mare Street, London E8 1EA ☎ 020 8356 3350 🖰 richa.kataria@hackney.gov.uk

Parking: Mr Seamus Adams, Head of Parking Services, 2 Hillman Street, London E8 1FB ☎ 020 8356 8333 🖰 seamus.adams@hackney.gov.uk

Partnerships: Ms Joanne Sumner Assistant Chief Officer, Town Hall, Mare Street, London E8 1EA ☎ 020 8356 3135 🖰 joanna.sumner@hackney.gov.uk

Personnel / HR: Mr Dan Paul Head of HR & OD, 280 Mare Street, London E8 1FB ☎ 020 8356 3110 🖰 dan.paul@hackney.gov.uk

Planning: Mr John Allen Assistant Director of Planning & Regulatory Services, 2 Hillman Street, London E8 1DY ☎ 020 8356 8134 🖰 john.allen@hackney.gov.uk

Procurement: Mr Chris Hudson, Assistant Director of Procurement & Fleet, 3rd Floor Keltan House, E8 4RU ☎ 020 8356 2725 🖷 020 8356 3037 ✉ chris.hudson@hackney.gov.uk

Public Libraries: Mr Ted Rogers Head of Libraries, Heritage & Culture, Hackney Service Centre, 1 Hillman Street, Hackney, London E8 1DY ☎ 020 8356 4782 ✉ edward.rogers@hackney.gov.uk

Recycling & Waste Minimisation: Mr Richard Gilbert Project Manager, Keltan House, 89-115 Mare Street, London E8 4RU ☎ 020 8356 4946 🖷 020 8356 4740 ✉ richard.gilbert@hackney.gov.uk

Regeneration: Mr Carl Welhan Interim Head of Regeneration Delivery, 2 Hillman Street, London E8 1DY ☎ 020 8356 3790 ✉ carl.welhan@hackney.gov.uk

Road Safety: Ms Maryann Allen Transport & Sustainable Engagement Manager, Hackney Service Centre, 1 Hillman Street, Hackney, London E8 1DY ☎ 020 8356 8184 🖷 020 8356 8263 ✉ maryann.allen@hackney.gov.uk

Social Services (Adult): Ms Kim Wright, Corporate Director of Health & Community Services, Town Hall, Mare Street, London E8 1EA ☎ 020 8356 7347 🖷 020 8356 7544 ✉ kim.wright@hackney.gov.uk

Social Services (Children): Ms Sheila Durr Assistant Director of Children's Social Care & Safeguarding, Hackney Service Centre, 1 Hillman Street, Hackney, London E8 1DY ☎ 020 8356 4603 🖷 020 8356 4740 ✉ sheila.durr@hackney.gov.uk

Social Services (Children): Mr Alan Wood, Corporate Director of Children & Young People's Services, The Learning Trust, 1 Reading Lane, London E8 1GQ ☎ 020 8820 7515 ✉ alan.wood@hackney.gov.uk

Public Health: Dr Penny Bevan Director - Public Health, Town Hall, Mare Street, London E8 1EA ✉ penny.bevan@hackney.gov.uk

Street Scene: Mr Andy Cunningham, Head of Streetscene, Keltan House, 89-115 Mare Street, London E8 4RU ☎ 020 8356 6657 ✉ andy.cunningham@hackney.gov.uk

Town Centre: Mr Carl Welhan Interim Head of Regeneration Delivery, 2 Hillman Street, London E8 1DY ☎ 020 8356 3790 ✉ carl.welhan@hackney.gov.uk

Traffic Management: Mr Suresh Prajapati Senior Enginner, Keltan House, 89 - 115 Mare Street, Hackney, London E8 4RU ☎ 020 8356 8374 ✉ suresh.prajapati@hackney.gov.uk

Transport: Mr Andy Cunningham, Head of Streetscene, Keltan House, 89-115 Mare Street, London E8 4RU ☎ 020 8356 6657 ✉ andy.cunningham@hackney.gov.uk

Transport: Mr Tom McCourt, Assistant Director of Public Realm, 2 Hillman Street, London E8 1FB ☎ 020 8356 8219 ✉ tom.mccourt@hackney.gov.uk

Transport Planner: Mr Paul Bowker Transport Planner, 300 Mare Street, London E8 3HE ☎ 020 8356 8123 ✉ paul.bowker@hackney.gov.uk

Waste Management: Mr John Wheatley, Head of Waste, Millfields Depot, London E5 0AR ☎ 0208 356 6690 ✉ john.wheatley@hackney.gov.uk

COUNCILLORS

***The Lord Mayor* Pipe**, Jules (LAB - London Borough of Hackney)

***Deputy Mayor* Linden**, Sophie (LAB - Hackney Central)
sophie.linden@hackney.gov.uk

Adams, Kam (LAB - Hoxton East & Shoreditch)

Adejare, Soraya (LAB - Dalston)
Soraya.Adejare@Hackney.gov.uk

Akhoon, Dawood (LD - Cazenove)
Dawood.Akhoon@hackney.gov.uk

Bell, Brian (LAB - Brownswood)
brian.bell@hackney.gov.uk

Bramble, Antoinette (LAB - London Fields)
Antoinette.Bramble@Hackney.gov.uk

Brett, Will (LAB - Victoria)
Will.Brett@Hackney.gov.uk

Buitekant, Barry (LAB - Haggerston)
barry.buitekant@hackney.gov.uk

Bunt, Laura (LAB - De Beauvoir)
Laura.Bunt@Hackney.gov.uk

Burke, Jon (LAB - Woodberry Down)
Jon.Burke@Hackney.gov.uk

Cameron, Sophie (LAB - Clissold)
Sophie.Cameron@Hackney.gov.uk

Chapman, Robert (LAB - Homerton)
Robert.Chapman@Hackney.gov.uk

Coban, Mete (LAB - Stoke Newington)
Mete.Coban@Hackney.gov.uk

Demirci, Feryal (LAB - Hoxton East & Shoreditch)
feryal.demirci@hackney.gov.uk

Desmond, Michael (LAB - Hackney Downs)
michael@desm.new.labour.org.uk

Ebbutt, Tom (LAB - Hoxton East & Shoreditch)
Tom.Ebbutt@Hackney.gov.uk

Etti, Sade (LAB - Clissold)
Sade.Etti@Hackney.gov.uk

Fajana-Thomas, Susan (LAB - Stoke Newington)
Susan.FajanaThomas@Hackney.gov.uk

Glanville, Philip (LAB - Hoxton West)
philip.glanville@hackney.gov.uk

Gordon, Margaret (LAB - Leabridge)
Margaret.Gordon@Hackney.gov.uk

Gregory, Michelle (LAB - Shacklewell)
Michelle.Gregory@Hackney.gov.uk

Hanson, Katie (LAB - Victoria)
katie.hanson@hackney.gov.uk

Hayhurst, Ben (LAB - Hackney Central)
ben.hayhurst@hackney.gov.uk

Hercock, Ned (LAB - Clissold)
Ned.Hercock@Hackney.gov.uk

Jacobson, Abraham (LD - Cazenove)
Abraham.Jacobson@Hackney.gov.uk

Kennedy, Christopher (LAB - Hackney Wick)
christopher.kennedy@hackney.gov.uk

Levy, Michael (CON - Springfield)

Lufkin, Richard (LAB - Shacklewell)
Richard.Lufkin@Hackney.gov.uk

McKenzie, Clayeon (LAB - Hoxton West)
clayeon.mckenzie@hackney.gov.uk

McShane, Jonathan (LAB - Haggerston)
jonathan.mcshane@hackney.gov.uk

Muir, Rick (LAB - Hackney Downs)
Rick.Muir@Hackney.gov.uk

Mulready, Sally (LAB - Homerton)
sally.mulready@hackney.gov.uk

Munn, Ann (LAB - Haggerston)
Ann.Munn@Hackney.gov.uk

Nicholson, Guy (LAB - Homerton)
guy.nicholson@hackney.gov.uk

Odze, Harvey (CON - Springfield)
Harvey.Odze@Hackney.gov.uk

Oguzkanli, Deniz (LAB - Leabridge)
deniz.oguzkanli@hackney.gov.uk

Ozsen, M Can (LAB - London Fields)
MCan.Ozsen@Hackney.gov.uk

Papier, Benzion (CON - Stamford Hill West)
benzion.papier@hackney.gov.uk

Patrick, Sharon (LAB - Kings Park)
sharon.patrick@hackney.gov.uk

Peters, James (LAB - De Beauvoir)
James.Peters@Hackney.gov.uk

Plouviez, Emma (LAB - London Fields)
emma.plouviez@hackney.gov.uk

Potter, Clare (LAB - Brownswood)
clare.potter@hackney.gov.uk

Rahilly, Tom (LAB - Kings Park)
Tom.Rahilly@Hackney.gov.uk

Rathbone, Ian (LAB - Leabridge)
Ian.Rathbone@Hackney.gov.uk

Rennison, Rebecca (LAB - Kings Park)
Rebecca.Rennison@Hackney.gov.uk

Rickard, Anna-Joy (LAB - Hackney Downs)
Anna-Joy.Rickard@Hackney.gov.uk

Sales, Rosemary (LAB - Stamford Hill West)
Rosemary.Sales@Hackney.gov.uk

Selman, Caroline (LAB - Woodberry Down)
Caroline.Selman@Hackney.gov.uk

Sharer, Ian (LD - Cazenove)
ian.sharer@Hackney.gov.uk

Sharman, Nick (LAB - Hackney Wick)
Nick.Sharman@Hackney.gov.uk

Snell, Peter (LAB - Dalston)
Peter.Snell@Hackney.gov.uk

Steinberger, Simche (CON - Springfield)
simche.steinberger@hackney.gov.uk

Stops, Vincent (LAB - Hackney Central)
vincent.stops@hackney.gov.uk

Taylor, Geoffrey (LAB - Victoria)
geoffrey.taylor@hackney.gov.uk

Thomson, Louisa (LAB - Stoke Newington)
Louisa.Thomson@hackney.gov.uk

Webb, Jessica (LAB - Hackney Wick)
jessica.webb@hackney.gov.uk

Williams, Carole (LAB - Hoxton West)
carole.williams@hackney.gov.uk

POLITICAL COMPOSITION
LAB: 51, CON: 4, LD: 3

COMMITTEE CHAIRS
Licensing: Ms Emma Plouviez

Pensions: Mr Robert Chapman

Halton U

Halton Borough Council, Municipal Building, Kingsway, Widnes WA8 7QF
☎ 0303 333 4300 🖷 0151 471 7301 hdl@halton.gov.uk
www.halton.gov.uk

FACTS AND FIGURES
Parliamentary Constituencies: Halton
EU Constituencies: North West
Election Frequency: Elections are by thirds

PRINCIPAL OFFICERS
Chief Executive: Mr David Parr, Chief Executive, Municipal Building, Kingsway, Widnes WA8 7QF ☎ 0151 511 6000
david.parr@halton.gov.uk

Senior Management: Mr Dwayne Johnson, Strategic Director - Health & Communtiy, Municipal Building, Kingsway, Widnes WA8 7QF ☎ 0151 511 6003 🖷 0151 471 7536
dwayne.johnson@halton.gov.uk

Senior Management: Mr Ian Leivesley, Strategic Director - Corporate & Policy, Municipal Building, Kingsway, Widnes WA8 7QF ☎ 0151 511 6002 ian.leivesley@halton.gov.uk

Senior Management: Mr Gerald Meehan Strategic Director - Environment, Municipal Building, Kingsway, Widnes WA8 7QF ☎ 0151 511 6004 🖷 0151 471 7304

Senior Management: Ms Eileen O'Meara Director - Public Health, Municipal Building, Kingsway, Widnes WA8 7QF
eileen.omeara@halton.gov.uk

Architect, Building / Property Services: Mr Wesley Rourke, Operational Director - Employment, Enterprise & Property, Corporate & Policy Directorate, Municipal Building, Kingsway, Widnes WA8 7QF ☎ 0151 511 8645 ✉ wesley.rourke@halton.gov.uk

Best Value: Mr Mike Foy Senior Performance Management Officer, Corporate & Policy Directorate, Municipal Building, Kingsway, Widnes WA8 7QF ☎ 0151 511 8081 🖷 0151 471 7301 ✉ mike.foy@halton.gov.uk

Building Control: Mr Mick Noone, Operational Director - Policy, Planning & Transportation, Municipal Building, Kingsway, Widnes WA8 7QF ☎ 0151 511 7604 ✉ mick.noone@halton.gov.uk

Catering Services: Mr Chris Patino, Operational Director - Communities & Environment, Select Security Stadium, Lowerhouse Lane, Widnes WA8 7DZ ☎ 0151 510 6000 ✉ chris.patino@halton.gov.uk

Children / Youth Services: Mr Gareth Jones Head of Service - Youth Offenders, Grosvenor House, Halton Lea, , Runcorn WA7 2WD ☎ 0151 511 7499 ✉ gareth.jones@halton.gov.uk

Children / Youth Services: Mr Gerald Meehan, Strategic Director - Children & Young People, Municipal Building, Kingsway, Widnes WA8 7QF ☎ 0151 511 6004 ✉ gerald.meehan@halton.gov.uk

Children / Youth Services: Mr Steve Nyakatawa Operational Director - Children & Young People, Grosvenor House, Halton Lea, , Runcorn WA7 2WD ☎ 0151 511 7344 ✉ steve.nyakatawa@halton.gov.uk

PR / Communications: Mrs Michelle Osborne Operational Director - Communications & Marketing, Municipal Building, Kingsway, Widnes WA8 7QF ☎ 0151 511 7723 ✉ michelle.osborne@halton.gov.uk

Community Safety: Mr Mick Andrews Community Safety Officer, 6-8 Church Street, Runcorn WA8 7LT ☎ 0151 511 7695

Computer Management: Mr Simon Riley, Operational Director - ICT Services, Municipal Building, Kingsway, Widnes WA8 7QF ☎ 0151 511 7000 🖷 0151 471 7302 ✉ simon.riley@halton.gov.uk

Contracts: Ms Lorraine Cox Operational Director - Procurement, Municipal Building, Kingsway, Widnes WA8 7QF ☎ 0151 511 7925 ✉ lorraine.cox@halton.gov.uk

Corporate Services: Mr Ian Leivesley, Strategic Director - Corporate & Policy, Municipal Building, Kingsway, Widnes WA8 7QF ☎ 0151 511 6002 ✉ ian.leivesley@halton.gov.uk

Education: Mr Gerald Meehan, Strategic Director - Children & Young People, Municipal Building, Kingsway, Widnes WA8 7QF ☎ 0151 511 6004 ✉ gerald.meehan@halton.gov.uk

E-Government: Mr Patrick Oliver, E-Government Development Team Leader, Municipal Building, Kingsway, Widnes WA8 7QF ☎ 0151 511 7110 ✉ pat.oliver@halton.gov.uk

Electoral Registration: Mrs Christine Lawley, Principal Electoral Services / Elections Officer, Corporate & Policy Directorate, Municipal Building, Kingsway, Widnes WA8 7QF ☎ 0151 511 8328 🖷 0151 471 7301 ✉ christine.lawley@halton.gov.uk

Emergency Planning: Mr Stephen Rimmer Head - Traffic Risk & Emergency Planning, Municipal Building, Kingsway, Widnes WA8 7QF ☎ 0151 511 7401 🖷 0151 471 7301 ✉ stephen.rimmer@halton.gov.uk

Environmental Health: Mr Dwayne Johnson, Strategic Director - Health & Communtiy, Municipal Building, Kingsway, Widnes WA8 7QF ☎ 0151 511 6003 🖷 0151 471 7536 ✉ dwayne.johnson@halton.gov.uk

Estates, Property & Valuation: Mr Wesley Rourke, Operational Director - Employment, Enterprise & Property, Corporate & Policy Directorate, Municipal Building, Kingsway, Widnes WA8 7QF ☎ 0151 511 8645 ✉ wesley.rourke@halton.gov.uk

Facilities: Mr Simon Webb Facilities Manager, Municipal Building, Kingsway, Widnes WA8 7QF ☎ 0151 511 8838 ✉ simon.webb@halton.gov.uk

Finance: Mr Ed Dawson Operational Director - Financial Services, Municipal Building, Kingsway, Widnes WA8 7QF ☎ 0151 511 7965 ✉ ed.dawson@halton.gov.uk

Finance: Mr Peter McCann Head - Halton Direct Link & Revenue & Benefits, Municipal Building, Kingsway, Widnes WA8 7QF ☎ 0151 511 8411 ✉ peter.mccann@halton.gov.uk

Fleet Management: Mr Chris Cullen Head - Operational Support Services, Lowerhouse Lane Depot, Lowerhouse Lane, Widnes WA8 7AW ☎ 0151 511 7937 ✉ chris.cullen@halton.gov.uk

Grounds Maintenance: Mr Tim Ward-Dutton Operational Spaces Manager, Municipal Building, Kingsway, Widnes WA8 7QF ☎ 01928 583913 ✉ tim.ward-dutton@halton.gov.uk

Health and Safety: Mr Tony Dean Principal Health & Safety Advisor, Municipal Building, Kingsway, Widnes WA8 7QF ☎ 0151 511 7967 ✉ tony.dean@halton.gov.uk

Highways: Mr Mick Noone, Operational Director - Policy, Planning & Transportation, Municipal Building, Kingsway, Widnes WA8 7QF ☎ 0151 511 7604 ✉ mick.noone@halton.gov.uk

Local Area Agreement: Ms Shelah Semoff Partnership Officer, Municipal Building, Kingsway, Widnes WA8 7QF ☎ 0151 511 8677 ✉ shelah.semoff@halton.gov.uk

Legal: Mr Mark Reaney Operational Director - Legal & Democratic Services, Municipal Building, Kingsway, Widnes WA8 7QF ☎ 0151 907 8300 🖷 0151 471 7301 ✉ mark.reaney@halton.gov.uk

Leisure and Cultural Services: Mr Chris Patino, Operational Director - Communities & Environment, Halton Stadium, Lowerhouse Lane, Widnes WA8 7DZ ☎ 0151 510 6000 ✉ chris.patino@halton.gov.uk

HALTON

Licensing: Mr Mark Reaney Operational Director - Legal & Democratic Services, Municipal Building, Kingsway, Widnes WA8 7QF ☎ 0151 511 6006 ✉ mark.reaney@halton.gov.uk

Lighting: Mr Stephen Rimmer Head - Traffic Risk & Emergency Planning, Municipal Building, Kingsway, Widnes WA8 7QF ☎ 0151 511 7401 🖷 0151 471 7301 ✉ stephen.rimmer@halton.gov.uk

Lottery Funding, Charity and Voluntary: Mr Wesley Rourke, Operational Director - Employment, Enterprise & Property, Corporate & Policy Directorate, Municipal Building, Kingsway, Widnes WA8 7QF ☎ 0151 511 8645 ✉ wesley.rourke@halton.gov.uk

Member Services: Mrs Christine Lawley, Principal Electoral Services / Elections Officer, Corporate & Policy Directorate, Municipal Building, Kingsway, Widnes WA8 7QF ☎ 0151 511 8328 🖷 0151 471 7301 ✉ christine.lawley@halton.gov.uk

Personnel / HR: Mr Richard Rout Divisional Manager - Human Resources & Learning Development, Municipal Building, Kingsway, Widnes WA8 7QF ☎ 0151 511 7826 ✉ richard.rout@halton.gov.uk

Planning: Mr Mick Noone, Operational Director - Policy, Planning & Transportation, Municipal Building, Kingsway, Widnes WA8 7QF ☎ 0151 511 7604 ✉ mick.noone@halton.gov.uk

Procurement: Ms Lorraine Cox Operational Director - Procurement, Municipal Building, Kingsway, Widnes WA8 7QF ☎ 0151 511 7925 ✉ lorraine.cox@halton.gov.uk

Public Libraries: Ms Paula Reilly-Cooper, Library Services Manager, Town Hall, Heath Road, Runcorn WA7 5TD ☎ 0151 511 8598 ✉ paula.reilly-cooper@halton.gov.uk

Recycling & Waste Minimisation: Mr Andy Horrocks, Recycling Officer, Lowerhouse Lane Depot, Lowerhouse Lane, Widnes WA8 7AW ☎ 0151 511 7520 🖷 0151 471 7305 ✉ andy.horrocks@halton.gov.uk

Road Safety: Mr Stephen Rimmer Head - Traffic Risk & Emergency Planning, Municipal Building, Kingsway, Widnes WA8 7QF ☎ 0151 511 7401 🖷 0151 471 7301 ✉ stephen.rimmer@halton.gov.uk

Social Services: Mr Dwayne Johnson, Strategic Director - Health & Communtiy, Municipal Building, Kingsway, Widnes WA8 7QF ☎ 0151 511 6003 🖷 0151 471 7536 ✉ dwayne.johnson@halton.gov.uk

Public Health: Ms Eileen O'Meara Director - Public Health, Municipal Building, Kingsway, Widnes WA8 7QF ✉ eileen.omeara@halton.gov.uk

Staff Training: Mr Richard Rout Divisional Manager - Human Resources & Learning Development, Municipal Building, Kingsway, Widnes WA8 7QF ☎ 0151 511 7826 ✉ richard.rout@halton.gov.uk

Traffic Management: Mr Stephen Rimmer Head - Traffic Risk & Emergency Planning, Municipal Building, Kingsway, Widnes WA8 7QF ☎ 0151 511 7401 🖷 0151 471 7301 ✉ stephen.rimmer@halton.gov.uk

Transport: Mr Mick Noone, Operational Director - Policy, Planning & Transportation, Municipal Building, Kingsway, Widnes WA8 7QF ☎ 0151 511 7604 ✉ mick.noone@halton.gov.uk

Transport Planner: Mr Mick Noone, Operational Director - Policy, Planning & Transportation, Municipal Building, Kingsway, Widnes WA8 7QF ☎ 0151 511 7604 ✉ mick.noone@halton.gov.uk

Waste Collection and Disposal: Mr Jimmy Unsworth, Head - Waste Management, Lowerhouse Lane Depot, Lowerhouse Lane, Widnes WA8 7AW ☎ 0151 511 7625 ✉ jimmy.Unsworth@halton.gov.uk

Waste Management: Mr Jimmy Unsworth, Head - Waste Management, Lowerhouse Lane Depot, Lowerhouse Lane, Widnes WA8 7AW ☎ 0151 511 7625 ✉ jimmy.Unsworth@halton.gov.uk

COUNCILLORS

***Mayor* Cargill**, Ellen (LAB - Halton Castle)
ellen.cargill@halton.gov.uk

***Deputy Mayor* Philbin**, Ged (LAB - Appleton)
ged.philbin@halton.gov.uk

***Leader of the Council* Polhill**, Rob (LAB - Halton View)
rob.polhill@halton.gov.uk

Baker, Sandra (LAB - Birchfield)
sandra.baker@halton.gov.uk

Bradshaw, Marjorie (CON - Daresbury)
marjorie.bradshaw@halton.gov.uk

Bradshaw, John (CON - Daresbury)
john.bradshaw@halton.gov.uk

Cargill, Dave (LAB - Norton South)
dave.cargill@halton.gov.uk

Cassidy, Lauren (LAB - Norton North)
Lauren.Cassidy@halton.gov.uk

Cole, Arthur (LAB - Halton Castle)
arthur.cole@halton.gov.uk

Dennett, Mark (LAB - Grange)
mark.dennett@halton.gov.uk

Edge, Susan (LAB - Appleton)
sue.edge@halton.gov.uk

Fry, Mike (LAB - Birchfield)
michael.fry@halton.gov.uk

Gerrard, Charlotte (LAB - Heath)
charlotte.gerrard@halton.gov.uk

Gerrard, John (LAB - Mersey)
john.gerrard@halton.gov.uk

Gilligan, Robert (LAB - Broadheath)
robert.gilligan@halton.gov.uk

Harris, Phil (LAB - Hough Green)
phil.harris@halton.gov.uk

Hignett, Pauline (LAB - Windmill House)
Pauline.Hignett2@halton.gov.uk

Hignett, Ron (LAB - Norton South)
ron.hignett@halton.gov.uk

Hill, Stan (LAB - Riverside)
Stan.Hill@halton.gov.uk

Hill, Valerie (LAB - Farnworth)
Valerie.Hill@halton.gov.uk

Horabin, Margaret (LAB - Kingsway)
margaret.horabin@halton.gov.uk

Howard, Harry (LAB - Halton Castle)
harry.howard@halton.gov.uk

Jones, Eddie (LAB - Appleton)
eddie.jones@halton.gov.uk

Lea, Darren (LAB - Grange)
Darren.Lea@halton.gov.uk

Lloyd-Jones, Martha (LAB - Norton South)
martha.lloydjones@halton.gov.uk

Lloyd-Jones, Peter (LAB - Norton North)
peter.lloydjones@halton.gov.uk

Loftus, Kath (LAB - Halton Lea)
kath.loftus@halton.gov.uk

Loftus, Chris (LAB - Beechwood)
chris.loftus@halton.gov.uk

Logan, Geoffrey (LAB - Beechwood)
geoffrey.logan@halton.gov.uk

Lowe, Joan (LAB - Grange)
joan.lowe@halton.gov.uk

Lowe, Alan (LAB - Halton Lea)
alan.lowe@halton.gov.uk

MacManus, Andrew (LAB - Farnworth)
andrew.macmanus@halton.gov.uk

McDermott, Tony (LAB - Broadheath)
tony.mcdermott@halton.gov.uk

McInerney, Angela (LAB - Farnworth)
angela.mcinerney@halton.gov.uk

McInerney, Tom (LAB - Halton View)
tom.mcinerney@halton.gov.uk

Morley, Keith (LAB - Broadheath)
keith.morley@halton.gov.uk

Nelson, Stef (LAB - Halton Brook)
stef.nelson@halton.gov.uk

Nolan, Paul (LAB - Hough Green)
paul.nolan@halton.gov.uk

Osborne, Shaun (LAB - Ditton)
shaun.osborne@halton.gov.uk

Parker, Stan (LAB - Halton View)
stan.parker@halton.gov.uk

Plumpton-Walsh, Carol (LAB - Halton Brook)
carol.plumptonwalsh@halton.gov.uk

Pumpton-Walsh, Norman (LAB - Mersey)
norman.plumptonwalsh@halton.gov.uk

Roberts, June (LAB - Kingsway)
june.roberts@halton.gov.uk

Roberts, Joe (LAB - Ditton)
joe.roberts@halton.gov.uk

Rowe, Christopher (LD - Heath)
christopher.rowe@halton.gov.uk

Sinnott, Pauline (LAB - Mersey)
Pauline.Sinnott2@halton.gov.uk

Stockton, John (LAB - Halton Brook)
john.stockton@halton.gov.uk

Stockton, Gareth (LD - Heath)
Gareth.Stockton@halton.gov.uk

Thompson, Dave (LAB - Halton Lea)
dave.thompson@halton.gov.uk

Wainwright, Kevan (LAB - Hough Green)
kevan.wainwright@halton.gov.uk

Wall, Andrea (LAB - Kingsway)
andrea.wall@halton.gov.uk

Wallace, Pamela (LAB - Riverside)
pamela.wallace@halton.gov.uk

Wharton, Mike (LAB - Hale)
mike.wharton@halton.gov.uk

Woolfall, Bill (LAB - Birchfield)
bill.woolfall2@halton.gov.uk

Wright, Marie (LAB - Ditton)
marie.wright@halton.gov.uk

Zygadllo, Geoff (LAB - Norton North)
geoff.zygadllo@halton.gov.uk

POLITICAL COMPOSITION

LAB: 52, LD: 2, CON: 2

COMMITTEE CHAIRS

Development Control: Mr Paul Nolan

Hambleton D

Hambleton District Council, Civic Centre, Stone Cross, Northallerton DL6 2UU
☎ 0845 121 1555 🖷 01609 767228 ✉ info@hambleton.gov.uk
💻 www.hambleton.gov.uk

FACTS AND FIGURES

Parliamentary Constituencies: Richmond (Yorks)
EU Constituencies: Yorkshire and the Humber
Election Frequency: Elections are of whole council

PRINCIPAL OFFICERS

Chief Executive: Mr Phil Morton Chief Executive, Civic Centre, Stone Cross, Northallerton DL6 2UU ☎ 01609 767022; 01609 767001 ✉ phil.morton@hambleton.gov.uk

Deputy Chief Executive: Mr Justin Ives Deputy Chief Executive & Director of Support Services, Civic Centre, Stone Cross, Northallerton DL6 2UU ☎ 01609 779977
✉ justin.ives@hambleton.gov.uk

Senior Management: Mr Dave Goodwin, Director of Customer & Leisure Services, Civic Centre, Stone Cross, Northallerton DL6 2UU
☎ 01609 779977 🖷 01609 767228
✉ dave.goodwin@hambleton.gov.uk

Senior Management: Mr Justin Ives Deputy Chief Executive & Director of Support Services, Civic Centre, Stone Cross, Northallerton DL6 2UU ☎ 01609 779977
✉ justin.ives@hambleton.gov.uk

HAMBLETON

Senior Management: Mr Michael Jewitt, Director of Environmental & Planning Services, Civic Centre, Stone Cross, Northallerton DL6 2UU ☎ 01609 779977 🖷 01609 767228 ✉ mick.jewitt@hambleton.gov.uk

Building Control: Mr Mark Harbottle Planning Manager, Civic Centre, Stone Cross, Northallerton DL6 2UU ☎ 01609 779977 ✉ mark.harbottle@hambleton.gov.uk

PR / Communications: Mrs Aly Thompson Communications Manager, Civic Centre, Stone Cross, Northallerton DL6 2UU ☎ 01609 767063 ✉ aly.thompson@hambleton.gov.uk

Community Safety: Ms Helen Kemp Head of Service - Customer & Economy, Civic Centre, Stone Cross, Northallerton DL6 2UU ☎ 01609 779977 ✉ helen.kemp@hambleton.gov.uk

Customer Service: Ms Sandra Hall Customer & Communications Manager, Civic Centre, Stone Cross, Northallerton DL6 2UU ☎ 01609 779977 ✉ sandra.hall@hambleton.gov.uk

Electoral Registration: Mr Gary Nelson Head of Service - Legal & Information, Civic Centre, Stone Cross, Northallerton DL6 2UU ☎ 01609 779977 ✉ gary.nelson@hambleton.gov.uk

Environmental / Technical Services: Mr Michael Jewitt, Director of Environmental & Planning Services, Civic Centre, Stone Cross, Northallerton DL6 2UU ☎ 01609 779977 🖷 01609 767228 ✉ mick.jewitt@hambleton.gov.uk

Environmental Health: Mr Philip Mepham Environmental Health Manager, Swale House, Frenchgate, Richmond DL10 4JE ☎ 01748 829100 🖷 01748 826186 ✉ philip.mepham@richmondshire.gov.uk

Finance: Mr Justin Ives Deputy Chief Executive & Director of Support Services, Civic Centre, Stone Cross, Northallerton DL6 2UU ☎ 01609 779977 ✉ justin.ives@hambleton.gov.uk

Treasury: Mr Justin Ives Deputy Chief Executive & Director of Support Services, Civic Centre, Stone Cross, Northallerton DL6 2UU ☎ 01609 779977 ✉ justin.ives@hambleton.gov.uk

Housing: Mr Michael Jewitt, Director of Environmental & Planning Services, Civic Centre, Stone Cross, Northallerton DL6 2UU ☎ 01609 779977 🖷 01609 767228 ✉ mick.jewitt@hambleton.gov.uk

Housing Maintenance: Mr Michael Jewitt, Director of Environmental & Planning Services, Civic Centre, Stone Cross, Northallerton DL6 2UU ☎ 01609 779977 🖷 01609 767228 ✉ mick.jewitt@hambleton.gov.uk

Local Area Agreement: Mr Michael Jewitt, Director of Environmental & Planning Services, Civic Centre, Stone Cross, Northallerton DL6 2UU ☎ 01609 779977 🖷 01609 767228 ✉ mick.jewitt@hambleton.gov.uk

Legal: Mr Gary Nelson Head of Service - Legal & Information, Civic Centre, Stone Cross, Northallerton DL6 2UU ☎ 01609 779977 ✉ gary.nelson@hambleton.gov.uk

Leisure and Cultural Services: Mr Dave Goodwin, Director of Customer & Leisure Services, Civic Centre, Stone Cross, Northallerton DL6 2UU ☎ 01609 779977 🖷 01609 767228 ✉ dave.goodwin@hambleton.gov.uk

Member Services: Mr Gary Nelson Head of Service - Legal & Information, Civic Centre, Stone Cross, Northallerton DL6 2UU ☎ 01609 779977 ✉ gary.nelson@hambleton.gov.uk

Planning: Mr Mark Harbottle Planning Manager, Civic Centre, Stone Cross, Northallerton DL6 2UU ☎ 01609 779977 ✉ mark.harbottle@hambleton.gov.uk

Recycling & Waste Minimisation: Mr Paul Staines Head of Service - Environment, Civic Centre, Stone Cross, Northallerton DL6 2UU ☎ 0845 121 1555 ✉ paul.staines@hambleton.gov.uk

Waste Collection and Disposal: Mr Paul Staines Head of Service - Environment, Civic Centre, Stone Cross, Northallerton DL6 2UU ☎ 0845 121 1555 ✉ paul.staines@hambleton.gov.uk

Waste Management: Mr Paul Staines Head of Service - Environment, Civic Centre, Stone Cross, Northallerton DL6 2UU ☎ 0845 121 1555 ✉ paul.staines@hambleton.gov.uk

COUNCILLORS

***Leader of the Council* Robson**, Mark (CON - Sowerby)
cllr.mark.robson@hambleton.gov.uk

***Deputy Leader of the Council* Wilkinson**, Peter (CON - Northallerton Broomfield)
cllr.peter.wilkinson@hambleton.gov.uk

Adamson, Derek (CON - Thirsk)
cllr.derek.adamson@hambleton.gov.uk

Baker, Robert (CON - Thorntons)
cllr.bob.baker@hambleton.gov.uk

Bardon, Peter (CON - Sowerby)
cllr.peter.bardon@hambleton.gov.uk

Barker, Arthur (CON - Leeming)
cllr.arthur.barker@hambleton.gov.uk

Billings, Ken (IND - Northallerton North)
cllr.ken.billings@hambleton.gov.uk

Blades, David (CON - Northallerton Broomfield)
cllr.david.blades@hambleton.gov.uk

Cookman, Christine (CON - Stillington)
cllr.christine.cookman@hambleton.gov.uk

Coulson, John (IND - Northallerton Central)
cllr.john.coulson@hambleton.gov.uk

Dadd, Gareth (CON - Thirsk)
cllr.gareth.dadd@hambleton.gov.uk

Dickins, Stephen (CON - Rudby)
cllr.stephen.dickins@hambleton.gov.uk

Ellis, Geoff (CON - Easingwold)
cllr.geoff.ellis@hambleton.gov.uk

Fortune, Bridget (CON - Rudby)
cllr.bridget.fortune@hambleton.gov.uk

Greenwell, Frances (CON - Great Ayton)
cllr.frances.greenwell@hambleton.gov.uk

Griffiths, Jackie (LD - Stokesley)
cllr.jackie.griffiths@hambleton.gov.uk

Griffiths, Bryn (LD - Stokesley)
cllr.bryn.griffiths@hambleton.gov.uk

Hall, Tony (CON - Northallerton Central)
cllr.tony.hall@hambleton.gov.uk

Hardisty, Kevin (CON - Romanby)
cllr.kevin.hardisty@hambleton.gov.uk

Hudson, Richard (CON - Great Ayton)
cllr.richard.hudson@hambleton.gov.uk

Hugill, David (CON - Swainby)
cllr.david.hugill@hambleton.gov.uk

Key, Gary (CON - Topcliffe)
cllr.garry.key@hambleton.gov.uk

Kirk, Ron (CON - Great Ayton)
cllr.ron.kirk@hambleton.gov.uk

Knapton, Nigel (CON - Tollerton)
cllr.nigel.knapton@hambleton.gov.uk

Les, Carl (CON - Bedale)
cllr.carl.les@hambleton.gov.uk

Noone, John (CON - Bedale)
cllr.john.noone@hambleton.gov.uk

Patmore, Caroline (CON - White Horse)
cllr.caroline.patmore@hambleton.gov.uk

Phillips, Brian (CON - Morton on Swale)
cllr.brian.phillips@hambleton.gov.uk

Prest, John (CON - Northallerton North)
cllr.john.prest@hambleton.gov.uk

Rigby, Mike (IND - Huby Sutton)
cllr.mike.rigby@hambleton.gov.uk

Robinson, Andrew (IND - Thirsk)
cllr.andrew.robinson@hambleton.gov.uk

Rooke, Chris (CON - Shipton)
cllr.chris.rooke@hambleton.gov.uk

Sanderson, Isobel (CON - Brompton)
cllr.isobel.sanderson@hambleton.gov.uk

Shepherd, Shirley (CON - Easingwold)

Skilbeck, Margaret (CON - Broughton and Greenhow)
cllr.margaret.skilbeck@hambleton.gov.uk

Smith, David (IND - Crakehall)
cllr.david.smith@hambleton.gov.uk

Smith, John (CON - Romanby)
cllr.john.smith@hambleton.gov.uk

Sowray, Peter (CON - Helperby)
cllr.peter.sowray@hambleton.gov.uk

Swales, Tim (CON - Osmotherley)
cllr.tim.swales@hambleton.gov.uk

Wake, Andy (CON - Stokesley)
cllr.andy.wake@hambleton.gov.uk

Watson, Stephen (CON - Cowtons)
cllr.stephen.watson@hambleton.gov.uk

Watson, Janet (CON - Whitestonecliffe)
cllr.janet.watson@hambleton.gov.uk

Webster, David (CON - Tanfield)
cllr.david.webster@hambleton.gov.uk

Wood, Anthony (CON - Leeming Bar)
cllr.anthony.wood@hambleton.gov.uk

POLITICAL COMPOSITION

CON: 37, IND: 5, LD: 2

Hammersmith & Fulham — L

Hammersmith & Fulham London Borough Council,
Hammersmith Town Hall, 7 King Street, London W6 9JU
☎ 020 8748 3020 🖷 020 8741 0307 ✉ information@lbhf.gov.uk
💻 www.lbhf.gov.uk

FACTS AND FIGURES

Parliamentary Constituencies: Hammersmith
EU Constituencies: London
Election Frequency: Elections are of whole council

PRINCIPAL OFFICERS

Chief Executive: Mr Nigel Pallace, Chief Executive, Town Hall Extension, King Street, London W6 9JU ☎ 020 8753 3000 🖷 020 8753 3397 ✉ nigel.pallace@lbhf.gov.uk

Senior Management: Ms Liz Bruce Tri-Borough Executive Director - Adult Social Care, Town Hall, King Street, London W6 9JU ☎ 020 8753 5166 ✉ liz.bruce@lbhf.gov.uk

Senior Management: Ms Lyn Carpenter Executive Director of Environment, Leisure & Residents' Services, Hammersmith Town Hall, 7 King Street, London W6 9JU ☎ 020 8753 5710 ✉ lyn.carpenter@lbhf.gov.uk

Senior Management: Mr Andrew Christie, Tri-Borough Executive Director - Children & Families, Cambridge House, London W6 0LE ☎ 020 8753 5002; 020 7361 2354; 020 7361 2229 ✉ andrew.christie@rbkc.gov.uk

Senior Management: Ms Meradin Peachey Director - Public Health, Westminster City Hall, 64 Victoria Street, London SW1E 6QP ☎ ✉ mpeachey@westminster.gov.uk

Senior Management: Ms Sue Redmond Interim Tri-Borough Executive Director of Adult Social Care, Westminster City Hall, 64 Victoria Street, London SW1E 6QP ☎ 020 8753 5001 ✉ sue.redmond@lbhf.gov.uk

Senior Management: Ms Heather Schroeder Acting Director of Community Services, Hammersmith Town Hall, 7 King Street, London W6 9JU ☎ 020 8748 3020 ✉ heather.schroeder@lbhf.gov.uk

Senior Management: Ms Jane West, Executive Director of Finance & Corporate Governance, Town Hall, King Street, London W6 9JU ☎ 020 8753 1900 🖷 020 8741 0307 ✉ jane.west@lbhf.gov.uk

Access Officer / Social Services (Disability): Mr Richard Holden Tri-Borough Head of Children With Disabilities, Westminster City Hall, 64 Victoria Street, London SW1E 6QP ☎ 020 7361 3751 ✉ richard.holden@rbkc.gov.uk

Access Officer / Social Services (Disability): Mr Malcolm Rose Team Leader, Westminster City Hall, 64 Victoria Street, London SW1E 6QP ☎ 020 7641 6617 mrose@westminster.gov.uk

Access Officer / Social Services (Disability): Ms Jill Vickers Interim Director of Adult Social Care Operations, 4th Floor, 77 Glenthorne Road, London W6 0LJ ☎ 020 8753 5007 jill.vickers@lbhf.gov.uk

Architect, Building / Property Services: Ms Maureen McDonald-Khan Director of Building & Property Management, Town Hall Extension, King Street, London W6 9JU ☎ 020 8753 4701 maureen.mcdonald-khan@lbhf.gov.uk

Building Control: Mr Jay Jayaweera, Head of Building Control, Town Hall Extension, King Street, London W6 9JU ☎ 020 8753 3424 🖷 020 8753 3367 jay.jayaweera@lbhf.gov.uk

Children / Youth Services: Mr Andrew Christie, Tri-Borough Executive Director - Children & Families, Cambridge House, London W6 0LE ☎ 020 8753 5002; 020 7361 2354; 020 7361 2229 andrew.christie@rbkc.gov.uk

Children / Youth Services: Ms Rachel Wright-Turner Tri-Borough Director of Strategic Commissioning for Children & Families, Westminster City Hall, 64 Victoria Street, London SW1E 6QP ☎ rachel.wright-turner@rbkc.gov.uk

Civil Registration: Ms Lyn Carpenter Executive Director of Environment, Leisure & Residents' Services, 77 Glenthorne Road, Hammersmith, London W6 0LJ ☎ 020 8753 5710 lyn.carpenter@lbhf.gov.uk

Civil Registration: Mr John Collins Director of H&F Direct, Town Hall, King Street, London W6 9JU ☎ 020 8753 1544 john.collins@lbhf.gov.uk

PR / Communications: Mr Mike Clarke Tri-Borough Director of Libraries & Archives, Town Hall, Hornton Street, London W8 7NX ☎ 020 7641 2199 mclarke1@westminster.gov.uk

PR / Communications: Mr Geoff Cowart Corporate Communications Manager, Hammersmith Town Hall, 7 King Street, London W6 9JU ☎ 020 8753 2012 geoff.cowart@lbhf.gov.uk

PR / Communications: Mr Simon Jones, Assistant Director of Communications & Policy, Town Hall, King Street, London W6 9JU ☎ 020 8748 3020 simon.jones@lbhf.gov.uk

PR / Communications: Ms Jane West, Executive Director of Finance & Corporate Governance, Town Hall, King Street, London W6 9JU ☎ 020 8753 1900 🖷 020 8741 0307 jane.west@lbhf.gov.uk

Community Planning: Ms Heather Schroeder Acting Director of Community Services, Hammersmith Town Hall, 7 King Street, London W6 9JU ☎ 020 8748 3020 heather.schroeder@lbhf.gov.uk

Community Safety: Mr David Page Bi-Borough Director of Safer Neighbourhoods, Hammersmith Town Hall, 7 King Street, London W6 9JU ☎ 020 8753 2125 david.page@lbhf.gov.uk

Computer Management: Mr Ed Garcez Tri-Borough Chief Information Officer, Town Hall, King Street, London W6 9JU ☎ 020 8753 2900 ed.garcez@lbhf.gov.uk

Computer Management: Ms Jackie Hudson Director of Procurement & IT Strategy, Hammersmith Town Hall, 7 King Street, London W6 9JU ☎ 020 8753 2946 🖷 020 8741 0307 jackie.hudson@lbhf.gov.uk

Consumer Protection and Trading Standards: Mr Nick Austin Bi-Borough Director of Environmental Health, Hammersmith Town Hall, 7 King Street, London W6 9JU ☎ 020 8753 3904; 020 7341 5600 nick.austin@brkc.gov.uk

Corporate Services: Ms Jane West, Executive Director of Finance & Corporate Governance, Town Hall, King Street, London W6 9JU ☎ 020 8753 1900 🖷 020 8741 0307 jane.west@lbhf.gov.uk

Economic Development: Ms Kim Dero Head of Economic Development, Town Hall Extension, King Street, London W6 9JU ☎ 020 8748 3020 kim.dero@lbhf.gov.uk

Education: Mr Andrew Christie, Tri-Borough Executive Director - Children & Families, Cambridge House, London W6 0LE ☎ 020 8753 5002; 020 7361 2354; 020 7361 2229 andrew.christie@rbkc.gov.uk

Education: Mr Ian Heggs Tri-Borough Director of Schools Commissioning, Cambridge House, Cambridge Grove, Hammersmith, London W6 0LE ☎ 020 7361 3332 ian.heggs@rbkc.gov.uk

E-Government: Ms Jackie Hudson Director of Procurement & IT Strategy, Hammersmith Town Hall, 7 King Street, London W6 9JU ☎ 020 8753 2946 🖷 020 8741 0307 jackie.hudson@lbhf.gov.uk

Electoral Registration: Ms Zoe Wilkins Electoral Services Manager, Hammersmith Town Hall, 7 King Street, London W6 9JU ☎ 020 8753 2175 zoe.wilkins@lbhf.gov.uk

Environmental Health: Mr Nick Austin Bi-Borough Director of Environmental Health, Hammersmith Town Hall, 7 King Street, London W6 9JU ☎ 020 8753 3904; 020 7341 5600 nick.austin@brkc.gov.uk

Estates, Property & Valuation: Ms Maureen McDonald-Khan Director of Building & Property Management, Town Hall Extension, King Street, London W6 9JU ☎ 020 8753 4701 maureen.mcdonald-khan@lbhf.gov.uk

Events Manager: Ms Helen Pinnington Events Manager, Hammersmith Town Hall, 7 King Street, London W6 9JU ☎ 020 8753 2104 helen.pinnington@lbhf.gov.uk

Facilities: Ms Adele Casey Technical Services Manager, Town Hall Extension, King Street, London W6 9JU ☎ 020 8753 2106 adele.casey@lbhf.gov.uk

Finance: Mr Jonathan Hunt Tri-Borough Director of Pensions & Treasury, Town Hall, King Street, London W6 9JU ☎ 020 7641 1804 jonathan.hunt@westminster.gov.uk

Finance: Mr Hitesh Jolapara, Bi-Borough Director of Finance, Town Hall, Hornton Street, London W8 7NX ☎ 020 7361 2316 🖷 020 7361 3716 ✉ hitesh.jolapara@rbkc.gov.uk

Finance: Ms Jane West, Executive Director of Finance & Corporate Governance, Town Hall, King Street, London W6 9JU ☎ 020 8753 1900 🖷 020 8741 0307 ✉ jane.west@lbhf.gov.uk

Treasury: Mr Jonathan Hunt Tri-Borough Director of Pensions & Treasury, Town Hall, King Street, London W6 9JU ☎ 020 7641 1804 ✉ jonathan.hunt@westminster.gov.uk

Pensions: Mr Jonathan Hunt Tri-Borough Director of Pensions & Treasury, Town Hall, King Street, London W6 9JU ☎ 020 7641 1804 ✉ jonathan.hunt@westminster.gov.uk

Pensions: Mr Halfield Jackman Pensions & Investments Manager, Treasury Department, Floor 16 West, Westminster City Council, 64 Victoria Street, London SW1E 6QP ☎ 020 8753 2560 ✉ halfield.jackman@lbhf.gov.uk

Fleet Management: Mr Roy Finan, Fleet Manager of Cleaner, Greener & Cultural Services, 25 Bagleys Lane, Fulham, London SW6 2QA ☎ 020 8753 3225 🖷 020 8753 3231 ✉ roy.finan@lbhf.gov.uk

Grounds Maintenance: Ms Lyn Carpenter Executive Director of Environment, Leisure & Residents' Services, 77 Glenthorne Road, Hammersmith, London W6 0LJ ☎ 020 8753 5710 ✉ lyn.carpenter@lbhf.gov.uk

Grounds Maintenance: Ms Sue Harris Bi-Borough Director - Environment, Leisure & Residents' Services, Hammersmith Town Hall, 7 King Street, London W6 9JU ☎ 020 8753 4295 ✉ sue.harris@lbhf.gov.uk

Health and Safety: Mr Nick Austin Bi-Borough Director of Environmental Health, Hammersmith Town Hall, 7 King Street, London W6 9JU ☎ 020 8753 3904; 020 7341 5600 ✉ nick.austin@brkc.gov.uk

Highways: Mr Mahmood Siddiqi Bi-Borough Director of Transport & Highways, Town Hall, Hornton Street, London W8 7NX ☎ 020 7361 3589; 020 8748 3020 ✉ mahmood.siddiqi@rbkc.gov.uk

Local Area Agreement: Mr Peter Smith Strategy Manager, Room 39, Hammersmith Town Hall, London W6 9JT ☎ 020 8753 2206 ✉ Peter.smith@lbhf.gov.uk

Legal: Mrs Tasnim Shawkat Director of Law, Town Hall, Hornton Street, London W8 7NX ☎ 020 7361 2257 ✉ tasnim.shawkat@rbkc.gov.uk

Leisure and Cultural Services: Ms Lyn Carpenter Executive Director of Environment, Leisure & Residents' Services, 77 Glenthorne Road, Hammersmith, London W6 0LJ ☎ 020 8753 5710 ✉ lyn.carpenter@lbhf.gov.uk

Leisure and Cultural Services: Ms Donna Pentelow Bi-Borough Head of Culture, Hammersmith Town Hall, 7 King Street, London W6 9JU ☎ 020 8753 2358; 020 8752 2358 🖷 020 8753 3713 ✉ donna.pentelow@lbhf.gov.uk

Licensing: Ms Sharon Baylis Bi-Borough Director of Customer & Business Development, Hammersmith Town Hall, 7 King Street, London W6 9JU ☎ 020 8753 1636 ✉ sharon.baylis@lbhf.gov.uk

Lottery Funding, Charity and Voluntary: Ms Sue Spiller Head of Community Investment, 145 King Street, Hammersmith, London W6 9XY ☎ 020 8753 2483 🖷 020 8741 4448 ✉ sue.spiller@lbhf.gov.uk

Member Services: Ms Lyn Anthony Head of Executive Services, Hammersmith Town Hall, 7 King Street, London W6 9JU ☎ 020 8753 1011 ✉ lyn.anthony@lbhf.gov.uk

Member Services: Ms Jane West, Executive Director of Finance & Corporate Governance, Town Hall, King Street, London W6 9JU ☎ 020 8753 1900 🖷 020 8741 0307 ✉ jane.west@lbhf.gov.uk

Parking: Mr David Taylor, Bi-Borough Head of Parking Services, PO Box 3387, London SW6 2QF ☎ 020 8753 3251 ✉ david.taylor@lbhf.gov.uk

Personnel / HR: Ms Debbie Morris Head of Facilities Management, Town Hall, King Street, London W6 9JU ☎ 020 7361 3189 ✉ debbiej.morris@rbkc.gov.uk

Personnel / HR: Ms Jane West, Executive Director of Finance & Corporate Governance, Town Hall, King Street, London W6 9JU ☎ 020 8753 1900 🖷 020 8741 0307 ✉ jane.west@lbhf.gov.uk

Procurement: Ms Jackie Hudson Director of Procurement & IT Strategy, Hammersmith Town Hall, 7 King Street, London W6 9JU ☎ 020 8753 2946 🖷 020 8741 0307 ✉ jackie.hudson@lbhf.gov.uk

Public Libraries: Ms Lyn Carpenter Executive Director of Environment, Leisure & Residents' Services, 77 Glenthorne Road, Hammersmith, London W6 0LJ ☎ 020 8753 5710 ✉ lyn.carpenter@lbhf.gov.uk

Public Libraries: Mr Mike Clarke Tri-Borough Director of Libraries & Archives, Town Hall, Hornton Street, London W8 7NX ☎ 020 7641 2199 ✉ mclarke1@westminster.gov.uk

Public Libraries: Mr Chris Lloyd Library Services Manager, Hammersmith Library, Shepherds Bush Road, London W6 7AT ☎ 020 8753 3811 🖷 020 8753 3815 ✉ chris.lloyd@lbhf.gov.uk

Recycling & Waste Minimisation: Ms Sue Harris Bi-Borough Director - Environment, Leisure & Residents' Services, Hammersmith Town Hall, 7 King Street, London W6 9JU ☎ 020 8753 4295 ✉ sue.harris@lbhf.gov.uk

Social Services: Ms Stella Baillie, Tri-Borough Director of Integrated Adult Social Care, 77 Glenthorne Road, Hammersmith, London W6 0LJ ☎ 020 7361 2398 ✉ stella.baillie@rbkc.gov.uk

Social Services: Ms Gaynor Driscoll Joint Commissioning Manager of Sexual Health, Westminster City Hall, 64 Victoria Street, London SW1E 6QP ☎ 020 7641 4000 ✉ gdriscoll@westminster.gov.uk

HAMMERSMITH & FULHAM

Social Services (Adult): Ms Jill Vickers Interim Director of Adult Social Care Operations, 4th Floor, 77 Glenthorne Road, London W6 0LJ ☎ 020 8753 5007 🖰 jill.vickers@lbhf.gov.uk

Social Services (Children): Mr Andrew Christie, Tri-Borough Executive Director - Children & Families, Cambridge House, London W6 0LE ☎ 020 8753 5002; 020 7361 2354; 020 7361 2229 🖰 andrew.christie@rbkc.gov.uk

Public Health: Ms Meradin Peachey Director - Public Health, Westminster City Hall, 64 Victoria Street, London SW1E 6QP 🖰 mpeachey@westminster.gov.uk

Staff Training: Ms Debbie Morris Head of Facilities Management, Town Hall, King Street, London W6 9JU ☎ 020 7361 3189 🖰 debbiej.morris@rbkc.gov.uk

Street Scene: Ms Lyn Carpenter Executive Director of Environment, Leisure & Residents' Services, 77 Glenthorne Road, Hammersmith, London W6 0LJ ☎ 020 8753 5710 🖰 lyn.carpenter@lbhf.gov.uk

Street Scene: Ms Sue Harris Bi-Borough Director - Environment, Leisure & Residents' Services, Hammersmith Town Hall, 7 King Street, London W6 9JU ☎ 020 8753 4295 🖰 sue.harris@lbhf.gov.uk

Sustainable Development: Ms Joan McGarvey, Bi-Borough Senior Policy Officer, Transport, Environment and Leisure Services, Council Offices, 37 Pembroke Road, London W8 6PW ☎ 020 7341 5173 🖷 020 7341 5145 🖰 joan.mcgarvey@rbkc.gov.uk

Town Centre: Ms Kim Dero Head of Economic Development, 145 King Street, Hammersmith, London W6 9JU ☎ 020 8748 3020 🖰 kim.dero@lbhf.gov.uk

Total Place: Mr Peter Smith Strategy Manager, Room 39, Hammersmith Town Hall, London W6 9JT ☎ 020 8753 2206 🖰 Peter.smith@lbhf.gov.uk

Waste Collection and Disposal: Ms Lyn Carpenter Executive Director of Environment, Leisure & Residents' Services, 77 Glenthorne Road, Hammersmith, London W6 0LJ ☎ 020 8753 5710 🖰 lyn.carpenter@lbhf.gov.uk

Waste Collection and Disposal: Ms Sue Harris Bi-Borough Director - Environment, Leisure & Residents' Services, Hammersmith Town Hall, 7 King Street, London W6 9JU ☎ 020 8753 4295 🖰 sue.harris@lbhf.gov.uk

Waste Management: Ms Lyn Carpenter Executive Director of Environment, Leisure & Residents' Services, 77 Glenthorne Road, Hammersmith, London W6 0LJ ☎ 020 8753 5710 🖰 lyn.carpenter@lbhf.gov.uk

Waste Management: Ms Sue Harris Bi-Borough Director - Environment, Leisure & Residents' Services, Hammersmith Town Hall, 7 King Street, London W6 9JU ☎ 020 8753 4295 🖰 sue.harris@lbhf.gov.uk

Waste Management: Ms Kathy May Bi-Borough Head of Waste & Street Enforcement, Council Offices, 37 Pembroke Road, London W8 6PW ☎ 020 7341 5616 🖰 kathy.may@rbkc.gov.uk

COUNCILLORS

***Mayor* Umeh**, Mercy (LAB - Shepherds Bush Green)
mercy.umeh@lbhf.gov.uk

***Deputy Mayor* Brown**, Daryl (LAB - North End)
daryl.brown@lbhf.gov.uk

***Leader of the Council* Cowan**, Stephen (LAB - Hammersmith Broadway)
stephen.cowan@lbhf.gov.uk

***Deputy Leader of the Council* Cartwright**, Michael (LAB - Hammersmith Broadway)
michael.cartwight@lbhf.gov.uk

***Group Leader* Smith**, Gregg (CON - Town)
greg.smith@lbhf.gov.uk

Adam, Michael (CON - Munster)
michael.adam@lbhf.gov.uk

Aherne, Colin (LAB - Wormholt and White City)
colin.aherne@lbhf.gov.uk

Alford, Adronie (CON - Munster)
adronie.alford@lbhf.gov.uk

Barlow, Hannah (LAB - Avonmore and Brook Green)
Hannah.Barlow@lbhf.gov.uk

Botterill, Nicholas (CON - Parsons Green and Walham)
nicholas.botterill@lbhf.gov.uk

Brown, Andrew (CON - Town)
andrew.brown@lbhf.gov.uk

Carlebach, Joe (CON - Avonmore and Brook Green)
joe.carlebach@lbhf.gov.uk

Cassidy, Iain (LAB - Fulham Reach)
Iain.Cassidy@lbhf.gov.uk

Chumnery, Elaine (LAB - College Park and Old Oak)
elaine.chumnery@lbhf.gov.uk

Coleman, Ben (LAB - Fulham Broadway)
ben.coleman@lbhf.gov.uk

Connell, Adam (LAB - Addison)
Adam.Connell@lbhf.gov.uk

Culhane, Larry (LAB - North End)
Larry.Culhane@lbhf.gov.uk

De'Ath, Alan (LAB - Fulham Broadway)
Alan.De'Ath@lbhf.gov.uk

Dewhirst, Charlie (CON - Ravenscourt Park)
charlie.dewhirst@lbhf.gov.uk

Donovan, Belinda (CON - Addison)
belinda.donovan@lbhf.gov.uk

Fennimore, Sue (LAB - Addison)
Sue.Fennimore@lbhf.gov.uk

Ffiske, Caroline (CON - Avonmmore and Brook Green)
Caroline.Ffiske@lbhf.gov.uk

Ginn, Marcus (CON - Palace Riverside)
marcus.ginn@lbhf.gov.uk

Hamilton, Steve (CON - Sands End)
steve.hamilton@lbhf.gov.uk

Harcourt, Wesley (LAB - College Park and Old Oak)
wesley.harcourt@lbhf.gov.uk

Hashem, Ali (LAB - North End)
Ali.Hashem@lbhf.gov.uk

Holder, Sharon (LAB - Fulham Broadway)
Sharon.Holder@lbhf.gov.uk

Homan, Lisa (LAB - Askew)
lisa.homan@lbhf.gov.uk

Ivimy, Lucy (CON - Ravenscourt Park)
lucy.ivimy@lbhf.gov.uk

Johnson, Donald (CON - Palace Riverside)
donald.johnson@lbhf.gov.uk

Jones, Andrew (LAB - Shepherds Bush Green)
andrew.jones@lbhf.gov.uk

Karmel, Alex (CON - Munster)
alex.karmel@lbhf.gov.uk

Largan, Robert (CON - Sands End)
robert.largan@lbhf.gov.uk

Law, Jane (CON - Sands End)
jane.law@lbhf.gov.uk

Loveday, Mark (CON - Parsons Green and Walham)
mark.loveday@lbhf.gov.uk

Lukey, Vivienne (LAB - Fulham Reach)
Vivienne.Lukey@lbhf.gov.uk

Macmillan, Sue (LAB - Wormholt and White City)
sue.macmillan@lbhf.gov.uk

Murphy, P J (LAB - Hammersmith Broadway)
pj.murphy@lbhf.gov.uk

Needham, Caroline (LAB - Askew)
caroline.needham@lbhf.gov.uk

Nsumbu, Viya (CON - Town)
Viya.Nsumbu@lbhf.gov.uk

Perez Shepherd, Natalia (LAB - Shepherds Bush Green)
Natalia.PerezShepherd@lbhf.gov.uk

Phibbs, Harry (CON - Ravenscourt Park)
harry.phibbs@lbhf.gov.uk

Schmid, Max (LAB - Wormholt and White City)
max.schmid@lbhf.gov.uk

Stainton, Frances (CON - Parsons Green and Walham)
frances.stainton@lbhf.gov.uk

Vaughan, Rory (LAB - Askew)
rory.vaughan@lbhf.gov.uk

Vincent, Guy (LAB - Fulham Reach)
Guy.Vincent@lbhf.gov.uk

POLITICAL COMPOSITION

LAB: 26, CON: 20

COMMITTEE CHAIRS

Adult Social Care: Mr Rory Vaughan

Audit: Mr Iain Cassidy

Finance & Delivery: Mr P J Murphy

Health & Wellbeing: Ms Vivienne Lukey

Licensing: Ms Natalia Perez Shepherd

Pensions: Mr Iain Cassidy

Hampshire C

Hampshire County Council, The Castle, Winchester SO23 8UJ
☎ 01962 841841 🖷 01962 867273 ✉ info@hants.gov.uk
💻 www.hants.gov.uk

FACTS AND FIGURES

Parliamentary Constituencies: Aldershot, Basingstoke, Eastleigh, Fareham, Gosport, Havant, Meon Valley, New Forest East, New Forest West, Southampton, Test, Winchester
EU Constituencies: South East
Election Frequency: Elections are of whole council

PRINCIPAL OFFICERS

Chief Executive: Mr Andrew Smith, Chief Executive, Elizabeth II Court, Winchester SO23 8UJ ☎ ; 01962 847300 ✉ andrew.j.smith@hants.gov.uk

Deputy Chief Executive: Mr John Coughlan, Deputy Chief Executive & Director of Children's Services, Elizabeth II Court, , Winchester SO23 8UG ☎ 01962 846400 ✉ john.coughlan@hants.gov.uk

Senior Management: Mr Paul Archer Director of Policy & Governance, Elizabeth II Court South, , Winchester SO23 8UJ ☎ 01962 846124 ✉ paul.archer@hants.gov.uk

Senior Management: Mr John Coughlan, Deputy Chief Executive & Director of Children's Services, Elizabeth II Court, , Winchester SO23 8UG ☎ 01962 846400 ✉ john.coughlan@hants.gov.uk

Senior Management: Mrs Gill Duncan Director of Adult Services, Elizabeth II Court, Winchester SO23 8UG ☎ 01962 847200 ✉ gill.duncan@hants.gov.uk

Senior Management: Mr Stuart Jarvis, Director of Economy, Transport & Environment, Elizabeth II Court, , Winchester SO23 8UD ☎ 01962 845260 ✉ stuart.jarvis@hants.gov.uk

Senior Management: Dr Ruth Milton Director - Public Health, The Castle, Winchester SO23 8UJ ✉ ruth.milton@hants.gov.uk

Senior Management: Ms Karen Murray Director of Culture, Communities & Business Services, Three Minsters House, 76 High Street, Winchester SO23 8UL ☎ 01962 847876 ✉ karen.murray@hants.gov.uk

Senior Management: Mrs Carolyn Williamson Director of Corporate Resources, Elizabeth II Court, Winchester SO23 8UJ ☎ 01962 847400 ✉ carolyn.williamson@hants.gov.uk

Access Officer / Social Services (Disability): Ms Ruth Dixon Deputy Director of Community Care Services & Commissioning, Elizabeth II Court, , Winchester SO23 8UG ☎ 01962 847260 ✉ ruth.dixon@hants.gov.uk

HAMPSHIRE

Access Officer / Social Services (Disability): Ms Camilla Gibson Equalities, Diversity & Inclusion Deputy Manager, Elizabeth II Court, Winchester SO23 8UQ ☎ 01962 845216 camilla.gibson@hants.gov.uk

Access Officer / Social Services (Disability): Ms Jessica Hutchinson Strategic Diversity & Inclusion Manager, Elizabeth Court, , Winchester SO23 8UQ ☎ 01962 845880 jessica.hutchinson@hants.gov.uk

Architect, Building / Property Services: Mr Steve Clow Assistant Director of Property Services, Three Minsters House, 76 High Street, Winchester SO23 8UL ☎ 01962 847858 steve.clow@hants.gov.uk

Best Value: Mr Gary Smith Head of Policy, Elizabeth II Court South, Winchester SO23 8UJ ☎ 01962 847402 gary.smith@hants.gov.uk

Building Control: Mr Steve Clow Assistant Director of Property Services, Three Minsters House, 76 High Street, Winchester SO23 8UL ☎ 01962 847858 steve.clow@hants.gov.uk

Catering Services: Ms Amanda Frost, Head of Catering Services 27-29 Market Street, Eastleigh SO53 5RG ☎ 02380 627729 amanda.frost@hants.gov.uk

Children / Youth Services: Mr John Coughlan, Deputy Chief Executive & Director of Children's Services, Elizabeth II Court, , Winchester SO23 8UG ☎ 01962 846400 john.coughlan@hants.gov.uk

Children / Youth Services: Mr Steve Crocker Deputy Director of Children & Families, Elizabeth II Court, Winchester SO23 8UG ☎ 01962 847991 steve.crocker@hants.gov.uk

Children / Youth Services: Mrs Felicity Roe Assistant Director of Access, Performance & Resources, Elizabeth II Court East, Winchester SO23 8UG ☎ 01962 846374 felicity.roe@hants.gov.uk

Civil Registration: Mrs Nicola Horsey Assistant Director of Community & Business Support, Three Ministers House, 76 High Street, Winchester SO23 8UL ☎ 01962 845423 nicola.horsey@hants.gov.uk

PR / Communications: Ms Kate Ball Communications Manager - Media, Elizabeth II Court South, Winchester SO23 8ZF ☎ 01962 847317 kate.ball@hants.gov.uk

PR / Communications: Ms Helen Gregory Communications Manager, Elizabeth II Court, Winchester SO23 8UJ ☎ 01962 847135 helen.gregory2@hants.gov.uk

PR / Communications: Ms Deborah Harkin Head of Performance & Communications, Elizabeth II Court, Winchester SO23 8UJ ☎ 01962 846699 deborah.harkin@hants.gov.uk

Community Planning: Mr Robert Ormerod, Community Strategy Manager, Elizabeth II Court, Winchester SO23 8UJ ☎ 01962 845122 robert.ormerod@hants.gov.uk

Community Safety: Mrs Nicola Horsey Assistant Director of Community & Business Support, Three Ministers House, 76 High Street, Winchester SO23 8UL ☎ 01962 845423 nicola.horsey@hants.gov.uk

Computer Management: Mr Jos Creese, Head of Information, Elizabeth II Court South, Winchester SO23 8UJ ☎ 01962 847436 jos.creese@hants.gov.uk

Consumer Protection and Trading Standards: Mrs Nicola Horsey Assistant Director of Community & Business Support, Three Ministers House, 76 High Street, Winchester SO23 8UL ☎ 01962 845423 nicola.horsey@hants.gov.uk

Contracts: Mr Neil Jones, Assistant Director of Business Services, Three Minsters House, 76 High Street, Winchester SO23 8UL ☎ 01962 846180 neil.jones@hants.gov.uk

Corporate Services: Mrs Barbara Beardwell Monitoring Officer & Head of Governance, Elizabeth II Court South, The Castle, Winchester SO23 8UJ ☎ 01962 845157 barbara.beardwell@hants.gov.uk

Corporate Services: Mr Sergio Sgambellone Head of Customer & Business Services, Elizabeth II Court South, Winchester SO23 8UJ ☎ 01962 847544 sergio.sgambellone@hants.gov.uk

Corporate Services: Mr Gordon Smith Corporate Information Services Manager, Elizabeth II Court South, Winchester SO23 8UJ ☎ 01962 846010 gordon.smith@hants.gov.uk

Corporate Services: Mr Richard White Head of Integrated Business Centre, Athelstan House, St. Clement Street, Winchester SO23 9DR ☎ 01962 813951 richard.white@hants.gov.uk

Customer Service: Mr Bob Wild Head of Corporate Customer Services, Parkway Offices, Wickham Road, Fareham PO16 7JL ☎ 01329 225335 bob.wild@hants.gov.uk

Economic Development: Mr David Fletcher Assistant Director of Economic Development, Elizabeth II Court West, Winchester SO23 8UG ☎ 01962 846125 david.fletcher@hants.gov.uk

Education: Mr John Clarke Deputy Director - Education & Inclusion, Elizabeth II Court, Winchester SO23 8UG ☎ 01962 846459 john.clarke@hants.gov.uk

E-Government: Mr Jos Creese, Head of Information, Elizabeth II Court, Winchester SO23 8UJ ☎ 01962 847436 jos.creese@hants.gov.uk

Emergency Planning: Mr Ian Hoult, Head of Emergency Planning & Resilience, Elizabeth II Court South, Winchester SO23 8UJ ☎ 01962 846840 🖷 01962 834525 ian.hoult@hants.gov.uk

Energy Management: Mr Chitra Nadarajah Environmental Strategy Manager, Elizabeth II Court, , Winchester SO23 8UD ☎ 01962 846771 chitra.nadarajah@hants.gov.uk

Environmental / Technical Services: Mr Stuart Jarvis, Director of Economy, Transport & Environment, Elizabeth II Court, , Winchester SO23 8UD ☎ 01962 845260 ✉ stuart.jarvis@hants.gov.uk

Environmental / Technical Services: Mrs Frances Martin Assistant Director - Waste, Planning & Environment, Elizabeth II Court, Winchester SO23 8UG ☎ 01962 845266 ✉ frances.martin@hants.gov.uk

Environmental / Technical Services: Mr James Strachan Assistant Director of Research & Resources, Elizabeth II Court, Winchester SO23 8UD ☎ 01962 846454 ✉ james.strachan@hants.gov.uk

Estates, Property & Valuation: Mr Steve Clow Assistant Director of Property Services, Three Minsters House, 76 High Street, Winchester SO23 8UL ☎ 01962 847858 ✉ steve.clow@hants.gov.uk

European Liaison: Ms Paddy Hillary Corporate Policy Manager, Elizabeth II Court, Winchester SO23 8UJ ☎ 01962 847391 ✉ paddy.hillary@hants.gov.uk

Events Manager: Ms Kathie Lock Head of Facilities Management, Three Ministers House, 76 High Street, Winchester SO23 8UG ☎ 01962 847779 ✉ kathie.lock@hants.gov.uk

Facilities: Ms Kathie Lock Head of Facilities Management, Three Ministers House, 76 High Street, Winchester SO23 8UG ☎ 01962 847779 ✉ kathie.lock@hants.gov.uk

Finance: Mr Rob Carr Head of Finance, Elizabeth II Court, Winchester SO23 8UJ ☎ 01962 847508 ✉ rob.carr@hants.gov.uk

Finance: Mr Nick Weaver Head of Pension Services & Transactions, Elizabeth II Court, Winchester SO23 8UB ☎ 01962 847584 ✉ nick.weaver@hants.gov.uk

Finance: Mrs Carolyn Williamson Director of Corporate Resources, Elizabeth II Court, Winchester SO23 8UJ ☎ 01962 847400 ✉ carolyn.williamson@hants.gov.uk

Fleet Management: Mr Paul Leaves Transport Management, Building C, Bar End Industrial Estate, Winchester SO23 9NR ☎ 01962 873933 ✉ paul.leaves@hants.gov.uk

Grounds Maintenance: Mr Steve Clow Assistant Director of Property Services, Three Minsters House, 76 High Street, Winchester SO23 8UL ☎ 01962 847858 ✉ steve.clow@hants.gov.uk

Health and Safety: Mr Peter Andrews Corporate Risk Manager, Elizabeth II Court South, Winchester SO23 8UJ ☎ 01962 847309 ✉ peter.andrews@hants.gov.uk

Highways: Mr Tim Lawton Head of Highways for the South & West Areas, Jacobs Gutter Lane, Totton, Southampton SO40 9QT ☎ 023 8042 7001 ✉ tim.lawton@hants.gov.uk

Highways: Mr Colin Taylor, Assistant Director of Highways, Traffic & Transport, Elizabeth II Court, Winchester SO23 8UD ☎ 01962 846753 ✉ colin.taylor@hants.gov.uk

Legal: Mr Kevin Gardner Head of Legal Services, Elizabeth II Court South, Winchester SO23 8UJ ☎ 01962 847381 ✉ kevin.gardner@hants.gov.uk

Leisure and Cultural Services: Ms Jo Heath Head of Countryside Service, Castle Avenue, Winchester SO23 8UJ ☎ 01962 847717 ✉ jo.heath@hants.gov.uk

Leisure and Cultural Services: Mrs Nicola Horsey Assistant Director of Community & Business Support, Three Ministers House, 76 High Street, Winchester SO23 8UL ☎ 01962 845423 ✉ nicola.horsey@hants.gov.uk

Leisure and Cultural Services: Ms Karen Murray Director of Culture, Communities & Business Services, Three Minsters House, 76 High Street, Winchester SO23 8UL ☎ 01962 847876 ✉ karen.murray@hants.gov.uk

Leisure and Cultural Services: Mr John Tickle Assistant Director of Culture & Heritage, Three Ministers House, 76 High Street, Winchester SO23 8UL ☎ 01962 846000 ✉ john.tickle@hants.gov.uk

Lifelong Learning: Mr George Allen Head of Adult & Community Learning, Elizabeth II Court, , Winchester SO23 8UG ☎ 01962 846943 ✉ george.allen@hants.gov.uk

Lighting: Mr Julian Higgins Assistant Highways Manager (ITS), HCC Street Lighting, PFI Office, Unit 1 Royal London Park, Flanders Road, Hedge End, Southampton SO30 2LG ☎ 01489 771772 ✉ julian.higgins@hants.gov.uk

Member Services: Mrs Debbie Vaughan Head of Democratic & Member Services, Elizabeth II Court South, Winchester SO23 8UJ ☎ 01962 847330 ✉ debbie.vaughan@hants.gov.uk

Partnerships: Ms Paddy Hillary Corporate Policy Manager, Elizabeth II Court South, Winchester SO23 8UJ ☎ 01962 847391 ✉ paddy.hillary@hants.gov.uk

Personnel / HR: Ms Jenny Lewis Head of HR & Workforce Development, Elizabeth Court II, Winchester SO23 8UJ ☎ 01962 841841 ✉ jenny.lewis@hants.gov.uk

Planning: Mr Chris Murray Head of Strategic Planning, Elizabeth II Court West, Winchester SO23 0UD ☎ 01962 846728 ✉ chris.murray@hants.gov.uk

Procurement: Mr Neil Jones, Assistant Director of Business Services, Three Ministers House, 76 High Street, Winchester SO23 8UL ☎ 01962 846180 ✉ neil.jones@hants.gov.uk

Procurement: Mr Shaun Le Picq Assistant Head of Transformation, Castle Avenue, Winchester SO23 8UL ☎ 01962 846216 ✉ shaun.lepicq@hants.gov.uk

Public Libraries: Mrs Nicola Horsey Assistant Director of Community & Business Support, Three Ministers House, 76 High Street, Winchester SO23 8UL ☎ 01962 845423 ✉ nicola.horsey@hants.gov.uk

HAMPSHIRE

Recycling & Waste Minimisation: Mr James Potter Head of Waste & Resource Management, Elizabeth Court II, Winchester SO23 8UD ☎ 01962 832275 ✉ james.potter@hants.gov.uk

Regeneration: Ms Emily Dickson Regeneration & Development Control Manager, Elizabeth II Court, Winchester SO23 0UD ☎ 01962 667941 ✉ emily.dickson@hants.gov.uk

Road Safety: Mr Marc Samways Traffic Management & Safety Manager, Elizabeth II Court West, Winchester SO23 8UD ☎ 01962 832238 ✉ marc.samways@hants.gov.uk

Social Services (Adult): Mr Ian Cross Area Director (West) Older People & Physical Disabilities, Elizabeth II Court, Winchester SO23 8UQ ☎ 01962 845815 ✉ ian.cross@hants.gov.uk

Social Services (Adult): Ms Ruth Dixon Deputy Director of Community Care Services & Commissioning, Elizabeth II Court, , Winchester SO23 8UG ☎ 01962 847260 ✉ ruth.dixon@hants.gov.uk

Social Services (Adult): Mrs Gill Duncan Director of Adult Services, Elizabeth II Court, Winchester SO23 8UG ☎ 01962 847200 ✉ gill.duncan@hants.gov.uk

Social Services (Adult): Mr Richard Ellis Deputy Director - Adult Services, Policy & Strategic Development, Elizabeth II Court, Winchester SO23 8UG ☎ 01962 847284 ✉ richard.ellis@hants.gov.uk

Social Services (Adult): Ms Camilla Gibson Equalities, Diversity & Inclusion Deputy Manager, Elizabeth II Court, Winchester SO23 8UQ ☎ 01962 845216 ✉ camilla.gibson@hants.gov.uk

Social Services (Adult): Ms Sharon Hardy Director of Operations (Nursing & Residential Care, In-House Services), Elizabeth II Court, Winchester SO23 0UD ☎ 01962 847294 ✉ sharon.hardy@hants.gov.uk

Social Services (Adult): Ms Sally Jones Area Director (South & East) Older People & Physical Disabilities, Elizabeth II Court, Winchester SO23 8UQ ☎ 023 9243 2091 ✉ sally.jones@hants.gov.uk

Social Services (Adult): Ms Sue Pidduck Area Director (North & East) Older People & Physical Disabilities, Elizabeth II Court, Winchester SO23 8UQ ☎ 01962 845295 ✉ sue.pidduck@hants.gov.uk

Social Services (Children): Mr John Coughlan, Director of Children's Services, Elizabeth II Court, Winchester SO23 8UD ☎ 01962 846400 ✉ john.coughlan@hants.gov.uk

Social Services (Children): Mr Steve Crocker Deputy Director of Children & Families, Elizabeth II Court, Winchester SO23 8UG ☎ 01962 847991 ✉ steve.crocker@hants.gov.uk

Social Services (Children): Mrs Felicity Roe Assistant Director of Access, Performance & Resources, Elizabeth II Court, Winchester SO23 8UG ☎ 01962 846374 ✉ felicity.roe@hants.gov.uk

Public Health: Dr Ruth Milton Director - Public Health, The Castle, Winchester SO23 8UJ ☎ ✉ ruth.milton@hants.gov.uk

Staff Training: Ms Helen Howe Commissioner for People Development, Regency House, 13 St Clement Street, Winchester SO23 9HH ☎ 01962 833016 ✉ helen.howe@hants.gov.uk

Sustainable Development: Mr Alan Williams Strategic Manager - Environment, Elizabeth II Court, Winchester SO23 8UG ☎ 01962 846827 ✉ alan.williams@hants.gov.uk

Tourism: Mr Andrew Bateman Tourism Manager, ElizabethII Court, Winchester SO23 8UD ☎ 01962 845478 ✉ andrew.bateman@hants.gov.uk

Traffic Management: Mr Adrian Gray Head of Highways (Traffic Management), Elizabeth II Court, Winchester SO23 8UD ☎ 01256 382409 ✉ adrian.gray@hants.gov.uk

Traffic Management: Mr Colin Taylor, Assistant Director of Highways, Traffic & Transport, Elizabeth II Court, Winchester SO23 8UD ☎ 01962 846753 ✉ colin.taylor@hants.gov.uk

Transport: Mr Tim Lawton Head of Highways for the South & West Areas, Jacobs Gutter Lane, Totton, Southampton SO40 9QT ☎ 023 8042 7001 ✉ tim.lawton@hants.gov.uk

Transport: Mr Peter Shelley Head of Passenger Transport, Capital House, 48 Andover Road, Winchester SO22 6AG ☎ 01962 847212 ✉ peter.shelley@hants.gov.uk

Transport Planner: Mr Keith Willcox Assistant Director - Strategic Transport, Elizabeth II Court West, Winchester SO23 8UD ☎ 01962 846997 ✉ keith.willcox@hants.gov.uk

Waste Collection and Disposal: Mr James Potter Head of Waste & Resource Management, Elizabeth Court II, Winchester SO23 8UD ☎ 01962 832275 ✉ james.potter@hants.gov.uk

Waste Management: Mr James Potter Head of Waste & Resource Management, Elizabeth Court II, Winchester SO23 8UD ☎ 01962 832275 ✉ james.potter@hants.gov.uk

COUNCILLORS

***Chair* Glen**, Jonathan (CON - Odiham)
jonathan.glen@hants.gov.uk

***Vice-Chair* Chapman**, Keith (CON - Calleva and Kingsclere)
keith.chapman@hants.gov.uk

***Leader of the Council* Perry**, Roy (CON - Romsey Extra)
roy.perry@hants.gov.uk

***Deputy Leader of the Council* Mans**, Keith (CON - Lyndhurst)
keith.mans@hants.gov.uk

Bailey, Phil (LD - Winchester Downlands)
phil.bailey@hants.gov.uk

Bennison, John (O - Church Crookham and Ewshot)
john.bennison@hants.gov.uk

Bolton, Ray (CON - Emsworth and St Faith's)
ray.bolton@hants.gov.uk

Briggs, Ann (CON - Waterloo and Stakes North)
ann.briggs@hants.gov.uk

Burgess, Rita (CON - Basingstoke South West)
rita.burgess@hants.gov.uk

Burgess, Graham (CON - Lee)
graham.burgess@hants.gov.uk

Carew, Adam (LD - Bordon, Whitehill and Lindford)
adam.carew@hants.gov.uk

Carter, Christopher (CON - Leesland and Town)
christopher.carter@hants.gov.uk

Chadd, Roz (CON - Farnborough North)
roz.chadd@hants.gov.uk

Chegwyn, Peter (LD - Hardway)
peter.chegwyn@hants.gov.uk

Choudhary, Charles (CON - Aldershot West)
charles.choudhary@hants.gov.uk

Clarke, Vaughan (CON - Petersfield Hangars)
vaughan.clarke@hants.gov.uk

Collett, Adrian (LD - Yateley East, Blackwater and Ancells)
adrian.collett@hants.gov.uk

Connor, Criss (LAB - Basingstoke Central)
criss.connor@hants.gov.uk

Cooper, Mark (LD - Romsey Town)
cllr.mark.cooper@hants.gov.uk

Cowper, Ferris (CON - Headley)
ferris.cowper@hants.gov.uk

Cully, Shaun (LAB - Bridgemary)
shaun.cully@hants.gov.uk

Davidovitz, Colin (CON - Chandlers Ford)
colin.dav@hants.gov.uk

Dowden, Alan (LD - Baddesley)
alan.dowden@hants.gov.uk

Edgar, Peter (CON - Leesland and Town)
peter.edgar@hants.gov.uk

England, Jacqui (IND - Lymington)
jacqui.england@hants.gov.uk

Evans, Keith (CON - Fareham Warsash)
keith.evans@hants.gov.uk

Fairhurst, Liz (CON - Bedhampton and Leigh Park)
liz.fairhurst@hants.gov.uk

Fawkes, Philip (UKIP - South Waterside)
philip.fawkes@hants.gov.uk

Finch, Ray (UKIP - Bedhampton and Leigh Park)
ray.finch@hants.gov.uk

Frankum, Jane (LAB - Basingstoke North)
jane.frankum@hants.gov.uk

Gibson, Andrew (CON - Test Valley Central)
andrew.gibson@hants.gov.uk

Greenwood, Chris (UKIP - Eastleigh West)
chris.greenwood@hants.gov.uk

Gurden, Brian (LD - Basingstoke South East)
brian.gurden@hants.gov.uk

Harrison, David (LD - Totton South and Marchwood)
david.harrison@hants.gov.uk

Harvey, Marge (CON - Catherington)
marge.harvey@hants.gov.uk

Heron, Edward (CON - Fordingbridge)
edward.heron@hants.gov.uk

Hockley, Geoffrey (CON - Fareham Titchfield)
geoff.hockley@hants.gov.uk

Hooke, Tony (UKIP - Andover South)
tony.hooke@hants.gov.uk

House, Keith (LD - Hamble)
keith.house@hants.gov.uk

Humby, Rob (CON - Bishops Waltham)
rob.humby@hants.gov.uk

Huxstep, Roger (CON - Meon Valley)
roger.huxstep@hants.gov.uk

Joy, Andrew (CON - Alton Town)
andrew.joy@hants.gov.uk

Keast, David (CON - Cowplain and Hart Plain)
david.keast@hants.gov.uk

Kemp-Gee, Mark (CON - Alton Rrual)
mark.kemp-gee@hants.gov.uk

Kendal, Mel (CON - New Milton)
mel.kendal@hants.gov.uk

Kryle, Rupert (LD - Botley and Hedge End)
rupert.kyrle@hants.gov.uk

Lagdon, Chris (UKIP - Totton North)
chris.lagdon@hants.gov.uk

Latham, Peter (CON - Fareham Town)
peter.latham@hants.gov.uk

Lovegrove, Warwick (LD - Tadley and Baughurst)
warwick.lovegrove@hants.gov.uk

Lyon, Martin (UKIP - Bishopstoke and Fair Oak)
martin.lyon@hants.gov.uk

Mather, Fiona (CON - Winchester Eastgate)
fiona.mather@hants.gov.uk

McIntosh, Robin (CON - Purbrook and Stakes South)
robin.mcintosh@hants.gov.uk

McNair Scott, Anna (CON - Candovers)
anna.mcnairscott@hants.gov.uk

Moon, Ken (CON - Petersfield Butser)
ken.moon@hants.gov.uk

Moore, Andy (UKIP - Eastleigh East)
andy.moore@hants.gov.uk

Pearce, Frank (CON - Hayling Island)
frank.pearce@hants.gov.uk

Porter, Jacqueline (LD - Itchen Valley)
jackie.porter@hants.gov.uk

Price, Roger (LD - Fareham Portchester)
roger.price@hants.gov.uk

Reid, Stephen (CON - Basingstoke North West)
stephen.reid@hants.gov.uk

Rice, Alan (CON - Milford and Hordle)
alan.rice@hants.gov.uk

Ringrow, George (CON - Fareham Town)
george.ringrow@hants.gov.uk

Rippon-Swaine, Steve (CON - Ringwood)
steve.rippon-swaine@hants.gov.uk

Rolt, Timothy (UKIP - Andover North)
timothy.rolt@hants.gov.uk

Rust, Frank (LAB - Aldershot East)
frank.rust@hants.gov.uk

Simpson, David (LD - Hartley Wintney, Eversley and Yateley West)
david.simpson@hants.gov.uk

Stallard, Patricia (CON - Winchester Southern Parishes)
members.support@hants.gov.uk

Staplehurst, Mark (UKIP - Farnborough West)
mark.staplehurst@hants.gov.uk

Still, Elaine (CON - Loddon)
elaine.still@hants.gov.uk

Tennent, Bruce (LD - West End and Hedge End Grange Park)
bruce.tennent@hants.gov.uk

Thacker, Tom (CON - Whitchurch and Clere)
tom.thacker@hants.gov.uk

Thornber, Ken (CON - Brockenhurst)
ken.thornber@hants.gov.uk

Tod, Martin (LD - Winchester Westgate)
martin.tod@hants.gov.uk

Wade, Malcolm (LD - Dibden And Hythe)
malcolm.wade@hants.gov.uk

Wall, John (CON - Farnborough South)
john.wall@hants.gov.uk

West, Pat (CON - Andover West)
pat.west@hants.gov.uk

Wheale, Sharyn (CON - Fleet)
sharyn.wheale@hants.gov.uk

Wood, Christopher (UKIP - Fareham Crofton)
christopher.wood@hants.gov.uk

Woodward, Seán (CON - Fareham Sarisbury)
sean.woodward@hants.gov.uk

POLITICAL COMPOSITION
CON: 45, LD: 17, UKIP: 10, LAB: 4, O: 1, IND: 1

Harborough D

Harborough District Council, The Symington Building, Adam & Eve Street, Market Harborough LE16 7AG
☎ 01858 828282 🖷 01858 821000 💻 www.harborough.gov.uk

FACTS AND FIGURES
Parliamentary Constituencies: Harborough, Leicestershire South, Rutland and Melton
EU Constituencies: East Midlands
Election Frequency: Elections are of whole council

PRINCIPAL OFFICERS
Senior Management: Mrs Ann Marie Hawkins Head of Community, Wellbeing & Partnerships, The Symington Building, Adam & Eve Street, Market Harborough LE16 7AG ☎ 01858 828282 ✉ a.hawkins@harborough.gov.uk

Senior Management: Mrs Beverley Jolly, Corporate Director - Resources, The Symington Building, Adam & Eve Street, Market Harborough LE16 7AG ☎ 01858 828282
✉ b.jolly@harborough.gov.uk

Senior Management: Mr Norman Proudfoot, Corporate Director - Community Resources, The Symington Building, Adam & Eve Street, Market Harborough LE16 7AG ☎ 01858 828282
✉ n.proudfoot@harborough.gov.uk

Senior Management: Mr Simon Riley Head of Financial Services & S151 Officer, The Symington Building, Adam & Eve Street, Market Harborough LE16 7AG ☎ 01858 828282

Senior Management: Mrs Verina Wenham Head of Legal & Democratic Services, The Symington Building, Adam & Eve Street, Market Harborough LE16 7AG ☎ 01858 821258
✉ v.wenham@harborough.gov.uk

Building Control: Mr Simon Costall Principal Building Control Officer, The Symington Building, Adam & Eve Street, Market Harborough LE16 7AG ☎ 01858 821142
✉ s.costall@harborough.gov.uk

Children / Youth Services: Ms Stella Renwick Children & Youth Officer, The Symington Building, Adam & Eve Street, Market Harborough LE16 7AG ☎ 01858 828282
✉ s.renwick@harborough.gov.uk

PR / Communications: Mrs Rachael Felts Communications & Customer Services Manager, The Symington Building, Adam & Eve Street, Market Harborough LE16 7AG ☎ 01858 821217
✉ r.felts@harborough.gov.uk

Community Safety: Mr Thomas Day Community Safety Officer, The Symington Building, Adam & Eve Street, Market Harborough LE16 7AG ☎ 01858 828282 ✉ t.day@harborough.gov.uk

Computer Management: Mr Chris James ICT Services Manager, The Symington Building, Adam & Eve Street, Market Harborough LE16 7AG ☎ 01858 821311 🖷 01858 821311
✉ c.james@harborough.gov.uk

Contracts: Mr Jonathan Ward-Langman Service Manager - Commissioning, The Symington Building, Adam & Eve Street, Market Harborough LE16 7AG ☎ 01858 828282
✉ j.ward-langman@harborough.gov.uk

Corporate Services: Mr Richard Ellis Service Manager - Corporate Services, The Symington Building, Adam & Eve Street, Market Harborough LE16 7AG ☎ 01858 821370 🖷 01858 821000
✉ r.ellis@harborough.gov.uk

Customer Service: Mrs Rachael Felts Communications & Customer Services Manager, The Symington Building, Adam & Eve Street, Market Harborough LE16 7AG ☎ 01858 821217
✉ r.felts@harborough.gov.uk

Economic Development: Mrs Heather Wakefield, Planning Enforcement Officer, The Symington Building, Adam & Eve Street, Market Harborough LE16 7AG ☎ 01858 828282
✉ h.wakefield@harborough.gov.uk

E-Government: Mr Chris James ICT Services Manager, The Symington Building, Adam & Eve Street, Market Harborough LE16 7AG ☎ 01858 821311 🖷 01858 821311 ✉ c.james@harborough.gov.uk

Electoral Registration: Ms Sheena Mortimer Electoral Services Manager, The Symington Building, Adam & Eve Street, Market Harborough LE16 7AG ☎ 01858 828282 🖷 01858 821311 ✉ s.mortimer@harborough.gov.uk

Emergency Planning: Mr Norman Proudfoot, Corporate Director - Community Resources, The Symington Building, Adam & Eve Street, Market Harborough LE16 7AG ☎ 01858 828282 ✉ n.proudfoot@harborough.gov.uk

Energy Management: Mr Graham Ladds, Energy Manager & Technical Officer, The Symington Building, Adam & Eve Street, Market Harborough LE16 7AG ☎ 01858 821328 🖷 01858 821002 ✉ g.ladds@harborough.gov.uk

Environmental / Technical Services: Ms Elaine Bird Regulatory Services Manager, The Symington Building, Adam & Eve Street, Market Harborough LE16 7AG ☎ 01858 821130 🖷 01858 821100 ✉ e.bird@harborough.gov.uk

Finance: Mr Simon Riley Head of Financial Services & S151 Officer, The Symington Building, Adam & Eve Street, Market Harborough LE16 7AG ☎ 01858 828282

Grounds Maintenance: Mr Matthew Bradford Contracted Service Manager, The Symington Building, Adam & Eve Street, Market Harborough LE16 7AG ☎ 01858 821290 ✉ m.bradford@harborough.gov.uk

Home Energy Conservation: Mr Graham Ladds, Energy Manager & Technical Officer, The Symington Building, Adam & Eve Street, Market Harborough LE16 7AG ☎ 01858 821328 🖷 01858 821002 ✉ g.ladds@harborough.gov.uk

Legal: Mrs Verina Wenham Head of Legal & Democratic Services, The Symington Building, Adam & Eve Street, Market Harborough LE16 7AG ☎ 01858 821258 ✉ v.wenham@harborough.gov.uk

Licensing: Ms Jessica Nichols Licensing Enforcement Officer, The Symington Building, Adam & Eve Street, Market Harborough LE16 7AG ☎ 01858 821172 ✉ j.nichols@harborough.gov.uk

Member Services: Ms Beth Murgatroyd, Principal Democratic Officer, The Symington Building, Adam & Eve Street, Market Harborough LE16 7AG ☎ 01858 821370 ✉ b.murgatroyd@harborough.gov.uk

Partnerships: Mrs Ann Marie Hawkins Head of Community, Wellbeing & Partnerships, The Symington Building, Adam & Eve Street, Market Harborough LE16 7AG ☎ 01858 828282 ✉ a.hawkins@harborough.gov.uk

Personnel / HR: Mrs Kate Frow Human Resources Manager, The Symington Building, Adam & Eve Street, Market Harborough LE16 7AG ☎ 01858 821303 🖷 01858 821306 ✉ k.frow@harborough.gov.uk

Planning: Mr Adrian Eastwood Development Control Service Manager, The Symington Building, Adam & Eve Street, Market Harborough LE16 7AG ☎ 01858 821142 🖷 01858 821097 ✉ a.eastwood@harborough.gov.uk

Recycling & Waste Minimisation: Mr Russell Smith, Senior Waste Management Officer, The Symington Building, Adam & Eve Street, Market Harborough LE16 7AG ☎ 01858 821177 ✉ r.smith@harborough.gov.uk

Regeneration: Mr Stephen Pointer Strategic Planning Services Manager, The Symington Building, Adam & Eve Street, Market Harborough LE16 7AG ☎ 01858 821168 ✉ s.pointer@harborough.gov.uk

Staff Training: Mrs Kate Frow Human Resources Manager, The Symington Building, Adam & Eve Street, Market Harborough LE16 7AG ☎ 01858 821303 🖷 01858 821306 ✉ k.frow@harborough.gov.uk

Street Scene: Mr Stephen Pointer Strategic Planning Services Manager, The Symington Building, Adam & Eve Street, Market Harborough LE16 7AG ☎ 01858 821168 ✉ s.pointer@harborough.gov.uk

Tourism: Mr Stephen Pointer Strategic Planning Services Manager, The Symington Building, Adam & Eve Street, Market Harborough LE16 7AG ☎ 01858 821168 ✉ s.pointer@harborough.gov.uk

Waste Collection and Disposal: Mr Russell Smith, Senior Waste Management Officer, The Symington Building, Adam & Eve Street, Market Harborough LE16 7AG ☎ 01858 821177 ✉ r.smith@harborough.gov.uk

Waste Management: Mr Russell Smith, Senior Waste Management Officer, The Symington Building, Adam & Eve Street, Market Harborough LE16 7AG ☎ 01858 821177 ✉ r.smith@harborough.gov.uk

COUNCILLORS

***Chair* Rook**, Michael (CON - Tilton)
m.rook@harborough.gov.uk

***Vice-Chair* Ackerley**, Janette (CON - Lutterworth - Swift)
j.ackerley@harborough.gov.uk

***Leader of the Council* Pain**, Blake (CON - Lubenham)
b.pain@harborough.gov.uk

***Deputy Leader of the Council* King**, Phillip (CON - Kibworth)
p.king@harborough.gov.uk

Bannister, Neil (CON - Dunton)
n.bannister@harborough.gov.uk

Beesley-Reynolds, Lynne (CON - Kibworth)
l.beesley-reynolds@harborough.gov.uk

Bilbie, Stephen (CON - Fleckney)
S.Bilbie@harborough.gov.uk

Bowles, Lesley (CON - Bosworth)
L.Bowles@harborough.gov.uk

Brodrick, Jo (CON - Market Harborough Welland)
j.brodrick@harborough.gov.uk

Burrell, Amanda (LD - Thurnby and Houghton)
a.burrell@harborough.gov.uk

Callis, Peter (LD - Market Harborough - Logan)
p.callis@harborough.gov.uk

Champion, Barry (CON - Market Harborough Great Bowden and Arden)
b.champion@harborough.gov.uk

Chapman, Elaine (CON - Lutterworth - Brookfield)
e.chapman@harborough.gov.uk

Dann, Paul (CON - Astley - Primethorpe)
p.dann@harborough.gov.uk

Dunton, Roger (LD - Market Harborough Welland)
r.dunton@harborough.gov.uk

Elliott, Peter (LD - Thurnby and Houghton)
p.elliott@harbourough.gov.uk

Evans, Derek (CON - Market Harborough - Little Bowden)
d.evans@harborough.gov.uk

Everett, John (CON - Misterton)
j.everett@harborough.gov.uk

Galton, Simon (LD - Thurnby and Houghton)
s.galton@harborough.gov.uk

Graves, Mark (CON - Astley - Astley)
m.graves@harborough.gov.uk

Hadkiss, Richard (CON - Market Harborough - Logan)
r.hadkiss@harborough.gov.uk

Hall, Neville (CON - Peatling)
npthall.knaptoft@gmail.com

Hallam, James (CON - Glen)
j.hallam@harborough.gov.uk

Hammond, Matthew (CON - Lutterworth - Springs)
m.hammond@harborough.gov.uk

Hill, Sarah (LD - Market Harborough Great Bowden and Arden)
s.hill@harborough.gov.uk

Holyoak, Christopher (CON - Kibworth)
c.holyoak@harborough.gov.uk

Knowles, Phil (LD - Market Harborough Great Bowden and Arden)
p.knowles@harborough.gov.uk

Liquorish, Bill (CON - Astley - Sutton)
w.liquorish@harborough.gov.uk

Modha, Sindy (CON - Billesdon)
S.Modha@harborough.gov.uk

Nunn, Amanda (CON - Market Harborough - Little Bowden)
A.Nunn@harborough.gov.uk

Page, Rosita (CON - Ullesthorpe)
r.page@harborough.gov.uk

Rickman, Michael (CON - Nevill)
M.Rickman@harborough.gov.uk

Robinson, Geraldine (CON - Lutterworth - Orchard)
g.robinson@harborough.gov.uk

Simpson, Julie (LD - Market Harborough Welland)
j.simpson@harborough.gov.uk

Spendlove-Mason, Grahame (CON - Glen)
g.spendlove-mason@harborough.gov.uk

Tomlin, Richard (CON - Astley - Broughton)
r.tomlin@harborough.gov.uk

Wood, Charmaine (CON - Fleckney)
c.wood@harborough.gov.uk

POLITICAL COMPOSITION
CON: 29, LD: 8

COMMITTEE CHAIRS
Planning: Mr Christopher Holyoak

Haringey L

Haringey London Borough Council, River Park House, 225 High Road, London N22 8HQ
☎ 020 8489 0000 ✉ customer.services@haringey.gov.uk
💻 www.haringey.gov.uk

FACTS AND FIGURES
Parliamentary Constituencies: Hornsey and Wood Green, Tottenham
EU Constituencies: London
Election Frequency: Elections are of whole council

PRINCIPAL OFFICERS
Chief Executive: Mr Nick Walkley Chief Executive, 5th Floor, River Park House, 225 High Road, London N22 8HQ ☎ 020 8489 2648 ✉ nick.walkley@haringey.gov.uk

Deputy Chief Executive: Ms Zina Etheridge Deputy Chief Executive, Level 5, River Park House, 225 High Road, London N22 8HQ ☎ 020 8489 8690 ✉ zina.etheridge@haringey.gov.uk

Senior Management: Dr Jeanelle de Gruchy Director - Public Health, 4th Floor, River Park House, 225 Station Road, London N22 8HQ ☎ 020 8489 5119 ✉ jeanelle.degruchy@haringey.gov.uk

Senior Management: Ms Tracie Evans Chief Operating Officer, Level 5, River Park House, 225 High Road, London N22 8HQ ☎ 020 8489 2688 ✉ tracie.evans@haringey.gov.uk

Senior Management: Ms Lyn Garner Director of Regeneration, Planning & Development, Level 4, River Park House, 225 High Road, London N22 8HQ ☎ 020 8489 4523 ✉ lyn.garner@haringey.gov.uk

Building Control: Mr Malcolm Greaves Head of Asset Management, 6th Floor, Level 6 Alexandra House, 10 Station Road, London N22 7TR ☎ 020 8489 2900 ✉ malcolm.greaves@haringey.gov.uk

Catering Services: Ms Marianna Clune-Georgiou, Head of Catering, Lea Valley Techno Park, London N17 9LN ☎ 020 8489 4643 ✉ marianna.clune-georgiou@haringey.gov.uk

Children / Youth Services: Mr Sean Segal Manager - Confernce Chair, Level 1, River Park House, 225 High Road, London N22 8HQ ☎ 020 8489 1177 ✉ sean.segal@haringey.gov.uk

Community Planning: Ms Claire Kowalska Community Safety Strategic Manager, 4th Floor, River Park House, 225 Station Road, London N22 8HQ

Computer Management: Mr David Airey Head of IT, 3rd Floor, River Park House, 225 High Road, London N22 8HQ ☎ 020 8489 4673 🖷 020 8489 3998 david.airey@haringey.gov.uk

Consumer Protection and Trading Standards: Mr Keith Betts, Service Manager for Commercial Enforcement, 1st Floor, Ashley Road, London N17 9LN ☎ 020 8849 5525

Contracts: Mr Hugh Sharkey Head of Procurement, 1st Floor, Alexandra House, 10 Station Road, London N22 7TR ☎ 020 8489 2120 hugh.sharkey@haringey.gov.uk

Corporate Services: Ms Helen Constantine Strategic Lead - Government & Business Improvement, 7th Floor, River Park House, 225 High Road, London N22 7SG ☎ 020 8489 3905 helen.constantine@haringey.gov.uk

Corporate Services: Mr Sanjay Mackintosh Head of Strategic Commissioning, River Park House, 225 High Road, London N22 8HQ

Electoral Registration: Mr George Cooper, Electoral Registration Manager, Civic Centre, Wood Green, High Road, London N22 8LE ☎ 020 8489 2976

Emergency Planning: Mr Andrew Meek, Emergency Planning Officer, Level 4, River Park House, 225 High Road, London N22 8HQ ☎ 020 8489 1164 andrew.meek@haringey.gov.uk

Events Manager: Ms Elena Pippou, Arts, Culture & Marketing Officer, Level 2, River Park House, 225 High Road, London N22 8HQ ☎ 020 8489 1419 elena.pippou@haringey.gov.uk

Pensions: Ms Janet Richards Pensions Manager, 5th Floor, Alexandra House, 10 Station Road, London N22 8HQ ☎ 020 8489 3824 janet.richards@haringey.gov.uk

Fleet Management: Mr Darren Butterfield, Transport Manager, Level 2, River Park House, 225 High Road, London N22 8HQ ☎ 020 8489 5786 darren.butterfield@haringey.gov.uk

Highways: Mr Peter Boddy Sustainable Transport Manager, 5th Floor, Alexandra House, London N22 7TR ☎ 020 8489 1765 peter.boddy@haringey.gov.uk

Highways: Ms Ann Cunningham Head of Traffic Management, Level 2, River Park House, 225 High Road, London N22 8HQ ☎ 020 8489 1355 ann.cunningham@haringey.gov.uk

Housing: Mr David Sherrington Director of Asset Management, 8th Floor, Alexandra House, 10 Station Road, London N22 7TR ☎ 020 8489 4487260 david.sherrington@haringey.gov.uk

Housing Maintenance: Mr Malcolm Greaves Head of Asset Management, 6th Floor, Level 6 Alexandra House, 10 Station Road, London N22 7TR ☎ 020 8489 2900 malcolm.greaves@haringey.gov.uk

Local Area Agreement: Ms Claire Kowalska Community Safety Strategic Manager, 4th Floor, River Park House, 225 Station Road, London N22 8HQ

Leisure and Cultural Services: Mr Simon Farrow Head of Client Services, Level 4, River Park House, 225 High Road, London N22 8HQ ☎ 020 8489 3639 simon.farrow@haringey.gov.uk

Lighting: Ms Wendy Thorgood Sustainable Transport Officer, 6th Floor, Alexandra House, 10 Station Road, London N22 7TR ☎ 020 8489 5351 wendy.thorgood@haringey.gov.uk

Lottery Funding, Charity and Voluntary: Ms Elena Pippou, Arts, Culture & Marketing Officer, Ground Floor, Hornsey Library, London N22 9JA ☎ 020 8489 1419 elena.pippou@haringey.gov.uk

Member Services: Mr Clifford Hart Cabinet Committees Manager, River Park House, 225 High Road, London N22 8HQ ☎ 020 8489 2922 clifford.hart@haringey.gov.uk

Personnel / HR: Ms Jacquie McGeachie Assistant Director of Human Resources, 5th Floor, Alexandra House, London N22 7TR ☎ 020 8489 3172 jacquie.mcgeachie@haringey.gov.uk

Planning: Ms Lyn Garner Director of Regeneration, Planning & Development, Level 4, River Park House, 225 High Road, London N22 8HQ ☎ 020 8489 4523 lyn.garner@haringey.gov.uk

Recycling & Waste Minimisation: Mr Stephen McDonnell Assistant Director - Environmental Services & Community Safety, Level 2, River Park House, 225 High Road, London N22 8HQ ☎ 020 8489 2485 stephen.mcdonnell@haringey.gov.uk

Regeneration: Ms Lyn Garner Director of Regeneration, Planning & Development, Level 4, River Park House, 225 High Road, London N22 8HQ ☎ 020 8489 4523 lyn.garner@haringey.gov.uk

Road Safety: Ms Denise Adolphe Smarter Travel Manager, Level 2, River Park House, 225 High Road, London N22 8HQ ☎ 020 8489 1128 denise.adolphe@haringey.gov.uk

Public Health: Dr Jeanelle de Gruchy Director - Public Health, River Park House, 225 High Road, London N22 8HQ ☎ 020 8489 5119 jeanelle.degruchy@haringey.gov.uk

Tourism: Ms Elena Pippou, Arts, Culture & Marketing Officer, Ground Floor, Hornsey Library, London N22 9JA ☎ 020 8489 1419 elena.pippou@haringey.gov.uk

Traffic Management: Mr Anthony Kennedy, Sustainable Transport Manager, 1st Floor, River Park House, 225 High Road, London N22 8HQ ☎ 020 8489 5351 tony.kennedy@haringey.gov.uk

Transport: Mr Pembe Hipolyte, Assistant Escort Team Manager, Level 2, River Park Road, 225 High Road, London N22 8HQ ☎ 020 8489 5629 🖷 020 8489 5647

HARINGEY

Waste Collection and Disposal: Mr Stephen McDonnell Assistant Director - Environmental Services & Community Safety, Level 2, River Park House, 225 High Road, London N22 8HQ
☎ 020 8489 2485 ✉ stephen.mcdonnell@haringey.gov.uk

Waste Management: Mr Stephen McDonnell Assistant Director - Environmental Services & Community Safety, Level 2, River Park House, 225 High Road, London N22 8HQ ☎ 020 8489 2485
✉ stephen.mcdonnell@haringey.gov.uk

COUNCILLORS

***Mayor* Mann**, Jennifer (LAB - Hornsey)
jennifer.mann@haringey.gov.uk

***Deputy Mayor* Ozbek**, Ali Gul (LAB - St Ann's)
aligul.ozbek@haringey.gov.uk

***Leader of the Council* Kober**, Claire (LAB - Seven Sisters)
claire.kober@haringey.gov.uk

***Deputy Leader of the Council* Vanier**, Bernice (LAB - Tottenham Green)
bernice.vanier@haringey.gov.uk

***Group Leader* Engert**, Gail (LD - Muswell Hill)
gail.engert@haringey.gov.uk

Woodside: Vacant

Adamou, Gina (LAB - Harringay)
gina.adamou@haringey.gov.uk

Adje, Charles (LAB - White Hart Lane)
charles.adje@haringey.gov.uk

Ahmet, Peray (LAB - Noel Park)
peray.ahmet@haringey.gov.uk

Akwasi-Ayisi, Eugene (LAB - West Green)
eugene.akwasi-ayisi@haringey.gov.uk

Amin, Kaushika (LAB - Northumberland Park)
kaushika.amin@haringey.gov.uk

Arthur, Jason (LAB - Crouch End)
jason.arthur@haringey.gov.uk

Basu, Dhiren (LAB - Seven Sisters)
dhiren.basu@haringey.gov.uk

Beacham, David (LD - Alexandra)
david.beacham@haringey.gov.uk

Berryman, Patrick (LAB - Fortis Green)
patrick.berryman@haringey.gov.uk

Bevan, John (LAB - Northumberland Park)
john.bevan@haringey.gov.uk

Blake, Barbara (LAB - St Ann's)
barbara.blake@haringey.gov.uk

Blake, Mark (LAB - Muswell Hill)
mark.blake@haringey.gov.uk

Bull, Gideon (LAB - White Hart Lane)
gideon.bull@haringey.gov.uk

Bull, Clare (LAB - Bounds Green)
clare.bull@haringey.gov.uk

Carroll, Vincent (LAB - Tottenham Hale)
vincent.carroll@haringey.gov.uk

Carter, Clive (LD - Highgate)
clive.carter@haringey.gov.uk

Christophides, Joanna (LAB - Bounds Green)
joanna.christophides@haringey.gov.uk

Connor, Pippa (LD - Muswell Hill)
pippa.connor@haringey.gov.uk

Demirci, Ali (LAB - Bounds Green)
ali.demirci@haringey.gov.uk

Diakides, Isidoros (LAB - Tottenham Green)
isidoros.dialides@haringey.gov.uk

Doron, Natan (LAB - Crouch End)
natan.doron@haringey.gov.uk

Ejiofer, Joseph (LAB - Bruce Grove)
joseph.ejiofer@haringey.gov.uk

Elliot, Sarah (LD - Crouch End)
sarah.elliott@haringey.gov.uk

Gallagher, Tim (LAB - Stroud Green)
tim.gallagher@haringey.gov.uk

Goldberg, Joe (LAB - Seven Sisters)
joe.goldberg@haringey.gov.uk

Griffith, Eddie (LAB - West Green)
eddie.griffith@haringey.gov.uk

Gunes, Makbule (LAB - Tottenham Green)
makbule.gunes@haringey.gov.uk

Hare, Bob (LD - Highgate)
bob.hare@haringey.gov.uk

Hearn, Kirsten (LAB - Stroud Green)
kirsten.hearn@haringey.gov.uk

Ibrahim, Emine (LAB - Harringay)
emine.ibrahim@haringey.gov.uk

Jogee, Adam (LAB - Hornsey)
adam.jogee@haringey.gov.uk

Mallett, Toni (LAB - West Green)
toni.mallett@haringey.gov.uk

Marshall, Denise (LAB - Noel Park)
denise.marshall@haringey.gov.uk

McNamara, Stuart (LAB - Bruce Grove)
stuart.mcnamara@haringey.gov.uk

McShane, Liz (LAB - Alexandra)
liz.mcshane@haringey.gov.uk

Morris, Liz (LD - Highgate)
liz.morris@haringey.gov.uk

Morton, Peter (LAB - St Ann's)
peter.morton@haringey.gov.uk

Newton, Martin (LD - Fortis Green)
martin.newton@haringey.gov.uk

Opoku, Felicia (LAB - Bruce Grove)
felicia.opoku@haringey.gov.uk

Patterson, James (LAB - Alexandra)
james.patterson@haringey.gov.uk

Peacock, Sheila (LAB - Northumberland Park)
sheila.peacock@haringey.gov.uk

Reith, Lorna (LAB - Tottenham Hale)
lorna.reith@haringey.gov.uk

Rice, Reg (LAB - Tottenham Hale)
reg.rice@haringey.gov.uk

Ross, Viv (LD - Fortis Green)
viv.ross@haringey.gov.uk

Ryan, James (LAB - Harringay)
james.ryan@haringey.gov.uk

Sahota, Raj (LAB - Stroud Green)
raj.sahota@haringey.gov.uk

Stennett, Anne (LAB - White Hart Lane)
anne.stennett@haringey.gov.uk

Strickland, Alan (LAB - Noel Park)
alan.strickland@haringey.gov.uk

Waters, Ann (LAB - Woodside)
ann.waters@haringey.gov.uk

Weston, Elin (LAB - Hornsey)
elin.weston@haringey.gov.uk

Wright, Charles (LAB - Woodside)
charles.wright@haringey.gov.uk

POLITICAL COMPOSITION
LAB: 47, LD: 9, Vacant: 1

COMMITTEE CHAIRS
Health & Wellbeing: Ms Claire Kober

Pensions: Ms Clare Bull

Harlow D

Harlow District Council, Civic Centre, The Water Gardens, Harlow CM20 1WG
☎ 01279 446611 🖷 01279 446767 ✉ contact@harlow.gov.uk
💻 www.harlow.gov.uk

FACTS AND FIGURES
Parliamentary Constituencies: Harlow
EU Constituencies: Eastern
Election Frequency: Elections are by thirds

PRINCIPAL OFFICERS
Chief Executive: Mr Malcolm Morley Chief Executive, Civic Centre, The Water Gardens, Harlow CM20 1WG ☎ 01279 446611 ✉ malcolm.morley@harlow.gov.uk

Senior Management: Mr Graham Branchett Chief Operating Officer, Civic Centre, The Water Gardens, Harlow CM20 1WG ☎ 01279 446611 ✉ graham.branchett@harlow.gov.uk

Architect, Building / Property Services: Mr Graeme Bloomer Head of Place, Civic Centre, The Water Gardens, Harlow CM20 1WG ☎ 01276 446270 ✉ graeme.bloomer@harlow.gov.uk

Building Control: Mr Graeme Bloomer Head of Place, Civic Centre, The Water Gardens, Harlow CM20 1WG ☎ 01276 446270 ✉ graeme.bloomer@harlow.gov.uk

Children / Youth Services: Ms Jane Greer Acting Head of Community Wellbeing, Civic Centre, The Water Gardens, Harlow CM20 1WG ☎ 01279 446410 ✉ jane.greer@harlow.gov.uk

PR / Communications: Ms Jane Greer Acting Head of Community Wellbeing, Civic Centre, The Water Gardens, Harlow CM20 1WG ☎ 01279 446410 ✉ jane.greer@harlow.gov.uk

Community Safety: Ms Jane Greer Acting Head of Community Wellbeing, Civic Centre, The Water Gardens, Harlow CM20 1WG ☎ 01279 446410 ✉ jane.greer@harlow.gov.uk

Computer Management: Mr Simon Freeman Head of Finance, Civic Centre, The Water Gardens, Harlow CM20 1WG ☎ 01279 446228 ✉ simon.freeman@harlow.gov.uk

Contracts: Mr Brian Keane Head of Governance, Civic Centre, The Water Gardens, Harlow CM20 1WG ☎ 01279 446037 ✉ brian.keane@harlow.gov.uk

Corporate Services: Mr Brian Keane Head of Governance, Civic Centre, The Water Gardens, Harlow CM20 1WG ☎ 01279 446037 ✉ brian.keane@harlow.gov.uk

Customer Service: Ms Jane Greer Acting Head of Community Wellbeing, Civic Centre, The Water Gardens, Harlow CM20 1WG ☎ 01279 446410 ✉ jane.greer@harlow.gov.uk

Economic Development: Ms Jane Greer Acting Head of Community Wellbeing, Civic Centre, The Water Gardens, Harlow CM20 1WG ☎ 01279 446410 ✉ jane.greer@harlow.gov.uk

Electoral Registration: Mr Brian Keane Head of Governance, Civic Centre, The Water Gardens, Harlow CM20 1WG ☎ 01279 446037 ✉ brian.keane@harlow.gov.uk

Emergency Planning: Mr Graeme Bloomer Head of Place, Civic Centre, The Water Gardens, Harlow CM20 1WG ☎ 01276 446270 ✉ graeme.bloomer@harlow.gov.uk

Energy Management: Mr Graeme Bloomer Head of Place, Civic Centre, The Water Gardens, Harlow CM20 1WG ☎ 01276 446270 ✉ graeme.bloomer@harlow.gov.uk

Environmental / Technical Services: Mr Graeme Bloomer Head of Place, Civic Centre, The Water Gardens, Harlow CM20 1WG ☎ 01276 446270 ✉ graeme.bloomer@harlow.gov.uk

Environmental Health: Mr Graeme Bloomer Head of Place, Civic Centre, The Water Gardens, Harlow CM20 1WG ☎ 01276 446270 ✉ graeme.bloomer@harlow.gov.uk

Estates, Property & Valuation: Mr Graeme Bloomer Head of Place, Civic Centre, The Water Gardens, Harlow CM20 1WG ☎ 01276 446270 ✉ graeme.bloomer@harlow.gov.uk

Facilities: Mr Graeme Bloomer Head of Place, Civic Centre, The Water Gardens, Harlow CM20 1WG ☎ 01276 446270 ✉ graeme.bloomer@harlow.gov.uk

Grounds Maintenance: Mr Graeme Bloomer Head of Place, Civic Centre, The Water Gardens, Harlow CM20 1WG ☎ 01276 446270 ✉ graeme.bloomer@harlow.gov.uk

Health and Safety: Mr Brian Keane Head of Governance, Civic Centre, The Water Gardens, Harlow CM20 1WG ☎ 01279 446037 brian.keane@harlow.gov.uk

Highways: Mr Graeme Bloomer Head of Place, Civic Centre, The Water Gardens, Harlow CM20 1WG ☎ 01276 446270 graeme.bloomer@harlow.gov.uk

Home Energy Conservation: Mr Graeme Bloomer Head of Place, Civic Centre, The Water Gardens, Harlow CM20 1WG ☎ 01276 446270 graeme.bloomer@harlow.gov.uk

Housing: Mr Andrew Murray Head of Housing, Civic Centre, The Water Gardens, Harlow SM20 1WG ☎ 01279 446676 andrew.murray@harlow.gov.uk

Housing Maintenance: Mr Andrew Murray Head of Housing, Civic Centre, The Water Gardens, Harlow SM20 1WG ☎ 01279 446676 andrew.murray@harlow.gov.uk

Legal: Mr Brian Keane Head of Governance, Civic Centre, The Water Gardens, Harlow CM20 1WG ☎ 01279 446037 brian.keane@harlow.gov.uk

Leisure and Cultural Services: Ms Jane Greer Acting Head of Community Wellbeing, Civic Centre, The Water Gardens, Harlow CM20 1WG ☎ 01279 446410 jane.greer@harlow.gov.uk

Licensing: Mr Graeme Bloomer Head of Place, Civic Centre, The Water Gardens, Harlow CM20 1WG ☎ 01276 446270 graeme.bloomer@harlow.gov.uk

Member Services: Mr Brian Keane Head of Governance, Civic Centre, The Water Gardens, Harlow CM20 1WG ☎ 01279 446037 brian.keane@harlow.gov.uk

Parking: Mr Graeme Bloomer Head of Place, Civic Centre, The Water Gardens, Harlow CM20 1WG ☎ 01276 446270 graeme.bloomer@harlow.gov.uk

Personnel / HR: Mr Brian Keane Head of Governance, Civic Centre, The Water Gardens, Harlow CM20 1WG ☎ 01279 446037 brian.keane@harlow.gov.uk

Planning: Mr Graeme Bloomer Head of Place, Civic Centre, The Water Gardens, Harlow CM20 1WG ☎ 01276 446270 graeme.bloomer@harlow.gov.uk

Procurement: Mr Brian Keane Head of Governance, Civic Centre, The Water Gardens, Harlow CM20 1WG ☎ 01279 446037 brian.keane@harlow.gov.uk

Recycling & Waste Minimisation: Mr Graeme Bloomer Head of Place, Civic Centre, The Water Gardens, Harlow CM20 1WG ☎ 01276 446270 graeme.bloomer@harlow.gov.uk

Regeneration: Ms Jane Greer Acting Head of Community Wellbeing, Civic Centre, The Water Gardens, Harlow CM20 1WG ☎ 01279 446410 jane.greer@harlow.gov.uk

Staff Training: Mr Brian Keane Head of Governance, Civic Centre, The Water Gardens, Harlow CM20 1WG ☎ 01279 446037 brian.keane@harlow.gov.uk

Street Scene: Mr Graeme Bloomer Head of Place, Civic Centre, The Water Gardens, Harlow CM20 1WG ☎ 01276 446270 graeme.bloomer@harlow.gov.uk

Town Centre: Ms Jane Greer Acting Head of Community Wellbeing, Civic Centre, The Water Gardens, Harlow CM20 1WG ☎ 01279 446410 jane.greer@harlow.gov.uk

Waste Collection and Disposal: Mr Graeme Bloomer Head of Place, Civic Centre, The Water Gardens, Harlow CM20 1WG ☎ 01276 446270 graeme.bloomer@harlow.gov.uk

Waste Management: Mr Graeme Bloomer Head of Place, Civic Centre, The Water Gardens, Harlow CM20 1WG ☎ 01276 446270 graeme.bloomer@harlow.gov.uk

COUNCILLORS

***Chair* Hall**, Tony (CON - Church Langley)
tony.hall@harlow.gov.uk

***Vice-Chair* Stevens**, Edna (LAB - Netteswell)
edna.stevens@harlow.gov.uk

***Leader of the Council* Clempner**, Jon (LAB - Little Parndon and Hare Street)
jon.clempner@harlow.gov.uk

***Deputy Leader of the Council* Toal**, Emma (LAB - Harlow Common)
emma.toal@harlow.gov.uk

Beckett, Ian (LAB - Bush Fair)
ian.beckett@harlow.gov.uk

Carter, Simon (CON - Church Langley)
simon.carter@harlow.gov.uk

Carter, David (CON - Great Parndon)
david.carter@harlow.gov.uk

Charles, Joel (CON - Old Harlow)
joel.charles@harlow.gov.uk

Churchill, Nick (CON - Sumners and Kingsmoor)
nick.churchill@harlow.gov.uk

Clark, Jean (LAB - Little Parndon and Hare Street)
jean.clark@harlow.gov.uk

Clempner, Karen (LAB - Toddbrook)

Cross, Jacqui (LAB - Mark Hall)
jacqui.cross@harlow.gov.uk

Danvers, Mike (LAB - Netteswell)
mike.danvers@harlow.gov.uk

Davis, Bob (LAB - Mark Hall)
bob.davis@harlow.gov.uk

Doku, Manny (LAB - Bush Fair)
emmanuel.doku@harlow.gov.uk

Durcan, Tony (LAB - Little Parndon and Hare Street)
anthony.durcan@harlow.gov.uk

Forman, Waida (LAB - Netteswell)
waida.forman@harlow.gov.uk

Hulcoop, Maggie (LAB - Harlow Common) maggie.hulcoop@harlow.gov.uk

Johnson, Eddie (CON - Great Parndon) eddie.johnson@harlow.gov.uk

Johnson, Andrew (CON - Church Langley) andrew.johnson@harlow.gov.uk

Johnson, Shona (CON - Great Parndon) Shona.johnson@harlow.gov.uk

Jolles, Muriel (CON - Old Harlow) muriel.jolles@harlow.gov.uk

Livings, Sue (CON - Old Harlow) sue.livings@harlow.gov.uk

Long, Dan (UKIP - Bush Fair) dan.long@harlow.gov.uk

McCabe, Patrick (LAB - Staple Tye) patrick.mccabe@harlow.gov.uk

Perrin, Russell (CON - Sumners and Kingsmoor) russell.perrin@harlow.gov.uk

Pryor, Bill (UKIP - Staple Tye) bill.pryor@harlow.gov.uk

Purton, Danny (LAB - Mark Hall) danny.purton@harlow.gov.uk

Souter, Clive (CON - Sumners and Kingsmoor) clive.souter@harlow.gov.uk

Strachan, John (LAB - Staple Tye) john.strachan@harlow.gov.uk

Truan, Rod (LAB - Toddbrook) rod.truan@harlow.gov.uk

Waite, Phil (LAB - Toddbrook) phil.waite@harlow.gov.uk

Wilkinson, Mark (LAB - Harlow Common) mark.wilkinson@harlow.gov.uk

POLITICAL COMPOSITION

LAB: 19, CON: 12, UKIP: 2

COMMITTEE CHAIRS

Audit & Standards: Mr Manny Doku

Development Management: Mr Phil Waite

Licensing: Ms Maggie Hulcoop

Harrogate D

Harrogate Borough Council, Council Offices, Crescent Gardens, Harrogate HG1 2SG
☎ 01423 500600 🖷 01423 556100 💻 www.harrogate.gov.uk

FACTS AND FIGURES

Parliamentary Constituencies: Harrogate and Knaresborough
EU Constituencies: Yorkshire and the Humber
Election Frequency: Elections are by thirds

PRINCIPAL OFFICERS

Chief Executive: Mr Wallace Sampson Chief Executive, PO Box 787, Harrogate HG1 9RW ☎ 01423 500600 ext. 56081 🖷 01423 556160 ✉ wallace.sampson@harrogate.gov.uk

Senior Management: Mr Nigel Avison, Director - Economy & Culture, PO Box 787, Harrogate HG1 9RW ☎ 01423 500600 ext. 56536 🖷 01423 556530 ✉ nigel.avison@harrogate.gov.uk

Senior Management: Mrs Rachel Bowles Director - Corporate Affairs, PO Box 787, Harrogate HG1 9RW ☎ 01423 500600 ext. 56705 🖷 01423 556100 ✉ rachel.bowles@harrogate.gov.uk

Senior Management: Mr Alan Jenks Director - Community, PO Box 787, Harrogate HG1 9RW ☎ 01423 500600 ext. 56849 🖷 01423 556810 ✉ alan.jenks@harrogate.gov.uk

Senior Management: Mr Simon Kent Director - Harrogate International Centre, Harrogate International Centre, Kings Road, Harrogate HG1 5LA ☎ 01423 537237 ✉ simon.kent@harrogate.gov.uk

Access Officer / Social Services (Disability): Mr Nigel Thompson, Chief Facilities Manager, PO Box 787, Harrogate HG1 9RW ☎ 01423 500600 ext. 56657 🖷 01423 556580 ✉ nigel.thompson-dts@harrogate.gov.uk

Architect, Building / Property Services: Mr Nigel Avison, Director - Economy & Culture, PO Box 787, Harrogate HG1 9RW ☎ 01423 500600 ext. 56536 🖷 01423 556530 ✉ nigel.avison@harrogate.gov.uk

Building Control: Mr John Fowler Chief Building Control Officer, PO Box 787, Harrogate HG1 9RW ☎ 01423 500600 ext. 56597 🖷 01423 556550 ✉ john.fowler@harrogate.gov.uk

PR / Communications: Mr Giles Latham Communications & Marketing Manager, PO Box 787, Harrogate HG1 9RW ☎ 01423 500600 ext. 58448 🖷 01423 556100 ✉ giles.latham@harrogate.gov.uk

Community Planning: Mr Alan Jenks Director - Community, PO Box 787, Harrogate HG1 9RW ☎ 01423 500600 ext. 56849 🖷 01423 556810 ✉ alan.jenks@harrogate.gov.uk

Community Safety: Mrs Nicky Garside Head of Safer Communities, PO Box 787, Harrogate HG1 9RW ☎ 01423 500600 ext. 56847 🖷 01423 556820 ✉ nicky.garside@harrogate.gov.uk

Community Safety: Mrs Julia Stack, Community Safety & CCTV Manager, PO Box 787, Harrogate HG1 9RW ☎ 01423 500600 ext. 56632 🖷 01423 556820 ✉ julia.stack@harrogate.gov.uk

Computer Management: Mr Mike Kenworthy Head of ICT & Customer Support, PO Box 787, Harrogate HG1 9RW ☎ 01423 500600 ext. 56073 ✉ mike.kenworthy@harrogate.gov.uk

Corporate Services: Mr Simon Kent Director - Harrogate International Centre, Harrogate International Centre, Kings Road, Harrogate HG1 5LA ☎ 01423 537237 ✉ simon.kent@harrogate.gov.uk

Customer Service: Mrs Christine Pyatt Corporate Customer Services Manager, PO Box 787, Harrogate HG1 9RW ☎ 01423 500600 ext. 56845 🖷 01423 556100 ✉ christine.pyatt@harrogate.gov.uk

HARROGATE

Direct Labour: Mr Patrick Kilburn, Head of Parks & Environmental Services, PO Box 787, Harrogate HG1 9RW ☎ 01423 500600 ext. 51106 🖶 01423 556810 🖱 patrick.kilburn@harrogate.gov.uk

Economic Development: Mr Nigel Avison, Director - Economy & Culture, PO Box 787, Harrogate HG1 9RW ☎ 01423 500600 ext. 56536 🖶 01423 556530 🖱 nigel.avison@harrogate.gov.uk

E-Government: Mr Mike Kenworthy Head of ICT & Customer Support, PO Box 787, Harrogate HG1 9RW ☎ 01423 500600 ext. 56073 🖱 mike.kenworthy@harrogate.gov.uk

Electoral Registration: Mrs Jennifer Norton Head of Legal & Governance, PO Box 787, Harrogate HG1 9RW ☎ 01423 500600 ext. 56036 🖱 jennifer.norton@harrogate.gov.uk

Emergency Planning: Mr Ian Speirs Civil Contingencies Officer, PO Box 787, Harrogate HG1 9RW ☎ 01423 500600 ext. 56014 🖱 ian.speirs@harrogate.gov.uk

Energy Management: Mr Nigel Avison, Director - Economy & Culture, PO Box 787, Harrogate HG1 9RW ☎ 01423 500600 ext. 56536 🖶 01423 556530 🖱 nigel.avison@harrogate.gov.uk

Environmental / Technical Services: Mr Patrick Kilburn, Head of Parks & Environmental Services, PO Box 787, Harrogate HG1 9RW ☎ 01423 500600 ext. 51106 🖶 01423 556810 🖱 patrick.kilburn@harrogate.gov.uk

Environmental Health: Mrs Nicky Garside Head of Safer Communities, PO Box 787, Harrogate HG1 9RW ☎ 01423 500600 ext. 56847 🖶 01423 556820 🖱 nicky.garside@harrogate.gov.uk

Environmental Health: Mr Alan Jenks Director - Community, PO Box 787, Harrogate HG1 9RW ☎ 01423 500600 ext. 56849 🖶 01423 556810 🖱 alan.jenks@harrogate.gov.uk

Estates, Property & Valuation: Mr Nigel Avison, Director - Economy & Culture, PO Box 787, Harrogate HG1 9RW ☎ 01423 500600 ext. 56536 🖶 01423 556530 🖱 nigel.avison@harrogate.gov.uk

European Liaison: Ms Genevieve Gillies, Economic Development Officer for Regeneration, PO Box 787, Harrogate HG1 9RW ☎ 01423 500600 ext. 56079 🖶 01423 556050 🖱 genevieve.gillies@harrogate.gov.uk

Finance: Mr Andrew Crookham Head of Finance, PO Box 787, Harrogate HG1 9RW ☎ 01423 500600 ext. 58473 🖱 andrew.crookham@harrogate.gov.uk

Fleet Management: Mr Alan Smith Transport Manager, PO Box 787, Harrogate HG1 9RW ☎ 01423 500600 ext. 56877 🖶 01423 530174 🖱 alan.smith@harrogate.gov.uk

Grounds Maintenance: Mr Patrick Kilburn, Head of Parks & Environmental Services, PO Box 787, Harrogate HG1 9RW ☎ 01423 500600 ext. 51106 🖶 01423 556810 🖱 patrick.kilburn@harrogate.gov.uk

Health and Safety: Miss Sarah Young Health & Safety Advisor, PO Box 787, Harrogate HG1 9RW ☎ 01423 500600 ext. 56078 🖶 01423 556180 🖱 sarah.young@harrogate.gov.uk

Home Energy Conservation: Mrs Jane Money, Environmental Strategy Manager, PO Box 787, Harrogate HG1 9RW ☎ 01423 500600 ext. 56801 🖶 01423 556720 🖱 jane.money@harrogate.gov.uk

Housing: Ms Madelaine Bell Head of Housing & Property, PO Box 787, Harrogate HG1 9RW ☎ 01423 500600 ext. 58352 🖱 madelaine.bell@harrogate.gov.uk

Housing: Mr Alan Jenks Director - Community, PO Box 787, Harrogate HG1 9RW ☎ 01423 500600 ext. 56849 🖶 01423 556810 🖱 alan.jenks@harrogate.gov.uk

Housing Maintenance: Mr Stephen Hargreaves, Property Services Manager, PO Box 787, Harrogate HG1 9RW ☎ 01423 500600 ext. 56907 🖱 stephen.hargreaves@harrogate.gov.uk

Legal: Mrs Jennifer Norton Head of Legal & Governance, PO Box 787, Harrogate HG1 9RW ☎ 01423 500600 ext. 56036 🖱 jennifer.norton@harrogate.gov.uk

Leisure and Cultural Services: Ms Lois Toyne Head of Culture, Tourism & Sports, PO Box 787, Harrogate HG1 9RW ☎ 01423 500600 ext. 56187 🖱 lois.toyne@harrogate.gov.uk

Licensing: Mr Gareth Bentley, Licensing & Occupational Safety Manager, PO Box 787, Harrogate HG1 9RW ☎ 01423 500600 ext. 51027 🖶 01423 556820 🖱 gareth.bentley@harrogate.gov.uk

Lighting: Mr David Oliver, Street Lighting Engineer, PO Box 787, Harrogate HG1 9RW ☎ 01423 500600 ext. 56544 🖱 david.oliver@harrogate.gov.uk

Lottery Funding, Charity and Voluntary: Mrs Jennifer Norton Head of Legal & Governance, PO Box 787, Harrogate HG1 9RW ☎ 01423 500600 ext. 56036 🖱 jennifer.norton@harrogate.gov.uk

Member Services: Mrs Jennifer Norton Head of Legal & Governance, PO Box 787, Harrogate HG1 9RW ☎ 01423 500600 ext. 56036 🖱 jennifer.norton@harrogate.gov.uk

Parking: Mrs Nicky Garside Head of Safer Communities, PO Box 787, Harrogate HG1 9RW ☎ 01423 500600 ext. 56847 🖶 01423 556820 🖱 nicky.garside@harrogate.gov.uk

Partnerships: Mrs Ann Byrne, Partnerships & Engagement Manager, PO Box 787, Harrogate HG1 9RW ☎ 01423 500600 ext. 56067 🖱 ann.byrne@harrogate.gov.uk

Personnel / HR: Ms Kay Atherton Head of Organisational Development & Improvement, PO Box 787, Harrogate HG1 9RW ☎ 01423 500600 ext. 58472 🖱 kay.atherton@harrogate.gov.uk

Planning: Mr Dave Allenby, Head of Planning & Development, PO Box 787, Harrogate HG1 9RW ☎ 01423 500600 ext. 56516 🖱 dave.allenby@harrogate.gov.uk

Procurement: Mrs Marion Wrightson Procurement Manager, PO Box 787, Harrogate HG1 9RW ☎ 01423 500600 ext. 56166 marion.wrightson@harrogate.gov.uk

Recycling & Waste Minimisation: Mrs Alex Rankin, Recycling & Promotions Officer, PO Box 787, Harrogate HG1 9RW ☎ 01423 500600 ext. 56965 🖷 01423 530174 alex.rankin@harrogate.gov.uk

Regeneration: Ms Genevieve Gillies, Economic Development Officer for Regeneration, PO Box 787, Harrogate HG1 9RW ☎ 01423 500600 ext. 56079 🖷 01423 556050 genevieve.gillies@harrogate.gov.uk

Sustainable Communities: Mrs Jane Money, Environmental Strategy Manager, PO Box 787, Harrogate HG1 9RW ☎ 01423 500600 ext. 56801 🖷 01423 556720 jane.money@harrogate.gov.uk

Sustainable Development: Mrs Jane Money, Environmental Strategy Manager, PO Box 787, Harrogate HG1 9RW ☎ 01423 500600 ext. 56801 🖷 01423 556720 jane.money@harrogate.gov.uk

Tourism: Mr Simon Kent Director - Harrogate International Centre, Harrogate International Centre, Kings Road, Harrogate HG1 5LA ☎ 01423 537237 simon.kent@harrogate.gov.uk

Tourism: Ms Helen Suckling Visitor Services Manager, PO Box 787, Harrogate HG1 9RW ☎ 01423 500600 ext. 37306 🖷 01423 537270 helen.suckling@harrogate.gov.uk

Transport: Mr Alan Smith Transport Manager, PO Box 787, Harrogate HG1 9RW ☎ 01423 500600 ext. 56877 🖷 01423 530174 alan.smith@harrogate.gov.uk

Waste Collection and Disposal: Mr Patrick Kilburn, Head of Parks & Environmental Services, PO Box 787, Harrogate HG1 9RW ☎ 01423 500600 ext. 51106 🖷 01423 556810 patrick.kilburn@harrogate.gov.uk

Waste Management: Mr Patrick Kilburn, Head of Parks & Environmental Services, PO Box 787, Harrogate HG1 9RW ☎ 01423 500600 ext. 51106 🖷 01423 556810 patrick.kilburn@harrogate.gov.uk

Children's Play Areas: Mrs Jennifer Love Technical Officer, PO Box 787, Harrogate HG1 9RW ☎ 01423 500600 ext. 51072 jennifer.love@harrogate.gov.uk

COUNCILLORS

***Mayor* Simms**, Nigel (CON - Mashamshire)
nigel.simms@harrogate.gov.uk

***Deputy Mayor* Travena**, Jennifer (LD - Granby)
jennifer.travena@harrogate.gov.uk

***Leader of the Council* Cooper**, Richard (CON - High Harrogate)
richard.cooper@harrogate.gov.uk

***Deputy Leader of the Council* Harrison**, Michael (CON - Killinghall)
michael.harrison@harrogate.gov.uk

Alton, Anthony (CON - Claro)
anthony.alton@harrogate.gov.uk

Atkinson, Margaret (CON - Kirkby Malzeard)
margaret.atkinson@harrogate.gov.uk

Bateman, Bernard (CON - Wathvale)
bernard.bateman@harrogate.gov.uk

Batt, John (CON - Knaresborough East)
john.batt@harrogate.gov.uk

Bayliss, Caroline (CON - Ribston)
caroline.bayliss@harrogate.gov.uk

Broadbank, Philip (LD - Starbeck)
philip.broadbank@harrogate.gov.uk

Brown, Nick (CON - Newby)
nick.brown@harrogate.gov.uk

Burnett, Rebecca (CON - Rossett)
rebecca.burnett@harrogate.gov.uk

Butterfield, Jean (CON - Low Harrogate)
jean.butterfield@harrogate.gov.uk

Chambers, Michael (CON - Ripon Spa)
mike.chambers@harrogate.gov.uk

Chapman, Trevor (LD - New Park)
trevor.chapman@harrogate.gov.uk

Clark, Jim (CON - Rossett)
jim.clark@harrogate.gov.uk

Ennis, John (CON - Low Harrogate)
john.ennis@harrogate.gov.uk

Fawcett, Shirley (CON - Spofforth with Lower Wharfedale)

Flynn, Helen (LD - Nidd Valley)
helen.flynn@harrogate.gov.uk

Fox, John (LD - Granby)
john.fox@harrogate.gov.uk

Fox, Ivor (CON - Knaresborough Scriven Park)
ivor.fox@harrogate.gov.uk

Galloway, Ian (CON - Bishop Monkton)
ian.galloway@harrogate.gov.uk

Goode, David (LD - Knaresborough King James)
david.goode@harrogate.gov.uk

Goss, Andrew (LD - Woodfield)
andrew.goss@harrogate.gov.uk

Haslam, Paul (CON - Bilton)
paul.haslam@harrogate.gov.uk

Hawke, Sid (IND - Ripon Minster)
sid.hawke@harrogate.gov.uk

Hill, Matthew (CON - Pannal)
matt.hill@harrogate.gov.uk

Hill, Christine (CON - Lower Nidderdale)
christine.hill@harrogate.gov.uk

Ireland, Philip (CON - Knaresborough King James)
phil.ireland@harrogate.gov.uk

Jackson, Steven (CON - Saltergate)
steven.jackson@harrogate.gov.uk

Johnson, Ben (CON - High Harrogate)
ben.johnson@harrogate.gov.uk

Jones, Anne (LD - Knaresborough Scriven Park)
anne.jones@harrogate.gov.uk

HARROGATE

Jones, Pat (CON - Stray)
Pat.Jones@harrogate.gov.uk

Law, Janet (LD - Starbeck)
janet.law@harrogate.gov.uk

Lewis, Chris (IND - Ouseburn)
chris.lewis@harrogate.gov.uk

Lumley, Stanley (CON - Pateley Bridge)
stanley.lumley@harrogate.gov.uk

Mackenzie, Don (CON - Harlow Moor)
don.mackenzie@harrogate.gov.uk

Mann, John (CON - Pannal)
john.mann@harrogate.gov.uk

Marsh, Pat (LD - Hookstone)
pat.marsh@harrogate.gov.uk

Martin, Stuart (CON - Ripon Moorside)
stuart.martin@harrogate.gov.uk

McHardy, Pauline (IND - Ripon Moorside)
pauline.mchardy@harrogate.gov.uk

Metcalfe, Zoe (CON - Ripon Minster)
zoe.metcalfe@harrogate.gov.uk

O'Neill, Robert (LD - Woodfield)
robert.oneill@harrogate.gov.uk

Rodgers, Val (LD - Bilton)
val.rodgers@harrogate.gov.uk

Ryder, Christine (CON - Washburn)
christine.ryder@harrogate.gov.uk

Savage, John (LIB - Marston Moor)
john.savage@harrogate.gov.uk

Skardon, Clare (LD - Hookstone)
membserv@harrogate.gov.uk

Skidmore, Alan (CON - Ripon Spa)
alan.skidmore@harrogate.gov.uk

Swift, Graham (CON - Saltergate)
graham.swift@harrogate.gov.uk

Theakston, Simon (CON - Harlow Moor)
simon.theakston@theakstons.co.uk

Trotter, Clifford (CON - Stray)
cliff.trotter@harrogate.gov.uk

Webber, Matthew (LD - New Park)
matthew.webber@harrogate.gov.uk

Willoughby, Christine (LD - Knaresborough East)
christine.willoughby@harrogate.gov.uk

Windass, Robert (CON - Boroughbridge)
cllr.windass@harrogate.gov.uk

POLITICAL COMPOSITION

CON: 35, LD: 15, IND: 3, LIB: 1

COMMITTEE CHAIRS

Devlopment: Mr Jim Clark

Licensing: Mr John Ennis

Planning: Mr John Mann

Harrow — L

Harrow London Borough Council, Civic Centre, Station Road, Harrow HA1 2XF
☎ 020 8863 5611 🖷 020 8424 1134 🖰 info@harrow.gov.uk
💻 www.harrow.gov.uk

FACTS AND FIGURES

Parliamentary Constituencies: Harrow East, Harrow West, Uxbridge and Ruislip South
EU Constituencies: London
Election Frequency: Elections are of whole council

PRINCIPAL OFFICERS

Chief Executive: Mr Michael Lockwood, Chief Executive, Civic Centre, Station Road, Harrow HA1 2XF ☎ 020 8424 1001 🖰 michael.lockwood@harrow.gov.uk

Senior Management: Ms Caroline Bruce Corporate Director - Environment & Enterprise, Civic Centre, Station Road, Harrow HA1 2XF

Senior Management: Mr Chris Spencer Corporate Director - Children & Families, Civic Centre, Station Road, Harrow HA1 2XF

Senior Management: Mr Tom Whiting Corporate Director - Resources, Civic Centre, Station Road, Harrow HA1 2XF ☎ 020 8863 5611 🖰 tom.whiting@harrow.gov.uk

Children / Youth Services: Ms Wendy Beeton Divisional Director - Integrated Early Years, Civic Centre, Station Road, Harrow HA1 2XF ☎ 020 8416 8830 🖰 wendy.beeton@harrow.gov.uk

Children / Youth Services: Ms Catherine Doran Corporate Director - Children's Services, Civic Centre, Station Road, Harrow HA1 2XF ☎ 020 8424 1356 🖰 catherine.doran@harrow.gov.uk

Children / Youth Services: Mr Richard Segalov Divisional Director - Integrated Early Years, Civic Centre, Station Road, Harrow HA1 2XF ☎ 020 8420 9344 🖰 richard.segalov@harrow.gov.uk

Civil Registration: Ms Elaine McEachron Registration & Support Services Manager, Civic Centre, Station Road, Harrow HA1 2XF ☎ 020 8424 1097 🖰 elaine.mceachron@harrow.gov.uk

PR / Communications: Ms Lindsay Coulson Head - Communications, Civic Centre, Station Road, Harrow HA1 2XF ☎ 020 8424 1292 🖰 linday.coulson@harrow.gov.uk

Community Planning: Ms Carol Yarde Head - Transformation, Community, Health & Wellbeing, Civic Centre, Station Road, Harrow HA1 2XF ☎ 020 8420 9660 🖰 carol.yarde@harrow.gov.uk

Community Safety: Mr Andew Howe Director - Public Health, Civic Centre, Station Road, Harrow HA1 2XF ☎ 020 8420 9501 🖰 andrew.how@harrow.gov.uk

Corporate Services: Mr Philip Hamberger Interim Head - Development & Improvement, Civic Centre, Station Road, Harrow HA1 2XF ☎ 020 8420 9298 🖰 philip.hamberger@harrow.gov.uk

Corporate Services: Mr Andy Parsons Interim Head - Property Service, Civic Centre, Station Road, Harrow HA1 2XF ☎ 020 8736 6106 ✉ andy.parsons@harrow.gov.uk

Customer Service: Ms Carol Cutler, Director - Business Transformation & Customer Service, Exchequer Building, Civic Centre, Station Road, Harrow HA1 2XF ☎ 020 8424 6701 ✉ carol.cutler@harrow.gov.uk

Economic Development: Mr Mark Billington Head of Service - Economic Development, Research & Enterprise, Civic Centre, Station Road, Harrow HA1 2XF ☎ 020 8736 6533 ✉ mark.billington@harrow.gov.uk

Education: Ms Leora Cruddes Divisional Director, Civic Centre, Station Road, Harrow HA1 2XF ☎ 020 8873 6523 ✉ leora.cruddes@harrow.gov.uk

Electoral Registration: Ms Elaine McEachron Registration & Support Services Manager, Civic Centre, Station Road, Harrow HA1 2XF ☎ 020 8424 1097 ✉ elaine.mceachron@harrow.gov.uk

Emergency Planning: Mr Kan Grover Service Manager - Emergency Planning & Business Continuity, Civic Centre, Station Road, Harrow HA1 2XF ☎ 020 8420 9319 ✉ kan.grover@harrow.gov.uk

Environmental / Technical Services: Mr John Edwards Divisional Director - Environmental Services, Civic Centre, Station Road, Harrow HA1 2XF ☎ 020 8736 6799 ✉ john.edwards@harrow.gov.uk

Finance: Ms Dawn Calvert Finance Director, Civic Centre, Station Road, Harrow HA1 2XF ☎ 020 8420 9269 ✉ dawn.calvert@harrow.gov.uk

Treasury: Mr George Bruce Treasury & Pension Fund Manager, Civic Centre, Station Road, Harrow HA1 2XF ☎ 020 8424 1170 ✉ george.bruce@harrow.gov.uk

Pensions: Mr George Bruce Treasury & Pension Fund Manager, Civic Centre, Station Road, Harrow HA1 2XF ☎ 020 8424 1170 ✉ george.bruce@harrow.gov.uk

Pensions: Mr Andrew Campion Interim Planned Investments Manager, Civic Centre, Station Road, Harrow HA1 2XF ☎ 020 8424 1339 ✉ andrew.campion@harrow.gov.uk

Pensions: Ms Maggie Challoner Interim Head - Asset Management Investments, Civic Centre, Station Road, Harrow HA1 2XF ☎ 020 8424 1473 ✉ maggie.challoner@harrow.gov.uk

Housing: Ms Lynne Pennington Divisional Director - Housing Services, Civic Centre, Station Road, Harrow HA1 2XF ☎ 020 8424 1998 ✉ lynne.pennington@harrow.gov.uk

Legal: Ms Jessica Farmer Head - Legal Practice, Civic Centre, Station Road, Harrow HA1 2XF ☎ 020 8424 1889 ✉ jessica.farmer@harrow.gov.uk

Legal: Mr Hugh Peart, Director - Legal & Governance Services, Civic Centre, Station Road, Harrow HA1 2XF ☎ 020 8424 1272 ✉ hugh.peart@harrow.gov.uk

Leisure and Cultural Services: Ms Marianne Locke Divisional Director - Community & Cultural Services, Civic Centre, Station Road, Harrow HA1 2XF ☎ 020 8736 6530 ✉ marianne.locke@harrow.gov.uk

Member Services: Ms Elaine McEachron Registration & Support Services Manager, Civic Centre, Station Road, Harrow HA1 2XF ☎ 020 8424 1097 ✉ elaine.mceachron@harrow.gov.uk

Partnerships: Mr Alex Dewsnap Divisional Director - Strategic Commissioning, Civic Centre, Station Road, Harrow HA1 2XF ☎ 020 8416 8250 ✉ alex.dewsnap@harrow.gov.uk

Personnel / HR: Mr Jon Turner, Divisional Director - HRD & Shared Services, Civic Centre, Station Road, Harrow HA1 2XF ☎ 020 8424 1225 ✉ jon.turner@harrow.gov.uk

Planning: Mr Phil Greenwood, Head of Service - Major Development Projects, Civic Centre, Station Road, Harrow HA1 2XF ☎ 020 8424 1166 ✉ phil.greenwood@harrow.gov.uk

Planning: Mr Stephen Kelly Divisional Director - Planning Services, Civic Centre, Station Road, Harrow HA1 2XF ☎ 020 8736 6149 ✉ stephen.kelly@harrow.gov.uk

Procurement: Mr John Edwards Divisional Director - Environmental Services, Civic Centre, Station Road, Harrow HA1 2XF ☎ 020 8736 6799 ✉ john.edwards@harrow.gov.uk

Social Services: Mr Roger Rickman Divisional Director - Special Needs Services, Civic Centre, Station Road, Harrow HA1 2XF ☎ 020 8966 6334 ✉ roger.rickman@harrow.gov.uk

Social Services (Adult): Ms Bernie Flaherty Director - Social Services, Civic Centre, Station Road, Harrow HA1 2XF ☎ 020 8863 5611 ✉ bernie.flaherty@harrow.gov.uk

Public Health: Dr Andrew Howe Director - Public Health, 27 Carnarvon Road, Barnet EN5 4LX ☎ 020 8359 3970 ✉ andrew.howe@harrow.gov.uk

Sustainable Communities: Mr John Edwards Divisional Director - Environmental Services, Civic Centre, Station Road, Harrow HA1 2XF ☎ 020 8736 6799 ✉ john.edwards@harrow.gov.uk

COUNCILLORS

***Mayor* Suresh**, Krishna (LAB - Rayners Lane)
krishna.suresh@harrow.gov.uk

***Deputy Mayor* Shah**, Rekha (LAB - Wealdstone)
rekha.shah@harrow.gov.uk

***Leader of the Council* Perry**, David (LAB - Marlborough)
david.perry@harrow.gov.uk

***Deputy Leader of the Council* Ferry**, Keith (LAB - Greenhill)
keith.ferry@harrow.gov.uk

HARROW

***Group Leader* Weston**, Georgia (IND - Headstone North)
georgia.weston@harrow.gov.uk

Ali, Ghazanfar (LAB - Greenhill)
ghazanfar.ali@harrow.gov.uk

Almond, Richard (CON - Pinner South)
richard.almond@harrow.gov.uk

Amadi, Chika (LAB - Edgware)
chika.amadi@harrow.gov.uk

Anderson, Susan (LAB - Greenhill)
sue.anderson@harrow.gov.uk

Anderson, Jeff (LAB - Rayners Lane)
jeff.anderson@harrow.gov.uk

Ashton, Marilyn (CON - Stanmore Park)
marilyn.ashton@harrow.gov.uk

Bath, Camilla (CON - Stanmore Park)
camilla.bath@harrow.gov.uk

Baxter, June (CON - Harrow on the Hill)
june.baxter@harrow.gov.uk

Bednell, Christine (CON - Stanmore Park)
christine.bednell@harrow.gov.uk

Bond, James (IND - Headstone North)
james.bond@harrow.gov.uk

Borio, Michael (LAB - Queensbury)
michael.borio@harrow.gov.uk

Brown, Simon (LAB - Headstone South)
simon.brown@harrow.gov.uk

Chana, Kamaljit (CON - Pinner South)
kamaljit.chana@harrow.gov.uk

Chauhan, Ramji (CON - Harrow Weald)
ramji.chauhan@harrow.gov.uk

Currie, Bob (LAB - Roxbourne)
bob.curie@harrow.gov.uk

Dattani, Niraj (LAB - Kenton East)
niraj.dattani@harrow.gov.uk

Davine, Margaret (LAB - Roxeth)
margaret.davine@harrow.gov.uk

Dooley, Josephine (LAB - Roxbourne)
josephine.dooley@harrow.gov.uk

Fitzpatrick, Pamela (LAB - Headstone South)
pamela.fitzpatrick@harrow.gov.uk

Greek, Stephen (CON - Harrow Weald)
stephen.greek@harrow.gov.uk

Green, Mitzi (LAB - Kenton East)
mitzi.green@harrow.gov.uk

Hall, Susan (CON - Hatch End)
susan.hall@harrow.gov.uk

Hearnden, Glen (LAB - Harrow on the Hill)
glen.hearnden@harrow.gov.uk

Henson, Graham (LAB - Roxbourne)
graham.henson@harrow.gov.uk

Hinkley, John (CON - Hatch End)
john.hinkley@harrow.gov.uk

Jogia, Ameet (CON - Canons)
ameet.jogia@harrow.gov.uk

Kara, Manji (CON - Belmont)
maji.kara@harrow.gov.uk

Kendler, Barry (LAB - Edgware)
barry.kendler@harrow.gov.uk

Lammiman, Jean (CON - Hatch End)
jean.lammiman@harrow.gov.uk

Macleod, Barry (CON - Harrow on the Hill)
barry.macloed@harrow.gov.uk

Marikar, Kairul (LAB - West Harrow)
kairul.marikar@harrow.gov.uk

Maru, Ajay (LAB - Kenton West)
ajay.maru@harrow.gov.uk

Miles, Jerry (LAB - Roxeth)
jerry.miles@harrow.gov.uk

Mithani, Vina (CON - Kenton West)
vina.mithani@harrow.gov.uk

Moshenson, Amir (CON - Canons)
amir.moshenson@harrow.gov.uk

Mote, Janet (CON - Headstone North)
janet.mote@harrow.gov.uk

Mote, Chris (CON - Pinner South)
chris.mote@harrow.gov.uk

Noyce, Chris (LD - Rayners Lane)
chris.noyce@harrow.gov.uk

O'Dell, Phillip (LAB - Wealdstone)
phillip.odell@harrow.gov.uk

Osborn, Paul (CON - Pinner)
paul.osborn@harrow.gov.uk

Parekh, Nitin (LAB - Edgware)
nitin.parekh@harrow.gov.uk

Parmar, Varsha (LAB - Marlborough)
varsha.parmar@harrow.gov.uk

Parmar, Mina (CON - Belmont)
mina.parmar@harrow.gov.uk

Patel, Pritesh (CON - Harrow Weald)
pritesh.patel@harrow.gov.uk

Patel, Primesh (LAB - Roxeth)
primesh.patel@harrow.gov.uk

Rabadia, Kantilal (CON - Kenton West)
kanti.rabadia@harrow.gov.uk

Ramchandani, Kiran (LAB - Queensbury)
kiran.ramchandani@harrow.gov.uk

Robson, Christine (LAB - West Harrow)
christine.robson@harrow.gov.uk

Seymour, Lynda (CON - Belmont)
lynda.seymour@harrow.gov.uk

Shah, Sachin (LAB - Queensbury)
sachin.shah@harrow.gov.uk

Shah, Aneka (LAB - Kenton East)
aneka.shah@harrow.gov.uk

Stevenson, Norman (CON - Pinner)
norman.stevenson@harrow.gov.uk

Suresh, Sasikala (LAB - Headstone South)
sasikala.suresh@harrow.gov.uk

Swersky, Adam (LAB - West Harrow)
adam.swersky@harrow.gov.uk

Thakker, Bharat (CON - Canons)
bharat.thakker@harrow.gov.uk

Weiss, Antonio (LAB - Marlborough)
antonio.weiss@harrow.gov.uk

Whitehead, Anne (LAB - Wealdstone)
anne.whitehead@harrow.gov.uk

Wright, Stephen (CON - Pinner)
stephen.wright@harrow.gov.uk

POLITICAL COMPOSITION

LAB: 34, CON: 26, IND: 2, LD: 1

COMMITTEE CHAIRS

Audit: Mr Antonio Weiss

Health & Wellbeing: Ms Anne Whitehead

Licensing: Ms Kairul Marikar

Pensions: Mr Adam Swersky

Planning: Mr Keith Ferry

Hart D

Hart District Council, Civic Offices, Harlington Way, Fleet GU51 4AE
☎ 01252 622122 🖷 01252 626886 ✉ enquiries@hart.gov.uk
🖳 www.hart.gov.uk

FACTS AND FIGURES

Parliamentary Constituencies: Hampshire North East
EU Constituencies: South East
Election Frequency: Elections are by thirds

PRINCIPAL OFFICERS

Chief Executive: Ms Patricia Hughes Joint Chief Executive, Civic Offices, Harlington Way, Fleet GU51 4AE ☎ 01252 622122 ✉ patricia.hughes@hart.gov.uk

Chief Executive: Mr Daryl Phillips Joint Chief Executive, Civic Offices, Harlington Way, Fleet GU51 4AE ☎ 01252 622122 ✉ daryl.phillips@hart.gov.uk

Senior Management: Ms Patricia Hughes Joint Chief Executive, Civic Offices, Harlington Way, Fleet GU51 4AE ☎ 01252 622122 ✉ patricia.hughes@hart.gov.uk

Senior Management: Mr Daryl Phillips Joint Chief Executive, Civic Offices, Harlington Way, Fleet GU51 4AE ☎ 01252 622122 ✉ daryl.phillips@hart.gov.uk

Architect, Building / Property Services: Mr John Elson, Head of Technical Services, Civic Offices, Harlington Way, Fleet GU51 4AE ☎ 01252 622122 ✉ john.elson@hart.gov.uk

Community Safety: Ms Caroline Ryan Community Safety Manager, Civic Offices, Harlington Way, Fleet GU51 4AE ☎ 01252 622122

Contracts: Mr John Elson, Head of Technical Services, Civic Offices, Harlington Way, Fleet GU51 4AE ☎ 01252 622122 ✉ john.elson@hart.gov.uk

Customer Service: Mrs Liz Squires Head of Revenues & Benefits, Civic Offices, Harlington Way, Fleet GU51 4AE ☎ 01252 622122 ✉ liz.squires@hart.gov.uk

Direct Labour: Ms Sarah Robinson, Waste & Recycling Manager, Springwell Lane Depot, Hartley Wintney RG27 8BW ☎ 01252 622122 ✉ sarah.robinson@hart.gov.uk

Electoral Registration: Mr Andy Tiffin Head of Democratic Services, Civic Offices, Harlington Way, Fleet GU51 4AE ☎ 01252 622122 ✉ andrew.tiffin@hart.gov.uk

Emergency Planning: Mr John Elson, Head of Technical Services, Civic Offices, Harlington Way, Fleet GU51 4AE ☎ 01252 622122 ✉ john.elson@hart.gov.uk

Energy Management: Mr John Elson, Head of Technical Services, Civic Offices, Harlington Way, Fleet GU51 4AE ☎ 01252 622122 ✉ john.elson@hart.gov.uk

Environmental / Technical Services: Mr John Elson, Head of Technical Services, Civic Offices, Harlington Way, Fleet GU51 4AE ☎ 01252 622122 ✉ john.elson@hart.gov.uk

Environmental Health: Mr Nick Steevens Head of Regulatory Services, Civic Offices, Harlington Way, Fleet GU51 4AE ☎ 01252 774296 ✉ nick.steevens@hart.gov.uk

Estates, Property & Valuation: Mr John Elson, Head of Technical Services, Civic Offices, Harlington Way, Fleet GU51 4AE ☎ 01252 622122 ✉ john.elson@hart.gov.uk

Facilities: Mr Matt Saunders, Building Manager, Civic Offices, Harlington Way, Fleet GU51 4AE ☎ 01252 622122 🖷 01252 774408 ✉ matt.saunders@hart.gov.uk

Finance: Mr Tony Higgins Head of Finance & S151 Officer, Civic Offices, Harlington Way, Fleet GU51 4AE ☎ 01252 622122 ✉ tony.higgins@hart.gov.uk

Treasury: Mr Tony Higgins Head of Finance & S151 Officer, Civic Offices, Harlington Way, Fleet GU51 4AE ☎ 01252 622122 ✉ tony.higgins@hart.gov.uk

Grounds Maintenance: Mr John Elson, Head of Technical Services, Civic Offices, Harlington Way, Fleet GU51 4AE ☎ 01252 622122 ✉ john.elson@hart.gov.uk

Health and Safety: Mr Paul Beaumont Principal Environmental Health Officer, Civic Offices, Harlington Way, Fleet GU51 4AE ☎ 01252 622122 ✉ paul.beaumont@hart.gov.uk

Highways: Mr John Elson, Head of Technical Services, Civic Offices, Harlington Way, Fleet GU51 4AE ☎ 01252 622122 ✉ john.elson@hart.gov.uk

HART

Housing: Mr Phil Turner Head of Housing, Civic Offices, Harlington Way, Fleet GU51 4AE ☎ 01252 774488 ✉ phil.turner@hart.gov.uk

Legal: Ms Melanie O'Sullivan Head of Shared Legal Services, Civic Offices, Harlington Way, Fleet GU51 4AE ☎ 01256 845402 ✉ melanie.o'sullivan@basingstoke.gov.uk

Leisure and Cultural Services: Mr Carl Westby, Head of Leisure, Civic Offices, Harlington Way, Fleet GU51 4AE ☎ 01252 622122 ✉ carl.westby@hart.gov.uk

Licensing: Ms Angela Semowa Licensing Officer, Civic Offices, Harlington Way, Fleet GU51 4AE ☎ 01252 622122 ✉ angela.semowa@hart.gov.uk

Member Services: Ms Gill Chapman Committee Clerk, Civic Offices, Harlington Way, Fleet GU51 4AE ☎ 01252 622122 ✉ gill.chapman@hart.gov.uk

Parking: Mr Geoff Hislop, Parking Manager, Civic Offices, Harlington Way, Fleet GU51 4AE ☎ 01252 622122 ✉ geoff.hislop@hart.gov.uk

Planning: Mr Daryl Phillips Joint Chief Executive, Civic Offices, Harlington Way, Fleet GU51 4AE ☎ 01252 622122 ✉ daryl.phillips@hart.gov.uk

Recycling & Waste Minimisation: Mr John Elson, Head of Technical Services, Civic Offices, Harlington Way, Fleet GU51 4AE ☎ 01252 622122 ✉ john.elson@hart.gov.uk

Recycling & Waste Minimisation: Mrs Sarah Robinson Waste & Recycling Manager, Civic Offices, London Road, Basingstoke RG21 4AH ☎ 01252 774426 🖷 01256 845200 ✉ sarah.robinson@hart.gov.uk

Road Safety: Mr John Elson, Head of Technical Services, Civic Offices, Harlington Way, Fleet GU51 4AE ☎ 01252 622122 ✉ john.elson@hart.gov.uk

Street Scene: Ms Sarah Robinson, Waste & Recycling Manager, Springwell Lane Depot, Hartley Wintney RG27 8BW ☎ 01252 622122 ✉ sarah.robinson@hart.gov.uk

Traffic Management: Mr John Elson, Head of Technical Services, Civic Offices, Harlington Way, Fleet GU51 4AE ☎ 01252 622122 ✉ john.elson@hart.gov.uk

Waste Collection and Disposal: Mr John Elson, Head of Technical Services, Civic Offices, Harlington Way, Fleet GU51 4AE ☎ 01252 622122 ✉ john.elson@hart.gov.uk

Waste Management: Ms Sarah Robinson, Waste & Recycling Manager, Springwell Lane Depot, Hartley Wintney RG27 8BW ☎ 01252 622122 ✉ sarah.robinson@hart.gov.uk

Children's Play Areas: Mr Adam Green Grounds & Countryside Manager, Civic Offices, Harlington Way, Fleet GU51 4AE ☎ 01252 622122 ✉ adam.green@hart.gov.uk

COUNCILLORS

***Chair* Oliver**, Alan (IND - Fleet Central)
alan.oliver@hart.gov.uk

***Leader of the Council* Parker**, Stephen (CON - Fleet East)
stephen.parker@hart.gov.uk

***Deputy Leader of the Council* Burchfield**, Brian (CON - Hook)
brian.burchfield@hart.gov.uk

Ambler, Simon (O - Church Crookham West)
simon.ambler@hart.gov.uk

Axam, Chris (R - Crookham East)
chris.axam@hart.gov.uk

Bailey, Stuart (LD - Yateley East)
stuart.bailey@hart.gov.uk

Billings, Myra (LD - Yateley West)
myra.billings@hart.gov.uk

Blewett, Brian (LD - Blackwater and Hawley)
brian.blewett@hart.gov.uk

Butler, Gill (O - Crookham East)
gill.butler@hart.gov.uk

Clarke, Tony (O - Crookham West & Ewshot)
tony.clarke@hart.gov.uk

Cockarill, Graham (LD - Yateley East)
graham.cockarill@hart.gov.uk

Collett, Adrian (LD - Blackwater and Hawley)
adrian.collett@hart.gov.uk

Crampton, Anne (CON - Hartley Wintney)
anne.crampton@hart.gov.uk

Crisp, Gerry (LD - Yateley West)
enquiries@hart.gov.uk

Crookes, Kenneth (CON - Odiham)
kenneth.crookes@hart.gov.uk

Dickens, Shawn (CON - Yateley West)
shawn.dickens@hart.gov.uk

Forster, Steve (CON - Fleet West)
steve.forster@hart.gov.uk

Gorys, Stephen (CON - Odiham)
stephen.gorys@hart.gov.uk

Gray, Alexander (CON - Fleet Central)
alex.gray@hart.gov.uk

Harward, Robert (LD - Blackwater and Hawley)
robert.harward@hart.gov.uk

Kennett, John (CON - Odiham)
john.kennett@hart.gov.uk

Kinnell, Sara (CON - Fleet West)
sara.kinnell@hart.gov.uk

Leeson, Robert (IND - Hook)
rob.leeson@hart.gov.uk

Lewis, Ian (CON - Fleet East)
ian.lewis@hart.gov.uk

Makepeace-Browne, Wendy (O - Fleet Central)
wendy.makepeace-brown@hart.gov.uk

Morris, Mike (CON - Hook)
mike.morris@hart.gov.uk

Neighbour, David (LD - Yateley East)
david.neighbour@hart.gov.uk

Radley, James (O - Crookham East)
james.radley@hart.gov.uk

Radley, Jenny (O - Crookham West & Ewshot)
jenny.radley@hart.gov.uk

Renshaw, Andrew (CON - Hartley Wintney)
andrew.renshaw@hart.gov.uk

Southern, Tim (CON - Hartley Wintney)
tim.southern@hart.gov.uk

Wheale, Sharyn (CON - Fleet East)
sharyn.wheale@hart.gov.uk

Woods, Richard (CON - Fleet West)
richard.woods@hart.gov.uk

POLITICAL COMPOSITION
CON: 16, LD: 8, O: 6, IND: 2, R: 1

COMMITTEE CHAIRS

Audit: Mr David Neighbour

Licensing: Mr Adrian Collett

Planning: Mr Simon Ambler

Hartlepool U

Hartlepool Borough Council, Civic Centre, Victoria Road, Hartlepool TS24 8AY
☎ 01429 266522 🖷 01429 523005
🖱 customer.service@hartlepool.gov.uk 💻 www.hartlepool.gov.uk

FACTS AND FIGURES
Parliamentary Constituencies: Hartlepool
EU Constituencies: North East
Election Frequency: Elections are by thirds

PRINCIPAL OFFICERS

Chief Executive: Ms Gill Alexander Chief Executive, Civic Centre, Victoria Road, Hartlepool TS24 8AY ☎ 01429 523001 🖱 gill.alexander@hartlepool.gov.uk

Assistant Chief Executive: Mr Andrew Atkin, Assistant Chief Executive, Civic Centre, Victoria Road, Hartlepool TS24 8AY ☎ 01429 523003 🖱 andrew.atkin@hartlepool.gov.uk

Senior Management: Mr Peter Devlin Chief Solicitor, Civic Centre, Victoria Road, Hartlepool TS24 8AY ☎ 01429 523003 🖷 01429 523856 🖱 peter.devlin@hartlepool.gov.uk

Senior Management: Mr Chris Little Chief Financial Officer, Civic Centre, Victoria Road, Hartlepool TS24 8AY ☎ 01429 523003 🖱 chris.little@hartlepool.gov.uk

Senior Management: Mrs Denise Ogden, Director of Regeneration & Neighbourhood Services, Civic Centre, Victoria Road, Hartlepool TS24 8AY ☎ 01429 523808 🖱 denise.ogden@hartlepool.gov.uk

Senior Management: Ms Louise Wallace Director - Public Health, Civic Centre, Victoria Road, Hartlepool TS24 8AY ☎ 01429 284030 🖱 louise.wallace@hartlepool.gov.uk

Best Value: Mr Andrew Atkin, Assistant Chief Executive, Civic Centre, Victoria Road, Hartlepool TS24 8AY ☎ 01429 523003 🖱 andrew.atkin@hartlepool.gov.uk

Children / Youth Services: Mr Mark Smith Head of Integrated Youth Support Services, Civic Centre, Victoria Road, Hartlepool TS24 8AY ☎ 01429 523901 🖱 mark.smith@hartlepool.gov.uk

Civil Registration: Ms Julie Howard Customer & Business Manager, Civic Centre, Victoria Road, Hartlepool TS24 8AY ☎ 01429 284354 🖱 julie.howard@hartlepool.gov.uk

PR / Communications: Mr Alastair Rae, Public Relations Officer, Civic Centre, Victoria Road, Hartlepool TS24 8AY ☎ 01429 523510 🖱 alastair.rae@hartlepool.gov.uk

Community Planning: Mr Damien Wilson Assistant Director of Regeneration & Planning, Civic Centre, Victoria Road, Hartlepool TS24 8AY ☎ 01429 523400 🖱 damien.wilson@hartlepool.gov.uk

Community Safety: Mrs Denise Ogden, Director of Regeneration & Neighbourhood Services, Civic Centre, Victoria Road, Hartlepool TS24 8AY ☎ 01429 523808 🖱 denise.ogden@hartlepool.gov.uk

Community Safety: Mr Damien Wilson Assistant Director of Regeneration & Planning, Civic Centre, Victoria Road, Hartlepool TS24 8AY ☎ 01429 523400 🖱 damien.wilson@hartlepool.gov.uk

Computer Management: Mr Andrew Atkin, Assistant Chief Executive, Civic Centre, Victoria Road, Hartlepool TS24 8AY ☎ 01429 523003 🖱 andrew.atkin@hartlepool.gov.uk

Consumer Protection and Trading Standards: Mr Ian Harrison Principal Trading Standards & Licensing Officer, Bryan Hanson House, Lynn Street, Hartlepool TS24 7BT ☎ 01429 523349 🖱 ian.harrison@hartlepool.gov.uk

Contracts: Mr David Hart Strategic Procurement Manager, Civic Centre, Victoria Road, Hartlepool TS24 8AY ☎ 01429 523495 🖱 david.hart@hartlepool.gov.uk

Corporate Services: Ms Julie Howard Customer & Business Manager, Civic Centre, Victoria Road, Hartlepool TS24 8AY ☎ 01429 284354 🖱 julie.howard@hartlepool.gov.uk

Customer Service: Ms Julie Howard Customer & Business Manager, Civic Centre, Victoria Road, Hartlepool TS24 8AY ☎ 01429 284354 🖱 julie.howard@hartlepool.gov.uk

Direct Labour: Ms Gill Alexander Chief Executive, Civic Centre, Victoria Road, Hartlepool TS24 8AY ☎ 01429 523001 🖱 gill.alexander@hartlepool.gov.uk

Economic Development: Mr Damien Wilson Assistant Director of Regeneration & Planning, Civic Centre, Victoria Road, Hartlepool TS24 8AY ☎ 01429 523400 🖱 damien.wilson@hartlepool.gov.uk

HARTLEPOOL

E-Government: Mr Andrew Atkin, Assistant Chief Executive, Civic Centre, Victoria Road, Hartlepool TS24 8AY ☎ 01429 523003 ✉ andrew.atkin@hartlepool.gov.uk

Electoral Registration: Mr Peter Devlin Chief Solicitor, Civic Centre, Victoria Road, Hartlepool TS24 8AY ☎ 01429 523003 ✉ peter.devlin@hartlepool.gov.uk

Emergency Planning: Mr Robin Beech Emergency Planning Officer, Emergency Planning Unit, Aurora Court, Barton Road, Riverside Park, Middlesbrough TS2 1RY ☎ 01642 232442 🖷 01642 224926 ✉ robin.beech@hartlepool.gov.uk

Environmental / Technical Services: Mr Alastair Smith, Assistant Director of Neighbourhoods, Civic Centre, Victoria Road, Hartlepool TS24 8AY ☎ 01429 523802 ✉ alastair.smith@hartlepool.gov.uk

Environmental Health: Mr Adrian Hurst Principal Environmental Health Officer, Civic Centre, Victoria Road, Hartlepool TS24 8AY ☎ 01429 523323 ✉ adrian.hurst@hartlepool.gov.uk

Estates, Property & Valuation: Mr Alastair Smith, Assistant Director of Neighbourhoods, Civic Centre, Victoria Road, Hartlepool TS24 8AY ☎ 01429 523802 ✉ alastair.smith@hartlepool.gov.uk

Finance: Mr Chris Little Chief Financial Officer, Civic Centre, Victoria Road, Hartlepool TS24 8AY ☎ 01429 523003 ✉ chris.little@hartlepool.gov.uk

Fleet Management: Mr Alastair Smith, Assistant Director of Neighbourhoods, Civic Centre, Victoria Road, Hartlepool TS24 8AY ☎ 01429 523802 ✉ alastair.smith@hartlepool.gov.uk

Grounds Maintenance: Mrs Denise Ogden, Director of Regeneration & Neighbourhood Services, Civic Centre, Victoria Road, Hartlepool TS24 8AY ☎ 01429 523808 ✉ denise.ogden@hartlepool.gov.uk

Health and Safety: Ms Rachel Price Health, Safety & Wellbeing Manager, Civic Centre, Victoria Road, Hartlepool TS24 8AY ☎ 01429 523560 ✉ rachel.price2@hartlepool.gov.uk

Highways: Mr Alastair Smith, Assistant Director of Neighbourhoods, Bryan Hanson House, Lynn Street, Hartlepool TS24 8BT ☎ 01429 523802 ✉ alastair.smith@hartlepool.gov.uk

Legal: Mr Peter Devlin Chief Solicitor, Civic Centre, Victoria Road, Hartlepool TS24 8AY ☎ 01429 523003 🖷 01429 523856 ✉ peter.devlin@hartlepool.gov.uk

Licensing: Mr Ian Harrison Principal Trading Standards & Licensing Officer, Bryan Hanson House, Lynn Street, Hartlepool TS24 7BT ☎ 01429 523349 ✉ ian.harrison@hartlepool.gov.uk

Lighting: Mr Bob Golightly Street Lighting Controller, Church Street, Hartlepool TS24 7BT ☎ 01429 523254 ✉ bob.golightly@hartlepool.gov.uk

Member Services: Mrs Lorraine Bennison Principal Registration & Members Services Officer, Civic Centre, Victoria Road, Hartlepool TS24 8AY ☎ 01429 523017 ✉ lorraine.bennison@hartlepool.gov.uk

Parking: Mr Alastair Smith, Assistant Director of Neighbourhoods, Civic Centre, Victoria Road, Hartlepool TS24 8AY ☎ 01429 523802 ✉ alastair.smith@hartlepool.gov.uk

Partnerships: Mrs Catherine Grimwood Performance & Partnerships Manager, Civic Centre, Victoria Road, Hartlepool TS24 8AY ☎ 01429 284322 ✉ catherine.grimwood@hartlepool.gov.uk

Procurement: Mr David Hart Strategic Procurement Manager, Civic Centre, Victoria Road, Hartlepool TS24 8AY ☎ 01429 523495 ✉ david.hart@hartlepool.gov.uk

Recycling & Waste Minimisation: Mrs Denise Ogden, Director of Regeneration & Neighbourhood Services, Civic Centre, Victoria Road, Hartlepool TS24 8AY ☎ 01429 523808 ✉ denise.ogden@hartlepool.gov.uk

Recycling & Waste Minimisation: Ms Fiona Srogi, Waste Services Officer, Church Street, Lynn Street Depot, Hartlepool TS24 7BT ☎ 01429 523829 ✉ fiona.srogi@hartlepool.gov.uk

Regeneration: Mr Damien Wilson Assistant Director of Regeneration & Planning, Civic Centre, Victoria Road, Hartlepool TS24 8AY ☎ 01429 523400 ✉ damien.wilson@hartlepool.gov.uk

Road Safety: Mr Paul Watson, Road Safety Officer, Church Street, Lynn Street Depot, Hartlepool TS24 7BT ☎ 01429 523590 🖷 01429 860830 ✉ paul.watson@hartlepool.gov.uk

Social Services (Adult): Ms Geraldine Martin Head of Adult Services, Civic Centre, Victoria Road, Hartlepool TS24 8AY ☎ 01429 266522 ✉ geraldine.martin@hartlepool.gov.uk

Social Services (Children): Mr Mark Smith Head of Integrated Youth Support Services, Civic Centre, Victoria Road, Hartlepool TS24 8AY ☎ 01429 523901 ✉ mark.smith@hartlepool.gov.uk

Public Health: Ms Louise Wallace Director - Public Health, Civic Centre, Victoria Road, Hartlepool TS24 8AY ☎ 01429 284030 ✉ louise.wallace@hartlepool.gov.uk

Street Scene: Mrs Denise Ogden, Director of Regeneration & Neighbourhood Services, Civic Centre, Victoria Road, Hartlepool TS24 8AY ☎ 01429 523808 ✉ denise.ogden@hartlepool.gov.uk

Sustainable Communities: Mr Damien Wilson Assistant Director of Regeneration & Planning, Civic Centre, Victoria Road, Hartlepool TS24 8AY ☎ 01429 523400 ✉ damien.wilson@hartlepool.gov.uk

Town Centre: Mrs Denise Ogden, Director of Regeneration & Neighbourhood Services, Civic Centre, Victoria Road, Hartlepool TS24 8AY ☎ 01429 523808 ✉ denise.ogden@hartlepool.gov.uk

Traffic Management: Mr Alastair Smith, Assistant Director of Neighbourhoods, Bryan Hanson House, Lynn Street, Hartlepool TS24 8BT ☎ 01429 523802 ✉ alastair.smith@hartlepool.gov.uk

Transport: Mr Alastair Smith, Assistant Director of Neighbourhoods, Bryan Hanson House, Lynn Street, Hartlepool TS24 8BT ☎ 01429 523802 ✉ alastair.smith@hartlepool.gov.uk

Transport Planner: Mr Alastair Smith, Assistant Director of Neighbourhoods, Civic Centre, Victoria Road, Hartlepool TS24 8AY ☎ 01429 523802 ✉ alastair.smith@hartlepool.gov.uk

Waste Collection and Disposal: Mrs Denise Ogden, Director of Regeneration & Neighbourhood Services, Civic Centre, Victoria Road, Hartlepool TS24 8AY ☎ 01429 523808 ✉ denise.ogden@hartlepool.gov.uk

Waste Management: Mrs Denise Ogden, Director of Regeneration & Neighbourhood Services, Civic Centre, Victoria Road, Hartlepool TS24 8AY ☎ 01429 523808 ✉ denise.ogden@hartlepool.gov.uk

COUNCILLORS

***Ceremonial Mayor* Fleet**, Mary (LAB - Jesmond)
mary.fleet@hartlepool.gov.uk

***Leader of the Council* Akers-Belcher**, Christopher (LAB - Foggy Furze)
christopher.akers-belcher@hartlepool.gov.uk

***Deputy Leader of the Council* Richardson**, Carl (LAB - Victoria)
carl.richardson@hartlepool.gov.uk

Ainslie, Jim (LAB - Headland & Harbour)
jim.ainslie@hartlepool.gov.uk

Akers-Belcher, Stephen (LAB - Manor House)
stephen.akers-belcher@hartlepool.gov.uk

Atkinson, Kelly (O - Seaton)
kelly.atkinson@hartlepool.gov.uk

Barclay, Allan (LAB - Manour House)
allan.barclay@hartlepool.gov.uk

Beck, Paul (LAB - Hart)
paul.beck@hartlepool.gov.uk

Belcher, Sandra (LAB - Jesmond)
sandra.belcher@hartlepool.gov.uk

Brash, Jonathan (IND - Burn Valley)
jonathan.brash@hartlepool.gov.uk

Clark, Alan (LAB - Fens & Rossmere)
alan.clark@hartlepool.gov.uk

Cook, Rob (LAB - De Bruce)
rob.cook@hartlepool.gov.uk

Cranney, Kevin (LAB - Foggy Furze)
kevin.cranney@hartlepool.gov.uk

Gibbon, Steve (IND - Fens & Rossmere)
steve.gibbon@hartlepool.gov.uk

Griffin, Sheila (LAB - De Bruce)
sheila.griffin@hartlepool.gov.uk

Hall, Gerald (LAB - Burn Valley)
gerard.hall@hartlepool.gov.uk

Hind, Thomas (UKIP - Seaton)
tom.hind@hartlepool.gov.uk

Jackson, Peter (LAB - Headland & Harbour)
peter.jackson@hartlepool.gov.uk

James, Marjorie (LAB - Manor House)
marjoriejames45@yahoo.co.uk

Lauderdale, John (IND - Burn Valley)
john.lauderdale@hartlepool.gov.uk

Lawton, Trisha (LAB - Victoria)
patirica.lawton@ntlworld.com

Lindridge, James (LAB - Fens & Rossmere)
jim.lindridge@hartlepool.gov.uk

Lyons, Brenda (CON - Rural West)
brenda.lyons@hartlepool.gov.uk

Martin-Wells, Ray (CON - Rural West)
ray.martin-wells@hartlepool.gov.uk

Morris, George (CON - Rural West)
george.morris@hartlepool.gov.uk

Riddle, David (IND - Hart)
david.riddle@hartlepool.gov.uk

Robinson, Jean (LAB - Hart)

Simmons, Chris (LAB - Victoria)
chris.simmons@hartlepool.gov.uk

Sirs, Kaylee (LAB - Foggy Furze)
kaylee.sirs@hartlepool.gov.uk

Springer, George (UKIP - Jesmond)
george.springer@hartlepool.gov.uk

Tempest, Sylvia (LAB - Headland & Harbour)
sylvia.tempest@hartlepool.gov.uk

Thomas, Stephen (LAB - De Bruce)
stephen.thomas@hartlepool.gov.uk

Thompson, Paul (IND - Seaton) paul.thompson@hartlepool.gov.uk

POLITICAL COMPOSITION

LAB: 22, IND: 5, CON: 3, UKIP: 2, O: 1

COMMITTEE CHAIRS

Adult Services: Mr Paul Beck

Adult Services: Mr Carl Richardson

Audit: Mr Ray Martin-Wells

Children Services: Mr Chris Simmons

Finance & Policy: Mr Christopher Akers-Belcher

Health & Wellbeing: Mr Christopher Akers-Belcher

Licensing: Mr George Morris

Planning: Mr Rob Cook

Hastings D

Hastings Borough Council, Town Hall, Queen's Road, Hastings TN34 1QR
☎ 01424 451066 🖷 01424 781743 💻 www.hastings.gov.uk

FACTS AND FIGURES

Parliamentary Constituencies: Hastings and Rye
EU Constituencies: South East
Election Frequency: Elections are biennial

PRINCIPAL OFFICERS

Chief Executive: Ms Jane Hartnell Director of Corporate Services & Governance (Head of Paid Service), Aquila House, Breeds Place, Hastings TB34 3UY ☎ 01424 451482 🖷 01424 451732 ✉ jhartnell@hastings.gov.uk

HASTINGS

Senior Management: Ms Monica Adams-Acton, Assistant Director - Regeneration & Culture, Aquila House, Breeds Place, Hastings TN34 3UY ☎ 01424 451749 🖷 01424 451749 ✉ madams-acton@hastings.gov.uk

Senior Management: Mr Peter Grace Assistant Director - Financial Services & Revenues, Aquila House, Breeds Place, Hastings TN34 3UY ☎ 01424 451503 🖷 01424 781515 ✉ pgrace@hastings.gov.uk

Senior Management: Mr Mike Hepworth Assistant Director - Environment & Place, Aquila House, Breeds Place, Hastings TN34 3UY ☎ 01424 783332 ✉ mhepworth@hastings.gov.uk

Senior Management: Mr Simon Hubbard, Director - Operational Services, Aquila House, Breeds Place, Hastings TN34 3UY ☎ 01424 451753 ✉ shubbard@hastings.gov.uk

Senior Management: Mr Andrew Palmer Assistant Director - Housing & Built Environment, Aquilia House, Breeds Place, Hastings TN34 3UY ☎ 01424 451316 🖷 01424 781305 ✉ apalmer@hastings.gov.uk

Architect, Building / Property Services: Mrs Amy Terry Estates Manager, Aquila House, Breeds Place, Hastings TN34 3UY ☎ 01424 451640 🖷 01424 451515 ✉ aterry@hastings.gov.uk

Best Value: Mr Tom Davies Chief Auditor, Town Hall, Queen's Road, Hastings TN34 1QR ☎ 01424 451524 ✉ tdavies@hastings.gov.uk

Building Control: Mr Brian Bristow Building Control Manager, Bexhill Town Hall, Bexhill-on-Sea TN39 3JX ☎ 01424 787680 ✉ brian.bristow@rother.gov.uk

Children / Youth Services: Mr Emile Tambeh Youth & Senior's Participation Officer, Town Hall, Queen's Road, Hastings TN34 1QR ☎ 01424 451760 ✉ etambeh@hastings.gov.uk

PR / Communications: Mr Kevin Boorman, Marketing & Major Projects Manager, Aquila House, Breeds Place, Hastings TN34 3UY ☎ 01424 451123 🖷 01424 781743 ✉ kboorman@hastings.gov.uk

Community Safety: Mr Mike Fagan Community Safety Manager, Aquila House, Breeds Place, Hastings TN34 3UY ☎ 01424 451438 ✉ mfagan@hastings.gov.uk

Computer Management: Mr Mark Bourne, Head of Information Technology, Aquila House, Breeds Place, Hastings TN34 3UY ☎ 01424 451414 🖷 01424 781401 ✉ mbourne@hastings.gov.uk

Corporate Services: Mr Stephen Dodson Accommodation & Transformation Manager, Town Hall, Queen's Road, Hastings TN34 1QR ☎ 01424 783326 ✉ sdodson@hastings.gov.uk

Customer Service: Ms Natasha Tewkesbury Corporate Customer Services Manager, Town Hall, Queen's Road, Hastings TN34 1QR ☎ 01424 451709 ✉ ntewkesbury@hastings.gov.uk

Economic Development: Ms Monica Adams-Acton, Assistant Director - Regeneration & Culture, Aquila House, Breeds Place, Hastings TN34 3UY ☎ 01424 451749 🖷 01424 451749 ✉ madams-acton@hastings.gov.uk

E-Government: Mr Mark Bourne, Head of Information Technology, Aquila House, Breeds Place, Hastings TN34 3UY ☎ 01424 451414 🖷 01424 781401 ✉ mbourne@hastings.gov.uk

Electoral Registration: Mrs Katrina Silverson Electoral Services Manager, Aquila House, Breeds Place, Hastings TN34 3UY ☎ 01424 451747 🖷 01424 451732 ✉ ksilverson@hastings.gov.uk

Emergency Planning: Mr Mike Hepworth Assistant Director - Environment & Place, Aquila House, Breeds Place, Hastings TN34 3UY ☎ 01424 783332 ✉ mhepworth@hastings.gov.uk

Environmental / Technical Services: Mr Mike Hepworth Assistant Director - Environment & Place, Aquila House, Breeds Place, Hastings TN34 3UY ☎ 01424 783332 ✉ mhepworth@hastings.gov.uk

Estates, Property & Valuation: Mrs Amy Terry Estates Manager, Aquila House, Breeds Place, Hastings TN34 3UY ☎ 01424 451640 🖷 01424 451515 ✉ aterry@hastings.gov.uk

Events Manager: Mr Kevin Boorman, Marketing & Major Projects Manager, Aquila House, Breeds Place, Hastings TN34 3UY ☎ 01424 451123 🖷 01424 781743 ✉ kboorman@hastings.gov.uk

Facilities: Mr Mike Hepworth Assistant Director - Environment & Place, Aquila House, Breeds Place, Hastings TN34 3UY ☎ 01424 783332 ✉ mhepworth@hastings.gov.uk

Finance: Mr Peter Grace Assistant Director - Financial Services & Revenues, Aquila House, Breeds Place, Hastings TN34 3UY ☎ 01424 451503 🖷 01424 781515 ✉ pgrace@hastings.gov.uk

Finance: Mr Alan Mitchell Chief Accountant, Town Hall, Queen's Road, Hastings TN34 1QR ☎ 01424 451520 🖷 01424 451515 ✉ amitchell@hastings.gov.uk

Treasury: Mr Alan Mitchell Chief Accountant, Town Hall, Queen's Road, Hastings TN34 1QR ☎ 01424 451520 🖷 01424 451515 ✉ amitchell@hastings.gov.uk

Grounds Maintenance: Mrs Virginia Gilbert Head of Amenities, Resorts & Leisure, Aquila House, Breeds Place, Hastings TN34 3UY ☎ 01424 451956 🖷 01424 451133 ✉ vgilbert@hastings.gov.uk

Health and Safety: Mr Mike Hepworth Assistant Director - Environment & Place, Aquila House, Breeds Place, Hastings TN34 3UY ☎ 01424 783332 ✉ mhepworth@hastings.gov.uk

Highways: Mr Mike Hepworth Assistant Director - Environment & Place, Aquila House, Breeds Place, Hastings TN34 3UY ☎ 01424 783332 ✉ mhepworth@hastings.gov.uk

Housing: Mr Andrew Palmer Assistant Director - Housing & Built Environment, Aquilia House, Breeds Place, Hastings TN34 3UY ☎ 01424 451316 🖷 01424 781305 ✉ apalmer@hastings.gov.uk

Legal: Ms Christine Barkshire-Jones Chief Legal Officer, Aquila House, Breeds Place, Hastings TN34 3UY ☎ 01424 451731 🖷 01424 781732 ✉ cbarkshire-jones@hastings.gov.uk

Leisure and Cultural Services: Ms Monica Adams-Acton, Assistant Director - Regeneration & Culture, Aquila House, Breeds Place, Hastings TN34 3UY ☎ 01424 451749 🖷 01424 451749 ✉ madams-acton@hastings.gov.uk

Licensing: Mr Bob Brown, Licensing Manager, Aquila House, Breeds Place, Hastings TN34 3UY ☎ 01424 783249 ✉ bbrown@hastings.gov.uk

Member Services: Mr Mark Horan Senior Corporate & Democratic Services Officer, Aquila House, Breeds Place, Hastings TB34 3UY ☎ 01424 451485 ✉ mhoran@hastings.gov.uk

Parking: Mr Mike Hepworth Assistant Director - Environment & Place, Aquila House, Breeds Place, Hastings TN34 3UY ☎ 01424 783332 ✉ mhepworth@hastings.gov.uk

Personnel / HR: Mrs Verna Connolly, Executive Manager - People, Customer & Business Support, Town Hall, Queen's Road, Hastings TN34 1QR ☎ 01424 451707 🖷 01424 451769 ✉ vconnolly@hastings.gov.uk

Planning: Mr Andrew Palmer Assistant Director - Housing & Built Environment, Aquila House, Breeds Place, Hastings TN34 3UY ☎ 01424 451316 🖷 01424 781305 ✉ apalmer@hastings.gov.uk

Recycling & Waste Minimisation: Mr Mike Hepworth Assistant Director - Environment & Place, Aquila House, Breeds Place, Hastings TN34 3UY ☎ 01424 783332 ✉ mhepworth@hastings.gov.uk

Regeneration: Ms Monica Adams-Acton, Assistant Director - Regeneration & Culture, Aquila House, Breeds Place, Hastings TN34 3UY ☎ 01424 451749 🖷 01424 451749 ✉ madams-acton@hastings.gov.uk

Staff Training: Mrs Verna Connolly, Executive Manager - People, Customer & Business Support, Town Hall, Queen's Road, Hastings TN34 1QR ☎ 01424 451707 🖷 01424 451769 ✉ vconnolly@hastings.gov.uk

Street Scene: Mr Mike Hepworth Assistant Director - Environment & Place, Aquila House, Breeds Place, Hastings TN34 3UY ☎ 01424 783332 ✉ mhepworth@hastings.gov.uk

Tourism: Mr Kevin Boorman, Marketing & Major Projects Manager, Aquila House, Breeds Place, Hastings TN34 3UY ☎ 01424 451123 🖷 01424 781743 ✉ kboorman@hastings.gov.uk

Town Centre: Mr Robert Woods, Town Centre Manager, Summerfields Business Centre, Bohemia Road, Hastings TN34 1UT ☎ 01424 205516 ✉ rwoods@hastings.gov.uk

Waste Collection and Disposal: Mr Mike Hepworth Assistant Director - Environment & Place, Aquila House, Breeds Place, Hastings TN34 3UY ☎ 01424 783332 ✉ mhepworth@hastings.gov.uk

Waste Management: Mr Richard Homewood, Director - Environmental Services, Aquila House, Breeds Place, Hastings TN34 3UY ☎ 01424 783200 ✉ rhomewood@hastings.gov.uk

Children's Play Areas: Mr Mike Hepworth Assistant Director - Environment & Place, Aquila House, Breeds Place, Hastings TN34 3UY ☎ 01424 783332 ✉ mhepworth@hastings.gov.uk

COUNCILLORS

***Leader of the Council* Chowney**, Peter (LAB - Tressell)
cllr.peter.chowney@hastings.gov.uk

***Deputy Leader of the Council* Forward**, Kim (LAB - Gensing)
cllr.kim.forward@hastings.gov.uk

Atkins, Liam (CON - Conquest)
cllr.liam.atkins@hastings.gov.uk

Batsford, Andy (LAB - St Helens)
cllr.andy.batsford@hastings.gov.uk

Beaney, Sue (LAB - Braybrooke)
cllr.sue.beaney@hastings.gov.uk

Beaver, Matthew (CON - West St Leonards)
cllr.matthew.beaver@hastings.gov.uk

Cartwright, Andrew (LAB - Gensing)
cllr.andrew.cartwright@hastings.gov.uk

Charlesworth, Maureen (CON - Maze Hill)
cllr.maureen.charlesworth@hastings.gov.uk

Charman, Tania (LAB - Tressell)
cllr.tania.charman@hastings.gov.uk

Clark, Lee (LAB - Castle)
cllr.lee.clark@hastings.gov.uk

Cooke, Robert (CON - Ashdown)
cllr.robert.cooke@hastings.gov.uk

Davies, Warren (LAB - Baird)
cllr.warren.davies@hastings.gov.uk

Dowling, Bruce (LAB - Hollington)
cllr.bruce.dowling@hastings.gov.uk

Edwards, Michael (CON - Ashdown)
cllr.mike.edwards@hastings.gov.uk

Fitzgerald, Colin (LAB - Silverhill)
cllr.colin.fitzgerald@hastings.gov.uk

Hodges, John (LAB - Old Hastings)
cllr.john.hodges@hastings.gov.uk

Howard, Mike (LAB - West St Leonards)
cllr.mike.howard@hastings.gov.uk

Lee, Rob (CON - Maze Hill)
cllr.rob.lee@hastings.gov.uk

Poole, Dawn (LAB - Old Hastings)
cllr.dawn.poole@hastings.gov.uk

Pragnell, Peter (CON - Conquest)
cllr.peter.pragnell@hastings.gov.uk

Roberts, Alan (LAB - Wishing Tree)
cllr.alan.roberts@hastings.gov.uk

Rogers, Judy (LAB - Castle)
cllr.judy.rogers@hastings.gov.uk

Sabetian, Dominic (LAB - Braybrooke)
cllr.dominic.sabetian@hastings.gov.uk

Scott, Philip (LAB - Wishing Tree)
cllr.philip.scott@hastings.gov.uk

Sinden, Nigel (LAB - Silverhill)
cllr.nigel.sinden@hastings.gov.uk

Street, Richard (LAB - Ore)
cllr.richard.street@hastings.gov.uk

Turner, Mike (LAB - Baird)
cllr.mike.turner@hastings.gov.uk

Webb, Trevor (LAB - Central St Leonards)
cllr.trevor.webb@hastings.gov.uk

Westley, Emily (LAB - Hollington)
cllr.emily.westley@hastings.gov.uk

Wincott, Michael (LAB - Ore)
cllr.michael.wincott@hastings.gov.uk

POLITICAL COMPOSITION
LAB: 23, CON: 7

COMMITTEE CHAIRS
Audit: Mr Matthew Beaver

Licensing: Mr Dominic Sabetian

Planning: Mr Richard Street

Havant D

Havant Borough Council, Public Service Plaza, Civic Centre Road, Havant PO9 2AX
☎ 023 9247 4174 🖷 023 9248 0263 💻 www.havant.gov.uk

FACTS AND FIGURES
Parliamentary Constituencies: Havant
EU Constituencies: South East
Election Frequency: Elections are by thirds

PRINCIPAL OFFICERS
Chief Executive: Ms Sandy Hopkins Joint Chief Executive, Public Service Plaza, Civic Centre Road, Havant PO9 2AX ☎ 023 9244 6150 🖷 023 9248 0263 🖰 sandy.hopkins@havant.gov.uk

Senior Management: Mr Tom Horwood, Executive Director, Public Service Plaza, Civic Centre Road, Havant PO9 2AX ☎ 01730 234025; 023 9244 6151 🖷 01730 267760; 023 9248 0263 🖰 tom.horwood@easthants.gov.uk

Senior Management: Ms Gill Kneller, Executive Director, Public Service Plaza, Civic Centre Road, Havant PO9 2AX ☎ 01730 234004; 023 9244 6151 🖷 01730 234012; 023 9248 0263 🖰 gill.kneller@easthants.gov.uk

Building Control: Mr Robin Seamer Building Control Team Leader, Public Service Plaza, Civic Centre Road, Havant PO9 2AX ☎ 023 9244 6578 🖰 robin.seamer@ehavant.gov.uk

PR / Communications: Mrs Dawn Adey Service Manager of Marketing & Customer Relations, Public Service Plaza, Civic Centre Road, Havant PO9 2AX ☎ 023 9244 6392 🖷 023 9248 0263 🖰 dawn.adey@havant.gov.uk

Community Safety: Mr Tim Pointer Community Team Leader, Public Service Plaza, Civic Centre Road, Havant PO9 2AX ☎ 023 9244 6606 🖷 023 8248 0263 🖰 tim.pointer@havant.gov.uk

Computer Management: Mr Craig Richards IT Partnerships Manager, Public Service Plaza, Civic Centre Road, Havant PO9 2AX ☎ 023 9244 6391 🖷 023 8248 0263 🖰 craig.richards@havant.gov.uk

Corporate Services: Ms Sandy Hopkins Joint Chief Executive, Public Service Plaza, Civic Centre Road, Havant PO9 2AX ☎ 023 9244 6150 🖷 023 9248 0263 🖰 sandy.hopkins@havant.gov.uk

Customer Service: Mrs Janice Newman, Customer Services Manager, Public Service Plaza, Civic Centre Road, Havant PO9 2AX ☎ 023 9244 6040 🖷 023 9248 0263 🖰 janice.newman@havant.gov.uk

Direct Labour: Mr Peter Vince, Operational Services Manager, Southmoor Depot, 2 Penner Road, Havant PO9 1QH ☎ 023 9244 5253 🖰 peter.vince@havant.gov.uk

Economic Development: Mr Jeff Crate, Business Development Officer of Team Leader, Public Service Plaza, Civic Centre Road, Havant PO9 2AX ☎ 023 9244 6615 🖷 023 9244 6545 🖰 jeff.crate@havant.gov.uk

E-Government: Mrs Susan Parker, Service Manager of Organisational Development, Public Service Plaza, Civic Centre Road, Havant PO9 2AX ☎ 023 9244 6493 🖷 023 9248 0263 🖰 susan.parker@havant.gov.uk

Electoral Registration: Mrs Jayne Day, Electoral Services Team Leader, Public Service Plaza, Civic Centre Road, Havant PO9 2AX ☎ 023 9244 6226 🖷 023 9248 0263 🖰 jayne.day@havant.gov.uk

Emergency Planning: Mr Stuart Pinkney, Safety & Emergency Planning Officer, Public Service Plaza, Civic Centre Road, Havant PO9 2AX ☎ 023 9244 6675 🖷 023 9244 6455 🖰 stuart.pinkney@havant.gov.uk

Energy Management: Mr Peter Gammage, Building Services Officer, Public Service Plaza, Civic Centre Road, Havant PO9 2AX ☎ 023 9248 6409 🖷 023 9248 6409 🖰 peter.gammage@havant.gov.uk

Environmental / Technical Services: Mr Steve Perkins Executive Head - Environmental Services, Southmoor Depot, 2 Penner Road, , Havant PO9 2AX ☎ 023 9244 6520 🖰 steve.perkins@havant.gov.uk

Environmental / Technical Services: Mr Peter Vince, Operational Services Manager, Southmoor Depot, 2 Penner Road, Havant PO9 1QH ☎ 023 9244 5253 🖰 peter.vince@havant.gov.uk

Environmental Health: Mrs Lorna Read Interim Service Manager - Environmental Health, Public Service Plaza, Civic Centre Road, , Havant PO9 1QH ☎ 023 9244 6665 🖰 lorna.read@havant.gov.uk

Estates, Property & Valuation: Mr Jon Sanders Service Manager of Facilities, Public Service Plaza, Civic Centre Road, Havant PO9 2AX ☎ 023 9244 6566 🖰 jon.sanders@easthants.gov.uk

European Liaison: Miss Hannah Newbury, Senior Solicitor, Public Service Plaza, Civic Centre Road, Havant PO9 2AX ☎ 023 9244 6213 🖷 023 9248 0263 ✉ hannah.newbury@havant.gov.uk

Facilities: Mr Neil Payne, Facilities Team Leader, Public Service Plaza, Civic Centre Road, Havant PO9 2AX ☎ 023 9244 6646 🖷 023 9244 6240 ✉ neil.payne@havant.gov.uk

Finance: Mrs Jane Eaton Executive Head of Governance, Logistics & S151 Officer, Public Service Plaza, Civic Centre Road, Havant PO9 2AX ☎ 01730 234035; 023 9244 6151 ✉ jane.eaton@havant.gov.uk

Treasury: Mrs Jane Eaton Executive Head of Governance, Logistics & S151 Officer, Public Service Plaza, Civic Centre Road, Havant PO9 2AX ☎ 01730 234035; 023 9244 6151 ✉ jane.eaton@havant.gov.uk

Fleet Management: Mr Peter Vince, Operational Services Manager, Southmoor Depot, 2 Penner Road, Havant PO9 1QH ☎ 023 9244 5253 ✉ peter.vince@havant.gov.uk

Grounds Maintenance: Mr Peter Vince, Operational Services Manager, Southmoor Depot, 2 Penner Road, Havant PO9 1QH ☎ 023 9244 5253 ✉ peter.vince@havant.gov.uk

Highways: Ms Michelle Green Parking & Traffic Management Team Leader, Public Service Plaza, Civic Centre Road, Havant Po9 2AX ☎ 023 9244 6462 🖷 023 9244 6455 ✉ michelle.green@havan.gov.uk

Home Energy Conservation: Mrs Pennie Brown Sustainability Adviser, Public Service Plaza, Civic Centre Road, Havant PO9 2AX ☎ 023 9244 6554 🖷 023 9248 0263 ✉ pennie.smith@havant.gov.uk

Housing: Ms Tracey Howard Service Manager of Housing, Public Service Plaza, Civic Centre Road, Havant PO9 2AX ☎ 023 9244 6626 🖷 023 9248 0263 ✉ tracey.howard@easthants.gov.uk

Legal: Mrs Jo Barden-Hernandez, Head of Legal Services, Public Service Plaza, Civic Centre Road, Havant PO9 2AX ☎ 01730 234068; 023 9244 6212 🖷 023 9248 0263 ✉ jo.barden-hernandez@easthants.gov.uk

Leisure and Cultural Services: Mr Tim Slater Executive Head of Communities, Public Service Plaza, Civic Centre Road, Havant PO9 2AX ☎ 023 9244 6276 ✉ tim.slater@havant.gov.uk

Licensing: Mrs Lorna Read Interim Service Manager - Environmental Health, Public Service Plaza, Civic Centre Road, , Havant PO9 1QH ☎ 023 9244 6665 ✉ lorna.read@havant.gov.uk

Lottery Funding, Charity and Voluntary: Mr Dan Grindey Service Management - Economic Development, Public Service Plaza, Civic Centre Road, Havant PO9 2AX ☎ 023 9244 6177 ✉ dan.grindey@havant.gov.uk

Member Services: Mrs Penny Milne Democratic Services Team Leader, Public Service Plaza, Civic Centre Road, Havant PO9 2AX ☎ 023 9244 6230 ✉ penny.milne@havant.gov.uk

Parking: Ms Michelle Green Parking & Traffic Management Team Leader, Public Service Plaza, Civic Centre Road, Havant PO9 2AX ☎ 023 9244 6462 🖷 023 9244 6455 ✉ michelle.green@havant.gov.uk

Partnerships: Mrs Nicki Conyard Community Regeneration Team Leader, Public Service Plaza, Civic Centre Road, Havant PO9 2AX ☎ 023 9244 6114 ✉ nicki.conyard@havant.gov.uk

Personnel / HR: Ms Caroline Tickner Service Manager of Human Resources, Public Service Plaza, Civic Centre Road, Havant PO9 2AX ☎ 023 9244 6160 🖷 023 9244 6684 ✉ caroline.tickner@havant.gov.uk

Planning: Mrs Julia Potter Executive Head of Economy & Planning, Public Service Plaza, Civic Centre Road, Havant PO9 2AX ☎ 01730 234376; 023 9244 6520 🖷 01730 234385; 023 9244 6588 ✉ julia.potter@easthants.gov.uk

Procurement: Ms Hilda Jackson, Procurement Team Manager, Public Service Plaza, Civic Centre Road, Havant PO9 2AX ☎ 023 9244 6396 🖷 023 9244 6240 ✉ hilda.jackson@havant.gov.uk

Recycling & Waste Minimisation: Mr Peter Vince, Operational Services Manager, Southmoor Depot, 2 Penner Road, Havant PO9 1QH ☎ 023 9244 5253 ✉ peter.vince@havant.gov.uk

Regeneration: Mrs Claire Hughes, Economic Development & Community Manager, Public Service Plaza, Civic Centre Road, Havant PO9 2AX ☎ 023 9244 5235 🖷 023 9249 8031 ✉ claire.hughes@havant.gov.uk

Staff Training: Ms Caroline Tickner Service Manager of Human Resources, Public Service Plaza, Civic Centre Road, Havant PO9 2AX ☎ 023 9244 6160 🖷 023 9244 6684 ✉ caroline.tickner@havant.gov.uk

Sustainable Communities: Mrs Claire Hughes, Economic Development & Community Manager, Public Service Plaza, Civic Centre Road, Havant PO9 2AX ☎ 023 9244 5235 🖷 023 9249 8031 ✉ claire.hughes@havant.gov.uk

Tourism: Mr Jeff Crate, Business Development Officer of Team Leader, Public Service Plaza, Civic Centre Road, Havant PO9 2AX ☎ 023 9244 6615 🖷 023 9244 6545 ✉ jeff.crate@havant.gov.uk

Town Centre: Mr Jeff Crate, Business Development Officer of Team Leader, Public Service Plaza, Civic Centre Road, Havant PO9 2AX ☎ 023 9244 6615 🖷 023 9244 6545 ✉ jeff.crate@havant.gov.uk

Traffic Management: Ms Michelle Green Parking & Traffic Management Team Leader, Public Service Plaza, Civic Centre Road, Havant PO9 2AX ☎ 023 9244 6462 🖷 023 9244 6455 ✉ michelle.green@havant.gov.uk

Transport: Mr Peter Vince, Operational Services Manager, Southmoor Depot, 2 Penner Road, Havant PO9 1QH ☎ 023 9244 5253 ✉ peter.vince@havant.gov.uk

HAVANT

Waste Collection and Disposal: Mr Peter Vince, Operational Services Manager, Southmoor Depot, 2 Penner Road, Havant PO9 1QH ☎ 023 9244 5253 ✉ peter.vince@havant.gov.uk

Waste Management: Mr Peter Vince, Operational Services Manager, Southmoor Depot, 2 Penner Road, Havant PO9 1QH ☎ 023 9244 5253 ✉ peter.vince@havant.gov.uk

COUNCILLORS

***Mayor* Turner**, Leah (CON - Hayling East)
leah.turner@havant.gov.uk

***Deputy Mayor* Ponsonby**, Faith (LD - Battins)
faith.ponsonby@havant.gov.uk

***Leader of the Council* Cheshire**, Michael (CON - Hart Plain)
michael.cheshire@havant.gov.uk

***Deputy Leader of the Council* Briggs**, Anthony (CON - Cowplain)
tony.briggs@havant.gov.uk

Bains, Narinda (CON - Cowplain)
Narinder./Baines@havant.gov.uk

Blackett, Gwendoline (CON - Purbrook)
gwen.blackett@havant.gov.uk

Branson, Jackie (CON - St Faith's)
jackie.branson@havant.gov.uk

Brown, Richard (LAB - Warren Park)
richard.brown@havant.gov.uk

Buckley, Paul (CON - Waterloo)
paul.buckley@havant.gov.uk

Cousins, Ralph (LAB - Battins)
ralph.cousins@havant.gov.uk

Cresswell, Rivka (CON - Emsworth)
Rivka.Cresswell@havant.gov.uk

Edwards, Frida (CON - Bondfields)
frida.edwards@havant.gov.uk

Fairhurst, Michael (CON - Barncroft)
mike.fairhurst@havant.gov.uk

Francis, Beryl (LAB - Warren Park)
beryl.francis@havant.gov.uk

Gibb-Gray, Brendan (CON - Emsworth)
brendan.gibb-gray@havant.gov.uk

Guest, David (CON - St Faith's)
david.guest@havant.gov.uk

Hart, Terence (LAB - Bondfields)
terry.hart@havant.gov.uk

Heard, Rory (CON - Stakes)
rory.heard@havant.gov.uk

Hughes, Gary (CON - Purbrook)
Gary.Hughes@havant.gov.uk

Keast, David (CON - Cowplain)
david.keast@havant.gov.uk

Kerrin, Garry (UKIP - Stakes)
garry.kerrin@havant.gov.uk

Lenaghan, Andrew (CON - Hayling West)
andrew.lenaghan@havant.gov.uk

Mackey, Colin (CON - Emsworth)
colin.mackey@havant.gov.uk

Patrick, Diana (CON - Stakes)
diana.patrick@havant.gov.uk

Perry, John (UKIP - Hayling East)
john.perry@havant.gov.uk

Pierce-Jones, Victor (CON - Hayling West)
victor.pierce-jones@havant.gov.uk

Pike, Tim (CON - St Faith's)
Tim.Pike@havant.gov.uk

Rees, Edward (CON - Bedhampton)
Edward.Rees@havant.gov.uk

Satchwell, Clare (CON - Hayling East)
Clare.Satchwell@Havant.gov.uk

Sceal, Mike (CON - Waterloo)
michael.sceal@havant.gov.uk

Shimbart, Elaine (CON - Hart Plain)
elaine.shimbart@havant.gov.uk

Shimbart, Gerald (CON - Hart Plain)
gerald.shimbart@havant.gov.uk

Smith, Kenneth (CON - Bedhampton)
ken.smith@havant.gov.uk

Smith, David (CON - Bedhampton)
david.smith@havant.gov.uk

Tarrant, Caren (CON - Purbrook)
caren.tarrant@havant.gov.uk

Wade, Peter (CON - Waterloo)
peter.wade@havant.gov.uk

Weeks, Yvonne (CON - Barncroft)
yvonne.weeks@havant.gov.uk

Wilson, Michael (CON - Hayling West)
michael.wilson@havant.gov.uk

POLITICAL COMPOSITION

CON: 31, LAB: 4, UKIP: 2, LD: 1

COMMITTEE CHAIRS

Audit: Mr Kenneth Smith

Development Management: Mr Paul Buckley

Havering L

Havering London Borough Council, Town Hall, Main Road, Romford RM1 3BD
☎ 01708 434343 🖷 01708 432424 ✉ info@havering.gov.uk
🖳 www.havering.gov.uk

FACTS AND FIGURES

Parliamentary Constituencies: Hornchurch and Upminster, Romford
EU Constituencies: London
Election Frequency: Elections are of whole council

PRINCIPAL OFFICERS

Chief Executive: Ms Cheryl Coppell, Chief Executive, Town Hall, Main Road, Romford RM1 3BD ☎ 01708 432062 🖷 01708 432068 ✉ cheryl.coppell@havering.gov.uk

Senior Management: Mr Andrew Blake-Herbert Group Director - Communities & Resources, Town Hall, Main Road, Romford RM1 3BD ☎ 01708 432218 ✉ andrew.blake-herbert@havering.gov.uk

Senior Management: Ms Deborah Hindson Managing Director - oneSource, Fourth Floor, Eastside, Newham, London E16 2QU ☎ 01708 30932 ✉ deborah.hindon@onesource.co.uk

Senior Management: Ms Joy Hollister Group Director of Children, Adults & Housing, Town Hall, Main Road, Romford RM1 3BD ☎ 01708 433804 ✉ joy.hollister@havering.gov.uk

Senior Management: Dr Sue Milner Director - Public Health, Town Hall, Main Road, Romford RM1 3BD ✉ sue.milner@havering.gov.uk

Architect, Building / Property Services: Mr Garry Green, Property Services Manager, Tollgate House, 96 - 98 Market Place, Romford RM1 3ER ☎ 01708 432566 ✉ garry.green@havering.gov.uk

Architect, Building / Property Services: Mr Andrew Skeggs Technical & Facilities Group Manager, River Chambers, 36 High Street, Romford RM1 1HR ☎ 01708 433600 ✉ andy.skeggs@havering.gov.uk

Best Value: Ms Claire Thompson Corporate Policy & Community Manager, Town Hall, Main Road, Romford RM1 3BD ☎ 01708 431003 ✉ claire.thompson@havering.gov.uk

Building Control: Mr Ronald Adams Building Control Team Leader, Town Hall, Main Road, Romford RM1 3BD ☎ 01708 432710 ✉ ron.adams@havering.gov.uk

Building Control: Mr Peter Berry Building Control Team Leader, Town Hall, Main Road, Romford RM1 3BD ☎ 01708 432707 ✉ peter.berry@havering.gov.uk

Catering Services: Mr Dennis Brewin Catering & Traded Services Manager, 7th Floor, Mercury House, Mercury Garden, Romford RM1 3AH ☎ 01708 433211 ✉ dennis.brewin@havering.gov.uk

Children / Youth Services: Ms Kathy Bundred Head of Children's Services, Mercury House, Mercury Gardens, Romford RM1 3SL ☎ 01708 433002 ✉ kathy.bundred@havering.gov.uk

Civil Registration: Ms Louise Edmonds Registration & Bereavement Services Manager, Langtons House, Billte Land, Hornchurch RM1 1XL ☎ 01708 433498 ✉ louise.edmonds@havering.gov.uk

PR / Communications: Mr Mark Leech Head of Communications, Town Hall, Main Road, Romford RM1 3BD ☎ 01708 434373 ✉ mark.leech@havering.gov.uk

Community Planning: Mr Patrick Keyes Head of Regulatory Services, Town Hall, Main Road, Romford RM1 3BD ☎ 01708 432720 ✉ patrick.keyes@havering.gov.uk

Community Safety: Ms Diane Egan Community Safety Team Leader, Town Hall, Main Road, Romford RM1 3BD ☎ 01708 432927 ✉ diane.eagan@havering.gov.uk

Computer Management: Mr Geoff Connell Director - ICT Services, Town Hall, Main Road, Romford RM1 3BD ☎ 01708 432226 ✉ geoff.connell@havering.gov.uk

Consumer Protection and Trading Standards: Mr John Wade, Public Protection Manager, Mercury House, Mercury Gardens, Romford RM1 3SL ☎ 01708 432748 ✉ john.wade@havering.gov.uk

Contracts: Mr Hassan Iqbal, Strategic Procurement Partner, Central Library, St Edwards Way, Romford RM1 3AR ☎ 01708 432541 ✉ hassan.iqbal@havering.gov.uk

Corporate Services: Mr Mark Butler Head of Asset Management, River Chambers, High Street, Romford RM1 1JD ☎ 01708 432947 ✉ mark.butler@havering.gov.uk

Corporate Services: Ms Nikki Richardson, Corporate Support Services Manager, Town Hall, Main Road, Romford RM1 3BD ☎ 01708 432170 ✉ nikki.richardson@havering.gov.uk

Customer Service: Ms Penny Nugent Customer Services Operations Manager, Mercury House, Mercury Gardens, Romford RM1 3SL ☎ 01708 434225 ✉ penny.nugent@havering.gov.uk

Economic Development: Mr Tom Dobrashian Head of Economic Development, Town Hall, Main Road, Romford RM1 3BD ☎ 01708 432583 ✉ tom.dobrashian@havering.gov.uk

Education: Ms Mary Pattinson Head of Learning & Achievement, Mercury House, Mercury Gardens, Romford RM1 3SL ☎ 01708 433808 ✉ mary.pattinson@havering.gov.uk

E-Government: Mr Geoff Connell Director - ICT Services, Town Hall, Main Road, Romford RM1 3BD ☎ 020 8430 2000; 020 8430 2000 ✉ geoff.connell@havering.gov.uk

Electoral Registration: Mr Ronald Adams Building Control Team Leader, Town Hall, Main Road, Romford RM1 3BD ☎ 01708 432710 ✉ ron.adams@havering.gov.uk

Emergency Planning: Mr Alan Clark Emergency Planning & Business Continuity Manager, Mercury House, Mercury Gardens, Romford RM1 3SL ☎ 01708 433206 ✉ alan.clark@havering.gov.uk

Energy Management: Mr Mark Lowers, Energy Strategy Team Leader, Mercury House, Mercury Gardens, Romford RM1 3SL ☎ 01708 432884 ✉ mark.lowers@havering.gov.uk

Environmental / Technical Services: Mr John Wade, Public Protection Manager, Mercury House, Mercury Gardens, Romford RM1 3SL ☎ 01708 432748 ✉ john.wade@havering.gov.uk

Environmental Health: Mr John Wade, Public Protection Manager, Mercury House, Mercury Gardens, Romford RM1 3SL ☎ 01708 432748 ✉ john.wade@havering.gov.uk

Estates, Property & Valuation: Mr Garry Green, Property Services Manager, Mercury House, Mercury Gardens, Romford RM1 3SL ☎ 01708 432566 ✉ garry.green@havering.gov.uk

HAVERING

Events Manager: Mr Michael Thomas Campaigns & Marketing Manager, Town Hall, Main Road, Romford RM1 3BD ☎ 01708 432427 ✉ michael.thomas@havering.gov.uk

Facilities: Mr Andrew Skeggs Technical & Facilities Group Manager, River Chambers, 36 High Street, Romford RM1 1HR ☎ 01708 433600 ✉ andy.skeggs@havering.gov.uk

Finance: Mr Andrew Blake-Herbert Group Director - Communities & Resources, Town Hall, Main Road, Romford RM1 3BD ☎ 01708 432218 ✉ andrew.blake-herbert@havering.gov.uk

Finance: Ms Gillian Clelland Managing Director - oneSource, 4th Floor, Eastside, Newham, London E16 2QU ☎ 01708 434656 ✉ gillian.cleland@onesource.co.uk

Pensions: Ms Tara Philpott Pensions Programme Manager, Central Library, St Edwards Way, Romford RM1 3AR ✉ tara.philpott@havering.gov.uk

Fleet Management: Mr Mark Butler Head of Asset Management, River Chambers, High Street, Romford RM1 1JD ☎ 01708 432947 ✉ mark.butler@havering.gov.uk

Grounds Maintenance: Mr Simon Parkinson, Head of Culture & Leisure Services, Stable Block, Langtons House, Billet Lane, Hornchurch RM11 1XJ ☎ 01708 434014 ✉ simon.parkinson@havering.gov.uk

Health and Safety: Mrs Susan Wilks Corporate Health & Safety and Support Manager, Mercury House, Mercury Gardens, Romford RM1 3SL ☎ 01708 432903 ✉ susan.wilks@havering.gov.uk

Highways: Mr Bob Wenman, Head of Street Care, Mercury House, Mercury Gardens, Romford RM1 3RX ☎ 01708 432898 ✉ bob.wenman@havering.gov.uk

Home Energy Conservation: Mr Mark Lowers, Energy Strategy Team Leader, Mercury House, Mercury Gardens, Romford RM1 3SL ☎ 01708 432884 ✉ mark.lowers@havering.gov.uk

Housing: Mr Brian Partridge Housing Needs & Strategy Manager, 2nd Floor, Mercury House, Mercury Garden, Romford RM1 3SL ☎ ✉ brian.partridge@havering.gov.uk

Housing: Mr Neil Stubbings Head of Homes & Housing, Mercury House, Mercury Gardens, Romford RM1 3RX ✉ neil.stubbings@havering.gov.uk

Housing Maintenance: Mr Kevin Hazelwood Property Services Manager, Homes and Housing Office, Chippenham Road, Harold Hill, Romford RM3 8YQ ☎ 01708 434091 ✉ kevin.hazelwood@havering.gov.uk

Local Area Agreement: Mr Brian Partridge Housing Needs & Strategy Manager, 2nd Floor, Mercury House, Mercury Garden, Romford RM1 3SL ✉ brian.partridge@havering.gov.uk

Legal: Mr Graham White Director - Legal & Governance, Third Floor Estates, Newham Dockside, London E16 2QU ✉ graham.white@havering.gov.uk

Leisure and Cultural Services: Mr Simon Parkinson, Head of Culture & Leisure Services, Stable Block, Langtons House, Billet Lane, Hornchurch RM11 1XJ ☎ 01708 434014 ✉ simon.parkinson@havering.gov.uk

Licensing: Ms Trudi Penman, Licensing & Health & Safety Manager, Mercury House, Mercury Gardens, Romford RM1 3SL ☎ 01708 432718 ✉ trudi.penman@havering.gov.uk

Lifelong Learning: Ms Joy Hollister Group Director of Children, Adults & Housing, Town Hall, Main Road, Romford RM1 3BD ☎ 01708 433804 ✉ joy.hollister@havering.gov.uk

Lifelong Learning: Mrs Mary Pattinson Head of Learning & Achievement, Mercury House, Mercury Gardens, Romford RM1 3SL ☎ 01708 433808 ✉ mary.pattinson@havering.gov.uk

Lighting: Mr Bob Wenman, Head of Street Care, Mercury House, Mercury Gardens, Romford RM1 3RX ☎ 01708 432898 ✉ bob.wenman@havering.gov.uk

Lottery Funding, Charity and Voluntary: Mr Tom Dobrashian Head of Economic Development, Town Hall, Main Road, Romford RM1 3BD ☎ 01708 432583 ✉ tom.dobrashian@havering.gov.uk

Member Services: Mr Andrew Beesley Administration Manager, Town Hall, Main Road, Romford RM1 3BD ☎ 01708 432437 ✉ andrew.beesley@havering.gov.uk

Parking: Mr David Pritchard, Group Manager of Traffic & Parking Control, Mercury House, Mercury Gardens, Romford RM1 3SL ☎ 01708 433123 ✉ david.pritchard@havering.gov.uk

Personnel / HR: Mrs Caroline Nugent Head of Strategic HR & OD, Central Library, St Edwards Way, Romford RM1 3AR ☎ 01708 432181 ✉ caroline.nugent@havering.gov.uk

Planning: Ms Helen Oakerbee Planning Manager - Planning Control, Town Hall, Main Road, Romford RM1 3BD ☎ 01708 432800 ✉ helen.oakerbees@havering.gov.uk

Public Libraries: Ms Ann Rennie Library Service Manager, Central Library, St Edwards Way, Romford RM1 3AR ☎ 01708 434922 ✉ ann.rennie@havering.gov.uk

Recycling & Waste Minimisation: Mr Paul Ellis, Group Manager - Waste Environment Services, Mercury House, Mercury Gardens, Romford RM1 3SL ☎ 01708 432966 ✉ paul.ellis@havering.gov.uk

Social Services: Ms Joy Hollister Group Director of Children, Adults & Housing, Town Hall, Main Road, Romford RM1 3BD ☎ 01708 433804 ✉ joy.hollister@havering.gov.uk

Social Services (Adult): Ms Barbara Nicholls Head - Adult Services, Town Hall, Main Road, Romford RM1 3BD ☎ 01708 433069 ✉ barbara.nicholls@havering.gov.uk

Social Services (Children): Ms Kathy Bundred Head of Children's Services, Mercury House, Mercury Gardens, Romford RM1 3SL ☎ 01708 433002 ✉ kathy.bundred@havering.gov.uk

Public Health: Dr Sue Milner Director - Public Health, Town Hall, Main Road, Romford RM1 3BD ✉ sue.milner@havering.gov.uk

Staff Training: Mr Mark Porter Operational HR Team Leader, Central Library, St Edwards Way, Romford RM1 3AR ☎ 01708 432989 ✉ mark.porter@havering.gov.uk

Street Scene: Mr Bob Wenman, Head of Street Care, Mercury House, Mercury Gardens, Romford RM1 3RX ☎ 01708 432898 ✉ bob.wenman@havering.gov.uk

Sustainable Development: Ms Sheri Lim Sustainability Officer, Mercury House, Mercury Gardens, Romford RM1 3SL ☎ 01708 432590 ✉ sheri.lim@havering.gov.uk

Tourism: Mr Tom Dobrashian Head of Economic Development, Town Hall, Main Road, Romford RM1 3BD ☎ 01708 432583 ✉ tom.dobrashian@havering.gov.uk

Town Centre: Mr Perry Brooker Town Centres Officer, Town Hall, Main Road, Romford RM1 3BD ☎ 01708 432577 ✉ perry.brooker@havering.gov.uk

Traffic Management: Mr Martyn Thomas Development & Transport Manager, Town Hall, Main Road, Romford RM1 3BD ☎ 01708 432845 ✉ martyn.thomas@havering.gov.uk

Transport: Mr Norman Webb Transport Operations Manager, Central Depot, Rainham Road, Hornchurch RM12 5BF ☎ 01708 433163 ✉ norman.webb@havering.gov.uk

Transport Planner: Mr Martyn Thomas Development & Transport Manager, Town Hall, Main Road, Romford RM1 3BD ☎ 01708 432845 ✉ martyn.thomas@havering.gov.uk

Waste Collection and Disposal: Mr Paul Ellis, Group Manager - Waste Environment Services, Mercury House, Mercury Gardens, Romford RM1 3SL ☎ 01708 432966 ✉ paul.ellis@havering.gov.uk

Waste Management: Mr Paul Ellis, Group Manager - Waste Environment Services, Mercury House, Mercury Gardens, Romford RM1 3SL ☎ 01708 432966 ✉ paul.ellis@havering.gov.uk

Waste Management: Mr Bob Wenman, Head of Street Care, Mercury House, Mercury Gardens, Romford RM1 3RX ☎ 01708 432898 ✉ bob.wenman@havering.gov.uk

Children's Play Areas: Mr Simon Parkinson, Head of Culture & Leisure Services, Stable Block, Langtons House, Billet Lane, Hornchurch RM11 1XJ ☎ 01708 434014 ✉ simon.parkinson@havering.gov.uk

COUNCILLORS

***Mayor* Eagling**, Brian (R - Harold Wood)
councillorbrian.eagling@havering.gov.uk

***Deputy Mayor* Crowder**, Philippa (CON - Pettits)
councillorPhilippa.Crowder@havering.gov.uk

***Leader of the Council* Ramsey**, Roger (CON - Emerson Park)
councillorroger.ramsey@havering.gov.uk

***Group Leader* Morgon**, Ray (R - Hacton)
councillorraymond.morgan@havering.gov.uk

***Group Leader* Tucker**, Jeffrey (R - Rainham and Wennington)
councillorjeffrey.tucker@havering.gov.uk

Alexander, June (R - Cranham)
councillorjune.alexander@havering.gov.uk

Barrett, Clarence (R - Cranham)
councillorclarence.barrett@havering.gov.uk

Benham, Robert (CON - Brooklands)
councillorrobert.benham@havering.gov.uk

Best, Ray (CON - Havering Park)
ray.best@havering.gov.uk

Brice-Thompson, Wendy (CON - Romford Town)
councillorwendy.bricethompson@havering.gov.uk

Burton, Michael Deon (R - South Hornchurch)
councillormichaeldeon.burton@havering.gov.uk

Chapman, Joshua (CON - Romford Town)
councillorjoshua.chapman@havering.gov.uk

Crowder, John (CON - Havering Park)
councillorJohn.Crowder@havering.gov.uk

Darvill, Keith (LAB - Heaton)
councillorkeith.darvill@havering.gov.uk

Davis, Meg (CON - Havering Park)
councillorMeg.Davis@havering.gov.uk

de Wulverton, Ian (UKIP - Heaton)
councillorIan.DeWulverton@havering.gov.uk

Dervish, Osman (CON - Pettits)
councillorosman.dervish@havering.gov.uk

Dodin, Nic (R - Hacton)
councillornic.dodin@havering.gov.uk

Donald, Alex (R - Harold Wood)
councillorAlex.Donald@havering.gov.uk

Durant, David (R - Rainham and Wennington)
councillordavid.durant@havering.gov.uk

Ford, Gillian (R - Cranham)
councillorgillian.ford@havering.gov.uk

Frost, Jason (CON - Mawneys)
councillorJason.Frost@havering.gov.uk

Ganly, Jody (R - Hylands)
councillorJody.Ganly@havering.gov.uk

Glanville, John (UKIP - Emerson Park)
councillorJohn.Glanville@havering.gov.uk

Hawthorn, Linda (R - Upminster)
councillorlinda.hawthorn@havering.gov.uk

Hyde, Philip (UKIP - Heaton)
councillorPhilip.Hyde@havering.gov.uk

Johnson, David (UKIP - Gooshays)
councillorDavid.Johnson@havering.gov.uk

Kelly, Steven (CON - Emerson Park)
councillorsteven.kelly@havering.gov.uk

Martin, Phil (UKIP - South Hornchurch)
councillorPhil.Martin@havering.gov.uk

Matthews, Barbara (R - Hacton)
councillorbarbara.matthews@havering.gov.uk

HAVERING

Misir, Robby (CON - Pettits)
councillorrobby.misir@havering.gov.uk

Mugglestone, Barry (R - Elm Park)
councillorBarry.Mugglestone@havering.gov.uk

Mylod, John (R - Saint Andrews)
councillorjohn.mylod@havering.gov.uk

Nunn, Stephanie (R - Elm Park)
councillorStephanie.Nunn@havering.gov.uk

Ower, Ron (R - Upminster)
councillorron.ower@havering.gov.uk

Pain, Gary (CON - Hylands)
councillorgary.pain@havering.gov.uk

Patel, Dilip (CON - Mawneys)
councillorDilip.Patel@havering.gov.uk

Persaud, Viddy (CON - Brooklands)
councillorViddy.Persaud@havering.gov.uk

Roberts, Keith (R - Rainham and Wennington)
councillorKeith.Roberts@havering.gov.uk

Rumble, Patricia (UKIP - Gooshays)
councillorPatricia.Rumble@havering.gov.uk

Smith, Carol (CON - Hylands)
councillorCarol.Smith@havering.gov.uk

Thompson, Frederick (CON - Romford Town)
councillorfrederick.thompson@havering.gov.uk

Trew, Linda (CON - Mawneys)
councillorlinda.trew@havering.gov.uk

Van den Hende, Linda (R - Upminster)
councillorlinda.vandenhende@havering.gov.uk

Wallace, Melvin (CON - Squirrel's Heath)
councillormelvin.wallace@havering.gov.uk

Webb, Lawrence (UKIP - Gooshays)
councillorlawrence.webb@havering.gov.uk

Westwood, Roger (CON - Brooklands)
councillorRobert.Westwood@havering.gov.uk

White, Michael (CON - Squirrel's Heath)
councillormichael.white@havering.gov.uk

White, Damian (CON - Squirrel's Heath)
councillordamian.white@havering.gov.uk

Whitney, Reg (R - Saint Andrews)
councillorReginald.Whitney@havering.gov.uk

Wilkes, Julie (R - Elm Park)
councillorJulie.Wilkes@havering.gov.uk

Williamson, Graham (R - South Hornchurch)
councillorGraham.Williamson@havering.gov.uk

Wise, Darren (R - Harold Wood)
councillorDarren.Wise@havering.gov.uk

Wood, John (R - Saint Andrews)
councillorjohn.wood@havering.gov.uk

POLITICAL COMPOSITION

R: 24, CON: 22, UKIP: 7, LAB: 1

COMMITTEE CHAIRS

Audit: Ms Viddy Persaud

Licensing: Ms Linda Van den Hende

Pensions: Mr John Crowder

Herefordshire U

Herefordshire Council, Plough Lane, Hereford HR4 0LE
☎ 01432 260000 🖷 01432 260286 ✉ info@herefordshire.gov.uk
💻 www.herefordshire.gov.uk

FACTS AND FIGURES

Parliamentary Constituencies: Hereford and Herefordshire South, Herefordshire North
EU Constituencies: West Midlands
Election Frequency: Elections are by thirds

PRINCIPAL OFFICERS

Chief Executive: Mr Alistair Neill Chief Executive, Plough Lane, Hereford HR1 1SH ☎ 01432 260044 ✉ alistair.neill@herefordshire.gov.uk

Senior Management: Ms Jo Davidson Director - Children's Wellbeing, Plough Lane, Hereford HR1 1SH ☎ 01432 260039 ✉ jdavidson@herefordshire.gov.uk

Senior Management: Mr Geoff Hughes, Director - Economy, Communities & Corporate, Plough Lane, Hereford HR1 1SH ☎ 01432 260695 ✉ ghughes@herefordshire.gov.uk

Senior Management: Mr Martin Samuels Director - Adults & Wellbeing, Plough Lane, Hereford HR4 0LE ☎ 01432 260339 ✉ martin.samuels@herefordshire.gov.uk

Senior Management: Mr Rod Thomson Director - Public Health, Plough Lane, Hereford HR1 1SH ☎ 01432 383783 ✉ rod.thomson@herefordshire.gov.uk

Children / Youth Services: Ms Jo Davidson Director - Children's Wellbeing, Plough Lane, Hereford HR1 1SH ☎ 01432 260039 ✉ jdavidson@herefordshire.gov.uk

PR / Communications: Ms Alex Floyd Head of Communications & Engagement, Plough Lane, Hereford HR4 0LE ☎ 01432 383510 ✉ alexandra.floyd@herefordshire.gov.uk

Community Safety: Ms Nina Bridges Sustainable Communities Manager, Plough Lane, Hereford HR4 0LE ☎ 01432 260624 ✉ nbridges@herefordshire.gov.uk

Consumer Protection and Trading Standards: Mr Mike Pigrem Head - Consumer & Business Protection, Blue School House, Blue School Street, Hereford HR1 2ZB ☎ 01432 261658 🖷 01432 261982 ✉ mpigrem@herefordshire.gov.uk

Customer Service: Mr Roger Horton Customer Services Area Manager, Franklin House, 4 Commercial Road, Hereford HR1 2BB ☎ 01432 383828 ✉ roger.horton@herefordshire.gov.uk

Economic Development: Mr Andrew Ashcroft, Assistant Director - Economic, Environment & Cultural Services, Blue School House, Blue School Street, Hereford HR1 2ZB ☎ 01432 383098 ✉ aashcroft@herefordshire.gov.uk

Education: Ms Lisa Fraser Head of Learning Achievement, Plough Lane, Hereford HR4 0LE ☎ 01432 383043 lfraser@herefordshire.gov.uk

Electoral Registration: Ms Colette Maund, Electoral Services Manager, Town Hall, St Owens Street, Hereford HR1 2PJ ☎ 01432 260696 🖷 01432 260114 cmaund@herefordshire.gov.uk

Emergency Planning: Ms Erica Hermon Corporate Services Statutory Manager, Shirehall, St Peter's Square, Hereford HR1 2HY ☎ 01432 261906 ehermon@herefordshire.gov.uk

Environmental / Technical Services: Mr Chris Jenner Environmental Services Manager, Blue School House, Blue School Street, Hereford HR1 2ZB ☎ 01432 261941 cjenner@herefordshire.gov.uk

Environmental Health: Mr Marc Willimont Head of Development Management & Environmental Health, Blue School House, Blue School Street, Hereford HR1 2ZB ☎ 01432 261986 mwillimont@herefordshire.gov.uk

Estates, Property & Valuation: Mr Tony Featherstone, Strategic Asset Manager, Plough Lane, Hereford HR4 0LE ☎ 01432 383368 afeatherstone@herefordshire.gov.uk

European Liaison: Ms Vinia Abesamis, Senior Policy & Funding Officer, Plough Lane, PO Box 4, Hereford HR4 0XH ☎ 01432 383031 🖷 01432 610677 vabesamis@herefordshire.gov.uk

Facilities: Mr Geoffrey Jones Property Operations Manager, Plough Lane, Hereford HR4 0LE ☎ 01432 261532 gjones@herefordshire.gov.uk

Finance: Mr Peter Robinson Director - Resources, Plough Lane, Hereford HR1 1SH ☎ 01432 383519 dpowell@herefordshire.gov.uk

Health and Safety: Mr Phil Chandler Health & Safety Advisor, Shirehall, St. Peter's Square, Hereford HR1 2HY ☎ 01432 260240 phil.chandler@herefordshire.gov.uk

Highways: Mr Richard Ball, Assistant Director - Placed Based Commissioning, Plough Lane, PO Box 236, Hereford HR4 0WZ ☎ 01432 260965 🖷 01432 383031 rball@herefordshire.gov.uk

Housing: Mr Sukhdev Dosanjhu Assistant Director - Homes & Community Services, Plough Lane, Hereford HR4 0LE ☎ 01432 383783 sukhdev.dosanjhu@herefordshire.gov.uk

Legal: Ms Erica Hermon Corporate Services Statutory Manager, Shirehall, St Peter's Square, Hereford HR1 2HY ☎ 01432 261906 ehermon@herefordshire.gov.uk

Leisure and Cultural Services: Mr Mick Ligema Cultural Services Manager, Plough Lane, Hereford HR4 0LE ☎ 01432 260631 mligema@herefordshire.gov.uk

Licensing: Mr Marc Willimont Head of Development Management & Environmental Health, Blue School House, Blue School Street, Hereford HR1 2ZB ☎ 01432 261986 mwillimont@herefordshire.gov.uk

Lifelong Learning: Ms Susan Cobourne Adult & Community Learning, Plough Lane, Hereford HR4 0LE ☎ 01432 383639 scobourne@herefordshire.gov.uk

Member Services: Mrs Michelle Price Governance Services, Shirehall, St. Peters Square, Hereford HR1 2HY ☎ 01432 260024 michelleprice@herefordshire.gov.uk

Personnel / HR: Ms TJ Postles Head of Workforce & OD, Plough Lane, PO Box 4, Hereford HR4 0XH ☎ 01432 261855 tjpostles@herefordshire.gov.uk

Planning: Mr Marc Willimont Head of Development Management & Environmental Health, Blue School House, Blue School Street, Hereford HR1 2ZB ☎ 01432 261986 mwillimont@herefordshire.gov.uk

Procurement: Mr Wayne Welsby Head - Commercial Services, Plough Lane, Hereford HR4 0LE ☎ 01432 261529 wwelsby@herefordshire.gov.uk

Public Libraries: Mr Jonathan Chedgzoy Libraries Manager, Plough Lane, Hereford HR4 0LE ☎ 01432 260557 jchedgzoy@herefordshire.gov.uk

Recycling & Waste Minimisation: Mr Kenton Vigus Waste Disposal Team Leader, Plough Lane, Hereford HR4 0LE ☎ 01432 260169 kvigus@herefordshire.gov.uk

Regeneration: Mr Nick Webster, Economic Development Manager, Plough Lane, Hereford HR4 0LE ☎ 01432 260601 nwebster@herefordshire.gov.uk

Road Safety: Mr Jeremy Callard Team Leader Transport Strategy, Plough Lane, Hereford HR4 0LE ☎ 01432 383437 amann@herefordshire.gov.uk

Social Services (Adult): Mr Martin Samuels Director - Adults & Wellbeing, Plough Lane, Hereford HR4 0LE ☎ 01432 260339 martin.samuels@herefordshire.gov.uk

Social Services (Children): Ms Jo Davidson Director - Children's Wellbeing, Plough Lane, Hereford HR1 1SH ☎ 01432 260039 jdavidson@herefordshire.gov.uk

Public Health: Mr Rod Thomson Director - Public Health, Plough Lane, Hereford HR1 1SH ☎ 01432 383783 rod.thomson@herefordshire.gov.uk

Staff Training: Ms TJ Postles Head of Workforce & OD, Plough Lane, PO Box 4, Hereford HR4 0XH ☎ 01432 261855 tjpostles@herefordshire.gov.uk

Transport: Mr Richard Ball, Assistant Director - Placed Based Commissioning, Plough Lane, PO Box 236, Hereford HR4 0WZ ☎ 01432 260965 🖷 01432 383031 rball@herefordshire.gov.uk

Waste Management: Mr Richard Wood Waste Services Manager, Plough Lane, PO Box 167, Hereford HR4 0WY ☎ 01432 383009 rnwood@hereford.gov.uk

HEREFORDSHIRE

COUNCILLORS

***Chair* Wilcox**, DB (CON - College)
bwilcox@herefordshire.gov.uk

***Vice-Chair* McCaull**, PJ (IND - Leominster South)
pmccaull@herefordshire.gov.uk

***Leader of the Council* Johnson**, AW (CON - Hope End)
ajohnson@herefordshire.gov.uk

***Deputy Leader of the Council* Morgan**, PM (CON - Bishops Frome & Cradley)
pmorgan@herefordshire.gov.uk

***Group Leader* James**, TM (LD - Kington)
tjames@herefordshire.gov.uk

***Group Leader* Matthews**, R (IND - Credenhill)
rmatthews@herefordshire.gov.uk

***Group Leader* Powers**, Anthony (IND - Greyfriars)
anthony.powers@herefordshire.gov.uk

Andrews, PA (LD - Widemarsh)
paandrews@herefordshire.gov.uk

Baker, Bruce (CON - Hampton)
bruce.baker@herefordshire.gov.uk

Bartlett, Jenny (GRN - Leominster East)
jenny.bartlett@herefordshire.gov.uk

Bowen, WLS (IND - Bircher)
sbowen@herefordshire.gov.uk

Bowes, Tracy (IND - Belmont Rural)
tracy.bowes@herefordshire.gov.uk

Bramer, H (CON - Penyard)
hbramer@herefordshire.gov.uk

Butler, Clive (CON - Bobblestock)
clive.butler@herefordshire.gov.uk

Chappell, ACR (IND - Hinton & Hunderton)
cchappell@herefordshire.gov.uk

Cooper, MJK (CON - Weobley)
mcooper2@herefordshire.gov.uk

Crockett, Pauline (IND - Queenswood)
pauline.crockett@herefordshire.gov.uk

Cutter, PGH (CON - Ross East)
pcutter@herefordshire.gov.uk

Durkin, BA (CON - Old Gore)
bdurkin@herefordshire.gov.uk

Edwards, PJ (IND - Newton Farm)
pjedwards@herefordshire.gov.uk

Gandy, Carole (CON - Mortimer)
carole.gandy@herefordshire.gov.uk

Greenow, DW (CON - Hagley)
dgreenow@herefordshire.gov.uk

Guthrie, KS (CON - Sutton Walls)
kguthrie@herefordshire.gov.uk

Hardwick, J (IND - Backbury)
jhardwick1@herefordshire.gov.uk

Harlow, David (CON - Birch)
david.harlow@herefordshire.gov.uk

Harvey, EPJ (IND - Ledbury North)
epjharvey@herefordshire.gov.uk

Holton, Emma (CON - Ledbury South)
emma.holton@herefordshire.gov.uk

Hyde, JA (CON - Ross North)
jhyde@herefordshire.gov.uk

Johnson, Jon (CON - Wormside)
jon.johnson@herefordshire.gov.uk

Kenyon, JLV (IND - Tupsley)
jkenyon@herefordshire.gov.uk

Lester, JG (CON - Three Crosses)
jlester@herefordshire.gov.uk

Lloyd-Hayes, MD (IND - Aylestone Hill)
mlloyd-hayes@herefordshire.gov.uk

Mansell, Mark (IND - Kings Acre)
mark.mansell@herefordshire.gov.uk

Mayo, RL (CON - Ross West)
rmayo@herefordshire.gov.uk

McEvilly, Mark (CON - Saxon Gate)
mark.mcevilly@herefordshire.gov.uk

Michael, SM (IND - Whitecross)
smichael@herefordshire.gov.uk

Newman, Paul (CON - Kerne Bridge)
paul.newman@herefordshire.gov.uk

Norman, FM (GRN - Leominster West)
fnorman@herefordshire.gov.uk

North, Cath (IND - Eign Hill)
cath.north@herefordshire.gov.uk

Phillips, RJ (CON - Arrow)
rjphillips@herefordshire.gov.uk

Powell, Graham (CON - Golden Valley South)
grahampowell@herefordshire.gov.uk

Price, PD (CON - Golden Valley North)
pprice@herefordshire.gov.uk

Rone, P (CON - Redhill)
prone@herefordshire.gov.uk

Round, Andrew (IND - Holmer)
andrew.round@herefordshire.gov.uk

Seldon, A (IND - Bromyard West)
aseldon@herefordshire.gov.uk

Shaw, Nigel (CON - Bromyard Bringsty)
nigel.shaw@herefordshire.gov.uk

Skelton, Clive (CON - Castle)
clive.skelton@herefordshire.gov.uk

Stone, J (CON - Leominster North & Rural)
jstone@herefordshire.gov.uk

Summers, David (IND - Dinedor Hill)
david.summers@herefordshire.gov.uk

Swinglehurst, Elissa (CON - Llangarron)
elissawinglehurst@tiscali.co.uk

Tawn, Len (IND - Central)
len.tawn@herefordshire.gov.uk

West, Andrew (IND - Ledbury West)
andrew.warmington@herefordshire.gov.uk

Williams, Steve (CON - Stoney Street)
steve.williams@herefordshire.gov.uk

POLITICAL COMPOSITION
CON: 29, IND: 20, LD: 2, GRN: 2

COMMITTEE CHAIRS
Audit & Governance: Mr BA Durkin

Health & Social Care: Ms PA Andrews

Planning: Mr PGH Cutter

Hertfordshire C

Hertfordshire County Council, County Hall, Pegs Lane, Hertford SG13 8DE
☎ 01992 555555 🖷 01992 555644 ✉ firstname.lastname@hertscc.gov.uk
💻 www.hertsdirect.org

FACTS AND FIGURES
Parliamentary Constituencies: Hertfordshire South West
EU Constituencies: Eastern
Election Frequency: Elections are of whole council

PRINCIPAL OFFICERS
Chief Executive: Mr John Wood, Chief Executive & Director of Environment, County Hall, Pegs Lane, Hertford SG13 8DF ☎ 01992 555601 🖷 01992 555505 ✉ john.wood@hertfordshire.gov.uk

Deputy Chief Executive: Mrs Sarah Pickup, Deputy Chief Executive, County Hall, Pegs Lane, Hertford SG13 8DE ☎ 01992 555601 🖷 01922 555505 ✉ sarah.pickup@hertfordshire.gov.uk

Senior Management: Ms Jenny Coles Director of Children's Services, County Hall, Pegs Lane, Hertford SG13 8DE ☎ 01992 555755 🖷 01992 555719 ✉ jenny.coles@hertfordshire.gov.uk

Senior Management: Mr Iain MacBeath Director - Health & Community Services, County Hall, Pegs Lane, Hertford SG13 8DE ☎ 01992 556363 🖷 01992 556323 ✉ iain.macbeath@hertfordshire.gov.uk

Senior Management: Mr Jim McManus Director of Public Health, County Hall, Pegs Lane, Hertford SG13 8DE ☎ 01438 845389 ✉ jim.mcmanus@hertfordshire.gov.uk

Senior Management: Mr Roy Wilsher Director of Community Protection & Chief Fire Officer, Service HQ, Old London Road, Hertford SG13 7LD ☎ 01992 507501 🖷 01992 503048 ✉ roy.wilsher@hertfordshire.gov.uk

Best Value: Ms Rebecca Price Head of Performance & Improvement, County Hall, Pegs Lane, Hertford SG13 8DE ☎ 01992 588746 🖷 01992 555930 ✉ rebecca.price@hertfordshire.gov.uk

Building Control: Ms Angela Bucksey Assistant Director - Property, County Hall, Pegs Lane, Hertford SG13 8DE ☎ 01992 556397 🖷 01992 555505 ✉ angela.bucksey@hertfordshire.gov.uk

Catering Services: Ms Lin O'Brien, Head of Hertfordshire Catering, Hertfordshire Business Services, The Mundells, Welwyn Garden City, Hertford AL7 1FT ☎ 01707 293510 ✉ lin.obrien@hertfordshire.gov.uk

Children / Youth Services: Mr Andrew Simmons Deputy Director - Children's Services & Education, County Hall, Pegs Lane, Hertford SG13 8DE ☎ 01992 555503 ✉ andrew.simmons@hertfordshire.gov.uk

Civil Registration: Mr Steve Charteris Head of Democratic & Statutory Services, The Old Courthouse, St Albans Road East, Hatfield AL10 0ES ☎ 01707 897375 🖷 01707 897379 ✉ steve.charteris@hertfordshire.gov.uk

PR / Communications: Ms Lindsay Coulson Head of Communications & Strategic Engagement, County Hall, Pegs Lane, Hertford SG13 8DE ☎ 01992 556655 🖷 01992 555647 ✉ lindsay.coulson@hertfordshire.gov.uk

Computer Management: Mr Stuart Bannerman-Campbell Assistant Director - Improvement & Technology, County Hall, Pegs Lane, Hertford SG13 8DE ☎ 01992 588397 🖷 01992 555505 ✉ stuart.campbell@hertfordshire.gov.uk

Consumer Protection and Trading Standards: Mr Guy Pratt, Assistant Director - Community Protection, Service HQ, Old London Road, Hertford SG13 7LD ☎ 01727 813849 🖷 01727 813829 ✉ guy.pratt@hertfordshire.gov.uk

Contracts: Mr Stuart Bannerman-Campbell Assistant Director - Improvement & Technology, County Hall, Pegs Lane, Hertford SG13 8DE ☎ 01992 588397 🖷 01992 555505 ✉ stuart.campbell@hertfordshire.gov.uk

Customer Service: Mr Michael Francis Head of Customer Service, County Hall, Pegs Lane, Hertford SG13 8DE ☎ 01992 556994 🖷 01992 588550 ✉ michael.francis@hertfordshire.gov.uk

Economic Development: Ms Jan Hayes-Griffin Assistant Director of Planning, Strategy & Communications, County Hall, Pegs Lane, Hertford SG13 8DE ☎ 01992 555203 🖷 01992 555505 ✉ jan.hayes-griffin@hertfordshire.gov.uk

Education: Mr Andrew Simmons Deputy Director - Children's Services & Education, County Hall, Pegs Lane, Hertford SG13 8DE ☎ 01992 555503 ✉ andrew.simmons@hertfordshire.gov.uk

E-Government: Mr Michael Francis Head of Customer Service, County Hall, Pegs Lane, Hertford SG13 8DE ☎ 01992 556994 🖷 01992 588550 ✉ michael.francis@hertfordshire.gov.uk

Electoral Registration: Mr Steve Charteris Head of Democratic & Statutory Services, The Old Courthouse, St Albans Road East, Hatfield AL10 0ES ☎ 01707 897375 🖷 01707 897379 ✉ steve.charteris@hertfordshire.gov.uk

Emergency Planning: Mr John Boulter, Head of Protection (Business), County Hall, Pegs Lane, Hertford SG13 8DE ☎ 01992 555951 ✉ john.boulter@hertfordshire.gov.uk

Estates, Property & Valuation: Ms Angela Bucksey Assistant Director - Property, County Hall, Pegs Lane, Hertford SG13 8DE ☎ 01992 556397 🖷 01992 555505 ✉ angela.bucksey@hertfordshire.gov.uk

HERTFORDSHIRE

Facilities: Ms Angela Bucksey Assistant Director - Property, County Hall, Pegs Lane, Hertford SG13 8DE ☎ 01992 556397 🖷 01992 555505 ✉ angela.bucksey@hertfordshire.gov.uk

Finance: Ms Claire Cook Assistant Director - Finance, County Hall, Pegs Lane, Hertford SG13 8DE ☎ 01992 555555 ✉ claire.cook@hertfordshire.gov.uk

Treasury: Ms Claire Cook Assistant Director - Finance, County Hall, Pegs Lane, Hertford SG13 8DE ☎ 01992 555555 ✉ claire.cook@hertfordshire.gov.uk

Fleet Management: Ms Angela Bucksey Assistant Director - Property, County Hall, Pegs Lane, Hertford SG13 8DE ☎ 01992 556397 🖷 01992 555505 ✉ angela.bucksey@hertfordshire.gov.uk

Health and Safety: Mr James Ottery Health & Safety Manager, County Hall, Pegs Lane, Hertford SG13 8DE ☎ 01992 556677 🖷 01992 555962 ✉ james.ottery@hertfordshire.gov.uk

Highways: Mr Rob Smith, Deputy Director - Environment, County Hall, Pegs Lane, Hertford SG13 8DE ☎ 01992 556121 🖷 01992 556106 ✉ rob.smith@hertfordshire.gov.uk

Legal: Ms Kathryn Pettitt Chief Legal Officer, County Hall, Pegs Lane, Hertford SG13 8DE ☎ 01992 555527 ✉ kathryn.pettitt@hertfordshire.gov.uk

Lifelong Learning: Mr Andrew Bignell Head of Libraries, Culture & Learning, County Hall, Pegs Lane, Hertford SG13 8DE ☎ 01992 588309 🖷 01707 281589 ✉ andrew.bignell@hertfordshire.gov.uk

Member Services: Mr Alex James Head - Corporate Policy & Business Support, County Hall, Pegs Lane, Hertford SG13 8DE ☎ 01992 588259 ✉ alex.james@hertfordshire.gov.uk

Partnerships: Ms Jan Hayes-Griffin Assistant Director of Planning, Strategy & Communications, County Hall, Pegs Lane, Hertford SG13 8DE ☎ 01992 555203 🖷 01992 555505 ✉ jan.hayes-griffin@hertfordshire.gov.uk

Personnel / HR: Ms Karen Grave Interim Head of Human Resources & Organisational Development, County Hall, Pegs Lane, Hertford SG13 8DE ☎ 01992 556653 ✉ karen.grave@hertfordshire.gov.uk

Planning: Ms Jan Hayes-Griffin Assistant Director of Planning, Strategy & Communications, County Hall, Pegs Lane, Hertford SG13 8DE ☎ 01992 555203 🖷 01992 555505 ✉ jan.hayes-griffin@hertfordshire.gov.uk

Procurement: Mr Stuart Bannerman-Campbell Assistant Director - Improvement & Technology, County Hall, Pegs Lane, Hertford SG13 8DE ☎ 01992 588397 🖷 01992 555505 ✉ stuart.campbell@hertfordshire.gov.uk

Public Libraries: Ms Taryn Pearson Assistant Director of Customer Services & Libraries, County Hall, Pegs Lane, Hertford SG13 8DE ☎ 01992 556351 ✉ taryn.pearson@hertfordshire.gov.uk

Recycling & Waste Minimisation: Mr Matthew King Head of Waste Management, County Hall, Pegs Lane, Hertford SG13 8DE ☎ 01992 556160 🖷 01992 556180 ✉ matthew.king@hertfordshire.gov.uk

Regeneration: Mr Jon Tiley, Business Manager - Spatial & Land Use Planning, County Hall, Pegs Lane, Hertford SG13 8DE ☎ 01992 556292 🖷 01992 556290 ✉ jonathan.tiley@hertfordshire.gov.uk

Road Safety: Mr Trevor Mason Safe & Sustainable Journeys Manager, County Hall, Pegs Lane, Hertford SG13 8DE ☎ 01992 556804 🖷 01992 556820 ✉ trevor.mason@hertfordshire.gov.uk

Social Services (Adult): Mr Earl Dutton, Assistant Director of Older People & Physically Disabled People, County Hall, Pegs Lane, Hertford SG13 8DE ☎ 01992 556301 🖷 01992 556323 ✉ earl.dutton@hertscc.gov.uk

Social Services (Adult): Mr Iain MacBeath Director - Health & Community Services, County Hall, Pegs Lane, Hertford SG13 8DE ☎ 01992 556363 🖷 01992 556323 ✉ iain.macbeath@hertfordshire.gov.uk

Social Services (Children): Ms Jenny Coles Director of Children's Services, County Hall, Pegs Lane, Hertford SG13 8DE ☎ 01992 555755 🖷 01992 555719 ✉ jenny.coles@hertfordshire.gov.uk

Staff Training: Ms Samantha Holliday Head of HR Learning & Organisational Development, County Hall, Pegs Lane, Hertford SG13 8DE ☎ 01438 845105 ✉ samantha.holliday@hertscc.gov.uk

Sustainable Communities: Mr John Rumble, Head - Environmental Resource Planning, County Hall, Pegs Lane, Hertford SG13 8DE ☎ 01992 556296 🖷 01992 556290 ✉ john.rumble@hertfordshire.gov.uk

Sustainable Development: Mr Jon Tiley, Business Manager - Spatial & Land Use Planning, County Hall, Pegs Lane, Hertford SG13 8DE ☎ 01992 556292 🖷 01992 556290 ✉ jonathan.tiley@hertfordshire.gov.uk

Transport: Mr Rob Smith, Deputy Director - Environment, County Hall, Pegs Lane, Hertford SG13 8DE ☎ 01992 556121 🖷 01992 556106 ✉ rob.smith@hertfordshire.gov.uk

Transport Planner: Ms Glenda Hardy Head of Admissions & Transport, County Hall, Pegs Lane, Hertford SG13 8DE ☎ 01438 737500 ✉ glenda.hardy@hertfordshire.gov.uk

Transport Planner: Mr Tom Hennessey Business Manager - Transport, Access & Safety, County Hall, Pegs Lane, Hertford SG13 8DE ☎ 01992 588385 ✉ tom.hennessey@hertfordshire.gov.uk

Waste Management: Mr Matthew King Head of Waste Management, County Hall, Pegs Lane, Hertford SG13 8DE ☎ 01992 556160 🖷 01992 556180 ✉ matthew.king@hertfordshire.gov.uk

COUNCILLORS

Leader of the Council **Gordon**, Robert (CON - Goffs Oak and Bury Green)
robert.gordon@hertscc.gov.uk

Deputy Leader of the Council **Hayward**, Chris (CON - Chorleywood)
christopher.hayward@hertscc.gov.uk

Andrews, David (CON - Ware North)
david.andrews@hertscc.gov.uk

Ashley, Derrick (CON - Hitchin South)
derrick.ashley@hertscc.gov.uk

Barfoot, John (CON - Bishop's Stortford East)
john.barfoot@hertscc.gov.uk

Barnard, David (CON - Hitchin Rural)
david.barnard@hertfordshire.gov.uk

Batson, Sherma (LAB - Broadwater)
sherma.batson@hertfordshire.gov.uk

Bedford, Sara (LD - Abbots Langley)
sara.bedford@hertfordshire.gov.uk

Beeching, Roger (CON - Sawbridgeworth)
roger.beeching@hertscc.gov.uk

Bell, Nigel (LAB - Vicarage Holywell)
nigel.bell@hertscc.gov.uk

Billing, Judi (LAB - Hitchin North)
judi.billing@hertfordshire.gov.uk

Bright, Morris (CON - Potters Bar West and Shenley)
morris.bright@hertfordshire.gov.uk

Button, Frances (CON - Oxhey Park)
frances.button@hertscc.gov.uk

Chesterman, Lynn (LAB - Welwyn Garden City South)
lynn.chesterman@sky.com

Cheswright, Rosemary (CON - Braughing)
rose.cheswright@hertfordshire.gov.uk

Churchard, Geoff (LD - Sandridge)
geoff.churchard@hertscc.gov.uk

Clapper, Caroline (CON - Watling)
caroline.clapper@hertscc.gov.uk

Cook, Maureen (LAB - Hatfield North)
maureen.cook@hertfordshire.gov.uk

Cowan, Malcolm (LD - Handside and Peartree)
malcolm.cowan@hertscc.gov.uk

Crawley, Maxine (CON - St Albans Rural)
maxine.crawley@hertscc.gov.uk

Crofton, Ken (CON - Hertford Rural)
ken.crofton@hertfordshire.gov.uk

Douris, Terry (CON - Hemel Hempstead North West)
terry.douris@hertscc.gov.uk

Drury, Steve (LD - Croxley)
david.drury@hertscc.gov.uk

Giles-Medhurst, Stephen (LD - Central Watford & Oxhey)
sgm@cix.co.uk

Gordon, Dreda (LAB - The Colneys)
dreda.gordon@hertfordshire.gov.uk

Hart, Dee (CON - Waltham Cross)
dee.hart@hertscc.gov.uk

Hastrick, Kareen (LD - Meriden Tudor)
kareen.hastrick@hertfordshire.gov.uk

Henry, Richard (LAB - St Nicholas)
richard.henry@hertfordshire.gov.uk

Heritage, Teresa (CON - Harpenden South West)
teresa.heritage@hertscc.gov.uk

Hewitt, David (CON - Cheshunt Central)
david.hewitt@hertscc.gov.uk

Hill, Fiona (CON - Royston)
fiona.hill@hertscc.gov.uk

Hollinghurst, Nicholas (LD - Tring)
nicholas.hollinghurst@hertscc.gov.uk

Hone, Terry (CON - Letchworth South)
terry.hone@hertfordshire.gov.uk

Hunter, Tony (CON - North Herts Rural)
tony.hunter@hertscc.gov.uk

Hutchings, Tim (CON - Hoddesdon North)
tim.hutchings@hertfordshire.gov.uk

Johnston, Sara (CON - Haldens)
sara.johnston@hertscc.gov.uk

Joynes, Anne (LAB - Callowland Leggatts)
acj276@btinternet.com

Kercher, Lorna (LAB - Letchworth North West)
lorna.kercher@sky.com

King, Amanda (LAB - Old Stevenage)
amanda.king@hertfordshire.gov.uk

King, Joan (LAB - South Oxhey)
joan.king@hertfordshire.gov.uk

Knell, Peter (CON - Potters Bar East)
peter.knell@hertfordshire.gov.uk

Lee, Aislinn (LD - St Stephen's)
aislinn.lee@hertscc.gov.uk

Lloyd, David (CON - Bridgewater)
david.lloyd@hertscc.gov.uk

Lloyd, John (LAB - Shephall)
john.lloyd@hertscc.gov.uk

Mason, Paul (CON - Flamstead End and Turnford)
paul.mason@hertfordshire.gov.uk

McAndrew, Graham (CON - Bishop's Stortford Rural)
graham.mcandrew@hertfordshire.gov.uk

McKay, Anthony (CON - Hemel Hempstead South East)
anthony.mckay@hertfordshire.gov.uk

Mills, Roma (LAB - St Albans North)
roma.mills@btinternet.com

Mills-Bishop, Mark (CON - Hatfield Rural)
mark.mills-bishop@hertfordshire.gov.uk

Muir, Michael (CON - Letchworth East and Baldock)
michael.muir@hertscc.gov.uk

O'Brien, Steve (CON - Bushey North)
steve.obrien@hertscc.gov.uk

Parker, Robin (LD - Chells)
robin.parker@hertscc.gov.uk

Plancey, Alan (CON - Borehamwood South)
alan.plancey@hertfordshire.gov.uk

Prowse, Robert (LD - St Albans East)
robert.prowse@hertscc.gov.uk

Quilty, Seamus (CON - Bushey South)
seamus.quilty@hertscc.gov.uk

Reay, Ian (CON - Berkhamsted)
ian.reay@hertscc.gov.uk

Reefe, Leon (LAB - Borehamwood North)
leon.reefe@hertfordshire.gov.uk

Roberts, Richard (CON - Kings Langley)
richard.roberts@hertscc.gov.uk

Ruffles, Peter (CON - St Andrews)
peter.ruffles@hertscc.gov.uk

Sangster, Ralph (CON - Rickmansworth)
ralph.sangster@hertfordshire.gov.uk

Scudder, Derek (LD - Woodside Stanborough)
derek.scudder@hertscc.gov.uk

Searing, Alan (CON - Hoddesdon South)
alan.searing@hertscc.gov.uk

Smith, Richard (CON - Welwyn)
richard.smith@hertscc.gov.uk

Stevenson, Andrew (CON - Hertford All Saints)
andrew.stevenson@hertfordshire.gov.uk

Stevenson, Andrew (CON - All Saints)
andrew.stevenson@hertfordshire.gov.uk

Taylor, Sharon (LAB - Bedwell)
sharon.taylor@stevenage.gov.uk

Taylor, Jeanette (CON - Ware South)
jeanette.taylor@hertfordshire.gov.uk

Thake, Richard (CON - Knebworth and Codicote)
richard.thake@hertscc.gov.uk

Tindell, Ron (LD - Hemel Hempstead St Pauls)
ron.tindall@hertscc.gov.uk

Walkington, Sandy (LD - St Albans South)
sandy.walkington@hertfordshire.gov.uk

Watkin, Mark (LD - Nascot Park)
mark.watkin@hertscc.gov.uk

White, Chris (LD - St Albans Central)
chriswhite@cix.co.uk

Williams, Andrew (CON - Hemel Hempstead East)
andrew.williams@hertscc.gov.uk

Williams, David (CON - Harpenden North East)
david.williams@hertfordshire.gov.uk

Woodward, Colin (CON - Bishop's Stortford West)
colin.woodward@hertscc.gov.uk

Wyatt-Lowe, William (CON - Hemel Hempstead Town)
william.wyatt-lowe@hertfordshire.gov.uk

Wyatt-Lowe, Colette (CON - Hemel Hempstead North)
colette.wyatt-lowe@hertscc.gov.uk

Zukowskyj, Paul (LD - Hatfield South)
paul.zukowskyj@hertfordshire.gov.uk

POLITICAL COMPOSITION

CON: 47, LD: 16, LAB: 15

COMMITTEE CHAIRS

Audit: Mr Andrew Williams

Development Control: Mr Ian Reay

Pensions: Mr Chris Hayward

Hertsmere D

Hertsmere Borough Council, Civic Office, Elstree Way, Borehamwood WD6 1WA
☎ 020 8207 2277 🖷 020 8207 7441 ✉ customer.services@hertsmere.gov.uk 💻 www.hertsmere.gov.uk

FACTS AND FIGURES

Parliamentary Constituencies: Hertsmere
EU Constituencies: Eastern
Election Frequency: Elections are by thirds

PRINCIPAL OFFICERS

Chief Executive: Mr Donald Graham Chief Executive, Civic Office, Elstree Way, Borehamwood WD6 1WA ☎ 020 8207 2277 🖷 020 8207 7441 ✉ donald.graham@hertsmere.gov.uk

Senior Management: Ms Sajida Bijle, Director - Resources, Civic Offices, Elstree Way, Borehamwood WD6 1WA ☎ 020 8207 2277 🖷 020 8207 7487 ✉ sajida.bijle@hertsmere.gov.uk

Senior Management: Mr Glen Wooldrige, Director - Environment, Civic Office, Elstree Way, Borehamwood WD6 1WA ☎ 020 8207 2277 ✉ environment@hertsmere.gov.uk

Architect, Building / Property Services: Mr Richard Stubbs Asset Manager, Civic Office, Elstree Way, Borehamwood WD6 1WA ☎ 020 8207 2277 🖷 020 8207 7441

PR / Communications: Ms Catherine Shepherd, Corporate Communications Manager, Civic Offices, Elstree Way, Borehamwood WD6 1WA ☎ 020 8207 2277 ✉ corporate.communications@hertsmere.gov.uk

Community Safety: Ms Valerie Kane Community Safety Manager, Civic Offices, Elstree Way, Borehamwood WD6 1WA ☎ 020 8207 7462 🖷 020 8207 7478 ✉ community.services@hertsmere.gov.uk

Computer Management: Ms Sajida Bijle, Director - Resources, Civic Office, Elstree Way, Borehamwood WD6 1WA ☎ 020 8207 2277 🖷 020 8207 7487 ✉ sajida.bijle@hertsmere.gov.uk

Contracts: Mr Andrew Harper, Procurement Manager, Civic Offices, Elstree Way, Borehamwood WD6 1WA ☎ 020 8207 2277; 01707 357371 ✉ a.harper@welhat.gov.uk

Corporate Services: Ms Hilary Shade, Head of Partnerships & Community Engagement, Civic Office, Elstree Way, Borehamwood WD6 1WA ☎ 020 8207 7519 🖷 020 8207 7499 ✉ corporate.support@hertsmere.gov.uk

Customer Service: Ms Judith Fear, Head of HR & Customer Services, Civic Offices, Elstree Way, Borehamwood WD6 1WA ☎ 020 8207 7475 🖷 020 8207 7550 ✉ human.resources@hertsmere.gov.uk

Customer Service: Mr Lee Gallagher, Customer Service Operation Manager, Civic Offices, Elstree Way, Borehamwood WD6 1WA ☎ 020 8207 2277 🖷 020 8207 7424 ✉ customer.services@hertsmere.gov.uk

Economic Development: Mr Glen Wooldrige, Director - Environment, Civic Office, Elstree Way, Borehamwood WD6 1WA ☎ 020 8207 2277 ✉ environment@hertsmere.gov.uk

Electoral Registration: Ms Jo Bateman Electoral Services Manager, Civic Office, Elstree Way, Borehamwood WD6 1WA ☎ 020 8207 7481 🖷 020 8207 7555 ✉ jo.bateman@hertsmere.gov.uk

Emergency Planning: Mr Chris Gascoine, Chief Environmental Health Officer, Civic Offices, Elstree Way, Borehamwood WD6 1WA ☎ 020 8207 7433 🖷 020 8207 7441 ✉ environmental.health@hertsmere.gov.uk

Emergency Planning: Mr Glen Wooldrige, Director - Environment, Civic Office, Elstree Way, Borehamwood WD6 1WA ☎ 020 8207 2277 ✉ environment@hertsmere.gov.uk

Environmental / Technical Services: Mr Simon Payton, Head of Engineering, Civic Offices, Elstree Way, Borehamwood WD6 1WA ☎ 020 8207 2277 🖷 020 8207 7441 ✉ engineering.services@hertsmere.gov.uk

Environmental Health: Mr Chris Gascoine, Chief Environmental Health Officer, Civic Offices, Elstree Way, Borehamwood WD6 1WA ☎ 020 8207 7433 🖷 020 8207 7441 ✉ environmental.health@hertsmere.gov.uk

Environmental Health: Mr Glen Wooldrige, Director - Environment, Civic Office, Elstree Way, Borehamwood WD6 1WA ☎ 020 8207 2277 ✉ environment@hertsmere.gov.uk

Estates, Property & Valuation: Mr Rob Ambler Estates Valuer, Civic Office, Elstree Way, Borehamwood WD6 1WA ☎ 020 8207 7486 🖷 020 8207 7499 ✉ estate.maintenance@hertsmere.gov.uk

Finance: Ms Sajida Bijle, Director - Resources, Civic Office, Elstree Way, Borehamwood WD6 1WA ☎ 020 8207 2277 🖷 020 8207 7487 ✉ sajida.bijle@hertsmere.gov.uk

Finance: Mr M Bunyan Head of Finance, Revenues, Benefits & IS, Civic Office, Elstree Way, Borehamwood WD6 1WA ☎ 020 8207 2277

Treasury: Mr James Woodward S151 Officer, Civic Office, Elstree Way, Borehamwood WD6 1WA ☎ 020 8207 2277 ✉ james.woodward@hertsmere.gov.uk

Fleet Management: Mr Steve Burton, Head of Waste & Street Scene, Civic Offices, Elstree Way, Borehamwood WD6 1WA ☎ 020 8207 2277 ✉ waste.management@hertsmere.gov.uk

Grounds Maintenance: Mr Steve Burton, Head of Waste & Street Scene, Civic Office, Elstree Way, Borehamwood WD6 1WA ☎ 020 8207 2277 ✉ waste.management@hertsmere.gov.uk

Housing: Mr Glen Wooldrige, Director - Environment, Civic Office, Elstree Way, Borehamwood WD6 1WA ☎ 020 8207 2277 ✉ environment@hertsmere.gov.uk

Legal: Ms Sajida Bijle, Director - Resources, Civic Office, Elstree Way, Borehamwood WD6 1WA ☎ 020 8207 2277 🖷 020 8207 7487 ✉ sajida.bijle@hertsmere.gov.uk

Licensing: Ms Sue Hardy, Principal Licensing Officer, Civic Office, Elstree Way, Borehamwood WD6 1WA ☎ 020 8207 7441 🖷 020 8207 7436 ✉ licensing.services@hertsmere.gov.uk

Licensing: Mr Glen Wooldrige, Director - Environment, Civic Office, Elstree Way, Borehamwood WD6 1WA ☎ 020 8207 2277 ✉ environment@hertsmere.gov.uk

Member Services: Ms Sajida Bijle, Director - Resources, Civic Office, Elstree Way, Borehamwood WD6 1WA ☎ 020 8207 2277 🖷 020 8207 7487 ✉ sajida.bijle@hertsmere.gov.uk

Parking: Mrs Clare Fensome, Parking Operations Manager, Civic Office, Elstree Way, Borehamwood WD6 1WA ☎ 020 7208 2277 ✉ cpz.department@hertsmere.gov.uk

Parking: Mr Glen Wooldrige, Director - Environment, Civic Office, Elstree Way, Borehamwood WD6 1WA ☎ 020 8207 2277 ✉ environment@hertsmere.gov.uk

Partnerships: Ms Hilary Shade, Head of Partnerships & Community Engagement, Civic Office, Elstree Way, Borehamwood WD6 1WA ☎ 020 8207 7519 🖷 020 8207 7499 ✉ corporate.support@hertsmere.gov.uk

Personnel / HR: Ms Sajida Bijle, Director - Resources, Civic Office, Elstree Way, Borehamwood WD6 1WA ☎ 020 8207 2277 🖷 020 8207 7487 ✉ sajida.bijle@hertsmere.gov.uk

Personnel / HR: Ms Judith Fear, Head of HR & Customer Services, Civic Offices, Elstree Way, Borehamwood WD6 1WA ☎ 020 8207 7475 🖷 020 8207 7550 ✉ human.resources@hertsmere.gov.uk

Planning: Mr Glen Wooldrige, Director - Environment, Civic Office, Elstree Way, Borehamwood WD6 1WA ☎ 020 8207 2277 ✉ environment@hertsmere.gov.uk

Procurement: Mr Andrew Harper, Procurement Manager, Civic Offices, Elstree Way, Borehamwood WD6 1WA ☎ 020 8207 2277; 01707 357371 ✉ a.harper@welhat.gov.uk

Recycling & Waste Minimisation: Mr Steve Burton, Head of Waste & Street Scene, Civic Offices, Elstree Way, Borehamwood WD6 1WA ☎ 020 8207 2277 ✉ waste.management@hertsmere.gov.uk

Recycling & Waste Minimisation: Mr Glen Wooldrige, Director - Environment, Civic Office, Elstree Way, Borehamwood WD6 1WA ☎ 020 8207 2277 ✉ environment@hertsmere.gov.uk

Staff Training: Ms Judith Fear, Head of HR & Customer Services, Civic Offices, Elstree Way, Borehamwood WD6 1WA ☎ 020 8207 7475 🖷 020 8207 7550 ✉ human.resources@hertsmere.gov.uk

Street Scene: Mr Steve Burton, Head of Waste & Street Scene, Civic Office, Elstree Way, Borehamwood WD6 1WA ☎ 020 8207 2277 ✉ waste.management@hertsmere.gov.uk

Street Scene: Mr Glen Wooldrige, Director - Environment, Civic Office, Elstree Way, Borehamwood WD6 1WA ☎ 020 8207 2277 ✉ environment@hertsmere.gov.uk

HERTSMERE

Sustainable Communities: Mr Chris Gascoine, Chief Environmental Health Officer, Civic Offices, Elstree Way, Borehamwood WD6 1WA ☎ 020 8207 7433 🖷 020 8207 7441 ✉ environmental.health@hertsmere.gov.uk

Tourism: Mr Lee Gallagher, Customer Service Operation Manager, Civic Offices, Elstree Way, Borehamwood WD6 1WA ☎ 020 8207 2277 🖷 020 8207 7424 ✉ customer.services@hertsmere.gov.uk

Waste Collection and Disposal: Mr Steve Burton, Head of Waste & Street Scene, Civic Offices, Elstree Way, Borehamwood WD6 1WA ☎ 020 8207 2277 ✉ waste.management@hertsmere.gov.uk

Waste Collection and Disposal: Mr Glen Wooldrige, Director - Environment, Civic Office, Elstree Way, Borehamwood WD6 1WA ☎ 020 8207 2277 ✉ environment@hertsmere.gov.uk

Waste Management: Mr Steve Burton, Head of Waste & Street Scene, Civic Offices, Elstree Way, Borehamwood WD6 1WA ☎ 020 8207 2277 ✉ waste.management@hertsmere.gov.uk

COUNCILLORS

***Mayor* Worster**, Martin (CON - Potters Bar Furzefield)
cllr.martin.worster@hertsmere.gov.uk

***Deputy Mayor* Rutledge**, Peter (CON - Bushey St James)
cllr.pete.rutledge@hertsmere.gov.uk

***Leader of the Council* Bright**, Morris (CON - Elstree)
cllr.morris.bright@hertsmere.gov.uk

***Deputy Leader of the Council* Graham**, John (CON - Aldenham East)
cllr.john.graham@hertsmere.gov.uk

Ash, Thomas (CON - Borehamwood Kenilworth)
cllr.thomas.ash@hertsmere.gov.uk

Barker, Cynthia (CON - Potters Bar Furzefield)
cllr.cynthia.barker@hertsmere.gov.uk

Batten, Brenda (CON - Bushey Heath)
cllr.brenda.batten@hertsmere.gov.uk

Brown, Susan (CON - Borehamwood Brookmeadow)
cllr.susan.brown@hertsmere.gov.uk

Burcombe, David (CON - Borehamwood Cowley Hill)
Cllr.David.Burcombe@hertsmere.gov.uk

Butler, Richard (LAB - Borehamwood Cowley Hill)
cllr.richard.butler@hertsmere.gov.uk

Choudhury, Pervez (CON - Bushey St James)
cllr.pervez.choudhury@hertsmere.gov.uk

Clapper, Caroline (CON - Aldenham West)
cllr.caroline.clapper@hertsmere.gov.uk

Cohen, Harvey (CON - Elstree)
cllr.harvey.cohen@hertsmere.gov.uk

Davis, Lawrence (CON - Bushey North)
cllr.lawrence.davis@hertsmere.gov.uk

Donne, John (CON - Potters Bar Parkfield)
cllr.john.donne@hertsmere.gov.uk

Eni, Victor (CON - Borehamwood Kenilworth)
Cllr.Victor.Eni@hertsmere.gov.uk

Goldstein, Charles (CON - Aldenham East)
cllr.charles.goldstein@hertsmere.gov.uk

Heywood, Jean (CON - Potters Bar Oakmere)
cllr.jean.heywood@hertsmere.gov.uk

Hodgson-Jones, Paul (CON - Potters Bar Parkfield)
cllr.paul.hodgson-jones@hertsmere.gov.uk

Keates, Carey (CON - Bushey St James)
cllr.carey.keates@hertsmere.gov.uk

Kelly, Charles (CON - Borehamwood Hillside)
cllr.charles.kelly@hertsmere.gov.uk

Knell, Peter (CON - Potters Bar Furzefield)
cllr.peter.knell@hertsmere.gov.uk

Lambert, David (CON - Aldenham West)
cllr.david.lambert@hertsmere.gov.uk

Lyon, Ruth (CON - Potters Bar Oakmere)
cllr.ruth.lyon@hertsmere.gov.uk

Merchant, Kashif (CON - Bushey North)
cllr.kashif.merchant@hertsmere.gov.uk

Morris, Paul (CON - Bushey Heath)
cllr.paul.morris@hertsmere.gov.uk

Plancey, Alan (CON - Borehamwood Brookmeadow)
Cllr.Alan.Plancey@hertsmere.gov.uk

Quilty, Seamus (CON - Bushey Heath)
cllr.seamus.quilty@hertsmere.gov.uk

Sachdev, Abhishek (CON - Potters Bar Parkfield)
cllr.abhishek.sachdev@hertsmere.gov.uk

Sachdev, Meenal (CON - Borehamwood Hillside)
Cllr.Meenal.Sachdev@hertsmere.gov.uk

Silver, Gary (CON - Borehamwood Brookmeadow)
cllr.gary.silver@hertsmere.gov.uk

Silver, Linda (CON - Bushey Park)
cllr.linda.silver@hertsmere.gov.uk

Spencer, Anthony (CON - Shenley)
cllr.anthony.spencer@hertsmere.gov.uk

Swallow, Penny (CON - Potters Bar Oakmere)
cllr.penny.swallow@hertsmere.gov.uk

Swerling, Anne (CON - Bushey Park)
cllr.anne.swerling@hertsmere.gov.uk

Turner, Farida (CON - Borehamwood Hillside)
cllr.fardia.turner@hertsmere.gov.uk

Vince, Michelle (LAB - Borehamwood Cowley Hill)
cllr.michelle.vince@hertsmere.gov.uk

Wayne, Peter (CON - Shenley)
cllr.peter.wayne@hertsmere.gov.uk

West, Jane (CON - Bushey North)
jane.west@hertsmere.gov.uk

POLITICAL COMPOSITION

CON: 37, LAB: 2

COMMITTEE CHAIRS

Audit: Mr Charles Goldstein

Licensing: Mr John Donne

Planning: Ms Linda Silver

High Peak D

High Peak Borough Council, Town Hall, Market Place, Buxton SK17 6EL
☎ 0845 129 7777 🖷 01663 751042 ✉ borough-council@highpeak.gov.uk
💻 www.highpeak.gov.uk

FACTS AND FIGURES

Parliamentary Constituencies: High Peak
EU Constituencies: East Midlands
Election Frequency: Elections are of whole council

PRINCIPAL OFFICERS

Chief Executive: Mr Simon Baker, Chief Executive, Town Hall, Market Place, Buxton SK17 6EL ☎ 01538 395400 🖷 01538 395474 ✉ simon.baker@highpeak.gov.uk

Senior Management: Mr Dai Larner Executive Director - Place, Town Hall, Market Place, Buxton SK17 6EL ☎ 01538 395400 ✉ dai.larner@highpeak.gov.uk

Senior Management: Mr Andrew Stokes, Executive Director - Transformation, Town Hall, Market Place, Buxton SK17 6EL ☎ 01538 395622 ✉ andrew.stokes@staffsmoorlands.gov.uk

Senior Management: Mr Mark Trillo, Executive Director - People, Moorlands House, Stockwell Street, Leek ST13 6HQ ☎ 01538 395623 🖷 01538 395474 ✉ mark.trillo@staffsmoorlands.gov.uk

Architect, Building / Property Services: Mr Paul Hare Assets Manager, Moorlands House, Stockwell Street, Leek ST13 6HQ ☎ 01538 395400 ✉ paul.hare@highpeak.gov.uk

Building Control: Mr Dai Larner Executive Director - Place, Town Hall, Market Place, Buxton SK17 6EL ☎ 01538 395400 ✉ dai.larner@highpeak.gov.uk

Building Control: Mr Robert Weaver Head of Regulatory Services, Moorlands House, Stockwell Street, Leek ST13 6HQ ☎ 01538 395400 ✉ robert.weaver@highpeak.gov.uk

PR / Communications: Miss Carolyn Sanders Press & Promotions Officer, Moorlands House, Stockwell Street, Leek ST13 6HQ ☎ 01538 395400 ✉ carolyn.sanders@highpeak.gov.uk

Community Planning: Mr Mark Forrester, Democratic & Community Services Manager, Moorlands House, Stockwell Street, Leek ST13 6HQ ☎ 01538 395768 🖷 01538 395474 ✉ mark.forrester@staffsmoorlands.gov.uk

Community Planning: Mr Dai Larner Executive Director - Place, Town Hall, Market Place, Buxton SK17 6EL ☎ 01538 395400 ✉ dai.larner@highpeak.gov.uk

Community Safety: Mr David Smith Community Safety & Enforcement Manager, Moorlands House, Stockwell Street, Leek ST13 6HQ ☎ 01538 395692 🖷 01538 395474 ✉ david.smith@staffsmoorlands.gov.uk

Computer Management: Ms Mary Walker Organisational Development & Transformation Manager, Town Hall, Market Place, Buxton SK17 6EL ☎ 01538 395400 ✉ mary.walker@highpeak.gov.uk

Economic Development: Ms Pranali Parikh Regeneration Manager, Moorlands House, Stockwell Street, Leek ST13 6HQ ☎ 01538 395400 ✉ pranali.parikh@highpeak.gov.uk

Environmental Health: Mr Dai Larner Executive Director - Place, Town Hall, Market Place, Buxton SK17 6EL ☎ 01538 395400 ✉ dai.larner@highpeak.gov.uk

Environmental Health: Mr Robert Weaver Head of Regulatory Services, Town Hall, Market Place, Buxton SK17 6EL ☎ 01538 395400 ✉ robert.weaver@highpeak.gov.uk

Estates, Property & Valuation: Mr Paul Hare Assets Manager, Moorlands House, Stockwell Street, Leek ST13 6HQ ☎ 01538 395400 ✉ paul.hare@highpeak.gov.uk

Facilities: Mr Paul Hare Assets Manager, Moorlands House, Stockwell Street, Leek ST13 6HQ ☎ 01538 395400 ✉ paul.hare@highpeak.gov.uk

Finance: Mr Andrew Stokes, Executive Director - Transformation, Moorlands House, Stockwell Street, Leek ST13 6HQ ☎ 01538 395622 ✉ andrew.stokes@staffsmoorlands.gov.uk

Grounds Maintenance: Ms Nicola Kemp Waste Collection Manager, Moorlands House, Stockwell Street, Leek ST13 6HQ ☎ 01538 395400 ✉ nicola.kemp@highpeak.gov.uk

Health and Safety: Mr David Owen Corporate Health & Safety Advisor, Moorlands House, Stockwell Street, Leek ST13 6HQ ☎ 01538 395595 🖷 01538 395474 ✉ david.owen@staffsmoorlands.gov.uk

Housing: Mr Dai Larner Executive Director - Place, Moorlands House, Stockwell Street, Leek ST13 6HQ ☎ 01538 395400 ✉ dai.larner@highpeak.gov.uk

Housing Maintenance: Mr Dai Larner Executive Director - Place, Moorlands House, Stockwell Street, Leek ST13 6HQ ☎ 01538 395400 ✉ dai.larner@highpeak.gov.uk

Local Area Agreement: Mr Mark Forrester, Democratic & Community Services Manager, Moorlands House, Stockwell Street, Leek ST13 6HQ ☎ 01538 395768 🖷 01538 395474 ✉ mark.forrester@staffsmoorlands.gov.uk

Legal: Mr Mark Trillo Executive Director - People, Moorlands House, Stockwell Street, Leek ST13 6HQ ☎ 01538 395623 ✉ mark.trillo@highpeak.gov.uk

Leisure and Cultural Services: Mr Terry Crawford Head of Visitor Services, Pavilion Gardens, Buxton SK17 6BE ☎ 01298 28400 Ext 4224 ✉ terry.crawford@highpeak.gov.uk

Licensing: Mr Robert Weaver Head of Regulatory Services, Moorlands House, Stockwell Street, Leek ST13 6HQ ☎ 01538 395400 ✉ robert.weaver@highpeak.gov.uk

Member Services: Mr Mark Forrester, Democratic & Community Services Manager, Moorlands House, Stockwell Street, Leek ST13 6HQ ☎ 01538 395768 🖷 01538 395474 ✉ mark.forrester@staffsmoorlands.gov.uk

HIGH PEAK

Member Services: Mr Linden Vernon Member Services Manager, Moorlands House, Stockwell Street, Leek ST13 6HQ ☎ 01538 395400 ✉ linden.vernon@highpeak.gov.uk

Parking: Mr Terry Crawford Visitor Services Manager, Pavilion Gardens, St John's Road, Buxton SK17 6XN ☎ 01298 284 00 ext 4224 ✉ terry.crawford@highpeak.gov.uk

Partnerships: Mr Mark Forrester, Democratic & Community Services Manager, Moorlands House, Stockwell Street, Leek ST13 6HQ ☎ 01538 395768 🖷 01538 395474 ✉ mark.forrester@staffsmoorlands.gov.uk

Personnel / HR: Ms Mary Walker Organisational Development & Transformation Manager, Town Hall, Market Place, Buxton SK17 6EL ☎ 01538 395400 ✉ mary.walker@highpeak.gov.uk

Planning: Mr Dai Larner Executive Director - Place, Town Hall, Market Place, Buxton SK17 6EL ☎ 01538 395400 ✉ dai.larner@highpeak.gov.uk

Planning: Mr Robert Weaver Head of Regulatory Services, Moorlands House, Stockwell Street, Leek ST13 6HQ ☎ 01538 395400 ✉ robert.weaver@highpeak.gov.uk

Procurement: Ms Claire Hazeldene Finance & Procurement Manager, Moorlands House, Stockwell Street, Leek ST13 6HQ ☎ 01538 395400 ✉ claire.hazeldene@highpeak.gov.uk

Recycling & Waste Minimisation: Ms Nicola Kemp Waste Collection Manager, Moorlands House, Stockwell Street, Leek ST13 6HQ ☎ 01538 395400 ✉ nicola.kemp@highpeak.gov.uk

Regeneration: Ms Pranali Parikh Regeneration Manager, Moorlands House, Stockwell Street, Leek ST13 6HQ ☎ 01538 395400 ✉ pranali.parikh@highpeak.gov.uk

Staff Training: Ms Mary Walker Organisational Development & Transformation Manager, Town Hall, Market Place, Buxton SK17 6EL ☎ 01538 395400 ✉ mary.walker@highpeak.gov.uk

Street Scene: Mrs Joy Redfern Street Scene Manager, Town Hall, Market Place, Buxton SK17 6EL ☎ 0845 129 7777 ✉ joy.redfern@highpeak.gov.uk

Sustainable Communities: Mr Mark Forrester, Democratic & Community Services Manager, Moorlands House, Stockwell Street, Leek ST13 6HQ ☎ 01538 395768 🖷 01538 395474 ✉ mark.forrester@staffsmoorlands.gov.uk

Tourism: Mr Terry Crawford Head of Visitor Services, Pavilion Gardens, Buxton SK17 6BE ☎ 01298 28400 Ext 4224 ✉ terry.crawford@highpeak.gov.uk

Tourism: Mr Dai Larner Executive Director - Place, Moorlands House, Stockwell Street, Leek ST13 6HQ ☎ 01538 395400 ✉ dai.larner@highpeak.gov.uk

Town Centre: Mr Dai Larner Executive Director - Place, Moorlands House, Stockwell Street, Leek ST13 6HQ ☎ 01538 395400 ✉ dai.larner@highpeak.gov.uk

Total Place: Mr Mark Forrester, Democratic & Community Services Manager, Moorlands House, Stockwell Street, Leek ST13 6HQ ☎ 01538 395768 🖷 01538 395474 ✉ mark.forrester@staffsmoorlands.gov.uk

Waste Collection and Disposal: Mr Keith Parker Head of Operational Services, Town Hall, Market Place, Buxton SK17 6EL ☎ 01538 395400 ✉ keith.parker@staffsmoorlands.gov.uk

Waste Management: Mr Keith Parker Head of Operational Services, Town Hall, Market Place, Buxton SK17 6EL ☎ 01538 395400 ✉ keith.parker@staffsmoorlands.gov.uk

COUNCILLORS

***Mayor* Young**, Stewart (CON - Chapel West)
Stewart.Young@highpeak.gov.uk

***Deputy Mayor* Boynton**, Colin (CON - Cote Heath)
colin.boynton@highpeak.gov.uk

***Leader of the Council* Ashton**, Tony (CON - Sett)
Tony.Ashton@highpeak.gov.uk

***Group Leader* Greenhalgh**, Damien (LAB - Howard Town)
damien.greenalgh@highpeak.gov.uk

***Group Leader* Lomax**, David (LD - Whaley Bridge)
david.lomax@highpeak.gov.uk

***Alderman* Kelly**, Ed (LAB - Hadfield North)
edward.kelly@highpeak/gov.uk

St John's: Vacant

Atkins, Ray (LD - New Mills West)
Raymond.Atkins@highpeak.gov.uk

Barrow, Alan (LAB - New Mills East)
Alan.Barrow@highpeak.gov.uk

Claff, Godfrey (LAB - Howard Town)
Godfrey.Claff@highpeak.gov.uk

Douglas, Jamie (CON - Old Glossop)
jamie.douglas@highpeak.gov.uk

Dowson, Lance (LAB - New Mills West)
Lance.Dowson@highpeak.gov.uk

Easter, Peter (CON - Hayfield)
peter.easter@highpeak.gov.uk

Flower, Samantha (CON - Burbage)
samantha.flower@highpeak.gov.uk

Fox, Andrew (CON - Whaley Bridge)
andrew.fox@highpeak.gov.uk

Grooby, Linda (CON - Cote Heath)
linda.grooby@highpeak.gov.uk

Haken, John (CON - Simmondley)
John.Haken@highpeak.gov.uk

Hardy, Paul (CON - Old Glossop)
paul.hardy@highpeak.gov.uk

Helliwell, Sarah (CON - Hope Valley)
sarah.helliwell@highpeak.gov.uk

Howe, Caroline (CON - Blackbrook)
caroline.howe@highpeak.gov.uk

Huddlestone, Ian (LAB - New Mills East)
ian.huddlestone@highpeak.gov.uk

Jenner, Pat (LAB - Tintwistle)
Pat.Jenner@highpeak.gov.uk

Johnson, Clive (CON - Corbar)
clive.johnson@highpeak.gov.uk

Kappes, John (CON - Blackbrock)
john.kappes@highpeak.gov.uk

Kemp, Tony (CON - Corbar)
Tony.Kemp@highpeak.gov.uk

Kerr, David (LAB - Stone Bench)
david.kerr@hhighpeak.gov.uk

Longos, Nick (LAB - Padfield)
nicholas.longos@highpeak.gov.uk

McCabe, Julie Ann (CON - Simmondley)
Julie.Mccabe@highpeak.gov.uk

McKeown, Anthony (LAB - Gamesley)
Anthony.McKeown@highpeak.gov.uk

McKeown, Robert (LAB - Hadfield South)
Robert.McKeown@highpeak.gov.uk

Oakley, Graham (LAB - Whitfield)
Graham.Oakley@highpeak.gov.uk

Perkins, Jim (CON - Chapel East)
jim.perkins@highpeak.gov.uk

Pritchard, John (IND - Whaley Bridge)
John.Pritchard@highpeak.gov.uk

Quinn, Rachael (LAB - Barms)
Rachael.Quinn@highpeak.gov.uk

Robbins, Daren (CON - Limestone Peak)
daren.robbins@highpeak.gov.uk

Siddall, Edward (LAB - Hadfield South)
Edward.Siddall@highpeak.gov.uk

Sizeland, Kath (CON - Chapel West)
kathleen.sizeland@highpeaks.gov.uk

Sloman, Fiona (LAB - Stone Bench)
Fiona.Sloman@highpeak.gov.uk

Stone, Matthew (LAB - Buxton Central)
matthew.stone@highpeak.gov.uk

Thrane, Emily (CON - Temple)
Emily.Thrane@highpeak.gov.uk

Todd, Jean (LAB - Buxton Central)
jean.todd@highpeak.gov.uk

Walton, John (CON - Hope Valley)
John.Walton@highpeak.gov.uk

Wharmby, Jean (CON - Dinting)
Jean.Wharmby@highpeak.gov.uk

POLITICAL COMPOSITION

CON: 22, LAB: 17, LD: 2, Vacant: 1, IND: 1

COMMITTEE CHAIRS

Audit: Mr John Pritchard

Development Control: Mr David Lomax

Licensing: Mr Jim Perkins

Highland S

Highland Council, Council Offices, Glenurquhart Road, Inverness IV3 5NX
☎ 01463 702000 🖷 01463 702182 🖳 www.highland.gov.uk

FACTS AND FIGURES

Parliamentary Constituencies: Caithness, Sutherland and Easter Ross, Inverness, Nairn, Badenoch and Strathspey, Ross, Skye and Lochaber
EU Constituencies: Scotland
Election Frequency: Elections are of whole council

PRINCIPAL OFFICERS

Chief Executive: Mr Steve Barron Chief Executive, Council Offices, Glenurquhart Road, Inverness IV3 5NX ☎ 01463 702837 🖷 01463 702879 ✉ steve.barron@highland.gov.uk

Assistant Chief Executive: Ms Michelle Morris Depute Chief Executive / Director of Corporate Development, Council Offices, Glenurquhart Road, Inverness IV3 5NX ☎ 01463 702845 🖷 01463 702879 ✉ michelle.morris@highland.gov.uk

Senior Management: Mr Bill Alexander Director of Care & Learning, Council Offices, Glenurquhart Road, Inverness IV3 5NX ☎ 01463 702860 ✉ bill.alexander@highland.gov.uk

Senior Management: Mr Stuart Black Director of Development & Infrastructure, Council Offices, Glenurquhart Road, Inverness IV3 5NX ☎ 01463 702251 🖷 01463 702298 ✉ stuart.black@highland.gov.uk

Senior Management: Mr William Gilfillan Director of Community Services, Council Offices, Glenurquhart Road, Inverness IV3 5NX ☎ 01463 252920 ✉ william.gilfillan@highland.gov.uk

Senior Management: Mr Derek Yule Director of Finance, Council Offices, Glenurquhart Road, Inverness IV3 5NX ☎ 01463 702301 🖷 01463 702310 ✉ derek.yule@highland.gov.uk

Architect, Building / Property Services: Mr David Goldie Head of Housing, Council Offices, Glenurquhart Road, Inverness IV3 5NX ☎ 01463 702864 ✉ david.goldie@highland.gov.uk

Building Control: Mr Glenn Campbell Building Standards Manager, Council Offices, Glenurquhart Road, Inverness IV3 5NX ☎ 01463 702561 ✉ glenn.campbell@highland.gov.uk

Catering Services: Mrs Norma Murray, Catering & Cleaning Manager, Ness House, Drummond School, Drummond Road, Inverness IV2 4NZ ☎ 01463 663307 🖷 01463 702828 ✉ norma.murray@highland.gov.uk

Children / Youth Services: Ms Sandra Campbell Head of Children's Services, Council Offices, Glenurquhart Road, Inverness IV3 5NX ☎ 01463 702819 ✉ sandra.campbell@highland.gov.uk

Civil Registration: Ms Diane Minty Chief Registrar, Highland Archive & Registration Office, Bught Road, Inverness IV3 5SS ☎ 01463 256402 ✉ diane.minty@highland.gov.uk

HIGHLAND

PR / Communications: Ms Alison MacNeill Acting Public Relations Manager, Council Offices, Glenurquhart Road, Inverness IV3 5NX ☎ 01463 702071 🖷 01463 702025 ✉ alison.macneill@highland.gov.uk

Community Planning: Ms Carron McDiarmid Head of Policy & Reform, Council Offices, Glenurquhart Road, Inverness IV3 5NX ☎ 01463 702952 ✉ carron.mcdiarmid@highland.gov.uk

Community Safety: Ms Isabelle Baikie Community Safety Officer, Council Offices, Glenurquhart Road, Inverness IV3 5NX ☎ 01463 702246 🖷 01463 702830 ✉ isabelle.baikie@highland.gov.uk

Computer Management: Mr John Grieve, Corporate ICT Manager, Council Offices, Glenurquhart Road, Inverness IV3 5NX ☎ 01463 702741 ✉ john.grieve@highland.gov.uk

Consumer Protection and Trading Standards: Mr Gordon Robb Trading Standards Manager, 38 Harbour Road, Inverness IV1 1UF ☎ 01463 228721 ✉ gordon.robb@highland.gov.uk

Contracts: Mr Finlay Macdonald Acting Head of Property, Council Offices, Glenurquhart Road, Inverness IV3 5NX ☎ 01463 702211 ✉ finlay.macdonald@highland.gov.uk

Corporate Services: Ms Michelle Morris Depute Chief Executive / Director of Corporate Development, Council Offices, Glenurquhart Road, Inverness IV3 5NX ☎ 01463 702845 🖷 01463 702879 ✉ michelle.morris@highland.gov.uk

Customer Service: Ms Tina Page Customer Services Manager, Council Offices, Glenurquhart Road, Inverness IV3 5NX ☎ 01463 702707 ✉ tina.page@highland.gov.uk

Economic Development: Mr Stuart Black Director of Development & Infrastructure, Council Offices, Glenurquhart Road, Inverness IV3 5NX ☎ 01463 702251 🖷 01463 702298 ✉ stuart.black@highland.gov.uk

Education: Mr Jim Steven Head of Education, Council Offices, Glenurquhart Road, Inverness IV3 5NX ☎ 01463 702804 ✉ jim.steven@highland.gov.uk

E-Government: Ms Vicki Nairn Head of Digital Transformation, Council Offices, Glenurquhart Road, Inverness IV3 5NX ☎ 01463 702848 ✉ vicki.nairn@highland.gov.uk

Electoral Registration: Mr John Bruce, Elections Manager, Council Offices, Dingwall IV15 9QN ☎ 01463 702017 ✉ john.bruce@highland.gov.uk

Emergency Planning: Mr Donald Norrie Emergency Planning & Business Continuity Manager, Council Offices, Glenurquhart Road, Inverness IV3 5NX ☎ 01463 713479 🖷 01463 243583 ✉ donald.norrie@highland.gov.uk

Energy Management: Mr Eddie Boyd Head of Energy & Engineering Services Manager, Council Offices, Glenurquhart Road, Inverness IV3 5NX ☎ 01463 255270 ✉ eddie.boyd@highland.gov.uk

Environmental Health: Dr Colin Clark Head of Environmental & Regulatory Services, Council Offices, Glenurquhart Road, Inverness IV3 5NX ☎ 01463 702527 ✉ colin.clark@highland.gov.uk

Estates, Property & Valuation: Mr Allan Maguire Head of Property Partnerships, Council Offices, Glenurquhart Road, Inverness IV3 5NX ☎ 01463 702528 🖷 01463 702885 ✉ allan.maguire@highland.gov.uk

European Liaison: Mr Gordon Summers Principal European Officer, Council Offices, Glenurquhart Road, Inverness IV3 5NX ☎ 01463 702508 🖷 01463 702830 ✉ gordon.summers@highland.gov.uk

Events Manager: Mr Gerry Reynolds, Events Officer, Town House, Inverness IV2 4SF ☎ 01463 724216 ✉ gerry.reynolds@highlands.gov.uk

Finance: Mr Derek Yule Director of Finance, Council Offices, Glenurquhart Road, Inverness IV3 5NX ☎ 01463 702301 🖷 01463 702310 ✉ derek.yule@highland.gov.uk

Pensions: Mr Charlie McCallum Payroll & Pensions Manager, Council Offices, Glenurquhart Road, Inverness IV3 5NX ☎ 01463 702000 ✉ charlie.mccallum@highland.gov.uk

Fleet Management: Mr Richard Evans Head of Roads & Transport, Council Offices, Glenurquhart Road, Inverness IV3 5NX ☎ 01463 252922 ✉ richard.evans@highland.gov.uk

Grounds Maintenance: Mr Richard Evans Head of Roads & Transport, Council Offices, Glenurquhart Road, Inverness IV3 5NX ☎ 01463 252922 ✉ richard.evans@highland.gov.uk

Health and Safety: Ms Gena Falconer, Occupational Health, Safety & Wellbeing Manager, Dochfour Drive, , Inverness IV3 5EB ☎ 01463 703094 🖷 01463 703090 ✉ gena.falconer@highland.gov.uk

Highways: Mr Richard Evans Head of Roads & Transport, Council Offices, Glenurquhart Road, Inverness IV3 5NX ☎ 01463 252922 ✉ richard.evans@highland.gov.uk

Home Energy Conservation: Mr Eddie Boyd Head of Energy & Engineering Services Manager, Council Offices, Glenurquhart Road, Inverness IV3 5NX ☎ 01463 255270 ✉ eddie.boyd@highland.gov.uk

Housing: Mr David Goldie Head of Housing, Council Offices, Glenurquhart Road, Inverness IV3 5NX ☎ 01463 702864 ✉ david.goldie@highland.gov.uk

Housing Maintenance: Mrs Caroline Campbell Performance & Building Maintenance Manager, Council Offices, Glenurquhart Road, Inverness IV3 5NX ☎ 01463 702610 ✉ caroline.campbell@highland.gov.uk

Legal: Mr Stewart Fraser Head of Corporate Governance, Council Offices, Glenurquhart Road, Inverness IV3 5NX ☎ 01463 702112 ✉ stewart.fraser@highland.gov.uk

Leisure and Cultural Services: Mr Ian Murray Chief Executive - High Life Highland, 12/13 Ardross Street, Inverness IV3 5NS ☎ 01463 663824 🖷 01463 663809 ian.murray@highland.gov.uk

Licensing: Mr Michael Elsey, Senior Licensing Officer, Town House, High Street, Inverness IV1 1JJ ☎ 01463 724298 🖷 01463 724300 michael.elsey@highland.gov.uk

Lottery Funding, Charity and Voluntary: Mrs Carron McDiarmid, Head of Policy & Reform, Council Offices, Glenurquhart Road, Inverness IV3 5NX ☎ 01463 702852 carron.mcdiarmid@highland.gov.uk

Member Services: Ms Julie MacLennan Democratic Services Manager, Council Offices, Glenurquhart Road, Inverness IV3 5NX ☎ 01463 702118 🖷 01463 702182 julie.maclennan@highland.gov.uk

Parking: Mr Richard Evans Head of Roads & Transport, Council Offices, Glenurquhart Road, Inverness IV3 5NX ☎ 01463 252922 richard.evans@highland.gov.uk

Personnel / HR: Mr John Batchelor, Head of People & Performance, Council Offices, Glenurquhart Road, Inverness IV3 5NX ☎ 01463 702056 🖷 01463 702062 john.batchelor@highland.gov.uk

Planning: Mr Stuart Black Director of Development & Infrastructure, Council Offices, Glenurquhart Road, Inverness IV3 5NX ☎ 01463 702251 🖷 01463 702298 stuart.black@highland.gov.uk

Procurement: Mr Ashley Gould, Head of Procurement, Floor 3, 21/23 Church Street, Inverness IV1 1DY ☎ 01463 785146 ashley.gould@highland.gov.uk

Public Libraries: Mr Douglas Wilby Head of Performance - High Life Highland, High Life Highland, 12 - 13 Ardross Street, Inverness IV3 5NS ☎ 01463 663800 douglas.wilby@highlifehighland.com

Recycling & Waste Minimisation: Dr Colin Clark Head of Environmental & Regulatory Services, Council Offices, Glenurquhart Road, Inverness IV3 5NX ☎ 01463 702527 colin.clark@highland.gov.uk

Regeneration: Mr Andy McCann Economy & Regeneration Manager, Council Offices, Glenurquhart Road, Inverness IV3 5NX ☎ 01463 702260 andy.mccann@highland.gov.uk

Road Safety: Mr Richard Evans Head of Roads & Transport, Council Offices, Glenurquhart Road, Inverness IV3 5NX ☎ 01463 252922 richard.evans@highland.gov.uk

Social Services: Ms Sandra Campbell Head of Children's Services, Council Offices, Glenurquhart Road, Inverness IV3 5NX ☎ 01463 702819 sandra.campbell@highland.gov.uk

Social Services (Children): Ms Sandra Campbell Head of Children's Services, Council Offices, Glenurquhart Road, Inverness IV3 5NX ☎ 01463 702819 sandra.campbell@highland.gov.uk

Staff Training: Ms Catherine Christie, Learning & Development Manager, Dochfour Drive, Inverness IV3 5EB ☎ 01463 703064 🖷 01463 703051 catherine.christie@highland.gov.uk

Sustainable Development: Ms Carron McDiarmid Head of Policy & Reform, Council Offices, Glenurquhart Road, Inverness IV3 5NX ☎ 01463 702952 carron.mcdiarmid@highland.gov.uk

Tourism: Mr Colin Simpson Principal Tourism & Film Co-ordinator, Council Offices, Glenurquhart Road, Inverness IV3 5NX ☎ 01463 702957 colin.simpson@highland.gov.uk

Town Centre: Mr David Haas City Manager, Town House, High Street, Inverness IV1 1JJ ☎ 01463 724201 david.haas@highland.gov.uk

Traffic Management: Mr Richard Evans Head of Roads & Transport, Council Offices, Glenurquhart Road, Inverness IV3 5NX ☎ 01463 252922 richard.evans@highland.gov.uk

Waste Collection and Disposal: Dr Colin Clark Head of Environmental & Regulatory Services, Council Offices, Glenurquhart Road, Inverness IV3 5NX ☎ 01463 702527 colin.clark@highland.gov.uk

Waste Management: Dr Colin Clark Head of Environmental & Regulatory Services, Council Offices, Glenurquhart Road, Inverness IV3 5NX ☎ 01463 702527 colin.clark@highland.gov.uk

COUNCILLORS

***Convener* McCallum**, Isobel (IND - Black Isle)
isobel.mccallum.cllr@highland.gov.uk

***Provost* Fraser**, Laurie (IND - Nairn)
laurie.fraser.cllr@highland.gov.uk

***Deputy Provost* Slater**, Jean (SNP - Inverness Ness-side)
jean.slater.cllr@highland.gov.uk

***Leader of the Council* Davidson**, Margaret (IND - Aird and Loch Ness)
margaret.davidson.cllr@highland.gov.uk

***Deputy Leader of the Council* Rhind**, Alasdair (IND - Tain and Easter Ross)
alasdair.rhind.cllr@highland.gov.uk

Alston, David (LD - Black Isle)
david.alston.cllr@highland.gov.uk

Balfour, Roddy (IND - Culloden and Ardersier)
roderick.balfour.cllr@highland.gov.uk

Barclay, Jennifer (IND - Black Isle)
jennifer.barclay.cllr@highland.gov.uk

Baxter, Andrew (IND - Fort William and Ardnamurchan)
andrew.baxter.cllr@highland.gov.uk

Bremner, David (IND - Landward Caithness)
david.bremner.cllr@highland.gov.uk

Brown, Ian (SNP - Inverness Millburn)
ian.brown.cllr@highland.gov.uk

Caddick, Carolyn (LD - Inverness South)
carolyn.caddick.cllr@highland.gov.uk

Campbell, Janet (IND - Inverness Central)
janet.campbell.cllr@highland.gov.uk

Campbell, Isabelle (IND - Wester Ross, Strathpeffer and Lochalsh)
isabelle.campbell.cllr@highland.gov.uk

HIGHLAND

Carmichael, Helen (IND - Aird and Loch Ness)
helen.carmichael.cllr@highland.gov.uk

Christie, Alasdair (LD - Inverness Ness-side)
alasdair.christie.cllr@highland.gov.uk

Clark, Bill (SNP - Caol and Mallaig)
bill.clark.cllr@highland.gov.uk

Cockburn, Ian (SNP - Wester Ross, Strathpeffer and Lochalsh)
ian.cockburn.cllr@highland.gov.uk

Coghill, Gillian (IND - Landward Caithness)
gillian.coghill.cllr@highland.gov.uk

Crawford, Jim (IND - Inverness South)
jim.crawford.cllr@highland.gov.uk

Donald, Norrie (IND - Inverness Ness-side)
norrie.donald.cllr@highland.gov.uk

Douglas, Jaci (IND - Badenoch and Strathspey)
jaci.douglas.cllr@highland.gov.uk

Duffy, Allan (SNP - Inverness West)
allan.duffy.cllr@highland.gov.uk

Fallows, David (SNP - Badenoch and Strathspey)
bill.fallows.cllr@highland.gov.uk

Farlow, George (SNP - North, West and Central Sutherland)
george.farlow.cllr@highland.gov.uk

Fernie, Bill (IND - Wick)
bill.fernie.cllr@highland.gov.uk

Finlayson, Mike (IND - Cromarty Firth)
michael.finlayson.cllr@highland.gov.uk

Ford, John (LAB - Culloden and Ardersier)
john.ford.cllr@highland.gov.uk

Fraser, Hamish (IND - Eilean a' Cheo)
hamish.fraser.cllr@highland.gov.uk

Fraser, Craig (SNP - Black Isle)
craig.fraser.cllr@highland.gov.uk

Fuller, Stephen (SNP - Nairn)
stephen.fuller.cllr@highland.gov.uk

Gordon, John (IND - Eilean a' Cheo)
john.gordon.cllr@highland.gov.uk

Gormley, Bren (SNP - Fort William and Ardnamurchan)
bren.gormley.cllr@highland.gov.uk

Gowans, Ken (SNP - Inverness South)
ken.gowans.cllr@highland.gov.uk

Graham, Alex (LD - Inverness West)
alex.graham.cllr@highland.gov.uk

Gray, Jimmy (LAB - Inverness Millburn)
jimmy.gray.cllr@highland.gov.uk

Green, Michael (IND - Nairn)
michael.green.cllr@highland.gov.uk

Greene, Richard (IND - Wester Ross, Strathpeffer and Lochalsh)
richard.greene.cllr@highland.gov.uk

Henderson, Allan (IND - Caol and Mallaig)
allan.henderson.cllr@highland.gov.uk

Hendry, Drew (SNP - Aird and Loch Ness)
drew.hendry.cllr@highland.gov.uk

Kerr, Donnie (IND - Inverness Central)
donnie.kerr.cllr@highland.gov.uk

Laird, Richard (SNP - Inverness Central)
richard.laird.cllr@highland.gov.uk

Lobban, Bill (SNP - Badenoch and Strathspey)
bill.loban.cllr@highland.gov.uk

MacDonald, Neil (LAB - Wick)
neil.macdonald.cllr@highland.gov.uk

MacDonald, Liz (SNP - Nairn)
liz.macdonald.cllr@highland.gov.uk

Mackay, Donnie (IND - Thurso)
donnie.mackay.cllr@highland.gov.uk

MacKay, Deirdre (LAB - East Sutherland and Edderton)
deirdre.mackay.cllr@highland.gov.uk

MacKay, Willie (IND - Landward Caithness)
willie.mackay.cllr@highland.gov.uk

MacKenzie, Graham (SNP - Dingwall and Seaforth)
graham.mackenzie.cllr@highland.gov.uk

MacKinnon, Alister (IND - Dingwall and Seaforth)
alister.mackinnon.cllr@highland.gov.uk

MacLean, Angela (LD - Dingwall and Seaforth)
angela.maclean.cllr@highland.gov.uk

MacLennan, Thomas (IND - Fort William and Ardnamurchan)
thomas.maclennan.cllr@highland.gov.uk

MacLeod, Kenneth (LD - Inverness Milburn)
kenneth.macleod.cllr@highland.gov.uk

McAlister, Bet (LAB - Inverness Central)
elizabeth.mcallister.cllr@highland.gov.uk

McGillivray, Jim (IND - East Sutherland and Edderton)
jim.mcgillivray.cllr@highland.gov.uk

Millar, Drew (LD - Eilean a' Cheo)
drew.millar.cllr@highland.gov.uk

Morrison, Hugh (IND - North, West and Central Sutherland)
hugh.morrison.cllr@highland.gov.uk

Munro, Linda (INDNA - North, West and Central Sutherland)
linda.munro.cllr@highland.gov.uk

Murphy, Brian (LAB - Fort William and Ardnamurchan)
brian.murphy.cllr@highland.gov.uk

Parr, Fraser (LAB - Inverness Ness-side)
fraser.parr.cllr@highland.gov.uk

Paterson, Margaret (IND - Dingwall and Seaforth)
margaret.paterson.cllr@highland.gov.uk

Phillips, Graham (SNP - East Sutherland and Edderton)
graham.phillips.cllr@highland.gov.uk

Prag, Thomas (LD - Inverness South)
thomas.prag.cllr@highland.gov.uk

Rattray, Martin (LD - Cromarty Firth)
martin.rattray.cllr@highland.gov.uk

Reiss, Matthew (IND - Landward Caithness)
matthew.reiss.cllr@highland.gov.uk

Renwick, Ian (SNP - Eilean a' Cheo)
ian.renwick.cllr@highland.gov.uk

Rimell, Gregor (SNP - Badenoch and Strathspey)
gregor.rimmel.cllr@highland.gov.uk

Robertson, Fiona (IND - Tain and Easter Ross)
fiona.robertson.cllr@highland.gov.uk

Rosie, John (IND - Thurso)
john.rosie2.cllr@highland.gov.uk

Ross, Graham (IND - Inverness West)
graham.ross.cllr@highland.gov.uk

Ross, Gail (SNP - Wick)
gail.ross.cllr@highland.gov.uk

Saxon, Roger (LAB - Thurso)
roger.saxon.cllr@highland.gov.uk

Sinclair, Audrey (IND - Wester Ross, Strathpeffer and Lochalsh)
audrey.sinclair.cllr@highland.gov.uk

Sinclair, Glynis (SNP - Culloden and Ardersier)
glynis.sinclair.cllr@highland.gov.uk

Smith, Maxine (SNP - Cromarty Firth)
maxine.smith.cllr@highland.gov.uk

Stephen, Kate (LD - Culloden and Ardersier)
kate.stephen.cllr@highland.gov.uk

Stone, Jamie (LD - Tain and Easter Ross)
jamie.stone.cllr@highland.gov.uk

Thompson, Ben (IND - Caol and Mallaig)
ben.thompson.cllr@highland.gov.uk

Wilson, Carolyn (IND - Cromarty Firth)
carolyn.wilson.cllr@highland.gov.uk

Wood, Hamish (LD - Aird and Loch Ness)
hamish.wood.cllr@highland.gov.uk

POLITICAL COMPOSITION

IND: 37, SNP: 22, LD: 12, LAB: 8, INDNA: 1

COMMITTEE CHAIRS

Audit: Mr Richard Laird

Education, Children & Adult Services: Mr Drew Millar

Licensing: Mr Ian Cockburn

Pensions: Mr David Fallows

Planning, Development & Infrastructure: Dr Audrey Sinclair

Hillingdon L

Hillingdon London Borough Council, Civic Centre, High Street, Uxbridge UB8 1UW
☎ 01895 250111 🖷 01895 273636 🖳 www.hillingdon.gov.uk

FACTS AND FIGURES

Parliamentary Constituencies: Hayes and Harlington, Ruislip-Northwood, Uxbridge and Ruislip South
EU Constituencies: London
Election Frequency: Elections are of whole council

PRINCIPAL OFFICERS

Chief Executive: Ms Fran Beasley Chief Executive & Corporate Director of Administration, Civic Centre, High Street, Uxbridge UB8 1UW ☎ 01895 250569 🖷 01895 277047 ✉ fbeasley@hillingdon.gov.uk

Deputy Chief Executive: Ms Jean Palmer, Deputy Chief Executive & Director of Residents' Services, Civic Centre, Uxbridge UB8 1UW ☎ 01895 250622 🖷 01895 250223 ✉ jean.palmer@hillingdon.gov.uk

Senior Management: Dr Sharon Daye Director - Public Health, Civic Centre, High Street, Uxbridge UB8 1UW ☎ 01895 556008 ✉ sdaye@hillingdon.gov.uk

Senior Management: Mr Paul Whaymand Director of Finance, Civic Centre, High Street, Uxbridge UB8 1UW ☎ 01895 250725 🖷 01895 277047 ✉ pwhaymand@hillingdon.gov.uk

Senior Management: Mr Tony Zaman Director of Adult Services / Interim Director of Children & Young People's Services, Civic Centre, High Street, Uxbridge UB8 1UW ☎ 01895 250506 ✉ tzaman@hillingdon.gov.uk

Access Officer / Social Services (Disability): Ms Clare Harris SEN Category Lead, Civic Centre, High Street, Uxbridge UB8 1UW ☎ 01895 277051 ✉ charris@hillingdon.gov.uk

Architect, Building / Property Services: Mr John Gill Estate Service Manager, Civic Centre, High Street, Uxbridge UB8 1UW ☎ 01895 277036 ✉ jgill3@hillingdon.gov.uk

Building Control: Mr James Rodger Head of Planning & Enforcement, Civic Centre, High Street, Uxbridge UB8 1UW ☎ 01895 220049 ✉ jrodger2@hillingdon.gov.uk

Catering Services: Ms Gwen Terry Contract Manager of FM Soft Services, Civic Centre, High Street, Uxbridge UB8 1UW ☎ 01895 250221 ✉ gterry@hillingdon.gov.uk

Children / Youth Services: Mr Tom Murphy, Service Manager of Early Intervention, Civic Centre, High Street, Uxbridge UB8 1UW ☎ 01895 558273 🖷 01895 250493 ✉ tmurphy@hillingdon.gov.uk

Civil Registration: Mr Mike Liddiard, Electoral & Registration Services Manager, Civic Centre, High Street, Uxbridge UB8 1UW ☎ 01895 250962 🖷 01805 250812 ✉ mliddiard@hillingdon.gov.uk

PR / Communications: Mr John Seekings Head of Corporate Communications, Civic Centre, High Street, Uxbridge UB8 1UW ☎ 01895 250822 ✉ jseekings@hillingdon.gov.uk

Community Safety: Mr Ed Shaylor Community Safety Team Service Manager, Civic Centre, High Street, Uxbridge UB8 1UW ☎ 01895 277532 ✉ eshaylor@hillingdon.gov.uk

Computer Management: Ms Shirley Clipp ICT Service Manager, Civic Centre, High Street, Uxbridge UB8 1UW ☎ 01895 250759 ✉ sclipp@hillingdon.gov.uk

Consumer Protection and Trading Standards: Miss Sue Pollitt Trading Standards Manager, Civic Centre, Uxbridge UB8 1UW ☎ 01895 277425 🖷 01895 277443 ✉ spollitt@hillingdon.gov.uk

Contracts: Mr Perry Scott Head of Corporate Procurement, Civic Centre, High Street, Uxbridge UB8 1UW ☎ 01895 556719 ✉ pscott@hillingdon.gov.uk

HILLINGDON

Customer Service: Ms Louise Forster Access Channel Manager, Civic Centre, High Street, Uxbridge UB8 1UW ☎ 01895 556021 🖷 01895 250869 ✉ lforster@hillingdon.gov.uk

Economic Development: Ms Inga Spencer Senior Economic Development Officer, Civic Centre, High Street, Uxbridge UB8 1UW ☎ 01895 250580 🖷 01895 250823 ✉ ispencer@hillingdon.gov.uk

Education: Mr Dan Kennedy Head of Business Performance, Policy & Standards, Education, Housing & Public Health, Civic Centre, High Street, Uxbridge UB8 1UW ☎ 01895 250495 ✉ dkennedy@hillingdon.gov.uk

Electoral Registration: Mr Mike Liddiard, Electoral & Registration Services Manager, Civic Centre, High Street, Uxbridge UB8 1UW ☎ 01895 250962 🖷 01805 250812 ✉ mliddiard@hillingdon.gov.uk

Emergency Planning: Mr Mike Price Service Manager - Civil Protection & Mortuary, Civic Centre, High Street, Uxbridge UB8 1UW ☎ 01895 277048 🖷 01895 556419 ✉ mprice@hillingdon.gov.uk

Energy Management: Mr Richard Coomber Energy Officer, Civic Centre, High Street, Uxbridge UB8 1UW ☎ 01895 556478 ✉ rcoomber@hillingdon.gov.uk

Estates, Property & Valuation: Mr John Gill Estate Service Manager, Civic Centre, High Street, Uxbridge UB8 1UW ☎ 01895 277036 ✉ jgill3@hillingdon.gov.uk

Events Manager: Ms Lyn Summers Project & Events Officer, Civic Centre, High Street, Uxbridge UB8 1UW ☎ 01895 556640 ✉ lsummers@hillingdon.gov.uk

Facilities: Mr John Ioanou Facilities Manager, Civic Centre, High Street, Uxbridge UB8 1UW ☎ 01895 250111 🖷 01895 250290 ✉ jioanouu@hillingdon.gov.uk

Finance: Mr Paul Whaymand Director of Finance, Civic Centre, High Street, Uxbridge UB8 1UW ☎ 01895 250725 🖷 01895 277047 ✉ pwhaymand@hillingdon.gov.uk

Pensions: Mr Ken Chisholm Corporate Pensions Manager, Civic Centre, High Street, Uxbridge UB8 1UW ☎ 01895 250847 ✉ ken.chisholm@hillingdon.gov.uk

Fleet Management: Mr Colin Russell, Waste Division Manager, Harlington Road Depot, Harlington Road, Hillingdon UB8 3EY ☎ 01895 556217 🖷 01895 2500103 ✉ crussell@hillingdon.gov.uk

Grounds Maintenance: Mr Paul Richards Head of Green Spaces, Sport & Culture, Civic Centre, High Street, Uxbridge UB8 1UW ☎ 01895 250814 ✉ prichards@hillingdon.gov.uk

Health and Safety: Ms Christine Barker Corporate Health & Safety Manager, Civic Centre, High Street, Uxbridge UB8 1UW ☎ 01895 277377 🖷 01895 250217 ✉ cbarker@hillingdon.gov.uk

Highways: Mr Chris Tasker Team Manager, Civic Centre, High Street, Uxbridge UB8 1UW ☎ 01895 250564 🖷 01895 277086 ✉ ctasker@hillingdon.gov.uk

Home Energy Conservation: Ms Jo Gill, Energy Efficiency Co-ordinator, Civic Centre, High Street, Uxbridge UB8 1UW ☎ 01895 277436 🖷 01895 277340 ✉ jgill@hillingdon.gov.uk

Housing: Mr Nigel Dicker Deputy Director - Residents' Services, Civic Centre, High Street, Uxbridge UB8 1UW ☎ 01895 250566 ✉ ndicker@hillingdon.gov.uk

Housing Maintenance: Mr Graham Ross Maintenance Contracts Officer, Civic Centre, High Street, Uxbridge UB8 1UW ☎ 01895 556642 ✉ gross@hillingdon.gov.uk

Legal: Mr Rajesh Alagh Borough Solicitor, Civic Centre, Uxbridge UB8 1UW ☎ 01895 250617 🖷 01895 277373 ✉ ralagh@hillingdon.gov.uk

Leisure and Cultural Services: Mr Nigel Dicker Deputy Director - Residents' Services, Civic Centre, High Street, Uxbridge UB8 1UW ☎ 01895 250566 ✉ ndicker@hillingdon.gov.uk

Leisure and Cultural Services: Mr James Rodger Head of Planning & Enforcement, Civic Centre, High Street, Uxbridge UB8 1UW ☎ 01895 220049 ✉ jrodger2@hillingdon.gov.uk

Licensing: Ms Stephanie Waterford Licensing Services Manager, Civic Centre, High Street, Uxbridge UB8 1UW ☎ 01895 277232 🖷 01895 250223 ✉ swaterford@hillingdon.gov.uk

Lifelong Learning: Ms Gill McLean Corporate Learning & Development Manager, Civic Centre, High Street, Uxbridge UB8 1UW ☎ 01895 277338 ✉ gmclean@hillingdon.gov.uk

Lighting: Mr Tim Edwards, Public Lighting Manager, Civic Centre, High Street, Uxbridge UB8 1UW ☎ 01895 277511 🖷 01895 277508 ✉ tedwards@hillingdon.gov.uk

Lottery Funding, Charity and Voluntary: Mr Nigel Cramb, Partnerships, Business & Community Engagement Manager, Civic Centre, Uxbridge UB8 1UW ☎ 01895 250394 🖷 01895 250823 ✉ ncramb@hillingdon.gov.uk

Member Services: Mr Lloyd White Head of Democratic Services, Civic Centre, High Street, Uxbridge UB8 1UW ☎ 01895 250636 🖷 01895 277373 ✉ lwhite@hillingdon.gov.uk

Parking: Mr Roy Clark, Parking Services Manager, Civic Centre, High Street, Uxbridge UB8 1UW ☎ 01895 277776 ✉ rclark@hillingdon.gov.uk

Partnerships: Mr Kevin Byrne Head of Policy & Partnerships, Civic Centre, High Street, Uxbridge UB8 1UW ☎ 01895 556063 ✉ kbyrne2@hillingdon.gov.uk

Personnel / HR: Ms Pauline Moore Head of Human Resources, Civic Centre, High Street, Uxbridge UB8 1UW ☎ 01895 556737 ✉ pmoore2@hillingdon.gov.uk

Planning: Mr James Rodger Head of Planning & Enforcement, Civic Centre, High Street, Uxbridge UB8 1UW ☎ 01895 220049 ✉ jrodger2@hillingdon.gov.uk

Procurement: Mr Perry Scott Head of Corporate Procurement, Civic Centre, High Street, Uxbridge UB8 1UW ☎ 01895 556719 pscott@hillingdon.gov.uk

Public Libraries: Mr Nigel Dicker Deputy Director - Residents' Services, Civic Centre, High Street, Uxbridge UB8 1UW ☎ 01895 250566 ndicker@hillingdon.gov.uk

Recycling & Waste Minimisation: Mr Colin Russell, Waste Division Manager, Harlington Road Depot, Harlington Road, Hillingdon UB8 3EY ☎ 01895 556217 🖷 01895 2500103 crussell@hillingdon.gov.uk

Road Safety: Mrs Mhairi Mansi Road Safety & School Travel Manager, Civic Centre, High Street, Uxbridge UB8 1UW ☎ 01895 250484 🖷 01895 277208 mstephens@hillingdon.gov.uk

Social Services: Mr Tony Zaman Director of Adult Services / Interim Director of Children & Young People's Services, Civic Centre, High Street, Uxbridge UB8 1UW ☎ 01895 250506 tzaman@hillingdon.gov.uk

Social Services (Adult): Mr Tony Zaman Director of Adult Services / Interim Director of Children & Young People's Services, Civic Centre, High Street, Uxbridge UB8 1UW ☎ 01895 250506 tzaman@hillingdon.gov.uk

Social Services (Children): Ms Lynne Adams Service Manager - Children's Resources, Civic Centre, High Street, Uxbridge UB8 1UW ☎ 01895 277867 ladams@hillingdon.gov.uk

Public Health: Dr Sharon Daye Director - Public Health, Civic Centre, High Street, Uxbridge UB8 1UW ☎ 01895 556008 sdaye@hillingdon.gov.uk

Staff Training: Ms Gill McLean Corporate Learning & Development Manager, Civic Centre, High Street, Uxbridge UB8 1UW ☎ 01895 277338 gmclean@hillingdon.gov.uk

Sustainable Communities: Mr Kevin Byrne Head of Policy & Partnerships, Civic Centre, High Street, Uxbridge UB8 1UW ☎ 01895 556063 kbyrne2@hillingdon.gov.uk

Town Centre: Mr David Knowles Transport & Projects Senior Manager, Civic Centre, High Street, Uxbridge UB8 1UW ☎ 01895 277598 dknowles@hillingdon.gov.uk

Traffic Management: Mr Colin Rider Highways Inspector, Civic Centre, High Street, Uxbridge UB8 1UW ☎ 01895 556133 crider@hillingdon.gov.uk

Transport: Mr Colin Russell, Waste Division Manager, Harlington Road Depot, Harlington Road, Hillingdon UB8 3EY ☎ 01895 556217 🖷 01895 2500103 crussell@hillingdon.gov.uk

Transport Planner: Ms Jales Tippell Deputy Director - Highways & Community Engagement, Civic Centre, High Street, Uxbridge UB8 1UW ☎ 01895 277468 jtippel@hillingdon.gov.uk

Total Place: Mr Kevin Byrne Head of Policy & Partnerships, Civic Centre, High Street, Uxbridge UB8 1UW ☎ 01895 556063 kbyrne2@hillingdon.gov.uk

Waste Collection and Disposal: Mr Colin Russell, Waste Division Manager, Harlington Road Depot, Harlington Road, Hillingdon UB8 3EY ☎ 01895 556217 🖷 01895 2500103 crussell@hillingdon.gov.uk

Waste Management: Mr Colin Russell, Waste Division Manager, Harlington Road Depot, Harlington Road, Hillingdon UB8 3EY ☎ 01895 556217 🖷 01895 2500103 crussell@hillingdon.gov.uk

Children's Play Areas: Mr Paul Richards Head of Green Spaces, Sport & Culture, Civic Centre, High Street, Uxbridge UB8 1UW ☎ 01895 250814 prichards@hillingdon.gov.uk

COUNCILLORS

***Mayor* Cooper**, Judith (CON - Uxbridge South)
JCooper@hillingdon.gov.uk

***Deputy Mayor* Hensley**, John (CON - Ickenham)
JHensley@hillingdon.gov.uk

***Leader of the Council* Puddifoot**, Ray (CON - Ickenham)
leader@hillingdon.gov.uk

***Deputy Leader of the Council* Simmonds**, David (CON - Ickenham)
DSimmonds@hillingdon.gov.uk

***Group Leader* Jarjussey**, Phoday (LAB - Botwell)
pjarjussey@hillingdon.gov.uk

Allen, Lynne (LAB - Townfield)
LAllen@hillingdon.gov.uk

Barnes, Teji (CON - Cavendish)
TBarnes@hillingdon.gov.uk

Bianco, Jonathan (CON - Northwood Hills)
JBianco@hillingdon.gov.uk

Birah, Mohinder (LAB - Yeading)
MBirah@hillingdon.gov.uk

Bridges, Wayne (CON - Hillingdon East)
Wbridges@hillingdon.gov.uk

Burles, Tony (LAB - Uxbridge South)
anthonyburles@hotmail.co.uk

Burrows, Keith (CON - Uxbridge South)
KBurrows@hillingdon.gov.uk

Chamdal, Roy (CON - Brunel)
RChamdal@hillingdon.gov.uk

Chapman, Alan (CON - Hillingdon East)
AChapman@hillingdon.gov.uk

Cooper, George (CON - Uxbridge North)
gcooper@hillingdon.gov.uk

Corthorne, Philip (CON - West Ruislip)
PCorthorne@hillingdon.gov.uk

Crowe, Brian (CON - West Ruislip)
bcrowe@hilingdon.gov.uk

Curling, Peter (LAB - Townfield)
PCurling@hillingdon.gov.uk

Dann, Catherine (CON - Eastcote and East Ruislip)
CDann@hillingdon.gov.uk

Davis, Peter (CON - Yiewsley)
PDavis@hillingdon.gov.uk

Denys, Nick (CON - Eastcote and East Ruislip)
NDenys@hillingdon.gov.uk

Dheer, Kanwal (LAB - Barnhill)
KDheer@hillingdon.gov.uk

Dhillon, Jazz (LAB - Pinkwell)
JDhillon@hillingdon.gov.uk

Dhot, Jas (LAB - Barnhill)
JDhot@hillingdon.gov.uk

Duducu, Jem (CON - South Ruislip)
JDuducu@hillingdon.gov.uk

Duncan, Janet (LAB - West Drayton)
JDuncan2@hillingdon.gov.uk

East, Beulah (LAB - Charville)
BeulahEast@hillingdon.gov.uk

Edwards, Ian (CON - Yiewsley)
IEdwards@hillingdon.gov.uk

Eginton, Tony (LAB - Barnhill)
TEginton@hillingdon.gov.uk

Flynn, Duncan (CON - Northwood Hills)
DFlynn@hillingdon.gov.uk

Fyfe, Neil (CON - Charville)
nfyfe@hillingdon.gov.uk

Gardner, Janet (LAB - Botwell)
jgardner@hillingdon.gov.uk

Garg, Narinder (LAB - Yeading)
NGarg@hillingdon.gov.uk

Gilham, Dominic (CON - West Drayton)
dgilham@hillingdon.gov.uk

Graham, Raymond (CON - Uxbridge North)
RGraham@hillingdon.gov.uk

Haggar, Becky (CON - Eastcote and East Ruislip)
BHaggar@hillingdon.gov.uk

Higgins, Henry (CON - Harefield)
HHiggins@hillingdon.gov.uk

Jackson, Pat (CON - Hillingdon East)
PJackson@hillingdon.gov.uk

Kauffman, Allan (CON - South Ruislip)
AKauffman2@hillingdon.gov.uk

Kelly, Judy (CON - South Ruislip)
JKelly@hillingdon.gov.uk

Khatra, Manjit (LAB - Heathrow Villages)
MKhatra@hillingdon.gov.uk

Khursheed, Mo (LAB - Botwell)
MKhursheed@hillingdon.gov.uk

Lakhmana, Kuldeep (LAB - Pinkwell)
KLakhmana@hillingdon.gov.uk

Lavery, Edward (CON - Cavendish)
ELavery@hillingdon.gov.uk

Lewis, Richard (CON - Northwood)
RLewis@hillingdon.gov.uk

Markham, Michael (CON - Manor)
MMarkham@hillingdon.gov.uk

Melvin, Carol (CON - Northwood)
CMelvin@hillingdon.gov.uk

Mills, Richard (CON - Brunel)
rmills2@hillingdon.gov.uk

Mills, Douglas (CON - Manor)
DMills@hillingdon.gov.uk

Money, Peter (LAB - Heathrow Villages)
PMoney@hillingdon.gov.uk

Morgan, John (CON - Northwood Hills)
jmorgan2@hillingdon.gov.uk

Morse, John (LAB - Pinkwell)
JMorse2@hillingdon.gov.uk

Nelson, June (LAB - Heathrow Villages)
JN`elson@hillingdon.gov.uk

O'Brien, Susan (CON - Manor)
so'brien@hillingdon.gov.uk

Oswell, John (LAB - Charville)
joswell@hillingdon.gov.uk

Palmer, Jane (CON - Harefield)
JPalmer3@hillingdon.gov.uk

Riley, John (CON - West Ruislip)
JRiley@hillingdon.gov.uk

Sansarpuri, Robin (LAB - Townfield)
rsansarpuri@hillingdon.gov.uk

Seaman-Digby, Scott (CON - Northwood)
scott@seaman-digby.com

Singh, Jagjit (LAB - Yeading)
JSingh2@hillingdon.gov.uk

Stead, Brian (CON - Brunel)
Bstead@hillingdon.gov.uk

Sweeting, Jan (LAB - West Drayton)
JSweeting@hillingdon.gov.uk

Wallana, Shehryar (CON - Yiewsley)
SWallana@hillingdon.gov.uk

White, Michael (CON - Cavendish)
mrwhite@hillingdon.gov.uk

Yarrow, David (CON - Uxbridge North)
DYarrow@hillingdon.gov.uk

POLITICAL COMPOSITION

CON: 42, LAB: 23

COMMITTEE CHAIRS

Children & Young People: Ms Jane Palmer

Health & Wellbeing: Mr Ray Puddifoot

Licensing: Mr Dominic Gilham

Pensions: Mr Philip Corthorne

Pensions: Mr David Simmonds

Hinckley & Bosworth D

Hinckley & Bosworth Borough Council, Council Offices, Hinckley Hub, Rugby Road, Hinckley LE10 0FR
☎ 01455 238141 🖷 01455 251172 🖳 www.hinckley-bosworth.gov.uk

FACTS AND FIGURES

Parliamentary Constituencies: Bosworth

EU Constituencies: East Midlands
Election Frequency: Elections are of whole council

PRINCIPAL OFFICERS

Chief Executive: Mr Steve Atkinson, Chief Executive, Council Offices, Hinckley Hub, Rugby Road, Hinckley LE10 0FR ☎ 01455 255606 🖷 01455 251172 🖱 steve.atkinson@hinckley-bosworth.gov.uk

Deputy Chief Executive: Mr Bill Cullen, Deputy Chief Executive for Community Direction, Council Offices, Hinckley Hub, Rugby Road, Hinckley LE10 0FR ☎ 01455 255676 🖷 01455 251172 🖱 bill.cullen@hinckley-bosworth.gov.uk

Deputy Chief Executive: Mr Sanjiv Kohli Deputy Chief Executive for Corporate Direction (S151 Officer), Council Offices, Hinckley Hub, Rugby Road, Hinckley LE10 0FR ☎ 01455 235607 🖱 sanjiv.kohli@hinckley-bosworth.gov.uk

Senior Management: Mr Rob Parkinson Chief Officer for Environmental Health, Council Offices, Hinckley Hub, Rugby Road, Hinckley LE10 0FR ☎ 01455 255641 🖷 01455 234590 🖱 rob.parkinson@hinckley-bosworth.gov.uk

Senior Management: Ms Katherine Plummer Chief Officer for Finance, Customer Services & Compliance, Council Offices, Hinckley Hub, Rugby Road, Hinckley LE10 0FR 🖱 katherine.plummer@hinckley-bosworth.gov.uk

Senior Management: Ms Sharon Stacey, Chief Officer for Housing, Community Safety & Partnerships, Council Offices, St Mary's Road, Hinckley LE10 1EQ ☎ 01455 255636 🖷 01455 251172 🖱 sharon.stacey@hinckley-bosworth.gov.uk

Senior Management: Mr Nic Thomas Chief Planning & Development Officer, Council Offices, Hinckley Hub, Rugby Road, Hinckley LE10 0FR ☎ 01455 255692 🖱 nic.thomas@hinckley-bosworth.gov.uk

Building Control: Mr Nic Thomas Chief Planning & Development Officer, Council Offices, Hinckley Hub, Rugby Road, Hinckley LE10 0FR ☎ 01455 255692 🖱 nic.thomas@hinckley-bosworth.gov.uk

Children / Youth Services: Ms Rebecca Ball Children & Young People's Strategic Co-ordinator, Council Offices, Hinckley Hub, Rugby Road, Hinckley LE10 0FR ☎ 01455 255937 🖷 01455 891505 🖱 rebecca.ball@hickley-bosworth.gov.uk

PR / Communications: Mrs Jacqueline Puffett, Communications & Promotions Officer, Council Offices, Hinckley Hub, Rugby Road, Hinckley LE10 0FR ☎ 01455 255630 🖷 01455 635692 🖱 jacqueline.puffett@hinckley-bosworth.gov.uk

Community Planning: Ms Edwina Grant Strategic & Community Planning Officer, Council Offices, Hinckley Hub, Rugby Road, Hinckley LE10 0FR ☎ 01455 255629 🖷 01455 255997 🖱 edwina.grant@hinckley-bosworth.gov.uk

Community Safety: Ms Sharon Stacey, Chief Officer for Housing, Community Safety & Partnerships, Council Offices, Hinckley Hub, Rugby Road, Hinckley LE10 0FR ☎ 01455 255636 🖷 01455 251172 🖱 sharon.stacey@hinckley-bosworth.gov.uk

Computer Management: Mr Paul Langham ICT Manager, Council Offices, Hinckley Hub, Rugby Road, Hinckley LE10 0FR ☎ 01455 255995 🖷 01455 255632 🖱 paul.langham@hinckley-bosworth.gov.uk

Contracts: Mrs Julie Kenny, Chief Officer - Corporate Governance & Housing Repair, Council Offices, Hinckley Hub, Rugby Road, Hinckley LE10 0FR ☎ 01455 255985 🖷 01455 251172 🖱 julie.kenny@hinckley-bosworth.gov.uk

Customer Service: Ms Lynn Fray Customer Services Manager, Council Offices, Hinckley Hub, Rugby Road, Hinckley LE10 0FR ☎ 01455 255625 🖷 01455 251172 🖱 lynn.fray@hinckley-bosworth.gov.uk

Economic Development: Mrs Judith Sturley Senior Economic Regeneration Officer, Council Offices, Hinckley Hub, Rugby Road, Hinckley LE10 0FR ☎ 01455 255855 🖷 01455 251172 🖱 judith.sturley@hinckley-bosworth.gov.uk

Energy Management: Mrs Jane Neachell Climate Change Officer, Council Offices, Hinckley Hub, Rugby Road, Hinckley LE10 0FR ☎ 01455 255947 🖷 01455 234590 🖱 jane.neachell@hinckley-bosworth.gov.uk

Environmental / Technical Services: Mr Rob Parkinson Chief Officer for Environmental Health, Council Offices, Hinckley Hub, Rugby Road, Hinckley LE10 0FR ☎ 01455 255641 🖷 01455 234590 🖱 rob.parkinson@hinckley-bosworth.gov.uk

Environmental Health: Mr Steven Merry Commercial Environmental Health Manager, Council Offices, Hinckley Hub, Rugby Road, Hinckley LE10 0FR ☎ 01455 255735 🖷 01455 234590 🖱 steven.merry@hinckley-bosworth.gov.uk

Environmental Health: Mr Rob Parkinson Chief Officer for Environmental Health, Council Offices, St Mary's Road, Hinckley LE10 1EQ ☎ 01455 255641 🖷 01455 234590 🖱 rob.parkinson@hinckley-bosworth.gov.uk

Estates, Property & Valuation: Mr Malcolm Evans, Estates & Assets Manager, Council Offices, Hinckley Hub, Rugby Road, Hinckley LE10 0FR ☎ 01455 255614 🖷 01455 251172 🖱 malcolm.evans@hinckley-bosworth.gov.uk

Events Manager: Ms Sarah Underwood Events Assistant, Council Offices, Hinckley Hub, Rugby Road, Hinckley LE10 0FR ☎ 01455 255784 🖱 sarah.underwood@hinckley-bosworth.gov.uk

Finance: Mr Sanjiv Kohli Deputy Chief Executive for Corporate Direction (S151 Officer), Council Offices, Hinckley Hub, Rugby Road, Hinckley LE10 0FR ☎ 01455 235607 🖱 sanjiv.kohli@hinckley-bosworth.gov.uk

Finance: Ms Katherine Plummer Chief Officer for Finance, Customer Services & Compliance, Council Offices, Hinckley Hub, Rugby Road, Hinckley LE10 0FR 🖱 katherine.plummer@hinckley-bosworth.gov.uk

Grounds Maintenance: Mrs Caroline Roffey Public Space Manager, The Depot, Middlefield Lane, Hinckley LE10 0RA ☎ 01455 255782 🖷 01455 891428 🖱 caroline.roffey@hinckley-bosworth.gov.uk

HINCKLEY & BOSWORTH

Health and Safety: Mr Adrian Wykes, Principal Safety, Health & Resilience Officer for Environmental Health, Council Offices, Hinckley Hub, Rugby Road, Hinckley LE10 0FR 🖷 01455 234590 🖰 adrian.wykes@hinckley-bosworth.gov.uk

Housing: Ms Sharon Stacey, Chief Officer for Housing, Community Safety & Partnerships, Council Offices, St Mary's Road, Hinckley LE10 1EQ ☎ 01455 255636 🖷 01455 251172 🖰 sharon.stacey@hinckley-bosworth.gov.uk

Housing Maintenance: Ms Sharon Stacey, Chief Officer for Housing, Community Safety & Partnerships, Council Offices, St Mary's Road, Hinckley LE10 1EQ ☎ 01455 255636 🖷 01455 251172 🖰 sharon.stacey@hinckley-bosworth.gov.uk

Legal: Ms Maria Memoli Legal Services Manager, Council Offices, Hinckley Hub, Rugby Road, Hinckley LE10 0FR ☎ 01455 255621 🖰 emma.horton@hinckley-bosworth.gov.uk

Leisure and Cultural Services: Mr Simon Jones, Cultural Services Manager, Council Offices, Hinckley Hub, Rugby Road, Hinckley LE10 0FR ☎ 01455 255699 🖷 01455 891505 🖰 simon.jones@hinckley-bosworth.gov.uk

Licensing: Mr Mark Brymer, Principal Licensing Officer, Council Offices, Hinckley Hub, Rugby Road, Hinckley LE10 0FR ☎ 01455 255645 🖷 ; 01455 234590 🖰 mark.brymer@hinckley-bosworth.gov.uk

Member Services: Miss Rebecca Owen Democratic Services Officer, Council Offices, Hinckley Hub, Rugby Road, Hinckley LE10 0FR ☎ 01455 255879 🖷 01455 635692 🖰 rebecca.owen@hinckley-bosworth.gov.uk

Personnel / HR: Mrs Julie Stay, Human Resources & Transformation Manager, Council Offices, Hinckley Hub, Rugby Road, Hinckley LE10 0FR ☎ 01455 255688 🖷 01455 255997 🖰 julie.stay@hinckley-bosworth.gov.uk

Planning: Mr Nic Thomas Chief Planning & Development Officer, Council Offices, Hinckley Hub, Rugby Road, Hinckley LE10 0FR ☎ 01455 255692 🖰 nic.thomas@hinckley-bosworth.gov.uk

Procurement: Mrs Julie Kenny, Chief Officer - Corporate Governance & Housing Repair, Council Offices, St Mary's Road, Hinckley LE10 1EQ ☎ 01455 255985 🖷 01455 251172 🖰 julie.kenny@hinckley-bosworth.gov.uk

Recycling & Waste Minimisation: Ms Jane Green Minimisation Officer, The Depot, Middlefield Lane, Hinckley LE10 0RA ☎ 01455 255980 🖷 01455 891428 🖰 jane.green@hinckley-bosworth.gov.uk

Regeneration: Mr Nic Thomas Chief Planning & Development Officer, Council Offices, Hinckley Hub, Rugby Road, Hinckley LE10 0FR ☎ 01455 255692 🖰 nic.thomas@hinckley-bosworth.gov.uk

Staff Training: Mrs Julie Stay, Human Resources & Transformation Manager, Council Offices, St Mary's Road, Hinckley LE10 1EQ ☎ 01455 255688 🖷 01455 255997 🖰 julie.stay@hinckley-bosworth.gov.uk

Street Scene: Mr Darren Moore Business Development & Waste Manager, Council Offices, Hinckley Hub, Rugby Road, Hinckley LE10 0FR ☎ 01455 255976 🖰 darren.moore@hinckley-bosworth.gov.uk

Tourism: Ms Lindsay Orton Creative Communites & Tourism Officer, Council Offices, Hinckley Hub, Rugby Road, Hinckley LE10 0FR ☎ 01455 255805 🖷 01455 891505 🖰 linday.orton@hinckley-bosworth.gov.uk

Town Centre: Mr Mark Hyrniw Town Centre Manager, Council Offices, Hinckley Hub, Rugby Road, Hinckley LE10 0FR ☎ 01455 255755 🖷 ; 01455 891505 🖰 ; mark.hryniw@hinckley-bosworth.gov.uk

COUNCILLORS

***Mayor* Richards**, Janice (CON - Earl Shilton)
janice.richards@hinckley-bosworth.gov.uk

***Deputy Mayor* Allen**, Richard (CON - Earl Shilton)
richard.allen@hinckley-bosworth.gov.uk

***Leader of the Council* Hall**, Mike (CON - Burbage Sketchley & Stretton)
mike.hall@hinckley-bosworth.gov.uk

***Deputy Leader of the Council* Morrell**, K (CON - Twycross & Witherley with Sheepy)
kevin.morrell@hinckley-bosworth.gov.uk

***Group Leader* Bray**, Stuart (LD - Hinckley Castle)
stuart.bray@hinckley-bosworth.gov.uk

Bessant, Paul (CON - Markfield, Stanton & Field Head)
paul.bessant@hinckley-bosworth.gov.uk

Bill, David (LD - Hinckley Clarendon)
david.bill@hinckley-bosworth.gov.uk

Boothby, Chris (CON - Ratby, Bagworth & Thornton)
chris.boothby@hinckley-bosworth.gov.uk

Camamile, Ruth (CON - Newbold Verdon with Desford & Peckleton)
ruth.camamile@hinckley-bosworth.gov.uk

Cartwright, Martin (LD - Groby)
martin.cartwright@hinckley-bosworth.gov.uk

Cook, Maureen (CON - Cadeby, Carlton & Market Bosworth with Shackerstone)
maureen.cook@hinckley-bosworth.gov.uk

Cope, Genesta (LD - Hinckley Trinity)
genesta.cope@hinckley-bosworth.gov.uk

Cope, David (LD - Hinckley Trinity)
david.cope@hinckley-bosworth.gov.uk

Crooks, William (LD - Barlestone, Nailstone and Obaston)
bill.crooks@hinckley-bosworth.gov.uk

Hodgkins, Lynda (LD - Hinckley De Montfort)
lynda.hodgkins@hinckley-bosworth.gov.uk

Hollick, Ted (LD - Groby)
ted.hollick@hinckley-bosworth.gov.uk

Kirby, Jan (CON - Hinckley De Montfort)
jan.kirby@hinckley-bosworth.gov.uk

Ladkin, Chris (CON - Earl Shilton)
chris.ladkin@hinckley-bosworth.gov.uk

Lay, Matthew (LAB - Markfield, Stanton & Field Head)
matthew.lay@hinckley-bosworth.gov.uk

Lynch, Keith (LD - Hinckley Clarendon)
keith.lynch@hinckley-bosworth.gov.uk

Nichols, Keith (LD - Hinckley De Montfort)
keith.nichols@hinckley-bosworth.gov.uk

Nickerson, Mark (CON - Burbage St Catherines & Lash Hill)
mark.nickerson@hinckley-bosworth.gov.uk

O'Shea, Ozzy (CON - Ratby, Bagworth & Thornton)
ozzy.oshea@hinckley-bosworth.gov.uk

Roberts, RB (CON - Barwell)
russel.roberts@hinckley-bosworth.gov.uk

Rooney, Stanley (CON - Burbage Sketchley & Stretton)
stanley.rooney@hinclkley_bosworth.gov.uk

Smith, Hazel (CON - Barwell)
hazel.smith@hinckley-bosworth.gov.uk

Surtees, Miriam (CON - Newbold Verdon with Desford & Peckleton)
miriam.surtees@hinckley-bosworth.gov.

Sutton, Brian (CON - Newbold Verdon with Desford & Peckleton)
brian.sutton@hinckley-bosworth.gov.uk

Taylor, Diane (LD - Hinckley Clarendon)
diane.taylor@hinckley-bosworth.gov.uk

Wallace, Peter (CON - Burbage St Catherines & Lash Hill)
peter.wallace@hinckley-bosworth.gov.uk

Ward, R (CON - Ambien)
reg.ward@hinckley-bosworth.gov.uk

Williams, Huw (CON - Barwell)
huw.williams@hinckley-bosworthuk

Witherford, Bronwen (LD - Hinckley Castle)
bron.witherford@hinckley-bosworth.gov.uk

Wright, Amanda (CON - Burbage Sketchley & Stretton)
amanda.wright@hinckley-bosworth.gov.uk

POLITICAL COMPOSITION

CON: 21, LD: 12, LAB: 1

COMMITTEE CHAIRS

Finance & Audit: Mrs Ruth Camamile

Licensing: Ms Hazel Smith

Planning: Mr R Ward

Horsham D

Horsham District Council, Parkside, Chart Way, Horsham RH12 1RL
☎ 01403 215100 🖷 01403 262985 contact@horsham.gov.uk
www.horsham.gov.uk

FACTS AND FIGURES

Parliamentary Constituencies: Arundel and South Downs, Horsham
EU Constituencies: South East
Election Frequency: Elections are of whole council

PRINCIPAL OFFICERS

Chief Executive: Mr Tom Crowley, Chief Executive, Parkside, Chart Way, Horsham RH12 1RL ☎ 01403 215102 🖷 01403 215145 tom.crowley@horsham.gov.uk

Senior Management: Mrs Natalie Brahma-Pearl Director - Community Services, Parkside, Chart Way, Horsham RH12 1RL ☎ 01403 215250

Senior Management: Mrs Katharine Eberhart Director - Corporate Resources, Parkside, Chart Way, Horsham RH12 1RL ☎ 01403 215300 🖷 01403 215371 katharine.eberhart@horsham.gov.uk

Senior Management: Mr Chris Lyons Director - Planning, Economic Development & Property, Parkside, Chart Way, Horsham RH12 1RL ☎ 01403 215401 chris.lyons@horsham.gov.uk

Access Officer / Social Services (Disability): Mr Stephen Shorrocks Building Control Manager, Parkside, Chart Way, Horsham RH12 1RL ☎ 01403 215500 🖷 01403 215198 stephen.shorrocks@horsham.gov.uk

Architect, Building / Property Services: Mr Brian Elliott Property & Facilities Manager, Parkside, Chart Way, Horsham RH12 1RL brian.elliott@horsham.gov.uk

Best Value: Mr Mark Pritchard Commissioning & Performance Manager, Parkside, Chart Way, Horsham RH12 1RL ☎ 01403 215110 mark.pritchard@horsham.gov.uk

Building Control: Mr Stephen Shorrocks Building Control Manager, Parkside, Chart Way, Horsham RH12 1RL ☎ 01403 215500 🖷 01403 215198 stephen.shorrocks@horsham.gov.uk

PR / Communications: Mrs Alison Turner Communications Manager, Parkside, Chart Way, Horsham RH12 1RL ☎ 01403 215549 🖷 01403 262985 alison.turner@horsham.gov.uk

Community Planning: Mrs Barbara Childs Spatial Planning Manager, Parkside, Chart Way, Horsham RH12 1RL ☎ 01403 215181

Community Safety: Mr Trevor Beadle Head of Community & Culture, Parkside, Chart Way, Horsham RH12 1RL ☎ 01403 215493 🖷 01403 262985 trevor.beadle@horsham.gov.uk

Community Safety: Mr Greg Charman Community Safety Manager, Parkside, Chart Way, Horsham RH12 1RL ☎ 01403 215124 greg.charman@horsham.gov.uk

Computer Management: Mr John Ross Head of CenSus ICT, Parkside, Chart Way, Horsham RH12 1RL ☎ 01403 215217 john.ross@horsham.gov.uk

Contracts: Mrs Katharine Eberhart Director - Corporate Resources, Parkside, Chart Way, Horsham RH12 1RL ☎ 01403 215301 🖷 01403 215371 katharine.eberhart@horsham.gov.uk

Customer Service: Mr David Plank Customer Services Manager, Parkside, Chart Way, Horsham RH12 1RL ☎ 01403 215371 david.plank@horsham.gov.uk

Economic Development: Ms Lynda Spain Economic Development Officer, Parkside, Chart Way, Horsham RH12 1RL ☎ 01403 215137 lynda.spain@horsham.gov.uk

E-Government: Mr John Ross Head of CenSus ICT, Parkside, Chart Way, Horsham RH12 1RL ☎ 01403 215217 john.ross@horsham.gov.uk

HORSHAM

Electoral Registration: Mrs Maxine Mears, Elections Services Officer, Parkside, Chart Way, Horsham RH12 1RL ☎ 01403 215126 🖷 01403 262985 🖰 maxine.mears@horsham.gov.uk

Emergency Planning: Mr Greg Charman Community Safety Manager, Parkside, Chart Way, Horsham RH12 1RL ☎ 01403 215124 🖰 greg.charman@horsham.gov.uk

Environmental Health: Mr John Batchelor Environmental Health, Parkside, Chart Way, Horsham RH12 1RL ☎ 01403 215417 🖰 john.batchelor@horsham.gov.uk

Estates, Property & Valuation: Mr Brian Elliott Property & Facilities Manager, Parkside, Chart Way, Horsham RH12 1RL 🖰 brian.elliott@horsham.gov.uk

Estates, Property & Valuation: Mr John Loxley, Estates Management & Valuation Surveyor, Parkside, Chart Way, Horsham RH12 1RL ☎ 01403 215483 🖷 01403 215487 🖰 john.loxley@horsham.gov.uk

Facilities: Mr Brian Elliott Property & Facilities Manager, Parkside, Chart Way, Horsham RH12 1RL 🖰 brian.elliott@horsham.gov.uk

Finance: Mrs Katharine Eberhart Director - Corporate Resources, Parkside, Chart Way, Horsham RH12 1RL ☎ 01403 215300 🖷 01403 215371 🖰 katharine.eberhart@horsham.gov.uk

Fleet Management: Mr John McArthur Street Scene & Fleet Manager, Parkside, Chart Way, Horsham RH12 1RL ☎ 01403 739388 🖰 john.mcarthur@horsham.gov.uk

Grounds Maintenance: Mr Evan Giles, Parks Services Manager, Parkside, Chart Way, Horsham RH12 1RL ☎ 01403 215257 🖷 01403 215268 🖰 evan.giles@horsham.gov.uk

Health and Safety: Mr Michael Marchant Corporate Safety Officer, Parkside, Chart Way, Horsham RH12 1RL ☎ 01403 215211 🖰 michael.marchant@horsham.gov.uk

Home Energy Conservation: Miss Gill Daniel, Environmental Co-ordination Officer, Parkside, Chart Way, Horsham RH12 1RL ☎ 01403 215281 🖷 01403 215467 🖰 gill.daniel@horsham.gov.uk

Housing: Mr Andrew Smith Strategic Housing Manager, Parkside, Chart Way, Horsham RH12 1RL ☎ 01403 215202 🖰 andrew.smith@horsham.gov.uk

Legal: Mr Paul Cummins Head of Legal & Democratic Services, Parkside, Chart Way, Horsham RH12 1RL ☎ 01403 215435 🖰 paul.cummins@horsham.gov.uk

Leisure and Cultural Services: Mr Trevor Beadle Head of Community & Culture, Parkside, Chart Way, Horsham RH12 1RL ☎ 01403 215493 🖷 01403 262985 🖰 trevor.beadle@horsham.gov.uk

Licensing: Mr John Batchelor Environmental Health, Parkside, Chart Way, Horsham RH12 1RL ☎ 01403 215417 🖰 john.batchelor@horsham.gov.uk

Member Services: Mr Paul Cummins Head of Legal & Democratic Services, Parkside, Chart Way, Horsham RH12 1RL ☎ 01403 215435 🖰 paul.cummins@horsham.gov.uk

Parking: Mr Ben Golds Parking Services Manager, Parkside, Chart Way, Horsham RH12 1RL ☎ 01403 215055 🖰 ben.golds@horsham.gov.uk

Personnel / HR: Mr Robert Laban Human Resources & Organisational Development Manager, Parkside, Chart Way, Horsham RH12 1RL ☎ 01403 215406 🖰 robert.laban@horsham.gov.uk

Planning: Mr Aidan Thatcher Development Manager, Parkside, Chart Way, Horsham RH12 1RL ☎ 01403 215167 🖰 aidan.thatcher@horsham.gov.uk

Procurement: Mr Roger Dennis Joint Procurement Officer, Parkside, Chart Way, Horsham RH12 1RL ☎ 01444 477254 🖰 rogerd@horsham.gov.uk

Staff Training: Mr Robert Laban Human Resources & Organisational Development Manager, Parkside, Chart Way, Horsham RH12 1RL ☎ 01403 215406 🖰 robert.laban@horsham.gov.uk

Street Scene: Mr John McArthur Street Scene & Fleet Manager, Parkside, Chart Way, Horsham RH12 1RL ☎ 01403 739388 🖰 john.mcarthur@horsham.gov.uk

Sustainable Communities: Mr Trevor Beadle Head of Community & Culture, Parkside, Chart Way, Horsham RH12 1RL ☎ 01403 215493 🖷 01403 262985 🖰 trevor.beadle@horsham.gov.uk

Sustainable Development: Mrs Barbara Childs Spatial Planning Manager, Parkside, Chart Way, Horsham RH12 1RL ☎ 01403 215181

Tourism: Mr Trevor Beadle Head of Community & Culture, Parkside, Chart Way, Horsham RH12 1RL ☎ 01403 215493 🖷 01403 262985 🖰 trevor.beadle@horsham.gov.uk

Town Centre: Mr Garry Mortimer-Cook, Town Centres Manager, Parkside, Chart Way, Horsham RH12 1RL ☎ 01403 215386 🖰 garry.mortimer-cook@horsham.gov.uk

Children's Play Areas: Mr Evan Giles, Parks Services Manager, Parkside, Chart Way, Horsham RH12 1RL ☎ 01403 215257 🖷 01403 215268 🖰 evan.giles@horsham.gov.uk

COUNCILLORS

***Leader of the Council* Dawe**, Ray (CON - Chantry (Amberley, Parham, Storrington and Sullington and Washington)) Ray.Dawe@horsham.gov.uk

Arthur, Roger (UKIP - Chanctonbury) roger.arthur@horsham.gov.uk

Bailey, John (CON - Rudgwick) John.Bailey@horsham.gov.uk

Baldwin, Andrew (CON - Holbrook East (North Horsham)) Andrew.Baldwin@horsham.gov.uk

Blackwall, John (CON - Chanctonbuty (Ashington, Thakeham, West Chiltington and Wiston)) John.Blackall@horsham.gov.uk

Bradnum, Toni (CON - Nuthurst (Lower Beeding and Nuthurst))
Toni.Bradnum@horsham.gov.uk

Britten, Alan (CON - Roffey North (North Horsham))
Alan.Britten@horsham.gov.uk

Burgess, Peter (CON - Holbrook West (Horsham Town and Holbrook West Ward of North Horsham))
peter.burgess@horsham.gov.uk

Burgess, Karen (CON - Holbrook East (North Horsham))
Karen.Burgess@horsham.gov.uk

Chidlow, John (CON - Southwater)
John.Chidlow@horsham.gov.uk

Chowen, Jonathan (CON - Cowfold, Shermanbury and West Grinstead)
Jonathan.Chowen@horsham.gov.uk

Circus, Philip (CON - Chanctonbury (Ashington, Thakeham, West Chiltington and Wiston))
Philip.Circus@horsham.gov.uk

Clarke, Roger (CON - Cowfold, Shermanbury and West Grinstead)
roger.clarke@horsham.gov.uk

Clarke, Paul (CON - Pulborough and Coldwaltham)
Paul.Clarke@horsham.gov.uk

Coldwell, David (CON - Bramber, Upper Beeding and Woodmancote)
David.Coldwell@horsham.gov.uk

Cornell, Roy (CON - Roffey South (Horsham Town and Roffey South Ward of North Horsham))
Roy.Cornell@horsham.gov.uk

Costin, Christine (LD - Trafalgar (Horsham Town))
Christine.Costin@horsham.gov.uk

Crosbie, Leonard (LD - Trafalgar (Horsham Town))
Leonard.Crosbie@horsham.gov.uk

Dancer, Johnathan (LD - Roffey North (North Horsham))
Johnathan.Dancer@horsham.gov.uk

Donnelly, Brian (CON - Pulborough and Coldwaltham)
Brian.Donnelly@horsham.gov.uk

French, Matthew (CON - Broadbridge Heath)
Matthew.French@horsham.gov.uk

Hogben, Tony (CON - Denne (Horsham Town))
Anthony.Hogben@horsham.gov.uk

Howard, Ian (CON - Southwater)
Ian.Howard@horsham.gov.uk

Jenkins, David (CON - Chanctonbury (Ashington, Thakeham, West Chiltington and Wiston))
David.Jenkins@horsham.gov.uk

Jupp, Nigel (CON - Billinghurst and Shipley)
Nigel.Jupp@horsham.gov.uk

Kitchen, Liz (CON - Rusper and Colgate)
Elizabeth.kitchen@horsham.gov.uk

Lee, Adrian (CON - Denne (Horsham Town))
Adrian.Lee@horsham.gov.uk

Lindsay, Gordon (CON - Billingshurst and Shipley)
Gordon.Lindsay@horsham.gov.uk

Lloyd, Tim (CON - Steyning (Steyning and Ashurst))
Timothy.Lloyd@horsham.gov.uk

Marshall, Paul (CON - Chantry (Amberley, Parham, Storrington & Sullington and Washington))
Paul.Marshall@horsham.gov.uk

Mitchell, Christian (CON - Holbrook West (Horsham Town and Holbrook West Ward of North Horsham))
Christian.Mitchell@horsham.gov.uk

Morgan, Mike (IND - Henfield (Henfield Parish))
mike.morgan@horsham.gov.uk

Murphy, Josh (CON - Horsham Park (Horsham Town))
Josh.Murphy@horsham.gov.uk

Newman, Godfrey (LD - Forest (Horsham Town))
Godfrey.Newman@horsham.gov.uk

O'Connell, Brian (CON - Henfield)
Brian.O'Connell@horsham.gov.uk

Relleen, Connor (CON - Horsham Park (Horsham Town))
Connor.Relleen@horsham.gov.uk

Ritchie, Stuart (CON - Itchingfield, Slinfold and Warnham)
Stuart.Ritchie@horsham.gov.uk

Rowbottom, Kate (CON - Billingshurst and Shipley)
Kate.Rowbottom@horsham.gov.uk

Sanson, Jim (CON - Chantry (Amberley, Parham, Storrington and Sullington and Washington))
jim.sanson@horsham.gov.uk

Skipp, David (LD - Horsham Park (Horsham Town))
David.Skipp@horsham.gov.uk

Staines, Ben (CON - Bramber,Upper Beeding and Woodmancote)
Ben.Staines@horsham.gov.uk

Torn, Simon (CON - Roffey South (Horsham Town and Roffey South Ward of North Horsham))
Simon.Torn@horsham.gov.uk

Vickers, Claire (CON - Southwater)
Claire.Vickers@horsham.gov.uk

Willett, Michael (CON - Steyning (Steyning & Ashurst))
Michael.Willett@horsham.gov.uk

Youtan, Tricia (CON - Itchingfield, Slinfold and Warnham)
Tricia.Youtan@horsham.gov.uk

POLITICAL COMPOSITION

CON: 38, LD: 5, UKIP: 1, IND: 1

Hounslow L

Hounslow London Borough Council, Civic Centre, Lampton Road, Hounslow TW3 4DN
☎ 020 8583 2000 🖷 020 8583 2592
information.ced@hounslow.gov.uk www.hounslow.gov.uk

FACTS AND FIGURES

Parliamentary Constituencies: Brentford and Isleworth, Feltham and Heston
EU Constituencies: London
Election Frequency: Elections are of whole council

PRINCIPAL OFFICERS

Chief Executive: Ms Mary Harpley Chief Executive, Civic Centre, Lampton Road, Hounslow TW3 4DN ☎ 020 8583 2012 🖷 202 8583 2013 mary.harpley@hounslow.gov.uk

Senior Management: Mr Alan Adams Director of Children's & Adults' Services, Civic Centre, Lampton Road, Hounslow TW3 4DN ☎ 020 8583 3500 alan.adams@hounslow.gov.uk

HOUNSLOW

Senior Management: Dr Imran Choudhury Assistant Director - Leisure & Public Health, Civic Centre, Lampton Road, Hounslow TW3 4DN ✉ imran.choudhury@hounslow.gov.uk

Senior Management: Mr Brendon Walsh Director of Regeneration, Economic Development & Environment, Civic Centre, Lampton Road, Hounslow TW3 4DN ☎ 020 8583 5331 ✉ brendon.walsh@hounslow.gov.uk

Best Value: Mr David Allum, Director of Corporate Services, Hounslow Homes, St Catherines House, 2 Hanworth Road, Feltham TW13 5AB ☎ 020 8583 3938 📠 020 8583 3730 ✉ david.allum@hounslowhomes.org.uk

Building Control: Ms Heather Cheesbrough Assistant Director of Strategic Planning, Regeneration & Economic Development, Civic Centre, Lampton Road, Hounslow TW3 4DN ☎ 020 8583 5328 ✉ heather.cheesbrough@hounslow.gov.uk

Building Control: Mr Paul Jackson Interim Head of Building Control, Civic Centre, Lampton Road, Hounslow TW3 4DN ☎ 020 8583 5402 ✉ paul.jackson@hounslow.gov.uk

Catering Services: Mr Nick Moore Interim General Manager of DSO Catering, Spring Grove House, West Thames College, Isleworth TW7 4HS ☎ 020 8583 2932 ✉ nick.moore@hounslow.gov.uk

Children / Youth Services: Mr Alan Adams Director of Children's & Adults' Services, Civic Centre, Lampton Road, Hounslow TW3 4DN ☎ 020 8583 3500 ✉ alan.adams@hounslow.gov.uk

Children / Youth Services: Mr Michael Marks Assistant Director of Early Intervention & Education, Civic Centre, Lampton Road, Hounslow TW3 4DN ☎ 020 8583 2903 ✉ michael.marks@hounslow.gov.uk

Civil Registration: Ms Susan Hayter Registration & Nationality Service Manager Superintendent Registrar, Civic Centre, Lampton Road, Hounslow TW3 4DN ☎ 020 8583 2086 ✉ susan.hayter@hounslow.gov.uk

PR / Communications: Mr Ian Tomkins Interim Head - Corporate Communications, Civic Centre, Lampton Road, Hounslow TW3 4DN ☎ 020 8583 2180 ✉ ian.tompkins@hounslow.gov.uk

Community Planning: Ms Merle Abbott Head of Inclusion, Civic Centre, Lampton Road, Hounslow TW3 4DN ☎ 020 8583 2788 ✉ merle.abbott@hounslow.gov.uk

Community Safety: Mr Aled Richards Assistant Director of Community Safety, Environment & Regulatory Services, Civic Centre, Lampton Road, Hounslow TW3 4DN ☎ 020 8583 4961 ✉ aled.richards@hounslow.gov.uk

Community Safety: Ms Kirti Sisodia, Head of Community Safety & Crime Reduction, Civic Centre, Lampton Road, Hounslow TW3 4DN ☎ 020 8583 2464 📠 020 8583 2466 ✉ kirti.sisodia@hounslow.gov.uk

Computer Management: Ms Barbara Munden Head of ICT, Civic Centre, Lampton Road, Hounslow TW3 4DN ☎ 020 8583 5950 ✉ barbara.munden@hounslow.gov.uk

Consumer Protection and Trading Standards: Mr Nigel Farmer, Head of Business Regulations, Civic Centre, Lampton Road, Hounslow TW3 4DN ☎ 020 8583 5147 📠 020 8583 5130 ✉ nigel.farmer@hounslow.gov.uk

Corporate Services: Ms Sarah Rayner Assistant Director of Supply Chain Management, Civic Centre, Lampton Road, Hounslow TW3 4DN ☎ 020 8583 5018 ✉ sarah.rayner@hounslow.gov.uk

Corporate Services: Ms Clare Saul Deputy Head of Corporate Communications, Civic Centre, Lampton Road, Hounslow TW3 4DN ☎ 020 8583 2186 ✉ clare.saul@hounslow.gov.uk

Customer Service: Ms Bukky McGlynn Acting Head of Customer Services, Civic Centre, Lampton Road, Hounslow TW3 4DN ☎ 020 8583 4504 ✉ bukky.mcglynn@hounslow.gov.uk

Customer Service: Mr David Palmer Head of Business Support, Civic Centre, Lampton Road, Hounslow TW3 4DN ☎ 020 8583 5300 ✉ david.palmer@hounslow.gov.uk

Direct Labour: Mr Sayeed Kadir, Director of Property Services for Hounslow Homes, Hounslow Homes, Civic Centre, Lampton Road, Hounslow TW3 4DN ☎ 020 8583 4301 📠 020 8583 3709 ✉ sayeed.kadir@hounslowhomes.org.uk

Economic Development: Ms Heather Cheesbrough Assistant Director of Strategic Planning, Regeneration & Economic Development, Civic Centre, Lampton Road, Hounslow TW3 4DN ☎ 020 8583 5328 ✉ heather.cheesbrough@hounslow.gov.uk

Economic Development: Mr Alan Hesketh Interim Principal Economic Development Officer, Civic Centre, Lampton Road, Hounslow TW3 4DN ☎ 020 8583 2420 ✉ alan.hesketh@hounslow.gov.uk

Economic Development: Mr Brendon Walsh Director of Regeneration, Economic Development & Environment, Civic Centre, Lampton Road, Hounslow TW3 4DN ☎ 020 8583 5331 ✉ brendon.walsh@hounslow.gov.uk

Education: Mr Alan Adams Director of Children's & Adults' Services, Civic Centre, Lampton Road, Hounslow TW3 4DN ☎ 020 8583 3500 ✉ alan.adams@hounslow.gov.uk

Education: Mr Michael Marks Assistant Director of Early Intervention & Education, Civic Centre, Lampton Road, Hounslow TW3 4DN ☎ 020 8583 2903 ✉ michael.marks@hounslow.gov.uk

E-Government: Ms Barbara Munden Head of ICT, Civic Centre, Lampton Road, Hounslow TW3 4DN ☎ 020 8583 5950 ✉ barbara.munden@hounslow.gov.uk

Electoral Registration: Ms Cassie Triggs Electoral Manager, Civic Centre, Lampton Road, Hounslow TW3 4DN ☎ 020 8583 2095 📠 020 8583 2055 ✉ cassie.triggs@hounslow.gov.uk

Emergency Planning: Mr Twm Palmer Interim Head of Emergency Planning, Civic Centre, Lampton Road, Hounslow TW3 4DN ☎ 020 8583 5019 ✉ twm.palmer@hounslow.gov.uk

Environmental / Technical Services: Mr Brendon Walsh Director of Regeneration, Economic Development & Environment, Civic Centre, Lampton Road, Hounslow TW3 4DN ☎ 020 8583 5331 ✉ brendon.walsh@hounslow.gov.uk

Environmental Health: Mr Gerry McCarthy Head of Pollution Control Team, Civic Centre, Lampton Road, Hounslow TW3 4DN ☎ 020 8583 5183 ✉ gerry.mccarthy@hounslow.gov.uk

Estates, Property & Valuation: Mr Ed Palmieri Interim Head of Property Management in Corporate Property, Civic Centre, Lampton Road, Hounslow TW3 4DN ☎ 020 8583 2500 ✉ ed.palmieri@hounslow.gov.uk

Events Manager: Ms Anita Bhangoo Events Manager, Civic Centre, Lampton Road, Hounslow TW3 4DN ☎ 020 8583 2547 ✉ anita.bhangoo@hounslow.gov.uk

Facilities: Ms Anna Harries, Head of Facilities, Civic Centre, Lampton Road, Hounslow TW3 4DN ☎ 020 8583 4079 🖷 020 8583 2488 ✉ anna.harries@hounslow.gov.uk

Finance: Ms Christine Holland Head of Central Finance (CED), Civic Centre, Lampton Road, Hounslow TW3 4DN ☎ 020 8583 2380 ✉ christine.holland@hounslow.gov.uk

Finance: Mr Robert Meldrum Head of Finance for Environment, Civic Centre, Lampton Road, Hounslow TW3 4DN ☎ 020 8583 5311 ✉ robert.meldrum@hounslow.gov.uk

Finance: Mr Clive Palfreyman Assistant Director for Strategic Finance, Civic Centre, Lampton Road, Hounslow TW3 4DN ☎ 020 8583 2430 ✉ clive.palfreyman@hounslow.gov.uk

Finance: Mr Alex Taylor Head of Finance & Accountancy (CSLL), Civic Centre, Lampton Road, Hounslow TW3 4DN ☎ 020 8583 2836 ✉ alex.taylor@hounslow.gov.uk

Pensions: Ms L Lorelei, Chief Technical Officer, Pensions & Investment, Civic Centre, Lampton Road, Hounslow TW3 4DN ☎ 020 8583 2310 ✉ lorelei.watson@hounslow.gov.uk

Pensions: Mr Neil Mason Pensions Officer, Civic Centre, Lampton Road, Hounslow TW3 4DN ☎ 020 8583 5635 ✉ neil.mason@hounslow.gov.uk

Fleet Management: Ms Sarah Rayner Assistant Director of Supply Chain Management, Civic Centre, Lampton Road, Hounslow TW3 4DN ☎ 020 8583 5018 ✉ sarah.rayner@hounslow.gov.uk

Grounds Maintenance: Mr Paul Bassi Leisure & Cultural Services Manager, Civic Centre, Lampton Road, Hounslow TW3 4DN ☎ 020 8583 6794 ✉ paul.bassi@hounslow.gov.uk

Health and Safety: Ms Geraldine Austen-Reed Lead Occupational Health & Safety Advisor, Civic Centre, Lampton Road, Hounslow TW3 4DN ☎ 020 8583 2000 ✉ geraldine.austen-reed@hounslow.gov.uk

Health and Safety: Mr Peter Matthew Assistant Director for Housing, Civic Centre, Lampton Road, Hounslow TW3 4DN ☎ 020 8583 2504 ✉ peter.matthew@hounslow.gov.uk

Health and Safety: Mr Aled Richards Assistant Director of Community Safety, Environment & Regulatory Services, Civic Centre, Lampton Road, Hounslow TW3 4DN ☎ 020 8583 4961 ✉ aled.richards@hounslow.gov.uk

Home Energy Conservation: Mr Charles Pipe, Energy Efficiency Advisor, Civic Centre, Lampton Road, Hounslow TW3 4DN ☎ 020 8583 3963 🖷 020 8583 3990 ✉ charles.pipe@hounslow.gov.uk

Housing: Mr Peter Matthew Assistant Director for Housing, Civic Centre, Lampton Road, Hounslow TW3 4DN ☎ 020 8583 2504 ✉ peter.matthew@hounslow.gov.uk

Housing: Ms Alison Simmons Assistant Director of Housing Strategy Services, Civic Centre, Lampton Road, Hounslow TW3 4DN ☎ 020 8583 3500 ✉ alison.simmons@hounslow.gov.uk

Housing Maintenance: Ms Orla Gallagher Interim Chief Executive - Houslow Housing, Civic Centre, Lampton Road, Hounslow TW3 4DN ☎ 020 8583 3707 🖷 020 8583 2592 ✉ orla.gallagher@hounslow.gov.uk

Local Area Agreement: Ms Helen Wilson Policy Officer, Civic Centre, Lampton Road, Hounslow TW3 4DN ☎ 020 8583 2461 ✉ helen.wilson@hounslow.gov.uk

Legal: Ms Caroline Eaton Monitoring Officer, Civic Centre, Lampton Road, Hounslow TW3 4DN ☎ 020 8583 2027 ✉ caroline.eaton@hounslow.gov.uk

Leisure and Cultural Services: Dr Imran Choudhury Assistant Director - Leisure & Public Health, Civic Centre, Lampton Road, Hounslow TW3 4DN ☎ ✉ imran.choudhury@hounslow.gov.uk

Leisure and Cultural Services: Mr Hamish Pringle Assistant Director of Leisure & Cultural Services, Civic Centre, Lampton Road, Hounslow TW3 4DN ☎ 202 8583 4647 ✉ Hamish.pringle@hounslow.gov.uk

Licensing: Mr Nigel Farmer, Head of Business Regulations, Civic Centre, Lampton Road, Hounslow TW3 4DN ☎ 020 8583 5147 🖷 020 8583 5130 ✉ nigel.farmer@hounslow.gov.uk

Lifelong Learning: Mr Alan Adams Director of Children's & Adults' Services, Civic Centre, Lampton Road, Hounslow TW3 4DN ☎ 020 8583 3500 ✉ alan.adams@hounslow.gov.uk

Lottery Funding, Charity and Voluntary: Ms Uttam Gujral, Head of Community Partnerships Unit, Civic Centre, Lampton Road, Hounslow TW3 4DN ☎ 020 8583 2455 🖷 020 8583 2466 ✉ uttam.gujral@hounslow.gov.uk

Member Services: Mr Ian Duke Head of Policy & Scrutiny, Civic Centre, Lampton Road, Hounslow TW3 4DN ☎ 020 8583 2191 ✉ ian.duke@hounslow.gov.uk

Member Services: Mr Thomas Ribbits Head of Democratic Services, Civic Centre, Lampton Road, Hounslow TW3 4DN ☎ 020 8583 2251 🖷 020 8583 2252 ✉ thomas.ribbits@hounslow.gov.uk

Parking: Mr Steve Stearn Interim Head of Parking, Civic Centre, Lampton Road, Hounslow TW3 4DN ☎ 020 8583 2000 steve.stearn@hounslow.gov.uk

Personnel / HR: Mr John Kitching Head of Human Resources, Civic Centre, Lampton Road, Hounslow TW3 4DN ☎ 020 8583 2287 john.kitching@hounslow.gov.uk

Personnel / HR: Mr John Walsh Assistant Director of Transformation & HR, Civic Centre, Lampton Road, Hounslow TW3 4DN ☎ 020 8583 2100 john.walsh@hounslow.gov.uk

Planning: Ms Heather Cheesbrough Assistant Director of Strategic Planning, Regeneration & Economic Development, Civic Centre, Lampton Road, Hounslow TW3 4DN ☎ 020 8583 5328 heather.cheesbrough@hounslow.gov.uk

Planning: Mr Brendon Walsh Director of Regeneration, Economic Development & Environment, Civic Centre, Lampton Road, Hounslow TW3 4DN ☎ 020 8583 5331 brendon.walsh@hounslow.gov.uk

Procurement: Mr Mark Pearson Head of Procurement, Civic Centre, Lampton Road, Hounslow TW3 4DN ☎ 020 8583 5763 mark.pearson@hounslow.gov.uk

Public Libraries: Mr Tim Douglas Leisure & Cultural Services Manager, Civic Centre, Lampton Road, Hounslow TW3 4DN ☎ 020 8583 3538 tim.douglas@hounslow.gov.uk

Recycling & Waste Minimisation: Mr Andrew Baker Interim Head of Waste & Recycling, Civic Centre, Lampton Road, Hounslow TW3 4DN ☎ 020 8583 5065 andrew.baker@hounslow.gov.uk

Regeneration: Ms Heather Cheesbrough Assistant Director of Strategic Planning, Regeneration & Economic Development, Civic Centre, Lampton Road, Hounslow TW3 4DN ☎ 020 8583 5328 heather.cheesbrough@hounslow.gov.uk

Regeneration: Mr Brendon Walsh Director of Regeneration, Economic Development & Environment, Civic Centre, Lampton Road, Hounslow TW3 4DN ☎ 020 8583 5331 brendon.walsh@hounslow.gov.uk

Road Safety: Mr Mark Frost Road Safety Manager, Civic Centre, Lampton Road, Hounslow TW3 4DN ☎ 020 8583 2000 mark.frost@hounslow.gov.uk

Social Services: Mr Mun Thong Phung Assistant Director - Adult Safeguarding, Social Care & Health, Civic Centre, Lampton Road, Hounslow TW3 4DN ☎ 020 8583 3593 mun-thong.phung@hounslow.gov.uk

Social Services (Adult): Mr Alan Adams Director of Children's & Adults' Services, Civic Centre, Lampton Road, Hounslow TW3 4DN ☎ 020 8583 3500 alan.adams@hounslow.gov.uk

Social Services (Adult): Ms Rachel Egan Assistant Director - Strategy, Planning & Transformation, Civic Centre, Lampton Road, Hounslow TW3 4DN ☎ 020 8583 3001 rachel.egan@hounslow.gov.uk

Social Services (Adult): Ms Mimi Konigsberg Director of Community Services, Civic Centre, Lampton Road, Hounslow TW3 4DN ☎ 020 8583 3500 🖷 020 8583 3077 mimi.konigsberg@hounslow.gov.uk

Social Services (Children): Ms Jacqui McShannon Assistant Director of Children's Safeguarding & Specialist Services, Civic Centre, Lampton Road, Hounslow TW3 4DN ☎ 020 8583 3002 jacqui.mcshannon@hounslow.gov.uk

Safeguarding: Mr Mun Thong Phung Assistant Director - Adult Safeguarding, Social Care & Health, Civic Centre, Lampton Road, Hounslow TW3 4DN ☎ 020 8583 3593 mun-thong.phung@hounslow.gov.uk

Public Health: Dr Imran Choudhury Assistant Director - Leisure & Public Health, Civic Centre, Lampton Road, Hounslow TW3 4DN ☎ imran.choudhury@hounslow.gov.uk

Sustainable Development: Mr Rob Gibson, Head of Environmental Strategy, Civic Centre, Lampton Road, Hounslow TW3 4DN ☎ 020 8583 5217 🖷 020 8583 5233 rob.gibson@hounslow.gov.uk

Traffic Management: Mr Mark Frost Road Safety Manager, Civic Centre, Lampton Road, Hounslow TW3 4DN ☎ 020 8583 2000 mark.frost@hounslow.gov.uk

Waste Collection and Disposal: Mr Andrew Baker Interim Head of Waste & Recycling, Civic Centre, Lampton Road, Hounslow TW3 4DN ☎ 020 8583 5065 andrew.baker@hounslow.gov.uk

Waste Management: Mr Andrew Baker Interim Head of Waste & Recycling, Civic Centre, Lampton Road, Hounslow TW3 4DN ☎ 020 8583 5065 andrew.baker@hounslow.gov.uk

COUNCILLORS

Leader of the Council **Curran**, Steve (LAB - Syon)
steve.curran@hounslow.gov.uk

Deputy Leader of the Council **Mann**, Amritpal (LAB - Heston East)
amrit.mann@hounslow.gov.uk

Anderson, Keith (LAB - Bedfont)
keith.anderson@hounslow.gov.uk

Atterton, Candice (LAB - Hanworth)
candice.atterton@hounslow.gov.uk

Atwal Hear, Harleen (LAB - Heston Central)
harleen.atwalhear@hounslow.gov.uk

Barwood, Felicity (CON - Chiswick Riverside)
felicity.barwood@hounslow.gov.uk

Bath, Lily (LAB - Heston West)
lily.bath@hounslow.gov.uk

Bath, Rajinder (LAB - Heston West)
rajinder.bath@hounslow.gov.uk

Bruce, Tom (LAB - Hounslow South)
tom.bruce@hounslow.gov.uk

Buttar, Manjit (LAB - Heston Central)
manjit.buttar@hounslow.gov.uk

Carey, Peter (CON - Osterley and Spring Grove)
peter.carey@hounslow.gov.uk

Chatt, John (LAB - Feltham North)
john.chatt@hounslow.gov.uk

Chaudhary, Samia (LAB - Hanworth)
samia.chaudhary@hounslow.gov.uk

Chopra, Bandna (LAB - Hounslow West)
bandna.chopra@hounslow.gov.uk

Christie, Sam (LAB - Bedfont)
sam.christie@hounslow.gov.uk

Collins, Mel (LAB - Brentford)
mel.collins@hounslow.gov.uk

Davies, Samantha (CON - Turnham Green)
samantha.davies@hounslow.gov.uk

Dennison, Theo (LAB - Syon)
theo.dennison@hounslow.gov.uk

Dunne, Katherine (LAB - Syon)
katherine.dunne@hounslow.gov.uk

Ellar, Colin (LAB - Hounslow Heath)
colin.ellar@hounslow.gov.uk

Foote, Richard (LAB - Hanworth)
richard.foote@hounslow.gov.uk

Green, Linda (LAB - Isleworth)
linda.green@hounslow.gov.uk

Grewal, Pritam (LAB - Hounslow Central)
pritam.grewal@hounslow.gov.uk

Grewal, Ajmer (LAB - Hounslow Central)
ajmer.grewal@hounslow.gov.uk

Grewal, Puneet (LAB - Hounslow West)
puneet.grewal@hounslow.gov.uk

Gupta, Sachin (LAB - Bedfont)
sachin.gupta@hounslow.gov.uk

Gurung, Bishnu Bahadur (LAB - Hanworth Park)
bishnu.gurung@hounslow.gov.uk

Hearn, Sam (CON - Chiswick Riverside)
sam.hearn@hounslow.gov.uk

Howe, Tina (LAB - Hanworth Park)
tina.howe@hounslow.gov.uk

Hughes, Elizabeth (LAB - Feltham West)
elizabeth.hughes@hounslow.gov.uk

Hughes, David (LAB - Feltham West)
david.hughes@hounslow.gov.uk

Kaur, Kamaljit (LAB - Heston East)
kamaljit.kaur@hounslow.gov.uk

Khan, Hanif (LAB - Hanworth Park)
hanif.khan@hounslow.gov.uk

Lal, Gurmail (LAB - Heston East)
gurmail.lal@hounslow.gov.uk

Lambert, Guy (LAB - Brentford)
guy.lambert@hounslow.gov.uk

Lee, Adrian (CON - Turnham Green)
adrian.lee@hounslow.gov.uk

Louki, Tony (LAB - Osterley and Spring Grove)
tony.louki@hounslow.gov.uk

Lynch, Paul (CON - Chiswick Riverside)
paul.lynch@hounslow.gov.uk

Malhotra, Mukesh (LAB - Hounslow Heath)
mukesh.malhotra@hounslow.gov.uk

Malik, Nisar (LAB - Hounslow Central)
nisar.malik@hounslow.gov.uk

Malik, Khulique (LAB - Feltham North)
khulique.malik@hounslow.gov.uk

Mayne, Ed (LAB - Isleworth)
ed.mayne@hounslow.gov.uk

McGregor, Gerald (CON - Chiswick Homefields)
gerald.mcgregor@hounslow.gov.uk

Mehrban, Shaida (LAB - Hounslow South)
shaida.mehrban@hounslow.gov.uk

Mir, Hina (LAB - Feltham North)
hina.mir@hounslow.gov.uk

Mitchell, Alan (LAB - Feltham West)
alan.mitchell@hounslow.gov.uk

O'Reilly, Sheila (CON - Osterley and Spring Grove)
sheila.o'reilly@hounslow.gov.uk

Oulds, Robert (CON - Chiswick Homefields)
robert.oulds@hounslow.gov.uk

Purewal, Surinder (LAB - Heston Central)
surinder.purewal@hounslow.gov.uk

Rajawat, Shantanu (LAB - Heston West)
Shantanu.Rajawat@hounslow.gov.uk

Saeed, Daanish (LAB - Cranford)
daanish.saeed@hounslow.gov.uk

Sampson, Sue (LAB - Isleworth)
sue.sampson@hounslow.gov.uk

Sangha, Sohan (LAB - Cranford)
sohan.sangha@hounslow.gov.uk

Savin, Myra (LAB - Brentford)
myra.savin@hounslow.gov.uk

Sharma, Jagdish (LAB - Hounslow West)
jagdish.sharma@hounslow.gov.uk

Smart, Corinna (LAB - Hounslow Heath)
corinna.smart@hounslow.gov.uk

Thompson, Peter (CON - Turnham Green)
peter.thompson@hounslow.gov.uk

Todd, John (CON - Chiswick Homefields)
john.todd@hounslow.gov.uk

Virdi, Gurpal (IND - Cranford)
gurpal.virdi1@hounslow.gov.uk

Whatley, Bob (LAB - Hounslow South)
bob.whatley@hounslow.gov.uk

POLITICAL COMPOSITION

LAB: 48, CON: 11, IND: 1

COMMITTEE CHAIRS

Audit: Mr Surinder Purewal

Health & Safety: Ms Katherine Dunne

Licensing: Mr David Hughes

Planning: Mr Bob Whatley

HUNTINGDONSHIRE

Huntingdonshire D

Huntingdonshire District Council, Pathfinder House, St. Mary's Street, Huntingdon PE29 3TN
☎ 01480 388388 🖷 01480 388099 ✉ mail@huntsdc.gov.uk
💻 www.huntsdc.gov.uk

FACTS AND FIGURES

Parliamentary Constituencies: Cambridgeshire North West, Huntingdon
EU Constituencies: Eastern
Election Frequency: Elections are by thirds

PRINCIPAL OFFICERS

Chief Executive: Ms Jo Lancaster Managing Director, Pathfinder House, St. Mary's Street, Huntingdon PE29 3TN ☎ 01480 388300 ✉ jo.lancaster@huntingdonshire.gov.uk

Senior Management: Mr Nigel McCurdy Corporate Director - Delivery, Pathfinder House, St. Mary's Street, Huntingdon PE29 3TN ☎ 01480 388332 🖷 01480 388099 ✉ nigel.mccurdy@huntingdonshire.gov.uk

Senior Management: Ms Julie Slatter Corporate Director - Services, Pathfinder House, St. Mary's Street, Huntingdon PE29 3TN ☎ 01480 388388 🖷 01480 388099 ✉ steve.couper@huntingdonshire.gov.uk

Architect, Building / Property Services: Mr Chris Stopford Head of Community Services, Pathfinder House, St. Mary's Street, Huntingdon PE29 3TN ☎ 01480 388280 🖷 01480 388099 ✉ chris.stopford@huntingdonshire.gov.uk

Building Control: Mr Chris Knights Building Control Manager, Pathfinder House, St. Mary's Street, Huntingdon PE29 3TN ☎ 01480 388449 🖷 01480 388099 ✉ chris.knights@huntingdonshire.gov.uk

PR / Communications: Mrs Donna Rocket Corporate Project Officer of Communications, Pathfinder House, St. Mary's Street, Huntingdon PE29 3TN ☎ 01480 388239 🖷 01480 388099 ✉ donna.rocket@huntingdonshire.gov.uk

Community Planning: Mr Dan Smith, Community Initiatives Manager, Pathfinder House, St. Mary's Street, Huntingdon PE29 3TN ☎ 01480 388377 🖷 01480 388099 ✉ dan.smith@huntingdonshire.gov.uk

Community Safety: Mrs Claudia Deeth, Team Leader of Community Safety, Pathfinder House, St. Mary's Street, Huntingdon PE29 3TN ☎ 01480 388233 🖷 01480 388099 ✉ claudia.deeth@huntingdonshire.gov.uk

Computer Management: Mr John Taylor Head of Customer Services, Pathfinder House, St. Mary's Street, Huntingdon PE29 3TN ☎ 01480 388119 🖷 01480 388099 ✉ john.taylor@huntingdonshire.gov.uk

Contracts: Mr Nigel Arkle Procurement Manager, Pathfinder House, St. Mary's Street, Huntingdon PE29 3TN ☎ 01480 388104 🖷 01480 388099 ✉ nigel.arkle@huntingdonshire.gov.uk

Corporate Services: Mr Adrian Dobbyne Corporate Team Manager, Pathfinder House, St. Mary's Street, Huntingdon PE29 3TN ☎ 01480 388100 🖷 01480 388099 ✉ adrian.dobbyne@huntingdonshire.gov.uk

Customer Service: Mr John Taylor Head of Customer Services, Pathfinder House, St. Mary's Street, Huntingdon PE29 3TN ☎ 01480 388119 🖷 01480 388099 ✉ john.taylor@huntingdonshire.gov.uk

Economic Development: Mr Andy Moffat Building Control Manager, Pathfinder House, St. Mary's Street, Huntingdon PE29 3TN ☎ 01480 388400 🖷 01480 388099 ✉ andy.moffatt@huntingdonshire.gov.uk

E-Government: Mr Joe Beddingfield Web & Systems Manager, Pathfinder House, St. Mary's Street, Huntingdon PE29 3TN ☎ 01480 388235 🖷 01480 388099 ✉ joe.beddingfield@huntingdonshire.gov.uk

Electoral Registration: Mrs Lisa Jablonska Elections & Democratic Services Manager, Pathfinder House, St. Mary's Street, Huntingdon PE29 3TN ☎ 01480 388004 🖷 01480 388099 ✉ lisa.jablonska@huntingdonshire.gov.uk

Emergency Planning: Mr Steven Howell Health, Safety & Emergency Planning Co-ordinator, Pathfinder House, St. Mary's Street, Huntingdon PE29 3TN ☎ 01480 38863 🖷 01480 388099 ✉ steven.howell@huntingdonshire.gov.uk

Energy Management: Mr Chris Jablonski, Team Leader - Environment, Pathfinder House, St. Mary's Street, Huntingdon PE29 3TN ☎ 01480 388368 🖷 01480 388099 ✉ chris.jablonski@huntingdonshire.gov.uk

Environmental / Technical Services: Mr Chris Stopford Head of Community Services, Pathfinder House, St. Mary's Street, Huntingdon PE29 3TN ☎ 01480 388280 🖷 01480 388099 ✉ chris.stopford@huntingdonshire.gov.uk

Environmental Health: Mr Chris Stopford Head of Community Services, Pathfinder House, St. Mary's Street, Huntingdon PE29 3TN ☎ 01480 388280 🖷 01480 388099 ✉ chris.stopford@huntingdonshire.gov.uk

Estates, Property & Valuation: Mr Bill Tilah Estates Management Surveyor, Pathfinder House, St. Mary's Street, Huntingdon PE29 3TN ☎ 01480 387086 🖷 01480 388099 ✉ bill.tilah@huntingdonshire.gov.uk

Facilities: Mr Gerry Ryan Facilities & Administration Manager, Pathfinder House, St. Mary's Street, Huntingdon PE29 3TN ☎ 01480 388425 🖷 01480 388099 ✉ gerry.ryan@huntingdonshire.gov.uk

Finance: Mr Clive Mason Head of Resources, Pathfinder House, St. Mary's Street, Huntingdon PE29 3TN ☎ 01480 388103 🖷 01480 388099 ✉ clive.mason@huntingdonshire.gov.uk

Fleet Management: Mr Gerry Ryan Facilities & Administration Manager, Pathfinder House, St. Mary's Street, Huntingdon PE29 3TN ☎ 01480 388425 🖷 01480 388099 ✉ gerry.ryan@huntingdonshire.gov.uk

Grounds Maintenance: Mr John Craig Green Space Manager, Pathfinder House, St. Mary's Street, Huntingdon PE29 3TN ☎ 01480 388638 🖷 01480 388099 ✉ john.craig@huntingdonshire.gov.uk

Health and Safety: Mr Andrew Radford Corporate Safety Advisor, Pathfinder House, St. Mary's Street, Huntingdon PE29 3TN ☎ 01480 388079 🖷 01480 388099 ✉ safety.advisor@huntingdonshire.gov.uk

Home Energy Conservation: Ms Julia Blackwell, Energy Efficiency Officer, Pathfinder House, St. Mary's Street, Huntingdon PE29 3TN ☎ 01480 388527 🖷 01480 388099 ✉ julia.blackwell@huntingdonshire.gov.uk

Housing: Mr John Taylor Head of Customer Services, Pathfinder House, St. Mary's Street, Huntingdon PE29 3TN ☎ 01480 388119 🖷 01480 388099 ✉ john.taylor@huntingdonshire.gov.uk

Housing Maintenance: Mr John Taylor Head of Customer Services, Pathfinder House, St. Mary's Street, Huntingdon PE29 3TN ☎ 01480 388119 🖷 01480 388099 ✉ john.taylor@huntingdonshire.gov.uk

Legal: Miss Shirley Tacey Solicitor, Pathfinder House, St. Mary's Street, Huntingdon PE29 3TN ☎ 01480 388023 🖷 01480 388099 ✉ shirley.tacey@huntingdonshire.gov.uk

Leisure and Cultural Services: Ms Jayne Wisely Head of Leisure & Health, Pathfinder House, St. Mary's Street, Huntingdon PE29 3TN ☎ 01480 388049 🖷 01480 388099 ✉ simon.bell@huntingdonshire.gov.uk

Licensing: Mrs Christine Allison Licensing Manager, Pathfinder House, St. Mary's Street, Huntingdon PE29 3TN ☎ 01480 388010 🖷 01480 388099 ✉ christine.allison@huntingdonshire.gov.uk

Lighting: Mrs Christine Allison Licensing Manager, Pathfinder House, St. Mary's Street, Huntingdon PE29 3TN ☎ 01480 388010 🖷 01480 388099 ✉ christine.allison@huntingdonshire.gov.uk

Lottery Funding, Charity and Voluntary: Mr Dan Smith, Community Initiatives Manager, Pathfinder House, St. Mary's Street, Huntingdon PE29 3TN ☎ 01480 388377 🖷 01480 388099 ✉ dan.smith@huntingdonshire.gov.uk

Member Services: Mrs Lisa Jablonska Elections & Democratic Services Manager, Pathfinder House, St. Mary's Street, Huntingdon PE29 3TN ☎ 01480 388004 🖷 01480 388099 ✉ lisa.jablonska@huntingdonshire.gov.uk

Parking: Mr Stuart Bell, Transportation Team Leader, Pathfinder House, St. Mary's Street, Huntingdon PE29 3TN ☎ 01480 388387 🖷 01480 388099 ✉ stuart.bell@huntingdonshire.gov.uk

Partnerships: Mr Adrian Dobbyne Corporate Team Manager, Pathfinder House, St. Mary's Street, Huntingdon PE29 3TN ☎ 01480 388100 🖷 01480 388099 ✉ adrian.dobbyne@huntingdonshire.gov.uk

Personnel / HR: Mr Daniel Buckridge Policy, Performance & Transformation Manager, Pathfinder House, St. Mary's Street, Huntingdon PE29 3TN ☎ 01480 388065 🖷 01480 388099 ✉ daniel.buckridge@huntingdonshire.gov.uk

Planning: Mr Andy Moffat Building Control Manager, Pathfinder House, St. Mary's Street, Huntingdon PE29 3TN ☎ 01480 388400 🖷 01480 388099 ✉ andy.moffatt@huntingdonshire.gov.uk

Procurement: Mr Nigel Arkle Procurement Manager, Pathfinder House, St. Mary's Street, Huntingdon PE29 3TN ☎ 01480 388104 🖷 01480 388099 ✉ nigel.arkle@huntingdonshire.gov.uk

Recycling & Waste Minimisation: Mr Chris Jablonski, Team Leader - Environment, Pathfinder House, St. Mary's Street, Huntingdon PE29 3TN ☎ 01480 388368 🖷 01480 388099 ✉ chris.jablonski@huntingdonshire.gov.uk

Regeneration: Mr Andy Moffat Building Control Manager, Pathfinder House, St. Mary's Street, Huntingdon PE29 3TN ☎ 01480 388400 🖷 01480 388099 ✉ andy.moffatt@huntingdonshire.gov.uk

Staff Training: Ms Lisa Morris Senior HR Advisor, Pathfinder House, St. Mary's Street, Huntingdon PE29 3TN ☎ 01480 388314 🖷 01480 388099 ✉ lisa.morris@huntingdonshire.gov.uk

Street Scene: Mrs Sonia Hansen, Street Scene Manager, Pathfinder House, St. Mary's Street, Huntingdon PE29 3TN ☎ 01480 388360 🖷 01480 388099 ✉ sonia.hansen@huntingdonshire.gov.uk

Sustainable Communities: Mr Dan Smith, Community Initiatives Manager, Pathfinder House, St. Mary's Street, Huntingdon PE29 3TN ☎ 01480 388377 🖷 01480 388099 ✉ dan.smith@huntingdonshire.gov.uk

Sustainable Development: Mr Paul Bland Planning Services Manager of Policy, Pathfinder House, St. Mary's Street, Huntingdon PE29 3TN ☎ 01480 388430 🖷 01480 388099 ✉ paul.bland@huntingdonshire.gov.uk

Town Centre: Mrs Sue Bedlow Corporate Team Manager, Pathfinder House, St. Mary's Street, Huntingdon PE29 3TN ☎ 01480 387096 🖷 01480 388099 ✉ susan.bedlow@huntingdonshire.gov.uk

Transport: Mr Stuart Bell, Transportation Team Leader, Pathfinder House, St. Mary's Street, Huntingdon PE29 3TN ☎ 01480 388387 🖷 01480 388099 ✉ stuart.bell@huntingdonshire.gov.uk

Transport Planner: Mr Stuart Bell, Transportation Team Leader, Pathfinder House, St. Mary's Street, Huntingdon PE29 3TN ☎ 01480 388387 🖷 01480 388099 ✉ stuart.bell@huntingdonshire.gov.uk

Waste Collection and Disposal: Mrs Beth Gordon Operations Manager, Pathfinder House, St. Mary's Street, Huntingdon PE29 3TN ☎ 01480 388720

HUNTINGDONSHIRE

Waste Management: Mrs Beth Gordon Operations Manager, Pathfinder House, St. Mary's Street, Huntingdon PE29 3TN
☎ 01480 388720

Children's Play Areas: Mr John Craig Green Space Manager, Pathfinder House, St. Mary's Street, Huntingdon PE29 3TN
☎ 01480 388638 🖷 01480 388099
 john.craig@huntingdonshire.gov.uk

COUNCILLORS

***Chair* Bucknell**, Peter (CON - Warboys and Bury)
peter.bucknell@huntingdonshire.gov.uk

***Vice-Chair* West**, Richard (CON - Gransden and The Offords)
richard.west@huntingdonshire.gov.uk

***Leader of the Council* Ablewhite**, Jason (CON - St Ives - East)
jason.ablewhite@huntingdonshire.gov.uk

***Deputy Leader of the Council* Howe**, Robin (CON - Upwood and The Raveleys)
robin.howe@huntingdonshire.gov.uk

***Group Leader* Churchill**, Ken (UKIP - Little Paxton)
ken.churchill@huntingdonshire.gov.uk

***Group Leader* Conboy**, Sarah (LD - Godmanchester)
sarah.conboy@huntingdonshire.gov.uk

Alban, Timothy (CON - Stilton)
tim.alban@huntingdonshire.gov.uk

Baker, Keith (CON - Alconbury and the Stukeleys)
keith.baker@huntingdonshire.gov.uk

Bates, Ian (CON - The Hemingfords)
ian.bates@huntingdonshire.gov.uk

Boddington, Barbara (CON - Gransden and The Offords)
barbara.boddington@huntingdonshire.gov.uk

Brown, Daryl (CON - Huntingdon East)
daryl.brown@huntingdonshire.gov.uk

Bull, Graham (CON - Somersham)
Graham.Bull@huntingdonshire.gov.uk

Butler, Eric (CON - Yaxley and Farcet)
eric.butler@huntsdc.gov.uk

Carter, Robin (CON - Earith)
roboin.carter@huntingdonshire.gov.uk

Cawley, Stephen (CON - Huntingdon West)
stephen.cawley@huntingdonshire.gov.uk

Chapman, Barry (CON - St Neots - Priory Park)
barry.chapman@huntingdonshire.gov.uk

Criswell, Steve (CON - Somersham)
steve.criswell@huntingdonshire.gov.uk

Curtis, Angela (CON - Warboys and Bury)
angie.curtis@huntingdonshire.gov.uk

Davies, John (CON - St Ives - South)
john.davies@huntingdonshire.gov.uk

Dew, Douglas (CON - The Hemingfords)
douglas.dew@huntingdonshire.gov.uk

Dickinson, Angie (CON - St Ives - South)
angie.dickinson@huntingdonshire.gov.uk

Duffy, Lisa (UKIP - Ramsey)
lisa.duffy@huntingdonshire.gov.uk

Farrer, Rodney (IND - St Neots - Eaton Ford)
bob.farrer@huntingdonshire.gov.uk

Francis, Mike (CON - Earith)
mike.francis@huntingdonshire.gov.uk

Fuller, Ryan (CON - St Ives - West)
ryan.fuller@huntingdonshire.gov.uk

Gardener, Ian (CON - St Neots - Priory Park)
ian.gardener@huntingdonshire.gov.uk

George, Leedo (LAB - Huntingdon North)
leedo.george@huntingdonshire.gov.uk

Giles, Derek (IND - St Neots - Eaton Socon)
derek.giles@huntingdonshire.gov.uk

Gray, Jonathan (CON - Kimbolton and Staughton)
jonathan.gray@huntingdonshire.gov.uk

Hansard, Andrew (CON - St Neots - Eynesbury)
andrew.hansard@huntingdonshire.gov.uk

Hardy, Andrew (UKIP - Huntingdon East)
andrew.hardy@huntingdonshire.gov.uk

Harrison, Roger (CON - St Neots - Eaton Socon)
roger.harrison@huntingdonshire.gov.uk

Harty, David (CON - St Neots - Eaton Ford)
david.harty@huntingdonshire.gov.uk

Hayward, Terry (IND - Buckden)
terry.hayward@huntingdonshire.gov.uk

Hyland, Barry (UKIP - Yaxley and Farcet)
barry.hyland@huntingdonshire.gov.uk

Jordan, Patricia (LD - Brampton)
patricia.jordan@huntingdonshire.gov.uk

Kadewere, Patrick (LAB - Huntingdon North)
patrick.kadewere@huntingdonshire.gov.uk

Kadic, Laine (CON - Godmanchester)
laine.kadic@huntingdonshire.gov.uk

Matthews, Rita (CON - Elton and Folksworth)
rita.matthews@huntingdonshire.gov.uk

Mead, David (CON - Fenstanton)
david.mead@huntingdonshire.gov.uk

Morris, John (LD - Brampton)
john.morris@huntingdonshire.gov.uk

Oliver, Mark (CON - Yaxley and Farcet)
mark.oliver@huntingdonshire.gov.uk

Palmer, John (CON - Ramsey)
john.palmer@huntingdonshire.gov.uk

Reeve, Peter (UKIP - Ramsey)
reeve@ukip.org

Reynolds, Deborah (CON - St Ives - East)
deborah.reynolds@huntingdonshire.gov.uk

Sanderson, Tom (CON - Huntingdon West)
tom.sanderson@huntingdonshire.gov.uk

Shellens, Michael (LD - Huntingdon East)
mike.shellens@huntingdonshire.gov.uk

Tuplin, Dick (IND - Sawtry)
dick.tuplin@huntingdonshire.gov.uk

Tysoe, Darren (CON - Sawtry)
darren.tysoe@huntingdonshire.gov.uk

Van De Kerkhove, Steven (IND - St Neots - Eynesbury)
steve.vandekerkhove@huntingdonshire.gov.uk

Wainwright, Karl (CON - St Neots - Eynesbury)
karl.wainwright@huntingdonshire.gov.uk

White, Jim (CON - Ellington)
jim.white@huntingdonshire.gov.uk

POLITICAL COMPOSITION

CON: 36, IND: 5, UKIP: 5, LD: 4, LAB: 2

COMMITTEE CHAIRS

Development Management: Mrs Barbara Boddington

Licensing: Mr Ryan Fuller

Hyndburn D

Hyndburn Borough Council, Scaitcliffe House, Ormerod Street, Accrington BB5 0PF
☎ 01254 388111 🖷 01254 392597 🖳 www.hyndburnbc.gov.uk

FACTS AND FIGURES

Parliamentary Constituencies: Hyndburn
EU Constituencies: North West
Election Frequency: Elections are by thirds

PRINCIPAL OFFICERS

Chief Executive: Mr David Welsby, Chief Executive, Scaitcliffe House, Ormerod Street, Accrington BB5 0PF ☎ 01254 388111 🖷 01254 380637 ✉ dave.welsby@hyndburnbc.gov.uk

Deputy Chief Executive: Mr Joe McIntyre, Deputy Chief Executive, Scaitcliffe House, Ormerod Street, Accrington BB5 0PF ☎ 01254 388111 🖷 01254 380637 ✉ joe.mcintyre@hyndburnbc.gov.uk

Senior Management: Ms Jane Ellis, Executive Director - Legal & Democratic Services, Scaitcliffe House, Ormerod Street, Accrington BB5 0PF ☎ 01254 388111 🖷 01254 380637 ✉ jane.ellis@hyndburnbc.gov.uk

Architect, Building / Property Services: Mrs Helen McCue-Melling Regeneration & Property Manager, Scaitcliffe House, Ormerod Street, Accrington BB5 0PF ☎ 01254 388111 🖷 01254 380122 ✉ helen.mccue-melling@hyndburnbc.gov.uk

Best Value: Mr Michael Walker, Corporate Performance Manager, Scaitcliffe House, Ormerod Street, Accrington BB5 0PF ☎ 01254 388111 🖷 01254 380637 ✉ michael.walker@hyndburnbc.gov.uk

Building Control: Mr Simon Prideaux Chief Planning & Transportation Officer, Scaitcliffe House, Ormerod Street, Accrington BB5 0PF ☎ 01254 388111 🖷 01254 391625 ✉ simon.prideaux@hyndburnbc.gov.uk

PR / Communications: Mrs Cathy Kierans, Senior Marketing & Communications Officer, Scaitcliffe House, Ormerod Street, Accrington BB5 0PF ☎ 01254 388111 🖷 01254 380637 ✉ cathy.kierans@hyndburnbc.gov.uk

Community Planning: Mr Rob Grigorjevs Head of Town Centre Development, Scaitcliffe House, Ormerod Street, Accrington BB5 0PF ☎ 01254 388111 🖷 01254 380122 ✉ rob.grigorjevs@hyndburnbc.gov.uk

Community Safety: Mr Michael Walker, Corporate Performance Manager, Scaitcliffe House, Ormerod Street, Accrington BB5 0PF ☎ 01254 388111 🖷 01254 380637 ✉ michael.walker@hyndburnbc.gov.uk

Computer Management: Mr Scott Gardner, ICT Manager, Scaitcliffe House, Ormerod Street, Accrington BB5 0PF ☎ 01254 388111 🖷 01254 380272 ✉ scott.gardner@hyndburnbc.gov.uk

Corporate Services: Mr David Welsby, Chief Executive, Scaitcliffe House, Ormerod Street, Accrington BB5 0PF ☎ 01254 388111 🖷 01254 380637 ✉ dave.welsby@hyndburnbc.gov.uk

Customer Service: Mrs Pauline Duckworth Head of Customer Services & Benefits, Town Hall, Blackburn Road, , Accrington BB5 1LA ☎ 01254 380200 ✉ pauline.duckworth@hyndburnbc.gov.uk

Customer Service: Mr Lee Middlehurst, Finance & Administration Manager, Town Hall, Blackburn Road, Accrington BB5 1LA ☎ 01254 388111 🖷 01254 392597 ✉ lee.middlehurst@hyndburnbc.gov.uk

E-Government: Mr Scott Gardner, ICT Manager, Scaitcliffe House, Ormerod Street, Accrington BB5 0PF ☎ 01254 388111 🖷 01254 380272 ✉ scott.gardner@hyndburnbc.gov.uk

Electoral Registration: Ms Karina Bilham Elections Officer, Scaitcliffe House, Ormerod Street, Accrington BB5 0PF ☎ 01254 388111 🖷 01254 392597 ✉ karina.billham@hyndburnbc.gov.uk

Emergency Planning: Mr Paul Fleck, Safety & Emergency Planning Officer, Willows Lane Depot, Willows Lane, Accrington BB5 0RT ☎ 01254 388111 🖷 01254 872250 ✉ paul.fleck@hyndburnbc.gov.uk

Energy Management: Mrs Helen McCue-Melling Regeneration & Property Manager, Scaitcliffe House, Ormerod Street, Accrington BB5 0PF ☎ 01254 388111 🖷 01254 380122 ✉ helen.mccue-melling@hyndburnbc.gov.uk

Environmental Health: Mr Tony Akrigg Head of Environmental Partnership, Willows Lane Depot, Willows Lane, Accrington BB5 0RT ☎ 01254 388111 🖷 01254 872250 ✉ tony.akrigg@hyndburnbc.gov.uk

Estates, Property & Valuation: Mrs Helen McCue-Melling Regeneration & Property Manager, Scaitcliffe House, Ormerod Street, Accrington BB5 0PF ☎ 01254 388111 🖷 01254 380122 ✉ helen.mccue-melling@hyndburnbc.gov.uk

Facilities: Mrs Helen McCue-Melling Regeneration & Property Manager, Scaitcliffe House, Ormerod Street, Accrington BB5 0PF ☎ 01254 388111 🖷 01254 380122 ✉ helen.mccue-melling@hyndburnbc.gov.uk

HYNDBURN

Finance: Mr Joe McIntyre, Deputy Chief Executive, Scaitcliffe House, Ormerod Street, Accrington BB5 0PF ☎ 01254 388111 🖷 01254 380637 ✉ joe.mcintyre@hyndburnbc.gov.uk

Fleet Management: Mr Steve Riley Head of Community Services, Willows Lane Depot, Willows Lane, Accrington BB5 0RT ☎ 01254 388111 🖷 01254 872250 ✉ steve.riley@hyndburnbc.gov.uk

Grounds Maintenance: Mr Craig Haraben Head of Parks & Cemeteries, Willows Lane Depot, Willows Lane, Accrington BB5 0RT ☎ 01254 388111 🖷 01254 872250 ✉ craig.haraben@hyndburndc.gov.uk

Health and Safety: Mr Paul Fleck, Safety & Emergency Planning Officer, Willows Lane Depot, Willows Lane, Accrington BB5 0RT ☎ 01254 388111 🖷 01254 872250 ✉ paul.fleck@hyndburnbc.gov.uk

Housing: Mr Denis Aldridge Housing Advice & Homeslessness Manager, Scaitcliffe House, Ormerod Street, Accrington BB5 0PF ☎ 01254 388111 🖷 01254 391625 ✉ denis.aldridge@hyndburnbc.gov.uk

Legal: Ms Jane Ellis, Executive Director - Legal & Democratic Services, Scaitcliffe House, Ormerod Street, Accrington BB5 0PF ☎ 01254 388111 🖷 01254 380637 ✉ jane.ellis@hyndburnbc.gov.uk

Leisure and Cultural Services: Mr Joe McIntyre, Deputy Chief Executive, Scaitcliffe House, Ormerod Street, Accrington BB5 0PF ☎ 01254 388111 🖷 01254 380637 ✉ joe.mcintyre@hyndburnbc.gov.uk

Licensing: Mr Howard Bee Licensing Manager, Scaitcliffe House, Ormerod Street, Accrington BB5 0PF ☎ 01254 388111 🖷 01254 386711 ✉ howard.bee@hyndburnbc.gov.uk

Member Services: Mrs Helen Gee, Member Services Manager, Scaitcliffe House, Ormerod Street, Accrington BB5 0PF ☎ 01254 388111 🖷 01254 380122 ✉ helen.gee@hyndburnbc.gov.uk

Partnerships: Mr Michael Walker, Corporate Performance Manager, Scaitcliffe House, Ormerod Street, Accrington BB5 0PF ☎ 01254 388111 🖷 01254 380637 ✉ michael.walker@hyndburnbc.gov.uk

Personnel / HR: Mrs Kirsten Burnett Head of Human Resources, Scaitcliffe House, Ormerod Street, Accrington BB5 0PF ☎ 01254 388111 🖷 01254 392597 ✉ kirsten.burnett@hyndburnbc.gov.uk

Planning: Mr Simon Prideaux Chief Planning & Transportation Officer, Scaitcliffe House, Ormerod Street, Accrington BB5 0PF ☎ 01254 388111 🖷 01254 391625 ✉ simon.prideaux@hyndburnbc.gov.uk

Procurement: Mr Derek Rydeheard, Administration Services Manager, Scaitcliffe House, Ormerod Street, Accrington BB5 0PF ☎ 01254 388111 🖷 01254 392597 ✉ derek.rydeheard@hyndburnbc.gov.uk

Recycling & Waste Minimisation: Mr Steve Riley Head of Community Services, Willows Lane Depot, Willows Lane, Accrington BB5 0RT ☎ 01254 388111 🖷 01254 872250 ✉ steve.riley@hyndburnbc.gov.uk

Regeneration: Mr Mark Hoyle Head of Regeneration & Housing, Scaitcliffe House, Ormerod Street, Accrington BB5 0PF ☎ 01254 388111 🖷 01254 380122 ✉ mark.hoyle@hyndburnbc.gov.uk

Staff Training: Mrs Kirsten Burnett Head of Human Resources, Scaitcliffe House, Ormerod Street, Accrington BB5 0PF ☎ 01254 388111 🖷 01254 392597 ✉ kirsten.burnett@hyndburnbc.gov.uk

Street Scene: Mr Steve Riley Head of Community Services, Willows Lane Depot, Willows Lane, Accrington BB5 0RT ☎ 01254 388111 🖷 01254 872250 ✉ steve.riley@hyndburnbc.gov.uk

Sustainable Communities: Mr Simon Prideaux Chief Planning & Transportation Officer, Scaitcliffe House, Ormerod Street, Accrington BB5 0PF ☎ 01254 388111 🖷 01254 391625 ✉ simon.prideaux@hyndburnbc.gov.uk

Sustainable Development: Ms Anne Hourican, Senior Environmental Initiatives Officer, Scaitcliffe House, Ormerod Street, Accrington BB5 0PF ☎ 01254 388111 🖷 01254 391625 ✉ anne.hourican@hyndburnbc.gov.uk

Town Centre: Mr Rob Grigorjevs Head of Town Centre Development, Scaitcliffe House, Ormerod Street, Accrington BB5 0PF ☎ 01254 388111 🖷 01254 380122 ✉ rob.grigorjevs@hyndburnbc.gov.uk

Waste Collection and Disposal: Mr Steve Riley Head of Community Services, Willows Lane Depot, Willows Lane, Accrington BB5 0RT ☎ 01254 388111 🖷 01254 872250 ✉ steve.riley@hyndburnbc.gov.uk

Waste Management: Mr Steve Riley Head of Community Services, Willows Lane Depot, Willows Lane, Accrington BB5 0RT ☎ 01254 388111 🖷 01254 872250 ✉ steve.riley@hyndburnbc.gov.uk

Children's Play Areas: Mr Craig Haraben Head of Parks & Cemeteries, Willows Lane Depot, Willows Lane, Accrington BB5 0RT ☎ 01254 388111 🖷 01254 872250 ✉ craig.haraben@hyndburndc.gov.uk

COUNCILLORS

***Mayor* Haworth**, Marlene (CON - St. Oswald's)
marlene.haworth@hyndburnbc.gov.uk

***Deputy Mayor* O'Kane**, Tim (LAB - Clayton-le-Moors)
tim.okane@hyndburnbc.gov.uk

***Leader of the Council* Parkinson**, Miles (LAB - Altham)
miles.parkinson@hyndburnbc.gov.uk

***Deputy Leader of the Council* Cox**, Paul (LAB - Milnshaw)
paul.cox@hyndburnbc.gov.uk

***Group Leader* Thompson**, Paul (UKIP - St. Oswald's)
paul.thompson@hyndburnbc.gov.uk

Addison, Judith (CON - Immanuel)
judith.addison@hyndburnfc.gov.uk

Allen, Lisa (CON - St. Oswald's)
lisa.allen@hyndburnbc.gov.uk

Ayub, Mohammad (LAB - Central)
mohammad.ayub@hyndburnbc.gov.uk

Aziz, Noordad (LAB - Netherton)
noordad.aziz@hyndburnbc.gov.uk

Britcliffe, Peter (CON - St. Andrew's)
peter.britcliffe@hyndburnbc.gov.uk

Cleary, Clare (LAB - Rishton)
clare.cleary@hyndburnbc.gov.uk

Cox, Loraine (LAB - Church)
loraine.cox@hyndburnbc.gov.uk

Dad, Munsif (LAB - Spring Hill)
munsif.dad@hyndburnbc.gov.uk

Dawson, Bernard (LAB - Huncoat)
b.dawson453@btinternet.com

Dobson, Tony (CON - Barnfield)
tdob@aol.com

Dwyer, Wendy (LAB - Peel)
wendy.dwyer@hyndburnbc.gov.uk

Fielding, Diane (LAB - Spring Hill)
enquiries@hyndburnbc.gov.uk

Fisher, Melissa (LAB - Clayton-le-Moors)
melissa.fisher@hyndburnbc.gov.uk

Fisher, Chris (LAB - Altham)
chris.fisher@hyndburnbc.gov.uk

Grayson, Harry (LAB - Rishton)
harry.grayson@hyndburnbc.gov.uk

Harrison, June (LAB - Barnfield)
june.harrison@hyndburnbc.gov.uk

Higgins, Eamonn (LAB - Huncoat)
eamonn.higgins@hyndburnbc.gov.uk

Hurn, Terry (CON - Baxenden)
terry.hurn@hyndburnbc.gov.uk

Khan, Abdul (LAB - Central)
abdul.khan@hyndburnbc.gov.uk

Livesey, Julie Anne (CON - Immanuel)
julie.livesey@hyndburnbc.gov.uk

Molineux, Gareth (LAB - Overton)
gareth.molineux@hyndburnbc.gov.uk

Molineux, Kerry (LAB - Overton)
kerry.molineux@hyndburnbc.gov.uk

Moss, Ken (LAB - Rishton)
ken.moss@hyndburnfc.gov.uk

Nedwell, Jenny (LAB - Overton)
jenny.nedwell@hyndburnbc.gov.uk

Parkinson, Bernadette (LAB - Netherton)
bernadette.parkinson@hyndburnbc.gov.uk

Pinder, Bill (LAB - St. Andrew's)
bill.pinder@hyndburnbc.gov.uk

Plummer, Joyce (LAB - Peel)
joyce.plummer@hyndburnbc.gov.uk

Pratt, Kath (CON - Baxenden)
kathleen.pratt@hyndburnbc.gov.uk

Pritchard, Malcolm (UKIP - Milnshaw)
malcolm.pritchard@hyndburnbc.gov.uk

Smith, Joan (LAB - Church)
cllrjoansmith@googlemail.com

POLITICAL COMPOSITION
LAB: 25, CON: 8, UKIP: 2

COMMITTEE CHAIRS

Audit: Mr Bill Pinder

Licensing: Ms Joyce Plummer

Planning: Mr Harry Grayson

Inverclyde S

Inverclyde Council, Municipal Buildings, Clyde Square, Greenock PA15 1LY
☎ 01475 717171 🖷 01475 712777 💻 www.inverclyde.gov.uk

FACTS AND FIGURES
Parliamentary Constituencies: Inverclyde
EU Constituencies: Scotland
Election Frequency: Elections are of whole council

PRINCIPAL OFFICERS

Chief Executive: Mr John Mundell, Chief Executive, Municipal Buildings, Clyde Square, Greenock PA15 1LY ☎ 01475 712701 🖷 01475 712777 ✉ chief.executive@inverclyde.gov.uk

Senior Management: Mr Aubrey Fawcett, Corporate Director - Environment, Regeneration & Resources, Municipal Buildings, Clyde Square, Greenock PA15 1LY ☎ 01475 712761 ✉ aubrey.fawcett@inverclyde.gov.uk

Senior Management: Mr Brian Moore Corporate Director - Community Health & Care Partnership, Dalrymple House, Dalrymple Street, Greenock PA15 1HT ☎ 01475 714015 🖷 01475 714060 ✉ brian.moore@inverclyde.gov.uk

Access Officer / Social Services (Disability): Mr Stuart Jamieson, Head of Regeneration & Planning, 6 Cathcart Square, Greenock PA15 1LS ☎ 01475 712402 🖷 01475 712468 ✉ stuart.jamieson@inverclyde.gov.uk

Building Control: Mr Nicolas McLaren Building Control Manager, Municipal Buildings, Clyde Square, Greenock PA15 1LY ☎ 01475 712403 🖷 01475 712465 ✉ nicolas.mclaren@inverclyde.gov.uk

Catering Services: Ms Elspeth Tierney, Facilities Services Manager, Municipal Buildings, Greenock PA15 1LY ☎ 01475 712449 ✉ elspeth.tierney@inverclyde.gov.uk

Civil Registration: Mr Ian Kearns, Registration Manager, 40 West Stewart Street, Greenock PA15 1YA ☎ 01475 714256 ✉ ian.kearns@inverclyde.gov.uk

PR / Communications: Mr George Barbour Corporate Communications Manager, Municipal Buildings, Clyde Square, Greenock PA15 1LY ☎ 01475 712385 ✉ george.barbour@inverclyde.gov.uk

Community Planning: Mr Aubrey Fawcett, Corporate Director - Environment, Regeneration & Resources, Municipal Buildings, Clyde Square, Greenock PA15 1LY ☎ 01475 712761 ✉ aubrey.fawcett@inverclyde.gov.uk

INVERCLYDE

Community Planning: Ms Miriam McKenna Strategic Partnership Manager, Municipal Buildings, Clyde Square, Greenock PA15 1LY ☎ 01475 712042 ✉ miriam.mckenna@inverclyde.gov.uk

Computer Management: Mr Allan McDonald Operations Manager, Municipal Buildings, Clyde Square, Greenock PA15 1LY ☎ 01475 712765 ✉ allan.mcdonald@inverclyde.gov.uk

Consumer Protection and Trading Standards: Mr John Arthur, Head of Safer & Inclusive Communities, West Stewart Street, Greenock PA15 1SN ☎ 01475 714263 🖷 01475 714253 ✉ john.arthur@inverclyde.gov.uk

Economic Development: Mr Stuart Jamieson, Head of Regeneration & Planning, 6 Cathcart Square, Greenock PA15 1LS ☎ 01475 712402 🖷 01475 712468 ✉ stuart.jamieson@inverclyde.gov.uk

Education: Ms Ruth Binks Head of Education, Municipal Buildings, Clyde Square, Greenock PA15 1LY ☎ 01475 712850 ✉ ruth.binks@inverclyde.gov.uk

Education: Ms Angela Edwards Head of Educational Planning & Culture, 105 Dalrymple Street, Greenock PA15 1LS ✉ angela.edwards@inverclyde.gov.uk

Emergency Planning: Mr Colin Pearson Civil Contingencies Officer, West Stewart Street, Greenock PA15 1SN ☎ 01475 714222 ✉ colin.pearson@inverclyde.gov.uk

Environmental Health: Mr John Arthur, Head of Safer & Inclusive Communities, West Stewart Street, Greenock PA15 1SN ☎ 01475 714263 🖷 01475 714253 ✉ john.arthur@inverclyde.gov.uk

Estates, Property & Valuation: Mrs Audrey Galloway, Asset Management Planning Manager, Cathcart House, Cathcart Sqaure, Greenock PA15 1LS ☎ 01475 712508 ✉ audrey.greenwood@inverclyde.gov.uk

European Liaison: Mr Stuart Jamieson, Head of Regeneration & Planning, 6 Cathcart Square, Greenock PA15 1LS ☎ 01475 712402 🖷 01475 712468 ✉ stuart.jamieson@inverclyde.gov.uk

Events Manager: Mr Stuart Jamieson, Head of Regeneration & Planning, 6 Cathcart Square, Greenock PA15 1LS ☎ 01475 712402 🖷 01475 712468 ✉ stuart.jamieson@inverclyde.gov.uk

Finance: Mr Alan Puckrin, Chief Financial Officer, Municipal Buildings, Clyde Square, Greenock PA15 1LY ☎ 01475 712223 🖷 01475 712288 ✉ alan.puckrin@inverclyde.gov.uk

Fleet Management: Mr John Williams Transport Manager, Municipal Buildings, Clyde Square, Greenock PA15 1LY ☎ 01475 717171 ✉

Grounds Maintenance: Mr William Rennie, Grounds Services Manager, Pottery Street, Greenock PA15 2UD ☎ 01475 714761 ✉ willie.rennie@inverclyde.gov.uk

Health and Safety: Ms Pauline Ramsay, Senior Health & Safety Officer, Personnel Services, Municipal Buildings, Clyde Square, Greenock PA15 1LY ☎ 01475 712717 🖷 01475 712726 ✉ pauline.ramsay@inverclyde.gov.uk

Highways: Mr Robert Graham, Environmental Services Manager Roads, Transport & Waste Services, 71 East Hamilton Street, Greenock PA15 2UA ☎ 01475 714800 🖷 01475 714825 ✉ robert.graham@inverclyde.gov.uk

Legal: Mr Gerard Malone Head of Legal & Democratic Services, Municipal Buildings, Clyde Square, Greenock PA15 1LY ☎ 01475 712139 ✉ gerard.malone@inverclyde.gov.uk

Leisure and Cultural Services: Mr Stuart Jamieson, Head of Regeneration & Planning, 6 Cathcart Square, Greenock PA15 1LS ☎ 01475 712402 🖷 01475 712468 ✉ stuart.jamieson@inverclyde.gov.uk

Lighting: Mr Robert Graham, Environmental Services Manager Roads, Transport & Waste Services, 71 East Hamilton Street, Greenock PA15 2UA ☎ 01475 714800 🖷 01475 714825 ✉ robert.graham@inverclyde.gov.uk

Lottery Funding, Charity and Voluntary: Mr Stuart Jamieson, Head of Regeneration & Planning, 6 Cathcart Square, Greenock PA15 1LS ☎ 01475 712402 🖷 01475 712468 ✉ stuart.jamieson@inverclyde.gov.uk

Personnel / HR: Mr Steven McNab Head of Organisational Development & Human Resources, Municipal Buildings, Clyde Square, Greenock PA15 1LY ☎ 01475 712015 ✉ steven.mcnab@inverclyde.gov.uk

Planning: Mr Stuart Jamieson, Head of Regeneration & Planning, 6 Cathcart Square, Greenock PA15 1LS ☎ 01475 712402 🖷 01475 712468 ✉ stuart.jamieson@inverclyde.gov.uk

Public Libraries: Mr Stuart Jamieson, Head of Regeneration & Planning, 6 Cathcart Sqaure, Greenock PA15 1LS ☎ 01475 712402 🖷 01475 712468 ✉ stuart.jamieson@inverclyde.gov.uk

Public Libraries: Ms Alana Ward Libraries Manager, Central Library, Clyde Square, Greenock PA15 1NB ☎ 01475 712347 ✉ alana.ward@inverclyde.gov.uk

Recycling & Waste Minimisation: Mr Drew Hall, Energy Manager, Environmental & Consumer Services, 40 West Stewart Street, Greenock PA15 1SN ☎ 01475 714272 🖷 01475 714216 ✉ drew.hall@inverclyde.gov.uk

Road Safety: Ms Margaret Dickson, Road Safety Training Officer, 71 East Hamilton Street, Greenock PA15 2UA ☎ 01475 714811 🖷 01475 714825 ✉ margaret.dickson@inverclyde.gov.uk

Social Services: Mr Brian Moore Corporate Director - Community Health & Care Partnership, Dalrymple House, Dalrymple Street, Greenock PA15 1HT ☎ 01475 714015 🖷 01475 714060 ✉ brian.moore@inverclyde.gov.uk

Social Services (Adult): Mr Brian Moore Corporate Director - Community Health & Care Partnership, Dalrymple House, Dalrymple Street, Greenock PA15 1HT ☎ 01475 714015 🖷 01475 714060 ✉ brian.moore@inverclyde.gov.uk

Social Services (Children): Ms Sharon McAlees Head of Children & Criminal Justic Services, Dalrymple House, Dalrymple Street, Greenock PA15 1UN ☎ 01475 714006 🖷 01475 712726 ✉ robert.murphy@inverclyde.gov.uk

Staff Training: Mrs Carol Reid, Project Manager, Municipal Buildings, Clyde Square, Greenock PA15 1LY ☎ 01475 712027 🖷 01475 712726 ✉ carol.reid@inverclyde.gov.uk

Street Scene: Mr William Rennie, Grounds Services Manager, Pottery Street, Greenock PA15 2UD ☎ 01475 714761 ✉ willie.rennie@inverclyde.gov.uk

Sustainable Development: Mr Drew Hall, Energy Manager, Environmental & Consumer Services, 40 West Stewart Street, Greenock PA15 1SN ☎ 01475 714272 🖷 01475 714216 ✉ drew.hall@inverclyde.gov.uk

Tourism: Mr Stuart Jamieson, Head of Regeneration & Planning, Business Store, Greenock PA15 1DE ☎ 01475 712402 🖷 01475 712468 ✉ stuart.jamieson@inverclyde.gov.uk

Traffic Management: Mr Robert Graham, Environmental Services Manager Roads, Transport & Waste Services, 71 East Hamilton Street, Greenock PA15 2UA ☎ 01475 714800 🖷 01475 714825 ✉ robert.graham@inverclyde.gov.uk

Transport: Mr John Williams Transport Manager, Pottery Street, Greenock PA15 2UH ☎ 01475 717171

Waste Collection and Disposal: Mr Ian Moffat Head of Environmental & Commercial Services, Pottery Street, Greenock PA15 2UH ☎ 01475 714760 🖷 01475 714770 ✉ ian.moffat@inverclyde.gov.uk

Waste Management: Mr Ian Moffat Head of Environmental & Commercial Services, Pottery Street, Greenock PA15 2UH ☎ 01475 714760 🖷 01475 714770 ✉ ian.moffat@inverclyde.gov.uk

COUNCILLORS

***Provost* McCormick**, Michael (LAB - Inverclyde East Central)
michael.mccormick@inverclyde.gov.uk

***Leader of the Council* McCabe**, Stephen (LAB - Inverclyde East)
stephen.mccabe@inverclyde.gov.uk

***Deputy Leader of the Council* Clocherty**, Jim (LAB - Inverclyde North)
jim.clocherty@inverclyde.gov.uk

Ahlfeld, Ronnie (IND - Inverclyde West)
ronnie.ahlfeld@inverclyde.gov.uk

Brennan, Martin (LAB - Inverclyde North)
martin.brennan@inverclyde.gov.uk

Brooks, Keith (SNP - Inverclyde South)
keith.brooks@inverclyde.gov.uk

Campbell-Sturgess, Math (SNP - Inverclyde North)
math.campbell@inverclyde.gov.uk

Dorrian, Gerry (LAB - Inverclyde South West)
gerry.dorrian@inverclyde.gov.uk

Grieve, Jim (SNP - Inverclyde East Central)
jim.grieve@inverclyde.gov.uk

Jones, Vaughan (IND - Inverclyde South)
vaughan.jones@inverclyde.gov.uk

Loughran, Terry (LAB - Inverclyde West)
terry.loughran@linverclyde.gov.uk

MacLeod, Jim (SNP - Inverclyde East)
jim.macleod@inverclyde.gov.uk

McColgan, James (LAB - Inverclyde East)
james.mccolgan@inverclyde.gov.uk

McEleny, Chris (SNP - Inverclyde West)
chris.mceleny@inverclyde.gov.uk

McIlwee, Joe (LAB - Inverclyde South)
joe.mcilwee@inverclyde.gov.uk

Moran, Robert (LAB - Inverclyde East Central)
robert.moran@inverclyde.gov.uk

Nelson, Innes (SNP - Inverclyde South West)
innes.nelson@inverclyde.gov.uk

Rebecchi, Luciano (LD - Inverclyde South West)
luciano.rebecchi@inverclyde.gov.uk

Shepherd, Kenny (LD - Inverclyde North)
kenny.shepherd@inverclyde.gov.uk

Wilson, David (CON - Inverclyde East)
david.wilson@inverclyde.gov.uk

POLITICAL COMPOSITION

LAB: 9, SNP: 6, LD: 2, IND: 2, CON: 1

COMMITTEE CHAIRS

Audit: Mr Luciano Rebecchi

Education & Communities: Mr Terry Loughran

Environment & Regeneration: Mr Michael McCormick

Planning: Mr David Wilson

Ipswich D

Ipswich Borough Council, Grafton House, 15 - 17 Russell Road, Ipswich IP1 2DE
☎ 01473 432000 🖷 01473 432522 ✉ enquiries@ipswich.gov.uk
🖳 www.ipswich.gov.uk

FACTS AND FIGURES

Parliamentary Constituencies: Ipswich
EU Constituencies: Eastern
Election Frequency: Elections are by thirds

PRINCIPAL OFFICERS

Chief Executive: Mr Russell Williams, Chief Executive, Grafton House, 15 - 17 Russell Road, Ipswich IP1 2DE ☎ 01473 433501 🖷 01473 432033 ✉ russell.williams@ipswich.gov.uk

Deputy Chief Executive: Ms Helen Pluck Chief Operating Officer / Deputy Chief Executive, Grafton House, 15 - 17 Russell Road, Ipswich IP1 2DE ☎ 01473 432002 🖷 01473 432033 ✉ helen.pluck@ipswich.gov.uk

Senior Management: Mr Ian Blofield, Head - Housing & Customer Service, Grafton House, 15-17 Russell Road, Ipswich IP1 2DE ☎ 01473 433710 🖷 01473 432033 ✉ ian.blofield@ipswich.gov.uk

Senior Management: Ms Evelyn Crossland Head - Shared Revenues Partnership, Grafton House, 15 - 17 Russell Road, Ipswich IP1 2DE ☎ 01473 433782 🖷 01473 432033 ✉ evelyn.cross@ipswich.gov.uk

Senior Management: Mr David Field, Head - Resource Management, Grafton House, 15 - 17 Russell Road, Ipswich IP1 2DE ☎ 01473 433859 🖷 01473 432033 ✉ david.field@ipswich.gov.uk

Senior Management: Mr Gordon Mole Head - Community & Cultural Services, Grafton House, 15 - 17 Russell Road, Ipswich IP1 2DE ☎ 01473 432060 🖷 01473 432033 ✉ gordon.mole@ipswich.gov.uk

Access Officer / Social Services (Disability): Mr Malcolm Brown Principal Building Control Surveyor, Grafton House, 15 - 17 Russell Road, Ipswich IP1 2DE ☎ 01473 432957 ✉ malcolm.brown@ipswich.gov.uk

Architect, Building / Property Services: Ms Emily Atack Operations Manager - Asset, Property & Economic Development, Grafton House, 15 - 17 Russell Road, Ipswich IP1 2DE ☎ 01473 432200 ✉ emily.atack@ipswich.gov.uk

Best Value: Mrs Vicky Moseley, Senior Performance & Projects Officer, Grafton House, 15-17 Russell Road, Ipswich IP1 2DE ☎ 01473 432044 ✉ vicky.moseley@ipswich.gov.uk

Building Control: Mr Malcolm Brown Principal Building Control Surveyor, Grafton House, 15 - 17 Russell Road, Ipswich IP1 2DE ☎ 01473 432957 ✉ malcolm.brown@ipswich.gov.uk

PR / Communications: Mr Max Stocker, Head - Communications & Design, Grafton House, 15-17 Russell Road, Ipswich IP1 2DE ☎ 01473 432035 ✉ max.stocker@ipswich.gov.uk

Community Planning: Mr Tibbs Pinter Assistant Operations Manager - Community Development & Diversity, Grafton House, 15 - 17 Russell Road, Ipswich IP1 2DE ☎ 01473 433436 ✉ tibbs.pinter@ipswich.gov.uk

Community Safety: Mr Mike Grimwood, Operations Manager - Community Safety & Licensing, Grafton House, 15-17 Russell Road, Ipswich IP1 2DE ☎ 01473 433052 ✉ mike.grimwood@ipswich.gov.uk

Computer Management: Mr Howard Gaskin IT Infrastructure Manager, Grafton House, 15 - 17 Russell Road, Ipswich IP1 2DE ☎ 01473 433891 ✉ howard.gaskin@ipswich.gov.uk

Contracts: Mr Kevin Oxborrow Operations Manager - Maintenance & Contracts, Gipping House, 7 Whittle Road, Hadleigh Road Industrial Estate, Ipswich IP1 2DE ☎ 01473 432414 ✉ kevin.oxborrow@ipswich.gov.uk

Corporate Services: Mr David Field, Head - Resource Management, Grafton House, 15 - 17 Russell Road, Ipswich IP1 2DE ☎ 01473 433859 🖷 01473 432033 ✉ david.field@ipswich.gov.uk

Economic Development: Mr Peter Lee Operations Manager - Economic Development, Grafton House, 15 - 17 Russell Road, Ipswich IP1 2DE ☎ 01473 432924 ✉ peter.lee@ipswich.gov.uk

Electoral Registration: Mr David Connors Team Leader - Business & Democratic Support, Grafton House, 15 - 17 Russell Road, Ipswich IP1 2DE ☎ 01473 432531 ✉ david.connors@ipswich.gov.uk

Environmental / Technical Services: Ms Donna Baldwin Operations Manager - Environmental Health, Grafton House, 15 - 17 Russell Road, Ipswich IP1 2DE ☎ 01473 433113 ✉ donna.baldwin@ipswich.gov.uk

Environmental Health: Ms Donna Baldwin Operations Manager - Environmental Health, Grafton House, 15 - 17 Russell Road, Ipswich IP1 2DE ☎ 01473 433113 ✉ donna.baldwin@ipswich.gov.uk

Estates, Property & Valuation: Mr Simon Unthank Principal Valuation Surveyor, Grafton House, 15 - 17 Russell Road, Ipswich IP1 2DE ☎ 01473 432212 🖷 01473 432974 ✉ simon.unthank@ipswich.gov.uk

Events Manager: Mr Jonathan Stephenson Operations Manager - Arts & Entertainments, Grafton House, 15 - 17 Russell Road, Ipswich IP1 2DE ☎ 01473 432217 ✉ jonathan.stephenson@ipswich.gov.uk

Finance: Mr Ian Blofield, Head - Housing & Customer Service, Grafton House, 15-17 Russell Road, Ipswich IP1 2DE ☎ 01473 433710 🖷 01473 432033 ✉ ian.blofield@ipswich.gov.uk

Finance: Mr Jon Hudson Operations Manager - Finance, Grafton House, 15 - 17 Russell Road, Ipswich IP1 2DE ☎ 01473 433740 ✉ jon.hudson@ipswich.gov.uk

Fleet Management: Ms Ondraya Plowman Vehicle Fleet Manager, Grafton House, 15 - 17 Russell Road, Ipswich IP1 2DE ☎ 01473 432430 ✉ ondraya.plowman@ipswich.gov.uk

Grounds Maintenance: Mr Eddie Peters Operations Manager - Streetcare, Gipping House, 7 Whittle Road, Hadleigh Road Industrial Estate, Ipswich IP2 0UH ☎ 01473 432412 ✉ eddie.peters@ipswich.gov.uk

Health and Safety: Mr Malcolm Earl Corporate Health & Safety Manager, Grafton House, 15 - 17 Russell Road, Ipswich IP1 2DE ☎ 01473 433435 ✉ malcolm.earl@ipswich.gov.uk

Home Energy Conservation: Mr Ian Blofield, Head - Housing & Customer Service, Grafton House, 15-17 Russell Road, Ipswich IP1 2DE ☎ 01473 433710 🖷 01473 432033 ✉ ian.blofield@ipswich.gov.uk

Housing: Mr Ian Blofield, Head - Housing & Customer Service, Grafton House, 15-17 Russell Road, Ipswich IP1 2DE ☎ 01473 433710 🖷 01473 432033 ✉ ian.blofield@ipswich.gov.uk

Housing Maintenance: Mr Ian Blofield, Head - Housing & Customer Service, Grafton House, 15-17 Russell Road, Ipswich IP1 2DE ☎ 01473 433710 🖷 01473 432033 ✉ ian.blofield@ipswich.gov.uk

Legal: Ms Pauline McBride Head - Legal & Democratic Services Manager, Grafton House, 15 - 17 Russell Road, Ipswich IP1 2DE ☎ 01473 4332323 ✉ pauline.mcbride@ipswich.gov.uk

Leisure and Cultural Services: Mr Gordon Mole Head - Community & Cultural Services, Grafton House, 15 - 17 Russell Road, Ipswich IP1 2DE ☎ 01473 432060 🖷 01473 432033 ✉ gordon.mole@ipswich.gov.uk

Licensing: Mr Mike Grimwood, Operations Manager - Community Safety & Licensing, Grafton House, 15-17 Russell Road, Ipswich IP1 2DE ☎ 01473 433052 ✉ mike.grimwood@ipswich.gov.uk

Member Services: Ms Janice Robinson Community Development & Democratic Operations Manager, Grafton House, 15 - 17 Russell Road, Ipswich IP1 2DE ☎ 01473 432510 ✉ janice.robinson@ipswich.gov.uk

Parking: Ms Mandy Chapman Assistant Manager - Car Parks, Gipping House, 7 Whittle Road, Hadleigh Road Industrial Estate, Ipswich IP2 0UH ☎ 01473 432849 ✉ mandy.chapman@ipswich.gov.uk

Planning: Mr Steve Miller Operations Manager - Development Control, Grafton House, 15 - 17 Russell Road, Ipswich IP1 2DE ☎ 01473 432903 ✉ steve.miller@ipswich.gov.uk

Procurement: Mr Andrew Beschizza, Procurement Manager, Grafton House, 15-17 Russell Road, Ipswich IP1 2DE ☎ 01473 433906 ✉ andrew.beschizza@ipswich.gov.uk

Recycling & Waste Minimisation: Mr Gordon Mole Head - Community & Cultural Services, Grafton House, 15 - 17 Russell Road, Ipswich IP1 2DE ☎ 01473 432060 🖷 01473 432033 ✉ gordon.mole@ipswich.gov.uk

Staff Training: Ms Katie Coupe, Employee Development Advisor, Grafton House, 15-17 Russell Road, Ipswich IP1 2DE ☎ 01473 433425 ✉ katie.coupe@ipswich.gov.uk

Street Scene: Ms Ondraya Plowman Vehicle Fleet Manager, Gipping House, 7 Whittle Road, Hadleigh Road Industrial Estate, Ipswich IP2 0UH ☎ 01473 432430 ✉ ondraya.plowman@ipswich.gov.uk

Sustainable Communities: Ms Janice Robinson Community Development & Democratic Operations Manager, Grafton House, 15 - 17 Russell Road, Ipswich IP1 2DE ☎ 01473 432510 ✉ janice.robinson@ipswich.gov.uk

Sustainable Development: Mr Robert Hobbs Planning Policy Team Leader, Grafton House, 15 - 17 Russell Road, Ipswich IP1 2DE ☎ 01473 432931 ✉ robert.hobbs@ipswich.gov.uk

Tourism: Mr David Stainer Tourist Centre Manager, Tourist Information Centre, St Stephens Church, St Stephens Lane, Ipswich IP1 1DP ☎ 01473 43078

Town Centre: Mr Peter Lee Operations Manager - Economic Development, Grafton House, 15 - 17 Russell Road, Ipswich IP1 2DE ☎ 01473 432924 ✉ peter.lee@ipswich.gov.uk

Waste Collection and Disposal: Mr Gordon Mole Head - Community & Cultural Services, Grafton House, 15 - 17 Russell Road, Ipswich IP1 2DE ☎ 01473 432060 🖷 01473 432033 ✉ gordon.mole@ipswich.gov.uk

Waste Management: Mr Gordon Mole Head - Community & Cultural Services, Grafton House, 15 - 17 Russell Road, Ipswich IP1 2DE ☎ 01473 432060 🖷 01473 432033 ✉ gordon.mole@ipswich.gov.uk

Children's Play Areas: Mr Eddie Peters Operations Manager - Streetcare, Gipping House, 7 Whittle Road, Hadleigh Road Industrial Estate, Ipswich IP2 0UH ☎ 01473 432412 ✉ eddie.peters@ipswich.gov.uk

COUNCILLORS

***Leader of the Council* Ellesmere**, David (LAB - Gipping)
david.ellesmere@councillors.ipswich.gov.uk

***Deputy Leader of the Council* Rudkin**, Bryony (LAB - Bridge)
bryony.rudkin@councillors.ipswich.gov.uk

Cann, Andrew (LD - St Margaret's)
andrew.cann@councillors.ipswich.gov.uk

Carnall, John (CON - Bixley)
john.carnall@councillors.ipswich.gov.uk

Cenci, Nadia (CON - Stoke Park)
nadia.cenci@councillors.ipswich.gov.uk

Chisholm, Glen (LAB - Stoke Park)
glen.chisholm@councillors.ipswich.gov.uk

Clarke, Hamil (LAB - Sprites)
hamil.clarke@councillors.ipswich.gov.uk

Cook, Martin (LAB - Gainsborough)
martin.cook@councillors.ipswich.gov.uk

Cook, John (LAB - Alexandra)
john.cook@councillors.ipswich.gov.uk

Darwin, Shelley (LAB - St John's)
shelley.darwin@councillors.ipswitch.gov.uk

Debman, George (CON - Holywells)
george.debman@councillors.ipswich.gov.uk

Elavalakan, Elango (LAB - St John's)
elango.elavalakan@councillors.ipswich.gov.uk

Fern, Roger (LAB - Sprites)
roger.fern@councillors.ipswich.gov.uk

Gage, Sandra (LAB - Rushmere)
sandra.gage@councillors.ipswich.gov.uk

Gardiner, Peter (LAB - Gipping)
peter.gardiner@councillors.ipswich.gov.uk

Gibbs, Julian (LAB - Westgate)
julian.gibbs@councillors.ipswich.gov.uk

Goldsmith, David (CON - Castle Hill)
david.goldsmith@councillors.ipswich.gov.uk

Goonan, Martin (LAB - Whitehouse)
martin.goonan@councillors.ipswich.gov.uk

IPSWICH

Grant, Albert (LAB - Whitehouse)
albert.grant@councillors.ipswich.gov.uk

Hall, Bob (CON - Sprites)
bob.hall@councillors.ipswich.gov.uk

Harsant, Elizabeth (CON - Holywells)
elizabeth.harsant@councillors.ipswich.gov.uk

Hopgood, Andi (LAB - Gainsborough)
andi.hopgood@coucillors.ipswich.gov.uk

Hyde-Chambers, Robin (CON - Stoke Park)
robin.hyde-chambers@councillors.ipswitchy.gov.uk

Ion, Stephen (CON - Rushmere)
stephen.ion@councillors.ipswitch gov.uk

Jones, Carole (LAB - Westgate)
carole.jones@councillors.ipswich.gov.uk

Knowles, Bill (LAB - Priory Heath)
bill.knowles@councillors.ipswich.gov.uk

Kreidewolf, Colin (LAB - Westgate)
colin.kreidewolf@councillors.ipswich.gov.uk

Leeder, Adam (LAB - Alexandra)
adam.leeder@councillors.ipswich.gov.uk

Lockington, Inga (LD - St Margaret's)
inga.lockington@councillors.ipswich.gov.uk

Macartney, Jeanette (LAB - Gipping)
jeanette.macartney@councillors.ipswich.gov.uk

Macdonald, Neil (LAB - St John's)
neil.macdonald@councillors.ipswich.gov.uk

Maguire, Daniel (LAB - Priory Heath)
daniel.maguire@councillors.ipswich.gov.uk

Meudec, Sophie (LAB - Whitton)
sophie.meudec@councillors.ipswich.gov.uk

Mowles, John (LAB - Gainsborough)
john.mowles@councillors.ipswich.gov.uk

Phillips, Edward (CON - Bixley)
edward.phillips@councillors.ipswich.gov.uk

Pope, Richard (CON - Bixley)
richard.pope@councillors.ipswitch.gov.uk

Powell, Jim (LAB - Bridge)
jim.powell@councillors.ipswich.gov.uk

Quinton, Bill (LAB - Priory Heath)
bill.quinton@councillors.ipswich.gov.uk

Reynolds, Lee (DUP - St Margarets)
lee.reynolds@councillors.ipswitcyh.gov.uk

Riley, Jane (LAB - Alexandra)
jane.riley@coucillors.ipswich.gov.uk

Ross, Alasdair (LAB - Rushmere)
alasdair.ross@councillors.ipswich.gov.uk

Smart, Phil (LAB - Bridge)
phil.smart@councillors.ipswich.gov.uk

Stewart, Pam (CON - Holywells)
pam.stewart@councillors.ipswich.gov.uk

Stewart, Chris (CON - Castle Hill)
chris.stewart@coucillors.ipswich.gov.uk

Vickery, Robin (CON - Castle Hill)
robin.vickery@councillors.ipswich.gov.uk

Whitton, Hugh (LAB - Whittton)
hugh.whittall@councillors.ipswitch.gov.uk

Wright, Colin (LAB - Whitehouse)
colin.wright@councillors.ipswich.gov.uk

Xhaferaj, Erion (CON - Whitton)
erion.xhaferaj@councillors.ipswitch.gov.uk

POLITICAL COMPOSITION

LAB: 31, CON: 14, LD: 2, DUP: 1

COMMITTEE CHAIRS

Audit: Mr John Cook

Licensing: Mr Roger Fern

Planning & Development: Mr Peter Gardiner

Isle of Anglesey W

Isle of Anglesey County Council, County Offices, Llangefni LL77 7TW
☎ 01248 750057 🖷 01248 750839 ✉ gjxce@anglesey.gov.uk
💻 www.anglesey.gov.uk

FACTS AND FIGURES

Parliamentary Constituencies: Ynys Mon
EU Constituencies: Wales
Election Frequency: Elections are of whole council

PRINCIPAL OFFICERS

Chief Executive: Dr Gwynne Jones Chief Executive, Swyddfa'r Sir, Llangefni LL77 7TW ☎ 01248 752102

Senior Management: Mrs Gwen Carrington Director of Community, Swyddfa'r Sir, Llangefni LL77 7TW ☎ 01248 752703 🖷 01248 752705 ✉ gwencarrington@ynysmon.gov.uk

Senior Management: Mr Arthur Owen, Director of Sustainable Development, Swyddfa'r Sir, Llangefni LL77 7TW ☎ 01248 752401 🖷 01248 752412 ✉ awopl@ynysmon.gov.uk

Access Officer / Social Services (Disability): Mrs Glenys Williams Team Leader - Disability Service, Swyddfa'r Sir, Llangefni LL7 7TW ☎ 01248 752771 🖷 01248 750107 ✉ gwxss@ynysmon.gov.uk

Architect, Building / Property Services: Mr Rhys Griffiths, Principal Surveyor, Swyddfa'r Sir, Llangefni LL77 7TW ☎ 01248 752161 🖷 01248 724839 ✉ rhghp@ynysmon.gov.uk

Best Value: Mr Gethin Morgan, Business Planning & Programme Manager, Swyddfa'r Sir, Llangefni LL77 7TW ☎ 01248 752111 🖷 01248 750839 ✉ grmce@ynysmon.gov.uk

Building Control: Mr Gareth Jones, Team Leader - Building Control, Swyddfa'r Sir, Llangefni LL77 7TW ☎ 01248 752220 🖷 01248 752232 ✉ gareth.jones@ynysmon.gov.uk

Children / Youth Services: Mrs Gwen Carrington Director of Community, Swyddfa'r Sir, Llangefni LL77 7TW ☎ 01248 752703 🖷 01248 752705 ✉ gwencarrington@ynysmon.gov.uk

Civil Registration: Ms Marian Wyn Griffiths, Superintendent Registrar, Shire Hall, Llangefni LL77 7TW ☎ 01248 752564 🖷 01248 723459 ✉ mgxcs@ynysmon.gov.uk

PR / Communications: Mr Gethin Jones, Communication Officer, Swyddfa'r Sir, Llangefni LL77 7TW ☎ 01248 752130 🖷 01248 750839 ✉ gjxce@ynysmon.gov.uk

Community Safety: Mrs Catherine Roberts, Community Safety Delivery Manager for Gwynedd and Anglesey, Adeilad Mona, Swyddfa'r Cyngor, Caernarfon LL75 1SH ☎ 01286 679047 🖷 01248 752880 ✉ CatherineERoberts@gwynedd.gov.uk

Computer Management: Mr John Thomas Business Transformation Manager, County Offices, Llangefni LL77 7TW ☎ 01248 75195911 ✉ johnthomas@ynysmon.gov.uk

Consumer Protection and Trading Standards: Mr David Riley, Chief Public Protection Officer, Swyddfa'r Sir, Llangefni LL77 7TW ☎ 01248 752841 🖷 01248 752880 ✉ daveriley@ynysmon.gov.uk

Contracts: Mrs Gwen Carrington Director of Community, Swyddfa'r Sir, Llangefni LL77 7TW ☎ 01248 752703 🖷 01248 752705 ✉ gwencarrington@ynysmon.gov.uk

Corporate Services: Ms Carys Edwards, Head of Profession - Human Resources, Swyddfa'r Sir, Llangefni LL77 7TW ☎ 01248 752502 🖷 01248 752583 ✉ cexcs@ynysmon.gov.uk

Economic Development: Mr Dylan Williams, Head of Economic & Community Regeneration, Anglesey Business Centre, Bryn Cefni Business Park, Llangefni LL77 7XA ☎ 01248 752499 🖷 01248 752192 ✉ dwxpl@ynysmon.gov.uk

Education: Mrs Delyth Molyneux Head of Service - Education, Parc Mount, Glanhwfa Road, Llangefni LL77 7EY ☎ 01248 752916 ✉ delythmolyneux@ynysmon.gov.uk

E-Government: Mr John Thomas Business Transformation Manager, County Offices, Llangefni LL77 7TW ☎ 01248 75195911 ✉ johnthomas@ynysmon.gov.uk

Electoral Registration: Ms Haulwen Ann Hughes, Electoral Services Officer, Anglesey Business Centre, Bryn Cefni Business Park, Llangefni LL77 7XA ☎ 01248 752519 ✉ haulwenhughes@ynysmon.gov.uk

Energy Management: Mr Adrian Williams Energy Manager, Swyddfa'r Sir, Llangefni LL77 7TW ☎ 01248 752249 🖷 01248 724839 ✉ awxht@ynysmon.gov.uk

Environmental / Technical Services: Mr Arthur Owen, Director of Sustainable Development, Swyddfa'r Sir, Llangefni LL77 7TW ☎ 01248 752401 🖷 01248 752412 ✉ awopl@ynysmon.gov.uk

Environmental Health: Mr David Riley, Chief Public Protection Officer, Swyddfa'r Sir, Llangefni LL77 7TW ☎ 01248 752841 🖷 01248 752880 ✉ daveriley@ynysmon.gov.uk

Estates, Property & Valuation: Mr Dylan Edwards Principal Valuation Officer, Swyddfa'r Sir, Llangefni LL77 7TW ☎ 01248 752277 ✉ tedwards@ynysmon.gov.uk

European Liaison: Mr Aled Prys Davies Principal Development Officer (Support & Funding), Anglesey Business Centre, Bryn Cefni Business Park, Llangefni LL77 7XA ☎ 01248 752479 🖷 01248 752192 ✉ apdpl@ynysmon.gov.uk

Events Manager: Mr Michael Thomas Senior Development Officer - Tourism & Marketing, Anglesey Business Centre, Bryn Cefni Business Park, Llangefni LL77 7XA ☎ 01248 752492 ✉ mptpl@ynysmon.gov.uk

Finance: Mr Richard Micklewright Interim Head of Function - Resources, County Offices, Llangefni LL77 7TW ☎ 01248 752601 🖷 01248 752696 ✉ richardmicklewright@ynysmon.gov.uk

Fleet Management: Mr Noel Roberts Fleet & Driver Manager, Swyddfa'r Sir, Llangefni LL77 7TW ☎ 01248 752375 🖷 01248 724839 ✉ rnrht@ynysmon.gov.uk

Grounds Maintenance: Mr Huw Percy, Chief Engineer (Maintenance), Swyddfa'r Sir, Llangefni LL77 7TW ☎ 01248 752371 🖷 01248 724839 ✉ hmpht@ynysmon.gov.uk

Health and Safety: Mr Stephen Nicol Health & Safety Team Leader, Swyddfa'r Sir, Llangefni LL77 7TW ☎ 01248 751884 🖷 01248 752880 ✉ snxpp@anglesey.gov.uk

Highways: Mr Huw Percy, Chief Engineer (Maintenance), Swyddfa'r Sir, Llangefni LL77 7TW ☎ 01248 752371 🖷 01248 724839 ✉ hmpht@ynysmon.gov.uk

Housing: Ms Shan Williams Head of Housing, Swyddfa'r Sir, Llangefni LL77 7TW ☎ 01248 725201 🖷 01248 752243; 01248 752233 ✉ slwhp@ynysmon.gov.uk

Legal: Ms Lynn Ball, Head of Function: Legal & Administration / Monitoring Officer, Swyddfa'r Sir, Llangefni LL77 7TW ☎ 01248 752586 🖷 01248 752132 ✉ lbxcs@ynysmon.gov.uk

Leisure and Cultural Services: Mrs Delyth Molyneux Head of Service - Education, Parc Mount, Glanhwfa Road, Llangefni LL77 7EY ☎ 01248 752916 ✉ delythmolyneux@ynysmon.gov.uk

Leisure and Cultural Services: Mr Dylan Williams, Head of Economic & Community Regeneration, Anglesey Business Centre, Bryn Cefni Business Park, Llangefni LL77 7XA ☎ 01248 752499 🖷 01248 752192 ✉ dwxpl@ynysmon.gov.uk

Licensing: Mr John Lloyd Senior Enforcement Officer (Licensing), Swyddfa'r Sir, Llangefni LL77 7TW ☎ 01248 752852 🖷 01248 752884 ✉ jelpp@ynysmon.gov.uk

Licensing: Mr Sion Lloyd Jones Operations Manager, Swyddfa'r Sir, Llangefni LL77 7EY ☎ 01248 752843 ✉ slhpp@ynysmon.gov.uk

Lifelong Learning: Mrs Delyth Molyneux Head of Service - Education, Parc Mount, Glanhwfa Road, Llangefni LL77 7EY ☎ 01248 752916 ✉ delythmolyneux@ynysmon.gov.uk

Lighting: Mr Eryl Davies Senior Engineer (Lighting), Swyddfa'r Sir, Llangefni LL77 7TW ☎ 01248 752393 ✉ ecdxht@ynysmon.gov.uk

ISLE OF ANGLESEY

Member Services: Mr Huw Jones Head of Democratic Services, Swyddfa'r Sir, Llangefni LL77 7TW ☎ 01248 752108 🖷 01248 750839 🖰 jhjce@ynysmon.gov.uk

Parking: Mr Alun Roberts, Decriminalised Parking Officer, Swyddfa'r Sir, Llangefni LL77 7TW ☎ 01248 752244 🖰 jarht@ynysmon.gov.uk

Personnel / HR: Ms Carys Edwards, Head of Profession - Human Resources, Swyddfa'r Sir, Llangefni LL77 7TW ☎ 01248 752502 🖷 01248 752583 🖰 cexcs@ynysmon.gov.uk

Planning: Mr Arthur Owen, Director of Sustainable Development, Swyddfa'r Sir, Llangefni LL77 7TW ☎ 01248 752401 🖷 01248 752412 🖰 awopl@ynysmon.gov.uk

Procurement: Mrs Sioned Rowlands Procurement Officer, Swyddfa'r Sir, Llangefni LL77 7TW ☎ 01248 752136 🖰 srxce@ynysmon.gov.uk

Public Libraries: Mrs Delyth Molyneux Head of Service - Education, Parc Mount, Glanhwfa Road, Llangefni LL77 7EY ☎ 01248 752916 🖰 delythmolyneux@ynysmon.gov.uk

Recycling & Waste Minimisation: Mr Meirion Edwards, Principal Waste Management Officer, Swyddfa'r Sir, Llangefni LL77 7TW ☎ 01248 752818 🖰 mpepp@ynysmon.gov.uk

Regeneration: Mr Dylan Williams, Head of Economic & Community Regeneration, Anglesey Business Centre, Bryn Cefni Business Park, Llangefni LL77 7XA ☎ 01248 752499 🖷 01248 752192 🖰 dwxpl@ynysmon.gov.uk

Road Safety: Mr Huw Percy, Chief Engineer (Maintenance), Swyddfa'r Sir, Llangefni LL77 7TW ☎ 01248 752371 🖷 01248 724839 🖰 hmpht@ynysmon.gov.uk

Social Services: Mrs Gwen Carrington Director of Community, Swyddfa'r Sir, Llangefni LL77 7TW ☎ 01248 752703 🖷 01248 752705 🖰 gwencarrington@ynysmon.gov.uk

Social Services (Adult): Mrs Gwen Carrington Director of Community, Swyddfa'r Sir, Llangefni LL77 7TW ☎ 01248 752703 🖷 01248 752705 🖰 gwencarrington@ynysmon.gov.uk

Social Services (Adult): Mr Alwyn Rhys Jones Head of Adult Services, County Offices, Llangefni LL77 7TW ☎ 01248 752707 🖰 alwynrhys-jones@ynysmon.gov.uk

Social Services (Children): Mrs Gwen Carrington Director of Community, Swyddfa'r Sir, Llangefni LL77 7TW ☎ 01248 752703 🖷 01248 752705 🖰 gwencarrington@ynysmon.gov.uk

Social Services (Children): Ms Anwen Huws Head of Children's Services, Swyddfa'r Sir, Llangefni LL77 7TW ☎ 01248 752797 🖰 amhss@ynysmon.gov.uk

Staff Training: Ms Carys Edwards, Head of Profession - Human Resources, Swyddfa'r Sir, Llangefni LL77 7TW ☎ 01248 752502 🖷 01248 752583 🖰 cexcs@ynysmon.gov.uk

Sustainable Development: Mr Arthur Owen, Director of Sustainable Development, Swyddfa'r Sir, Llangefni LL77 7TW ☎ 01248 752401 🖷 01248 752412 🖰 awopl@ynysmon.gov.uk

Tourism: Mr Iwan Huws Tourism & Maritime Manager, Anglesey Business Centre, Bryn Cefni Business Park, Llangefni LL77 7TW ☎ 01248 752493 🖰 gihpl@anglesey.gov.uk

Traffic Management: Mr Huw Percy, Chief Engineer (Maintenance), Swyddfa'r Sir, Llangefni LL77 7TW ☎ 01248 752371 🖷 01248 724839 🖰 hmpht@ynysmon.gov.uk

Transport: Mr Dewi Roberts, Chief Engineer (Transportation), Swyddfa'r Sir, Llangefni LL77 7TW ☎ 01248 752457 🖷 01248 724839 🖰 dwrpl@ynysmon.gov.uk

Transport Planner: Mr Huw Percy, Chief Engineer (Maintenance), Swyddfa'r Sir, Llangefni LL77 7TW ☎ 01248 752371 🖷 01248 724839 🖰 hmpht@ynysmon.gov.uk

Waste Collection and Disposal: Mr Meirion Edwards, Principal Waste Management Officer, Swyddfa'r Sir, Llangefni LL77 7TW ☎ 01248 752860 🖷 01248 752880 🖰 mpepp@ynysmon.gov.uk

Waste Collection and Disposal: Ms Carys Wyn Roberts, Contract Supervisor, Swyddfa'r Sir, Llangefni LL77 7TW ☎ 01248 752860 🖷 01248 752880 🖰 cwrpp@anglesey.gov.uk

Waste Management: Mr Meirion Edwards, Principal Waste Management Officer, Swyddfa'r Sir, Llangefni LL77 7TW ☎ 01248 752860 🖷 01248 752880 🖰 mpepp@ynysmon.gov.uk

COUNCILLORS

***Leader of the Council* Williams**, Ieuan (IND - Lligwy)
ieuanwilliams@anglesey.gov.uk

***Deputy Leader of the Council* Roberts**, J Arwel (LAB - Caergybi)
johnarwelroberts@anglesey.gov.uk

Davies, Lewis (PC - Seiriol)
lewisdavies@anglesey.gov.uk

Dew, Richard (IND - Llifon)
richarddew@anglesey.gov.uk

Evans, Jim (IND - Aethwy)
jimevans@anglesey.gov.uk

Evans, Jeffrey (IND - Ynys Gybi)
jeffreyevans@anglesey.gov.uk

Griffith, Ann (PC - Bro Aberffraw)
anngriffith@anglesey.gov.uk

Griffith, John (PC - Talybolion)
johngriffith@anglesey.gov.uk

Hughes, Kenneth (IND - Talybolion)
kennethphughes@anglesey.gov.uk

Hughes, Derlwyn Rees (IND - Lligwy)
derlwynrhughes@anglesey.gov.uk

Hughes, Vaughan (PC - Lligwy)
vaughanhughes@anglesey.gov.uk

Hughes, Victor (IND - Bro Rhosyr)
tvictor.hughes@anglesey.gov.uk

Hughes, Williams (IND - Twrcelyn)
wthau@anglesey.gov.uk

Hughes, Trefor (PC - Ynys Gybi)
treforlloydhughes@anglesey.gov.uk

Huws, Llinos Medi (PC - Talybolion)
llinosmedihuws@anglesey.gov.uk

Jones, Carwyn (PC - Seiriol)
carwyneliasjones@anglesey.gov.uk

Jones, Gwilym (IND - Llifon)
gwilymojones@anglesey.gov.uk

Jones, Hywel Eifion (IND - Bro Rhosyr)
hyweleifionjones@anglesey.gov.uk

Jones, Robert Llewelyn (INDNA - Caergybi)
robertljones@anglesey.gov.uk

Jones, Raymond (IND - Caergybi)
raymondjones@anglesey.gov.uk

Jones, R.Meirion (PC - Aethwy)
rmeirionjones@anglesey.gov.uk

Jones, Aled (INDNA - Twrcelyn)
aledmjones@anglesey.gov.uk

Jones, Richard (IND - Twrcelyn)
richardowainjones@anglesey.gov.uk

Mummery, Alun (PC - Aethwy)
alunwmummery@anglesey.gov.uk

Parry, Robert (PC - Canolbarth Môn)
bobparry@anglesey.gov.uk

Rees, Dylan (PC - Canolbarth Môn)
dylanrees@anglesey.gov.uk

Roberts, Nicola (PC - Canolbarth Môn)
nicolaroberts@anglesey.gov.uk

Rogers, Peter (IND - Bro Aberffraw)
peterrogers@anglesey.gov.uk

Rowlands, Alwyn (LAB - Seiriol)
alwynrowlands@anglesey.gov.uk

Thomas, Dafydd (IND - Ynys Gybi)
dafyddrhysthomas@anglesey.gov.uk

POLITICAL COMPOSITION
IND: 14, PC: 12, INDNA: 2, LAB: 2

COMMITTEE CHAIRS

Audit & Governance: Mr Robert Llewelyn Jones

Licensing: Mr Williams Hughes

Isle of Wight U

Isle of Wight Council, County Hall, High Street, Newport PO30 1UD
☎ 01983 821000 🖷 01983 823333 🖰 customer.services@iow.gov.uk
💻 www.iwight.com

FACTS AND FIGURES
Parliamentary Constituencies: Isle of Wight
EU Constituencies: South East
Election Frequency: Elections are of whole council

PRINCIPAL OFFICERS

Chief Executive: Mr David Burbage Managing Director & Head of Paid Service, County Hall, High Street, Newport PO30 1UD
☎ 01983 821000 ext 6211 🖰 david.burbage@iow.gov.uk

Deputy Chief Executive: Mr John Metcalfe Assistant Director - Economic Development, Tourism & Leisure, County Hall, High Street, Newport PO30 1UD ☎ 01983 821000 ext 6211
🖰 john.metcalf@iow.gov.uk

Architect, Building / Property Services: Mr Ashley Curzon Strategic Manager - Economic Development & Asset Management, County Hall, High Street, Newport PO30 1UD ☎ 01983 821000 ext 6210 🖰 ashley.curzon@iow.gov.uk

Building Control: Mr John Lutas, Building Control Manager, Seaclose, Fairlee Road, Newport PO30 2QS ☎ 01983 821000
🖷 01983 823851 🖰 john.lutas@iow.gov.uk

Civil Registration: Mrs Sharon Crews Celebratory & Registration Service Manager, Seaclose Offices, Fairlee Road, Newport PO30 2QS ☎ 01983 821000 🖰 janice.lord@iow.gov.uk

PR / Communications: Mrs Helen Wheller Media Team Leader, County Hall, High Street, Newport PO30 1UD ☎ 01983 821000
🖰 helen.wheller@iow.gov.uk

Community Planning: Mr Martin Elliott Director - Adult Social Care, County Hall, High Street, Newport PO30 1UD
☎ 01983 821000 🖰 martin.elliott@iow.gov.uk

Computer Management: Mr Gavin Muncaster Strategic Manager - ICT & Digital Services, Bugle House, High Street, Newport PO30 1UD ☎ 01983 821000 🖷 01983 823501
🖰 gavin.muncaster@iow.gov.uk

Consumer Protection and Trading Standards: Mr Mike Cleary Senior Trading Standards Manager, Jubilee Stores, The Quay, Newport PO30 2EH ☎ 01983 821000 🖰 mike.cleary@iow.gov.uk

Contracts: Mrs Sue Dasant Strategic Manager - Procurement & Contract, County Hall, High Street, Newport PO30 1UD
☎ 01983 821000 🖰 sue.dasant@iow.gov.uk

Customer Service: Mrs Sharon Betts Shared Service Manager, Westbridge Centre, Brading Road, Ryde PO33 1QS
☎ 01983 821000 🖰 sharon.betts@iow.gov.uk

Economic Development: Mr John Metcalfe Head of Economic Development, Tourism & Leisure, County Hall, High Street, Newport PO30 1UD ☎ 01983 821000 🖰 john.metcalf@iow.gov.uk

E-Government: Mr Gavin Muncaster Strategic Manager - ICT & Digital Services, Bugle House, High Street, Newport PO30 1UD
☎ 01983 821000 🖷 01983 823501 🖰 gavin.muncaster@iow.gov.uk

Electoral Registration: Mr Clive Joynes, Election & Land Charges Manager, County Hall, High Street, Newport PO30 1UD
☎ 01983 823341 🖷 01983 823344 🖰 clive.joynes@iow.gov.uk

ISLE OF WIGHT

Emergency Planning: Mr Darren Steed Resilience Manager, County Hall, High Street, Newport PO30 1UD ☎ 01983 823314 🖷 01983 521636 🖰 darren.steed@iow.gov.uk

Energy Management: Mr Timothy Watson Energy Manager, County Hall, High Street, Newport PO30 1UD ☎ 01983 821000 🖷 01983 822763 🖰 timothy.watson@iow.gov.uk

Estates, Property & Valuation: Miss Andrea Jenkins Senior Estates Manager, County Hall, High Street, Newport PO30 1UD ☎ 01983 823263 🖷 01983 822763 🖰 andrea.jenkins@iow.gov.uk

Events Manager: Miss Elaine Cesar Senior Events Officer, County Hall, High Street, Newport PO30 1UD ☎ 01983 821000 🖰 elaine.cesar@iow.gov.uk

Facilities: Mrs Ruth Jones Facilities Manager, County Hall, High Street, Newport PO30 1UD ☎ 01983 821000 🖰 ruth.jones@iow.gov.uk

Finance: Mr Stuart Fraser Head of Finance & Section 151, County Hall, High Street, Newport PO30 1UD ☎ 01983 821000 🖰 stuart.fraser@iow.gov.uk

Treasury: Mrs Jo Thistlewood Technical Finance Officer, County Hall, High Street, Newport PO30 1UD ☎ 01983 821000 🖰 jo.thistlewood@iow.gov.uk

Pensions: Mr Graham Fahy HR Support & Pensions Manager, Westbridge Centre, Brading Road, Ryde PO33 1QS ☎ 01983 821000 🖰 graham.fahy@iow.gov.uk

Fleet Management: Mr Nick Symes Fleet Manager, Cemetery Hill, Carisbrooke, Newport PO30 1YS ☎ 01983 823786 🖰 nick.symes@iow.gov.uk

Grounds Maintenance: Mr Matthew Chatfield Parks & Countryside Manager, County Hall, High Street, Newport PO30 1UD ☎ 01983 821000 🖷 01983 823841 🖰 matthew.chatfield@iow.gov.uk

Health and Safety: Mr Anthony Thorn Strategic Lead - People Management Service, County Hall, High Street, Newport PO30 1UD ☎ 01983 821000 🖰 anthony.thorn@iow.gov.uk

Highways: Mr Antony Cooke Highways PFI Contract Programme Manager, Enterprise House, St Cross Buisness Park, Newport PO30 5WB ☎ 01983 821000 🖷 01983 520563 🖰 antony.cook@iow.gov.uk

Housing: Mrs Wendy Perera Head of Planning & Regulatory Services, County Hall, High Street, Newport PO30 1UD ☎ 01983 821000 🖰 wendy.perera@iow.gov.uk

Legal: Mrs Helen Miles Strategic Manager & Deputy Monitoring Officer, County Hall, High Street, Newport PO30 1UD ☎ 01983 821000 🖰 helen.miles@iow.gov.uk

Leisure and Cultural Services: Mr Lee Matthews, Recreation & Public Spaces Manager, County Hall, High Street, Newport PO30 1UD ☎ 01983 823815 🖷 01983 823841 🖰 lee.matthews@iow.gov.uk

Licensing: Mr Kevin Winchcombe Principal Licensing Officer, Jubilee Stores, The Quay, Newport PO30 2EH ☎ 01983 821000 🖷 01983 823171 🖰 kevin.winchcombe@iow.gov.uk

Lifelong Learning: Mrs Sarah Teague Commissioner for Learning & Development, Carnival Learning Centre, Westridge, PO33 1QS ☎ 01983 817280 🖰 sarah.teague@iow.gov.uk

Member Services: Mrs Jo Cooke Business Hub Manager - Members & Governance, County Hall, High Street, Newport PO30 1UD ☎ 01983 821000 🖰 jo.cooke@iow.gov.uk

Parking: Mr Mark Downer Parking Operations Manager, Enterprise House, Newport PO30 5WB ☎ 01983 821000 🖰 mark.downer@iow.gov.uk

Partnerships: Ms Astrid Davies, Commissioning Manager, County Hall, High Street, Newport PO30 1UD ☎ 01983 823804 🖷 01983 823535 🖰 astrid.davies@iow.gov.uk

Personnel / HR: Mrs Claire Shand, Head - Human Resources & Organisational Change, County Hall, High Street, Newport PO30 1UD ☎ 01983 823120 🖷 01983 823012 🖰 claire.shand@iow.gov.uk

Planning: Mrs Wendy Perera Head of Planning & Regulatory Services, County Hall, High Street, Newport PO30 1UD ☎ 01983 821000 🖰 wendy.perera@iow.gov.uk

Procurement: Mrs Sue Dasant Strategic Manager - Procurement & Contract, County Hall, High Street, Newport PO30 1UD ☎ 01983 821000 🖰 sue.dasant@iow.gov.uk

Public Libraries: Mr Rob Jones Libraries Officer, 5 Mariners Way, Somerton Industrial Estate, Cowes PO31 8PD ☎ 01983 203885 🖰 rob.jones@iow.gov.uk

Recycling & Waste Minimisation: Ms Laura Kay Principal Waste Policy & Delivery Manager, County Hall, High Street, Newport PO30 1UD ☎ 01983 823777 🖷 01983 520563 🖰 laura.kay@iow.gov.uk

Road Safety: Mrs Tracey Webb Senior Road Safety Officer, Sandown Fire Station, East Yar Road, Newport PO36 9AX ☎ 01983 408263 🖰 tracey.webb@iow.gov.uk

Social Services: Mr Martin Elliott Director - Adult Social Care, County Hall, High Street, Newport PO30 1UD ☎ 01983 821000 🖰 martin.elliott@iow.gov.uk

Public Health: Prof Rida Elkheir Director - Public Health, County Hall, High Street, Newport PO30 1UD ☎ 🖰 rida.elkheir@iow.gov.uk

Staff Training: Mr Charles Charalambous Commissioning Manager, The Carnival Learning Centre, Westridge, Brading Road, Ryde PO33 1QS ☎ 01983 821000 🖰 charles.charalambous@iow.gov.uk

Sustainable Development: Mr Jim Fawcett Principal Officer - Environment, County Hall, High Street, Newport PO30 1UD ☎ 01983 821000 🖰 ashley.curzon@iow.gov.uk

Tourism: Mr Ashley Curzon Strategic Manager - Economic Development & Asset Management, County Hall, High Street, Newport PO30 1UD ☎ 01983 821000 ext 6210 ✉ ashley.curzon@iow.gov.uk

Transport Planner: Mr Chris Wells, Principal Policy Planning Officer - Highways & Transport, Enterprise House, St Cross Business Park, Newport PO30 5WB ☎ 01983 821000 ✉ chris.wells@iow.gov.uk

Waste Collection and Disposal: Mr Mike Ackrill Principal Waste & Contracts Officer, County Hall, High Street, Newport PO30 1UD ☎ 01983 821000 ✉ mike.ackrill@iow.gov.uk

Waste Management: Mr Mike Ackrill Principal Waste & Contracts Officer, County Hall, High Street, Newport PO30 1UD ☎ 01983 821000 ✉ mike.ackrill@iow.gov.uk

COUNCILLORS

***Leader of the Council* Bacon**, Jonathan (IND - Brading, St.Helens & Bembridge)
Jonathan.Bacon@iow.gov.uk

***Deputy Leader of the Council* Stubbings**, Stephen (IND - Ventnor West)
stephen.stubbings@iow.gov.uk

Baker-Smith, Julia (IND - Whippingham & Osborne)
juliawhippinghamosborne@hotmail.co.uk

Barry, Reginald (LD - Nettlestone and Seaview)
regbarry@outlook.com

Bertie, Paul (CON - Cowes North)
paul.bertie@iow.gov.uk

Blezzard, Robert (IND - Sandown North)
bob.blezzard@iow.gov.uk

Bloomfield, Raymond (CON - Lake South)
ray.bloomfield@iow.gov.uk

Chapman, Charles (IND - Ryde South)
charles.chapman@iow.gov.uk

Downer, Rodney (IND - Godshill and Wroxhall)
rodney.downer@iow.gov.uk

Eccles, David (CON - Freshwater North)
david.eccles@iow.gov.uk

Fuller, Paul (IND - Cowes West and Gurnard)
paulfulleriw@gmail.com

Gauntlett, Conrad (CON - Havenstreet, Ashey & Haylands)

Gilbey, Jonathan (IND - Shanklin Central)
jonathan.gilbey@iow.gov.uk

Hillard, Luisa (IND - East Cowes)
luisa.hillard@iow.gov.uk

Hobart, John (CON - Carisbrooke)
john.hobart@iow.gov.uk

Hollands, Alan (LAB - Lake North)
alan.hollands@btinternet.com

Hollis, Richard (CON - Parkhurst)
Richard.Hollis@iow.gov.uk

Howe, John (LD - Totland)
John.Howe@iow.gov.uk

Hutchinson, Stuart (CON - West Wight)
stu.hutch@btinternet.com

Jones-Evans, Julie (CON - Newport Central)
Julie.Jones-Evans@iow.gov.uk

Jordan, Philip (IND - Ryde North West)
phil.jordan@iow.gov.uk

Kendall, Gordon (IND - Brading, St Helens & Bembridge)
gordon.kendall@tiscali.co.uk

Lumley, Geoff (LAB - Newport East)
geofflumley2@gmail.com

Medland, John (IND - Freshwater South)
john.medland@iow.gov.uk

Nicholson, John (CON - Cowes South & Northwood)
cllr.john.nicholson@btconnect.com

Peacey-Wilcox, Lora (CON - Cowes Medina)
lora@onwight.net

Perks, Graham (UKIP - Ventnor East)
graham.perks@iow.gov.uk

Pitcher, Daryll (UKIP - Wootton Bridge)
daryll.pitcher@iow.gov.uk

Price, Matthew (CON - Newport North)
matthew.price@iow.gov.uk

Priest, Richard (IND - Shanklin South)
richard.priest@iow.gov.uk

Richards, Colin (IND - Arreton & Newchurch)
colin.richards@iow.gov.uk

Seely, Robert (CON - Central Wight)
bob.seely@iow.gov.uk

Smart, Shirley (IND - Newport South)
shirley.smart@iow.gov.uk

Stephens, Ian (IND - Ryde West)
ian.stephens@iow.gov.uk

Stewart, David (CON - Chale Niton & Whitwell)
david.stewart@iow.gov.uk

Ward, Ian (CON - Sandown South)
ian.ward@iow.gov.uk

Warlow, Ivor (IND - Binstead and Fishbourne)
ivor.warlow@iow.gov.uk

Whitby-Smith, Roger (IND - Ryde East)
roger.whitbysmith@iow.gov.uk

Whitehouse, Christopher (CON - Newport West)
chris.whitehouse@iow.gov.uk

Whittle, Wayne (CON - Ryde North East)
Wayne.Whittle@iow.gov.uk

POLITICAL COMPOSITION

IND: 18, CON: 16, LAB: 2, LD: 2, UKIP: 2

COMMITTEE CHAIRS

Audit: Mr Stuart Hutchinson

Licensing: Miss Julie Jones-Evans

Planning: Ms Julia Baker-Smith

Scrutiny: Mr David Stewart

ISLINGTON

Islington L

Islington London Borough Council, Town Hall, Upper Street, London N1 2UD
☎ 020 7527 2000 🖷 020 7527 5001 ✉ contact@islington.gov.uk
💻 www.islington.gov.uk

FACTS AND FIGURES

Parliamentary Constituencies: Islington North, Islington South and Finsbury
EU Constituencies: London
Election Frequency: Elections are of whole council

PRINCIPAL OFFICERS

Chief Executive: Ms Lesley Seary Chief Executive, Town Hall, Upper Street, London N1 2UD ☎ 020 7527 3062 ✉ lesley.seary@islington.gov.uk

Assistant Chief Executive: Ms Lela Kogbara ACE - Strategy & Partnerships, Room G16, Town Hall, Upper Street, London N1 2UD ☎ ; 020 7527 3120 🖷 020 7527 3013 ✉ lela.kogbara@islington.gov.uk

Assistant Chief Executive: Ms Debra Norman ACE - Governance & HR, Town Hall, Upper Street, London N1 2UD ☎ 020 7527 6096 🖷 020 7527 3267 ✉ debra.norman@islington.gov.uk

Senior Management: Ms Julie Billett Director - Public Health, Town Hall, Upper Street, London N1 2UD ☎ 020 7527 1221 ✉ julie.billett@islington.gov.uk

Senior Management: Ms Cathy Blair Interim Corporate Director - Children's Services, Town Hall, Upper Street, London N1 2UD ☎ 020 7527 5624 ✉ cathy.blair@islington.gov.uk

Senior Management: Mr Mike Curtis, Corporate Director - Finance & Resources, 7 Newington Barrow Way, London N7 7EP ☎ 020 7527 2294 🖷 020 7527 2407 ✉ mike.curtis@islington.gov.uk

Senior Management: Mr Sean McLaughlin Corporate Director - Housing & Adult Social Services, 338-346 Goswell Road, London EC1V 7LQ ☎ 020 7527 8178 🖷 020 7527 8362 ✉ sean.mclaughlin@islington.gov.uk

Senior Management: Mr Kevin O'Leary, Corporate Director - Environment & Regeneration, 222 Upper Street, London N1 1XR ☎ 020 7527 2350 🖷 020 7527 2731 ✉ kevin.oleary@islington.gov.uk

Access Officer / Social Services (Disability): Mr Sean McLaughlin Corporate Director - Housing & Adult Social Services, 338-346 Goswell Road, London EC1V 7LQ ☎ 020 7527 8178 🖷 020 7527 8362 ✉ sean.mclaughlin@islington.gov.uk

Building Control: Ms Jan Hart, Service Director - Public Protection & Development Management, 222 Upper Street, London N1 1XR ☎ 020 7527 3193 🖷 020 7527 3375 ✉ jan.hart@islington.gov.uk

Children / Youth Services: Ms Eleanor Schooling Corporate Director - Children's Services, 222 Upper Street, London N1 1YA ☎ 020 7527 5624 ✉ eleanor.schooling@islington.gov.uk

Civil Registration: Mr Besserat Atsehaba Superintendent Registrar, Town Hall, Upper Street, London N1 2UD ☎ 020 7527 6357 🖷 020 7527 6308 ✉ besserat.atsehaba@islington.gov.uk

PR / Communications: Ms Lela Kogbara ACE - Strategy & Partnerships, Room G16, Town Hall, Upper Street, London N1 2UD ☎ 020 7527 3120 🖷 020 7527 3013 ✉ lela.kogbara@islington.gov.uk

Community Safety: Mr Alva Bailey, Head of Service - Community Safety, Room 116, 222 Upper Street, London N1 1XR ☎ 020 7527 3135 🖷 020 7527 3098 ✉ alva.bailey@islington.gov.uk

Computer Management: Ms Emma Marinos, Director - Digital Services & Transformation, Town Hall, Upper Street, London N1 2UD ☎ 020 7527 3467 🖷 020 7527 3291 ✉ emma.marinos@islington.gov.uk

Consumer Protection and Trading Standards: Ms Jan Hart, Service Director - Public Protection & Development Management, 222 Upper Street, London N1 1XR ☎ 020 7527 3193 🖷 020 7527 3375 ✉ jan.hart@islington.gov.uk

Contracts: Mr Peter Hurlock Head of Strategic Procurement, 7 Newington Barrow Way, Finsbury Park, , London N7 7EP ☎ 020 7257 3131 ✉ peter.hurlock@islington.gov.uk

Customer Service: Mr Martin Bevis Assistant Director - Financial Operations & Customer Services, 222 Upper Street, London N1 7XR ☎ 020 7527 2000 🖷 0207 527 5454 ✉ martin.bevis@islington.gov.uk

Economic Development: Ms Lela Kogbara ACE - Strategy & Partnerships, Room G16, Town Hall, Upper Street, London N1 2UD ☎ 020 7527 3120 🖷 020 7527 3013 ✉ lela.kogbara@islington.gov.uk

Education: Ms Eleanor Schooling Corporate Director - Children's Services, 222 Upper Street, London N1 1YA ☎ 020 7527 5624 ✉ eleanor.schooling@islington.gov.uk

E-Government: Ms Emma Marinos, Director - Digital Services & Transformation, Town Hall, Upper Street, London N1 2UD ☎ 020 7527 3467 🖷 020 7527 3291 ✉ emma.marinos@islington.gov.uk

Electoral Registration: Mr Andrew Smith, Electoral Services Manager, Town Hall, Upper Street, London N1 2UD ☎ 020 7527 3085 🖷 020 7527 3289 ✉ andrew.smith@islington.gov.uk

Emergency Planning: Mr Andy French, Principal Emergency Planning Officer, 222 Upper Street, London N1 1XE ☎ 020 7527 3195 🖷 020 7527 3375 ✉ andy.french@islington.gov.uk

Environmental / Technical Services: Mr Kevin O'Leary, Corporate Director - Environment & Regeneration, 222 Upper Street, London N1 1XR ☎ 020 7527 2350 🖷 020 7527 2731 ✉ kevin.oleary@islington.gov.uk

Environmental Health: Ms Jan Hart, Service Director - Public Protection & Development Management, 222 Upper Street, London N1 1XE ☎ 020 7527 3193 🖷 020 7527 3375 ✉ jan.hart@islington.gov.uk

Facilities: Ms Beverley Densham Head - Accommodation & Facilities, 7 Newington Barrow Way, Finsbury Park, Islington, London N7 7EP ☎ 020 7527 4052 beverley.densham@islington.gov.uk

Finance: Mr Mike Curtis, Corporate Director - Finance & Resources, 222 Upper Street, London N1 1XR ☎ 020 7527 2294 🖷 020 7527 2407 mike.curtis@islington.gov.uk

Finance: Mr Alan Layton, Director - Financial Management, 222 Upper Street, London N1 1XR ☎ 020 7527 2835 🖷 020 7527 2407 alan.layton@islington.gov.uk

Treasury: Mr Mike Curtis, Corporate Director - Finance & Resources, 7 Newington Barrow Way, London N7 7EP ☎ 020 7527 2294 🖷 020 7527 2407 mike.curtis@islington.gov.uk

Pensions: Mr Stephen Rogers, Pensions Manager, 7 Newington Barrow Way, Finsbury Park, , London N7 7EP ☎ 020 7527 2028 stephen.rogers@islington.gov.uk

Fleet Management: Mr Kenny Wilks Head of Street Environmental Services, 1 Cottage Road, London N7 8TP ☎ 020 7527 4534 kenny.wilks@islington.gov.uk

Grounds Maintenance: Mr Andrew Bedford Parks & Open Spaces Manager, Clocktower Office, 36 North Road, London N7 9TU ☎ 020 7527 3287 andrew.bedford@islington.gov.uk

Health and Safety: Ms Beverley Densham Head - Accommodation & Facilities, 7 Newington Barrow Way, Finsbury Park, Islington, London N7 7EP ☎ 020 7527 4052 beverley.densham@islington.gov.uk

Highways: Mr Bram Kainth, Director - Public Realm, 222 Upper Street, London N1 1XR ☎ 020 7527 2949 🖷 020 7527 2145 bram.kainth@islington.gov.uk

Home Energy Conservation: Ms Lucy Padfield, Energy Services Manager, Energy Centre, 222 Upper Street, London N1 1RE ☎ 020 7527 2501 🖷 020 7527 2332 lucy.padfield@islington.gov.uk

Housing: Mr Sean McLaughlin Corporate Director - Housing & Adult Social Services, 338-346 Goswell Road, London EC1V 7LQ ☎ 020 7527 8178 🖷 020 7527 8362 sean.mclaughlin@islington.gov.uk

Local Area Agreement: Ms Anette Hobart Corporate Partnership & Performance Manager, Town Hall, Upper Street, London N1 2UD ☎ 020 7527 3244 annette.hobart@islington.gov.uk

Legal: Ms Debra Norman ACE - Governance & HR, Town Hall, Upper Street, London N1 2UD ☎ 020 7527 6096 🖷 020 7527 3267 debra.norman@islington.gov.uk

Licensing: Ms Jan Hart, Service Director - Public Protection & Development Management, 222 Upper Street, London N1 1RE ☎ 020 7527 3193 🖷 020 7527 3375 jan.hart@islington.gov.uk

Lighting: Mr Bram Kainth, Director - Public Realm, 222 Upper Street, London N1 1XR ☎ 020 7527 2949 🖷 020 7527 2145 bram.kainth@islington.gov.uk

Member Services: Mr John Lynch, Head - Democratic Services, Town Hall, Upper Street, London N1 2UD ☎ 020 7527 3002 🖷 020 7527 3092 john.lynch@islington.gov.uk

Parking: Mr Bram Kainth, Director - Public Realm, 222 Upper Street, London N1 1XR ☎ 020 7527 2949 🖷 020 7527 2145 bram.kainth@islington.gov.uk

Personnel / HR: Ms Debra Norman ACE - Governance & HR, Town Hall, Upper Street, London N1 2UD ☎ 020 7527 6096 🖷 020 7527 3267 debra.norman@islington.gov.uk

Planning: Ms Karen Sullivan Service Director - Planning & Development, 222 Upper Street, London N1 1XR ☎ 020 7527 2730 karen.sullivan@islington.gov.uk

Public Libraries: Ms Rosemary Doyle, Head of Library & Cultural Services, Fieldway Crescent, London N5 1PF ☎ 020 7619 6903 🖷 020 7619 6906 rosemary.doyle@islington.gov.uk

Recycling & Waste Minimisation: Mr Bram Kainth, Director - Public Realm, 222 Upper Street, London N1 1XR ☎ 020 7527 2949 🖷 020 7527 2145 bram.kainth@islington.gov.uk

Road Safety: Mr Bram Kainth, Director - Public Realm, 222 Upper Street, London N1 1XR ☎ 020 7527 2949 🖷 020 7527 2145 bram.kainth@islington.gov.uk

Social Services (Adult): Mr Sean McLaughlin Corporate Director - Housing & Adult Social Services, 338-346 Goswell Road, London EC1V 7LQ ☎ 020 7527 8178 🖷 020 7527 8362 sean.mclaughlin@islington.gov.uk

Social Services (Children): Ms Eleanor Schooling Corporate Director - Children's Services, 222 Upper Street, London N1 1YA ☎ 020 7527 5624 eleanor.schooling@islington.gov.uk

Public Health: Ms Julie Billett Director - Public Health, Town Hall, Upper Street, London N1 2UD ☎ 020 7527 1221 julie.billett@islington.gov.uk

Street Scene: Mr Bram Kainth, Director - Public Realm, 222 Upper Street, London N1 1XR ☎ 020 7527 2949 🖷 020 7527 2145 bram.kainth@islington.gov.uk

Traffic Management: Mr Bram Kainth, Director - Public Realm, 222 Upper Street, London N1 1XR ☎ 020 7527 2949 🖷 020 7527 2145 bram.kainth@islington.gov.uk

Transport: Mr Bram Kainth, Director - Public Realm, 222 Upper Street, London N1 1XR ☎ 020 7527 2949 🖷 020 7527 2145 bram.kainth@islington.gov.uk

Transport Planner: Ms Karen Sullivan Service Director - Planning & Development, 222 Upper Street, London N1 1XR ☎ 020 7527 2730 karen.sullivan@islington.gov.uk

Waste Collection and Disposal: Mr Bram Kainth, Director - Public Realm, 222 Upper Street, London N1 1XR ☎ 020 7527 2949 🖷 020 7527 2145 bram.kainth@islington.gov.uk

ISLINGTON

Waste Management: Mr Bram Kainth, Director - Public Realm, 222 Upper Street, London N1 1XR ☎ 020 7527 2949 🖷 020 7527 2145 ✉ bram.kainth@islington.gov.uk

COUNCILLORS

***Mayor* Greening**, Richard (LAB - Highbury West)
richard.greening@islington.gov.uk

***Deputy Mayor* Fletcher**, Kat (LAB - St. George's)
kat.fletcher@islington.gov.uk

***Leader of the Council* Watts**, Richard (LAB - Tollington)
richard.watts@islington.gov.uk

***Deputy Leader of the Council* Burgess**, Janet (LAB - Junction)
janet.burgess@islington.gov.uk

Andrews, Raphael (LAB - Clerkenwell)
raphael.andrews@islington.gov.uk

Caluori, Joe (LAB - Mildmay)
joe.caluori@islington.gov.uk

Chowdhury, Jilani (LAB - Barnsbury)
jilani.chowdhury@islington.gov.uk

Comer- Schwartz, Kaya (LAB - Junction)
kaya.comerschwartz@islington.gov.uk

Convery, Paul (LAB - Caledonian)
paul.convery@islington.gov.uk

Court, James (LAB - Clerkenwell)
james.court@islington.gov.uk

Debono, Theresa (LAB - Highbury West)
theresa.debono@islington.gov.uk

Diner, Alex (LAB - Canonbury)
alex.diner@islington.gov.uk

Donovan, Alice (LAB - Clerkenwell)
alice.donovan@islington.gov.uk

Doolan, Gary (LAB - St. Peters)
gary.doolan@islington.gov.uk

Erdogan, Aysegul (LAB - Highbury East)
aysegul.erdogan@islington.gov.uk

Gallagher, Troy (LAB - Bunhill)
troy.gallagher@islington.gov.uk

Gantly, Osh (LAB - Highbury East)
osh.gantly@islington.gov.uk

Gill, Satnam (LAB - St. George's)
satnam.gill@islington.gov.uk

Hamitouche, Mouna (LAB - Barnsbury)
mouna.hamitouche@islington.gov.uk

Heather, Gary (LAB - Finsbury Park)
gary.heather@islington.gov.uk

Hull, Andy (LAB - Highbury West)
andy.hull@islington.gov.uk

Ismail, Rakhia (LAB - Holloway)
rakhia.ismail@islington.gov.uk

Jeapes, Clare (LAB - Canonbury)
clare.jeapes@islington.gov.uk

Kaseki, Jean Roger (LAB - Tollington)
jean.kaseki@islington.gov.uk

Kay, Jenny (LAB - Mildmay)
jenny.kay@islington.gov.uk

Khan, Robert (LAB - Bunhill)
robert.khan@islington.gov.uk

Klute, Martin (LAB - St. Peters)
martin.klute@islington.gov.uk

Murray, James (LAB - Barnsbury)
james.murray@islington.gov.uk

Nicholls, Tim (LAB - Junction)
tim.nicholls@islingtong.gov.uk

O'Halloran, Una (LAB - Caledonian)
una.o'halloran@islington.gov.uk

O'Sullivan, Michael (LAB - Finsbury Park)
mick.o'sullivan@islington.gov.uk

Parker, Olly (LAB - Mildmay)
olly.parker@islington.gov.uk

Perry, Alice (LAB - St. Peters)
alice.perry@islington.gov.uk

Perry, Rupert (LAB - Caledonian)
rupert.perry@islington.gov.uk

Picknell, Angela (LAB - St. Marys)
angela.picknell@islington.gov.uk

Poole, Gary (LAB - St. Mary's)
gary.poole@islington.gov.uk

Poyser, Dave (LAB - Hillrise)
dave.poyser@islington.gov.uk

Russell, Caroline (GRN - Highbury East)
caroline.russell@islington.gov.uk

Safi Ngongo, Michelline (LAB - Hillrise)
michelline.mgongo@islington.gov.uk

Shaikh, Asima (LAB - Finsbury Park)
asima.shaikh@islington.gov.uk

Smith, Paul (LAB - Holloway)
paul.smith@islington.gov.uk

Spall, Marian (LAB - Hillrise)
marian.spall@islington.gov.uk

Turan, Nurullah (LAB - St. Mary's)
nurullah.turan@islington.gov.uk

Ward, Nick (LAB - St. George's)
nick.ward@islington.gov.uk

Ward, Diarmaid (LAB - Holloway)
diarmaid.ward@islington.gov.uk

Wayne, Nick (LAB - Canonbury)
nick.wayne@islington.gov.uk

Webbe, Claudia (LAB - Bunhill)
claudia.webbe@islington.gov.uk

Williamson, Flora (LAB - Tollington)
flora.williamson@islington.gov.uk

POLITICAL COMPOSITION

LAB: 47, GRN: 1

COMMITTEE CHAIRS

Audit: Mr Satnam Gill

Licensing: Ms Flora Williamson

Planning: Mr Robert Khan

Kensington & Chelsea L

The Royal Borough of Kensington & Chelsea Council, Town Hall, Hornton Street, London W8 7NX
☎ 020 7361 3000 🖷 020 7938 1445 🖳 www.rbkc.gov.uk

FACTS AND FIGURES

Parliamentary Constituencies: Chelsea and Fulham, Kensington
EU Constituencies: London
Election Frequency: Elections are of whole council

PRINCIPAL OFFICERS

Chief Executive: Mr Nicholas Holgate, Town Clerk, Town Hall, Hornton Street, London W8 7NX ☎ 020 8753 2001; 020 7361 2299 🖷 020 8741 0307; 020 7361 2764 ✉ nicholas.holgate@rbkc.gov.uk

Senior Management: Ms Liz Bruce , Tri-Borough Executive Director - Adult Social Care, Town Hall, King Street, London W6 9JU ☎ 020 8753 5166 ✉ liz.bruce@lbhf.gov.uk

Senior Management: Mr Andrew Christie, Tri-Borough Executive Director - Children & Families, Town Hall, Hornton Street, London W8 7NX ☎ 020 8753 5002; 020 7361 2354; 020 7361 2229 ✉ andrew.christie@rbkc.gov.uk

Senior Management: Ms Sue Harris , Bi-Borough Director - Environment, Leisure & Residents' Services, Town Hall, King Street, London W6 0LJ ☎ 020 8753 4295 ✉ sue.harris@lbhf.gov.uk

Senior Management: Mr Tony Redpath, Director of Strategy & Local Services, Town Hall, Hornton Street, London W8 7NX ☎ 020 7361 3174 ✉ tony.redpath@rbkc.gov.uk

Senior Management: Mr Graham Stallwood , Director - Planning & Borough Development, Town Hall, Hornton Street, London W8 7NX ☎ 020 7361 2075 ✉ graham.stallwood@brkc.gov.uk

Access Officer / Social Services (Disability): Mr Richard Holden , Tri-Borough Head of Children With Disabilities, Westminster City Hall, 64 Victoria Street, London SW1E 6QP ☎ 020 7361 3751 ✉ richard.holden@rbkc.gov.uk

Access Officer / Social Services (Disability): Mr Malcolm Rose , Team Leader, Westminster City Hall, 64 Victoria Street, London SW1E 6QP ☎ 020 7641 6617 ✉ mrose@westminster.gov.uk

Building Control: Mr John Allen , Building Control Manager, Town Hall, Hornton Street, London W8 7NX ☎ 020 7361 3802 ✉ john.allen@rbkc.gov.uk

Building Control: Mr Graham Stallwood , Director - Planning & Borough Development, Town Hall, Hornton Street, London W8 7NX ☎ 020 7361 2075 ✉ graham.stallwood@brkc.gov.uk

Children / Youth Services: Mr Andrew Christie, Tri-Borough Executive Director - Children & Families, Town Hall, Hornton Street, London W8 7NX ☎ 020 8753 5002; 020 7361 2354; 020 7361 2229 ✉ andrew.christie@rbkc.gov.uk

Children / Youth Services: Ms Rachel Wright-Turner , Tri-Borough Director of Strategic Commissioning for Children & Families, Westminster City Hall, 64 Victoria Street, London SW1E 6QP ✉ rachel.wright-turner@rbkc.gov.uk

Civil Registration: Mr Steven Lord , Superintendent Registrar, Chelsea Registrar Office, Kings Road, London SW3 5EE ☎ 020 7361 4107 ✉ steven.lord@rbkc.gov.uk

PR / Communications: Mr Martin Fitzpatrick, Head of Media & Communications, Town Hall, Hornton Street, London W8 7NX ☎ 020 7361 3585 🖷 020 7937 9670 ✉ martin.fitzpatrick@rbkc.gov.uk

Community Safety: Mr David Page , Bi-Borough Director of Safer Neighbourhoods, Town Hall, King Street, London W6 9JU ☎ 020 8753 2125 ✉ david.page@lbhf.gov.uk

Computer Management: Mr Ed Garcez , Tri-Borough Chief Information Officer, Town Hall, King Street, London W6 9JU ☎ 020 8753 2900 ✉ ed.garcez@lbhf.gov.uk

Contracts: Mr Roger van Goethem , Procurement & Commercial Manager, Town Hall, Hornton Street, London W8 7NX ☎ 020 7361 3345 ✉ roger.vangoethem@rbkc.gov.uk

Corporate Services: Ms Debbie Morris , Head of Facilities Management, Town Hall, Hornton Street, London W8 7NX ☎ 020 7361 3189 ✉ debbiej.morris@rbkc.gov.uk

Customer Service: Mr Ray Brown, Director of Customer Access, Town Hall, Hornton Street, London W8 7NX ☎ 020 7361 3291 🖷 020 7368 0246 ✉ ray.brown@rbkc.gov.uk

Economic Development: Mr Graham Hart , Regeneration Manager, Town Hall, Hornton Street, London W8 7NX ☎ 020 7631 3336 🖷 020 7361 2764 ✉ graham.hart@rbkc.gov.uk

Education: Mr Andrew Christie, Tri-Borough Executive Director - Children & Families, Town Hall, Hornton Street, London W8 7NX ☎ 020 8753 5002; 020 7361 2354; 020 7361 2229 ✉ andrew.christie@rbkc.gov.uk

Education: Mr Ian Heggs , Tri-Borough Director of Schools Commissioning, Town Hall, Hornton Street, London W8 7NX ☎ 020 7361 3332 ✉ ian.heggs@rbkc.gov.uk

E-Government: Mr Barry Holloway , Head of Information Systems, Town Hall, Hornton Street, London W8 7NX ☎ 020 7361 2042 🖷 020 7361 2754 ✉ barry.holloway@rbkc.gov.uk

Electoral Registration: Mrs Susan Loynes , Electoral Services Manager, Town Hall, Hornton Street, London W8 7NX ☎ 020 7361 3931 ✉ susan.loynes@rbkc.gov.uk

Emergency Planning: Mr David Kerry, Contingency Planning Manager, Town Hall, Hornton Street, London W8 7NX ☎ 020 7361 2139 🖷 020 7361 2573 ✉ david.kerry@rbkc.gov.uk

Energy Management: Ms Debbie Morris , Head of Facilities Management, Town Hall, King Street, London W6 9JU ☎ 020 7361 3189 ✉ debbiej.morris@rbkc.gov.uk

Environmental Health: Mr Nick Austin , Bi-Borough Director of Environmental Health, Council Offices, 37 Pembroke Road, London W6 6PW ☎ 020 8753 3904; 020 7341 5600 ✉ nick.austin@brkc.gov.uk

Estates, Property & Valuation: Mr Michael Clark , Director of Corporate Property & Customer Services, Town Hall, Hornton Street, London W8 7NX ☎ 07960 579967 🖷 020 7361 2008 ✉ michael.clark@rbkc.gov.uk

Facilities: Ms Debbie Morris , Head of Facilities Management, Town Hall, King Street, London W6 9JU ☎ 020 7361 3189 ✉ debbiej.morris@rbkc.gov.uk

Finance: Mr Nicholas Holgate , Town Clerk & Executive Director of Finance, Town Hall, Hornton Street, London W8 7NX ☎ 020 7361 2384 🖷 020 7361 3716 ✉ nicholas.holgate@rbkc.gov.uk

Finance: Mr Hitesh Jolapara, Bi-Borough Director of Finance, Town Hall, Hornton Street, London W8 7NX ☎ 020 7361 2316 🖷 020 7361 3716 ✉ hitesh.jolapara@rbkc.gov.uk

Pensions: Mrs Maria Bailey , Pensions Manager, Town Hall, Hornton Street, London W8 7NX ☎ 020 7361 3000 ✉ maria.bailey@rbkc.gov.uk

Pensions: Mr Jonathan Hunt , Tri-Borough Director of Pensions & Treasury, Town Hall, King Street, London W6 9JU ☎ 020 7641 1804 ✉ jonathan.hunt@westminster.gov.uk

Health and Safety: Mr Gary Mann , Health & Safety Officer, Town Hall, Hornton Street, London W8 7NX ☎ 020 7361 3733 🖷 020 7361 2676 ✉ gary.mann@rbkc.gov.uk

Highways: Mr Mahmood Siddiqi , Bi-Borough Director of Transport & Highways, Town Hall, Hornton Street, London W8 7NX ☎ 020 7361 3589; 020 8748 3020 ✉ mahmood.siddiqi@rbkc.gov.uk

Housing: Ms Laura Johnson , Director of Housing, Town Hall, Hornton Street, London W8 7NX ☎ 020 7361 2362 ✉ laura.johnson@rbkc.gov.uk

Housing Maintenance: Mr Nick Austin , Bi-Borough Director of Environmental Health, Council Offices, 37 Pembroke Road, London W6 6PW ☎ 020 8753 3904; 020 7341 5600 ✉ nick.austin@brkc.gov.uk

Legal: Mrs Tasnim Shawkat , Director of Law, Town Hall, Hornton Street, London W8 7NX ☎ 020 7361 2257 ✉ tasnim.shawkat@rbkc.gov.uk

Leisure and Cultural Services: Mr Ullash Karia , Head of Leisure & Parks, The Stableyard, Holland Park, Ilchester Place, London W8 6LU ☎ 020 7938 8171 ✉ ullash.karia@rbkc.gov.uk

Leisure and Cultural Services: Ms Donna Pentelow , Bi-Borough Head of Culture, Town Hall, King Street, London W6 0LJ ☎ 020 8753 2358; 020 8752 2358 🖷 020 8753 3713 ✉ donna.pentelow@lbhf.gov.uk

Licensing: Mr Patrick Crowley, Licensing Team Manager, Council Offices, 37 Pembroke Road, London W8 6PW ☎ 020 7341 5601 🖷 020 7368 0231 ✉ patrick.crowley@rbkc.gov.uk

Lighting: Mr Derek Mahon , Senior Lighting Engineer, Council Offices, 37 Pembroke Road, London W8 6PW ☎ 020 7341 5254 ✉ derek.mahon@rbkc.gov.uk

Lottery Funding, Charity and Voluntary: Mrs Lucy Ashdown , Funding & Partnerships Officer, Town Hall, Hornton Street, London W8 7NX ☎ 020 7361 2509 ✉ lucy.ashdown@rbkc.gov.uk

Parking: Mr David Taylor, Bi-Borough Head of Parking Services, PO Box 3387, London SW6 2QF ☎ 020 8753 3251 ✉ david.taylor@lbhf.gov.uk

Partnerships: Mr Stephen Morgan , Community Engagement Manager, Town Hall, Hornton Street, London W8 7NX ☎ 020 7854 5852 ✉ stephen.morgan@rbkc.gov.uk

Personnel / HR: Ms Debbie Morris , Head of Facilities Management, Town Hall, Hornton Street, London W8 7NX ☎ 020 7361 3189 ✉ debbiej.morris@rbkc.gov.uk

Planning: Mr Graham Stallwood , Director - Planning & Borough Development, Town Hall, Hornton Street, London W8 7NX ☎ 020 7361 2075 ✉ graham.stallwood@brkc.gov.uk

Procurement: Mr Andrew Lee, Head of Strategic Procurement, Town Hall, Hornton Street, London W8 7NX ☎ 020 7361 2674 ✉ andrew.lee@rbkc.gov.uk

Public Libraries: Mr Mike Clarke , Tri-Borough Director of Libraries & Archives, Town Hall, Hornton Street, London W8 7NX ☎ 020 7641 2199 ✉ mclarke1@westminster.gov.uk

Recycling & Waste Minimisation: Ms Sue Harris , Bi-Borough Director - Environment, Leisure & Residents' Services, Town Hall, King Street, London W6 0LJ ☎ 020 8753 4295 ✉ sue.harris@lbhf.gov.uk

Regeneration: Mr Graham Hart , Regeneration Manager, Town Hall, Hornton Street, London W8 7NX ☎ 020 7631 3336 🖷 020 7361 2764 ✉ graham.hart@rbkc.gov.uk

Road Safety: Mr Neil Simpson , Road Safety Manager, Council Offices, 37 Pembroke Road, London W8 6PW ☎ 020 7361 3628 ✉ neil.simpson@rbkc.gov.uk

Social Services: Ms Stella Baillie, Tri-Borough Director of Integrated Adult Social Care, Town Hall, Hornton Street, London W8 7NX ☎ 020 7361 2398 ✉ stella.baillie@rbkc.gov.uk

Social Services: Ms Gaynor Driscoll , Joint Commissioning Manager of Sexual Health, Westminster City Hall, 64 Victoria Street, London SW1E 6QP ☎ 020 7641 4000 ✉ gdriscoll@westminster.gov.uk

Social Services (Children): Mr Andrew Christie, Tri-Borough Executive Director - Children & Families, Town Hall, Hornton Street, London W8 7NX ☎ 020 8753 5002; 020 7361 2354; 020 7361 2229 ✉ andrew.christie@rbkc.gov.uk

Staff Training: Mr Nick Alcock, Corporate Learning & Development Manager, Council Offices, 37 Pembroke Road, London W8 6PW ☎ 020 7341 5130 ✉ nick.alcock@rbkc.gov.uk

Sustainable Communities: Mr Tony Redpath, Director of Strategy & Local Services, Town Hall, Hornton Street, London W8 7NX ☎ 020 7361 3174 ✉ tony.redpath@rbkc.gov.uk

Sustainable Development: Ms Joan McGarvey, Bi-Borough Senior Policy Officer, Transport, Environment and Leisure Services, Council Offices, 37 Pembroke Road, London W8 6PW ☎ 020 7341 5173 🖷 020 7341 5145 ✉ joan.mcgarvey@rbkc.gov.uk

Town Centre: Ms Joanna Hammond , Neighbourhood Planning Manager, Town Hall, Hornton Street, London W8 7NX ☎ 020 7361 2061 ✉ joanna.hammond@rbkc.gov.uk

Transport Planner: Mr Mark Chetwynd , Chief Transport Policy Officer, Town Hall, Hornton Street, London W8 7NX ☎ 020 7361 3747 ✉ mark.chetwynd@rbkc.gov.uk

Waste Management: Ms Kathy May , Bi-Borough Head of Waste & Street Enforcement, Council Offices, 37 Pembroke Road, London W8 6PW ☎ 020 7341 5616 ✉ kathy.may@rbkc.gov.uk

COUNCILLORS

***Mayor* Freeman**, Robert (CON - Campden)
mayor@rbkc.gov.uk

***Deputy Mayor* Rossi**, Marie-Therese (CON - Redcliffe)
cllr.rossi@rbkc.gov.uk

***Leader of the Council* Paget-Brown**, Nicholas (CON - Brompton & Hans Town)
cllr.paget-brown@rbkc.gov.uk

***Deputy Leader of the Council* Feilding-Mellen**, Rock (CON - Holland)
cllr.feilding-mellen@rbkc.gov.uk

Ahern, Tim (CON - Campden)
cllr.ahern@rbkc.gov.uk

Allison, Eve (CON - St Helen's)
cllr.allison@rbkc.gov.uk

Aouane, Fenella (CON - Earl's Court)
cllr.aouane@rbkc.gov.uk

Atkinson, Robert (LAB - Notting Dale)
cllr.r.atkinson@rbkc.gov.uk

Bakhtiar, Mohammed (LAB - St Helen's)
cllr.bakhtiar@rbkc.gov.uk

Berrill-Cox, Adrian (CON - Chelsea Riverside)
cllr.berrill-cox@rbkc.gov.uk

Blakeman, Judith (LAB - Notting Dale)
cllr.blakeman@rbkc.gov.uk

Borwick, Victoria (CON - Abingdon)
cllr.borwick@rbkc.gov.uk

Campbell, Elizabeth (CON - Royal Hospital)
cllr.e.campbell@rbkc.gov.uk

Campbell, Barbara (CON - Pembridge)
cllr.campbell@rbkc.gov.uk

Campion, David (CON - Pembridge)
cllr.campion@rbkc.gov.uk

Coates, Anthony (CON - Courtfield)
cllr.coates@rbkc.gov.uk

Coleridge, Timothy (CON - Brompton & Hans Town)
cllr.colleridge@rbkc.gov.uk

Collinson, Deborah (CON - Holland)
cllr.collinson@rbkc.gov.uk

Condon-Simmonds, Maighread (CON - Chelsea Riverside)
cllr.condon-simmonds@rbkc.gov.uk

Dent Coad, Emma (LAB - Golborne)
cllr.dentcoad@rbkc.gov.uk

Faulks, Catherine (CON - Campden)
cllr.faulks@rbkc.gov.uk

Gardner, Joanna (CON - Abingdon)
cllr.gardner@rbkc.gov.uk

Hargreaves, Gerard (CON - Chelsea Riverside)
cllr.hargreaves@rbkc.gov.uk

Healy, Pat (LAB - Dalgarno)
cllr.healy@rbkc.gov.uk

Husband, James (CON - Abingdon)
cllr.husband@rbkc.gov.uk

Lasharie, Beinazir (LAB - Notting Dale)
cllr.lasharie@rbkc.gov.uk

Lightfoot, Warwick (CON - Holland)
cllr.lightfoot@rbkc.gov.uk

Lindsay, David (CON - Norland)
cllr.lindsay@rbkc.gov.uk

Littler, Harrison (LAB - Colville)
cllr.littler@rbkc.gov.uk

Lomas, Andrew (LAB - Colville)
cllr.lomas@rbkc.gov.uk

Mackover, Sam (CON - Queen's Gate)
Cllr.mackover@rbkc.gov.uk

Marshall, Quentin (CON - Courtfield)
cllr.marshall@rbkc.gov.uk

Mason, Pat (LAB - Golborne)
cllr.mason@rbkc.gov.uk

Mills, Julie (CON - Norland)
cllr.mills@rbkc.gov.uk

Moylan, Daniel (CON - Queen's Gate)
cllr.moylan@rbkc.gov.uk

Nicholls, David (CON - Redcliffe)
cllr.nicholls@rbkc.gov.uk

Palmer, Matthew (CON - Queen's Gate)
cllr.palmer@rbkc.gov.uk

Pascall, Will (CON - Stanley)
cllr.pascall@rbkc.gov.uk

Powell, Bevan (LAB - Golborne)
cllr.powell@rbkc.gov.uk

KENSINGTON & CHELSEA

Press, Monica (LAB - Colville)
cllr.press@rbkc.gov.uk

Rinker, Andrew (CON - Royal Hospital)
cllr.rinker@rbkc.gov.uk

Rutherford, Elizabeth (CON - Courtfield)
cllr.rutherford@rbkc.gov.uk

Spalding, Malcolm (CON - Earl's Court)
cllr.spalding@rbkc.gov.uk

Taylor-Smith, Kim (CON - Stanley)
cllr.taylor-smith@rbkc.gov.uk

Thompson, Robert (LAB - Dalgarno)
cllr.thompson@rbkc.gov.uk

Wade, Linda (LD - Earl's Court)
cllr.wade@rbkc.gov.uk

Warrick, Paul (CON - Stanley)
cllr.warrick@rbkc.gov.uk

Weale, Mary (CON - Brompton & Hans Town)
cllr.weale@rbkc.gov.uk

Will, Emma (CON - Royal Hospital)
cllr.will@rbkc.gov.uk

Williams, Charles (CON - Redcliffe)
cllr.williams@rbkc.gov.uk

POLITICAL COMPOSITION

CON: 37, LAB: 12, LD: 1

COMMITTEE CHAIRS

Audit & Transparency: Mr Paul Warrick

Family & Children's Services: Mr David Lindsay

Licensing: Ms Julie Mills

Planning: Mr Paul Warrick

Kent C

Kent County Council, Sessions House, County Hall, Maidstone ME14 1XQ
☎ 0845 824 7247 🖷 01622 759905 🖳 www.kent.gov.uk

FACTS AND FIGURES

Parliamentary Constituencies: Thanet North, Thanet South
EU Constituencies: South East
Election Frequency: Elections are of whole council

PRINCIPAL OFFICERS

Chief Executive: Mr David Cockburn , Head of Paid Service & Corporate Director of Business Strategy & Support, Sessions House, County Hall, Maidstone ME14 1XQ ☎ 03000 410001 david.cockburn@kent.gov.uk

Senior Management: Ms Amanda Beer , Corporate Director of Engagement, Organisation, Development & Design, Sessions House, County Hall, Maidstone ME14 1XQ ☎ 03000 415835 amanda.beer@kent.gov.uk

Senior Management: Ms Barbara Cooper , Corporate Director of Growth, Environment & Transport, Invicta House, County Hall, Maidstone ME14 1XX ☎ 03000 415981 barbara.cooper@kent.gov.uk

Senior Management: Mr Andrew Ireland , Corporate Director of Social Care, Health & Wellbeing, Sessions House, County Hall, Maidstone ME14 1XQ ☎ 03000 416297 andrew.ireland@kent.gov.uk

Senior Management: Mr Patrick Leeson , Corporate Director of Education & Young People's Services, Sessions House, County Hall, Maidstone ME14 1XQ ☎ 03000 416384 patrick.leeson@kent.gov.uk

Senior Management: Mr Andrew Scott-Clark , Director of Public Health, Sessions House, County Hall, Maidstone ME14 1XQ ☎ 03000 416659 andrew.scott-clark@kent.gov.uk

Senior Management: Mr Geoff Wild, Director of Governance & Law, Sessions House, County Hall, Maidstone ME14 1XQ ☎ 03000 416840 geoff.wild@kent.gov.uk

Senior Management: Mr Andy Wood , Corporate Director of Finance & Procurement, Sessions House, County Hall, Maidstone ME14 1XQ ☎ 03000 416854 andy.wood@kent.gov.uk

Architect, Building / Property Services: Mr Paul Kennedy, Business Change Manager, Sessions House, County Hall, Maidstone ME14 1XQ ☎ 03000 410240 paul.kennedy@kent.gov.uk

Building Control: Ms Rebecca Spore , Director of Infrastructure, Sessions House, County Hall, Maidstone ME14 1XQ ☎ 03000 416716 rebecca.spore@kent.gov.uk

Children / Youth Services: Mr Patrick Leeson , Corporate Director of Education & Young People's Services, Sessions House, County Hall, Maidstone ME14 1XQ ☎ 03000 416384 patrick.leeson@kent.gov.uk

Civil Registration: Ms Angela Slaven , Interim Director, Sessions House, County Hall, Maidstone ME14 1XQ ☎ 03000 419518 angela.slaven@kent.gov.uk

Community Safety: Mr Shafik Peerbux , Community Safety & Partnership Manager, Sessions House, County Hall, Maidstone ME14 1XQ ☎ 03000 413431 shafik.peerbux@kent.gov.uk

Computer Management: Mr Paul Day , Interim Director of ICT, Sessions House, County Hall, Maidstone ME14 1XQ ☎ 03000 414150 paul.day@kent.gov.uk

Consumer Protection and Trading Standards: Mr Mike Overbeke , Head of Public Protection, 8 Abbey Wood Road, Kingshill, West Malling ME19 4YT ☎ 03000 413427 mike.overbeke@kent.gov.uk

Customer Service: Ms Jane Kendal , Head of Service for Customer Relationship, Sessions House, County Hall, Maidstone ME14 1XQ ☎ 03000 417108 jane.kendal@kent.gov.uk

Economic Development: Mr David Cockburn , Head of Paid Service & Corporate Director of Business Strategy & Support, Sessions House, County Hall, Maidstone ME14 1XQ
☎ 03000 410001 ✉ david.cockburn@kent.gov.uk

Economic Development: Ms Barbara Cooper , Corporate Director of Growth, Environment & Transport, Invicta House, County Hall, Maidstone ME14 1XX ☎ 03000 415981
✉ barbara.cooper@kent.gov.uk

Education: Mr Scott Bagshaw , Head of Admissions & Transport, Sessions House, County Hall, Maidstone ME14 1XQ
☎ 03000 415798 ✉ scott.bagshaw@kent.gov.uk

Education: Mr Patrick Leeson , Corporate Director of Education & Young People's Services, Sessions House, County Hall, Maidstone ME14 1XQ ☎ 03000 416384 ✉ patrick.leeson@kent.gov.uk

Environmental Health: Mr Andrew Scott-Clark , Director of Public Health, Sessions House, County Hall, Maidstone ME14 1XQ
☎ 03000 416659 ✉ andrew.scott-clark@kent.gov.uk

European Liaison: Mr Dafydd Pugh , Head of Brussels Office, Kent Brussels Office, International House, 45 Rue du Commerce, Brussels, B- 1000 ☎ 00322 504 0750 ✉ dafydd.pugh@kent.gov.uk

Events Manager: Mrs Deborah Malthouse, Events Manager, Sessions House, County Hall, Maidstone ME14 1XQ
☎ 03000 416426 ✉ deborah.malthouse@kent.gov.uk

Facilities: Mr Martin Benson , Kent Facilities (Amey), Sessions House, County Hall, Maidstone ME14 1XQ ☎ 03000 415842

Pensions: Ms Barbara Cheatler , Pensions Manager, Brenchley House, Week Street, Maidstone ME14 1RF ☎ 03000 415270
✉ barbara.cheatler@kent.gov.uk

Grounds Maintenance: Mr Richard Kilvington, Business Manager, Aylesford Depot, Aylesford ME20 7HB ☎ 01622 605025
✉ richard.kilvington@kent.gov.uk

Health and Safety: Ms Helen Bale, Corporate Health & Safety Manager, Sessions House, County Hall, Maidstone ME14 1XQ
☎ 03000 417239 ✉ helen.bale@kent.gov.uk

Highways: Mr John Burr , Director of Highways & Transportation, Invicta House, County Hall, Maidstone ME14 1XX ☎ 03000 411626
✉ john.burr@kent.gov.uk

Legal: Mr Geoff Wild, Director of Governance & Law, Sessions House, County Hall, Maidstone ME14 1XQ ☎ 03000 416840
✉ geoff.wild@kent.gov.uk

Member Services: Mr Peter Sass , Head of Democratic Services & Local Leadership, Sessions House, County Hall, Maidstone ME14 1XQ ☎ 03000 416647 ✉ peter.sass@kent.gov.uk

Personnel / HR: Ms Amanda Beer , Corporate Director of Engagement, Organisation, Development & Design, Sessions House, County Hall, Maidstone ME14 1XQ ☎ 03000 415835
✉ amanda.beer@kent.gov.uk

Planning: Mr Paul Crick , Director of Environment, Planning & Enforcement, Invicta House, County Hall, Maidstone ME14 1XX
☎ 03000 413356 ✉ paul.crick@kent.gov.uk

Planning: Mr Jerry Crossley , Planning Team Leader, Sessions House, County Hall, Maidstone ME14 1XQ ☎ 03000 413357
✉ jerry.crossley@kent.gov.uk

Planning: Mrs Sharon Thompson , Head of Planning Applications, Invicta House, County Hall, Maidstone ME14 1XX ☎ 03000 413468
✉ sharon.thompson@kent.gov.uk

Procurement: Mr Nick Vickers , Head of Financial Management, Sessions House, County Hall, Maidstone ME14 1XQ
☎ 03000 416797 ✉ nick.vickers@kent.gov.uk

Public Libraries: Ms Angela Slaven , Interim Director, Sessions House, County Hall, Maidstone ME14 1XQ ☎ 03000 419518
✉ angela.slaven@kent.gov.uk

Social Services: Mr Andrew Ireland , Corporate Director of Social Care, Health & Wellbeing, Sessions House, County Hall, Maidstone ME14 1XQ ☎ 03000 416297 ✉ andrew.ireland@kent.gov.uk

Social Services: Mr Mark Lobban , Director of Strategic Commissioning, 3rd Floor, Brenchley House, Week Street, Maidstone ME14 1RF ☎ 03000 415393 ✉ mark.lobban@kent.gov.uk

Social Services: Ms Penny Southern , Director of Learning Disability & Mental Health FSC, Brenchley House, Week Street, Maidstone ME14 1RF ☎ 03000 415505 ✉ penny.southern@kent.gov.uk

Social Services (Adult): Ms Anne Tidmarsh , Director, Brenchley House, Maidstone ME14 1RF ✉ anne.tidmarsh@kent.gov.uk

Social Services (Children): Ms Jean Imray , Director of Specialist Children's Services, Sessions House, County Hall, Maidstone ME14 1XQ ☎ 01622 221573 🖷 01622 694091
✉ jean.imray@kent.gov.uk

Public Health: Mr Andrew Scott-Clark , Director of Public Health, Sessions House, County Hall, Maidstone ME14 1XQ
☎ 03000 416659 ✉ andrew.scott-clark@kent.gov.uk

Staff Training: Mrs Coral Ingleton , Senior Learning & Development Manager, Sessions House, County Hall, Maidstone ME14 1XQ ☎ 03000 416296 ✉ coral.ingleton@kent.gov.uk

Tourism: Ms Frances Warrington, Head of Tourism, Invicta House, County Hall, Maidstone ME14 1XX ☎ 01622 221923 🖷 01622 691418
✉ frances.warrington@kent.gov.uk

Transport: Mr David Hall , Future Highways Manager, 1st Floor, Invicta House, County Hall, Maidstone ME14 1XX ☎ 01622 221081
🖷 01622 691028 ✉ david.hall@kent.gov.uk

Waste Management: Ms Caroline Arnold, Head of Waste Management, Waste Management, Block H, The Forstal, Beddow Way, Maidstone ME20 7BT ☎ 01622 605990 🖷 01622 605999
✉ caroline.arnold@kent.gov.uk

KENT

COUNCILLORS

Leader of the Council **Carter**, Paul (CON - Maidstone Rural North)
paul.carter@kent.gov.uk

Deputy Leader of the Council **Simmonds**, John (CON - Canterbury West)
john.simmonds@kent.gov.uk

Group Leader **Latchford**, Roger (UKIP - Birchington and Villages)
roger.latchford@kent.gov.uk

Allen, Ann (CON - Wilmington)
ann.allen@kent.gov.uk

Angell, Mike (CON - Ashford Rural South)
mike.angell@kent.gov.uk

Baldock, Mike (UKIP - Swale West)
mike.baldock@kent.gov.uk

Balfour, Matthew (CON - Malling Rural East)
matthew.balfour@kent.gov.uk

Bird, Rob (LD - Maidstone Central)
rob.bird@kent.gov.uk

Birkby, Hod (UKIP - Folkestone West)
hod.birkby@kent.gov.uk

Bond, Nicholas (UKIP - Herne Bay)
nicholas.bond@kent.gov.uk

Bowles, Andrew (CON - Swale East)
andrew.bowles@kent.gov.uk

Brazier, David (CON - Sevenoaks North East)
david.brazier@kent.gov.uk

Brivio, Pam (LAB - Dover Town)
pam.brivio@kent.gov.uk

Brookbank, Robert (CON - Swanley)
robert.brookbank@kent.gov.uk

Burgess, Lee (UKIP - Swale Central)
lee.burgess@kent.gov.uk

Caller, Colin (LAB - Gravesham East)
colin.caller@kent.gov.uk

Carey, Susan (CON - Elham Valley)
susan.carey@kent.gov.uk

Chard, Nick (CON - Sevenoaks East)
nick.chard@kent.gov.uk

Chittenden, Ian (LD - Maidstone North East)
ian.chittenden@kent.gov.uk

Clark, Brian (LD - Maidstone South)
brian.clark@kent.gov.uk

Cole, Penny (CON - Dartford East)
penny.cole@kent.gov.uk

Cooke, Gary (CON - Maidstone South East)
gary.cooke@kent.gov.uk

Cowan, Gordon (LAB - Dover Town)
gordon.cowan@kent.gov.uk

Crabtree, Margaret (CON - Sevenoaks Central)
margaret.crabtree@kent.gov.uk

Cribbon, Jane (LAB - Gravesham East)
jane.cribben@kent.gov.uk

Crowther, Adrian (UKIP - Sheppey)
adrian.crowther@kent.gov.uk

Dagger, Valerie (CON - Malling West)
valerie.dagger@kent.gov.uk

Daley, Dan (LD - Maidstone Central)
dan.daley@kent.gov.uk

Dance, Mark (CON - Whitstable)
mark.dance@kent.gov.uk

Davies, John (CON - Tunbridge Wells West)
john.davies@kent.gov.uk

Dean, Trudy (LD - Malling Central)
trudy.dean@kent.gov.uk

Eddy, Mike (LAB - Deal)
mike.eddy@kent.gov.uk

Elenor, Jeff (UKIP - Margate West)
jeffrey.elenor@kent.gov.uk

Elenor, Mo (UKIP - Margate and Cliftonville)
mo.elenor@kent.gov.uk

Gates, Tom (CON - Faversham)
tom.gates@kent.gov.uk

Gibbens, Graham (CON - Canterbury City North East)
graham.gibbens@kent.gov.uk

Gough, Roger (CON - Darent Valley)
roger.gough@kent.gov.uk

Harman, Peter (R - Swanscombe and greenhithe)
peter.harman@kent.gov.uk

Harrison, Mike (CON - Whitstable)
mike.harrison@kent.gov.uk

Harrison, Angela (LAB - Sheerness)
angela.harrison@kent.gov.uk

Heale, Martyn (UKIP - Ramsgate)
martyn.heale@kent.gov.uk

Hill, Michael (CON - Tenterden)
michael.hill@kent.gov.uk

Hoare, Chris (UKIP - Tunbridge Wells East)
christopher.hoare@kent.gov.uk

Hohler, Sarah (CON - Malling North)
sarah.hohler@kent.gov.uk

Holden, Seán (CON - Cranbrook)
sean.holden@kent.gov.uk

Homewood, Peter (CON - Malling Rural North East)
peter.homewood@kent.gov.uk

Hotson, Eric (CON - Maidstone Rural South)
eric.hotson@kent.gov.uk

Howes, Sue (LAB - Northfleet and Gravesend West)
sue.howes@kent.gov.uk

King, Alex (CON - Tunbridge Wells Rural)
alex.king@kent.gov.uk

Kite, Jeremy (CON - Dartford Rural)
jeremy.kite@kent.gov.uk

Koowaree, George (LD - Ashford East)
george.koowaree@kent.gov.uk

Long, Richard (CON - Tonbridge)
richard.long1@kent.gov.uk

Lymer, Geoff (CON - Dover West)
geoff.lymer@kent.gov.uk

MacDowall, Brian (UKIP - Herne Bay)
brian.macdowall@kent.gov.uk

Maddison, Tom (LAB - Dartford North East)
tom.maddison@kent.gov.uk

Manion, Steve (CON - Dover North)
steve.manion@kent.gov.uk

Marsh, Alan (CON - Herne and Sturry)
alan.marsh@kent.gov.uk

McKenna, Frank (UKIP - Folkestone North East)
frank.mckenna@kent.gov.uk

Neaves, Bob (UKIP - Folkestone South)
bob.neaves@kent.gov.uk

Northey, Michael (CON - Canterbury South East)
michael.northey@kent.gov.uk

Oakford, Peter (CON - Tunbridge Wells North)
peter.oakford@kent.gov.uk

Ozog, Jan (CON - Dartford West)
jan.ozog@kent.gov.uk

Parry, Richard (CON - Sevenoaks West)
richard.parry@kent.gov.uk

Pearman, Clive (CON - Sevenoaks South)
clive.pearman@kent.gov.uk

Ridings, Leyland (CON - Sandwich)
leyland.ridings@kent.gov.uk

Rowbotham, Eileen (LAB - Deal)
eileen.rowbotham@kent.gov.uk

Scholes, James (CON - Tunbridge Wells South)
james.scholes@kent.gov.uk

Scobie, William (LAB - Margate and Cliftonville)
william.scobie@kent.gov.uk

Shonk, Trevor (UKIP - Ramsgate)
trevor.shonk@kent.gov.uk

Simkins, Charlie (CON - Ashford Rural West)
charlie.simkins@kent.ac.uk

Smith, Christopher (CON - Tonbridge)
chris.smith@kent.gov.uk

Smyth, Derek (LAB - Ashford South)
derek.smyth@kent.gov.uk

Stockell, Paulina (CON - Maidstone Rural West)
paulina.stockell@kent.gov.uk

Sweetland, Bryan (CON - Gravesham Rural)
bryan.sweetland@kent.gov.uk

Terry, Alan (UKIP - Broadstairs and Sir Moses Montefiore)
alan.terry@kent.gov.uk

Thandi, Narinderjit (LAB - Northfleet and Gravesend West)
narinderjit.thandi@kent.gov.uk

Truelove, Roger (LAB - Swale Central)
roger.truelove@kent.gov.uk

Vye, Martin (LD - Canterbury City South West)
martin.vye@kent.gov.uk

Waters, Carole (CON - Romney Marsh)
carole.waters@kent.gov.uk

Wedgebury, Jim (CON - Ashford Central)
jim.wedgebury@kent.gov.uk

Whittle, Jenny (CON - Maidstone Rural East)
jenny.whittle2@kent.gov.uk

Whybrow, Martin (GRN - Hythe)
martin.whybrow@kent.gov.uk

Wickham, Andrew (CON - Ashford Rural East)
andrew.wickham@kent.gov.uk

Wiltshire, Zita (UKIP - Broadstairs and Sir Moses Montefiore)
zita.wiltshire@kent.gov.uk

POLITICAL COMPOSITION

CON: 46, UKIP: 16, LAB: 13, LD: 7, R: 1, GRN: 1

COMMITTEE CHAIRS

Adult Social Care & Health: Mr Christopher Smith

Audit & Governance: Mr Richard Long

Children's Social Care & Health: Mrs Ann Allen

Environment & Transport: Mrs Paulina Stockell

Health & Wellbeing: Mr Roger Gough

Planning: Mr John Davies

Kettering D

Kettering Borough Council, Municipal Offices, Bowling Green Road, Kettering NN15 7QX
☎ 01536 410333 🖷 01536 410795 🖳 www.kettering.gov.uk

FACTS AND FIGURES

Parliamentary Constituencies: Kettering
EU Constituencies: East Midlands
Election Frequency: Elections are of whole council

PRINCIPAL OFFICERS

Chief Executive: Mr David Cook , Chief Executive, Municipal Offices, Bowling Green Road, Kettering NN15 7QX ☎ 01536 534205 🖷 01536 534218 ✉ davidcook@kettering.gov.uk

Deputy Chief Executive: Mr Martin Hammond, Deputy Chief Executive, Municipal Offices, Bowling Green Road, Kettering NN15 7QX ☎ 01536 534210 🖷 01536 315116 ✉ martinhammond@kettering.gov.uk

Deputy Chief Executive: Mr Graham Soulsby, Deputy Chief Executive & Chief Financial Officer, Municipal Offices, Bowling Green Road, Kettering NN15 7QX ☎ 01536 532413 🖷 01536 315116 ✉ grahamsoulsby@kettering.gov.uk

Assistant Chief Executive: Ms Lisa Hyde , Assistant Chief Executive, Municipal Offices, Bowling Green Road, Kettering NN15 7QX ☎ 01536 534342 🖷 01536 534218 ✉ lisahyde@kettering.gov.uk

Best Value: Mr Guy Holloway, Head - Corporate Development & IT, Municipal Offices, Bowling Green Road, Kettering NN15 7QX ☎ 01536 534243 ✉ guyholloway@kettering.gov.uk

Building Control: Mr Robert Harbour , Head - Development Services, Municipal Offices, Bowling Green Road, Kettering NN15 7QX ☎ 01536 534126 ✉ robertharbour@kettering.gov.uk

PR / Communications: Mr Guy Holloway , Head - Corporate Development, Municipal Offices, Bowling Green Road, Kettering NN15 7QX ☎ 01536 534243 ✉ guyholloway@kettering.gov.uk

Community Planning: Mr Robert Harbour , Head - Development Services, Municipal Offices, Bowling Green Road, Kettering NN15 7QX ☎ 01536 534126 ✉ robertharbour@kettering.gov.uk

Community Safety: Mrs Shirley Plenderleith , Head - Community Services, Municipal Offices, Bowling Green Road, Kettering NN15 7QX ☎ 01536 535696 ✉ shirleyplenderleith@kettering.gov.uk

Computer Management: Mr Guy Holloway, Head - Corporate Development & IT, Municipal Offices, Bowling Green Road, Kettering NN15 7QX ☎ 01536 534243 ✉ guyholloway@kettering.gov.uk

Corporate Services: Mr Guy Holloway, Head - Corporate Development & IT, Municipal Offices, Bowling Green Road, Kettering NN15 7QX ☎ 01536 534243 ✉ guyholloway@kettering.gov.uk

Customer Service: Mrs Julie Trahern , Head - Income & Debt Management, Municipal Offices, Bowling Green Road, Kettering NN15 7QX ☎ 01536 532428 ✉ julietrahern@kettering.gov.uk

E-Government: Mr Guy Holloway , Head - Corporate Development, Municipal Offices, Bowling Green Road, Kettering NN15 7QX ☎ 01536 534243 ✉ guyholloway@kettering.gov.uk

Electoral Registration: Ms Sue Lyons , Head - Democratic & Legal Services, Municipal Offices, Bowling Green Road, Kettering NN15 7QX ☎ 01536 534209; 01536 543209 ✉ suelyons@kettering.gov.uk

Emergency Planning: Mr Brendan Coleman , Head - Environmental Care Services, 4 Robinson Way, Telford Way Industrial Estate, Kettering NN16 8PP ☎ 01536 534460 ✉ brendancoleman@kettering.gov.uk

Environmental Health: Mrs Shirley Plenderleith , Head - Community Services, Municipal Offices, Bowling Green Road, Kettering NN15 7QX ☎ 01536 535696 ✉ shirleyplenderleith@kettering.gov.uk

Estates, Property & Valuation: Ms Sue Lyons , Head - Democratic & Legal Services, Municipal Offices, Bowling Green Road, Kettering NN15 7QX ☎ 01536 534209; 01536 543209 ✉ suelyons@kettering.gov.uk

Facilities: Mr Guy Holloway , Head - Corporate Development, Municipal Offices, Bowling Green Road, Kettering NN15 7QX ☎ 01536 534243 ✉ guyholloway@kettering.gov.uk

Finance: Mr Mark Dickenson , Acting Head - Finance, Municipal Offices, Bowling Green Road, Kettering NN15 7QX ☎ 01536 534303 ✉ markdickenson@kettering.gov.uk

Finance: Mr Graham Soulsby, Deputy Chief Executive & Chief Financial Officer, Municipal Offices, Bowling Green Road, Kettering NN15 7QX ☎ 01536 532413 🖷 01536 315116 ✉ grahamsoulsby@kettering.gov.uk

Fleet Management: Mr Brendan Coleman , Head - Environmental Care Services, 4 Robinson Way, Telford Way Industrial Estate, Kettering NN16 8PP ☎ 01536 534460 ✉ brendancoleman@kettering.gov.uk

Grounds Maintenance: Mr Brendan Coleman , Head - Environmental Care Services, 4 Robinson Way, Telford Way Industrial Estate, Kettering NN16 8PP ☎ 01536 534460 ✉ brendancoleman@kettering.gov.uk

Health and Safety: Mr Brendan Coleman , Head - Environmental Care Services, 4 Robinson Way, Telford Way Industrial Estate, Kettering NN16 8PP ☎ 01536 534460 ✉ brendancoleman@kettering.gov.uk

Home Energy Conservation: Mrs Shirley Plenderleith , Head - Community Services, Municipal Offices, Bowling Green Road, Kettering NN15 7QX ☎ 01536 535696 ✉ shirleyplenderleith@kettering.gov.uk

Housing: Mr John Conway, Head - Housing, Municipal Offices, Bowling Green Road, Kettering NN15 7QX ☎ 01536 534288 ✉ johnconway@kettering.gov.uk

Housing Maintenance: Mr John Conway, Head - Housing, Municipal Offices, Bowling Green Road, Kettering NN15 7QX ☎ 01536 534288 ✉ johnconway@kettering.gov.uk

Legal: Ms Sue Lyons , Head - Democratic & Legal Services, Municipal Offices, Bowling Green Road, Kettering NN15 7QX ☎ 01536 534209; 01536 543209 ✉ suelyons@kettering.gov.uk

Leisure and Cultural Services: Ms Val Hitchman, Head - Community Services, Municipal Offices, Bowling Green Road, Kettering NN15 7QX ☎ 01536 534392 ✉ valeriehitchman@kettering.gov.uk

Licensing: Mrs Shirley Plenderleith , Head - Community Services, Municipal Offices, Bowling Green Road, Kettering NN15 7QX ☎ 01536 535696 ✉ shirleyplenderleith@kettering.gov.uk

Lighting: Mr Brendan Coleman , Head - Environmental Care Services, 4 Robinson Way, Telford Way Industrial Estate, Kettering NN16 8PP ☎ 01536 534460 ✉ brendancoleman@kettering.gov.uk

Lottery Funding, Charity and Voluntary: Ms Val Hitchman, Head - Community Services, Municipal Offices, Bowling Green Road, Kettering NN15 7QX ☎ 01536 534392 ✉ valeriehitchman@kettering.gov.uk

Member Services: Ms Sue Lyons , Head - Democratic & Legal Services, Municipal Offices, Bowling Green Road, Kettering NN15 7QX ☎ 01536 534209; 01536 543209 ✉ suelyons@kettering.gov.uk

Parking: Mrs Shirley Plenderleith , Head - Community Services, Municipal Offices, Bowling Green Road, Kettering NN15 7QX ☎ 01536 535696 ✉ shirleyplenderleith@kettering.gov.uk

Personnel / HR: Ms Sam Maher , Interim Head - HR, Municipal Offices, Bowling Green Road, Kettering NN15 7QX ☎ 01536 534214 ✉ sammaher@kettering.gov.uk

Planning: Mr Robert Harbour , Head - Development Services, Municipal Offices, Bowling Green Road, Kettering NN15 7QX ☎ 01536 534126 ✉ robertharbour@kettering.gov.uk

Procurement: Mr Guy Holloway, Head - Corporate Development & IT, Municipal Offices, Bowling Green Road, Kettering NN15 7QX ☎ 01536 534243 ✉ guyholloway@kettering.gov.uk

Recycling & Waste Minimisation: Mr Brendan Coleman , Head - Environmental Care Services, 4 Robinson Way, Telford Way Industrial Estate, Kettering NN16 8PP ☎ 01536 534460 ✉ brendancoleman@kettering.gov.uk

Staff Training: Ms Sam Maher , Interim Head - HR, Municipal Offices, Bowling Green Road, Kettering NN15 7QX ☎ 01536 534214 ✉ sammaher@kettering.gov.uk

Street Scene: Mr Brendan Coleman , Head - Environmental Care Services, 4 Robinson Way, Telford Way Industrial Estate, Kettering NN16 8PP ☎ 01536 534460 ✉ brendancoleman@kettering.gov.uk

Sustainable Communities: Mr Robert Harbour , Head - Development Services, Municipal Offices, Bowling Green Road, Kettering NN15 7QX ☎ 01536 534126 ✉ robertharbour@kettering.gov.uk

Sustainable Development: Mr Robert Harbour , Head - Development Services, Municipal Offices, Bowling Green Road, Kettering NN15 7QX ☎ 01536 534126 ✉ robertharbour@kettering.gov.uk

Waste Collection and Disposal: Mr Brendan Coleman , Head - Environmental Care Services, 4 Robinson Way, Telford Way Industrial Estate, Kettering NN16 8PP ☎ 01536 534460 ✉ brendancoleman@kettering.gov.uk

Waste Management: Mr Brendan Coleman , Head - Environmental Care Services, 4 Robinson Way, Telford Way Industrial Estate, Kettering NN16 8PP ☎ 01536 534460 ✉ brendancoleman@kettering.gov.uk

COUNCILLORS

***Mayor* Derbyshire**, June (CON - Desborough Loatland)
junederbyshire@kettering.gov.uk

***Deputy Mayor* Edwards**, Scott (CON - St Michaels and Wicksteed)
scottedwards@kettering.gov.uk

***Leader of the Council* Roberts**, Russell (CON - Barton)
russellroberts@kettering.gov.uk

***Deputy Leader of the Council* Bunday**, Lloyd (CON - Ise Lodge)
lloydbunday@kettering.gov.uk

***Group Leader* West**, Johnathon (LAB - Northfield)
jonathanwest@kettering.gov.uk

Adams, Linda (LAB - Avondale Grange)
lindaadams@kettering.gov.uk

Bain, Duncan (CON - Pipers Hill)
duncanbain@kettering.gov.uk

Bellamy, Steve (CON - Barton)
stevebellamy@kettering.gov.uk

Brown, Michael (CON - Brambleside)
michaelbrown@kettering.gov.uk

Burton, James (CON - All Saint)
jamesburton@kettering.gov.uk

Davies, Ashely (CON - Brambleside)
ashdavies@kettering.gov.uk

Dearing, Mark (CON - Desborough Loatland)
markdearing@kettering.gov.uk

Don, Maggie (LAB - St Michaels and Wicksteed)
maggiedon2@kettering.gov.uk

Freer, Terry (CON - St Peter's)
terryfreer@kettering.gov.uk

Groome, Ruth (IND - Burton Latimer)
ruthgroome@kettering.gov.uk

Hakewill, Jim (CON - Slade)
jimhakewill@kettering.gov.uk

Henson, Jenny (CON - St Michaels and Wicksteed)
jennyhenson@kettering.gov.uk

Hollobone, Philip (CON - Ise Lodge)
philip.hollobone.mp@parliament.uk

Howes, David (CON - Welland)
davidhowes@kettering.gov.uk

Lee, Anne (LAB - Pipers Hill)
annelee@kettering.gov.uk

Lynch, Shirley (CON - Ise Lodge)
shirleylynch@kettering.gov.uk

Malin, Mary (CON - St Peter's)
marymalin@kettering.gov.uk

Mills, Alan (LAB - Rothwell)
alanmills@kettering.gov.uk

Mitchell, Clark (LAB - Avondale Grange)
clarkmitchell@kettering.gov.uk

Moreton, Cliff (CON - Slade)
cliffmoreton@kettering.gov.uk

Rowley, Mark (CON - Queen Eleanor and Buccleuch)
markrowley@kettering.gov.uk

Scrimshaw, Mike (LAB - William Knibb)
mikescrimshaw@kettering.gov.uk

Smith, Jan (CON - Burton Latimer)
jansmith@kettering.gov.uk

Soans, Dave (CON - Desborough St Giles)
davesoans@kettering.gov.uk

Sumpter, Karl (CON - Rothwell)

Talbot, Margaret (CON - Rothwell)
margarettalbot@kettering.gov.uk

Tebbutt, Mike (CON - Desborough St Giles)
miketebbutt@kettering.gov.uk

Thurland, Lesley (CON - All Saints)
lesleythurland@kettering.gov.uk

Titcombe, Gregory (CON - All Saints)
gregtitcombe@kettering.gov.uk

Watts, Keli (LAB - William Knibb)
keliwatts@kettering.gov.uk

Zanger, Derek (CON - Burton Latimer)
derekzanger@kettering.gov.uk

POLITICAL COMPOSITION
CON: 27, LAB: 8, IND: 1

COMMITTEE CHAIRS
Licensing: Mrs Margaret Talbot

Planning: Mrs Shirley Lynch

King's Lynn & West Norfolk D

Borough Council of King's Lynn & West Norfolk, Chapel Street, King's Lynn PE30 1EX
☎ 01553 616200 🖷 01553 691663 ✉ contact@west-norfolk.gov.uk
💻 www.west-norfolk.gov.uk

FACTS AND FIGURES
Parliamentary Constituencies: Norfolk North West, Norfolk South West
EU Constituencies: Eastern
Election Frequency: Elections are of whole council

PRINCIPAL OFFICERS
Chief Executive: Mr Ray Harding, Chief Executive, King's Court, Chapel Street, King's Lynn PE30 1EX ☎ 01553 616245 🖷 01553 616736 ✉ ray.harding@west-norfolk.gov.uk

Senior Management: Mr Chris Bamfield, Executive Director - Commercial Services, King's Court, Chapel Street, King's Lynn PE30 1EX ☎ 01553 616648 🖷 01553 616640 ✉ chris.bamfield@west-norfolk.gov.uk

Senior Management: Mrs Debbie Gates, Executive Director - Central Services, King's Court, Chapel Street, King's Lynn PE30 1EX ☎ 01553 616605 🖷 01553 616728 ✉ debbie.gates@west-norfolk.gov.uk

Senior Management: Mr Geoff Hall, Executive Director - Environment & Planning, King's Court, Chapel Street, King's Lynn PE30 1EX ☎ 01553 616618 🖷 01553 616652 ✉ geoff.hall@west-norfolk.gov.uk

Access Officer / Social Services (Disability): Mrs Allison Bingham, Building Technician, King's Court, Chapel Street, King's Lynn PE30 1EX ☎ 01553 616743 ✉ allison.bingham@west-norfolk.gov.uk

Architect, Building / Property Services: Mr Matthew Henry, Property Services Manager, King's Court, Chapel Street, King's Lynn PE30 1EX ☎ 01553 616272 🖷 01553 616682 ✉ matthew.henry@west-norfolk.gov.uk

Best Value: Mr Ian Burbidge, Policy & Performance Manager, King's Court, Chapel Street, King's Lynn PE30 1EX ☎ 01553 616722 🖷 01553 616680 ✉ ian.burbidge@west-norfolk.gov.uk

Building Control: Mr Geoff Hall, Executive Director - Environment & Planning, King's Court, Chapel Street, King's Lynn PE30 1EX ☎ 01553 616618 🖷 01553 616652 ✉ geoff.hall@west-norfolk.gov.uk

PR / Communications: Mrs Sharon Clifton , Communications Manager, King's Court, Chapel Street, King's Lynn PE30 1EX ☎ 01553 616711 ✉ sharon.clifton@west-norfolk.gov.uk

Community Planning: Mrs Debbie Gates, Executive Director - Central Services, King's Court, Chapel Street, King's Lynn PE30 1EX ☎ 01553 616605 🖷 01553 616728 ✉ debbie.gates@west-norfolk.gov.uk

Computer Management: Mrs Debbie Gates, Executive Director - Central Services, King's Court, Chapel Street, King's Lynn PE30 1EX ☎ 01553 616605 🖷 01553 616728 ✉ debbie.gates@west-norfolk.gov.uk

Contracts: Ms Lorraine Gore , Assistant Director - Finance, King's Court, Chapel Street, King's Lynn PE30 1EX ☎ 01553 616432 ✉ lorraine.gore@west-norfolk.gov.uk

Corporate Services: Mr Ray Harding, Chief Executive, King's Court, Chapel Street, King's Lynn PE30 1EX ☎ 01553 616245 🖷 01553 616736 ✉ ray.harding@west-norfolk.gov.uk

Customer Service: Mrs Debbie Gates, Executive Director - Central Services, King's Court, Chapel Street, King's Lynn PE30 1EX ☎ 01553 616605 🖷 01553 616728 ✉ debbie.gates@west-norfolk.gov.uk

Economic Development: Mr Geoff Hall, Executive Director - Environment & Planning, King's Court, Chapel Street, King's Lynn PE30 1EX ☎ 01553 616618 🖷 01553 616652 ✉ geoff.hall@west-norfolk.gov.uk

E-Government: Mrs Debbie Gates, Executive Director - Central Services, King's Court, Chapel Street, King's Lynn PE30 1EX ☎ 01553 616605 🖷 01553 616728 ✉ debbie.gates@west-norfolk.gov.uk

Electoral Registration: Mrs Sam Winter, Democratic Services Manager, King's Court, Chapel Street, King's Lynn PE30 1EX ☎ 01553 616327 🖷 01553 616758 ✉ sam.winter@west-norfolk.gov.uk

Emergency Planning: Mr Geoff Hall, Executive Director - Environment & Planning, King's Court, Chapel Street, King's Lynn PE30 1EX ☎ 01553 616618 🖷 01553 616652 ✉ geoff.hall@west-norfolk.gov.uk

Environmental Health: Mr Geoff Hall, Executive Director - Environment & Planning, King's Court, Chapel Street, King's Lynn PE30 1EX ☎ 01553 616618 🖷 01553 616652 ✉ geoff.hall@west-norfolk.gov.uk

Estates, Property & Valuation: Mr Matthew Henry, Property Services Manager, King's Court, Chapel Street, King's Lynn PE30 1EX ☎ 01553 616272 🖷 01553 616682 ✉ matthew.henry@west-norfolk.gov.uk

European Liaison: Mr Ostap Paparega , Regeneration & Economic Development Manager, King's Court, Chapel Street, King's Lynn PE30 1EX ☎ 01553 616890 🖷 01553 775726 ✉ ostap.paparega@west-norfolk.gov.uk

Events Manager: Mr Chris Bamfield, Executive Director - Commercial Services, King's Court, Chapel Street, King's Lynn PE30 1EX ☎ 01553 616648 🖷 01553 616640 ✉ chris.bamfield@west-norfolk.gov.uk

Finance: Ms Lorraine Gore , Assistant Director - Finance, King's Court, Chapel Street, King's Lynn PE30 1EX ☎ 01553 616432 ✉ lorraine.gore@west-norfolk.gov.uk

Treasury: Mr Geoff Hall, Executive Director - Environment & Planning, King's Court, Chapel Street, King's Lynn PE30 1EX ☎ 01553 616618 🖷 01553 616652 ✉ geoff.hall@west-norfolk.gov.uk

Fleet Management: Mr Nathan Johnson, Public & Open Space Manager, King's Court, Chapel Street, King's Lynn PE30 1EX ☎ 01553 780780 🖷 01553 771657 ✉ nathan.johnson@west-norfolk.gov.uk

Grounds Maintenance: Mr Nathan Johnson, Public & Open Space Manager, King's Court, Chapel Street, King's Lynn PE30 1EX ☎ 01553 780780 🖷 01553 771657 ✉ nathan.johnson@west-norfolk.gov.uk

Health and Safety: Mr Dave Clack , Safety & Welfare Adviser, King's Court, Chapel Street, King's Lynn PE30 1EX ☎ 01553 616368 🖷 01553 616680 ✉ dave.clack@west-norfolk.gov.uk

Home Energy Conservation: Mr Tony Howell, Housing Officer, King's Court, Chapel Street, King's Lynn PE30 1EX ☎ 01553 616469 🖷 01553 775142 ✉ tony.howell@west-norfolk.gov.uk

Housing: Mr Duncan Hall , Strategic Housing & Community Safety Manager, King's Court, Chapel Street, King's Lynn PE30 1EX ☎ 01553 616445 ✉ duncan.hall@west-norfolk.gov.uk

Legal: Ms Emma Duncan , Legal Services Manager, King's Court, Chapel Street, King's Lynn PE30 1EX ☎ 01553 616270 ✉ emma.duncan@west-norfolk.gov.uk

Leisure and Cultural Services: Mr Chris Bamfield, Executive Director - Commercial Services, King's Court, Chapel Street, King's Lynn PE30 1EX ☎ 01553 616648 🖷 01553 616640 ✉ chris.bamfield@west-norfolk.gov.uk

Lottery Funding, Charity and Voluntary: Mr Ian Burbidge, Policy & Performance Manager, King's Court, Chapel Street, King's Lynn PE30 1EX ☎ 01553 616722 🖷 01553 616680 ✉ ian.burbidge@west-norfolk.gov.uk

Member Services: Mrs Sam Winter, Democratic Services Manager, King's Court, Chapel Street, King's Lynn PE30 1EX ☎ 01553 616327 🖷 01553 616758 ✉ sam.winter@west-norfolk.gov.uk

Parking: Mr Martin Chisholm , Business Manager - Commercial Services, King's Court, Chapel Street, King's Lynn PE30 1EX ☎ 01553 616650 ✉ martin.chisholm@west-norfolk.gov.uk

Partnerships: Mr Ian Burbidge, Policy & Performance Manager, King's Court, Chapel Street, King's Lynn PE30 1EX ☎ 01553 616722 🖷 01553 616680 ✉ ian.burbidge@west-norfolk.gov.uk

Personnel / HR: Mrs Debbie Gates, Executive Director - Central Services, King's Court, Chapel Street, King's Lynn PE30 1EX ☎ 01553 616605 🖷 01553 616728 ✉ debbie.gates@west-norfolk.gov.uk

Planning: Mr Geoff Hall, Executive Director - Environment & Planning, King's Court, Chapel Street, King's Lynn PE30 1EX ☎ 01553 616618 🖷 01553 616652 ✉ geoff.hall@west-norfolk.gov.uk

Procurement: Mr Toby Cowper , Principal Accountant, King's Court, Chapel Street, King's Lynn PE30 1EX ☎ 01553 616248 🖷 01553 616565 ✉ toby.cowper@west-norfolk.gov.uk

Recycling & Waste Minimisation: Mr Chris Bamfield, Executive Director - Commercial Services, King's Court, Chapel Street, King's Lynn PE30 1EX ☎ 01553 616648 🖷 01553 616640 ✉ chris.bamfield@west-norfolk.gov.uk

Recycling & Waste Minimisation: Mr Nathan Johnson, Public & Open Space Manager, King's Court, Chapel Street, King's Lynn PE30 1EX ☎ 01553 780780 🖷 01553 771657 ✉ nathan.johnson@west-norfolk.gov.uk

Regeneration: Mr Ostap Paparega , Regeneration & Economic Development Manager, King's Court, Chapel Street, King's Lynn PE30 1EX ☎ 01553 616890 🖷 01553 775726 ✉ ostap.paparega@west-norfolk.gov.uk

Staff Training: Miss Becky Box, Personnel Manager, King's Court, Chapel Street, King's Lynn PE30 1EX ☎ 01553 616502 🖷 01553 616680 ✉ becky.box@west-norfolk.gov.uk

Street Scene: Mr Nathan Johnson, Public & Open Space Manager, King's Court, Chapel Street, King's Lynn PE30 1EX ☎ 01553 780780 🖷 01553 771657 ✉ nathan.johnson@west-norfolk.gov.uk

Sustainable Communities: Mr Geoff Hall, Executive Director - Environment & Planning, King's Court, Chapel Street, King's Lynn PE30 1EX ☎ 01553 616618 🖷 01553 616652 ✉ geoff.hall@west-norfolk.gov.uk

Sustainable Development: Mr Geoff Hall, Executive Director - Environment & Planning, King's Court, Chapel Street, King's Lynn PE30 1EX ☎ 01553 616618 🖷 01553 616652 ✉ geoff.hall@west-norfolk.gov.uk

Tourism: Mr Tim Humphreys, Tourism Manager, King's Court, Chapel Street, King's Lynn PE30 1EX ☎ 01553 616643 🖷 01553 775726 ✉ tim.humphreys@west-norfolk.gov.uk

Town Centre: Mr Alistair Cox, Town Centre Manager, King's Court, Chapel Street, King's Lynn PE30 1EX ☎ 01553 616739 🖷 01553 775726 ✉ alistair.cox@west-norfolk.gov.uk

Waste Collection and Disposal: Mr Nathan Johnson, Public & Open Space Manager, King's Court, Chapel Street, King's Lynn PE30 1EX ☎ 01553 780780 🖷 01553 771657 ✉ nathan.johnson@west-norfolk.gov.uk

Waste Management: Mr Chris Bamfield, Executive Director - Commercial Services, King's Court, Chapel Street, King's Lynn PE30 1EX ☎ 01553 616648 🖷 01553 616640 ✉ chris.bamfield@west-norfolk.gov.uk

COUNCILLORS

***Mayor* Manning**, Colin (CON - Heacham)
cllr.colin.manning@west-norfolk.gov.uk

***Deputy Mayor* Whitby**, David (CON - Clenchwarton)
cllr.david.whitby@west-norfolk.gov.uk

***Leader of the Council* Daubney**, Nick (CON - South Wootton)
cllr.nick.daubney@west-norfolk.gov.uk

***Deputy Leader of the Council* Beales**, Alistair (CON - Gayton)
cllr.alistair.beales@west-norfolk.gov.uk

Anota, Bal (CON - West Winch)
cllr.baljinder.anota@west-norfolk.gov.uk

Ayres, Barry (CON - St Lawrence)
cllr.barry.ayres@west-norfolk.gov.uk

Bambridge, Lesley (CON - St Margarets with St Nicholas)
cllr.lesley.bambridge@west-norfolk.gov.uk

Baylis, Michael (CON - East Rudham)
cllr.baron.horsbrugh@west-norfolk.gov.uk

Beal, Paul (CON - Hunstanton)
cllr.paul.beal@west-norfolk.gov.uk

Bird, Richard (IND - Hunstanton)
cllr.richard.bird@west-norfolk.gov.uk

Blunt, Richard (CON - Walpole)
cllr.richard.blunt@west-norfolk.gov.uk

Bower, Carol (CON - Hunstanton)
cllr.carol.bower@west.norfolk.gov.uk

Bubb, Anthony (LD - Dersingham)
cllr.tony.bubb@west-norfolk.gov.uk

Collingham, Judy (CON - Dersingham)
cllr.judith.collingham@west-norfolk.gov.uk

Collop, John (LAB - Gaywood Chase)
cllr.john.collop@west-norfolk.gov.uk

Collop, Sandra (LAB - Gaywood Chase)
cllr.sandra.collop@west-norfolk.gov.uk

Colvin, Peter (CON - Heacham)
cllr.peter.colvin@west-norfolk.gov.uk

Crofts, Chris (CON - Emneth with Outwell)
cllr.chris.crofts@west-norfolk.gov.uk

Devereux, Ian (CON - Snettisham)
cllr.ian.devereux@west-norfolk.gov.uk

Fraser, Susan (CON - Grimston)
cllr.susan.fraser@west-norfolk.gov.uk

Gidney, Peter (CON - West Winch)
cllr.peter.gidney@west-norfolk.gov.uk

Gourlay, Ian (LAB - Fairstead)
cllr.ian.gourlay@west-norfolk.gov.uk

Groom, Roy (CON - Walton)
cllr.roy.groom@west-norfolk.gov.uk

Hipperson, Geoffrey (CON - Airfield)
cllr.geoffrey.hipperson@west-norfolk.gov.uk

Hodson, Peter (CON - Watlington)
cllr.peter.hodson@west-norfolk.gov.uk

Hopkins, Marcus (IND - Wiggenhall)
cllr.marcus.hopkins@west-norfolk.gov.uk

Howard, Greville (CON - North Wootton)
cllr.greville.howard@west-norfolk.gov.uk

Howland, Michael (CON - Airfield)
cllr.michael.howland@west-norfolk.gov.uk

Humphrey, Harry (CON - Emneth with Outwell)
cllr.harry.humphrey@west-norfolk.gov.uk

Joyce, Charles (LAB - Lynn, South & West)
cllr.charles.joyce@west-norfolk.gov.uk

Kittow, Claire (LAB - St Margarets with St Nicholas)
cllr.claire.kittow@west-norfolk.gov.uk

Kunes, Paul (CON - Spellowfields)
cllr.paul.kunes@west-norfolk.gov.uk

Lawrence, Adrian (CON - Denton)
cllr.adrian.lawrence@west-norfolk.gov.uk

Long, Brian (CON - Mershe Lande)
cllr.brian.long@west-norfolk.gov.uk

McGuiness, Gary (LAB - Lynn, South & West)
cllr.gary.mcguiness@west-norfolk.gov.uk

Mellish, Kathy (CON - Downham Old Town)
cllr.kathy.mellish@west-norfolk.gov.uk

Middleton, Graham (CON - Gaywood Old)
cllr.graham.middleton@west-norfolk.gov.uk

Moriarty, James (LAB - Priory)
cllr.james.moriarty@west-norfolk.gov.uk

Morrison, Andrew (CON - Docking)
cllr.andrew.morrison@west-norfolk.gov.uk

Nockolds, Elizabeth (CON - South Wootton)
cllr.elizabeth.nockolds@west-norfolk.gov.uk

Peake, Mick (CON - Denton)
cllr.mick.peake@west-norfolk.gov.uk

Pope, David (CON - Upwell and Delph)
cllr.david.pope@west-norfolk.gov.uk

Rochford, Patrick (CON - Gaywood North Bank)
cllr.patrick.rochford@west-norfolk.gov.uk

Sampson, Colin (CON - Wissey)
cllr.colin.sampson@west-norfolk.gov.uk

Sandell, Sam (CON - Burnham)
cllr.sam.sandell@west-norfolk.gov.uk

Shorting, Mark (CON - Gaywood North Bank)
cllr.mark.shorting@west-norfolk.gov.uk

Smith, Thomas (CON - Gaywood North Bank)
cllr.thomas.smith@west-norfolk.gov.uk

Spikings, Vivienne (CON - Upwell and Delph)
cllr.vivienne.spikings@west-norfolk.gov.uk

Squire, Sandra (CON - Wimbotsham with Fincham)
cllr.sandra.squire@west-norfolk.gov.uk

Storey, Martin (CON - Denton)
cllr.martin.storey@west-norfolk.gov.uk

Tilbury, Mike (IND - Valley Hill)
cllr.mike.tilbury@west-norfolk.gov.uk

Tyler, Donald (CON - South Downham)
cllr.donald.tyler@west-norfolk.gov.uk

Tyler, Andy (LAB - Lynn North)
cllr.andy.tyler@west-norfolk.gov.uk

Wareham, Geoff (CON - North Downham)
cllr.geoff.wareham@west-norfolk.gov.uk

Watson, Elizabeth (CON - Brancaster)
cllr.elizabeth.watson@west-norfolk.gov.uk

Westrop, Jacqueline (CON - East Downham)
cllr.jackqueline.westrop@west-norfolk.gov.uk

White, Anthony (CON - Hilgay with Denver)
cllr.tony.white@west-norfolk.gov.uk

Wilkinson, Margaret (LAB - Fairstead)
cllr.margaret.wilkinson@west-norfolk.gov.uk

Wing-Pentelow, Toby (CON - Springwood)
cllr.toby.pentelow@west-norfolk.gov.uk

Wright, Avril (CON - Snettisham)

Young, Sheila (CON - Spellowfields)
cllr.sheila.young@west-norfolk.gov.uk

POLITICAL COMPOSITION

CON: 48, LAB: 9, IND: 3, LD: 1

Kingston upon Hull City U

Kingston upon Hull City Council, Guildhall, Alfred Gelder Street, Hull HU1 2AA
☎ 01482 609100 ✉ info@hullcc.gov.uk 💻 www.hullcc.gov.uk

FACTS AND FIGURES

Parliamentary Constituencies: Hull East, Hull North, Hull West and Hessle
EU Constituencies: Yorkshire and the Humber
Election Frequency: Elections are by thirds

PRINCIPAL OFFICERS

Chief Executive: Mr Matt Jukes , Chief Operating Officer, The Guildhall, Alfred Gelder Street, Hull HU1 2AA ☎ 01482 616320 ✉ matt.jukes@hullcc.gov.uk

Senior Management: Mr Brendan Arnold , Director - Resources & City Treasurer, The Guildhall, Alfred Gelder Street, Hull HU1 2AA ☎ 01482 614812 ✉ brendan.arnold@hullcc.gov.uk

Senior Management: Miss Trish Dalby, Corporate Director , The Guildhall, Alfred Gelder Street, Hull HU1 2AA ☎ 01482 615000 🖷 01482 613111 ✉ trish.dalby@hullcc.gov.uk

Senior Management: Mr Milorad Vasic , Director - Children & Family Services, The Guildhall, Alfred Gelder Street, Hull HU1 2AA ☎ 01482 613232 ✉ milorad.vasic@hullcc.gov.uk

Senior Management: Mrs Julia Weldon , Director - Public Health, The Guildhall, Alfred Gelder Street, Hull HU1 2AA ☎ 01482 616324 ✉ julia.weldon@hullcc.gov.uk

Access Officer / Social Services (Disability): Ms Alison Barker , City Adults Social Care Manager, Brunswick Huse, Strand Close, Beverley Road, Hull HU2 9DB ☎ 01482 616308 🖷 01483 616162 ✉ alison.barker@hullcc.gov.uk

Access Officer / Social Services (Disability): Ms Tracy Harsley , CitySafe & Early Intervention Manager, Brunswick House, Strand Close, Bevereley Road, Hull HU2 9DB ☎ 01482 616039 ✉ tracy.harsley@hullcc.go.uk

Architect, Building / Property Services: Mr Nick Howbridge , City Property & Assets Manager, The Myton Centre, William Street, Hull HU1 2SP ☎ 01482 331038 ✉ nick.howbridge@hullcc.gov.uk

Building Control: Mr Nick Howbridge , City Property & Assets Manager, The Myton Centre, William Street, Hull HU1 2SP ☎ 01482 331038 ✉ nick.howbridge@hullcc.gov.uk

Children / Youth Services: Miss Vanessa Harvey-Samuel , City Learning & Skills Manager, Brunswick House, Strand Close, Bevereley Road, Hull HU2 9DB ☎ 01482 616094 ✉ vanessa.harvey-samuel@hullcc.gov.uk

Children / Youth Services: Mr Milorad Vasic , Director - Children & Family Services, The Guildhall, Alfred Gelder Street, Hull HU1 2AA ☎ 01482 613232 ✉ milorad.vasic@hullcc.gov.uk

Civil Registration: Mr Andy Brown, City Customer Services Manager, Guildhall, Alfred Gelder Street, Hull HU1 2AA ☎ 01482 613444 🖷 01482 613562 ✉ andy.brown@hullcc.gov.uk

PR / Communications: Mr Nathan Turner , Assistant City Manager - Regeneration & Policy, Guildhall, Alfred Gelder Street, Hull HU1 2AA ☎ 01482 613175 ✉ nathan.turner@hullcc.gov.uk

Community Safety: Ms Tracy Harsley , CitySafe & Early Intervention Manager, Brunswick House, Strand Close, Bevereley Road, Hull HU2 9DB ☎ 01482 616039 ✉ tracy.harsley@hullcc.go.uk

Computer Management: Mr Brendan Arnold , Director - Resources & City Treasurer, The Guildhall, Alfred Gelder Street, Hull HU1 2AA ☎ 01482 614812 ✉ brendan.arnold@hullcc.gov.uk

Consumer Protection and Trading Standards: Ms Tracy Harsley , CitySafe & Early Intervention Manager, Brunswick House, Strand Close, Bevereley Road, Hull HU2 9DB ☎ 01482 616039 ✉ tracy.harsley@hullcc.go.uk

Customer Service: Mr Andy Brown, City Customer Services Manager, Guildhall, Alfred Gelder Street, Hull HU1 2AA ☎ 01482 613444 🖷 01482 613562 ✉ andy.brown@hullcc.gov.uk

Economic Development: Mr Mark Jones, City Economic Development & Regeneration Manager, The Guildhall, Alfred Gelder Street, Hull HU1 2AA ☎ 01482 615128 🖷 01482 612160 ✉ mark.jones@hullcc.gov.uk

Education: Miss Vanessa Harvey-Samuel , City Learning & Skills Manager, Brunswick House, Strand Close, Bevereley Road, Hull HU2 9DB ☎ 01482 616094 ✉ vanessa.harvey-samuel@hullcc.gov.uk

KINGSTON UPON HULL CITY

Education: Mr Milorad Vasic , Director - Children & Family Services, The Guildhall, Alfred Gelder Street, Hull HU1 2AA ☎ 01482 613232 ✉ milorad.vasic@hullcc.gov.uk

E-Government: Mr Brendan Arnold , Director - Resources & City Treasurer, The Guildhall, Alfred Gelder Street, Hull HU1 2AA ☎ 01482 614812 ✉ brendan.arnold@hullcc.gov.uk

Electoral Registration: Mr Ian Anderson , Town Clerk (& Monitoring Officer), Guildhall, Alfred Gelder Street, Hull HU1 2AA ☎ 01482 613233 🖷 01482 613081 ✉ ian.anderson@hullcc.gov.uk

Emergency Planning: Mr Andy Brown, City Customer Services Manager, Guildhall, Alfred Gelder Street, Hull HU1 2AA ☎ 01482 613444 🖷 01482 613562 ✉ andy.brown@hullcc.gov.uk

Emergency Planning: Miss Trish Dalby, Corporate Director , The Guildhall, Alfred Gelder Street, Hull HU1 2AA ☎ 01482 615000 🖷 01482 613111 ✉ trish.dalby@hullcc.gov.uk

Energy Management: Mr Brendan Arnold , Director - Resources & City Treasurer, The Guildhall, Alfred Gelder Street, Hull HU1 2AA ☎ 01482 614812 ✉ brendan.arnold@hullcc.gov.uk

Environmental / Technical Services: Mr Andy Burton , City Streetscene Manager, Staveley House, Stockholme Road Depot, Hull HU7 0XW ☎ 01482 614002 ✉ andy.burton@hullcc.gov.uk

Environmental / Technical Services: Ms Tracy Harsley , CitySafe & Early Intervention Manager, Brunswick House, Strand Close, Bevereley Road, Hull HU2 9DB ☎ 01482 616039 ✉ tracy.harsley@hullcc.go.uk

Environmental Health: Ms Tracy Harsley , CitySafe & Early Intervention Manager, Brunswick House, Strand Close, Bevereley Road, Hull HU2 9DB ☎ 01482 616039 ✉ tracy.harsley@hullcc.go.uk

Estates, Property & Valuation: Mr Nick Howbridge , City Property & Assets Manager, The Myton Centre, William Street, Hull HU1 2SP ☎ 01482 331038 ✉ nick.howbridge@hullcc.gov.uk

European Liaison: Mr Mark Jones, City Economic Development & Regeneration Manager, The Guildhall, Alfred Gelder Street, Hull HU1 2AA ☎ 01482 615128 🖷 01482 612160 ✉ mark.jones@hullcc.gov.uk

Events Manager: Mr Mark Jones, City Economic Development & Regeneration Manager, The Guildhall, Alfred Gelder Street, Hull HU1 2AA ☎ 01482 615128 🖷 01482 612160 ✉ mark.jones@hullcc.gov.uk

Facilities: Mr Brendan Arnold , Director - Resources & City Treasurer, The Guildhall, Alfred Gelder Street, Hull HU1 2AA ☎ 01482 614812 ✉ brendan.arnold@hullcc.gov.uk

Finance: Mr Brendan Arnold , Director - Resources & City Treasurer, The Guildhall, Alfred Gelder Street, Hull HU1 2AA ☎ 01482 614812 ✉ brendan.arnold@hullcc.gov.uk

Fleet Management: Mr Andy Burton , City Streetscene Manager, Staveley House, Stockholme Road Depot, Hull HU7 0XW ☎ 01482 614002 ✉ andy.burton@hullcc.gov.uk

Grounds Maintenance: Mr Andy Burton , City Streetscene Manager, Staveley House, Stockholme Road Depot, Hull HU7 0XW ☎ 01482 614002 ✉ andy.burton@hullcc.gov.uk

Highways: Mr Andy Burton , City Streetscene Manager, Staveley House, Stockholme Road Depot, Hull HU7 0XW ☎ 01482 614002 ✉ andy.burton@hullcc.gov.uk

Housing Maintenance: Mrs Laura Carr , City Neighbourhoods & Housing Manager, 5th Floor, Kingston House, Bond Street, Hull HU1 3ER ☎ 01482 612645 ✉ laura.carr@hullcc.gov.uk

Legal: Mr Ian Anderson , Town Clerk (& Monitoring Officer), Guildhall, Alfred Gelder Street, Hull HU1 2AA ☎ 01482 613233 🖷 01482 613081 ✉ ian.anderson@hullcc.gov.uk

Leisure and Cultural Services: Mr Mitch Upfold , Hull Culture & Leisure Services Managing Director, Dock Office Chambers, New Cross Street, Hull HU1 3DU ☎ 01482 614778 ✉ mitch.upfold@hullcc.gov.uk

Licensing: Ms Tracy Harsley , CitySafe & Early Intervention Manager, Brunswick House, Strand Close, Bevereley Road, Hull HU2 9DB ☎ 01482 616039 ✉ tracy.harsley@hullcc.go.uk

Lifelong Learning: Miss Vanessa Harvey-Samuel , City Learning & Skills Manager, Brunswick House, Strand Close, Bevereley Road, Hull HU2 9DB ☎ 01482 616094 ✉ vanessa.harvey-samuel@hullcc.gov.uk

Lifelong Learning: Mr Milorad Vasic , Director of Children & Family Services, The Guildhall, Alfred Gelder Street, Hull HU1 2AA ☎ 01482 615101 ✉ Milorad.Vasic@hullcc.gov.uk

Lighting: Mr Andy Burton , City Streetscene Manager, Staveley House, Stockholme Road Depot, Hull HU7 0XW ☎ 01482 614002 ✉ andy.burton@hullcc.gov.uk

Member Services: Mr Ian Anderson , Town Clerk (& Monitoring Officer), Guildhall, Alfred Gelder Street, Hull HU1 2AA ☎ 01482 613233 🖷 01482 613081 ✉ ian.anderson@hullcc.gov.uk

Parking: Mr Andy Burton , City Streetscene Manager, Staveley House, Stockholme Road Depot, Hull HU7 0XW ☎ 01482 614002 ✉ andy.burton@hullcc.gov.uk

Personnel / HR: Mrs Jacqui Blesic , City HR Manager, The Guildhall, Alfred Gelder Street, Hull HU1 2AA ☎ 01482 613044 ✉ jacqui.blesic@hullcc.gov.uk

Planning: Mr Mark Jones, City Economic Development & Regeneration Manager, The Guildhall, Alfred Gelder Street, Hull HU1 2AA ☎ 01482 615128 🖷 01482 612160 ✉ mark.jones@hullcc.gov.uk

Procurement: Mr Ian Anderson , Town Clerk (& Monitoring Officer), Guildhall, Alfred Gelder Street, Hull HU1 2AA ☎ 01482 613233 🖷 01482 613081 ✉ ian.anderson@hullcc.gov.uk

Public Libraries: Mr Andy Brown, City Customer Services Manager, Guildhall, Alfred Gelder Street, Hull HU1 2AA ☎ 01482 613444 🖷 01482 613562 ✉ andy.brown@hullcc.gov.uk

Recycling & Waste Minimisation: Mr Andy Burton , City Streetscene Manager, Staveley House, Stockholme Road Depot, Hull HU7 0XW ☎ 01482 614002 ✉ andy.burton@hullcc.gov.uk

Regeneration: Mr Mark Jones, City Economic Development & Regeneration Manager, The Guildhall, Alfred Gelder Street, Hull HU1 2AA ☎ 01482 615128 🖷 01482 612160 ✉ mark.jones@hullcc.gov.uk

Road Safety: Mr Andy Burton , City Streetscene Manager, Staveley House, Stockholme Road Depot, Hull HU7 0XW ☎ 01482 614002 ✉ andy.burton@hullcc.gov.uk

Social Services: Mr Milorad Vasic , Director of Children & Family Services, The Guildhall, Alfred Gelder Street, Hull HU1 2AA ☎ 01482 615101 ✉ Milorad.Vasic@hullcc.gov.uk

Social Services (Adult): Ms Alison Barker , City Adults Social Care Manager, Brunswick Huse, Strand Close, Beverley Road, Hull HU2 9DB ☎ 01482 616308 🖷 01483 616162 ✉ alison.barker@hullcc.gov.uk

Social Services (Children): Mr Jon Plant, City Children Safeguarding Manager, Brunswick House, Strand Close, Bevereley Road, Hull HU2 9DB ☎ 01482 616004 🖷 01482 616107 ✉ jon.plant@hullcc.gov.uk

Social Services (Children): Mr Milorad Vasic , Director of Children & Family Services, The Guildhall, Alfred Gelder Street, Hull HU1 2AA ☎ 01482 615101 ✉ Milorad.Vasic@hullcc.gov.uk

Public Health: Mrs Julia Weldon , Director - Public Health, The Guildhall, Alfred Gelder Street, Hull HU1 2AA ☎ 01482 616324 ✉ julia.weldon@hullcc.gov.uk

Staff Training: Mrs Jacqui Blesic , City HR Manager, The Guildhall, Alfred Gelder Street, Hull HU1 2AA ☎ 01482 613044 ✉ jacqui.blesic@hullcc.gov.uk

Street Scene: Mr Andy Burton , City Streetscene Manager, Staveley House, Stockholme Road Depot, Hull HU7 0XW ☎ 01482 614002 ✉ andy.burton@hullcc.gov.uk

Sustainable Communities: Mr Mark Jones, City Economic Development & Regeneration Manager, The Guildhall, Alfred Gelder Street, Hull HU1 2AA ☎ 01482 615128 🖷 01482 612160 ✉ mark.jones@hullcc.gov.uk

Sustainable Development: Mr Mark Jones, City Economic Development & Regeneration Manager, The Guildhall, Alfred Gelder Street, Hull HU1 2AA ☎ 01482 615128 🖷 01482 612160 ✉ mark.jones@hullcc.gov.uk

Tourism: Mr Mark Jones, City Economic Development & Regeneration Manager, The Guildhall, Alfred Gelder Street, Hull HU1 2AA ☎ 01482 615128 🖷 01482 612160 ✉ mark.jones@hullcc.gov.uk

Town Centre: Mr Mark Jones, City Economic Development & Regeneration Manager, The Guildhall, Alfred Gelder Street, Hull HU1 2AA ☎ 01482 615128 🖷 01482 612160 ✉ mark.jones@hullcc.gov.uk

Traffic Management: Mr Andy Burton , City Streetscene Manager, Staveley House, Stockholme Road Depot, Hull HU7 0XW ☎ 01482 614002 ✉ andy.burton@hullcc.gov.uk

Waste Collection and Disposal: Mr Andy Burton , City Streetscene Manager, Staveley House, Stockholme Road Depot, Hull HU7 0XW ☎ 01482 614002 ✉ andy.burton@hullcc.gov.uk

Waste Management: Mr Andy Burton , City Streetscene Manager, Staveley House, Stockholme Road Depot, Hull HU7 0XW ☎ 01482 614002 ✉ andy.burton@hullcc.gov.uk

COUNCILLORS

***Leader of the Council* Brady**, Stephen (LAB - Southcoates West)
councillor.brady@hullcc.gov.uk

***Deputy Leader of the Council* Hale**, Daren (LAB - St Andrews)
councillor.hale@hullcc.gov.uk

Abbott, John (CON - Bricknell)
councillor.abbott@hullcc.gov.uk

Allen, Pete (LAB - Pickering)
councillor.allen@hullcc.gov.uk

Armstrong, Suzanne (LAB - Ings)
councillor.armstrong@hullcc.gov.uk

Barrett, Richard (UKIP - Southcoates East)
councillor.barrett@hullcc.gov.uk

Bayes, Steven (LAB - Orchard Park and Greenwood)
steven.bayes@hullcc.gov.uk

Belcher, Sharon (LAB - Marfleet)
councillor.belcher@hullcc.gov.uk

Bell, Abigail (LD - Pickering)
councillor.bell@hullcc.gov.uk

Black, John (LAB - Longhill)
councillor.black@hullcc.gov.uk

Brabazon, Marjorie (LAB - Avenue)
councillor.brabazon@hullcc.gov.uk

Brown, Danny (LAB - Kings Park)
councillor.brown@hullcc.gov.uk

Chambers, Linda (LD - Drypool)
councillor.chambers@hullcc.gov.uk

Chaytor, Sean (LAB - Marfleet)
councillor.chaytor@hullcc.gov.uk

Clark, Peter (LAB - Bransholme East)
councillor.p.clark@hullcc.gov.uk

Clark, Alan (LAB - Newington)
councillor.clark@hullcc.gov.uk

KINGSTON UPON HULL CITY

Clarkson, Carol (LAB - Longhill)
councillor.clarkson@hullcc.gov.uk

Clay, Helena (LD - Boothferry)
councillor.woods@hullcc.gov.uk

Conner, Julia (LAB - Orchard Park and Greenwood)
councillor.conner@hullcc.gov.uk

Craker, Dave (LAB - Sutton)
councillor.craker@hullcc.gov.uk

Dad, Jackie (LD - Holderness)
councillor.dad@hullcc.gov.uk

Dorton, Andy (LAB - Avenue)
councillor.dorton@hullcc.gov.uk

Fareham, John (CON - Bricknell)
councillor.fareham@hullcc.gov.uk

Fudge, Nadine (LAB - St Andrews)
councillor.fudge@hullcc.gov.uk

Fudge, Leanne (LAB - Derringham)
councillor.fudge2@hullcc.gov.uk

Gardiner, Alan (LAB - Ings)
councillor.gardiner@hullcc.gov.uk

Geraghty, Terry (LAB - Orchard Park and Greenwood)
councillor.geraghty@hullcc.gov.uk

Glew, Mary (LAB - Southcoates West)
councillor.glew@hullcc.gov.uk

Harrison, Anita (LAB - Bransholme East)
councillor.harrison@hullcc.gov.uk

Hatcher, Diana (LD - Drypool)
councillor.hatcher@hullcc.gov.uk

Herrera-Richmond, Haraldo (LAB - Boothferry)
councillor.herrara-richmond@hullcc.gov.uk

Hewitt, John (LAB - Longhill)
councillor.j.hewitt@hullcc.gov.uk

Inglis, Colin (LAB - Myton)
councillor.inglis@hullcc.gov.uk

Jones, Rilba (LAB - Myton)
councillor.jones@hullcc.gov.uk

Keal, Terry (LD - Sutton)
councillor.keal@hullcc.gov.uk

Kennett, Gill (LAB - Holderness)
councillor.kennett@hullcc.gov.uk

Korczak Fields, Joyce (LAB - University)
councillor.KorczakFields@hullcc.gov.uk

Lunn, Gwen (LAB - Newland)
councillor.lunn@hullcc.gov.uk

Mancey, Martin (LAB - Myton)
councillor.mancey@hullcc.gov.uk

Mann, Eliza (LD - Derringham)
councillor.mann@hullcc.gov.uk

Mathieson, Karen (LD - Beverely)
councillor.mathieson@hullcc.gov.uk

McCobb, David (LD - Beverley)
councillor.mccobb@hullcc.gov.uk

McVie, Tom (LAB - Southcoates East)
councillor.mcvie@hullcc.gov.uk

Nicola, Rosie (LAB - Avenue)
councillor.nicola@hullcc.gov.uk

O'Mullane, Helene (LAB - Bransholme West)
councillor.o'mullane@hullcc.gov.uk

Pantelakis, Rosemary (LAB - Marfleet)
councillor.pantelakis@hullcc.gov.uk

Payne, Cheryl (LD - Derringham)
councillor.c.payne@hullcc.gov.uk

Payne, Ruth (LD - Boothferry)
councillor.r.payne@hullcc.gov.uk

Petrini, Lynn (LAB - Newington)
councillor.petrini@hullcc.gov.uk

Quinn, Charles (LD - Kings Park)
councillor.quinn@hullcc.gov.uk

Ross, Michael (LD - Newland)
councillor.ross@hullcc.gov.uk

Spencer, Helena (LAB - Newington)
councillor.spencer@hullcc.gov.uk

Sumpton, Christopher (LAB - Holderness)
councillor.sumpton@hullcc.gov.uk

Thomas, Claire (LD - Pickering)
councillor.thomas@hullcc.gov.uk

Thompson, Mike (LAB - Ings)
councillor.thompson@hullcc.gov.uk

Turner, Ken (LAB - Sutton)
councillor.turner@hullcc.gov.uk

Webster, Phil (LAB - Bransholme West)
councillor.webster@hullcc.gov.uk

Williams, Adam (LD - Drypool)
councillor.williams@hullcc.gov.uk

Wilson, Steve (LAB - University)
councillor.wilson@hullcc.gov.uk

POLITICAL COMPOSITION

LAB: 41, LD: 15, CON: 2, UKIP: 1

Kingston upon Thames L

Royal Borough of Kingston upon Thames Council, Guildhall 1, High Street, Kingston upon Thames KT1 1EU
☎ 020 8547 5757 🖳 www.kingston.gov.uk

FACTS AND FIGURES

Parliamentary Constituencies: Kingston and Surbiton, Richmond Park
EU Constituencies: London
Election Frequency: Elections are of whole council

PRINCIPAL OFFICERS

Chief Executive: Mr Bruce McDonald, Chief Executive, Guildhall, Kingston upon Thames KT1 1EU ☎ 020 8547 5150
🖷 020 8547 5012 🖰 bruce.mcdonald@rbk.kingston.gov.uk

Senior Management: Dr Jonathan Hildebrand , Director - Public Health, Guildhall 1, High Street, Kingston upon Thames KT1 1EU
☎ 020 8547 6800 🖰 jonathan.hildebrand@rbk.kingston.gov.uk

Senior Management: Ms Sue Redmond , Interim Director - Adult Services, Guildhall 2, High Street, Kingston upon Thames KT1 1EU ☎ 020 8547 6000 🖷 020 8547 6086 ✉ sue.redmond@kingston.gov.uk

Senior Management: Mr Roy Thompson , Director - Place, Guildhall 1, High Street, Kingston upon Thames KT1 1EU ☎ 020 8547 5343 ✉ roy.thompson@rbk.kingston.gov.uk

Senior Management: Mrs Sheila West, Executive Head - Organisational Development & Strategic Business, Guildhall 2, Kingston upon Thames KT1 1EU ☎ 020 8547 5153 🖷 020 8547 5188 ✉ sheila.west@rbk.kingston.gov.uk

Senior Management: Mr Leigh Whitehouse , Director - Finance, Guildhall 2, Kingston upon Thames KT1 1EU ☎ 020 8547 5570 🖷 020 8547 5925 ✉ leigh.whitehouse@rbk.kingston.gov.uk

Architect, Building / Property Services: Mr Karl Limbert , Head of Property, Guildhall 2, High Street, Kingston upon Thames KT1 1EU ☎ 020 8547 5155 ✉ karl.limbert@kingston.gov.uk

Best Value: Mr Chris Morgan , Capability Lead - Commissioning, Guildhall 1, High Street, Kingston upon Thames KT1 1EU ☎ 020 8547 5300 ✉ chris.morgan@rbk.kingston.gov.uk

Children / Youth Services: Ms Alison Twynam , Assistant Director of Social Care - Achieving for Children, Civic Centre, 44 York Street, Twickenham TW1 3BZ ✉ a.twynam@richmond.gov.uk

Civil Registration: Mr Dennis Mulligan, Registration Manager & Superintendent Registrar, The Register Office, 35 Coombe Road, Kingston upon Thames KT2 7BA ☎ 020 8547 6191 🖷 020 8547 6188 ✉ dennis.mulligan@rbk.kingston.gov.uk

PR / Communications: Mr John Haynes , Team Leader - Communications, Guildhall, Kingston upon Thames KT1 1EU ☎ 020 8547 4710 🖷 020 8547 5012 ✉ john.haynes@kingston.gov.uk

Community Planning: Mr Gary Walsh , Capability Lead - Community, Guildhall 1, High Street, Kingston upon Thames KT1 1EU ☎ 020 8547 4698 ✉ gary.walsh@rbk.kingston.gov.uk

Community Safety: Ms Marion Todd , Safer Kingston Partnership Manager, Guildhall 1, High Street, Kingston upon Thames KT1 1EU ☎ 020 8547 5039 ✉ marion.todd@rbk.kingston.gov.uk

Computer Management: Mr Rob Miller , Head of Shared ICT Service, Guildhall 2, High Street, Kingston upon Thames KT1 1EU ✉ rob.miller@kingston.gov.uk

Consumer Protection and Trading Standards: Mr Mark Reed , Interim Service Manager - Environmental Health & Trading Standards, Guildhall 2, High Street, Kingston upon Thames KT1 1EU ☎ 020 8547 5513 🖷 020 8547 5515 ✉ markreed@kingston.gov.uk

Contracts: Mr Chris Morgan , Capability Lead - Commissioning, Guildhall 1, High Street, Kingston upon Thames KT1 1EU ☎ 020 8547 5300 ✉ chris.morgan@rbk.kingston.gov.uk

Customer Service: Mr Russell Anthony , Transitional Service Manager - Customer Contact, Guildhall 1, High Street, Kingston upon Thames KT1 1EU ☎ 020 8547 5393 ✉ russell.anthony@rbk.kingston.gov.uk

Economic Development: Mr Andrew Sherville , Team Leader - Business Community Sector, Guildhall 1, High Street, Kingston upon Thames KT1 1EU ☎ 020 8547 5025 ✉ andrew.sherville@kingston.gov.uk

E-Government: Mr Rob Miller , Head of Shared ICT Service, Guildhall 2, High Street, Kingston upon Thames KT1 1EU ✉ rob.miller@kingston.gov.uk

Electoral Registration: Mr Andrew Bessant , Head - Corporate Governance, Guildhall 1, High Street, Kingston upon Thames KT1 1EU ☎ 020 8547 4628 🖷 020 8547 5125 ✉ andrew.bessant@rbk.kingston.gov.uk

Electoral Registration: Mr Gareth Harrington , Manager - Electoral Services, Guildhall, High Street, Kingston upon Thames KT1 1EU ☎ 020 8547 5035 🖷 020 8547 5099 ✉ gareth.harrington@rbk.kingston.gov.uk

Emergency Planning: Mr Chris Begley , Contingency Planning Manager, Guildhall 1, High Street, Kingston upon Thames KT1 1EU ☎ 020 8547 5400 🖷 020 8547 6224 ✉ chris.begley@kingston.gov.uk

Environmental / Technical Services: Mrs Shifa Mustafa , Interim Head of Environment, Guildhall 2, High Street, Kingston upon Thames KT1 1EU ☎ 020 8547 4705 ✉ shifa.mustafa@kingston.gov.uk

Environmental / Technical Services: Mr Mark Reed , Interim Service Manager - Environmental Health & Trading Standards, Guildhall 2, High Street, Kingston upon Thames KT1 1EU ☎ 020 8547 5513 🖷 020 8547 5515 ✉ markreed@kingston.gov.uk

Estates, Property & Valuation: Mr Karl Limbert , Head of Property, Guildhall 2, High Street, Kingston upon Thames KT1 1EU ☎ 020 8547 5155 ✉ karl.limbert@kingston.gov.uk

European Liaison: Ms Brigitte Pfender, International Partnerships Co-ordinator, Guildhall, Kingston upon Thames KT1 1EU ☎ 020 8547 5009 🖷 020 8547 5125 ✉ brigitte.pfender@rbk.kingston.gov.uk

Finance: Mr Jeremy Randall , Head of Finance - Strategy & Accounting, Guildhall 2, High Street, Kingston upon Thames KT1 1EU ☎ 020 8547 5572 ✉ jeremy.randall@rbk.kingston.gov.uk

Finance: Mr Leigh Whitehouse , Director - Finance, Guildhall 2, Kingston upon Thames KT1 1EU ☎ 020 8547 5570 🖷 020 8547 5925 ✉ leigh.whitehouse@rbk.kingston.gov.uk

Treasury: Mrs Rachel Howard , Finance Strategy Capability Lead, Guildhall 2, High Street, Kingston upon Thames KT1 1EU ☎ 020 8547 5625 ✉ rachel.howard@rbk.kingston.gov.uk

KINGSTON UPON THAMES

Pensions: Mr Paul Godfrey , Senior Finance Analyst, Guildhall 2, High Street, Kingston upon Thames KT1 1EU ☎ 020 8547 5621 ✉ paul.godfrey@kingston.gov.uk

Pensions: Ms Sue Grimstead , Pensions Manager, Guildhall 1, High Street, Kingston upon Thames KT1 1EU ☎ 0208 547 5614 ✉ sue.grimstead@rbk.kingston.gov.uk

Grounds Maintenance: Ms Marie-Claire Edwards , Service Manager - Green Spaces, Guildhall 2, Kingston upon Thames KT1 1EU ☎ 020 8547 5372 ✉ marie-claire.edwards@rbk.kingston.gov.uk

Health and Safety: Ms Lorna Mansell, Occupational Health & Safety Manager, Guildhall, Kingston upon Thames KT1 1EU ☎ 020 8547 5187 🖷 020 8547 5186 ✉ lorna.mansell@rbk.kingston.gov.uk

Housing: Mr Darren Walsh , Head of Housing, Guildhall 2, Kingston upon Thames KT1 1EU ☎ 020 8547 5430 ✉ darren.welsh@kingston.gov.uk

Local Area Agreement: Mr Kevin Mitchell , Capability Lead - Strategy, Guildhall 1, High Street, Kingston upon Thames KT1 1EU ☎ 020 8547 5982 ✉ kevin.mitchell@rbk.kingston.gov.uk

Legal: Mr Nick Bishop, Corporate Solicitor, Guildhall, Kingston upon Thames KT1 1EU ☎ 020 8547 5110 🖷 020 8547 5127 ✉ nick.bishop@rbk.kingston.gov.uk

Leisure and Cultural Services: Mrs Vivienne Bennett , Head of Culture, Guildhall 2, Kingston upon Thames KT1 1EU ☎ 020 8547 5267 🖷 020 8547 5213 ✉ vivienne.bennett@kingston.gov.uk

Lifelong Learning: Mrs Vivienne Bennett , Head of Culture, Guildhall 2, Kingston upon Thames KT1 1EU ☎ 020 8547 5267 🖷 020 8547 5213 ✉ vivienne.bennett@kingston.gov.uk

Lifelong Learning: Mr Ian Dodds , Director - Standards & Improvements, Achieving for Children, Regal House, London Road, Twickenham TW1 3BQ ☎ 020 8831 6116 🖷 020 8891 7714 ✉ ian.dodds@richmond.gov.uk

Lottery Funding, Charity and Voluntary: Ms Jill Darling , Team Leader - Voluntary Sector & Business Community, Guildhall, High Street, Kingston upon Thames KT1 1EU ☎ 020 8547 5124 ✉ jill.darling@rbk.kingston.gov.uk

Member Services: Mr Andrew Bessant, Head - Corporate Governance, Guildhall, Kingston upon Thames KT1 1EU ☎ 020 8547 4628 ✉ andrew.bessant@rbk.kingston.gov.uk

Parking: Mr Mehmet Mazhar , Interim Service Manager - Traffic Management & Design, Guildhall 2, High Street, Kingston upon Thames KT1 1EU ☎ 020 8547 5943 ✉ mehmet.mazhar@kingston.gov.uk

Personnel / HR: Mrs Sheila West, Executive Head - Organisational Development & Strategic Business, Guildhall 2, Kingston upon Thames KT1 1EU ☎ 020 8547 5153 🖷 020 8547 5188 ✉ sheila.west@rbk.kingston.gov.uk

Planning: Mr Viv Evans , Head of Planning & Transportation, Guildhall 2, High Street, Kingston upon Thames KT1 1EU ☎ 020 8547 5933 ✉ viv.evans@kingston.gov.uk

Procurement: Mr Chris Morgan , Capability Lead - Commissioning, Guildhall 1, High Street, Kingston upon Thames KT1 1EU ☎ 020 8547 5300 ✉ chris.morgan@rbk.kingston.gov.uk

Public Libraries: Mrs Vivienne Bennett , Head of Culture, Guildhall 2, Kingston upon Thames KT1 1EU ☎ 020 8547 5267 🖷 020 8547 5213 ✉ vivienne.bennett@kingston.gov.uk

Public Libraries: Ms Grace McElwee , Strategic Manager of Libraries & Heritage Services, Kingston Library, Fairfield Road, Kingston upon Thames KT1 2PS ☎ 020 8547 6423 🖷 020 8547 6426 ✉ grace.mcelwee@rbk.kingston.gov.uk

Recycling & Waste Minimisation: Mrs Shifa Mustafa , Interim Head of Environment, Guildhall 2, High Street, Kingston upon Thames KT1 1EU ☎ 020 8547 4705 ✉ shifa.mustafa@kingston.gov.uk

Road Safety: Mr Mehmet Mazhar , Interim Service Manager - Traffic Management & Design, Guildhall 2, High Street, Kingston upon Thames KT1 1EU ☎ 020 8547 5943 ✉ mehmet.mazhar@kingston.gov.uk

Social Services: Ms Sue Redmond , Interim Director - Adult Services, Guildhall 2, High Street, Kingston upon Thames KT1 1EU ☎ 020 8547 6000 🖷 020 8547 6086 ✉ sue.redmond@kingston.gov.uk

Social Services (Adult): Ms Sue Redmond , Interim Director - Adult Services, Guildhall 2, High Street, Kingston upon Thames KT1 1EU ☎ 020 8547 6000 🖷 020 8547 6086 ✉ sue.redmond@kingston.gov.uk

Public Health: Dr Jonathan Hildebrand , Director - Public Health, Guildhall 1, High Street, Kingston upon Thames KT1 1EU ☎ 020 8547 6800 ✉ jonathan.hildebrand@rbk.kingston.gov.uk

Staff Training: Mrs Sheila West, Executive Head - Organisational Development & Strategic Business, Guildhall 2, Kingston upon Thames KT1 1EU ☎ 020 8547 5153 🖷 020 8547 5188 ✉ sheila.west@rbk.kingston.gov.uk

Street Scene: Mr Dalton Cenac , Service Manager - Street Scene, Guildhamm 2, High Street, Kingston upon Thames KT1 1EU ☎ 020 8547 5895 ✉ dalton.cenac@kingston.gov.uk

Sustainable Communities: Ms Paula Tribe , Relationship Manager - Place, Guildhall, High Street, Kingston upon Thames KT1 1EU ☎ 020 8547 5421 ✉ paula.tribe@kingston.gov.uk

Town Centre: Ms Ros Morgan , Kingston Town Centre Manager, 3rd Floor, Neville House, 55 Eden Street, Kingston upon Thames KT1 1EU ☎ 020 8547 1221

Traffic Management: Mr Mehmet Mazhar , Interim Service Manager - Traffic Management & Design, Guildhall 2, High Street, Kingston upon Thames KT1 1EU ☎ 020 8547 5943 ✉ mehmet.mazhar@kingston.gov.uk

Waste Collection and Disposal: Mrs Shifa Mustafa , Interim Head of Environment, Guildhall 2, High Street, Kingston upon Thames KT1 1EU ☎ 020 8547 4705 ✉ shifa.mustafa@kingston.gov.uk

COUNCILLORS

***Mayor* Arora**, Roy (CON - Coombe Vale)
roy.arora@kingston.gov.uk

***Deputy Mayor* Clark**, Mary (CON - Old Malden)
mary.clark@kingston.gov.uk

***Leader of the Council* Davis**, Kevin (CON - Old Malden)
kevin.davis@kingston.gov.uk

***Deputy Leader of the Council* Wallooppillai**, Gaj (CON - Coombe Hill)
gaj.wallooppillai@councillors.kingston.gov.uk

***Group Leader* Cottington**, Linsey (LAB - Norbiton)
linsey.cottington@kingston.gov.uk

***Group Leader* Green**, Elizabeth (LD - St Marks)
liz.green@councillors.kingston.gov.uk

Abraham, Sushila (LD - Berrylands)
sushila.abraham@councillors.kingston.gov.uk

Austin, Geoff (CON - Canbury)
geoffrey.Austin@councillors.kingston.gov.uk

Ayles, John (LD - Surbiton Hill)
john.ayles@councillors.kingston.gov.uk

Bamford, Patricia (LD - Chessington South)
patricia.bamford@councillors.kingston.gov.uk

Bass, Rowena (CON - Coombe Hill)
rowena.bass@kingston.gov.uk

Bedforth, Paul (CON - Beverley)
paul.bedforth@kingston.gov.uk

Brisbane, Bill (LD - Norbiton)
bill.brisbane@kingston.gov.uk

Chase, Clive (LD - Chessington North and Hook)
clive.chase@kingston.gov.uk

Cheetham, Jack (CON - St James)
jack.cheetham@kingston.gov.uk

Craig, Andrea (CON - Canbury)
andrea.craig@councillors.kingston.gov.uk

Cunningham, David (CON - Tudor)
david.cunningham@councillors.kingston.gov.uk

Davies, Tom (LD - Tolworth & Hook Rise)
tom.davies@kingston.gov.uk

Day, Andrew (CON - Chessington North and Hook)
andrew.day@councillors.kingston.gov.uk

Doyle, Phil (CON - Grove)
phil.doyle@kingston.gov.uk

Fraser, David (CON - Old Malden)
david.fraser@councillors.kingston.gov.uk

Gander, Hilary (LD - Surbiton Hill)
hilary.gander@kingston.gov.uk

George, Ian (CON - Alexandra)
ian.george@kingston.gov.uk

Glasspool, David (CON - Canbury)
david.glasspool@kingston.gov.uk

Griffin, Sheila (LAB - Norbiton)
sheila.griffin@kingston.gov.uk

Hayes, Chris (CON - Alexandra)
chris.hayes@kingston.gov.uk

Head, Mike (CON - Berrylands)
mike.head@kingston.gov.uk

Hudson, Richard (CON - Alexandra)
richard.hudson@councillors.kingston.gov.uk

Humphrey, Eric (CON - Coombe Hill)
eric.humphrey@councillors.kingston.gov.uk

Johnson, Andy (CON - Berrylands)
andy.johnson@kingston.gov.uk

Mirza, Shiraz (LD - Chessington South)
shiraz.mirza@councillors.kingston.gov.uk

Moll, Rebekah (LD - Grove)
rebekah.moll@kingston.gov.uk

Netley, Maria (CON - Tudor)
maria.netley@kingston.gov.uk

Pandya, Raju (CON - Beverley)
raju.pandya@kingston.gov.uk

Patel, Priyen (CON - St James's)
priyen.patel@councillors.kingston.gov.uk

Paton, Terry (CON - Beverley)
terry.paton@councillors.kingston.gov.uk

Pickering, Julie (CON - Coombe Vale)
julie.pickering@councillors.kingston.gov.uk

Reid, Rachel (LD - Chessington South)
rachel.reid@councillors.kingston.gov.uk

Roberts, Cathy (CON - Coombe Vale)
cathy.roberts@kingston.gov.uk

Rolfe, Lorraine (LD - Tolworth and Hook Rise)
lorraine.rolfe@kingston.gov.uk

Scantlebury, Hugh (CON - Tudor)
hugh.scantlebury@kingston.gov.uk

Self, Malcolm (LD - Surbiton Hill)
malcolm.self@councillors.kingston.gov.uk

Smith, Ken (CON - St James's)
ken.smith@councillors.kingston.gov.uk

Thayalan, Thay (LD - Tolworth and Hook Rise)
thay.thayalan@kingston.gov.uk

Thompson, Margaret (LD - Chessington North and Hook)
margaret.thompson@councillors.kingston.gov.uk

White, Diane (LD - St Marks)
diane.white@kingston.gov.uk

Yoganathan, Yogan (LD - St Marks)
yogan.yoganathan@councillors.kingston.gov.uk

POLITICAL COMPOSITION

CON: 28, LD: 17, LAB: 2

COMMITTEE CHAIRS

Audit: Ms Rowena Bass

Development: Mr Richard Hudson

Health & Wellbeing: Mr Kevin Davis

Licensing: Mr Phil Doyle

Pensions: Mr Eric Humphrey

Policy & Finance: Mr Eric Humphrey

Kirklees M

Kirklees Metropolitan Council, Civic Centre 3, Market Street, Huddersfield HD1 1WG
☎ 01484 221000 🖷 01484 221777
performance.communication@kirklees.gov.uk
www.kirklees.gov.uk

FACTS AND FIGURES

Parliamentary Constituencies: Batley and Spen, Colne Valley, Dewsbury, Huddersfield, Wakefield
EU Constituencies: Yorkshire and the Humber
Election Frequency: Elections are by thirds

PRINCIPAL OFFICERS

Chief Executive: Mr Adrian Lythgo , Chief Executive, 1st Floor, Civic Centre 3, Market Street, Huddersfield HD1 2TG ☎ 01484 221000 🖷 01484 221065 adrian.lythgo@kirklees.gov.uk

Senior Management: Ms Jacqui Gedman, Director - Place, Civic Centre 3, Market Street, Huddersfield HD1 1WG ☎ 01484 221000 🖷 01484 221645 jacqui.gedman@kirklees.gov.uk

Senior Management: Mrs Alison O'Sullivan, Director - Children & Adults, Ground Floor, Civic Centre 1, High Street, Huddersfield HD1 2NF ☎ 01484 221000 🖷 01484 225237 alison.o'sullivan@kirklees.gov.uk

Senior Management: Ms Ruth Redfern , Director - Communities, Transformation & Change, Civic Centre 3, Market Street, Huddersfield HD1 1WG

Senior Management: Mr David Smith , Director - Resources, Civic Centre 3, Market Street, Huddersfield HD1 1WG ☎ 01484 221000 david.smith@kirklees.gov.uk

Senior Management: Ms Rachel Spencer-Henshall , Director - Public Health, Civic Centre 3, Market Street, Huddersfield HD1 1WG rachael.spencer-henshall@kirklees.gov.uk

Catering Services: Ms Annette Bird , Schools FM Manager, Civic Centre 3, Market Street, Huddersfield HD1 1WG ☎ 01484 221000 annette.bird@kirklees.gov.uk

Civil Registration: Ms Lesley Hewitson , Superintendent Registrar, Register Office, Wellington Street, Dewsbury WF13 1LY ☎ 01924 324880

PR / Communications: Mr Alun Ireland , Publicity & Media Manager, Civic Centre 3, Market Street, Huddersfield HD1 1WG ☎ 01484 221000

Community Safety: Ms Carol Gilchrist , Head of Safe & Cohesive Communities, Civic Centre 3, Market Street, Huddersfield HD1 1WG ☎ 01484 221000 carol.gilchrist@kirklees.gov.uk

Computer Management: Mr Andy Bramall , Head of IT, Civic Centre 3, Market Street, Huddersfield HD1 1WG ☎ 01484 221000 andy.bramall@kirklees.gov.uk

Consumer Protection and Trading Standards: Mr Graham Hebblethwaite, Chief Officer, West Yorkshire Joint Services, West Yorkshire Joint Services, PO Box 5, Nepshaw Lane South, Morley LS27 0QP ☎ 0113 253 0241

Contracts: Mr Keith Smith , Assistant Director - Personalisation & Commissioning, Gateway to Care, 3rd Floor, Market Street, Huddersfield HD1 2HG ☎ 01484 221000 keith.smith@kirklees.gov.uk

Corporate Services: Ms Julie Fothergill , Policy Unit Manager, Civic Centre 3, Market Street, Huddersfield HD1 1WG ☎ 01484 221783 julie.fothergill@kirklees.gov.uk

Corporate Services: Mr John Heneghan , Policy Unit Manager, Civic Centre 3, Market Street, Huddersfield HD1 1WG ☎ 01484 221779 john.henegham@kirklees.gov.uk

Customer Service: Ms Jane Brady , Assistant Director - Resources, Civic Centre 1, High Street, Huddersfield HD1 2NF ☎ 01484 221000 jane.brady@kirklees.gov.uk

Electoral Registration: Ms Susan Hutson, Electoral Services Manager, 49-51 Huddersfield Road, Holmfirth HD9 3ER ☎ 01484 222403 🖷 01484 222450 susan.hutson@kirklees.gov.uk

Emergency Planning: Mr Sean Westerby, Corporate Safety / Resilience Team Manager, Emergency Planning, Kirkgate Buildings, Byram Street, Huddersfield HD1 1BY ☎ 01484 226414 🖷 01484 224883 sean.westerby@kirklees.gov.uk

Environmental / Technical Services: Mr Rob Dalby , Environmental Protection Manager, Flint Street, Fartown, Huddersfield HD1 6LG ☎ 01484 226403 🖷 01484 226409 rob.dalby@kirkless.gov.uk

Environmental Health: Mr Rob Dalby , Environmental Protection Manager, Flint Street, Fartown, Huddersfield HD1 6LG ☎ 01484 226403 🖷 01484 226409 rob.dalby@kirkless.gov.uk

Estates, Property & Valuation: Ms Joanne Bartholomew, Assistant Director - Physical Resources & Procurement, Design & Property Service, Kirkgate Buildings, Byram street, Huddersfield HD1 4SA ☎ 01484 226052 joanne.bartholomew@kirklees.gov.uk

European Liaison: Mr Chris Rowe , Policy Officer, Civic Centre 3, Market Street, Huddersfield HD1 1WG ☎ 01484 221000 chris.rowe@kirklees.gov.uk

Facilities: Ms Joanne Bartholomew, Assistant Director - Physical Resources & Procurement, Design & Property Service, Kirkgate Buildings, Byram street, Huddersfield HD1 4SA ☎ 01484 226052 joanne.bartholomew@kirklees.gov.uk

Fleet Management: Mr Darren Fletcher , Fleet Manager, Civic Centre 3, Market Street, Huddersfield HD1 1WG ☎ 01484 221000 darren.fletcher@kirklees.gov.uk

Grounds Maintenance: Mr John Fletcher, Assistant Head of Service, Parks & Open Spaces, Culture & Leisure Services, The Stadium Business and Leisure Complex, Stadium Way, Huddersfield HD1 6PG ☎ 01484 221000 🖷 01484 234144 john.fletcher@kirklees.gov.uk

Highways: Ms Jacqui Gedman, Director - Place, E & T Highways & Transportation, Flint Street, Huddersfield HD1 6LG ☎ 01484 221000 🖷 01484 221645 jacqui.gedman@kirklees.gov.uk

Housing: Ms Kim Brear, Assistant Director - Streetscene & Housing, Civic Centre 1, 4th Floor South, High Street, Huddersfield HD1 2NF ☎ 01484 221487 🖷 01484 221250 kim.brear@kirklees.gov.uk

Local Area Agreement: Ms Julie Fothergill , Policy Unit Manager, Civic Centre 3, Market Street, Huddersfield HD1 1WG ☎ 01484 221783 julie.fothergill@kirklees.gov.uk

Legal: Ms Julie Muscroft , Assistant Director - Legal Governance & Monitoring, Civic Centre 3, Market Street, Huddersfield HD1 1WG ☎ 01484 221720 julie.muscroft@kirklees.gov.uk

Leisure and Cultural Services: Ms Kimiyo Rickett, Assistant Director of Communities & Leisure, The Stadium Business and Leisure Complex, Stadium Way, Huddersfield HD1 6PG ☎ 01484 234002 🖷 01484 234014 kimiyo.rickett@kirklees.gov.uk

Licensing: Ms Catherine Walter , Licensing Manager, Flint Street Depot, Flint Street, Fartown, Huddersfield HD1 6LG ☎ 01484 221000 catherine.walter@kirklees.gov.uk

Parking: Mr Neil Tootill , Operational Manager, Corporation Yard, Mayman Lane, Batley WF17 7TA ☎ 01484 222858 neil.tootill@kirklees.gov.uk

Personnel / HR: Ms Rosemary Gibson , Head of HR, Civic Centre 3, Market Street, Huddersfield HD1 1WG ☎ 01484 221000 rosemary.gibson@kirklees.gov.uk

Planning: Mr Paul Kemp , Assistant Director - Commissioning & Safeguarding Assurance, Ground Floor, Civic Centre 1, High Street, Huddersfield HD1 2NF ☎ 01484 221000 paul.kemp@kirklees.gov.uk

Planning: Mr Keith Smith , Assistant Director - Personalisation & Commissioning, Gateway to Care, 3rd Floor, Market Street, Huddersfield HD1 2HG ☎ 01484 221000 keith.smith@kirklees.gov.uk

Procurement: Ms Joanne Bartholomew, Assistant Director - Physical Resources & Procurement, Kirkgate Buildings, Byram Street, Huddersfield HD1 1BY ☎ 01484 226052 joanne.bartholomew@kirklees.gov.uk

Public Libraries: Ms Jane Brady , Assistant Director - Resources, Civic Centre 1, High Street, Huddersfield HD1 2NF ☎ 01484 221000 jane.brady@kirklees.gov.uk

Recycling & Waste Minimisation: Mr Dave McMahon, Environmental Projects Manager, Vine Street Depot, Leeds Road, Huddersfield HD1 6NT ☎ 01484 223116 🖷 01484 223155 dave.mcmahon@kirklees.gov.uk

Regeneration: Ms Jacqui Gedman, Director - Place, Civic Centre 3, Market Street, Huddersfield HD1 1WG ☎ 01484 221000 🖷 01484 221645 jacqui.gedman@kirklees.gov.uk

Road Safety: Ms Cath Bottomley , Unit Manager - Business Support, Flint Street, Fartown, Huddersfield HD1 6LG ☎ 01484 225552 cath.bottomley@kirklees.gov.uk

Social Services: Mr Paul Johnson, Assistant Director - Family Support & Protection Services, Ground Floor, Civic Centre 1, High Street, Huddersfield HD1 2NF ☎ 01484 225331 🖷 01484 225188 paul.johnson@kirklees.gov.uk

Social Services (Adult): Mr Keith Smith , Assistant Director - Personalisation & Commissioning, Gateway to Care, 3rd Floor, Market Street, Huddersfield HD1 2HG ☎ 01484 221000 keith.smith@kirklees.gov.uk

Social Services (Children): Mrs Alison O'Sullivan, Director - Children & Adults, Ground Floor, Civic Centre 1, High Street, Huddersfield HD1 2NF ☎ 01484 221000 🖷 01484 225237 alison.o'sullivan@kirklees.gov.uk

Public Health: Ms Rachel Spencer-Henshall , Director - Public Health, Civic Centre 3, Market Street, Huddersfield HD1 1WG rachael.spencer-henshall@kirklees.gov.uk

Street Scene: Ms Kim Brear, Assistant Director - Streetscene & Housing, Civic Centre 1, 4th Floor South, High Street, Huddersfield HD1 2NF ☎ 01484 221487 🖷 01484 221250 kim.brear@kirklees.gov.uk

Tourism: Ms Jess Newbould, Senior Tourism Officer, Economic Development Service, Civic Centre 3, Huddersfield HD1 2EY ☎ 01484 221675 jess.newbould@kirklees.gov.uk

Town Centre: Ms Jayne Pearson , Town Centre Manager, Queensgate Market, Princess Alexandra Walk, Huddersfield HD1 2SU ☎ 01484 223357 jayne.pearson@kirklees.gov.uk

Waste Collection and Disposal: Mr Will Acornley , Head of Waste, Recycling & Transport, Riverbank Court, Wakefield Road, Huddersfield HD5 9AA ☎ 01484 223146 🖷 01484 223155 will.acornley@kirklees.gov.uk

COUNCILLORS

***Mayor* Kane**, Paul (LAB - Dewsbury East)
paul.kane@kirklees.gov.uk

***Deputy Mayor* Dodds**, Jim (CON - Denby Dale)
jim.dodds@kirklees.gov.uk

***Leader of the Council* Sheard**, David (LAB - Heckmondwike)
david.sheard@kirklees.gov.uk

***Deputy Leader of the Council* Calvert**, Jean (LAB - Ashbrow)
jean.calvert@kirklees.gov.uk

KIRKLEES

***Group Leader* Light**, Robert (CON - Birstall and Birkenshaw)
robert.light@kirklees.gov.uk

***Group Leader* Turner**, Nicola (LD - Colne Valley)
nicola.turner@kirklees.gov.uk

Ahmed, Masood (LAB - Dewsbury South)
masoodg.ahmed@kirklees.gov.uk

Akhtar, Mahmood (LAB - Batley East)
mahmood.akhtar@kirklees.gov.uk

Allison, Karen (GRN - Newsome)
karen.allison@kirklees.gov.uk

Alvy, Simon (LAB - Liversedge and Gomersal)
simon.alvy@kirklees.gov.uk

Armer, Bill (CON - Kirkburton)
bill.armer@kirklees.gov.uk

Barraclough, Robert (GRN - Kirkburton)
robertw.barraclough@kirklees.gov.uk

Bellamy, Donna (CON - Colne Valley)
donna.bellamy@kirklees.gov.uk

Bolt, Martyn (CON - Mirfield)
martyn.bolt@kirklees.gov.uk

Burke, Cahal (LD - Lindley)
cahal.burke@kirklees.gov.uk

Cooper, Andrew (GRN - Newsome)
andrew.cooper@kirklees.gov.uk

Dad, Nosheen (LAB - Dewsbury South)
nosheen.dad@kirklees.gov.uk

Firth, Donald (CON - Holme Valley South)
donald.firth@kirklees.gov.uk

Firth, Eric (LAB - Dewsbury East)
eric.firth@kirklees.gov.uk

Greaves, Charles (IND - Holme Valley North)
charles.greaves@kirklees.gov.uk

Hall, Steve (LAB - Heckmondwike)
steve.hall@kirklees.gov.uk

Hall, David (CON - Liversedge and Gomersal)
david.hall@kirklees.gov.uk

Hemingway, Mark (CON - Lindley)
mark.hemingway@kirklees.gov.uk

Hill, Erin (LAB - Crosland Moor and Netherton)
erin.hill@kirklees.gov.uk

Holmes, Lisa (CON - Liversedge and Gomersal)
lisa.holmes@kirklees.gov.uk

Holroyd-Doveton, Edgar (IND - Holme Valley North)
edgar.holroyd-doveton@kirklees.gov.uk

Hughes, Judith (LAB - Almondbury)
judith.hughes@kirklees.gov.uk

Hussain, Mumtaz (LAB - Dewsbury West)
mumtaz.hussain@kirklees.gov.uk

Iredale, Christine (LD - Golcar)
christine.iredale@kirklees.gov.uk

Kendrick, Viv (LAB - Heckmondwike)
viv.kendrick@kirklees.gov.uk

Khan, Murarrat (LAB - Dalton)
mussarat.khan@kirklees.gov.uk

Lawson, John Craig (LD - Cleckheaton)
john.lawson@kirklees.gov.uk

Lees-Hamilton, Vivien (CON - Mirfield)
vivien.lees-hamilton@kirklees.gov.uk

Lowe, Gwen (LAB - Batley West)
gwen.lowe@kirklees.gov.uk

Lyons, Terry (IND - Holme Valley North)
terry.lyons@kirklees.gov.uk

Marchington, Andrew (LD - Golcar)
andrew.marchington@kirklees.gov.uk

Mather, Naheed (LAB - Dalton)
naheed.mather@kirklees.gov.uk

Mayet, Hanif (LAB - Batley East)
hanif.mayet@kirklees.gov.uk

McBride, Peter (LAB - Dalton)
peter.mcbride@kirklees.gov.uk

O'Donovan, Darren (LAB - Dewsbury West)
darren.odonovan@kirklees.gov.uk

O'Neill, Peter (LAB - Batley West)
peter.o'neill@kirklees.gov.uk

Palfreeman, Andrew (CON - Birstall and Birkenshaw)
andrew.palfreeman@kirklees.gov.uk

Pandor, Shabir (LAB - Batley West)
shabir.pandor@kirklees.gov.uk

Patel, Abdul (LAB - Dewsbury South)
abdul.patel@kirklees.gov.uk

Patrick, Nigel (CON - Holme Valley South)
nigel.patrick@kirklees.gov.uk

Pattison, Carole (LAB - Greenhead)
carole.pattison@kirklees.gov.uk

Pinnock, Amanda (LAB - Ashbrow)
amanda.pinnock@kirklees.gov.uk

Pinnock, Kath (LD - Cleckheaton)
kath.pinnock@kirklees.gov.uk

Pinnock, Andrew (LD - Cleckheaton)
andrew.pinnock@kirklees.gov.uk

Richards, Hilary (LAB - Golcar)
hilary.richards@kirklees.gov.uk

Ridgway, David (LD - Colne Valley)
david.ridgway@kirklees.gov.uk

Rowling, Karen (LAB - Dewsbury West)
karen.rowling@kirklees.gov.uk

Sarwar, Mohammad (LAB - Crosland Moor and Netherton)
mohammad.sarwar@kirklees.gov.uk

Scott, Phil (LD - Almondbury)
phil.scott@kirklees.gov.uk

Scott, Cathy (LAB - Dewsbury East)
cathy.scott@kirklees.gov.uk

Sims, Ken (CON - Holme Valley South)
kenneth.sims@kirklees.gov.uk

Smaje, Liz (CON - Birstall and Birkenshaw)
elizabeth.smaje@kirklees.gov.uk

Smith, Ken (LAB - Ashbrow)
ken.smith@kirklees.gov.uk

Sokhal, Mohan (LAB - Greenhead)
mohan.sokhal@kirklees.gov.uk

Stewart-Turner, Julie (GRN - Newsome)
julie.stewart-turner@kirklees.gov.uk

Stubley, Amanda (LAB - Batley East)
amanda.stubley@kirklees.gov.uk

Taylor, Kathleen (CON - Mirfield)
kath.taylor@kirklees.gov.uk

Taylor, John (CON - Kirkburton)
johnj.taylor@kirklees.gov.uk

Turner, Graham (LAB - Denby Dale)
graham.turner@kirklees.gov.uk

Ullah, Sheikh (LAB - Greenhead)
sheikh.ullah@kirklees.gov.uk

Walton, Molly (LAB - Crosland Moor and Netherton)
molly.walton@kirklees.gov.uk

Watson, Michael (CON - Denby Dale)
michael.watson@kirklees.gov.uk

Wilkinson, Linda (LD - Almondbury)
linda.wilkinson@kirklees.gov.uk

Wilson, Gemma (CON - Lindley)
gemma.wilson@kirklees.gov.uk

POLITICAL COMPOSITION

LAB: 34, CON: 18, LD: 10, GRN: 4, IND: 3

COMMITTEE CHAIRS

Health & Wellbeing: Ms Viv Kendrick

Licensing: Mr Ken Smith

Planning: Mr Steve Hall

Knowsley M

Knowsley Metropolitan Borough Council, Municipal Buildings, Archway Road, Huyton L36 9UX
☎ 0151 489 6000 🖷 0151 443 3507 🖳 www.knowsley.gov.uk

FACTS AND FIGURES

Parliamentary Constituencies: Garston and Halewood, Knowsley
EU Constituencies: North West
Election Frequency: Elections are by thirds

PRINCIPAL OFFICERS

Chief Executive: Mr Mike Harden, Chief Executive, PO Box 24, Municipal Buildings, Archway Road, Huyton L36 9UX ☎ 0151 443 3772 🖷 0151 443 3557 ✉ mike.harden@knowsley.gov.uk

Senior Management: Mr Matthew Ashton , Assistant Executive Director of Public Health & Wellbeing, Municipal Buildings, Archway Road, Huyton L36 9UX ☎ 0151 443 4844 ✉ matthew.ashton@knowsley.gov.uk

Architect, Building / Property Services: Mr Stuart Barnes , Head of Planning, PO Box 26, Municipal Buildings, Archway Road, Huyton L36 9FB ☎ 0151 443 2303 ✉ stuart.barnes@knowsley.gov.uk

Architect, Building / Property Services: Mr Ian Capper , Head of Property & Development, Municipal Buildings, Archway Road, Huyton L36 9UX ☎ 0151 443 2220 ✉ ian.capper@knowsley.gov.uk

Catering Services: Mr Jon Dyson , Head of Commercial Services, Yorkon Building, Archway Road, Huyton L36 9YX ☎ 0151 443 2407 🖷 01514 432467 ✉ jon.dyson@knowsley.gov.uk

Civil Registration: Ms Pauline Douglas , Superintendent Registrar, Council Offices, High Street, Prescot L34 3LH ☎ 0151 443 5299 ✉ pauline.douglas@knowsley.gov.uk

Community Safety: Ms Jemma Jones , Interim Senior Legal Advisor - Crime & Disorder, Yorkon Building, Archway Road, Huyton L36 9UX ☎ 0151 443 4683 ✉ jemma.jones@knowsley.gov.uk

Computer Management: Mr Andrew Garden , Head of IT, Civic Way, Westmoreland Road, Huyton L36 9GD ☎ 0151 443 3487 🖷 0151 4433814 ✉ andrew.garden@knowsley.gov.uk

Consumer Protection and Trading Standards: Mr Mike Leyden , Better Regulations & Compliance Manager, Yorkon Buildings, Archway Road, Huyton L36 9UX ☎ 0151 443 4744 ✉ mike.leyden@knowsley.gov.uk

Contracts: Ms Deborah Lee , Head of Exchequer Services, Kirkby Municipal Buildings, Cherryfield Drive, Kirkby L32 1TX ☎ 0151 443 4163 🖷 0151 443 5407 ✉ deborah.lee@knowsley.gov.uk

Corporate Services: Mrs Dawn Boyer , Head of Corporate Services, Nutgrove Villa, Westmorland Road, Huyton, Liverpool L36 6GA ☎ 0151 443 4165 ✉ dawn.boyer@knowsley.gov.uk

Customer Service: Mr Phil Aspinall , Head of Customer Services, Municipal Buildings, Archway Road, Huyton L36 9UX ☎ 0151 443 3378 ✉ phil.aspinall@knowsley.gov.uk

Economic Development: Mr Barry Fawcett , Head of Housing & Economic Development, Yorkon Building, Archway Road, Huyton L36 9UX ☎ 0151 443 2251 ✉ barry.fawcett@knowsley.gov.uk

Education: Ms Maria Taylor , Head of Schools & Educational Attainment, Municipal Buildings, Archway Road, Huyton L36 9UX ☎ 0151 443 5614 ✉ maria.taylor@knowsley.gov.uk

E-Government: Mr Andrew Garden , Head of IT, Civic Way, Westmoreland Road, Huyton L36 9GD ☎ 0151 443 3487 🖷 0151 4433814 ✉ andrew.garden@knowsley.gov.uk

Electoral Registration: Ms Cheryl Ryder, Elections Officer, Democratic Services, Municipal Buildings, Archway Road, Huyton L36 9UX ☎ 0151 489 6000 ✉ cheryl.ryder@knowsley.gov.uk

Emergency Planning: Mr Brian Toolan, Head of Risk & Resilience, Civic Way, Westmorland Road, Huyton L36 9GD ☎ 0151 443 3601 ✉ brian.toolan@knowsley.gov.uk

Energy Management: Mr John Burns , Energy Conservation Officer, Municipal Buildings, Archway Road, Huyton L36 9UX ☎ 0151 443 2201 ✉ john.burns@knowsley.gov.uk

KNOWSLEY

Environmental / Technical Services: Mr John Flaherty , Executive Director - Place, Municipal Buildings, Archway Road, Huyton L36 9UX ☎ 0151 443 2410 ✉ john.flaherty@knowsley.gov.uk

Environmental Health: Ms Tracy Dickinson, Head of Environmental Health & Consumer Protection, 2nd Floor, Yorkon Building, Archway Road, Huyton L36 9FB ☎ 0151 443 4732 🖷 0151 289 7488 ✉ tracy.dickinson@knowsley.gov.uk

Estates, Property & Valuation: Mr Ian Capper , Head of Property & Development, Municipal Buildings, Archway Road, Huyton L36 9UX ☎ 0151 443 2220 ✉ ian.capper@knowsley.gov.uk

Facilities: Mr Jon Dyson , Head of Commercial Services, Yorkon Building, Archway Road, Huyton L36 9YX ☎ 0151 443 2407 🖷 01514 432467 ✉ jon.dyson@knowsley.gov.uk

Finance: Mr James Duncan , Executive Director of Resources, PO Box 24, Municipal Buildings, Archway Road, Huyton L36 9YZ ☎ 0151 443 3407 ✉ james.duncan@knowsley.gov.uk

Fleet Management: Mrs Julie Mallon , Head of Streetscene, Fleet & Logistics Services, Municipal Buildings, Archway Road, Huyton L36 9UX ☎ 0151 443 2412 🖷 0151 443 2467 ✉ julie.mallon@knowsley.gov.uk

Fleet Management: Mr Andy Millar , Transportation, Road Safety & Travel Plans Manager, PO Box 26, Municipal Buildings, Archway Road, Huyton L36 9FB ☎ 0151 443 2235 ✉ andy.millar@knowsley.gov.uk

Grounds Maintenance: Ms Denise Best , Operations Manager (Streetscene), Stretton Way, Huyton L36 6JF ☎ 0151 443 2427 ✉ denise.best@knowsley.gov.uk

Highways: Mr Andy Millar , Transportation, Road Safety & Travel Plans Manager, Yorkon Building, Archway Way, Huyton L36 9FB ☎ 0151 443 2235 ✉ andy.millar@knowsley.gov.uk

Home Energy Conservation: Mr Dale Milburn , Assistant Executive Director of Economic Development, Yorkon Building, Archway Road, Huyton L36 9FB ☎ 0151 443 2290 ✉ dale.milburn@knowsley.gov.uk

Housing: Ms Lisa Harris , Assistant Executive Director of Regeneration & Housing, Yorkon Building, Archway Road, Huyton L36 9FB ☎ 0151 443 2377 ✉ lisa.harris@knowsley.gov.uk

Local Area Agreement: Mr Justin Thompson , Assistant Executive Director of Neghbourhoods, PO Box 21, Municipal Buildings, Archway Road, Huyton L36 9YU ☎ 0151 443 3397 ✉ justin.thompson@knowsley.gov.uk

Legal: Mr Mike Dearing , Head of Legal Services, PO Box 21, Municipal Buildings, Archway Road, Huyton L36 9YU ☎ 0151 443 3762 ✉ mike.dearing@knowsley.gov.uk

Leisure and Cultural Services: Mr Kevin Schofield , Head of Leisure & Provider Services, Municipal Buildings, Archway Road, Huyton L36 9UX ☎ 0151 443 3493 ✉ kevin.schofield@knowsley.gov.uk

Leisure and Cultural Services: Ms Paula Williams , Head of Culture & Libraries, Municipal Buildings, Archway Road, Huyton L36 9UX ☎ 0151 443 3468 ✉ paula.williams@knowsley.gov.uk

Licensing: Mr Alan Shone , Consumer Protection Manager, Yorkon Building, Archway Road, Huyton L36 9YU ☎ 0151 443 2798 🖷 0151 443 5438 ✉ alan.shone@knowsley.gov.uk

Lighting: Ms Michele Grey , Street Lighting Co-ordinator, PO Box 26, Municipal Buildings, Archway Road, Huyton L36 9FB ☎ 0151 443 3170 ✉ michele.grey@knowlsey.gov.uk

Member Services: Ms Yvonne Ledgerton, Assistant Executive Director of Governance, PO Box 21, Municipal Buildings, Archway Road, Huyton L36 9UX ☎ 0151 443 3609 🖷 0151 482 1262 ✉ yvonne.ledgerton@knowsley.gov.uk

Parking: Mr Steve Myers , Town Centres Investment Manager, York Building, Archway Road, Huyton L36 9FB ☎ 0151 443 2298 ✉ steve.myers@knowsley.gov.uk

Partnerships: Mr Justin Thompson , Service Director - Neighbourhoods, Yorkon Building, Archway Road, Huyton L36 9YU ☎ 0151 443 3397 🖷 0151 4433030 ✉ justin.thompson@knowsley.gov.uk

Personnel / HR: Mr Dave Turner , Head of Human Resources, Civic Way, Westmorland Road, Huyton L36 9GD ☎ 0151 443 2951 ✉ dave.turner@knowsley.gov.uk

Planning: Mr Stuart Barnes , Head of Planning, PO Box 26, Municipal Buildings, Archway Road, Huyton L36 9FB ☎ 0151 443 2303 ✉ stuart.barnes@knowsley.gov.uk

Procurement: Mr Liam Power , Procurement Manager, Municipal Buildings, Archway Road, Huyton L36 9UX ☎ 0151 443 4169 ✉ laim.power@knowsley.gov.uk

Public Libraries: Ms Paula Williams , Head of Culture & Libraries, Municipal Buildings, Archway Road, Huyton L36 9UX ☎ 0151 443 3468 ✉ paula.williams@knowsley.gov.uk

Recycling & Waste Minimisation: Mr Jon Dyson , Head of Commercial Services, Yorkon Buildings, Archway Road, Huyton L36 9YU ☎ 0151 443 2407 🖷 01514 432467 ✉ jon.dyson@knowsley.gov.uk

Regeneration: Ms Lisa Harris , Assistant Executive Director of Regeneration & Housing, Yorkon Building, Archway Road, Huyton L36 9FB ☎ 0151 443 2377 ✉ lisa.harris@knowsley.gov.uk

Road Safety: Mr Andy Millar , Transportation, Road Safety & Travel Plans Manager, PO Box 26, Municipal Buildings, Archway Road, Huyton L36 9FB ☎ 0151 443 2235 ✉ andy.millar@knowsley.gov.uk

Social Services (Adult): Ms Julie Moss , Assistant Executive Director of Adult Social Care, Municipal Buildings, Archway Road, Huyton L36 9UX ☎ 0151 443 4486 ✉ julie.moss@knowsley.gov.uk

Social Services (Children): Mr Peter Murphy , Assistant Executive Director of Children's Social Care, Municipal Buildings, Archway Road, Huyton L36 9UX ☎ 0151 443 3024 ✉ peter.murphy@knowsley.gov.uk

Public Health: Mr Matthew Ashton , Assistant Executive Director of Public Health & Wellbeing, Municipal Buildings, Archway Road, Huyton L36 9UX ☎ 0151 443 4844 ✉ matthew.ashton@knowsley.gov.uk

Street Scene: Mrs Julie Mallon , Head of Streetscene, Fleet & Logistics Services, Municipal Buildings, Archway Road, Huyton L36 9UX ☎ 0151 443 2412 🖷 0151 443 2467 ✉ julie.mallon@knowsley.gov.uk

Sustainable Development: Mr Rupert Casey , Head of Sustainable Resources, Stretton Way, Archway Road, Huyton L36 6JF ☎ 0151 443 2411 ✉ rupert.casey@knowsley.gov.uk

Town Centre: Ms Lisa Harris , Assistant Executive Director of Regeneration & Housing, Yorkon Building, Archway Road, Huyton L36 9FB ☎ 0151 443 2377 ✉ lisa.harris@knowsley.gov.uk

Traffic Management: Mr Sean Traynor , Head of Highways & Traffic, Municipal Buildings, Archway Road, Huyton L36 9UX ☎ 0151 443 2332 ✉ sean.traynor@knowsley.gov.uk

Transport: Mr Andy Millar , Transportation, Road Safety & Travel Plans Manager, PO Box 26, Municipal Buildings, Archway Road, Huyton L36 9FB ☎ 0151 443 2235 ✉ andy.millar@knowsley.gov.uk

Waste Management: Mr Jon Dyson , Head of Commercial Services, Yorkon Building, Archway Road, Huyton L36 9YU ☎ 0151 443 2407 🖷 01514 432467 ✉ jon.dyson@knowsley.gov.uk

COUNCILLORS

Leader of the Council **Moorhead**, Andy (LAB - St Bartholomew's)
andy.moorhead@knowsley.gov.uk

Allen, Denise (LAB - Prescot East)
denise.allen@knowsley.gov.uk

Arnall, Del (LAB - Park)
del.arnall@knowsley.gov.uk

Aston, Jayne (LAB - Cherryfield)
jayne.aston@knowsley.gov.uk

Bannon, Christine (LAB - Roby)
christine.bannon@knowsley.gov.uk

Baum, Dennis (LAB - Stockbridge)
dennis.baum@knowsley.gov.uk

Boland, Peter (LAB - St Gabriel's)
peter.boland@knowsley.gov.uk

Brennan, Bill (LAB - Kirby Central)
bill.brennan@knowsley.gov.uk

Brennan, Tony (LAB - Shelvington)
tony.brennan@knowsley.gov.uk

Byron, Terry (LAB - Whiston South)
terry.byron@knowsley.gov.uk

Connor, Edward (LAB - Northwood)
eddie.connor@knowsley.gov.uk

Cunningham, Tony (LAB - St Bartholomew's)
tony.cunningham@knowsley.gov.uk

Dobbie, Dave (LAB - Park)
dave.dobbie@knowsley.gov.uk

Donnelly, John (LAB - Stockbridge)
john.donnelly@knowsley.gov.uk

Finneran, Edna (LAB - Halewood North)
edna.finneran@knowsley.gov.uk

Flanders, Adam (LAB - Prescot West)
adam.flanders@knowsley.gov.uk

Flatley, Gillian (LAB - Prescot East)
gillian.flatley@knowsley.gov.uk

Flute, Alan John (LAB - Halewood West)
alan.flute@knowlsey.gov.uk

Gaffney, Ron (LAB - Whiston North)
ron.gaffney@knowsley.gov.uk

Gaffney, Sandra (LAB - Whiston North)
sandra.gaffney@knowsley.gov.uk

Garland, Terence (LAB - Northwood)
terence.garland@knowsley.gov.uk

Grannell, Ted (LAB - Cherryfield)
ted.grannell@knowsley.gov.uk

Greer, John (LAB - Park)
john.greer@knowsley.gov.uk

Halpin, Ray (LAB - Shevington)
ray.halpin@knowsley.gov.uk

Harris, Jackie (LAB - Kirkby Central)
jackie.harris@knowsley.gov.uk

Harris, Tina (LAB - Halewood South)
tina.harris@knowsley.gov.uk

Harvey, Margaret (LAB - Roby)
margaret.harvey@knowsley.gov.uk

Harvey, Tony (LAB - Longview)
tony.harvey@knowsley.gov.uk

Harvey, Allan (LAB - Halewood South)
allan.harvey@knowsley.gov.uk

Hogg, Norman (LAB - Halewood West)
norman.hogg@knowsley.gov.uk

Kearns, Mike (LAB - Prescot West)
mike.kearns@knowsley.gov.uk

Keats, Jean (LAB - Whitefield)
jean.keats@knowsley.gov.uk

Keats, Norman (LAB - Whitefield)
norman.keats@knowsley.gov.uk

Kelly, Pauline (LAB - Whiston North)
pauline.kelly@knowsley.gov.uk

Lamb, Victoria (LAB - St Michael's)
vickie.lamb@knowsley.gov.uk

Lee, Samuel (LAB - Longview)
sammy.lee@knowsley.gov.uk

Lilly, Joan (LAB - St Michael's)
joan.lilly@knowsley.gov.uk

Lonergan, David (LAB - Cherryfield)
david.lonergan@knowsley.gov.uk

KNOWSLEY

Maguire, Bob (LAB - Swanside)
bob.maguire@knowsley.gov.uk

McGlashan, Ken (LAB - Page Moss)
ken.mcglashan@knowsley.gov.uk

McNeill, Veronica (LAB - Page Moss)
veronica.mcneill@knowsley.gov.uk

Moorhead, Kay (LAB - St Michael's)
kay.moorhead@knowsley.gov.uk

Morgan, Graham (LAB - Roby)
graham.morgan@knowsley.gov.uk

Murphy, Michael (LAB - Northwood)
michael.murphy@knowsley.gov.uk

Newman, Tony (LAB - Whiston South)
tony.newman@knowsley.gov.uk

O'Hare, Brian (LAB - St Gabriel's)
brian.o'hare@knowsley.gov.uk

O'Hare, Christina (LAB - St Bartholomew's)
christine.ohare@knowsley.gov.uk

O'Keeffe, Steff (LAB - Prescot East)
steff.o'keefe@knowsley.gov.uk

O'Keeffe, Lynn (LAB - Prescot West)
lynn.o'keefe@knowsley.gov.uk

O'Mara, Margi (LAB - Longview)
margi.o'mara@knowsley.gov.uk

Powell, Terry (LAB - Halewood North)
terry.powell@knowsley.gov.uk

Powell, Shelley (LAB - Halewood North)
shelley.powell@knowsley.gov.uk

Round, Ron (LAB - Swanside)
ron.round@knowsley.gov.uk

See, Gary (LAB - Halewood South)
gary.see@knowsley.gov.uk

Sharp, Malcolm (LAB - Shevington)
malcolm.sharp@knowsley.gov.uk

Smith, Ros (LAB - Whitefield)
ros.smith@knowsley.gov.uk

Stuart, Marie (LAB - Kirkby Central)
marie.stuart@knowsley.gov.uk

Swann, Bob (LAB - Halewood West)
bob.swann@knowsley.gov.uk

Tully, Dave (LAB - Page Moss)
dave.tully@knowsley.gov.uk

Walsh, Frank (LD - St Gabriel's)
frank.walsh@knowsley.gov.uk

Weightman, Bill (LAB - Stockbridge)
bill.weightman@knowsley.gov.uk

Williams, David (LAB - Whiston South)
david.williams@knowsley.gov.uk

Wright, Graham (LAB - Swanside)
graham.wright@knowsley.gov.uk

POLITICAL COMPOSITION
LAB: 62, LD: 1

COMMITTEE CHAIRS

Adults & Childrens Wellbeing: Ms Del Arnall

Audit: Mrs Pauline Kelly

Finance: Mr Terry Byron

Licensing: Ms Lynn O'Keeffe

Planning: Ms Margaret Harvey

Lambeth L

London Borough of Lambeth, Lambeth Town Hall, Brixton Hill, London SW2 1RW
☎ 020 7926 1000 💻 www.lambeth.gov.uk

FACTS AND FIGURES
Parliamentary Constituencies: Dulwich and West Norwood, Streatham, Vauxhall
EU Constituencies: London
Election Frequency: Elections are of whole council

PRINCIPAL OFFICERS

Chief Executive: Mr Sean Harriss , Chief Executive, Lambeth Town Hall, Brixton Hill, London SW2 1RW ☎ 020 7926 1000 🖱 sharriss@lambeth.gov.uk

Senior Management: Ms Jackie Belton , Strategic Director - Corporate Resources, Lambeth Town Hall, Brixton Hill, London SW2 1RW ☎ 020 7926 9673 🖱 jbelton@lambeth.gov.uk

Senior Management: Ms Helen Charlesworth , Strategic Director - Children, Adults & Health, Phoenix House, 40 Wandsworth Road, London SW8 2LL ☎ 020 7926 1000 🖱 hcharlesworth@lambeth.gov.uk

Senior Management: Ms Sue Foster , Strategic Director - Delivery, Hambrook House, Porden Road, London SW2 5RW ☎ 020 7926 3426 🖱 sfoster1@lambeth.gov.uk

Senior Management: Dr Ruth Wallis , Director - Public Health, 160 Tooley Street, London SE1 2QH 🖱 ruth.wallis@southwark.gov.uk

Access Officer / Social Services (Disability): Mr Dominic Stanton, Assistant Director - Adult Social Care, 6th Floor, Phoenix House, 10 Wandsworth Road, London SW8 2LL ☎ 020 7926 4515 🖱 dstanton@lambeth.gov.uk

PR / Communications: Mr Julian Ellerby , Divisional Director - Campaigns & Communications, Lambeth Town Hall, Brixton Hill, London SW2 1RW ☎ 020 7926 1273 🖷 020 7926 2839 🖱 jellerby@lambeth.gov.uk

Community Planning: Mr David Joyce , Assistant Director - Planning & Development, Phoenix House, 10 Wandsworth Road, London SW8 2LL ☎ 020 7926 1109 🖱 djoyce@lambeth.gov.uk

Community Safety: Ms Ann Corbett , Assistant Director - Community Safety, 205 Stockwell Road, Brixton, London SW9 9SL ☎ 020 7926 2898 🖱 acorbett@lambeth.gov.uk

Consumer Protection and Trading Standards: Mr Robert Gardner, Head of Trading Standards, 2 Herne Hill Road, Brixton Hill, London SE24 0AU ☎ 020 7926 6122

Electoral Registration: Mr Jamie Baker , Electoral & Civic Services Manager, Lambeth Town Hall, Brixton Hill, London SW2 1RW ☎ 020 7926 2307 ✉ jbaker1@lambeth.gov.uk

Emergency Planning: Mr Jo Couzens , Emergency Response Planning Officer, Lambeth Town Hall, Brixton Hill, London SW2 1RW ☎ 020 7926 6162 🖷 020 7926 6150 ✉ jcouzens@lambeth.gov.uk

Environmental / Technical Services: Ms Sue Foster , Strategic Director - Delivery, Hambrook House, Porden Road, London SW2 5RW ☎ 020 7926 3426 ✉ sfoster1@lambeth.gov.uk

Estates, Property & Valuation: Mr Uzo Nwanze, Head of VAMS (Transformation), Lambeth Town Hall, Brixton Hill, London SW2 1RW ☎ 020 7926 9929 🖷 020 7926 9357 ✉ unwanze@lambeth.gov.uk

Pensions: Mrs Linda Osborne , Pensions Manager, Phoenix House, 10 Wandsworth Road, London SW8 2LL ☎ 020 7926 1000 ✉ losborne1@lambeth.gov.uk

Highways: Mr Raj Mistry , Head of Parking Services, 234 - 244 Stockwell Road, Brixton, London SW9 9SP ☎ 020 7926 6263 ✉ rmistry@lambeth.gov.uk

Housing: Ms Sue Foster , Strategic Director - Delivery, Hambrook House, Porden Road, London SW2 5RW ☎ 020 7926 3426 ✉ sfoster1@lambeth.gov.uk

Legal: Mr Mark Hynes, Director - Corporate Affairs, Lambeth Town Hall, Brixton Hill, London SW2 1RW ☎ 020 7926 2433

Member Services: Mr David Burn, Head - Democratic Services & Scrutiny, Lambeth Town Hall, Brixton Hill, London SW2 1RW ☎ 020 7926 2186 🖷 020 7929 2755 ✉ dburn@lambeth.gov.uk

Parking: Mr Raj Mistry , Head of Parking Services, 234 - 244 Stockwell Road, Brixton, London SW9 9SP ☎ 020 7926 6263 ✉ rmistry@lambeth.gov.uk

Personnel / HR: Ms Nana Amoa-Buahin, Divisional Director - HR & OD, Phoenix House, 10 Wandsworth Road, London SW2 1RW ☎ 020 7926 0068 🖷 020 7926 9518 ✉ namoa-buahin@lambeth.gov.uk

Regeneration: Ms Sue Foster , Strategic Director - Delivery, Hambrook House, Porden Road, London SW2 5RW ☎ 020 7926 3426 ✉ sfoster1@lambeth.gov.uk

Public Health: Dr Ruth Wallis , Director - Public Health, 160 Tooley Street, London SE1 2QH ✉ ruth.wallis@southwark.gov.uk

Street Scene: Mr Raj Mistry , Head of Parking Services, 234 - 244 Stockwell Road, Brixton, London SW9 9SP ☎ 020 7926 6263 ✉ rmistry@lambeth.gov.uk

COUNCILLORS

***Mayor* Anyanwu**, Donatus (LAB - Coldharbour)
DAnyanwu@lambeth.gov.uk

***Deputy Mayor* Jaffer**, Saleha (LAB - St. Leonard's)
SJaffer@lambeth.gov.uk

***Leader of the Council* Peck**, Lib (LAB - Thornton)
lpeck@lambeth.gov.uk

***Deputy Leader of the Council* McGlone**, Paul (LAB - Ferndale)
pmcglone@lambeth.gov.uk

***Deputy Leader of the Council* Walker**, Imogen (LAB - Stockwell)
iwalker@lambeth.gov.uk

Adilypour, Danial (LAB - Streatham South)
DAdilypour@lambeth.gov.uk

Agdomar, Michelle (LAB - Herne Hill)
MAgdomar@lambeth.gov.uk

Ainslie, Scott (GRN - St. Leonard's)
streathamgreenparty@gmail.com

Aminu, Adedamola (LAB - Tulse Hill)
aaminu@lambeth.gov.uk

Amos, David (LAB - Prince's)
DAmos@lambeth.gov.uk

Atkins, Mary (LAB - Tulse Hill)
MAtkins@lambeth.gov.uk

Atkins, Liz (LAB - Streatham Hill)
LAtkins@lambeth.gov.uk

Bennett, Matthew (LAB - Gipsy Hill)
mpbennett@lambeth.gov.uk

Bigham, Alex (LAB - Stockwell)
abigham@lambeth.gov.uk

Birley, Anna (LAB - Thurlow Park)
ABirley@lambeth.gov.uk

Brathwaite, Jennifer (LAB - Gipsy Hill)
jbrathwaite@lambeth.gov.uk

Bray, Linda (LAB - Clapham Town)
LBray@lambeth.gov.uk

Briggs, Tim (CON - Clapham Common)
tbriggs@lambeth.gov.uk

Cameron, Marcia (LAB - Tulse Hill)
mcameron@lambeth.gov.uk

Chowdhury, Rezina (LAB - Streatham Hill)
RChowdhury@lambeth.gov.uk

Clark, Malcolm (LAB - Streatham Wells)
MClark@lambeth.gov.uk

Cowell, Fred (LAB - Thurlow Park)
FCowell@lambeth.gov.uk

Craig, Kevin (LAB - Bishop's)
kcraigh@lambeth.gov.uk

Davie, Edward (LAB - Thornton)
edavie@lambeth.gov.uk

de Cordova, Marsha (LAB - Larkhall)
MdeCordova@lambeth.gov.uk

Deckers Dowber, Max (LAB - Thurlow Park)
MDeckersdowber@lambeth.gov.uk

Dickson, Jim (LAB - Herne Hill)
jdickson@lambeth.gov.uk

Dyer, Jacqui (LAB - Vassall)
jdyer3@lambeth.gov.uk

Edbrooke, Jane (LAB - Oval)
jedbrooke@lambeth.gov.uk

Eshalomi, Florence (LAB - Brixton Hill)
FEshalomi@lambeth.gov.uk

Francis, Niranjan (LAB - Gipsy Hill)
nrfrancis@lambeth.gov.uk

Gadsby, Paul (LAB - Vassall)
PGadsby@lambeth.gov.uk

Gallop, Annie (LAB - Vassall)
AGallop@lambeth.gov.uk

Garden, Adrian (LAB - Brixton Hill)
agarden@lambeth.gov.uk

Gentry, Bernard (CON - Clapham Common)
BGentry@lambeth.gov.uk

Haselden, Nigel (LAB - Clapham Town)
nhaselden@lambeth.gov.uk

Heywood, Rachel (LAB - Coldharbour)
rheywood@lambeth.gov.uk

Hill, Robert (LAB - St. Leonard's)
RHill@lambeth.gov.uk

Holborn, Jack (LAB - Herne Hill)
JHolborn@lambeth.gov.uk

Holland, Claire (LAB - Oval)
CHolland@lambeth.gov.uk

Hopkins, Jack (LAB - Oval)
jhopkins@lambeth.gov.uk

Kazantzis, John (LAB - Streatham South)
JKazantzis@lambeth.gov.uk

Kind, Ben (LAB - Bishop's)
BKind@lambeth.gov.uk

McClure, Vaila (LAB - Prince's)
VMcClure@lambeth.gov.uk

Meldrum, Jackie (LAB - Knight's Hill)
jmeldrum@lambeth.gov.uk

Morris, Diana (LAB - Thornton)
dmmorris@lambeth.gov.uk

Mosley, Jennie (LAB - Bishop's)
JMosley@lambeth.gov.uk

Nathanson, Louise (CON - Clapham Common)
LNathanson@lambeth.gov.uk

Parr, Matt (LAB - Coldharbour)
mparr1@lambeth.gov.uk

Pickard, Jane (LAB - Knight's Hill)
jpickard@lambeth.gov.uk

Prentice, Sally (LAB - Ferndale)
SPrentice@lambeth.gov.uk

Rosa, Guilherme (LAB - Stockwell)
GRosa@lambeth.gov.uk

Sabharwal, Neil (LAB - Ferndale)
nsabharwal@lambeth.gov.uk

Seedat, Mohammed (LAB - Streatham Wells)
MSeedat@lambeth.gov.uk

Simpson, Iain (LAB - Streatham Hill)
ISimpson@lambeth.gov.uk

Simpson, Joanne (LAB - Prince's)
JSimpson2@lambeth.gov.uk

Tiedemann, Martin (LAB - Brixton Hill)
Mtiedemann@lambeth.gov.uk

Treppass, Amélie (LAB - Streatham Wells)
ATreppass@lambeth.gov.uk

Valcarcel, Christiana (LAB - Larkhall)
cvalcarcel@lambeth.gov.uk

Wellbelove, Christopher (LAB - Clapham Town)
cllrwellbelove@gmail.com

Wilcox, Clair (LAB - Streatham South)
CWilcox@lambeth.gov.uk

Wilson, Andrew (LAB - Larkhall)
AWilson5@lambeth.gov.uk

Winifred, Sonia (LAB - Knights Hill)
Swinifred@lambeth.gov.uk

POLITICAL COMPOSITION

LAB: 59, CON: 3, GRN: 1

COMMITTEE CHAIRS

Health & Wellbeing: Mr Jim Dickson

Licensing: Mr Adrian Garden

Licensing: Ms Michelle Agdomar

Planning: Mr Diana Morris

Lancashire C

Lancashire County Council, PO Box 78, County Hall, Preston PR1 8XJ
☎ 0845 053 0000 🖷 01722 533553 ✉ enquiries@lancashire.gov.uk
💻 www.lancashire.gov.uk

FACTS AND FIGURES

Parliamentary Constituencies: Burnley, Chorley, Fylde, Hyndburn, Morecambe and Lunesdale, Pendle, Preston, Ribble Valley, Rossendale and Darwen, South Ribble
EU Constituencies: North West
Election Frequency: Elections are of whole council

PRINCIPAL OFFICERS

Chief Executive: Ms Jo Turton , Chief Executive, PO Box 61, County Hall, Preston PR1 0LD ☎ 01772 536260
✉ jo.turton@lancashire.gov.uk

Assistant Chief Executive: Mr Steve Browne, Corporate Director - Commissioning & Deputy Chief Executive, PO Box 78, County Hall, Preston PR1 8XJ ☎ 01772 534121
✉ steve.browne@lancashire.gov.uk

Senior Management: Mr Phil Barrett , Director - Community Services, PO Box 78, County Hall, Preston PR1 8XJ
☎ 01772 538222 ✉ phil.barrett@lancashire.gov.uk

Senior Management: Mr George Graham , Director - Pension Fund, PO Box 78, County Hall, Preston PR1 8XJ ☎ 01772 538102
✉ george.graham@lancashire.gov.uk

Senior Management: Mr Mike Jenson , Chief Investment Officer, PO Box 78, County Hall, Preston PR1 8XJ ☎ 01772 534742 ✉ mike.jenson@lancashire.gov.uk

Senior Management: Dr Sakthi Karunanithi , Director - Public Health & Wellbeing, PO Box 78, County Hall, Preston PR1 8XJ ☎ 01772 536287 ✉ sakthi.karunanithi@lancashire.gov.uk

Senior Management: Mr Martin Kelly , Director - Economic Development, PO Box 78, County Hall, Preston PR1 8XJ ☎ 01772 536197 ✉ martin.kelly@lancashire.gov.uk

Senior Management: Mr Mike Kirby , Director - Corporate Commissioning, PO Box 78, County Hall, Preston PR1 8XJ ☎ 01772 534660 ✉ mike.kirby@lancashire.gov.uk

Senior Management: Ms Lisa Kitto , Director - Corporate Services, PO Box 78, County Hall, Preston PR1 8XJ ☎ 01772 534757 ✉ lisa.kitto@lancashire.gov.uk

Senior Management: Mr Damon Lawrenson , Director - Financial Resources, PO Box 78, County Hall, Preston PR1 8XJ ☎ 01772 534715 ✉ damon.lawrenson@lancashire.gov.uk

Senior Management: Mr Tony Pounder , Director - Adult Services, PO Box 78, County Hall, Preston PR1 8XJ ☎ 01772 531553 ✉ tony.pounder@lancashire.gov.uk

Senior Management: Ms Sue Procter , Director - Programmes & Project Management, PO Box 78, County Hall, Preston PR1 8XJ ☎ 01772 539493 ✉ sue.procter@lancashire.gov.uk

Senior Management: Ms Laura Sales , Director - Legal, Democratic & Governance, PO Box 78, County Hall, Preston PR1 8XJ ☎ 01772 533375 ✉ laura.sales@lancashire.gov.uk

Senior Management: Mr Bob Stott , Director - Children's Services, PO Box 78, County Hall, Preston PR1 8XJ ☎ 01772 531652 ✉ bob.stott@lancashire.gov.uk

Senior Management: Mr Eddie Sutton , Director - Development & Corporate Services, PO Box 78, County Hall, Preston PR1 8XJ ☎ 01772 533475 ✉ eddie.sutton@lancashire.gov.uk

Senior Management: Ms Louise Taylor , Corporate Director - Operations & Delivery, PO Box 78, County Hall, Preston PR1 8XJ ☎ 01772 534121 ✉ louise.taylor@lancashire.gov.uk

Senior Management: Mr Ian Young , Director - Governance, Finance & Public Services, PO Box 78, County Hall, Preston PR1 8XJ ☎ 01772 533531 ✉ ian.young@lancashire.gov.uk

Architect, Building / Property Services: Mr Shaun Capper , Head of Service - Design & Construction, Cuerdan Way, Bamber Bridge, Preston PR5 6BF ☎ 01772 530251 ✉ shaun.capper@lancashire.gov.uk

Children / Youth Services: Ms Diane Booth , Head of Service - Children's Social Care, PO Box 78, County Hall, Preston PR1 8XJ ☎ 01282 470129 ✉ diane.booth@lancashire.gov.uk

Children / Youth Services: Mr Bob Stott , Director - Children's Services, PO Box 78, County Hall, Preston PR1 8XJ ☎ 01772 531652 ✉ bob.stott@lancashire.gov.uk

Children / Youth Services: Ms Louise Taylor , Corporate Director - Operations & Delivery, PO Box 78, County Hall, Preston PR1 8XJ ☎ 01772 534121 ✉ louise.taylor@lancashire.gov.uk

Civil Registration: Ms Julie Bell , Head of Service - Libraries, Museums, Culture & Registrars, Park Hotel, East Cliff, Preston PR1 3EA ☎ 01772 536727 ✉ julie.bell@lancashire.gov.uk

PR / Communications: Mr Tim Seamans , Head of Service - Communications, Corporate Communications Group, County Hall, Preston PR1 8XJ ☎ 01772 530760 ✉ tim.seamans@lancashire.gov.uk

Community Planning: Mr Phil Barrett , Director - Community Services, PO Box 78, County Hall, Preston PR1 8XJ ☎ 01772 538222 ✉ phil.barrett@lancashire.gov.uk

Consumer Protection and Trading Standards: Mr Paul Noone, Assistant Director of Trading Standards Service, County Hall, Preston PR1 0LD ☎ 01772 534123 ✉ paul.noone@lancashire.gov.uk

Corporate Services: Ms Lisa Kitto , Director - Corporate Services, PO Box 78, County Hall, Preston PR1 8XJ ☎ 01772 534757 ✉ lisa.kitto@lancashire.gov.uk

Corporate Services: Ms Ruth Lowry , Head of Service - Internal Audit, PO Box 78, County Hall, Preston PR1 8XJ ☎ 01772 534898 ✉ ruth.lowry@lancashire.gov.uk

Corporate Services: Ms Sue Procter , Director - Programmes & Project Management, PO Box 78, County Hall, Preston PR1 8XJ ☎ 01772 539493 ✉ sue.procter@lancashire.gov.uk

Economic Development: Mr Martin Kelly , Director - Economic Development, PO Box 78, County Hall, Preston PR1 8XJ ☎ 01772 536197 ✉ martin.kelly@lancashire.gov.uk

Education: Mr Brendan Lee , Head of Service - Special Educational Needs & Disabilty, PO Box 78, County Hall, Preston PR1 8XJ ☎ 01772 538323 ✉ brendan.lee@lancashire.gov.uk

Emergency Planning: Mr Alan Wilton , Head of Service - Emergency Planning & Resilience, PO Box 78, County Hall, Preston PR1 8XJ ☎ 01772 537902 ✉ alan.wilton@lancashire.gov.uk

Environmental / Technical Services: Mr Andrew Mullaney, Head of Service - Planning & Environment, PO Box 78, County Hall, Preston PR1 8XJ ☎ 01772 534190 ✉ andrew.mullaney@lancashire.gov.uk

Environmental Health: Mr Paul Noone , Head of Service - Trading Standards & Scientific Services, PO Box 78, County Hall, Preston PR1 8XJ ☎ 01772 534123 ✉ steve.scott@lancashire.gov.uk

Estates, Property & Valuation: Mr Gary Pearse , Head of Service - Estates, PO Box 78, County Hall, Preston PR1 8XJ ☎ 01772 533903 ✉ gary.pearse@lancashire.gov.uk

LANCASHIRE

Finance: Mr Damon Lawrenson , Director - Financial Resources, PO Box 78, County Hall, Preston PR1 8XJ ☎ 01772 534715 ✉ damon.lawrenson@lancashire.gov.uk

Finance: Mr Ian Young , Director - Governance, Finance & Public Services, PO Box 78, County Hall, Preston PR1 8XJ ☎ 01772 533531 ✉ ian.young@lancashire.gov.uk

Pensions: Mr George Graham , Director - Pension Fund, PO Box 78, County Hall, Preston PR1 8XJ ☎ 01772 538102 ✉ george.graham@lancashire.gov.uk

Pensions: Mr Mike Jenson , Chief Investment Officer, PO Box 78, County Hall, Preston PR1 8XJ ☎ 01772 534742 ✉ mike.jenson@lancashire.gov.uk

Highways: Mr Shaun Capper , Head of Service - Design & Construction, Cuerdan Way, Bamber Bridge, Preston PR5 6BF ☎ 01772 530251 ✉ shaun.capper@lancashire.gov.uk

Highways: Mr Phil Durnell , Head of Service - Highways, PO Box 78, County Hall, Preston PR1 8XJ ☎ 01772 538502 ✉ phil.durnell@lancashire.gov.uk

Legal: Ms Laura Sales , Director - Legal, Democratic & Governance, PO Box 78, County Hall, Preston PR1 8XJ ☎ 01772 533375 ✉ laura.sales@lancashire.gov.uk

Leisure and Cultural Services: Ms Julie Bell , Head of Service - Libraries, Museums, Culture & Registrars, Park Hotel, East Cliff, Preston PR1 3EA ☎ 01772 536727 ✉ julie.bell@lancashire.gov.uk

Member Services: Ms Laura Sales , Director - Legal, Democratic & Governance, PO Box 78, County Hall, Preston PR1 8XJ ☎ 01772 533375 ✉ laura.sales@lancashire.gov.uk

Member Services: Mr Ian Young , Director - Governance, Finance & Public Services, PO Box 78, County Hall, Preston PR1 8XJ ☎ 01772 533531 ✉ ian.young@lancashire.gov.uk

Personnel / HR: Ms Deborah Barrow , Head of Service - Human Resources, PO Box 78, County Hall, Preston PR1 8XJ ☎ 01772 535805 ✉ deborah.burrows@lancashire.gov.uk

Planning: Mr Andrew Mullaney , Head of Service - Planning & Environment, PO Box 78, County Hall, Preston PR1 8XJ ☎ 01772 534190 ✉ andrew.mullaney@lancashire.gov.uk

Public Libraries: Ms Julie Bell , Head of Service - Libraries, Museums, Culture & Registrars, Park Hotel, East Cliff, Preston PR1 3EA ☎ 01772 536727 ✉ julie.bell@lancashire.gov.uk

Recycling & Waste Minimisation: Ms Sue Procter, Assistant Director of Environmental Services (Area East), LCC Highways Office, Highways Depot, Willows Lane, Accrington BB5 0RT ☎ 01254 770985 ✉ susan.procter@lancashire.gov.uk

Recycling & Waste Minimisation: Mr Steve Scott , Head of Service - Trading Standards & Scientific Services, PO Box 78, County Hall, Preston PR1 8XJ ☎ 01772 533755 ✉ steve.scott@lancashire.gov.uk

Social Services: Mr Brendan Lee , Head of Service - Special Educational Needs & Disabilty, PO Box 78, County Hall, Preston PR1 8XJ ☎ 01772 538323 ✉ brendan.lee@lancashire.gov.uk

Social Services: Ms Catherine Whalley , Head of Service - Social Care, PO Box 78, County Hall, Preston PR1 8XJ ☎ 07816 971177 ✉ catherine.whalley@lancashire.gov.uk

Social Services (Adult): Mr Tony Pounder , Director - Adult Services, PO Box 78, County Hall, Preston PR1 8XJ ☎ 01772 531553 ✉ tony.pounder@lancashire.gov.uk

Social Services (Adult): Ms Liz Wilde , Head of Service - Older People, PO Box 78, County Hall, Preston PR1 8XJ ☎ 07887 831031 ✉ liz.wilde@lancashire.gov.uk

Social Services (Children): Ms Diane Booth , Head of Service - Children's Social Care, PO Box 78, County Hall, Preston PR1 8XJ ☎ 01282 470129 ✉ diane.booth@lancashire.gov.uk

Social Services (Children): Mr Bob Stott , Director - Children's Services, PO Box 78, County Hall, Preston PR1 8XJ ☎ 01772 531652 ✉ bob.stott@lancashire.gov.uk

Fostering & Adoption: Ms Barbara Bath , Head of Service - Apodtion, Fostering & Residential, PO Box 78, County Hall, Preston PR1 8XJ ☎ 01772 535491 ✉ barbara.bath@lancashire.gov.uk

Safeguarding: Ms Charlotte Hammond , Head of Service - Safeguarding, PO Box 78, County Hall, Preston PR1 8XJ ☎ 0777 133 8882 ✉ charlotte.hammond@lancashire.gov.uk

Public Health: Dr Sakthi Karunanithi , Director - Public Health & Wellbeing, PO Box 78, County Hall, Preston PR1 8XJ ☎ 01772 536287 ✉ sakthi.karunanithi@lancashire.gov.uk

Transport: Mr Oliver Starkey, Head of Service - Public & Integrated Transport, PO Box 78, County Hall, Preston PR1 8XJ ☎ 01772 534619 ✉ oliver.starkey@lancashire.gov.uk

Transport Planner: Mr Oliver Starkey, Head of Service - Public & Integrated Transport, PO Box 78, County Hall, Preston PR1 8XJ ☎ 01772 534619 ✉ oliver.starkey@lancashire.gov.uk

Waste Collection and Disposal: Mr Steve Scott , Head of Service - Trading Standards & Scientific Services, PO Box 78, County Hall, Preston PR1 8XJ ☎ 01772 533755 ✉ steve.scott@lancashire.gov.uk

COUNCILLORS

***Leader of the Council* Mein**, Jennifer (LAB - Preston South East)
jennifer.mein@lancashire.gov.uk

***Deputy Leader of the Council* Borrow**, David (LAB - Preston North West)
david.borrow@lancashire.gov.uk

Aldridge, Terence (LAB - Skelmersdale Central)
terry.aldridge@lancashire.gov.uk

Ali, Azhar (LAB - Nelson South)
azhar.ali@lancashire.gov.uk

Ashton, Timothy (CON - Lytham)
tim.ashton@lancashire.gov.uk

Atkinson, Albert (CON - Ribble Valley North East)
albert.atkinson@lancashire.gov.uk

Barnes, Alyson (LAB - Rossendale North)
alyson.barnes@lancashire.gov.uk

Barron, Malcolm (CON - West Lancashire North)
malcolm.barron@lancashire.gov.uk

Beavers, Lorraine (LAB - Fleetwood West)
lorraine.beavers@lancashire.gov.uk

Brindle, Margaret (LD - Burnley Rural)
margaret.brindle@lancashire.gov.uk

Britcliffe, Peter (CON - Oswaldtwistle)
peter.britcliffe@lancashire.gov.uk

Brown, Terry (LAB - Chorley East)
terry.brown@lancashire.gov.uk

Brown, Ian (CON - Clitheroe)
ian.brown2@lancashire.gov.uk

Brown, Ken (CON - Heysham)
ken.brown@lancashire.gov.uk

Buckley, Peter (CON - St Annes North)
peter.buckley@lancashire.gov.uk

Burns, Terry (LAB - Burnley North East)
terry.burns@lancashire.gov.uk

Charles, Susie (CON - Lancaster Rural East)
susie.charles@lancashire.gov.uk

Cheetham, Anne (CON - Rossendale South)
anne.cheetham@lancashire.gov.uk

Clempson, Alf (CON - Poulton-le-Fylde)
alf.clempson@lancashire.gov.uk

Clifford, Dareen (LAB - Morecambe South)
darren.clifford@lancashire.gov.uk

Craig-Wilson, Fabian (CON - St Annes South)
fabian.craig-wilson@lancashire.gov.uk

Crompton, Carl (LAB - Preston Central South)
carl.crompton@lancashire.gov.uk

Dad, Munsif (LAB - Accrington West)
munsif.dad@lancashire.gov.uk

Dawson, Bernard (LAB - Accrington South)
bernard.dawson@lancashire.gov.uk

De Molfetta, Francesco (LAB - Preston Central North)
francesco.demolfetta@lancashire.gov.uk

Dereli, Cynthia (LAB - West Lancashire West)
cynthia.dereli@lancashire.gov.uk

Devaney, Michael (CON - Chorley Rural North)
michael.devaney@lancashire.gov.uk

Dowding, Gina (GRN - Lancaster Central)
gina.dowding@lancashire.gov.uk

Driver, Geoff (CON - Preston North)
geoff.driver@lancashire.gov.uk

Ellard, Kevin (LAB - Preston East)
kevin.ellard@lancashire.gov.uk

Frills, John (LAB - Skelmersdale East)
john.frills@lancashire.gov.uk

Gibson, Julie (LAB - Skelmersdale West)
julie.gibson@lancashire.gov.uk

Gooch, Graham (CON - South Ribble Rural West)
graham.gooch@lancashire.gov.uk

Green, Michael (CON - Leyland South West)
mike.france@lancashire.gov.uk

Hanson, Janice (LAB - Morecambe West)
janice.hanson@lancashire.gov.uk

Hassan, Misfar (LAB - Burnley Central East)
misfar.hassan@lancashire.gov.uk

Hayhurst, Paul (IND - Fylde West)
paul.hayhurst@lancashire.gov.uk

Henig, Chris (LAB - Lancaster South East)
chris.henig@lancashire.gov.uk

Hennessy, Nikki (LAB - Ormskirk West)
nikki.hennessy2@lancashire.gov.uk

Holgate, Steven (LAB - Chorley West)
steve.holgate@lancashire.gov.uk

Howarth, David (LD - Penwortham North)
david.howarth2@lancashire.gov.uk

Iddon, Keith (CON - Chorley Rural West)
keith.iddon@lancashire.gov.uk

Iqbal, Mohammed (LAB - Brierfield and Nelson North)
mohammed.iqbal@lancashire.gov.uk

James, Alycia (CON - Lancaster Rural North)
alycia.james@lancashire.gov.uk

Johnstone, Marcus (LAB - Padiham and Burnley West)
marcus.johnstone@lancashire.gov.uk

Jones, Anthony (CON - Morecambe North)
anthony.jones@lancashire.gov.uk

Kay, Andrea (CON - Thornton Cleveleys North)
andrea.kay@lancashire.gov.uk

Lawrenson, Jim (CON - Thornton Cleveleys Central)
jim.lawrenson@lancashire.co.uk

Lord, Dorothy (LD - Pendal Central)
dorothy.lord@lancashire.gov.uk

Martin, Tony (LAB - Burnley Central West)
tony.martin@lancashire.gov.uk

Molineux, Gareth (LAB - Great Harwood)
gareth.molineux@lancashire.gov.uk

Motala, Yousuf (LAB - Preston City)
yousuf.motala@lancashire.gov.uk

Murray, Bev (LAB - Chorley South)
bev.murray@lancashire.gov.uk

Newman-Thompson, Richard (LAB - Lancaster East)
richard.newman-thompson@lancashire.gov.uk

Oades, Liz (IND - Fylde East)
liz.oades@lancashire.gov.uk

Oakes, Jackie (LAB - Rossendale East)
jackie.oakes@lancashire.gov.uk

O'Toole, David (CON - West Lancashire South)
david.o'toole@lancashire.gov.uk

Otter, Mike (CON - Farington)
mike.otter@lancashire.gov.uk

Parkinson, Miles (LAB - Rishton and Clayton-Le-Moors)
miles.parkinson@lancashire.gov.uk

Penney, Nicola (LAB - Skerton)
niki.penney@lancashire.gov.uk

Perkins, Sandra (IND - Garstang)
sandra.perkins@lancashire.gov.uk

Perks, Mark (CON - Chorley North)
mark.perks@lancashire.gov.uk

Pritchard, Clare (LAB - Accrington North)
clare.pritchard@lancashire.gov.uk

Prynn, Sue (LAB - Penwortham South)
sue.prynn@lancashire.gov.uk

Rigby, Paul (CON - Fylde South)
paul.rigby@lancashire.gov.uk

Schofield, Alan (CON - Ribble Valley South West)
alan.schofield@lancashire.gov.uk

Sedgewick, Keith (CON - Preston North East)
keith.sedgewick@lancashire.gov.uk

Serridge, Sean (LAB - Whitworth)
sean.serridge@lancashire.gov.uk

Shedwick, John (CON - Amounderness)
john.shedwick@lancashire.gov.uk

Shewan, Ron (LAB - Fleetwood East)
ron.shewan@lancashire.gov.uk

Smith, David (CON - Longridge with Bowland)
david.smith@lancashire.gov.uk

Snape, Kim (LAB - Chorley Rural East)
kim.snape@lancashire.gov.uk

Stansfield, David (CON - Rossendale West)
dave.stansfield@lancashire.gov.uk

Sumner, Jeff (LD - Burnley South West)
jeff.sumner@lancashire.gov.uk

Taylor, Vivien (CON - Wyre Side)
vivien.taylor@lancashire.gov.uk

Tomlinson, Matthew (LAB - Leyland Central)
matthew.tomlinson@lancashire.gov.uk

Wakeford, Christian (CON - Pendle West)
christian.wakeford@lancashire.gov.uk

Watts, David (LAB - Bamber Bridge and Walton le Dale)
dave.watts@lancashire.gov.uk

Westley, David (CON - West Lancashire East)
david.westley@lancashire.gov.uk

Whipp, David (LD - West Craven)
david.whipp@lancashire.gov.uk

White, Paul (CON - Pendle East)
paul.white@lancashire.gov.uk

Wilkins, George (CON - Preston Rural)
george.wilkins@lancashire.gov.uk

Winlow, Bill (LD - Preston West)
bill.winlow@lancashire.gov.uk

Yates, Barrie (CON - South Ribble Rural East)
barrie.yates2@lancashire.gov.uk

POLITICAL COMPOSITION

LAB: 39, CON: 35, LD: 6, IND: 3, GRN: 1

COMMITTEE CHAIRS

Audit & Governance: Mr Terry Brown

Development Control: Mr Munsif Dad

Pensions: Mr Kevin Ellard

Lancaster City — D

Lancaster City Council, Town Hall, Dalton Square, Lancaster LA1 1PJ
☎ 01524 582000 🖷 01524 582979
customerservices@lancaster.gov.uk 🖳 www.lancaster.gov.uk

FACTS AND FIGURES

Parliamentary Constituencies: Lancaster and Fleetwood
EU Constituencies: North West
Election Frequency: Elections are of whole council

PRINCIPAL OFFICERS

Chief Executive: Mr Mark Cullinan, Chief Executive, Town Hall, Dalton Square, Lancaster LA1 1PJ ☎ 01524 582011 🖷 01524 582042 chiefexecutive@lancaster.gov.uk

Senior Management: Mr Mark Davies, Chief Officer - Environment, White Lund Depot, White Lund Industrial Estate, Morecambe LA3 3DT ☎ 01524 582401 🖷 01524 582401 mdavies@lancaster.gov.uk

Senior Management: Mr Andrew Dobson, Chief Officer - Regeneration & Planning, Town Hall, Marine Road, Morecambe LA4 4AF ☎ 01524 582303 🖷 01524 582323 adobson@lancaster.gov.uk

Senior Management: Ms Suzanne Lodge, Chief Officer - Health & Housing, Town Hall, Marine Road, Morecambe LA4 4AF ☎ 01524 582709 🖷 01524 582701 slodge@lancaster.gov.uk

Senior Management: Ms Nadine Muschamp, Chief Officer - Resources (S151 Officer), Town Hall, Dalton Square, Lancaster LA1 1PJ ☎ 01524 582117 🖷 01524 582160 nmuschamp@lancaster.gov.uk

Senior Management: Mrs Sarah Taylor, Chief Officer - Governance (Monitoring Officer), Town Hall, Dalton Square, Lancaster LA1 1PJ ☎ 01524 582025 🖷 01524 582030 staylor@lancaster.gov.uk

Architect, Building / Property Services: Ms Nadine Muschamp, Chief Officer - Resources (S151 Officer), Town Hall, Dalton Square, Lancaster LA1 1PJ ☎ 01524 582117 🖷 01524 582160 nmuschamp@lancaster.gov.uk

Building Control: Mr Andrew Dobson, Chief Officer - Regeneration & Planning, Town Hall, Marine Road, Morecambe LA4 4AF ☎ 01524 582303 🖷 01524 582323 adobson@lancaster.gov.uk

PR / Communications: Mr Michael Hill , Communications & Marketing Team Leader, Town Hall, Dalton Square, Lancaster LA1 1PJ ☎ 0524 582041 mhill@lancaster.gov.uk

Community Planning: Mr Andrew Dobson, Chief Officer - Regeneration & Planning, Town Hall, Marine Road, Morecambe LA4 4AF ☎ 01524 582303 🖷 01524 582323 ✉ adobson@lancaster.gov.uk

Community Safety: Mr Mark Davies, Chief Officer - Environment, White Lund Depot, White Lund Industrial Estate, Morecambe LA3 3DT ☎ 01524 582401 🖷 01524 582401 ✉ mdavies@lancaster.gov.uk

Computer Management: Mr Chris Riley , Applications Manager for ICT Services, Town Hall, Dalton Square, Lancaster LA1 1PJ ☎ 01524 582106 🖷 01524 582171 ✉ cjriley@lancaster.gov.uk

Consumer Protection and Trading Standards: Ms Suzanne Lodge, Chief Officer - Health & Housing, Town Hall, Marine Road, Morecambe LA4 4AF ☎ 01524 582709 🖷 01524 582701 ✉ slodge@lancaster.gov.uk

Contracts: Mr Mark Davies, Chief Officer - Environment, White Lund Depot, White Lund Industrial Estate, Morecambe LA3 3DT ☎ 01524 582401 🖷 ; 01524 582401 ✉ mdavies@lancaster.gov.uk

Corporate Services: Mr Mark Cullinan, Chief Executive, Town Hall, Dalton Square, Lancaster LA1 1PJ ☎ 01524 582011 🖷 01524 582042 ✉ chiefexecutive@lancaster.gov.uk

Customer Service: Ms Alison McGurk , Customer Service & Visitor Information Centre Manager, Town Hall, Dalton Square, Lancaster LA1 1PJ ☎ 01524 582399 🖷 01524 582979 ✉ amcgurk@lancaster.gov.uk

Direct Labour: Mr Mark Davies, Chief Officer - Environment, White Lund Depot, White Lund Industrial Estate, Morecambe LA3 3DT ☎ 01524 582401 🖷 01524 582401 ✉ mdavies@lancaster.gov.uk

Economic Development: Mr Andrew Dobson, Chief Officer - Regeneration & Planning, Town Hall, Marine Road, Morecambe LA4 4AF ☎ 01524 582303 🖷 01524 582323 ✉ adobson@lancaster.gov.uk

Electoral Registration: Mrs Sarah Taylor, Chief Officer - Governance (Monitoring Officer), Town Hall, Dalton Square, Lancaster LA1 1PJ ☎ 01524 582025 🖷 01524 582030 ✉ staylor@lancaster.gov.uk

Emergency Planning: Mr Mark Bartlett, Civil Contingencies Officer, Town Hall, Marine Road, Morecambe LA4 4AF ☎ 01524 582680 🖷 01524 582709 ✉ mbartlett@lancaster.gov.uk

Energy Management: Ms Suzanne Lodge, Chief Officer - Health & Housing, Town Hall, Marine Road, Morecambe LA4 4AF ☎ 01524 582709 🖷 01524 582701 ✉ slodge@lancaster.gov.uk

Environmental / Technical Services: Mr Mark Davies, Chief Officer - Environment, White Lund Depot, White Lund Industrial Estate, Morecambe LA3 3DT ☎ 01524 582401 🖷 01524 582401 ✉ mdavies@lancaster.gov.uk

Environmental Health: Ms Suzanne Lodge, Chief Officer - Health & Housing, Town Hall, Marine Road, Morecambe LA4 4AF ☎ 01524 582709 🖷 01524 582701 ✉ slodge@lancaster.gov.uk

Estates, Property & Valuation: Mr Andrew Dobson, Chief Officer - Regeneration & Planning, Town Hall, Marine Road, Morecambe LA4 4AF ☎ 01524 582303 🖷 01524 582323 ✉ adobson@lancaster.gov.uk

European Liaison: Mrs Sarah Taylor, Chief Officer - Governance (Monitoring Officer), Town Hall, Dalton Square, Lancaster LA1 1PJ ☎ 01524 582025 🖷 01524 582030 ✉ staylor@lancaster.gov.uk

Events Manager: Mr Andrew Dobson, Chief Officer - Regeneration & Planning, Town Hall, Marine Road, Morecambe LA4 4AF ☎ 01524 582303 🖷 01524 582323 ✉ adobson@lancaster.gov.uk

Facilities: Ms Nadine Muschamp, Chief Officer - Resources (S151 Officer), Town Hall, Dalton Square, Lancaster LA1 1PJ ☎ 01524 582117 🖷 ; 01524 582160 ✉ nmuschamp@lancaster.gov.uk

Finance: Ms Nadine Muschamp, Chief Officer - Resources (S151 Officer), Town Hall, Dalton Square, Lancaster LA1 1PJ ☎ 01524 582117 🖷 ; 01524 582160 ✉ nmuschamp@lancaster.gov.uk

Fleet Management: Mr Mark Davies, Chief Officer - Environment, White Lund Depot, White Lund Industrial Estate, Morecambe LA3 3DT ☎ 01524 582401 🖷 ; 01524 582401 ✉ mdavies@lancaster.gov.uk

Grounds Maintenance: Mr Mark Davies, Chief Officer - Environment, White Lund Depot, White Lund Industrial Estate, Morecambe LA3 3DT ☎ 01524 582401 🖷 01524 582401 ✉ mdavies@lancaster.gov.uk

Health and Safety: Ms Suzanne Lodge, Chief Officer - Health & Housing, Town Hall, Marine Road, Morecambe LA4 4AF ☎ 01524 582709 🖷 01524 582701 ✉ slodge@lancaster.gov.uk

Highways: Mr Mark Davies, Chief Officer - Environment, White Lund Depot, White Lund Industrial Estate, Morecambe LA3 3DT ☎ 01524 582401 🖷 ; 01524 582401 ✉ mdavies@lancaster.gov.uk

Housing: Ms Suzanne Lodge, Chief Officer - Health & Housing, Town Hall, Marine Road, Morecambe LA4 4AF ☎ 01524 582709 🖷 01524 582701 ✉ slodge@lancaster.gov.uk

Housing Maintenance: Ms Suzanne Lodge, Chief Officer - Health & Housing, Town Hall, Marine Road, Morecambe LA4 4AF ☎ 01524 582709 🖷 01524 582701 ✉ slodge@lancaster.gov.uk

Legal: Mrs Sarah Taylor, Chief Officer - Governance (Monitoring Officer), Town Hall, Dalton Square, Lancaster LA1 1PJ ☎ 01524 582025 🖷 01524 582030 ✉ staylor@lancaster.gov.uk

Leisure and Cultural Services: Ms Suzanne Lodge, Chief Officer - Health & Housing, Town Hall, Marine Road, Morecambe LA4 4AF ☎ 01524 582709 🖷 01524 582701 ✉ slodge@lancaster.gov.uk

Licensing: Mrs Sarah Taylor, Chief Officer - Governance (Monitoring Officer), Town Hall, Dalton Square, Lancaster LA1 1PJ ☎ 01524 582025 🖷 01524 582030 ✉ staylor@lancaster.gov.uk

LANCASTER CITY

Lighting: Mr Mark Davies, Chief Officer - Environment, White Lund Depot, White Lund Industrial Estate, Morecambe LA3 3DT ☎ 01524 582401 🖷 ; 01524 582401 ✉ mdavies@lancaster.gov.uk

Member Services: Mrs Sarah Taylor, Chief Officer - Governance (Monitoring Officer), Town Hall, Dalton Square, Lancaster LA1 1PJ ☎ 01524 582025 🖷 01524 582030 ✉ staylor@lancaster.gov.uk

Parking: Mr Mark Davies, Chief Officer - Environment, White Lund Depot, White Lund Industrial Estate, Morecambe LA3 3DT ☎ 01524 582401 🖷 ; 01524 582401 ✉ mdavies@lancaster.gov.uk

Personnel / HR: Mrs Sarah Taylor, Chief Officer - Governance (Monitoring Officer), Town Hall, Dalton Square, Lancaster LA1 1PJ ☎ 01524 582025 🖷 01524 582030 ✉ staylor@lancaster.gov.uk

Planning: Mr Andrew Dobson, Chief Officer - Regeneration & Planning, Town Hall, Marine Road, Morecambe LA4 4AF ☎ 01524 582303 🖷 01524 582323 ✉ adobson@lancaster.gov.uk

Procurement: Ms Nadine Muschamp, Chief Officer - Resources (S151 Officer), Town Hall, Dalton Square, Lancaster LA1 1PJ ☎ 01524 582117 🖷 01524 582160 ✉ nmuschamp@lancaster.gov.uk

Recycling & Waste Minimisation: Mr Mark Davies, Chief Officer - Environment, White Lund Depot, White Lund Industrial Estate, Morecambe LA3 3DT ☎ 01524 582401 🖷 01524 582401 ✉ mdavies@lancaster.gov.uk

Regeneration: Mr Andrew Dobson, Chief Officer - Regeneration & Planning, Town Hall, Marine Road, Morecambe LA4 4AF ☎ 01524 582303 🖷 01524 582323 ✉ adobson@lancaster.gov.uk

Staff Training: Mrs Sarah Taylor, Chief Officer - Governance (Monitoring Officer), Town Hall, Dalton Square, Lancaster LA1 1PJ ☎ 01524 582025 🖷 01524 582030 ✉ staylor@lancaster.gov.uk

Street Scene: Mr Mark Davies, Chief Officer - Environment, White Lund Depot, White Lund Industrial Estate, Morecambe LA3 3DT ☎ 01524 582401 🖷 ; 01524 582401 ✉ mdavies@lancaster.gov.uk

Sustainable Development: Mr Andrew Dobson, Chief Officer - Regeneration & Planning, Town Hall, Marine Road, Morecambe LA4 4AF ☎ 01524 582303 🖷 01524 582323 ✉ adobson@lancaster.gov.uk

Tourism: Mr Andrew Dobson, Chief Officer - Regeneration & Planning, Town Hall, Marine Road, Morecambe LA4 4AF ☎ 01524 582303 🖷 01524 582323 ✉ adobson@lancaster.gov.uk

Town Centre: Mr Andrew Dobson, Chief Officer - Regeneration & Planning, Town Hall, Marine Road, Morecambe LA4 4AF ☎ 01524 582303 🖷 01524 582323 ✉ adobson@lancaster.gov.uk

Waste Collection and Disposal: Mr Mark Davies, Chief Officer - Environment, White Lund Depot, White Lund Industrial Estate, Morecambe LA3 3DT ☎ 01524 582401 🖷 01524 582401 ✉ mdavies@lancaster.gov.uk

Waste Management: Mr Mark Davies, Chief Officer - Environment, White Lund Depot, White Lund Industrial Estate, Morecambe LA3 3DT ☎ 01524 582401 🖷 01524 582401 ✉ mdavies@lancaster.gov.uk

COUNCILLORS

***Mayor* Barry**, Jon (GRN - Marsh)
jbarry@lancaster.gov.uk

***Deputy Mayor* Jackson**, Caroline (GRN - Bulk)
cjackson@lancaster.gov.uk

***Leader of the Council* Blamire**, Eileen (LAB - John O'Gaunt)
eblamire@lancaster.gov.uk

***Deputy Leader of the Council* Hanson**, Janice (LAB - Harbour)
jhanson@lancaster.gov.uk

***Group Leader* Williamson**, Peter (CON - Upper Lune Valley)
pwilliamson@lancaster.gov.uk

Armstrong, Sam (GRN - University & Scotforth)
starmstrong@lancaster.gov.uk

Ashworth, June (IND - Bare)
jashworth@lancaster.gov.uk

Atkinson, Lucy (LAB - University & Scotforth)
latkinson@lancaster.gov.uk

Bateson, Stuart (CON - Heysham South)
sbateson@lancaster.gov.uk

Biddulph, Alan (LAB - Heysham South)
abiddulph@lancaster.gov.uk

Brayshaw, Carla (LAB - Heysham Central)
cbrayshaw@lancaster.gov.uk

Brookes, Dave (GRN - Castle)
dbrookes@lancaster.gov.uk

Brown, Tracy (LAB - Westgate)
tmbrown@lancaster.gov.uk

Bryning, Abbott (LAB - Skerton East)
abryning@lancaster.gov.uk

Charlies, Susie (CON - Ellel)
scharles@lancaster.gov.uk

Clifford, Darren (LAB - Harbour)
dclifford@lancaster.gov.uk

Cooper, Brett (CON - Bare)
bcooper@lancaster.gov.uk

Cozler, Claire (LAB - Westgate)
ccozler@lancaster.gov.uk

Denwood, Sheila (LAB - Scotforth West)
sdenwood@lancaster.gov.uk

Devey, Rob (LAB - Skerton West)
rdevey@lancaster.gov.uk

Edwards, Charlie (CON - Bare)
cedwards@lancaster.gov.uk

Gardiner, Andrew (CON - Overton)
agardiner@lancaster.gov.uk

Goodrich, Nigel (CON - Silverdale)
ngoodrich@lancaster.gov.uk

Guilding, Melanie (CON - Carnforth & Millhead)
mguilding@lancaster.gov.uk

Hall, Janet (LAB - Skerton East)
jhall@lancaster.gov.uk

Hamilton-Cox, Tim (GRN - Bulk)
thamiltoncox@lancaster.gov.uk

Hartley, Colin (LAB - Heysham South)
chartley@lancaster.gov.uk

Helme, Helen (CON - Ellel)
hhelme@lancaster.gov.uk

Hughes, Brendan (LAB - Poulton)
bhughes@lancaster.gov.uk

Jackson, Joan (CON - Lower Lune Valley)
jjackson@lancaster.gov.uk

Kay, Andrew (GRN - Bulk)
akay@lancaster.gov.uk

Kershaw, Ronnie (LAB - Scotforth West)
rkershaw@lancaster.gov.uk

Knight, Geoff (IND - Heysham Central)
gknight@lancaster.gov.uk

Leadbetter, Christopher (CON - Carnforth & Millhead)
cleadbetter@lancaster.gov.uk

Leyshon, James (LAB - Scotforth East)
jleyshon@lancaster.gov.uk

Leytham, Karen (LAB - Skerton West)
kleytham@lancaster.gov.uk

Mace, Roger (CON - Kellet)
rmace@lancaster.gov.uk

Mann, Matt (LAB - University & Scotforth)
mmann@lancaster.gov.uk

Metcalfe, Terrie (LAB - Poulton)
tmetcalfe@lancaster.gov.uk

Mills, Abi (GRN - Scotforth West)
amills@lancaster.gov.uk

Newman-Thompson, Richard (LAB - John O'Gaunt)
richard.newman-thompson@lancashire.gov.uk

Novell, Rebecca (GRN - Marsh)
rnovell@lancaster.gov.uk

Parkinson, Jane (CON - Lower Lune Valley)
japarkinson@lancaster.gov.uk

Pattison, Margaret (LAB - Heysham North)
mpattison@lancaster.gov.uk

Redfern, Robert (LAB - Skerton East)
rredfern@lancaster.gov.uk

Rogerson, Sylvia (CON - Bolton & Slyne)
srogerson@lancaster.gov.uk

Sands, Ron (LAB - Heysham North)
rsands@lancaster.gov.uk

Scott, Elizabeth (LAB - John O'Gaunt)
lscott@lancaster.gov.uk

Sherlock, Roger (LAB - Skerton West)
rsherlock@lancaster.gov.uk

Smith, David (LAB - Westgate)
dasmith@lancaster.gov.uk

Sykes, Susan (CON - Warton)
ssykes@lancaster.gov.uk

Thomas, Malcolm (CON - Bolton & Slyne)
jthomas@lancaster.gov.uk

Warriner, Andrew (LAB - Torrisholme)
awarriner@lancaster.gov.uk

Whitaker, David (LAB - Harbour)
dwhitaker@lancaster.gov.uk

Whitehead, Anne (LAB - Scotforth East)
pawhitehead@lancaster.gov.uk

Wild, John (CON - Bolton & Slyne)
jwild@lancaster.gov.uk

Williamson, Phillippa (CON - Torrisholme)
phwilliamson@lancaster.gov.uk

Wilson, Nicholas (GRN - Castle)
nwilkinson@lancaster.gov.uk

Woodruff, Paul (IND - Halton-with-Aughton)
pwoodruff@lancaster.gov.uk

Yates, Peter (CON - Carnforth & Millhead)
pyates@lancaster.gov.uk

POLITICAL COMPOSITION
LAB: 29, CON: 19, GRN: 9, IND: 3

COMMITTEE CHAIRS
Audit: Mr Matt Mann

Audit: Ms Susan Sykes

Licensing: Ms Terrie Metcalfe

Leeds City M

Leeds City Council, Civic Hall, Leeds LS1 1UR
☎ 0113 222 4444 ✉ general.enquiries@leeds.gov.uk
💻 www.leeds.gov.uk

FACTS AND FIGURES
Parliamentary Constituencies: Elmet and Rothwell, Leeds Central, Leeds East, Leeds North East, Leeds North West, Leeds West, Morley and Outwood, Normanton, Pontefract and Castleford, Pudsey
EU Constituencies: Yorkshire and the Humber
Election Frequency: Elections are by thirds

PRINCIPAL OFFICERS
Chief Executive: Mr Tom Riordan , Chief Executive, Chief Executive's Office, 3rd Floor East, Civic Hall, Leeds LS1 1UR
☎ 0113 247 4554 ✉ tom.riordan@leeds.gov.uk

Deputy Chief Executive: Mr Alan Gay, Deputy Chief Executive & Director of Resources, Civic Hall, Calverley Street, Leeds LS1 1UR
☎ 0113 247 4226 🖷 0113 247 4346 ✉ alan.gay@leeds.gov.uk

Assistant Chief Executive: Mr James Rogers, Assistant Chief Executive (Citizens & Communities), 3rd Floor East, Civic Hall, Calverley Street, Leeds LS1 1UR ☎ 0113 224 3579 🖷 0113 247 4870 ✉ james.rogers@leeds.gov.uk

Senior Management: Dr Ian Cameron , Executive Director - Public Health, 3rd Floor East, Civic Hall, Calverley Street, Leeds LS1 1UR ☎ 0113 395 2810 ✉ ian.cameron@leeds.gov.uk

LEEDS CITY

Senior Management: Mr Neil Evans, Director - Environment & Neighbourhoods, 4th Floor West, Merrion House, Leeds LS1 1UR ☎ 0113 247 4721 🖷 0113 247 4721 🖰 neil.evans@leeds.gov.uk

Senior Management: Mr Martin Farrington, Director - City Development, The Leonardo Building, 2 Rossington Street, Leeds LS2 8HB ☎ 0113 224 3816 🖷 0113 247 7748 🖰 martin.farrington@leeds.gov.uk

Senior Management: Mr Nigel Richardson , Director - Children's Services, 3rd Floor, St. Georges House, Leeds LS1 3DL ☎ 0113 378 3687 🖰 nigel.richasrdson@leeds.gov.uk

Senior Management: Ms Cath Roff , Director of Adult Social Care, Civic Hall, Leeds LS1 1UR 🖰 cath.roff@ledds.gov.uk

Senior Management: Ms Catherine Witham , City Solicitor, Civic Hall, Leeds LS1 1UR ☎ 0113 247 4537 🖰 catherine.witham@leeds.gov.uk

Access Officer / Social Services (Disability): Ms Shona McFarlane , Chief Officer Access & Care Delivery, 2nd Floor, Enterprise House, Leeds LS1 2LE ☎ 0113 378 3884 🖰 shona.mcfarlane@leeds.gov.uk

Architect, Building / Property Services: Mr Martin Farrington, Director - City Development, The Leonardo Building, 2 Rossington Street, Leeds LS2 8HB ☎ 0113 224 3816 🖷 0113 247 7748 🖰 martin.farrington@leeds.gov.uk

Best Value: Mr Alan Gay, Deputy Chief Executive & Director of Resources, Civic Hall, Calverley Street, Leeds LS1 1UR ☎ 0113 247 4226 🖷 0113 247 4346 🖰 alan.gay@leeds.gov.uk

Building Control: Mr Martin Farrington, Director - City Development, The Leonardo Building, 2 Rossington Street, Leeds LS2 8HB ☎ 0113 224 3816 🖷 0113 247 7748 🖰 martin.farrington@leeds.gov.uk

Catering Services: Ms Sarah Martin , Head of Property & Fleet Services, Commercial Services, Seacroft Ring Road Depot, Ring Road, Seacroft, Leeds LS14 1NZ ☎ 0113 378 2358 🖰 sarah.martin@leeds.gov.uk

Children / Youth Services: Mr Jim Hopkinson , Head of Service - Targetted Services, 3rd Floor, St. Georges House, Leeds LS1 3DL ☎ 0113 378 3689 🖰 jim.hopkinson@leeds.gov.uk

Children / Youth Services: Mr Nigel Richardson , Director - Children's Services, 3rd Floor, St. Georges House, Leeds LS1 3DL ☎ 0113 378 3687 🖰 nigel.richasrdson@leeds.gov.uk

Civil Registration: Mr James Rogers, Assistant Chief Executive (Citizens & Communities), Civic Hall, Leeds LS1 1UR ☎ 0113 224 3579 🖷 0113 247 4870 🖰 james.rogers@leeds.gov.uk

PR / Communications: Ms Dee Reid , Head of Communications, Planning Policy & Improvement, Communications Team, 4th Floor West, Civic Hall, Leeds LS1 1UR ☎ 0113 247 5427; 0113 247 5427 🖰 dee.reid@leeds.gov.uk; dee.reid@leeds.gov.uk

Community Planning: Mr James Rogers, Assistant Chief Executive (Citizens & Communities), 3rd Floor East, Civic Hall, Calverley Street, Leeds LS1 1UR ☎ 0113 224 3579 🖷 0113 247 4870 🖰 james.rogers@leeds.gov.uk

Community Safety: Mr Neil Evans, Director - Environment & Neighbourhoods, 4th Floor West, Merrion House, Leeds LS1 1UR ☎ 0113 247 4721 🖷 0113 247 4721 🖰 neil.evans@leeds.gov.uk

Computer Management: Mr Alan Gay, Deputy Chief Executive & Director of Resources, Civic Hall, Calverley Street, Leeds LS1 1UR ☎ 0113 247 4226 🖷 0113 247 4346 🖰 alan.gay@leeds.gov.uk

Computer Management: Mr Dylan Roberts , Chief ICT Officer, Apex Centre, Apex Way, Leeds LS11 5LT ☎ 0113 395 1515 🖰 dylan.roberts@leeds.gov.uk

Contracts: Mr David Outram , Chief Officer (Strategy & Resources), St George House, 40 Great George Street, Leeds LS1 3DL ☎ 0113 395 2463 🖰 david.outram@leeds.gov.uk

Corporate Services: Mr Alan Gay, Deputy Chief Executive & Director of Resources, Civic Hall, Calverley Street, Leeds LS1 1UR ☎ 0113 247 4226 🖷 0113 247 4346 🖰 alan.gay@leeds.gov.uk

Corporate Services: Ms Mariana Pexton , Chief Officer (Strategy & Improvement), 3rd Floor East, Civic Hall, Calverley Street, Leeds LS1 1UR ☎ 0113 376 0001 🖰 mariana.pexton@leeds.gov.uk

Customer Service: Mr Lee Hemsworth , Chief Officer (Customer Access), West Gate, Ground Floor, 6 Grace Street, Leeds LS1 2RP ☎ 0113 376002 🖰 lee.hemsworth@leeds.gov.uk

Customer Service: Ms Susan Murray , Head of Customer Contact, Westgate, 6 Grace Street, Leeds LS1 2RP ☎ 0113 376 0012 🖰 susan.murray@leeds.gov.uk

Customer Service: Mr James Rogers, Assistant Chief Executive (Citizens & Communities), 3rd Floor East, Civic Hall, Calverley Street, Leeds LS1 1UR ☎ 0113 224 3579 🖷 0113 247 4870 🖰 james.rogers@leeds.gov.uk

Economic Development: Mr Tom Bridges , Chief Officer - Economy & Regeneration, The Leonardo Building, Level 6, 2 Rossington Street, Leeds LS2 8HD ☎ 0113 224 3735 🖰 tom.bridges@leeds.gov.uk

Economic Development: Ms Sue Burgess , Head of Markets Service, Kirkgate Market, 34 George Street, Leeds LS2 7HY ☎ 0113 378 1950 🖰

Education: Mr Nigel Richardson , Director - Children's Services, Childrens Services, 6th Floor East, Civic Hall, Leeds LS2 8DT ☎ 0113 378 3687 🖰 nigel.richasrdson@leeds.gov.uk

E-Government: Mr James Rogers, Assistant Chief Executive (Citizens & Communities), 3rd Floor East, Civic Hall, Calverley Street, Leeds LS1 1UR ☎ 0113 224 3579 🖷 0113 247 4870 🖰 james.rogers@leeds.gov.uk

Electoral Registration: Ms Susanna Benton , Electoral Services Manager, Town Hall, The Headrow, Leeds LS1 3AD
☎ 0113 247 6727 ✉ susanna.benton@leeds.gov.uk

Emergency Planning: Mr Nigel Street , Principal Officer - Resilience & Emergencies, Civic Hall, Leeds LS1 1UR
☎ 0113 247 4341 ✉ nigel.street@leeds.gov.uk

Energy Management: Mr Peter Lynes , Senior Asset Management Officer, Thoresby House, Level 5SE, 2 Rossington Street, Leeds LS2 8HD ☎ 0113 247 5536
✉ peter.lynes@leeds.gov.uk

Environmental / Technical Services: Ms Helen Freeman, Chief Officer (Environmental Action), Level 2 Southside, Thoresby House, Rossington Street, Leeds LS2 8HD ☎ 0113 247 8888
🖷 0113 224 3543 ✉ helen.freeman@leeds.gov.uk

Environmental Health: Ms Helen Freeman, Chief Officer (Environmental Action), Level 2 Southside, Thoresby House, Rossington Street, Leeds LS2 8HD ☎ 0113 247 8888
🖷 0113 224 3543 ✉ helen.freeman@leeds.gov.uk

Estates, Property & Valuation: Mr Martin Farrington, Director - City Development, The Leonardo Building, 2 Rossington Street, Leeds LS2 8HB ☎ 0113 224 3816 🖷 0113 247 7748
✉ martin.farrington@leeds.gov.uk

Events Manager: Mr Paul Footitt , Events Manager, 1st Floor, Town Hall, Headrow, Leeds LS1 3AD ☎ 0113 224 3600
✉ paul.footitt@leeds.gov.uk

Facilities: Ms Sarah Martin , Head of Property & Fleet Services, Commercial Services, Seacroft Ring Road Depot, Ring Road, Seacroft, Leeds LS14 1NZ ☎ 0113 378 2358
✉ sarah.martin@leeds.gov.uk

Finance: Mr Alan Gay, Deputy Chief Executive & Director of Resources, Civic Hall, Calverley Street, Leeds LS1 1UR
☎ 0113 247 4226 🖷 0113 247 4346 ✉ alan.gay@leeds.gov.uk

Fleet Management: Mr Terence Pycroft , Head of Fleet Services, 255a York Road, Leeds LS9 7QQ ☎ 0113 378 1440
✉ terry.pycroft@leeds.gov.uk

Grounds Maintenance: Mr Neil Evans, Director - Environment & Neighbourhoods, 4th Floor West, Merrion House, Leeds LS1 1UR
☎ 0113 247 4721 🖷 0113 247 4721 ✉ neil.evans@leeds.gov.uk

Grounds Maintenance: Ms Sarah Martin , Head of Property & Fleet Services, Commercial Services, Seacroft Ring Road Depot, Ring Road, Seacroft, Leeds LS14 1NZ ☎ 0113 378 2358
✉ sarah.martin@leeds.gov.uk

Health and Safety: Ms Lorraine Hallam, Chief Officer (Human Resources), Civic Hall, Calverley Street, Leeds LS1 1UR ☎ 0113 395 1600 ✉ lorraine.hallam@leeds.gov.uk

Highways: Mr Gary Bartlett , Chief Highways Officer, Civic Hall, Leeds LS1 1UR ☎ 0113 247 5319 ✉ gary.bartlett@leeds.gov.uk

Highways: Mr Martin Farrington, Director - City Development, The Leonardo Building, 2 Rossington Street, Leeds LS2 8HB
☎ 0113 224 3816 🖷 0113 247 7748 ✉ martin.farrington@leeds.gov.uk

Home Energy Conservation: Mr George Munson , Senior Programme Leader (Environment & Housing), 2nd Floor, St. Georges Hall, Leeds LS1 3DL ☎ 0113 395 1767
✉ george.munson@leeds.gov.uk

Housing: Mr Neil Evans, Director - Environment & Neighbourhoods, 4th Floor West, Merrion House, Leeds LS1 1UR
☎ 0113 247 4721 🖷 0113 247 4721 ✉ neil.evans@leeds.gov.uk

Housing Maintenance: Mr Simon Costigan , Chief Officer - Property & Contract, Civic Hall, Leeds LS1 1UR ☎ 0113 318 1337
✉ simon.costigan@leeds.gov.uk

Local Area Agreement: Ms Mariana Pexton , Chief Officer (Strategy & Improvement), 3rd Floor East, Civic Hall, Calverley Street, Leeds LS1 1UR ☎ 0113 376 0001
✉ mariana.pexton@leeds.gov.uk

Legal: Ms Catherine Witham , City Solicitor, Civic Hall, Leeds LS1 1UR ☎ 0113 247 4537 ✉ catherine.witham@leeds.gov.uk

Leisure and Cultural Services: Mr Martin Farrington, Director - City Development, The Leonardo Building, 2 Rossington Street, Leeds LS2 8HB ☎ 0113 224 3816 🖷 0113 247 7748
✉ martin.farrington@leeds.gov.uk

Leisure and Cultural Services: Mr Cluny Macpherson , Chief Officer - Culture & Sport, Leonardo Building, 6th Floor, 2 Rossington Street, Leeds LS2 8HD ✉ cluny.macpherson@leeds.gov.uk

Licensing: Mr James Rogers, Assistant Chief Executive (Citizens & Communities), 3rd Floor East, Civic Hall, Calverley Street, Leeds LS1 1UR ☎ 0113 224 3579 🖷 0113 247 4870
✉ james.rogers@leeds.gov.uk

Lifelong Learning: Mr Nigel Richardson , Director - Children's Services, 3rd Floor, St. Georges House, Leeds LS1 3DL
☎ 0113 378 3687 ✉ nigel.richasrdson@leeds.gov.uk

Lighting: Mr Martin Farrington, Director - City Development, The Leonardo Building, 2 Rossington Street, Leeds LS2 8HB ☎ 0113 224 3816 🖷 0113 247 7748 ✉ martin.farrington@leeds.gov.uk

Lottery Funding, Charity and Voluntary: Mr James Rogers, Assistant Chief Executive (Citizens & Communities), 3rd Floor East, Civic Hall, Calverley Street, Leeds LS1 1UR ☎ 0113 224 3579
🖷 0113 247 4870 ✉ james.rogers@leeds.gov.uk

Member Services: Mr Ian Cornick , Head of Civic & Member Support, Civic Hall, Leeds LS1 1UR ☎ 0113 224 3206
✉ ian.cornick@leeds.gov.uk

Member Services: Mr Andy Hodson , Head of Governance Services, Corporate Governance, 4th Floor West, Civic Hall, Leeds LS1 1UR ☎ 0113 224 3208 ✉ andy.hodson@leeds.gov.uk

LEEDS CITY

Member Services: Mr Peter Marrington , Head of Scrutiny & Member Development, Civic Hall, Leeds LS1 1UR ☎ 0113 395 1151 ✉ peter.marrington@leeds.gov.uk

Member Services: Ms Catherine Witham , City Solicitor, Civic Hall, Leeds LS1 1UR ☎ 0113 247 4537 ✉ catherine.witham@leeds.gov.uk

Parking: Mr Neil Evans, Director - Environment & Neighbourhoods, 4th Floor West, Merrion House, Leeds LS1 1UR ☎ 0113 247 4721 🖷 0113 247 4721 ✉ neil.evans@leeds.gov.uk

Partnerships: Mr Alan Gay, Deputy Chief Executive & Director of Resources, Civic Hall, Calverley Street, Leeds LS1 1UR ☎ 0113 247 4226 🖷 0113 247 4346 ✉ alan.gay@leeds.gov.uk

Partnerships: Mr James Rogers, Assistant Chief Executive (Citizens & Communities), 3rd Floor East, Civic Hall, Calverley Street, Leeds LS1 1UR ☎ 0113 224 3579 🖷 0113 247 4870 ✉ james.rogers@leeds.gov.uk

Personnel / HR: Mr Alan Gay, Deputy Chief Executive & Director of Resources, Civic Hall, Calverley Street, Leeds LS1 1UR ☎ 0113 247 4226 🖷 0113 247 4346 ✉ alan.gay@leeds.gov.uk

Personnel / HR: Ms Lorraine Hallam, Chief Officer (Human Resources), Civic Hall, Calverley Street, Leeds LS1 1UR ☎ 0113 395 1600 ✉ lorraine.hallam@leeds.gov.uk

Planning: Mr Martin Farrington, Director - City Development, The Leonardo Building, 2 Rossington Street, Leeds LS2 8HB ☎ 0113 224 3816 🖷 0113 247 7748 ✉ martin.farrington@leeds.gov.uk

Procurement: Mr Alan Gay, Deputy Chief Executive & Director of Resources, Civic Hall, Calverley Street, Leeds LS1 1UR ☎ 0113 247 4226 🖷 0113 247 4346 ✉ alan.gay@leeds.gov.uk

Procurement: Mr David Outram , Chief Officer (Strategy & Resources), St George House, 40 Great George Street, Leeds LS1 3DL ☎ 0113 395 2463 ✉ david.outram@leeds.gov.uk

Public Libraries: Mr Martin Farrington, Director - City Development, The Leonardo Building, 2 Rossington Street, Leeds LS2 8HB ☎ 0113 224 3816 🖷 0113 247 7748 ✉ martin.farrington@leeds.gov.uk

Public Libraries: Mr Cluny Macpherson , Chief Officer - Culture & Sport, Leonardo Building, 6th Floor, 2 Rossington Street, Leeds LS2 8HD ✉ cluny.macpherson@leeds.gov.uk

Recycling & Waste Minimisation: Mrs Susan Upton , Chief Officer (Waste Management), Level 2 Southside, Thoresby House, Rossington Street, Leeds LS2 8HD ☎ 0113 247 8888 ✉ susan.upton@leeds.gov.uk

Regeneration: Mr Tom Bridges , Chief Officer - Economy & Regeneration, The Leonardo Building, Level 6, 2 Rossington Street, Leeds LS2 8HD ☎ 0113 224 3735 ✉ tom.bridges@leeds.gov.uk

Road Safety: Mr Gary Bartlett , Chief Highways Officer, Civic Hall, Leeds LS1 1UR ☎ 0113 247 5319 ✉ gary.bartlett@leeds.gov.uk

Social Services: Ms Cath Roff , Director of Adult Social Care, Civic Hall, Leeds LS1 1UR ✉ cath.roff@ledds.gov.uk

Social Services (Adult): Ms Cath Roff , Director of Adult Social Care, Civic Hall, Leeds LS1 1UR ✉ cath.roff@ledds.gov.uk

Social Services (Children): Mr Nigel Richardson , Director - Children's Services, 3rd Floor, St. Georges House, Leeds LS1 3DL ☎ 0113 378 3687 ✉ nigel.richasrdson@leeds.gov.uk

Public Health: Dr Ian Cameron , Executive Director - Public Health, Civic Hall, Leeds LS1 1UR ☎ 0113 395 2810 ✉ ian.cameron@leeds.gov.uk

Staff Training: Ms Lorraine Hallam, Chief Officer (Human Resources), 3rd Floor West, Civic Hall, Leeds LS1 1UR ☎ 0113 395 1600 ✉ lorraine.hallam@leeds.gov.uk

Street Scene: Mr Neil Evans, Director - Environment & Neighbourhoods, 4th Floor West, Merrion House, Leeds LS1 1UR ☎ 0113 247 4721 🖷 0113 247 4721 ✉ neil.evans@leeds.gov.uk

Street Scene: Ms Helen Freeman, Chief Officer (Environmental Action), Level 2 Southside, Thoresby House, Rossington Street, Leeds LS2 8HD ☎ 0113 247 8888 🖷 0113 224 3543 ✉ helen.freeman@leeds.gov.uk

Sustainable Communities: Mr James Rogers, Assistant Chief Executive (Citizens & Communities), 3rd Floor East, Civic Hall, Calverley Street, Leeds LS1 1UR ☎ 0113 224 3579 🖷 0113 247 4870 ✉ james.rogers@leeds.gov.uk

Sustainable Development: Mr Tim Hill , Chief Planning Officer, The Leonardo Building, 2 Rossington Street, Leeds LS2 8HD ☎ 0113 247 8177 ✉ tim.hill@leeds.gov.uk

Tourism: Mr Tom Bridges , Chief Officer - Economy & Regeneration, The Leonardo Building, Level 6, 2 Rossington Street, Leeds LS2 8HD ☎ 0113 224 3735 ✉ tom.bridges@leeds.gov.uk

Town Centre: Mr John Ebo , City Centre Manager, Leonardo Buidling, 2 Rossington Street, Leeds LS2 8HD ☎ 0113 247 4714 ✉ john.ebo@leeds.gov.uk

Traffic Management: Mr Gary Bartlett , Chief Highways Officer, Civic Hall, Leeds LS1 1UR ☎ 0113 247 5319 ✉ gary.bartlett@leeds.gov.uk

Transport: Ms Julie Meakin, Chief Commercial Services Officer, Seacroft Ring Road Depot, Ring Road, Seacroft, Leeds LS14 1NZ ☎ 0113 214 9568 ✉ julie.meakin@leeds.gov.uk

Transport Planner: Mr Gary Bartlett , Chief Highways Officer, Civic Hall, Leeds LS1 1UR ☎ 0113 247 5319 ✉ gary.bartlett@leeds.gov.uk

Waste Collection and Disposal: Mrs Susan Upton , Chief Officer (Waste Management), Level 2 Southside, Thoresby House, Rossington Street, Leeds LS2 8HD ☎ 0113 247 8888 ✉ susan.upton@leeds.gov.uk

Waste Management: Mr Tom Smith , Head of Environmental Services, 1st Floor, Dewsbury Road One Stop, 190 Dewsbury Road, Leeds LS11 6PF ☎ 0113 395 1395 ✉ tom.smith@leeds.gov.uk

COUNCILLORS

***Leader of the Council* Blake**, Judith (LAB - Middleton Park)
judith.blake@leeds.gov.uk

***Deputy Leader of the Council* Lewis**, James (LAB - Kippax and Methley)
james.lewis@leeds.gov.uk

***Deputy Leader of the Council* Yeadon**, Lucinda (LAB - Kirkstall)
lucinda.yeadon@leeds.gov.uk

***Group Leader* Blackburn**, David (GRN - Farnley and Wortley)
cllr.david.blackburn@leeds.gov.uk

***Group Leader* Carter**, Andrew (CON - Calverley and Farsley)
andrew.carter@leeds.gov.uk

***Group Leader* Finnigan**, Robert (IND - Morley North)
robert.finnigan@leeds.gov.uk

***Group Leader* Golton**, Stewart (LD - Rothwell)
stewart.golton@leeds.gov.uk

Akhtar, Javaid (LAB - Hyde Park and Woodhouse)
javaid.akhtar@leeds.gov.uk

Anderson, Barry (CON - Adel and Wharfedale)
barry.anderson@leeds.gov.uk

Anderson, Caroline (CON - Adel and Wharfedale)
caroline.anderson@leeds.gov.uk

Bentley, Sue (LD - Weetwood)
sue.bentley@leeds.gov.uk

Bentley, Jonathan (LD - Weetwood)
jonathan.bentley@leeds.gov.uk

Blackburn, Ann (GRN - Farnley and Wortley)
ann.blackburn@leeds.gov.uk

Bruce, Karen (LAB - Rothwell)
karen.bruce@leeds.gov.uk

Buckley, Neil (CON - Alwoodley)
neil.buckley@leeds.gov.uk

Campbell, Colin (LD - Otley and Yeadon)
colin.campbell@leeds.gov.uk

Carter, Amanda (CON - Calverley and Farsley)

Castle, Ann (CON - Harewood)
ann.castle@leeds.gov.uk

Chapman, Judith (LD - Weetwood)
judith.m.chapman@leeds.gov.uk

Charlwood, Rebecca (LAB - Moortown)
rebecca.charlwood@leeds.gov.uk

Cleasby, Brian (LD - Horsforth)
brian.cleasby@leeds.gov.uk

Cohen, Daniel (CON - Alwoodley)
daniel.cohen@leeds.gov.uk

Collins, Dawn (CON - Horsforth)
dawn.collins2@leeds.gov.uk

Congreve, David (LAB - Beeston and Holbeck)
david.congreve@leeds.gov.uk

Coulson, Mick (LAB - Pudsey)
mick.coulson@leeds.gov.uk

Coupar, Debra (LAB - Cross Gates and Whinmoor)
debra.coupar@leeds.gov.uk

Cummins, Judith (LAB - Temple Newsam)
judith.cummins@leeds.gov.uk

Davey, Patrick (LAB - City and Hunslet)
patrick.davey@leeds.gov.uk

Dawson, Neil (LAB - Morley South)
neil.dawson@leeds.gov.uk

Dobson, Mark (LAB - Garforth and Swillington)
mark.dobson@leeds.gov.uk

Dobson, Catherine (LAB - Killingbeck and Seacroft)

Downes, Ryk (LD - Otley and Yeadon)
ryk.downes@leeds.gov.uk

Dowson, Jane (LAB - Chapel Allerton)
jane.dowson@leeds.gov.uk

Dunn, Jack (LAB - Ardsley and Robin Hood)
jack.dunn@leeds.gov.uk

Elliott, Judith (IND - Morley South)
judith.elliott@leeds.gov.uk

Flynn, Billy (CON - Adel and Wharfedale)
billy.flynn@leeds.gov.uk

Gabriel, Angela (LAB - Beeston and Holbeck)
angela.gabriel@leeds.gov.uk

Gettings, Bob (IND - Morley North)
robert.gettings@leeds.gov.uk

Grahame, Ronald (LAB - Burmantofts and Richmond Hill)
ronald.grahame@leeds.gov.uk

Grahame, Pauleen (LAB - Cross Gates and Whinmoor)
pauleen.grahame@leeds.gov.uk

Groves, Kim (LAB - Middleton Park)
kim.groves@leeds.gov.uk

Gruen, Peter (LAB - Cross Gates and Whinmoor)
peter.gruen@leeds.gov.uk

Gruen, Caroline (LAB - Bramley and Stanningley)

Hamilton, Sharon (LAB - Moortown)
sharon.hamilton@leeds.gov.uk

Harland, Mary (LAB - Kippax and Methley)

Harper, Gerry (LAB - Hyde Park and Woodhouse)
gerald.harper@leeds.gov.uk

Harrand, Peter (CON - Alwoodley)
peter.harrand@leeds.gov.uk

Harrington, Roger (LAB - Gipton and Harehills)

Hayden, Helen (LAB - Temple Newsam)

Heselwood, Julie (LAB - Bramley and Stanningley)

Hussain, Arif (LAB - Gipton and Harehills)
arif.hussain@leeds.gov.uk

Hussain, Ghulam (LAB - Roundhay)
ghulam.hussain@leeds.gov.uk

Hyde, Graham (LAB - Killingbeck and Seacroft)
graham.hyde@leeds.gov.uk

LEEDS CITY

Illingworth, John (LAB - Kirkstall)
john.illingworth@leeds.gov.uk

Ingham, Maureen (LAB - Burmantofts and Richmond Hill)

Iqbal, Mohammed (LAB - City and Hunslet)
mohammed.iqbal@leeds.gov.uk

Jarosz, Josephine (LAB - Pudsey)
josephine.jarosz@leeds.gov.uk

Khan, Asghar (LAB - Burmantofts and Richmond Hill)
asghar.khan@leeds.gov.uk

Lamb, Alan (CON - Wetherby)
alan.lamb@leeds.gov.uk

Latty, Pat (CON - Guiseley and Rawdon)
patricia.latty@leeds.gov.uk

Latty, Graham (CON - Guiseley and Rawdon)
graham.latty@leeds.gov.uk

Lay, Sandy (LD - Otley and Yeadon)
sandy.lay@leeds.gov.uk

Leadley, Tom (IND - Morley North)
thomas.leadley@leeds.gov.uk

Lewis, Richard (LAB - Pudsey)
richard.lewis@leeds.gov.uk

Lowe, Alison (LAB - Armley)
alison.lowe@leeds.gov.uk

Lyons, Michael (LAB - Temple Newsam)
michael.lyons@leeds.gov.uk

Macniven, Christine (LAB - Roundhay)
christine.macniven@leeds.gov.uk

Magsood, Kamila (LAB - Gipton and Harehills)
kamila.maqsood@leeds.gov.uk

McKenna, Andrea (LAB - Garforth and Swillington)
andrea.mckenna@leeds.gov.uk

McKenna, James (LAB - Armley)
james.mckenna@leeds.gov.uk

McKenna, Stuart (LAB - Garforth and Swillington)
stuart.mckenna@leeds.gov.uk

Mulherin, Lisa (LAB - Ardsley and Robin Hood)
lisa.mulherin@leeds.gov.uk

Nagle, David (LAB - Rothwell)
david.nagle@leeds.gov.uk

Nash, Elizabeth (LAB - City and Hunslet)
elizabeth.nash@leeds.gov.uk

Ogilvie, Adam (LAB - Beeston and Holbeck)
adam.ogilvie@leeds.gov.uk

Procter, Rachael (CON - Harewood)
rachael.procter@leeds.gov.uk

Procter, John (CON - Wetherby)
john.procter@leeds.gov.uk

Pryor, Jonathan (LAB - Headingley)
jonathan.pryor@leeds.gov.uk

Rafique, Mohammed (LAB - Chapel Allerton)
cllr.mohammed.rafique@leeds.gov.uk

Renshaw, Karen (LAB - Ardsley and Robin Hood)
karen.renshaw@leeds.gov.uk

Ritchie, Kevin (LAB - Bramley and Stanningley)
kevin.ritchie@leeds.gov.uk

Robinson, Matthew (CON - Harewood)
matthew.robinson@leeds.gov.uk

Selby, Brian (LAB - Killingbeck and Seacroft)
brian.selby@leeds.gov.uk

Smart, Alice (LAB - Armley)
alice.smart@leeds.gov.uk

Sobel, Alex (LAB - Moortown)
alex.sobel@leeds.gov.uk

Taylor, Eileen (LAB - Chapel Allerton)
eileen.taylor@leeds.gov.uk

Towler, Christine (LAB - Hyde Park and Woodhouse)

Townsley, Christopher (LD - Horsforth)
christopher.townsley@leeds.gov.uk

Truswell, Paul (LAB - Middleton Park)
paul.truswell@leeds.gov.uk

Urry, Bill (LAB - Roundhay)
bill.urry@leeds.gov.uk

Varley, Shirley (IND - Morley South)
shirley.varley@leeds.gov.uk

Venner, Fiona (LAB - Kirkstall)
fiona.venner@leeds.gov.uk

Wadsworth, Paul (CON - Guiseley and Rawdon)
paul.wadsworth@leeds.gov.uk

Wakefield, Keith (LAB - Kippax and Methley)
keith.wakefield@leeds.gov.uk

Walker, Janette (LAB - Headingley)
janette.walker@leeds.gov.uk

Walshaw, Neil (LAB - Headingley)
neil.walshaw@leeds.gov.uk

Wilford, Terry (GRN - Farnley and Wortley)
terry.wilford@leeds.gov.uk

Wilkinson, Gerald (CON - Wetherby)
gerald.wilkinson@leeds.gov.uk

Wood, Rod (CON - Calverley and Farsley)
roderic.wood@leeds.gov.uk

POLITICAL COMPOSITION
LAB: 63, CON: 19, LD: 9, IND: 5, GRN: 3

COMMITTEE CHAIRS
Corporate Governance & Audit: Mr Ghulam Hussain

Health & Wellbeing: Ms Lisa Mulherin

Licensing: Ms Mary Harland

Leicester City U

Leicester City Council, City Hall, 115 Charles Street, Leicester LE1 1FZ

☎ 0116 254 9922 🖷 0116 254 5531 💻 www.leicester.gov.uk

FACTS AND FIGURES
Parliamentary Constituencies: Leicester East, Leicester South,

Leicester West
EU Constituencies: East Midlands
Election Frequency: Elections are of whole council

PRINCIPAL OFFICERS

Chief Executive: Mr Andy Keeling , Chief Operating Officer, City Hall, 115 Charles Street, Leicester LE1 1FZ ☎ 0116 454 0112 ✉ andy.keeling@leicester.gov.uk

Senior Management: Mr John Leach , Director - Local Services, City Hall, 115 Charles Street, Leicester LE1 1FZ ☎ 0116 454 1828 ✉ john.leach@leicester.gov.uk

Senior Management: Ms Ruth Tennant , Director - Public Health, City Hall, 115 Charles Street, Leicester LE1 1FZ ☎ 0116 454 0237 ✉ ruth.tennant@leicester.gov.uk

Access Officer / Social Services (Disability): Ms Tracie Rees, Director - Care Services & Commissioning, City Hall, 115 Charles Street, Leicester LE1 1FZ ☎ 0116 454 2301 ✉ tracie.rees@leicester.gov.uk

Architect, Building / Property Services: Mr Andrew Smith , Director - Planning, Transport & Economic Development, City Hall, 115 Charles Street, Leicester LE1 1FZ ☎ 0116 454 2801 ✉ andrewl.smith@leicester.gov.uk

Catering Services: Ms Jane Faulks , Education Catering Manager, 90 Leycroft Road, Leicester LE4 1BZ ☎ 0116 454 5067 ✉ jane.faulk@leicester.gov.uk

Children / Youth Services: Ms Frances Craven , Strategic Director - Children, City Hall, 115 Charles Street, Leicester LE1 1FZ ☎ 0116 454 0124 ✉ frances.craven@leicester.gov.uk

Children / Youth Services: Ms Jane Winterbone , Interim Director - Learning, Quality & Performance, City Hall, 115 Charles Street, Leicester LE1 1FZ ☎ 0116 252 7701 ✉ jane.winterbone@leicester.gov.uk

Civil Registration: Mr Kevin Lewis , Registration Service Manager, Town Hall, Town Hall Square, Leicester LE1 9BG ☎ 0845 045 0901 ✉ lewk001@leicester.gov.uk

PR / Communications: Ms Deborah Reynolds , Media & PR Manager, City Hall, 115 Charles Street, Leicester LE1 1FZ ☎ 0116 454 4151 ✉ debra.reynolds@leicester.gov.uk

Community Safety: Ms Daxa Pancholi , Head of Community Safety, City Hall, 115 Charles Street, Leicester LE1 1FZ ☎ 0116 454 0203 🖷 0116 285 6241 ✉ daxa.pancholi@leicester.gov.uk

Computer Management: Mr Carl Skidmore , City Information Officer, City Hall, 115 Charles Street, Leicester LE1 1FZ ☎ 0116 454 1166 ✉ carl.skidmore@leicester.gov.uk

Consumer Protection and Trading Standards: Mr Roman Leszczyszyn, Head of Regulatory Services, New Walk Centre, Welford Place, Leicester LE1 6ZG ☎ 0116 454 3191 ✉ roman.leszczyszyn@leicester.gov.uk

Corporate Services: Ms Miranda Cannon , Director - Delivery, Communications & Political Governance, City Hall, 115 Charles Street, Leicester LE1 1FZ ☎ 0116 454 0102 ✉ miranda.cannon@leicester.gov.uk

Customer Service: Mrs Caroline Jackson , Head of Revenues & Customer Support, City Hall, 115 Charles Street, Leicester LE1 1FZ ☎ 0116 454 2501 ✉ caroline.jackson@leicester.gov.uk

Economic Development: Mr Andrew Smith , Director - Planning, Transport & Economic Development, City Hall, 115 Charles Street, Leicester LE1 1FZ ☎ 0116 454 2801 ✉ andrewl.smith@leicester.gov.uk

E-Government: Mr Carl Skidmore , City Information Officer, City Hall, 115 Charles Street, Leicester LE1 1FZ ☎ 0116 454 1166 ✉ carl.skidmore@leicester.gov.uk

Electoral Registration: Ms Alison Saxby, Electoral Services Manager, York House, Granby Street, Leicester LE1 6FB ☎ 0116 299 5965 🖷 0116 247 0863 ✉ alison.saxby@leicester.gov.uk

Emergency Planning: Mr Martin Halse , Resilience Manager, City Hall, 115 Charles Street, Leicester LE1 1FZ ☎ 0116 238 5001 🖷 0116 252 6749 ✉ martin.halse@leicester.gov.uk

Energy Management: Mr Nicholas Morris , Head of Energy Services, 2 - 4 Market Place South, Leicester LE1 5HB ☎ 0116 454 2229 ✉ nicholas.morris@leicester.gov.uk

Environmental Health: Mr John Leach , Director - Local Services, City Hall, 115 Charles Street, Leicester LE1 1FZ ☎ 0116 454 1828 ✉ john.leach@leicester.gov.uk

Estates, Property & Valuation: Mr Neil Gamble , Head of Property, City Hall, 115 Charles Street, Leicester LE1 1FZ ☎ 0116 454 2104 ✉ neil.gamble@leicester.gov.uk

European Liaison: Mrs Joanne Ives, Policy, Partnerships & Programmes Manager, City Hall, 115 Charles Street, Leicester LE1 1FZ ☎ 0116 454 2934 🖷 0116 254 3720 ✉ joanne.ives@leicester.gov.uk

Events Manager: Ms Maggie Shutt, Festivals & Events Manager, Wellington House, Wellington Street, Leicester LE1 6HL ☎ 0116 454 3601 🖷 0116 299 5979 ✉ maggie.shutt@leicester.gov.uk

Facilities: Mr Wyndham Price , Corporate Premises Manager, City Hall, 115 Charles Street, Leicester LE1 1FZ ☎ 0116 454 2189 ✉ wyndham.price@leicester.gov.uk

Finance: Ms Alison Greenhill , Director - Finance, City Hall, 115 Charles Street, Leicester LE1 1FZ ☎ 0116 454 4001 ✉ alison.greenhill@leicester.gov.uk

Grounds Maintenance: Mr Stewart Doughty , Head of Parks & Open Space, Abbey Park, Abbey Park Road, Leicester LE4 5AQ ☎ 0116 233 3020 ✉ stewart.doughty@leicester.gov.uk

Health and Safety: Mr Martin Southam , Head of Health & Safety, City Hall, 115 Charles Street, Leicester LE1 1FZ ☎ 0116 454 4307 ✉ martin.southam@leicester.gov.uk

Highways: Mr Martin Fletcher , Head of Highways, Leycroft Road, Leicester LE4 1BZ ☎ 0116 454 4965 ✉ martin.fletcher@leicester.gov.uk

Home Energy Conservation: Mr Mike Richardson, Home Energy Team Leader, 35 Rowsley Street, Leicester LE5 5JP ☎ 0116 454 3781 ✉ richm002@leicester.gov.uk

Housing: Ms Ann Branson , Director of Housing, Ian Marlow Centre, Blackbird Road, Leicester LE4 0AR ☎ 0116 454 5101 ✉ ann.branson@leicester.gov.uk

Housing Maintenance: Ms Ann Branson , Director of Housing, Ian Marlow Centre, Blackbird Road, Leicester LE4 0AR ☎ 0116 454 5101 ✉ ann.branson@leicester.gov.uk

Housing Maintenance: Mr Ian Craig, Head of Direct Services, Housing Department, Blackbird Road, Leicester LE4 0AR ☎ 0116 454 5211 🖷 0116 251 8998 ✉ craii001@leicester.gov.uk

Legal: Mr Kamal Adatia , City Barrister & Head of Standards, 16 New Walk, Leicester LE1 6UB ☎ 0116 454 1401 ✉ kamal.adatia@leicester.gov.uk

Leisure and Cultural Services: Ms Liz Blyth , Director of Cultural & Neighbourhood Services, City Hall, 115 Charles Street, Leicester LE1 1FZ ☎ 0116 454 3501 ✉ liz.blyth@leicester.gov.uk

Leisure and Cultural Services: Ms Sarah Levitt, Head of Arts & Museums, City Hall, 115 Charles Street, Leicester LE1 1FZ ☎ 0116 454 3521 ✉ sarah.levitt@leicester.gov.uk

Leisure and Cultural Services: Ms Margaret Mernagh , Interim Head of Sports Services, City Hall, 115 Charles Street, Leicester LE1 1FZ ☎ 0116 454 3511 ✉ margaret.mernagh@leicester.gov.uk

Licensing: Mr Mike Broster, Head of Licensing & Pollution Control, New Walk Centre, Welford Place, Leicester LE1 6ZG ☎ 0116 454 3041 ✉ mike.broster@leicester.gov.uk

Personnel / HR: Ms Stephanie Holloway , Head of HR, Sovereign House, Princess Road West, Leicester LE1 6TR ☎ 0116 454 431 ✉ stephanie.holloway@leicester.gov.uk

Planning: Mr Andrew Smith , Director - Planning, Transport & Economic Development, City Hall, 115 Charles Street, Leicester LE1 1FZ ☎ 0116 454 2801 ✉ andrewl.smith@leicester.gov.uk

Procurement: Mr Neil Bayliss , Head of Procurement, City Hall, 115 Charles Street, Leicester LE1 1FZ ☎ 0116 454 4021 ✉ neil.bayliss@leicester.gov.uk

Public Libraries: Mr Adrian Wills , Head of Libraries & Information Services, City Hall, 115 Charles Street, Leicester LE1 1FZ ☎ 0116 454 3541 ✉ adrian.wills@leicester.gov.uk

Recycling & Waste Minimisation: Mr Geoff Soden , Waste Services Manager, City Hall, 115 Charles Street, Leicester LE1 1FZ ☎ 0116 454 6732 ✉ geoff.soden@leicester.gov.uk

Social Services: Ms Clair Pyper , Interim Director - Children, Young People & Families, City Hall, 115 Charles Street, Leicester LE1 1FZ ☎ 0116 454 0125 ✉ clair.pyper@leicester.gov.uk

Social Services: Ms Ruth Tennant , Director - Public Health, City Hall, 115 Charles Street, Leicester LE1 1FZ ☎ 0116 454 0237 ✉ ruth.tennant@leicester.gov.uk

Social Services (Adult): Ms Ruth Lake , Director - Adult Social Care & Safeguarding, City Hall, 115 Charles Street, Leicester LE1 1FZ ☎ 0116 454 5551 ✉ ruth.lake@leicester.gov.uk

Social Services (Children): Ms Clair Pyper , Interim Director - Children, Young People & Families, City Hall, 115 Charles Street, Leicester LE1 1FZ ☎ 0116 454 0125 ✉ clair.pyper@leicester.gov.uk

Public Health: Ms Ruth Tennant , Director - Public Health, City Hall, 115 Charles Street, Leicester LE1 1FZ ☎ 0116 454 0237 ✉ ruth.tennant@leicester.gov.uk

Staff Training: Mr Paul McChrystal , Head of Learning & Development, Sovereign House, Princess Road West, Leicester LE1 6TR ☎ 0116 454 2751 ✉ paul.mcchrystal@leicester.gov.uk

Street Scene: Mr John Leach , Director - Local Services, City Hall, 115 Charles Street, Leicester LE1 1FZ ☎ 0116 454 1828 ✉ john.leach@leicester.gov.uk

Sustainable Communities: Ms Carol Brass, Team Leader - Environment Team, 16 New Walk, Leicester LE1 6UB ☎ 0116 252 6732 🖷 0116 255 9053 ✉ carol.brass@leicester.gov.uk

Sustainable Communities: Ms Anna Dodd, Team Leader - Environment Team, New Walk Centre, Welford Place, Leicester LE1 6ZG ☎ 0116 252 6732 🖷 0116 255 9053 ✉ anna.dodd@leicester.gov.uk

Town Centre: Ms Sarah Harrison , Director of City Centre, York House, Granby Street, Leicester LE1 6FB ☎ 0116 222 3329 ✉ sarahmharrison@leicester.gov.uk

Waste Management: Mr Geoff Soden , Waste Services Manager, City Hall, 115 Charles Street, Leicester LE1 1FZ ☎ 0116 454 6732 ✉ geoff.soden@leicester.gov.uk

COUNCILLORS

***Mayor* Soulsby**, Peter (LAB - City Mayor)
peter.soulsby@leicester.gov.uk

Aldred, Teresa (LAB - Thurncourt)
teresa.aldred@leicester.gov.uk

Alfonso, Dawn (LAB - Fosse)
dawn.alfonso@leicester.gov.uk

Aqbany, Hanif (LAB - Wycliffe)
hanif.aqbany@leicester.gov.uk

Bajaj, Deepak (LAB - Evington)
deepak.bajaj@leicester.gov.uk

Barton, Susan (LAB - Western)
susan.barton@leicester.gov.uk

Bhavsar, Harshad (LAB - Abbey)
harshad.bhavsar@leicester.gov.uk

Byrne, Annette (LAB - Abbey)
annette.byrne@leicester.gov.uk

Cank, Diane (LAB - Troon)
diane.cank@leicester.gov.uk

Cassidy, Ted (LAB - Fosse)

Chapman, Lucy (LAB - Stoneygate)

Chohan, Mansukhlal (LAB - Belgrave)
mo.chohan@leicester.gov.uk

Chowdhury, Shofiqul (LAB - Spinney Hills)
shofiqul.chowdhury@leicester.gov.uk

Clair, Piara (LAB - Rushey Mead)
piara.singhclair@leicester.gov.uk

Clarke, Adam (LAB - Aylestone)
adam.clarke@leicester.gov.uk

Cleaver, Virginia (LAB - Eyres Monsell)
virginia.cleaver@leicester.gov.uk

Cole, George (LAB - Western)
george.cole@leicester.gov.uk

Connelly, Andrew (LAB - Westcotes)
andy.connelly@leicester.gov.uk

Corrall, Stephen (LAB - Braunston Park and Rowley Fields)
stephen.corrall@leicester.gov.uk

Cutkelvin, Elly (LAB - Saffron)
elly.cutkelvin@leicester.gov.uk

Dawood, Mohammed (LAB - Wycliffe)
councillor.mohammed.dawood@leicester.gov.uk

Dempster, Vi (LAB - Humberstone and Hamilton)
vi.dempster@leicester.gov.uk

Fonseca, Luis (LAB - North Evington)
luis.fonseca@leicester.gov.uk

Govind, Ratilal (LAB - Evington)
ratilal.govind@leicester.gov.uk

Grant, Ross (CON - Knighton)
ross.grant@leicester.gov.uk

Gugnani, Inderjit (LAB - Knighton)
inderjit.gugnani@leicester.gov.uk

Halford, Elaine (LAB - Braunston Park and Rowley Fields)
elaine.halford@leicester.gov.uk

Hunter, Sue (LAB - Evington)
councillor.sue.hunter@leicester.gov.uk

Joshi, Rashmikant (LAB - Humberstone and Hamilton)
rashmikant.joshi@leicester.gov.uk

Khote, Jean (LAB - North Evington)
jean.khote@leicester.gov.uk

Kitterick, Patrick (LAB - Castle)
patrick.kitterick@btinternet.com

Malik, Mustafa (LAB - Spinney Hills)

Master, Kirk (LAB - Stoneygate)
kirk.master@leicester.gov.uk

Moore, Lynn (LAB - Knighton)
councillor.lynn.moore@leicester.gov.uk

Newcombe, Paul (LAB - Thurncourt)
paul.newcombe@leicester.gov.uk

Osman, Abdul Razak (LAB - North Evington)
abdul.osman@leicester.gov.uk

Palmer, Rory (LAB - Eyres Monsell)
rory.palmer@leicester.gov.uk

Patel, Rita (LAB - Rushey Mead)
councillor.rita.patel@leicester.gov.uk

Porter, Nigel (LD - Aylestone)
nigel.porter@leicester.gov.uk

Rae Bhatia, Hemant (LAB - Beaumont Leys)
hemant.raebhatia@leicester.gov.uk

Riyait, Vijay Singh (LAB - Abbey)
vijay.rayait@leicester.gov.uk

Russell, Sarah (LAB - Westcotes)
sarah.russell@leicester.gov.uk

Sandhu, Gurinder Singh (LAB - Humberstone and Hamilton)

Sangster, Deborah (LAB - Castle)
deborah.sangster@leicester.gov.uk

Senior, Lynn (LAB - Castle)
lynn.senior@leicester.gov.uk

Shelton, Bill (LAB - Saffron)
bill.shelton@leicester.gov.uk

Singh, Baljit (LAB - Troon)
baljit.singh@leicester.gov.uk

Singh Johal, Kulwinder (LAB - Braunston Park and Rowley Fields)
kulwinder.singhjoha.@leicester.gov.uk

Sood, Manjula (LAB - Belgrave)
manjula.sood@leicester.gov.uk

Thalukdar, Aminur (LAB - Stoneygate)
aminur.thalukdar@leicester.gov.uk

Thomas, John (LAB - Belgrave)
john.thomas@leicester.gov.uk

Unsworth, Malcolm (LAB - Western)
malcolm.unsworth@leicester.gov.uk

Waddington, Susan (LAB - Beaumont Leys)
sue.waddington@leicester.gov.uk

Westley, Paul (LAB - Beaumont Leys)
paul.westley@leicester.gov.uk

Willmott, Ross (LAB - Rushey Mead)members.services@leicester.gov.uk

POLITICAL COMPOSITION
LAB: 53, LD: 1, CON: 1

Leicestershire C

Leicestershire County Council, County Hall, Glenfield, Leicester LE3 8TF
☎ 0116 232 3232 🖷 0116 305 6260; 0116 265 6260
information@leics.gov.uk 💻 www.leics.gov.uk

FACTS AND FIGURES
EU Constituencies: East Midlands
Election Frequency: Elections are of whole council

LEICESTERSHIRE

PRINCIPAL OFFICERS

Chief Executive: Mr John Sinnott, Chief Executive, County Hall, Glenfield, Leicester LE3 8RA ☎ 0116 305 6001 🖷 0116 305 6221 ✉ john.sinnott@leics.gov.uk

Assistant Chief Executive: Mr Tom Purnell, Assistant Chief Executive, County Hall, Glenfield, Leicester LE3 8RA ☎ 0116 305 7019 🖷 0116 305 7271 ✉ tom.purnell@leics.gov.uk

Senior Management: Mr Phil Crossland , Director of Environment & Transport, County Hall, Glenfield, Leicester LE3 8TF ☎ 0116 305 7000 🖷 0116 305 7962 ✉ phil.crossland@leics.gov.uk

Senior Management: Mrs Lesley Hagger , Director of Children & Young People's Services, County Hall, Glenfield, Leicester LE3 8TF ☎ 0116 305 6340 🖷 0116305 6332 ✉ lesley.hagger@leicds.gov.uk

Senior Management: Mr Brian Roberts, Director of Corporate Resources, County Hall, Glenfield, Leicester LE3 8RA ☎ 0116 305 7830 🖷 0116 305 7833 ✉ brian.roberts@leic.gov.uk

Senior Management: Mr Mike Sandys , Director - Public Health, County Hall, Glenfield, Leicester LE3 8TF ☎ 0116 305 4239 ✉ mike.sandys@leics.gov.uk

Access Officer / Social Services (Disability): Ms Heather Pick , Head of Service of Promoting Independence, County Hall, Glenfield, Leicester LE3 8TF ☎ 0116 305 7458 🖷 0116 305 7460 ✉ heather.pick@leics.gov.uk

Architect, Building / Property Services: Mr Richard Tebbatt , Technical Manager, County Hall, Glenfield, Leicester LE3 8TF ☎ 0116 305 6886 🖷 0116 305 6722 ✉ richard.tebbatt@leics.gov.uk

Catering Services: Ms Carol Harris, Food & Nutrition Manager, County Hall, Glenfield, Leicester LE3 8TF ☎ 0116 305 9242 ✉ carol.harris@leics.gov.uk

Catering Services: Ms Wendy Philp, School Food Service Manager, County Hall, Glenfield, Leicester LE3 8TF ☎ 0116 305 5770 ✉ wendy.philp@leics.gov.uk

Catering Services: Mr Phil Smith , Catering Manager, County Hall, Glenfield, Leicester LE3 8TF ☎ 0116 305 6115 ✉ phil.smith@leics.gov.uk

Children / Youth Services: Mrs Lesley Hagger , Director of Children & Young People's Services, County Hall, Glenfield, Leicester LE3 8TF ☎ 0116 305 6340 🖷 0116305 6332 ✉ lesley.hagger@leicds.gov.uk

Children / Youth Services: Mr Walter McCulloch , Assistant Director of Children's Social Care, County Hall, Glenfield, Leicester LE3 8TF ☎ 0116 3057441 ✉ walter.mcculloch@leics.gov.uk

Children / Youth Services: Mrs Jane Moore , Head of Youth Justice & Safer Communities, County Hall, Glenfield, Leicester LE3 8TF ☎ 0116 305 2649 🖷 0116 305 6260 ✉ jane.moore@leics.gov.uk

Civil Registration: Mrs Amanda Bettany , County Superintendent Registrar, County Hall, Glenfield, Leicester LE3 8TF ☎ 0116 605 6585 🖷 0116 305 6580 ✉ amanda.bettany@leics.gov.uk

PR / Communications: Ms Joanna Morrison , Corporate Communications Manager, County Hall, Glenfield, Leicester LE3 8TF ☎ 0116 305 5850 🖷 0116 305 6266 ✉ joanna.morrison@leics.gov.uk

Community Planning: Mr Tom Purnell, Assistant Chief Executive, County Hall, Glenfield, Leicester LE3 8RA ☎ 0116 305 7019 🖷 0116 305 7271 ✉ tom.purnell@leics.gov.uk

Community Safety: Mrs Gurjit Samra-Rai, Community Safety Manager, County Hall, Glenfield, Leicester LE3 8RA ☎ 0116 305 6056 🖷 0116 305 6260 ✉ grai@leics.gov.uk

Computer Management: Mr Manjit Saroya , Head of ICT Services, County Hall, Glenfield, Leicester LE3 8TF ☎ 0116 305 7780 🖷 0116 305 7721 ✉ manjit.saroya@leics.gov.uk

Consumer Protection and Trading Standards: Mr David Bull, Head of Regulatory Services, County Hall, Glenfield, Leicester LE3 8RN ☎ 0116 305 7572 🖷 0116 305 7370 ✉ david.bull@leics.gov.uk

Consumer Protection and Trading Standards: Mr Keith Regan , Trading Standards Manager, County Hall, Glenfield, Leicester LE3 8TF ☎ 0116 305 6533 ✉ keith.regan@leics.gov.uk

Customer Service: Mrs Rachael Stone-Browning, Customer Services Manager, County Hall, Glenfield, Leicester LE3 8RA ☎ 0116 305 6227 🖷 0116 305 0006 ✉ rachael.stone-browning@leics.gov.uk

Education: Mr David Atterbury, Education Officer of Strategic Services, County Hall, Glenfield, Leicester LE3 8TF ☎ 0116 305 7729 🖷 0116 305 6332 ✉ david.atterbury@leics.gov.uk

Education: Mrs Lesley Hagger , Director of Children & Young People's Services, County Hall, Glenfield, Leicester LE3 8TF ☎ 0116 305 6340 🖷 0116305 6332 ✉ lesley.hagger@leicds.gov.uk

E-Government: Mr Manjit Saroya , Head of ICT Services, County Hall, Glenfield, Leicester LE3 8TF ☎ 0116 305 7780 🖷 0116 305 7721 ✉ manjit.saroya@leics.gov.uk

Electoral Registration: Mr Mohammed Seedat , Head of Democratic Services & Administration, County Hall, Glenfield, Leicester LE3 8TF ☎ 0116 305 6037 🖷 0116 305 6260 ✉ mo.seedat@leics.gov.uk

Emergency Planning: Ms Fiona Holbourn, Head of Procurement & Resilience, County Hall, Glenfield, Leicester LE3 8RB ☎ 0116 305 6185 ✉ fiona.holbourn@leics.gov.uk

Energy Management: Mr Graham Read , Corporate Facilities Manager, County Hall, Glenfield, Leicester LE3 8TF ☎ 0116 305 6278 🖷 0116 288 1674 ✉ graham.read@leics.gov.uk

Environmental / Technical Services: Ms Holly Field , Assistant Director of Environment, County Hall, Glenfield, Leicester LE3 8TF ☎ 0116 305 8101 ✉ holly.field@leics.gov.uk

Estates, Property & Valuation: Mr Graham Read , Corporate Facilities Manager, County Hall, Glenfield, Leicester LE3 8TF ☎ 0116 305 6278 🖷 0116 288 1674 ✉ graham.read@leics.gov.uk

European Liaison: Ms Nicole Rickard , Team Leader of Policy & Partnerships, County Hall, Glenfield, Leicester LE3 8RA ☎ 0116 305 6977 🖷 0116 305 7271 ✉ nicole.rickard@leics.gov.uk

Facilities: Mr Graham Read , Corporate Facilities Manager, County Hall, Glenfield, Leicester LE3 8TF ☎ 0116 305 6278 🖷 0116 288 1674 ✉ graham.read@leics.gov.uk

Finance: Mr Brian Roberts, Director of Corporate Resources, County Hall, Glenfield, Leicester LE3 8RA ☎ 0116 305 7830 🖷 0116 305 7833 ✉ brian.roberts@leic.gov.uk

Finance: Mr Chris Tambini , Assistant Director - Strategic Finance & Procurement, County Hall, Glenfield, Leicester LE3 8TF ☎ 0116 305 6199 ✉ chris.tambini@leics.gov.uk

Pensions: Mr Ian Howe , Pensions Manager, County Hall, Glenfield, Leicester LE3 8TF ☎ 0116 305 6945 ✉ ian.howe@leics.gov.uk

Pensions: Mr Colin Pratt , Pension Investments Officer, County Hall, Glenfield, Leicester LE3 8TF ☎ 0116 305 7656 ✉ colin.pratt@leics.gov.uk

Fleet Management: Mr David Atterbury, Education Officer of Strategic Services, County Hall, Glenfield, Leicester LE3 8TF ☎ 0116 305 7729 🖷 0116 305 6332 ✉ david.atterbury@leics.gov.uk

Fleet Management: Mr Tony Kirk , Group Manager of Passenger Transport Unit, County Hall, Glenfield, Leicester LE3 8TF ☎ 0116 305 6270 🖷 0116 305 7181 ✉ tony.kirk@leics.gov.uk

Grounds Maintenance: Mr Graham Read , Corporate Facilities Manager, County Hall, Glenfield, Leicester LE3 8TF ☎ 0116 305 6278 🖷 0116 288 1674 ✉ graham.read@leics.gov.uk

Health and Safety: Mr Colin Jones , Health, Safety & Wellbeing Manager, County Hall, Glenfield, Leicester LE3 8TF ☎ 0116 305 7552 ✉ colin.jones@leics.gov.uk

Highways: Mr Phil Crossland , Director of Environment & Transport, County Hall, Glenfield, Leicester LE3 8TF ☎ 0116 305 7000 🖷 0116 305 7962 ✉ phil.crossland@leics.gov.uk

Local Area Agreement: Mr John Wright , Senior Policy & Performance Officer, County Hall, Glenfield, Leicester LE3 8TF ☎ 0116 305 7041 ✉ john.r.wright@leics.gov.uk

Legal: Mr Andrew James , Interim Head of Legal Services, County Hall, Glenfield, Leicester LE3 8TF ☎ 0116 305 6007 ✉ andrew.james@leics.gov.uk

Leisure and Cultural Services: Mr John Byrne , Sports Co-ordinator, County Hall, Glenfield, Leicester LE3 8RA ☎ 01509 564852 ✉ j.byrne2@lboro.ac.uk

Leisure and Cultural Services: Ms Franne Wills , Assistant Director of Communities, County Hall, Glenfield, Leicester LE3 8TF ☎ 0116 305 0692 ✉ franne.wills@leics.gov.uk

Lifelong Learning: Ms Franne Wills , Assistant Director of Communities, County Hall, Glenfield, Leicester LE3 8TF ☎ 0116 305 0692 ✉ franne.wills@leics.gov.uk

Lighting: Mr Mark Stevens, Assistant Director of Highways, County Hall, Glenfield, Leicester LE3 8RA ☎ 0116 305 7966 🖷 0116 305 7962 ✉ mark.stevens@leics.gov.uk

Member Services: Ms Liz Clark , Assistant Director - Strategic ICT & Communications, County Hall, Glenfield, Leicester LE3 8TF ☎ 0116 305 6236 ✉ liz.clark@leics.gov.uk

Member Services: Mr Mohammed Seedat , Head of Democratic Services & Administration, County Hall, Glenfield, Leicester LE3 8TF ☎ 0116 305 6037 🖷 0116 305 6260 ✉ mo.seedat@leics.gov.uk

Partnerships: Mr Tom Purnell, Assistant Chief Executive, County Hall, Glenfield, Leicester LE3 8RA ☎ 0116 305 7019 🖷 0116 305 7271 ✉ tom.purnell@leics.gov.uk

Personnel / HR: Mr Gordon McFarlane , Assistant Director - Corporate Services & Transformation, County Hall, Glenfield, Leicester LE3 8TF ☎ 0116 305 6123 ✉ gordon.mcfarlane@leics.gov.uk

Planning: Mr Lonek Wojtulewicz, Head of Planning Historic & Natural Environment, County Hall, Glenfield, Leicester LE3 8TE ☎ 0116 305 7040 🖷 0116 305 7297 ✉ lonek.wojtulewicz@leics.gov.uk

Procurement: Ms Fiona Holbourn, Head of Procurement & Resilience, County Hall, Glenfield, Leicester LE3 8RB ☎ 0116 305 6185 ✉ fiona.holbourn@leics.gov.uk

Public Libraries: Mr Nigel Thomas , Service Delivery Manager, County Hall, Glenfield, Leicester LE3 8TF ☎ 0116 305 7379 🖷 0116 305 7370 ✉ nigel.thomas@leics.gov.uk

Recycling & Waste Minimisation: Ms Holly Field, Assistant Director of Environment, County Hall, Glenfield, Leicester LE3 8RJ ☎ 0116 305 8101 🖷 0116 305 8128 ✉ holly.field@leics.gov.uk

Regeneration: Mr Derk Van Der Wardt , Group Manager of Communities & Places, County Hall, Glenfield, Leicester LE3 8TF ☎ 0116 305 7581 ✉ derk.vanderwardt@leics.gov.uk

Road Safety: Mr Nigel Horsley , Team Manager, Road Safety & Travel Awareness, County Hall, Glenfield, Leicester LE3 8TF ☎ 0116 305 7227 ✉ nigel.horsley@leics.gov.uk

Social Services: Mr Mick Connell, Director of Adults & Communities, County Hall, Glenfield, Leicester LE3 8RA ☎ 0116 305 7454 🖷 0116 305 7460 ✉ mick.connell@leics.gov.uk

Social Services (Children): Mr Walter McCulloch , Assistant Director of Children's Social Care, County Hall, Glenfield, Leicester LE3 8TF ☎ 0116 305 7441 ✉ walter.mcculloch@leics.gov.uk

LEICESTERSHIRE

Public Health: Mr Mike Sandys , Director - Public Health, County Hall, Glenfield, Leicester LE3 8TF ☎ 0116 305 4239 ✉ mike.sandys@leics.gov.uk

Staff Training: Ms Jennifer Penfold , Learning & Development Manager, County Hall, Glenfield, Leicester LE3 8TF ☎ 0116 305 5615 🖷 0116 305 6285 ✉ jennifer.penfold@leics.gov.uk

Tourism: Ms Joanna Morrison , Corporate Communications Manager, County Hall, Glenfield, Leicester LE3 8TF ☎ 0116 305 5850 🖷 0116 305 6266 ✉ joanna.morrison@leics.gov.uk

Transport: Mr Phil Crossland , Director of Environment & Transport, County Hall, Glenfield, Leicester LE3 8TF ☎ 0116 305 7000 🖷 0116 305 7962 ✉ phil.crossland@leics.gov.uk

Transport Planner: Mr Paul Sheard , Group Manager of Transport Planning, County Hall, Glenfield, Leicester LE3 8RJ ☎ 0116 305 7191 ✉ paul.sheard@leics.gov.uk

Total Place: Mr Simon Lawrence , Programme Manager, County Hall, Glenfield, Leicester LE3 8TF ☎ 0116 305 7243 ✉ simon.lawrence@leics.gov.uk

Waste Collection and Disposal: Ms Holly Field, Assistant Director of Environment, County Hall, Glenfield, Leicester LE3 8RJ ☎ 0116 305 8101 🖷 0116 305 8128 ✉ holly.field@leics.gov.uk

Waste Management: Mr Phil Crossland , Director of Environment & Transport, County Hall, Glenfield, Leicester LE3 8TF ☎ 0116 305 7000 🖷 0116 305 7962 ✉ phil.crossland@leics.gov.uk

Waste Management: Ms Holly Field, Assistant Director of Environment, County Hall, Glenfield, Leicester LE3 8RJ ☎ 0116 305 8101 🖷 0116 305 8128 ✉ holly.field@leics.gov.uk

COUNCILLORS

Leader of the Council **Rushton**, Nicholas (CON - Valley)
nicholas.rushton@leics.gov.uk

Deputy Leader of the Council **Rhodes**, Byron (CON - Belvoir)
byron.rhodes@leics.gov.uk

Bently, Iain (CON - Birstall)
iain.bentley@leics.gov.uk

Bill, David (LD - Hinckley)
david.bill@leics.gov.uk

Blunt, Richard (CON - Kirby Muxloe and Leicester Forest)
richard.blunt@leics.gov.uk

Boulter, Bill (LD - Wigston South)
bill.boulter@leics.gov.uk

Bray, Stuart (LD - Burbage Castle)
stuart.bray@leics.gov.uk

Camamile, Ruth (CON - Mallory)
ruth.camamile@leics.gov.uk

Charlesworth, Michael (LD - Wigston Busloe)
michael.charlesworth@leics.gov.uk

Coxon, John (CON - Ashby de la Zouch)
john.coxon@leics.gov.uk

Dickinson, Jackie (CON - Enderby Meridian)
jackie.dickinson@leics.gov.uk

Enynon, Terri (LAB - Coalville)
terri.enyon@leics.gov.uk

Feltham, Kevin (CON - Gartree)
kevin.feltham@leics.gov.uk

Fox, Jo (LAB - Braunstone Town)
jo.fox@leics.gov.uk

Galton, Simon (LD - Launde)
simon.galton@leics.gov.uk

Gamble, Dean (LD - Oadby)
dean.gamble@leics.gov.uk

Hampson, Stephen (CON - Syston Ridgeway)
stephen.hampson@leics.gov.uk

Hart, Graham (CON - Bruntingthorpe)
graham.hart@leics.gov.uk

Hill, Sarah (LD - Market Harborough East)
sarah.hill@leics.gov.uk

Houseman, David (CON - Syston Fosse)
dave.houseman@leics.gov.uk

Hunt, Max (LAB - Loughborough North West)
max.hunt@leics.gov.uk

Jennings, David (CON - Cosby & Countesthorpe)
david.jennings@leics.gov.uk

Kaufman, Jeffrey (LD - Oadby)
jeffrey.kaufman@leics.gov.uk

Kershaw, Tony (CON - Quorn and Barrow)
tony.kershaw@leics.gov.uk

Knaggs, Kate (LAB - Thurmaston)
kate.knaggs@leics.gov.uk

Lewis, Peter (CON - Loughborough South West)
peter.lewis@leics.gov.uk

Liquorish, Bill (CON - Broughton Astley)
bill.liquorish@leics.gov.uk

Lloydall, Helen (LD - Wigston Poplars)
helen.lloydall@leics.gov.uk

Lynch, Keith (LD - Burbage Castle)
keith.lynch@leics.gov.uk

Miah, Jewel (LAB - Loughborough East)
jewel.miah@leics.gov.uk

Mullaney, Michael (LD - Hinckley)
michael.mullaney@leics.gov.uk

Newton, Betty (LAB - Loughborough North)
betty.newton@leics.gov.uk

Orson, Joseph (CON - Asfordby)
joe.orson@leics.gov.uk

Osborne, Peter (CON - Rothley & Mountsorrel)
peter.osborne@leics.gov.uk

O'Shea, Ozzy (CON - Groby and Ratby)
ozzy.o'shea@leics.gov.uk

Ould, Ivan (CON - Market Bosworth)
ivan.ould@leics.gov.uk

Page, Rosita (CON - Lutterworth)
rosita.page@leics.gov.uk

Pain, Blake (CON - Market Harborough West & Foxton)
blake.pain@leics.gov.uk

Pearson, Alan (CON - Melton South)
alan.pearson@leics.gov.uk

Pendleton, Trevor (CON - Castle Donington)
trevor.pendleton@leics.gov.uk

Posnett, Pam (CON - Melton North)
pam.posnett@leics.gov.uk

Radford, Christine (CON - Shepshed)
christine.radford@leics.gov.uk

Richards, Janice (CON - Earl Shilton)
janice.richards@leics.gov.uk

Richardson, Terry (CON - Narborough & Whetstone)
terry.richardson@leics.gov.uk

Sharp, Robert (LAB - Loughborough South)
robert.sharp@leics.gov.uk

Sheahan, Sean (LAB - Forest & Measham)
sean.sheahan@leics.gov.uk

Shepherd, Richard (CON - Sileby and The WOlds)
richard.shepherd@leics.gov.uk

Snartt, David (CON - Bradgate)
david.snartt@leics.gov.uk

Spence, Leon (LAB - Whitwick)
leon.spence@leics.gov.uk

Sprason, David (UKIP - Markfield Desford & Thornton)
david.sprason@leics.gov.uk

Walsh, Geoff (LD - Blaby and Glen Parva)
geoff.walsh@leics.gov.uk

White, Ernie (CON - Stanton Croft & Normanton)
ernie.white@leics.gov.uk

Worman, Heather (LAB - Ibstock & Appleby)
heather.worman@leics.gov.uk

Wyatt, Michael (LD - Warren Hills)
michael.wyatt@leics.gov.uk

Yates, Lynton (UKIP - Glenfields)
lynton.yates@leics.gov.uk

POLITICAL COMPOSITION

CON: 30, LD: 13, LAB: 10, UKIP: 2

COMMITTEE CHAIRS

Environment & Transport: Mr David Jennings

Health & Wellbeing: Mr Ernie White

Lewes D

Lewes District Council, Lewes House, 32 High Street, Lewes BN7 2LX
☎ 01273 471600 💻 www.lewes.gov.uk

FACTS AND FIGURES

Parliamentary Constituencies: Lewes
EU Constituencies: South East
Election Frequency: Elections are of whole council

PRINCIPAL OFFICERS

Chief Executive: Ms Jenny Rowlands , Chief Executive, Lewes House, 32 High Street, Lewes BN7 2LX ☎ 01273 471600 ✉ jenny.rowlands@lewes.gov.uk

Senior Management: Mr John Magness, Director - Finance, Southover House, Southover Road, Lewes BN7 1AB ☎ 01273 484467 🖷 01273 484233 ✉ john.magness@lewes.gov.uk

Senior Management: Ms Gillian Marston , Director - Service Delivery, Southover House, Southover Road, Lewes BN7 1AB ☎ 01273 471600 ✉ gillian.marston@lewes.gov.uk

Access Officer / Social Services (Disability): Ms Sue Dunkley, Access Officer, Southover House, Southover Road, Lewes BN7 1AB ☎ 01273 481121 🖷 01273 484452 ✉ sue.dunkley@lewes.gov.uk

Architect, Building / Property Services: Mr Andy Chequers , Corporate Head - Housing Services, Lewes House, 32 High Street, Lewes BN7 2LX ☎ 01273 484380 🖷 01273 484431 ✉ andy.chequers@lewes.gov.uk

Best Value: Mr David Heath, Head - Audit & Performance, 4 Fisher Street, Lewes BN7 2DQ ☎ 01273 471600 🖷 01273 484090 ✉ david.heath@lewes.gov.uk

Building Control: Mr Roger Carsons , Head - Building Control, Planning and Environment Services, PO Box 2707, Southover House, Southover Road, Lewes BN7 1AB ☎ 01273 481120 🖷 01273 484442 ✉ roger.carsons@lewes.gov.uk

PR / Communications: Ms Liz Lacon, Press Officer, Lewes House, 32 High Street, Lewes BN7 2LX ☎ 01273 484141 🖷 01273 484254 ✉ liz.lacon@lewes.gov.uk

Computer Management: Ms Kalpna Dice , Head of IT Department, Lewes House, 32 High Street, Lewes BN7 2LX ☎ 01273 471600 ✉ kalpna.dice@lewes.gov.uk

Contracts: Mr John Magness, Director - Finance, Southover House, Southover Road, Lewes BN7 1AB ☎ 01273 484467 🖷 01273 484233 ✉ john.magness@lewes.gov.uk

Customer Service: Mr David Parry , Senior Customer Services Assistant, Southover House, Southover Road, Lewes BN7 1AB ☎ 01273 486031 ✉ david.parry@lewes.gov.uk

Economic Development: Ms Gillian Marston , Director - Service Delivery, Southover House, Southover Road, Lewes BN7 1AB ☎ 01273 471600 ✉ gillian.marston@lewes.gov.uk

Electoral Registration: Mr Steven Andrews, Electoral Services Manager, Lewes House, 32 High Street, Lewes BN7 2LX ☎ 01273 484117 ✉ steven.andrews@lewes.gov.uk

Emergency Planning: Mr Ian Hodgson , Emergency Planning Officer, Southover House, Southover Road, Lewes BN7 1AB ☎ 01273 486334 ✉ ian.hodgson@lewes.gov.uk

Emergency Planning: Ms Gillian Marston , Director - Service Delivery, Southover House, Southover Road, Lewes BN7 1AB ☎ 01273 471600 ✉ gillian.marston@lewes.gov.uk

Environmental / Technical Services: Mr Tim Bartlett , Environmental Health Manager, Lewes House, 32 High Street, Lewes BN7 2LX ☎ 01273 486082 ✉ tim.bartlett@lewes.gov.uk

Environmental Health: Mr Tim Bartlett , Environmental Health Manager, Lewes House, 32 High Street, Lewes BN7 2LX ☎ 01273 486082 ✉ tim.bartlett@lewes.gov.uk

Finance: Mr John Magness, Director - Finance, Southover House, Southover Road, Lewes BN7 1AB ☎ 01273 484467 🖷 01273 484233 ✉ john.magness@lewes.gov.uk

Finance: Mr Ian Morris , Head - Revenues & Benefits, Lewes House, 32 High Street, Lewes BN7 2LX ☎ 01273 484079 ✉ ian.morris@lewes.gov.uk

Grounds Maintenance: Mr Andy Frost, Parks Manager, Southover House, Southover Road, Lewes BN7 1AB ☎ 01273 484398 ✉ andy.frost@lewes.gov.uk

Health and Safety: Mr Matthew Britnell , Safety Officer, Lewes House, 32 High Street, Lewes BN7 2LX ☎ 01273 486106 ✉ matthew.britnell@lewes.gov.uk

Housing: Ms Jo Jacks , Housing Needs Officer, Fisher Street, Lewes BN7 2DQ ☎ 01273 486144 ✉ jo.jacks@lewes.gov.uk

Housing: Mr John Magness, Director - Finance, Southover House, Southover Road, Lewes BN7 1AB ☎ 01273 484467 🖷 01273 484233 ✉ john.magness@lewes.gov.uk

Housing Maintenance: Mr Andy Chequers , Corporate Head - Housing Services, Lewes House, 32 High Street, Lewes BN7 2LX ☎ 01273 484380 🖷 01273 484431 ✉ andy.chequers@lewes.gov.uk

Legal: Ms Celia Cullen , Director - Shared Legal Services Unit, Lewes House, 32 High Street, Lewes BN7 2LX ☎ 01273 471600 ✉ celia.cullen@lewes.gov.uk

Legal: Ms Catherine Knight, Assistant Director - Corporate Services, Lewes House, 32 High Street, Lewes BN7 2LX ☎ 01273 481116 🖷 01273 484121 ✉ catherine.knight@lewes.gov.uk

Licensing: Ms Gillian Marston , Director - Service Delivery, Southover House, Southover Road, Lewes BN7 1AB ☎ 01273 471600 ✉ gillian.marston@lewes.gov.uk

Member Services: Ms Rachel Allan , Performance & Committee Officer, Lewes House, 32 High Street, Lewes BN7 2LX ☎ 01273 486228 ✉ rachel.allan@lewes.gov.uk

Planning: Ms Gillian Marston , Director - Service Delivery, Southover House, Southover Road, Lewes BN7 1AB ☎ 01273 471600 ✉ gillian.marston@lewes.gov.uk

Recycling & Waste Minimisation: Ms Julia Black, Community Recycling Officer, Community Recycling Centre, 20 North Street, Lewes BN7 2PE ☎ 01273 486268 🖷 01273 486619 ✉ julia.black@lewes.gov.uk

Staff Training: Ms Helen Knight , HR Manager, Lewes House, 32 High Street, Lewes BN7 2LX ☎ 01273 481365 ✉ helen.knight@lewes.gov.uk

Staff Training: Ms Jill Yeates, Health & Safety Officer, Lewes House, 32 High Street, Lewes BN7 2LX ☎ 01273 486276 🖷 01273 484233 ✉ jill.yeates@lewes.gov.uk

Sustainable Communities: Mr Tim Bartlett , Environmental Health Manager, Lewes House, 32 High Street, Lewes BN7 2LX ☎ 01273 486082 ✉ tim.bartlett@lewes.gov.uk

Sustainable Development: Mr Greg Martin , Waste Operations Manager, Community Recycling Centre, 20 North Street, Lewes BN7 2PE ☎ 01273 486423 ✉ greg.martin@lewes.gov.uk

Waste Collection and Disposal: Mr Greg Martin , Waste Operations Manager, Community Recycling Centre, 20 North Street, Lewes BN7 2PE ☎ 01273 486423 ✉ greg.martin@lewes.gov.uk

Waste Management: Mr Greg Martin , Waste Operations Manager, Community Recycling Centre, 20 North Street, Lewes BN7 2PE ☎ 01273 486423 ✉ greg.martin@lewes.gov.uk

COUNCILLORS

***Chair* O'Keeffe**, Ruth (IND - Lewes Priory)
rok@supanet.com

***Vice-Chair* Robertson**, Robbie (CON - Peacehaven West)
robbie.robertson@lewes.gov.uk

***Leader of the Council* Blackman**, Rob (CON - Seaford West)
rob.blackman@lewes.gov.uk

***Deputy Leader of the Council* Smith**, Andy (CON - East Saltdean and Telscombe Cliffs)
cllr.andysmith.ldc@gmail.com

***Group Leader* Osborne**, Sarah (LD - Plumpton Streat East Chiltington & St John Without)
sarah.osborne2@lewes.gov.uk

***Group Leader* Rowell**, Tony (GRN - Lewes Priory)
tony.rowell@lewes.gov.uk

Adeniji, Sam (CON - Seaford South)
sam.adeniji@lewes.gov.uk

Amy, Graham (LD - Newhaven Denton and Meeching)
graham.amy@lewes.gov.uk

Barnes, Simon (UKIP - Newhaven Denton and Meeching)
simon.barnes@lewes.gov.uk

Botting, Wayne (CON - East Saltdean and Telscombe Cliffs)
wayne.botting@lewes.gov.uk

Bovington, Bill (CON - Seaford Central)
bill.bovington@lewes.gov.uk

Carr, Julie (LD - Newhaven Valley)
julie.carr@lewes.gov.uk

Carter, Joanna (GRN - Lewes Bridge)
joanna.carter@lewes.gov.uk

Catlin, Stephen (IND - Lewes Priory)
stephen.catlin@lewes.gov.uk

Chartier, Michael (LD - Lewes Castle)
michael.cartier@lewes.gov.uk

Cooper, Daisy (LD - Lewes Bridge)
daisy.cooper@lewes.gov.uk

Davy, Sharon (CON - Chailey and Wivelsfield)
sharon.davy@lewes.gov.uk

Enever, Nigel (CON - Peacehaven East)
nigel.enever@lewes.gov.uk

Franklin, Paul (CON - Seaford North)
paul.franklin@lewes.gov.uk

Gander, Paul (CON - Ouse Valley and Ringmer)
paul.gander@lewes.gov.uk

Gardiner, Peter (LD - Ouse Valley and Ringmer)
peter.gardiner@lewes.gov.uk

Gauntlett, Stephen (LD - Seaford Central)
stephen.gauntlett@lewes.gov.uk

Giles, Bill (CON - Newhaven Denton and Meeching)
bill.giles@lewes.gov.uk

Harrison-Hicks, Jacqueline (CON - Peacehaven East)
jmharricks@btinternet.com

Honeyman, Olivia (LD - Seaford South)
olivia.honeyman@lewes.gov.uk

Ient, Vic (LD - Kingston)
vic.ient@lewes.gov.uk

Jones, Tom (CON - Ditchling and Westmerton)
tom.jones@lewes.gov.uk

Lambert, Alex (LD - Seaford North)
alex.lambert@lewes.gov.uk

Linington, Isabelle (CON - Barcombe and Hamsey)
isabelle.linington@lewes.gov.uk

Lorraine, Andy (CON - Peacehaven North)
andy.lorraine@lewes.gov.uk

Maskell, Ron (CON - East Saltdean and Telscombe Cliffs)
cllr.ronmaskell@gmail.com

Merry, Elayne (CON - Peacehaven North)
elayne.merry@lewes.gov.uk

Murray, Susan (GRN - Lewes Castle)
susan.murray@lewes.gov.uk

Neave, Dave (CON - Peacehaven West)
david.neave@lewes.gov.uk

Nicholson, Tony (CON - Seaford East)
tony.angela@btinternet.com

Peterson, Julian (CON - Seaford East)
julian.peterson@lewes.gov.uk

Saunders, Steve (LD - Newhaven Valley)
steve.saunders@lewes.gov.uk

Sheppard, Jim (CON - Newick)
j.sheppard3@btinternet.com

Sugarman, Cyril (CON - Chailey and Wivelsfield)
cyril.sugarman@lewes.gov.uk

Turner, Richard (CON - Ouse Valley and Ringmer)
richard.turner@lewes.gov.uk

Wallraven, Linda (CON - Seaford West)
linda.wallraven@lewes.gov.uk

POLITICAL COMPOSITION

CON: 24, LD: 11, GRN: 3, IND: 2, UKIP: 1

COMMITTEE CHAIRS

Audit: Mr Michael Chartier

Licensing: Mr Sam Adeniji

Planning: Ms Sharon Davy

Lewisham L

Lewisham London Borough Council, Civic Suite, Town Hall, London SE6 4RU
☎ 020 8314 6000 💻 www.lewisham.gov.uk

FACTS AND FIGURES

Parliamentary Constituencies: Lewisham Deptford, Lewisham East, Lewisham West and Penge
EU Constituencies: London
Election Frequency: Elections are of whole council

PRINCIPAL OFFICERS

Chief Executive: Mr Barry Quirk, Chief Executive, 5th Floor, Laurence House, 1 Catford Road, London SE6 4RU ☎ 020 8314 6445 🖷 020 8314 3028 ✉ barry.quirk@lewisham.gov.uk

Senior Management: Ms Aileen Buckton, Executive Director of Community Services, 5th Floor, Laurence House, 1 Catford Road, London SE6 4RU ☎ 020 8314 8107 🖷 020 8314 3023 ✉ aileen.buckton@lewisham.gov.uk

Senior Management: Dr Danny Ruta , Director - Public Health, Laurence House, 1 Catford Road, London SE6 4RU ☎ 020 8314 9094 ✉ danny.ruta@lewisham.gov.uk

Senior Management: Ms Janet Senior, Executive Director for Resources & Regeneration, 5th Floor, Laurence House, 1 Catford Road, London SE6 4RU ☎ 020 8314 8013 🖷 020 8314 3046 ✉ janet.senior@lewisham.gov.uk

Senior Management: Mr Kevin Sheehan , Executive Director of Customer Services, 5th Floor, Laurence House, 1 Catford Road, London SE6 4RU ☎ 020 8314 6800 ✉ kevin.sheehan@lewisham.gov.uk

Senior Management: Ms Sara Williams , Executive Director of Children & Young People, Laurence House, 1 Catford Road, London SE6 4RU ☎ 020 8314 8527 ✉ sara.williams@lewisham.gov.uk

Architect, Building / Property Services: Ms Annettal Crossley Head of Property Services, 2nd Floor, Laurence House, 1 Catford Road, London SE6 4RU ☎ 020 8314 9222 ✉ annettal.crossley@lewisham.gov.uk

Best Value: Mr Barrie Neal, Head of Corporate Policy & Governance, 5th Floor, Laurence House, 1 Catford Road, London SE6 4RU ☎ 020 8314 9852 ✉ barrie.neal@lewisham.gov.uk

Building Control: Mr Thiru Moolan , Civil & Structural Engineering Manager, 4th Floor, Laurence House, 1 Catford Road, London SE6 4RU ✉ building.control@lewisham.gov.uk

LEWISHAM

Children / Youth Services: Mr Alan Docksey , Head of Resources CYP, 3rd Floor, Laurence House, 1 Cartford Road, London SE6 4RU ☎ 020 8314 3582 alan.docksey@lewisham.gov.uk

Children / Youth Services: Ms Sara Williams , Executive Director of Children & Young People, Laurence House, 1 Catford Road, London SE6 4RU ☎ 020 8314 8527 sara.williams@lewisham.gov.uk

Civil Registration: Mr Glynne Harris , Superintendent Registrar, Registrar Office, Lewisham High Street, London SE13 4RU ☎ 020 8690 2128 🖷 020 8314 1078 glynne.harris@lewisham.gov.uk

Civil Registration: Ms Renee Hayles , Head of Land Charges, 5th Floor, Laurence House, 1 Catford Road, London SE6 4RU ☎ 020 8314 6078 renee.hayles@lewisham.gov.uk

PR / Communications: Mr Adrian Wardle , Head of Communications, Civic Suite, Town Hall, London SE6 4RU ☎ 020 8314 6087 🖷 020 8314 3120 adrian.wardle@lewisham.gov.uk

Community Planning: Ms Liz Dart , Head of Culture & Community Development, Laurence House, 1 Catford Road, London SE6 4RU ☎ 020 8314 6000 liz.dart@lewisham.gov.uk

Community Safety: Mr Gary Connors , Crime Enforcement Regulation Team Service Manager, Mercia Grove, Lewisham, London SE13 7EZ ☎ 020 8314 9773 gary.connors@lewisham.gov.uk

Community Safety: Ms Geeta Subramaniam , Head of Crime Reduction & Supporting People, 5th Floor, Laurence House, 1 Catford Road, London SE6 4RU ☎ 020 8314 9509 geeta.subramaniam@lewisham.gov.uk

Computer Management: Mr Duncan Dewhurst , Head of Service Change & Technology, 5th Floor, Laurence House, 1 Catford Road, London SE6 4RU ☎ 07875 082430 duncan.dewhurst@lewisham.gov.uk

Consumer Protection and Trading Standards: Mr Gary Connors , Crime Enforcement Regulation Team Service Manager, Mercia Grove, Lewisham, London SE13 7EZ ☎ 020 8314 9773 gary.connors@lewisham.gov.uk

Customer Service: Mr Kevin Sheehan , Executive Director of Customer Services, 5th Floor, Laurence House, 1 Catford Road, London SE6 4RU ☎ 020 8314 6800 kevin.sheehan@lewisham.gov.uk

Economic Development: Mr Kevin Turner , Economic Development Manager, Laurence House, 1 Catford Road, London SE6 4RU ☎ 020 8314 8229 🖷 020 8314 3129 kevin.turner@lewisham.gov.uk

Education: Ms Louise Comely , Head of Inclusion Service, Kaleidoscope, 4th Floor, 32 Rushey Green, London SE6 4JF ☎ 020 7138 1432 louise.comely@lewisham.gov.uk

Education: Ms Sara Williams , Executive Director of Children & Young People, Laurence House, 1 Catford Road, London SE6 4RU ☎ 020 8314 8527 sara.williams@lewisham.gov.uk

Electoral Registration: Ms Kath Nicholson, Head of Law, 5th Floor, Laurence House, 1 Catford Road, London SE6 4RU ☎ 020 8314 7648 🖷 020 8314 3107 kath.nicholson@lewisham.gov.uk

Emergency Planning: Mr John Brown, Principal Emergency Planning Officer, 5th Floor, Laurence House, 1 Catford Road , London SE6 4RU ☎ 020 8314 8579 🖷 020 8314 3155

Energy Management: Mr Martin O'Brien , Sustainability Officer, Laurence House, 1 Catford Road, London SE6 4RU ☎ 020 8314 6605 martin.o'brien@lewisham.gov.uk

Environmental / Technical Services: Mr Nigel Tyrell, Head of Environment, Wearside Service Centre, Wearside Road, London SE13 7EZ ☎ 020 8314 6000 nigel.tyrell@lewisham.gov.uk

Estates, Property & Valuation: Mr Rob Holmans , Head of Programme Management & Property, Laurence House, 1 Catford Road, London SE6 4RU ☎ 020 8314 6000 rob.holmes@lewisham.gov.uk

European Liaison: Ms Nicola Marven , International Partnerships & Projects Officer, Civic Suite, Town Hall, London SE6 4RU ☎ 020 8324 7227 nicola.marven@lewisham.gov.uk

Events Manager: Ms Carmel Langstaff , Head of Arts & Entertainment, 5th Floor, Laurence House, 1 Catford Road, London SE6 4RU ☎ 020 8314 7729 carmel.langstaff@lewisham.gov.uk

Events Manager: Mr Andy Thomas , Cultural Development Manager, 5th Floor, Laurence House, 1 Catford Road, London SE6 4RU ☎ 020 8314 6000 andy.thomas@lewisham.gov.uk

Facilities: Ms Annnettal Crossley , Head of Property Services, 2nd Floor, Laurence House, 1 Catford Road, London SE6 4RU ☎ 020 8314 9222 annettal.crossley@lewisham.gov.uk

Finance: Ms Janet Senior, Executive Director for Resources & Regeneration, 5th Floor, Laurence House, 1 Catford Road, London SE6 4RU ☎ 020 8314 8013 🖷 020 8314 3046 janet.senior@lewisham.gov.uk

Pensions: Mr Tim O'Connor , Pensions Manager, 5th Floor, Laurence House, 1 Catford Road, London SE6 4RU ☎ 020 8314 7142 tim.o'connor@lewisham.gov.uk

Pensions: Mr Selwyn Thompson , Pension Investment Manager, 5th Floor, Laurence House, 1 Catford Road, London SE6 4RU ☎ 020 8314 6932 selwyn.thompson@lewisham.gov.uk

Fleet Management: Mr Martin Champkins, Service Unit Manager of Lewisham Door to Door, Lewisham Town Hall, London SE6 4RU ☎ 020 8314 0991 🖷 020 8314 2190 martin.champkins@lewisham.gov.uk

Health and Safety: Mr David Austin , Head of Corporate Resources, 3rd Floor, Town Hall, London SE6 4RU ☎ 020 8314 8914 🖷 020 8314 3448 ✉ david.austin@lewisham.gov.uk

Housing: Ms Genevieve Macklin , Head of Strategic Housing, 5th Floor, Laurence House, 1 Catford Road, London SE6 4RU ☎ 020 8314 6057 ✉ genevieve.macklin@lewisham.gov.uk

Local Area Agreement: Ms Fenella Beckman , Strategic Partnership Manager, Civic Suite, Town Hall, London SE6 4RU ☎ 020 8314 8632 ✉ Fenella.Beckman@lewisham.gov.uk

Legal: Ms Kath Nicholson, Head of Law, 5th Floor, Laurence House, 1 Catford Road, London SE6 4RU ☎ 020 8314 7648 🖷 020 8314 3107 ✉ kath.nicholson@lewisham.gov.uk

Leisure and Cultural Services: Mr Andy Thomas , Cultural Development Manager, 5th Floor, Laurence House, 1 Catford Road, London SE6 4RU ☎ 020 8314 6000 ✉ andy.thomas@lewisham.gov.uk

Licensing: Mr Gary Connors , Crime Enforcement Regulation Team Service Manager, Mercia Grove, Lewisham, London SE13 7EZ ☎ 020 8314 9773 ✉ gary.connors@lewisham.gov.uk

Lottery Funding, Charity and Voluntary: Mr Paul Hadfield , Enterprise Development Manager, 5th Floor, Laurence House, 1 Catford Road, London SE6 4RU ☎ 020 8314 8022 🖷 020 8314 3129 ✉ paul.hadfield@lewisham.gov.uk

Member Services: Mr Kevin Flaherty, Head of Business & Committee , Civic Suite, Town Hall, London SE6 4RU ☎ 020 8314 8824 🖷 020 8314 3111 ✉ kevin.flaherty@lewisham.gov.uk

Member Services: Mr Derek Johnson , Business & Civic Co-ordinator, Civic Suite, Town Hall, London SE6 4RU ☎ 020 8314 8636 🖷 020 8314 3111 ✉ derek.johnson@lewisham.gov.uk

Parking: Ms Lesley Brooks, Service Group Manager of Travel Demand, Wearside Depot, Lewisham, London SE13 7EZ ☎ 020 8314 6000 🖷 020 8690 6083 ✉ lesley.brooks@lewisham.gov.uk

Partnerships: Mr Paul Aladenika , Head of Policy & Partnerships, 5th Floor, Laurence House, 1 Catford Road, London SE6 4RU ☎ 020 8314 7148 ✉ paul.aladenika@lewisham.gov.uk

Personnel / HR: Mr Andreas Ghosh , Head of Personnel & Development, 5th Floor, Laurence House, 1 Catford Road, London SE6 4RU ☎ 020 8314 7519 🖷 020 8314 3071 ✉ andreas.ghosh@lewisham.gov.uk

Planning: Mr John Miller, Head of Planning Services, 5th Floor, Laurence House, 1 Catford Road, London SE6 4RU ☎ 020 8314 8706 🖷 020 8314 3127 ✉ john.miller@lewisham.gov.uk

Public Libraries: Mr Gerald Jones , Head of Community Education, 2nd Floor, Laurence House, 1 Catford Road, London SE5 4RU ☎ 020 8314 6189 ✉ gerald.jones@lewisham.gov.uk

Public Libraries: Mr Antonio Rizzo , Head of Libraries, 2nd Floor, Laurence House, 1 Catford Road, London SE13 6LG ☎ 020 8314 8025 ✉ antonio.rizzo@lewisham.gov.uk

Recycling & Waste Minimisation: Ms Sam Kirk, Strategic Waste & Environment Manager, Wearside Service Centre, Wearside Road, London SE13 7EZ ☎ 020 8314 2076 🖷 020 8314 2128 ✉ sam.kirk@lewisham.gov.uk

Road Safety: Ms Lesley Brooks, Service Group Manager of Travel Demand, Wearside Depot, Lewisham, London SE13 7EZ ☎ 020 8314 6000 🖷 020 8690 6083 ✉ lesley.brooks@lewisham.gov.uk

Social Services: Ms Alison Beck , Head of Bereavement Services, Lewisham Crematorium, Verdant Lane, London SE16 1TP ☎ 020 8314 6000 ✉ alison.beck@lewisham.gov.uk

Social Services: Ms Aileen Buckton, Executive Director of Community Services, 5th Floor, Laurence House, 1 Catford Road, London SE6 4RU ☎ 020 8314 8107 🖷 020 8314 3023 ✉ aileen.buckton@lewisham.gov.uk

Social Services: Mr Alan Docksey , Head of Resources - Social Care, 3rd Floor, Laurence House, 1 Cartford Road, London SE6 4RU ☎ 020 8314 3582 ✉ alan.docksey@lewisham.gov.uk

Social Services: Ms Sarah Wainer, Head of Performance & Strategy in Adult Care & Health, 5th Floor, Laurence House, 1 Catford Road, London SE6 4RU ☎ 020 8314 9611 🖷 020 8314 3023 ✉ sarah.wainer@lewisham.gov.uk

Social Services (Children): Mr Alastair Pettigrew , Interim Director - Children's Social Care, Civic Suite, Town Hall, London SE6 4RU ☎ 020 8314 8140 ✉ alastair.pettigrew@lewisham.gov.uk

Public Health: Dr Danny Ruta , Director - Public Health, Civic Suite, Town Hall, London SE6 4RU ☎ 020 8314 9094 ✉ danny.ruta@lewisham.gov.uk

Staff Training: Mr Andrew Jacobs , Organisational Learning & Talent Manager, Lewisham Town Hall, London SE6 4RU ☎ 020 8314 6035 ✉ andrew.jacobs@lewisham.gov.uk

Street Scene: Mr Ian Ransom , Transport Service Group Manager, Wearside Service Centre, Wearside Road, London SE13 7EZ ☎ 020 8314 6000 ✉ ian.ransom@lewisham.gov.uk

Sustainable Communities: Mr Martin O'Brien , Sustainability Officer, 5th Floor, Laurence House, 1 Catford Road, London SE6 4RU ☎ 020 8314 6605 ✉ martin.o'brien@lewisham.gov.uk

Sustainable Development: Mr Martin O'Brien , Sustainability Officer, 5th Floor, Laurence House, 1 Catford Road, London SE6 4RU ☎ 020 8314 6605 ✉ martin.o'brien@lewisham.gov.uk

Tourism: Mr Kevin Turner , Economic Development Manager, Laurence House, 1 Catford Road, London SE6 4RU ☎ 020 8314 8229 🖷 020 8314 3129 ✉ kevin.turner@lewisham.gov.uk

LEWISHAM

Waste Collection and Disposal: Mr Michael Bryan, Group Service Manager - Refuse, Wearside Service Centre, Wearside Road, London SE13 7EZ ☎ 020 8314 2113 🖷 020 8314 2043 ✉ michael.bryan@lewisham.gov.uk

Waste Collection and Disposal: Ms Sam Kirk, Strategic Waste & Environment Manager, Wearside Service Centre, Wearside Road, London SE13 7EZ ☎ 020 8314 2076 🖷 020 8314 2128 ✉ sam.kirk@lewisham.gov.uk

Waste Management: Ms Sam Kirk, Strategic Waste & Environment Manager, Wearside Service Centre, Wearside Road, London SE13 7EZ ☎ 020 8314 2076 🖷 020 8314 2128 ✉ sam.kirk@lewisham.gov.uk

COUNCILLORS

***Chair* Adefiranye**, Obajimi (LAB - Brockley)
cllr_obajimi.adefiranye@lewisham.gov.uk

***Vice-Chair* Till**, Alan (LAB - Perry Vale)
cllr_alan.till@lewisham.gov.uk

***Mayor* Bullock**, Steve (LAB - London Borough of Lewisham)
steve.bullock@lewisham.gov.uk

***Deputy Mayor* Smith**, Alan (LAB - Catford South)
cllr_alan.smith@lewisham.gov.uk

Amrani, Abdeslam (LAB - Catford South)
cllr_abdeslam.amrani@lewisham.gov.uk

Barnham, Chris (LAB - Crofton Park)
cllr_chris.barnham@lewisham.gov.uk

Bell, Paul (LAB - Telegraph Hill)
cllr_paul.bell@lewisham.gov.uk

Bernards, Peter (LAB - Forest Hill)
cllr_peter.bernards@lewisham.gov.uk

Best, Chris (LAB - Sydenham)
cllr_chris.best@lewisham.gov.uk

Bonavia, Kevin (LAB - Blackheath)
cllr_kevin.bonavia@lewisham.gov.uk

Bourne, Andre (LAB - Downham)
cllr_andre.bourne@lewisham.gov.uk

Britton, David (LAB - Downham)
david.britton17@hotmail.com

Brown, Bill (LAB - Ladywell)
cllr_bill.brown@lewisham.gov.uk

Clarke, Suzannah (LAB - Grove Park)
cllr_suzannah.clarke@lewisham.gov.uk

Coughlin, John (GRN - Brockley)
cllr_john.coughlin@lewisham.gov.uk

Curran, Liam (LAB - Sydenham)
cllr_liam.curran@lewisham.gov.uk

Daby, Janet (LAB - Whitefoot)
cllr_janet.daby@lewisham.gov.uk

Dacres, Brenda (LAB - New Cross)
cllr_brenda.dacres@lewisham.gov.uk

De Ryk, Amanda (LD - Blackheath)
cllr_amanda.deryk@lewisham.gov.uk

Dromey, Joe (LAB - New Cross)
cllr_joe.dromey@lewisham.gov.uk

Egan, Damien (LAB - Lewisham Central)
damien.egan@lewisham.gov.uk

Elliott, Colin (LAB - Grove Park)
cllr_colin.elliott@lewisham.gov.uk

Hall, Alan (LAB - Bellingham)
cllr_alan.hall@lewisham.gov.uk

Handley, Carl (LAB - Ladywell)
cllr_carlrichard.handley@lewisham.gov.uk

Hilton, Maja (LAB - Forest Hill)
cllr_maja.hilton@lewisham.gov.uk

Hooks, Simon (LAB - Lee Green)
cllr_simon.hooks@lewisham.gov.uk

Ibitson, Ami (LAB - Bellingham)
cllr_ami.ibitson@lewisham.gov.uk

Ingleby, Mark (LAB - Whitefoot)
cllr_mark.ingleby@lewisham.gov.uk

Jeffrey, Stella (LAB - Lewisham Central)
cllr_stella.jeffrey@lewisham.gov.uk

Johnston-Franklin, Liz (LAB - Ladywell)
cllr_liz.johnston-franklin@lewisham.gov.uk

Kennedy, Alicia (LAB - Brockley)
cllr_alicia.kennedy@lewisham.gov.uk

Kennedy, Roy (LAB - Crofton Park)
cllr_roy.kennedy@lewisham.gov.uk

Klier, Helen (LAB - Rushey Green)
cllr_helen.klier@lewisham.gov.uk

Mallory, Jim (LAB - Lee Green)
cllr_jim.mallory@lewisham.gov.uk

Maslin, Paul (LAB - New Cross)
cllr_paul.maslin@lewisham.gov.uk

Michael, David (LAB - Evelyn)
cllr_david.michael@lewisham.gov.uk

Millbank, Joan (LAB - Telegraph Hill)
cllr_joan.millbank@lewisham.gov.uk

Milne, Jamie (LAB - Evelyn)
cllr_jamie.milne@lewisham.gov.uk

Moore, Hilary (LAB - Grove Park)
cllr_hilary.moore@lewisham.gov.uk

Morrison, Pauline (LAB - Crofton Park)
cllr_pauline.morrison@lewisham.gov.uk

Muldoon, John (LAB - Rushey Green)
cllr_john.muldoon@lewisham.gov.uk

Ogunbadewa, Olurotimi (LAB - Downham)
cllr_olurotimi.ogunbadewa@lewisham.gov.uk

Onikosi, Rachel (LAB - Sydenham)
cllr_rachel.onikosi@lewisham.gov.uk

Onuegbu, Crada (LAB - Evelyn)
cllr_crada.onuegbu@lewisham.gov.uk

Paschoud, Jacq (LAB - Bellingham)
cllr_jacq.paschoud@lewisham.gov.uk

Paschoud, John (LAB - Perry Vale)
cllr_john.paschoud@lewisham.gov.uk

Raven, Pat (LAB - Lee Green)
cllr_pat.raven@lewisham.gov.uk

Reid, Joan (LAB - Lewisham Central)
cllr_joan.reid@lewisham.gov.uk

Siddorn, Gareth (LAB - Blackheath)
cllr_gareth.siddorn@lewisham.gov.uk

Slater, Jonathan (LAB - Whitefoot)
cllr_jonathan.slater@lewisham.gov.uk

Sorba, Luke (LAB - Telegraph Hill)
cllr_luke.sorba@lewisham.gov.uk

Stamirowski, Eva (LAB - Catford South)
cllr_eva.stamirowski@lewisham.gov.uk

Upex, Paul (LAB - Forest Hill)
cllr_paul.upex@lewisham.gov.uk

Walsh, James-J (LAB - Rushey Green)
cllr_james-j.walsh@lewisham.gov.uk

Wise, Susan (LAB - Perry Vale)
cllr_susan.wise@lewisham.gov.uk

POLITICAL COMPOSITION

LAB: 53, LD: 1, GRN: 1

COMMITTEE CHAIRS

Children & Young Peole: Ms Hilary Moore

Licensing: Ms Eva Stamirowski

Sustainable Deveopment: Mr Liam Curran

Lichfield D

Lichfield District Council, District Council House, Frog Lane, Lichfield WS13 6ZB
☎ 01543 308000 🖷 01543 309899 ✉ enquiries@lichfielddc.gov.uk
🖳 www.lichfielddc.gov.uk

FACTS AND FIGURES

Parliamentary Constituencies: Lichfield, Tamworth
EU Constituencies: West Midlands
Election Frequency: Elections are of whole council

PRINCIPAL OFFICERS

Chief Executive: Ms Diane Tilley , Chief Executive, District Council House, Frog Lane, Lichfield WS13 6ZB ☎ 01543 308001 🖷 01543 308049 ✉ diane.tilley@lichfielddc.gov.uk

Senior Management: Mr Richard King , Strategic Director - Democratic, Development & Legal Services, District Council House, Frog Lane, Lichfield WS13 6YU ☎ 01543 308060 🖷 01543 308200 ✉ richard.king@lichfielddc.gov.uk

Senior Management: Mrs Jane Kitchen, Director - Finance, Revenues & Benefits, District Council House, Frog Lane, Lichfield WS13 6YU ☎ 01543 308770 ✉ jane.kitchen@lichfielddc.gov.uk

Senior Management: Mrs Helen Titterton, Strategic Director - Community, Housing & Health, District Council House, Frog Lane, Lichfield WS13 6ZE ☎ 01543 308700 🖷 01543 308712 ✉ helen.titterton@lichfielddc.gov.uk

Senior Management: Mr Neil Turner , Director - Leisure & Parks, District Council House, Frog Lane, Lichfield WS13 6ZD ☎ 01543 308761

Architect, Building / Property Services: Mr John Brown, Land & Property Manager, District Council House, Frog Lane, Lichfield WS13 6YU ☎ 01543 308061 🖷 01543 309899 ✉ john.brown@lichfielddc.gov.uk

Architect, Building / Property Services: Mr Richard King, Strategic Director - Democratic Development & Legal Services, District Council House, Frog Lane, Lichfield WS13 6YU ☎ 01543 308060 🖷 01543 309899 ✉ richard.king@lichfielddc.gov.uk

Building Control: Mr Ged Cooper, Building Control Manager, District Council House, Frog Lane, Lichfield WS13 6YZ ☎ 01543 308155 🖷 01543 308161 ✉ ged.cooper@lichfielddc.gov.uk

Building Control: Mr Richard King , Strategic Director - Democratic, Development & Legal Services, District Council House, Frog Lane, Lichfield WS13 6YU ☎ 01543 308060 🖷 01543 308200 ✉ richard.king@lichfielddc.gov.uk

PR / Communications: Mr Richard King, Strategic Director - Democratic Development & Legal Services, District Council House, Frog Lane, Lichfield WS13 6YU ☎ 01543 308060 🖷 01543 309899 ✉ richard.king@lichfielddc.gov.uk

PR / Communications: Ms Elizabeth Thatcher, Communications & Tourism Manager, District Council House, Frog Lane, Lichfield WS13 6ZD ☎ 01543 308781 🖷 01543 308780 ✉ elizabeth.thatcher@lichfielddc.gov.uk

Community Planning: Mr Richard King, Strategic Director - Democratic Development & Legal Services, District Council House, Frog Lane, Lichfield WS13 6YU ☎ 01543 308060 🖷 01543 309899 ✉ richard.king@lichfielddc.gov.uk

Community Planning: Mrs Helen Titterton, Strategic Director - Community, Housing & Health, District Council House, Frog Lane, Lichfield WS13 6ZE ☎ 01543 308700 🖷 01543 308712 ✉ helen.titterton@lichfielddc.gov.uk

Community Safety: Ms Jenni Coleman, Community Safety Officer, Donegal House, Bore Street, Lichfield WS13 6NE ☎ 01543 308005 🖷 01543 308211 ✉ jenni.coleman@lichfielddc.gov.uk

Community Safety: Mrs Helen Titterton, Strategic Director - Community, Housing & Health, District Council House, Frog Lane, Lichfield WS13 6ZE ☎ 01543 308700 🖷 01543 308712 ✉ helen.titterton@lichfielddc.gov.uk

Computer Management: Mr Kevin Sleeman , E-Business & Information Strategy Manager, District Council House, Frog Lane, Lichfield WS13 6ZF ☎ 01543 308120 ✉ kevin.sleeman@lichfield.gov.uk

Contracts: Mr Richard King, Strategic Director - Democratic Development & Legal Services, District Council House, Frog Lane, Lichfield WS13 6YU ☎ 01543 308060 🖷 01543 309899 ✉ richard.king@lichfielddc.gov.uk

LICHFIELD

Corporate Services: Mr Richard King, Strategic Director - Democratic Development & Legal Services, District Council House, Frog Lane, Lichfield WS13 6YU ☎ 01543 308060 🖷 01543 309899 ✉ richard.king@lichfielddc.gov.uk

Customer Service: Mrs Helen Titterton, Strategic Director - Community, Housing & Health, District Council House, Frog Lane, Lichfield WS13 6ZE ☎ 01543 308700 🖷 01543 308712 ✉ helen.titterton@lichfielddc.gov.uk

Customer Service: Mrs Ysanne Williams, Customer Services Manager, District Council House, Frog Lane, Lichfield WS13 6ZF ☎ 01543 308738 ✉ ysanne.williams@lichfielddc.gov.uk

Economic Development: Mr Richard King , Strategic Director - Democratic, Development & Legal Services, District Council House, Frog Lane, Lichfield WS13 6YU ☎ 01543 308060 🖷 01543 308200 ✉ richard.king@lichfielddc.gov.uk

Economic Development: Mr James Roberts, Economic Development & Enterprise Manager, Marmion House, Lichfield Street, Tamworth B79 7BZ ☎ 01827 709204 🖷 01827 709271 ✉ james-roberts@tamworth.gov.uk

E-Government: Mr Kevin Sleeman , E-Business & Information Strategy Manager, District Council House, Frog Lane, Lichfield WS13 6ZF ☎ 01543 308120 ✉ kevin.sleeman@lichfielddc.gov.uk

Electoral Registration: Mr Richard King, Strategic Director - Democratic Development & Legal Services, District Council House, Frog Lane, Lichfield WS13 6YU ☎ 01543 308060 🖷 01543 309899 ✉ richard.king@lichfielddc.gov.uk

Electoral Registration: Ms Sarah Pearce, Licensing & Electoral Services Manager, District Council House, Frog Lane, Lichfield WS13 6YU ☎ 01543 308008 🖷 01543 309899 ✉ sarah.pearce@lichfielddc.gov.uk

Emergency Planning: Mr Steve Berry , Civil Contingencies Officer, District Council House, Frog Lane, Lichfield WS13 6ZB ☎ 01543 308070 ✉ steve.berry@lichfielddc.gov.uk

Energy Management: Mr Richard King, Strategic Director - Democratic Development & Legal Services, District Council House, Frog Lane, Lichfield WS13 6YU ☎ 01543 308060 🖷 01543 309899 ✉ richard.king@lichfielddc.gov.uk

Energy Management: Mrs Helen Titterton, Strategic Director - Community, Housing & Health, District Council House, Frog Lane, Lichfield WS13 6ZE ☎ 01543 308700 🖷 01543 308712 ✉ helen.titterton@lichfielddc.gov.uk

Environmental / Technical Services: Mrs Helen Titterton, Strategic Director - Community, Housing & Health, District Council House, Frog Lane, Lichfield WS13 6ZE ☎ 01543 308700 🖷 01543 308712 ✉ helen.titterton@lichfielddc.gov.uk

Environmental Health: Mr Gareth Davies , Environmental Health Manager, District Council House, Frog Lane, Lichfield WS13 6ZB ☎ 01543 308741 🖷 01543 308728 ✉ gareth.davies@lichfielddc.gov.uk

Environmental Health: Mrs Helen Titterton, Strategic Director - Community, Housing & Health, District Council House, Frog Lane, Lichfield WS13 6ZE ☎ 01543 308700 🖷 01543 308712 ✉ helen.titterton@lichfielddc.gov.uk

Estates, Property & Valuation: Mr John Brown, Land & Property Manager, District Council House, Frog Lane, Lichfield WS13 6YU ☎ 01543 308061 🖷 01543 309899 ✉ john.brown@lichfielddc.gov.uk

Estates, Property & Valuation: Mr Richard King, Strategic Director - Democratic Development & Legal Services, District Council House, Frog Lane, Lichfield WS13 6YU ☎ 01543 308060 🖷 01543 309899 ✉ richard.king@lichfielddc.gov.uk

Finance: Mrs Jane Kitchen, Director - Finance, Revenues & Benefits, District Council House, Frog Lane, Lichfield WS13 6YU ☎ 01543 308770 ✉ jane.kitchen@lichfielddc.gov.uk

Fleet Management: Mr Gary Brownridge , Streetscene & Fleet Manager, District Council House, Frog Lane, Lichfield WS13 6ZB ☎ 01543 687572 🖷 01543 687588 ✉ gary.brownridge@lichfielddc.gov.uk

Grounds Maintenance: Mr Gary Brownridge , Streetscene & Fleet Manager, District Council House, Frog Lane, Lichfield WS13 6ZB ☎ 01543 687572 🖷 01543 687588 ✉ gary.brownridge@lichfielddc.gov.uk

Health and Safety: Mr Steve Langston , Health & Safety Manager, District Council House, Frog Lane, Lichfield WS13 6ZF ☎ 01543 308107; 01827 709224 🖷 01543 308103; 01827 709271 ✉ steven.langston@lichfielddc.gov.uk

Health and Safety: Mrs Helen Titterton, Strategic Director - Community, Housing & Health, District Council House, Frog Lane, Lichfield WS13 6ZE ☎ 01543 308700 🖷 01543 308712 ✉ helen.titterton@lichfielddc.gov.uk

Health and Safety: Mr Neil Turner , Director - Leisure & Parks, District Council House, Frog Lane, Lichfield WS13 6ZD ☎ 01543 308761

Home Energy Conservation: Mrs Helen Titterton, Strategic Director - Community, Housing & Health, District Council House, Frog Lane, Lichfield WS13 6ZE ☎ 01543 308700 🖷 01543 308712 ✉ helen.titterton@lichfielddc.gov.uk

Housing: Mrs Helen Titterton, Strategic Director - Community, Housing & Health, District Council House, Frog Lane, Lichfield WS13 6ZE ☎ 01543 308700 🖷 01543 308712 ✉ helen.titterton@lichfielddc.gov.uk

Legal: Mr Richard King , Strategic Director - Democratic, Development & Legal Services, District Council House, Frog Lane, Lichfield WS13 6ZB ☎ 01543 308060 🖷 01543 308200 ✉ richard.king@lichfielddc.gov.uk

Legal: Ms Baljit Nahal , Solicitor/Monitoring Officer, District Council House, Frog Lane, Lichfield WS13 6YU ☎ 01543 308002 ✉ bal.nahal@lichfielddc.gov.uk

Leisure and Cultural Services: Mr Neil Turner , Director - Leisure & Parks, District Council House, Frog Lane, Lichfield WS13 6ZD ☎ 01543 308761

Licensing: Mr Richard King , Strategic Director - Democratic, Development & Legal Services, District Council House, Frog Lane, Lichfield WS13 6YU ☎ 01543 308060 🖷 01543 308200 ✉ richard.king@lichfielddc.gov.uk

Licensing: Ms Sarah Pearce, Licensing & Electoral Services Manager, District Council House, Frog Lane, Lichfield WS13 6YU ☎ 01543 308008 🖷 01543 309899 ✉ sarah.pearce@lichfieddc.gov.uk

Lottery Funding, Charity and Voluntary: Mr Clive Gibbons , Housing Services Manager, District Council House, Frog Lane, Lichfield WS13 6ZB ☎ 01543 308702 🖷 01543 308712 ✉ clive.gibbons@lichfielddc.gov.uk

Member Services: Mr Richard King , Strategic Director - Democratic, Development & Legal Services, District Council House, Frog Lane, Lichfield WS13 6YU ☎ 01543 308060 🖷 01543 308200 ✉ richard.king@lichfielddc.gov.uk

Member Services: Ms Baljit Nahal , Solicitor/Monitoring Officer, District Council House, Frog Lane, Lichfield WS13 6YU ☎ 01543 308002 ✉ bal.nahal@lichfielddc.gov.uk

Parking: Mr Craig Jordan , Development Executive, District Council House, Frog Lane, Lichfield WS13 6ZB ☎ 01543 308202 🖷 01543 308200 ✉ craig.jordan@lichfielddc.gov.uk

Personnel / HR: Mrs Cathy Pepper, Personnel Manager, District Council House, Frog Lane, Lichfield WS13 6ZF ☎ 01543 308112 🖷 01543 308103 ✉ cathy.pepper@lichfielddc.gov.uk

Personnel / HR: Ms Diane Tilley, Chief Executive, District Council House, Frog Lane, Lichfield WS13 6ZB ☎ 01543 308001 🖷 01543 308049 ✉ diane.tilley@lichfielddc.gov.uk

Planning: Mr Richard King, Strategic Director - Democratic Development & Legal Services, District Council House, Frog Lane, Lichfield WS13 6YU ☎ 01543 308060 🖷 01543 309899 ✉ richard.king@lichfielddc.gov.uk

Procurement: Mrs Jane Kitchen, Director - Finance, Revenues & Benefits, District Council House, Frog Lane, Lichfield WS13 6YU ☎ 01543 308770 ✉ jane.kitchen@lichfielddc.gov.uk

Recycling & Waste Minimisation: Mr Nigel Harris , Waste & Environmental Protection Manager, Lichfield District Council, Reliant Way, Burntwood Business Park, Zone 2, Burntwood WS7 3JH ☎ 01543 687549 ✉ nigel.harris@lichfielddc.gov.uk

Regeneration: Mr Richard King , Strategic Director - Democratic, Development & Legal Services, District Council House, Frog Lane, Lichfield WS13 6YU ☎ 01543 308060 🖷 01543 308200 ✉ richard.king@lichfielddc.gov.uk

Street Scene: Mr Gary Brownridge , Streetscene & Fleet Manager, District Council House, Frog Lane, Lichfield WS13 6ZB ☎ 01543 687572 🖷 01543 687588 ✉ gary.brownridge@lichfielddc.gov.uk

Sustainable Communities: Mrs Helen Titterton, Strategic Director - Community, Housing & Health, District Council House, Frog Lane, Lichfield WS13 6ZE ☎ 01543 308700 🖷 01543 308712 ✉ helen.titterton@lichfielddc.gov.uk

Sustainable Development: Mr Richard King , Strategic Director - Democratic, Development & Legal Services, District Council House, Frog Lane, Lichfield WS13 6YU ☎ 01543 308060 🖷 01543 308200 ✉ richard.king@lichfielddc.gov.uk

Tourism: Ms Elizabeth Thatcher, Communications & Tourism Manager, District Council House, Frog Lane, Lichfield WS13 6ZD ☎ 01543 308781 🖷 01543 308780 ✉ elizabeth.thatcher@lichfielddc.gov.uk

Waste Collection and Disposal: Mr Nigel Harris , Waste & Environmental Protection Manager, Lichfield District Council, Reliant Way, Burntwood Business Park, Zone 2, Burntwood WS7 3JH ☎ 01543 687549 ✉ nigel.harris@lichfielddc.gov.uk

Waste Management: Mr Nigel Harris , Waste & Environmental Protection Manager, Lichfield District Council, Reliant Way, Burntwood Business Park, Zone 2, Burntwood WS7 3JH ☎ 01543 687549 ✉ nigel.harris@lichfielddc.gov.uk

Children's Play Areas: Mr Neil Turner , Director - Leisure & Parks, District Council House, Frog Lane, Lichfield WS13 6ZD ☎ 01543 308761

COUNCILLORS

***Leader of the Council* Wilcox**, Michael (CON - Alrewas and Fradley)
michael.wilcox@lichfielddc.gov.uk

***Deputy Leader of the Council* Pritchard**, Ian (CON - Kings Bromley)
ian.pritchard@lichfielddc.gov.uk

Allsopp, Jeanette (CON - Boley Park)
jeanette.allsopp@lichfielddc.gov.uk

Arnold, Susan (CON - Mease and Tame)
susan.arnold@lichfielddc.gov.uk

Awty, Bob (CON - Leomansley)
bob.awty@lichfielddc.gov.uk

Bacon, Brian (CON - Curborough)
brain.bacon@lochfielddc.gov.uk

Bacon, Norma (CON - Curborough)
norma.bacon@lichfielddc.gov.uk

Barnett, Shirley Ann (CON - Colton and Mavesyn Ridware)
shirley.barnett@lichfielddc.gov.uk

Bland, Marion (LD - Chadsmead)
marion.bland@lichfielddc.gov.uk

Boyle, Gwyneth (CON - St. John's)
gwyneth.boyle@lichfielddc.gov.uk

Constable, Brenda (CON - All Saints)
brenda.constable@lichfielddc.gov.uk

Constable, Douglas (CON - Highfield)
douglas.constable@lichfielddc.gov.uk

Cox, Richard (CON - Armitage with Handsacre)
richard.cox@lichfielddc.gov.uk

LICHFIELD

Derrick, Bernard (CON - Stowe)
bernard.derrick@lichfielddc.gov.uk

Drinkwater, Eric (LAB - Chase Terrace)
eric.drinkwater@lichfielddc.gov.uk

Eadie, Iain (CON - Leomansley)
iain.eadie@lichfielddc.gov.uk

Eagland, Janet (CON - Boley Park)
janet.eagland@lichfielddc.gov.uk

Evans, Diane (LAB - Boney Hay)
diane.evans@lichfielddc.gov.uk

Fisher, Helen (CON - Highfield)
helen.fisher@lichfielddc.gov.uk

Flowith, Louise (CON - Little Aston)
louise.flowith@lichfielddc.gov.uk

Greatorex, Colin (CON - Stowe)
colin.greatorex@lichfielddc.gov.uk

Hancocks, Rita (CON - Shenstone)
rita.hancocks@lichfielddc.gov.uk

Heath, Russell (LAB - Boney Hay)
russell.heath@lichfielddc.gov.uk

Hogan, Paul (CON - Alrewas and Fradley)
paul.hogan@lichfielddc.gov.uk

Humphreys, Ken (CON - All Saints)
kenneth.humphreys@lichfielddc.gov.uk

Isaacs, Donald (LAB - Summerfield)
donald.isaacs@lichfielddc.gov.uk

Leytham, David (CON - Curborough)
david.leytham@lichfielddc.gov.uk

Marshall, Thomas (CON - Armitage with Handsacre)
thomas.marshall@lichfielddc.gov.uk

Mosson, Richard (CON - Burntwood Central)
richard.mosson@lichfielddc.gov.uk

Mynott, Glen (LAB - Fazeley)
glen.mynott@lichfielddc.gov.uk

Norman, Steve (LAB - Summerfield)
steven.norman@lichfielddc.gov.uk

Pearce, Alan (CON - Fazeley)
alan.pearce@lichfielddc.gov.uk

Perkins, Ellen (CON - Mease and Tame)
ellen.perkins@lichfielddc.gov.uk

Powell, Joseph (CON - Little Aston)
joseph.powell@lichfielddc.gov.uk

Pullen, Doug (CON - Fazeley)
doug.pullen@lichfield.gov.uk

Richards, Valerie (CON - Hammerwich)
val.richards@lichfielddc.gov.uk

Roberts, Neil (CON - Longdon)
neil.roberts@lichfielddc.gov.uk

Salter, David (CON - Shenstone)
david.salter@lichfielddc.gov.uk

Smedley, David (CON - Stowe)
david.smedley@lichfielddc.gov.uk

Smith, David (CON - Stonnall)
david.smith@lichfielddc.gov.uk

Smith, Andrew (CON - Leomansley)
andrew.smith@lichfielddc.gov.uk

Spruce, Christopher (CON - St. John's)
christopher.spruce@lichfielddc.gov.uk

Stanhope, Margaret (CON - Alrewas and Fradley)
margaret.stanhope@lichfielddc.gov.uk

Strachan, Robert (CON - Whittington)
rob.strachan@lichfield.gov.uk

Taylor, Stephen (LAB - Chasetown)
stephen.taylor@lichfielddc.gov.uk

Thomas, Terry (CON - CHadsmead)
terry.thomas@lichfielddc.gov.uk

Tittley, Martyn (CON - Armitage with Handsacre)
martyn.tittley@lichfielddc.gov.uk

Tranter, Heather (CON - Burntwood Central)
heather.tranter@lichfielddc.gov.uk

Walker, John (LAB - Chase Terrace)
johnthomas.walker@lichfielddc.gov.uk

Warfield, Mark (CON - Boley Park)
mark.warfield@lichfielddc.gov.uk

White, Alan (CON - Whittington)
alan.white@lichfielddc.gov.uk

Wilks, John (CON - St. John's)
john.wilks@lichfielddc.gov.uk

Willis-Croft, Keith (LAB - Chasetown)
keith.willis-croft@lichfielddc.gov.uk

Wilson, Brett (CON - Hammerwich)
brett.wilson@lichfielddc.gov.uk

Woodward, Susan (LAB - Chase Terrace)
susan.woodward@lichfielddc.gov.uk

Yeates, Brian (CON - Bourne Vale)
brian.yeates@lichfielddc.gov.uk

POLITICAL COMPOSITION

CON: 45, LAB: 10, LD: 1

Lincoln City D

Lincoln City Council, City Hall, Beaumont Fee, Lincoln LN1 1DD
☎ 01522 881188 🖷 01522 521736 email@lincoln.gov.uk
www.lincoln.gov.uk

FACTS AND FIGURES

Parliamentary Constituencies: Lincoln
EU Constituencies: East Midlands
Election Frequency: Elections are by thirds

PRINCIPAL OFFICERS

Chief Executive: Mrs Angela Andrews , Interim Chief Executive (Director of Resources), City Hall, Beaumont Fee, Lincoln LN1 1DD ☎ 01522 873292 🖷 01522 542569 angela.andrews@lincoln.gov.uk

Senior Management: Mrs Angela Andrews , Interim Chief Executive (Director of Resources), City Hall, Beaumont Fee, Lincoln LN1 1DD ☎ 01522 873292 🖷 01522 542569 angela.andrews@lincoln.gov.uk

Senior Management: Mr John Latham, Director of Development & Environmental Services, City Hall, Beaumont Fee, Lincoln LN1 1DD ☎ 01522 873471 🖷 01522 567934 🖰 john.latham@lincoln.gov.uk

Senior Management: Mr Bob Ledger , Director of Housing & Community Services, City Hall, Beaumont Fee, Lincoln LN1 1DD

Building Control: Mr Marcus Tasker , Principal Building Control Officer, City Hall, Beaumont Fee, Lincoln LN1 1DD ☎ 01522 873429 🖰 marcus.tasker@lincoln.gov.uk

PR / Communications: Mr Steven Welsby , Communications Manager, City Hall, Beaumont Fee, Lincoln LN1 1DD ☎ 01522 873318 🖷 01522 521736 🖰 steven.welsby@lincoln.gov.uk

Community Planning: Mr John Latham, Director of Development & Environmental Services, City Hall, Beaumont Fee, Lincoln LN1 1DD ☎ 01522 873471 🖷 01522 567934 🖰 john.latham@lincoln.gov.uk

Community Safety: Mr John Latham, Director of Development & Environmental Services, City Hall, Beaumont Fee, Lincoln LN1 1DD ☎ 01522 873471 🖷 01522 567934 🖰 john.latham@lincoln.gov.uk

Computer Management: Mr Matt Smith, Business Development & IT Manager, City Hall, Beaumont Fee, Lincoln LN1 1DD ☎ 01522 873308 🖷 01522 560049 🖰 matt.smith@lincoln.gov.uk

Corporate Services: Mr Simon Walters , Assistant Director of Corporate Review & Development, City Hall, Beaumont Fee, Lincoln LN1 1DD ☎ 01522 873866 🖷 01522 521736 🖰 simon.walters@lincoln.gov.uk

Corporate Services: Mrs Carolyn Wheater , Assistant Director of Corporate Support Services, City Hall, Beaumont Fee, Lincoln LN1 1DD ☎ 01522 873323 🖷 01522 542569 🖰 carolyn.wheater@lincoln.gov.uk

Customer Service: Ms Joanne Crookes , Customer Services Manager, City Hall, Beaumont Fee, Lincoln LN1 1DD ☎ 01522 873407 🖷 01522 542569 🖰 joanne.crookes@lincoln.gov.uk

Economic Development: Ms Kate Ellis , Assistant Director - Planning & Regeneration, City Hall, Beaumont Fee, Lincoln LN1 1DD ☎ 01522 873824 🖷 01522 560049 🖰 kate.ellis@lincoln.gov.uk

E-Government: Mr Matt Smith, Business Development & IT Manager, City Hall, Beaumont Fee, Lincoln LN1 1DD ☎ 01522 873308 🖷 01522 560049 🖰 matt.smith@lincoln.gov.uk

Electoral Registration: Mr Steve Swain, Principal Democratic Services Officer, City Hall, Beaumont Fee, Lincoln LN1 1DD ☎ 01522 873439 🖷 01522 542569 🖰 steve.swain@lincoln.gov.uk

Emergency Planning: Mr John Latham, Director of Development & Environmental Services, City Hall, Beaumont Fee, Lincoln LN1 1DD ☎ 01522 873471 🖷 01522 567934 🖰 john.latham@lincoln.gov.uk

Energy Management: Mr David Bowskill, Housing Energy Officer, City Hall, Beaumont Fee, Lincoln LN1 1DD ☎ 01522 873377 🖷 01522 510822 🖰 david.bowskill@lincoln.gov.uk

Environmental Health: Ms Sara Boothright, Food, Health & Safety Manager, City Hall, Beaumont Fee, Lincoln LN1 1DD ☎ 01522 873314 🖷 01522 546702 🖰 sara.boothright@lincoln.gov.uk

Estates, Property & Valuation: Mr Mark Wheater , Strategic Property Services Manager, City Hall, Beaumont Fee, Lincoln LN1 1DD ☎ 01522 873513 🖰 mark.wheater@lincoln.gov.uk

European Liaison: Ms Michelle Smith , Senior Programme Managements Officer, City Hall, Beaumont Fee, Lincoln LN1 1DD ☎ 01522 873329 🖷 01522 567934 🖰 michelle.smith@lincoln.gov.uk

Events Manager: Ms Claire Thompson , Principal Events & Culture Officer, City Hall, Beaumont Fee, Lincoln LN1 1DD ☎ 01522 873540 🖰 claire.thompson@lincoln.gov.uk

Finance: Mrs Angela Andrews , Interim Chief Executive (Director of Resources), City Hall, Beaumont Fee, Lincoln LN1 1DD ☎ 01522 873292 🖷 01522 542569 🖰 angela.andrews@lincoln.gov.uk

Grounds Maintenance: Mr Dave Charysz, Open Spaces Officer, City Hall, Beaumont Fee, Lincoln LN1 1DE ☎ 01522 873414 🖷 01522 560049 🖰 dave.charysz@lincoln.gov.uk

Health and Safety: Ms Sara Boothright, Food, Health & Safety Manager, City Hall, Beaumont Fee, Lincoln LN1 1DD ☎ 01522 873314 🖷 01522 546702 🖰 sara.boothright@lincoln.gov.uk

Home Energy Conservation: Mr David Bowskill, Housing Energy Officer, City Hall, Beaumont Fee, Lincoln LN1 1DD ☎ 01522 873377 🖷 01522 510822 🖰 david.bowskill@lincoln.gov.uk

Housing: Ms Karen Talbot , Assistant Director of Housing, City Hall, Beaumont Fee, Lincoln LN1 1DD ☎ 01522 873532 🖰 karen.talbot@lincoln.gov.uk

Housing Maintenance: Mr Matthew Hillman , Acting City Maintenance Manager, City Hall, Beaumont Fee, Lincoln LN1 1DD ☎ 01522 873639 🖰 matthew.hillman@lincoln.gov.uk

Legal: Ms Carolyn Wheater , Head of Corporate Support Services, City Hall, Beaumont Fee, Lincoln LN1 1DD ☎ 01522 873323 🖷 01522 521736 🖰 carolyn.wheater@lincoln.gov.uk

Leisure and Cultural Services: Mr Steve Bird, Assistant Director of Communities & Street Scene, City Hall, Beaumont Fee, Lincoln LN1 1DH ☎ 01522 873421 🖷 01522 546702 🖰 steve.bird@lincoln.gov.uk

Leisure and Cultural Services: Mr Simon Colburn , Assistant Director of Health & Environmental Services, City Hall, Beaumont Fee, Lincoln LN1 1DD ☎ 01522 873241 🖰 simon.colburn@lincoln.gov.uk

Licensing: Mr Kevin Barron, Licensing Manager, City Hall, Beaumont Fee, Lincoln LN1 1DD ☎ 01522 873564 🖷 01522 542569 🖰 kevin.barron@lincoln.gov.uk

Lifelong Learning: Ms Jane Newman , Work Based Learning Manager, City Hall, Beaumont Fee, Lincoln LN1 1DD ☎ 01522 873807 🖰 jane.newman@lincoln.gov.uk

LINCOLN CITY

Lottery Funding, Charity and Voluntary: Ms Michelle Smith , Senior Programme Managements Officer, City Hall, Beaumont Fee, Lincoln LN1 1DD ☎ 01522 873329 🖷 01522 567934 🖰 michelle.smith@lincoln.gov.uk

Member Services: Mr Steve Swain, Principal Democratic Services Officer, City Hall, Beaumont Fee, Lincoln LN1 1DD ☎ 01522 873439 🖷 01522 542569 🖰 steve.swain@lincoln.gov.uk

Parking: Mr Steve Lockwood, Leisure, Sport & City Services Manager, City Hall, Beaumont Fee, Lincoln LN1 1DD ☎ 01522 873520 🖰 steve.lockwood@lincoln.gov.uk

Partnerships: Mr Simon Walters , Assistant Director of Corporate Review & Development, City Hall, Beaumont Fee, Lincoln LN1 1DD ☎ 01522 873866 🖷 01522 521736 🖰 simon.walters@lincoln.gov.uk

Personnel / HR: Mrs Carolyn Wheater , Assistant Director of Corporate Support Services, City Hall, Beaumont Fee, Lincoln LN1 1DD ☎ 01522 873323 🖷 01522 542569 🖰 carolyn.wheater@lincoln.gov.uk

Planning: Ms Kate Ellis , Assistant Director - Planning & Regeneration, City Hall, Beaumont Fee, Lincoln LN1 1DD ☎ 01522 873824 🖷 01522 560049 🖰 kate.ellis@lincoln.gov.uk

Procurement: Ms Jaclyn Gibson , Assistant Director of Business Development & Finance, City Hall, Beaumont Fee, Lincoln LN1 1DD ☎ 01522 873258 🖷 01522 542569 🖰 jaclyn.gibson@lincoln.gov.uk

Street Scene: Ms Caroline Bird , Community Services Manager, City Hall, Beaumont Fee, Lincoln LN1 1DD ☎ 01522 873405 🖰 caroline.bird@lincoln.gov.uk

Sustainable Communities: Mr Simon Walters , Assistant Director of Corporate Review & Development, City Hall, Beaumont Fee, Lincoln LN1 1DD ☎ 01522 873866 🖷 01522 521736 🖰 simon.walters@lincoln.gov.uk

Waste Collection and Disposal: Mr Steve Bird, Assistant Director of Communities & Street Scene, City Hall, Beaumont Fee, Lincoln LN1 1DH ☎ 01522 873421 🖷 01522 546702 🖰 steve.bird@lincoln.gov.uk

Waste Management: Ms Caroline Bird , Community Services Manager, City Hall, Beaumont Fee, Lincoln LN1 1DD ☎ 01522 873405 🖰 caroline.bird@lincoln.gov.uk

COUNCILLORS

***Mayor* Kerry**, Andrew (CON - Hartsolme)
andrew.kerry@lincoln.gov.uk

***Leader of the Council* Metcalfe**, Richard (LAB - Glebe)
richard.metcalfe@lincoln.gov.uk

***Deputy Leader of the Council* Nannestad**, Donald (LAB - Castle)
donald.nannestad@lincoln.gov.uk

***Group Leader* Hills**, Ronald (CON - Hartsolme)
ronald.hills@lincoln.gov.uk

Bilton, Bill (LAB - Bracebridge)
bill.bilton@lincoln.gov.uk

Brothwell, Kathleen (LAB - Abbey)
kathleen.brothwell@lincoln.gov.uk

Burke, Sue (LAB - Minster)
sue.burke@lincoln.gov.uk

Burke, Chris (LAB - Park)
chris.burke@lincoln.gov.uk

Bushell, Bob (LAB - Moorland)
bob.bushell@lincoln.gov.uk

Charlesworth, Brent (LAB - Park)
brent.charlesworth@lincoln.gov.uk

Clayton-Hewson, Gill (LAB - Boultham)
gillclayton-hewson@lincoln.gov.uk

Daniel, Carol (LAB - Minster)
carol.daniel@lincoln.gov.uk

Ellis, Geoff (LAB - Moorland)
geoff.ellis@lincoln.gov.uk

Gray, Tony (LAB - Birchwood)
tony.gray@lincoln.gov.uk

Hanrahan, Jim (LAB - Castle)
jim.hanrahan@lincoln.gov.uk

Hewson, Gary (LAB - Boultham)
gary.hewson@lincoln.gov.uk

Jackson, David (LAB - Park)
david.jackson@lincoln.gov.uk

Kirk, Jackie (LAB - Glebe)
jackie.kirk@lincoln.gov.uk

Kirk, Rosanne (LAB - Birchwood)
rosanne.kirk@lincoln.gov.uk

Lee, Karen (LAB - Carholme)
karen.lee@lincoln.gov.uk

Maxwell, Liz (LAB - Minster)
liz.maxwell@lincoln.gov.uk

McNulty, Adrianna (LAB - Moorland)
adrianna.mcnulty@lincoln.gov.uk

Murray, Neil (LAB - Carholme)
neil.murray@lincoln.gov.uk

Riddick, Marika (CON - Hartsolme)
marika.riddick@lincoln.gov.uk

Smith, Fay (LAB - Abbey)
fay.smith@lincoln.gov.uk

Speakman, Tony (LAB - Carholme)
tony.speakman@lincoln.gov.uk

Strengiel, Edmund (CON - Birchwood)
edmund.strengiel@lincoln.gov.uk

Toofany, Ralph (LAB - Boultham)
ralph.toofany@lincoln.gov.uk

Vaughan, Patrick (LAB - Glebe)
pat.vaughan@lincoln.gov.uk

Weaver, Keith (CON - Bracebridge)
keith.weaver@lincoln.gov.uk

West, Peter (LAB - Abbey)
peter.west@lincoln.gov.uk

Wilson, Matthew (CON - Bracebridge)
matthew.wilson@lincoln.gov.uk

Woolley, Loraine (LAB - Castle)
loraine.woolley@lincoln.gov.uk

POLITICAL COMPOSITION

LAB: 27, CON: 6

COMMITTEE CHAIRS

Audit: Mr Tony Speakman

Licensing: Ms Kathleen Brothwell

Planning: Mr Jim Hanrahan

Lincolnshire C

Lincolnshire County Council, County Offices, Newland, Lincoln LN1 1YL
☎ 01522 552222 🖷 01522 516137
customer_services@lincolnshire.gov.uk 💻 www.lincolnshire.gov.uk

FACTS AND FIGURES

EU Constituencies: East Midlands
Election Frequency: Elections are of whole council

PRINCIPAL OFFICERS

Chief Executive: Mr Tony McArdle, Chief Executive, County Offices, Newland, Lincoln LN1 1YL ☎ 01522 552001 🖷 01522 552004 tony.mcardle@lincolnshire.gov.uk

Senior Management: Ms Debbie Barnes , Executive Director - Children's Services, County Offices, Newland, Lincoln LN1 1YL ☎ 01552 553201 debbie.barnes@lincolnshire.gov.uk

Senior Management: Mr Glen Garrod , Director - Adult Social Services, Orchard House, Orchard Street, Lincoln LN1 1BA ☎ 01522 552808 🖷 01522 554025 glen.garrod@lincolnshire.gov.uk

Senior Management: Ms Judith Hetherington-Smith , Chief Information & Commissioning Officer, County Offices, Newland, Lincoln LN1 1YL ☎ 01522 553603 judith.hetheringtonsmith@lincolnshire.gov.uk

Senior Management: Dr Tony Hill , Executive Director - Public Health, County Offices, Newland, Lincoln LN1 1YL ☎ 01552 553960 🖷 01522 553200 tony.hill@lincolnshire.gov.uk

Senior Management: Mr Pete Moore, Executive Director - Finance & Public Protection, County Offices, Newland, Lincoln LN1 1YL ☎ 01522 553602 🖷 01522 553962 pete.moore@lincolnshire.gov.uk

Senior Management: Mr Richard Wills, Executive Director - Environment & Economy, County Offices, Newland, Lincoln LN1 1YL ☎ 01522 553000 🖷 01522 512335 richard.wills@lincolnshire.gov.uk

Access Officer / Social Services (Disability): Mr Glen Garrod, Director - Adult Social Services, Orchard House, Orchard Street, Lincoln LN1 1BA ☎ 01522 552808 🖷 01522 554025 glen.garrod@lincolnshire.gov.uk

Architect, Building / Property Services: Mr Kevin Kendall, County Property Officer, County Offices, Newland, Lincoln LN1 1YL ☎ 01552 553099 🖷 01522 541561 kevin.kendall@lincolnshire.gov.uk

Best Value: Mr George Spiteri , Strategic Commercial & Performance Manager, County Offices, Newland, Lincoln LN1 1YL ☎ 01522 552120 george.spiteri@lincolnshire.gov.uk

Catering Services: Mrs Claire Blackbourn, Assistant Catering Services Manager, Mill House (3rd Floor), Brayford Wharf North, Lincoln LN1 1YT ☎ 01522 836554 🖷 01522 516061 claire.blackbourn@mouchel-lincoln.com

Children / Youth Services: Mr Stuart Carlton , Assistant Director - Lead Early Help, County Offices, Newland, Lincoln LN1 1YL ☎ 01552 554051 stuart.carlton@lincolnshire.gov.uk

Civil Registration: Ms Donna Sharp , County Services Manager, Lindum Road, Lincoln LN2 1NN ☎ 01522 554052 🖷 01522 589524 donna.sharp@lincolnshire.gov.uk

PR / Communications: Ms Karen Spencer , Strategic Communications & Digital Engagement Manager, County Offices, Newland, Lincoln LN1 1YL ☎ 01522 552303 karen.spencer@lincolnshire.gov.uk

Community Safety: Mr Mark Housley , County Officer - Public Protection, Room 35, Myle Cross Centre, Lincoln LN2 4EL ☎ 01522 554593 mark.housley@lincolnshire.gov.uk

Computer Management: Mr Simon Oliver , Chief Technology Officer, Orchard House, Orchard Street, Lincoln LN2 4EL ☎ 01522 555596 simon.oliver@lincolnshire.gov.uk

Consumer Protection and Trading Standards: Mrs Sara Barry, Safer Communities Manager, Myle Cross Centre, Lincoln LN2 4EL ☎ 01522 552499 sara.barry@lincolnshire.gov.uk

Contracts: Ms Sophie Reeve , Chief Commercial Officer, Orchard House, Orchard Street, Lincoln LN1 1BA ☎ 01522 552578 sophie.reeve@lincolnshire.gov.uk

Corporate Services: Mr Pete Moore, Executive Director - Finance & Public Protection, County Offices, Newland, Lincoln LN1 1YL ☎ 01522 553602 🖷 01522 553962 pete.moore@lincolnshire.gov.uk

Customer Service: Mrs Zoe Butler , Head of Customer Services, SERCO, Thomas Parker House, 13 - 14 Silver Street, Lincoln LN2 1DY ☎ 01522 550002 zoe.butler@lincolnshire.gov.uk

Economic Development: Mr Justin Brown, Enterprise Commissioner, Witham Park House, Waterside South, Lincoln LN5 7JN ☎ 01522 550630 🖷 01522 516720 justin.brown@lincolnshire.gov.uk

Education: Ms Debbie Barnes , Executive Director - Children's Services, County Offices, Newland, Lincoln LN1 1YL ☎ 01552 553201 debbie.barnes@lincolnshire.gov.uk

LINCOLNSHIRE

E-Government: Ms Judith Hetherington-Smith , Chief Information & Commissioning Officer, Business Modernisation Unit, County Offices, Newland, Lincoln LN1 1YL ☎ 01522 553603 ⌨ judith.hetheringtonsmith@lincolnshire.gov.uk

Emergency Planning: Mr David Powell , Head - Emergency Planning, Fire and Rescue Headquarters, South Park Avenue, Lincoln LN5 8EL ☎ 01522 582224 🖷 01522 519318 ⌨ david.powell@lincoln.fire-uk.org

Energy Management: Mr Kevin Kendall , County Property Officer, County Offices, Newland, Lincoln LN1 1YL ☎ 01552 553099 🖷 01522 541561 ⌨ kevin.kendall@lincolnshire.gov.uk

Environmental / Technical Services: Mr Richard Wills, Executive Director - Environment & Economy, City Hall, Beaumont Fee, Lincoln LN1 1DN ☎ 01522 553000 🖷 01522 512335 ⌨ richard.wills@lincolnshire.gov.uk

Environmental Health: Mr Sean Kent , Group Manager - Environmental Services, Witham Park House, Waterside South, Lincoln LN5 7JN ☎ 01522 554833 🖷 01522 554840 ⌨ sean.kent@lincolnshire.gov.uk

Estates, Property & Valuation: Mr Kevin Kendall , County Property Officer, County Offices, Newland, Lincoln LN1 1YL ☎ 01552 553099 🖷 01522 541561 ⌨ kevin.kendall@lincolnshire.gov.uk

European Liaison: Ms Susannah Lewis , Funding & Regeneration Team Leader, Witham Park House, Waterside South, Lincoln LN5 7JN ☎ 01522 550638 ⌨ susannah.lewis@lincolnshire.gov.uk

Events Manager: Mr Mark Stoneham, Events Manager, County Offices, Newland, Lincoln LN1 1YL ☎ 01522 552118 🖷 01522 552323 ⌨ mark.stoneham@lincolnshire.gov.uk

Finance: Mr David Forbes, County Finance Officer, Orchard House, Orchard Street, Lincoln LN1 1YZ ☎ 01522 553642 ⌨ david.forbes@lincolnshire.gov.uk

Finance: Mr Pete Moore, Executive Director - Finance & Public Protection, County Offices, Newland, Lincoln LN1 1YL ☎ 01522 553602 🖷 01522 553962 ⌨ pete.moore@lincolnshire.gov.uk

Treasury: Ms Jo Ray , Pensions & Treasury Manager, Orchard House, Orchard Street, Lincoln LN1 1YZ ☎ 01522 553656 ⌨ jo.ray@lincolnshire.gov.uk

Pensions: Ms Jo Ray , Pensions & Treasury Manager, Orchard House, Orchard Street, Lincoln LN1 1YZ ☎ 01522 553656 ⌨ jo.ray@lincolnshire.gov.uk

Fleet Management: Mr David J Davies , Principal Maintenance Engineer & County Fleet Manager, Unit 7, Witham Park House, Waterside South, Lincoln LN5 7JN ☎ 01522 553080 🖷 01522 553149 ⌨ davidj.davies@lincolnshire.gov.uk

Health and Safety: Ms Sarah Danes , Strategic Risk Manager, County Offices, Newland, Lincoln LN1 1YL ☎ 01522 552206 ⌨ sarah.danes@lincolnshire.gov.uk

Highways: Mr Steve Willis , Chief Operating Officer - Development Services, Witham Park House, Waterside South, Lincoln LN5 7JN ☎ 01522 554848 ⌨ steve.willis@lincolnshire.gov.uk

Legal: Mr David Coleman , Chief Legal Officer, 45 - 49 Newland, Lincoln LN1 1XZ ☎ 01522 552542 🖷 01522 552588 ⌨ david.coleman@lincolnshire.gov.uk

Leisure and Cultural Services: Mr Jonathan Platt , County Libraries & Heritage Manager, 15 - 17 The Avenue, Lincoln LN1 1PD ☎ 01522 550586 ⌨ jonathan.platt@lincolnshire.gov.uk

Lifelong Learning: Ms Thea Croxall , Principal Commissioning Officer - Learning, Eastgate Centre, 105 Eastgate, Sleaford NG34 7EN ☎ 01522 550381 ⌨ thea.croxall@lincolnshire.gov.uk

Lighting: Mr Stan Hall, Principal Engineer - Street Lighting, Crown House, Grantham Street, Lincoln LN2 1BD ☎ 01522 555572 🖷 01522 553068 ⌨ stan.hall@lincolnshire.gov.uk

Lottery Funding, Charity and Voluntary: Ms Wendy Moore , Funding & Community Grants Officer, Orchard House, Orchard Street, Lincoln LN1 1YL ☎ 01522 552223 ⌨ wendy.moore@lincolnshire.gov.uk

Member Services: Mr Nigel West , Democratic Services Manager, County Offices, Newland, Lincoln LN1 1YL ☎ 01522 552840 🖷 01522 552004 ⌨ nigel.west@lincolnshire.gov.uk

Parking: Mr Mick Phoenix , Parking Services Manager, Unit 7, Witham Park House, Waterside South, Lincoln LN5 7JN ☎ 01522 552105 ⌨ mick.phoenix@lincoln.gov.uk

Personnel / HR: Mrs Fiona Thompson , Service Manager - People, County Offices, Newland, Lincoln LN1 1YL ☎ 01522 552207 🖷 01522 516010 ⌨ fiona.thompson@lincolnshire.gov.uk

Planning: Mr Andrew Gutherson , County Commissioner for Economy & Place, Witham Park House, Waterside South, Lincoln LN5 7JN ☎ 01522 554827 🖷 01522 554829 ⌨ andy.gutherson@lincolnshire.gov.uk

Procurement: Ms Sophie Reeve , Chief Commercial Officer, Orchard House, Orchard Street, Lincoln LN1 1BA ☎ 01522 552578 ⌨ sophie.reeve@lincolnshire.gov.uk

Public Libraries: Mr Jonathan Platt , County Libraries & Heritage Manager, 15 - 17 The Avenue, Lincoln LN1 1PD ☎ 01522 550586 ⌨ jonathan.platt@lincolnshire.gov.uk

Recycling & Waste Minimisation: Mr Sean Kent , Group Manager - Environmental Services, Witham Park House, Waterside South, Lincoln LN5 7JN ☎ 01522 554833 🖷 01522 554840 ⌨ sean.kent@lincolnshire.gov.uk

Regeneration: Mr Paul Wheatley , Group Manager - Economic Delivery, Ground Floor, City Hall, Beaumont Fee, Lincoln LN1 1DD ☎ 01522 550600 ⌨ paul.wheatley@lincolnshire.gov.uk

Regeneration: Mr Steve Willis , Chief Operating Officer - Development Services, Witham Park House, Waterside South, Lincoln LN5 7JN ☎ 01522 554848 ⌨ steve.willis@lincolnshire.gov.uk

Road Safety: Mr Richard Greener, Partnership Development Manager, The Pelham Centre, Lincoln LN5 8HE ☎ 01522 805801 🖷 01522 805803 ✉ richard.greener@lincolnshire.gov.uk

Social Services (Adult): Mr Justin Hackney , Chief Commissioning Officer - Joint Commissioning Specialist Services, Orchard House, Orchard Street, Lincoln LN2 1BA ☎ 01522 554259 ✉ justin.hackney@lincolnshire.gov.uk

Social Services (Adult): Mr Pete Sidgwick , Chief Commissioning Officer - Frail, Elderly & Long-Term Conditions, Orchard House, Orchard Street, Lincoln LN1 1BA ☎ 01522 552211 ✉ pete.sidgwick@lincolnshire.gov.uk

Social Services (Children): Ms Debbie Barnes , Executive Director - Children's Services, County Offices, Newland, Lincoln LN1 1YL ☎ 01552 553201 ✉ debbie.barnes@lincolnshire.gov.uk

Staff Training: Mrs Fiona Thompson , Service Manager - People, County Offices, Newland, Lincoln LN1 1YL ☎ 01522 552207 🖷 01522 516010 ✉ fiona.thompson@lincolnshire.gov.uk

Sustainable Development: Mr Douglas Robinson, Sustainability Team Leader, Witham Park House, Waterside South, Lincoln LN5 7JN ☎ 01522 554816 🖷 01522 554840 ✉ douglas.robinson@lincolnshire.gov.uk

Tourism: Ms Mary Powell, Tourism & Development Manager, Unit 4, Witham Park House, Waterside South, Lincoln LN5 7JN ☎ 01522 550612 🖷 01522 516720 ✉ mary.powell@lincolnshire.gov.uk

Traffic Management: Mr Steve Willis , Chief Operating Officer - Development Services, Witham Park House, Waterside South, Lincoln LN5 7JN ☎ 01522 554848 ✉ steve.willis@lincolnshire.gov.uk

Transport: Ms Anita Ruffle , Group Manager - Passenger Transport Unit, Crown House, Grantham Street, Lincoln LN2 1BD ☎ 01522 553147 ✉ anita.ruffle@lincolnshire.gov.uk

Transport Planner: Ms Anita Ruffle , Group Manager - Passenger Transport Unit, Crown House, Grantham Street, Lincoln LN2 1BD ☎ 01522 553147 ✉ anita.ruffle@lincolnshire.gov.uk

Waste Collection and Disposal: Mr Sean Kent , Group Manager - Environmental Services, Witham Park House, Waterside South, Lincoln LN5 7JN ☎ 01522 554833 🖷 01522 554840 ✉ sean.kent@lincolnshire.gov.uk

Waste Management: Mr Sean Kent , Group Manager - Environmental Services, Witham Park House, Waterside South, Lincoln LN5 7JN ☎ 01522 554833 🖷 01522 554840 ✉ sean.kent@lincolnshire.gov.uk

COUNCILLORS

***Chair* Webb**, William (CON - Holbeach Rural)
cllrw.webb@lincolnshire.gov.uk

***Vice-Chair* Trollope-Bellew**, Martin (CON - Stamford Rural)
cllrt.trollopebellew@lincolnshire.gov.uk

***Leader of the Council* Hill**, Martin (CON - Folkingham Rural)
cllrm.hill@lincolnshire.gov.uk

***Deputy Leader of the Council* Bradwell**, Patricia (CON - Billinghay and Metheringham)
cllrp.bradwell@lincolnshire.gov.uk

Adams, Bob (CON - Colsterworth Rural)
cllrb.adams@lincolnshire.gov.uk

Allan, Mark (IND - Sleaford)
cllrm.allan@lincolnshire.gov.uk

Aron, Bill (IND - Horncastle and Tetford)
cllrb.aron@lincolnshire.gov.uk

Austin, Alison (IND - Boston South)
cllra.austin@lincolnshire.gov.uk

Ayling, Victoria (UKIP - Spilsby Fen)
cllrv.ayling@lincolnshire.gov.uk

Beaver, John (IND - Gainsborough Hill)
cllrj.beaver@lincolnshire.gov.uk

Brailsford, David (CON - Stamford West)
cllrd.brailsford@lincolnshire.gov.uk

Brewis, Christopher (IND - Sutton Elloe)
cllrc.brewis@lincolnshire.gov.uk

Bridges, Anthony (CON - Louth Rural North)
cllrt.bridges@lincolnshire.gov.uk

Brockway, Jacqueline (CON - Nettleham and Saxilby)
cllrj.brockway@lincolnshire.gov.uk

Brookes, Michael (CON - Boston Rural)
cllrm.brookes@lincolnshire.gov.uk

Clarke, Kevin (LAB - Lincoln Boultham)
cllrk.clarke@lincolnshire.gov.uk

Davie, Colin (CON - Ingoldmells Rural)
cllrc.davie@lincolnshire.gov.uk

Davies, Richard (CON - Grantham North West)
cllrr.davies@lincolnshire.gov.uk

Dilks, Philip (LAB - Deeping St. James)
cllrp.dilks@lincolnshire.gov.uk

Dodds, Sarah (LAB - Louth North)
cllrs.dodds@lincolnshire.gov.uk

Ellis, Geoffrey (LAB - Lincoln Moorland)
cllrg.ellis@lincolnshire.gov.uk

Fairman, Richard (UKIP - Spalding East and Moulton)
cllrr.faiman@lincolnshire.gov.uk

Fleetwood, Ian (CON - Bardney and Cherry Willingham)
cllri.fleetwood@lincolnshire.gov.uk

Foulkes, Robert (UKIP - Stamford North)
cllrr.foulkes@lincolnshire.gov.uk

Hagues, Andrew (CON - Sleaford West and Leasingham)
cllra.hagues@lincolnshire.gov.uk

Hough, John (LAB - Louth South)
cllrj.hough@lincolnshire.gov.uk

Hoyes, Denis (CON - Woodhall Spa and Wragby)
cllrd.hoyes@lincolnshire.gov.uk

Hunter-Clarke, Dean (UKIP - Skegness North)
cllrd.hunter-clarke@lincolnshire.gov.uk

Hunter-Clarke, Robin (UKIP - Skegness South)
cllrr.hunter-clarke@lincolnshire.gov.uk

Jackson, Nev (LAB - Lincoln Park)
cllrn.jackson@lincolnshire.gov.uk

Jesson, Alan (UKIP - Spalding South)
cllra.jesson@lincolnshire.gov.uk

LINCOLNSHIRE

Jones, Marc (CON - Lincoln Bracebridge)
cllrm.jones@lincolnshire.gov.uk

Keimach, Burt (CON - Market Rasen Wolds)
cllrb.keimach@lincolnshire.gov.uk

Keywood-Wainwright, Tiggs (IND - Boston North West)
cllrt.keywood-wainwright@lincolnshire.gov.uk

Kinch, Stuart (CON - Gainsborough Rural South)
cllrs.kinch@lincolnshire.gov.uk

Kirk, Rosanne (LAB - Lincoln Birchwood)
cllrr.kirk@lincolnshire.gov.uk

Mair, Colin (UKIP - Tattershall Castle)
cllrc.mair@lincolnshire.gov.uk

Marfleet, Hugo (CON - Louth Wolds)
cllrh.marfleet@lincolnshire.gov.uk

Marriott, John (LD - Hykeham Forum)
cllrj.marriott@lincolnshire.gov.uk

McAuley, Robert (IND - Boston West)
cllrb.mcauley@lincolnshire.gov.uk

McNally, Daniel (UKIP - Louth Marsh)
cllrd.mcnally@lincolnshire.gov.uk

Morgan, Dawn (LAB - Grantham South)
cllrc.morgan@lincolnshire.gov.uk

Murray, Neil (LAB - Lincoln Glebe)
cllrn.murray@lincolnshire.gov.uk

Newton, Angela (IND - Spalding West)
cllra.newton@lincolnshire.gov.uk

O'Connor, Pat (LD - Gainsborough Trent)
cllrp.oconnor@lincolnshire.gov.uk

Overton, Marianne (IND - Branston and Navenby)
cllrm.overton@lincolnshire.gov.uk

Oxby, Ron (CON - Heighington and Washingborough)
cllrr.oxby@lincolnshire.gov.uk

Pain, Christopher (IND - Wainfleet and Burgh)
cllrc.pain@lincolnshire.gov.uk

Palmer, Stephen (IND - Alford and Sutton)
cllrs.palmer@lincolnshire.gov.uk

Parker, Robert (LAB - Lincoln West)
cllrr.parker@lincolnshire.gov.uk

Pepper, Nigel (CON - Crowland and Whaplode)
cllrn.pepper@lincolnshire.gov.uk

Phillips, Raymond (CON - Bassingham Rural)
cllrr.phillips@lincolnshire.gov.uk

Powell, Helen (IND - Bourne Castle)
cllrh.powell@lincolnshire.gov.uk

Ransome, Sue (UKIP - Boston East)
cllrs.ransome@lincolnshire.gov.uk

Ransome, Elizabeth (UKIP - Boston Fishtoft)
cllre.ransome@lincolnshire.gov.uk

Ransome, Felicity (UKIP - Boston Coastal)
cllrf.ransome@lincolnshire.gov.uk

Rawlins, Sue (CON - Welton Rural)
cllrs.rawlins@lincolnshire.gov.uk

Renshaw, Judith (LAB - Lincoln North)
cllrj.renshaw@lincolnshire.gov.uk

Renshaw, Robin (LAB - Lincoln East)
cllrr.renshaw@lincolnshire.gov.uk

Reynolds, Anne (UKIP - Mablethorpe)
cllra.reynolds@lincolnshire.gov.uk

Robinson, Peter (CON - Market Deeping & West Deeping)
cllrp.robinson@lincolnshire.gov.uk

Rollings, Lesley Anne (LD - Scotter Rural)

Shore, Reg (LD - Skellingthorpe and Hykeham South)
cllrr.shore@lincolnshire.gov.uk

Smith, Nicola (UKIP - Lincoln Hartsholme)
cllrj.smith@lincolnshire.gov.uk

Sneath, Elizabeth (CON - Spalding Elloe)
cllre.sneath@lincolnshire.gov.uk

Strange, Charles (CON - Ancholme Cliff)
cllrc.strange@lincolnshire.gov.uk

Talbot, Christine (CON - Bracebridge Heath and Waddington)
cllrc.talbot@lincolnshire.gov.uk

Turner, Tony (CON - North Wolds)
cllra.turner@lincolnshire.gov.uk

Tweedale, Stuart (CON - Ruskington and Cranwell)
cllrs.tweedale@lincolnshire.gov.uk

Whittington, Mark (CON - Grantham Barrowby)
cllrm.whittington@lincolnshire.gov.uk

Wood, Paul (IND - Hough)
cllrp.wood@lincolnshire.gov.uk

Woolley, Sue (CON - Bourne Abbey)
cllrs.woolley@lincolnshire.gov.uk

Wootten, Ray (CON - Grantham North)
cllrr.wootten@lincolnshire.gov.uk

Wootten, Linda (CON - Grantham East)
cllrl.wootten@lincolnshire.gov.uk

Worth, Charles (CON - Holbeach)
cllrn.worth@lincolnshire.gov.uk

Wray, Susan (CON - Donington Rural)
cllrs.wray@lincolnshire.gov.uk

Young, Barry
(CON - Sleaford Rural South)
cllrb.young@lincolnshire.gov.uk

POLITICAL COMPOSITION

CON: 35, IND: 13, UKIP: 13, LAB: 12, LD: 4

COMMITTEE CHAIRS

Audit: Mrs Sue Rawlins

Children & Young People: Mr John Hough

Health & Wellbeing: Mrs Sue Woolley

Pensions: Mr Mark Allan

Planning & Regulation: Mr Ian Fleetwood

Lisburn City & Castlereagh District N

Lisburn City & Castlereagh District, Island Civic Centre, The Island, Lisburn BT27 4RL

PRINCIPAL OFFICERS

Chief Executive: Dr Theresa Donaldson , Chief Executive, Island Civic Centre, The Island, Lisburn BT27 4RL

Senior Management: Mr Adrian Donaldson , Director of Corporate Services, Island Civic Centre, The Island, Lisburn BT27 4RL ☎ 028 9244 7528 adriand@lisburncastlereagh.gov.uk

Senior Management: Mr Colin McClintock , Director of Development & Planning, Island Civic Centre, The Island, Lisburn BT27 4RL ☎ 028 9244 7202 colin.mcclintock@lisburncastlereagh.gov.uk

Senior Management: Ms Heather Moore , Director of Environmental Services, Island Civic Centre, The Island, Lisburn BT27 4RL ☎ 028 9244 7393 heather.moore@lisburncastlereagh.gov.uk

Senior Management: Mr Jim Rose , Director of Leisure & Community Services, Island Civic Centre, The Island, Lisburn BT27 4RL ☎ 028 9244 7203 jim.rose@lisburncastlereagh.gov.uk

Community Planning: Mr Jim Rose , Director of Leisure & Community Services, Island Civic Centre, The Island, Lisburn BT27 4RL ☎ 028 9244 7203 jim.rose@lisburncastlereagh.gov.uk

Corporate Services: Mr Adrian Donaldson , Director of Corporate Services, Island Civic Centre, The Island, Lisburn BT27 4RL ☎ 028 9244 7528 adriand@lisburncastlereagh.gov.uk

Environmental / Technical Services: Ms Heather Moore, Director of Environmental Services, Island Civic Centre, The Island, Lisburn BT27 4RL ☎ 028 9244 7393 heather.moore@lisburncastlereagh.gov.uk

Environmental Health: Ms Heather Moore, Director of Environmental Services, Island Civic Centre, The Island, Lisburn BT27 4RL ☎ 028 9244 7393 heather.moore@lisburncastlereagh.gov.uk

Leisure and Cultural Services: Mr Jim Rose , Director of Leisure & Community Services, Island Civic Centre, The Island, Lisburn BT27 4RL ☎ 028 9244 7203 jim.rose@lisburncastlereagh.gov.uk

Planning: Mr Colin McClintock , Director of Development & Planning, Island Civic Centre, The Island, Lisburn BT27 4RL ☎ 028 9244 7202 colin.mcclintock@lisburncastlereagh.gov.uk

COUNCILLORS

Anderson, Nathan (DUP - Castlereagh South)
nathan.anderson@lisburncastlereagh.gov.uk

Baird, James (UUP - Downshire East)
james.baird@lisburncastlereagh.gov.uk

Beckett, Thomas (DUP - Killultagh)
thomas.beckett@lisburncastlereagh.gov.uk

Bloomfield, Brian (UUP - Lisburn North)
brian.bloomfield@lisburncastlereagh.gov.uk

Butler, Robbie (UUP - Killultagh)
robbie.butler@lisburncastlereagh.gov.uk

Carson, Scott (DUP - Lisburn North)
scott.carson@lisburncastlereagh.gov.uk

Catney, Patrick (SDLP - Killultagh)
pat.catney@lisburncastlereagh.gov.uk

Dillon, James (UUP - Downshire West)
jim.dillon@lisburncastlereagh.gov.uk

Drysdale, David (DUP - Castlereagh East)
david.drysdale@lisburncastlereagh.gov.uk

Ewart, Allan (DUP - Downshire West)
allan.ewart@lisburncastlereagh.gov.uk

Ewing, Andrew (DUP - Lisburn South)
andrew.ewing@lisburncastlereagh.gov.uk

Gallen, John (SDLP - Castlereagh South)
john.gallen@lisburncastlereagh.gov.uk

Gawaith, Owen (O - Downshire West)
owen.gawaith@lisburncastlereagh.gov.uk

Girvin, Andrew (O - Castlereagh East)
andrew.girvan@lisburncastlereagh.gov.uk

Givan, Alan (DUP - Lisburn South)
alan.givan@lisburncastlereagh.gov.uk

Gray, Janet (DUP - Downshire East)
janet.gray@lisburncastlereagh.gov.uk

Grehan, Amanda (O - Lisburn South)
amanda.grehan@lisburncastlereagh.gov.uk

Harvey, Brian (SDLP - Castlereagh South)
brian.harvey@lisburncastlereagh.gov.uk

Henderson, Michael (UUP - Castlereagh South)
michael.henderson@lisburncastlereagh.gov.uk

Jeffers, Tommy (DUP - Castlereagh East)
tommy.jeffers@lisburncastlereagh.gov.uk

Kamble, Vasundhara (O - Castlereagh South)
vasundhara.kamble@lisburncastlereagh.gov.uk

Leathem, William (DUP - Killultagh)
william.leathem@lisburncastlereagh.gov.uk

Legge, Hazel (UUP - Castlereagh East)
hazel.legge@lisburncastlereagh.gov.uk

Mackin, Uel (DUP - Downshire East)
uel.mackin@lisburncastlereagh.gov.uk

Mallon, Ben (DUP - Castlereagh South)
ben.mallon@lisburncastlereagh.gov.uk

Martin, Stephen (O - Lisburn North)
stephen.martin@lisburncastlereagh.gov.uk

McCarthy, Jonny (O - Lisburn North)
johnny.mccarthy@lisburncastlereagh.gov.uk

McIntyre, Aaron (O - Downshire East)
aaron.mcintyre@lisburncastlereagh.gov.uk

Mitchell, Tim (UUP - Lisburn South)
tim.mitchell@lisburncastlereagh.gov.uk

Morrow, Tim (O - Castlereagh East)
tim.morrow@lisburncastlereagh.gov.uk

Palmer, John (DUP - Downshire West)
john.palmer@lisburncastlereagh.gov.uk

Palmer, Jenny (DUP - Lisburn North)
jenny.palmer@lisburncastlereagh.gov.uk

Poots, Luke (DUP - Downshire East)
luke.poots@lisburncastlereagh.gov.uk

Porter, Paul (DUP - Lisburn South)
paul.porter@lisburncastlereagh.gov.uk

Redpath, Alexander (UUP - Downshire West)
alexander.redpath@lisburncastlereagh.gov.uk

Rice, Geraldine (O - Castlereagh South)
geraldine.rice@lisburncastlereagh.gov.uk

Skillen, Sharon (DUP - Castlereagh East)
sharon.skillen@lisburncastlereagh.gov.uk

Tinsley, James (DUP - Killultagh)
james.tinsley@lisburncastlereagh.gov.uk

Tolerton, Margaret (DUP - Lisburn North)
margaret.tolerton@lisburncastlereagh.gov.uk

Walker, Rhoda (DUP - Lisburn South)
rhoda.walker@lisburncastlereagh.gov.uk

POLITICAL COMPOSITION
DUP: 20, O: 9, UUP: 8, SDLP: 3

Liverpool City M

Liverpool City Council, Municipal Buildings, Dale Street, Liverpool L69 2DH
☎ 0151 233 3000 ✉ liverpool.direct@liverpool.gov.uk
💻 www.liverpool.gov.uk

FACTS AND FIGURES
Parliamentary Constituencies: Liverpool, Riverside, Liverpool, Walton, Liverpool, Wavertree, Liverpool, West Derby
EU Constituencies: North West
Election Frequency: Elections are by thirds

PRINCIPAL OFFICERS
Chief Executive: Mr Ged Fitzgerald , Chief Executive, Labour Group Office, Municipal Buildings, Dale Street, Liverpool L69 2DH
☎ 0151 225 3602 ✉ ged.fitzgerald@liverpool.gov.uk

Senior Management: Ms Sandra Davies , Interim Director - Public Health, Labour Group Office, Municipal Buildings, Dale Street, Liverpool L69 2DH ☎ 0151 233 1106
✉ sandra.davies@liverpool.gov.uk

Senior Management: Ms Becky Hellard , Director of Finance & Resources, Room 14, Municipal Buildings, Dale Street, Liverpool L69 2DH ☎ 0151 225 2347 ✉ becky.hellard@liverpool.gov.uk

Senior Management: Mr Samih Kalakeche , Director of Adult Services & Health, 2nd Floor, Millennium House, Victoria Street, Liverpool L1 6LD ☎ 0151 223 4213
✉ samih.kalakeche@liverpool.gov.uk

Senior Management: Mr Nick Kavanagh , Director of Regeneration & Employment, 3rd Floor, Millennium House, Victoria Street, Liverpool L1 6LD ☎ 0151 233 6715
✉ nick.kavanagh@liverpool.gov.uk

Senior Management: Ms Colette O'Brien , Director of Children & Young People's Services, 2nd Floor, Millennium House, 60 Victoria Street, Liverpool L1 6JF ☎ 0151 233 2799 🖷 0151 233 4200
✉ colette.o'brien@liverpool.gov.uk

Senior Management: Mr Ron Odunaiya , Director of Community Services, 1st Floor, Management Suite, Millennium House, Victoria Street, Liverpool L1 6LD ☎ 0151 233 4415
✉ ron.odunaiya@liverpool.gov.uk

Catering Services: Ms Suzanne Halsall, Catering Business Manager, Dyson Hall, Dyson Hall Drive, Liverpool L9 7HA
☎ 0151 225 5021 🖷 0151 225 5148 ✉ suzanne.halsall@liverpool.gov.uk

Children / Youth Services: Ms Colette O'Brien , Director of Children & Young People's Services, 2nd Floor, Millennium House, 60 Victoria Street, Liverpool L1 6JF ☎ 0151 233 2799 🖷 0151 233 4200 ✉ colette.o'brien@liverpool.gov.uk

Civil Registration: Ms Patricia Dobie , Superintendent Registrar, The Register Office, Heritage Entrance, St. George's Hall, St. George's Place, Liverpool L1 1JJ ☎ 0151 225 5719 🖷 0151 707 8793
✉ patricia.dobie@liverpool.gov.uk

PR / Communications: Mr Paul Johnston , Communications Manager, Municipal Buildings, Dale Street, Liverpool LR 2DH
☎ 0151 225 5517 🖷 0151 225 5510 ✉ paul.johnston@liverpool.gov.uk

Community Planning: Mr Mark Kitts, Assistant Director of Regeneration, Municipal Buildings, Dale Street, Liverpool L2 2DH
☎ 0151 233 4202 🖷 0151 225 3959 ✉ mark.kitts@liverpool.gov.uk

Community Safety: Mr Ron Odunaiya , Director of Community Services, 1st Floor, Management Suite, Millennium House, Victoria Street, Liverpool L1 6LD ☎ 0151 233 4415
✉ ron.odunaiya@liverpool.gov.uk

Consumer Protection and Trading Standards: Mr Dale Willis , Cemeteries, Crematoria & Mortuary Manager, 3rd Floor, Millennium House, Victoria Street, Liverpool L1 6LD ☎ 0151 233 4202
✉ dale.willis@liverpool.gov.uk

Economic Development: Mr Nick Kavanagh , Director of Regeneration & Employment, 3rd Floor Millennium House, Victoria Street, Liverpool L1 6LD ☎ 0151 233 6715
✉ nick.kavanagh@liverpool.gov.uk

Education: Ms Colette O'Brien , Director of Children & Young People's Services, 2nd Floor, Millennium House, 60 Victoria Street, Liverpool L1 6JF ☎ 0151 233 2799 🖷 0151 233 4200
✉ colette.o'brien@liverpool.gov.uk

Electoral Registration: Mr Stephen Barker , Electoral Services Manager, Room 230, Municipal Buildings, Dale Street, Liverpool L2 2DH ☎ 0151 225 3519 🖷 0151 225 2365
✉ stephen.barker@liverpool.gov.uk

Emergency Planning: Mr Jamie Riley , Emergency Planning Officer, Brougham Terrace, West Derby Road, Liverpool L6 1AE
☎ 0151 225 6017 🖷 0151 225 6039 ✉ jamie.riley@liverpool.gov.uk

Environmental Health: Mr Chris Lomas, Divisional Manager - Licensing & Public Protection, Municipal Buildings, Dale Street, Liverpool L2 2DH ☎ 0151 225 6056 🖱 chris.lomas@liverpool.gov.uk

European Liaison: Mr Martin Eyres , Head of European Programmes, Chief Executive's Office, Municipal Buildings, Dale Street, Liverpool L2 2DH ☎ 0151 225 3023 🖷 0151 233 6386 🖱 martin.eyres@liverpool.gov.uk

Events Manager: Mrs Judith Feather , Head of Events, The Capital Building, 10th Floor, 39 Old Hall Street, Liverpool L3 9PP ☎ 0151 600 2909 🖱 judith.feather@liverpool.gov.uk

Facilities: Mr Tony Wylie, Premises Manager, Ground Floor, Mucipal Buildings, Dale Street, Liverpool L2 2DH ☎ 0151 225 2217 🖷 0151 225 2218 🖱 tony.wylie@liverpool.gov.uk

Finance: Ms Becky Hellard , Director of Finance & Resources, Room 14, Municipal Buildings, Dale Street, Liverpool L69 2DH ☎ 0151 225 2347 🖱 becky.hellard@liverpool.gov.uk

Finance: Mr Tim Povall , Head of Finance, Ground Floor, Municipal Buildings, Dale Street, Liverpool L2 2DH ☎ 0151 225 2345 🖱 tim.povall@liverpool.gov.uk

Fleet Management: Mr John Carrington, Fleet Services Manager, Newton Road Depot, Liverpool L2 2DH ☎ 0151 233 6504 🖷 0151 233 6517 🖱 john.carrington@liverpool.gov.uk

Highways: Mr Steven Holcroft, Transportation Divisional Manager, 4th Floor, Millennium House, 60 Victoria Street, Liverpool L2 2DH ☎ 0151 233 8130 🖱 steven.holcroft@liverpool.gov.uk

Home Energy Conservation: Mr Brendan Peurcell, Head of Energy Management, Room 106, Municipal Buildings, Dale Street, Liverpool L69 2DH ☎ 0151 225 2473 🖷 0151 225 2218 🖱 brendan.purcell@liverpool.gov.uk

Housing: Mr Mark Kitts, Assistant Director of Regeneration, Municipal Buildings, Dale Street, Liverpool L2 2DH ☎ 0151 233 4202 🖷 0151 225 3959 🖱 mark.kitts@liverpool.gov.uk

Legal: Mrs Jeanette McLoughlin , City Solicitor & Monitoring Officer, Labour Group Office, Municipal Buildings, Dale Street, Liverpool L69 2DH ☎ 0151 225 6795 🖷 0151 225 2392 🖱 jeanette.mcloughlin@liverpool.gov.uk

Leisure and Cultural Services: Mrs Claire McColgan , Assistant Director of Culture & Tourism, The Capital Building, 10th Floor, 39 Old Hall Street, Liverpool L3 9PP ☎ 0151 600 2956 🖱 claire.mccolgan@liverpool.gov.uk

Licensing: Mr John McHale , Interim Director of Licensing, Room 216, Municipal Buildings, Dale Street, Liverpool L2 2DH ☎ 0151 233 4415 🖱 john.mchale@liverpool.gov.uk

Lighting: Mr Steven Holcroft, Transportation Divisional Manager, 4th Floor, Millennium House, 60 Victoria Street, Liverpool L2 2DH ☎ 0151 233 8130 🖱 steven.holcroft@liverpool.gov.uk

Member Services: Mr Chris Walsh, Head of Democratic Services, Municipal Buildings, Dale Street, Liverpool L2 2DH ☎ 0151 225 2432 🖷 0151 225 2427 🖱 chris.walsh@liverpool.gov.uk

Parking: Mr Roy Tunstall, Parking Services Manager, 5 Crosshall Street, Liverpool L2 2DH ☎ 0151 233 3011 🖷 0151 225 2488 🖱 roy.tunstall@liverpool.gov.uk

Partnerships: Ms Catherine Garnell , Assistant Chief Executive, Municipal Buildings, Dale Street, Liverpool L2 2DH ☎ 0151 225 2877 🖷 0151 255 6313 🖱 catherine.garnell@liverpool.gov.uk

Personnel / HR: Ms Colette Hannay , Head of Human Resources & Payroll Services, 6th Floor, Venture Place, 13 - 17 Sir Thomas Street, Liverpool L1 6BW ☎ 0151 233 3000 🖱 colette.hannay@liverpool.gov.uk

Planning: Mr David Hughes , Head of Planning, 3rd Floor, Millennium House, 60 Victoria Street, Liverpool L1 6AJ ☎ 0151 233 5666 🖱 david.hughes@liverpool.gov.uk

Public Libraries: Ms Joyce Little, Head of Libraries & Information Services, Municipal Buildings, Dale Street, Liverpool L2 2DH ☎ 0151 233 6346 🖷 0151 233 6399 🖱 joyce.little@liverpool.gov.uk

Recycling & Waste Minimisation: Mr Andrew McCartan , Environmental Services Manager, 1st Floor, Millennium House, Victoria Street, Liverpool L69 1JB ☎ 0151 233 6380 🖱 andrew.mccartan@liverpool.gov.uk

Regeneration: Mr Nick Kavanagh , Director of Regeneration & Employment, 3rd Floor Millennium House, Victoria Street, Liverpool L1 6LD ☎ 0151 233 6715 🖱 nick.kavanagh@liverpool.gov.uk

Road Safety: Mr David Ng , Team Leader - Road Safety Services, PO Box 981, Municipal Buildings, Liverpool L69 1JB ☎ 0151 233 2386 🖷 0151 233 2384 🖱 david.ng@liverpool.gov.uk

Social Services: Mrs Bernie Brown , Assistant Director of Education & Children's Services, 2nd Floor, Millennium House, 60 Victoria Street, Liverpool L1 6JF 🖱 bernie.brown@liverpool.gov.uk

Social Services (Adult): Mr Samih Kalakeche , Director of Adult Services & Health, 2nd Floor, Millennium House, Victoria Street, Liverpool L1 6JQ ☎ 0151 223 4213 🖱 samih.kalakeche@liverpool.gov.uk

Social Services (Children): Ms Liz Mekki , Divisional Manager of Children's Safeguarding, Team 2, 2nd Floor, Millennium House, 60 Victoria Street, Liverpool L1 6JF ☎ 0151 233 4174 🖷 0151 233 4222 🖱 liz.mekki@liverpool.gov.uk

Public Health: Ms Sandra Davies , Interim Director - Public Health, Labour Group Office, Municipal Buildings, Dale Street, Liverpool L69 2DH ☎ 0151 233 1106 🖱 sandra.davies@liverpool.gov.uk

Sustainable Development: Mr Mark Kitts, Assistant Director of Regeneration, Municipal Buildings, Dale Street, Liverpool L2 2DH ☎ 0151 233 4202 🖷 0151 225 3959 🖱 mark.kitts@liverpool.gov.uk

LIVERPOOL CITY

Tourism: Mr Keith Blundell, Director - Blue Chip Tourism & Liverpool Destination Services, The Capital Building, 39 Old Hall Street, Liverpool L3 9PP ☎ 0151 233 6363 🖷 0151 233 6333

Town Centre: Mr Mike Cockburn , City Centre Manager, 1st Floor, Millennium House, 60 Victoria Street, Liverpool L1 6JE ☎ 0151 233 5327 ✉ mike.cockburn@liverpool.gov.uk

Traffic Management: Mr Steven Holcroft, Transportation Divisional Manager, 4th Floor, Millennium House, 60 Victoria Street, Liverpool L2 2DH ☎ 0151 233 8130 ✉ steven.holcroft@liverpool.gov.uk

Transport: Mr Steven Holcroft, Transportation Divisional Manager, 4th Floor, Millennium House, 60 Victoria Street, Liverpool L2 2DH ☎ 0151 233 8130 ✉ steven.holcroft@liverpool.gov.uk

Transport Planner: Mr Steven Holcroft, Transportation Divisional Manager, 4th Floor, Millennium House, 60 Victoria Street, Liverpool L2 2DH ☎ 0151 233 8130 ✉ steven.holcroft@liverpool.gov.uk

Waste Collection and Disposal: Mr Chris Lomas, Divisional Manager - Licensing & Public Protection, Municipal Buildings, Dale Street, Liverpool L2 2DH ☎ 0151 225 6056 ✉ chris.lomas@liverpool.gov.uk

Waste Management: Mr Chris Lomas, Divisional Manager - Licensing & Public Protection, Municipal Buildings, Dale Street, Liverpool L2 2DH ☎ 0151 225 6056 ✉ chris.lomas@liverpool.gov.uk

COUNCILLORS

***Mayor* Anderson**, Joe (LAB - No Ward)
mayor@liverpool.gov.uk

***Deputy Mayor* O'Byrne**, Ann (LAB - Warbreck)
ann.o'byrne@liverpool.gov.uk

Aspinall, Mary (LAB - Cressington)
mary.aspinall@liverpool.gov.uk

Banks, Christine (LAB - Central)
christine.banks2@liverpool.gov.uk

Barrington, Daniel (LAB - West Derby)
daniel.barrington@liverpool.gov.uk

Beaumont, Tim (LAB - Picton)
tim.beaumont@liverpool.gov.uk

Brant, Paul (LAB - Fazakerley)
paul.brant@liverpool.gov.uk

Brennan, Peter (LAB - Old Swan)
peter.brennan2@liverpool.gov.uk

Brown, Lawrence (GRN - Greenbank)
lawrence.brown@liverpool.gov.uk

Caine, Debbie (LAB - Norris Green)
Debbie.Caine@loverpool.gov.uk

Calvert, Joanne (LAB - Old Swan)
joanne.calvert@liverpool.gov.uk

Casstles, Helen (LAB - Wavertree)
helen.casstles@liverpool.gov.uk

Clarke, Peter (LAB - Fazakerley)
peter.clarke@liverpool.gov.uk

Concepcion, Tony (LAB - Yew Tree)

Connor, Sharon (LAB - Allerton and Hunts Cross)
sharon.connor@liverpool.gov.uk

Corbett, Jane (LAB - Everton)
jane.corbett@liverpool.gov.uk

Corrigan, Michelle (LAB - Riverside)
michelle.corrigan@liverpool.gov.uk

Coyne, John (GRN - St Michaels)
john.coyne@liverpool.gov.uk

Crofts, Nick (LAB - Knotty Ash)
nick.crofts@liverpool.gov.uk

Crone, Thomas (GRN - St Michaels)
thomas.crone@liverpool.gov.uk

Cummins, Martin (IND - Croxteth)
martin.cummins@liverpool.gov.uk

Dean, Alan (LAB - Princes Park)
alan.dean@liverpool.gov.uk

Dowling, Adele (LAB - Anfield)
adele.dowling@liverpool.gov.uk

Dowling, Brian (LAB - Anfield)
brian.dowling@liverpool.gov.uk

Foxley, Andrew (LAB - Mossley Hill)
Andrew.Foxley@liverpool.gov.uk

Fraenkel, Beatrice (LAB - Kirkdale)
beatrice.fraenkel@liverpool.gov.uk

Francis, Ian (LAB - Anfield)
ian.francis@liverpool.gov.uk

Gladden, Roz (LAB - Clubmoor)
roz.gladden@liverpool.gov.uk

Gladden, Roy (LAB - County)
roy.gladden@liverpool.gov.uk

Glare, Claire (LAB - Belle Vale)
claire.glare@liverpool.gov.uk

Hanratty, Dave (LAB - Fazakerley)
dave.hanratty@liverpool.gov.uk

Hanson, Joseph (LAB - Kirkdale)
joseph.hanson@liverpool.gov.uk

Harrison, Cheryl (LAB - Warbreck)
cheryl.harrison@liverpool.gov.uk

Heron, Sue (LAB - Kensington and Fairfield)
sue.heron@liverpool.gov.uk

Hinnigan, Lynnie (LAB - Cressington)
lynnie.hinnigan@liverpool.gov.uk

Hirschfield, Ruth (LAB - Childwall)
ruth.hirschfield@liverpool.gov.uk

Hont, Frank (LAB - Childwall)
frank.hont@liverpool.gov.uk

Hughes, Dan (LAB - Allerton and Hunts Cross)
dan.hughes@liverpool.gov.uk

Hurley, Patrick (LAB - Mossley Hill)
patrick.hurley@liverpool.gov.uk

Jennings, Sarah (GRN - St Michaels)
sarah.jennings@liverpool.gov.uk

Jolly, Rosie (LD - Wavertree)
rosie.jolly@liverpool.gov.uk

Jones, Bill (LAB - Cressington)
bill.jones@liverpool.gov.uk

Kemp, Richard (LD - Church)
richard.kemp@liverpool.gov.uk

Kemp, Erica (LD - Church)
erica.kemp@liverpool.gov.uk

Kennedy, Malcolm (LAB - Kirkdale)
malcolm.kennedy@liverpool.gov.uk

Kent, Janet (LAB - Belle Vale)
janet.kent@liverpool.gov.uk

Knight, Doreen (LAB - Speke-Garston)
doreen.knight@liverpool.gov.uk

Kushner, Barry (LAB - Norris Green)
barry.kushner@liverpool.gov.uk

Kushner, Joann (LAB - Croxteth)

Mace, Barbara (LD - Woolton)
barbara.mace@liverpool.gov.uk

McAlley, Colin (LAB - Woolton)
colin.mcalley@liverpool.gov.uk

McIntosh, John (LAB - Everton)
john.mcintosh@liverpool.gov.uk

McLinden, Richard (LAB - Warbreck)
richard.mclinden@liverpool.gov.uk

Millar, Gary (LD - Old Swan)
gary.millar@liverpool.gov.uk

Mitchell, Peter (LAB - Croxteth)
peter.mitchell@liverpool.gov.uk

Moore, Timothy (LAB - Princes Park)
timothy.moore@liverpool.gov.uk

Morrison, Kevin (LIB - Tuebrook and Stoneycroft)
kevin.morrison@liverpool.gov.uk

Morrison, Jake (IND - Wavertree)
jake.morrison@liverpool.gov.uk

Munby, Steve (LAB - Riverside)
stephen.munby@liverpool.gov.uk

Murray, Barbara (LAB - Yew Tree)
barbara.murray@liverpool.gov.uk

Nicholas, Nathalie (LAB - Picton)
nathalie.nicholas@liverpool.gov.uk

Noakes, James (LAB - Clubmoor)
james.noakes@liverpool.gov.uk

Norris, Mark (LAB - Woolton)
mark.norris@liverpool.gov.uk

O'Byrne, Rachael (LAB - Allerton and Hunts Cross)
rachael.o'byrne@liverpool.gov.uk

Orr, Lana (LAB - West Derby)
lana.orr@liverpool.gov.uk

Owen, Eryl (LAB - County)
eryl.owen@liverpool.gov.uk

Prendergast, Frank (LAB - Everton)
frank.prendergast@liverpool.gov.uk

Prince, John (LAB - Yew Tree)
john.prince@liverpool.gov.uk

Qadir, Abdul (LAB - Picton)
abdul.qadir@liverpool.gov.uk

Radford, Steve (LIB - Tuebrook and Stoneycroft)
northwestliberalparty@hotmail.co.uk

Rainey, Irene (LAB - Clubmoor)
irene.rainey@liverpool.gov.uk

Rasmussen, Mary (LAB - Speke-Garston)
mary.rasmussen@liverpool.gov.uk

Roberts, James (LAB - Greenbank)
james.roberts2@liverpool.gov.uk

Robertson-Collins, Laura (LAB - Greenbank)
laura.robertson-collins@liverpool.gov.uk

Robinson, Liam (LAB - Kensington and Fairfield)
liam.robinson@liverpool.gov.uk

Rothery, Anna (LAB - Princes Park)
anna.rothery@liverpool.gov.uk

Simon, Wendy (LAB - Kensington and Fairfield)
wendy.simon@liverpool.gov.uk

Small, Nick (LAB - Central)
nick.small@liverpool.gov.uk

Spurrell, Emily (LAB - Mossley Hill)
emily.spurrell@liverpool.gov.uk

Strickland, Colin (LAB - Speke-Garston)
colin.strickland@liverpool.gov.uk

Sullivan, Sharon (LAB - Central)
sharon.sullivan@liverpool.gov.uk

Taylor, Ged (LAB - Knotty Ash)
ged.taylor@liverpool.gov.uk

Taylor, Jacqui (LAB - Knotty Ash)

Thomas, Pam (LAB - West Derby)
pamela.thomas@liverpool.gov.uk

Walker, Alan (LAB - Norris Green)
alan.walker@liverpool.gov.uk

Walton, Pauline (LAB - Belle Vale)
pauline.walton@liverpool.gov.uk

Wenstone, Richard (LAB - Church)
richard.wenstone@liverpool.gov.uk

Williams, Hazel (LIB - Tuebrook and Stoneycroft)
hazel.williams@liverpool.gov.uk

Wolfson, Jeremy (LAB - Childwall)
jeremy.wolfson@liverpool.gov.uk

Wood, Hetty (LAB - Riverside)
hetty.wood@liverpool.gov.uk

Woodhouse, Gerard (LAB - County)
gerard.woodhouse@liverpool.gov.uk

POLITICAL COMPOSITION

LAB: 77, LD: 5, GRN: 4, LIB: 3, IND: 2

COMMITTEE CHAIRS

Audit: Mr Frank Prendergast

Licensing: Ms Christine Banks

Planning: Mr John McIntosh

LUTON

Luton Borough Council, Town Hall, Luton LU1 2BQ
☎ 01582 546000 🖷 01582 546680 🖳 www.luton.gov.uk

FACTS AND FIGURES

Parliamentary Constituencies: Luton North, Luton South
EU Constituencies: Eastern
Election Frequency: Elections are of whole council

PRINCIPAL OFFICERS

Chief Executive: Mr Trevor Holden , Chief Executive, Town Hall, Luton LU1 2BQ ☎ 01582 546015 🖷 01582 546680 ✉ chiefexec@luton.gov.uk

Senior Management: Mr Colin Chick, Director - Environment & Regeneration, 2nd Floor, Town Hall, Luton LU1 2BQ ☎ 01582 546301 🖷 01582 546975 ✉ colin.chick@luton.gov.uk

Senior Management: Ms Pam Garraway , Director - Housing & Community Living, 3rd Floor, Unity House, 111 Stuart Street, Luton LU1 5NP ☎ 01582 547500 🖷 01582 547733 ✉ pam.garraway@luton.gov.uk

Senior Management: Mr Robin Porter , Director - Commercial & Transformation Services, 3rd Floor, Town Hall, Luton LU1 2BQ ☎ 01582 548205 ✉ robin.porter@luton.gov.uk

Senior Management: Ms Sally Rowe , Director - Children & Learning, Town Hall, Luton LU1 2BQ ☎ 01582 547500 🖷 01582 547733 ✉ pam.garraway@luton.gov.uk

Senior Management: Ms Gerry Taylor , Director - Public Health, 4th Floor, Unity House, 111 Stuart Street, Luton LU1 2NP ☎ 01582 548448 🖷 01582 548451 ✉ gerry.taylor@luton.gov.uk

Architect, Building / Property Services: Mr Roger Kirk , Head of Capital & Asset Management, 3rd Floor, Apex House, 30-34 Upper George Street, Luton LU1 2RD ☎ 01582 548268 ✉ roger.kirk@luton.gov.uk

Best Value: Ms Nicola Perry , Head of Policy & Performance, Ground Floor, Town Hall, Luton LU1 2BQ ☎ 01582 546073 🖷 01582 546680 ✉ HOPP@luton.gov.uk

Building Control: Mr Chris Pagdin , Head of Planning, Town Hall, Luton LU1 2BQ ☎ 01582 546329 🖷 01582 547138 ✉ chris.pagdin@luton.gov.uk

Catering Services: Mr Ferri Fassihi, General Catering Manager, Luton Learning and Resource Centre, Strangers Way, Luton LU1 ☎ 01582 538211 🖷 01582 538226 ✉ feraidoun.fassihi@luton.gov.uk

Children / Youth Services: Mr Nick Chamberlain, Early Intervention Service Manager, 1st Floor, Unity House, 111 Stuart Street, Luton LU1 5NP ☎ 01582 548057 🖷 01582 548232 ✉ nicholas.chamberlain@luton.gov.uk

Children / Youth Services: Ms Sally Rowe , Director - Children & Learning, Town Hall, Luton LU1 2BQ ☎ 01582 547500 🖷 01582 547733 ✉ pam.garraway@luton.gov.uk

Civil Registration: Ms Angela Claridge , Head of HR & Monitoring Officer, 2nd Floor, Apex House, 30-34 Upper George Street, Luton LU1 2RD ☎ 01582 546291 🖷 01582 546994 ✉ angela.claridge@luton.gov.uk

PR / Communications: Mr Rob Leigh , Head of Communications, 1st Floor, Town Hall Annexe, Luton LU1 2BQ ☎ 01582 546035 ✉ rob.leigh@luton.gov.uk

Community Planning: Ms Laura Church, Head of Business & Consumer Services, 2nd Floor, Town Hall, Luton LU1 2BQ ☎ 01582 546433 🖷 01582 546971 ✉ laura.church@luton.gov.uk

Community Safety: Ms Vicky Hayes , Community Safety & Anti-Social Behaviour Officer, Luton Police Station, Buxton Road, Luton LU4 8AU ☎ 01582 394177 ✉ vicky.hayes@luton.gov.uk

Contracts: Mr Chris Addey, Corporate Procurement Manager, 2nd Floor - Stuart House, Upper George Street, Luton LU1 2RD ☎ 01582 546867 🖷 01582 546850 ✉ addeyc@luton.gov.uk

Corporate Services: Mr Robin Porter , Director - Commercial & Transformation Services, Ground Floor, Unity House, 111 Stuart Street, Luton LU1 2NP ☎ 01582 548205 ✉ robin.porter@luton.gov.uk

Customer Service: Ms Sue Nelson , Head of Revenues & Customer Service, Ground Floor, Unity House, Town Hall, Luton LU1 2BQ ☎ 01582 547094 ✉ sue.nelson@luton.gov.uk

Direct Labour: Ms Mo Harkin , Head of Housing, 2nd Floor, Unity House, 111 Stuart Street, Luton LU1 5NP ☎ 01582 546202 🖷 01582 547733 ✉ HOHSG@luton.gov.uk

Economic Development: Ms Laura Church, Head of Business & Consumer Services, 1st Floor - Stuart House, Upper George Street, Luton LU1 2RD ☎ 01582 546433 🖷 01582 546971 ✉ laura.church@luton.gov.uk

Education: Ms Sally Rowe , Director - Children & Learning, Town Hall, Luton LU1 2BQ ☎ 01582 547500 🖷 01582 547733 ✉ pam.garraway@luton.gov.uk

Electoral Registration: Mr Sam Freer , Electoral Services Manager, 1st Floor, Town Hall, Luton LU1 2BQ ☎ 01582 546088 🖷 01582 546680 ✉ sam.freer@luton.gov.uk

Emergency Planning: Mr Anthony Green , Civil Protection Officer, 1st Floor, Town Hall Annexe, Luton LU1 2BQ ☎ 01582 547240 🖷 01582 547058 ✉ anthony.green@luton.gov.uk

Environmental / Technical Services: Mr Colin Chick, Director - Environment & Regeneration, 2nd Floor, Town Hall, Luton LU1 2BQ ☎ 01582 546301 🖷 01582 546975 ✉ colin.chick@luton.gov.uk

Environmental Health: Ms Laura Church, Head of Business & Consumer Services, 1st Floor - Stuart House, Upper George Street, Luton LU1 2RD ☎ 01582 546433 🖷 01582 546971 ✉ laura.church@luton.gov.uk

Finance: Mr David Kempson, Head of Corporate Finance, 2nd Floor, Wesley House, Chapel Street, Luton LU1 2SE ☎ 01582 546087 ✉ david.kempson@luton.gov.uk

Fleet Management: Mr Simon Smith , Transport Manager, Central Depot, Kingsway, Luton LU4 8AU ☎ 01582 546877 🖷 01582 546883 🖰 simon.smith@luton.gov.uk

Grounds Maintenance: Mr Barry Timms, Parks & Cemeteries Manager, Wardown Park Offices, Luton LU2 7HA ☎ 01582 546702 🖷 01582 546894 🖰 barry.timms@luton.gov.uk

Health and Safety: Ms Caron Owens, Corporate Health & Safety Manager, 2nd Floor, Clemiston House, 14 Upper George Street, Luton LU1 2RP ☎ 01582 546299 🖷 01582 546350 🖰 caron.owens@luton.gov.uk

Highways: Mr Alex Constantinides , Head of Engineering & Street Services, 2nd Floor, Town Hall, Luton LU1 2BQ ☎ 01582 546619 🖷 01582 546649 🖰 alex.constantinides@luton.gov.uk

Housing: Ms Pam Garraway , Director - Housing & Community Living, Unity House, 111 Stuart Street, Luton LU1 5NP ☎ 01582 547500 🖷 01582 547733 🖰 pam.garraway@luton.gov.uk

Housing: Ms Mo Harkin , Head of Housing, 2nd Floor, Unity House, 111 Stuart Street, Luton LU1 5NP ☎ 01582 546202 🖷 01582 547733 🖰 HOHSG@luton.gov.uk

Local Area Agreement: Ms Nicola Perry , Head of Policy & Performance, Ground Floor, Town Hall, Luton LU1 2BQ ☎ 01582 546073 🖷 01582 546680 🖰 HOPP@luton.gov.uk

Legal: Ms Angela Claridge , Head of HR & Monitoring Officer, Apex House, Luton LU1 2RD ☎ 01582 546291 🖷 01582 546994 🖰 angela.claridge@luton.gov.uk

Leisure and Cultural Services: Ms Maggie Appleton , Leisure & Cultural Services Manager, Central Library, Luton LU1 2BQ ☎ 01582 546000 🖰 maggie.appleton@luton.gov.uk

Licensing: Ms Laura Church, Head of Business & Consumer Services, 1st Floor - Stuart House, Upper George Street, Luton LU1 2RD ☎ 01582 546433 🖷 01582 546971 🖰 laura.church@luton.gov.uk

Lifelong Learning: Ms Sally Rowe , Director - Children & Learning, Town Hall, Luton LU1 2BQ ☎ 01582 547500 🖷 01582 547733 🖰 pam.garraway@luton.gov.uk

Lighting: Mr Alex Constantinides , Head of Engineering & Street Services, 2nd Floor, Town Hall, Luton LU1 2BQ ☎ 01582 546619 🖷 01582 546649 🖰 alex.constantinides@luton.gov.uk

Lighting: Mr Graham Turner, Highways Maintenance Services Manager, 4th Floor, Town Hall, Luton LU1 2BQ ☎ 01582 546257 🖷 01582 547177 🖰 graham.turner@luton.gov.uk

Member Services: Ms Debbie Janes, Democratic Services Manager, Town Hall, Luton LU1 2BQ ☎ 01582 546038 🖷 01582 547143 🖰 deborah.janes@luton.gov.uk

Parking: Mr Tony Stefano , Parking Operations Manager, Town Hall, Luton LU1 2BQ ☎ 01582 548521 🖷 01582 548522 🖰 tony.stefano@luton.gov.uk

Personnel / HR: Ms Angela Claridge , Head of HR & Monitoring Officer, 2nd Floor, Apex House, 30-34 Upper George Street, Luton LU1 2RD ☎ 01582 546291 🖷 01582 546994 🖰 angela.claridge@luton.gov.uk

Planning: Mr Chris Pagdin , Head of Planning, Town Hall, Luton LU1 2BQ ☎ 01582 546329 🖷 01582 547138 🖰 chris.pagdin@luton.gov.uk

Procurement: Mr William Clapp , Head of Procurement & Shared Services, Town Hall, Luton LU1 2BQ ☎ 01582 546867 🖰 william.clapp@luton.gov.uk

Regeneration: Ms Laura Church, Head of Business & Consumer Services, 2nd Floor, Town Hall, George Street, Luton LU1 2RD ☎ 01582 546433 🖷 01582 546971 🖰 laura.church@luton.gov.uk

Road Safety: Mr Alex Constantinides , Head of Engineering & Street Services, 2nd Floor, Town Hall, Luton LU1 2BQ ☎ 01582 546619 🖷 01582 546649 🖰 alex.constantinides@luton.gov.uk

Social Services (Adult): Ms Pam Garraway , Director - Housing & Community Living, Unity House, 111 Stuart Street, Luton LU1 5NP ☎ 01582 547500 🖷 01582 547733 🖰 pam.garraway@luton.gov.uk

Social Services (Adult): Ms Maud O'Leary , Head of Adult Social Care, 2nd Floor, Unity House, 111 Stuart Street, Luton LU1 5NP ☎ 01582 547503 🖷 01582 547733 🖰 maud.oleary@luton.gov.uk

Social Services (Children): Ms Jo Fisher , Head of Area Integrated Services, 3rd Floor, Unity House, 111 Stuart Street, Luton LU1 5NP ☎ 01582 548006 🖷 01582 548220 🖰 joanne.fisher@luton.gov.uk

Social Services (Children): Ms Sally Rowe , Director - Children & Learning, Town Hall, Luton LU1 2BQ ☎ 01582 547500 🖷 01582 547733 🖰 pam.garraway@luton.gov.uk

Public Health: Ms Gerry Taylor , Director - Public Health, 4th Floor, Unity House, 111 Stuart Street, Luton LU1 2NP ☎ 01582 548448 🖷 01582 548451 🖰 gerry.taylor@luton.gov.uk

Staff Training: Ms Lesley McNeill , Learning & Development Manager, Ground Floor, Apex House, 30 - 34 George Street, Luton LU1 2RD ☎ 01582 547556 🖷 01582 547753 🖰 lesley.mcneill@luton.gov.uk

Street Scene: Mr Alex Constantinides , Head of Engineering & Street Services, 2nd Floor, Town Hall, Luton LU1 2BQ ☎ 01582 546619 🖷 01582 546649 🖰 alex.constantinides@luton.gov.uk

Sustainable Communities: Mr Colin Chick, Director - Environment & Regeneration, Town Hall, Luton LU1 2BQ ☎ 01582 546301 🖷 01582 546975 🖰 colin.chick@luton.gov.uk

Sustainable Communities: Ms Laura Church, Head of Business & Consumer Services, 2nd Floor, Town Hall, Luton LU1 2BQ ☎ 01582 546433 🖷 01582 546971 🖰 laura.church@luton.gov.uk

Sustainable Development: Mr Colin Chick, Director - Environment & Regeneration, Town Hall, Luton LU1 2BQ ☎ 01582 546301 🖷 01582 546975 🖰 colin.chick@luton.gov.uk

Sustainable Development: Ms Laura Church, Head of Business & Consumer Services, 2nd Floor, Town Hall, Luton LU1 2BQ ☎ 01582 546433 🖷 01582 546971 ⌨ laura.church@luton.gov.uk

Tourism: Ms Laura Church, Head of Business & Consumer Services, 2nd Floor, Town Hall, Luton LU1 2BQ ☎ 01582 546433 🖷 01582 546971 ⌨ laura.church@luton.gov.uk

Town Centre: Mr Mal Hussain , Team Leader, 2nd Floor, 2 - 12 Victoria Street, Luton LU1 2UA ☎ 01582 547227 🖷 01582 546971

Traffic Management: Mr Jonathan Palmer, Traffic & Asset Manager, 4th Floor, Town Hall, Luton LU1 2BQ ☎ 01582 546686 🖷 01582 547177 ⌨ jonathan.palmer@luton.gov.uk

Transport: Mr Simon Smith , Transport Manager, Central Depot, Kingsway, Luton LU4 8AU ☎ 01582 546877 🖷 01582 546883 ⌨ simon.smith@luton.gov.uk

Transport Planner: Mr Alex Constantinides , Head of Engineering & Street Services, 2nd Floor, Town Hall, Luton LU1 2BQ ☎ 01582 546619 🖷 01582 546649 ⌨ alex.constantinides@luton.gov.uk

Total Place: Mr Robin Porter , Director - Commercial & Transformation Services, Ground Floor, Unity House, 111 Stuart Street, Luton LU1 2NP ☎ 01582 548205 ⌨ robin.porter@luton.gov.uk

Waste Management: Mr Shaun Askins , Head of Waste Management, Central Depot, Luton LU4 8AU ☎ 01582 546807 🖷 01582 546895 ⌨

COUNCILLORS

***Mayor* Taylor**, Dave (LAB - Farley)
dave.taylor@luton.gov.uk

***Deputy Mayor* Saleem**, Sameera (LAB - Leagrave)
sameera.saleem@luton.gov.uk

***Leader of the Council* Simmons**, Hazel (LAB - Lewsey)
hazel.simmons@luton.gov.uk

***Deputy Leader of the Council* Timoney**, Sian (LAB - Farley)
sian.timoney@luton.gov.uk

Agbley, David (LAB - South)
david.agbley@luton.gov.uk

Akbar, Waheed (LAB - Leagrave)
waheed.akbar@luton.gov.uk

Ashraf, Mohammed (LAB - Dallow)
mohammed.ashraf@luton.gov.uk

Ayub, Mohammad (LAB - Biscot)
mohammad.ayub@luton.gov.uk

Ayub, Naseem (LAB - Biscot)
naseem.ayub@luton.gov.uk

Baker, John (CON - Round Green)
john.baker@luton.gov.uk

Burnett, Jacqui (LAB - Lewsey)
jacqueline.burnett@luton.gov.uk

Campbell, Gilbert (CON - Bramingham)
gilbert.campbell@luton.gov.uk

Castleman, Paul (LAB - South)
paul.castleman@luton.gov.uk

Chapman, Peter (LD - Wigmore)
peter.chapman@luton.gov.uk

Chowdhury, Irak (LAB - Round Green)
irak.chowdhury@luton.gov.uk

Davis, Roy J (LAB - Northwell)
roy.davis@luton.gov.uk

Dolling, Michael (LD - Stopsley)
michael.dolling@luton.gov.uk

Dolling, Meryl (LD - Stopsley)
meryl.dolling@luton.gov.uk

Farooq, Mohammed (LAB - Dallow)
mohammed.farooq@luton.gov.uk

Franks, David (LD - Barnfield)
david.franks@luton.gov.uk

Garrett, Michael (CON - Icknield)
michael.garrett@luton.gov.uk

Green, Fiona (LAB - Sundon Park)
fiona.green@luton.gov.uk

Gurbuz, Aysegul (LAB - High Town)
aysegul.gurbuz@luton.gov.uk

Hopkins, Rachel (LAB - Barnfield)
rachel.hopkins@luton.gov.uk

Hussain, Mahmood (LAB - Farley)
mahmood.hussain@luton.gov.uk

Keens, Terry (LD - Crawley)
terry.keens@luton.gov.uk

Khan, Aslam (LAB - Lewsey)
aslam.khan@luton.gov.uk

Khan, Tahir (LAB - Biscot)
tahir.khan@luton.gov.uk

Lewis, Stephen (LAB - Limbury)
stephen.lewis@luton.gov.uk

Malcolm, Andrew (LAB - High Town)
andrew.malcolm@luton.gov.uk

Malik, Tahir (LAB - Challney)
tahir.malik@luton.gov.uk

Moles, Diane (LD - Wigmore)
diane.moles@luton.gov.uk

O'Callaghan, Amy (LAB - South)
amy.ocallaghan@luton.gov.uk

Pedersen, Anna (LD - Sundon Park)
anna.pedersen@luton.gov.uk

Petts, Jeff (CON - Icknield)
jeff.petts@luton.gov.uk

Rafiq, Nazia (LAB - Dallow)
nazia.rafiq@luton.gov.uk

Rathore, Asma (LAB - Saints)
asma.rathore@luton.gov.uk

Riaz, Mohammed (LAB - Saints)
mohammed.riaz@luton.gov.uk

Rivers, Mark (LAB - Round Green)
mark.rivers@luton.gov.uk

Roden, Sheila (LAB - Leagrave)
sheila.roden@luton.gov.uk

Rowlands, Jennifer (LAB - Limbury)
jennifer.rowlands@luton.gov.uk

Saleem, Raja (LAB - Saints)
raja.saleem@luton.gov.uk

Shaw, Tom (LAB - Challney)
tom.shaw@luton.gov.uk

Skepelhorn, Alan (LD - Wigmore)
alan.skepelhorn@luton.gov.uk

Taylor, James (LAB - Crawley)
james.taylor@luton.gov.uk

Waheed, Yasmin (LAB - Challney)
yasmin.waheed@luton.gov.uk

Worlding, Don (LAB - Northwell)
don.worlding@luton.gov.uk

Young, John (CON - Bramingham)
john.young@luton.gov.uk

POLITICAL COMPOSITION
LAB: 35, LD: 8, CON: 5

COMMITTEE CHAIRS
Audit & Governance: Mr David Agbley

Licensing: Mr Mark Rivers

Maidstone D

Maidstone Borough Council, Maidstone House, King Street, Maidstone ME15 6JQ
☎ 01622 602000 🖱 💻 www.maidstone.gov.uk

FACTS AND FIGURES
Parliamentary Constituencies: Faversham & Mid Kent, Maidstone and the Weald
EU Constituencies: South East
Election Frequency: Elections are by thirds

PRINCIPAL OFFICERS
Chief Executive: Mrs Alison Broom , Chief Executive, Maidstone House, King Street, Maidstone ME15 6JQ ☎ 01622 602019 🖷 01622 602226 🖱 alisonbroom@maidstone.gov.uk

Senior Management: Ms Zena Cooke , Director of Regeneration & Communities (S151 Officer), Maidstone House, King Street, Maidstone ME15 6JQ

Senior Management: Mr David Edwards, Director of Environment & Shared Services, Maidstone House, King Street, Maidstone ME15 6JQ ☎ 01622 602797 🖷 01622 602974 🖱 davidedwards@maidstone.gov.uk

Senior Management: Mr Paul Taylor , Mid Kent Services Director, Maidstone House, King Street, Maidstone ME15 6JQ ☎ 01622 602663 🖱 paultaylor@maidstone.gov.uk

Architect, Building / Property Services: Mr David Tibbit, Property & Procurement Manager, Maidstone House, King Street, Maidstone ME15 6JQ ☎ 01622 602361 🖷 01622 602029 🖱 davidtibbit@maidstone.gov.uk

Best Value: Miss Georgia Hawkes, Service Improvement Manager, Maidstone House, King Street, Maidstone ME15 6JQ ☎ 01622 602168 🖱 georgiahawkes@maidstone.gov.uk

Building Control: Mr David Harrison, Emergency Planning Officer, Maidstone House, King Street, Maidstone ME12 6JQ ☎ 01622 602034 🖱 davidharrison@maidstone.gov.uk

PR / Communications: Mr Roger Adley, Communications Manager, Maidstone House, King Street, Maidstone ME15 6JQ ☎ 01622 602758 🖷 01622 602226

Community Safety: Mr John Littlemore, Head of Housing & Community Services, Maidstone House, King Street, Maidstone ME15 6JQ ☎ 01622 602207 🖷 01622 602974 🖱 johnlittlemore@maidstone.gov.uk

Computer Management: Mr Tony Bullock , Chief Technology Officer, Maidstone House, King Street, Maidstone ME15 6JQ ☎ 01622 602915 🖱 tonybullock@maidstone.gov.uk

Computer Management: Mr Andrew Cole , Head of ICT Shared Services, Maidstone House, King Street, Maidstone ME15 6JQ 🖱 andrew.cole@tunbridgewells.gov.uk

Computer Management: Mr Dave Lindsay, Chief Information Officer, Maidstone House, King Street, Maidstone ME15 6JQ ☎ 01622 602156 🖷 01622 602970 🖱 davelindsay@maidstone.gov.uk

Contracts: Mr David Tibbit, Property & Procurement Manager, Maidstone House, King Street, Maidstone ME15 6JQ ☎ 01622 602361 🖷 01622 602029 🖱 davidtibbit@maidstone.gov.uk

Corporate Services: Mr Paul Riley , Head of Finance & Resources, Maidstone House, King Street, Maidstone ME15 6JQ ☎ 01622 602396 🖱 paulriley@maidstone.gov.uk

Customer Service: Mr Paul Riley , Head of Finance & Resources, Maidstone House, King Street, Maidstone ME15 6JQ ☎ 01622 602396 🖱 paulriley@maidstone.gov.uk

Economic Development: Mrs Dawn Hudd , Head of Commercial & Economic Development, Maidstone House, King Street, Maidstone ME15 6JQ ☎ 01622 602336 🖱 dawnhudd@maidstone.gov.uk

E-Government: Mr Dave Lindsay, Chief Information Officer, Maidstone House, King Street, Maidstone ME15 6JQ ☎ 01622 602156 🖷 01622 602970 🖱 davelindsay@maidstone.gov.uk

Electoral Registration: Mrs Kathy Hildidge , Interim Electoral Services Manager, Maidstone House, King Street, Maidstone ME15 6JQ ☎ 01622 602023 🖱 kathyhildidge@maidstone.gov.uk

MAIDSTONE

Emergency Planning: Mr David Harrison, Emergency Planning Officer, Maidstone House, King Street, Maidstone ME12 6JQ ☎ 01622 602034 ✉ davidharrison@maidstone.gov.uk

Energy Management: Mr David Tibbit, Property & Procurement Manager, Maidstone House, King Street, Maidstone ME15 6JQ ☎ 01622 602361 🖷 01622 602029 ✉ davidtibbit@maidstone.gov.uk

Environmental Health: Mr John Littlemore, Head of Housing & Community Services, Maidstone House, King Street, Maidstone ME15 6JQ ☎ 01622 602207 🖷 01622 602974 ✉ johnlittlemore@maidstone.gov.uk

Estates, Property & Valuation: Mr David Tibbit, Property & Procurement Manager, Maidstone House, King Street, Maidstone ME15 6JQ ☎ 01622 602361 🖷 01622 602029 ✉ davidtibbit@maidstone.gov.uk

Facilities: Ms Lisa Cook , Facilities & Corporate Support Manager, Maidstone House, King Street, Maidstone ME15 6JQ ☎ 01622 602236 ✉ lisacook@maidstone.gov.uk

Finance: Mr Paul Riley , Head of Finance & Resources, Maidstone House, King Street, Maidstone ME15 6JQ ☎ 01622 602396 ✉ paulriley@maidstone.gov.uk

Fleet Management: Mrs Jennifer Shepherd , Waste & Street Scene Manager, Maidstone House, King Street, Maidstone ME15 6JQ ☎ 01622 602400 🖷 01622 602972 ✉ jennifershepherd@maidstone.gov.uk

Health and Safety: Mr Alistair Barker , Corporate Health & Safety Manager, Maidstone House, King Street, Maidstone ME15 6JQ ☎ 01622 605308 🖷 01622 602972 ✉ alastairbarker@maidstone.gov.uk

Housing: Mr John Littlemore, Head of Housing & Community Services, Maidstone House, King Street, Maidstone ME15 6JQ ☎ 01622 602207 🖷 01622 602974 ✉ johnlittlemore@maidstone.gov.uk

Legal: Mr John Scarborough , Head of Legal Services, Maidstone House, King Street, Maidstone ME15 6JQ ☎ 01795 417527 ✉ john.scarborough@midkent.gov.uk

Leisure and Cultural Services: Mrs Dawn Hudd , Head of Commercial & Economic Development, Maidstone House, King Street, Maidstone ME15 6JQ ☎ 01622 602336 ✉ dawnhudd@maidstone.gov.uk

Licensing: Mr John Littlemore, Head of Housing & Community Services, Maidstone House, King Street, Maidstone ME15 6JQ ☎ 01622 602207 🖷 01622 602974 ✉ johnlittlemore@maidstone.gov.uk

Licensing: Mrs Claire Perry , Licensing Partnership Manager, Council Offices, Argyle Road, Sevenoaks TN13 1HG ☎ 01732 227325; 07970 731616 ✉ claire.perry@tunbridgewells.gov.uk

Member Services: Mrs Angela Woodhouse , Head of Policy & Communications, Maidstone House, King Street, Maidstone ME15 6JQ ☎ 01622 602620 🖷 01622 692246 ✉ angelawoodhouse@maidstone.gov.uk

Parking: Mr Jeff Kitson, Parking Services Manager, Maidstone House, King Street, Maidstone ME15 6JQ ☎ 01622 602376 ✉ jeffkitson@maidstone.gov.uk

Partnerships: Mr Paul Taylor , Mid Kent Services Director, Maidstone House, King Street, Maidstone ME15 6JQ ☎ 01622 602663 ✉ paultaylor@maidstone.gov.uk

Personnel / HR: Ms Dena Smart, Head of HR Shared Services, Maidstone House, King Street, Maidstone ME15 6JQ ☎ 01622 602712 🖷 01622 602974 ✉ denasmart@maidstone.gov.uk

Planning: Mr Rob Jarman, Head of Planning & Development, Maidstone House, King Street, Maidstone ME15 6JQ ☎ 01622 602214 🖷 01622 602974 ✉ robjarman@maidstone.gov.uk

Procurement: Mr Stephen Trigg, Procurement Manager, Maidstone House, King Street, Maidstone ME15 6JQ ☎ 01622 602811 ✉ stephentrigg@maidstone.gov.uk

Recycling & Waste Minimisation: Mrs Jennifer Shepherd , Waste & Street Scene Manager, Maidstone House, King Street, Maidstone ME15 6JQ ☎ 01622 602400 🖷 01622 602972 ✉ jennifershepherd@maidstone.gov.uk

Regeneration: Mrs Dawn Hudd , Head of Commercial & Economic Development, Maidstone House, King Street, Maidstone ME15 6JQ ☎ 01622 602336 ✉ dawnhudd@maidstone.gov.uk

Staff Training: Mrs Catherine Harrison , Learning & Development Manager, Maidstone House, King Street, Maidstone ME15 6JQ ☎ 01622 602349 🖷 01622 602974 ✉ catherineharrison@maidstone.gov.uk

Sustainable Communities: Mr John Littlemore, Head of Housing & Community Services, Maidstone House, King Street, Maidstone ME15 6JQ ☎ 01622 602207 🖷 01622 602974 ✉ johnlittlemore@maidstone.gov.uk

Sustainable Development: Mr Rob Jarman, Head of Planning & Development, Maidstone House, King Street, Maidstone ME15 6JQ ☎ 01622 602214 🖷 01622 602974 ✉ robjarman@maidstone.gov.uk

Tourism: Mrs Laura Dickson , Tourism Manager, Maidstone House, King Street, Maidstone ME15 6JQ ☎ 01622 602510 🖷 01622 602970 ✉ lauradickson@maidstone.gov.uk

Town Centre: Mr Andrew Davy, The Management Suite, Chequers Centre, Pads Hill, Maidstone ME15 6AL

Waste Collection and Disposal: Mrs Jennifer Shepherd , Waste & Street Scene Manager, Maidstone House, King Street, Maidstone ME15 6JQ ☎ 01622 602400 🖷 01622 602972 ✉ jennifershepherd@maidstone.gov.uk

COUNCILLORS

***Mayor* Moriarty**, Daniel (IND - Park Wood)
danielmoriarty@maidstone.gov.uk

***Leader of the Council* Wilson**, Fran (LD - High Street)
franwilson@maidstone.gov.uk

Ash, Richard (CON - Bearsted)
richardash@maidstone.gov.uk

Blackmore, Annabelle (CON - Marden and Yalding)
annabelleblackmore@maidstone.gov.uk

Boughton, Matt (CON - Fant)

Brice, Louise (CON - Staplehurst)
louisebrice@maidstone.gov.uk

Burton, David (CON - Marden and Yalding)
david.burton@burtons.uk.com

Butler, Derek (CON - Boxley)
derekbutler@maidstone.gov.uk

Chittenden, Ian (LD - South)
inachittenden@maidstone.gov.uk

Clark, Brian (LD - South)
brianclark@maidstone.gov.uk

Cox, Martin (LD - East)
martincox@maidstone.gov.uk

Cuming, Mike (CON - Bearsted)
mikecuming@maidstone.gov.uk

Daley, Dan (LD - Allington)
dandaley@maidstone.gov.uk

de Wiggondene, Nick (CON - Detling and Thurnham)
nickdewiggondene@maidstone.gov.uk

Ells, Simon (UKIP - Shepway North)
simonells@maidstone.gov.uk

English, Clive (LD - HIgh Street)
cliveenglish@maidstone.gov.uk

Fissenden, Nikki (LD - East)
nicolafissenden@maidstone.gov.uk

Fort, Gill (CON - Leeds)
gillfort@maidstone.gov.uk

Garland, Christopher (CON - Shepway North)
christophergarland@maidstone.gov.uk

Gooch, Fay (IND - Barming)
faygooch@maidstone.gov.uk

Greer, Malcolm (CON - Boxley)
malcolmgreer@hazelwoodbox.fsnet.co.uk

Grigg, Susan (LD - Loose)
susangrigg@maidstone.gov.uk

Harper, Paul (LAB - Fant)
paulharper@maidstone.gov.uk

Harwood, Tony (LD - North)
tonyharwood@maidstone.gov.uk

Hemsley, Michael (CON - North)
michaelhemsley@maidstone.gov.uk

Hinder, Wendy (CON - Boxley)
wendyhinder@maidstone.gov.uk

Joy, Denise (LD - HIgh Street)
denisejoy@maidstone.gov.uk

Mckay, Malcolm (LAB - Shepway South)
malcolmmckay@maidstone.gov.uk

McLoughlin, Steve (CON - Marden and Yalding)
stevemcloughlin@maidstone.gov.uk

Mortimer, Derek (LD - South)
DerekMortimer@maidstone.gov.uk

Mortimer, Brian (LD - Coxheath and Hunton)
brianmortimer@maidstone.gov.uk

Munford, Steve (IND - Boughton Monchelsea and Chart Sutton)
stevemunford@maidstone.gov.uk

Naghi, David (LD - East)
davidnaghi@maidstone.gov.uk

Newton, Gordon (IND - Downswood and Otham)
gordonnewton@maidstone.gov.uk

Paine, Stephen (CON - Fant)
stephenpaine@maidstone.gov.uk

Parvin, Daphne (CON - North Downs)
daphneparvin@maidstone.gov.uk

Paterson, Jenni (LD - North)

Perry, John (CON - Staplehurst)
johnperry@maidstone.gov.uk

Pickett, David (LD - Bridge)
davidpickett@maidstone.gov.uk

Ring, Marion (CON - Shepway North)
marionring@maidstone.gov.uk

Robertson, Cynthia (LD - Allington)
cynthiarobertson@maidstone.gov.uk

Ross, James (CON - Bridge)
jamesross@maidstone.gov.uk

Round, Martin (CON - Headcorn)
martinround@maidstone.gov.uk

Sams, Janetta (IND - Harrietsham and Lenham)

Sams, Tom (IND - Harrietsham and Lenham)
tomsams@maidstone.gov.uk

Sargeant, Dave (UKIP - Shepway South)
davesargeant@maidstone.gov.uk

Springett, Val (CON - Bearsted)
valspringett@maidstone.gov.uk

Stockell, Pauline (CON - Sutton Valence and Langley)
paulinastockell@maidstone.gov.uk

Thick, Richard (CON - Headcorn)
richardthick@maidstone.gov.uk

Vizzard, Bryan (LD - Heath)
bryanvizzard@maidstone.gov.uk

Watson, Belinda (LD - Allington)
belindawatson@maidstone.gov.uk

Webb, Richard (LD - Coxheath and Hunton)
richardwebb@maidstone.gov.uk

Webster, Jade (CON - Park Wood)
jadewebster@maidstone.gov.uk

Willis, James (LD - Heath)
jameswills@maidstone.gov.uk

Wilson, John A
(CON - Coxheath and Hunton)
johnawilson@maidstone.gov.uk

POLITICAL COMPOSITION
CON: 25, LD: 20, IND: 6, LAB: 2, UKIP: 2

MAIDSTONE

COMMITTEE CHAIRS

Communities, Housing & Environment: Ms Marion Ring

Licensing: Mrs Wendy Hinder

Planning: Mr Clive English

Maldon D

Maldon District Council, District Council Offices, Princes Road, Maldon CM9 7DL
☎ 01621 854477 🖷 01621 852575 💻 www.maldon.gov.uk

FACTS AND FIGURES

Parliamentary Constituencies: Maldon
EU Constituencies: Eastern
Election Frequency: Elections are of whole council

PRINCIPAL OFFICERS

Chief Executive: Ms Fiona Marshall, Chief Executive, Council Offices, Princes Road, Maldon CM9 5DL ☎ 01621 854477 🖷 01621 852575 fiona.marshall@maldon.gov.uk

Senior Management: Mr Richard Holmes, Director of Customers & Community, District Council Offices, Princes Road, Maldon CM9 7DL ☎ 01621 875752 richard.holmes@maldon.gov.uk

Senior Management: Mr Simon Meecham , Director of Planning & Regulatory Services, District Council Offices, Princes Road, Maldon CM9 7DL

Senior Management: Ms Ka Ng , Director of Resources, District Council Offices, Princes Road, Maldon CM9 7DL

Access Officer / Social Services (Disability): Mr Norman Wright, Part-Time Access Officer, Princes Road, Maldon CM9 5DL ☎ 01621 854477 norman.wright@maldon.gov.uk

Building Control: Mr Anthony Nelson , Interim Building Control Team Leader, District Council Offices, Princes Road, Maldon CM9 7DL ☎ 01621 854477 anthony.nelson@maldon.gov.uk

PR / Communications: Mr Russell Dawes , Communications Manager, Council Offices, Princes Road, Maldon CM9 5DL ☎ 01621 854477 russell.dawes@maldon.gov.uk

Community Safety: Mr Richard Holmes, Director of Customers & Community, District Council Offices, Princes Road, Maldon CM9 7DL ☎ 01621 875752 richard.holmes@maldon.gov.uk

Community Safety: Mrs Chris Rust , Community Safety & LSP Co-ordinator, District Council Offices, Princes Road, Maldon CM9 7DL ☎ 01621 854477 chris.rust@maldon.gov.uk

Computer Management: Mr Ray Ware , IT Manager, District Council Offices, Princes Road, Maldon CM9 7DL ☎ 01621 854477 ray.ware@maldon.gov.uk

Customer Service: Mrs Sue Green , Customers Manager, District Council Offices, Princes Road, Maldon CM9 7DL ☎ 01621 854477 sue.green@maldon.gov.uk

Direct Labour: Mr Steve Krolzig, Maintenance Officer, District Council Offices, Princes Road, Maldon CM9 7DL ☎ 01621 875826 steve.krolzig@maldon.gov.uk

Economic Development: Mrs Kerry Martin , Economic Development Manager, District Council Offices, Princes Road, Maldon CM9 7DL ☎ 01621 875853 kerry.martin@maldon.gov.uk

E-Government: Mr Simon Mitchell, IT Team Leader, Council Offices, Princes Road, Maldon CM9 5DL ☎ 01621 854477 simon.mitchell@maldon.gov.uk

Electoral Registration: Ms Lynda Elsegood, Elections Management Officer, Council Offices, Princes Road, Maldon CM9 5DL ☎ 01621 854477 🖷 01621 852575 lynda.elsegood@maldon.gov.uk

Electoral Registration: Mrs Melissa Kelly , Head of Customers & Facilities, District Council Offices, Princes Road, Maldon CM9 7DL ☎ 01621 854477 melissa.kelly@maldon.gov.uk

Emergency Planning: Mr Richard Holmes, Director of Customers & Community, District Council Offices, Princes Road, Maldon CM9 7DL ☎ 01621 875752 richard.holmes@maldon.gov.uk

Energy Management: Mrs Shirley Hall , Environment Team Leader, Council Offices, Princes Road, Maldon CM9 7DL ☎ 01621 854477 🖷 01621 852575 shirley.hall@maldon.gov.uk

Environmental / Technical Services: Mrs Gill Gibson, Commercial Environmental Health Team Leader, Council Offices, Princes Road, Maldon CM9 5DL ☎ 01621 854477 gillian.gibson@maldon.gov.uk

Environmental / Technical Services: Mr Ian Haines, Environmental Manager, Council Offices, Princes Road, Maldon CM9 5DL ☎ 01621 854477 🖷 01621 852575 ian.haines@maldon.gov.uk

Environmental Health: Mrs Gill Gibson, Commercial Environmental Health Team Leader, Council Offices, Princes Road, Maldon CM9 5DL ☎ 01621 854477 gillian.gibson@maldon.gov.uk

Environmental Health: Mr Ian Haines, Environmental Manager, Council Offices, Princes Road, Maldon CM9 5DL ☎ 01621 854477 🖷 01621 852575 ian.haines@maldon.gov.uk

Estates, Property & Valuation: Mr David Rust , Senior Technical Officer, District Council Offices, Princes Road, Maldon CM9 7DL ☎ 01621 854477 david.rust@maldon.gov.uk

Events Manager: Miss Alexis Brown , Tourism & Events Manager, District Council Offices, Princes Road, Maldon CM9 7DL ☎ 01621 856503 alexis.brown@maldon.gov.uk

Facilities: Mr Jonathan Stevens , Facilities Manager, District Council Offices, Princes Road, Maldon CM9 7DL ☎ 01621 854477 jonathan.stevens@maldon.gov.uk

Finance: Ms Ka Ng , Director of Resources, District Council Offices, Princes Road, Maldon CM9 7DL

Grounds Maintenance: Mr Ben Brown , Tourism, Countryside & Coast Manager, District Council Offices, Princes Road, Maldon CM9 7DL ☎ 01621 875752 ✉ ben.brown@maldon.gov.uk

Grounds Maintenance: Mr Steve Krolzig, Maintenance Officer, District Council Offices, Princes Road, Maldon CM9 7DL ☎ 01621 875826 ✉ steve.krolzig@maldon.gov.uk

Health and Safety: Mrs Gill Gibson, Commercial Environmental Health Team Leader, Council Offices, Princes Road, Maldon CM9 5DL ☎ 01621 854477 ✉ gillian.gibson@maldon.gov.uk

Housing: Mr Paul Gayler , Strategic Housing Manager, District Council Offices, Princes Road, Maldon CM9 7DL ☎ 01621 854477 ✉ paul.gayler@maldon.gov.uk

Legal: Mrs Melissa Kelly , Head of Customers & Facilities, District Council Offices, Princes Road, Maldon CM9 7DL ☎ 01621 854477 ✉ melissa.kelly@maldon.gov.uk

Leisure and Cultural Services: Mr Richard Heard, Director of Customers & Community, District Council Offices, Princes Road, Maldon CM9 7DL ☎ 01621 875838 ✉ richard.heard@maldon.gov.uk

Leisure and Cultural Services: Mr Richard Holmes, Director of Customers & Community, District Council Offices, Princes Road, Maldon CM9 7DL ☎ 01621 875752 ✉ richard.holmes@maldon.gov.uk

Lottery Funding, Charity and Voluntary: Ms Ka Ng , Director of Resources, District Council Offices, Princes Road, Maldon CM9 7DL

Member Services: Mrs Val Downes, PA to the Leader, Council Offices, Princes Road, Maldon CM9 7DL ☎ 01621 854477 🖷 01621 875757 ✉ val.downes@maldon.gov.uk

Parking: Mr Richard Holmes, Director of Customers & Community, District Council Offices, Princes Road, Maldon CM9 7DL ☎ 01621 875752 ✉ richard.holmes@maldon.gov.uk

Personnel / HR: Mrs Dawn Moyse , Group Manager - People, Policy & Performance, District Council Offices, Princes Road, Maldon CM9 7DL ☎ 01621 854477 ✉ dawn.moyse@maldon.gov.uk

Planning: Mr Nick Fenwick , Interim Planning Services Manager, District Council Offices, Princes Road, Maldon CM9 7DL ☎ 01621 854477 ✉ nick.fenwick@maldon.gov.uk

Recycling & Waste Minimisation: Mr Ian Haines, Environmental Manager, Council Offices, Princes Road, Maldon CM9 5DL ☎ 01621 854477 🖷 01621 852575 ✉ ian.haines@maldon.gov.uk

Staff Training: Mrs Dawn Moyse , Group Manager - People, Policy & Performance, District Council Offices, Princes Road, Maldon CM9 7DL ☎ 01621 854477 ✉ dawn.moyse@maldon.gov.uk

Street Scene: Mrs Karen Bomford, Community & Living Manager, District Council Offices, Princes Road, Maldon CM9 7DL ☎ 01621 854477 🖷 01621 842665

Sustainable Communities: Mr Richard Holmes, Director of Customers & Community, District Council Offices, Princes Road, Maldon CM9 7DL ☎ 01621 875752 ✉ richard.holmes@maldon.gov.uk

Waste Collection and Disposal: Mrs Karen Bomford, Community & Living Manager, District Council Offices, Princes Road, Maldon CM9 7DL ☎ 01621 854477 🖷 01621 842665

Waste Management: Mrs Karen Bomford, Community & Living Manager, District Council Offices, Princes Road, Maldon CM9 7DL ☎ 01621 854477 🖷 01621 842665

COUNCILLORS

***Chair* Elliott**, Peter (CON - Burnham-on-Crouch South)
cllr.peter.elliott@maldon.gov.uk

***Vice-Chair* Bass**, Henry (CON - Wickham Bishops and Woodham)
cllr.henry.bass@maldon.gov.uk

***Leader of the Council* Lewis**, Miriam (CON - Heybridge West)
cllr.miriam.lewis@maldon.gov.uk

***Deputy Leader of the Council* Durham**, Mark (CON - Wickham Bishops and Woodham)
cllr.mark.durham@maldon.gov.uk

***Group Leader* Beale**, Brian (IND - Southminster)
cllr.brian.beale@maldon.gov.uk

Acevedo, Beverley (UKIP - Althorne)
cllr.beverley.acevedo@maldon.gov.uk

Archer, John (CON - Purleigh)
cllr.john.archer@maldon.gov.uk

Bamford, Elaine (CON - Tolleshunt D'Arcy)
cllr.elaine.bamford@maldon.gov.uk

Beale, Anne (CON - Heybridge East)
cllr.anne.beale@maldon.gov.uk

Boyce, Robert (CON - Althorne)
cllr.bob.boyce@maldon.gov.uk

Cain, Andrew (CON - Maldon South)
cllr.andrew.cain@maldon.gov.uk

Channer, Penny (CON - Mayland)
cllr.penny.channer@maldon.gov.uk

Dewick, Richard (CON - Tillingham)
cllr.richard.dewick@maldon.gov.uk

Dobson, Ian (CON - Heybridge West)
cllr.ian.dobson@maldon.gov.uk

Elliott, Helen (CON - Burnham-on-Crouch North)
cllr.helen.elliott@maldon.gov.uk

Fluker, Adrian (CON - Southminster)
cllr.adrian.fluker@maldon.gov.uk

Harker, Bryan (CON - Heybridge East)
cllr.bryan.harker@maldon.gov.uk

Harker, Brenda (CON - Maldon South)
cllr.brenda.harker@maldon.gov.uk

Heard, Mark (IND - Maldon West)
cllr.mark.heard@maldon.gov.uk

Helm, Michael (CON - Mayland)
cllr.michael.helm@maldon.gov.uk

Keys, John (CON - Great Totham)
cllr.john.keys@maldon.gov.uk

MacKenzie, Charles (CON - Maldon West)
cllr.charles.mackenzie@maldon.gov.uk

Pearlman, Michael (CON - Maldon North)
cllr.michael.pearlman@maldon.gov.uk

Pratt, Ron (CON - Burnham-on-Crouch South)
cllr.ron.pratt@maldon.gov.uk

Pudney, Neil (CON - Burnham-on-Crouch North)
cllr.neil.pudney@maldon.gov.uk

Savage, Stephen (CON - Maldon East)
cllr.stephen.savage@maldon.gov.uk

Shrimpton, Tony (CON - Maldon North)
cllr.tony.shrimpton@maldon.gov.uk

Sismey, David (CON - Great Totham)
cllr.david.sismey@maldon.gov.uk

St. Joseph, Andrew (CON - Tollesbury)
cllr.andrew.st.joseph@maldon.gov.uk

Thompson, Maddie (CON - Tolleshunt D'Arcy)
cllr.maddie.thompson@maldon.gov.uk

White, Sue (CON - Purleigh)
cllr.sue.white@maldon.gov.uk

POLITICAL COMPOSITION
CON: 28, IND: 2, UKIP: 1

COMMITTEE CHAIRS

Audit: Mr Bryan Harker

Planning & Licensing: Mrs Penny Channer

Malvern Hills D

Malvern Hills District Council, Council House, Avenue Road, Malvern WR14 3AF
☎ 01684 862151 🖷 01684 862473 ✉ contactus@malvernhills.gov.uk
💻 www.malvernhills.gov.uk

FACTS AND FIGURES
EU Constituencies: West Midlands
Election Frequency: Elections are of whole council

PRINCIPAL OFFICERS

Chief Executive: Mr Jack Hegarty , Chief Executive, Council House, Avenue Road, Malvern WR14 3AF ☎ 01684 862338

Deputy Chief Executive: Mr Andy Baldwin , Deputy Chief Executive - Head of Resources, Council House, Avenue Road, Malvern WR14 3AF ☎ 01684 862236 ✉ andy.baldwin@malvernhills.gov.uk

Senior Management: Mr Ivor Pumfrey, Acting Head of Regulatory Services, Council House, Avenue Road, Malvern WR14 3AF ☎ 01684 862296 ✉ ivor.pumfrey@malvernhills.gov.uk

Senior Management: Mr John Williams, Head of Policy & Governance, Council House, Avenue Road, Malvern WR14 3AF ☎ 01684 862227 ✉ john.williams@malvernhills.gov.uk

Senior Management: Mr Gary Williams, Head of Planning & Housing, Council House, Avenue Road, Malvern WR14 2TB ☎ 01684 862293 ✉ gary.williams@malvernhills.gov.uk

Best Value: Mr John Williams, Head of Policy & Governance, Council House, Avenue Road, Malvern WR14 3AF ☎ 01684 862227 ✉ john.williams@malvernhills.gov.uk

Community Planning: Mr Gary Williams, Head of Planning & Housing, Council House, Avenue Road, Malvern WR14 2TB ☎ 01684 862293 ✉ gary.williams@malvernhills.gov.uk

Computer Management: Mr Andy Baldwin , Deputy Chief Executive - Head of Resources, Council House, Avenue Road, Malvern WR14 3AF ☎ 01684 862236 ✉ andy.baldwin@malvernhills.gov.uk

Contracts: Mr John Williams, Head of Policy & Governance, Council House, Avenue Road, Malvern WR14 3AF ☎ 01684 862227 ✉ john.williams@malvernhills.gov.uk

Corporate Services: Mr John Williams, Head of Policy & Governance, Council House, Avenue Road, Malvern WR14 3AF ☎ 01684 862227 ✉ john.williams@malvernhills.gov.uk

Customer Service: Mr Ivor Pumfrey, Acting Head of Regulatory Services, Council House, Avenue Road, Malvern WR14 3AF ☎ 01684 862296 ✉ ivor.pumfrey@malvernhills.gov.uk

Economic Development: Mr Phil Merrick , Head of Economic Development, Council House, Avenue Road, Malvern WR14 3AF ☎ 01684 862199 ✉ phil.merrick@malvernhills.gov.uk

Emergency Planning: Mr Ivor Pumfrey, Acting Head of Regulatory Services, Council House, Avenue Road, Malvern WR14 3AF ☎ 01684 862296 ✉ ivor.pumfrey@malvernhills.gov.uk

Emergency Planning: Mr John Williams, Head of Policy & Governance, Council House, Avenue Road, Malvern WR14 3AF ☎ 01684 862227 ✉ john.williams@malvernhills.gov.uk

Estates, Property & Valuation: Mr Andy Baldwin , Deputy Chief Executive - Head of Resources, Council House, Avenue Road, Malvern WR14 3AF ☎ 01684 862236 ✉ andy.baldwin@malvernhills.gov.uk

Facilities: Mr Andy Baldwin , Deputy Chief Executive - Head of Resources, Council House, Avenue Road, Malvern WR14 3AF ☎ 01684 862236 ✉ andy.baldwin@malvernhills.gov.uk

Finance: Mr Andy Baldwin , Deputy Chief Executive - Head of Resources, Council House, Avenue Road, Malvern WR14 3AF ☎ 01684 862236 ✉ andy.baldwin@malvernhills.gov.uk

Housing: Mr Gary Williams, Head of Planning & Housing, Council House, Avenue Road, Malvern WR14 2TB ☎ 01684 862293 ✉ gary.williams@malvernhills.gov.uk

Legal: Mr John Williams, Head of Policy & Governance, Council House, Avenue Road, Malvern WR14 3AF ☎ 01684 862227 ✉ john.williams@malvernhills.gov.uk

Leisure and Cultural Services: Mr Ivor Pumfrey, Acting Head of Regulatory Services, Council House, Avenue Road, Malvern WR14 3AF ☎ 01684 862296 ✉ ivor.pumfrey@malvernhills.gov.uk

Licensing: Mr Ivor Pumfrey, Acting Head of Regulatory Services, Council House, Avenue Road, Malvern WR14 3AF ☎ 01684 862296 ✉ ivor.pumfrey@malvernhills.gov.uk

Member Services: Mr John Williams, Head of Policy & Governance, Council House, Avenue Road, Malvern WR14 3AF ☎ 01684 862227 ✉ john.williams@malvernhills.gov.uk

Personnel / HR: Mr Andy Baldwin , Deputy Chief Executive - Head of Resources, Council House, Avenue Road, Malvern WR14 3AF ☎ 01684 862236 ✉ andy.baldwin@malvernhills.gov.uk

Planning: Mr Gary Williams, Head of Planning & Housing, Council House, Avenue Road, Malvern WR14 2TB ☎ 01684 862293 ✉ gary.williams@malvernhills.gov.uk

Waste Collection and Disposal: Mr Ivor Pumfrey, Acting Head of Regulatory Services, Council House, Avenue Road, Malvern WR14 3AF ☎ 01684 862296 ✉ ivor.pumfrey@malvernhills.gov.uk

COUNCILLORS

***Chair* Williams**, Barbara (CON - Martley)
barbara.williams@malvernhillsdc.net

***Vice-Chair* Raine**, John (GRN - West)
john.raine@malvernhillsdc.net

***Leader of the Council* Grove**, Phillip (CON - Tenbury)
phillip.grove@malvernhillsdc.net

***Deputy Leader of the Council* Behan**, Bronwen (CON - Longdon)
bronwen.behan@malvernhillsdc.net

***Group Leader* Roskams**, Julian (GRN - West)
julian.roskams@malvernhillsdc.net

Baker, Melanie (CON - Chase)
melanie.baker@malvernhillsdc.net

Baker, Tony (CON - Dyson Perrins)
tony.baker@malvernhillsdc.net

Bovey, Caroline (LD - Pickersleigh)
caroline.bovey@malvernhillsdc.net

Campbell, Hannah (CON - Priory)
hannah.campbell@malvernhillsdc.net

Campbell, Jill (IND - Wells)
jill.campbell@malvernhillsdc.net

Chambers, David (CON - Broadheath)
david.chambers@malvernhillsdc.net

Clarke, Dean (IND - Hallow)
drcmhdc@gamil.com

Cumming, Paul (CON - Woodbury)
paul.cumming@malvernhillsdc.net

Cumming, Pam (CON - Baldwin)
pam.cumming@malvernhillsdc.net

Davies, Mick (IND - Morton)
mick.davies@malvernhillsdc.net

Dell, Chris (CON - Lindbridge)
chris.dell@malvernhillsdc.net

Farmer, Gill (CON - Teme Valley)
gill.farmer@malvernhillsdc.net

Godwin, Douglas (CON - Broadheath)
douglas.godwin@malvernhillsdc.net

Halling, Leanne (CON - Pickersleigh)
leanne.halling@malvernhillsdc.net

Hall-Jones, Roger (CON - Priory)
roger.hall-jones@malvernhillsdc.net

Harrison, David (IND - Kempsey)
david.harrison@malvernhillsdc.net

Hung Chan, Kwai (LD - Link)
kwai.hung.chang@malvernhillsdc.net

Kerby, Robert (CON - Link)
robert.kerby@malvernhillsdc.net

Massey, Rebecca (CON - Chase)
rebecca.massey@malvernhillsdc.net

Michael, John (IND - Kempsey)
john.michael@malvernhillsdc.net

Morgan, Andrea (CON - Upton and Hanley)
andrea.morgan@malvernhillsdc.net

Morgan, Mike (CON - Upton and Hanley)
mike.morgan@malvernhillsdc.net

Myatt, Val (LD - Pickersleigh)
val.myatt@malvernhillsdc.net

Newman, Elaine (LD - Powick)
elaine.newman@malvernhillsdc.net

O'Donnell, Chris (CON - Wells)
chris.odonnell@malvernhillsdc.net

O'Donnell, James (CON - Chase)
james.odonnell@malvernhillsdc.net

Owenson, Jeremy (CON - Ripple)
jeremy.owenson@malvernhillsdc.net

Penn, Tony (CON - Tenbury)
tony.penn@malvernhillsdc.net

Reed, Chris (GRN - Dyson Perrins)
chris.reed@malvernhillsdc.net

Rouse, Sarah (IND - Alfrick and Leigh)
sarah.rouse@malvernhillsdc.net

Warburton, Anthony (IND - Alfrick and Leigh)
anthony.warburton@malvernhillsdc.net

Watkins, David (CON - Link)
david.watkins@malvernhillsdc.net

Wells, Tom (LD - Powick)
talwells@btinernet.com

POLITICAL COMPOSITION

CON: 23, IND: 7, LD: 5, GRN: 3

COMMITTEE CHAIRS

Audit: Mr David Watkins

Planning: Ms Melanie Baker

MANCHESTER CITY

Manchester City M

Manchester City Council, Manchester City Council, Town Hall, Albert Square, Manchester M60 2LA
☎ 0161 234 5000 manchester@manchester.gov.uk
www.manchester.gov.uk

FACTS AND FIGURES

Parliamentary Constituencies: Blackley and Broughton, Manchester Central, Manchester, Gorton, Manchester, Withington, Wythenshawe and Sale East
EU Constituencies: North West
Election Frequency: Elections are by thirds

PRINCIPAL OFFICERS

Chief Executive: Sir Howard Bernstein, Chief Executive, Manchester City Council, Town Hall, Albert Square, Manchester M60 2LA ☎ 0161 234 3006 🖷 0161 234 3098 h.bernstein@manchester.gov.uk

Deputy Chief Executive: Mr Geoff Little, Deputy Chief Executive of People, Manchester City Council, Town Hall, Albert Square, Manchester M60 2LA ☎ 0161 234 3280 🖷 0161 236 2959 g.little@manchester.gov.uk

Deputy Chief Executive: Ms Sara Todd, Deputy Chief Executive of Growth & Neighbourhoods, Manchester City Council, Town Hall, Albert Square, Manchester M60 2LA ☎ 0161 234 3286 🖷 0161 234 2959 s.todd@manchester.gov.uk

Assistant Chief Executive: Mr Sean McGonigle , Assistant Chief Executive - Growth, Manchester City Council, Town Hall, Albert Square, Manchester M60 2LA ☎ 0161 234 4821 🖷 0161 234 7118 s.mcgonigle@manchester.gov.uk

Senior Management: Ms Carol Culley , Deputy City Treasurer, Manchester City Council, Town Hall, Albert Square, Manchester M60 2LA ☎ 0161 234 3406 🖷 0161 234 3435 c.culley@manchester.gov.uk

Senior Management: Mr John Edwards , Director - Education & Skills, Manchester City Council, Town Hall, Albert Square, Manchester M60 2LA ☎ 0161 234 4314 🖷 0161 276 7629 j.edwards@manchester.gov.uk

Senior Management: Ms Sharon Kemp , Strategic Director - Reform, Manchester City Council, Town Hall, Albert Square, Manchester M60 2LA ☎ 0161 234 1145 🖷 0161 234 3435 s.kemp@manchester.gov.uk

Senior Management: Mr Richard Paver, City Treasurer, Manchester City Council, Town Hall, Albert Square, Manchester M60 2LA ☎ 0161 234 3564 🖷 0161 274 7015 r.paver@manchester.gov.uk

Senior Management: Mr David Regan , Director of Public Health, Manchester City Council, Town Hall, Albert Square, Manchester M60 2LA ☎ 0161 234 5000 d.regan@manchester.gov.uk

Senior Management: Ms Gladys Rhodes-White , Interim Strategic Director - Children & Commissioning Services, Manchester City Council, Town Hall, Albert Square, Manchester M60 2LA ☎ 0161 234 3804 🖷 0161 276 7629 g.rhodeswhite@manchester.gov.uk

Senior Management: Mr Eddie Smith , Strategic Director - Strategic Development, Manchester City Council, Town Hall, Albert Square, Manchester M60 2LA ☎ 0161 234 3030 e.smith@manchester.gov.uk

Senior Management: Ms Hazel Summers , Acting Strategic Director - Adult Social Services, Manchester City Council, Town Hall, Albert Square, Manchester M60 2LA ☎ 0161 234 5000 h.summers@manchester.gov.uk

Senior Management: Ms Liz Treacy, City Solicitor, Manchester City Council, Town Hall, Albert Square, Manchester M60 2LA ☎ 0161 234 3339 🖷 0161 234 3098 l.treacy@manchester.gov.uk

Access Officer / Social Services (Disability): Ms Kathleen Weaver , Head of Customer Access, Manchester City Council, Town Hall, Albert Square, Manchester M60 2LA ☎ 0161 234 3745 k.weaver1@manchester.gov.uk

Architect, Building / Property Services: Mr Eddie Smith , Strategic Director - Strategic Development, Manchester City Council, Town Hall, Albert Square, Manchester M60 2LA ☎ 0161 234 3030 e.smith@manchester.gov.uk

Best Value: Ms Sarah Henry , Head of Public Intelligence & Performance, Manchester City Council, Town Hall, Albert Square, Manchester M60 2LA ☎ 0161 234 1012 🖷 0161 274 0025 s.henry@manchester.gov.uk

Building Control: Ms Julie Roscoe , Head of Planning, Licensing & Building Control, Manchester City Council, Town Hall, Albert Square, Manchester M60 2LA ☎ 0161 234 4552 🖷 0161 234 4508 j.roscoe@manchester.gov.uk

Children / Youth Services: Ms Gladys Rhodes-White , Interim Strategic Director - Children & Commissioning Services, Manchester City Council, Town Hall, Albert Square, Manchester M60 2LA ☎ 0161 234 3804 🖷 0161 276 7629 g.rhodeswhite@manchester.gov.uk

Civil Registration: Mr Jonathan Kershners , Registration & Coroners Service Manager, Manchester City Council, Town Hall, Albert Square, Manchester M60 2LA ☎ 0161 234 5566 🖷 0161 234 5528 j.kershner@manchester.gov.uk

PR / Communications: Ms Sharon Kemp , Strategic Director - Reform, Manchester City Council, Town Hall, Albert Square, Manchester M60 2LA ☎ 0161 234 1145 🖷 0161 234 3435 s.kemp@manchester.gov.uk

Community Safety: Ms Fiona Sharkey , Strategic Lead - Compliance/Community Safety, Manchester City Council, Town Hall, Albert Square, Manchester M60 2LA ☎ 0161 957 8379 🖷 0161 856 2130 fiona.sharkey@manchester.gov.uk

Computer Management: Mr Bob Brown , Interim Chief Information Officer, Manchester City Council, Town Hall, Albert Square, Manchester M60 2LA ☎ 0161 234 5998 b.brown1@manchester.gov.uk

Consumer Protection and Trading Standards: Ms Fiona Sharkey , Strategic Lead - Compliance/Community Safety, Manchester City Council, Town Hall, Albert Square, Manchester M60 2LA ☎ 0161 957 8379 🖷 0161 856 2130 fiona.sharkey@manchester.gov.uk

Contracts: Mr Ian Brown, Head of Corporate Procurement, Manchester City Council, Town Hall, Albert Square, Manchester M60 2LA ☎ 0161 234 3255 🖷 0161 274 7015 i.brown@manchester.gov.uk

Corporate Services: Mr Richard Paver, City Treasurer, Manchester City Council, Town Hall, Albert Square, Manchester M60 2LA ☎ 0161 234 3564 🖷 0161 274 7015 r.paver@manchester.gov.uk

Customer Service: Mr Lee Owen , Head of Customer Services, Manchester City Council, Town Hall, Albert Square, Manchester M60 2LA ☎ 0161 245 7525 l.owen@manchester.gov.uk

Direct Labour: Mr Mike Brogan , Operations Manager, Manchester City Council, Hopper Street Depot, Ardwick, Manchester M12 6LA ☎ 0161 908 5800 🖷 0161 908 5858 m.brogan@manchester.gov.uk

Economic Development: Ms Angela Harrington , Head of Work & Skills, Manchester City Council, Town Hall, Albert Square, Manchester M60 2LA ☎ 0161 234 1501 🖷 0161 274 0036 a.harrington@manchester.gov.uk

E-Government: Ms Jennifer Green , Head of Communications Content & Strategy, Manchester City Council, Town Hall, Albert Square, Manchester M60 2LA ☎ 0161 234 4420 j.green1@manchester.gov.uk

Electoral Registration: Ms Kate Brown , Electoral Services Programme Manager, Manchester City Council, Town Hall, Albert Square, Manchester M60 2LA ☎ 0161 234 3147 k.brown3@manchester.gov.uk

Emergency Planning: Ms Fiona Worrall , Director - Neighbourhood Delivery, Manchester City Council, Town Hall, Albert Square, Manchester M60 2LA ☎ 0161 234 3926 fiona.worrall@manchester.gov.uk

Energy Management: Mr Walter Dooley, Group Energy Manager, Manchester City Council, Town Hall, Albert Square, Manchester M60 2LA ☎ 0161 234 3633 🖷 0161 236 0357 w.dooley@manchester.gov.uk

Environmental / Technical Services: Ms Jessica Bowles , Head of Policy, Partnerships & Research, Manchester City Council, Town Hall, Albert Square, Manchester M60 2LA ☎ 0161 234 5000 j.bowles@manchester.gov.uk

Environmental Health: Ms Janet Shaw , Citywide Support Team Lead, Manchester City Council, Town Hall, Albert Square, Manchester M60 2LA ☎ 0161 234 1587 🖷 0161 274 7239 j.shaw@manchester.gov.uk

Estates, Property & Valuation: Mr Eddie Smith , Strategic Director - Strategic Development, Manchester City Council, Town Hall, Albert Square, Manchester M60 2LA ☎ 0161 234 3030 e.smith@manchester.gov.uk

European Liaison: Ms Jessica Bowles , Head of Policy, Partnerships & Research, Manchester City Council, Town Hall, Albert Square, Manchester M60 2LA ☎ 0161 234 5000 j.bowles@manchester.gov.uk

Events Manager: Mr Mike Parrott , Head of Events, Manchester City Council, Town Hall, Albert Square, Manchester M60 2LA ☎ 0161 234 5242 m.parrott@manchester.gov.uk

Facilities: Mr Steven Southern , Senior Facilites Manager, New Smithfield Market, Whitworth Street East, Bradford, Manchester M11 2NQ ☎ 0161 234 5242 🖷 0161 274 7277 s.southern@manchester.gov.uk

Finance: Mr Richard Paver, City Treasurer, Manchester City Council, Town Hall, Albert Square, Manchester M60 2LA ☎ 0161 234 3564 🖷 0161 274 7015 r.paver@manchester.gov.uk

Treasury: Ms Carol Culley , Deputy City Treasurer, Manchester City Council, Town Hall, Albert Square, Manchester M60 2LA ☎ 0161 234 3406 🖷 0161 234 3435 c.culley@manchester.gov.uk

Fleet Management: Ms Rachel Christie , Strategic Lead - Public Realm, Manchester City Council, Town Hall, Albert Square, Manchester M60 2LA ☎ 0161 856 3237 🖷 0161 234 7245 r.christie@manchester.gov.uk

Health and Safety: Mr Simon Gardiner, Health & Safety Manager, Manchester City Council, Town Hall, Albert Square, Manchester M60 2LA ☎ 0161 234 5260 🖷 0161 274 7002 s.gardiner@manchester.gov.uk

Highways: Mr Kevin Gillham , Citywide Highway Manager, Manchester City Council, Town Hall, Albert Square, Manchester M60 2LA ☎ 0161 234 5148 🖷 0161 908 5716 k.gillham@manchester.gov.uk

Housing: Mr Paul Beardmore , Director of Housing, Manchester City Council, Town Hall, Albert Square, Manchester M60 2LA ☎ 0161 234 4811 🖷 0161 234 4232 p.beardmore@manchester.gov.uk

Local Area Agreement: Ms Jessica Bowles , Head of Policy, Partnerships & Research, Manchester City Council, Town Hall, Albert Square, Manchester M60 2LA ☎ 0161 234 5000 j.bowles@manchester.gov.uk

Legal: Ms Jacqueline Dennis , Head of Legal Services, Manchester City Council, Town Hall, Albert Square, Manchester M60 2LA ☎ 0161 234 3053 🖷 0161 274 0041 j.dennis@manchester.gov.uk

MANCHESTER CITY

Legal: Ms Liz Treacy, City Solicitor, Manchester City Council, Town Hall, Albert Square, Manchester M60 2LA ☎ 0161 234 3339 🖷 0161 234 3098 ✉ l.treacy@manchester.gov.uk

Leisure and Cultural Services: Mr Neil Fairlamb , Strategic Leads - Parks/Leisure/Events, Manchester City Council, Town Hall, Albert Square, Manchester M60 2LA ☎ 0161 219 2539 ✉ n.fairlamb@manchester.gov.uk

Leisure and Cultural Services: Mr Neil MacInnes , Strategic Lead - Library/Galleries/Culture, Manchester City Council, Town Hall, Albert Square, Manchester M60 2LA ☎ 0161 234 1392 🖷 0161 274 7053 ✉ n.macinnes@libraries.manchester.gov.uk

Licensing: Ms Julie Roscoe , Head of Planning, Licensing & Building Control, Manchester City Council, Town Hall, Albert Square, Manchester M60 2LA ☎ 0161 234 4552 🖷 0161 234 4508 ✉ j.roscoe@manchester.gov.uk

Lifelong Learning: Ms Julie Rushton , Head of Manchester Adult Education Service, Manchester City Council, Town Hall, Albert Square, Manchester M60 2LA ☎ 0161 234 5679 🖷 0161 205 6729 ✉ j.rushton@manchester.gov.uk

Lighting: Mr Kevin Gillham , Citywide Highway Manager, Manchester City Council, Town Hall, Albert Square, Manchester M60 2LA ☎ 0161 234 5148 🖷 0161 908 5716 ✉ k.gillham@manchester.gov.uk

Lottery Funding, Charity and Voluntary: Ms Liz Goodger , Commissioning Manager, Manchester City Council, Town Hall, Albert Square, Manchester M60 2LA ☎ 0161 234 1285 ✉ l.goodger@manchester.gov.uk

Member Services: Ms Nicola Fernley , Head of Member Services, Manchester City Council, Town Hall, Albert Square, Manchester M60 2LA ☎ 0161 234 4289 🖷 0161 274 7009 ✉ n.fernley@manchester.gov.uk

Partnerships: Ms Jessica Bowles , Head of Policy, Partnerships & Research, Manchester City Council, Town Hall, Albert Square, Manchester M60 2LA ☎ 0161 234 5000 ✉ j.bowles@manchester.gov.uk

Personnel / HR: Ms Sharon Kemp , Strategic Director - Reform, Manchester City Council, Town Hall, Albert Square, Manchester M60 2LA ☎ 0161 234 1145 🖷 0161 234 3435 ✉ s.kemp@manchester.gov.uk

Planning: Ms Julie Roscoe , Head of Planning, Licensing & Building Control, Manchester City Council, Town Hall, Albert Square, Manchester M60 2LA ☎ 0161 234 4552 🖷 0161 234 4508 ✉ j.roscoe@manchester.gov.uk

Procurement: Mr Ian Brown, Head of Corporate Procurement, Manchester City Council, Town Hall, Albert Square, Manchester M60 2LA ☎ 0161 234 3255 🖷 0161 274 7015 ✉ i.brown@manchester.gov.uk

Public Libraries: Mr Neil MacInnes , Strategic Lead - Library/ Galleries/Culture, Manchester City Council, Town Hall, Albert Square, Manchester M60 2LA ☎ 0161 234 1392 🖷 0161 274 7053 ✉ n.macinnes@libraries.manchester.gov.uk

Recycling & Waste Minimisation: Mr Mark Glynn , Strategic Lead - Waste/Recycling/Street Cleansing, South Neighbourhood Delivery Team, West Didsbury Police Station, Chorlton Park, Manchester M20 2ES ☎ 0161 234 5501 ✉ m.glynn@manchester.gov.uk

Regeneration: Ms Fiona Worrall , Director - Neighbourhood Delivery, Manchester City Council, Town Hall, Albert Square, Manchester M60 2LA ☎ 0161 234 3926 ✉ fiona.worrall@manchester.gov.uk

Road Safety: Mr Kevin Gillham , Citywide Highway Manager, Manchester City Council, Town Hall, Albert Square, Manchester M60 2LA ☎ 0161 234 5148 🖷 0161 908 5716 ✉ k.gillham@manchester.gov.uk

Road Safety: Mr Kent Wells , Service Manager, Manchester City Council, Town Hall, Albert Square, Manchester M60 2LA ☎ 0161 245 7440 🖷 0151 274 7242 ✉ k.wells@manchester.gov.uk

Social Services (Adult): Ms Hazel Summers , Acting Strategic Director - Adult Social Services, Manchester City Council, Town Hall, Albert Square, Manchester M60 2LA ☎ 0161 234 5000 ✉ h.summers@manchester.gov.uk

Public Health: Mr David Regan , Director of Public Health, Manchester City Council, Town Hall, Albert Square, Manchester M60 2LA ☎ 0161 234 5000 ✉ d.regan@manchester.gov.uk

Staff Training: Ms Caroline Powell , Strategic Business Partner, Manchester City Council, Town Hall, Albert Square, Manchester M60 2LA ☎ 0161 234 6522 ✉ c.powell@manchester.gov.uk

Street Scene: Ms Rachel Christie , Strategic Lead - Public Realm, Central Park Polic Station, Northampton Road, Manchester M40 5BQ ☎ 0161 856 3237 🖷 0161 234 7245 ✉ r.christie@manchester.gov.uk

Sustainable Communities: Ms Fiona Worrall , Director - Neighbourhood Delivery, Manchester City Council, Town Hall, Albert Square, Manchester M60 2LA ☎ 0161 234 3926 ✉ fiona.worrall@manchester.gov.uk

Town Centre: Ms Angela Whitehead , City Centre Delivery Manager, Bootle Street Police Station, Bootle Street, Manchester M2 5GU ☎ 0161 856 3001 ✉ a.whitehead@manchester.gov.uk

Traffic Management: Mr Kevin Gillham , Citywide Highway Manager, Manchester City Council, Town Hall, Albert Square, Manchester M60 2LA ☎ 0161 234 5148 🖷 0161 908 5716 ✉ k.gillham@manchester.gov.uk

Transport: Mr Gary Campin , Fleet Manager, Manchester City Council, Town Hall, Albert Square, Manchester M60 2LA ☎ 0161 957 8419 🖷 0161 274 7239 ✉ g.campin@manchester.gov.uk

Transport Planner: Mr Kevin Gillham , Citywide Highway Manager, Manchester City Council, Town Hall, Albert Square, Manchester M60 2LA ☎ 0161 234 5148 🖷 0161 908 5716 ✉ k.gillham@manchester.gov.uk

Waste Management: Mr Kevin Gillham , Citywide Highway Manager, Manchester City Council, Town Hall, Albert Square, Manchester M60 2LA ☎ 0161 234 5148 🖷 0161 908 5716
k.gillham@manchester.gov.uk

COUNCILLORS

***The Lord Mayor* Murphy**, Paul (LAB - Moston)
cllr.p.murphy@manchester.gov.uk

***Leader of the Council* Leese**, Richard (LAB - Crumpsall)
cllr.r.leese@manchester.gov.uk

***Deputy Leader of the Council* Murphy**, Sue (LAB - Brooklands)
cllr.s.murphy@manchester.gov.uk

***Deputy Leader of the Council* Priest**, Bernard (LAB - Ardwick)
cllr.b.priest@manchester.gov.uk

Adams, Bridie (LAB - Didsbury East)
cllr.b.adams@manhester.gov.uk

Akbar, Rabnawaz (LAB - Rusholme)
cllr.r.akbar@manchester.gov.uk

Ali, Shaukat (LAB - Cheetham)
cllr.shaukat.ali@manchester.gov.uk

Ali, Ahmed (LAB - Rusholme)
cllr.a.ali@manchester.gov.uk

Ali, Azra (LAB - Burnage)
cllr.azra.ali@manchester.gov.uk

Ali, Sameem (LAB - Moss Side)
cllr.s.ali@manchester.gov.uk

Ali, Nasrin (LAB - Levenshulme)
cllr.n.ali@manchester.gov.uk

Amesbury, Michael Lee (LAB - Fallowfield)
cllr.m.amesbury@manchester.gov.uk

Andrews, Paul (LAB - Baguley)
cllr.p.andrews@manchester.gov.uk

Appleby, Paula (LAB - Moston)
cllr.p.appleby@manchester.gov.uk

Austin, Carl (LAB - Burnage)
cllr.c.austin@manchester.gov.uk

Barrett, Hugh (LAB - Sharston)
cllr.h.barrett@manchester.gov.uk

Battle, Rosa (LAB - Bradford)
cllr.r.battle@manchester.gov.uk

Bridges, Garry (LAB - Old Moat)
cllr.g.bridges@manchester.gov.uk

Chappell, Kate (LAB - Rusholme)
cllr.k.chappell@manchester.gov.uk

Chohan, Abid (LAB - Longsight)
cllr.a.chohan@manchester.gov.uk

Collins, Sandra (LAB - Harpurhey)
cllr.s.collins@manchester.gov.uk

Connolly, Julie (LAB - Cheetham)
cllr.j.connolly@manchester.gov.uk

Cookson, Peter (LAB - Gorton South)
cllr.p.cookson@manchester.gov.uk

Cooley, Susan (LAB - Brooklands)
cllr.s.cooley@manchester.gov.uk

Cox, Alistair (LAB - Moss Side)
cllr.a.cox@manchester.gov.uk

Craig, Bev (LAB - Burnage)
cllr.b.craig@manchester.gov.uk

Curley, Basil (LAB - Charlestown)
cllr.b.curley@manchester.gov.uk

Dar, Yasmine (LAB - Moston)
cllr.y.dar@manchester.gov.uk

Davies, Joan (LAB - City Centre)
cllr.j.davies@mamchester.gov.uk

Ellison, David (LAB - Didsbury West)
cllr.d.ellison@manchester.gov.uk

Evans, Glynn (LAB - Brooklands)
cllr.g.evans@manchester.gov.uk

Farrell, John (LAB - Higher Blackley)
cllr.j.farrell@manchester.gov.uk

Fender, Andrew (LAB - Old Moat)
cllr.a.fender@manchester.gov.uk

Flanagan, John (LAB - Miles Platting and Newton Heath)
cll.j.flanagan@manchester.gov.uk

Fletcher-Hackwood, Grace (LAB - Fallowfield)
cllr.g.fletcher-hackwood@manchester.gov.uk

Gillard, Daniel (LAB - Withington)
cllr.d.gillard@manchester.gov.uk

Green, Joanne (LAB - Harpurhey)
cllr.j.green@manchester.gov.uk

Grimshaw, Carmine (LAB - Miles Platting and Newton Heath)
cllr.c.grimshaw@manchester.gov.uk

Hackett, Mark (LAB - Charlestown)
cllr.m.hackett@manchester.gov.uk

Hacking, John (LAB - Chorlton)
cllr.j.hacking@manchester.gov.uk

Hassan, Naeem (LAB - Cheetham)
cllr.n.hassan@manchester.gov.uk

Hewitson, Tina (LAB - Ardwick)
cllr.t.hewitson@manchester.gov.uk

Hitchen, June (LAB - Miles Platting and Newton Heath)
cllr.j.hitchen@manchester.gov.uk

Hughes, Jon (LAB - Gorton North)
cllr.j.hughes@manchester.gov.uk

Igbon, Lee-Ann (LAB - Hulme)
cllr.l.igbon@manchester.gov.uk

Judge, Sarah (LAB - Woodhouse Park)
cllr.s.judge@manchester.gov.uk

Judge, Thomas (LAB - Sharston)
cllr.t.judge@manchester.gov.uk

Kamal, Afia (LAB - Gorton North)
cllr.a.kamal@manchester.gov.uk

Karney, Patrick (LAB - Harpurhey)
cllr.p.karney@manchester.gov.uk

Kirkpartick, Veronica (LAB - Charlestown)
cllr.v.kirkpatrick@manchester.gov.uk

Knowles, Beth (LAB - City Centre)
cllr.b.knowles@manchester.gov.uk

MANCHESTER CITY

Lanchbury, Shelley (LAB - Higher Blackley)
cllr.s.lanchbury@machester.gov.uk

Lone, Amina (LAB - Hulme)
cllr.a.lone@manchester.gov.uk

Longsden, John (LAB - Bradford)
cllr.j.longsden@manchester.gov.uk

Loughman, Mick (LAB - Ancoats and Clayton)
cllr.m.loughman@manchester.gov.uk

Ludford, Donna (LAB - Ancoats and Clayton)
cllr.d.ludford@manchester.gov.uk

Manco, Ollie (LAB - Ancoats and Clayton)
cllr.o.manco@manchester.gov.uk

Marshall, Beth (LAB - Crumpsall)
cllr.b.marshall@manchester.gov.uk

Midgley, Joanna (LAB - Chorlton Park)
cllr.j.midgley@manchester.gov.uk

Monaghan, Madeleine (LAB - Sharston)
cllr.m.monaghan@manchester.gov.uk

Moore, Rebecca (LAB - Withington)
cllr.r.moore@manchester.gov.uk

Murphy, Nigel (LAB - Hulme)
cllr.n.murphy@manchester.gov.uk

Newman, Sheila (LAB - Chorlton)
cllr.s.newman@manchester.gov.uk

Newman, Eddy (LAB - Woodhouse Park)
cllr.e.newman@manchester.gov.uk

Noor, Dzidra (LAB - Levenshulme)
cllr.d.noor@manchester.gov.uk

Ollerhead, Carl (LAB - Didsbury West)
Cllr.c.ollerhead@manchester.gov.uk

O'Neil, Brian (LAB - Woodhouse Park)
cllr.brian.oneil@manchester.gov.uk

Paul, Chris (LAB - Withington)
cllr.c.paul@manchester.gov.uk

Peel, Kevin (LAB - City Centre)
cllr.k.peel@manchester.gov.uk

Pritchard, Jon-Leigh (LAB - Crumpsall)
cllr.j.pritchard@manchester.gov.uk

Rahman, Luthfur (LAB - Longsight)
cllr.l.rahman@manchester.gov.uk

Raikes, Luke (LAB - Baguley)
cllr.l.raikes@manchester.gov.uk

Rawlins, Tracey (LAB - Baguley)
cllr.t.rawlins@manchester.gov.uk

Rawson, Dave (LAB - Chorlton Park)
cllr.d.rawson@manchester.gov.uk

Razaq, Aftab (LAB - Whalley Range)
cllr.a.razaq@manchester.gov.uk

Reeves, Suzannah (LAB - Old Moat)
cllr.s.reeves@manchester.gov.uk

Reid, Julie (LAB - Gorton South)
cllr.j.reid@manchester.gov.uk

Richards, Suzanne (LAB - Longsight)
cllr.s.richards@manchester.gov.uk

Rowles, Emily (LAB - Moss Side)
cllr.e.rowles@manchester.gov.uk

Royle, David (LAB - Fallowfield)
cllr.d.royle@manchester.gov.uk

Russell, Sarah (LAB - Northenden)
cllr.s.russell@manchester.gov.uk

Sheikh, Basat (LAB - Levenshulme)
cllr.b.sheikh@manchester.gov.uk

Shilton-Godwin, Mandie (LAB - Chorlton Park)
cllr.m.shiltongodwin@manchester.gov.uk

Shone, Fran (LAB - Northenden)
cllr.f.shone@manchester.gov.uk

Siddiqi, Nilofar (LAB - Gorton North)
cllr.n.siddiqi@manchester.gov.uk

Simcock, Andrew (LAB - Didsbury East)
cllr.a.simcock@manchester.gov.uk

Smitheman, Mavis (LAB - Ardwick)
mave@smitheman1.demon.co.uk

Stogia, Angeliki (LAB - Whalley Range)
cllr.a.stogia@manchester.gov.uk

Stone, Bernard (LAB - Gorton South)
cllr.b.stone@manchester.gov.uk

Strong, Matt (LAB - Chorlton)
cllr.m.strong@manchester.gov.uk

Swannick, Neil (LAB - Bradford)
cllr.n.swannick@manchester.gov.uk

Teubler, Josie (LAB - Didsbury West)
cllr.j.teubler@manchester.gov.uk

Trotman, Anna (LAB - Higher Blackley)
cllr.a.trotman@manchester.gov.uk

Watson, Mary (LAB - Whalley Range)
cllr.m.watson@manchester.gov.uk

Webb, Chris (LAB - Northenden)
cllr.c.webb@manchester.gov.uk

Wilson, James (LAB - Didsbury East)
cllr.j.wilson@manchester.gov.uk

POLITICAL COMPOSITION
LAB: 96

COMMITTEE CHAIRS
Audit: Mr Mark Hackett

Licensing: Mr John Longsden

Planning & Highways: Mr Mick Loughman

Young People & Children: Ms Julie Reid

Mansfield D

Mansfield District Council, Civic Centre, Chesterfield Road South, Mansfield NG19 7BH
☎ 01623 463463 🖷 01623 463900 mdc@mansfield.gov.uk
www.mansfield.gov.uk

FACTS AND FIGURES
Parliamentary Constituencies: Mansfield

EU Constituencies: East Midlands
Election Frequency: Elections are of whole council

PRINCIPAL OFFICERS

Chief Executive: Mrs Bev Smith , Interim Chief Operating Officer (Corporate Director - Regeneration & Regulation), Civic Centre, Chesterfield Road South, Mansfield NG19 7BH ☎ 01623 463463 bsmith@mansfield.gov.uk

Senior Management: Mr Ajman Ali , Corporate Director - Housing & Environment, Civic Centre, Chesterfield Road South, Mansfield NG19 7BH ☎ 01623 463463 🖷 01623 463900 aali@mansfield.gov.uk

Senior Management: Mrs Bev Smith , Interim Chief Operating Officer (Corporate Director - Regeneration & Regulation), Civic Centre, Chesterfield Road South, Mansfield NG19 7BH ☎ 01623 463463 bsmith@mansfield.gov.uk

Access Officer / Social Services (Disability): Ms Sharon Allman , Equality & Diversity Research Officer, Mansfield District Council, Civic Centre, Chesterfield Road South, Mansfield NG19 7BH ☎ 01623 463042 sallman@mansfield.gov.uk

Architect, Building / Property Services: Mr Philip Colledge, Principal General Practice Surveyor & Corporate Asset Manager, Civic Centre, Chesterfield Road South, Mansfield NG19 7BH ☎ 01623 463463 🖷 01623 463900 pcolledge@mansfield.gov.uk

Architect, Building / Property Services: Mr Brian Holmes, Architecture & Facilities Manager, Civic Centre, Chesterfield Road South, Mansfield NG19 7BH ☎ 01623 463463 bholmes@mansfield.gov.uk

Architect, Building / Property Services: Mr Steve Melhuish , Group Architect, Civic Centre, Chesterfield Road South, Mansfield NG19 7BH ☎ 01623 463463 smelhuish@mansfield.gov.uk

Building Control: Mr Martyn Saxton, Head of Planning, Community Safety & Regulatory Services, Civic Centre, Chesterfield Road South, Mansfield NG19 7BH ☎ 01623 463208 msaxton@mansfield.gov.uk

PR / Communications: Ms Donna Ellis , Marketing & Communications Manager, Civic Centre, Chesterfield Road South, Mansfield NG19 7BH ☎ 01623 463463 🖷 01623 463900 dellis@mansfield.gov.uk

Community Planning: Mr M Robinson , Head of Regeneration, Leisure & Marketing, Civic Centre, Chesterfield Road South, Mansfield NG19 7BH ☎ 01623 463900 mrobinson@mansfield.gov.uk

Community Safety: Mrs Bev Smith , Corporate Director of Regeneration & Regulation, Civic Centre, Chesterfield Road South, Mansfield NG19 7BH ☎ 01623 463463 🖷 01623 463900 bsmith@mansfield.gov.uk

Computer Management: Mrs Christine Marsh, ICT Manager, Civic Centre, Chesterfield Road South, Mansfield NG19 7BH ☎ 01623 463463 🖷 01623 463900 cmarsh@mansfield.gov.uk

Contracts: Mr Ajman Ali , Corporate Director - Housing & Environment, Civic Centre, Chesterfield Road South, Mansfield NG19 7BH ☎ 01623 463463 🖷 01623 463900 aali@mansfield.gov.uk

Corporate Services: Mrs Ruth Marlow, Managing Director, Civic Centre, Chesterfield Road South, Mansfield NG19 7BH ☎ 01623 463366 🖷 01623 463999 rmarlow@mansfield.gov.uk

Customer Service: Mr Mick Andrews , Head of Finance, Property & Revenue Services, Civic Centre, Chesterfield Road South, Mansfield NG19 7BH ☎ 01623 463031 🖷 01623 463900 mandrews@mansfield.gov.uk

Direct Labour: Mr Martyn Thurman, Head of Neighbourhood Services, Civic Centre, Chesterfield Road South, Mansfield NG19 7BH ☎ 01623 463463 🖷 01623 463900 mthurman@mansfield.gov.uk

Economic Development: Mr M Robinson , Head of Regeneration, Leisure & Marketing, Civic Centre, Chesterfield Road South, Mansfield NG19 7BH ☎ 01623 463900 mrobinson@mansfield.gov.uk

E-Government: Mrs Christine Marsh, ICT Manager, Civic Centre, Chesterfield Road South, Mansfield NG19 7BH ☎ 01623 463463 🖷 01623 463900 cmarsh@mansfield.gov.uk

Electoral Registration: Ms Julie Jevons, Electoral Services Manager, Civic Centre, Chesterfield Road South, Mansfield NG19 7BH ☎ 01623 463463 Extn 3394 🖷 01623 463900 jjevons@mansfield.gov.uk

Emergency Planning: Mrs Bev Smith , Corporate Director of Regeneration & Regulation, Civic Centre, Chesterfield Road South, Mansfield NG19 7BH ☎ 01623 463463 🖷 01623 463900 bsmith@mansfield.gov.uk

Energy Management: Mr Ajman Ali , Corporate Director - Housing & Environment, Civic Centre, Chesterfield Road South, Mansfield NG19 7BH ☎ 01623 463463 🖷 01623 463900 aali@mansfield.gov.uk

Environmental / Technical Services: Mr Ajman Ali , Corporate Director - Housing & Environment, Civic Centre, Chesterfield Road South, Mansfield NG19 7BH ☎ 01623 463463 🖷 01623 463900 aali@mansfield.gov.uk

Environmental / Technical Services: Mr Martyn Thurman, Head of Neighbourhood Services, Civic Centre, Chesterfield Road South, Mansfield NG19 7BH ☎ 01623 463463 🖷 01623 463900 mthurman@mansfield.gov.uk

Environmental Health: Mr Chris Rowlston, Environmental Health Manager, Civic Centre, Chesterfield Road South, Mansfield NG19 7BH ☎ 01623 463038 crowlston@mansfield.gov.uk

Estates, Property & Valuation: Mr Philip Colledge, Principal General Practice Surveyor & Corporate Asset Manager, Civic Centre, Chesterfield Road South, Mansfield NG19 7BH ☎ 01623 463463 🖷 01623 463900 pcolledge@mansfield.gov.uk

MANSFIELD

Events Manager: Mr Kevan Poyntz , Town Centre Manager, Civic Centre, Chesterfield Road South, Mansfield NG19 7BH ☎ 01623 653350 ✉ kpoyntz@mansfield.gov.uk

Finance: Mr Mick Andrews , Head of Finance, Property & Revenue Services, Civic Centre, Chesterfield Road South, Mansfield NG19 7BH ☎ 01623 463031 🖷 01623 463900 ✉ mandrews@mansfield.gov.uk

Fleet Management: Mr George Farrell , Fleet Manager, Hermitage Lane Depot, Hermitage Lane, Mansfield NG18 5GU ☎ 01623 463093 ✉ gfarrell@mansfield.gov.uk

Grounds Maintenance: Mr Martyn Thurman, Head of Neighbourhood Services, Civic Centre, Chesterfield Road South, Mansfield NG19 7BH ☎ 01623 463463 🖷 01623 463900 ✉ mthurman@mansfield.gov.uk

Health and Safety: Mrs Bev Smith , Corporate Director of Regeneration & Regulation, Civic Centre, Chesterfield Road South, Mansfield NG19 7BH ☎ 01623 463463 🖷 01623 463900 ✉ bsmith@mansfield.gov.uk

Home Energy Conservation: Mr Ajman Ali , Corporate Director - Housing & Environment, Civic Centre, Chesterfield Road South, Mansfield NG19 7BH ☎ 01623 463463 🖷 01623 463900 ✉ aali@mansfield.gov.uk

Housing: Ms Hayley Barsby , Head of Housing, Civic Centre, Chesterfield Road South, Mansfield NG19 7BH ☎ 01623 463463 🖷 01623 463900 ✉ hbarsby@mansfield.gov.uk

Housing Maintenance: Mr Andrew Johnson , Housing Repairs, Civic Centre, Chesterfield Road South, Mansfield NG19 7BH ☎ 01623 463463 (extn 1)

Legal: Mr Martyn Saxton , Head of Planning & Regulatory Services, Civic Centre, Chesterfield Road South, Mansfield NG19 7BH ☎ 01623 463463 🖷 01623 463900 ✉ msaxton@mansfield.gov.uk

Leisure and Cultural Services: Mr M Robinson , Head of Regeneration, Leisure & Marketing, Civic Centre, Chesterfield Road South, Mansfield NG19 7BH ☎ 01623 463900 ✉ mrobinson@mansfield.gov.uk

Licensing: Ms Samantha Yates , Licensing Manager, Civic Centre, Chesterfield Road South, Mansfield NG19 7BH ☎ 01623 463463 ✉ syates@mansfield.gov.uk

Lighting: Mr Martyn Thurman, Head of Neighbourhood Services, Civic Centre, Chesterfield Road South, Mansfield NG19 7BH ☎ 01623 463463 🖷 01623 463900 ✉ mthurman@mansfield.gov.uk

Member Services: Mr Mark Pemberton, Democratic Services Manager, Civic Centre, Chesterfield Road South, Mansfield NG19 7BH ☎ 01623 463463 🖷 01623 463900 ✉ mpemberton@mansfield.gov.uk

Parking: Mr Kevan Poyntz , Town Centre Manager, Civic Centre, Chesterfield Road South, Mansfield NG19 7BH ☎ 01623 653350 ✉ kpoyntz@mansfield.gov.uk

Partnerships: Mrs Bev Smith , Interim Chief Operating Officer (Corporate Director - Regeneration & Regulation), Civic Centre, Chesterfield Road South, Mansfield NG19 7BH ☎ 01623 463463 ✉ bsmith@mansfield.gov.uk

Personnel / HR: Mrs Mariam Amos , HR Manager, Council Offices, Urban Road, Kirkby-in-Ashfield NG17 8DA ☎ 01623 663032 ✉ mamos@mansfield.gov.uk

Planning: Mr Martyn Saxton, Head of Planning, Community Safety & Regulatory Services, Civic Centre, Chesterfield Road South, Mansfield NG19 7BH ☎ 01623 463208 ✉ msaxton@mansfield.gov.uk

Procurement: Mr Mick Andrews , Head of Finance, Property & Revenue Services, Civic Centre, Chesterfield Road South, Mansfield NG19 7BH ☎ 01623 463031 🖷 01623 463900 ✉ mandrews@mansfield.gov.uk

Recycling & Waste Minimisation: Mr Martyn Thurman, Head of Neighbourhood Services, Civic Centre, Chesterfield Road South, Mansfield NG19 7BH ☎ 01623 463463 🖷 01623 463900 ✉ mthurman@mansfield.gov.uk

Regeneration: Mr M Robinson , Head of Regeneration, Leisure & Marketing, Civic Centre, Chesterfield Road South, Mansfield NG19 7BH ☎ 01623 463900 ✉ mrobinson@mansfield.gov.uk

Staff Training: Mrs Lorraine Powney , Principal Learning & Development Adviser, Civic Centre, Chesterfield Road South, Mansfield NG19 7BH ☎ 01623 463250 🖷 01623 463900 ✉ lpowney@mansfield.gov.uk

Street Scene: Mr Martyn Thurman, Head of Neighbourhood Services, Civic Centre, Chesterfield Road South, Mansfield NG19 7BH ☎ 01623 463463 🖷 01623 463900 ✉ mthurman@mansfield.gov.uk

Sustainable Communities: Mrs Ruth Marlow, Managing Director, Civic Centre, Chesterfield Road South, Mansfield NG19 7BH ☎ 01623 463366 🖷 01623 463999 ✉ rmarlow@mansfield.gov.uk

Town Centre: Mr Kevan Poyntz , Town Centre Manager, Civic Centre, Chesterfield Road South, Mansfield NG19 7BH ☎ 01623 653350 ✉ kpoyntz@mansfield.gov.uk

Waste Collection and Disposal: Mr Martyn Thurman, Head of Neighbourhood Services, Civic Centre, Chesterfield Road South, Mansfield NG19 7BH ☎ 01623 463463 🖷 01623 463900 ✉ mthurman@mansfield.gov.uk

Waste Management: Mr Martyn Thurman, Head of Neighbourhood Services, Civic Centre, Chesterfield Road South, Mansfield NG19 7BH ☎ 01623 463463 🖷 01623 463900 ✉ mthurman@mansfield.gov.uk

COUNCILLORS

***Mayor* Allsop**, Kate (IND - Mayor's Ward)
kallsop@mansfield.gov.uk

Adey, Sharron (LAB - Netherfield)
sadey@mansfield.gov.uk

Answer, Barry (UKIP - Abbott)
banswer@mansfield.gov.uk

Atherton, Katrina (LAB - Manor)
katherton@mansfield.gov.uk

Barton, Mick (IND - Maun Valley)
mbarton@mansfield.gov.uk

Bennet, Nicholas (LAB - Kingsway)
nbennett@mansfield.gov.uk

Bosnjak, Joyce (LAB - Hornby)
jbosnjak@mansfield.gov.uk

Brown, Kevin (IND - Oakham)
brownk@mansfield.gov.uk

Clay, Terry (LAB - Brick Kiln)
tclay@mansfield.gov.uk

Crawford, Peter (LAB - Warsop Carrs)
pcrawford@mansfield.gov.uk

Drewett, Bill (IND - Ling Forest)
bdrewett@mansfield.gov.uk

Fisher, Amanda (LAB - Woodhouse)
afisher@mansfield.gov.uk

Garner, Stephen (IND - Racecourse)
sgarner@mansfield.gov.uk

Harvey, S (IND - Kingswalk)
sharvey@mansfield.gov.uk

Higgins, Sally (LAB - Ladybrook)
shiggins@mansfield.gov.uk

Hopewell, Vaughan (LAB - Oak Tree)
vhopewell@mansfield.gov.uk

Jelley, Ron (IND - Grange Farm)
rjelley@mansfield.gov.uk

Kerr, John (LAB - Market Warsop)
jkerr@mansfield.gov.uk

Lohan, Brian (LAB - Portland)
blohan@mansfield.gov.uk

McCallum, S (LAB - Sherwood)
smccallum@mansfield.gov.uk

Norman, Ann (LAB - Park Hall)
anorman@mansfield.gov.uk

Probert, Lee (LAB - Yeoman Hill)
lprobert@mansfield.gov.uk

Richardson, Stuart (LAB - Penniment)
srichardson@mansfield.gov.uk

Rickersey, Stewart (IND - Eakring)
srickersey@mansfield.gov.uk

Saunders, Dave (IND - Sandhurst)
dsaunders@mansfield.gov.uk

Sheppard, Ian (IND - Broomhill)
isheppard@mansfield.gov.uk

Sissons, Andy (IND - Newgate)
asissons@mansfield.gov.uk

Smart, John (LAB - Ransom Wood)
jsmart@mansfield.gov.uk

Smith, David (IND - Woodlands)
dmsmith@mansfield.gov.uk

Sutcliffe, Roger (IND - Lindhurst)
rsutcliffe@mansfield.gov.uk

Tristram, Andrew (IND - Berry Hill)
atristram@mansfield.gov.uk

Walker, Sidney (UKIP - Newlands)
swalker@mansfield.gov.uk

Wallace, Stuart (IND - Carr Bank)
swallace@mansfield.gov.uk

Ward, Sonya (LAB - Bull Farm & Pleasley Hill)
sward@mansfield.gov.uk

Wetton, Andy (LAB - Meden)
jwetton@mansfield.gov.uk

Wright, Lesley (LAB - Peafields)
lwright@mansfield.gov.uk

Wright, Martin (IND - Holly)
mwright@mansfield.gov.uk

POLITICAL COMPOSITION

LAB: 19, IND: 16, UKIP: 2

Medway U

Medway Council, Civic Headquarters, Gun Wharf, Dock Road, Chatham ME4 4TR
☎ 01634 306000 🖷 01634 332756 ✉ info@medway.gov.uk
🖳 www.medway.gov.uk

FACTS AND FIGURES

Parliamentary Constituencies: Chatham and Aylesford, Gillingham and Rainham, Rochester and Strood
EU Constituencies: South East
Election Frequency: Elections are of whole council

PRINCIPAL OFFICERS

Chief Executive: Mr Neil Davies, Chief Executive, Civic Headquarters, Gun Wharf, Dock Road, Chatham ME4 4TR
☎ 01634 332705 ✉ neil.davies@medway.gov.uk

Senior Management: Mr Richard Hicks , Acting Director - Regeneration, Community & Culture, Civic Headquarters, Gun Wharf, Dock Road, Chatham ME4 4TR ☎ 01634 338108
🖷 01634 332743 ✉ richard.hicks@medway.gov.uk

Senior Management: Ms Barbara Peacock , Director - Children & Adults, Civic Headquarters, Gun Wharf, Dock Road, Chatham ME4 4TR ☎ 01634 331011 🖷 01634 332848
✉ barbara.peacock@medway.gov.uk

Access Officer / Social Services (Disability): Ms Jackie Challis, Joint Physical Disability Manager, Civic Headquarters, Gun Wharf, Dock Road, Chatham ME4 4TR ☎ 01634 331272
✉ jackie.challis@medway.gov.uk

Access Officer / Social Services (Disability): Ms Amanda Dean, Joint Physical Disability Manager, Civic Headquarters, Gun Wharf, Dock Road, Chatham ME4 4TR ☎ 01634 331272
✉ amanda.dean@medway.gov.uk

Architect, Building / Property Services: Mr Rob Dennis , Head - Property & Capital Projects, Civic Headquarters, Gun Wharf, Dock Road, Chatham ME4 4TR ☎ 01634 332880 ✉ rob.dennis@medway.gov.uk

Building Control: Mr Tony Van Veghel, South Thames Gateway Building Control Partnership Director, Compass Centre, Chatham Maritime, Chatham ME4 4YH ☎ 01634 331552 🖷 01634 331624 ✉ tony.vanveghel@medway.gov.uk

Children / Youth Services: Ms Barbara Peacock , Director - Children & Adults, Civic Headquarters, Gun Wharf, Dock Road, Chatham ME4 4TR ☎ 01634 331011 🖷 01634 332848 ✉ barbara.peacock@medway.gov.uk

Civil Registration: Mr Paul Edwards, Bereavement & Registration Services Manager, Medway Crematorium, Upper Robin Hood Lane, Blue Bell Hill, Chatham ME5 9QU ☎ 01634 331352 ✉ paul.edwards@medway.gov.uk

PR / Communications: Ms Charlotte Edwards , Marketing Communications Manager, Civic Headquarters, Gun Wharf, Dock Road, Chatham ME4 4TR ☎ 01634 323449 ✉ charlotte.edwards@medway.gov.uk

PR / Communications: Ms Stephanie Goad, Assistant Director - Communications, Performance & Partnerships, Civic Headquarters, Gun Wharf, Dock Road, Chatham ME4 4TR ☎ 01634 332737 🖷 01634 332743 ✉ stephanie.goad@medway.gov.uk

Community Safety: Mr Tim England , Head - Safer Communities, Civic Headquarters, Gun Wharf, Dock Road, Chatham ME4 4TR ☎ 01634 333534 🖷 01634 333117 ✉ tim.england@medway.gov.uk

Computer Management: Ms Moira Bragg, Head - ICT, Civic Headquarters, Gun Wharf, Dock Road, Chatham ME4 4TR ☎ 01634 332087 🖷 01634 332881 ✉ moira.bragg@medway.gov.uk

Consumer Protection and Trading Standards: Mr Andy McGrath , Assistant Director, Civic Headquarters, Gun Wharf, Dock Road, Chatham ME4 4TR ☎ 01634 331376 🖷 01634 331613 ✉ andy.mcgrath@medway.gov.uk

Corporate Services: Mr Perry Holmes , Assistant Director, Civic Headquarters, Gun Wharf, Dock Road, Chatham ME4 4TR ☎ 01634 332133 ✉ perry.holmes@medway.gov.uk

Customer Service: Mr Martin Garlick , Head - Customer Contact, Civic Headquarters, Gun Wharf, Dock Road, Chatham ME4 4TR ☎ 01634 338771 ✉ martin.garlick@medway.gov.uk

Economic Development: Ms Frances Toomey , Head - Regeneration & Economic Development, Civic Headquarters, Gun Wharf, Dock Road, Chatham ME4 4TR ☎ 01634 338119 ✉ frances.toomey@medway.gov.uk

Education: Ms Pauline Maddison , Acting Assistant Director, Civic Headquarters, Gun Wharf, Dock Road, Chatham ME4 4TR ☎ 01634 331013 ✉ pauline.maddison@medway.gov.uk

E-Government: Ms Moira Bragg, Head - ICT, Civic Headquarters, Gun Wharf, Dock Road, Chatham ME4 4TR ☎ 01634 332087 🖷 01634 332881 ✉ moira.bragg@medway.gov.uk

Electoral Registration: Ms Jane Ringham, Head - Elections & Member Services, Civic Headquarters, Gun Wharf, Dock Road, Chatham ME4 4TR ☎ 01634 332864 🖷 01634 332862 ✉ jane.ringham@medway.gov.uk

Emergency Planning: Ms Angela Wilkins, Emergency Planning Manager, Civic Headquarters, Gun Wharf, Dock Road, Chatham ME4 4TR ☎ 01634 333542 🖷 01634 331720 ✉ angela.wilkins@medway.gov.uk

Energy Management: Mr Rob Dennis , Head - Property & Capital Projects, Civic Headquarters, Gun Wharf, Dock Road, Chatham ME4 4TR ☎ 01634 332880 ✉ rob.dennis@medway.gov.uk

Environmental / Technical Services: Mr Andy McGrath , Assistant Director, Civic Headquarters, Gun Wharf, Dock Road, Chatham ME4 4TR ☎ 01634 331376 🖷 01634 331613 ✉ andy.mcgrath@medway.gov.uk

Environmental Health: Mr Andy McGrath , Assistant Director, Civic Headquarters, Gun Wharf, Dock Road, Chatham ME4 4TR ☎ 01634 331376 🖷 01634 331613 ✉ andy.mcgrath@medway.gov.uk

Estates, Property & Valuation: Mr Rob Dennis , Head - Property & Capital Projects, Civic Headquarters, Gun Wharf, Dock Road, Chatham ME4 4TR ☎ 01634 332880 ✉ rob.dennis@medway.gov.uk

European Liaison: Ms Frances Toomey , Head - Regeneration & Economic Development, Civic Headquarters, Gun Wharf, Dock Road, Chatham ME4 4TR ☎ 01634 338119 ✉ frances.toomey@medway.gov.uk

Events Manager: Mr Carl Madjitey, Head - Festivals, Arts, Theatres & Events, Civic Headquarters, Gun Wharf, Dock Road, Chatham ME4 4TR ☎ 01634 338114 ✉ carl.madjitey@medway.gov.uk

Facilities: Mr Rob Dennis , Head - Property & Capital Projects, Civic Headquarters, Gun Wharf, Dock Road, Chatham ME4 4TR ☎ 01634 332880 ✉ rob.dennis@medway.gov.uk

Finance: Mr Phil Watts , Chief Finance Officer, Civic Headquarters, Gun Wharf, Dock Road, Chatham ME4 4TR ☎ 01634 332220 ✉ phil.watts@medway.gov.uk

Grounds Maintenance: Mr Simon Swift , Head - Greenspaces, Heritage & Libraries, Civic Headquarters, Gun Wharf, Dock Road, Chatham ME4 4TR ☎ 01634 331276 ✉ simon.swift@medway.gov.uk

Health and Safety: Ms Lynette Rispoli, Corporate Health & Safety Manager, Civic Headquarters, Gun Wharf, Dock Road, Chatham ME4 4TR ☎ 01634 333011 ✉ lynette.rispoli@medway.gov.uk

Highways: Mr Phil Moore, Head - Highways, Maintenance & Parking, Civic Centre, Rochester ME2 4AU ☎ 01634 331146 🖷 01634 331759 ✉ phil.moore@medway.gov.uk

Housing: Mr Matthew Gough , Head - Strategic Housing, Civic Headquarters, Gun Wharf, Dock Road, Chatham ME4 4TR ☎ 01634 333177 ✉ matthew.gough@medway.gov.uk

Housing Maintenance: Mr Marc Blowers , Head - Housing Management, Civic Headquarters, Gun Wharf, Dock Road, Chatham ME4 4TR ☎ 01634 334382 ✉ marc.blowers@medway.gov.uk

Leisure and Cultural Services: Mr Richard Hicks , Acting Director - Regeneration, Community & Culture, Civic Headquarters, Gun Wharf, Dock Road, Chatham ME4 4TR ☎ 01634 338108 🖷 01634 332743 ✉ richard.hicks@medway.gov.uk

Licensing: Ms Alison Poulson, Local Land Charges & Licensing Manager, Civic Headquarters, Gun Wharf, Dock Road, Chatham ME4 4TR ☎ 01634 332774 ✉ alison.poulson@medway.gov.uk

Lifelong Learning: Ms Carol Traxler , Head - Adult Education & Community Learning, Medway Adult Learning Service, Eastgate, Rochester ME1 1EW ☎ 01634 338442 ✉ carol.taxler@medway.gov.uk

Lighting: Mr Phil Moore, Head - Highways, Maintenance & Parking, Civic Centre, Rochester ME2 4AU ☎ 01634 331146 🖷 01634 331759 ✉ phil.moore@medway.gov.uk

Member Services: Ms Jane Ringham, Head - Elections & Member Services, Civic Headquarters, Gun Wharf, Dock Road, Chatham ME4 4TR ☎ 01634 332864 🖷 01634 332862 ✉ jane.ringham@medway.gov.uk

Parking: Ms Rubena Hafizi , Parking Manager, Civic Centre, Strood, Rochester ME2 4AU ☎ 01634 331725 🖷 01634 331777 ✉ rubena.hafizi@medway.gov.uk

Partnerships: Ms Stephanie Goad, Assistant Director - Communications, Performance & Partnerships, Civic Headquarters, Gun Wharf, Dock Road, Chatham ME4 4TR ☎ 01634 332737 🖷 01634 332743 ✉ stephanie.goad@medway.gov.uk

Personnel / HR: Ms Tricia Palmer, Assistant Director - Organisational Services, Civic Headquarters, Gun Wharf, Dock Road, Chatham ME4 4TR ☎ 01634 332343 🖷 01634 332858 ✉ tricia.palmer@medway.gov.uk

Planning: Mr Stephen Gaimster, Assistant Director - Housing & Regeneration, Civic Headquarters, Gun Wharf, Dock Road, Chatham ME4 4TR ☎ 01634 331192 🖷 01634 331184 ✉ stephen.gaimster@medway.gov.uk

Planning: Mr Dave Harris, Development Control Manager, Civic Headquarters, Gun Wharf, Dock Road, Chatham ME4 4TR ☎ 01634 331575 🖷 01634 331184 ✉ dave.harris@medway.gov.uk

Procurement: Mr Perry Holmes , Assistant Director, Civic Headquarters, Gun Wharf, Dock Road, Chatham ME4 4TR ☎ 01634 332133 ✉ perry.holmes@medway.gov.uk

Public Libraries: Mr Simon Swift , Head - Greenspaces, Heritage & Libraries, Civic Headquarters, Gun Wharf, Dock Road, Chatham ME4 4TR ☎ 01634 331276 ✉ simon.swift@medway.gov.uk

Recycling & Waste Minimisation: Ms Sarah Dagwell, Head - Waste Services Operational, Civic Centre, Rochester ME2 4AU ☎ 01634 331597 🖷 01634 331720 ✉ sarah.dagwell@medway.gov.uk

Regeneration: Mr Richard Hicks , Acting Director - Regeneration, Community & Culture, Civic Headquarters, Gun Wharf, Dock Road, Chatham ME4 4TR ☎ 01634 338108 🖷 01634 332743 ✉ richard.hicks@medway.gov.uk

Social Services: Mr Ian Sutherland , Deputy Director - Adult Social Care, Civic Headquarters, Gun Wharf, Dock Road, Chatham ME4 4TR ☎ 01634 331212 ✉ ian.sutherland@medway.gov.uk

Social Services (Adult): Mr Ian Sutherland , Deputy Director - Adult Social Care, Civic Headquarters, Gun Wharf, Dock Road, Chatham ME4 4TR ☎ 01634 331212 ✉ ian.sutherland@medway.gov.uk

Social Services (Children): Mr Phil Watson , Assistant Director - Children's Social Care, Civic Headquarters, Gun Wharf, Dock Road, Chatham ME4 4TR ☎ 01634 331215 ✉ phil.watson@medway.gov.uk

Public Health: Ms Alison Barnett , Director - Public Health, Civic Headquarters, Gun Wharf, Dock Road, Chatham ME4 4TR ☎ 01273 336032 ✉ alison.barnett@medway.gov.uk

Staff Training: Mrs Carrie McKenzie , Head of Organisational Charge, Civic Headquarters, Gun Wharf, Dock Road, Chatham ME4 4TR ☎ 01634 332261 ✉ carrie.mckenzie@medway.gov.uk

Street Scene: Mr Andy McGrath , Assistant Director, Civic Headquarters, Gun Wharf, Dock Road, Chatham ME4 4TR ☎ 01634 331376 🖷 01634 331613 ✉ andy.mcgrath@medway.gov.uk

Sustainable Communities: Mr Stephen Gaimster, Assistant Director - Housing & Regeneration, Civic Headquarters, Gun Wharf, Dock Road, Chatham ME4 4TR ☎ 01634 331192 🖷 01634 331184 ✉ stephen.gaimster@medway.gov.uk

Sustainable Development: Mr Stephen Gaimster, Assistant Director - Housing & Regeneration, Civic Headquarters, Gun Wharf, Dock Road, Chatham ME4 4TR ☎ 01634 331192 🖷 01634 331184 ✉ stephen.gaimster@medway.gov.uk

Tourism: Mr Bob Dimond , Head - Sport, Leisure & Tourism, Civic Headquarters, Gun Wharf, Dock Road, Chatham ME4 4TR ☎ 01634 338238 ✉ bob.dimond@medway.gov.uk

Town Centre: Mr Stephen Gaimster, Assistant Director - Housing & Regeneration, Civic Headquarters, Gun Wharf, Dock Road, Chatham ME4 4TR ☎ 01634 331192 🖷 01634 331184 ✉ stephen.gaimster@medway.gov.uk

Traffic Management: Mr Martin Morris , Traffic Management Manager, Civic Headquarters, Gun Wharf, Dock Road, Chatham ME4 4TR ☎ 01634 331148 ✉ martin.morris@medway.gov.uk

Transport: Mr Steve Hewlett, Head - Integrated Transport, Civic Headquarters, Gun Wharf, Dock Road, Chatham ME4 4TR ☎ 01634 331103 🖷 01634 331729 ✉ steve.hewlett@medway.gov.uk

Transport Planner: Mr Steve Hewlett, Head - Integrated Transport, Civic Headquarters, Gun Wharf, Dock Road, Chatham ME4 4TR ☎ 01634 331103 🖷 01634 331729 ✉ steve.hewlett@medway.gov.uk

MEDWAY

Waste Collection and Disposal: Ms Michelle Chambers, Contract Services Manager, Civic Centre, Rochester ME2 4AU ☎ 01634 333008 🖷 01634 331720 michelle.chambers@medway.gov.uk

Waste Collection and Disposal: Ms Sarah Dagwell, Head - Waste Services Operational, Civic Centre, Rochester ME2 4AU ☎ 01634 331597 🖷 01634 331720 sarah.dagwell@medway.gov.uk

Waste Management: Ms Sarah Dagwell, Head - Waste Services Operational, Civic Centre, Rochester ME2 4AU ☎ 01634 331597 🖷 01634 331720 sarah.dagwell@medway.gov.uk

Children's Play Areas: Mr Simon Swift , Head - Greenspaces, Heritage & Libraries, Civic Headquarters, Gun Wharf, Dock Road, Chatham ME4 4TR ☎ 01634 331276 simon.swift@medway.gov.uk

COUNCILLORS

***Mayor* Kemp**, Barry (CON - Rainham Central)
barryjkemp@hotmail.com

***Deputy Mayor* Iles**, Steve (CON - Strood North)
steve.iles@live.co.uk

***Leader of the Council* Jarrett**, Alan (CON - Lordswood and Capstone)
alan.jarrett@medway.gov.uk

***Deputy Leader of the Council* Doe**, Howard (CON - Rainham South)
howard.doe@blueyonder.co.uk

***Group Leader* Freshwater**, Roy (UKIP - Peninsula)
royfreshwater@hotmail.co.uk

***Group Leader* Maple**, Vince (LAB - Chatham Central)
vince.maple@medway.gov.uk

Avey, John (CON - Strood South)
johnavey838@btinternet.com

Bhutia, Tashi (CON - Princes Park)
tashi747@gmail.com

Bowler, Nicholas (LAB - Rochester East)
nickbowler89@btinternet.com

Brake, David (CON - Walderslade)
david.brake@medway.gov.uk

Brown-Reckless, Catriona (UKIP - Strood South)
catriona.reckless@medway.gov.uk

Carr, David (CON - Rainham North)
david-j-carr@hotmail.co.uk

Chambers, Rodney (CON - Hempstead and Wigmore)
rodney.chambers@medway.gov.uk

Chambers, Diane (CON - Hempstead and Wigmore)
diane.chambers@medway.gov.uk

Chishti, Rehman (CON - Rainham Central)
rehman.chishti.mp@parliament.uk

Chitty, Jane (CON - Strood North)
jane.chitty@medway.gov.uk

Clarke, Trevor (CON - Rochester South and Horsted)
trevorclarke@blueyonder.co.uk

Cooper, Pat (IND - Gillingham North)
patecooper@virginmedia.com

Craven, Sam (LAB - Luton and Wayfield)
samcraven2010@hotmail.co.uk

Etheridge, Gary (CON - Strood Rural)
medway48@yahoo.co.uk

Fearn, Matt (CON - Cuxton and Halling)
matt_fearn@hotmail.com

Filmer, Philip (CON - Peninsula)
phil.filmer@medway.gov.uk

Franklin, Michael (CON - Luton and Wayfield)
mikefranklin@blueyonder.co.uk

Gilry, Dorte (LAB - Twydall)
gilry.dorte@gmail.com

Godwin, Paul (LAB - Chatham Central)
paul.godwin@medway.gov.uk

Griffin, Sylvia (CON - Rochester South and Horsted)
sylvia_brian@btinternet.com

Griffiths, Glyn (LAB - Twydall)
glyngriff@blueyonder.co.uk

Gulvi, Adrian (CON - Walderslade)
avhgulvin@btinternet.com

Hall, Phil (CON - Strood North)
phil.hall@medway.gov.uk

Hicks, Peter (CON - Strood Rural)
peterhicks690@yahoo.co.uk

Howard, Anne-Claire (CON - Twydall)
anneclaire4twydall@gmail.com

Johnson, Clive (LAB - Gillingham South)
clive.johnson@medway.gov.uk

Joy, Mark (IND - Strood South)
mpjoystroodsouth@gmail.com

Khan, Naushabah (LAB - Gillingham South)
naushabah.khan@medway.gov.uk

Mackness, Andrew (CON - River)
andrewmackness@live.co.uk

McDonald, Dan (LAB - Gillingham South)
dan.mcdonald@medway.gov.uk

Murray, Teresa (LAB - Rochester East)
teresamurraytm@aol.com

O'Brien, Mike (CON - Rainham Central)
mikeobrien155@blueyonder.co.uk

Opara, Gloria (CON - Princes Park)
gloria.opara@medway.gov.uk

Osborne, Tristan (LAB - Luton and Wayfield)
tris.osborne@gmail.com

Pendergast, Mick (UKIP - Peninsula)
mick.pendergast@medway.gov.uk

Potter, Martin (CON - Rainham North)
mpotter.rainham@gmail.com

Price, Adam (LAB - Gillingham North)
adam.price@medway.gov.uk

Purdy, Wendy (CON - Watling)
Johnpurdy@btinternet.com

Royle, David (CON - Rainham South)
david.royle94@btinernet.com

Saroy, Asha (CON - Watling)
cllrsaroy@outlook.com

Shaw, Julie (LAB - Chatham Central)
shaw9089@btinternet.com

Stamp, Andy (LAB - Gillingham North)
andy.stamp@medway.gov.uk

Tejan, Habib (CON - River)
habibtejan@live.co.uk

Tolhurst, Kelly (CON - Rochester West)
kellytolhurst@hotmail.co.uk

Tranter, Stuart (CON - Rochester West)
stuart-tranter@btconnect.com

Turpin, Rupert (CON - Rochester South and Horsted)
cllrturpin@gmail.com

Wicks, Les (CON - Rainham South)
les.wicks@hotmail.com

Wildey, David (CON - Lordswood and Capstone)
david.wiley@medway.gov.uk

Williams, John (CON - Strood Rural)
johnwilliams@freeavalon.co.uk

POLITICAL COMPOSITION

CON: 36, LAB: 14, UKIP: 3, IND: 2

COMMITTEE CHAIRS

Audit: Mr Barry Kemp

Health & Adult Social Care: Mr Trevor Clarke

Licensing & Safety: Mrs Diane Chambers

Planning: Mrs Diane Chambers

Melton D

Melton Borough Council, Parkside, Station Approach, Burton Street, Melton Mowbray LE13 1GH
☎ 01664 502502 🖷 01664 410283 🖳 www.melton.gov.uk

FACTS AND FIGURES

Parliamentary Constituencies: Rutland and Melton
EU Constituencies: East Midlands
Election Frequency: Elections are of whole council

PRINCIPAL OFFICERS

Chief Executive: Mrs Lynn Aisbett, Chief Executive, Parkside, Station Approach, Burton Street, Melton Mowbray LE13 1GH ☎ 01664 502502 ⌂ laisbett@melton.gov.uk

Senior Management: Mr Keith Aubrey , Strategic Director, Parkside, Station Approach, Burton Street, Melton Mowbray LE13 1GH

Senior Management: Mrs Dawn Garton, Head of Central Services, Parkside, Station Approach, Burton Street, Melton Mowbray LE13 1GH ☎ 01664 502502 ⌂ dgarton@melton.gov.uk

Senior Management: Ms Christine Marshall , Strategic Director, Parkside, Station Approach, Burton Street, Melton Mowbray LE13 1GH ☎ 01664 502502 🖷 01664 410283 ⌂ cmarshall@melton.gov.uk

Senior Management: Mr Harrinder Rai, Head of Communities & Neighbourhoods, Parkside, Station Approach, Burton Street, Melton Mowbray LE13 1GH ☎ 01664 502502 🖷 01664 410283 ⌂ hrai@melton.gov.uk

Senior Management: Mrs Angela Tebbutt, Head of Communications, Parkside, Station Approach, Burton Street, Melton Mowbray LE13 1GH ☎ 01664 502502 🖷 01664 410283 ⌂ atebbutt@melton.gov.uk

Senior Management: Mr Jim Worley, Head of Regulatory Services, Parkside, Station Approach, Burton Street, Melton Mowbray LE13 1GH ☎ 01664 502502 🖷 01664 410283 ⌂ jworley@melton.gov.uk

Architect, Building / Property Services: Mr David Blanchard, Corporate Property Officer, Parkside, Station Approach, Burton Street, Melton Mowbray LE13 1GH ☎ 01664 502502 ⌂ dblanchard@melton.gov.uk

Building Control: Mr Jim Worley, Head of Regulatory Services, Parkside, Station Approach, Burton Street, Melton Mowbray LE13 1GH ☎ 01664 502502 🖷 01664 410283 ⌂ jworley@melton.gov.uk

PR / Communications: Mrs Angela Tebbutt, Head of Communications, Parkside, Station Approach, Burton Street, Melton Mowbray LE13 1GH ☎ 01664 502502 🖷 01664 410283 ⌂ atebbutt@melton.gov.uk

Community Planning: Mr Harrinder Rai, Head of Communities & Neighbourhoods, Parkside, Station Approach, Burton Street, Melton Mowbray LE13 1GH ☎ 01664 502502 🖷 01664 410283 ⌂ hrai@melton.gov.uk

Community Safety: Mr Harrinder Rai, Head of Communities & Neighbourhoods, Parkside, Station Approach, Burton Street, Melton Mowbray LE13 1GH ☎ 01664 502502 🖷 01664 410283 ⌂ hrai@melton.gov.uk

Computer Management: Mr Paul Langham , IT Client Manager, Parkside, Station Approach, Burton Street, Melton Mowbray LE13 1GH ☎ 01455 255995 ⌂ plangham@melton.gov.uk

Contracts: Mr Tony Hall, Head of Welland Procurement, Parkside, Station Approach, Burton Street, Melton Mowbray LE13 1GH ☎ 01664 502502 ⌂ thall@melton.gov.uk

Customer Service: Mrs Angela Tebbutt, Head of Communications, Parkside, Station Approach, Burton Street, Melton Mowbray LE13 1GH ☎ 01664 502502 🖷 01664 410283 ⌂ atebbutt@melton.gov.uk

Economic Development: Mr Harrinder Rai, Head of Communities & Neighbourhoods, Parkside, Station Approach, Burton Street, Melton Mowbray LE13 1GH ☎ 01664 502502 🖷 01664 410283 ⌂ hrai@melton.gov.uk

Electoral Registration: Ms Sally Renwick, Elections Officer, Parkside, Station Approach, Burton Street, Melton Mowbray LE13 1GH ☎ 01664 502502 ⌂ srenwick@melton.gov.uk

Emergency Planning: Mr Jim Worley, Head of Regulatory Services, Parkside, Station Approach, Burton Street, Melton Mowbray LE13 1GH ☎ 01664 502502 🖷 01664 410283 ✉ jworley@melton.gov.uk

Environmental Health: Mrs Victoria Clarke, Environment Protection & Safety Manager, Parkside, Station Approach, Burton Street, Melton Mowbray LE13 1GH ☎ 01664 502502 🖷 01664 410283 ✉ vclarke@melton.gov.uk

Estates, Property & Valuation: Mr David Blanchard, Corporate Property Officer, Parkside, Station Approach, Burton Street, Melton Mowbray LE13 1GH ☎ 01664 502502 ✉ dblanchard@melton.gov.uk

Events Manager: Ms Lisa Hammond, Joint Town Centre Manager, Parkside, Station Approach, Burton Street, Melton Mowbray LE13 1GH ☎ 01664 502502 ✉ lhammond@melton.gov.uk

Facilities: Mr Stephen Richardson , Facilities Manager, Parkside, Station Approach, Burton Street, Melton Mowbray LE13 1GH ☎ 01664 502502 ✉ srichardson@melton.gov.uk

Finance: Mrs Dawn Garton, Head of Central Services, Parkside, Station Approach, Burton Street, Melton Mowbray LE13 1GH ☎ 01664 502502 ✉ dgarton@melton.gov.uk

Grounds Maintenance: Mr Ramon Selvon, Waste & Grounds Maintenance Manager, Parkside, Station Approach, Burton Street, Melton Mowbray LE13 1GH ☎ 01664 502502 ✉ rselvon@melton.gov.uk

Health and Safety: Mr Chris Morris , HR & Health & Safety Officer, Parkside, Station Approach, Burton Street, Melton Mowbray LE13 1GH ☎ 01664 502502 ✉ sburton@melton.gov.uk

Home Energy Conservation: Mrs Victoria Clarke, Environment Protection & Safety Manager, Parkside, Station Approach, Burton Street, Melton Mowbray LE13 1GH ☎ 01664 502502 🖷 01664 410283 ✉ vclarke@melton.gov.uk

Housing: Mr Harrinder Rai, Head of Communities & Neighbourhoods, Parkside, Station Approach, Burton Street, Melton Mowbray LE13 1GH ☎ 01664 502502 🖷 01664 410283 ✉ hrai@melton.gov.uk

Housing Maintenance: Mr Harrinder Rai, Head of Communities & Neighbourhoods, Parkside, Station Approach, Burton Street, Melton Mowbray LE13 1GH ☎ 01664 502502 🖷 01664 410283 ✉ hrai@melton.gov.uk

Legal: Ms Verina Wenham , Solicitor to the Council, Parkside, Station Approach, Burton Street, Melton Mowbray LE13 1GH ☎ 01664 502502 🖷 01664 410283 ✉ vwenham@melton.gov.uk

Leisure and Cultural Services: Mr Ronan Browne, People Manager, Parkside, Station Approach, Burton Street, Melton Mowbray LE13 1GH ☎ 01664 502502 🖷 01664 410283 ✉ rbrowne@melton.gov.uk

Licensing: Mrs E Holdsworth , Licensing Officer, Parkside, Station Approach, Burton Street, Melton Mowbray LE13 1GH ☎ 01664 502502 ✉ eholdsworth@melton.gov.uk

Licensing: Mr Jim Worley, Head of Regulatory Services, Parkside, Station Approach, Burton Street, Melton Mowbray LE13 1GH ☎ 01664 502502 🖷 01664 410283 ✉ jworley@melton.gov.uk

Lottery Funding, Charity and Voluntary: Mr Harrinder Rai, Head of Communities & Neighbourhoods, Parkside, Station Approach, Burton Street, Melton Mowbray LE13 1GH ☎ 01664 502502 🖷 01664 410283 ✉ hrai@melton.gov.uk

Member Services: Mrs Angela Tebbutt, Head of Communications, Parkside, Station Approach, Burton Street, Melton Mowbray LE13 1GH ☎ 01664 502502 🖷 01664 410283 ✉ atebbutt@melton.gov.uk

Parking: Mr David Blanchard, Corporate Property Officer, Parkside, Station Approach, Burton Street, Melton Mowbray LE13 1GH ☎ 01664 502502 ✉ dblanchard@melton.gov.uk

Personnel / HR: Mrs Angela Tebbutt, Head of Communications, Parkside, Station Approach, Burton Street, Melton Mowbray LE13 1GH ☎ 01664 502502 🖷 01664 410283 ✉ atebbutt@melton.gov.uk

Planning: Mr Jim Worley, Head of Regulatory Services, Parkside, Station Approach, Burton Street, Melton Mowbray LE13 1GH ☎ 01664 502502 🖷 01664 410283 ✉ jworley@melton.gov.uk

Procurement: Mr Tony Hall, Head of Welland Procurement, Parkside, Station Approach, Burton Street, Melton Mowbray LE13 1GH ☎ 01664 502502 ✉ thall@melton.gov.uk

Recycling & Waste Minimisation: Ms Amanda Hume , Environmental Services Officer, Parkside, Station Approach, Burton Street, Melton Mowbray LE13 1GH ☎ 01664 502502 🖷 01664 410283 ✉ ahume@melton.gov.uk

Recycling & Waste Minimisation: Mr Ramon Selvon, Waste & Grounds Maintenance Manager, Parkside, Station Approach, Burton Street, Melton Mowbray LE13 1GH ☎ 01664 502502 ✉ rselvon@melton.gov.uk

Regeneration: Mr Harrinder Rai, Head of Communities & Neighbourhoods, Parkside, Station Approach, Burton Street, Melton Mowbray LE13 1GH ☎ 01664 502502 🖷 01664 410283 ✉ hrai@melton.gov.uk

Staff Training: Mrs Sarah-Jane O'Connor, HR & Communications Manager, Parkside, Station Approach, Burton Street, Melton Mowbray LE13 1GH ☎ 01664 502502 🖷 01664 410283 ✉ soconnor@melton.gov.uk

Sustainable Communities: Mr Harrinder Rai, Head of Communities & Neighbourhoods, Parkside, Station Approach, Burton Street, Melton Mowbray LE13 1GH ☎ 01664 502502 🖷 01664 410283 ✉ hrai@melton.gov.uk

Sustainable Development: Mr Harrinder Rai, Head of Communities & Neighbourhoods, Parkside, Station Approach, Burton Street, Melton Mowbray LE13 1GH ☎ 01664 502502 🖷 01664 410283 ✉ hrai@melton.gov.uk

Tourism: Mr Harrinder Rai, Head of Communities & Neighbourhoods, Parkside, Station Approach, Burton Street, Melton Mowbray LE13 1GH ☎ 01664 502502 🖷 01664 410283 ✉ hrai@melton.gov.uk

Town Centre: Ms Shelagh Core , Joint Town Centre Manager, Parkside, Station Approach, Burton Street, Melton Mowbray LE13 1GH ☎ 01664 502502 ✉ score@melton.gov.uk

Town Centre: Ms Lisa Hammond, Joint Town Centre Manager, Parkside, Station Approach, Burton Street, Melton Mowbray LE13 1GH ☎ 01664 502502 ✉ lhammond@melton.gov.uk

Transport: Mr Jim Worley, Head of Regulatory Services, Parkside, Station Approach, Burton Street, Melton Mowbray LE13 1GH ☎ 01664 502502 🖷 01664 410283 ✉ jworley@melton.gov.uk

Waste Collection and Disposal: Mr Jim Worley, Head of Regulatory Services, Parkside, Station Approach, Burton Street, Melton Mowbray LE13 1GH ☎ 01664 502502 🖷 01664 410283 ✉ jworley@melton.gov.uk

Waste Management: Mr Ramon Selvon, Waste & Grounds Maintenance Manager, Parkside, Station Approach, Burton Street, Melton Mowbray LE13 1GH ☎ 01664 502502 ✉ rselvon@melton.gov.uk

Waste Management: Mr Jim Worley, Head of Regulatory Services, Parkside, Station Approach, Burton Street, Melton Mowbray LE13 1GH ☎ 01664 502502 🖷 01664 410283 ✉ jworley@melton.gov.uk

COUNCILLORS

***Mayor* Douglas**, Jeanne (CON - Melton Craven)
jdouglas@melton.gov.uk

***Deputy Mayor* Lumley**, Simon (CON - Melton Newport)
slumley@melton.gov.uk

***Leader of the Council* Rhodes**, Byron (CON - Long Clawson and Stathern)
brhodes@leics.gov.uk

***Deputy Leader of the Council* Posnett**, Pam (CON - Melton Newport)
pposnett@melton.gov.uk

Baguley, Pam (CON - Long Clawson and Stathern)
pbaguley@melton.gov.uk

Bains, Tejpal (CON - Melton Sysonby)
tbains@melton.gov.uk

Beaken, Tracy (CON - Melton Craven)
tbeaken@melton.gov.uk

Botterill, Gerald (CON - Croxton Kerrial)
gbotterill@melton.gov.uk

Chandler, Pru (CON - Bottesford)
pchandler@melton.gov.uk

Culley, Tina (IND - Melton Egerton)
tculley@melton.gov.uk

Cumbers, Pat (CON - Melton Dorian)
pcumbers@melton.gov.uk

de Burle, Ronnie (CON - Ashfordby)
rdeburle@melton.gov.uk

Faulkner, Peter (CON - Melton Egerton)
pfaulkner@melton.gov.uk

Glancy, Margaret (CON - Melton Newport)
mglancy@melton.gov.uk

Graham, Malise (CON - Wymondham)
mgraham@melton.gov.uk

Greenow, Tom (CON - Melton Warwick)
tgreenow@melton.gov.uk

Higgins, Leigh (CON - Somerby)
lhiggins@melton.gov.uk

Holmes, Elaine (IND - Waltham on the Wolds)
eholmes@melton.gov.uk

Hurrell, Julia (CON - Melton Warwick)
jhurrell@melton.gov.uk

Hutchinson, Edward (IND - Frisby on the Wreake)
ehutchinson@melton.gov.uk

Illingworth, John (CON - Melton Sysonby)
jillingworth@melton.gov.uk

Manderson, Val (CON - Melton Sysonby)
vmanderson@melton.gov.uk

Orson, Joe (CON - Old Dalby)
jorson@melton.gov.uk

Pearson, Alan (CON - Melton Dorian)
apearson@melton.gov.uk

Sheldon, Mal (CON - Ashfordby)
msheldon@melton.gov.uk

Simpson, Janet (CON - Gaddesby)
janetsimpson@melton.gov.uk

Wright, David (CON - Bottesford)
dwright@melton.gov.uk

Wyatt, John (CON - Melton Dorian)
jwyatt@melton.gov.uk

POLITICAL COMPOSITION

CON: 25, IND: 3

COMMITTEE CHAIRS

Finance & Admin: Mr Byron Rhodes

Licensing: Mr John Wyatt

Planning: Mr John Illingworth

Mendip D

Mendip District Council, Council Offices, Cannards Grave Road, Shepton Mallet BA4 5BT
☎ 0300 303 8588 ✉ customerservices@mendip.gov.uk
🖳 www.mendip.gov.uk

FACTS AND FIGURES

Parliamentary Constituencies: Wells
EU Constituencies: South West
Election Frequency: Elections are of whole council

PRINCIPAL OFFICERS

Chief Executive: Mr Stuart Brown, Chief Executive, Mendip District Council, Cannards Grave Road, Shepton Mallet BA4 5BT
☎ 01749 648999 ✉ stuart.brown@mendip.gov.uk

MENDIP

Senior Management: Mrs Tracy Aarons, Corporate Manager - Built Environment, Council Offices, Cannards Grave Road, Shepton Mallet BA4 5BT ☎ 0300 303 8588 🖷 01749 344050 ✉ tracy.aarons@mendip.gov.uk

Senior Management: Mrs Chris Atkinson, Corporate Manager - Access to Services, Council Offices, Cannards Grave Road, Shepton Mallet BA4 5BT ☎ 01749 648999 🖷 01749 341542 ✉ chris.atkinson@mendip.gov.uk

Senior Management: Mr Stuart Cave , Corporate Manager - Regulatory Services, Mendip District Council, Cannards Grave Road, Shepton Mallet BA4 5BT ☎ 01749 648999 ✉ stuart.cave@mendip.gov.uk

Senior Management: Mrs Donna Nolan , Corporate Manager - Governance & Public Spaces, Mendip District Council, Cannards Grave Road, Shepton Mallet BA4 5BT ☎ 01749 648999 ✉ donna.nolan@mendip.gov.uk

Building Control: Mrs Tracy Aarons, Corporate Manager - Built Environment, Council Offices, Cannards Grave Road, Shepton Mallet BA4 5BT ☎ 0300 303 8588 🖷 01749 344050 ✉ tracy.aarons@mendip.gov.uk

PR / Communications: Mr Matt Smith , Senior Communications Officer, Council Offices, Cannards Grave Road, Shepton Mallet BA4 5BT ☎ 0300 303 8588 ✉ matthew.smith@mendip.gov.uk

Contracts: Mrs Chris Atkinson, Corporate Manager - Access to Services, Council Offices, Cannards Grave Road, Shepton Mallet BA4 5BT ☎ 01749 648999 🖷 01749 341542 ✉ chris.atkinson@mendip.gov.uk

Corporate Services: Mrs Chris Atkinson, Corporate Manager - Access to Services, Council Offices, Cannards Grave Road, Shepton Mallet BA4 5BT ☎ 01749 648999 🖷 01749 341542 ✉ chris.atkinson@mendip.gov.uk

Customer Service: Mrs Chris Atkinson, Corporate Manager - Access to Services, Council Offices, Cannards Grave Road, Shepton Mallet BA4 5BT ☎ 01749 648999 🖷 01749 341542 ✉ chris.atkinson@mendip.gov.uk

Economic Development: Mr Stuart Cave , Corporate Manager - Regulatory Services, Mendip District Council, Cannards Grave Road, Shepton Mallet BA4 5BT ☎ 01749 648999 ✉ stuart.cave@mendip.gov.uk

Electoral Registration: Mr Steve Lake , Electoral Services Manager, Mendip District Council, Cannards Grave Road, Shepton Mallet BA4 5BT ☎ 01749 648999 ✉ steven.lake@capita.co.uk

Environmental Health: Mrs Claire Malcolmson , Compliance Team Manager, Mendip District Council, Cannards Grave Road, Shepton Mallet BA4 5BT ☎ 01749 648999 ✉ claire.malcolmson@mendip.gov.uk

Finance: Mr Paul Deal , Section 151 Officer, Council Offices, Cannards Grave Road, Shepton Mallet BA4 5BT ☎ 01749 648999 ✉ paul.deal@mendip.gov.uk

Health and Safety: Mr Stuart Finney , Operational Assets Team Manager, Council Offices, Cannards Grave Road, Shepton Mallet BA4 5BT ☎ 01749 648999 ✉ stuart.finney@mendip.gov.uk

Housing: Mrs Tracy Aarons, Corporate Manager - Built Environment, Council Offices, Cannards Grave Road, Shepton Mallet BA4 5BT ☎ 0300 303 8588 🖷 01749 344050 ✉ tracy.aarons@mendip.gov.uk

Legal: Mrs Donna Nolan , Corporate Manager - Governance & Public Spaces, Mendip District Council, Cannards Grave Road, Shepton Mallet BA4 5BT ☎ 01749 648999 ✉ donna.nolan@mendip.gov.uk

Licensing: Mr Jason Kirkwood, Licensing Manager, Council Offices, Cannards Grave Road, Shepton Mallet BA4 5BT ☎ 01749 648999 🖷 01749 344050 ✉ jason.kirkwood@mendip.gov.uk

Member Services: Mrs Claire Dicken, Member Support Officer, Council Offices, Cannards Grave Road, Shepton Mallet BA4 5BT ☎ 01749 648999 🖷 01749 341542 ✉ claire.dicken@mendip.gov.uk

Personnel / HR: Mr Rob North , HR Manager, Council Offices, Cannards Grave Road, Shepton Mallet BA4 5BT ☎ 01749 648999 ✉ rob.north@mendip.gov.uk

Planning: Mrs Tracy Aarons, Corporate Manager - Built Environment, Council Offices, Cannards Grave Road, Shepton Mallet BA4 5BT ☎ 0300 303 8588 🖷 01749 344050 ✉ tracy.aarons@mendip.gov.uk

Procurement: Mr Geoff Thompson , Corporate Services Team Manager, Council Offices, Cannards Grave Road, Shepton Mallet BA4 5BT ☎ 01749 648999 ✉ geoff.thompson@mendip.gov.uk

Staff Training: Ms Fiona Fowler , Personnel Officer, Council Offices, Cannards Grave Road, Shepton Mallet BA4 5BT ☎ 0300 303 8588 🖷 01749 344050 ✉ fiona.fowler@mendip.gov.uk

COUNCILLORS

***Chair* Marsh**, Jeannette (CON - Shepton East) cllr.marsh@mendip.gov.uk

***Vice-Chair* Drewe**, Edward (CON - Ammerdown) Cllr.Drewe@mendip.gov.uk

***Leader of the Council* Siggs**, Harvey (CON - Wells St Cuthberts) cllr.siggs@mendip.gov.uk

***Deputy Leader of the Council* Killen**, Tom (CON - Chewton Mendip and Ston Easton) cllr.killen@mendip.gov.uk

***Group Leader* Sprawson-White**, Helen (LD - Frome Oakfield) Cllr.Sprawson-White@mendip.gov.uk

Beale, Joanna (CON - Frome Berkley Down)

Beha, Bryan (LD - Street South) Cllr.Beha@mendip.gov.uk

Berry, Eve (CON - Frome Berkley Down)

Boyden, Adam (LD - Frome College) Cllr.Boyden@mendip.gov.uk

Bradshaw, Peter (CON - Creech)
Cllr.Bradshaw@mendip.gov.uk

Brunsdon, John (CON - Glastonbury St Edmund's)
cllr.brunsdon@mendip.gov.uk

Carter, Rachel (CON - Ashwick, Chilcompton and Stratton Ward)
cllr.rcarter@mendip.gov.uk

Carter, John (CON - Street North)
Cllr.Carter@mendip.gov.uk

Coles, John (CON - Glastonbury St John's)
cllr.coles@mendip.gov.uk

Collins, Shane (GRN - Frome Keyford)

Cottle, Nick (LD - Glastonbury St Edmund's)
Cllr.Cottle@mendip.gov.uk

Davies, Simon (CON - Shepton West)

Falle, Stina (GRN - Frome Market)

Greenhalgh, John (CON - The Pennards and Ditcheat)

Ham, Philip (CON - Coleford and Holcombe)
cllr.ham@mendip.gov.uk

Harris, Des (GRN - Frome Market)

Height, Bente (CON - Shepton East)
Cllr.Height@mendip.gov.uk

Henderson, Steve (CON - Glastonbury St Benedict's)

Hewitt-Cooper, Nigel (CON - Croscombe and Pilton)
cllr.hewitt-cooper@mendip.gov.uk

Hooton, Damon (LD - Frome Park)
cllr.hooton@mendip.gov.uk

Horsfall, Alvin (LD - Frome Keyford)
cllr.horsfall@mendip.gov.uk

Hudson, Claire (LD - Frome Park)
cllr.hudson@mendip.gov.uk

Hughes, Lloyd (IND - Street South)
cllr.hughes@mendip.gov.uk

Mackenzie, Roy (LD - Wells St Thomas)

Mockford, Clive (CON - Beckington and Selwood)

Napper, Terry (CON - Street West)
Cllr.Napper@mendip.gov.uk

Noel, Graham (CON - Moor)
Cllr.Noel@mendip.gov.uk

North, John (CON - Wells Central)
Cllr.North@mendip.gov.uk

Oliver, Linda (CON - Rode and Norton St Phillip)
cllr.loliver@mendip.gov.uk

Osman, John (CON - Wells St Cuthburts)
Cllr.Osman@mendip.gov.uk

Parham, John (CON - Shepton West)
cllr.parham@mendip.gov.uk

Pullin, Mike (CON - St Cuthbert Out North)

Rice, Timothy (CON - Street North)

Rideout, Mike (CON - Frome College)

Sen, Adam (LD - Street North)

Skidmore, Dick (CON - No Ward)

Taylor, Nigel (CON - Wookey and St Cuthbert Out West)
Cllr.Taylor@mendip.gov.uk

Townsend, Alan (CON - Coleford and Holcombe)

Unwin, Daniel (LD - Wells St Thomas')
cllr.unwin@mendip.gov.uk

van Dyk, David (CON - Cranmore, Doulting and Nunney)

Woollcombe-Adams, Nigel (CON - Butleigh and Baltonsborough)
Cllr.Woollcombe-Adams@mendip.gov.uk

Wyke, Ros (LD - Rodney and Westbury)

POLITICAL COMPOSITION

CON: 32, LD: 11, GRN: 3, IND: 1

COMMITTEE CHAIRS

Audit: Mr John North

Licensing: Mr Peter Bradshaw

Planning: Mr Nigel Hewitt-Cooper

Merthyr Tydfil W

Merthyr Tydfil County Borough Council, Civic Centre, Castle Street, Merthyr Tydfil CF47 8AN
☎ 01685 725000 🖷 01685 722146 ✉ customer.care@merthyr.gov.uk
💻 www.merthyr.gov.uk

FACTS AND FIGURES

Parliamentary Constituencies: Merthyr Tydfil and Rhymney
EU Constituencies: Wales
Election Frequency: Elections are of whole council

PRINCIPAL OFFICERS

Chief Executive: Mr Gareth Chapman, Chief Executive, Civic Centre, Castle Street, Merthyr Tydfil CF47 8AN ☎ 01685 725208 ✉ gareth.chapman@merthyr.gov.uk

Assistant Chief Executive: Mr Ellis Cooper, Corporate Director, Civic Centre, Castle Street, Merthyr Tydfil CF47 8AN ☎ 01685 726295 ✉ ellis.cooper@merthyr.gov.uk

Senior Management: Miss Lorraine Buck , Corporate Director, Civic Centre, Castle Street, Merthyr Tydfil CF47 8AN ☎ 01685 724621 ✉ lorraine.buck@merthyr.gov.uk

Senior Management: Mr Ellis Cooper, Corporate Director, Civic Centre, Castle Street, Merthyr Tydfil CF47 8AN ☎ 01685 726295 ✉ ellis.cooper@merthyr.gov.uk

Access Officer / Social Services (Disability): Ms Lisa Emerson , Asset Manager, Ty Keir Hardie, Riverside Court, Avenue de Clichy, Merthyr Tydfil CF47 8XD ☎ 01685 725000 ✉ lisa.emerson@merthyr.gov.uk

Architect, Building / Property Services: Ms Cheryllee Evans, Head of Property Services & Estates, Unit 5, Triangle Business Park, Pentrebach, Merthyr Tydfil CF48 4TQ ☎ 01685 725290 ✉ cheryllee.evans@merthyr.gov.uk

MERTHYR TYDFIL

Building Control: Mr Ken Bateman, Group Leader - Building Control, Unit 5, Triangle Business Park, Pentrebach, Merthyr Tydfil CF4 4TQ ☎ 01685 726257 🖷 01685 382698 🖰 ken.bateman@merthyr.gov.uk

Catering Services: Ms Edwina Pickering , Acting Team Leader - Catering Service, Unit 5, Triangle Business Park, Pentrebach, Merthyr Tydfil CF48 4TQ ☎ 01685 725000 🖰 edwina.pickering@merthyr.gov.uk

Children / Youth Services: Mr Ian Benbow , Head - Adult & Family Social Regeneration, Civic Centre, Castle Street, Merthyr Tydfil CF47 8AN ☎ 01685 724602 🖰 ian.benbow@merthyr.gov.uk

Children / Youth Services: Mr Chris Hole , Head - Youth Service, Civic Centre, Castle Street, Merthyr Tydfil CF47 8AN ☎ 01685 725000 🖷 01685 721795 🖰 chris.hole@merthyr.gov.uk

Civil Registration: Mrs Dianne Green, Superintendent Registrar, Register Office, Ty Penderyn, 26 High Street, Merthyr Tydfil CF47 8DP ☎ 01685 725000 🖰 dianne.green@merthyr.gov.uk

PR / Communications: Mrs Ceri Dinham , Team Leader - Corporate Communications, Civic Centre, Castle Street, Merthyr Tydfil CF47 8AN ☎ 01685 725483 🖰 corporate.communications@merthyr.gov.uk

Community Planning: Ms Judith Jones , Head of Planning, Unit 5, Triangle Business Park, Pentrebach, Merthyr Tydfil CF48 4TQ ☎ 01685 725000 🖰 judith.jones@merthyr.gov.uk

Community Safety: Ms Judith Jones , Head of Planning, Unit 5, Triangle Business Park, Pentrebach, Merthyr Tydfil CF48 4TQ ☎ 01685 725000 🖰 judith.jones@merthyr.gov.uk

Computer Management: Mr Richard Evans , ICT Manager, Civic Centre, Castle Street, Merthyr Tydfil CF47 8AN ☎ 01685 725000 🖰 richard.evans@merthyr.gov.uk

Consumer Protection and Trading Standards: Mr Paul Lewis, Trading Standards Manager, Civic Centre, Castle Street, Merthyr Tydfil CF47 8AN ☎ 01685 725000 🖰 paul.lewis@merthyr.gov.uk

Consumer Protection and Trading Standards: Mr Steve Peters, Head of Public Protection, Civic Centre, Castle Street, Merthyr Tydfil CF47 8AN ☎ 01685 725030 🖷 01685 374201 🖰 steve.peters@merthyr.gov.uk

Contracts: Mr Ellis Cooper, Corporate Director, Civic Centre, Castle Street, Merthyr Tydfil CF47 8AN ☎ 01685 726295 🖰 ellis.cooper@merthyr.gov.uk

Contracts: Mr Paul Davies , Procurement & Efficiency Officer, Unit 5, Triangle Business Park, Pentrebach, Merthyr Tydfil CF48 4TQ ☎ 01685 724904 🖰 paul.davies@merthyr.gov.uk

Corporate Services: Mr Mark Thomas , Head of Corporate Services, Civic Centre, Castle Street, Merthyr Tydfil CF47 8AN ☎ 01685 725000 🖰 mark.thomas@merthyr.gov.uk

Customer Service: Mr Gregg Edwards , Customer & Corporate Support Manager, Civic Centre, Castle Street, Merthyr Tydfil CF47 8AN ☎ 01685 725000 🖰 gregg.edwards@merthyr.gov.uk

Direct Labour: Mrs Cherylee Evans , Chief Officer - Neighbourhood Services, Civic Centre, Castle Street, Merthyr Tydfil CF47 8AN ☎ 01685 725000 🖰 cherylee.evans@merthyr.gov.uk

Economic Development: Mr Chris Long , Business Support & Tourism Manager, Unit 5, Triangle Business Park, Pentrebach, Merthyr Tydfil CF48 4TQ ☎ 01685 725079 🖷 01685 723751 🖰 chris.long@merthyr.gov.uk

Economic Development: Mr Alyn Owen, Chief Officer - Regeneration, Unit 5, Triangle Business Park, Pentrebach, Merthyr Tydfil CF48 4QT ☎ 01625 725303 🖷 01685 723751 🖰 alyn.owen@merthyr.gov.uk

Education: Mrs Dorothy Haines , Chief Officer - Learning, Civic Centre, Castle Street, Merthyr Tydfil CF47 8AN ☎ 01685 724621 🖰 dorothy.haines@merthyr.gov.uk

E-Government: Mr Ellis Cooper, Corporate Director, Civic Centre, Castle Street, Merthyr Tydfil CF47 8AN ☎ 01685 726295 🖰 ellis.cooper@merthyr.gov.uk

Electoral Registration: Ms Ann Taylor, Democratic Services Manager, Civic Centre, Castle Street, Merthyr Tydfil CF47 8AN ☎ 01685 725202 🖷 01685 374397 🖰 ann.taylor@merthyr.gov.uk

Emergency Planning: Mr Robert Gough, Emergency Planning / Local Resilience Unit Manager, Unit 5, Triangle Business Park, Pentrebach, Merthyr Tydfil CF48 4TQ ☎ 01685 725162 🖷 01685 387740 🖰 robert.gough@merthyr.gov.uk

Energy Management: Mr James Edwards, Energy Officer, Unit 5, Triangle Business Park, Pentrebach, Merthyr Tydfil CF48 4TQ ☎ 01685 726208 🖷 01685 383168 🖰 james.edwards@merthyr.gov.uk

Energy Management: Mrs Cherylee Evans , Chief Officer - Neighbourhood Services, Civic Centre, Castle Street, Merthyr Tydfil CF47 8AN ☎ 01685 725000 🖰 cherylee.evans@merthyr.gov.uk

Environmental / Technical Services: Mrs Cherylee Evans , Chief Officer - Neighbourhood Services, Civic Centre, Castle Street, Merthyr Tydfil CF47 8AN ☎ 01685 725000 🖰 cherylee.evans@merthyr.gov.uk

Environmental Health: Mr Steve Peters, Head of Public Protection, Civic Centre, Castle Street, Merthyr Tydfil CF47 8AN ☎ 01685 725030 🖷 01685 374201 🖰 steve.peters@merthyr.gov.uk

Estates, Property & Valuation: Ms Lisa Emerson , Asset Manager, Unit 5, Triangle Business Park, Pentrebach, Merthyr Tydfil CF48 4TQ ☎ 01685 725000 🖰 lisa.emerson@merthyr.gov.uk

European Liaison: Mr Alyn Owen, Chief Officer - Regeneration, Unit 5, Triangle Business Park, Pentrebach, Merthyr Tydfil CF48 4QT ☎ 01625 725303 🖷 01685 723751 🖰 alyn.owen@merthyr.gov.uk

Finance: Mr Steve Jones , Head of Finance, Civic Centre, Castle Street, Merthyr Tydfil CF47 8AN ☎ 01685 725000 ✉ steve.jones@merthyr.gov.uk

Fleet Management: Mr Paul Davies, Fleet Manager, Unit 20, Merthyr Industrial Estate, Pentrebach, Merthyr Tydfil CF48 4DR ☎ 01685 725000 🖷 01685 387982 ✉ paul.davies@merthyr.gov.uk

Grounds Maintenance: Mrs Cherylee Evans , Chief Officer - Neighbourhood Services, Civic Centre, Castle Street, Merthyr Tydfil CF47 8AN ☎ 01685 725000 ✉ cherylee.evans@merthyr.gov.uk

Health and Safety: Mr Alyn Dinham, Occupational Health & Safety Officer, Civic Centre, Castle Street, Merthyr Tydfil CF47 8AN ☎ 01685 724677 🖷 01685 725055 ✉ alyn.dinham@merthyr.gov.uk

Highways: Mr Jeremy Morgan , Head - Engineering, Unit 20, Merthyr Industrial Park, Pentrebach, Merthyr Tydfil CF48 4DR ☎ 01685 726253 ✉ jeremy.morgan@merthyr.gov.uk

Housing: Mr Steve Peters, Head of Public Protection, Civic Centre, Castle Street, Merthyr Tydfil CF47 8AN ☎ 01685 725030 🖷 01685 374201 ✉ steve.peters@merthyr.gov.uk

Legal: Mrs Carys Kennedy, Head - Legal Services, Civic Centre, Castle Street, Merthyr Tydfil CF47 8AN ☎ 01685 725454 🖷 01685 725060 ✉ carys.kennedy@merthyr.gov.uk

Leisure and Cultural Services: Mr Richard Marsh , Manager - Leisure, Culture & Environment, Civic Centre, Castle Street, Merthyr Tydfil CF47 8AN ☎ 01685 725273 ✉ richard.marsh@merthyr.gov.uk

Licensing: Mr Paul Lewis , Trading Standards Manager, Civic Centre, Castle Street, Merthyr Tydfil CF47 8AN ☎ 01685 725000 ✉ paul.lewis@merthyr.gov.uk

Lifelong Learning: Mrs Dorothy Haines , Chief Officer - Learning, Civic Centre, Castle Street, Merthyr Tydfil CF47 8AN ☎ 01685 724621 ✉ dorothy.haines@merthyr.gov.uk

Lighting: Mr Jeremy Morgan , Head - Engineering, Unit 20, Merthyr Industrial Estate, Pentrebach, Merthyr Tydfil CF48 4DR ☎ 01685 726253 ✉ jeremy.morgan@merthyr.gov.uk

Member Services: Ms Ann Taylor, Democratic Services Manager, Civic Centre, Castle Street, Merthyr Tydfil CF47 8AN ☎ 01685 725202 🖷 01685 374397 ✉ ann.taylor@merthyr.gov.uk

Parking: Mr Gregg Edwards , Customer & Corporate Support Manager, Civic Centre, Castle Street, Merthyr Tydfil CF47 8AN ☎ 01685 725000 ✉ gregg.edwards@merthyr.gov.uk

Partnerships: Mr Mark Thomas , Head of Corporate Services, Civic Centre, Castle Street, Merthyr Tydfil CF47 8AN ☎ 01685 725000 ✉ mark.thomas@merthyr.gov.uk

Personnel / HR: Mr David Jones , Payroll Officer, Unit 5, Triangle Business Park, Pentrebach, Merthyr Tydfil CF48 4TQ ☎ 01685 725325 ✉ david.jones@merthyr.gov.uk

Personnel / HR: Ms Lisa Jones , Head of HR, Civic Centre, Castle Street, Merthyr Tydfil CF47 8AN ☎ 01685 725000 ✉ lisa.jones@merthyr.gov.uk

Planning: Ms Judith Jones , Head of Planning, Unit 5, Triangle Business Park, Pentrebach, Merthyr Tydfil CF48 4TQ ☎ 01685 725000 ✉ judith.jones@merthyr.gov.uk

Procurement: Mr Paul Davies , Procurement & Efficiency Officer, Unit 5, Triangle Business Park, Pentrebach, Merthyr Tydfil CF48 4TQ ☎ 01685 724904 ✉ paul.davies@merthyr.gov.uk

Public Libraries: Ms Sian Antony , Libraries Manager, Central Library, High Street, Merthyr Tydfil CF47 8AF ☎ 01685 353480 ✉ sian.antony@merthyr.gov.uk

Public Libraries: Ms Jane Selwood , Libraries Manager, Central Library, High Street, Merthyr Tydfil CF47 8AF ☎ 01685 353480 ✉ jane.selwood@merthyr.gov.uk

Recycling & Waste Minimisation: Ms Valerie Steel, Waste Services Officer, Unit 4, Pentrebach Industrial Park, Pentrebach, Merthyr Tydfil CF48 4DR ☎ 01685 725478 🖷 01685 725024 ✉ val.steel@merthyr.gov.uk

Regeneration: Mr Alyn Owen, Chief Officer - Regeneration, Unit 5, Triangle Business Park, Pentrebach, Merthyr Tydfil CF48 4QT ☎ 01625 725303 🖷 01685 723751 ✉ alyn.owen@merthyr.gov.uk

Road Safety: Ms Lisa Clement-Williams , Road Safety Officer, Unit 20, Merthyr Industrial Estate, Pentrebach, Merthyr Tydfil CF48 4DR ☎ 01685 726286 ✉ lisa.clement-williams@merthyr.gov.uk

Social Services (Adult): Mr Mark Anderton , Head of Adult Social Services, Unit 20, Merthyr Industrial Estate, Pentrebach, Merthyr Tydfil CF48 4DR ☎ 01685 725000 ✉ mark.anderton@merthyr.gov.uk

Social Services (Children): Mrs Annabel Lloyd , Head of Children's Services, Unit 20, Merthyr Industrial Estate, Pentrebach, Merthyr Tydfil CF48 4DR ☎ 01685 725000 ✉ annabel.lloyd@merthyr.gov.uk

Town Centre: Mrs Rhian Prosser, Town Centre Manager, Unit 5, Triangle Business Park, Pentrebach, Merthyr Tydfil CF48 4TQ ☎ 01685 725106 ✉ rhian.prosser@merthyr.gov.uk

Traffic Management: Mr Martin Stark, Traffic Management Engineer, Unit 20, Merthyr Industrial Park, Pentrebach, Merthyr Tydfil CF48 4DR ☎ 01685 726287 🖷 01685 387982 ✉ martin.stark@merthyr.gov.uk

Transport: Mr Martin Stark, Traffic Management Engineer, Unit 20, Merthyr Industrial Park, Pentrebach, Merthyr Tydfil CF48 4DR ☎ 01685 726287 🖷 01685 387982 ✉ martin.stark@merthyr.gov.uk

COUNCILLORS

***Mayor* Isaac**, David (LAB - Penydarren)
david.isaac@merthyr.gov.uk

***Deputy Mayor* Davies**, Margaret (LAB - Cyfarthfa)
margaret.davies@merthyr.gov.uk

MERTHYR TYDFIL

***Leader of the Council* Toomey**, Brendan (LAB - Park)
brendan.toomey@merthyr.gov.uk

***Deputy Leader of the Council* Williams**, Phil (LAB - Dowlais)
phil.williams@merthyr.gov.uk

***Group Leader* Thomas**, Richard (IND - Treharris)
richard.thomas@merthyr.gov.uk

Barrett, Howard (IND - Vaynor)
howard.barrett@merthyr.gov.uk

Barry, Chris (LAB - Park)
chris.barry@merthyr.gov.uk

Braithwaite, Rhonda (LAB - Gurnos)
rhonda.braithwaite@merthyr.gov.uk

Brown, Paul (IND - Cyfarthfa)
paul.brown@merthyr.gov.uk

Carter, Brent (LAB - Plymouth)
brent.carter@merthyr.gov.uk

Chaplin, Tony (LAB - Cyfarthfa)
tony.chaplin@merthyr.gov.uk

Davies, David (LAB - Town)
david.davies3@merthyr.gov.uk

Galsworthy, Ernie (LAB - Treharris)
ernie.galsworthy@merthyr.gov.uk

Jones, Harvey (LAB - Plymouth)
harvey.jones@merthyr.gov.uk

Jones, Allan (IND - Penydarren)
allan.jones@merthyr.gov.uk

Jones, David (LAB - Town)
david.jones2@merthyr.gov.uk

Jones, Clive (LAB - Park)
clive.jones@merthyr.gov.uk

Jones, Gareth (IND - Bedlinog)
gareth.jones1@merthyr.gov.uk

Lewis, Gareth (LAB - Plymouth)
gareth.lewis@merthyr.gov.uk

Lewis, Tom (LAB - Dowlais)
tom.lewis@merthyr.gov.uk

Mansbridge, Brian (LAB - Merthyr Vale)
brian.mansbridge@merthyr.gov.uk

Matthews, Linda (LAB - Town)
linda.matthews@merthyr.gov.uk

McCarthy, John (LAB - Penydarren)
john.mccarthy@merthyr.gov.uk

Moran, Kate (LAB - Treharris)
kate.moran@merthyr.gov.uk

Mytton, Lisa (IND - Vaynor)
lisa.mytton@merthyr.gov.uk

O'Neill, Mike (LAB - Gurnos)
mike.o'neill@merthyr.gov.uk

Roberts, Darren (LAB - Merthyr Vale)
darren.roberts@merthyr.gov.uk

Slater, Sian (LAB - Town)
sian.slater@hotmail.com

Smart, Leighton (IND - Bedlinog)
leighton.smart@merthyr.gov.uk

Smith, Bill (LAB - Gurnos)
bill.smith@merthyr.gov.uk

Thomas, Raymond (LAB - Dowlais)
ray.thomas@merthyr.gov.uk

Tovey, Clive (IND - Gurnos)
clive.tovey@merthyr.gov.uk

Williams, Simon (LAB - Dowlais)
simon.williams@merthyr.gov.uk

POLITICAL COMPOSITION

LAB: 25, IND: 8

COMMITTEE CHAIRS

Audit: Mr Richard Thomas

Licensing: Mr Clive Jones

Merton L

London Borough of Merton, Merton Civic Centre, London Road, Morden SM4 5DX
☎ 020 8274 4901 🖷 020 8545 0446 ✉ communications@merton.gov.uk
🖳 www.merton.gov.uk

FACTS AND FIGURES

Parliamentary Constituencies: Mitcham and Morden, Wimbledon
EU Constituencies: London
Election Frequency: Elections are of whole council

PRINCIPAL OFFICERS

Chief Executive: Mr Ged Curran, Chief Executive, Merton Civic Centre, London Road, Morden SM4 5DX ☎ 020 8545 3332 ✉ ged.curran@merton.gov.uk

Senior Management: Dr Kay Eilbert , Director - Public Health, Merton Civic Centre, London Road, Morden SM4 5DX ☎ 020 8545 4836 ✉ kay.eilbert@merton.gov.uk

Senior Management: Ms Caroline Holland, Director - Corporate Services, Merton Civic Centre, London Road, Morden SM4 5DX ☎ 020 8545 3450 🖷 020 8543 3952 ✉ caroline.holland@merton.gov.uk

Senior Management: Mr Chris Lee , Director - Environment & Regeneration, Merton Civic Centre, London Road, Morden SM4 5DX ☎ 020 8545 3050 🖷 020 8545 4105 ✉ chris.lee@merton.gov.uk

Senior Management: Ms Yvette Stanley , Director - Children, Schools & Families, Merton Civic Centre, London Road, Morden SM4 5DX ☎ 020 8545 3251 🖷 020 8545 3443 ✉ yvette.stanley@merton.gov.uk

Senior Management: Mr Simon Williams , Director - Community & Housing, Merton Civic Centre, London Road, Morden SM4 5DX ☎ 020 8545 3680 ✉ simon.williams@merton.gov.uk

Architect, Building / Property Services: Mr Howard Joy, Property Management & Review Manager, Merton Civic Centre, London Road, Morden SM4 5DX ☎ 020 8545 3083 ✉ howard.joy@merton.gov.uk

Architect, Building / Property Services: Mr James McGinlay, Head - Sustainable Communities, Merton Civic Centre, London Road, Morden SM4 5DX ☎ 020 8545 4154 ✉ james.mcginlay@merton.gov.uk

Building Control: Mr John Hill , Head - Public Protection & Development, Merton Civic Centre, London Road, Morden SM4 5DX ☎ 020 8545 3052 🖷 020 8545 4105 ✉ john.hill@merton.gov.uk

Building Control: Mr Chris Lee , Director - Environment & Regeneration, Merton Civic Centre, London Road, Morden SM4 5DX ☎ 020 8545 3050 🖷 020 8545 4105 ✉ chris.lee@merton.gov.uk

Building Control: Mr Trevor McIntosh, Building Control Liaison Officer, Merton Civic Centre, London Road, Morden SM4 5DX ☎ 020 8545 3121 🖷 020 8545 6085 ✉ trevor.mcintosh@merton.gov.uk

Catering Services: Mrs Christine Humphries, Corporate Contracts & Technical Administration Manager, Merton Civic Centre, London Road, Morden SM4 5DX ☎ 020 8545 3510 🖷 020 8545 3572 ✉ christine.humphries@merton.gov.uk

Children / Youth Services: Mr Paul Angeli , Assistant Director - Children's Social Care & Youth Inclusion, Merton Civic Centre, London Road, Morden SM4 5DX ☎ 020 8545 3376 ✉ paul.angeli@merton.gov.uk

Children / Youth Services: Mr Paul Ballatt , Head - Commissioning, Strategy & Performance, Merton Civic Centre, London Road, Morden SM4 5DX ☎ 020 8545 4066 ✉ paul.ballatt@merton.gov.uk

Children / Youth Services: Ms Allison Jones , Service Manager – Early Years, Merton Civic Centre, London Road, Morden SM4 5DX ☎ 020 8545 3796 ✉ allison.jones@merton.gov.uk

Children / Youth Services: Ms Janet Martin , Head - Education, Merton Civic Centre, London Road, Morden SM4 5DX ☎ 020 8545 4060 ✉ janet.martin@merton.gov.uk

Children / Youth Services: Ms Lisa Richardson , Service Support Manager - Permanence, LAC & Care Leavers, Merton Civic Centre, London Road, Morden SM4 5DX ☎ 020 8545 4288 ✉ lisa.richardson@merton.gov.uk

Children / Youth Services: Ms Kate Saksena , Manager - Merton School Improvement, Merton Civic Centre, London Road, Morden SM4 5DX ☎ 020 8545 3806 ✉ kate.saksena@merton.gov.uk

Children / Youth Services: Ms Yvette Stanley , Director - Children, Schools & Families, Merton Civic Centre, London Road, Morden SM4 5DX ☎ 020 8545 3251 🖷 020 8545 3443 ✉ yvette.stanley@merton.gov.uk

PR / Communications: Ms Sophie Poole, Head - Communications, Merton Civic Centre, London Road, Morden SM4 5DX ☎ 020 8545 3181 🖷 020 8545 0446 ✉ sophie.poole@merton.gov.uk

Computer Management: Mr Mark Humphries , Assistant Director - Infrastructure & Transactions, Merton Civic Centre, London Road, Morden SM4 5DX ☎ 020 8545 3193 ✉ mark.humphries@merton.gov.uk

Consumer Protection and Trading Standards: Mr Ian Murrell , Environmental Health, Trading Standards & Licensing Manager, Merton Civic Centre, London Road, Morden SM4 5DX ☎ 020 8545 3859 ✉ ian.murrell@merton.gov.uk

Contracts: Mr Paul Ballatt , Head - Commissioning, Strategy & Performance, Merton Civic Centre, London Road, Morden SM4 5DX ☎ 020 8545 4066 ✉ paul.ballatt@merton.gov.uk

Contracts: Mrs Christine Humphries, Corporate Contracts & Technical Administration Manager, Merton Civic Centre, London Road, Morden SM4 5DX ☎ 020 8545 3510 🖷 020 8545 3572 ✉ christine.humphries@merton.gov.uk

Corporate Services: Ms Caroline Holland, Director - Corporate Services, Merton Civic Centre, London Road, Morden SM4 5DX ☎ 020 8545 3450 🖷 020 8543 3952 ✉ caroline.holland@merton.gov.uk

Corporate Services: Mr Dean Shoesmith , Joint Executive Head of Human Resources, Merton Civic Centre, London Road, Morden SM4 5DX ☎ 020 8545 3370 ✉ dean.shoesmith@merton.gov.uk

Customer Service: Mr Sean Cunniffe , Head - Customer Contact, Merton Civic Centre, London Road, Morden SM4 5DX ☎ 020 8274 4928 ✉ sean.cunniffe@merton.gov.uk

Education: Ms Janet Martin , Head - Education, Merton Civic Centre, London Road, Morden SM4 5DX ☎ 020 8545 4060 ✉ janet.martin@merton.gov.uk

Education: Ms Yvette Stanley , Director - Children, Schools & Families, Merton Civic Centre, London Road, Morden SM4 5DX ☎ 020 8545 3251 🖷 020 8545 3443 ✉ yvette.stanley@merton.gov.uk

Education: Ms Yvonne Tomlin , Head - Community Education, Merton Civic Centre, London Road, Morden SM4 5DX ☎ 020 8274 5236 ✉ yvonne.tomlin@merton.gov.uk

Electoral Registration: Mr Paul Evans , Assistant Director of Corporate Governance & Head of Shared Legal Services, Clifford House, 67C St Helier Avenue, Morden SM4 6HY ☎ 020 8545 3338 ✉ paul.evans@merton.gov.uk

Emergency Planning: Mr Adam Viccari , Head - Corporate Safety Services, Merton Civic Centre, London Road, Morden SM4 5DX ☎ 020 8545 4803 ✉ adam.viccari@merton.gov.uk

Environmental Health: Mr Chris Lee , Director - Environment & Regeneration, Merton Civic Centre, London Road, Morden SM4 5DX ☎ 020 8545 3050 🖷 020 8545 4105 ✉ chris.lee@merton.gov.uk

Environmental Health: Mr Ian Murrell , Environmental Health, Trading Standards & Licensing Manager, Merton Civic Centre, London Road, Morden SM4 5DX ☎ 020 8545 3859 ✉ ian.murrell@merton.gov.uk

MERTON

Estates, Property & Valuation: Mr Howard Joy, Property Management & Review Manager, Merton Civic Centre, London Road, Morden SM4 5DX ☎ 020 8545 3083 ✉ howard.joy@merton.gov.uk

Facilities: Mrs Christine Humphries, Corporate Contracts & Technical Administration Manager, Merton Civic Centre, London Road, Morden SM4 5DX ☎ 020 8545 3510 🖷 020 8545 3572 ✉ christine.humphries@merton.gov.uk

Finance: Ms Fariba Barron , Finance Placements Manager, Merton Civic Centre, London Road, Morden SM4 5DX ☎ 020 8454 4262 ✉ fariba.barron@merton.gov.uk

Finance: Mr Paul Dale , Interim Assistant Director - Resources, Merton Civic Centre, London Road, Morden SM4 5DX ☎ 020 8545 3458 ✉ paul.dale@merton.gov.uk

Treasury: Ms Miriam Adams , Interim Treasury & Insurance Manager, Merton Civic Centre, London Road, Morden SM4 5DX ☎ 020 8545 3642 ✉ miriam.adams@merton.gov.uk

Fleet Management: Mr Cormac Stokes , Head - Street Scene & Waste, Merton Civic Centre, London Road, Morden SM4 5DX ☎ 020 8545 3190 🖷 020 8545 4105 ✉ cormac.stokes@merton.gov.uk

Grounds Maintenance: Mr Doug Napier , Leisure & Culture Greenspaces Manager, Merton Civic Centre, London Road, Morden SM4 5DX ☎ 020 8545 3657 ✉ doug.napier@merton.gov.uk

Highways: Mr Mario Lecordier , Traffic & Highways Service Manager, Merton Civic Centre, London Road, Morden SM4 5DX ☎ 020 8545 3202 🖷 020 8545 3199 ✉ mario.lecordier@merton.gov.uk

Highways: Mr Cormac Stokes , Head - Street Scene & Waste, Merton Civic Centre, London Road, Morden SM4 5DX ☎ 020 8545 3190 🖷 020 8545 4105 ✉ cormac.stokes@merton.gov.uk

Housing: Mr Simon Williams, Director - Community & Housing, Merton Civic Centre, London Road, Morden SM4 5DX ☎ 020 8545 3680 ✉ simon.williams@merton.gov.uk

Legal: Mr Paul Evans , Assistant Director of Corporate Governance & Head of Shared Legal Services, Clifford House, 67C St Helier Avenue, Morden SM4 6HY ☎ 020 8545 3338 ✉ paul.evans@merton.gov.uk

Leisure and Cultural Services: Mr Anthony Hopkins, Head - Libraries & Heritage Services, Merton Civic Centre, London Road, Morden SM4 5DX ☎ 020 8545 3770 ✉ anthony.hopkins@merton.gov.uk

Leisure and Cultural Services: Ms Christine Parsloe , Manager - Culture Development, Merton Civic Centre, London Road, Morden SM4 5DX ☎ 020 8545 3669 ✉ christine.parsloe@merton.gov.uk

Licensing: Mr Ian Murrell , Environmental Health, Trading Standards & Licensing Manager, Merton Civic Centre, London Road, Morden SM4 5DX ☎ 020 8545 3859 ✉ ian.murrell@merton.gov.uk

Lifelong Learning: Ms Yvonne Tomlin , Head - Community Education, Merton Civic Centre, London Road, Morden SM4 5DX ☎ 020 8274 5236 ✉ yvonne.tomlin@merton.gov.uk

Lighting: Mr Cormac Stokes , Head - Street Scene & Waste, Merton Civic Centre, London Road, Morden SM4 5DX ☎ 020 8545 3190 🖷 020 8545 4105 ✉ cormac.stokes@merton.gov.uk

Parking: Mr John Hill , Head - Public Protection & Development, Merton Civic Centre, London Road, Morden SM4 5DX ☎ 020 8545 3052 🖷 020 8545 4105 ✉ john.hill@merton.gov.uk

Personnel / HR: Mr Dean Shoesmith , Joint Executive Head of Human Resources, Merton Civic Centre, London Road, Morden SM4 5DX ☎ 020 8545 3370 ✉ dean.shoesmith@merton.gov.uk

Procurement: Mr Tom Procter , Manager - Contracts & School Organisation, Merton Civic Centre, London Road, Morden SM4 5DX ☎ 020 8545 3306 ✉ tom.procter@merton.gov.uk

Procurement: Mr Peter Stone , Head - Procurement, Merton Civic Centre, London Road, Morden SM4 5DX ☎ 020 8545 3736 ✉ peter.stone@merton.gov.uk

Public Libraries: Mr Anthony Hopkins, Head - Libraries & Heritage Services, Merton Civic Centre, London Road, Morden SM4 5DX ☎ 020 8545 3770 ✉ anthony.hopkins@merton.gov.uk

Recycling & Waste Minimisation: Mr Cormac Stokes , Head - Street Scene & Waste, Merton Civic Centre, London Road, Morden SM4 5DX ☎ 020 8545 3190 🖷 020 8545 4105 ✉ cormac.stokes@merton.gov.uk

Regeneration: Mr James McGinlay , Head - Sustainable Communities, Merton Civic Centre, London Road, Morden SM4 5DX ☎ 020 8545 4154 ✉ james.mcginlay@merton.gov.uk

Social Services: Ms Marcia Whitehall-Smith , Service Manager – Community Support, Merton Civic Centre, London Road, Morden SM4 5DX ☎ 020 8545 4631 ✉ marcia.white-hallsmith@merton.gov.uk

Social Services (Children): Ms Naheed Chaudhry , Service Manager - Policy, Planning & Performance, Merton Civic Centre, London Road, Morden SM4 5DX ☎ 020 8545 4090 ✉ naheed.chaudhry@merton.gov.uk

Social Services (Children): Mr Lee Hopkins , Service Manger - Safeguarding, Children's Standards & Training, Merton Civic Centre, London Road, Morden SM4 5DX ☎ 020 8274 4993 ✉ lee.hopkins@merton.gov.uk

Social Services (Children): Mr Keith Shipman , Manager - Education & Inclusion, Merton Civic Centre, London Road, Morden SM4 5DX ☎ 020 8545 3546 ✉ keith.shipman@merton.gov.uk

Social Services (Children): Ms Leanne Wallder , Joint Commissioning Manager - Children & Families, Merton Civic Centre, London Road, Morden SM4 5DX ☎ 020 8545 3591 ✉ leanne.wallder@merton.gov.uk

Public Health: Dr Kay Eilbert , Director - Public Health, Merton Civic Centre, London Road, Morden SM4 5DX ☎ 020 8545 4836 ✉ kay.eilbert@merton.gov.uk

Staff Training: Mr Dean Shoesmith , Joint Executive Head of Human Resources, Merton Civic Centre, London Road, Morden SM4 5DX ☎ 020 8545 3370 ✉ dean.shoesmith@merton.gov.uk

Street Scene: Mr Cormac Stokes , Head - Street Scene & Waste, Merton Civic Centre, London Road, Morden SM4 5DX ☎ 020 8545 3190 🖷 020 8545 4105 ✉ cormac.stokes@merton.gov.uk

Sustainable Communities: Mr James McGinlay , Head - Sustainable Communities, Merton Civic Centre, London Road, Morden SM4 5DX ☎ 020 8545 4154 ✉ james.mcginlay@merton.gov.uk

Sustainable Development: Mr John Hill , Head - Public Protection & Development, Merton Civic Centre, London Road, Morden SM4 5DX ☎ 020 8545 3052 🖷 020 8545 4105 ✉ john.hill@merton.gov.uk

Sustainable Development: Mr James McGinlay , Head - Sustainable Communities, Merton Civic Centre, London Road, Morden SM4 5DX ☎ 020 8545 4154 ✉ james.mcginlay@merton.gov.uk

Town Centre: Mr John Hill , Head - Public Protection & Development, Merton Civic Centre, London Road, Morden SM4 5DX ☎ 020 8545 3052 🖷 020 8545 4105 ✉ john.hill@merton.gov.uk

Traffic Management: Mr Cormac Stokes , Head - Street Scene & Waste, Merton Civic Centre, London Road, Morden SM4 5DX ☎ 020 8545 3190 🖷 020 8545 4105 ✉ cormac.stokes@merton.gov.uk

Transport: Mr Cormac Stokes , Head - Street Scene & Waste, Merton Civic Centre, London Road, Morden SM4 5DX ☎ 020 8545 3190 🖷 020 8545 4105 ✉ cormac.stokes@merton.gov.uk

Transport Planner: Mr Cormac Stokes , Head - Street Scene & Waste, Merton Civic Centre, London Road, Morden SM4 5DX ☎ 020 8545 3190 🖷 020 8545 4105 ✉ cormac.stokes@merton.gov.uk

Waste Collection and Disposal: Mr Brian McLoughlin, Waste Operations Manager, Merton Civic Centre, London Road, Morden SM4 5DX ☎ 020 8274 4936 🖷 020 8545 3942 ✉ brian.mcloughlin@merton.gov.uk

Waste Collection and Disposal: Mr Cormac Stokes , Head - Street Scene & Waste, Merton Civic Centre, London Road, Morden SM4 5DX ☎ 020 8545 3190 🖷 020 8545 4105 ✉ cormac.stokes@merton.gov.uk

Waste Management: Mr Brian McLoughlin, Waste Operations Manager, Merton Civic Centre, London Road, Morden SM4 5DX ☎ 020 8274 4936 🖷 020 8545 3942 ✉ brian.mcloughlin@merton.gov.uk

COUNCILLORS

***Mayor* Chung**, David (LAB - Longthornton)
david.chung@merton.gov.uk

***Deputy Mayor* Cowper**, Pauline (LAB - Cannon Hill)
pauline.cowper@merton.gov.uk

***Leader of the Council* Alambritis**, Stephen (LAB - Ravensbury)
stephen.alambritis@merton.gov.uk

***Deputy Leader of the Council* Allison**, Mark (LAB - Lavender Fields)
mark.allison@merton.gov.uk

Akyigyina, Agatha (LAB - Figge's Marsh)
agatha.akyigyina@merton.gov.uk

Anderson, Stan (LAB - Lower Morden)
stan.anderson@merton.gov.uk

Attawar, Laxmi (LAB - Colliers Wood)
laxmi.attawar@merton.gov.uk

Badenoch, Hamish (CON - Village)
hamish.badenoch@merton.gov.uk

Bowcott, John (CON - Village)
john.bowcott@merton.gov.uk

Bull, Michael (CON - Dundonald)
michael.bull@merton.gov.uk

Bush, Adam (CON - Raynes Park)
adam.bush@merton.gov.uk

Byers, Tobin (LAB - Cannon Hill)
tobin.byers@merton.gov.uk

Chirico, Charlie (CON - Trinity)
charlie.chirico@merton.gov.uk

Cooper-Marbiah, Caroline (LAB - Colliers Wood)
Caroline.Cooper-Marbiah@merton.gov.uk

Crowe, Stephen (CON - Raynes Park)
stephen.crowe@merton.gov.uk

Curtin, Mary (LAB - Lower Morden)
mary.curtin@merton.gov.uk

Dean, David (CON - Dundonald)
david.dean@merton.gov.uk

Dehaney, John (LAB - Graveney)
john.dehaney@merton.gov.uk

Draper, Nick (LAB - Colliers Wood)
nick.draper@merton.gov.uk

Foley, Edward (R - Merton Park)
edward.foley@merton.gov.uk

Fraser, Brenda (LAB - Longthornton)
brenda.fraser@merton.gov.uk

Gadzama, Fidelis (LAB - Cannon Hill)
fidelis.gadzama@merton.gov.uk

Garrod, Ross (LAB - Lavender Fields)
ross.garrod@merton.gov.uk

Grocott, Suzanne (CON - Dundonald)
suzanne.grocott@merton.gov.uk

Hanna, Jeff (LAB - Pollards Hill)
jeff.hanna@merton.gov.uk

Henry, Joan (LAB - Pollards Hill)
joan.henry@merton.gov.uk

Holden, Daniel (CON - Hillside)
daniel.holden@merton.gov.uk

Holmes, James (CON - Trinity)
james.holmes@merton.gov.uk

Howard, Janice (CON - Wimbledon Park)
janice.howard@merton.gov.uk

Jeanes, Mary-Jane (LD - West Barnes)
mary-jane.jeanes@merton.gov.uk

Jones, Philip (LAB - Ravensbury)
philip.jones@merton.gov.uk

Jones, Abigail (LAB - Abbey)
abigail.jones@merton.gov.uk

Judge, Andrew (LAB - Abbey)
andrew.judge@merton.gov.uk

Kenny, Sally (LAB - Lower Morden)
sally.kenny@labour.gov.uk

Kirby, Linda (LAB - Graveney)
linda.kirby@merton.gov.uk

Latif, Najeeb (CON - Village)
najeeb.latif@merton.gov.uk

Lewis-Lavender, Gilli (CON - West Barnes)
gilli.lewis-lavender@merton.gov.uk

Lewis-Lavender, Brian (CON - West Barnes)
brian.lewis-lavender@merton.gov.uk

Macauley, Edith (LAB - Lavender Fields)
edith.macauley@merton.gov.uk

Makin, Russell (LAB - Cricket Green)
russell.makin@merton.gov.uk

Martin, Maxi (LAB - St. Helier)
maxi.martin@merton.gov.uk

McCabe, Peter (LAB - Ravensbury)
peter.mccabe@merton.gov.uk

Moulton, Oonagh (CON - Wimbledon Park)
oonagh.moulton@merton.gov.uk

Munn, Ian (LAB - Cricket Green)
ian.munn@merton.gov.uk

Neep, Katy (LAB - Abbey)
katy.neep@merton.gov.uk

Pearce, Dennis (LAB - St. Helier)
dennis.pearce@merton.gov.uk

Sargeant, John (R - Merton Park)
john.sargeant@merton.gov.uk

Saunders, Judy (LAB - Cricket Green)
judy.saunders@merton.gov.uk

Simpson, David (CON - Hillside)
david.simpson@merton.gov.uk

Skeete, Marsie (LAB - Longthornton)
marsie.skeete@merton.gov.uk

Southgate, Peter (R - Merton Park)
peter.southgate@merton.gov.uk

Stanford, Geraldine (LAB - Figge's Marsh)
geraldine.stanord@merton.gov.uk

Taylor, Linda (CON - Wimbledon Park)
linda.taylor@merton.gov.uk

Uddin, Imran (LAB - St. Helier)
imran.uddin@merton.gov.uk

Udeh, Gregory (LAB - Graveney)
gregory.udeh@merton.gov.uk

Walker, Peter (LAB - Figge's Marsh)
peter.walker@merton.gov.uk

West, Jill (CON - Raynes Park)
jill.west@merton.gov.uk

Whelton, Martin (LAB - Pollards Hill)
martin.whelton@merton.gov.uk

Williams, David (CON - Hillside)
david.williams@merton.gov.uk

POLITICAL COMPOSITION

LAB: 36, CON: 19, R: 3, LD: 1

COMMITTEE CHAIRS

Health & Wellbeing: Ms Caroline Cooper-Marbiah

Licensing: Mr Jeff Hanna

Planning: Ms Linda Kirby

Mid & East Antrim District Council N

Mid & East Antrim District Council, The Braid, 1 - 29 Bridge Street, Ballymena BT43 5EJ

PRINCIPAL OFFICERS

Chief Executive: Ms Anne Donaghy , Chief Executive, The Braid, 1 - 29 Bridge Street, Ballymena BT43 5EJ

Senior Management: Mrs Sandra Cole , Director of Finance & Governance, The Braid, 1 - 29 Bridge Street, Ballymena BT43 5EJ
sandra.cole@midandeastantrim.gov.uk

Senior Management: Mrs Karen Hargan , Director of Organisation Development & Community Planning, The Braid, 1 - 29 Bridge Street, Ballymena BT43 5EJ
karen.hargan@midandeastantrim.gov.uk

Senior Management: Mr Philip Thompson , Director of Operations, The Braid, 1 - 29 Bridge Street, Ballymena BT43 5EJ
philip.thompson@midandeastantrim.gov.uk

Community Planning: Mrs Karen Hargan , Director of Organisation Development & Community Planning, The Braid, 1 - 29 Bridge Street, Ballymena BT43 5EJ
karen.hargan@midandeastantrim.gov.uk

Corporate Services: Mr Philip Thompson , Director of Operations, The Braid, 1 - 29 Bridge Street, Ballymena BT43 5EJ
philip.thompson@midandeastantrim.gov.uk

Finance: Mrs Sandra Cole , Director of Finance & Governance, The Braid, 1 - 29 Bridge Street, Ballymena BT43 5EJ
sandra.cole@midandeastantrim.gov.uk

Personnel / HR: Mrs Karen Hargan , Director of Organisation Development & Community Planning, The Braid, 1 - 29 Bridge Street, Ballymena BT43 5EJ
karen.hargan@midandeastantrim.gov.uk

COUNCILLORS

Adger, Beth (DUP - Braid)
cr.adger@ballymena.gov.uk

Anderson, Donna (O - Ballymena)
cllr.anderson@midandeastantrim.gov.uk

Ashe, Billy (DUP - Carrick Castle)
billy.ashe@carrickfergus.org

Beattie, May (DUP - Knockagh)
may.beattie@carrickfergus.org

Brown, James (IND - Carrick Castle)

Carson, John (DUP - Ballymena)
cllr.carson@ballymena.gov.uk

Cherry, Robin (UUP - Braid)
ald.cherry@ballymena.gov.uk

Clyde, Beth (DUP - Braid)
beth.clyde@ballymena.gov.uk

Gaston, Timothy (O - Bannside)
cr.gaston@ballymena.gov.uk

Glover, Reuben (DUP - Ballymena)
cllr.glover@midandeastantrim.gov.uk

Hanna, Sam (DUP - Braid)
ald.hanna@ballymena.gov.uk

Hardy, Patrice (SF - Bannside)
cllr.hardy@midandeastantrim.gov.uk

Henry, Billy (DUP - Bannside)
billy.henry@ballymena.gov.uk

Henry, James (IND - Ballymena)
cr.jhenry@ballymena.gov.uk

Johnston, Cheryl (DUP - Carrick Castle)
cllr.johnston@midandeastantrim.gov.uk

Jordan, Noel (UKIP - Carrick Castle)
cllr.jordan@midandeastantrim.gov.uk

Logan, Robert (ALL - Larne Lough)
cllr.logan@midandeastantrim.org

Lyons, Gordon (DUP - Coast Road)
cllr.lyons@midandeastantrim.gov.uk

Maguire, Paul (SF - Braid)
paul.maguire@ballymenacouncil.org

McCaughey, William (DUP - Braid)
clr.mccaughey@ballymena.gov.uk

McClurg, Lynn (DUP - Knockagh)
lynn.mcclurg@carrickfergus.org

McDonald, Stewart (O - Bannside)
cllr.mcdonald@midandeastantrim.gov.uk

McKeen, Gregg (DUP - Larne Lough)
gregg.mckeen@larne.gov.uk

McKeown, James (SF - Coast Road)
james.mckeown@larne.gov.uk

McKinty, Mark (UUP - Larne Lough)
mark.mckinty@larne.gov.uk

McNeilly, William (UUP - Bannside)
cr.mcneilly@ballymena.gov.uk

Millar, Lindsay (UUP - Knockagh)
cllr.millar@midandeastantrim.org

Morrow, Maureen (UUP - Coast Road)
maureen.morrow@larne.gov.uk

Mulvenna, Geraldine (ALL - Coast Road)
geraldine.mulvenna@larne.gov.uk

Nicholl, Tommy (DUP - Bannside)
crt.nicholl@ballymena.gov.uk

Nicholl, Stephen (UUP - Ballymena)
cllr.snichol@midandeastantrim.gov.uk

O'Loan, Declan (SDLP - Ballymena)
cr.o'loan@ballymena.gov.uk

Reid, Paul (DUP - Larne Lough)
cllr.reid@midandeastantrim.gov.uk

Sinclair, Paul (ALL - Knockagh)
cllr.sinclair@midandeastantrim.org

Stewart, John (UUP - Carrick Castle)
john.stewart@carrickfergus.org

Wales, Audrey (DUP - Ballymena)
cr.wales@ballymena.gov.uk

Wilson, Andrew (UUP - Knockagh)
andrew.wilson@carrickfergus.org

Wilson, Ruth (O - Coast Road)
cllr.rwilson@midandeastantrim.gov.uk

Wilson, Andrew (UUP - Larne Lough)
cllr.andyparkwilson@midandeastantrim.gov.uk

POLITICAL COMPOSITION

DUP: 16, UUP: 9, O: 4, SF: 3, ALL: 3, IND: 2, SDLP: 1, UKIP: 1

Mid Devon D

Mid Devon District Council, Phoenix House, Phoenix Lane, Tiverton EX16 6PP
☎ 01884 255255 🖷 01884 234318 ✉ chiefexec@middevon.gov.uk
💻 www.middevon.gov.uk

FACTS AND FIGURES

Parliamentary Constituencies: Devon Central, Tiverton and Honiton
EU Constituencies: South West
Election Frequency: Elections are of whole council

PRINCIPAL OFFICERS

Chief Executive: Mr Kevin Finan , Chief Executive, Phoenix House, Phoenix Lane, Tiverton EX16 6PP ☎ 01884 234201 ✉ kfinan@middevon.gov.uk

Senior Management: Mrs Jenny Clifford , Head of Planning & Regeneration, Phoenix House, Phoenix Lane, Tiverton EX16 6PP ☎ 01884 234346 ✉ jclifford@middevon.gov.uk

Senior Management: Mrs Christina Cross, Head of Business Information Services, Phoenix House, Phoenix Lane, Tiverton EX16 6PP ☎ 01884 234912 ✉ ccross@middevon.gov.uk

Senior Management: Mr Andrew Jarrett , Head of Finance, Phoenix House, Phoenix Lane, Tiverton EX16 6PP ☎ 01884 234242 ✉ ajarrett@middevon.gov.uk

MID DEVON

Senior Management: Mrs Jill May , Head of HR & Development, Phoenix House, Phoenix Lane, Tiverton EX16 6PP ☎ 01884 234381 🖰 jmay@middevon.gov.uk

Senior Management: Ms Liz Reeves, Head of Customer Services, Phoenix House, Phoenix Lane, Tiverton EX16 6PP ☎ 01884 234371 🖰 lreeves@middevon.gov.uk

Senior Management: Mr Nick Sanderson, Head of Housing & Property Services, Phoenix House, Phoenix Lane, Tiverton EX16 6PP ☎ 01884 234960 🖰 nsanderson@middevon.gov.uk

Senior Management: Mrs Amy Tregellas, Head of Communities & Governance, Phoenix House, Phoenix Lane, Tiverton EX16 6PP ☎ 01884 234246 🖰 atregellas@middevon.gov.uk

Architect, Building / Property Services: Mr Nick Sanderson, Head of Housing & Property Services, Phoenix House, Phoenix Lane, Tiverton EX16 6PP ☎ 01884 234960 🖰 nsanderson@middevon.gov.uk

Building Control: Mrs Jenny Clifford , Head of Planning & Regeneration, Phoenix House, Phoenix Lane, Tiverton EX16 6PP ☎ 01884 234346 🖰 jclifford@middevon.gov.uk

Children / Youth Services: Mr John Bodley-Scott, Community Development Officer, Phoenix House, Phoenix Lane, Tiverton EX16 6PP ☎ 01884 234363 🖰 jbodleyscott@middevon.gov.uk

PR / Communications: Mr Andrew Lacey, Communications & Reputation Manager, Phoenix House, Phoenix Lane, Tiverton EX16 6PP ☎ 01884 234232 🖰 alacey@middevon.gov.uk

Community Planning: Mr John Bodley-Scott, Community Development Officer, Phoenix House, Phoenix Lane, Tiverton EX16 6PP ☎ 01884 234363 🖰 jbodleyscott@middevon.gov.uk

Community Safety: Mrs Julia Ryder, Community Safety & Emergency Planning Officer, Phoenix House, Phoenix Lane, Tiverton EX16 6PP ☎ 01884 234997 🖰 jryder@middevon.gov.uk

Computer Management: Mrs Christina Cross, Head of Business Information Services, Phoenix House, Phoenix Lane, Tiverton EX16 6PP ☎ 01884 234912 🖰 ccross@middevon.gov.uk

Contracts: Mrs Chanelle Busby , Procurement Manager, Phoenix House, Phoenix Lane, Tiverton EX16 6PP ☎ 01884 234228 🖰 cwhite@middevon.gov.uk

Corporate Services: Mr Kevin Finan , Chief Executive, Phoenix House, Phoenix Lane, Tiverton EX16 6PP ☎ 01884 234201 🖰 kfinan@middevon.gov.uk

Customer Service: Ms Liz Reeves, Head of Customer Services, Phoenix House, Phoenix Lane, Tiverton EX16 6PP ☎ 01884 234371 🖰 lreeves@middevon.gov.uk

Economic Development: Mr Gordon Cleaver, Regeneration Manager, Phoenix House, Phoenix Lane, Tiverton EX16 6PP ☎ 01884 234368 🖰 gcleaver@middevon.gov.uk

E-Government: Mrs Christina Cross, Head of Business Information Services, Phoenix House, Phoenix Lane, Tiverton EX16 6PP ☎ 01884 234912 🖰 ccross@middevon.gov.uk

Electoral Registration: Miss Jackie Stoneman, Electoral Services Officer, Phoenix House, Phoenix Lane, Tiverton EX16 6PP ☎ 01884 234214 🖰 jstoneman@middevon.gov.uk

Emergency Planning: Mrs Julia Ryder, Community Safety & Emergency Planning Officer, Phoenix House, Phoenix Lane, Tiverton EX16 6PP ☎ 01884 234997 🖰 jryder@middevon.gov.uk

Energy Management: Mr Andrew Busby, Property Services Manager, Phoenix House, Phoenix Lane, Tiverton EX16 6PP ☎ 01884 234948 🖰 abusby@middevon.gov.uk

Environmental Health: Mr Simon Newcombe, Public Health Manager, Phoenix House, Phoenix Lane, Tiverton EX16 6PP ☎ 01884 244615 🖰 snewcombe@middevon.gov.uk

Estates, Property & Valuation: Mr Nick Sanderson, Head of Housing & Property Services, Phoenix House, Phoenix Lane, Tiverton EX16 6PP ☎ 01884 234960 🖰 nsanderson@middevon.gov.uk

European Liaison: Mr Gordon Cleaver, Regeneration Manager, Phoenix House, Phoenix Lane, Tiverton EX16 6PP ☎ 01884 234368 🖰 gcleaver@middevon.gov.uk

Facilities: Mr Andrew Busby, Property Services Manager, Phoenix House, Phoenix Lane, Tiverton EX16 6PP ☎ 01884 234948 🖰 abusby@middevon.gov.uk

Finance: Mr Andrew Jarrett , Head of Finance, Phoenix House, Phoenix Lane, Tiverton EX16 6PP ☎ 01884 234242 🖰 ajarrett@middevon.gov.uk

Fleet Management: Mr Stuart Noyce , Waste Services Manager, Phoenix House, Phoenix Lane, Tiverton EX16 6PP ☎ 01884 244635 🖰 snoyce@middevon.gov.uk

Grounds Maintenance: Mr Andrew Busby, Property Services Manager, Phoenix House, Phoenix Lane, Tiverton EX16 6PP ☎ 01884 234948 🖰 abusby@middevon.gov.uk

Health and Safety: Mr Michael Lowe , Health & Safety Officer, Phoenix House, Phoenix Lane, Tiverton EX16 6PP ☎ 01884 234395 🖰 mlowe@middevon.gov.uk

Housing: Mrs Claire Fry , Housing Services Manager, Phoenix House, Phoenix Lane, Tiverton EX16 6PP ☎ 01884 234386 🖰 cfry@middevon.gov.uk

Housing Maintenance: Mr Mark Baglow , Housing Maintenance Manager, Phoenix House, Phoenix Lane, Tiverton EX16 6PP ☎ 01884 233011 🖰 mbaglow@middevon.gov.uk

Legal: Mr Simon Johnson, Legal Services Manager, Phoenix House, Phoenix Lane, Tiverton EX16 6PP ☎ 01884 234210 🖰 sjohnson@middevon.gov.uk

Leisure and Cultural Services: Miss Samantha Bennion , Leisure Services Manager, Phoenix House, Phoenix Lane, Tiverton EX16 6PP ☎ 01884 234902 ✉ sbennion@middevon.gov.uk

Licensing: Mr Tom Keating , Licensing Officer, Phoenix House, Phoenix Lane, Tiverton EX16 6PP ☎ 01884 244618 ✉ tkeating@middevon.gov.uk

Lottery Funding, Charity and Voluntary: Mr Paul Tucker, Grants Officer, Phoenix House, Phoenix Lane, Tiverton EX16 6PP ☎ 01884 234930 ✉ ptucker@middevon.gov.uk

Member Services: Mrs Amy Tregellas, Head of Communities & Governance, Phoenix House, Phoenix Lane, Tiverton EX16 6PP ☎ 01884 234246 ✉ atregellas@middevon.gov.uk

Parking: Mr Stuart Noyce , Waste Services Manager, Phoenix House, Phoenix Lane, Tiverton EX16 6PP ☎ 01884 244635 ✉ snoyce@middevon.gov.uk

Personnel / HR: Mrs Jill May , Head of HR & Development, Phoenix House, Phoenix Lane, Tiverton EX16 6PP ☎ 01884 234381 ✉ jmay@middevon.gov.uk

Planning: Mrs Jenny Clifford , Head of Planning & Regeneration, Phoenix House, Phoenix Lane, Tiverton EX16 6PP ☎ 01884 234346 ✉ jclifford@middevon.gov.uk

Procurement: Mrs Chanelle Busby , Procurement Manager, Phoenix House, Phoenix Lane, Tiverton EX16 6PP ☎ 01884 234228 ✉ cwhite@middevon.gov.uk

Recycling & Waste Minimisation: Mr Stuart Noyce , Waste Services Manager, Phoenix House, Phoenix Lane, Tiverton EX16 6PP ☎ 01884 244635 ✉ snoyce@middevon.gov.uk

Regeneration: Mr Gordon Cleaver, Regeneration Manager, Phoenix House, Phoenix Lane, Tiverton EX16 6PP ☎ 01884 234368 ✉ gcleaver@middevon.gov.uk

Staff Training: Ms Julia Bickley , Learning & Development Officer, Phoenix House, Phoenix Lane, Tiverton EX16 6PP ☎ 01884 234381 ✉ jbickley@middevon.gov.uk

Street Scene: Mr Stuart Noyce , Waste Services Manager, Phoenix House, Phoenix Lane, Tiverton EX16 6PP ☎ 01884 244635 ✉ snoyce@middevon.gov.uk

Sustainable Communities: Mr John Bodley-Scott, Community Development Officer, Phoenix House, Phoenix Lane, Tiverton EX16 6PP ☎ 01884 234363 ✉ jbodleyscott@middevon.gov.uk

Tourism: Mr Gordon Cleaver, Regeneration Manager, Phoenix House, Phoenix Lane, Tiverton EX16 6PP ☎ 01884 234368 ✉ gcleaver@middevon.gov.uk

Waste Collection and Disposal: Mr Stuart Noyce , Waste Services Manager, Phoenix House, Phoenix Lane, Tiverton EX16 6PP ☎ 01884 244635 ✉ snoyce@middevon.gov.uk

Waste Management: Mr Stuart Noyce , Waste Services Manager, Phoenix House, Phoenix Lane, Tiverton EX16 6PP ☎ 01884 244635 ✉ snoyce@middevon.gov.uk

Children's Play Areas: Mr Andrew Busby, Property Services Manager, Phoenix House, Phoenix Lane, Tiverton EX16 6PP ☎ 01884 234948 ✉ abusby@middevon.gov.uk

COUNCILLORS

***Chair* Daw**, John (CON - Taw)
jdaw@middevon.gov.uk

***Deputy Chair* Hughes**, Glanmor (CON - Upper Culm)
ghughes@middevon.gov.uk

***Leader of the Council* Eginton**, Clive (CON - Taw Vale)
ceginton@middevon.gov.uk

Andrews, Eileen (IND - Cullompton South)
eandrews@middevon.gov.uk

Bainbridge, Heather (CON - Canonsleigh)
hbainbridge@middevon.gov.uk

Berry, Rosemary (CON - Cullompton Outer)
rberry@middevon.gov.uk

Binks, Judi (CON - Sandford and Creedy)
jbink@middevon.gov.uk

Busch, Karl (CON - Cullompton North)
kbusch@middeveon.gov.uk

Chesterton, Richard (CON - Lower Culm)
rchesterton@middevon.gov.uk

Collis, Christine (CON - Canonsleigh)
ccollis@middevon.gov.uk

Colthorpe, Polly (CON - Way)
pcolthorpe@middevon.gov.uk

Coren, Derek (CON - Yeo)
dcoren@middevon.gov.uk

Davey, Neal (CON - Lowman)
ndavey@middevon.gov.uk

Daw, Chris (CON - Cranmore)
cdaw@middevon.gov.uk

Deed, Bob (CON - Cadbury)
bdeed@middevon.gov.uk

Doe, Jill (CON - Lower Culm)
jdoe@middevon.gov.uk

Dolley, Ron (UKIP - Westexe)
rdolley@middevon.gov.uk

Downes, John (LD - Boniface)
jdownes@middevon.gov.uk

Evans, Bob (CON - Lower Culm)
revans@middevon.gov.uk

Flaws, Steve (CON - Westexe)
sflaws@middevon.gov.uk

Griggs, Sue (CON - Cranmore)
sgriggs@middevon.gov.uk

Hare-Scott, Peter (CON - Newbrooke)
pharescott@middevon.gov.uk

Heal, Peter (CON - Yeo)
pheal@middevon.gov.uk

Hull, Brenda (CON - Castle)
bhull@middevon.gov.uk

Knowles, Dennis (IND - Lowman)
dknowles@middevon.gov.uk

Letch, Frank (LD - Lawrence)
fletch@middevon.gov.uk

Moore, Andrew (CON - Clare and Shuttern)
amoore@middevon.gov.uk

Radford, Ray (CON - Halberton and Uplowman)
rradford@middevon.gov.uk

Roach, Jenny (LIB - Silverton)
jroach@middevon.gov.uk

Rosamond, Frank (IND - Upper Culm)
frosamond@middevon.gov.uk

Slade, Colin (CON - Lowman)
cslade@middevon.gov.uk

Slade, Clarrisa (CON - Cranmore)
cslade@middevon.gov.uk

Slade, Elizabeth (CON - Castle)

Smith, Johnathan (UKIP - Westexe)
jsmith@middevon.gov.uk

Snow, Terry (IND - Cullompton South)
tsnow@middevon.gov.uk

Squire, John (CON - Upper Yeo)
jsquire@middevon.gov.uk

Squires, Margaret (CON - Sandford and Creedy)
msquires@middevon.gov.uk

Stanley, Raymond (CON - Clare and Shuttern)
rstanley@middevon.gov.uk

Taylor, Luke (LD - Bradninch)
ntaylor@middevon.gov.uk

Way, Nick (LD - Boniface)
nway@middevon.gov.uk

Woollatt, Nikki (IND - Cullompton North)
nwoollatt@middevon.gov.uk

Wright, Bob (IND - Lawrence)
bwright@middevon.gov.uk

POLITICAL COMPOSITION

CON: 29, IND: 6, LD: 4, UKIP: 2, LIB: 1

COMMITTEE CHAIRS

Audit: Mr Bob Evans

Mid Suffolk D

Mid Suffolk District Council, Council Offices, 131 High Street, Needham Market IP6 8DL
☎ 01449 724500 🖷 01449 724696
🖳 www.midsuffolk.gov.uk

FACTS AND FIGURES

Parliamentary Constituencies: Bury St. Edmunds
EU Constituencies: Eastern
Election Frequency: Elections are of whole council

PRINCIPAL OFFICERS

Chief Executive: Mrs Charlie Adan , Chief Executive, Council Offices, 131 High Street, Needham Market, Ipswich IP6 8DL
☎ 01473 825710 🖷 01473 825742
🖰 charlie.adan@baberghmidsuffolk.gov.uk

Senior Management: Ms Lindsay Barker , Strategic Director - Place, Council Offices, 131 High Street, Needham Market IP6 8DL
☎ 01473 825844 🖷 01473 825742 🖰 lindsay.barker@midsuffolk.gov.uk; lindsay.barker@baberghmidsuffolk.gov.uk

Senior Management: Mr Mike Evans , Strategic Director - People, Council Offices, 131 High Street, Needham Market IP6 8DL
☎ 01473 825746 🖷 01473 825742 🖰 michael.evans@misuffolk.gov.uk; michael.evans@baberghmidsuffolk.gov.uk

Senior Management: Mr Mike Hammond , Interim Director - Transformation, Council Offices, Corks Lane, Hadleigh, Ipswich IP7 6SJ ☎ 01473 825750 🖷 01473 825742
🖰 mike.hammond@babergh.gov.uk

Senior Management: Mr Andrew Hunkin , Strategic Director - Corporate, Council Offices, 131 High Street, Needham Market IP6 8DL ☎ 01473 825820 🖷 01473 825742
🖰 andrew.hunkin@baberghmidsuffolk.gov.uk

Best Value: Mr Peter Quirk , Head - Corporate Organisation, Council Offices, 131 High Street, Needham Market IP6 8DL
☎ 01473 825829 🖷 01473 825742
🖰 peter.quirk@baberghmidsuffolk.gov.uk

Building Control: Mr Peter Burrows , Head - Economy, Council Offices, Corks Lane, Hadleigh, Ipswich IP7 6SJ ☎ 01449 724503
🖷 01449 724514 🖰 peter.burrows@baberghmidsuffolk.gov.uk

Building Control: Mr Gary Starling , Corporate Manager - Building Control, Council Offices, 131 High Street, Needham Market IP6 8DL ☎ 01473 825856 🖷 01473 825708
🖰 gary.starling@baberghmidsuffolk.gov.uk

PR / Communications: Mr Paul Simon , Corporate Manager - Communications, Council Offices, Corks Lane, Hadleigh IP7 6SJ
☎ 01473 826634 🖷 01473 825742
🖰 paul.simon@baberghmidsuffolk.gov.uk

Community Planning: Ms Sue Clements , Corporate Manager - Strong Communities, Council Offices, Corks Lane, Hadleigh, Ipswich IP7 6SJ ☎ 01449 724657 🖷 01449 724655
🖰 sue.clemments@baberghmidsuffolk.gov.uk

Community Safety: Ms Peta Jones , Corporate Manager - Safe Communities, Council Offices, 131 High Street, Needham Market IP6 8DL ☎ 01449 724642 🖷 01449 724655
🖰 peta.jones@baberghmidsuffolk.gov.uk

Computer Management: Mr Carl Reeder , Corporate Manager - Information Management & ICT, Council Offices, 131 High Street, Needham Market IP6 8DL ☎ 01473 825790
🖰 carl.reeder@baberghmidsuffolk.gov.uk

Contracts: Mrs Rachel Hodson-Gibbons , Corporate Manager - Commissioning, Council Offices, 131 High Street, Needham Market IP6 8DL ☎ 01449 724587 rachel.hodson-gibbons@baberghmidsuffolk.gov.uk

Corporate Services: Ms Suki Binjal , Monitoring Officer, Council Offices, Corks Lane, Hadleigh, Ipswich IP7 6SJ ☎ 01473 825729 suki.binjal@baberghmidsuffolk.gov.uk

Corporate Services: Mr Andrew Hunkin, Strategic Director - Corporate, Council Offices, Corks Lane, Hadleigh IP7 6SJ ☎ 01473 825820 🖷 01473 823742 andrew.hunkin@baberghmidsuffolk.gov.uk

Corporate Services: Mr Peter Quirk , Head - Corporate Organisation, Council Offices, 131 High Street, Needham Market IP6 8DL ☎ 01473 825829 🖷 01473 825742 peter.quirk@baberghmidsuffolk.gov.uk

Corporate Services: Ms Katherine Steel , Head - Corporate Resources, Council Offices, 131 High Street, Needham Market IP6 8DL ☎ 01473 826649 🖷 01473 825742 katherine.steel@baberghmidsuffolk.gov.uk

Customer Service: Mr David Cleary , Corporate Manager - Customer Services, Council Offices, Corks Lane, Hadleigh IP7 6SJ ☎ 01473 825722 david.cleary@baberghmidsuffolk.gov.uk

Direct Labour: Mr Ryan Jones , Corporate Manager - Asset Management Operations, Council Offices, 131 High Street, Needham Market IP6 8DL ☎ 01473 825787 🖷 01473 825770 ryan.jones@baberghmidsuffolk.gov.uk

Economic Development: Mr David Benham, Corporate Manager - Economic Development & Tourism, Council Offices, 131 High Street, Needham Market IP6 8DL ☎ 01449 724649 🖷 01449 724655 david.benham@baberghmidsuffolk.gov.uk

Economic Development: Mrs Sue Dawes , Economic Development Technical Officer, Council Offices, Corks Lane, Hadleigh, Ipswich IP7 6SJ ☎ 01473 825868 🖷 01473 825708 sue.dawes@baberghmidsuffolk.gov.uk

E-Government: Mr Carl Reeder , Corporate Manager - Information Management & ICT, Council Offices, 131 High Street, Needham Market IP6 8DL ☎ 01473 825790 carl.reeder@baberghmidsuffolk.gov.uk

Electoral Registration: Mr Philip Tallent, Corporate Manager - Elections & Electoral Management, Council Offices, 131 High Street, Needham Market IP6 8DL ☎ 01473 825891 🖷 01473 825742 philip.tallent@baberghmidsuffolk.gov.uk

Emergency Planning: Ms Sue Herne , Emergency Planning Responsive Officer, Council Offices, 131 High Street, Needham Market, Ipswich IP6 8DL ☎ 01449 724851 🖷 01449 724655 sue.herne@baberghmidsuffolk.gov.uk

Energy Management: Mr Chris Fry , Head - Environment, Council Offices, 131 High Street, Needham Market IP6 8DL ☎ 01473 826649 🖷 01473 825742 chris.fry@baberghmidsuffolk.gov.uk

Environmental / Technical Services: Mr Ryan Jones , Corporate Manager - Asset Management Operations, Council Offices, 131 High Street, Needham Market IP6 8DL ☎ 01473 825787 🖷 01473 825770 ryan.jones@baberghmidsuffolk.gov.uk

Environmental Health: Mr James Buckingham , Corporate Manager - Environmental Protection, Council Offices, 131 High Street, Needham Market IP6 8DL ☎ 01473 825880 🖷 01473 825738 james.buckingham@midsuffolk.gov.uk; james.buckingham@baberghmidsuffolk.gov.uk

Environmental Health: Mr Chris Fry , Head - Environment, Council Offices, Corks Lane, Hadleigh, Ipswich IP7 6SJ ☎ 01473 826649 🖷 01473 825742 chris.fry@baberghmidsuffolk.gov.uk

Estates, Property & Valuation: Mr Ryan Jones , Corporate Manager - Asset Management Operations, Council Offices, 131 High Street, Needham Market IP6 8DL ☎ 01473 825787 🖷 01473 825770 ryan.jones@baberghmidsuffolk.gov.uk

European Liaison: Mr Jonathan Free , Head - Communities, Council Offices, 131 High Street, Needham Market IP6 8DL ☎ 01473 826649 🖷 01473 825742 jonathan.free@baberghmidsuffolk.gov.uk

Facilities: Mr Ryan Jones , Corporate Manager - Asset Management Operations, Council Offices, 131 High Street, Needham Market IP6 8DL ☎ 01473 825787 🖷 01473 825770 ryan.jones@baberghmidsuffolk.gov.uk

Finance: Ms Katherine Steel , Head - Corporate Resources, Council Offices, 131 High Street, Needham Market IP6 8DL ☎ 01473 826649 🖷 01473 825742 katherine.steel@baberghmidsuffolk.gov.uk

Treasury: Mr John Moyles , Corporate Manager - Financial Services & Treasury, Council Offices, Corks Lane, Hadleigh, Ipswich IP7 6SJ ☎ 01473 825819 john.moyles@baberghmidsuffolk.gov.uk

Fleet Management: Mr Ryan Jones , Corporate Manager - Asset Management Operations, Council Offices, 131 High Street, Needham Market IP6 8DL ☎ 01473 825787 🖷 01473 825770 ryan.jones@baberghmidsuffolk.gov.uk

Grounds Maintenance: Mr Peter Garrett , Corporate Manager - Public Realm, Council Offices, Corks Lane, Hadleigh, Ipswich IP7 6SJ ☎ 01473 826615 🖷 01473 823594 ryan.jones@baberghmidsuffolk.gov.uk

Health and Safety: Mr Kevin Collins , Joint Corporate Health & Safety Officer, Council Offices, 131 High Street, Needham Market IP6 8DL ☎ 01449 724704 kevin.collins@baberghmidsuffolk.gov.uk

Home Energy Conservation: Mr James Buckingham , Corporate Manager - Environmental Protection, Council Offices, 131 High Street, Needham Market IP6 8DL ☎ 01473 825880 🖷 01473 825738 james.buckingham@midsuffolk.gov.uk; james.buckingham@baberghmidsuffolk.gov.uk

Housing: Mr Martin King , Head - Housing, Council Offices, 131 High Street, Needham Market IP6 8DL ☎ 01473 826649 🖷 01473 825742 martin.king@midsuffolk.gov.uk; martin.king@baberghmidsuffolk.gov.uk

MID SUFFOLK

Housing Maintenance: Mr Ryan Jones , Corporate Manager - Asset Management Operations, Council Offices, 131 High Street, Needham Market IP6 8DL ☎ 01473 825787 🖷 01473 825770 ✉ ryan.jones@baberghmidsuffolk.gov.uk

Legal: Ms Suki Binjal , Monitoring Officer, Council Offices, Corks Lane, Hadleigh, Ipswich IP7 6SJ ☎ 01473 825729 ✉ suki.binjal@baberghmidsuffolk.gov.uk

Leisure and Cultural Services: Mr Jonathan Free , Head - Communities, Council Offices, 131 High Street, Needham Market IP6 8DL ☎ 01473 826649 🖷 01473 825742 ✉ jonathan.free@baberghmidsuffolk.gov.uk

Leisure and Cultural Services: Mr Jonathan Seed , Corporate Manager - Healthy Communities, Council Offices, 131 High Street, Needham Market IP6 8DL ☎ 01449 724857 🖷 01449 724655 ✉ jonathan.seed@baberghmidsuffolk.gov.uk

Licensing: Mr Lee Carvell , Corporate Manager - Licensing, Council Offices, 131 High Street, Needham Market IP6 8DL ☎ 01473 825719 ✉ lee.carvell@baberghmidsuffolk.gov.uk

Lottery Funding, Charity and Voluntary: Ms Sue Clements , Corporate Manager - Strong Communities, Council Offices, Corks Lane, Hadleigh, Ipswich IP7 6SJ ☎ 01449 724657 🖷 01449 724655 ✉ sue.clemments@baberghmidsuffolk.gov.uk

Member Services: Mr Peter Quirk , Head - Corporate Organisation, Council Offices, 131 High Street, Needham Market IP6 8DL ☎ 01473 825829 🖷 01473 825742 ✉ peter.quirk@baberghmidsuffolk.gov.uk

Parking: Mr Chris Fry , Head - Environment, Council Offices, 131 High Street, Needham Market IP6 8DL ☎ 01473 826649 🖷 01473 825742 ✉ chris.fry@baberghmidsuffolk.gov.uk

Partnerships: Ms Sue Clements , Corporate Manager - Strong Communities, Council Offices, Corks Lane, Hadleigh, Ipswich IP7 6SJ ☎ 01449 724657 🖷 01449 724655 ✉ sue.clemments@baberghmidsuffolk.gov.uk

Personnel / HR: Ms Carla Doyle , Corporate Manager - Organisational Development, Council Offices, Corks Lane, Hadleigh, Ipswich IP7 6SJ ☎ 01473 825744 🖷 01473 825742 ✉ carla.doyle@baberghmidsuffolk.gov.uk

Planning: Mr Philip Isbell , Corporate Manager - Development Management, Council Offices, 131 High Street, Needham Market IP6 8DL ☎ 01449 724537 ✉ philip.isbell@midsuffolk.gov.uk

Procurement: Mrs Rachel Hodson-Gibbons , Corporate Manager - Commissioning, Council Offices, 131 High Street, Needham Market IP6 8DL ☎ 01449 724587 ✉ rachel.hodson-gibbons@baberghmidsuffolk.gov.uk

Recycling & Waste Minimisation: Mr Oliver Faiers , Corporate Manager - Waste, Council Offices, Corks Lane, Hadleigh, Ipswich IP7 6SJ ☎ 01449 778621 ✉ oliver.faiers@baberghmidsuffolk.gov.uk

Regeneration: Mr David Benham, Corporate Manager - Economic Development & Tourism, Council Offices, 131 High Street, Needham Market IP6 8DL ☎ 01449 724649 🖷 01449 724655 ✉ david.benham@baberghmidsuffolk.gov.uk

Staff Training: Ms Carla Doyle , Corporate Manager - Organisational Development, Council Offices, Corks Lane, Hadleigh, Ipswich IP7 6SJ ☎ 01473 825744 🖷 01473 825742 ✉ carla.doyle@baberghmidsuffolk.gov.uk

Sustainable Communities: Mr Rich Cooke , Corporate Manager - Spatial Planning Policy, Council Offices, Corks Lane, Hadleigh IP7 6SJ ☎ 01473 825775 ✉ rich.cooke@babergh.gov.uk

Sustainable Communities: Mr Jonathan Free , Head - Communities, Council Offices, Corks Lane, Hadleigh, Ipswich IP7 6SJ ☎ 01473 826649 🖷 01473 825742 ✉ jonathan.free@baberghmidsuffolk.gov.uk

Sustainable Development: Mr Chris Fry , Head - Environment, Council Offices, 131 High Street, Needham Market IP6 8DL ☎ 01473 826649 🖷 01473 825742 ✉ chris.fry@baberghmidsuffolk.gov.uk

Tourism: Mr David Benham, Corporate Manager - Economic Development & Tourism, Council Offices, 131 High Street, Needham Market IP6 8DL ☎ 01449 724649 🖷 01449 724655 ✉ david.benham@baberghmidsuffolk.gov.uk

Waste Collection and Disposal: Mr Oliver Faiers , Corporate Manager - Waste, Council Offices, Corks Lane, Hadleigh, Ipswich IP7 6SJ ☎ 01449 778621 ✉ oliver.faiers@baberghmidsuffolk.gov.uk

Waste Management: Mr Oliver Faiers , Corporate Manager - Waste, Council Offices, Corks Lane, Hadleigh, Ipswich IP7 6SJ ☎ 01449 778621 ✉ oliver.faiers@baberghmidsuffolk.gov.uk

Children's Play Areas: Mr Chris Fry , Head - Environment, Council Offices, 131 High Street, Needham Market IP6 8DL ☎ 01473 826649 🖷 01473 825742 ✉ chris.fry@baberghmidsuffolk.gov.uk

COUNCILLORS

***Chair* Osborne**, Derek (CON - Rickinghall & Walsham)

***Leader of the Council* Haley**, Derrick (CON - Thurston & Hessett)
derrick.haley@midsuffolk.gov.uk

***Deputy Leader of the Council* Gowrley**, Nick (CON - Stowmarket South)
nick.gowrley@midsuffolk.gov.uk

***Group Leader* Otton**, Penny (LD - Rattlesden)
penny.otton@midsuffolk.gov.uk

Barker, Roy (CON - Badwell Ash)
roy.barker@midsuffolk.gov.uk

Brewster, Gerard (IND - Stowmarket South)
gerard.brewster@midsuffolk.gov.uk

Burn, David (CON - Palgrave)
david.burn@midsuffolk.gov.uk

Card, David (CON - Barking & Somersham)
david.card@midsuffolk.gov.uk

Caston, James (CON - Claydon & Barham)
james.caston@midsuffolk.gov.uk

Curran, Marilyn (CON - Fressingfield)
marilyn.curran@midsuffolk.gov.uk

Eburne, Rachel (GRN - Haughley & Wetherden)
rachel.eburne@midsuffolk.gov.uk

Ekpenyong, Paul (CON - Stowmarket Central)
paul.ekpenyong@midsuffolk.gov.uk

Field, John (LD - Bramford & Blakenham)
john.field@midsuffolk.gov.uk

Flatman, Charles (IND - Eye)
charles.flatman@midsuffolk.gov.uk

Flatman, Julie (CON - Stradbroke & Laxfield)

Fleming, Jessica (CON - Rickinghall & Walsham)

Gibson-Harries, Elizabeth (CON - Hoxne)
elizabeth.gibson-harries@midsuffolk.gov.uk

Green, Gary (CON - Stowmarket North)
gary.green@midsuffolk.gov.uk

Guthrie, Kathie (CON - Debenham)
kathie.guthrie@midsuffolk.gov.uk

Hicks, Matthew (CON - Worlingworth)
matthew.hicks@midsuffolk.gov.uk

Horn, Glen (CON - Wetheringsett)
glen.horn@midsuffolk.gov.uk

Humphreys, Barry (CON - Stowmarket North)

Jewson, Esther (CON - Thurston & Hessett)
esther.jewson@midsuffolk.gov.uk

Kearsley, Diana (CON - Gislingham)
diana.kearsley@midsuffolk.gov.uk

Levantis, John (CON - Elmswell & Norton)
john.levantis@midsuffolk.gov.uk

Mansel, Sarah (GRN - Elmswell & Norton)
sarah.mansel@midsuffok.gov.uk

Marchant, Wendy (LD - Needham Market)
wendy.marchant@midsuffolk.gov.uk

Matthissen, John (GRN - Onehouse)
john.matthissen@midsuffolk.gov.uk

Mayes, Lesley (CON - Stowmarket Central)

Morley, Suzie (CON - The Stonhams)
suzie.morley@midsuffolk.gov.uk

Muller, Dave (CON - Stowmarket North)
dave.muller@midsuffolk.gov.uk

Norris, Mike (LD - Needham Market)
mike.norris@midsuffolk.gov.uk

Passmore, Tim (CON - Helmingham & Coddenham)
timothy.passmore@midsuffolk.gov.uk

Storey, Jane (CON - Woolpit)
jane.storey@midsuffolk.gov.uk

Stringer, Andrew (GRN - Mendlesham)
andrew.stringer@midsuffolk.gov.uk

Welham, Keith (GRN - Stowupland)
keith.welham@midsuffolk.gov.uk

Welsby, Kevin (CON - Bramford & Blakenham)
kevin.welsby@midsuffolk.gov.uk

Whitehead, John (CON - Claydon & Barham)
john.whitehead@midsuffolk.gov.uk

Whybrow, David (CON - Ringshall)
david.whybrow@midsuffolk.gov.uk

Wilshaw, Jill (CON - Bacton & Old Newton)
jill.wilshaw@midsuffolk.gov.uk

POLITICAL COMPOSITION

CON: 29, GRN: 5, LD: 4, IND: 2

COMMITTEE CHAIRS

Audit: Mrs Elizabeth Gibson-Harries

Licensing: Mrs Kathie Guthrie

Mid Sussex D

Mid Sussex District Council, Oaklands, Oaklands Road, Haywards Heath RH16 1SS
☎ 01444 458166 🖷 01444 450027 ✉ enquiries@midsussex.gov.uk
💻 www.midsussex.gov.uk

FACTS AND FIGURES

EU Constituencies: South East

Election Frequency: Elections are of whole council

PRINCIPAL OFFICERS

Chief Executive: Ms Kathryn Hall , Chief Executive, Mid Sussex District Council, Oaklands, Oaklands Road, Haywards Heath RH16 1SS ☎ 01444 477498 🖷 01444 477236 ✉ kathryn.hall@midsussex.gov.uk

Assistant Chief Executive: Miss Judy Holmes , Assistant Chief Executive, Oaklands, Oaklands Road, Haywards Heath RH16 1SS ☎ 0144 477015 ✉ judy.holmes@midsussex.gov.uk

Senior Management: Mr Tom Clark, Solicitor to the Council, Mid Sussex District Council, Oaklands, Oaklands Road, Haywards Heath RH16 1SS ☎ 01444 477459 ✉ tom.clark@midsussex.gov.uk

Senior Management: Mr Mark Fisher , Head of Leisure & Sustainability, Oaklands, Oaklands Road, Haywards Heath RH16 1SS ☎ 01444 477367 ✉ mark.fisher@midsussex.gov.uk

Senior Management: Mr Simon Hughes , Head of Digital & Customer Services, Oaklands, Oaklands Road, Haywards Heath RH16 1SS ✉ simon.hughes@midsussex.gov.uk

Senior Management: Mrs Lynne Standing, Head of Housing, Environmental Health & Building Control, Oaklands, Oaklands Road, Haywards Heath RH16 1SS ☎ 01444 477411 🖷 01444 417965 ✉ lynne.standing@midsussex.gov.uk

Senior Management: Mr Peter Stuart, Head of HR & Finance, Oaklands, Oaklands Road, Haywards Heath RH16 1SS ☎ 01444 477315 ✉ peter.stuart@midsussex.gov.uk

MID SUSSEX

Senior Management: Ms Claire Tester , Head of Planning & Economic Promotion, Oaklands, Oaklands Road, Haywards Heath RH16 1SS ☎ 01444 477322 ✉ claire.tester@midsussex.gov.uk

Building Control: Mrs Yvonne Leddy , Business Unit Leader for Environmental Health & Building Control, Oaklands, Oaklands Road, Haywards Heath RH16 1SS ☎ 01444 477300 ✉ yvonne.leddy@midsussex.gov.uk

Children / Youth Services: Ms Susannah Conway , Young Persons' Development Officer, Oaklands, Oaklands Road, Haywards Heath RH16 1SS ☎ 01444 477518 ✉ susannah.conway@midsussex.gov.uk

PR / Communications: Mrs Diane Talbot , Business Unit Leader for Customer Services & Communications, Oaklands, Oaklands Road, Haywards Heath RH16 1SS ☎ 01444 477387 ✉ diane.talbot@midsussex.gov.uk

Community Planning: Ms Lucie Venables , Senior Community Partnership Officer, Oaklands, Oaklands Road, Haywards Heath RH16 1SS ☎ 01444 477204 🖷 01444 477507 ✉ lucie.venables@midsussex.gov.uk

Community Safety: Ms Nicola Jackson , Community Safety Officer, Oaklands, Oaklands Road, Haywards Heath RH16 1SS ☎ 01444 477550 🖷 01444 417965 ✉ nicolette.russell@midsussex.gov.uk

Computer Management: Mr Mark Gawley , CenSus IT Operations Manager, Horsham DC, Parkside, Chart Way, Horsham RH12 1PL ☎ 01903 221477; 01903 221197 ✉ mark.gawley@adur-worthing.gov.uk

Contracts: Mr Ian Gifford , Property & Asset Manager, Oaklands, Oaklands Road, Haywards Heath RH16 1SS ☎ 01444 477490 ✉ ian.gifford@midsussex.gov.uk

Corporate Services: Miss Judy Holmes , Assistant Chief Executive, Oaklands, Oaklands Road, Haywards Heath RH16 1SS ☎ 0144 477015 ✉ judy.holmes@midsussex.gov.uk

Customer Service: Ms Karen Speirs , Senior Customer Services Officer, Oaklands, Oaklands Road, Haywards Heath RH16 1SS ☎ 01444 477510 ✉ karen.speirs@midsussex.gov.uk

Economic Development: Ms Claire Tester , Head of Planning & Economic Promotion, Oaklands, Oaklands Road, Haywards Heath RH16 1SS ☎ 01444 477322 ✉ claire.tester@midsussex.gov.uk

Electoral Registration: Mr Terry Stanley , Senior Elections Officer, Oaklands, Oaklands Road, Haywards Heath RH16 1SS ☎ 01444 477415 ✉ terry.stanley@midsussex.gov.uk

Emergency Planning: Mr Ben Toogood , Emergency Planning & Outdoor Services Manager, Oaklands, Oaklands Road, Haywards Heath RH16 1SS ☎ 01444 477379 ✉ ben.toogood@midsussex.gov.uk

Energy Management: Mr Ian Gifford , Property & Asset Manager, Oaklands, Oaklands Road, Haywards Heath RH16 1SS ☎ 01444 477490 ✉ ian.gifford@midsussex.gov.uk

Environmental Health: Mrs Yvonne Leddy , Business Unit Leader for Environmental Health & Building Control, Oaklands, Oaklands Road, Haywards Heath RH16 1SS ☎ 01444 477300 ✉ yvonne.leddy@midsussex.gov.uk

Estates, Property & Valuation: Ms Emma Grundy , Property & Asset Manager, Oaklands, Oaklands Road, Haywards Heath RH16 1SS ☎ 01444 477490 ✉ emma.grundy@midsussex.gov.uk

Facilities: Mr David Harper, Business Unit Leader for Waste & Outdoor Services, Oaklands, Oaklands Road, Haywards Heath RH16 1SS ☎ 01444 477487 🖷 01444 450027 ✉ david.harper@midsussex.gov.uk

Finance: Mr Peter Stuart, Head of HR & Finance, Oaklands, Oaklands Road, Haywards Heath RH16 1SS ☎ 01444 477315 ✉ peter.stuart@midsussex.gov.uk

Grounds Maintenance: Mr Rupert Browning, Business Unit Leader for Landscapes, Oaklands, Oaklands Road, Haywards Heath RH16 1SS ☎ 01444 477374 🖷 01444 477464 ✉ rupert.browning@midsussex.gov.uk

Health and Safety: Mr Scott Wakely , Corporate Safety & Technical Services Officer, Oaklands, Oaklands Road, Haywards Heath RH16 1SS ☎ 01444 477002 ✉ scott.wakely@midsussex.gov.uk

Home Energy Conservation: Ms Celia Austin , Sustainability Officer, Oaklands, Oaklands Road, Haywards Heath RH16 1SS ☎ 01444 477370 ✉ celia.austin@midsussex.gov.uk

Housing: Mrs Lynne Standing, Head of Housing, Environmental Health & Building Control, Oaklands, Oaklands Road, Haywards Heath RH16 1SS ☎ 01444 477411 🖷 01444 417965 ✉ lynne.standing@midsussex.gov.uk

Legal: Mr Tom Clark, Solicitor to the Council, Mid Sussex District Council, Oaklands, Oaklands Road, Haywards Heath RH16 1SS ☎ 01444 477459 ✉ tom.clark@midsussex.gov.uk

Leisure and Cultural Services: Mr Mark Fisher , Head of Leisure & Sustainability, Oaklands, Oaklands Road, Haywards Heath RH16 1SS ☎ 01444 477367 ✉ mark.fisher@midsussex.gov.uk

Licensing: Mr Paul Thornton, Senior Licensing Officer, Oaklands, Oaklands Road, Haywards Heath RH16 1SS ☎ 01444 477428 ✉ paul.thornton@midsussex.gov.uk

Member Services: Ms Hannah Martin , Senior Member Services Officer, Oaklands, Oaklands Road, Haywards Heath RH16 1SS ☎ 01444 477111 ✉ hannah.martin@midsussex.gov.uk

Parking: Mrs Sue Rees , Parking Services Manager, Mid Sussex District Council, Oaklands, Oaklands Road, Haywards Heath RH16 1SS ☎ 01444 477586 ✉ sue.rees@midsussex.gov.uk

Partnerships: Mr Terry Standing , Business Unit Leader - Member Performance & Partnerships, Oaklands, Oaklands Road, Haywards Heath RH16 1SS ☎ 01444 477514 ✉ tim.cusack@midsussex.gov.uk

Personnel / HR: Mr Peter Stuart, Head of HR & Finance, Oaklands, Oaklands Road, Haywards Heath RH16 1SS ☎ 01444 477315 ✉ peter.stuart@midsussex.gov.uk

Planning: Ms Claire Tester , Head of Planning & Economic Promotion, Oaklands, Oaklands Road, Haywards Heath RH16 1SS ☎ 01444 477322 ✉ claire.tester@midsussex.gov.uk

Procurement: Mr Roger Dennis , Joint Procurement Officer, Oaklands, Oaklands Road, Haywards Heath RH16 1SS ☎ 01444 477254 ✉ rogerd@horsham.gov.uk

Recycling & Waste Minimisation: Mr David Harper, Business Unit Leader for Waste & Outdoor Services, Oaklands, Oaklands Road, Haywards Heath RH16 1SS ☎ 01444 477487 🖷 01444 450027 ✉ david.harper@midsussex.gov.uk

Staff Training: Ms Emma Jackson, Personnel & Training Officer, Oaklands, Oaklands Road, Haywards Heath RH16 1SS ☎ 01444 477276 🖷 01444 450027 ✉ emma.jackson@midsussex.gov.uk

Sustainable Communities: Mr Simon Hardy , Business Unit Leader for Community Services & Culture, Oaklands, Oaklands Road, Haywards Heath RH16 1SS ☎ 01444 477454 🖷 01444 477461 ✉ simon.hardy@midsussex.gov.uk

Sustainable Development: Ms Celia Austin , Sustainability Officer, Oaklands, Oaklands Road, Haywards Heath RH16 1SS ☎ 01444 477370 ✉ celia.austin@midsussex.gov.uk

Waste Collection and Disposal: Mr David Harper, Business Unit Leader for Waste & Outdoor Services, Oaklands, Oaklands Road, Haywards Heath RH16 1SS ☎ 01444 477487 🖷 01444 450027 ✉ david.harper@midsussex.gov.uk

Waste Management: Mr David Harper, Business Unit Leader for Waste & Outdoor Services, Oaklands, Oaklands Road, Haywards Heath RH16 1SS ☎ 01444 477487 🖷 01444 450027 ✉ david.harper@midsussex.gov.uk

Children's Play Areas: Mr Rupert Browning, Business Unit Leader for Landscapes, Oaklands, Oaklands Road, Haywards Heath RH16 1SS ☎ 01444 477374 🖷 01444 477464 ✉ rupert.browning@midsussex.gov.uk

COUNCILLORS

***Chair* Reed**, Peter (CON - East Grinstead - Ashplats)
peter.reed@midsussex.gov.uk

***Vice-Chair* Forbes**, Bruce (CON - Crawley Down and Turners Hill)
Bruce.Forbes@midsussex.gov.uk

***Leader of the Council* Wall**, Garry (CON - Haywards Heath - Franklands)
Garry.wall@midsussex.gov.uk

***Deputy Leader of the Council* Ash-Edwards**, Jonathan (CON - Haywards Heath - Heath)
jonathan.ash-edwards@midsussex.gov.uk

Allen, John (CON - Bolney)
john.allen@midsussex.gov.uk

Barrett-Miles, Andrew (CON - Burgess Hill - Dunstall)
andrew.barrett-miles@midsussex.gov.uk

Belsey, Margaret (CON - East Grinstead - Baldwins)
Margaret.Belsey@midsussex.gov.uk

Belsey, John (CON - Ashurst Wood)
john.belsey@midsuusex.gov.uk

Belsey, Edward (CON - East Grinstead - Herontye)
Edward.Belsey@midsussex.gov.uk

Bennett, Liz (CON - East Grinstead - Ashplats)
liz.bennett@midsussex.gov.uk

Boutrup, Anne (CON - Haywards Heath - Ashenground)
anne.boutrup@midsussex.gov.uk

Bradbury, Pete (CON - Cuckfield)
pete.bradbury@midsussex.gov.uk

Brunsdon, Heidi (CON - East Grinstead - Imberhorne)
heidi.brunsdon@midsussex.gov.uk

Burke, Kevin (CON - Hassocks)
kevin.burke@midsussex.gov.uk

Catharine, Cherry (CON - Burgess Hill - Leylands)
Cherry.Catharine@midsussex.gov.uk

Cherry, Richard (CON - Burgess Hill - Meeds)
richard.cherry@midsussex.gov.uk

Clarke, Rod (CON - Haywards Heath - Franklands)
rod.clarke@midsussex.gov.uk

Coote, Philip (CON - Crawley Down and Turners Hill)
Phillip.Coote@midsussex.gov.uk

de Mierre, Ruth (CON - Haywards Heath - Bentswood)
Ruth.DeMierre@midsussex.gov.uk

Dorey, Tony (CON - Copthorne and Worth)
tony.dorey@midsussex.gov.uk

Dorking, David (CON - Haywards Heath - Bentswood)
David.Dorking@midsussex.gov.uk

Ellis, Sandy (CON - Haywards Heath - Heath)
sandra.ellis@midsussex.gov.uk

Hansford, Steven (CON - Burgess Hill - Victoria)
steven.hansford@midsussex.gov.uk

Heard, Ginny (CON - Burgess Hill - Franklands)
Ginny.Heard@midsussex.gov.uk

Hersey, Margaret (CON - Lindfield)
margaret.hersey@midsussex.gov.uk

Hersey, Christopher (CON - High Weald)
chris.hersey@midsussex.gov.uk

Holden, Colin (CON - Burgess Hill - St Andrews)
colin.holden@midsussex.gov.uk

Jones, Anne (CON - Burgess Hill - Meeds)
anne.jones@midsussex.gov.uk

King, Chris (CON - Burgess Hill - Franklands)
chris.king@midsussex.gov.uk

Knight, Jim (CON - Haywards Heath - Lucastes)
jim.knight@midsussex.gov.uk

Landriani, Jacqui (CON - Burgess Hill - Dunstall)
jacqui.landriani@midsussex.gov.uk

Lea, Andrew (CON - Lindfield)
andrew.lea@midsussex.gov.uk

Lea, Anthea (CON - Lindfield)
anthea.lea@midsussex.gov.uk

MID SUSSEX

MacNaughton, Andrew (CON - Ardingly and Balcombe)
andrew.macnaughton@midsussex.gov.uk

Mainstone, Bob (LD - East Grinstead - Imberhorne)
Bob.Mainstone@midsussex.gov.uk

Marples, Gordon (CON - Hassocks)
gordon.marples@midsussex.gov.uk

Marsh, Gary (CON - Ardingly and Balcombe)
gary.marsh@midsussex.gov.uk

Martin, Peter (CON - Hassocks)
peter.martin@midsussex.gov.uk

Matthews, Edward (CON - Copthorne and Worth)
edward.matthews@midsussex.gov.uk

Mockford, Norman (CON - East Grinstead - Town)
norman.mockford@midsussex.gov.uk

Moore, Pru (CON - Burgess Hill - Leylands)
pru.moore@midsussex.gov.uk

Mundin, Howard (CON - Haywards Heath - Ashenground)
howard.mundin@midsussex.gov.uk

Page, Kirsty (CON - Burgess Hill - St Andrews)
kirsty.page@midsussex.gov.uk

Rawlinson, Geoff (CON - Haywards Heath - Lucastes)
Geoff.Rawlinson@midsussex.gov.uk

Salisbury, Robert (CON - Cuckfield)
robert.salisbury@midsussex.gov.uk

Stockwell, Linda (CON - High Weald)
linda.stockwell@midsussex.gov.uk

Sweatman, Dick (CON - East Grinstead - Herontye)
Dick.Sweatman@midsussex.gov.uk

Thomas-Atkin, Mandy (CON - Burgess Hill - Victoria)
mandy.thomas-atkin@midsussex.gov.uk

Trumble, Colin (CON - Hurstpierpoint and Downs)
Colin.Trumble@midsussex.gov.uk

Walker, Neville (CON - Crawley Down and Turners Hill)
Neville.Walker@midsussex.gov.uk

Watts Williams, Anthony (CON - Hurstpierpoint and Downs)
AnthonyWattsWilliams@midsussex.gov.uk

Webster, Norman (CON - East Grinstead - Baldwins)
Norman.Webster@midsussex.gov.uk

Wilkinson, John (CON - Hurstpierpoint and Downs)
john.wilkinson@midsussex.gov.uk

Wyan, Peter (CON - East Grinstead - Town)
peter.wyan@midsussex.gov.uk

POLITICAL COMPOSITION

CON: 53, LD: 1

COMMITTEE CHAIRS

Audit: Mr Andrew Lea

Licensing: Mr Jim Knight

Planning: Mr Robert Salisbury

Mid Ulster District, Mid Ulster Transition Committee, Change Management Office, c/o Dungannon & South Tyrone Borough Council, Circular Road, Dungannon BT71 6DT
☎ 028 8772 0300 philip.moffett@dungannon.gov.uk
www.midulstercouncil.org

PRINCIPAL OFFICERS

Chief Executive: Mr Anthony Tohill , Chief Executive, Mid Ulster Transition Committee, Change Management Office, c/o Dungannon & South Tyrone Borough Council, Circular Road, Dungannon BT71 6DT

Senior Management: Dr Chris Boomer , Planning Manager, Mid Ulster Transition Committee, Change Management Office, c/o Dungannon & South Tyrone Borough Council, Circular Road, Dungannon BT71 6DT ☎ 03000 132132
chris.boomer@midulstercouncil.org

Senior Management: Ms Anne-Marie Campbell , Director of Culture & Leisure, Mid Ulster Transition Committee, Change Management Office, c/o Dungannon & South Tyrone Borough Council, Circular Road, Dungannon BT71 6DT ☎ 03000 132132
annemarie.campbell@midulstercouncil.org

Senior Management: Ms Marissa Canavan , Lead HR Officer, Mid Ulster Transition Committee, Change Management Office, c/o Dungannon & South Tyrone Borough Council, Circular Road, Dungannon BT71 6DT ☎ 03000 132132
marissa.canavan@midulstercouncil.org

Senior Management: Mr Andrew Cassells , Director of Environment & Property, Mid Ulster Transition Committee, Change Management Office, c/o Dungannon & South Tyrone Borough Council, Circular Road, Dungannon BT71 6DT ☎ 03000 132132
andrew.cassells@midulstercouncil.org

Senior Management: Mr Mark Kelso , Director of Public Health & Infrastructure, Mid Ulster Transition Committee, Change Management Office, c/o Dungannon & South Tyrone Borough Council, Circular Road, Dungannon BT71 6DT ☎ 03000 132132
mark.kelso@midulstercouncil.org

Senior Management: Mr Adrian McCreesh , Director of Business & Communities, Mid Ulster Transition Committee, Change Management Office, c/o Dungannon & South Tyrone Borough Council, Circular Road, Dungannon BT71 6DT ☎ 03000 132132
adrian.mccreesh@midulstercouncil.org

Senior Management: Mr JJ Tohill , Lead Finance Officer, Mid Ulster Transition Committee, Change Management Office, c/o Dungannon & South Tyrone Borough Council, Circular Road, Dungannon BT71 6DT ☎ 03000 132132
jj.tohill@midulstercouncil.org

Architect, Building / Property Services: Mr Terry Scullion , Head of Property Services, Mid Ulster Transition Committee, Change Management Office, c/o Dungannon & South Tyrone Borough Council, Circular Road, Dungannon BT71 6DT ☎ 03000 132132 terry.scullion@midulstercouncil.org

Building Control: Mr Willie Wilkinson , Head of Building Control, Mid Ulster Transition Committee, Change Management Office, c/o Dungannon & South Tyrone Borough Council, Circular Road, Dungannon BT71 6DT ☎ 03000 132132 🖱 willie.wilkinson@midulstercouncil.org

Community Planning: Ms Claire Linney , Head of Community Development, Mid Ulster Transition Committee, Change Management Office, c/o Dungannon & South Tyrone Borough Council, Circular Road, Dungannon BT71 6DT ☎ 03000 132132 🖱 claire.linney@midulstercouncil.org

Computer Management: Mr Barry O'Hagan , Head of ICT, Mid Ulster Transition Committee, Change Management Office, c/o Dungannon & South Tyrone Borough Council, Circular Road, Dungannon BT71 6DT ☎ 03000 132132 🖱 barry.ohagan@midulstercouncil.org

Corporate Services: Mr Adrian McCreesh , Director of Business & Communities, Mid Ulster Transition Committee, Change Management Office, c/o Dungannon & South Tyrone Borough Council, Circular Road, Dungannon BT71 6DT ☎ 03000 132132 🖱 adrian.mccreesh@midulstercouncil.org

Corporate Services: Mr Philip Moffett , Change Manager, Mid Ulster Transition Committee, Change Management Office, c/o Dungannon & South Tyrone Borough Council, Circular Road, Dungannon BT71 6DT

Economic Development: Ms Fiona McKeown , Head of Economic Development, Mid Ulster Transition Committee, Change Management Office, c/o Dungannon & South Tyrone Borough Council, Circular Road, Dungannon BT71 6DT ☎ 03000 132132 🖱 fiona.mckeown@midulstercouncil.org

Environmental / Technical Services: Mr Andrew Cassells , Director of Environment & Property, Mid Ulster Transition Committee, Change Management Office, c/o Dungannon & South Tyrone Borough Council, Circular Road, Dungannon BT71 6DT ☎ 03000 132132 🖱 andrew.cassells@midulstercouncil.org

Environmental / Technical Services: Mr Raymond Lowry , Head of Technical Services, Mid Ulster Transition Committee, Change Management Office, c/o Dungannon & South Tyrone Borough Council, Circular Road, Dungannon BT71 6DT ☎ 03000 132132 🖱 raymond.lowry@midulstercouncil.org

Environmental / Technical Services: Mr Mark McAdoo , Head of Environmental Services, Mid Ulster Transition Committee, Change Management Office, c/o Dungannon & South Tyrone Borough Council, Circular Road, Dungannon BT71 6DT ☎ 03000 132132 🖱 mark.mcadoo@midulstercouncil.org

Environmental Health: Mr Andrew Cassells , Director of Environment & Property, Mid Ulster Transition Committee, Change Management Office, c/o Dungannon & South Tyrone Borough Council, Circular Road, Dungannon BT71 6DT ☎ 03000 132132 🖱 andrew.cassells@midulstercouncil.org

Environmental Health: Ms Fiona McClements , Head of Environmental Health, Mid Ulster Transition Committee, Change Management Office, c/o Dungannon & South Tyrone Borough Council, Circular Road, Dungannon BT71 6DT ☎ 03000 132132 🖱 fiona.mcclements@midulstercouncil.org

Finance: Ms Paula Keer , Head of Finance, Mid Ulster Transition Committee, Change Management Office, c/o Dungannon & South Tyrone Borough Council, Circular Road, Dungannon BT71 6DT ☎ 03000 132132 🖱 paula.kerr@midulstercouncil.org

Finance: Mr JJ Tohill , Lead Finance Officer, Mid Ulster Transition Committee, Change Management Office, c/o Dungannon & South Tyrone Borough Council, Circular Road, Dungannon BT71 6DT ☎ 03000 132132 🖱 jj.tohill@midulstercouncil.org

Leisure and Cultural Services: Ms Anne-Marie Campbell , Director of Culture & Leisure, Mid Ulster Transition Committee, Change Management Office, c/o Dungannon & South Tyrone Borough Council, Circular Road, Dungannon BT71 6DT ☎ 03000 132132 🖱 annemarie.campbell@midulstercouncil.org

Personnel / HR: Ms Marissa Canavan , Lead HR Officer, Mid Ulster Transition Committee, Change Management Office, c/o Dungannon & South Tyrone Borough Council, Circular Road, Dungannon BT71 6DT ☎ 03000 132132 🖱 marissa.canavan@midulstercouncil.org

Personnel / HR: Ms Geraldine Dyson , Head of HR, Mid Ulster Transition Committee, Change Management Office, c/o Dungannon & South Tyrone Borough Council, Circular Road, Dungannon BT71 6DT ☎ 03000 132132 🖱 geraldine.dyson@midulstercouncil.org

Planning: Dr Chris Boomer , Planning Manager, Mid Ulster Transition Committee, Change Management Office, c/o Dungannon & South Tyrone Borough Council, Circular Road, Dungannon BT71 6DT ☎ 03000 132132 🖱 chris.boomer@midulstercouncil.org

Planning: Mr Melvin Brown , Head of Development Management, Mid Ulster Transition Committee, Change Management Office, c/o Dungannon & South Tyrone Borough Council, Circular Road, Dungannon BT71 6DT ☎ 03000 132132 🖱 melvin.brown@midulstercouncil.org

Public Health: Mr Mark Kelso , Director of Public Health & Infrastructure, Mid Ulster Transition Committee, Change Management Office, c/o Dungannon & South Tyrone Borough Council, Circular Road, Dungannon BT71 6DT ☎ 03000 132132 🖱 mark.kelso@midulstercouncil.org

Tourism: Mr Michael Browne , Head of Tourism, Mid Ulster Transition Committee, Change Management Office, c/o Dungannon & South Tyrone Borough Council, Circular Road, Dungannon BT71 6DT ☎ 03000 132132 🖱 michael.browne@midulstercouncil.org

COUNCILLORS

Ashton, Kim (DUP - Dungannon)
kim.ashton@dstbc.org

Bateson, Peter (SF - Moyola)
peadardebath@gmail.com

Bell, Gavin (SF - Cookstown)
gavin.bell.sf@gmail.com

Buchanan, Wilbert (DUP - Cookstown)
william774@btinternet.com

Burton, Frances (DUP - Clogher Valley)
frances.burton@dstbc.org

Clarke, Sean (SF - Magherafelt)
clerke@hotmail.com

Cuddy, Walter (UUP - Dungannon)
walter.cuddy@dstbc.org

Cuthbertson, Clement (DUP - Dungannon)
clementcuthbertson@hotmail.co.uk

Dillon, Linda (SF - Torrent)
linda.dillon81@gmail.com

Elattar, Catherine (SF - Moyola)
celattar@yahoo.ie

Forde, Anne (DUP - Moyola)
cllr.forde@magherafelt.gov.uk

Gildernew, Phelim (SF - Clogher Valley)
phelim.gildernew@dstbc.org

Gillespie, Mickey (SF - Torrent)
michael.gillespie@dstbc.org

Glasgow, Mark (UUP - Cookstown)
mark814glasgow@btinternet.com

Kearney, Martin (SDLP - Carntogher)
kearney768@btinternet.com

Mallaghan, Cáthal (SF - Cookstown)
cathalmallaghan@hotmail.com

McAleer, Sharon (SDLP - Clogher Valley)
sharonmcaleer.sdlp@gmail.com

McEldowney, Kate (SF - Carntogher)
kate.mceldowney@yahoo.ie

McFlynn, Christine (SDLP - Magherafelt)
christine.mcflynn@cookstown.gov.uk

McGinley, Ronan (SF - Torrent)
ronanmcginley@ymail.com

McGuigan, Brian (SF - Carntogher)
bmcguigan52@yahoo.ie

McGuigan, Sean (SF - Clogher Valley)
sean.mcguigan@dstbc.org

McKinney, Derek (UUP - Moyola)
derekmckinney71@gmail.com

McLean, Paul (DUP - Magherafelt)
mcleanpaul@me.com

McNamee, John (SF - Cookstown)
john.mcnamee@cookstown.gov.uk

McPeake, Seán (SF - Carntogher)
seanmcpeake@hotmail.com

Molloy, Dominic (SF - Dungannon)
domonic.molloy@dstbc.org

Monteith, Barry (IND - Dungannon)
barry.monteith@dstbc.org

Mullen, Denise (SDLP - Dungannon)
denise.mullen.125@gmail.com

Mulligan, Robert (UUP - Clogher Valley)
robert.mulligan@dstbc.org

O'Neill, Caoimhe (SF - Moyola)
caoimheoneill01@yahoo.com

O'Neill, Joe (SF - Torrent)
joe.oneill@dstbc.org

Quinn, Malachy (SDLP - Torrent)
malachyquinn@hotmail.com

Quinn, Tony (SDLP - Cookstown)
tony.quinn@cookstown.gov.uk

Reid, Kenneth (UUP - Torrent)
kenneth.reid@dstbc.org

Robinson, Wills (DUP - Clogher Valley)
wills.robinson@dstbc.org

Shiels, James (DUP - Carntogher)
jamesshiels817@gmail.com

Shiels, George (UUP - Magherafelt)
g.shiels49@btinternet.com

Totten, Darren (SF - Magherafelt)
darrentotten34@gmail.com

Wilson, Trevor (UUP - Cookstown)
trevor@8theash.freeserve.co.uk

POLITICAL COMPOSITION
SF: 18, DUP: 8, UUP: 7, SDLP: 6, IND: 1

Middlesbrough U

Middlesbrough Council, Town Hall, Middlesbrough TS1 2QQ
☎ 01642 245432 🖳 www.middlesbrough.gov.uk

FACTS AND FIGURES
Parliamentary Constituencies: Middlesbrough
EU Constituencies: North East
Election Frequency: Elections are of whole council

PRINCIPAL OFFICERS
Chief Executive: Mr Mike Robinson , Chief Executive, PO Box 500, Civic Centre, Middlesbrough TS1 9FT ☎ 01642 729101 🖷 01642728970 ✉ mike_robinson@middlesbrough.gov.uk

Senior Management: Mrs Richenda Broad , Executive Director - Wellbeing, Care & Learning, PO Box 151, Civic Centre, Middlesbrough TS1 9FU ☎ 01642 729500 🖷 01642 729969 ✉ richenda_broad@middlesbrough.gov.uk

Senior Management: Mr Kevin Parkes , Executive Director - Economic Development & Communities, PO Box 506, Civic Centre, Middlesbrough TS1 9FY ☎ 01642 729301 🖷 01642 729978 ✉ kevin_parkes@middlesbrough.gov.uk

Senior Management: Mr Tony Parkinson , Executive Director - Commercial & Corporate Services, PO Box 505, Civic Centre, Middlesbrough TS1 9FZ ☎ 01642 729046 ✉ tony_parkinson@middlesbrough.gov.uk

Access Officer / Social Services (Disability): Mr Mike Sharman , Assessment & Care Manager, PO Box 151, Civic Centre, Middlesbrough TS1 9FU ☎ 01642 729012 ✉ mike_sharman@middlebrough.gov.uk

Architect, Building / Property Services: Mr Ian McConville , Highway Management, Maintenance & Design Manager, PO Box 502, Vancouver House, Gurney Street, Middlesbrough TS1 9FW ☎ 01642 728160 ✉ ian_mcconville@middlebrough.gov.uk

Building Control: Mr Kevin Wood , Building Control Group Leader, PO Box 506, Civic Centre, Middlesbrough TS1 9FY ☎ 01642 729473 ✉ kevin_wood@middlesbrough.gov.uk

Catering Services: Mrs Angela Blower, Catering Manager, Central Depot, Cargo Fleet Lane, Middlesbrough TS3 8AL ☎ 01642 728030 🖷 01642 728965 ✉ angela_blower@middlesbrough.gov.uk

Children / Youth Services: Mrs Richenda Broad , Executive Director - Wellbeing, Care & Learning, PO Box 151, Civic Centre, Middlesbrough TS1 9FU ☎ 01642 729500 🖷 01642 729969 ✉ richenda_broad@middlesbrough.gov.uk

Civil Registration: Ms Christine Green , Registration Services Manager, Register Office, Corporation Road, Middlesbrough TS1 2DA ☎ 01642 729457 ✉ christine_green@middlesbrough.gov.uk

PR / Communications: Mrs Debbie Robinson , Communications Manager, PO Box 500, Civic Centre, Middlesbrough TS1 9FY ☎ 01642 729205 🖷 01642 729660 ✉ debbie_robinson@servicemiddlesbrough.gov.uk

Community Safety: Mrs Sharon Thomas , Assistant Director - Economic Development, PO Box 506, Civic Centre, Middlesbrough TS1 9FY ☎ 01642 729600 ✉ sharon_thomas@middlesbrough.gov.uk

Computer Management: Mr Andy Evans , IT Manager, Vancouver House, Middlesbrough TS1 9FY ☎ 01642 727801 ✉ andy.evans@mouchel-middlesbrough.gov.uk

Consumer Protection and Trading Standards: Mr John Wells , Public Protection Operations Manager, Vancouver House, Middlesbrough TS1 1LY ☎ 01642 728221 ✉ john_wells@middlesbrough.gov.uk

Contracts: Ms Claire Walker , Strategic Commissioning & Procurement Worker, Civic Centre, Middlesbrough TS1 9FT ☎ 01642 728415 ✉ claire_walker@middlesbrough.gov.uk

Corporate Services: Mr Tony Parkinson , Executive Director - Commercial & Corporate Services, PO Box 505, Civic Centre, Middlesbrough TS1 9FZ ☎ 01642 729046 ✉ tony_parkinson@middlesbrough.gov.uk

Customer Service: Mr Andy Unsworth , Customer Services Manager, Vancouver House, 50 Corporation Road, Middlesbrough TS1 2RH ☎ 01642 726104 ✉ andy.unsworth@mouchel-middlesbrough.gov.uk

Economic Development: Mrs Yaffa Philips , Economic Development Officer, PO Box 506, Civic Centre, Middlesbrough TS1 9FY ☎ 01642 729139 ✉ yaffa_phillips@middlesbrough.gov.uk

Economic Development: Ms Sharon Thomas , Assistant Director - Economic Development, PO Box 506, Civic Centre, Middlesbrough TS1 9FY ☎ 01642 729600 🖷 01642 729978 ✉ sharon_thomas@middlesbrough.gov.uk

Education: Mrs Richenda Broad , Executive Director - Wellbeing, Care & Learning, PO Box 151, Civic Centre, Middlesbrough TS1 9FU ☎ 01642 729500 🖷 01642 729969 ✉ richenda_broad@middlesbrough.gov.uk

Education: Mr Paul Wilson , Head of Education ICT, Rede House, Middlesbrough TS1 1LY ☎ 01642 727609

E-Government: Ms Julia Coxon , ICT Strategy & Projects Manager, PO Box 500, Civic Centre, Middlesbrough TS1 9FZ ☎ 01642 729628 ✉ julia_coxon@middlesbrough.gov.uk

Electoral Registration: Mr John Stuart , Senior Electoral Services Manager, PO Box 503, Civic Centre, Middlesbrough TS1 9FX ☎ 01642 729772 🖷 01642 729882 ✉ john_stuart@middlesbrough.gov.uk

Emergency Planning: Mr Edward Kunonga , Assistant Director - Improving Public Health & Director - Public Health, PO Box 505, Town Hall, Middlesbrough TS1 9FZ ☎ 01642 728020 ✉ edward_kunonga@middlesbrough.gov.uk

Energy Management: Mr Gareth Lonsbrough , Asset Manager, Civic Centre, Middlesbrough TS1 9FT ☎ 01642 729270 ✉ gavin_lonsbrough@middlesbrough.gov.uk

Environmental / Technical Services: Mr Tom Punton, Assistant Director - Environment, Property & Commercial Services, PO Box 506, Civic Centre, Middlesbrough TS1 9FY ☎ 01642 728300 ✉ tom_punton@middlesbrough.gov.uk

Environmental Health: Mrs Judith Hedgley , Environmental Health Manager, Vancouver House, Middlesbrough TS1 9FW ☎ 01642 728215 ✉ judith_hedgley@middlesbrough.gov.uk

Estates, Property & Valuation: Mr Tim Wake , Principal Estates Surveyor, PO Box 506, Civic Centre, Middlesbrough TS1 9FY ☎ 01642 729107 ✉ tim.wake@middlesbrough.gov.uk

Finance: Mr Paul Slocombe, Chief Finance Officer and Assistant Director - Finance & Investment, PO Box 506, Civic Centre, Middlesbrough TS1 9GA ☎ 01642 729032 🖷 01642 729983 ✉ paul_slocombe@middlesbrough.gov.uk

Pensions: Mr Mike Hopwood , Head of Pensions, PO Box 340, Middlesbrough TS1 2XP ☎ 01642 727778 🖷 01642 727989 ✉ mike_hopwood@middlesbrough.gov.uk

Fleet Management: Mr Tom Punton, Assistant Director - Environment, Property & Commercial Services, PO Box 506, Civic Centre, Middlesbrough TS1 9FY ☎ 01642 728300 ✉ tom_punton@middlesbrough.gov.uk

Grounds Maintenance: Mr Tom Punton, Assistant Director - Environment, Property & Commercial Services, PO Box 506, Civic Centre, Middlesbrough TS1 9FY ☎ 01642 728300 ✉ tom_punton@middlesbrough.gov.uk

Health and Safety: Mr Ian Campbell, Health & Safety Advisor, 4th Floor, Vancouver House, Gurney Street, Middlesbrough TS1 1JL ☎ 01642 727414 ✉ ian.campbell@mouchel-middlesbrough.com

Highways: Mr Derek Gittins , Head of Transport & Infrastructure, PO Box 502, Vancouver House, Gurney Street, Middlesbrough TS1 9FW ☎ 01642 728636 ✉ derek_gittins@middlesbrough.gov.uk

MIDDLESBROUGH

Housing: Ms Sharon Thomas , Assistant Director - Economic Development, PO Box 506, Civic Centre, Middlesbrough TS1 9FY ☎ 01642 729600 🖷 01642 729978 ✉ sharon_thomas@middlesbrough.gov.uk

Legal: Mr Bryn Roberts , Legal Services Manager, Town Hall, Middlesbrough TS1 2QQ ☎ 01642 729738 ✉ bryn_roberts@middlesbrough.gov.uk

Leisure and Cultural Services: Ms Anne Besford , Cultural Services Manager, PO Box 504, Town Hall, Middlesbrough TS1 9FY ☎ 01642 729703 ✉ anne_besford@middlesbrough.gov.uk

Licensing: Mr Tim Hodgkinson, Principal Licensing Officer, PO Box 502, Vancouver House, Gurney Street, Middlesbrough TS1 9FW ☎ 01642 728720 🖷 01642 728902 ✉ tim_hodgkinson@middlesbrough.gov.uk

Lottery Funding, Charity and Voluntary: Mr Martin Harvey , Community Infrastructure Manager, PO Box 506, Civic Centre, Middlesbrough TS1 9FY ☎ 01642 729254 ✉ martin_harvey@middlesbrough.gov.uk

Member Services: Mr Nigel Sayer , Head of Democratic Services, PO Box 503, Town Hall, Middlesbrough TS1 9FX ☎ 01642 729031 ✉ nigel_sayer@middlesbrough.gov.uk

Parking: Mr Derek Gittins , Head of Transport & Infrastructure, PO Box 502, Vancouver House, Gurney Street, Middlesbrough TS1 9FW ☎ 01642 728636 ✉ derek_gittins@middlesbrough.gov.uk

Partnerships: Mr John Polson , Partnership Manager, PO Box 500, Civic Centre, Middlesbrough TS1 9FT ☎ 01642 729017 ✉ john_polson@middlesbrough.gov.uk

Personnel / HR: Mrs Karen Whitmore , Assistant Director - Organisation & Governance, PO Box 500, Civic Centre, Middlesbrough TS1 9FT ☎ 01642 729117 ✉ karen_whitmore@middlesbrough.gov.uk

Planning: Mrs Sharon Thomas , Assistant Director - Economic Development, PO Box 506, Civic Centre, Middlesbrough TS1 9FY ☎ 01642 729600 ✉ sharon_thomas@middlesbrough.gov.uk

Procurement: Mr Paul Slocombe, Chief Finance Officer and Assistant Director - Finance & Investment, PO Box 506, Civic Centre, Middlesbrough TS1 9GA ☎ 01642 729032 🖷 01642 729983 ✉ paul_slocombe@middlesbrough.gov.uk

Public Libraries: Mr Martin Harvey , Community Infrastructure Manager, PO Box 506, Civic Centre, Middlesbrough TS1 9FY ☎ 01642 729254 ✉ martin_harvey@middlesbrough.gov.uk

Recycling & Waste Minimisation: Mr Ken Sherwood, Waste & Environmental Strategy Manager, PO Box 502, Vancouver House, Gurney Street, Middlesbrough TS1 9FW ☎ 01642 728514 ✉ ken_sherwood@middlesbrough.gov.uk

Regeneration: Mr Kevin Parkes , Executive Director - Economic Development & Communities, PO Box 506, Civic Centre, Middlesbrough TS1 9FY ☎ 01642 729301 🖷 01642 729978 ✉ kevin_parkes@middlesbrough.gov.uk

Road Safety: Mr Derek Gittins , Head of Transport & Infrastructure, PO Box 502, Vancouver House, Gurney Street, Middlesbrough TA1 9FW ☎ 01642 728636 ✉ derek_gittins@middlesbrough.gov.uk

Social Services: Mrs Richenda Broad , Executive Director - Wellbeing, Care & Learning, PO Box 151, Civic Centre, Middlesbrough TS1 9FU ☎ 01642 729500 🖷 01642 729969 ✉ richenda_broad@middlesbrough.gov.uk

Social Services (Adult): Mrs Richenda Broad , Executive Director - Wellbeing, Care & Learning, PO Box 151, Civic Centre, Middlesbrough TS1 9FU ☎ 01642 729500 🖷 01642 729969 ✉ richenda_broad@middlesbrough.gov.uk

Public Health: Mr Edward Kunonga , Assistant Director - Improving Public Health & Director - Public Health, PO Box 505, Town Hall, Middlesbrough TS1 9FZ ☎ 01642 728020 ✉ edward_kunonga@middlesbrough.gov.uk

Staff Training: Ms Jill Brown , Organisational Development Project Officer, PO Box 500, Civic Centre, Middlesbrough TS1 9FT ☎ 01642 729130 ✉ jill_brown@middlesbrough.gov.uk

Street Scene: Mr Tom Punton, Assistant Director - Environment, Property & Commercial Services, PO Box 506, Civic Centre, Middlesbrough TS1 9FY ☎ 01642 728300 ✉ tom_punton@middlesbrough.gov.uk

Sustainable Development: Mr Richard Horniman , Assistant Director - Supporting Communities, PO Box 504, Civic Centre, Middlesbrough TS1 9FY ☎ 01642 729538 ✉ richard_horniman@middlebrough.gov.uk

Tourism: Mrs Yaffa Philips , Economic Development Officer, PO Box 506, Civic Centre, Middlesbrough TS1 9FY ☎ 01642 729139 ✉ yaffa_phillips@middlesbrough.gov.uk

Traffic Management: Mr Derek Gittins , Head of Transport & Infrastructure, PO Box 502, Vancouver House, Gurney Street, Middlesbrough TS1 9FW ☎ 01642 728636 ✉ derek_gittins@middlesbrough.gov.uk

Transport: Mr Derek Gittins , Head of Transport & Infrastructure, PO Box 502, Vancouver House, Gurney Street, Middlesbrough TS1 9FW ☎ 01642 728636 ✉ derek_gittins@middlesbrough.gov.uk

Transport Planner: Mr Derek Gittins , Head of Transport & Infrastructure, PO Box 502, Vancouver House, Gurney Street, Middlesbrough TS1 9FW ☎ 01642 728636 ✉ derek_gittins@middlesbrough.gov.uk

Total Place: Mr Martin Harvey , Community Infrastructure Manager, PO Box 506, Civic Centre, Middlesbrough TS1 9FY ☎ 01642 729254 ✉ martin_harvey@middlesbrough.gov.uk

Waste Collection and Disposal: Mr Ken Sherwood, Waste & Environmental Strategy Manager, PO Box 502, Vancouver House, Gurney Street, Middlesbrough TS1 9FW ☎ 01642 728514 ✉ ken_sherwood@middlesbrough.gov.uk

Waste Management: Mr Ken Sherwood, Waste & Environmental Strategy Manager, PO Box 502, Vancouver House, Gurney Street, Middlesbrough TS1 9FW ☎ 01642 728514
✉ ken_sherwood@middlesbrough.gov.uk

COUNCILLORS

***Chair* Bloundele**, Stephen (LAB - Linthorpe)
stephen_bloundele@middlesbrough.gov.uk

***Vice-Chair* Brady**, Bob (LAB - Newport)
bob_brady@middlesbrough.gov.uk

***Mayor* Budd**, David (LAB - No Ward)
mayor@middlesbrough.gov.uk

***Deputy Mayor* Rooney**, Charles (LAB - Longlands & Beechwood)
charles_rooney@middlesbrough.gov.uk

Arundale, Ronald (CON - Kader)
ronald_arundale@middlesbrough.gov.uk

Biswas, Shamal (LAB - Acklam)
shamal_biswas@middlesbrough.gov.uk

Blyth, Jordan (LAB - Kader)
jordan_blyth@middlesbrough.gov.uk

Brunton, Janice (LAB - Coulby Newham)
janice_brunton@middlesbrough.gov.uk

Carr, Michael (LAB - Ladgate)
mike_carr@middlesbrough.gov.uk

Cole, John (LAB - Coulby Newham)
john_cole@middlesbrough.gov.uk

Coupe, David (CON - Stainton & Thornton)
david_coupe@middlesbrough.gov.uk

Cox, Peter (IND - Park End & Beckfield)
peter_cox@middlesbrough.gov.uk

Culley, Joe (LAB - Coulby Newham)
joe_culley@middlesbrough.gov.uk

Davison, Dorothy (IND - Marton East)
dorothy_davison@middlesbrough.gov.uk

Dean, Sheila (LAB - Acklam)
sheila_dean@middlesbrough.gov.uk

Dryden, Eddie (LAB - Berwick Hills & Pallister)
eddie_dryden@middlesbrough.gov.uk

Goodchild, June (LAB - Ladgate)
june_goodchild@middlesbrough.gov.uk

Harvey, Tracy (LAB - Newport)
cllrtracy_harvey@middlesbrough.gov.uk

Hellaoui, Alma (LAB - Newport)
alma_hellaoui@middlesbrough.gov.uk

Higgins, Teresa (LAB - Longlands & Beechwood)
teresa_higgins@middlesbrough.gov.uk

Hobson, Christine (CON - Marton West)
chris_hobson@middlesbrough.gov.uk

Hobson, John (CON - Marton West)
john_hobson@middlesbrough.gov.uk

Hubbard, Brian (IND - Park End & Beckfield)
brian_hubbard@middlesbrough.gov.uk

Hussain, Naweed (LAB - Linthorpe)
naweed_hussain@middlesbrough.gov.uk

Lawton, Terry (LAB - Brambles & Thorntree)
terence_lawton@middlesbrough.gov.uk

Lewis, Linda (LAB - Central)
linda_lewis@middlesbrough.gov.uk

Mawston, Tom (IND - Marton East)
tom_mawston@middlesbrough.gov.uk

McCabe, Dennis (IND - Trimdon)
dennis_mccabe@middlesbrough.gov.uk

McGee, Julie (LAB - Berwick Hills & Pallister)
julie_mcgee@middlesbrough.gov.uk

McGloin, Lesley (IND - Nunthorpe)
lesley_mcgloin@middlesbrough.gov.uk

McIntyre, Frances (LAB - Park)
fraces_mcintyre@middlesbrough.gov.uk

McTigue, Joan (IND - Longlands & Beechwood)
joan_mctigue@middlesbrough.gov.uk

Purvis, Peter (LAB - Brambles & Thorntree)
peter_purvis@middlesbrough.gov.uk

Purvis, Geraldine (LAB - Brambles & Thorntree)
geraldine_purvis@middlesbrough.gov.uk

Rathmell, Jon (IND - Nunthorpe)
jon_rathmell@middlesbrough.gov.uk

Rooney, Denise (LAB - Ayresome)
denise_rooney@middlesbrough.gov.uk

Rostron, Julia (LAB - Park)
julia_rostron@middlesbrough.gov.uk

Saunders, Michael (IND - Park End & Beckfield)
michael_saunders@middlesbrough.gov.uk

Shan, Ansab (LAB - Central)
ansab_shan@middlesbrough.gov.uk

Sharrocks, Jean (LAB - Trimdon)
jean_sharrocks@middlesbrough.gov.uk

Taylor, Bernard (LAB - Ayresome)
bernard_taylor@middlesbrough.gov.uk

Thompson, Michael (LAB - Berwick Hills & Pallister)
mick_thompson@middlesbrough.gov.uk

Uddin, Zafar (LAB - Central)
zafar_uddin@middlesbrough.gov.uk

Walker, Nicola (LAB - Hemlington)
nicola_walker@middlesbrough.gov.uk

Walker, Jeanette (LAB - Hemlington)
jeanette_walker@middlesbrough.gov.uk

Walters, Margaret (LAB - Park)
margaret_walters@middlesbrough.gov.uk

Young, Lewis (LAB - North Ormesby)
lewis_young@middlesbrough.gov.uk

POLITICAL COMPOSITION

LAB: 34, IND: 9, CON: 4

COMMITTEE CHAIRS

Audit: Mr Peter Purvis

Licensing: Mr Bernard Taylor

Planning & Development: Mr John Cole

MIDLOTHIAN

Midlothian S

Midlothian Council, Midlothian House, 40-46 Buccleuch Street, Dalkeith EH22 1DN
☎ 0131 270 7500 🖷 0131 271 3050 ✉ enquiries@midlothian.gov.uk 💻 www.midlothian.gov.uk

FACTS AND FIGURES

Parliamentary Constituencies: Midlothian
EU Constituencies: Scotland
Election Frequency: Elections are of whole council

PRINCIPAL OFFICERS

Chief Executive: Mr Kenneth Lawrie , Chief Executive, Midlothian House, 40-46 Buccleuch Street, Dalkeith EH22 1DN
☎ 0131 271 3002 ✉ kenneth.lawrie@midlothian.gov.uk

Senior Management: Mr John Blair, Director of Resources, Midlothian House, Buccleuch Street, Dalkeith EH22 1DJ
☎ 0131 271 3102 ✉ john.blair@midlothian.gov.uk

Senior Management: Ms Eibhlin McHugh , Joint Director of Health & Social Care, Fairfield House, 8 Lothian Road, Dalkeith EH22 3ZH ☎ 0131 271 3605 ✉ eibhlin.mchugh@midlothian.gov.uk

Senior Management: Mrs Mary Smith , Director of Education, Communities & Economy, Fairfield House, 8 Lothian Road, Dalkeith EH22 3ZG ☎ 0131 271 3718 ✉ mary.smith@midlothian.gov.uk

Access Officer / Social Services (Disability): Ms Jo Foley , Service Manager - Resources, Fairfield House, 8 Lothian Road, Dalkeith EH22 3ZG ☎ 0131 271 3792 ✉ jo.foley@midlothian.gov.uk

Access Officer / Social Services (Disability): Ms Alison White, Head of Adult & Social Care, Fairfield House, 8 Lothian Road, Dalkeith EH22 3ZH ☎ 0131 271 3605
✉ alison.white@midlothian.gov.uk

Architect, Building / Property Services: Mr Garry Sheret , Head of Property & Facilities Management, Midlothian House, Buccleuch Street, Dalkeith EH22 1DN ☎ 0131 561 5249
✉ garry.sheret@midlothian.gov.uk

Best Value: Ms Nancy Brown , Tranformation Programme Manager, Midlothian House, 40-46 Buccleuch Street, Dalkeith EH22 1DN ☎ 0131 271 3444 ✉ nancy.brown@midlothian.gov.uk

Building Control: Mr John Delamar , Building Standards Manager, Fairfield House, 8 Lothian Road, Dalkeith EH22 1DJ
☎ 0131 271 3322 ✉ john.delamar@midlothian.gov.uk

Building Control: Mr Ian Johnson , Head of Communities & Economy, Fairfield House, 8 Lothian Road, Dalkeith EH22 3ZQ
☎ 0131 271 3460 ✉ ian.johnson@midlothian.gov.uk

Catering Services: Ms Margaret McKenzie , Catering Services Manager, Midlothian House, 40-46 Buccleuch Street, Dalkeith EH22 1DN ☎ 0131 561 5314 ✉ margaret.mckenzie@midlothian.gov.uk

Children / Youth Services: Ms Joan Tranent , Head of Children's Services, Fairfield House, 8 Lothian Road, Dalkeith EH22 3ZG ☎ 0131 271 3721 ✉ joan.tranent@midlothian.gov.uk

Children / Youth Services: Ms Grace Vickers , Head of Education, Fairfield House, 8 Lothian Road, Dalkeith EH22 3ZG
☎ 0131 271 3719 ✉ grace.vickers@midlothian.gov.uk

Civil Registration: Ms Jane Milne , Customer Service Manager, Buccleuch House, 1 White Hart Street, Dalkeith EH22 1AE ☎ 0131 271 3971 ✉ jane.milne@midlothian.gov.uk

PR / Communications: Ms Ranaa Ahmed , Public Relations Officer, 29 Jarnac Court, Dalkeith EH22 1HU ☎ 0131 271 3423
✉ ranaa.ahmed@midlothian.gov.uk

PR / Communications: Ms Lynn Cochrane , Senior Public Relations Officer, 29 Jarnac Court, Dalkeith EH22 1HU ☎ 0131 271 3294 ✉ lynn.cochrane@midlothian.gov.uk

Community Planning: Mr Alasdair Mathers, Communities & Performance Manager, Fairfield House, 8 Lothian Road, Dalkeith EH22 3ZG ☎ 0131 271 3438 ✉ alasdair.mathers@midlothian.gov.uk

Community Safety: Mr Kevin Anderson , Head of Customer & Housing Services, Buccleuch House, 1 White Hart Street, Dalkeith EH22 1AE ☎ 0131 271 3615 ✉ kevin.anderson@midlothian.gov.uk

Community Safety: Ms Rosie Kendall , Community Safety Manager, Fairfield House, 8 Lothian Road, Dalkeith EH22 3ZG
☎ 0131 271 6654 ✉ rosie.kendall@midlothian.gov.uk

Community Safety: Ms Eibhlin McHugh , Joint Director of Health & Social Care, Fairfield House, 8 Lothian Road, Dalkeith EH22 3ZH
☎ 0131 271 3605 ✉ eibhlin.mchugh@midlothian.gov.uk

Computer Management: Mr Phil Timoney , Digital Services Manager, Midlothian House, 40-46 Buccleuch Street, Dalkeith EH22 1DN ☎ 0131 271 3030 ✉ phil.timoney@midlothian.gov.uk

Consumer Protection and Trading Standards: Mr Ian Johnson , Head of Communities & Economy, Fairfield House, 8 Lothian Road, Dalkeith EH22 3ZQ ☎ 0131 271 3460
✉ ian.johnson@midlothian.gov.uk

Consumer Protection and Trading Standards: Mr Stephen Thomson , Principal Trading Standards & Laboratory Manager, Fairfield House, 8 Lothian Road, Dalkeith EH22 3ZG ☎ 0131 271 3553 ✉ stephen.thomson@midlothian.gov.uk

Contracts: Mr Iain Johnston , Procurement Manager, Midlothian House, 40-46 Buccleuch Street, Dalkeith EH22 1DN ☎ 0131 271 3102 ✉ iain.johnston@midlothian.gov.uk

Corporate Services: Mr John Blair, Director of Resources, Midlothian House, Buccleuch Street, Dalkeith EH22 1DJ ☎ 0131 271 3102 ✉ john.blair@midlothian.gov.uk

Customer Service: Ms Jane Milne , Customer Service Manager, Buccleuch House, 1 White Hart Street, Dalkeith EH22 1AE
☎ 0131 271 3971 ✉ jane.milne@midlothian.gov.uk

Direct Labour: Mr Ricky Moffat , Head of Commercial Operations, Midlothian House, 40-46 Buccleuch Street, Dalkeith EH22 1DN
☎ 0131 561 5306 ✉ ricky.moffat@midlothian.gov.uk

Direct Labour: Mr Garry Sheret , Head of Property & Facilities Management, Midlothian House, Buccleuch Street, Dalkeith EH22 1DN ☎ 0131 561 5249 garry.sheret@midlothian.gov.uk

Economic Development: Mr Ian Johnson , Head of Communities & Economy, Fairfield House, 8 Lothian Road, Dalkeith EH22 3ZQ ☎ 0131 271 3460 ian.johnson@midlothian.gov.uk

Education: Ms Grace Vickers , Head of Education, Fairfield House, 8 Lothian Road, Dalkeith EH22 3ZG ☎ 0131 271 3719 grace.vickers@midlothian.gov.uk

E-Government: Mr Phil Timoney , Digital Services Manager, Midlothian House, 40-46 Buccleuch Street, Dalkeith EH22 1DN ☎ 0131 271 3030 phil.timoney@midlothian.gov.uk

Electoral Registration: Mr John Blair, Director of Resources, Midlothian House, Buccleuch Street, Dalkeith EH22 1DJ ☎ 0131 271 3102 john.blair@midlothian.gov.uk

Electoral Registration: Mr Allan Brown, Electoral Officer, Midlothian House, Buccleuch Street, Dalkeith EH22 1DN ☎ 0131 271 3255 allan.brown@midlothian.gov.uk

Emergency Planning: Mr John Blair, Director of Resources, Midlothian House, Buccleuch Street, Dalkeith EH22 1DJ ☎ 0131 271 3102 john.blair@midlothian.gov.uk

Emergency Planning: Mrs Jane Young, Contingency Planning Officer, 1 Eskdaill Court, Dalkeith EH22 1AG ☎ 0131 271 3078 jane.young@midlothian.gov.uk

Energy Management: Mr Garry Sheret , Head of Property & Facilities Management, Midlothian House, Buccleuch Street, Dalkeith EH22 1DN ☎ 0131 561 5249 garry.sheret@midlothian.gov.uk

Environmental / Technical Services: Ms Edel Ryan , Group Manager of Environmental Health, Fairfield House, 8 Lothian Street, Dalkeith EH22 3ZG ☎ 0131 271 3742 edel.ryan@midlothian.gov.uk

Environmental Health: Mr Ian Johnson , Head of Communities & Economy, Fairfield House, 8 Lothian Road, Dalkeith EH22 3ZQ ☎ 0131 271 3460 ian.johnson@midlothian.gov.uk

Environmental Health: Ms Edel Ryan , Group Manager of Environmental Health, Fairfield House, 8 Lothian Street, Dalkeith EH22 3ZH ☎ 0131 271 3742 edel.ryan@midlothian.gov.uk

Estates, Property & Valuation: Mr Gareth Davies , Property Manager, Fairfield House, 8 Lothian Road, Dalkeith EH22 3ZH ☎ 0131 271 3495 gareth.davies@midlothian.gov.uk

Estates, Property & Valuation: Mr Garry Sheret , Head of Property & Facilities Management, Midlothian House, Buccleuch Street, Dalkeith EH22 1DN ☎ 0131 561 5249 garry.sheret@midlothian.gov.uk

Events Manager: Mr Ricky Moffat , Head of Commercial Operations, Midlothian House, 40-46 Buccleuch Street, Dalkeith EH22 1DN ☎ 0131 561 5306 ricky.moffat@midlothian.gov.uk

Facilities: Mr Garry Sheret , Head of Property & Facilities Management, Midlothian House, Buccleuch Street, Dalkeith EH22 1DN ☎ 0131 561 5249 garry.sheret@midlothian.gov.uk

Finance: Mr Gary Fairley , Head of Finance & Integrated Service Support, Midlothian House, 40-46 Buccleuch Street, Dalkeith EH22 1DN ☎ 0131 271 3110 gary.fairley@midlothian.gov.uk

Fleet Management: Mr Trevor Docherty , Business Manager - Travel & Fleet, Midlothian House, 40-46 Buccleuch Street, Dalkeith EH22 1DN ☎ 0131 561 5448 trevor.docherty@midlothian.gov.uk

Grounds Maintenance: Mr Justin Venton , Land & Countryside Manager, Midlothian House, 40-46 Buccleuch Street, Dalkeith EH22 1DN ☎ 0131 561 5220 justin.venton@midlothian.gov.uk

Health and Safety: Mr Chris Lawson , Risk Manager, 1 Eskdaill Court, Dalkeith EH22 1AG ☎ 0131 271 3069 chris.lawson@midlothian.gov.uk

Highways: Mr Neil Dougall , Road Services Manager, Midlothian House, 40-46 Buccleuch Street, Dalkeith EH22 1DN ☎ 0131 561 5215 neil.dougall@midlothian.gov.uk

Home Energy Conservation: Mr William Jackson , Building Services Manager, Stobhill Depot, 40a Stobhill Road, Newtongrange, Dalkeith EH22 4NU ☎ 0131 561 5310 billy.jackson@midlothian.gov.uk

Housing: Mr Kevin Anderson , Head of Customer & Housing Services, Buccleuch House, 1 White Hart Street, Dalkeith EH22 1AE ☎ 0131 271 3615 kevin.anderson@midlothian.gov.uk

Housing: Mr Stephen Clark , Group Manager - Performance & Housing Strategy, Buccleuch House, 1 White Hart Street, Dalkeith EH22 1AE ☎ 0131 271 3506 stephen.clark@midlothian.gov.uk

Housing Maintenance: Mr William Jackson , Building Services Manager, Stobhill Depot, 40a Stobhill Road, Newtongrange, Dalkeith EH22 4NU ☎ 0131 561 5310 billy.jackson@midlothian.gov.uk

Legal: Mr Alan Turpie , Legal Services Manager, Midlothian House, 40-46 Buccleuch Street, Dalkeith EH22 1DN ☎ 0131 271 3667 alan.turpie@midlothian.gov.uk

Leisure and Cultural Services: Mr Garry Sheret , Head of Property & Facilities Management, Midlothian House, Buccleuch Street, Dalkeith EH22 1DN ☎ 0131 561 5249 garry.sheret@midlothian.gov.uk

Licensing: Mr Alan Turpie , Legal Services Manager, Midlothian House, 40-46 Buccleuch Street, Dalkeith EH22 1DN ☎ 0131 271 3667 alan.turpie@midlothian.gov.uk

Lifelong Learning: Ms Annette Lang , Manager - Lifelong Learning & Employability, Fairfield House, 8 Lothian Street, Dalkeith EH22 3ZG ☎ 0131 271 3923 annette.lang@midlothian.gov.uk

Lighting: Mr Keith Slight, Lighting Manager, Midlothian House, Buccleuch Street, Dalkeith EH22 1DN ☎ 0131 561 5222 keith.slight@midlothian.gov.uk

MIDLOTHIAN

Lottery Funding, Charity and Voluntary: Mr Alasdair Mathers, Communities & Performance Manager, 1 Eskdail Court, Dalkeith EH22 1AG ☎ 0131 271 3438 ✉ alasdair.mathers@midlothian.gov.uk

Member Services: Mr Kyle Clark-Hay , Democratic & Document Services Manager, Midlothian House, 40-46 Buccleuch Street, Dalkeith EH22 1DN ☎ 0131 270 5796 ✉ kyle.clark-hay@midlothian.gov.uk

Parking: Mr Neil Dougall , Road Services Manager, Midlothian House, 40-46 Buccleuch Street, Dalkeith EH22 1DN ☎ 0131 561 5215 ✉ neil.dougall@midlothian.gov.uk

Partnerships: Mr John Blair, Director of Resources, Midlothian House, Buccleuch Street, Dalkeith EH22 1DJ ☎ 0131 271 3102 ✉ john.blair@midlothian.gov.uk

Personnel / HR: Mr Gary Fairley , Head of Finance & Integrated Service Support, Midlothian House, 40-46 Buccleuch Street, Dalkeith EH22 1DN ☎ 0131 271 3110 ✉ gary.fairley@midlothian.gov.uk

Personnel / HR: Ms Marina Naylor , Organisational Development HR Manager, Midlothian House, 40-46 Buccleuch Street, Dalkeith EH22 1DN ☎ 0131 271 3988 ✉ marina.naylor@midlothian.gov.uk

Planning: Mr Ian Johnson , Head of Communities & Economy, Fairfield House, 8 Lothian Road, Dalkeith EH22 3ZQ ☎ 0131 271 3460 ✉ ian.johnson@midlothian.gov.uk

Procurement: Mr Iain Johnston , Procurement Manager, Midlothian House, 40-46 Buccleuch Street, Dalkeith EH22 1DN ☎ 0131 271 3102 ✉ iain.johnston@midlothian.gov.uk

Public Libraries: Ms Jane Milne , Customer Service Manager, Buccleuch House, 1 White Hart Street, Dalkeith EH22 1AE ☎ 0131 271 3971 ✉ jane.milne@midlothian.gov.uk

Recycling & Waste Minimisation: Mr Phil Riddell , Business Manager - Waste & Fleet Services, Stobhill Depot, 40a Stobhill Road, Newtongrange, Dalkeith EH22 4NU ☎ 0131 561 5300 ✉ phil.riddell@midlothian.gov.uk

Regeneration: Mr Alasdair Mathers, Communities & Performance Manager, 1 Eskdail Court, Dalkeith EH22 1AG ☎ 0131 271 3438 ✉ alasdair.mathers@midlothian.gov.uk

Road Safety: Mr Neil Dougall , Road Services Manager, Midlothian House, 40-46 Buccleuch Street, Dalkeith EH22 1DN ☎ 0131 561 5215 ✉ neil.dougall@midlothian.gov.uk

Social Services: Ms Eibhlin McHugh , Joint Director of Health & Social Care, Fairfield House, 8 Lothian Road, Dalkeith EH22 3ZH ☎ 0131 271 3605 ✉ eibhlin.mchugh@midlothian.gov.uk

Social Services (Adult): Ms Alison White , Head of Adult & Social Care, Fairfield House, 8 Lothian Road, Dalkeith EH22 3ZH ☎ 0131 271 3605 ✉ alison.white@midlothian.gov.uk

Social Services (Children): Ms Joan Tranent , Head of Children's Services, Fairfield House, 8 Lothian Road, Dalkeith EH22 3ZG ☎ 0131 271 3721 ✉ joan.tranent@midlothian.gov.uk

Staff Training: Ms Marina Naylor , Organisational Development HR Manager, Midlothian House, 40-46 Buccleuch Street, Dalkeith EH22 1DN ☎ 0131 271 3988 ✉ marina.naylor@midlothian.gov.uk

Sustainable Communities: Mr Alasdair Mathers, Communities & Performance Manager, 1 Eskdail Court, Dalkeith EH22 1AG ☎ 0131 271 3438 ✉ alasdair.mathers@midlothian.gov.uk

Sustainable Development: Mr Ian Johnson , Head of Communities & Economy, Fairfield House, 8 Lothian Road, Dalkeith EH22 3ZQ ☎ 0131 271 3460 ✉ ian.johnson@midlothian.gov.uk

Tourism: Mr John Beveridge , Economic Development Manager, Fairfield House, 8 Lothian Street, Dalkeith EH22 3ZG ☎ 0131 271 3431 ✉ john.beveridge@midlothian.gov.uk

Town Centre: Mr Garry Sheret , Head of Property & Facilities Management, Midlothian House, Buccleuch Street, Dalkeith EH22 1DN ☎ 0131 561 5249 ✉ garry.sheret@midlothian.gov.uk

Traffic Management: Mr Neil Dougall , Road Services Manager, Midlothian House, 40-46 Buccleuch Street, Dalkeith EH22 1DN ☎ 0131 561 5215 ✉ neil.dougall@midlothian.gov.uk

Transport: Mr Trevor Docherty , Business Manager - Travel & Fleet, Midlothian House, 40-46 Buccleuch Street, Dalkeith EH22 1DN ☎ 0131 561 5448 ✉ trevor.docherty@midlothian.gov.uk

Transport Planner: Mr Neil Dougall , Road Services Manager, Midlothian House, 40-46 Buccleuch Street, Dalkeith EH22 1DN ☎ 0131 561 5215 ✉ neil.dougall@midlothian.gov.uk

Waste Collection and Disposal: Mr Ricky Moffat , Head of Commercial Operations, Midlothian House, 40-46 Buccleuch Street, Dalkeith EH22 1DN ☎ 0131 561 5306 ✉ ricky.moffat@midlothian.gov.uk

Waste Management: Mr Phil Riddell , Business Manager - Waste & Fleet Services, Stobhill Depot, 40a Stobhill Road, Newtongrange, Dalkeith EH22 4NU ☎ 0131 561 5300 ✉ phil.riddell@midlothian.gov.uk

Children's Play Areas: Mr Justin Venton , Land & Countryside Manager, Midlothian House, 40-46 Buccleuch Street, Dalkeith EH22 1DN ☎ 0131 561 5220 ✉ justin.venton@midlothian.gov.uk

COUNCILLORS

***Provost* Wallace**, Joe (SNP - Penicuik)
joe.wallace@midlothian.gov.uk

***Leader of the Council* Johnstone**, Catherine (SNP - Midlothian South)
catherine.johnstone@midlothian.gov.uk

***Deputy Leader of the Council* Constable**, Bob (SNP - Bonnyrigg)
bob.constable@midlothian.gov.uk

Baxter, Ian (SGP - Bonnyrigg)
ian.baxter@midlothian.gov.uk

Beattie, Lisa (SNP - Midlothian East)
lisa.beattie@midlothian.gov.uk

Bennett, Alex (LAB - Dalkeith)
alex.bennett@midlothian.gov.uk

Bryant, Jim (SNP - Dalkeith)
jim.bryant@midlothian.gov.uk

Coventry, Andrew (SNP - Midlothian West)
andrew.coventry@midlothian.gov.uk

de Vink, Peter (IND - Midlothian East)
peter.deVink@midlothian.gov.uk

Imrie, Russell (LAB - Midlothian West)
russell.imrie@midlothian.gov.uk

Milligan, Derek (LAB - Bonyrigg)
derek.milligan@midlothian.gov.uk

Montgomery, Adam (LAB - Penicuik)
adam.montgomery@midlothian.gov.uk

Muirhead, Jim (LAB - Midlothian South)
jim.muirhead@midlothian.gov.uk

Parry, Kelly (SNP - Midlothian West)

Pottinger, Bryan (LAB - Midlothian South)
bryan.pottinger@midlothian.gov.uk

Rosie, Derek (SNP - Penicuik)
derek.rosie@midlothian.gov.uk

Russell, Margot (LAB - Dalkeith)
margot.russell@midlothian.gov.uk

Young, Kenny (LAB - Midlothian East)
Kenny.Young@midlothian.gov.uk

POLITICAL COMPOSITION

LAB: 8, SNP: 8, IND: 1, SGP: 1

Milton Keynes U

Milton Keynes Council, Civic Offices, 1 Saxon Gate East, Milton Keynes MK9 3EJ
☎ 01908 691691 🖷 01908 252456
firstname.lastname@milton-keynes.gov.uk
www.milton-keynes.gov.uk

FACTS AND FIGURES

Parliamentary Constituencies: Milton Keynes North, Milton Keynes South
EU Constituencies: South East
Election Frequency: Elections are by thirds

PRINCIPAL OFFICERS

Chief Executive: Ms Carole Mills , Chief Executive, Civic Offices, 1 Saxon Gate East, Milton Keynes MK9 3EJ ☎ 01908 252200 carole.mills@milton-keynes.gov.uk

Senior Management: Mr Michael Bracey , Corporate Director - People, Saxon Court, 502 Avebury Boulevard, Milton Keynes MK9 3HS ☎ 01908 258041 🖷 01908 252456 michael.bracey@milton-keynes.gov.uk

Senior Management: Mr Tim Hannam , Corporate Director - Resources, Saxon Court, 502 Avebury Boulevard, Milton Keynes MK9 3HS ☎ 01908 252756 tim.hannam@milton-keynes.gov.uk

Senior Management: Mr Duncan Sharkey , Corporate Director - Place, Civic Offices, 1 Saxon Gate East, Milton Keynes MK9 3EJ duncan.sharkey@milton-keynes.gov.uk

Access Officer / Social Services (Disability): Ms Amanda Griffiths , Head of Learning Disability Services, Tower Drive Centre, Tower Drive, Neath Hill, Milton Keynes MK14 6NA ☎ 01908 253042 🖷 01908 253185 amanda.griffiths@milton-keynes.gov.uk

Architect, Building / Property Services: Mr Mark Dolling , Capital Programme Director, Saxon Court, 502 Avebury Blvd, Milton Keynes MK9 3HS ☎ 01908 253375 mark.dolling@milton-keynes.gov.uk

Building Control: Mr Neil Allen , Head of Environmental Services, Civic Offices, 1 Saxon Gate East, Milton Keynes MK9 3EJ ☎ 01908 252365 🖷 01908 252319 neil.allen@milton-keynes.gov.uk

Children / Youth Services: Mr Michael Bracey , Corporate Director - People, Saxon Court, 502 Avebury Boulevard, Milton Keynes MK9 3HS ☎ 01908 258041 🖷 01908 252456 michael.bracey@milton-keynes.gov.uk

Children / Youth Services: Ms Nicky Rayner , Service Director - Children & Families, Civic Offices, 1 Saxon Gate East, Milton Keynes MK9 3EJ ☎ 01908 253121 nicky.rayner@milton-keynes.gov.uk

Civil Registration: Ms Yvette Medri , Registration Services Manager, Bracknell House, Aylesbury Street, Bletchley MK2 2BE ☎ 01908 372101 yvette.medri@milton-keynes.gov.uk

PR / Communications: Ms Kellie Evans , Corporate Communications Manager, Civic Offices, 1 Saxon Gate East, Milton Keynes MK9 3EJ ☎ 01908 252413 🖷 01908 252768 kellie.evans@milton-keynes.gov.uk

Community Planning: Mr Bob Wilson , Development Plans Manager, Civic Offices, 1 Saxon Gate East, Milton Keynes MK9 3EJ ☎ 01908 252480 bob.wilson@milton-keynes.gov.uk

Community Safety: Mr Colin Wilderspin , Head of Community Safety, Civic Offices, 1 Saxon Gate East, Milton Keynes MK9 3EJ ☎ 01908 254533 colin.wilderspin@milton-keynes.gov.uk

Computer Management: Ms Hazel Lewis , Service Delivery Manager, Saxon Court, 502 Avebury Blvd, Milton Keynes MK9 3HS ☎ 01908 254117 hazel.lewis@milton-keynes.gov.uk

Consumer Protection and Trading Standards: Mr Chris Londy , Head of Environmental Health & Trading Standards, Civic Offices, 1 Saxon Gate East, Milton Keynes MK9 3EJ ☎ 01908 252327 chris.londy@milton-keynes.gov.uk

Contracts: Mr Mick Hancock , Assistant Director of Joint Commissioning & Contracts, Civic Offices, 1 Saxon Gate East, Milton Keynes MK9 3EJ ☎ 01908 257967 mick.hancock@milton-keynes.gov.uk

Contracts: Ms Catharine Southern , Head of Strategic Procurement, Civic Offices, 1 Saxon Gate East, Milton Keynes MK9 3EJ ☎ 01908 254780 catharine.southern@milton-keynes.gov.uk

MILTON KEYNES

Corporate Services: Mr Tim Hannam , Corporate Director - Resources, Saxon Court, 502 Avebury Boulevard, Milton Keynes MK9 3HS ☎ 01908 252756 ✉ tim.hannam@milton-keynes.gov.uk

Customer Service: Ms Rebecca Peck , Head of Customer Service, Civic Offices, 1 Saxon Gate East, Milton Keynes MK9 3EJ ☎ 01908 253930 ✉ rebecca.peck@milton-keynes.gov.uk

Direct Labour: Mr Mike Hainge , Service Director - Public Realm Service Group, Civic Offices, 1 Saxon Gate East, Milton Keynes MK9 3EJ ☎ 01908 254258 ✉ mike.hainge@milton-keynes.gov.uk

Economic Development: Ms Pam Gosal , Corporate Head of Economic Development, Civic Offices, 1 Saxon Gate East, Milton Keynes MK9 3EJ ☎ 01908 252192 ✉ pam.gosal@milton-keynes.gov.uk

Education: Mr Michael Bracey , Corporate Director - People, Saxon Court, 502 Avebury Boulevard, Milton Keynes MK9 3HS ☎ 01908 258041 🖷 01908 252456 ✉ michael.bracey@milton-keynes.gov.uk

E-Government: Mr Paul Wheeler , Head of ICT Strategic Development, Saxon Court, 502 Avebury Blvd, Milton Keynes MK9 3HS ☎ 01908 254148 ✉ paul.wheeler@milton-keynes.gov.uk

Electoral Registration: Ms June Allen , Member & Electoral Services Manager, Civic Offices, 1 Saxon Gate East, Milton Keynes MK9 3EJ ☎ 01908 254844 🖷 01908 252511 ✉ june.allen@milton-keynes.gov.uk

Emergency Planning: Mr Chris Londy , Head of Environmental Health & Trading Standards, Civic Offices, 1 Saxon Gate East, Milton Keynes MK9 3EJ ☎ 01908 252327 ✉ chris.londy@milton-keynes.gov.uk

Energy Management: Mr Jeremy Draper, Senior Practitioner, Civic Offices, 1 Saxon Gate East, Milton Keynes MK9 3EJ ☎ 01908 252652 🖷 01908 252575 ✉ jeremy.draper@milton-keynes.gov.uk

Environmental / Technical Services: Mr Mike Hainge , Service Director - Public Realm Service Group, Civic Offices, 1 Saxon Gate East, Milton Keynes MK9 3EJ ☎ 01908 254258 ✉ mike.hainge@milton-keynes.gov.uk

Environmental Health: Mr Chris Londy , Head of Environmental Health & Trading Standards, Civic Offices, 1 Saxon Gate East, Milton Keynes MK9 3EJ ☎ 01908 252327 ✉ chris.londy@milton-keynes.gov.uk

Estates, Property & Valuation: Mr Mark Dolling , Capital Programme Director, Saxon Court, 502 Avebury Blvd, Milton Keynes MK9 3HS ☎ 01908 253375 ✉ mark.dolling@milton-keynes.gov.uk

Facilities: Ms Yvonne Mullens, Facilities Manager , Saxon Court, 502 Avebury Boulevard, Milton Keynes MK9 3HS ☎ 01908 253627 🖷 01908 252456 ✉ yvonne.mullens@milton-keynes.gov.uk

Finance: Ms Nicole Jones , Service Director - Finance & Resources, Saxon Court, 502 Avebury Blvd, Milton Keynes MK9 3HS ☎ 01908 252079 ✉ nicole.jones@milton-keynes.gov.uk

Grounds Maintenance: Mr Andy Hudson, Head of Environment & Waste, Civic Offices, 1 Saxon Gate East, Milton Keynes MK9 3EJ ☎ 01908 252577 🖷 01908 252575 ✉ andy.hudson@milton-keynes.gov.uk

Health and Safety: Mr Chris Londy , Head of Environmental Health & Trading Standards, Civic Offices, 1 Saxon Gate East, Milton Keynes MK9 3EJ ☎ 01908 252327 ✉ chris.londy@milton-keynes.gov.uk

Highways: Mr David Hall , Interim Head of Highways, Synergy Park, Chesney Wold, Bleak Hall, Milton Keynes NK6 1LY ☎ 01908 252411 ✉ david.hall@milton-keynes.gov.uk

Home Energy Conservation: Mr Jeremy Draper, Senior Practitioner, Civic Offices, 1 Saxon Gate East, Milton Keynes MK9 3EJ ☎ 01908 252652 🖷 01908 252575 ✉ jeremy.draper@milton-keynes.gov.uk

Housing: Ms Jane Reed , Service Director - Housing & Communities, Civic Offices, 1 Saxon Gate East, Milton Keynes MK9 3EJ ☎ 01908 252782 ✉ jane.reed@milton-keynes.gov.uk

Housing Maintenance: Ms Clare Dowds , Head of Repairs, Property Transport & Public Access, Civic Offices, 1 Saxon Gate East, Milton Keynes MK9 3EJ ☎ 01908 252782 ✉ clare.dowds@milton-keynes.gov.uk

Legal: Mr Stephen Gerrard , Interim Service Director - Legal & Democratic Services, Civic Offices, 1 Saxon Gate East, Milton Keynes MK9 3EJ ☎ 01908 252385 🖷 01908 52600 ✉ stephen.gerrard@milton-keynes.gov.uk

Leisure and Cultural Services: Mr Paul Sanders, Assistant Director of Community Facilities Unit, Community Wellbeing, Saxon Court, 502 Avebury Avenue, Milton Keynes MK9 3HS ☎ 01908 253639 🖷 01908 253304 ✉ paul.sanders@milton-keynes.gov.uk

Licensing: Mr Neil Allen , Head of Environmental Services, Civic Offices, 1 Saxon Gate East, Milton Keynes MK9 3EJ ☎ 01908 252365 🖷 01908 252319 ✉ neil.allen@milton-keynes.gov.uk

Lifelong Learning: Mr Michael Bracey , Corporate Director - People, Saxon Court, 502 Avebury Boulevard, Milton Keynes MK9 3HS ☎ 01908 258041 🖷 01908 252456 ✉ michael.bracey@milton-keynes.gov.uk

Lighting: Mr Chris Hales , Street Lighting Engineer, Saxon Court, 502 Avebury Boulevard, Milton Keynes MK6 1HS ☎ 01908 252825 🖷 01908 252822 ✉ chris.hales@milton-keynes.gov.uk

Lottery Funding, Charity and Voluntary: Mr Paul Sanders, Assistant Director of Community Facilities Unit, Saxon Court, 502 Avebury Boulevard, Milton Keynes MK6 1NE ☎ 01908 253639 🖷 01908 253304 ✉ paul.sanders@milton-keynes.gov.uk

Member Services: Ms June Allen , Member & Electoral Services Manager, Civic Offices, 1 Saxon Gate East, Milton Keynes MK9 3EJ ☎ 01908 254844 🖷 01908 252511 ✉ june.allen@milton-keynes.gov.uk

Parking: Ms Sara Bailey , Parking Strategy Manager, Civic Offices, 1 Saxon Gate East, Milton Keynes MK9 3EJ ☎ 01908 252198 🖷 01908 252456 ✉ sara.bailey@milton-keynes.gov.uk

Partnerships: Ms Sarah Gonsalves , Head of Policy & Performance, Civic Offices, 1 Saxon Gate East, Milton Keynes MK9 3EJ ☎ 01908 253099 🖷 01908 252768 ✉ sarah.gonsalves@milton-keynes.gov.uk

Personnel / HR: Ms Catherine Weir , HR Service Delivery Manager, Saxon Court, 502 Avebury Boulevard, Milton Keynes MK9 3HS ☎ 01908 253913 ✉ catherine.weir@milton-keynes.gov.uk

Planning: Mr David Hackford , Interim Assistant Director - Planning & Transport, Civic Offices, 1 Saxon Gate East, Milton Keynes MK9 3EJ ☎ 01908 252492 ✉ david.hackford@milton-keynes.gov.uk

Procurement: Ms Catharine Southern , Head of Strategic Procurement, Civic Offices, 1 Saxon Gate East, Milton Keynes MK9 3EJ ☎ 01908 254780 ✉ catharine.southern@milton-keynes.gov.uk

Public Libraries: Ms Helen Boult , Library Services Manager, CMK Library, 555 Silbury Blvd, Milton Keynes MK9 3HL ☎ 01908 254068 ✉ helen.boult@milton-keynes.gov.uk

Recycling & Waste Minimisation: Mr Andy Hudson, Head of Environment & Waste, Civic Offices, 1 Saxon Gate East, Milton Keynes MK9 3EJ ☎ 01908 252577 🖷 01908 252575 ✉ andy.hudson@milton-keynes.gov.uk

Regeneration: Ms Kathryn Eames , Corporate Manager - Regeneration, Civic Offices, 1 Saxon Gate East, Milton Keynes MK9 3EJ ☎ 01908 254788 ✉ kathryn.eames@milton-keynes.gov.uk

Regeneration: Mr Duncan Sharkey , Corporate Director - Place, Civic Offices, 1 Saxon Gate East, Milton Keynes MK9 3EJ ✉ duncan.sharkey@milton-keynes.gov.uk

Road Safety: Mr Adrian Carden , Road Safety Team Leader, Civic Offices, 1 Saxon Gate East, Milton Keynes MK9 3EJ ☎ 01908 252764 ✉ adrian.carden@milton-keynes.gov.uk

Social Services: Mr Michael Bracey , Corporate Director - People, Saxon Court, 502 Avebury Boulevard, Milton Keynes MK9 3HS ☎ 01908 258041 🖷 01908 252456 ✉ michael.bracey@milton-keynes.gov.uk

Social Services: Ms Suzanne Joyner , Strategic Director - Adult Social Care & Health Partnerships, Civic Offices, 1 Saxon Gate East, Milton Keynes MK9 3EJ ☎ 01908 257973 ✉ suzanne.joyner@milton-keynes.gov.uk

Social Services (Adult): Ms Victoria Collins , Assistant Director - Physical Disability, Older People's Services & Care Act Lead, Civic Offices, 1 Saxon Gate East, Milton Keynes MK9 3EJ ☎ 01908 253508 ✉ victoria.collins@milton-keynes.gov.uk

Social Services (Children): Ms Nicky Rayner , Service Director - Children & Families, Civic Offices, 1 Saxon Gate East, Milton Keynes MK9 3EJ ☎ 01908 253121 ✉ nicky.rayner@milton-keynes.gov.uk

Public Health: Ms Muriel Scott , Director - Public Health, 7 Hadleigh Close, Putnoe, Bedford MK41 8JW ☎ 0300 300 5616 ✉ muriel.scott@centralbedfordshire.gov.uk

Staff Training: Ms Catherine Weir , HR Service Delivery Manager, Saxon Court, 502 Avebury Boulevard, Milton Keynes MK9 3HS ☎ 01908 253913 ✉ catherine.weir@milton-keynes.gov.uk

Sustainable Communities: Mr Geoff Snelson, Director of Strategy, Civic Offices, 1 Saxon Gate East, Milton Keynes MK9 3EJ ☎ 01908 252665 🖷 01908 252768 ✉ geoff.snelson@milton-keynes.gov.uk

Sustainable Development: Mr Andrew Horner , Head of Development Management, Civic Offices, 1 Saxon Gate East, Milton Keynes MK9 3EJ ☎ 01908 252609 ✉ andrew.horner@milton-keynes.gov.uk

Traffic Management: Mr David Hall , Interim Head of Highways, Synergy Park, Chesney Wold, Bleak Hall, Milton Keynes NK6 1LY ☎ 01908 252411 ✉ david.hall@milton-keynes.gov.uk

Transport: Mr Andrew Coleman , Passenger Transport Manager, Civic Offices, 1 Saxon Gate East, Milton Keynes MK9 3EJ ☎ 01908 254739 🖷 01908 252302 ✉ andrew.coleman@milton-keynes.gov.uk

Transport: Mr Brian Matthews , Head of Transportation Services, Civic Offices, 1 Saxon Gate East, Milton Keynes MK9 3EJ ☎ 01908 252064 🖷 01908 252456 ✉ brian.matthews@milton-keynes.gov.uk

Transport Planner: Mr David Lawson , Transport Policy & Programme Manager, Civic Offices, 1 Saxon Gate East, Milton Keynes MK9 3EJ ☎ 01908 252510 🖷 01908 252302 ✉ david.lawson@milton-keynes.gov.uk

Waste Collection and Disposal: Mr Andy Hudson, Head of Environment & Waste, Civic Offices, 1 Saxon Gate East, Milton Keynes MK9 3EJ ☎ 01908 252577 🖷 01908 252575 ✉ andy.hudson@milton-keynes.gov.uk

Waste Management: Mr Andy Hudson, Head of Environment & Waste, Civic Offices, 1 Saxon Gate East, Milton Keynes MK9 3EJ ☎ 01908 252577 🖷 01908 252575 ✉ andy.hudson@milton-keynes.gov.uk

COUNCILLORS

***Mayor* McLean**, Keith (CON - Olney)
keith.mclean@milton-keynes.gov.uk

***Deputy Mayor* Coventry**, Stephen (LAB - Woughton and Fishermead)
cllrstevencoventry@talktalk.net

***Leader of the Council* Marland**, Peter (LAB - Wolverton)
peter.marland@milton-keynes.gov.uk

***Deputy Leader of the Council* O'Neill**, Hannah (LAB - Woughton and Fishermead)
hannah.o'neill@milton-keynes.gov.uk

***Group Leader* McCall**, Douglas (LD - Newport Pagnell South)
douglas.mccall@milton-keynes.gov.uk

Alexander, Paul (LD - Newport Pagnell South)
Paul.Alexander@milton-keynes.gov.uk

MILTON KEYNES

Bald, Edith (CON - Tattenhoe)
edith.bald@milton-keynes.gov.uk

Baume, Carole (LAB - Bletchley East)
carole.baume@milton-keynes.gov.uk

Betteley, Sarah (LAB - Central Milton Keynes)
sarah.betteley@milton-keynes.gov.uk

Bint, John (CON - Broughton)
john.bint@milton-keynes.gov.uk

Brackenbury, Ric (LD - Campbell Park and Old Woughton)
ric.brackenbury@milton-keynes.gov.uk

Bradburn, Robin (LD - Bradwell)
robin.bradburn@milton-keynes.gov.uk

Bramall, Alice (CON - Danesborough and Walton)
alice.bramall@milton-keynes.gov.uk

Brunning, Denise (CON - Stony Stratford)
Denise.Brunning@milton-keynes.gov.uk

Buckley, Andrew (CON - Monkston)
andrew.buckley@milton-keynes.gov.uk

Burke, Margaret (LAB - Stantonbury)
margaret.burke@milton-keynes.gov.uk

Cannon, Peter (LD - Shenley Brook End)
peter.cannon@milton-keynes.gov.uk

Clancy, Ann (CON - Bletchley Park)
ann.clancy@milton-keynes.gov.uk

Clifton, Matthew (LAB - Loughton and Shenley)
matthew.clifton@milton-keynes.gov.uk

Crooks, Samuel (LD - Broughton)
sam.crooks@milton-keynes.gov.uk

Dransfield, Andrew (CON - Loughton and Shenley)
andy.dransfield@milton-keynes.gov.uk

Eastman, Derek (LD - Newport Pagnell South)
derek.eastman@milton-keynes.gov.uk

Exon, Robert (LD - Bradwell)
robert.exon@milton-keynes.gov.uk

Ferrans, Jennie (LD - Monkston)
jenni.ferans@milton-keynes.gov.uk

Ganatra, Hiten (CON - Shenley Brook End)
hiten.ganatra@milton-keynes.gov.uk

Geaney, Maggie (CON - Bletchley West)
maggie.geaney@milton-keynes.gov.uk

Geary, Andrew (CON - Newport Pagnell North and Hanslope)
andrew.geary@milton-keynes.gov.uk

Geary, Peter (CON - Olney)
peter.geary@milton-keynes.gov.uk

Gifford, Liz (LAB - Stony Stratford)
liz.gifford@milton-keynes.gov.uk

Gifford, Robert (LAB - Stony Stratford)
robert.gifford@milton-keynes.gov.uk

Gowans, Martin (LAB - Bletchley Park)
martin.gowans@milton-keynes.gov.uk

Green, Jeannette (CON - Newport Pagnell North and Hanslope)
jeanette.green@milton-keynes.gov.uk

Hopkins, Victoria (CON - Danesborough and Walton)
victoria.hopkins@milton-keynes.gov.uk

Hopkins, David (CON - Danesborough and Walton)
david.hopkins@milton-keynes.gov.uk

Hosking, David (CON - Olney)
david.hosking@milton-keynes.gov.uk

Khan, Mohammed (LAB - Bletchley East)
mohammed.khan@milton-keynes.gov.uk

Legg, Mick (LAB - Bletchley West)
michael.legg@yahoo.com

Lewis, David (LAB - Bradwell)
david.lewis@milton-keynes.gov.uk

Long, Nigel (LAB - Bletchley West)
nigel.long@milton-keynes.gov.uk

McCall, Isobel (LD - Campbell Park and Old Woughton)
isobel.mccall@milton-keynes.gov.uk

McDonald, Peter (CON - Campbell Park and Old Woughton)
peter.mcdonald@milton-keynes.gov.uk

McKenzie, Gladstone (LAB - Bletchley Park)
gladstone.mckenzie@milton-keynes.gov.uk

McPake, Vanessa (LD - Monkston)
vanessa.mcpake@milton-keynes.gov.uk

Middleton, Robert (LAB - Wolverton)
robert.middleton@milton-keynes.gov.uk

Miles, Norman (LAB - Wolverton)
norman.miles@milton-keynes.gov.uk

Morla, Geetha (CON - Tattenhoe)
geetha.morla@milton-keynes.gov.uk

Morris, Catriona (CON - Broughton)
catriona.morris@milton-keynes.gov.uk

Nolan, Zoe (LAB - Loughton and Shenley)
zoe.nolan@milton-keynes.gov.uk

Patey-Smith, Lynn (CON - Newport Pagnell North and Hanslope)
lynn.patey-smith@milton-keynes.gov.uk

Small, Gerald (CON - Tattenhoe)
gerald.small@milton-keynes.gov.uk

Walker, Alex (CON - Stantonbury)
alex.walker@milton-keynes.gov.uk

Wallis, Pauline (LAB - Central Milton Keynes)
Pauline.Wallis@milton-keynes.gov.uk

Webb, Alan (LAB - Bletchley East)
alan.webb@milton-keynes.gov.uk

White, Brian (LAB - Stantonbury)
brian.white@milton-keynes.gov.uk

Williams, Paul (LAB - Central Milton Keynes)
Paul.Williams@milton-keynes.gov.uk

Williams, Chris (LD - Shenley Brook End)
chris.williams1@milton-keynes.gov.uk

Wilson, Kevin (LAB - Woughton and Fishermead)
kevin.wilson@milton-keynes.gov.uk

POLITICAL COMPOSITION

LAB: 23, CON: 22, LD: 12

COMMITTEE CHAIRS

Audit: Mr Peter McDonald

Children & Young People: Mr Samuel Crooks

Development Control: Mr Andrew Geary

Economy, Growth & Regeneration: Ms Isobel McCall

Health & Adult Social Care: Ms Alice Bramall

Standards: Ms Denise Brunning

Mole Valley D

Mole Valley District Council, Pippbrook, Dorking RH4 1SJ
☎ 01306 885001 🖷 01306 876821 ✉ info@molevalley.gov.uk
💻 www.molevalley.gov.uk

FACTS AND FIGURES

Parliamentary Constituencies: Mole Valley
EU Constituencies: South East
Election Frequency: Elections are by thirds

PRINCIPAL OFFICERS

Chief Executive: Ms Yvonne Rees, Chief Executive (Mole Valley) Strategic Director of Customers & Communities (Surrey), Pippbrook, Dorking RH4 1SJ ☎ 01306 879101 ✉ yvonne.rees@molevalley.gov.uk

Deputy Chief Executive: Mr Nick Gray , Deputy Chief Executive, Pippbrook, Dorking RH4 1SJ ☎ 01306 879307 🖷 01306 876821 ✉ nick.gray@molevalley.gov.uk

Senior Management: Mr Richard Burrows , Corporate Head of Service, Pippbrook, Dorking RH4 1SJ ☎ 01306 879156 ✉ richard.burrows@molevalley.gov.uk

Senior Management: Mr Paul Feehily , Interim Corporate Head of Service, Pippbrook, Dorking RH4 1SJ ☎ 01306 879237 ✉ paul.feehily@molevalley.gov.uk

Senior Management: Mrs Angela Griffiths, Corporate Head of Service - Democratic & Legal, Pippbrook, Dorking RH4 1SJ ☎ 01306 879133 🖷 01306 879302 ✉ angela.griffiths@molevalley.gov.uk

Senior Management: Mr Graeme Kane , Corporate Head of Service, Pippbrook, Dorking RH4 1SJ ☎ 01306 870622 🖷 01306 876321 ✉ graeme.kane@molevalley.gov.uk

Senior Management: Mrs Rachel O'Reilly, Corporate Head of Service, Pippbrook, Dorking RH4 1SJ ☎ 01306 879358 🖷 01306 876821 ✉ rachel.o'reilly@molevalley.gov.uk

Senior Management: Mr Steve Ruddy , Corporate Head of Service - Environment, Pippbrook, Dorking RH4 1SJ ☎ 01306 879225 ✉ steve.ruddy@molevalley.gov.uk

Access Officer / Social Services (Disability): Mrs Rachel O'Reilly, Corporate Head of Service, Pippbrook, Dorking RH4 1SJ ☎ 01306 879358 🖷 01306 876821 ✉ rachel.o'reilly@molevalley.gov.uk

Architect, Building / Property Services: Mr Richard Burrows , Corporate Head of Service, Pippbrook, Dorking RH4 1SJ ☎ 01306 879156 ✉ richard.burrows@molevalley.gov.uk

Building Control: Mr Andrew Winton , Building Control Manager, Pippbrook, Dorking RH4 1SJ ☎ 01306 879252 🖷 01306 876821 ✉ andrew.winton@molevalley.gov.uk

Children / Youth Services: Mrs Rachel O'Reilly, Corporate Head of Service, Pippbrook, Dorking RH4 1SJ ☎ 01306 879358 🖷 01306 876821 ✉ rachel.o'reilly@molevalley.gov.uk

PR / Communications: Mrs Louise Bircher , Customer Service & Communications Manager, Pippbrook, Dorking RH4 1SJ ☎ 01306 879155 🖷 01306 876821 ✉ louise.bircher@molevalley.gov.uk

Community Planning: Mrs Rachel O'Reilly, Corporate Head of Service, Pippbrook, Dorking RH4 1SJ ☎ 01306 879358 🖷 01306 876821 ✉ rachel.o'reilly@molevalley.gov.uk

Community Safety: Mrs Rachel O'Reilly, Corporate Head of Service, Pippbrook, Dorking RH4 1SJ ☎ 01306 879358 🖷 01306 876821 ✉ rachel.o'reilly@molevalley.gov.uk

Computer Management: Mr Robert Thomas, Head of Information Technology, Pippbrook, Dorking RH4 1SJ ☎ 01306 879171 🖷 01306 876821 ✉ bob.thomas@molevalley.gov.uk

Consumer Protection and Trading Standards: Mr Steve Ruddy , Corporate Head of Service - Environment, Pippbrook, Dorking RH4 1SJ ☎ 01306 879225 ✉ steve.ruddy@molevalley.gov.uk

Contracts: Mr Richard Burrows , Corporate Head of Service, Pippbrook, Dorking RH4 1SJ ☎ 01306 879156 ✉ richard.burrows@molevalley.gov.uk

Corporate Services: Ms Yvonne Rees, Chief Executive (Mole Valley) Strategic Director of Customers & Communities (Surrey), Pippbrook, Dorking RH4 1SJ ☎ 01306 879101 ✉ yvonne.rees@molevalley.gov.uk

Customer Service: Mrs Louise Bircher , Customer Service & Communications Manager, Pippbrook, Dorking RH4 1SJ ☎ 01306 879155 🖷 01306 876821 ✉ louise.bircher@molevalley.gov.uk

Economic Development: Ms Sandra Grant , Economic Unit Manager, Pippbrook, Dorking RH4 1SJ ☎ 01306 655017 🖷 01306 742359 ✉ sandra.grant@molevalley.gov.uk

Electoral Registration: Mrs Arabella Davies , Democratic Services Manager, Pippbrook, Dorking RH4 1SJ ☎ 01306 879137 🖷 01306 879302 ✉ arabella.davies@molevalley.gov.uk

Emergency Planning: Mrs Angela Griffiths, Corporate Head of Service - Democratic & Legal, Pippbrook, Dorking RH4 1SJ ☎ 01306 879133 🖷 01306 879302 ✉ angela.griffiths@molevalley.gov.uk

Energy Management: Mr Steve Ruddy , Corporate Head of Service - Environment, Pippbrook, Dorking RH4 1SJ ☎ 01306 879225 ✉ steve.ruddy@molevalley.gov.uk

Environmental / Technical Services: Mr Steve Ruddy , Corporate Head of Service - Environment, Pippbrook, Dorking RH4 1SJ ☎ 01306 879225 ✉ steve.ruddy@molevalley.gov.uk

MOLE VALLEY

Environmental Health: Mr Steve Ruddy , Corporate Head of Service - Environment, Pippbrook, Dorking RH4 1SJ ☎ 01306 879225 ✉ steve.ruddy@molevalley.gov.uk

Estates, Property & Valuation: Mr Richard Burrows , Corporate Head of Service, Pippbrook, Dorking RH4 1SJ ☎ 01306 879156 ✉ richard.burrows@molevalley.gov.uk

Facilities: Mr Jason Hughes, Senior Engineer & IT Co-ordinator, Pippbrook, Dorking RH4 1SJ ☎ 01306 879184 🖷 01306 876821 ✉ jason.hughes@molevalley.gov.uk

Finance: Mr Nick Gray , Deputy Chief Executive, Pippbrook, Dorking RH4 1SJ ☎ 01306 879307 🖷 01306 876821 ✉ nick.gray@molevalley.gov.uk

Grounds Maintenance: Mr Paul Anderson , Parks & Parking Manager, Pippbrook, Dorking RH4 1SJ ☎ 01306 870613 🖷 01306 876821 ✉ paul.anderson@molevalley.gov.uk

Health and Safety: Mrs Angela Griffiths, Corporate Head of Service - Democratic & Legal, Pippbrook, Dorking RH4 1SJ ☎ 01306 879133 🖷 01306 879302 ✉ angela.griffiths@molevalley.gov.uk

Home Energy Conservation: Mr Steve Ruddy , Corporate Head of Service - Environment, Pippbrook, Dorking RH4 1SJ ☎ 01306 879225 ✉ steve.ruddy@molevalley.gov.uk

Housing: Ms Alison Wilks , Strategic Housing Manager, Pippbrook, Dorking RH4 1SJ ☎ 01306 870645 🖷 01306 876321 ✉ alison.wilks@molevalley.gov.uk

Housing Maintenance: Ms Alison Wilks , Strategic Housing Manager, Pippbrook, Dorking RH4 1SJ ☎ 01306 870645 🖷 01306 876321 ✉ alison.wilks@molevalley.gov.uk

Legal: Mr Chris Harris , Legal Services Manager (Solicitor), Pippbrook, Dorking RH4 1SJ ☎ 01306 879130 🖷 01306 876821 ✉ christopher.harris@molevalley.gov.uk

Leisure and Cultural Services: Mr Richard Burrows , Corporate Head of Service, Pippbrook, Dorking RH4 1SJ ☎ 01306 879156 ✉ richard.burrows@molevalley.gov.uk

Licensing: Mr John Pleasance , Senior Licensing Officer, Pippbrook, Dorking RH4 1SJ ☎ 01306 879351 🖷 01306 876321 ✉ john.pleasance@molevalley.gov.uk

Lottery Funding, Charity and Voluntary: Mrs Rachel O'Reilly, Corporate Head of Service, Pippbrook, Dorking RH4 1SJ ☎ 01306 879358 🖷 01306 876821 ✉ rachel.o'reilly@molevalley.gov.uk

Member Services: Mrs Angela Griffiths, Corporate Head of Service - Democratic & Legal, Pippbrook, Dorking RH4 1SJ ☎ 01306 879133 🖷 01306 879302 ✉ angela.griffiths@molevalley.gov.uk

Parking: Mr Paul Anderson , Parks & Parking Manager, Pippbrook, Dorking RH4 1SJ ☎ 01306 870613 🖷 01306 876821 ✉ paul.anderson@molevalley.gov.uk

Partnerships: Mrs Rachel O'Reilly, Corporate Head of Service, Pippbrook, Dorking RH4 1SJ ☎ 01306 879358 🖷 01306 876821 ✉ rachel.o'reilly@molevalley.gov.uk

Personnel / HR: Ms Kate Ivackovic , HR Manager, Pippbrook, Dorking RH4 1SJ ☎ 01306 879360 🖷 01306 876821 ✉ kate.ivackovic@molevalley.gov.uk

Planning: Mr Jack Straw, Planning Policy Manager, Pippbrook, Dorking RH4 1SJ ☎ 01306 879246 🖷 01306 876821 ✉ jack.straw@molevalley.gov.uk

Procurement: Mr Richard Burrows , Corporate Head of Service, Pippbrook, Dorking RH4 1SJ ☎ 01306 879156 ✉ richard.burrows@molevalley.gov.uk

Recycling & Waste Minimisation: Mr Josh Lambe , Recycling Manager, Pippbrook, Dorking RH4 1SJ ☎ 01306 879118 ✉ josh.lambe@molevalley.gov.uk

Staff Training: Ms Kate Ivackovic , HR Manager, Pippbrook, Dorking RH4 1SJ ☎ 01306 879360 🖷 01306 876821 ✉ kate.ivackovic@molevalley.gov.uk

Street Scene: Mr Rod Shaw, Prinicipal Conservation Officer, Pippbrook, Dorking RH4 1SJ ☎ 01306 879247 ✉ rod.shaw@molevalley.gov.uk

Sustainable Communities: Mr Steve Ruddy , Corporate Head of Service - Environment, Pippbrook, Dorking RH4 1SJ ☎ 01306 879225 ✉ steve.ruddy@molevalley.gov.uk

Sustainable Development: Mr Steve Ruddy , Corporate Head of Service - Environment, Pippbrook, Dorking RH4 1SJ ☎ 01306 879225 ✉ steve.ruddy@molevalley.gov.uk

Town Centre: Ms Sandra Grant, Dorking Town Centre Manager, Dorking Town Centre Management, c/o Barclays Bank Plc, 87/99 High Street, Dorking RH4 1AN ☎ 01306 655017 🖷 01306 742359 ✉ sandra.grant@molevalley.gov.uk

Town Centre: Mrs Lucy Hanson, Leatherhead Town Centre Manager, Fairmount House, Bull Hill, Leatherhead KT22 7AH ☎ 01372 363652 🖷 01372 363652 ✉ lucy.hanson@molevalley.gov.uk

Waste Collection and Disposal: Mr Steve Ruddy , Corporate Head of Service - Environment, Pippbrook, Dorking RH4 1SJ ☎ 01306 879225 ✉ steve.ruddy@molevalley.gov.uk

Waste Management: Mr Steve Ruddy , Corporate Head of Service - Environment, Pippbrook, Dorking RH4 1SJ ☎ 01306 879225 ✉ steve.ruddy@molevalley.gov.uk

Children's Play Areas: Mr Paul Anderson , Parks & Parking Manager, Pippbrook, Dorking RH4 1SJ ☎ 01306 870613 🖷 01306 876821 ✉ paul.anderson@molevalley.gov.uk

COUNCILLORS

***Chair* Aboud**, Emile (CON - Fetcham West)
cllr.aboud@molevalley.gov.uk

***Vice-Chair* Cooksey**, Margaret (LD - Dorking South)
cllr.margaretcooksey@molevalley.gov.uk

***Leader of the Council* Townsend**, Chris (IND - Ashtead Park)
cllr.townsend@molevalley.gov.uk

***Deputy Leader of the Council* Friend**, James (CON - Westcott)
cllr.friend@molevalley.gov.uk

Ashton, Tim (CON - Leatherhead South)
cllr.ashton@molevalley.gov.uk

Botting, Lucy (CON - Bookham North)
cllr.botting@molevalley.gov.uk

Brooks, Lynne (CON - Fetcham East)
Cllr.LynneBrooks@molevalley.gov.uk

Brooks, Stella (LD - Bookham South)
cllr.brooks@molevalley.gov.uk

Chandler, John (NP - Bookham South)
cllr.chandler@molevalley.gov.uk

Cooksey, Stephen (LD - Dorking South)
cllr.cooksey@molevalley.gov.uk

Cooper, Mary (IND - Ashtead Village)
cllr.cooper@molevalley.gov.uk

Curran, Clare (CON - Bookham North)
cllr.curran@molevalley.gov.uk

Dickson, Rosemary (CON - Leatherhead South)
cllr.dickson@molevalley.gov.uk

Draper, David (LD - Dorking North)
cllr.draper@molevalley.gov.uk

Elderton, Paul (LD - Dorking North)
paul.elderton@virgin.net

Hancock, Paula (IND - Ashtead Common)
cllr.hancock@molevalley.gov.uk

Haque, Raj (LD - Fetcham West)
cllr.haque@molevalley.gov.uk

Homewood, Valerie (LD - Beare Green)
cllr.valeriehomewood@molevalley.gov.uk

Huggins, Mary (CON - Capel, Leigh and Newdigate)
cllr.huggins@molevalley.gov.uk

Hunt, Chris (CON - Ashtead Village)
cllr.hunt@molevalley.gov.uk

Hurst, Roger (LD - Mickleham, Westhumble and Pixham)
cllr.hurst@molevalley.gov.uk

Jones, Howard (CON - Leatherhead North)
cllr.jones@molevalley.gov.uk

Lewis-Carr, Bridget (LD - Leatherhead North)
cllr.lewis-carr@molevalley.gov.uk

Ling, Simon (IND - Ashtead Village)
cllr.ling@molevalley.gov.uk

Longhurst, Mick (LD - Holmwoods)
cllr.longhurst@molevalley.gov.uk

Loretto, Tim (LD - Dorking South)
cllr.loretto@molevalley.gov.uk

Michael, Vivienne (CON - Okewood)
cllr.michael@molevalley.gov.uk

Mir, David (CON - Leith Hill)
cllr.mir@molevalley.gov.uk

Monkman, Wayne (LD - Holmwoods)
cllr.monkman@molevalley.gov.uk

Muggeridge, John (CON - Brockham, Betchwood and Buckland)
cllr.muggeridge@molevalley.gov.uk

Musgrove, Stephen (UKIP - Holmwoods)
cllr.musgrove@molevalley.gov.uk

Newman, Paul (CON - Bookham North)
cllr.newman@molevalley.gov.uk

Northcott, John (IND - Ashtead Common)
cllr.northcott@molevalley.gov.uk

Osborne-Patterson, Corinna (CON - Capel, Leigh and Newdigate)
Cllr.Osborne-Patterson@molevalley.gov.uk

Patel, Jatin (CON - Bookham South)
cllr.patel@molevalley.gov.uk

Potter, Paul (LD - Brockham, Betchworth and Buckland)
cllr.potter@molevalley.gov.uk

Preedy, David (LD - Box Hill and Headley)
cllr.preedy@molevalley.gov.uk

Seed, Sarah (CON - Fetcham East)
cllr.seed@molevalley.gov.uk

Shimmin, Philippa (LD - Leatherhead North)
cllr.shimmin@molevalley.gov.uk

Stanyard, Peter (IND - Ashtead Park)
cllr.stanyard@molevalley.gov.uk

Yarwood, Charles (CON - Charlwood)
cllr.yarwood@molevalley.gov.uk

POLITICAL COMPOSITION
CON: 18, LD: 15, IND: 6, NP: 1, UKIP: 1

Monmouthshire W

Monmouthshire County Council, County Hall, Rhadyr, Usk NP15 1GA
☎ 01633 644644 🖷 01633 644666 ✉ feedback@monmouthshire.gov.uk
💻 www.monmouthshire.gov.uk

FACTS AND FIGURES
Parliamentary Constituencies: Monmouth
EU Constituencies: Wales
Election Frequency: Elections are of whole council

PRINCIPAL OFFICERS
Chief Executive: Mr Paul Matthews , Chief Executive, County Hall, Rhadyr, Usk NP15 1GA ☎ 01633 644644
✉ paulmatthews@monmouthshire.gov.uk

Senior Management: Ms Kellie Beirne , Chief Officer - Enterprise, County Hall, Rhadyr, Usk NP15 1GA ☎ 01633 644468
✉ kelliebeirne@monmouthshire.gov.uk

Senior Management: Mr Simon Burch , Chief Officer - Health & Social Care, County Hall, Rhadyr, Usk NP15 1GA ☎ 01633 644601
🖷 01633 644577 ✉ simonburch@monmouthshire.gov.uk

MONMOUTHSHIRE

Senior Management: Mr Peter Davies , Head of Commercial & People Development, County Hall, Rhadyr, Usk NP15 1GA ☎ 01633 644644 🖷 01633 644294 ✉ peterdavies@monmouthshire.gov.uk

Senior Management: Ms Tracey Harry , Head of Democracy & Regulatory Services, County Hall, Rhadyr, Usk NP15 1GA

Senior Management: Mr Roger Hoggins, Head - Operations, County Hall, Rhadyr, Usk NP15 1GA ☎ 01633 644134 🖷 01633 644144 ✉ rogerhoggins@monmouthshire.gov.uk

Senior Management: Ms Sarah McGuiness , Chief Officer - Children & Young People, County Hall, Rhadyr, Usk NP15 1GA ☎ 01633 644644 🖷 01633 644488 ✉ sarahmcguiness@monmouthshire.gov.uk

Senior Management: Mr Will McLean , Head - Policy & Engagement, County Hall, Rhadyr, Usk NP15 1GA

Senior Management: Mrs Joy Robson , Head - Finance & Section 151 Officer, County Hall, Rhadyr, Usk NP15 1GA ☎ 01633 644644 🖷 01633 644270 ✉ joyrobson@monmouthshire.gov.uk

Access Officer / Social Services (Disability): Mr Alan Burkitt , Policy Officer - Equalities & Welsh Language, County Hall, Rhadyr, Usk NP15 1GA ☎ 01633 644644 ✉ alanburkitt@monmouthshire.gov.uk

Architect, Building / Property Services: Mr Rob O'Dwyer , Head of Property Services & Facilities Manager, Innovation House, Wales 1 Business Park, Newport Road, Magor, Caldicot NP26 3DG ☎ 01633 644452 ✉ roberto'dwyer@monmouthshire.gov.uk

Building Control: Mr Philip Thomas , Development Control Manager, County Hall, Rhadyr, Usk NP15 1GA ☎ 01633 644644 ✉ philipthomas@monmouthshire.gov.uk

Children / Youth Services: Ms Tracey Jelfs , Interim Head of Children's Services, County Hall, Rhadyr, Usk NP15 1GA ☎ 01633 644571 🖷 01633 644577 ✉ traceyjelfs@monmouthshire.gov.uk

Civil Registration: Ms Sally Morgan , Registration Service Manager, County Hall, Rhadyr, Usk NP15 1GA ☎ 01873 735468 ✉ sallymorgan@monmouthshire.gov.uk

PR / Communications: Ms Abigale Barton , Communications & Engagement Manager, County Hall, Rhadyr, Usk NP15 1GA ☎ 01633 644644 ✉ abigalebarton@monmouthshire.gov.uk

Community Planning: Ms Deb Hill-Howells , Head of Community Led Delivery, County Hall, Rhadyr, Usk NP15 1GA ☎ 01633 644281 ✉ debrahill-howells@monmouthshire.gov.uk

Computer Management: Ms Sian Hayward , Digital & Technology Manager, County Hall, Rhadyr, Usk NP15 1GA ☎ 01633 644309 ✉ sianhayward@monmouthshire.gov.uk

Contracts: Mr Roger Hoggins, Head - Operations, County Hall, Rhadyr, Usk NP15 1GA ☎ 01633 644134 🖷 01633 644144 ✉ rogerhoggins@monmouthshire.gov.uk

Direct Labour: Mr Roger Hoggins, Head - Operations, County Hall, Rhadyr, Usk NP15 1GA ☎ 01633 644134 🖷 01633 644144 ✉ rogerhoggins@monmouthshire.gov.uk

Economic Development: Ms Cath Fallon , Head of Economy & Enterprise, County Hall, Rhadyr, Usk NP15 1GA ☎ 01633 748316 ✉ cathfallon@monmouthshire.gov.uk

Education: Ms Sarah McGuiness , Chief Officer - Children & Young People, County Hall, Rhadyr, Usk NP15 1GA ☎ 01633 644644 🖷 01633 644488 ✉ sarahmcguiness@monmouthshire.gov.uk

E-Government: Mr Peter Davies , Head of Commercial & People Development, County Hall, Rhadyr, Usk NP15 1GA ☎ 01633 644644 🖷 01633 644294 ✉ peterdavies@monmouthshire.gov.uk

Energy Management: Mr Roger Hoggins, Head - Operations, County Hall, Rhadyr, Usk NP15 1GA ☎ 01633 644134 🖷 01633 644144 ✉ rogerhoggins@monmouthshire.gov.uk

Events Manager: Mr Dan Davies , Enterprise Coordinator, County Hall, Rhadyr, Usk NP15 1GA ☎ 01633 644044 ✉ dandavies@monmouthshire.gov.uk

Facilities: Mr Rob O'Dwyer , Head of Property Services & Facilities Manager, County Hall, Rhadyr, Usk NP15 1GA ☎ 01633 644452 ✉ roberto'dwyer@monmouthshire.gov.uk

Finance: Mrs Joy Robson , Head - Finance & Section 151 Officer, County Hall, Rhadyr, Usk NP15 1GA ☎ 01633 644644 🖷 01633 644270 ✉ joyrobson@monmouthshire.gov.uk

Fleet Management: Ms Deb Jackson , Transport Manager, County Hall, Rhadyr, Usk NP15 1GA ☎ 01291 691312 ✉ debjackson@monmouthshire.gov.uk

Grounds Maintenance: Mr Roger Hoggins, Head - Operations, County Hall, Rhadyr, Usk NP15 1GA ☎ 01633 644134 🖷 01633 644144 ✉ rogerhoggins@monmouthshire.gov.uk

Health and Safety: Mr Laurence Dawkins , Safety Manager, County Hall, Rhadyr, Usk NP15 1GA ☎ 01633 644196 🖷 01633 644666 ✉ laurencedawkins@monmouthshire.gov.uk

Highways: Mr Tony Wallen , Head of Highways & Flood Management, County Hall, Rhadyr, Usk NP15 1GA ☎ 01633 889220 ✉ tonywallen@monmouthshire.gov.uk

Home Energy Conservation: Mr John Parfitt , Housing Renewals & Careline Manager, County Hall, Rhadyr, Usk NP15 1GA ☎ ; 01633 644681 ✉ johnparfitt@monmouthshire.gov.uk

Housing: Mr Ian Bakewell , Housing & Regeneration Manager, County Hall, Rhadyr, Usk NP15 1GA ☎ 01633 644479 🖷 01633 644577 ✉ ian.blakewell@monmouthshire.gov.uk

Housing Maintenance: Mr Ian Bakewell , Housing & Regeneration Manager, County Hall, Rhadyr, Usk NP15 1GA ☎ 01633 644479 🖷 01633 644577 ✉ ian.blakewell@monmouthshire.gov.uk

Legal: Mr Rob Tranter , Monitoring Officer/Head of Legal Services, County Hall, Rhadyr, Usk NP15 1GA ☎ 01633 644064 ✉ robtranter@monmouthshire.gov.uk

Leisure and Cultural Services: Mr Ian Saunders , Head of Tourism, Leisure & Culture, County Hall, Rhadyr, Usk NP15 1GA ☎ 01633 644499 ✉ iansaunders@monmouthshire.gov.uk

Licensing: Ms Linda O'Gorman, Principal Licensing Officer, County Hall, Rhadyr, Usk NP15 1GA ☎ 01633 644214 ✉ lindaogorman@monmouthshire.gov.uk

Lifelong Learning: Ms Sarah McGuiness , Chief Officer - Children & Young People, County Hall, Rhadyr, Usk NP15 1GA ☎ 01633 644644 🖷 01633 644488 ✉ sarahmcguiness@monmouthshire.gov.uk

Member Services: Mr John Pearson , Local Democracy Manager, County Hall, Rhadyr, Usk NP15 1GA ☎ 01633 644978 ✉ johnpearson@monmouthshire.gov.uk

Parking: Mr Roger Hoggins, Head - Operations, County Hall, Rhadyr, Usk NP15 1GA ☎ 01633 644134 🖷 01633 644144 ✉ rogerhoggins@monmouthshire.gov.uk

Personnel / HR: Mr Peter Davies , Head of Commercial & People Development, County Hall, Rhadyr, Usk NP15 1GA ☎ 01633 644644 🖷 01633 644294 ✉ peterdavies@monmouthshire.gov.uk

Public Libraries: Ms Ann Jones , Libraries, Museums & Art Manager, County Hall, Rhadyr, Usk NP15 1GA ✉ annjones@monmouthshire.gov.uk

Recycling & Waste Minimisation: Ms Rachel Jowitt , Head of Waste & Street Services, County Hall, Rhadyr, Usk NP15 1GA ☎ 01633 748326 ✉ racheljowitt@monmouthshire.gov.uk

Regeneration: Ms Kellie Beirne , Chief Officer - Enterprise, County Hall, Rhadyr, Usk NP15 1GA ☎ 01633 644468 ✉ kelliebeirne@monmouthshire.gov.uk

Road Safety: Mr Paul Keeble , Traffic & Network Manager, County Hall, Rhadyr, Usk NP15 1GA ☎ 01633 644644 ✉ paulkeeble@monmouthshire.gov.uk

Social Services: Mr Simon Burch , Chief Officer - Health & Social Care, County Hall, Rhadyr, Usk NP15 1GA ☎ 01633 644601 🖷 01633 644577 ✉ simonburch@monmouthshire.gov.uk

Social Services (Adult): Ms Julie Boothroyd , Head of Adult Services, County Hall, Rhadyr, Usk NP15 1GA ☎ 01633 644601 🖷 01633 644577 ✉ julieboothroyd@monmouthshire.gov.uk

Social Services (Children): Ms Tracey Jelfs , Interim Head of Children's Services, County Hall, Rhadyr, Usk NP15 1GA ☎ 01633 644571 🖷 01633 644577 ✉ traceyjelfs@monmouthshire.gov.uk

Staff Training: Mr John McConnachie , Training Lead, County Hall, Rhadyr, Usk NP15 1GA ☎ 01873 735453 ✉ johnmcconnachie@monmouthshire.gov.uk

Street Scene: Ms Rachel Jowitt , Head of Waste & Street Services, County Hall, Rhadyr, Usk NP15 1GA ☎ 01633 748326 ✉ racheljowitt@monmouthshire.gov.uk

Sustainable Communities: Ms Kellie Beirne , Chief Officer - Enterprise, County Hall, Rhadyr, Usk NP15 1GA ☎ 01633 644468 ✉ kelliebeirne@monmouthshire.gov.uk

Sustainable Development: Ms Hazel Clatworthy, Sustainable Community Officer, County Hall, Rhadyr, Usk NP15 1GA ☎ 01633 644843 🖷 01633 644200 ✉ hazelclatworthy@monmouthshire.gov.uk

Tourism: Ms Nicola Smith , Tourism Officer, County Hall, Rhadyr, Usk NP15 1GA ☎ 01633 644847 🖷 01633 644800 ✉ nicolasmith@monmouthshire.gov.uk

Traffic Management: Mr Paul Keeble , Traffic & Network Manager, County Hall, Rhadyr, Usk NP15 1GA ☎ 01633 644644 ✉ paulkeeble@monmouthshire.gov.uk

Transport: Mr Richard Cope , Passenger Transport Unit Manager, County Hall, Rhadyr, Usk NP15 1GA ☎ 01633 644745 ✉ richardcope@monmouthshire.gov.uk

Transport Planner: Mr Christian Achmidt , Transport Planning & Policy Officer, County Hall, Rhadyr, Usk NP15 1GA ☎ 01633 644727 ✉ christianschmidt@monmouthshire.gov.uk

Total Place: Ms Deb Hill-Howells , Head of Community Led Delivery, County Hall, Rhadyr, Usk NP15 1GA ☎ 01633 644281 ✉ debrahill-howells@monmouthshire.gov.uk

Waste Collection and Disposal: Ms Rachel Jowitt , Head of Waste & Street Services, County Hall, Rhadyr, Usk NP15 1GA ☎ 01633 748326 ✉ racheljowitt@monmouthshire.gov.uk

Waste Management: Ms Rachel Jowitt , Head of Waste & Street Services, County Hall, Rhadyr, Usk NP15 1GA ☎ 01633 748326 ✉ racheljowitt@monmouthshire.gov.uk

Children's Play Areas: Mr Tim Bradfield , Recreation Officer, County Hall, Rhadyr, Usk NP15 1GA ☎ 01633 644136 ✉ timbradfield@monmouthshire.gov.uk

COUNCILLORS

***Chair* Strong**, Brian (CON - Usk)
brianstrong@monmouthshire.gov.uk

***Vice-Chair* Higginson**, Jim (LAB - Severn)
ronhigginson@monmouthshire.gov.uk

***Leader of the Council* Fox**, Peter (CON - Portskewett)
peterfox@monmouthshire.gov.uk

Batrouni, Dimitri (LAB - St. Christopher's)
dimitribatrouni@monmouthshire.gov.uk

Blakebrough, Debby (IND - Trellech United)
debbyblakebrough@monmouthshire.gov.uk

Burrows, Geoffrey (CON - Mitchel Troy)
geoffburrows@monmouthsire.gov.uk

Chapman, Ralph (IND - Mardy)
ralphchapman@monmouthshire.gov.uk

MONMOUTHSHIRE

Clarke, Peter (CON - Llangybi Fawr)
peterclarke@monmouthshire.gov.uk

Crook, Jessica (LAB - The Elms)
jessicacrook@monmouthshire.gov.uk

Dovey, David (CON - St. Kingsmark)
daviddovey@monmouthshire.gov.uk

Down, Graham (IND - Shirenewton)
grahamdown@monmouthshire.gov.uk

Easson, Tony (LAB - Dewstow)
anthonyeasson@monmouthshire.gov.uk

Edwards, Douglas (LD - Grofield)
douglasedwards@monmouthshire.gov.uk

Edwards, Ruth (CON - Llantilio Crossenny)
ruthedwards@monmouthshire.gov.uk

Evans, David (LAB - West End)
davidevans2@monmouthshire.gov.uk

Farley, Peter (LAB - St Mary's)
peterfarley@monmouhshire.gov.uk

George, James (LAB - Lansdown)
jamesgeorge@monmouthshire.gov.uk

Greenland, Robert (CON - Devauden)
robertgreenland@monmouthshire.gov.uk

Guppy, Linda (LD - Rogiet)
lindaguppy@monmouthshire.gov.uk

Hacket Pain, Liz (CON - Wyesham)
lizhacketpain@monmouthshire.gov.uk

Harris, Roger (LAB - Croesonen)
rogerharris@monmouthshire.gov.uk

Hayward, Robert (IND - Dixton with Osbaston)
bobhayward@monmouthshire.gov.uk

Hickman, Martin (CON - Llanfoist Fawr)
martinhickman@monmouthshire.gov.uk

Hobson, Phil (LD - Larkfield)
philhobson@monmouthshire.gov.uk

Howard, Giles (CON - Llanelly Hill)
gileshoward@monmouthshire.gov.uk

Howarth, Simon (IND - Llanelly Hill)
simonhowarth@monmouthshire.gov.uk

Jones, Bryan (CON - Goetre Fawr)
bryanjones@monmouthshire.gov.uk

Jones, Sara (CON - Llanover)
sarajones2@monmouthshire.gov.uk

Jones, Penny (CON - Raglan)
pennyjones@monmouthshire.gov.uk

Jones, David (IND - Crucorney)
davidhughesjones@monmouthshire.gov.uk

Jordan, Paul (CON - Cantref)
pauljordan@monmouthshire.gov.uk

Marshall, John (IND - Green Lane)
johnmarshall@monmouthshire.gov.uk

Murphy, Phil (CON - Caerwent)
philmurphy@monmouthshire.gov.uk

Powell, Maureen (CON - Castle)
maureenpowell@monmouthshire.gov.uk

Prosser, John (CON - Priory)
johnprosser@monmouthshire.gov.uk

Smith, Val (IND - Llanbadoc)
valsmith@monmouthshire.gov.uk

Taylor, Frances (IND - Mill)
francestaylor@monmouthdhire.gov.uk

Watts, Pauline (LAB - Caldicot Castle)
paulinewatts@monmouthshire.gov.uk

Watts, Armand (LAB - Thornwell)
armandwatts@monmouthshire.gov.uk

Webb, Ann (CON - St. Arvans)
annwebb@monmouthshire.gov.uk

White, Susan (CON - Overmonnow)
susanwhite@monmouthshire.gov.uk

Williams, Kevin (LAB - Llanwenarth Ultra)
kevinwilliams@monmouthshire.gov.uk

Wintle, Alan (IND - Drybirdge)
alanwintle@monmouthshire.gov.uk

POLITICAL COMPOSITION

CON: 19, LAB: 11, IND: 10, LD: 3

COMMITTEE CHAIRS

Licensing & Regulatory: Ms Linda Guppy

Planning: Ms Ruth Edwards

Moray S

Moray Council, Council Offices, High Street, Elgin IV30 1BX
☎ 01343 543451 🖷 01343 540399 🖳 www.moray.gov.uk

FACTS AND FIGURES

Parliamentary Constituencies: Moray
EU Constituencies: Scotland
Election Frequency: Elections are of whole council

PRINCIPAL OFFICERS

Chief Executive: Mr Roddy Burns, Chief Executive, Council Offices, High Street, Elgin IV30 1BX ☎ 01343 563001 🖷 01343 563990 ✉ roddy.burns@moray.gov.uk

Senior Management: Mr Richard Anderson , Head of Housing & Property, Council Offices, High Street, Elgin IV30 1BX ☎ 01343 563532 ✉ richard.anderson@moray.gov.uk

Senior Management: Mr Stephen Cooper , Head of Direct Services, PO Box 6760, Elgin IV30 9BX ☎ 01343 563777 ✉ stephen.p.cooper@moray.gov.uk

Senior Management: Ms Vivienne Cross , Acting Head of Schools & Curriculum Development, Council Offices, High Street, Elgin IV30 1BX ☎ 01343 563411 ✉ vivienne.cross@moray.gov.uk

Senior Management: Mr Laurence Findlay , Corporate Director - Education & Social Care, Council Office, High Street, Elgin IV30 1BX ☎ 01343 563530 🖷 01343 563390 ✉ laurence.findlay@moray.gov.uk

Senior Management: Ms Pam Gowans , Chief Officer - Moray Health & Social Care Partnership, Council Offices, High Street, Elgin IV30 1BX ☎ 01343 563552 🖷 01343 563990 ✉ pamela.gowans@moray.gov.uk

Senior Management: Mr Jim Grant , Head of Development Services, Council Offices, High Street, Elgin IV30 1BX ☎ 01343 563262 🖷 01343 563990 ✉ jim.grant@moray.gov.uk

Senior Management: Mrs Rhona Gunn , Acting Corporate Director - Economic Development, Planning & Infrastructure, Council Offices, High Street, Elgin IV30 1BX ☎ 01343 563152 🖷 01343 563990 ✉ rhona.gunn@moray.gov.uk

Senior Management: Mr Graham Jarvis , Head of Lifelong Learning, Culture & Sport, Council Offices, High Street, Elgin IV30 1BX ☎ 01343 563365 ✉ graham.jarvis@moray.gov.uk

Senior Management: Ms Susan Maclaren , Head of Integrated Children's Services, Council Offices, High Street, Elgin IV30 1BX ☎ 01343 563584 ✉ susan.maclaren@moray.gov.uk

Senior Management: Mr Alasdair McEachan , Acting Head of Legal & Democratic Services, Council Offices, High Street, Elgin IV30 1BX ☎ 01343 563080 ✉ alasdair.mceachan@moray.gov.uk

Senior Management: Mr Mark Palmer, Corporate Director - Corporate Services, Council Offices, High Street, Elgin IV30 1BX ☎ 01343 563103 🖷 01343 563990 ✉ mark.palmer@moray.gov.uk

Senior Management: Mrs Denise Whitworth, Head of Human Resources & ICT, Council Offices, High Street, Elgin IV30 1BX ☎ 01343 563060 ✉ denise.whitworth@moray.gov.uk

Senior Management: Ms Margaret Wilson , Head of Financial Services, Council Offices, High Street, Elgin IV30 1BX ✉ margaret.wilson@moray.gov.uk

Architect, Building / Property Services: Mr Moray Mcleod , Design Manager, Council Offices, High Street, Elgin IV30 1BX ☎ 01343 563727 ✉ moray.mcleod@moray.gov.uk

Architect, Building / Property Services: Mr Eddie Milne , Property Resources Manager, Council Office, High Street, Elgin IV30 1BX ☎ 01343 563708 ✉ eddie.milne@moray.gov.uk

Best Value: Mrs Bridget Mustard, Corporate Policy Unit Manager, Council Offices, High Street, Elgin IV30 1BX ☎ 01343 563048 🖷 01343 540399 ✉ bridget.mustard@moray.gov.uk

Building Control: Mr Kevan Sturgeon , Building Standards Manager, Council Offices, High Street, Elgin IV30 1BX ☎ 01343 563269 🖷 01343 563990 ✉ kevan.sturgeon@moray.gov.uk

Catering Services: Ms Pearl Gray, Catering Officer, PO Box 6760, Elgin IV30 9BX ☎ 01343 557086 ✉ pearl.gray@moray.gov.uk

Children / Youth Services: Ms Susan Maclaren , Head of Integrated Children's Services, Council Offices, High Street, Elgin IV30 1BX ☎ 01343 563584 ✉ susan.maclaren@moray.gov.uk

Civil Registration: Mrs Heather Greig , Senior Registrar, 240 High Street, Elgin IV30 1BA ☎ 01343 554600 ✉ heather.greig@moray.gov.uk

PR / Communications: Mr Peter Jones, PR & Communications Officer, Council Offices, High Street, Elgin IV30 1BX ☎ 01343 563601 🖷 01343 563311 ✉ peter.jones@moray.gov.uk

Community Planning: Mrs Bridget Mustard, Corporate Policy Unit Manager, Council Offices, High Street, Elgin IV30 1BX ☎ 01343 563048 ✉ bridget.mustard@moray.gov.uk

Community Safety: Mrs Jane Mackie , Head of Community Care, The Moray Council, Spynie Hospital, Elgin IV30 5PW ☎ 01343 567127 ✉ jane.mackie@moray.gov.uk

Community Safety: Mr Kev McPherson , Partnership Development Officer, Council Offices, High Street, Elgin IV30 1BX ☎ 01343 563316 ✉ kev.mcpherson@moray.gov.uk

Computer Management: Ms Denise Whitworth, Head of Human Resources & ICT, Council Offices, High Street, Elgin IV30 1BX ☎ 01343 563060 ✉ denise.whitworth@moray.gov.uk

Consumer Protection and Trading Standards: Mr Peter Adamson , Trading Standards Manager, Council Offices, High Street, Elgin IV30 1BX ☎ 01343 563940 🖷 01343 563990 ✉ peter.adamson@moray.gov.uk

Contracts: Mr Ian Bruce, Environmental Protection Manager, PO Box 6760, Elgin IV30 9BX ☎ 01343 557040 ✉ brucei@moray.gov.uk

Customer Service: Mr Eric Bell , Customer Services Manager, Council Offices, High Street, Elgin IV30 1BX ☎ 01343 563107 ✉ eric.bell@moray.gov.uk

Direct Labour: Mr Michael Rollo, Building Services Manager, The DLO Depot, Mosstodloch, IV30 1TY ☎ 01343 823043 ✉ mike.rollo@moray.gov.uk

Economic Development: Mr Gordon Sutherland , Planning & Economic Development Manager, Council Offices, High Street, Elgin IV30 1BX ☎ 01343 563278 🖷 01343 563990 ✉ gordon.sutherland@moray.gov.uk

Education: Mr Laurence Findlay , Corporate Director - Education & Social Care, Council Office, High Street, Elgin IV30 1BX ☎ 01343 563530 🖷 01343 563390 ✉ laurence.findlay@moray.gov.uk

Electoral Registration: Mr Roddy Burns, Chief Executive, Council Offices, High Street, Elgin IV30 1BX ☎ 01343 563001 🖷 01343 563990 ✉ roddy.burns@moray.gov.uk

Emergency Planning: Mrs Donna McLean , Emergency Planning Officer, Council Offices, High Street, Elgin IV30 1BX ☎ 01343 563865 ✉ donna.mclean@moray.gov.uk

Energy Management: Mr Moray MacLeod, Design Manager, Council Offices, High Street, Elgin IV30 1BX ☎ 01343 563727 ✉ moray.macleod@moray.gov.uk

MORAY

Environmental / Technical Services: Mr Jim Grant , Head of Development Services, Council Offices, High Street, Elgin IV30 1BX 01343 563262 01343 563990 jim.grant@moray.gov.uk

Environmental Health: Ms Karen Sievewright , Environmental Health Manager, Council Offices, High Street, Elgin IV30 1BX 01343 563356 01343 563990 karen.sievewright@moray.gov.uk

Estates, Property & Valuation: Mr Stuart Beveridge , Estates Manager, Council Offices, High Street, Elgin IV30 1BX 01343 563257 stuart.beveridge@moray.gov.uk

Facilities: Mrs Susan May , Operational Support Officer, PO Box 6760, Elgin IV30 9BX 01343 557088 susan.may@moray.gov.uk

Finance: Ms Margaret Wilson , Head of Financial Services, Council Offices, High Street, Elgin IV30 1BX 01343 563102 margaret.wilson@moray.gov.uk

Fleet Management: Mr Leslie Thomson, Fleet Services Manager, PO Box 6760, Elgin IV30 9BX 01343 557051 leslie.thomson@moray.gov.uk

Grounds Maintenance: Mr Ken Kennedy , Lands & Parks Officer, PO Box 6760, Elgin IV30 9BX 01343 557051 ken.kennedy@moray.gov.uk

Health and Safety: Mr Doug Reid, Health & Safety Manager, Council Offices, High Street, Elgin IV30 1BX 01343 563073 doug.reid@moray.gov.uk

Highways: Mr Stephen Cooper , Head of Direct Services, PO Box 6760, Elgin IV30 9BX 01343 563777 stephen.p.cooper@moray.gov.uk

Housing: Mr Richard Anderson , Head of Housing & Property, Council Offices, High Street, Elgin IV30 1BX 01343 563532 richard.anderson@moray.gov.uk

Housing Maintenance: Mr John MacDonald , Asset Manager, Council Offices, High Street, Elgin IV30 1BX 0343 563743 john.macdonald@moray.gov.uk

Legal: Mr Alasdair McEachan , Acting Head of Legal & Democratic Services, Council Offices, High Street, Elgin IV30 1BX 01343 563080 alasdair.mceachan@moray.gov.uk

Leisure and Cultural Services: Mr Nick Goodchild, Educational Resources Manager, Council Offices, High Street, Elgin IV30 1BX 01343 563401 goodchn@moray.gov.uk

Licensing: Mr Alasdair McEachan , Acting Head of Legal & Democratic Services, Council Offices, High Street, Elgin IV30 1BX 01343 563080 alasdair.mceachan@moray.gov.uk

Lifelong Learning: Mr Graham Jarvis , Head of Lifelong Learning, Culture & Sport, Council Offices, High Street, Elgin IV30 1BX 01343 563365 graham.jarvis@moray.gov.uk

Lighting: Mr Bill Ross , Roads Maintenance Manager, PO Box 6760, Elgin IV30 9BX 01343 557303 bill.ross@moray.gov.uk

Member Services: Mr Roddy Burns, Chief Executive, Council Offices, High Street, Elgin IV30 1BX 01343 563001 01343 563990 roddy.burns@moray.gov.uk

Parking: Mrs Nicola Moss , Transportation Manager, PO Box 6760, Elgin IV30 9BX 01343 563785 nicola.moss@moray.gov.uk

Partnerships: Mr Peter Jones, PR & Communications Officer, Council Offices, High Street, Elgin IV30 1BX 01343 563601 01343 563311 peter.jones@moray.gov.uk

Partnerships: Mrs Bridget Mustard, Corporate Policy Unit Manager, Council Offices, High Street, Elgin IV30 1BX 01343 563048 01343 540399 bridget.mustard@moray.gov.uk

Personnel / HR: Ms Denise Whitworth, Head of Human Resources & ICT, Council Offices, High Street, Elgin IV30 1BX 01343 563060 denise.whitworth@moray.gov.uk

Planning: Mrs Beverley Smith , Manager - Development Management, Council Offices, High Street, Elgin IV30 1BX 01343 563276 01343 563990 beverley.smith@moray.gov.uk

Procurement: Mrs Diane Beattie , Payments Manager, Council Offices, High Street, Elgin IV30 1BX 01343 563136 diane.beattie@moray.gov.uk

Public Libraries: Mr Alistair Campbell, Principal Librarian, Council Offices, High Street, Elgin IV30 1BX 01343 562610 sheila.campbell@moray.gov.uk

Recycling & Waste Minimisation: Mr Ian Bruce, Environmental Protection Manager, PO Box 6760, Elgin IV30 9BX 01343 557040 brucei@moray.gov.uk

Recycling & Waste Minimisation: Mr Stephen Cooper , Head of Direct Services, PO Box 6760, Elgin IV30 9BX 01343 563777 stephen.p.cooper@moray.gov.uk

Road Safety: Mr Dave Malpas , Senior Engineer - Traffic, PO Box 6760, Elgin IV30 9BX 01343 563780 dave.malpas@moray.gov.uk

Social Services: Ms Susan Maclaren , Head of Integrated Children's Services, Council Offices, High Street, Elgin IV30 1BX 01343 563584 susan.maclaren@moray.gov.uk

Social Services (Adult): Mrs Jane Mackie , Head of Community Care, The Moray Council, Spynie Hospital, Elgin IV30 5PW 01343 567127 jane.mackie@moray.gov.uk

Social Services (Children): Ms Susan Maclaren , Head of Integrated Children's Services, Council Offices, High Street, Elgin IV30 1BX 01343 563584 susan.maclaren@moray.gov.uk

Staff Training: Ms Carol Sheridan, Employee Development Manager, Council Offices, 149 High Street, Elgin IV30 1BX 01343 563070 carol.sheridan@moray.gov.uk

Traffic Management: Mr Dave Malpas , Senior Engineer - Traffic, PO Box 6760, Elgin IV30 9BX ☎ 01343 563780 ✉ dave.malpas@moray.gov.uk

Transport: Mr Stephen Cooper , Head of Direct Services, PO Box 6760, Elgin IV30 9BX ☎ 01343 563777 ✉ stephen.p.cooper@moray.gov.uk

Transport: Mrs Nicola Moss , Transportation Manager, PO Box 6760, Elgin IV30 9BX ☎ 01343 563785 ✉ nicola.moss@moray.gov.uk

Waste Collection and Disposal: Mr Ian Bruce, Environmental Protection Manager, PO Box 6760, Elgin IV30 9BX ☎ 01343 557040 ✉ brucei@moray.gov.uk

Waste Management: Mr Ian Bruce, Environmental Protection Manager, PO Box 6760, Elgin IV30 9BX ☎ 01343 557040 ✉ brucei@moray.gov.uk

Children's Play Areas: Mr Ken Kennedy , Lands & Parks Officer, PO Box 6760, Elgin IV30 9BX ☎ 01343 557051 ✉ ken.kennedy@moray.gov.uk

COUNCILLORS

***Convener* Wright**, Allan (CON - Heldon and Laich)
allan.wright@moray.gov.uk

***Leader of the Council* Cree**, Stewart (IND - Keith and Cullen)
stewart.cree@moray.gov.uk

Alexander, George (IND - Forres)
george.alexander@moray.gov.uk

Allan, James (CON - Elgin City South)
james.allan@moray.gov.uk

Coull, Gary (SNP - Keith and Cullen)
gary.coull@moray.gov.uk

Cowe, John (IND - Heldon and Laich)
john.cowe@moray.gov.uk

Cowie, Gordon (IND - Buckie)
gordon.cowie@moray.gov.uk

Creswell, Lorna (IND - Forres)
lorna.creswell@moray.gov.uk

Divers, John (SNP - Elgin City South)
john.divers@moray.gov.uk

Gowans, Patsy (SNP - Elgin City North)
patsy.gowans@moray.gov.uk

Howe, Margo (SNP - Fochabers Lhanbryde)
margo.howe@moray.gov.uk

Leadbitter, Graham (SNP - Elgin City South)
graham.leadbitter@moray.gov.uk

McConachie, Michael (SNP - Speyside Glenlivet)
michael.mcconachie@moray.gov.uk

McDonald, Gordon (SNP - Buckie)
gordon.mcdonald@moray.gov.uk

McGillivray, Eric (IND - Heldon and Laich)
eric.mcgillivray@moray.gov.uk

McLean, Aaron (SNP - Forres)
aaron.mclean@moray.gov.uk

Morton, Sean (LAB - Fochabers Lhanbryde)
sean.morton@moray.gov.uk

Murdoch, Fiona (IND - Speyside Glenlivet)
fiona.murdoch@moray.gov.uk

Paul, Pearl (SNP - Speyside Glenlivet)
pearl.paul@moray.gov.uk

Reid, Kirsty (SNP - Elgin City North)
kirsty.reid@moray.gov.uk

Ross, Douglas (CON - Fochabers Lhanbryde)
douglas.ross@moray.gov.uk

Shand, Michael (SNP - Elgin City North)
mike.shand@moray.gov.uk

Shepherd, Ronald (IND - Keith and Cullen)
ronald.shepherd@moray.gov.uk

Skene, Anne (IND - Forres)
anne.skene@moray.gov.uk

Tuke, Chris (IND - Heldon and Laich)
chris.tuke@moray.gov.uk

Warren, Sonya (SNP - Buckie)
sonya.warren@moray.gov.uk

POLITICAL COMPOSITION

SNP: 12, IND: 10, CON: 3, LAB: 1

COMMITTEE CHAIRS

Audit & Scrutiny: Mr Gordon McDonald

Health & Social Care: Ms Lorna Creswell

Licensing: Mr Ronald Shepherd

Planning & Regulatory Services: Mr Chris Tuke

Neath Port Talbot W

Neath Port Talbot County Borough Council, Civic Centre, Port Talbot SA13 1PJ
☎ 01639 763333 🖷 01639 763444 💻 www.npt.gov.uk

FACTS AND FIGURES

Parliamentary Constituencies: Aberavon, Neath
EU Constituencies: Wales
Election Frequency: Elections are of whole council

PRINCIPAL OFFICERS

Chief Executive: Mr Steven Phillips , Chief Executive, Civic Centre, Port Talbot SA13 1PJ

Senior Management: Mr Aled Evans, Corporate Director of Education, Leisure & Lifelong Learning, Civic Centre, Port Talbot SA13 1PJ ☎ 01639 763298 ✉ a.evans@npt.gov.uk

Senior Management: Mr Nick Jarman, Corporate Director of Social Services, Health & Housing, Port Talbot Civic Centre, Port Talbot SA13 1PJ ☎ 01639 763333; 01639 763279 ✉ n.jarman@npt.gov.uk

NEATH PORT TALBOT

Senior Management: Mr Hywel Jenkins, Corporate Director of Finance & Corporate Services, Civic Centre, Port Talbot SA13 1PJ ☎ 01639 763252 🖱 h.jenkins@npt.gov.uk

Senior Management: Mr Gareth Nutt, Corporate Director of Environment, The Quays, Brunel Way, Baglan Energy Park, Neath SA11 2GG ☎ 01639 686668 🖱 g.nutt@npt.gov.uk

Architect, Building / Property Services: Mr Simon Brennan , Head of Property & Regeneration, The Quays, Brunel Way, Baglan Energy Park, Neath SA11 2GG ☎ 01639 686370 🖱 s.brennan@npt.gov.uk

Best Value: Mrs Karen Jones , Head of Corporate Strategy & Democratic Services, Civic Centre, Port Talbot SA13 1PJ ☎ 01639 763713 🖱 k.jones3@npt.gov.uk

Building Control: Mrs Nicola Pearce, Head of Planning, The Quays, Brunel Way, Baglan Energy Park, Neath SA11 2GG ☎ 01639 686681 🖱 n.pearce@npt.gov.uk

Catering Services: Mr Andrew Thomas, Head of Support Services & Commissioning Development, Civic Centre, Port Talbot SA13 1PJ ☎ 01639 763791 🖱 a.d.thomas@npt.gov.uk

Children / Youth Services: Mr Aled Evans, Corporate Director of Education, Leisure & Lifelong Learning, Civic Centre, Port Talbot SA13 1PJ ☎ 01639 763298 🖱 a.evans@npt.gov.uk

Civil Registration: Mr David Michael , Head of Legal & Democratic Services & Monitoring Officer, Civic Centre, Port Talbot SA13 1PJ ☎ 01639 763368 🖱 d.michael@npt.gov.uk

Community Planning: Mrs Karen Jones , Head of Corporate Strategy & Democratic Services, Civic Centre, Port Talbot SA13 1PJ ☎ 01639 763713 🖱 k.jones3@npt.gov.uk

Computer Management: Mr Stephen John , Head of ICT, The Quays, Brunel Way, Baglan Energy Park, Neath SA11 2GG ☎ 01639 686218 🖱 s.john@npt.gov.uk

Consumer Protection and Trading Standards: Ms Angela Thomas , Head of Business Strategy & Public Protection, Civic Centre, Port Talbot SA13 1PJ ☎ 01639 763794 🖱 a.j.thomas@npt.gov.uk

Contracts: Mr David Rees, Head of Financial Services, Aberavon House, Port Talbot SA13 1PJ ☎ 01639 763646 🖱 d.rees1@npt.gov.uk

Corporate Services: Mr Hywel Jenkins, Corporate Director of Finance & Corporate Services, Civic Centre, Port Talbot SA13 1PJ ☎ 01639 763252 🖱 h.jenkins@npt.gov.uk

Corporate Services: Mrs Karen Jones , Head of Corporate Strategy & Democratic Services, Civic Centre, Port Talbot SA13 1PJ ☎ 01639 763713 🖱 k.jones3@npt.gov.uk

Customer Service: Mrs Karen Jones , Head of Corporate Strategy & Democratic Services, Civic Centre, Port Talbot SA13 1PJ ☎ 01639 763713 🖱 k.jones3@npt.gov.uk

Economic Development: Mr Simon Brennan , Head of Property & Regeneration, The Quays, Brunel Way, Baglan Energy Park, Neath SA11 2GG ☎ 01639 686370 🖱 s.brennan@npt.gov.uk

Education: Mr Aled Evans, Corporate Director of Education, Leisure & Lifelong Learning, Civic Centre, Port Talbot SA13 1PJ ☎ 01639 763298 🖱 a.evans@npt.gov.uk

E-Government: Mr Hywel Jenkins, Corporate Director of Finance & Corporate Services, Civic Centre, Port Talbot SA13 1PJ ☎ 01639 763252 🖱 h.jenkins@npt.gov.uk

Electoral Registration: Mr Rhys George , Electoral Registration Officer, Civic Centre, Port Talbot SA13 1PJ ☎ 01639 763719; 01639 763323 🖱 r.j.george@npt.gov.uk

Emergency Planning: Mrs Sheenagh Rees , Head of Human Resources, Civic Centre, Port Talbot SA13 1PJ ☎ 01639 763315 🖱 s.rees5@npt.gov.uk

Energy Management: Mr Simon Brennan , Head of Property & Regeneration, The Quays, Brunel Way, Baglan Energy Park, Neath SA11 2GG ☎ 01639 686370 🖱 s.brennan@npt.gov.uk

Environmental / Technical Services: Mr Simon Brennan , Head of Property & Regeneration, The Quays, Brunel Way, Baglan Energy Park, Neath SA11 2GG ☎ 01639 686370 🖱 s.brennan@npt.gov.uk

Environmental Health: Ms Angela Thomas , Head of Business Strategy & Public Protection, Civic Centre, Port Talbot SA13 1PJ ☎ 01639 763794 🖱 a.j.thomas@npt.gov.uk

Estates, Property & Valuation: Mr Simon Brennan , Head of Property & Regeneration, The Quays, Brunel Way, Baglan Energy Park, Neath SA11 2GG ☎ 01639 686370 🖱 s.brennan@npt.gov.uk

European Liaison: Mr Gareth Nutt, Corporate Director of Environment, The Quays, Brunel Way, Baglan Energy Park, Neath SA11 2GG ☎ 01639 686668 🖱 g.nutt@npt.gov.uk

Facilities: Mr Simon Brennan , Head of Property & Regeneration, The Quays, Brunel Way, Baglan Energy Park, Neath SA11 2GG ☎ 01639 686370 🖱 s.brennan@npt.gov.uk

Finance: Mr Hywel Jenkins, Corporate Director of Finance & Corporate Services, Civic Centre, Port Talbot SA13 1PJ ☎ 01639 763252 🖱 h.jenkins@npt.gov.uk

Fleet Management: Mr Mike Roberts, Head of Streetcare, The Quays, Brunel Way, Baglan Energy Park, Neath SA11 2GG ☎ 01639 686966 🖱 m.roberts@npt.gov.uk

Grounds Maintenance: Mr Mike Roberts, Head of Streetcare, The Quays, Brunel Way, Baglan Energy Park, Neath SA11 2GG ☎ 01639 686966 🖱 m.roberts@npt.gov.uk

Health and Safety: Mrs Sheenagh Rees , Head of Human Resources, Civic Centre, Port Talbot SA13 1PJ ☎ 01639 763315 🖱 s.rees5@npt.gov.uk

Highways: Mr David Griffiths , Head of Engineering & Transport, The Quays, Brunel Way, Baglan Energy Park, Neath SA11 2GG ☎ 01639 686340 ✉ d.w.griffiths@npt.gov.uk

Legal: Mr David Michael , Head of Legal & Democratic Services & Monitoring Officer, Civic Centre, Port Talbot SA13 1PJ ☎ 01639 763368 ✉ d.michael@npt.gov.uk

Leisure and Cultural Services: Mr Andrew Thomas, Head of Support Services & Commissioning Development, Civic Centre, Port Talbot SA13 1PJ ☎ 01639 763791 ✉ a.d.thomas@npt.gov.uk

Licensing: Mr David Michael , Head of Legal & Democratic Services & Monitoring Officer, Civic Centre, Port Talbot SA13 1PJ ☎ 01639 763368 ✉ d.michael@npt.gov.uk

Lifelong Learning: Mr Chris Millis , Head of Planning & Performance, Civic Centre, Port Talbot SA13 1PJ ☎ 01639 763226 ✉ c.d.millis@npt.gov.uk

Lighting: Mr Mike Roberts, Head of Streetcare, The Quays, Brunel Way, Baglan Energy Park, Neath SA11 2GG ☎ 01639 686966 ✉ m.roberts@npt.gov.uk

Member Services: Mrs Karen Jones , Head of Change Management and Innovation, Civic Centre, Port Talbot SA13 1PJ ☎ 01639 763713 ✉ k.jones3@npt.gov.uk

Member Services: Mr David Michael , Head of Legal & Democratic Services & Monitoring Officer, Civic Centre, Port Talbot SA13 1PJ ☎ 01639 763368 ✉ d.michael@npt.gov.uk

Parking: Mr David Griffiths , Head of Engineering & Transport, The Quays, Brunel Way, Baglan Energy Park, Neath SA11 2GG ☎ 01639 686340 ✉ d.w.griffiths@npt.gov.uk

Partnerships: Mr Aled Evans, Corporate Director of Education, Leisure & Lifelong Learning, Civic Centre, Port Talbot SA13 1PJ ☎ 01639 763298 ✉ a.evans@npt.gov.uk

Personnel / HR: Mrs Sheenagh Rees , Head of Human Resources, Civic Centre, Port Talbot SA13 1PJ ☎ 01639 763315 ✉ s.rees5@npt.gov.uk

Planning: Mrs Nicola Pearce, Head of Planning, The Quays, Brunel Way, Baglan Energy Park, Neath SA11 2GG ☎ 01639 686681 ✉ n.pearce@npt.gov.uk

Procurement: Mr David Rees, Head of Financial Services, Aberavon House, Port Talbot SA13 1PJ ☎ 01639 763646 ✉ d.rees1@npt.gov.uk

Public Libraries: Mr Andrew Thomas, Head of Support Services & Commissioning Development, Civic Centre, Port Talbot SA13 1PJ ☎ 01639 763791 ✉ a.d.thomas@npt.gov.uk

Recycling & Waste Minimisation: Mr Mike Roberts, Head of Streetcare, The Quays, Brunel Way, Baglan Energy Park, Neath SA11 2GG ☎ 01639 686966 ✉ m.roberts@npt.gov.uk

Regeneration: Mr Simon Brennan , Head of Property & Regeneration, The Quays, Brunel Way, Baglan Energy Park, Neath SA11 2GG ☎ 01639 686370 ✉ s.brennan@npt.gov.uk

Road Safety: Mr David Griffiths , Head of Engineering & Transport, The Quays, Brunel Way, Baglan Energy Park, Neath SA11 2GG ☎ 01639 686340 ✉ d.w.griffiths@npt.gov.uk

Social Services: Mr Nick Jarman, Corporate Director of Social Services, Health & Housing, Port Talbot Civic Centre, Port Talbot SA13 1PJ ☎ 01639 763333; 01639 763279 ✉ n.jarman@npt.gov.uk

Social Services (Adult): Ms Claire Marchant , Head of Community Care & Housing Services, Civic Centre, Port Talbot SA13 1PJ ☎ 01639 763287 ✉ c.marchant@npt.gov.uk

Social Services (Children): Mrs Andrew Jarrett , Head of Children & Young People Services, Civic Centre, Port Talbot SA13 1PJ ☎ 01639 763283 ✉ a.jarrett@npt.gov.uk

Staff Training: Mrs Sheenagh Rees , Head of Human Resources, Civic Centre, Port Talbot SA13 1PJ ☎ 01639 763315 ✉ s.rees5@npt.gov.uk

Street Scene: Mr Mike Roberts, Head of Streetcare, The Quays, Brunel Way, Baglan Energy Park, Neath SA11 2GG ☎ 01639 686966 ✉ m.roberts@npt.gov.uk

Sustainable Communities: Ms Claire Marchant , Head of Community Care & Housing Services, Civic Centre, Port Talbot SA13 1PJ ☎ 01639 763287 ✉ c.marchant@npt.gov.uk

Sustainable Communities: Mrs Nicola Pearce, Head of Planning, The Quays, Brunel Way, Baglan Energy Park, Neath SA11 2GG ☎ 01639 686681 ✉ n.pearce@npt.gov.uk

Sustainable Development: Mrs Nicola Pearce, Head of Planning, The Quays, Brunel Way, Baglan Energy Park, Neath SA11 2GG ☎ 01639 686681 ✉ n.pearce@npt.gov.uk

Town Centre: Ms Gemma Nesbitt , Neath Town Centre Manager, The Quays, Brunel Way, Baglan Energy Park, Neath SA11 1PJ ☎ 01639 686413

Traffic Management: Mr David Griffiths , Head of Engineering & Transport, The Quays, Brunel Way, Baglan Energy Park, Neath SA11 2GG ☎ 01639 686340 ✉ d.w.griffiths@npt.gov.uk

Transport: Mr David Griffiths , Head of Engineering & Transport, The Quays, Brunel Way, Baglan Energy Park, Neath SA11 2GG ☎ 01639 686340 ✉ d.w.griffiths@npt.gov.uk

Waste Collection and Disposal: Mr Mike Roberts, Head of Streetcare, The Quays, Brunel Way, Baglan Energy Park, Neath SA11 2GG ☎ 01639 686966 ✉ m.roberts@npt.gov.uk

Waste Management: Mr Mike Roberts, Head of Streetcare, The Quays, Brunel Way, Baglan Energy Park, Neath SA11 2GG ☎ 01639 686966 ✉ m.roberts@npt.gov.uk

NEATH PORT TALBOT

COUNCILLORS

***Mayor* Davies**, Arthur (LAB - Coedffranc Central)
cllr.a.p.h.davies@npt.gov.uk

***Deputy Mayor* Penry**, Sheila (LAB - Neath East)
cllr.s.m.penry@npt.gov.uk

***Leader of the Council* Thomas**, Alun (LAB - Onllwyn)
leader@npt.gov.uk

***Deputy Leader of the Council* Rees**, Peter (LAB - Neath South)
cllr.p.rees@npt.gov.uk

Bebell, Harry (LAB - Coedffranc West)
cllr.h.m.bebell@npt.gov.uk

Bebell, Paula (LAB - Coedffranc Central)
cllr.p.bebell@npt.gov.uk

Bryant, John (PC - Bryncoch North)
cllr.j.r.bryant@npt.gov.uk

Carter, Alan (LAB - Cimla)
cllr.a.carter@npt.gov.uk

Chaves, Audrey (LAB - Sandfields West)
cllr.a.chaves@npt.gov.uk

Clement-Williams, Carol (LAB - Baglan)
cllr.c.clement@npt.gov.uk

Crowley, Matthew (LAB - Sandfields East)
cllr.c.m.crowley@npt.gov.uk

Davies, Rosalyn (PC - Godre'rgraig)
cllr.r.davies@npt.gov.uk

Davies, Des (LAB - Resolven)
cllr.d.w.davies@npt.gov.uk

Dudley, Janice (PC - Bryncoch South)
cllr.j.dudley@npt.gov.uk

Ellis, Martin (IND - Pelenna)
cllr.m.ellis@npt.gov.uk

Evans, James (LAB - Sandfields West)
cllr.j.s.evans@npt.gov.uk

Golding, Ceri (LAB - Aberavon)
cllr.c.p.golding@npt.gov.uk

Greenaway, Paul (LAB - Baglan)
cllr.p.greenaway@npt.gov.uk

Harvey, Mike (LAB - Coedffranc North)
cllr.m.harvey@npt.gov.uk

Hunt, Steve (IND - Seven Sisters)
cllr.s.k.hunt@npt.gov.uk

James, Ian (LAB - Port Talbot)
cllr.i.b.james@npt.gov.uk

James, Rob (LAB - Bryncoch South)
cllr.r.james@npt.gov.uk

James, Mike (LAB - Pontardawe)
cllr.m.l.james@npt.gov.uk

James, Lella (IND - Sandfields East)
cllr.l.h.james@npt.gov.uk

James, Hugh (LAB - Briton Ferry West)
cllr.h.n.james@npt.gov.uk

Jenkins, Andrew (LAB - Neath South)
cllr.a.jenkins@npt.gov.uk

Jones, Doreen (LAB - Aberdulais)
cllr.d.jones@npt.gov.uk

Jones, Eddie (LAB - Glynneath)
cllr.e.e.jones@npt.gov.uk

Jones, Mark (LAB - Aberavon)
cllr.m.jones@npt.gov.uk

Jones, Rob (LAB - Margam)
cllr.r.g.jones@npt.gov.uk

Jones, Scott (LAB - Cymmer)
cllr.s.jones@npt.gov.uk

Keogh, Dennis (LAB - Port Talbot)
cllr.d.keogh@npt.gov.uk

Latham, Edward (LAB - Sandfields East)
cllr.e.v.latham@npt.gov.uk

Lewis, Marian (LAB - Bryn and Cwmavon)
cllr.m.a.lewis@npt.gov.uk

Lewis, David (INDNA - Allt-Wen)
cllr.d.lewis@npt.gov.uk

Llewellyn, Alun (PC - Ystalyfera)
cllr.a.llewellyn@npt.gov.uk

Lloyd, Kristine (LAB - Cwmllynfell)
cllr.k.lloyd@npt.gov.uk

Lockyer, Alan Richard (LAB - Neath North)
cllr.a.r.lockyer@npt.gov.uk

Miller, John (LAB - Neath East)
cllr.j.miller@npt.gov.uk

Miller, Sandra (LAB - Neath East)
cllr.s.miller@npt.gov.uk

Morgan, Del (PC - Glynneath)
cllr.j.d.morgan@npt.gov.uk

Morgan, Colin (INDNA - Briton Ferry East)
cllr.c.morgan@npt.gov.uk

Morgans, Cari (LAB - Tonna)
cllr.c.morgans@npt.gov.uk

Paddison, Suzanne (LAB - Sandfields West)
cllr.s.paddison@npt.gov.uk

Pearson, Karen (LAB - Crynant)
cllr.k.pearson@npt.gov.uk

Peters, Martin (PC - Dyffryn)
cllr.d.m.peters@npt.gov.uk

Phillips, Rebecca (PC - Trebanos)
cllr.r.phillips@npt.gov.uk

Protheroe, Mark (LAB - Neath North)
cllr.m.protheroe@npt.gov.uk

Purcell, Linet (PC - Pontardawe)
cllr.l.purcell@npt.gov.uk

Rahaman, Saifur (LAB - Port Talbot)
cllr.s.rahaman@npt.gov.uk

Rawlings, Glyn (LAB - Glyncorrwg)
cllr.h.g.rawlings@npt.gov.uk

Richards, Peter (LAB - Baglan)
cllr.p.d.richards@npt.gov.uk

Rogers, John (LAB - Tai-Bach)
cllr.j.rogers@npt.gov.uk

Siddley, Alf (LAB - Blaengwrach)
cllr.a.j.siddley@npt.gov.uk

Taylor, Anthony J (LAB - Tai-Bach)
cllr.a.j.taylor@npt.gov.uk

Taylor, Anthony (IND - Aberavon)
cllr.a.taylor@npt.gov.uk

Thomas, Alex (LAB - Rhos)
cllr.a.l.thomas@npt.gov.uk

Thomas, Ralph (LAB - Gwynfi)
cllr.r.thomas@npt.gov.uk

Warman, John (LD - Cimla)
cllr.j.warman@npt.gov.uk

Whitelock, Dave (LAB - Bryn and Cwmavon)
cllr.d.whitelock@npt.gov.uk

Williams, David (LAB - Bryn and Cwmavon)
cllr.i.d.williams@npt.gov.uk

Williams, Lynda (LAB - Gwaun-Cae-Gurwen)
cllr.l.g.williams@npt.gov.uk

Wingrave, Annette (LAB - Cadoxton)
cllr.a.wingrave@npt.gov.uk

Woolcock, Arwyn (LAB - Lower Brynamman)
cllr.a.n.woolcock@npt.gov.uk

POLITICAL COMPOSITION
LAB: 49, PC: 8, IND: 4, INDNA: 2, LD: 1

COMMITTEE CHAIRS
Audit: Mrs Lella James

Planning: Mr Rob Jones

Registration & Licensing: Mr Glyn Rawlings

New Forest D

New Forest District Council, Appletree Court, Beaulieu Road, Lyndhurst SO43 7PA
☎ 023 8028 5000 🖷 023 8028 5555 🖳 www.newforest.gov.uk

FACTS AND FIGURES
Parliamentary Constituencies: New Forest East, New Forest West
EU Constituencies: South East
Election Frequency: Elections are of whole council

PRINCIPAL OFFICERS
Chief Executive: Mr Dave Yates, Chief Executive, Appletree Court, Beaulieu Road, Lyndhurst SO43 7PA ☎ 023 8028 5588 🖷 023 8028 5555 ✉ dave.yates@nfdc.gov.uk

Senior Management: Mr Robert Jackson , Executive Director, Appletree Court, Beaulieu Road, Lyndhurst SO43 7PA ☎ 023 8028 5588 🖷 023 8028 5555 ✉ bob.jackson@nfdc.gov.uk

Senior Management: Mr John Mascall, Executive Director, Appletree Court, Beaulieu Road, Lyndhurst SO43 7PA ☎ 023 8028 5588 🖷 023 8028 5555 ✉ john.mascall@nfdc.gov.uk

Access Officer / Social Services (Disability): Mrs Catherine Granville , HR Operations Manager, Appletree Court, Beaulieu Road, Lyndhurst SO43 7PA ☎ 023 8028 5588 🖷 023 8028 5555 ✉ catherine.granville@nfdc.gov.uk

Architect, Building / Property Services: Mr Geoff Bettle , Head of Property Services, Marsh Lane Depot, Marsh Lane, Lymington SO41 9BX ☎ 023 8028 5588 🖷 023 8028 5076 ✉ geoff.bettle@nfdc.gov.uk

Best Value: Mr Robert Jackson , Executive Director, Appletree Court, Beaulieu Road, Lyndhurst SO43 7PA ☎ 023 8028 5588 🖷 023 8028 5555 ✉ bob.jackson@nfdc.gov.uk

Building Control: Mr John Brian , Building Control Manager, Appletree Court, Beaulieu Road, Lyndhurst SO43 7PA ☎ 023 8028 5588 🖷 023 8028 5370 ✉ john.brian@nfdc.gov.uk

PR / Communications: Mrs Sara Hamilton , Corporate Communications Manager, Appletree Court, Beaulieu Road, Lyndhurst SO43 7PA ☎ 023 8028 5588 ✉ sara.hamilton@nfdc.gov.uk

Community Safety: Mrs Annie Righton, Head of Public Health & Community Safety, Appletree Court, Beaulieu Road, Lyndhurst SO43 7PA ☎ 023 8028 5588 🖷 023 8028 5370 ✉ annie.righton@nfdc.gov.uk

Computer Management: Mr Ken Connolly, Head of ICT Services, Appletree Court, Beaulieu Road, Lyndhurst SO43 7PA ☎ 023 8028 5588 🖷 023 8028 5555 ✉ ken.connolly@nfdc.gov.uk

Contracts: Mr David Ruskell , Procurement & Contract Monitoring Officer, Marsh Lane Depot, Marsh Lane, Lymington SO41 9BX ☎ 023 8028 5588 🖷 023 8028 5076 ✉ david.ruskell@nfdc.gov.uk

Customer Service: Mr Glynne Miles, Head of Housing & Customer Services, Appletree Court, Beaulieu Road, Lyndhurst SO43 7PA ☎ 023 8028 5588 🖷 023 8028 5386 ✉ glynne.miles@nfdc.gov.uk

Direct Labour: Mr Colin Read , Head of Environment Services, Marsh Lane Depot, Marsh Lane, Lymington SO41 9BX ☎ 023 8028 5588 🖷 023 8028 5052 ✉ colin.read@nfdc.gov.uk

Economic Development: Mr Martin Devine, Head of Leisure & Employment, Appletree Court, Beaulieu Road, Lyndhurst SO43 7PA ☎ 023 8028 5588 🖷 023 8028 5555 ✉ martin.devine@nfdc.gov.uk

E-Government: Mr Ken Connolly, Head of ICT Services, Appletree Court, Beaulieu Road, Lyndhurst SO43 7PA ☎ 023 8028 5588 🖷 023 8028 5555 ✉ ken.connolly@nfdc.gov.uk

Electoral Registration: Mrs Rosemary Rutins, Democratic Services Manager, Appletree Court, Beaulieu Road, Lyndhurst SO43 7PA ☎ 023 8028 5588 🖷 023 8028 5555 ✉ rosemary.rutins@nfdc.gov.uk

Emergency Planning: Mrs Annie Righton, Head of Public Health & Community Safety, Appletree Court, Beaulieu Road, Lyndhurst SO43 7PA ☎ 023 8028 5588 🖷 023 8028 5370 ✉ annie.righton@nfdc.gov.uk

Energy Management: Mr Geoff Bettle , Head of Property Services, Marsh Lane Depot, Marsh Lane, Lymington SO41 9BX ☎ 023 8028 5588 🖷 023 8028 5076 ✉ geoff.bettle@nfdc.gov.uk

Environmental / Technical Services: Mr Colin Read , Head of Environment Services, Marsh Lane Depot, Marsh Lane, Lymington SO41 9BX ☎ 023 8028 5588 🖷 023 8028 5052 🖰 colin.read@nfdc.gov.uk

Environmental Health: Mrs Annie Righton, Head of Public Health & Community Safety, Appletree Court, Beaulieu Road, Lyndhurst SO43 7PA ☎ 023 8028 5588 🖷 023 8028 5370 🖰 annie.righton@nfdc.gov.uk

Estates, Property & Valuation: Mr Andy Groom, Valuer, Appletree Court, Beaulieu Road, Lyndhurst SO43 7PA ☎ 023 8028 5588 🖷 023 8028 5370 🖰 andy.groom@nfdc.gov.uk

Facilities: Mr Geoff Bettle , Head of Property Services, Marsh Lane Depot, Marsh Lane, Lymington SO41 9BX ☎ 023 8028 5588 🖷 023 8028 5076 🖰 geoff.bettle@nfdc.gov.uk

Finance: Mr Robert Jackson , Executive Director, Appletree Court, Beaulieu Road, Lyndhurst SO43 7PA ☎ 023 8028 5588 🖷 023 8028 5555 🖰 bob.jackson@nfdc.gov.uk

Fleet Management: Mr Colin Read , Head of Environment Services, Marsh Lane Depot, Marsh Lane, Lymington SO41 9BX ☎ 023 8028 5588 🖷 023 8028 5052 🖰 colin.read@nfdc.gov.uk

Grounds Maintenance: Mr Colin Read , Head of Environment Services, Marsh Lane Depot, Marsh Lane, Lymington SO41 9BX ☎ 023 8028 5588 🖷 023 8028 5052 🖰 colin.read@nfdc.gov.uk

Health and Safety: Mrs Rebecca Drummond , Performance Improvement Manager, Appletree Court, Beaulieu Road, Lyndhurst SO43 7PA ☎ 023 8028 5588 🖷 023 8028 5555 🖰 rebecca.drummond@nfdc.gov.uk

Highways: Mr Chris Elliott , Head of Planning & Transportation, Appletree Court, Beaulieu Road, Lyndhurst SO43 7PA ☎ 023 8028 5588 🖷 023 8028 5370 🖰 chris.elliott@nfdc.gov.uk

Home Energy Conservation: Ms Emma Waterman , Energy & Environment Officer, Appletree Court, Beaulieu Road, Lyndhurst SO43 7PA ☎ 023 8028 5588 🖷 023 8028 5370 🖰 emma.waterman@nfdc.gov.uk

Housing: Mr Glynne Miles, Head of Housing & Customer Services, Appletree Court, Beaulieu Road, Lyndhurst SO43 7PA ☎ 023 8028 5588 🖷 023 8028 5386 🖰 glynne.miles@nfdc.gov.uk

Housing Maintenance: Mr Glynne Miles, Head of Housing & Customer Services, Appletree Court, Beaulieu Road, Lyndhurst SO43 7PA ☎ 023 8028 5588 🖷 023 8028 5386 🖰 glynne.miles@nfdc.gov.uk

Legal: Ms Grainne O'Rourke, Head of Legal & Democratic Services, Appletree Court, Beaulieu Road, Lyndhurst SO43 7PA ☎ 023 8028 5588 🖷 023 8028 5555 🖰 grainne.o'rourke@nfdc.gov.uk

Leisure and Cultural Services: Mr Martin Devine, Head of Leisure & Employment, Appletree Court, Beaulieu Road, Lyndhurst SO43 7PA ☎ 023 8028 5588 🖷 023 8028 5555 🖰 martin.devine@nfdc.gov.uk

Licensing: Mr Paul Weston , Licensing Manager, Appletree Court, Beaulieu Road, Lyndhurst SO43 7PA ☎ 023 8028 5588 🖷 023 8028 5370 🖰 paul.weston@nfdc.gov.uk

Lighting: Mr Allan Ellis, Assistant Engineer, Appletree Court, Beaulieu Road, Lyndhurst SO43 7PA ☎ 023 8028 5588 🖷 023 8028 5370 🖰 allan.ellis@nfdc.gov.uk

Lottery Funding, Charity and Voluntary: Mr Martin Devine, Head of Leisure & Employment, Appletree Court, Beaulieu Road, Lyndhurst SO43 7PA ☎ 023 8028 5588 🖷 023 8028 5555 🖰 martin.devine@nfdc.gov.uk

Member Services: Ms Grainne O'Rourke, Head of Legal & Democratic Services, Appletree Court, Beaulieu Road, Lyndhurst SO43 7PA ☎ 023 8028 5588 🖷 023 8028 5555 🖰 grainne.o'rourke@nfdc.gov.uk

Parking: Mr John Bull, Parking Manager, Town Hall, Avenue Road, Lymington SO41 9ZG ☎ 023 8028 5588 🖷 023 8028 5755 🖰 john.bull@nfdc.gov.uk

Personnel / HR: Mrs Manjit Sandhu, Head of Human Resources, Appletree Court, Beaulieu Road, Lyndhurst SO43 7PA ☎ 023 8028 5482 🖷 023 8028 5405 🖰 manjit.sandhu@nfdc.gov.uk

Planning: Mr Chris Elliott , Head of Planning & Transportation, Appletree Court, Beaulieu Road, Lyndhurst SO43 7PA ☎ 023 8028 5588 🖷 023 8028 5370 🖰 chris.elliott@nfdc.gov.uk

Procurement: Mr Ian Smoker , Procurement Manager, Marsh Lane Depot, Marsh Lane, Lymington SO41 9BX ☎ 023 8028 5588 🖷 023 8028 5076 🖰 ian.smoker@nfdc.gov.uk

Recycling & Waste Minimisation: Mr Colin Read , Head of Environment Services, Marsh Lane Depot, Marsh Lane, Lymington SO41 9BX ☎ 023 8028 5588 🖷 023 8028 5052 🖰 colin.read@nfdc.gov.uk

Road Safety: Mr Chris Elliott , Head of Planning & Transportation, Appletree Court, Beaulieu Road, Lyndhurst SO43 7PA ☎ 023 8028 5588 🖷 023 8028 5370 🖰 chris.elliott@nfdc.gov.uk

Staff Training: Mrs Zoe Ormerod , Human Resources Advisor, Appletree Court, Beaulieu Road, Lyndhurst SO43 7PA ☎ 023 8028 5588 🖷 023 8028 5555 🖰 zoe.ormerod@nfdc.gov.uk

Street Scene: Mr Colin Read , Head of Environment Services, Marsh Lane Depot, Marsh Lane, Lymington SO41 9BX ☎ 023 8028 5588 🖷 023 8028 5052 🖰 colin.read@nfdc.gov.uk

Tourism: Mr Anthony Climpson, Employment & Tourism Manager, Appletree Court, Beaulieu Road, Lyndhurst SO43 7PA ☎ 023 8028 5588 🖷 023 8028 5555 🖰 anthony.climpson@nfdc.gov.uk

Traffic Management: Mr Chris Elliott , Head of Planning & Transportation, Appletree Court, Beaulieu Road, Lyndhurst SO43 7PA ☎ 023 8028 5588 🖷 023 8028 5370 🖰 chris.elliott@nfdc.gov.uk

Transport Planner: Mr Chris Elliott , Head of Planning & Transportation, Appletree Court, Beaulieu Road, Lyndhurst SO43 7PA ☎ 023 8028 5588 🖷 023 8028 5370 ✉ chris.elliott@nfdc.gov.uk

Waste Collection and Disposal: Mr Colin Read , Head of Environment Services, Marsh Lane Depot, Marsh Lane, Lymington SO41 9BX ☎ 023 8028 5588 🖷 023 8028 5052 ✉ colin.read@nfdc.gov.uk

Waste Management: Mr Colin Read , Head of Environment Services, Marsh Lane Depot, Marsh Lane, Lymington SO41 9BX ☎ 023 8028 5588 🖷 023 8028 5052 ✉ colin.read@nfdc.gov.uk

COUNCILLORS

***Chair* Hoare**, Alison (CON - Marchwood)
alison.hoare@newforest.gov.uk

***Vice-Chair* Beck**, Goff (CON - Barton)
goff.beck@newforest.gov.uk

***Leader of the Council* Rickman**, Barry (CON - Boldre and Sway)
barry.rickman@newforest.gov.uk

***Deputy Leader of the Council* Heron**, Edward (CON - Downlands and Forest)
edward.heron@newforest.gov.uk

Alvey, Alan (CON - Holbury and North Blackfield)
alan.alvey@newforest.gov.uk

Andrews, Diane (CON - Bramshaw, Copythorne North and Minstead)
diane.andrews@newforest.gov.uk

Andrews, Bill (CON - Dibden and Hythe East)
bill.andrews@newforest.gov.uk

Armstrong, Peter (CON - Butts Ash and Dibden Purlieu)
peter.armstrong@newforest.gov.uk

Beeton, Sophie (CON - Milford)
sophie.beeton@newforest.gov.uk

Bellows, Roxy (CON - Fordingbridge)
roxanne.bellows@newforest.gov.uk

Bennison, Sue (CON - Marchwood)
sue.bennison@newforest.gov.uk

Binns, James (CON - Butts Ash and Dibden Purlieu)
james.binns@newforest.gov.uk

Blunden, Geoffrey (CON - Becton)
geoffrey.blunden@newforest.gov.uk

Britton, Dean (CON - Totton North)
dean.britton@newforest.gov.uk

Brooks, Di (CON - Totton West)
di.brooks@newforest.gov.uk

Carpenter, Fran (CON - Hordle)
fran.carpenter@newforest.gov.uk

Cerasoli, Louise (CON - Totton Central)
louise.cerasoli@newforest.gov.uk

Clarke, Steve (CON - Milton)
steve.clarke@newforest.gov.uk

Cleary, Jill (CON - Fernhill)
jill.cleary@newforest.gov.uk

Coombes, Ian (CON - Totton East)
ian.coombes@newforest.gov.uk

Crisell, Kate (CON - Furzedown and Hardley)
kate.crisell@newforest.gov.uk

Davies, Steve (CON - Milton)
stevep.davies@newforest.gov.uk

Davis, Arthur (CON - Totton East)
arthur.davis@newforest.gov.uk

Dow, Bill (CON - Forest North West)
bill.dow@newforest.gov.uk

Ford, Christine (CON - Ringwood North)
christine.ford@newforest.gov.uk

Frampton, Richard (CON - Bransgore and Burley)
richard.frampton@newforest.gov.uk

Glass, Allan (CON - Holbury and North Blackfield)
allan.glass@newforest.gov.uk

Harris, Michael (CON - Brockenhurst and Forest South East)
michael.harris@newforest.gov.uk

Harris, Len (CON - Totton South)
len.harris@newforest.gov.uk

Harrison, David (LD - Totton South)
david.harrison@newforest.gov.uk

Heron, Jeremy (CON - Ringwood South)
jeremy.heron@newforest.gov.uk

Holding, Maureen (CON - Brockenhurst and Forest South East)
maureen.holding@newforest.gov.uk

Jackman, Penny (CON - Pennington)
penny.jackman@newforest.gov.uk

Kendal, Melville (CON - Milford)
melville.kendal@newforest.gov.uk

Lane, Emma (CON - Ringwood East and Sopley)
emma.lane@newforest.gov.uk

Lovelace, Penny (CON - Hordle)
penny.lovelace@newforest.gov.uk

Lucas, Brian (CON - Totton Central)
brian.lucas@newforest.gov.uk

McEvoy, Alexis (CON - Fawley, Blackfield and Langley)
alexis.mcevoy@newforest.gov.uk

Olliff-Cooper, John (CON - Buckland)
john.olliff-cooper@newforest.gov.uk

O'Sullivan, Alan (CON - Barton)
alan.osullivan@newforest.gov.uk

Penman, Neville (CON - Totton North)
neville.penman@newforest.gov.uk

Penson, Alan (CON - Lymington Town)
alan.penson@newforest.gov.uk

Poole, Dan (CON - Dibden and Hythe East)
dan.poole@newforest.gov.uk

Puttock, Leslie (CON - Ashurst, Copythorne South and Netley Marsh)
leslie.puttock@newforest.gov.uk

Rippon-Swaine, Steve (CON - Ringwood South)
steve.rippon-swain@newforest.gov.uk

Rostand, Anna (CON - Lymington Town)
anna.rostand@newforest.gov.uk

Russell, David (CON - Totton West)
david.russell@newforest.gov.uk

Sevier, Ann (CON - Fordingbridge)
ann.sevier@newforest.gov.uk

Steele, Mark (CON - Bransgore and Burley)
mark.steele@newforest.gov.uk

Thierry, Michael (CON - Ringwood North)
michael.thierry@newforest.gov.uk

Thorne, Beverley (CON - Hythe West and Langdown)
beverley.thorne@newforest.gov.uk

Tipp, Derek (CON - Ashurst, Copythorne South and Netley Marsh)
derek.tipp@newforest.gov.uk

Tungate, Neil (CON - Bashley)
neil.tungate@newforest.gov.uk

Wade, Alex (LD - Hythe West and Langdown)
alex.wade@newforest.gov.uk

Wappet, Bob (CON - Fawley, Blackfield and Langley)
bob.wappet@newforest.gov.uk

Ward, Christine (CON - Becton)
christine.ward@newforest.gov.uk

Ward, John (CON - Fernhill)
johngward@newforest.gov.uk

White, Michael (CON - Pennington)
michael.white@newforest.gov.uk

Wise, Colin (CON - **re and Sway)**
colin.wise@newforest.gov.uk

Wyeth, Pat (CON - Lyndhurst)
pat.wyeth@newforest.gov.uk

POLITICAL COMPOSITION

CON: 58, LD: 2

COMMITTEE CHAIRS

Audit: Mr Alan O'Sullivan

General Purposes & Licensing: Mr Steve Clarke

Planning Development Control: Mrs Diane Andrews

Newark & Sherwood D

Newark & Sherwood District Council, Kelham Hall, Newark NG23 5QX
☎ 01636 650000 🖷 01636 655229 ✉ corporate@nsdc.info
💻 www.newark-sherwooddc.gov.uk

FACTS AND FIGURES

Parliamentary Constituencies: Newark, Sherwood
EU Constituencies: East Midlands
Election Frequency: Elections are of whole council

PRINCIPAL OFFICERS

Chief Executive: Mr Andrew Muter, Chief Executive, Kelham Hall, Newark NG23 5QX ☎ 01636 650000 ✉ andrew.muter@nsdc.info

Deputy Chief Executive: Mrs Kirsty Cole, Deputy Chief Executive, Kelham Hall, Newark NG23 5QX ☎ 01636 650000 ✉ kirsty.cole@nsdc.info

Senior Management: Mr David Dickinson, Director - Resources, Kelham Hall, Newark NG23 5QX ☎ 01636 650000 ✉ david.dickinson@nsdc.info

Senior Management: Mr Matthew Finch , Director - Customers, Kelham Hall, Newark NG23 5QX

Senior Management: Mr Andy Statham, Director - Community, Kelham Hall, Newark NG23 5QX ☎ 01636 650000 ✉ andy.statham@nsdc.info

Senior Management: Mrs Karen White, Director - Safety, Kelham Hall, Newark NG23 5QX ☎ 01636 650000 ✉ karen.white@nsdc.info

Architect, Building / Property Services: Mr David Best , Deputy Business Manager - Asset Management, Kelham Hall, Newark NG23 5QX ✉ david.best@nsdc.info

Building Control: Mr David Jones , Building Control Manager, Kelham Hall, Newark NG23 5QX ☎ 01636 650000 ✉ dave.jones@nsdc.info

PR / Communications: Ms Jill Simpson , Business Manager - Customer Services, Kelham Hall, Newark NG23 5QX ☎ 01636 650000 ✉ jill.simpson@nsdc.info

Community Safety: Ms Lisa Lancaster , Business Manager - Community Safety, Kelham Hall, Newark NG23 5QX ☎ 01636 650000 ✉ lisa.lancaster@nsdc.info

Computer Management: Mrs Sharon Parkinson , Business Manager - ICT, Kelham Hall, Newark NG23 5QX ☎ 01636 650000 ✉ sharon.parkinson@nsdc.info

Corporate Services: Mrs Kirsty Cole, Deputy Chief Executive, Kelham Hall, Newark NG23 5QX ☎ 01636 650000 ✉ kirsty.cole@nsdc.info

Customer Service: Ms Jill Simpson , Business Manager - Customer Services, Kelham Hall, Newark NG23 5QX ☎ 01636 650000 ✉ jill.simpson@nsdc.info

Economic Development: Mrs Julie Reader-Sullivan , Business Manager - Economic Development, Kelham Hall, Newark NG23 5QX ✉ julie.reader-sullivan@nsdc.info

Electoral Registration: Mr Mark Jurejko, Elections Manager, Kelham Hall, Newark NG23 5QX ☎ 01636 650000 ✉ mark.jurejko@nsdc.info

Emergency Planning: Ms Lisa Lancaster , Business Manager - Community Safety, Kelham Hall, Newark NG23 5QX ☎ 01636 650000 ✉ lisa.lancaster@nsdc.info

Environmental / Technical Services: Mr Andy Statham, Director - Community, Kelham Hall, Newark NG23 5QX ☎ 01636 650000 ✉ andy.statham@nsdc.info

Environmental Health: Mr Alan Batty , Business Manager - Environmental Health, Kelham Hall, Newark NG23 5QX ☎ 01636 650000 ✉ alan.batty@nsdc.info

Estates, Property & Valuation: Mr David Best , Deputy Business Manager - Asset Management, Kelham Hall, Newark NG23 5QX ✉ david.best@nsdc.info

Finance: Mr David Dickinson, Director - Resources, Kelham Hall, Newark NG23 5QX ☎ 01636 650000 ✉ david.dickinson@nsdc.info

Fleet Management: Mr Andrew Kirk, Business Manager - Waste, Litter & Recycling, Kelham Hall, Newark NG23 5QX ☎ 01636 650000 ✉ andrew.kirk@nsdc.info

Grounds Maintenance: Mr Philip Beard, Business Manager - Parks & Amenities, Kelham Hall, Newark NG23 5QX ☎ 01636 650000 🖷 01636 655705 ✉ philip.beard@nsdc.info

Health and Safety: Ms Lisa Lancaster , Business Manager - Community Safety, Kelham Hall, Newark NG23 5QX ☎ 01636 650000 ✉ lisa.lancaster@nsdc.info

Housing: Mr Rob Main , Strategic Housing Manager, Kelham Hall, Newark NG23 5QX ☎ 01636 650000 ✉ rob.main@nsdc.info

Legal: Mrs Karen White, Director - Safety, Kelham Hall, Newark NG23 5QX ☎ 01636 650000 ✉ karen.white@nsdc.info

Leisure and Cultural Services: Mr Andy Carolan, Principal Manager - Leisure Centres, Kelham Hall, Newark NG23 5QX ☎ 01636 650000 ✉ andy.carolan@nsdc.info

Licensing: Mr Alan Batty , Business Manager - Environmental Health, Kelham Hall, Newark NG23 5QX ☎ 01636 650000 ✉ alan.batty@nsdc.info

Lifelong Learning: Mrs Tracey Mellors , Business Manager - Human Resources, Kelham Hall, Newark NG23 5QX ☎ 01636 650000 ✉ tracey.mellors@nsdc.info

Lottery Funding, Charity and Voluntary: Mr Andy Hardy , Business Manager - Community, Arts & Sports, Kelham Hall, Newark NG23 5QX ☎ 01636 650000 ✉ andy.hardy@nsdc.info

Member Services: Mr Nigel Hill, Business Manager - Democratic Services, Kelham Hall, Newark NG23 5QX ☎ 01636 650000 ✉ nigel.hill@nsdc.info

Parking: Mr Ian Harrison , Business Manager - Markets & Car Parks, Kelham Hall, Newark NG23 5QX ✉ ian.harrison@nsdc.info

Personnel / HR: Mrs Tracey Mellors , Business Manager - Human Resources, Kelham Hall, Newark NG23 5QX ☎ 01636 650000 ✉ tracey.mellors@nsdc.info

Planning: Mr Matthew Lamb , Business Manager - Development, Kelham Hall, Newark NG23 5QX ☎ 01636 650000 ✉ matt.lamb@nsdc.info

Procurement: Mr John King , Business Manager - Procurement, Kelham Hall, Newark NG23 5QX ☎ 01636 650000 ✉ john.king@nsdc.info

Recycling & Waste Minimisation: Mr Andrew Kirk, Business Manager - Waste, Litter & Recycling, Kelham Hall, Newark NG23 5QX ☎ 01636 650000 ✉ andrew.kirk@nsdc.info

Staff Training: Mrs Tracey Mellors , Business Manager - Human Resources, Kelham Hall, Newark NG23 5QX ☎ 01636 650000 ✉ tracey.mellors@nsdc.info

Transport: Mr Andrew Kirk, Business Manager - Waste, Litter & Recycling, Kelham Hall, Newark NG23 5QX ☎ 01636 650000 ✉ andrew.kirk@nsdc.info

Waste Collection and Disposal: Mr Andrew Kirk, Business Manager - Waste, Litter & Recycling, Kelham Hall, Newark NG23 5QX ☎ 01636 650000 ✉ andrew.kirk@nsdc.info

Waste Management: Mr Andrew Kirk, Business Manager - Waste, Litter & Recycling, Kelham Hall, Newark NG23 5QX ☎ 01636 650000 ✉ andrew.kirk@nsdc.info

COUNCILLORS

***Chair* Walker**, Ivor (CON - Farndon and Fernwood)
ivor.walker@surfree.co.uk

***Vice-Chair* Roberts**, Tony (CON - Beacon)
tony.roberts@newark-sherwooddc.gov.uk

***Leader of the Council* Blaney**, Roger (CON - Trent)
roger.blaney@newark-sherwooddc.gov.uk

***Deputy Leader of the Council* Lloyd**, David (CON - Beacon)
david.lloyd2@newark-sherwooddc.gov.uk

***Group Leader* Dawn**, Gill (IND - Bridge)
gill.dawn@newark-sherwooddc.gov.uk

***Group Leader* Truswell**, Abbie (LAB - Ollerton)
abbie.truswell@newark-sherwooddc.gov.uk

Arnold, Kathleen (LAB - Rainworth South and Blidworth)
kathleen.arnold@newark-sherwooddc.gov.uk

Batey, Derek (LAB - Ollerton)
derek.batey@newark-sherwooddc.gov.uk

Brooks, Celia (LAB - Edwinstowe and Clipstone)
celia.brooks@newark-sherwooddc.gov.uk

Brooks, Gordon (CON - Balderton South)
gordon.brooks@newark-sherwooddc.gov.uk

Brooks, Betty (CON - Balderton South)
betty.brooks@newark-sherwooddc.gov.uk

Brown, Irene (IND - Bridge)
irene.brown@newark-sherwooddc.gov.uk

Buttery, Mark (LAB - Rainworth North and Rufford)
mark.buttery@newark-sherwooddc.gov.uk

Clarke, David (CON - Collingham)
davidj.clarke@newark-sherwooddc.gov.uk

Cope, Max (CON - Devon)
max.cope@newark-sherwooddc.gov.uk

Crowe, Rita (CON - Beacon)
rita.crowe@newark-sherwooddc.gov.uk

Crowe, Bob (CON - Devon)
bob.crowe@newark-sherwooddc.gov.uk

Dobson, Maureen (IND - Collingham)
maureen.dobson@newark-sherwooddc.gov.uk

Duncan, Peter (CON - Devon)
peter.duncan@newark-sherwooddc.gov.uk

Girling, Keith (CON - Castle)
keith.girling@newark-sherwooddc.gov.uk

Handley, Paul (CON - Southwell)
paul.handley@newark-sherwooddc.gov.uk

Jackson, Roger (CON - Dover Beck)
roger.jackson@newark-sherwooddc.gov.uk

Laughton, Bruce (CON - Southwell)
bruce.laughton@newark-sherwooddc.gov.uk

Lee, Johno (CON - Balderton North and Coddington)
johno.lee@newark-sherwooddc.gov.uk

Michael, Sylvia (CON - Sutton-on-Trent)
sylvia.michael@newark-sherwooddc.gov.uk

Mison, Neill (CON - Farndon and Fernwood)
neill.mison@newark-sherwooddc.gov.uk

Payne, David (CON - Balderton North and Coddington)
david.payne@newark-sherwooddc.gov.uk

Peacock, Paul (LAB - Edwinstowe and Clipstone)
paul.peacock@newark-sherwooddc.gov.uk

Rainbow, Penny (CON - Southwell)
penny.rainbow@newark-sherwooddc.gov.uk

Saddington, Susan (CON - Muskham)
susan.saddington@newark-sherwooddc.gov.uk

Soar, Sheila (LAB - Bilsthorpe)
sheila.soar@newark-sherwooddc.gov.uk

Staples, David (LAB - Boughton)
david.staples@newark-sherwooddc.gov.uk

Taylor, Frank (CON - Farnsfield)
frank.taylor@newark-sherwooddc.gov.uk

Thompson, Dave (LAB - Edwinstowe and Clipstone)
david.thompson@newark-sherwooddc.gov.uk

Tift, Linda (LAB - Rainworth North and Rufford)
linda.tift@newark-sherwooddc.gov.uk

Walker, Keith (CON - Farndon and Fernwood)
keith.walker@newark-sherwooddc.gov.uk

Wells, Benjamin (LAB - Ollerton)
benjamin.wells@newark-sherwooddc.gov.uk

Wendels, Tim (CON - Lowdham)tim.wendels@newark-sherwooddc.gov.uk

Woodhead, Yvonne (LAB - Rainworth South and Blidworth)
yvonne.woodhead@newark-sherwooddc.gov.uk

POLITICAL COMPOSITION

CON: 24, LAB: 12, IND: 3

COMMITTEE CHAIRS

Audits & Accounts: Mrs Sylvia Michael

General Purposes: Mrs Rita Crowe

Licensing: Mrs Rita Crowe

Planning: Mr David Payne

Newcastle upon Tyne City M

Newcastle upon Tyne City Council, Civic Centre, Newcastle upon Tyne NE1 8QH
☎ 0191 232 8520 🖷 0191 211 4942 💻 www.newcastle.gov.uk

FACTS AND FIGURES

Parliamentary Constituencies: Newcastle Central, Newcastle East, Newcastle North
EU Constituencies: North East
Election Frequency: Elections are by thirds

PRINCIPAL OFFICERS

Chief Executive: Ms Pat Ritchie , Chief Executive, Civic Centre, Newcastle upon Tyne NE1 8QH ☎ 0191 278 7878
pat.ritchie@newcastle.gov.uk

Assistant Chief Executive: Mr Andrew Lewis , Assistant Chief Executive, Civic Centre, Newcastle upon Tyne NE1 8QH
☎ 0191 211 5681 andrew.lewis@newcastle.gov.uk

Senior Management: Mr Tony Kirkham , Director of Resources, Civic Centre, Newcastle upon Tyne NE1 8QH ☎ 0191 211 5226
tony.kirkham@newcastle.gov.uk

Senior Management: Mr Michael Murphy , Director of Communities, Civic Centre, Newcastle upon Tyne NE1 8QH
☎ 0191 211 5950 michael.murphy@newcastle.gov.uk

Senior Management: Mr Tom Warburton , Director of Investment & Development, Civic Centre, Newcastle upon Tyne NE1 8QH
☎ 0191 211 5660 tom.warburton@newcastle.gov.uk

Senior Management: Mr Ewen Weir , Director of Wellbeing, Care & Learning, Civic Centre, Newcastle upon Tyne NE1 8QH
☎ 0191 211 5478 🖷 0191 211 4955 ewen.weir@newcastle.gov.uk

Access Officer / Social Services (Disability): Mr Neil Swinney, Access Officer, Civic Centre, Newcastle upon Tyne NE1 8QH
☎ 0191 211 6804 neil.swinney@newcastle.gov.uk

Architect, Building / Property Services: Mr Stuart Turnbull , Service Manager - Architecture & Building Design Services, Civic Centre, Newcastle upon Tyne NE1 8QH ☎ 0191 278 3277
stuart.turnbull@newcastle.gov.uk

Building Control: Mr David Ewles , Head of Building Control, Civic Centre, Newcastle upon Tyne NE1 8QH ☎ 0191 211 6180
david.n.ewles@newcastle.gov.uk

Catering Services: Ms Tracey Cuthbert , Service Manager - Civic Facilities, Civic Centre, Newcastle upon Tyne NE1 8QH
☎ 0191 211 6940 tracey.cuthbert@newcastle.gov.uk

Children / Youth Services: Mr Mick McCracken , Assistant Director - Family Insights, Civic Centre, Newcastle upon Tyne NE1 8QH ☎ 0191 211 6307 mick.mccracken@newcastle.gov.uk

Civil Registration: Ms Julie Cable , Customer Contact Specialist, Civic Centre, Newcastle upon Tyne NE1 8QH ☎ 0191 211 5006
julie.cable@newcastle.gov.uk

PR / Communications: Mr Steve Park , Assistant Director - Policy, Communication & Performance, Civic Centre, Newcastle upon Tyne NE1 8QH ☎ 0191 211 5071 🖷 0191 211 4888 ✉ steve.park@newcastle.gov.uk

Community Planning: Mr Neil Quinn , Co-operative Communities Service Manager, Civic Centre, Newcastle upon Tyne NE1 8QH ☎ 0191 277 3615 ✉ neil.quinn@newcastle.gov.uk

Community Safety: Ms Robyn Thomas, Service Manager - Community Safety, Civic Centre, Newcastle upon Tyne NE1 8QH ☎ 0191 277 7835 ✉ robyn.thomas@newcastle.gov.uk

Computer Management: Mr James Lowden , ICT Services Manager, Civic Centre, Newcastle upon Tyne NE1 8QH ☎ 0191 277 7282 ✉ james.lowden@newcastle.gov.uk

Consumer Protection and Trading Standards: Mr Stephen Savage, Assistant Director - Public Safety & Regulation, Civic Centre, Newcastle upon Tyne NE1 8QH ☎ 0191 211 6101 ✉ stephen.savage@newcastle.gov.uk

Contracts: Ms Rachel Baillie , Assistant Director - Commissioning & Procurement, Civic Centre, Newcastle upon Tyne NE1 8QH ☎ 0191 211 6458 ✉ rachel.baillie@newcastle.gov.uk

Corporate Services: Mr Tony Kirkham , Director of Resources, Civic Centre, Newcastle upon Tyne NE1 8QH ☎ 0191 211 5226 ✉ tony.kirkham@newcastle.gov.uk

Customer Service: Ms Diane Scott , Service Manager - Customer Contact, Civic Centre, Newcastle upon Tyne NE1 8QH ☎ 0191 277 7580 ✉ diane.scott@newcastle.gov.uk

Direct Labour: Mr Michael Murphy , Director of Communities, Civic Centre, Newcastle upon Tyne NE1 8QH ☎ 0191 211 5950 ✉ michael.murphy@newcastle.gov.uk

Economic Development: Mr Rob Hamilton , Economic Development Principal Advisor, Civic Centre, Newcastle upon Tyne NE1 8QH ☎ 0191 277 8947 ✉ rob.hamilton@newcastle.gov.uk

Education: Mr Martin Surtees , Assistant Director - Education, Civic Centre, Newcastle upon Tyne NE99 2BN ☎ 0191 211 5300 ✉ martin.surtees@newcastle.gov.uk

Education: Mr Ewen Weir , Director of Wellbeing, Care & Learning, Civic Centre, Newcastle upon Tyne NE1 8QH ☎ 0191 211 5478 🖷 0191 211 4955 ✉ ewen.weir@newcastle.gov.uk

E-Government: Mr James Lowden , ICT Services Manager, Civic Centre, Newcastle upon Tyne NE99 2BN ☎ 0191 277 7282 ✉ james.lowden@newcastle.gov.uk

Electoral Registration: Mr Ian Humphries , Principal Electoral & Members Service Officer, Civic Centre, Newcastle upon Tyne NE1 8QH ☎ 0191 277 7175 ✉ ian.humphries@newcastle.gov.uk

Emergency Planning: Mr Stephen Savage, Assistant Director - Public Safety & Regulation, Civic Centre, Newcastle upon Tyne NE1 8PB ☎ 0191 211 6101 ✉ stephen.savage@newcastle.gov.uk

Energy Management: Mr Simon Johnson , Senior Neighbourhood Manager - Energy Services, Allendale House, Newcastle upon Tyne NE6 2SZ ☎ 0191 278 3449 ✉ simon.johnson@newcastle.gov.uk

Environmental / Technical Services: Mr Michael Murphy , Director of Communities, Civic Centre, Newcastle upon Tyne NE1 8QH ☎ 0191 211 5950 ✉ michael.murphy@newcastle.gov.uk

Environmental Health: Mr Stephen Savage, Assistant Director - Public Safety & Regulation, Civic Centre, Newcastle upon Tyne NE1 8QH ☎ 0191 211 6101 ✉ stephen.savage@newcastle.gov.uk

Estates, Property & Valuation: Mr Paul Scaplehorn , Strategic Property Services Manager, Civic Centre, Newcastle upon Tyne NE1 8QH ☎ 0191 211 5505 ✉ paul.scaplehorn@newcastle.gov.uk

European Liaison: Mr Steve Park , Assistant Director - Policy, Communication & Performance, Civic Centre, Newcastle upon Tyne NE1 8QH ☎ 0191 211 5071 🖷 0191 211 4888 ✉ steve.park@newcastle.gov.uk

Events Manager: Mr Stephen Savage, Assistant Director - Public Safety & Regulation, Civic Centre, Newcastle upon Tyne NE1 8QH ☎ 0191 211 6101 ✉ stephen.savage@newcastle.gov.uk

Facilities: Ms Christine Herriot , Head of Facilities Services Civic Management, Civic Centre, Newcastle upon Tyne NE99 2BN ☎ 0191 277 7665 🖷 0191 277 7662 ✉ christine.herriot@newcastle.gov.uk

Finance: Mr Tony Kirkham , Director of Resources, Civic Centre, Newcastle upon Tyne NE1 8QH ☎ 0191 211 5226 ✉ tony.kirkham@newcastle.gov.uk

Fleet Management: Mr Peter Morton , City Transport Manager, Newington Road West, Newcastle upon Tyne NE5 6BD ☎ 0191 278 3901 ✉ peter.morton@newcastle.gov.uk

Grounds Maintenance: Mr Michael Murphy , Director of Communities, Civic Centre, Newcastle upon Tyne NE1 8QH ☎ 0191 211 5950 ✉ michael.murphy@newcastle.gov.uk

Health and Safety: Ms Katherine Chapman , Team Manager - Health & Safety, Civic Centre, Newcastle upon Tyne NE1 8QH ☎ 0191 211 5211 ✉ katherine.chapman@newcastle.gov.uk

Highways: Mr Michael Murphy, Director of Communities, Civic Centre, Newcastle upon Tyne NE1 8QH ☎ 0191 211 5950 ✉ michael.murphy@newcastle.gov.uk

Home Energy Conservation: Mr Simon Johnson , Senior Neighbourhood Manager - Energy Services, Room FF17, Allendale Road, Newcastle upon Tyne NE64 2SZ ☎ 0191 278 3449 ✉ simon.johnson@newcastle.gov.uk

Housing: Mr Mick Firth , Senior Specialist - Advisor, Civic Centre, Newcastle upon Tyne NE1 8QH ☎ 0191 211 5627 ✉ mick.firth@newcastle.gov.uk

NEWCASTLE UPON TYNE CITY

Housing Maintenance: Mr Mick Firth , Senior Specialist - Advisor, Civic Centre, Newcastle upon Tyne NE1 8QH
☎ 0191 211 5627 ✉ mick.firth@newcastle.gov.uk

Local Area Agreement: Mr Phil Hunter , Senior Specialist, Civic Centre, Newcastle upon Tyne NE1 8QH ☎ 0191 277 7802
✉ philip.hunter@newcastle.gov.uk

Legal: Mr John Softly , Assistant Director - Legal Services, Civic Centre, Newcastle upon Tyne NE1 8QH ☎ 0191 277 7047
✉ john.softly@newcastle.gov.uk

Leisure and Cultural Services: Mr David Fay , Head of Service - Libraries & Leisure, City Library, Newcastle upon Tyne NE1 8AX
☎ 0191 277 4152 ✉ david.fay@newcastle.gov.uk

Licensing: Mr Stephen Savage, Assistant Director - Public Safety & Regulation, Civic Centre, Newcastle upon Tyne NE1 8QH
☎ 0191 211 6101 ✉ stephen.savage@newcastle.gov.uk

Lifelong Learning: Mr Tony Durcan, Assistant Director - Customers, Culture & Skills, Civic Centre, Newcastle upon Tyne NE1 8QH ☎ 0191 211 5383 ✉ tony.durcan@newcastle.gov.uk

Lighting: Mr Michael Murphy, Director of Communities, Civic Centre, Newcastle upon Tyne NE1 8QH ☎ 0191 211 5950
✉ michael.murphy@newcastle.gov.uk

Member Services: Ms Linda Scott , Service Manager - Democratic Services, Civic Centre, Newcastle upon Tyne NE1 8QH
☎ 0191 211 5101 ✉ linda.scott@newcastle.gov.uk

Parking: Mr Stephen Savage, Assistant Director - Public Safety & Regulation, Civic Centre, Newcastle upon Tyne NE1 8QH ☎ 0191 211 6101 ✉ stephen.savage@newcastle.gov.uk

Personnel / HR: Ms Pam Perry , Assistant Director - Human Resources, Civic Centre, Newcastle upon Tyne NE1 8QH
☎ 0191 211 5246 ✉ pam.perry@newcastle.gov.uk

Planning: Ms Kath Lawless , Assistant Director - Planning, Civic Centre, Newcastle upon Tyne NE1 8QH ☎ 0191 211 5629
✉ kath.lawless@newcastle.gov.uk

Procurement: Ms Rachel Baillie , Assistant Director - Commissioning & Procurement, Civic Centre, Newcastle upon Tyne NE1 8QH ☎ 0191 211 6458 ✉ rachel.baillie@newcastle.gov.uk

Public Libraries: Mr Tony Durcan, Assistant Director - Customers, Culture & Skills, Civic Centre, Newcastle upon Tyne NE1 8QH
☎ 0191 211 5383 ✉ tony.durcan@newcastle.gov.uk

Recycling & Waste Minimisation: Mr Michael Murphy , Director of Communities, Civic Centre, Newcastle upon Tyne NE1 8QH
☎ 0191 211 5950 ✉ michael.murphy@newcastle.gov.uk

Regeneration: Mr Tom Warburton , Director of Investment & Development, Civic Centre, Newcastle upon Tyne NE1 8QH
☎ 0191 211 5660 ✉ tom.warburton@newcastle.gov.uk

Road Safety: Mr Michael Murphy, Director of Communities, Civic Centre, Newcastle upon Tyne NE1 8QH ☎ 0191 211 5950
✉ michael.murphy@newcastle.gov.uk

Social Services: Mr Ewen Weir , Director of Wellbeing, Care & Learning, Civic Centre, Newcastle upon Tyne NE99 1RD
☎ 0191 211 5478 🖷 0191 211 4955 ✉ ewen.weir@newcastle.gov.uk

Social Services (Adult): Ms Cathy Bull , Assistant Director - Social Care, Civic Centre, Newcastle upon Tyne NE1 8QH
☎ 0191 211 6318 ✉ cathy.bull@newcastle.gov.uk

Social Services (Children): Mr Mick McCracken , Assistant Director - Family Insights, Civic Centre, Newcastle upon Tyne NE1 8QH ☎ 0191 211 6307 ✉ mick.mccracken@newcastle.gov.uk

Staff Training: Ms Pam Perry , Assistant Director - Human Resources, Civic Centre, Newcastle upon Tyne NE1 8QH
☎ 0191 211 5246 ✉ pam.perry@newcastle.gov.uk

Street Scene: Mr Tom Warburton , Director of Investment & Development, Civic Centre, Newcastle upon Tyne NE1 8QH
☎ 0191 211 5660 ✉ tom.warburton@newcastle.gov.uk

Sustainable Communities: Mr Neil Quinn , Co-operative Communities Service Manager, Civic Centre, Newcastle upon Tyne NE1 8QH ☎ 0191 277 3615 ✉ neil.quinn@newcastle.gov.uk

Sustainable Development: Mr Tom Warburton , Director of Investment & Development, Civic Centre, Newcastle upon Tyne NE1 8QH ☎ 0191 211 5660 ✉ tom.warburton@newcastle.gov.uk

Tourism: Mr Andrew Rothwell , Culture & Tourism Manager, Civic Centre, Newcastle upon Tyne NE1 8QH ☎ 0191 211 5610
✉ andrew.rothwell@newcastle.gov.uk

Town Centre: Mr Andrew Lewis , Assistant Chief Executive, Civic Centre, Newcastle upon Tyne NE1 8QH ☎ 0191 211 5681
✉ andrew.lewis@newcastle.gov.uk

Traffic Management: Mr Michael Murphy, Director of Communities, Civic Centre, Newcastle upon Tyne NE1 8QH
☎ 0191 211 5950 ✉ michael.murphy@newcastle.gov.uk

Transport: Mr Peter Morton , City Transport Manager, Newington Road West, Newcastle upon Tyne NE5 6BD ☎ 0191 278 3901
✉ peter.morton@newcastle.gov.uk

Transport Planner: Mr Mark Wilson , Regional Transport Principal Advisor, Civic Centre, Newcastle upon Tyne NE1 8QH
☎ 0191 211 5679 ✉ mark.wilson@newcastle.gov.uk

Total Place: Mr Andrew Lewis , Assistant Chief Executive, Civic Centre, Newcastle upon Tyne NE1 8QH ☎ 0191 211 5681
✉ andrew.lewis@newcastle.gov.uk

Waste Collection and Disposal: Mr Michael Murphy, Director of Communities, Civic Centre, Newcastle upon Tyne NE1 8QH
☎ 0191 211 5950 ✉ michael.murphy@newcastle.gov.uk

Waste Management: Mr Michael Murphy, Director of Communities, Civic Centre, Newcastle upon Tyne NE1 8QH
☎ 0191 211 5950 michael.murphy@newcastle.gov.uk

Children's Play Areas: Mr Mick McCracken , Assistant Director - Family Insights, Civic Centre, Newcastle upon Tyne NE1 8QH
☎ 0191 211 6307 mick.mccracken@newcastle.gov.uk

COUNCILLORS

***Sheriff* Stephenson**, Hazel (LAB - Benwell and Scotswood)
hazel.stephenson@newcastle.gov.uk

***Leader of the Council* Forbes**, Nick (LAB - Westgate)
nick.forbes@newcastle.gov.uk

***Deputy Leader of the Council* McCarty**, Joyce (LAB - Wingrove)
joyce.mccarty@newcastle.gov.uk

Ahad, Dipu (LAB - Elswick)
dipu.ahad@newcastle.gov.uk

Ainsley, Arlene (LAB - South Jesmond)
arlene.ainsley@newcastle.gov.uk

Ali, Irim (LAB - Wingrove)
irim.ali@newcastle.gov.uk

Allen, Pauline (LD - Parklands)
pauline.allen@newcastle.gov.uk

Allibhai, Kerry (LAB - South Jesmond)
kerry.allibhai@newcastle.gov.uk

Allison, George (LAB - Byker)
george.allison@newcastle.gov.uk

Ashby, Robin (LD - Parklands)
robin.asby@newcastle.gov.uk

Bartlett, Christopher (LAB - South Heaton)
christopher.bartlett@newcastle.gov.uk

Beecham, Jeremy (LAB - Benwell and Scotswood)
jeremybeecham@blueyonder.co.uk

Bell, Ged (LAB - Kenton)
ged.bell@newcastle.gov.uk

Bird, Simon (LAB - Denton)
simon.bird@newcastle.gov.uk

Bowman, Mick (LAB - North Heaton)
mick.bowman@newcastle.gov.uk

Breakey, Peter (LD - North Jesmond)
peter.breakey@newcastle.gov.uk

Burke, Michael (LAB - Denton)
michael.burke@newcastle.gov.uk

Cook, David (LAB - Lemington)
david.cook@newcastle.gov.uk

Corbett, Bill (IND - Westerhope)
bill.corbett@newcastle.gov.uk

Cott, Nick (LD - West Gosforth)
nick.cott@newcastle.gov.uk

Davis, Melissa (LAB - Denton)
melissa.davis@newcastle.gov.uk

Denholm, David (LAB - Walkergate)
david.denholm@newcastle.gov.uk

Donnelly, Marc (IND - Westerhope)
marc.donnelly@newcastle.gov.uk

Down, David (LD - Parklands)
david.down@newcastle.gov.uk

Dunn, Veronica (LAB - Byker)
veronica.dunn@newcastle.gov.uk

Fairlie, Stephen (LAB - Newburn)
steve.fairlie@newcastle.gov.uk

Faulkner, David (LD - Fawdon)
david.faulkner@newcastle.gov.uk

Franks, Hilary (LAB - Newburn)
hilary.franks@newcastle.gov.uk

Gallagher, Henry (LD - East Gosforth)
henry.gallagher@newcastle.gov.uk

Graham, Ian (LD - Castle)
ian.graham@newcastle.gov.uk

Higgins, Robert (LAB - Benwell and Scotswood)
rob.higgins@newcastle.gov.uk

Hillicks, Pat (IND - Westerhope)
pat.hillicks@newcastle.gov.uk

Hindmarsh, Brenda (LD - Fawdon)
brenda.hindmarsh@newcastle.gov.uk

Huddart, Doreen (LD - North Heaton)
doreen.huddart@newcastle.gov.uk

Hunter, Brian (LAB - Castle)
brian.hunter@newcastle.gov.uk

Jones, Denise (LAB - South Heaton)
denise.jones@newcastle.gov.uk

Kane, Gareth (LD - Ouseburn)
gareth.kane@newcastle.gov.uk

Kemp, Nick (LAB - Byker)
nick.kemp@newcastle.gov.uk

Kilgour, Karen (LAB - Fenham)
karen.kilgour@newcastle.gov.uk

Kingsland, Joanne (LAB - Westgate)
joanne.kingsland@newcastle.gov.uk

Lambert, Stephen (LAB - Kenton)
stephen.lambert@newcastle.gov.uk

Leggott, Peter (LD - East Gosforth)
peter.leggott@newcastle.gov.uk

Lower, Anita (LD - Castle)
anita.lower@newcastle.gov.uk

Lowson, Maureen (LAB - Walkergate)
maureen.lowson@newcastle.gov.uk

McGuinness, Kim (LAB - Lemington)
kim.mcguinness@newcastle.gov.uk

Mendelson, Felicity (LAB - South Jesmond)
felicity.mendelson@newcastle.gov.uk

O'Brien, Geoff (LAB - Westgate)
geoff.obrien@newcastle.gov.uk

Pattison, George (LAB - Woolsington)
george.pattison@newcastle.gov.uk

Pattison, Sharon (LAB - Woolsington)
sharon.pattison@newcastle.gov.uk

NEWCASTLE UPON TYNE CITY

Pearson, Sue (LAB - Blakelaw)
sue.pearson@newcastle.gov.uk

Perry, Dan (LAB - North Jesmond)
dan.perry@newcastle.gov.uk

Phillipson, Barry (LAB - Lemington)
barry.phillipson@newcastle.gov.uk

Powers, Stephen (LAB - Ouseburn)
stephen.powers@newcastle.gov.uk

Psallidas, Stephen (LD - Ouseburn)
stephen.psallidas@newcastle.gov.uk

Rahman, Habib (LAB - Elswick)
habib.rahman@newcastle.gov.uk

Renton, Bob (LD - Dene)
bob.renton@newcastle.gov.uk

Riley, Ben (LAB - Blakelaw)
ben.riley@newcastle.gov.uk

Robinson, Jacqui (LAB - Woolsington)
jacqui.robinson@newcastle.gov.uk

Robinson, Karen (LD - Dene)
karen.robinson@newcastle.gov.uk

Schofield, Ann (LAB - Elswick)
ann.schofield@newcastle.gov.uk

Shepherd, Bill (LD - West Gosforth)
william.shepherd@newcastle.gov.uk

Slesenger, David (LD - East Gosforth)
david.slesenger@newcastle.gov.uk

Slesenger, Jaqueline (LD - West Gosforth)
jacqueline.slesenger@newcastle.gov.uk

Stockdale, David (LAB - Blakelaw)
david.stockdale@newcastle.gov.uk

Stokel-Walker, John (LAB - Walker)
john.stokel-walker@newcastle.gov.uk

Stone, Greg (LD - North Heaton)
greg.stone@newcastle.gov.uk

Streather, Jane (LAB - Kenton)
jane.streather@newcastle.gov.uk

Talbot, Marion (LAB - Fenham)
marion.talbot@newcastle.gov.uk

Taylor, Wendy (LD - Dene)
wendy.taylor@newcastle.gov.uk

Tinnion, Antoine (LAB - Fawdon)
antoine.tinnion@newcastle.gov.uk

Todd, Nigel (LAB - Wingrove)
nigel.todd@newcastle.gov.uk

Tokell, Ian (LAB - Fenham)
ian.tokell@newcastle.gov.uk

Walker, Catherine (LD - North Jesmond)
catherine.walker@newcastle.gov.uk

White, Sophie (LAB - South Heaton)
sophie.white@newcastle.gov.uk

Wood, Margaret (LAB - Walker)
margaret.wood@newcastle.gov.uk

Wood, Stevie (LAB - Walkergate)
stephen.wood@newcastle.gov.uk

Wood, Dave (LAB - Walker)
dave.wood@newcastle.gov.uk

Wright, Linda (LAB - Newburn)
linda.wright@newcastle.gov.uk

POLITICAL COMPOSITION
LAB: 53, LD: 22, IND: 3

COMMITTEE CHAIRS

Licensing: Mr George Pattison

Planning: Mr George Allison

Newcastle-under-Lyme D

Newcastle-under-Lyme Borough Council, Civic Offices, Merrial Street, Newcastle-under-Lyme ST5 2AG
☎ 01782 717717 🖷 01782 711032 💻 www.newcastle-staffs.gov.uk

FACTS AND FIGURES
Parliamentary Constituencies: Newcastle-under-Lyme, Stoke-on-Trent North, Stone
EU Constituencies: West Midlands
Election Frequency: Elections are by thirds

PRINCIPAL OFFICERS

Chief Executive: Mr John Sellgren , Chief Executive, Civic Offices, Merrial Street, Newcastle-under-Lyme ST5 2AG

Senior Management: Mr Dave Adams, Executive Director - Operational Services, Civic Offices, Merrial Street, Newcastle-under-Lyme ST5 2AG ☎ 01782 742504 🖷 01782 713252 🖰 dave.adams@newcastle-staffs.gov.uk

Senior Management: Mr Neale Clifton, Executive Director - Regeneration & Development, Civic Offices, Merrial Street, Newcastle-under-Lyme ST5 2AG ☎ 01782 742401 🖷 01782 714303 🖰 neale.clifton@newcastle-staffs.gov.uk

Senior Management: Mr Kelvin Turner , Executive Director - Resources, Support Services & S151 Officer, Civic Offices, Merrial Street, Newcastle-under-Lyme ST5 2AG ☎ 01782 742106 🖰 kelvin.turner@newcastle-staffs.gov.uk

Architect, Building / Property Services: Mr Graham Williams , Head of Assets & Regeneration, Civic Offices, Merrial Street, Newcastle-under-Lyme ST5 2AG ☎ 01782 742370 🖷 01782 714303 🖰 graham.williams@newcastle-staffs.gov.uk

Building Control: Mr Guy Benson , Head - Planning & Development, Civic Offices, Merrial Street, Newcastle-under-Lyme ST5 2AG ☎ 01782 744440 🖰 guy.benson@newcastle-staffs.gov.uk

PR / Communications: Mr Phil Jones, Head - Communications, Civic Offices, Merrial Street, Newcastle-under-Lyme ST5 2AG ☎ 01782 742271 🖰 phil.jones@newcastle-staffs.gov.uk

Community Safety: Mrs Sarah Moore , Partnerships Manager, Civic Offices, Merrial Street, Newcastle-under-Lyme ST5 2AG ☎ 01782 742496 🖷 01782 714303 🖰 sarah.moore@newcastle-staffs.gov.uk

Computer Management: Mr David Elkington , ICT Operations & Development Manager, Civic Offices, Merrial Street, Newcastle-under-Lyme ST5 2AG ☎ 01782 742472 🖷 01782 714303 david.elkington@newcastle-staffs.gov.uk

Computer Management: Mrs Jeannette Hilton , Head - Customer Services & ICT Services, Civic Offices, Merrial Street, Newcastle-under-Lyme ST5 2AG ☎ 01782 742470 jeannette.hilton@newcastle-staffs.gov.uk

Contracts: Mr Roger Tait , Head - Operations, Civic Offices, Merrial Street, Newcastle-under-Lyme ST5 2AG ☎ 01782 742632 🖷 01782 713251 roger.tait@newcastle-staffs.gov.uk

Corporate Services: Mr Kelvin Turner , Executive Director - Resources, Support Services & S151 Officer, Civic Offices, Merrial Street, Newcastle-under-Lyme ST5 2AG ☎ 01782 742106 kelvin.turner@newcastle-staffs.gov.uk

Customer Service: Mrs Jeannette Hilton , Head - Customer Services & ICT Services, Civic Offices, Merrial Street, Newcastle-under-Lyme ST5 2AG ☎ 01782 742470 jeannette.hilton@newcastle-staffs.gov.uk

Direct Labour: Mr Paul Pickerill , Streetscene Manager, Civic Offices, Merrial Street, Newcastle-under-Lyme ST5 2AG ☎ 01782 744760

Economic Development: Mr Simon Smith, Regeneration & Economic Development Manager, Civic Offices, Merrial Street, Newcastle-under-Lyme ST5 2AG ☎ 01782 742460 🖷 01782 714303 simon.smith@newcastle-staffs.gov.uk

Electoral Registration: Miss Julia Cleary , Democratic Services Manager, Civic Offices, Merrial Street, Newcastle-under-Lyme ST5 2AG ☎ 01782 742227 🖷 01782 711032 julia.cleary@newcastle-staffs.gov.uk

Emergency Planning: Mr Graham Williams , Head of Assets & Regeneration, Civic Offices, Merrial Street, Newcastle-under-Lyme ST5 2AG ☎ 01782 742370 🖷 01782 714303 graham.williams@newcastle-staffs.gov.uk

Energy Management: Mr Graham Williams , Head of Assets & Regeneration, Civic Offices, Merrial Street, Newcastle-under-Lyme ST5 2AG ☎ 01782 742370 🖷 01782 714303 graham.williams@newcastle-staffs.gov.uk

Environmental Health: Miss Nesta Barker , Head of Environmental Health Services, Civic Offices, Merrial Street, Newcastle-under-Lyme ST5 2AG ☎ 01782 742732 🖷 01782 714303 nesta.barker@newcastle-staffs.gov.uk

European Liaison: Mr Simon Smith, Regeneration & Economic Development Manager, Civic Offices, Merrial Street, Newcastle-under-Lyme ST5 2AG ☎ 01782 742460 🖷 01782 714303 simon.smith@newcastle-staffs.gov.uk

Events Manager: Mrs Janet Baddeley , Communications Manager, Civic Offices, Merrial Street, Newcastle-under-Lyme ST5 2AG ☎ 01782 742605 janet.baddeley@newcastle-staffs.gov.uk

Facilities: Mr Julian Lythgo , Facilities Manager, Civic Offices, Merrial Street, Newcastle-under-Lyme ST5 2AG ☎ 01782 742368 julian.lythgo@newcastle-staff.gov.uk

Finance: Mr Dave Roberts , Head - Finance, Civic Offices, Merrial Street, Newcastle-under-Lyme ST5 2AG ☎ 01782 742111 dave.roberts@newcastle-staffs.gov.uk

Finance: Mr Kelvin Turner , Executive Director - Resources, Support Services & S151 Officer, Civic Offices, Merrial Street, Newcastle-under-Lyme ST5 2AG ☎ 01782 742106 kelvin.turner@newcastle-staffs.gov.uk

Treasury: Mr Kelvin Turner , Executive Director - Resources, Support Services & S151 Officer, Civic Offices, Merrial Street, Newcastle-under-Lyme ST5 2AG ☎ 01782 742106 kelvin.turner@newcastle-staffs.gov.uk

Fleet Management: Mr Trevor Nicoll , Head of Recycling & Fleet Services, Civic Offices, Merrial Street, Newcastle-under-Lyme ST5 2AG ☎ 01782 742155 🖷 01782 713252 trevor.nicoll@newcastle-staffs.gov.uk

Grounds Maintenance: Mr Roger Tait , Head - Operations, Civic Offices, Merrial Street, Newcastle-under-Lyme ST5 2AG ☎ 01782 742632 🖷 01782 713251 roger.tait@newcastle-staffs.gov.uk

Health and Safety: Ms Claire Dodd , Corporate Health & Safety Officer, Civic Offices, Merrial Street, Newcastle-under-Lyme ST5 2AG ☎ 01782 742262 claire.dodd@newcastle-staffs.gov.uk

Home Energy Conservation: Mr Michael O'Connor , Principal Environmental Health Officer, Civic Offices, Merrial Street, Newcastle-under-Lyme ST5 2AG ☎ 01782 742564 🖷 01782 713252 mike.o'connor@newcastle-staffs.gov.uk

Housing: Mr Neale Clifton, Executive Director - Regeneration & Development, Civic Offices, Merrial Street, Newcastle-under-Lyme ST5 2AG ☎ 01782 742401 🖷 01782 714303 neale.clifton@newcastle-staffs.gov.uk

Housing: Mrs Joanne Halliday , Head - Housing, Civic Offices, Merrial Street, Newcastle-under-Lyme ST5 2AG ☎ 01782 742451 🖷 01782 714303 joanne.halliday@newcastle-staffs.gov.uk

Legal: Mr Mark Bailey , Head of Business Improvement, Central Services & Partnerships, Civic Offices, Merrial Street, Newcastle-under-Lyme ST5 2AG ☎ 01782 742751 mark.bailey@newcastle-staffs.gov.uk

Leisure and Cultural Services: Mr Robert Foster , Head - Leisure & Cultural Services, Civic Offices, Merrial Street, Newcastle-under-Lyme ST5 2AG ☎ 01782 742636 🖷 01782 713252 robert.foster@newcastle-staffs.gov.uk

Licensing: Miss Julia Cleary , Democratic Services Manager, Civic Offices, Merrial Street, Newcastle-under-Lyme ST5 2AG ☎ 01782 742227 🖷 01782 711032 julia.cleary@newcastle-staffs.gov.uk

Lottery Funding, Charity and Voluntary: Mr Robert Foster , Head - Leisure & Cultural Services, Civic Offices, Merrial Street, Newcastle-under-Lyme ST5 2AG ☎ 01782 742636 🖷 01782 713252 robert.foster@newcastle-staffs.gov.uk

NEWCASTLE-UNDER-LYME

Member Services: Miss Julia Cleary , Democratic Services Manager, Civic Offices, Merrial Street, Newcastle-under-Lyme ST5 2AG ☎ 01782 742227 🖷 01782 711032 🖰 julia.cleary@newcastle-staffs.gov.uk

Parking: Mr Graham Williams , Head of Assets & Regeneration, Civic Offices, Merrial Street, Newcastle-under-Lyme ST5 2AG ☎ 01782 742370 🖷 01782 714303 🖰 graham.williams@newcastle-staffs.gov.uk

Partnerships: Mrs Sarah Moore , Partnerships Manager, Civic Offices, Merrial Street, Newcastle-under-Lyme ST5 2AG ☎ 01782 742496 🖷 01782 714303 🖰 sarah.moore@newcastle-staffs.gov.uk

Personnel / HR: Mrs Sarah Taylor , Acting Head of Human Resources, Civic Offices, Merrial Street, Newcastle-under-Lyme ST5 2AG ☎ 01782 742261 🖷 01782 711032 🖰 sarah.taylor@newcastle-staffs.gov.uk

Planning: Mr Guy Benson , Head - Planning & Development, Civic Offices, Merrial Street, Newcastle-under-Lyme ST5 2AG ☎ 01782 744440 🖰 guy.benson@newcastle-staffs.gov.uk

Procurement: Mr Simon Sowerby , Procurement Officer, Civic Offices, Merrial Street, Newcastle-under-Lyme ST5 2AG ☎ 01782 742756 🖷 01782 711032 🖰

Recycling & Waste Minimisation: Mr Trevor Nicoll , Head of Recycling & Fleet Services, Civic Offices, Merrial Street, Newcastle-under-Lyme ST5 2AG ☎ 01782 742155 🖷 01782 713252 🖰 trevor.nicoll@newcastle-staffs.gov.uk

Regeneration: Mr Neale Clifton, Executive Director - Regeneration & Development, Civic Offices, Merrial Street, Newcastle-under-Lyme ST5 2AG ☎ 01782 742401 🖷 01782 714303 🖰 neale.clifton@newcastle-staffs.gov.uk

Staff Training: Mrs Sarah Taylor , Acting Head of Human Resources, Civic Offices, Merrial Street, Newcastle-under-Lyme ST5 2AG ☎ 01782 742261 🖷 01782 711032 🖰 sarah.taylor@newcastle-staffs.gov.uk

Street Scene: Mr Paul Pickerill , Streetscene Manager, Civic Offices, Merrial Street, Newcastle-under-Lyme ST5 2AG ☎ 01782 744760 🖰

Sustainable Communities: Mr Neale Clifton , Executive Director - Regeneration & Development, Civic Offices, Merrial Street, Newcastle-under-Lyme ST5 2AG ☎ 01782 742401 🖷 01782 714303 🖰 neale.clifton@newcastle-staffs.gov.uk

Sustainable Development: Mr Neale Clifton , Executive Director - Regeneration & Development, Civic Offices, Merrial Street, Newcastle-under-Lyme ST5 2AG ☎ 01782 742401 🖷 01782 714303 🖰 neale.clifton@newcastle-staffs.gov.uk

Tourism: Mr Phil Jones, Head - Communications, Civic Offices, Merrial Street, Newcastle-under-Lyme ST5 2AG ☎ 01782 742271 🖰 phil.jones@newcastle-staffs.gov.uk

Transport: Mr Stephen Gee , Transport Manager, Central Depot, Knutton Lane, Newcastle-under-Lyme ST5 2SL ☎ 01782 742712 🖷 01782 713179 🖰 stephen.gee@newcastle-staffs.gov.uk

Transport Planner: Mr Stephen Gee , Transport Manager, Central Depot, Knutton Lane, Newcastle-under-Lyme ST5 2SL ☎ 01782 742712 🖷 01782 713179 🖰 stephen.gee@newcastle-staffs.gov.uk

Waste Collection and Disposal: Mr Trevor Nicoll , Head of Recycling & Fleet Services, Civic Offices, Merrial Street, Newcastle-under-Lyme ST5 2AG ☎ 01782 742155 🖷 01782 713252 🖰 trevor.nicoll@newcastle-staffs.gov.uk

Waste Management: Mr Trevor Nicoll , Head of Recycling & Fleet Services, Civic Offices, Merrial Street, Newcastle-under-Lyme ST5 2AG ☎ 01782 742155 🖷 01782 713252 🖰 trevor.nicoll@newcastle-staffs.gov.uk

Waste Management: Mr Paul Pickerill , Streetscene Manager, Civic Offices, Merrial Street, Newcastle-under-Lyme ST5 2AG ☎ 01782 744760

COUNCILLORS

***Mayor* Hambleton**, Sandra (LAB - Bradwell)
sandra.hambleton@newcastle-staffs.gov.uk

***Deputy Mayor* Wilkes**, Ian (LD - Audley and Bignall End)
ian.wilkes@newcastle-staffs.gov.uk

***Leader of the Council* Shenton**, Elizabeth (LAB - Town)
elizabeth.shenton@newcastle-staffs.gov.uk

***Deputy Leader of the Council* Turner**, Terry (LAB - Kidsgrove)
terry.turner@newcastle-staffs.gov.uk

***Group Leader* Huckfield**, Derrick (UKIP - Knutton and Silverdale)

***Group Leader* Owen**, Kenneth (UKIP - Holditch)

***Group Leader* Reddish**, Marion (LD - Thistleberry)
marion.reddish@newcastle-staffs.gov.uk

***Group Leader* Sweeney**, Stephen (CON - Clayton)
stephen.sweeney@newcastle-staffs.gov.uk

Allport, David (LAB - Talke)
david.allport@newcastle-staffs.gov.uk

Astle, Margaret (LAB - Kidsgrove)
margaret.astle@kidsgrove.info

Bailey, Reginald (LAB - Kidsgrove)
reginald.bailey@newcastle-staffs.gov.uk

Baker, Sophia (LAB - Holditch)
sophia.baker@newcastle-staffs.gov.uk

Bates, Elsie (LAB - Newchapel)
elsie.bates@newcastle-staffs.gov.uk

Beech, Ann (LAB - Audley and Bignall End)
ann.beech@newcastle-staffs.gov.uk

Braithwaite, Eileen (IND - Silverdale and Parksite)

Burgess, Silvia (LAB - Butt Lane)
silvia.burgess@newcastle-staffs.gov.uk

Cooper, Julie (CON - Porthill)
julie.cooper@newcastle-staffs.gov.uk

Cooper, John (CON - Porthill)
john.cooper@newcastle-staffs.gov.uk

Dymond, Sylvia (LAB - Butt Lane)
sylviadymond@talktalk.net

Eagles, Tony (LAB - Knutton and Silverdale)
tony.eagles@newcastle-staffs.gov.uk

Eastwood, Colin (LAB - Wolstanton)
colin.eastwood@newcastle-staffs.gov.uk

Fear, Andrew (CON - Seabridge)
andrew.fear@newcastle-staffs.gov.uk

Frankish, Avril (CON - Halmer End)
avril@frankish.org

Hailstones, Peter (CON - Seabridge)
peter.hailstones@newcastle-staffs.gov.uk

Hailstones, Linda (CON - Westlands)
linda.hailstones@newcastle-staffs.gov.uk

Hambleton, Trevor (LAB - Bradwell)
trevor.hambleton@newcastle-staffs.gov.uk

Harper, David (UKIP - Chesterton)

Heesom, Gillian (CON - Westlands)
gillian.heesom@newcastle-staffs.gov.uk

Holland, Mark (CON - Westlands)
mark.holland@newcastle-staffs.gov.uk

Johnson, Trevor (CON - Wolstanton)
trevorgjohnson@aol.com

Johnson, Hilda (LAB - Chesterton)
hilda.johnson@newcastle-staffs.gov.uk

Kearon, Tony (LAB - Keele)
tony.kearon@newcastle-staffs.gov.uk

Loades, David (CON - Loggerheads and Whitmore)
david.loades@newcastle-staffs.gov.uk

Mancey, Chloe (CON - Seabridge)
chloe.mancey@newcastle-staffs.gov.uk

Matthews, Ian (CON - May Bank)
ian.matthews@newcastle-staffs.gov.uk

Naylon, Wenslie (GRN - Keele)

Northcott, Paul (CON - Loggerheads and Whitmore)

Parker, Andrew (CON - Clayton)
mradp76@yahoo.com

Peers, Tracey (CON - Loggerheads and Whitmore)
tracey.peers@newcastle-staffs.gov.uk

Pickup, Sarah (LAB - Ravenscliffe)
s44ahg@gmail.com

Plant, Glyn (LAB - Bradwell)
glyn.plant@newcastle-staffs.gov.uk

Proctor, Bert (LAB - Audley and Bignall End)

Robinson, Kyle (LAB - Butt Lane)
kyle.robinson@newcastle-staffs.gov.uk

Rout, Amelia (LAB - Silverdale and Parksite)
amelia.rout@newcastle-staffs.gov.uk

Simpson, Sandra (LAB - Chesterton)
sandra.simpson@newcastle-staffs.gov.uk

Stringer, David (LAB - Ravenscliffe)
david.stringer@newcastle-staffs.gov.uk

Stubbs, Mike (LAB - Talke)
mike.stubbs@newcastle-staffs.gov.uk

Tagg, John (CON - May Bank)
john.tagg@newcastle-staffs.gov.uk

Tagg, Simon (CON - May Bank)
simon.tagg@newcastle-staffs.gov.uk

Walklate, June (LD - Thistleberry)
june.walklate@newcastle-staffs.gov.uk

Wallace, Robert (LAB - Town)

Waring, Paul (LAB - Newchapel)
paul.waring@newcastle-staffs.gov.uk

Welsh, Billy (LD - Madeley)
billy.welsh@newcastle-staffs.gov.uk

Wemyss, Andrew (LD - Halmer End)
andrew.wemyss@newcastle-staffs.gov.uk

White, Simon (LD - Madeley)
simon.white@newcastle-staffs.gov.uk

Williams, John (LAB - Cross Heath)
john.williams@newcastle-staffs.gov.uk

Williams, Gillian (LAB - Cross Heath)
gillian.williams@newcastle-staffs.gov.uk

Winfield, Joan (LAB - Cross Heath)
joan.winfield@newcastle-staffs.gov.uk

Wing, Lucinda (CON - Thistleberry)
lucinda.wing@newcastle-staffs.gov.uk

Woolley, David (UKIP - Wolstanton)

POLITICAL COMPOSITION

LAB: 29, CON: 19, LD: 6, UKIP: 4, GRN: 1, IND: 1

COMMITTEE CHAIRS

Audit: Ms Sarah Pickup

Health & Wellbeing: Mr Colin Eastwood

Licensing: Mr Trevor Hambleton

Planning: Miss Sophia Baker

Newham L

Newham London Borough Council, Newham Dockside, 1000 Dockside Road, Royal Albert Dock, London E16 2QU
☎ 020 8430 2000 firstname.lastname@newham.gov.uk
www.newham.gov.uk

FACTS AND FIGURES

Parliamentary Constituencies: East Ham, West Ham
EU Constituencies: London
Election Frequency: Elections are of whole council

PRINCIPAL OFFICERS

Chief Executive: Mr Kim Bromley-Derry , Chief Executive, Newham Dockside, 1000 Dockside Road, Royal Albert Dock, London E16 2QU ☎ 020 8430 2000
kim.bromley-derry@newham.gov.uk

Assistant Chief Executive: Mr Tony Clements , Assistant Chief Executive - External Partnerships, Newham Dockside, 1000 Dockside Road, Royal Albert Dock, London E16 2QU ☎ 020 8430 2000 tony.clements@newham.gov.uk

NEWHAM

Assistant Chief Executive: Mr Douglas Trainer , Head of Communications, Newham Dockside, 1000 Dockside Road, Royal Albert Dock, London E16 2QU ☎ 020 8430 2000 ✉ douglas.trainer@newham.gov.uk

Senior Management: Mrs Deborah Hindson , Managing Director of oneSource, Newham Dockside, 1000 Dockside Road, Royal Albert Dock, London E16 2QU ☎ 020 8430 2000 ✉ deborah.hindson@newham.gov.uk

Senior Management: Ms Meradin Peachey , Director - Public Health, Newham Dockside, 1000 Dockside Road, Royal Albert Dock, London E16 2QU ☎ 020 8430 2000 ✉ meradin.peachey@newham.gov.uk

Access Officer / Social Services (Disability): Miss Grainne Siggins , Director of Adult Social Care, Newham Dockside, 1000 Dockside Road, Royal Albert Dock, London E16 2QU ✉ grainne.siggins@newham.gov.uk

Architect, Building / Property Services: Ms Zoe Power , Acting Director of Business Systems, Property & Commercial Development, Newham Dockside, 1000 Dockside Road, Royal Albert Dock, London E16 2QU ☎ 020 8460 2000 ✉ zoe.power@newham.gov.uk

Building Control: Mr Terry Harvey , Building Control Team Manager, Newham Dockside, 1000 Dockside Road, Royal Albert Dock, London E16 2QU ☎ 020 3373 4692 ✉ terry.harvey@newham.gov.uk

Catering Services: Mr John Ledgley, Head of Newham Catering & Cleaning Services, Newham Catering, 242 Fernhill Street , London E16 2HZ ☎ 020 8430 2000 ✉ john.ledgley@newham.gov.uk

Children / Youth Services: Mr James Thomas , Director - Children's Services, Newham Dockside, 1000 Dockside Road, Royal Albert Dock, London E16 2QU ☎ 020 8430 2000 ✉ james.thomas@newham.gov.uk

Civil Registration: Ms Lynne Cummings, Superintendent Registrar, Newham Register Office, 207 Plashet Grove, London E6 1BT ☎ 020 8430 3616 ✉ lynne.cummings@newham.gov.uk

PR / Communications: Mr Gary Bird , Deputy Head of Communications, Newham Dockside, 1000 Dockside Road, Royal Albert Dock, London E16 2QU ☎ 020 8430 2000 ✉ gary.bird@newham.gov.uk

Community Planning: Mr Damian Atkinson , Head of Commissioning (Community Neighbourhoods), Newham Dockside, 1000 Dockside Road, Royal Albert Dock, London E16 2QU ☎ 020 8430 2000 ✉ damian.atkinson@newham.gov.uk

Community Safety: Mr Nick Bracken , Director of Enforcement & Safety, Newham Dockside, 1000 Dockside Road, Royal Albert Dock, London E16 2QU ☎ 020 8430 2000 ✉ nick.bracken@newham.gov.uk

Computer Management: Mr Geoff Connell , Director - ICT Services, Newham Dockside, 1000 Dockside Road, Royal Albert Dock, London E16 2QU ☎ 020 8430 2000; 020 8430 2000 ✉ geoff.connell@havering.gov.uk

Consumer Protection and Trading Standards: Ms Sheila Roberts , Enforcement Manager (Special Operations), Newham Dockside, 1000 Dockside Road, Royal Albert Dock, London E16 2QU ☎ 020 3373 7914 ✉ sheila.roberts@newham.gov.uk

Contracts: Mr David Pridmore , Head of Procurement, Newham Dockside, 1000 Dockside Road, Royal Albert Dock, London E16 2QU ☎ 020 8430 2000 ✉ david.pridmore@newham.gov.uk

Customer Service: Mr Chris Boylett , Head of Customer Transactions, Newham Dockside, 1000 Dockside Road, Royal Albert Dock, London E16 2QU ☎ 020 8430 2000 ✉ chris.boylett@newham.gov.uk

Economic Development: Ms Deirdra Armsby , Director - Strategic Planning, Regeneration & Olympic Legacy, Newham Dockside, 1000 Dockside Road, Royal Albert Dock, London E16 2QU ☎ 020 8430 2000 ✉ deirdra.armsby@newham.gov.uk

Education: Mr James Thomas , Director - Children's Services, Newham Dockside, 1000 Dockside Road, Royal Albert Dock, London E16 2QU ☎ 020 8430 2000 ✉ james.thomas@newham.gov.uk

Electoral Registration: Mr Paul Libreri , Head of Registration & Electoral Services, East Ham Town Hall, 324 Barking Road, London E6 2RP ☎ 020 8430 2000 ✉ paul.libreri@newham.gov.uk

Emergency Planning: Mr Russell Bryan , Operational Manager, Newham Dockside, 1000 Dockside Road, Royal Albert Dock, London E16 2QU ☎ 020 8430 2000 ✉ russell.bryan@newham.gov.uk

Environmental / Technical Services: Mr Gary Alderson , Director - Environmental Services, Newham Dockside, 1000 Dockside Road, Royal Albert Dock, London E16 2QU ☎ 020 8430 2000 ✉ gary.alderson@newham.gov.uk

Environmental Health: Mr Russell Bryan , Operational Manager, Newham Dockside, 1000 Dockside Road, Royal Albert Dock, London E16 2QU ☎ 020 8430 2000 ✉ russell.bryan@newham.gov.uk

Estates, Property & Valuation: Mr David Beament , Acting Head of Property Valuation, Newham Dockside, 1000 Dockside Road, Royal Albert Dock, London E16 2QU ☎ 020 8430 2000 ✉ david.beament@newham.gov.uk

Events Manager: Mrs Sue Meiners , Head of Events & Sponsorship, Newham Dockside, 1000 Dockside Road, Royal Albert Dock, London E16 2QU ☎ 020 8430 2000 ✉ sue.meiners@newham.gov.uk

Facilities: Mr Les Hayward , Head of Facilities Management, Newham Dockside, 1000 Dockside Road, Royal Albert Dock, London E16 2QU ☎ 020 8430 2000 ✉ les.haywood@onesource.gov.uk

Finance: Mrs Deborah Hindson , Managing Director of oneSource, Newham Dockside, 1000 Dockside Road, Royal Albert Dock, London E16 2QU ☎ 020 8430 2000 ✉ deborah.hindson@newham.gov.uk

Finance: Mr Roy Noland , Head of Financial Control, Newham Dockside, 1000 Dockside Road, Royal Albert Dock, London E16 2QU ☎ 020 8430 2000 ✉ roy.nolan@newham.gov.uk

Pensions: Mr Ian Weavers , Pensions Manager, Newham Dockside, 1000 Dockside Road, Royal Albert Dock, London E16 2QU ☎ 020 3373 8408 ✉ ian.weavers@newham.gov.uk

Fleet Management: Mr Bob Smith , Transport Team Manager, Central Depot, Folkestone Road, London E6 4BX ☎ 020 8430 2000 ✉ bob.smith@newham.gov.uk

Grounds Maintenance: Mr Peter Gay , Head of Greenspace & Estate Services, Newham Dockside, 1000 Dockside Road, Royal Albert Dock, London E16 2QU ☎ 020 3373 1996 ✉ peter.gay@newham.gov.uk

Health and Safety: Mr Garry Fisher , Assistant Head of HR (Health & Safety), Newham Dockside, 1000 Dockside Road, Royal Albert Dock, London E16 2QU ☎ 020 8430 2000 ✉ garry.fisher@newham.gov.uk

Highways: Mr John Biden , Head of Traffic & Transportation, Newham Dockside, 1000 Dockside Road, Royal Albert Dock, London E16 2QU ☎ 020 8430 2000 ✉ john.biden@newham.gov.uk

Home Energy Conservation: Mr Simon Throp , Head of Property Services, Bridge House, 320 High Street North, London E15 1EP ☎ 020 8430 2000 ✉ simon.throp@newham.gov.uk

Housing: Mr John East , Director of Community Infrastructure, Newham Dockside, 1000 Dockside Road, Royal Albert Dock, London E16 2QU ☎ 020 8430 2000 ✉ john.east@newham.gov.uk

Housing Maintenance: Mr John East , Director of Community Infrastructure, Newham Dockside, 1000 Dockside Road, Royal Albert Dock, London E16 2QU ☎ 020 8430 2000 ✉ john.east@newham.gov.uk

Legal: Mr Graham White , Director - Legal & Governance, Newham Dockside, 1000 Dockside Road, Royal Albert Dock, London E16 2QU ☎ 020 8430 2000 ✉ graham.white@havering.gov.uk

Licensing: Ms Sheila Roberts , Enforcement Manager (Special Operations), Newham Dockside, 1000 Dockside Road, Royal Albert Dock, London E16 2QU ☎ 020 3373 7914 ✉ sheila.roberts@newham.gov.uk

Lifelong Learning: Mr Steve Cameron , Head of Achievement & Employability, Connexions, 51 Broadway, London E15 4BQ ☎ 020 8430 2000 ✉ steve.cameron@newham.gov.uk

Lighting: Mr Jaspal Sehmi , Structural Services Manager, Newham Dockside, 1000 Dockside Road, Royal Albert Dock, London E16 2QU ☎ 020 8430 2000 ✉ jaspal.sehmi@newham.gov.uk

Parking: Mr Laurence Courtney , Head of Parking, Newham Dockside, 1000 Dockside Road, Royal Albert Dock, London E16 2QU ☎ 020 8430 2000 ✉ laurence.courtney@newham.gov.uk

Personnel / HR: Mrs Jan Douglas , Deputy Director of Strategic People Services, Newham Dockside, 1000 Dockside Road, Royal Albert Dock, London E16 2QU ☎ 020 8430 2000 ✉ jan.douglas@newham.gov.uk

Planning: Ms Deirdra Armsby , Director - Strategic Planning, Regeneration & Olympic Legacy, Newham Dockside, 1000 Dockside Road, Royal Albert Dock, London E16 2QU ☎ 020 8430 2000 ✉ deirdra.armsby@newham.gov.uk

Procurement: Mr David Pridmore , Head of Procurement, Newham Dockside, 1000 Dockside Road, Royal Albert Dock, London E16 2QU ☎ 020 8430 2000 ✉ david.pridmore@newham.gov.uk

Public Libraries: Mr Damian Atkinson , Head of Commissioning (Community Neighbourhoods), Newham Dockside, 1000 Dockside Road, Royal Albert Dock, London E16 2QU ☎ 020 8430 2000 ✉ damian.atkinson@newham.gov.uk

Recycling & Waste Minimisation: Mr Gary Alderson , Director - Environmental Services, Newham Dockside, 1000 Dockside Road, Royal Albert Dock, London E16 2QU ☎ 020 8430 2000 ✉ gary.alderson@newham.gov.uk

Regeneration: Ms Deirdra Armsby , Director - Strategic Planning, Regeneration & Olympic Legacy, Newham Dockside, 1000 Dockside Road, Royal Albert Dock, London E16 2QU ☎ 020 8430 2000 ✉ deirdra.armsby@newham.gov.uk

Road Safety: Mr John Biden , Head of Traffic & Transportation, Newham Dockside, 1000 Dockside Road, Royal Albert Dock, London E16 2QU ☎ 020 8430 2000 ✉ john.biden@newham.gov.uk

Social Services (Adult): Miss Grainne Siggins , Director of Adult Social Care, Newham Dockside, 1000 Dockside Road, Royal Albert Dock, London E16 2QU ✉ grainne.siggins@newham.gov.uk

Social Services (Children): Mr James Thomas , Director - Children's Services, Newham Dockside, 1000 Dockside Road, Royal Albert Dock, London E16 2QU ☎ 020 8430 2000 ✉ james.thomas@newham.gov.uk

Public Health: Ms Meradin Peachey , Director - Public Health, Newham Dockside, 1000 Dockside Road, Royal Albert Dock, London E16 2QU ☎ 020 8430 2000 ✉ meradin.peachey@newham.gov.uk

Staff Training: Mrs Jan Douglas , Deputy Director of Strategic People Services, Newham Dockside, 1000 Dockside Road, Royal Albert Dock, London E16 2QU ☎ 020 8430 2000 ✉ jan.douglas@newham.gov.uk

Town Centre: Ms Deirdra Armsby , Director - Strategic Planning, Regeneration & Olympic Legacy, Newham Dockside, 1000 Dockside Road, Royal Albert Dock, London E16 2QU ☎ 020 8430 2000 ✉ deirdra.armsby@newham.gov.uk

Traffic Management: Mr John Biden , Head of Traffic & Transportation, Newham Dockside, 1000 Dockside Road, Royal Albert Dock, London E16 2QU ☎ 020 8430 2000 ✉ john.biden@newham.gov.uk

Transport: Mr John Biden , Head of Traffic & Transportation, Newham Dockside, 1000 Dockside Road, Royal Albert Dock, London E16 2QU ☎ 020 8430 2000 ✉ john.biden@newham.gov.uk

NEWHAM

Transport Planner: Mr John Biden , Head of Traffic & Transportation, Newham Dockside, 1000 Dockside Road, Royal Albert Dock, London E16 2QU ☎ 020 8430 2000
john.biden@newham.gov.uk

Waste Collection and Disposal: Mr Jarlath Griffin , Head of Operations, Newham Dockside, 1000 Dockside Road, Royal Albert Dock, London E16 2QU ☎ 020 8430 2000
jarlath.griffin@newham.gov.uk

Waste Management: Mr Gary Alderson , Director - Environmental Services, Newham Dockside, 1000 Dockside Road, Royal Albert Dock, London E16 2QU ☎ 020 8430 2000
gary.alderson@newham.gov.uk

COUNCILLORS

***Mayor* Wales**, Robin (LAB - No Ward)
Mayor@newham.gov.uk

***Deputy Mayor* Hudson**, Lester (LAB - Wall End)
lester.hudson@newham.gov.uk

Abdulmuhit, Hanif (LAB - Green Street West)
hanif.abdulmuhit@newham.gov.uk

Akiwowo, Seyi (LAB - Forest Gate North)
seyi.akiwowo@newham.gov.uk

Alarice, Aleen (LAB - Plaistow South)
aleen.alarice@newham.gov.uk

Alexander, Jose (LAB - Green Street East)
jose.alexander@newham.gov.uk

Baikie, Andrew (LAB - Little Ilford)
andrew.baikie@newham.gov.uk

Beckles, James (LAB - Plaistow North)
james.beckles@newham.gov.uk

Bourne, Freda (LAB - West Ham)
freda.bourne@newham.gov.uk

Brayshaw, Steve (LAB - Royal Docks)
steve.brayshaw@newham.gov.uk

Chowdhury, Ayesha (LAB - Beckton)
ayesha.chowdhury@newham.gov.uk

Christie, David (LAB - Beckton)
david.christie@newham.gov.uk

Clark, Ken (LAB - Little Ilford)
ken.clark@newham.gov.uk

Clarke, Frances (LAB - Wall End)
frances.clarke@newham.gov.uk

Collier, Bryan (LAB - Canning Town South)
bryan.collier@newham.gov.uk

Corbett, Ian (LAB - East Ham Central)
ian.corbett@newham.gov.uk

Corbett, Jo (LAB - Manor Park)
jo.corbett@newham.gov.uk

Crawford, Richard (LAB - Stratford and New Town)
richard.crawford@newham.gov.uk

Desai, Unmesh (LAB - East Ham Central)
unmesh.desai@newham.gov.uk

Easter, Ann (LAB - Canning Town North)
ann.easter@newham.gov.uk

Fiaz, Rokhsana (LAB - Custom House)
rokhsana.fiaz@newham.gov.uk

Fiberesima, Charity (LAB - Boleyn)
charity.fiberesima@newham.gov.uk

Furness, Clive (LAB - Canning Town North)
clive.furness@newham.gov.uk

Gray, John (LAB - West Ham)
john.gray@newham.gov.uk

Griffiths, Alan (LAB - Canning Town South)
alan.griffiths@newham.gov.uk

Gulamussen, Zuber (LAB - East Ham North)
zuber.gulamussen@newham.gov.uk

Holland, Patricia (LAB - Custom House)
patricia.holland@newham.gov.uk

Hussain, Forhad (LAB - Plaistow North)
forhad.hussain@newham.gov.uk

Ibrahim, Idris (LAB - Green Street West)
idris.ibrahim@newham.gov.uk

Khan, Obaid (LAB - Boleyn)
obaid.khan@newham.gov.uk

Laguda, Joy (LAB - Plaistow North)
joy.laguda@newham.gov.uk

Marriott, Julianne (LAB - East Ham Central)
julianne.marriott@newham.gov.uk

Masters, Susan (LAB - East Ham South)
susan.masters@newham.gov.uk

McAlmont, Anthony (LAB - Royal Docks)
anthony.mcalmont@newham.gov.uk

McAuley, Conor (LAB - Custom House)
conor.mcauley@newham.gov.uk

McLean, Charlene (LAB - Stratford and New Town)
charlene.mclean@newham.gov.uk

Murphy, Patrick (LAB - Royal Docks)
patrick.murphy@newham.gov.uk

Nazeer, Farah (LAB - Little Ilford)
farah.nazeer@newham.gov.uk

Nekiwala, Firoza (LAB - East Ham North)
firoza.nekiwala@newham.gov.uk

Noor, Ahmed (LAB - Plaistow South)
ahmed.noor@newham.gov.uk

Patel, Mas (LAB - Forest Gate South)
mas.patel@newham.gov.uk

Patel, Mukesh (LAB - Green Street East)
mukesh.patel@newham.gov.uk

Patel, Salim (LAB - Manor Park)
salim.patel@newham.gov.uk

Paul, Terence (LAB - Stratford and New Town)
terence.paul@newham.gov.uk

Peppiatt, Quintin (LAB - East Ham South)
quintin.peppiatt@newham.gov.uk

Rahman, Rohima (LAB - Green Street East)
rohima.rahman@newham.gov.uk

Rahman, Tahmina (LAB - Green Street West)
tahmina.rahman@newham.gov.uk

Robinson, Ellie (LAB - Forest Gate North)
ellie.robinson@newham.gov.uk

Sathianesan, Paul (LAB - East Ham North)
paul.sathianesan@newham.gov.uk

Scoresby, Kay (LAB - Canning Town North)
kay.scoresby@newham.gov.uk

Shah, Lakmini (LAB - East Ham South)
lakmini.shah@newham.gov.uk

Singh, Amarjit (LAB - Manor Park)
amarjit.singh@newham.gov.uk

Sparrowhawk, Ted (LAB - Wall End)
ted.sparrowhawk@newham.gov.uk

Thomas, Sheila (LAB - Canning Town South)
sheila.thomas@newham.gov.uk

Tripp, Rachel (LAB - Forest Gate North)
rachel.tripp@newham.gov.uk

Vaughan, Winston (LAB - Forest Gate South)
winston.vaughan@newham.gov.uk

Virdee, Harvinder (LAB - Boleyn)
harvinder.virdee@newham.gov.uk

Walls, Dianne (LAB - Forest Gate South)
dianne.walls@newham.gov.uk

Whitworth, John (LAB - West Ham)
john.whitworth@newham.gov.uk

Wilson, Neil (LAB - Plaistow South)
neil.wilson@newham.gov.uk

Wilson, Toni (LAB - Beckton)
toni.wilson@newham.gov.uk

POLITICAL COMPOSITION
LAB: 61

COMMITTEE CHAIRS

Audit: Mr Lester Hudson

Children & Young People: Ms Kay Scoresby

Development: Mr Mukesh Patel

Development: Mr Ken Clark

Health & Social Care: Ms Dianne Walls

Health & Wellbeing: Mr Clive Furness

Licensing: Mr Ian Corbett

Newport City W

Newport City Council, Civic Centre, Newport NP20 4UR
☎ 01633 656656 🖷 01633 656611 ✉ info@newport.gov.uk
🖳 www.newport.gov.uk

FACTS AND FIGURES
Parliamentary Constituencies: Newport East , Newport West
EU Constituencies: Wales
Election Frequency: Elections are of whole council

PRINCIPAL OFFICERS

Chief Executive: Mr Will Godfrey , Chief Executive, Civic Centre, Newport NP20 4UR ☎ 01633 232002 ✉ will.godfrey@newport.gov.uk

Assistant Chief Executive: Ms Sheila Davies , Strategic Director - Place, Civic Centre, Newport NP20 4UR ☎ 01633 232501 ✉ sheila.davies@newport.gov.uk

Assistant Chief Executive: Mr Mike Nicholson , Strategic Director - People, Civic Centre, Newport NP20 4UR ☎ 01633 656656 ✉ mike.nicholson@newport.gov.uk

Children / Youth Services: Mr Mike Lewis , Museums & Heritage Officer, Civic Centre, Newport NP20 4UR ☎ 01633 235249 ✉ mike.lewis@newport.gov.uk

Civil Registration: Ms Shan Jenkins , Registration Services Manager, Register Office, The Mansion House, 4 Stow Park Circle, Newport NP20 4HE ☎ 01633 414774

PR / Communications: Mr Jonathan Hollins , Communications & Marketing Manager, Civic Centre, Newport NP20 4UR ☎ 01633 210454 ✉ jonathan.hollins@newport.gov.uk

Community Safety: Ms Helen Wilkie, Public Protection Manager, Civic Centre, Newport NP20 4UR ☎ 01633 851695 ✉ helen.wilkie@newport.gov.uk

Computer Management: Mr Mark Neilson, Head of Customer & Digital Innovation, Civic Centre, Newport NP20 4UR ☎ 01633 851563 ✉ mark.neilson@newport.gov.uk

Consumer Protection and Trading Standards: Ms Helen Wilkie, Public Protection Manager, Civic Centre, Newport NP20 4UR ☎ 01633 851695 ✉ helen.wilkie@newport.gov.uk

Customer Service: Ms Leanne Rowlands , Customer Services Manager, Information Station, Old Station Building, Queensway, Newport NP20 4AX ☎ 01633 851560 ✉ leanne.rowlands@newport.gov.uk

Economic Development: Ms Sheila Davies , Strategic Director - Place, Civic Centre, Newport NP20 4UR ☎ 01633 232501 ✉ sheila.davies@newport.gov.uk

Education: Mr James Harris , Chief Education Officer, Civic Centre, Newport NP20 4UR ☎ 01495 355419; 01633 232258 🖷 01495 355900 ✉ james.harris@newport.gov.uk

E-Government: Mr Mark Neilson, Head of Customer & Digital Innovation, Civic Centre, Newport NP20 4UR ☎ 01633 851563 ✉ mark.neilson@newport.gov.uk

Electoral Registration: Mr Phillip Johnson , Electoral Registration Manager, Civic Centre, Newport NP20 4UR ☎ 01633 210742 ✉ phillip.johnson@newport.gov.uk

Emergency Planning: Mr Alan Young, Civil Contingencies Manager, Civic Centre, Newport NP20 4UR ☎ 01633 210591 ✉ alan.young@newport.gov.uk

Environmental Health: Ms Helen Wilkie, Public Protection Manager, Civic Centre, Newport NP20 4UR ☎ 01633 851695 ✉ helen.wilkie@newport.gov.uk

NEWPORT CITY

Finance: Mr Meirion Rushworth , Head of Finance, Civic Centre, Newport NP20 4UR ☎ 01633 210644 ✉ meirion.rushworth@newport.gov.uk

Grounds Maintenance: Mr Philip Matley , Interim Head of Streetscene, Civic Centre, Newport NP20 4UR ☎ 01633 656656 ✉ philip.matley@newport.gov.uk

Health and Safety: Ms Debra Wood-Lawson , Head of People & Business Changes, Civic Centre, Newport NP20 4UR ☎ 01633 210954 ✉ debra.wood-lawson@newport.gov.uk

Highways: Mr Philip Matley , Interim Head of Streetscene, Civic Centre, Newport NP20 4UR ☎ 01633 656656 ✉ philip.matley@newport.gov.uk

Housing: Mr Mike Jones , Housing & Property Manager, Civic Centre, Newport NP20 4UR ☎ 01633 210603 ✉ mike.jones@newport.gov.uk

Legal: Mr Gareth Price, Head of Law & Regulations, Civic Centre, Newport NP20 4UR ☎ 01633 210726 ✉ gareth.price@newport.gov.uk

Licensing: Ms Helen Wilkie, Public Protection Manager, Civic Centre, Newport NP20 4UR ☎ 01633 851695 ✉ helen.wilkie@newport.gov.uk

Lighting: Mr Philip Matley , Interim Head of Streetscene, Civic Centre, Newport NP20 4UR ☎ 01633 656656 ✉ philip.matley@newport.gov.uk

Member Services: Mr Richard Jefferies , Chief Democratic Services Officer, Civic Centre, Newport NP20 4UR ☎ 01633 210729 ✉ richard.jefferies@newport.gov.uk

Partnerships: Mr Rhys Cornwall , Framework Partnership Manager, Civic Centre, Newport NP20 4UR ☎ 01633 210649 ✉ rhys.cornwall@newport.gov.uk

Personnel / HR: Ms Debra Wood-Lawson , Head of People & Business Changes, Civic Centre, Newport NP20 4UR ☎ 01633 210954 ✉ debra.wood-lawson@newport.gov.uk

Procurement: Mr Richard Leake , Strategic Procurement Officer, Civic Centre, Newport NP20 4UR ☎ 01633 210686 ✉ richard.leake@newport.gov.uk

Recycling & Waste Minimisation: Mr Malcolm Lane, Environmental Services Manager, Civic Centre, Newport NP20 4UR ☎ 01633 232709 ✉ malcolm.lane@newport.gov.uk

Regeneration: Ms Sheila Davies , Strategic Director - Place, Civic Centre, Newport NP20 4UR ☎ 01633 232501 ✉ sheila.davies@newport.gov.uk

Social Services: Mr Mike Nicholson , Strategic Director - People, Civic Centre, Newport NP20 4UR ☎ 01633 656656 ✉ mike.nicholson@newport.gov.uk

Social Services (Adult): Mr Jonathan Griffiths , Head of Adult & Community Services, Civic Centre, Newport NP20 4UR ☎ 01633 210241 ✉ jonathan.griffiths@newport.gov.uk

Social Services (Children): Ms Sally Jenkins , Integrated Head of Children & Family Services, Civic Centre, Newport NP20 4UR ☎ 01633 210725 ✉ sally.jenkins@newport.gov.uk

Staff Training: Ms Debra Wood-Lawson , Head of People & Business Changes, Civic Centre, Newport NP20 4UR ☎ 01633 210954 ✉ debra.wood-lawson@newport.gov.uk

Street Scene: Mr John Lamb , Head of Streetscene, Civic Centre, Newport NP20 4UR

Tourism: Ms Lynne Richards, Tourism Officer, Civic Centre, Newport NP20 4UR ☎ 01633 233327 ✉ lynne.richards@newport.gov.uk

Transport: Ms Tracy McAdam , Integrated Transport Unit Manager, Telford Depot, Newport NP19 0ES ☎ 01633 851738 ✉ tracy.mcadam@newport.gov.uk

Waste Collection and Disposal: Mr Malcolm Lane, Environmental Services Manager, Civic Centre, Newport NP20 4UR ☎ 01633 232709 ✉ malcolm.lane@newport.gov.uk

Waste Management: Mr Malcolm Lane, Environmental Services Manager, Civic Centre, Newport NP20 4UR ☎ 01633 232709 ✉ malcolm.lane@newport.gov.uk

Children's Play Areas: Mr Mike McGow , Parks & Outdoor Recreation Manager, Civic Centre, Newport NP20 4UR ☎ 01633 232830 ✉ mike.mcgow@newport.gov.uk

COUNCILLORS

***Mayor* Thomas**, Herbert (LAB - Gaer)
herbert.thomas@newport.gov.uk

***Deputy Mayor* Thomas**, Kate (LAB - Stow Hill)
kate.thomas@newport.gov.uk

***Leader of the Council* Bright**, Bob (LAB - Ringland)
bob.bright@newport.gov.uk

***Deputy Leader of the Council* Truman**, Ray (LAB - Alway)
ray.truman@newport.gov.uk

Ali, Omar (LAB - Pillgwenlly)
omar.ali@newport.gov.uk

Al-Nuaimi, Miqdad (LAB - Stow Hill)
miqdad.al-nuaimi@newport.gov.uk

Atwell, David (CON - Langstone)
david.atwell@newport.gov.uk

Bond, Tom (LAB - Rogerstone)
tom.bond@newport.gov.uk

Cockeram, Paul (LAB - Shaftesbury)
paul.cokeram@newport.gov.uk

Cornelious, Margaret (CON - Graig)
margaret.cornelious@newport.gov.uk

Corten, Emma (LAB - Ringland)
emma.corten@newport.gov.uk

Critchley, Ken (LAB - Liswerry)
ken.critchley@newport.gov.uk

Davies, Deb (LAB - Beechwood)
deborah.davies@newport.gov.uk

Delahaye, Val (LAB - Bettws)
valerie.delahaye@newport.gov.uk

Evans, Matthew (CON - Allt-yr-yn)
matthew.evans@newport.gov.uk

Evans, Chris (LAB - Rogerstone)
chris.evans@newport.gov.uk

Ferris, Charles (CON - Allt-yr-yn)
charles.ferris@newport.gov.uk

Fouweather, David (CON - Allt-yr-yn)
david.fouweather@newport.gov.uk

Garland, Emma (LAB - St. Julians)
emma.garland@newport.gov.uk

Giles, Gail (LAB - Caerleon)
gail.giles@newport.gov.uk

Guy, John (LAB - Alway)
john.guy@newport.gov.uk

Hannon, Paul (LAB - Beechwood)
paul.hannon@newport.gov.uk

Harvey, Debbie (LAB - Alway)
debbie.harvey@newport.gov.uk

Hayat, Ibrahim (LAB - Pillgwenlly)
ibrahim.hayat@newport.gov.uk

Huntley, Paul (LAB - Caerleon)
paul.huntley@newport.gov.uk

Hutchings, Rhys (LAB - St. Julians)
rhys.hutchings@newport.gov.uk

Jeavons, Roger (LAB - Liswerry)
roger.jeavons@newport.gov.uk

Jenkins, Christine (LAB - Victoria)
christine.jenkins@newport.gov.uk

Kellaway, Martyn (CON - Llanwern)
martyn.kellaway@newport.gov.uk

Linton, Malcolm (LAB - Ringland)
malcolm.linton@newport.gov.uk

Maxfield, Christine (LAB - Malpas)
christine.maxfield@newport.gov.uk

Mayer, David (LAB - Malpas)
david.mayer@newport.gov.uk

Mlewa, Sally (LAB - Rogerstone)
sally.mlewa@newport.gov.uk

Mogford, Ray (CON - Langstone)
ray.mogford@newport.gov.uk

Morris, Allan (LAB - Liswerry)
allan.morris@newport.gov.uk

Mudd, Jane (LAB - Malpas)
jane.mudd@newport.gov.uk

Poole, Bob (LAB - Shaftesbury)
bob.poole@newport.gov.uk

Rahman, Majid (LAB - Victoria)
majid.rahman@newport.gov.uk

Richards, John (LAB - Liswerry)
john.richards@newport.gov.uk

Spencer, Mark (LAB - Beechwood)
mark.spencer@newport.gov.uk

Suller, Tom (CON - Marshfield)
tom.suller@newport.gov.uk

Suller, Cliff (LAB - Caerleon)
cliff.suller@newport.gov.uk

Townsend, Ed (LD - St. Julians)
ed.townsend@newport.gov.uk

Trigg, Noel (IND - Bettws)
.oel.trigg@newport.gov.uk

Watkins, Trevor (LAB - Tredegar Park)
trevor.watkins@newport.gov.uk

Whitcutt, Mark (LAB - Gaer)
mark.whitcutt@newport.gov.uk

White, Richard (CON - Marshfield)
richard.white@newport.gov.uk

Whitehead, Kevin (IND - Bettws)
kevin.whitehead@newport.gov.uk

Wilcox, Deborah (LAB - Gaer)
debbie.wilcox@newport.gov.uk

Williams, David (CON - Graig)
david.williams@newport.gov.uk

POLITICAL COMPOSITION

LAB: 37, CON: 10, IND: 2, LD: 1

COMMITTEE CHAIRS

Licensing: Mr Cliff Suller

Planning: Mr Paul Huntley

Planning & Development: Mr David Atwell

Newry City, Mourne & Down District N

Newry City, Mourne & Down District, Newry City, Mourne & Down District, Monaghan Row, Newry BT35 8DJ
☎ 03000 132233 info@nmandd.org www.newrymournedown.org

PRINCIPAL OFFICERS

Chief Executive: Mr Liam Hannaway , Chief Executive, Newry City, Mourne & Down District, Monaghan Row, Newry BT35 8DJ

Senior Management: Mr Eddy Curtis , Strategic Planning & Performance Director, Newry City, Mourne & Down District, Monaghan Row, Newry BT35 8DJ

Senior Management: Mr M Lipsett , Director of Community Engagement, Health & Wellbeing & Leisure, Newry City, Mourne & Down District, Monaghan Row, Newry BT35 8DJ

Senior Management: Ms Canice O'Rourke , Director of Environmental Services, Newry City, Mourne & Down District, Monaghan Row, Newry BT35 8DJ

NEWRY CITY, MOURNE & DOWN DISTRICT

Senior Management: Mrs Marie Ward , Group Chief Building Control Officer, Newry City, Mourne & Down District, Monaghan Row, Newry BT35 8DJ

Building Control: Mrs Marie Ward , Group Chief Building Control Officer, Newry City, Mourne & Down District, Monaghan Row, Newry BT35 8DJ

Corporate Services: Mr J McBride , Change Manager, Newry City, Mourne & Down District, Monaghan Row, Newry BT35 8DJ

Environmental / Technical Services: Ms Canice O'Rourke , Director of Environmental Services, Newry City, Mourne & Down District, Monaghan Row, Newry BT35 8DJ

Leisure and Cultural Services: Mr M Lipsett , Director of Community Engagement, Health & Wellbeing & Leisure, Newry City, Mourne & Down District, Monaghan Row, Newry BT35 8DJ

Planning: Mr Eddy Curtis , Strategic Planning & Performance Director, Newry City, Mourne & Down District, Monaghan Row, Newry BT35 8DJ

COUNCILLORS

***Mayor* Hughes**, Daire (SF - Fews)
daire.hughes@sinnfein.ie

***Deputy Mayor* Quinn**, Brian (SDLP - The Mournes)
brian.quinn@newryandmourne.gov.uk

Burns, William (DUP - The Mournes)
william.burns@newryandmourne.gov.uk

Carr, Michael (SDLP - Crotlieve)
michael.carr@newryandmourne.gov.uk

Casey, Charlie (SF - Newry Town)
charlie.casey@newryandmourne.gov.uk

Curran, Brendan (IND - Newry Town)
brendan.curran@newryandmourne.gov.uk

Donnelly, Geraldine (SDLP - Slieve Gullion)
geraldine.donnelly@newryandmourne.gov.uk

Doran, Sean (SF - The Mournes)
sean.doran@newryandmourne.gov.uk

Ennis, Sinead (SF - Crotlieve)
sinead.ennis@sinnfein.ie

Feehan, John (SDLP - Fews)
john.feehan@newryandmourne.gov.uk

Feely, Frank (SDLP - Newry Town)
frank.feely@newryandmourne.gov.uk

Fitzpatrick, Gillian (SDLP - Crotlieve)
gillian.fitzpatrick@newryandmourne.gov.uk

Flynn, A (SF - Slieve Gullion)

Harte, Valerie (SF - Newry Town)
valerie.harte@newryandmourne.gov.uk

Hearty, Terry (SF - Slieve Gullion)
terry.hearty@newryandmourne.gov.uk

Hyland, David (IND - Newry Town)
david.hyland@newryandmourne.gov.uk

Kimmins, Liz (SF - Slieve Gullion)
liz.kimmins@sinnfien.ie

Larkin, Mickey (SF - Slieve Gullion)
micky.larkin@sinnfien.ie

McArdle, John (SDLP - Newry Town)
john.mcardle@newryandmourne.gov.uk

McAteer, Declan (SDLP - Crotlieve)
declan.mcateer@newryandmourne.gov.uk

McGreevy, Connaire (SDLP - Crotlieve)
connaire.mcgreevy@newryandmourne.gov.uk

McKee, Harold (UUP - The Mournes)
harold.mckee@newryandmourne.gov.uk

Moffett, A (UUP - Fews)

Mulgrew, Roisin (SF - Fews)
roisin.mulgrew@sinnfein.ie

Murphy, Mick (SF - Crotlieve)
mick.murphy@newryandmourne.gov.uk

Ó Muirí, Barry (SF - Fews)
barra.omuiri@sinnfein.ie

Patterson, Jackie (IND - Newry Town)
jackie.patterson@newryandmourne.gov.uk

Reilly, Henry (UKIP - The Mournes)
henry.reilly@newryandmourne.gov.uk

Ruane, Michael (SF - Crotlieve)
michael.ruane@newryandmourne.gov.uk

Taylor, David (UUP - Fews)
david.taylor@newryandmourne.gov.uk

POLITICAL COMPOSITION

SF: 13, SDLP: 9, IND: 3, UUP: 3, DUP: 1, UKIP: 1

Norfolk C

Norfolk County Council, County Hall, Martineau Lane, Norwich NR1 2DH
☎ 0344 800 8020 🖷 0844 800 8012 ✉ information@norfolk.gov.uk
💻 www.norfolk.gov.uk

FACTS AND FIGURES

Parliamentary Constituencies: Broadland, Great Yarmouth, Norfolk Mid, Norfolk North, Norfolk North West, Norfolk South, Norfolk South West, Norwich North, Norwich South
EU Constituencies: Eastern
Election Frequency: Elections are of whole council

PRINCIPAL OFFICERS

Chief Executive: Dr Wendy Thomson , Managing Director, County Hall, Martineau Lane, Norwich NR1 2DH ☎ 01603 222000 ✉ wendy.thomson@norfolk.gov.uk

Senior Management: Mr Harold Bodmer , Executive Director - Adult Social Services, County Hall, Martineau Lane, Norwich NR1 2DH ☎ 01603 223175 🖷 01603 222301 ✉ harold.bodmer@norfolk.gov.uk

Senior Management: Ms Anne Gibson, Executive Director - Resources, County Hall, Martineau Lane, Norwich NR1 2DH ☎ 01603 222609 ✉ anne.gibson@norfolk.gov.uk

Senior Management: Mr Tom McCabe , Executive Director - Community & Environmental Services, County Hall, Martineau Lane, Norwich NR1 2DH ☎ 01603 222500 ✉ tom.mccabe@norfolk.gov.uk

Senior Management: Mr Michael Rosen , Executive Director - Children's Services, County Hall, Martineau Lane, Norwich NR1 2DH ☎ 01603 222600 ✉ michael.rosen@norfolk.gov.uk

Senior Management: Dr Louise Smith , Director - Public Health, County Hall, Martineau Lane, Norwich NR1 2DH ☎ 01603 638304 ✉ lousie.smith@norfolk.gov.uk

Senior Management: Mr Peter Timmins , Executive Director - Finance, County Hall, Martineau Lane, Norwich NR1 2DH ☎ 01603 222400 🖷 01603 222694 ✉ peter.timmins@norfolk.gov.uk

Access Officer / Social Services (Disability): Mr Harold Bodmer , Executive Director - Adult Social Services, County Hall, Martineau Lane, Norwich NR1 2DH ☎ 01603 223175 🖷 01603 222301 ✉ harold.bodmer@norfolk.gov.uk

Architect, Building / Property Services: Mr Michael Britch, Managing Director - NPS & Norse Group, Lancaster House, 16 Central Avenue, St Andrews Business Park, Norwich NR7 0HR ☎ 01603 706100 🖷 01603 706102 ✉ mike.britch@nps.co.uk

Catering Services: Mr Peter Hawes, Managing Director - NORSE Commercial Services, Fifers Lane, 280 Fifers Lane, Norwich NR6 6EQ ☎ 01603 894271 ✉ peter.hawes@ncsgrp.co.uk

Children / Youth Services: Mr Gordon Boyd , Assistant Director - Education, County Hall, Martineau Lane, Norwich NR1 2DH ☎ 01603 223492 ✉ gordon.boyd@norfolk.gov.uk

Children / Youth Services: Mr Don Evans , Assistant Director - Performance & Challenge, County Hall, Martineau Lane, Norwich NR1 2DH ☎ 01603 223909 ✉ don.evans@norfolk.gov.uk

Children / Youth Services: Mr Owen Jenkins , Finance Business Partner (Children's Services), County Hall, Martineau Lane, Norwich NR1 2DH ☎ 01603 223160 ✉ owen.jenkins2@norfolk.gov.uk

Children / Youth Services: Ms Cathy Mouser , Assistant Director - Social Work, County Hall, Martineau Lane, Norwich NR1 2DH ☎ 01603 217653 ✉ cathy.mouse@norfolk.gov.uk

Children / Youth Services: Mr Michael Rosen , Executive Director - Children's Services, County Hall, Martineau Lane, Norwich NR1 2DH ☎ 01603 222600 ✉ michael.rosen@norfolk.gov.uk

Children / Youth Services: Ms Elly Starling , Lead HR & OD Business Partner, County Hall, Martineau Lane, Norwich NR1 2DH ☎ 01603 223476 ✉ elly.starling@norfolk.gov.uk

Children / Youth Services: Mr Sal Thirlway , Assistant Director - Early Help, County Hall, Martineau Lane, Norwich NR1 2DH ☎ 01603 223747 ✉ sal.thirlway@norfolk.gov.uk

Civil Registration: Mrs Caroline Clarke , Regulatory Manager, County Hall, Martineau Lane, Norwich NR1 2DH ☎ 01603 222949 ✉ caroline.clarke@norfolk.gov.uk

Civil Registration: Ms Jacqueline Lake , Senior Coroner, 69-75 Thorpe Road, Norwich NR1 1UA ☎ 01603 663302 ✉ norfolk@coroner.norfolk.gov.uk

PR / Communications: Ms Christine Birchall , Manager - Corporate Communications & Marketing, County Hall, Martineau Lane, Norwich NR1 2DH ☎ 01603 222843 🖷 01603 222602 ✉ christine.birchall@norfolk.gov.uk

PR / Communications: Mr Mark Langlands, Media & Public Affairs Manager, County Hall, Martineau Lane, Norwich NR1 2DH ☎ 01603 228888 🖷 01603 222602 ✉ mark.langlands@norfolk.gov.uk

Community Planning: Ms Jo Richardson , Manager - Corporate Planning & Partnerships Manager, County Hall, Martineau Lane, Norwich NR1 2DH ☎ 01603 223816 ✉ jo.richardson@norfolk.gov.uk

Community Safety: Mr Nigel Williams , Chief Fire Officer, F&R Service Headquarters, Whitegates, Hethersett, Norwich NR9 3DN ☎ 0300 123 1386 ✉ nigel.williams@fire.norfolk.gov.uk

Computer Management: Mr Steve Leggetter , Head of ICT, County Hall, Martineau Lane, Norwich NR1 2DH ☎ 0344 800 8020 ✉ steve.leggetter@norfolk.gov.uk

Consumer Protection and Trading Standards: Mrs Sophie Leney , Trading Standards Manager, County Hall, Martineau Lane, Norwich NR1 2DH ☎ 01603 224275 ✉ sophie.leney@norfolk.gov.uk

Contracts: Mr Al Collier , Head - Procurement, County Hall, Martineau Lane, Norwich NR1 2DH ☎ 01603 223372 ✉ al.collier@norfolk.gov.uk

Corporate Services: Mrs Debbie Bartlett , Head - Business Intelligence & Performance, County Hall, Martineau Lane, Norwich NR1 2DH ☎ 01603 222475 ✉ debbie.bartlett@norfolk.gov.uk

Customer Service: Ms Ceri Summer , Customer Access & Development Manager, County Hall, Martineau Lane, Norwich NR1 2DH ☎ 01603 223398 ✉ ceri.summer@norfolk.gov.uk

Direct Labour: Mr Peter Hawes, Managing Director - NORSE Commercial Services, The Annex, County Hall, Norwich NR1 2UQ ☎ 01603 894271 ✉ peter.hawes@ncsgrp.co.uk

Economic Development: Ms Fiona McDiarmid , Assistant Director - Economic Development & Strategy, County Hall, Martineau Lane, Norwich NR1 2DH ☎ 01603 223810 🖷 01603 223345 ✉ fiona.mcdiarmid@norfolk.gov.uk

Education: Mr Richard Snowden , Head - Schools Admissions Service, County Hall, Martineau Lane, Norwich NR1 2DH ☎ 01603 223489 ✉ richard.snowden@norfolk.gov.uk

Emergency Planning: Mr Nigel Williams , Chief Fire Officer, F&R Service Headquarters, Whitegates, Hethersett, Norwich NR9 3DN ☎ 0300 123 1386 ✉ nigel.williams@fire.norfolk.gov.uk

Energy Management: Mr David Collinson, Assistant Director - Community & Environmental Services, County Hall, Martineau Lane, Norwich NR1 2DH ☎ 01603 222253 🖷 01603 222889 ✉ david.collinson@norfolk.gov.uk

NORFOLK

Estates, Property & Valuation: Mr Michael Britch, Managing Director - NPS & Norse Group, Lancaster House, 16 Central Avenue, St Andrews Business Park, Norwich NR7 0HR ☎ 01603 706100 🖷 01603 706102 🖱 mike.britch@nps.co.uk

European Liaison: Ms Karen Gibson , Partnership & Delivery Manager, County Hall, Martineau Lane, Norwich NR1 2DH ☎ 01603 222598 🖱 karen.gibson@norfolk.gov.uk

Facilities: Mr Graham Wray, Facilities Manager, NPS Property Consultants Ltd, Building Surveying Group, Martineau Lane, Norwich NR1 1DH ☎ 01603 222554 🖱 graham.wray@nps.gov.uk

Finance: Mr Peter Timmins , Executive Director - Finance, County Hall, Martineau Lane, Norwich NR1 2DH ☎ 01603 222400 🖷 01603 222694 🖱 peter.timmins@norfolk.gov.uk

Pensions: Ms Nicola Mark , Head - Norfolk Pension Fund, Laurence House, 5 St Andrews Hill, Norwich NR2 1AD ☎ 01603 222171 🖱 nicola.mark@norfolk.gov.uk

Fleet Management: Ms Cheryl Hewett , Business Travel Manager, County Hall, Martineau Lane, Norwich NR1 2DH ☎ 01603 223229 🖱 cheryl.hewett@norfolk.gov.uk

Health and Safety: Ms Derryth Wright , Health, Safety & Well-Being Manager, County Hall, Martineau Lane, Norwich NR1 2DH ☎ 01603 222912 🖱 derryth.wright@norfolk.gov.uk

Highways: Ms Tracy Jessop , Assistant Director - Highways & Transport, County Hall, Martineau Lane, Norwich NR1 2DH ☎ 01603 223831 🖱 tracy.jessop@norfolk.gov.uk

Legal: Ms Victoria McNeill, Practice Director, County Hall, Martineau Lane, Norwich NR1 2DH ☎ 01603 223415 🖷 01603 222899 🖱 victoria.mcneill@norfolk.gov.uk

Leisure and Cultural Services: Mrs Jennifer Holland, Assistant Director - Community & Environmental Services & Head of Libraries, County Hall, Martineau Lane, Norwich NR1 2UA ☎ 01603 222272 🖷 01603 222422 🖱 jennifer.holland@norfolk.gov.uk

Leisure and Cultural Services: Mr Steve Miller , Head of Norfolk Museums Service, Shirehall, Norwich NR1 3JQ ☎ 01603 493620 🖱 steve.miller@norfolk.gov.uk

Lifelong Learning: Ms Kerry Furness , Organisation Development Manager, County Hall, Martineau Lane, Norwich NR1 2DH ☎ 01603 222909 🖱 kerry.furness@norfolk.gov.uk

Lifelong Learning: Mrs Jennifer Holland, Assistant Director - Community & Environmental Services & Head of Libraries, County Hall, Martineau Lane, Norwich NR1 2UA ☎ 01603 222272 🖷 01603 222422 🖱 jennifer.holland@norfolk.gov.uk

Lighting: Mr Nick Tupper , Highways Maintenance Manager, County Hall, Martineau Lane, Norwich NR1 2DH ☎ 01603 224290 🖱 nick.tupper@norfolk.gov.uk

Member Services: Mr Chris Walton , Head - Democratic Services, County Hall, Martineau Lane, Norwich NR1 2DH ☎ 01603 222620 🖱 chris.walton@norfolk.gov.uk

Partnerships: Mrs Debbie Bartlett , Head - Business Intelligence & Performance, County Hall, Martineau Lane, Norwich NR1 2DH ☎ 01603 222475 🖱 debbie.bartlett@norfolk.gov.uk

Personnel / HR: Ms Audrey Sharp , Acting Head - Human Resources, County Hall, Martineau Lane, Norwich NR1 2DH ☎ 01603 222796 🖷 01603 222970 🖱 audrey.sharp@norfolk.gov.uk

Planning: Mr Tom McCabe , Executive Director - Community & Environmental Services, County Hall, Martineau Lane, Norwich NR1 2DH ☎ 01603 222500 🖱 tom.mccabe@norfolk.gov.uk

Procurement: Mr Al Collier , Head - Procurement, County Hall, Martineau Lane, Norwich NR1 2DH ☎ 01603 223372 🖱 al.collier@norfolk.gov.uk

Public Libraries: Mrs Jennifer Holland, Assistant Director - Community & Environmental Services & Head of Libraries, County Hall, Martineau Lane, Norwich NR1 2UA ☎ 01603 222272 🖷 01603 222422 🖱 jennifer.holland@norfolk.gov.uk

Public Libraries: Mr Gary Tuson , County Archivist, County Hall, Martineau Lane, Norwich NR1 2DH ☎ 01603 222003 🖱 gary.tuson@norfolk.gov.uk

Recycling & Waste Minimisation: Mr David Collinson, Assistant Director - Community & Environmental Services, County Hall, Martineau Lane, Norwich NR1 2DH ☎ 01603 222253 🖷 01603 222889 🖱 david.collinson@norfolk.gov.uk

Regeneration: Ms Fiona McDiarmid , Assistant Director - Economic Development & Strategy, County Hall, Martineau Lane, Norwich NR1 2DH ☎ 01603 223810 🖷 01603 223345 🖱 fiona.mcdiarmid@norfolk.gov.uk

Road Safety: Mr Iain Temperton, Team Manager - Casualty Reduction, Education & Development, County Hall, Martineau Lane, Norwich NR1 2SG ☎ 01603 223348 🖷 01603 222024 🖱 iain.temperton@norfolk.gov.uk

Social Services (Adult): Ms Lorrayne Barrett , Director of Integrated Services, County Hall, Martineau Lane, Norwich NR1 2DH ☎ 01493 448171 🖱 lorrayne.barrett@norfolk.gov.uk

Social Services (Adult): Mr Harold Bodmer, Executive Director - Adult Social Services, County Hall, Martineau Lane, Norwich NR1 2DH ☎ 01603 223175 🖷 01603 222301 🖱 harold.bodmer@norfolk.gov.uk

Social Services (Adult): Ms Lorna Bright , Assistant Director - Social Work & Occupational Therapy, County Hall, Martineau Lane, Norwich NR1 2DH ☎ 01602 223960 🖱 lorna.bright@norfolk.gov.uk

Social Services (Adult): Ms Janice Dane , Assistant Director - Early Help & Prevention, County Hall, Martineau Lane, Norwich NR1 2DH ☎ 01603 223438 🖱 janice.dane@norfolk.gov.uk

Social Services (Adult): Ms Catherine Underwood , Director - Integrated Commissioning, County Hall, Martineau Lane, Norwich NR1 2DH ☎ 01603 224378 🖱 catherine.underwood@norfolk.gov.uk

Public Health: Ms Lucy Macleod , Interim Director - Public Health, County Hall, Martineau Lane, Norwich NR1 2DH ☎ 01603 638304 ✉ lucy.macleod@norfolk.gov.uk

Transport Planner: Ms Tracy Jessop , Assistant Director - Highways & Transport, County Hall, Martineau Lane, Norwich NR1 2DH ☎ 01603 223831 ✉ tracy.jessop@norfolk.gov.uk

Waste Collection and Disposal: Mr Paul Borrett, Waste & Energy Manager, County Hall, Martineau Lane, Norwich NR1 2SG ☎ 01603 222197 ✉ paul.borrett@norfolk.gov.uk

Waste Management: Mr David Collinson, Assistant Director - Community & Environmental Services, County Hall, Martineau Lane, Norwich NR1 2DH ☎ 01603 222253 🖷 01603 222889 ✉ david.collinson@norfolk.gov.uk

COUNCILLORS

***Leader of the Council* Nobbs**, George (LAB - Crome)
george.nobbs@norfolk.gov.uk

***Deputy Leader of the Council* Roper**, Daniel (LD - Hevingham and Spixworth)
daniel.roper@norfolk.gov.uk

***Group Leader* Bearman**, Richard (GRN - Mancroft)
richard.bearman@norfolk.gov.uk

***Group Leader* Coke**, Richard (UKIP - Gayton and Nar Valley)
richard.coke@norfolk.gov.uk

***Group Leader* FitzPatrick**, Tom (CON - Fakenham)
tom.fitzpatrick@norfolk.gov.uk

***Group Leader* Kemp**, Alexanrda (IND - Clenchwarton and King's Lynn South)
alexandra.kemp@norfolk.gov.uk

***Group Leader* Strong**, Marie (LD - Wells)
marie.strong@norfolk.gov.uk

Adams, Anthony (CON - Drayton and Horsford)
anthony.adams@norfolk.gov.uk

Agnew, Stephen (UKIP - Marshland North)
stephen.agnew@norfolk.gov.uk

Aldred, Colin (UKIP - Lothingland)
colin.aldred@norfolk.gov.uk

Askew, Stephen (CON - Guiltcross)
stephen.askew@norfolk.gov.uk

Baker, Michael (UKIP - Holt)
michael.baker@norfolk.gov.uk

Bird, Richard (IND - North Coast)
richard.bird@norfolk.gov.uk

Borrett, Bill (CON - Elmham and Mattishall)
bill.borrett@norfolk.gov.uk

Boswell, Andrew (GRN - Nelson)
andrew.boswell@norfolk.gov.uk

Bremner, Bert (LAB - University)
bert.bremner@norfolk.gov.uk

Brociek-Coulton, Julie (LAB - Sewell)
julie.brociek-coulton@norfolk.gov.uk

Byrne, Alexander (CON - Attleborough)
alexander.byrne@norfolk.gov.uk

Carttiss, Michael (CON - West Flegg)

Castle, Mick (LAB - Yarmouth North and Central)
mick.castle@norfolk.gov.uk

Chamberlin, Jennifer (CON - Diss and Roydon)
jennifer.chamberlin@norfolk.gov.uk

Chenery of Horsbrugh, Michael (CON - Docking)
michael.chenery@norfolk.gov.uk

Childs, Jonathon (UKIP - East Flegg)
jonathon.childs@norfolk.gov.uk

Clancy, Stuart (CON - Taverham)
stuart.clancy@norfolk.gov.uk

Collis, David (LAB - King's Lynn North and Central)
david.collis@norfolk.gov.uk

Corlett, Emma (LAB - Town Close)
emma.corlett@norfolk.gov.uk

Cox, Hilary (CON - Cromer)
hilary.cox@norfolk.gov.uk

Crawford, Denis (UKIP - Thetford East)
denis.crawford@norfolk.gov.uk

Dearnley, Adrian (GRN - Thorpe Hamlet)
adrian.dearnley@norfolk.gov.uk

Dewsbury, Margaret (CON - Hingham)
margaret.dewsbury@norfolk.gov.uk

Dixon, Nigel (CON - Hoveton and Stalham)
nigel.dixon@norfolk.gov.uk

Dobson, John (CON - Dersingham)
john.dobson@norfolk.gov.uk

East, Tim (LD - Costessey)
tim.east@norfolk.gov.uk

Foulger, Colin (CON - Forehoe)
colin.foulger@norfolk.gov.uk

Garrod, Tom (CON - Wroxham)
thomas.garrod@norfolk.gov.uk

Gilmour, Paul (UKIP - Dereham South)
paul.gilmour@norfolk.gov.uk

Grey, Alan (UKIP - Breydon)
alan.grey@norfolk.gov.uk

Gurney, Shelagh (CON - Hellesdon)
shelagh.gurney@norfolk.gov.uk

Hacon, Pat (LAB - Caister-on-Sea)
pat.hacon@norfolk.gov.uk

Hannah, Brian (LD - Sheringham)
brian.hannah@norfolk.gov.uk

Harrison, David (LD - Aylsham)
david.harrison@norfolk.gov.uk

Hebborn, Stan (UKIP - Watton)
stan.hebborn@norfolk.gov.uk

Humphrey, Harry (CON - Marshland South)
harry.humphrey@norfolk.gov.uk

Iles, Brian (CON - Acle)
brian.iles@norfolk.gov.uk

Jermy, Terry (LAB - Thetford West)
terry.jermy@norfolk.gov.uk

Jordan, Cliff (CON - Yare and All Saints)
cliff.jordan@norfolk.gov.uk

Joyce, James (LD - Reepham)
james.joyce@norfolk.gov.uk

Kiddle-Morris, Mark (CON - Necton and Launditch)
mark.kiddle-morris@norfolk.gov.uk

Law, Jason (CON - Freebridge Lynn)
jason.law@norfolk.gov.uk

Leggett, Judy (CON - Old Catton)
judy.leggett@norfolk.gov.uk

Long, Brian (CON - Fincham)
brian.long@norfolk.gov.uk

Mackie, Ian (CON - Thorpe St Andrew)
ian.mackie@norfolk.gov.uk

Monson, Ian (CON - The Brecks)
ian.monson@norfolk.gov.uk

Mooney, Joe (CON - Wymondham)
joe.mooney@norfolk.gov.uk

Morgan, Elizabeth (GRN - Wensum)
elizabeth.morgan@norfolk.gov.uk

Morphew, Steve (LAB - Catton Grove)
steve.morphew@norfolk.gov.uk

Northam, Wyndham (CON - Mundesley)
wyndham.northam@norfolk.gov.uk

Parkinson-Hare, Rex (UKIP - Yarmouth Nelson and Southtown)
rex.parkinson-hare@norfolk.gov.uk

Perkins, Jim (UKIP - Gaywood North and Central)
jim.perkins@norfolk.gov.uk

Plant, Graham (CON - Gorleston St Andrews)

Proctor, Andrew (CON - Blofield and Brundall)
andrew.proctor@norfolk.gov.uk

Ramsbotham, David (UKIP - Melton Constable)
david.ramsbotham@norfolk.gov.uk

Richmond, William (CON - Dereham North)
william.richmond@norfolk.gov.uk

Rumsby, Christine (LAB - Mile Cross)

Sands, Mike (LAB - Bowthorpe)
mike.sands@norfolk.gov.uk

Seward, Eric (LD - North Walsham East)
eric.seward@norfolk.gov.uk

Shaw, Nigel (CON - Woodside)
nigel.shaw@norfolk.gov.uk

Smith, Roger (CON - Henstead)
roger.smith@norfolk.gov.uk

Smyth, Paul (UKIP - Swaffham)
paul.smyth@norfolk.gov.uk

Somerville, Margaret (CON - Clavering)
margaret.somerville@norfolk.gov.uk

Spratt, Beverley (CON - West Depwade)
beverley.spratt@norfolk.gov.uk

Storey, Martin (CON - Feltwell)
martin.storey@norfolk.gov.uk

Thomas, Alison (CON - Long Stratton)
alison.thomas@norfolk.gov.uk

Thomas, David (LD - South Smallburgh)
david.thomas@norfolk.gov.uk

Timewell, John (LD - North Walsham West and Erpingham)
john.timewell@norfolk.gov.uk

Virgo, Judith (CON - Humbleyard)
judith.virgo@norfolk.gov.uk

Walker, Colleen (LAB - Magdalen)
colleen.walker@norfolk.gov.uk

Ward, John (CON - Sprowston)
john.ward@norfolk.gov.uk

Watkins, Brian (LD - Eaton)
brian.watkins@norfolk.gov.uk

Whitaker, Sue (LAB - Lakenham)
sue.whitaker@norfolk.gov.uk

White, Anthony (CON - Downham Market)
anthony.white@norfolk.gov.uk

Wilby, Martin (CON - East Depwade)
martin.wilby@norfolk.gov.uk

Wilkinson, Margaret (LAB - Gaywood South)
margaret.wilkinson@norfolk.gov.uk

POLITICAL COMPOSITION
CON: 40, LAB: 14, UKIP: 13, LD: 10, GRN: 4, IND: 2

COMMITTEE CHAIRS
Adult Social Care: Ms Sue Whitaker

Audit: Mr Ian Mackie

Children's Services: Mr James Joyce

Pensions: Mr Steve Morphew

Planning: Mr Brian Long

North Ayrshire S

North Ayrshire Council, Cunninghame House, Irvine KA12 8EE
☎ 0845 603 0590 🖷 01294 324144 ✉ contactus@north-ayrshire.gov.uk
💻 www.north-ayrshire.gov.uk

FACTS AND FIGURES
Parliamentary Constituencies: Ayrshire North and Arran
EU Constituencies: Scotland
Election Frequency: Elections are of whole council

PRINCIPAL OFFICERS
Chief Executive: Ms Elma Murray , Chief Executive, Cunninghame House, Irvine KA12 8EE ☎ 01294 324124 🖷 01294 324114
✉ asproul@north-ayrshire.gov.uk

Senior Management: Mr John Butcher , Executive Director - Education & Youth Employment, Cunninghame House, Irvine KA12 8EE

Senior Management: Ms Iona Colvin , Executive Director - Health & Social Care Partnership, Cunninghame House, Irvine KA12 8EE ☎ 01294 317725 🖷 01294 317702
✉ icolvin@north-ayreshire.gov.uk

Senior Management: Mr Andrew Fraser , Head of Service - Democratic Services, Cunninghame House, Irvine KA12 8EE ☎ 01294 324125 🖷 01294 324144 ✉ afraser@north-ayrshire.gov.uk

Senior Management: Ms Laura Friel , Executive Director - Finance & Corporate Support, Cunninghame House, Irvine KA12 8EE ☎ 01294 324152 🖷 01294 324544 ✉ lfriel@north-ayrshire.gov.uk

Senior Management: Mr Craig Hatton , Executive Director - Place, Cunninghame House, Irvine KA12 8EE ☎ 01294 541514 🖷 01294 541504 ✉ chatton@north-ayrshire.gov.uk

Senior Management: Ms Karen Yeomans , Executive Director - Economy & Communities, Cunninghame House, Irvine KA12 8EE ☎ 01294 324308 🖷 01294 324309 ✉ karenyeomans@north-ayrshire.gov.uk

Access Officer / Social Services (Disability): Ms Louise Kirk, Access Officer, Cunninghame House, Irvine KA12 8EE ☎ 01294 324766 🖷 01294 324372 ✉ lkirk@north-ayrshire.gov.uk

Architect, Building / Property Services: Ms Yvonne Baulk , Head of Physical Environment, Cunninghame House, Irvine KA12 8EE ☎ 01294 324514 🖷 01294 324544 ✉ jdickie@north-ayreshire.gov.uk

Best Value: Mr Andrew Fraser , Head of Service - Democratic Services, Cunninghame House, Irvine KA12 8EE ☎ 01294 324125 🖷 01294 324144 ✉ afraser@north-ayrshire.gov.uk

Building Control: Mr Scott McKenzie , Senior Manager - Protective Services, Cunninghame House, Irvine KA12 8EE ☎ 01294 324347 🖷 01294 324301 ✉ smckenzie@north-ayreshire.gov.uk

Catering Services: Mr Ken Campbell , Facilities Manager, Montgomerie House, 2A Byrehill Drive, West Byrehill Industrial Estate, Kilwinning KA13 6HN ☎ 01294 541523 🖷 01294 541564 ✉ kcampbell@north-ayrshire.gov.u

Children / Youth Services: Mr John McKnight, Senior Manager - Community & Development, Cunninghame House, Irvine KA12 8EE ☎ 01294 468035 🖷 01294 602938 ✉ jmcknight@north-ayrshire.gov.uk

Children / Youth Services: Dr Audrey Sutton , Head of Community & Culture, Cunninghame House, Irvine KA12 8EE ☎ 01294 324414 🖷 01294 324444 ✉ asutton@north-ayrshire.gov.uk

PR / Communications: Ms Lynne McEwan , Corporate Communications Manager, Cunninghame House, Irvine KA12 8EE ☎ 01294 324117 🖷 01294 324154 ✉ lmcewan@north-ayreshire.gov.uk

Community Planning: Ms Morna Rae , Community Planning Team Leader, Cunninghame House, Irvine KA12 8EE ☎ 01294 324117 🖷 01294 324144 ✉ mrae@north-ayreshire.gov.uk

Community Safety: Mr Pat Kelly , Temporary Principal Officer ASB / Community Safety Services, Cunninghame House, Irvine KA12 8EE ☎ 01294 314672 ✉ pkelly@northayrshire.gov.uk

Computer Management: Mr Alan Blakely , IT Manager, Cunninghame House, Irvine KA12 8EE ☎ 01294 324272 🖷 01294 324274 ✉ ablakely@north-ayrshire.gov.uk

Consumer Protection and Trading Standards: Mr Andy Moynihan, Team Manager (Trading Standards), Bridgegate House, Bridgegate, Irvine KA12 8BD ☎ 01294 310117 🖷 01294 310104 ✉ amoynihan@north-ayrshire.gov.uk

Contracts: Mr Andrew Fraser , Head of Service - Democratic Services, Cunninghame House, Irvine KA12 8EE ☎ 01294 324125 🖷 01294 324144 ✉ afraser@north-ayrshire.gov.uk

Corporate Services: Mr Andrew Fraser , Head of Service - Democratic Services, Cunninghame House, Irvine KA12 8EE ☎ 01294 324125 🖷 01294 324144 ✉ afraser@north-ayrshire.gov.uk

Customer Service: Ms Esther Gunn , Customer Services Manager, Bridgegate House, Irvine KA12 8DB ☎ 01294 323690 🖷 01294 323974 ✉ egunn@north-ayrshire.gov.uk

Economic Development: Ms Karen Yeomans , Executive Director - Economy & Communities, Cunninghame House, Irvine KA12 8EE ☎ 01294 324308 🖷 01294 324309 ✉ karenyeomans@north-ayrshire.gov.uk

Electoral Registration: Ms Elma Murray , Chief Executive, Cunninghame House, Irvine KA12 8EE ☎ 01294 324124 🖷 01294 324114 ✉ asproul@north-ayrshire.gov.uk

Emergency Planning: Ms Jane McGeorge , Civil Contingencies Co-ordinator, Ayrshire Civil Contingencies Team, Building 372, Alpha Freight Area, Robertson Road, Glasgow Prestwick Airport, Prestwick KA9 2PL ☎ 01292 692182 🖷 01292 692184 ✉ jmcgeorge@north-ayrshire.gov.uk

Energy Management: Ms Jennifer Wraith , Senior Energy Officer, Perceton House, Irvine KA11 2AL ✉ jwraith@north-ayrshire.gov.uk

Environmental / Technical Services: Ms Karen Yeomans , Executive Director - Economy & Communities, Cunninghame House, Irvine KA12 8EE ☎ 01294 324308 🖷 01294 324309 ✉ karenyeomans@north-ayrshire.gov.uk

Environmental Health: Mr Hugh McGhee , Team Manager - Public Health & Pollution, Cunninghame House, Irvine KA12 8EE ☎ 01294 324392 🖷 01294 324360 ✉ hmcghee@north-ayreshire.gov.uk

Estates, Property & Valuation: Mr Alastair Ross , Asset Manager, Cunninghame House, Irvine KA12 8EE ✉ aross@north-ayreshire.gov.uk

European Liaison: Ms Linda Aird, European Officer, Perceton House, Irvine KA11 2AL ☎ 01294 225195 🖷 01294 225184 ✉ lindaaird@north-ayrshire.gov.uk

Events Manager: Ms Pauline Palmer , Senior Communications Officer - Marketing & Events, Cunninghame House, Irvine KA12 8EE ☎ 01294 324158 🖷 01294 324154 ✉ ppalmer@north-ayreshire.gov.uk

NORTH AYRSHIRE

Finance: Ms Laura Friel , Executive Director - Finance & Corporate Support, Cunninghame House, Irvine KA12 8EE ☎ 01294 324152 🖷 01294 324544 ✉ lfriel@north-ayrshire.gov.uk

Fleet Management: Mr Gordon Mitchell , Transport Manager, Montgomerie House, 2A Byrehill Drive, West Byrehill Industrial Estate, Kilwinning KA13 6HN ☎ 01294 541601 🖷 01294 551604 ✉ gmitchell@north-ayreshire.gov.uk

Grounds Maintenance: Mr Wallace Turpie , Operations Manager - Sreetscene, Perceton House, Irvine KA11 2AL ☎ 01294 324653 🖷 01294 225244 ✉ chatton@north-ayreshire.gov.uk

Health and Safety: Ms Catherine Reilly , Team Manager - Food, Health & Safety, Cunninghame House, Irvine KA12 8EE ☎ 01294 324355 ✉ creilly@north-ayrshire.gov.uk

Home Energy Conservation: Ms Jennifer Wraith , Senior Energy Officer, Perceton House, Irvine KA11 2AL ✉ jwraith@north-ayrshire.gov.uk

Housing: Ms Yvonne Baulk , Head of Physical Environment, Cunninghame House, Irvine KA12 8EE ☎ 01294 324514 🖷 01294 324544 ✉ jdickie@north-ayreshire.gov.uk

Housing Maintenance: Mr Michael McIntosh , Senior Mantainence Officer, Perceton House, Irvine KA11 2AL ☎ 01294 225078 ✉ mmcintosh@north-ayreshire.gov.uk

Legal: Mr Andrew Fraser , Head of Service - Democratic Services, Cunninghame House, Irvine KA12 8EE ☎ 01294 324125 🖷 01294 324144 ✉ afraser@north-ayrshire.gov.uk

Licensing: Mr William O'Brien , Senior Solicitor - Licensing, District Court & Licensing Office, Townshouse, Irvine KA12 0AZ ☎ 01294 311998 🖷 01294 312170 ✉ nalexander@north-ayreshire.gov.uk

Lighting: Ms Karen Yeomans , Executive Director - Economy & Communities, Cunninghame House, Irvine KA12 8EE ☎ 01294 324308 🖷 01294 324309 ✉ karenyeomans@north-ayrshire.gov.uk

Member Services: Mr Andrew Fraser , Head of Service - Democratic Services, Cunninghame House, Irvine KA12 8EE ☎ 01294 324125 🖷 01294 324144 ✉ afraser@north-ayrshire.gov.uk

Parking: Mr David Lodge , Supervisory Engineer, Cunninghame House, Irvine KA12 8EE ☎ 01294 324744 🖷 01294 324344 ✉ dlodge@north-ayreshire.gov.uk

Personnel / HR: Mr Gavin Macgregor , Head of Human Resources & Organisational Development, Cunninghame House, Irvine KA12 8EE ☎ 01294 324651 🖷 01294 324664 ✉ gmacgregor@north-ayrshire.gov.uk

Planning: Mr James Miller, Senior Manager - Planning, Cunninghame House, Irvine KA12 8EE ☎ 01294 324315 🖷 01294 324372 ✉ jmiller@north-ayrshire.gov.uk

Procurement: Ms Laura Friel , Executive Director - Finance & Corporate Support, Cunninghame House, Irvine KA12 8EE ☎ 01294 324152 🖷 01294 324544 ✉ lfriel@north-ayrshire.gov.uk

Recycling & Waste Minimisation: Mr David Mackay , Waste Services Manager, Cunninghame House, Irvine KA12 8EE ☎ 01294 541525 🖷 01294 541544 ✉ dmackay@north-ayreshire.gov.uk

Regeneration: Ms Karen Yeomans , Executive Director - Economy & Communities, Cunninghame House, Irvine KA12 8EE ☎ 01294 324308 🖷 01294 324309 ✉ karenyeomans@north-ayrshire.gov.uk

Road Safety: Ms Karen Yeomans , Executive Director - Economy & Communities, Cunninghame House, Irvine KA12 8EE ☎ 01294 324308 🖷 01294 324309 ✉ karenyeomans@north-ayrshire.gov.uk

Social Services: Ms Iona Colvin , Executive Director - Health & Social Care Partnership, Cunninghame House, Irvine KA12 8EE ☎ 01294 317725 🖷 01294 317702 ✉ icolvin@north-ayreshire.gov.uk

Social Services (Adult): Mr David Rowland , Head of Service - Health & Community Care, Cunninghame House, Irvine KA12 8EE ✉ drowland@north-ayrshire.gov.uk

Social Services (Children): Mr Stephen Brown , Head of Service - Children, Families & Criminal Justice Services, Cunninghame House, Irvine KA12 8EE ☎ 01294 317727 ✉ sbrown@north-ayrshire.gov.uk

Staff Training: Mr Gavin Macgregor , Head of Human Resources & Organisational Development, Cunninghame House, Irvine KA12 8EE ☎ 01294 324651 🖷 01294 324664 ✉ gmacgregor@north-ayrshire.gov.uk

Street Scene: Mr Russell McCutcheon , Head of Environment & Related Services, Montgomerie House, 2A Byrehill Drive, West Byrehill Industrial Estate, Kilwinning KA13 6HN ☎ 01294 541570 🖷 01294 541504 ✉ russellmccutcheon@north-ayrshire.gov.uk

Sustainable Communities: Ms Karen Yeomans , Executive Director - Economy & Communities, Cunninghame House, Irvine KA12 8EE ☎ 01294 324308 🖷 01294 324309 ✉ karenyeomans@north-ayrshire.gov.uk

Sustainable Development: Ms Karen Yeomans , Executive Director - Economy & Communities, Cunninghame House, Irvine KA12 8EE ☎ 01294 324308 🖷 01294 324309 ✉ karenyeomans@north-ayrshire.gov.uk

Tourism: Ms Karen Yeomans , Executive Director - Economy & Communities, Cunninghame House, Irvine KA12 8EE ☎ 01294 324308 🖷 01294 324309 ✉ karenyeomans@north-ayrshire.gov.uk

Town Centre: Mr George Hunter , Town Centre Manager, Perceton House, Irvine KA11 2AL ☎ 01294 225177 🖷 01294 225184 ✉ ghunter@north-ayrshire.gov.uk

Traffic Management: Mr Crawford Forsyth , Assistant Transportation Manager, Perceton House, Irvine KA11 2AL ☎ 01294 225100 ✉ cforsyth@north-ayreshire.gov.uk

Waste Collection and Disposal: Mr Russell McCutcheon , Head of Environment & Related Services, Montgomerie House, 2A Byrehill Drive, West Byrehill Industrial Estate, Kilwinning KA13 6HN ☎ 01294 541570 🖷 01294 541504 ✉ russellmccutcheon@north-ayrshire.gov.uk

Waste Management: Mr Russell McCutcheon , Head of Environment & Related Services, Montgomerie House, 2A Byrehill Drive, West Byrehill Industrial Estate, Kilwinning KA13 6HN
☎ 01294 541570 🖷 01294 541504
🖱 russellmccutcheon@north-ayrshire.gov.uk

Children's Play Areas: Mr Wallace Turpie , Operations Manager - Sreetscene, Perceton House, Irvine KA11 2AL ☎ 01294 324653
🖷 01294 225244 🖱 chatton@north-ayreshire.gov.uk

COUNCILLORS

***Provost* Sturgeon**, Joan (SNP - Irvine East)
jsturgeon@north-ayrshire.gov.uk

***Leader of the Council* Gibson**, Willie (SNP - Saltcoats and Stevenston)
wjrgibson@north-ayrshire.gov.uk

***Deputy Leader of the Council* Hill**, Alan (SNP - North Coast and Cumbraes)
alanhill@north-ayrshire.gov.uk

Barr, Robert (IND - Dalry and West Kilbride)
rbarr@north-ayrshire.gov.uk

Bell, John (LAB - Kilbirnie and Beith)
jbell@north-ayrshire.gov.uk

Brown, Matthew (SNP - Irvine West)
mbrown@north-ayrshire.gov.uk

Bruce, John (SNP - Ardrossan and Arran)
johnbruce@north-ayrshire.gov.uk

Burns, Marie (SNP - Irvine East)
marieburns@north-ayrshire.gov.uk

Clarkson, Ian (LAB - Irvine West)
Iclarkson@north-ayrshire.gov.uk

Cullinane, Joe (LAB - Kilwinning)
joecullinane@north-ayrshire.gov.uk

Dickson, Anthea (SNP - Kilbirnie and Beith)
antheadickson@north-ayrshire.gov.uk

Easdale, John (LAB - Irvine East)
johneasdale@north-ayrshire.gov.uk

Ferguson, John (SNP - Kilwinning)
fergusonjohn@north-ayrshire.gov.uk

Gallagher, Alex (LAB - North Coast and Cumbraes)
agallagher@north-ayrshire.gov.uk

Gurney, Anthony (SNP - Ardrossan and Arran)
agurney@north-ayrshire.gov.uk

Highgate, Jean (IND - Kilbirnie and Beith)
jhighgate@north-ayrshire.gov.uk

Hunter, John (IND - Ardrossan and Arran)
jhunter@north-ayrshire.gov.uk

Maguire, Ruth (SNP - Irvine West)
ruthmaguire@north-ayrshire.gov.uk

Marshall, Tom (O - North Coast and Cumbraes)
tommarshall@north-ayrshire.gov.uk

McLardy, Elizabeth (IND - Dalry and West Kilbride)
emclardy@north-ayrshire.gov.uk

McLean, Grace (SNP - North Coast and Cumbraes)
gracemclean@north-ayrshire.gov.uk

McMillan, Catherine (SNP - Dalry and West Kilbride)
catherinemcmillan@north-ayrshire.gov.uk

McNamara, Peter (LAB - Ardrossan and Arran)
pmcnamara@north-ayrshire.gov.uk

McNichol, Ronnie (IND - Saltcoats and Stevenston)
rmcnicol@north-ayrshire.gov.uk

Montgomerie, Jim (LAB - Saltcoats and Stevenston)
jimmontgomerie@north-ayrshire.gov.uk

Munro, Alan (LAB - Saltcoats and Stevenston)
amunro@north-ayrshire.gov.uk

Oldfather, Irene (LAB - Irvine East)
ireneoldfather@north-ayrshire.gov.uk

O'Neill, David (LAB - Irvine West)
doneill@north-ayrshire.gov.uk

Reid, Donald (LAB - Kilwinning)
donaldreid@north-ayrshire.gov.uk

Steel, Robert (IND - Kilwinning)
robertsteel@north-ayrshire.gov.uk

POLITICAL COMPOSITION

SNP: 12, LAB: 11, IND: 6, O: 1

COMMITTEE CHAIRS

Audit: Mr Peter McNamara

Planning: Mr Matthew Brown

North Devon D

North Devon District Council, Lynton House, Commercial Road, Barnstaple EX31 1DG
☎ 01271 327711 🖷 01271 388451 🖱 info@northdevon.gov.uk
💻 www.northdevon.gov.uk

FACTS AND FIGURES

EU Constituencies: South West
Election Frequency: Elections are of whole council

PRINCIPAL OFFICERS

Chief Executive: Mr Mike Mansell, Chief Executive, Lynton House, Commercial Road, Barnstaple EX31 1DG ☎ 01271 388252
🖷 01271 343968 🖱 mike.mansell@northdevon.gov.uk

Senior Management: Ms Diana Hill, Head of Property & Technical Services, Lynton House, Commercial Road, Barnstaple EX31 1DG ☎ 01271 388377 🖷 01271 388268
🖱 diana.hill@northdevon.gov.uk

Senior Management: Mr Jeremy Mann, Head of Environmental Health & Housing Services, Lynton House, Commercial Road, Barnstaple EX31 1DG ☎ 01271 388341 🖷 01271 388328
🖱 jeremy.mann@northdevon.gov.uk

Senior Management: Mr Ricky McCormack, Head of Waste & Recycling Services, Lynton House, Commercial Road, Barnstaple EX31 1DG ☎ 01271 388503 🖱 ricky.mccormack@northdevon.gov.uk

NORTH DEVON

Senior Management: Mr Ken Miles , Head of Legal & Monitoring Officer, Lynton House, Commercial Road, Barnstaple EX31 1DG ☎ 01271 388266 ✉ ken.miles@northdevon.gov.uk

Senior Management: Mr John Triggs , Head of Financial Services, Lynton House, Commercial Road, Barnstaple EX31 1DG ☎ 01271 388221 ✉ jon.triggs@northdevon.gov.uk

Architect, Building / Property Services: Ms Diana Hill, Head of Property & Technical Services, Lynton House, Commercial Road, Barnstaple EX31 1DG ☎ 01271 388377 🖷 01271 388268 ✉ diana.hill@northdevon.gov.uk

Building Control: Mr Mike Tucker , Building Control Team Leader, Lynton House, Commercial Road, Barnstaple EX31 1DG ☎ 01271 388400 ✉ mike.tucker@northdevon.gov.uk

PR / Communications: Mrs Claire Holm, Customer & Corporate Communications Manager, Lynton House, Commercial Road, Barnstaple EX31 1DG ☎ 01271 388239 🖷 01271 329433 ✉ claire.holm@northdevon.gov.uk

Community Safety: Ms Amanda Palmer, Community Safety Officer, Lynton House, Commercial Road, Barnstaple EX31 1DG ☎ 01271 335241 ✉ amanda.palmer@northdevon.gov.uk

Computer Management: Mrs Christina Cross , Head of Business Information Services, Lynton House, Commercial Road, Barnstaple EX31 1DG ☎ 01271 388226 ✉ christina.cross@northdevon.gov.uk

Contracts: Mr Mike Mansell, Chief Executive, Lynton House, Commercial Road, Barnstaple EX31 1DG ☎ 01271 388252 🖷 01271 343968 ✉ mike.mansell@northdevon.gov.uk

Customer Service: Mrs Claire Holm, Customer & Corporate Communications Manager, Lynton House, Commercial Road, Barnstaple EX31 1DG ☎ 01271 388239 🖷 01271 329433 ✉ claire.holm@northdevon.gov.uk

Direct Labour: Mr Ricky McCormack, Head of Waste & Recycling Services, Lynton House, Commercial Road, Barnstaple EX31 1DG ☎ 01271 388503 ✉ ricky.mccormack@northdevon.gov.uk

Economic Development: Ms Ellen Vernon , Economic Regeneration Officer, Lynton House, Commercial Road, Barnstaple EX31 1DG ☎ 01271 388368 ✉ ellen.vernon@northdevon.gov.uk

E-Government: Mrs Christina Cross , Head of Business Information Services, Lynton House, Commercial Road, Barnstaple EX31 1DG ☎ 01271 388226 ✉ christina.cross@northdevon.gov.uk

Electoral Registration: Mrs Judith Dark, Electoral Services Officer, Lynton House, Commercial Road, Barnstaple EX31 1DG ☎ 01271 388277 ✉ judith.dark@northdevon.gov.uk

Emergency Planning: Mr Andrew Millie, Environmental Protection & Emergency Planning Manager, Lynton House, Commercial Road, Barnstaple EX31 1DG ☎ 01271 388334 🖷 01271 388328 ✉ andrew.millie@northdevon.gov.uk

Energy Management: Ms Diana Hill, Head of Property & Technical Services, Lynton House, Commercial Road, Barnstaple EX31 1DG ☎ 01271 388377 🖷 01271 388268 ✉ diana.hill@northdevon.gov.uk

Environmental Health: Mr Jeremy Mann, Head of Environmental Health & Housing Services, Lynton House, Commercial Road, Barnstaple EX31 1DG ☎ 01271 388341 🖷 01271 388328 ✉ jeremy.mann@northdevon.gov.uk

Estates, Property & Valuation: Ms Diana Hill, Head of Property & Technical Services, Lynton House, Commercial Road, Barnstaple EX31 1DG ☎ 01271 388377 🖷 01271 388268 ✉ diana.hill@northdevon.gov.uk

Facilities: Ms Diana Hill, Head of Property & Technical Services, Lynton House, Commercial Road, Barnstaple EX31 1DG ☎ 01271 388377 🖷 01271 388268 ✉ diana.hill@northdevon.gov.uk

Finance: Mr John Triggs , Head of Financial Services, Lynton House, Commercial Road, Barnstaple EX31 1DG ☎ 01271 388221 ✉ jon.triggs@northdevon.gov.uk

Grounds Maintenance: Mr Mark Kentell , Contracts Delivery Manager, Lynton House, Commercial Road, Barnstaple EX31 1DG ☎ 01271 327711 ✉ mark.kentell@northdevon.gov.uk

Health and Safety: Mr Mike Ballard , Health & Safety Advisor, Lynton House, Commercial Road, Barnstaple EX31 1DG ☎ 01271 327711 ✉ mike.ballard@northdevon.gov.uk

Home Energy Conservation: Mr Jeremy Mann, Head of Environmental Health & Housing Services, Lynton House, Commercial Road, Barnstaple EX31 1DG ☎ 01271 388341 🖷 01271 388328 ✉ jeremy.mann@northdevon.gov.uk

Housing: Mr Jeremy Mann, Head of Environmental Health & Housing Services, Lynton House, Commercial Road, Barnstaple EX31 1DG ☎ 01271 388341 🖷 01271 388328 ✉ jeremy.mann@northdevon.gov.uk

Legal: Mr Ken Miles , Head of Legal & Monitoring Officer, Lynton House, Commercial Road, Barnstaple EX31 1DG ☎ 01271 388266 ✉ ken.miles@northdevon.gov.uk

Leisure and Cultural Services: Mr Mark Kentell , Contracts Delivery Manager, Lynton House, Commercial Road, Barnstaple EX31 1DG ☎ 01271 327711 ✉ mark.kentell@northdevon.gov.uk

Licensing: Miss Katy Nicholls , Licensing Manager, Lynton House, Commercial Road, Barnstaple EX31 1DG ☎ 01271 388312 🖷 01271 388328 ✉ katy.nicholls@northdevon.gov.uk

Lifelong Learning: Mrs Nikki Gordon , Human Resources Manager, Lynton House, Commercial Road, Barnstaple EX31 1DG ☎ 01271 388548 🖷 01271 343968 ✉ nikki.gordon@northdevon.gov.uk

Lottery Funding, Charity and Voluntary: Mrs Lorna Jones , Community Grants & Funding Officer, Lynton House, Commercial Road, Barnstaple EX31 1DG ☎ 01271 388327 🖷 01271 343968 ✉ lorna.jones@northdevon.gov.uk

Member Services: Mrs Bev Triggs , Senior Member Services Officer, Lynton House, Commercial Road, Barnstaple EX31 1DG ☎ 01271 388254 ✉ bev.triggs@northdevon.gov.uk

Parking: Mr Martin Williams , Procurement & Service Delivery Manager, Lynton House, Commercial Road, Barnstaple EX31 1DG ☎ 01271 388273 ✉ martin.williams@northdevon.gov.uk

Personnel / HR: Mrs Nikki Gordon , Human Resources Manager, Lynton House, Commercial Road, Barnstaple EX31 1DG ☎ 01271 388548 🖷 01271 343968 ✉ nikki.gordon@northdevon.gov.uk

Planning: Mr Mike Kelly , Planning Manager, Lynton House, Commercial Road, Barnstaple EX31 1DG ☎ 01271 388439 ✉ mike.kelly@northdevon.gov.uk

Procurement: Mr Martin Williams , Procurement & Service Delivery Manager, Lynton House, Commercial Road, Barnstaple EX31 1DG ☎ 01271 388273 ✉ martin.williams@northdevon.gov.uk

Recycling & Waste Minimisation: Mr Ricky McCormack, Head of Waste & Recycling Services, Lynton House, Commercial Road, Barnstaple EX31 1DG ☎ 01271 388503 ✉ ricky.mccormack@northdevon.gov.uk

Staff Training: Mrs Nikki Gordon , Human Resources Manager, Lynton House, Commercial Road, Barnstaple EX31 1DG ☎ 01271 388548 🖷 01271 343968 ✉ nikki.gordon@northdevon.gov.uk

Waste Collection and Disposal: Mr Ricky McCormack, Head of Waste & Recycling Services, Lynton House, Commercial Road, Barnstaple EX31 1DG ☎ 01271 388503 ✉ ricky.mccormack@northdevon.gov.uk

Waste Management: Mr Ricky McCormack, Head of Waste & Recycling Services, Lynton House, Commercial Road, Barnstaple EX31 1DG ☎ 01271 388503 ✉ ricky.mccormack@northdevon.gov.uk

Children's Play Areas: Mr Mark Kentell , Contracts Delivery Manager, Lynton House, Commercial Road, Barnstaple EX31 1DG ☎ 01271 327711 ✉ mark.kentell@northdevon.gov.uk

COUNCILLORS

***Chair* Fowler**, Geoffery (LD - Ilfracombe (West))
geoffrey.fowler@northdevon.gov.uk

***Vice-Chair* Wilkinson**, Malcolm (LD - Georgeham and Mortehoe)
malcolm.wilkinson@northdevon.gov.uk

***Leader of the Council* Greenslade**, Brian (LD - Barnstaple (Pilton))
brian.greenslade@northdevon.gov.uk

Barker, Pat (CON - Georgeham and Mortehoe)
pat.barker@northdevon.gov.uk

Biederman, Frank (IND - Fremington)
frank.biederman@northdevon.gov.uk

Bradford, Adam (LD - Barnstaple (Central))
adam.bradford@northdevon.gov.uk

Brailey, David (CON - Barnstaple (Longbridge))
david.brailey@northdevon.gov.uk

Brown, Lesley (LD - Barnstaple (Yeo Valley))
lesley.brown@northdevon.gov.uk

Cann, Rodney (INDNA - Bickington and Roundswell)
rodney.cann@northdevon.gov.uk

Chesters, Jasmine (CON - Braunton (West))
jasmine.chesters@northdevon.gov.uk

Chugg, Caroline (CON - Braunton (West))
caroline.chugg@northdevon.gov.uk

Clark, Julia (INDNA - Combe Martin)
julia.clark@northdevon.gov.uk

Crabb, Paul (CON - Ilfracombe (Central))
paul.crabb@northdevon.gov.uk

Croft, Sue (CON - Chulmleigh)
sue.croft@northdevon.gov.uk

Davis, Andrea (CON - Heanton Punchardon)
andrea.davis@northdevon.gov.uk

Edgell, Richard (CON - North Molton)
richard.edgell@northdevon.gov.uk

Edmunds, Mike (IND - Ilfracombe (East))
mike.edmunds@northdevon.gov.uk

Flynn, Jaqueline (CON - Barnstaple (Longbridge))
jacqueline.flynn@northdevon.gov.uk

Gubb, Yvette (INDNA - Combe Martin)
yvette.gubb@northdevon.gov.uk

Gurney, Julian (LD - Lynton and Lynmouth)
julian.gurney@northdevon.gov.uk

Harrison, Michael (CON - Barnstaple (Newport))
henry.harrison@northdevon.gov.uk

Haywood, Sue (LD - Barnstaple (Forches and Whiddon Valley))
suzanne.haywood@northdevon.gov.uk

Hockin, Brian (INDNA - Bickington and Roundswell)
brian.hockin@northdevon.gov.uk

Hunt, Julie (LD - Barnstaple (Forches and Whiddon Valley))
julie.hunt@northdevon.gov.uk

Lane, Glyn (CON - Landkey, Swimbridge and Taw)
glyn.lane@northdevon.gov.uk

Ley, Eric (IND - Bishops Nympton)
eric.ley@northdevon.gov.uk

Lucas, Douglas (CON - Brauton East)
douglas.lucas@northdevon.gov.uk

Luggar, David (CON - Landkey, Swimbridge and Taw)
david.luggar@northdevon.gov.uk

Manuel, Mair (LD - Barnstaple (Pilton))
mair.manuel@northdevon.gov.uk

Mathews, John (CON - Barnstaple (Newport))
john.mathews@northdevon.gov.uk

Moore, John (INDNA - South Molton)
john.moore@northdevon.gov.uk

Moores, Brian (CON - Instow)
brian.moores@northdevon.gov.uk

Payne, Colin (LD - Barnstaple (Yeo Valley))
colin.payne@northdevon.gov.uk

Prowse, Malcolm (INDNA - Bratton Fleming)
malcolm.prowse@northdevon.gov.uk

NORTH DEVON

Spear, Derrick (LD - Braunton East)
derrick.spear@northdevon.gov.uk

Tucker, Frederick (LD - Marwood)
frederick.tucker@northdevon.gov.uk

Turner, Christopher (IND - Fremington)
chris.turner@northdevon.gov.uk

Webb, Philip (CON - Ilfracombe (West))
philip.webb@northdevon.gov.uk

Webber, Faye (LD - Barnstaple (Central))
faye.webber@northdevon.gov.uk

White, Walter (IND - Chittlehampton)
walter.white@northdevon.gov.uk

Worden, David (LD - South Molton)
david.worden@northdevon.gov.uk

Yabsley, Paul (CON - Ilfracombe (Central))
paul.yabsley@northdevon.gov.uk

Yabsley, Jeremy (CON - Witheridge Ward)
jeremy.yabsley@northdevon.gov.uk

POLITICAL COMPOSITION

CON: 18, LD: 14, INDNA: 6, IND: 5

COMMITTEE CHAIRS

Audit: Mr Adam Bradford

Licensing: Mr Frederick Tucker

Planning: Mr Eric Ley

North Dorset D

North Dorset District Council, Nordon, Salisbury Road, Blandford Forum DT11 7LL
☎ 01258 454111 🖷 01258 480179 💻 www.north-dorset.gov.uk

FACTS AND FIGURES

Parliamentary Constituencies: Dorset North
EU Constituencies: South West
Election Frequency: Elections are of whole council

PRINCIPAL OFFICERS

Chief Executive: Mr Matt Prosser , Chief Executive, Tri-Council Partnership, South Walks House, South Walks Road, Dorchester DT1 1UZ ☎ 01305 251010 🖰 d.clarke@weymouth.gov.uk

Assistant Chief Executive: Mr Stuart Caundle , Assistant Chief Executive, South Walks House, South Walks Road, Dorchester DT1 1UZ ☎ 01258 484010 🖰 scaundle@north-dorset.co.uk

Senior Management: Mr Martin Hamilton , Strategic Director, South Walks House, South Walks Road, Dorchester DT1 1UZ ☎ 01305 838086 🖰 m.hamilton@westdorset-weymouth.gov.uk

Senior Management: Mr Stephen Hill , Strategic Director, South Walks House, South Walks Road, Dorchester DT1 1UZ ☎ 01258 484034 🖰 shill@north-dorset.gov.uk

Senior Management: Mr Jason Vaughan, Strategic Director & S151 Officer, South Walks House, South Walks Road, Dorchester DT1 1UZ ☎ 01305 838233 🖰 j.vaughan@westdorset-weymouth.gov.uk

Best Value: Mr Drystan Gatrell , Business Information Analyst, Nordon, Salisbury Road, Blandford Forum DT11 7LL ☎ 01258 484056 🖷 01258 480007 🖰 dgatrell@north-dorset.gov.uk

Building Control: Mr Kerry Pitt-Kerby, Environment & Private Sector Housing Team Leader, Nordon, Salisbury Road, Blandford Forum DT11 7LL ☎ 01258 484311 🖷 01258 480179 🖰 kpittkerby@north-dorset.gov.uk

Community Planning: Mr Hugh de Longh , Community Planning Officer, Nordon, Salisbury Road, Blandford Forum DT11 7LL ☎ 01258 484025 🖷 01258 480179

Community Safety: Mr John Bartlett , Community Safety Policy Officer, Nordon, Salisbury Road, Blandford Forum DT11 7LL ☎ 01258 484368 🖰 jbartlett@north-dorset.gov.uk

Computer Management: Mr Bryan Alford, Business Technology Solutions Advisor, Nordon, Salisbury Road, Blandford Forum DT11 7LL ☎ 01258 484073 🖷 01258 480007 🖰 balford@north-dorset.gov.uk

Customer Service: Ms Emma Edgeley-Long , Business Change Co-ordinator, Nordon, Salisbury Road, Blandford Forum DT11 7LL ☎ 01258 484053 🖰 eedgeley-long@north-dorset.gov.uk

E-Government: Mr Bryan Alford, Business Technology Solutions Advisor, Nordon, Salisbury Road, Blandford Forum DT11 7LL ☎ 01258 484073 🖷 01258 480007 🖰 balford@north-dorset.gov.uk

Electoral Registration: Ms Jacqui Andrews , Democratic Services Manager, Nordon, Salisbury Road, Blandford Forum DT11 7LL ☎ 01258 484325 🖷 01258 480179 🖰 jandrews@north-dorset.gov.uk

Emergency Planning: Mr Roger Frost, Food Safety & Licensing Manager, Nordon, Salisbury Road, Blandford Forum DT11 7LL ☎ 01258 484316 🖷 01258 480179 🖰 rfrost@north-dorset.gov.uk

Energy Management: Mr Kevin Morris, Environment, Land, Property & Commissioning Manager, Nordon, Salisbury Road, Blandford Forum DT11 7LL ☎ 01258 484276 🖷 01258 480179 🖰 kmorris@north-dorset.gov.uk

Environmental / Technical Services: Mr Mike Coker, Principal Technical Officer, Nordon, Salisbury Road, Blandford Forum DT11 7LL ☎ 01258 484275 🖷 01258 480179 🖰 mcoker@north-dorset.gov.uk

Environmental Health: Mr Roger Frost, Food Safety & Licensing Manager, Nordon, Salisbury Road, Blandford Forum DT11 7LL ☎ 01258 484316 🖷 01258 480179 🖰 rfrost@north-dorset.gov.uk

Environmental Health: Mr Kerry Pitt-Kerby, Environment & Private Sector Housing Team Leader, Nordon, Salisbury Road, Blandford Forum DT11 7LL ☎ 01258 484311 🖷 01258 480179 🖰 kpittkerby@north-dorset.gov.uk

Estates, Property & Valuation: Mr Kevin Morris, Environment, Land, Property & Commissioning Manager, Nordon, Salisbury Road, Blandford Forum DT11 7LL ☎ 01258 484276 🖷 01258 480179 🖰 kmorris@north-dorset.gov.uk

Facilities: Mr Kevin Morris, Environment, Land, Property & Commissioning Manager, Nordon, Salisbury Road, Blandford Forum DT11 7LL ☎ 01258 484276 🖷 01258 480179 ✉ kmorris@north-dorset.gov.uk

Finance: Mr Ian Milne , Finance Manager, Nordon, Salisbury Road, Blandford Forum DT11 7LL ☎ 01258 484115 ✉ imilne@north-dorset.gov.uk

Finance: Mr Jason Vaughan, Strategic Director & S151 Officer, South Walks House, South Walks Road, Dorchester DT1 1UZ ☎ 01305 838233; 01305 251010 ✉ j.vaughan@westdorset-weymouth.gov.uk

Health and Safety: Mr Roger Frost, Food Safety & Licensing Manager, Nordon, Salisbury Road, Blandford Forum DT11 7LL ☎ 01258 484316 🖷 01258 480179 ✉ rfrost@north-dorset.gov.uk

Home Energy Conservation: Mr Kerry Pitt-Kerby, Environment & Private Sector Housing Team Leader, Nordon, Salisbury Road, Blandford Forum DT11 7LL ☎ 01258 484311 🖷 01258 480179 ✉ kpittkerby@north-dorset.gov.uk

Housing: Ms Sarah How , Senior Housing Needs Officer, Nordon, Salisbury Road, Blandford Forum DT11 7LL ☎ 01258 484386 🖷 01258 480179 ✉ show@north-dorset.gov.uk

Legal: Mr Robert Firth , Legal Services Manager & Commissioning Manager, Nordon, Salisbury Road, Blandford Forum DT11 7LL ☎ 01258 484364 ✉ rfirth@north-dorset.gov.uk

Leisure and Cultural Services: Mr Kevin Morris, Environment, Land, Property & Commissioning Manager, Nordon, Salisbury Road, Blandford Forum DT11 7LL ☎ 01258 484276 🖷 01258 480179 ✉ kmorris@north-dorset.gov.uk

Licensing: Mr Peter Davies , Senior Licensing Officer, Nordon, Salisbury Road, Blandford Forum DT11 7LL ☎ 01258 484014 🖷 01258 480179 ✉ pdavies@north-dorset.gov.uk

Member Services: Ms Jacqui Andrews , Democratic Services Manager, Nordon, Salisbury Road, Blandford Forum DT11 7LL ☎ 01258 484325 🖷 01258 480179 ✉ jandrews@north-dorset.gov.uk

Parking: Mr Kevin Morris, Environment, Land, Property & Commissioning Manager, Nordon, Salisbury Road, Blandford Forum DT11 7LL ☎ 01258 484276 🖷 01258 480179 ✉ kmorris@north-dorset.gov.uk

Personnel / HR: Ms Bobbie Bragg, Senior Personnel Advisor, Nordon, Salisbury Road, Blandford Forum DT11 7LL ☎ 01258 454032 🖷 01258 484037 ✉ bbragg@north-dorset.gov.uk

Planning: Mr John Hammond , Development Services Manager, Nordon, Salisbury Road, Blandford Forum DT11 7LL ☎ 01258 484202 🖷 01258 480179 ✉ jhammond@north-dorset.gov.uk

Recycling & Waste Minimisation: Mr Robert Firth , Legal Services Manager & Commissioning Manager, Nordon, Salisbury Road, Blandford Forum DT11 7LL ☎ 01258 484364 ✉ rfirth@north-dorset.gov.uk

Regeneration: Mr Hugh de Longh , Community Planning Officer, Nordon, Salisbury Road, Blandford Forum DT11 7LL ☎ 01258 484025 🖷 01258 480179

Staff Training: Ms Bobbie Bragg, Senior Personnel Advisor, Nordon, Salisbury Road, Blandford Forum DT11 7LL ☎ 01258 454032 🖷 01258 484037 ✉ bbragg@north-dorset.gov.uk

Sustainable Communities: Mr Kevin Morris, Environment, Land, Property & Commissioning Manager, Nordon, Salisbury Road, Blandford Forum DT11 7LL ☎ 01258 484276 🖷 01258 480179 ✉ kmorris@north-dorset.gov.uk

Sustainable Development: Mr Paul McIntosh , Sustainability Officer, Nordon, Salisbury Road, Blandford Forum DT11 7LL ☎ 01258 484019 🖷 01258 480179 ✉ pmcintosh@north-dorset.gov.uk

Waste Collection and Disposal: Mr Robert Firth , Legal Services Manager & Commissioning Manager, Nordon, Salisbury Road, Blandford Forum DT11 7LL ☎ 01258 484364 ✉ rfirth@north-dorset.gov.uk

Waste Management: Mr Robert Firth , Legal Services Manager & Commissioning Manager, Nordon, Salisbury Road, Blandford Forum DT11 7LL ☎ 01258 484364 ✉ rfirth@north-dorset.gov.uk

COUNCILLORS

***Chair* Fox**, Victor (CON - Sturminster Newton)
victorfox187@btinternet.com

***Vice-Chair* Burch**, Audrey (CON - Bulbarrow)
audreyburch01@googlemail.com

***Leader of the Council* Croney**, Deborah (CON - Hill Forts)
hillfortsward@hotmail.co.uk

***Deputy Leader of the Council* Carr-Jones**, Graham (CON - Blackmore)
grahamcarrjones@aol.com

Batstone, Pauline (CON - Lydden Vale)
cllr.p.batstone@btinternet.com

Batty-Smith, Bill (CON - Blackmore)
w.battysmith@readingfans.co.uk

Beer, Derek (LD - Shaftesbury Central)

Butler, Esme (IND - Blandford Damory Down)
esbutler@sky.com

Cattaway, Andrew (CON - Motcombe & Bourton)
cattaways@tinyworld.co.uk

Cooper, Barrie (LD - Blandford Langton St Leonards)

Dowden, Charles (CON - Stours & Marnhull)
charles.dowden010@btinternet.com

Francis, Jo (CON - Shaftesbury East)
francisja@icloud.com

Gould, Mike (CON - Gillingham Town)
mgould@emf-ltd.co.uk

Jefferson, Gary (CON - Shaftesbury West)
gpjefferson@gmail.com

Jespersen, Sherry (CON - Hill Forts)
cllr.s.jespersen@btinternet.com

NORTH DORSET

Kerby, Andrew (CON - Riversdale & Portman)
cllr.akerby@north-dorset.gov.uk

Langham, Catherine (CON - The Beacon)
cel@langhamfarm.co.uk

Leonard, Mark (CON - Blandford Hilltop)
markleonard4hilltop@gmail.com

Milstead, David (LD - Gillingham Town)
david.milsted@virgin.net

Parker, Emma (CON - Abbey)
emmaparker77@hotmail.co.uk

Pothecary, Val (CON - Gillingham Town)
vpothecary@tiscali.co.uk

Pritchard, Simon (IND - Shaftesbury East)
cllrpritchard@hotmail.co.uk

Ridout, Belinda (CON - Gillingham Rural)
cllr.belindaridout@talktalk.net

Roake, Michael (CON - Sturminster Newton)
mroake5179@aol.com

Schwier, James (CON - Hill Forts)
hillfortsward@hotmail.co.uk

Skipwith, Deirdre (CON - Lower Tarrants)
deirdreskipwith@hotmail.co.uk

Somper, Jane (CON - Abbey)
janesomper@hotmail.co.uk

Stayt, John (CON - Riversdale & Portman)
john.stayt@btinternet.com

Stayt, Jackie (CON - Blanford Old Town)
jackiestayt@uwclub.net

Tanner, John (LD - Blandford Station)
jjtanners@hotmail.com

Walsh, David (CON - Gillingham Rural)
cllr.davidwalsh@talktalk.net

Westbrook, Jane (CON - Stours & Marnhull)
westbrookjane@yahoo.co.uk

Williams, Peter (CON - Motcombe & Bourton)
peterwilliams53@gmail.com

POLITICAL COMPOSITION

CON: 27, LD: 4, IND: 2

COMMITTEE CHAIRS

Accounts & Audit: Mrs Audrey Burch

Development Management: Mr Bill Batty-Smith

North Down & Ards District Council N

North Down & Ards District Council, North Down Borough Council, Town Hall, The Castle, Bangor BT20 4BT
☎ 028 9127 8034 enquiries@northdownandards.gov.uk
www.northdownandards.gov.uk

PRINCIPAL OFFICERS

Chief Executive: Mr Stephen Reid , Chief Executive, North Down Borough Council, Town Hall, The Castle, Bangor BT20 4BT

Senior Management: Mr Graeme Bannister , Director of Community & Wellbeing, North Down Borough Council, Town Hall, The Castle, Bangor BT20 4BT

Senior Management: Mr Dave Clarke , Director of Finance, North Down Borough Council, Town Hall, The Castle, Bangor BT20 4BT

Senior Management: Mr David Lindsay , Director of Environment, North Down Borough Council, Town Hall, The Castle, Bangor BT20 4BT

Senior Management: Ms Christine Mahon , Director of Regeneration, Development & Planning, North Down Borough Council, Town Hall, The Castle, Bangor BT20 4BT

Senior Management: Ms Wendy Monson , Director of Organisational Development & Administration, North Down Borough Council, Town Hall, The Castle, Bangor BT20 4BT

Community Planning: Mr Graeme Bannister , Director of Community & Wellbeing, North Down Borough Council, Town Hall, The Castle, Bangor BT20 4BT

Corporate Services: Ms Claire Jackson , Lead Officer - Corporate Communications, North Down Borough Council, Town Hall, The Castle, Bangor BT20 4BT

Corporate Services: Ms Gillian McCready , Local Government Reform Manager, North Down Borough Council, Town Hall, The Castle, Bangor BT20 4BT

Environmental / Technical Services: Mr David Lindsay , Director of Environment, North Down Borough Council, Town Hall, The Castle, Bangor BT20 4BT

Finance: Mr Dave Clarke , Director of Finance, North Down Borough Council, Town Hall, The Castle, Bangor BT20 4BT

Member Services: Ms Jayne Taylor , Member Services, North Down Borough Council, Town Hall, The Castle, Bangor BT20 4BT

Personnel / HR: Ms Wendy Monson , Director of Organisational Development & Administration, North Down Borough Council, Town Hall, The Castle, Bangor BT20 4BT

Planning: Ms Christine Mahon , Director of Regeneration, Development & Planning, North Down Borough Council, Town Hall, The Castle, Bangor BT20 4BT

Regeneration: Ms Christine Mahon , Director of Regeneration, Development & Planning, North Down Borough Council, Town Hall, The Castle, Bangor BT20 4BT

COUNCILLORS

***Leader of the Council* Graham**, Alan (DUP - Bangor West)
alan.graham@northdownandards.gov.uk

***Deputy Leader of the Council* Fletcher**, James (UUP - Comber)
james.fletcher@northdownandards.gov.uk

Adair, Robert (DUP - Ards Peninsula)
robert.adair@northdownandards.gov.uk

Allen, Daniel (UUP - Holywood & Clandeboye)
daniel.allen@northdownandards.gov.uk

Anderson, Stuart (ALL - Bangor Central)
stuart.anderson@northdownandards.gov.uk

Armstrong, Kellie (ALL - Ards Peninsula)
kellie.armstrong@northdownandards.gov.uk

Armstrong-Cotter, Naomi (DUP - Newtownards)
naomi.armstrong@northdownandards.gov.uk

Barry, John (GRN - Holywood & Clandeboye)
john.barry@northdownandards.gov.uk

Boyle, Joe (SDLP - Ards Peninsula)
joe.boyle@northdownandards.gov.uk

Brooks, Mark (UUP - Bangor East & Donaghadee)
mark.brooks@northdownandards.gov.uk

Carson, Angus (UUP - Ards Peninsula)
angus.carson@northdownandards.gov.uk

Cathcart, Alistair (DUP - Bangor Central)
alistair.cathcart@northdownandards.gov.uk

Chambers, Alan (IND - Bangor East & Donaghadee)
alan.chambers@northdownandards.gov.uk

Comber, Stephen (O - Comber)
stephen.coopers@northdownandards.gov.uk

Cummings, Trevor (DUP - Comber)
trevor.cummings@northdownandards.gov.uk

Dunne, Stephen (DUP - Holywood & Clandeboye)
stephen.dunne@northdownandards.gov.uk

Edmund, Nigel (DUP - Ards Peninsula)
nigel.edmund@northdownandards.gov.uk

Ferguson, Katherine (UUP - Newtownards)
katherine.ferguson@northdownandards.gov.uk

Gibson, Robert (DUP - Comber)
robert.gibson@northdownandards.gov.uk

Gilmour, Jennifer (DUP - Holywood & Clandeboye)
jennifer.gilmour@northdownandards.gov.uk

Girvan, Deborah (ALL - Comber)
deborah.given@northdownandards.gov.uk

Henry, Ian (UUP - Bangor Central)
ian.henry@northdownandards.gov.uk

Irvine, Wesley (DUP - Bangor Central)
wesley.irvine@northdownandards.gov.uk

Keery, Bill (DUP - Bangor East & Donaghadee)
bill.keery@northdownandards.gov.uk

Kennedy, Colin (DUP - Newtownards)
colin.kennedy@northdownandards.gov.uk

Leslie, Alan (DUP - Bangor West)
alan.leslie@northdownandards.gov.uk

Martin, Peter (DUP - Bangor East & Donaghadee)
peter.martin@northdownandards.gov.uk

McClean, Carl (UUP - Bangor Central)
carl.mcclean@northdownandards.gov.uk

McDowell, Alan (ALL - Newtownards)
alan.mcdowell@northdownandards.gov.uk

McIlveen, Stephen (DUP - Newtownards)
stephen.mcilveen@northdownandards.gov.uk

Menagh, Jimmy (IND - Newtownards)
jimmy.menagh@northdownandards.gov.uk

Muir, Andrew (ALL - Holywood & Clandeboye)
andrew.muir@northdownandards.gov.uk

Roberts, Paul (GRN - Bangor West)
paul.roberts@northdownandards.gov.uk

Robinson, Noelle (IND - Bangor Central)
noelle.robinson@northdownandards.gov.uk

Smart, Richard (UUP - Newtownards)
richard.smart@northdownandards.gov.uk

Smith, Marion (UUP - Bangor West)
marion.smith@northdownandards.gov.uk

Smith, Tom (DUP - Bangor East & Donaghadee)
tom.smith@northdownandards.gov.uk

Thompson, Eddie (DUP - Ards Peninsula)
eddie.thompson@northdownandards.gov.uk

Walker, Gavin (ALL - Bangor East & Donaghadee)
gavin.walker@northdownandards.gov.uk

Wilson, Scott (ALL - Bangor West)
scott.wilson@northdownandards.gov.uk

POLITICAL COMPOSITION

DUP: 17, UUP: 9, ALL: 7, IND: 3, GRN: 2, O: 1, SDLP: 1

COMMITTEE CHAIRS

Finance & Resources: Mr Angus Carson

Planning: Mr Robert Gibson

Strategic Services: Mr Alan McDowell

North East Derbyshire D

North East Derbyshire District Council, 2013 Mill Lane, Wingerworth, Chesterfield S42 6NG
☎ 01246 231111 🖷 01246 550213; 01246 550213
enquiries@ne-derbyshire.gov.uk 💻 www.ne-derbyshire.gov.uk

FACTS AND FIGURES

Parliamentary Constituencies: Derbyshire North East
EU Constituencies: East Midlands
Election Frequency: Elections are of whole council

PRINCIPAL OFFICERS

Chief Executive: Mr Wes Lumley, Joint Chief Executive Officer, 2013 Mill Lane, Wingerworth, Chesterfield S42 6NG ☎ 01246 217155 wes.lumley@bolsover.gov.uk

Senior Management: Mr Paul Hackett , Joint Executive Director - Transformation, 2013 Mill Lane, Wingerworth, Chesterfield S42 6NG ☎ 01246 217543 paul.hackett@ne-derbyshire.gov.uk

Senior Management: Mr Bryan Mason , Joint Executive Director - Operations, 2013 Mill Lane, Wingerworth, Chesterfield S42 6NG ☎ 01246 242431 bryan.mason@ne-derbyshire.gov.uk

NORTH EAST DERBYSHIRE

Architect, Building / Property Services: Ms Sue Cooper , Estates Officer, 2013 Mill Lane, Wingerworth, Chesterfield S42 6NG ☎ 01246 217195 🖷 01246 217446 ✉ sue.cooper@ne-derbyshire.gov.uk

Best Value: Mrs Jane Foley, Joint Assistant Director - Customer Service & Improvement, 2013 Mill Lane, Wingerworth, Chesterfield S42 6NG ☎ 01246 242343; 01246 217029 🖷 01246 242423; 01246 217442 ✉ jane.foley@bolsover.gov.uk

Building Control: Mr Malcolm Clinton , Business Manager, 2013 Mill Lane, Wingerworth, Chesterfield S42 6NG ☎ 01246 345817; 01246 354900 ✉ malcolm.clinton@ne-derbyshire.gov.uk; malcolm.clinton@bcnconsultancy.co.uk

Children / Youth Services: Mrs Rebecca Slack , Housing Strategy & Enabling Manager, 2013 Mill Lane, Wingerworth, Chesterfield S42 6NG ☎ 01246 217289 ✉ rebecca.slack@ne-derbyshire.gov.uk

PR / Communications: Mr Scott Chambers , Communications Officer, 2013 Mill Lane, Wingerworth, Chesterfield S42 6NG ☎ 01246 217692 ✉ scott.chambers@bolsover.gov.uk

Community Planning: Mr Adrian Kirkham , Planning Services Manager, 2013 Mill Lane, Wingerworth, Chesterfield S42 6NG ☎ 01246 217591 ✉ adrian.kirkham@ne-derbyshire.gov.uk

Community Safety: Ms Faye Green , Community Safety Manager, 2013 Mill Lane, Wingerworth, Chesterfield S42 6NG ☎ 01246 217015 ✉ faye.green@ne-derbyshire.gov.uk

Computer Management: Mr Nick Blaney , Joint IT Services Manager, 2013 Mill Lane, Wingerworth, Chesterfield S42 6NG ☎ 01246 217103; 01246 217103; 01246 717097 ✉ nick.blaney@ne-derbyshire.gov.uk

Contracts: Mr Bryan Mason , Joint Executive Director - Operations, 2013 Mill Lane, Wingerworth, Chesterfield S42 6NG ☎ 01246 242431 ✉ bryan.mason@ne-derbyshire.gov.uk

Corporate Services: Mrs Sarah Sternberg , Joint Assistant Director - Governance & Monitoring Officer, 2013 Mill Lane, Wingerworth, Chesterfield S42 6NG ☎ 01246 217057 🖷 01246 217442 ✉ sarah.sternberg@bolsover.gov.uk

Customer Service: Mrs Jane Foley , Joint Assistant Director - Customer Services & Improvement, 2013 Mill Lane, Wingerworth, Chesterfield S42 6NG ☎ 01246 217029 ✉ jane.foley@bolsover.gov.uk

Customer Service: Ms Rachael Pope , Customer Services Operational Manager, 2013 Mill Lane, Wingerworth, Chesterfield S42 6NG ☎ 01246 217658 ✉ rachael.pope@ne-derbyshire.gov.uk

Economic Development: Mrs Allison Westray-Chapman , Joint Assistant Director - Economic Growth, 2013 Mill Lane, Wingerworth, Chesterfield S42 6NG ☎ 01246 217199 ✉ allison.westray-chapman@ne-derbyshire.gov.uk

E-Government: Mrs Sarah Sternberg , Joint Assistant Director - Governance & Monitoring Officer, 2013 Mill Lane, Wingerworth, Chesterfield S42 6NG ☎ 01246 217057 🖷 01246 217442 ✉ sarah.sternberg@bolsover.gov.uk

Electoral Registration: Mrs Sarah Sternberg , Joint Assistant Director - Governance & Monitoring Officer, 2013 Mill Lane, Wingerworth, Chesterfield S42 6NG ☎ 01246 217057 🖷 01246 217442 ✉ sarah.sternberg@bolsover.gov.uk

Emergency Planning: Mr Paul Hackett , Joint Executive Director - Transformation, 2013 Mill Lane, Wingerworth, Chesterfield S42 6NG ☎ 01246 217543 ✉ paul.hackett@ne-derbyshire.gov.uk

Emergency Planning: Mr Lee Hickin , Joint Assistant Director - Leisure, 2013 Mill Lane, Wingerworth, Chesterfield S42 6NG ☎ 01246 217218 ✉ lee.hickin@bolsover.gov.uk

Energy Management: Mr Paul Hackett, Joint Executive Director - Transformation, 2013 Mill Lane, Wingerworth, Chesterfield S42 6NG ☎ 01246 217543 ✉ paul.hackett@ne-derbyshire.gov.uk

Environmental / Technical Services: Mr James Arnold , Joint Assistant Director - Planning & Environmental Health, 2013 Mill Lane, Wingerworth, Chesterfield S42 6NG ☎ 01246 217436 ✉ james.arnold@bolsover.gov.uk

Environmental Health: Mr James Arnold , Joint Assistant Director - Planning & Environmental Health, 2013 Mill Lane, Wingerworth, Chesterfield S42 6NG ☎ 01246 217436 ✉ james.arnold@bolsover.gov.uk

Estates, Property & Valuation: Mr Dave Broom , Architect, 2013 Mill Lane, Wingerworth, Chesterfield S42 6NG ☎ 01246 217374 ✉ david.broom@ne-derbyshire.gov.uk

Estates, Property & Valuation: Mr Robert Walker , Property Services Officer, 2013 Mill Lane, Wingerworth, Chesterfield S42 6NG ☎ 01246 217588 🖷 01246 217446 ✉ robert.walker@ne-derbyshire.gov.uk

Facilities: Mr Dave Broom , Architect, 2013 Mill Lane, Wingerworth, Chesterfield S42 6NG ☎ 01246 217374 ✉ david.broom@ne-derbyshire.gov.uk

Facilities: Mr Robert Walker , Property Services Officer, 2013 Mill Lane, Wingerworth, Chesterfield S42 6NG ☎ 01246 217588 🖷 01246 217446 ✉ robert.walker@ne-derbyshire.gov.uk

Finance: Ms Dawn Clarke , Joint Assistant Director - Finance, Revenues & Benefits, 2013 Mill Lane, Wingerworth, Chesterfield S42 6NG ☎ 01246 217658 ✉ dawn.clarke@ne-derbyshire.gov.uk

Finance: Mr Bryan Mason , Joint Executive Director - Operations, 2013 Mill Lane, Wingerworth, Chesterfield S42 6NG ☎ 01246 242431 ✉ bryan.mason@ne-derbyshire.gov.uk

Fleet Management: Mr Steve Brunt , Joint Assistant Director - Street Scene, 2013 Mill Lane, Wingerworth, Chesterfield S42 6NG ☎ 01246 217264 ✉ steve.brunt@ne-derbyshire.gov.uk

Grounds Maintenance: Mr Steve Brunt , Joint Assistant Director - Street Scene, 2013 Mill Lane, Wingerworth, Chesterfield S42 6NG ☎ 01246 217264 ✉ steve.brunt@ne-derbyshire.gov.uk

Grounds Maintenance: Mr Darren Mitchell , Grounds Maintenance Manager, 2013 Mill Lane, Wingerworth, Chesterfield S42 6NG ☎ 01246 217285 🖷 01246 217464 ✉ darren.mitchell@ne-derbyshire.gov.uk

Health and Safety: Mrs Angela Grundy , Joint Assistant Director - Human Resources & Payroll, 2013 Mill Lane, Wingerworth, Chesterfield S42 6NG ☎ 01246 242411; 01246 217009 ✉ angela.grundy@ne-derbyshire.gov.uk

Health and Safety: Mr Paul Hackett, Joint Executive Director - Transformation, 2013 Mill Lane, Wingerworth, Chesterfield S42 6NG ☎ 01246 217543 ✉ paul.hackett@ne-derbyshire.gov.uk

Health and Safety: Mr Mark Spotswood , Health & Safety Advisor, 2013 Mill Lane, Wingerworth, Chesterfield S42 6NG ✉ mark.spotswood@bolsover.gov.uk

Housing: Ms Lorraine Shaw , Managing Director - Rykneld Homes, 2013 Mill Lane, Wingerworth, Chesterfield S42 6NG ☎ 01246 217808 ✉ lorraine.shaw@rykneldhomes.org.uk

Legal: Mrs Naomi Smith , Principal Solicitor, 2013 Mill Lane, Wingerworth, Chesterfield S42 6NG ☎ 01246 237141 ✉ naomi.smith@ne-derbyshire.gov.uk

Leisure and Cultural Services: Mr Paul Hackett , Joint Executive Director - Transformation, 2013 Mill Lane, Wingerworth, Chesterfield S42 6NG ☎ 01246 217543 ✉ paul.hackett@ne-derbyshire.gov.uk

Leisure and Cultural Services: Mr Lee Hickin , Joint Assistant Director - Leisure, 2013 Mill Lane, Wingerworth, Chesterfield S42 6NG ☎ 01246 217218 ✉ lee.hickin@bolsover.gov.uk

Licensing: Mr John Chambers, Licensing Co-ordinator, 2013 Mill Lane, Wingerworth, Chesterfield S42 6NG ☎ 01246 217216 🖷 01246 217447 ✉ john.chambers@ne-derbyshire.gov.uk

Lottery Funding, Charity and Voluntary: Ms Dawn Clarke , Joint Assistant Director - Finance, Revenues & Benefits, 2013 Mill Lane, Wingerworth, Chesterfield S42 6NG ☎ 01246 217658 ✉ dawn.clarke@ne-derbyshire.gov.uk

Member Services: Mrs Sarah Sternberg , Joint Assistant Director - Governance & Monitoring Officer, 2013 Mill Lane, Wingerworth, Chesterfield S42 6NG ☎ 01246 217057 🖷 01246 217442 ✉ sarah.sternberg@bolsover.gov.uk

Partnerships: Mr Sam Ulyatt , Policy Officer, 2013 Mill Lane, Wingerworth, Chesterfield S42 6NG ☎ 01246 217014 ✉ sam.ulyatt@ne-derbyshire.gov.uk

Personnel / HR: Mrs Angela Grundy , Joint Assistant Director - Human Resources & Payroll, 2013 Mill Lane, Wingerworth, Chesterfield S42 6NG ☎ 01246 242411; 01246 217009 ✉ angela.grundy@ne-derbyshire.gov.uk

Planning: Mr James Arnold , Joint Assistant Director - Planning & Environmental Health, 2013 Mill Lane, Wingerworth, Chesterfield S42 6NG ☎ 01246 217436 ✉ james.arnold@bolsover.gov.uk

Planning: Mr Adrian Kirkham , Planning Services Manager, 2013 Mill Lane, Wingerworth, Chesterfield S42 6NG ☎ 01246 217591 ✉ adrian.kirkham@ne-derbyshire.gov.uk

Procurement: Mr Bryan Mason , Joint Executive Director - Operations, 2013 Mill Lane, Wingerworth, Chesterfield S42 6NG ☎ 01246 242431 ✉ bryan.mason@ne-derbyshire.gov.uk

Recycling & Waste Minimisation: Mr Steve Jowett , Joint Waste & Recycling Manager, 2013 Mill Lane, Wingerworth, Chesterfield S42 6NG ☎ 01246 217266 🖷 01246 217442 ✉ steve.jowett@ne-derbyshire.gov.uk

Regeneration: Mr Wes Lumley, Joint Chief Executive Officer, 2013 Mill Lane, Wingerworth, Chesterfield S42 6NG ☎ 01246 217155 ✉ wes.lumley@bolsover.gov.uk

Regeneration: Mrs Allison Westray-Chapman , Joint Assistant Director - Economic Growth, 2013 Mill Lane, Wingerworth, Chesterfield S42 6NG ☎ 01246 217199 ✉ allison.westray-chapman@ne-derbyshire.gov.uk

Staff Training: Mrs Angela Grundy , Joint Assistant Director - Human Resources, 2013 Mill Lane, Wingerworth, Chesterfield S42 6NG ☎ 01246 217009 ✉ angela.grundy@ne-derbyshire.gov.uk

Street Scene: Mr Steve Brunt , Joint Assistant Director - Streetscene, 2013 Mill Lane, Wingerworth, Chesterfield S42 6NG ☎ 01246 217264 ✉ steve.brunt@ne-derbyshire.gov.uk

Sustainable Communities: Mrs Debbie Whitehead , Consultation & Community Involvement Officer, 2013 Mill Lane, Wingerworth, Chesterfield S42 6NG ☎ 01246 217018 ✉ debbie.whitehead@ne-derbyshire.gov.uk

Sustainable Development: Mrs Jane Foley, Joint Assistant Director - Customer Service & Improvement, 2013 Mill Lane, Wingerworth, Chesterfield S42 6NG ☎ 01246 242343; 01246 217029 🖷 01246 242423; 01246 217442 ✉ jane.foley@bolsover.gov.uk

Transport: Mr Steve Brunt , Joint Assistant Director - Street Scene, 2013 Mill Lane, Wingerworth, Chesterfield S42 6NG ☎ 01246 217264 ✉ steve.brunt@ne-derbyshire.gov.uk

Waste Collection and Disposal: Mr Steve Brunt , Joint Assistant Director - Streetscene, 2013 Mill Lane, Wingerworth, Chesterfield S42 6NG ☎ 01246 217264 ✉ steve.brunt@ne-derbyshire.gov.uk

Waste Management: Mr Steve Brunt , Streetscene Manager, 2013 Mill Lane, Wingerworth, Chesterfield S42 6NG ☎ 01246 217624 ✉ steve.brunt@ne-derbyshire.gov.uk

COUNCILLORS

Leader of the Council **Baxter**, Graham (LAB - Dronfield North) cllr.baxter@ne-derbyshire.gov.uk

Deputy Leader of the Council **Hill**, Elizabeth (LAB - Grassmoor) cllr.hill@ne-derbyshire.gov.uk

Antcliff, Pat (CON - Wingerworth)

NORTH EAST DERBYSHIRE

Armitage, William (CON - Ashover)

Austen, Jane (LAB - Eckington North)

Barker, Nigel (LAB - North Wingfield Central)
nigel.barker@ne-derbyshire.gov.uk

Barnes, Barry (LAB - Shirland)

Barry, Jayne (LAB - North Wingfield Central)

Blanshard, Liz (CON - Dronfield South)

Boyle, Shay (LAB - Sutton)

Butler, Geoff (LAB - Pilsley and Morton)

Cooper, Andrew (IND - Pilsley and Morton)
andrew.cooper@ne-derbyshire.gov.uk

Cupit, Charlotte (CON - Shirland)

Dale, Alex (CON - Coal Aston)

Elliott, Peter (CON - Brampton and Walton)
peter.elliot@ne-derbyshire.gov.uk

Ellis, Stuart (CON - Wingerworth)
stuart.ellis@ne-derbyshire.gov.uk

Emmens, Michelle (CON - Gosforth Valley)

Foster, Mark (CON - Dronfield Woodhouse)

Foster, Angelique (CON - Dronfield South)

Garrett, Alan (LAB - Killamarsh West)
alan.garrett@ne-derbyshire.gov.uk

Gordon, Michael (LAB - Ridgeway and Marsh Lane)
cllr.gordon@ne-derbyshire.gov.uk

Griffin-Chappel, Gary (CON - Coal Aston)

Hall, Roger (CON - Dronfield Woodhouse)

Hill, Julie (LAB - Grassmoor)

Holmes, Patricia (LAB - Pilsley and Morton)
patricia.holmes@ne-derbyshire.gov.uk

Huckerby, Carol (CON - Barlow and Holmesfield)
carol.huckerby@ne-derbyshire.gov.uk

Hunt, Clive (LAB - Eckington South)
clive.hunt@ne-derbyshire.gov.uk

Kerry, Patrick (LAB - Sutton)
patrick.kerry@ne-derbyshire.gov.uk

Laws, Harold (LAB - Killamarsh East)

Lewis, Barry (CON - Wingerworth)

Lilley, Jeff (LAB - North Wingfield Central)

Lilleyman, Wayne (LAB - Tupton)

Mansbridge, Ted (LAB - Clay Cross South)

Morley, Geoff (LAB - Clay Cross North)
cllr.morley@ne-derbyshire.gov.uk

Peters, Stephen (LAB - Tupton)

Powell, Alan (CON - Gosforth Valley)

Reader, Tracy (LAB - Clay Cross North)

Rice, William (LAB - Killamarsh West)
billy.rice@ne-derbyshire.gov.uk

Ridgway, Jacqueline (LAB - Eckington South)

Ridgway, Brian (LAB - Renishaw)
brian.ridgway@ne-derbyshire.gov.uk

Robinson, Lilian (LAB - Killamarsh West)

Rouse, Kathy (LAB - Clay Cross North)

Skinner, Derrick (LAB - Shirland)

Smith, Christine (LAB - Dronfield North)
christine.smith@ne-derbyshire.gov.uk

Smith, Rosie (LAB - Unstone)

Stone, Lee (LAB - Holmewood and Heath)
lee.stone@ne-derbyshire.gov.uk

Tait, Kevin (CON - Dronfield South)

Thacker, Martin (CON - Brampton and Walton)
martin.thacker@ne-derbyshire.gov.uk

Tite, Catherine (LAB - Eckington North)

Welton, Richard (CON - Gosforth Valley)

Williams, Patricia (LAB - Holmewood and Heath)
patricia.williams@ne-derbyshire.gov.uk

Windle, John (LAB - Killamarsh East)
john.windle@ne-derbyshire.gov.uk

Wright, Brian (LAB - Clay Cross South)
brian.wright@ne-derbyshire.gov.uk

POLITICAL COMPOSITION

LAB: 34, CON: 18, IND: 1

North East Lincolnshire U

North East Lincolnshire Council, Municipal Offices, Town Hall Square, Grimsby DN31 1HU
☎ 01472 313131 🖳 www.nelincs.gov.uk

FACTS AND FIGURES

Parliamentary Constituencies: Cleethorpes, Great Grimsby
EU Constituencies: Yorkshire and the Humber
Election Frequency: Elections are by thirds

PRINCIPAL OFFICERS

Chief Executive: Mr Rob Walsh, Chief Executive, Municipal Offices, Town Hall Square, Grimsby DN31 1HU ☎ 01472 323870 🖷 01472 323917 rob.walsh@nelincs.gov.uk

Deputy Chief Executive: Ms Joanne Hewson , Deputy Chief Executive - Communities, Municipal Offices, Town Hall Square, Grimsby DN31 1HU ☎ 01472 323021 joanne.hewson@nelincs.gov.uk

Senior Management: Ms Angela Blake , Director - Economy & Growth, Municipal Offices, Town Hall Square, Grimsby DN31 1HU ☎ 01472 324741 angela.blake@nelincs.gov.uk

Senior Management: Ms Bev Compton , Assistant Director - Adult Services & Health Improvement, Municipal Offices, Town Hall Square, Grimsby DN31 1HU ☎ 01472 326126 beverley.compton@nelincs.gov.uk

Senior Management: Mr Paul Cordy , Assistant Director - Children's Services, Municipal Offices, Town Hall Square, Grimsby DN31 1HU ☎ 01472 323255 ✉ paul.cordy@nelincs.gov.uk

Senior Management: Ms Helen Isaacs , Assistant Director - Governance & Democracy, Municipal Offices, Town Hall Square, Grimsby DN31 1HU ☎ 01472 326127 ✉ helen.isaacs@nelincs.gov.uk

Senior Management: Ms Sally Jack , Assistant Director - Joint Delivery, Municipal Offices, Town Hall Square, Grimsby DN31 1HU ☎ 01472 325631 🖷 01472 323030 ✉ sally.jack@nelincs.gov.uk

Senior Management: Mr Steve Kay , Assistant Director - Early Intervention, Municipal Offices, Town Hall Square, Grimsby DN31 1HU ☎ 01472 323266 ✉ steve.kay@nelincs.gov.uk

Senior Management: Mr Tony Maione , Assistant Director - Law (Monitoring Officer), Municipal Offices, Town Hall Square, Grimsby DN31 1HU ☎ 01472 324016 ✉ tony.maione@nelincs.gov.uk

Senior Management: Mr Tony Neul, Assistant Director - Environment, Municipal Offices, Town Hall Square, Grimsby DN31 1HU ☎ 01472 323989 ✉ tony.neul@nelincs.gov.uk

Senior Management: Mr Stephen Pintus , Director - Public Health, Municipal Offices, Town Hall Square, Grimsby DN31 1HU ☎ 01472 324012 ✉ stephen.pintus@nelincs.gov.uk

Senior Management: Ms Sharon Wroot , Director - Finance, Municipal Offices, Town Hall Square, Grimsby DN31 1HU ☎ 01472 324423 ✉ sharon.wroot@nelincs.gov.uk

Architect, Building / Property Services: Mr Dave Gelder, Deputy Head of Architecture, Origin 2, Origin Way, Europarc, Grimsby DN37 9TZ ☎ 01472 324450 ✉ david.gelder@nelincs.gov.uk

Building Control: Mr Mark Cawood , Planning & Building Control Manager, Origin 1, Origin Way, Europarc, Grimsby DN37 9TZ ☎ 01472 323280 ✉ mark.cawood@nelincs.gov.uk

Children / Youth Services: Mr Steve Kay , Assistant Director - Early Intervention, Municipal Offices, Town Hall Square, Grimsby DN31 1HU ☎ 01472 323266 ✉ steve.kay@nelincs.gov.uk

Civil Registration: Mrs Tracy Frisby , Registrars & Civic Services Team Manager, Cleethorpes Town Hall, Knoll Street, Grimsby DN35 8LN ☎ 01472 324860 ✉ tracy.riley@nelincs.gov.uk

PR / Communications: Mr Iain Lovell , Head of Communications, Print & Marketing, Municipal Offices, Town Hall Square, Grimsby DN31 1HU ☎ 01472 325960 ✉ iain.lovell@nelincs.gov.uk

Community Safety: Mr Spencer Hunt , Service Manager Safer Communities, The Elms, 22 Abbey Road, Grimsby DN32 0HW ☎ 01472 325939 ✉ spencer.hunt@neclincs.gov.uk

Computer Management: Mr Paul Hudson , ICT Group Manager, Civic Offices, Knoll Street, Cleethorpes DN35 8LN ☎ 01472 323977 ✉ paul.hudson@nelincs.gov.uk

Consumer Protection and Trading Standards: Mr Neil Clark , Trading Standards Manager, Municipal Offices, Town Hall Square, Grimsby DN31 1HU ☎ 01472 324805 ✉ neil.clark@nelincs.gov.uk

Contracts: Ms Debbie Dales , Contract & Commercial Service Manager, St. James House, Grimsby DN31 1EP ☎ 01472 324153 ✉ debbie.dales@nelincs.gov.uk

Corporate Services: Ms Sharon Wroot , Director - Finance, Municipal Offices, Town Hall Square, Grimsby DN31 1HU ☎ 01472 324423 ✉ sharon.wroot@nelincs.gov.uk

Customer Service: Ms Susan Simpson , Communities, Customer & Business Suppoer Services Manager, Municipal Offices, Town Hall Square, Grimsby DN31 1HU ☎ 01472 323757 ✉ susan.simpson@nelincs.gov.uk

Economic Development: Mr Damien Jaines-White, Service Manager - Economic Development, Municipal Offices, Town Hall Square, Grimsby DN31 1HU ☎ 01472 324674 🖷 01472 326402 ✉ damien.jaines-white@nelincs.gov.uk

Education: Ms Joanne Hewson , Deputy Chief Executive - Communities, Municipal Offices, Town Hall Square, Grimsby DN31 1HU ☎ 01472 323021 ✉ joanne.hewson@nelincs.gov.uk

Electoral Registration: Mr Stephen McGrath , Elections & Complaints Team Manager, Municipal Offices, Town Hall Square, Grimsby DN31 1HU ☎ 01472 324160 🖷 01472 324132 ✉ stephen.mcgrath@nelincs.gov.uk

Emergency Planning: Mr James Mason, Assistant Emergency Planning Manager, Fishing Hetetage Centre, Alexandra Dock, Grimsby DN31 1UZ ☎ 01472 324829 🖷 01472 324411 ✉ james.mason@nelincs.gov.uk

Energy Management: Mr Tony Neul, Assistant Director - Environment, Municipal Offices, Town Hall Square, Grimsby DN31 1HU ☎ 01472 323989 ✉ tony.neul@nelincs.gov.uk

Environmental / Technical Services: Mr Neil Beeken , Food Health Manager, Thrunscoe Centre, Highgate, Cleethorpes DN35 8NX ☎ 01472 324773 🖷 01472 324767 ✉ neil.beeken@nelincs.gov.uk

Environmental Health: Mr Neil Beeken , Food Health Manager, Municipal Offices, Town Hall Square, Grimsby DN31 1HU ☎ 01472 324773 🖷 01472 324767 ✉ neil.beeken@nelincs.gov.uk

Estates, Property & Valuation: Ms Wendy Fisher , Assets Service Manager, Municipal Offices, Town Hall Square, Grimsby DN31 1HU ☎ 01472 323132 ✉ wendy.fisher@nelincs.gov.uk

Events Manager: Ms Sue Marshall , Operations Manager - Cultural Services, Fishing Heritage Centre, Grimsby DN31 1UZ ☎ 01472 323640 ✉ sue.marshall@nelincs.gov.uk

Facilities: Mr Paul Thorpe , Building & Facilities Operations Manager, Origin 2, Origin Way, Europarc, Grimsby DN37 9TZ ☎ 01472 324782 ✉ paul.thorpe@nelincs.gov.uk

Finance: Ms Sharon Wroot , Director - Finance, Municipal Offices, Town Hall Square, Grimsby DN31 1HU ☎ 01472 324423 sharon.wroot@nelincs.gov.uk

Fleet Management: Mr Glenn Greetham, Head of Neighbourhood Operations, Doughty Road Depot, Grimsby DN32 0LL ☎ 01472 325709 glenn.greetham@nelincs.gov.uk

Grounds Maintenance: Mr Glenn Greetham, Head of Neighbourhood Operations, Doughty Road Depot, Grimsby DN32 0LL ☎ 01472 325709 glenn.greetham@nelincs.gov.uk

Health and Safety: Mr Mark Smith , Occupational Health & Safety Manager, Civic Offices, Knoll Street, Grimsby DN35 8LN ☎ 01472 324071 mark.smith@nelincs.gov.uk

Highways: Mr Marcus Asquith , Head of Highways & Transport, Origin 2, Origin Way, Europarc, Grimsby DN37 9TZ ☎ 01472 336676 🖷 01472 325657 marcus.asquith@nelincs.gov.uk

Home Energy Conservation: Ms Debra Fox, Home Energy Promotions Officer, Origin 1, 1 Origin Way, Europarc, Grimsby DN37 9TZ ☎ 01472 324782 debra.fox@nelincs.gov.uk

Housing: Ms Debbie Fagan , Service Manager - Strategic Housing, Acorn Business Park, Unit 5, Moss Road, Grimsby DN32 0LT
☎ 01472 324977 debbie.fagan@nelincs.gov.uk

Legal: Mr Tony Maione , Assistant Director - Law (Monitoring Officer), Municipal Offices, Town Hall Square, Grimsby DN31 1HU ☎ 01472 324016 tony.maione@nelincs.gov.uk

Leisure and Cultural Services: Ms Sue Marshall , Operations Manager - Cultural Services, Fishing Heritage Centre, Grimsby DN31 1UZ ☎ 01472 323640 sue.marshall@nelincs.gov.uk

Licensing: Mr Adrian Moody, Licensing Manager, Municipal Offices, Town Hall Square, Grimsby DN31 1HU ☎ 01472 324759 adrian.moody@nelincs.gov.uk

Lighting: Mr Marcus Asquith , Head of Highways & Transport, Municipal Offices, Town Hall Square, Grimsby DN31 1HU ☎ 01472 336676 🖷 01472 325657 marcus.asquith@nelincs.gov.uk

Member Services: Mr Paul Windley , Democratic & Scrutiny Team Manager, Municipal Offices, Town Hall Square, Grimsby DN31 1HU ☎ 01472 324121 paul.windley@nelincs.gov.uk

Parking: Mr Christopher Mayall , CEO Supervisor, Municipal Offices, Town Hall Square, Grimsby DN31 1HU ☎ 01472 324379 christopher.mayall@nelincs.gov.uk

Personnel / HR: Ms Sue Walton , HR Group Manager, Civic Offices, Knoll Street, Cleethorpes DN35 8LN ☎ 01472 323259 sue.walton@nelincs.gov.uk

Planning: Mr Jake Newby , Lead Officer for Planning, Acorn Business, Unit 5, Moss Road, Grimsby DN32 0LT ☎ 01472 324227 jake.newby@nelincs.gov.uk

Procurement: Ms Rachel Devaney , Partnerships, Contract Management & Compliance Specialist, Central Library, Town Hall Square, Grimsby DN31 1HG ☎ 01472 324153 rachel.devaney@nelincs.gov.uk

Public Libraries: Mr Steve Hipkins, Head of Cultural Services, Central Library, Town Hall Square, Grimsby DN31 1HG ☎ 01472 323611 🖷 01472 323618 steve.hipkins@nelincs.gov.uk

Recycling & Waste Minimisation: Mr Tony Neul, Assistant Director - Environment, Origin 1, Europarc, Grimsby DN37 9TZ ☎ 01472 323989 tony.neul@nelincs.gov.uk

Road Safety: Mr Marcus Asquith , Head of Highways & Transport, Municipal Offices, Town Hall Square, Grimsby DN31 1HU ☎ 01472 336676 🖷 01472 325657 marcus.asquith@nelincs.gov.uk

Social Services: Ms Joanne Hewson , Deputy Chief Executive - Communities, Municipal Offices, Town Hall Square, Grimsby DN31 1HU ☎ 01472 323021 joanne.hewson@nelincs.gov.uk

Social Services (Adult): Ms Joanne Hewson , Deputy Chief Executive - Communities, Municipal Offices, Town Hall Square, Grimsby DN31 1HU ☎ 01472 323021 joanne.hewson@nelincs.gov.uk

Social Services (Children): Mr Paul Cordy , Assistant Director - Children's Services, Municipal Offices, Town Hall Square, Grimsby DN31 1HU ☎ 01472 323255 paul.cordy@nelincs.gov.uk

Public Health: Mr Stephen Pintus , Director - Public Health, Municipal Offices, Town Hall Square, Grimsby DN31 1HU ☎ 01472 324012 stephen.pintus@nelincs.gov.uk

Staff Training: Ms Debbie Walden , Learning & Development Team Manager, Civic Offices, Knoll Street, Cleethorpes DN34 5TD ☎ 01472 324059 deborah.walden@nelincs.gov.uk

Street Scene: Mr Tony Neul, Assistant Director - Environment, Origin 1, Europarc, Grimsby DN37 9TZ ☎ 01472 323989 tony.neul@nelincs.gov.uk

Sustainable Communities: Ms Joanne Hewson , Deputy Chief Executive - Communities, Municipal Offices, Town Hall Square, Grimsby DN31 1HU ☎ 01472 323021 joanne.hewson@nelincs.gov.uk

Tourism: Ms Sue Marshall , Operations Manager - Cultural Services, Fishing Heritage Centre, Grimsby DN31 1UZ ☎ 01472 323640 sue.marshall@nelincs.gov.uk

Traffic Management: Mr Marcus Asquith , Head of Highways & Transport, Municipal Offices, Town Hall Square, Grimsby DN31 1HU ☎ 01472 336676 🖷 01472 325657 marcus.asquith@nelincs.gov.uk

Transport: Mr Marcus Asquith , Head of Highways & Transport, Municipal Offices, Town Hall Square, Grimsby DN31 1HU ☎ 01472 336676 🖷 01472 325657 marcus.asquith@nelincs.gov.uk

Transport Planner: Mr Marcus Asquith , Head of Highways & Transport, Municipal Offices, Town Hall Square, Grimsby DN31 1HU
☎ 01472 336676 🖷 01472 325657 ✉ marcus.asquith@nelincs.gov.uk

Waste Collection and Disposal: Mr Tony Neul, Assistant Director - Environment, Origin 1, Europarc, Grimsby DN37 9TZ
☎ 01472 323989 ✉ tony.neul@nelincs.gov.uk

Waste Management: Mr Tony Neul, Assistant Director - Environment, Origin 1, Europarc, Grimsby DN37 9TZ
☎ 01472 323989 ✉ tony.neul@nelincs.gov.uk

COUNCILLORS

***Mayor* Barber**, Clifford (LD - Freshney)
cliff.barber@nelincs.gov.uk

***Deputy Mayor* McGilligan-Fell**, Christina (LD - Park)
christina.mcgilliganfell@nelincs.gov.uk

***Leader of the Council* Oxby**, Ray (LAB - South)
ray.oxby@nelincs.gov.uk

***Deputy Leader of the Council* Hyldon-King**, Jane (LAB - Yarborough)
jane.hyldon-king@nelincs.gov.uk

Barrow, Matthew (LAB - Park)
matthew.barrow@nelincs.gov.uk

Beasant, Stephen (LD - East Marsh)
steve.beasant@nelincs.gov.uk

Bishell, Becci (UKIP - East Marsh)
rebecca.bishell@nelincs.gov.uk

Bolton, David (LAB - Immingham)
david.bolton@nelincs.gov.uk

Bramley, Jane (UKIP - South)
jane.bramley@nelincs.gov.uk

Brookes, Keith (CON - Haverstoe)
keith.brookes@nelincs.gov.uk

Brown, Matthew (LAB - Croft Baker)
matthew.brown@nelincs.gov.uk

Burton, Mike (LAB - Immingham)
mike.burton@nelincs.gov.uk

Cairns, James (UKIP - Yarborough)
james.cairns@nelincs.gov.uk

Chase, Hazel (LAB - Sidney Sussex)
hazel.chase@nelincs.gov.uk

Colquhoun, Iain (CON - Waltham)
iain.colquhoun@nelincs.gov.uk

Cracknell, Margaret (CON - Haverstoe)
margaret.cracknell@nelincs.gov.uk

De Freitas, Andrew (LD - Park)
andrew.defreitas@nelincs.gov.uk

Dickerson, Melanie (CON - Wolds)
melaine.dickerson@nelincs.gov.uk

Fenty, John (CON - Humberston and New Waltham)
john.fenty@ntlworld.com

Harness, Stephen (UKIP - Humberston and New Waltham)
stephen.harness@nelincs.gov.uk

Hasthorpe, David (CON - Wolds)
david.hasthorpe@nelincs.gov.uk

Hudson, Henry (UKIP - Scartho)
henry.hudson@nelincs.gov.uk

Jackson, Philip (CON - Waltham)
philip.jackson@nelincs.gov.uk

James, Rosalind (LAB - Heneage)
ros.james@nelincs.gov.uk

Lindley, Ian (CON - Scartho)
ian.lindley@nelincs.gov.uk

Mickleburgh, Tim (LAB - West Marsh)
tim.mickleburgh@nelincs.gov.uk

Parkinson, Bill (CON - Haverstoe)
bill.parkinson@nelincs.gov.uk

Patrick, Matthew (LAB - Heneage)
matthew.patrick@nelincs.gov.uk

Pettigrew, Nick (UKIP - Freshney)
nick.pettigrew@nelincs.gov.uk

Shaw, Christopher (LAB - Sidney Sussex)
chris.shaw@nelincs.gov.uk

Shepherd, Ron (UKIP - Scartho)
ron.shepherd@nelincs.gov.uk

Shreeve, Stan (CON - Humberston and New Waltham)
stanley.shreeve@nelincs.gov.uk

Stanland, Chris (LAB - South)
christopher.stanland@nelincs.gov.uk

Stinson, Matt (UKIP - Sidney Sussex)
matt.stinson@nelincs.gov.uk

Stockton, John (UKIP - Heneage)
john.stockton@nelincs.gov.uk

Sutton, Ray (LAB - Freshney)
ray.sutton@nelincs.gov.uk

Thurogood, Terry (LAB - Croft Baker)
terry.thurogood@nelincs.gov.uk

Walker, Terry (LAB - East Marsh)
terry.walker@nelincs.gov.uk

Watson, David (LAB - Immingham)
dave.watson@nelincs.gov.uk

Wheatley, Peter (LAB - Yarborough)
peter.wheatley@nelincs.gov.uk

Wilson, Karl (LAB - West Marsh)
karl.wilson@nelincs.gov.uk

POLITICAL COMPOSITION

LAB: 18, CON: 10, UKIP: 9, LD: 4

COMMITTEE CHAIRS

Audit & Governance: Mr Stan Shreeve

Children & Young People: Mr Ian Lindley

Planning: Mr Philip Jackson

Regeneration, Environment & Housing: Mr Matt Stinson

NORTH HERTFORDSHIRE

North Hertfordshire D

North Hertfordshire District Council, Council Offices, Gernon Road, Letchworth SG6 3JF
☎ 01462 474000 🖷 01462 474559 or 01462 474227
💻 www.north-herts.gov.uk

FACTS AND FIGURES

Parliamentary Constituencies: Hertfordshire North East, Hitchin and Harpenden
EU Constituencies: Eastern
Election Frequency: Elections are by thirds

PRINCIPAL OFFICERS

Chief Executive: Mr David Scholes, Chief Executive & Strategic Director of Planning, Housing & Enterprise, Council Offices, Gernon Road, Letchworth SG6 3JF ☎ 01462 474836
🖱 david.scholes@north-herts.gov.uk

Senior Management: Mrs Norma Atlay, Strategic Director of Finance, Policy & Governance, Council Offices, Gernon Road, Letchworth SG6 3JF ☎ 01462 474297 🖷 01462 474396
🖱 norma.atlay@north-herts.gov.uk

Senior Management: Mr John Robinson, Strategic Director of Customer Services, Council Offices, Gernon Road, Letchworth SG6 3JF ☎ 01462 474655 🖷 01462 474633
🖱 john.robinson@north-herts.gov.uk

Best Value: Ms Fiona Timms , Performance & Risk Manager, Council Offices, Gernon Road, Letchworth SG6 3JF
☎ 01462 474251 🖷 01462 474396 🖱 fiona.timms@north-herts.gov.uk

Building Control: Mr Ian Fullstone, Head of Development & Building Control, Council Offices, Gernon Road, Letchworth SG6 3HU ☎ 01462 474480 🖱 ian.fullstone@north-herts.gov.uk

Children / Youth Services: Mrs Helen Rae , Children's & Young People's Development Manager, Council Offices, Gernon Road, Letchworth SG6 3JF ☎ 01462 474333
🖱 helen.rae@north-herts.gov.uk

PR / Communications: Ms Sarah Dobor , Communications Manager, Council Offices, Gernon Road, Letchworth SG6 3JF
☎ 01462 474552 🖱 sarah.dobor@north-herts.gov.uk

Community Safety: Ms Rebecca Coates , Community Safety Manager, Council Offices, Gernon Road, Letchworth SG6 3JF
☎ 01462 474504 🖱 rebecca.coates@north-herts.gov.uk

Computer Management: Mr Vic Godfrey, Information Technology Manager, Town Lodge, Gernon Road, Letchworth SG6 3HN
☎ 01462 474455 🖷 01462 474396 🖱 vic.godfrey@north-herts.gov.uk

Corporate Services: Ms Liz Green, Head of Policy & Community Services, Council Offices, Gernon Road, Letchworth SG6 3JF
☎ 01462 474230 🖱 liz.green@north-herts.gov.uk

Corporate Services: Mr John Robinson, Strategic Director of Customer Services, Council Offices, Gernon Road, Letchworth SG6 3JF ☎ 01462 474655 🖷 01462 474633
🖱 john.robinson@north-herts.gov.uk

Customer Service: Ms Johanne Dufficy , Customer Services Manager, Council Offices, Gernon Road, Letchworth SG6 3JF
☎ 01462 474555 🖱 johanne.dufficy@north-herts.gov.uk

E-Government: Mr Gavin Midgley , Website Manager, Council Offices, Gernon Road, Letchworth SG6 3JF
🖱 gavin.midgley@north-herts.gov.uk

Electoral Registration: Mr David Miley, Democratic Services Manager, Council Offices, Gernon Road, Letchworth SG6 3JF
☎ 01462 474208 🖷 01462 474227 🖱 david.miley@north-herts.gov.uk

Emergency Planning: Mr Derek Wootton, Emergency Planning Officer, Council Offices, Gernon Road, Letchworth SG6 3JF
☎ 01462 474246 🖱 derek.wootton@north-herts.gov.uk

Environmental / Technical Services: Mr Vaughan Watson, Head of Leisure & Environmental Services, Council Offices, Gernon Road, Letchworth SG6 3JF ☎ 01462 474641 🖷 01462 474500
🖱 vaughan.watson@north-herts.gov.uk

Environmental Health: Mr Peter Carey , Head of Housing & Public Protection, Council Offices, Gernon Road, Letchworth SG6 3JF ☎ 01462 474293 🖱 peter.carey@north-herts.gov.uk

Finance: Mrs Norma Atlay, Strategic Director of Finance, Policy & Governance, Council Offices, Gernon Road, Letchworth SG6 3JF
☎ 01462 474297 🖷 01462 474396
🖱 norma.atlay@north-herts.gov.uk

Finance: Mr Andrew Cavanagh , Head of Finance Performance & Asset Management, Council Offices, Gernon Road, Letchworth SG6 3JF ☎ 01462 474247 🖱 andrew.cavanagh@north-herts.gov.uk

Treasury: Mr Tim Neil , Accounting & Treasury Manager, Council Offices, Gernon Road, Letchworth SG6 3JF ☎ 01462 474461
🖱 tim.neil@north-herts.gov.uk

Fleet Management: Ms Chloe Hipwood , Service Manager of Waste Management, Council Offices, Gernon Road, Letchworth SG6 3JF ☎ 01462 474304 🖱 chloe.hipwood@north-herts.gov.uk

Grounds Maintenance: Mr Andrew Mills, Service Manager of Grounds Maintenance, Council Offices, Gernon Road, Letchworth SG6 3TR ☎ 01462 474272 🖱 andrew.mills@north-herts.gov.uk

Health and Safety: Mr Les Davidson , Health & Safety Officer, Council Offices, Gernon Road, Letchworth SG6 3TR
☎ 01462 474600 🖱 les.davidson@north-herts.gov.uk

Legal: Ms Katie White , Corporate Legal Manager & Monitoring Officer, Council Offices, Gernon Road, Letchworth SG6 3JF
☎ 01462 474315 🖱 katie.white@north-herts.gov.uk

Leisure and Cultural Services: Mrs Ros Allwood , Cultural Services Manager, Council Offices, Gernon Road, Letchworth SG6 3JF ☎ 01462 435197 🖱 ros.allwood@north-herts.gov.uk

Leisure and Cultural Services: Mr Vaughan Watson, Head of Leisure & Environmental Services, Council Offices, Gernon Road, Letchworth SG6 3JF ☎ 01462 474641 🖷 01462 474500
🖱 vaughan.watson@north-herts.gov.uk

Licensing: Mr Steven Cobb , Licensing & Enforcement Manager, Council Offices, Gernon Road, Letchworth SG6 3JF ☎ 01462 474370 🖷 01462 474409 ✉ steven.cobb@north-herts.gov.uk

Member Services: Mr Ian Gourlay , Senior Committee & Member Services Officer, Council Offices, Gernon Road, Letchworth SG6 3JF ☎ 01462 474641 ✉ ian.gourlay@north-herts.gov.uk

Member Services: Mr David Miley, Democratic Services Manager, Council Offices, Gernon Road, Letchworth SG6 3JF ☎ 01462 474208 🖷 01462 474227 ✉ david.miley@north-herts.gov.uk

Parking: Mr Steve Crowley , Contracts & Projects Manager, Council Offices, Gernon Road, Letchworth SG6 3JF ☎ 01462 474211 ✉ steve.crowley@north-herts.gov.uk

Partnerships: Ms Liz Green, Head of Policy & Community Services, Council Offices, Gernon Road, Letchworth SG6 3JF ☎ 01462 474230 ✉ liz.green@north-herts.gov.uk

Personnel / HR: Mrs Kerry Shorrocks, Corporate Human Resources Manager, Council Offices, Gernon Road, Letchworth SG6 3JF ☎ 01462 474224 ✉ kerry.shorrocks@north-herts.gov.uk

Planning: Ms Louise Symes , Strategy Planning & Enterprise Manager, Council Offices, Gernon Road, Letchworth SG6 3JF ☎ 01462 474836 ✉ louise.symes@north-herts.gov.uk

Recycling & Waste Minimisation: Ms Chloe Hipwood , Service Manager of Waste Management, Council Offices, Gernon Road, Letchworth SG6 3JF ☎ 01462 474304 ✉ chloe.hipwood@north-herts.gov.uk

Staff Training: Mrs Vicky Jobling , Learning & Development Manager, Council Offices, Gernon Road, Letchworth SG6 3JF ☎ 01462 474435 ✉ victoria.jobling@north-herts.gov.uk

Sustainable Communities: Mr Stuart Izzard , Community Development Manager, Council Offices, Gernon Road, Letchworth SG6 3JF ☎ 01462 474439 ✉ stuart.izzard@north-herts.gov.uk

Waste Collection and Disposal: Ms Chloe Hipwood , Service Manager of Waste Management, Council Offices, Gernon Road, Letchworth SG6 3JF ☎ 01462 474304 ✉ chloe.hipwood@north-herts.gov.uk

Children's Play Areas: Mr Steve Geach , Parks & Countryside Development Manager, Council Offices, Gernon Road, Letchworth SG6 3JF ☎ 01462 474641 ✉ steve.geach@north-herts.gov.uk

COUNCILLORS

***Chair* Shakespeare-Smith**, Raymond (CON - Hitchin Walsworth)
rayss83@hotmail.com

***Vice-Chair* Booth**, John (CON - Letchworth South East)
john.booth@north-herts.gov.uk

***Vice-Chair* Hone**, Terry (CON - Letchworth South West)
terry.hone@north-herts.gov.uk

***Leader of the Council* Needham**, Lynda (CON - Letchworth South West)
lynda.needham@north-herts.gov.uk

***Group Leader* Jarvis**, Sal (LD - Chesfield)
sal@sjarvis.co.uk

***Group Leader* Radcliffe**, Frank (LAB - Hitchin Oughton)
frank.radcliffe@north-herts.gov.uk

Ashley, Allison (CON - Hitchin Priory)
allison_priory@yahoo.co.uk

Bardett, Alan (CON - Knebworth)
alanbardett1@btinternet.com

Barnard, David (CON - Hitchwood, Offa and Hoo)
david.barnard@north-herts.gov.uk

Billing, Clare (LAB - Letchworth Grange)
clare.billing@north-herts.gov.uk

Billing, Judi (LAB - Hitchin Bearton)
judi.billing@north-herts.gov.uk

Bishop, John (CON - Kimpton)
john.bishop@north-herts.gov.uk

Burt, Peter (CON - Royston Heath)
peter.burt@north-herts.gov.uk

Cunningham, Julian (CON - Letchworth South East)
julian.cunningham@ntlworld.com

Davidson, Bill (CON - Royston Meridian)
bill.davidson@north-herts.gov.uk

Frost, Faye (CON - Hitchwood, Offa and Hoo)

Gray, Jane (CON - Codicote)
jg@abboptshay.com

Green, Jean (CON - Royston Palace)
jean.green@north-herts.gov.uk

Grindal, Gary (LAB - Letchworth Wilbury)
gary.grindal@north-herts.gov.uk

Harris, Nicola (CON - Hitchin Highbury)
nicola.harris@north-herts.gov.uk

Harris, John (CON - Baldock East)
john.harris@north-herts.gov.uk

Harwood, Simon (CON - Hitchin Highbury)
simon.harwood@north-herts.gov.uk

Hemingway, Steve (CON - Knebworth)
steve.hemingway@north-herts.gov.uk

Henry, Cathryn (CON - Chesfield)
cathryn.henry@north-herts.gov.uk

Henry, Cathryn (CON - Chesfield)
cathryn.henry@north-herts.gov.uk

Hill, Fiona (CON - Royston Heath)
fiona.hill@north-herts.gov.uk

Hunter, Tony (CON - Royston Meridian)
tony.hunter@hertscc.gov.uk

Jarvis, Steve (LD - Weston and Sandon)
steve.jarvis@north-herts.gov.uk

Kercher, Lorna (LAB - Letchworth East)
lorna.kercher@north-herts.gov.uk

Kirby, Joan (LAB - Hitchin Oughton)

Leal-Bennett, David (CON - Hitchin Highbury)
david.leal-bennett@north-herts.gov.uk

Levett, David (CON - Letchworth South East)
david@dlevett.co.uk

NORTH HERTFORDSHIRE

Lewis, Ben (CON - Royston Palace)
ben.lewis@north-herts.gov.uk

Lovewell, Bernard (CON - Hitchin Walsworth)
bernard.lovewell@north-herts.gov.uk

Lunn, Sandra (LAB - Letchworth Grange)
sandra.lunn@north-herts.gov.uk

Mantle, Ian (LAB - Letchworth East)
ian.mantle@north-herts.gov.uk

Marment, Paul (CON - Letchworth Grange)
paul.marment@north-herts.gov.uk

McNally, Jim (CON - Baldock Town)
jim.mcnally@north-herts.gov.uk

Millard, Alan (CON - Hitchin Walsworth)
alanjmillard@yahoo.com

Morris, Gerald (CON - Ermine)
gerald.morris@north-herts.gov.uk

Muir, Michael (CON - Baldock Town)
michael.muir@hertscc.gov.uk

Paterson, Janine (CON - Arbury)
janine.paterson@north-herts.gov.uk

Rice, Mike (CON - Letchworth South West)
mike.rice@ntlworld.com

Sangha, Deepak (LAB - Letchworth Wilbury)
deepak.sangha@north-herts.gov.uk

Segalini, Deborah (LAB - Hitchin Bearton)
deborah.segalini@north-herts.gov.uk

Smith, Adrian (LAB - Hitchin Bearton)
adrian.smith@north-herts.gov.uk

Spencer-Smith, Harry (CON - Cadwell)
harry.spencer-smith@north-herts.gov.uk

Strong, Claire (CON - Hitchwood, Offa and Hoo)

Thake, Richard (CON - Hitchin Priory)
richard.thake@north-herts.gov.uk

Weeks, Michael (CON - Baldock Town)
michael.weeks@north-herts.gov.uk

POLITICAL COMPOSITION

CON: 37, LAB: 11, LD: 2

COMMITTEE CHAIRS

Finance, Audit & Risk: Mr Michael Weeks

Licensing: Mr Michael Muir

Planning: Mr David Barnard

North Kesteven D

North Kesteven District Council, District Council Offices, Kesteven Street, Sleaford NG34 7EF
☎ 01529 414155 🖷 01529 413956
customer_services@n-kesteven.gov.uk 💻 www.n-kesteven.gov.uk

FACTS AND FIGURES

Parliamentary Constituencies: Sleaford and North Hykeham
EU Constituencies: East Midlands
Election Frequency: Elections are of whole council

PRINCIPAL OFFICERS

Chief Executive: Mr Ian Fytche, Chief Executive, District Council Offices, Kesteven Street, Sleaford NG34 7EF ☎ 01529 414155
ian_fytche@n-kesteven.gov.uk

Deputy Chief Executive: Miss Karen Bradford , Deputy Chief Executive, District Council Offices, Kesteven Street, Sleaford NG34 7EF ☎ 01529 414155 karen_bradford@n-kesteven.gov.uk

Senior Management: Ms Michelle Carrington, Head of Corporate & Customer Services, District Council Offices, Kesteven Street, Sleaford NG34 7EF ☎ 01529 414155
michelle_carrington@n-kesteven.gov.uk

Senior Management: Mr Michael Kelleher , Head of Housing & Property Services, District Council Offices, Kesteven Street, Sleaford NG34 7EF ☎ 01529 414155
michael_kelleher@n-kesteven.gov.uk

Senior Management: Mr Andrew McDonough, Head of Development, Economic & Cultural Services, District Council Offices, Kesteven Street, Sleaford NG34 7EF ☎ 01529 414155
andrew_mcdonough@n-kesteven.gov.uk

Senior Management: Mr Philip Roberts, Corporate Director, District Council Offices, Kesteven Street, Sleaford NG34 7EF
☎ 01529 414155 philip_roberts@n-kesteven.gov.uk

Senior Management: Mr Russell Stone , Head of Finance & Resources, District Council Offices, Kesteven Street, Sleaford NG34 7EF ☎ 01529 414155 russell_stone@n-kesteven.gov.uk

Senior Management: Mr Mark Taylor, Head of Environment & Public Protection, District Council Offices, Kesteven Street, Sleaford NG34 7EF ☎ 01529 414155; 01476 406080 🖷 01476 406000
mark_taylor@n-kesteven.gov.uk

Architect, Building / Property Services: Mr Michael Gadd, Property Services Manager, District Council Offices, Kesteven Street, Sleaford NG34 7EF ☎ 01529 414155
michael_gadd@n-kesteven.gov.uk

Building Control: Mr Paul Weldon , Building Control Manager & Access Officer, District Council Offices, Kesteven Street, Sleaford NG34 7EF ☎ 01529 414155 paul_weldon@n-kesteven.gov.uk

PR / Communications: Mr Jason Hippisley , Press & Publications Officer, District Council Offices, Kesteven Street, Sleaford NG34 7EF ☎ 01529 414155
jason_hippisley@n-kesteven.gov.uk

Community Planning: Ms Luisa McIntosh , Community Partnerships Manager, District Council Offices, Kesteven Street, Sleaford NG34 7EF ☎ 01529 414155
luisa_mcintosh@n-kesteven.gov.uk

Community Safety: Mrs Heidi Ryder , Community Safety Officer, District Council Offices, Kesteven Street, Sleaford NG34 7EF
☎ 01529 414155 heidi_ryder@n-kesteven.gov.uk

Computer Management: Ms Michelle Carrington, Head of Corporate & Customer Services, District Council Offices, Kesteven Street, Sleaford NG34 7EF ☎ 01529 414155 ✉ michelle_carrington@n-kesteven.gov.uk

Computer Management: Mr Gareth Kinton , Information Technology Manager, District Council Offices, Kesteven Street, Sleaford NG34 7EF ☎ 01529 414155 ✉ gareth_kinton@n-kesteven.gov.uk

Contracts: Mr Michael Gadd, Property Services Manager, District Council Offices, Kesteven Street, Sleaford NG34 7EF ☎ 01529 414155 ✉ michael_gadd@n-kesteven.gov.uk

Corporate Services: Ms Michelle Carrington, Head of Corporate & Customer Services, District Council Offices, Kesteven Street, Sleaford NG34 7EF ☎ 01529 414155 ✉ michelle_carrington@n-kesteven.gov.uk

Customer Service: Ms Michelle Carrington, Head of Corporate & Customer Services, District Council Offices, Kesteven Street, Sleaford NG34 7EF ☎ 01529 414155 ✉ michelle_carrington@n-kesteven.gov.uk

Economic Development: Mr Alan Gray , Economic Development Manager, District Council Offices, Kesteven Street, Sleaford NG34 7EF ☎ 01529 414155 ✉ alan.gray@n-kesteven.gov.uk

Electoral Registration: Mrs Marcella Heath , Democratic Services Manager, District Council Offices, Kesteven Street, Sleaford NG34 7EF ☎ 01529 414155 ✉ marcella_heath@n-kesteven.gov.uk

Electoral Registration: Mrs Gill Hopkins , Electoral Services Manager, District Council Offices, Kesteven Street, Sleaford NG34 7EF ☎ 01529 414155 ✉ gill_hopkins@n-kesteven.gov.uk

Emergency Planning: Ms Sarah Golembiewski , Corporate Health, Safety & Emergency Planning Officer, District Council Offices, Kesteven Street, Sleaford NG34 7EF ☎ 01529 414155 ✉ sarah_golembiewski@n-kesteven.gov.uk

Energy Management: Mr Michael Gadd, Property Services Manager, District Council Offices, Kesteven Street, Sleaford NG34 7EF ☎ 01529 414155 ✉ michael_gadd@n-kesteven.gov.uk

Environmental Health: Mr Mark Taylor, Head of Environment & Public Protection, District Council Offices, Kesteven Street, Sleaford NG34 7EF ☎ 01529 414155; 01476 406080 🖷 01476 406000 ✉ mark_taylor@n-kesteven.gov.uk

Estates, Property & Valuation: Mr Michael Gadd, Property Services Manager, District Council Offices, Kesteven Street, Sleaford NG34 7EF ☎ 01529 414155 ✉ michael_gadd@n-kesteven.gov.uk

Finance: Mr Russell Stone , Head of Finance & Resources, District Council Offices, Kesteven Street, Sleaford NG34 7EF ☎ 01529 414155 ✉ russell_stone@n-kesteven.gov.uk

Grounds Maintenance: Miss Nina Camm , Environmental Manager, District Council Offices, Kesteven Street, Sleaford NG34 7EF ☎ 01529 414155 ✉ nina_camm@n-kesteven.gov.uk

Health and Safety: Ms Sarah Golembiewski , Corporate Health, Safety & Emergency Planning Officer, District Council Offices, Kesteven Street, Sleaford NG34 7EF ☎ 01529 414155 ✉ sarah_golembiewski@n-kesteven.gov.uk

Housing: Mr Michael Kelleher , Head of Housing & Property Services, District Council Offices, Kesteven Street, Sleaford NG34 7EF ☎ 01529 414155 ✉ michael_kelleher@n-kesteven.gov.uk

Housing Maintenance: Mr Michael Gadd, Property Services Manager, District Council Offices, Kesteven Street, Sleaford NG34 7EF ☎ 01529 414155 ✉ michael_gadd@n-kesteven.gov.uk

Leisure and Cultural Services: Mr Mike Lock, Leisure & Cultural Services Manager, District Council Offices, Kesteven Street, Sleaford NG34 7EF ☎ 01529 414155 ✉ mike_lock@n-kesteven.gov.uk

Licensing: Mr David Harper , Licensing Manager, District Council Offices, Kesteven Street, Sleaford NG34 7EF ☎ 01529 414155 ✉ david_harper@n-kesteven.gov.uk

Lighting: Mr Russell Shortland, Design & Maintenance Manager, District Council Offices, Kesteven Street, Sleaford NG34 7EF ☎ 01529 414155 ✉ russell_shortland@n-kesteven.gov.uk

Lottery Funding, Charity and Voluntary: Miss Karen Bradford, Deputy Chief Executive, District Council Offices, Kesteven Street, Sleaford NG34 7EF ☎ 01529 414155 ✉ karen_bradford@n-kesteven.gov.uk

Member Services: Miss Pauline Collett , Civic Officer, District Council Offices, Kesteven Street, Sleaford NG34 7EF ☎ 01529 414155 ✉ pauline_collett@n-kesteven.gov.uk

Member Services: Mrs Marcella Heath , Democratic Services Manager, District Council Offices, Kesteven Street, Sleaford NG34 7EF ☎ 01529 414155 ✉ marcella_heath@n-kesteven.gov.uk

Personnel / HR: Ms Christine Cooper , Human Resources Manager, District Council Offices, Kesteven Street, Sleaford NG34 7EF ☎ 01529 414155 ✉ christine_cooper@n-kesteven.gov.uk

Planning: Mr Andrew McDonough, Head of Development, Economic & Cultural Services, District Council Offices, Kesteven Street, Sleaford NG34 7EF ☎ ; 01529 414155 ✉ andrew_mcdonough@n-kesteven.gov.uk

Recycling & Waste Minimisation: Miss Nina Camm , Environmental Manager, District Council Offices, Kesteven Street, Sleaford NG34 7EF ☎ 01529 414155 ✉ nina_camm@n-kesteven.gov.uk

Staff Training: Ms Christine Cooper , Human Resources Manager, District Council Offices, Kesteven Street, Sleaford NG34 7EF ☎ 01529 414155 ✉ christine_cooper@n-kesteven.gov.uk

Street Scene: Miss Nina Camm , Environmental Manager, District Council Offices, Kesteven Street, Sleaford NG34 7EF ☎ 01529 414155 ✉ nina_camm@n-kesteven.gov.uk

NORTH KESTEVEN

Sustainable Communities: Mr Andrew McDonough, Head of Development, Economic & Cultural Services, District Council Offices, Kesteven Street, Sleaford NG34 7EF ☎ 01529 414155 ✉ andrew_mcdonough@n-kesteven.gov.uk

Sustainable Development: Mrs Bonnie Bond , Sustainability Co-ordination Officer, District Council Offices, Kesteven Street, Sleaford NG34 7EF ☎ 01529 414155 ✉ bonnie_bond@n-kesteven.gov.uk

Tourism: Mr Andrew McDonough, Head of Development, Economic & Cultural Services, District Council Offices, Kesteven Street, Sleaford NG34 7EF ☎ 01529 414155 ✉ andrew_mcdonough@n-kesteven.gov.uk

Waste Collection and Disposal: Miss Nina Camm, Environmental Manager, District Council Offices, Kesteven Street, Sleaford NG34 7EF ☎ 01529 414155 ✉ nina_camm@n-kesteven.gov.uk

Waste Management: Miss Nina Camm , Environmental Manager, District Council Offices, Kesteven Street, Sleaford NG34 7EF ☎ 01529 414155 ✉ nina_camm@n-kesteven.gov.uk

COUNCILLORS

***Chair* Ogden**, Gill (CON - Billinghay, Martin and North Kyme)
cllr_gill_ogden@n-kesteven.gov.uk

***Vice-Chair* Money**, John (CON - Metheringham)
cllr_john_money@n-kesteven.gov.uk

***Leader of the Council* Brighton**, Marion (CON - Heighington and Washingborough)
cllr_marion_brighton@n-kesteven.gov.uk

***Deputy Leader of the Council* Gallagher**, Mike (CON - Bracebridge Heath and Waddington East)
cllr_mike_gallagher@n-kesteven.gov.uk

Appleby, Sally (CON - Eagle, Swinderby and Witham St Hughs)
Cllr_Sally_Appleby@n-kesteven.gov.uk

Barrett, Kay (LD - North Hykeham Forum)
cllr_kay_barrett@n-kesteven.gov.uk

Boston, Terry (CON - Ruskington)
cllr_terry_boston@n-kesteven.gov.uk

Burley, Peter (CON - Bracebridge Heath and Waddington East)
Cllr_Peter_Burley@n-kesteven.gov.uk

Carrington, Ian (CON - Heighington and Washingborough)
cllr_ian_carrington@n-kesteven.gov.uk

Cawrey, Lindsey (CON - Bracebridge Heath and Waddington East)
Cllr_Lindsey_Cawrey@n-kesteven.gov.uk

Clarke, Andrea (CON - North Hykeham Mill)
Cllr_Andrea_Clarke@n-kesteven.gov.uk

Conning, Tim (CON - Sleaford Quarrington and Mareham)
Cllr_Tim_Conning@n-kesteven.gov.uk

Conway, Laura (IND - Cliff Villages)
Cllr_Laura_Conway@n-kesteven.gov.uk

Cook, Kate (CON - Osbournby)
cllr_kate_cook@n-kesteven.gov.uk

Cucksey, Ray (CON - Branston)
cllr_ray_cucksey@n-kesteven.gov.uk

Dolby, Keith (IND - Sleaford Castle)
Cllr_Keith_Dolby@n-kesteven.gov.uk

Fields, Steve (IND - Sleaford Westholme)
cllr_steve_fields@n-kesteven.gov.uk

Goldson, Chris (IND - Skellingthorpe)
cllr_chris_goldson@n-kesteven.gov.uk

Harrison, Julia (CON - Kirkby La Thorpe and South Kyme)
cllr_julia_harrison@n-kesteven.gov.uk

Hazelwood, Geoff (CON - Sleaford Quarrington and Mareham)
Cllr_Geoffrey_Hazelwood@n-kesteven.gov.uk

Howe, Sue (CON - Bassingham and Brant Broughton)
Cllr_Sue_Howe@n-kesteven.gov.uk

Jackson, Glenville (IND - Sleaford Holdingham)

Kendrick, Rob (CON - Metheringham)
Cllr_Rob_Kendrick@n-kesteven.gov.uk

Lee, Wallace (LD - North Hykeham Memorial)
Cllr_Wallace_Lee@n-kesteven.gov.uk

Lindgren, Peter (IND - Branston)
cllr_Peter_Lungren@n-kesteven.gov.uk

Little, Ross (CON - North Hykeham Witham)
Cllr_Ross_Little@n-kesteven.gov.uk

Matthan, Susanna (IND - Billinghay, Martin and North Kyme)
cllr_Susabba_Matthan@n-kesteven.gov.uk

Ogden, Stewart (CON - Heckington Rural)
cllr_stewart_ogden@n-kesteven.gov.uk

Overton, Marianne (IND - Cliff Villages)
cllr_marianne_overton@n-kesteven.gov.uk

Oxby, Ron (CON - Heighington and Washingborough)
cllr_ron_oxby@n-kesteven.gov.uk

Pannell, Shirley (IND - Skellingthorpe)
cllr_shirley_pannell@n-kesteven.gov.uk

Pearce, Sarah (CON - Ashby De La Launde and Cranwell)
cllr_sarah_pearse@n-kesteven.gov.uk

Pennell, Lance (CON - Waddington West)
cllr_lance_pennell@n-kesteven.gov.uk

Suffield, Mark (IND - Sleaford Quarrington and Mareham)
cllr_mark_suffield@n-kesteven.gov.uk

Suiter, David (IND - Sleaford Navigation)
Cllr_David_Suiter@n-kesteven.gov.uk

Tarry, Sally (CON - Heckington Rural)
cllr_sally_tarry@n-kesteven.gov.uk

Waring, Susan (CON - Leasingham and Rauceby)
Cllr_Susan_Waring@n-kesteven.gov.uk

Wells, Barbara (IND - Eagle, Swinderby and Witham St Hughs)
cllr_barbara_wells@n-kesteven.gov.uk

Whittaker, Pam (CON - North Hykeham Moor)
cllr_pam_whittaker@n-kesteven.gov.uk

Whittle, Geoffrey (CON - Ashby De La Launde and Cranwell)
Cllr_Geoffrey_Whittle@n-kesteven.gov.uk

Woodman, Pat (IND - Bassingham and Brant Broughton)
cllr_pat_woodman@n-kesteven.gov.uk

Wright, Richard (CON - Ruskington)
Cllr_Richard_Wright@n-kesteven.gov.uk

POLITICAL COMPOSITION
CON: 27, IND: 13, LD: 2

COMMITTEE CHAIRS

Audit: Mrs Susan Waring

Licensing: Mr Lance Pennell

Planning: Mrs Pat Woodman

North Lanarkshire S

North Lanarkshire Council, Civic Centre, Motherwell ML1 1AB
☎ 01698 302222 🖷 01698 275125 💻 www.northlan.gov.uk

FACTS AND FIGURES
Parliamentary Constituencies: Airdrie and Shotts, Coatbridge, Chryston & Bellshill, Cumbernauld, Kilsyth and Kirkintilloch East, Motherwell & Wishaw
EU Constituencies:
Election Frequency: Elections are of whole council

PRINCIPAL OFFICERS

Chief Executive: Mr Paul Jukes, Chief Executive, Civic Centre, Motherwell ML1 1AB ☎ 01698 302452 🖷 01698 264116 🖱 jukesp@northlan.gov.uk

Senior Management: Mr Alistair Crichton, Executive Director of Finance & Customer Service , Civic Centre, Motherwell ML1 1AB ☎ 01698 302200 🖷 01698 264116 🖱 crichtona@northlan.gov.uk

Senior Management: Mr Duncan Mackay , Executive Director - Housing & Social Work Services, Scott House, 73-77 Merry Street, Motherwell ML1 1JE ☎ 01698 332024 🖱 mackayd@northlan.gov.uk

Senior Management: Ms June Murray , Executive Director of Corporate Services, Civic Centre, Motherwell ML1 1AB ☎ 01698 302344 🖱 murrayj@northlan.gov.uk

Senior Management: Mr Andrew Sutherland , Executive Director of Learning & Leisure Services, Civic Centre, Motherwell ML1 1AB ☎ 01698 302222

Senior Management: Mr Kenneth Wilson, Interim Executive Director of Environmental Services (Head of Land Services), Buchanan Business Park, Stepps , Glasgow G33 6HR ☎ 01698 302222 🖱 wilsonk@northlan.gov.uk

Access Officer / Social Services (Disability): Mr Dilini Wilkinson, Community Care Senior (Older Adults), 122 Bank Street, Coatbridge ML5 1ET ☎ 01236 622202 🖷 01698 332179 🖱 wilkinsondi@northlan.gov.uk

Building Control: Mr David Provan, Business Building Standards Manager, Fleming House , 2 Tryst Road, Cumbernauld G67 1JW ☎ 01698 812369 🖷 01236 618099 🖱 provand@northlan.gov.uk

Catering Services: Ms Lynda Donnelly , First Stop Shop Manager, Civic Centre, Motherwell ML1 1AB ☎ 01236 856466 🖱 donnellyly@northlan.gov.uk

Children / Youth Services: Ms Alison Gordon , Head of Social Work Services, Scott House, 73 - 77 Merry Street, Motherwell ML1 1JE ☎ 01698 332001 🖱 gordonal@northlan.gov.uk

Civil Registration: Ms June Murray , Executive Director of Corporate Services, Civic Centre, Motherwell ML1 1AB ☎ 01698 302344 🖱 murrayj@northlan.gov.uk

PR / Communications: Mr Stephen Penman , Head of Corporate Communications & Marketing, Civic Centre, Motherwell ML1 1AB ☎ 01698 302591 🖱 penmanste@northlan.gov.uk

Computer Management: Mrs Irene McKelvey, Head of E-Government & Service Development , Civic Centre, Motherwell ML1 1AB ☎ 01698 302532 🖷 01698 403011 🖱 mckelveyi@northlan.gov.uk

Consumer Protection and Trading Standards: Mr Paul Bannister , Trading Standards Manager, Fleming House, 2 Tryst Road, Cumbernauld G67 1JW ☎ 01236 856460 🖱 bannisterp@northlan.gov.uk

Corporate Services: Mr Brian Cook , Head of Revenue Services, Dalziel Building, 7 Scott Street, Motherwell ML1 1PN ☎ 01698 403929 🖱 cookb@northlan.gov.uk

Corporate Services: Ms June Murray , Executive Director of Corporate Services, Civic Centre, Motherwell ML1 1AB ☎ 01698 302344 🖱 murrayj@northlan.gov.uk

Economic Development: Ms Shirley Linton , Head of Planning & Regeneration, Civic Centre, Motherwell ML1 1AB ☎ 01236 632650 🖱 lintons@northlan.gov.uk

Education: Ms Isabelle Boyd , Head of Service - Standards & Inclusion, Municipal Buildings, Kildonan Street, Coatbridge ML5 3BT ☎ 01236 812279 🖱 boydisab@northlan.gov.uk

Education: Mr James McKinstry , Head of Education Provision, Civic Centre, Motherwell ML1 1AB ☎ 01698 302222 🖱 mckinstryj@northlan.gov.uk

Education: Mr Andrew Sutherland , Executive Director of Learning & Leisure Services, Civic Centre, Motherwell ML1 1AB ☎ 01698 302222

E-Government: Mrs Irene McKelvey, Head of E-Government & Service Development , Civic Centre, Motherwell ML1 1AB ☎ 01698 302532 🖷 01698 403011 🖱 mckelveyi@northlan.gov.uk

Emergency Planning: Ms Aileen McMann , Contingency Planning Officer, Civic Centre, Motherwell ML1 1AB ☎ 07939 280125 🖱 mcmanna@northlan.gov.uk

Environmental / Technical Services: Mr Paul Jukes, Chief Executive, Civic Centre, Motherwell ML1 1AB ☎ 01698 302452 🖷 01698 264116 🖱 jukesp@northlan.gov.uk

Environmental Health: Mr Paul Jukes, Chief Executive, Civic Centre, Motherwell ML1 1AB ☎ 01698 302452 🖷 01698 264116 🖱 jukesp@northlan.gov.uk

NORTH LANARKSHIRE

Estates, Property & Valuation: Mr Eric Hislop , Asset & Support Manager, Civic Centre, Motherwell ML1 1AB ☎ 01698 302372 ✉ hislope@snorthlan.gov.uk

Facilities: Mr Graham Patrick , Head of Facility Support Services, Buchanan Tower, Stepps, Glasgow G33 6HR ☎ 01698 302222 ✉ patrickg@northlan.gov.uk

Finance: Mr Alistair Crichton, Executive Director of Finance & Customer Service , Civic Centre, Motherwell ML1 1AB ☎ 01698 302200 🖷 01698 264116 ✉ crichtona@northlan.gov.uk

Finance: Mr Paul Hughes , Head of Financial Services, Civic Centre, Motherwell ML1 1AB ☎ 01698 302275 ✉ hughesp@northlan.gov.uk

Grounds Maintenance: Mr Ken Forbes , Business Manager (Environment & Cemeteries), Old Edinburgh Road, Belshill ML4 3JS ☎ 01698 506310 ✉ forbesk@northlan.gov.uk

Health and Safety: Mr Stuart Hamilton, Principal Health & Safety Officer, Civic Centre, Motherwell ML1 1AB ☎ 01698 302368 🖷 01698 230278 ✉ hamiltonst@northlan.gov.uk

Housing: Ms Elaine McHugh , Head of Housing Services, Civic Centre, Motherwell ML1 1AB ☎ 01698 302222 ✉ elaine.mchugh@northlan.gov.uk

Housing Maintenance: Mr Des Murray , Head of Housing Property, Civic Centre, Motherwell ML1 1AB ☎ 01698 524758 ✉ murraydes@northlan.gov.uk

Leisure and Cultural Services: Mr Andrew Sutherland , Executive Director of Learning & Leisure Services, Civic Centre, Motherwell ML1 1AB ☎ 01698 302222

Licensing: Mr Paul Guidi , Acting Managing Solicitor, Civic Centre, Motherwell ML1 1AB ☎ 01698 302294 ✉ guidip@northlan.gov.uk

Lifelong Learning: Ms L McMurrich , Head of Community Information & Learning, Municipal Buildings, Kildonan Street, Coatbridge ML5 3BT ☎ 01236 812338 ✉ mcmurrichl@northlan.gov.uk

Lifelong Learning: Mr Andrew Sutherland , Executive Director of Learning & Leisure Services, Civic Centre, Motherwell ML1 1AB ☎ 01698 302222

Lighting: Mr Colin Nimmo , Lighting Design Manager, Civic Centre, Motherwell ML1 1AB ☎ 01236 616217 ✉ nimmoc@northlan.gov.uk

Personnel / HR: Ms Iris Wylie, Head of Human Resources , Civic Centre, Motherwell ML1 1AB ☎ 01698 302215 🖷 01698 230387 ✉ wyliei@northlan.gov.uk

Planning: Mr Paul Jukes, Chief Executive, Civic Centre, Motherwell ML1 1AB ☎ 01698 302452 🖷 01698 264116 ✉ jukesp@northlan.gov.uk

Planning: Ms Shirley Linton , Head of Planning & Regeneration, Civic Centre, Motherwell ML1 1AB ☎ 01236 632650 ✉ lintons@northlan.gov.uk

Procurement: Ms Audrey Telfer, Senior Procurement Officer, Dalziel House, 7 Scott Street, Motherwell ML1 1PN ☎ 01698 403954 ✉ telfera@northlan.gov.uk

Public Libraries: Ms Gemma Alexander , Libraries & Information Manager, Civic Centre, Motherwell ML1 1AB ☎ 01698 332604 ✉ alexanderg@northlan.gov.uk

Regeneration: Mr Paul Jukes, Chief Executive, Civic Centre, Motherwell ML1 1AB ☎ 01698 302452 🖷 01698 264116 ✉ jukesp@northlan.gov.uk

Regeneration: Ms Shirley Linton , Head of Planning & Regeneration, Civic Centre, Motherwell ML1 1AB ☎ 01236 632650 ✉ lintons@northlan.gov.uk

Social Services: Mr Duncan Mackay , Executive Director - Housing & Social Work Services, Scott House, 73-77 Merry Street, Motherwell ML1 1JE ☎ 01698 332024 ✉ mackayd@northlan.gov.uk

Staff Training: Ms Heather Liddle, Principal Training Officer , Civic Centre, Motherwell ML1 1AB ☎ 01698 302097 🖷 01698 230278 ✉ liddleh@northlan.gov.uk

Street Scene: Mr David Cullen , Joint Cleansing Services Manager, Bellshill Complex, Old Edinburgh Road, Bellshill ML4 3JF ☎ 01698 506271 🖷 01698 302044 ✉ cullend@northlan.gov.uk

Street Scene: Mr Harry Morgan , Joint Cleansing Services Manager, Bellshill Complex, Old Edinburgh Road, Bellshill ML4 3JF ☎ 01698 506271 🖷 01698 302044 ✉ morganh@northlan.gov.uk

Sustainable Development: Mr David Baxter, Assistant Business Manager, Fleming House, 2 Tryst Road, Cumbernauld G67 1JW ☎ 01236 616243 🖷 01236 616232 ✉ baxterd@northlan.gov.uk

Town Centre: Mr Jack Duffy, Town Centre Manager (Cumbernauld), Town Centre Initiatives Ltd, Coatbridge ML5 3EL ☎ 01263 638444 ✉ duffyja@northlan.gov.uk

Town Centre: Ms Anne Flood, Town Centre Manager, Town Centre Initiatives Ltd, Coatbridge ML5 3EL ☎ 01263 638443 ✉ flooda@northlan.gov.uk

Traffic Management: Mr John Marran, Business Manager (Road Strategy & Assets), Fleming House, 2 Tryst Road, Cumbernauld G67 1JW ☎ 01236 616253 🖷 01236 616232 ✉ marranj@northlan.gov.uk

Transport: Mr Graham Mackay, Head of Roads & Transportation, Fleming House, 2 Tryst Road, Cumbernauld G67 1JW ☎ 01236 616202 🖷 01236 616232 ✉ mackaygd@northlan.gov.uk

Transport Planner: Mr Graham Mackay, Head of Roads & Transportation, Buchanan Tower, Stepps, Glasgow G33 6HR ☎ 01236 616202 🖷 01236 616232 ✉ mackaygd@northlan.gov.uk

Waste Collection and Disposal: Mr Kenneth Wilson, Interim Executive Director of Environmental Services (Head of Land Services), Buchanan Business Park, Stepps , Glasgow G33 6HR ☎ 01698 302222 ✉ wilsonk@northlan.gov.uk

Waste Management: Mr Kenneth Wilson, Interim Executive Director of Environmental Services (Head of Land Services), Buchanan Business Park, Stepps , Glasgow G33 6HR
☎ 01698 302222 ✉ wilsonk@northlan.gov.uk

COUNCILLORS

***Provost* Robertson**, James (LAB - Fortissat)
robertsonj@northlan.gov.uk

Baird, David (SNP - Mossend and Holytown)
bairddavid@northlan.gov.uk

Beveridge, Alan (SNP - Airdrie North)
beveridgeal@northlan.gov.uk

Brooks, James (LAB - Coatbridge South)
brooksj@northlan.gov.uk

Burrows, Robert (LAB - Thorniewood)
BurrowsR@northlan.gov.uk

Cefferty, Charles (IND - Fortissat)
ceffertyc@northlan.gov.uk

Chadha, Balwant Singh (LAB - Cumbernauld North)
chadhab@northlan.gov.uk

Clinch, Alan (LAB - Murdostoun)
clincha@northlan.gov.uk

Cochrane, Thomas (SNP - Fortissat)
cochraneth@northlan.gov.uk

Coyle, Sophia (SNP - Airdrie North)
CoyleS@northlan.gov.uk

Coyle, Michael (SNP - Airdrie South)
coylem@northlan.gov.uk

Coyle, Agnes (SNP - Airdrie South)
coylea@northlan.gov.uk

Coyle, James (LAB - Mossend and Holytown)
coylej@northlan.gov.uk

Curley, Thomas (LAB - Airdrie South)
curleyt@northlan.gov.uk

Curran, Harry (LAB - Belshill)
curranh@northlan.gov.uk

Docherty, Kevin (LAB - Coatbridge West)
Dochertyke@northlan.gov.uk

Fagan, David (LAB - Airdrie South)
cllr.david.fagan@googlemail.com

Farooq, Shahid (SNP - Motherwell North)
farooqs@northlan.gov.uk

Goldie, William (SNP - Cumbernauld South)
GoldieW@northlan.gov.uk

Graham, Alan (LAB - Cumbernauld South)
grahamallan@northlan.gov.uk

Grant, Stephen (LAB - Abronhill, Kildrum and the Village)
grantst@northlan.gov.uk

Griffin, Stephanie (LAB - Cumbernauld South)
muirsteph@northlan.gov.uk

Harmon, Kaye (LAB - Motherwell South East and Ravenscraig)
harmonk@northlan.gov.uk

Higgins, John (LAB - Coatbridge South)
higginsjoh@northlan.gov.uk

Hogg, William (LAB - Strathkelvin)
hoggw@northlan.gov.uk

Hogg, Paddy (SNP - Cumbernauld South)
hoggp@northlan.gov.uk

Hume, Jim (SNP - Wishaw)
humej@northlan.gov.uk

Irvine, Elizabeth (SNP - Abronhill, Kildrum and the Village)
irvinee@northlan.gov.uk

Johnston, Tom (SNP - Abronhill, Kildrum and the Village)
johnstont@northlan.gov.uk

Jones, Jean (LAB - Kilsyth)
jonesj@northlan.gov.uk

Kelly, Paul (LAB - Motherwell West)
kellyp2@northlan.gov.uk

Logue, James (LAB - Airdrie Central)
loguej@northlan.gov.uk

Love, Samuel (LAB - Wishaw)
lovesam@northlan.gov.uk

Lunny, Thomas (LAB - Motherwell South East and Ravenscraig)
lunnyt@northlan.gov.uk

Lyle, Marina (SNP - Belshill)
lylem@northlan.gov.uk

MacGregor, Fulton (SNP - Coatbridge North and Glenboig)
macgregorful@northlan.gov.uk

Majid, Imtiaz (SNP - Coatbridge South)
majidi@northlan.gov.uk

Masterton, Alan (SNP - Cumbernauld North)
mastertona@northlan.gov.uk

McAnulty, Julie (SNP - Coatbridge North and Glenboig)
macnultyj@northlan.oov.uk

McCabe, James (LAB - Thorniewood)
mccabej@northlan.gov.uk

McCulloch, Barry (LAB - Cumbernauld North)
mccullochb@northlan.gov.uk

McGlinchey, Frances (IND - Strathkelvin)
mcglincheyf@northlan.gov.uk

McGuigan, Harry (LAB - Belshill)
mcguiganh@northlan.gov.uk

McKay, Frank (LAB - Wishaw)
mckayf@northlan.gov.uk

McKendrick, Robert (IND - Murdostoun)
mckendrickr@northlan.gov.uk

McKenna, Helen (LAB - Motherwell North)
McKennaH@northlan.gov.uk

McLaren, John (LAB - Strathkelvin)
mclarenjohn@northlan.gov.uk

McNally, Frank (LAB - Mossend and Holytown)
mcnallyf@northlan.gov.uk

McPake, Michael (LAB - Coatbridge North and Glenboig)
mcpakemi@northlan.gov.uk

McVey, Heather (LAB - Kilsyth)
mcveyh@northlan.gov.uk

Morgan, Thomas (LAB - Airdrie North)
morgant@northlan.gov.uk

NORTH LANARKSHIRE

Nolan, Peter (LAB - Motherwell North)
nolanp@northlan.gov.uk

O'Brien, Alan (IND - Cumbernauld North)
obrienal@northlan.gov.uk

O'Rorke, Gary (LAB - Motherwell South East and Ravenscraig)
ororkeg@northlan.gov.uk

O'Rourke, Pat (LAB - Motherwell North)

Ross, Michael (LAB - Motherwell West)
rossm@northlan.gov.uk

Shevlin, Nicky (LAB - Murdostoun)
shevlinn@northlan.gov.uk

Shields, William (LAB - Coatbridge North and Glenboig)
shieldsb@northlan.gov.uk

Smith, James (LAB - Coatbridge West)
smithjam@northlan.gov.uk

Spowart, Andrew (LAB - Airdrie North)
spowarta@northlan.gov.uk

Stevenson, Alan (SNP - Kilsyth)
stevensonal@northlan.gov.uk

Stocks, David (SNP - Airdrie Central)
stocksd@northlan.gov.uk

Sullivan, Peter (LAB - Airdrie Central)
sullivanp@northlan.gov.uk

Taggart, John (SNP - Murdostoun)
taggartjo@northlan.gov.uk

Valentine, Annette (SNP - Motherwell West)
valentinean@northlan.gov.uk

Valentine, Alan (SNP - Motherwell South East and Ravenscraig)
valentinea@northlan.gov.uk

Wallace, Brian (LAB - Strathkelvin)
wallaceb@northlan.gov.uk

Welsh, Paul (SNP - Coatbridge West)
welshp@northlan.gov.uk

POLITICAL COMPOSITION

LAB: 41, SNP: 23, IND: 4

COMMITTEE CHAIRS

Audit & Governance: Mr Gary O'Rorke

Housing & Social Work: Mr Samuel Love

Licensing: Mr Peter Nolan

Planning & Transportation: Mr James Coyle

North Lincolnshire U

North Lincolnshire Council, Pittwood House, Ashby Road, Scunthorpe DN16 1AB
☎ 01724 296296 🖷 01724 296079
pittwoodreception@northlincs.gov.uk
www.northlincs.gov.uk

FACTS AND FIGURES

Parliamentary Constituencies: Brigg and Goole, Scunthorpe
EU Constituencies: East Midlands
Election Frequency: Elections are of whole council

PRINCIPAL OFFICERS

Chief Executive: Mr Simon Driver, Chief Executive, Civic Centre, Ashby Road, Scunthorpe DN16 1AB ☎ 01724 296000 🖷 01724 296005 simon.driver@northlincs.gov.uk

Senior Management: Ms Frances Cunning , Director - Public Health, Pittwood House, Ashby Road, Scunthorpe DN16 1AB frances.cunning@northlincs.gov.uk

Access Officer / Social Services (Disability): Ms Denise Hyde, Director - People, Civic Centre, Ashby Road, Scunthorpe DN16 1AB ☎ 01724 296406 🖷 01724 296404 denise.hyde@northlincs.gov.uk

Architect, Building / Property Services: Mr Peter Williams, Director - Places, Civic Centre, Ashby Road, Scunthorpe DN16 1AB ☎ 01724 296710 🖷 01724 296770 peter.williams@northlincs.gov.uk

Best Value: Mr Jason Whaler, Assistant Director - Business Support, Civic Centre, Ashby Road, Scunthorpe DN16 1AB ☎ 01724 296018 🖷 01724 296030 jason.whaler@northlincs.gov.uk

Building Control: Mr Marcus Walker , Assistant Director - Planning & Regeneration, Civic Centre, Ashby Road, Scunthorpe DN16 1AB ☎ 01724 297305 🖷 01724 297899 marcus.walker@northlincs.gov.uk

Catering Services: Mrs Sharon Seddon, Head - Catering & Cleaning, Church Square House, Scunthorpe DN15 6NL ☎ 01724 297922 sharon.seddon@northlincs.gov.uk

Children / Youth Services: Mr Mick Gibbs , Assistant Director - Children's Services, Hewson House, Station Road, Brigg DN20 8XJ ☎ 01724 296410 mick.gibbs@northlincs.gov.uk

Children / Youth Services: Ms Denise Hyde, Director - People, Civic Centre, Ashby Road, Scunthorpe DN16 1AB ☎ 01724 296406 🖷 01724 296404 denise.hyde@northlincs.gov.uk

Civil Registration: Mrs Alison Prestwood, Head - Registration Service, Civic Centre, Ashby Road, Scunthorpe DN16 1AB ☎ 01724 298555 alison.prestwood@northlincs.gov.uk

PR / Communications: Mr Chris Skinner , Head - Communications, Civic Centre, Ashby Road, Scunthorpe DN16 1AB ☎ 01724 296301 chris.skinner@northlincs.gov.uk

Community Planning: Mr David Hey , Head - Stronger Communities, Civic Centre, Ashby Road, Scunthorpe DN16 1AB ☎ 01724 296646 dave.hey@northlincs.gov.uk

Community Safety: Mr Stuart Minto , Head - Safer Neighbourhoods, Shelford House, Scunthorpe DN15 6NU ☎ 01724 244654 stuart.minto@northlincs.gov.uk

Computer Management: Mr Martin Oglesby , Head - IT Services, Cary Lane, Brigg DN15 6XQ ☎ 01724 296266 martin.oglesby@northlincs.gov.uk

Consumer Protection and Trading Standards: Mr Richard Copley , Trading Standards & Licensing Manager, Church Square House, Scunthorpe DL15 6QX ☎ 01724 297649 richard.copley@northlincs.gov.uk

Contracts: Mr Jason Whaler, Assistant Director - Business Support, Civic Centre, Ashby Road, Scunthorpe DN16 1AB ☎ 01724 296018 🖷 01724 296030 🖰 jason.whaler@northlincs.gov.uk

Corporate Services: Mr Paul Taylor , Head - Asset Management, Hewson House, Station Road, Brigg DN20 8XJ ☎ 01724 297477 🖰 paul.taylor@northlincs.gov.uk

Customer Service: Miss Helen Rowe , Assistant Director - Customer Services, Civic Centre, Ashby Road, Scunthorpe DN16 1AB ☎ 01724 297667 🖰 helen.rowe@northlincs.gov.uk

Economic Development: Mr Marcus Walker , Assistant Director - Planning & Regeneration, Civic Centre, Ashby Road, Scunthorpe DN16 1AB ☎ 01724 297305 🖷 01724 297899 🖰 marcus.walker@northlincs.gov.uk

Education: Mr Peter Thorpe , Assistant Director - Education, Civic Centre, Ashby Road, Scunthorpe DN16 1AB ☎ 01724 297188 🖰 peter.thorpe@northlincs.gov.uk

E-Government: Mr Jason Whaler, Assistant Director - Business Support, Civic Centre, Ashby Road, Scunthorpe DN16 1AB ☎ 01724 296018 🖷 01724 296030 🖰 jason.whaler@northlincs.gov.uk

Electoral Registration: Mrs Anthia Taylor , Electoral Registrations Officer, Civic Centre, Ashby Road, Scunthorpe DN16 1AB ☎ 01724 296248 🖰 anthia.taylor@northlincs.gov.uk

Emergency Planning: Mr Chris Wilson , Emergency Planning Officer, Humber Emergency Planning Service, Church Square House, Scunthorpe DN15 6NL ☎ 01724 297406 🖰 chris.wilson@northlincs.gov.uk

Energy Management: Mr Craig Stapleton , Energy Manager, Church Square House, Scunthorpe DN15 6NL ☎ 01724 296514 🖰 craig.stapleton@northlincs.gov.uk

Environmental / Technical Services: Mr Trevor Laming , Assistant Director - Technical & Environmental Services, Civic Centre, Ashby Road, Scunthorpe DN16 1AB ☎ 01724 297603 🖷 01724 297333 🖰 trevor.laming@northlincs.gov.uk

Environmental Health: Mr Trevor Laming , Assistant Director - Technical & Environmental Services, Civic Centre, Ashby Road, Scunthorpe DN16 1AB ☎ 01724 297603 🖷 01724 297333 🖰 trevor.laming@northlincs.gov.uk

Estates, Property & Valuation: Mr Paul Nicholson , Estates & Valuations Manager, Hewson House, Station Road, Brigg DN20 8XY ☎ 01724 296789 🖰 paul.nicholson@northlincs.gov.uk

European Liaison: Mr Marcus Walker , Assistant Director - Planning & Regeneration, Civic Centre, Ashby Road, Scunthorpe DN16 1AB ☎ 01724 297305 🖷 01724 297899 🖰 marcus.walker@northlincs.gov.uk

Events Manager: Ms Margaret Price , Senior Tourism & Event Management Officer, Civic Centre, Ashby Road, Scunthorpe DN16 1AB ☎ 01724 297356 🖰 margaret.price@northlincs.gov.uk

Facilities: Miss Helen Rowe , Assistant Director - Customer Services, Civic Centre, Ashby Road, Scunthorpe DN16 1AB ☎ 01724 297667 🖰 helen.rowe@northlincs.gov.uk

Finance: Mr Mike Wedgewood, Director - Policy & Resources, Civic Centre, Ashby Road, Scunthorpe DN16 1AB ☎ 01724 296012 🖷 01724 296030 🖰 mike.wedgewood@northlincs.gov.uk

Fleet Management: Mr Chris Matthews , Assistant Director - Community Services, Civic Centre, Ashby Road, Scunthorpe DN16 1AB ☎ 01724 297366 🖷 01724 297880 🖰 chris.matthews@northlincs.gov.uk

Grounds Maintenance: Mr Chris Matthews , Assistant Director - Community Services, Civic Centre, Ashby Road, Scunthorpe DN16 1AB ☎ 01724 297366 🖷 01724 297880 🖰 chris.matthews@northlincs.gov.uk

Health and Safety: Mr Martin Burns , Health & Safety Manager, Civic Centre, Ashby Road, Scunthorpe DN16 1AB ☎ 01724 297594 🖰 martin.burns@northlincs.gov.uk

Highways: Mr Chris Matthews , Assistant Director - Community Services, Civic Centre, Ashby Road, Scunthorpe DN16 1AB ☎ 01724 297366 🖷 01724 297880 🖰 chris.matthews@northlincs.gov.uk

Home Energy Conservation: Mr Trevor Laming , Assistant Director - Technical & Environmental Services, Civic Centre, Ashby Road, Scunthorpe DN16 1AB ☎ 01724 297603 🖷 01724 297333 🖰 trevor.laming@northlincs.gov.uk

Housing: Mr Trevor Laming , Assistant Director - Technical & Environmental Services, Civic Centre, Ashby Road, Scunthorpe DN16 1AB ☎ 01724 297603 🖷 01724 297333 🖰 trevor.laming@northlincs.gov.uk

Legal: Mr Will Bell , Assistant Director - Legal & Democratic, Civic Centre, Ashby Road, Scunthorpe DN16 1AB ☎ 01724 296204 🖰 will.bell@northlincs.gov.uk

Leisure and Cultural Services: Miss Helen Rowe , Assistant Director - Customer Services, Civic Centre, Ashby Road, Scunthorpe DN16 1AB ☎ 01724 297667 🖰 helen.rowe@northlincs.gov.uk

Licensing: Mr Trevor Laming , Assistant Director - Technical & Environmental Services, Civic Centre, Ashby Road, Scunthorpe DN16 1AB ☎ 01724 297603 🖷 01724 297333 🖰 trevor.laming@northlincs.gov.uk

Lifelong Learning: Miss Helen Rowe , Assistant Director - Customer Services, Civic Centre, Ashby Road, Scunthorpe DN16 1AB ☎ 01724 297667 🖰 helen.rowe@northlincs.gov.uk

Lighting: Mr Chris Matthews , Assistant Director - Community Services, Civic Centre, Ashby Road, Scunthorpe DN16 1AB ☎ 01724 297366 🖷 01724 297880 🖰 chris.matthews@northlincs.gov.uk

Member Services: Mr Mel Holmes, Head - Democratic Services, Civic Centre, Ashby Road, Scunthorpe DN16 1AB ☎ 01724 296230 🖷 01724 281705 🖰 mel.holmes@northlincs.gov.uk

NORTH LINCOLNSHIRE

Parking: Mr Marcus Walker , Assistant Director - Planning & Regeneration, Civic Centre, Ashby Road, Scunthorpe DN16 1AB ☎ 01724 297305 🖷 01724 297899 ✉ marcus.walker@northlincs.gov.uk

Partnerships: Miss Rachel Johnson, Business Strategy & Transformation Manager, Civic Centre, Ashby Road, Scunthorpe DN16 1AB ☎ 01724 296391 ✉ rachel.johnson@northlincs.gov.uk

Personnel / HR: Mrs Helen Manderson , Assistant Director - Human Resources, Civic Centre, Ashby Road, Scunthorpe DN16 1AB ☎ 01724 296310 🖷 01724 296339 ✉ helen.manderson@northlincs.gov.uk

Planning: Mr Phil Wallis, Head - Development Management, Civic Centre, Ashby Road, Scunthorpe DN16 1AB ☎ 01724 297492 ✉ philip.wallis@northlincs.gov.uk

Procurement: Mr Jason Whaler, Assistant Director - Business Support, Civic Centre, Ashby Road, Scunthorpe DN16 1AB ☎ 01724 296018 🖷 01724 296030 ✉ jason.whaler@northlincs.gov.uk

Public Libraries: Miss Helen Rowe , Assistant Director - Customer Services, Civic Centre, Ashby Road, Scunthorpe DN16 1AB ☎ 01724 297667 ✉ helen.rowe@northlincs.gov.uk

Recycling & Waste Minimisation: Mr Chris Matthews , Assistant Director - Community Services, Civic Centre, Ashby Road, Scunthorpe DN16 1AB ☎ 01724 297366 🖷 01724 297880 ✉ chris.matthews@northlincs.gov.uk

Regeneration: Mr Marcus Walker , Assistant Director - Planning & Regeneration, Civic Centre, Ashby Road, Scunthorpe DN16 1AB ☎ 01724 297305 🖷 01724 297899 ✉ marcus.walker@northlincs.gov.uk

Road Safety: Mr Chris Matthews , Assistant Director - Community Services, Civic Centre, Ashby Road, Scunthorpe DN16 1AB ☎ 01724 297366 🖷 01724 297880 ✉ chris.matthews@northlincs.gov.uk

Social Services (Adult): Ms Karen Pavey , Assistant Director - Adult Services, Civic Centre, Ashby Road, Scunthorpe DN16 1AB ☎ 01724 296420 ✉ karen.pavey@northlincs.gov.uk

Social Services (Children): Ms Denise Hyde, Director - People, Civic Centre, Ashby Road, Scunthorpe DN16 1AB ☎ 01724 296406 🖷 01724 296404 ✉ denise.hyde@northlincs.gov.uk

Public Health: Ms Frances Cunning , Director - Public Health, Pittwood House, Ashby Road, Scunthorpe DN16 1AB ✉ frances.cunning@northlincs.gov.uk

Staff Training: Mrs Christine Wilkinson, Strategic Workforce Lead (Organisational & Commercial Development), Civic Centre, Ashby Road, Scunthorpe DN16 1AB ☎ 01724 296322 🖷 01724 296339 ✉ christine.wilkinson@northlincs.gov.uk

Street Scene: Mr Chris Matthews , Assistant Director - Community Services, Civic Centre, Ashby Road, Scunthorpe DN16 1AB ☎ 01724 297366 🖷 01724 297880 ✉ chris.matthews@northlincs.gov.uk

Sustainable Communities: Mr David Hey , Head - Stronger Communities, Civic Centre, Ashby Road, Scunthorpe DN16 1AB ☎ 01724 296646 ✉ dave.hey@northlincs.gov.uk

Sustainable Development: Mr Tim Allen, Environment Team Manager, Church Square House, PO Box 42, Scunthorpe DN15 6XQ ☎ 01724 297387 🖷 01724 297870 ✉ tim.allen@northlincs.gov.uk

Tourism: Ms Margaret Price , Senior Tourism & Event Management Officer, Civic Centre, Ashby Road, Scunthorpe DN16 1AB ☎ 01724 297356 ✉ margaret.price@northlincs.gov.uk

Town Centre: Mr Peter Williams, Director - Places, Civic Centre, Ashby Road, Scunthorpe DN16 1AB ☎ 01724 296710 🖷 01724 296770 ✉ peter.williams@northlincs.gov.uk

Traffic Management: Mr Chris Matthews , Assistant Director - Community Services, Civic Centre, Ashby Road, Scunthorpe DN16 1AB ☎ 01724 297366 🖷 01724 297880 ✉ chris.matthews@northlincs.gov.uk

Transport: Miss Jodie Booth , Team Manager - Transport Planning, Hewson House, Station Road, Scunthorpe DN20 8XJ ☎ 01724 297373 🖷 01724 297899 ✉ jodie.booth@northlincs.gov.uk

Transport Planner: Miss Jodie Booth , Team Manager - Transport Planning, Hewson House, Station Road, Scunthorpe DN20 8XJ ☎ 01724 297373 🖷 01724 297899 ✉ jodie.booth@northlincs.gov.uk

Waste Collection and Disposal: Mr John Coates , Head of Waste Services, North Linc Council, Cottage Beck Road, Scunthorpe DN16 1TS ☎ 01724 297901 ✉ john.coates@northlincs.gov.uk

Waste Management: Mr John Coates , Head of Waste Services, North Linc Council, Cottage Beck Road, Scunthorpe DN16 1TS ☎ 01724 297901 ✉ john.coates@northlincs.gov.uk

Children's Play Areas: Mr Tom Coburn , Head - Sport, Leisure & Culture, Hewson House, Station Road, Brigg DN20 8XJ ☎ 01724 297260 ✉ tom.coburn@northlincs.gov.uk

COUNCILLORS

***Mayor* Rowson**, Helen (CON - Burton Upon Stather and Winterton)
Cllr.HelenRowson@northlincs.gov.uk

***Deputy Mayor* Foster**, Trevor (CON - Ridge)
Cllr.TrevorFoster@northlincs.gov.uk

***Leader of the Council* Redfern**, Liz (CON - Axholme Central)
Cllr.LizRedfern@northlincs.gov.uk

Ali, Mashook (LAB - Town)
Cllr.mashookali@northlincs.gov.uk

Allcock, Ron (CON - Axholme South)
Cllr.RonAllcock@northlincs.gov.uk

Armiger, Margaret (CON - Bottesford)
Cllr.margaretarmiger@northlincs.gov.uk

Armitage, Susan (LAB - Brumby)
Cllr.SueArmitage@northlincs.gov.uk

Bainbridge, Sandra (LAB - Frodingham)
cllr.sandrabainbridge@northlincs.gov.uk

Briggs, John (CON - Axholme North)
Cllr.JohnBriggs@northlincs.gov.uk

Carlile, Pauline (LAB - Brumby)
paulinecarlile@aol.com

Clark, Peter (CON - Ferry)
Cllr.PeterClark@northlincs.gov.uk

Collinson, John (LAB - Ashby)
Cllr.JohnCollinson@northlincs.gov.uk

Davison, Andrea (LAB - Ashby)
cllAndreaDavison@aol.com

Davison, John (CON - Bottesford)
Cllr.johndavison@northlincs.gov.uk

Ellerby, Anthony (LAB - Frodingham)
cllr.tonyellerby@northlincs.gov.uk

England, John (CON - Ridge)

Evison, Jonathan (CON - Barton)
Cllr.JonathanEvison@northlincs.gov.uk

Foster, Len (LAB - Brumby)
len.k.foster@northlincs.gov.uk

Glover, Ivan (CON - Broughton & Appleby)
Cllr.IvanGlover@northlincs.gov.uk

Godfrey, Susan (LAB - Kingsway with Lincoln Gardens)
Cllr.SusanGodfrey@northlincs.gov.uk

Gosling, Antony (LAB - Kingsway with Lincoln Gardens)
cllr.tonygosling@northlincs.gov.uk

Grant, Michael (LAB - Ashby)
Cllr.MickGrant@northlincs.gov.uk

Hannigan, Richard (CON - Ferry)
Cllr.richardhannigan@northlincs.gov.uk

Kataria, Haque Nawaz (LAB - Town)
Cllr.HaqueKataria@northlincs.gov.uk

Kirk, Mark (LAB - Crosby and Park)
mark.kirk@northlincs.gov.uk

Longcake, Derek (CON - Bottesford)
Cllr.dereklongcake@northlincs.gov.uk

Marper, Elaine (CON - Burton Upon Stather and Winterton)
Cllr.ElaineMarper@northlincs.gov.uk

Mumby-Croft, Holly (CON - Broughton & Appleby)
Cllr.hollymumby-croft@northlincs.gov.uk

Ogg, Ralph (CON - Burton Upon Stather and Winterton)
Cllr.RalphOgg@northlincs.gov.uk

Oldfield, David (LAB - Burringham and Gunness)
Cllr.DaveOldfield@northlincs.gov.uk

O'Sullivan, Christine (LAB - Crosby and Park)
cllr.christineo'sullivan@northlincs.gov.uk

Perry, Barbara (LAB - Crosby & Park)
Cllr.barbaraperry@northlincs.gov.uk

Poole, Neil (CON - Ridge)
cllr.NeilPoole@northlinks.gov.uk

Reed, Julie (CON - Axholme North)
Cllr.juliereed@northlincs.gov.uk

Robinson, David (CON - Axholme Central)
Cllr.DavidRobinson@northlincs.gov.uk

Rose, David (CON - Axholme South)
Cllr.davidrose@northlincs.gov.uk

Sherwood, Carl (CON - Brigg and Wolds)
Cllr.CarlSherwood@northlincs.gov.uk

Sherwood, Nigel (CON - Brigg and Wolds)
Cllr.NigelSherwood@northlincs.gov.uk

Vickers, Keith (CON - Barton)
Cllr.KeithVickers@northlincs.gov.uk

Vickers, Paul (CON - Barton)
Cllr.PaulVickers@northlinks.gov.uk

Waltham, Rob (CON - Brigg and Wolds)
rob.waltham@northlincs.gov.uk

Well, David (CON - Ferry)
Cllr.DavidWell@northlincs.gov.uk

Wilson, Stuart (LAB - Kingsway with Lincoln Gardens)
Cllr.stuartwilson@northlincs.gov.uk

POLITICAL COMPOSITION
CON: 26, LAB: 17

COMMITTEE CHAIRS
Audit: Mr Peter Clark

Health & Wellbeing: Mr Rob Waltham

Licensing: Mr Keith Vickers

Planning: Mr Nigel Sherwood

North Norfolk D

North Norfolk District Council, Council Offices, Holt Road, Cromer NR27 9EN
☎ 01263 513811 🖷 01263 515042 ✉ districtcouncil@north-norfolk.gov.uk
🖳 www.northnorfolk.org

FACTS AND FIGURES
Parliamentary Constituencies: Norfolk North
EU Constituencies: Eastern
Election Frequency: Elections are of whole council

PRINCIPAL OFFICERS
Chief Executive: Mrs Sheila Oxtoby, Chief Executive, Council Offices, Holt Road, Cromer NR27 9EN ☎ 01263 516000 🖷 01263 515042 ✉ sheila.oxtoby@north-norfolk.gov.uk

Senior Management: Mr Nick Baker, Corporate Director, Council Offices, Holt Road, Cromer NR27 9EN ☎ 01263 516221 🖷 01263 515042 ✉ nick.baker@north-norfolk.gov.uk

Senior Management: Mr Steve Blatch, Corporate Director, Council Offices, Holt Road, Cromer NR27 9EN ☎ 01263 516232 🖷 01263 515042 ✉ steve.blatch@north-norfolk.gov.uk

Architect, Building / Property Services: Mr Tony Turner , Property Manager, Council Offices, Holt Road, Cromer NR27 9EN ☎ 01263 516196 🖷 01263 515042 ✉ tony.turner@north-norfolk.gov.uk

Building Control: Mr Stuart Tate , Building Control Manager, Council Offices, Holt Road, Cromer NR27 9EN ☎ 01263 516132 🖷 01263 514802 ✉ stuart.tate@north-norfolk.gov.uk

NORTH NORFOLK

Catering Services: Mrs Maxine Collis , Property Business Manager, Council Offices, Holt Road, Cromer NR27 9EN ☎ 01263 516256 🖷 01263 515042 🖱 maxine.collis@north-norfolk.gov.uk

PR / Communications: Mrs Sue Lawson , Communications & PR Manager, Council Offices, Holt Road, Cromer NR27 9EN ☎ 01263 516344 🖷 01263 515042 🖱 sue.lawson@north-norfolk.gov.uk

Community Safety: Mr Stephen Hems , Head of Environmental Health, Council Offices, Holt Road, Cromer NR27 9EN ☎ 01263 516182 🖷 01263 515042 🖱 steve.hems@north-norfolk.gov.uk

Computer Management: Mrs Helen Mitchell, ICT Manager, Council Offices, Holt Road, Cromer NR27 9EN ☎ 01263 515042 🖱 helen.mitchell@north-norfolk.gov.uk

Customer Service: Mr David Williams , Customer Services Manager, Council Offices, Holt Road, Cromer NR27 9EN ☎ 01263 516415 🖷 01263 515042 🖱 david.williams@north-norfolk.gov.uk

Economic Development: Mr Robert Young , Head of Economic & Community Development, Council Offices, Holt Road, Cromer NR27 9EN ☎ 01263 516162 🖷 01263 515042 🖱 robert.young@north-norfolk.gov.uk

E-Government: Mr Sean Kelly , Head of Business Transformation, Council Offices, Holt Road, Cromer NR27 9EN ☎ 01263 516276 🖷 01263 515042 🖱 sean.kelly@north-norfolk.gov.uk

Electoral Registration: Ms Suzanne Taylor , Electoral Services Manager, Council Offices, Holt Road, Cromer NR27 9EN ☎ 01263 516046 🖷 01263 515042 🖱 suzanne.taylor@north-norfolk.gov.uk

Emergency Planning: Mr Stephen Hems , Head of Environmental Health, Council Offices, Holt Road, Cromer NR27 9EN ☎ 01263 516182 🖷 01263 515042 🖱 steve.hems@north-norfolk.gov.uk

Environmental / Technical Services: Mr Stephen Hems , Head of Environmental Health, Council Offices, Holt Road, Cromer NR27 9EN ☎ 01263 516182 🖷 01263 515042 🖱 steve.hems@north-norfolk.gov.uk

Environmental Health: Mr Stephen Hems , Head of Environmental Health, Council Offices, Holt Road, Cromer NR27 9EN ☎ 01263 516182 🖷 01263 515042 🖱 steve.hems@north-norfolk.gov.uk

Estates, Property & Valuation: Mr Martin Green , Estates & Valuation Manager, Council Offices, Holt Road, Cromer NR27 9EN ☎ 01263 516049 🖷 01263 515042 🖱 martin.green@north-norfolk.gov.uk

European Liaison: Mr Robert Young , Head of Economic & Community Development, Council Offices, Holt Road, Cromer NR27 9EN ☎ 01263 516162 🖷 01263 515042 🖱 robert.young@north-norfolk.gov.uk

Facilities: Mr Tony Turner , Property Manager, Council Offices, Holt Road, Cromer NR27 9EN ☎ 01263 516196 🖷 01263 515042 🖱 tony.turner@north-norfolk.gov.uk

Finance: Miss Karen Sly, Head of Finance, Council Offices, Holt Road, Cromer NR27 9EN ☎ 01263 516243 🖷 01263 515042 🖱 karen.sly@north-norfolk.gov.uk

Treasury: Ms Caz Williams , Team Leader for the Exchequer, Council Offices, Holt Road, Cromer NR27 9EN ☎ 01263 516063 🖷 01263 515042 🖱 caz.williams@north-norfolk.gov.uk

Fleet Management: Mrs Julie Cooke, Head of Organisational Development, Council Offices, Holt Road, Cromer NR27 9EN ☎ 01263 516040 🖷 01263 515042 🖱 julie.cooke@north-norfolk.gov.uk

Grounds Maintenance: Mr Karl Read, Sports & Leisure Services Manager, Council Offices, Holt Road, Cromer NR27 9EN ☎ 01263 516002 🖷 01263 515042 🖱 karl.read@north-norfolk.gov.uk

Health and Safety: Mr Stephen Hems , Head of Environmental Health, Council Offices, Holt Road, Cromer NR27 9EN ☎ 01263 516182 🖷 01263 515042 🖱 steve.hems@north-norfolk.gov.uk

Housing: Mr Robert Young , Head of Economic & Community Development, Council Offices, Holt Road, Cromer NR27 9EN ☎ 01263 516162 🖷 01263 515042 🖱 robert.young@north-norfolk.gov.uk

Legal: Mrs Emma Duncan, Head of Legal, Council Offices, Holt Road, Cromer NR27 9EN ☎ 01263 516045 🖷 01263 515042 🖱 emma.duncan@north-norfolk.gov.uk

Leisure and Cultural Services: Mr Karl Read, Sports & Leisure Services Manager, Council Offices, Holt Road, Cromer NR27 9EN ☎ 01263 516002 🖷 01263 515042 🖱 karl.read@north-norfolk.gov.uk

Licensing: Mr Stephen Hems , Head of Environmental Health, Council Offices, Holt Road, Cromer NR27 9EN ☎ 01263 516182 🖷 01263 515042 🖱 steve.hems@north-norfolk.gov.uk

Lifelong Learning: Mr Robert Young , Head of Economic & Community Development, Council Offices, Holt Road, Cromer NR27 9EN ☎ 01263 516162 🖷 01263 515042 🖱 robert.young@north-norfolk.gov.uk

Member Services: Mrs Emma Denny , Team Leader - Democratic Services, Council Offices, Holt Road, Cromer NR27 9EN ☎ 01263 516010 🖷 01263 515042 🖱 emma.denny@north-norfolk.gov.uk

Parking: Mrs Maxine Collis , Property Business Manager, Council Offices, Holt Road, Cromer NR27 9EN ☎ 01263 516256 🖷 01263 515042 🖱 maxine.collis@north-norfolk.gov.uk

Partnerships: Mr Robert Young , Head of Economic & Community Development, Council Offices, Holt Road, Cromer NR27 9EN ☎ 01263 516162 🖷 01263 515042 🖱 robert.young@north-norfolk.gov.uk

Personnel / HR: Mrs Julie Cooke, Head of Organisational Development, Council Offices, Holt Road, Cromer NR27 9EN ☎ 01263 516040 🖷 01263 515042 🖱 julie.cooke@north-norfolk.gov.uk

Planning: Mrs Nicola Baker , Head of Planning, Council Offices, Holt Road, Cromer NR27 9EN ☎ 01263 516135 🖷 01263 515042 🖱 nicola.baker@north-norfolk.gov.uk

Recycling & Waste Minimisation: Mr Stephen Hems , Head of Environmental Health, Council Offices, Holt Road, Cromer NR27 9EN ☎ 01263 516182 🖷 01263 515042 🖰 steve.hems@north-norfolk.gov.uk

Staff Training: Mrs Julie Cooke, Head of Organisational Development, Council Offices, Holt Road, Cromer NR27 9EN ☎ 01263 516040 🖷 01263 515042 🖰 julie.cooke@north-norfolk.gov.uk

Sustainable Communities: Mr Robert Young , Head of Economic & Community Development, Council Offices, Holt Road, Cromer NR27 9EN ☎ 01263 516162 🖷 01263 515042 🖰 robert.young@north-norfolk.gov.uk

Tourism: Mr Robert Young , Head of Economic & Community Development, Council Offices, Holt Road, Cromer NR27 9EN ☎ 01263 516162 🖷 01263 515042 🖰 robert.young@north-norfolk.gov.uk

Waste Collection and Disposal: Mr Scott Martin , Environmental Services Manager, Council Offices, Holt Road, Cromer NR27 9EN ☎ 01263 516341 🖷 01263 515042 🖰 scott.martin@north-norfolk.gov.uk

Waste Management: Mr Stephen Hems , Head of Environmental Health, Council Offices, Holt Road, Cromer NR27 9EN ☎ 01263 516182 🖷 01263 515042 🖰 steve.hems@north-norfolk.gov.uk

Children's Play Areas: Mr Paul Ingham , Parks & Countryside Manager, Council Offices, Holt Road, Cromer NR27 9EN ☎ 01263 516001 🖷 01263 515042 🖰 paul.ingham@north-norfolk.gov.uk

COUNCILLORS

***Chair* Claussen-Reynolds**, Annie (CON - Lancaster North)
annie.claussen-reynolds@north-norfolk.gov.uk

***Vice-Chair* Lee**, John (CON - Suffield Park)
john.lee@north-norfolk.gov.uk

***Leader of the Council* FitzPatrick**, Tom (CON - Walsingham)
tom.fitzpatrick@north-norfolk.gov.uk

***Deputy Leader of the Council* Fitch-Tillett**, Angie (CON - Poppyland)
angie.fitch-tillett@north-norfolk.gov.uk

***Group Leader* Seward**, Eric (LD - North Walsham North)
eric.seward@north-norfolk.gov.uk

***Group Leader* Wells**, Andrew (LD - Glaven)
andrew.wells@north-norfolk.gov.uk

Arnold, Sue (CON - Roughton)
sue.arnold@north-norfolk.gov.uk

Butikofer, Sarah (LD - The Runtons)
sarah.butikofer@north-norfolk.gov.uk

Coppack, Nicholas (CON - Gaunt)
nicolas.coppack@north-norfolk.gov.uk

Cox, Hilary (CON - Cromer)
Hilary.cox@north-norfolk.gov.uk

Dixon, Nigel (CON - Hoveton)
nigel.dixon@north-norfolk.gov.uk

English, Jenny (CON - Briston)
jenny.english@north-norfolk.gov.uk

Fitzpatrick, Vincent (CON - Priory)
vincent.fitzpatrick@north-norfolk.gov.uk

Gay, Virginia (LD - North Walsham West)
v.gay@virgin.net

Green, Ann (CON - Wensum)
ann.green@north-norfolk.gov.uk

Grove-Jones, Pauline (LD - Stalham and Sutton)
pauline.grove-jones@north-norfolk.gov.uk

Hannah, Brian (LD - Sheringham North)
brian.hannah@north-norfolk.gov.uk

Hester, Simon (CON - Priory)
simon.hester@north-norfolk.gov.uk

High, Philip (LD - Holt)
philip.high@north-norfolk.gov.uk

Jarvis, Ben (CON - Waterside)
benjamin.jarvis@north-norfolk.gov.uk

Knowles, Michael (CON - Chaucer)
mike.knowles@north-norfolk.gov.uk

Lloyd, Nigel (LD - North Walsham)
nigel.lloyd@north-norfolk.gov.uk

McGoun, Barbara (LD - St Benet)
barbara.mcgoun@north-norfolk.gov.uk

Moore, Ann (LD - North Walsham North)
ann.moore@north-norfolk.gov.uk

Moore, Peter (LD - North Walsham East)
cllrpetermoore@aol.com

Northam, Wyndham (CON - Mundesley)
wyndham.northam@north-norfolk.gov.uk

Oliver, Judy (CON - Sheringham South)
judy.oliver@north-norfolk.gov.uk

Palmer, Becky (CON - The Raynhams)
becky.palmer@north-norfolk.gov.uk

Pearce, Nigel (CON - Suffield Park)

Perry-Warnes, Georgie (CON - Corpusty)
georgie.perry-warnes@north-norfolk.gov.uk

Price, Richard (CON - Waxham)
Richard.Price@norwich-norfolk.gov.uk

Prior, Maggie (CON - Holt)
maggie.prior@north-norfolk.gov.uk

Punchard, Jeremy (CON - Lancaster South)
jeremy.punchard@north-norfolk.gov.uk

Rest, John (CON - Lancaster South)
john.arest@north-norfolk.gov.uk

Reynolds, Roy (CON - Lancaster North)
roy.reynolds@north-norfolk.gov.uk

Rice, Paul (CON - Waterside)
paul.rice@north-norfolk.gov.uk

Shaw, Simon (CON - Scottow)
simon.shaw@north-norfolk.gov.uk

Shepherd, Richard (CON - Sheringham South)
richard.shepherd@north-norfolk.gov.uk

Smith, Norman (CON - Erpingham)
norman.smith@north-norfolk.gov.uk

Smith, Douglas (CON - Sheringham North)
doug.smith@norton-norfolk@gov.uk

Smith, Barry (CON - Mundesley)
barry.smith@north-norfolk.gov.uk

Stevens, Robert (CON - Stalham and Sutton)

Uprichard, Vivienne (LD - North Walsham East)
vivienne.uprichard@north-norfolk.gov.uk

Walker, Lee (LD - Happisburgh)
gbeachkidz@btinternet.com

Ward, Steven (CON - Lancaster South)
steven.ward@north-norfolk.gov.uk

Williams, Glyn (CON - Worstead)
glyn.williams@north-norfolk.gov.uk

Yiasimi, Andreas (LD - Cromer Town)
andreas.yiasimi@north-norfolk.gov.uk

Young, David (LD - High Heath)
david.young@north-norfolk.gov.uk

POLITICAL COMPOSITION

CON: 33, LD: 15

COMMITTEE CHAIRS

Audit: Mr Vincent Fitzpatrick

Development: Mr Roy Reynolds

Licensing: Mr Richard Price

North Somerset U

North Somerset Council, Town Hall, Walliscote Grove Road, Weston-super-Mare BS23 1UJ
☎ 01934 888888 🖷 01934 888822
✉ firstname.surname@n-somerset.gov.uk 💻 www.n-somerset.gov.uk

FACTS AND FIGURES

Parliamentary Constituencies: Weston-super-Mare
EU Constituencies: South West
Election Frequency: Elections are of whole council

PRINCIPAL OFFICERS

Chief Executive: Mr Mike Jackson, Chief Executive Officer, Town Hall, Walliscote Grove Road, Weston-super-Mare BS23 1UJ
☎ 01934 634972 🖷 01934 888822 ✉ mike.jackson@n-somerset.gov.uk

Senior Management: Ms Sheila Smith , Director - People & Communities, Town Hall, Walliscote Grove Road, Weston-super-Mare BS23 1UJ ☎ 01934 888830 ✉ sheila.smith@n-somerset.gov.uk

Senior Management: Mr David Turner, Director - Development & Environment, Town Hall, Walliscote Grove Road, Weston-super-Mare BS23 1UJ ☎ 01934 888885 ✉ david.turner@n-somerset.gov.uk

Access Officer / Social Services (Disability): Mr Anthony Rylands, Disability Equality Access Officer, Town Hall, Walliscote Grove Road, Weston-super-Mare BS23 1UJ ☎ 01934 634989
✉ anthony.rylands@n-somerset.gov.uk

Architect, Building / Property Services: Mr Mark McSweeney , Property Services Manager, Town Hall, Walliscote Grove Road, Weston-super-Mare BS23 1UJ ☎ 01275 882920
✉ mark.mcsweeney@n-somerset.gov.uk

Best Value: Mr Paul Morris, Head - Performance Improvement & Human Resources, Town Hall, Walliscote Grove Road, Weston-super-Mare BS23 1UJ ☎ 01934 888843
✉ paul.morris@n-somerset.gov.uk

Building Control: Mr Jason Beale , Service Development Manager, Town Hall, Walliscote Grove Road, Weston-super-Mare BS23 1UJ ☎ 01275 888811 ✉ jason.beale@n-somerset.gov.uk

Catering Services: Mrs Lynda Mitchell, Commissioning & Contracts Manager, Town Hall, Walliscote Grove Road, Weston-super-Mare BS23 1UJ ☎ 01275 888319
✉ lynda.mitchell@n-somerset.gov.uk

Children / Youth Services: Ms Sheila Smith , Director - People & Communities, Town Hall, Walliscote Grove Road, Weston-super-Mare BS23 1UJ ☎ 01934 888830 ✉ sheila.smith@n-somerset.gov.uk

Civil Registration: Mr Richard Tucker , Superintendent Registrar, Town Hall, Walliscote Grove Road, Weston-super-Mare BS23 1UJ
☎ 01934 627552 ✉ richard.tucker@n-somerset.gov.uk

PR / Communications: Mrs Vanessa Andrews , Marketing & Communications Manager, Town Hall, Walliscote Grove Road, Weston-super-Mare BS23 1UJ ☎ 01275 888728
✉ vanessa.andrews@n-somerset.gov.uk

Community Planning: Mr Michael Reep , Planning Policy Manager, Town Hall, Walliscote Grove Road, Weston-super-Mare BS23 1UJ ☎ 01934 426775 ✉ michael.reep@n-somerset.gov.uk

Community Safety: Ms Jo Mercer , Community Safety & Drug Action Team Manager, Town Hall, Walliscote Grove Road, Weston-super-Mare BS23 1UJ ☎ 01934 426880
✉ jo.mercer@n-somerset.gov.uk

Computer Management: Mr Mike Riggall , Strategic ICT Client Manager, Town Hall, Walliscote Grove Road, Weston-super-Mare BS23 1UJ ☎ 01934 426385 ✉ mike.riggall@n-somerset.gov.uk

Consumer Protection and Trading Standards: Ms Mandy Bishop, Assistant Director - Operations, Town Hall, Walliscote Grove Road, Weston-super-Mare BS23 1UJ ☎ 01275 882806
✉ mandy.bishop@n-somerset.gov.uk

Contracts: Mr Simon Farnsworth , Commercial & Contracts Manager, Town Hall, Walliscote Grove Road, Weston-super-Mare BS23 1UJ ☎ 01275 882963 ✉ simon.farnsworth@n-somerset.gov.uk

Customer Service: Ms Simone Woolley , Customer Services Manager, Town Hall, Walliscote Grove Road, Weston-super-Mare BS23 1UJ ☎ 01934 427370 ✉ simon.woolley@n-somerset.gov.uk

Economic Development: Mr Simon Gregory, Economic Development Service Manager, Town Hall, Walliscote Grove Road, Weston-super-Mare BS23 1UJ ☎ 01934 426327
✉ simon.gregory@n-somerset.gov.uk

Education: Ms Jane Routledge , Interim Head - Learning & Achievement, Town Hall, Walliscote Grove Road, Weston-super-Mare BS23 1UJ ☎ 01275 884427
✉ jane.routledge@n-somerset.gov.uk

Electoral Registration: Mr Mike Jones, Electoral Services Manager, Town Hall, Walliscote Grove Road, Weston-super-Mare BS23 1UJ ☎ 01934 634903 mike.jones@n-somerset.gov.uk

Emergency Planning: Mr Ian Wilson , Emergency Management Officer, Town Hall, Walliscote Grove Road, Weston-super-Mare BS23 1UJ ☎ 01934 426706 ian.wilson2@n-somerset.gov.uk

Energy Management: Mr Steve Hodges, Mechanical, Electrical & Energy Manager, Town Hall, Walliscote Grove Road, Weston-super-Mare BS23 1UJ ☎ 01934 634710 steve.hodges@n-somerset.gov.uk

Environmental Health: Ms Mandy Bishop, Assistant Director - Operations, Town Hall, Walliscote Grove Road, Weston-super-Mare BS23 1UJ ☎ 01275 882806 mandy.bishop@n-somerset.gov.uk

Estates, Property & Valuation: Mr Malcolm Coe , Head - Finance & Property, Town Hall, Walliscote Grove Road, Weston-super-Mare BS23 1UJ ☎ 01934 634619 malcolm.coe@n-somerset.gov.uk

Events Manager: Mr Darren Fairchild , Seafront & Events Service Manager, Town Hall, Walliscote Grove Road, Weston-super-Mare BS23 1UJ ☎ 01934 427274 darren.fairchild@n-somerset.gov.uk

Finance: Mr Malcolm Coe , Head - Finance & Property, Town Hall, Walliscote Grove Road, Weston-super-Mare BS23 1UJ ☎ 01934 634619 malcolm.coe@n-somerset.gov.uk

Fleet Management: Mr Carl Nicholson , Fleet Supervisor, Town Hall, Walliscote Grove Road, Weston-super-Mare BS23 1UJ ☎ 01275 882935 carl.nicholson@n-somerset.gov.uk

Grounds Maintenance: Mr Ed McKay , Parks & Streetscene Contracts Officer, Town Hall, Walliscote Grove Road, Weston-super-Mare BS23 1UJ ☎ 01934 427681 edward.mckay@n-somerset.gov.uk

Health and Safety: Ms Cate Sampson , Health & Safety Manager, Town Hall, Walliscote Grove Road, Weston-super-Mare BS23 1UJ ☎ 01934 888632 cate.sampson@n-somerset.gov.uk

Highways: Mr Frank Cox, Highway Service Manager, Town Hall, Walliscote Grove Road, Weston-super-Mare BS23 1UJ ☎ 01934 426784 frank.cox@n-somerset.gov.uk

Highways: Mr Colin Medus, Head - Highways & Transport, Town Hall, Walliscote Grove Road, Weston-super-Mare BS23 1UJ ☎ 01934 426498 colin.medus@n-somerset.gov.uk

Home Energy Conservation: Ms Kim Herivel, Home Energy Efficiency Officer, Town Hall, Walliscote Grove Road, Weston-super-Mare BS23 1UJ ☎ 01934 426686 kim.herivel@n-somerset.gov.uk

Housing: Mr Mark Hughes , Head - Housing, Town Hall, Walliscote Grove Road, Weston-super-Mare BS23 1UJ ☎ 01934 426320 mark.hughes@n-somerset.gov.uk

Local Area Agreement: Ms Rhiannon Jones , Policy Development Officer, Town Hall, Walliscote Grove Road, Weston-super-Mare BS23 1UJ ☎ 01275 884204 rhiannon.jones@n-somerset.gov.uk

Legal: Mr Nick Brain , Head - Legal & Democratic Services, Town Hall, Walliscote Grove Road, Weston-super-Mare BS23 1UJ ☎ 01934 634929 nick.brain@n-somerset.gov.uk

Leisure and Cultural Services: Ms Mandy Bishop, Assistant Director - Operations, Town Hall, Walliscote Grove Road, Weston-super-Mare BS23 1UJ ☎ 01275 882806 mandy.bishop@n-somerset.gov.uk

Licensing: Ms Mandy Bishop, Assistant Director - Operations, Town Hall, Walliscote Grove Road, Weston-super-Mare BS23 1UJ ☎ 01275 882806 mandy.bishop@n-somerset.gov.uk

Lifelong Learning: Ms Jill Croskell , Community Learning Team Manager, Town Hall, Walliscote Grove Road, Weston-super-Mare BS23 1UJ ☎ 01934 426105 jill.croskell@n-somerset.gov.uk

Lighting: Mr Darren Coffin-Smith , Highways & Transport Asset Manager, Town Hall, Walliscote Grove Road, Weston-super-Mare BS23 1UJ ☎ 01275 888548 darren.coffin-smith@n-somerset.gov.uk

Lottery Funding, Charity and Voluntary: Ms Lorraine Bush , Policy & Partnerships Development Officer, Town Hall, Walliscote Grove Road, Weston-super-Mare BS23 1UJ ☎ 01934 634888 lorraine.bush@n-somerset.gov.uk

Member Services: Ms Fiona Robertson , Deputy Head - Legal & Democratic Services, Town Hall, Walliscote Grove Road, Weston-super-Mare BS23 1UJ ☎ 01934 634686 fiona.robertson@n-somerset.gov.uk

Parking: Mr Allan Taylor , Car Parking Services Manager, Town Hall, Walliscote Grove Road, Weston-super-Mare BS23 1UJ ☎ 01934 427293 allan.taylor@n-somerset.gov.uk

Partnerships: Mr Richard Penska , Head - Support Services Partnership, Town Hall, Walliscote Grove Road, Weston-super-Mare BS23 1UJ ☎ 01275 884256 richard.penska@n-somerset.gov.uk

Personnel / HR: Mr Paul Morris, Head - Performance Improvement & Human Resources, Town Hall, Walliscote Grove Road, Weston-super-Mare BS23 1UJ ☎ 01934 888843 paul.morris@n-somerset.gov.uk

Planning: Mr Richard Kent, Head - Development Management, Town Hall, Walliscote Grove Road, Weston-super-Mare BS23 1UJ ☎ 01275 888811 richard.kent@n-somerset.gov.uk

Public Libraries: Mr Andy Brisley, Libraries & Information Service Manager, Town Hall, Walliscote Grove Road, Weston-super-Mare BS23 1UJ ☎ 01934 426658 andy.brisley@n-somerset.gov.uk

Recycling & Waste Minimisation: Mr Colin Russell , Recycling & Waste Service Manager, Town Hall, Walliscote Grove Road, Weston-super-Mare BS23 1UJ ☎ 01934 888802 colin.russell@n-somerset.gov.uk

NORTH SOMERSET

Regeneration: Mr Karuna Tharmananthar , Deputy Director - Development & Environment, Town Hall, Walliscote Grove Road, Weston-super-Mare BS23 1UJ ☎ 01275 888886 ✉ karuna.tharmananthar@n-somerset.gov.uk

Road Safety: Mr Frank Cox, Highway Service Manager, Town Hall, Walliscote Grove Road, Weston-super-Mare BS23 1UJ ☎ 01934 426784 ✉ frank.cox@n-somerset.gov.uk

Social Services (Children): Mr Eifion Price , Assistant Director - Support & Safeguarding, Town Hall, Walliscote Grove Road, Weston-super-Mare BS23 1UJ ☎ 01275 884392 ✉ eifion.price@n-somerset.gov.uk

Safeguarding: Mr Eifion Price , Assistant Director - Support & Safeguarding, Town Hall, Walliscote Grove Road, Weston-super-Mare BS23 1UJ ☎ 01275 884392 ✉ eifion.price@n-somerset.gov.uk

Public Health: Ms Natalie Field , Interim Director - Public Health, Town Hall, Walliscote Grove Road, Weston-super-Mare BS23 1UJ ☎ 01275 885132 ✉ natalie.field@n-somerset.gov.uk

Staff Training: Mr Paul Morris, Head - Performance Improvement & Human Resources, Town Hall, Weston-super-Mare BS23 1AE ☎ 01934 888843 ✉ paul.morris@n-somerset.gov.uk

Street Scene: Mr John Flannigan , Community & Enforcement Service Manager, Town Hall, Walliscote Grove Road, Weston-super-Mare BS23 1UJ ☎ 01934 427346 ✉ john.flannigan@n-somerset.gov.uk

Sustainable Communities: Mr David Turner, Director - Development & Environment, Town Hall, Walliscote Grove Road, Weston-super-Mare BS23 1UJ ☎ 01934 888885 ✉ david.turner@n-somerset.gov.uk

Sustainable Development: Mr Michael Reep , Planning Policy Manager, Town Hall, Walliscote Grove Road, Weston-super-Mare BS23 1UJ ☎ 01934 426775 ✉ michael.reep@n-somerset.gov.uk

Tourism: Mr Simon Gregory, Economic Development Service Manager, Town Hall, Walliscote Grove Road, Weston-super-Mare BS23 1UJ ☎ 01934 426327 ✉ simon.gregory@n-somerset.gov.uk

Town Centre: Mr Mark MacGregor , Head - Streets & Open Spaces, Town Hall, Walliscote Grove Road, Weston-super-Mare BS23 1UJ ☎ 01934 888802 ✉ mark.macgregor@n-somerset.gov.uk

Traffic Management: Mr Frank Cox, Highway Service Manager, Town Hall, Walliscote Grove Road, Weston-super-Mare BS23 1UJ ☎ 01934 426784 ✉ frank.cox@n-somerset.gov.uk

Transport: Ms Bella Fortune , Transportation Service Manager, Town Hall, Walliscote Grove Road, Weston-super-Mare BS23 1UJ ☎ 01934 427540 ✉ bella.fortune@n-somerset.gov.uk

Transport Planner: Ms Bella Fortune , Transportation Service Manager, Town Hall, Walliscote Grove Road, Weston-super-Mare BS23 1UJ ☎ 01934 427540 ✉ bella.fortune@n-somerset.gov.uk

Waste Collection and Disposal: Mr John Carson , Recycling & Waste Contracts Manager, Town Hall, Walliscote Grove Road, Weston-super-Mare BS23 1UJ ☎ 01934 427401 ✉ john.carson@n-somerset.gov.uk

Waste Management: Mr Colin Russell , Recycling & Waste Service Manager, Town Hall, Walliscote Grove Road, Weston-super-Mare BS23 1UJ ☎ 01934 888802 ✉ colin.russell@n-somerset.gov.uk

Children's Play Areas: Mr Ed McKay , Parks & Streetscene Contracts Officer, Town Hall, Walliscote Grove Road, Weston-super-Mare BS23 1UJ ☎ 01934 427681 ✉ edward.mckay@n-somerset.gov.uk

COUNCILLORS

***Chair* Cave**, Charles (CON - Long Ashton)
charles.cave@n-somerset.gov.uk

***Vice-Chair* Crockford-Hawley**, John (LD - Weston-super-Mare Hillside)
john.crockford-hawley@n-somerset.gov.uk

***Leader of the Council* Ashton**, Nigel (CON - Gordano Valley)
nigel.ashton@n-somerset.gov.uk

***Deputy Leader of the Council* ap Rees**, Elfan (CON - Hutton & Locking)
elfan.ap.rees@n-somerset.gov.uk

Baker, Felicity (CON - Portishead West)
felicity.baker@n-somerset.gov.uk

Barber, Jan (CON - Nailsea Youngwood)
jan.barber@n-somerset.gov.uk

Barclay, Karen (IND - Backwell)
karen.barclay@n-somerset.gov.uk

Bell, Mike (LD - Weston-super-Mare Central)
mike.bell@n-somerset.gov.uk

Blades, Chris (CON - Clevedon West)
christopher.blades@n-somerset.gov.uk

Blades, Ericka (CON - Clevedon Yeo)
ericka.blades@n-somerset.gov.uk

Blatchford, Mary (CON - Nailsea Yeo)
mary.blatchford@n-somerset.gov.uk

Bryant, Peter (CON - Weston-super-Mare Uphill)
peter.bryantcouncillor@n-somerset.gov.uk

Burden, Peter (CON - Portishead South)
peter.burden@n-somerset.gov.uk

Canniford, Mark (LD - Weston-super-Mare Hillside)
mark.canniford@n-somerset.gov.uk

Clayton, James (LAB - Weston-super-Mare Bournville)
james.clayton@n-somerset.gov.uk

Cleland, Robert (CON - Weston-super-Mare Mid Worle)
robert.cleland@n-somerset.gov.uk

Codling, Sarah (CON - Weston-super-Mare Winterstoke)
sarah.codling@n-somerset.gov.uk

Cole, Andy (IND - Nailsea Golden Valley)
andy.cole@n-somerset.gov.uk

Crew, Peter (CON - Weston-super-Mare South Worle)
peter.crew@n-somerset.gov.uk

Davies, Donald (IND - Pill)
donald.davies@n-somerset.gov.uk

Garner, Bob (CON - Clevedon South)
bob.garner@n-somerset.gov.uk

Hadley, Judith (CON - Yatton)
judith.hadley@n-somerset.gov.uk

Hall, Colin (CON - Clevedon Walton)
colin.hall@n-somerset.gov.uk

Harley, Ann (CON - Banwell & Winscombe)
ann.harley@n-somerset.gov.uk

Hitchins, David (CON - Weston-super-Mare South Worle)
david.hitchins@n-somerset.gov.uk

Iles, Jill (CON - Yatton)
jill.iles@n-somerset.gov.uk

Jacobs, Ruth (CON - Wick St Lawrence & St George's)
ruth.jacobs@n-somerset.gov.uk

Jolley, David (CON - Portishead West)
david.jolley@n-somerset.gov.uk

Knight, Reyna (CON - Portishead North)
reyna.knight@n-somerset.gov.uk

Leimdorfer, Tom (GRN - Congresbury & Puxton)
tom.leimdorfer@n-somerset.gov.uk

Ley-Morgan, John (IND - Weston-super-Mare Uphill)
john.ley-morgan@n-somerset.gov.uk

Mead, Derek (IND - Weston-super-Mare North Worle)
derek.mead@n-somerset.gov.uk

Nightingale, Richard (CON - Weston-super-Mare Central)
richard.nightingale@n-somerset.gov.uk

O'Brien, Jerry (CON - Banwell & Winscombe)

Oyns, David (CON - Portishead East)
david.oyns@n-somerset.gov.uk

Parker, Ian (LAB - Weston-super-Mare Bournville)
ian.parker@n-somerset.gov.uk

Pasley, David (CON - Portishead East)
david.pasley@n-somerset.gov.uk

Payne, Dawn (CON - Weston-super-Mare Winterstoke)
dawn.payne@n-somerset.gov.uk

Pepperall, Marcia (CON - Weston-super-Mare North Worle)
marcia.pepperall@n-somerset.gov.uk

Pilgrim, Lisa (CON - Weston-super-Mare Kewstoke)
lisa.pilgrim@n-somerset.gov.uk

Porter, Terry (CON - Hutton & Locking)
terry.porter@n-somerset.gov.uk

Shopland, David (IND - Clevedon East)

Stowey, Kate (CON - Long Ashton)
kate.stowey@n-somerset.gov.uk

Tonkin, James (IND - Nailsea West End)
james.tonkin@n-somerset.gov.uk

Tucker, Richard (LAB - Weston-super-Mare Milton)
richard.tucker@n-somerset.gov.uk

Wells, Elizabeth (CON - Blagdon and Churchill)

Williams, Martin (CON - Weston-super-Mare Milton)
martin.williams@n-somerset.gov.uk

Willis, Roz (CON - Weston-super-Mare Kewstoke)
roz.willis@n-somerset.gov.uk

Wilton, Nick (CON - Winford)
nick.wilton@n-somerset.gov.uk

Yamanaka, Deborah (LD - Wrington)
deborah.yamanaka@n-somerset.gov.uk

POLITICAL COMPOSITION

CON: 35, IND: 7, LD: 4, LAB: 3, GRN: 1

North Tyneside M

North Tyneside Metropolitan Borough Council, Quadrant, The Silverlink North, Cobalt Business Park, North Tyneside, NE27 0BY
☎ 0845 200 0101 💻 www.northtyneside.gov.uk

FACTS AND FIGURES

Parliamentary Constituencies: Tynemouth, Tyneside North
EU Constituencies: North East
Election Frequency: Elections are by thirds

PRINCIPAL OFFICERS

Chief Executive: Mr Patrick Melia , Chief Executive & S151 Officer, Quadrant, The Silverlink North, Cobalt Business Park, North Tyneside, NE27 0BY ☎ 0191 643 2001 🖷 0191 643 2431
✉ patrick.melia@northtyneside.gov.uk

Deputy Chief Executive: Mr Paul Hanson, Deputy Chief Executive, Quadrant, The Silverlink North, Cobalt Business Park, NE27 0BY ☎ 0191 643 7001 🖷 0191 643 2431
✉ paul.hanson@northtyneside.gov.uk

Senior Management: Mr Paul Buie , Head of Business & Economic Development, Quadrant, The Silverlink North, Cobalt Business Park, North Tyneside, NE27 0BY ☎ 0191 643 6402
✉ paul.buie@northtyneside.gov.uk

Senior Management: Ms Wendy Burke , Interim Director of Public Health, Quadrant, The Silverlink North, Cobalt Business Park, North Tyneside, NE27 0BY ☎ 0191 643 2104
✉ wendy.burke@northtyneside.gov.uk

Senior Management: Ms Lisa Clark , Head of Commercial Services & Business Re-design, Quadrant, The Silverlink North, Cobalt Business Park, North Tyneside, NE27 0BY ☎ 0191 643 7760
✉ lisa.clark@northtyneside.gov.uk

Senior Management: Ms Vivienne Geary, Head of Law & Governance, Quadrant, The Silverlink North, Cobalt Business Park, North Tyneside, NE27 0BY ☎ 0191 643 5339 🖷 0191 643 2431
✉ vivienne.geary@northtyneside.gov.uk

Senior Management: Ms Jean Griffiths , Head of Children, Young People & Learning, Quadrant, The Silverlink North, Cobalt Business Park, North Tyneside, NE27 0BY ☎ 0191 643 7070
✉ jean.griffiths@northtyneside.gov.uk

Senior Management: Mr Ben Kaner , Head of Digital Strategy, Quadrant, The Silverlink North, Cobalt Business Park, North Tyneside, NE27 0BY ☎ 0191 643 7760
✉ ben.kaner@northtyneside.gov.uk

NORTH TYNESIDE

Senior Management: Mrs Jackie Laughton , Head of Corporate Strategy, Quadrant, The Silverlink North, Cobalt Business Park, North Tyneside, NE27 0BY ☎ 0191 643 7070 🖷 0191 643 2427 🖰 jacqueline.laughton@northtyneside.gov.uk

Senior Management: Ms Alison Lazazzera, Head of Human Resources & Organisation Development, Quadrant, The Silverlink North, Cobalt Business Park, North Tyneside, NE27 0BY ☎ 0191 643 5012 🖰 alison.lazazzera@northtyneside.gov.uk

Senior Management: Mr Mark Longstaff , Head of Commissioning & Investment, Quadrant West, The Silverlink North, Cobalt Business Park, North Tyneside, NE27 0BY ☎ 0191 643 8091 🖰 mark.longstaff@northtyneside.gov.uk

Senior Management: Mrs Jacqui Old , Head of Adult Social Care, Quadrant, The Silverlink North, Cobalt Business Park, North Tyneside, NE27 0BY ☎ 0191 643 7317 🖷 0191 643 1776 🖰 jacqui.old@northtyneside.gov.uk

Senior Management: Mr Phil Scott, Head of Environment, Housing & Leisure, Quadrant, The Silverlink North, 2nd Floor, Quadrant West, Cobalt Business Park, NE27 0BY ☎ 0191 643 7295 🖷 0191 643 2414 🖰 phil.scott@northtyneside.gov.uk

Building Control: Mr Colin MacDonald, Senior Manager - Technical & Regulatory Services, Quadrant, The Silverlink North, Cobalt Business Park, North Tyneside, NE27 0BY ☎ 0191 643 6620 🖷 0191 643 2391 🖰 colin.macdonald@northtyneside.gov.uk

Catering Services: Ms Barbara Patterson, Catering Manager, Quadrant, The Silverlink North, Cobalt Business Park, North Tyneside, NE27 0BY ☎ 0191 643 8340 🖷 0191 643 2408 🖰 barbara.patterson@northtyneside.gov.uk

Children / Youth Services: Ms Jill Baker , Senior Manager - Early Help & Vulnerable Families, Quadrant, The Silverlink North, Cobalt Business Park, North Tyneside, NE27 0BY ☎ 0191 643 6462 🖰 jill.baker2@northtyneside.gov.uk

Civil Registration: Ms Christine Lois, Registration Service Manager, Maritime Chambers, Howard Street, North Shields NE30 1LZ ☎ 0191 643 6790 🖰 christine.lois@northtyneside.gov.uk

PR / Communications: Mrs Jeanette Hedley , Communications & Engagement Manager, Quadrant, The Silverlink North, Cobalt Business Park, North Tyneside, NE27 0BY ☎ 0191 643 5077 🖷 0191 643 2431 🖰 jeanette.hedley@northtyneside.gov.uk

Community Safety: Ms Lindsey Horwood , Resilience & Security Manager, Quadrant, The Silverlink North, Cobalt Business Park, North Tyneside, NE27 0BY ☎ 0191 643 6483 🖰 lindsey.horwood@northtyneside.gov.uk

Computer Management: Mr Ben Kaner , Head of Digital Strategy, Quadrant, The Silverlink North, Cobalt Business Park, North Tyneside, NE27 0BY ☎ 0191 643 7760 🖰 ben.kaner@northtyneside.gov.uk

Consumer Protection and Trading Standards: Mr Colin MacDonald, Senior Manager - Technical & Regulatory Services, Quadrant, The Silverlink North, Cobalt Business Park, North Tyneside, NE27 0BY ☎ 0191 643 6620 🖷 0191 643 2391 🖰 colin.macdonald@northtyneside.gov.uk

Customer Service: Ms Lisa Clark , Head of Commercial Services & Business Re-design, Quadrant, The Silverlink North, Cobalt Business Park, North Tyneside, NE27 0BY ☎ 0191 643 7760 🖰 lisa.clark@northtyneside.gov.uk

Economic Development: Mr Paul Buie , Head of Business & Economic Development, Quadrant, The Silverlink North, Cobalt Business Park, North Tyneside, NE27 0BY ☎ 0191 643 6402 🖰 paul.buie@northtyneside.gov.uk

Education: Mrs Jean Griffiths , Head of Children, Young People & Learning, Quadrant, The Silverlink North, Cobalt Business Park, North Tyneside, NE27 0BY ☎ 0191 643 8782 🖷 0191 643 2431 🖰 jean.griffiths@northtyneside.gov.uk

E-Government: Mrs Jackie Laughton , Head of Corporate Strategy, Quadrant, The Silverlink North, Cobalt Business Park, North Tyneside, NE27 0BY ☎ 0191 643 7070 🖷 0191 643 2427 🖰 jacqueline.laughton@northtyneside.gov.uk

Electoral Registration: Ms Joanne McGregor , Manager of Law & Governance, Quadrant, The Silverlink North, Cobalt Business Park, North Tyneside, NE27 0BY ☎ 0191 643 5350 🖰 joanne.mcgregor@northtyneside.gov.uk

Emergency Planning: Mr Phil Scott, Head of Environment, Housing & Leisure, Quadrant, The Silverlink North, 2nd Floor, Quadrant West, Cobalt Business Park, NE27 0BY ☎ 0191 643 7295 🖷 0191 643 2414 🖰 phil.scott@northtyneside.gov.uk

Energy Management: Mr Phil Scott, Head of Environment, Housing & Leisure, Quadrant, The Silverlink North, 2nd Floor, Quadrant West, Cobalt Business Park, NE27 0BY ☎ 0191 643 7295 🖷 0191 643 2414 🖰 phil.scott@northtyneside.gov.uk

Environmental / Technical Services: Mr Phil Scott, Head of Environment, Housing & Leisure, Quadrant, The Silverlink North, 2nd Floor, Quadrant West, Cobalt Business Park, NE27 0BY ☎ 0191 643 7295 🖷 0191 643 2414 🖰 phil.scott@northtyneside.gov.uk

Environmental Health: Mr Colin MacDonald, Senior Manager - Technical & Regulatory Services, Quadrant, The Silverlink North, Cobalt Business Park, North Tyneside, NE27 0BY ☎ 0191 643 6620 🖷 0191 643 2391 🖰 colin.macdonald@northtyneside.gov.uk

Estates, Property & Valuation: Mr Niall Cathie , Strategic Asset Manager, Quadrant, The Silverlink North, Cobalt Business Park, North Tyneside, NE27 0BY ☎ 0191 643 6517 🖰 niall.cathie@northtyneside.gov.uk

European Liaison: Ms Melissa Wells , Policy & Intelligence Advisor, Quadrant, The Silverlink North, Cobalt Business Park, North Tyneside, NE27 0BY ☎ 0191 643 6412 🖰 melissa.wells@northtyneside.gov.uk

Events Manager: Mr Peter Warne, Tourism & Events Development Manager, Town Hall, High Street East, Wallsend NE28 7RR ☎ 0191 643 7411 🖷 0191 643 2406 🖰 pete.warne@northtyneside.gov.uk

Facilities: Mr Niall Cathie , Strategic Asset Manager, Quadrant, The Silverlink North, Cobalt Business Park, North Tyneside, NE27 0BY ☎ 0191 643 6517 🖰 niall.cathie@northtyneside.gov.uk

Finance: Mrs Janice Gillespie , Senior Manager - Corporate Finance, Quadrant, The Silverlink North, Cobalt Business Park, North Tyneside, NE27 0BY ☎ 0191 643 5701 🖷 0191 643 2431 ✉ janice.gillespie@northtyneside.gov.uk

Fleet Management: Mr Steve Helyer , Senior Manager - Fleet, Security & Building Cleaning, Quadrant, The Silverlink North, Cobalt Business Park, North Tyneside, NE27 0BY ☎ 0191 643 6490 🖷 0191 643 2414 ✉ steve.helyer@northtyneside.gov.uk

Grounds Maintenance: Mr Phil Scott, Head of Environment, Housing & Leisure, Quadrant, The Silverlink North, 2nd Floor, Quadrant West, Cobalt Business Park, NE27 0BY ☎ 0191 643 7295 🖷 0191 643 2414 ✉ phil.scott@northtyneside.gov.uk

Health and Safety: Ms Alison Lazazzera, Head of Human Resources & Organisation Development, Quadrant, The Silverlink North, Cobalt Business Park, North Tyneside, NE27 0BY ☎ 0191 643 5012 ✉ alison.lazazzera@northtyneside.gov.uk

Highways: Mr Colin MacDonald, Senior Manager - Technical & Regulatory Services, Quadrant, The Silverlink North, Cobalt Business Park, North Tyneside, NE27 0BY ☎ 0191 643 6620 🖷 0191 643 2391 ✉ colin.macdonald@northtyneside.gov.uk

Housing: Mr Phil Scott, Head of Environment, Housing & Leisure, Quadrant, The Silverlink North, 2nd Floor, Quadrant West, Cobalt Business Park, NE27 0BY ☎ 0191 643 7295 🖷 0191 643 2414 ✉ phil.scott@northtyneside.gov.uk

Housing Maintenance: Mr Paul Worth , Operations Manager - Housing Services, Quadrant, The Silverlink North, Cobalt Business Park, North Tyneside, NE27 0BY ☎ 0191 643 7554 🖷 0191 643 2412 ✉ paul.worth@northtyneside.gov.uk

Local Area Agreement: Mr Craig Anderson , Manager - Policy & Performance, Quadrant, The Silverlink North, Cobalt Business Park, North Tyneside, NE27 0BY ☎ 0191 643 5621 🖷 0191 643 2431 ✉ craig.anderson@northtyneside.gov.uk

Legal: Ms Vivienne Geary, Head of Law & Governance, Quadrant, The Silverlink North, Cobalt Business Park, North Tyneside, NE27 0BY ☎ 0191 643 5339 🖷 0191 643 2431 ✉ vivienne.geary@northtyneside.gov.uk

Leisure and Cultural Services: Mr Phil Scott, Head of Environment, Housing & Leisure, Quadrant, The Silverlink North, 2nd Floor, Quadrant West, Cobalt Business Park, NE27 0BY ☎ 0191 643 7295 🖷 0191 643 2414 ✉ phil.scott@northtyneside.gov.uk

Leisure and Cultural Services: Mr Paul Youlden, Senior Manager - Sport & Leisure, Quadrant, The Silverlink North, Cobalt Business Park, North Tyneside, NE27 0BY ☎ 0191 643 7430 🖷 0191 200 6696 ✉ paul.youlden@northtyneside.gov.uk

Licensing: Mr Colin MacDonald, Senior Manager - Technical & Regulatory Services, Quadrant, The Silverlink North, Cobalt Business Park, North Tyneside, NE27 0BY ☎ 0191 643 6620 🖷 0191 643 2391 ✉ colin.macdonald@northtyneside.gov.uk

Lifelong Learning: Mrs Jean Griffiths , Head of Children, Young People & Learning, Quadrant, The Silverlink North, Cobalt Business Park, North Tyneside, NE27 0BY ☎ 0191 643 8782 🖷 0191 643 2431 ✉ jean.griffiths@northtyneside.gov.uk

Lottery Funding, Charity and Voluntary: Mrs Jackie Laughton , Head of Corporate Strategy, Quadrant, The Silverlink North, Cobalt Business Park, North Tyneside, NE27 0BY ☎ 0191 643 7070 🖷 0191 643 2427 ✉ jacqueline.laughton@northtyneside.gov.uk

Member Services: Ms Yvette Monaghan , Customer, Member & Governor Services Manager, Quadrant, The Silverlink North, Cobalt Business Park, North Tyneside, NE27 0BY ☎ 0191 643 5361 🖷 0191 643 2415 ✉ yvette.monaghan@northtyneside.gov.uk

Parking: Mr Colin MacDonald, Senior Manager - Technical & Regulatory Services, Quadrant, The Silverlink North, Cobalt Business Park, North Tyneside, NE27 0BY ☎ 0191 643 6620 🖷 0191 643 2391 ✉ colin.macdonald@northtyneside.gov.uk

Partnerships: Mrs Jackie Laughton , Head of Corporate Strategy, Quadrant, The Silverlink North, Cobalt Business Park, North Tyneside, NE27 0BY ☎ 0191 643 7070 🖷 0191 643 2427 ✉ jacqueline.laughton@northtyneside.gov.uk

Personnel / HR: Ms Alison Lazazzera , Strategic HR Manager, Quadrant, The Silverlink North, Cobalt Business Park, NE27 0BY ☎ 0191 643 5012 ✉ alison.lazazzera@northtyneside.gov.uk

Planning: Mr Colin MacDonald, Senior Manager - Technical & Regulatory Services, Quadrant, The Silverlink North, Cobalt Business Park, North Tyneside, NE27 0BY ☎ 0191 643 6620 🖷 0191 643 2391 ✉ colin.macdonald@northtyneside.gov.uk

Procurement: Ms Allison Mitchell , Senior Manager - Internal Assurance & Risk Assessment, Quadrant, The Silverlink North, Cobalt Business Park, North Tyneside, NE27 0BY ☎ 0191 643 5720 ✉ allison.mitchell@northtyneside.gov.uk

Public Libraries: Mr Steve Bishop , Senior Manager - Cultural Services, Quadrant, The Silverlink North, Cobalt Business Park, North Tyneside, NE27 0BY ☎ 0191 643 7410 ✉ steve.bishop@nothtyneside.gov.uk

Recycling & Waste Minimisation: Ms Samantha Dand , Senior Manager - Local Environment Services, Quadrant, The Silverlink North, Cobalt Business Park, North Tyneside, NE27 0BY ☎ 0191 643 7294 🖷 0191 643 2414 ✉ samantha.dand@northtyneside.gov.uk

Regeneration: Mr Francis Lowes , Senior Manager - Investment & Regeneration, Quadrant, The Silverlink North, Cobalt Business Park, North Tyneside, NE27 0BY ☎ 0191 643 6421 ✉ francis.lowes@northtyneside.gov.uk

Road Safety: Mr Colin MacDonald, Senior Manager - Technical & Regulatory Services, Quadrant, The Silverlink North, Cobalt Business Park, North Tyneside, NE27 0BY ☎ 0191 643 6620 🖷 0191 643 2391 ✉ colin.macdonald@northtyneside.gov.uk

Social Services (Adult): Mrs Jacqui Old , Head of Adult Social Care, Quadrant, The Silverlink North, Cobalt Business Park, North Tyneside, NE27 0BY ☎ 0191 643 7317 🖷 0191 643 1776 ✉ jacqui.old@northtyneside.gov.uk

Social Services (Children): Mrs Jean Griffiths , Head of Children, Young People & Learning, Quadrant, The Silverlink North, Cobalt Business Park, North Tyneside, NE27 0BY ☎ 0191 643 8782 🖷 0191 643 2431 ✉ jean.griffiths@northtyneside.gov.uk

NORTH TYNESIDE

Public Health: Ms Wendy Burke , Interim Director of Public Health, Quadrant, The Silverlink North, Cobalt Business Park, North Tyneside, NE27 0BY ☎ 0191 643 2104 wendy.burke@northtyneside.gov.uk

Staff Training: Ms Alison Lazazzera , Strategic HR Manager, Quadrant, The Silverlink North, Cobalt Business Park, NE27 0BY ☎ 0191 643 5012 alison.lazazzera@northtyneside.gov.uk

Sustainable Communities: Mr Phil Scott, Head of Environment, Housing & Leisure, Quadrant, The Silverlink North, 2nd Floor, Quadrant West, Cobalt Business Park, NE27 0BY ☎ 0191 643 7295 🖷 0191 643 2414 phil.scott@northtyneside.gov.uk

Sustainable Development: Mr Paul Nelson , Environmental Sustainability Manager, Quadrant, The Silverlink North, Cobalt Business Park, North Tyneside, NE27 0BY ☎ 0191 643 6467 🖷 0191 643 2141 paul.nelson@northtyneside.gov.uk

Tourism: Mr Peter Warne, Tourism & Events Development Manager, Town Hall, High Street East, Wallsend NE28 7RR ☎ 0191 643 7411 🖷 0191 643 2406 pete.warne@northtyneside.gov.uk

Town Centre: Mr John Fleet , Town Centres Manager, Quadrant, The Silverlink North, Cobalt Business Park, NE27 0BY ☎ 0191 643 6419 john.fleet@northtyneside.gov.uk

Traffic Management: Mr Colin MacDonald, Senior Manager - Technical & Regulatory Services, Quadrant, The Silverlink North, Cobalt Business Park, North Tyneside, NE27 0BY ☎ 0191 643 6620 🖷 0191 643 2391 colin.macdonald@northtyneside.gov.uk

Total Place: Mrs Jackie Laughton , Head of Corporate Strategy, Quadrant, The Silverlink North, Cobalt Business Park, North Tyneside, NE27 0BY ☎ 0191 643 7070 🖷 0191 643 2427 jacqueline.laughton@northtyneside.gov.uk

Waste Collection and Disposal: Mr Phil Scott, Head of Environment, Housing & Leisure, Quadrant, The Silverlink North, Cobalt Business Park, North Tyneside, NE27 0BY ☎ 0191 643 7295 🖷 0191 643 2414 phil.scott@northtyneside.gov.uk

Waste Management: Mr Phil Scott, Head of Environment, Housing & Leisure, Quadrant, The Silverlink North, Cobalt Business Park, North Tyneside, NE27 0BY ☎ 0191 643 7295 🖷 0191 643 2414 phil.scott@northtyneside.gov.uk

Children's Play Areas: Ms Samantha Dand , Senior Manager - Local Environment Services, Quadrant, The Silverlink North, Cobalt Business Park, North Tyneside, NE27 0BY ☎ 0191 643 7294 🖷 0191 643 2414 samantha.dand@northtyneside.gov.uk

COUNCILLORS

***Directly Elected Mayor* Redfern**, Norma (LAB - No Ward)

***Deputy Mayor* Pickard**, Bruce (LAB - Riverside)
bruce.pickard@northtyneside.gov.uk

Allan, Jim (LAB - Camperdown)
jim.allan@ea-direct.com

Arkle, Anne (LAB - Camperdown)
anne.arkle@northtyneside.gov.uk

Austin, Alison (CON - Monkseaton North)
alison.austin@northtyneside.gov.uk

Barrie, Ken (CON - Cullercoats)
ken.barrie@northtyneside.gov.uk

Bell, Linda (LAB - Wallsend)
linda.bell@northtyneside.gov.uk

Bell, Gary (LAB - Killingworth)
gary.bell@northtyneside.gov.uk

Bolger, Karen (LAB - Tynemouth)
karen.bolgercllr@northtyneside.gov.uk

Brooks, Pamela (LAB - Preston)
p.brooks@live.co.uk

Burdis, Carole (LAB - Valley)
carole.burdis@northtyneside.gov.uk

Burdis, Brian (LAB - Valley)
valleycllrs@hotmail.com

Cassidy, Joanne (LAB - Weetslade)
joanne.cassidy@northtyneside.gov.uk

Clark, Karen (LAB - Longbenton)
karen.clark@northtyneside.gov.uk

Cox, Steve (LAB - Collingwood)
cllrstevecox@gmail.com

Darke, Linda (LAB - Killingworth)
linda.darke@northtyneside.gov.uk

Darke, Eddie (LAB - Longbenton)
eddie.darke@northtyneside.gov.uk

Davis, Cath (LAB - Preston)
cath.davis@northtyneside.gov.uk

Day, Sarah (LAB - Tynemouth)
sarah.day@northtyneside.gov.uk

Drummond, Davey (LAB - Monkseaton South)
davey.drummond@northtyneside.gov.uk

Earley, Peter (LAB - Benton)
peter.earley@northtyneside.gov.uk

Glindon, Ray (LAB - Camperdown)
ray.glindon@northtyneside.gov.uk

Graham, Sandra (LAB - Whitley Bay)
sandra.graham@northtyneside.gov.uk

Grayson, Ian (CON - Monkseaton South)
igrayson@hotmail.com

Green, Muriel (LAB - Weetslade)
muriel.green@northtyneside.gov.uk

Hall, Margaret (LAB - Whitley Bay)
margaret.hall@northtyneside.gov.uk

Harrison, John (LAB - Howdon)
john.harrison@northtyneside.gov.uk

Hodson, Edwin (CON - St Mary's)
edwin.hodson@northtyneside.gov.uk

Hunter, Janet (LAB - Benton)
janet.hunter@northtyneside.gov.uk

Hunter, John (LAB - Howdon)
john.hunter@northtyneside.gov.uk

Huscroft, Marian (LD - Northumberland)

Huscroft, Nigel (LD - Northumberland)

Johnson, Carl (LAB - Battle Hill)
carl.johnson@northtyneside.gov.uk

Lilly, David (CON - Tynemouth)
david.lilly@nothtyneside.gov.uk

Lott, Frank (LAB - Riverside)
frank.lott@northtyneside.gov.uk

Lott, Wendy (LAB - Riverside)
wendy.lott@northtyneside.gov.uk

Madden, Gary (LAB - Wallsend)
gary.madden@northtyneside.gov.uk

Madden, Maureen (LAB - Howdon)
maureen.madden@northtyneside.gov.uk

Mason, Paul (CON - Monkseaton North)
paul.mason@northtyneside.gov.uk

McGarr, David (LAB - Battle Hill)
david.mcgarr@northtyneside.gov.uk

McIntyre, Pam (CON - St Mary's)
pam.mcintyre@northtyneside.gov.uk

McMeekan, David (LAB - Cullercoats)
david.mcmeekan@northtyneside.gov.uk

McMullen, Anthony (LAB - Weetslade)
anthony.mcmullen@northtyneside.gov.uk

Miller, Leslie (CON - Monkseaton North)
les.miller@northtyneside.gov.uk

Mortimer, Shirley (CON - Cullercoats)
shirley.mortimer@northtyneside.gov.uk

Mulvenna, Tommy (LAB - Valley)
tommy.mulvenna@northtyneside.gov.uk

Munby, Joan (LAB - Monkseaton South)
joan.munby@northtyneside.gov.uk

Newman, Andy (LAB - Northumberland)
andy.newman@northtyneside.gov.uk

Oliver, Pat (LAB - Benton)
pat.oliver@northtyneside.gov.uk

Osborne, Kate (LAB - Preston)
kate.osborne@northtyneside.gov.uk

O'Shea, John (LAB - Whitley Bay)
john.o'shea@northtyneside.gov.uk

Percy, Alan (LAB - Chirton)
alan.percy@northtyneside.gov.uk

Pickard, Jeanette (LAB - Collingwood)
jeanette.pickard@northtyneside.gov.uk

Rankin, Martin (LAB - Collingwood)
martin.rankin@northtyneside.gov.uk

Reynolds, Margaret (LAB - Chirton)
margaret.reynolds@northtyneside.gov.uk

Spillard, Lesley (LAB - Battle Hill)
lesley.spillard@northtyneside.gov.uk

Stirling, John (LAB - Chirton)
john.stirling@northtyneside.gov.uk

Thirlaway, Matthew (LAB - Wallsend)
matthew.thirlaway@northtyneside.gov.uk

Waggott-Fairley, Alison (LAB - Killingworth)
alison.waggott-fairley@northtyneside.gov.uk

Walker, Joan (LAB - Longbenton)
joan.walker@northtyneside.gov.uk

Wallace, Judith (CON - St Mary's)
judith.wallace@northtyneside.gov.uk

POLITICAL COMPOSITION
LAB: 49, CON: 10, LD: 2

North Warwickshire D

North Warwickshire Borough Council, The Council House, South Street, Atherstone CV9 1DE
☎ 01827 715341 🖷 01827 719225
customerservices@northwarks.gov.uk 💻 www.northwarks.gov.uk

FACTS AND FIGURES
Parliamentary Constituencies: Warwickshire North
EU Constituencies: West Midlands
Election Frequency: Elections are of whole council

PRINCIPAL OFFICERS

Chief Executive: Mr Jerry Hutchinson, Chief Executive, Old Bank House, 129 Long Street, Atherstone CV9 1DE ☎ 01827 715341 jerryhutchinson@northwarks.gov.uk

Deputy Chief Executive: Mr Chris Brewer, Deputy Chief Executive, The Council House, South Street, Atherstone CV9 1DE ☎ 01827 715341 chrisbrewer@northwarks.gov.uk

Assistant Chief Executive: Mr Steve Maxey , Assistant Chief Executive & Solicitor to the Council, The Council House, South Street, Atherstone CV9 1DE ☎ 01827 719438; 01827 715341 stevemaxey@northwarks.gov.uk

Assistant Chief Executive: Mr Bob Trahern , Assistant Chief Executive - Community Services, The Council House, South Street, Atherstone CV9 1DE ☎ 01827 715341 🖷 01827 719225 bobtrahern@northwarks.gov.uk

Building Control: Mr Kevin Bunsell , Head of Building Control, Town Hall, Nuneaton CV11 5AA ☎ 024 7637 6521 kevin.bunsell@nuneatonandbedworth.gov.uk

PR / Communications: Miss Karen Barrow, Communications & PR Officer, The Council House, South Street, Atherstone CV9 1DE ☎ 01827 719309 karenbarrow@northwarks.gov.uk

Community Planning: Mr Jerry Hutchinson, Chief Executive, Old Bank House, 129 Long Street, Atherstone CV9 1DE ☎ 01827 715341 jerryhutchinson@northwarks.gov.uk

Community Safety: Mr Robert Beggs, Policy Support Manager, The Council House, South Street, Atherstone CV9 1DE ☎ 01827 719238 robertbeggs@northwarks.gov.uk

Computer Management: Ms Linda Bird, Assistant Director - Corporate Services, The Council House, South Street, Atherstone CV9 1DE ☎ 01827 719327 🖷 01827 719225 lindabird@northwarks.gov.uk

NORTH WARWICKSHIRE

Corporate Services: Ms Linda Bird, Assistant Director - Corporate Services, The Council House, South Street, Atherstone CV9 1DE ☎ 01827 719327 🖷 01827 719225 ✉ lindabird@northwarks.gov.uk

Customer Service: Mr Bob Trahern , Assistant Chief Executive - Community Services, The Council House, South Street, Atherstone CV9 1DE ☎ ; 01827 715341 🖷 01827 719225 ✉ bobtrahern@northwarks.gov.uk

E-Government: Ms Linda Bird, Assistant Director - Corporate Services, The Council House, South Street, Atherstone CV9 1DE ☎ 01827 719327 🖷 01827 719225 ✉ lindabird@northwarks.gov.uk

Electoral Registration: Mr David Harris, Democratic Services Manager, Old Bank House, 129 Long Street, Atherstone CV9 1DE ☎ 01827 719222 ✉ davidharris@northwarks.gov.uk

Emergency Planning: Mr Robert Beggs, Policy Support Manager, The Council House, South Street, Atherstone CV9 1DE ☎ 01827 719238 ✉ robertbeggs@northwarks.gov.uk

Energy Management: Mr David Baxendale , Environmental Health Manager, The Council House, South Street, Atherstone CV9 1DE ☎ 01827 719322 ✉ davidbaxendale@northwarks.gov.uk

Environmental / Technical Services: Mr Richard Dobbs, Assistant Director - Streetscape, The Council House, South Street, Atherstone CV9 1DE ☎ 01827 719440 ✉ richarddobbs@northwarks.gov.uk

Environmental Health: Mr Steve Whiles , Environmental Health Manager, Old Bank House, South Street, Atherstone CV9 1DE ☎ 01827 715341 ✉ stephenwhiles@northwarks.gov.uk

Facilities: Mr Chris Jones, Facilities Management Manager, The Council House, South Street, Atherstone CV9 1DE ☎ 01827 719265 ✉ chrisjones@northwarks.gov.uk

Finance: Mr Chris Brewer, Deputy Chief Executive, The Council House, South Street, Atherstone CV9 1DE ☎ 01827 715341 ✉ chrisbrewer@northwarks.gov.uk

Fleet Management: Mr Richard Dobbs, Assistant Director - Streetscape, The Council House, South Street, Atherstone CV9 1DE ☎ 01827 719440 ✉ richarddobbs@northwarks.gov.uk

Grounds Maintenance: Mr Richard Dobbs, Assistant Director - Streetscape, The Council House, South Street, Atherstone CV9 1DE ☎ 01827 719440 ✉ richarddobbs@northwarks.gov.uk

Health and Safety: Miss Kerry Drakeley , HR Officer, Old Bank House, Long Street, Atherstone CV9 1DE ☎ 01827 719300 ✉ kerrydrakeley@northwarks.gov.uk

Home Energy Conservation: Mr David Baxendale, Environmental Health Manager, The Council House, South Street, Atherstone CV9 1DE ☎ 01827 719322 ✉ davidbaxendale@northwarks.gov.uk

Housing: Ms Angela Coates , Assistant Director - Housing, The Council House, South Street, Atherstone CV9 1DE ☎ 01827 715341 ✉ angelacoates@northwarks.gov.uk

Housing Maintenance: Mr Martin Juggins , Responsive Repairs Manager - Operations, Sheepy Road Depot, Atherstone CV9 1HH ☎ 01827 719308 ✉ martinjuggins@northwarks.gov.uk

Legal: Mr Steve Maxey , Assistant Chief Executive & Solicitor to the Council, The Council House, South Street, Atherstone CV9 1DE ☎ 01827 719438; 01827 715341 ✉ stevemaxey@northwarks.gov.uk

Leisure and Cultural Services: Mr Simon Powell, Assistant Director - Leisure & Community Development, The Council House, South Street, Atherstone CV9 1DE ☎ 01827 715341 ✉ simonpowell@northwarks.gov.uk

Licensing: Mr Phil Wortley , Licensing Enforcement Officer, Old Bank House, 129 Long Street, Atherstone CV9 1DE ☎ 01827 719482 ✉ philwortley@northwarks.gov.uk

Lottery Funding, Charity and Voluntary: Ms Jaki Douglas, Partnership & Development Manager, The Council House, South Street, Atherstone CV9 1DE ☎ 01827 719492 ✉ jakidouglas@northwarks.gov.uk

Member Services: Mr David Harris, Democratic Services Manager, Old Bank House, 129 Long Street, Atherstone CV9 1DE ☎ 01827 719222 ✉ davidharris@northwarks.gov.uk

Parking: Mr Richard Dobbs, Assistant Director - Streetscape, The Council House, South Street, Atherstone CV9 1DE ☎ 01827 719440 ✉ richarddobbs@northwarks.gov.uk

Partnerships: Ms Jaki Douglas, Partnership & Development Manager, The Council House, South Street, Atherstone CV9 1DE ☎ 01827 719492 ✉ jakidouglas@northwarks.gov.uk

Personnel / HR: Ms Sue Garner, Assistant Director - Finance & HR, The Council House, South Street, Atherstone CV9 1DE ☎ 01827 719374 🖷 01827 719225 ✉ suegarner@northwarks.gov.uk

Personnel / HR: Ms Janis McCulloch , HR Manager, Old Bank House, Long Street, Atherstone CV9 1DE ☎ 01827 719236 🖷 01827 719225 ✉ janismcculloch@northwarks.gov.uk

Planning: Mr Jeff Brown , Head - Development Control, The Council House, South Street, Atherstone CV9 1DE ☎ 01827 719310 🖷 01827 719363 ✉ jeffbrown@northwarks.gov.uk

Procurement: Mrs Elayne Cooper, Procurement Manager, The Council House, South Street, Atherstone CV9 1DE ☎ 01827 719203 🖷 01827 719225 ✉ elaynecooper@northwarks.gov.uk

Recycling & Waste Minimisation: Mr Richard Dobbs, Assistant Director - Streetscape, The Council House, South Street, Atherstone CV9 1DE ☎ 01827 719440 ✉ richarddobbs@northwarks.gov.uk

Regeneration: Mrs Rachel Stephens , Community Development Officer - Rural Regeneration, The Council House, South Street, Atherstone CV9 1DE ☎ 01827 719301 ✉ rachelstephens@northwarks.gov.uk

Staff Training: Ms Sue Garner, Assistant Director - Finance & HR, The Council House, South Street, Atherstone CV9 1DE ☎ 01827 719374 🖷 01827 719225 🖰 suegarner@northwarks.gov.uk

Street Scene: Mr Richard Dobbs, Assistant Director - Streetscape, The Council House, South Street, Atherstone CV9 1DE ☎ 01827 719440 🖰 richarddobbs@northwarks.gov.uk

Sustainable Communities: Mrs Julie Taylor, Senior Policy Support Officer, The Council House, South Street, Atherstone CV9 1DE ☎ 01827 719437 🖰 julietaylor@northwarks.gov.uk

Sustainable Development: Mrs Julie Taylor, Senior Policy Support Officer, Old Bank House, 129 Long Street, Atherstone CV9 1DE ☎ 01827 719437 🖰 julietaylor@northwarks.gov.uk

Waste Collection and Disposal: Mr Richard Dobbs, Assistant Director - Streetscape, The Council House, South Street, Atherstone CV9 1DE ☎ 01827 719440 🖰 richarddobbs@northwarks.gov.uk

Waste Management: Mr Richard Dobbs, Assistant Director - Streetscape, The Council House, South Street, Atherstone CV9 1DE ☎ 01827 719440 🖰 richarddobbs@northwarks.gov.uk

Children's Play Areas: Ms Alethea Wilson , Landscape Manager, The Council House, South Street, Atherstone CV9 1DE ☎ 01827 715341 🖰 aletheawilson@northwarks.gov.uk

COUNCILLORS

***Mayor* Davis**, Martin (CON - Atherstone South and Mancetter) martindavis@northwarks.gov.uk

***Deputy Mayor* Smitten**, John (CON - Polesworth West) johnsmitten@northwarks.gov.uk

***Leader of the Council* Humphreys**, David (CON - Newton Regis and Warton) davidhumphreys@northwarks.gov.uk

***Deputy Leader of the Council* Wright**, David (CON - Fillongley) davidwright@northwarks.gov.uk

Bell, Margaret (CON - Hartshill) margaretbell@northwarks.gov.uk

Chambers, Jacky (LAB - Dordon) jackychambers@northwarks.gov.uk

Clews, Denise (CON - Atherstone South and Mancetter) deniseclews@northwarks.gov.uk

Davey, Patrick (CON - Newton Regis and Warton) patrickdavey@northwarks.gov.uk

Dirveiks, Neil (LAB - Atherstone Central) neildirveiks@northwarks.gov.uk

Dirveiks, Lorna (LAB - Atherstone Central) lornadirveiks@northwarks.gov.uk

Farrell, Adam (LAB - Coleshill North) adamfarrell@northwarks.gov.uk

Ferro, Dominic (LAB - Coleshill North) dominicferro@northwarks.gov.uk

Hanratty, Sue (CON - Polesworth West) suehanratty@northwarks.gov.uk

Hayfield, Colin (CON - Arley and Whitacre) colinhayfield@northwarks.gov.uk

Henney, Brian (LAB - Hartshill) brianhenney@northwarks.gov.uk

Ingram, Stacey (CON - Coleshill South) staceyingram@northwarks.gov.uk

Jarvis, Ray (CON - Atherstone North) rayjarvis@northwarks.gov.uk

Jenns, Andy (CON - Kingsbury) andyjenns@northwarks.gov.uk

Jones, Mark (CON - Coleshill South) markjones@northwarks.gov.uk

Lea, Joan (CON - Curdworth) joanlea@northwarks.gov.uk

Lewis, Ann (LAB - Hurley and Wood End) annlewis@northwarks.gov.uk

Morson, Peter (LAB - Dordon) petermorson@northwarks.gov.uk

Moss, Brian (LAB - Kingsbury) brianmoss@northwarks.gov.uk

Payne, Raymond (CON - Water Orton) raymondpayne@northwarks.gov.uk

Phillips, Hayden (LAB - Hurley and Wood End) haydenphillips@northwarks.gov.uk

Reilly, David (CON - Water Orton) davidreilly@northwarks.gov.uk

Simpson, Mark (CON - Arley and Whitacre) marksimpson@northwarks.gov.uk

Singh, Mejar (CON - Atherstone North) mejarsingh@northwarks.gov.uk

Smith, Leslie (CON - Fillongley) lessmith@northwarks.gov.uk

Stanley, Michael (LAB - Polesworth East) mickstanley@northwarks.gov.uk

Stanley, Emma (LAB - Polesworth East) emmastanley@northwarks.gov.uk

Sweet, Ray (LAB - Baddesley Ensor and Grendon) raysweet@northwarks.gov.uk

Waters, Terry (CON - Curdworth) terrywaters@northwarks.gov.uk

Watkins, Andrew (CON - Arley and Whitacre) andrewwatkins@northwarks.gov.uk

Wright, Andy (CON - Baddesley Ensor and Grendon) andywright@northwarks.gov.uk

POLITICAL COMPOSITION

CON: 22, LAB: 13

COMMITTEE CHAIRS

Licensing: Mr Mark Jones

North West Leicestershire D

North West Leicestershire District Council, Council Offices, Coalville LE67 3FJ
☎ 01530 454545 🖷 01530 454506
customer.services@nwleicestershire.gov.uk 💻 www.nwleics.gov.uk

FACTS AND FIGURES

Parliamentary Constituencies: Leicestershire North West
EU Constituencies: East Midlands
Election Frequency: Elections are of whole council

PRINCIPAL OFFICERS

Chief Executive: Miss Christine Fisher, Chief Executive, Council Offices, Coalville LE67 3FJ ☎ 01530 454502 christine.fisher@nwleicestershire.gov.uk

Deputy Chief Executive: Mr Steve Bambrick, Director of Services & Deputy Chief Executive, Council Offices, Coalville LE67 3FJ ☎ 01530 454555 steve.bambrick@nwleicestershire.gov.uk

Senior Management: Mr Steve Bambrick, Director of Services & Deputy Chief Executive, Council Offices, Coalville LE67 3FJ ☎ 01530 454555 steve.bambrick@nwleicestershire.gov.uk

Senior Management: Mr Ray Bowmer , Head of Finance, Council Offices, Coalville LE67 3FJ ☎ 01530 454520 ray.bowmer@nwleicestershire.gov.uk

Senior Management: Mr Glyn Jones , Director of Housing, Council Offices, Coalville LE67 3FJ ☎ 01530 454819 glyn.jones@nwleicestershire.gov.uk

Senior Management: Mr Mike Murphy, Human Resources Team Manager, Council Offices, Coalville LE67 3FJ ☎ 01530 454518 mike.murphy@nwleicestershire.gov.uk

Senior Management: Miss Elizabeth Warhurst, Head of Legal & Support Services, Council Offices, Coalville LE67 3FJ ☎ 01530 454762 elizabeth.warhurst@nwleicestershire.gov.uk

Building Control: Mr Steve Bambrick, Director of Services & Deputy Chief Executive, Council Offices, Coalville LE67 3FJ ☎ 01530 454555 steve.bambrick@nwleicestershire.gov.uk

Building Control: Mr David Darlington, Building Control Manager, Council Offices, Coalville LE67 3FJ ☎ 01530 454691 david.darlington@nwleicestershire.gov.uk

Children / Youth Services: Mr John Richardson, Head of Community Services, Council Offices, Coalville LE67 3FJ ☎ 01530 454832 john.richardson@nwleicestershire.gov.uk

PR / Communications: Ms Caroline Ashman , Communications Team Leader, Council Offices, Coalville LE67 3FJ ☎ 01530 454546 caroline.ashman@nwleicestershire.gov.uk

Community Planning: Mr John Richardson, Head of Community Services, Council Offices, Coalville LE67 3FJ ☎ 01530 454832 john.richardson@nwleicestershire.gov.uk

Computer Management: Mr Mike Harding , ICT Team Manager, Council Offices, Coalville LE67 3FJ ☎ 01530 454716 mike.harding@nwleicestershire.gov.uk

Corporate Services: Mrs Lisa Cotton , Senior Auditor, Council Offices, Coalville LE67 3FJ ☎ 01530 454728 lisa.cotton@nwleicestershire.gov.uk

Customer Service: Mr Steve McCue , Customer Team Manager, Council Offices, Coalville LE67 3FJ ☎ 01530 454557 steve.mccue@nwleicestershire.gov.uk

Customer Service: Miss Elizabeth Warhurst, Head of Legal & Support Services, Council Offices, Coalville LE67 3FJ ☎ 01530 454762 elizabeth.warhurst@nwleicestershire.gov.uk

Electoral Registration: Mrs Louise Beeston, Electoral Services Officer, Council Offices, Coalville LE67 3FJ ☎ 01530 454512 louise.beeston@nwleicestershire.gov.uk

Electoral Registration: Miss Christine Fisher, Chief Executive, Council Offices, Coalville LE67 3FJ ☎ 01530 454502 christine.fisher@nwleicestershire.gov.uk

Electoral Registration: Mrs Melanie Phillips , Democratic & Support Services Team Manager, Whitwick Road, Coalville LE67 3FJ ☎ 01530 454511 melaine.phillips@nwleicestershire.gov.uk

Emergency Planning: Mr Mike Murphy, Human Resources Team Manager, Council Offices, Coalville LE67 3FJ ☎ 01530 454518 mike.murphy@nwleicestershire.gov.uk

Environmental Health: Miss Christine Fisher, Chief Executive, Council Offices, Coalville LE67 3FJ ☎ 01530 454502 christine.fisher@nwleicestershire.gov.uk

Environmental Health: Mr Lee Mansfield, Environmental Health Team Manager, Council Offices, Coalville LE67 3FJ ☎ 01530 454610 lee.mansfield@nwleicestershire.gov.uk

Environmental Health: Miss Elizabeth Warhurst, Head of Legal & Support Services, Council Offices, Coalville LE67 3FJ ☎ 01530 454762 elizabeth.warhurst@nwleicestershire.gov.uk

Estates, Property & Valuation: Mr Simon Harvey , Property Asset Manager, Council Offices, Coalville LE67 3FJ ☎ 01530 454550 simon.harvey@nwleicestershire.gov.uk

Events Manager: Mr Goff Lewis , Cultural Services Team Manager, Council Offices, Coalville LE67 3FJ ☎ 01530 454601 goff.lewis@nwleicestershire.gov.uk

Finance: Mr Ray Bowmer , Head of Finance, Council Offices, Coalville LE67 3FJ ☎ 01530 454520 ray.bowmer@nwleicestershire.gov.uk

Fleet Management: Mr Charlie Clarke , Transport Manager, Council Offices, Coalville LE67 3FJ ☎ 01530 454629 charlie.clarke@nwleicestershire.gov.uk

Grounds Maintenance: Mr Jason Knight , Leisure Services Team Manager, Council Offices, Coalville LE67 3FJ ☎ 01530 454602

Health and Safety: Mr Ian Bennett , Health & Safety Officer, Council Offices, Coalville LE67 3FJ ☎ 01530 454522 ✉ ian.bennett@nwleicestershire.gov.uk

Housing: Mrs Sue Hallam , Strategic Housing Team Manager, Council Offices, Coalville LE67 3FJ ☎ 01530 454612 ✉ sue.hallam@nwleicestershire.gov.uk

Housing: Mrs Amanda Harper , Housing Management Team Manager, Council Offices, Coalville LE67 3FJ ☎ 01530 454808 ✉ amanda.harper@nwleicestershire.gov.uk

Housing: Mr Glyn Jones , Director of Housing, Council Offices, Coalville LE67 3FJ ☎ 01530 454819 ✉ glyn.jones@nwleicestershire.gov.uk

Housing: Mr Christopher Lambert , Head of Housing, Council Offices, Coalville LE67 3FJ ☎ 01530 454780 ✉ chris.lambert@nwleicestershire.gov.uk

Housing Maintenance: Mr Neil Barks , Interim Housing Maintenance Team Manager, Council Offices, Coalville LE67 3FJ ☎ 01530 454849 ✉ neil.barks@nwleicestershire.gov.uk

Legal: Miss Elizabeth Warhurst, Head of Legal & Support Services, Council Offices, Coalville LE67 3FJ ☎ 01530 454762 ✉ elizabeth.warhurst@nwleicestershire.gov.uk

Leisure and Cultural Services: Mr Steve Bambrick, Director of Services & Deputy Chief Executive, Council Offices, Coalville LE67 3FJ ☎ 01530 454555 ✉ steve.bambrick@nwleicestershire.gov.uk

Leisure and Cultural Services: Mr Jason Knight , Leisure Services Team Manager, Council Offices, Coalville LE67 3FJ ☎ 01530 454602 ✉

Leisure and Cultural Services: Mr Goff Lewis , Cultural Services Team Manager, Council Offices, Coalville LE67 3FJ ☎ 01530 454601 ✉ goff.lewis@nwleicestershire.gov.uk

Leisure and Cultural Services: Mr John Richardson, Head of Community Services, Council Offices, Coalville LE67 3FJ ☎ 01530 454832 ✉ john.richardson@nwleicestershire.gov.uk

Licensing: Mr Lee Mansfield, Environmental Health Team Manager, Council Offices, Coalville LE67 3FJ ☎ 01530 454610 ✉ lee.mansfield@nwleicestershire.gov.uk

Member Services: Mrs Melanie Phillips , Democratic & Support Services Team Manager, Council Offices, Coalville LE67 3FJ ☎ 01530 454511 ✉ melanie.phillips@nwleicestershire.gov.uk

Member Services: Miss Elizabeth Warhurst, Head of Legal & Support Services, Council Offices, Coalville LE67 3FJ ☎ 01530 454762 ✉ elizabeth.warhurst@nwleicestershire.gov.uk

Personnel / HR: Mr Mike Murphy, Human Resources Team Manager, Council Offices, Coalville LE67 3FJ ☎ 01530 454518 ✉ mike.murphy@nwleicestershire.gov.uk

Planning: Mr Steve Bambrick, Director of Services & Deputy Chief Executive, Council Offices, Coalville LE67 3FJ ☎ 01530 454555 ✉ steve.bambrick@nwleicestershire.gov.uk

Planning: Mr Chris Elston , Planning & Development Team Manager, Council Offices, Coalville LE67 3FJ ☎ 01530 454668 ✉ chris.elston@nwleicestershire.gov.uk

Planning: Mr Jim Newton , Head of Regeneration & Planning, Council Offices, Coalville LE67 3FJ ☎ 01530 454782 ✉ jim.newton@nwleicestershire.gov.uk

Procurement: Miss Anna Wright , Financial Services Team Manager, Council Offices, Coalville LE67 3FJ ☎ 01530 454492 ✉ anna.wright@nwleicestershire.gov.uk

Recycling & Waste Minimisation: Mr Paul Coates , Waste Services Team Manager, Council Offices, Coalville LE67 3FJ ☎ 01530 454663 ✉ paul.coates@nwleicestershire.gov.uk

Regeneration: Mr Ian Nelson , Head of Planning Policy, Council Offices, Coalville LE67 3FJ ☎ 01530 454676 ✉ ian.nelson@nwleicestershire.gov.uk

Regeneration: Mr Jim Newton , Head of Regeneration & Planning, Council Offices, Coalville LE67 3FJ ☎ 01530 454782 ✉ jim.newton@nwleicestershire.gov.uk

Street Scene: Ms Clare Proudfoot , Street Action Team Manager, Council Offices, Coalville LE67 3FJ ☎ 01530 454564 🖷 01530 454506 ✉ clare.proudfoot@nwleicestershire.gov.uk

Waste Collection and Disposal: Mr Paul Coates , Waste Services Team Manager, Council Offices, Coalville LE67 3FJ ☎ 01530 454545 ✉

Waste Management: Mr Paul Coates , Waste Services Team Manager, Council Offices, Coalville LE67 3FJ ☎ 01530 454663 ✉ paul.coates@nwleicestershire.gov.uk

Waste Management: Mr John Richardson, Head of Community Services, Council Offices, Coalville LE67 3FJ ☎ 01530 454832 ✉ john.richardson@nwleicestershire.gov.uk

Children's Play Areas: Mr Jason Knight , Leisure Services Team Manager, Council Offices, Coalville LE67 3FJ ☎ 01530 454602

COUNCILLORS

***Chair* Bridges**, John (CON - Ashby Woulds) john.bridges@nwleicestershire.gov.uk

***Vice-Chair* Cotterill**, John (CON - Coalville East) john.cotterill@nwleicestershire.gov.uk

***Leader of the Council* Blunt**, Richard (CON - Appleby) richard.blunt@nwleicestershire.gov.uk

NORTH WEST LEICESTERSHIRE

***Deputy Leader of the Council* Smith**, Alison (CON - Daleacre Hill)
alison.smith@nwleicestershire.gov.uk

***Group Leader* Neilson**, Tom (LAB - Measham South)
tom.neilson@nwleicestershire.gov.uk

Adams, Ron (LAB - Broom Leys)
ronnie.adams@nwleicestershire.gov.uk

Allman, Graham (CON - Ashby Money Hill)
graham.allman@mwleicestershire.gov.uk

Ashman, Robert (CON - Oakthorpe & Donisthorpe)
robert.ashman@nwleicestershire.gov.uk

Bayliss, Roger (CON - Ashby Holywell)
roger.bayliss@nwleicestershire.gov.uk

Boam, Russell (CON - Valley)
russell.boam@nwleicestershire.gov.uk

Canny, Rachel (IND - Castle Donington Central)
rachelmcanny@gmail.com

Clarke, Nick (LAB - Greenhill)
nick.clarke@nwleicestershire.gov.uk

Clarke, John (CON - Ibstock West)
john.clarke@nwleicestershire.gov.uk

Coxon, John (CON - Ashby Castle)
john.coxon@nwleicestershire.gov.uk

Everitt, David (LAB - Thringstone)
david.everitt@nwleicestershire.gov.uk

Eynon, Terri (LAB - Hugglescote St Mary's)
terri.eynon@nwleicestershire.gov.uk

Fenning, Felix (LAB - Ibstock East)
felix.fenning@nwleicestershire.gov.uk

Geary, John (LAB - Snibston South)
john.geary@nwleicestershire.gov.uk

Gillard, Stuart (CON - Hermitage)
stuart.gillard@nwleicestershire.gov.uk

Gillard, Tony (CON - Holly Hayes)
tony.gillard@nwleicestershire.gov.uk

Goacher, Louise (CON - Thornborough)
louise.goacher@nwleicestershire.gov.uk

Harrison, Dan (CON - Castle Donington Park)
daniel.harrison@nwleicestershire.gov.uk

Hoult, Jim (CON - Ashby Ivanhoe)
jim.hoult@nwleicestershire.gov.uk

Hoult, Gill (CON - Measham North)
gill.hoult@nwleicestershire.gov.uk

Johnson, Russell (LAB - Hugglescote St John's)
russell.johnson@nwleicestershire.gov.uk

Jones, Geraint (CON - Ashby Willesley)
geraint.jones@nwleicestershire.gov.uk

Legrys, John (LAB - Coalville West)
john.legrys@nwleicestershire.gov.uk

McKendrick, Susuan (LAB - Blackfordby)
susan.mckendrick@nwleicestershire.gov.uk

Merrie, Keith (CON - Ellistown & Battlefleet)
keith.merrie@nwleicestershire.gov.uk

Pendleton, Trevor (CON - Kegworth)
trevor.pendleton@nwleicestershire.gov.uk

Purver, Paula (CON - Snibston North)
paula.purver@nwleicestershire.gov.uk

Richichi, Virge (CON - Sence Valley)
virge.richichi@icloud.co.uk

Rushton, Nicholas (CON - Long Whatton & Diseworth)
nicholas.rushton@leics.gov.uk

Saffell, Tony (IND - Castle Donington Castle)
tony.saffell@donington.me.uk

Smith, Nigel (CON - Ravenstone & Packington)
nigel.smith@nwleicestershire.gov.uk

Specht, Michael (CON - Bardon)
michael.specht@nwleicestershire.gov.uk

Stevenson, David (CON - Worthington & Breedon)
david.stevenson@nwleicestershire.gov.uk

Wyatt, Michael (LD - Castle Rock)
michael.wyatt@nwleicestershire.gov.uk

POLITICAL COMPOSITION

CON: 25, LAB: 10, IND: 2, LD: 1

COMMITTEE CHAIRS

Audit & Governance: Mr John Cotterill

Licensing: Mr Nigel Smith

Planning: Mr David Stevenson

North Yorkshire C

North Yorkshire County Council, County Hall, Northallerton DL7 8AD
☎ 0845 872 7374 🖷 01609 778199 🖳 www.northyorks.gov.uk

FACTS AND FIGURES

Parliamentary Constituencies: Harrogate and Knaresborough, Richmond (Yorks), Scarborough and Whitby, Skipton and Ripon
EU Constituencies: Yorkshire and the Humber
Election Frequency: Elections are of whole council

PRINCIPAL OFFICERS

Chief Executive: Mr Richard Flinton, Chief Executive, County Hall, Northallerton DL7 8AD ☎ 01609 532444 🖷 01609 778199
richard.flinton@northyorks.gov.uk

Senior Management: Mr David Bowe, Corporate Director - Business & Environmental Services, County Hall, Northallerton DL7 8AD ☎ 01609 532128 🖷 01609 760794
david.bowe@northyorks.gov.uk

Senior Management: Mrs Justine Brooksbank, Assistant Chief Executive - Business Support, County Hall, Northallerton DL7 8AD ☎ 01609 532103 🖷 01609 779938
justine.brooksbank@northyorks.gov.uk

Senior Management: Mr Peter Dwyer , Corporate Director - Children & Young People's Services, County Hall, Northallerton DL7 8AD ☎ 01609 532146 🖷 01609 773756
pete.dwyer@northyorks.gov.uk

Senior Management: Mr Gary Fielding , Corporate Director - Strategic Resources, County Hall, Northallerton DL7 8AD ☎ 01609 533304 🖷 01609 778199 ✉ gary.fielding@northyorks.gov.uk

Senior Management: Mr Barry Khan , Assistant Chief Executive - Legal & Democratic Services, County Hall, Northallerton DL7 8AD ☎ 01609 532173 ✉ barry.khan@northyorks.gov.uk

Senior Management: Mrs Mary Weastell , Assistant Chief Executive - Customer Services, County Hall, Northallerton DL7 8AD ☎ 01609 537411 ✉ mary.weastell@northyorks.gov.uk

Senior Management: Mr Richard Webb , Corporate Director - Health & Adult Services, County Hall, Northallerton DL7 8AD ☎ 01609 532139 ✉ richard.webb@northyorks.gov.uk

Architect, Building / Property Services: Mr Jon Holden , Assistant Director - Strategic Resources, County Hall, Northallerton DL7 8AD ☎ 01609 534076 ✉ jon.holden@northyorks.gov.uk

Catering Services: Mr Nick Postma, Client Catering Manager, County Hall, Northallerton DL7 8AD ☎ 01609 532167 ✉ nick.postma@northyorks.gov.uk

Civil Registration: Mr Robin Mair , General Manager - Registration, Archives & Coroners, Library Headquarters, 21 Grammar School Lane, Northallerton DL7 8AD ☎ 01609 533806 🖷 01609 780793 ✉ robin.mair@northyorks.gov.uk

PR / Communications: Ms Helen Edwards , Head - Communications, County Hall, Northallerton DL7 8AD ☎ 01609 532104 ✉ helen.edwards@northyorks.gov.uk

Community Planning: Mr Neil Irving , Assistant Director - Policy & Partnerships, County Hall, Northallerton DL7 8AD ☎ 01609 533489 🖷 01609 778199 ✉ neil.irving@northyorks.gov.uk

Community Safety: Mr Neil Irving , Assistant Director - Policy & Partnerships, County Hall, Northallerton DL7 8AD ☎ 01609 533489 🖷 01609 778199 ✉ neil.irving@northyorks.gov.uk

Computer Management: Mr Robert Ling , Assistant Director - Technology & Change, County Hall, Northallerton DL7 8AD ☎ 01609 533476 ✉ robert.ling@northyorks.gov.uk

Consumer Protection and Trading Standards: Mr Graham Venn, Assistant Director - Trading Standards & Planning Services, Thornfield Business Park, Standard Way, Northallerton DL6 2XQ ☎ 01609 766408 🖷 01609 780970 ✉ graham.venn@northyorks.gov.uk

Contracts: Mr Simon Toplass , Head of Procurement & Contract Manager, County Hall, Northallerton DL7 8AD ☎ 01609 797419 ✉ simon.toplass@northyorks.gov.uk

Customer Service: Ms Sarah Foley , Head of Customer Services, County Hall, Northallerton DL7 8AD ☎ 01609 533872 ✉ sarah.foley@northyorks.gov.uk

Economic Development: Mr James Farrar , Assistant Director - Economic & Partnerships Unit, County Hall, Northallerton DL7 8AD ☎ 01609 533598 ✉ james.farrar@northyorks.gov.uk

Education: Mr Peter Dwyer , Corporate Director - Children & Young People's Services, County Hall, Northallerton DL7 8AD ☎ 01609 532146 🖷 01609 773756 ✉ pete.dwyer@northyorks.gov.uk

E-Government: Ms Lucy Darwin , Systems Manager, County Hall, Northallerton DL7 8AD ☎ 01609 533337

Electoral Registration: Ms Josie O'Dowd , Democratic Services Manager, County Hall, Northallerton DL7 8AD ☎ 01609 532591 🖷 01609 532343 ✉ josie.o'dowd@northyorks.gov.uk

Emergency Planning: Mr Tom Knox , Head - Emergency Planning, County Hall, Northallerton DL7 8AD ☎ 01609 532110 ✉ tom.knox@northyorks.gov.uk

Energy Management: Ms Karen Atkinson , Energy Officer, County Hall, Northallerton DL7 8AD ☎ 01609 535775 ✉ karen.p.atkinson@northyorks.gov.uk

European Liaison: Mr James Farrar , Assistant Director - Economic & Partnerships Unit, County Hall, Northallerton DL7 8AD ☎ 01609 533598 ✉ james.farrar@northyorks.gov.uk

Facilities: Mrs Karen Adamson , Corporate Property Operations Manager, County Hall, Northallerton DL7 8AD ☎ 01609 535288 ✉ karen.adamson@northyorks.gov.uk

Finance: Mr Gary Fielding , Corporate Director - Strategic Resources, County Hall, Northallerton DL7 8AD ☎ 01609 533304 🖷 01609 778199 ✉ gary.fielding@northyorks.gov.uk

Treasury: Mr Gary Fielding , Corporate Director - Strategic Resources, County Hall, Northallerton DL7 8AD ☎ 01609 533304 🖷 01609 778199 ✉ gary.fielding@northyorks.gov.uk

Pensions: Mr Tom Morrison , Principal Accountant - Pension Investment Officer, County Hall, Northallerton DL7 8AD ☎ 0845 872 7374 ✉ tom.morrison@northyorks.gov.uk

Fleet Management: Mr Richard Owens , Assistant Director - Integrated Passenger Transport, County Hall, Northallerton DL7 8AD ☎ 01609 535660 ✉ richard.owens@northyorks.gov.uk

Grounds Maintenance: Mrs Karen Adamson , Corporate Property Operations Manager, County Hall, Northallerton DL7 8AD ☎ 01609 535288 ✉ karen.adamson@northyorks.gov.uk

Health and Safety: Mr Dominic Passman, Head - Health & Safety Risk Management, County Hall, Northallerton DL7 8AD ☎ 01609 532594 🖷 01609 780733 ✉ dominic.passman@northyorks.gov.uk

Highways: Mr Barrie Mason , Assistant Director - Highways & Transportation, County Hall, Northallerton DL7 8AD ☎ 01609 532137 🖷 01609 779838 ✉ barrie.mason@northyorks.gov.uk

Legal: Mr Barry Khan , Assistant Chief Executive - Legal & Democratic Services, County Hall, Northallerton DL7 8AD ☎ 01609 532173 ✉ barry.khan@northyorks.gov.uk

NORTH YORKSHIRE

Lighting: Mr Paul Gilmore, Road Lighting Team Leader, County Hall, Northallerton DL7 8AD ☎ 01609 532946 🖷 01609 532772 paul.gilmore@northyorks.gov.uk

Lottery Funding, Charity and Voluntary: Ms Marie-Ann Jackson , Head of Stronger Communities, County Hall, Northallerton DL7 8AD ☎ 01609 532925 marie-ann.jackson@northyorks.gov.uk

Member Services: Mrs Amanda Fry , Staff Officer to Chief Executive, County Hall, Northallerton DL7 8AD ☎ 01609 532705 🖷 01609 778199 amanda.fry@northyorks.gov.uk

Partnerships: Mr Neil Irving , Assistant Director - Policy & Partnerships, County Hall, Northallerton DL7 8AD ☎ 01609 533489 🖷 01609 778199 neil.irving@northyorks.gov.uk

Personnel / HR: Mrs Justine Brooksbank, Assistant Chief Executive - Business Support, County Hall, Northallerton DL7 8AD ☎ 01609 532103 🖷 01609 779938 justine.brooksbank@northyorks.gov.uk

Planning: Mr Ian Fielding, Assistant Director - Waste Management, County Hall, Northallerton DL7 8AD ☎ 01609 532161 🖷 01609 532474 ian.fielding@northyorks.gov.uk

Procurement: Mr Simon Toplass , Head of Procurement & Contract Manager, County Hall, Northallerton DL7 8AD ☎ 01609 797419 simon.toplass@northyorks.gov.uk

Public Libraries: Ms Julie Blaisdale, Assistant Director - Information Services, County Hall, Northallerton DL7 8AD ☎ 01609 533494 🖷 01609 780793 julie.blaisdale@northyorks.gov.uk

Recycling & Waste Minimisation: Mr Ian Fielding, Assistant Director - Waste Management, County Hall, Northallerton DL7 8AD ☎ 01609 532161 🖷 01609 532474 ian.fielding@northyorks.gov.uk

Road Safety: Mr Allan McVeigh , Traffic Management & Road Safety Group Manager, County Hall, Northallerton DL7 8AD ☎ 01609 532847 🖷 01609 779838 allan.mcveigh@northyorks.gov.uk

Social Services (Adult): Ms Anne-Marie Lubanski , Assistant Director - Care & Support, Adult Social Care Operations, County Hall, Northallerton DL7 8AD anne-marie.lubanski@northyorks.gov.uk

Social Services (Children): Ms Judith Hay , Assistant Director - Children's Social Care, County Hall, Northallerton DL7 8AD ☎ 01609 533569 judith.hay@northyorks.gov.uk

Public Health: Dr Lincoln Sargeant , Director - Public Health, County Hall, Northallerton DL7 8AD

Staff Training: Ms Tracy Harrison , Head of Training & Learning, County Hall, Northallerton DL7 8AD ☎ 01609 533125 tracy.harrison@northyorks.gov.uk

Tourism: Mr James Farrar , Assistant Director - Economic & Partnerships Unit, County Hall, Northallerton DL7 8AD ☎ 01609 533598 james.farrar@northyorks.gov.uk

Traffic Management: Mr Barrie Mason , Assistant Director - Highways & Transportation, County Hall, Northallerton DL7 8AD ☎ 01609 532137 🖷 01609 779838 barrie.mason@northyorks.gov.uk

Transport Planner: Mr Richard Owens , Assistant Director - Integrated Passenger Transport, County Hall, Northallerton DL7 8AD ☎ 01609 535660 richard.owens@northyorks.gov.uk

Waste Management: Mr Ian Fielding, Assistant Director - Waste Management, County Hall, Northallerton DL7 8AD ☎ 01609 532161 🖷 01609 532474 ian.fielding@northyorks.gov.uk

COUNCILLORS

***Leader of the Council* Les**, Carl (CON - Catterick Bridge)
cllr.carl.les@northyorks.gov.uk

***Deputy Leader of the Council* Dadd**, Gareth (CON - Thirsk)
cllr.gareth.dadd@northyorks.gov.uk

Arnold, Val (CON - Kirkbymoorside)
cllr.val.arnold@northyorks.gov.uk

Atkinson, Margaret (CON - Masham and Fountains)
cllr.margaret.atkinson@northyorks.gov.uk

Backhouse, Andrew (CON - Newby)
cllr.andrew.backhouse@northyorks.gov.uk

Baker, Robert (CON - Sowerby)
cllr.robert.baker@northyorks.gov.uk

Barker, Arthur (CON - Swale)
cllr.arthur.barker@northyorks.gov.uk

Barrett, Philip (IND - South Craven)
cllr.philip.barrett@northyorks.gov.uk

Bastiman, Derek (CON - Scalby and the Coast)
cllr.derek.bastiman@northyorks.gov.uk

Bateman, Bernard (CON - Ripon North)
cllr.bernard.bateman@northyorks.gov.uk

Billing, David (LAB - Woodlands)
cllr.david.billing@northyorks.gov.uk

Blackburn, John (CON - Hertford and Cayton)
cllr.john.blackburn@scarborough.gov.uk

Blackie, John (IND - Upper Dales)
cllr.john.blackie@northyorks.gov.uk

Blades, David (CON - Romanby and Broomfield)
cllr.david.blades@northyorks.gov.uk

Broadbent, Eric (LAB - Northstead)
cllr.eric.broadbent@northyorks.gov.uk

Burr, Lindsay (LD - Malton)
cllr.lindsay.burr@northyorks.gov.uk

Butterfield, Jean (CON - Harrogate Central)
cllr.jean.butterfield@northyorks.gov.uk

Casling, Elizabeth (CON - Escrick)
cllr.elizabeth.casling@northyorks.gov.uk

Chance, David (CON - Whitby Mayfield cum Mulgrave)
cllr.david.chance@northyorks.gov.uk

Clark, Jim (CON - Harrogate Harlow)
cllr.jim.clark@northyorks.gov.uk

Clark, John (LIB - Pickering)
cllr.john.clark@northyorks.gov.uk

Cooper, Richard (CON - Harrogate Central)
cllr.richard.cooper@northyorks.gov.uk

Cross, Sam (UKIP - Filey)
cllr.sam.cross@northyorks.gov.uk

de Courcey-Bayley, Margaret-Ann (LD - Harrogate Starbeck)
cllr.margaret-ann.decourcey-bayley@northyorks.gov.uk

Ennis, John (CON - Harrogate Oatlands)
cllr.john.ennis@northyorks.gov.uk

Fort, John (CON - Pateley Bridge)
cllr.john.fort@northyorks.gov.uk

Goss, Andrew (LD - Harrogate Bilton and Nidd Gorge)
cllr.andrew.goss@northyorks.gov.uk

Grant, Helen (IND - Central Richmondshire)
cllr.helen.grant@northyorks.gov.uk

Griffiths, Bryn (LD - Stokesley)
cllr.bryn.griffiths@northyorks.gov.uk

Hall, Tony (CON - Northallerton)
cllr.tony.hall@northyorks.gov.uk

Harrison, Michael (CON - Lower Nidderdale and Bishop Monkton)
cllr.michael.harrison@northyorks.gov.uk

Harrison-Topham, Roger (CON - Middle Dales)
cllr.roger.harrison-topham@northyorks.gov.uk

Heseltine, Robert (IND - Skipton East)
cllr.robert.heseltine@northyorks.gov.uk

Heseltine, Michael (CON - Richmondshire North)
cllr.michael.heseltine@northyorks.gov.uk

Horton, Peter (IND - Ripon South)
cllr.peter.horton@northyorks.gov.uk

Hoult, Bill (LD - Knaresborough)
cllr.bill.hoult@northyorks.gov.uk

Ireton, David (CON - North Craven)
cllr.david.ireton@northyorks.gov.uk

Jeffels, David (CON - Seamer and Derwent Valley)
cllr.david.jeffles@scarborough.gov.uk

Jefferson, Janet (IND - Castle)
cllr.janet.jefferson@northyorks.gov.uk

Jones, Anne (LD - Knaresborough)
cllr.anne.jones@northyorks.gov.uk

Jordan, Mike (CON - South Selby)
cllr.mike.jordan@northyorks.gov.uk

Lee, Andrew (CON - Cawood and Saxton)
cllr.andrew.lee@northyorks.gov.uk

Lunn, Clifford (CON - Selby Brayton)
cllr.cliff.lunn@northyorks.gov.uk

Mackenzie, Don (CON - Harrogate Saltergate)
cllr.don.mackenzie@northyorks.gov.uk

Marsden, Penny (IND - Weaponness and Ramshill)
cllr.penny.marsden@northyorks.gov.uk

Marshall, Shelagh (CON - Mid Craven)
cllr.shelagh.marshall@northyorks.gov.uk

Marshall, Brian (LAB - Selby Barlby)
cllr.brian.marshall@northyorks.gov.uk

McCartney, John (IND - Osgoldcross)
cllr.john.mccartney@northyorks.gov.uk

Metcalfe, Chris (CON - Tadcaster)
cllr.chris.metcalfe@northyorks.gov.uk

Moorehouse, Heather (CON - Great Ayton)
cllr.heather.moorehouse@northyorks.gov.uk

Mulligan, Patrick (CON - Airedale)
cllr.patrick.mulligan@northyorks.gov.uk

Packham, Robert (LAB - Sherburn in Elmet)
cllr.robert.packham@northyorks.gov.uk

Parsons, Stuart (LD - Richmond)
cllr.stuart.parsons@northyorks.gov.uk

Patmore, Caroline (CON - Stillington)
cllr.caroline.patmore@northyorks.gov.uk

Pearson, Christopher (CON - Mid Selby)
cllr.chris.pearson@northyorks.gov.uk

Plant, Joe (CON - Whitby Streonshalh)
cllr.joe.plant@northyorks.gov.uk

Randerson, Anthony (LAB - Eastfield and Osgodby)
cllr.tony.randerson@northyorks.gov.uk

Ritchie, John (LAB - Falsgrave and Stepney)
cllr.john.ritchie@northyorks.gov.uk

Sanderson, Janet (CON - Thornton Dale and The Wolds)
cllr.janet.sanderson@northyorks.gov.uk

Savage, John (LIB - Ainsty)
cllr.john.savage@northyorks.gov.uk

Shaw-Wright, Steven (LAB - Selby Barlby)
cllr.steven.shaw-wright@northyorks.gov.uk

Shields, Elizabeth (LD - Norton)
cllr.elizabeth.shields@northyorks.gov.uk

Simister, David (UKIP - Harrogate Bilton and Nidd Gorge)
cllr.david.simister@northyorks.gov.uk

Solloway, Andy (IND - Skipton West)
Cllr.Andy.Solloway@northyorks.gov.uk

Sowray, Peter (CON - Easingwold)
cllr.peter.sowray@northyorks.gov.uk

Swales, Timothy (CON - North Hambleton)
cllr.tim.swales@northyorks.gov.uk

Swiers, Helen (CON - Esk Valley)
cllr.helen.swiers@northyorks.gov.uk

Trotter, Cliff (CON - Pannal and Lower Wharfedale)
cllr.cliff.trotter@northyorks.gov.uk

Weighell, John (CON - Bedale)
cllr.john.weighell@northyorks.gov.uk

Welch, Richard (CON - Ribblesdale)
cllr.richard.welch@northyorks.gov.uk

Windass, Robert (CON - Boroughbridge)
cllr.robert.windass@northyorks.gov.uk

Wood, Clare (CON - Hovingham and Sheriff Hutton)
cllr.clare.wood@northyorks.gov.uk

POLITICAL COMPOSITION

CON: 44, IND: 9, LD: 8, LAB: 7, LIB: 2, UKIP: 2

NORTHAMPTON

Northampton D

Northampton Borough Council, The Guildhall, St Giles Square, Northampton NN1 1DE
☎ 0300 330 7000 🖷 01604 837395 ✉ enquiries@northampton.gov.uk
💻 www.northampton.gov.uk

FACTS AND FIGURES

Parliamentary Constituencies: Northampton North, Northampton South
EU Constituencies: East Midlands
Election Frequency: Elections are of whole council

PRINCIPAL OFFICERS

Chief Executive: Mr David Kennedy, Chief Executive, The Guildhall, St Giles Square, Northampton NN1 1DE ☎ 01604 837726 ✉ dkennedy@northampton.gov.uk

Senior Management: Mr Steven Boyes , Director - Regeneration, Enterprise & Planning, The Guildhall, St Giles Square, Northampton NN1 1DE ☎ 01604 838531 ✉ sboyes@northampton.gov.uk

Senior Management: Mr Francis Fernandes, Borough Secretary & Monitoring Officer, The Guildhall, Northampton NN1 1DE ☎ 01604 837334 ✉ ffernandes@northampton.gov.uk

Senior Management: Ms Julie Seddon , Director - Customers & Communities, The Guildhall, St Giles Square, Northampton NN1 1DE ☎ 01604 837379 ✉ julieseddon@northampton.gov.uk

Building Control: Mr Lee Hunter , Building Control Manager, The Guildhall, St Giles Square, Northampton NN1 1DE ☎ 01604 838920 ✉ lhunter@northampton.gov.uk

PR / Communications: Ms Deborah Denton , Communications Manager, The Guildhall, St Giles Square, Northampton NN1 1DE ☎ 01604 837393 ✉ ddenton@northampton.gov.uk

Community Safety: Ms Debbie Ferguson , Community Safety Partnership Manager, The Guildhall, St Giles Square, Northampton NN1 1DE ☎ 01604 838731 ✉ dferguson@northampton.gov.uk

Corporate Services: Mr Francis Fernandes, Borough Secretary & Monitoring Officer, The Guildhall, Northampton NN1 1DE ☎ 01604 837334 ✉ ffernandes@northampton.gov.uk

Customer Service: Ms Marion Goodman , Head of Customer & Cultural Services, The Guildhall, St Giles Square, Northampton NN1 1DE ☎ 01604 838273 ✉ mgoodman@northampton.gov.uk

Economic Development: Mr Steven Boyes , Director - Regeneration, Enterprise & Planning, The Guildhall, St Giles Square, Northampton NN1 1DE ☎ 01604 838531 ✉ sboyes@northampton.gov.uk

E-Government: Ms Marion Goodman , Head of Customer & Cultural Services, The Guildhall, St Giles Square, Northampton NN1 1DE ☎ 01604 838273 ✉ mgoodman@northampton.gov.uk

Electoral Registration: Ms Jackie Thoy , Electoral Services Administrator, The Guildhall, St Giles Square, Northampton NN1 1DE ☎ 01604 837111 ✉ jthoy@northampton.gov.uk

Emergency Planning: Mr Aaron Goddard , Emergency Planning Officer, The Guildhall, St Giles Square, Northampton NN1 1DE ☎ 01604 837589 ✉ agoddard@northampton.gov.uk

Environmental / Technical Services: Ms Ruth Austen , Environment Health Manager, The Guildhall, St Giles Square, Northampton NN1 1DE ☎ 01604 837794 ✉ rausten@northampton.gov.uk

Environmental Health: Ms Ruth Austen , Environment Health Manager, The Guildhall, St Giles Square, Northampton NN1 1DE ☎ 01604 837794 ✉ rausten@northampton.gov.uk

Estates, Property & Valuation: Mr Andrew Meakin , Interim Corporate Asset Manager, The Guildhall, St Giles Square, Northampton NN1 1DE ☎ 01604 838761 ✉ ameakin@northampton.gov.uk

Facilities: Ms Shelley Parker , Facilities Manager, The Guildhall, St Giles Square, Northampton NN1 1DE ☎ 01604 837362 ✉ sparker@northampton.gov.uk

Finance: Mr Glenn Hammons , Chief Finance Officer & S151 Officer, The Guildhall, St Giles Square, Northampton NN1 1DE ☎ 01604 366521 ✉ ghammons@northampton.gov.uk

Housing: Mr Phil Harris , Head of Housing & Wellbeing, The Guildhall, St Giles Square, Northampton NN1 1DE ☎ 01604 837666 ✉ pharris@northampton.gov.uk

Legal: Mr Francis Fernandes, Borough Secretary & Monitoring Officer, The Guildhall, Northampton NN1 1DE ☎ 01604 837334 ✉ ffernandes@northampton.gov.uk

Leisure and Cultural Services: Ms Julie Seddon , Director - Customers & Communities, The Guildhall, St Giles Square, Northampton NN1 1DE ☎ 01604 837379 ✉ julieseddon@northampton.gov.uk

Licensing: Ms Julie Seddon , Director - Customers & Communities, The Guildhall, St Giles Square, Northampton NN1 1DE ☎ 01604 837379 ✉ julieseddon@northampton.gov.uk

Lottery Funding, Charity and Voluntary: Mrs Victoria Rockall , Partnerships & Communities Manager, The Guildhall, St Giles Square, Northampton NN1 1DE ☎ 01604 837074 ✉ vrockall@northampton.gov.uk

Member Services: Mr Francis Fernandes, Borough Secretary & Monitoring Officer, The Guildhall, Northampton NN1 1DE ☎ 01604 837334 ✉ ffernandes@northampton.gov.uk

Parking: Mr Derrick Simpson , Town Centre Manager, The Guildhall, St Giles Square, Northampton NN1 1DE ☎ 01604 838953 ✉ dsimpson@northampton.gov.uk

Partnerships: Mrs Victoria Rockall , Partnerships & Communities Manager, The Guildhall, St Giles Square, Northampton NN1 1DE ☎ 01604 837074 ✉ vrockall@northampton.gov.uk

Planning: Mr David Hackforth , Interim Head of Planning, The Guildhall, St Giles Square, Northampton NN1 1DE ☎ 01604 838921 ✉ dhackforth@northampton.gov.uk

Regeneration: Mr Richard Lawrence , Head of Service, Regeneration, Enterprise & Planning, The Guildhall, St Giles Square, Northampton NN1 1DE ✉ rlawrence@northampton.gov.uk

Town Centre: Mr Derrick Simpson , Town Centre Manager, The Guildhall, St Giles Square, Northampton NN1 1DE ☎ 01604 838953 ✉ dsimpson@northampton.gov.uk

Waste Collection and Disposal: Ms Julie Seddon , Director - Customers & Communities, The Guildhall, St Giles Square, Northampton NN1 1DE ☎ 01604 837379 ✉ julieseddon@northampton.gov.uk

Waste Management: Ms Julie Seddon , Director - Customers & Communities, The Guildhall, St Giles Square, Northampton NN1 1DE ☎ 01604 837379 ✉ julieseddon@northampton.gov.uk

Children's Play Areas: Ms Julie Seddon , Director - Customers & Communities, The Guildhall, St Giles Square, Northampton NN1 1DE ☎ 01604 837379 ✉ julieseddon@northampton.gov.uk

COUNCILLORS

***Mayor* Flavell**, Penelope (CON - Rushmills)
cllr.pflavell@northampton.gov.uk

***Deputy Mayor* Malpas**, Christopher (CON - Billing)
cllr.cmalpas@northampton.gov.uk

***Leader of the Council* Markham**, Mary (CON - Park)
cllr.mmarkham@northampton.gov.uk

***Group Leader* Stone**, Danielle (LAB - Castle)
cllr.dstone@northampton.gov.uk

Ansell, Tony (CON - Abington)
cllr.tansell@northampton.gov.uk

Ashraf, Rufia (LAB - St James)

Azizur Rahman, Mohammed (CON - Spring Park)
cllr.maziz@northampton.gov.uk

Beardsworth, Sally (LD - Kingsthorpe)
cllr.sbeardsworth@northampton.gov.uk

Birch, Jane (LAB - Trinity)
cllr.jbirch@northampton.gov.uk

Bottwood, Alan (CON - Upton)
cllr.abottwood@northampton.gov.uk

Cali, Muna (LAB - Castle)
cllr.mcali@northampton.gov.uk

Caswell, John (CON - New Duston)
cllr.jcaswell@northampton.gov.uk

Choudary, Nazim (LAB - St Davids)
cllr.nchoudary@northampton.gov.uk

Chunga, Clemennt (LAB - Brookside)
cllr.cchunga@northampton.gov.uk

Clubard, Vicky (LAB - Delapre & Briar Hill)
cllr.vclubard@northampton.gov.uk

Davenport, Julie (LAB - Delapre & Briar Hill)
cllr.jdavenport@northampton.gov.uk

Duffy, Janice (LAB - Talavera)
cllr.jduffy@northampton.gov.uk

Eales, Terrie (LAB - Kings Heath)
cllr.teales@northampton.gov.uk

Eales, Gareth (LAB - Spencer)
cllr.geales@northampton.gov.uk

Eldred, Brandon (CON - East Hunsbury)
cllr.beldred@northampton.gov.uk

Golby, Matthew (CON - New Duston)
cllr.mgolby@northampton.gov.uk

Gowen, Elizabeth (LAB - Eastfield)
cllr.egowen@northampton.gov.uk

Hadland, Tim (CON - Old Duston)
cllr.thadland@northampton.gov.uk

Hallam, Mike (CON - Parklands)
cllr.mhallam@northampton.gov.uk

Haque (Enam), Anamul (LAB - Castle)
cllr.ahaque@northampton.gov.uk

Hibbert, Stephen (CON - Riverside)
cllr.shibbert@northampton.gov.uk

Hill, Michael (CON - Nene Valley)
northamptonhill@yahoo.com

Hill, James (CON - Rectory Farm)
cllr.jhill@northampton.gov.uk

Kilbride, Andrew (CON - Billing)
cllr.akilbridge@northampton.gov.uk

King, Anna (CON - Phippsville)
cllr.aking@northampton.gov.uk

Lane, Jamie (CON - Boothville)
cllr.jlane@northampton.gov.uk

Larratt, Phil (CON - East Hunsbury)
cllr.plarratt@northampton.gov.uk

Lynch, Matthew (CON - Westone)
cllr.mlynch@northampton.gov.uk

Marriott, Les (LAB - Semilong)
cllr.lmarriott@northampton.gov.uk

McCutcheon, Arthur (LAB - Headlands)
amccutcheon@northampton.gov.uk

Meredith, Dennis (LD - Talavera)
cllr.dmeredith@northampton.gov.uk

Nunn, Jonathan (CON - Nene Valley)
cllr.jnunn@northampton.gov.uk

Oldham, Brian (CON - West Hunsbury)
cllr.**ham@northampton.gov.uk**

Parekh, Nilesh (CON - Sunnyside)
cllr.nparekh@northampton.gov.uk

Patel, Suresh (CON - Old Duston)
cllr.spatel@northampton.gov.uk

Russell, Catherine (LAB - Kingsley)
cllr.crussell@northampton.gov.uk

Sargeant, Brian (CON - Upton)
cllr.bsargeant@northampton.gov.uk

Shaw, Samual (CON - Obelisk)
cllr.sshaw@northampton.gov.uk

Smith, Zoe (LAB - Abington)
cllr.zsmith@northampton.gov.uk

Walker, Graham (CON - Delapre & Briar Hill)
cllr.gwalker@northampton.gov.uk

POLITICAL COMPOSITION
CON: 26, LAB: 17, LD: 2

COMMITTEE CHAIRS
Audit: Mr Jonathan Nunn

Development: Mr Mike Hallam

Licensing: Mr Brian Sargeant

Planning: Mr Brian Oldham

Northamptonshire C

Northamptonshire County Council, County Hall, Northampton NN1 1AN
☎ 0300 126 1000 🖷 01604 236223 💻 www.northamptonshire.gov.uk

FACTS AND FIGURES
EU Constituencies: East Midlands

Election Frequency: Elections are of whole council

PRINCIPAL OFFICERS
Chief Executive: Mr Paul Blantern , Chief Executive, County Hall, Northampton NN1 1AN ☎ 01604 367100 🖷 01604 366652 🖰 pblantern@northamptonshire.gov.uk

Senior Management: Akeem Ali , Director - Public Health, County Hall, Northampton NN1 1AN 🖰 aali@northamptonshire.gov.uk

Senior Management: Mr Paul Blantern , Chief Executive, County Hall, Northampton NN1 1AN ☎ 01604 367100 🖷 01604 366652 🖰 pblantern@northamptonshire.gov.uk

Senior Management: Mr Tony Ciaburro , Director of Environment, Development & Transport, County Hall, Northampton NN1 1AN ☎ 01604 366740 🖷 01604 366652 🖰 tciaburro@northamptonshire.gov.uk

Senior Management: Mrs Carolyn Kus , Director of Adult Social Care Services, Room 72, County Hall, Northampton NN1 1AN ☎ 01604 367670 🖷 01604 366652 🖰 ckus@northamptonshire.gov.uk

Access Officer / Social Services (Disability): Ms Palvinder Kudhail , Assistant Director - Early Help & Prevention, County Hall, Northampton NN1 1AN ☎ 01604 367561 🖰 pkudhail@northamptonshire.gov.uk

Architect, Building / Property Services: Mr James Wheeler , Head of Property Services (Strategic Asset Manager), County Hall, Northampton NN1 1AN ☎ 01604 366447 🖷 01604 366970 🖰 jwheeler@northamptonshire.gov.uk

Building Control: Mr James Wheeler , Head of Property Services (Strategic Asset Manager), County Hall, Northampton NN1 1AN ☎ 01604 366447 🖷 01604 366970 🖰 jwheeler@northamptonshire.gov.uk

Children / Youth Services: Satinder Gautam , Assistant Director of Safeguarding & Children's Services, County Hall, Northampton NN1 1AN ☎ 01604 366004 🖰 sgautam@northamptonshire.gov.uk

Civil Registration: Mr Jeremy Rawlings , Registration Service Manager, County Hall, Northampton NN1 1AN ☎ 0300 126 1010 🖰 jrawlings@northamptonshire.gov.uk

PR / Communications: Mr Simon Deacon , Head of Communications & Marketing, Room 90, County Hall, Northampton NN1 1AN ☎ 01604 367323 🖷 01604 237255 🖰 sdeacon@northamptonshire.gov.uk

Community Planning: Mr Roy Boulton, Assistant Director of Environmental & Planning, County Hall, Northampton NN1 1AN ☎ 01604 366056 🖰 rboulton@northamptonshire.gov.uk

Community Safety: Ms Deborah Mahon , Safe & Sustainable Communities Manager, County Hall, Northampton NN1 1AN ☎ 01604 367596 🖰 dmahon@northamptonshire.gov.uk

Computer Management: Mr Ian Farrar , Head of IT, County Hall, Northampton NN1 1AN ☎ 0300 126 1000 🖰 ifarrar@cambridge.gov.uk

Consumer Protection and Trading Standards: Mr David Hedger , Trading Standards Manager, Trading Standards, Wootton Hall Park, Northampton NN4 0GB ☎ 01604 362498 🖰 dhedger@northamptonshire.gov.uk

Contracts: Mr Matt Bowmer , Director of Finance, County Hall, Northampton NN1 1AN ☎ 01604 366550 🖰 m.bowmer@northamptonshire.gov.uk

Corporate Services: Ms Alison Parry , Head of Commercial Management, County Hall, Northampton NN1 1AN ☎ 01604 366838 🖰 aparry@northamptonshire.gov.uk

Customer Service: Ms Leanne Hanwell , Head of CSC, County Hall, Northampton NN1 1AN ☎ 01604 367952 🖰 lhanwell@northamptonshire.gov.uk

Economic Development: Mr Tony Ciaburro , Director of Environment, Development & Transport, County Hall, Northampton NN1 1AN ☎ 01604 366740 🖷 01604 366652 🖰 tciaburro@northamptonshire.gov.uk

Education: Mr Alex Hopkins , Director of Children, Families & Education, County Hall, Northampton NN1 1AN ☎ 01604 366359 🖷 01604 236550 🖰 aghopkins@northamptonshire.gov.uk

E-Government: Mr Matt Bowmer , Director of Finance, County Hall, Northampton NN1 1AN ☎ 01604 366550 🖰 m.bowmer@northamptonshire.gov.uk

Emergency Planning: Mr Matthew Hoy , Emergency Planning Manager, County Hall, Northampton NN1 1AN ☎ 01604 361348 ✉ mhoy@northamptonshire.gov.uk

Energy Management: Dr Darren Perry , Strategic Leader of Energy & Carbon Management, County Hall, Northampton NN1 1AN ☎ 01604 366948 ✉ daperry@northamptonshire.gov.uk

Estates, Property & Valuation: Mr Jeffrey Snell , Estates Operations Manager, County Hall, Northampton NN1 1AN ☎ 01604 236447 🖷 01604 236979 ✉ jsnell@northamptonshire.gov.uk

European Liaison: Mr Tony Ciaburro , Director of Environment, Development & Transport, PO Box 93, County Hall, Northampton NN1 1AN ☎ 01604 366740 🖷 01604 366652 ✉ tciaburro@northamptonshire.gov.uk

Facilities: Ms Catherine Kimmett , Facilities Manager, County Hall, Northampton NN1 1AN ✉ ckimmet@northamptonshire.gov.uk

Finance: Mr Matt Bowmer , Director of Finance, County Hall, Northampton NN1 1AN ☎ 01604 366550 ✉ m.bowmer@northamptonshire.gov.uk

Pensions: Mr Paul Tysoe , Group Accountant for the Pension Fund, John Dryden House, 8-10 The Lakes, Northampton NN4 7DD ☎ 01604 368671 ✉ p.tysoe@northamptonshire.gov.uk

Pensions: Mr Mark Whitby , Head of Pensions Operations, John Dryden House, 8 - 10 The Lakes, Northampton NN4 7DD ☎ 01604 366636 ✉ mwhitby@northamptonshire.gov.uk

Grounds Maintenance: Mr James Wheeler , Head of Property Services (Strategic Asset Manager), County Hall, Northampton NN1 1AN ☎ 01604 366447 🖷 01604 366970 ✉ jwheeler@northamptonshire.gov.uk

Health and Safety: Ms Sue Stagg, Health & Safety Manager, County Hall, Northampton NN1 1AN ☎ 01604 366447 🖷 01604 367359 ✉ sstagg@northamptonshire.gov.uk

Highways: Mr David Farquhar , Assistant Director of Highways, Transport & Infrastructure, County Hall, Northampton NN1 1AN ☎ 01604 654401 ✉ dfarquhar@northamptonshire.gov.uk

Local Area Agreement: Mr Peter McLaren, Head of Partnership Support Unit, County Hall, Northampton NN1 1AN ☎ 01604 237106 🖷 01604 237675 ✉ pmclaren@northamptonshire.gov.uk

Leisure and Cultural Services: Ms Janet Doran , Assistant Director of Place, Transformation & Wellbeing, County Hall, Northampton NN1 1AN ☎ 01604 366023 🖷 01604 237600 ✉ jdoran@northamptonshire.gov.uk

Licensing: Mr David Hedger , Trading Standards Manager, Trading Standards, Wootton Hall Park, Northampton NN4 0GB ☎ 01604 362498 ✉ dhedger@northamptonshire.gov.uk

Lighting: Mr Geoff Emmins, Highways Maintenance Manager, Riverside House, Riverside Way, Bedford Road, Northampton NN1 5NX ☎ 01604 654481 ✉ gemmins@northamptonshire.gov.uk

Lottery Funding, Charity and Voluntary: Mr Thomas Tansey , Third Sector Liaison, County Hall, Northampton NN1 1AN ☎ 01604 366025 ✉ ttansey@northamptonshire.gov.uk

Member Services: Mr Quentin Baker , Director of Law, Property & Governance, County Hall, Northampton NN1 1AN ☎ 0300 126 1000 ✉ qbaker@cambridgeshire.gov.uk

Parking: Mr David Farquhar , Assistant Director of Highways, Transport & Infrastructure, Riverside House, Riverside Way, Bedford Road, Northampton NN1 5NX ☎ 01604 654401 ✉ dfarquhar@northamptonshire.gov.uk

Personnel / HR: Mrs Christine Reed, Director of People, Transformation & Transactional Services, PO Box 93, County Hall, Northampton NN1 1AN ☎ 01604 367291 ✉ creed@northamptonshire.gov.uk

Planning: Mr Roy Boulton, Assistant Director of Environmental & Planning, PO Box 93, County Hall, Northampton NN1 1AN ☎ 01604 366056 ✉ rboulton@northamptonshire.gov.uk

Procurement: Mr Paul White, Head of Shared Services & Procurement, PO Box 93, County Hall, Northampton NN1 1DN ☎ 01604 236465 ✉ pwhite@northamptonshire.gov.uk

Public Libraries: Ms Jane Battye , Customer & Library Service Manager, County Hall, Northampton NN1 1AN ✉ jbattye@northamptonshire.gov.uk

Recycling & Waste Minimisation: Mr Wade Siddiqui , Manager of Waste Management, County Hall, Northampton NN1 1AN ☎ 01604 367147 🖷 01604 237331 ✉ wsiddiqui@northamptonshire.gov.uk

Regeneration: Mr Tony Ciaburro , Director of Environment, Development & Transport, PO Box 93, County Hall, Northampton NN1 1AN ☎ 01604 366740 🖷 01604 366652 ✉ tciaburro@northamptonshire.gov.uk

Road Safety: Mr John Spencer , Team Leader for Road Safety & Sustainability, Riverside Way, Bedford Road, Northampton NN1 5NX ☎ 01604 654430 🖷 01604 654455 ✉ jspencer@mqwsp.co.uk

Social Services: Mrs Carolyn Kus , Director of Adult Social Care Services, Room 72, County Hall, Northampton NN1 1AN ☎ 01604 367670 🖷 01604 366652 ✉ ckus@northamptonshire.gov.uk

Social Services (Adult): Mrs Carolyn Kus , Director of Adult Social Care Services, Room 72, County Hall, Northampton NN1 1AN ☎ 01604 367670 🖷 01604 366652 ✉ ckus@northamptonshire.gov.uk

Social Services (Children): Mr Alex Hopkins , Director of Children, Families & Education, County Hall, Northampton NN1 1AN ☎ 01604 366359 🖷 01604 236550 ✉ aghopkins@northamptonshire.gov.uk

Public Health: Akeem Ali , Director - Public Health, County Hall, Northampton NN1 1AN ✉ aali@northamptonshire.gov.uk

NORTHAMPTONSHIRE

Staff Training: Ms Barbara Barrett , Head of Organisational & Workplace Development, John Dryden House, Northampton NN4 7YD ☎ 01604 362075 ✉ bbarrett@northamptonshire.gov.uk

Sustainable Communities: Mr Tony Ciaburro , Director of Environment, Development & Transport, PO Box 93, County Hall, Northampton NN1 1AN ☎ 01604 366740 🖷 01604 366652 ✉ tciaburro@northamptonshire.gov.uk

Sustainable Development: Mr Tony Ciaburro , Director of Environment, Development & Transport, PO Box 93, County Hall, Northampton NN1 1AN ☎ 01604 366740 🖷 01604 366652 ✉ tciaburro@northamptonshire.gov.uk

Tourism: Ms Sue Grace, Assistant Director of Customer & Communities, PO Box 93, County Hall, Northampton NN1 1AN ☎ 01604 366806 🖷 01604 237600 ✉ sgrace@northamptonshire.gov.uk

Traffic Management: Mr David Farquhar , Assistant Director of Highways, Transport & Infrastructure, Riverside House, Riverside Way, Bedford Road, Northampton NN1 5NX ☎ 01604 654401 ✉ dfarquhar@northamptonshire.gov.uk

Transport: Mr David Farquhar , Assistant Director of Highways, Transport & Infrastructure, Riverside House, Riverside Way, Bedford Road, Northampton NN1 5NX ☎ 01604 654401 ✉ dfarquhar@northamptonshire.gov.uk

Transport Planner: Mr David Farquhar , Assistant Director of Highways, Transport & Infrastructure, Riverside House, Riverside Way, Bedford Road, Northampton NN1 5NX ☎ 01604 654401 ✉ dfarquhar@northamptonshire.gov.uk

Waste Collection and Disposal: Mr Wade Siddiqui , Manager of Waste Management, County Hall, Northampton NN1 1AN ☎ 01604 367147 🖷 01604 237331 ✉ wsiddiqui@northamptonshire.gov.uk

Waste Management: Mr Wade Siddiqui , Manager of Waste Management, County Hall, Northampton NN1 1AN ☎ 01604 367147 🖷 01604 237331 ✉ wsiddiqui@northamptonshire.gov.uk

COUNCILLORS

***Leader of the Council* Harker**, Jim (CON - Ise)
jharker@northamptonshire.gov.uk

***Deputy Leader of the Council* Smith**, Heather (CON - Oundle)
hsmith@northamptonshire.gov.uk

Beardsworth, Sally (LD - Kingsthorpe South)
sbeardsworth@northamptonshire.gov.uk

Bell, Paul (CON - Earls Barton)
pbell@northamptonshire.gov.uk

Brackenbury, Wendy (CON - Thrapston)
wbrackenbury@northamptonshire.gov.uk

Brookfield, Julie (LAB - Corby West)
jbrookfield@northamptonshire.gov.uk

Broomfield, Jim (UKIP - Brackley)
jbroomfield@northamptonshire.gov.uk

Brown, Robin (CON - Woodford & Weedon)
rwbrown@northamptonshire.gov.uk

Brown, Michael (UKIP - Kingsthorpe North)
mibrown@northamptonshire.gov.uk

Butcher, Mary (LAB - Oakley)
mbutcher@northamptonshire.gov.uk

Clarke, Michael (CON - Hackleton & Grange Park)
mclarke@northamptonshire.gov.uk

Collyer, Adam (UKIP - Daventry West)
acollyer@northamptonshire.gov.uk

Coombe, Elizabeth (LAB - Brickhill & Queensway)
ecoombe@northamptonshire.gov.uk

Eales, Gareth (LAB - Dallington Spencer)
gaeales@northamptonshire.gov.uk

Glynane, Brendan (LD - Delapre & Rushmere)
bglynane@northamptonshire.gov.uk

Golby, Matthew (CON - Duston West & St Crispin)
mgolby@northamptonshire.gov.uk

Gonzalez De Savage, Andrew (CON - East Hunsbury & Shelfleys)
adesavage@northamptonshire.gov.uk

Groome, Christopher (IND - Burton & Broughton)
cgroome@northamptonshire.gov.uk

Hakewill, James (CON - Rothwell & Mawsley)
jhakewill@northamptonshire.gov.uk

Hales, Eileen (LAB - Windmill)
eihales@northamptonshire.gov.uk

Hallam, Mike (CON - Boothville & Parklands)
mhallam@northamptonshire.gov.uk

Heggs, Stan (CON - Corby Rural)
sheggs@northamptonshire.gov.uk

Hills, Alan (CON - Daventry East)
ahills@northamptonshire.gov.uk

Homer, Sue (CON - Irchester)
shomer@northamptonshire.gov.uk

Hope, Jill (LD - Sixfields)
jhope@northamptonshire.gov.uk

Hughes, Sylvia (CON - Irthlingborough)
shughes@northamptonshire.gov.uk

Hughes, Dudley (CON - Raunds)
dhughes@northanptonshire.gov.uk

Irving-Swift, Cecile (CON - Brixworth)

Kirkbride, Joan (CON - Bugbrooke)
jkirkbride@northamptonshire.gov.uk

Larratt, Phill (CON - Nene Valley)
cllr.plarratt@northampton.gov.uk

Lawman, Graham (CON - Croyland & Swanspool)
gmlawman@northamptonshire.gov.uk

Lawson, Derek (CON - Higham Ferrers)
dlawson@northamptonshire.gov.uk

Legg, Stephen (CON - Riverside Park)
slegg@northamtonshire.gov.uk

Lofts, Chris (LD - Towcester & Roade)

Longley, Malcolm (CON - Braunston & Crick)

Mackintosh, David (CON - Billing & Rectory Farm)
dmackintosh@northamptonshire.gov.uk

Matthews, Allan (CON - Desborough)
amatthews@northamptonshire.gov.uk

McCutcheon, Arthur (LAB - Headlands)
amccutcheon@northamptonshire.gov.uk

McGhee, John (LAB - Kingswood)
jmcghee@northamptonshire.gov.uk

Mercer, Andy (CON - Rushden South)
amercer@northamptonshire.gov.uk

Meredith, Dennis (LD - Talavera)
dmeredith@northamptonshire.gov.uk

Morris, Ian (CON - Silverstone)
imorris@northamptonshire.gov.uk

Osborne, Steve (CON - Long Buckby)
sjosborne@northamptonshire.gov.uk

Parker, Bill (CON - Clover Hill)
bparker@northamptonshire.gov.uk

Patel, Suresh (CON - Duston East)
supatel@northamptonshire.gov.uk

Patel, Bhupendra (CON - Finedon)
bpatel@northamptonshire.gov.uk

Roberts, Russell (CON - Wicksteed)
rroberts@northamptonshire.gov.uk

Sawbridge, Ron (CON - Middleton Cheney)

Scott, Bob (LAB - Lloyds)
bascott@northamptonshire.gov.uk

Scrimshaw, Mick (LAB - Northall)
mscrimshaw@northamptonshire.gov.uk

Shephard, Judith (CON - Moulton)
jshephard@northamptonshire.gov.uk

Stone, Danielle (LAB - Abington & Phippsville)
dstone@northamptonshire.gov.uk

Strachan, Winston (LAB - Castle)
wstrachan@northamptonshire.gov.uk

Tye, Michael (CON - Rushden Pemberton West)
mtye@northamptonshire.gov.uk

Uldall, Sarah (LD - St George)
suldall@northamptonshire.gov.uk

Walker, Allen (CON - Deanshanger)
awalker@northamptonshire.gov.uk

Waters, Malcolm (CON - Hatton Park)
mwaters@northamptonshire.gov.uk

POLITICAL COMPOSITION

CON: 36, LAB: 11, LD: 6, UKIP: 3, IND: 1

COMMITTEE CHAIRS

Development Control: Mr Ian Morris

Finance & Resources: Mr James Hakewill

Northumberland U

Northumberland Council, County Hall, Morpeth NE61 2EF
☎ 0845 600 6400 🖷 01670 534117 ✉ ask@northumberland.gov.uk
🖳 www.northumberland.gov.uk

FACTS AND FIGURES

Parliamentary Constituencies: Berwick-upon-Tweed, Blyth Valley, Hexham, Wansbeck
EU Constituencies: North East
Election Frequency: Elections are of whole council

PRINCIPAL OFFICERS

Senior Management: Mrs Daljit Lally , Executive Director - Wellbeing & Community Health Services, County Hall, Morpeth NE61 2EF ☎ 01670 622682 🖷 01670 620223 ✉ daljit.lally@northumberland.gcsx.gov.uk

Senior Management: Mr Steve Mason , Lead Executive Director, County Hall, Morpeth NE61 2EF ☎ 01670 622929 🖷 01670 620223 ✉ steven.mason@northumberland.gov.uk

Senior Management: Mr Geoff Paul , Director of Planning, Economy & Housing, County Hall, Morpeth NE61 2EF ☎ 01670 622388 🖷 01670 620223 ✉ geoff.paul@northumberland.gov.uk

Architect, Building / Property Services: Mr Paul Leo , Head of Strategic Estates, County Hall, Morpeth NE61 2EF ☎ 01670 623105 🖷 01670 620223 ✉ paul.leo@northumberland.gov.uk

Building Control: Mr Philip Soderquest , Head of Public Protection, County Hall, Morpeth NE61 2EF ☎ 01670 623696 🖷 01670 620223 ✉ philip.soderquest@northumberland.gcsx.gov.uk

Children / Youth Services: Mr Roger Edwardson , Head of Service - Education Support, County Hall, Morpeth NE61 2EF ☎ 01670 620311 🖷 01670 511413 ✉ roger.edwardson@northumberland.gov.uk

Civil Registration: Mrs Lorraine Dewison , Registration & Coronial Manager, County Hall, Morpeth NE61 2EF ☎ 01670 622544 🖷 01670 620223 ✉ lorraine.dewison@northumberland.gov.uk

Community Safety: Mr Alex Bennett , Chief Fire Officer, Fire & Rescue Service Headquarters, West Hartford Business Park, Cramlington NE23 3JP ☎ 01670 621112 ✉ alex.bennett@northumberland.gov.uk

Computer Management: Mr Neil Arnold , Information Services Manager, County Hall, Morpeth NE61 2EF ☎ 01670 623238 🖷 01670 620223 ✉ neil.arnold@northumberland.gov.uk

Consumer Protection and Trading Standards: Mr Philip Soderquest , Head of Public Protection, County Hall, Morpeth NE61 2EF ☎ 01670 623696 🖷 01670 620223 ✉ philip.soderquest@northumberland.gcsx.gov.uk

Contracts: Mr Steve Mason , Lead Executive Director, County Hall, Morpeth NE61 2EF ☎ 01670 622929 🖷 01670 620223 ✉ steven.mason@northumberland.gov.uk

Corporate Services: Mrs Alison Elsdon , Head of Corporate Services, County Hall, Morpeth NE61 2EF ☎ 01670 622168 🖷 01670 620223 ✉ alison.elsdon@nothumberland.gov.uk

Customer Service: Mr Colin Logan , Head of Financial & Customer Services, County Hall, Morpeth NE61 2EF ☎ 01670 622926 🖷 01670 620223 ✉ colin.logan@northumberland.gov.uk

NORTHUMBERLAND

Education: Mr John Clark , Head of Planning & Organisation, County Hall, Morpeth NE61 2EF ☎ 01670 624049 🖷 01670 620223 ✉ john.clark@northumberland.gov.uk

E-Government: Mr Neil Arnold , Information Services Manager, County Hall, Morpeth NE61 2EF ☎ 01670 623238 🖷 01670 620223 ✉ neil.arnold@northumberland.gov.uk

Electoral Registration: Mr Geoff Paul , Director of Planning, Economy & Housing, County Hall, Morpeth NE61 2EF ☎ 01670 622388 🖷 01670 620223 ✉ geoff.paul@northumberland.gov.uk

Emergency Planning: Mr Alex Bennett , Chief Fire Officer, Fire & Rescue Service Headquarters, West Hartford Business Park, Cramlington NE23 3JP ☎ 01670 621112 ✉ alex.bennett@northumberland.gov.uk

Energy Management: Mr Peter McArdle , Energy Officer, County Hall, Morpeth NE61 2EF ☎ 01670 622317 🖷 01670 511413 ✉ peter.mcardle@northumberland.gov.uk

Environmental Health: Mr Philip Soderquest , Head of Public Protection, County Hall, Morpeth NE61 2EF ☎ 01670 623696 🖷 01670 620223 ✉ philip.soderquest@northumberland.gcsx.gov.uk

Estates, Property & Valuation: Mr Paul Leo , Head of Strategic Estates, County Hall, Morpeth NE61 2EF ☎ 01670 623105 🖷 01670 620223 ✉ paul.leo@northumberland.gov.uk

Finance: Mr Steve Mason , Lead Executive Director, County Hall, Morpeth NE61 2EF ☎ 01670 622929 🖷 01670 620223 ✉ steven.mason@northumberland.gov.uk

Pensions: Ms Marion Fryatt , Team Leader - Pensions, County Hall, Morpeth NE61 2EF ☎ 01670 623568 ✉ marion.fryatt@northumberland.gov.uk

Pensions: Ms Clare Gorman , Senior Accountant, County Hall, Morpeth NE61 2EF ☎ 01670 623579 ✉ clare.gorman@northumberland.gov.uk

Pensions: Mr Alan Whittle , Head of Pension Administration, County Hall, Morpeth NE61 2EF ☎ 01670 623569 🖷 01670 620223 ✉ alan.whittle@northumberland.gov.uk

Fleet Management: Mr Paul Jones , Head of Neighbourhood Services, County Hall, Morpeth NE61 2EF ☎ 01670 623432 🖷 01670 620223 ✉ paul.jones@northumberland.gscx.gov.uk

Grounds Maintenance: Mr Paul Jones , Head of Neighbourhood Services, County Hall, Morpeth NE61 2EF ☎ 01670 623432 🖷 01670 620223 ✉ paul.jones@northumberland.gscx.gov.uk

Health and Safety: Mr John Froud , Corporate Health & Safety Manager, County Hall, Morpeth NE61 2EF ☎ 01670 623806 🖷 01670 620223 ✉ john.froud@northumberland.gov.uk

Highways: Mr Paul Jones , Head of Neighbourhood Services, County Hall, Morpeth NE61 2EF ☎ 01670 623432 🖷 01670 620223 ✉ paul.jones@northumberland.gscx.gov.uk

Housing: Mr Geoff Paul , Director of Planning, Economy & Housing, County Hall, Morpeth NE61 2EF ☎ 01670 622388 🖷 01670 620223 ✉ geoff.paul@northumberland.gov.uk

Housing Maintenance: Mr Kevin Lowry , Managing Director of Homes for Northumberland, Civic Centre, Renwick Road, Blyth NE24 2BX ☎ 01670 622871 ✉ kevin.lowry@hfn.uk.com

Legal: Mr Liam Henry , Legal Services Manager, County Hall, Morpeth NE61 2EF ☎ 01670 623324 🖷 01670 620223 ✉ liam.henry@northumberland.gov.uk

Leisure and Cultural Services: Mr Bruce Ledger , Chief Executive - Active Northumberland, Active Northumberland, Concordia Leisure Centre, Cramlington NE23 6YB ☎ 01670 622237 ✉ bledger@activenorthumberland.org.uk

Licensing: Mr Philip Soderquest , Head of Public Protection, County Hall, Morpeth NE61 2EF ☎ 01670 623696 🖷 01670 620223 ✉ philip.soderquest@northumberland.gcsx.gov.uk

Lifelong Learning: Ms Elaine O'Conner , Head of Employability & Skills, County Hall, Morpeth NE61 2EF ☎ 01670 622806 🖷 01670 620223 ✉ elaine.o'conner@northumberland.gov.uk

Lifelong Learning: Ms Heather Thomas , Head of Service, County Hall, Morpeth NE61 2EF ☎ 01670 622107 🖷 01670 620223 ✉ heather.thomas@northumberland.gov.uk

Lighting: Mr Paul Jones , Head of Neighbourhood Services, County Hall, Morpeth NE61 2EF ☎ 01670 623432 🖷 01670 620223 ✉ paul.jones@northumberland.gscx.gov.uk

Member Services: Mrs Jackie Roll , Democratic Services Manager, County Hall, Morpeth NE61 2EF ☎ 01670 622603 🖷 01670 620233 ✉ jackie.roll@northumberland.gov.uk

Parking: Mr David Laux , Head of Technical Services, County Hall, Morpeth NE61 2EF ☎ 01670 623139 ✉ david.laux@northumberland.gcsx.gov.uk

Planning: Mrs Karen Ledger , Head of Planning & Housing Services, County Hall, Morpeth NE61 2EF ☎ 01670 623430 🖷 01670 620223 ✉ karen.ledger@northumberland.gov.uk

Procurement: Ms Teresa Palmer , Shared Head of Procurement, County Hall, Morpeth NE61 2EF ☎ 01670 622357 🖷 01670 620223 ✉ teresa.palmer@northumberland.gov.uk

Public Libraries: Mr Nigel Walsh , Service Manager - Culture, Heritage & Libraries, County Hall, Morpeth NE61 2EF ☎ 01670 624753 ✉ nwalsh@activenorthumberland.gov.uk

Recycling & Waste Minimisation: Mr Paul Jones , Head of Neighbourhood Services, County Hall, Morpeth NE61 2EF ☎ 01670 623432 🖷 01670 620223 ✉ paul.jones@northumberland.gscx.gov.uk

Road Safety: Mr David Laux , Head of Technical Services, County Hall, Morpeth NE61 2EF ☎ 01670 623139 ✉ david.laux@northumberland.gcsx.gov.uk

Social Services (Adult): Mrs Daljit Lally , Executive Director - Wellbeing & Community Health Services, County Hall, Morpeth NE61 2EF ☎ 01670 622682 🖷 01670 620223 daljit.lally@northumberland.gcsx.gov.uk

Social Services (Children): Mrs Daljit Lally , Executive Director - Wellbeing & Community Health Services, County Hall, Morpeth NE61 2EF ☎ 01670 622682 🖷 01670 620223 daljit.lally@northumberland.gcsx.gov.uk

Public Health: Mr Philip Soderquest , Head of Public Protection, County Hall, Morpeth NE61 2EF ☎ 01670 623696 🖷 01670 620223 philip.soderquest@northumberland.gcsx.gov.uk

Staff Training: Mr Paul Brooks , Learning & OD Manager, County Hall, Morpeth NE61 2EF ☎ 01670 623142 🖷 01670 620223 paul.brooks@northumberland.gov.uk

Street Scene: Mr David Laux , Head of Technical Services, County Hall, Morpeth NE61 2EF ☎ 01670 623139 david.laux@northumberland.gcsx.gov.uk

Sustainable Development: Mrs Karen Ledger , Head of Planning & Housing Services, County Hall, Morpeth NE61 2EF ☎ 01670 623430 🖷 01670 620223 karen.ledger@northumberland.gov.uk

Tourism: Mr Nigel Walsh , Service Manager - Culture, Heritage & Libraries, County Hall, Morpeth NE61 2EF ☎ 01670 624753 nwalsh@activenorthumberland.gov.uk

Traffic Management: Mr David Laux , Head of Technical Services, County Hall, Morpeth NE61 2EF ☎ 01670 623139 david.laux@northumberland.gcsx.gov.uk

Transport: Mr David Laux , Head of Technical Services, County Hall, Morpeth NE61 2EF ☎ 01670 623139 david.laux@northumberland.gcsx.gov.uk

Transport Planner: Mr David Laux , Head of Technical Services, County Hall, Morpeth NE61 2EF ☎ 01670 623139 david.laux@northumberland.gcsx.gov.uk

Waste Collection and Disposal: Mr Paul Jones , Head of Neighbourhood Services, County Hall, Morpeth NE61 2EF ☎ 01670 623432 🖷 01670 620223 paul.jones@northumberland.gscx.gov.uk

Waste Management: Mr Paul Jones , Head of Neighbourhood Services, County Hall, Morpeth NE61 2EF ☎ 01670 623432 🖷 01670 620223 paul.jones@northumberland.gscx.gov.uk

COUNCILLORS

***Leader of the Council* Davey**, Grant (LAB - Kitty Brewster)
Grant.Davey@northumberland.gov.uk

***Deputy Leader of the Council* Ledger**, David (LAB - Choppington)
David.Ledger@northumberland.gov.uk

***Group Leader* Jackson**, Peter (CON - Ponteland South with Heddon)
Peter.Jackson@northumberland.gov.uk

Arckless, George (LAB - Amble)
Robert.Arckless99@northumberland.gov.uk

Armstrong, Eileen (CON - Ponteland East & Stannington)
Eileen.Armstrong@northumberland.gov.uk

Bawn, David (CON - Morpeth North)
David.Bawn@northumberland.gov.uk

Bridgett, Steven (INDNA - Rothbury)
Steven.Bridgett@northumberland.gov.uk

Burt, Eileen (LAB - Prudhoe North)
Eileen.Burt@northumberland.gov.uk

Cairns, Heather (LD - Alnwick)
Heather.Cairns@northumberland.gov.uk

Cairns, Kate (LD - Longhoughton)
Kate.Cairns@northumberland.gov.uk

Campbell, Deirdre (LAB - Newsham)

Cartie, Eileen (LAB - Wensleydale)
Eileen.Carter@northumberland.gov.uk

Castle, Gordon (IND - Alnwick)
Gordon.Castle@northumberland.gov.uk

Cessford, Colin (CON - Hexham West)
Colin.Cessford@northumberland.gov.uk

Dale, Anne (IND - Stocksfield & Broomhaugh)
Anne.Dale@northumberland.gov.uk

Daley, Wayne (CON - Cramlington North)
Wayne.Daley@northumberland.gov.uk

Davey, Susan (LAB - Cowpen)
Susan.Davey@northumberland.gov.uk

Dickinson, Scott (LAB - Druridge Bay)
Scott.Dickinson@northumberland.gov.uk

Dodd, Richard (CON - Ponteland North)
Richard.Dodd@northumberland.gov.uk

Douglas, Milburn (IND - Lynemouth)
Milburn.Douglas@northumberland.gov.uk

Dungworth, Susan (LAB - Hartley)
Susan.Dungworth@northumberland.gov.uk

Fearon, Jean (CON - Corbridge)
Jean.Fearon@northumberland.gov.uk

Flux, Barry (CON - Cramlington West)
Barry.Flux@northumberland.gov.uk

Foster, Julie (LAB - Stakeford)
JulieD.Foster@northumberland.gov.uk

Gallacher, Brian (LAB - Haydon)
Brian.Gallacher@northumberland.gov.uk

Gibson, Rupert (CON - Humshaugh)
Rupert.Gibson@northumberland.gov.uk

Gobin, Jeff (LAB - Sleekburn)

Graham, Kathy (LAB - Cramlington Village)
Kathy.Graham@northumberland.gov.uk

Grimshaw, Lynne (LAB - Bothal)
Lynne.Grimshaw@northumberland.gov.uk

Hepple, Allan (LAB - Cramlington South East)
Allan.Hepple@northumberland.gov.uk

Homer, Cath (CON - Hexham East)
Cath.Homer@northumberland.gov.uk

Horncastle, Colin (CON - South Tynedale)
Colin.Horncastle@northumberland.gov.uk

Hunter, Elizabeth (LD - Berwick West with Ord)
Isabel.Hunter@northumberland.gov.uk

Hutchinson, Ian (CON - Haltwhistle)
Ian.Hutchinson@northumberland.gov.uk

Johnstone, Terry (LAB - Bedlington West)
Terry.Johnstone@northumberland.gov.uk

Jones, Gavin (LD - Berwick North)
Gavin.Jones@northumberland.gov.uk

Jones, Veronica (CON - Ponteland West)
Veronica.Jones@northumberland.gov.uk

Kelly, Paul (IND - Bywell)
Paul.Kelly@northumberland.gov.uk

Lang, Jim (LAB - Seaton with Newbiggin West)
Jim.Lang@northumberland.gov.uk

Lindley, Ian (IND - Morpeth Stobhill)
Ian.Lindley@northumberland.gov.uk

Murray, Anthony (CON - Wooler)
Anthony.Murray99@northumberland.gov.uk

Nisbet, Kath (LAB - Croft)
Kath.Nisbet@northumberland.gov.uk

Parry, Ken (LAB - Hirst)
Ken.Parry@northumberland.gov.uk

Pidcock, Bernard (LAB - Holywell)
Bernard.Pidcock@northumberland.gov.uk

Pidcock, Laura (LAB - Cramlington Eastfield)
Laura.Pidcock@northumberland.gov.uk

Purvis, Mark (LAB - College)
mark.purvis@northumberland.gov.uk

Reid, Tony (LAB - Prudhoe South)
Tony.Reid@northumberland.gov.uk

Reid, Jeff (LD - Plessey)
Jeff.Reid@northumberland.gov.uk

Richards, Margaret (LAB - Seghill with Seaton Delaval)
Margaret.Richards01@northumberland.gov.uk

Rickerby, Lesley (LD - South Blyth)
Lesley.Rickerby@northumberland.gov.uk

Riddle, John (CON - Bellingham)
John.Riddle@northumberland.gov.uk

Robson, Terry (CON - Hexham Central with Acomb)
Terry.Robson@northumberland.gov.uk

Sambrook, Alan (LAB - Pegswood)
Alan.Sambrook@northumberland.gov.uk

Sanderson, Glen (CON - Longhorsley)
Glen.Sanderson@northumberland.gov.uk

Sharp, Alan (LD - Haydon & Hadrian)
Alan.Sharp@northumberland.gov.uk

Simpson, Elizabeth (LAB - Newbiggin Central & East)
Elizabeth.Simpson@northumberland.gov.uk

Smith, James (LD - Berwick East)
James.Smith@northumberland.gov.uk

Swithenbank, Ian (LAB - Cramlington East)
Ian.Switchenbank@northumberland.gov.uk

Tebbutt, Andrew (LD - Morpeth Kirkhill)
Andrew.Tebbutt@northumberland.gov.uk

Thorne, Trevor (CON - Shilbottle)
embletonhall@btinternet.com

Tyler, Valerie (LAB - Bedlington East)
Valerie.Tyler@northumberland.gov.uk

Wallace, Alyson (LAB - Bedlington Central)
Alyson.Wallace@northumberland.gov.uk

Watkin, Richard (LD - Norham & Islandshires)
DouWatkin@aol.com

Watson, Jeffrey (IND - Amble West & Warkworth)
Jeffrey.Watson@northumberland.gov.uk

Webb, Gordon (LAB - Isabella)
Gordon.Webb@northumberland.gov.uk

Wilson, Thomas (LAB - Ashington Central)
Thomas.Wilson@northumberland.gov.uk

Woodman, John (CON - Bamburgh)
John.Woodman@northumberland.gov.uk

POLITICAL COMPOSITION

LAB: 31, CON: 19, LD: 10, IND: 6, INDNA: 1

COMMITTEE CHAIRS

Audit: Mrs Anne Dale

Family & Children's Services: Mr Bernard Pidcock

Health & Wellbeing: Mr Scott Dickinson

Housing: Mr Ken Parry

Pensions: Mr Tony Reid

Planning: Mr Paul Kelly

Norwich City D

Norwich City Council, City Hall, St. Peter's Street, Norwich NR2 1NH
☎ 0344 980 3333 ✉ info@norwich.gov.uk 🖳 www.norwich.gov.uk

FACTS AND FIGURES

Parliamentary Constituencies: Norwich North, Norwich South
EU Constituencies: Eastern
Election Frequency: Elections are by thirds

PRINCIPAL OFFICERS

Chief Executive: Ms Laura McGillivray, Chief Executive, City Hall, St. Peter's Street, Norwich NR2 1NH ☎ 01603 212001 🖷 01603 213001 ✉ lauramcgillivray@norwich.gov.uk

Senior Management: Mr Anthony Bull, Executive Head - Business Relationship Management & Democracy, City Hall, St. Peter's Street, Norwich NR2 1NH ☎ 01603 212326 ✉ anthonybull@norwich.gov.uk

Senior Management: Mr David Moorcroft , Executive Head - Regeneration & Development, City Hall, St. Peter's Street, Norwich NR2 1NH ☎ 01603 212225 ✉ davidmoorcroft@norwich.gov.uk

Senior Management: Mr Russell O'Keefe , Executive Head - Strategy, People & Neighbourhoods, Norwich City Council, St. Peter's Street, Norwich NR2 1NH ☎ 01603 212908 ✉ russello'keefe@norwich.gov.uk

Senior Management: Ms Nikki Rotsos, Executive Head - Service, Customers, Communications & Culture, City Hall, St. Peter's Street, Norwich NR2 1NH ☎ 01603 212211 ✉ nikkirotsos@norwich.gov.uk

Access Officer / Social Services (Disability): Mr David Moorcroft , Executive Head - Regeneration & Development, City Hall, St. Peter's Street, Norwich NR2 1NH ☎ 01603 212225 ✉ davidmoorcroft@norwich.gov.uk

Architect, Building / Property Services: Mr David Moorcroft , Executive Head - Regeneration & Development, City Hall, St. Peter's Street, Norwich NR2 1NH ☎ 01603 212225 ✉ davidmoorcroft@norwich.gov.uk

Best Value: Mr Russell O'Keefe , Executive Head - Strategy, People & Neighbourhoods, Norwich City Council, St. Peter's Street, Norwich NR2 1NH ☎ 01603 212908 ✉ russello'keefe@norwich.gov.uk

Building Control: Mr David Moorcroft , Executive Head - Regeneration & Development, City Hall, St. Peter's Street, Norwich NR2 1NH ☎ 01603 212225 ✉ davidmoorcroft@norwich.gov.uk

Building Control: Mr Graham Nelson , Head of Planning Services, City Hall, St. Peter's Street, Norwich NR2 1NH ☎ 01603 212530 ✉ grahamnelson@norwich.gov.uk

PR / Communications: Mr Richard Balls , Communications Manager, City Hall, St. Peter's Street, Norwich NR2 1NH ☎ 01603 212991 ✉ richardballs@norwich.gov.uk

Community Planning: Mr Bob Cronk, Head of Local Neighbourhood Services, City Hall, St Peter's Street, Norwich NR2 1NH ☎ 01603 212373 🖷 01603 212380 ✉ bobcronk@norwich.gov.uk

Community Planning: Mr David Moorcroft , Executive Head - Regeneration & Development, City Hall, St. Peter's Street, Norwich NR2 1NH ☎ 01603 212225 ✉ davidmoorcroft@norwich.gov.uk

Community Safety: Mr Bob Cronk, Head of Local Neighbourhood Services, City Hall, St Peter's Street, Norwich NR2 1NH ☎ 01603 212373 🖷 01603 212380 ✉ bobcronk@norwich.gov.uk

Community Safety: Mr David Moorcroft , Executive Head - Regeneration & Development, City Hall, St. Peter's Street, Norwich NR2 1NH ☎ 01603 212225 ✉ davidmoorcroft@norwich.gov.uk

Computer Management: Mr Anthony Bull, Executive Head - Business Relationship Management & Democracy, City Hall, St. Peter's Street, Norwich NR2 1NH ☎ 01603 212326 ✉ anthonybull@norwich.gov.uk

Contracts: Mr Anthony Bull, Executive Head - Business Relationship Management & Democracy, City Hall, St. Peter's Street, Norwich NR2 1NH ☎ 01603 212326 ✉ anthonybull@norwich.gov.uk

Corporate Services: Mr Russell O'Keefe , Executive Head - Strategy, People & Neighbourhoods, Norwich City Council, City Hall, St Peter's Street, Norwich NR2 1NH ☎ 01603 212908 ✉ russello'keefe@norwich.gov.uk

Customer Service: Ms Tina Bailey, Head of Customer Services, City Hall, St. Peter's Street, Norwich NR2 1NH ☎ 01603 212759 ✉ tinabailey@norwich.gov.uk

Economic Development: Ms Ellen Tilney , Economic Development Manager, City Hall, St. Peter's Street, Norwich NR2 1NH ☎ 01603 212225 ✉ ellentilney@norwich.gov.uk

E-Government: Ms Jane Rogers , Systems Support Team Leader, City Hall, St. Peter's Street, Norwich NR2 1NH ☎ 0344 980 3333

Electoral Registration: Mr Stuart Guthrie , Electoral Services Manager, City Hall, St. Peter's Street, Norwich NR2 1NH ☎ 01603 212055 ✉ stuartguthrie@norwich.gov.uk

Emergency Planning: Ms Teresa Cannon , Emergency Planning Manager, City Hall, St. Peter's Street, Norwich NR2 1NH ☎ 01603 212474 ✉ teresacanon@norwich.gov.uk

Environmental / Technical Services: Mr Adrian Akester, Head of Citywide Services, City Hall, St. Peter's Street, Norwich NR2 1NH ☎ 01603 213521 ✉ adrianakester@norwich.gov.uk

Environmental Health: Mr Michael Stephenson , Public Protection Manager, City Hall, St. Peter's Street, Norwich NR2 1NH ☎ 01603 212283 ✉ michaelstephenson@norwich.gov.uk

Estates, Property & Valuation: Mr Andy Watt , Head of City Development Services, City Hall, St. Peter's Street, Norwich NR2 1NH ☎ 01603 212691 ✉ andywatt@norwich.gov.uk

Events Manager: Ms Helen Selleck , Culture & Events Manager, City Hall, St. Peter's Street, Norwich NR2 1NH ☎ 01603 212317 ✉ helenselleck@norwich.gov.uk

Facilities: Mr Eamonn Pellican , Facilities Manager - NPS Norwich, City Hall, St. Peter's Street, Norwich NR2 1NH ☎ 0344 980 3333 ✉ eamonn.pellican@nps.co.uk

Finance: Ms Justine Hartley , Head of Finance - LGSS, City Hall, St. Peter's Street, Norwich NR2 1NH ☎ 01603 212440 ✉ justinehartley@norwich.gov.uk

Grounds Maintenance: Mr Adrian Akester, Head of Citywide Services, City Hall, St. Peter's Street, Norwich NR2 1NH ☎ 01603 213521 ✉ adrianakester@norwich.gov.uk

Health and Safety: Mr Adrian Akester, Head of Citywide Services, City Hall, St. Peter's Street, Norwich NR2 1NH ☎ 01603 213521 ✉ adrianakester@norwich.gov.uk

Highways: Mr Andy Watt , Head of City Development Services, City Hall, St. Peter's Street, Norwich NR2 1NH ☎ 01603 212691 ✉ andywatt@norwich.gov.uk

NORWICH CITY

Home Energy Conservation: Mr Richard Wilson , Environmental Strategy Manager, City Hall, St. Peter's Street, Norwich NR2 1NH ☎ 01603 212312 ✉ richardwilson@norwich.gov.uk

Housing: Mrs Tracy John , Head of Neigbourhood & Strategic Housing, Norwich City Council, City Hall, St Peter's Street, Norwich NR2 1NH ☎ 01603 212939 ✉ tracyjohn@norwich.gov.uk

Leisure and Cultural Services: Ms Nikki Rotsos , Executive Head of Customers, Communications & Culture, City Hall, St. Peter's Street, Norwich NR2 1NH ☎ 01603 212211 🖷 01603 212010 ✉ nikkirotsos@norwich.gov.uk

Licensing: Mr Adrian Akester, Head of Citywide Services, City Hall, St. Peter's Street, Norwich NR2 1NH ☎ 01603 213521 ✉ adrianakester@norwich.gov.uk

Lottery Funding, Charity and Voluntary: Mr Bob Cronk, Head of Local Neighbourhood Services, City Hall, St Peter's Street, Norwich NR2 1NH ☎ 01603 212373 🖷 01603 212380 ✉ bobcronk@norwich.gov.uk

Member Services: Mr Andy Emms , Democratic Services Manager, City Hall, St. Peter's Street, Norwich NR2 1NH ☎ 01603 212459 ✉ andyemms@norwich.gov.uk

Parking: Mr Andy Watt , Head of City Development Services, City Hall, St. Peter's Street, Norwich NR2 1NH ☎ 01603 212691 ✉ andywatt@norwich.gov.uk

Personnel / HR: Mrs Dawn Bradshaw , Head of HR & Learning, City Hall, Norwich, NR2 1NH, Norwich NR2 1NH ☎ 01603 212434 ✉ dawnbradshaw@norwich.gov.uk

Planning: Mr Graham Nelson , Head of Planning, City Hall, St. Peter's Street, Norwich NR2 1NH ☎ 01603 212530 ✉ grahamnelson@norwich.gov.uk

Procurement: Mr Anthony Bull, Executive Head - Business Relationship Management & Democracy, City Hall, St. Peter's Street, Norwich NR2 1NH ☎ 01603 212326 ✉ anthonybull@norwich.gov.uk

Recycling & Waste Minimisation: Mr Adrian Akester, Head of Citywide Services, City Hall, St. Peter's Street, Norwich NR2 1NH ☎ 01603 213521 ✉ adrianakester@norwich.gov.uk

Regeneration: Mr Andy Watt , Head of City Development Services, City Hall, St. Peter's Street, Norwich NR2 1NH ☎ 01603 212691 ✉ andywatt@norwich.gov.uk

Road Safety: Mr Andy Watt , Head of City Development Services, City Hall, St. Peter's Street, Norwich NR2 1NH ☎ 01603 212691 ✉ andywatt@norwich.gov.uk

Street Scene: Mr Adrian Akester , Head of Citywide Services, City Hall, St. Peter's Street, Norwich NR2 1NH ☎ 01603 213521 ✉ adrianakester@norwich.gov.uk

Street Scene: Mr Andy Watt , Head of City Development Services, City Hall, St. Peter's Street, Norwich NR2 1NH ☎ 01603 212691 ✉ andywatt@norwich.gov.uk

Sustainable Communities: Mr David Moorcroft , Executive Head - Regeneration & Development, City Hall, St. Peter's Street, Norwich NR2 1NH ☎ 01603 212225 ✉ davidmoorcroft@norwich.gov.uk

Tourism: Ms Michelle Hurren , Tourist Development Manager, City Hall, St. Peter's Street, Norwich NR2 1NH ☎ 01603 212211 🖷 01603 212010 ✉ michellehurren@norwich.gov.uk

Traffic Management: Mr Andy Watt , Head of City Development Services, City Hall, St. Peter's Street, Norwich NR2 1NH ☎ 01603 212396 ✉ andywatt@norwich.gov.uk

Transport: Mr David Moorcroft , Executive Head - Regeneration & Development, City Hall, St. Peter's Street, Norwich NR2 1NH ☎ 01603 212225 ✉ davidmoorcroft@norwich.gov.uk

Transport: Mr Andy Watt , Head of City Development Services, City Hall, St. Peter's Street, Norwich NR2 1NH ☎ 01603 212396 ✉ andywatt@norwich.gov.uk

Transport Planner: Mr David Moorcroft , Executive Head - Regeneration & Development, City Hall, St. Peter's Street, Norwich NR2 1NH ☎ 01603 212225 ✉ davidmoorcroft@norwich.gov.uk

Transport Planner: Mr Andy Watt , City Development Services, City Hall, St. Peter's Street, Norwich NR2 1NH ☎ 01603 212396 ✉ andywatt@norwich.gov.uk

Waste Collection and Disposal: Mr Adrian Akester , Head of Citywide Services, City Hall, St. Peter's Street, Norwich NR2 1NH ☎ 01603 213521 ✉ adrianakester@norwich.gov.uk

Waste Management: Mr Adrian Akester, Head of Citywide Services, City Hall, St. Peter's Street, Norwich NR2 1NH ☎ 01603 213521 ✉ adrianakester@norwich.gov.uk

Children's Play Areas: Mr Simon Meek , Parks & Open Spaces Manager, City Hall, St. Peter's Street, Norwich NR2 1NH ☎ 01603 212403 ✉ simonmeek@norwich.gov.uk

COUNCILLORS

***Leader of the Council* Waters**, Alan (LAB - Crome)
a.waters@cllr.norwich.gov.uk

***Deputy Leader of the Council* Harris**, Gail (LAB - Catton Grove)
g.harris@cllr.norwich.gov.uk

Ackroyd, Carolyne (LD - Eaton)
c.ackroyd@cllr.norwich.gov.uk

Arthur, Brenda (LAB - University)
b.arthur@cllr.norwich.gov.uk

Blunt, Neil (GRN - Wensum)
n.blunt@cllr.norwich.gov.uk

Bogelein, Sandra (GRN - Wensum)
s.bogelein@cllr.norwich.gov.uk

Boswell, Andrew (GRN - Nelson)
a.boswell@cllr.norwich.gov.uk

Bradford, David (LAB - Crome)
d.bradford@cllr.norwich.gov.uk

Bremner, Bert (LAB - University)
b.bremner@cllr.norwich.gov.uk

Brociek-Coulton, Julie (LAB - Sewell)
j.brociekcoulton@cllr.norwich.gov.uk

Button, Sally (LAB - Bowthorpe)
s.button@cllr.norwich.gov.uk

Carlo, Denise (GRN - Nelson)
d.carlo@cllr.norwich.gov.uk

Coleshill, Ed (LAB - Sewell)
e.coleshill@cllr.norwich.gov.uk

Driver, Keith (LAB - Lakenham)
k.driver@cllr.norwich.gov.uk

Grahame, Lesley (GRN - Thorpe Hamlet)
l.grahame@cllr.norwich.gov.uk

Haynes, Ash (GRN - Town Close)
a.haynes@cllr.norwich.gov.uk

Henderson, Jo (GRN - Thorpe Hamlet)
j.henderson@cllr.norwich.gov.uk

Herries, Chris (LAB - Lakenham)
c.herries@cllr.norwich.gov.uk

Howard, Lucy (GRN - Mancroft)
l.howard@cllr.norwich.gov.uk

Jackson, Simeon (GRN - Mancroft)
s.jackson@cllr.norwich.gov.uk

Jones, Tim (GRN - Nelson)
t.jones@cllr.norwich.gov.uk

Kendrick, Paul (LAB - Catton Grove)
p.kendrick@cllr.norwich.gov.uk

Lubbock, Judith (LD - Eaton)
j.lubbock@cllr.norwich.gov.uk

Manning, Patrick (LAB - Lakenham)
p.manning@cllr.norwich.gov.uk

Maxwell, Marion (LAB - Crome)
m.maxwell@cllr.norwich.gov.uk

Neale, Paul (GRN - Town Close)
p.neale@cllr.norwich.gov.uk

Packer, Matthew (LAB - Sewell)
m.packer@cllr.norwich.gov.uk

Peek, Martin (LAB - Wensum)
m.peek@cllr.norwich.gov.uk

Price, Ben (GRN - Thorpe Hamlet)
b.price@cllr.norwich.gov.uk

Raby, David (GRN - Town Close)
d.raby@cllr.norwich.gov.uk

Ryan, Roger (LAB - University)
r.ryan@cllr.norwich.gov.uk

Sands, Susan (LAB - Bowthorpe)
s.sands@cllr.norwich.gov.uk

Sands, Mike (LAB - Bowthorpe)
m.sands@cllr.norwich.gov.uk

Schmierer, Martin (GRN - Mancroft)
m.schmierer@cllr.norwich.gov.uk

Stonard, Mike (LAB - Catton Grove)
m.stonard@cllr.norwich.gov.uk

Thomas, Vaughan (LAB - Mile Cross)
vaughan.thomas@cllr.norwich.gov.uk

Thomas, Vivien (LAB - Mile Cross)
vivien.thomas@cllr.norwich.gov.uk

Woollard, Charmain (LAB - Mile Cross)
c.woollard@cllr.norwich.gov.uk

Wright, James (LD - Eaton)
j.wright@cllr.norwich.gov.uk

POLITICAL COMPOSITION
LAB: 22, GRN: 14, LD: 3

COMMITTEE CHAIRS
Audit: Mr Paul Neale

Licensing: Ms Sally Button

Planning: Mr Mike Sands

Nottingham City U

Nottingham City Council, Loxley House, Station Street, Nottingham NG2 3NG
☎ 0115 915 5555 🖷 0115 915 4636 💻 www.nottinghamcity.gov.uk

FACTS AND FIGURES
Parliamentary Constituencies: Nottingham East, Nottingham North, Nottingham South
EU Constituencies: East Midlands
Election Frequency: Elections are of whole council

PRINCIPAL OFFICERS
Chief Executive: Mr Ian Curryer , Chief Executive, Loxley House, Station Street, Nottingham NG2 3NG ☎ 0115 876 3600
🖱 ian.curryer@nottinghamcity.gov.uk

Deputy Chief Executive: Mr David Bishop , Deputy Chief Executive - Corporate Director - Development & Growth, Loxley House, Station Street, Nottingham NG2 3NG ☎ 0115 876 3758
🖱 david.bishop@nottinghamcity.gov.uk

Senior Management: Ms Alison Michalska , Corporate Director - Children & Adults, Loxley House, Station Street, Nottingham NG2 3NG ☎ 0115 876 3332 🖱 alison.michalska@nottinghamcity.gov.uk

Senior Management: Mr Andy Vaughan , Strategic Director - Commercial & Neighbourhood Services, Loxley House, Station Street, Nottingham NG2 3NG ☎ 0115 876 5627
🖱 andy.vaughan@nottinghamcity.gov.uk

Building Control: Mr Robert De Rosa , Acting Head - Building Control, Loxley House, Station Street, Nottingham NG2 3NG
☎ 0115 876 4026 🖱 robert.derosa@nottinghamcity.gov.uk

Catering Services: Ms Liz Dobson, Head - Catering & Cleaning Services, Medway Building, Eastcroft Depot, London Road, Nottingham NG2 3AH ☎ 0115 876 1731 🖷 0115 876 1747
🖱 liz.dobson@nottinghamcity.gov.uk

Children / Youth Services: Mrs Candida Brudenell , Strategic Director - Early Intervention, Loxley House, Station Street, Nottingham NG2 3NG ☎ 0115 876 3609 ✉ candida.brudenell@nottinghamcity.gov.uk

Civil Registration: Ms Lucy Lee , Head of Civic Coronial & Celebratory Services, The Council House, Old Market Square, Nottingham NG1 2DT ☎ 0115 876 5480 ✉ lucy.lee@nottinghamcity.gov.uk

Community Safety: Ms Emma Orrock , Business Development Manager, Central Police Station, North Church Street, Nottingham NG1 4BH ☎ 0115 967 0999 ✉ emma.orrock@nottinghamcity.gov.uk

Computer Management: Mr Simon Salmon , Head of IT, Loxley House, Station Street, Nottingham NG2 3NG ☎ 0115 876 2301 ✉ simon.salmon@nottinghamcity.gov.uk

Consumer Protection and Trading Standards: Mr Richard Antcliff , Chief Licensing, Trading Standards & ASB Officer, Loxley House, Station Street, Nottingham NG2 3NG ☎ 0115 967 0999 ✉ richard.antcliff@nottinghamshire.pnn.police.uk

Customer Service: Ms Lynne North , Senior Customer Services Officer, Loxley House, Station Street, Nottingham NG2 3NG ☎ 0115 876 4950 ✉ lynne.north@nottinghamcity.gov.uk

Economic Development: Mr Chris Henning , Director - Economic Development, Loxley House, Station Street, Nottingham NG2 3NG ☎ 0115 876 4906 ✉ chris.henning@nottinghamcity.gov.uk

Education: Ms Alison Michalska , Corporate Director - Children & Adults, Loxley House, Station Street, Nottingham NG2 3NG ☎ 0115 876 3332 ✉ alison.michalska@nottinghamcity.gov.uk

Electoral Registration: Ms Sarah Wilson , Chief Elections Officer, Loxley House, Station Street, Nottingham NG2 3NG ☎ 0115 876 4308 ✉ sarah.wilson@nottinghamcity.gov.uk

Emergency Planning: Mr Paul Millward, Head - Resilience, Island Block, The Guildhall, Nottingham NG1 4BT ☎ 0115 876 2980 🖷 0115 876 3132 ✉ paul.millward@nottinghamcity.gov.uk

Energy Management: Ms Gail Scholes , Head - Energy Services, Loxley House, Station Street, Nottingham NG2 3NG ☎ 0115 876 5652 ✉ gail.scholes@nottinghamcity.gov.uk

Environmental Health: Mr Andy Vaughan , Strategic Director - Commercial & Neighbourhood Services, Loxley House, Station Street, Nottingham NG2 3NG ☎ 0115 876 5627 ✉ andy.vaughan@nottinghamcity.gov.uk

European Liaison: Mr John Connelly, Head - Regional & International Team, Loxley House, Station Street, Nottingham NG2 3NG ☎ 0115 876 4490 🖷 0115 876 3132 ✉ john.connelly@nottinghamcity.gov.uk

Events Manager: Ms Kate Collins , Conference & Events Manager, Royal Centre, Theatre Square, Nottingham NG1 5ND ☎ 0115 989 5530 ✉ kate.collins@nottinghamcity.gov.uk

Facilities: Mr Gary Shaw , FM Manager, Loxley House, Station Street, Nottingham NG2 3NG ☎ 0115 876 3098 ✉ gary.shaw@nottinghamcity.gov.uk

Fleet Management: Mr Tony Hall , Fleet Operations Manager, Humber Building, Eastcroft Depot, London Road, Nottingham NG2 3AH ☎ 0115 876 2198 ✉ tony.hall@nottinghamcity.gov.uk

Highways: Mr Chris Keane , Head of Highway & Energy Infrastructure, Humber Building, Eastcroft Depot, London Road, Nottingham NG2 3AH ☎ 0115 876 1363 ✉ chris.keane@nottinghamcity.gov.uk

Housing: Ms Gill Moy , Director - Housing, Loxley House, Station Street, Nottingham NG2 3NG ☎ 0115 915 7430 🖷 0115 915 5349 ✉ gill.moy@nottinghamcityhomes.org.uk

Legal: Mr Glen O'Connell , Director - Legal & Democratic Services & Monitoring Officer, Loxley House, Station Street, Nottingham NG2 3NG ☎ 0115 876 4330 🖷 0115 876 3132 ✉ glen.oconnell@nottinghamcity.gov.uk

Leisure and Cultural Services: Mr Nigel Hawkins , Head - Culture & Libraries, Loxley House, Station Street, Nottingham NG2 3NG ☎ 0115 876 4969 ✉ nigel.hawkins@nottinghamcity.gov.uk

Licensing: Ms Angela Rawson , Manager - Licensing, Tamar Building, Eastcroft Depot, London Road, Nottingham NG2 3AH ☎ 0115 876 1749 ✉ angela.rawson@nottinghamcity.gov.uk

Member Services: Ms Debra La Mola, Head - Democratic Services, Loxley House, Station Street, Nottingham NG2 3NG ☎ 0115 876 4292 🖷 0115 915 4812 ✉ debra.lamola@nottinghamcity.gov.uk

Parking: Mr Pete Mitchell , Head - Licensing, Permits & Regulations, Central Police Station, North Church Street, Nottingham NG1 4BH ☎ 0300 300 9999 🖷 0115 915 2258 ✉ pete.mitchell@nottinghamshire.pnn.police.uk

Planning: Ms Sue Flack , Director - Planning & Transport, Loxley House, Station Street, Nottingham NG2 3NG ☎ 0115 876 5896 ✉ sue.flack@nottinghamcity.gov.uk

Procurement: Ms Jo Pettifor , Strategic Procurement Manager, Loxley House, Station Street, Nottingham NG2 3NG ☎ 0115 876 5026 ✉ jo.pettifor@nottinghamcity.gov.uk

Recycling & Waste Minimisation: Mr Daniel Ayrton , Commercial Operations Manager, Tyne Building, Eastcroft Depot, London Road, Nottingham NG2 3AH ☎ 0115 876 1830 ✉ daniel.ayrton@nottinghamcity.gov.uk

Regeneration: Ms Gill Callingham , Regeneration Specialist, Loxley House, Station Street, Nottingham NG2 3NG ☎ 0115 876 3469 ✉ gill.callingham@nottinghamcity.gov.uk

Road Safety: Mr Francis Ashton , Service Manager - Accident Investigation Traffic & Safety, Loxley House, Station Street, Nottingham NG2 3NG ☎ 0115 876 5224 ✉ francis.ashton@nottinghamcity.gov.uk

Social Services: Ms Helen Jones , Director - Adult Social Care, Loxley House, Station Street, Nottingham NG2 3NG ☎ 0115 876 3504 helen.jones@nottinghamcity.gov.uk

Social Services (Adult): Ms Helen Jones , Director - Adult Social Care, Loxley House, Station Street, Nottingham NG2 3NG ☎ 0115 876 3504 helen.jones@nottinghamcity.gov.uk

Social Services (Children): Ms Helen Blackman , Director - Children's Social Care, Loxley House, Station Street, Nottingham NG2 3NG ☎ 0115 876 4710 helen.blackman@nottinghamcity.gov.uk

Public Health: Dr Chris Kenny , Director - Public Health, Loxley House, Station Street, Nottingham NG2 3NG ☎ 0115 876 5419 chris.kenny@nottscc.gov.uk

Staff Training: Ms Denise Willis , Development Manager, Loxley House, Station Street, Nottingham NG2 3NG ☎ 0115 876 3463 denise.willis@nottinghamcity.gov.uk

Street Scene: Mr Dave Halstead , Head - Neighbourhood Operations & Deputy Director of Commercial & Neighbourhood Services, Loxley House, Station Street, Nottingham NG2 3NG ☎ 0115 876 5634 dave.halstead@nottinghamcity.gov.uk

Tourism: Mr Simon Redgate , Tourism Centre Manager, Nottingham Tourist Centre, 1-4 Smithy Row, Nottingham NG1 2BY ☎ 0115 876 2969 simon.redgate@nottinghamcity.gov.uk

Traffic Management: Ms Caroline Nash , Service Manager - Traffic Management, Loxley House, Station Street, Nottingham NG2 3NG ☎ 0115 876 5243 🖷 0115 915 6550 caroline.nash@nottinghamcity.gov.uk

Transport: Mr Adrian Hill , Head - Commercial Development, Loxley House, Station Street, Nottingham NG2 3NG ☎ 0115 876 5632 adrian.hill@nottinghamcity.gov.uk

Transport Planner: Ms Kerry Perruzza , Senior Transport Planner, Loxley House, Station Street, Nottingham NG2 3NG ☎ 0115 876 3947 kerry.perruzza@nottinghamcity.gov.uk

Transport Planner: Mr Robert Smith , Senior Transport Planner, Loxley House, Station Street, Nottingham NG2 3NG ☎ 0115 876 3604 robert.smith@nottinghamcity.gov.uk

Waste Collection and Disposal: Mr Paul Marshall , Manager - Waste Operations, Tyne House, Eastcroft Depot, London Road, Nottingham NG2 3AH ☎ 0115 876 1834 paul.marshall@nottinghamcity.gov.uk

Waste Management: Mr Paul Marshall , Manager - Waste Operations, Tyne House, Eastcroft Depot, London Road, Nottingham NG2 3AH ☎ 0115 876 1834 paul.marshall@nottinghamcity.gov.uk

COUNCILLORS

***The Lord Mayor* Morris**, Jackie (LAB - Bulwell)
jackie.morris@nottinghamcity.gov.uk

***Sheriff* Saghir**, Mohammed (LAB - Leen Valley)
cllrmohammed.saghir@nottinghamcity.gov.uk

***Leader of the Council* Collins**, Jon (LAB - St Ann's)
jon.collins@nottinghamcity.gov.uk

***Deputy Leader of the Council* Chapman**, Graham (LAB - Aspley)
graham.chapman@nottinghamcity.gov.uk

***Group Leader* Culley**, Georgina (CON - Wollaton West)
georgina.culley@nottinghamcity.gov.uk

Ali, Liaqat (LAB - Radford and Park)
liaqat.ali@nottinghamcity.gov.uk

Armstrong, Jim (CON - Wollaton West)
jim.armstrong@nottinghamcity.gov.uk

Arnold, Cat (LAB - Basford)
cat.arnold@nottinghamcity.gov.uk

Ayoola, Leslie (LAB - Mapperley)
leslie.ayoola@nottinghamcity.gov.uk

Aziz, Ilyas (LAB - Radford and Park)
ilyas.aziz@nottinghamcity.gov.uk

Ball, Alex (LAB - Sherwood)
alex.ball@nottinghamcity.gov.uk

Battlemuch, Steve (LAB - Wollaton West)
steve.battlemuch@nottinghamcity.gov.uk

Bryan, Merlita (LAB - Arboretum)
merlita.bryan@nottinghamcity.gov.uk

Campbell, Eunice (LAB - Bulwell Forest)
eunice.campbell@nottinghamcity.gov.uk

Choudhry, Azad (LAB - Arboretum)
azad.choudhry@nottinghamcity.gov.uk

Clark, Alan (LAB - Bulwell Forest)
alan.clark@nottinghamcity.gov.uk

Cook, Josh (LAB - Clifton North)
josh.cook@nottinghamcity.gov.uk

Edwards, Michael (LAB - Bridge)
michael.edwards@nottinghamcity.gov.uk

Ferguson, Pat (LAB - Clifton North)
pat.ferguson@nottinghamcity.gov.uk

Gibson, Chris (LAB - Clifton South)
chris.gibson@nottinghamcity.gov.uk

Grocock, Brian (LAB - Bestwood)
brian.grocock@nottinghamcity.gov.uk

Hartshorne, John (LAB - Bulwell)
john.hartshorne@nottinghamcity.gov.uk

Healy, Rosemary (LAB - Mapperley)
rosemary.healy@nottinghamcity.gov.uk

Heaton, Nicola (LAB - Bridge)
nicola.heaton@nottinghamcity.gov.uk

Ibrahim, Mohammed (LAB - Berridge)
mohammed.ibrahim@nottinghamcity.gov.uk

Ifediora, Patience (LAB - Aspley)
patience.ifediora@nottinghamcity.gov.uk

Jenkins, Corall (LAB - Clifton South)
corall.jenkins@nottinghamcity.gov.uk

Jenkins, Glyn (LAB - Leen Valley)
glyn.jenkins@nottinghamcity.gov.uk

Johnson, Sue (LAB - St Ann's)
sue.johnson@nottinghamcity.gov.uk

Jones, Carole-Ann (LAB - Berridge)
carole-ann.jones@nottinghamcity.gov.uk

Khan, Neghat Nawaz (LAB - Dales)
neghat.khan@nottinghamcity.gov.uk

Khan, Gul (LAB - Dales)
gul.khan@nottinghamcity.gov.uk

Klein, Ginny (LAB - Bulwell)
ginny.klein@nottinghamcity.gov.uk

Liversidge, David (LAB - St Ann's)
dave.liversidge@nottinghamcity.gov.uk

Longford, Sally (LAB - Wollaton East and Lenton Abbey)
sally.longford@nottinghamcity.gov.uk

McCulloch, Carole (LAB - Aspley)
carole.mcculloch@nottinghamcity.gov.uk

McDonald, Nick (LAB - Bulwell Forest)
nick.mcdonald@nottinghamcity.gov.uk

Mellen, David (LAB - Dales)
david.mellen@nottinghamcity.gov.uk

Neal, Toby (LAB - Berridge)
toby.neal@nottinghamcity.gov.uk

Norris, Alex (LAB - Basford)
alex.norris@nottinghamcity.gov.uk

Parbutt, Brian (LAB - Sherwood)
brian.parbutt@nottinghamcity.gov.uk

Peach, Anne (LAB - Radford and Park)
anne.peach@nottinghamcity.gov.uk

Piper, Sarah (LAB - Dunkirk and Lenton)
sarah.piper@nottinghamcity.gov.uk

Rule, Andrew (CON - Clifton North)
andrew.rule@nottinghamcity.gov.uk

Smith, Wendy (LAB - Bilborough)
wendy.smith@nottinghamcity.gov.uk

Smith, David (LAB - Bestwood)
cllr-david smith@nottinghamcity.gov.uk

Tansley, Chris (LAB - Mapperley)
chris.tansley@nottinghamcity.gov.uk

Trimble, David (LAB - Dunkirk and Lenton)
dave.trimble@nottinghamcity.gov.uk

Urquhart, Jane (LAB - Sherwood)
jane.arquhart@nottinghamcity.gov.uk

Watson, Marcia (LAB - Bilborough)
marcia.watson@nottinghamcity.gov.uk

Webster, Sam (LAB - Wollaton East and Lenton Abbey)
sam.webster@nottinghamcity.gov.uk

Wildgust, Mick (LAB - Bestwood)
mick.wildgust@nottinghamcity.gov.uk

Wood, Malcolm (LAB - Bilborough)
malcolm.wood@nottinghamcity.gov.uk

Woodings, Linda (LAB - Basford)
linda.wooding@nottinghamcity.gov.uk

Young, Steve (LAB - Clifton South)
steve.young@nottinghamcity.gov.uk

POLITICAL COMPOSITION
LAB: 52, CON: 3

COMMITTEE CHAIRS
Audit: Ms Sarah Piper

Health & Wellbeing: Mr Alex Norris

Licensing: Mr Brian Grocock

Planning: Mr Chris Gibson

Nottinghamshire C

Nottinghamshire County Council, County Hall, West Bridgford NG2 7QP
☎ 0115 982 3823 🖷 0115 971 7945 ✉ enquiries@nottscc.gov.uk
💻 www.nottinghamshire.gov.uk

FACTS AND FIGURES
EU Constituencies: East Midlands
Election Frequency: Elections are of whole council

PRINCIPAL OFFICERS
Chief Executive: Mr Anthony May , Chief Executive, County Hall, West Bridgford NG2 7QP ☎ 0115 977 3582
✉ anthony.may@nottscc.gov.uk

Deputy Chief Executive: Mr David Pearson, Corporate Director - Adult Social Care, Health & Public Protection, County Hall, West Bridgford NG2 7QP ☎ 0115 977 4636
✉ david.pearson@nottscc.gov.uk

Senior Management: Ms Jayne Francis-Ward , Corporate Director - Policy, Planning & Corporate Services, County Hall, West Bridgford NG2 7QP ☎ 0115 977 3478
✉ jayne.francis-ward@nottscc.gov.uk

Senior Management: Mr Tim Gregory , Corporate Director - Environment & Resources, County Hall, West Bridgford NG2 7QP ☎ 0115 977 3404 ✉ tim.gregory@nottscc.gov.uk

Senior Management: Mr Derek Higton , Acting Corporate Director - Children, Families & Cultural Services, County Hall, West Bridgford NG2 7QP ☎ 0115 977 3498
✉ derek.higton@nottscc.gov.uk

Senior Management: Dr Chris Kenny , Director - Public Health, County Hall, West Bridgford NG2 7QP ☎ 0115 876 5419
✉ chris.kenny@nottscc.gov.uk

Senior Management: Mr David Pearson, Corporate Director - Adult Social Care, Health & Public Protection, County Hall, West Bridgford NG2 7QP ☎ 0115 977 4636
✉ david.pearson@nottscc.gov.uk

Access Officer / Social Services (Disability): Mr Paul McKay, Service Director - Access & Public Protection, County Hall, West Bridgford NG2 7QP ☎ 0115 977 3909
✉ paul.mckay@nottscc.gov.uk

Architect, Building / Property Services: Mr Tim Gregory , Corporate Director - Environment & Resources, County Hall, West Bridgford NG2 7QP ☎ 0115 977 3404 ✉ tim.gregory@nottscc.gov.uk

Architect, Building / Property Services: Mr Jas Hundal , Service Director - Transport, Property & Environment, Trent Bridge House, Fox Road, West Bridgford NG2 6BJ ☎ 0115 977 4257 ✉ jas.hundal@nottscc.gov.uk

Catering Services: Mr Jas Hundal , Service Director - Transport, Property & Environment, Trent Bridge House, Fox Road, West Bridgford NG2 6BJ ☎ 0115 977 4257 ✉ jas.hundal@nottscc.gov.uk

Catering Services: Mr Kevin McKay, Group Manager - Catering & Facilities Management, County Hall, West Bridgford NG2 7QP ☎ 0115 977 4369 ✉ kevin.mckay@nottscc.gov.uk

Children / Youth Services: Mr Steve Edwards , Service Director - Children's Social Care, County Hall, West Bridgford NG2 7QP ☎ 0115 977 4782 🖷 0115 977 2420 ✉ steve.edwards@nottscc.gov.uk

Children / Youth Services: Mr Derek Higton , Acting Corporate Director - Children, Families & Cultural Services, County Hall, West Bridgford NG2 7QP ☎ 0115 977 3498 ✉ derek.higton@nottscc.gov.uk

Children / Youth Services: Mr Chris Warren , Group Manager - Young People's Service, County Hall, West Bridgford NG2 7QP ☎ 0115 977 4430 ✉ christopher.warren@nottscc.gov.uk

Civil Registration: Mr Rob Fisher, Group Manager - Emergency Management & Registration, County Hall, West Bridgford NG2 7QP ☎ 0115 977 3681 ✉ rob.fisher@nottscc.gov.uk

Civil Registration: Mr Paul McKay, Service Director - Access & Public Protection, County Hall, West Bridgford NG2 7QP ☎ 0115 977 3909 ✉ paul.mckay@nottscc.gov.uk

PR / Communications: Mr Martin Done , Service Director - Communications & Marketing, County Hall, West Bridgford NG2 7QP ☎ 0115 977 2026 ✉ martin.done@nottscc.gov.uk

Community Planning: Ms Sally Gill , Group Manager - Planning, Community & Voluntary Team, County Hall, West Bridgford NG2 7QP ☎ 0115 993 2608 ✉ sally.gill@nottscc.gov.uk

Computer Management: Mr Tim Gregory , Corporate Director - Environment & Resources, County Hall, West Bridgford NG2 7QP ☎ 0115 977 3404 ✉ tim.gregory@nottscc.gov.uk

Computer Management: Mr Ivor Nicholson , Service Director - ICT, County Hall, West Bridgford NG2 7QP ☎ 0115 977 3300 ✉ ivor.nicholson@nottscc.gov.uk

Consumer Protection and Trading Standards: Mr Paul McKay, Service Director - Access & Public Protection, County Hall, West Bridgford NG2 7QP ☎ 0115 977 3909 ✉ paul.mckay@nottscc.gov.uk

Contracts: Ms Clare Winter , Group Manager - Procurement, County Hall, West Bridgford NG2 7QP ☎ 0115 977 2619 ✉ clare.winter@nottscc.gov.uk

Corporate Services: Ms Jayne Francis-Ward , Corporate Director - Policy, Planning & Corporate Services, County Hall, West Bridgford NG2 7QP ☎ 0115 977 3478 ✉ jayne.francis-ward@nottscc.gov.uk

Corporate Services: Ms Celia Morris , Group Manager - Corporate Strategy, Trent Bridge House, Fox Road, West Bridgford NG2 6BJ ☎ 0115 977 2043 ✉ celia.morris@nottscc.gov.uk

Customer Service: Ms Marie Rowney , Group Manager - Customer Services, Customer Service Centre, Mercury House, Little Oak Drive, Sherwood Business Park, Nottingham NG15 0DR ☎ 01623 434901 ✉ marie.rowney@nottscc.gov.uk

Customer Service: Ms Marjorie Toward , Service Director - HR & Customer Services, County Hall, West Bridgford NG2 7QP ☎ 0115 977 4404 ✉ marje.toward@nottscc.gov.uk

Economic Development: Mr Matthew Lockley , Team Manager - Economic Development, County Hall, West Bridgford NG2 7QP ☎ 0115 977 2446 ✉ matthew.lockley@nottscc.gov.uk

Education: Mr Derek Higton , Acting Corporate Director - Children, Families & Cultural Services, County Hall, West Bridgford NG2 7QP ☎ 0115 977 3498 ✉ derek.higton@nottscc.gov.uk

Education: Mr John Slater, Service Director - Education Standards & Inclusion, County Hall, West Bridgford NG2 7QP ☎ 0115 977 3589 🖷 0115 981 2824 ✉ john.slater@nottscc.gov.uk

E-Government: Mr Ivor Nicholson , Service Director - ICT, County Hall, West Bridgford NG2 7QP ☎ 0115 977 3300 ✉ ivor.nicholson@nottscc.gov.uk

Emergency Planning: Mr Rob Fisher, Group Manager - Emergency Management & Registration, County Hall, West Bridgford NG2 7QP ☎ 0115 977 3681 ✉ rob.fisher@nottscc.gov.uk

Emergency Planning: Mr Paul McKay, Service Director - Access & Public Protection, County Hall, West Bridgford NG2 7QP ☎ 0115 977 3909 ✉ paul.mckay@nottscc.gov.uk

Energy Management: Mr Mick Allen , Group Manager - Waste & Energy Management, Trent Bridge House, Fox Road, West Bridgford NG2 6BJ ☎ 0115 977 4684 ✉ mick.allen@nottscc.gov.uk

Estates, Property & Valuation: Mr Jas Hundal , Service Director - Transport, Property & Environment, Trent Bridge House, Fox Road, West Bridgford NG2 6BJ ☎ 0115 977 4257 ✉ jas.hundal@nottscc.gov.uk

Facilities: Mr Kevin McKay, Group Manager - Catering & Facilities Management, Trent Bridge House, Fox Road, West Bridgford NG2 6BJ ☎ 0115 977 4369 ✉ kevin.mckay@nottscc.gov.uk

Treasury: Ms Jane Gannon , Finance Officer, County Hall, West Bridgford NG2 7QP ☎ 0115 977 4176 ✉ jane.gannon@nottscc.gov.uk

Pensions: Mr Simon Cunnington , Senior Accountant, Pensions Office, Business Support Centre, County Hall, West Bridgford NG2 7QP ☎ 0115 977 2581 ✉ simon.cunnington@nottsc.gov.uk

Pensions: Mr John Fairbanks , Pensions Manager, BSC, Oak House, Ruddington Fields Business Park, Ruddington, Nottingham NG11 6JW ☎ 0115 846 3347 ✉ john.fairbanks@nottsc.gov.uk

Fleet Management: Mr Neil Hodgson , Acting Service Director - Highways, Trent Bridge House, Fox Road, West Bridgford NG2 6BJ ☎ 0115 977 2720 ✉ neil.hodgson@nottscc.gov.uk

Grounds Maintenance: Mr Neil Hodgson , Acting Service Director - Highways, Trent Bridge House, Fox Road, West Bridgford NG2 6BJ ☎ 0115 977 2720 ✉ neil.hodgson@nottscc.gov.uk

Health and Safety: Mr John Nilan , Team Manager - Health & Safety, Lawn View House, Station Road, Sutton-in-Ashfield NG17 5GA ☎ 01623 434560 ✉ john.nilan@nottscc.gov.uk

Highways: Mr Neil Hodgson , Acting Service Director - Highways, Trent Bridge House, Fox Road, West Bridgford NG2 6BJ ☎ 0115 977 2720 ✉ neil.hodgson@nottscc.gov.uk

Legal: Ms Heather Dickinson , Group Manager - Legal Services, County Hall, West Bridgford NG2 7QP ☎ 0115 977 4835 ✉ heather.dickinson@nottscc.gov.uk

Legal: Ms Jayne Francis-Ward , Corporate Director - Policy, Planning & Corporate Services, County Hall, West Bridgford NG2 7QP ☎ 0115 977 3478 ✉ jayne.francis-ward@nottscc.gov.uk

Leisure and Cultural Services: Mr Steve Bradley , Group Manager - Cultural & Enrichment Services, County Hall, West Bridgford NG2 7QP ☎ 0115 977 2715 ✉ steve.bradley@nottscc.gov.uk

Leisure and Cultural Services: Mr Derek Higton , Service Director - Youth, Families & Culture, County Hall, West Bridgford NG2 7QP ☎ 0115 977 3498 ✉ derek.higton@nottscc.gov.uk

Lifelong Learning: Mr Peter Gaw , Group Manager - Libraries, Archives, Information & Learning, County Hall, West Bridgford NG2 7QP ☎ 0115 977 4201 ✉ peter.gaw@nottscc.gov.uk

Lifelong Learning: Ms Sue Green, Adult & Community Learning Services Manager, County Hall, West Bridgford NG2 7QP ☎ 0115 977 2875 ✉ sue.green@nottscc.gov.uk

Lighting: Mr Neil Hodgson , Acting Service Director - Highways, Trent Bridge House, Fox Road, West Bridgford NG2 6BJ ☎ 0115 977 2720 ✉ neil.hodgson@nottscc.gov.uk

Lighting: Mr Gary Wood , Group Manager - Transport Policy & Programmes, Trent Bridge House, Fox Road, West Bridgford NG2 6BJ ☎ 0115 977 4270 ✉ gary.wood@nottscc.gov.uk

Member Services: Mr Keith Ford , Team Manager - Democratic Services, County Hall, West Bridgford NG2 7QP ☎ 0115 977 2590 ✉ keith.ford@nottscc.gov.uk

Parking: Mr Peter Goode , Traffic Manager, County Hall, West Bridgford NG2 7QP ☎ 0115 977 4269 ✉ peter.goode@nottscc.gov.uk

Personnel / HR: Mr Tim Gregory , Corporate Director - Environment & Resources, County Hall, West Bridgford NG2 7QP ☎ 0115 977 3404 ✉ tim.gregory@nottscc.gov.uk

Personnel / HR: Ms Marjorie Toward , Service Director - HR & Customer Services, County Hall, West Bridgford NG2 7QP ☎ 0115 977 4404 ✉ marje.toward@nottscc.gov.uk

Planning: Ms Sally Gill , Group Manager - Planning, Community & Voluntary Team, County Hall, West Bridgford NG2 7QP ☎ 0115 993 2608 ✉ sally.gill@nottscc.gov.uk

Procurement: Ms Clare Winter , Group Manager - Procurement, County Hall, West Bridgford NG2 7QP ☎ 0115 977 2619 ✉ clare.winter@nottscc.gov.uk

Public Libraries: Mr Peter Gaw , Group Manager - Libraries, Archives, Information & Learning, County Hall, West Bridgford NG2 7QP ☎ 0115 977 4201 ✉ peter.gaw@nottscc.gov.uk

Recycling & Waste Minimisation: Mr Mick Allen , Group Manager - Waste & Energy Management, Trent Bridge House, Fox Road, West Bridgford NG2 6BJ ☎ 0115 977 4684 ✉ mick.allen@nottscc.gov.uk

Regeneration: Mr Matthew Lockley , Team Manager - Economic Development, County Hall, West Bridgford NG2 7QP ☎ 0115 977 2446 ✉ matthew.lockley@nottscc.gov.uk

Road Safety: Ms Suzanne Heydon , Group Manager - Highway Safety, Trent Bridge House, Fox Road, West Bridgford NG2 6BJ ☎ 0115 977 4487 ✉ suzanne.heydon@nottscc.gov.uk

Social Services: Mr David Pearson, Corporate Director - Adult Social Care, Health & Public Protection, County Hall, West Bridgford NG2 7QP ☎ 0115 977 4636 ✉ david.pearson@nottscc.gov.uk

Social Services (Adult): Ms Caroline Baria , Service Director - South Nottinghamshire, County Hall, West Bridgford NG2 7QP ☎ 0115 977 3985 ✉ caroline.baria@nottscc.gov.uk

Social Services (Adult): Ms Sue Batty , Acting Service Director - Mid & North Nottinghamshire, County Hall, West Bridgford NG2 7QP ☎ 0115 977 4876 ✉ sue.batty@nottscc.gov.uk

Social Services (Children): Mr Steve Edwards , Service Director - Children's Social Care, County Hall, West Bridgford NG2 7QP ☎ 0115 977 4782 🖷 0115 977 2420 ✉ steve.edwards@nottscc.gov.uk

Social Services (Children): Mr Derek Higton , Acting Corporate Director - Children, Families & Cultural Services, County Hall, West Bridgford NG2 7QP ☎ 0115 977 3498 ✉ derek.higton@nottscc.gov.uk

Social Services (Children): Ms Pam Rosseter , Group Manager - Safeguarding & Independent Review, County Hall, West Bridgford NG2 7QP ☎ 0115 977 3921 ✉ pam.rosseter@nottscc.gov.uk

Public Health: Miss Sarah Everest , Senior Public Health & Commissioning Manager, County Hall, West Bridgford NG2 7QP

Public Health: Dr Chris Kenny , Director - Public Health, County Hall, West Bridgford NG2 7QP ☎ 0115 876 5419 ✉ chris.kenny@nottscc.gov.uk

Staff Training: Ms Marjorie Toward , Service Director - HR & Customer Services, County Hall, West Bridgford NG2 7QP ☎ 0115 977 4404 ✉ marje.toward@nottscc.gov.uk

Tourism: Mr Steve Bradley , Group Manager - Cultural & Enrichment Services, County Hall, West Bridgford NG2 7QP ☎ 0115 977 2715 ✉ steve.bradley@nottscc.gov.uk

Tourism: Mr Derek Higton , Acting Corporate Director - Children, Families & Cultural Services, County Hall, West Bridgford NG2 7QP ☎ 0115 977 3498 ✉ derek.higton@nottscc.gov.uk

Traffic Management: Mr Chris Charnley , Group Manager - Highways Management, County Hall, West Bridgford NG2 7QP ☎ 0115 977 2065 ✉ chris.charnley@nottscc.gov.uk

Traffic Management: Mr Peter Goode , Traffic Manager, County Hall, West Bridgford NG2 7QP ☎ 0115 977 4269 ✉ peter.goode@nottscc.gov.uk

Transport: Mr Neil Hodgson , Acting Service Director - Highways, Trent Bridge House, Fox Road, West Bridgford NG2 6BJ ☎ 0115 977 2720 ✉ neil.hodgson@nottscc.gov.uk

Transport Planner: Mr Mark Hudson , Group Manager - Transport & Travel Services, County Hall, West Bridgford NG2 7QP ☎ 0115 977 4519 ✉ mark.hudson@nottscc.gov.uk

Transport Planner: Mr Gary Wood , Group Manager - Transport Policy & Programmes, Trent Bridge House, Fox Road, West Bridgford NG2 6BJ ☎ 0115 977 4270 ✉ gary.wood@nottscc.gov.uk

Waste Management: Mr Mick Allen , Group Manager - Waste & Energy Management, Trent Bridge House, Fox Road, West Bridgford NG2 6BJ ☎ 0115 977 4684 ✉ mick.allen@nottscc.gov.uk

COUNCILLORS

***Chair* Fielding**, Sybil (LAB - Worksop North)
cllr.sybil.fielding@nottscc.gov.uk

***Leader of the Council* Rhodes**, Alan (LAB - Worksop North East and Carlton)
cllr.alan.rhodes@nottscc.gov.uk

***Deputy Leader of the Council* Bosnjak**, Joyce (LAB - Mansfield North)
cllr.joyce.bosnjak@nottscc.gov.uk

Adair, Reg (CON - Ruddington)
cllr.reg.adair@nottscc.gov.uk

Allan, Pauline (LAB - Arnold North)
cllr.pauline.allan@nottscc.gov.uk

Allan, Roy (LAB - Arnold South)
cllr.roy.allan@nottscc.gov.uk

Allin, John (LAB - Warsop)
cllr.john.allin@nottscc.gov.uk

Barnfather, Chris (CON - Newstead)
cllr.chris.barnfather@nottscc.gov.uk

Bell, Alan (LAB - Mansfield East)
cllr.alan.bell@nottscc.gov.uk

Brooks, Nikki (LAB - Carlton East)
cllr.nicki.brooks@nottscc.gov.uk

Brown, Andrew (CON - Soar Valley)
cllr.andrew1.brown@nottscc.gov.uk

Butler, Richard (CON - Cotgrave)
cllr.richard.butler@nottscc.gov.uk

Calvert, Steve (LAB - West Bridgford Central & South)
cllr.steve.calvert@nottscc.gov.uk

Campbell, Ian (LAB - Retford West)
cllr.ian.campbell@nottscc.gov.uk

Carr, Steve (LD - Beeston North)
cllr.steve.carr@nottscc.gov.uk

Carroll, Steve (LAB - Sutton in Ashfield East)
cllr.steven.carroll@nottscc.gov.uk

Clarke, John (LAB - Carlton East)
cllr.john.clarke@nottscc.gov.uk

Cottee, John (CON - Keyworth)
cllr.john.cottee@nottscc.gov.uk

Creamer, Jim (LAB - Carlton West)
cllr.jim.creamer@nottscc.gov.uk

Cutts, Kay (CON - Radcliffe-on-Trent)
cllr.katherine.cutts@nottscc.gov.uk

Dobson, Maureen (IND - Collingham)
cllr.maureen.dobson@nottscc.gov.uk

Doddy, John (CON - Chilwell and Toton)

Elliot, Boyd (CON - Calverton)
cllr.boyd.elliot@nottscc.gov.uk

Foale, Kate (LAB - Beeston South & Attenborough)
cllr.kate.foale@nottscc.gov.uk

Garner, Stephen (IND - Mansfield South)
cllr.stephen.garner@nottscc.gov.uk

Gilfoyle, Glynn (LAB - Worksop East)
cllr.glyn.gilfoyle@nottscc.gov.uk

Greaves, Kevin (LAB - Worksop West)
cllr.kevin.greaves@nottscc.gov.uk

Grice, Alice (LAB - Hucknall)
cllr.alice.grice@nottscc.gov.uk

Handley, John (CON - Beauvale)
cllr.john.handley@nottscc.gov.uk

Harwood, Colleen (LAB - Mansfield East)
cllr.collen.harwood@nottscc.gov.uk

Heptinstall, Stan (LD - Bramcote and Stapleford)
cllr.stan.heptinstall@nottscc.gov.uk

Hollis, Tom (LD - Sutton in Ashfield West)
tom@aldmail.co.uk

Jackson, Roger (CON - Farnsfield & Lowdham)
cllr.roger.jackson@nottscc.gov.uk

Jackson, Richard (CON - Chilwell and Toton)
cllr.richard.jackson@nottscc.gov.uk

Kirkham, David (LAB - Sutton in Ashfield Central)
cllr.david.kirkham@nottscc.gov.uk

Knight, John (LAB - Kirkby in Ashfield North)
cllr.john.knight@nottscc.gov.uk

Langton, Darren (LAB - Mansfield West)
cllr.darren.langton@nottscc.gov.uk

Laughton, Bruce (CON - Southwell and Caunton)
cllr.bruce.laughton@nottscc.gov.uk

Longdon, Keith (LD - Eastwood)
cllr.keith.longdon@nottscc.gov.uk

Madden, Rachel (LD - Kirkby in Ashfield South)
cllr.rachel.madden@nottscc.gov.uk

Meale, Diana (LAB - Mansfield West)
cllr.diana.meale@nottscc.gov.uk

Ogle, John (CON - Tuxford)
cllr.john.ogle@nottscc.gov.uk

Owen, Philip (CON - Nuthall)
cllr.philip.owen@nottscc.gov.uk

Payne, Michael (LAB - Arnold North)
cllr.michael.payne@nottscc.gov.uk

Peck, John (LAB - Rufford)
cllr.john.peck@nottscc.gov.uk

Place, Sheila (LAB - Blyth and Harworth)
cllr.sheila.place@nottscc.gov.uk

Plant, Liz (LAB - West Bridgford Central & South)
cllr.liz.plant@nottscc.gov.uk

Pringle, Mike (LAB - Ollerton)
cllr.mike.pringle@nottscc.gov.uk

Pulk, Darrell (LAB - Carlton West)
cllr.darrell.pulk@nottscc.gov.uk

Rigby, Ken (LD - Kimberley and Trowell)
cllr.ken.rigby@nottscc.gov.uk

Roberts, Tony (CON - Newark West)
cllr.tony.roberts@nottscc.gov.uk

Saddington, Sue (CON - Farndon and Muskham)
cllr.susan.saddington@nottscc.gov.uk

Sissons, Andy (IND - Mansfield South)
cllr.andy.sissons@nottscc.gov.uk

Skelding, Pamela (LAB - Retford East)
cllr.pamela.skelding@nottscc.gov.uk

Suthers, Martin (CON - Bingham)
cllr.martin.suthers@nottscc.gov.uk

Tsimbiridis, Parry (LAB - Mansfield North)
cllr.parry.tsimbiridis@nottscc.gov.uk

Turner, Gail (IND - Selston)
cllr.gail.turner@nottscc.gov.uk

Walker, Keith (CON - Balderton)
cllr.keith.walker@nottscc.gov.uk

Wallace, Stuart (CON - Newark East)
cllr.stuart.wallace@nottscc.gov.uk

Weisz, Muriel (LAB - Arnold South)
cllr.muriel.weisz@nottscc.gov.uk

Wheeler, Gordon (CON - West Bridgford West)
cllr.gordon.wheeler@nottscc.gov.uk

Wilkinson, John (LAB - Hucknall)
cllr.john.hucknall@nottscc.gov.uk

Williams, Jacky (LD - Bramcote and Stapleford)
cllr.jacky.williams@nottscc.gov.uk

Wilmott, John (LAB - Hucknall)
cllr.john.wilmott@nottscc.gov.uk

Woodhead, Yvonne (LAB - Blidworth)
cllr.yvonne.woodhead@nottscc.gov.uk

Yates, Liz (CON - Misterton)
cllr.liz.yates@nottscc.gov.uk

Zadrozny, Jason (LD - Sutton in Ashfield North)
cllr.jason.zadrozny@nottscc.gov.uk

POLITICAL COMPOSITION
LAB: 34, CON: 21, LD: 8, IND: 4

COMMITTEE CHAIRS
Adult Social Care & Health: Ms Muriel Weisz

Audit: Mr Keith Walker

Children & Young People: Mr John Peck

Economic Development: Ms Diana Meale

Health & Wellbeing: Ms Joyce Bosnjak

Planning & Licensing: Mr John Wilkinson

Transport & Highways: Mr Kevin Greaves

Nuneaton & Bedworth D

Nuneaton & Bedworth Borough Council, Town Hall, Nuneaton CV11 5AA
☎ 024 7637 6376 🖷 024 7637 6583
💻 www.nuneatonandbedworth.gov.uk

FACTS AND FIGURES
Parliamentary Constituencies: Nuneaton
EU Constituencies: West Midlands
Election Frequency: Elections are biennial

PRINCIPAL OFFICERS
Chief Executive: Mr Alan Franks , Managing Director, Town Hall, Nuneaton CV11 5AA ☎ 024 7637 6438
🖱 alan.franks@nuneatonandbedworth.gov.uk

Senior Management: Mr Brent Davis, Director of Assets & Street Services, Council House, Nuneaton CV11 5AA ☎ 024 7637 6347
🖷 024 7637 6465 🖱 brent.davis@nuneatonandbedworth.gov.uk

Senior Management: Mrs Dawn Dawson, Director of Housing & Communities, Town Hall, Nuneaton CV11 5AA ☎ 024 7637 6408
🖱 dawn.dawson@nuneatonandbedworth.gov.uk

Senior Management: Mrs Simone Donaghy , Director of Corporate Finance & Procurement, Town Hall, Nuneaton CV11 5AA ☎ 024 7637 6264 🖱 simone.donaghy@nuneatonandbedworth.gov.uk

Senior Management: Mr Ian Powell, Director of Regeneration & Public Protection, Town Hall, Nuneaton CV11 5AA ☎ 024 7637 6396
🖷 0870 608 9492 🖱 ian.powell@nuneatonandbedworth.gov.uk

Senior Management: Mr Philip Richardson, Director of Governance & Recreation, Town Hall, Nuneaton CV11 5AA ☎ 024 7637 6233 🖷 0870 608 9457 ✉ philip.richardson@nuneatonandbedworth.gov.uk

Senior Management: Ms Chris Tydeman , Director of Business Improvement, Town Hall, Nuneaton CV11 5AA

Architect, Building / Property Services: Mr Brent Davis, Director of Assets & Street Services, Council House, Nuneaton CV11 5AA ☎ 024 7637 6347 🖷 024 7637 6465 ✉ brent.davis@nuneatonandbedworth.gov.uk

Building Control: Mr Kevin Bunsell , Head of Building Control, Town Hall, Nuneaton CV11 5AA ☎ 024 7637 6521 ✉ kevin.bunsell@nuneatonandbedworth.gov.uk

PR / Communications: Mr Andrew Daw , Communications & Events Manager, Town Hall, Nuneaton CV11 5AA ☎ 024 7637 6372 ✉ andrew.daw@nuneatonandbedworth.gov.uk

Corporate Services: Mrs Linda Downes , Head of Internal Audit, Town Hall, Nuneaton CV11 5AA ☎ 024 7637 6260 ✉ linda.downes@nuneatonandbedworth.gov.uk

Economic Development: Mr Les Snowdon, Head of Estates & Town Centres, Town Hall, Nuneaton CV11 5AA ☎ 024 7637 6376 ✉ les.snowdon@nuneatonandbedworth.gov.uk

Electoral Registration: Mrs Debbie Davies , Principal Democratic Services Offices, Town Hall, Nuneaton CV11 5AA ☎ 024 7637 6221 ✉ debbie.davies@nuneatonandbedworth.gov.uk

Environmental Health: Mr Ian Powell, Director of Regeneration & Public Protection, Town Hall, Nuneaton CV11 5AA ☎ 024 7637 6396 🖷 0870 608 9492 ✉ ian.powell@nuneatonandbedworth.gov.uk

Estates, Property & Valuation: Mr Les Snowdon, Head of Estates & Town Centres, Town Hall, Nuneaton CV11 5AA ☎ 024 7637 6376 ✉ les.snowdon@nuneatonandbedworth.gov.uk

Events Manager: Mr Andrew Daw , Communications & Events Manager, Town Hall, Nuneaton CV11 5AA ☎ 024 7637 6372 ✉ andrew.daw@nuneatonandbedworth.gov.uk

Treasury: Mr Craig Pugh , Treasury & Technical Manager, Council House, Nuneaton CV11 5AA ☎ 024 7637 6376 ✉ craig.pugh@nuneatonandbedworth.gov.uk

Health and Safety: Mr John Ashton , Health & Safety Manager, Town Hall, Nuneaton CV11 5AA ☎ 024 7637 6213 ✉ john.ashton@nuneatonandbedworth.gov.uk

Housing Maintenance: Mr Brent Davis, Director of Assets & Street Services, Council House, Nuneaton CV11 5AA ☎ 024 7637 6347 🖷 024 7637 6465 ✉ brent.davis@nuneatonandbedworth.gov.uk

Legal: Mr Philip Richardson, Director of Governance & Recreation, Town Hall, Nuneaton CV11 5AA ☎ 024 7637 6233 🖷 0870 608 9457 ✉ philip.richardson@nuneatonandbedworth.gov.uk

Licensing: Mr Ian Powell, Director of Regeneration & Public Protection, Town Hall, Nuneaton CV11 5AA ☎ 024 7637 6396 🖷 0870 608 9492 ✉ ian.powell@nuneatonandbedworth.gov.uk

Member Services: Mrs Pam Matthews , Senior Democratic Services Officer, Town Hall, Nuneaton CV11 5AA ☎ 024 7637 6204 ✉ pam.matthews@nuneatonandbedworth.gov.uk

Recycling & Waste Minimisation: Ms Sue Cummine , Waste Reduction & Compliance Officer, St. Mary's Road Depot, Nuneaton CV11 5AR ☎ 024 7637 6025 ✉ sue.cummine@nuneatonandbedworth.gov.uk

Waste Collection and Disposal: Mr Glen McGrandle , Head of Waste & Transport, St Mary's Road Depot, Nuneaton CV11 5AA ☎ 024 7637 6049 ✉ glen.mcgrandle@nuneatonandbedworth.gov.uk

Waste Management: Mr Glen McGrandle , Head of Waste & Transport, St Mary's Road Depot, Nuneaton CV11 5AA ☎ 024 7637 6049 ✉ glen.mcgrandle@nuneatonandbedworth.gov.uk

COUNCILLORS

***Mayor* Longden**, Barry (LAB - Kingswood)
barry.longden@nuneatonandbedworth.gov.uk

***Deputy Mayor* Sheppard**, Jill (LAB - Abbey)
jill.sheppard@nuneatonandbedworth.gov.uk

***Leader of the Council* Harvey**, Dennis (LAB - Camp Hill)
dennis.harvey@nuneatonandbedworth.gov.uk

***Deputy Leader of the Council* Jackson**, Julie (LAB - Wem Brook)
julie.jackson@nuneatonandbedworth.gov.uk

Aldington, Danny (LAB - Heath)
danny.aldington@nuneatonandbedworth.gov.uk

Beaumont, John (LAB - Bulkington)
john.beaumont@nuneatonandbedworth.gov.uk

Bennett, Christine (LAB - Galley Common)
christine.bennett@nuneatonbedworth.gov.uk

Bonner, Ian (GRN - Weddington)
ian.bonner@nuneatonbedworth.gov.uk

Copland, Robert (LAB - Poplar)
bob.copland@nuneatonandbedworth.gov.uk

Doherty, Terry (LAB - Bulkington)
terry.doherty@nuneatonandbedworth.gov.uk

Doughty, Sara (LAB - Exhall)
sara.doughty@nuneatonandbedworth.gov.uk

Elliott, Tricia (LAB - Bar Pool)
patricia.elliott@nuneatonandbedworth.gov.uk

Foster, James (CON - St Nicholas)
james.foster@nuneatonandbedworth.gov.uk

Fowler, Dianne (LAB - Slough)
dianne.fowler@nuneatonandbedworth.gov.uk

Glass, John (LAB - Poplar)
john.glass@nuneatonandbedworth.gov.uk

Grant, Nicholas (CON - Whitestone)
nick.grant@nuneatonandbedworth.gov.uk

Hancox, William (LAB - Bede)
bill.hancox@nuneatonandbedworth.gov.uk

NUNEATON & BEDWORTH

Hawkes, Brian (LAB - Heath)
brian.hawkes@nuneatonandbedworth.gov.uk

Haynes, John (LAB - Bede)
john.haynes@nuneatonandbedworth.gov.uk

Hickling, Paul (LAB - Galley Common)
paul.hickling@nuneatonandbedworth.gov.uk

Kondakor, Keith (GRN - Weddington)
keith.kondakor@nuneatonandbedworth.gov.uk

Lloyd, Anthony (LAB - Slough)
anthony.lloyd@nuneatonandbedworth.gov.uk

Lloyd, Ian (LAB - Camp Hill)
ian.lloyd@nuneatonandbedworth.gov.uk

Margrave, Sam (LAB - Attleborough)
sam.margrave@nuneatonandbedworth.gov.uk

Navarro, Don (LAB - Arbury)
don.navarro@nuneatonandbedworth.gov.uk

Phillips, Caroline (LAB - Arbury)
caroline.phillips@nuneatonandbedworth.gov.uk

Phillips, Neil (LAB - Abbey)
neil.phillips@nuneatonandbedworth.gov.uk

Pomfrett, Gwynne (LAB - Bar Pool)
gwynne.pomfrett@nuneatonandbedworth.gov.uk

Sheppard, Tracy (LAB - Wem Brook)
tracy.sheppard@nuneatonbedworth.gov.uk

Tandy, June (LAB - Attleborough)
june.tandy@nuneatonandbedworth.gov.uk

Taylor, Roma (LAB - Exhall)
roma.taylor@nuneatonandbedworth.gov.uk

Tromans, Rob (CON - St Nicholas)
robert.tromans@nuneatonandbedworth.gov.uk

Watkins, Christopher (LAB - Kingswood)
christopher.watkins@nuneatonandbedworth.gov.uk

Wilson, Kristofer (CON - Whitestone)
kristofer.wilson@nuneatonandbedworth.gov.uk

POLITICAL COMPOSITION

LAB: 28, CON: 4, GRN: 2

COMMITTEE CHAIRS

Audit: Mr John Haynes

Licensing: Mr Robert Copland

Planning Applications: Mr William Hancox

Oadby & Wigston D

Oadby & Wigston Borough Council, Council Offices, Station Road, Wigston LE18 2DR
☎ 0116 288 8961 🖷 0116 288 7828
🖳 www.oadby-wigston.gov.uk

FACTS AND FIGURES

Parliamentary Constituencies: Harborough
EU Constituencies: East Midlands
Election Frequency: Elections are of whole council

PRINCIPAL OFFICERS

Chief Executive: Mr Mark Hall , Chief Executive, Council Offices, Station Road, Wigston LE18 2DR ☎ 0116 257 2600
🖷 0116 288 7828 ✉ mark.hall@oadby-wigston.gov.uk

Senior Management: Mrs Anne Court, Director of Service Delivery, Council Offices, Station Road, Wigston LE18 2DR ☎ 0116 257 2602 🖷 0116 288 7828 ✉ anne.court1@oadby-wigston.gov.uk

Community Planning: Mrs Anita Pathak-Mould , Head of Community, Council Offices, Station Road, Wigston LE18 2DR
☎ 0116 257 2674 ✉ anita.pathak-mould@oadby-wigston.gov.uk

Community Safety: Mrs Anita Pathak-Mould , Head of Community, Council Offices, Station Road, Wigston LE18 2DR
☎ 0116 257 2674 ✉ anita.pathak-mould@oadby-wigston.gov.uk

Computer Management: Mr Paul Langham , ICT Manager, Council Offices, Station Road, Wigston LE18 2DR ☎ 01455 255995
🖷 0116 288 7828 ✉ paul.langham@oadby-wigston.gov.uk

Corporate Services: Mrs Kalv Garcha , Head of Corporate Resources, Council Offices, Station Road, Wigston LE18 2DR
☎ 0116 257 2626 ✉ kalv.garcha@oadby-wigston.gov.uk

Economic Development: Adrian Thorpe , Planning Policy and Regeneration Manager, Council Offices, Station Road, Wigston LE18 2DR ☎ 0116 257 2645 ✉ adrian.thorpe@oadby-wigston.gov.uk

Emergency Planning: Ms Avril Lennox, Leisure Development Officer, Brocks Hill Country Park, Oadby LE2 5JJ ☎ 0116 257 2735
🖷 0116 288 7828 ✉ avril.lennox@oadby-wigston.gov.uk

Environmental Health: Mrs Anita Pathak-Mould , Head of Community, Council Offices, Station Road, Wigston LE18 2DR
☎ 0116 257 2674 ✉ anita.pathak-mould@oadby-wigston.gov.uk

Fleet Management: Brian Kew , Depot Manager, The Depot, Wigston Road, Oadby LE2 5JE ☎ 0116 257 2830
✉ brian.kew@oadby-wigston.gov.uk

Grounds Maintenance: Brian Kew , Depot Manager, The Depot, Wigston Road, Oadby LE2 5JE ☎ 0116 257 2830
✉ brian.kew@oadby-wigston.gov.uk

Health and Safety: Mrs Kalv Garcha , Head of Corporate Resources, Council Offices, Station Road, Wigston LE18 2DR
☎ 0116 257 2626 ✉ kalv.garcha@oadby-wigston.gov.uk

Housing: Mrs Anita Pathak-Mould , Head of Community, Council Offices, Station Road, Wigston LE18 2DR ☎ 0116 257 2674
✉ anita.pathak-mould@oadby-wigston.gov.uk

Housing Maintenance: Mrs Anita Pathak-Mould , Head of Community, Council Offices, Station Road, Wigston LE18 2DR
☎ 0116 257 2674 ✉ anita.pathak-mould@oadby-wigston.gov.uk

Legal: Mrs Kalv Garcha , Head of Corporate Resources, Council Offices, Station Road, Wigston LE18 2DR ☎ 0116 257 2626
✉ kalv.garcha@oadby-wigston.gov.uk

Leisure and Cultural Services: Ms Avril Lennox, Leisure Development Officer, Brocks Hill Country Park, Washbrook Lane, Oadby LE2 5JJ ☎ 0116 257 2735 🖷 0116 288 7828 ✉ avril.lennox@oadby-wigston.gov.uk

Licensing: Mrs Kalv Garcha , Head of Corporate Resources, Council Offices, Station Road, Wigston LE18 2DR ☎ 0116 257 2626 ✉ kalv.garcha@oadby-wigston.gov.uk

Member Services: Mrs Anne Court, Director of Service Delivery, Council Offices, Station Road, Wigston LE18 2DR ☎ 0116 257 2602 🖷 0116 288 7828 ✉ anne.court1@oadby-wigston.gov.uk

Parking: Ms Margaret Smith , Administration & Facilities Manager, The Depot, Wigston Road, Oadby LE2 5JE ☎ 0116 257 2832 ✉ margaret.smith@oadby-wigston.gov.uk

Personnel / HR: Mrs Kalv Garcha , Head of Corporate Resources, Council Offices, Station Road, Wigston LE18 2DR ☎ 0116 257 2626 ✉ kalv.garcha@oadby-wigston.gov.uk

Planning: Chris Forrett , Planning Control Manager, Council Offices, Station Road, Wigston LE18 2DR ☎ 0116 257 2710 ✉ chris.forrett@oadby-wigston.gov.uk

Procurement: Mr Paul Loveday , Head of Finance, Council Offices, Station Road, Wigston LE18 2DR ☎ 0116 257 2750 🖷 0116 288 7828 ✉ paul.loveday@oadby-wigston.gov.uk

Recycling & Waste Minimisation: Ms Karen Parkes , Recycling Co-ordinator, The Depot, Wigston Road, Oadby LE2 5JE ☎ 0116 257 2841 ✉ karen.parkes@oadby-wigston.gov.uk

Regeneration: Adrian Thorpe , Planning Policy and Regeneration Manager, Council Offices, Station Road, Wigston LE18 2DR ☎ 0116 257 2645 ✉ adrian.thorpe@oadby-wigston.gov.uk

Staff Training: Mrs Kalv Garcha , Head of Corporate Resources, Council Offices, Station Road, Wigston LE18 2DR ☎ 0116 257 2626 ✉ kalv.garcha@oadby-wigston.gov.uk

Sustainable Communities: Mrs Anita Pathak-Mould , Head of Community, Council Offices, Station Road, Wigston LE18 2DR ☎ 0116 257 2674 ✉ anita.pathak-mould@oadby-wigston.gov.uk

Town Centre: Adrian Thorpe , Planning Policy and Economic Development Manager, Council Offices, Station Road, Wigston LE18 2DR ☎ 0116 257 2645 ✉ adrian.thorpe@oadby-wigston.gov.uk

Waste Collection and Disposal: Brian Kew , Depot Manager, The Depot, Wigston Road, Oadby LE2 5JE ☎ 0116 257 2830 ✉ brian.kew@oadby-wigston.gov.uk

Waste Management: Brian Kew , Depot Manager, The Depot, Wigston Road, Oadby LE2 5JE ☎ 0116 257 2830 ✉ brian.kew@oadby-wigston.gov.uk

Children's Play Areas: Ms Margaret Smith , Administration & Facilities Manager, The Depot, Wigston Road, Oadby LE2 5JE ☎ 0116 257 2832 ✉ margaret.smith@oadby-wigston.gov.uk

COUNCILLORS

***Mayor* Darr**, Latif (LD - Oadby Brocks Hill)
latif.darr@oadby-wigston.gov.uk

***Deputy Mayor* Eaton**, Robert (LD - Wigston Meadowcourt)
robert.eaton@oadby-wigston.gov.uk

***Leader of the Council* Boyce**, John (LD - South Wigston)
john.boyce@oadby-wigston.gov.uk

***Deputy Leader of the Council* Charlesworth**, Michael (LD - Wigston All Saints)
michael.charlesworth@oadby-wigston.gov.uk

Atwal, Gurpal (LAB - Oadby Uplands)
gurpal.atwal@oadby-wigston.gov.uk

Barr, Ted (CON - Wigston Meadowcourt)
ted.barr@oadby-wigston.gov.uk

Bentley, Lee (LD - Wigston All Saints)
lee.bentley@oadby-wigston.gov.uk

Bond, Anne (CON - Oadby St Peters)
anne.bond@oadby-wigston.gov.uk

Boulter, Bill (LD - Wigston Fields)
bill.boulter@oadby-wigston.gov.uk

Broadley, Linda (LD - Wigston St Wolstans)
linda.broadley@oadby-wigston.gov.uk

Broadley, Frank (LD - Wigston St Wolstans)
frank.broadley@oadby-wigston.gov.uk

Carter, David (LD - Oadby St Peters)
david.carter@oadby-wigston.gov.uk

Chalk, Kerree (LD - Wigston St Wolstans)
Kerree.chalk@oadby-wigston.gov.uk

Chamberlain, Marie (LD - Wigston Meadowcourt)
marie.chamberlain@oadby-wigston.gov.uk

Dave, Bhupendra (CON - Oadby Woodlands)
bhupendra.dave@oadby-wigston.gov.uk

Eaton, Lynda (LD - Wigston All Saints)
lynda.eaton@oadby-wigston.gov.uk

Fahey, Bob (CON - Oadby Grange)
bob.fahey@oadby-wigston.gov.uk

Gamble, Dean (LD - Oadby Woodlands)
dean.gamble@oadby-wigston.gov.uk

Haq, Samia (LD - Oadby Uplands)
samia.haq@oadby-wigston.gov.uk

Kaufman, Jeffrey (LD - Oadby Brocks Hill)
jeffrey.kaufman@oadby-wigston.gov.uk

Khong, Teck (CON - Oadby Grange)
teck.khong@oadby-wigston.gov.uk

Loydall, Kevin (LD - Wigston Fields)
kevin.loydall@oadby-wigston.gov.uk

Loydall, Helen (LD - Wigston Fields)
helen.loydall@oadby-wigston.gov.uk

Morris, Sharon (LD - South Wigston)
sharon.morris@oadby-wigston.gov.uk

Morris, Richard (LD - South Wigston)
richard.morris@oadby-wigston.gov.uk

Thakor, Ravendra (CON - Oadby Grange)
ravendra.thakor@oadby-wigston.gov.uk

POLITICAL COMPOSITION
LD: 19, CON: 6, LAB: 1

COMMITTEE CHAIRS
Development Control: Mr Lee Bentley

Licensing & Regulatory: Mrs Helen Loydall

Oldham M

Oldham Metropolitan Borough Council, Civic Centre, West Street, Oldham OL1 1UG
☎ 0161 770 3000 🖷 0161 770 5185 💻 www.oldham.gov.uk

FACTS AND FIGURES
Parliamentary Constituencies: Ashton under Lyne, Oldham East and Saddleworth, Oldham West and Royton
EU Constituencies: North West
Election Frequency: Elections are by thirds

PRINCIPAL OFFICERS
Chief Executive: Dr Carolyn Wilkins , Chief Executive, Civic Centre, West Street, Oldham OL1 1UG ☎ 0161 770 4190 carolyn.wilkins@oldham.gov.uk

Senior Management: Ms Emma Alexander , Executive Director - Corporate & Commercial Services, Civic Centre, West Street, Oldham OL1 1UW ☎ 0161 770 5157 emma.alexander@oldham.gov.uk

Senior Management: Ms Maggie Kufeldt , Executive Director - Health & Wellbeing, Civic Centre, West Street, Oldham OL1 1UG ☎ 0161 770 4208 maggie.kufeldt@oldham.gov.uk

Senior Management: Ms Helen Lockwood , Executive Director - Neighbourhoods & Co-operatives, Civic Centre, West Street, Oldham OL1 1UG ☎ 0161 770 1848 helen.lockwood@oldham.gov.uk

Senior Management: Ms Elaine McLean , Executive Director - Economy & Skills, Civic Centre, West Street, Oldham OL1 1UW ☎ 0161 770 4079 elaine.mclean@oldham.gov.uk

Senior Management: Mr Tom Stannard , Director - Enterprise & Skills, Civic Centre, West Street, Oldham OL1 1UG tom.stannard@oldham.gov.uk

Building Control: Mr John Rooney , Interim Head of Planning & Infrastructure, Civic Centre, West Street, Oldham OL1 1UG ☎ 0161 770 4558 john.rooney@oldham.gov.uk

Catering Services: Ms Anne Burns , Catering Manager, Civic Centre, West Street, Oldham OL1 1UG ☎ 0161 770 4262 anne.burns@oldham.gov.uk

Children / Youth Services: Mr Neil Consterdine , Head of Integrated Youth, Civic Centre, West Street, Oldham OL1 1UG ☎ 0161 770 8734 neil.consterdine@oldham.gov.uk

Children / Youth Services: Ms Kim Scragg , Director of Safeguarding, Civic Centre, West Street, Oldham OL1 1UG ☎ 0161 770 4751 kim.scragg@oldham.gov.uk

Civil Registration: Ms Marina Brown , Registration Services Manager, Chadderton Town Hall, Oldham OL9 6PP ☎ 0161 770 8963 marina.brown@oldham.gov.uk

PR / Communications: Mrs Shelley Kipling , Head of Communications, Room 437, Civic Centre, West Street, Oldham OL1 1UG ☎ 0161 770 3792 🖷 0161 770 4045 shelley.kipling@oldham.gov.uk

PR / Communications: Mr Carl Marsden , Head of Communications, Room 437, Civic Centre, West Street, Oldham OL1 1UG ☎ 0161 770 4323 carl.marsden@oldham.gov.uk

Community Safety: Ms Jill Beaumont , Director of Community Services, Civic Centre, West Street, Oldham OL1 1UG ☎ 0161 770 4778 jill.beaumont@oldham.gov.uk

Computer Management: Ms Helen Gerling , Interim Director - Commercial & Transformational Services, Civic Centre, West Street, Oldham OL1 1UG ☎ 0161 770 3468 helen.gerling@oldham.gov.uk

Consumer Protection and Trading Standards: Ms Carol Brown, Director - Environmental Services, Civic Centre, West Street, Oldham OL1 1UG ☎ 0161 770 4452 carol.brown@oldham.gov.uk

Contracts: Mrs Karen Lowes , Head of Strategic Sourcing, Civic Centre, West Street, Oldham OL1 1UG ☎ 0161 770 4936 karen.lowes@oldham.gov.uk

Corporate Services: Mr Mark Reynolds, Director of Policy & Governance, Civic Centre, West Street, Oldham OL1 1UG ☎ 0161 770 5147 mark.reynolds@oldham.gov.uk

Customer Service: Ms Suzanne Heywood , Head of Customer & Business Support Services, PO Box 160, Civic Centre, West Street, Oldham OL1 1UG ☎ 0161 770 4905 suzanne.heywood@oldham.gov.uk

Economic Development: Mr Darren Jones , Director - Economic Development, Oldham Business Centre, Cromwell Street, Oldham OL1 1BB ☎ 0161 770 4002 darren.jones@oldham.gov.uk

Education: Mr Steve Edwards , Interim Director - Education & Early Years, Civic Centre, West Street, Oldham OL1 1UG ☎ 0161 770 4089 steve.edwards@oldham.gov.uk

Electoral Registration: Ms Julie Bruce , Head of Elections & Land Charges, Civic Centre, West Street, Oldham OL1 1UG ☎ 0161 770 4712 julie.bruce@oldham.gov.uk

Environmental Health: Mr Neil Crabtree , Head of Service - Public Protection, Sir Robert Peacock House, Vulcan Street, Oldham OL4 1LA ☎ 0161 770 4141 neil.crabtree@oldham.gov.uk

European Liaison: Mr Dave Catherall , Principal Officer - External Funding, Civic Centre, West Street, Oldham OL1 1UG ☎ 0161 770 5165 dave.catherall@oldham.gov.uk

Events Manager: Mr Mark Reynolds, Director of Policy & Governance, Civic Centre, West Street, Oldham OL1 1UG ☎ 0161 770 5147 mark.reynolds@oldham.gov.uk

Facilities: Mr Peter Wood , Head of Facilities Management, Civic Centre, West Street, Oldham OL1 1UG ☎ 0161 770 4028 peter.wood@oldham.gov.uk

Finance: Ms Anne Ryans , Interim Director of Finance, PO Box 196, Civic Centre, West Street, Oldham OL1 1UG ☎ 0161 770 4902 anne.ryans@oldham.gov.uk

Fleet Management: Mr Craig Dale , Head of Service - Highways, Operations, Waste & Fleet Management, Civic Centre, West Street, Oldham OL1 1UG ☎ 0161 770 4441 craig.dale@oldham.gov.uk

Grounds Maintenance: Mr Glenn Dale , Group Manager - Environmental Services, Alexandra Park, Oldham OL8 2BN ☎ 0161 770 4065 glenn.dale@oldham.gov.uk

Housing: Ms Carol Brown, Director - Environmental Services, Civic Centre, West Street, Oldham OL1 1UG ☎ 0161 770 4452 carol.brown@oldham.gov.uk

Legal: Mr Paul Entwistle , Director of Legal Services, PO Box 33, Civic Centre, West Street, Oldham OL1 1UL ☎ 0161 770 4822 paul.entwistle@oldham.gov.uk

Leisure and Cultural Services: Ms Sheena MacFarlane, Head of Heritage Libraries & Art, PO Box 335, Civic Centre, West Street, Oldham OL1 1XJ ☎ 0161 770 4664 🖷 0161 770 4652 sheena.macfarlane@oldham.gov.uk

Licensing: Mr John Garforth , Licensing Manager & Trading Standards, Sir Robert Peacock House, Vulcan Street, Oldham OL1 4LA ☎ 0161 770 5026 john.garforth@oldham.gov.uk

Lifelong Learning: Ms Lynda Fairhurst , Head of Lifelong Learning Services, Civic Centre, West Street, Oldham OL1 1UG ☎ 0161 770 8055 lynda.fairhurst@oldham.gov.uk

Lighting: Mr John McAuley , PFI Lighting Manager, Lees Road Depot, Lees Road, Oldham OL4 1HD ☎ 0161 770 1669 john.mcauley@oldhamrochdalestreetlights.gov.uk

Member Services: Mr Paul Entwistle , Director of Legal Services, PO Box 33, Civic Centre, West Street, Oldham OL1 1UL ☎ 0161 770 4822 paul.entwistle@oldham.gov.uk

Personnel / HR: Ms Dianne Frost , Director - People Services, Civic Centre, West Street, Oldham OL1 1UG ☎ 0161 770 4965 dianne.frost@oldham.gov.uk

Planning: Mr John Rooney , Interim Head of Planning & Infrastructure, Civic Centre, West Street, Oldham OL1 1UG ☎ 0161 770 4558 john.rooney@oldham.gov.uk

Procurement: Mrs Karen Lowes , Head of Strategic Sourcing, Civic Centre, West Street, Oldham OL1 1UG ☎ 0161 770 4936 karen.lowes@oldham.gov.uk

Public Libraries: Ms Sheena MacFarlane, Head of Heritage Libraries & Art, PO Box 335, Civic Centre, West Street, Oldham OL1 1XJ ☎ 0161 770 4664 🖷 0161 770 4652 sheena.macfarlane@oldham.gov.uk

Recycling & Waste Minimisation: Mr Craig Dale , Head of Service - Highways, Operations, Waste & Fleet Management, Civic Centre, West Street, Oldham OL1 1UG ☎ 0161 770 4441 craig.dale@oldham.gov.uk

Regeneration: Ms Imogen Fuller , Principal Regeneration Officer, Civic Centre, West Street, Oldham OL1 1UG ☎ 0161 770 5164 imogen.fuller@oldham.gov.uk

Regeneration: Mr Tom Stannard , Director - Enterprise & Skills, Civic Centre, West Street, Oldham OL1 1UG tom.stannard@oldham.gov.uk

Road Safety: Mr Gary Sutcliffe , Principal Engineer, Henshaw House, Cheapside, Oldham OL1 1NY ☎ 0161 770 3046 gary.sutcliffe@oldham.gov.uk

Social Services (Adult): Mr Paul Grubic , Director of Adults' Services, Civic Centre, West Street, Oldham OL1 1UG ☎ 0161 770 4317 paul.grubic@oldham.gov.uk

Social Services (Children): Ms Kim Scragg , Director of Safeguarding, Civic Centre, West Street, Oldham OL1 1UG ☎ 0161 770 4751 kim.scragg@oldham.gov.uk

Staff Training: Mr John Fraine , Business Partner - Adults & Children's Sector, Ashwood House, Ellen Street, Oldham OL9 6QR ☎ 0161 770 8709 john.fraine@oldham.gov.uk

Street Scene: Mr Glenn Dale , Group Manager - Environmental Services, Alexandra Park, Oldham OL8 2BN ☎ 0161 770 4065 glenn.dale@oldham.gov.uk

Town Centre: Ms Sara Hewitt , Town Centre Manager, Level 3, Business Centre, Cromwell Street, Oldham OL1 1BB ☎ 0161 770 5282 🖷 0161 770 8306 sara.hewitt@oldham.gov.uk

Waste Collection and Disposal: Mr Craig Dale , Head of Service - Highways, Operations, Waste & Fleet Management, Civic Centre, West Street, Oldham OL1 1UG ☎ 0161 770 4441 craig.dale@oldham.gov.uk

Waste Management: Mr Craig Dale , Head of Service - Highways, Operations, Waste & Fleet Management, Moorhey Street Depot, Moorhey Street, Oldham OL4 1JF ☎ 0161 770 4441 craig.dale@oldham.gov.uk

COUNCILLORS

***Mayor* Ur-Rehman**, Ateeque (LAB - Medlock Vale)
ateeque.urrehman@oldham.gov.uk

***Deputy Mayor* Heffernan**, Derek (LD - Saddleworth North)
derek.heffenan@oldham.gov.uk

***Leader of the Council* McMahon**, Jim (LAB - Failsworth East)
cllr.j.mcmahon@oldham.gov.uk

***Deputy Leader of the Council* Stretton**, Jean (LAB - Hollinwood)
jean.stretton@oldham.gov.uk

Ahmed, Riaz (LAB - Waterhead)
riaz.ahmad@oldham.gov.uk

OLDHAM

Akhtar, Shoab (LAB - Werneth)
shoab.akhtar@oldham.gov.uk

Alexander, Ginny (LAB - St. James)
ginny.alexander@oldham.gov.uk

Alexander, Adrian (LAB - Saddleworth West & Lees)
cllr.a.alexander@oldham.gov.uk

Ali, Mohon (LAB - Chadderton North)
mohon.ali@oldham.gov.uk

Ames, Brian (LAB - Hollinwood)
brian.ames@oldham.gov.uk

Azad, Montaz Ali (LAB - Coldhurst)
cllr.m.azad@oldham.gov.uk

Ball, Cath (LAB - St. James)
cath.ball@oldham.gov.uk

Bashforth, Marie (LAB - Royton South)
marie.bashforth@oldham.gov.uk

Bashforth, Steven (LAB - Royton South)
steven.bashforth@oldham.gov.uk

Bates, Warren (UKIP - Failsworth West)
warren.bates@oldham.gov.uk

Blyth, Rod (LD - Shaw)
rod.blyth@oldham.gov.uk

Briggs, Norman (LAB - Failsworth East)
norman.briggs@oldham.gov.uk

Brownridge, Barbara (LAB - Chadderton North)
barbara.brownridge@oldham.gov.uk

Chadderton, Amanda (LAB - Royton South)
amanda.chadderton@oldham.gov.uk

Chauhan, Zahid (LAB - Alexandra)
zahid.chauhan@oldham.gov.uk

Cosgrove, Angela (LAB - St. James)
angela.cosgrove@oldham.gov.uk

Dawson, David (LAB - Failsworth East)
david.dawson@oldham.gov.uk

Dean, Peter (LAB - Waterhead)
cllr.p.dean@oldham.gov.uk

Dearden, Susan (LAB - Chadderton Central)
susan.dearden@oldham.gov.uk

Fielding, Sean (LAB - Failsworth West)
sean.fielding@oldham.gov.uk

Garry, Elaine (LAB - Failsworth West)
elaine.garry@oldham.gov.uk

Gloster, Chris (LD - Shaw)
chris.gloster@oldham.gov.uk

Haque, Fazlul (LAB - Chadderton North)
fazlul.haque@oldham.gov.uk

Harkness, Garth (LD - Saddleworth North)
garth.harkness@oldham.gov.uk

Harrison, Jenny (LAB - Alexandra)
Cllr.J.Harrison@oldham.gov.uk

Hibbert, David (LAB - Chadderton South)
david.hibbert@oldham.gov.uk

Hudson, John (CON - Saddleworth South)
john.hudson@oldham.gov.uk

Hussain, Fida (LAB - Werneth)
fida.hussain@oldham.gov.uk

Iqbal, Javid (LAB - Werneth)
javid.iqbal@oldham.gov.uk

Jabbar, Abdul (LAB - Coldhurst)
abdul.jabbar@oldham.gov.uk

Judge, Bernard (LAB - Royton North)
bernard.judge@oldham.gov.uk

Kirkham, Nikki (IND - Saddleworth North)
nikki.kirkham@oldham.gov.uk

Klonowski, Peter (UKIP - Saddleworth West & Lees)
peter.klonowski@oldham.gov.uk

Larkin, Tony (LAB - Royton North)
tony.larkin@oldham.gov.uk

Malik, Abdul (LAB - Coldhurst)
abdul.malik@oldham.gov.uk

McCann, John (LD - Saddleworth South)
john.mccann@oldham.gov.uk

McLaren, Colin (LAB - Chadderton Central)
colin.mclaren@oldham.gov.uk

Moores, Eddie (LAB - Chadderton Central)
cllr.e.moores@oldham.gov.uk

Murphy, Dave (LD - Crompton)
dave.murphy@oldham.gov.uk

Mushtaq, Shaid (LAB - Alexandra)
shaid.mushtaq@oldham.gov.uk

Price, Vita (LAB - Waterhead)
vita.price@oldham.gov.uk

Qumer, Shadab (LAB - St. Mary's)
shadab.qumer@oldham.gov.uk

Rehman, Kaiser (LAB - Medlock Vale)
cllr.k.rehman@oldham.gov.uk

Roberts, Hannah (LAB - Royton North)
hannah.roberts@oldham.gov.uk

Salamat, Ali Aqueel (LAB - St. Mary's)
a.a.salamat@oldham.gov.uk

Sedgwick, Val (LD - Saddleworth West & Lees)
val.sedgwick@oldham.gov.uk

Shah, Arooj (LAB - St. Mary's)
arooj.shah@oldham.gov.uk

Sheldon, Graham (CON - Saddleworth South)
cllr.g.sheldon@oldham.gov.uk

Shuttleworth, Graham (LAB - Chadderton South)
cllr.g.shuttleworth@oldham.gov.uk

Sykes, Howard (LD - Shaw)
howard.sykes@oldham.gov.uk

Toor, Yasmin (LAB - Medlock Vale)
yasmin.toor@oldham.gov.uk

Turner, Julia (LD - Crompton)
Julia.Turner@oldham.gov.uk

Williams, Steve (LAB - Hollinwood)
cllr.s.williams@oldham.gov.uk

Williamson, Diane (LD - Crompton)
diane.williamson@oldham.gov.uk

Wrigglesworth, Joy (LAB - Chadderton South)
joy.wrigglesworth@oldham.gov.uk

POLITICAL COMPOSITION

LAB: 45, LD: 10, UKIP: 2, CON: 2, IND: 1

COMMITTEE CHAIRS

Licensing: Mr Abdul Malik
Planning: Mr Steven Bashforth

Orkney S

Orkney Islands Council, Council Offices, School Place, Kirkwall KW15 1NY
☎ 01856 873535 🖷 01856 874615 ✉ customerservice@orkney.gov.uk
💻 www.orkney.gov.uk

FACTS AND FIGURES

Parliamentary Constituencies: Orkney and Shetland
EU Constituencies: Scotland
Election Frequency: Elections are of whole council

PRINCIPAL OFFICERS

Chief Executive: Mr Alistair Buchan , Chief Executive, Council Offices, School Place, Kirkwall KW15 1NY ☎ 01856 873535 🖷 01865 876158 ✉ chief.executive@orkney.gov.uk

Access Officer / Social Services (Disability): Mr Tom McGuire , Service Manager, Council Offices, School Place, Kirkwall KW15 1NY ☎ 01856 873535 🖷 01856 886453 ✉ tom.mcguire@nhs.net

Architect, Building / Property Services: Mrs Jan Falconer , Head of Strategic Development & Regeneration, Council Offices, School Place, Kirkwall KW15 1NY ☎ 01856 873535 ext 2714 🖷 01856 876094 ✉ jan.falconer@orkney.gov.uk

Best Value: Mr Jim Love, Corporate Services Officer, Council Offices, School Place, Kirkwall KW15 1NY ☎ 01856 873535 ✉ jim.love@orkney.gov.uk

Building Control: Mr Jack Leslie, Principal Building Standards Officer, Council Offices, School Place, Kirkwall KW15 1NY ☎ 01856 873535 🖷 01856 886451 ✉ jack.leslie@orkney.gov.uk

Catering Services: Ms Anne Harrison, Catering Manager, St Rognvald Street, Kirkwall KW15 1PR ☎ 01856 879238 🖷 01856 879239 ✉ anne.harrison@orkney.gov.uk

Children / Youth Services: Ms Marie O'Sullivan , Head of Children's Service, Criminal Justice & Primary Care, Council Offices, School Place, Kirkwall KW15 1NY ☎ 01856 873535 🖷 01856 886453 ✉ marie.osullivan@nhs.net

Civil Registration: Ms Patricia Breck , Senior Registrar, Council Offices, School Place, Kirkwall KW15 1NY ☎ 01856 873535 ✉ patricia.breck@orkney.gov.uk

PR / Communications: Mr David Hartley , Communications Officer, Council Offices, School Place, Kirkwall KW15 1NY ☎ 01856 873535 🖷 01856 874615 ✉ david.hartley@orkney.gov.uk

Community Planning: Ms Hannah Thomson , Community Planning Officer, Council Offices, School Place, Kirkwall KW15 1NY ☎ 01856 873535 ✉ hannah.thomson@orkney.gov.uk

Computer Management: Mr Robert Horrobin, Customer First Manager, 9 King Street, Kirkwall, Orkney KW15 1JF ☎ 01856 873535 🖷 01856 876158 ✉ robert.horrobin@orkney.gov.uk

Consumer Protection and Trading Standards: Mr Gary Foubister, Trading Standards Manager, Council Offices, School Place, Kirkwall KW15 1NY ☎ 01856 873535 🖷 01856 886450 ✉ gary.foubister@orkney.gov.uk

Contracts: Mr Gavin Barr , Executive Director of Development & Infrastructure, Council Offices, School Place, Kirkwall KW15 1NY ☎ 01856 873535 🖷 01856 876094 ✉ gavin.barr@orkney.gov.uk

Corporate Services: Mrs Gillian Morrison, Executive Director of Corporate Services, Council Offices, School Place, Kirkwall KW15 1NY ☎ 01856 873535 🖷 01856 876158 ✉ gillian.morrison@orkney.gov.uk

Corporate Services: Ms Dawn Sherwood , Head of IT & Support Services, Council Offices, School Place, Kirkwall KW15 1NY ☎ 01856 873535 ✉ dawn.sherwood@orkney.gov.uk

Customer Service: Mrs Catherine Foubister , Customer Services Manager, Council Offices, School Place, Kirkwall KW15 1NY ☎ 01856 873535 ✉ catherine.foubister@orkney.gov.uk

Direct Labour: Mr Gavin Barr , Executive Director of Development & Infrastructure, Council Offices, School Place, Kirkwall KW15 1NY ☎ 01856 873535 🖷 01856 876094 ✉ gavin.barr@orkney.gov.uk

Economic Development: Mrs Jan Falconer , Head of Strategic Development & Regeneration, Council Offices, School Place, Kirkwall KW15 1NY ☎ 01856 873535 ext 2714 🖷 01856 876094 ✉ jan.falconer@orkney.gov.uk

Education: Mr Wilfred Weir , Executive Director of Education, Leisure & Housing, Council Offices, School Place, Kirkwall KW15 1NY ☎ 01856 873535 ✉ wilf.weir@orkney.gov.uk

E-Government: Mr Robert Horrobin, Customer First Manager, 9 King Street, Kirkwall, Orkney KW15 1JF ☎ 01856 873535 🖷 01856 876158 ✉ robert.horrobin@orkney.gov.uk

Electoral Registration: Mr Michael Forbes , Electoral Registration Officer, Charlotte House, Commercial Road, Lerwick, Shetland ZE1 0LX ☎ 01595 745700 🖷 01595 745710 ✉ ero@shetland.gov.uk

Emergency Planning: Mr Malcolm Russell, Safety & Contingencies Manager, Council Offices, School Place, Kirkwall KW15 1NY ☎ 01856 873535 🖷 01856 874615 ✉ malcolm.russell@orkney.gov.uk

Energy Management: Mr Alistair Morton , Energy & Utilities Officer, Council Offices, School Place, Kirkwall KW15 1NY ☎ 01856 873535 🖷 01856 876094 ✉ alistair.morton@orkney.gov.uk

ORKNEY

Environmental / Technical Services: Mr Gavin Barr , Executive Director of Development & Infrastructure, Council Offices, School Place, Kirkwall KW15 1NY ☎ 01856 873535 🖷 01856 876094 ✉ gavin.barr@orkney.gov.uk

Environmental Health: Mr David Brown , Environmental Health Manager, Council Offices, School Place, Kirkwall KW15 1NY ☎ 01856 873535 🖷 01856 876450 ✉ david.brown@orkney.gov.uk

Estates, Property & Valuation: Mr Graeme Christie , Estates Manager, Council Offices, School Place, Kirkwall KW15 1NY ☎ 01856 873535 🖷 01856 876094 ✉ graeme.christie@orkney.gov.uk

European Liaison: Miss Phyllis Harvey, European Liaison Officer, Council Offices, School Place, Kirkwall KW15 1NY ☎ 01856 873535 🖷 01856 875846 ✉ phyllis.harvey@orkney.gov.uk

Facilities: Mr Gwyn Evans, Facilities Manager, Council Offices, School Place, Kirkwall KW15 1NY ☎ 01856 873535 🖷 01856 876094 ✉ gwyn.evans@orkney.gov.uk

Finance: Mr Gareth Waterson , Head of Finance, Council Offices, School Place, Kirkwall KW15 1NY ☎ 01856 873535 🖷 01856 876158 ✉ finance@orkney.gov.uk

Pensions: Mr Bryan Hay , Pensions Manager, Council Offices, School Place, Kirkwall KW15 1NY ☎ 01856 873535 🖷 01856 876158 ✉ bryan.hay@orkney.gov.uk

Fleet Management: Mr Kenny Copland , Fleet Manager, Council Offices, School Place, Kirkwall KW15 1NY ☎ 01856 872311 🖷 01856 874311 ✉ kenny.copland@orkney.gov.uk

Grounds Maintenance: Mr Peter Bevan , Engineering Services Manager, Council Offices, School Place, Kirkwall KW15 1NY ☎ 01856 873535 🖷 01856 876094 ✉ peter.bevan@orkney.gov.uk

Health and Safety: Mr Malcolm Russell, Safety & Contingencies Manager, Council Offices, School Place, Kirkwall KW15 1NY ☎ 01856 873535 🖷 01856 874615 ✉ malcolm.russell@orkney.gov.uk

Highways: Mr Darren Richardson , Head of Roads & Environmental Services, Council Offices, School Place, Kirkwall KW15 1NY ☎ 01856 873535 🖷 01856 876094 ✉ darren.richardson@orkney.gov.uk

Housing: Ms Frances Troup , Head of Housing & Homelessness, Council Offices, School Place, Kirkwall KW15 1NY ☎ 01856 873535 ✉ frances.troup@orkney.gov.uk

Housing Maintenance: Ms Frances Troup , Head of Housing & Homelessness, Council Offices, School Place, Kirkwall KW15 1NY ☎ 01856 873535 ✉ frances.troup@orkney.gov.uk

Legal: Mr Fraser Bell , Head of Legal Services, Council Offices, School Place, Kirkwall KW15 1NY ☎ 01856 873535 🖷 01856 874615 ✉ fraser.bell@orkney.gov.uk

Leisure and Cultural Services: Ms Karen Greaves , Head of Leisure & Lifelong Learning, Council Offices, School Place, Kirkwall KW15 1NY ☎ 01856 873535 🖷 01856 870302 ✉ karen.greaves@orkney.gov.uk

Licensing: Mr Fraser Bell , Head of Legal Services, Council Offices, School Place, Kirkwall KW15 1NY ☎ 01856 873535 🖷 01856 874615 ✉ fraser.bell@orkney.gov.uk

Lifelong Learning: Ms Karen Greaves , Head of Leisure & Lifelong Learning, Council Offices, School Place, Kirkwall KW15 1NY ☎ 01856 873535 🖷 01856 870302 ✉ karen.greaves@orkney.gov.uk

Lighting: Mr Darren Richardson , Head of Roads & Environmental Services, Council Offices, School Place, Kirkwall KW15 1NY ☎ 01856 873535 🖷 01856 876094 ✉ darren.richardson@orkney.gov.uk

Member Services: Mrs Maureen Spence, Democratic Services Manager, Council Offices, School Place, Kirkwall KW15 1NY ☎ 01856 873535 🖷 01856 871604 ✉ maureen.spence@orkney.gov.uk

Parking: Mr Darren Richardson , Head of Roads & Environmental Services, Council Offices, School Place, Kirkwall KW15 1NY ☎ 01856 873535 🖷 01856 876094 ✉ darren.richardson@orkney.gov.uk

Personnel / HR: Mr Andrew Groundwater , Head of HR & Performance, Council Offices, School Place, Kirkwall KW15 1NY ☎ 01856 873535 🖷 01856 888779 ✉ andrew.groundwater@orkney.gov.uk

Planning: Mr Roddy Mackay, Head of Planning & Regulatory Services, Council Offices, School Place, Kirkwall KW15 1NX ☎ 01856 873535 🖷 01856 886451 ✉ roddy.mackay@orkney.gov.uk

Procurement: Mr Gary Butler , Procurement Manager, Council Offices, School Place, Kirkwall KW15 1NY ☎ 01856 873535 🖷 01856 876158 ✉ gary.butler@orkney.gov.uk

Public Libraries: Mr Gary Amos, Library & Archive Manager, The Orkney Library & Archive, Junction Road, Kirkwall KW15 1AG ☎ 01856 873166 🖷 01856 875260 ✉ gary.amos@orkneylibrary.org.uk

Recycling & Waste Minimisation: Ms Maria Cuthbertson , Waste Services Manager, Council Offices, School Place, Kirkwall KW15 1NY ☎ 01856 873535 ext 2702 🖷 01856 876094 ✉ maria.cuthbertson@orkney.gov.uk

Regeneration: Mrs Jan Falconer , Head of Strategic Development & Regeneration, Council Offices, School Place, Kirkwall KW15 1NY ☎ 01856 873535 ext 2714 🖷 01856 876094 ✉ jan.falconer@orkney.gov.uk

Road Safety: Mrs Yvonne Scott , Community Safety Officer, Council Offices, School Place, Kirkwall KW15 1NY ☎ 01856 873535 ✉ yvonne.scott@orkney.gov.uk

Social Services (Adult): Ms Caroline Sinclair , Head of Health & Community Care, Council Offices, School Place, Kirkwall KW15 1NY ☎ 01856 873535 🖷 01856 876453 ✉ caroline.sinclair@orkney.gov.uk

Social Services (Children): Ms Marie O'Sullivan , Head of Children's Service, Criminal Justice & Primary Care, Council Offices, School Place, Kirkwall KW15 1NY ☎ 01856 873535 🖷 01856 886453 ✉ marie.osullivan@nhs.net

Staff Training: Mrs Alison Skea , Learning & Development Manager, Council Offices, School Place, Kirkwall KW15 1NY ☎ 01856 873535 ✉ alison.skea@orkney.gov.uk

Sustainable Development: Mrs Jan Falconer , Head of Strategic Development & Regeneration, Council Offices, School Place, Kirkwall KW15 1NY ☎ 01856 873535 ext 2714 🖷 01856 876094 🖰 jan.falconer@orkney.gov.uk

Sustainable Development: Mr Roddy Mackay, Head of Planning & Regulatory Services, Council Offices, School Place, Kirkwall KW15 1NX ☎ 01856 873535 🖷 01856 886451 🖰 roddy.mackay@orkney.gov.uk

Tourism: Mrs Jan Falconer , Head of Strategic Development & Regeneration, Council Offices, School Place, Kirkwall KW15 1NY ☎ 01856 873535 ext 2714 🖷 01856 876094 🖰 jan.falconer@orkney.gov.uk

Traffic Management: Mr Darren Richardson , Head of Roads & Environmental Services, Council Offices, School Place, Kirkwall KW15 1NY ☎ 01856 873535 🖷 01856 876094 🖰 darren.richardson@orkney.gov.uk

Transport: Ms Laura Cromarty , Transport Manager, Council Offices, School Place, Kirkwall KW15 1NY ☎ 01856 873535 🖰 laura.cromarty@orkney.gov.uk

Transport Planner: Ms Phyllis Towrie , Transport Planner, Council Offices, School Place, Kirkwall KW15 1NY ☎ 01856 873535 🖷 01856 886466 🖰 phyllis.towrie@orkney.gov.uk

Waste Collection and Disposal: Ms Maria Cuthbertson , Waste Services Manager, Council Offices, School Place, Kirkwall KW15 1NY ☎ 01856 873535 ext 2702 🖷 01856 876094 🖰 maria.cuthbertson@orkney.gov.uk

Waste Management: Ms Maria Cuthbertson , Waste Services Manager, Council Offices, School Place, Kirkwall KW15 1NY ☎ 01856 873535 ext 2702 🖷 01856 876094 🖰 maria.cuthbertson@orkney.gov.uk

Children's Play Areas: Mr Gary Burton , Sports & Leisure Manager, Council Offices, School Place, Kirkwall KW15 1NY ☎ 01856 883535 ext 2440 🖰 gary.burton@orkney.gov.uk

COUNCILLORS

***Convener* Heddle**, Steven (IND - Kirkwall East)
steven.heddle@orkney.gov.uk

Annal, Janice (IND - Kirkwall East)
janice.annal@orkney.gov.uk

Clackson, Stephen (IND - North Isles)
stephen.clackson@orkney.gov.uk

Clouston, Alan (IND - Kirkwall West & Orphir)
alan.clouston@orkney.gov.uk

Crichton, Rob (IND - Stromness & South Isles)
rob.crichton@orkney.gov.uk

Davidson, Maurice (IND - Stromness & South Isles)
maurice.davidson@orkney.gov.uk

Drever, Andrew (IND - East Mainland, South Ronaldsay & Burray)
andrew.drever@orkney.gov.uk

Foubister, Jim (IND - East Midland, South Ronaldsay & Burray)
james.foubister@orkney.gov.uk

Hagan, Stephen (IND - North Isles)
stephen.hagan@orkney.com

Johnston, Harvey (IND - West Mainland)
harvey.johnston@orkney.gov.uk

Madge, Russ (IND - East Mainland, South Ronaldsay & Burray)
russ.madge@orkney.gov.uk

Manson, Leslie (IND - Kirkwall West & Orphir)
cllr.leslie.manson@orkney.gov.uk

Moar, Jimmy (IND - West Mainland)
james.moar@orkney.gov.uk

Richards, John (IND - Kirkwall West & Orphir)
john.richards@orkney.gov.uk

Shearer, Gwenda (IND - Kirkwall East)
gwenda.shearer@orkney.gov.uk

Sinclair, Graham (IND - North Isles)
graham.sinclair@orkney.gov.uk

Stockan, James (IND - Stromness & South Isles)
james.stockan@orkney.gov.uk

Stout, Bill (IND - Kirkwall East)
bill.stout@orkney.gov.uk

Tierney, Owen (IND - West Mainland)
owen.tierney@orkney.gov.uk

Tullock, David (IND - Kirkwall West & Orphir)
david.tullock@orkney.gov.uk

POLITICAL COMPOSITION

IND: 20

COMMITTEE CHAIRS

Development & Infrastructure: Mr James Stockan

Education, Leisure & Housing: Mr Harvey Johnston

Monitoring & Audit: Mr David Tullock

Planning: Mr Rob Crichton

Oxford City D

Oxford City Council, Town Hall, St. Aldate's, Oxford OX1 1BX
☎ 01865 249811 🖳 www.oxford.gov.uk

FACTS AND FIGURES

Parliamentary Constituencies: Oxford East, Oxford West and Abingdon
EU Constituencies: South East
Election Frequency: Elections are biennial

PRINCIPAL OFFICERS

Chief Executive: Mr Peter Sloman , Chief Executive, Town Hall, St. Aldate's, Oxford OX1 1BX ☎ 01865 252354 🖰 psloman@oxford.gov.uk

Assistant Chief Executive: Ms Caroline Green , Assistant Chief Executive, Town Hall, St. Aldate's, Oxford OX1 1BX 🖰 cgreen@oxford.gov.uk

Senior Management: Mr David Edwards , Executive Director - City Regeneration, Town Hall, St. Aldate's, Oxford OX1 1BX ☎ 01865 252463 🖰 dedwards@oxford.gov.uk

OXFORD CITY

Senior Management: Mr Tim Sadler , Executive Director - Community Services, Town Hall, St. Aldate's, Oxford OX1 1BX ☎ 01865 252313 🖷 01865 252256 ✉ tsadler@oxford.gov.uk

Senior Management: Ms Jacqueline Yates , Executive Director - Organisational Development & Corporate Services, Town Hall, St. Aldate's, Oxford OX1 1BX

Community Safety: Mr Richard Adams, Community Safety Manager, Town Hall, St. Aldate's, Oxford OX1 1BX ☎ 01865 252283 🖷 01865 252066 ✉ rjadams@oxford.gov.uk

Customer Service: Ms Helen Bishop , Head - Customer Services, Town Hall, St. Aldate's, Oxford OX1 1BX ☎ 01865 858650 ✉ hbishop@oxford.gov.uk

Direct Labour: Mr Graham Bourton, Head - Direct Services, Cowley Marsh Depot, Marsh Road, Oxford OX4 2HH ☎ 01865 252974 ✉ gbourton@oxford.gov.uk

E-Government: Mr Christopher Lee , Web Contact Manager, Town Hall, St. Aldate's, Oxford OX1 1BX ☎ 01865 249811 ✉ clee@oxford.gov.uk

Electoral Registration: Mr Martin John, Electoral Services Manager, Town Hall, St. Aldate's, Oxford OX1 1BX ☎ 01865 252518 ✉ mjohn@oxford.gov.uk

Finance: Mr Nigel Kennedy , Head - Finance, Town Hall, St. Aldate's, Oxford OX1 1BX ☎ 01865 252708 ✉ nkennedy@oxford.gov.uk

Treasury: Ms Anna Winship , Treasury & VAT Manager, St Aldgate's Chambers, 109 - 113 St Aldgate's, Oxford OX1 1DS ☎ 01865 252517 ✉ awinship@oxford.gov.uk

Grounds Maintenance: Mr Stuart Fitzsimmons , Parks & Open Spaces Manager, Cutteslowe Park, Oxford OX2 8ES ☎ 01865 467270 ✉ sfitzsimmons@oxford.gov.uk

Highways: Mr Shaun Hatton , Highways Manager, Town Hall, St. Aldate's, Oxford OX1 1BX ☎ 01865 249811 ✉ shatton@oxford.gov.uk

Home Energy Conservation: Mr Paul Robinson , Team Leader - Energy & Climate Change, St Aldate's Chambers, St Aldate's, Oxford OX1 1DS ☎ 01865 252541 🖷 01865 252344 ✉ probinson@oxford.gov.uk

Housing Maintenance: Mr Graham Bourton, Head - Direct Services, Cowley Marsh Depot, Marsh Road, Oxford OX4 2HH ☎ 01865 252974 ✉ gbourton@oxford.gov.uk

Legal: Mr Jeremy Thomas, Head - Law & Governance, Town Hall, St. Aldate's, Oxford OX1 1BX ☎ 01865 252224 ✉ jthomas@oxford.gov.uk

Leisure and Cultural Services: Mr Ian Brooke , Head - Leisure & Parks, Bury Knowle House, Oxford OX3 9RG ☎ 01865 467232 ✉ ibrooke@oxford.gov.uk

Parking: Mr Jason Munro , Car Parks Manager, Town Hall, St. Aldate's, Oxford OX1 1BX ☎ 01865 252125 ✉ jmunro@oxford.gov.uk

Partnerships: Mrs Val Johnson, Partnership Development Manager, Town Hall, St. Aldate's, Oxford OX1 1BX ☎ 01865 252209 ✉ vjohnson@oxford.gov.uk

Recycling & Waste Minimisation: Mr Robert Brown , Waste & Recycling Development Officer, Cowley Marsh Depot, Marsh Road, Oxford OX4 2HH ☎ 01865 252955 ✉ Rbrown@oxford.gov.uk

Regeneration: Mr David Edwards , Executive Director - City Regeneration, Town Hall, St. Aldate's, Oxford OX1 1BX ☎ 01865 252463 ✉ dedwards@oxford.gov.uk

Street Scene: Mr Andrew Wright , Street Scene Area Manager, Cowley Marsh Depot, Marsh Road, Oxford OX4 2HH ☎ 01865 282967 ✉ awright@oxford.gov.uk

Transport: Mr Paul Einon , Fleet & Maintenance Manager, Town Hall, St. Aldate's, Oxford OX1 1BX ☎ 01865 252928 ✉ peinon@oxford.gov.uk

Transport Planner: Mr Paul Einon , Fleet & Maintenance Manager, Town Hall, St. Aldate's, Oxford OX1 1BX ☎ 01865 252928 ✉ peinon@oxford.gov.uk

Waste Collection and Disposal: Mr David Huddle , Street Scene Area Manager, Cowley Marsh Depot, Marsh Road, Oxford OX4 2HH ☎ 01865 252955 ✉ dhuddle@oxford.gov.uk

Waste Management: Mr Robert Brown , Waste & Recycling Development Officer, Cowley Marsh Depot, Marsh Road, Oxford OX4 2HH ☎ 01865 282955 ✉ rbrown@oxford.gov.uk

COUNCILLORS

***The Lord Mayor* Humberstone**, Rae (LAB - Blackbird Leys)
cllrrhumberstone@oxford.gov.uk

***Deputy Lord Mayor* Cook**, Colin (LAB - Jericho and Osney)
cllrccook@oxford.gov.uk

***Sheriff* Malik**, Sajjad (LAB - Cowley Marsh)
cllrsmalik@oxford.gov.uk

***Leader of the Council* Price**, Bob (LAB - Hinksey Park)
cllrbprice@oxford.gov.uk

***Deputy Leader of the Council* Turner**, Ed (LAB - Rose Hill and Iffley)
cllreturner@oxford.gov.uk

***Group Leader* Fooks**, Jean (LD - Summertown)
cllrjfooks@oxford.gov.uk

***Group Leader* Simmons**, Craig (GRN - St. Mary's)
cllrcsimmons@oxford.gov.uk

Abbasi, Mohammed (LAB - Cowley Marsh)
cllrmabbasi@oxford.gov.uk

Altaf-Khan, Mohammed (LD - Headington)
cllrmaltaf-khan@oxford.gov.uk

Anwar, Farida (LAB - Headington Hill & Northway)
cllrfanwar@oxford.gov.uk

Benjamin, Elise (GRN - Iffley Fields)
cllrebenjamin@oxford.gov.uk

Brandt, Ruthi (GRN - Carfax)
cllrrbrandt@oxford.gov.uk

Brown, Susan (LAB - Churchill)
cllrsbrown@oxford.gov.uk

Clark, Bev (LAB - St. Clement's)
cllrbclack@oxford.gov.uk

Clarkson, Mary (LAB - Marston)
cllrmclarkson@oxford.gov.uk

Coulter, Van (LAB - Barton and Sandhills)
cllrvcoulter@oxford.gov.uk

Darke, Roy (LAB - Headington Hill & Northway)
cllrrdarke@oxford.gov.uk

Fry, James (LAB - North)
cllrjfry@oxford.gov.uk

Goddard, Stephen (LD - Wolvercote)
cllrsgoddard@oxford.gov.uk

Gotch, Michael (LD - Wolvercote)
cllrmgotch@oxford.gov.uk

Grant, Andrew (LD - Summertown)
cllragrant@oxford.gov.uk

Haines, Mick (IND - Marston)
cllrmhaines@oxford.gov.uk

Hayes, Tom (LAB - St. Clement's)
cllrthayes@oxford.gov.uk

Henwood, David (LAB - Cowley)
cllrdhenwood@oxford.gov.uk

Hollick, Sam (GRN - Holywell)
cllrshollick@oxford.gov.uk

Hollingsworth, Alex (LAB - Carfax)
cllrahollingsworth@oxford.gov.uk

Kennedy, Pat (LAB - Lye Valley)
cllrpkennedy@oxford.gov.uk

Lloyd-Shogbesan, Ben (LAB - Lye Valley)
cllrblloyd-shogbesan@oxford.gov.uk

Lygo, Mark (LAB - Churchill)
cllrmlygo@oxford.gov.uk

Munkonge, Chewe (LAB - Quarry & Risinghurst)
cllrcmunkonge@oxford.gov.uk

Paule, Michelle (LAB - Rose Hill and Iffley)
cllrmpaule@oxford.gov.uk

Pressel, Susanna (LAB - Jericho and Osney)
cllrspressel@oxford.gov.uk

Rowley, Mike (LAB - Barton and Sandhills)
cllrmrowley@oxford.gov.uk

Royce, Gwynneth (LD - St. Margaret's)
cllrgroyce@oxford.gov.uk

Sanders, Gillian (LAB - Littlemore)
cllrgsanders@oxford.gov.uk

Seamons, Scott (LAB - Northfield Brook)
cllrsseamons@oxford.gov.uk

Simm, Christine (LAB - Cowley)
cllrcsimm@oxford.gov.uk

Sinclair, Dee (LAB - Quarry and Risinghurst)
cllrdsinclair@oxford.gov.uk

Smith, Linda (LAB - Blackbird Leys)
cllrlsmith@oxford.gov.uk

Tanner, John (LAB - Littlemore)
cllrjtanner@oxford.gov.uk

Tarver, Richard (LAB - Iffley Fields)
cllrrtarver@oxford.gov.uk

Taylor, Sian (LAB - Northfield Brook)
cllrstaylor@oxford.gov.uk

Thomas, David (GRN - Holywell)
cllrdthomas@oxford.gov.uk

Upton, Louise (LAB - North)
cllrlupton@oxford.gov.uk

van Nooijen, Oscar (LAB - Hinksey Park)
cllrovannooijen@oxford.gov.uk

Wade, Elizabeth (LD - St. Margaret's)
cllrlwade@oxford.gov.uk

Wilkinson, Ruth (LD - Headington)
cllrrwilkinson@oxford.gov.uk

Wolff, Dick (GRN - St. Mary's)
cllrdwolff@oxford.gov.uk

POLITICAL COMPOSITION

LAB: 33, LD: 8, GRN: 6, IND: 1

COMMITTEE CHAIRS

Audit & Governance: Mr James Fry

General Purposes Licensing: Ms Mary Clarkson

Housing: Ms Linda Smith

Oxfordshire C

Oxfordshire County Council, County Hall, New Road, Oxford OX1 1ND
☎ 01865 792422 ✉ online@oxfordshire.gov.uk
💻 www.oxfordshire.gov.uk

FACTS AND FIGURES

Parliamentary Constituencies: Banbury, Henley, Oxford East, Oxford West and Abingdon, Wantage, Witney
EU Constituencies: South East
Election Frequency: Elections are of whole council

PRINCIPAL OFFICERS

Chief Executive: Mr Peter Clark, Head of Law & Governance & Head of Paid Service, County Hall, New Road, Oxford OX1 1ND
☎ 01865 323907 ✉ peter.clark@oxfordshire.gov.uk

Senior Management: Mr Jim Leivers , Director for Children's Services, County Hall, New Road, Oxford OX1 1ND ☎ 01865 815122
✉ jim.lievers@oxfordshire.gov.uk

Senior Management: Mr Jonathan McWilliam , Director of Public Health, County Hall, New Road, Oxford OX1 1ND ☎ 01865 325004
✉ jonathan.mcwilliam@oxfordshire.gov.uk

Senior Management: Ms Sue Scane , Director for Environment & Economy, County Hall, New Road, Oxford OX1 1ND
☎ 01865 816399 ✉ sue.scane@oxfordshire.gov.uk

Access Officer / Social Services (Disability): Mr John Jackson, Director of Adult Social Services & Director of Strategy & Transformation, County Hall, New Road, Oxford OX1 1ND ☎ 01865 323574 ✉ john.jackson@oxfordshire.gov.uk

Architect, Building / Property Services: Mr Mark Kemp , Deputy Director - Commercial, County Hall, New Road, Oxford OX1 1ND ☎ 01865 815845 ✉ mark.kemp@oxfordshire.gov.uk

Children / Youth Services: Mr Jim Leivers , Director for Children's Services, County Hall, New Road, Oxford OX1 1ND ☎ 01865 815122 ✉ jim.lievers@oxfordshire.gov.uk

Children / Youth Services: Ms Rebecca Matthews , Interim Deputy Director - Education & Early Intervention, County Hall, New Road, Oxford OX1 1ND ☎ 01865 815125 ✉ rebecca.matthews@oxfordshire.gov.uk

Civil Registration: Mrs Jacquie Bugeja , Head of Registration & Coroner Services, 1 Tidmarsh Lane, Oxford OX1 1NS ☎ 01865 816288 ✉ jacquie.bugeja@oxfordshire.gov.uk

PR / Communications: Mr Eddie Gibb , Head of Communications, County Hall, New Road, Oxford OX1 1ND ☎ 01865 896198 ✉ eddie.gibb@oxfordshire.gov.uk

Community Safety: Mr David Etheridge , Chief Fire Officer & Head of Community Safety, County Hall, New Road, Oxford OX1 1ND ☎ 01865 855205 🖷 01865 855241 ✉ david.etheridge@oxfordshire.gov.uk

Computer Management: Mr Martyn Ward , Service Manager ICT Business Delivery, Unipart House, Garsington Road, Oxford OX4 2GQ ☎ 07786 691134 ✉ martyn.ward@oxfordshire.gov.uk

Consumer Protection and Trading Standards: Mr Richard Webb , Trading Standards & Community Safety Manager, Graham Hill House, Electric Avenue, Ferry Hinksey Road, Oxford OX2 0BY ☎ 01865 815791 ✉ richard.webb@oxfordshire.gov.uk

Contracts: Ms Kate Terroni , Deputy Director - Joint Commissioning, County Hall, New Road, Oxford OX1 1ND ☎ 01865 815792 ✉ kate.terroni@oxfordshire.gov.uk

Customer Service: Mr Graham Shaw , Deputy Director for Oxfordshire Customer Services, Unipart House, Garsington Road, Oxford OX4 2GQ ☎ 07939 069084 ✉ graham.shaw@oxfordshire.gov.uk

Economic Development: Ms Bev Hindle , Deputy Director - Strategy & Infrastructure Planning, County Hall, New Road, Oxford OX1 1ND ☎ 01865 815113 ✉ bev.hindle@oxfordshire.gov.uk

Education: Ms Rebecca Matthews , Interim Deputy Director - Education & Early Intervention, County Hall, New Road, Oxford OX1 1ND ☎ 01865 815125 ✉ rebecca.matthews@oxfordshire.gov.uk

E-Government: Mr Graham Shaw , Deputy Director for Oxfordshire Customer Services, Unipart House, Garsington Road, Oxford OX4 2GQ ☎ 07939 069084 ✉ graham.shaw@oxfordshire.gov.uk

Emergency Planning: Ms Carol MacKay , Principal Emergency Planning Officer, Woodeaton Manor Lodge, Oxford OX3 9GU ☎ 01865 323763 ✉ carol.mackay@oxfordshire.gov.uk

Energy Management: Ms Bev Hindle , Deputy Director - Strategy & Infrastructure Planning, County Hall, New Road, Oxford OX1 1ND ☎ 01865 815113 ✉ bev.hindle@oxfordshire.gov.uk

Environmental / Technical Services: Ms Bev Hindle , Deputy Director - Strategy & Infrastructure Planning, County Hall, New Road, Oxford OX1 1ND ☎ 01865 815113 ✉ bev.hindle@oxfordshire.gov.uk

Estates, Property & Valuation: Mr Mark Kemp , Deputy Director - Commercial, County Hall, New Road, Oxford OX1 1ND ☎ 01865 815845 ✉ mark.kemp@oxfordshire.gov.uk

Facilities: Mr Mark Kemp , Deputy Director - Commercial, County Hall, New Road, Oxford OX1 1ND ☎ 01865 815845 ✉ mark.kemp@oxfordshire.gov.uk

Finance: Ms Lorna Baxter , Chief Finance Officer, County Hall, New Road, Oxford OX1 1ND ☎ 01865 323971 ✉ lorna.baxter@oxfordshire.gov.uk

Treasury: Ms Lorna Baxter , Chief Finance Officer, County Hall, New Road, Oxford OX1 1ND ☎ 01865 323971 ✉ lorna.baxter@oxfordshire.gov.uk

Pensions: Ms Sally Fox , Pensions Services Manager, Pension Services, Oxfordshire County Council, Unipart House, Garsington Road, Oxford oX4 2GQ ☎ 01865 797111 ✉ sally.fox@oxfordshire.gov.uk

Pensions: Ms Donna Ross , Principal Financial Manager, Treasury & Pension Fund Investment Team, Oxfordshire County Council, 3rd Floor, County Hall, New Road, Oxford OX1 1ND ☎ 01865 323976 ✉ donna.ross@oxfordshire.gov.uk

Health and Safety: Ms Sue Corrigan , County HR Manager, County Hall, New Road, Oxford OX1 1ND ☎ 01865 810280

Highways: Mr Mark Kemp , Deputy Director - Commercial, County Hall, New Road, Oxford OX1 1ND ☎ 01865 815845 ✉ mark.kemp@oxfordshire.gov.uk

Legal: Mr Peter Clark, Head of Law & Governance & Head of Paid Service, County Hall, New Road, Oxford OX1 1ND ☎ 01865 323907 ✉ peter.clark@oxfordshire.gov.uk

Legal: Mr Nick Graham , Deputy Head of Law & Culture, County Hall, New Road, Oxford OX1 1ND ✉ nick.graham@oxfordshire.gov.uk

Leisure and Cultural Services: Mr Nick Graham , Deputy Head of Law & Culture, County Hall, New Road, Oxford OX1 1ND ✉ nick.graham@oxfordshire.gov.uk

Member Services: Mr Peter Clark, Head of Law & Governance & Head of Paid Service, County Hall, New Road, Oxford OX1 1ND ☎ 01865 323907 ✉ peter.clark@oxfordshire.gov.uk

Partnerships: Mr John Courouble , Research & Intelligence Manager, County Hall, New Road, Oxford OX1 1ND ☎ 01865 896163 ✉ john.courouble@oxfordshire.gov.uk

Partnerships: Ms Maggie Scott , Head of Policy, County Hall, New Road, Oxford OX1 1ND ☎ 01865 816061 maggie.scott@oxfordshire.gov.uk

Personnel / HR: Mr Steve Munn, Chief Human Resources Officer, County Hall, New Road, Oxford OX1 1ND ☎ 01865 815191 steve.munn@oxfordshire.gov.uk

Planning: Ms Bev Hindle , Deputy Director - Strategy & Infrastructure Planning, County Hall, New Road, Oxford OX1 1ND ☎ 01865 815113 bev.hindle@oxfordshire.gov.uk

Procurement: Mr Graham Collins , Interim County Procurement officer, County Hall, New Road, Oxford OX1 1ND ☎ 01865 323111 graham.collins@oxfordshire.gov.uk

Public Libraries: Ms Karen Warren , Cultural Services Manager, Oxford Central Library, Westgate, Oxford OX1 1DJ ☎ 01865 322580 karen.warren@oxfordshire.gov.uk

Recycling & Waste Minimisation: Ms Bev Hindle , Deputy Director - Strategy & Infrastructure Planning, County Hall, New Road, Oxford OX1 1ND ☎ 01865 815113 bev.hindle@oxfordshire.gov.uk

Road Safety: Mr Mark Kemp , Deputy Director - Commercial, County Hall, New Road, Oxford OX1 1ND ☎ 01865 815845 mark.kemp@oxfordshire.gov.uk

Social Services: Mr John Jackson, Director of Adult Social Services & Director of Strategy & Transformation, County Hall, New Road, Oxford OX1 1ND ☎ 01865 323574 john.jackson@oxfordshire.gov.uk

Social Services (Adult): Ms Seona Douglas , Deputy Director for Adult Social Care, County Hall, New Road, Oxford OX1 1ND ☎ 01865 323570

Social Services (Children): Ms Lucy Butler , Deputy Director for Children's Social Care & YOS, County Hall, New Road, Oxford OX1 1ND ☎ 01865 815165 lucy.butler@oxfordshire.gov.uk

Public Health: Mr Jonathan McWilliam , Director of Public Health, County Hall, New Road, Oxford OX1 1ND ☎ 01865 325004 jonathan.mcwilliam@oxfordshire.gov.uk

Staff Training: Ms Karen Hopwood , Learning & Development Manager, County Hall, New Road, Oxford OX1 1ND ☎ 07557 082597 karen.hopwood@oxfordshire.gov.uk

Sustainable Communities: Ms Bev Hindle , Deputy Director - Strategy & Infrastructure Planning, County Hall, New Road, Oxford OX1 1ND ☎ 01865 815113 bev.hindle@oxfordshire.gov.uk

Sustainable Development: Ms Bev Hindle , Deputy Director - Strategy & Infrastructure Planning, County Hall, New Road, Oxford OX1 1ND ☎ 01865 815113 bev.hindle@oxfordshire.gov.uk

Sustainable Development: Ms Sue Scane , Director for Environment & Economy, County Hall, New Road, Oxford OX1 1ND ☎ 01865 816399 sue.scane@oxfordshire.gov.uk

Traffic Management: Mr Mark Kemp , Deputy Director - Commercial, County Hall, New Road, Oxford OX1 1ND ☎ 01865 815845 mark.kemp@oxfordshire.gov.uk

Transport: Mr Mark Kemp , Deputy Director - Commercial, County Hall, New Road, Oxford OX1 1ND ☎ 01865 815845 mark.kemp@oxfordshire.gov.uk

Transport Planner: Ms Bev Hindle , Deputy Director - Strategy & Infrastructure Planning, County Hall, New Road, Oxford OX1 1ND ☎ 01865 815113 bev.hindle@oxfordshire.gov.uk

Waste Management: Mr Mark Kemp , Deputy Director - Commercial, County Hall, New Road, Oxford OX1 1ND ☎ 01865 815845 mark.kemp@oxfordshire.gov.uk

COUNCILLORS

***Chair* Sanders**, John (LAB - Cowley)
john.sanders@oxfordshire.gov.uk

***Vice-Chair* Waine**, Michael (CON - Bicester Town)
michael.waine@oxfordshire.gov.uk

***Leader of the Council* Hudspeth**, Ian (CON - Woodstock)
ian.hudspeth@oxfordshire.gov.uk

***Deputy Leader of the Council* Rose**, Rodney (CON - Charlbury & Wychwood)
rodney.rose@oxfordshire.gov.uk

Atkins, Lynda (IND - Wallingford)
lynda.atkins@oxfordshire.gov.uk

Azad, Jamila (LAB - St Clement's & Cowley Marsh)
jamila.azad@oxfordshire.gov.uk

Bartholomew, David (CON - Sonning Common)
david.bartholomew@oxfordshire.gov.uk

Beal, Mike (LAB - Banbury Grimsbury & Castle)
mike.beal@oxfordshire.gov.uk

Billington, Maurice (CON - Kidlington South)
maurice.billington@oxfordshire.gov.uk

Brighouse, Liz (LAB - Churchill & Lye Valley)
liz.brighouse@oxfordshire.gov.uk

Bulmer, Kevin (CON - Goring)
kevin.bulmer@oxfordshire.gov.uk

Carter, Nick (CON - Thame & Chinnor)
nick.carter@oxfordshire.gov.uk

Chapman, Louise (CON - Hanborough & Minster Lovell)
louise.chapman@oxfordshire.gov.uk

Cherry, Mark (LAB - Banbury Calthorpe)
mark.cherry@oxfordshire.gov.uk

Christie, John (LAB - Banbury Ruscote)
john.christie@oxfordshire.gov.uk

Coates, Sam (GRN - University Park)
sam.coates@oxfordshire.gov.uk

Constance, Yvonne (CON - Shrivenham)
yvonne.constance@oxfordshire.gov.uk

Curran, Steve (LAB - Leys)
stephen.curran@oxfordshire.gov.uk

Dhesi, Surinder (LAB - Banbury Hardwick)
surinder.dhesi@oxfordshire.gov.uk

Fatemian, Arash (CON - Deddington)
arash.fatemian@oxfordshire.gov.uk

Fawcett, Neil (LD - Abingdon South)
neil.fawcett@oxfordshire.gov.uk

Fooks, Jean (LD - Wolvercote & Summertown)
jean.fooks@oxfordshire.gov.uk

Fulljames, Catherine (CON - Ploughley)
catherine.fulljames@oxfordshire.gov.uk

Gearing, Anthony (CON - Kirtlington & Kidlington North)
anthony.gearing@oxfordshire.gov.uk

Godden, Janet (LD - North Hinksey)
janet.godden@oxfordshire.gov.uk

Gray, Mark (IND - Benson & Cholsey)
mark.gray2@oxfordshire.gov.uk

Greene, Patrick (CON - Didcot East & Hagbourne)
patrick.greene@oxfordshire.gov.uk

Hallchurch, Tim (CON - Otmoor)
timothy.hallchurch@oxfordshire.gov.uk

Handley, Pete (CON - Carterton South & West)
peter.handley@oxfordshire.gov.uk

Hannaby, Jenny (LD - Grove & Wantage)
jenny.hannaby@oxfordshire.gov.uk

Hards, Nick (LAB - Didcot West)
nick.hards@oxfordshire.gov.uk

Harris, Neville (INDNA - Didcot Ladygrove)
nevhar@aol.com

Harrod, Steve (CON - Chalgrove & Watlington)
steve.harrod@oxfordshire.gov.uk

Heathcoat, Judith (CON - Faringdon)
judith.heathcoat@oxfordshire.gov.uk

Hibbert-Biles, Hilary (CON - Chipping Norton)
hilary.biles@oxfordshire.gov.uk

Howson, John (LD - St Margaret's)
john.howson@oxfordshire.gov.uk

Johnston, Bob (LD - Kennington & Radley)
bob.johnston@oxfordshire.gov.uk

Langridge, Richard (CON - Witney North & East)
richard.langridge@oxfordshire.gov.uk

Lilly, Stewart (CON - Hendreds & Harwell)
stewart.lilly@oxfordshire.gov.uk

Lindsay-Gale, Lorraine (CON - Berinsfield & Garsington)
lorraine.lindsay-gale@oxfordshire.gov.uk

Lovatt, Sandy (CON - Abingdon North)
sandy.lovatt@oxfordshire.gov.uk

Lygo, Mark (LAB - Marston & Northway)
mark.lygo@oxfordshire.gov.uk

Mallon, Kieron (CON - Bloxham & Easington)

Matthew, Charles (CON - Eynsham)
charles.matthew@oxfordshire.gov.uk

Mills, James (CON - Witney West & Bampton)
james.mills@oxfordshire.gov.uk

Nimmo Smith, David (CON - Henley-on-Thames)
david.nimmo-smith@oxfordshire.gov.uk

Owen, Neil (CON - Burford & Carterton North)
neil.owen@oxfordshire.gov.uk

Patrick, Zoé (LD - Grove & Wantage)
zoe.patrick@oxfordshire.gov.uk

Phillips, Glynis (LAB - Barton, Sandhills & Risinghurst)
glynis.phillips@oxfordshire.gov.uk

Pressel, Susanna (LAB - Jericho & Osney)
susanna.pressel@oxfordshire.gov.uk

Price, Laura (LAB - Witney South & Central)
laura.price@oxfordshire.gov.uk

Purse, Anne (LD - Wheatley)
anne.purse@oxfordshire.gov.uk

Reynolds, George (CON - Wroxton & Hook Norton)
george.reynolds@oxfordshire.gov.uk

Rooke, Alison (LD - Abingdon East)
alison.rooke@oxfordshire.gov.uk

Sanders, Gill (LAB - Rose Hill & Littlemore)
gill.sanders@oxfordshire.gov.uk

Sibley, Les (IND - Bicester West)
les.sibley@oxfordshire.gov.uk

Smith, Roz (LD - Headington & Quarry)
roz.smith@oxfordshire.gov.uk

Stratford, Lawrie (CON - Bicester North)
lawrie.stratford@oxfordshire.gov.uk

Tanner, John (LAB - Isis)
john.tanner@oxfordshire.gov.uk

Tilley, Melinda (CON - Kingston & Cumnor)
melinda.tilley@oxfordshire.gov.uk

Webber, Richard (LD - Sutton Courtenay & Marcham)
richard.webber@oxfordshire.gov.uk

Williams, David (GRN - Iffley Fields & St Mary's)
david.williams@oxfordshire.gov.uk

Wilmshurst, David (CON - Thame & Chinnor)
david.wilmshurst@oxfordshire.gov.uk

POLITICAL COMPOSITION

CON: 31, LAB: 15, LD: 11, IND: 3, GRN: 2, INDNA: 1

COMMITTEE CHAIRS

Audit & Governance: Mr David Wilmshurst

Pensions: Mr Stewart Lilly

Planning & Regulation: Mrs Catherine Fulljames

Pembrokeshire W

Pembrokeshire County Council, County Hall, Haverfordwest
SA61 1TP
☎ 01437 764551 🖷 01437 775303 enquiries@pembrokeshire.gov.uk
www.pembrokeshire.gov.uk

FACTS AND FIGURES

Parliamentary Constituencies: Carmarthen West and South Pembrokeshire, Preseli Pembrokeshire
EU Constituencies: Wales
Election Frequency: Elections are of whole council

PRINCIPAL OFFICERS

Chief Executive: Mr Ian Westley, Chief Executive, County Hall, Haverfordwest SA61 1TP ☎ 01437 764551 ian.westley@pembrokeshire.gov.uk

Deputy Chief Executive: Dr Ben Pykett , Deputy Chief Executive, County Hall, Haverfordwest SA61 1TP ☎ 01437 764551 ben.pykett@pembrokeshire.gov.uk

Senior Management: Ms Kate Evan-Hughes , Director - Children & Schools, County Hall, Haverfordwest SA61 1TP ☎ 01437 764551 kate.evanhughes@pembrokeshire.gov.uk

Senior Management: Dr Steven Jones , Director - Development, County Hall, Haverfordwest SA61 1TP ☎ 01437 764551 steven_jones@pembrokeshire.gov.uk

Senior Management: Mrs Pam Marsden , Director - Social Services & Leisure, County Hall, Haverfordwest SA61 1TP ☎ 01437 764551 pam.marsden@pembrokeshire.gov.uk

Access Officer / Social Services (Disability): Mr Alan Hunt, Access Officer, County Hall, Haverfordwest SA61 1TP ☎ 01437 764551 alan.hunt@pembrokeshire.gov.uk

Architect, Building / Property Services: Mr Barry Cooke , Head of Property, County Hall, Haverfordwest SA61 1TP ☎ 01437 764551 barry.cooke@pembrokeshire.gov.uk

Best Value: Dr Ben Pykett , Deputy Chief Executive, County Hall, Haverfordwest SA61 1TP ☎ 01437 764551 ben.pykett@pembrokeshire.gov.uk

Building Control: Mr David Fitzsimon , Head of Planning, County Hall, Haverfordwest SA61 1TP ☎ 01437 764551 david.fitzsimon@pembrokeshire.gov.uk

Catering Services: Mr Ian Eynon , Head of Business Services, County Hall, Haverfordwest SA61 1TP ☎ 01437 764451 ian.eynon@pembrokeshire.gov.uk

Children / Youth Services: Ms Kate Evan-Hughes , Director - Children & Schools, County Hall, Haverfordwest SA61 1TP ☎ 01437 764551 kate.evanhughes@pembrokeshire.gov.uk

Children / Youth Services: Ms Allison Parkinson , Head of Children's Services, County Hall, Haverfordwest SA61 1TP ☎ 01437 764551 allison.parkinson@pembrokeshire.gov.uk

Civil Registration: Mr Ceri Davies , Head of Human Resources, County Hall, Haverfordwest SA61 1TP ☎ 01437 764551 ceri.davies@pembrokeshire.gov.uk

PR / Communications: Mr Len Mullins , Press & Public Relations Manager, County Hall, Haverfordwest SA61 1TP ☎ 01437 764551 len.mullins@pembrokeshire.gov.uk

PR / Communications: Dr Ben Pykett , Deputy Chief Executive, County Hall, Haverfordwest SA61 1TP ☎ 01437 764551 ben.pykett@pembrokeshire.gov.uk

Community Planning: Dr Ben Pykett , Deputy Chief Executive, County Hall, Haverfordwest SA61 1TP ☎ 01437 764551 ben.pykett@pembrokeshire.gov.uk

Community Safety: Mr Mark Elliott , Head of Public Protection, County Hall, Haverfordwest SA61 1TP ☎ 01437 764551 mark.elliott@pembrokeshire.gov.uk

Computer Management: Mr John Roberts , Head of Information Technology & Central Support Services, County Hall, Haverfordwest SA61 1TP ☎ 01437 764551 john.roberts@pembrokeshire.gov.uk

Consumer Protection and Trading Standards: Mr Mark Elliott , Head of Public Protection, County Hall, Haverfordwest SA61 1TP ☎ 01437 764551 mark.elliott@pembrokeshire.gov.uk

Contracts: Mr Paul Ashley-Jones, Head of Procurement, County Hall, Haverfordwest SA61 1TP ☎ 01437 764551 🖷 01437 776510 paul.ashley-jones@pembrokeshire.gov.uk

Corporate Services: Dr Ben Pykett , Deputy Chief Executive, County Hall, Haverfordwest SA61 1TP ☎ 01437 764551 ben.pykett@pembrokeshire.gov.uk

Customer Service: Dr Ben Pykett , Deputy Chief Executive, County Hall, Haverfordwest SA61 1TP ☎ 01437 764551 ben.pykett@pembrokeshire.gov.uk

Economic Development: Mr Martin White , Head of Regeneration, County Hall, Haverfordwest SA61 1TP ☎ 01437 764551 martin.white@pembrokeshire.gov.uk

Education: Ms Kate Evan-Hughes , Director - Children & Schools, County Hall, Haverfordwest SA61 1TP ☎ 01437 764551 kate.evanhughes@pembrokeshire.gov.uk

Education: Mr Ian Eynon , Head of Business Services, County Hall, Haverfordwest SA61 1TP ☎ 01437 764451 ian.eynon@pembrokeshire.gov.uk

Education: Mr James White , Head of Performance & Community, County Hall, Haverfordwest SA61 1TP james.white@pembrokeshire.gov.uk

E-Government: Mr John Roberts , Head of Information Technology & Central Support Services, County Hall, Haverfordwest SA61 1TP ☎ 01437 764551 john.roberts@pembrokeshire.gov.uk

Electoral Registration: Mr Glynne Morgan, Electoral Services Manager, County Hall, Haverfordwest SA61 1TP ☎ 01437 764551 glynne.morgan@pembrokeshire.gov.uk

Emergency Planning: Mr Richard Brown, Head of Environment & Civil Contingencies, County Hall, Haverfordwest SA61 1TP ☎ 01437 764551 richard.brown@pembrokeshire.gov.uk

Energy Management: Mr Darren Thomas, Head of Highways & Construction, County Hall, Haverfordwest SA61 1TP ☎ 01437 764551 🖷 01437 775008 darren.thomas@pembrokeshire.gov.uk

Environmental / Technical Services: Mr Ian Westley, Chief Executive, County Hall, Haverfordwest SA61 1TP ☎ 01437 764551 🖱 ian.westley@pembrokeshire.gov.uk

Environmental Health: Mr Mark Elliott , Head of Public Protection, County Hall, Haverfordwest SA61 1TP ☎ 01437 764551 🖱 mark.elliott@pembrokeshire.gov.uk

Estates, Property & Valuation: Mr Barry Cooke , Head of Property, County Hall, Haverfordwest SA61 1TP ☎ 01437 764551 🖱 barry.cooke@pembrokeshire.gov.uk

European Liaison: Mr Gwyn Evans, European Manager, County Hall, Haverfordwest SA61 1TP ☎ 01437 764551 🖶 01437 776184 🖱 gwyn.evans@pembrokeshire.gov.uk

Facilities: Mr Gareth Howells, Facilities Manager, County Hall, Haverfordwest SA61 1TP ☎ 01437 764551 🖶 01437 775303 🖱 gareth.howells@pembrokeshire.gov.uk

Finance: Mr Jonathan Haswell , Chief Finance Officer, County Hall, Haverfordwest SA61 1TP ☎ 01437 764551 🖱 jonathan.haswell@pembrokeshire.gov.uk

Finance: Mr Kerry Macdermott , Head of Revenue Services, County Hall, Haverfordwest SA61 1TP ☎ 01437 775755 🖱 kerry.macdermott@pembrokeshire.gov.uk

Fleet Management: Mr Hubert Mathias, Transport & Fleet Manager, County Hall, Haverfordwest SA61 1TP ☎ 01437 764551 🖱 hubert.mathias@pembrokeshire.gov.uk

Grounds Maintenance: Mr Richard Brown, Head of Environment & Civil Contingencies, County Hall, Haverfordwest SA61 1TP ☎ 01437 764551 🖱 richard.brown@pembrokeshire.gov.uk

Grounds Maintenance: Mr Glenville Codd , Area Maintenance Manager for the South, County Hall, Haverfordwest SA61 1TP ☎ 01437 764551 🖱 glenville.codd@pembrokeshire.gov.uk

Health and Safety: Mr Paul Eades , Risk Manager & Business Continuity, County Hall, Haverfordwest SA61 1TP ☎ 01437 764551 🖱 paul.eades@pembrokeshire.gov.uk

Highways: Mr Darren Thomas, Head of Highways & Construction, County Hall, Haverfordwest SA61 1TP ☎ 01437 764551 🖶 01437 775008 🖱 darren.thomas@pembrokeshire.gov.uk

Home Energy Conservation: Mr Steven Keating , Energy Manager, County Hall, Haverfordwest SA61 1TP ☎ 01437 764551 🖱 steve.keating@pembrokeshire.gov.uk

Housing: Mrs Lyn Hambidge , Head of Housing , County Hall, Haverfordwest SA61 1TP ☎ 01437 764551 🖱 lyn.hambidge@pembrokeshire.gov.uk

Housing Maintenance: Mrs Lyn Hambidge , Head of Housing , County Hall, Haverfordwest SA61 1TP ☎ 01437 764551 🖱 lyn.hambidge@pembrokeshire.gov.uk

Local Area Agreement: Dr Ben Pykett , Deputy Chief Executive, County Hall, Haverfordwest SA61 1TP ☎ 01437 764551 🖱 ben.pykett@pembrokeshire.gov.uk

Legal: Ms Claire Incledon , Head of Legal & Committee Services, County Hall, Haverfordwest SA61 1TP ☎ 01437 764551 🖱 claire.incledon@pembrokeshire.gov.uk

Leisure and Cultural Services: Mr Mike Cavanagh , Head of Cultural Services, County Hall, Haverfordwest SA61 1TP ☎ 01437 764551 🖱 mike.cavanagh@pembrokeshire.gov.uk

Leisure and Cultural Services: Mr Chris Payne , Leisure Services Manager, County Hall, Haverfordwest SA61 1TP ☎ 01437 764551 🖶 01437 775303 🖱 chris.payne@pembrokeshire.gov.uk

Licensing: Mr Mark Elliott , Head of Public Protection, County Hall, Haverfordwest SA61 1TP ☎ 01437 764551 🖱 mark.elliott@pembrokeshire.gov.uk

Lifelong Learning: Mr James White , Head of Performance & Community, County Hall, Haverfordwest SA61 1TP 🖱 james.white@pembrokeshire.gov.uk

Lighting: Mr Darren Thomas, Head of Highways & Construction, County Hall, Haverfordwest SA61 1TP ☎ 01437 764551 🖶 01437 775008 🖱 darren.thomas@pembrokeshire.gov.uk

Lottery Funding, Charity and Voluntary: Dr Ben Pykett , Deputy Chief Executive, County Hall, Haverfordwest SA61 1TP ☎ 01437 764551 🖱 ben.pykett@pembrokeshire.gov.uk

Member Services: Ms Claire Incledon , Head of Legal & Committee Services, County Hall, Haverfordwest SA61 1TP ☎ 01437 764551 🖱 claire.incledon@pembrokeshire.gov.uk

Parking: Mr Marc Owen , Streetcare Manager, County Hall, Haverfordwest SA61 1TP ☎ 01437 764551 🖱 marc.owen@pembrokeshire.gov.uk

Partnerships: Dr Ben Pykett , Deputy Chief Executive, County Hall, Haverfordwest SA61 1TP ☎ 01437 764551 🖱 ben.pykett@pembrokeshire.gov.uk

Personnel / HR: Mr Ceri Davies , Head of Human Resources, County Hall, Haverfordwest SA61 1TP ☎ 01437 764551 🖱 ceri.davies@pembrokeshire.gov.uk

Planning: Mr David Fitzsimon , Head of Planning, County Hall, Haverfordwest SA61 1TP ☎ 01437 764551 🖱 david.fitzsimon@pembrokeshire.gov.uk

Planning: Dr Steven Jones , Director - Development, County Hall, Haverfordwest SA61 1TP ☎ 01437 764551 🖱 steven_jones@pembrokeshire.gov.uk

Procurement: Mr Paul Ashley-Jones, Head of Procurement, County Hall, Haverfordwest SA61 1TP ☎ 01437 764551 🖶 01437 776510 🖱 paul.ashley-jones@pembrokeshire.gov.uk

Public Libraries: Mr Mike Cavanagh , Head of Cultural Services, County Hall, Haverfordwest SA61 1TP ☎ 01437 764551 ✉ mike.cavanagh@pembrokeshire.gov.uk

Recycling & Waste Minimisation: Mr Richard Brown, Head of Environment & Civil Contingencies, County Hall, Haverfordwest SA61 1TP ☎ 01437 764551 ✉ richard.brown@pembrokeshire.gov.uk

Regeneration: Mr Martin White , Head of Regeneration, County Hall, Haverfordwest SA61 1TP ☎ 01437 764551 ✉ martin.white@pembrokeshire.gov.uk

Road Safety: Ms Kirstie-Anne Donoghue , Road Safety Officer, County Hall, Haverfordwest SA61 1TP ☎ 01437 764551 🖷 01437 775008 ✉ kirstie-anne.donoghue@pembrokeshire.gov.uk

Social Services: Mrs Pam Marsden , Director - Social Services & Leisure, County Hall, Haverfordwest SA61 1TP ☎ 01437 764551 ✉ pam.marsden@pembrokeshire.gov.uk

Social Services (Adult): Ms Ellen Law , Acting Head of Adult Care, County Hall, Haverfordwest SA61 1TP ☎ 01437 754551 ✉ ellen.law@pembrokeshire.gov.uk

Social Services (Children): Ms Allison Parkinson , Head of Children's Services, County Hall, Haverfordwest SA61 1TP ☎ 01437 764551 ✉ allison.parkinson@pembrokeshire.gov.uk

Staff Training: Mrs Sue Swan , Learning & Development Manager, County Hall, Haverfordwest SA61 1TP ☎ 01437 764551 ✉ sue.swan@pembrokeshire.gov.uk

Street Scene: Mr Darren Thomas, Head of Highways & Construction, County Hall, Haverfordwest SA61 1TP ☎ 01437 764551 🖷 01437 775008 ✉ darren.thomas@pembrokeshire.gov.uk

Sustainable Communities: Dr Steven Jones , Director - Development, County Hall, Haverfordwest SA61 1TP ☎ 01437 764551 ✉ steven_jones@pembrokeshire.gov.uk

Sustainable Development: Dr Steven Jones , Director - Development, County Hall, Haverfordwest SA61 1TP ☎ 01437 764551 ✉ steven_jones@pembrokeshire.gov.uk

Tourism: Mr Martin White , Head of Regeneration, County Hall, Haverfordwest SA61 1TP ☎ 01437 764551 ✉ martin.white@pembrokeshire.gov.uk

Town Centre: Dr Steven Jones , Director of Development, County Hall, Haverfordwest SA61 1TP ☎ 01437 764551 ✉ steven_jones@pembrokeshire.gov.uk

Traffic Management: Mr Darren Thomas, Head of Highways & Construction, County Hall, Haverfordwest SA61 1TP ☎ 01437 764551 🖷 01437 775008 ✉ darren.thomas@pembrokeshire.gov.uk

Transport: Mr Hubert Mathias, Transport & Fleet Manager, County Hall, Haverfordwest SA61 1TP ☎ 01437 764551 ✉ hubert.mathias@pembrokeshire.gov.uk

Transport Planner: Mr Darren Thomas, Head of Highways & Construction, County Hall, Haverfordwest SA61 1TP ☎ 01437 764551 🖷 01437 775008 ✉ darren.thomas@pembrokeshire.gov.uk

Total Place: Dr Ben Pykett , Deputy Chief Executive, County Hall, Haverfordwest SA61 1TP ☎ 01437 764551 ✉ ben.pykett@pembrokeshire.gov.uk

Waste Collection and Disposal: Mr Richard Brown, Head of Environment & Civil Contingencies, County Hall, Haverfordwest SA61 1TP ☎ 01437 764551 ✉ richard.brown@pembrokeshire.gov.uk

Waste Management: Mr Richard Brown, Head of Environment & Civil Contingencies, County Hall, Haverfordwest SA61 1TP ☎ 01437 764551 ✉ richard.brown@pembrokeshire.gov.uk

Children's Play Areas: Mr Richard Brown, Head of Environment & Civil Contingencies, County Hall, Haverfordwest SA61 1TP ☎ 01437 764551 ✉ richard.brown@pembrokeshire.gov.uk

COUNCILLORS

***Chair* Evans**, Wynne (IND - Narberth)
cllr.wynne.evans@pembrokeshire.gov.uk

***Vice-Chair* Brinsden**, John Anthony (INDNA - Amroth)
brinsden-2@supanet.com

***Leader of the Council* Adams**, James (IND - Camrose)
cllr.jamie.adams@pembrokeshire.gov.uk

***Deputy Leader of the Council* Lewis**, Keith (IND - Crymych)
cllr.keith.lewis@pembrokeshire.gov.uk

***Group Leader* Howlett**, David (CON - Wiston)
cllr.david.howlett@pembrokeshire.gov.uk

***Group Leader* Kilmister**, Bob (IND - Dinas Cross)
cllr.bob.kilmister@pembrokeshire.gov.uk

***Group Leader* Miller**, Paul (LAB - Neyland West)
cllr.paul.miller@pembrokeshire.gov.uk

***Group Leader* Williams**, Michael (PC - Tenby North)
cllr.michael.williams@pembrokeshire.gov.uk

Allen-Mirehouse, John (IND - Hundleton)
cllr.john.allen-mirehouse@pembrokeshire.gov.uk

Baker, Philip (NP - Saundersfoot)
cllr.phil.baker@pembrokeshire.gov.uk

Bowen, Roderick (PC - Clydau)
cllr.rod.bowen@pembrokeshire.gov.uk

Bryan, David (CON - Haverfordwest Priory)
cllr.david.bryan@pembrokeshire.gov.uk

Bush, Daphne (IND - Pembroke St. Mary South)
cllr.daphne.bush@pembrokeshire.gov.uk

Davies, John Thomas (IND - Cilgerran)
john.cwmbetws@virgin.net

Davies, Pat (LAB - Fishguard: North West)
cllr.pat.davies@pembrokeshire.gov.uk

Edwards, David Mark (IND - Haverfordwest Prendergast)
cllr.mark.edwards@pembrokeshire.gov.uk

Evans, Mike (NP - Tenby South)
sumo.evans@hotmail.co.uk

PEMBROKESHIRE

Frayling, Lyndon (IND - Haverfordwest Garth)
cllr.lyndon.frayling@pembrokeshire.gov.uk

George, Huw (IND - Maenclochog)
cllr.huw.george@pembrokeshire.gov.uk

Hall, Brian (IND - Pembroke Dock Market)
cllr.brian.hall@pembrokeshire.gov.uk

Hancock, Simon (LAB - Neyland East)
simon615@btinternet.com

Harries, Paul (IND - Newport)
cllr.paul.harries@pembrokeshire.gov.uk

Havard, Umelda (IND - Merlins Bridge)
cllr.umelda.havard@pembrokeshire.gov.uk

Hodgson, Tessa (NP - Lamphey)
cllr.tessa.hodgson@pembrokeshire.gov.uk

Hudson, Stanley (CON - Milford North)
cllr.stanley.hudson@pembrokeshire.gov.uk

James, Owen (NP - Scleddau)
cllr.owen.james@pembrokeshire.gov.uk

James, Mike (IND - St Dogmaels)
cllr.mike.james@pembrokeshire.gov.uk

Jenkins, Lyn (IND - Solva)
cllr.lyn.jenkins@pembrokeshire.gov.uk

John, Michael (IND - Llangwm)
cllr.michael.john@pembrokeshire.gov.uk

Joseph, Stephen (NP - Milford Central)
cllr.stephen.joseph@pembrokeshire.gov.uk

Kidney, Phillip (NP - Manorbier)
cllr.phillip.kidney@pembrokeshire.gov.uk

Lee, Alison (NP - Pembroke Dock Central)
cllr.alison.lee@pembrokeshire.gov.uk

Lewis, Robert (IND - Martletwy)
cllr.rob.lewis@pembrokeshire.gov.uk

Llewellyn, Pearl (IND - Pembroke Monkton)
cllr.pearl.llewellyn@pembrokeshire.gov.uk

Lloyd, David (NP - St. Davids)
cllr.david.lloyd@pembrokeshire.gov.uk

Morgan, Peter (IND - The Havens)
cllr.peter.morgan@pembrokeshire.gov.uk

Morse, Elwyn (IND - Narberth Rural)
cllr.elwyn.morse@pembrokeshire.gov.uk

Neale, David (IND - Carew)
cllr.david.neale@pembrokeshire.gov.uk

Nutting, Jonathan (IND - Pembroke St Michael)
cllr.jonathan.nutting@pembrokeshire.gov.uk

Owens, Reg (IND - St. Ishmaels)
cllr.reg.owens@pembrokeshire.gov.uk

Pepper, Myles (IND - Fishguard: North East)
cllr.myles.pepper@pembrokeshire.gov.uk

Perkins, Susan (IND - Pembroke Dock Llanion)
cllr.susan.perkins@pembrokeshire.gov.uk

Preston, Jonathan (PC - Penally)
cllr.jonathan.preston@pembrokeshire.gov.uk

Price, Gwilym (LAB - Goodwick)
cllr.gwilym.price@pembrokeshire.gov.uk

Pugh, David (IND - Kilgetty / Begelly)
cllr.david.pugh@pembrokeshire.gov.uk

Rees, David (IND - Llanrhian)
cllr.david.rees@pembrokeshire.gov.uk

Richards, Thomas (IND - Letterston)
cllr.tom.richards@pembrokeshire.gov.uk

Rowlands, Ken (IND - Johnston)
cllr.ken.rowlands@pembrokeshire.gov.uk

Simpson, David (NP - Lampeter Velfrey)
cllr.david.simpson@pembrokeshire.gov.uk

Sinnett, Rhys (PC - Milford West)
cllr.rhys.sinnett@pembrokeshire.gov.uk

Stock, Peter (INDNA - Haverfordwest Portfield)
cllr.peter.stock@pembrokeshire.gov.uk

Stoddart, Robert Michael (NP - Milford Hakin)
cllr.mike.stoddart@pembrokeshire.gov.uk

Stoddart, Vivien (NP - Milford Hubberston)
vivien.stoddart@virgin.net

Summons, Robert (IND - Burton)
cllr.rob.summons@pembrokeshire.gov.uk

Tudor, Thomas (LAB - Haverfordwest Castle)
cllr.thomas.tudor@pembrokeshire.gov.uk

Wilcox, Anthony (LAB - Pembroke Dock Pennar)
cllr.tony.wilcox@pembrokeshire.gov.uk

Williams, William (IND - Pembroke St. Mary North)
cllr.arwyn.williams@pembrokeshire.gov.uk

Williams, Jacob (INDNA - East Williamston)
jw@jacobwilliams.com

Woodham, Guy (LAB - Milford East)
cllr.guy.woodham@pembrokeshire.gov.uk

Yelland, Steve (IND - Rudbaxton)
cllr.steve.yelland@pembrokeshire.gov.uk

POLITICAL COMPOSITION

IND: 32, NP: 11, LAB: 7, PC: 4, CON: 3, INDNA: 3

COMMITTEE CHAIRS

Licensing: Ms Daphne Bush

Planning: Mr Myles Pepper

Pendle D

Pendle Borough Council, Town Hall, Market Street, Nelson BB9 7LG
☎ 01282 661661 🖷 01282 661630 💻 www.pendle.gov.uk

FACTS AND FIGURES

Parliamentary Constituencies: Pendle
EU Constituencies: North West
Election Frequency: Elections are by thirds

PRINCIPAL OFFICERS

Senior Management: Mr Dean Langton, Strategic Director, Town Hall, Market Street, Nelson BB9 7LG ☎ 01282 661602 🖷 01282 661601 ✉ dean.langton@pendle.gov.uk

Senior Management: Mr Philip Mousdale, Corporate Director, Town Hall, Market Street, Nelson BB9 7LG ☎ 01282 661634 🖷 01282 661601 ✉ philip.mousdale@pendle.gov.uk

Architect, Building / Property Services: Ms Sharon Livesey, Head of Property Services, Number One Market Street, Nelson BB9 7LJ ☎ 01282 878937 🖷 01282 661940 ✉ sharon.livesey@liberata.com

Building Control: Mr Neil Watson, Planning, Building Control & Licensing Services Manager, Town Hall, Market Street, Nelson BB9 7LG ☎ 01282 661706 🖷 01282 661720 ✉ neil.watson@pendle.gov.uk

PR / Communications: Ms Alice Barnett , Principal Communications Officer, Town Hall, Market Street, Nelson BB9 7LG ☎ 01282 661780

Community Planning: Mr Peter Atkinson , Neighbourhood Services Manager, Elliott House, 9 Market Square, Nelson BB9 0LX ☎ 01282 661063 🖷 01282 661043 ✉ peter.atkinson@pendle.gov.uk

Community Safety: Mr Geoff Whitehead, Localities, Communities and Policy Supervisor, Elliott House, 9 Market Square, Nelson BB9 0LX ☎ 01282 661660 🖷 01282 661043 ✉ geoff.whitehead@pendle.gov.uk

Computer Management: Mr Peter Rushton , ICT Service Delivery Manager, Number One Market Street, Nelson BB9 7LJ ☎ 01282 878984 🖷 01282 661811 ✉ peter.rushton@liberata.com

Customer Service: Ms Vicky McGurk , Pendle Service Delivery Manager, Liberata UK Ltd, Manor Lane, Sheffield S2 1TR ☎ 01282 878501 ✉ vicky.mcgurk@liberata.com

Economic Development: Ms Julie Whittaker , Housing, Health & Economic Development Services Manager, Elliott House, 9 Market Square, Nelson BB9 0LX ☎ 01282 661038 🖷 01282 661043 ✉ julie.whittaker@pendle.gov.uk

E-Government: Mr Peter Rushton , ICT Service Delivery Manager, Number One Market Street, Nelson BB9 7LJ ☎ 01282 878984 🖷 01282 661811 ✉ peter.rushton@liberata.com

Electoral Registration: Ms Gillian Turpin , Elections & Registration Manager, Town Hall, Market Street, Nelson BB9 7LG ☎ 01282 661919 ✉ gillian.turpin@pendle.gov.uk

Emergency Planning: Mr David Walker , Environmental Services Manager, Fleet Street Depot, Nelson BB9 7YQ ☎ 01282 661746 🖷 01282 661750 ✉ david.walker@pendle.gov.uk

Energy Management: Ms Sharon Livesey, Head of Property Services, Number One Market Street, Nelson BB9 7LJ ☎ 01282 878937 🖷 01282 661940 ✉ sharon.livesey@liberata.com

Environmental Health: Ms Julie Whittaker , Housing, Health & Economic Development Services Manager, Elliott House, 9 Market Square, Nelson BB9 0LX ☎ 01282 661038 🖷 01282 661043 ✉ julie.whittaker@pendle.gov.uk

Environmental Health: Ms Julie Whittaker , Housing, Health & Economic Development Services Manager, Elliott House, 9 Market Square, Nelson BB9 0LX ☎ 01282 661038 🖷 01282 661043 ✉ julie.whittaker@pendle.gov.uk

Estates, Property & Valuation: Ms Sharon Livesey, Head of Property Services, Number One Market Street, Nelson BB9 7LJ ☎ 01282 878937 🖷 01282 661940 ✉ sharon.livesey@liberata.com

Events Manager: Mr Michael Williams , Tourism Officer, Elliott House, 9 Market Square, Nelson BB9 0LX ☎ 01282 661963 🖷 01282 661881 ✉ michael.williams@pendle.gov.uk

Finance: Mr Vince Green , Financial Services Manager, Elliott House, 9 Market Square, Nelson BB9 0LX ☎ 01282 661867 ✉ vince.green@pendle.gov.uk

Fleet Management: Mr David Walker , Environmental Services Manager, Fleet Street Depot, Nelson BB9 7YQ ☎ 01282 661746 🖷 01282 661750 ✉ david.walker@pendle.gov.uk

Grounds Maintenance: Mr Keith Higson , Parks Technical Officer, Fleet Street Depot, Nelson BB9 7YQ ☎ 01282 661597 ✉ keith.higson@pendle.gov.uk

Health and Safety: Mr David Walker , Environmental Services Manager, Fleet Street Depot, Nelson BB9 7YQ ☎ 01282 661746 🖷 01282 661750 ✉ david.walker@pendle.gov.uk

Home Energy Conservation: Ms Julie Whittaker , Housing, Health & Economic Development Services Manager, Elliott House, 9 Market Square, Nelson BB9 0LX ☎ 01282 661038 🖷 01282 661043 ✉ julie.whittaker@pendle.gov.uk

Housing: Ms Julie Whittaker , Housing, Health & Economic Development Services Manager, Elliott House, 9 Market Square, Nelson BB9 0LX ☎ 01282 661038 🖷 01282 661043 ✉ julie.whittaker@pendle.gov.uk

Legal: Mr Richard Townson, Democratic & Legal Manager, Town Hall, Market Street, Nelson BB9 7LG ☎ 01282 661650 🖷 01282 661630 ✉ richard.townson@pendle.gov.uk

Leisure and Cultural Services: Mr Phil Storey, Chief Executive of Pendle Leisure Trust, Colne Town Hall, Albert Road, Colne BB8 0AQ ☎ 01282 661224 🖷 01282 661221 ✉ phil.storey@pendleleisuretrust.co.uk

Licensing: Mr Neil Watson, Planning, Building Control & Licensing Services Manager, Town Hall, Market Street, Nelson BB9 7LG ☎ 01282 661706 🖷 01282 661720 ✉ neil.watson@pendle.gov.uk

Lifelong Learning: Mr Simon Tisdale , Learning & Organisational Development Officer, Number One, Market Street, Nelson BB9 7LJ ☎ 01282 878805 ✉ simon.tisdale@liberata.com

Member Services: Mrs Jane Watson , Senior Committee Administrator, Town Hall, Market Street, Nelson BB9 7LG ☎ 01282 661648 ✉ jane.watson@pendle.gov.uk

PENDLE

Parking: Mrs Sandra Farnell , Transport & Co-ordination Manager, Elliott House, 9 Market Square, Nelson BB9 0LX ☎ 01282 661053 ✉ sandra.farnell@pendle.gov.uk

Personnel / HR: Ms Lesley Ritchie , Human Resources Manager, Number One Market Square, Nelson BB9 7LJ ☎ 01282 878800 🖷 01282 661700 ✉ lesley.ritchie@liberata.gov.uk

Planning: Mr Neil Watson, Planning, Building Control & Licensing Services Manager, Town Hall, Market Street, Nelson BB9 7LG ☎ 01282 661706 🖷 01282 661720 ✉ neil.watson@pendle.gov.uk

Procurement: Mr Vince Green , Financial Services Manager, Elliott House, 9 Market Square, Nelson BB9 0LX ☎ 01282 661867 ✉ vince.green@pendle.gov.uk

Recycling & Waste Minimisation: Mr David Walker, Environmental Services Manager, Fleet Street Depot, Nelson BB9 7YQ ☎ 01282 661746 🖷 01282 661750 ✉ david.walker@pendle.gov.uk

Regeneration: Ms Julie Whittaker , Housing, Health & Economic Development Services Manager, Elliott House, 9 Market Square, Nelson BB9 0LX ☎ 01282 661038 🖷 01282 661043 ✉ julie.whittaker@pendle.gov.uk

Staff Training: Ms Lesley Ritchie , Human Resources Manager, Number One Market Square, Nelson BB9 7LJ ☎ 01282 878800 🖷 01282 661700 ✉ lesley.ritchie@liberata.gov.uk

Tourism: Mr Michael Williams , Tourism Officer, Elliott House, 9 Market Square, Nelson BB9 0LX ☎ 01282 661963 🖷 01282 661881 ✉ michael.williams@pendle.gov.uk

Town Centre: Ms Hannah Latty , Town Centres Officer, Elliott House, 9 Market Square, Nelson BB9 0LX ☎ 01282 661677 ✉ hannah.latty@pendle.gov.uk

Waste Collection and Disposal: Mr David Walker, Environmental Services Manager, Fleet Street Depot, Nelson BB9 7YQ ☎ 01282 661746 🖷 01282 661750 ✉ david.walker@pendle.gov.uk

Waste Management: Mr David Walker , Environmental Services Manager, Fleet Street Depot, Nelson BB9 7YQ ☎ 01282 661746 🖷 01282 661750 ✉ david.walker@pendle.gov.uk

Children's Play Areas: Mr Keith Higson , Parks Technical Officer, Fleet Street Depot, Nelson BB9 7YQ ☎ 01282 661597 ✉ keith.higson@pendle.gov.uk

COUNCILLORS

***Mayor* Ahmed**, Nawaz (LAB - Brierfield)
mna2010@hotmail.co.uk

***Deputy Mayor* Carroll**, Rosemary (CON - Earby)
rosemary@carro-step.co.uk

***Leader of the Council* Iqbal**, Mohammed (LAB - Bradley)
mohammed.iqbal@pendle.gov.uk

***Deputy Leader of the Council* Greaves**, Tony (LD - Waterside)
tonygreaves@cix.co.uk

Adams, Marjorie (LD - Coates)
adamsmarjorie7@gmail.com

Ahmed, Nadeem (LD - Whitefield)
nadeem.ahmed@pendle.gov.uk

Allen, Robert (LAB - Reedley)
robert.allen@pendle.gov.uk

Ammer, Mohammed (LAB - Southfield)
mammer786@aol.com

Ansar, Eileen (LAB - Clover Hill)

Arshad, Mohammed (LAB - Brierfield)
mohammed.arshad@pendle.gov.uk

Ashraf, Naeem (LAB - Brierfield)
naeem.ashraf@pendle.gov.uk

Aziz, Abdul (CON - Walverden)
abdul.aziz@pendle.gov.uk

Benson, Smith (CON - Horsfield)

Blackburn, Wayne (LAB - Clover Hill)
wblackburn@outlook.com

Butterworth, Neil (CON - Horsfield)
neil14@live.co.uk

Clegg, David (LD - Vivary Bridge)
david.clegg@pendle.gov.uk

Cockburn-Price, Sarah (CON - Boulsworth)
sarah@cockburn-price.com

Cooney, Tommy (CON - Marsden)
tommy.cooney@pendle.gov.uk

Cooney, Joe (CON - Vivary Bridge)
joe.cooney@pendle.gov.uk

Crossley, Linda (CON - Barrowford)
linda.crossley@pendle.gov.uk

Davy, Lyle (CON - Coates)
lyledavy@hotmail.com

Foxley, Margaret (CON - Boulsworth)
margaret@foxley5.orangehome.co.uk

Goulthrop, Mike (CON - Earby)
msgoulthrop@hotmail.co.uk

Hanif, Mohammad (LAB - Reedley)
hanifbtc@gmail.com

Hartley, Ken (LD - Craven)
kenknhrt@gmai.com

Henderson, Julie (LAB - Walverden)
julie.henderson@pendle.gov.uk

Horsfield, Morris (CON - Earby)

Iqbal, Yasser (LAB - Reedley)
yasser.iqbal@hotmail.co.uk

Jowett, Christopher (CON - Barrowford)
chrisjowett@icloud.com

Lord, Dorothy (LD - Waterside)
dorothy.lord@lancashire.gov.uk

Mahmood, Asjad (LAB - Whitefield)
asjad.mahmood@pendle.gov.uk

McEvoy, Noel (CON - Blacko and Higherford)
noel.mcevoy@pendle.gov.uk

Milner, Richard (LD - Craven)
chubbyrugby@btinternet.com

Newman, Brian (LD - Old Laund Booth) brian.newman@pendle.gov.uk

Nixon, Jonathan (CON - Horsfield) jonathan.nixon@pendle.gov.uk

Parker, Brian (BNP - Marsden) brian.parker@pendle.gov.uk

Roach, Graham (LD - Waterside) graham.roach@pendle.gov.uk

Sakib, Mohammad (LAB - Bradley) mohammadsakib@hotmail.co.uk

Shore, Kathleen (LAB - Clover Hill)

Starkie, James (CON - Higham and Pendleside) james.starkie@pendle.gov.uk

Teall, Claire (LD - Coates) cteall05@aol.com

Tweedie, Ian (LAB - Vivary Bridge) ian.tweedie@pendle.gov.uk

Wakeford, Christian (CON - Barrowford) christian.wakeford@lancashire.gov.uk

Waugh, Graham (CON - Foulridge) grwaugh@yahoo.co.uk

Whalley, David (LAB - Southfield) david.whalley@pendle.gov.uk

Whipp, David (LD - Craven) david.whipp@pendle.gov.uk

White, Paul (CON - Boulsworth) cllrwhite@icloud.com

Wicks, Sheila (LAB - Southfield) sheila.wicks@pendle.gov.uk

Younis, Nadeem (LAB - Bradley) nadeem.younis@pendle.gov.uk

POLITICAL COMPOSITION

CON: 19, LAB: 18, LD: 11, BNP: 1

COMMITTEE CHAIRS

Accounts & Audit: Mr Robert Allen

Development Management: Mr Ken Hartley

Licensing: Ms Eileen Ansar

Perth & Kinross S

Perth & Kinross Council, Perth & Kinross Council, 2 High Street, Perth PH1 5PH
☎ 01738 475000 🖷 01738 475710 ✉ enquiries@pkc.gov.uk
🖳 www.pkc.gov.uk

FACTS AND FIGURES

Parliamentary Constituencies: Ochil and Perthshire South, Perth and Perthshire North
EU Constituencies: Scotland
Election Frequency: Elections are of whole council

PRINCIPAL OFFICERS

Chief Executive: Ms Bernadette Malone, Chief Executive, Council Buildings, 2 High Street, Perth PH1 5PH ☎ 01738 475009 🖷 01738 475008 ✉ chiefexec@pkc.gov.uk

Deputy Chief Executive: Mr John Fyffe , Depute Chief Executive & Executive Director for Education & Children's Services, Council Buildings, 2 High Street, Perth PH1 5PH ☎ 01738 475445 🖷 01738 475510 ✉ jfyffe@pkc.gov.uk

Senior Management: Mr Jim Valentine, Executive Director of Environment, 2 High Street, Perth PH1 5GD ☎ 01738 476502 🖷 01738 475310 ✉ jvalentine@pkc.gov.uk

Senior Management: Mr John Walker, Executive Director of Housing & Community Care, 2 High Street, Perth PH1 5GD ☎ 01738 476001 ✉ jwalker@pkc.gov.uk

Access Officer / Social Services (Disability): Mr John Gilruth, Head of Community Care, Council Buildings, 2 High Street, Perth PH1 5PH ☎ 01738 476711

Architect, Building / Property Services: Mr Stephen Crawford, Head of Property Services, Pullar House, 35 Kinnoull Street, Perth PH1 5GD ☎ 01738 476503 ✉ scrawford@pkc.gov.uk

Building Control: Mr David Littlejohn , Head of Planning & Regeneration, Pullar House, 35 Pullar House, Perth PH1 5GD ☎ 01738 477942 🖷 01738 475955 ✉ dlittlejohn@pkc.gov.uk

Children / Youth Services: Mr Bill Atkinson, Depute Director, Pullar House, 35 Kinnoull Street, Perth PH1 5GD ☎ 01738 476204 🖷 01738 476210 ✉ batkinson@pkc.gov.uk

Civil Registration: Mrs Gillian Taylor, Head of Democratic Services, Council Buildings, 2 High Street, Perth PH1 5PH ☎ 01738 475135 🖷 01738 475008 ✉ gataylor@pkc.gov.uk

PR / Communications: Mrs Gillian Taylor, Head of Democratic Services, Council Buildings, 2 High Street, Perth PH1 5PH ☎ 01738 475135 🖷 01738 475008 ✉ gataylor@pkc.gov.uk

Community Planning: Mr John Fyffe , Depute Chief Executive & Executive Director for Education & Children's Services, Perth & Kinross Council, 2 High Street, Perth PH1 5PH ☎ 01738 475445 🖷 01738 475510 ✉ jfyffe@pkc.gov.uk

Community Safety: Mr John Walker, Executive Director of Housing & Community Care, Pullar House, 35 Pullar House, Perth PH1 5GD ☎ 01738 476001 ✉ jwalker@pkc.gov.uk

Computer Management: Mr Alan Taylor , Head of Finance & Support Services, Pullar House, 35 Pullar Street, Perth PH1 5GD ☎ 01738 476702

Consumer Protection and Trading Standards: Mr Keith McNamara , Head of Environmental & Consumer Services, Pullar House, 35 Pullar House, Perth PH1 5GD ☎ 01738 476404 🖷 01738 475310 ✉ kdmcnamara@pkc.gov.uk

Contracts: Mr Ian Innes, Head of Legal Services, Council Buildings, 2 High Street, Perth PH1 5PH ☎ 01738 475103 🖷 01738 475910 ✉ iinnes@pkc.gov.uk

Customer Service: Mr John Walker, Executive Director of Housing & Community Care, Pullar House, 35 Kinnoull Street, Perth PH1 5GD ☎ 01738 476001 ✉ jwalker@pkc.gov.uk

Economic Development: Mr David Littlejohn , Head of Planning & Regeneration, Pullar House, 35 Pullar House, Perth PH1 5GD ☎ 01738 477942 🖷 01738 475955 ✉ dlittlejohn@pkc.gov.uk

Education: Ms S Devlin , Head of Education Services (Primary), Pullar House, 35 Kinnoull Street, Perth PH1 5GD ☎ 01738 476312 ✉ sdevlin@pkc.gov.uk

Education: Mr John Fyffe , Depute Chief Executive & Executive Director for Education & Children's Services, Perth & Kinross Council, 2 High Street, Perth PH1 5PH ☎ 01738 475445 🖷 01738 475510 ✉ jfyffe@pkc.gov.uk

Education: Mr P McAvoy , Head of Education Services (Secondary), Pullar House, 35 Kinnoull Street, Perth PH1 5GD ☎ 01738 476387 ✉ pmcavoy@pkc.gov.uk

Electoral Registration: Ms Bernadette Malone, Chief Executive, Council Buildings, 2 High Street, Perth PH1 5PH ☎ 01738 475009 🖷 01738 475008 ✉ chiefexec@pkc.gov.uk

Emergency Planning: Mr Jim Valentine, Executive Director of Environment, 2 High Street, Perth PH1 5GD ☎ 01738 476502 🖷 01738 475310 ✉ jvalentine@pkc.gov.uk

Energy Management: Mr David Littlejohn , Head of Planning & Regeneration, Pullar House, 35 Pullar House, Perth PH1 5GD ☎ 01738 477942 🖷 01738 475955 ✉ dlittlejohn@pkc.gov.uk

Environmental / Technical Services: Mr Jim Valentine, Executive Director of Environment, 2 High Street, Perth PH1 5GD ☎ 01738 476502 🖷 01738 475310 ✉ jvalentine@pkc.gov.uk

Environmental Health: Mr Keith McNamara , Head of Environmental & Consumer Services, Pullar House, 35 Pullar House, Perth PH1 5GD ☎ 01738 476404 🖷 01738 475310 ✉ kdmcnamara@pkc.gov.uk

Estates, Property & Valuation: Mr Stephen Crawford , Head of Property Services, Pullar House, 35 Kinnoull Street, Perth PH1 5GD ☎ 01738 476503 ✉ scrawford@pkc.gov.uk

European Liaison: Mr David Littlejohn , Head of Planning & Regeneration, Pullar House, 35 Pullar House, Perth PH1 5GD ☎ 01738 477942 🖷 01738 475955 ✉ dlittlejohn@pkc.gov.uk

Events Manager: Mr David Littlejohn , Head of Planning & Regeneration, Pullar House, 35 Pullar House, Perth PH1 5GD ☎ 01738 477942 🖷 01738 475955 ✉ dlittlejohn@pkc.gov.uk

Facilities: Mr Stephen Crawford , Head of Property Services, Pullar House, 35 Kinnoull Street, Perth PH1 5GD ☎ 01738 476503 ✉ scrawford@pkc.gov.uk

Finance: Mr John Symon, Head of Finance, Council Buildings, 2 High Street, Perth PH1 5PH ☎ 01738 475504 🖷 01738 475110 ✉ jsymon@pkc.gov.uk

Fleet Management: Mrs Barbara Renton , Depute Director (Environment), 2 High Street, Perth PH1 5PH ☎ 01738 476505 🖷 01738 476510 ✉ brenton@pkc.gov.uk

Grounds Maintenance: Mrs Barbara Renton , Depute Director (Environment), 2 High Street, Perth PH1 5PH ☎ 01738 476505 🖷 01738 476510 ✉ brenton@pkc.gov.uk

Health and Safety: Mr Stuart Mackenzie , Head of Performance & Resources, Pullar House, 35 Pullar House, Perth PH1 5GD ☎ 01738 475531 🖷 01738 476510 ✉ smackenzie@pkc.gov.uk

Highways: Mrs Barbara Renton , Depute Director (Environment), 2 High Street, Perth PH1 5PH ☎ 01738 476505 🖷 01738 476510 ✉ brenton@pkc.gov.uk

Home Energy Conservation: Mr Jim Valentine, Executive Director of Environment, 2 High Street, Perth PH1 5GD ☎ 01738 476502 🖷 01738 475310 ✉ jvalentine@pkc.gov.uk

Housing: Ms Lorna Cameron , Head of Housing & Strategic Commissioning, 2 High Street, Perth PH1 5GD ☎ 01738 476705

Housing: Mr John Walker, Executive Director of Housing & Community Care, 2 High Street, Perth PH1 5GD ☎ 01738 476001 ✉ jwalker@pkc.gov.uk

Housing Maintenance: Ms Lorna Cameron , Head of Housing & Strategic Commissioning, Perth & Kinross Council, 2 High Street, Perth PH1 5PH ☎ 01738 476705 ✉ lecameron@pkc.gov.uk

Housing Maintenance: Mr John Walker, Executive Director of Housing & Community Care, 2 High Street, Perth PH1 5GD ☎ 01738 476001 ✉ jwalker@pkc.gov.uk

Local Area Agreement: Mr Jim Valentine, Executive Director of Environment, 2 High Street, Perth PH1 5GD ☎ 01738 476502 🖷 01738 475310 ✉ jvalentine@pkc.gov.uk

Legal: Mr Ian Innes, Head of Legal Services, Council Buildings, 2 High Street, Perth PH1 5PH ☎ 01738 475103 🖷 01738 475910 ✉ iinnes@pkc.gov.uk

Leisure and Cultural Services: Ms Fiona Robertson , Head of Communities & Cultural Services, Pullar House, 35 Pullar House, Perth PH1 5GD ☎ 01738 476313 🖷 01738 476210 ✉ fionarobertson@pkc.gov.uk

Licensing: Mr Ian Innes, Head of Legal Services, Council Buildings, 2 High Street, Perth PH1 5PH ☎ 01738 475103 🖷 01738 475910 ✉ iinnes@pkc.gov.uk

Lifelong Learning: Ms Fiona Robertson , Head of Communities & Cultural Services, Pullar House, 35 Pullar House, Perth PH1 5GD ☎ 01738 476313 🖷 01738 476210 ✉ fionarobertson@pkc.gov.uk

Lottery Funding, Charity and Voluntary: Mr David Littlejohn , Head of Planning & Regeneration, Pullar House, 35 Pullar House, Perth PH1 5GD ☎ 01738 477942 🖷 01738 475955 ✉ dlittlejohn@pkc.gov.uk

Member Services: Mrs Gillian Taylor, Head of Democratic Services, Council Buildings, 2 High Street, Perth PH1 5PH ☎ 01738 475135 🖷 01738 475008 ✉ gataylor@pkc.gov.uk

Parking: Mrs Barbara Renton , Depute Director (Environment), 2 High Street, Perth PH1 5PH ☎ 01738 476505 🖷 01738 476510 ✉ brenton@pkc.gov.uk

Planning: Mr David Littlejohn , Head of Planning & Regeneration, Pullar House, 35 Pullar House, Perth PH1 5GD ☎ 01738 477942 🖷 01738 475955 ✉ dlittlejohn@pkc.gov.uk

Procurement: Ms Lorna Cameron , Head of Housing & Strategic Commissioning, Perth & Kinross Council, 2 High Street, Perth PH1 5PH ☎ 01738 476705 ✉ lecameron@pkc.gov.uk

Public Libraries: Ms Fiona Robertson , Head of Communities & Cultural Services, Pullar House, 35 Pullar House, Perth PH1 5GD ☎ 01738 476313 🖷 01738 476210 ✉ fionarobertson@pkc.gov.uk

Recycling & Waste Minimisation: Mr Keith McNamara , Head of Environmental & Consumer Services, Pullar House, 35 Pullar House, Perth PH1 5GD ☎ 01738 476404 🖷 01738 475310 ✉ kdmcnamara@pkc.gov.uk

Regeneration: Mr David Littlejohn , Head of Planning & Regeneration, Pullar House, 35 Pullar House, Perth PH1 5GD ☎ 01738 477942 🖷 01738 475955 ✉ dlittlejohn@pkc.gov.uk

Road Safety: Mrs Barbara Renton , Depute Director (Environment), 2 High Street, Perth PH1 5PH ☎ 01738 476505 🖷 01738 476510 ✉ brenton@pkc.gov.uk

Social Services: Mr John Gilruth , Depute Director, 2 High Street, Perth PH2 5PH ☎ 01738 476711 🖷 01738 476010 ✉ jgilruth@pkc.gov.uk

Social Services (Adult): Mr John Gilruth , Head of Community Care, 2 High Street, Perth PH1 5GD ☎ 01738 476711

Social Services (Children): Mr Bill Atkinson, Depute Director, Pullar House, 35 Kinnoull Street, Perth PH1 5GD ☎ 01738 476204 🖷 01738 476210 ✉ batkinson@pkc.gov.uk

Social Services (Children): Mr John Gilruth , Head of Community Care, Pullar House, 35 Pullar House, Perth PH1 5GD ☎ 01738 476711

Staff Training: Mrs Karen Donaldson , Corporate Human Resources Manager, 2 High Street, Perth PH1 5PH ☎ 01738 475430 ✉ kadonaldson@pkc.gov.uk

Tourism: Mr David Littlejohn , Head of Planning & Regeneration, Pullar House, 35 Pullar House, Perth PH1 5GD ☎ 01738 477942 🖷 01738 475955 ✉ dlittlejohn@pkc.gov.uk

Town Centre: Mr David Littlejohn , Head of Planning & Regeneration, Pullar House, 35 Pullar House, Perth PH1 5GD ☎ 01738 477942 🖷 01738 475955 ✉ dlittlejohn@pkc.gov.uk

Traffic Management: Mrs Barbara Renton , Depute Director (Environment), 2 High Street, Perth PH1 5PH ☎ 01738 476505 🖷 01738 476510 ✉ brenton@pkc.gov.uk

Transport: Mrs Barbara Renton , Depute Director (Environment), 2 High Street, Perth PH1 5PH ☎ 01738 476505 🖷 01738 476510 ✉ brenton@pkc.gov.uk

Waste Collection and Disposal: Mr Keith McNamara , Head of Environmental & Consumer Services, Pullar House, 35 Pullar House, Perth PH1 5GD ☎ 01738 476404 🖷 01738 475310 ✉ kdmcnamara@pkc.gov.uk

Waste Management: Mr Keith McNamara , Head of Environmental & Consumer Services, Pullar House, 35 Pullar House, Perth PH1 5GD ☎ 01738 476404 🖷 01738 475310 ✉ kdmcnamara@pkc.gov.uk

COUNCILLORS

***Provost* Grant**, Liz (SNP - Blairgowrie & Glens)
egrant@pkc.gov.uk

***Deputy Provost* Band**, Bob (SNP - Perth City South)
bband@pkc.gov.uk

***Leader of the Council* Miller**, Ian (SNP - Strathmore)
imiller@pkc.gov.uk

***Deputy Leader of the Council* Grant**, Alan (SNP - Strathmore)
adgrant@pkc.gov.uk

***Group Leader* Barrett**, Peter (LD - Perth City Centre)
pabarrett@pkc.gov.uk

***Group Leader* Cuthbert**, Dave (IND - Kinross shire)
dcuthbert@pkc.gov.uk

***Group Leader* MacLellan**, Archie (LAB - Perth City Centre)
aamaclellan@pkc.gov.uk

***Group Leader* Roberts**, Mac (CON - Carse of Gowrie)
mroberts@pkc.gov.uk

Anderson, Henry (SNP - Almond & Earn)
handerson@pkc.gov.uk

Barnacle, Michael (IND - Kinross shire)
mbarnacle@pkc.gov.uk

Brock, Rhona (IND - Strathearn)
rbrock@pkc.gov.uk

Campbell, Ian (CON - Highland)
icampbell@pkc.gov.uk

Cowan, Ann (CON - Strathearn)
acowan@pkc.gov.uk

Doogan, Dave (SNP - Perth City North)
ddoogan@pkc.gov.uk

Ellis, Bob (SNP - Blairgowrie & Glens)
rellis@pkc.gov.uk

Flynn, John (LAB - Perth City North)
jmflynn@pkc.gov.uk

Gaunt, Ann (LD - Strathallan)
agaunt@pkc.gov.uk

Giacopazzi, Joe (SNP - Kinross shire)
jgiacopazzi@pkc.gov.uk

Gillies, Callum (LAB - Perth City North)
cgillies@pkc.gov.uk

Gray, Tom (SNP - Strathallan)
tomgray@pkc.gov.uk

Howie, Kate (SNP - Highland)
khowie@pkc.gov.uk

Jack, Alan (IND - Almond & Earn)
hajack@pkc.gov.uk

Kellas, John (SNP - Strathtay)
jkellas@pkc.gov.uk

Laing, Grant (SNP - Strathtay)
glaing@pkc.gov.uk

Livingstone, Alan (CON - Almond & Earn)
alivingstone@pkc.gov.uk

Lyle, Murray (CON - Strathallan)
mlyle@pkc.gov.uk

Maclachlan, Elspeth (SNP - Perth City North)
emaclachlan@pkc.gov.uk

Melloy, Dennis (CON - Strathmore)
dmelloy@pkc.gov.uk

Munro, Alistair (LAB - Perth City South)
alistairmunro@pkc.gov.uk

Parrott, Andrew (SNP - Perth City Centre)
aparrott@pkc.gov.uk

Pover, Douglas (SNP - Carse of Gowrie)
dpover@pkc.gov.uk

Robertson, Willie (LD - Kinross shire)
wrobertson@pkc.gov.uk

Shiers, Caroline (CON - Blairgowrie & Glens)
cshiers@pkc.gov.uk

Simpson, Lewis (LD - Strathmore)
lddsimpson@pkc.gov.uk

Stewart, Alexander (CON - Perth City South)
astewart@pkc.gov.uk

Stewart, Heather (CON - Perth City Centre)
heatherstewart@pkc.gov.uk

Vaughan, Barbara (CON - Strathtay)
bvaughan@pkc.gov.uk

Walker, Gordon (SNP - Carse of Gowrie)
gordonwalker@pkc.gov.uk

Williamson, Mike (SNP - Highland)
mwilliamson@pkc.gov.uk

Wilson, Willie (LD - Perth City South)
wowilson@pkc.gov.uk

Younger, Anne (SNP - Strathearn)
ayounger@pkc.gov.uk

POLITICAL COMPOSITION
SNP: 18, CON: 10, LD: 5, IND: 4, LAB: 4

COMMITTEE CHAIRS

Audit: Ms Barbara Vaughan

Development Management: Mr Tom Gray

Licensing: Mr Bob Ellis

Peterborough City U

Peterborough City Council, Town Hall, Bridge Street, Peterborough PE1 1HG
☎ 01733 747474 🖷 01733 452537 ✉ ask@peterborough.gov.uk
💻 www.peterborough.gov.uk

FACTS AND FIGURES
Parliamentary Constituencies: Cambridgeshire North West, Peterborough
EU Constituencies: Eastern
Election Frequency: Elections are by thirds

PRINCIPAL OFFICERS

Chief Executive: Mrs Gillian Beasley, Chief Executive, Town Hall, Bridge Street, Peterborough PE1 1HL ☎ 01733 452390 🖷 01733 452694 ✉ gillian.beasley@peterborough.gov.uk

Senior Management: Mr John Harrison, Corporate Director of Resources, Town Hall, Bridge Street, Peterborough PE1 1HG ☎ 01733 452520 ✉ john.harrison@peterborough.gov.uk

Senior Management: Mr Simon Machen , Corporate Director of Growth & Regeneration, Town Hall, Bridge Street, Peterborough PE1 1HG ☎ 01733 453475 🖷 01733 453505 ✉ simon.machen@peterborough.gov.uk

Senior Management: Ms Wendi Ogle-Welbourn , Corporate Director of People & Communities, Bayard Place, Broadway, Peterborough PE1 1FB ☎ 01733 863749 ✉ wendi.ogle-welbourn@peterborough.gov.uk

Senior Management: Dr Liz Robin , Director of Public Health, Town Hall, Bridge Street, Peterborough PE1 1HG ☎ 01733 207175 ✉ liz.robin@peterborough.gov.u

Senior Management: Ms Kim Sawyer , Director of Governance, Town Hall, Bridge Street, Peterborough PE1 1HG ☎ 01733 452361 ✉ kim.sawyer@peterborough.gov.uk

Architect, Building / Property Services: Mr Richard Porter , Head of Strategic Property, Manor Drive, Paston Parkway, Peterborough PE4 7AP ☎ 01733 384544 ✉ richard.porter@peterborough.gov.uk

Architect, Building / Property Services: Mr Martin Raper, Account Director, Amey, Nursery Lane, Fengate, Peterborough PE1 5BG ☎ 01733 425325 ✉ martin.raper@amey.gov.uk

Building Control: Mr Kevin Dawson, Head of Resilience, Town Hall, Bridge Street, Peterborough PE1 1HG ☎ 01733 453464 🖷 01733 453505 ✉ kevin.dawson@peterborough.gov.uk

Building Control: Mr Nick Harding , Head of Planning, Transport & Engineering Services, Town Hall, Bridge Street, Peterborough PE1 1HG ☎ 01733 454441 ✉ nicholas.harding@peterborough.gov.uk

Building Control: Ms Melissa Shaw , Head of Service Management, Enterprise Peterborough, Nursery Lane, Fengate, Peterborough PE1 5BG ☎ 01733 425325 🖷 01733 425326 ✉ melissa.shaw@enterprisepeterborough.co.uk

Catering Services: Ms Melissa Shaw , Head of Service Management, Enterprise Peterborough, Nursery Lane, Fengate, Peterborough PE1 5BG ☎ 01733 425325 🖷 01733 425326 🖱 melissa.shaw@enterprisepeterborough.co.uk

Children / Youth Services: Mrs Alison Bennett , Head of Service, Quality Assurance & Safeguarding, Bayard Place, Broadway, Peterborough PE1 1FB ☎ 01733 863627 🖱 alison.bennett@peterborough.gov.uk

Children / Youth Services: Mr Iain Easton , Head of Youth Offending Service, Youth Offending Service, 13/15 Cavell Court, Lincoln Road, Peterborough PE1 ZRJ ☎ 01733 864237 🖷 01733 864220 🖱 iain.easton@peterborough.gov.uk

Civil Registration: Ms Ruth Hodson , Registration Manager, Register Office, 33 Thorpe Road, Peterborough PE3 6AB ☎ 01733 864640 🖱 ruth.hodson@peterborough.gov.uk

PR / Communications: Ms Rachael Thornton , Head of Communications, Town Hall, Bridge Street, Peterborough PE1 1HQ ☎ 01733 452477 🖱 rachael.thornton@peterborough.gov.uk

Community Planning: Mr Adrian Chapman, Service Director - Adult Services & Communities, Bayard Place, Broadway, Peterborough PE1 1HZ ☎ 01733 863887 🖱 adrian.chapman@peterborough.gov.uk

Community Safety: Mr Adrian Chapman, Service Director - Adult Services & Communities, Bayard Place, Broadway, Peterborough PE1 1HZ ☎ 01733 863887 🖱 adrian.chapman@peterborough.gov.uk

Computer Management: Mr Richard Godfrey , Assistant Director - Digital Peterborough, Town Hall, Bridge Street, Peterborough PE1 1HG ☎ 01733 317989 🖱 richard.godfrey@peterborough.gov.uk

Contracts: Mr Andy Cox , Senior Contracts & Partnership Manager, Town Hall, Bridge Street, Peterborough PE1 1HG ☎ 01733 452465 🖱 andy.cox@peterborough.gov.uk

Corporate Services: Mr John Harrison, Corporate Director of Resources, Town Hall, Bridge Street, Peterborough PE1 1HG ☎ 01733 452520 🖱 john.harrison@peterborough.gov.uk

Corporate Services: Mr Richard Hodgson , Head of Strategic Projects, Town Hall, Bridge Street, Peterborough PE1 1HG ☎ 01733 384535 🖱 richard.hodgson@peterborough.gov.uk

Corporate Services: Mr Steven Pilsworth , Head of Strategic Finance, Town Hall, Bridge Street, Peterborough PE1 1HG ☎ 01733 384564 🖷 01733 384585 🖱 steven.pilsworth@peterborough.gov.uk

Customer Service: Mr Mark Sandhu , Head of Customer Services, Customer Service Centre, Bayard Place, Broadway, Peterborough PE1 1FZ ☎ 01733 296321 🖷 01733 354396 🖱 mark.sandhu@serco.com

Economic Development: Mr Steve Bowyer , Acting Chief Executive, Peters Court, City Road, Peterborough PE1 1SA ☎ 01733 317489 🖱 steve.bowyer@peterborough.gov.uk

Education: Mr Jonathan Lewis , Assistant Director Education & Resources, Children's Services Dept, Bayard Place, Broadway, Peterborough PE1 1FB ☎ 01733 863912 🖷 01733 863935 🖱 jonathan.lewis@peterborough.gov.uk

E-Government: Mr Richard Godfrey , Assistant Director - Digital Peterborough, Town Hall, Bridge Street, Peterborough PE1 1HG ☎ 01733 317989 🖱 richard.godfrey@peterborough.gov.uk

Electoral Registration: Mr Mark Emson , Electoral Services Officer, Town Hall, Bridge Street, Peterborough PE1 1HG ☎ 01733 452282 🖱 mark.emson@peterborough.gov.uk

Electoral Registration: Ms Rachel Parnell , Compliance Manager (Elections), Town Hall, Bridge Street, Peterborough PE1 1HG ☎ 01733 452277 🖱 rachel.parnell@peterborough.gov.uk

Emergency Planning: Mr Kevin Dawson, Head of Resilience, Town Hall, Bridge Street, Peterborough PE1 1HG ☎ 01733 453464 🖷 01733 453505 🖱 kevin.dawson@peterborough.gov.uk

Environmental / Technical Services: Mr Simon Machen , Director of Growth & Regeneration, Town Hall, Bridge Street, Peterborough PE1 1HG ☎ 01733 453475 🖷 01733 453505 🖱 simon.machen@peterborough.gov.uk

Environmental Health: Mr Peter Gell , Strategic Regulatory Services Manager, Bayard Place, Broadway, Peterborough PE1 1HZ ☎ 01733 453419 🖱 peter.gell@peterborough.gov.uk

Estates, Property & Valuation: Mr Richard Porter , Head of Strategic Property, Manor Drive, Paston Parkway, Peterborough PE4 7AP ☎ 01733 384544 🖱 richard.porter@peterborough.gov.uk

European Liaison: Ms Annette Joyce, Head of Commercial Operations, Town Hall, Bridge Street, Peterborough PE1 1HG ☎ 01733 452280 🖱 annette.joyce@peterborough.gov.uk

Events Manager: Ms Annette Joyce, Head of Commercial Operations, Town Hall, Bridge Street, Peterborough PE1 1HG ☎ 01733 452280 🖱 annette.joyce@peterborough.gov.uk

Facilities: Ms Sue Scott , Premises Manager, Manor Drive, Paston Parkway, Peterborough PE4 7AP ☎ 01733 384542 🖷 01733 207100 🖱 sue.scott@peterborough.gov.uk

Finance: Mr John Harrison, Corporate Director of Resources, Town Hall, Bridge Street, Peterborough PE1 1HG ☎ 01733 452520 🖱 john.harrison@peterborough.gov.uk

Grounds Maintenance: Mr Martin Raper , Account Director, Amey, Nursery Lane, Fengate, Peterborough PE1 5BG ☎ 01733 425325 🖱 martin.raper@amey.gov.uk

Health and Safety: Mr Andy Baker , Health & Safety Adviser, Town Hall, Bridge Street, Peterborough PE1 1HG ☎ 01733 453526 🖱 andy.baker@peterborough.gov.uk

Highways: Mr Peter Tebb, Network & Traffic Manager, Dodson House, Fengate, Peterborough PE1 5FS ☎ 01733 453519 🖷 01733 453444 🖱 peter.tebb@peterborough.gov.uk

PETERBOROUGH CITY

Housing: Ms Belinda Child , Head of Housing & Health Improvement, Bayard Place, Broadway, Peterborough PE1 1HZ ☎ 01733 863769 ✉ belinda.child@peterborough.gov.uk

Local Area Agreement: Mr Richard Astle , Director of GPP, 25 Priestgate, Peterborough PE1 1JL ☎ 01733 207340 ✉ richard@gpp-peterborough.org.uk

Legal: Ms Kim Sawyer , Director of Governance, Town Hall, Bridge Street, Peterborough PE1 1HG ☎ 01733 452361 ✉ kim.sawyer@peterborough.gov.uk

Leisure and Cultural Services: Mr Kevin Tighe, Head of Cultural Services, Vivacity, Central Library, Broadway, Peterborough PE1 1HZ ☎ 01733 863784 ✉ kevin.tighe@vivacity-peterborough.com

Licensing: Mr Adrian Day , Licensing Manager, Bayard Place, Broadway, Peterborough PE1 1HZ ☎ 01733 454437 🖷 01733 453518 ✉ adrian.day@peterborough.gov.uk

Lifelong Learning: Mrs Lou Williams , Service Director - Children's Services & Safeguarding, Bayard Place, Broadway, Peterborough PE1 1FB ☎ 01733 863606 ✉ lou.williams@peterborough.gov.uk

Lighting: Mr Mark Speed , Transport & Infrastructure Planning Manager, Town Hall, Bridge Street, Peterborough PE1 1HG ☎ 01733 317471 ✉ mark.speed@peterborough.gov.uk

Member Services: Ms Kim Sawyer , Director of Governance, Town Hall, Bridge Street, Peterborough PE1 1HG ☎ 01733 452361 ✉ kim.sawyer@peterborough.gov.uk

Parking: Mr Darren Bell , Parking Operations Manager, Town Hall, Bridge Street, Peterborough PE1 1HG ☎ 01733 452375 ✉ darren.bell@peterborough.gov.uk

Partnerships: Mr Dominic Hudson , Strategic Partnerships Manager, Town Hall, Bridge Street, Peterborough PE1 1HG ☎ 01733 452384 ✉ dominic.hudson@peterborough.gov.uk

Personnel / HR: Mrs Mandy Pullen , Acting Head of Human Resources, Town Hall, Bridge Street, Peterborough PE1 1HG ☎ 01733 863628 ✉ mandy.pullen@peterborough.gov.uk

Planning: Mr Simon Machen , Director of Growth & Regeneration, Town Hall, Bridge Street, Peterborough PE1 1HG ☎ 01733 453475 🖷 01733 453505 ✉ simon.machen@peterborough.gov.uk

Procurement: Mr Andy Cox , Senior Contracts & Partnership Manager, Town Hall, Bridge Street, Peterborough PE1 1HG ☎ 01733 452465 ✉ andy.cox@peterborough.gov.uk

Public Libraries: Ms Heather Walton, Library & Customer Services Manager, Vivacity, Central Library, Broadway, Peterborough PE1 1HZ ☎ 01733 864271 🖷 01733 319140 ✉ heather.walton@vivacity-peterborough.com

Recycling & Waste Minimisation: Mr Richard Pearn , Waste Partnership Manager, Town Hall, Bridge Street, Peterborough PE1 1HG ☎ 01733 864739 ✉ richard.pearn@peterborough.gov.uk

Regeneration: Mr Simon Machen , Director of Growth & Regeneration, Town Hall, Bridge Street, Peterborough PE1 1HG ☎ 01733 453475 🖷 01733 453505 ✉ simon.machen@peterborough.gov.uk

Road Safety: Ms Clair George, Road Safety Officer, Bayard Place, Broadway, Peterborough PE1 1ZX ☎ 01733 453576 🖷 01733 453444 ✉ clair.george@peterborough.gov.uk

Road Safety: Mr Peter Tebb, Network & Traffic Manager, Town Hall, Bridge Street, Peterborough PE1 1HG ☎ 01733 453519 🖷 01733 453444 ✉ peter.tebb@peterborough.gov.uk

Social Services (Adult): Mr Adrian Chapman, Service Director - Adult Services & Communities, Bayard Place, Broadway, Peterborough PE1 1HZ ☎ 01733 863887 ✉ adrian.chapman@peterborough.gov.uk

Social Services (Children): Mrs Lou Williams , Service Director - Children's Services & Safeguarding, Bayard Place, Broadway, Peterborough PE1 1FB ☎ 01733 863606 ✉ lou.williams@peterborough.gov.uk

Public Health: Dr Liz Robin , Director of Public Health, Town Hall, Bridge Street, Peterborough PE1 1HG ☎ 01733 207175 ✉ liz.robin@peterborough.gov.u

Staff Training: Mr Colin Wilson , Training & Development Manager, Town Hall, Bridge Street, Peterborough PE1 1HG ☎ 01733 864626 🖷 01733 384511 ✉ colin.wilson@peterborough.gov.uk

Street Scene: Mr Martin Raper , Account Director, Amey, Nursery Lane, Fengate, Peterborough PE1 5BG ☎ 01733 425325 ✉ martin.raper@amey.gov.uk

Sustainable Communities: Ms Wendi Ogle-Welbourn , Corporate Director of People & Communities, Bayard Place, Broadway, Peterborough PE1 1FB ☎ 01733 863749 ✉ wendi.ogle-welbourn@peterborough.gov.uk

Sustainable Development: Mr Simon Machen , Director of Growth & Regeneration, Town Hall, Bridge Street, Peterborough PE1 1HG ☎ 01733 453475 🖷 01733 453505 ✉ simon.machen@peterborough.gov.uk

Tourism: Ms Annette Joyce, Head of Commercial Operations, City Centre Services, Town Hall, Bridge Street, Peterborough PE1 1HG ☎ 01733 452280 ✉ annette.joyce@peterborough.gov.uk

Town Centre: Ms Annette Joyce, Head of Commercial Operations, Town Hall, Bridge Street, Peterborough PE1 1HG ☎ 01733 452280 ✉ annette.joyce@peterborough.gov.uk

Traffic Management: Mr Simon Machen , Director of Growth & Regeneration, Town Hall, Bridge Street, Peterborough PE1 1HG ☎ 01733 453475 🖷 01733 453505 ✉ simon.machen@peterborough.gov.uk

Transport: Mr Mark Speed , Transport & Infrastructure Planning Manager, Town Hall, Bridge Street, Peterborough PE1 1HG ☎ 01733 317471 ✉ mark.speed@peterborough.gov.uk

Transport Planner: Mr Mark Speed , Transport & Infrastructure Planning Manager, Town Hall, Bridge Street, Peterborough PE1 1HG ☎ 01733 317471 ✉ mark.speed@peterborough.gov.uk

Total Place: Ms Annette Joyce, Head of Commercial Operations, Town Hall, Bridge Street, Peterborough PE1 1HG ☎ 01733 452280 ✉ annette.joyce@peterborough.gov.uk

Waste Collection and Disposal: Mr Martin Raper , Account Director, Amey, Nursery Lane, Fengate, Peterborough PE1 5BG ☎ 01733 425325 ✉ martin.raper@amey.gov.uk

Waste Management: Mr Richard Pearn , Waste Partnership Manager, Town Hall, Bridge Street, Peterborough PE1 1HG ☎ 01733 864739 ✉ richard.pearn@peterborough.gov.uk

Children's Play Areas: Mrs Denise Noble , Voyager Area Manager, Bayard Place, Broadway, Peterborough PE1 1FB ☎ 01733 742581 ✉ denise.noble@peterborough.gov.uk

COUNCILLORS

***Mayor* Peach**, John (CON - Park)
john.peach@peterborough.gov.uk

***Deputy Mayor* Khan**, Nazim (LAB - Central)
nazim.khan@peterborough.gov.uk

***Leader of the Council* Holdich**, John (CON - Glinton and Wittering)
john.holdich@peterborough.gov.uk

***Deputy Leader of the Council* Fitzgerald**, Wayne (CON - West)
wayne.fitzgerald@peterborough.gov.uk

***Group Leader* Ash**, Chris (LIB - Dogsthorpe)
chris.ash@peterborough.gov.uk

***Group Leader* Jamil**, Mohammed (LAB - Central)
mohammed.jamil@peterborough.gov.uk

***Group Leader* Okonkowski**, John (UKIP - Orton Longueville)
john.okonkowski@peterborough.gov.uk

Aitken, Kim (CON - Orton Waterville)
kim.aitken@peterborough.gov.uk

Bisby, Ray (CON - Stanground Central)
ray.bisby@peterborough.gov.uk

Brown, Richard (CON - Eye and Thorney)
richard.brown@peterborough.gov.uk

Casey, Graham (CON - Orton Longueville)
graham.casey@peterborough.gov.uk

Coles, Andy (CON - Bretton South)
andy.coles@peterborough.gov.uk

Davidson, Julia (LD - Werrington South)
julia.davidson@peterborough.gov.uk

Elsey, Gavin (CON - Orton Waterville)
gavin.elsey@peterborough.gov.uk

Faustino, Pedro (CON - Fletton and Woodston)
pedro.faustino@peterborough.gov.uk

Ferris, Richard (LAB - Park)
richard.ferris@peterborough.gov.uk

Forbes, Lisa (LAB - Orton Longueville)
lisa.forbes@peterborough.gov.uk

Fower, Darren (LD - Werrington South)
darren.fower@peterborough.gov.uk

Fox, Judith (IND - Werrington North)
judy.fox@peterborough.gov.uk

Fox, John (IND - Werrington North)
john.fox@peterborough.gov.uk

Fox, Frances (UKIP - Paston)
frances.fox@peterborough.gov.uk

Harper, Chris (CON - Stanground East)
chris.harper@peterborough.gov.uk

Harrington, David (IND - Newborough)
david.harrington@peterborough.gov.uk

Herdman, Roger (UKIP - Bretton North)
roger.herdman@peterborough.gov.uk

Hiller, Peter (CON - Northborough)
peter.hiller@peterborough.gov.uk

Iqbal, Azher (CON - East)
azher.iqbal@peterborough.gov.uk

Johnson, Jo (LAB - East)
jo.johnson@peterborough.gov.uk

Knowles, John (LAB - Paston)
john.knowles@peterborough.gov.uk

Lamb, Diane (CON - Glinton and Wittering)
diane.lamb@peterborough.gov.uk

Lane, Stephen (IND - Werrington North)
stephen.lane@peterborough.gov.uk

Maqbool, Yasmeen (CON - West)
yasmeen.maqbool@peterborough.gov.uk

Martin, Stuart (LAB - Bretton North)
stuart.martin@peterborough.gov.uk

Miners, Adrian (LIB - Dogsthorpe)
adrian.miners@peterborough.gov.uk

Murphy, Ed (LAB - Ravensthorpe)
ed.murphy@peterborough.gov.uk

Nadeem, Mohammed (CON - Central)
mohammed.nadeem@peterborough.gov.uk

Nawaz, Gul (CON - Ravensthorpe)
gul.nawaz@peterborough.gov.uk

North, Nigel (CON - Orton with Hampton)
nigel.north@peterborough.gov.uk

Over, David (CON - Barnack)
david.over@peterborough.gov.uk

Rush, Brian (CON - Stanground Central)
brian.rush@peterborough.gov.uk

Saltmarsh, Bella (LIB - Dogsthorpe)
bella.saltmarsh@peterborough.gov.uk

Sanders, David (CON - Eye and Thorney)
david.sanders@peterborough.gov.uk

Sandford, Nick (LD - Walton)
nick.sandford@peterborough.gov.uk

Scott, Sheila (CON - Orton with Hampton)
sheila.scott@peterborough.gov.uk

Seaton, David (CON - Orton with Hampton)
david.seaton@peterborough.gov.uk

PETERBOROUGH CITY

Serluca, Lucia (CON - Fletton and Woodston)
lucia.serluca@peterborough.gov.uk

Shabbir, Nabil (LAB - East)
nabil.shabbir@peterborough.gov.uk

Shaheed, Asif (LD - Walton)
asif.shaheed@peterborough.gov.uk

Sharp, Keith (IND - North)
keith.sharp@peterborough.gov.uk

Shearman, John (LAB - Park)
john.shearman@peterborough.gov.uk

Stokes, June (CON - Orton Waterville)
june.stokes@peterborough.gov.uk

Swift, Charles (IND - North)
charles.swift@peterborough.gov.uk

Sylvester, Ann (LAB - Bretton North)
ann.sylvester@peterborough.gov.uk

Thacker, Paula (CON - Werrington South)
paula.thacker@peterborough.gov.uk

Thulbourn, Nick (LAB - Fletton and Woodston)
nick.thulbourn@peterborough.gov.uk

Whitby, John (UKIP - Stanground Central)
john.whitby@peterborough.gov.uk

Yonga, Jonas (LAB - Paston)
jonas.yonga@peterborough.gov.uk

POLITICAL COMPOSITION

CON: 26, LAB: 13, IND: 6, LD: 4, UKIP: 4, LIB: 3

COMMITTEE CHAIRS

Audit: Mr Andy Coles

Health & Wellbeing: Mr John Holdich

Licensing: Ms Paula Thacker

Planning & Environmental Protection: Mr Chris Harper

Plymouth City U

Plymouth City Council, Civic Centre, Royal Parade, Plymouth PL1 2AA
☎ 01752 668000 🖷 01752 304880 ✉ info@plymouth.gov.uk
💻 www.plymouth.gov.uk

FACTS AND FIGURES

EU Constituencies: South West
Election Frequency: Elections are by thirds

PRINCIPAL OFFICERS

Chief Executive: Ms Tracey Lee , Chief Executive, Ballard House, West Hoe Road, Plymouth PL1 3BJ ☎ 01752 668000 ✉ tracey.lee@plymouth.gov.uk

Assistant Chief Executive: Mr Giles Perritt , Assistant Chief Executive, Plymouth City Council, Plymouth PL1 2AA ☎ 01752 668000 ✉ giles.peritt@plymouth.gov.uk

Senior Management: Ms Lesa Annear , Director for Transformation, Civic Centre, Royal Parade, Plymouth PL1 2AA

Senior Management: Mrs Carole Burgoyne , Director for People, Plymouth City Council, Plymouth PL1 2AA ☎ 01752 668000 ✉ carole.burgoyne@plymouth.gov.uk

Senior Management: Mr Kelechi Nnoaham , Director of Public Health, Plymouth City Council, Plymouth PL1 2AA ☎ 01752 668000 ✉ kelechi.nnoaham@plymouth.gov.uk

Senior Management: Mr Anthony Payne , Director for Place, Plymouth City Council, Plymouth PL1 2AA ☎ 01752 668000 ✉ anthony.payne@plymouth.gov.uk

Architect, Building / Property Services: Mr Anthony Payne , Director for Place, Plymouth City Council, Plymouth PL1 2AA ☎ 01752 668000 ✉ anthony.payne@plymouth.gov.uk

Building Control: Mr Paul Barnard, Assistant Director for Strategic Planning & Infrastructure, Plymouth City Counil, Plymouth PL1 2AA ☎ 01752 668000 ✉ paul.barnard@plymouth.gov.uk

Catering Services: Mr Brad Pearce , Education Catering Manager, Plymouth City Council, Plymouth PL1 2AA ☎ 01752 668000 ✉ brad.pearce@plymouth.gov.uk

Children / Youth Services: Ms Judith Harwood , Assistant Director for Education, Learning & Families, Plymouth City Council, Plymouth PL1 2AA ☎ 01752 668000 ✉ judith.harwood@plymouth.gov.uk

Civil Registration: Ms Karen Ward, Registration Services Manager, Registrars Office, Lockyer Street, Plymouth PL1 2AA ☎ 01752 307223 🖷 01752 256046 ✉ karen.ward@plymouth.gov.uk

PR / Communications: Mr Richard Longford, Head of Communications, Plymouth City Council, Plymouth PL1 2AA ☎ 01752 305405 ✉ richard.longford@plymouth.gov.uk

Community Safety: Mr Peter Aley, Head of Community Services, Plymouth City Council, Plymouth PL1 2AA ☎ 01752 668000 ✉ pete.aley@plymouth.gov.uk

Consumer Protection and Trading Standards: Mr Robin Carton, Public Protection Service Manager, Plymouth City Council, Plymouth PL1 2AA ☎ 01752 668000 ✉ robin.carton@plymouth.gov.uk

Contracts: Mr Martin Collins , Strategic Procurement Manager, Civic Centre, Royal Parade, Plymouth PL1 2AA ☎ 01752 668000 ✉ martin.collins@plymouth.gov.uk

Customer Service: Ms Faye Batchelor-Hambleton , Assistant Director for Customer Services, Plymouth City Council, Plymouth PL1 2AA ☎ 01752 668000

Economic Development: Mr David Draffan , Assistant Director for Economic Development, Plymouth City Council, Plymouth PL1 2AA ☎ 01752 668000 ✉ david.draffan@plymouth.gov.uk

Education: Ms Judith Harwood , Assistant Director for Education, Learning & Families, Plymouth City Council, Plymouth PL1 2AA ☎ 01752 668000 ✉ judith.harwood@plymouth.gov.uk

Electoral Registration: Mr Nigel Spilsbury, Electoral Services Manager, Plymouth City Council, Plymouth PL1 2AA ☎ 01752 668000 nigel.spilsbury@plymouth.gov.uk

Emergency Planning: Mr Scott Senior, Civil Protection Manager, Plymouth City Council, Plymouth PL1 2AA ☎ 01752 668000 scott.senior@plymouth.gov.uk

Energy Management: Mr Robin Carton, Public Protection Service Manager, Plymouth City Council, Plymouth PL1 2AA ☎ 01752 668000 robin.carton@plymouth.gov.uk

Environmental Health: Mr Robin Carton, Public Protection Service Manager, Plymouth City Council, Plymouth PL1 2AA ☎ 01752 668000 robin.carton@plymouth.gov.uk

Facilities: Mr Chris Trevitt , Head of Capital Assets, Plymouth City Council, Plymouth PL1 2AA ☎ 01752 668000 chris.trevitt@plymouth.gov.uk

Fleet Management: Mr John Simpson , Fleet & Garage Manager, Prince Rock Depot, Macadam Road, Plymouth PL4 0RZ ☎ 01752 668000 john.simpson@plymouth.gov.uk

Grounds Maintenance: Mr Gareth Harrison-Poole , Street Cleansing & Grounds Manager, Prince Rock Depot, Macadam Road, Plymouth PL4 0RZ ☎ 01752 668000 gareth.harrison-poole@plymouth.gov.uk

Health and Safety: Ms Emma Rose , Head of Health, Safety & Wellbeing, Plymouth City Council, Plymouth PL1 2AA ☎ 01752 668000 emma.rose@plymouth.gov.uk

Highways: Mr Adrian Trim , Head of Highways, Parks & Maritime Services, Plymouth City Council, Plymouth PL1 2AA ☎ 01752 668000 adrian.trim@plymouth.gov.uk

Housing: Mr Stuart Palmer , Assistant Director for Homes & Communities, Plymouth City Council, Plymouth PL1 2AA ☎ 01752 668000 stuart.palmer@plymouth.gov.uk

Legal: Mr David Shepperd , Head of Legal Services, Plymouth City Council, Plymouth PL1 2AA ☎ 01752 668000 david.shepperd@plymouth.gov.uk

Leisure and Cultural Services: Ms Nicola Moyle , Head of Arts & Heritage, Plymouth City Council, Plymouth PL1 2AA ☎ 01752 668000 nicola.moyle@plymouth.gov.uk

Licensing: Mr Robin Carton, Public Protection Service Manager, Plymouth City Council, Plymouth PL1 2AA ☎ 01752 668000 robin.carton@plymouth.gov.uk

Member Services: Ms Judith Shore , Democratic & Member Services Manager, Plymouth City Council, Plymouth PL1 2AA ☎ 01752 668000 judith.shore@plymouth.gov.uk

Parking: Mr Mike Artherton , Parking & Marine Service Manager, Plymouth City Council, Plymouth PL1 2AA ☎ 01752 668000 mike.artherton@plymouth.gov.uk

Personnel / HR: Mr Giles Perritt , Assistant Chief Executive, Plymouth City Council, Plymouth PL1 2AA ☎ 01752 668000 giles.peritt@plymouth.gov.uk

Planning: Mr Paul Barnard, Assistant Director for Strategic Planning & Infrastructure, Plymouth City Council, Plymouth PL1 2AA ☎ 01752 668000 paul.barnard@plymouth.gov.uk

Procurement: Mr Martin Collins , Strategic Procurement Manager, Civic Centre, Royal Parade, Plymouth PL1 2AA ☎ 01752 668000 martin.collins@plymouth.gov.uk

Recycling & Waste Minimisation: Mr Gareth Harrison-Poole, Street Cleansing & Grounds Manager, Prince Rock Depot, Macadam Road, Plymouth PL4 0RZ ☎ 01752 668000 gareth.harrison-poole@plymouth.gov.uk

Regeneration: Mr Anthony Payne , Director for Place, Plymouth City Council, Plymouth PL1 2AA ☎ 01752 668000 anthony.payne@plymouth.gov.uk

Road Safety: Ms Susan Keith , Road Safety Officer, Plymouth City Council, Plymouth PL1 2AA ☎ 01752 668000 susan.keith@plymouth.gov.uk

Social Services (Adult): Mr David Simpkins , Assistant Director for Co-operative Commissioning & Adult Social Care, Plymouth City Council, Plymouth PL1 2AA ☎ 01752 668000 dave.simpkins@plymouth.gov.uk

Social Services (Children): Ms Alison Botham , Assistant Director for Children's Social Care, Plymouth City Council, Plymouth PL1 2AA ☎ 01752 668000 alison.botham@plymouth.gov.uk

Public Health: Mr Kelechi Nnoaham , Director of Public Health, Plymouth City Council, Plymouth PL1 2AA ☎ 01752 668000 kelechi.nnoaham@plymouth.gov.uk

Street Scene: Mr Gareth Harrison-Poole , Street Cleansing & Grounds Manager, Prince Rock Depot, Macadam Road, Plymouth PL4 0RZ ☎ 01752 668000 gareth.harrison-poole@plymouth.gov.uk

Tourism: Mr David Draffan , Assistant Director for Economic Development, Plymouth City Council, Plymouth PL1 2AA ☎ 01752 668000 david.draffan@plymouth.gov.uk

Town Centre: Mr Stephen Krause , City Centre Manager - Plymouth City Centre Company, Plymouth City Council, Plymouth PL1 2AA ☎ 01752 668000 stefan.krause@plymouth.gov.uk

Traffic Management: Mr Adrian Trim , Head of Highways, Parks & Maritime Services, Plymouth City Council, Plymouth PL1 2AA ☎ 01752 668000 adrian.trim@plymouth.gov.uk

Transport Planner: Mr Philip Heseltine , Head of Integrated Transport, Plymouth City Council, Plymouth PL1 2AA ☎ 01752 668000 philip.heseltine@plymouth.gov.uk

Waste Collection and Disposal: Mr Simon Dale , Assistant Director of Street Scene Services (Interim), Plymouth City Council, Plymouth PL1 2AA ☎ 01752 668000 simon.dale@plymouth.gov.uk

PLYMOUTH CITY

Waste Management: Mr Gareth Harrison-Poole , Street Cleansing & Grounds Manager, Prince Rock Depot, Macadam Road, Plymouth PL4 0RZ ☎ 01752 668000
gareth.harrison-poole@plymouth.gov.uk

Children's Play Areas: Mr Gareth Harrison-Poole , Street Cleansing & Grounds Manager, Prince Rock Depot, Macadam Road, Plymouth PL4 0RZ ☎ 01752 668000
gareth.harrison-poole@plymouth.gov.uk

COUNCILLORS

***The Lord Mayor* Mahony**, John (CON - Peverell)
john.mahony@plymouth.gov.uk

***Deputy Lord Mayor* Ball**, Richard (CON - Compton)
richard.ball@plymouth.gov.uk

***Leader of the Council* Evans**, Tudor (LAB - Ham)
tudor.evans@plymouth.gov.uk

***Deputy Leader of the Council* Smith**, Peter (LAB - Honicknowle)
peter.smith@plymouth.gov.uk

***Group Leader* Bowyer**, Ian (CON - Eggbuckland)
ian.bowyer@plymouth.gov.uk

Aspinall, Mary (LAB - Sutton and Mount Gould)
mary.aspinall@plymouth.gov.uk

Beer, Terri (CON - Plympton Erle)
terri.beer@plymouth.gov.uk

Bowie, Sally (LAB - St Budeaux)
sally.bowie@plymouth.gov.uk

Bowyer, Lynda (CON - Eggbuckland)
lynda.bowyer@plymouth.gov.uk

Bridgeman, Maddi (UKIP - Moor View)
maddi.bridgeman@plymouth.gov.uk

Churchill, Nigel (CON - Plymstock Dunstone)
nigel.churchill@plymouth.gov.uk

Coker, Mark (LAB - Devonport)
mark.coker@plymouth.gov.uk

Damarell, Danny (LAB - St Budeaux)
danny.damarell@plymouth.gov.uk

Dann, Sue (LAB - Sutton and Mount Gould)
sue.dann@plymouth.gov.uk

Darcy, Ian (CON - Plympton Erle)
ian.darcy@plymouth.gov.uk

Davey, Philippa (LAB - Stoke)
philippa.davey@plymouth.gov.uk

Davey, Sam (LAB - Stoke)
sam.davey@plymouth.gov.uk

Deacon, Mark (CON - Southway)
mark.deacon@plymouth.gov.uk

Downie, David (CON - Budshead)
dave.downie@plymouth.gov.uk

Drean, Jonathan (CON - Budshead)
jonathan.drean@plymouth.gov.uk

Fletcher, David (CON - Compton)
david.fletcher@plymouth.gov.uk

Foster, Wendy (CON - Plymstock Radford)
wendy.foster@plymouth.gov.uk

Foster, Ken (CON - Plymstock Radford)
kenneth.foster@plymouth.gov.uk

Fox, Mike (LAB - Moor View)
mike.fox@plymouth.gov.uk

Fry, Ted (CON - Compton)
ted.fry@plymouth.gov.uk

Hendy, Neil (LAB - Efford and Lipson)
neil.hendy@plymouth.gov.uk

James, David (CON - Plympton St Mary)
david.i.james@plymouth.gov.uk

Jarvis, Paul (LAB - Eggbuckland)
paul.jarvis@plymouth.gov.uk

Jordan, Glenn (CON - Plympton Chaddlewood)
glenn.jordan@plymouth.gov.uk

Kelly, Nick (CON - Moor View)
nick.kelly@plymouth.gov.uk

Leaves, Martin (CON - Peverell)
martin.leaves@plymouth.gov.uk

Leaves, Michael (CON - Plymstock Radford)
michael.leaves@plymouth.gov.uk

Leaves, Samantha (CON - Plympton St Mary)
samantha.leaves@plymouth.gov.uk

Lowry, Mark (LAB - Honicknowle)
mark.lowry@plymouth.gov.uk

McDonald, Susan (LAB - St Peter and the Waterfront)
susan.mcdonald@plymouth.gov.uk

Morris, Jonny (LAB - Southway)
jonny.morris@plymouth.gov.uk

Murphy, Pauline (LAB - Efford and Lipson)
pauline.murphy@plymouth.gov.uk

Nicholson, Patrick (CON - Plympton St Mary)
patrick.nicholson@plymouth.gov.uk

Nicholson, Patricia (CON - Peverell)
patricia.nicholson@plymouth.gov.uk

Parker, Lorraine (LAB - Southway)
lorraine.parker@plymouth.gov.uk

Penberthy, Chris (LAB - St Peter and the Waterfront)
chris.penberthy@plymouth.gov.uk

Pengelly, Vivien (CON - Plymstock Dunstone)
vivien.pengelly@plymouth.gov.uk

Rennie, Eddie (LAB - Sutton and Mount Gould)
eddie.rennie@plymouth.gov.uk

Ricketts, Steven (CON - Drake)
steven.ricketts@plymouth.gov.uk

Riley, John (UKIP - Honicknowle)
john.riley@plymouth.gov.uk

Salter, David (CON - Plympton Chaddlewood)
david.salter@plymouth.gov.uk

Singh, Chaz (LAB - Drake)
chaz.singh@plymouth.gov.uk

Sparling, Michael (LAB - Stoke)
mike.sparling@plymouth.gov.uk

Stevens, William (LAB - Devonport)
william.stevens@plymouth.gov.uk

Storer, Christopher (UKIP - Ham)
chris.storer@plymouth.gov.uk

Taylor, Kate (LAB - Devonport)
Kate.taylor@plymouth.gov.uk

Taylor, John (LAB - Budshead)
jon.taylor@plymouth.gov.uk

Tuffin, Ian (LAB - St Peter and the Waterfront)
ian.tuffin@plymouth.gov.uk

Tuohy, Tina (LAB - Ham)
tina.tuohy@plymouth.gov.uk

Vincent, Brian (LAB - Efford and Lipson)
brian.vincent@plymouth.gov.uk

Wheeler, George (LAB - St Budeaux)
george.wheeler@plymouth.gov.uk

Wigens, Kevin (CON - Plymstock Dunstone)
kevin.wigens@plymouth.gov.uk

POLITICAL COMPOSITION

LAB: 28, CON: 26, UKIP: 3

COMMITTEE CHAIRS

Audit: Ms Lorraine Parker

Licensing: Mr Eddie Rennie

Planning: Mr William Stevens

Planning: Ms Tina Tuohy

Planning: Mr Patrick Nicholson

Poole U

Borough of Poole, Civic Centre, Poole BH15 2RU
☎ 01202 633633 🖷 01202 633706 enquiries@poole.gov.uk
www.boroughofpoole.com

FACTS AND FIGURES

Parliamentary Constituencies: Dorset Mid and Poole North, Poole
EU Constituencies: South West
Election Frequency: Elections are of whole council

PRINCIPAL OFFICERS

Chief Executive: Mr Andrew Flockhart , Interim Chief Executive, Civic Centre, Poole BH15 2RU ☎ 01202 633201 a.flockhart@poole.gov.uk

Deputy Chief Executive: Ms Jan Thurgood, Strategic Director for People, Civic Centre, Poole BH15 2RU ☎ 01202 633207 j.thurgood@poole.gov.uk

Senior Management: Ms Sophia Callaghan , Assistant Director - Public Health, Civic Centre Annexe, Poole BH15 2RU ☎ 01202 611107 s.callaghan@poole.gov.uk

Senior Management: Mrs Kate Ryan , Strategic Director for Place, Civic Centre, Poole BH15 2RU ☎ 01202 633202 k.ryan@poole.gov.uk

Access Officer / Social Services (Disability): Mr David Vitty, Head of Adult Social Care - Services, Civic Centre Annexe, Poole BH15 2RU ☎ 01202 261132 d.vitty@poole.gov.uk

Architect, Building / Property Services: Mr Adam Richens, Head of Financial Services, Civic Centre, Poole BH15 2RU ☎ 01202 633183 🖷 01202 633811 a.richens@poole.gov.uk

Best Value: Ms Bridget West, Corporate Communications & Information Manager, Civic Centre, Poole BH15 2RU ☎ 01202 633085 🖷 01202 633899 bridget.west@poole.gov.uk

Building Control: Mr Stephen Thorne , Head of Planning & Regeneration Services, Civic Centre, Poole BH15 2RU ☎ 01202 633327 🖷 01202 633345 s.thorne@poole.gov.uk

Catering Services: Ms Tina Hayter , Executive Catering Manager, Crown Buildings 4th Floor, Civic Centre, Poole BH15 2RU ☎ 01202 261178 🖷 01202 261001 t.hayter@poole.gov.uk

Children / Youth Services: Mrs Vicky Wales , Head of Children, Young People & Learning, The Dolphin Centre, Poole BH15 1SZ ☎ 01202 262251 v.wales@poole.gov.uk

Civil Registration: Mr Tim Martin, Interim Corporate Strategy Team Manager, Civic Centre, Poole BH15 2RU ☎ 01202 633021 🖷 01202 633040 t.martin@poole.gov.uk

PR / Communications: Mr Ian Turner , Communications Manager, Civic Centre, Poole BH15 2RU ☎ 01202 633269 l.turner@poole.gov.uk

Community Planning: Mr Tim Martin, Interim Corporate Strategy Team Manager, Civic Centre, Poole BH15 2RU ☎ 01202 633021 🖷 01202 633040 t.martin@poole.gov.uk

Community Safety: Mrs Anthi Minhinnick , Community Safety Partnership Manager, Civic Centre, Poole BH15 2RU ☎ 01202 223320 a.minhinnick@poole.gov.uk

Computer Management: Mrs Katie Lacey, Head of ICT & Customer Support, Civic Centre, Poole BH15 2RU ☎ 01202 633156 k.lacey@poole.gov.uk

Consumer Protection and Trading Standards: Mr Shaun Robson, Head of Environmental & Consumer Protection, Unit 1, Newfields Business Park, 2 Stinsford Road, Poole BH17 0NF ☎ 01202 261701 🖷 01202 262240 s.robson@poole.gov.uk

Contracts: Mr Adam Richens , Head of Financial Services, Civic Centre, Poole BH15 2RU ☎ 01202 633183 🖷 01202 633811 a.richens@poole.gov.uk

Customer Service: Mrs Katie Lacey, Head of ICT & Customer Support, Civic Centre, Poole BH15 2RU ☎ 01202 633156 k.lacey@poole.gov.uk

Economic Development: Mr Stephen Thorne , Head of Planning & Regeneration Services, Civic Centre, Poole BH15 2RU ☎ 01202 633327 🖷 01202 633345 s.thorne@poole.gov.uk

POOLE

Education: Mrs Vicky Wales , Head of Children, Young People & Learning, The Dolphin Centre, Poole BH15 1SZ ☎ 01202 262251 ✉ v.wales@poole.gov.uk

Electoral Registration: Mr Paul Morris, Registration Services Manager, Room 157, Civic Centre, Poole BH15 2RH ☎ 01202 633028 🖷 01202 633094 ✉ p.morris@poole.gov.uk

Emergency Planning: Mr Adam Richens , Head of Financial Services, Civic Centre, Poole BH15 2RU ☎ 01202 633183 🖷 01202 633811 ✉ a.richens@poole.gov.uk

Energy Management: Mr Julian Collins, Corporate Energy Conservation Officer, Civic Centre, Poole BH15 2RU ☎ 01202 261219 🖷 01202 261211 ✉ j.collins@poole.gov.uk

Environmental / Technical Services: Mr Shaun Robson, Head of Environmental & Consumer Protection, Unit 1, Newfields Business Park, 2 Stinsford Road, Poole BH17 0NF ☎ 01202 261701 🖷 01202 262240 ✉ s.robson@poole.gov.uk

Environmental Health: Mr Shaun Robson, Head of Environmental & Consumer Protection, Unit 1, Newfields Business Park, 2 Stinsford Road, Poole BH17 0NF ☎ 01202 261701 🖷 01202 262240 ✉ s.robson@poole.gov.uk

Estates, Property & Valuation: Mr Adam Richens , Head of Financial Services, Civic Centre, Poole BH15 2RU ☎ 01202 633183 🖷 01202 633811 ✉ a.richens@poole.gov.uk

European Liaison: Mr Stephen Thorne , Head of Planning & Regeneration Services, Civic Centre, Poole BH15 2RU ☎ 01202 633327 🖷 01202 633345 ✉ s.thorne@poole.gov.uk

Facilities: Mr Julian McLaughlin , Head of Transportation Services, Civic Centre, Poole BH15 2RU ☎ 01202 262143 ✉ julian.mclaughlin@poole.gov.uk

Finance: Mr Adam Richens , Head of Financial Services, Civic Centre, Poole BH15 2RU ☎ 01202 633183 🖷 01202 633811 ✉ a.richens@poole.gov.uk

Fleet Management: Mr Shaun Robson, Head of Environmental & Consumer Protection, Unit 1, Newfields Business Park, 2 Stinsford Road, Poole BH17 0NF ☎ 01202 261701 🖷 01202 262240 ✉ s.robson@poole.gov.uk

Grounds Maintenance: Mr Kevin McErlane, Head of Culture & Community Learning, Poole Central Library, The Dolphin Centre, Poole BH15 1QE ☎ 01202 262400 🖷 01202 262431 ✉ k.mcerlane@poole.gov.uk

Health and Safety: Mr Vincent Axford , Health & Safety Officer, Unit 1, Newfields Business Park, 2 Stinsford Road, Poole BH17 0NF ☎ 01202 633463 🖷 01202 633477 ✉ v.axford@poole.gov.uk

Highways: Mr Julian McLaughlin , Head of Transportation Services, Civic Centre, Poole BH15 2RU ☎ 01202 262143 ✉ julian.mclaughlin@poole.gov.uk

Home Energy Conservation: Mr Paul Cooling , Carbon Reduction Manager, Civic Centre, Poole BH15 2RU ☎ 01202 633719 ✉ p.cooling@poole.gov.uk

Housing: Ms Cally Antill , Head of Housing & Community Services, Civic Centre, Poole BH15 2RU ☎ 01202 633440 ✉ c.antill@poole.gov.uk

Housing Maintenance: Mr Joe Logan , Head of Poole Housing Partnership (PHP) Ltd, Poole Housing Partnership (PHP) Ltd, Beech House, 28 - 30 Wimbourne Road, Poole BH15 2BU ☎ 01202 264444

Local Area Agreement: Mr Tim Martin, Interim Corporate Strategy Team Manager, Civic Centre, Poole BH15 2RU ☎ 01202 633021 🖷 01202 633040 ✉ t.martin@poole.gov.uk

Legal: Mr Tim Martin, Interim Corporate Strategy Team Manager, Civic Centre, Poole BH15 2RU ☎ 01202 633021 🖷 01202 633040 ✉ t.martin@poole.gov.uk

Leisure and Cultural Services: Mr Kevin McErlane, Head of Culture & Community Learning, Poole Central Library, The Dolphin Centre, Poole BH15 1QE ☎ 01202 262400 🖷 01202 262431 ✉ k.mcerlane@poole.gov.uk

Licensing: Mr Shaun Robson, Head of Environmental & Consumer Protection, Unit 1, Newfields Business Park, 2 Stinsford Road, Poole BH17 0NF ☎ 01202 261701 🖷 01202 262240 ✉ s.robson@poole.gov.uk

Lifelong Learning: Mr Kevin McErlane, Head of Culture & Community Learning, Poole Central Library, The Dolphin Centre, Poole BH15 1QE ☎ 01202 262400 🖷 01202 262431 ✉ k.mcerlane@poole.gov.uk

Lighting: Mr Julian McLaughlin , Head of Transportation Services, Civic Centre, Poole BH15 2RU ☎ 01202 262143 ✉ julian.mclaughlin@poole.gov.uk

Lottery Funding, Charity and Voluntary: Mr Kevin McErlane, Head of Culture & Community Learning, Poole Central Library, The Dolphin Centre, Poole BH15 1QE ☎ 01202 262400 🖷 01202 262431 ✉ k.mcerlane@poole.gov.uk

Lottery Funding, Charity and Voluntary: Ms Karen Naylor, Principal Officer Planning & Quality Assurance, Crown Buildings 3rd Floor, Poole BH15 2RU ☎ 01202 261130 🖷 01202 261161 ✉ k.naylor@poole.gov.uk

Member Services: Miss Pauline Gill, Democratic Services Manager, Civic Centre, Poole BH15 2RU ☎ 01202 633043 🖷 01202 633040 ✉ p.gill@poole.gov.uk

Parking: Mr Julian McLaughlin , Head of Transportation Services, Civic Centre, Poole BH15 2RU ☎ 01202 262143 ✉ julian.mclaughlin@poole.gov.uk

Partnerships: Mr Tim Martin, Interim Corporate Strategy Team Manager, Civic Centre, Poole BH15 2RU ☎ 01202 633021 🖷 01202 633040 ✉ t.martin@poole.gov.uk

Personnel / HR: Mr Carl Wilcox , Head of Human Resources, Civic Centre, Poole BH15 2RU ☎ 01202 633452 🖷 01202 633477 ✉ c.wilcox@poole.gov.uk

Planning: Mr Stephen Thorne , Head of Planning & Regeneration Services, Civic Centre, Poole BH15 2RU ☎ 01202 633327 🖷 01202 633345 ✉ s.thorne@poole.gov.uk

Procurement: Mr Adam Richens , Head of Financial Services, Civic Centre, Poole BH15 2RU ☎ 01202 633183 🖷 01202 633811 ✉ a.richens@poole.gov.uk

Public Libraries: Mr Kevin McErlane, Head of Culture & Community Learning, Poole Central Library, The Dolphin Centre, Poole BH15 1QE ☎ 01202 262400 🖷 01202 262431 ✉ k.mcerlane@poole.gov.uk

Recycling & Waste Minimisation: Ms Ruzina Begum , Waste Management Officer, Unit 1, New Field Business Park, Stinsford Road, Poole BH17 0NF ☎ 01202 261742 🖷 01202 261717 ✉ r.begum@poole.gov.uk

Regeneration: Mr Stephen Thorne , Head of Planning & Regeneration Services, Civic Centre, Poole BH15 2RU ☎ 01202 633327 🖷 01202 633345 ✉ s.thorne@poole.gov.uk

Road Safety: Mr Julian McLaughlin , Head of Transportation Services, Civic Centre, Poole BH15 2RU ☎ 01202 262143 ✉ julian.mclaughlin@poole.gov.uk

Social Services: Ms Jan Thurgood, Strategic Director for People, Civic Centre, Poole BH15 2RU ☎ 01202 633207 ✉ j.thurgood@poole.gov.uk

Social Services (Adult): Mr Phil Hornsby , Head of Commissioning & Improvement (People Services), Crown Buildings, 4th Floor, Civic Centre, Poole BH15 2RU ☎ 01202 261030 ✉ p.hornsby@poole.gov.uk

Social Services (Adult): Mr David Vitty , Head of Adult Social Care - Services, Civic Centre Annexe, Poole BH15 2RU ☎ 01202 261132 ✉ d.vitty@poole.gov.uk

Social Services (Children): Ms Gerry Moore, Head of Children & Young People's Social Care, 14a Commercial Road, Poole BH15 0JW ☎ 01202 714715 🖷 01202 715589 ✉ gerry.moore@poole.gov.uk

Public Health: Ms Sophia Callaghan , Assistant Director - Public Health, Civic Centre Annexe, Poole BH15 2RU ☎ 01202 611107 ✉ s.callaghan@poole.gov.uk

Staff Training: Mr Carl Wilcox , Head of Human Resources, Civic Centre, Poole BH15 2RU ☎ 01202 633452 🖷 01202 633477 ✉ c.wilcox@poole.gov.uk

Street Scene: Mr Shaun Robson, Head of Environmental & Consumer Protection, Unit 1, Newfields Business Park, 2 Stinsford Road, Poole BH17 0NF ☎ 01202 261701 🖷 01202 262240 ✉ s.robson@poole.gov.uk

Sustainable Communities: Ms Jan Thurgood, Strategic Director for People, Civic Centre, Poole BH15 2RU ☎ 01202 633207 ✉ j.thurgood@poole.gov.uk

Sustainable Development: Mrs Kate Ryan , Strategic Director for Place, Civic Centre, Poole BH15 2RU ☎ 01202 633202 ✉ k.ryan@poole.gov.uk

Tourism: Mr Graham Richardson, Tourism Manager, Enefco House, Visitor Welcome Centre, 19 Strand Street, The Quay, Poole BH15 1HE ☎ 01202 262539 🖷 01202 262684 ✉ g.richardson@pooletourism.com

Town Centre: Mr Graham Richardson, Tourism Manager, Enefco House, Visitor Welcome Centre, 19 Strand Street, The Quay, Poole BH15 1HE ☎ 01202 262539 🖷 01202 262684 ✉ g.richardson@pooletourism.com

Traffic Management: Mr Julian McLaughlin , Head of Transportation Services, Civic Centre, Poole BH15 2RU ☎ 01202 262143 ✉ julian.mclaughlin@poole.gov.uk

Transport: Mr Julian McLaughlin , Head of Transportation Services, Civic Centre, Poole BH15 2RU ☎ 01202 262143 ✉ julian.mclaughlin@poole.gov.uk

Transport Planner: Mr Julian McLaughlin , Head of Transportation Services, Civic Centre, Poole BH15 2RU ☎ 01202 262143 ✉ julian.mclaughlin@poole.gov.uk

Waste Collection and Disposal: Mr Shaun Robson, Head of Environmental & Consumer Protection, Unit 1, Newfields Business Park, 2 Stinsford Road, Poole BH17 0NF ☎ 01202 261701 🖷 01202 262240 ✉ s.robson@poole.gov.uk

Waste Management: Mr Shaun Robson, Head of Environmental & Consumer Protection, Unit 1, Newfields Business Park, 2 Stinsford Road, Poole BH17 0NF ☎ 01202 261701 🖷 01202 262240 ✉ s.robson@poole.gov.uk

Children's Play Areas: Mr Kevin McErlane, Head of Culture & Community Learning, Poole Central Library, The Dolphin Centre, Poole BH15 1QE ☎ 01202 262400 🖷 01202 262431 ✉ k.mcerlane@poole.gov.uk

COUNCILLORS

***Mayor* Stribley**, Ann (CON - Parkstone)
a.stribley@poole.gov.uk

***Deputy Mayor* Adams**, Peter (CON - Oakdale)
p.adams@poole.gov.uk

***Leader of the Council* Walton**, Janet (CON - Oakdale)
j.walton@poole.gov.uk

***Deputy Leader of the Council* Haines**, May (CON - Canford Cliffs)
m.haines@poole.gov.uk

Atkinson, Elaine (CON - Penn Hill)
elaine.atkinson@poole.gov.uk

Bagwell, Julie (IND - Hamworthy West)
j.bagwell@poole.gov.uk

Brooke, Michael (LD - Broadstone)
m.brooke@poole.gov.uk

Brown, David (LD - Merley and Bearwood)
d.brown@poole.gov.uk

Burden, Les (CON - Creekmoor)
l.burden@poole.gov.uk

Butt, Judy (CON - Creekmoor)
j.butt@poole.gov.uk

Challinor, John (CON - Parkstone)
j.challinor@poole.gov.uk

Dion, Xena (CON - Penn Hill)
x.dion@poole.gov.uk

Eades, Phillip (LD - Branksome West)
p.eades@poole.gov.uk

Farrell, Malcolm (CON - Newtown)
m.farrell@poole.gov.uk

Fisher, Mike (UKIP - Alderney)
m.fisher@poole.gov.uk

Gabriel, Sean (CON - Canford Heath West)
s.gabriel@poole.gov.uk

Garner-White, Andy (CON - Pooel Town)
a.garner-white@poole.gov.uk

Gupta, Vishal (CON - Hamworthy East)
v.gupta@poole.gov.uk

Hadley, Andy (IND - Poole Town)
a.hadley@poole.gov.uk

Hodges, Jennie (LD - Canford Heath East)
j.hodges@poole.gov.uk

Howell, Mark (IND - Poole Town)
m.howel@poole.gov.uk

Iyengar, Mohan (CON - Canford Cliffs)
m.iyengar@poole.gov.uk

Le Poidevin, Marion (LD - Branksome West)
m.lepoidevin@gov.uk

Mellor, Drew (CON - Branksome East)
d.mellor@poole.gov.uk

Moore, Sandra (LD - Canford Heath East)
s.moore@poole.gov.uk

Newell, David (CON - Broadstone)
d.newell@poole.gov.uk

Newell, Jane (CON - Merley and Bearwood)
j.newell@poole.gov.uk

Parker, Ron (CON - Penn Hill)
r.parker@poole.gov.uk

Pawlowski, Peter (CON - Canford Cliffs)
p.pawlowski@poole.gov.uk

Pope, Marion (CON - Merley and Bearwood)
m.pope@poole.gov.uk

Potter, Ian (CON - Oakdale)
i.potter@poole.gov.uk

Rampton, John (CON - Creekmoor)
j.rampton@poole.gov.uk

Rampton, Karen (CON - Branksome East)
k.rampton@poole.gov.uk

Russell, Louise (CON - Alderney)
l.russell@poole.gov.uk

Tindle, Ray (CON - Canford Heath West)
r.tindle@poole.gov.uk

Tomlin, Joanne (CON - Broadstone)
j.tomlin@poole.gov.uk

Trent, Russell (CON - Alderney)
r.trent@poole.gov.uk

White, Michael (CON - Hamworthy East)
mike.white@poole.gov.uk

Wilkins, Michael (CON - Hamworthy West)
m.wilkins@poole.gov.uk

Williams, Emma (CON - Parkstone)
e.williams@poole.gov.uk

Wilson, Lindsay (CON - Newtown)
lindsay.wilson@poole.giv.uk

Wilson, Graham (LD - Newtown)
g.wilson@poole.gov.uk

POLITICAL COMPOSITION
CON: 31, LD: 7, IND: 3, UKIP: 1

COMMITTEE CHAIRS
Planning: Mr Peter Pawlowski

Portsmouth City U

Portsmouth City Council, Civic Offices, Guildhall Square, Portsmouth PO1 2AL
☎ 023 9282 2251 🖷 023 9282 8441 🖳 www.portsmouth.gov.uk

FACTS AND FIGURES
Parliamentary Constituencies: Portsmouth North, Portsmouth South
EU Constituencies: South East
Election Frequency: Elections are by thirds

PRINCIPAL OFFICERS
Chief Executive: Mr David Williams, Chief Executive, Civic Offices, Guildhall Square, Portsmouth PO1 2AL ☎ 023 9283 4009 ✉ david.williams@portsmouthcc.gov.uk

Deputy Chief Executive: Mr Michael Lawther, Deputy Chief Executive & City Solicitor, Civic Offices, Guildhall Square, Portsmouth PO1 2AL ☎ 023 9284 1116 ✉ michael.lawther@portsmouthcc.gov.uk

Senior Management: Dr Janet Maxwell , Director - Public Health, Civic Offices, Guildhall Square, Portsmouth PO1 2AL ✉ janet.maxwell@portsmouthcc.gov.uk

Senior Management: Ms Di Smith , Interim Strategic Director - Children's Services, Civic Offices, Guildhall Square, Portsmouth PO1 2AL ☎ 023 9284 1202 ✉ di.smith@portsmouthcc.gov.uk

Senior Management: Ms Kathy Wadsworth , Strategic Director and Director of Regeneration, Civic Offices, Guildhall Square, Portsmouth PO1 2AL ☎ 023 9283 4295 ✉ kathy.wadsworth@portsmouthcc.gov.uk

Access Officer / Social Services (Disability): Ms Gina Perryman , Equality Advisor, Civic Offices, Guildhall Square, Portsmouth PO1 2AL ☎ 023 9283 4789 ✉ gina.perryman@portsmouthcc.gov.uk

Architect, Building / Property Services: Mr Alan Langridge , Team Leader - Quantity Surveyors, Civic Offices, Guildhall Square, Portsmouth PO1 2AL ☎ 023 9283 4731 🖷 023 9283 4966 ✉ alan.langridge@portsmouthcc.gov.uk

Civil Registration: Ms Lorraine Porter , Superintendent Registrar, Births, Deaths & Marriages, Milldam House, Burnaby Road, Portsmouth PO1 3AF ☎ 023 9282 9041 🖷 023 9283 1996 ✉ lorraine.porter@portsmouthcc.gov.uk

PR / Communications: Mr Lee Todd , Communications Manager, Civic Offices, Guildhall Square, Portsmouth PO1 2AL ✉ lee.todd@portsmouthcc.gov.uk

Community Planning: Mr Paddy May , Corporate Strategy Manager, Civic Offices, Guildhall Square, Portsmouth PO1 2AL ☎ 023 9283 4020 ✉ paddy.may@portsmouthcc.gov.uk

Community Safety: Ms Rachael Dalby, Head of Community Safety, Civic Offices, Guildhall Square, Portsmouth PO1 2AL ☎ 023 9283 4040 ✉ rachael.dalby@portsmouthcc.gov.uk

Computer Management: Mr Chris Ward , Head of Information & Solutions, Civic Offices, Guildhall Square, Portsmouth PO1 2AL ☎ 023 9283 4423 ✉ chris.ward@portsmouthcc.gov.uk

Consumer Protection and Trading Standards: Mr Peter Emmett , Trading Standards Manager, Civic Offices, Guildhall Square, Portsmouth PO1 2AL ☎ 023 9284 1291 ✉ peter.emmett@portsmouthcc.gov.uk

Corporate Services: Mr Jon Bell , Director of HR, Legal & Performance, Civic Offices, Guildhall Square, Portsmouth PO1 2AL ☎ 023 8782 ✉ jon.bell@portsmouthcc.gov.uk

Customer Service: Ms Louise Wilders, Head of Customer, Community & Democratic Services, Civic Offices, Guildhall Square, Portsmouth PO1 2AL ☎ 023 9268 8545 ✉ louise.wilders@portsmouthcc.gov.uk

Economic Development: Mr Stephen Baily, Head of City Development & Cultural Services, Civic Offices, Guildhall Square, Portsmouth PO1 2AL ☎ 023 9283 4399 ✉ stephen.baily@portsmouthcc.gov.uk

Emergency Planning: Ms Cindy Jones , Civil Contingencies Manager, Civic Offices, Guildhall Square, Portsmouth PO1 2AL ☎ 023 9268 8050 ✉ cindy.jones@portsmouthcc.gov.uk

Environmental Health: Mr Richard Lee , Environmental Health Manager, Civic Offices, Guildhall Square, Portsmouth PO1 2AL ☎ 023 9283 4857 ✉ richard.lee@portsmouthcc.gov.uk

Events Manager: Ms Claire Looney , Partnership & Commissioning Manager, Civic Offices, Guildhall Square, Portsmouth PO1 2AL ☎ 023 9283 4185 ✉ claire.looney@portsmouthcc.gov.uk

Facilities: Ms Michelle Miller , Landlord Services, Civic Offices, Guildhall Square, Portsmouth PO1 2AL ☎ 023 9283 4992 ✉ michelle.miller@portsmouthcc.gov.uk

Finance: Mr Chris Ward , Head of Information & Solutions, Civic Offices, Guildhall Square, Portsmouth PO1 2AL ☎ 023 9283 4423 ✉ chris.ward@portsmouthcc.gov.uk

Fleet Management: Mr Michael Vickers , Transport Manager, Civic Offices, Guildhall Square, Portsmouth PO1 2AL ☎ 023 9283 4684 ✉ michael.vickers@portsmouthcc.gov.uk

Grounds Maintenance: Mr Seamus Meyer, Strategic Project Manager, Civic Offices, Guildhall Square, Portsmouth PO1 2AL ☎ 023 9283 4163 ✉ seamus.meyer@portsmouthcc.gov.uk

Housing: Mr Owen Buckwell, Director of Property & Housing, Civic Offices, Guildhall Square, Portsmouth PO1 2AL ☎ 023 9283 4503 ✉ owen.buckwell@portsmouthcc.gov.uk

Local Area Agreement: Mr Paddy May , Corporate Strategy Manager, Civic Offices, Guildhall Square, Portsmouth PO1 2AL ☎ 023 9283 4020 ✉ paddy.may@portsmouthcc.gov.uk

Legal: Mr Michael Lawther, Deputy Chief Executive & City Solicitor, Civic Offices, Guildhall Square, Portsmouth PO1 2AL ☎ 023 9284 1116 ✉ michael.lawther@portsmouthcc.gov.uk

Leisure and Cultural Services: Mr Stephen Baily, Head of City Development & Cultural Services, Civic Offices, Guildhall Square, Portsmouth PO1 2AL ☎ 023 9283 4399 ✉ stephen.baily@portsmouthcc.gov.uk

Licensing: Mrs Nicki Humphreys, Licensing Manager, Civic Offices, Guildhall Square, Portsmouth PO1 2AL ☎ 023 9283 4604 ✉ licensing@portsmouthcc.gov.uk

Lifelong Learning: Ms Jan Paterson , Head of Learning & Development, Civic Offices, Guildhall Square, Portsmouth PO1 2AL ☎ 023 9283 4458 ✉ jan.paterson@portsmouthcc.gov.uk

Lighting: Ms Jane Tume , PFI Contract Manager, Civic Offices, Guildhall Square, Portsmouth PO1 2AL ☎ 023 9283 4667 ✉ jane.tume@portsmouthcc.gov.uk

Parking: Mr Michael Robinson , Parking Manager, Civic Offices, Guildhall Square, Portsmouth PO1 2AL ☎ 023 9268 8497 ✉ michael.robinson@portsmouthcc.gov.uk

Personnel / HR: Mr Jon Bell , Director of HR, Legal & Performance, Civic Offices, Guildhall Square, Portsmouth PO1 2AL ☎ 023 8782 ✉ jon.bell@portsmouthcc.gov.uk

Planning: Ms Claire Upton-Brown , City Development Manager, Civic Offices, Guildhall Square, Portsmouth PO1 2AL ✉ claire.upton-brown@portsmouthcc.gov.uk

Procurement: Mr Greg Povey , Assistant Director of Contract, Procurement & Commercial, Civic Offices, Guildhall Square, Portsmouth PO1 2AL ☎ 023 9283 4406 ✉ grey.povey@portsmouthcc.gov.uk

PORTSMOUTH CITY

Public Libraries: Ms Lindy Elliott , Library Services Manager, Civic Offices, Guildhall Square, Portsmouth PO1 2AL ☎ 023 9268 8058 lindy.elliott@portsmouthcc.gov.uk

Recycling & Waste Minimisation: Mr Paul Fielding , Assistant Head of Service - Environment & Recreation, Civic Offices, Guildhall Square, Portsmouth PO1 2AL ☎ 023 9283 4625 🖷 023 9284 1561 paul.fielding@portsmouthcc.gov.uk

Social Services (Adult): Mr Robert Watt, Head of Adult Social Care, Civic Offices, Guildhall Square, Portsmouth PO1 2AL ☎ 023 9284 1160 robert.watt@portsmouthcc.gov.uk

Social Services (Children): Mr Stephen Kitchman , Head of Children's Social Care & Safeguarding, Civic Offices, Guildhall Square, Portsmouth PO1 2AL ☎ 023 9284 1154 🖷 023 9284 1158 stephen.kitchman@portsmouthcc.gov.uk

Public Health: Dr Janet Maxwell , Director - Public Health, Civic Offices, Guildhall Square, Portsmouth PO1 2AL janet.maxwell@portsmouthcc.gov.uk

Staff Training: Ms Liz Aplin , Operational Training Manager, Civic Offices, Guildhall Square, Portsmouth PO1 2AL ☎ 023 9268 8551 liz.aplin@portsmouthcc.gov.uk

Street Scene: Mr Paul Fielding , Assistant Head of Service - Environment & Recreation, Civic Offices, Guildhall Square, Portsmouth PO1 2AL ☎ 023 9283 4625 🖷 023 9284 1561 paul.fielding@portsmouthcc.gov.uk

Tourism: Ms Jane Singh , Visitor Services & Development Manager, Civic Offices, Guildhall Square, Portsmouth PO1 2AL ☎ 023 9283 4636 jane.singh@portsmouthcc.gov.uk

Town Centre: Mr Barry Walker, City Centre Manager, Civic Offices, Guildhall Square, Portsmouth PO1 2AL ☎ 023 6133 4529 barry.walker@portsmouthcc.gov.uk

Waste Collection and Disposal: Mr Paul Fielding , Assistant Head of Service - Environment & Recreation, Civic Offices, Guildhall Square, Portsmouth PO1 2AL ☎ 023 9283 4625 🖷 023 9284 1561 paul.fielding@portsmouthcc.gov.uk

COUNCILLORS

***The Lord Mayor* Jonas**, Frank (CON - Hilsea)
cllr.frank.jonas@portsmouthcc.gov.uk

***Deputy Lord Mayor* Fuller**, David (LD - Fratton)
cllr.david.fuller@portsmouthcc.gov.uk

***Leader of the Council* Jones**, Donna (CON - Hilsea)
Cllr.Donna.Jones@portsmouthcc.gov.uk

***Deputy Leader of the Council* Stubbs**, Luke (CON - Eastney and Craneswater)
cllr.luke.stubbs@portsmouthcc.gov.uk

***Group Leader* Ferrett**, John (LAB - Paulsgrove)
Cllr.John.Ferrett@portsmouthcc.gov.uk

***Group Leader* Galloway**, Colin (UKIP - Nelson)
cllr_galloway@outlook.com

***Group Leader* Vernon-Jackson**, Gerald (LD - Milton)
geraldvj@gmail.com

Ashmore, Dave (LD - Fratton)
cllr.dave.ashmore@portsmouthcc.gov.uk

Bosher, Simon (CON - Drayton and Farlington)
Cllr.Simon.Bosher@portsmouthcc.gov.uk

Brent, Jennie (CON - Eastney and Craneswater)
cllr.jennie.brent@portsmouthcc.gov.uk

Brent, Ryan (CON - St Thomas)
cllr.ryan.brent@portsmouthcc.gov.uk

Chowdhury, Yahiya (LAB - Charles Dickens)
cllr.yahiya.chowdhury@portmsouthcc.gov.uk

Denny, Alicia (UKIP - Copnor)
a.denny.ukipcopnor@gmail.com

Dowling, Ben (LD - Milton)
btldowling@yahoo.co.uk

Ellcome, Ken (CON - Drayton and Farlington)
Cllr.Ken.Ellcome@portsmouthcc.gov.uk

Ferrett, Ken (LAB - Nelson)
cllr.ken.ferrett@portsmouthcc.gov.uk

Foster, Margaret (LD - Charles Dickens)
Cllr.Margaret.Foster@portsmouthcc.gov.uk

Godier, Paul (UKIP - Charles Dickens)
cllr.paul.godier@portsmouthcc.gov.uk

Gray, Aiden (LAB - Cosham)
Cllr.Aiden.Gray@portsmouthcc.gov.uk

Harris, Scott (CON - Hilsea)
cllr.scott.harris@portsmouthcc.gov.uk

Hastins, Steve (UKIP - Baffins)
cllr_hastings@outlook.com

Hockaday, Hannah (CON - Cosham)
hannah.hockaday@me.com

Horton, Suzy (LD - Central Southsea)
cllr.suzy.horton@portsmouthcc.gov.uk

Hunt, Lee (LD - Central Southsea)
Cllr.Lee.Hunt@portsmouthcc.gov.uk

Lyon, Ian (CON - Nelson)
cllr.ian.lyon@portsmouthcc.gov.uk

Mason, Hugh (LD - St Jude)
Cllr.Hugh.Mason@portsmouthcc.gov.uk

Mason, Lee (CON - Cosham)
Cllr.Lee.Mason@portsmouthcc.gov.uk

New, Gemma (CON - Paulsgrove)
cllr.gemma.new@portsmouthcc.gov.uk

New, Robert (CON - Copnor)
Cllr.Robert.New@portsmouthcc.gov.uk

Potter, Stuart (UKIP - Paulsgrove)
cllr_potter@ukipportsmouth.org

Purvis, Will (LD - Milton)
Cllr.Will.Purvis@portsmouthcc.gov.uk

Sanders, Darren (LD - Baffins)
Cllr.Darren.Sanders@portsmouthcc.gov.uk

Smith, Phil (LD - Central Southsea)
Cllr.Phil.Smith@portsmouthcc.gov.uk

Stagg, Lynne (LD - Baffins)
Cllr.Lynne.Stagg@portsmouthcc.gov.uk

Stockdale, Sandra (LD - St Thomas)
Cllr.Sandra.Stockdale@portsmouthcc.gov.uk

Swan, Julie (UKIP - Fratton)
cllrswan@outlook.com

Symes, Linda (CON - St Jude)
cllr.linda.symes@portsmouthcc.gov.uk

Tompkins, David (CON - St Jude)
cllr.david.tomkins@portsmouthcc.gov.uk

Wemyss, Steve (CON - Drayton and Farlington)
cllr.Steve.Wemyss@portsmouthcc.gov.uk

Winnington, Matthew (LD - Eastney and Craneswater)
Cllr.Matthew.Winnington@portsmouthcc.gov.uk

Wood, Rob (LD - St Thomas)
cllr.rob.wood@portsmouthcc.gov.uk

Young, Neil (CON - Copnor)
Cllr.Neill.Young@portsmouthcc.gov.uk

POLITICAL COMPOSITION

CON: 17, LD: 15, UKIP: 6, LAB: 4

COMMITTEE CHAIRS

Education, Children & Young People: Mr Will Purvis

Governance & Audit: Mr Simon Bosher

Planning: Mr Aiden Gray

Powys W

Powys County Council, County Hall, Llandrindod Wells LD1 5LG
☎ 01597 826000 🖷 01597 826230 🖳 www.powys.gov.uk

FACTS AND FIGURES

Parliamentary Constituencies: Brecon and Radnorshire, Montgomeryshire
EU Constituencies: Wales
Election Frequency: Elections are of whole council

PRINCIPAL OFFICERS

Chief Executive: Mr Jeremy Patterson, Chief Executive, County Hall, Llandrindod Wells LD1 5LG ☎ 01597 826082 🖷 01597 826220 ✉ jeremy.patterson@powys.gov.uk

Senior Management: Mr Paul Griffiths, Strategic Director - Place, County Hall, Llandrindod Wells LD1 5LG ☎ 01597 826464 ✉ paul.griffiths@powys.gov.uk

Senior Management: Ms Amanda Lewis , Strategic Director - People, County Hall, Llandrindod Wells LD1 5LG ☎ 01597 826906 ✉ amanda.lewis@powys.gov.uk

Senior Management: Mr Nick Philpott, Director of Change & Governance, County Hall, Llandrindod Wells LD1 5LG ☎ 01597 826093 ✉ nick.philpott@powys.gov.uk

Senior Management: Mr Clive Pinney, Solicitor to the Council, County Hall, Llandrindod Wells LD1 5LG ☎ 01597 826746 ✉ clive.pinney@powys.gov.uk

Senior Management: Mr David Powell , Strategic Director - Resources, County Hall, Llandrindod Wells LD1 5LG ☎ 01597 826729 ✉ david.powell@powys.gov.uk

Architect, Building / Property Services: Ms Sarah Jowett , Senior Manager - Regeneration & Property, County Hall, Llandrindod Wells LD1 5LG ☎ 01597 826553 ✉ sarah.jowett@powys.gov.uk

Best Value: Mr Nick Philpott, Director of Change & Governance, County Hall, Llandrindod Wells Ld1 5LG ☎ 01597 826093 ✉ nick.philpott@powys.gov.uk

Building Control: Ms Heather Jones , Professional Lead - Building Control, County Hall, Llandrindod Wells LD1 5LG ☎ 01597 827752 ✉ heather.jones@powys.gov.uk

Catering Services: Mr Jason Rawbone , Principal Catering Officer, The Gwalia, Llandrindod Wells LD1 6AA ☎ 01597 827291 ✉ jason.rawbone@powys.gov.uk

Civil Registration: Ms Bronwyn Curnow , Registration Services Manager, County Hall, Llandrindod Wells LD1 5LG ☎ 01597 827468 ✉ bronwyn.curnow@powys.gov.uk

PR / Communications: Ms Anya Richards , Senior Communications Manager, County Hall, Llandrindod Wells LD1 5LG ☎ 01597 826089 ✉ anya.richards@powys.gov.uk

Computer Management: Mr Allen Hart , Information & Customer Services Manager, County Hall, Llandrindod Wells LD1 5LG ☎ 01597 826090 ✉ allen.hart@powys.gov.uk

Consumer Protection and Trading Standards: Mr Ken Yorston , Senior Manager - Regulatory Services, County Hall, Llandrindod Wells LD1 5LG ☎ 01597 826570 ✉ ken.yorston@powys.gov.uk

Customer Service: Mr Allen Hart , Information & Customer Services Manager, County Hall, Llandrindod Wells LD1 5LG ☎ 01597 826090 ✉ allen.hart@powys.gov.uk

Economic Development: Ms Susan Bolter , Head of Regeneration Property & Commissioning, County Hall, Llandrindod Wells LD1 5LG ☎ 01597 826195 ✉ susan.bolter@powys.gov.uk

Education: Mr Ian Roberts , Head of Schools, County Hall, Llandrindod Wells LD1 5LG ☎ 01597 826422 ✉ ian.roberts@powys.gov.uk

Electoral Registration: Ms Sandra Matthews , Principal Elections Officer, County Hall, Llandrindod Wells LD1 5LG ☎ 01597 826747 🖷 01597 826220 ✉ sandra.matthews@powys.gov.uk

Emergency Planning: Mr Wayne Jones , Prinicpal Emergency Planning Officer, County Hall, Llandrindod Wells LD1 5LG ☎ 01597 826000 ✉

Energy Management: Mr Gareth Richards , Energy Management Officer, County Hall, Llandrindod Wells LD1 5LG ☎ 01597 826629 ✉ garethr@powys.gov.uk

POWYS

Environmental Health: Ms Nia Hughes , Professional Lead Environmental Health, Neuadd Maldwyn, Welshpool SY21 7AS ☎ 01938 551299 ✉ nia.hughes@powys.gov.uk

Estates, Property & Valuation: Ms Susan Bolter , Head of Regeneration Property & Commissioning, County Hall, Llandrindod Wells LD1 5LG ☎ 01597 826195 ✉ susan.bolter@powys.gov.uk

European Liaison: Ms Kay Francis , European & External Funding Officer, The Gwalia, Llandrindod Wells LD1 6AA ☎ 01597 826180 ✉ kay.francis@powys.gov.uk

Facilities: Mr Neil Clutton , Property Manager, County Hall, Llandrindod Wells LD1 5LG ☎ 01597 826595 ✉ neil.clutton@powys.gov.uk

Finance: Mr David Powell , Strategic Director - Resources, County Hall, Llandrindod Wells LD1 5LG ☎ 01597 826729 ✉ david.powell@powys.gov.uk

Pensions: Mr Joe Rollin , Pensions Manager, County Hall, Llandrindod Wells LD1 5LG ☎ 01597 826306 ✉ joe.rollin@powys.gov.uk

Fleet Management: Mr Tim Washington , Interim Fleet Manager, County Hall, Llandrindod Wells LD1 5LG ☎ 01597 829846 ✉ tim.washington@powys.gov.uk

Housing: Mr Simon Inkson , Head of Housing, County Hall, Llandrindod Wells LD1 5LG ☎ 01597 826639 ✉ simon.inkson@powys.gov.uk

Housing Maintenance: Mr Dafydd Evans , Senior Manager - Housing Solutions, Neuadd Maldwyn, Severn Road, Welshpool SY21 7AS ☎ 01938 551214 ✉ dafydd.evans@powys.gov.uk

Legal: Mr Clive Pinney, Solicitor to the Council, County Hall, Llandrindod Wells LD1 5LG ☎ 01597 826746 ✉ clive.pinney@powys.gov.uk

Leisure and Cultural Services: Mr Paul Griffiths, Strategic Director - Place, County Hall, Llandrindod Wells LD1 5LG ☎ 01597 826464 ✉ paul.griffiths@powys.gov.uk

Member Services: Mr Wyn Richards , Head of Democratic Services, County Hall, Llandrindod Wells LD1 5LG ☎ 01597 826375 ✉ wyn.richards@powys.gov.uk

Personnel / HR: Mr Jason Lewis , Head of Professional Services & Commissioning, County Hall, Llandrindod Wells LD1 5LG ☎ 01597 826318 ✉ jason.lewis@powys.gov.uk

Planning: Mr Gwilym Davies , Lead Professional Development Management, County Hall, Llandrindod Wells LD1 5LG ☎ 01597 827344 ✉ gwilym.davies@powys.gov.uk

Procurement: Ms Gail Jones , Professional Lead - Commercial Services, County Hall, Llandrindod Wells LD1 5LG ☎ 01597 826326 ✉ gail.jones@powys.gov.uk

Recycling & Waste Minimisation: Mr Ashley Collins , Waste Services Manager, County Hall, Llandrindod Wells LD1 5LG ☎ 01597 826974 ✉ ashley.collins@powys.gov.uk

Regeneration: Ms Susan Bolter , Head of Regeneration Property & Commissioning, County Hall, Llandrindod Wells LD1 5LG ☎ 01597 826195 ✉ susan.bolter@powys.gov.uk

Road Safety: Mr Tony Caine , Road Safety & Traffic Systems Manager, County Hall, Llandrindod Wells LD1 5LG ☎ 0845 607 6652 ✉ tony.caine@powys.gov.uk

Social Services: Ms Amanda Lewis , Strategic Director - People, County Hall, Llandrindod Wells LD1 5LG ☎ 01597 826906 ✉ amanda.lewis@powys.gov.uk

Social Services (Adult): Ms Joy Garfitt , Head of Adult Services, County Hall, Llandrindod Wells LD1 5LG ☎ 01597 826578 ✉ joy.garfitt@powys.gov.uk

Social Services (Children): Ms Pauline Higham , Head of Children's Services, 1 High Street, Llandrindod Wells LD1 6AG ☎ 01597 827084 ✉ pauline.higham@powys.gov.uk

Staff Training: Ms Sarah Powell , Professional Lead - Culture & Leadership Development, County Hall, Llandrindod Wells LD1 5LG ☎ 01597 826762 ✉ sarah.powell@powys.gov.uk

Sustainable Development: Ms Heather Delonnette, Sustainable Development Co-ordinator, County Hall, Llandrindod Wells LD1 5LG ☎ 01597 826165 ✉ heather.delonnette@powys.gov.uk

Tourism: Ms Julie Lewis , Tourism Officer, Brecon Tourist Information Centre, Cattle Market Car Park, Brecon LD3 9DA ☎ 01874 612275 ✉ julie.lewis@powys.gov.uk

Traffic Management: Mr Tony Caine , Road Safety & Traffic Systems Manager, County Hall, Llandrindod Wells LD1 5LG ☎ 0845 607 6652 ✉ tony.caine@powys.gov.uk

Transport: Mr John Forsey , Transport Passenger Manager, County Hall, Llandrindod Wells LD1 5LG ☎ 01597 826642 ✉ john.forsey@powys.gov.uk

Transport Planner: Mr John Forsey , Transport Passenger Manager, County Hall, Llandrindod Wells LD1 5LG ☎ 01597 826642 ✉ john.forsey@powys.gov.uk

Waste Collection and Disposal: Mr Ashley Collins , Waste Services Manager, County Hall, Llandrindod Wells LD1 5LG ☎ 01597 826974 ✉ ashley.collins@powys.gov.uk

Waste Management: Mr Ashley Collins , Waste Services Manager, County Hall, Llandrindod Wells LD1 5LG ☎ 01597 826974 ✉ ashley.collins@powys.gov.uk

COUNCILLORS

***Leader of the Council* Thomas**, Barry (IND - Llanfihangel) cllr.barry.thomas@powys.gov.uk

Alexander, Myfanwy (IND - Banwy)
cllr.myfanwy.alexander@powys.gov.uk

Ashton, Paul (LD - St Mary)
cllr.paul.ashton@powys.gov.uk

Bailey, Dawn (IND - Trewern)
cllr.dawn.bailey@powys.gov.uk

Banks, Garry (LD - Presteigne)
cllr.garry.banks@powys.gov.uk

Bowker, Gemma-Jane (LD - Newton Llanwchaiarn North)
cllr.gemma.jane.bowker@powys.gov.uk

Brown, Graham (IND - Llandrinio)
cllr.graham.brown@powys.gov.uk

Brunt, John (IND - Beguildy)
cllr.john.brunt@powys.gov.uk

Corfield, Linda (IND - Forden)
cllr.linda.corfield@powys.gov.uk

Curry, Kelvyn (LD - Rhayader)
cllr.kelvyn.curry@powys.gov.uk

Davies, Dai (IND - Berriew)
cllr.dai.davies@powys.gov.uk

Davies, Aled (CON - Llanrhaeadr-ym-Mochnant / Llansilin)
cllr.aled.davies@powys.gov.uk

Davies, Chris (CON - Glasbury)
cllr.chris.davies@powys.gov.uk

Davies, Stephen (IND - Bronllys)
cllr.stephen.davies@powys.gov.uk

Davies, Rachel (IND - Caersws)
cllr.rachel.davies@powys.gov.uk

Davies, Sandra (LAB - Cwm-Twrch)
cllr.sandra.davies@powys.gov.uk

Davies, Melanie (IND - Llangors)
cllr.melanie.davies@powys.gov.uk

Davies, Roche (IND - Llandinam)
cllr.roche.davies@powys.gov.uk

Dorrance, Matthew (LAB - St John)
cllr.matthew.dorrance@powys.gov.uk

Evans, David (IND - Nantmel)
cllr.david.evans@powys.gov.uk

Evans, Viola (IND - Llanfair Caereinion)
cllr.viola.evans@powys.gov.uk

Evans, John (IND - Llanyre)
cllr.john.evans@powys.gov.uk

Fitzpatrick, Liam (IND - Talybont-on-Usk)
cllr.liam.fitzpatrick@powys.gov.uk

George, Russell (CON - Newtown Central)
cllr.russell.george@powys.gov.uk

Harris, Rosemarie (NP - Llangynidr)
cllr.rosemarie.harris@powys.gov.uk

Harris, Peter (CON - Newtown Llanllwchaiarn West)
cllr.peter.harris@powys.gov.uk

Hayes, Stephen (IND - Montgomery)
cllr.stephen.hayes@powys.gov.uk

Holloway, Ann (IND - Welshpool Llanerchyddol)
cllr.ann.holloway@powys.gov.uk

Holmes, Jeff (LD - Llangattock)
cllr.jeff.holmes@powys.gov.uk

Hopkins, Geraint (IND - Gwernyfed)
cllr.geraint.hopkins@powys.gov.uk

Jones, Dai (IND - Llanbrynmair)
cllr.dai.jones@powys.gov.uk

Jones, Graham (CON - Blaen Hafren)
cllr.graham.jones@powys.gov.uk

Jones, Joy (LD - Newtown East)
cllr.joy.jones@powys.gov.uk

Jones, Michael (IND - Churchstoke)
cllr.michael.john.jones@powys.gov.uk

Jones, Arwel (IND - Llandysilio)
cllr.arwel.jones@powys.gov.uk

Jones, Wynne (IND - Dolforwyn)
cllr.wynne.jones@powys.gov.uk

Jones, Michael (IND - Old Radnor)
cllr.michael.jones@powys.gov.uk

Jones, Eldrydd (IND - Meifod)
cllr.eldrydd.jones@powys.gov.uk

Jones, David (IND - Guilsfield)
cllr.david.jones@powys.gov.uk

Jump, Francesca (LD - Welshpool Gungrog)
cllr.francesca.jump@powys.gov.uk

Lewis, Peter (CON - Llanfyllin)
cllr.peter.lewis@powys.gov.uk

Lewis, Hywel (IND - Llangunllo)
cllr.hywel.lewis@powys.gov.uk

Mackenzie, Maureen (LD - Llanelwedd)
cllr.maureen.mackenzie@powys.gov.uk

Mayor, Darren (NP - Llanwddyn)
cllr.darren.mayor@powys.gov.uk

McNicholas, Susan (LAB - Ynescedwyn)
cllr.susan.mcnicholas@powys.gov.uk

Medlicott, Peter (IND - Knighton)
cllr.peter.medlicott@powys.gov.uk

Meredith, David (LAB - St David Within)
cllr.david.meredith@powys.gov.uk

Mills, Bob (IND - Newtown South)
cllr.bob.mills@powys.gov.uk

Morgan, Gareth (IND - Llanidloes)
cllr.gareth.morgan@powys.gov.uk

Morgan, Evan (IND - Maescar / Llywel)
cllr.evan.morgan@powys.gov.uk

Morris, John (LD - Crickhowell)
cllr.john.morris@powys.gov.uk

Powell, William (LD - Talgarth)
cllr.william.powell@powys.gov.uk

Powell, John (IND - Llanbadarn Fawr)
cllr.john.powell@powys.gov.uk

Price, David (IND - Llanafanfawr)
cllr.david.price@powys.gov.uk

Price, Gary (CON - Llandrindod North)
cllr.gary.price@powys.gov.uk

Pritchard, Philip (IND - Welshpool Castle)
cllr.phil.pritchard@powys.gov.uk

Ratcliffe, Gareth (IND - Hay)
cllr.gareth.ratcliffe@powys.gov.uk

Roberts-Jones, Kath (IND - Kerry)
cllr.kath.roberts-jones@powys.gov.uk

Shearer, Joy (IND - Rhiwcynon)
cllr.joy.shearer@powys.gov.uk

Silk, Kathryn (LD - Bwlch)
cllr.kathryn.silk@powys.gov.uk

Tampin, Keith (IND - Llandrindod East/Llandrindod West)
cllr.keith.tampin@powys.gov.uk

Thomas, David (LAB - Tawe Uchaf)
cllr.david.thomas@powys.gov.uk

Thomas, Gwynfor (CON - Llansanffraid)
cllr.gwynfor.thomas@powys.gov.uk

Thomas, Tony (IND - Felin-fach)
cllr.tony.thomas@powys.gov.uk

Thomas, Gillian (IND - Yscir)
cllr.gillian.thomas@powys.gov.uk

Turner, Tom (CON - Llandrindod South)
cllr.tom.turner@powys.gov.uk

Van-Rees, Tim (IND - Llanwrtyd Wells)
cllr.tim.van-rees@powys.gov.uk

Vaughan, Gwilym (IND - Glantwymyn)
cllr.gwilym.vaughan@powys.gov.uk

Williams, Michael (IND - Machynlleth)
cllr.michael.williams@powys.gov.uk

Williams, Huw (NP - Ystradgynlais)
cllr.huw.williams@powys.gov.uk

Williams, Sarah (LAB - Aber-craf)
cllr.sarah.williams@powys.gov.uk

Williams, Gwilym (CON - Disserth and Trecoed)
cllr.gwilym.williams@powys.gov.uk

York, Avril (IND - Builth)
cllr.avril.york@powys.gov.uk

POLITICAL COMPOSITION
IND: 43, LD: 11, CON: 10, LAB: 6, NP: 3

Preston D

Preston City Council, Town Hall, Lancaster Road, Preston PR1 2RL
☎ 01772 906900 🖷 01772 906901 ✉ info@preston.gov.uk
🖳 www.preston.gov.uk

FACTS AND FIGURES
Parliamentary Constituencies: Preston
EU Constituencies: North West
Election Frequency: Elections are by thirds

PRINCIPAL OFFICERS
Chief Executive: Ms Lorraine Norris, Chief Executive, Town Hall, Lancaster Road, Preston PR1 2RL ☎ 01772 906101 🖷 01772 906366 ✉ l.norris@preston.gov.uk

Assistant Chief Executive: Mr Derek Whyte, Assistant Chief Executive, Town Hall, Lancaster Road, Preston PR1 2RL ☎ 01772 903430 ✉ d.whyte@preston.gov.uk

Senior Management: Mrs Alison Brown, Director of Corporate Services, Town Hall, Lancaster Road, Preston PR1 2RL ☎ 01772 906197 ✉ a.brown@preston.gov.uk

Senior Management: Mr Neil Fairhurst, Director of Customer Services, PO Box 10, Town Hall, Lancaster Road, Preston PR1 2RL ☎ 01772 906197 ✉ n.fairhurst@preston.gov.uk

Senior Management: Mr Chris Hayward , Director of Development, Lancastria House, Preston PR1 2RH ☎ 01772 906171 ✉ c.hayward@preston.gov.uk

Senior Management: Mr Adrian Phillips, Director of Environment, Lancastria House, Lancaster Road, Preston PR1 2RH ☎ 01772 906171 ✉ a.phillips@preston.gov.uk

Best Value: Ms Jenny Rowlands , Senior Performance Advisor, Town Hall, Lancaster Road, Preston PR1 2RL ☎ 01772 906605 ✉ j.rowlands@preston.gov.uk

Building Control: Mr D Tomlinson , Head of Building Services, Town Hall, Lancaster Road, Preston PR1 2RL ☎ 01772 906536 ✉ d.tomlinson@preston.gov.uk

PR / Communications: Mr Stephen Parkinson, Head of Communications, Town Hall, Lancaster Road, Preston PR1 2RL ☎ 01772 906464 🖷 01771 906822 ✉ s.parkinson@preston.gov.uk

Community Safety: Mrs Michelle Pilling, Community Safety Manager, MAPS Team, Preston Police Preston, Lancaster Road North, Preston PR1 2SA ☎ 01772 209796 ✉ m.pilling@preston.gov.uk

Computer Management: Mr Neil Fairhurst, Director of Customer Services, Town Hall, Lancaster Road, Preston PR1 2RL ☎ 01772 906197 ✉ n.fairhurst@preston.gov.uk

Contracts: Ms Caron Parmenter , Head of Legal Services, Town Hall, Lancaster Road, Preston PR1 2RL ☎ 01772 906373 ✉ c.parmenter@preston.gov.uk

Corporate Services: Mrs Alison Brown, Director of Corporate Services, Town Hall, Lancaster Road, Preston PR1 2RL ☎ 01772 906197 ✉ a.brown@preston.gov.uk

Customer Service: Mr Peter Kerry, Call Centre Manager, Town Hall, Lancaster Road, Preston PR1 2RL ☎ 01772 906939 🖷 01772 906336 ✉ p.kerry@preston.gov.uk

Direct Labour: Mr Adrian Phillips, Director of Environment, Lancastria House, Lancaster Road, Preston PR1 2RH ☎ 01772 906171 ✉ a.phillips@preston.gov.uk

Economic Development: Mr Derek Whyte, Assistant Chief Executive, Town Hall, Lancaster Road, Preston PR1 2RL ☎ 01772 903430 ✉ d.whyte@preston.gov.uk

E-Government: Mr Neil Fairhurst, Director of Customer Services, Town Hall, Lancaster Road, Preston PR1 2RL ☎ 01772 906197 ✉ n.fairhurst@preston.gov.uk

Electoral Registration: Mr Peter Welsh , Head of Electoral Services, Town Hall, Lancaster Road, Preston PR1 2RL ☎ 01772 906115 ✉ p.welsh@preston.gov.uk

Emergency Planning: Mr Alan Murray, Emergency Planning Officer, Town Hall, Lancaster Road, Preston PR1 2RL ☎ 01772 906162 🖷 01772 906822 ✉ a.murray@preston.gov.uk

Energy Management: Mr Adrian Phillips, Director of Environment, Town Hall, Lancaster Road, Preston PR1 2RL ☎ 01772 906171 ✉ a.phillips@preston.gov.uk

Environmental Health: Mr Craig Sharp, Chief Environmental Health Officer, Town Hall, Lancaster Road, Preston PR1 2RL ☎ 01772 906301 ✉ c.sharp@preston.gov.uk

Estates, Property & Valuation: Mr Derek Woods , Head of Property Management, Town Hall, Lancaster Road, Preston PR1 2RL ☎ 01772 906519 ✉ d.woods@preston.gov.uk

European Liaison: Mr Derek Whyte, Assistant Chief Executive, Town Hall, Lancaster Road, Preston PR1 2RL ☎ 01772 903430 ✉ d.whyte@preston.gov.uk

Events Manager: Mr Tim Joel , Events Manager, Town Hall, Lancaster Road, Preston PR1 2RL ☎ 01772 903660 ✉ t.joel@preston.gov.uk

Facilities: Mr Adrian Phillips, Director of Environment, Town Hall, Lancaster Road, Preston PR1 2RL ☎ 01772 906171 ✉ a.phillips@preston.gov.uk

Finance: Mr A Robinson , Head of Shared Services, Town Hall, Lancaster Road, Preston PR1 2RL ☎ 01772 906023 ✉ a.robinson@preston.gov.uk

Finance: Ms Jackie Wilding , City Treasurer, Town Hall, Lancaster Road, Preston PR1 2RL ☎ 01772 906808 ✉ j.wilding@prestong.gov.uk

Fleet Management: Mr Adrian Phillips, Director of Environment, Town Hall, Lancaster Road, Preston PR1 2RL ☎ 01772 906171 ✉ a.phillips@preston.gov.uk

Grounds Maintenance: Mr Matt Kelly , Head of Parks & Horticultural Services, Argyll Road, Preston PR1 6JY ☎ 01772 906141 🖷 01772 558488 ✉ m.kelly@preston.gov.uk

Health and Safety: Ms Lesley Routh, Health & Safety Manager, Town Hall, Lancaster Road, Preston PR1 2RL ☎ 01772 906385 🖷 01772 906822 ✉ l.routh@preston.gov.uk

Home Energy Conservation: Mr Craig Sharp, Chief Environmental Health Officer, Town Hall, Lancaster Road, Preston PR1 2RL ☎ 01772 906301 ✉ c.sharp@preston.gov.uk

Housing: Mr Craig Sharp, Chief Environmental Health Officer, Town Hall, Lancaster Road, Preston PR1 2RL ☎ 01772 906301 ✉ c.sharp@preston.gov.uk

Legal: Ms Caron Parmenter , Head of Legal Services, Town Hall, Lancaster Road, Preston PR1 2RL ☎ 01772 906373 ✉ c.parmenter@preston.gov.uk

Leisure and Cultural Services: Mr Jimmy Khan , Head of Sport & Leisure, Town Hall, Lancaster Road, Preston PR1 2RL ☎ 01772 903126 ✉ j.khan@preston.gov.uk

Leisure and Cultural Services: Ms A M Walker , Head of Arts & Heritage Services, Harris Museum, Market Square, Preston PR1 2PP ☎ 01772 906105 ✉ a.walker@preston.gov.uk

Licensing: Mr Mike Thorpe, Head of Licensing Services, Town Hall, Lancaster Road, Preston PR1 2RL ☎ 01772 906114 ✉ m.thorpe@preston.gov.uk

Lottery Funding, Charity and Voluntary: Ms Jennifer Carthy , Neighbourhood Manager, Town Hall, Lancaster Road, Preston PR1 2RL ☎ 01772 903425 ✉ j.carthy@preston.gov.uk

Member Services: Ms Julie Grundy , Head of Member Services, Town Hall, Lancaster Road, Preston PR1 2RL ☎ 01772 906112 ✉ j.grundy@preston.gov.uk

Parking: Mr Mick Tickle , Building Cleaning & Parking Manager, Town Hall, Lancaster Road, Preston PR1 2RL ☎ 01772 906256 ✉ m.tickle@preston.gov.uk

Partnerships: Ms Jenny Rowlands , Senior Performance Advisor, Town Hall, Lancaster Road, Preston PR1 2RL ☎ 01772 906605 ✉ j.rowlands@preston.gov.uk

Personnel / HR: Mrs Alison Brown, Director of Corporate Services, Town Hall, Lancaster Road, Preston PR1 2RL ☎ 01772 906197 ✉ a.brown@preston.gov.uk

Planning: Mr Chris Hayward , Director of Development, Lancastria House, Preston PR1 2RH ☎ 01772 906171 ✉ c.hayward@preston.gov.uk

Procurement: Mr Mervyn Sheppard , Corporate Projects Legal Advisor, Town Hall, Lancaster Road, Preston PR1 2RL ☎ 01772 906104 ✉ m.sheppard@preston.gov.uk

Recycling & Waste Minimisation: Ms Debbie Slater , Senior Recycling & Waste Management Officer, Argyll Road, Preston PR1 6JY ☎ 01772 906786 ✉ d.slater@preston.gov.uk

Regeneration: Mr Derek Whyte, Assistant Chief Executive, Town Hall, Lancaster Road, Preston PR1 2RL ☎ 01772 903430 ✉ d.whyte@preston.gov.uk

Staff Training: Mrs Steph Hayes , Training & Development Manager, Town Hall, Lancaster Road, Preston PR1 2RL ☎ 01772 906399 🖷 01772 906822 ✉ s.hayes@preston.gov.uk

PRESTON

Street Scene: Mr Mark Taylor , Deputy Head of Parks, Street Scene & Transport, Argyll Road, Preston PR1 6JY ☎ 01772 906219 ✉ m.a.taylor@preston.gov.uk

Tourism: Ms Rita Whitlock , Visitor Information Centre Manager, Guild Hall, Lancaster Road, Preston PR1 1HT ☎ 01772 903215 ✉ r.whitlock@preston.gov.uk

Transport: Mr Adrian Phillips, Director of Environment, Town Hall, Lancaster Road, Preston PR1 2RL ☎ 01772 906171 ✉ a.phillips@preston.gov.uk

Waste Collection and Disposal: Mr Adrian Phillips, Director of Environment, Town Hall, Lancaster Road, Preston PR1 2RL ☎ 01772 906171 ✉ a.phillips@preston.gov.uk

Waste Management: Mr Adrian Phillips, Director of Environment, Town Hall, Lancaster Road, Preston PR1 2RL ☎ 01772 906171 ✉ a.phillips@preston.gov.uk

COUNCILLORS

***Mayor* McManus**, Margaret (CON - Sharoe Green)
cllr.m.mcmanus@preston.gov.uk

***Deputy Mayor* Collins**, John (LAB - Moor Park)
cllr.j.collins@preston.gov.uk

***Leader of the Council* Rankin**, Peter John (LAB - Tulketh)

***Deputy Leader of the Council* Swindells**, John (LAB - University)

Abram, Christine (CON - Lea)
cllr.c.abram@preston.gov.uk

Afrin, Veronica (LAB - St Matthew's)
cllr.v.afrin@preston.gov.uk

Atkins, Elizabeth (LAB - Ashton)
cllr.e.atkins@preston.gov.uk

Bax, Ismail (LAB - Deepdale)
cllr.i.bax@preston.gov.uk

Borrow, David (LAB - Moor Park)
cllr.d.borrow@preston.gov.uk

Boswell, Robert (LAB - Tulketh)
cllr.r.boswell@preston.gov.uk

Brown, Matthew (LAB - Tulketh)
cllr.m.brown@preston.gov.uk

Brown, Pauline (LD - Ingol)
cllr.p.brown@preston.gov.uk

Browne, John (LAB - Brookfield)
cllr.j.browne@preston.gov.uk

Cartwright, Neil (CON - Preston Rural East)
cllr.n.cartwright@preston.gov.uk

Cartwright, Terry (IND - Deepdale)
cllr.t.cartwright@preston.gov.uk

Cartwright, Kathleen (CON - College)
cllr.b.cartwright@preston.gov.uk

Corker, Philip (LAB - Brookfield)
cllr.p.corker@preston.gov.uk

Coupland, Zafar (LAB - Fishwick)
cllr.z.coupland@preston.gov.uk

Crompton, Linda (LAB - Riversway)
cllr.l.crompton@preston.gov.uk

Crompton, Carl (LAB - University)
cllr.c.crompton@preston.gov.uk

Crowe, Phil (LAB - Larches)
cllr.p.crowe@preston.gov.uk

Darby, Neil (LD - Ingol)
cllr.n.darby@preston.gov.uk

Davies, Thomas (CON - Preston Rural East)
cllr.t.davies@preston.gov.uk

Desai, Salim (LAB - Town Centre)
cllr.s.desai@preston.gov.uk

Dewhurst, Daniel (CON - Lea)
cllr.d.dewhurst@preston.gov.uk

Eaves, Nerys (LAB - Brookfield)
cllr.n.eaves@preston.gov.uk

Edmondson, Rowena (CON - Greyfriars)
cllr.r.edmondson@preston.gov.uk

Faruki, Anis (LAB - St George's)
cllr.a.faruki@preston.gov.uk

Gale, Drew (LAB - Town Centre)
cllr.d.gale@preston.gov.uk

Gildert, Sonia (CON - Sharoe Green)
cllr.s.gildert@preston.gov.uk

Greenhalgh, Stuart (CON - Garrison)
cllr.s.greenhalgh@preston.gov.uk

Hammond, David (CON - Greyfriars)
cllr.d.hammond@preston.gov.uk

Hart, Trevor (CON - Lea)
cllr.t.hart@preston.gov.uk

Hull, James (LAB - St George's)
cllr.j.hull@preston.gov.uk

Iqbal, Javed (LAB - St. Matthew's)
cllr.j.iqbal@preston.gov.uk

Jeffrey, Jason (LD - Ingol)
cllr.j.jeffrey@preston.gov.uk

Kelly, Peter (LAB - Riversway)
cllr.p.kelly@preston.gov.uk

Leach, Charlotte (CON - Garrison)
cllr.c.leach@preston.gov.uk

Leeming, Roy (LAB - St Matthew's)
cllr.r.leeming@preston.gov.uk

Moore, Damien (CON - Greyfriars)
cllr.d.moore@preston.gov.uk

Moss, Peter (LAB - Riversway)
cllr.p.moss@preston.gov.uk

Mullen, Stephen (LD - Cadley)
cllr.s.mullen@preston.gov.uk

Patel, Yakub (LAB - Town Centre)
cllr.y.patel@preston.gov.uk

Pomfret, Nicholas (LAB - Ribbleton)
cllr.n.pomfret@preston.gov.uk

Potter, John (LD - Cadley)
cllr.j.potter@preston.gov.uk

Rawlinson, Martyn (LAB - Fishwick)
cllr.m.rawlinson@preston.gov.uk

Rollo, Brian (LAB - Ribbleton)
cllr.b.rollo@preston.gov.uk

Routeledge, Mark (LAB - Ashton)
cllr.m.routledge@preston.gov.uk

Saksena, Jonathan (LAB - Ribbleton)
cllr.j.saksena@preston.gov.uk

Seddon, Harry (CON - College)
cllr.h.seddon@preston.gov.uk

Smith, Lona (CON - Preston Rural North)
cllr.l.smith@preston.gov.uk

Thomas, Christine (CON - Garrison)
cllr.c.thomas@preston.gov.uk

Thompson, Stephen (CON - Preston Rural North)
cllr.s.thompson@preston.gov.uk

Walker, David (CON - Sharoe Green)
cllr.d.walker@preston.gov.uk

Whittam, Susan (CON - Preston Rural North)
cllr.s.whittam@preston.gov.uk

Yates, Mark (LAB - Larches)
cllr.m.yates@preston.gov.uk

Yates, Rebecca (LAB - Larches)
cllr.r.yates@preston.gov.uk

POLITICAL COMPOSITION
LAB: 32, CON: 19, LD: 5, IND: 1

COMMITTEE CHAIRS
Audit: Mr Damien Moore

Licensing: Mr John Browne

Planning: Mr Brian Rollo

Purbeck D

Purbeck District Council, Westport House, Worgret Road, Wareham BH20 4PP
☎ 01929 556561 🖷 01929 552688 ✉ enquiries@purbeck-dc.gov.uk
💻 www.purbeck.gov.uk

FACTS AND FIGURES
Parliamentary Constituencies: Dorset Mid and Poole North, Dorset South
EU Constituencies: South West
Election Frequency: Elections are by thirds

PRINCIPAL OFFICERS
Chief Executive: Mr Steve Mackenzie, Chief Executive, Westport House, Worgret Road, Wareham BH20 4PP ☎ 01929 557233 🖷 01929 552688 ✉ stevemackenzie@purbeck-dc.gov.uk

Senior Management: Ms Bridget Downton , General Manager - Planning & Community Services, Westport House, Worgret Road, Wareham BH20 4PP ☎ 01929 557268 🖷 01929 552688 ✉ bridgetdownton@purbeck-dc.gov.uk

Senior Management: Mrs Sue Joyce, General Manager - Resources, Westport House, Worgret Road, Wareham BH20 4PP ☎ 01929 557321 🖷 01929 552688 ✉ suejoyce@purbeck-dc.gov.uk

Best Value: Ms Jane Hay, Performance & Information Officer, Westport House, Worgret Road, Wareham BH20 4PP ☎ 01929 557325 🖷 01929 552688 ✉ janehay@purbeck-dc.gov.uk

Building Control: Mr David Kitcatt , Building Control Manager, Westport House, Worgret Road, Wareham BH20 4PP ☎ 01929 557272 ✉ davidkitcatt@purbeck-dc.gov.uk

PR / Communications: Miss Claire Lodge , Communications Officer, Westport House, Worgret Road, Wareham BH20 4PP ☎ 01929 557201 🖷 01929 552688 ✉ clairelodge@purbeck-dc.gov.uk

Community Planning: Ms Bridget Downton , General Manager - Planning & Community Services, Westport House, Worgret Road, Wareham BH20 4PP ☎ 01929 557268 🖷 01929 552688 ✉ bridgetdownton@purbeck-dc.gov.uk

Computer Management: Mr Paul Gammon , IT Manager, Westport House, Worgret Road, Wareham BH20 4PP ☎ 01929 557316 🖷 01929 552688 ✉ paulgammon@purbeck-dc.gov.uk

Contracts: Mrs Jacquie Hall, Property & Procurement Team Leader, Westport House, Worgret Road, Wareham BH20 4PP ☎ 01929 557299 🖷 01929 552688 ✉ jacquiehall@purbeck-dc.gov.uk

Corporate Services: Ms Jane Hay, Performance & Information Officer, Westport House, Worgret Road, Wareham BH20 4PP ☎ 01929 557325 🖷 01929 552688 ✉ janehay@purbeck-dc.gov.uk

Customer Service: Ms Sharon Attwater , Customer Services Team Leader, Westport House, Worgret Road, Wareham BH20 4PP ☎ 01929 557250 ✉ sharonattwater@purbeck-dc.gov.uk

Economic Development: Mr Richard Wilson , Environmental Design Manager, Westport House, Worgret Road, Wareham BH20 4PP ☎ 01929 557320 🖷 01929 552688 ✉ richardwilson@purbeck-dc.gov.uk

E-Government: Mr Paul Gammon , IT Manager, Westport House, Worgret Road, Wareham BH20 4PP ☎ 01929 557316 🖷 01929 552688 ✉ paulgammon@purbeck-dc.gov.uk

Electoral Registration: Ms Kirsty Riglar , Democratic & Electoral Services Manager, Westport House, Worgret Road, Wareham BH20 4PP ☎ 01929 557221 🖷 01929 552668 ✉ kirstyriglar@purbeck-dc.gov.uk

Emergency Planning: Ms Kirsty Riglar , Democratic & Electoral Services Manager, Westport House, Worgret Road, Wareham BH20 4PP ☎ 01929 557221 🖷 01929 552668 ✉ kirstyriglar@purbeck-dc.gov.uk

Energy Management: Ms Laura Brewer , Public Health Manager, Westport House, Worgret Road, Wareham BH20 4PP ☎ 01929 557275 ✉ laurabrewer@purbeck-dc.gov.uk

Environmental / Technical Services: Ms Laura Brewer , Public Health Manager, Westport House, Worgret Road, Wareham BH20 4PP ☎ 01929 557275 ✉ laurabrewer@purbeck-dc.gov.uk

PURBECK

Environmental / Technical Services: Mr Richard Conway , Environment Manager, Westport House, Worgret Road, Wareham BH20 4PP ☎ 01929 557267 🖷 01929 552668 🖰 richardconway@purbeck-dc.gov.uk

Environmental Health: Ms Laura Brewer , Public Health Manager, Westport House, Worgret Road, Wareham BH20 4PP ☎ 01929 557275 🖰 laurabrewer@purbeck-dc.gov.uk

Environmental Health: Mr Richard Conway , Environment Manager, Westport House, Worgret Road, Wareham BH20 4PP ☎ 01929 557267 🖷 01929 552668 🖰 richardconway@purbeck-dc.gov.uk

Estates, Property & Valuation: Mrs Jacquie Hall, Property & Procurement Team Leader, Westport House, Worgret Road, Wareham BH20 4PP ☎ 01929 557299 🖷 01929 552688 🖰 jacquiehall@purbeck-dc.gov.uk

Facilities: Mrs Jacquie Hall, Property & Procurement Team Leader, Westport House, Worgret Road, Wareham BH20 4PP ☎ 01929 557299 🖷 01929 552688 🖰 jacquiehall@purbeck-dc.gov.uk

Finance: Mrs Sue Joyce, General Manager - Resources, Westport House, Worgret Road, Wareham BH20 4PP ☎ 01929 557321 🖷 01929 552688 🖰 suejoyce@purbeck-dc.gov.uk

Grounds Maintenance: Mr Richard Conway , Environment Manager, Westport House, Worgret Road, Wareham BH20 4PP ☎ 01929 557267 🖷 01929 552668 🖰 richardconway@purbeck-dc.gov.uk

Health and Safety: Mr Alfred Agbonlahor, Health & Safety Adviser, Westport House, Worgret Road, Wareham BH20 4PP ☎ 01929 557390 🖷 01929 552668 🖰 alfredagbonlahor@purbeck-dc.gov.uk

Housing: Ms Fiona Brown , Housing Manager, Westport House, Worgret Road, Wareham BH20 4PP ☎ 01929 557310 🖷 01929 552668 🖰 fionabrown@purbeck-dc.gov.uk

Legal: Mr David Fairbairn , Solicitor to the Council / Monitoring Officer, Westport House, Worgret Road, Wareham BH20 4PP ☎ 01929 557223 🖷 01929 552688 🖰 davidfairbairn@purbeck-dc.gov.uk

Licensing: Ms Claire Meakin , Licensing Officer, Westport House, Worgret Road, Wareham BH20 4PP ☎ 01929 557220 🖰 clairemeakin@purbeck-dc.gov.uk

Member Services: Ms Kirsty Riglar , Democratic & Electoral Services Manager, Westport House, Worgret Road, Wareham BH20 4PP ☎ 01929 557221 🖷 01929 552668 🖰 kirstyriglar@purbeck-dc.gov.uk

Partnerships: Mr Steve Mackenzie, Chief Executive, Westport House, Worgret Road, Wareham BH20 4PP ☎ 01929 557233 🖷 01929 552688 🖰 stevemackenzie@purbeck-dc.gov.uk

Personnel / HR: Mrs Christine Dewey, Human Resources Manager, Westport House, Worgret Road, Wareham BH20 4PP ☎ 01929 557204 🖷 01929 552688 🖰 christinedewey@purbeck-dc.gov.uk

Planning: Ms Bridget Downton , General Manager - Planning & Community Services, Westport House, Worgret Road, Wareham BH20 4PP ☎ 01929 557268 🖷 01929 552688 🖰 bridgetdownton@purbeck-dc.gov.uk

Procurement: Mrs Jacquie Hall, Property & Procurement Team Leader, Westport House, Worgret Road, Wareham BH20 4PP ☎ 01929 557299 🖷 01929 552688 🖰 jacquiehall@purbeck-dc.gov.uk

Regeneration: Mr Richard Wilson , Environmental Design Manager, Westport House, Worgret Road, Wareham BH20 4PP ☎ 01929 557320 🖷 01929 552688 🖰 richardwilson@purbeck-dc.gov.uk

Staff Training: Mrs Christine Dewey, Human Resources Manager, Westport House, Worgret Road, Wareham BH20 4PP ☎ 01929 557204 🖷 01929 552688 🖰 christinedewey@purbeck-dc.gov.uk

Sustainable Communities: Ms Anna Lee , General Manager - Planning & Community Services, Westport House, Worgret Road, Wareham BH20 4PP ☎ 01929 557339 🖰 annalee@purbeck-dc.gov.uk

Sustainable Development: Ms Anna Lee , General Manager - Planning & Community Services, Westport House, Worgret Road, Wareham BH20 4PP ☎ 01929 557339 🖰 annalee@purbeck-dc.gov.uk

Tourism: Ms Alison Turnock , Natural Heritage & Tourism Manager, Westport House, Worgret Road, Wareham BH20 4PP ☎ 01929 557337 🖷 01929 552688 🖰 alisonturnock@purbeck-dc.gov.uk

COUNCILLORS

***Chair* Trite**, Bill (CON - Swanage North)
swanbase.w@virgin.net

***Vice-Chair* Pratt**, Mike (CON - Swanage South)
Marmike24@hotmail.com

***Leader of the Council* Suttle**, Gary (CON - Swanage South)
gary.suttle@gmsuttle.co.uk

***Deputy Leader of the Council* Quinn**, Barry (CON - West Purbeck)
Cllr.Quinn@purbeck-dc.gov.uk

Barnes, Malcolm (CON - Winfrith)
Cllr.Barnes@purbeck-dc.gov.uk

Budd, David (LD - Wareham)
cllr.budd@purbeck-dc.gov.uk

Colvey, Martyn (LD - Lytchett Matravers)
martyn@colvey.tv

Critchley, Keith (LD - Wareham)
Cllr.Critchley@purbeck-dc.gov.uk

Dragon, Nigel (IND - Castle)
Cllr.Dragon@purbeck-dc.gov.uk

Drane, Fred (LD - Lytchett Minster and Upton East)
f.h.drane@dorsetcc.gov.uk

Ezzard, Beryl (LD - St. Martin)
cllr.ezzard@purbeck-dc.gov.uk

Goldsack, Simon (LD - Wool)
srbgoldsack@aol.com

Green, Keith (LD - St. Martin)
Cllr.Green@purbeck-dc.gov.uk

Holmes, Graham (LD - Wool)
Graham30kwk@talktalk.net

Johns, Paul (CON - Lytchett Minster and Upton West)
paul.johns12@btinternet.com

Kenward, Bridget (CON - Creech Barrow)
cllr.kenward@purbeck-dc.gov.uk

Lovell, Mike (CON - Langton)
mwjlovell@gmail.com

Marsh, Gloria (CON - Swanage North)
Cllr.Marsh@purbeck-dc.gov.uk

Osmond, Eric (LD - Wareham)
cllrosmond@gmail.com

Patrick, Ali (CON - Swanage South)
ali@patrickswanage.co.uk

Pipe, Bill (CON - Lytchett Minster and Upton West)
magpiebillpipe@freeuk.com

Taylor, John (LD - Lytchett Matravers)
Cllr.Taylor@purbeck-dc.gov.uk

Tilling, Carol (LD - Lytchett Minster and Upton East)
cllrcaroltilling@gmail.com

Wharf, Peter (CON - Bere Regis)
peter.wharf@btopenworld.com

POLITICAL COMPOSITION

CON: 12, LD: 11, IND: 1

Reading U

Reading Borough Council, Civic Offices, Bridge Street, Reading RG1 2LU
☎ 0118 937 3737 🖷 0118 958 9770
forename.surname@reading.gov.uk 💻 www.reading.gov.uk

FACTS AND FIGURES

Parliamentary Constituencies: Reading East, Reading West
EU Constituencies: South East
Election Frequency: Elections are by thirds

PRINCIPAL OFFICERS

Chief Executive: Mr Ian Wardle , Managing Director, Civic Offices, Bridge Street, Reading RG1 2LU ian.wardle@reading.gov.uk

Senior Management: Ms Alison Bell, Director of Environment & Neighbourhood Services, Civic Offices, Bridge Street, Reading RG1 2LU ☎ 0118 937 2457 alison.bell@reading.gov.uk

Senior Management: Mrs Zoe Hanim, Head of Customer Services, Civic Offices, Bridge Street, Reading RG1 2LU ☎ 0118 937 2173 🖷 0118 937 2155 zoe.hanim@reading.gov.uk

Access Officer / Social Services (Disability): Mrs Zoe Hanim, Head of Customer Services, Civic Offices, Bridge Street, Reading RG1 2LU ☎ 0118 937 2173 🖷 0118 937 2155 zoe.hanim@reading.gov.uk

Best Value: Mrs Zoe Hanim, Head of Customer Services, Civic Offices, Bridge Street, Reading RG1 2LU ☎ 0118 937 2173 🖷 0118 937 2155 zoe.hanim@reading.gov.uk

Civil Registration: Mr Matthew Golledge , Trading Standards Manager, Civic Offices, Bridge Street, Reading RG1 2LU ☎ 0118 937 2497 🖷 0118 937 2557 matthew.golledge@reading.gov.uk

Community Planning: Mr Grant Thornton, Head of Economic & Cultural Development, Civic Offices, Bridge Street, Reading RG1 2LU ☎ 0118 937 2416 🖷 0118 937 2155 grant.thornton@reading.gov.uk

Computer Management: Mr John Barnfield , ICT Manager, Civic Offices, Bridge Street, Reading RG1 2LU ☎ 0118 937 7286 john.barnfield@reading.gov.uk

Customer Service: Mrs Zoe Hanim, Head of Customer Services, Civic Offices, Bridge Street, Reading RG1 2LU ☎ 0118 937 2173 🖷 0118 937 2155 zoe.hanim@reading.gov.uk

Education: Mr Kevin McDaniel , Head of Education & Commissioning Services, Civic Offices, Bridge Street, Reading RG1 2LU ☎ 0118 937 4240 kevin.mcdaniel@reading.gov.uk

E-Government: Mrs Zoe Hanim, Head of Customer Services, Civic Offices, Bridge Street, Reading RG1 2LU ☎ 0118 937 2173 🖷 0118 937 2155 zoe.hanim@reading.gov.uk

Electoral Registration: Mrs Julie Kempen, Electoral Services Manager, Civic Offices, Bridge Street, Reading RG1 2LU ☎ 0118 937 2731 🖷 0118 937 2591 julie.kempen@reading.gov.uk

Emergency Planning: Mr Brett Dyson, Emergency Planning & Risk Officer, Civic Offices, Bridge Street, Reading RG1 2LU ☎ 0118 937 2235 🖷 0118 397 2559 brett.dyson@reading.gov.uk

Energy Management: Mr Ben Burfoot , Sustainability Manager, Civic Offices, Bridge Street, Reading RG1 2LU ☎ 0118 937 2232 🖷 0118 937 2155 ben.burfoot@reading.ac.uk

Estates, Property & Valuation: Mr Bruce Tindall, Head of Development, Civic Offices, Bridge Street, Reading RG1 2LU ☎ 0118 937 2594 🖷 0118 937 2767 bruce.tindall@reading.gov.uk

European Liaison: Mr Grant Thornton, Head of Economic & Cultural Development, Civic Offices, Bridge Street, Reading RG1 2LU ☎ 0118 937 2416 🖷 0118 937 2155 grant.thornton@reading.gov.uk

Facilities: Ms Jan Sagoo, Head of Civic Services / New Civic Project, Civic Offices, Bridge Street, Reading RG1 2LU ☎ 0118 937 2304 🖷 0118 937 2591 jan.sagoo@reading.gov.uk

Finance: Mr Alan Cross, Head of Finance, Civic Offices, Bridge Street, Reading RG1 2LU ☎ 0118 937 2058 🖷 0118 937 2278 alan.cross@reading.gov.uk

Finance: Mr Dave Fisher, Chief Accountant, Civic Offices, Bridge Street, Reading RG1 2LU ☎ 0118 937 2747 🖷 0118 937 2278 dave.fisher@reading.gov.uk

READING

Fleet Management: Ms Michelle Crick , Neighbourhood Services Support Manager, 19 Bennet Road, Reading RG2 0QX ☎ 0118 937 3993 ✉ peter.butler@reading.gov.uk

Health and Safety: Mr Robin Pringle, Corporate Safety & Workforce Development, Civic Offices, Bridge Street, Reading RG1 2LU ☎ 0118 937 2519 ✉ robin.pringle@reading.gov.uk

Highways: Mr Vaughan Norris, Highways Manager, Civic Offices, Bridge Street, Reading RG1 2LU ☎ 0118 937 2669 🖷 0119 937 2609 ✉ vaughan.norris@reading.gov.uk

Home Energy Conservation: Mr Paul Taylor, Housing Stock Regeneration Manager, 6 Darwin Close, Reading RG2 0RB ☎ 0118 939 0224 🖷 0118 975 3334 ✉ paul.taylor@reading.gov.uk

Housing: Mr Phil Eldridge , Property Services Manager, Civic Offices, Bridge Street, Reading RG1 2LU ☎ 0118 937 2266 🖷 0118 937 2052 ✉ phil.eldridge@reading.gov.uk

Housing Maintenance: Mr Phil Eldridge , Property Services Manager, Civic Offices, Bridge Street, Reading RG1 2LU ☎ 0118 937 2266 🖷 0118 937 2052 ✉ phil.eldridge@reading.gov.uk

Local Area Agreement: Mrs Zoe Hanim, Head of Customer Services, Civic Offices, Bridge Street, Reading RG1 2LU ☎ 0118 937 2173 🖷 0118 937 2155 ✉ zoe.hanim@reading.gov.uk

Legal: Mr Christopher Brooks, Head of Legal & Democratic Services, Civic Offices, Bridge Street, Reading RG1 2LU ☎ 0118 937 2602 🖷 0118 937 2767 ✉ chris.brooks@reading.gov.uk

Leisure and Cultural Services: Mr Rhodri Thomas , Museum & Town Hall General Manager, Reading Central Library, Abbey Square, Reading RG1 3BQ ☎ 0118 937 3943 🖷 0118 956 6719 ✉ rhodri.thomas@reading.gov.uk

Licensing: Ms Clare Bradley, Environmental Health Manager (Licensing & Environmental Protection), Civic Offices, Bridge Street, Reading RG1 2LU ☎ 0118 937 2322 🖷 0118 937 2557 ✉ clare.bradley@reading.gov.uk

Lighting: Mr Vaughan Norris, Highways Manager, Civic Offices, Bridge Street, Reading RG1 2LU ☎ 0118 937 2669 🖷 0119 937 2609 ✉ vaughan.norris@reading.gov.uk

Lottery Funding, Charity and Voluntary: Ms Irene Cameron, Team Leader - Funding Services, Civic Offices, Bridge Street, Reading RG1 2LU ☎ 0118 937 2387 🖷 0118 939 0155 ✉ irene.cameron@reading.gov.uk

Member Services: Ms Jan Sagoo, Head of Civic Services / New Civic Project, Civic Offices, Bridge Street, Reading RG1 2LU ☎ 0118 937 2304 🖷 0118 937 2591 ✉ jan.sagoo@reading.gov.uk

Parking: Mr Mark Smith , Head of Transportation & Streetcare, Civic Offices, Bridge Street, Reading RG1 2LU ☎ 0118 937 2813 ✉ mark.smith@reading.gov.uk

Partnerships: Ms Sarah Gee , Head of Housing, Neighbourhoods & Communities, Civic Offices, Bridge Street, Reading RG1 2LU ☎ 0118 937 2973 🖷 0118 937 2786 ✉ sarah.gee@reading.gov.uk

Planning: Ms Alison Bell, Director of Environment & Neighbourhood Services, Civic Offices, Bridge Street, Reading RG1 2LU ☎ 0118 937 2457 ✉ alison.bell@reading.gov.uk

Procurement: Mr John Littlefair , Procurement & Partnership Manager, Civic Offices, Bridge Street, Reading RG1 2LU ☎ 0118 937 2748 🖷 0118 958 0278 ✉ andy.allen@reading.gov.uk

Recycling & Waste Minimisation: Mr Oliver Burt, Project Manager, 2-4 Darwin Close, Reading RG2 0RB ☎ 0118 937 3990 ✉ oliver.burt@reading.gov.uk

Regeneration: Mr Chris Bloomfield , Neighbourhood Regeneration Manager, Civic Offices, Bridge Street, Reading RG1 2LU ☎ 0118 937 2176 🖷 0118 937 2155 ✉ chris.bloomfield@reading.gov.uk

Road Safety: Mr Simon Beasley, Network & Parking Services Manager, Civic Offices, Bridge Street, Reading RG1 2LU ☎ 0118 937 2228 🖷 0118 937 2633 ✉ simon.beasley@reading.gov.uk

Social Services: Ms Sue Gosling , CRT Business Support Team Leader, Civic Offices, Bridge Street, Reading RG1 2LU ☎ 0118 937 3676 🖷 0118 955 3744 ✉ sue.gosling@reading.gov.uk

Public Health: Ms Asmat Nisa , Consultant in Public Health, Civic Offices, Bridge Street, Reading RG1 2LU ☎ 0118 937 2115 ✉ asmat.nisa@reading.gov.uk

Staff Training: Mr Russell Gabini , Organisational & Workforce Development Manager, Civic Offices, Bridge Street, Reading RG1 2LU ☎ 0118 937 2115 ✉ russell.gabini@reading.gov.uk

Street Scene: Mr Chris Camfield, Street Environment Manager, 19 Bennetts Road, Reading RG2 0QX ☎ 0118 937 2040 ✉ chris.camfield@reading.gov.uk

Sustainable Communities: Mr Ben Burfoot , Sustainability Manager, Civic Offices, Bridge Street, Reading RG1 2LU ☎ 0118 937 2232 🖷 0118 937 2155 ✉ ben.burfoot@reading.ac.uk

Sustainable Development: Mr Ben Burfoot , Sustainability Manager, Civic Offices, Bridge Street, Reading RG1 2LU ☎ 0118 937 2232 🖷 0118 937 2155 ✉ ben.burfoot@reading.ac.uk

Tourism: Ms Sue Brackley, Economic Development Manager, Reading Central Library, Abbey Square, Reading RG1 3BQ ☎ 0118 900 1624 🖷 0118 939 9885 ✉ sue.brackley@reading.gov.uk

Traffic Management: Mr Simon Beasley, Network & Parking Services Manager, Civic Offices, Bridge Street, Reading RG1 2LU ☎ 0118 937 2228 🖷 0118 937 2633 ✉ simon.beasley@reading.gov.uk

Waste Collection and Disposal: Mr Oliver Burt, Project Manager, 2-4 Darwin Close, Reading RG2 0RB ☎ 0118 937 3990 ✉ oliver.burt@reading.gov.uk

Waste Collection and Disposal: Mr Chris Green, Waste Operations Manager, 2-4 Darwin Close, Reading RG2 0RB ☎ 0118 937 3950 ✉ chris.green@reading.gov.uk

COUNCILLORS

***Mayor* Hacker**, Sarah (LAB - Battle)
Sarah-Jane.Hacker@reading.gov.uk

***Deputy Mayor* Ayub**, Mohammed (LAB - Abbey)
Mohammed.Ayub@reading.gov.uk

***Leader of the Council* Lovelock**, Jo (LAB - Norcot)
Jo.Lovelock@reading.gov.uk

***Deputy Leader of the Council* Page**, Tony (LAB - Abbey)
Tony.Page@reading.gov;uk

***Group Leader* Duveen**, Ricky (LD - Tilehurst)
Ricky.Duveen@reading.gov.uk

***Group Leader* Skeats**, Jeanette (CON - Thames)
Jeanette.Skeats@reading.gov.uk

***Group Leader* White**, Rob (GRN - Park)
Rob.White@reading.gov.uk

Absolom, David (LAB - Redlands)
David.Absolom@reading.gov.uk

Absolom, Debs (LAB - Norcot)
Debs.Absolom@reading.gov.uk

Ballsdon, Isobel (CON - Mapledurham)
Isobel.Ballsden@reading.gov.uk

Chrisp, Rachael (LAB - Caversham)
Rachael.Crisp@reading.gov.uk

Davies, Richard (LAB - Caversham)
Richard.Davies@reading.gov.uk

Dennis, Glenn (LAB - Kentwood)
Glann.Dennis@reading.gov.uk

Eden, Rachel (LAB - Whitley)
Reachel.Eden@reading.gov.uk

Edwards, Kelly (LAB - Whitley)
Kelly.Edwards@reading.gov.uk

Edwards, Deborah (LAB - Southcote)
Deborah.Edwards@reading.gov.uk

Ennis, John (LAB - Southcote)
John.Ennis@reading.gov.uk

Gavin, Jan (LAB - Redlands)
Jan.Gavin@reading.gov.uk

Gittings, Paul (LAB - Minster)
Paul.Gittings@reading.gov.uk

Grashoff, Clare (CON - Peppard)
Clare.Grashoff@reading.gov.uk

Hopper, Ed (CON - Thames)
Ed.Hopper@reading.gov.uk

Hoskin, Graeme (LAB - Norcot)
Graeme.Hoskin@reading.gov.uk

James, Sophia (LAB - Katesgrove)
Sophia.James@reading.gov.uk

Jones, Tony (LAB - Redlands)
Tony.Jones@reading.gov.uk

Khan, Gul (LAB - Battle)
Gul.Khan@reading.gov.uk

Lawrence, Matt (LAB - Southcote)
Matt.Lawrence@reading.gov.uk

Livingston, Marian (LAB - Minster)
Marian.Livingston@reading.gov.uk

Maskell, Chris (LAB - Battle)
Chris.Maskell@reading.gov.uk

McDonald, Claire (CON - Caversham)
Claire.McDonald@reading.gov.uk

McElligott, Eileen (LAB - Church)
Eileen.McElligott@reading.gov.uk

O'Connell, Meri (LD - Tilehurst)
Meri.O'Connell@reading.vo.uk

Orton, Mike (LAB - Whitley)
Mike.Orton@reading.gov.uk

Pearce, Ashley (LAB - Church)
Ashley.Pearce@reaind.gov.uk

Robinson, Simon (CON - Peppard)
Simon.Robinson@reading.gov.uk

Rodda, Matt (LAB - Katesgrove)
Matt.Rodda@reading.gov.uk

Singh, Daya Pal (LAB - Kentwood)
Daya.Pal.Singh@reading.gov.uk

Stanford-Beale, Jane (CON - Peppard)
Jane.Stanford-Beale@reading.gov.uk

Steele, Tom (CON - Kentwood)
Tom.Steele@reading.gov.uk

Stevens, David (CON - Thames)
David.Stevens@reading.gov.uk

Terry, Liz (LAB - Minster)
Liz.Terry@reading.gov.uk

Tickner, Bet (LAB - Abbey)
Bet.Tickner@reading.gov.uk

Vickers, Sandra (CON - Tilehurst)
Sandra.Vickers@reading.gov.uk

Whitham, Jamie (GRN - Park)
jamie.whitham@reading.gov.uk

Williams, Josh (GRN - Park)
Josh.Williams@reading.gov.uk

Williams, Rose (LAB - Katesgrove)
Rose.Williams@reading.gov.uk

Woodward, Paul (LAB - Church)
Paul.Woodward@reading.gov.uk

POLITICAL COMPOSITION

LAB: 31, CON: 10, GRN: 3, LD: 2

COMMITTEE CHAIRS

Planning: Mr David Absolom

Redbridge L

Redbridge London Borough Council, Town Hall, High Road, Ilford IG1 1DD
☎ 020 8554 5000 customer.cc@redbridge.gov.uk
www.redbridge.gov.uk

FACTS AND FIGURES

Parliamentary Constituencies: Chingford and Woodford, Ilford

REDBRIDGE

North, Ilford South, Leyton and Wanstead
EU Constituencies: London
Election Frequency: Elections are of whole council

PRINCIPAL OFFICERS

Chief Executive: Mr Roger Hampson , Chief Executive, Town Hall, High Road, Ilford IG1 1DD ☎ 020 8708 2100 ✉ roger.hampson@redbridge.gov.uk

Senior Management: Mr Simon Barry , Director of Environment & Community Services, Town Hall, High Road, Ilford IG1 1DD ☎ 020 8708 3567 ✉ simon.barry@redbridge.gov.uk

Senior Management: Mr Simon Goodwin , Borough Solicitor & Secretary, Town Hall, High Road, Ilford IG1 1DD ☎ 020 8708 2201 ✉ simon.goodwin@redbridge.gov.uk

Senior Management: Ms Vicky Hobart , Director - Public Health, Lynton House, 255 - 259 High Road, Ilford IG1 1NY ☎ 020 8708 5731 ✉ vicky.hobart@redbridge.gov.uk

Senior Management: Mr John Powell , Director of Adult Social Services, Health & Wellbeing, Lynton House, 255 - 259 High Road, Ilford IG1 1NY ☎ 020 8708 5535 ✉ john.powell@redbridge.gov.uk

Senior Management: Ms Pat Reynolds, Director of Children's Services, Lynton House, 255-259 High Road, Ilford IG1 1NY ☎ 020 8708 3100 ✉ pat.reynolds@redbridge.gov.uk

Senior Management: Mr Richard Szadziewski , Interim Director of Finance & Resources, Lynton House, 255 - 259 High Road, Ilford IG1 1NY ☎ 020 8708 3588 ✉ richard.szadziewski@redbridge.gov.uk

Access Officer / Social Services (Disability): Ms Leila Hussain , Interim Principal Officer - Access, Wellbeing & Support, Lynton House, 255 - 259 High Road, Ilford IG1 1NY ☎ 020 8708 5169 ✉ leila.hussain@redbridge.gov.uk

Architect, Building / Property Services: Mr Fred Steel , Head of Building Services, Lynton House, 255-259 High Road, Ilford IG1 1NY ☎ 020 8708 3514 ✉ fred.steel@redbridge.gov.uk

Building Control: Mr Amrik Notta, Head of Building Control, Town Hall, High Road, Ilford IG1 1DD ☎ 020 8708 2521 ✉ amrik.notta@redbridge.gov.uk

Catering Services: Ms Therese Hamshaw , Catering Manager, PO Box 2, Town Hall, High Road, Ilford IG1 1DD ☎ 020 8708 2003 ✉ therese.hamshaw@redbridge.gov.uk

Children / Youth Services: Ms Pat Reynolds, Director of Children's Services, Lynton House, 255 - 299 High Road, Ilford IG1 1NY ☎ 020 8708 3100 ✉ pat.reynolds@redbridge.gov.uk

Civil Registration: Ms Christine Casson , Deputy Superintendent Registration Services, Queen Victoria House, 794 Cranbrook Road, Barkingside, Ilford IG6 1JS ☎ 020 8708 7123 ✉ christine.casson@redbridge.gov.uk

PR / Communications: Ms Kirsty Tobin , Head of Marketing & Communications, Town Hall, High Road, Ilford IG1 1DD ☎ 020 8708 3766 ✉ kirsty.tobin@redbridge.gov.uk

Community Safety: Ms Kathy Nixon, Chief Community Safety & Enforcement Officer / Transformation Programme Lead, Town Hall, High Road, Ilford IG1 1DD ☎ 020 8708 5996 ✉ kathy.nixon@redbridge.gov.uk

Computer Management: Mr Lee Edwards, Chief ICT Officer, 17/23 Clements Road, Ilford IG1 1AG ☎ 020 8708 4100 ✉ lee.edwards@redbridge.gov.uk

Consumer Protection and Trading Standards: Mr Alan Drake, Head of Community Protection & Enforcement, 8 Perth Terrace, Perth Road, Ilford IG2 6AT ☎ 020 8708 5490 ✉ alan.drake@redbridge.gov.uk

Contracts: Mr Bill Leharne Interim Head of Strategic Procurement, Lynton House, 255 - 259 High Road, Ilford IG1 1NY ☎ 020 8708 3711 ✉ bill.leharne@redbridge.gov.uk

Corporate Services: Mr Kevin Wackett , Head of Parks & Open Spaces, 210 Wash Lodge, Cranbrook Road, Ilford IG1 4TG ☎ 020 8708 3223 ✉ kevin.wackett@visionrcl.org.uk

Customer Service: Mr Peter Ratnarajah , Chief Payments, Benefits & Customer Services Officer, 22 - 26 Clements Road, Ilford IG1 1BD ☎ 020 8708 4519 ✉ peter.ratnarajah@redbridge.gov.uk

Direct Labour: Mr Dave Cuthell , Chief Environmental Services Officer, Ley Street Depot, Ley Street, Ilford IG2 7QX ☎ 020 8708 5019 ✉ david.cuthell@redbridge.gov.uk

Economic Development: Mr Mark Lucas , Head of Inward Investment & Enterprise, Town Hall, High Road, Ilford IG1 1DD ☎ 020 8708 2143 ✉ mark.lucas@redbridge.gov.uk

Education: Mr Martin Baker , Interim Chief Officer - Learning & School Improvement, Lynton House, 255-259 High Road, Ilford IG1 1NY ☎ 020 8708 3056 ✉ martin.baker@redbridge.gov.uk

Education: Ms Ronke Martins-Taylor , Chief Services to Young People Officer, Lynton House, 255-259 High Road, Ilford IG1 1NY ☎ 020 8708 3378 ✉ ronke.martins-taylor@redbridge.gov.uk

Education: Mr John O'Keefe , Chief Education Planning & Resources Officer, Lynton House, 255-259 High Road, Ilford IG1 1NY ☎ 020 8708 3117 ✉ john.okeefe@redbridge.gov.uk

Education: Ms Pat Reynolds, Director of Children's Services, Lynton House, 255-259 High Road, Ilford IG1 1NY ☎ 020 8708 3100 ✉ pat.reynolds@redbridge.gov.uk

E-Government: Mr Lee Edwards , Chief ICT Officer, 17-23 Clements Road, Ilford IG1 1AG ☎ 020 8708 4100 ✉ lee.edwards@redbridge.gov.uk

Electoral Registration: Mr George Sullivan, Electoral Services Manager, Queen Victoria House, 794 Cranbrook Road, Barkingside, Ilford IG6 1JS ☎ 020 8708 7170 ✉ george.sullivan@redbridge.gov.uk

Emergency Planning: Mr Jeremy Reynolds , Emergency Planning & Business Continuity Manager, Redbridge Control Centre, Ley Street Depot, Ley Street, Ilford IG2 7QX ☎ 020 8708 5520 ✉ jeremy.reynolds@redbridge.gov.uk

Energy Management: Mr Garry Proctor , Mechanical Services Management, Lynton House, 255 - 259 High Road, Ilford IG1 1NY ☎ 020 8708 3324 ✉ garry.proctor@redbridge.gov.uk

Environmental Health: Mr Themis Skouros , Environmental Protection Manager, Lynton House, 255 - 258 High Road, Ilford IG1 1NY ☎ 020 8708 5687 ✉ themis.skouros@redbridge.gov.uk

Estates, Property & Valuation: Mr David Pethen , Head of Estates & Asset Management, Lynton House, 255-259 High Road, Ilford IG1 1NY ☎ 020 8708 3215 ✉ david.pethen@redbridge.gov.uk

Facilities: Mr Dyfrig Walters , Head of Facilities Management, Town Hall, High Road, Ilford IG1 1DD ☎ 020 8708 3960 ✉ dyfrig.walters@redbridge.gov.uk

Finance: Mr Mark Green , Chief Financial Services Officer, Lynton House, 255-259 High Road, Ilford IG1 1NY ☎ 020 8708 3013 ✉ mark.green@redbridge.gov.uk

Finance: Mr Richard Szadziewski , Interim Director of Finance & Resources, Lynton House, 255 - 259 High Road, Ilford IG1 1NY ☎ 020 8708 3588 ✉ richard.szadziewski@redbridge.gov.uk

Pensions: Mr Doug Falconer , Pensions Manager, HR - Pensions, Lynton House, 255-259 High Road, Ilford IG1 1NY ☎ 020 8708 3549 ✉ doug.falconer@redbridge.gov.uk

Pensions: Mrs Hilary Taylor , Principal Finance Officer, Lynton House, 255-259 High Road, Ilford IG1 1NY ☎ 020 8708 3021 ✉ hilary.taylor@redbridge.gov.uk

Fleet Management: Mr Eddie Cross, Head of Transport Engineering Service, Ley Street Depot, Ley Street, Ilford IG2 7QX ☎ 020 8708 5212 ✉ eddie.cross@redbridge.gov.uk

Health and Safety: Mr Ian Wringe , Health & Safety Manager, Lynton House, 255 - 259 High Road, Ilford IG1 1NY ☎ 020 8708 3152 ✉ ian.wringe@redbridge.gov.uk

Highways: Mr Cliff Woolnoth , Head of Engineering, Lynton House, 255-259 High Road, Ilford IG1 1NY ☎ 020 8708 3570 ✉ cliff.woolnoth@redbridge.gov.uk

Housing: Ms Elaine Gosling , Head of Housing Management, West Housing Office, 152 Broadmead Road, Woodford Green, Ilford IG8 0AG ☎ 020 8708 7657 ✉ elaine.gosling@redbridge.gov.uk

Housing Maintenance: Ms Ola Akinfe , Interim Head of Asset Management (Housing), West Housing Office, 152 Broadmead Road, Woodford Green, Ilford IG8 0AG ☎ 020 8708 8305 ✉ ola.akinfe@redbridge.gov.uk

Housing Maintenance: Mr Fred Steel , Head of Building Services, Lynton House, 255-259 High Road, Ilford IG1 1NY ☎ 020 8708 3514 ✉ fred.steel@redbridge.gov.uk

Local Area Agreement: Mr John Turkson , Principal Officer - Community Partnerships, Ley Street House, 497 - 499 Ley Street, Ilford IG2 7QX ☎ 020 8708 2381 ✉ john.turkson@redbridge.gov.uk

Legal: Mr Simon Goodwin , Borough Solicitor & Secretary, Town Hall, High Road, Ilford IG1 1DD ☎ 020 8708 2201 ✉ simon.goodwin@redbridge.gov.uk

Leisure and Cultural Services: Mr Iain Varah, Chief Executive, Central Library, Clements Road, Ilford IG1 1EA ☎ 020 8708 2012 ✉ iain.varah@visionrcl.org.uk

Licensing: Mr Alan Drake, Head of Community Protection & Enforcement, 8 Perth Terrace, Perth Road, Ilford IG2 6AT ☎ 020 8708 5490 ✉ alan.drake@redbridge.gov.uk

Lifelong Learning: Mr Iain Varah, Chief Executive, Central Library, Clements Road, Ilford IG1 1EA ☎ 020 8708 2012 ✉ iain.varah@visionrcl.org.uk

Lighting: Mr Cliff Woolnoth , Head of Engineering, Lynton House, 255-259 High Road, Ilford IG1 1NY ☎ 020 8708 3570 ✉ cliff.woolnoth@redbridge.gov.uk

Member Services: Mr Tony Prescod , Head of Constitutional Services, Town Hall, High Road, Ilford IG1 1DD ☎ 020 8708 2204 ✉ tony.prescod@redbridge.gov.uk

Parking: Mr Cameron Findlay , Parking Manager, Town Hall, High Road, Ilford IG1 1DD ☎ 020 8708 3027 ✉ cameron.findlay@redbridge.gov.uk

Partnerships: Mr John Turkson , Community Partnerships Manager, Ley Street House, 497 - 499 Ley Street, Ilford IG2 7QX ☎ 020 8708 2381 ✉ john.turkson@redbridge.gov.uk

Personnel / HR: Ms Marj Keddy, Chief Human Resources Officer, Lynton House, 255-259 High Road, Ilford IG1 1NY ☎ 020 8708 3974 ✉ marj.keddy@redbridge.gov.uk

Personnel / HR: Mr Richard Szadziewski , Interim Director of Finance & Resources, Lynton House, 255 - 259 High Road, Ilford IG1 1NY ☎ 020 8708 3588 ✉ richard.szadziewski@redbridge.gov.uk

Planning: Mr Mark Lucas , Head of Inward Investment & Enterprise, Town Hall, High Road, Ilford IG1 1DD ☎ 020 8708 2143 ✉ mark.lucas@redbridge.gov.uk

Procurement: Mr Bill Leharne , Interim Head of Strategic Procurement, Lynton House, 255 - 259 High Road, Ilford IG1 1NY ☎ 020 8708 3711 ✉ bill.leharne@redbridge.gov.uk

Public Libraries: Mr Gareth Morley , Head of Culture & Libraries, Lynton House, 255-259 High Road, Ilford IG1 1NY ☎ 020 8708 3426 ✉ gareth.morley@visionrcl.org.uk

Recycling & Waste Minimisation: Mr Tom Lawrence , Recycling Manager, Ley Street Depot, Ley Street, Ilford IG2 7QX ☎ 020 8708 5517 ✉ tom.lawrence@redbridge.gov.uk

REDBRIDGE

Regeneration: Mr Mark Lucas , Head of Inward Investment & Enterprise, Town Hall, High Road, Ilford IG1 1DD ☎ 020 8708 2143 🖱 mark.lucas@redbridge.gov.uk

Regeneration: Ms Alison Young , Chief Planning & Regeneration Officer, Town Hall, High Road, Ilford IG1 1DD ☎ 020 8708 2067 🖱 alison.young@redbridge.gov.uk

Road Safety: Ms Jane Arthur, Group Manager of Road Safety, Lynton House, 255-259 High Road, Ilford IG1 1NY ☎ 020 8708 3971 🖱 jane.arthur@redbridge.gov.uk

Social Services (Adult): Mr John Powell , Director of Adult Social Services, Health & Wellbeing, Ley Street House, 497-499 Ley Street, Ilford IG2 7QX ☎ 020 8708 5535 🖱 john.powell@redbridge.gov.uk

Social Services (Children): Mrs Caroline Cutts , Chief Children & Families Officer, Lynton House, 255 - 259 High Road, Ilford IG1 1NY ☎ 020 8708 5304 🖱 caroline.cutts@redbridge.gov.uk

Social Services (Children): Ms Pat Reynolds, Director of Children's Services, Lynton House, 255-259 High Road, Ilford IG1 1NY ☎ 020 8708 3100 🖱 pat.reynolds@redbridge.gov.uk

Public Health: Ms Vicky Hobart , Director - Public Health, Town Hall, Forest Road, London E17 4JF ☎ 020 8708 5731 🖱 vicky.hobart@redbridge.gov.uk

Staff Training: Ms Ann Butler , Workforce Development Manager, Lynton House, 255-259 High Road, Ilford IG1 1NY ☎ 020 8708 3446 🖱 ann.butler@redbridge.gov.uk

Street Scene: Mr Russell Ward , Head of Environmental Services, Ley Street Depot, Ley Street, Ilford IG2 7QX ☎ 020 8708 5511 🖱 russell.ward@redbridge.gov.uk

Town Centre: Ms Gillian Balfe , Town Centre & BID Manager, Room 21, Town Hall, High Road, Ilford IG1 1DD ☎ 020 8708 2563 🖱 gillian.balfe@redbridge.gov.uk

Town Centre: Ms Rubie Charalambous , Ilford Town Centre Manager, The Management Suite, The Exchange Mall, High Road, Ilford IG1 1RS ☎ 020 8553 3000 🖱 rubie.charalambous@theexchangeilford.gov.uk

Traffic Management: Mr Syed Hussain , Traffic Group Manager, Lynton House, 255-259 High Road, Ilford IG1 1NY ☎ 020 8708 3651 🖱 syed.hussain@redbridge.gov.uk

Transport: Mr Cliff Woolnoth , Head of Engineering, Lynton House, 255-259 High Road, Ilford IG1 1NY ☎ 020 8708 3570 🖱 cliff.woolnoth@redbridge.gov.uk

Transport Planner: Mr Cliff Woolnoth , Head of Engineering, Lynton House, 255-259 High Road, Ilford IG1 1NY ☎ 020 8708 3570 🖱 cliff.woolnoth@redbridge.gov.uk

Waste Collection and Disposal: Mr Dave Cuthell , Chief Environmental Services Officer, Ley Street Depot, Ley Street, Ilford IG2 7QX ☎ 020 8708 5019 🖱 david.cuthell@redbridge.gov.uk

Waste Management: Mr Dave Cuthell , Chief Environmental Services Officer, Ley Street Depot, Ley Street, Ilford IG2 7QX ☎ 020 8708 5019 🖱 david.cuthell@redbridge.gov.uk

COUNCILLORS

***Mayor* White**, Barbara (LAB - Goodmayes)
barbara.white@redbridge.gov.uk

***Leader of the Council* Athwal**, Jas (LAB - Mayfield)
jas.athwal@redbridge.gov.uk

***Deputy Leader of the Council* Norman**, Elaine (LAB - Newbury)
elaine.norman@redbridge.gov.uk

***Group Leader* Bond**, Ian (LD - Roding)
ian.bond@redbridge.gov.uk

***Group Leader* Canal**, Paul (CON - Bridge)
paul.canal@redbridge.gov.uk

Ahmad, Shakil (LAB - Loxford)
shakil.ahmad@redbridge.gov.uk

Ahmed, Mohammed (LAB - Loxford)
mohammed.ahmed@redbridge.gov.uk

Ahmed, Mushtaq (LAB - Cranbrook)
mushtaq.ahmed@redbridge.gov.uk

Bain, Sheila (LAB - Wanstead)
sheila.bain@redbridge.gov.uk

Bellwood, Stuart (LAB - Seven Kings)
stuart.bellwood@redbridge.gov.uk

Best, Emma (CON - Church End)
emma.best@redbridge.gov.uk

Bhamra, Gurdial (LAB - Clayhall)
Gurdial.bhamra@redbridge.gov.uk

Blaber, Sarah (CON - Roding)
sarah.blaber@redbridge.gov.uk

Bola, Varinder (LAB - Cranbrook)
varinder.singhbola@redbridge.gov.uk

Bromiley, David (CON - Fullwell)
david.bromiley@redbridge.gov.uk

Chaudhary, Mahboob (CON - Cranbrook)
mahboob.chaudhary@redbridge.gov.uk

Choudhary, Aziz (LAB - Chadwell)
aziz.choudhary@redbridge.gov.uk

Chowdhury, Khayer (LAB - Valentines)
khayer.chowdhury@redbridge.gov.uk

Cleaver, Hugh (LD - Church End)
Hugh.cleaver@redbridge.gov.uk

Cole, Robert (CON - Clayhall)
robert.cole@redbridge.gov.uk

Coomb, Helen (LAB - Clementswood)
helen.coomb@redbridge.gov.uk

Cronin, Colin (CON - Snaresbrook)
colin.cronin@redbridge.gov.uk

Cummins, Christopher (CON - Snaresbrook)
christopher.cummins@redbridge.gov.uk

Deakins, Gwyneth (LD - Roding)
gwyneth.deakins@redbridge.gov.uk

Dunn, Michelle (CON - Wanstead)
michelle.dunn@redbridge.gov.uk

Emmett, Roy (LAB - Hainault)
roy.emmett@redbridge.gov.uk

Fairley-Churchill, John (CON - Bridge)
john.fairley-churchill@redbridge.gov.uk

Flint, Kay (LAB - Mayfield)
kay.flint@redbridge.gov.uk

Haran, Jeevah (CON - Fullwell)
jeevah.haran@redbridge.gov.uk

Hatfull, Ross (LAB - Valentines)
ross.hatfull@redbridge.gov.uk

Hayes, Nicholas (CON - Fullwell)
nicholas.hayes@redbridge.gov.uk

Hehir, Joe (LAB - Hainault)
joe.hehir@redbridge.gov.uk

Howard, John (LAB - Aldborough)
john.howard@redbridge.gov.uk

Huggett, Linda (CON - Monkhams)
linda.huggett@redbridge.gov.uk

Hussain, Farah (LAB - Valentines)
farah.hussain@redbridge.gov.uk

Hussain, Zulfiqar (LAB - Clementswood)
cllr.hussain@redbridge.gov.uk

Javed, Muhammed (LAB - Clementswood)
muhammed.javed@redbridge.gov.uk

Jeyaranjan, Thavathuray (LAB - Newbury)
thavathuray.jeyaranjan@redbridge.gov.uk

Jones, Bert (LAB - Goodmayes)
bert.jones@redbridge.gov.uk

Kaur-Thiara, Debbie (LAB - Aldborough)
debbie.Kaur-thiara@redbridge.gov.uk

Kissin, Ashley (CON - Barkingside)
ashley.kissin@redbridge.gov.uk

Lambert, Brian (CON - Fairlop)
brian.lambert@redbridge.gov.uk

Littlewood, Robert (LAB - Seven Kings)
bob.littlewood@redbridge.gov.uk

McLaren, Tom (CON - Church End)
tom.mclaren@redbridge.gov.uk

Merry, Paul (LAB - Wanstead)
paul.merry@redbridge.gov.uk

Nijjar, Baldesh (LAB - Seven Kings)
baldesh.nijjar@redbridge.gov.uk

Nolan, Suzanne (CON - Snaresbrook)
suzanne.nolan@redbridge.gov.uk

O'Shea, James (CON - Monkhams)
cllr.o'shea@redbridge.gov.uk

Packer, Karen (CON - Barkingside)
karen.packer@redbridge.gov.uk

Parkash, Ayodhiya (LAB - Mayfield)
ayodhiya.parkash@redbridge.gov.uk

Prince, Keith (CON - Barkingside)
keith.prince@redbridge.gov.uk

Rai, Kam (LAB - Goodmayes)
kam.rai@redbridge.gov.uk

Rashid, Taifur (LAB - Loxford)
taifur.rashid@redbridge.gov.uk

Ryan, Joyce (CON - Fairlop)

Sachs, Anne (LAB - Chadwell)
anne.sachs@redbridge.gov.uk

Santos, Mark (LAB - Hainault)
mark.santos@redbridge.gov.uk

Sharma, Dev (LAB - Newbury)
dev.sharma@redbridge.gov.uk

Sharpe, Tom (CON - Fairlop)
tom.sharpe@redbridge.gov.uk

Stark, Michael (CON - Monkhams)
michael.stark@redbridge.gov.uk

Streeting, Wes (LAB - Aldborough)
wes.streeting@redbridge.gov.uk

Turbefield, Robin (CON - Bridge)
robin.turbefield@redbridge.gov.uk

Weinberg, Alan (CON - Clayhall)
alan.weinberg@redbridge.gov.uk

Zammett, Neil (LAB - Chadwell)
neil.zammett@redbridge.gov.uk

POLITICAL COMPOSITION

LAB: 35, CON: 25, LD: 3

COMMITTEE CHAIRS

Children & Young People: Mr Robert Littlewood

Pensions: Ms Elaine Norman

Redcar & Cleveland U

Redcar & Cleveland Borough Council, Town Hall, Fabian Road, South Bank, Redcar TS6 9AR
☎ 01642 774774 💻 www.redcar-cleveland.gov.uk

FACTS AND FIGURES

Parliamentary Constituencies: Middlesbrough South and Cleveland East, Redcar
EU Constituencies: North East
Election Frequency: Elections are of whole council

PRINCIPAL OFFICERS

Chief Executive: Ms Amanda Skelton , Chief Executive, Redcar and Cleveland House, Kirkleatham Street, Redcar TS10 1RT
☎ 01642 444003 🖶 01642 444004
amanda.skelton@redcar-cleveland.gov.uk

Senior Management: Mr Gerry Brough , Corporate Director of Regeneration Services, Redcar and Cleveland House, Kirkleatham Street, Redcar TS10 1RT ☎ 01642 444258
gerry.brough@redcar-cleveland.gov.uk

Senior Management: Mr Mike Greene , Assistant Director - Neighbourhoods & Customer Services, Redcar and Cleveland House, Kirkleatham Street, Redcar TS10 1RT ☎ 01642 444346
mike.greene@redcar-cleveland.gov.uk

REDCAR & CLEVELAND

Senior Management: Mrs Pauline Kavanagh, Assistant Director - Organisational Change, Redcar and Cleveland House, Kirkleatham Street, Redcar TS10 1RT ☎ 01642 444021 🖷 01642 771284 ✉ pauline.kavanagh@redcar-cleveland.gov.uk

Senior Management: Mr Mark Ladyman , Assistant Director - Regeneration, Redcar and Cleveland House, Kirkleatham Street, Redcar TS10 1RT ☎ 01642 444322 ✉ mark.ladyman@redcar-cleveland.gov.uk

Senior Management: Mr John Sampson , Corporate Director of Corporate Resources, Redcar and Cleveland House, Kirkleatham Street, Redcar TS10 1RT ☎ 01642 771144 ✉ john.sampson@redcar-cleveland.gov.uk

Senior Management: Ms Barbara Shaw, Corporate Director of People's Services, Seafield House, Kirkleatham Street, Redcar TS10 1SP ☎ 01642 771674 🖷 01642 771670 ✉ barbara.shaw@redcar-cleveland.gov.uk

Architect, Building / Property Services: Mrs Sarah Lamont , Asset Manager, Belmont House, Recotry Lane, Guisborough TS14 7FD ☎ 01642 776951 ✉ sarah.lamont@redcar-cleveland.gov.uk

Building Control: Mr Mike Pengilley , Principal Building Control Surveyor, Redcar & Cleveland House, Kirkleatham Street, Redcar TS10 1RT ☎ 01287 612358 🖷 01287 612367 ✉ mike.pengilley@redcar-cleveland.gov.uk

Children / Youth Services: Mr Chris Daniel , Assistant Director - Children & Families, Seafield House, Kirkleatham Street, Redcar TS10 1SP ☎ 01642 771673 ✉ chris.daniel@redcar-cleveland.gov.uk

Children / Youth Services: Miss Agnes Scott , Team Manager - Youth & Community, 25k Centre, Ayton Drive, Redcar TS10 4EW ☎ 01642 777544 ✉ aggie.scott@redcar-cleveland.gov.uk

Civil Registration: Mr Peter Wilson , Superintendent Registrar, Redcar Heart, Ridley Street, Redcar TS10 1RT ☎ 01642 444648 ✉ peter.wilson@redcar-cleveland.gov.uk

PR / Communications: Mrs Miranda Sykes , Communications & Media Manager, Redcar and Cleveland House, Kirkleatham Street, Redcar TS10 1RT ☎ 01642 444458 ✉ miranda.sykes@redcar-cleveland.gov.uk

Computer Management: Mrs Sarah Lamont , Corporate Resources, Belmont House, Rectory Lane, Guisborough TS14 7FD ☎ 01642 776951 ✉ sarah.lamont@redcar-cleveland.gov.uk

Consumer Protection and Trading Standards: Mr Julian Sorrell , Principal Trading Standards Officer, Belmont House, Rectory Lane, Guisborough TS14 7FD ☎ 01287 612322 ✉ julian.sorrell@redcar-cleveland.gov.uk

Contracts: Mrs Deborah Thorne , Commissioning & Procurement Manager, Belmont House, Rectory Lane, Guisborough TS14 7FD ☎ 01642 771256 🖷 01642 771143 ✉ deborah.thorne@redcar-cleveland.gov.uk

Corporate Services: Mr John Sampson , Corporate Director of Corporate Resources, Redcar and Cleveland House, Kirkleatham Street, Redcar TS10 1RT ☎ 01642 771144 ✉ john.sampson@redcar-cleveland.gov.uk

Customer Service: Mr Mike Fleming , Contact Centre Manager, Redcar and Cleveland House, Kirkleatham Street, Redcar TS10 1RT ☎ 01642 495382 ✉ mike.fleming@redcar-cleveland.gov.uk

Economic Development: Mr Gerry Brough , Corporate Director of Regeneration Services, Redcar and Cleveland House, Kirkleatham Street, Redcar TS10 1RT ☎ 01642 444258 ✉ gerry.brough@redcar-cleveland.gov.uk

Education: Mr John Anthony , Head of Learning & Achievement, Seafield House, Kirkleatham Street, Redcar TS10 1SP ☎ 01642 444342 ✉ john.anthony@redcar-cleveland.gov.uk

Electoral Registration: Mrs Sue Bridges , Principal Governance Officer, Redcar Heart, Ridley Street, Redcar TS10 1RT ☎ 01642 444092 ✉ sue.bridges@redcar-cleveland.gov.uk

Emergency Planning: Mr Stuart Marshall, Emergency Planning Officer, Redcar & Cleveland House, Kirkleatham Street, Redcar TS10 1RT ☎ 01642 444202 ✉ stuart.marshall@redcar-cleveland.gov.uk

Energy Management: Mr Stewart Kerr , Energy Management Specialist, Fairway House, Limerick Road, Dormanstown, Redcar TS10 5JU ☎ 01642 771288 ✉ stewart.kerr@redcar-cleveland.gov.uk

Environmental / Technical Services: Ms Tracy Hilton , Principal Officer - Environmental Protection, Belmont House, Rectory Lane, Guisborough TS14 7FD ☎ 01287 612420 ✉ tracy.hilton@redcar-cleveland.gov.uk

Environmental Health: Mrs Vikki Bell , Principal Environmental Health Officer, Belmont House, Rectory Lane, Guisborough TS14 7FD ☎ 01287 612404 ✉ vikki.bell@redcar-cleveland.gov.uk

Estates, Property & Valuation: Mrs Sarah Lamont , Asset Manager, Belmont House, Recotry Lane, Guisborough TS14 7FD ☎ 01642 776951 ✉ sarah.lamont@redcar-cleveland.gov.uk

Events Manager: Mr Malcolm Armstrong , Cultural Services Manager, Bellamy Pavilion, Kirkleatham, Redcar TS10 5NW ☎ 01642 496422 ✉ malcolm.armstrong@redcar-cleveland.gov.uk

Facilities: Mr Brian Stephenson , Building Manager, Fairway House, Limerick Road, Dormanstown, Redcar TS10 5JU ☎ 01642 776905 ✉ brian.stephenson@redcar-cleveland.gov.uk

Finance: Mr John Sampson , Corporate Director of Corporate Resources, Redcar and Cleveland House, Kirkleatham Street, Redcar TS10 1RT ☎ 01642 771144 ✉ john.sampson@redcar-cleveland.gov.uk

Fleet Management: Mr Colin Bowley , Waste & Fleet Manager, Fairway House, Limerick Road, Dormanstown, Redcar TS10 5JU ☎ 01642 776909 ✉ colin.bowley@redcar-cleveland.gov.uk

Grounds Maintenance: Mr Gary Cummins , Streetscene Operations Manager, Fairway House, Limerick Road, Dormanstown, Redcar TS10 5JU ☎ 01642 776960 gary.cummins@redcar-cleveland.gov.uk

Health and Safety: Mr John Summers, Health & Safety Manager, Belmont House, Rectory Lane, Guisborough TS14 7FD ☎ 01642 444064 john.summers@redcar-cleveland.gov.uk

Highways: Mr Paul Campbell , Assistant Director - Regeneration, Redcar & Cleveland House, Kirkleatham Street, Redcar TS10 1RT ☎ 01642 444242 paul.campbell@redcar-cleveland.gov.uk

Home Energy Conservation: Mr Stewart Kerr , Energy Management Specialist, Fairway House, Limerick Road, Dormanstown, Redcar TS10 5JU ☎ 01642 771288 stewart.kerr@redcar-cleveland.gov.uk

Housing: Mr Roger Kay , Housing Strategy Lead, Redcar and Cleveland House, Kirkleatham Street, Redcar TS10 1RT ☎ 01287 612450 roger.kay@redcar-cleveland.gov.uk

Local Area Agreement: Mr Rob Mitchell , Head of Policy & Performance, Redcar and Cleveland House, Kirkleatham Street, Redcar TS10 1RT ☎ 01642 444507 rob.mitchell@redcar-cleveland.gov.uk

Legal: Mr Gerard Tompkinson , Legal & Governance Manager, Redcar Heart, Ridley Street, Redcar TS10 1RT ☎ 01642 444536 gerard.tompkinson@redcar-cleveland.gov.uk

Leisure and Cultural Services: Mr Malcolm Armstrong , Cultural Services Manager, Bellamy Pavilion, Kirkleatham, Redcar TS10 5NW ☎ 01642 496422 malcolm.armstrong@redcar-cleveland.gov.uk

Licensing: Mr Stephen Brown , Principal Licensing Officer, Belmont House, Rectory Lane, Guisborough TS14 7FD ☎ 01287 612402 stephen.brown@redcar-cleveland.gov.uk

Lighting: Mr Adrian Miller , Regulatory Services Manager, Belmont House, Rectory Lane, Guisborough TS14 7FD ☎ 01287 612454 adrian.miller@redcar-cleveland.gov.uk

Member Services: Mr Gerard Tompkinson , Legal & Governance Manager, Redcar Heart, Ridley Street, Redcar TS10 1RT ☎ 01642 444536 gerard.tompkinson@redcar-cleveland.gov.uk

Parking: Mr Stephen Brown , Principal Licensing Officer, Belmont House, Rectory Lane, Guisborough TS14 7FD ☎ 01287 612402 stephen.brown@redcar-cleveland.gov.uk

Partnerships: Ms Val Mitchell , Stronger Communities Manager, Redcar & Cleveland House, Kirkleatham Street, Redcar TS10 1RT ☎ 01642 776948 val.mitchell@redcar-cleveland.gov.uk

Personnel / HR: Mrs Pauline Kavanagh, Assistant Director - Organisational Change, Redcar and Cleveland House, Kirkleatham Street, Redcar TS10 1RT ☎ 01642 444021 🖷 01642 771284 pauline.kavanagh@redcar-cleveland.gov.uk

Planning: Mr Alex Conti , Planning Strategy Team Leader, Redcar & Cleveland House, Kirkleatham Street, Redcar TS10 1RT ☎ 01287 612353 alex.conti@redcar-cleveland.gov.uk

Procurement: Mrs Deborah Thorne , Commissioning & Procurement Manager, Redcar & Cleveland House, Kirkleatham Street, Redcar TS10 1RT ☎ 01642 771256 🖷 01642 771143 deborah.thorne@redcar-cleveland.gov.uk

Public Libraries: Mr Gary Cummins , Streetscene Operations Manager, Fairway House, Limerick Road, Dormanstown, Redcar TS10 5JU ☎ 01642 776960 gary.cummins@redcar-cleveland.gov.uk

Recycling & Waste Minimisation: Mr Anthony Smith, Waste, Recyling & Fleet Operations Manager, Fairway House, Limerick Road, Dormanstown, Redcar TS10 5JU ☎ 01642 776971 anthony.smith@redcar-cleveland.gov.uk

Regeneration: Mr Gerry Brough , Corporate Director of Regeneration Services, Redcar and Cleveland House, Kirkleatham Street, Redcar TS10 1RT ☎ 01642 444258 gerry.brough@redcar-cleveland.gov.uk

Social Services: Ms Barbara Shaw, Corporate Director of People's Services, Seafield House, Kirkleatham Street, Redcar TS10 1SP ☎ 01642 771674 🖷 01642 771670 barbara.shaw@redcar-cleveland.gov.uk

Social Services (Adult): Mr Patrick Rice , Assistant Director - Commissioning Adults, Seafield House, Kirkleatham Street, Redcar TS10 1SP ☎ 01642 771676 patrick.rice@redcar-cleveland.gov.uk

Social Services (Children): Mr Chris Daniel , Assistant Director - Children & Families, Seafield House, Kirkleatham Street, Redcar TS10 1SP ☎ 01642 771673 chris.daniel@redcar-cleveland.gov.uk

Public Health: Dr Toks Sangowawa , Clinical Director - Public Health, Seafield House, Kirkleatham Street, Redcar TS10 1SP toks.sangowawa@redcar-cleveland.gov.uk

Staff Training: Mrs Angela Wright , Workforce Development Manager, Belmont House, Rectory Lane, Guisborough TS14 7FD ☎ 01642 444523 angela.wright@redcar-cleveland.gov.uk

Street Scene: Mr Gary Cummins , Streetscene Operations Manager, Fairway House, Limerick Road, Dormanstown, Redcar TS10 5JU ☎ 01642 776960 gary.cummins@redcar-cleveland.gov.uk

Sustainable Communities: Mr Gerry Brough , Corporate Director of Regeneration Services, Redcar and Cleveland House, Kirkleatham Street, Redcar TS10 1RT ☎ 01642 444258 gerry.brough@redcar-cleveland.gov.uk

Sustainable Development: Mr Gerry Brough , Corporate Director of Regeneration Services, Redcar and Cleveland House, Kirkleatham Street, Redcar TS10 1RT ☎ 01642 444258 gerry.brough@redcar-cleveland.gov.uk

Tourism: Mr Malcolm Armstrong , Cultural Services Manager, Bellamy Pavilion, Kirkleatham, Redcar TS10 5NW ☎ 01642 496422 malcolm.armstrong@redcar-cleveland.gov.uk

REDCAR & CLEVELAND

Town Centre: Ms Jane Hierons , Visitor & Town Centre Team Leader, Redcar and Cleveland House, Kirkleatham Street, Redcar TS10 1RT ☎ 01642 771180 ✉ jane.hierons@redcar-cleveland.gov.uk

Traffic Management: Mr Colin Bowley , Waste & Fleet Manager, Fleet Depot, Limerick Road, Dormanstown, Redcar TS10 5JU ☎ 01642 776909 ✉ colin.bowley@redcar-cleveland.gov.uk

Transport: Mr Colin Bowley , Waste & Fleet Manager, Fleet Depot, Limerick Road, Dormanstown, Redcar TS10 5JU ☎ 01642 776909 ✉ colin.bowley@redcar-cleveland.gov.uk

Transport Planner: Mr Colin Bowley , Waste & Fleet Manager, Fleet Depot, Limerick Road, Dormanstown, Redcar TS10 5JU ☎ 01642 776909 ✉ colin.bowley@redcar-cleveland.gov.uk

Total Place: Mr Rob Mitchell , Head of Policy & Performance, Redcar and Cleveland House, Kirkleatham Street, Redcar TS10 1RT ☎ 01642 444507 ✉ rob.mitchell@redcar-cleveland.gov.uk

Waste Collection and Disposal: Mr Anthony Smith, Waste, Recyling & Fleet Operations Manager, Fleet Depot, Limerick Road, Dormanstown, Redcar TS10 5JU ☎ 01642 776971 ✉ anthony.smith@redcar-cleveland.gov.uk

Waste Management: Mr Anthony Smith, Waste, Recyling & Fleet Operations Manager, Fairway House, Limerick Road, Dormanstown, Redcar TS10 5JU ☎ 01642 776971 ✉ anthony.smith@redcar-cleveland.gov.uk

COUNCILLORS

***Mayor* Forster**, Brenda (LAB - Kirkleatham)
Brenda.forster@redcar-cleveland.gov.uk

***Leader of the Council* Jeffrey**, Sue (LAB - South Bank)
sue.jeffrey@redcar-cleveland.gov.uk

***Deputy Leader of the Council* Walsh**, David (LAB - Skelton)
dave.walsh@redcar-cleveland.gov.uk

Abbott, Christopher (LD - Newcomen)
Chris.Abbott@redcar-cleveland.gov.uk

Ayre, Billy (LAB - Normanby)
billy.ayre@redcar-cleveland.gov.uk

Baldwin, Neil (LAB - Coatham)
neil.baldwin@redcar-cleveland.gov.uk

Bebdelow, Neil (LAB - South Bank)
neil.bendelow@redcar-cleveland.gov.uk

Brown, Alec (LAB - Dormanstown)
alc.brown@redcar-cleveland.gov.uk

Cawley, Ceri (LAB - Dormanstown)
cari.cawley@redcar-cleveland.gov.uk

Clarke, Bill (IND - Guisborough)
bill.clarke@redcar-cleveland.gov.uk

Cooney, Norah (CON - Longbeck)
Norah.Cooney@redcar-cleveland.gov.uk

Davies, Wayne (IND - Loftus)
wayne.davies@redcar-cleveland.gov.uk

Dennis, Brian (LAB - Normanby)
brian.dennis@redcar-cleveland.gov.uk

Dick, Michael (LAB - Brotton)
michael.dick@redcar-cleveland.gov.uk

Findley, Mike (IND - Longbeck)
mike.findley@redcar-cleveland.gov.uk

Firman, Kevin (LAB - Kirkleatham)
kevin.firman@redcar-cleveland.gov.uk

Foggo, Chris (CON - Skelton)
cliff.fogg@redcar-cleveland.gov.uk

Foley-McCormack, Chris (LAB - Normanby)
chris.foley-mccormack@redcar_cleveland.gov.uk

Goddard, Ray (LAB - Dormanstown)
ray.goddard@redcar-cleveland.gov.uk

Griffiths, Malcolm (CON - Brotton)
malcolm.griffiths@redcar-cleveland.gov.uk

Halton, Valerie (CON - Hutton)
valerie.halton@redcar-cleveland.gov.uk

Hannaway, Craig (LAB - Saltburn)
craig.hannaway@redcar-cleveland.gov.uk

Harding, Lisa (LD - West Dyke)
lisa.harding@redcar-cleveland.gov.uk

Higgins, Ann (IND - Eston)

Hodgson, Robert (LAB - Teesville)
robert.hodgson@redcar-cleveland.gov.uk

Holyoake, Shelagh (LAB - Guisborough)
shelagh.holyoake@redcar-cleveland.gov.uk

Hunt, Barry (IND - Brotton)
barry.hunt@redcar-cleveland.gov.uk

Jackson, Eric (LAB - Loftus)
eric.jackson@redcar-cleveland.gov.uk

Jeffery, Graham (CON - Hutton)
graham.jeffery@redcar-cleveland.gov.uk

Jeffery, Carole (CON - Westworth)
carole.jeffery@redcar-cleveland.gov.uk

Jeffrey, Ian (LAB - South Bank)
ian.jeffrey@redcar-cleveland.gov.uk

Jones, Chris (LD - West Dyke)
chris.jones@redcar-cleveland.gov.uk

Kay, Steve (O - Lockwood)
steve.kay@redcar-cleveland.gov.uk

King, Karen (LD - St Germains)
karen.king@redcar-cleveland.gov.uk

Lanigan, Mary (IND - Loftus)
mary.lanigan@redcar-cleveland.gov.uk

Mason, Josh (LD - Zetland)
josh.mason@redcar-cleveland.gov.uk

Massey, Christopher (LAB - Eston)
christopher.massey@redcar-cleveland.gov.uk

McLuckie, Helen (LAB - Skelton)
helen.mccluckie@redcar-cleveland.gov.uk

Moses, Marjorie (LD - St Germains)
Marjorie.Moses@redcar-cleveland.gov.uk

Nightingale, Glyn (LD - Ormesby)
glyn.nightingale@redcar-cleveland.gov.uk

Nightingale, Irene (LD - Ormesby)
Irene.nightingale@redcar-cleveland.gov.uk

Norton, Bob (LAB - Teesville)
bob.norton@redcar-cleveland.gov.uk

O'Brien, Neil (LAB - Zetland)
neil.obrien@redcar-cleveland.gov.uk

Ovens, Mary (LD - West Dyke)
mary.ovens@redcar-cleveland.gov.uk

Pallister, Lynn (LAB - Grangetown)
lynn.pallister@redcar-cleveland.gov.uk

Quartermain, Carl (LAB - Coatham)
carl.quartermain@redcar-cleveland.co.uk

Quigley, Dale (LAB - Kirkleatham)
dale.quigley@redcar-cleveland.gov.uk

Reed, Leanne (LAB - Teesville)
leanne.reed@redcar-cleveland.gov.uk

Smith, Stuart (IND - Saltburn)
stuart.smith@redcar-cleveland.gov.uk

Spencer, Peter (CON - Hutton)
peter.spencer@redcar-cleveland.gov.uk

Stainthorpe, Jade (LAB - Grangetown)
jade.stainthorpe@redcar-cleveland.gov.uk

Teasdale, Dennis (CON - Guisborough)
dennis.teasdale@redcar-cleveland.gov.uk

Thomson, Philip (CON - Saltburn)
Philip.thomson@redcar-cleveland.gov.uk

Turner, Steve (UKIP - Longbeck)
steve.turner@redcar-cleveland.gov.uk

Watts, Anne (CON - Westworth)
anne.watts@redcar-cleveland.gov.uk

Wells, Billy (LAB - Newcomen)
billy.wells@redcar-cleveland.gov.uk

Williams, Geraldine (LAB - Eston)
geraldine.williams@redcar-cleveland.gov.uk

Wilson, Ann (LD - Ormesby)
ann.s.wilson@redcar-cleveland.gov.uk

Wilson, Margaret (LD - St Germains)
margaret.Wilson@redcar-cleveland.gov.uk

POLITICAL COMPOSITION
LAB: 29, LD: 11, CON: 10, IND: 7, O: 1, UKIP: 1

COMMITTEE CHAIRS
Governance: Mr Ray Goddard

Health & Wellbeing: Mrs Sue Jeffrey

Redditch D

Redditch, Town Hall, Walter Stranz Square, Redditch B98 8AH
☎ 01527 64252 🖷 01527 65216 🖱 corporate@redditch.gov.uk
💻 www.redditchbc.gov.uk

FACTS AND FIGURES
Parliamentary Constituencies: Redditch
EU Constituencies: West Midlands
Election Frequency: Elections are by thirds

PRINCIPAL OFFICERS
Chief Executive: Mr Kevin Dicks, Chief Executive, Town Hall, Walter Stranz Square, Redditch B98 8AH ☎ 01527 881400; 01527 64252 🖷 01527 881212; 01527 65216
🖱 k.dicks@bromsgroveandredditch.gov.uk

Deputy Chief Executive: Mrs Susan Hanley, Strategic Director & Deputy Chief Executive, Town Hall, Walter Stranz Square, Redditch B98 8AH ☎ 01527 64252 Extn 3601; 01527 881483 🖷 01527 65216
🖱 s.hanley@bromsgroveandredditch.gov.uk

Senior Management: Ms Jayne Pickering , Strategic Director & S151 Officer, Town Hall, Walter Stranz Square, Redditch B98 8AH
☎ 01527 64252; 01527 881207 🖷 01527 65216
🖱 j.pickering@bromsgroveandredditch.gov.uk

Building Control: Mr Adrian Wyre , Principal Building Control Surveyor, The Council House, Burcot Lane, Bromsgrove B60 1AA
☎ 01562 732532 🖱 a.wyre@bromsgroveandredditch.gov.uk

Children / Youth Services: Mr John Godwin , Head of Leisure, Town Hall, Walter Stranz Square, Redditch B98 8AH ☎ 01527 64252; 01527 881762 🖷 01527 65216
🖱 j.godwin@bromsgroveandredditch.gov.uk

PR / Communications: Mrs Anne-Marie Harley, Communications & Publicity Manager, Town Hall, Walter Stranz Square, Redditch B98 8AH ☎ 01527 881651; 01527 65252 🖷 01527 881212; 01527 65216 🖱 a.harley@bromsgroveandredditch.gov.uk

Community Planning: Ms Ruth Bamford , Head of Planning & Regeneration Services, Town Hall, Walter Stranz Square, Redditch B98 8AH ☎ 01527 64252 Extn 3201; 01527 64252 ext. 3201
🖷 01527 65216 🖱 r.bamford@bromsgroveandredditch.gov.uk

Community Safety: Mrs Judith Willis , Acting Head of Community Services, Town Hall, Walter Stranz Square, Redditch B98 8AH
☎ 01527 64252 🖷 01527 65216
🖱 judith.willis@bromsgroveandredditch.gov.uk

Contracts: Ms Jayne Pickering , Strategic Director & S151 Officer, Town Hall, Walter Stranz Square, Redditch B98 8AH
☎ 01527 64252; 01527 881207 🖷 01527 65216
🖱 j.pickering@bromsgroveandredditch.gov.uk

Corporate Services: Ms Jayne Pickering , Strategic Director & S151 Officer, Town Hall, Walter Stranz Square, Redditch B98 8AH
☎ 01527 64252; 01527 881207 🖷 01527 65216
🖱 j.pickering@bromsgroveandredditch.gov.uk

Customer Service: Ms Amanda de Warr , Head of Customer Services, Town Hall, Walter Stranz Square, Redditch B98 8AH
☎ 01527 64252; 01527 881241 🖷 01527 65216
🖱 a.dewarr@bromsgroveandredditch.gov.uk

Economic Development: Ms Ruth Bamford , Head of Planning & Regeneration Services, Town Hall, Walter Stranz Square, Redditch B98 8AH ☎ 01527 64252 Extn 3201; 01527 64252 ext. 3201
🖷 01527 65216 🖱 r.bamford@bromsgroveandredditch.gov.uk

REDDITCH

Economic Development: Mr Steve Singleton, Economic Development Manager - North Worcestershire, Wyre Forest House, Finepoint Way, Kidderminster DY11 7WF ☎ 01562 732168 ✉ steve.singleton@wyreforestdc.gov.uk

E-Government: Mrs Deb Poole , Head of Business Transformation, Town Hall, Walter Stranz Square, Redditch B98 8AH ☎ 01527 64252 🖷 01527 65216 ✉ d.poole@bromsgroveandredditch.gov.uk

Emergency Planning: Mr Derek Allen, Strategic Housing Manager, The Council House, Burcot Lane, Bromsgrove B60 1AA ☎ 01527 881278 🖷 01527 881414 ✉ d.allen@bromsgroveandredditch.gov.uk

Emergency Planning: Ms Rebecca Pritchard , North Worcestershire Civil Contingencies & Resilience Manager, Civic Centre, New Street, Stourport DY13 8UJ ✉ r.pritchard@bromsgroveandredditch.gov.uk

Energy Management: Ms Jayne Pickering , Strategic Director & S151 Officer, Town Hall, Walter Stranz Square, Redditch B98 8AH ☎ 01527 64252; 01527 881207 🖷 01527 65216 ✉ j.pickering@bromsgroveandredditch.gov.uk

Environmental / Technical Services: Mr Guy Revans, Head of Environmental Services, Town Hall, Walter Stranz Square, Redditch B98 8AH ☎ 01527 64252; 01527 64252 ext. 3292 🖷 01527 65216 ✉ g.revans@bromsgroveandredditch.gov.uk

Environmental Health: Mr Guy Revans, Head of Environmental Services, Town Hall, Walter Stranz Square, Redditch B98 8AH ☎ 01527 64252; 01527 64252 ext. 3292 🖷 01527 65216 ✉ g.revans@bromsgroveandredditch.gov.uk

Events Manager: Mr Ray Cooke , Leisure Services Manager, Town Hall, Walter Stranz Square, Redditch B98 8AH ☎ 01527 64252 Extn 3248 🖷 01527 65216 ✉ r.cooke@redditchbc.gov.uk

Events Manager: Mr Hugh Moseley, Arts Development & Special Events Officer, The Council House, Burcot Lane, Bromsgrove B60 1AA ☎ 01527 881381 ✉ h.mosley@bromsgroveandredditch.gov.uk

Finance: Ms Sam Morgan , Finance Manager, Town Hall, Walter Stranz Square, Redditch B98 8AH ☎ 01527 64252 ✉ sam.morgan@bromsgroveandredditch.gov.uk

Finance: Ms Jayne Pickering , Strategic Director & S151 Officer, Town Hall, Walter Stranz Square, Redditch B98 8AH ☎ 01527 64252; 01527 881207 🖷 01527 65216 ✉ j.pickering@bromsgroveandredditch.gov.uk

Fleet Management: Mr Paul Mills , Transport & Supplies Manager, Town Hall, Walter Stranz Square, Redditch B98 8AH ☎ 01527 64252 🖷 01527 65216 ✉ p.mills@bromsgroveandredditch.gov.uk

Grounds Maintenance: Mr Guy Revans, Head of Environmental Services, Town Hall, Walter Stranz Square, Redditch B98 8AH ☎ 01527 64252; 01527 64252 ext. 3292 🖷 01527 65216 ✉ g.revans@bromsgroveandredditch.gov.uk

Health and Safety: Ms Becky Barr , Human Resources Manager, Town Hall, Walter Stranz Square, Redditch B98 8AH ☎ 01527 64252 🖷 01527 65216 ✉ b.talbot@redditchbc.gov.uk

Home Energy Conservation: Mr Guy Revans, Head of Environmental Services, Town Hall, Walter Stranz Square, Redditch B98 8AH ☎ 01527 64252; 01527 64252 ext. 3292 🖷 01527 65216 ✉ g.revans@bromsgroveandredditch.gov.uk

Housing: Mrs Liz Tompkin , Head of Housing, Town Hall, Walter Stranz Square, Redditch B98 8AH ☎ 01527 64252 ext. 3304 🖷 01527 65216 ✉ l.tompkin@bromsgrove.gov.uk

Housing Maintenance: Mrs Liz Tompkin , Head of Housing, Town Hall, Walter Stranz Square, Redditch B98 8AH ☎ 01527 64252 ext. 3304 🖷 01527 65216 ✉ l.tompkin@bromsgrove.gov.uk

Legal: Mrs Claire Felton , Head of Legal, Equalities & Democratic Services, Town Hall, Walter Stranz Square, Redditch B98 8AH ☎ 01572 64252; 01527 881429 🖷 01527 65216; 01527 881414 ✉ c.felton@bromsgroveandredditch.gov.uk

Leisure and Cultural Services: Mr John Godwin , Head of Leisure, Town Hall, Walter Stranz Square, Redditch B98 8AH ☎ 01527 64252; 01527 881762 🖷 01527 65216 ✉ j.godwin@bromsgroveandredditch.gov.uk

Lottery Funding, Charity and Voluntary: Mrs Judith Willis , Acting Head of Community Services, Town Hall, Walter Stranz Square, Redditch B98 8AH ☎ 01527 64252 🖷 01527 65216 ✉ judith.willis@bromsgroveandredditch.gov.uk

Member Services: Mrs Sheena Jones, Democratic Services Manager, The Council House, Burcot Lane, Bromsgrove B60 1AA ☎ 01527 01527 548240 🖷 01527 881414 ✉ s.jones@bromsgroveandredditch.gov.uk

Parking: Mr Peter Liddington, Civil Enforcement Parking Officer, Town Hall, Walter Stranz Square, Redditch B98 8AH ☎ 01527 64252 🖷 01527 65216 ✉ p.liddington@redditchbc.gov.uk

Partnerships: Mrs Rebecca Dunn , Policy Manager, Bromsgrove District Council, The Council House, Burcot Lane, Bromsgrove B66 1AA ☎ 01527 881616 ✉ r.dunn@bromsgroveandredditch.gov.uk

Personnel / HR: Ms Becky Barr , Human Resources Manager, Town Hall, Walter Stranz Square, Redditch B98 8AH ☎ 01527 64252 🖷 01527 65216 ✉ b.talbot@redditchbc.gov.uk

Planning: Ms Ruth Bamford , Head of Planning & Regeneration Services, Town Hall, Walter Stranz Square, Redditch B98 8AH ☎ 01527 64252 Extn 3201; 01527 64252 ext. 3201 🖷 01527 65216 ✉ r.bamford@bromsgroveandredditch.gov.uk

Procurement: Ms Carmen Young , Procurement Officer, Town Hall, Walter Stranz Square, Redditch B98 8AH ☎ 01527 64252 ✉ c.young@bromsgroveandredditch.gov.uk

Recycling & Waste Minimisation: Mr Guy Revans, Head of Environmental Services, Town Hall, Walter Stranz Square, Redditch B98 8AH ☎ 01527 64252; 01527 64252 ext. 3292 🖷 01527 65216 ✉ g.revans@bromsgroveandredditch.gov.uk

Regeneration: Ms Ruth Bamford , Head of Planning & Regeneration Services, Town Hall, Walter Stranz Square, Redditch B98 8AH ☎ 01527 64252 Extn 3201; 01527 64252 ext. 3201 🖷 01527 65216 ✉ r.bamford@bromsgroveandredditch.gov.uk

Staff Training: Ms Becky Barr , Human Resources Manager, Town Hall, Walter Stranz Square, Redditch B98 8AH ☎ 01527 64252 🖷 01527 65216 ✉ b.talbot@redditchbc.gov.uk

Street Scene: Mr Guy Revans, Head of Environmental Services, Town Hall, Walter Stranz Square, Redditch B98 8AH ☎ 01527 64252; 01527 64252 ext. 3292 🖷 01527 65216 ✉ g.revans@bromsgroveandredditch.gov.uk

Town Centre: Ms Ruth Bamford , Head of Planning & Regeneration Services, Town Hall, Walter Stranz Square, Redditch B98 8AH ☎ 01527 64252 Extn 3201; 01527 64252 ext. 3201 🖷 01527 65216 ✉ r.bamford@bromsgroveandredditch.gov.uk

Transport: Mr Paul Mills , Transport & Supplies Manager, Town Hall, Walter Stranz Square, Redditch B98 8AH ☎ 01527 64252 🖷 01527 65216 ✉ p.mills@bromsgroveandredditch.gov.uk

Transport Planner: Mr Paul Mills , Transport & Supplies Manager, Town Hall, Walter Stranz Square, Redditch B98 8AH ☎ 01527 64252 🖷 01527 65216 ✉ p.mills@bromsgroveandredditch.gov.uk

Waste Collection and Disposal: Mr Guy Revans, Head of Environmental Services, Town Hall, Walter Stranz Square, Redditch B98 8AH ☎ 01527 64252; 01527 64252 ext. 3292 🖷 01527 65216 ✉ g.revans@bromsgroveandredditch.gov.uk

Waste Management: Mr Guy Revans, Head of Environmental Services, Town Hall, Walter Stranz Square, Redditch B98 8AH ☎ 01527 64252; 01527 64252 ext. 3292 🖷 01527 65216 ✉ g.revans@bromsgroveandredditch.gov.uk

Children's Play Areas: Mr John Godwin , Head of Leisure, Town Hall, Walter Stranz Square, Redditch B98 8AH ☎ 01527 64252; 01527 881762 🖷 01527 65216 ✉ j.godwin@bromsgroveandredditch.gov.uk

COUNCILLORS

***Mayor* Hill**, Pattie (LAB - Batchley & Brockhill)
pattie.hill@redditchbc.gov.uk

***Deputy Mayor* Baker**, Joe (LAB - Greenlands)
joe.baker@redditchbc.gov.uk

***Leader of the Council* Hartnett**, Bill (LAB - Church Hill)
bill.hartnett@redditchbc.gov.uk

***Deputy Leader of the Council* Chance**, Greg (LAB - Central)
greg.chance@redditchbc.gov.uk

Baker-Price, Tom (CON - Headless Corss & Oakenshaw)

Bennett, Roger (CON - Headless Cross & Oakenshaw)
roger.bennett@redditchbc.gov.uk

Brookes, Natalie (LAB - Batchley & Brockhill)
natalie.brookes@redditchbc.gov.uk

Brunner, Juliet (CON - Matchborough)
juliet.brunner@redditchbc.gov.uk

Bush, David (CON - West)
david.bush@redditchbc.gov.uk

Chalk, Michael (CON - Abbey)
michael.chalk@redditchbc.gov.uk

Clayton, Anita (CON - Batchley & Bockhill)

Clayton, Brandon (CON - Astwood Bank & Feckenham)
brandon.clayton@redditchbc.gov.uk

Dormer, Mathew (CON - West)
matthew.dormer@redditchbc.gov.uk

Fisher, John (LAB - Matchborough)
john.fisher@redditchbc.gov.uk

Fry, Andy (LAB - Lodge Park)
andy.fry@redditchbc.gov.uk

Hopkins, Gay (CON - Headless Cross & Oakenshaw)
gay.hopkins@redditchbc.gov.uk

King, Wanda (LAB - Greenlands)
wanda.king@redditchbc.gov.uk

Potter, Jane (CON - Astwood Bank & Feckenham)
jane.potter@redditchbc.gov.uk

Prosser, Gareth (CON - Crabbs Cross)
gareth.prosser@redditchbc.gov.uk

Pulsford, Antonia (CON - Winyates)
antonia.pulsford@redditchbc.gov.uk

Shurmer, Mark (LAB - Lodge Park)
mark.shurmer@redditchbc.gov.uk

Smith, Yvonne (LAB - Winyates)
yvonne.smith@redditchbc.gov.uk

Smith, Rachael (LAB - Abbey)
rachael.smith@redditchbc.gov.uk

Swansborough, Paul (UKIP - Winyates)
paul.swansborough@redditchbc.gov.uk

Taylor, Debbie (LAB - Central)
debbie.taylor@redditchbc.gov.uk

Thain, David (CON - Crabbs Cross)
david.thain@redditchbc.gov.uk

Wheeler, Jennifer (LAB - Greenlands)

Witherspoon, Pat (LAB - Church Hill)
pat.witherspoon@redditchbc.gov.uk

Wood-Ford, Nina (LAB - Church Hill)
nina.wood-ford@redditchbc.gov.uk

POLITICAL COMPOSITION

LAB: 15, CON: 13, UKIP: 1

COMMITTEE CHAIRS

Audit: Mr David Thain

Licensing: Mrs Pat Witherspoon

Planning: Cllr Andy Fry

Reigate & Banstead D

Reigate & Banstead Borough Council, Town Hall, Castlefield Road, Reigate RH2 0SH
☎ 01737 276000 🖷 01737 276718
✉ customer.services@reigate-banstead.gov.uk
🖳 www.reigate-banstead.gov.uk

REIGATE & BANSTEAD

FACTS AND FIGURES

Parliamentary Constituencies: Reigate
EU Constituencies: South East
Election Frequency: Elections are by thirds

PRINCIPAL OFFICERS

Chief Executive: Mr John Jory , Chief Executive, Town Hall, Castlefield Road, Reigate RH2 0SH ☎ 01737 276151 mary.nicholls@reigate-banstead.gov.uk

Deputy Chief Executive: Ms Kathy O'Leary , Deputy Chief Executive, Town Hall, Castlefield Road, Reigate RH2 0SH ☎ 07373 276512 kathy.oleary@reigate-banstead.gov.uk

Architect, Building / Property Services: Mr John Reed , Property Manager, Town Hall, Castlefield Road, Reigate RH2 0SH ☎ 01737 276571 🖷 01737 276070 john.reed@reigate-banstead.gov.uk

Building Control: Mr Peter Tonge , Environmental & Community Regulation Manager, Town Hall, Castlefield Road, Reigate RH2 0SH ☎ 01737 276209 peter.tonge@reigate-banstead.gov.uk

PR / Communications: Ms Fiona Cullen , Communications, Information & Change Manager, Town Hall, Castlefield Road, Reigate RH2 0SH ☎ 01737 276296 communications@reigate-banstead.gov.uk

Community Planning: Mr Simon Bland, Business & Community Engagement Manager, Town Hall, Castlefield Road, Reigate RH2 0SH ☎ 01737 276303 🖷 01737 276404 simon.bland@reigate-banstead.gov.uk

Community Safety: Mrs Debbie Stitt, Community Safety Manager, Town Hall, Castlefield Road, Reigate RH2 0SH ☎ 01737 276305 🖷 01737 276739 debbie.stitt@reigate-banstead.gov.uk

Computer Management: Ms Fiona Cullen , Communications, Information & Change Manager, Town Hall, Castlefield Road, Reigate RH2 0SH ☎ 01737 276296 communications@reigate-banstead.gov.uk

Contracts: Mr Michael Graham , Legal Services Manager, Town Hall, Castlefield Road, Reigate RH2 0SH ☎ 01737 276106 michael.graham@reigate-banstead.gov.uk

Corporate Services: Mr Gavin Handford , Head of Corporate Development, Town Hall, Castlefield Road, Reigate RH2 0SH ☎ 01737 276027 gavin.handford@reigate-banstead.gov.uk

Customer Service: Ms Fiona Cullen , Communications, Information & Change Manager, Town Hall, Castlefield Road, Reigate RH2 0SH ☎ 01737 276296 communications@reigate-banstead.gov.uk

Economic Development: Mr Simon Bland, Business & Community Engagement Manager, Town Hall, Castlefield Road, Reigate RH2 0SH ☎ 01737 276303 🖷 01737 276404 simon.bland@reigate-banstead.gov.uk

E-Government: Ms Fiona Cullen , Communications, Information & Change Manager, Town Hall, Castlefield Road, Reigate RH2 0SH ☎ 01737 276296 communications@reigate-banstead.gov.uk

Electoral Registration: Ms Sally Crawford , Electoral Services Manager, Town Hall, Castlefield Road, Reigate RH2 0SH ☎ 01737 276440 sally.crawford@reigate-banstead.gov.uk

Emergency Planning: Mr Gavin Handford , Head of Corporate Development, Town Hall, Castlefield Road, Reigate RH2 0SH ☎ 01737 276027 gavin.handford@reigate-banstead.gov.uk

Energy Management: Mr John Reed , Property Manager, Town Hall, Castlefield Road, Reigate RH2 0SH ☎ 01737 276571 🖷 01737 276070 john.reed@reigate-banstead.gov.uk

Environmental / Technical Services: Ms Kathy O'Leary , Deputy Chief Executive, Town Hall, Castlefield Road, Reigate RH2 0SH ☎ 07373 276512 kathy.oleary@reigate-banstead.gov.uk

Environmental Health: Mr Peter Tonge , Environmental & Community Regulation Manager, Town Hall, Castlefield Road, Reigate RH2 0SH ☎ 01737 276209 peter.tonge@reigate-banstead.gov.uk

Estates, Property & Valuation: Mr John Reed , Property Manager, Town Hall, Castlefield Road, Reigate RH2 0SH ☎ 01737 276571 🖷 01737 276070 john.reed@reigate-banstead.gov.uk

Facilities: Mr John Reed , Property Manager, Town Hall, Castlefield Road, Reigate RH2 0SH ☎ 01737 276571 🖷 01737 276070 john.reed@reigate-banstead.gov.uk

Finance: Mr Bill Pallett , Finance Manager, Town Hall, Castlefield Road, Reigate RH2 0SH ☎ 01737 276560 🖷 01737 276513 bill.pallett@reigate-banstead.gov.uk

Fleet Management: Mr Ken Dodds , Transport Fleet Manager, Town Hall, Castlefield Road, Reigate RH2 0SH ☎ 01737 276614 🖷 01737 276641 ken.dodds@reigate-banstead.gov.uk

Grounds Maintenance: Mr Emanuel Flecken , Parks & Countryside Manager, Town Hall, Castlefield Road, Reigate RH2 0SH ☎ 01737 276226 emanuel.flecken@reigate-banstead.gov.uk

Health and Safety: Ms Mari Roberts-Wood , People & Welfare Manager, Town Hall, Castlefield Road, Reigate RH2 0SH ☎ 01737 276030 mari.roberts-wood@reigate-banstead.gov.uk

Housing: Ms Mari Roberts-Wood , People & Welfare Manager, Town Hall, Castlefield Road, Reigate RH2 0SH ☎ 01737 276030 mari.roberts-wood@reigate-banstead.gov.uk

Legal: Mr Michael Graham , Legal Services Manager, Town Hall, Castlefield Road, Reigate RH2 0SH ☎ 01737 276106 michael.graham@reigate-banstead.gov.uk

Leisure and Cultural Services: Mr Tom Kealey , Leisure & Wellbeing Manager, Town Hall, Castlefield Road, Reigate RH2 0SH ☎ 01737 276840 tom.kealey@reigate-banstead.gov.uk

Licensing: Mr Ben Murray , Team Leader, Town Hall, Castlefield Road, Reigate RH2 0SH ☎ 01737 276069 ben.murray@reigate-banstead.gov.uk

Lottery Funding, Charity and Voluntary: Mr Simon Bland, Business & Community Engagement Manager, Town Hall, Castlefield Road, Reigate RH2 0SH ☎ 01737 276303 🖷 01737 276404 ✉ simon.bland@reigate-banstead.gov.uk

Member Services: Mr Gavin Handford , Head of Corporate Development, Town Hall, Castlefield Road, Reigate RH2 0SH ☎ 01737 276027 ✉ gavin.handford@reigate-banstead.gov.uk

Parking: Mr Gavin Handford , Head of Corporate Development, Town Hall, Castlefield Road, Reigate RH2 0SH ☎ 01737 276027 ✉ gavin.handford@reigate-banstead.gov.uk

Personnel / HR: Ms Mari Roberts-Wood , People & Welfare Manager, Town Hall, Castlefield Road, Reigate RH2 0SH ☎ 01737 276030 ✉ mari.roberts-wood@reigate-banstead.gov.uk

Planning: Ms Luci Mould , Places & Planning Manager, Town Hall, Castlefield Road, Reigate RH2 0SH ☎ 01737 276214 ✉ luci.mould@reigate-banstead.gov.uk

Procurement: Mr Bill Pallett , Finance Manager, Town Hall, Castlefield Road, Reigate RH2 0SH ☎ 01737 276560 🖷 01737 276513 ✉ bill.pallett@reigate-banstead.gov.uk

Recycling & Waste Minimisation: Mr Frank Etheridge , Recycling & Cleansing Manager, Town Hall, Castlefield Road, Reigate RH2 0SH ☎ 01737 276219 ✉ frank.etheridge@reigate-banstead.gov.uk

Regeneration: Ms Luci Mould , Places & Planning Manager, Town Hall, Castlefield Road, Reigate RH2 0SH ☎ 01737 276214 ✉ luci.mould@reigate-banstead.gov.uk

Staff Training: Ms Mari Roberts-Wood , People & Welfare Manager, Town Hall, Castlefield Road, Reigate RH2 0SH ☎ 01737 276030 ✉ mari.roberts-wood@reigate-banstead.gov.uk

Street Scene: Mr Frank Etheridge , Recycling & Cleansing Manager, Town Hall, Castlefield Road, Reigate RH2 0SH ☎ 01737 276219 ✉ frank.etheridge@reigate-banstead.gov.uk

Sustainable Communities: Ms Luci Mould , Places & Planning Manager, Town Hall, Castlefield Road, Reigate RH2 0SH ☎ 01737 276214 ✉ luci.mould@reigate-banstead.gov.uk

Sustainable Development: Ms Luci Mould , Places & Planning Manager, Town Hall, Castlefield Road, Reigate RH2 0SH ☎ 01737 276214 ✉ luci.mould@reigate-banstead.gov.uk

Waste Collection and Disposal: Mr Frank Etheridge , Recycling & Cleansing Manager, Town Hall, Castlefield Road, Reigate RH2 0SH ☎ 01737 276219 ✉ frank.etheridge@reigate-banstead.gov.uk

Children's Play Areas: Mr Emanuel Flecken , Parks & Countryside Manager, Town Hall, Castlefield Road, Reigate RH2 0SH ☎ 01737 276226 ✉ emanuel.flecken@reigate-banstead.gov.uk

COUNCILLORS

***Mayor* Spiers**, Joan (CON - Kingswood with Burgh Heath)
cllr.spiers@reigate-banstead.gov.uk

***Deputy Mayor* Powell**, David (CON - Horley West)
Cllr.Powell@reigate-banstead.gov.uk

***Leader of the Council* Broad**, Victor (CON - Tadworth and Walton)
cllr.broad@reigate-banstead.gov.uk

***Deputy Leader of the Council* Kay**, Allen (CON - Horley Central)
cllr.kay@reigate-banstead.gov.uk

Absalom, Rosemary (CON - Reigate Central)
cllr.absalom@reigate-banstead.gov.uk

Allcard, Derek (CON - South Park and Woodhatch)
cllr.allcard@reigate-banstead.gov.uk

Blacker, Michael (CON - Reigate Central)

Bramhall, Natalie (CON - Redhill West)
Cllr.MrsBramhall@reigate-banstead.gov.uk

Bramhall, Stephen (CON - South Park and Woodhatch)
cllr.bramhall@reigate-banstead.gov.uk

Bray, Jill (R - Tattenhams)
cllr.bray@reigate-banstead.gov.uk

Brunt, Mark (CON - Merstham)
cllr.brunt@reigate-banstead.gov.uk

Clarke, James (CON - Tadworth and Walton)
cllr.clarke@reigate-banstead.gov.uk

Coad, Richard (CON - Redhill East)
cllr.coad@reigate-banstead.gov.uk

Crome, Graeme (CON - Merstham)
cllr.crome@reigate-banstead.gov.uk

Durrant, James (CON - Earlswood and Whitbushes)
Cllr.Durrant@reigate-banstead.gov.uk

Ellacott, Julian (CON - Redhill West)

Essex, Jonathan (GRN - Redhill East)
Cllr.Essex@reigate-banstead.gov.uk

Foreman, Keith (CON - Chipstead, Hooley and Woodmansterne)
Cllr.Foreman@reigate-banstead.gov.uk

Godden, John (CON - Meadvale and St John's)
cllr.godden@reigate-banstead.gov.uk

Grant-Duff, Zully (CON - Reigate Hill)
cllr.grant-duff@reigate-banstead.gov.uk

Hack, Lynne (CON - Banstead Village)
Cllr.hack@reigate-banstead.gov.uk

Harper, Robert (R - Tattenhams)
cllr.harper@reigate-banstead.gov.uk

Harris, Norman (R - Nork)
cllr.norman.harris@reigate-banstead.gov.uk

Harrison, Nicholas (R - Tattenhams)
cllr.harrison@reigate-banstead.gov.uk

Horwood, Alexander (CON - Horley West)
Cllr.Horwood@reigate-banstead.gov.uk

Humphreys, Eddy (CON - Banstead Village)
Cllr.Humphreys@reigate-banstead.gov.uk

Jackson, David (CON - Horley West)
cllr.jackson@reigate-banstead.gov.uk

Kelly, Frank (CON - Merstham)
Cllr.Kelly@reigate-banstead.gov.uk

Knight, Graham (CON - Horley East)
Cllr.Knight@reigate-banstead.gov.uk

Kulka, Stephen (LD - Meadvale and St John's)
cllr.kulka@reigate-banstead.gov.uk

Lynch, Andrew (CON - Horley Central)
cllr.lynch@reigate-banstead.gov.uk

Mantle, Richard (IND - Chipstead, Hooley and Woodmansterne)
cllr.mantle@reigate-banstead.gov.uk

Mill, Rosalind (CON - Kingswood with Burgh Heath)
cllr.mill@reigate-banstead.gov.uk

Newstead, Roger (CON - Reigate Hill)
cllr.newstead@reigate-banstead.gov.uk

Parnall, Simon (CON - Kingswood with Burgh Heath)
Cllr.Parnall@reigate-banstead.gov.uk

Paul, Jamie (CON - Preston)
cllr.paul@reigate-banstead.gov.uk

Pay, David (CON - Redhill West)
cllr.pay@reigate-banstead.gov.uk

Renton, Rita (CON - Earlswood and Whitebushes)
Cllr.Renton@reigate-banstead.gov.uk

Rickman, Simon (CON - South Park and Woodhatch)

Ross-Tomlin, Dorothy (CON - Salfords and Sidlow)
cllr.ross-tomlin@reigate-banstead.gov.uk

Schofield, Tony (CON - Horley East)

Selby, Michael (R - Nork)
cllr.selby@reigate-banstead.gov.uk

Shillinglaw, Patsy (CON - Meadvale and St John's)
Cllr.Shillinglaw@reigate-banstead.gov.uk

Stead, Brian (R - Nork)
cllr.stead@reigate-banstead.gov.uk

Stephenson, John (CON - Chipstead, Hooley and Woodmansterne)
Cllr.Stephenson@reigate-banstead.gov.uk

Stevens, Christian (UKIP - Horley Central)
cllr.stevens@reigate-banstead.gov.uk

Thompson, Barbara (CON - Earlswood and Whitebushes)
Cllr.Thomson@reigate-banstead.gov.uk

Truscott, Bryan (GRN - Redhill East)
Cllr.Trusctoo@reigate-banstead.gov.uk

Turner, Rachel (CON - Tadworth and Walton)
cllr.turner@reigate-banstead.gov.uk

Walsh, Samuel (CON - Banstead Village)
cllr.walsh@reigate-banstead.gov.uk

Whinney, Christopher (IND - Reigate Central)
cllr.whinney@reigate-banstead.gov.uk

POLITICAL COMPOSITION

CON: 39, R: 6, GRN: 2, IND: 2, LD: 1, UKIP: 1

Renfrewshire S

Renfrewshire Council, Renfrewshire House, Cotton Street, Paisley PA1 1UJ
☎ 0141 842 5000 🖷 0141 840 3335
✉ chiefexec@renfrewshire.gov.uk 🖳 www.renfrewshire.gov.uk

FACTS AND FIGURES

Parliamentary Constituencies: Paisley and Renfrewshire North, Paisley and Renfrewshire South
EU Constituencies: Scotland
Election Frequency: Elections are of whole council

PRINCIPAL OFFICERS

Chief Executive: Ms Sandra Black, Chief Executive, Renfrewshire House, Cotton Street, Paisley PA1 1TR ☎ 0141 618 7355 🖷 0141 842 5055 ✉ sandra.black@renfrewshire.gov.uk

Senior Management: Ms Mary Crearie , Director of Development & Housing Services, Renfrewshire House, Cotton Street, Paisley PA1 1JD ☎ 0141 618 6256 🖷 0141 842 5552 ✉ mary.crearie@renfrewshire.gov.uk

Senior Management: Mrs Shona MacDougall, Director of Community Resources, Renfrewshire House, Cotton Street, Paisley PA1 1BU ☎ 0141 618 7626 🖷 0141 840 3233 ✉ shona.i.macdougall@renfrewshire.gov.uk

Senior Management: Mr Peter Macleod , Director of Children's Services, Renfrewshire House, Cotton Street, Paisley PA1 1TZ ☎ 0141 842 5167 🖷 0141 842 5144 ✉ peter.macleod@renfrewshire.gov.uk

Senior Management: Mr Alan Russell , Director - Finance & Resources, Renfrewshire House, Cotton Street, Paisley PA1 1UJ ☎ 0141 618 7363 ✉ alan.russell@renfrewshire.gov.uk

Access Officer / Social Services (Disability): Mr Peter Macleod , Director of Children's Services, Renfrewshire House, Cotton Street, Paisley PA1 1TZ ☎ 0141 842 5167 🖷 0141 842 5144 ✉ peter.macleod@renfrewshire.gov.uk

Architect, Building / Property Services: Mr Joe Lynch , Head of Property, Renfrewshire House, Cotton Street, Paisley PA1 1UJ ☎ 0141 618 6159 ✉ joe.lynch@renfrewshire.gov.uk

Building Control: Ms Mary Crearie , Director of Development & Housing Services, Renfrewshire House, Cotton Street, Paisley PA1 1JD ☎ 0141 618 6256 🖷 0141 842 5552 ✉ mary.crearie@renfrewshire.gov.uk

Catering Services: Mrs Shona MacDougall, Director of Community Resources, Renfrewshire House, Cotton Street, Paisley PA1 1BU ☎ 0141 618 7626 🖷 0141 840 3233 ✉ shona.i.macdougall@renfrewshire.gov.uk

Children / Youth Services: Ms Dorothy Hawthorn , Head of Child Care & Criminal Justice, Renfrewshire House, Cotton Street, Paisley PA1 1UJ ☎ 0141 618 6827 ✉ dorothy.hawthorn@renfrewshire.gsx.gov.uk

Civil Registration: Mr Ken Graham, Head of Corporate Governance, Renfrewshire House, Cotton Street, Paisley PA1 1TR ☎ 0141 618 7360 🖷 0141 840 3635 ✉ ken.graham@renfrewshire.gov.uk

PR / Communications: Ms Annette McCann , Head of Communications, Renfrewshire House, Cotton Street, Paisley PA1 1WU ☎ 0141 618 4707 ✉ annette.mccann@renfrewshire.gov.uk

Community Safety: Mrs Shona MacDougall, Director of Community Resources, Renfrewshire House, Cotton Street, Paisley PA1 1BU ☎ 0141 618 7626 🖶 0141 840 3233 shona.i.macdougall@renfrewshire.gov.uk

Community Safety: Mr Oliver Reid, Service Manager, Renfrewshire House, Cotton Street, Paisley PA1 1WU ☎ 0141 618 7352 🖶 0141 840 3349 oliver.reid@renfrewshire.gov.uk

Computer Management: Mr Patrick Murray , Head of ICT, Renfrewshire House, Cotton Street, Paisley PA1 1UJ patrick.murray@renfrewshire.gcsx.gov.uk

Consumer Protection and Trading Standards: Mrs Shona MacDougall, Director of Community Resources, Renfrewshire House, Cotton Street, Paisley PA1 1BU ☎ 0141 618 7626 🖶 0141 840 3233 shona.i.macdougall@renfrewshire.gov.uk

Contracts: Mr Ken Graham, Head of Corporate Governance, Renfrewshire House, Cotton Street, Paisley PA1 1TR ☎ 0141 618 7360 🖶 0141 840 3635 ken.graham@renfrewshire.gov.uk

Corporate Services: Mr Alan Russell , Director - Finance & Resources, Renfrewshire House, Cotton Street, Paisley PA1 1UJ ☎ 0141 618 7363 alan.russell@renfrewshire.gov.uk

Customer Service: Ms Rhona McGrath , Head of Business Services, Renfrewshire House, Cotton Street, Paisley PA1 1UJ ☎ 0141 618 6879 rhona.mcgrath@renfrewshire.gcsx.gov.uk

Economic Development: Ms Mary Crearie , Director of Development & Housing Services, Renfrewshire House, Cotton Street, Paisley PA1 1JD ☎ 0141 618 6256 🖶 0141 842 5552 mary.crearie@renfrewshire.gov.uk

Education: Mr Peter Macleod , Director of Children's Services, Renfrewshire House, Cotton Street, Paisley PA1 1TZ ☎ 0141 842 5167 🖶 0141 842 5144 peter.macleod@renfrewshire.gov.uk

Electoral Registration: Mr Alasdair MacTaggart , Assessor & Electoral Registration Officer, 16 Glasgow Road, Paisley PA1 3QF ☎ 0141 618 5903 alasdair.mactaggar@renfrewshire-vjb.gov.uk

Emergency Planning: Mr David Mair , Senior Civil Contingencies Officer, Renfrewshire House, Cotton Street, Paisley PA1 1WB ☎ 0141 618 7403 david.mair@renfrewshire.gsx.gov.uk

Energy Management: Ms Mary Crearie , Director of Development & Housing Services, Renfrewshire House, Cotton Street, Paisley PA1 1JD ☎ 0141 618 6256 🖶 0141 842 5552 mary.crearie@renfrewshire.gov.uk

Environmental / Technical Services: Ms Mary Crearie , Director of Development & Housing Services, Renfrewshire House, Cotton Street, Paisley PA1 1JD ☎ 0141 618 6256 🖶 0141 842 5552 mary.crearie@renfrewshire.gov.uk

Environmental Health: Mrs Shona MacDougall, Director of Community Resources, Renfrewshire House, Cotton Street, Paisley PA1 1BU ☎ 0141 618 7626 🖶 0141 840 3233 shona.i.macdougall@renfrewshire.gov.uk

Estates, Property & Valuation: Mr Frank Hughes , Asset Manager, Renfrewshire House, Cotton Street, Paisley PA1 1UJ ☎ 0141 618 6175 frank.hughes@renfrewshire.gov.uk

European Liaison: Ms Ruth Cooper , Economic Development Manager, Renfrewshire House, Cotton Street, Paisley PA1 1LL ☎ 0141 842 5000 ruth.cooper@renfrewshire.gov.uk

Facilities: Ms Diane Leask , Head of Facilities Management, Renfrewshire House, Cotton Street, Paisley PA1 1UJ ☎ 0141 618 4672 diane.leask@renfrewshire.gov.uk

Finance: Mr Alan Russell , Director - Finance & Resources, Renfrewshire House, Cotton Street, Paisley PA1 1UJ ☎ 0141 618 7363 alan.russell@renfrewshire.gov.uk

Fleet Management: Mr Scott Allan , Head of Amenity Services, Renfrewshire House, Cotton Street, Paisley PA1 1UJ ☎ 0141 618 7932 scott.allan@renfrewshire.gov.uk

Grounds Maintenance: Mrs Shona MacDougall, Director of Community Resources, Renfrewshire House, Cotton Street, Paisley PA1 1BU ☎ 0141 618 7626 🖶 0141 840 3233 shona.i.macdougall@renfrewshire.gov.uk

Health and Safety: Mr David Marshall , Head of HR & Organisational Development, Renfrewshire House, Cotton Street, Paisley PA1 1TS ☎ 0141 618 7359 🖶 0141 848 5420 david.marshall@renfrewshire.gov.uk

Highways: Mr Scott Allan , Head of Amenity Services, Renfrewshire House, Cotton Street, Paisley PA1 1UJ ☎ 0141 618 7932 scott.allan@renfrewshire.gov.uk

Home Energy Conservation: Ms Mary Crearie , Director of Development & Housing Services, Renfrewshire House, Cotton Street, Paisley PA1 1JD ☎ 0141 618 6256 🖶 0141 842 5552 mary.crearie@renfrewshire.gov.uk

Housing: Ms Mary Crearie , Director of Development & Housing Services, Renfrewshire House, Cotton Street, Paisley PA1 1JD ☎ 0141 618 6256 🖶 0141 842 5552 mary.crearie@renfrewshire.gov.uk

Housing Maintenance: Mr Frank Hughes , Asset Manager, Renfrewshire House, Cotton Street, Paisley PA1 1UJ ☎ 0141 618 6175 frank.hughes@renfrewshire.gov.uk

Legal: Mr Ken Graham, Head of Corporate Governance, Renfrewshire House, Cotton Street, Paisley PA1 1TR ☎ 0141 618 7360 🖶 0141 840 3635 ken.graham@renfrewshire.gov.uk

Leisure and Cultural Services: Mrs Joyce McKellar , Chief Executive, Renfrewshire House, Cotton Street, Paisley PA1 1TR ☎ 0141 618 7191 joyce.mckellar@renfrewshire.gsx.gov.uk

Licensing: Mr Ken Graham, Head of Corporate Governance, Renfrewshire House, Cotton Street, Paisley PA1 1TR ☎ 0141 618 7360 🖶 0141 840 3635 ken.graham@renfrewshire.gov.uk

Lifelong Learning: Mr Peter Macleod , Director of Children's Services, Renfrewshire House, Cotton Street, Paisley PA1 1TZ ☎ 0141 842 5167 🖷 0141 842 5144 peter.macleod@renfrewshire.gov.uk

Lighting: Mr Scott Allan , Head of Amenity Services, Renfrewshire House, Cotton Street, Paisley PA1 1UJ ☎ 0141 618 7932 scott.allan@renfrewshire.gov.uk

Member Services: Mr Ken Graham, Head of Corporate Governance, Renfrewshire House, Cotton Street, Paisley PA1 1TR ☎ 0141 618 7360 🖷 0141 840 3635 ken.graham@renfrewshire.gov.uk

Parking: Mr Scott Allan , Head of Amenity Services, Renfrewshire House, Cotton Street, Paisley PA1 1UJ ☎ 0141 618 7932 scott.allan@renfrewshire.gov.uk

Personnel / HR: Mr David Marshall , Head of HR & Organisational Development, Renfrewshire House, Cotton Street, Paisley PA1 1TS ☎ 0141 618 7359 🖷 0141 848 5420 david.marshall@renfrewshire.gov.uk

Planning: Ms Mary Crearie , Director of Development & Housing Services, Renfrewshire House, Cotton Street, Paisley PA1 1JD ☎ 0141 618 6256 🖷 0141 842 5552 mary.crearie@renfrewshire.gov.uk

Procurement: Mr David Amos , Head of Policy & Commissioning, Renfrewshire House, Cotton Street, Paisley PA1 1UJ ☎ 0141 618 4702 david.amos@renfrewshire.gov.uk

Public Libraries: Mrs Joyce McKellar , Chief Executive, Renfrewshire House, Cotton Street, Paisley PA1 1TR ☎ 0141 618 7191 joyce.mckellar@renfrewshire.gsx.gov.uk

Recycling & Waste Minimisation: Mrs Shona MacDougall, Director of Community Resources, Renfrewshire House, Cotton Street, Paisley PA1 1BU ☎ 0141 618 7626 🖷 0141 840 3233 shona.i.macdougall@renfrewshire.gov.uk

Regeneration: Mr Alasdair Morrison , Head of Regeneration, Renfrewshire House, Cotton Street, Paisley PA1 1UJ

Road Safety: Mr Scott Allan , Head of Amenity Services, Renfrewshire House, Cotton Street, Paisley PA1 1UJ ☎ 0141 618 7932 scott.allan@renfrewshire.gov.uk

Social Services: Mr Peter Macleod , Director of Social Work, Renfrewshire House, Cotton Street, Paisley PA1 1TZ ☎ 0141 618 6829 🖷 0141 842 5144 peter.macleod@renfrewshire.gov.uk

Social Services (Adult): Mr David Leese , Chief Officer Designate, Renfrewshire House, Cotton Street, Paisley PA1 1UJ ☎ 0141 618 7648 david.leese@ggc.scot.nhs.uk

Social Services (Children): Mr Peter Macleod , Director of Children's Services, Renfrewshire House, Cotton Street, Paisley PA1 1TZ ☎ 0141 842 5167 🖷 0141 842 5144 peter.macleod@renfrewshire.gov.uk

Staff Training: Mr David Marshall , Head of HR & Organisational Development, Renfrewshire House, Cotton Street, Paisley PA1 1TS ☎ 0141 618 7359 🖷 0141 848 5420 david.marshall@renfrewshire.gov.uk

Street Scene: Mr Scott Allan , Head of Amenity Services, Renfrewshire House, Cotton Street, Paisley PA1 1UJ ☎ 0141 618 7932 scott.allan@renfrewshire.gov.uk

Town Centre: Ms Amanda Moulson , Town Centre's Project Manager, Renfrewshire House, Cotton Street, Paisley PA1 1LL ☎ 0141 618 7857 🖷 0141 842 5833 amanda.moulson@renfrewshire.gov.uk

Traffic Management: Mr Scott Allan , Head of Amenity Services, Renfrewshire House, Cotton Street, Paisley PA1 1UJ ☎ 0141 618 7932 scott.allan@renfrewshire.gov.uk

Transport: Mr Scott Allan , Head of Amenity Services, Renfrewshire House, Cotton Street, Paisley PA1 1UJ ☎ 0141 618 7932 scott.allan@renfrewshire.gov.uk

Transport: Mrs Shona MacDougall, Director of Community Resources, Renfrewshire House, Cotton Street, Paisley PA1 1BU ☎ 0141 618 7626 🖷 0141 840 3233 shona.i.macdougall@renfrewshire.gov.uk

Transport Planner: Mr Scott Allan , Head of Amenity Services, Renfrewshire House, Cotton Street, Paisley PA1 1UJ ☎ 0141 618 7932 scott.allan@renfrewshire.gov.uk

Waste Collection and Disposal: Mrs Shona MacDougall, Director of Community Resources, Renfrewshire House, Cotton Street, Paisley PA1 1BU ☎ 0141 618 7626 🖷 0141 840 3233 shona.i.macdougall@renfrewshire.gov.uk

Waste Management: Mrs Shona MacDougall, Director of Community Resources, Renfrewshire House, Cotton Street, Paisley PA1 1BU ☎ 0141 618 7626 🖷 0141 840 3233 shona.i.macdougall@renfrewshire.gov.uk

COUNCILLORS

***Provost* Hall**, Anne (LAB - Houston, Crosslee and Linwood)
cllr.anne.hall@renfrewshire.gov.uk

Bibby, Derek (LAB - Johnstone North, Kilbarchan and Lochwinnoch)
cllr.derek.bibby@renfrewshire.gov.uk

Brown, Maria (SNP - Bishopton, Bridge of Weir and Langbank)
cllr.maria.brown@renfrewshire.gov.uk

Brown, Bill (LAB - Renfrew North)
cllr.bill.brown@renfrewshire.gov.uk

Caldwell, John (LAB - Johnstone South, Elderslie and Howwood)
cllr.john.caldwell@renfrewshire.gov.uk

Cameron, Lorraine (SNP - Paisley South West)
cllr.lorraine.cameron@renfrewshire.gov.uk

Clark, Stuart (LAB - Houston, Crosslee and Linwood)
cllr.stuart.clark@renfrewshire.gov.uk

Devine, Eddie (LAB - Paisley South)
cllr.eddie.devine@renfrewshire.gov.uk

Devine, Margaret (LAB - Renfrew South and Gallowhill)
cllr.margaret.devine@renfrewshire.gov.uk

Doig, Audrey (SNP - Houston, Crosslee and Linwood)
cllr.audrey.doig@renfrewshire.gov.uk

Doig, Andy (SNP - Johnstone North, Kilbarchan and Lochwinnoch)
cllr.andy.doig@renfrewshire.gov.uk

Gilmour, Christopher (LAB - Johnstone North, Kilbarchan and Lochwinnoch)
cllr.christopher.gilmour@renfrewshire.gov.uk

Glen, Roy (LAB - Paisley South)
cllr.roy.glen@renfrewshire.gov.uk

Grady, Eddie (LAB - Renfrew South and Gallowhill)
cllr.eddie.grady@renfrewshire.gov.uk

Harte, Jim (LAB - Erskine and Inchinnan)
cllr.james.harte@renfrewshire.gov.uk

Henry, Jacqueline (LAB - Paisley South West)
cllr.jacqueline.henry@renfrewshire.gov.uk

Holmes, Michael (LAB - Bishopton, Bridge of Weir and Langbank)
cllr.michael.holmes@renfrewshire.gov.uk

Hood, John (LAB - Johnstone South, Elderslie and Howwood)
cllr.john.hood@renfrewshire.gov.uk

Kelly, Terry (LAB - Paisley North West)
cllr.terry.kelly@renfrewshire.gov.uk

Lawson, Brian (SNP - Paisley East and Ralston)
cllr.brian.lawson@renfrewshire.gov.uk

Mack, Paul (IND - Paisley South)
cllr.paul.mack@renfrewshire.gov.uk

MacLaren, Kenny (SNP - Paisley North West)
cllr.kenny.maclaren@renfrewshire.gov.uk

Maclaren, James (CON - Bishopton, Bridge of Weir and Langbank)
cllr.james.maclaren@renfrewshire.gov.uk

MacLaren, Mags (SNP - Paisley North West)
cllr.mags.maclaren@renfrewshire.gov.uk

Macmillan, Mark (LAB - Paisley South West)
cllr.mark.macmillan@renfrewshire.gov.uk

McCartin, Eileen (LD - Paisley South West)
cllr.eileen.mccartin@renfrewshire.gov.uk

McEwan, Cathy (SNP - Renfrew South and Gallowhill)
cllr.cathy.mcewan@renfrewshire.gov.uk

McGee, Stephen (SNP - Johnstone South, Elderslie and Howwood)
cllr.stephen.mcgee@renfrewshire.gov.uk

McGurk, Marie (SNP - Paisley South)
cllr.marie.mcgurk@renfrewshire.gov.uk

McMillan, Iain (LAB - Johnstone South, Elderslie and Howwood)
cllr.iain.mcmillan@renfrewshire.gov.uk

McQuade, James (SNP - Erskine and Inchinnan)
cllr.james.mcquade@renfrewshire.gov.uk

Mullin, Sam (LAB - Erskine and Inchinnan)
cllr.sam.mullin@renfrewshire.gov.uk

Murrin, Alexander (LAB - Renfrew North)
cllr.alex.murrin@renfrewshire.gov.uk

Mylet, Will (SNP - Paisley East and Ralston)
cllr.will.mylet@renfrewshire.gov.uk

Nicolson, Iain (SNP - Erskine and Inchinnan)
cllr.iain.nicholson@renfrewshire.gov.uk

Noon, Allan (SNP - Houston, Crosslee and Linwood)
cllr.allan.noon@renfrewshire.gov.uk

Perrie, Bill (SNP - Renfrew North)
cllr.bill.perrie@renfrewshire.gov.uk

Sharkey, Jim (LAB - Paisley East and Ralston)
cllr.jim.sharkey@renfrewshire.gov.uk

Sharkey, Maureen (LAB - Paisley East and Ralston)
cllr.maureen.sharkey@renfrewshire.gov.uk

Williams, Thomas (LAB - Paisley North West)
cllr.tommy.williams@renfrewshire.gov.uk

POLITICAL COMPOSITION

LAB: 22, SNP: 15, LD: 1, CON: 1, IND: 1

COMMITTEE CHAIRS

Planning & Property: Mr Terry Kelly

Social Work, Health & Wellbeing: Mr Iain McMillan

Rhondda Cynon Taff W

Rhondda Cynon Taff County Borough Council, The Pavilions, Cambrian Park, Clydach Vale, Tonypandy CF40 2XX
☎ 01443 424000 🖷 01443 424034 🖳 www.rhondda-cynon-taff.gov.uk

FACTS AND FIGURES

Parliamentary Constituencies: Cynon Valley, Pontypridd, Rhondda
EU Constituencies: Wales
Election Frequency: Elections are of whole council

PRINCIPAL OFFICERS

Chief Executive: Mr Chris Bradshaw , Interim Chief Executive, The Pavilions, Cambrian Park, Clydach Vale, Tonypandy CF40 2XX
☎ 01443 424026 🖷 01443 424027
🖰 christopher.d.bradshaw@rctcbc.gov.uk

Senior Management: Mr Gio Isingrini , Group Director - Community & Children's Services, The Pavilions, Cambrian Park, Clydach Vale, Tonypandy CF40 2XX ☎ 01443 424140 🖷 01443 424027 🖰 gio.isingrini@rctcbc.gov.uk

Senior Management: Mr Christopher Lee, Group Director - Corporate & Frontline Services, The Pavilions, Cambrian Park, Clydach Vale, Tonypandy CF40 2XX ☎ 01443 424026 🖷 01443 424027 🖰 christopher.d.lee@rctcbc.gov.uk

Senior Management: Mr Paul Lucas , Director - Legal & Democratic Services, The Pavilions, Cambrian Park, Clydach Vale, Tonypandy CF40 2XX ☎ 01443 424105 🖷 01443 424027
🖰 paul.j.lucas@rctcbc.gov.uk

Senior Management: Mr Tony Wilkins, Director - Human Resources, The Pavilions, Cambrian Park, Clydach Vale, CF40 2XX
☎ 01443 424166 🖷 01443 424025 🖰 tony.wilkins@rctcbc.gov.uk

Architect, Building / Property Services: Mr Colin Atyeo, Director - Corporate Estates, Valleys Innovation Centre, Navigation Park, Abercynon, Mountain Ash CF44 4SN ☎ 01443 744555 🖷 01443 744557 🖰 colin.m.atyeo@rctcbc.gov.uk

Best Value: Mr Paul Griffiths , Service Director - Performance & Improvement, Bronwydd, Porth CF39 9DL ☎ 01443 680609 🖰 d.paul.griffiths@rctcbc.gov.uk

Building Control: Mr Neil Parfitt , Building Control - Business Manager, Sardis House, Sardis Road, Pontypridd CF37 1DU ☎ 01443 494845 🖷 01443 494774 🖰 neil.parfitt@rctcbc.gov.uk

Catering Services: Mrs Anne Bull, Head of Catering Services & Schools Facilities Services, Ty Trevithick, Abercynon, Mountain Ash CF45 4UQ ☎ 01443 744155 🖷 01443 744290 🖰 anne.bull@rctcbc.gov.uk

Children / Youth Services: Mr Andrew Gwynn , Service Director - Children's Services, Unit 3, Ty Pennant, Catherine Street, Pontypridd CF45 4UQ ☎ 01443 495118 🖷 01443 406290 🖰 andrew.v.gwynn@rctcbc.gov.uk

Children / Youth Services: Mr Derek James , Engagement & Participation Team Leader, Ty Trevithick, Abercynon, Mountain Ash CF45 4UQ ☎ 01443 744105 🖷 01443 744039 🖰 derek.james@rctcbc.gov.uk

Civil Registration: Ms Lynda Parry , Superintendent Registrar, Municipal Buildings, Gelliwastad Road, Pontypridd CF37 2DP ☎ 01443 486869 🖷 01443 494040 🖰 lynda.m.parry@rctcbc.gov.uk

PR / Communications: Mr Christian Hanagan , Service Director - Cabinet Office & PR, The Pavilions, Cambrian Park, Clydach Vale, Tonypandy CF40 2XX ☎ 01443 424005 🖷 01443 424004 🖰 christian.sj.hanagan@rctcbc.gov.uk

Community Safety: Mr Andrew Mallin , Community Safety & Partnership Coordinator, Ty Elai, Dinas Isaf Industrial Estate, Williamstown, Tonypandy CF40 1NY ☎ 01443 425640 🖷 01443 425301 🖰 andrew.mallin@rctcbc.gov.uk

Computer Management: Mr Leigh Gripton, Director of Customer Care & ICT, Ty Elai, Dinas Isaf Industrial Estate, Williamstown, Tonypandy CF40 1NY ☎ 01443 444400 🖰 leigh.f.gripton@rctcbc.gov.uk

Computer Management: Mr Tim Jones , Head of ICT, Ty Elai, Dinas Isaf Industrial Estate, Williamstown, Tonypandy CF40 1NY ☎ 01443 444458 🖰 tim.d.jones@rctcbc.gov.uk

Consumer Protection and Trading Standards: Mr Tony O'Leary , Trading Standards Manager, Ty Elai, Dinas Isaf Industrial Estate, Williamstown, Tonypandy CF40 1NY ☎ 01443 445337 🖷 01443 425301 🖰 tonyoleary@rctcbc.gov.uk

Corporate Services: Mr Christopher Lee, Group Director - Corporate & Frontline Services, The Pavilions, Cambrian Park, Clydach Vale, Tonypandy CF40 2XX ☎ 01443 424026 🖷 01443 424027 🖰 christopher.d.lee@rctcbc.gov.uk

Customer Service: Mrs Roseann Edwards , Head of Customer Care, Ty Elai, Dinas Isaf Industrial Estate, Williamstown, Tonypandy CF40 1NY ☎ 01443 444402 🖰 roseann.edwards@rctcbc.gov.uk

Economic Development: Ms Jane Cook, Director of Regeneration & Planning, Floor 5, Unit 3, Ty Pennant, Catherine Street, Pontypridd CF37 2TB ☎ 01443 495161 🖷 01443 407725 🖰 jane.cook@rctcbc.gov.uk

Education: Mrs Esther Thomas , Service Director - Schools & Community, Ty Trevithick, Abercynon, Tonypandy CF45 4UQ ☎ 01443 744009 🖷 01443 744023 🖰 esther.k.thomas@rctcbc.gov.uk

E-Government: Mr Leigh Gripton, Director of Customer Care & ICT, Ty Elai, Dinas Isaf Industrial Esate, Williamstown, Tonypandy CF40 1NY ☎ 01443 444400 🖰 leigh.f.gripton@rctcbc.gov.uk

Electoral Registration: Mr Mark Green , Business Support Manager, Maritime Business Park, Maritime Industrial Estate, Pontypridd CF37 1NY ☎ 01443 490100 🖷 01443 485776 🖰 william.m.green@rctcbc.gov.uk

Emergency Planning: Mr Ian Woodland , Resilience & Sustainability Lead Advisor, Sardis House, Sardis Road, Pontypridd CF37 1DU ☎ 01685 727478 🖰 ian.woodland@rctcbc.gov.uk

Energy Management: Mr Joseph Pearson , Energy Compliance Officer, Valleys Innovation Centre, Navigation Park, Abercynon, Mountain Ash CF37 1DU ☎ 01443 744416 🖷 01443 744466 🖰 joseph.s.pearson@rctcbc.gov.uk

Environmental Health: Mr Clive Osmond , Senior Environmental Health Officer, Ty Elai, Dina Isaf Industrial Estate, Williamstown, Tonypandy CF40 1NY ☎ 01443 425380 🖷 01443 425301 🖰 clive.g.osmond@rctcbc.gov.uk

Estates, Property & Valuation: Mr Colin Atyeo, Director - Corporate Estates, Valleys Innovation Centre, Navigation Park, Abercynon, Mountain Ash CF45 4SN ☎ 01443 744555 🖷 01443 744557 🖰 colin.m.atyeo@rctcbc.gov.uk

Events Manager: Mr Ian Christopher , Strategic Manager, The Pavilions, Cambrian Park, Clydach Vale, Tonypandy CF40 2XX ☎ 0143 424017 🖰 ian.christopher@rctcbc.gov.uk

Facilities: Ms Jackie Jones , Facilities Cleaning Manager, Ty Glantaf, Unit B23, Taff Falls Road, Treforest Industrial Estate, Pontypridd CF37 5TT ☎ 01443 827705 🖷 01443 844310 🖰 jackie.m.jones@rctcbc.gov.uk

Finance: Mr Barrie Davies , Director - Financial Services, Bronwydd House, Porth CF39 9DL ☎ 01443 680559 🖷 01443 680504 🖰 barrie.j.davies@rctcbc.gov.uk

Pensions: Mr Ian Traylor , Head of Service - Payroll, Pensions & Payments, Bronwydd House, Porth CF39 9DL ☎ 01443 680591 🖷 01443 680717 🖰 ian.f.taylor@rctcbc.gov.uk

Fleet Management: Mrs Julie Waites, Fleet Manager, Ty Glantaf, Unit B23, Taff Falls Road, Treforest Industrial Estate, Pontypridd CF37 5TT ☎ 01443 827730 🖷 01443 827760 🖰 julie.y.waites@rctcbc.gov.uk

Health and Safety: Mr Mike Murphy , Health & Safety Advisor, Ty Elai, Dinas Isaf Industrial Estate, Williamstown, Tonypandy CF40 1NY ☎ 01443 425536 🖷 01443 444534 ✉ mike.murphy@rctcbc.gov.uk

Highways: Mr Roger Waters , Service Director - Highways & Streetcare, Sardis House, Sardis Road, Pontypridd CF37 1DU ☎ 01443 494702 🖷 01443 491414 ✉ roger.j.waters@rctcbc.gov.uk

Housing: Mr Phillip Howells , Head of Community Housing Services, Ty Elai, Dinas Isaf Industrial Estate, Williamstown, Tonypandy CF40 1NY ☎ 01443 425746 ✉ phillip.howells@rctcbc.gov.uk

Local Area Agreement: Mr Simon Gale , Service Director Planning, Sardis House, Sardis Road, Pontypridd CF37 1DU ☎ 01443 494716 🖷 01443 494799 ✉ simon.gale@rctcbc.gov.uk

Legal: Mr Paul Lucas , Director - Legal & Democratic Services, The Pavilions, Cambrian Park, Clydach Vale, Tonypandy CF40 2XX ☎ 01443 424105 🖷 01443 424027 ✉ paul.j.lucas@rctcbc.gov.uk

Leisure and Cultural Services: Mr Dave Batten, Head of Leisure, Parks & Countryside, Ty Elai, Dinas Isaf Industrial Estate, Williamstown, Tonypandy CF40 1NY ☎ 01443 425592 🖷 01443 425080 ✉ david.c.batten@rctcbc.gov.uk

Leisure and Cultural Services: Mrs Strinda Davies , Head of Arts Service, Rhondda Heritage Park, Lewis Merthyr Colliery, Coed Cae Road, Trehafod, Mountain Ash CF37 7NP ☎ 01443 682036 ✉ strinda.p.davies@rctcbc.gov.uk

Licensing: Mrs Meryl Williams , Licensing Manager, Ty Elai, Dinas Isaf Industrial Estate, Williamstown, Tonypandy CF40 1NY ☎ 01443 425361 🖷 01443 425301 ✉ meryl.d.williams@rctcbc.gov.uk

Lifelong Learning: Mrs Esther Thomas , Service Director - Schools & Community, Ty Trevithick, Abercynon, Tonypandy CF45 4UQ ☎ 01443 744009 🖷 01443 744023 ✉ esther.k.thomas@rctcbc.gov.uk

Lighting: Mr Mark Anderson , Senior Engineer - Street Lighting, Sardis House, Sardis Road, Pontypridd CF37 1DU ☎ 01443 494792 ✉ mark.anderson@rctcbc.gov.uk

Lottery Funding, Charity and Voluntary: Mr Peter Mortimer, Regeneration & Resources Manager, Level 5, Unit 3, Ty Pennant, Catherine Street, Pontypridd CF37 2TB ☎ 01443 490407 🖷 01443 407725 ✉ peter.j.mortimer@rctcbc.gov.uk

Member Services: Mrs Karyl May , Democratic Services Manager, The Pavilions, Cambrian Park, Clydach Vale, Tonypandy CF40 2XX ☎ 01443 424045 🖷 01443 424115 ✉ karyl.may@rctcbc.gov.uk

Parking: Mr Alistair Critchlow , Parking Services & Streetworks Manager, Sardis House, Sardis Road, Pontypridd CF37 1DU ☎ 01443 494751 🖷 01443 494778 ✉ alistair.critchlow@rctcbc.gov.uk

Personnel / HR: Mr Tony Wilkins, Director - Human Resources, The Pavilions, Cambrian Park, Clydach Vale, CF40 2XX ☎ 01443 424166 🖷 01443 424025 ✉ tony.wilkins@rctcbc.gov.uk

Planning: Mr Simon Gale , Service Director Planning, Sardis House, Sardis Road, Pontypridd CF37 1DU ☎ 01443 494716 🖷 01443 494799 ✉ simon.gale@rctcbc.gov.uk

Procurement: Mr Vince Hanly, Service Director Procurement, Bronwydd, Porth CF39 9DL ☎ 01443 680538 🖷 01443 680787 ✉ vince.hanly@rctcbc.gov.uk

Public Libraries: Mrs Wendy Edwards , Head of Community Learning, Ty Trevithick, Abercynon, Mountain Ash CF45 4UQ ☎ 01443 744111 ✉ wendy.edwards@rctcbc.gov.uk

Recycling & Waste Minimisation: Mr Nigel Wheeler, Service Director of Street Care, Ty Glantaf, Unit B23, Taff Falls Road, Treforest Industrial Estate, Pontypridd CF37 5TT ☎ 01443 827707 🖷 01443 827730 ✉ nigel.wheeler@rctcbc.gov.uk

Regeneration: Ms Jane Cook, Director of Regeneration & Planning, Floor 5, Unit 3, Ty Pennant, Catherine Street, Pontypridd CF37 2TB ☎ 01443 495161 🖷 01443 407725 ✉ jane.cook@rctcbc.gov.uk

Road Safety: Ms Jessica White , Road Safety Manager, Sardis House, Sardis Road, Pontypridd CF37 1DU ☎ 01443 494785 ✉ jessica.j.white@rctcbc.gov.uk

Social Services: Mr Gio Isingrini , Group Director - Community & Children's Services, The Pavilions, Cambrian Park, Clydach Vale, Tonypandy CF40 2XX ☎ 01443 424140 🖷 01443 424027 ✉ gio.isingrini@rctcbc.gov.uk

Social Services (Adult): Mr Bob Gatis, Service Director - Adult Locality & Short Term Intervention, Ty Elai, Dinas Isaf Industrial Estate, Williamstown, Tonypandy CF40 1NY ☎ 01443 425401 🖷 01443 425440 ✉ robert.e.gatis@rctcbc.gov.uk

Social Services (Children): Mr Andrew Gwynn , Service Director - Children's Services, Unit 3, Ty Pennant, Catherine Street, Pontypridd CF45 4UQ ☎ 01443 495118 🖷 01443 406290 ✉ andrew.v.gwynn@rctcbc.gov.uk

Staff Training: Ms Deborah Hughes , Head of Organisational Development, The Pavilions, Cambrian Park, Clydach Vale, Tonypandy CF40 2XX ☎ 01443 424103 🖷 01443 424025 ✉ deborah.hughes@rctcbc.gov.uk

Street Scene: Mr Steve Owen , Head of Street Care, Ty Glantaf, Unit B23, Taff Falls Road, Treforest Industrial Estate, Pontypridd CF37 5TT ☎ 01443 827702 🖷 01143 827730 ✉ steve.owen@rctcbc.gov.uk

Sustainable Development: Mr Ian Woodland , Resilience & Sustainability Lead Advisor, Sardis House, Sardis Road, Pontypridd CF37 1DU ☎ 01685 727478 ✉ ian.woodland@rctcbc.gov.uk

Tourism: Ms Luan Oestrich , Tourism Manager, The Pavilions, Cambrian Park, Clydach Vale, Tonypandy CF40 2XX ☎ 01443 424009 🖷 01443 425553 ✉ luan.oestrich@rctcbc.gov.uk

Town Centre: Mr Adrian Evans , Town Centre Strategy Manager, Floor 5, Unit 3, Ty Pennant, Catherine Street, Pontypridd CF32 2TB ☎ 01443 490409 🖷 01443 407725 ✉ adrian.evans@rctcbc.gov.uk

RHONDDA CYNON TAFF

Transport: Mr Charlie Nelson , Transportation Manager, Sardis House, Sardis Road, Pontypridd CF37 1DU ☎ 01443 494818 🖷 01443 494875 ✉ charlie.e.nelson@rctcbc.gov.uk

Transport Planner: Mr Adrian Morgan , Strategic Transport Planner, Sardis House, Sardis Road, Pontypridd CF37 1DU ☎ 01443 494714 ✉ adrian.c.morgan@rctcbc.gov.uk

Waste Collection and Disposal: Ms Lynette Beddow , Trade Waste & Recycling Officer, Ty Glantaf, Unti B23, Taff Falls Road, Treforest Industrial Estate, Pontypridd CF37 5TT ☎ 01443 827721 🖷 01443 827730 ✉ lynette.beddow@rctcbc.gov.uk

Waste Management: Ms Nicola Jones , Waste Services Officer, Ty Glantaf, Unit B23, Taff Falls Road, Treforest Industrial Estate, Pontypridd CF37 5TT ☎ 01443 827720 🖷 01443 827730 ✉ nicola.jones@rctcbc.gov.uk

Children's Play Areas: Ms Lisa Austin , Play & Recreation Facilities Manager, Unit H3/H4, Coed Cae Lane Industrial Estate, Pontyclun CF72 9HG ☎ 01443 233967 ✉ lisa.austin@rctcbc.gov.uk

COUNCILLORS

***Leader of the Council* Morgan**, Andrew (LAB - Mountain Ash West)
andrew.morgan2@rhondda-cynon-taff.gov.uk

***Deputy Leader of the Council* Montague**, Keiron (LAB - Maerdy)

Adams, Mark (LAB - Tylorstown)
lewis.m.adams@rhondda-cynon-taff.gov.uk

Baccara, Paul (IND - Talbot Green)
paul.baccara@rhondda-cynon-taff.gov.uk

Bates, Teressa (LAB - Hawthorn)
teressa.a.bates@rhondda-cynon-taff.gov.uk

Bevan, Robert (LAB - Tylorstown)
robert.bevan@rhondda-cynon-taff.gov.uk

Boggis, Helen (LAB - Penywaun)
Helen.Boggis@rhondda-cynon-taff.gov.uk

Bonetto, Jill (LAB - Taffs Well)
Jill.Bonetto@rhondda-cynon-taff.gov.uk

Bradwick, Steven (LAB - Aberdare East)
steven.a.bradwick@rhondda-cynon-taff.gov.uk

Bunnage, Jacqui (LAB - Llantwit Fardre)
Jacqui.Bunnage@rhondda-cynon-taff.gov.uk

Calvert, Anita (LAB - Aberaman South)
Anita.Calvert@rhondda-cynon-taff.gov.uk

Cannon, Paul (LAB - Ystrad)
paul.cannon@rhondda-cynon-taff.gov.uk

Carter, Steve Laurence (LAB - Pontypridd Town)

Cass, Joyce (LAB - Graig)
joyce.cass@rhondda-cynon-taff.gov.uk

Crimmings, Ann (LAB - Aberdare West with Llwydcoed)
ann.crimmings@rhondda-cynon-taff.gov.uk

David, John (LAB - Tonteg)
john.david@rhondda-cynon-taff.gov.uk

Davies, Annette (LAB - Ferndale)
annette.davies@rhondda-cynon-taff.gov.uk

Davies, Albert (LAB - Abercynon)
alby.davies@rhondda-cynon-taff.gov.uk

Davies, Cennard (PC - Treorchy)

Davies, Geraint (PC - Treherbert)
geraint.r.davies@btconnect.com

Davies, Margaret (LAB - Porth)
margaret.davies2@rhondda-cynon-taff.gov.uk

Davies, John (LAB - Aberdare West with Llwydcoed)
John.Davies2@rhondda-cynon-taff.gov.uk

De Vet, Linda (LAB - Aberaman North)
linda.devet@rhondda-cynon-taff.gov.uk

Elliott, Jeffrey (LAB - Cwmbach)
Jeffrey.Elliott@rhondda-cynon-taff.gov.uk

Evans, Sheryl (LAB - Aberaman North)
sheryl.m.evans@rctcbc.gov.uk

Evans-Fear, Sera (PC - Treorchy)
treorci@yahoo.com

Forey, Michael (LAB - Aberdare East)
mike.forey@rhondda-cynon-taff.gov.uk

Fox, Adam (LAB - Penrhiwceiber)
adam.s.fox@rhondda-cynon-taff.gov.uk

Griffiths, Margaret (LAB - Pontyclun)
Margaret.Griffiths@rhondda-cynon-taff.gov.uk

Griffiths, Paul (LAB - Pontyclun)
Paul.Griffiths@rhondda-cynon-taff.gov.uk

Hanagan, Eudine (LAB - Tonyrefail West)

Holmes, Glynne (LAB - Llantrisant Town)
glynne.holmes@rhondda-cynon-taff.gov.uk

Hopkins, Geraint (LAB - Llanharan)
geraint.e.hopkins@rhondda-cynon-taff.gov.uk

Howe, Philip (IND - Ferndale)
Philip.Howe@rhondda-cynon-taff.gov.uk

James, Joel (CON - Llantwit Fardre)
joel.s.james@rhondda-cynon-taff.gov.uk

Jarman, Pauline (PC - Mountain Ash East)

Jones, Sylvia (LAB - Llwynpia)
sylvia.j.jones@rhondda-cynon-taff.gov.uk

Langford, Lionel (LAB - Ynyshir)
lionel.langford@rhondda-cynon-taff.gov.uk

Lewis, Rhys (LAB - Abercynon)
Rhys.Lewis@rhondda-cynon-taff.gov.uk

Leyshon, Christina (LAB - Rhondda)
christina.leyshon@rhondda-cynon-taff.gov.uk

Lloyd, Simon (LAB - Mountain Ash West)
simon.lloyd@rhondda-cynon-taff.gov.uk

McDonald, Robert (LAB - Tonyrefail East)
robert.mcdonald@rhondda-cynon-taff.gov.uk

Middle, Craig (LAB - Tonypandy)
craig.j.middle@rhondda-cynon-taff.gov.uk

Morgan, Karen (PC - Hirwaun)
karen.morgan2@rhondda-cynon-taff.gov.uk

Morgan, Barrie (LAB - Cilfynydd)
barrie.j.morgan@rhondda-cynon-taff.gov.uk

Norris, Mark (LAB - Cwm Clydach)
mark.a.norris@rhondda-cynon-taff.gov.uk

Pearce, Irene Elizabeth (PC - Treherbert)
Irene.E.Pearce@rhondda-cynon-taff.gov.uk

Pickering, Sue (LAB - Ynysybwl)
Sue.Pickering@rhondda-cynon-taff.gov.uk

Powderhill, Steve (LAB - Treforest)
Steve.Powderhill@rhondda-cynon-taff.gov.uk

Powell, Michael (LD - Trallwng)
michael.j.powell@rhondda-cynon-taff.gov.uk

Privett, Kenneth (LAB - Penygraig)

Rees, Sharon (LAB - Aberdare West with Llwydcoed)
Sharon.Rees2@rhondda-cynon-taff.gov.uk

Rees-Owen, Shelley (PC - Pentre)
Shelley.Rees-Owen@rhondda-cynon-taff.gov.uk

Roberts, Aurfron (LAB - Gilfach Goch)
aurfron.roberts@rhondda-cynon-taff.gov.uk

Rosser, Joy (LAB - Trealaw)

Smith, Graham (LAB - Porth)
Graham.Smith@rhondda-cynon-taff.gov.uk

Smith, Robert (LAB - Rhondda)
robert.w.smith@rhondda-cynon-taff.gov.uk

Stacey, Graham (LAB - Church Village)
graham.stacey@rhondda-cynon-taff.gov.uk

Stephens, Barry (LAB - Llanharry)
Barry.Stephens2@rhondda-cynon-taff.gov.uk

Tegg, Margaret (LAB - Cymmer)
margaret.tegg@rhondda-cynon-taff.gov.uk

Thomas, Graham (LAB - Rhigos)
Graham.P.Thomas@rhondda-cynon-taff.gov.uk

Turner, Roger (LAB - Brynna)
roger.k.turner@rhondda-cynon-taff.gov.uk

Walker, Lyndon (IND - Tonteg)
Lyndon.Walker@rhondda-cynon-taff.gov.uk

Ward, Jane (LAB - Penrhiwceiber)
jane.ward@rhondda-cynon-taff.gov.uk

Wasley, Paul (IND - Tonyrefail East)
Paul.Wasley@rhondda-cynon-taff.gov.uk

Watts, John (LAB - Ystrad)
malcolm.j.watts@rhondda-cynon-taff.gov.uk

Weaver, Maureen (PC - Pentre)
Maureenowen54@gmail.com

Webber, Maureen (LAB - Rhydfelin Central)
maureen.webber@rhondda-cynon-taff.gov.uk

Webster, Emyr John (PC - Treorchy)
Emry.J.Webster@rhondda-cynon-taff.gov.uk

Weeks, Dennis (LAB - Penygraig)
william.d.weeks@rhondda-cynon-taff.gov.uk

Williams, Doug (LAB - Glyncoch)
doug.williams@rhondda-cynon-taff.gov.uk

Williams, Christopher (LAB - Cymmer)
christopher.j.williams3@rhondda-cynon-taff.gov.uk

Williams, Tina (LAB - Aberaman South)
Tina.Williams@rhondda-cynon-taff.gov.uk

Willis, Clayton (LAB - Tyn-y-Nant)
clayton.j.willis@rhondda-cynon-taff.gov.uk

Yeo, Richard (LAB - Beddau)
Richard.Yeo@rhondda-cynon-taff.gov.uk

POLITICAL COMPOSITION
LAB: 60, PC: 9, IND: 4, CON: 1, LD: 1

COMMITTEE CHAIRS
Children & Young People: Ms Christina Leyshon

Development Control: Mr Graham Stacey

Education & Lifelong Learning: Ms Christina Leyshon

Health & Wellbeing: Mr Robert Smith

Licensing: Mr Adam Fox

Ribble Valley D

Ribble Valley Borough Council, Council Offices, Church Walk, Clitheroe BB7 2RA
☎ 01200 425111 🖷 01200 414488 ✉ contact@ribblevalley.gov.uk
💻 www.ribblevalley.gov.uk

FACTS AND FIGURES
Parliamentary Constituencies: Ribble Valley
EU Constituencies: North West
Election Frequency: Elections are of whole council

PRINCIPAL OFFICERS
Chief Executive: Mr Marshal Scott , Chief Executive, Council Offices, Church Walk, Clitheroe BB7 2RA ☎ 01200 425111 🖷 01200 414488

Senior Management: Mr John Heap, Director of Community Services, Council Offices, Church Walk, Clitheroe BB7 2RA ☎ 01200 425111 🖷 01200 414488 ✉ john.heap@ribblevalley.gov.uk

Senior Management: Ms Jane Pearson , Director - Resources, Council Offices, Church Walk, Clitheroe BB7 2RA ☎ 01200 425111 ✉ jane.pearson@ribblevalley.gov.uk

Architect, Building / Property Services: Mr Adrian Harper , Head of Engineering, Council Offices, Church Walk, Clitheroe BB7 2RA ☎ 01200 425111 ✉ adrian.harper@ribblevalley.gov.uk

Architect, Building / Property Services: Mr Tim Lynas , Principal Surveyor, Council Offices, Church Walk, Clitheroe BB7 2RA ☎ 01200 425111 ✉ tim.lynas@ribblevalley.gov.uk

Best Value: Ms Jane Pearson , Director - Resources, Council Offices, Church Walk, Clitheroe BB7 2RA ☎ 01200 425111 ✉ jane.pearson@ribblevalley.gov.uk

Building Control: Mr James Russell , Head of Environmental Health, Council Offices, Church Walk, Clitheroe BB7 2RA ☎ 01200 425111 🖷 01200 414488 ✉ james.russell@ribblevalley.gov.uk

RIBBLE VALLEY

PR / Communications: Ms Theresa Sanderson, Corporate Communications Officer, Council Offices, Church Walk, Clitheroe BB7 2RA ☎ 01200 425111 🖷 01200 414488 ✉ theresa.sanderson@ribblevalley.gov.uk

PR / Communications: Mrs Michelle Smith, Head of HR, Council Offices, Church Walk, Clitheroe BB7 2RA ☎ 01200 425111 🖷 01200 414488 ✉ michelle.smith@ribblevalley.gov.uk

Community Planning: Mr Colin Hirst, Head of Regeneration & Housing, Council Offices, Church Walk, Clitheroe BB7 2RA ☎ 01200 425111 🖷 01200 414487 ✉ colin.hirst@ribblevalley.gov.uk

Computer Management: Mr Stuart Haworth , ICT Manager, Council Offices, Church Walk, Clitheroe BB7 2RA ☎ 01200 425111

Consumer Protection and Trading Standards: Mr James Russell , Head of Environmental Health, Council Offices, Church Walk, Clitheroe BB7 2RA ☎ 01200 425111 🖷 01200 414488 ✉ james.russell@ribblevalley.gov.uk

Contracts: Mr Adrian Harper , Head of Engineering, Council Offices, Church Walk, Clitheroe BB7 2RA ☎ 01200 425111 ✉ adrian.harper@ribblevalley.gov.uk

Contracts: Mr John Heap, Director of Community Services, Council Offices, Church Walk, Clitheroe BB7 2RA ☎ 01200 425111 🖷 01200 414488 ✉ john.heap@ribblevalley.gov.uk

Customer Service: Ms Toni Bates , Customer Services Supporter, Council Offices, Church Walk, Clitheroe BB7 2RA ☎ 01200 425111 ✉ toni.bates@ribblevalley.gov.uk

Direct Labour: Mr Adrian Harper , Head of Engineering, Council Offices, Church Walk, Clitheroe BB7 2RA ☎ 01200 425111 ✉ adrian.harper@ribblevalley.gov.uk

Electoral Registration: Mrs Diane Rice, Head of Legal & Democratic Services, Council Offices, Church Walk, Clitheroe BB7 2RA ☎ 01200 425111 🖷 01200 414488 ✉ diane.rice@ribblevalley.gov.uk

Emergency Planning: Mr Chris Shuttleworth, Building Control Surveyor, Council Offices, Church Walk, Clitheroe BB7 2RA ☎ 01200 425111 🖷 01200 414488 ✉ chris.shuttleworth@ribblevalley.gov.uk

Energy Management: Mr Tim Lynas , Principal Surveyor, Council Offices, Church Walk, Clitheroe BB7 2RA ☎ 01200 425111 ✉ tim.lynas@ribblevalley.gov.uk

Environmental Health: Mr James Russell , Head of Environmental Health, Council Offices, Church Walk, Clitheroe BB7 2RA ☎ 01200 425111 🖷 01200 414488 ✉ james.russell@ribblevalley.gov.uk

Events Manager: Mr Tom Pridmore , Tourism & Events Officer, Council Offices, Church Walk, Clitheroe BB7 2RA ☎ 01200 425111 ✉ tom.pridmore@ribblevalley.gov.uk

Finance: Mr Lawson Oddie , Head of Financial Services, Council Offices, Church Walk, Clitheroe BB7 2RA ☎ 01200 425111 ✉ lawson.oddie.ribblevalley.gov.uk

Finance: Ms Jane Pearson , Director - Resources, Council Offices, Church Walk, Clitheroe BB7 2RA ☎ 01200 425111 ✉ jane.pearson@ribblevalley.gov.uk

Grounds Maintenance: Mr Alan Boyer, Amenity Cleansing Manager, Council Offices, Church Walk, Clitheroe BB7 2RA ☎ 01200 425111 🖷 01200 414488 ✉ alan.boyer@ribblevalley.gov.uk

Health and Safety: Mr Phil Dodd, Health & Safety Officer, Council Offices, Church Walk, Clitheroe BB7 2RA ☎ 01200 425111 🖷 01200 414488 ✉ phil.dodd@ribblevalley.gov.uk

Health and Safety: Mrs Michelle Smith, Head of HR, Council Offices, Church Walk, Clitheroe BB7 2RA ☎ 01200 425111 🖷 01200 414488 ✉ michelle.smith@ribblevalley.gov.uk

Housing: Mr Colin Hirst, Head of Regeneration & Housing, Council Offices, Church Walk, Clitheroe BB7 2RA ☎ 01200 425111 🖷 01200 414487 ✉ colin.hirst@ribblevalley.gov.uk

Housing Maintenance: Ms Rachael Stott , Housing Strategy Officer, Council Offices, Church Walk, Clitheroe BB7 2RA ☎ 01200 425111 ✉ rachael.stott@ribblevalley.gov.uk

Local Area Agreement: Mr Colin Hirst, Head of Regeneration & Housing, Council Offices, Church Walk, Clitheroe BB7 2RA ☎ 01200 425111 🖷 01200 414487 ✉ colin.hirst@ribblevalley.gov.uk

Legal: Mrs Diane Rice, Head of Legal & Democratic Services, Council Offices, Church Walk, Clitheroe BB7 2RA ☎ 01200 425111 🖷 01200 414488 ✉ diane.rice@ribblevalley.gov.uk

Leisure and Cultural Services: Mr Mark Beveridge , Head of Cultural & Leisure Services, Council Offices, Church Walk, Clitheroe BB7 2RA ☎ 01200 425111 🖷 01200 414488 ✉ mark.beveridge@ribblevalley.gov.uk

Licensing: Mrs Diane Rice, Head of Legal & Democratic Services, Council Offices, Church Walk, Clitheroe BB7 2RA ☎ 01200 425111 🖷 01200 414488 ✉ diane.rice@ribblevalley.gov.uk

Lifelong Learning: Mrs Michelle Smith, Head of HR, Council Offices, Church Walk, Clitheroe BB7 2RA ☎ 01200 425111 🖷 01200 414488 ✉ michelle.smith@ribblevalley.gov.uk

Lottery Funding, Charity and Voluntary: Mr Mark Beveridge , Head of Cultural & Leisure Services, Council Offices, Church Walk, Clitheroe BB7 2RA ☎ 01200 425111 🖷 01200 414488 ✉ mark.beveridge@ribblevalley.gov.uk

Member Services: Mrs Diane Rice, Head of Legal & Democratic Services, Council Offices, Church Walk, Clitheroe BB7 2RA ☎ 01200 425111 🖷 01200 414488 ✉ diane.rice@ribblevalley.gov.uk

Personnel / HR: Mrs Michelle Smith, Head of HR, Council Offices, Church Walk, Clitheroe BB7 2RA ☎ 01200 425111 🖷 01200 414488 ✉ michelle.smith@ribblevalley.gov.uk

Planning: Mr John Macholc , Head of Planning Services, Ribble Valley Borough Council, Church Walk, Clitheroe BB7 2RA ☎ 01200 425111 🖷 01200 414488 ✉ john.macholc@ribblevalley.gov.uk

Procurement: Ms Jane Pearson , Director - Resources, Council Offices, Church Walk, Clitheroe BB7 2RA ☎ 01200 425111 ✉ jane.pearson@ribblevalley.gov.uk

Recycling & Waste Minimisation: Mr Adrian Harper , Head of Engineering, Council Offices, Church Walk, Clitheroe BB7 2RA ☎ 01200 425111 ✉ adrian.harper@ribblevalley.gov.uk

Recycling & Waste Minimisation: Mr John Heap, Director of Community Services, Council Offices, Church Walk, Clitheroe BB7 2RA ☎ 01200 425111 🖷 01200 414488 ✉ john.heap@ribblevalley.gov.uk

Recycling & Waste Minimisation: Mr Peter McGeorge, Waste Management Officer, Council Offices, Church Walk, Clitheroe BB7 2RA ☎ 01200 425111 🖷 01200 414488 ✉ peter.mcgeorge@ribblevalley.gov.uk

Regeneration: Mr Colin Hirst, Head of Regeneration & Housing, Council Offices, Church Walk, Clitheroe BB7 2RA ☎ 01200 425111 🖷 01200 414487 ✉ colin.hirst@ribblevalley.gov.uk

Staff Training: Mrs Michelle Smith, Head of HR, Council Offices, Church Walk, Clitheroe BB7 2RA ☎ 01200 425111 🖷 01200 414488 ✉ michelle.smith@ribblevalley.gov.uk

Street Scene: Mr Adrian Harper , Head of Engineering, Council Offices, Church Walk, Clitheroe BB7 2RA ☎ 01200 425111 ✉ adrian.harper@ribblevalley.gov.uk

Sustainable Communities: Mr Colin Hirst, Head of Regeneration & Housing, Council Offices, Church Walk, Clitheroe BB7 2RA ☎ 01200 425111 🖷 01200 414487 ✉ colin.hirst@ribblevalley.gov.uk

Tourism: Mr Mark Beveridge , Head of Cultural & Leisure Services, Council Offices, Church Walk, Clitheroe BB7 2RA ☎ 01200 425111 🖷 01200 414488 ✉ mark.beveridge@ribblevalley.gov.uk

Tourism: Mr Tom Pridmore , Tourism & Events Officer, Council Offices, Church Walk, Clitheroe BB7 2RA ☎ 01200 425111 ✉ tom.pridmore@ribblevalley.gov.uk

Waste Collection and Disposal: Mr Adrian Harper , Head of Engineering, Council Offices, Church Walk, Clitheroe BB7 2RA ☎ 01200 425111 ✉ adrian.harper@ribblevalley.gov.uk

Waste Collection and Disposal: Mr John Heap, Director of Community Services, Council Offices, Church Walk, Clitheroe BB7 2RA ☎ 01200 425111 🖷 01200 414488 ✉ john.heap@ribblevalley.gov.uk

Waste Management: Mr Adrian Harper , Head of Engineering, Council Offices, Church Walk, Clitheroe BB7 2RA ☎ 01200 425111 ✉ adrian.harper@ribblevalley.gov.uk

Waste Management: Mr John Heap, Director of Community Services, Council Offices, Church Walk, Clitheroe BB7 2RA ☎ 01200 425111 🖷 01200 414488 ✉ john.heap@ribblevalley.gov.uk

Waste Management: Mr Peter McGeorge, Waste Management Officer, Council Offices, Church Walk, Clitheroe BB7 2RA ☎ 01200 425111 🖷 01200 414488 ✉ peter.mcgeorge@ribblevalley.gov.uk

Children's Play Areas: Mr Adrian Harper , Head of Engineering, Council Offices, Church Walk, Clitheroe BB7 2RA ☎ 01200 425111 ✉ adrian.harper@ribblevalley.gov.uk

COUNCILLORS

***Mayor* Hilton**, Bridget (CON - Waddington and West Bradford) cllr.hilton@ribblevalley.gov.uk

***Leader of the Council* Hirst**, Stuart (CON - Wilpshire) cllr.hirst@ribblevalley.gov.uk

Ainsworth, Peter (CON - Clayton-le-Dale with Ramsgreave) cllr.ainsworth@ribblevalley.gov.uk

Alcock, Janet (CON - Aighton, Bailey and Chaigley)

Atkinson, Stephen (CON - Billington and Old Langho) cllr.atkinson@ribblevalley.gov.uk

Bennett, Richard (CON - Read and Simonstone) cllr.bennett@ribblevalley.gov.uk

Bibby, Susan (CON - Wilpshire) cllr.bibby@ribblevalley.gov.uk

Brown, Alison (CON - Langho) cllr.abrown@ribblevalley.gov.uk

Brown, Ian (CON - Salthill) cllr.brown@ribblevalley.gov.uk

Brunskill, Stella (CON - Mellor) cllr.brunskill@ribblevalley.gov.uk

Carefoot, Stuart (CON - Derby and Thornley) cllr.carefoot@ribblevalley.gov.uk

Dobson, Paula (CON - Langho) cllr.dobson@ribblevalley.gov.uk

Dowson, Pamela (CON - Salthill) cllr.dowson@ribblevalley.gov.uk

Elms, Rosemary (CON - Bowland, Newton and Slaidburn) cllr.elms@ribblevalley.gov.uk

Elms, Paul (CON - Waddington and West Bradford) cllr.pelms@ribblevalley.gov.uk

Fenton, Maureen (LAB - Edisford and Low Moor) cllr.fenton@ribblevalley.gov.uk

French, Mark (LD - Littlemoor) cllr.french@ribblevalley.gov.uk

Geldard, Graham (CON - St Marys) cllr.geldard@ribblevalley.gov.uk

Graves, Lesley (CON - Read and Simonstone) cllr.graves@ribblevalley.gov.uk

Hargreaves, Ruth (LD - St Marys) cllr.hargreaves@ribblevalley.gov.uk

Hill, Terry (CON - Whalley) cllr.thill@ribblevalley.gov.uk

Hind, Sue (CON - Edisford and Low Moor) cllr.shind@ribblevalley.gov.uk

Hind, Ken (CON - Dilworth) cllr.hind@ribblevalley.gov.uk

RIBBLE VALLEY

Holgate, Joyce (CON - Whalley)
cllr.holgate@ribblevalley.gov.uk

Hore, Simon (CON - Chipping)
cllr.hore@ribblevalley.gov.uk

Knox, Susan (LD - Littlemoor)
cllr.sknox@ribblevalley.gov.uk

Knox, Allan (LD - Primrose)
cllr.knox@ribblevalley.gov.uk

Mirfin, Ged (CON - Billington and Old Langho)
cllr.mirfin@ribblevalley.gov.uk

Newmark, Richard (CON - Sabden)
cllr.newmark@ribblevalley.gov.uk

Robinson, Mary (LD - Primrose)
cllr.robinson@ribblevalley.gov.uk

Rogerson, James (IND - Alston and Hothersall)
cllr.rogerson@ribblevalley.gov.uk

Sayers, Ian (CON - Ribchester)
cllr.sayers@ribblevalley.gov.uk

Scott, Gary (CON - Chatburn)
cllr.scott@ribblevalley.gov.uk

Sherras, Richard (CON - Gisburn and Rimington)
cllr.sherras@ribblevalley.gov.uk

Smith, David (CON - Alston and Hothersall)
cllr.smith@ribblevalley.gov.uk

Swarbrick, Rupert (CON - Dilworth)
cllr.swarbrick@ribblevalley.gov.uk

Taylor, Doreen (CON - Clayton-le-Dale with Ramsgreave)
cllr.dtaylor@ribblevalley.gov.uk

Thompson, Robert (CON - Wiswell and Pendleton)
cllr.thompson@ribblevalley.gov.uk

Walsh, Noel (CON - Mellor)
cllr.walsh@ribblevalley.gov.uk

White, Jim (CON - Derby and Thornley)
cllr.white@ribblevalley.gov.uk

POLITICAL COMPOSITION

CON: 33, LD: 5, IND: 1, LAB: 1

Richmond upon Thames L

Richmond upon Thames London Borough Council, Civic Centre, 44 York Street, Twickenham TW1 3BZ
☎ 020 8891 1411 ✉ press-pr@richmond.gov.uk 🖳 www.richmond.gov.uk

FACTS AND FIGURES

Parliamentary Constituencies: Richmond Park, Twickenham
EU Constituencies: London
Election Frequency: Elections are of whole council

PRINCIPAL OFFICERS

Chief Executive: Ms Gillian Norton, Chief Executive, Civic Centre, 44 York Street, Twickenham TW1 3BZ ☎ 020 8891 1411 🖷 020 8891 7703 ✉ g.norton@richmond.gov.uk

Senior Management: Mr Paul Chadwick, Director of Environment, Civic Centre, 44 York Street, Twickenham TW1 3BZ ☎ 020 8891 7870 🖷 020 8891 7361 ✉ p.chadwick@richmond.gov.uk

Senior Management: Ms Cathy Kerr , Director of Adult & Community Services, Civic Centre, 44 York Street, Twickenham TW1 3BZ ☎ 020 8891 7360 🖷 020 8891 7703 ✉ cathy.kerr@richmond.gov.uk

Senior Management: Mr Mark Maidment, Director of Finance & Corporate Services, Civic Centre, 44 York Street, Twickenham TW1 3BZ ☎ 020 8891 7171 🖷 020 8891 7333 ✉ m.maidment@richmond.gov.uk

Senior Management: Mr Nick Whitfield , Chief Executive Officer - Achieving for Children, Civic Centre, 44 York Street, Twickenham TW1 3BZ ☎ 020 8891 7906 🖷 020 8831 6216 ✉ nick.whitfield@richmond.gov.uk

Senior Management: Dr Dagmar Zeuner , Director - Public Health, Civic Centre, 44 York Street, Twickenham TW1 3BZ ☎ 020 8734 3013 ✉ dagmar.zeuner@richmond.gov.uk

Architect, Building / Property Services: Mr Paul Chadwick, Director of Environment, Civic Centre, 44 York Street, Twickenham TW1 3BZ ☎ 020 8891 7870 🖷 020 8891 7361 ✉ p.chadwick@richmond.gov.uk

Best Value: Ms Gill Ford , Head of Performance & Quality Assurance, Civic Centre, 44 York Street, Twickenham TW1 3BZ ☎ 020 8487 5016 🖷 020 8487 5026 ✉ g.ford@richmond.gov.uk

Building Control: Mr David Batsford, Head of Building Control, 2nd Floor, Civic Centre, 44 York Street, Twickenham TW1 3BZ ☎ 020 8891 7346 🖷 020 8891 7347 ✉ d.batsford@richmond.gov.uk

Children / Youth Services: Ms Alison Twynam , Assistant Director of Social Care - Achieving for Children, Civic Centre, 44 York Street, Twickenham TW1 3BZ ✉ a.twynam@richmond.gov.uk

Civil Registration: Miss Alison Parr , Superintendent Registrar, Register Office, 1 Spring Terrace, Richmond TW9 1LW ☎ 0845 612 2660 🖷 020 8940 8226 ✉ alison.parr@richmond.gov.uk

PR / Communications: Mrs Elinor Firth , Head of Communications, Civic Centre, 44 York Street, Twickenham TW1 3BZ ☎ 020 8487 5159 🖷 020 8891 7718 ✉ e.firth@richmond.gov.uk

PR / Communications: Ms Katrina Waite , Community Engagement Manager, Civic Centre, 44 York Street, Twickenham TW1 3BZ ☎ 020 8831 6289 ✉ katrina.waite@richmond.gov.uk

Community Planning: Ms Mandy Skinner , Assistant Director of Commissioning, Corporate Policy & Strategy, Civic Centre, 44 York Street, Twickenham TW1 3BZ ☎ 020 8891 7929 🖷 020 8891 7703 ✉ mandy.skinner@richmond.gov.uk

Community Planning: Ms Katrina Waite , Community Engagement Manager, Civic Centre, 44 York Street, Twickenham TW1 3BZ ☎ 020 8831 6289 ✉ katrina.waite@richmond.gov.uk

Community Safety: Ms Natasha Allen , Community Safety Manager, Civic Centre, 44 York Street, Twickenham TW1 3BZ ☎ 020 8487 5349 ✉ natasha.allen@richmond.gov.uk

Computer Management: Mr Adrian Boylan , Head of ICT, Civic Centre, 44 York Street, Twickenham TW1 3BZ ☎ 020 8891 7917 ✉ a.boylan@richmond.gov.uk

Computer Management: Mr Mike Gravatt, Assistant Director of Finance & Corporate Services, Civic Centre, 44 York Street, Twickenham TW1 3BZ ☎ 020 8891 7238 🖷 020 8891 7233 ✉ m.gravatt@richmond.gov.uk

Consumer Protection and Trading Standards: Mr Paul Foster, Head of Regulatory Services Partnership, Civic Centre, 44 York Street, Twickenham TW1 3BZ ☎ 020 8545 3077 ✉ paul.foster@merton.gov.uk

Consumer Protection and Trading Standards: Mr Paul Foster, Head of Regulatory Services Partnership, Civic Centre, 44 York Street, Twickenham TW1 3BZ ☎ 020 8545 3077 ✉ paul.foster@merton.gov.uk

Corporate Services: Ms Gill Ford , Head of Performance & Quality Assurance, Civic Centre, 44 York Street, Twickenham TW1 3BZ ☎ 020 8487 5016 🖷 020 8487 5026 ✉ g.ford@richmond.gov.uk

Corporate Services: Mrs Carol McBean , Head of Corporate Partnership & Policy, Civic Centre, 44 York Street, Twickenham TW1 3BZ ☎ 020 8831 6231 ✉ c.macbean@richmond.gov.uk

Corporate Services: Mr Graham Russell , Assistant Director of Finance & Corporate Services, Civic Centre, 44 York Street, Twickenham TW1 3BZ ☎ 020 8891 7226 ✉ g.russell@richmond.gov.uk

Customer Service: Mr Simon Batchelor, Head of Customer Services, Civic Centre, 44 York Street, Twickenham TW1 3BZ ☎ 020 8487 5219 ✉ simon.batchelor@richmond.gov.uk

Direct Labour: Mr Andrew Darvill, Assistant Director of Highways & Transport, Civic Centre, 44 York Street, Twickenham TW1 3BZ ☎ 020 8891 7070 🖷 020 8891 7923 ✉ a.darvill@richmond.gov.uk

Economic Development: Mr Sean Gillen , Economic Development Manager, Civic Centre, 44 York Street, Twickenham TW1 3BZ ☎ 020 8831 6219 🖷 020 8891 7347 ✉ sean.gillen@richmond.gov.uk

Education: Mr Nick Whitfield , Chief Executive Officer - Achieving for Children, Civic Centre, 44 York Street, Twickenham TW1 3BZ ☎ 020 8891 7906 🖷 020 8831 6216 ✉ nick.whitfield@richmond.gov.uk

E-Government: Mr Mike Gravatt, Assistant Director of Finance & Corporate Services, Civic Centre, 44 York Street, Twickenham TW1 3BZ ☎ 020 8891 7238 🖷 020 8891 7233 ✉ m.gravatt@richmond.gov.uk

Electoral Registration: Ms Cathy Potter , Head of Electoral Services, York House, Richmond Road, Twickenham TW1 3AA ☎ 020 8891 7784 ✉ cathy.potter@richmond.gov.uk

Emergency Planning: Mr Jon Robinson , Health, Safety & Resilience Advisor, Civic Centre, 44 York Street, Twickenham TW1 3BZ ☎ 020 8891 7111 🖷 020 8891 7858 ✉ jonathan.robinson@richmond.gov.uk

Energy Management: Miss Ishbel Murray , Assistant Director of Environment, Property, Parks & Sustainability, Civic Centre, 44 York Street, Twickenham TW1 3BZ ☎ 020 8891 7310 ✉ ishbel.murray@richmond.gov.uk

Environmental / Technical Services: Mr Jon Freer , Assistant Director of Environment, Civic Centre, 44 York Street, Twickenham TW1 3BZ ☎ 020 8891 7319 ✉ j.freer@richmond.gov.uk

Environmental Health: Mr Paul Foster , Head of Regulatory Services Partnership, Civic Centre, 44 York Street, Twickenham TW1 3BZ ☎ 020 8545 3077 ✉ paul.foster@merton.gov.uk

Environmental Health: Mr Paul Foster , Head of Regulatory Services Partnership, Civic Centre, 44 York Street, Twickenham TW1 3BZ ☎ 020 8545 3077 ✉ paul.foster@merton.gov.uk

Estates, Property & Valuation: Mr Paul Chadwick, Director of Environment, Civic Centre, 44 York Street, Twickenham TW1 3BZ ☎ 020 8891 7870 🖷 020 8891 7361 ✉ p.chadwick@richmond.gov.uk

Estates, Property & Valuation: Mr Peter Southcombe , Head of Estates & Valuation, Civic Centre, 44 York Street, Twickenham TW1 3BZ ☎ 020 8487 5118 🖷 020 8487 5125 ✉ p.southcombe@richmond.gov.uk

Events Manager: Ms Laura Steele , Community Events Manager, Civic Centre, 44 York Street, Twickenham TW1 3BZ ☎ 020 8891 7074 ✉ laura.steele@richmond.gov.uk

Facilities: Mr Paul Cook , Corporate Facilities Manager, Civic Centre, 44 York Street, Twickenham TW1 3BZ ☎ 020 8891 7463 🖷 020 8891 7858 ✉ p.cook@richmond.gov.uk

Finance: Mr Mike Gravatt, Assistant Director of Finance & Corporate Services, Civic Centre, 44 York Street, Twickenham TW1 3BZ ☎ 020 8891 7238 🖷 020 8891 7233 ✉ m.gravatt@richmond.gov.uk

Finance: Mr Mark Maidment, Director of Finance & Corporate Services, York House Annexe, York House, Twickenham TW1 3AA ☎ 020 8891 7171 🖷 020 8891 7333 ✉ m.maidment@richmond.gov.uk

Treasury: Ms Sue Cornwell , Treasury Manager, Ground Floor, Civic Centre, 44 York Street, Twickenham TW1 3BZ ☎ 020 8891 7252 ✉ s.cornwell@richmond.gov.uk

Pensions: Ms Collette Hollands , Pensions Manager, Civic Centre, 44 York Street, Twickenham TW1 3BZ ☎ 020 8871 6510 ✉ c.hollands@wandsworth.gov.uk

Fleet Management: Mr Andrew Darvill, Assistant Director of Highways & Transport, Civic Centre, 44 York Street, Twickenham TW1 3BZ ☎ 020 8891 7070 🖷 020 8891 7923 ✉ a.darvill@richmond.gov.uk

Grounds Maintenance: Mr Paul Chadwick, Director of Environment, Civic Centre, 44 York Street, Twickenham TW1 3BZ ☎ 020 8891 7870 🖷 020 8891 7361 ✉ p.chadwick@richmond.gov.uk

Health and Safety: Mr Jon Robinson , Health, Safety & Resilience Advisor, Civic Centre, 44 York Street, Twickenham TW1 3BZ ☎ 020 8891 7111 🖷 020 8891 7858 ✉ jonathan.robinson@richmond.gov.uk

Highways: Mr Andrew Darvill, Assistant Director of Highways & Transport, Civic Centre, 44 York Street, Twickenham TW1 3BZ ☎ 020 8891 7070 🖷 020 8891 7923 ✉ a.darvill@richmond.gov.uk

Home Energy Conservation: Mr Colin Coomber , Energy Efficiency Co-ordinator, Civic Centre, 44 York Street, Twickenham TW1 3BZ ☎ 020 8891 7663 🖷 020 8831 6404 ✉ c.coomber@richmond.gov.uk

Housing: Mr Brian Castle, Assistant Director of Community Service Operations, Civic Centre, 44 York Street, Twickenham TW1 3BZ ☎ 020 8891 7482 🖷 020 8891 7792 ✉ b.castle@richmond.gov.uk

Housing: Mr Ken Emerson , Head of Housing Operations, Civic Centre, 44 York Street, Twickenham TW1 3BZ ☎ 020 8831 6406 🖷 020 8891 7403 ✉ k.emerson@richmond.gov.uk

Local Area Agreement: Ms Carol MacBean , Head of Strategy & Policy, Civic Centre, 44 York Street, Twickenham TW1 3BZ ☎ 020 8831 6231 ✉ c.macbean@richmond.gov.uk

Legal: Mr Paul Evans , Assistant Director of Corporate Governance & Head of Shared Legal Services, 1st Floor, Gifford House Legal Services, 67c St Helier Avenue, Morden SM4 6HY ☎ 020 8545 3338 ✉ paul.evans@merton.gov.uk

Leisure and Cultural Services: Mr Colin Sinclair , Head of Sport & Fitness, Regal House, London Road, Twickenham TW1 3QB ☎ 020 8831 6140 🖷 020 8891 7904 ✉ c.sinclair@richmond.gov.uk

Leisure and Cultural Services: Mr Nick Whitfield , Chief Executive Officer - Achieving for Children, Civic Centre, 44 York Street, Twickenham TW1 3BZ ☎ 020 8891 7906 🖷 020 8831 6216 ✉ nick.whitfield@richmond.gov.uk

Licensing: Mr Paul Foster , Head of Regulatory Services Partnership, Civic Centre, 44 York Street, Twickenham TW1 3BZ ☎ 020 8545 3077 ✉ paul.foster@merton.gov.uk

Lifelong Learning: Mr Ian Dodds , Director - Standards & Improvements, Achieving for Children, Regal House, London Road, Twickenham TW1 3BQ ☎ 020 8831 6116 🖷 020 8891 7714 ✉ ian.dodds@richmond.gov.uk

Lighting: Mr Andrew Darvill, Assistant Director of Highways & Transport, Civic Centre, 44 York Street, Twickenham TW1 3BZ ☎ 020 8891 7070 🖷 020 8891 7923 ✉ a.darvill@richmond.gov.uk

Member Services: Ms Kathryn Thomas , Head of Democratic Services, York House, Richmond Road, Twickenham TW1 3AA ☎ 020 8891 7860 🖷 020 8891 7701 ✉ kathryn.thomas@richmond.gov.uk

Parking: Mr Andrew Darvill, Assistant Director of Highways & Transport, Civic Centre, 44 York Street, Twickenham TW1 3BZ ☎ 020 8891 7070 🖷 020 8891 7923 ✉ a.darvill@richmond.gov.uk

Personnel / HR: Ms Sheila West , Corporate Head of Human Resources for Kingston & Richmond, Guildhall 1, High Street, Kingston upon Thames KT1 1EU ☎ 020 8547 5153 ✉ sheila.west@rbk.kingston.gov.uk

Planning: Mr Robert Angus , Head of Development & Enforcement, Civic Centre, 44 York Street, Twickenham TW1 3BZ ☎ 020 8891 7271 🖷 020 8891 7789 ✉ r.angus@richmond.gov.uk

Procurement: Mr Nick Richmond-Smith , Head of Procurement, Civic Centre, 44 York Street, Twickenham TW1 3BZ ☎ 020 8891 7175 ✉ nick.richmond-smith@richmond.gov.uk

Public Libraries: Mr Mike Gravatt, Assistant Director of Finance & Corporate Services, Civic Centre, 44 York Street, Twickenham TW1 3BZ ☎ 020 8891 7238 🖷 020 8891 7233 ✉ m.gravatt@richmond.gov.uk

Recycling & Waste Minimisation: Mr Jon Freer , Assistant Director of Development and Street Scene, Civic Centre, 44 York Street, Twickenham TW1 3BZ ☎ 020 8891 7319 🖷 020 8891 7787 ✉ j.freer@richmond.gov.uk

Recycling & Waste Minimisation: Mr David Ingham , Waste Minimisation Officer, Central Depot, Langhorn Drive, Twickenham TW2 7SG ☎ 020 8487 5239 ✉ d.ingham@richmond.gov.uk

Regeneration: Mr Philip Wealthy , Head of Policy & Design, Civic Centre, 44 York Street, Twickenham TW1 3BZ ☎ 020 8891 7320 🖷 020 8891 7703 ✉ p.wealthy@richmond.gov.uk

Road Safety: Mr Sam Merison , Principal Safety Education Officer, Civic Centre, 44 York Street, Twickenham TW1 3BZ ☎ 020 8487 5356 ✉ sam.merison@richmond.gov.uk

Social Services: Ms Cathy Kerr , Director of Adult & Community Services, Civic Centre, 44 York Street, Twickenham TW1 3BZ ☎ 020 8891 7360 🖷 020 8891 7703 ✉ cathy.kerr@richmond.gov.uk

Social Services (Adult): Mr Derek Oliver , Assistant Director of Community Care Services, Civic Centre, 44 York Street, Twickenham TW1 3BZ ☎ 020 8891 7608 ✉ derek.oliver@richmond.gov.uk

Social Services (Children): Ms Alison Twynam , Assistant Director of Social Care - Achieving for Children, Civic Centre, 44 York Street, Twickenham TW1 3BZ ✉ a.twynam@richmond.gov.uk

Public Health: Dr Dagmar Zeuner , Director - Public Health, Civic Centre, 44 York Street, Twickenham TW1 3BZ ☎ 020 8734 3013 ✉ dagmar.zeuner@richmond.gov.uk

Street Scene: Mr Jon Freer , Assistant Director of Development and Street Scene, Civic Centre, 44 York Street, Twickenham TW1 3BZ ☎ 020 8891 7319 🖷 020 8891 7787 ✉ j.freer@richmond.gov.uk

Sustainable Communities: Mr Robert Angus , Head of Development & Enforcement, Civic Centre, 44 York Street, Twickenham TW1 3BZ ☎ 020 8891 7271 🖷 020 8891 7789 ✉ r.angus@richmond.gov.uk

Sustainable Development: Miss Ishbel Murray , Assistant Director of Environment, Property, Parks & Sustainability, Civic Centre, 44 York Street, Twickenham TW1 3BZ ☎ 020 8891 7310 ✉ ishbel.murray@richmond.gov.uk

Tourism: Ms Angela Ivey, Principal Tourism & Marketing Manager, Civic Centre, 44 York Street, Twickenham TW1 3BZ ☎ 020 8487 5047 🖷 020 8891 7347 ✉ a.ivey@richmond.gov.uk

Traffic Management: Mr Andrew Darvill, Assistant Director of Highways & Transport, Civic Centre, 44 York Street, Twickenham TW1 3BZ ☎ 020 8891 7070 🖷 020 8891 7923 ✉ a.darvill@richmond.gov.uk

Transport: Mr Andrew Darvill, Assistant Director of Highways & Transport, Civic Centre, 44 York Street, Twickenham TW1 3BZ ☎ 020 8891 7070 🖷 020 8891 7923 ✉ a.darvill@richmond.gov.uk

Transport Planner: Mr Andrew Darvill, Assistant Director of Highways & Transport, Civic Centre, 44 York Street, Twickenham TW1 3BZ ☎ 020 8891 7070 🖷 020 8891 7923 ✉ a.darvill@richmond.gov.uk

Waste Collection and Disposal: Mr Jon Freer , Assistant Director of Environment, Civic Centre, 44 York Street, Twickenham TW1 3BZ ☎ 020 8891 7319 ✉ j.freer@richmond.gov.uk

Waste Management: Mr Jon Freer , Assistant Director of Environment, Civic Centre, 44 York Street, Twickenham TW1 3BZ ☎ 020 8891 7319 ✉ j.freer@richmond.gov.uk

Children's Play Areas: Mr David Allister , Head of Parks & Open Spaces, Civic Centre, 44 York Street, Twickenham TW1 3BZ ☎ 020 8831 6135 ✉ d.allister@richmond.gov.uk

COUNCILLORS

***Mayor* Seymour**, Martin (CON - Hampton North)
cllr.mseymour@richmond.gov.uk

***Deputy Mayor* Loveland**, Jean (CON - Ham, Petersham and Richmond Riverside)
cllr.jloveland@richmond.gov.uk

***Leader of the Council* True**, Nicholas (CON - East Sheen)
cllr.lordtrue@richmond.gov.uk

***Deputy Leader of the Council* Samuel**, Geoffrey (CON - Hampton North)
cllr.gsamuel@richmond.gov.uk

***Group Leader* Roberts**, Gareth (LD - Hampton)
cllr.groberts@richmond.gov.uk

Acton, Geoff (LD - St Margaret's and North Twickenham)
cllr.gacton@richmond.gov.uk

Allen, Piers (LD - West Twickenham)
cllr.pallen@richmond.gov.uk

Arbour, Tony (CON - Hampton Wick)
cllr.tarbour@richmond.gov.uk

Avon, Paul (CON - Mortlake and Barnes Common)
cllr.pavon@richmond.gov.uk

Blakemore, Lisa (CON - North Richmond)
cllr.lblakemore@richmond.gov.uk

Bond, Meena (CON - Kew)
cllr.mbond@richmond.gov.uk

Boulton, Jane (CON - West Twickenham)
cllr.jboulton@richmond.gov.uk

Boyle, Mark (CON - Fulwell and Hampton Hill)
cllr.mboyle@richmond.gov.uk

Buckwell, Peter (CON - South Richmond)
cllr.pbuckwell@richmond.gov.uk

Butler, Margaret (CON - North Richmond)
cllr.mbutler@richmond.gov.uk

Butler, Alan (CON - Heathfield)
cllr.abutler@richmond.gov.uk

Cardy, Jonathan (LD - Fulwell and Hampton Hill)
cllr.jcardy@richmond.gov.uk

Chappell, Susan (CON - Twickenham Riverside)
cllr.schappell@richmond.gov.uk

Churchill, Jennifer (LD - Teddington)
cllr.jchurchill@richmond.gov.uk

Coombs, John (LD - Heathfield)
cllr.jcoombs@richmond.gov.uk

Curran, Gemma (CON - Mortlake and Barnes Common)
cllr.gcurran@richmond.gov.uk

Dias, Benedict (CON - Twickenham Riverside)
cllr.bdias@richmond.gov.uk

Ehmann, Alexander (LD - St Margaret's and North Twickenham)
cllr.aehmann@richmond.gov.uk

Elengorn, Martin (LD - Teddington)
cllr.melengorn@richmond.gov.uk

Elliot, Gareth (CON - Whitton)
cllr.gelliot@richmond.gov.uk

Elloy, Jerry (LD - Fulwell and Hampton Hill)
cllr.jelloy@richmond.gov.uk

Evans, Gareth (CON - Hampton Wick)
cllr.gevans@richmond.gov.uk

Fleming, Pamela (CON - South Richmond)
cllr.pfleming@richmond.gov.uk

Frost, Penelope (LD - Ham, Petersham and Richmond Riverside)
cllr.pfrost@richmond.gov.uk

Hambidge, Annie (CON - Heathfield)
cllr.ahambidge@richmond.gov.uk

Head, Clare (CON - South Twickenham)
cllr.chead@richmond.gov.uk

Healy, Grant (CON - Whitton)
cllr.ghealy@richmond.gov.uk

Hill, Helen (CON - Twickenham Riverside)
cllr.hhill@richmond.gov.uk

Hodgins, Paul (CON - Barnes)
cllr.phodgins@richmond.gov.uk

Horner, Monica (CON - Kew)
cllr.mhorner@richmond.gov.uk

Howard, Kate (CON - Hampton North)
cllr.khoward@richmond.gov.uk

Jaeger, Liz (LD - Whitton)
cllr.ljaeger@richmond.gov.uk

Khosa, Ben (LD - St Margaret's and North Twickenham)
cllr.bkhosa@richmond.gov.uk

Knight, Stephen (LD - Teddington)
cllr.sknight@richmond.gov.uk

Lee-Parsons, Helen (LD - West Twickenham)
cllr.hlee-parsons@richmond.gov.uk

Linnette, David (CON - Kew)
cllr.dlinnette@richmond.gov.uk

Locke, Geraldine (LD - Hampton Wick)

Marcel, Brian (CON - East Sheen)
cllr.bmarcel@richmond.gov.uk

Marlow, David (CON - South Twickenham)
cllr.dmarlow@richmond.gov.uk

Martin, Richard (CON - Mortlake and Barnes Common)
cllr.rmartin@richmond.gov.uk

Nicholson, Suzette (LD - Hampton)
cllr.snicholson@richmond.gov.uk

O'Malley, Thomas (CON - South Richmond)
cllr.tomalley@richmond.gov.uk

Palmer, Rita (CON - Barnes)
cllr.rpalmer@richmond.gov.uk

Percival, Christine (CON - Barnes)
cllr.cpercival@richmond.gov.uk

Porter, David (CON - South Twickenham)
cllr.dporter@richmond.gov.uk

Sale, Petra (CON - Hampton)
cllr.psale@richmond.gov.uk

Speak, Stephen (CON - North Richmond)
democratic.services@richmond.gov.uk

Thompson, Robert (CON - East Sheen)
cllr.rthompson@richmond.gov.uk

Tippett, Sarah (CON - Ham, Petersham and Richmond Riverside)
cllr.stippett@richmond.gov.uk

POLITICAL COMPOSITION
CON: 38, LD: 16

COMMITTEE CHAIRS

Audit: Mr Jonathan Cardy

Health & Wellbeing: Ms Christine Percival

Pensions: Mr Geoff Acton

Planning: Ms Gemma Curran

Richmondshire D

Richmondshire District Council, Swale House, Frenchgate, Richmond DL10 4JE
☎ 01748 829100 🖷 01748 825071 ✉ enquiries@richmondshire.gov.uk
💻 www.richmondshire.gov.uk

FACTS AND FIGURES
Parliamentary Constituencies: Richmond (Yorks)
EU Constituencies: Yorkshire and the Humber
Election Frequency: Elections are of whole council

PRINCIPAL OFFICERS

Chief Executive: Mr Tony Clark, Managing Director, Mercury House, Station Road, Richmond DL10 4JX ☎ 01748 829100 🖷 01748 826186 ✉ tony.clark@richmondshire.gov.uk

Senior Management: Mr Colin Dales, Corporate Director - Operational Services, Mercury House, Station Road, Richmond DL10 4JX ☎ 01748 829100 🖷 01748 826186 ✉ colin.dales@richmondshire.gov.uk

Senior Management: Mr Callum McKeon, Corporate Director - Strategy & Regulatory / Monitoring Officer, Mercury House, Station Road, Richmond DL10 4JX ☎ 01748 829100 🖷 01748 826186 ✉ callum.mckeon@richmondshire.gov.uk

Senior Management: Ms Sian Moore , Corporate Director - Resources & S151 Officer, Mercury House, Station Road, Richmond DL10 4JX ☎ 01748 829100 🖷 01748 826186 ✉ sian.moore@richmondshire.gov.uk

Community Safety: Ms Pat Wilson, Business & Community Safety Manager, Mercury House, Station Road, Richmond DL10 4JX ☎ 01748 829100 🖷 01748 826186 ✉ pat.wilson@richmondshire.gov.uk

Computer Management: Mr Graeme Thistlethwaite , ICT & Business Change Manager, Mercury House, Station Road, Richmond DL10 4JX ☎ 01748 829100 ✉ graeme.thistlethwaite@richmondshire.gov.uk

Customer Service: Ms Carole Dew , Customer Services Manager, Mercury House, Station Road, Richmond DL10 4JX ☎ 01748 829100 🖷 01748 826186 ✉ carole.dew@richmondshire.gov.uk

Electoral Registration: Ms Sandra Hullah, Electoral Services Officer, Mercury House, Station Road, Richmond DL10 4JX ☎ 01748 829100 🖷 01748 826186 ✉ sandra.hullah@richmondshire.gov.uk

Emergency Planning: Mr Callum McKeon, Corporate Director - Strategy & Regulatory / Monitoring Officer, Mercury House, Station Road, Richmond DL10 4JX ☎ 01748 829100 🖷 01748 826186 ✉ callum.mckeon@richmondshire.gov.uk

Environmental Health: Mr Stuart Wears , Environmental Health Manager, Mercury House, Station Road, Richmond DL10 4JX ☎ 01748 829100 ✉ stuart.wears@richmondshire.gov.uk

Finance: Ms Sian Moore , Corporate Director - Resources & S151 Officer, Mercury House, Station Road, Richmond DL10 4JX ☎ 01748 829100 🖷 01748 826186 ✉ sian.moore@richmondshire.gov.uk

Grounds Maintenance: Mr Gary Hudson, Open Spaces & Amenities Manager, Mercury House, Station Road, Richmond DL10 4JX ☎ 01748 829100 🖷 01748 826186 ✉ gary.hudson@richmondshire.gov.uk

Health and Safety: Mr Tim Burrows , Health & Safety Advisor, Mercury House, Station Road, Richmond DL10 4JX ☎ 01748 829100 🖷 01748 826186 ✉ tim.burrows@richmondshire.gov.uk

Housing: Mr Colin Dales, Corporate Director - Operational Services, Mercury House, Station Road, Richmond DL10 4JX ☎ 01748 829100 🖷 01748 826186 ✉ colin.dales@richmondshire.gov.uk

Housing Maintenance: Ms Sara Smith , Landlord Services Manager, Mercury House, Station Road, Richmond DL10 4JX ☎ 01748 829100 🖷 01748 826186 ✉ sara.smith@richmondshire.gov.uk

Leisure and Cultural Services: Mr Colin Dales, Corporate Director - Operational Services, Mercury House, Station Road, Richmond DL10 4JX ☎ 01748 829100 🖷 01748 826186 ✉ colin.dales@richmondshire.gov.uk

Licensing: Mr Stuart Wears , Environmental Health Manager, Mercury House, Station Road, Richmond DL10 4JX ☎ 01748 829100 ✉ stuart.wears@richmondshire.gov.uk

Member Services: Mr Michael Dowson, Democratic Services Manager, Mercury House, Station Road, Richmond DL10 4JX ☎ 01748 829100 🖷 01748 826186 ✉ michael.dowson@richmondshire.gov.uk

Parking: Mr Gary Hudson, Open Spaces & Amenities Manager, Mercury House, Station Road, Richmond DL10 4JX ☎ 01748 829100 🖷 01748 826186 ✉ gary.hudson@richmondshire.gov.uk

Personnel / HR: Ms Laura Sellers , Interim HR & Payroll Manager, Mercury House, Station Road, Richmond DL10 4JX ☎ 01718 829100 ✉ laura.sellers@richmondshire.gov.uk

Planning: Mr Peter Featherstone, Planning & Development Manager, Mercury House, Station Road, Richmond DL10 4JX ☎ 01748 829100 🖷 01748 826186 ✉ peter.featherstone@richmondshire.gov.uk

Recycling & Waste Minimisation: Ms Amanda Dyson , Waste & Recycling Manager, Mercury House, Station Road, Richmond DL10 4JX ☎ 01748 829100 ✉ amanda.dyson@richmondshire.gov.uk

Street Scene: Mr Terry Thorpe , Transport & Street Scene Manager, Mercury House, Station Road, Richmond DL10 4JX ☎ 01748 829100 ✉ terry.thorpe@richmondshire.gov.uk

Transport: Mr Terry Thorpe , Transport & Street Scene Manager, Mercury House, Station Road, Richmond DL10 4JX ☎ 01748 829100 ✉ terry.thorpe@richmondshire.gov.uk

Waste Collection and Disposal: Ms Amanda Dyson , Waste & Recycling Manager, Mercury House, Station Road, Richmond DL10 4JX ☎ 01748 829100 ✉ amanda.dyson@richmondshire.gov.uk

COUNCILLORS

***Chair* Robinson**, John (LD - Richmond Central) cllr.j.robinson@richmondshire.gov.uk

***Leader of the Council* Peacock**, Yvonne (CON - Addlebrough) cllr.y.peacock@richmondshire.gov.uk

***Deputy Leader of the Council* Threlfall**, Ian (CON - Brompton on Swale and Scorton) cllr.i.threlfall@richmondshire.gov.uk

Amsden, John (IND - Bolton Castle) cllr.j.amsden@richmondshire.gov.uk

Beal, Richard (IND - Reeth and Arkengarthdale) cllr.r.beal@richmondshire.gov.uk

Blackie, John (IND - Hawes and High Abbotside) cllr.j.blackie@richmondshire.gov.uk

Blows, Richard (CON - Swaledale) cllr.r.blows@richmondshire.gov.uk

Cameron, Jamie (CON - Newsham with Eppleby) cllr.j.cameron@richmondshire.gov.uk

Cullen, Paul (IND - Hipswell) cllr.p.cullen@richmondshire.gov.uk

Curran DL, Linda (IND - Richmond West) cllr.l.curran@richmondshire.gov.uk

Dale, Angie (IND - Colburn) cllr.a.dale@richmondshire.gov.uk

Dawson, Campbell (CON - Barton) cllr.c.dawson@richmondshire.gov.uk

Duff, Tony (CON - Leyburn) cllr.t.duff@richmondshire.gov.uk

Fairhurst, Susan (CON - Middleham) cllr.s.fairhurst@richmondshire.gov.uk

Gibbs, Sam (CON - Croft) cllr.s.gibbs@richmondshire.gov.uk

Gill, Danny (CON - Brompton on Swale and Scorton) cllr.d.gill@richmondshire.gov.uk

Glover, William (CON - Colburn) cllr.w.glover@richmondshire.gov.uk

Grant, Helen (IND - Scotton) cllr.h.grant@richmondshire.gov.uk

Grose, Lawrence (CON - Hipswell) cllr.l.grose@richmondshire.gov.uk

Heslop, William (IND - Gilling) cllr.w.heslop@richmondshire.gov.uk

Kirby, Karen (CON - Richmond East) cllr.k.kirby@richmondshire.gov.uk

Linehan, Geoffrey (CON - Hornby Castle) cllr.g.linehan@richmondshire.gov.uk

Lord, Russel (IND - Richmond East) cllr.r.lord@richmondshire.gov.uk

Middlemiss, Patricia (CON - Scotton) cllr.p.middlemiss@richmondshire.gov.uk

Ormston, Richard (CON - Lower Wensleydale) cllr.r.ormston@richmondshire.gov.uk

Parsons, Stuart (IND - Richmond West) cllr.s.parsons@richmondshire.gov.uk

Partridge, Bev (CON - Colburn) cllr.b.partridge@richmondshire.gov.uk

Pelton, Tony (IND - Catterick) cllr.t.pelton@richmondshire.gov.uk

Sankey, Derek (CON - Catterick)

Sedgwick, Karin (CON - Leyburn)
cllr.k.sedgwick@richmondshire.gov.uk

Thompson, Angus (CON - Middleton Tyas)
cllr.a.thompson@richmondshire.gov.uk

Thornton-Berry, Caroline (CON - Penhill)
cllr.c.thornton-berry@richmondshire.gov.uk

Wilson-Petch, Jimmy (CON - Melsonby)
cllr.j.wilson-petch@richmondshire.gov.uk

World, Clive (LD - Richmond Central)
cllr.c.world@richmondshire.gov.uk

POLITICAL COMPOSITION
CON: 21, IND: 11, LD: 2

COMMITTEE CHAIRS

Audit, Governance & Standards: Mr Geoffrey Linehan

Licensing: Mr Jimmy Wilson-Petch

Rochdale M

Rochdale Metropolitan Borough Council, Municipal Offices, Smith Street, Rochdale OL16 1LQ
☎ 01706 647474 council@rochdale.gov.uk www.rochdale.gov.uk

FACTS AND FIGURES
Parliamentary Constituencies: Heywood and Middleton, Rochdale
EU Constituencies: North West
Election Frequency: Elections are by thirds

PRINCIPAL OFFICERS

Chief Executive: Mr Steve Rumbelow , Chief Executive, Municipal Offices, Smith Street, Rochdale OL16 1LQ ☎ 01706 924703
steve.rumbelow@rochdale.gov.uk

Senior Management: Ms Sheila Downey , Director of Adult Services, Floor 3, Number One Riverside, Smith Street, Rochdale OL16 1XU ☎ 01706 922975 sheila.downey@rochdale.gov.uk

Senior Management: Ms Gail Hopper , Director of Children's Services, Floor 4, Number One Riverside, Smith Street, Rochdale OL16 1XU ☎ 01706 825000 gail.hopper@rochdale.gov.uk

Senior Management: Mrs Pauline Kane , Director of Finance, Floor 2, Number One Riverside, Smith Street, Rochdale OL16 1XU
☎ 01706 925002 pauline.kane@rochdale.gov.uk

Senior Management: Mr Julian Massel , Interim Head of Customers & Corporate, Floor 2, Number One Riverside, Smith Street, Rochdale OL16 1XU ☎ 01706 925015
julian.massel@rochdale.gov.uk

Senior Management: Ms Wendy Meston , Interim Director - Public Health, Municipal Offices, Smith Street, Rochdale OL16 1LQ
wendy.meston@rochdale.gov.uk

Senior Management: Mr Mark Widdup, Director of Economy & Environment, Green Lane, Heywood OL10 2DY ☎ 01706 925284
mark.widdup@rochdale.gov.uk

Access Officer / Social Services (Disability): Ms Sheila Downey , Director of Adult Services, Floor 3, Number One Riverside, Smith Street, Rochdale OL16 1XU ☎ 01706 922975
sheila.downey@rochdale.gov.uk

Architect, Building / Property Services: Mr Len Windle , Senior Property Manager - Technical, Floor 4, Number One Riverside, Smith Street, Rochdale OL16 1XU ☎ 01706 923346
len.windle@rochdale.gov.uk

Building Control: Mr David Oakes , Building Control Manager, Floor 3, Number One Riverside, Smith Street, Rochdale OL16 1XU
☎ 01706 924324 david.oakes@rochdale.gov.uk

Catering Services: Mr Peter Gurney , Facilities Manager - Catering, Green Lane, Heywood, Rochdale OL10 2DY
☎ 01706 925775 peter.gurney@rochdale.gov.uk

Children / Youth Services: Ms Sandra Bowness , Assistant Director, Floor 4, Number One Riverside, Smith Street, Rochdale OL16 1XU ☎ 01706 925159 sandra.bowness@rochdale.gov.uk

Civil Registration: Mrs Aileen Bollard , Superintendent Registrar, PO Box 15, Ground Floor, Town Hall, Rochdale OL16 1AB
☎ 01706 924779 aileen.bollard@rochdale.gov.uk

PR / Communications: Mr Danny Brierley , Public Relations Manager, Floor 2, Number One Riverside, Smith Street, Rochdale OL16 1XU ☎ 01706 925724 danny.brierley@rochdale.gov.uk

Community Safety: Ms Jeanette Staley , Community Safety Manager, Floor 3, Number One Riverside, Smith Street, Rochdale OL16 1XU ☎ 01706 924987 jeanette.staley@rochdale.gov.uk

Consumer Protection and Trading Standards: Mr Andy Glover, Chief Public Protection Officer, Floor 3, Number One Riverside, Smith Street, Rochdale OL16 1XU ☎ 01706 924105
🖷 01706 924185 andy.glover@rochdale.gov.uk

Corporate Services: Mr Julian Massel , Interim Head of Customers & Corporate, Floor 2, Number One Riverside, Smith Street, Rochdale OL16 1XU ☎ 01706 925015
julian.massel@rochdale.gov.uk

Customer Service: Mr Julian Massel , Interim Head of Customers & Corporate, Floor 2, Number One Riverside, Smith Street, Rochdale OL16 1XU ☎ 01706 925015
julian.massel@rochdale.gov.uk

Economic Development: Ms Susan Ayres, Economic Affairs Manager, Floor 3, Number One Riverside, Smith Street, Rochdale OL16 1XU ☎ 01706 925636 susan.ayres@rochdale.gov.uk

Education: Ms Gail Hopper , Director of Children's Services, Floor 4, Number One Riverside, Smith Street, Rochdale OL16 1XU
☎ 01706 825000 gail.hopper@rochdale.gov.uk

Electoral Registration: Mrs Clare Poole, Electoral Services Manager, Floor 2, Number One Riverside, Smith Street, Rochdale OL16 1XU ☎ 01706 924759 🖷 0844 963 2311
clare.poole@rochdale.gov.uk

Emergency Planning: Ms Jeanette Staley , Community Safety Manager, Floor 3, Number One Riverside, Smith Street, Rochdale OL16 1XU ☎ 01706 924987 ✉ jeanette.staley@rochdale.gov.uk

Energy Management: Ms Donna Bowler , Head of Highways, Property & Strategic Housing, Floor 4, Number One Riverside, Smith Street, Rochdale OL16 1XU ☎ 01706 924849 ✉ donna.bowler@rochdale.gov.uk

Environmental / Technical Services: Mr Mark Widdup, Director of Economy & Environment, Green Lane, Heywood OL10 2DY ☎ 01706 925284 ✉ mark.widdup@rochdale.gov.uk

Environmental Health: Ms Nicola Rogers , Environmental Health Manager, Floor 3, Number One Riverside, Smith Street, Rochdale OL16 1XU ☎ 01706 924124 ✉ nicola.rogers@rochdale.gov.uk

Estates, Property & Valuation: Mr Peter Gregory , Senior Property Manager - Estates, Floor 4, Number One Riverside, Smith Street, Rochdale OL16 1XU ☎ 01706 923271 ✉ peter.gregory@rochdale.gov.uk

Facilities: Ms Donna Bowler , Head of Highways, Property & Strategic Housing, Floor 4, Number One Riverside, Smith Street, Rochdale OL16 1XU ☎ 01706 924849 ✉ donna.bowler@rochdale.gov.uk

Finance: Mrs Pauline Kane , Director of Finance, Floor 2, Number One Riverside, Smith Street, Rochdale OL16 1XU ☎ 01706 925002 ✉ pauline.kane@rochdale.gov.uk

Fleet Management: Mr Martin Taylor , Service Manager - Environmental Management, Green Lane, Heywood, Rochdale OL10 2DY ☎ 01706 922004 ✉ martin.taylor@rochdale.gov.uk

Grounds Maintenance: Mr Martin Taylor , Service Manager - Environmental Management, Green Lane, Heywood, Rochdale OL10 2DY ☎ 01706 922004 ✉ martin.taylor@rochdale.gov.uk

Health and Safety: Ms Nancy Wilson , Corporate Safety Adviser, Brook House, Oldham Road, Middleton, Manchester M24 1AY ☎ 01706 925057 ✉ nancy.wilson@rochdale.gov.uk

Highways: Mr Steve Reay , Highways Manager, Floor 4, Number One Riverside, Smith Street, Rochdale OL16 1XU ☎ 01706 924461 ✉ steve.reay@rochdale.gov.uk

Home Energy Conservation: Ms Donna Bowler , Head of Highways, Property & Strategic Housing, Floor 4, Number One Riverside, Smith Street, Rochdale OL16 1XU ☎ 01706 924849 ✉ donna.bowler@rochdale.gov.uk

Housing: Ms Donna Bowler , Head of Highways, Property & Strategic Housing, Floor 4, Number One Riverside, Smith Street, Rochdale OL16 1XU ☎ 01706 924849 ✉ donna.bowler@rochdale.gov.uk

Legal: Mr David Wilcocks , Head of Legal & Governance Reform, Brook House, Oldham Road, Middleton, Manchester M24 1AY ☎ 01706 924703 ✉ david.wilcocks@rochdale.gov.uk

Leisure and Cultural Services: Mrs Pauline Kane , Director of Finance, Floor 2, Number One Riverside, Smith Street, Rochdale OL16 1XU ☎ 01706 925002 ✉ pauline.kane@rochdale.gov.uk

Licensing: Mrs Beverley Wilkinson , Licensing Manager, Floor 3, Number One Riverside, Smith Street, Rochdale OL16 1XU ☎ 01706 924178 ✉ beverley.wilkinson@rochdale.gov.uk

Lifelong Learning: Ms Sandra Bowness , Assistant Director, Floor 4, Number One Riverside, Smith Street, Rochdale OL16 1XU ☎ 01706 925159 ✉ sandra.bowness@rochdale.gov.uk

Lighting: Mr Jonathan Hartley , Street Lighting Client Team Manager, Floor 4, Number One Riverside, Smith Street, Rochdale OL16 1XU ☎ 0161 770 1681 ✉ jonathan.hartley@rochdale.gov.uk

Member Services: Mr Mark Hardman , Townships & Governance Manager, Floor 2, Number One Riverside, Smith Street, Rochdale OL16 1XU ☎ 01706 824704 ✉ mark.hardman@rochdale.gov.uk

Parking: Ms Julie Rushton , Parking Team Leader, Floor 4, Number One Riverside, Smith Street, Rochdale OL16 1XU ☎ 01706 924464 ✉ julie.rushton@rochdale.gov.uk

Personnel / HR: Ms Susan Blundell , Head of HR, Floor 2, Number One Riverside, Smith Street, Rochdale OL16 1XU ☎ 01706 925603 📠 01706 925656 ✉ susan.blundell@rochdale.gov.uk

Planning: Mr Mark Robinson , Development Control Manager, Floor 3, Number One Riverside, Smith Street, Rochdale OL16 1XU ☎ 01706 924308 📠 01706 924185 ✉ mark.robinson@rochdale.gov.uk

Procurement: Mrs Pauline Kane , Director of Finance, Floor 2, Number One Riverside, Smith Street, Rochdale OL16 1XU ☎ 01706 925002 ✉ pauline.kane@rochdale.gov.uk

Public Libraries: Mr Julian Massel , Interim Head of Customers & Corporate, Floor 2, Number One Riverside, Smith Street, Rochdale OL16 1XU ☎ 01706 925015 ✉ julian.massel@rochdale.gov.uk

Recycling & Waste Minimisation: Mr Martin Taylor , Service Manager - Environmental Management, Green Lane, Heywood, Rochdale OL10 2DY ☎ 01706 922004 ✉ martin.taylor@rochdale.gov.uk

Road Safety: Mr Tony Lees , Road Safety Team Leader, Floor 4, Number One Riverside, Smith Street, Rochdale OL16 1XU ☎ 01706 924582 📠 01706 921666 ✉ tony.lees@rochdale.gov.uk

Social Services (Adult): Ms Sheila Downey , Director of Adult Services, Floor 3, Number One Riverside, Smith Street, Rochdale OL16 1XU ☎ 01706 922975 ✉ sheila.downey@rochdale.gov.uk

Social Services (Children): Mr Paul Marshall , Assistant Director - Children's Social Care, Floor 4, Number One Riverside, Smith Street, Rochdale OL16 1XU ☎ 01706 925203 ✉ paul.marshall@rochdale.gov.uk

Public Health: Ms Wendy Meston , Interim Director - Public Health, Municipal Offices, Smith Street, Rochdale OL16 1LQ ✉ wendy.meston@rochdale.gov.uk

Staff Training: Ms Fiona Nuttall , Organisational Development Manager, Floor 2, Number One Riverside, Smith Street, Rochdale OL16 1XU ☎ 01706 922406 ✉ fiona.nuttall@rochdale.gov.uk

Street Scene: Mr Martin Taylor , Service Manager - Environmental Management, Green Lane, Heywood, Rochdale OL10 2DY ☎ 01706 922004 ✉ martin.taylor@rochdale.gov.uk

Sustainable Development: Mr Barnaby Fryer , Sustainability & Climate Change Team Leader, Floor 3, Number One Riverside, Smith Street, Rochdale OL16 1XU ☎ 01706 922047 ✉ barnaby.fryer@rochdale.gov.uk

Tourism: Ms Susan Ayres, Economic Affairs Manager, Floor 3, Number One Riverside, Smith Street, Rochdale OL16 1XU ☎ 01706 925636 ✉ susan.ayres@rochdale.gov.uk

Town Centre: Ms Debbie O'Brien, Town Centre Manager, 17A Baillie Street, Rochdale OL16 1JA ☎ 01706 926676 🖷 01706 718848 ✉ debbie@rochdaletcm.co.uk

Transport: Mr Martin Taylor , Service Manager - Environmental Management, Green Lane, Heywood, Rochdale OL10 2DY ☎ 01706 922004 ✉ martin.taylor@rochdale.gov.uk

Waste Collection and Disposal: Mr Martin Taylor , Service Manager - Environmental Management, Green Lane, Heywood, Rochdale OL10 2DY ☎ 01706 922004 ✉ martin.taylor@rochdale.gov.uk

Waste Management: Mr Martin Taylor , Service Manager - Environmental Management, Green Lane, Heywood, Rochdale OL10 2DY ☎ 01706 922004 ✉ martin.taylor@rochdale.gov.uk

Children's Play Areas: Mr Martin Taylor , Service Manager - Environmental Management, Green Lane, Heywood, Rochdale OL10 2DY ☎ 01706 922004 ✉ martin.taylor@rochdale.gov.uk

COUNCILLORS

***Mayor* Biant**, Surinder (LAB - Spotland and Falinge)
surinder.biant@rochdale.gov.uk

***Deputy Mayor* Dutton**, Raymond (LAB - North Heywood)
raymond.dutton@rochdale.gov.uk

***Leader of the Council* Farnell**, Richard (LAB - Balderstone and Kirkholt)
richard.farnell@rochdale.gov.uk

***Deputy Leader of the Council* Williams**, Peter (LAB - South Middleton)
peter.williams@rochdale.gov.uk

***Group Leader* Dearnley**, Ashley (CON - Wardle and West Littleborough)
ashley.dearnley@rochdale.gov.uk

Ahmed, Shefali (IND - Spotland and Falinge)
shefali.ahmed@rochdale.gov.uk

Ahmed, Shakil (LAB - Kingsway)
shakil.ahmed@rochdale.gov.uk

Ahmed, Iftikhar (LAB - Central Rochdale)
iftikhar.ahmed@rochdale.gov.uk

Ahmed, Ali (LAB - Central Rochdale)
ali.ahmed@rochdale.gov.uk

Ali, Daalat (LAB - Kingsway)
daalat.ali@rochdale.gov.uk

Ali, Sultan (LAB - Central Rochdale)
sultan.ali@rochdale.gov.uk

Bell, Andy (LAB - South Middleton)
andrew.bell@rochdale.gov.uk

Beswick, Jacqueline (LAB - West Heywood)
jacqui.beswick@rochdale.gov.uk

Biant, Cecile (LAB - Spotland and Falinge)
cecile.biant@rochdale.gov.uk

Blundell, John (LAB - Smallbridge and Firgrove)
john.blundell@rochdale.gov.uk

Boriss, Malcolm (LAB - East Middleton)
malcolm.boriss@rochdale.gov.uk

Brett, Allen (LAB - Milnrow and Newhey)
allen.brett@rochdale.gov.uk

Brosnan, Lynne (LAB - Kingsway)
lynne.brosnan@rochdale.gov.uk

Burke, Philip (LAB - West Middleton)
philip.burke@rochdale.gov.uk

Butterworth, Neil (LAB - Milnrow and Newhey)
neil.butterworth@rochdale.gov.uk

Clegg, Robert (CON - Wardle and West Littleborough)
robert.clegg@rochdale.gov.uk

Duckworth, Ian (CON - Bamford)
ian.duckworth@rochdale.gov.uk

Emmott, Susan (LAB - Hopwood Hall)
susan.emmott@rochdale.gov.uk

Emmott, Neil (LAB - West Middleton)
neil.emmott@rochdale.gov.uk

Emsley, Janet (LAB - Littleborough Lakeside)
janet.emsley@rochdale.gov.uk

Furlong, Christopher (LAB - North Middleton)
christopher.furlong@rochdale.gov.uk

Gartside, James (CON - Norden)
james.gartside@rochdale.gov.uk

Gartside, Jane (CON - Bamford)
jane.gartside@rochdale.gov.uk

Greenall, Pat (LAB - North Middleton)
pat.greenall@rochdale.gov.uk

Hartley, John (LAB - Littleborough Lakeside)
john.hartley@rochdale.gov.uk

Heakin, Kieran (LAB - Healey)
kieran.heakin@rochdale.gov.uk

Holly, Michael (CON - Norden)
michael.holly@rochdale.gov.uk

Hornby, Jean (LAB - Castleton)
jean.hornby@rochdale.gov.uk

Hussain, Aftab (LAB - Smallbridge and Firgrove)
aftab.hussain2@rochdale.gov.uk

Joinson, Peter (LAB - South Middleton)
peter.joinson@rochdale.gov.uk

Kelly, Andy (LD - Milnrow and Newhey)
andy.kelly@rochdale.gov.uk

Lambert, Colin (LAB - West Heywood)
colin.lambert@rochdale.gov.uk

Linden, Terry (LAB - Milkstone and Deeplish)
terry.linden@rochdale.gov.uk

Martin, Donna (LAB - East Middleton)
donna.martin@rochdale.gov.uk

McCarthy, Alan (LAB - West Heywood)
alanmmccarthy@btinternet.com

Meredith, Daniel (LAB - Balderstone and Kirkholt)
daniel.meredith@rochdale.gov.uk

Mir, Amna (LAB - Smallbridge and Firgrove)
amna.mir@rochdale.gov.uk

Murphy, Lily (LAB - West Middleton)
lil.murphy@rochdale.gov.uk

Nickson, Kathleen (LAB - Balderstone and Kirkholt)
kathleen.nickson@rochdale.gov.uk

O'Neill, Shaun (LAB - Healey)
shaun.o'neill@rochdale.gov.uk

O'Rourke, Liam (LAB - North Heywood)
liam.o'rourke@rochdale.gov.uk

Paolucci-Escobar, Rina (CON - Wardle and West Littleborough)
rina.paolucci@rochdale.gov.uk

Rashid, Aasim (LAB - Castleton)
aasim.rashid@rochdale.gov.uk

Robinson, Linda (LAB - Hopwood Hall)
linda.robinson@rochdale.gov.uk

Rowbotham, Sara (LAB - North Middleton)
sara.rowbotham@rochdale.gov.uk

Rush, Peter (LD - North Heywood)
peter.rush@rochdale.gov.uk

Sheerin, Billy (LAB - Castleton)
billy.sheerin@rochdale.gov.uk

Stott, Ann (CON - Littleborough Lakeside)
ann.stott2@rochdale.gov.uk

Sullivan, Patricia (CON - Bamford)
patricia.sullivan@rochdale.gov.uk

Wardle, Carol (LAB - Hopwood Hall)
carolwardle1@gmail.com

Wazir, Shah (LAB - Healey)
shah.wazir@rochdale.gov.uk

West, June (LAB - East Middleton)
june.west@rochdale.gov.uk

Winkler, Peter (CON - Norden)
peter.winkler@rochdale.gov.uk

Zaheer, Sameena (LAB - Milkstone and Deeplish)
sameena.zaheer@rochdale.gov.uk

Zaman, Mohammed (LAB - Milkstone and Deeplish)
mohammed.zaman@rochdale.gov.uk

POLITICAL COMPOSITION

LAB: 47, CON: 10, LD: 2, IND: 1

COMMITTEE CHAIRS

Audit & Governance: Mr Liam O'Rourke

Communities, Regeneration & Environment: Mr Neil Butterworth

Health, Schools & Care: Ms Sara Rowbotham

Planning & Licensing: Ms Carol Wardle

Rochford — D

Rochford District Council, Council Offices, South Street, Rochford SS4 1BW
☎ 01702 546366 🖷 01702 545737 ✉ information@rochford.gov.uk
💻 www.rochford.gov.uk

FACTS AND FIGURES

Parliamentary Constituencies: Rayleigh and Wickford, Rochford and Southend East
EU Constituencies: Eastern
Election Frequency: Elections are by thirds

PRINCIPAL OFFICERS

Chief Executive: Mr Amar Dave , Chief Executive, Council Offices, South Street, Rochford SS4 1BW ☎ 01702 546366 🖷 01702 545737 ✉ amar.dave@rochford.gov.uk

Senior Management: Mr John Bostock , Head of Finance, Council Offices, South Street, Rochford SS4 1BW ☎ 01702 546366 ✉ john.bostock@rochford.gov.uk

Senior Management: Ms Karen Bridge , Electoral Services Manager, Council Offices, South Street, Rochford SS4 1BW ☎ 01702 546336 🖷 01702 545737 ✉ karen.bridge@rochford.gov.uk

Senior Management: Mr Matt Harwood-White , Assistant Director - Commercial Services, Council Offices, South Street, Rochford SS4 1BW ☎ 01702 546366 ✉ matt.harwoodwhite@rochford.gov.uk

Senior Management: Mr Marcus Hotten , Assistant Director - Environmental Services, Council Offices, South Street, Rochford SS4 1BW ☎ 01702 546366 ✉ marcus.hotten@rochford.gov.uk

Senior Management: Mr Nicholas Khan , Director, Council Offices, South Street, Rochford SS4 1BW ☎ 01702 318169 ✉ nicholas.khan@rochford.gov.uk

Senior Management: Ms Angela Law , Assistant Director - Legal Services (Interim), Council Offices, South Street, Rochford SS4 1BW ☎ 01702 546366 ✉ angela.law@rochford.gov.uk

Senior Management: Mr Andrew Mowbray , Assistant Director - Transformational Services, Council Offices, South Street, Rochford SS4 1BW ☎ 01702 546366 ✉ andrew.mowbray@rochford.gov.uk

Senior Management: Mr Joseph Raveendran , Assistant Director - Resources Services (Interim), Council Offices, South Street, Rochford SS4 1BW ☎ 01702 546366 ✉ joseph.raveendram@rochford.gov.uk

Senior Management: Mr Shaun Scrutton, Director, Council Offices, South Street, Rochford SS4 1BW ☎ 01702 318100 ✉ shaun.scrutton@rochford.gov.uk

ROCHFORD

Senior Management: Mrs Dawn Tribe , Assistant Director - Customer, Revenues & Benefits Services, Council Offices, South Street, Rochford SS4 1BW ☎ 01702 546366 🖱 dawn.tribe@rochford.gov.uk

Building Control: Mr Allan Taylor , Building Control Manager, Council Offices, South Street, Rochford SS4 1BW ☎ 01702 546366 🖷 01702 318181 🖱 allan.taylor@rochford.gov.uk

PR / Communications: Mrs Claudia McClellan, People & Policy Unit Manager, Council Offices, South Street, Rochford SS4 1BW ☎ ; 01702 546366 🖱 claudia.mcclellan@rochford.gov.uk

Community Safety: Mr Jeremy Bourne, Head of Community Services, Council Offices, South Street, Rochford SS4 1BW ☎ 01702 546366 🖷 01702 545737 🖱 jeremy.bourne@rochford.gov.uk

Computer Management: Mr Shaun Scrutton, Director, Council Offices, South Street, Rochford SS4 1BW ☎ 01702 318100 🖱 shaun.scrutton@rochford.gov.uk

Customer Service: Mr Jeremy Bourne, Head of Community Services, Council Offices, South Street, Rochford SS4 1BW ☎ 01702 546366 🖷 01702 545737 🖱 jeremy.bourne@rochford.gov.uk

Economic Development: Mr Shaun Scrutton, Director, Council Offices, South Street, Rochford SS4 1BW ☎ 01702 318100 🖱 shaun.scrutton@rochford.gov.uk

E-Government: Mr Shaun Scrutton, Director, Council Offices, South Street, Rochford SS4 1BW ☎ 01702 318100 🖱 shaun.scrutton@rochford.gov.uk

Electoral Registration: Ms Karen Bridge , Electoral Services Manager, Council Offices, South Street, Rochford SS4 1BW ☎ 01702 546336 🖷 01702 545737 🖱 karen.bridge@rochford.gov.uk

Emergency Planning: Mr Jeff Stacey , Emergency Planning & Business Continuity Officer, Council Offices, South Street, Rochford SS4 1BW ☎ 01702 546366 🖷 01702 318183 🖱 jeff.stacey@rochford.gov.uk

Energy Management: Mr Alan Thomas , Asset Manager, Council Offices, South Street, Rochford SS4 1BW ☎ 01702 546366 🖱 alan.thomas@rochford.gov.uk

Environmental / Technical Services: Mr Richard Evans, Head of Environmental Services, Council Offices, South Street, Rochford SS4 1BW ☎ 01702 546366 🖱 richard.evans@rochford.gov.uk

Environmental Health: Mr Richard Evans, Head of Environmental Services, Council Offices, South Street, Rochford SS4 1BW ☎ 01702 546366 🖱 richard.evans@rochford.gov.uk

Estates, Property & Valuation: Mr Alan Thomas , Asset Manager, Council Offices, South Street, Rochford SS4 1BW ☎ 01702 546366 🖱 alan.thomas@rochford.gov.uk

Treasury: Mr Matthew Petley , Senior Accountant, Council Offices, South Street, Rochford SS4 1BW ☎ 01702 546366 🖱 matthewpetley@rochford.gov.uk

Grounds Maintenance: Mr Richard Evans, Head of Environmental Services, Council Offices, South Street, Rochford SS4 1BW ☎ 01702 546366 🖱 richard.evans@rochford.gov.uk

Health and Safety: Mr David Connor , Health & Safety Officer, Council Offices, South Street, Rochford SS4 1BW ☎ 01702 546366 🖱 david.connor@rochford.gov.uk

Home Energy Conservation: Mr Steve Neville , Strategic Housing Manager, Council Offices, South Street, Rochford SS4 1BW ☎ 01702 546366 🖱 steve.neville@rochford.gov.uk

Housing: Mr Jeremy Bourne, Head of Community Services, Council Offices, South Street, Rochford SS4 1BW ☎ 01702 546366 🖷 01702 545737 🖱 jeremy.bourne@rochford.gov.uk

Legal: Mr Albert Bugeja , Head of Legal, Estates and Member Services, Council Offices, South Street, Rochford SS4 1BW ☎ 01702 318130 🖷 01702 545737 🖱 albert.bugeja@rochford.gov.uk

Leisure and Cultural Services: Mr Jeremy Bourne, Head of Community Services, Council Offices, South Street, Rochford SS4 1BW ☎ 01702 546366 🖷 01702 545737 🖱 jeremy.bourne@rochford.gov.uk

Licensing: Mr Richard Evans, Head of Environmental Services, Council Offices, South Street, Rochford SS4 1BW ☎ 01702 546366 🖱 richard.evans@rochford.gov.uk

Member Services: Mr John Bostock , Member Services Manager, Council Offices, South Street, Rochford SS4 1BW ☎ 01702 546366 🖷 01702 545737 🖱 john.bostock@rochford.gov.uk

Parking: Mr Shaun Scrutton, Director, Council Offices, South Street, Rochford SS4 1BW ☎ 01702 318100 🖱 shaun.scrutton@rochford.gov.uk

Personnel / HR: Mrs Claudia McClellan, People & Policy Unit Manager, Council Offices, South Street, Rochford SS4 1BW ☎ 01702 546366 🖱 claudia.mcclellan@rochford.gov.uk

Planning: Mr Shaun Scrutton, Director, Council Offices, South Street, Rochford SS4 1BW ☎ 01702 318100 🖱 shaun.scrutton@rochford.gov.uk

Recycling & Waste Minimisation: Mr Richard Evans, Head of Environmental Services, Council Offices, South Street, Rochford SS4 1BW ☎ 01702 546366 🖱 richard.evans@rochford.gov.uk

Regeneration: Mr Shaun Scrutton, Director, Council Offices, South Street, Rochford SS4 1BW ☎ 01702 318100 🖱 shaun.scrutton@rochford.gov.uk

Staff Training: Mrs Claudia McClellan, People & Policy Unit Manager, Council Offices, South Street, Rochford SS4 1BW ☎ 01702 546366 🖱 claudia.mcclellan@rochford.gov.uk

Street Scene: Mr Richard Evans, Head of Environmental Services, Council Offices, South Street, Rochford SS4 1BW ☎ 01702 546366 🖱 richard.evans@rochford.gov.uk

Waste Collection and Disposal: Mr Richard Evans, Head of Environmental Services, Council Offices, South Street, Rochford SS4 1BW ☎ 01702 546366 ✉ richard.evans@rochford.gov.uk

Waste Management: Mr Richard Evans, Head of Environmental Services, Council Offices, South Street, Rochford SS4 1BW ☎ 01702 546366 ✉ richard.evans@rochford.gov.uk

COUNCILLORS

***Chair* Glynn**, Heather (CON - Hawkwell South)
cllrheather.glynn@rochford.gov.uk

***Vice-Chair* Lawmon**, Jack (CON - Wheatley)
cllrjack.lawmon@rochford.gov.uk

***Leader of the Council* Cutmore**, Terry (CON - Ashingdon and Canewdon)
cllrterry.cutmore@rochford.gov.uk

***Deputy Leader of the Council* Hudson**, Keith (CON - Hockley Central)
cllrkeith.hudson@rochford.gov.uk

***Group Leader* Black**, Chris (LD - Downhall and Rawreth)
cllrchris.black@rochford.gov.uk

***Group Leader* Hayter**, John (UKIP - Trinity)
cllrjohn.hayter@rochford.gov.uk

Burton, Jamie (UKIP - Grange)
cllrjamie.burton@rochford.gov.uk

Butcher, Lesley (CON - Hawkwell North)
cllrlesley.butcher@rochford.gov.uk

Carter, Michael (CON - Hockley North)
cllrmichael.carter@rochford.gov.uk

Dray, Robin (CON - Whitehouse)
cllrrobin.dray@rochford.gov.uk

Gibson, Jerry (LAB - Rochford)
cllrjerry.gibson@rochford.gov.uk

Gordon, Keith (CON - Rochford)
cllrkeith.gordon@rochford.gov.uk

Griffin, John (CON - Wheatley)
cllrjohn.griffin@rochford.gov.uk

Hale, Angela (CON - Hullbridge)
cllrangela.hale@rochford.gov.uk

Hazlewood, Brian (CON - Hockley Central)
cllrbrian.hazlewood@rochford.gov.uk

Hookway, Neil (UKIP - Foulness and Great Wakering)
cllrneil.hookway@rochford.gov.uk

Hoy, Michael (GRN - Hullbridge)
cllr.michael.hoy@rochford.gov.uk

Hoy, Diane (GRN - Hullbridge)
cllrdiane.hoy@rochford.gov.uk

Ioannou, George (CON - Ashingdon and Canewdon)
cllrgeorge.ioannou@rochford.gov.uk

Lucas-Gill, Gillian (CON - Rochford)
cllrgillian.lucas-gill@rochford.gov.uk

Lumley, June (LD - Grange)
cllrjune.lumley@rochford.gov.uk

Maddocks, Malcolm (CON - Hockley West)
cllrmalcolm.maddocks@rochford.gov.uk

Mason, John (R - Hawkwell West)
cllrjohn.mason@rochford.gov.uk

Mason, Christine (R - Hawkwell West)
cllrchristine.mason@rochford.gov.uk

McPherson, Jo (CON - Hawkwell North)
cllrjo.mcpherson@rochford.gov.uk

Merrick, David (CON - Lodge)
cllrdavid.merrick@rochford.gov.uk

Mockford, Joan (CON - Sweyne Park)
cllrjoan.mockford@rochford.gov.uk

Oatham, Ron (LD - Downhall and Rawreth)
cllrron.oatham@rochford.gov.uk

Pavelin, Carol (CON - Sweyne Park)
cllrcarol.pavelin@rochford.gov.uk

Roe, Cheryl (CON - Rayleigh Central)
cllrcheryl.roe@rochford.gov.uk

Seagers, Colin (CON - Foulness and Great Wakering)
cllrcolin.seagers@rochford.gov.uk

Smith, Simon (CON - Whitehouse)
cllrsimon.smith@rochford.gov.uk

Spencer, Margaret (CON - Rayleigh Central)
cllrmargaret.spencer@rochford.gov.uk

Sperring, Dave (CON - Trinity)
cllrdave.sperring@rochford.gov.uk

Steptoe, Mike (CON - Barling and Sutton)
cllrmike.steptoe@rochford.gov.uk

Ward, Ian (CON - Lodge)
cllrian.ward@rochford.gov.uk

Webb, Mike (CON - Hawkwell South)
cllrmike.webb@rochford.gov.uk

Weston, Carole (CON - Hockley Central)
cllrcarole.weston@rochford.gov.uk

Wilkins, Barbara (CON - Foulness and Great Wakering)
cllrbarbara.wilkins@rochford.gov.uk

POLITICAL COMPOSITION

CON: 28, LD: 3, UKIP: 3, R: 2, GRN: 2, LAB: 1

COMMITTEE CHAIRS

Audit: Mrs Joan Mockford

Development: Mr Colin Seagers

Licensing: Mrs Carole Weston

Rossendale D

Rossendale Borough Council, Business Centre, Futures Park, Newchurch Road, Bacup OL13 0BB
☎ 01706 217777 🖷 01706 224504
✉ generalenquiries@rossendalebc.gov.uk 🖳 www.rossendale.gov.uk

FACTS AND FIGURES

Parliamentary Constituencies: Hyndburn, Rossendale and Darwen
EU Constituencies: North West
Election Frequency: Elections are by thirds

ROSSENDALE

PRINCIPAL OFFICERS

Chief Executive: Mr Stuart Sugarman , Chief Executive, The Business Centre, Futures Park, Newchurch Road, Bacup OL13 0BB ☎ 01706 252440 🖷 01706 873577 ✉ stuartsugarman@rossendalebc.gov.uk

Senior Management: Mr Andrew Buckle, Head of Customer Services & ICT, The Business Centre, Futures Park, Newchurch Road, Bacup OL13 0BB ☎ 01706 238606 🖷 01706 873577 ✉ andrewbuckle@rossendalebc.gov.uk

Senior Management: Mr Steve Jackson , Head of Health, Housing & Regeneration, The Business Centre, Futures Park, Newchurch Road, Bacup OL13 0BB ☎ 01706 252404 🖷 01706 873577 ✉ stephenjackson@rossendalebc.gov.uk

Senior Management: Mr Joe Kennedy , Head of Operations, Henrietta Street Depot, Bacup OL13 0AR ☎ 01706 252519 ✉ josephkennedy@rossendalebc.gov.uk

Senior Management: Mr Phil Seddon , Head of Finance & Property, The Business Centre, Futures Park, Newchurch Road, Bacup OL13 0BB ☎ 01706 252465 🖷 01706 873577 ✉ philseddon@rossendalebc.gov.uk

Architect, Building / Property Services: Mr Lee Childs, Property & Facilities Services Officer, The Busníess Centre, Futures Park, Bacup OL13 0BB ☎ 01706 252527 🖷 01706 873577 ✉ leechilds@rossendalebc.gov.uk

Architect, Building / Property Services: Mr Mike Forster, Property Services Manager, The Business Centre, Futures Park, Newchurch Road, Bacup OL13 0BB ☎ 01706 252442 🖷 01706 873577 ✉ michael.forster@rossendalebc.gov.uk

Building Control: Mr Alan Dixon, District Building Control Officer, The Business Centre, Futures Park, Newchurch Road, Bacup OL13 0BB ☎ 01706 252525 ✉ alandixon@rossendalebc.gov.uk

Building Control: Mr Andrew Pearson , District Building Control Officer, The Business Centre, Futures Park, Newchurch Road, Bacup OL13 0BB ☎ 01706 252524 ✉ andrewpearson@rossendalebc.gov.uk

PR / Communications: Ms Katie Gee , Corporate Officer, Business Centre, Futures Park, Newchurch Road, Bacup OL13 0BB ☎ 01706 252554 🖷 01706 873577 ✉ katiegee@rossendalebc.gov.uk

Computer Management: Mr Andrew Buckle, Head of Customer Services & ICT, The Business Centre, Futures Park, Newchurch Road, Bacup OL13 0BB ☎ 01706 238606 🖷 01706 873577 ✉ andrewbuckle@rossendalebc.gov.uk

Consumer Protection and Trading Standards: Ms Tracy Brzozowski, Licensing & Enforcement Manager, The Business Centre, Futures Park, Newchurch Road, Bacup OL13 0BB ☎ 01706 238602 ✉ tracybrzozowski@rossendalebc.gov.uk

Contracts: Mr Stuart Sugarman , Chief Executive, The Business Centre, Futures Park, Newchurch Road, Bacup OL13 0BB ☎ 01706 252440 🖷 01706 873577 ✉ stuartsugarman@rossendalebc.gov.uk

Customer Service: Mr Andrew Buckle, Head of Customer Services & ICT, The Business Centre, Futures Park, Newchurch Road, Bacup OL13 0BB ☎ 01706 238606 🖷 01706 873577 ✉ andrewbuckle@rossendalebc.gov.uk

Economic Development: Mr Steve Jackson , Head of Health, Housing & Regeneration, The Business Centre, Futures Park, Newchurch Road, Bacup OL13 0BB ☎ 01706 252404 🖷 01706 873577 ✉ stephenjackson@rossendalebc.gov.uk

Economic Development: Mr David Presto , Economic Development & External Funding Manager, Business Centre, Futures Park, Newchurch Road, Bacup OL13 0BB ☎ 01706 252477 🖷 01706 873577 ✉ davidpresto@rossendalebc.gov.uk

E-Government: Mr Andrew Buckle, Head of Customer Services & ICT, The Business Centre, Futures Park, Newchurch Road, Bacup OL13 0BB ☎ 01706 238606 🖷 01706 873577 ✉ andrewbuckle@rossendalebc.gov.uk

Electoral Registration: Ms Joanne Smith, Elections Manager , The Business Centre, Futures Park, Newchurch Road, Bacup OL13 0BB ☎ 01706 252461 ✉ joannesmith@rossendalebc.gov.uk

Emergency Planning: Mr Phil Seddon , Head of Finance & Property, The Business Centre, Futures Park, Newchurch Road, Bacup OL13 0BB ☎ 01706 252465 🖷 01706 873577 ✉ philseddon@rossendalebc.gov.uk

Energy Management: Mr Lee Childs, Property & Facilities Services Officer, The Busniess Centre, Futures Park, Bacup OL13 0BB ☎ 01706 252527 🖷 01706 873577 ✉ leechilds@rossendalebc.gov.uk

Energy Management: Mr Mike Forster, Property Services Manager, The Business Centre, Futures Park, Newchurch Road, Bacup OL13 0BB ☎ 01706 252442 🖷 01706 873577 ✉ michael.forster@rossendalebc.gov.uk

Environmental / Technical Services: Mr Joe Kennedy , Head of Operations, Henrietta Street Depot, Bacup OL13 0AR ☎ 01706 252519 ✉ josephkennedy@rossendalebc.gov.uk

Environmental Health: Mr Steve Jackson , Head of Health, Housing & Regeneration, The Business Centre, Futures Park, Newchurch Road, Bacup OL13 0BB ☎ 01706 252404 🖷 01706 873577 ✉ stephenjackson@rossendalebc.gov.uk

Estates, Property & Valuation: Mr Lee Childs, Property & Facilities Services Officer, The Busniess Centre, Futures Park, Bacup OL13 0BB ☎ 01706 252527 🖷 01706 873577 ✉ leechilds@rossendalebc.gov.uk

Estates, Property & Valuation: Mr Mike Forster, Property Services Manager, The Business Centre, Futures Park, Newchurch Road, Bacup OL13 0BB ☎ 01706 252442 🖷 01706 873577 ✉ michael.forster@rossendalebc.gov.uk

Events Manager: Ms Katie Gee , Corporate Officer, Business Centre, Futures Park, Newchurch Road, Bacup OL13 0BB ☎ 01706 252554 🖷 01706 873577 ✉ katiegee@rossendalebc.gov.uk

Facilities: Mr Lee Childs, Property & Facilities Services Officer, The Busniess Centre, Futures Park, Bacup OL13 0BB ☎ 01706 252527 🖷 01706 873577 🖱 leechilds@rossendalebc.gov.uk

Facilities: Mr Mike Forster, Property Services Manager, The Business Centre, Futures Park, Newchurch Road, Bacup OL13 0BB ☎ 01706 252442 🖷 01706 873577 🖱 michael.forster@rossendalebc.gov.uk

Finance: Mr Phil Seddon , Head of Finance & Property, The Business Centre, Futures Park, Newchurch Road, Bacup OL13 0BB ☎ 01706 252465 🖷 01706 873577 🖱 philseddon@rossendalebc.gov.uk

Fleet Management: Ms Christine Chadderton, Transport Co-ordinator, Henrietta Street Depot, Bacup OL13 0AR ☎ 01706 878660 🖱 christinechadderton@rossendalebc.gov.uk

Fleet Management: Mr Joe Kennedy , Head of Operations, Henrietta Street Depot, Bacup OL13 0AR ☎ 01706 252519 🖱 josephkennedy@rossendalebc.gov.uk

Grounds Maintenance: Mr Joe Kennedy , Head of Operations, Henrietta Street Depot, Bacup OL13 0AR ☎ 01706 252519 🖱 josephkennedy@rossendalebc.gov.uk

Health and Safety: Mr Steve Tomlinson , Health & Safety Officer, Business Centre, Futures Park, Newchurch Road, Bacup OL13 0BB ☎ 01706 873577 🖱 stevetomlinson@rossendalebc.gov.uk

Home Energy Conservation: Mr Steve Jackson , Head of Health, Housing & Regeneration, The Business Centre, Futures Park, Newchurch Road, Bacup OL13 0BB ☎ 01706 252404 🖷 01706 873577 🖱 stephenjackson@rossendalebc.gov.uk

Housing: Mr Steve Jackson , Head of Health, Housing & Regeneration, The Business Centre, Futures Park, Newchurch Road, Bacup OL13 0BB ☎ 01706 252404 🖷 01706 873577 🖱 stephenjackson@rossendalebc.gov.uk

Legal: Mr Stuart Sugarman , Chief Executive, The Business Centre, Futures Park, Newchurch Road, Bacup OL13 0BB ☎ 01706 252440 🖷 01706 873577 🖱 stuartsugarman@rossendalebc.gov.uk

Leisure and Cultural Services: Mr Martin Kay, General Manager, Business Centre, Futures Park, Newchurch Road, Bacup OL13 0BB ☎ 01706 242319 🖱 martin.kay@rltrust.co.uk

Licensing: Ms Tracy Brzozowski, Licensing & Enforcement Manager, The Business Centre, Futures Park, Newchurch Road, Bacup OL13 0BB ☎ 01706 238602 🖱 tracybrzozowski@rossendalebc.gov.uk

Lifelong Learning: Mrs Clare Law, HR Manager, The Business Centre, Futures Park, Newchurch Road, Bacup OL13 0BB ☎ 01706 252457 🖷 01706 873577 🖱 clarelaw@rossendalebc.gov.uk

Member Services: Mrs Carolyn Sharples , Committee & Member Services Manager, The Business Centre, Futures Park, Newchurch Road, Bacup OL13 0BB ☎ 01706 252422 🖷 01706 873577 🖱 carolynsharples@rossendalebc.gov.uk

Personnel / HR: Mrs Clare Law, HR Manager, The Business Centre, Futures Park, Newchurch Road, Bacup OL13 0BB ☎ 01706 252457 🖷 01706 873577 🖱 clarelaw@rossendalebc.gov.uk

Planning: Mr Stephen Stray , Planning Manager, The Business Centre, Futures Park, Newchurch Road, Bacup OL13 0BB ☎ 01706 252420 🖱 stephenstray@rossendalebc.gov.uk

Procurement: Mr Phil Seddon , Head of Finance & Property, The Business Centre, Futures Park, Newchurch Road, Bacup OL13 0BB ☎ 01706 252465 🖷 01706 873577 🖱 philseddon@rossendalebc.gov.uk

Recycling & Waste Minimisation: Mr Joe Kennedy , Head of Operations, Henrietta Street Depot, Bacup OL13 0AR ☎ 01706 252519 🖱 josephkennedy@rossendalebc.gov.uk

Regeneration: Mr Steve Jackson , Head of Health, Housing & Regeneration, The Business Centre, Futures Park, Newchurch Road, Bacup OL13 0BB ☎ 01706 252404 🖷 01706 873577 🖱 stephenjackson@rossendalebc.gov.uk

Regeneration: Mr David Presto , Economic Development & External Funding Manager, Business Centre, Futures Park, Newchurch Road, Bacup OL13 0BB ☎ 01706 252477 🖷 01706 873577 🖱 davidpresto@rossendalebc.gov.uk

Staff Training: Mrs Clare Law, HR Manager, The Business Centre, Futures Park, Newchurch Road, Bacup OL13 0BB ☎ 01706 252457 🖷 01706 873577 🖱 clarelaw@rossendalebc.gov.uk

Street Scene: Mr Joe Kennedy , Head of Operations, Henrietta Street Depot, Bacup OL13 0AR ☎ 01706 252519 🖱 josephkennedy@rossendalebc.gov.uk

Sustainable Development: Mr David Presto , Economic Development & External Funding Manager, Business Centre, Futures Park, Newchurch Road, Bacup OL13 0BB ☎ 01706 252477 🖷 01706 873577 🖱 davidpresto@rossendalebc.gov.uk

Sustainable Development: Mr Stephen Stray , Planning Manager, The Business Centre, Futures Park, Newchurch Road, Bacup OL13 0BB ☎ 01706 252420 🖱 stephenstray@rossendalebc.gov.uk

Tourism: Mr Steve Jackson , Head of Health, Housing & Regeneration, The Business Centre, Futures Park, Newchurch Road, Bacup OL13 0BB ☎ 01706 252404 🖷 01706 873577 🖱 stephenjackson@rossendalebc.gov.uk

Tourism: Mr David Presto , Economic Development & External Funding Manager, Business Centre, Futures Park, Newchurch Road, Bacup OL13 0BB ☎ 01706 252477 🖷 01706 873577 🖱 davidpresto@rossendalebc.gov.uk

Town Centre: Mr Steve Jackson , Head of Health, Housing & Regeneration, The Business Centre, Futures Park, Newchurch Road, Bacup OL13 0BB ☎ 01706 252404 🖷 01706 873577 🖱 stephenjackson@rossendalebc.gov.uk

Town Centre: Mr David Presto , Economic Development & External Funding Manager, Business Centre, Futures Park, Newchurch Road, Bacup OL13 0BB ☎ 01706 252477 🖷 01706 873577 🖱 davidpresto@rossendalebc.gov.uk

Transport: Ms Christine Chadderton, Transport Co-ordinator, Henrietta Street Depot, Bacup OL13 0AR ☎ 01706 878660 ✉ christinechadderton@rossendalebc.gov.uk

Waste Collection and Disposal: Mr Joe Kennedy , Head of Operations, Henrietta Street Depot, Bacup OL13 0AR ☎ 01706 252519 ✉ josephkennedy@rossendalebc.gov.uk

Waste Management: Mr Joe Kennedy , Head of Operations, Henrietta Street Depot, Bacup OL13 0AR ☎ 01706 252519 ✉ josephkennedy@rossendalebc.gov.uk

COUNCILLORS

***Mayor* Procter**, Marilyn (LAB - Worsley)
marilynprocter@rossendalebc.gov.uk

***Deputy Mayor* Morris**, Granville (CON - Greenfield)
granvillemorris@rossendalebc.gov.uk

***Leader of the Council* Barnes**, Alyson (LAB - Goodshaw)
alysonbarnes@rossendalebc.gov.uk

***Deputy Leader of the Council* Lamb**, Christine (LAB - Stacksteads)
christinelamb@rossendalebc.gov.uk

***Group Leader* Smith**, Darryl (CON - Eden)
darrylsmith@rossendalebc.gov.uk

Ashworth, Barbara (LAB - Greensclough)
barbaraashworth@rossendalebc.gov.uk

Barnes, Lynda (CON - Facit and Shawforth)
lyndabarnes@rossendalebc.gov.uk

Bleakley, Caroline (LAB - Hareholme)
carolinebleakley@rossendalebc.gov.uk

Cheetham, Anne (CON - Eden)
annecheetham@rossendalebc.gov.uk

Collinge, Sarah (CON - Whitewell)
sarahcollinge@rossendalebc.gov.uk

Crawforth, Colin (LAB - Hareholme)
colincrawforth@rossendalebc.gov.uk

de Souza, Madeline (IND - Facit and Shawforth)
madelinedesouza@rossendalebc.gov.uk

Eaton, James (CON - Greensclough)
jameseaton@rossendalebc.gov.uk

Eaton, Janet (CON - Irwell)
janeteaton@rossendalebc.gov.uk

Essex, Brian (CON - Helmshore)
brianessex@rossendalebc.gov.uk

Evans, Peter (CON - Helmshore)
peterevans@rossendalebc.gov.uk

Farrington, Dorothy (LAB - Goodshaw)
dorothyfarrington@rossendalebc.gov.uk

Fletcher, Andrea (LAB - Cribden)
andreafletcher@rossendalebc.gov.uk

Graham, Janet (CON - Cribden)
janetgraham@rossendalebc.gov.uk

Haworth, Tony (CON - Helmshore)
tonyhaworth@rossendalebc.gov.uk

Hughes, Steve (LAB - Irwell)
stevehughes@rossendalebc.gov.uk

Kempson, Karl (CON - Whitewell)
karlkempson@rossendalebc.gov.uk

Kenyon, Ann (LAB - Worsley)
annkenyon@rossendalebc.gov.uk

Knowles, Roy (LAB - Longholme)
royknowles@rossendalebc.gov.uk

Lythgoe, Adrian (LAB - Worsley)
adrianlythgoe@rossendalebc.gov.uk

Marriott, Patrick (LAB - Hareholme)
patrickmarriott@rossendalebc.gov.uk

McMahon, Annie (LAB - Longholme)
anniemcmahon@rossendalebc.gov.uk

Neal, Alan (IND - Healey and Whitworth)
alanneal@rossendalebc.gov.uk

Oakes, Jackie (LAB - Stacksteads)
jackieoakes@rossendalebc.gov.uk

Robertson, Amanda (LAB - Whitewell)
amandarobertson@rossendalebc.gov.uk

Sandiford, Gladys (CON - Greenfield)
gladyssandiford@rossendalebc.gov.uk

Serridge, Sean (LAB - Healey and Whitworth)
seanserridge@rossendalebc.gov.uk

Shipley, Annabel (CON - Greenfield)
annabelshipley@rossendalebc.gov.uk

Smallridge, Sam (LAB - Longholme)
samsmallridge@rossendalebc.gov.uk

Smith, Michelle (LAB - Irwell)
michellesmith@rossendalebc.gov.uk

Steen, Peter (CON - Greensclough)
petersteen@rossendalebc.gov.uk

POLITICAL COMPOSITION

LAB: 19, CON: 15, IND: 2

COMMITTEE CHAIRS

Audit & Accounts: Mr Roy Knowles

Development Control: Ms Jackie Oakes

Licensing: Mr Colin Crawforth

Rother D

Rother District Council, Town Hall, Bexhill-on-Sea TN39 3JX
☎ 01424 787878 🖷 01424 787879 ✉ chiefexec@rother.gov.uk
💻 www.rother.gov.uk

FACTS AND FIGURES

Parliamentary Constituencies: Bexhill and Battle
EU Constituencies: South East
Election Frequency: Elections are of whole council

PRINCIPAL OFFICERS

Senior Management: Mr Malcolm Johnston , Executive Director - Resources & Head of Paid Service, Town Hall, Bexhill-on-Sea TN39 3JX ☎ 01424 787000 🖷 01424 787879 ✉ malcolm.johnston@rother.gov.uk

Senior Management: Dr Anthony Leonard , Executive Director - Business Operations & Head of Paid Service, Town Hall, Bexhill-on-Sea TN39 3JX ☎ 01424 787500 🖷 01424 787520

Best Value: Ms Joanne Wright, Policy Officer, Town Hall, Bexhill-on-Sea TN39 3JX ☎ 01424 787816 🖷 01424 787879 🖱 joanne.wright@rother.gov.uk.

Building Control: Mr Jonathan Cornell , Building Control Manager, Town Hall, Bexhill-on-Sea TN39 3JX ☎ 01424 787680 🖷 01424 787657 🖱 jonathan.cornell@rother.gov.uk

Building Control: Mr Jonathan Cornell , Chief Building Control Officer, Town Hall, Bexhill-on-Sea TN39 3JX ☎ 01424 787670 🖱 jonathan.cornell@rother.gov.uk

Community Planning: Mrs Brenda Mason, Service Manager - Community & Economy, Town Hall, Bexhill-on-Sea TN39 3JX ☎ 01424 787000 🖷 01424 787520 🖱 brenda.mason@rother.gov.uk

Computer Management: Mr John Collins, Manager for Corporate HR, Town Hall, Bexhill-on-Sea TN39 3JX ☎ 01424 787000 🖷 01424 787000 🖱 john.collins@rother.gov.uk

Corporate Services: Ms Suzanne Collins , Head of Corporate Services, Town Hall, Bexhill-on-Sea TN39 3JX ☎ 01424 787835 🖷 01424 787879 🖱 suzanne.collins@rother.gov.uk

Customer Service: Mr Mark Adams , Customer Services Officer, Town Hall, Bexhill-on-Sea TN39 3JX ☎ 01424 787000 🖱 mark.adams@rother.gov.uk

Economic Development: Mr Graham Burgess, Head of Regeneration, Town Hall, Bexhill-on-Sea TN39 3JX ☎ 01424 787000 🖱 graham.burgess@rother.gov.uk

Electoral Registration: Ms Suzanne Collins , Head of Corporate Services, Town Hall, Bexhill-on-Sea TN39 3JX ☎ 01424 787835 🖷 01424 787879 🖱 suzanne.collins@rother.gov.uk

Environmental Health: Mr Richard Parker-Harding, Head of Environmental Health, 14 Beeching Road, Bexhill-on-Sea TN39 3LG 🖱 richard.parker-harding@rother.gov.uk

Estates, Property & Valuation: Ms Suzanne Collins , Head of Corporate Services, Town Hall, Bexhill-on-Sea TN39 3JX ☎ 01424 787835 🖷 01424 787879 🖱 suzanne.collins@rother.gov.uk

Facilities: Ms Kim Ross , Head of Amenities, Town Hall, Bexhill-on-Sea TN39 3JX ☎ 01424 787000 🖱 kim.ross@rother.gov.uk

Finance: Mr Malcolm Johnston , Executive Director - Resources & Head of Paid Service, Town Hall, Bexhill-on-Sea TN39 3JX ☎ 01424 787000 🖷 01424 787879 🖱 malcolm.johnston@rother.gov.uk

Finance: Mr Robin Vennard , Head of Finance, Town Hall, Bexhill-on-Sea TN39 3JX ☎ 01424 787000 🖱 robin.vennard@rother.gov.uk

Treasury: Mr Clive Jefferson , Treasurer, Town Hall, Bexhill-on-Sea TN39 3JX ☎ 01424 787000 🖱 clive.jefferson@rother.gov.uk

Health and Safety: Mr John Collins, Manager for Corporate HR, Town Hall, Bexhill-on-Sea TN39 3JX ☎ 01424 787000 🖷 01424 787000 🖱 john.collins@rother.gov.uk

Housing: Mr Martin Bolton , Housing Needs Manager, Town Hall, Bexhill-on-Sea TN39 3JX ☎ 01424 787000 🖱 martin.bolton@rother.gov.uk

Legal: Ms Suzanne Collins , Head of Corporate Services, Town Hall, Bexhill-on-Sea TN39 3JX ☎ 01424 787835 🖷 01424 787879 🖱 suzanne.collins@rother.gov.uk

Leisure and Cultural Services: Ms Kim Ross , Head of Amenities, Town Hall, Bexhill-on-Sea TN39 3JX ☎ 01424 787000 🖱 kim.ross@rother.gov.uk

Licensing: Mr Richard Parker-Harding, Head of Environmental Health, 14 Beeching Road, Bexhill-on-Sea TN39 3LG 🖱 richard.parker-harding@rother.gov.uk

Member Services: Ms Suzanne Collins , Head of Corporate Services, Town Hall, Bexhill-on-Sea TN39 3JX ☎ 01424 787835 🖷 01424 787879 🖱 suzanne.collins@rother.gov.uk

Parking: Ms Kim Ross , Head of Amenities, Town Hall, Bexhill-on-Sea TN39 3JX ☎ 01424 787000 🖱 kim.ross@rother.gov.uk

Personnel / HR: Mr John Collins, Manager for Corporate HR, Town Hall, Bexhill-on-Sea TN39 3JX ☎ 01424 787000 🖷 01424 787000 🖱 john.collins@rother.gov.uk

Planning: Mr Tim Hickling , Manager for Strategy & Planning, Town Hall, Bexhill-on-Sea TN39 3JX ☎ 01424 787000 🖱 tim.hickling@rother.gov.uk

Recycling & Waste Minimisation: Ms Kim Ross , Head of Amenities, 14 Beeching Road, Bexhill-on-Sea TN39 3LG ☎ 01424 787000 🖱 kim.ross@rother.gov.uk

Regeneration: Mr Graham Burgess, Head of Regeneration, Town Hall, Bexhill-on-Sea TN39 3JX ☎ 01424 787000 🖱 graham.burgess@rother.gov.uk

Staff Training: Mr John Collins, Manager for Corporate HR, Town Hall, Bexhill-on-Sea TN39 3JX ☎ 01424 787000 🖷 01424 787000 🖱 john.collins@rother.gov.uk

Sustainable Communities: Mrs Brenda Mason, Service Manager - Community & Economy, Town Hall, Bexhill-on-Sea TN39 3JX ☎ 01424 787000 🖷 01424 787520 🖱 brenda.mason@rother.gov.uk

Sustainable Development: Mrs Brenda Mason, Service Manager - Community & Economy, Town Hall, Bexhill-on-Sea TN39 3JX ☎ 01424 787000 🖷 01424 787520 🖱 brenda.mason@rother.gov.uk

Tourism: Mr Graham Burgess, Head of Regeneration, Town Hall, Bexhill-on-Sea TN39 3JX ☎ 01424 787000 🖱 graham.burgess@rother.gov.uk

COUNCILLORS

***Chair* Carroll**, James (CON - Bexhill Sidley) cllr.jim.carroll@rother.gov.uk

***Vice-Chair* Osborne**, Paul (CON - Eastern Rother)
cllr.paul.osborne@rother.gov.uk

***Mayor* Watson**, Maurice (LAB - Bexhill Sidley)
cllr.maurice.watson@rother.gov.uk

***Leader of the Council* Maynard**, Carl (CON - Brede Valley)
cllr.carl.maynard@rother.gov.uk

***Deputy Leader of the Council* Kenward**, Martin (CON - Bexhill Kewhurst)
cllr.martin.kenward@rother.gov.uk

***Group Leader* Field**, Kathryn (LD - Battle)
cllr.kathryn.field@rother.ac.uk

Ampthill, (CON - Rye)
cllr.lord.ampthill@rother.gov.uk

Azad, Abul (CON - Bexhill Central)
cllr.abul.azad@rother.gov.uk

Barnes, Mary (CON - Ticehurst & Etchingham)
cllr.mary.barnes@rother.gov.uk

Bird, Roger (CON - Marsham)
cllr.roger.bird@rother.gov.uk

Browne, Graham (CON - Salehurst)
cllr.graham.browne@rother.gov.uk

Carroll, Richard (CON - Bexhill Central)
cllr.richard.carroll@rother.gov.uk

Clark, Charles (IND - Bexhill St Michaels)
cllr.charles.clark@rother.gov.uk

Curtis, Gary (CON - Crowhurst)
cllr.gary.curtis@rother.gov.uk

Dixon, Kevin (LD - Battle)
cllr.kevin.dixon@rother.gov.uk

Douart, Patrick (CON - Bexhill Sackville)
cllr.patrick.douart@rother.gov.uk

Earl, Stuart (IND - Bexhill St Marks)
cllr.stuart.earl@rother.gov.uk

Elford, Simon (CON - Bexhill St Michaels)
cllr.simon.elford@rother.gov.uk

Elliston, Robert (CON - Ticehurst and Etchingham)
cllr.robert.elliston@rother.gov.uk

Ganly, Anthony (CON - Ewhurst and Sedlescombe)
cllr.tony.ganly@rother.gov.uk

George, Bridget (CON - Bexhill St Stephens)
cllr.bridget.george@rother.gov.uk

Graham, Tom (CON - Bexhill St Marks)
cllr.tom.graham@rother.gov.uk

Hart, Sally-Ann (CON - Eastern Rother)
cllr.sally-ann.hart@rother.gov.uk

Hollidge, Ian (CON - Bexhill Sackville)
cllr.ian.hollidge@rother.gov.uk

Hughes, Joyce (CON - Bexhill Central)
cllr.joy.hughes@rother.gov.uk

Jenkins, Ian (CON - Rother Levels)
cllr.ian.jenkins@rother.gov.uk

Johnson, Jonathan (CON - Brede Valley)
cllr.jonathon.johnson@rother.gov.uk

Johnson, Gillian (CON - Bexhill Old Town)
cllr.gillian.johnson@rother.gov.uk

Kentfield, Brian (CON - Bexhill Kewhurst)
cllr.brian.kentfield@rother.gov.uk

Kirby-Green, Eleanor (CON - Darwell)
cllr.eleanor.kirby-green@rother.gov.uk

Mansi, Tony (IND - Bexhill Collington)
cllr.tony.mansi@rother.gov.uk

Mooney, Martin (CON - Rother Levels)
cllr.martin.mooney@rother.gov.uk

Oliver, Douglas (IND - Bexhill Collington)
cllr.doug.oliver@rother.gov.uk

Potts, Jacqueline (CON - Bexhill Old Town)
cllr.jacqueline.potts@rother.gov.uk

Prochak, Susan (LD - Salehurst)
cllr.susan.prochak@rother.gov.uk

Rowlinson, Emily (CON - Darwell)
cllr.emily.rowlinson@rother.gov.uk

Saint, Chris (CON - Marsham)
cllr.chris.saint@rother.gov.uk

Stevens, Gennette (CON - Rye)
cllr.gennette.stevens@rother.gov.uk

POLITICAL COMPOSITION

CON: 30, IND: 4, LD: 3, LAB: 1

COMMITTEE CHAIRS

Audit: Mr Martin Mooney

Licensing: Mr Simon Elford

Planning: Mr Brian Kentfield

Rotherham M

Rotherham Metropolitan Borough Council, Riverside House, Main Street, Rotherham S60 1AE
☎ 01709 382121 🖳 www.rotherham.gov.uk

FACTS AND FIGURES

Parliamentary Constituencies: Rother Valley, Rotherham, Wentworth and Dearne
EU Constituencies: Yorkshire and the Humber
Election Frequency: Elections are by thirds

PRINCIPAL OFFICERS

Chief Executive: Ms Stella Manzie , Managing Director (Commissioner), Riverside House, Main Street, Rotherham S60 1AE ☎ 01709 822770 ✉ stella.manzie@rotherham.gov.uk

Senior Management: Ms Teresa Roche , Director - Public Health, Riverside House, Main Street, Rotherham S60 1AE ☎ 01709 255845 ✉ teresa.roche@rotherham.gov.uk

Senior Management: Mr Ian Thomas , Strategic Director - Children's Services, Riverside House, Main Street, Rotherham S60 1AE ☎ 01709 822506 ✉ ian.thomas@rotherham.gov.uk

Access Officer / Social Services (Disability): Mr Stuart Carr , Disability Co-ordinator, Riverside House, Main Street, Rotherham S60 1AE ☎ 01709 254022 ✉ stuart.carr@rotherham.gov.uk

Building Control: Mr Bruce Carter , Building Control Manager, Riverside House, Main Street, Rotherham S60 1AE ☎ 01709 829841 ✉ bruce.carter@rotherham.gov.uk

Catering Services: Mr Kim Phillips , Principal Catering Officer, Riverside House, Main Street, Rotherham S60 1AE ☎ 01709 254025 ✉ kim.phillips@rotherham.gov.uk

Children / Youth Services: Ms Karen Borthwick , Head of Schools Effectiveness Service, Riverside House, Main Street, Rotherham S60 1AE ☎ 01709 334075 ✉ karen.borthwick@rotherham.gov.uk

Children / Youth Services: Mr Ian Thomas , Strategic Director - Children's Services, Riverside House, Main Street, Rotherham S60 1AE ☎ 01709 822506 ✉ ian.thomas@rotherham.gov.uk

Civil Registration: Ms Louise Sennitt , Superintendant Registrar, Riverside House, Main Street, Rotherham S60 1AE ☎ 01709 822896

PR / Communications: Mrs Tracy Holmes, Head - Communications, Riverside House, Main Street, Rotherham S60 1AE ☎ 01709 822735 🖷 01709 822730 ✉ tracy.holmes@rotherham.gov.uk

Community Safety: Mr Steve Parry , Neighbourhood Crime & Justice Manager, Riverside House, Main Street, Rotherham S60 1AE ☎ 01709 334565 🖷 01709 334568 ✉ steve.parry@rotherham.gov.uk

Consumer Protection and Trading Standards: Mrs Janice Manning, Principal Officer - Environmental Health, Riverside House, Main Street, Rotherham S60 1AE ☎ 01709 823126 🖷 01709 823150 ✉ janice.manning@rotherham.gov.uk

Corporate Services: Mr Justin Homer , Head of Policy Improvement & Partnerships, Riverside House, Main Street, Rotherham S60 1AE ☎ 01709 823618 ✉ justin.homer@rotherham.gov.uk

Customer Service: Ms Zoe Oxley , Customer & Cultural Services Officer, Riverside House, Main Street, Rotherham S60 1AE ☎ 01709 334283 ✉ zoe.oxley@rotherham.gov.uk

Economic Development: Mr Karl Battersby, Strategic Director - Environment & Development Services, Riverside House, Main Street, Rotherham S60 1AE ☎ 01709 823801 🖷 01709 372530 ✉ karl.battersby@rotherham.gov.uk

Economic Development: Mr Paul Woodcock , Director - Planning & Regeneration, Riverside House, Main Street, Rotherham S60 1AE ☎ 01709 822971 🖷 01709 372530 ✉ paul.woodcock@rotherham.gov.uk

Education: Ms Karen Borthwick , Head of Schools Effectiveness Service, Riverside House, Main Street, Rotherham S60 1AE ☎ 01709 334075 ✉ karen.borthwick@rotherham.gov.uk

Electoral Registration: Ms Mags Evers , Elections & Registration Officer, Riverside House, Main Street, Rotherham S60 1AE ☎ 01709 823518 🖷 01709 367343 ✉ mags.evers@rotherham.gov.uk

Emergency Planning: Ms Claire Hanson , Interim Emergency & Safety Manager, Riverside House, Main Street, Rotherham S60 1AE ☎ 01709 823787 ✉ claire.hanson@rotherham.gov.uk

Energy Management: Mr David Rhodes, Environmental Officer, Riverside House, Main Street, Rotherham S60 1AE ☎ 01709 822166 ✉ david.rhodes@rotherham.gov.uk

Environmental Health: Mr Mark Ford , Safer Neighbourhoods Manager, Riverside House, Main Street, Rotherham S60 1AE ☎ 01709 254951 🖷 01709 823430 ✉ mark.ford@rotherham.gov.uk

Estates, Property & Valuation: Mr Paul Smith , Corporate Property Manager, Riverside House, Main Street, Rotherham S60 1AE ☎ 01709 254061 ✉ paul.smith@rotherham.gov.uk

Estates, Property & Valuation: Mr Dave Stimpson , Valuation Manager, Riverside House, Main Street, Rotherham S60 1AE ☎ 01709 254057 ✉ dave.stimpson@rotherham.gov.uk

European Liaison: Mr Michael Holmes , Policy & Partnerships Officer, Riverside House, Main Street, Rotherham S60 1AE ☎ 01709 254417 ✉ michael.holmes@rotherham.gov.uk

Events Manager: Ms Marie Hayes , Events & Promotion Manager, Riverside House, Maint Street, Rotherham S60 1AE ☎ 01709 255501 ✉ marie.hayes@rotherham.gov.uk

Facilities: Mr Stuart Carr , Facilities Manager, Riverside House, Main Street, Rotherham S60 1AE ☎ 01709 254021 ✉ stuart.carr@rotherham.gov.uk

Finance: Mr Stuart Booth , Interim Strategic Director - Resources, Riverside House, Main Street, Rotherham S60 1AE ☎ 01709 822034 ✉ stuart.booth@rotherham.gov.uk

Finance: Mr Pete Hudson , Chief Finance Officer, Riverside House, Main Street, Rotherham S60 1AE ☎ 01709 822032 ✉ peter.hudson@rotherham.gov.uk

Health and Safety: Mr Neil Perry , Principal Health & Safety Officer, Riverside House, Main Street, Rotherham S60 1AE ☎ 01709 822131 ✉ neil.perry@rotherham.gov.uk

Highways: Mr Colin Knight , Network Manager, Riverside House, Main Street, Rotherham S60 1AE ☎ 01709 822828 ✉ colin.knight@rotherham.gov.uk

Home Energy Conservation: Mr Paul Maplethorpe, Manager - Affordable Warmth & Sustainable Energy Co-ordinator, Riverside House, Main Street, Rotherham S60 1AE ☎ 01709 334964 ✉ paul.maplethorpe@rotherham.gov.uk

Housing: Mr Dave Richmond , Director - Housing & Neighbourhood Services, Riverside House, Main Street, Rotherham S60 1AE ☎ 01709 823100 ✉ dave.richmond@rotherham.gov.uk

Legal: Mrs Jacqueline Collins , Director - Legal & Democratic Services, Riverside Houe, Main Street, Rotherham S60 1AE ☎ 01709 255768 ✉ jacqueline.collins@rotherham.gov.uk

Leisure and Cultural Services: Ms Elenore Fisher , Head - Cultural Services, Riverside House, Main Street, Rotherham S60 1AE ☎ 01709 823623 ✉ elenore.fisher@rotherham.gov.uk

Leisure and Cultural Services: Mr Steve Hallsworth , Leisure Services Manager, Riverside House, Main Street, Rotherham S60 1AE ☎ 01709 822483 ✉ steve.hallsworth@rotherham.gov.uk

Licensing: Ms Janette Hicks , Licensing Manager, Riverside House, Main Street, Rotherham S60 1AE ☎ 01709 822524 ✉ jenette.hicks@rotherham.gov.uk

Lifelong Learning: Ms Karen Borthwick , Head of Schools Effectiveness Service, Riverside House, Main Street, Rotherham S60 1AE ☎ 01709 334075 ✉ karen.borthwick@rotherham.gov.uk

Lighting: Mr David Burton, Director - Streetpride, Riverside House, Main Street, Rotherham S60 1AE ☎ 01709 382121 ✉ david.burton@rotherham.gov.uk

Lottery Funding, Charity and Voluntary: Ms Carole Haywood , Manager - Policy & Partnerships, Riverside House, Main Street, Rotherham S60 1AE ☎ 01709 254435 ✉ carole.haywood@rotherham.gov.uk

Member Services: Ms Debbie Pons , Principal Democratic Services Officer, Town Hall, Moorgate Road, Rotherham S60 2TH ☎ 01709 822054 ✉ debbie.pons@rotherham.gov.uk

Parking: Mr Martin Beard , Parking Services Manager, Riverside House, Main Street, Rotherham S60 1AN ☎ 01709 822929 🖷 01709 373987 ✉ martin.beard@rotherham.gov.uk

Partnerships: Ms Carole Haywood , Manager - Policy & Partnerships, Riverside House, Main Street, Rotherham S60 1AE ☎ 01709 254435 ✉ carole.haywood@rotherham.gov.uk

Personnel / HR: Mr Simon Cooper , Director - HR, Riverside House, Main Street, Rotherham S60 1AE ☎ 01709 823745 🖷 01709 372530 ✉ simon.cooper@rotherham.gov.uk

Planning: Mr Karl Battersby, Strategic Director - Environment & Development Services, Riverside House, Main Street, Rotherham S60 1AN ☎ 01709 823801 🖷 01709 372530 ✉ karl.battersby@rotherham.gov.uk

Procurement: Mr Simon Bradley , Service Leader, Riverside House, Main Street, Rotherham S60 1AE ☎ 01709 334138 ✉ simon.bradley@rotherham.gov.uk

Public Libraries: Ms Elenore Fisher , Head - Cultural Services, Riverside House, Main Street, Rotherham S60 1AE ☎ 01709 823623 ✉ elenore.fisher@rotherham.gov.uk

Recycling & Waste Minimisation: Mr Adrian Gabriel, Waste Strategy Manager, Hellaby Depot, Sandbeck Way, Hellaby, Rotherham S66 8QL ☎ 01709 823108 🖷 01709 823120 ✉ adrian.gabriel@rotherham.gov.uk

Regeneration: Mr Paul Woodcock , Director - Planning & Regeneration, Riverside House, Main Street, Rotherham S60 1AE ☎ 01709 822971 🖷 01709 372530 ✉ paul.woodcock@rotherham.gov.uk

Social Services (Adult): Mr Graeme Betts , Director - Health & Wellbeing, Riverside House, Main Street, Rotherham S60 1AE ☎ 01709 823928 ✉ graeme.betts@rotherham.gov.uk

Social Services (Adult): Ms Sam Newton , Director - Asset & Care Management, Riverside House, Main Street, Rotherham S60 1AE ☎ 01709 824062 ✉ sam.newton@rotherham.gov.uk

Social Services (Children): Ms Jane Parfrement , Director - Safeguarding Children, Riverside House, Main Street, Rotherham S60 1AE ☎ 01709 823905 ✉ jane.parfremont@rotherham.gov.uk

Public Health: Ms Teresa Roche , Director - Public Health, Riverside House, Main Street, Rotherham S60 1AE ☎ 01709 255845 ✉ teresa.roche@rotherham.gov.uk

Staff Training: Mrs Tracey Parkin , Human Resources Manager, Riverside House, Main Street, Rotherham S60 1AE ☎ 01709 823742 🖷 01709 823744 ✉ tracey.parkin@rotherham.gov.uk

Street Scene: Mr David Burton, Director - Streetpride, Riverside House, Main Street, Rotherham S60 1AE ☎ 01709 382121 ✉ david.burton@rotherham.gov.uk

Town Centre: Ms Bernadette Rushton , Town Centre Manager, Riverside House, Main Street, Rotherham S60 1AE ☎ 01709 254888 ✉ bernadette.rushton@rotherham.gov.uk

Traffic Management: Mr Ian Ashmore, Principal Traffic Office, Riverside House, Main Street, Rotherham S60 1AN ☎ 01709 822825 🖷 01709 822370 ✉ ian.ashmore@rotherham.gov.uk

Transport: Mr Colin Knight , Network Manager, Riverside House, Main Street, Rotherham S60 1AE ☎ 01709 822828 ✉ colin.knight@rotherham.gov.uk

Transport Planner: Mr Colin Knight , Network Manager, Riverside House, Main Street, Rotherham S60 1AE ☎ 01709 822828 ✉ colin.knight@rotherham.gov.uk

Waste Collection and Disposal: Mr Adrian Gabriel, Waste Strategy Manager, Hellaby Depot, Sandbeck Way, Hellaby, Rotherham S66 8QL ☎ 01709 823108 🖷 01709 823120 ✉ adrian.gabriel@rotherham.gov.uk

Waste Management: Mr Adrian Gabriel, Waste Strategy Manager, Hellaby Depot, Sandbeck Way, Hellaby, Rotherham S66 8QL ☎ 01709 823108 🖷 01709 823120 ✉ adrian.gabriel@rotherham.gov.uk

COUNCILLORS

***Mayor* Clark**, Maggi (LAB - Keppel)
maggi.clark@rotherham.gov.uk

***Deputy Mayor* Middleton**, Christopher (CON - Sitwell)
christopher.middleton@rotherham.gov.uk

***Leader of the Council* Read**, Chris (LAB - Wickersley)
chris.read@rotherham.gov.uk

***Deputy Leader of the Council* Watson**, Gordon (LAB - Wales)
gordon.watson@rotherham.gov.uk

***Group Leader* Vines**, Caven (UKIP - Rawmarsh)
caven.vines@rotherham.gov.uk

Ahmed, Shabana (LAB - Brinsworth and Catcliffe)
shabana.ahmed@rotherham.gov.uk

Alam, Saghir (LAB - Boston Castle)
saghir.alam@rotherham.gov.uk

Ali, Shaukat (LAB - Rotherham East)
shaukat.ali@rotherham.gov.uk

Astbury, Lauren (LAB - Hellaby)
lauren.astbury@rotherham.gov.uk

Atkin, Alan (LAB - Wath)
alan.aitken@rotherham.gov.uk

Beaumont, Christine (LAB - Maltby)
christine.beaumont@rotherham.gov.uk

Beck, Dominic (LAB - Wales)
dominic.beck@rotherham.gov.uk

Buckley, Alan (LAB - Brinsworth and Catcliffe)
alan.buckley@rotherham.gov.uk

Burton, Josephine (LAB - Anston and Woodsetts)
josephine.burton@rotherham.gov.uk

Cowles, Allen (UKIP - Sitwell)
allen.cowles@rotherham.gov.uk

Currie, Simon (LAB - Valley)
simon.currie@rotherham.gov.uk

Cutts, David (UKIP - Keppel)
dave.cutts@rotherham.gov.uk

Elliot, Jayne (LAB - Wath)
jayne.elliot@rotherham.gov.uk

Ellis, Sue (LAB - Wickersley)
sue.ellis@rotherham.gov.uk

Evans, Simon (LAB - Rawmarsh)
simon.evans@rotherham.gov.uk

Finnie, Ian (UKIP - Dinnington)
ian.finnie@rotherham.gov.uk

Fleming, Richard (UKIP - Hellaby)
richard.fleming@rotherham.gov.uk

Godfrey, Maggie (LAB - Maltby)
maggie.godfrey@rotherham.gov.uk

Gosling, Alan (LAB - Wath)
alan.gosling@rotherham.gov.uk

Hague, Paul (UKIP - Keppel)
paul.hague@rotherham.gov.uk

Hamilton, Jane (LAB - Hoober)
jane.hamilton@rotherham.gov.uk

Hoddinott, Emma (LAB - Wickersley)
emma.hoddinott@rotherham.gov.uk

Hughes, Darren (LAB - Rother Vale)
darren.hughes@rotherham.gov.uk

Hunter, Lee (UKIP - Wingfield)
lee.hunter@rotherham.gov.uk

Jepson, Clive (IND - Anston and Woodsetts)
clive.jepson@rotherham.gov.uk

Johnson, Lindsay (LAB - Wingfield)
lindsay.johnston@rotherham.gov.uk

Jones, Ian (LAB - Rotherham West)
ian.jones@rotherham.gov.uk

Khan, Tajamal (LAB - Rotherham East)
tajamal.khan@rotherham.gov.uk

Lelliott, Denise (LAB - Rother Vale)
denise.lelliott@rotherham.gov.uk

Mallinder, Jeanette (LAB - Dinnington)
jeanette.mallinder@rotherham.gov.uk

McNeely, Rose (LAB - Boston Castle)
rose.mcneely@rotherham.gov.uk

Parker, Martyn (IND - Silverwood)
martyn.parker@rotherham.gov.uk

Pickering, Dave (LAB - Valley)
Dave.pickering@rotherham.gov.uk

Pitchley, Lyndsay (LAB - Holderness)
lyndsay.pitchley@rotherham.gov.uk

Price, Richard (LAB - Wingfield)
richard.price@rotherham.gov.uk

Reeder, Kathleen (UKIP - Valley)
kath.reeder@rotherham.gov.uk

Reynolds, Greg (UKIP - Rother Vale)
greg.reynolds@rotherham.gov.uk

Robinson, Christopher (LAB - Holderness)
chris-cllr.robinson@rotherham.gov.uk

Roche, David (LAB - Hoober)
david.roche@rotherham.gov.uk

Roddison, Andrew (LAB - Brinsworth and Catcliffe)
andrew.roddison@rotherham.gov.uk

Rose, Eve (LAB - Swinton)
eve.rose@rotherham.gov.uk

Rosling, Jon (LAB - Silverwood)
jon.rosling@rotherham.gov.uk

Rushforth, Amy (LAB - Maltby)
amy.rushworth@rotherham.gov.uk

Russell, Gwendoline (LAB - Silverwood)
ann.russell@rotherham.gov.uk

Sansom, Stuart (LAB - Swinton)
stuart.sansome@rotherham.gov.uk

Sims, Kath (LAB - Rotherham West)
kath.sims@rotherham.gov.uk

Smith, Gerald (LAB - Holderness)
gerald.smith@rotherham.gov.uk

Steele, Brian (LAB - Hoober)
brian.steele@rotherham.gov.uk

Taylor, Robert (LAB - Anston and Woodsetts)
robert.taylor@rotherham.gov.uk

Turner, Julie (UKIP - Sitwell)
julie.turner@rotherham.gov.uk

Turner, John (UKIP - Hellaby)
john.turner@rotherham.gov.uk

Tweed, Simon (LAB - Dinnington)
simon.tweed@rotherham.gov.uk

Vines, Maureen (UKIP - Rotherham West)
maureen.vines@rotherham.gov.uk

Wallis, Emma (LAB - Rotherham East)
emma.wallis@rotherham.gov.uk

Whelbourn, Glyn (LAB - Rawmarsh)
glyn.whelbourn@rotherham.gov.uk

Whysall, Jennifer (LAB - Wales)
jennifer.whysall@rotherham.gov.uk

Wyatt, Ken (LAB - Swinton)
ken.wyatt@rotherham.gov.uk

Yasseen, Taiba (LAB - Boston Castle)
taiba.yasseen@rotherham.gov.uk

POLITICAL COMPOSITION
LAB: 48, UKIP: 12, IND: 2, CON: 1

COMMITTEE CHAIRS
Audit: Mr Ken Wyatt

Children, Young People & Families: Ms Christine Beaumont

Licensing: Ms Sue Ellis

Planning: Mr Alan Atkin

Rugby D

Rugby Borough Council, Town Hall, Evreux Way, Rugby CV21 2RR
☎ 01788 533533 🖷 01788 533565 ✉ the.council@rugby.gov.uk
💻 www.rugby.gov.uk

FACTS AND FIGURES
Parliamentary Constituencies: Nuneaton, Rugby
EU Constituencies: West Midlands
Election Frequency: Elections are by thirds

PRINCIPAL OFFICERS
Chief Executive: Mr Ian Davis , Executive Director, Town Hall, Evreux Way, Rugby CV21 2RR ☎ 01788 533700 ✉ ian.davis@rugby.gov.uk

Chief Executive: Mr Adam Norburn, Executive Director, Town Hall, Evreux Way, Rugby CV21 2RR ☎ 01788 533550 🖷 01788 533409 ✉ adam.norburn@rugby.gov.uk

Senior Management: Mr Rob Black , Head of Planning & Recreation, Town Hall, Evreux Way, Rugby CV21 2RR

Senior Management: Mrs Raj Chand , Head of Customer & Information Services, Town Hall, Evreux Way, Rugby CV21 2RR ☎ 01788 533870 ✉ raj.chand@rugby.gov.uk

Senior Management: Mrs Mannie Grewal Ketley , Head of Resources, Town Hall, Evreux Way, Rugby CV21 2RR ✉ manniegrewalketley@rugby.gov.uk

Senior Management: Mr Doug Jones , Head of Business Transformation, Town Hall, Evreux Way, Rugby CV21 2RR ☎ 01788 533668 ✉ doug.jones@rugby.gov.uk

Senior Management: Mr Sean Lawson, Head of Environmental Services, Town Hall, Evreux Way, Rugby CV21 2RR ☎ 01788 533737 ✉ sean.lawson@rugby.gov.uk

Senior Management: Mr Steven Shanahan, Head of Housing & Property, Town Hall, Evreux Way, Rugby CV21 2RR ☎ 01788 533801 ✉ steven.shanahan@rugby.gov.uk

Best Value: Mr Doug Jones , Head of Business Transformation, Town Hall, Evreux Way, Rugby CV21 2LB ☎ 01788 533668 ✉ doug.jones@rugby.gov.uk

PR / Communications: Mr Matthew Deaves , Communication, Consultation & Information Manager, Town Hall, Evreux Way, Rugby CV21 2RR ☎ 01788 533562 ✉ matthew.deaves@rugby.gov.uk

Community Planning: Mrs Raj Chand , Head of Customer & Information Services, Town Hall, Evreux Way, Rugby CV21 2RR ☎ 01788 533870 ✉ raj.chand@rugby.gov.uk

Community Safety: Mr David Burrows , Regulatory Services Manager, Town Hall, Evreux Way, Rugby CV21 2RR ☎ 01788 533806 ✉ david.burrows@rugby.gov.uk

Computer Management: Mrs Raj Chand , Head of Customer & Information Services, Town Hall, Evreux Way, Rugby CV21 2RR ☎ 01788 533870 ✉ raj.chand@rugby.gov.uk

Customer Service: Mrs Raj Chand , Head of Customer & Information Services, Town Hall, Evreux Way, Rugby CV21 2RR ☎ 01788 533870 ✉ raj.chand@rugby.gov.uk

Direct Labour: Mr Sean Lawson, Head of Environmental Services, Town Hall, Evreux Way, Rugby CV21 2RR ☎ 01788 533737 ✉ sean.lawson@rugby.gov.uk

Economic Development: Mr Michael Beirne , Economic Development Officer, Town Hall, Evreux Way, Rugby CV21 2RR ☎ 01788 533752 ✉ michael.beirne@rugby.gov.uk

E-Government: Mr Doug Jones , Head of Business Transformation, Town Hall, Evreux Way, Rugby CV21 2RR ☎ 01788 533668 ✉ doug.jones@rugby.gov.uk

Electoral Registration: Mrs Sandy Veal , Electoral Services Officer, Town Hall, Evreux Way, Rugby CV21 2RR ☎ 01788 533595 ✉ sandy.veal@rugby.gov.uk

Emergency Planning: Mr Sean Lawson, Head of Environmental Services, Town Hall, Evreux Way, Rugby CV21 2RR ☎ 01788 533737 ✉ sean.lawson@rugby.gov.uk

Environmental / Technical Services: Mr Sean Lawson, Head of Environmental Services, Town Hall, Evreux Way, Rugby CV21 2RR ☎ 01788 533737 ✉ sean.lawson@rugby.gov.uk

Environmental / Technical Services: Mr Chris Worman , Parks & Grounds Manager, Town Hall, Evreux Way, Rugby CV21 2RR ☎ 01788 533706 ✉ chris.worman@rugby.gov.uk

Environmental Health: Mr Sean Lawson, Head of Environmental Services, Town Hall, Evreux Way, Rugby CV21 2RR ☎ 01788 533737 ✉ sean.lawson@rugby.gov.uk

Estates, Property & Valuation: Mr Steven Shanahan, Head of Housing & Property, Town Hall, Evreux Way, Rugby CV21 2RR ☎ 01788 533801 steven.shanahan@rugby.gov.uk

Finance: Mrs Mannie Grewal Ketley , Head of Resources, Town Hall, Evreux Way, Rugby CV21 2RR manniegrewalketley@rugby.gov.uk

Grounds Maintenance: Mr Chris Worman , Parks & Grounds Manager, Town Hall, Evreux Way, Rugby CV21 2RR ☎ 01788 533706 chris.worman@rugby.gov.uk

Health and Safety: Mr Sean Lawson, Head of Environmental Services, Town Hall, Evreux Way, Rugby CV21 2RR ☎ 01788 533737 sean.lawson@rugby.gov.uk

Housing: Mr Steven Shanahan, Head of Housing & Property, Town Hall, Evreux Way, Rugby CV21 2RR ☎ 01788 533801 steven.shanahan@rugby.gov.uk

Housing Maintenance: Mr Steven Shanahan, Head of Housing & Property, Town Hall, Evreux Way, Rugby CV21 2RR ☎ 01788 533801 steven.shanahan@rugby.gov.uk

Legal: Mrs Deborah Tyrrell , Legal Manager, Town Hall, Evreux Way, Rugby CV21 2RR ☎ 01788 533510 deborah.tyrrell@rugby.gov.uk

Leisure and Cultural Services: Mrs Raj Chand , Head of Customer & Information Services, Town Hall, Evreux Way, Rugby CV21 2RR ☎ 01788 533870 raj.chand@rugby.gov.uk

Licensing: Mr Sean Lawson, Head of Environmental Services, Town Hall, Evreux Way, Rugby CV21 2RR ☎ 01788 533737 sean.lawson@rugby.gov.uk

Member Services: Mr Steve Garrison, Democratic Services Manager , Town Hall, Evreux Way, Rugby CV21 2RR ☎ 01788 533521 steve.garrison@rugby.gov.uk

Parking: Mr David Burrows , Regulatory Services Manager, Town Hall, Evreux Way, Rugby CV21 2RR ☎ 01788 533806 david.burrows@rugby.gov.uk

Personnel / HR: Ms Suzanne Turner , Human Resources Manager, Town Hall, Evreux Way, Rugby CV21 2RR ☎ 01788 533570 suzanne.turner@rugby.gov.uk

Planning: Mr Nick Freer , Planning Services Manager, Town Hall, Evreux Way, Rugby CV21 2RR ☎ 01788 533737 nick.freer@rugby.gov.uk

Procurement: Mr Doug Jones , Head of Business Transformation, Town Hall, Evreux Way, Rugby CV21 2RR ☎ 01788 533668 doug.jones@rugby.gov.uk

Recycling & Waste Minimisation: Mr Sean Lawson, Head of Environmental Services, Town Hall, Evreux Way, Rugby CV21 2RR ☎ 01788 533737 sean.lawson@rugby.gov.uk

Staff Training: Ms Elaine McGladdery , Learning & Organisational Development Officer, Town Hall, Evreux Way, Rugby CV21 2RR ☎ 01788 533574 elaine.mcgladdery@rugby.gov.uk

Street Scene: Mr Sean Lawson, Head of Environmental Services, Town Hall, Evreux Way, Rugby CV21 2RR ☎ 01788 533737 sean.lawson@rugby.gov.uk

Sustainable Communities: Mr Ian Davis , Executive Director, Town Hall, Evreux Way, Rugby CV21 2RR ☎ 01788 533700 ian.davis@rugby.gov.uk

Sustainable Development: Ms Sarah Fisher , Forward Planning Manager, Town Hall, Evreux Way, Rugby CV21 2RR ☎ 01788 533668 sarah.fisher@rugby.gov.uk

Tourism: Mrs Nikki Grange , Arts Heritage & Tourism Manager, Rugby Art Gallery & Museum, Little Elborow Street, Rugby CV21 3BZ ☎ 01788 533203 nikki.grange@rugby.gov.uk

Waste Collection and Disposal: Mr Sean Lawson, Head of Environmental Services, Town Hall, Evreux Way, Rugby CV21 2RR ☎ 01788 533737 sean.lawson@rugby.gov.uk

Waste Management: Mr Sean Lawson, Head of Environmental Services, Town Hall, Evreux Way, Rugby CV21 2RR ☎ 01788 533737 sean.lawson@rugby.gov.uk

COUNCILLORS

***Mayor* Dodd**, Richard (LD - Paddox)
richard.dodd@rugby.gov.uk

***Deputy Mayor* Bragg**, Sally (CON - Wolston & the Lawfords)
sally.bragg@rugby.gov.uk

***Leader of the Council* Stokes**, Michael (CON - Admirals & Cawston)
michael.stokes@rugby.gov.uk

***Group Leader* Edwards**, Claire (LAB - Newbold & Brownsover)
claire.edwards@rugby.gov.uk

***Group Leader* Roodhouse**, Jerry (LD - Paddox)
jerry.roodhouse@rugby.gov.uk

A'Barrow, Julie (CON - Bilton)
julie.abarrow@rugby.gov.uk

Allen, Nigel (CON - Hillmorton)
nigel.allen@rugby.gov.uk

Avis, Tina (LAB - New Bilton)
tina.avis@rugby.gov.uk

Avis, Howard (LAB - Rokeby & Overslade)
bluesteel@fsmail.net

Birkett, Steven (LAB - New Bilton)
StevenWBirkett@hotmail.com

Buckley, Jim (CON - Hillmorton)
jim.buckley@rugby.gov.uk

Butlin, Peter (CON - Admirals & Cawston)
peter.butlin@rugby.gov.uk

Cade, Chris (CON - Bilton)
chris.cade@rugby.gov.uk

Coles, Andy (LAB - Newbold& Brownsover)
andy.coles@rugby.gov.uk

Crane, Emma (CON - Leam Valley)
emma.crane@rugby.gov.uk

Ellis, David (CON - Wolston & the Lawfords)
david.ellis@rugby.gov.uk

Garcia, Belinda (CON - Revel & Binley Woods)
belindagb@aol.com

Gillias, Anthony (CON - Revel & Binley Woods)
anthony.gillias@rugby.gov.uk

Hunt, Leigh (CON - Clifton, Newton & Churchover)
leigh.hunt@rugby.gov.uk

Keeling, Dale (LD - Eastlands)
dale.keeling@rugby.gov.uk

Lawrence, Kathryn (CON - Hillmorton)
kathryn.lawrence@rugby.gov.uk

Lewis, Bill (LD - Rokeby & Overslade)
bill.lewis@rugby.gov.uk

Mahoney, Tom (LAB - Benn)
tom.mahoney@rugby.gov.uk

Mistry, Ish (LAB - New Bilton)
ishmistry@hotmail.co.uk

Nash, Marion (LD - Rokeby & Overslade)
marion.nash@rugbylibdems.org.uk

New, Noreen (LD - Paddox)
noreen.new@rugby.gov.uk

O'Rourke, Maggie (LAB - Benn)
maggie.o'rourke@rugby.gov.uk

Pacey-Day, Chris (CON - Wolvey & Shilton)
chris@hi-tekdial.co.uk

Parker, Lisa (CON - Bilton)
lisa.parker@rugby.gov.uk

Poole, Derek (CON - Wolston & the Lawfords)
derek.poole@rugby.gov.uk

Robbins, Carolyn (CON - Coton & Boughton)
carolyn.robbins@rugby.gov.uk

Roberts, Deepah (IND - Dunsmore)
deepah.roberts@rugby.gov.uk

Roberts, Howard (IND - Dunsmore)
howard.roberts@rugby.gov.uk

Roodhouse, Sue (LD - Eastlands)
sue.roodhouse@rugby.gov.uk

Sandison, Neil (LD - Eastlands)
neil.sandison@rugby.gov.uk

Shera, Jim (LAB - Benn)
jim.shera@rugby.gov.uk

Simpson-Vince, Jill (CON - Coton & Boughton)
jill.simpson-vince@rugby.gov.uk

Srivastava, Ramesh (LAB - Newbold & Brownsover)
ramesh.srivastava@rugby.gov.uk

Taylor, Helen (CON - Coton & Boughton)
helen.taylor@rugby.gov.uk

Timms, Heather (CON - Revel & Binley Woods)
heather.timms@rugby.gov.uk

Watson-Merret, Carolyn (CON - Dunsmore)
cagsie@rugby.gov.uk

Williams, Mark (CON - Admirals & Cawston)
mark.williams@rugby.gov.uk

POLITICAL COMPOSITION
CON: 22, LAB: 10, LD: 8, IND: 2

COMMITTEE CHAIRS
Licensing: Ms Kathryn Lawrence

Planning: Mrs Carolyn Robbins

Runnymede D

Runnymede Borough Council, Civic Centre, Station Road, Addlestone KT15 2AH
☎ 01932 838383 🖷 01932 838384
generalenquiries@runnymede.gov.uk 💻 www.runnymede.gov.uk

FACTS AND FIGURES
Parliamentary Constituencies: Runnymede and Weybridge
EU Constituencies: South East
Election Frequency: Elections are by thirds

PRINCIPAL OFFICERS
Chief Executive: Mr Paul Turrell , Chief Executive, Civic Centre, Station Road, Addlestone KT15 2AH ☎ 01932 425500 🖷 01932 838384 paul.turrell@runnymede.gov.uk

Assistant Chief Executive: Mr Peter Sims, Assistant Chief Executive, Civic Offices, Station Road, Addlestone KT15 2AH ☎ 01932 425100 🖷 ; 01932 838384 peter.sims@runnymede.gov.uk

Senior Management: Mr Mario Leo , Corporate Head - Law & Governance, Civic Centre, Station Road, Addlestone KT15 2AH ☎ 01932 425640 🖷 01932 838384 mario.leo@runnymede.gov.uk

Senior Management: Mr Ian Maguire , Corporate Head - Planning & Environmental Services, Civic Centre, Station Road, Addlestone KT15 2AH ☎ 01932 415240 🖷 01932 838384 ian.maguire@runnymede.gov.uk

Senior Management: Mrs Jane Margetts , Corporate Head - Housing & Community Development, Civic Centre, Station Road, Addlestone KT15 2AH ☎ 01932 425824 🖷 01932 838384 jane.margetts@runnymede.gov.uk

Senior Management: Mr Peter McKenzie , Corporate Head - Resources, Civic Centre, Station Road, Addlestone KT15 2AH ☎ 01932 425320 🖷 01932 838384 peter.mckenzie@runnymede.gov.uk

Senior Management: Ms Sarah Walsh , Head of Strategy, Civic Centre, Station Road, Addlestone KT15 2AH

Architect, Building / Property Services: Mr Richard Webb , Principal Building Services Manager, Civic Centre, Station Road, Addlestone KT15 2AH ☎ 01932 425171 🖷 01932 838384 richard.webb@runnymede.gov.uk

Building Control: Mr David Jones , Building Control Manager, Civic Centre, Station Road, Addlestone KT15 2AH ☎ 01932 425160 🖷 01932 838384 david.jones@runnymede.gov.uk

PR / Communications: Ms Emma Hamilton , Communications Officer, Civic Centre, Station Road, Addlestone KT15 2AH ☎ 01932 425504 ✉ emma.hamilton@runnymede.gov.uk

Community Safety: Ms Shazia Sarwar , Community Safety Officer, Civic Centre, Station Road, Addlestone KT15 2AH ☎ 01932 425065 ✉ shazia.sarwar@runnymede.gov.uk

Computer Management: Mrs Helen Dunn , Head of ICT, Civic Centre, Station Road, Addlestone KT15 2AH ☎ 01932 425550; 01748 451499 ✉ helen.dunn@runnymede.gov.uk

Contracts: Mr Paul French , Head of Financial Services, Civic Centre, Station Road, Addlestone KT15 2AH ☎ 01932 425336 🖷 01932 838384 ✉ paul.french@runnymede.gov.uk

Customer Service: Mrs Julie Kitchenside , Customer Services Manager, Civic Centre, Station Road, Addlestone KT15 2AH ☎ 01932 425130 ✉ julie.kitchenside@runnymede.gov.uk

Economic Development: Mr Paul Turrell , Chief Executive, Civic Centre, Station Road, Addlestone KT15 2AH ☎ 01932 425500 🖷 01932 838384 ✉ paul.turrell@runnymede.gov.uk

E-Government: Mrs Helen Dunn , Head of ICT, Civic Centre, Station Road, Addlestone KT15 2AH ☎ 01932 425550; 01748 451499 ✉ helen.dunn@runnymede.gov.uk

Electoral Registration: Mrs Sam Clifton , Election Services Manager, Civic Centre, Station Road, Addlestone KT15 2AH ☎ 01932 425650 🖷 01932 838384 ✉ sam.clifton@runnymede.gov.uk

Emergency Planning: Mr Nicholas Moon , Risk & Resilience Manager, Civic Centre, Station Road, Addlestone KT15 2AH ☎ 01932 425178; 01784 451499 🖷 01932 838384 ✉ nick.moon@runnymede.gov.uk

Energy Management: Mr Richard Webb , Principal Building Services Manager, Civic Centre, Station Road, Addlestone KT15 2AH ☎ 01932 425171 🖷 01932 838384 ✉ richard.webb@runnymede.gov.uk

Environmental / Technical Services: Mr Ian Maguire , Corporate Head - Planning & Environmental Services, Civic Centre, Station Road, Addlestone KT15 2AH ☎ 01932 415240 🖷 01932 838384 ✉ ian.maguire@runnymede.gov.uk

Environmental Health: Mr Ian Maguire , Corporate Head - Planning & Environmental Services, Civic Centre, Station Road, Addlestone KT15 2AH ☎ 01932 415240 🖷 01932 838384 ✉ ian.maguire@runnymede.gov.uk

Estates, Property & Valuation: Mr David Yetton , Assistant Valuer, Civic Centre, Station Road, Addlestone KT15 2AH ☎ 01932 425696 ✉ david.yetton@runnymede.gov.uk

Facilities: Mr Richard Webb , Principal Building Services Manager, Civic Centre, Station Road, Addlestone KT15 2AH ☎ 01932 425171 🖷 01932 838384 ✉ richard.webb@runnymede.gov.uk

Finance: Mr Peter McKenzie , Corporate Head - Resources, Civic Centre, Station Road, Addlestone KT15 2AH ☎ 01932 425320 🖷 01932 838384 ✉ peter.mckenzie@runnymede.gov.uk

Fleet Management: Mr Alan Potter , Transport Officer, Chertsey Depot, Ford Road, Chertsey KT16 8HG ☎ 01932 425770 🖷 01932 425771 ✉ alan.potter@runnymede.gov.uk

Grounds Maintenance: Mr Peter Winfield, Community Development Manager - Green Space, Civic Offices, Station Road, Addlestone KT15 2AH ☎ 01932 425673 🖷 01932 838384 ✉ peter.winfield@runnymede.gov.uk

Highways: Mr Ian Maguire , Corporate Head - Planning & Environmental Services, Civic Centre, Station Road, Addlestone KT15 2AH ☎ 01932 415240 🖷 01932 838384 ✉ ian.maguire@runnymede.gov.uk

Home Energy Conservation: Mrs Verena Boxall , Energy Project Manager, Civic Centre, Station Road, Addlestone KT15 2AH ☎ 01932 425172 🖷 01932 838384 ✉ verena.boxall@runnymede.gov.uk

Housing: Mrs Jane Margetts , Corporate Head - Housing & Community Development, Civic Centre, Station Road, Addlestone KT15 2AH ☎ 01932 425824 🖷 01932 838384 ✉ jane.margetts@runnymede.gov.uk

Housing Maintenance: Mr Andrew Davidson , Housing Maintenance Manager, Civic Centre, Station Road, Addlestone KT15 2AH ☎ 01932 425840 🖷 01932 838384 ✉ andrew.davidson@runnymede.gov.uk

Legal: Mr Mario Leo , Corporate Head - Law & Governance, Civic Centre, Station Road, Addlestone KT15 2AH ☎ 01932 425640 🖷 01932 838384 ✉ mario.leo@runnymede.gov.uk

Leisure and Cultural Services: Mr Chris Hunt, Head of Community Development, Civic Centre, Station Road, Addlestone KT15 2AH ☎ 01932 425670 🖷 01938 838384 ✉ chris.hunt@runnymede.gov.uk

Licensing: Mr Robert Smith , Licensing Officer, Civic Centre, Station Road, Addlestone KT15 2AH ☎ 01932 425722 🖷 01932 838384 ✉ robert.smith@runnymede.gov.uk

Lighting: Mr Paul Sebego , Electrical Works Supervisor, Chertsey Depot, Ford Road, KT16 8HG ☎ 01932 425773 🖷 01932 425771 ✉ paul.sebego@runnymede.gov.uk

Member Services: Mr Bernard Fleckney , Democratic Services Manager, Civic Centre, Station Road, Addlestone KT15 2AH ☎ 01932 425620 🖷 01932 838384 ✉ bernard.fleckney@runnymede.gov.uk

Parking: Mr Ian Maguire , Corporate Head - Planning & Environmental Services, Civic Centre, Station Road, Addlestone KT15 2AH ☎ 01932 415240 🖷 01932 838384 ✉ ian.maguire@runnymede.gov.uk

Partnerships: Mrs Suzanne Stronge , Community Partnership Officer, Civic Centre, Station Road, Addlestone KT15 2AH ☎ 01932 425869 🖷 01932 838384 ✉ suzanne.stronge@runnymede.gov.uk

RUNNYMEDE

Personnel / HR: Ms Jan Hunt , Head of HR, Civic Centre, Station Road, Addlestone KT15 2AH ☎ 01932 425510 ✉ jan.hunt@runnymede.gov.uk

Planning: Mr Ian Maguire , Corporate Head - Planning & Environmental Services, Civic Centre, Station Road, Addlestone KT15 2AH ☎ 01932 415240 🖷 01932 838384 ✉ ian.maguire@runnymede.gov.uk

Procurement: Mr Paul French , Head of Financial Services, Civic Centre, Station Road, Addlestone KT15 2AH ☎ 01932 425336 🖷 01932 838384 ✉ paul.french@runnymede.gov.uk

Recycling & Waste Minimisation: Mr Ian Maguire , Corporate Head - Planning & Environmental Services, Civic Centre, Station Road, Addlestone KT15 2AH ☎ 01932 415240 🖷 01932 838384 ✉ ian.maguire@runnymede.gov.uk

Regeneration: Mr Paul Turrell , Chief Executive, Civic Centre, Station Road, Addlestone KT15 2AH ☎ 01932 425500 🖷 01932 838384 ✉ paul.turrell@runnymede.gov.uk

Staff Training: Mrs Angela Brown, Human Resources Officer, Civic Offices, Station Road, Addlestone KT15 2AH ☎ 01932 425513 🖷 01932 838384 ✉ angela.brown@runnymede.gov.uk

Street Scene: Mr Ian Maguire , Corporate Head - Planning & Environmental Services, Civic Centre, Station Road, Addlestone KT15 2AH ☎ 01932 415240 🖷 01932 838384 ✉ ian.maguire@runnymede.gov.uk

Tourism: Mr Chris Hunt, Head of Community Development, Civic Centre, Station Road, Addlestone KT15 2AH ☎ 01932 425670 🖷 01938 838384 ✉ chris.hunt@runnymede.gov.uk

Town Centre: Mr Ian Maguire , Corporate Head - Planning & Environmental Services, Civic Centre, Station Road, Addlestone KT15 2AH ☎ 01932 415240 🖷 01932 838384 ✉ ian.maguire@runnymede.gov.uk

Transport: Mr Alan Potter , Transport Officer, Chertsey Depot, Ford Road, Chertsey KT16 8HG ☎ 01932 425770 🖷 01932 425771 ✉ alan.potter@runnymede.gov.uk

Waste Collection and Disposal: Mr Dave Stedman , Direct Services Organisation Manager, Chertsey Depot, Ford Road, Chertsey KT16 8HG ☎ 01932 425760 🖷 01932 425771 ✉ dave.stedman@runnymede.gov.uk

Waste Management: Mr Dave Stedman , Direct Services Organisation Manager, Chertsey Depot, Ford Road, Chertsey KT16 8HG ☎ 01932 425760 🖷 01932 425771 ✉ dave.stedman@runnymede.gov.uk

COUNCILLORS

***Mayor* Cotty**, Derek (CON - Chertsey Meads)
cllr.derek.cotty@runnymede.gov.uk

***Deputy Mayor* Alderson**, Alan (R - Egham Town)
cllr.alan.alderson@runnymede.gov.uk

***Leader of the Council* Roberts**, Patrick (CON - Englefield Green East) cllr.patrick.roberts@runnymede.gov.uk

***Deputy Leader of the Council* Meares**, Hugh (CON - Englefield Green West)
cllr.hugh.meares@runnymede.gov.uk

***Group Leader* Gill**, Elaine (R - Thorpe)
cllr.elaine.gill@runnymede.gov.uk

Ashmore, John (R - Egham Town)
cllr.john.ashmore@runnymede.gov.uk

Broadhead, Jim (CON - Addlestone North)
cllr.jim.broadhead@runnymede.gov.uk

Butterfield, Howard (CON - Foxhills)
cllr.howard.butterfield@runnymede.gov.uk

Chaudhri, Iftikhar (CON - Foxhills)
cllr.iftikhar.chaudhri@runnymede.gov.uk

Clarke, Dolsie (CON - Chertsey St Ann's)
cllr.dolsie.clarke@runnymede.gov.uk

Dicks, Terry (CON - Chertsey South and Row Town)
cllr.terry.dicks@runnymede.gov.uk

Dunster, Valerie (CON - Woodham)
cllr.valerie.dunster@runnymede.gov.uk

Edis, Richard (CON - Chertsey St Ann's)
cllr.richard.edis@runnymede.gov.uk

Edwards, John (CON - Chertsey South and Row Town)
cllr.john.edwards@runnymede.gov.uk

Furey, John (CON - Addlestone Bourneside)
cllr.john.furey@runnymede.gov.uk

Gillham, Linda (R - Thorpe)
cllr.linda.gillham@runnymede.gov.uk

Gracey, Jacqui (CON - New Haw)
cllr.jacqui.gracey@runnymede.gov.uk

Harnden, Margaret (R - Thorpe)
cllr.margaret.harnden@runnymede.gov.uk

Heath, Marisa (CON - Englefield Green East)
cllr.marisa.heath@runnymede.gov.uk

Khalique, Dannielle (CON - Foxhills)
cllr.danniellekhalique@runnymede.gov.uk

Kingerley, Gail (CON - Woodham)
cllr.gail.kingerley@runnymede.gov.uk

Knight, David (R - Egham Town)
cllr.david.knight@runnymede.gov.uk

Kusneraitis, Michael (CON - Englefield Green West)
cllr.michael.kusneraitis@runnymede.gov.uk

Lay, Yvonna (CON - Egham Hythe)
cllr.yvonna.lay@runnymede.gov.uk

Mackay, Stewart (CON - Addlestone North)
cllr.stewart.mackay@runnymede.gov.uk

Mackin, Robert (CON - Woodham)
cllr.robert.mackin@runnymede.gov.uk

Maddox, Mark (CON - New Haw)
cllr.mark.maddox@runnymeade.gov.uk

Nuti, Mark (CON - Chertsey Meads)
cllr.mark.nuti@runnymede.gov.uk

Parr, David (CON - Addlestone North)
cllr.david.parr@runnymede.gov.uk

Pitt, Barry (CON - Chertsey South and Row Town)
cllr.barry.pitt@runnymede.gov.uk

Prescot, Nick (CON - Englefield Green West)
cllr.nick.prescot@runnymede.gov.uk

Roberts, Margaret (CON - Virginia Water)
cllr.margaret.roberts@runnymede.gov.uk

Saise-Marshall, Shannon (CON - Chertsey St Ann's)
cllr.shannon.saise-marshall@runnymede.gov.uk

Simmons, Cherith (CON - Addlestone Bourneside)
cllr.cherith.simmons@runnymede.gov.uk

Sohi, Japneet (CON - Englefield Green East)
cllr.japneet.sohi@runnymede.gov.uk

Sohi, Parshotam (CON - Virginia Water)
cllr.parshotam.sohi@runnymede.gov.uk

Tollett, Adrian (CON - New Haw)
cllr.adrian.tollett@runnymede.gov.uk

Tuley, Paul (CON - Chertsey Meads)
cllr.paul.tuley@runnymede.gov.uk

Waddell, Peter (CON - Addlestone Bourneside)
cllr.peter.waddell@runnymede.gov.uk

Warner, Gill (CON - Egham Hythe)
cllr.gill.warner@runnymede.gov.uk

Wase-Rogers, Nick (CON - Virginia Waters)
cllr.nick.wase-rogers@runnymede.gov.uk

Wilson, Jonathan (CON - Egham Hythe)
cllr.jonathan.wilson@runnymede.gov.uk

POLITICAL COMPOSITION

CON: 36, R: 6

COMMITTEE CHAIRS

Audit: Mr Jim Broadhead

Licensing: Mr David Parr

Planning: Ms Gail Kingerley

Rushcliffe D

Rushcliffe Borough Council, Civic Centre, Pavilion Road, West Bridgford NG2 5FE
☎ 0115 981 9911 🖷 0115 945 5882 ✉ customerservices@rushcliffe.gov.uk
🖳 www.rushcliffe.gov.uk

FACTS AND FIGURES

Parliamentary Constituencies: Rushcliffe
EU Constituencies: East Midlands
Election Frequency: Elections are of whole council

PRINCIPAL OFFICERS

Chief Executive: Mr Allen Graham, Chief Executive, Civic Centre, Pavilion Road, West Bridgford NG2 5FE ☎ 0115 914 8349 🖷 0115 914 8431 ✉ agraham@rushcliffe.gov.uk

Deputy Chief Executive: Mr Dan Swaine , Executive Manager - Operations & Corporate Governance, Civic Centre, Pavilion Road, West Bridgford NG2 5FE ☎ 0115 914 8343 🖷 0115 945 5882 ✉ dswaine@rushcliffe.gov.uk

Senior Management: Mr David Banks , Executive Manager - Neighbourhoods, Civic Centre, Pavilion Road, West Bridgford NG2 5FE ☎ 0115 914 8438 ✉ dbanks@rushcliffe.gov.uk

Senior Management: Ms Kath Marriott , Executive Manager - Transformation, Civic Centre, Pavilion Road, West Bridgford NG2 5FE ☎ 0115 914 8291 🖷 0115 945 5882 ✉ kmarriott@rushcliffe.gov.uk

Senior Management: Mr David Mitchell, Executive Manager - Communities, Civic Centre, Pavilion Road, West Bridgford NG2 5FE ☎ 0115 914 8267 🖷 0115 945 5882 ✉ dmitchell@rushcliffe.gov.uk

Senior Management: Mr Peter Streed , Executive Manager - Finance & Commercial, Civic Centre, Pavilion Road, West Bridgford NG2 5FE ☎ 0115 914 8567 🖷 0115 945 5882 ✉ psteed@rushcliffe.gov.uk

Senior Management: Mr Dan Swaine , Executive Manager - Operations & Corporate Governance, Civic Centre, Pavilion Road, West Bridgford NG2 5FE ☎ 0115 914 8343 🖷 0115 945 5882 ✉ dswaine@rushcliffe.gov.uk

Architect, Building / Property Services: Mr Adrian Hutson , Construction & Energy Manager, Civic Centre, Pavilion Road, West Bridgford NG2 5FE ☎ 0115 914 8442 🖷 0115 945 5882 ✉ ahutson@rushcliffe.gov.uk

PR / Communications: Mrs Nicky Mee, Communications Manager, Civic Centre, Pavilion Road, West Bridgford NG2 5FE ☎ 0115 914 8555 🖷 0115 945 5882 ✉ nmee@rushcliffe.gov.uk

Community Safety: Mr Ben Adams , Neighbourhood Manager, Civic Centre, Pavilion Road, West Bridgford NG2 5FE ☎ 0115 914 8487 🖷 0115 945 5882 ✉ badams@rushcliffe.gov.uk

Computer Management: Mr Greg Dwyer , ICT Service Delivery Manager, Civic Centre, Pavilion Road, West Bridgford NG2 5FE ☎ 0115 914 8411 🖷 0115 945 5882 ✉ gdwyer@rushcliffe.gov.uk

Corporate Services: Mr Dan Swaine , Executive Manager - Operations & Corporate Governance, Civic Centre, Pavilion Road, West Bridgford NG2 5FE ☎ 0115 914 8343 🖷 0115 945 5882 ✉ dswaine@rushcliffe.gov.uk

Customer Service: Ms Shirley Woltman, Customer Services Manager, Civic Centre, Pavilion Road, West Bridgford NG2 5FE ☎ 0115 981 9911 🖷 0115 945 5882 ✉ swoltman@rushcliffe.gov.uk

Electoral Registration: Mr Jeff Saxby, Elections & Corporate Information Manager, Civic Centre, Pavilion Road, West Bridgford NG2 5FE ☎ 0115 981 9216 🖷 0115 945 5882 ✉ jsaxby@rushcliffe.gov.uk

Emergency Planning: Ms Karen Emery , Emergency Planning Officer, Civic Centre, Pavilion Road, West Bridgford NG2 5FE ☎ 0115 977 3678 ✉ kemery@rushcliffe.gov.uk

Environmental Health: Mr David Banks , Executive Manager - Neighbourhoods, Civic Centre, Pavilion Road, West Bridgford NG2 5FE ☎ 0115 914 8438 ✉ dbanks@rushcliffe.gov.uk

Estates, Property & Valuation: Mr Adrian Hutson , Construction & Energy Manager, Civic Centre, Pavilion Road, West Bridgford NG2 5FE ☎ 0115 914 8442 🖷 0115 945 5882 ✉ ahutson@rushcliffe.gov.uk

Events Manager: Miss Nicola Pearson , Arts & Events Officer, Civic Centre, Pavilion Road, West Bridgford NG2 5FE ☎ 0115 914 8320 🖷 0115 945 5882 ✉ npearson@rushcliffe.gov.uk

Fleet Management: Mr Darryl Burch , Waste & Fleet Operations Manager, Civic Centre, Pavilion Road, West Bridgford NG2 5FE ☎ 0115 914 8405 🖷 0115 945 5882 ✉ dburch@rushcliffe.gov.uk

Grounds Maintenance: Ms Donna Dwyer , Strategic Housing Manager, Civic Centre, Pavilion Road, West Bridgford NG2 5FE ☎ 0115 914 8275 🖷 0115 945 5882 ✉ ddwyer@rushcliffe.gov.uk

Health and Safety: Ms Joanne Wilkinson, Health & Safety Advisor, Civic Centre, Pavilion Road, West Bridgford NG2 5FE ☎ 0115 914 8561 🖷 0115 945 5882 ✉ jwilkinson@rushcliffe.gov.uk

Housing: Ms Donna Dwyer , Strategic Housing Manager, Civic Centre, Pavilion Road, West Bridgford NG2 5FE ☎ 0115 914 8275 🖷 0115 945 5882 ✉ ddwyer@rushcliffe.gov.uk

Legal: Mr Paul Cox, Borough Solicitor, Civic Centre, Pavilion Road, West Bridgford NG2 5FE ☎ 0115 914 8215 🖷 0115 945 5882 ✉ pcox@rushcliffe.gov.uk

Leisure and Cultural Services: Mr Craig Taylor , Cultural Services Manager, Civic Centre, Pavilion Road, West Bridgford NG2 5FE ☎ 0115 914 8345 🖷 0115 914 8452 ✉ ctaylor@rushcliffe.gov.uk

Licensing: Mr Ben Adams , Neighbourhood Manager, Civic Centre, Pavilion Road, West Bridgford NG2 5FE ☎ 0115 914 8487 🖷 0115 945 5882 ✉ badams@rushcliffe.gov.uk

Member Services: Ms Vivien Nightingale , Member Services Manager, Civic Centre, Pavilion Road, West Bridgford NG2 5FE ☎ 0115 914 8481 ✉ vnightingale@rushcliffe.gov.uk

Partnerships: Mr David Mitchell, Executive Manager - Communities, Civic Centre, Pavilion Road, West Bridgford NG2 5FE ☎ 0115 914 8267 🖷 0115 945 5882 ✉ dmitchell@rushcliffe.gov.uk

Personnel / HR: Mrs Juli Hicks , Strategic Human Resources Manager, Civic Centre, Pavilion Road, West Bridgford NG2 5FE ☎ 0115 914 8316 🖷 0115 945 5882 ✉ jhicks@rushcliffe.gov.uk

Planning: Mr Andrew Pegram , Development Control Manager, Civic Centre, Pavilion Road, West Bridgford NG2 5FE ☎ 0115 914 8598 🖷 0115 945 5882 ✉ apegram@rushcliffe.gov.uk

Procurement: Ms Emma Galloway , Procurement Officer, Civic Centre, Pavilion Road, West Bridgford NG2 5FE ✉ egalloway@rushcliffe.gov.uk

Recycling & Waste Minimisation: Mr Darryl Burch , Waste & Fleet Operations Manager, Civic Centre, Pavilion Road, West Bridgford NG2 5FE ☎ 0115 914 8405 🖷 0115 945 5882 ✉ dburch@rushcliffe.gov.uk

Staff Training: Mrs Juli Hicks , Strategic Human Resources Manager, Civic Centre, Pavilion Road, West Bridgford NG2 5FE ☎ 0115 914 8316 🖷 0115 945 5882 ✉ jhicks@rushcliffe.gov.uk

Waste Collection and Disposal: Mr Darryl Burch , Waste & Fleet Operations Manager, Civic Centre, Pavilion Road, West Bridgford NG2 5FE ☎ 0115 914 8405 🖷 0115 945 5882 ✉ dburch@rushcliffe.gov.uk

Waste Management: Mr Darryl Burch , Waste & Fleet Operations Manager, Civic Centre, Pavilion Road, West Bridgford NG2 5FE ☎ 0115 914 8405 🖷 0115 945 5882 ✉ dburch@rushcliffe.gov.uk

Children's Play Areas: Mr Craig Taylor , Cultural Services Manager, Civic Centre, Pavilion Road, West Bridgford NG2 5FE ☎ 0115 914 8345 🖷 0115 914 8452 ✉ ctaylor@rushcliffe.gov.uk

COUNCILLORS

***Mayor* Purdue-Horan**, Francis (CON - Bingham West)
Cllr.Fpurdue-Horan@rushcliffe.gov.uk

***Deputy Mayor* Davidson**, George (IND - Bingham East)
Cllr.Davidison@rushcliffe.gov.uk

***Leader of the Council* Clarke**, Neil (CON - Radcliffe on Trent)
cllr.nclarke@rushcliffe.gov.uk

***Deputy Leader of the Council* Robinson**, Simon (CON - Edwalton)
cllr.srobinson@rushcliffe.gov.uk

Adair, Reginald (CON - Bunny)
Cllr.Radair@rushcliffe.gov.uk

Beardsall, Kevin (CON - Edwalton)
cllr.kbeardsall@rushcliffe.gov.uk

Brown, Andrew (CON - Sutton Bonington)
cllr.abrown@rushcliffe.gov.uk

Buckle, Martin (CON - Ruddington)
cllr.mbuckle@rushcliffe.gov.uk

Buschman, Brian (CON - Abbey)
Cllr.Bbuschman@rushcliffe.gov.uk

Butler, Richard (CON - Cotgrave)
Cllr.RLButler@rushcliffe.gov.uk

Chewings, Hayley (LAB - Cotgrave)
Cllr.hchewings@rushcliffe.gov.uk

Combellack, Tina (CON - Nevile & Langar)
cllr.tcombellack@rushcliffe.gov.uk

Cooper, Leslie (CON - Gamston South)
cllr.lcooper@rushcliffe.gov.uk

Cottee, John (CON - Keyworth & Wolds)
cllr.jcottee@rushcliffe.gov.uk

Dickinson, Angela (CON - Abbey)
Cllr.adickinson@rushcliffe.gov.uk

Donoghue, Julie (CON - Lutterell)
cllr.jdonoghue@rushcliffe.gov.uk

Edwards, Martin (LAB - Lutterell)
cllr.medwards@rushcliffe.gov.uk

Edyvean, Andrew (CON - Keyworth & Wolds)
cllr.aedyvean@rushcliffe.gov.uk

Greenwood, Jean (CON - Ruddington)
cllr.jgreenwood@rushcliffe.gov.uk

Hetherington, Ronald (CON - Leake)
cllr.rhetherington.gov.uk

Hull, Susan (IND - Bingham East)
Cllr.Shull@rushcliffe.gov.uk

Inglis, Robert (CON - Keyworth & Wolds)
cllr.ringlis@rushcliffe.gov.uk

Jeffreys, Christine (CON - Cotgrave)
Cllr.Cjeffreys:rushcliffe.gov.uk

Jones, Rod (LD - Musters)
cllr.rjones@rushcliffe.gov.uk

Khan, Karrar (LD - Musters)
cllr.kkhan@rushcliffe.gov.uk

Lawrence, Nigel (CON - East Bridgford)
cllr.nlawrence@rushcliffe.gov.uk

Lungley, John (CON - Ruddington)
cllr.jlungley@rushcliffe.gov.uk

MacInnes, Alistair (LAB - Trent Bridge)
cllr.amacinnes@rushcliffe.gov.uk

Males, Marie (CON - Leake)
cllr.mmales@rushcliffe.gov.uk

Mallender, Richard (GRN - Lady Bay)
cllr.rmallender@rushcliffe.gov.uk

Mallender, Susan (GRN - Lady Bay)
cllrsmallender@rushcliffe.gov.uk

Mason, Debbie (CON - Tollerton)
cllr.dmason@rushcliffe.gov.uk

Matthews, Stuart (CON - Gotham)
cllr.smatthews@rushcliffe.gov.uk

Moore, Gordon (CON - Cropwell)
cllr.gmoore@rushcliffe.gov.uk

Pell, Adeline (CON - Thoroton)
cllr.apell@rushcliffe.gov.uk

Phillips, Alan (CON - Compton Acres)
Cllr.Aphillips@rushcliffe.gov.uk

Plant, Liz (LAB - Trent Bridge)
cllr.eplant@rushcliffe.gov.uk

Smith, Jean (CON - Radcliffe on Trent)
cllr.jsmith@rushcliffe.gov.uk

Stockwood, John (CON - Bingham West)
Cllr.Jstockwood@rushcliffe.gov.uk

Suthers, Martin (CON - Cranmer)
Cllr.MSuthers@rushcliffe.gov.uk

Thurman, John (CON - Leake) cllr.jthurman@rushcliffe.gov.uk

Upton, Roger (CON - Radcliffe on Trent)
cllr.rupton@rushcliffe.gov.uk

Wheeler, Douglas (CON - Compton Acres)
Cllr.Dwheeler@rushcliffe.gov.uk

Wheeler, Jonathan (CON - Gamston North)
cllr.jwheeler@rushcliffe.gov.uk

POLITICAL COMPOSITION

CON: 34, LAB: 4, LD: 2, GRN: 2, IND: 2

Rushmoor D

Rushmoor Borough Council, Council Offices, Farnborough Road, Farnborough GU14 7JU
☎ 01252 398399 🖷 01252 524017 🖳 www.rushmoor.gov.uk

FACTS AND FIGURES

Parliamentary Constituencies: Aldershot
EU Constituencies: South East
Election Frequency: Elections are by thirds

PRINCIPAL OFFICERS

Chief Executive: Mr Andrew Lloyd, Chief Executive, Council Offices, Farnborough Road, Farnborough GU14 7JU ☎ 01252 398396 🖷 01252 524017 ✉ andrew.lloyd@rushmoor.gov.uk

Deputy Chief Executive: Mr David Quirk, Corporate Director, Council Offices, Farnborough Road, Farnborough GU14 7JU ☎ 01252 398100 🖷 01252 524017 ✉ david.quirk@rushmoor.gov.uk

Senior Management: Mr Ian Harrison , Corporate Director, Council Offices, Farnborough Road, Farnborough GU14 7JU ☎ 01252 398401 🖷 01252 524017 ✉ ian.harrison@rushmoor.gov.uk

Senior Management: Mr David Quirk, Corporate Director, Council Offices, Farnborough Road, Farnborough GU14 7JU ☎ 01252 398100 🖷 01252 524017 ✉ david.quirk@rushmoor.gov.uk

Architect, Building / Property Services: Mr John Curtis , Building Surveyor, Council Offices, Farnborough Road, Farnborough GU14 7JU ☎ 01252 398414 ✉ john.curtis@rushmoor.gov.uk

Best Value: Mrs Karen Edwards, Head of Strategy, Engagement & Organisational Development, Council Offices, Farnborough Road, Farnborough GU14 7JU ☎ 01252 398800 ✉ karen.edwards@rushmoor.gov.uk

Building Control: Mr Geoff Saker, Chief Building Control Officer, Council Offices, Farnborough Road, Farnborough GU14 7JU ☎ 01252 398720 🖷 01252 398726 ✉ geoff.saker@rushmoor.gov.uk

Children / Youth Services: Ms Debbie Wall, Leisure Development Officer, Council Offices, Farnborough Road, Farnborough GU14 7JU ☎ 01252 398745 🖷 01252 398765 ✉ debbie.wall@rushmoor.gov.uk

PR / Communications: Miss Gill Chisnall, Corporate Communications Manager , Council Offices, Farnborough Road, Farnborough GU14 7JU ☎ 01252 398744 🖷 01252 398806 ✉ gill.chisnall@rushmoor.gov.uk

Community Planning: Mrs Karen Edwards, Head of Strategy, Engagement & Organisational Development, Council Offices, Farnborough Road, Farnborough GU14 7JU ☎ 01252 398800 ✉ karen.edwards@rushmoor.gov.uk

Community Safety: Mr Peter Amies, Head of Community & Environmental Services, Council Offices, Farnborough Road, Farnborough GU14 7JU ☎ 01252 398750 🖷 01252 398765 ✉ peter.amies@rushmoor.gov.uk

Computer Management: Mr Nick Harding, Head of Information Technology & Facilities Services, Council Offices, Farnborough Road, Farnborough GU14 7JU ☎ 01252 398650 ✉ nick.harding@rushmoor.gov.uk

Contracts: Mr Peter Amies, Head of Community & Environmental Services, Council Offices, Farnborough Road, Farnborough GU14 7JU ☎ 01252 398750 🖷 01252 398765 ✉ peter.amies@rushmoor.gov.uk

Corporate Services: Ms Amanda Fahey , Head of Financial Services & Chief Finance Officer, Council Offices, Farnborough Road, Farnborough GU14 7JU ☎ 01252 398440 ✉ amanda.fahey@rushmoor.gov.uk

Customer Service: Mr Andrew Colver, Head of Democratic & Customer Services, Council Offices, Farnborough Road, Farnborough GU14 7JU ☎ 01252 398820 🖷 01252 524017 ✉ andrew.colver@rushmoor.gov.uk

Economic Development: Mr Keith Holland, Head of Planning Services, Council Offices, Farnborough Road, Farnborough GU14 7JU ☎ 01252 398790 🖷 01252 398668 ✉ keith.holland@rushmoor.gov.uk

E-Government: Mrs Karen Edwards, Head of Strategy, Engagement & Organisational Development, Council Offices, Farnborough Road, Farnborough GU14 7JU ☎ 01252 398800 ✉ karen.edwards@rushmoor.gov.uk

Electoral Registration: Mr Andrew Colver, Head of Democratic & Customer Services, Council Offices, Farnborough Road, Farnborough GU14 7JU ☎ 01252 398820 🖷 01252 524017 ✉ andrew.colver@rushmoor.gov.uk

Emergency Planning: Mr Jon Rundle, Head of Strategy, Performance & Partnership Management, Council Offices, Farnborough Road, Farnborough GU14 7JU ☎ 01252 398801 🖷 01252 398806 ✉ jon.rundle@rushmoor.gov.uk

Energy Management: Mr Les Murrell , Energy & Environment Manager, Council Offices, Farnborough Road, Farnborough GU14 7JU ☎ 01252 398538 ✉ les.murrell@rushmoor.gov.uk

Environmental / Technical Services: Miss Qamer Yasin , Head of Environmental Health & Housing Services, Council Offices, Farnborough Road, Farnborough GU14 7JU ☎ 01252 398640 🖷 01252 398552 ✉ qamer.yasin@rushmoor.gov.uk

Environmental Health: Miss Qamer Yasin , Head of Environmental Health & Housing Services, Council Offices, Farnborough Road, Farnborough GU14 7JU ☎ 01252 398640 🖷 01252 398552 ✉ qamer.yasin@rushmoor.gov.uk

Estates, Property & Valuation: Mrs Ann Greaves , Solicitor to the Council, Council Offices, Farnborough Road, Farnborough GU14 7JU ☎ 01252 398600 ✉ ann.greaves@rushmoor.gov.uk

European Liaison: Mr Peter Amies, Head of Community & Environmental Services, Council Offices, Farnborough Road, Farnborough GU14 7JU ☎ 01252 398750 🖷 01252 398765 ✉ peter.amies@rushmoor.gov.uk

Events Manager: Miss Gill Chisnall, Corporate Communications Manager , Council Offices, Farnborough Road, Farnborough GU14 7JU ☎ 01252 398744 🖷 01252 398806 ✉ gill.chisnall@rushmoor.gov.uk

Facilities: Mr Nick Harding, Head of Information Technology & Facilities Services, Council Offices, Farnborough Road, Farnborough GU14 7JU ☎ 01252 398650 ✉ nick.harding@rushmoor.gov.uk

Facilities: Mrs Sheila MacFarlane, Facilities Manager, Council Offices, Farnborough Road, Farnborough GU14 7JU ☎ 01252 398480 🖷 01252 524017 ✉ sheila.macfarlane@rushmoor.gov.uk

Finance: Ms Amanda Fahey , Head of Financial Services & Chief Finance Officer, Council Offices, Farnborough Road, Farnborough GU14 7JU ☎ 01252 398440 ✉ amanda.fahey@rushmoor.gov.uk

Grounds Maintenance: Mr Andy Ford, Parks Development Officer, Council Offices, Farnborough Road, Farnborough GU14 7JU ☎ 01252 398771 ✉ andy.ford@rushmoor.gov.uk

Health and Safety: Mr Roger Sanders , Health & Safety Officer, Council Offices, Farnborough Road, Farnborough GU14 7JU ☎ 01252 398160 ✉ roger.sanders@rushmoor.gov.uk

Home Energy Conservation: Mr Les Murrell , Energy & Environment Manager, Council Offices, Farnborough Road, Farnborough GU14 7JU ☎ 01252 398538 ✉ les.murrell@rushmoor.gov.uk

Housing: Miss Qamer Yasin , Head of Environmental Health & Housing Services, Council Offices, Farnborough Road, Farnborough GU14 7JU ☎ 01252 398640 🖷 01252 398552 ✉ qamer.yasin@rushmoor.gov.uk

Legal: Mrs Ann Greaves , Solicitor to the Council, Council Offices, Farnborough Road, Farnborough GU14 7JU ☎ 01252 398600 ✉ ann.greaves@rushmoor.gov.uk

Leisure and Cultural Services: Mr Peter Amies, Head of Community & Environmental Services, Council Offices, Farnborough Road, Farnborough GU14 7JU ☎ 01252 398750 🖷 01252 398765 ✉ peter.amies@rushmoor.gov.uk

Licensing: Mr John McNab , Environmental Health Manager of Licensing, Council Offices, Farnborough Road, Farnborough GU14 7JU ☎ 01252 398886 ✉ john.mcnab@rushmoor.gov.uk

Lifelong Learning: Mrs Karen Edwards, Head of Strategy, Engagement & Organisational Development, Council Offices, Farnborough Road, Farnborough GU14 7JU ☎ 01252 398800 ✉ karen.edwards@rushmoor.gov.uk

Lottery Funding, Charity and Voluntary: Mr Peter Amies, Head of Community & Environmental Services, Council Offices, Farnborough Road, Farnborough GU14 7JU ☎ 01252 398750 🖷 01252 398765 ✉ peter.amies@rushmoor.gov.uk

Member Services: Mr Andrew Colver, Head of Democratic & Customer Services, Council Offices, Farnborough Road, Farnborough GU14 7JU ☎ 01252 398820 🖷 01252 524017 ✉ andrew.colver@rushmoor.gov.uk

Parking: Mrs Kirsty Hosey , Parking Manager, Council Offices, Farnborough Road, Farnborough GU14 7JU ☎ 01252 398510 ✉ kirsty.hosey@rushmoor.gov.uk

Partnerships: Miss Annie Denton , Strategic Partnership Officer, Council Offices, Farnborough Road, Farnborough GU14 7JU ☎ 01252 398221 ✉ annie.denton@rushmoor.gov.uk

Personnel / HR: Mrs Karen Edwards, Head of Strategy, Engagement & Organisational Development, Council Offices, Farnborough Road, Farnborough GU14 7JU ☎ 01252 398800 ✉ karen.edwards@rushmoor.gov.uk

Planning: Mr Keith Holland, Head of Planning Services, Council Offices, Farnborough Road, Farnborough GU14 7JU ☎ 01252 398790 🖷 01252 398668 ✉ keith.holland@rushmoor.gov.uk

Procurement: Mrs Karen Edwards, Head of Strategy, Engagement & Organisational Development, Council Offices, Farnborough Road, Farnborough GU14 7JU ☎ 01252 398800 ✉ karen.edwards@rushmoor.gov.uk

Recycling & Waste Minimisation: Mr James Duggin , Contracts Manager, Council Offices, Farnborough Road, Farnborough GU14 7JU ☎ 01252 398167 ✉ james.duggin@rushmoor.gov.uk

Regeneration: Mrs Debbie Whitcombe , Regeneration Officer, Council Offices, Farnborough Road, Farnborough GU14 7JU ☎ 01252 398793 ✉ debbie.whitcombe@rushmoor.gov.uk

Staff Training: Mrs Sarah Barron , Principal Personnel Officer, Council Offices, Farnborough Road, Farnborough GU14 7JU ☎ 01252 398421 🖷 01252 398094 ✉ sarah.barron@rushmoor.gov.uk

Sustainable Communities: Mr Les Murrell , Energy & Environment Manager, Council Offices, Farnborough Road, Farnborough GU14 7JU ☎ 01252 398538 ✉ les.murrell@rushmoor.gov.uk

Sustainable Development: Mr Les Murrell , Energy & Environment Manager, Council Offices, Farnborough Road, Farnborough GU14 7JU ☎ 01252 398538 ✉ les.murrell@rushmoor.gov.uk

Tourism: Mr Peter Amies, Head of Community & Environmental Services, Council Offices, Farnborough Road, Farnborough GU14 7JU ☎ 01252 398750 🖷 01252 398765 ✉ peter.amies@rushmoor.gov.uk

Town Centre: Mr Keith Holland, Head of Planning Services, Council Offices, Farnborough Road, Farnborough GU14 7JU ☎ 01252 398790 🖷 01252 398668 ✉ keith.holland@rushmoor.gov.uk

Traffic Management: Mr John Trusler , Principal Engineer, Council Offices, Farnborough Road, Farnborough GU14 7JU ☎ 01252 398377 ✉ john.trusler@rushmoor.gov.uk

Waste Collection and Disposal: Mr James Duggin , Contracts Manager, Council Offices, Farnborough Road, Farnborough GU14 7JU ☎ 01252 398167 ✉ james.duggin@rushmoor.gov.uk

Waste Management: Mr James Duggin , Contracts Manager, Council Offices, Farnborough Road, Farnborough GU14 7JU ☎ 01252 398167 ✉ james.duggin@rushmoor.gov.uk

COUNCILLORS

***Mayor* Tennant**, Martin (CON - Cove and Southwood)
martin.tennant@rushmoor.gov.uk

***Deputy Mayor* Vosper**, Jacqui (CON - St. John's)
jacqui.vosper@rushmoor.gov.uk

***Leader of the Council* Moyle**, Peter (CON - St. John's)
peter.moyle@rushmoor.gov.uk

***Deputy Leader of the Council* Muschamp**, Ken (CON - Fernhill)
ken@laulind.co.uk

***Group Leader* Staplehurst**, Mark (UKIP - West Heath)
ukip.westheath@virginmedia.com

Bedford, Diane (CON - St. Mark's)
diane.bedford@tiscali.co.uk

Bell, David (UKIP - West Heath)
dave.bell100@ntworld.com

Bridgeman, Terry (LAB - Aldershot Park)
bridgemanterry@yahoo.co.uk

Carter, Sue (CON - Cove and Southwood)
sue.carter@rushmoor.gov.uk

Choudhary, Sophia (CON - Rowhill)
sophia.choudhary@rushmoor.gov.uk

Choudhary, Charles (CON - Rowhill)
charles.choudhary@btinternet.com

Clifford, David (CON - Empress)
david.clifford@rushmoor.gov.uk

Cooper, Rod (CON - West Heath)
rod.cooper@rushmoor.gov.uk

Corps, Liz (CON - St. Mark's)
liz.corps@ntlworld.com

Crawford, Alex (LAB - Wellington)
alex.crawford06@btinternet.com

Crerar, Peter (CON - Manor Park)
peter_crerar@btinternet.com

Dibble, Sue (LAB - North Town)
sue.dibble@rushmoor.gov.uk

Dibble, Keith (LAB - North Town)
keith.dibble@rushmoor.gov.uk

Dibbs, Roland (CON - Knellwood)
rlgdibbs@aol.com

Evans, Jennifer (LAB - Wellington)
evans.jenniferevans@gmail.com

Ferrier, Alan (CON - Fernhill)
alan.ferrier@rushmoor.gov.uk

Gladstone, David (CON - St. Mark's)
gladstone.conservative@gmail.com

Grattan, Clive (LAB - Cherrywood)
clive.grattan@rushmoor.gov.uk

Hughes, Ron (CON - Manor Park)
rhandi@btinternet.com

Hurst, Barbara (CON - St. John's)
barbara@pbhurst.com

Jackman, Adam (CON - Knellwood)
adam@jackman.org.uk

Jones, Barry (LAB - Cherrywood)
barry.jones@rushmoor.gov.uk

Lyon, Gareth (CON - Empress)
gareth.lyon@rushmoor.gov.uk

Marsh, John (CON - Fernhill)
johnmarsh@ntlworld.com

Masterson, Stephen (CON - Cove and Southwood)
steve@stationroad1958.fsnet.co.uk

Newell, Adrian (CON - Aldershot Park)
adriannewell@msn.com

Preece, Jeremy (LAB - Wellington)
jeremy.preece@rushmoor.gov.uk

Roberts, Mike (LAB - Aldershot Park)
mike.roberts@rushmoor.gov.uk

Rust, Frank (LAB - North Town)
frank.rust@rushmoor.gov.uk

Smith, Mike (CON - Empress)
mdsmithrushmoor@gmail.com

Taylor, Paul (CON - Knellwood)
paul.taylor@rsuhmoor.gov.uk

Taylor, Les (LAB - Cherrywood)
les.taylor@rushmoor.gov.uk

Thomas, Bruce (CON - Manor Park)
bruce.thomas@ntlworld.com

Welch, David (CON - Rowhill)
david.welch@rushmoor.gov.uk

POLITICAL COMPOSITION
CON: 26, LAB: 11, UKIP: 2

COMMITTEE CHAIRS

Licensing: Mr Martin Tennant

Licensing: Mr Alan Ferrier

Rutland U

Rutland County Council, Council Offices, Catmose, Oakham LE15 6HP
☎ 01572 722577 🖷 01572 758307 ✉ enquiries@rutland.gov.uk
🖳 www.rutland.gov.uk

FACTS AND FIGURES
Parliamentary Constituencies: Rutland and Melton
EU Constituencies: East Midlands
Election Frequency: Elections are of whole council

PRINCIPAL OFFICERS

Chief Executive: Mrs Helen Briggs, Chief Executive, Council Offices, Catmose, Oakham LE15 6HP ☎ 01572 758203 🖷 01572 758385 ✉ hbriggs@rutland.gov.uk

Deputy Chief Executive: Dr Tim O'Neill , Deputy Chief Executive & Director - People, Council Offices, Catmose, Oakham LE15 6HP ☎ 01572 758402 ✉ toneill@rutland.gov.uk

Senior Management: Mr Dave Brown , Director - Places, Environment, Planning & Transport, Council Offices, Catmose, Oakham LE15 6HP ☎ 01572 758461 🖷 01572 724378 ✉ dbrown@rutland.gov.uk

Senior Management: Ms Debbie Mogg , Director - Resources, Council Offices, Catmose, Oakham LE15 6HP ☎ 01572 758358 ✉ dmogg@rutland.gov.uk

Senior Management: Dr Tim O'Neill , Deputy Chief Executive & Director - People, Council Offices, Catmose, Oakham LE15 6HP ☎ 01572 758402 ✉ toneill@rutland.gov.uk

Senior Management: Mr Paul Phillipson , Director - Places, Development & Economy, Council Offices, Catmose, Oakham LE15 6HP ☎ 01572 758226 ✉ lwakeford@rutland.gov.uk

Architect, Building / Property Services: Mr Paul Phillipson , Operational Director - Places, Council Offices, Catmose, Oakham LE15 6HP ☎ 01572 722577 🖷 01572 758377 ✉ pphillipson@rutland.gov.uk

Building Control: Mr Paul Phillipson , Operational Director - Places, Council Offices, Catmose, Oakham LE15 6HP ☎ 01572 722577 🖷 01572 758377 ✉ pphillipson@rutland.gov.uk

Children / Youth Services: Dr Tim O'Neill , Deputy Chief Executive & Director - People, Council Offices, Catmose, Oakham LE15 6HP ☎ 01572 758402 ✉ toneill@rutland.gov.uk

Civil Registration: Ms Tricia Goodchild, Superintendent Registrar, Council Offices, Catmose, Oakham LE15 6HP ☎ 01572 722577 ✉ tgoodchild@rutland.gov.uk

PR / Communications: Mr Mat Waik , Strategic Communications Advisor, Council Offices, Catmose, Oakham LE15 6HP ☎ 01572 758328 🖷 01572 758385 ✉ mwaik@rutland.gov.uk

Community Safety: Mr Hugh Crouch , Senior Community Safety Officer, Council Offices, Catmose, Oakham LE15 6HP ☎ 01572 756655 ✉ hcrouch@rutland.gov.uk

Computer Management: Mr Mark Poole , Interim Head - IT, Council Offices, Catmose, Oakham LE15 6HP ☎ 01572 758360 ✉ mpoole@rutland.gov.uk

Consumer Protection and Trading Standards: Mr Paul Phillipson , Operational Director - Places, Council Offices, Catmose, Oakham LE15 6HP ☎ 01572 722577 🖷 01572 758377 ✉ pphillipson@rutland.gov.uk

Contracts: Ms Louise Gallagher , Team Manager - Contracts, Council Offices, Catmose, Oakham LE15 6HP ☎ 01572 758292 🖷 01572 758307 ✉ lgallagher@rutland.gov.uk

Corporate Services: Ms Debbie Mogg , Director - Resources, Council Offices, Catmose, Oakham LE15 6HP ☎ 01572 758358 ✉ dmogg@rutland.gov.uk

Customer Service: Mr Jay Khetani , Customer Services Manager, Council Offices, Catmose, Oakham LE15 6HP ☎ 01572 758326 ✉ jkhetani@rutland.gov.uk

Economic Development: Ms Libby Kingsley , Senior Economic Development Manager, Council Offices, Catmose, Oakham LE15 6HP ☎ 01572 722577 ✉ lkingsley@rutland.gov.uk

Education: Dr Tim O'Neill , Deputy Chief Executive & Director - People, Council Offices, Catmose, Oakham LE15 6HP ☎ 01572 758402 ✉ toneill@rutland.gov.uk

Electoral Registration: Ms Samantha Ramsey , Electoral Services Officer, Council Offices, Catmose, Oakham LE15 6HP ☎ 01572 758461 ✉ dbrown@rutland.gov.uk

Emergency Planning: Mr Dave Brown , Director - Places, Environment, Planning & Transport, Council Offices, Catmose, Oakham LE15 6HP ☎ 01572 758461 🖷 01572 724378 ✉ dbrown@rutland.gov.uk

Environmental Health: Mr Mark Loran , Senior Environmental Health Officer, Council Offices, Catmose, Oakham LE15 6HP ☎ 01572 758430 ✉ mloran@rutland.gov.uk

Estates, Property & Valuation: Mr Paul Phillipson , Operational Director - Places, Council Offices, Catmose, Oakham LE15 6HP ☎ 01572 722577 🖷 01572 758377 ✉ pphillipson@rutland.gov.uk

Finance: Ms Andrea Grinney , Head of Revenues & Benefits, Council Offices, Catmose, Oakham LE15 6HP ☎ 01572 722577 ✉ agrinney@rutland.gov.uk

Finance: Ms Debbie Mogg , Director - Resources, Council Offices, Catmose, Oakham LE15 6HP ☎ 01572 758358 ✉ dmogg@rutland.gov.uk

Grounds Maintenance: Mr Neil Tomlinson , Senior Highways Officer, Council Offices, Catmose, Oakham LE15 6HP ☎ 01572 758342 ✉ ntomlinson@rutland.gov.uk

Health and Safety: Mr Iain Watt , Corporate Health & Safety Officer, Council Offices, Catmose, Oakham LE15 6HP ☎ 01572 722577 ✉ iwatt@rutland.gov.uk

Highways: Mr Dave Brown , Director - Places, Environment, Planning & Transport, Council Offices, Catmose, Oakham LE15 6HP ☎ 01572 758461 🖷 01572 724378 ✉ dbrown@rutland.gov.uk

Legal: Mrs Diane Baker, Head of Corporate Governance, Council Offices, Catmose, Oakham LE15 6HP ☎ 01572 758202 🖷 01572 758307 ✉ dbaker@rutland.gov.uk

Leisure and Cultural Services: Mr Robert Clayton , Head of Culture & Leisure, Council Offices, Catmose, Oakham LE15 6HP ☎ 01572 758435 ✉ rclayton@rutland.gov.uk

Licensing: Mr John Dwyer , Licensing Officer, Council Offices, Catmose, Oakham LE15 6HP ✉ jdwyer@rutland.gov.uk

Lifelong Learning: Mr Mark Fowler , Head of Service - Lifelong Learning, Council Offices, Catmose, Oakham LE15 6HP ☎ 01572 722577 🖷 01572 758307 ✉ mfowler@rutland.gov.uk

Lighting: Mr Neil Tomlinson , Senior Highways Officer, Council Offices, Catmose, Oakham LE15 6HP ☎ 01572 758342 ✉ ntomlinson@rutland.gov.uk

Member Services: Mrs Diane Baker, Head of Corporate Governance, Council Offices, Catmose, Oakham LE15 6HP ☎ 01572 758202 🖷 01572 758307 ✉ dbaker@rutland.gov.uk

Parking: Ms Joanna Fraser , Parking Officer, Council Offices, Catmose, Oakham LE15 6HP ☎ 01572 72277 ✉ jfraser@rutland.gov.uk

Personnel / HR: Ms Carol Snell , Senior HR Adviser, Council Offices, Catmose, Oakham LE15 6HP ☎ 01572 722577 🖷 01572 758307 ✉ csnell@rutland.gov.uk

Planning: Mr Dave Brown , Director - Places, Environment, Planning & Transport, Council Offices, Catmose, Oakham LE15 6HP ☎ 01572 758461 🖷 01572 724378 ✉ dbrown@rutland.gov.uk

Public Libraries: Mr Robert Clayton , Head of Culture & Leisure, Council Offices, Catmose, Oakham LE15 6HP ☎ 01572 758435 ✉ rclayton@rutland.gov.uk

Recycling & Waste Minimisation: Mr Mark Loran , Senior Environmental Health Officer, Council Offices, Catmose, Oakham LE15 6HP ☎ 01572 758430 ✉ mloran@rutland.gov.uk

Road Safety: Mr Dave Brown , Director - Places, Environment, Planning & Transport, Council Offices, Catmose, Oakham LE15 6HP ☎ 01572 758461 🖷 01572 724378 ✉ dbrown@rutland.gov.uk

Social Services: Dr Tim O'Neill , Deputy Chief Executive & Director - People, Council Offices, Catmose, Oakham LE15 6HP ☎ 01572 758402 ✉ toneill@rutland.gov.uk

Social Services (Adult): Dr Tim O'Neill , Deputy Chief Executive & Director - People, Council Offices, Catmose, Oakham LE15 6HP ☎ 01572 758402 ✉ toneill@rutland.gov.uk

Social Services (Children): Dr Tim O'Neill , Deputy Chief Executive & Director - People, Council Offices, Catmose, Oakham LE15 6HP ☎ 01572 758402 ✉ toneill@rutland.gov.uk

Staff Training: Ms Carol Snell , Senior HR Adviser, Council Offices, Catmose, Oakham LE15 6HP ☎ 01572 722577 🖷 01572 758307 ✉ csnell@rutland.gov.uk

Street Scene: Ms Suzi Parfrement-Pollard , Street Scene Officer, Council Offices, Catmose, Oakham LE15 6HP ☎ 01572 758286 ✉ sparfrementpollard@rutland.gov.uk

Tourism: Ms Sarah Beresford , Tourism Officer, Council Offices, Catmose, Oakham LE15 6HP ☎ 01572 720921 🖷 01572 758307 ✉ sberesford@rutland.gov.uk

Traffic Management: Mr Neil Tomlinson , Senior Highways Officer, Council Offices, Catmose, Oakham LE15 6HP ☎ 01572 758342 ✉ ntomlinson@rutland.gov.uk

Transport: Mrs Emma Odabas , Group Manager - Transport & Accessibility, Council Offices, Catmose, Oakham LE15 6HP ☎ 01572 720923 ✉ eodabas@rutland.gov.uk

Transport Planner: Mrs Emma Odabas , Group Manager - Transport & Accessibility, Council Offices, Catmose, Oakham LE15 6HP ☎ 01572 720923 ✉ eodabas@rutland.gov.uk

Waste Collection and Disposal: Mr Mark Loran , Senior Environmental Health Officer, Council Offices, Catmose, Oakham LE15 6HP ☎ 01572 758430 ✉ mloran@rutland.gov.uk

Waste Management: Mr Mark Loran , Senior Environmental Health Officer, Council Offices, Catmose, Oakham LE15 6HP ☎ 01572 758430 ✉ mloran@rutland.gov.uk

COUNCILLORS

***Chair* Bool**, Kenneth (CON - Normanton)
kbool@rutland.gov.uk

***Vice-Chair* Baines**, Edward (CON - Martinsthorpe)
ebaines@rutland.gov.uk

***Leader of the Council* Begy**, Roger (CON - Greetham)
rbegy@rutland.gov.uk

***Deputy Leader of the Council* King**, Terry (CON - Exton)
tking@rutland.gov.uk

Asplin, Sam (LD - Whissendine)
sasplin@rutland.gov.uk

Bird, Oliver (IND - Oakham South West)
obird@rutland.gov.uk

Burkitt, Rachel (CON - Uppingham)
rburkitt@rutland.gov.uk

Callaghan, Ben (IND - Oakham South East)
bcallaghan@rutland.gov.uk

Clifton, Richard (CON - Oakham South West)
rclifton@rutland.gov.uk

Conde, Gary (CON - Ketton)
gconde@rutland.gov.uk

Cross, William (CON - Braunston and Belton)
wcross@rutland.gov.uk

Dale, Jeffrey (IND - Oakham North East)
jdale@rutland.gov.uk

Foster, Richard (CON - Cottesmore)
rfoster@rutland.gov.uk

Gale, Richard (IND - Oakham North West)
rgale@rutland.gov.uk

Hemsley, Oliver (CON - Langham)
ohemsley@rutland.gov.uk

Lammie, James (CON - Lyddington)
jlammie@rutland.gov.uk

MacDuff, Diane (CON - Ketton)
dmacduff@rutland.gov.uk

Mann, Alistair (CON - Oakham North West)
amann@rutland.gov.uk

Mathias, Tony (CON - Oakham South East)
tmathias@rutland.gov.uk

Oxley, Marc (IND - Uppingham)
moxley@rutland.gov.uk

Parsons, Chris (IND - Ryhall and Casterton)
cparsons@rutland.gov.uk

Stephenson, Lucy (CON - Uppingham)
lstephenson@rutland.gov.uk

Stewart, Andrew (CON - Cottesmore)
astewart@rutland.gov.uk

Waller, Gale (LD - Normanton)
gwaller@rutland.gov.uk

Walters, Alan (IND - Oakham North East)
awalters@rutland.gov.uk

Wilby, David (CON - Ryhall and Casterton)
dwilby@rutland.gov.uk

POLITICAL COMPOSITION

CON: 17, IND: 7, LD: 2

COMMITTEE CHAIRS

Adults & Health: Mrs Lucy Stephenson

Audit: Mrs Diane MacDuff

Children: Mr Jeffrey Dale

Development Control: Mr Edward Baines

Licensing: Mr Alan Walters

Ryedale D

Ryedale District Council, Ryedale House, Malton YO17 7HH
☎ 01653 600666 🖷 01653 696801 ✉ info@ryedale.gov.uk
💻 www.ryedale.gov.uk

FACTS AND FIGURES

Parliamentary Constituencies: Thirsk & Malton
EU Constituencies: Yorkshire and the Humber
Election Frequency: Elections are of whole council

PRINCIPAL OFFICERS

Chief Executive: Ms Janet Waggott, Chief Executive, Ryedale House, Malton YO17 7HH ☎ 01653 600666 🖷 01653 600175 ✉ janet.waggott@ryedale.gov.uk

Senior Management: Mr Gary Housden, Head of Planning & Housing, Ryedale House, Malton YO17 7HH ☎ 01653 600666 🖷 01653 696801 ✉ gary.housden@ryedale.gov.uk

Senior Management: Mr Peter Johnson , Finance Manager, Ryedale House, Malton YO17 7HH ☎ 01653 600666 ext 385 🖷 01653 696801 ✉ peter.johnson@ryedale.gov.uk

Senior Management: Mr Phil Long , Corporate Director, Ryedale House, Malton YO17 7HH ☎ 01653 600666 Extn 461 ✉ phil.long@ryedale.gov.uk

Senior Management: Mr Julian Rudd, Head of Economy & Infrastructure, Ryedale House, Malton YO17 7HH ☎ 01653 600666 Ext 218 🖷 01653 696801 ✉ julian.rudd@ryedale.gov.uk

Senior Management: Mrs Clare Slater, Head of Corporate Services, Ryedale House, Malton YO17 7HH ☎ 01653 600666 🖷 01653 696801 ✉ clare.slater@ryedale.gov.uk

Senior Management: Mr Anthony Winship, Council Solicitor, Ryedale House, Malton YO17 7HH ☎ 01653 600666 Ext 267 🖷 01653 696801 ✉ anthony.winship@ryedale.gov.uk

Architect, Building / Property Services: Mrs Beckie Bennett , Head of Environment, Streetscene & Facilities, Ryedale House, Malton YO17 7HH ☎ 01653 600666 Extn 483 ✉ beckie.bennett@ryedale.gov.uk

Best Value: Mrs Clare Slater, Head of Corporate Services, Ryedale House, Malton YO17 7HH ☎ 01653 600666 🖷 01653 696801 ✉ clare.slater@ryedale.gov.uk

Building Control: Mr Les Chapman, Building Control Manager, The Suite 2, Coxwold House, Easingwold Business Park, Easingwold, York YO61 3FB ☎ 01904 720281 🖷 01904 720282 ✉ les.chapman@ryedale.gov.uk

PR / Communications: Ms Jill Baldwin, Media Relations Officer, Ryedale House, Malton YO17 7HH ☎ 01653 600666 🖷 01653 696801 ✉ jill.baldwin@ryedale.gov.uk

PR / Communications: Mrs Clare Slater, Head of Corporate Services, Ryedale House, Malton YO17 7HH ☎ 01653 600666 🖷 01653 696801 ✉ clare.slater@ryedale.gov.uk

Community Planning: Mrs Jos Holmes, Economy Manager, Ryedale House, Malton YO17 7HH ☎ 01653 600666 Ext 240 🖷 01653 696801 ✉ jos.holmes@ryedale.gov.uk

Community Planning: Mrs Clare Slater, Head of Corporate Services, Ryedale House, Malton YO17 7HH ☎ 01653 600666 🖷 01653 696801 ✉ clare.slater@ryedale.gov.uk

Community Safety: Ms Gail Cook, Technical Support Officer , Ryedale House, Malton YO17 7HH ☎ 01653 600666 Ext 314 ✉ gail.cook@ryedale.gov.uk

Computer Management: Mrs Beckie Bennett , Head of Environment, Streetscene & Facilities, Ryedale House, Malton YO17 7HH ☎ 01653 600666 Extn 483 ✉ beckie.bennett@ryedale.gov.uk

Corporate Services: Mrs Clare Slater, Head of Corporate Services, Ryedale House, Malton YO17 7HH ☎ 01653 600666 🖷 01653 696801 ✉ clare.slater@ryedale.gov.uk

Corporate Services: Ms Janet Waggott, Chief Executive, Ryedale House, Malton YO17 7HH ☎ 01653 600666 🖷 01653 600175 ✉ janet.waggott@ryedale.gov.uk

Customer Service: Angela Jones , Business Support Manager, Ryedale House, Malton YO17 7HH ☎ 01653 600666 🖷 01653 696801 ✉ angela.jones@ryedale.gov.uk

Customer Service: Mrs Clare Slater, Head of Corporate Services, Ryedale House, Malton YO17 7HH ☎ 01653 600666 🖷 01653 696801 ✉ clare.slater@ryedale.gov.uk

Economic Development: Mr Julian Rudd, Head of Economy & Infrastructure, Ryedale House, Malton YO17 7HH ☎ 01653 600666 Ext 218 🖷 01653 696801 ✉ julian.rudd@ryedale.gov.uk

E-Government: Mr Phil Long, Head of Streetscene & Environment, Ryedale House, Malton YO17 7HH ☎ 01653 600666 ✉ phil.long@ryedale.gov.uk

Electoral Registration: Mr Simon Copley , Democratic Services Manager, Ryedale House, Malton YO17 7HH ☎ 01653 600666 Ext 277 🖷 01653 696801 ✉ simon.copley@ryedale.gov.uk

Emergency Planning: Mr Phil Long , Corporate Director, Ryedale House, Malton YO17 7HH ☎ 01653 600666 Extn 461 ✉ phil.long@ryedale.gov.uk

Environmental / Technical Services: Mrs Beckie Bennett , Head of Environment, Streetscene & Facilities, Ryedale House, Malton YO17 7HH ☎ 01653 600666 Extn 483 ✉ beckie.bennett@ryedale.gov.uk

Environmental Health: Mr Steven Richmond, Environmental Health Manager, Ryedale House, Malton YO17 7HH ☎ 01653 600666 Ext 247 🖷 01653 600764 ✉ steve.richmond@ryedale.gov.uk

European Liaison: Mr Julian Rudd, Head of Economy & Infrastructure, Ryedale House, Malton YO17 7HH ☎ 01653 600666 Ext 218 🖷 01653 696801 ✉ julian.rudd@ryedale.gov.uk

Events Manager: Mrs Jos Holmes, Economy Manager, Ryedale House, Malton YO17 7HH ☎ 01653 600666 Ext 240 🖷 01653 696801 ✉ jos.holmes@ryedale.gov.uk

Facilities: Mrs Beckie Bennett , Head of Environment, Streetscene & Facilities, Ryedale House, Malton YO17 7HH ☎ 01653 600666 Extn 483 ✉ beckie.bennett@ryedale.gov.uk

Fleet Management: Mrs Beckie Bennett , Head of Environment, Streetscene & Facilities, Ryedale House, Malton YO17 7HH ☎ 01653 600666 Extn 483 ✉ beckie.bennett@ryedale.gov.uk

Grounds Maintenance: Mrs Beckie Bennett , Head of Environment, Streetscene & Facilities, Ryedale House, Malton YO17 7HH ☎ 01653 600666 Extn 483 ✉ beckie.bennett@ryedale.gov.uk

Grounds Maintenance: Mrs Beckie Bennett , Head of Environment, Streetscene & Facilities, Ryedale House, Malton YO17 7HH ☎ 01653 600666 Extn 483 ✉ beckie.bennett@ryedale.gov.uk

Home Energy Conservation: Mr John Brown, Environmental & Recycling Officer, Central Depot, Showfield Lane Industrial Estate, Malton Y017 0BY ☎ 01653 600666 🖷 01653 690737 ✉ john.brown@ryedale.gov.uk

Housing: Mr Gary Housden, Head of Planning & Housing, Ryedale House, Malton YO17 7HH ☎ 01653 600666 🖷 01653 696801 ✉ gary.housden@ryedale.gov.uk

Housing: Ms Kim Robertshaw , Housing Services Manager, Ryedale House, Malton YO17 7HH ☎ 01653 600666 ✉ kim.robertshaw@ryedale.gov.uk

Legal: Mr Anthony Winship, Council Solicitor, Ryedale House, Malton YO17 7HH ☎ 01653 600666 Ext 267 🖷 01653 696801 ✉ anthony.winship@ryedale.gov.uk

Leisure and Cultural Services: Mr Steven Richmond, Environmental Health Manager, Ryedale House, Malton YO17 7HH ☎ 01653 600666 Ext 247 🖷 01653 600764 ✉ steve.richmond@ryedale.gov.uk

Licensing: Mr Steven Richmond, Environmental Health Manager, Ryedale House, Malton YO17 7HH ☎ 01653 600666 Ext 247 🖷 01653 600764 ✉ steve.richmond@ryedale.gov.uk

Lottery Funding, Charity and Voluntary: Mrs Jos Holmes, Economy Manager, Ryedale House, Malton YO17 7HH ☎ 01653 600666 Ext 240 🖷 01653 696801 ✉ jos.holmes@ryedale.gov.uk

Member Services: Mr Simon Copley , Democratic Services Manager, Ryedale House, Malton YO17 7HH ☎ 01653 600666 Ext 277 🖷 01653 696801 ✉ simon.copley@ryedale.gov.uk

Member Services: Mrs Clare Slater, Head of Corporate Services, Ryedale House, Malton YO17 7HH ☎ 01653 600666 🖷 01653 696801 ✉ clare.slater@ryedale.gov.uk

Parking: Mrs Beckie Bennett , Head of Environment, Streetscene & Facilities, Ryedale House, Malton YO17 7HH ☎ 01653 600666 Extn 483 ✉ beckie.bennett@ryedale.gov.uk

Partnerships: Mrs Clare Slater, Head of Corporate Services, Ryedale House, Malton YO17 7HH ☎ 01653 600666 🖷 01653 696801 ✉ clare.slater@ryedale.gov.uk

Personnel / HR: Mrs Denise Hewitt , Human Resources Manager, Ryedale House, Malton YO17 7HH ☎ 01653 600666 ✉ denise.hewitt@ryedale.gov.uk

Planning: Mr Gary Housden, Head of Planning & Housing, Ryedale House, Malton YO17 7HH ☎ 01653 600666 🖷 01653 696801 ✉ gary.housden@ryedale.gov.uk

Procurement: Mrs Clare Slater, Head of Corporate Services, Ryedale House, Malton YO17 7HH ☎ 01653 600666 🖷 01653 696801 ✉ clare.slater@ryedale.gov.uk

Recycling & Waste Minimisation: Mr John Brown, Environmental & Recycling Officer, Central Depot, Showfield Lane Industrial Estate, Malton Y017 0BY ☎ 01653 600666 🖷 01653 690737 ✉ john.brown@ryedale.gov.uk

Regeneration: Mr Julian Rudd, Head of Economy & Infrastructure, Ryedale House, Malton YO17 7HH ☎ 01653 600666 Ext 218 🖷 01653 696801 ✉ julian.rudd@ryedale.gov.uk

Staff Training: Mrs Denise Hewitt , Human Resources Manager, Ryedale House, Malton YO17 7HH ☎ 01653 600666 ✉ denise.hewitt@ryedale.gov.uk

Street Scene: Mrs Beckie Bennett , Head of Environment, Streetscene & Facilities, Ryedale House, Malton YO17 7HH ☎ 01653 600666 Extn 483 ✉ beckie.bennett@ryedale.gov.uk

Sustainable Communities: Mr Julian Rudd, Head of Economy & Infrastructure, Ryedale House, Malton YO17 7HH ☎ 01653 600666 Ext 218 🖷 01653 696801 ✉ julian.rudd@ryedale.gov.uk

Sustainable Development: Mr John Brown, Environmental & Recycling Officer, Central Depot, Showfield Lane Industrial Estate, Malton Y017 0BY ☎ 01653 600666 🖷 01653 690737 ✉ john.brown@ryedale.gov.uk

Tourism: Mrs Jos Holmes, Economy Manager, Ryedale House, Malton YO17 7HH ☎ 01653 600666 Ext 240 🖷 01653 696801 ✉ jos.holmes@ryedale.gov.uk

Town Centre: Mr Julian Rudd, Head of Economy & Infrastructure, Ryedale House, Malton YO17 7HH ☎ 01653 600666 Ext 218 🖷 01653 696801 ✉ julian.rudd@ryedale.gov.uk

Transport: Mrs Beckie Bennett , Head of Environment, Streetscene & Facilities, Ryedale House, Malton YO17 7HH ☎ 01653 600666 Extn 483 ✉ beckie.bennett@ryedale.gov.uk

Waste Collection and Disposal: Mrs Beckie Bennett , Head of Environment, Streetscene & Facilities, Ryedale House, Malton YO17 7HH ☎ 01653 600666 Extn 483 ✉ beckie.bennett@ryedale.gov.uk

Waste Collection and Disposal: Mrs Beckie Bennett , Head of Environment, Streetscene & Facilities, Ryedale House, Malton YO17 7HH ☎ 01653 600666 Extn 483 ✉ beckie.bennett@ryedale.gov.uk

Waste Management: Mrs Beckie Bennett , Head of Environment, Streetscene & Facilities, Ryedale House, Malton YO17 7HH ☎ 01653 600666 Extn 483 ✉ beckie.bennett@ryedale.gov.uk

COUNCILLORS

***Chair* Arnold**, V (CON - Sinnington)

***Vice-Chair* Gardiner**, B (CON - Kirkbymoorside)

***Leader of the Council* Cowling**, Linda (CON - Pickering West)
cllr.linda.cowling@ryedale.gov.uk

***Group Leader* Burr**, Lindsay (IND - Malton)
cllr.lindsay.burr@ryedale.gov.uk

***Group Leader* Clark**, John (LIB - Cropton)
cllr.john.clark@ryedale.gov.uk

***Group Leader* Shields**, Elizabeth (LD - Norton East)
cllr.elizabeth.shields@ryedale.gov.uk

***Group Leader* Wainwright**, Robert (IND - Hovingham)
cllr.robert.wainwright@ryedale.gov.uk

Acomb, Geoffrey (CON - Thornton Dale)
cllr.geoffrey.acomb@ryedale.gov.uk

Andrews, Paul (IND - Malton)

Andrews, Joy (LD - Pickering East)

Arnold, Steve (CON - Helmsley)
cllr.stephen.arnold@ryedale.gov.uk

Bailey, James (CON - Ampleforth)
cllr.james.bailey@ryedale.gov.uk

Cleary, M (CON - Derwent)

Cussons, David (CON - Kirkbymoorside)
cllr.david.cussons@ryedale.gov.uk

Duncan, K C (CON - Norton East)

Evans, P (CON - Derwent)

Farnell, F A (CON - Amotherby)

Frank, Janet (CON - Dales)
cllr.janet.frank@ryedale.gov.uk

Goodrick, C (CON - Ryedale South West)
cllr.caroline.goodrick@ryedale.gov.uk

Hope, Eric (CON - Sheriff Hutton)
cllr.eric.hope@ryedale.gov.uk

Ives, Luke (CON - Norton West)
cllr.luke.ives@ryedale.gov.uk

Jainu-Dean, T (CON - Wolds)

Jowitt, E (IND - Jowitt)

Keal, Dinah (LD - Norton West)
cllr.dinah.keal@ryedale.gov.uk

Maud, Brian (IND - Rillington)
cllr.brian.maud@ryedale.gov.uk

Oxley, W (CON - Pickering East)

Raper, John (CON - Sherburn)
cllr.john.raper@ryedale.gov.uk

Sanderson, Janet (CON - Thornton Dale)
cllr.janet.sanderson@ryedale.gov.uk

Thornton, T (LIB - Pickering West)

Wildress, John (CON - Helmsley)
cllr.john.wildress@ryedale.gov.uk

POLITICAL COMPOSITION
CON: 20, IND: 5, LD: 3, LIB: 2

COMMITTEE CHAIRS

Licensing: Mr Eric Hope

Planning: Mr John Wildress

Salford City M

Salford City Council, Salford Civic Centre, Chorley Road, Swinton, Salford M27 5FJ
☎ 0161 794 4711 🖷 0161 793 3043 💻 www.salford.gov.uk

FACTS AND FIGURES
Parliamentary Constituencies: Blackley and Broughton, Salford and Eccles, Worsley and Eccles South
EU Constituencies: North West
Election Frequency: Elections are by thirds

PRINCIPAL OFFICERS

Chief Executive: Mr Jim Taylor , City Director, Salford Civic Centre, Chorley Road, Swinton, Salford M27 5FJ ☎ 0161 793 3400 ✉ jim.taylor@salford.gov.uk

Senior Management: Mr Ben Dolan , Strategic Director of Environment & Community Safety, Salford Civic Centre, Chorley Road, Swinton, Salford M27 5FJ ☎ 0161 925 1112 🖷 0161 920 8481 ✉ ben.dolan@salford.gov.uk

Senior Management: Ms Sue Lightup , Strategic Director of Community, Health & Social Care, Salford Civic Centre, Chorley Road, Swinton, Salford M27 5FJ ☎ 0161 793 2200 ✉ sue.lightup@salford.gov.uk

Senior Management: Ms Charlotte Ramsden , Strategic Director - Children's Services, Unity House, Chorley Road, Swinton M27 5AW ☎ 0161 778 0130 ✉ charlotte.ramsden@salford.gov.uk

Architect, Building / Property Services: Mr Les Woolhouse , Building Surveying Manager, Urban Vision Partnership, Emerson House, Albert Street, Eccles M30 0TE ☎ 0161 779 4961 ✉ les.woolhouse@urbanvision.org.uk

Building Control: Mr Dave Jolley, Director of Planning & Building Control, Urban Vision Partnership Ltd, Emerson House, Albert Street, Eccles M30 0TE ☎ 0161 604 7784 🖷 0161 779 6002 ✉ dave.jolley@urbanvision.org.uk

Catering Services: Mr Dominic Clarke , Head of Service - Citywide & Community Services, Turnpike House, 631 Eccles New Road, Salford M50 1SW ☎ 0161 925 1109 ✉ dominic.clarke@salford.gov.uk

Children / Youth Services: Ms Eileen Buchan , Head of Integrated Youth Support Services, Salford Opportunity Centre, 2 Paddington Close, Churchill Way, Salford M6 5PL ☎ 0161 603 6834 🖷 0161 603 6840 ✉ eileen.buchan@salford.gov.uk

Civil Registration: Ms Rebecca Roberts , Superintendent Registrar, Salford Civic Centre, Chorley Road, Swinton M27 5FJ ☎ 0161 603 6880 🖷 0161 603 6892 ✉ rebecca.roberts@salford.gov.uk

PR / Communications: Ms Debbie Brown , Director - Service Reform & Development, Salford Civic Centre, Chorley Road, Swinton, Salford M27 5FJ ☎ 0161 607 8600 ✉ debbie.brown@salford.gov.uk

PR / Communications: Ms Sue Hill , Head of Communications, Salford Civic Centre, Chorley Road, Swinton, Salford M27 5FJ ☎ 0161 793 2600 ✉ sue.hill@salford.gov.uk

Community Planning: Mr Mark Reeves , Deputy Director - Environment & Community Safety, Salford Civic Centre, Chorley Road, Swinton, Salford M27 5FJ ☎ 0161 925 1113 🖷 0161 920 8481 ✉ mark.reeves@salford.gov.uk

Community Safety: Mr Mark Reeves , Deputy Director - Environment & Community Safety, Salford Civic Centre, Chorley Road, Swinton, Salford M27 5FJ ☎ 0161 925 1113 🖷 0161 920 8481 ✉ mark.reeves@salford.gov.uk

Computer Management: Mr David Hunter , Assistant Director of Corporate ICT, Salford Civic Centre, Chorley Road, Swinton M27 5FJ ☎ 0161 793 3911 ✉ david.hunter@salford.gov.uk

Consumer Protection and Trading Standards: Mr John Wooderson , Head of Service for Regulatory Services, Salford Civic Centre, Chorley Road, Swinton, Salford M27 5FJ ☎ 0161 793 2623 ✉ john.wooderson@salford.gov.uk

Contracts: Mr Andrew White , Procurement Manager, Unity House, Chorley Road, Swinton M27 5AW ☎ 0161 607 6295 ✉ andrew.white@salford.gov.uk

Customer Service: Mr John Tanner, Assistant Director of Customer Services, Unity House, Chorley Road, Swinton M27 5DA ☎ 0161 793 3364 ✉ john.tanner@salford.gov.uk

SALFORD CITY

Economic Development: Mr Bernie Vaudrey , Head of Business & Funding, Salford Civic Centre, Chorley Road, Swinton, Salford M27 5FJ ☎ 0161 793 2283 ✉ bernie.vaudrey@salford.gov.uk

Education: Ms Cathy Starbuck , Assistant Director - Children's Services, Unity House, Chorley Road, Swinton M27 5AW ☎ 0161 778 0183 ✉ cathy.starbuck@salford.gov.uk

E-Government: Mr David Hunter, Assistant Director of Corporate ICT, Salford Civic Centre, Chorley Road, Swinton M27 5FJ ☎ 0161 793 3911 ✉ david.hunter@salford.gov.uk

Electoral Registration: Mr Neil Watts , Principal Democratic Services Advisor of Elections, Salford Civic Centre, Chorley Road, Swinton M27 5FJ ☎ 0161 793 3446 ✉ neil.watts@salford.gov.uk

Emergency Planning: Mr David Hunter, Assistant Director of Corporate ICT, Salford Civic Centre, Chorley Road, Swinton M27 5FJ ☎ 0161 793 3911 ✉ david.hunter@salford.gov.uk

Energy Management: Mr Majid Maqbool , Energy Manager, 4th Floor, Emmerson House, Eccles M30 0TE ☎ 0161 607 6987 ✉ majid.maqbool@salford.gov.uk

Environmental Health: Mr John Wooderson , Head of Service for Regulatory Services, Salford Civic Centre, Chorley Road, Swinton, Salford M27 5FJ ☎ 0161 793 2623 ✉ john.wooderson@salford.gov.uk

Estates, Property & Valuation: Mr Richard Wynne, Director of Property & Development, Emerson House, Albert Street, Eccles M30 0TE ☎ 0161 779 6127 ✉ richard.wynne@urbanvision.org.uk

European Liaison: Mr Ian Thompson , Funding & Development Officer, Salford Civic Centre, Chorley Road, Swinton, Salford M27 5FJ ☎ 0161 793 2415 ✉ ian.thompson@salford.gov.uk

Events Manager: Mrs Lindsey Hebden, Tourism Marketing Manager, Salford Civic Centre, Chorley Road, Swinton M27 5FJ ☎ 0161 793 2375 ✉ lindsey.hebden@salford.gov.uk

Facilities: Mr David Horsler , Head of Facilities Management, Salford Civic Centre, Chorley Road, Swinton, Salford M27 5FJ ☎ 0161 607 6994 ✉ david.horsler@salford.gov.uk

Finance: Mr Neil Thornton , Director of Finance & Corporate Business, Unity House, Chorley Road, Swinton M27 5AW ☎ 0161 686 6200 ✉ neil.thornton@salford.gov.uk

Fleet Management: Mr Terry Dixie, Head of Services for Transportation, Turnpike House, 631 Eccles New Road, Salford M50 1SW ☎ 0161 925 1046 ✉ terry.dixie@salford.gov.uk

Grounds Maintenance: Mr David Seager , Assistant Director of Operational & Commercial Services, Salford Civic Centre, Chorley Road, Swinton, Salford M27 5FJ ☎ 0161 925 1115 🖷 0161 920 8481 ✉ david.seager@salford.gov.uk

Health and Safety: Mr John Wooderson , Head of Service for Regulatory Services, Salford Civic Centre, Chorley Road, Swinton, Salford M27 5FJ ☎ 0161 793 2623 ✉ john.wooderson@salford.gov.uk

Highways: Mr Shoaib Mohammaed , Director of Engineering, Emerson House, Albert Street, Eccles M30 0TE ☎ 0161 779 4800 ✉ shoaib.mohammaed@capita.co.uk

Home Energy Conservation: Mr Leslie Laws, Principal Officer for Affordable Warmth, Salford Civic Centre, Chorley Road, Swinton, Salford M27 5BY ☎ 0161 793 2264 🖷 0161 793 3377 ✉ leslie.laws@salford.gov.uk

Housing: Mrs Sarah Clayton , Head of Service for Strategy & Enabling, Salford Civic Centre, Chorley Road, Swinton M27 5BY ☎ 0161 793 2366 ✉ sarah,clayton@salford.gov.uk

Housing Maintenance: Mr Paul Lister , Maintenance Manager, Diamond House, 2 Peel Cross Road, Salford M5 4BT ☎ 0161 779 8899 🖷 0161 779 8977 ✉ paul.lister@salixhomes.org

Legal: Mr Ben Dolan , Strategic Director of Environment & Community Safety, Salford Civic Centre, Chorley Road, Swinton, Salford M27 5FJ ☎ 0161 925 1112 🖷 0161 920 8481 ✉ ben.dolan@salford.gov.uk

Leisure and Cultural Services: Mr David Seager , Assistant Director of Operational & Commercial Services, Salford Civic Centre, Chorley Road, Swinton, Salford M27 5FJ ☎ 0161 925 1115 🖷 0161 920 8481 ✉ david.seager@salford.gov.uk

Licensing: Mr John Wooderson , Head of Service for Regulatory Services, Salford Civic Centre, Chorley Road, Swinton, Salford M27 5FJ ☎ 0161 793 2623 ✉ john.wooderson@salford.gov.uk

Lighting: Mr Ian Darlington , Lighting Manager, Emerson House, Albert Street, Eccles M30 0TE ☎ 07825 937395 ✉ ian.darlington@urbanvision.org.uk

Lottery Funding, Charity and Voluntary: Ms Sue Ford , Funding & Development Manager, Salford Civic Centre, Chorley Road, Swinton M27 5BY ☎ 0161 793 3443 🖷 0161 793 2477 ✉ sue.ford@salford.gov.uk

Member Services: Mrs Karen Lucas , Principal Democratic Services Advisor, Salford Civic Centre, Chorley Road, Swinton M27 5FJ ☎ 0161 793 3318 ✉ karen.lucas@aslford.gov.uk

Parking: Mr William Earnshaw , Group Engineer - Parking Services, Emerson House, Eccles M30 0TE ☎ 0161 779 4924 ✉ william.earnshaw@urbanvision.org.uk

Personnel / HR: Ms Sam Betts , Assistant Director of Human Resources, Salford Civic Centre, Chorley Road, Swinton, Salford M27 5FJ ☎ 0161 607 8600 ✉ samantha.betts@salford.gov.uk

Planning: Mr Christopher Findley, Assistant Director of Planning, Salford Civic Centre, Chorley Road, Swinton, Salford M27 5BY ☎ 0161 793 3654 ✉ chris.findley@salford.gov.uk

Procurement: Mr Andrew White , Procurement Manager, Unity House, Chorley Road, Swinton M27 5AW ☎ 0161 607 6295 ✉ andrew.white@salford.gov.uk

Public Libraries: Ms Sarah Spence, Libraries & Information Services Manager, Salford Civic Centre, Chorley Road, Swinton M27 5DA ☎ 0161 778 0840 ✉ sarah.spence@scll.co.uk

Recycling & Waste Minimisation: Mr David Seager , Assistant Director of Operational & Commercial Services, Salford Civic Centre, Chorley Road, Swinton, Salford M27 5FJ ☎ 0161 925 1115 🖷 0161 920 8481 ✉ david.seager@salford.gov.uk

Regeneration: Ms Karen Hirst , Development Director, Salford Civic Centre, Chorley Road, Swinton M27 5FJ ☎ 0161 686 7411 ✉ karen.hirst@salford.gov.uk

Road Safety: Mr Brad Green , Engineering Manager, Emerson House, Albert Street, Eccles M30 0TE ☎ 01925 418333 ✉ brad.green@capita.co.uk

Social Services: Ms Sharon Hubber , Interim Assistant Director - Specialist Services, Unity House, Chorley Road, Swinton M27 5AW ☎ 0161 603 4311 ✉ sharon.hubber@salford.gov.uk

Social Services (Adult): Mr Dave Clemmett , Assistant Director of Operations, Salford Civic Centre, Chorley Road, Swinton M27 5BY ☎ 0161 793 2051 ✉ dave.clemmett@salford.gov.uk

Social Services (Adult): Mr Keith Darragh , Assistant Director of Resources, Salford Civic Centre, Chorley Road, Swinton M27 5BY ☎ 0161 793 3225 ✉ keith.darragh@salford.gov.uk

Social Services (Children): Ms Amanda Amesbury , Head of Service, Unity House, Chorley Road, Swinton M27 5AW ☎ 0161 603 4546 ✉ amanda.amesbury@salford.gov.uk

Public Health: Ms Debbie Brown , Director - Service Reform & Development, Unity House, Chorley Road, Swinton M27 5AW ☎ 0161 607 8600 ✉ debbie.brown@salford.gov.uk

Public Health: Mr David Herne , Director of Public Health, Unity House, Chorley Road, Swinton M27 5AW ☎ 0161 793 3518 ✉ david.herne@salford.gov.uk

Public Health: Ms Jacquie Russell , Assistant Director - Strategy & Change, Unity House, Chorley Road, Swinton M27 5AW ☎ 0161 793 3577 ✉ jacquie.russell@salford.gov.uk

Staff Training: Ms Sam Betts , Assistant Director of Human Resources, Salford Civic Centre, Chorley Road, Swinton, Salford M27 5FJ ☎ 0161 607 8600 ✉ samantha.betts@salford.gov.uk

Street Scene: Mrs Sinead Hayes , Street Works Manager, Emerson House, Albert House, Eccles M30 0TE ☎ 0161 779 6151 ✉ sinead.hayes@urbanvision.org.uk

Sustainable Communities: Mr Ben Dolan , Strategic Director of Environment & Community Safety, Salford Civic Centre, Chorley Road, Swinton, Salford M27 5FJ ☎ 0161 920 8400 🖷 0161 920 8481 ✉ ben.dolan@salford.gov.uk

Sustainable Development: Mr Christopher Findley, Assistant Director of Planning, Salford Civic Centre, Chorley Road, Swinton, Salford M27 5BY ☎ 0161 793 3654 ✉ chris.findley@salford.gov.uk

Tourism: Mrs Lindsey Hebden, Tourism Marketing Manager, Salford Civic Centre, Chorley Road, Swinton M27 5FJ ☎ 0161 793 2375 ✉ lindsey.hebden@salford.gov.uk

Town Centre: Ms Elaine Davis , Senior Development Manager, Salford Civic Centre, Chorley Road, Swinton, Salford M27 5FJ ☎ 0161 686 7420 ✉ elaine.davis@salford.gov.uk

Traffic Management: Mr Brad Green , Engineering Manager, Emerson House, Albert Street, Eccles M30 0TE ☎ 01925 418333 ✉ brad.green@capita.co.uk

Transport: Mr Terry Dixie, Head of Services for Transportation, Turnpike House, 631 Eccles New Road, Salford M50 1SW ☎ 0161 925 1046 ✉ terry.dixie@salford.gov.uk

Transport Planner: Mr Lee Evans , Transportation Engineer, Salford Civic Centre, Chorley Road, Swinton, Salford M27 5FJ ☎ 0161 793 3081 ✉ lee.evans@salford.gov.uk

Waste Collection and Disposal: Mr David Seager , Assistant Director of Operational & Commercial Services, Salford Civic Centre, Chorley Road, Swinton, Salford M27 5FJ ☎ 0161 925 1115 🖷 0161 920 8481 ✉ david.seager@salford.gov.uk

Waste Management: Mr David Seager , Assistant Director of Operational & Commercial Services, Salford Civic Centre, Chorley Road, Swinton, Salford M27 5FJ ☎ 0161 925 1115 🖷 0161 920 8481 ✉ david.seager@salford.gov.uk

COUNCILLORS

***Ceremonial Mayor* Dobbs**, Peter (LAB - Ordsall)
Councillor.Dobbs@salford.gov.uk

***Ceremonial Deputy Mayor* Garrido**, Karen (CON - Worsley)
councillor.garrido@salford.gov.uk

***Mayor* Stewart**, Ian
citymayor@salford.gov.uk

***Deputy Mayor* Lancaster**, David (LAB - Winton)
Councillor.Lancaster@salford.gov.uk

***Group Leader* Turner**, Les (CON - Walkden South)
councillor.turner@salford.gov.uk

Antrobus, Derek (LAB - Swinton North)
Councillor.Antrobus@salford.gov.uk

Balkind, Howard (LAB - Swinton South)
councillor.balkind@salford.gov.uk

Barnes, Michele (LAB - Barton)
councillor.barnes@salford.gov.uk

Bellamy, Sammie (LAB - Walkden North)
Councillor.Bellamy@salford.gov.uk

Blower, Neil (LAB - Swinton South)
councillor.blower@salford.gov.uk

Boshell, Paula (LAB - Winton)
councillor.boshell@salford.gov.uk

Brocklehurst, Adrian (LAB - Walkden North)
councillor.brocklehurst@salford.gov.uk

Burch, Tanya (LAB - Ordsall)
councillor.burch@salford.gov.uk

SALFORD CITY

Burgoyne, Eric (LAB - Little Hulton)
Councillor.EBurgoyne@salford.gov.uk

Cheetham, Andy (CON - Boothstown and Ellenbrook)
councillor.cheetham@salford.gov.uk

Clarkson, Christopher (CON - Worsley)
councillor.clarkson@salford.gov.uk

Coen, Stephen (LAB - Irwell Riverside)
councillor.coen@salford.gov.uk

Collinson, Jillian (CON - Boothstown and Ellenbrook)
councillor.collinson@salford.gov.uk

Compton, Graham (CON - Worsley)
councillor.compton@salford.gov.uk

Connor, Peter (LAB - Kersal)
councillor.connor@salford.gov.uk

Critchley, Richard (LAB - Walkden South)
councillor.critchley@salford.gov.uk

Davies, Harry (LAB - Kersal)
Councillor.Davies@salford.gov.uk

Dawson, Jim (LAB - Swinton North)
Councillor.Dawson@salford.gov.uk

Dennett, Paul (LAB - Langworthy)
councillor.dennett@salford.gov.uk

Dirir, Sareda (LAB - Claremont)
councillor.dirir@salford.gov.uk

Ferguson, John (LAB - Pendlebury)
councillor.ferguson@salford.gov.uk

Garrido, Robin (CON - Boothstown and Ellenbrook)
councillor.rgarrido@salford.gov.uk

Hamilton, Jane (LAB - Irwell Riverside)
councillor.hamilton@salford.gov.uk

Hesling, Stephen (LAB - Weaste and Seedley)
councillor.hesling@salford.gov.uk

Hinds, Bill (LAB - Swinton North)
Councillor.Hinds@salford.gov.uk

Hudson, Christine (LAB - Cadishead)
councillor.hudson@salford.gov.uk

Humphreys, Ann-Marie (LAB - Kersal)
councillor.humphreys@salford.gov.uk

Hunt, Jimmy (LAB - Cadishead)
councillor.hunt@salford.gov.uk

Jolley, David (LAB - Barton)
councillor.jolley@salford.gov.uk

Jones, Roger (LAB - Irlam)
councillor.jones@salford.gov.uk

Kelly, Tracy (LAB - Irlam)
councillor.kelly@salford.gov.uk

King, Jim (LAB - Broughton)
Councillor.King@salford.gov.uk

Lea, Bernard (LAB - Pendlebury)
Councillor.BLea@salford.gov.uk

Lewis, Kate (LAB - Little Hutton)
councillor.lewis@salford.gov.uk

Lindley, Iain (CON - Walkden South)
councillor.lindley@salford.gov.uk

Mashiter, Ray (LAB - Ordsall)
councillor.mashiter@salford.gov.uk

McIntyre, Charles (LAB - Broughton)
Councillor.Mcintyre@salford.gov.uk

Merrett, Gina (LAB - Swinton South)
councillor.merrett@salford.gov.uk

Merry, John (LAB - Broughton)
Councillor.Merry@salford.gov.uk

Morris, Margaret (LAB - Winton)
Councillor.Morris@salford.gov.uk

Mullen, John (LAB - Barton)
councillor.mullen@salford.gov.uk

Murphy, Joe (LAB - Claremont)
councillor.jmurphy@salford.gov.uk

Ord, Stephen (LAB - Irwell Riverside)
councillor.ord@salford.gov.uk

Pugh, Sue (LAB - Claremont)
councillor.pugh@salford.gov.uk

Reynolds, Gina (LAB - Langworthy)
councillor.reynolds@salford.gov.uk

Ryan, Brendan (LAB - Walkden North)
councillor.bryan@salford.gov.uk

Ryan, Patricia (LAB - Little Hulton)
councillor.ryan@salford.gov.uk

Stone, Lisa (LAB - Eccles)
councillor.stone@salford.gov.uk

Taylor, Peter (LAB - Irlam)
Councillor.Taylor@salford.gov.uk

Walsh, John (LAB - Cadishead)
councillor.walsh@salford.gov.uk

Warmisham, John (LAB - Langworthy)
councillor.warmisham@salford.gov.uk

Warner, Barry (LAB - Pendlebury)
Councillor.Warner@salford.gov.uk

Wheeler, Michael (LAB - Eccles)
councillor.wheeler@salford.gov.uk

Wheeler, Peter (LAB - Eccles)
councillor.pwheeler@salford.gov.uk

Wilson, Paul (LAB - Weaste and Seedley)
councillor.p.wilson@salford.gov.uk

Wilson, Ronnie (LAB - Weaste and Seedley)
councillor.rwilson@salford.gov.uk

POLITICAL COMPOSITION
LAB: 53, CON: 8

COMMITTEE CHAIRS
Children: Ms Tracy Kelly

Health & Adults: Ms Margaret Morris

Planning: Mr Ray Mashiter

Sandwell M

Sandwell Metropolitan Borough Council, Sandwell Council House, Oldbury B69 3DE
☎ 0121 569 2200 🖷 0121 569 3100 ✉ smbc@sandwell.gov.uk
🖳 www.sandwell.gov.uk

FACTS AND FIGURES

Parliamentary Constituencies: Halesowen and Rowley Regis, Warley, West Bromwich East, West Bromwich West
EU Constituencies: West Midlands
Election Frequency: Elections are by thirds

PRINCIPAL OFFICERS

Chief Executive: Mr Jan Britton, Chief Executive, Sandwell Council House, Oldbury B69 3DE ☎ 0121 569 3500 ✉ jan_britton@sandwell.gov.uk

Assistant Chief Executive: Ms Melanie Dudley , Assistant Chief Executive, Sandwell Council House, Oldbury B69 3DE ☎ 0121 569 3548 ✉ melanie_dudley@sandwell.gov.uk

Senior Management: Mr Brian Aldridge , Service Director - Learning Directorate, Sandwell Council House, Oldbury B69 3DE ☎ 0121 569 8325 ✉ brian_aldridge@sandwell.gov.uk

Senior Management: Ms Jyoti Atri , Director - Public Health, Sandwell Council House, Oldbury B69 3DE ☎ 0845 352 7645 ✉ jyoti_atri@sandwell.gov.uk

Senior Management: Ms Kerry Bollister , Director - Homes & Communities, Sandwell Council House, Oldbury B69 3DE ☎ 0121 569 5062 ✉ kerry_bollister@sandwell.gov.uk

Senior Management: Mr Nick Bubalo , Area Director - Regeneration & Economy / Area Director - West Bromwich & Smethwick, Sandwell Council House, Oldbury B69 3DE ☎ 0121 569 4253 ✉ nick_bubalo@sandwell.gov.uk

Senior Management: Ms Melanie Dudley , Assistant Chief Executive, Sandwell Council House, Oldbury B69 3DE ☎ 0121 569 3548 ✉ melanie_dudley@sandwell.gov.uk

Senior Management: Mr Steve Handley, Director - Street Scene, Sandwell Council House, Oldbury B69 3DE ☎ 0121 569 3718 ✉ steve_handley@sandwell.gov.uk

Senior Management: Mr Adrian Scarrott , Director - Neighbourhoods, Sandwell Council House, Oldbury B69 3DE ☎ 0121 569 5034 ✉ adrian_scarrott@sandwell.gov.uk

Senior Management: Mrs Neeraj Sharma, Director - Governance & Risk, Sandwell Council House, Oldbury B69 3DE ☎ 0121 569 3172 ✉ neeraj_sharma@sandwell.gov.uk

Senior Management: Mr David Stevens , Director - Adult Social Care, Sandwell Council House, Oldbury B69 3DE ☎ 0121 569 5887 ✉ david_stevens@sandwell.gov.uk

Senior Management: Mr Simon White , Director - Children's Services, Sandwell Council House, Oldbury B69 3DE ☎ 0121 569 8204 ✉ simon_white@sandwell.gov.uk

Access Officer / Social Services (Disability): Mr David Dwyer, Assistant Access Officer, Sandwell Council House, Oldbury B69 3DE ☎ 0121 569 3413 ✉ david_dwyer@sandwell.gov.uk

Building Control: Mr John Baker , Development & Regulatory Services Manager, Sandwell Council House, Oldbury B69 3DE ☎ 0121 569 4037 ✉ john_baker@sandwell.gov.uk

Catering Services: Ms Tracey Pace , Sandwell Inspired Partnership Service, Sandwell Council House, Oldbury B69 3DE ☎ 0121 296 3000 ✉ tracey_pace@sandwell.gov.uk

Children / Youth Services: Mr Charlie Spencer , Divisional Manager -Targeted Youth Support, Sandwell Council House, Oldbury B69 3DE ☎ 0845 352 7701 ✉ charlie_spencer@sandwell.gov.uk

Civil Registration: Mr Paul Sheldon, Registration Services Manager, Sandwell Register Office, Highfields, High Street, West Bromwich B70 8RJ ☎ 0121 569 2471 🖷 0121 569 2473 ✉ paul_sheldon@sandwell.gov.uk

PR / Communications: Mr Steve Harrison , Plain English Champion, Sandwell Council House, Oldbury B69 3DE ☎ 0121 569 3033 ✉ steve_harrison@sandwell.gov.uk

Community Planning: Ms Philippa Smith , Spacial Policy & Development Manager, Sandwell Council House, Oldbury B69 3DE ☎ 0121 569 4195 ✉ philippa_smith@sandwell.gov.uk

Community Safety: Mr Mark Peniket , General Manager - Neighbourhood Services, Sandwell Council House, Oldbury B69 3DE ☎ 0121 569 6040 ✉ mark_peniket@sandwell.gov.uk

Computer Management: Mr Andy Nicholls , ICT Strategy & Client Manager, Sandwell Council House, Oldbury B69 3DE ☎ 0121 569 3371 ✉ andy_nicholls@sandwell.gov.uk

Consumer Protection and Trading Standards: Ms Kerry Bollister , Director - Homes & Communities, Sandwell Council House, Oldbury B69 3DE ☎ 0121 569 5062 ✉ kerry_bollister@sandwell.gov.uk

Corporate Services: Ms Melanie Dudley , Assistant Chief Executive, Sandwell Council House, Oldbury B69 3DE ☎ 0121 569 3548 ✉ melanie_dudley@sandwell.gov.uk

Education: Mr Brian Aldridge , Service Director - Learning Directorate, Sandwell Council House, Oldbury B69 3DE ☎ 0121 569 8325 ✉ brian_aldridge@sandwell.gov.uk

Electoral Registration: Mr Philip Hardy , Electoral Services Manager, PO Box 2374, Sandwell Council House, Oldbury B69 3DE ☎ 0121 569 3244 ✉ philip_hardy@sandwell.gov.uk

Emergency Planning: Mr Alan Boyd , Resilience Manager, Sandwell Council House, Oldbury B69 3DE ☎ 0121 569 3060; 0121 569 3983 ✉ alan_boyd@sandwell.gov.uk

Environmental / Technical Services: Mr Mark Rowley , Environment Services Manager, Shidas Lane, Oldbury B69 2BP ☎ 0121 569 4117 ✉ mark_rowley@sandwell.gov.uk

Environmental Health: Mr Mark Rowley , Environment Services Manager, Shidas Lane, Oldbury B69 2BP ☎ 0121 569 4117 mark_rowley@sandwell.gov.uk

Estates, Property & Valuation: Mr Mark Peniket , General Manager - Neighbourhood Services, Sandwell Council House, Oldbury B69 3DE ☎ 0121 569 6040 mark_peniket@sandwell.gov.uk

Events Manager: Mr Tony Potter, Events & Projects Manager, Sandwell Valley Park Farm, Slaters Lane, West Bromwich B71 4BG ☎ 0121 553 0220 🖷 0121 569 4704 tony_potter@sandwell.gov.uk

Facilities: Ms Christine Bailey , Facilities Services Manager, Sandwell Council House, Oldbury B69 3DE ☎ 0121 569 3941 🖷 0121 569 3938 christine_bailey@sandwell.gov.uk

Fleet Management: Ms Carole Bishop, Fleet Manager, Transport Depot, Waterfall Lane, Cradley Heath B64 6RL ☎ 0121 569 6846 🖷 0121 559 5819 carole_bishop@sandwell.gov.uk

Health and Safety: Mr Chris Wiliiams , Health, Safety & Welfare Manager, PO Box 2374, Sandwell Council House, Oldbury B69 3DE ☎ 0121 569 8328 chris_williams@sandwell.gov.uk

Highways: Mr Irfan Choudry , Highways Service Manager, Sandwell Council House, Oldbury B69 3DE ☎ 0121 569 1857 irfan_choudry@sandwell.gov.uk

Housing: Ms Kate Lloyd , Services Manager - Housing Strategy & Partnerships, Sandwell Council House, Oldbury B69 3DE ☎ 0121 569 5016 Kate_lloyd@sandwell.gov.uk

Housing Maintenance: Mr Steve Greenhouse , Housing Repairs Service Manager, Operations & Development Centre, Roway Lane, Oldbury B69 3ES ☎ 0121 569 6441 steve_greenhouse@sandwell.gov.uk

Legal: Mrs Neeraj Sharma, Director - Governance & Risk, Sandwell Council House, PO Box 2374, Oldbury B69 3DE ☎ 0121 569 3172 neeraj_sharma@sandwell.gov.uk

Leisure and Cultural Services: Mr Paul Slater , Chief Executive - Sandwell Leisure Trust, Castlemill, Burnt Tree, Tipton DY4 7UF ☎ 0121 521 4422 paul_slater@sandwell.gov.uk

Licensing: Mr Steve Handley, Director - Street Scene, Sandwell Council House, Oldbury B69 3DE ☎ 0121 569 3718 steve_handley@sandwell.gov.uk

Lifelong Learning: Mr Brian Aldridge , Service Director - Learning Directorate, Sandwell Council House, Oldbury B69 3DE ☎ 0121 569 8325 brian_aldridge@sandwell.gov.uk

Lottery Funding, Charity and Voluntary: Ms Heather Chinner , Voluntary Sector Liason & Development Manager, Sandwell Council House, Oldbury B69 3DE ☎ 0121 569 3020 heather_chinner@sandwell.gov.uk

Member Services: Mr Rob Hevican , Member Services Manager, Sandwell Council House, Oldbury B69 3DE ☎ 0121 569 3043 robert_hevican@sandwell.gov.uk

Parking: Mr Steve Handley, Director - Street Scene, Sandwell Council House, Oldbury B69 3DE ☎ 0121 569 3718 steve_handley@sandwell.gov.uk

Personnel / HR: Ms Cathi Dodd , Service Manager - Improvement & Efficiency / Strategic HR, Sandwell Council House, Oldbury B69 3DE ☎ 0121 569 3289 cathi_dodd@sandwell.gov.uk

Planning: Mr Nick Bubalo , Area Director - Regeneration & Economy / Area Director - West Bromwich & Smethwick, Sandwell Council House, Oldbury B69 3DE ☎ 0121 569 4253 nick_bubalo@sandwell.gov.uk

Procurement: Mr Neil Whitehouse , Senior Category Manager, Sandwell Council House, Oldbury B69 3DE ☎ 0121 569 3625 neil_whitehouse@sandwell.gov.uk

Public Libraries: Mr Jim Wells , Service Lead - Leisure, Culture & Lifelong Learning, Sandwell Council House, Oldbury B69 3DE ☎ 0121 569 8242 jim_wells@sandwell.gov.uk

Recycling & Waste Minimisation: Mr Mark Rowley , Environment Services Manager, Shidas Lane, Oldbury B69 2BP ☎ 0121 569 4117 mark_rowley@sandwell.gov.uk

Regeneration: Mr Nick Bubalo , Area Director - Regeneration & Economy / Area Director - West Bromwich & Smethwick, Sandwell Council House, Oldbury B69 3DE ☎ 0121 569 4253 nick_bubalo@sandwell.gov.uk

Road Safety: Mr Irfan Choudry , Highways Service Manager, Sandwell Council House, Oldbury B69 3DE ☎ 0121 569 1857 irfan_choudry@sandwell.gov.uk

Social Services: Mr Simon White , Director - Children's Services, Sandwell Council House, Oldbury B69 3DE ☎ 0121 569 8204 simon_white@sandwell.gov.uk

Social Services (Adult): Mr David Stevens , Director - Adult Social Care, Sandwell Council House, Oldbury B69 3DE ☎ 0121 569 5887 david_stevens@sandwell.gov.uk

Public Health: Ms Jyoti Atri , Director - Public Health, Sandwell Council House, Oldbury B69 3DE ☎ 0845 352 7645 jyoti_atri@sandwell.gov.uk

Staff Training: Ms Melanie Dudley , Assistant Chief Executive, Sandwell Council House, Oldbury B69 3DE ☎ 0121 569 3548 melanie_dudley@sandwell.gov.uk

Street Scene: Mr Steve Handley, Director - Street Scene, Sandwell Council House, Oldbury B69 3DE ☎ 0121 569 3718 steve_handley@sandwell.gov.uk

Sustainable Communities: Mr Gary Bowman , Service Manager - Area Working, Sandwell Council House, Oldbury B69 3DE ☎ 0121 569 3447 gary_bowman@sandwell.gov.uk

Sustainable Development: Mr John Baker , Development & Regulatory Services Manager, Sandwell Council House, Oldbury B69 3DE ☎ 0121 569 4037 john_baker@sandwell.gov.uk

Tourism: Mr Jim Wells , Service Lead - Leisure, Culture & Lifelong Learning, Sandwell Council House, Oldbury B69 3DE
☎ 0121 569 8242 ✉ jim_wells@sandwell.gov.uk

Town Centre: Mr John Baker , Development & Regulatory Services Manager, Sandwell Council House, Oldbury B69 3DE
☎ 0121 569 4037 ✉ john_baker@sandwell.gov.uk

Traffic Management: Mr Irfan Choudry , Highways Service Manager, Sandwell Council House, Oldbury B69 3DE ☎ 0121 569 1857 ✉ irfan_choudry@sandwell.gov.uk

Waste Collection and Disposal: Mr Mark Rowley , Environment Services Manager, Shidas Lane, Oldbury B69 2BP ☎ 0121 569 4117 ✉ mark_rowley@sandwell.gov.uk

Waste Management: Mr Mark Rowley , Environment Services Manager, Shidas Lane, Oldbury B69 2BP ☎ 0121 569 4117 ✉ mark_rowley@sandwell.gov.uk

Children's Play Areas: Mr John Satchwell , Parks & Countryside Services Manager, Sandwell Council House, Oldbury B69 3DE
☎ 0121 569 6812 ✉ john_satchwell@sandwell.gov.uk

COUNCILLORS

Leader of the Council **Cooper**, Darren (LAB - Soho and Victoria)
darren_cooper@sandwell.gov.uk

Deputy Leader of the Council **Eling**, Steve (LAB - Abbey)
steve_eling@sandwell.gov.uk

Ahmed, Zahoor (LAB - St Pauls)
zahoor_ahmed@sandwell.gov.uk

Allcock, Keith (LAB - Newton)

Allen, Peter (LAB - Great Bridge)
peter_allen@sandwell.gov.uk

Ashman, Lorraine (LAB - Tividale)
lorraine_ashman@sandwell.gov.uk

Bawa, Babu (LAB - St Pauls)

Carmichael, Kerrie (LAB - Blackheath)
blackheathlabour@hotmail.co.uk

Cherrington, Bill (LAB - Princes End)
bill_cherrington@sandwell.gov.uk

Costigan, Elaine (LAB - Wednesbury North)
elainecostigan@hotmail.co.uk

Crompton, Maria (LAB - Tividale)
maria_crompton@sandwell.gov.uk

Crumpton, Trevor (LAB - Old Warley)
t.crumpton@talktalk.net

Crumpton, Susan (LAB - Old Warley)
sue_crumpton@cllr.sandwell.org.uk

Davies, Yvonne (LAB - Langley)
ydavies16@btinternet.com

Davies, Patricia (LAB - Hateley Heath)
patdavies2006@yahoo.co.uk

Davies, Sharon (LAB - Langley)
cllrsharon_davies@sandwell.gov.uk

Davies, Keith (LAB - Smethwick)
keithdavies2004@yahoo.co.uk

Dhallu, Bawa (LAB - West Bromwich Central)
bawa_singhdhallu@cllr.sandwell.org.uk

Downing, Susan (LAB - Oldbury)

Edis, Joy (LAB - Friar Park)

Edwards, John (LAB - Greets Green and Lyng)
john.e@pep.org.uk

Evans, Susan (LAB - Rowley)
susan_eaves@sandwell.gov.uk

Frazer, Kim (LAB - West Bromwich Central)
kimfrazer5225@yahoo.com

Frear, Steven (LAB - Bristnall)
steven.frear@btinternet.com

Garrett, Philip (UKIP - Princes End)
philip_garrett@sandwell.gov.uk

Gavan, Bill (LAB - Langley)
bill_gavan@sandwell.gov.uk

Giles, Elizabeth (LAB - Charlemont with Grove Vale)
elizabeth_giles@cllr.sandwell.gov.uk

Gill, Preet (LAB - St Pauls)
preet_kaurgill@sandwell.gov.uk

Goult, Carol (LAB - Bristnall)
carol_goult@cllr.sandwell.org.uk

Hackett, Simon (LAB - Friar Park)
simon_hackett@sandwell.gov.uk

Hadley, Joanne (LAB - Great Bridge)

Haque, Ahmadul (LAB - Tipton Green)

Hartwell, Suzanne (LAB - Oldbury)
suzanne_hartwell@cllr.sandwell.gov.uk

Hevican, Sandra (LAB - Tividale)
sandra_hevican@sandwell.gov.uk

Horton, Linda (LAB - Smethwick)
linda_horton@sandwell.gov.uk

Horton, Roger (LAB - Soho and Victoria)
councillor@lrhorton.freeserve.co.uk

Hosell, Shirley (LAB - Great Barr with Yew Tree)
shirley_hosell@sandwell.gov.uk

Hosell, David (LAB - Newton)
hoselld@blueyonder.co.uk

Hughes, Pam (LAB - Wednesbury South)
pam_hughes@sandwell.gov.uk

Hughes, Peter (LAB - Wednesbury North)
cllrpeter_hughes@sandwell.gov.uk

Hussain, Mahboob (LAB - Oldbury)
mahoob_hussain@sandwell.gov.uk

Jaron, Ann (LAB - Abbey)
ann_jaron@sandwell.gov.uk

Jarvis, Ann (LAB - Bristnall)
ann_jarvis@sandwell.gov.uk

Jones, Ian (LAB - Tipton Green)
ian_jones@sandwell.gov.uk

Jones, Stephen (LAB - Princes End)
cllrstephen_jones@sandwell.gov.uk

SANDWELL

Jones, Olwen (LAB - Wednesbury South)
olwen.jones53@gmail.com

Khatun, Syeda (LAB - Tipton Green)

Lewis, Geoffrey (LAB - Friar Park)
geoffreyjlewis@fsmail.net

Lloyd, Bob (LAB - Wednesbury South)
bob_lloyd@sandwell.gov.uk

Marshall, Richard (LAB - Smethwick)
richard_marshall@sandwell.gov.uk

Meehan, Tony (LAB - Wednesbury North)
tony_meehan@sandwell.gov.uk

Melia, Steve (LAB - Great Barr with Yew Tree)
smelia5751@aol.com

Moore, Paul (LAB - Hateley Heath)
paul_moore@sandwell.gov.uk

Phillips, Sue (LAB - Charlemont with Grove Vale)
sue_phillips@sandwell.gov.uk

Piper, Bob (LAB - Abbey)
bob.piper@gmail.com

Preece, Liam (LAB - Charlemont with Grove Vale)
liam_preece@sandwell.gov.uk

Price, Robert (LAB - Blackheath)
robert_price@cllr.sandwell.org.uk

Price, Barbara (LAB - Rowley)
councillor-mrs@bprice31.freeserve.co.uk

Price, Robert (LAB - Blackheath)
councillor@bprice31.freeserve.co.uk

Rouf, Mohammed (LAB - Soho and Victoria)

Rowley, Derek (LAB - Great Bridge)
derek_rowley@sandwell.gov.uk

Sandars, Paul (LAB - Hateley Heath)
sandarspaul@hotmail.com

Shackleton, Ann (LAB - Cradley Heath and Old Hill)
ann_shackleton@sandwell.gov.uk

Sidhu, Gurcharan (LAB - Greets Green and Lyng)

Tagger, Mohinder (LAB - West Bromwich Central)

Taylor, Jackie (LAB - Greets Green and Lyng)
jackie_taylor@sandwell.gov.uk

Tipper, John (LAB - Cradley Heath and Old Hill)
john_tipper@sandwell.gov.uk

Tranter, Chris (LAB - Rowley)
chris_tranter@sandwell.gov.uk

Trow, Steve (LAB - Old Warley)
stevetrow@blueyonder.co.uk

Underhill, Joyce (LAB - Newton)
joyceunderhill@btinternet.com

Webb, Julie (LAB - Cradley Heath and Old Hill)
juliewebb55@hotmail.com

Worsey, Christopher (LAB - Great Barr with Yew Tree)
chirs_worsey@sandwell.gov.uk

POLITICAL COMPOSITION
LAB: 71, UKIP: 1

COMMITTEE CHAIRS

Audit: Mr Gurcharan Sidhu

Children's Services & Education: Mrs Joyce Underhill

Health & Adult Social Care: Mr Paul Sandars

Licensing: Mr Peter Allen

Planning: Mr Steven Frear

Scarborough D

Scarborough Borough Council, Town Hall, St. Nicholas Street, Scarborough YO11 2HG
☎ 01723 232323 ✉ ce@scarborough.gov.uk
www.scarborough.gov.uk

FACTS AND FIGURES
Parliamentary Constituencies: Scarborough and Whitby
EU Constituencies: Yorkshire and the Humber
Election Frequency: Elections are of whole council

PRINCIPAL OFFICERS

Chief Executive: Mr Jim Dillon, Chief Executive, Town Hall, St. Nicholas Street, Scarborough YO11 2HG ☎ 01723 232300 ✉ jim.dillon@scarborough.gov.uk

Deputy Chief Executive: Mrs Hilary Jones , Deputy Chief Executive, Town Hall, St. Nicholas Street, Scarborough YO11 2HG ☎ 01723 232342 ✉ hilary.jones@scarborough.gov.uk

Senior Management: Mrs Lisa Dixon , Head of Democratic & Legal Services, Town Hall, St. Nicholas Street, Scarborough YO11 2HG ☎ 01723 232350 ✉ lisa.dixon@scarborough.gov.uk

Senior Management: Mr Nick Edwards , Director of Business Support, Town Hall, St. Nicholas Street, Scarborough YO11 2HG ☎ 01723 232410 ✉ nick.edwards@scarborough.gov.uk

Senior Management: Mr Andy Skelton, Director of Service Delivery, Town Hall, St. Nicholas Street, Scarborough YO11 2HG ☎ 01723 232493 ✉ andy.skelton@scarborough.gov.uk

Architect, Building / Property Services: Mr Martin Pedley , Asset & Risk Manager, Town Hall, St. Nicholas Street, Scarborough YO11 2HG ☎ 01723 232359 ✉ martin.pedley@scarborough.gov.uk

PR / Communications: Ms Gabrielle Jandzio, Communications Officer, Town Hall, St. Nicholas Street, Scarborough YO11 2HG ☎ 01723 232306 ✉ gabrielle.jandzio@scarborough.gov.uk

Community Safety: Ms Jo Ireland , Customers, Communities & Partnerships Manager, Town Hall, St. Nicholas Street, Scarborough YO11 2HG ☎ 01723 234315 ✉ jo.ireland@scarborough.gov.uk

Computer Management: Mr Greg Harper , ICT Delivery Manager, Town Hall, St. Nicholas Street, Scarborough YO11 2HG ☎ 01723 384333 ✉ greg.harper@scarborough.gov.uk

Contracts: Miss Rebecca Jackson , Legal Services Manager, Town Hall, St. Nicholas Street, Scarborough YO11 2HG ☎ 01723 232352 ✉ rebecca.jackson@scarborough.gov.uk

Customer Service: Ms Jo Ireland , Customers, Communities & Partnerships Manager, Town Hall, St. Nicholas Street, Scarborough YO11 2HG ☎ 01723 234315 ✉ jo.ireland@scarborough.gov.uk

Economic Development: Mr David Kelly , Economic Development Manager, Town Hall, St. Nicholas Street, Scarborough YO11 2HG ☎ 01723 232321 ✉ david.kelly@scarborough.gov.uk

E-Government: Mr Greg Harper , ICT Delivery Manager, Town Hall, St. Nicholas Street, Scarborough YO11 2HG ☎ 01723 384333 ✉ greg.harper@scarborough.gov.uk

Electoral Registration: Miss Kerry Russett , Office Manager - Legal & Democratic, Town Hall, St. Nicholas Street, Scarborough YO11 2HG ☎ 01723 383506 ✉ kerry.russett@scarborough.gov.uk

Emergency Planning: Mr Paul Thompson , Operations, Transport & Countryside Manager, Dean Road Depot, Scarborough YO12 7QS ☎ 01723 383112 ✉ paul.thompson@scarborough.gov.uk

Energy Management: Mr Jeremy Carter , Energy Manager, Town Hall, St. Nicholas Street, Scarborough YO11 2HG ☎ 01723 223243 ✉ jeremy.carter@scarborough.gov.uk

Environmental / Technical Services: Mr Andy Skelton, Director of Service Delivery, Town Hall, St. Nicholas Street, Scarborough YO11 2HG ☎ 01723 232493 ✉ andy.skelton@scarborough.gov.uk

Environmental Health: Mr Andy Skelton, Director of Service Delivery, Town Hall, St. Nicholas Street, Scarborough YO11 2HG ☎ 01723 232493 ✉ andy.skelton@scarborough.gov.uk

Estates, Property & Valuation: Mr Martin Pedley , Asset & Risk Manager, Town Hall, St. Nicholas Street, Scarborough YO11 2HG ☎ 01723 232359 ✉ martin.pedley@scarborough.gov.uk

Events Manager: Ms Rowena Marsden , Culture, Events & Filming Officer, Town Hall, St. Nicholas Street, Scarborough YO11 2HG ☎ 01723 383615 ✉ rowena.marsden@scarborough.gov.uk

Facilities: Mr Martin Pedley , Asset & Risk Manager, Town Hall, St. Nicholas Street, Scarborough YO11 2HG ☎ 01723 232359 ✉ martin.pedley@scarborough.gov.uk

Finance: Mr Nick Edwards , Director of Business Support, Town Hall, St. Nicholas Street, Scarborough YO11 2HG ☎ 01723 232410 ✉ nick.edwards@scarborough.gov.uk

Fleet Management: Mr Paul Thompson , Operations, Transport & Countryside Manager, Dean Road Depot, Scarborough YO12 7QS ☎ 01723 383112 ✉ paul.thompson@scarborough.gov.uk

Grounds Maintenance: Mr Paul Thompson , Operations, Transport & Countryside Manager, Dean Road Depot, Scarborough YO12 7QS ☎ 01723 383112 ✉ paul.thompson@scarborough.gov.uk

Health and Safety: Mr Robert Webster , Health & Safety Officer, Town Hall, St. Nicholas Street, Scarborough YO11 2HG ☎ 01723 232101 ✉ robert.webster@scarborough.gov.uk

Housing: Mr Andrew Rowe , Housing Manager, Town Hall, St. Nicholas Street, Scarborough YO11 2HG ☎ 01723 383598 ✉ andrew.rowe@scarborough.gov.uk

Legal: Miss Rebecca Jackson , Legal Services Manager, Town Hall, St. Nicholas Street, Scarborough YO11 2HG ☎ 01723 232352 ✉ rebecca.jackson@scarborough.gov.uk

Leisure and Cultural Services: Mr Andrew Williams , Leisure Manager, Town Hall, St. Nicholas Street, Scarborough YO11 2HG ☎ 01723 383610 ✉ andrew.williams@scarborough.gov.uk

Licensing: Ms Una Faithfull, Licensing Manager, Town Hall, St. Nicholas Street, Scarborough YO11 2HG ☎ 01723 232522 ✉ una.faithfull@scarborough.gov.uk

Lottery Funding, Charity and Voluntary: Ms Rowena Marsden, Culture, Events & Filming Officer, Town Hall, St. Nicholas Street, Scarborough YO11 2HG ☎ 01723 383615 ✉ rowena.marsden@scarborough.gov.uk

Member Services: Mr David Kitson , Regulatory & Governance Manager, Town Hall, St. Nicholas Street, Scarborough YO11 2HG ☎ 01723 234319 ✉ david.kitson@scarborough.gov.uk

Parking: Mr Stuart Clark , Parking CCTV & Venues Manager, Town Hall, St. Nicholas Street, Scarborough YO11 2HG ☎ 01723 383582 ✉ stuart.clark@scarborough.gov.uk

Partnerships: Ms Jo Ireland , Customers, Communities & Partnerships Manager, Town Hall, St. Nicholas Street, Scarborough YO11 2HG ☎ 01723 234315 ✉ jo.ireland@scarborough.gov.uk

Personnel / HR: Mrs Elaine Blades , Human Resources Manager, Town Hall, St. Nicholas Street, Scarborough YO11 2HG ☎ 01723 383560 ✉ elaine.blades@scarborough.gov.uk

Planning: Mr David Walker , Planning Manager, Town Hall, St. Nicholas Street, Scarborough YO11 2HG ☎ 01723 232438 ✉ david.walker@scarborough.gov.uk

Procurement: Mr David Gomersall , Procurement Officer, Town Hall, St. Nicholas Street, Scarborough YO11 2HG ☎ 01723 232344 ✉ david.gomersall@scarborough.gov.uk

Recycling & Waste Minimisation: Mr Harry Briggs , Environment, Enforcement & Contract Manager, Dean Road Depot, Scarborough YO12 7QS ☎ 01723 383189 ✉ harry.briggs@scarborough.gov.uk

Regeneration: Mr David Kelly , Economic Development Manager, Town Hall, St. Nicholas Street, Scarborough YO11 2HG ☎ 01723 232321 ✉ david.kelly@scarborough.gov.uk

Staff Training: Mr Roger Paterson , Principal HR Officer, Town Hall, St. Nicholas Street, Scarborough YO11 2HG ☎ 01723 232314 ✉ roger.paterson@scarborough.gov.uk

Street Scene: Mr Paul Thompson , Operations, Transport & Countryside Manager, Dean Road Depot, Scarborough YO12 7QS ☎ 01723 383112 ✉ paul.thompson@scarborough.gov.uk

SCARBOROUGH

Sustainable Communities: Ms Jo Ireland , Customers, Communities & Partnerships Manager, Town Hall, St. Nicholas Street, Scarborough YO11 2HG ☎ 01723 234315 ✉ jo.ireland@scarborough.gov.uk

Tourism: Mrs Janet Deacon , Tourism Manager, Town Hall, St. Nicholas Street, Scarborough YO11 2HG ☎ 01723 232570 ✉ janet.deacon@scarborough.gov.uk

Town Centre: Mr Nick Taylor , Investment Manager, Town Hall, St. Nicholas Street, Scarborough YO11 2HG ☎ 01723 232440 ✉ nick.taylor@scarborough.gov.uk

Traffic Management: Mr Stuart Clark , Parking CCTV & Venues Manager, Town Hall, St. Nicholas Street, Scarborough YO11 2HG ☎ 01723 383582 ✉ stuart.clark@scarborough.gov.uk

Transport: Mr Paul Thompson , Operations, Transport & Countryside Manager, Dean Road Depot, Scarborough YO12 7QS ☎ 01723 383112 ✉ paul.thompson@scarborough.gov.uk

Transport Planner: Mr Paul Thompson , Operations, Transport & Countryside Manager, Dean Road Depot, Scarborough YO12 7QS ☎ 01723 383112 ✉ paul.thompson@scarborough.gov.uk

Waste Collection and Disposal: Mr Paul Thompson , Operations, Transport & Countryside Manager, Dean Road Depot, Scarborough YO12 7QS ☎ 01723 383112 ✉ paul.thompson@scarborough.gov.uk

Waste Management: Mr Paul Thompson , Operations, Transport & Countryside Manager, Dean Road Depot, Scarborough YO12 7QS ☎ 01723 383112 ✉ paul.thompson@scarborough.gov.uk

COUNCILLORS

***Mayor* Fox**, Thomas (CON - Weaponness)
cllr.tom.fox@scarborough.gov.uk

***Deputy Mayor* Ritchie**, John (LAB - Falsgrave Park)
cllr.john.ritchie@scarborough.gov.uk

***Leader of the Council* Bastiman**, Derek (CON - Scalby)
cllr.derek.bastiman@scarborough.gov.uk

Abbot, Alf (CON - Whitby West Cliff)
cllr.alf.abbott@scarborough.gov.uk

Allanson, Godfrey (CON - Hertford)
cllr.godgrey.allanson@scarborough.gov.uk

Backhouse, Luke (CON - Newby)
cllr.luke.backhouse@scarborough.gov.uk

Backhouse, Andrew (CON - Lindhead)
cllr.andrew.backhouse@scarborough.gov.uk

Barnett, Rob (LAB - Streonshalh)
cllr.rob.barnett@scarborough.gov.uk

Bastiman, Lynn (CON - Stepney)
cllr.lynn.bastiman@scarborough.gov.uk

Billing, David (LAB - Central)
cllr.david.billing@scarborough.gov.uk

Broadbent, Eric (LAB - Central)
cllr.eric.broadbent@scarborough.gov.uk

Chance, David (CON - Mayfield)
clld.david.chance@scarborough.gov.uk

Chatt, William (IND - Woodlands)
cllr.bill.chatt@scarborough.gov.uk

Cluer, Dilys (GRN - Stepney)
cllr.dilys.cluer@scarborough.gov.uk

Cockerill, Mike (IND - Filey)
cllr.mike.cockerill@scarborough.gov.uk

Cooling, Liz (LAB - Falsgrave Park)
cllr.liz.cooling@scarborough.gov.uk

Coulson, Guy (CON - Esk Valley)
cllr.guy.coulson@scarborough.gov.uk

Cross, Sam (UKIP - Filey)
cllr.sam.cross@scarborough.gov.uk

Cross, Paul (LAB - Castle)
cllr.paul.cross@scarborough.gov.uk

Dennett, Gerald (LAB - Mayfield)
cllr.gerald.dennett@scarborough.gov.uk

Dodds, Jonathan (UKIP - Eastfield)
cllr.jonathan.dodds@scarborough.gov.uk

Donohue-Moncrieff, Michelle (CON - Hertford)
cllr.michelle.donohue-moncrieff@scarborough.gov.uk

Green, Simon (CON - Cayton)
cllr.simon.green@scarborough.gov.uk

Haddington, Colin (UKIP - Filey)
cllr.colin.haddington@scarborough.gov.uk

Harland, Marie (CON - Mulgrave)
cllr.marie.harland@scarborough.gov.uk

Inman, Vanda (LAB - Newby)
cllr.vanda.inman@scarborough.gov.uk

Jeffels, David (CON - Derwent Valley)
cllr.david.jeffels@scarborough.gov.uk

Jefferson, Janet (IND - Castle)
cllr.janet.jefferson@scarborough.gov.uk

Jenkinson, Andrew (CON - Newby)
cllr.andrew.jenkinson@scarborough.gov.uk

Lynskey, Hazel (CON - Scalby)
cllr.hazel.lynskey@scarborough.gov.uk

Mallory, Helen (CON - Seamer)
cllr.helen.mallory@scarborough.gov.uk

Maw, Carl (LAB - Northstead)
cllr.carl.maw@scarborough.gov.uk

Moody, Richard (LAB - Woodlands)
cllr.richard.moody@scarborough.gov.uk

Mortimer, Jane (CON - Flyingdales)
cllr.jane.mortimer@scarborough.gov.uk

Murphy, Roxanne (UKIP - Seamer)
cllr.roxanne.murphy@scarborough.gov.uk

Murphy, Norman (UKIP - Northstead)
cllr.norman.murphy@scarborough.gov.uk

Nock, John (CON - Mulgrave)
cllr.john.nock@scarborough.gov.uk

Pearson, Clive (CON - Danby)
cllr.clive.pearson@scarborough.gov.uk

Phillips, Heather (CON - Derwent Valley)
cllr.heather.phillips@scarborough.gov.uk

Plant, Joseph (CON - Whitby West Cliff)
cllr.joseph.plant@scarborough.gov.uk

Price, Neil (LAB - North Bay)
cllr.neil.price@scarborough.gov.uk

Randerson, Tony (LAB - Eastfield)
cllr.tony.randerson@scarborough.gov.uk

Siddons, Steve (LAB - Ramshill)
cllr.steve.siddens@scarborough.gov.uk

Smith, Martin (CON - North Bay)
cllr.martin.smith@scarborough.gov.uk

Swiers, Roberta (CON - Cayton)
cllr.roberta.swiers@scarborough.gov.uk

Trumper, Phillip (CON - Esk Valley)
cllr.phil.trumper@scarborough.gov.uk

Turner, Sandra (CON - Streonshalh)
cllr.sandra.turner@scarborough.gov.uk

Vesey, Mark (GRN - Ramshill)
cllr.mark.vesey@scarborough.gov.uk

Walsh, Callam (CON - Weaponness)
cllr.callam.walsh@scarborough.gov.uk

Warburton, John (LAB - Eastfield)
cllr.john.warburton@scarborough.gov.uk

POLITICAL COMPOSITION
CON: 26, LAB: 14, UKIP: 5, IND: 3, GRN: 2

COMMITTEE CHAIRS
Audit: Mr David Chance

Licensing: Mr Martin Smith

Planning & Development: Mrs Jane Mortimer

Scottish Borders S

Scottish Borders Council, Council Headquarters, Newtown St. Boswells, Melrose TD6 0SA
☎ 01835 824000 🖷 01835 825001 ✉ enquiries@scotborders.gov.uk
💻 www.scotborders.gov.uk

FACTS AND FIGURES
Parliamentary Constituencies: Berwickshire, Roxburgh and Selkirk, Dumfriesshire, Clydesdale and Tweedale
EU Constituencies: Scotland
Election Frequency: Elections are of whole council

PRINCIPAL OFFICERS
Chief Executive: Ms Tracey Logan, Chief Executive, Council Headquarters, Newtown St. Boswells, Melrose TD6 0SA
☎ 01835 825055 ✉ tracey.logan@scotborders.gov.uk

Deputy Chief Executive: Mr Philip Barr , Depute Chief Executive - Place, Council Headquarters, Newtown St. Boswells, Melrose TD6 0SA ☎ 01835 825132 ✉ philip.barr@scotborders.gov.uk

Deputy Chief Executive: Ms Jeanette McDiarmid , Depute Chief Executive - People, Council Headquarters, Newtown St. Boswells, Melrose TD6 0SA ☎ 01835 825217
✉ jeanette.mcdiarmid@scotborders.gov.uk

Assistant Chief Executive: Ms Jenny Wilkinson , Clerk to the Council, Council Headquarters, Newtown St. Boswells, Melrose TD6 0SA ☎ 01835 825004 ✉ jjwilkinson@scotborder.gov.uk

Senior Management: Mr Eric Baijal , Director of Public Health, Council Headquarters, Newtown St. Boswells, Melrose TD6 0SA
☎ 01835 826554 ✉ eric.baijal@scotborders.gov.uk

Senior Management: Mrs Jenni Craig , Service Director - Neighbourhood Services, Council Headquarters, Newtown St. Boswells, Melrose TD6 0SA ☎ 01835 825013
✉ jcraig@scotborders.gov.uk

Senior Management: Mr David Cressey , Service Director - Strategy & Policy, Council Headquarters, Newtown St. Boswells, Melrose TD6 0SA ☎ 01835 825082 ✉ dcressey@scotborders.gov.uk

Senior Management: Mr Rob Dickson , Corporate Transformation & Service Director, Council Headquarters, Newtown St. Boswells, Melrose TD6 0SA ☎ 01835 825075 🖷 01835 825158
✉ rob.dickson@scotborders.gov.uk

Senior Management: Mr Andrew Drummond-Hunt , Service Director - Commercial Services, Council Headquarters, Newtown St. Boswells, Melrose TD6 0SA ☎ 01835 826672 🖷 01835 825158
✉ adrummond-hunt@scotborders.gov.uk

Senior Management: Mr Brian Frater, Service Director - Regulatory Services, Council Headquarters, Newtown St. Boswells, Melrose TD6 0SA ☎ 01835 825067 🖷 01835 825158
✉ bfrater@scotborders.gov.uk

Senior Management: Ms Clair Hepburn , Chief Officer - Human Resources, Council Headquarters, Newtown St. Boswells, Melrose TD6 0SA ☎ 01835 826667 ✉ chepburn@scotborders.gov.uk

Senior Management: Mr David Robertson , Chief Financial Officer, Council Headquarters, Newtown St. Boswells, Melrose TD6 0SA ☎ 01835 825012 ✉ david.robertson@scotborders.gov.uk

Senior Management: Mrs Elaine Torrance , Chief Social Work Officer, Council Headquarters, Newtown St. Boswells, Melrose TD6 0SA ☎ 01835 825084 ✉ etorrance@scotborders.gov.uk

Senior Management: Mr Martin Wanless , Powered Planning Manager, Council Headquarters, Newtown St. Boswells, Melrose TD6 0SA ☎ 01835 825063 ✉ mwanless@scotborders.gov.uk

Architect, Building / Property Services: Mr Andrew Drummond-Hunt , Service Director - Commercial Services, Council Headquarters, Newtown St. Boswells, Melrose TD6 0SA ☎ 01835 826672 🖷 01835 825158 ✉ adrummond-hunt@scotborders.gov.uk

Architect, Building / Property Services: Mr Paul Frankland, Design Manager, Council Headquarters, Newtown St. Boswells, Melrose TD6 0SA ☎ 01835 825179 ✉ pfrankland@scotborders.gov.uk

SCOTTISH BORDERS

Architect, Building / Property Services: Mr Stuart Mawson , Property Manager, Council Headquarters, Newtown St. Boswells, Melrose TD6 0SA ☎ 01835 826550 stuart.mawson@scotborders.gov.uk

Building Control: Mr John Hayward , Development Standards Manager, Council Headquarters, Newtown St. Boswells, Melrose TD6 0SA ☎ 01835 825068 jhayward@scotborders.gov.uk

Catering Services: Mr Alastair McIntyre , Catering & Services Manager, Council Headquarters, Newtown St. Boswells, Melrose TD6 0SA ☎ 01835 826564 amcintyre@scotborders.gov.uk

Children / Youth Services: Mrs Elaine Torrance , Chief Social Work Officer, Council Headquarters, Newtown St. Boswells, Melrose TD6 0SA ☎ 01835 825084 etorrance@scotborders.gov.uk

Civil Registration: Ms Lisa Lauder , Chief Registrar, Council Headquarters, Newtown St. Boswells, Melrose TD6 0SA ☎ 01450 364710 🖷 01450 364711 llauder@scotborders.gov.uk

PR / Communications: Ms Tracey Graham , Communications & Partnerships Manager, Council Headquarters, Newtown St. Boswells, Melrose TD6 0SA ☎ 01835 826592 tgraham@scotborders.gov.uk

Community Planning: Ms Shona Smith , Communities & Partnerships Manager, Council Headquarters, Newtown St. Boswells, Melrose TD6 0SA ☎ 01835 825054 smsmith@scotborders.gov.uk

Community Safety: Mr Kenny Simpson , Chief Inspector Police Scotland / Safer Communities Manager, Council Headquarters, Newtown St. Boswells, Melrose TD6 0SA ☎ 01835 828228 kenneth.simpson@scotborders.gov.uk

Computer Management: Mr Stewart Meldrum , Corporate IT Manager, Council Headquarters, Newtown St. Boswells, Melrose TD6 0SA ☎ 01835 825046 smeldrum@scotborders.gov.uk

Consumer Protection and Trading Standards: Mr Anthony Carson , Regulatory Services Manager, Council Headquarters, Newtown St. Boswells, Melrose TD6 0SA ☎ 00835 825142 acarson@scotborders.gov.uk

Customer Service: Mr Les Grant , Customer Services Manager, Council Headquarters, Newtown St. Boswells, Melrose TD6 0SA ☎ 01835 825547 lgrant@scotborders.gov.uk

Direct Labour: Mr Brian Park , SBC Contracts Manager, Council Headquarters, Newtown St. Boswells, Melrose TD6 0SA ☎ 01835 825926 bpark@scotborders.gov.uk

Economic Development: Mr Bryan McGrath, Chief Officer - Economic Development, Council Headquarters, Newtown St. Boswells, Melrose TD6 0SA ☎ 01835 826525 bmcgrath@scotborders.gov.uk

Education: Ms Yvonne McCracken , Chief Officer - Strategy & Policy Development: Children & Young People, Council Headquarters, Newtown St. Boswells, Melrose TD6 0SA ☎ 01835 825455 ymccracken@scotborders.gov.uk

Education: Mrs Jackie Swanston , Chief Officer - Schools, Council Headquarters, Newtown St. Boswells, Melrose TD6 0SA ☎ 01835 825092 jswanston@scotborders.gov.uk

Electoral Registration: Mr Mark Dickson , Assessor & Electoral Registration Officer, Council Headquarters, Newtown St. Boswells, Melrose TD6 0SA ☎ 01835 825100 mdickson@scotborders.gov.uk

Emergency Planning: Mr Jim Fraser , Emergency Planning Officer, Council Headquarters, Newtown St. Boswells, Melrose TD6 0SA ☎ 01835 825056 jfraser@scotborders.gov.uk

Energy Management: Mr Stuart Mawson , Property Manager, Council Headquarters, Newtown St. Boswells, Melrose TD6 0SA ☎ 01835 826550 stuart.mawson@scotborders.gov.uk

Environmental Health: Mr Anthony Carson , Regulatory Services Manager, Council Headquarters, Newtown St. Boswells, Melrose TD6 0SA ☎ 00835 825142 acarson@scotborders.gov.uk

Estates, Property & Valuation: Mr Neil Hastie , Estates Manager, Council Headquarters, Newtown St. Boswells, Melrose TD6 0SA ☎ 01835 825167 nhastie@scotborders.gov.uk

European Liaison: Mr Douglas Scott, Senior Policy Advisor, Council Headquarters, Newtown St. Boswells, Melrose TD6 0SA ☎ 01835 824000 dscott@scotborders.gov.uk

Events Manager: Ms Jane Warcup, Events Officer - Strategy Development, Council Headquarters, Newtown St. Boswells, Melrose TD6 0SA ☎ 01835 825060 jwarcup@scotborders.gov.uk

Facilities: Mr John Gray , Cleaning & Facilities Manager, Council Headquarters, Newtown St. Boswells, Melrose TD6 0SA ☎ 01835 826670 john.gray@scotborders.gov.uk

Finance: Mr David Robertson , Chief Financial Officer, Council Headquarters, Newtown St. Boswells, Melrose TD6 0SA ☎ 01835 825012 david.robertson@scotborders.gov.uk

Pensions: Mr Ian Angus , HR Shared Services Manager, Council Headquarters, Newtown St. Boswells, Melrose TD6 0SA ☎ 01835 824000 iangus@scotborders.gov.uk

Fleet Management: Mr John Martin , Fleet Manager, Council Headquarters, Newtown St. Boswells, Melrose TD6 0SA ☎ 01835 825119 jmartin@scotborders.gov.uk

Grounds Maintenance: Mr Kenny Hastings , Neighbourhood Operating Manager, Council Headquarters, Newtown St. Boswells, Melrose TD6 0SA ☎ 01835 825507 khastings@scotborders.gov.uk

Health and Safety: Mr Rob Dickson , Corporate Transformation & Service Director, Council Headquarters, Newtown St. Boswells, Melrose TD6 0SA ☎ 01835 825075 🖷 01835 825158 rob.dickson@scotborders.gov.uk

Highways: Mr Colin Ovens , Infrastructure Manager, Council Headquarters, Newtown St. Boswells, Melrose TD6 0SA ☎ 01835 826635 covens@scotborders.gov.uk

Home Energy Conservation: Ms Cathie Fancy , Group Manager of Housing Strategy & Services, Council Headquarters, Newtown St. Boswells, Melrose TD6 0SA ☎ 01835 825080 ✉ cfancy@scotborders.gov.uk

Housing: Mr David Cressey , Service Director - Strategy & Policy, Council Headquarters, Newtown St. Boswells, Melrose TD6 0SA ☎ 01835 825082 ✉ dcressey@scotborders.gov.uk

Local Area Agreement: Mr David Cressey , Service Director - Strategy & Policy, Council Headquarters, Newtown St. Boswells, Melrose TD6 0SA ☎ 01835 825082 ✉ dcressey@scotborders.gov.uk

Legal: Ms Nuala McKinley , Chief Legal Officer, Council Headquarters, Newtown St. Boswells, Melrose TD6 0SA ☎ 01835 825220 ✉ nmckinley@scotborders.gov.uk

Leisure and Cultural Services: Mr Rob Dickson , Corporate Transformation & Service Director, Council Headquarters, Newtown St. Boswells, Melrose TD6 0SA ☎ 01835 825075 🖷 01835 825158 ✉ rob.dickson@scotborders.gov.uk

Licensing: Ms Anne Isles, Legal & Licensing Services Manager, Council Buildings, Albert Place, Galashiels TD1 3AW ☎ 01835 825002 ✉ aisles@scotborders.gov.uk

Lighting: Mr Brian Young , Network Manager, Council Headquarters, Newtown St. Boswells, Melrose TD6 0SA ☎ 01835 825178 🖷 01835 825158 ✉ byoung@scotborders.gov.uk

Lottery Funding, Charity and Voluntary: Ms Jean Robertson, Funding & Project Officer, Council Headquarters, Newtown St. Boswells, Melrose TD6 0SA ☎ 01835 824000 ✉ jarobertson@scotborders.gov.uk

Member Services: Ms Pauline Bolson, Democratic Services Officer, Council Headquarters, Newtown St. Boswells, Melrose TD6 0SA ☎ 01835 826053 ✉ pbolson@scotborders.gov.uk

Parking: Mr Brian Young , Network Manager, Council Headquarters, Newtown St. Boswells, Melrose TD6 0SA ☎ 01835 825178 🖷 01835 825158 ✉ byoung@scotborders.gov.uk

Partnerships: Ms Shona Smith , Communities & Partnerships Manager, Council Headquarters, Newtown St. Boswells, Melrose TD6 0SA ☎ 01835 825054 ✉ smsmith@scotborders.gov.uk

Personnel / HR: Ms Clair Hepburn , Chief Officer - Human Resources, Council Headquarters, Newtown St. Boswells, Melrose TD6 0SA ☎ 01835 826667 ✉ chepburn@scotborders.gov.uk

Planning: Mr John Hayward , Development Standards Manager, Council Headquarters, Newtown St. Boswells, Melrose TD6 0SA ☎ 01835 825068 ✉ jhayward@scotborders.gov.uk

Procurement: Ms Kathryn Dickson , Procurement Manager, Council Headquarters, Newtown St. Boswells, Melrose TD6 0SA ☎ 01835 826646 ✉ kathryn.dickson@scotborders.gov.uk

Public Libraries: Mr Ian Brown , Community Services Business Manager, Council Headquarters, Newtown St. Boswells, Melrose TD6 0SA ☎ 01835 826606 ✉ iabrown@scotborders.gov.uk

Recycling & Waste Minimisation: Mr Ross Sharp-Dent, Waste Manager, Council Headquarters, Newtown St. Boswells, Melrose TD6 0SA ☎ 01835 825111 ✉ rsharp-dent@scotborders.gov.uk

Regeneration: Mr Bryan McGrath, Chief Officer - Economic Development, Council Headquarters, Newtown St. Boswells, Melrose TD6 0SA ☎ 01835 826525 ✉ bmcgrath@scotborders.gov.uk

Road Safety: Mr Colin Ovens , Infrastructure Manager, Council Headquarters, Newtown St. Boswells, Melrose TD6 0SA ☎ 01835 826635 ✉ covens@scotborders.gov.uk

Social Services: Mrs Elaine Torrance , Chief Social Work Officer, Council Headquarters, Newtown St. Boswells, Melrose TD6 0SA ☎ 01835 825084 ✉ etorrance@scotborders.gov.uk

Social Services (Adult): Mrs Elaine Torrance , Chief Social Work Officer, Council Headquarters, Newtown St. Boswells, Melrose TD6 0SA ☎ 01835 825084 ✉ etorrance@scotborders.gov.uk

Street Scene: Mr Kenny Hastings , Neighbourhood Operating Manager, Council Headquarters, Newtown St. Boswells, Melrose TD6 0SA ☎ 01835 825507 ✉ khastings@scotborders.gov.uk

Sustainable Communities: Mr Douglas Scott, Senior Policy Advisor, Council Headquarters, Newtown St. Boswells, Melrose TD6 0SA ☎ 01835 824000 ✉ dscott@scotborders.gov.uk

Sustainable Development: Mr Bryan McGrath, Chief Officer - Economic Development, Council Headquarters, Newtown St. Boswells, Melrose TD6 0SA ☎ 01835 826525 ✉ bmcgrath@scotborders.gov.uk

Tourism: Mr Bryan McGrath, Chief Officer - Economic Development, Council Headquarters, Newtown St. Boswells, Melrose TD6 0SA ☎ 01835 826525 ✉ bmcgrath@scotborders.gov.uk

Town Centre: Mr Bryan McGrath, Chief Officer - Economic Development, Council Headquarters, Newtown St. Boswells, Melrose TD6 0SA ☎ 01835 826525 ✉ bmcgrath@scotborders.gov.uk

Traffic Management: Mr Brian Young , Network Manager, Council Headquarters, Newtown St. Boswells, Melrose TD6 0SA ☎ 01835 825178 🖷 01835 825158 ✉ byoung@scotborders.gov.uk

Transport Planner: Mr Graeme Johnstone , Principal Officer - Strategic Transport, Council Headquarters, Newtown St. Boswells, Melrose TD6 0SA ☎ 01835 825138 🖷 01835 825158 ✉ gjohnstone@scotborders.gov.uk

Waste Collection and Disposal: Mr Ross Sharp-Dent, Waste Manager, Council Headquarters, Newtown St. Boswells, Melrose TD6 0SA ☎ 01835 825111 ✉ rsharp-dent@scotborders.gov.uk

Waste Management: Mrs Jenni Craig , Service Director - Neighbourhood Services, Council Headquarters, Newtown St. Boswells, Melrose TD6 0SA ☎ 01835 825013 ✉ jcraig@scotborders.gov.uk

Children's Play Areas: Mrs Jenni Craig , Service Director - Neighbourhood Services, Council Headquarters, Newtown St. Boswells, Melrose TD6 0SA ☎ 01835 825013 ✉ jcraig@scotborders.gov.uk

SCOTTISH BORDERS

COUNCILLORS

***Convener* Garvie**, Graham (LD - Tweedale East)
ggarvie@scotborders.gov.uk

***Vice Convener* Brown**, Jim (SNP - Jedburgh and District)
jbrown@scotborders.gov.uk

***Leader of the Council* Parker**, David (IND - Leaderdale and Melrose)
dparker@scotborders.gov.uk

***Deputy Leader of the Council* Mitchell**, John (SNP - Galashiels and District)
jmitchell@scotborders.gov.uk

***Group Leader* Aitchison**, Sandy (IND - Galashiels and District)
saitchison@scotborders.gov.uk

***Group Leader* Ballantyne**, Michelle (CON - Selkirkshire)
michelle.ballantyne@scotborders.gov.uk

Archibald, Willie (SNP - Tweedale West)
warchibald@scotborders.gov.uk

Bell, Stuart (SNP - Tweedale East)
stuart.bell@scotborders.gov.uk

Bhatia, Catriona (LD - Tweedale West)
cbhatia@scotborders.gov.uk

Campbell, Joan (SNP - East Berwickshire)
joan.campbell@scotborders.gov.uk

Cockburn, Keith (CON - Tweedale West)
keith.cockburn@scotborders.gov.uk

Cook, Michael (IND - East Berwickshire)
mcook@scotborders.gov.uk

Cranston, Alastair (SNP - Hawick and Denholm)
alastair.cranston@scotborders.gov.uk

Davidson, Vicky (LD - Selkirkshire)
vdavidson@scotborders.gov.uk

Edgar, Gordon (IND - Selkirkshire)
gordon.edgar@scotborders.gov.uk

Fullarton, Jim (CON - East Berwickshire)
jfullarton@scotborders.gov.uk

Gillespie, Iain (IND - Leaderdale and Melrose)
iain.gillespie@scotborders.gov.uk

Greenwell, John (CON - Mid Berwickshire)
john.greenwell@scotborders.gov.uk

Herd, Bill (SNP - Galashiels and District)
bherd@scotborders.gov.uk

Logan, Gavin (CON - Tweedale East)
glogan@scotborders.gov.uk

Marshall, Stuart (IND - Hawick and Denholm)
smarshall@scotborders.gov.uk

McAteer, Watson (IND - Hawick and Denholm)
watson.mcateer@scotborders.gov.uk

Moffat, Donald (SNP - Mid Berwickshire)
dmoffat@scotborders.gov.uk

Mountford, Simon (CON - Kelso and District)
simon.mountford@scotborders.gov.uk

Nicol, Alec (LD - Kelso and District)
anicol@scotborders.gov.uk

Paterson, David (IND - Hawick and Hermitage)
dpaterson@scotborders.gov.uk

Renton, Frances (LD - Mid Berwickshire)
frenton@scotborders.gov.uk

Scott, Sandy (CON - Jedburgh and District)
sandyscott@scotborders.gov.uk

Smith, Ron (LD - Hawick and Hermitage)
rsmith@scotborders.gov.uk

Stewart, Rory (IND - Jedburgh and District)
rory.stewart@scotborders.gov.uk

Torrance, Jim (SNP - Leaderdale and Melrose)
jim.torrance@scotborders.gov.uk

Turnbull, George (CON - Hawick and Hermitage)
gturnbull@scotborders.gov.uk

Weatherston, Tom (CON - Kelso and District)
tweatherston@scotborders.gov.uk

White, Bill (IND - Galashiels and District)
bill.white@scotborders.gov.uk

POLITICAL COMPOSITION

IND: 10, CON: 9, SNP: 9, LD: 6

COMMITTEE CHAIRS

Audit: Ms Michelle Ballantyne

Licensing: Mr Willie Archibald

Pensions: Mr Bill White

Planning & Building Standards: Mr Ron Smith

Standards: Mr Alec Nicol

Sedgemoor D

Sedgemoor District Council, Bridgwater House, King Square, Bridgwater TA6 3AR
☎ 0845 408 2540 🖷 01278 446412 💻 www.sedgemoor.gov.uk

FACTS AND FIGURES

Parliamentary Constituencies: Bridgwater and Somerset West, Wells
EU Constituencies: South West
Election Frequency: Elections are of whole council

PRINCIPAL OFFICERS

Chief Executive: Mr Kerry Rickards, Chief Executive, Bridgwater House, King Square, Bridgwater TA6 3AR ☎ 01278 435423 kerry.rickards@sedgemoor.gov.uk

Senior Management: Mr Doug Bamsey, Corporate Director, Bridgwater House, King Square, Bridgwater TA6 3AR ☎ 01278 435435 doug.bamsey@sedgemoor.gov.uk

Senior Management: Mr Bob Brown, Corporate Director, Bridgwater House, King Square, Bridgwater TA6 3AR ☎ 01278 435327 bob.brown@sedgemoor.gov.uk

Senior Management: Mrs Allison Griffin, Corporate Director, Bridgwater House, King Square, Bridgwater TA6 3AR ☎ 01278 435741 allison.griffin@sedgemoor.gov.uk

Architect, Building / Property Services: Mr Tim Mander, Estates, Property & Valuation Officer, Bridgwater House, King Square, Bridgwater TA6 3AR ☎ 01278 435435 ✉ tim.mander@sedgemoor.gov.uk

Best Value: Mr Robin Starr, Information Officer , Bridgwater House, King Square, Bridgwater TA6 3AR ☎ 01278 435435 ✉ robin.starr@sedgemoor.gov.uk

PR / Communications: Ms Claire Faun, Corporate Relations Manager, Bridgwater House, King Square, Bridgwater TA6 3AR ☎ 01278 435320 ✉ pressoffice@sedgemoor.gov.uk

PR / Communications: Mrs Samantha Taylor , Community Relations Officer, Sedgemoor District Council, King Square, Bridgwater TA6 3AR ☎ 01278 435517 ✉ sam.taylor@sedgemoor.gov.uk

Community Planning: Ms Julie Cooper , Team Leader - Environment and Climate Change, SDC, Bridgwater House, King Square, Bridgwater TA6 3AR ☎ 01278 435425 ✉ julie.cooper@sedgemoor.gov.uk

Community Planning: Mrs Claire Pearce, Group Manager - Strategy & Business Services, Bridgwater House, King Square, Bridgwater TA6 3AR ☎ 01278 435435 ✉ claire.pearce@sedgemoor.gov.uk

Community Safety: Mrs Kristy Blackwell , Community Safety & Environmental Services Officer, Bridgwater House, King Square, Bridgwater TA6 3AR ☎ 01278 435435 ✉ kristy.blackwell@sedgemoor.gov.uk

Computer Management: Mr Paul Davidson, Head - E-Government, Bridgwater House, King Square, Bridgwater TA6 3AR ☎ 01278 435435 ✉ paul.davidson@sedgemoor.gov.uk

Computer Management: Mr Craig Wilkins , Head of Information Systems, Sedgemoor District Council, King Square, Bridgwater TA6 3AR ☎ 01278 435435 ✉ craig.wilkins@sedgemoor.gov.uk

Contracts: Mrs Joanna Hutchins , Procurement Officer, Sedgemoor District Council, King Square, Bridgwater TA6 3AR ☎ 01278 435435 ✉ joanna.hutchins@sedgemoor.gov.uk

Contracts: Ms Melanie Wellman, Group Manager - Legal & Procurement, Bridgwater House, King Square, Bridgwater TA6 3AR ☎ 01278 435435 ✉ melanie.wellman@sedgemoor.gov.uk

Corporate Services: Mr Julian Street , Group Manager, Bridgwater House, King Square, Bridgwater TA6 3AR ☎ 01278 435435 ✉ julian.street@sedgemoor.gov.uk

Customer Service: Mrs Viv Reading , Customer Contact Manager, Sedgemoor District Council, King Square, Bridgwater TA6 3AR ☎ 01278 435435 ✉ viv.reading@sedgemoor.gov.uk

Economic Development: Mrs Claire Pearce, Group Manager - Strategy & Business Services, Bridgwater House, King Square, Bridgwater TA6 3AR ☎ 01278 435435 ✉ claire.pearce@sedgemoor.gov.uk

E-Government: Mr Paul Davidson, Head - E-Government, Bridgwater House, King Square, Bridgwater TA6 3AR ☎ 01278 435435 ✉ paul.davidson@sedgemoor.gov.uk

Electoral Registration: Mrs Louise Potter , Electoral Services Officer, Bridgwater House, King Square, Bridgwater TA6 3AR ☎ 01278 435435 ✉ louise.potter@sedgemoor.gov.uk

Emergency Planning: Mrs Sarah Dowden , Team Leader - Food and Safety, Bridgwater House, King Square, Bridgwater TA6 3AR ☎ 01278 435748 ✉ sarah.dowden@sedgemoor.gov.uk

Energy Management: Mr David Baxter, Street Housing Manager, Bridgwater House, King Square, Bridgwater TA6 3AR ☎ 01278 435435 ✉ david.baxter@sedgemoor.gov.uk

Energy Management: Ms Julie Cooper , Team Leader- Environment and Climate change, SDC, Bridgwater House, King Square, Bridgwater TA6 3AR ☎ 01278 435435 ✉ julie.cooper@sedgemoor.gov.uk

Environmental / Technical Services: Mr Adrian Gardner, Group Manager - Environmental Health, Bridgwater House, King Square, Bridgwater TA6 3AR ☎ 01278 435435 ✉ adrian.gardner@sedgemoor.gov.uk

Estates, Property & Valuation: Mr Tim Mander, Estates, Property & Valuation Officer, Bridgwater House, King Square, Bridgwater TA6 3AR ☎ 01278 435435 ✉ tim.mander@sedgemoor.gov.uk

Facilities: Mr Bill Smith , Facilities Manager, Bridgwater House, King Square, Bridgwater TA6 3AR ☎ 01278 435435 ✉ bill.smith@sedgemoor.gov.uk

Finance: Mrs Alison Turner, Group Finance & Section 151 Manager, Bridgwater House, King Square, Bridgwater TA6 3AR ☎ 01278 435426 ✉ alison.turner@sedgemoor.gov.uk

Fleet Management: Mr Bob Kondys, Transport Supervisor, Bridgwater House, King Square, Bridgwater TA6 3AR ☎ 01278 435435 ✉ bob.kondys@sedgemoor.gov.uk

Grounds Maintenance: Mr Richard Stokes, Interim Operations Manager - Clear Surroundings, Bridgwater House, King Square, Bridgwater TA6 3AR ☎ 01278 435435 ✉ richard.stokes@sedgemoor.gov.uk

Health and Safety: Mr Derrick Cox, Corporate Health & Safety Officer, Bridgwater House, King Square, Bridgwater TA6 3AR ☎ 01278 435435 ✉ derrick.cox@sedgemoor.gov.uk

Home Energy Conservation: Mr David Baxter, Street Housing Manager, Bridgwater House, King Square, Bridgwater TA6 3AR ☎ 01278 435435 ✉ david.baxter@sedgemoor.gov.uk

Home Energy Conservation: Ms Julie Cooper , Team Leader Stronger Communities and Environment, Sedgemoor District Council, King Square, Bridgwater TA6 3AR ☎ 01278 435435 ✉ julie.cooper@sedgemoor.gov.uk

Housing: Mr David Baxter, Street Housing Manager, Bridgwater House, King Square, Bridgwater TA6 3AR ☎ 01278 435435 ✉ david.baxter@sedgemoor.gov.uk

Housing: Mr Adrian Gardner, Group Manager - Environmental Health, Bridgwater House, King Square, Bridgwater TA6 3AR ☎ 01278 435435 ✉ adrian.gardner@sedgemoor.gov.uk

Housing Maintenance: Mr Stephen Bennett, Partnering Manager, Bridgwater House, King Square, Bridgwater TA6 3AR ✉ stephen.bennett@sedgemoor.gov.uk

Legal: Ms Melanie Wellman, Group Manager - Legal & Procurement, Bridgwater House, King Square, Bridgwater TA6 3AR ☎ 01278 435435 ✉ melanie.wellman@sedgemoor.gov.uk

Leisure and Cultural Services: Mr Scott Mason, Parks Project Officer, Bridgwater House, King Square, Bridgwater TA6 3AR ☎ 01278 435435 ✉ scott.mason@sedgemoor.gov.uk

Licensing: Mr Alan Weldon, Licensing and Fraud Manager, Bridgwater House, King Square, Bridgwater TA6 3AR ☎ 01278 435435 ✉ alan.weldon@sedgemoor.gov.uk

Member Services: Mr Andrew Melhuish , Democratic Services Team Leader, Sedgemoor District Council, King Square, Bridgwater TA6 3AR ☎ 01278 435435 ✉ andrew.melhuish@sedgemoor.gov.uk

Parking: Mr Tom Dougall , Transportation Officer, Bridgwater House, King Square, Bridgwater TA6 3AR ☎ 01278 435435 ✉ tom.dougal@sedgemoor.gov.uk

Personnel / HR: Mrs Clare Johnson, Training & Development Manager, Bridgwater House, King Square, Bridgwater TA6 3AR ☎ 01278 435435 ✉ clare.johnson@sedgemoor.gov.uk

Planning: Mr Stuart Houlet , Service Manager, Bridgwater House, King Square, Bridgwater TA6 3AR ☎ 01278 435435 ✉ stuart.houlet@sedgemoor.gov.uk

Planning: Mrs Claire Pearce, Group Manager - Strategy & Business Services, Bridgwater House, King Square, Bridgwater TA6 3AR ☎ 01278 435435 ✉ claire.pearce@sedgemoor.gov.uk

Procurement: Ms Melanie Wellman, Group Manager - Legal & Procurement, Bridgwater House, King Square, Bridgwater TA6 3AR ☎ 01278 435435 ✉ melanie.wellman@sedgemoor.gov.uk

Recycling & Waste Minimisation: Mr Adrian Gardner, Group Manager - Environmental Health, Bridgwater House, King Square, Bridgwater TA6 3AR ☎ 01278 435435 ✉ adrian.gardner@sedgemoor.gov.uk

Regeneration: Mr Doug Bamsey, Corporate Director, Bridgwater House, King Square, Bridgwater TA6 3AR ☎ 01278 435435 ✉ doug.bamsey@sedgemoor.gov.uk

Staff Training: Mrs Caroline Derrick , Training & Development Manager, Bridgwater House, King Square, Bridgwater TA6 3AR ☎ 01278 435435 ✉ caroline.derrick@sedgemoor.gov.uk

Sustainable Communities: Ms Julie Cooper , Team Leader Stronger Communities and Environment, Bridgwater House, King Square, Bridgwater TA6 3AR ☎ 01278 435435 ✉ julie.cooper@sedgemoor.gov.uk

Sustainable Development: Mrs Claire Pearce, Group Manager - Strategy & Business Services, Bridgwater House, King Square, Bridgwater TA6 3AR ☎ 01278 435435 ✉ claire.pearce@sedgemoor.gov.uk

Tourism: Mrs Victoria Banham , Tourism Officer, Bridgwater House, King Square, Bridgwater TA6 3AR ☎ 01278 435435 ✉ victoria.banham@sedgemoor.gov.uk

Town Centre: Mrs Allison Griffin , Corporate Director, Sedgemoor District Council, King Square, Bridgwater TA6 3AR ☎ 01278 435435 ✉ allison.griffin@sedgemoor.gov.uk

Transport: Mr Bob Kondys, Transport Supervisor, Bridgwater House, King Square, Bridgwater TA6 3AR ☎ 01278 435435 ✉ bob.kondys@sedgemoor.gov.uk

Transport Planner: Mr Tom Dougall , Transportation Officer, Bridgwater House, King Square, Bridgwater TA6 3AR ☎ 01278 435435 ✉ tom.dougal@sedgemoor.gov.uk

Waste Collection and Disposal: Mr Adrian Gardner, Group Manager - Environmental Health, Bridgwater House, King Square, Bridgwater TA6 3AR ☎ 01278 435435 ✉ adrian.gardner@sedgemoor.gov.uk

Waste Management: Mr Adrian Gardner, Group Manager - Environmental Health, Bridgwater House, King Square, Bridgwater TA6 3AR ☎ 01278 435435 ✉ adrian.gardner@sedgemoor.gov.uk

Children's Play Areas: Mr Scott Mason, Parks Project Officer, Bridgwater House, King Square, Bridgwater TA6 3AR ☎ 01278 435435 ✉ scott.mason@sedgemoor.gov.uk

Children's Play Areas: Mrs Marina Turner , Parks Officer, Bridgwater House, King Square, Bridgwater TA6 3AR ☎ 01278 435435 ✉ marina.turner@sedgemoor.gov.uk

COUNCILLORS

***Chair* Dyer**, Ian (CON - Cannington & Wembdon)
ian.dyer@sedgemoor.gov.uk

***Vice-Chair* Cresswell**, Mike (CON - Bridgwater Fairfax)
mike.cresswell@sedgemoor.gov.uk

***Leader of the Council* McGinty**, Duncan (CON - East Polden)
duncan.mcginty@sedgemoor.gov.uk

***Deputy Leader of the Council* Hill**, Dawn (CON - Cheddar & Shipham)
dawn.hill@sedgemoor.gov.uk

***Group Leader* Corke**, Lorna (UKIP - Highbridge & Burnham Marine)
lorna.corke@sedgemoor.gov.uk

***Group Leader* Lerry**, Mick (LAB - Bridgwater Victoria)
michael.lerry@sedgemoor.gov.uk

Alder, Derek (CON - King's Isle)
derek.alder@sedgemoor.gov.uk

Bown, Ann (CON - Cannington & Wembdon)
ann.bown@sedgemoor.gov.uk

Bradford, Alan (CON - North Petherton)
alan.bradford@sedgemoor.gov.uk

Brown, Moira (LAB - Bridgwater Eastover)
moira.brown@sedgemoor.gov.uk

Burnett, Cheryl (CON - Burnham North)
cheryl.burnett@sedgemoor.gov.uk

Burridge-Clayton, Peter (CON - Burnham North)
peter.clayton@sedgemoor.gov.uk

Caswell, Rachael (CON - Bridgwater Wyndham)
rachael.caswell@sedgemoor.gov.uk

Caswell, Michael (CON - Quantocks)
michael.caswell@sedgemoor.gov.uk

Clarke, Michael (CON - Burnham Central)
michael.clarke@sedgemoor.gov.uk

Clarke, Maria (CON - Burnham Central)
maria.clarke@sedgemoor.gov.uk

Costello, Polly (CON - Wedmore & Mark)
polly.costello@sedgemoor.gov.uk

Denbee, John (CON - Axevale)
john.denbee@sedgemoor.gov.uk

Downing, Peter (CON - Cheddar & Shipham)
peter.downing@sedgemoor.gov.uk

Duddridge, Lance (CON - Bridgwater Victoria)
lance.duddridge@sedgemoor.gov.uk

Facey, Mike (CON - Burnham Central)
mike.facey@sedgemoor.gov.uk

Filmer, Bob (CON - Knoll)
bob.filmer@sedgemoor.gov.uk

Fraser, Anne (CON - North Petherton)
anne.fraser@sedgemoor.gov.uk

Gilling, Andrew (CON - Knoll)
andrew.gilling@sedgemoor.gov.uk

Glassford, Alex (LAB - Bridgwater Fairfax)
alex.glassford@sedgemoor.gov.uk

Granter, Graham (LAB - Bridgwater Fairfax)
graham.granter@sedgemoor.gov.uk

Grimes, Tony (CON - Berrow)
tony.grimes@sedgemoor.gov.uk

Hamlin, Alison (CON - Puriton & Woolavington)
alison.hamlin@sedgemoor.gov.uk

Healey, Mark (CON - Puriton & Woolavington)
mark.healey@sedgemoor.gov.uk

Herbert, Paul (CON - Burnham North)
paul.herbert@sedgemoor.gov.uk

Hinckes, Wes (LAB - Bridgwater Hamp)
wes.hinckes@sedgemoor.gov.uk

Human, Will (CON - Wedmore & Mark)
will.human@sedgemoor.gov.uk

Keen, Janet (CON - Highbridge & Burnham Marine)
janet.keen@sedgemoor.gov.uk

Keen, Roger (CON - Highbridge & Burnham Marine)
roger.keen@sedgemoor.gov.uk

Kingham, Stuart (CON - West Polden)
stuart.kingham@sedgemoor.gov.uk

Loveridge, Dave (LAB - Bridgwater Eastover)
david.loveridge@sedgemoor.gov.uk

Moore, Adrian (LAB - Bridgwater Hamp)
adrian.moore@sedgemoor.gov.uk

Pay, Julie (CON - Quantocks)
julie.pay@sedgemoor.gov.uk

Pearce, Kathy (LAB - Bridgwater Westover)
kathy.pearce@sedgemoor.gov.uk

Perry, Liz (CON - King's Isle)
liz.perry@sedgemoor.gov.uk

Redman, Leigh (LAB - Bridgwater Dunwear)
leigh.redman@sedgemoor.gov.uk

Revans, Bill (LD - North Petherton)
bill.revans@sedgemoor.gov.uk

Savage, Jeff (CON - Cheddar & Shipham)
jeff.savage@sedgemoor.gov.uk

Scammell, Richard (UKIP - Bridgwater Dunwear)
richard.scammell@sedgmoor.gov.uk

Scott, Liz (CON - Axevale)
liz.scott@sedgemoor.gov.uk

Slocombe, Gill (CON - Bridgwater Wyndham)
gill.slocombe@sedgemoor.gov.uk

Smedley, Brian (LAB - Bridgwater Westover)
brian.smedley@sedgemoor.gov.uk

Woodman, John (CON - Huntspill & Pawlett)
john.woodman@sedgemoor.gov.uk

POLITICAL COMPOSITION

CON: 35, LAB: 10, UKIP: 2, LD: 1

COMMITTEE CHAIRS

Audit & Governance: Ms Julie Pay

Development: Mr Bob Filmer

Licensing & General Purposes: Mr Jeff Savage

Standards: Mr John Woodman

Sefton M

Sefton Metropolitan Borough Council, Town Hall, Southport PR8 1DA

☎ 01704 533133 🖷 0151 934 2293 💻 www.sefton.gov.uk

FACTS AND FIGURES

Parliamentary Constituencies: Bootle, Sefton Central, Southport
EU Constituencies: North West
Election Frequency: Elections are by thirds

PRINCIPAL OFFICERS

Chief Executive: Mrs Margaret Carney , Chief Executive, Town Hall, Southport PR8 1DA ☎ 0151 934 2057 🖷 0151 934 2268 margaret.carney@sefton.gov.uk

SEFTON

Senior Management: Mr Graham Bayliss, Head of Service - Corporate Support, 2nd Floor, Magdalen House, Bootle L20 3NJ ☎ 0151 934 2721 🖷 0151 934 4600 ✉ graham.bayliss@sefton.gov.uk

Senior Management: Mr Jim Black , Head of Service - Locality Services, Hawthorne Road Depot, Hawthorne Road, Bootle L20 9PR ☎ 0151 288 6133 🖷 0151 285 5217 ✉ jim.black@sefton.gov.uk

Senior Management: Mr Dwayne Johnson , Director of Social Care & Health, Merton House, Stanley Road, Bootle L20 3DL ☎ 0151 934 4900 🖷 0151 934 3697 ✉ dwayne.johnson@sefton.gov.uk

Senior Management: Mr Alan Lunt , Head of Service - Regeneration & Housing, Magdalen House, 30 Trinity Road, Bootle L20 3NJ ☎ 0151 934 4580 🖷 0151 934 4876 ✉ alan.lunt@sefton.gov.uk

Senior Management: Mr Colin Pettigrew , Head of Service - Children's Social Care, 9th Floor Merton House, Stanley Road, Bootle L20 3JA ☎ 0151 934 3333 🖷 0151 934 3520 ✉ colin.pettigrew@sefton.gov.uk

Children / Youth Services: Mr Colin Pettigrew , Head of Service - Children's Social Care, 9th Floor Merton House, Stanley Road, Bootle L20 3JA ☎ 0151 934 3333 🖷 0151 934 3520 ✉ colin.pettigrew@sefton.gov.uk

Civil Registration: Ms Jill Coule , Head of Service - Regulation & Compliance, Ground Floor, Magdalen House, 30 Trinity Road, Bootle L20 3NJ ☎ 0151 934 2031 🖷 0151 934 2195 ✉ jill.coule@sefton.gov.uk

Community Safety: Ms Andrea Watts , Head of Service - Communities, Town Hall, Southport PR8 1DA ☎ 0151 934 2030 ✉ andrea.watts@sefton.gov.uk

Computer Management: Ms Margaret Rawding , Head of Finance & ICT Strategy, 4th Floor, Magdalen House, 30 Trinity Road, Bootle L20 3NJ ☎ 0151 934 4082 🖷 0151 934 4560 ✉ margaret.rawding@sefton.gov.uk

Consumer Protection and Trading Standards: Ms Jill Coule, Head of Service - Regulation & Compliance, Ground Floor, Magdalen House, 30 Trinity Road, Bootle L20 3NJ ☎ 0151 934 2031 🖷 0151 934 2195 ✉ jill.coule@sefton.gov.uk

Contracts: Ms Jill Coule , Head of Service - Regulation & Compliance, Ground Floor, Magdalen House, 30 Trinity Road, Bootle L20 3NJ ☎ 0151 934 2031 🖷 0151 934 2195 ✉ jill.coule@sefton.gov.uk

Corporate Services: Mr Graham Bayliss, Head of Service - Corporate Support, Magdalen House, 30 Trinity Road, Bootle L20 3NJ ☎ 0151 934 2721 🖷 0151 934 4600 ✉ graham.bayliss@sefton.gov.uk

Economic Development: Mr Mark Long , Head of Service - Inward Investment & Employment, Investment Centre, 375 Stanley Road, Bootle L20 5EF ☎ 0151 934 3471 🖷 0151 934 3449 ✉ mark.long@sefton.gov.uk

Education: Mr Mike McSorley , Head of Service - Schools & Families, Town Hall, Southport PR8 1DA ☎ 01704 533133 ✉ mike.mcsorley@sefton.gov.uk

Electoral Registration: Ms Jill Coule , Head of Service - Regulation & Compliance, Ground Floor, Magdalen House, 30 Trinity Road, Bootle L20 3NJ ☎ 0151 934 2031 🖷 0151 934 2195 ✉ jill.coule@sefton.gov.uk

Energy Management: Mr Alan Lunt , Head of Service - Regeneration & Housing, Magdalen House, 30 Trinity Road, Bootle L20 3NJ ☎ 0151 934 4580 🖷 0151 934 4876 ✉ alan.lunt@sefton.gov.uk

Environmental / Technical Services: Mr Alan Lunt , Head of Service - Regeneration & Housing, Magdalen House, 30 Trinity Road, Bootle L20 3NJ ☎ 0151 934 4580 🖷 0151 934 4876 ✉ alan.lunt@sefton.gov.uk

Environmental Health: Ms Jill Coule , Head of Service - Regulation & Compliance, Ground Floor, Magdalen House, 30 Trinity Road, Bootle L20 3NJ ☎ 0151 934 2031 🖷 0151 934 2195 ✉ jill.coule@sefton.gov.uk

European Liaison: Mr Mark Long , Head of Service - Inward Investment & Employment, Investment Centre, 375 Stanley Road, Bootle L20 5EF ☎ 0151 934 3471 🖷 0151 934 3449 ✉ mark.long@sefton.gov.uk

Facilities: Mr Alan Lunt , Head of Service - Regeneration & Housing, Magdalen House, 30 Trinity Road, Bootle L20 3NJ ☎ 0151 934 4580 🖷 0151 934 4876 ✉ alan.lunt@sefton.gov.uk

Finance: Ms Margaret Rawding , Head of Finance & ICT Strategy, 4th Floor, Magdalen House, 30 Trinity Road, Bootle L20 3NJ ☎ 0151 934 4082 🖷 0151 934 4560 ✉ margaret.rawding@sefton.gov.uk

Fleet Management: Mr Jim Black , Head of Service - Locality Services, Hawthorne Road Depot, Hawthorne Road, Bootle L20 9PR ☎ 0151 288 6133 🖷 0151 285 5217 ✉ jim.black@sefton.gov.uk

Health and Safety: Mr Graham Bayliss, Head of Service - Corporate Support, Magdalen House, 30 Trinity Road, Bootle L20 3NJ ☎ 0151 934 2721 🖷 0151 934 4600 ✉ graham.bayliss@sefton.gov.uk

Highways: Mr Jim Black , Head of Service - Locality Services, Hawthorne Road Depot, Hawthorne Road, Bootle L20 9PR ☎ 0151 288 6133 🖷 0151 285 5217 ✉ jim.black@sefton.gov.uk

Legal: Ms Jill Coule , Head of Service - Regulation & Compliance, Ground Floor, Magdalen House, 30 Trinity Road, Bootle L20 3NJ ☎ 0151 934 2031 🖷 0151 934 2195 ✉ jill.coule@sefton.gov.uk

Licensing: Ms Jill Coule , Head of Service - Regulation & Compliance, Ground Floor, Magdalen House, 30 Trinity Road, Bootle L20 3NJ ☎ 0151 934 2031 🖷 0151 934 2195 ✉ jill.coule@sefton.gov.uk

Lifelong Learning: Mr Mike McSorley , Head of Service - Schools & Families, Town Hall, Southport PR8 1DA ☎ 01704 533133 ✉ mike.mcsorley@sefton.gov.uk

Member Services: Ms Jill Coule , Head of Service - Regulation & Compliance, Ground Floor, Magdalen House, 30 Trinity Road, Bootle L20 3NJ ☎ 0151 934 2031 🖷 0151 934 2195 ✉ jill.coule@sefton.gov.uk

Parking: Ms Jill Coule , Head of Service - Regulation & Compliance, Ground Floor, Magdalen House, 30 Trinity Road, Bootle L20 3NJ ☎ 0151 934 2031 🖷 0151 934 2195 ✉ jill.coule@sefton.gov.uk

Personnel / HR: Mr Mark Dale , Head of Corporate Personnel, 2nd Floor, Magdalen House, 30 Trinity Road, Bootle L20 3NJ ☎ 0151 934 3949 🖷 0151 934 3396 ✉ mark.dale@sefton.gov.uk

Planning: Mr Alan Lunt , Head of Service - Regeneration & Housing, Magdalen House, 30 Trinity Road, Bootle L20 3NJ ☎ 0151 934 4580 🖷 0151 934 4876 ✉ alan.lunt@sefton.gov.uk

Procurement: Ms Margaret Rawding , Head of Finance & ICT Strategy, 4th Floor, Magdalen House, 30 Trinity Road, Bootle L20 3NJ ☎ 0151 934 4082 🖷 0151 934 4560 ✉ margaret.rawding@sefton.gov.uk

Public Libraries: Ms Andrea Watts , Head of Service - Communities, Town Hall, Southport PR8 1DA ☎ 0151 934 2030 ✉ andrea.watts@sefton.gov.uk

Recycling & Waste Minimisation: Mr Andrew Walker , Head of Service - Locality Services, Hawthorne Road Depot, Hawthorne Road, Bootle L20 9PR ☎ 0151 288 6159 ✉ andrew.walker@sefton.gov.uk

Regeneration: Mr Alan Lunt , Head of Service - Regeneration & Housing, Magdalen House, 30 Trinity Road, Bootle L20 3NJ ☎ 0151 934 4580 🖷 0151 934 4876 ✉ alan.lunt@sefton.gov.uk

Social Services (Adult): Mr Dwayne Johnson , Director of Social Care & Health, Merton House, Stanley Road, Bootle L20 3DL ☎ 0151 934 4900 🖷 0151 934 3697 ✉ dwayne.johnson@sefton.gov.uk

Social Services (Adult): Ms Tina Wilkins , Head of Service - Adult Social Care, Town Hall, Southport PR8 1DA ☎ 01704 533133 ✉ tina.wilkins@sefton.gov.uk

Social Services (Children): Mr Colin Pettigrew , Head of Service - Children's Social Care, 9th Floor Merton House, Stanley Road, Bootle L20 3JA ☎ 0151 934 3333 🖷 0151 934 3520 ✉ colin.pettigrew@sefton.gov.uk

Staff Training: Mr Mark Dale , Head of Corporate Personnel, 2nd Floor, Magdalen House, 30 Trinity Road, Bootle L20 3NJ ☎ 0151 934 3949 🖷 0151 934 3396 ✉ joan.matthews@sefton.gov.uk; mark.dale@sefton.gov.uk

Sustainable Development: Mr Alan Lunt , Head of Service - Regeneration & Housing, Magdalen House, 30 Trinity Road, Bootle L20 3NJ ☎ 0151 934 4580 🖷 0151 934 4876 ✉ alan.lunt@sefton.gov.uk

Tourism: Mr Mark Long , Head of Service - Inward Investment & Employment, Investment Centre, 375 Stanley Road, Bootle L20 5EF ☎ 0151 934 3471 🖷 0151 934 3449 ✉ mark.long@sefton.gov.uk

Waste Collection and Disposal: Mr Andrew Walker , Head of Service - Locality Services, Hawthorne Road Depot, Hawthorne Road, Bootle L20 9PR ☎ 0151 288 6159 ✉ andrew.walker@sefton.gov.uk

Waste Management: Mr Jim Black , Head of Service - Locality Services, Hawthorne Road Depot, Hawthorne Road, Bootle L20 9PR ☎ 0151 288 6133 🖷 0151 285 5217 ✉ jim.black@sefton.gov.uk

Children's Play Areas: Ms Andrea Watts , Head of Service - Communities, Town Hall, Southport PR8 1DA ☎ 0151 934 2030 ✉ andrea.watts@sefton.gov.uk

COUNCILLORS

***Vice-Chair* Cluskey**, Kevin (LAB - Ford)
kevin.cluskey@councillors.sefton.gov.uk

***Mayor* Kermode**, Stephen (LAB - Park)
stephen.kermode@councillors.sefton.gov.uk

***Leader of the Council* Maher**, Ian (LAB - Netherton and Orrell)
ian.maher@councillors.sefton.gov.uk

***Deputy Leader of the Council* Fairclough**, John (LAB - Linacre)
john.fairclough@councillors.sefton.gov.uk

***Group Leader* Jones**, Terry (CON - Ainsdale)
terry.jones@councillors.sefton.gov.uk

Ashton, Nigel (LD - Meols)
nigel.ashton@councillors.sefton.gov.uk

Atkinson, Marion (LAB - Molyneux)
marion.atkinson@councillors.sefton.gov.uk

Ball, Pat (CON - Dukes)
pat.ball@councillors.sefton.gov.uk

Barton, Jo (LD - Meols)
jo.barton@councillors.sefton.gov.uk

Barton, David (CON - Dukes)
david.barton@councillors.sefton.gov.uk

Bennett, Veronica (LAB - Blundellsands)
veronica.bennett@councillors.sefton.gov.uk

Bennett, Maria (O - Ravenmeols)
maria.bennett@councillors.sefton.gov.uk

Bliss, Harry (CON - Cambridge)
harry.bliss@councillors.sefton.gov.uk

Booth, Mike (LD - Kew)
mike.booth@councillors.sefton.gov.uk

Bradshaw, Susan (LAB - Netherton and Orrell)
susan.bradshaw@councillors.sefton.gov.uk

Brennan, Robert (LAB - Netherton and Orrell)
robert.brennan@councillors.sefton.gov.uk

Brodie-Browne, Iain (LD - Birkdale)
iain.brodie.brown@councillors.sefton.gov.uk

Burns, June (LAB - Park)
june.burns@councillors.sefton.gov.uk

Byrom, Leslie (LAB - Victoria)
les.byrom@councillors.sefton.gov.uk

Carr, Anthony (LAB - Molyneux)
anthony.carr@councillors.sefton.gov.uk

Carragher, Clare (LAB - Manor)
clare.carragher@councillors.sefton.gov.uk

Cummins, Paul (LAB - Church)
paul.cummins@councillors.sefton.gov.uk

SEFTON

Dams, Andy (LAB - Blundellsands)
andy.dams@councillors.sefton.gov.uk

Dawson, Tony (LD - Dukes)
tony.dawson@councillors.sefton.gov.uk

Dodd, John (LD - Meols)
john.dodd@councillors.sefton.gov.uk

Dowd, Peter (LAB - St. Oswald)
peter.dowd@councillors.sefton.gov.uk

Dutton, Denise (CON - Harington)
denise.dutton@councillors.sefton.gov.uk

Fearn, Maureen (LD - Kew)
maureen.fearn@councillors.sefton.gov.uk

Fearn of Southport, Ronnie (LD - Norwood)
libdems@sefton.gov.uk

Friel, Gordon (LAB - Linacre)
gordon.friel@councillors.sefton.gov.uk

Gatherer, Lynn (LAB - Sudell)
lynn.gatherer@councillors.sefton.gov.uk

Grace, Janet (LAB - Victoria)
janet.grace@councillors.sefton.gov.uk

Hale, Tim (LAB - Ravenmeols)
tim.hale@councillors.sefton.gov.uk

Hands, Richard (LD - Birkdale)
richard.hands@councillors.sefton.gov.uk

Hardy, Patricia (LAB - Litherland)
patricia.hardy@councillors.sefton.gov.uk

Hartill, Ted (CON - Ainsdale)
ted.hartill@councillors.sefton.gov.uk

Jamieson, Simon (CON - Harington)
simon.jamieson@councillors.sefton.gov.uk

Keith, Pat (LD - Cambridge)
pat.keith@councillors.sefton.gov.uk

Kelly, John (LAB - Litherland)
john.kelly@councillors.sefton.gov.uk

Kelly, John (LAB - Manor)
john.joseph.kelly@councillors.sefton.gov.uk

Kerrigan, Doreen (LAB - Linacre)
doreen.kerrigan@councillors.sefton.gov.uk

Killen, Nina (LAB - Harington)
nina.killen@councillors.sefton.gov.uk

Lappin, Paulette (LAB - Ford)
paulette.lappin@councillors.sefton.gov.uk

Lewis, Daniel (LD - Norwood)
daniel.lewis@councillors.sefton.gov.uk

Lewis, Daniel (LAB - Blundellsands)
Dan.T.Lewis@councillors.sefton.gov.uk

Mahon, James (LAB - St. Oswald)
james.mahon@councillors.sefton.gov.uk

McGinnity, Steve (LAB - Manor)
steve.mcginnity@councillors.sefton.gov.uk

McGuire, Sue (LD - Cambridge)
sue.mcguire@councillors.sefton.gov.uk

McKinley, Patrick (LAB - Sudell)
patrick.mckinley@councillors.sefton.gov.uk

Moncur, Ian (LAB - Ford)
ian.moncur@councillors.sefton.gov.uk

Murphy, Paula (LAB - Molyneux)
paula.murphy@councillors.sefton.gov.uk

O'Brien, Michael (LAB - Derby)
michael.o'brien@councillors.sefton.gov.uk

Owens, Robert (LAB - Sudell)
robert.owens@councillors.sefton.gov.uk

Page, Catie (LAB - Ravenmeols)
catie.page@councillors.sefton.gov.uk

Preece, Haydn (LD - Ainsdale)
preecehay@aol.com

Robinson, Dave (LAB - Derby)
dave.robinson@councillors.sefton.gov.uk

Roche, Michael (LAB - Victoria)
michael.roche@councillors.sefton.gov.uk

Sayers, John (LAB - Park)
john.sayers@councillors.sefton.gov.uk

Shaw, Simon (LD - Birkdale)
simon.shaw@councillors.sefton.gov.uk

Spencer, Paula (LAB - St. Oswald)
paula.spencer@councillors.sefton.gov.uk

Thompson, Anne (LAB - Derby)
anne.thompson@councillors.sefton.gov.uk

Tweed, Paul (LAB - Litherland)
paul.tweed@councillors.sefton.gov.uk

Veidman, Daren (LAB - Church)
daren.veidman@councillors.sefton.gov.uk

Weavers, Frederick (LD - Kew)
frederick.weavers@councillors.sefton.gov.uk

Webster, Veronica (LAB - Church)
veronica.webster@councillors.sefton.gov.uk

Welsh, Marianne (LD - Norwood)
marianne.welsh@councillors.sefton.gov.uk

POLITICAL COMPOSITION

LAB: 42, LD: 16, CON: 7, O: 1

COMMITTEE CHAIRS

Audit & Governance: Mr Robert Brennan

Licensing & Regulatory: Ms Doreen Kerrigan

Planning: Mr Daren Veidman

Selby D

Selby District Council, Civic Centre, Doncaster Road, Selby YO8 9FT
☎ 01757 705101 🖷 01757 292176
info@selby.gov.uk
www.selby.gov.uk

FACTS AND FIGURES

Parliamentary Constituencies: Selby and Ainsty
EU Constituencies: Yorkshire and the Humber
Election Frequency: Elections are of whole council

PRINCIPAL OFFICERS

Chief Executive: Ms Mary Weastell , Chief Executive - Selby/ Assistant Chief Executive - North Yorkshire, Civic Centre, Doncaster Road, Selby YO8 9FT ☎ 01757 292001 🖷 01757 292035 mweastell@selby.gov.uk

Deputy Chief Executive: Mr Jonathan Lund, Deputy Chief Executive, Civic Centre, Portholme Road, Selby YO8 4SB ☎ 01757 292056 jlund@selby.gov.uk

Senior Management: Mrs Janette Barlow, Director - Access Selby, Civic Centre, Doncaster Road, Selby YO8 9FT ☎ 01757 290220 🖷 01757 292229 jbarlow@selby.gov.uk

Senior Management: Mr Keith Dawson , Director - Access Selby, Civic Centre, Doncaster Road, Selby YO8 9FT ☎ 01757 292053 🖷 01757 292229 kdawson@selby.gov.uk

Senior Management: Mrs Karen Iveson, Executive Director & S151 Officer, Civic Centre, Portholme Road, Selby YO8 4SB ☎ 01757 292056 🖷 01757 292035 kiveson@selby.gov.uk

Senior Management: Mrs Rose Norris , Executive Director, Civic Centre, Doncaster Road, Selby YO8 9FT ☎ 01757 705101 🖷 01757 292035 rnorris@selby.gov.uk

Senior Management: Mr Mark Steward, Managing Director - Access Selby, Civic Centre, Portholme Road, Selby YO8 4SB ☎ 01757 292053 🖷 01757 292229 msteward@selby.gov.uk

Architect, Building / Property Services: Mrs Eileen Scothern , Business Manager, Civic Centre, Doncaster Road, Selby YO8 9FT ☎ 01757 705101 🖷 01757 292229 escothern@selby.gov.uk

Building Control: Mr Les Chapman, Building Control Manager, Suite 2, North Yorkshire Building Control, Coxwold House, Easingwold Business Park, Easingwold, York YO16 3FB ☎ 01347 822703 lchapman@selby.gov.uk

PR / Communications: Mr Mike James , Lead Officer - Marketing & Communications, Civic Centre, Doncaster Road, Selby YO8 9FT ☎ 01757 705101 🖷 01757 292229 mjames@selby.gov.uk

Community Planning: Mrs Rose Norris , Executive Director, Civic Centre, Portholme Road, Selby YO8 4SB ☎ 01757 705101 🖷 01757 292035 rnorris@selby.gov.uk

Computer Management: Mr Glenn Shelley , Business Manager, Civic Centre, Doncaster Road, Selby YO8 9FT ☎ 01757 292007 🖷 01757 292035 gshelley@selby.gov.uk

Contracts: Mr Keith Cadman , Lead Officer - Contracts, Civic Centre, Doncaster Road, Selby YO8 9FT ☎ 01757 705101 🖷 01757 292229 kcadman@selby.gov.uk

Customer Service: Mr Simon Parkinson , Lead Officer - Community Support Team, Civic Centre, Doncaster Road, Selby YO8 9FT ☎ 01757 705101 🖷 01757 292229 sparkinson@selby.gov.uk

Economic Development: Mrs Eileen Scothern , Business Manager, Civic Centre, Doncaster Road, Selby YO8 9FT ☎ 01757 705101 🖷 01757 292229 escothern@selby.gov.uk

E-Government: Mr Chris Smith , Lead Officer - Data & Systems, Civic Centre, Doncaster Road, Selby YO8 9FT ☎ 01757 705101 🖷 01757 292229 csmith@selby.gov.uk

Electoral Registration: Mrs Janice Senior , Business Support Supervisor, Civic Centre, Doncaster Road, Selby YO8 9FT ☎ 01757 705101 🖷 01757 292229 jsenior@selby.gov.uk

Emergency Planning: Mr Dean Richardson, Business Manager, Civic Centre, Doncaster Road, Selby YO8 9FT ☎ 01757 705101 🖷 01757 292229 drichardson@selby.gov.uk

Environmental / Technical Services: Mr Wayne Palmer , Lead Officer - Environmental Health & Housing, Civic Centre, Doncaster Road, Selby YO8 9FT ☎ 01757 705101 🖷 01757 292229 wpalmer@selby.gov.uk

Environmental Health: Mr Wayne Palmer , Lead Officer - Environmental Health & Housing, Civic Centre, Doncaster Road, Selby YO8 9FT ☎ 01757 705101 🖷 01757 292229 wpalmer@selby.gov.uk

Estates, Property & Valuation: Mr Dave Maycock , Lead Officer - Assets, Civic Centre, Doncaster Road, Selby YO8 9FT ☎ 01757 705101 🖷 01757 292229 dmaycock@selby.gov.uk

Finance: Mrs Karen Iveson, Executive Director & S151 Officer, Civic Centre, Portholme Road, Selby YO8 4SB ☎ 01757 292056 🖷 01757 292035 kiveson@selby.gov.uk

Health and Safety: Ms Jackie Humphries , Lead Officer - HR, Civic Centre, Doncaster Road, Selby YO8 9FT ☎ 01757 705101 🖷 01757 292229 jhumphries@selby.gov.uk

Housing: Mr Wayne Palmer , Lead Officer - Environmental Health & Housing, Civic Centre, Doncaster Road, Selby YO8 9FT ☎ 01757 705101 🖷 01757 292229 wpalmer@selby.gov.uk

Housing Maintenance: Mr Dave Maycock , Lead Officer - Assets, Civic Centre, Doncaster Road, Selby YO8 9FT ☎ 01757 705101 🖷 01757 292229 dmaycock@selby.gov.uk

Legal: Mrs Gillian Marshall , Solicitor to the Council, Civic Centre, Doncaster Road, Selby YO8 9FT ☎ 01757 705101 🖷 01757 292229 gmarshall@selby.gov.uk

Leisure and Cultural Services: Mr Keith Cadman , Lead Officer - Contracts, Civic Centre, Doncaster Road, Selby YO8 9FT ☎ 01757 705101 🖷 01757 292229 kcadman@selby.gov.uk

Licensing: Ms Helen McNeil , Lead Officer - Debt Control & Enforcement, Civic Centre, Doncaster Road, Selby YO8 9FT ☎ 01757 705101 🖷 01757 292229 hmcneil@selby.gov.uk

Member Services: Mr Palbinder Mann , Democratic Services Manager, Civic Centre, Doncaster Road, Selby YO8 9FT ☎ 01757 705101 pmann@selby.gov.uk

Parking: Mr Keith Cadman , Lead Officer - Contracts, Civic Centre, Doncaster Road, Selby YO8 9FT ☎ 01757 705101 🖷 01757 292229 kcadman@selby.gov.uk

SELBY

Partnerships: Mr Keith Cadman , Lead Officer - Contracts, Civic Centre, Doncaster Road, Selby YO8 9FT ☎ 01757 705101 🖷 01757 292229 🖱 kcadman@selby.gov.uk

Personnel / HR: Ms Jackie Humphries , Lead Officer - HR, Civic Centre, Doncaster Road, Selby YO8 9FT ☎ 01757 705101 🖷 01757 292229 🖱 jhumphries@selby.gov.uk

Planning: Mr Richard Sunter , Lead Officer - Planning, Civic Centre, Doncaster Road, Selby YO8 9FT ☎ 01757 705101 🖷 01757 292229 🖱 rsunter@selby.gov.uk

Procurement: Mr Keith Cadman , Lead Officer - Contracts, Civic Centre, Doncaster Road, Selby YO8 9FT ☎ 01757 705101 🖷 01757 292229 🖱 kcadman@selby.gov.uk

Recycling & Waste Minimisation: Mr Keith Cadman , Lead Officer - Contracts, Civic Centre, Doncaster Road, Selby YO8 9FT ☎ 01757 705101 🖷 01757 292229 🖱 kcadman@selby.gov.uk

Regeneration: Mrs Eileen Scothern , Business Manager, Civic Centre, Doncaster Road, Selby YO8 9FT ☎ 01757 705101 🖷 01757 292229 🖱 escothern@selby.gov.uk

Staff Training: Ms Jackie Humphries , Lead Officer - HR, Civic Centre, Doncaster Road, Selby YO8 9FT ☎ 01757 705101 🖷 01757 292229 🖱 jhumphries@selby.gov.uk

Street Scene: Mr Keith Cadman , Lead Officer - Contracts, Civic Centre, Doncaster Road, Selby YO8 9FT ☎ 01757 705101 🖷 01757 292229 🖱 kcadman@selby.gov.uk

Waste Collection and Disposal: Mr Keith Cadman , Lead Officer - Contracts, Civic Centre, Doncaster Road, Selby YO8 9FT ☎ 01757 705101 🖷 01757 292229 🖱 kcadman@selby.gov.uk

Waste Management: Mr Keith Cadman , Lead Officer - Contracts, Civic Centre, Doncaster Road, Selby YO8 9FT ☎ 01757 705101 🖷 01757 292229 🖱 kcadman@selby.gov.uk

COUNCILLORS

***Chair* Sweeting**, Richard (CON - Tadcaster) rsweeting@selby.gov.uk

***Leader of the Council* Crane**, Mark (CON - Brayton) mcrane@selby.gov.uk

***Deputy Leader of the Council* Mackman**, John (CON - Monk Fryston with South Milford) jmackman@selby.gov.uk

Arthur, Karl (CON - Derwent) karthur@selby.gov.uk

Buckle, David (CON - Sherburn in Elmet) dbuckle@selby.gov.uk

Casling, Liz (CON - Escrick) cllr.elizabeth.casling@northyorks.gov.uk

Cattanach, John (CON - Cawood with Wistow) jcattanach@Selby.gov.uk

Chilvers, Ian (CON - Brayton) ichilvers@selby.gov.uk

Chilvers, Judith (CON - Selby West) jchilvers@selby.gov.uk

Crawford, Jack (LAB - Byram & Brotherton) jcrawford@selby.gov.uk

Deans, James Thomas (CON - Derwent) jdeans@selby.gov.uk

Duckett, Stephanie (LAB - Barlby Village) sduckett@selby.gov.uk

Ellis, Keith (CON - Appleton Roebuck & Church Fenton) kellis@selby.gov.uk

Hobson, Mel (CON - Sherburn in Elmet) cllrmhobson@selby.gov.uk

Hutchinson, David (CON - South Milford) dhutchinson@selby.gov.uk

Jordan, Mike (CON - Camblesforth & Carlton) mjordan@selby.gov.uk

Lunn, Clifford (CON - Thorpe Willoughby) clunn@selby.gov.uk

Mackay, Donald (CON - Tadcaster) dbain-macay@selby.gov.uk

Marshall, Brian (LAB - Selby East) cllr.brian.marshall@northyorks.gov.uk

McCartney, Mary (IND - Eggborough) mmccartney@selby.gov.uk

Metcalfe, Christopher (CON - Tadcaster) cllr.chris.metcalfe@northyorks.gov.uk

Musgrave, Richard (CON - Appleton Roebuck & Church Fenton) rmusgrave@selby.gov.uk

Nichols, Wendy (LAB - Selby East) wnichols@selby.gov.uk

Packham, Robert (LAB - Sherburn in Elmet) cllrbpackham@selby.gov.uk

Pearson, Christopher (CON - Hambleton) cllr.chris.pearson@northyorks.gov.uk

Peart, Dave (CON - Camblesforth & Carlton) dpeart@selby.gov.uk

Reynolds, Ian (CON - Riccall) cllrireynolds@selby.gov.uk

Shaw-Wright, Jennifer (LAB - Selby West) jshawwright@selby.gov.uk

Thurlow, Anthony Jude (LAB - Selby West)

Welch, Paul (LAB - Selby East) pwelch@selby.gov.uk

White, Debbie (CON - Whitley) dewhite@selby.gov.uk

POLITICAL COMPOSITION

CON: 22, LAB: 8, IND: 1

COMMITTEE CHAIRS

Audit & Governance: Mr Mike Jordan

Licensing: Mr Christopher Pearson

Planning: Mr John Cattanach

Policy Review: Mr James Thomas Deans

Sevenoaks D

Sevenoaks District Council, Council Offices, Argyle Road, Sevenoaks TN13 1HG
☎ 01732 227000 🖷 01732 740693
communications@sevenoaks.gov.uk 💻 www.sevenoaks.gov.uk

FACTS AND FIGURES

Parliamentary Constituencies: Dartford, Sevenoaks, Tonbridge and Malling
EU Constituencies: South East
Election Frequency: Elections are of whole council

PRINCIPAL OFFICERS

Chief Executive: Dr Pav Ramewal, Chief Executive, Council Offices, Argyle Road, Sevenoaks TN13 1HG ☎ 01732 227000 pav.ramewal@sevenoaks.gov.uk

Senior Management: Mrs Lesley Bowles , Chief Officer - Communities & Business, Council Offices, Argyle Road, Sevenoaks TN13 1HG ☎ 01732 227000 lesley.bowles@sevenoaks.gov.uk

Senior Management: Mr Jim Carrington-West , Chief Officer - Corporate Support, Council Offices, Argyle Road, Sevenoaks TN13 1HG ☎ 01732 227000 jim.carrington-west@sevenoaks.gov.uk

Senior Management: Mr Richard Morris , Chief Planning Officer, Council Offices, Argyle Road, Sevenoaks TN13 1HG ☎ 01732 277000 richard.morris@worcester.gov.uk

Senior Management: Ms Christine Nuttall, Chief Officer - Legal & Governance, Council Offices, Argyle Road, Sevenoaks TN13 1HG ☎ 01732 227000 christine.nuttall@sevenoaks.gov.uk

Senior Management: Mr Adrian Rowbotham , Chief Finance Officer, Council Offices, Argyle Road, Sevenoaks TN13 1HG ☎ 01732 227000 adrian.rowbotham@sevenoaks.gov.uk

Senior Management: Mrs Pat Smith, Chief Housing Officer, Council Offices, Argyle Road, Sevenoaks TN13 1HG ☎ 01732 227355 🖷 01732 451332 pat.smith@sevenoaks.gov.uk

Senior Management: Mr Richard Wilson, Chief Officer - Environmental & Operational Services, Council Offices, Argyle Road, Sevenoaks TN13 1HG ☎ 01732 227000 richard.wilson@sevenoaks.gov.uk

Architect, Building / Property Services: Miss Emma Vincent , Property & Facilities Manager, Council Offices, Argyle Road, Sevenoaks TN13 1HG ☎ 01732 227000 emma.vincent@sevenoaks.gov.uk

Building Control: Mr Kevin Tomsett , Head of Parking & Surveying, Council Offices, Argyle Road, Sevenoaks TN13 1HG ☎ 01732 227000 kevin.tomsett@sevenoaks.gov.uk

PR / Communications: Mr Daniel Whitmarsh, Communications & Consultation Manager, Council Offices, Argyle Road, Sevenoaks TN13 1HG ☎ 01732 227000 daniel.whitmarsh@sevenoaks.gov.uk

Community Planning: Mr Alan Whiting, Community Planning & Projects Officer, Council Offices, Argyle Road, Sevenoaks TN13 1HG ☎ 01732 227000 alan.whiting@sevenoaks.gov.uk

Community Safety: Ms Kelly Webb, Community Safety Co-ordinator, Council Offices, Argyle Road, Sevenoaks TN13 1HG ☎ 01732 227000 kelly.webb@sevenoaks.gov.uk

Computer Management: Mr Jim Carrington-West , Chief Officer - Corporate Support, Council Offices, Argyle Road, Sevenoaks TN13 1HG ☎ 01732 227000 jim.carrington-west@sevenoaks.gov.uk

Contracts: Ms Christine Nuttall, Chief Officer - Legal & Governance, Council Offices, Argyle Road, Sevenoaks TN13 1HG ☎ 01732 227000 christine.nuttall@sevenoaks.gov.uk

Customer Service: Mrs Amy Wilton , Contact Centre Manager, Council Offices, Argyle Road, Sevenoaks TN13 1HG ☎ 01732 227000 amy.wilton@sevenoaks.gov.uk

Direct Labour: Mr Ian Finch , Head of Direct Services, Sevenoaks Direct Services, Dunbrik Depot, 2 Main Road, Sundridge, Sevenoaks TN14 6EP ☎ 01732 227000 ian.finch@sevenoaks.gov.uk

Economic Development: Mr Mark Bradbury , Head of Economic Development, Council Offices, Argyle Road, Sevenoaks TN13 1HG ☎ 01732 227000 mark.bradbury@sevenoaks.gov.uk

Electoral Registration: Mr Christian Everett , Electoral Services Manager, Council Offices, Argyle Road, Sevenoaks TN13 1HG ☎ 01732 227000 christian.everett@sevenoaks.gov.uk

Emergency Planning: Mr Kevin Tomsett , Head of Parking & Surveying, Council Offices, Argyle Road, Sevenoaks TN13 1HG ☎ 01732 227000 kevin.tomsett@sevenoaks.gov.uk

Environmental / Technical Services: Mr Richard Wilson, Chief Officer - Environmental & Operational Services, Council Offices, Argyle Road, Sevenoaks TN13 1HG ☎ 01732 227000 richard.wilson@sevenoaks.gov.uk

Environmental Health: Mrs Annie Sargent, Environmental Health Manager, Dartford Borough Council, Civic Centre, Home Gardens, Dartford DA1 1DR ☎ 01322 343434 🖷 01322 343422 annie.sargent@dartford.gov.uk

Estates, Property & Valuation: Mr Mark Bradbury , Head of Economic Development, Council Offices, Argyle Road, Sevenoaks TN13 1HG ☎ 01732 227000 mark.bradbury@sevenoaks.gov.uk

Facilities: Miss Emma Vincent , Property & Facilities Manager, Council Offices, Argyle Road, Sevenoaks TN13 1HG ☎ 01732 227000 emma.vincent@sevenoaks.gov.uk

Finance: Mr Adrian Rowbotham , Chief Finance Officer, Council Offices, Argyle Road, Sevenoaks TN13 1HG ☎ 01732 227000 adrian.rowbotham@sevenoaks.gov.uk

Grounds Maintenance: Mr David Boorman , Senior Parking & Amenities Officer, Council Offices, Argyle Road, Sevenoaks TN13 1HG ☎ 01732 227000 david.boorman@sevenoaks.gov.uk

Health and Safety: Mr Richard Wilson, Chief Officer - Environmental & Operational Services, Council Offices, Argyle Road, Sevenoaks TN13 1HG ☎ 01732 227000 richard.wilson@sevenoaks.gov.uk

Home Energy Conservation: Mr Daniel Shaw , Energy Conservation & Initiatives Officer, Council Offices, Argyle Road, Sevenoaks TN13 1HG ☎ 01732 227000 ✉ daniel.shaw@sevenoaks.gov.uk

Housing: Mrs Pat Smith, Chief Housing Officer, Council Offices, Argyle Road, Sevenoaks TN13 1HG ☎ 01732 227355 🖷 01732 451332 ✉ pat.smith@sevenoaks.gov.uk

Local Area Agreement: Mrs Lesley Bowles , Chief Officer - Communities & Business, Council Offices, Argyle Road, Sevenoaks TN13 1HG ☎ 01732 227000 ✉ lesley.bowles@sevenoaks.gov.uk

Legal: Ms Christine Nuttall, Chief Officer - Legal & Governance, Council Offices, Argyle Road, Sevenoaks TN13 1HG ☎ 01732 227000 ✉ christine.nuttall@sevenoaks.gov.uk

Leisure and Cultural Services: Mrs Hayley Brooks , Health & Leisure Manager, Council Offices, Argyle Road, Sevenoaks TN13 1HG ☎ 01732 227000 ✉ hayley.brooks@sevenoaks.gov.uk

Licensing: Mrs Claire Perry , Licensing Partnership Manager, Council Offices, Argyle Road, Sevenoaks TN13 1HG ☎ 01732 227325; 07970 731616 ✉ claire.perry@tunbridgewells.gov.uk

Lottery Funding, Charity and Voluntary: Mrs Lesley Bowles , Chief Officer - Communities & Business, Council Offices, Argyle Road, Sevenoaks TN13 1HG ☎ 01732 227000 ✉ lesley.bowles@sevenoaks.gov.uk

Member Services: Mrs Philippa Gibbs , Democratic Services Manager, Council Offices, Argyle Road, Sevenoaks TN13 1HG ☎ 01732 227000 ✉ philippa.gibbs@sevenoaks.gov.uk

Parking: Mr John Strachan , Parking Manager, Council Offices, Argyle Road, Sevenoaks TN13 1HG ☎ 01732 227000 ✉ john.strachan@sevenoaks.gov.uk

Personnel / HR: Mrs Nuala Beattie , Human Resources Manager, Council Offices, Argyle Road, Sevenoaks TN13 1HG ☎ 01732 227000 ✉ nuala.beattie@sevenoaks.gov.uk

Planning: Mr Richard Morris , Chief Planning Officer, Council Offices, Argyle Road, Sevenoaks TN13 1HG ☎ 01732 277000 ✉ richard.morris@worcester.gov.uk

Procurement: Mr Bami Cole, Audit, Risk & Anti-Fraud Manager, Dartford Borough Council, Civic Centre, Home Gardens, Dartford DA1 1DR ☎ ; 01322 343023 ✉ ; bami.cole@dartford.gov.uk

Recycling & Waste Minimisation: Mr Ian Finch , Head of Direct Services, Sevenoaks Direct Services, Dunbrik Depot, 2 Main Road, Sundridge, Sevenoaks TN14 6EP ☎ 01732 227000 ✉ ian.finch@sevenoaks.gov.uk

Staff Training: Mrs Nuala Beattie , Human Resources Manager, Council Offices, Argyle Road, Sevenoaks TN13 1HG ☎ 01732 227000 ✉ nuala.beattie@sevenoaks.gov.uk

Street Scene: Mr Ian Finch , Head of Direct Services, Sevenoaks Direct Services, Dunbrik Depot, 2 Main Road, Sundridge, Sevenoaks TN14 6EP ☎ 01732 227000 ✉ ian.finch@sevenoaks.gov.uk

Tourism: Mrs Hayley Brooks , Health & Leisure Manager, Council Offices, Argyle Road, Sevenoaks TN13 1HG ☎ 01732 227000 ✉ hayley.brooks@sevenoaks.gov.uk

Transport: Mr Kenneth Naylor , Transport Manager, Sevenoaks Direct Services, Dunbrik Depot, 2 Main Road, Sundridge, Sevenoaks TN14 6EP ☎ 01959 567000 ✉ kenneth.naylor@sevenoaks.gov.uk

Waste Collection and Disposal: Mr Ian Finch , Head of Direct Services, Sevenoaks Direct Services, Dunbrik Depot, 2 Main Road, Sundridge, Sevenoaks TN14 6EP ☎ 01732 227000 ✉ ian.finch@sevenoaks.gov.uk

Waste Management: Mr Richard Wilson, Chief Officer - Environmental & Operational Services, Council Offices, Argyle Road, Sevenoaks TN13 1HG ☎ 01732 227000 ✉ richard.wilson@sevenoaks.gov.uk

Children's Play Areas: Mr David Boorman , Senior Parking & Amenities Officer, Council Offices, Argyle Road, Sevenoaks TN13 1HG ☎ 01732 227000 ✉ david.boorman@sevenoaks.gov.uk

COUNCILLORS

***Chair* McGarvey**, Philip (CON - Farningham, Horton Kirby & South Darenth)
cllr.mcgarvey@sevenoaks.gov.uk

***Vice-Chair* Raikes**, Simon (CON - Sevenoaks Town & St. John's)
cllr.raikes@sevenoaks.gov.uk

***Leader of the Council* Fleming**, Peter (CON - Sevenoaks Town & St. John's)
cllr.fleming@tory.co.uk

***Deputy Leader of the Council* Lowe**, Michelle (CON - Otford & Shoreham)
cllr.lowe@sevenoaks.gov.uk

Abraham, Lawrence (CON - Hartley & Hodsoll Street)
cllr.abraham@sevenoaks.gov.uk

Ball, Laurence (CON - Swanley White Oak)
cllr.ball@sevenoaks.gov.uk

Barnes, John (CON - Swanley Christchurch & Swanley Village)
cllr.barnes@sevenoaks.gov.uk

Bayley, Kim (CON - Dunton Green & Riverhead)
cllr.bayley@sevenoaks.oov.uk

Bosley, Ian (CON - Fawkham & West Kingsdown)
cllr.bosley@sevenoaks.gov.uk

Bosley, Patricia (CON - Fawkham & West Kingsdown)
cllrp.bosley@sevenoaks.gov.uk

Brookbank, Robert (CON - Swanley Christchurch & Swanley Village)
cllr.brookbank@sevenoaks.gov.uk

Brown, Cameron (CON - Dunton Green & Riverhead)
cllr.brown@sevenoaks.gov.uk

Canet, Merilyn (LD - Sevenoaks Northern)
cllr.canet@sevenoaks.gov.uk

Clack, Graham (CON - Sevenoaks Town & St. John's)
cllr.clack@sevenoaks.gov.uk

Clark, Cameron (CON - Ash & New Ash Green)
cllr.c.clark@sevenoaks.gov.uk

Cooke, Patrick (CON - Penshurst, Forcombe & Chiddingstone)
cllr.cooke@sevenoaks.gov.uk

Dickins, Matthew (CON - Cowden & Hever)
cllr.dickins@sevenoaks.gov.uk

Dyball, Lesley (CON - Swanley St Mary's)
cllr.dyball@sevenoaks.gov.uk

Edwards-Winser, John (CON - Otford & Shoreham)
cllr.edwards-winser@sevenoaks.gov.uk

Esler, Diana (CON - Westerham and Crockham Hill)
cllr.esler@sevenoaks.gov.uk

Eyre, Andrew (CON - Sevenoaks Kippington)
cllr.eyre@sevenoaks.gov.uk

Firth, Anna (CON - Brasted, Chevening & Sundridge)
cllr.firth@sevenoaks.gov.uk

Gaywood, James (CON - Hartley & Hodsoll Street)
cllr.gaywood@sevenoaks.gov.uk

Grint, John (CON - Halstead, Knockholt & Badgers Mount)
cllr.grint@sevenoaks.gov.uk

Halford, James (CON - Swanley White Oak)

Hogarth, Roderick (CON - Seal & Weald)
cllr.hogarth@sevenoaks.gov.uk

Hogg, Michael (LAB - Swanley St. Mary's)
cllr.hogg@sevenoaks.gov.uk

Horwood, Michael (CON - Eynsford)
cllr.horwood@sevenoaks.gov.uk

Hunter, Avril (CON - Sevenoaks Kippington)
cllr.hunter@sevenoaks.gov.uk

Kelly, John (CON - Hartley & Hodsoll Street)
cllr.kelly@sevenoaks.gov.uk

Kitchener, Darren (IND - Hextable)
darrenkitchener@outlook.com

Krogdahl, Jonathan (CON - Sevenoaks Northern)
jkrogdahl@hotmail.com

Lake, Peter (CON - Leigh & Chiddingstone Causeway)
cllr.lake@sevenoaks.gov.uk

Layland, Alan (CON - Edenbridge South & West)
cllr.layland@sevenoaks.gov.uk

Lindsay, Stephen (UKIP - Crockenhill & Well Hill)
cllr.lindsay@sevenoaks.gov.uk

London, James (CON - Brasted, Chevening & Sundridge)
cllr.london@sevenoaks.gov.uk

Maskell, Kevin (CON - Westerham and Crockham Hill)
cllr.maskell@sevenoaks.gov.uk

McArthur, Margot (CON - Edenbridge South & West)
cllr.mcarthur@sevenoaks.gov.uk

McGregor, Stuart (CON - Edenbridge North & East)
cllr.mcgregor@sevenoaks.gov.uk

Morris, Dee (CON - Hextable)
cllr.morris@sevenoaks.gov.uk

Parkin, Faye (CON - Fawkham & West Kingsdown)
cllr.parkin@sevenoaks.gov.uk

Parson, Edward (CON - Sevenoaks Eastern)
cllr.parson@sevenoaks.gov.uk

Pearsall, Claire (CON - Ash & New Ash Green)
cllr.pearsall@sevenoaks.gov.uk

Pett, Alan (CON - Ash & New Ash Green)
cllr.pett@sevenoaks.gov.uk

Piper, Robert (CON - Brasted, Chevening & Sundridge)
cllr.piper@sevenoaks.gov.uk

Purves, Elizabeth (LD - Sevenoaks Eastern)
cllr.purves@sevenoaks.gov.uk

Reay, Simon (CON - Kemsing)
cllr.reay@sevenoaks.gov.uk

Rosen, Nina (CON - Swanley White Oak)
cllr.rosen@sevenoaks.gov.uk

Scholey, John (CON - Edenbridge North & East)
cllr.scholey@sevenoaks.gov.uk

Searles, Tony (CON - Swanley Christchurch & Swanley Villlage)
cllr.searles@sevenoaks.gov.uk

Stack, Lorraine (CON - Kemsing)
cllr.stack@sevenoaks.gov.uk

Tennessee, Ingrid (CON - Farningham, Horton Kirby & South Darenth)
cllr.tennessee@sevenoaks.gov.uk

Thornton, Julia (CON - Seal & Weald)
cllr.thornton@sevenoaks.gov.uk

Williamson, Gary (CON - Halstead, Knockholt & Badgers Mount)
cllr.williamson@sevenoaks.gov.uk

POLITICAL COMPOSITION

CON: 49, LD: 2, UKIP: 1, IND: 1, LAB: 1

COMMITTEE CHAIRS

Audit: Mr John Grint

Development Control: Mr Gary Williamson

Licensing: Mrs Dee Morris

Sheffield City M

Sheffield City Council, Town Hall, Pinstone Street, Sheffield S1 2DB
☎ 0114 273 4567 🖳 www.sheffield.gov.uk

FACTS AND FIGURES

Parliamentary Constituencies: Sheffield Brightside and Hillsborough, Sheffield South East, Sheffield, Central, Sheffield, Hallam, Sheffield, Heeley
EU Constituencies: Yorkshire and the Humber
Election Frequency: Elections are by thirds

PRINCIPAL OFFICERS

Chief Executive: Mr John Mothersole , Chief Executive, Room 126, Town Hall, Pinstone Street, Sheffield S1 2HH ☎ 0114 273 4002 🖷 0114 273 6644 🖰 john.mothersole@sheffield.gov.uk

Senior Management: Mr Simon Green , Executive Director of Place, Room 212, Town Hall, Pinstone Street, Sheffield S1 2HH ☎ 0114 273 4201 🖰 simon.green@sheffield.gov.uk

SHEFFIELD CITY

Senior Management: Mr James Henderson , Director of Policy, Performance & Communications, Town Hall, Pinstone Street, Sheffield S1 2HH ☎ 0114 273 5015 ✉ james.henderson@sheffield.gov.uk

Senior Management: Ms Jayne Ludlam, Executive Director of Children, Young People & Families, Room 140, Town Hall, Pinstone Street, Sheffield S1 2HH ☎ 0114 273 5726 ✉ jayne.ludlam@sheffield.gov.uk

Senior Management: Ms Laraine Manley, Executive Director - Communities, Room 208, Town Hall, Pinstone Street, Sheffield S1 2HH ☎ 0114 273 4300 ✉ laraine.manley@sheffield.gov.uk

Senior Management: Mr Eugene Walker , Interim Executive Director - Resources, Town Hall, Pinstone Street, Sheffield S1 2DB ☎ 0114 273 5167 ✉ eugene.walker@sheffield.gov.uk

Access Officer / Social Services (Disability): Mr Brian Messider, Disability Access Officer, 4th Floor, Howden House, Union Street, Sheffield S1 2SH ☎ 0114 273 4197 ✉ brian.messider@sheffield.gov.uk

Architect, Building / Property Services: Mr Nalin Seneviratne , Director of Capital & Major Projects, 4th Floor, Howden House, 1 Union Street, Sheffield S1 2SH ☎ 0114 205 7017 ✉ nalin.seneviratne@sheffield.gov.uk

Building Control: Mr Ralph Bennett , Chief Building Control Manager, Town Hall, Pinstone Street, Sheffield S1 2DB ☎ 0114 2734485 ✉ ralph.bennett@sheffield.gov.uk

Catering Services: Mr Mark Cummins, Operations Manager, Town Hall, Pinstone Street, Sheffield S1 2HH ☎ 0114 273 4537 ✉ mark.cummins@kier.gov.uk

Children / Youth Services: Ms Jayne Ludlam, Executive Director of Children, Young People & Families, Room 140, Town Hall, Pinstone Street, Sheffield S1 2HH ☎ 0114 273 5726 ✉ jayne.ludlam@sheffield.gov.uk

Civil Registration: Mrs Samantha Williams , Register Office Manager, Town Hall, Pinstone Street, Sheffield S1 2DB ☎ 0114 203 9434 🖷 0114 275 9965 ✉ samantha.williams@sheffield.gov.uk

PR / Communications: Mr James Henderson , Director of Policy, Performance & Communications, Town Hall, Pinstone Street, Sheffield S1 2HH ☎ 0114 273 5015 ✉ james.henderson@sheffield.gov.uk

Community Planning: Ms Dawn Shaw , Head of Libraries & Community Services, Floor 9, West Wing, Moorfield Building, 1 Moorfoot, Sheffield S1 4PL ☎ 0114 273 4486 ✉ dawn.shaw@sheffield.gov.uk

Community Safety: Ms Sarah Banks , Head of Safer Communities, New Bank House, Queen Street, Sheffield S1 2WA ☎ 0114 273 6605 ✉ sarah.banks@sheffield.gov.uk

Computer Management: Mrs Aline Hayes , Interim Director of ICT, Town Hall, Pinstone Street, Sheffield S1 2DB ☎ 0114 273 6818 ✉ aline.hayes@sheffield.gov.uk

Consumer Protection and Trading Standards: Mr Philip Glaves , Principal Officer - Consumer Affairs, 2-10 Carbrook Hall Road, Sheffield S9 2DB ☎ 0114 273 6284 ✉ philip.glaves@sheffield.gov.uk

Contracts: Mrs Marianne Betts , Director of Commercial Services, Level 2, North Wing, Morfoot Building, 1 Moorfoot, Sheffield S1 4PL ☎ 0114 205 7303 ✉ marianne.betts@sheffield.gov.uk

Customer Service: Ms Julie Toner, Director of Human Resources, Room 216C, Town Hall, Pinstone Street, Sheffield S1 2HH ☎ 0114 273 4081 ✉ julie.toner@sheffield.gov.uk

Economic Development: Mr Edward Highfield , Director of Creative Sheffield, Fountain Precinct, Balm Green, Sheffield S1 2JA ☎ 0114 223 2349 ✉ edward.highfield@sheffield.gov.uk

Education: Ms Jayne Ludlam, Executive Director of Children, Young People & Families, Room 140, Town Hall, Pinstone Street, Sheffield S1 2HH ☎ 0114 273 5726 ✉ jayne.ludlam@sheffield.gov.uk

Electoral Registration: Mr John Tomlinson , Electoral Services Manager, Room LG42, Town Hall, Pinstone Street, Sheffield S1 2HH ☎ 0114 273 4091 🖷 0114 273 4092 ✉ john.tomlinson@sheffield.gov.uk

Emergency Planning: Mr Keith Bradley , Emergency Planning Officer, Bailey House, Rawmarsh Road, Rotherham S60 1TD ☎ 01709 255356 ✉ keith.bradley@sheffield.gov.uk

Energy Management: Mr Chris Trotter , Energy & Utility Manager, Level 3, East Wing, Morfoot Building, Sheffield S1 4PL ☎ 0114 273 4562 ✉ chris.trotter@sheffield.gov.uk

Environmental / Technical Services: Mr Simon Green , Executive Director of Place, Room 212, Town Hall, Pinstone Street, Sheffield S1 2HH ☎ 0114 273 4201 ✉ simon.green@sheffield.gov.uk

Environmental Health: Mr Mick Crofts , Director of Business Strategy & Regulation, 4th Floor, Howden House, 1 Union Street, Sheffield S1 2SH ☎ 0114 205 5776 ✉ mick.crofts@sheffield.gov.uk

Estates, Property & Valuation: Mr Nalin Seneviratne , Director of Capital & Major Projects, 4th Floor, Howden House, 1 Union Street, Sheffield S1 2SH ☎ 0114 205 7017 ✉ nalin.seneviratne@sheffield.gov.uk

Events Manager: Ms Natasha Wagstaff, Events Manager, Town Hall, Pinstone Street, Sheffield S1 2HH ☎ 0114 273 6620 ✉ natasha.wagstaff@sheffield.gov.uk

Facilities: Mr Neil Dawson , Director - Transport & Facilities Management, Staniforth Road, Sheffield S9 3GZ ☎ 0114 203 7592 ✉ neil.dawson@sheffield.gov.uk

Finance: Mr Eugene Walker , Interim Executive Director - Resources, Town Hall, Pinstone Street, Sheffield S1 2DB ☎ 0114 273 5167 ✉ eugene.walker@sheffield.gov.uk

Fleet Management: Mr Neil Dawson , Director - Transport & Facilities Management, Staniforth Road, Sheffield S9 3GZ ☎ 0114 203 7592 ✉ neil.dawson@sheffield.gov.uk

Grounds Maintenance: Mr Paul Billington , Director of Culture & Environment, 5th Floor, Howden House, Union Street, Sheffield S1 2SH ☎ 0114 273 4700 ✉ paul.billington@sheffield.gov.uk

Health and Safety: Mr Steve Clark, Acting Human Resources Service Manager, Room 205, Town Hall, Pinstone Street, Sheffield S1 2HH ☎ 0114 273 4796 ✉ steve.clark@sheffield.gov.uk

Highways: Mr Steve Robinson , Head of Highway Maintenance, 4th Floor, Howden House, Union Street, Sheffield S1 2SH ☎ 0114 273 5553 ✉ steve.robinson@sheffield.gov.uk

Home Energy Conservation: Mr Robert Almond , Policy & Project Delivery Manager, Level 3, East Wing, Morfoot Building, Sheffield S1 4PL ☎ 0114 273 4193 ✉ robert.almond@sheffield.gov.uk

Housing: Ms Janet Sharpe , Director of Housing & Neighbourhood Service, Floor 9, West Wing, Moorfield Building, 1 Moorfoot, Sheffield S1 4PL ☎ 0114 273 5493 ✉ janet.sharpe@sheffield.gov.uk

Housing Maintenance: Mr Neil Piper , Project Officer, 4th Floor, Howden House, 1 Union Street, Sheffield S1 2SH ☎ 0114 273 4617 ✉ neil.piper@sheffield.gov.uk

Local Area Agreement: Mr David Hewitt , Corporate Performance Officer, Level 3, West Wing, Moorfoot Building, 1 Moorfoot, Sheffield S1 4PL ☎ 0114 273 5773 ✉ david.hewitt@sheffield.gov.uk

Legal: Ms Gillian Duckworth , Director of Legal & Governance / Monitoring Officer, 5th Floor, Howden House, Union Street, Sheffield S1 2SH ☎ 0114 273 4018 ✉ gillian.duckworth@sheffield.gov.uk

Leisure and Cultural Services: Mr Paul Billington , Director of Culture & Environment, Central Library, Surrey Street, Sheffield S1 1XZ ☎ 0114 273 4700 ✉ paul.billington@sheffield.gov.uk

Licensing: Mr Steve Lonnia, Chief Licensing Officer, Block C, Staniforth Road Depot, 609 Staniforth Road, Sheffield S9 3GZ ☎ 0114 205 3798 🖷 0114 273 5003 ✉ stephen.lonnia@sheffield.gov.uk

Lifelong Learning: Mr Tony Tweedy , Director of Lifelong Learning, Skills & Employment, 145 Crookesmoor Road, Sheffield S6 3FP ☎ 0114 229 6140 ✉ tony.tweedy@sheffield.gov.uk

Lighting: Mr Steve Robinson , Head of Highway Maintenance, 4th Floor, Howden House, Union Street, Sheffield S1 2SH ☎ 0114 273 5553 ✉ steve.robinson@sheffield.gov.uk

Lottery Funding, Charity and Voluntary: Ms Dawn Shaw, Head of Libraries & Community Services, Floor 9, West Wing, Moorfield Building, 1 Moorfoot, Sheffield S1 4PL ☎ 0114 273 4486 ✉ dawn.shaw@sheffield.gov.uk

Member Services: Mr Jason Dietsch , Head of Member Services, G13, Town Hall, Pinstone Street, Sheffield S1 2HH ☎ 0114 273 4117 ✉ jason.dietsch@sheffield.gov.uk

Member Services: Mr Paul Robinson , Head of Democratic Services - Council & Members, G13, Town Hall, Pinstone Street, Sheffield S1 2HH ☎ 0114 273 4029 ✉ paul.robinson@sheffield.gov.uk

Parking: Mr Moaz Khan , Interim Head of Transport, Traffic & Parking Services, 5th Floor, Howden House, Union Street, Sheffield S1 2SH ☎ 0114 273 6135 ✉ moaz.khan@sheffield.gov.uk

Partnerships: Mrs Marianne Betts , Director of Commercial Services, Level 2, North Wing, Morfoot Building, 1 Moorfoot, Sheffield S1 4PL ☎ 0114 205 7303 ✉ marianne.betts@sheffield.gov.uk

Personnel / HR: Ms Julie Toner, Director of Human Resources, Room 216C, Town Hall, Pinstone Street, Sheffield S1 2HH ☎ 0114 273 4081 ✉ julie.toner@sheffield.gov.uk

Planning: Mr David Caulfield , Director - Regeneration & Development Services, Floor 5 Howden House, Union Street, Sheffield S1 2SH ☎ 0114 273 5499 ✉ david.caulfield@sheffield.gov.uk

Planning: Mr Simon Green , Executive Director of Place, Room 212, Town Hall, Pinstone Street, Sheffield S1 2HH ☎ 0114 273 4201 ✉ simon.green@sheffield.gov.uk

Procurement: Mrs Marianne Betts , Director of Commercial Services, Level 2, North Wing, Morfoot Building, 1 Moorfoot, Sheffield S1 4PL ☎ 0114 205 7303 ✉ marianne.betts@sheffield.gov.uk

Public Libraries: Ms Dawn Shaw, Head of Libraries & Community Services, Floor 9, West Wing, Moorfield Building, 1 Moorfoot, Sheffield S1 4PL ☎ 0114 273 4486 ✉ dawn.shaw@sheffield.gov.uk

Recycling & Waste Minimisation: Ms Gillian Charters , Head of Waste Management, Town Hall, Pinstone Street, Sheffield S1 2DB ☎ 0114 203 7528 ✉ gillian.charters@sheffield.gov.uk

Regeneration: Mr Simon Ogden , Head of City Development Division, Floor 4, Howden House, 1 Union Street, Sheffield S1 2SH ☎ 0114 273 4189 ✉ simon.ogden@sheffield.gov.uk

Road Safety: Mr Moaz Khan , Interim Head of Transport, Traffic & Parking Services, 5th Floor, Howden House, Union Street, Sheffield S1 2SH ☎ 0114 273 6135 ✉ moaz.khan@sheffield.gov.uk

Social Services: Ms Laraine Manley, Executive Director - Communities, Room 208, Town Hall, Pinstone Street, Sheffield S1 2HH ☎ 0114 273 4300 ✉ laraine.manley@sheffield.gov.uk

Social Services (Adult): Ms Moira Wilson , Interim Director - Care & Support, Floor 9, Moorfoot Building, 1 Moorfoot, Sheffield S1 4PL ☎ 0114 273 4605 ✉ moira.wilson@sheffield.gov.uk

Social Services (Children): Ms Jayne Ludlam, Executive Director of Children, Young People & Families, Room 140, Town Hall, Pinstone Street, Sheffield S1 2HH ☎ 0114 273 5726 ✉ jayne.ludlam@sheffield.gov.uk

Public Health: Dr Stephen Horsley , Interim Director of Public Health, Town Hall, Pinstone Street, Sheffield S1 2DB ☎ 0114 205 7462 ✉ stephen.horsley@sheffield.gcsx.gov.uk

Staff Training: Ms Julie Toner, Director of Human Resources, Room 216C, Town Hall, Pinstone Street, Sheffield S1 2HH ☎ 0114 273 4081 ✉ julie.toner@sheffield.gov.uk

SHEFFIELD CITY

Street Scene: Mr Steve Robinson , Head of Highway Maintenance, 4th Floor, Howden House, Union Street, Sheffield S1 2SH ☎ 0114 273 5553 steve.robinson@sheffield.gov.uk

Sustainable Communities: Ms Laraine Manley, Executive Director - Communities, Room 208, Town Hall, Pinstone Street, Sheffield S1 2HH ☎ 0114 273 4300 laraine.manley@sheffield.gov.uk

Sustainable Development: Mr Nalin Seneviratne , Director of Capital & Major Projects, 4th Floor, Howden House, 1 Union Street, Sheffield S1 2SH ☎ 0114 205 7017 nalin.seneviratne@sheffield.gov.uk

Tourism: Miss Wendy Ulyett , Marketing Manager - Visitor Economy, 11 Broad Street, Sheffield S1 2BQ ☎ 0114 273 4129 wendy.ulyett@sheffield.gov.uk

Town Centre: Mr Richard Eyre , Head of City Centre Management & Major Events, Town Hall, Pinstone Street, Sheffield S1 2HH ☎ 0114 273 4704 richard.eyre@sheffield.gov.uk

Traffic Management: Mr Moaz Khan , Interim Head of Transport, Traffic & Parking Services, 5th Floor, Howden House, Union Street, Sheffield S1 2SH ☎ 0114 273 6135 moaz.khan@sheffield.gov.uk

Transport: Mr Stephen Ash , Assistant Transport Services Manager, Staniforth Road, Sheffield S9 3GZ ☎ 0114 203 7056 stephen.ash@sheffield.gov.uk

Transport Planner: Mr Moaz Khan , Interim Head of Transport, Traffic & Parking Services, 5th Floor, Howden House, Union Street, Sheffield S1 2SH ☎ 0114 273 6135 moaz.khan@sheffield.gov.uk

Waste Collection and Disposal: Ms Gillian Charters , Head of Waste Management, Town Hall, Pinstone Street, Sheffield S1 2DB ☎ 0114 203 7528 gillian.charters@sheffield.gov.uk

Waste Management: Ms Gillian Charters , Head of Waste Management, Town Hall, Pinstone Street, Sheffield S1 2DB ☎ 0114 203 7528 gillian.charters@sheffield.gov.uk

Children's Play Areas: Mr Paul Billington , Director of Culture & Environment, 5th Floor, Howden House, Union Street, Sheffield S1 2SH ☎ 0114 273 4700 paul.billington@sheffield.gov.uk

COUNCILLORS

***The Lord Mayor* Hussain**, Talib (LAB - Burngreave)
talib.hussain@sheffield.gov.uk

***Deputy Lord Mayor* Fox**, Denise (LAB - Birley)
denise.fox@sheffield.gov.uk

***Leader of the Council* Dore**, Julie (LAB - Arbourthorne)
julie.dore@sheffield.gov.uk

***Deputy Leader of the Council* Bramall**, Leigh (LAB - Southey)
leigh.bramall@sheffield.gov.uk

***Group Leader* Clarkson**, Jack (UKIP - Stocksbridge and Upper Don)
jack.clarkson@sheffield.gov.uk

***Group Leader* Murphy**, Robert (GRN - Central)
robert.murphy@sheffield.gov.uk

***Group Leader* Ross**, Colin (LD - Dore and Totley)
colin.ross@sheffield.gov.uk

Akther, Nasima (LAB - Nether Edge)
nasima.akther@sheffield.gov.uk

Alston, Sue (LD - Fulwood)
sue.alston@sheffield.gov.uk

Andrews, Pauline (UKIP - East Ecclesfield)
pauline.andrews@sheffield.gov.uk

Armstrong, Jenny (LAB - Manor Castle)
jennifer.armstrong2@sheffield.gov.uk

Auckland, Ian (LD - Graves Park)
ian.auckland@sheffield.gov.uk

Ayris, Steve (LD - Graves Park)
steve.ayris@sheffield.gov.uk

Baker, David (LD - Stannington)
david.baker@sheffield.gov.uk

Baker, Penny (LD - Ecclesall)
penny.baker@sheffield.gov.uk

Barker, David (LAB - Mosborough)
david.barker@sheffield.gov.uk

Blake, Olivia (LAB - Walkley)
olivia.blake@sheffield.gov.uk

Bond, Nikki (LAB - Nether Edge)
nikki.bond@sheffield.gov.uk

Booker, John (UKIP - West Ecclesfield)
john.booker@sheffield.gov.uk

Bowler, Isobel (LAB - Mosborough)
isobel.bowler@sheffield.gov.uk

Campbell, John (LAB - Richmond)
john.campbell@sheffield.gov.uk

Condliffe, Katie (LD - Stannington)
katie.condliffe@sheffield.gov.uk

Constance, Sheila (LAB - Firth Park)
sheila.constance@sheffield.gov.uk

Crowther, Richard (LAB - Stocksbridge and Upper Don)
richard.crowther@sheffield.gov.uk

Curran, Ben (LAB - Walkley)
ben.curran@sheffield.gov.uk

Dagnall, Lewis (LAB - Central)
lewis.dagnall@sheffield.gov.uk

Damms, Tony (LAB - Southey)
anthony.damms@sheffield.gov.uk

Davis, Keith (UKIP - Stocksbridge and Upper Don)
keith.davis@sheffield.gov.uk

Davison, Roger (LD - Ecclesall)
roger.davison@sheffield.gov.uk

Downing, Tony (LAB - Mosborough)
tony.downing@sheffield.gov.uk

Drabble, Mike (LAB - Arbourthorne)
mike.drabble@sheffield.gov.uk

Drayton, Jackie (LAB - Burngreave)
jackie.drayton@sheffield.gov.uk

Dunn, Jayne (LAB - Broomhill)
jayne.dunn@sheffield.gov.uk

Fox, Terry (LAB - Manor Castle)
terry.fox2@sheffield.gov.uk

Frost, Rob (LD - Crookes)
rob.frost@sheffield.gov.uk

Furniss, Gill (LAB - Southey)
gill.furniss@sheffield.gov.uk

Gibson, Neale (LAB - Walkley)
neale.gibson@sheffield.gov.uk

Gledhill, Julie (LAB - Beauchief and Greenhill)
julie.gledhill@sheffield.gov.uk

Hurst, Adam (LAB - West Ecclesfield)
adam.hurst@sheffield.gov.uk

Hurst, Dianne (LAB - Darnall)
dianne.hurst@sheffield.gov.uk

Hussain, Ibrar (LAB - Burngreave)
ibrar.hussain@sheffield.gov.uk

Iqbal, Mazher (LAB - Darnall)
mazher.iqbal@sheffield.gov.uk

Johnson, Bob (LAB - Hillsborough)
robert.johnson2@sheffield.gov.uk

Jones, Steve (LAB - Gleadless Valley)
steve.jones@sheffield.gov.uk

Law, Alan (LAB - Firth Park)
alan.law@sheffield.gov.uk

Lea, Mary (LAB - Darnall)
mary.lea@sheffield.gov.uk

Lindars-Hammond, George (LAB - Hillsborough)
george.lindars-hammond@sheffield.gov.uk

Lodge, Bryan (LAB - Birley)
bryan.lodge@sheffield.gov.uk

Marken, Aodan (GRN - Broomhill)
aodan.marken@sheffield.gov.uk

Maroof, Mohammad (LAB - Nether Edge)
mohammad.maroof@sheffield.gov.uk

McDonald, Cate (LAB - Gleadless Valley)
cate.mcdonald@sheffield.gov.uk

McGowen, Karen (LAB - Birley)
karen.mcgowan@sheffield.gov.uk

Midgley, Pat (LAB - Manor Castle)
patricia.midgley@sheffield.gov.uk

Mirfin-Boukouris, Helen (LAB - Beighton)
helen.mirfin-boukouris@sheffield.gov.uk

Mohammed, Shaffaq (LD - Ecclesall)
shaffaq.mohammed@sheffield.gov.uk

Munn, Roy (LAB - Beauchief and Greenhill)
roy.munn@sheffield.gov.uk

Murphy, Anne (LAB - Crookes)
anne.murphy@sheffield.gov.uk

Otten, Joe (LD - Dore and Totley)
joe.otten@sheffield.gov.uk

Paszek, Josie (LAB - Hillsborough)
josie.paszek@sheffield.gov.uk

Peace, Chris (LAB - Gleadless Valley)
chris.peace@sheffield.gov.uk

Price, Peter (LAB - Shiregreen and Brightside)
peter.price@sheffield.gov.uk

Priestley, Vickie (LD - Stannington)
vickie.priestley@sheffield.gov.uk

Reaney, Denise (LD - Graves Park)
denise.reaney@sheffield.gov.uk

Richards, Sioned-Mair (LAB - Shiregreen and Brightside)
sm.richards@sheffield.gov.uk

Rippon, Peter (LAB - Shiregreen and Brightside)
peter.rippon@sheffield.gov.uk

Rooney, Mick (LAB - Woodhouse)
michael.rooney@sheffield.gov.uk

Rooney, Lynn (LAB - Richmond)
lynn.rooney@sheffield.gov.uk

Rosling-Josephs, Chris (LAB - Beighton)
c.rosling-josephs@sheffield.gov.uk

Sangar, Andrew (LD - Fulwood)
andrew.sangar@sheffield.gov.uk

Satur, Ray (LAB - Woodhouse)
raymond.satur@sheffield.gov.uk

Satur, Jackie (LAB - Woodhouse)
jackie.satur@sheffield.gov.uk

Saunders, Ian (LAB - Beighton)
ian.saunders@sheffield.gov.uk

Scott, Jack (LAB - Arbourthorne)
jack.scott@sheffield.gov.uk

Shaw, Richard (LD - Beauchief and Greenhill)
richard.shaw@sheffield.gov.uk

Smalley, Sarah Jane (GRN - Central)
sarahjane.smalley@sheffield.gov.uk

Smith, Martin (LD - Dore and Totley)
martin.smith@sheffield.gov.uk

Smith, Geoff (LAB - Crookes)
geoff.smith2@sheffield.gov.uk

Sykes, Zoe (LAB - West Ecclesfield)
zoe.sykes@sheffield.gov.uk

Weatherall, Gary (LAB - Firth Park)
garry.weatherall@sheffield.gov.uk

Webster, Brian (GRN - Broomhill)
brian.webster@sheffield.gov.uk

Wilson, Steve (LAB - East Ecclesfield)
steven.wilson@sheffield.gov.uk

Wood, Paul (LAB - Richmond)
paul.wood3@sheffield.gov.uk

Woodcraft, Cliff (LD - Fulwood) cliff.woodcraft@sheffield.gov.uk

Wright, Joyce (LAB - East Ecclesfield)
joyce.wright@sheffield.gov.uk

POLITICAL COMPOSITION

LAB: 59, LD: 17, GRN: 4, UKIP: 4

COMMITTEE CHAIRS

Audit: Mr Steve Jones

Standards: Mr Bryan Lodge

Shepway D

Shepway District Council, Civic Centre, Castle Hill Avenue, Folkestone CT20 2QY
☎ 01303 853000 🖷 01303 245978 ✉ sdc@shepway.gov.uk
💻 www.shepway.gov.uk

FACTS AND FIGURES

Parliamentary Constituencies: Folkestone and Hythe
EU Constituencies: South East
Election Frequency: Elections are of whole council

PRINCIPAL OFFICERS

Chief Executive: Mr Alistair Stewart, Chief Executive, Civic Centre, Castle Hill Avenue, Folkestone CT20 2QY ☎ 01303 853203 🖷 01303 853255 ✉ alistair.stewart@shepway.gov.uk

Deputy Chief Executive: Ms Kathryn Beldon, Deputy Chief Executive, Civic Centre, Castle Hill Avenue, Folkestone CT20 2QY ☎ 01303 853263 🖷 01303 853293 ✉ kathryn.beldon@shepway.gov.uk

Senior Management: Dr Susan Priest , Corporate Director - Operations, Civic Centre, Castle Hill Avenue, Folkestone CT20 2QY

Architect, Building / Property Services: Mr Paul Marshall , Estate Management Officer, Civic Centre, Castle Hill Avenue, Folkestone CT20 2QY ☎ 01303 853439 🖷 01303 245978 ✉ paul.marshall@shepway.gov.uk

Building Control: Mr Nick Lewington , Principal Building Control Officer, Civic Centre, Castle Hill Avenue, Folkestone CT20 2QY ☎ 01303 853478 🖷 01303 258288 ✉ nick.lewington@shepway.gov.uk

Children / Youth Services: Mrs Tamasin Jarrett, Community Development Officer, Civic Centre, Castle Hill Avenue, Folkestone CT20 2QY ☎ 01303 853277 🖷 01303 853502 ✉ tamasin.jarrett@shepway.gov.uk

PR / Communications: Ms Sandy Fleming , Media Officer, Civic Centre, Castle Hill Avenue, Folkestone CT20 2QY ☎ 01303 853507 🖷 01303 245978 ✉ sandy.fleming@shepway.gov.uk

Community Planning: Mr Christopher Lewis , Head of Planning Services, Civic Centre, Castle Hill Avenue, Folkestone CT20 2QY ☎ 01303 853456 🖷 01303 858288 ✉ chris.lewis@shepway.gov.uk

Community Safety: Ms Jyotsna Leney, Community Safety Manager, Civic Centre, Castle Hill Avenue, Folkestone CT20 2QY ☎ 01303 853460 🖷 01303 853388 ✉ jyotsna.leney@shepway.gov.uk

Computer Management: Mr Steve Makin , ICT Contacts Officer, Civic Centre, Castle Hill Avenue, Folkestone CT20 2QY ☎ 01303 853541 🖷 01303 853412 ✉ steve.makin@shepway.gov.uk

Consumer Protection and Trading Standards: Mr Steve Courts , Principal Environmental Health Officer, Civic Centre, Castle Hill Avenue, Folkestone CT20 2QY ☎ 01303 853295 ✉ steve.courts@shepway.gov.uk

Contracts: Mr Andy Rush , Corporate Contracts Manager, Civic Centre, Castle Hill Avenue, Folkestone CT20 2QY ☎ 01303 853271 🖷 01303 254978 ✉ andy.rush@shepway.gov.uk

Corporate Services: Mr Jeremy Chambers , Corporate Director - Strategic Operations, Civic Centre, Castle Hill Avenue, Folkestone CT20 2QY ☎ 01303 853263 🖷 01303 853255 ✉ jeremy.chambers@shepway.gov.uk

Customer Service: Mr Jason Couch , Head of Customer Contact, Civic Centre, Castle Hill Avenue, Folkestone CT20 2QY ☎ 01303 853678 🖷 01303 245978 ✉ jason.couch@shepway.gov.uk

Economic Development: Mr David Shore, Planning Policy & Economic Development Manager, Civic Centre, Castle Hill Avenue, Folkestone CT20 2QY ☎ 01303 853459 🖷 01303 853502 ✉ david.shore@shepway.gov.uk

Emergency Planning: Miss Amy Golder , Policy Assistant, Civic Centre, Castle Hill Avenue, Folkestone CT20 2QY ☎ 01303 853254 🖷 01303 245978 ✉ amy.golder@shepway.gov.uk

Environmental / Technical Services: Mr Roger Walton , Head of Environmental Services, Civic Centre, Castle Hill Avenue, Folkestone CT20 2QY ☎ 01303 247385 🖷 01303 247385 ✉ roger.walton@shepway.gov.uk

Environmental Health: Mr Arthur Atkins, Principal Environmental Health Officer, Civic Centre, Castle Hill Avenue, Folkestone CT20 2QY ☎ 01303 853242 🖷 01303 852294 ✉ arthur.atkins@shepway.gov.uk

Facilities: Mrs Sarah House , Senior Front Office Officer, Civic Centre, Castle Hill Avenue, Folkestone CT20 2QY ☎ 01303 853336 ✉ sarah.house@shepway.gov.uk

Finance: Mrs Odette Collard-Woolmer , Head of Finance, Civic Centre, Castle Hill Avenue, Folkestone CT20 2QY ☎ 01303 853371 ✉ odette.collard-woolmer@shepway.gov.uk

Housing: Mr Bob Porter , Head of Communities, Civic Centre, Castle Hill Avenue, Folkestone CT20 2QY ☎ 01303 853333 🖷 01303 853774 ✉ bob.porter@shepway.gov.uk

Legal: Ms Estelle Culligan , Legal Services Manager, Civic Centre, Castle Hill Avenue, Folkestone CT20 2QY ☎ 01303 853539 🖷 01303 853388 ✉ estelle.culligan@shepway.gov.uk

Parking: Mr Fred Miller , Transportation Manager, Civic Centre, Castle Hill Avenue, Folkestone CT20 2QY ☎ 01303 853207 🖷 01303 853548 ✉ fred.miller@shepway.gov.uk

Personnel / HR: Mrs Andrina Smith , Strategic HR Manager, Civic Centre, Castle Hill Avenue, Folkestone CT20 2QY ☎ 01303 853405 🖷 01303 245978 ✉ andrina.smith@shepway.gov.uk

Procurement: Mrs Margaret Creed , Procurement Manager, Civic Centre, Castle Hill Avenue, Folkestone CT20 2QY ☎ 01303 853377 🖷 01303 583293 ✉ margaret.creed@shepway.gov.uk

Staff Training: Mrs Jo Gage , HR Business Partner of Organisational Development, Civic Centre, Castle Hill Avenue, Folkestone CT20 2QY ☎ 01303 853322 🖷 01303 245978 ✉ jo.gage@shepway.gov.uk

COUNCILLORS

***Chair* Holben**, Janet (CON - Sandgate & West Folkestone)
janet.holben@shepway.gov.uk

***Vice-Chair* Owen**, David (CON - Hythe)
david.owen@shepway.gov.uk

***Leader of the Council* Monk**, David (CON - Folkestone Central)
david.monk@shepway.gov.uk

***Deputy Leader of the Council* Hollingsbee**, Jennifer (CON - North Downs West)
jennifer.hollingsbee@shepway.gov.uk

***Group Leader* Lawes**, Mary (UKIP - Folkestone Harbour)
mary.lawes@shepway.gov.uk

Berry, Anne (CON - Broadmead)
annecllr.berry@shepway.gov.uk

Carey, Susan (CON - North Downs West)
susan.carey@shepway.gov.uk

Collier, John (CON - Cheriton)
john.collier@shepway.gov.uk

Dearden, Malcolm (CON - Hythe)
malcolm.dearden@shepway.gov.uk

Ewart-James, Alan (CON - Hythe)
alan.ewart-james@shepway.gov.uk

Gane, Peter (CON - Cheriton)
peter.gane@shepway.gov.uk

Goddard, Clive (CON - Walland & Denge Marsh)
clive.goddard@shepway.gov.uk

Godfrey, David (CON - North Downs East)
david.godfrey@shepway.gov.uk

Govett, Susie (UKIP - New Romney)
susie.govett@shepway.gov.uk

Jeffrey, Claire (LAB - East Folkestone)
claire.jeffrey@shepway.gov.uk

Laws, Len (UKIP - Walland & Denge Marsh)
len.laws@shepway.gov.uk

Love, Rory (CON - Sandgate & West Folkestone)
rory.love@shepway.gov.uk

Lyons, Michael (CON - Hythe Rural)
michael.lyons@shepway.gov.uk

Martin, Phillip (CON - North Downs East)
philip.martin@shepway.gov.uk

McKenna, Frank (UKIP - East Folkestone)
frank.mckenna@shepway.gov.uk

Meyers, Ian (UKIP - Romney Marsh)

Pascoe, Richard (CON - Folkestone Central)
richard.pascoe@shepway.gov.uk

Peacock, Paul (CON - Hythe Rural)
paul.peacock@shepway.gov.uk

Peall, Stuart (CON - North Downs East)
stuart.peall@shepway.gov.uk

Robinson, Damon (UKIP - Cheriton)
damon.robinson@shepway.gov.uk

Sacre, Carol (UKIP - East Folkestone)
carolo.sacre@shepway.gov.uk

Simmons, Peter (CON - New Romney)
peter.simmons@shepway.gov.uk

Wallace, Susan (CON - Folkestone Harbour)
susan.wallace@shepway.gov.uk

Wheeler, Rodica (CON - Folkestone Central)
rodica.wheeler@shepway.gov.uk

Wilkins, Roger (CON - Romney Marsh)
roger.wilkins@shepway.gov.uk

POLITICAL COMPOSITION

CON: 22, UKIP: 7, LAB: 1

COMMITTEE CHAIRS

Audit & Standards: Mr Peter Simmons

Development Control: Mr Clive Goddard

Licensing: Mr Michael Lyons

Shetland S

Shetland Islands Council, Office Headquarters, 8 North Ness Business Park, Lerwick ZE1 0LZ
☎ 01595 693535 🖷 01595 744509 ✉ info@shetland.gov.uk
💻 www.shetland.gov.uk

FACTS AND FIGURES

Parliamentary Constituencies: Orkney and Shetland
EU Constituencies: Scotland
Election Frequency: Elections are of whole council

PRINCIPAL OFFICERS

Chief Executive: Mr Mark Boden , Chief Executive, Office Headquarters, 8 North Ness Business park, Lerwick ZE1 0LZ
☎ 01595 744500 ✉ chief.executive@shetland.gov.uk

Architect, Building / Property Services: Mr Robert Sinclair , Executive Manager - Capital Programmes, Office Headquarters, 8 North Ness Business Park, Lerwick ZE1 0LZ ☎ 01595 744144
✉ robert.sinclair@shetland.gov.uk

Architect, Building / Property Services: Mr Carl Symons , Executive Manager - Estate Operations, Gremista, Lerwick ZE1 0PX
☎ 015959 744100 ✉ carl.symons@shetland.gov.uk

Best Value: Mr Crawford McIntyre , Executive Manager - Audit, Risk & Improvement, Office Headquarters, 8 North Ness Business Park, Lerwick ZE1 0LZ ☎ 01595 744546
✉ crawford.mcintyre@shetland.gov.uk

Building Control: Mr Iain McDiarmid, Executive Manager - Planning, Grantfield, Lerwick ZE1 0NT ☎ 01595 744813
🖷 01595 744804 ✉ planning@shetland.gov.uk

Catering Services: Mrs Lynda Duck, Catering & Cleaning Manager, Hayfield House, Hayfield Lane, Lerwick ZE1 0QD
☎ 01595 744129 🖷 01595 744010 ✉ lynda.duck@shetland.gov.uk

SHETLAND

Children / Youth Services: Mrs Helen Budge, Director - Children's Services, Hayfield House, Hayfield Lane, Lerwick ZE1 0QD ☎ 01595 744064 🖷 01595 744010 🖰 helen.budge@shetland.gov.uk

Civil Registration: Mrs Marilyn Williamson, Chief Registrar, Town Hall, Lerwick ZE1 0QD ☎ 01595 744562 🖷 01595 744585 🖰 registrar@shetland.gov.uk

Community Planning: Ms Vaila Simpson , Executive Manager - Community Planning & Development, Solarhus, 3 North Ness Business Park, Lerwick ZE1 0LZ ☎ 01595 744375 🖰 vaila.simpson@shetland.gov.uk

Community Safety: Ms Sara Fox , Community Safety Officer, Office Headquarters, 8 North Ness Business Park, Lerwick ZE1 0LZ 🖰 sara.fox@shetland.gov.uk

Computer Management: Mrs Susan Msalila , Executive Manager - ICT, Garthspool, Lerwick ZE1 0NP ☎ 01595 744763 🖰 susan.msalila@shetland.gov.uk

Consumer Protection and Trading Standards: Mr David Marsh, Service Manager - Trading Standards, Charlotte House, Commercial Road, Lerwick ZE1 0LX ☎ 01595 744862 🖷 01595 744804 🖰 trading.standards@shetland.gov.uk

Contracts: Mr Colin Black, Procurement Manager, Office Headquarters, 8 North Ness Business park, Lerwick ZE1 0LZ ☎ 01595 744595 🖷 ; 01595 744136 🖰 colin.black@shetland.gov.uk

Corporate Services: Ms Christine Ferguson, Director - Corporate Services, Office Headquarters, 8 North Ness Business Park, Lerwick ZE1 0LZ ☎ ; 01595 743819 🖷 ; 01595 744321 🖰 christine.ferguson@shetland.gov.uk

Direct Labour: Mr Carl Symons , Executive Manager - Estate Operations, Gremista, Lerwick ZE1 0PX ☎ 015959 744100 🖰 carl.symons@shetland.gov.uk

Economic Development: Mr Neil Grant, Director - Development Services, Solarhus, 3 North Ness Business Park, Lerwick ZE1 0LZ ☎ ; 01595 744968 🖷 01595 744961 🖰 mail.development@shetland.gov.uk

Education: Mrs Helen Budge, Director - Children's Services, Hayfield House, Hayfield Lane, Lerwick ZE1 0QD ☎ 01595 744064 🖷 01595 744010 🖰 helen.budge@shetland.gov.uk

Electoral Registration: Mr Michael Forbes , Electoral Registration Officer, Charlotte House, Commercial Road, Lerwick, Shetland ZE1 0LX ☎ 01595 745700 🖷 01595 745710 🖰 ero@shetland.gov.uk

Electoral Registration: Mr Jan-Robert Riise, Executive Manager - Governance & Law, Office Headquarters, 8 North Ness Business park, Lerwick ZE1 0LZ ☎ ; 01595 744551 🖷 01595 744585 🖰 legal@shetland.gov.uk

Emergency Planning: Ms Ingrid Gall , Emergency Planning & Resilience Officer, 20 Commercial Road, Lerwick ZE2 0LX ☎ 01595 744740 🖰 emergency.planning@shetland.gov.uk

Energy Management: Mrs Mary Lisk, Environmental Management Officer, Gremista, Lerwick ZE1 0LX ☎ 01595 744818 🖷 ; 01595 744177 🖰 mary.lisk@shetland.gov.uk

Energy Management: Mr John Simpson, Energy Manager, Gremista, Lerwick ZE1 0PX ☎ 01595 744819 🖷 01595 744804 🖰 john.simpson@shetland.gov.uk

Environmental Health: Mrs Margaret Sandison , Director - Infrastructure, Gremista, Lerwick ZE1 0PX ☎ 01595 744841 🖰 margaret.sandison@shetland.gov.uk

European Liaison: Miss Sally Spence, Project Manager, Solarhus 3, North Ness Business Centre, Lerwick ZE1 0LZ ☎ 01595 744915 🖷 01595 744961 🖰 sally.spence@shetland.gov.uk

Events Manager: Ms Nicola Halcrow , Events Co-ordinator, Solarhus 3, North Ness Business Park, Lerwick ZE1 0LZ ☎ 01595 744944 🖷 01595 744961 🖰 nicola.halcrow@shetland.gov.uk

Finance: Mr Steve Whyte , Executive Manager - Finance, Office Headquarters, 8 North Ness Business Park, Lerwick ZE1 0LZ ☎ 01595 744607 🖰 steve.whyte@shetland.gov.uk

Treasury: Mr Steve Whyte , Executive Manager - Finance, Office Headquarters, 8 North Ness Business Park, Lerwick ZE1 0LZ ☎ 01595 744607 🖰 steve.whyte@shetland.gov.uk

Pensions: Ms Mary Smith , Team Leader - Expenditure, Office Headquarters, 8 North Ness Business Park, Lerwick ZE1 0LZ ☎ 01595 744669 🖰 mary.smith@shetland.gov.uk

Fleet Management: Mr Michael Craigie , Executive Manager - Transport Planning, 6 North Ness Business Park, Lerwick ZE1 0LZ ☎ 01595 744160 🖷 01595 744880 🖰 michael.craigie@shetland.gov.uk

Health and Safety: Mrs Fiona Johnson, Safety Manager, Office Headquarters, 8 North Ness Business park, Lerwick ZE1 0LZ ☎ 01595 744567 🖷 01595 744585 🖰 fiona.johnson@shetland.gov.uk

Highways: Mr Dave Coupe , Executive Manager - Roads Maintenance, Gremista, Lerwick ZE1 0PX ☎ 01595 744104 🖰 dave.coupe@shetland.gov.uk

Home Energy Conservation: Mr John Simpson, Energy Manager, Gremista, Lerwick ZE1 0PX ☎ 01595 744819 🖷 01595 744804 🖰 john.simpson@shetland.gov.uk

Housing: Mrs Anita Jamieson , Executive Manager - Housing, 6 North Ness Business Park, Lerwick ZE1 0LZ ☎ 01595 744360 🖷 01595 744395 🖰 housing@shetland.gov.uk

Housing Maintenance: Mrs Anita Jamieson , Executive Manager - Housing, 6 North Ness Business Park, Lerwick ZE1 0LZ ☎ 01595 744360 🖷 01595 744395 🖰 housing@shetland.gov.uk

Legal: Ms Susan Brunton , Team Leader - Legal, Office Headquarters, 8 North Ness Business park, Lerwick ZE1 0LZ ☎ 01595 744550 🖰 susan.brunton@shetland.gov.uk

Leisure and Cultural Services: Mr Neil Watt, Executive Manager - Sport & Leisure, Hayfield House, Hayfield Lane, Lerwick ZE1 0QD ☎ 01595 744046 🖷 01595 744056 🖱 neil.watt@shetland.gov.uk

Licensing: Mr Jan-Robert Riise, Executive Manager - Governance & Law, Office Headquarters, 8 North Ness Business Park, Lerwick ZE1 OLZ ☎ ; 01595 744551 🖷 01595 744585 🖱 legal@shetland.gov.uk

Lifelong Learning: Ms June Porter , Team Leader - Community Development, Office Headquarters, 8 North Ness Business Park, Lerwick ZE1 0LZ ☎ 01595 743880 🖱 june.porter@shetland.gov.uk

Lighting: Mr Dave Coupe , Executive Manager - Roads Maintenance, Gremista, Lerwick ZE1 0PX ☎ 01595 744104 🖱 dave.coupe@shetland.gov.uk

Lighting: Mr Dave Coupe , Executive Manager - Roads Maintenance, Gremista, Lerwick ZE1 0PX ☎ 01595 744104 🖱 dave.coupe@shetland.gov.uk

Member Services: Ms Anita Arthur , Members Support Officer, Town Hall, Lerwick ZE1 0HB ☎ 01595 744505 🖱 leah.colyer@shetland.gov.uk

Parking: Mr Dave Coupe , Executive Manager - Roads Maintenance, Gremista, Lerwick ZE1 0PX ☎ 01595 744104 🖱 dave.coupe@shetland.gov.uk

Personnel / HR: Ms Denise Bell, Executive Manager - Human Resources, Office Headquarters, 8 North Ness Business park, Lerwick ZE1 0LZ ☎ 01595 744573 🖷 01595 743959 🖱 denise.bell@shetland.gov.uk

Planning: Mr Iain McDiarmid, Executive Manager - Planning, Grantfield, Lerwick ZE1 0NT ☎ ; 01595 744813 🖷 01595 744804 🖱 planning@shetland.gov.uk

Procurement: Mr Colin Black, Procurement Manager, Office Headquarters, 8 North Ness Business park, Lerwick ZE1 0LZ ☎ 01595 744595 🖷 ; 01595 744136 🖱 colin.black@shetland.gov.uk

Public Libraries: Ms Karen Fraser , Library & Information Services Manager, Shetland Libary, Lower Hillhead, Lerwick ZE1 0EL ☎ 01595 743868 🖱 karen.fraser@shetland.gov.uk

Recycling & Waste Minimisation: Mrs Mary Lisk, Environmental Management Officer, Grantfield, Lerwick ZE1 0NT ☎ 01595 744818 🖷 ; 01595 744177 🖱 mary.lisk@shetland.gov.uk

Regeneration: Mr Neil Grant, Director - Development Services, Office Headquarters, 8 North Ness Business Park, Lerwick ZE1 0LZ ☎ 01595 744968 🖷 01595 744961 🖱 mail.development@shetland.gov.uk

Road Safety: Mr Dave Coupe , Executive Manager - Roads Maintenance, Gremista, Lerwick ZE1 0PX ☎ 01595 744104 🖱 dave.coupe@shetland.gov.uk

Social Services (Adult): Ms Christine Ferguson, Director - Corporate Services, Kanterstead Office, Seafield Road, Lerwick ZE1 0WZ ☎ 01595 743819 🖷 01595 744321 🖱 christine.ferguson@shetland.gov.uk

Social Services (Adult): Mr Stephen Morgan , Executive Manager - Community Care, Grantfield, Lerwick ZE1 0NT ☎ 01595 744400 🖱 stephen.morgan@shetland.gov.uk

Staff Training: Mr Tommy Coutts , Short Course Manager, North Gremista Industrial Estate, Lerwick ZE1 0PX ☎ 01595 744744 🖱 thomas.coutts@shetland.gov.uk

Sustainable Communities: Mr Douglas Irvine, Executive Manager - Economic Development, Solarhus 3, North Ness Business Park, Lerwick ZE1 0LZ ☎ 01595 744932 🖷 01595 744961 🖱 douglas.irvine@shetland.gov.uk

Sustainable Development: Mr Austin Taylor, Development Plans & Heritage Team Leader, Office Headquarters, 8 North Ness Business Park, Lerwick ZE1 0LZ ☎ 01595 744833 🖱 john.taylor@shetland.gov.uk

Tourism: Mrs Linda Coutts, Project Manager, Solarhus 3, North Ness Business Park, Lerwick ZE1 0LZ ☎ 01595 744943 🖷 01595 744961 🖱 linda.coutts@shetland.gov.uk

Town Centre: Mr Iain McDiarmid, Executive Manager - Planning, Grantfield, Lerwick ZE1 0NT ☎ ; 01595 744813 🖷 01595 744804 🖱 planning@shetland.gov.uk

Traffic Management: Mr Dave Coupe , Executive Manager - Roads Maintenance, Gremista, Lerwick ZE1 0PX ☎ 01595 744104 🖱 dave.coupe@shetland.gov.uk

Transport: Mr Michael Craigie , Executive Manager - Transport Planning, Office Headquarters, 8 North Ness Business park, Lerwick ZE1 0LZ ☎ 01595 744160 🖷 01595 744880 🖱 michael.craigie@shetland.gov.uk

Transport Planner: Mr Michael Craigie , Executive Manager - Transport Planning, Office Headquarters, 8 North Ness Business park, Lerwick ZE1 0LZ ☎ 01595 744160 🖷 01595 744880 🖱 michael.craigie@shetland.gov.uk

COUNCILLORS

***Convener* Bell**, Malcolm (IND - Lerwick North)
convener@shetland.gov.uk

***Deputy Convener* Smith**, Cecil (IND - Lerwick South)
cecil.smith@shetland.gov.uk

***Deputy Leader of the Council* Fox**, Billy (IND - Shetland South)
billy.fox@shetland.gov.uk

***Group Leader* Robinson**, Gary (IND - Shetland West)
gary.robinson@shetland.gov.uk

Burgess, Mark (NP - Shetland Central)
mark.burgess@shetland.gov.uk

Campbell, Peter (IND - Lerwick South)
peter.campbell@shetland.gov.uk

Cleaver, Gary (IND - North Isles)
gary.cleaver@shetland.gov.uk

Cooper, Alastair (IND - Shetland North)
alastair.cooper@shetland.gov.uk

Coutts, Steven (NP - North Isles)
steven.coutts@shetland.gov.uk

SHETLAND

Duncan, Allison (IND - Shetland South)
allison.duncan@shetland.gov.uk

Henderson, Robert S (IND - North Isles)
robert.henderson@shetland.gov.uk

Manson, Andrea (IND - Shetland North)
andrea.manson@shetland.gov.uk

Ratter, Drew (NP - Shetland North)
drew.ratter@shetland.gov.uk

Robertson, Frank (IND - Shetland West)
frank.robertson@shetland.gov.uk

Sandison, Davie (IND - Shetland Central)
davie.sandison@shetland.gov.uk

Smith, George (IND - Shetland South)
george.smith@shetland.gov.uk

Smith, Theo (IND - Shetland West)
theo.smith@shetland.gov.uk

Stout, Michael (IND - Lerwick North)
michael.stout@shetland.gov.uk

Westlake, Amanda (IND - Lerwick South)
amanda.westlake@shetland.gov.uk

Wills, Jonathan (IND - Lerwick South)
jonathanwills47@gmail.com

Wishart, Vaila (IND - Shetland Central)
vaila.wishart@shetland.gov.uk

Wishart, Allan (IND - Lerwick North)
allan.wishart@shetland.gov.uk

POLITICAL COMPOSITION

IND: 19, NP: 3

COMMITTEE CHAIRS

Audit: Mr Allison Duncan

Licensing: Cllr George Smith

Planning: Mr Frank Robertson

Shropshire Unitary U

Shropshire Council, Shirehall, Abbey Foregate, Shrewsbury SY2 6ND
☎ 0345 678 9000 🖱 customer.service@shropshire.gov.uk
💻 www.shropshire.gov.uk

FACTS AND FIGURES

Parliamentary Constituencies: Ludlow, Shrewsbury and Atcham, Shropshire North, Wrekin, The
EU Constituencies:
Election Frequency:

PRINCIPAL OFFICERS

Chief Executive: Mr Clive Wright , Chief Executive, Shirehall, Abbey Foregate, Shrewsbury SY2 6ND 🖱 clive.wright@shropshire.gov.uk

Senior Management: Ms Nicki Beardmore , Director of Resources & Support, Shirehall, Abbey Foregate, Shrewsbury SY2 6ND ☎ 01743 252134 🖱 nicki.beardmore@shropshire.gov.uk

Senior Management: Ms Karen Bradshaw , Director of Children's Services, Shirehall, Abbey Foregate, Shrewsbury SY2 6ND ☎ 01743 254201 🖱 karen.bradshaw@shropshire.gov.uk

Senior Management: Mr George Candler , Director of Commissioning, Shirehall, Abbey Foregate, Shrewsbury SY2 6ND ☎ 01743 255003 🖱 george.candler@shropshire.gov.uk

Senior Management: Mr Stephen Chandler , Director of Adult Services, Shirehall, Abbey Foregate, Shrewsbury SY2 6ND ☎ 01743 253704 🖱 stephen.chandler@shropshire.gov.uk

Senior Management: Prof Rod Thomson , Director of Public Health, Shirehall, Abbey Foregate, Shrewsbury SY2 6ND 🖱 rod.thomson@shropshire.gov.uk

Building Control: Mr Stephen Rigney , Principal Building Control Surveyor, Shirehall, Abbey Foregate, Shrewsbury SY2 6ND ☎ 01743 255985 🖱 stephen.rigney@shropshire.gov.uk

Children / Youth Services: Ms Karen Bradshaw , Director of Children's Services, Shirehall, Abbey Foregate, Shrewsbury SY2 6ND ☎ 01743 254201 🖱 karen.bradshaw@shropshire.gov.uk

PR / Communications: Mr Nigel Bishop , Head of Customer Involvement, Shirehall, Abbey Foregate, Shrewsbury SY2 6ND ☎ 01743 252348 🖱 nigel.bishop@shropshire.gov.uk

Community Planning: Mr Nigel Bishop , Head of Customer Involvement, Shirehall, Abbey Foregate, Shrewsbury SY2 6ND ☎ 01743 252348 🖱 nigel.bishop@shropshire.gov.uk

Computer Management: Mr Barry Wilkinson , Head of Programme Management, Systems & Transition, Shirehall, Abbey Foregate, Shrewsbury SY2 6ND 🖱 barry.wilkinson@shropshire.gov.uk

Customer Service: Mr Nigel Bishop , Head of Customer Involvement, Shirehall, Abbey Foregate, Shrewsbury SY2 6ND ☎ 01743 252348 🖱 nigel.bishop@shropshire.gov.uk

Economic Development: Mr Andy Evans , Head of Business Growth & Prosperity, Shirehall, Abbey Foregate, Shrewsbury SY2 6ND ☎ 01743 253033 🖱 andrew.m.evans@shropshire.gov.uk

Education: Ms Karen Bradshaw , Director of Children's Services, Shirehall, Abbey Foregate, Shrewsbury SY2 6ND ☎ 01743 254201 🖱 karen.bradshaw@shropshire.gov.uk

Electoral Registration: Mrs Stacey Ijewsky , Elections Officer, Shirehall, Abbey Foregate, Shrewsbury SY2 6ND ☎ 01743 252334 🖱 stacey.ijewsky@shropshire.gov.uk

Electoral Registration: Ms Claire Porter , Head of Legal, Strategy & Democratic Services, Shirehall, Abbey Foregate, Shrewsbury SY2 6ND ☎ 01743 252763 🖱 claire.porter@shropshire.gov.uk

Emergency Planning: Ms Angie Beechey , Risk & Insurance Manager, Shirehall, Abbey Foregate, Shrewsbury SY2 6ND ☎ 01743 252073 🖱 angela.beechey@shropshire.gov.uk

Environmental Health: Mr Paul McGreary , Head of Public Protection, Shirehall, Abbey Foregate, Shrewsbury SY2 6ND ☎ 01743 253868 ✉ paul.mcgreary@shropshire.gov.uk

Estates, Property & Valuation: Ms Steph Jackson , Head of Commercial Services, Shirehall, Abbey Foregate, Shrewsbury SY2 6ND ☎ 01743 256127

Facilities: Ms Steph Jackson , Head of Commercial Services, Shirehall, Abbey Foregate, Shrewsbury SY2 6ND ☎ 01743 256127

Finance: Mr James Walton , Head of Finance, Governance & Assurance (S151 Officer), Shirehall, Abbey Foregate, Shrewsbury SY2 6ND ☎ 01743 252007 ✉ james.walton@shropshire.gov.uk

Treasury: Mr James Walton , Head of Finance, Governance & Assurance (S151 Officer), Shirehall, Abbey Foregate, Shrewsbury SY2 6ND ☎ 01743 252007 ✉ james.walton@shropshire.gov.uk

Pensions: Ms Debbie Sharp , Pensions Manager, Shirehall, Abbey Foregate, Shrewsbury SY2 6ND ☎ 01743 252192 ✉ debbie.sharp@shropshire.gov.uk

Highways: Mr Chris Edwards , Area Commissioner, Shirehall, Abbey Foregate, Shrewsbury SY2 6ND ☎ 01746 255478 ✉ chris.edwards@shropshire.gov.uk

Legal: Ms Claire Porter , Head of Legal, Strategy & Democratic Services, Shirehall, Abbey Foregate, Shrewsbury SY2 6ND ☎ 01743 252763 ✉ claire.porter@shropshire.gov.uk

Leisure and Cultural Services: Mr George Candler , Director of Commissioning, Shirehall, Abbey Foregate, Shrewsbury SY2 6ND ☎ 01743 255003 ✉ george.candler@shropshire.gov.uk

Licensing: Mr Paul McGreary , Head of Public Protection, Shirehall, Abbey Foregate, Shrewsbury SY2 6ND ☎ 01743 253868 ✉ paul.mcgreary@shropshire.gov.uk

Member Services: Ms Penny Chamberlain , Principal Committee Officer, Shirehall, Abbey Foregate, Shrewsbury SY2 6ND ☎ 01743 252729 ✉ penny.chamberlain@shropshire.gov.uk

Member Services: Ms Claire Porter , Head of Legal, Strategy & Democratic Services, Shirehall, Abbey Foregate, Shrewsbury SY2 6ND ☎ 01743 252763 ✉ claire.porter@shropshire.gov.uk

Partnerships: Mr George Candler , Director of Commissioning, Shirehall, Abbey Foregate, Shrewsbury SY2 6ND ☎ 01743 255003 ✉ george.candler@shropshire.gov.uk

Personnel / HR: Ms Michelle Leith , Head of Human Resources, Shirehall, Abbey Foregate, Shrewsbury SY2 6ND ☎ 01743 252804 ✉ michelle.leith@shropshire.gov.uk

Planning: Mr Ian Kilby , Development Manager, Shirehall, Abbey Foregate, Shrewsbury SY2 6ND ✉ ian.kilby@shropshire.gov.uk

Recycling & Waste Minimisation: Mr Tim Smith , Area Commissioner - North, Shirehall, Abbey Foregate, Shrewsbury SY2 6ND ☎ 01743 252411 ✉ tim.smith@shropshire.gov.uk

Regeneration: Mr Andy Evans , Head of Business Growth & Prosperity, Shirehall, Abbey Foregate, Shrewsbury SY2 6ND ☎ 01743 253033 ✉ andrew.m.evans@shropshire.gov.uk

Social Services: Mr Andy Begley , Head of Adult Social Care Operations, Shirehall, Abbey Foregate, Shrewsbury SY2 6ND ☎ 01743 252421 ✉ andy.begley@shropshire.gov.uk

Social Services (Adult): Mr Stephen Chandler , Director of Adult Services, Shirehall, Abbey Foregate, Shrewsbury SY2 6ND ☎ 01743 253704 ✉ stephen.chandler@shropshire.gov.uk

Social Services (Children): Ms Karen Bradshaw , Director of Children's Services, The Guildhall, Frankwell Quay, Shrewsbury SY3 8HQ ☎ 01743 254201 ✉ karen.bradshaw@shropshire.gov.uk

Social Services (Children): Ms Anne Cribbin , Head of Education Improvement & Efficiency, Shirehall, Abbey Foregate, Shrewsbury SY2 6ND ☎ 01743 254566 ✉ anne.cribbin@shropshire.gov.uk

Public Health: Prof Rod Thomson , Director of Public Health, Shirehall, Abbey Foregate, Shrewsbury SY2 6ND ✉ rod.thomson@shropshire.gov.uk

Staff Training: Ms Michelle Leith , Head of Human Resources, Shirehall, Abbey Foregate, Shrewsbury SY2 6ND ☎ 01743 252804 ✉ michelle.leith@shropshire.gov.uk

Transport: Mr Ron Buzzacott , Highways & Transport Manager, Shirehall, Abbey Foregate, Shrewsbury SY2 6ND ☎ 01743 255469 ✉ ron.buzzacott@shropshire.gov.uk

Waste Management: Mr Larry Wolfe , Head of Waste Management, Shirehall, Abbey Foregate, Shrewsbury SY2 6ND ☎ 01743 255995 ✉ larry.wolfe@shropshire.gov.uk

COUNCILLORS

Chair **Pate**, Malcolm (CON - Albrighton)
malcolm.pate@shropshire.gov.uk

Leader of the Council **Barrow**, Keith (CON - Oswestry South)
keith.barrow@shropshire.gov.uk

Deputy Leader of the Council **Charmley**, Stephen (CON - Whittington)
steve.charmley@shropshire.gov.uk

Group Leader **Dee**, Pauline (IND - Wem)
pauline.dee@shropshire.gov.uk

Group Leader **Evans**, Roger (LD - Longden)
roger.evans@shropshire.gov.uk

Group Leader **Mosley**, Alan (LAB - Castlefields & Ditherington)
alan.mosley@shropshire.gov.uk

Adams, Peter (CON - Bowbrook)
peter.m.adams@shropshire.gov.uk

Bannerman, Andrew (LD - Coton Hill & Quarry)
andrew.bannerman@shropshire.gov.uk

Bardsley, Nicholas (CON - Ruyton & Baschurch)
nick.bardsley@shropshire.gov.uk

SHROPSHIRE UNITARY

Barker, Timothy (CON - Burnell)
tim.baker@shropshire.gov.uk

Barnes, Charlotte (LD - Bishop's Castle)
charlotte.barnes@shropshire.gov.uk

Barrow, Joyce (CON - St Oswald)
joyce.barrow@shropshire.gov.uk

Bebb, Tudor (CON - Minsterley)
tudor.bebb@shropshire.gov.uk

Biggins, Thomas (CON - Whitchurch North)
thomas.biggins@shropshire.gov.uk

Boddington, Andy (LD - Ludlow North)
andy.boddington@shropshire.gov.uk

Bushell, Vernon (LAB - Harlescott)
vernon.bushell@shropshire.gov.uk

Butler, Gwilym (CON - Cleobury Mortimer)
gwilym.butler@shropshire.gov.uk

Cadwallader, John (CON - Market Drayton East)
john.cadwallader@shropshire.gov.uk

Calder, Karen (CON - Hodnet)
karen.calder@shropshire.gov.uk

Carroll, Dean (CON - Bagley)
dean.carroll@shropshire.gov.uk

Chapman, Lee (CON - Church Stretton & Craven Arms)
lee.chapman@shropshire.gov.uk

Chebsey, Anne (LD - Porthill)
anne.chebsey@shropshire.gov.uk

Cherrington, Peter (IND - Oswestry East)
peter.cherrington@shropshire.gov.uk

Clarke, Ted (LAB - Bayston Hill, Column & Sutton)
ted.clarke@shropshire.gov.uk

Dakin, Gerald (CON - Whitchurch South)
gerald.dakin@shropshire.gov.uk

Davenport, Steve (CON - St Martin's)
steve.davenport@shropshire.gov.uk

Davies, Andrew (CON - Cheswardine)
andrew.b.davies@shropshire.gov.uk

Evans, David (CON - Church Stretton & Craven Arms)
david.evans@shropshire.gov.uk

Everall, John (CON - Tern)
john.everall@shropshire.gov.uk

Fraser, Hannah (LD - Abbey)
hannah.fraser@shropshire.gov.uk

Hartin, Nigel (LD - Clun)
nigel.hartin@shropshire.gov.uk

Hartley, Ann (CON - Ellesmere Urban)
ann.hartley@shropshire.gov.uk

Huffer, Tracey (LD - Ludlow East)
tracey.huffer@shropshire.gov.uk

Huffer, Richard (LD - Clee)
richard.huffer@shropshire.gov.uk

Hughes, Roger (CON - Market Drayton West)
roger.hughes@shropshire.gov.uk

Hunt, Vincent (CON - Oswestry West)
vince.hunt@shropshire.gov.uk

Hurst-Knight, John (CON - Bridgnorth West & Tasley)
john.hurst-knight@shropshire.gov.uk

Jones, Jean (LAB - Broseley)
jean.e.jones@shropshire.gov.uk

Jones, Simon (CON - Shawbury)
simon.p.jones@shropshire.gov.uk

Kenny, Miles (LD - Underdale)
miles.kenny@shropshire.gov.uk

Kidd, Heather (LD - Chirbury & Worthen)
heather.kidd@shropshire.gov.uk

Lea, Christian (CON - Bridgnorth East & Astley Abbots)
christian.lea@shropshire.gov.uk

Lloyd, David (CON - Gobowen, Selattyn & Weston Rhyn)
david.lloyd@shropshire.gov.uk

Macey, Robert (CON - Gobowen, Selattyn & Weston Rhyn)
robert.macey@shropshire.gov.uk

Mackenzie, Jane (LAB - Bayston Hill, Column & Sutton)
jane.mackenzie@shropshire.gov.uk

Mellings, Christopher (LD - Wem)
chris.mellings@shropshire.gov.uk

Minnery, David (CON - Market Drayton West)
david.minnery@shropshire.gov.uk

Moseley, Pamela (LAB - Monkmoor)
pam.moseley@shropshire.gov.uk

Motley, Cecilia (CON - Corvedale)
cecilia.motley@shropshire.gov.uk

Mullock, Peggy (CON - Whitchurch North)
peggy.mullock@shropshire.gov.uk

Nutting, Peter (CON - Copthorne)
peter.nutting@shropshire.gov.uk

Owen, Mike (CON - Meole)
mike.owen@shropshire.gov.uk

Pardy, Kevin (LAB - Sundorne)
kevin.pardy@shropshire.gov.uk

Parr, William (CON - Bridgnorth East & Astley Abbots)
william.parr@shropshire.gov.uk

Parry, Vivienne (LD - Ludlow South)
vivienne.parry@shropshire.gov.uk

Price, John (CON - Oswestry East)
john.price@shropshire.gov.uk

Price, Malcolm (CON - Battlefield)
malcolm.price@shropshire.gov.uk

Roberts, David (CON - Loton)
david.roberts@shropshire.gov.uk

Roberts, Keith (CON - Radbrook)
keith.roberts@shropshire.gov.uk

Shineton, Madge (IND - Cleobury Mortimer)
madge.shineton@shropshire.gov.uk

Tandy, Jon (LAB - Bayston Hill, Column & Sutton)
jon.tandy@shropshire.gov.uk

Tindall, Robert (CON - Brown Clee)
robert.tindal@shropshire.gov.uk

Tremellen, Dave (INDNA - Highley)
dave.tremellen@shropshire.gov.uk

Turley, Kevin (IND - Shifnal North)
kevin.turley@shropshire.gov.uk

Turner, David (CON - Much Wenlock)
david.turner@shropshire.gov.uk

Walpole, Arthur (CON - Llanymynech)
arthur.walpole@shropshire.gov.uk

West, Stuart (CON - Shifnal South & Cosford)
stuart.west@shropshire.gov.uk

Wild, Claire (CON - Severn Valley)
claire.wild@shropshire.gov.uk

Williams, Brian (CON - The Meres)
brian.williams@shropshire.gov.uk

Williams, Mansel (LAB - Belle Vue)
mansel.williams@shropshire.gov.uk

Winwood, Les (CON - Bridgnorth West & Tasley)
les.winwood@shropshire.gov.uk

Wood, Michael (CON - Worfield)
michael.wood@shropshire.gov.uk

Woodward, Tina (CON - Alveley & Claverley)
tina.woodward@shropshire.gov.uk

Wynn, Paul (CON - Prees)
paul.wynn@shropshire.gov.uk

POLITICAL COMPOSITION

CON: 47, LD: 13, LAB: 9, IND: 4, INDNA: 1

COMMITTEE CHAIRS

Audit: Mr Brian Williams

Health & Adult Social Care: Mr Gerald Dakin

Health & Wellbeing: Mrs Karen Calder

Licensing: Mr Michael Wood

Slough U

Slough Borough Council, St Martin's Place, Bath Road, Slough SL1 3UQ
☎ 01753 552288 🖷 01753 692499 🖳 www.slough.gov.uk

FACTS AND FIGURES

Parliamentary Constituencies: Slough, Windsor
EU Constituencies: South East
Election Frequency: Elections are by thirds

PRINCIPAL OFFICERS

Chief Executive: Ms Ruth Bagley, Chief Executive, St Martin's Place, Bath Road, Slough SL1 3UQ ☎ 01753 875000 🖷 01753 875058 ✉ ruth.bagley@slough.gov.uk

Senior Management: Mr Roger Parkin, Director - Customer & Community Services, St Martin's Place, Bath Road, Slough SL1 3UQ ☎ 01753 875207 ✉ roger.parkin@slough.gov.uk

Senior Management: Ms Sarah Richards , Strategic Director - Regeneration, Housing & Resources, St Martin's Place, Bath Road, Slough SL1 3UQ ☎ 01753 875301 ✉ sarah.richards@slough.gov.uk

Senior Management: Ms Jane Wood , Strategic Director - Wellbeing, St Martin's Place, Bath Road, Slough SL1 3UF ☎ 01753 875751 ✉ jane.wood@slough.gov.uk

Architect, Building / Property Services: Mr Adrian Thomas , Property Manager, St Martin's Place, Bath Road, Slough SL1 3UQ ☎ 01753 875446 🖷 01753 875691 ✉ adrian.thomas@slough.gov.uk

Best Value: Mr Kevin Gordon , Assistant Director of Professional Services, St Martin's Place, Bath Road, Slough SL1 3UQ ☎ 01753 875213 🖷 01753 875659 ✉ kevin.gordon@slough.gov.uk

Building Control: Mr Sanjay Dhuna, Head of Building Control & Planning, St Martin's Place, Bath Road, Slough SL1 3UQ ☎ 01753 875810 🖷 01753 875809 ✉ sanjay.dhuna@slough.gov.uk

Children / Youth Services: Ms Jane Wood , Strategic Director - Wellbeing, St Martin's Place, Bath Road, Slough SL1 3UF ☎ 01753 875751 ✉ jane.wood@slough.gov.uk

Civil Registration: Mr Roger Parkin, Director - Customer & Community Services, St Martin's Place, Bath Road, Slough SL1 3UQ ☎ 01753 875207 ✉ roger.parkin@slough.gov.uk

PR / Communications: Mrs Kate Pratt , Communications Manager, St Martin's Place, Bath Road, Slough SL1 3UQ ☎ 01753 875088 ✉ kate.pratt@slough.gov.uk

Community Safety: Ms Louise Asby , Community Safety Manager, St Martin's Place, Bath Road, Slough SL1 3UQ ☎ 01753 875146 ✉ louise.asby@slough.gov.uk

Computer Management: Mr Simon Pallett , Head of Information Systems & Technology, St Martin's Place, Bath Road, Slough SL1 3UQ ☎ 01753 875095 🖷 01753 875897 ✉ simon.pallett@slough.gov.uk

Consumer Protection and Trading Standards: Ms Ginny DeHaan , Head of Consumer Protection & Business Compliance, St Martin's Place, Bath Road, Slough SL1 3UQ ☎ 01753 477912 ✉ ginny.dehaan@slough.gov.uk

Contracts: Ms Amardip Healy , Head of Legal Services, St Martin's Place, Bath Road, Slough SL1 3UQ ☎ 01753 875035 🖷 01753 875183 ✉ amardip.healy@slough.gov.uk

Corporate Services: Ms Sarah Richards , Strategic Director - Regeneration, Housing & Resources, St Martin's Place, Bath Road, Slough SL1 3UQ ☎ 01753 875301 ✉ sarah.richards@slough.gov.uk

Education: Mr Tony Browne , Head of School Services, St Martin's Place, Bath Road, Slough SL1 3UQ ☎ 01753 875717 ✉ tony.browne@slough.gov.uk

Education: Ms Jane Wood , Strategic Director - Wellbeing, St Martin's Place, Bath Road, Slough SL1 3UF ☎ 01753 875751 ✉ jane.wood@slough.gov.uk

E-Government: Mr Roger Parkin, Director - Customer & Community Services, St Martin's Place, Bath Road, Slough SL1 3UQ ☎ 01753 875207 ✉ roger.parkin@slough.gov.uk

SLOUGH

Electoral Registration: Ms Melanie Dark-Gale, Election Services Manager, St Martin's Place, Bath Road, Slough SL1 3UQ ☎ 01753 477236 🖷 01753 875331 🖱 melanie.dark-gale@slough.gov.uk

Emergency Planning: Mr Dean Trussler , Emergency Planning Officer, St Martin's Place, Bath Road, Slough SL1 3UQ ☎ 01753 875131 🖷 01753 694515 🖱 dean.trussler@slough.gov.uk

Environmental Health: Ms Ginny DeHaan , Head of Consumer Protection & Business Compliance, St Martin's Place, Bath Road, Slough SL1 3UQ ☎ 01753 477912 🖱 ginny.dehaan@slough.gov.uk

Estates, Property & Valuation: Mr Adrian Thomas , Property Manager, St Martin's Place, Bath Road, Slough SL1 3UQ ☎ 01753 875446 🖷 01753 875691 🖱 adrian.thomas@slough.gov.uk

Events Manager: Ms Lynsey Hellewell , Communication Project Officer, St Martin's Place, Bath Road, Slough SL1 3UQ ☎ 01753 875194 🖱 lynsey.hellewell@slough.gov.uk

Facilities: Ms Charan Dhillon, Head of Facilities Management, St Martin's Place, Bath Road, Slough SL1 3UF ☎ 01753 845945 🖷 01753 875691 🖱 charan.dhillon@slough.gov.uk

Finance: Mr Joseph Holmes , Assistant Director of Finance & Audit, St Martin's Place, Bath Road, Slough SL1 3UQ ☎ 01753 875358 🖱 joseph.holmes@slough.gov.uk

Health and Safety: Mr Robin Pringle , Health & Safety Manager, St Martin's Place, Bath Road, Slough SL1 3UQ ☎ 01753 875763 🖷 01753 478645 🖱 robin.pringle@slough.gov.uk

Highways: Mr Alex Deans , Head of Highways Engineering, St Martin's Place, Bath Road, Slough SL1 3UQ ☎ 01753 575633 🖱 alexander.deans@slough.gov.uk

Housing: Mr Neil Aves , Assistant Director - Housing Environment, The Centre, Farnham Road, Slough SL1 4UT ☎ 01753 875527 🖱 neil.aves@slough.gov.uk

Housing Maintenance: Mr Neil Aves , Assistant Director - Housing Environment, The Centre, Farnham Road, Slough SL1 4UT ☎ 01753 875527 🖱 neil.aves@slough.gov.uk

Legal: Ms Amardip Healy , Head of Legal Services, St Martin's Place, Bath Road, Slough SL1 3UQ ☎ 01753 875035 🖷 01753 875183 🖱 amardip.healy@slough.gov.uk

Leisure and Cultural Services: Mr Ketain Gandi , Head of Wellbeing & Community, St Martin's Place, Bath Road, Slough SL1 3UQ ☎ 01753 696099 🖱 ketain.gandi@slough.gov.uk

Licensing: Mr Michael Sims , Licensing Manager, St Martin's Place, Bath Road, Slough SL1 3UQ ☎ 01753 477387 🖱 michael.sims@slough.gov.uk

Lifelong Learning: Mr Philip Wright , Head of Learning & Community, St Martin's Place, Bath Road, Slough SL1 3UF ☎ 01753 875741 🖷 01753 875419 🖱 philip.wright@slough.gov.uk

Lighting: Mr Steve Brocklebank , Principal Engineer of Drainage & Lighting, St Martin's Place, Bath Road, Slough SL1 3UQ ☎ 01753 875625 🖷 01753 875660 🖱 steve.brocklebank@slough.gov.uk

Lottery Funding, Charity and Voluntary: Mr Alex Bowman , Strategic Commissioning Manager, St Martin's Place, Bath Road, Slough SL1 3UQ ☎ 01753 474037 🖱 alex.bowman@slough.gov.uk

Parking: Mr Garry Sullivan, Team Leader of Traffic Development, St Martin's Place, Bath Road, Slough SL1 3UQ ☎ 01753 477337 🖱 garry.sullivan@slough.gov.uk

Partnerships: Mr Gurpreet Anand , Assistant Director - Commissioning & Procurement, St Martin's Place, Bath Road, Slough SL1 3UQ ☎ 01753 875285 🖱 gurpreet.anand@slough.gov.uk

Personnel / HR: Mr Kevin Gordon , Assistant Director of Professional Services, St Martin's Place, Bath Road, Slough SL1 3UQ ☎ 01753 875213 🖷 01753 875659 🖱 kevin.gordon@slough.gov.uk

Planning: Mr Paul Stimpson , Strategic Lead - Planning Policy & Projects, St Martin's Place, Bath Road, Slough SL1 3UQ ☎ 01753 875820 🖷 01753 875623 🖱 paul.stimpson@slough.gov.uk

Procurement: Mr Gurpreet Anand , Assistant Director - Commissioning & Procurement, St Martin's Place, Bath Road, Slough SL1 3UQ ☎ 01753 875285 🖱 gurpreet.anand@slough.gov.uk

Public Libraries: Ms Claire Skeates , Service Development Manager, St Martin's Place, Bath Road, Slough SL1 3UQ ☎ 01753 875578 🖱 claire.skeates@slough.gov.uk

Recycling & Waste Minimisation: Mr Nicholas Hannon , Team Leader - Waste & Environment, St Martin's Place, Bath Road, Slough SL1 3UQ ☎ 01753 875275 🖱 nicholas.hannon@slough.gov.uk

Road Safety: Ms Lynsey Brookfield , Engineer - Traffic Engineering, St Martin's Place, Bath Road, Slough SL1 3UQ ☎ 01753 875622 🖱 lynsey.brookfield@slough.gov.uk

Social Services: Ms Jane Wood , Strategic Director - Wellbeing, St Martin's Place, Bath Road, Slough SL1 3UF ☎ 01753 875751 🖱 jane.wood@slough.gov.uk

Social Services (Adult): Mr Alan Sinclair , Assistant Director - Adult Social Care, St Martin's Place, Bath Road, Slough SL1 3UQ ☎ 01753 875752 🖱 alan.sinclair@slough.gov.uk

Social Services (Children): Ms Kitty Ferris , Assistant Director - Children, Young People & Families, St Martin's Place, Bath Road, Slough SL1 3UQ ☎ 01753 690901 🖱 kitty.ferris@slough.gov.uk

Public Health: Dr Lise Llewellyn , Director - Public Health, Easthampstead House, Town Square, Bracknell RG12 1AQ 🖱 lise.llewellyn@bracknell-forest.gov.uk

Street Scene: Ms Sarah Richards , Strategic Director - Regeneration, Housing & Resources, St Martin's Place, Bath Road, Slough SL1 3UQ ☎ 01753 875301 🖱 sarah.richards@slough.gov.uk

Tourism: Mrs Kate Pratt , Communications Manager, St Martin's Place, Bath Road, Slough SL1 3UQ ☎ 01753 875088 ✉ kate.pratt@slough.gov.uk

Traffic Management: Mr Alex Deans , Head of Highways Engineering, St Martin's Place, Bath Road, Slough SL1 3UQ ☎ 01753 575633 ✉ alexander.deans@slough.gov.uk

Transport: Mr Savio DeCruz , Acting Head of Transport, St Martin's Place, Bath Road, Slough SL1 3UQ ☎ 01753 875640 ✉ savio.decruz@slough.gov.uk

Transport Planner: Mr Joe Carter , Assistant Director - Assets, Infrastructure & Regeneration, St Martin's Place, Bath Road, Slough SL1 3UQ ☎ 01753 575653 ✉ joe.carter@slough.gov.uk

Waste Collection and Disposal: Mr Nicholas Hannon , Team Leader - Waste & Environment, St Martin's Place, Bath Road, Slough SL1 3UQ ☎ 01753 875275 ✉ nicholas.hannon@slough.gov.uk

Waste Management: Mr Nicholas Hannon , Team Leader - Waste & Environment, St Martin's Place, Bath Road, Slough SL1 3UQ ☎ 01753 875275 ✉ nicholas.hannon@slough.gov.uk

Children's Play Areas: Mr Ollie Kelly , Parks & Open Spaces Manager, St Martin's Place, Bath Road, Slough SL1 3UQ ☎ 01753 875252 ✉ ollie.kelly@slough.gov.uk

COUNCILLORS

***Mayor* Rasib**, Mohammed (LAB - Farnham)
mohammed.rasib@slough.gov.uk

***Deputy Mayor* Dhaliwal**, Arvind (LAB - Elliman)
arvind.dhaliwal@slough.gov.uk

***Leader of the Council* Anderson**, Robert (LAB - Britwell & Northborough)
rob.anderson@slough.gov.uk

***Deputy Leader of the Council* Swindlehurst**, James (LAB - Cippenham Green)
james.swindlehurst@slough.gov.uk

Abe, Frank (CON - Langley St. Mary's)
abe14uk@hotmail.com

Ajaib, Zaffar (LAB - Central)
zaffar.ajaib@slough.gov.uk

Bains, Rayman (CON - Upton)
rayman.bains@slough.gov.uk

Bal, Joginder (LAB - Farnham)
joginder.bal@slough.gov.uk

Brooker, Preston (LAB - Langley Kederminster)
preston.brooker@slough.gov.uk

Carter, Martin (LAB - Britwell & Northborough)
martin.carter@slough.gov.uk

Chahal, Wal (CON - Upton)
wal.chahal@slough.gov.uk

Chaudhry, Shafiq (LAB - Central)
shafiq.chaudhry@slough.gov.uk

Cheema, Avtar (LAB - Colnbrook with Poyle)
avtar.cheema@slough.gov.uk

Chohan, Nimrit (LAB - Cippenham Meadows)
nimrit.chohan@slough.gov.uk

Coad, Diana (CON - Langley St. Mary's)
dianacoad@aol.com

Dar, Haqeeq (LAB - Wexham Lea)
haqeeq.dar@slough.gov.uk

Davis, Roger (LAB - Cippenham Green)
roger_rebel40@hotmail.com

Dhaliwal, Amarpreet (CON - Upton)
amarpreet.dhaliwal@slough.gov.uk

Dhillon, Antreev (LAB - Baylis and Stoke)
antreev.dhillon@slough.gov.uk

Holledge, Michael (LAB - Langley Kederminster)
michael.holledge@slough.gov.uk

Holledge, Nora (LAB - Cippenham Green)
nora.holledge@slough.gov.uk

Hussain, Sabia (LAB - Chalvey)
sabiahussain786@gmail.com

Malik, Sandra (LAB - Wexham Lea)
sandymalik5@yahoo.co.uk

Mann, Pavitar (LAB - Central)
pavy2@hotmail.com

Mansoor, Fatima (LAB - Elliman)
fatima.mansoor@slough.gov.uk

Matloob, Fiza (LAB - Baylis and Stoke)
fizamatloob@yahoo.co.uk

Morris, Darren (CON - Haymill & Lynch Hill)
darren.morris@slough.gov.uk

Munawar, Sohail (LAB - Elliman)
sohail.munawar@slough.gov.uk

Nazir, Mohammed (LAB - Baylis and Stoke)
mohammed.nazir@slough.gov.uk

Pantelic, Natasa (LAB - Cippenham Meadows)
natasa.pantelic@slough.gov.uk

Parmar, Satpal (LAB - Cippenham Meadows)
satpal.parmar@slough.gov.uk

Plenty, Ted (LAB - Foxborough)
ted.plenty@slough.gov.uk

Rana, Mandeep (LAB - Langley Kedermister)
mandeep.rana@slough.gov.uk

Sandhu, Rajinder (CON - Upton)
rajinder.sandhu@slough.gov.uk

Shah, Ishrat (LAB - Foxborough)
ishrat08@hotmail.co.uk

Sharif, Mohamemd (LAB - Chalvey)
gbsharim@yahoo.co.uk

Smith, Dexter (CON - Colnbrook with Poyle)
dexter.j.smith@btinternet.com

Sohal, Paul (LAB - Wexham Lea)
Sohal51@aol.com

Strutton, Wayne (CON - Haymill & Lynch Hill)
w.strutton@sky.com

Usmani, Khaula (LAB - Chalvey)
khaula.usmani@slough.gov.uk

Wright, Anna (CON - Haymill & Lynch Hill)
anna.s.wright@hotmail.com

Zarait, Raja (LAB - Chalvey)
raja.zarait@slough.gov.uk

POLITICAL COMPOSITION
LAB: 32, CON: 10

COMMITTEE CHAIRS

Audit & Corporate Governance: Mr Nimrit Chohan

Education & Children's Services: Mr Joginder Bal

Licensing: Mr Roger Davis

Planning: Mr Haqeeq Dar

Solihull M

Solihull Metropolitan Borough Council, Solihull Metropolitan Borough Council, PO Box 18, Council House, Solihull B91 9QS
☎ 0121 704 6000 🖷 0121 704 6114 ✉ connectcc@solihull.gov.uk
💻 www.solihull.gov.uk

FACTS AND FIGURES
Parliamentary Constituencies: Meriden, Solihull
EU Constituencies: West Midlands
Election Frequency: Elections are by thirds

PRINCIPAL OFFICERS

Chief Executive: Mr Nick Page , Chief Executive, Solihull Metropolitan Borough Council, PO Box 18, Council House, Solihull B91 9QS

Senior Management: Ms Anne Brereton , Director - Managed Growth, Solihull Metropolitan Borough Council, PO Box 18, Council House, Solihull B91 9QS ☎ 0121 704 6364
✉ abrereton@solihull.gov.uk

Senior Management: Ms Sally Hodges , Director - Children's Services & Skills, Solihull Metropolitan Borough Council, PO Box 18, Council House, Solihull B91 9QS ☎ 0121 704 6734
✉ sally.hodges@solihull.gov.uk

Senior Management: Mr Ian James , Director - Communities & Adult Social Care, Solihull Metropolitan Borough Council, PO Box 18, Council House, Solihull B91 9QS ☎ 0121 704 6317
✉ ian.james@solihull.gov.uk

Senior Management: Mr Paul Johnson , Director - Resources, Solihull Metropolitan Borough Council, PO Box 18, Council House, Solihull B91 9QS ☎ 0121 704 6194 ✉ pjohnson@solihull.gov.uk

Senior Management: Mr Philip Lloyd-Williams , Director - Governance, Solihull Metropolitan Borough Council, PO Box 18, Council House, Solihull B91 9QS ☎ 0121 704 6721
✉ plwilliams@solihull.gov.uk

Senior Management: Mr Philip Mayhew , Director - Business Change, Solihull Metropolitan Borough Council, PO Box 18, Council House, Solihull B91 9QS ☎ 0121 704 6652
✉ pmayhew@solihull.gov.uk

Senior Management: Dr Stephen Munday , Director - Public Health & Commissioning, Solihull Metropolitan Borough Council, PO Box 18, Council House, Solihull B91 9QS ☎ 0121 704 6187
✉ stephen.munday@solihull.gov.uk

Access Officer / Social Services (Disability): Ms Clare Shannon , Head of Disability Services, Solihull Metropolitan Borough Council, PO Box 18, Council House, Solihull B91 9QS
☎ 0121 709 7043 ✉ clare.shannon@solihull.gov.uk

Children / Youth Services: Mr Adam Scott , Service Director - Children, Young People & Families, Solihull Metropolitan Borough Council, PO Box 18, Council House, Solihull B91 9QS
☎ 0121 704 8325 ✉ adam.scott@solihull.gov.uk

PR / Communications: Ms Deborah Martin-Williams , Head - Communications, Solihull Metropolitan Borough Council, PO Box 18, Council House, Solihull B91 9QS ☎ 0121 704 6772
✉ dmartinwilliams@solihull.gov.uk

Community Planning: Mr Faisal Hussain , Head - Community & Voluntary Relations, Solihull Metropolitan Borough Council, PO Box 18, Council House, Solihull B91 9QS ☎ 0121 704 8541
✉ fhussain@solihull.gov.uk

Community Safety: Ms Caroline Naven , Head - Neighbourhood Services, Solihull Metropolitan Borough Council, PO Box 18, Council House, Solihull B91 9QS ☎ 0121 704 8753 ✉ cnaven@solihull.gov.uk

Computer Management: Mr Steve Halliday , Head - ICT, Solihull Metropolitan Borough Council, PO Box 18, Council House, Solihull B91 9QS ☎ 0121 704 6196 ✉ shalliday@solihull.gov.uk

Customer Service: Ms Emma Mayhew , Head - Customer Services, Solihull Metropolitan Borough Council, PO Box 18, Council House, Solihull B91 9QS ☎ 0121 704 8667 ✉ emayhew@solihull.gov.uk

Education: Mr Chris Palmer , Assistant Director - Learning & Achievement, Solihull Metropolitan Borough Council, PO Box 18, Council House, Solihull B91 9QS ☎ 0121 704 8282
✉ chrispalmer@solihull.gov.uk

Environmental / Technical Services: Mr Jim Harte, Assistant Director - Highways, Neighbourhoods & Environment Services, Solihull Metropolitan Borough Council, PO Box 18, Council House, Solihull B91 9QS ☎ 0121 704 6453 ✉ jharte@solihull.gov.uk

Facilities: Mr Paul Evans , Head - Corporate Property Services, Solihull Metropolitan Borough Council, PO Box 18, Council House, Solihull B91 9QS ☎ 0121 704 6494 ✉ pevans@solihull.gov.uk

Finance: Mr Paul Johnson , Director - Resources, Solihull Metropolitan Borough Council, PO Box 18, Council House, Solihull B91 9QS ☎ 0121 704 6194 ✉ pjohnson@solihull.gov.uk

Treasury: Ms Samantha Gilbert , Head - Financial Operations, Solihull Metropolitan Borough Council, PO Box 18, Council House, Solihull B91 9QS ☎ 0121 704 6278 ✉ sgilbert@solihull.gov.uk

Grounds Maintenance: Mr Alan Brown , Head - Environmental Services, Solihull Metropolitan Borough Council, PO Box 18, Council House, Solihull B91 9QS ☎ 0121 704 8334 ✉ albrown@solihull.gov.uk

Highways: Mr Jim Harte, Assistant Director - Highways, Neighbourhoods & Environment Services, Solihull Metropolitan Borough Council, PO Box 18, Council House, Solihull B91 9QS ☎ 0121 704 6453 🖱 jharte@solihull.gov.uk

Highways: Mr Ashley Prior , Head - Highway Services, Solihull Metropolitan Borough Council, PO Box 18, Council House, Solihull B91 9QS ☎ 0121 704 8558 🖱 ashley.prior@solihull.gov.uk

Housing: Ms Anne Brereton , Director - Managed Growth, Solihull Metropolitan Borough Council, PO Box 18, Council House, Solihull B91 9QS ☎ 0121 704 6364 🖱 abrereton@solihull.gov.uk

Housing: Mr Ken Harrison , Head - Policy & Spatial Planning, Solihull Metropolitan Borough Council, PO Box 18, Council House, Solihull B91 9QS ☎ 0121 704 8320 🖱 ken.harrison@solihull.gov.uk

Legal: Mr Philip Lloyd-Williams , Director - Governance, Solihull Metropolitan Borough Council, PO Box 18, Council House, Solihull B91 9QS ☎ 0121 704 6721 🖱 plwilliams@solihull.gov.uk

Leisure and Cultural Services: Ms Caroline Naven , Head - Neighbourhood Services, Solihull Metropolitan Borough Council, PO Box 18, Council House, Solihull B91 9QS ☎ 0121 704 8753 🖱 cnaven@solihull.gov.uk

Lighting: Mr Ashley Prior , Head - Highway Services, Solihull Metropolitan Borough Council, PO Box 18, Council House, Solihull B91 9QS ☎ 0121 704 8558 🖱 ashley.prior@solihull.gov.uk

Member Services: Mr Philip Lloyd-Williams , Director - Governance, Solihull Metropolitan Borough Council, PO Box 18, Council House, Solihull B91 9QS ☎ 0121 704 6721 🖱 plwilliams@solihull.gov.uk

Member Services: Ms Deborah Merry , Head - Democratic Services, Solihull Metropolitan Borough Council, PO Box 18, Council House, Solihull B91 9QS ☎ 0121 704 6022 🖱 dmerry@solihull.gov.uk

Parking: Mr Ashley Prior , Head - Highway Services, Solihull Metropolitan Borough Council, PO Box 18, Council House, Solihull B91 9QS ☎ 0121 704 8558 🖱 ashley.prior@solihull.gov.uk

Partnerships: Ms Melanie Lockey , Head - Partnership Commissioning, Solihull Metropolitan Borough Council, PO Box 18, Council House, Solihull B91 9QS ☎ 0121 704 8403 🖱 mlockey@solihull.gov.uk

Personnel / HR: Mr Adrian Cattell , Head - Human Resources, Solihull Metropolitan Borough Council, PO Box 18, Council House, Solihull B91 9QS ☎ 0121 704 6038 🖱 acattell@solihull.gov.uk

Personnel / HR: Ms Viv Lawrence , Head - Organisational & Workforce Development, Solihull Metropolitan Borough Council, PO Box 18, Council House, Solihull B91 9QS ☎ 0121 704 6524 🖱 vlawrence@solihull.gov.uk

Planning: Mr Ken Harrison , Head - Policy & Spatial Planning, Solihull Metropolitan Borough Council, PO Box 18, Council House, Solihull B91 9QS ☎ 0121 704 8320 🖱 ken.harrison@solihull.gov.uk

Planning: Mr Martin Taylor , Head - Design & Development Management Services, Solihull Metropolitan Borough Council, PO Box 18, Council House, Solihull B91 9QS ☎ 0121 704 6311 🖱 martin.taylor@solihull.gov.uk

Procurement: Ms Liz Welton , Head - Procurement, Solihull Metropolitan Borough Council, PO Box 18, Council House, Solihull B91 9QS ☎ 0121 704 6088 🖱 lizwelton@solihull.gov.uk

Public Libraries: Ms Tracey Cox, Head - Libraries, Solihull Metropolitan Borough Council, PO Box 18, Council House, Solihull B91 9QS ☎ 0121 704 6945 🖱 tcox@solihull.gov.uk

Recycling & Waste Minimisation: Mr Alan Brown , Head - Environmental Services, Solihull Metropolitan Borough Council, PO Box 18, Council House, Solihull B91 9QS ☎ 0121 704 8334 🖱 albrown@solihull.gov.uk

Regeneration: Ms Anne Brereton , Director - Managed Growth, Solihull Metropolitan Borough Council, PO Box 18, Council House, Solihull B91 9QS ☎ 0121 704 6364 🖱 abrereton@solihull.gov.uk

Road Safety: Mr Ashley Prior , Head - Highway Services, Solihull Metropolitan Borough Council, PO Box 18, Council House, Solihull B91 9QS ☎ 0121 704 8558 🖱 ashley.prior@solihull.gov.uk

Social Services (Adult): Ms Susan Dale , Assistant Director - Adult Social Care, Solihull Metropolitan Borough Council, PO Box 18, Council House, Solihull B91 9QS ☎ 0121 704 6667 🖱 susan.dale@solihull.gov.uk

Social Services (Adult): Mr Ian James , Director - Communities & Adult Social Care, Solihull Metropolitan Borough Council, PO Box 18, Council House, Solihull B91 9QS ☎ 0121 704 6317 🖱 ian.james@solihull.gov.uk

Social Services (Children): Mr Philip Mayhew , Director - Business Change, Solihull Metropolitan Borough Council, PO Box 18, Council House, Solihull B91 9QS ☎ 0121 704 6652 🖱 pmayhew@solihull.gov.uk

Social Services (Children): Ms Tina Russell , Head - Children in Need, Solihull Metropolitan Borough Council, PO Box 18, Council House, Solihull B91 9QS ☎ 0121 788 4534 🖱 tinarussell@solihull.gov.uk

Social Services (Children): Mr Adam Scott , Service Director - Children, Young People & Families, Solihull Metropolitan Borough Council, PO Box 18, Council House, Solihull B91 9QS ☎ 0121 704 8325 🖱 adam.scott@solihull.gov.uk

Fostering & Adoption: Ms Jane Wilton , Head - Children in Care, Solihull Metropolitan Borough Council, PO Box 18, Council House, Solihull B91 9QS ☎ 0121 788 4227 🖱 jwilton@solihull.gov.uk

Looked after Children: Ms Jane Wilton , Head - Children in Care, Solihull Metropolitan Borough Council, PO Box 18, Council House, Solihull B91 9QS ☎ 0121 788 4227 🖱 jwilton@solihull.gov.uk

Childrens Social Care: Mr Philip Mayhew , Director - Business Change, Solihull Metropolitan Borough Council, PO Box 18, Council House, Solihull B91 9QS ☎ 0121 704 6652 🖱 pmayhew@solihull.gov.uk

SOLIHULL

Public Health: Dr Stephen Munday , Director - Public Health & Commissioning, Solihull Metropolitan Borough Council, PO Box 18, Council House, Solihull B91 9QS ☎ 0121 704 6187 ✉ stephen.munday@solihull.gov.uk

Staff Training: Ms Viv Lawrence , Head - Organisational & Workforce Development, Solihull Metropolitan Borough Council, PO Box 18, Council House, Solihull B91 9QS ☎ 0121 704 6524 ✉ vlawrence@solihull.gov.uk

Town Centre: Ms Caroline Naven , Head - Neighbourhood Services, Solihull Metropolitan Borough Council, PO Box 18, Council House, Solihull B91 9QS ☎ 0121 704 8753 ✉ cnaven@solihull.gov.uk

Traffic Management: Mr Ashley Prior , Head - Highway Services, Solihull Metropolitan Borough Council, PO Box 18, Council House, Solihull B91 9QS ☎ 0121 704 8558 ✉ ashley.prior@solihull.gov.uk

Waste Collection and Disposal: Mr Alan Brown , Head - Environmental Services, Solihull Metropolitan Borough Council, PO Box 18, Council House, Solihull B91 9QS ☎ 0121 704 8334 ✉ albrown@solihull.gov.uk

Waste Management: Mr Alan Brown , Head - Environmental Services, Solihull Metropolitan Borough Council, PO Box 18, Council House, Solihull B91 9QS ☎ 0121 704 8334 ✉ albrown@solihull.gov.uk

COUNCILLORS

***Mayor* Slater**, Glenis (LD - Elmdon)
gslater@solhihull.gov.uk

***Deputy Mayor* Wild**, Kate (CON - St Alphege)
kwild@solihull.gov.uk

***Leader of the Council* Sleigh**, Robert (CON - Bickenhill)
rsleigh@solihull.gov.uk

***Deputy Leader of the Council* Courts**, Ian (CON - Dorridge and Hockley Heath)
icourts@solihull.gov.uk

***Group Leader* Burn**, James (GRN - Chelmsey Wood)
james.burn@solihull.gov.uk

***Group Leader* Hall**, Robert (UKIP - Kingshurst and Fordbridge)
robert.hall@solihull.gov.uk

***Group Leader* Windmill**, John (LD - Olton)
jwindmill@solihull.gov.uk

Allen, Howard (GRN - Shirley West)
hallen@solihull.gov.uk

Allport, Gary (CON - Shirley South)
gallport@solihull.gov.uk

Allsopp, Ken (CON - Meriden)
kallsopp@solihull.gov.uk

Bassett, Margaret (CON - Silhill)
margaret.bassett@solihull.gov.uk

Bell, David (CON - Meriden)
dbell@aolihull.gov.uk

Brown, Linda (IND - Blythe)
linda.brown@solihull.gov.uk

Chamberlain, Irene (LD - Lyndon)
ichamberlain@solihull.gov.uk

Davis, Stuart (CON - St Alphege)
sdavis@solihull.gov.uk

Dicicco, Tony (CON - Meriden)
tony.dicicco@solihull.gov.uk

Evans, Debbie (UKIP - Kingshurst and Fordbridge)
debra.evans@solihull.gov.uk

Grinsell, Robert (CON - Olton)
robert.grinsell@solihull.gov.uk

Grinsell, Karen (CON - Shirley East)
karen.grinsall@solihull.gov.uk

Hawkins, Ken (CON - Blythe)
khawkins@solihull.gov.uk

Hewings, Martin (LD - Elmdon)
mhewings@solihull.gov.uk

Hodgson, Andrew (GRN - Shirley South)
ahodgson@solihull.gov.uk

Hodgson, Tim (GRN - Shirley West)
tim.hodgson@solihull.gov.uk

Hogarth, Peter (CON - Silhill)
phogarth@solihull.gov.uk

Holl-Allen, Diana (CON - Knowle)
dhollallen@solihull.gov.uk

Holmes, Brian (CON - Shirley West)
brian.holmes@solihull.gov.uk

Holt, Stephen (GRN - Smith's Wood)
stephen.holt@solihull.gov.uk

Holt, Richard (CON - Blythe)
richard.holt@solihull.gov.uk

Hulland, Robert (CON - Silhill)
rhulland@solihull.gov.uk

Hulland, Julie (CON - Lyndon)
julie.hulland@solihull.gov.uk

Ludlow, Tony (LD - Lyndon)
anthony.ludlow@solihull.gov.uk

Mackenzie, Annette (CON - Shirley East)
annette.mackenzie@solihull.gov.uk

Mackiewicz, Andrew (CON - Dorridge and Hockley Heath)
amackiewicz@solihull.gov.uk

Macnaughton, Karl (GRN - Chelmsley Wood)
kmacnaughton@solihull.gov.uk

McCarthy, Martin (CON - Elmdon)
martin.mccarthy@solihull.gov.uk

Meeson, Ken (CON - Dorridge and Hockley Heath)
kmeeson@solihull.gov.uk

Nash, Florence (LAB - Kingshurst and Fordbridge)
flo.nash@solihull.gov.uk

O'Kane, Claire Louise (LD - Olton)
claire.okane@solihull.gov.uk

Parker, Mark (CON - Shirley East)
mparker@solihull.gov.uk

Potts, Jeffrey (CON - Knowle)
jpotts@solihull.gov.uk

Rebeiro, Alan (CON - Knowle)
arebeiro@solihull.gov.uk

Richards, Ted (CON - Castle Bromwich)
grichards@solihull.gov.uk

Robinson, Michael (CON - Castle Bromwich)
mrobinson@solihull.gov.uk

Rolf, Alison (CON - Bickenhill)
alison.rolf@solihull.gov.uk

Ryan, Jim (CON - Bickenhill)
jiryan@solihull.gov.uk

Sandison, Angela (CON - Shirley South)
angela.sandison@solihull.gov.uk

Sheridan, Michael (GRN - Smith's Wood)
msheridan@solihull.gov.uk

Sleigh, Gail (CON - Castle Bromwich)
gsleigh@solihull.gov.uk

Tildesley, Joe (CON - St Alphege)
joetildesley@solihull.gov.uk

Williams, Chris (GRN - Chelmsley Wood)
chris.williams@solihull.gov.uk

Wilson, Mark (GRN - Smith's Wood)
mark.wilson@solihull.gov.uk

POLITICAL COMPOSITION
CON: 32, GRN: 9, LD: 6, UKIP: 2, IND: 1, LAB: 1

COMMITTEE CHAIRS
Children's Services, Education & Skills: Mr Andrew Mackiewicz

Health & Adult Social Care: Mrs Gail Sleigh

Planning: Mr David Bell

Somerset C

Somerset County Council, County Hall, Taunton TA1 4DY
☎ 0845 345 9166 🖷 01823 355258 info@somerset.gov.uk
www.somerset.gov.uk

FACTS AND FIGURES
Parliamentary Constituencies: Somerset North, Somerset North East
EU Constituencies: South West
Election Frequency: Elections are of whole council

PRINCIPAL OFFICERS
Chief Executive: Mr Patrick Flaherty , Chief Executive, County Hall, Taunton TA1 4DY ☎ 01823 359001 pflherty@somerset.gov.uk

Senior Management: Ms Trudi Grant , Director - Public Health, County Hall, Taunton TA1 4DY tgrant@somerset.gov.uk

Access Officer / Social Services (Disability): Mr David Dick , Learning Disabilities Operations Director, County Hall, Taunton TA1 4DY ☎ 01823 356794 ddick@somerset.gov.uk

Children / Youth Services: Mr Julian Wooster , Director of Children's Services, County Hall, Taunton TA1 4DY ☎ 01823 355886 jwooster@somerset.gov.uk

PR / Communications: Mr Mark Ford , Head of Communications, County Hall, Taunton TA1 4DY ☎ 01823 357143 mford@somerset.gov.uk

PR / Communications: Ms Deborah Porter , Deputy Head of Communications, County Hall, Taunton TA1 4DY ☎ 01823 355018 dporter@somerset.gov.uk

Community Safety: Ms Lucy Macready , Commissioning Manager of Community Safety, County Hall, Taunton TA1 4DY ☎ 01823 357114 lmacready@somerset.gov.uk

Computer Management: Mr Alan Webb , Strategic Manager of ICT Lead & Client, County Hall, Taunton TA1 4DY ☎ 01823 355293 awebb@somerset.gov.uk

Contracts: Ms Donna Fitzgerald , Strategic Manager of Business Client, County Hall, Taunton TA1 4DY ☎ 01823 355243 dmfitzgerald@somerset.gov.uk

Corporate Services: Mr Richard Williams , Business Development Director, County Hall, Taunton TA1 4DY ☎ 01823 355036 rowilliams@somerset.gov.uk

Economic Development: Mr Paul Hickson , Strategic Manager of Economy & Planning, County Hall, Taunton TA1 4DY ☎ 01823 355661 phickson@somerset.gov.uk

Education: Mr Paul Nugent , Learning & Achievement Operations Director, County Hall, Taunton TA1 4DY ☎ 01823 356891 pnugent@somerset.gov.uk

E-Government: Mr Alan Webb , Strategic Manager of ICT Lead & Client, County Hall, Taunton TA1 4DY ☎ 01823 355293 awebb@somerset.gov.uk

Electoral Registration: Mr Julian Gale , Strategic Manager of Governance & Risk, County Hall, Taunton TA1 4DY ☎ 01823 359047 jjgale@somerset.gov.uk

Emergency Planning: Ms Nicola Dawson , Civil Contingencies Manager, County Hall, Taunton TA2 8LQ ☎ 01823 364612 ndawson@somerset.gov.uk

Estates, Property & Valuation: Mr James Stubbs , Strategic Manager of Property, County Hall, Taunton TA1 4DY ☎ 01823 355364 jstubbs@somerset.gov.uk

European Liaison: Mr Jamshid Ahmadi, Service Manager of Economy Commissioning, County Hall, Taunton TA1 4DY ☎ 01823 356131 jahmadi@somerset.gov.uk

Facilities: Ms Heidi Boyle, Facilities Manager, County Hall, Taunton TA1 4DY ☎ 01823 365524 hboyle@somerset.gov.uk

Finance: Mr Kevin Nacey, Finance & Performance Director, County Hall, Taunton TA1 4DY ☎ 01823 355213 kbnacey@somerset.gov.uk

Pensions: Ms Catherine Drew , Service Manager of Pensions, County Hall, Taunton TA1 4DY ☎ 01823 355466 ✉ cmdrew@somerset.gov.uk

Pensions: Ms Claire Druce , Senior Pension Investments Officer, County Hall, Taunton TA1 4DY ☎ 01823 355449 ✉ cdruce@somerset.gov.uk

Health and Safety: Mr Brian Oldham, Operations Manager of Health & Safety, County Hall, Taunton TA1 4DY ☎ 01823 355089 🖷 01823 355521 ✉ **ham@somerset.gov.uk**

Highways: Mr Geoff Dight , Strategic Manager of Highways Maintenance, County Hall, Taunton TA1 4DY ☎ 01823 483064 ✉ gdight@somerset.gov.uk

Legal: Mrs Honor Clarke , Deputy County Solicitor, County Hall, Taunton TA1 4DY ☎ 01823 355012 ✉ HCClarke@somerset.gov.uk

Lifelong Learning: Ms Ros Pither , Strategic Manager of Learning, County Hall, Taunton TA1 4DY ☎ 01823 357867 ✉ rpither@somerset.gov.uk

Lighting: Mr Stephen Parkinson , Service Manager of Traffic Control & Lighting, County Hall, Taunton TA1 4DY ☎ 0845 345 9166 ✉ sparkinson@somerset.gov.uk

Member Services: Mr Julian Gale , Strategic Manager of Governance & Risk, County Hall, Taunton TA1 4DY ☎ 01823 359047 ✉ jjgale@somerset.gov.uk

Personnel / HR: Mr Richard Crouch, Group Director of Operations, County Hall, Taunton TA1 4DY ☎ 01823 355074 ✉ rmcrouch@somerset.gov.uk

Planning: Mr Philip Higginbottom , Service Manager of Planning Control, County Hall, Taunton TA1 4DY ☎ 01823 356939 ✉ phigginbottom@somerset.gov.uk

Procurement: Ms Donna Fitzgerald , Strategic Manager of Business Client, County Hall, Taunton TA1 4DY ☎ 01823 355243 ✉ dmfitzgerald@somerset.gov.uk

Public Libraries: Ms Sue Crowley , Strategic Manager of Library Services, County Hall, Taunton TA1 4DY ☎ 01278 458373 ✉ sacrowley@somerset.gov.uk

Recycling & Waste Minimisation: Mr Steve Read , Managing Director of Somerset Waste Partnership, Monmouth House, Blackbrook Park Avenue, Taunton TA1 2PX ☎ 01823 625708 ✉ sread@somerset.gov.uk

Regeneration: Ms Paula Hewitt , Lead Commissioner of Economic & Community Infrastructure, County Hall, Taunton TA1 4DY ☎ 01823 356020 ✉ prhewitt@somerset.gov.uk

Road Safety: Mr Terrance Beale , Service Manager of Road Safety, County Hall, Taunton TA1 4DY ☎ 01823 340014 ✉ tbeale@somerset.gov.uk

Social Services (Adult): Ms Clare Steel , Lead Commissioner of Adults & Health, County Hall, Taunton TA1 4DY ☎ 01823 355100 ✉ csteel@somerset.gov.uk

Social Services (Children): Mr Julian Wooster , Director of Children's Services, County Hall, Taunton TA1 4DY ☎ 01823 355886 ✉ jwooster@somerset.gov.uk

Public Health: Ms Trudi Grant , Director - Public Health, County Hall, Taunton TA1 4DY ✉ tgrant@somerset.gov.uk

Staff Training: Mr Hugh Griffith , Strategic Manager of HR Organisational Development, County Hall, Taunton TA1 4DY ☎ 01823 356124 ✉ dhgriffith@somerset.gov.uk

Tourism: Mr Paul Hickson , Strategic Manager of Economy & Planning, County Hall, Taunton TA1 4DY ☎ 01823 355661 ✉ phickson@somerset.gov.uk

Traffic Management: Ms Beverley Norman , Service Manager of Traffic Mangement, County Hall, Taunton TA1 4DY ☎ 01823 358089 ✉ bjnorman@somerset.gov.uk

Transport: Mr Phil Lowndes , Strategic Manager of Traffic & Transport Development, County Hall, Taunton TA1 4DY ☎ 01823 356139 ✉ aplowndes@somerset.gov.uk

Transport Planner: Mr Mike O'Dowd-Jones , Strategic Manager of Highways & Transport, County Hall, Taunton TA1 4DY ☎ 01823 356238 ✉ modowdjones@somerset.gov.uk

Waste Collection and Disposal: Mr Steve Read , Managing Director of Somerset Waste Partnership, Monmouth House, Blackbrook Park Avenue, Taunton TA1 2PX ☎ 01823 625708 ✉ sread@somerset.gov.uk

Waste Management: Mr Steve Read , Managing Director of Somerset Waste Partnership, Monmouth House, Blackbrook Park Avenue, Taunton TA1 2PX ☎ 01823 625708 ✉ sread@somerset.gov.uk

COUNCILLORS

***Chair* Lawrence**, Christine (CON - Dunster)
cmlawrence@somerset.gov.uk

***Vice-Chair* Noel**, Graham (CON - Mendip West)
gnoel@somerset.gov.uk

***Leader of the Council* Osman**, John (CON - Wells)
jdosman@somerset.gov.uk

***Deputy Leader of the Council* Hall**, David (CON - Bridgwater East & Bawdrip)
dhall@somerset.gov.uk

***Group Leader* Dimmick**, Alan (UKIP - Yeovil Central)
adimmick@somerset.gov.uk

Adkins, Michael (CON - Taunton North)
madkins@somerset.gov.uk

Bailey, John (LD - Martock)
jabailey@somerset.gov.uk

Baker, Justine (LD - Bishops Hull & Taunton West)
jmbaker@somerset.gov.uk

Bown, Ann (CON - Bridgwater West)
aebown@somerset.gov.uk

Brown, Richard (CON - North Petherton)
rjbrown@somerset.gov.uk

Burridge-Clayton, Peter (CON - Burnham on Sea North)
pburridgeclayton@somerset.gov.uk

Coles, Simon (LD - Taunton East)
scoles@somerset.gov.uk

Crabb, Samuel (LD - Brympton)
sdcrabb@somerset.gov.uk

Davies, Hugh (IND - Watchet & Stogursey)
hdavies@somerset.gov.uk

Denbee, John (CON - Brent)
jdenbee@somerset.gov.uk

Dyke, John (LD - Crewkerne)
jdyke@somerset.gov.uk

Edney, John (CON - Cannington)
jedney@somerset.gov.uk

Fothergill, David (CON - Monkton & North Curry)
djafothergill@somerset.gov.uk

Fysh, Marcus (CON - Coker)
mfysh@somerset.gov.uk

Gloak, Alan (LD - Glastonbury & Street)
afgloak@somerset.gov.uk

Govier, Andrew (LAB - Wellington)
ajgovier@somerset.gov.uk

Greene, David (IND - Yeovil South)
dagreene@somerset.gov.uk

Groskop, Anna (CON - Wincanton & Bruton)
amgroskop@somerset.gov.uk

Ham, Philip (CON - Mendip Central & East)
pjham@somerset.gov.uk

Healey, Mark (CON - Huntspill)
mhealey@somerset.gov.uk

Henley, Ross (LD - Blackdown & Neroche)
rlhenley@somerset.gov.uk

Hill, Dawn (CON - Cheddar)
dmhill@somerset.gov.uk

Horsfall, Alvin (LD - Frome East)
ajhorsfall@somerset.gov.uk

Hunt, James (CON - Upper Tone)
jahunt@somerset.gov.uk

Huxtable, David (CON - King Alfred)
djhuxtable@somerset.gov.uk

Le Hardy, Christopher (CON - South Petherton & Islemoor)
clehardy@somerset.gov.uk

Lewis, Michael (CON - Castle Cary)
mblewis@somerset.gov.uk

Lock, Jane (LD - Yeovil West)
jlock@somerset.gov.uk

Lock, Tony (LD - Yeovil East)
tlock@somerset.gov.uk

Loveridge, David (LAB - Bridgwater North & Central)
dloveridge@somerset.gov.uk

Napper, Terry (CON - Glastonbury & Street)
twenapper@somerset.gov.uk

Nicholson, Frances (CON - Dulverton & Exmoor)
fmnicholson@somerset.gov.uk

Oliver, Linda (CON - Frome North)
loliver@somerset.gov.uk

Parham, John (CON - Shepton Mallet)
jparham@somerset.gov.uk

Pearson, Nigel (UKIP - Chard North)
ncpearson@somerset.gov.uk

Prior-Sankey, Hazel (LD - Taunton South)
hrprior-sankey@somerset.gov.uk

Redman, Leigh (LAB - Bridgwater South)
lredman@somerset.gov.uk

Rigby, Mike (IND - Lydeard) msrigby@somerset.gov.uk

Ruddle, Dean (CON - Somerton)
ddruddle@somerset.gov.uk

Shortland, Jill (LD - Chard South)
jcshortland@somerset.gov.uk

Siggs, Harvey (CON - Mendip North West)
hsiggs@somerset.gov.uk

Venner, Terry (UKIP - Minehead)
tvenner@somerset.gov.uk

Vijeh, Linda (CON - Ilminster) lpvijeh@somerset.gov.uk

Wallace, William (CON - Blackmoor Vale)
wwallace@somerset.gov.uk

Wedderkopp, Danny (LD - Taunton Fairwater)
dwedderkopp@somerset.gov.uk

Wedderkopp, Alan (LD - Comeytrowe & Trull)
awedderkopp@somerset.gov.uk

Woodman, John (CON - Highbridge & Burnham South)
jwoodman@somerset.gov.uk

Woollcombe-Adams, Nigel (CON - Mendip South)
nwoollcombeadams@somerset.gov.uk

Yeomans, Derek (CON - Curry Rivel & Langport)
dnyeomans@somerset.gov.uk

POLITICAL COMPOSITION

CON: 31, LD: 14, UKIP: 3, IND: 3, LAB: 3

COMMITTEE CHAIRS

Audit: Mrs Dawn Hill

Health & Wellbeing: Miss Ann Bown

South Ayrshire S

South Ayrshire Council, County Buildings, Wellington Square, Ayr KA7 1DR
☎ 0300 123 0900 🖷 01292 612143 🖳 www.south-ayrshire.gov.uk

FACTS AND FIGURES

Parliamentary Constituencies: Ayr, Carrick and Cumnock, Ayrshire Central
EU Constituencies: Scotland
Election Frequency: Elections are of whole council

SOUTH AYRSHIRE

PRINCIPAL OFFICERS

Chief Executive: Mrs Eileen Howat, Chief Executive, County Buildings, Wellington Square, Ayr KA7 1DR ☎ 01292 612612 ✉ eileen.howat@south-ayrshire.gov.uk

Senior Management: Ms Valerie Andrews , Executive Director - Resources, Governance & Organisation, County Buildings, Wellington Square, Ayr KA7 1DR ☎ 01292 612466 🖷 01292 612455 ✉ valerie.andrews@south-ayrshire.gov.uk

Senior Management: Ms Lesley Bloomer , Executive Director - Economy, Neighbourhood & Environment, County Buildings, Wellington Square, Ayr KA7 1DR ☎ 01290 612185 ✉ lesley.bloomer@south-ayrshire.gov.uk

Senior Management: Mr Tim Eltringham , Director - Health & Social Care, County Buildings, Wellington Square, Ayr KA7 1DR ☎ 01292 612419 ✉ tim.eltringham@south-ayreshire.gov.uk

Senior Management: Mr Douglas Hutchinson , Director - Educational Services, County Buildings, Wellington Square, Ayr KA7 1DR ☎ 01292 621134 ✉ douglas.hutchinson@south-ayrshire.gov.uk

Architect, Building / Property Services: Ms Lesley Bloomer, Executive Director - Economy, Neighbourhood & Environment, County Buildings, Wellington Square, Ayr KA7 1DR ☎ 01290 612185 ✉ lesley.bloomer@south-ayrshire.gov.uk

Best Value: Ms Claire Monaghan , Head of Communities, County Buildings, Wellington Square, Ayr KA7 1DR ☎ 01292 612757 🖷 01292 612158 ✉ claire.monaghan@south-ayrshire.gov.uk

Building Control: Mr Mike Newall , Head of Neighbourhood Services, Burns House, Burns Statue Square, Ayr KA7 1UT ☎ 01292 616231 ✉ mike.newall@south-ayrshire.gov.uk

Catering Services: Ms Jennifer Rodden , Facilities Manager, County Buildings, Wellington Square, Ayr KA7 1DR ☎ 01292 616045 ✉ jennifer.rodden@south-ayrshire.gov.uk

Children / Youth Services: Ms Paula Godfrey , Head of Children's Healthcare & Criminal Justice, County Buildings, Wellington Square, Ayr KA7 1DR ☎ 01292 642244 ✉ paula.godfrey@south-ayrshire.gov.uk

PR / Communications: Ms Claire Monaghan , Head of Communities, County Buildings, Wellington Square, Ayr KA7 1DR ☎ 01292 612757 🖷 01292 612158 ✉ claire.monaghan@south-ayrshire.gov.uk

Community Planning: Ms Claire Monaghan , Head of Communities, County Buildings, Wellington Square, Ayr KA7 1DR ☎ 01292 612757 🖷 01292 612158 ✉ claire.monaghan@south-ayrshire.gov.uk

Community Safety: Ms Linda Warwick , Community Safety Co-ordinator, County Buildings, Wellington Square, Ayr KA7 1DR ☎ 01292 559403 ✉ linda.warwick@south-ayrshire.gov.uk

Computer Management: Mr Gordon Muir, ICT Strategy Officer, County Buildings, Wellington Square, Ayr KA7 1DR ☎ 01292 612731 🖷 01292 6121402 ✉ gordon.muir@south-ayrshire.gov.uk

Consumer Protection and Trading Standards: Mr Mike Newall , Head of Neighbourhood Services, Burns House, Burns Statue Square, Ayr KA7 1UT ☎ 01292 616231 ✉ mike.newall@south-ayrshire.gov.uk

Contracts: Mr Donald Gillies , Head of Property & Risk, County Buildings, Wellington Square, Ayr KA7 1DR ☎ 01292 612777 ✉ donald.gillies@south-ayrshire.gov.uk

Corporate Services: Mrs Eileen Howat, Chief Executive, County Buildings, Wellington Square, Ayr KA7 1DR ☎ 01292 612612 ✉ eileen.howat@south-ayrshire.gov.uk

Customer Service: Ms Kate O'Hagan , Head of Employee & Customer Services, County Buildings, Wellington Square, Ayr KA7 1DR ☎ 01292 612696 ✉ kate.ohagan@south-ayrshire.gov.uk

Economic Development: Mr Mark Hastings , Enterprise Manager, Burns House, Burns Statue Square, Ayr KA7 1UT ☎ 01292 616347 ✉ mark.hastings@south-ayrshire.gov.uk

Education: Mr Douglas Hutchinson , Director - Educational Services, County Buildings, Wellington Square, Ayr KA7 1DR ☎ 01292 621134 ✉ douglas.hutchinson@south-ayrshire.gov.uk

E-Government: Mrs Eileen Howat, Chief Executive, County Buildings, Wellington Square, Ayr KA7 1DR ☎ 01292 612612 ✉ eileen.howat@south-ayrshire.gov.uk

Electoral Registration: Ms Helen McPhee , Assessor & Electoral Registration Officer, County Buildings, Wellington Square, Ayr KA7 1DR ☎ 01292 612540 ✉ helen.mcphee@south-ayrshire.gov.uk

Emergency Planning: Mr David Whyte , Civil Contingencies Manager, Prestwick Airport, Building 372 Alpha Freight Area, Robertson Road, Prestwick KA9 2PL ☎ 01292 692180 🖷 01292 692184 ✉ david.whyte@south-ayrshire.gov.uk

Environmental / Technical Services: Ms Lesley Bloomer , Executive Director - Economy, Neighbourhood & Environment, County Buildings, Wellington Square, Ayr KA7 1DR ☎ 01290 612185 ✉ lesley.bloomer@south-ayrshire.gov.uk

Environmental Health: Mr David Thomson , Trading Standards & Environmental Health Manager, River Terrace, Ayr KA8 0BJ ☎ 01292 616055 ✉ david.thomson@south-ayrshire.gov.uk

Estates, Property & Valuation: Mr Donald Gillies , Head of Property & Risk, County Buildings, Wellington Square, Ayr KA7 1DR ☎ 01292 612777 ✉ donald.gillies@south-ayrshire.gov.uk

European Liaison: Ms Claire Monaghan , Head of Communities, County Buildings, Wellington Square, Ayr KA7 1DR ☎ 01292 612757 🖷 01292 612158 ✉ claire.monaghan@south-ayrshire.gov.uk

Events Manager: Mr Mark Hastings , Enterprise Manager, Burns House, Burns Statue Square, Ayr KA7 1UT ☎ 01292 616347 ✉ mark.hastings@south-ayrshire.gov.uk

Facilities: Ms Jennifer Rodden , Facilities Manager, County Buildings, Wellington Square, Ayr KA7 1DR ☎ 01292 616045 ✉ jennifer.rodden@south-ayrshire.gov.uk

Finance: Mr Tim Baulk , Head of Service, County Buildings, Wellington Square, Ayr KA7 1DR Tel 01292 612620 Email tim.baulk@south-ayrshire.gov.uk

Fleet Management: Mr Mike Newall , Head of Neighbourhood Services, Burns House, Burns Statue Square, Ayr KA7 1UT Tel 01292 616231 Email mike.newall@south-ayrshire.gov.uk

Grounds Maintenance: Mr Kenny Dalrymple , Neighbourhood Services Manager, Burns House, Burns Statue Square, Ayr KA7 1UT Tel 01292 612041 Fax 01292 616284 Email kenny.dalrymple@south-ayrshire.gov.uk

Health and Safety: Ms Kate O'Hagan , Head of Employee & Customer Services, County Buildings, Wellington Square, Ayr KA7 1DR Tel 01292 612696 Email kate.ohagan@south-ayrshire.gov.uk

Highways: Mr Mike Newall , Head of Neighbourhood Services, Burns House, Burns Statue Square, Ayr KA7 1UT Tel 01292 616231 Email mike.newall@south-ayrshire.gov.uk

Housing: Mr Kenny Leinster , Head of Community Health & Care Services, County Buildings, Wellington Square, Ayr KA7 1DR Tel 01292 612735 Fax 01292 612258 Email kenny.leinster@south-ayrshire.gov.uk

Housing Maintenance: Ms Lesley Bloomer , Executive Director - Economy, Neighbourhood & Environment, County Buildings, Wellington Square, Ayr KA7 1DR Tel 01290 612185 Email lesley.bloomer@south-ayrshire.gov.uk

Local Area Agreement: Ms Claire Monaghan , Head of Communities, County Buildings, Wellington Square, Ayr KA7 1DR Tel 01292 612757 Fax 01292 612158 Email claire.monaghan@south-ayrshire.gov.uk

Legal: Mr Ralf Riddiough , Head of Legal & Democratic Services, County Buildings, Wellington Square, Ayr KA7 1DR Tel 01292 612245 Email ralf.riddiough@south-ayrshire.gov.uk

Leisure and Cultural Services: Mrs Jill Cronin , Head of Development & Leisure, County Buildings, Wellington Square, Ayr KA7 1DR Tel 01292 612473 Fax 01292 612261 Email jill.cronin@south-ayrshire.gov.uk

Licensing: Mr Ralf Riddiough , Head of Legal & Democratic Services, County Buildings, Wellington Square, Ayr KA7 1DR Tel 01292 612245 Email ralf.riddiough@south-ayrshire.gov.uk

Lifelong Learning: Mr Douglas Hutchinson , Director - Educational Services, County Buildings, Wellington Square, Ayr KA7 1DR Tel 01292 621134 Email douglas.hutchinson@south-ayrshire.gov.uk

Lottery Funding, Charity and Voluntary: Mr David Sherlock , Improvement Manager, County Buildings, Wellington Square, Ayr KA7 1DR Tel 01292 612197 Email david.sherlock@south-ayrshire.gov.uk

Member Services: Mr Ralf Riddiough , Head of Legal & Democratic Services, County Buildings, Wellington Square, Ayr KA7 1DR Tel 01292 612245 Email ralf.riddiough@south-ayrshire.gov.uk

Parking: Mr Mike Newall , Head of Neighbourhood Services, Burns House, Burns Statue Square, Ayr KA7 1UT Tel 01292 616231 Email mike.newall@south-ayrshire.gov.uk

Partnerships: Ms Claire Monaghan , Head of Communities, County Buildings, Wellington Square, Ayr KA7 1DR Tel 01292 612757 Fax 01292 612158 Email claire.monaghan@south-ayrshire.gov.uk

Personnel / HR: Ms Kate O'Hagan , Head of Employee & Customer Services, County Buildings, Wellington Square, Ayr KA7 1DR Tel 01292 612696 Email kate.ohagan@south-ayrshire.gov.uk

Planning: Ms Christina Cox , Planning Manager, Burns House, Burns Statue Square, Ayr KA7 1UT Tel 01292 616234 Email christina.cox@south-ayrshire.gov.uk

Procurement: Mr Ralf Riddiough , Head of Legal & Democratic Services, County Buildings, Wellington Square, Ayr KA7 1DR Tel 01292 612245 Email ralf.riddiough@south-ayrshire.gov.uk

Public Libraries: Mrs Jill Cronin , Head of Development & Leisure, County Buildings, Wellington Square, Ayr KA7 1DR Tel 01292 612473 Fax 01292 612261 Email jill.cronin@south-ayrshire.gov.uk

Recycling & Waste Minimisation: Mr Kenny Dalrymple , Neighbourhood Services Manager, Burns House, Burns Statue Square, Ayr KA7 1UT Tel 01292 612041 Fax 01292 616284 Email kenny.dalrymple@south-ayrshire.gov.uk

Regeneration: Mrs Jill Cronin , Head of Development & Leisure, County Buildings, Wellington Square, Ayr KA7 1DR Tel 01292 612473 Fax 01292 612261 Email jill.cronin@south-ayrshire.gov.uk

Road Safety: Mrs Mary Garrett , Road Safety Officer, Ayrshire Roads Alliance, Burns House, Burns Statue Square, Ayr KA7 1UT Tel 01563 576448 Email mary.garrett@south-atyshire.gov.uk

Social Services: Mr Tim Eltringham , Director - Health & Social Care, County Buildings, Wellington Square, Ayr KA7 1DR Tel 01292 612419 Email tim.eltringham@south-ayreshire.gov.uk

Social Services (Adult): Mr Kenny Leinster , Head of Community Health & Care Services, County Buildings, Wellington Square, Ayr KA7 1DR Tel 01292 612735 Fax 01292 612258 Email kenny.leinster@south-ayrshire.gov.uk

Social Services (Children): Ms Paula Godfrey , Head of Children's Healthcare & Criminal Justice, County Buildings, Wellington Square, Ayr KA7 1DR Tel 01292 642244 Email paula.godfrey@south-ayrshire.gov.uk

Staff Training: Ms Kate O'Hagan , Head of Employee & Customer Services, County Buildings, Wellington Square, Ayr KA7 1DR Tel 01292 612696 Email kate.ohagan@south-ayrshire.gov.uk

Sustainable Communities: Ms Claire Monaghan , Head of Communities, County Buildings, Wellington Square, Ayr KA7 1DR Tel 01292 612757 Fax 01292 612158 Email claire.monaghan@south-ayrshire.gov.uk

SOUTH AYRSHIRE

Sustainable Development: Ms Claire Monaghan , Head of Communities, County Buildings, Wellington Square, Ayr KA7 1DR
☎ 01292 612757 🖷 01292 612158
🖰 claire.monaghan@south-ayrshire.gov.uk

Tourism: Mr Mark Hastings , Enterprise Manager, Burns House, Burns Statue Square, Ayr KA7 1UT ☎ 01292 616347
🖰 mark.hastings@south-ayrshire.gov.uk

Town Centre: Mr David Bell , Managing Director of Ayr Renaissance, County Buildings, Wellington Square, Ayr KA7 1DR
☎ 01292 612477 🖰 david.bell@south-ayrshire.gov.uk

Transport: Mr Mike Newall , Head of Neighbourhood Services, Burns House, Burns Statue Square, Ayr KA7 1UT ☎ 01292 616231
🖰 mike.newall@south-ayrshire.gov.uk

Waste Collection and Disposal: Mr Kenny Dalrymple , Neighbourhood Services Manager, Burns House, Burns Statue Square, Ayr KA7 1UT ☎ 01292 612041 🖷 01292 616284
🖰 kenny.dalrymple@south-ayrshire.gov.uk

Waste Management: Mr Kenny Dalrymple , Neighbourhood Services Manager, Burns House, Burns Statue Square, Ayr KA7 1UT ☎ 01292 612041 🖷 01292 616284
🖰 kenny.dalrymple@south-ayrshire.gov.uk

COUNCILLORS

***Provost* Moonie**, Helen (LAB - Prestwick)
helen.moonie@south-ayrshire.gov.uk

***Deputy Provost* Kilpatrick**, Mary (CON - Ayr East)
mary.kilpatrick@south-ayrshire.gov.uk

***Leader of the Council* McIntosh**, Bill (CON - Troon)
bill.mcintosh@south-ayrshire.gov.uk

***Deputy Leader of the Council* McDowall**, John (LAB - Girvan and South Carrick)
john.mcdowall@south-ayrshire.gov.uk

Allan, John (SNP - Kyle)
john.allan@south-ayrshire.gov.uk

Campbell, Andy (LAB - Kyle)
andy.campbell@south-ayrshire.gov.uk

Campbell, Douglas (SNP - Ayr North)
douglas.campbell@south-ayrshire.gov.uk

Cavana, Ian (LAB - Ayr North)
ian.cavana@south-ayrshire.gov.uk

Clark, Alec (IND - Girvan and South Carrick)
alec.clark@south-ayrshire.gov.uk

Cochrane, Ian (SNP - Prestwick)
ian.cochrane@south-ayrshire.gov.uk

Connolly, Brian (IND - Maybole, North Carrick and Coylton)
brian.connolly@south-ayrshire.gov.uk

Convery, Peter (CON - Troon)
peter.convery@south-ayrshire.gov.uk

Darwent, Kirsty (LAB - Ayr West)
kirsty.darwent@south-ayrshire.gov.uk

Davies, Hywel (IND - Kyle)
hywel.davies@south-ayrshire.gov.uk

Dorans, Allan (SNP - Ayr West)
allan.dorans@south-ayrshire.gov.uk

Douglas, Ian (SNP - Ayr East)
ian.douglas@south-ayrshire.gov.uk

Galbraith, Ann (CON - Maybole, North Carrick and Coylton)
ann.galbraith@south-ayrshire.gov.uk

Goldie, Sandra (LAB - Maybole, North Carrick and Coylton)
sandra.goldie@south-ayrshire.gov.uk

Grant, Bill (CON - Ayr West)
bill.grant@south-ayrshire.gov.uk

Grant, William (SNP - Maybole, North Carrick and Coylton)
william.grant@south-ayrshire.gov.uk

Hampton, John (CON - Ayr North)
john.hampton@south-ayrshire.gov.uk

Hunter, Hugh (CON - Prestwick)
hugh.hunter@south-ayrshire.gov.uk

McFarlane, Nan (SNP - Troon)
nan.mcfarlane@south-ayrshire.gov.uk

McGinley, Brian (LAB - Ayr East)
brian.mcginley@south-ayrshire.gov.uk

Miller, Rita (LAB - Ayr North)
rita.miller@south-ayrshire.gov.uk

Oattes, Alec (SNP - Girvan and South Carrick)
alec.oattes@south-ayrshire.gov.uk

Reid, Robin (CON - Ayr West)
robin.reid@south-ayrshire.gov.uk

Saxton, Phil (LAB - Troon)
philip.saxton@south-ayrshire.gov.uk

Toner, Margaret (CON - Prestwick)
margaret.toner@south-ayrshire.gov.uk

POLITICAL COMPOSITION

CON: 9, LAB: 9, SNP: 8, IND: 3

South Bucks D

South Bucks District Council, Council Offices, Capswood, Oxford Road, Denham UB9 4LH
☎ 01895 837200 🖷 01895 837277 🖰 sbdc@southbucks.gov.uk
💻 www.southbucks.gov.uk

FACTS AND FIGURES

Parliamentary Constituencies: Beaconsfield
EU Constituencies: South East
Election Frequency: Elections are of whole council

PRINCIPAL OFFICERS

Chief Executive: Mr Bob Smith, Interim Chief Executive (Director of Services), Council Offices, Capswood, Oxford Road, Denham UB9 4LH ☎ 01895 837367; 01494 732178 🖷 01494 586506
🖰 bsmith@chiltern.gov.uk

Senior Management: Mr Jim Burness, Director of Resources, Council Offices, Capswood, Oxford Road, Denham UB9 4LH
☎ 01895 837367; 01494 732905 🖰 jburness@chiltern.gov.uk

Senior Management: Mr Bob Smith, Interim Chief Executive (Director of Services), Council Offices, Capswood, Oxford Road, Denham UB9 4LH ☎ 01895 837367; 01494 732178 🖷 01494 586506 🖱 bsmith@chiltern.gov.uk

Architect, Building / Property Services: Mr Bob Smith, Interim Chief Executive (Director of Services), Council Offices, Capswood, Oxford Road, Denham UB9 4LH ☎ 01895 837367; 01494 732178 🖷 01494 586506 🖱 bsmith@chiltern.gov.uk

Building Control: Mr Bob Smith, Interim Chief Executive (Director of Services), Council Offices, Capswood, Oxford Road, Denham UB9 4LH ☎ 01895 837367; 01494 732178 🖷 01494 586506 🖱 bsmith@chiltern.gov.uk

Children / Youth Services: Mrs Rachael Winfield, Community & Partnerships Officer, Council Offices, Capswood, Oxford Road, Denham UB9 4LH ☎ 01895 837318 🖱 rachael.winfield@southbucks.gov.uk

PR / Communications: Mrs Rachel Prance , Community & Partnerships Officer, Council Offices, King George V Road, Amersham HP6 5AW ☎ 01494 732903 🖷 01494 586506 🖱 rprance@chiltern.gov.uk

Community Safety: Mr Martin Holt, Head of Healthy Communities, Council Offices, King George V Road, Amersham HP6 5AW ☎ 01494 732055 🖷 01494 586504 🖱 mholt@chiltern.gov.uk

Computer Management: Mr Jim Burness, Director of Resources, Council Offices, Capswood, Oxford Road, Denham UB9 4LH ☎ 01895 837367; 01494 732905 🖱 jburness@chiltern.gov.uk

Computer Management: Mrs Simonette Dixon, Head of Business Support, Council Offices, King George V Road, Amersham HP6 5AW ☎ 01494 732087 🖷 01494 586509 🖱 sdixon@chiltern.gov.uk

Contracts: Mr Bob Smith, Interim Chief Executive (Director of Services), Council Offices, Capswood, Oxford Road, Denham UB9 4LH ☎ 01895 837367; 01494 732178 🖷 01494 586506 🖱 bsmith@chiltern.gov.uk

Corporate Services: Mr Jim Burness, Director of Resources, Council Offices, Capswood, Oxford Road, Denham UB9 4LH ☎ 01895 837367; 01494 732905 🖱 jburness@chiltern.gov.uk

Customer Service: Mrs Nicola Ellis , Head of Customer Services, Council Offices, King George V Road, Amersham HP6 5AW ☎ 01494 732231 🖱 nellis@chiltern.gov.uk

Economic Development: Mr Bob Smith, Interim Chief Executive (Director of Services), Council Offices, Capswood, Oxford Road, Denham UB9 4LH ☎ 01895 837367; 01494 732178 🖷 01494 586506 🖱 bsmith@chiltern.gov.uk

Electoral Registration: Mrs Joanna Swift, Head of Legal & Democratic Services, Council Offices, Capswood, Oxford Road, Denham UB9 4LH ☎ 01895 837229; 01494 732761 🖱 jswift@chiltern.gov.uk

Electoral Registration: Mrs Kulvinder Tumber, Democratic & Electoral Services Manager, Council Offices, Capswood, Oxford Road, Denham UB9 4LH ☎ 01895 837225 🖱 kully.tumber@southbucks.gov.uk

Emergency Planning: Mr Dave Gilmour, Environmental Health Manager, Council Offices, Capswood, Oxford Road, Denham UB9 4LH ☎ 01895 837200 🖱 david.gilmour@southbucks.gov.uk

Energy Management: Mr Bob Smith, Interim Chief Executive (Director of Services), Council Offices, Capswood, Oxford Road, Denham UB9 4LH ☎ 01895 837367; 01494 732178 🖷 01494 586506 🖱 bsmith@chiltern.gov.uk

Environmental / Technical Services: Mr Peter Beckford , Head of Sustainable Development, Council Offices, Capswood, Oxford Road, Denham UB9 4LH ☎ 01895 837208; 01494 732036 🖱 pbeckford@chiltern.gov.uk

Environmental / Technical Services: Mr Chris Marchant , Head of Environment, Council Offices, Capswood, Oxford Road, Denham UB9 4LH ☎ 01895 837360; 01494 732250 🖱 cmarchant@chiltern.gov.uk

Environmental / Technical Services: Mr Bob Smith, Interim Chief Executive (Director of Services), Council Offices, Capswood, Oxford Road, Denham UB9 4LH ☎ 01895 837367; 01494 732178 🖷 01494 586506 🖱 bsmith@chiltern.gov.uk

Environmental Health: Mr Martin Holt, Head of Healthy Communities, Council Offices, King George V Road, Amersham HP6 5AW ☎ 01494 732055 🖷 01494 586504 🖱 mholt@chiltern.gov.uk

Environmental Health: Mr Bob Smith, Interim Chief Executive (Director of Services), Council Offices, Capswood, Oxford Road, Denham UB9 4LH ☎ 01895 837367; 01494 732178 🖷 01494 586506 🖱 bsmith@chiltern.gov.uk

Estates, Property & Valuation: Mr Bob Smith, Interim Chief Executive (Director of Services), Council Offices, Capswood, Oxford Road, Denham UB9 4LH ☎ 01895 837367; 01494 732178 🖷 01494 586506 🖱 bsmith@chiltern.gov.uk

Facilities: Mr Andrew Crow, Facilities Manager, Council Offices, Capswood, Oxford Road, Denham UB9 4LH ☎ 01895 837200 🖱 andrew.crow@southbucks.gov.uk

Finance: Mr Jim Burness, Director of Resources, Council Offices, Capswood, Oxford Road, Denham UB9 4LH ☎ 01895 837367; 01494 732905 🖱 jburness@chiltern.gov.uk

Finance: Mr Rodney Fincham , Head of Finance, Council Offices, Capswood, Oxford Road, Denham UB9 4LH ☎ 01895 837268 🖱 rodney.fincham@southbucks.gov.uk

Health and Safety: Mr Bob Smith, Interim Chief Executive (Director of Services), Council Offices, Capswood, Oxford Road, Denham UB9 4LH ☎ 01895 837367; 01494 732178 🖷 01494 586506 🖱 bsmith@chiltern.gov.uk

SOUTH BUCKS

Housing: Mr Bob Smith, Interim Chief Executive (Director of Services), Council Offices, Capswood, Oxford Road, Denham UB9 4LH ☎ 01895 837367; 01494 732178 🖷 01494 586506 🖱 bsmith@chiltern.gov.uk

Legal: Mrs Joanna Swift, Head of Legal & Democratic Services, Council Offices, Capswood, Oxford Road, Denham UB9 4LH ☎ 01895 837229; 01494 732761 🖱 jswift@chiltern.gov.uk

Leisure and Cultural Services: Mr Martin Holt, Head of Healthy Communities, Council Offices, King George V Road, Amersham HP6 5AW ☎ 01494 732055 🖷 01494 586504 🖱 mholt@chiltern.gov.uk

Licensing: Mr Bob Smith, Interim Chief Executive (Director of Services), Council Offices, Capswood, Oxford Road, Denham UB9 4LH ☎ 01895 837367; 01494 732178 🖷 01494 586506 🖱 bsmith@chiltern.gov.uk

Member Services: Mrs Kulvinder Tumber, Democratic & Electoral Services Manager, Council Offices, Capswood, Oxford Road, Denham UB9 4LH ☎ 01895 837225 🖱 kully.tumber@southbucks.gov.uk

Parking: Mr Chris Marchant , Head of Environment, Council Offices, Capswood, Oxford Road, Denham UB9 4LH ☎ 01895 837360; 01494 732250 🖱 cmarchant@chiltern.gov.uk

Partnerships: Mrs Rachel Prance , Community & Partnerships Officer, Council Offices, King George V Road, Amersham HP6 5AW ☎ 01494 732903 🖷 01494 586506 🖱 rprance@chiltern.gov.uk

Personnel / HR: Ms Judy Benson , HR Manager, Council Offices, Capswood, Oxford Road, Denham UB9 4LH ☎ 01895 837334 🖱 judy.benson@southbucks.gov.uk

Planning: Mr Bob Smith, Interim Chief Executive (Director of Services), Council Offices, Capswood, Oxford Road, Denham UB9 4LH ☎ 01895 837367; 01494 732178 🖷 01494 586506 🖱 bsmith@chiltern.gov.uk

Procurement: Mr Rodney Fincham , Head of Finance, Council Offices, Capswood, Oxford Road, Denham UB9 4LH ☎ 01895 837268 🖱 rodney.fincham@southbucks.gov.uk

Recycling & Waste Minimisation: Mr Bob Smith, Interim Chief Executive (Director of Services), Council Offices, Capswood, Oxford Road, Denham UB9 4LH ☎ 01895 837367; 01494 732178 🖷 01494 586506 🖱 bsmith@chiltern.gov.uk

Regeneration: Mr Peter Beckford , Head of Sustainable Development, Council Offices, Capswood, Oxford Road, Denham UB9 4LH ☎ 01895 837208; 01494 732036 🖱 pbeckford@chiltern.gov.uk

Sustainable Communities: Mr Martin Holt, Head of Healthy Communities, Council Offices, King George V Road, Amersham HP6 5AW ☎ 01494 732055 🖷 01494 586504 🖱 mholt@chiltern.gov.uk

Sustainable Development: Mr Bob Smith, Interim Chief Executive (Director of Services), Council Offices, Capswood, Oxford Road, Denham UB9 4LH ☎ 01895 837367; 01494 732178 🖷 01494 586506 🖱 bsmith@chiltern.gov.uk

Waste Collection and Disposal: Mr Bob Smith, Interim Chief Executive (Director of Services), Council Offices, Capswood, Oxford Road, Denham UB9 4LH ☎ 01895 837367; 01494 732178 🖷 01494 586506 🖱 bsmith@chiltern.gov.uk

Waste Management: Mr Bob Smith, Interim Chief Executive (Director of Services), Council Offices, Capswood, Oxford Road, Denham UB9 4LH ☎ 01895 837367; 01494 732178 🖷 01494 586506 🖱 bsmith@chiltern.gov.uk

COUNCILLORS

***Chair* Smith**, Duncan (CON - Gerrards Cross)
cllr.duncan.smith@southbucks.gov.uk

***Leader of the Council* Bagge**, Ralph (CON - Stoke Poges)
cllr.ralph.bagge@southbucks.gov.uk

***Deputy Leader of the Council* Naylor**, Nick (CON - Burnham Church & Beeches)
cllr.nick.naylor@southbucks.gov.uk

Anthony, David (CON - Farnham & Hedgerley)
cllr.david.anthony@southbucks.gov.uk

Bastiman, Philip (CON - Beaconsfield West)
cllr.philip.bastiman@southbucks.gov.uk

Bradford, Malcolm (CON - Wexham & Fulmer)
cllr.malcolm.bradford@southbucks.gov.uk

Chhokar, Santokh (CON - Gerrards Cross)
cllr.santokh.chhokar@southbucks.gov.uk

Dhillon, Dev (CON - Farnham & Hedgerley)
cllr.dev.dhillon@southbucks.gov.uk

Egleton, Trevor (CON - Stoke Poges)
cllr.trevor.egleton@southbucks.gov.uk

Gibbs, Barbara (CON - Gerrards Cross)
cllr.barbara.gibbs@southbucks.gov.uk

Griffin, Paul (IND - Iver Village & Richings Park)
cllr.paul.griffin@southbucks.gov.uk

Hardin, Barry (CON - Denham)
cllr.barry.harding@southbucks.gov.uk

Hazell, Lin (CON - Burnham Church & Beeches)
cllr.lin.hazell@southbucks.gov.uk

Hogan, Patrick (CON - Beaconsfield West)
cllr.patrick.hogan@southbucks.gov.uk

Hollis, Guy (CON - Denham)
cllr.guy.hollis@southbucks.gov.uk

Jordan, Jilly (CON - Iver Village & Richings Park)
cllr.jilly.jordan@southbucks.gov.uk

Kelly, Paul (CON - Burnham Church & Beeches)
cllr.paul.kelly@southbucks.gov.uk

Lowen-Cooper, Jacquetta (CON - Beaconsfield South)
cllr.jacquetta.lowen-cooper@southbucks.gov.uk

Matthews, Wendy (CON - Iver Village & Richings Park)
cllr.wendy.matthews@southbucks.gov.uk

Pepler, David (CON - Burnham Lent Rise & Taplow)
cllr.david.pepler@southbucks.gov.uk

Read, John (CON - Beaconsfield South)
cllr.john.read@southbucks.gov.uk

Reed, Roger (CON - Denham)
cllr.roger.reed@southbucks.gov.uk

Samson, Alan (CON - Burnham Lent Rise & Taplow)
cllr.alan.samson@southbucks.gov.uk

Sandy, George (CON - Burnham Lent Rise & Taplow)
cllr.george.sandy@southbucks.gov.uk

Sangster, Ray (CON - Iver Heath)
cllr.ray.sangster@southbucks.gov.uk

Sullivan, Luisa (CON - Iver Heath)
cllr.luisa.sullivan@southbucks.gov.uk

Vincent, David (CON - Farnham & Hedgerley)
cllr.david.vincent@southbucks.gov.uk

Walters, Alan (CON - Beaconsfield North)
cllr.alan.walters@southbucks.gov.uk

POLITICAL COMPOSITION
CON: 27, IND: 1

COMMITTEE CHAIRS
Audit: Mr Malcolm Bradford

Licensing: Mr Alan Walters

Planning: Mrs Jacquetta Lowen-Cooper

South Cambridgeshire D

South Cambridgeshire District Council, South Cambridgeshire Hall, Cambourne Business Park, Cambourne, Cambridge CB23 6EA
☎ 03450 450500 🖷 01954 713149 ✉ scdc@scambs.gov.uk
💻 www.scambs.gov.uk

FACTS AND FIGURES
Parliamentary Constituencies: Cambridgeshire South, Cambridgeshire South East
EU Constituencies: Eastern
Election Frequency: Elections are by thirds

PRINCIPAL OFFICERS
Chief Executive: Mrs Jean Hunter , Chief Executive, South Cambridgeshire Hall, Cambourne Business Park, Cambourne, Cambridge CB23 6EA ☎ 01954 713081 ✉ jean.hunter@scambs.gov.uk

Deputy Chief Executive: Mr Alex Colyer , Executive Director of Corporate Services & S151 Officer, South Cambridgeshire Hall, Cambourne Business Park, Cambourne, Cambridge CB23 6EA ☎ 01954 713023 ✉ alex.colyer@scambs.gov.uk

Senior Management: Mr Mike Hill , Director - Health & Environmental Services, South Cambridgeshire Hall, Cambourne Business Park, Cambourne, Cambridge CB23 6EA ☎ 03450 450500 🖷 01954 713248 ✉ mike.hill@scambs.gov.uk

Senior Management: Mr Stephen Hills , Director - Affordable Homes, South Cambridgeshire Hall, Cambourne Business Park, Cambourne, Cambridge CB23 6EA ☎ 03450 450500 ✉ stephen.hills@scambs.gov.uk

Senior Management: Ms Jo Mills , Director - Planning & New Communities, South Cambridgeshire Hall, Cambourne Business Park, Cambourne, Cambridge CB23 6EA

Best Value: Mr John Garnham , Head of Finance, Policy & Performance, South Cambridgeshire Hall, Cambourne Business Park, Cambourne, Cambridge CB23 6EA ☎ 03450 450500 ✉ john.garnham@scambs.gov.uk

Best Value: Mr Sean Missin, Procurement Officer, South Cambridgeshire Hall, Cambourne Business Park, Cambourne, Cambridge CB3 6EA ☎ 01954 713378 ✉ sean.missin@scambs.gov.uk

Building Control: Mr Andrew Dearlove , Interim Building Control Manager, South Cambridgeshire Hall, Cambourne Business Park, Cambourne, Cambridge CB23 6EA ☎ 03450 450450 ✉ andrew.dearlove@scambs.gov.uk

Catering Services: Mrs Eileen Simmons , Catering Manager, South Cambridgeshire Hall, Cambourne Business Park, Cambourne, Cambridge CB23 6EA ☎ 03450 450 500 ✉ eileen.simmons@scambs.gov.uk

PR / Communications: Mr Gareth Bell , Communications Manager, South Cambridgeshire Hall, Cambourne Business Park, Cambourne, Cambridge CB23 6EA ☎ 03450 450500 ✉ gareth.bell@scambs.gov.uk

Community Safety: Mr Phil Aldis , Community Safety Officer, South Cambridgeshire District Council, South Cambridgeshire Hall, Cambourne, Cambridge CB23 6EA ☎ 03450 450 500 ✉ phil.aldis@scambs.gov.uk

Computer Management: Mr Stephen Rayment, Head of ICT, South Cambridgeshire Hall, Cambourne Business Park, Cambourne, Cambridge CB23 6EA ☎ 03450 450 500 🖷 01954 713234 ✉ steve.rayment@scambs.gov.uk

Contracts: Mr Paul Quigley, Environment Services Manager, South Cambridgeshire Hall, Cambourne Business Park, Cambourne, Cambridge CB23 6EA ☎ 03450 450 500 🖷 01954 713248 ✉ paul.quigley@scambs.gov.uk

Customer Service: Miss Rachael Fox-Jackson , Customer Contact Manager, South Cambridgeshire Hall, Cambourne Business Park, Cambourne, Cambridge CB23 6EA ☎ 03450 450500 ✉ rachael.fox-jackson@scambs.gov.uk

Economic Development: Mrs Caroline Hunt , Planning Policy Manager, South Cambridgeshire Hall, Cambourne Business Park, Cambourne, Cambridge CB23 6EA ☎ 03450 450 500 ✉ caroline.hunt@scambs.gov.uk

E-Government: Mr Stephen Rayment, Head of ICT, South Cambridgeshire Hall, Cambourne Business Park, Cambourne, Cambridge CB23 6EA ☎ 03450 450 500 🖷 01954 713234 ✉ steve.rayment@scambs.gov.uk

Electoral Registration: Mr Andrew Francis , Electoral & Support Services Manager, South Cambridgeshire Hall, Cambourne Business Park, Cambourne, Cambridge CB23 6EA ☎ 03450 450 500 ✉ andrew.francis@scambs.gov.uk

SOUTH CAMBRIDGESHIRE

Emergency Planning: Mr Mike Hill , Director - Health & Environmental Services, South Cambridgeshire Hall, Cambourne Business Park, Cambourne, Cambridge CB23 6EA ☎ 03450 450500 🖷 01954 713248 ✉ mike.hill@scambs.gov.uk

Energy Management: Ms Siobhan Mellon , Partnerships Officer, South Cambridgeshire Hall, Cambourne Business Park, Cambourne, Cambridge CB23 6EA ☎ 03450 450500 ✉ siobhan.mellon@scambs.gov.uk

Environmental / Technical Services: Mr Paul Quigley, Environment Services Manager, South Cambridgeshire Hall, Cambourne Business Park, Cambourne, Cambridge CB23 6EA ☎ 03450 450 500 🖷 01954 713248 ✉ paul.quigley@scambs.gov.uk

Environmental Health: Mr Paul Quigley, Environment Services Manager, South Cambridgeshire Hall, Cambourne Business Park, Cambourne, Cambridge CB23 6EA ☎ 03450 450 500 🖷 01954 713248 ✉ paul.quigley@scambs.gov.uk

Facilities: Mr Michael Turner , Facilities Manager, South Cambridgeshire Hall, Cambourne Business Park, Cambourne, Cambridge CB23 6EA ☎ 03450 450500 ✉ michael.turner@scambs.gov.uk

Finance: Mr Alex Colyer , Executive Director of Corporate Services & S151 Officer, South Cambridgeshire Hall, Cambourne Business Park, Cambourne, Cambridge CB23 6EA ☎ 01954 713023 ✉ alex.colyer@scambs.gov.uk

Home Energy Conservation: Mr Paul Quigley, Environment Services Manager, South Cambridgeshire Hall, Cambourne Business Park, Cambourne, Cambridge CB23 6EA ☎ 03450 450 500 🖷 01954 713248 ✉ paul.quigley@scambs.gov.uk

Housing: Ms Anita Goddard , Housing Services Manager, South Cambridgeshire Hall, Cambourne Business Park, Cambourne, Cambridge CB23 6EA ☎ 03450 450 500 ✉ anita.goddard@scambs.gov.uk

Housing: Mr Stephen Hills , Director - Affordable Homes, South Cambridgeshire Hall, Cambourne Business Park, Cambourne, Cambridge CB23 6EA ☎ 03450 450500 ✉ stephen.hills@scambs.gov.uk

Housing Maintenance: Ms Anita Goddard , Housing Services Manager, South Cambridgeshire Hall, Cambourne Business Park, Cambourne, Cambridge CB23 6EA ☎ 03450 450 500 ✉ anita.goddard@scambs.gov.uk

Housing Maintenance: Mr Stephen Hills , Director - Affordable Homes, South Cambridgeshire Hall, Cambourne Business Park, Cambourne, Cambridge CB23 6EA ☎ 03450 450500 ✉ stephen.hills@scambs.gov.uk

Legal: Mrs Fiona McMillan , Head of Legal & Democratic Services, South Cambridgeshire District Council, South Cambridgeshire Hall, Cambourne, Cambridge CB23 6EA ☎ 03450 450500 ✉ fiona.mcmillan@scambs.gov.uk

Licensing: Mr Myles Bebbington, Licensing Officer, South Cambridgeshire Hall, Cambourne Business Park, Cambourne, Cambridge CB23 6EA ☎ 03450 450 500 🖷 01954 713248 ✉ myles.bebbington@scambs.gov.uk

Lighting: Mr Paul Quigley, Environment Services Manager, South Cambridgeshire Hall, Cambourne Business Park, Cambourne, Cambridge CB23 6EA ☎ 03450 450 500 🖷 01954 713248 ✉ paul.quigley@scambs.gov.uk

Member Services: Mr Graham Watts , Democratic Services Manager, South Cambridgeshire Hall, Cambourne Business Park, Cambourne, Cambridge CB23 6EA ☎ 03450 450450 ✉ graham.watts@scambs.gov.uk

Partnerships: Ms Gemma Barron , Partnerships Manager, South Cambridgeshire Hall, Cambourne Business Park, Cambourne, Cambridge CB23 6EA ☎ 03450 450500 ✉ gemma.barron@scambs.gov.uk

Personnel / HR: Ms Susan Gardner Craig, Human Resources Manager, South Cambridgeshire Hall, Cambourne Business Park, Cambourne, Cambridge CB3 6EA ☎ 03450 450 500 ✉ susan.gardnercraig@scambs.gov.uk

Planning: Mrs Caroline Hunt , Planning Policy Manager, South Cambridgeshire Hall, Cambourne Business Park, Cambourne, Cambridge CB23 6EA ☎ 03450 450 500 ✉ caroline.hunt@scambs.gov.uk

Procurement: Mr Sean Missin, Procurement Officer, South Cambridgeshire Hall, Cambourne Business Park, Cambourne, Cambridge CB23 6EA ☎ 01954 713378 ✉ sean.missin@scambs.gov.uk

Recycling & Waste Minimisation: Mr Paul Quigley, Environment Services Manager, South Cambridgeshire Hall, Cambourne Business Park, Cambourne, Cambridge CB23 6EA ☎ 03450 450 500 🖷 01954 713248 ✉ paul.quigley@scambs.gov.uk

Staff Training: Ms Susan Gardner Craig, Human Resources Manager, South Cambridgeshire Hall, Cambourne Business Park, Cambourne, Cambridge CB3 6EA ☎ 03450 450 500 ✉ susan.gardnercraig@scambs.gov.uk

Sustainable Communities: Mr Richard Hales , Strategic Sustainability Officer, South Cambridgeshire District Council, South Cambridgeshire Hall, Cambourne, Cambridge CB23 6EA ☎ 03450 450500 ✉ richard.hales@scambs.gov.uk

Transport Planner: Mr Jonathan Dixon, Principal Planning Policy Officer of Transport, South Cambridgeshire Hall, Cambourne Business Park, Cambourne, Cambridge CB3 6EA ☎ 03450 450 500 ✉ jonathan.dixon@scambs.gov.uk

COUNCILLORS

***Chair* Ellington**, Sue (CON - Swavesey)
cllr.ellington@scambs.gov.uk

***Vice-Chair* McCraith**, David (CON - Bassingbourn)
cllr.mccraith@scambs.gov.uk

***Leader of the Council* Manning**, Ray (CON - Willingham & Over)
cllr.manning@scambs.gov.uk

***Deputy Leader of the Council* Edwards**, Simon (CON - Cottenham)
cllr.edwards@scambs.gov.uk

***Group Leader* De Lacey**, Douglas (IND - Girton)
cllr.delacey@scambs.gov.uk

***Group Leader* Smith**, Bridget (LD - Gamlingay)
cllr.smithbz@scambs.gov.uk

Bard, David (CON - Sawston)
cllr.bard@scambs.gov.uk

Barrett, Val (CON - Melbourn)
cllr.barrettvm@scambs.gov.uk

Batchelor, Henry (LD - Linton)

Bradnam, Anna (LD - Milton)

Burkitt, Francis (CON - Barton)
cllr.burkitt@scambs.gov.uk

Burling, Brian (CON - Willingham and Over)
cllr.burling@scambs.gov.uk

Bygott, Thomas (CON - Girton)
cllr.bygott@scambs.gov.uk

Cathcart, Nigel (LAB - Bassingbourn)
cllr.cathcart@scambs.gov.uk

Chamberlain, Grenville (CON - Hardwick)

Chuffley, Kevin (CON - Sawston)

Cone, Graham (CON - Fulbourn)

Corney, Pippa (CON - Willingham and Over)
cllr.corney@scambs.gov.uk

Cross, Christopher (CON - Histon and Impington)

Davies, Neil (IND - Histon and Impington)
cllr.davies@scambs.gov.uk

Fraser, Andrew (CON - Balsham)
cllr.fraser@scambs.gov.uk

Hales, Jose (LD - Melbourn)
cllr.hales@scambs.gov.uk

Hall, Roger (CON - Bar Hill)
cllr.hall@scambs.gov.uk

Harford, Lynda (CON - Cottenham)
cllr.harford@scambs.gov.uk

Hart, Philippa (LD - Meldreth)

Hawkins, Tumi (LD - Caldecote)
cllr.hawkins@scambs.gov.uk

Hickford, Roger (CON - Linton)
cllr.hickford@scambs.gov.uk

Hockney, James (CON - Waterbeach)
cllr.hockney@scambs.gov.uk

Howell, Mark (CON - Papworth and Elsworth)
cllr.howell@scambs.gov.uk

Hunt, Caroline (CON - Teversham)
cllr.hunt@scambs.gov.uk

Johnson, Peter (CON - Waterbeach)
cllr.johnson@scambs.gov.uk

Kindersley, Sebastian (LD - Gamlingay)
cllr.kindersley@scambs.gov.uk

Lockwood, Janet (LD - Harston and Hauxton)
cllr.lockwood@scambs.gov.uk

Loynes, Mervyn (CON - Bourn)

Martin, Mick (CON - Duxford)
cllr.martin@scambs.gov.uk

Matthews, Raymond (CON - Sawston)
cllr.matthews@scambs.gov.uk

Morgan, David (CON - Bourn)

Murfitt, Cicely (IND - The Mordens)
cllr.murfitt@scambs.gov.uk

Nightingale, Charles (CON - The Shelfords and Stapleford)
cllr.nightingale@scambs.gov.uk

O'Brien, Des (CON - Bourn)

Orgee, Tony (CON - The Abingtons)
cllr.orgee@scambs.gov.uk

Page, Robin (IND - Haslingfield and the Eversdens)
cllr.page@scambs.gov.uk

Riley, Alex (CON - Longstanton)
cllr.riley@scambs.gov.uk

Roberts, Deborah (IND - Fowlmere and Foxton)
cllr.roberts@scambs.gov.uk

Scott, Tim (CON - Comberton)

Shelton, Ben (CON - The Shelfords and Stapleford)
cllr.shelton@scambs.gov.uk

Smith, Hazel (LD - Milton)
cllr.smithhm@scambs.gov.uk

Stonham, Edd (IND - Histon and Impington)
cllr.stonham@scambs.gov.uk

Topping, Peter (CON - Whittlesford)
cllr.topping@scambs.gov.uk

Turner, Robert (CON - The Wilbrahams)
cllr.turner@scambs.gov.uk

Turner, Richard (CON - Balsham)

Van de Weyer, Aidan (LD - Orwell & Barrington)
cllr.vandeweyer@scambs.gov.uk

Waters, Bunty (CON - Bar Hill)
cllr.waters@scambs.gov.uk

Whiteman-Downes, David (CON - The Shelfords and Stapleford)
cllr.whiteman-downes@scambs.gov.uk

Williams, John G (LD - Fulbourn)
cllr.williamsjg@scambs.gov.uk

Wotherspoon, Tim (CON - Cottenham)
cllr.wotherspoon@scambs.gov.uk

Wright, Nick (CON - Papworth and Elsworth)
cllr.wright@scambs.gov.uk

POLITICAL COMPOSITION

CON: 39, LD: 11, IND: 6, LAB: 1

COMMITTEE CHAIRS

Licensing: Mr Andrew Fraser

Licensing: Mr Alex Riley

Planning: Mrs Lynda Harford

SOUTH DERBYSHIRE

South Derbyshire D

South Derbyshire District Council, Civic Offices, Civic Way, Swadlincote DE11 0AH
☎ 01283 221000 🖷 01283 550128 civic.offices@south-derbys.gov.uk
www.south-derbys.gov.uk

FACTS AND FIGURES

Parliamentary Constituencies: Derbyshire South
EU Constituencies: East Midlands
Election Frequency: Elections are of whole council

PRINCIPAL OFFICERS

Chief Executive: Mr Frank McArdle , Chief Executive, Civic Offices, Civic Way, Swadlincote DE11 0AH ☎ 01283 595702 🖷 01283 595854 frank.mcardle@south-derbys.gov.uk

Senior Management: Mr Stuart Batchelor, Director - Community & Planning Services, Civic Offices, Civic Way, Swadlincote DE11 0AH ☎ 01283 595820 🖷 01283 595854 stuart.batchelor@south-derbys.gov.uk

Senior Management: Mr Mike Haynes , Director - Housing & Environmental Services, Civic Offices, Civic Way, Swadlincote DE11 0AH ☎ 01283 595775 🖷 01283 595852 mike.haynes@south-derbys.gov.uk

Senior Management: Mrs Ardip Kaur , Monitoring Officer & Council Solicitor, Civic Offices, Civic Way, Swadlincote DE11 0AH ☎ 01283 595715 ardip.kaur@south-derbys.gov.uk

Senior Management: Mr Kevin Stackhouse, Director - Finance & Corporate Services, Civic Offices, Civic Way, Swadlincote DE11 0AH ☎ 01283 595811 🖷 01283 595854 kevin.stackhouse@south-derbys.gov.uk

Building Control: Mr Stuart Batchelor, Director - Community & Planning Services, Civic Offices, Civic Way, Swadlincote DE11 0AH ☎ 01283 595820 🖷 01283 595854 stuart.batchelor@south-derbys.gov.uk

PR / Communications: Mr Keith Bull , Head of Communications, Civic Offices, Civic Way, Swadlincote DE11 0AH ☎ 01283 818705 keith.bull@northgate-is.com

Community Safety: Mr Stuart Batchelor, Director - Community & Planning Services, Civic Offices, Civic Way, Swadlincote DE11 0AH ☎ 01283 595820 🖷 01283 595854 stuart.batchelor@south-derbys.gov.uk

Computer Management: Mr Mark Sabin , ICT Service Delivery Manager, Civic Offices, Civic Way, Swadlincote DE11 0AH ☎ 01283 595703 🖷 01283 595720 mark.sabin@northgate-is.com

Corporate Services: Mr Kevin Stackhouse, Director - Finance & Corporate Services, Civic Offices, Civic Way, Swadlincote DE11 0AH ☎ 01283 595811 🖷 01283 595854 kevin.stackhouse@south-derbys.gov.uk

Customer Service: Mrs Angela Leese , Customer Contact Manager, Civic Offices, Civic Way, Swadlincote DE11 0AH ☎ 01283 595989 🖷 01283 595964 angela.leese@northgate-is.com

Direct Labour: Mr Mike Haynes , Director - Housing & Environmental Services, Civic Offices, Civic Way, Swadlincote DE11 0AH ☎ 01283 595775 🖷 01283 595852 mike.haynes@south-derbys.gov.uk

Economic Development: Mr Mike Roylance , Economic Development Manager, Civic Offices, Civic Way, Swadlincote DE11 0AH ☎ 01283 595725 🖷 01283 595864 mike.roylance@south-derbys.gov.uk

E-Government: Mr Mark Sabin , ICT Service Delivery Manager, Civic Offices, Civic Way, Swadlincote DE11 0AH ☎ 01283 595703 🖷 01283 595720 mark.sabin@northgate-is.com

Electoral Registration: Mr Frank McArdle , Chief Executive, Civic Offices, Civic Way, Swadlincote DE11 0AH ☎ 01283 595702 🖷 01283 595854 frank.mcardle@south-derbys.gov.uk

Emergency Planning: Mr Frank McArdle , Chief Executive, Civic Offices, Civic Way, Swadlincote DE11 0AH ☎ 01283 595702 🖷 01283 595854 frank.mcardle@south-derbys.gov.uk

Environmental / Technical Services: Mr Mike Haynes , Director - Housing & Environmental Services, Civic Offices, Civic Way, Swadlincote DE11 0AH ☎ 01283 595775 🖷 01283 595852 mike.haynes@south-derbys.gov.uk

Environmental Health: Mr Matthew Holford , Environmental Health Manager, Civic Offices, Civic Way, Swadlincote DE11 0AH ☎ 01283 595856 🖷 01283 595852 matthew.holford@south-derbys.gov.uk

Estates, Property & Valuation: Mr Steve Baker , Corporate Asset Manager, Civic Offices, Civic Way, Swadlincote DE11 0AH ☎ 01283 595965 🖷 01283 595854 steve.baker@south-derbys.gov.uk

European Liaison: Mr Frank McArdle , Chief Executive, Civic Offices, Civic Way, Swadlincote DE11 0AH ☎ 01283 595702 🖷 01283 595854 frank.mcardle@south-derbys.gov.uk

Finance: Mr Kevin Stackhouse, Director - Finance & Corporate Services, Civic Offices, Civic Way, Swadlincote DE11 0AH ☎ 01283 595811 🖷 01283 595854 kevin.stackhouse@south-derbys.gov.uk

Treasury: Mr Kevin Stackhouse, Director - Finance & Corporate Services, Civic Offices, Civic Way, Swadlincote DE11 0AH ☎ 01283 595811 🖷 01283 595854 kevin.stackhouse@south-derbys.gov.uk

Grounds Maintenance: Mr Mike Haynes , Director - Housing & Environmental Services, Civic Offices, Civic Way, Swadlincote DE11 0AH ☎ 01283 595775 🖷 01283 595852 mike.haynes@south-derbys.gov.uk

Health and Safety: Mr David Clamp, Head of Organisational Development, Civic Offices, Civic Way, Swadlincote DE11 0AH ☎ 01283 595729 🖷 01283 595854 david.clamp@northgate-is.com

Home Energy Conservation: Mr Mike Haynes , Director - Housing & Environmental Services, Civic Offices, Civic Way, Swadlincote DE11 0AH ☎ 01283 595775 🖷 01283 595852 mike.haynes@south-derbys.gov.uk

Housing: Mr Mike Haynes , Director - Housing & Environmental Services, Civic Offices, Civic Way, Swadlincote DE11 0AH ☎ 01283 595775 🖷 01283 595852 ✉ mike.haynes@south-derbys.gov.uk

Housing Maintenance: Mr Mike Haynes , Director - Housing & Environmental Services, Civic Offices, Civic Way, Swadlincote DE11 0AH ☎ 01283 595775 🖷 01283 595852 ✉ mike.haynes@south-derbys.gov.uk

Legal: Mrs Ardip Kaur , Monitoring Officer & Council Solicitor, Civic Offices, Civic Way, Swadlincote DE11 0AH ☎ 01283 595715 ✉ ardip.kaur@south-derbys.gov.uk

Leisure and Cultural Services: Mr Stuart Batchelor, Director - Community & Planning Services, Civic Offices, Civic Way, Swadlincote DE11 0AH ☎ 01283 595820 🖷 01283 595854 ✉ stuart.batchelor@south-derbys.gov.uk

Licensing: Mrs Ardip Kaur , Monitoring Officer & Council Solicitor, Civic Offices, Civic Way, Swadlincote DE11 0AH ☎ 01283 595715 ✉ ardip.kaur@south-derbys.gov.uk

Lifelong Learning: Mrs Ardip Kaur , Monitoring Officer & Council Solicitor, Civic Offices, Civic Way, Swadlincote DE11 0AH ☎ 01283 595715 ✉ ardip.kaur@south-derbys.gov.uk

Lottery Funding, Charity and Voluntary: Mr Stuart Batchelor, Director - Community & Planning Services, Civic Offices, Civic Way, Swadlincote DE11 0AH ☎ 01283 595820 🖷 01283 595854 ✉ stuart.batchelor@south-derbys.gov.uk

Member Services: Mrs Ardip Kaur , Monitoring Officer & Council Solicitor, Civic Offices, Civic Way, Swadlincote DE11 0AH ☎ 01283 595715 ✉ ardip.kaur@south-derbys.gov.uk

Partnerships: Mr Kevin Stackhouse, Director - Finance & Corporate Services, Civic Offices, Civic Way, Swadlincote DE11 0AH ☎ 01283 595811 🖷 01283 595854 ✉ kevin.stackhouse@south-derbys.gov.uk

Personnel / HR: Mr David Clamp, Head of Organisational Development, Civic Offices, Civic Way, Swadlincote DE11 0AH ☎ 01283 595729 🖷 01283 595854 ✉ david.clamp@northgate-is.com

Planning: Mr Stuart Batchelor, Director - Community & Planning Services, Civic Offices, Civic Way, Swadlincote DE11 0AH ☎ 01283 595820 🖷 01283 595854 ✉ stuart.batchelor@south-derbys.gov.uk

Procurement: Mr Kevin Stackhouse, Director - Finance & Corporate Services, Civic Offices, Civic Way, Swadlincote DE11 0AH ☎ 01283 595811 🖷 01283 595854 ✉ kevin.stackhouse@south-derbys.gov.uk

Recycling & Waste Minimisation: Mr Mike Haynes , Director - Housing & Environmental Services, Civic Offices, Civic Way, Swadlincote DE11 0AH ☎ 01283 595775 🖷 01283 595852 ✉ mike.haynes@south-derbys.gov.uk

Staff Training: Mr David Clamp, Head of Organisational Development, Civic Offices, Civic Way, Swadlincote DE11 0AH ☎ 01283 595729 🖷 01283 595854 ✉ david.clamp@northgate-is.com

Sustainable Development: Mr Stuart Batchelor, Director - Community & Planning Services, Civic Offices, Civic Way, Swadlincote DE11 0AH ☎ 01283 595820 🖷 01283 595854 ✉ stuart.batchelor@south-derbys.gov.uk

Tourism: Mr Mike Roylance , Economic Development Manager, Civic Offices, Civic Way, Swadlincote DE11 0AH ☎ 01283 595725 🖷 01283 595864 ✉ mike.roylance@south-derbys.gov.uk

Waste Collection and Disposal: Mr Mike Haynes , Director - Housing & Environmental Services, Civic Offices, Civic Way, Swadlincote DE11 0AH ☎ 01283 595775 🖷 01283 595852 ✉ mike.haynes@south-derbys.gov.uk

Waste Management: Mr Mike Haynes , Director - Housing & Environmental Services, Civic Offices, Civic Way, Swadlincote DE11 0AH ☎ 01283 595775 🖷 01283 595852 ✉ mike.haynes@south-derbys.gov.uk

COUNCILLORS

Leader of the Council **Wheeler**, Robert (CON - Linton)
bob.wheeler@south-derbys.gov.uk

Atkin, Neil (CON - Aston)
neil.atkin@south-derbys.gov.uk

Bambrick, Sean (LAB - Newhall and Stanton)
sean.bambrick@south-derbys.gov.uk

Billings, Andy (CON - Hilton)
andy.billings@south-derbys.gov.uk

Brown, Lisa (CON - Etwall)
lisa.brown@south-derbys.gov.uk

Chahal, Manjit (LAB - Stenson)
manji.chahal@south-derbys.gov.uk

Coe, Kim (CON - Woodville)
kim.coe@south-derbys.gov.uk

Coe, Robert (CON - Swadlincote)
robert.coe@south-derbys.gov.uk

Coyle, Hilary (CON - Aston)
hilary.coyle@south-derbys.gov.uk

Dunn, Paul (LAB - Midway)
paul.dunn@south-derbys.gov.uk

Farrington, Gillian (CON - Woodville)
gillian.farrington@south-derbys.gov.uk

Ford, Martyn (CON - Willington and Findern)
martyn.ford@south-derbys.gov.uk

Grant, John (CON - Linton)
john.grant@south-derbys.gov.uk

Hall, Margaret (CON - Seales)
margaret.hall@south-derbys.gov.uk

Harrison, John (CON - Melbourne)
john.harrison@south-derbys.gov.uk

Hewlett, Jim (CON - Melbourne)
jim.hewlett@south-derbys.gov.uk

MacPherson, Andrew (CON - Willington and Findern)

Muller, David (CON - Etwall)
david.muller@south-derbys.gov.uk

SOUTH DERBYSHIRE

Murray, Patrick (CON - Seales)
pat.murray@south-derbys.gov.uk

Patten, Julie (CON - Hilton)
julie.patten@south-derbys.gov.uk

Pearson, Robert (LAB - Midway)
rob.pearson@south-derbys.gov.uk

Plenderleith, Amy (CON - Hilton)
amy.plenderleith@south-derbys.gov.uk

Rhind, Gordon (LAB - Church Gresley)
gordon.rhind@south-derbys.gov.uk

Richards, Kevin (LAB - Newhall and Stanton)
kevin.richards@south-derbys.gov.uk

Roberts, Andy (CON - Hatton)
andy.roberts@south-derbys.gov.uk

Shepherd, David (LAB - Stenson)
david.shepherd@south-derbys.gov.uk

Smith, Peter (CON - Repton)
peter.smith@south-derbys.gov.uk

Southerd, Trevor (LAB - Church Gresley)
trevor.southerd@south-derbys.gov.uk

Stanton, Michael (CON - Repton)
michael.stanton@south-derbys.gov.uk

Stuart, Linda (LAB - Newhall and Stanton)
linda.stuart@south-derbys.gov.uk

Swann, Stuart (CON - Church Gresley)
stuart.swann@south-derbys.gov.uk

Taylor, Stephen (LAB - Woodville)
stephen.taylor@south-derbys.gov.uk

Tilley, Neil (LAB - Swadlincote)
neil.tilley@south-derbys.gov.uk

Watson, Peter (CON - Aston)
peter.watson@south-derbys.gov.uk

Wilkins, Peter (LAB - Midway)
peter.wilkins@south-derbys.gov.uk

Wyatt, Sandra (CON - Swadlincote)
sandra.wyatt@south-derbys.gov.uk

POLITICAL COMPOSITION
CON: 24, LAB: 12

COMMITTEE CHAIRS
Planning: Mr Andy Roberts

South Gloucestershire U

South Gloucestershire Council, The Council Offices, Badminton Road, Yate BS37 5AF
☎ 01454 868686 🖷 01454 863067
mailbox@southglos.gov.uk
www.southglos.gov.uk

FACTS AND FIGURES
Parliamentary Constituencies: Bristol North West, Filton and Bradley Stoke, Kingswood, Thornbury and Yate
EU Constituencies: South West
Election Frequency: Elections are of whole council

PRINCIPAL OFFICERS

Chief Executive: Mrs Amanda Deeks, Chief Executive, The Council Offices, Badminton Road, Yate BS37 5AF ☎ 01454 863851 🖷 01454 863855 amanda.deeks@southglos.gov.uk

Deputy Chief Executive: Mr David Perry, Director of Corporate Services, The Council Offices, Badminton Road, Yate BS37 5AF ☎ 01454 865001 🖷 01454 863855 dave.perry@southglos.gov.uk

Senior Management: Dr Mark Pietroni , Interim Director - Public Health, The Council Offices, Badminton Road, Yate BS37 5AF ☎ 014554 864200 directorofpublichealth@southglos.gov.uk

Access Officer / Social Services (Disability): Ms Alice Cleaveland , Access Officer, The Council Offices, Badminton Road, Yate BS37 5AF ☎ 01454 863860 🖷 01454 868150 alice.cleaveland@southglos.gov.uk

Architect, Building / Property Services: Mr Stephen Lewis , Head of ICT, The Council Offices, Badminton Road, Yate BS37 5AF ☎ 01454 865070 stephen.lewis@southglos.gov.uk

Best Value: Ms Sue Covello , Transformation & Efficiency Manager, The Council Offices, Badminton Road, Yate BS37 5AF ☎ 01454 864703 sue.covello@southglos.gov.uk

Building Control: Mr Brian Glasson , Head of Strategic Planning & Housing, The Council Offices, Badminton Road, Yate BS37 5AF ☎ 01454 863535 🖷 01454 863737 brian.glasson@southglos.gov.uk

Catering Services: Ms Kay Knight, Head of Traded & Support Services, The Council Offices, Badminton Road, Yate BS37 5AF ☎ 01454 863246 🖷 01454 863998 kay.knight@southglos.gov.uk

Children / Youth Services: Ms Geri Palfreeman , Service Manager of Preventative Services, Kingswood Locality Hub, High Street, Kingswood BS15 9TR ☎ 01454 863152 geri.palfreeman@southglos.gov.uk

Civil Registration: Ms Chris Benstock , Superintendent Registrar, The Council Offices, Badminton Road, Yate BS37 5AF ☎ 01454 863604 chris.benson@southglos.gov.uk

PR / Communications: Mr Daniel Ward , Senior External Communications Officer, The Council Offices, Badminton Road, Yate BS37 5AF ☎ 01454 863291 daniel.ward@southglos.gov.uk

Community Planning: Ms Marian Jones , Community Engagement Team Leader, The Council Offices, Badminton Road, Yate BS37 5AF ☎ 01454 865839 🖷 01454 868535 marian.jones@southglos.gov.uk

Community Safety: Mr Robert Walsh , Head of Safe Strong Communities, The Council Offices, Badminton Road, Yate BS37 5AF ☎ 01454 865818 robert.walsh@southglos.gov.uk

Computer Management: Mr Stephen Lewis , Head of ICT, The Council Offices, Badminton Road, Yate BS37 5AF ☎ 01454 865070 stephen.lewis@southglos.gov.uk

Contracts: Ms Sue Covello , Transformation & Efficiency Manager, The Council Offices, Badminton Road, Yate BS37 5AF ☎ 01454 864703 ✉ sue.covello@southglos.gov.uk

Corporate Services: Mr Andrew Birch , Deputy Head of Finance, The Council Offices, Badminton Road, Yate BS37 5AF ☎ 01454 865985 ✉ andrew.birch@southglos.gov.uk

Corporate Services: Mr Martin Dear , Head of Business Support, The Council Offices, Badminton Road, Yate BS37 5AF ☎ 01454 863197 ✉ martin.dear@southglos.gov.uk

Corporate Services: Mr Mike Hayesman , Head of Finance & Customer Services, The Council Offices, Badminton Road, Yate BS37 5AF ☎ 01454 865290 ✉ mike.hayesman@southglos.gov.uk

Corporate Services: Ms Clare Medland , Head of Strategy Development, The Council Offices, Badminton Road, Yate BS37 5AF ☎ 01454 863239 ✉ clare.medland@southglos.gov.uk

Corporate Services: Mr David Perry, Director of Corporate Services, The Council Offices, Badminton Road, Yate BS37 5AF ☎ 01454 865001 🖷 01454 863855 ✉ dave.perry@southglos.gov.uk

Customer Service: Ms Tracy Allison , Head of Integrated Locality Children's Services, The Council Offices, Badminton Road, Yate BS37 5AF ☎ 01454 863254 ✉ tracy.allison@southglos.gov.uk

Customer Service: Mr Jim Anderson , Team Manager of Preventative Services, Kingswood Hub, High Street, Kingswood BS15 9TR ☎ 01454 863799 ✉ jim.anderson@southglos.gov.uk

Customer Service: Mr Mike Hayesman , Head of Finance & Customer Services, The Council Offices, Badminton Road, Yate BS37 5AF ☎ 01454 865290 ✉ mike.hayesman@southglos.gov.uk

Customer Service: Ms Denise Porter , Head of Adult Social Care & Housing, The Council Offices, Badminton Road, Yate BS37 5AF ☎ 01454 866325 ✉ denise.porter@southglos.gov.uk

Direct Labour: Mr Mark King, Head of Street Care, Broad Lane Offices, Engine Common Lane, Yate BS37 7PN ☎ 01454 863912 🖷 01454 865812 ✉ mark.king@southglos.gov.uk

Economic Development: Mr Steve Evans, Director of Environment & Community Services, The Council Offices, Badminton Road, Yate BS37 5AF ☎ 01454 865811 🖷 01454 865812 ✉ steve.evans@southglos.gov.uk

Education: Ms Susannah Hill , Interim Head of Education, Skills & Learning, The Council Offices, Badminton Road, Yate BS37 5AF ☎ 01454 863271 ✉ susannah.hill@southglos.gov.uk

Education: Mr Peter Murphy, Director for Children, Adults & Health, The Council Offices, Badminton Road, Yate BS37 5AF ☎ 01454 863253 🖷 01454 863264 ✉ peter.murphy@southglos.gov.uk

E-Government: Mr Stephen Lewis , Head of ICT, The Council Offices, Badminton Road, Yate BS37 5AF ☎ 01454 865070 ✉ stephen.lewis@southglos.gov.uk

Electoral Registration: Ms Natalie Carr , Democratic Services Group Manager, The Council Offices, Badminton Road, Yate BS37 5AF ☎ 01454 868198 🖷 01454 864661 ✉ natalie.carr@southglos.gov.uk

Emergency Planning: Mr Simon Hailwood, Senior Emergency Planning Officer, The Council Offices, Badminton Road, Yate BS37 5AF ☎ 01454 863869 ✉ simon.hailwood@southglos.gov.uk

Energy Management: Mr Sean Prior , Senior Energy Engineer, The Council Offices, Badminton Road, Yate BS37 5AF ☎ 01454 865141 🖷 01454 865069 ✉ sean.prior@southglos.gov.uk

Environmental / Technical Services: Mr Gerald Madden , Health Manager, The Council Offices, Badminton Road, Yate BS37 5AF ☎ 01454 863569 🖷 01454 863642 ✉ gerald.madden@southglos.gov.uk

Environmental Health: Mr Brian Glasson , Head of Strategic Planning & Housing, The Council Offices, Badminton Road, Yate BS37 5AF ☎ 01454 863535 🖷 01454 863737 ✉ brian.glasson@southglos.gov.uk

Environmental Health: Mr Chris Taylor, Environmental Protection Manager, The Council Offices, Badminton Road, Yate BS37 5AF ☎ 01454 863474 🖷 01454 863484 ✉ chris.taylor@southglos.gov.uk

Estates, Property & Valuation: Mr Mike Hayesman , Head of Finance & Customer Services, The Council Offices, Badminton Road, Yate BS37 5AF ☎ 01454 865290 ✉ mike.hayesman@southglos.gov.uk

European Liaison: Mr George Kousouros , Community Project Manager, The Council Offices, Badminton Road, Yate BS37 5AF ☎ 01454 868152 🖷 01454 868150 ✉ george.kousouros@southglos.gov.uk

Facilities: Mr Andrew Davies , Facilities Officer, The Council Offices, Badminton Road, Yate BS37 5AF ☎ 01454 865058 ✉ andrew.davies@southglos.gov.uk

Finance: Mr Andy Brown , Head of Finance & Customer Services, The Council Offices, Badminton Road, Yate BS37 5AF ☎ 01454 863410 🖷 01454 864473 ✉ andy.brown@southglos.gov.uk

Finance: Ms Janet Faire , Head of Operational Support, The Council Offices, Badminton Road, Yate BS37 5AF ☎ 01454 865841 ✉ janet.faire@southglos.gov.uk

Finance: Mr Mike Hayesman , Head of Finance & Customer Services, The Council Offices, Badminton Road, Yate BS37 5AF ☎ 01454 865290 ✉ mike.hayesman@southglos.gov.uk

Finance: Mr David Perry, Director of Corporate Services, The Council Offices, Badminton Road, Yate BS37 5AF ☎ 01454 865001 🖷 01454 863855 ✉ dave.perry@southglos.gov.uk

Fleet Management: Mr Colin Shepherd , Fleet Operations Manager for Transport, Broad Lane Offices, Engine Common Lane, Yate BS37 7PN ☎ 01454 863918 ✉ colin.shepherd@southglos.gov.uk

Grounds Maintenance: Mr Simon Spedding , Group Manager - Design & Operations, Broad Lane Offices, Engine Common Lane, Yate BS37 7PN ☎ 01454 863971 🖷 01454 865819 ✉ simon.spedding@southglos.gov.uk

Health and Safety: Mr Tom Magnone, Health & Safety Manager, The Council Offices, Badminton Road, Yate BS37 5AF ☎ 01454 863096 🖷 01454 863071 ✉ tom.magnone@southglos.gov.uk

Highways: Mr Steve Evans, Director of Environment & Community Services, Broad Lane Offices, Engine Common Lane, Yate BS37 7PN ☎ 01454 865811 🖷 01454 865812 ✉ steve.evans@southglos.gov.uk

Highways: Mr Chris Sane, Head of Transport & Strategic Projects, The Council Offices, Badminton Road, Yate BS37 5AF ☎ 01454 863402 ✉ chris.sane@southglos.gov.uk

Home Energy Conservation: Ms Debby Paice, Home Energy Co-ordinator (Enabling), The Council Offices, High Street, Kingswood BS15 9TR ☎ 01454 865453 🖷 01454 865555 ✉ debby.paice@southglos.gov.uk

Housing: Mr Jon Shaw , Head of Strategy & Commissioning, The Council Offices, Badminton Road, Yate BS37 5AF ☎ 01454 865547 ✉ jon.shaw@southglos.gov.uk

Local Area Agreement: Mrs Yvonne Davis , Strategic Partnerships & Planning Manager, The Council Offices, Badminton Road, Yate BS37 5AF ☎ 01454 863865 ✉ yvonne.davis@southglos.gov.uk

Legal: Mr John McCormack, Head of Legal & Democratic Services & Monitoring, The Council Offices, Badminton Road, Yate BS37 5AF ☎ 01454 865980 ✉ john.mccormack@southglos.gov.uk

Leisure and Cultural Services: Mr Steve Evans, Director of Environment & Community Services, The Council Offices, Badminton Road, Yate BS37 5AF ☎ 01454 865811 🖷 01454 865812 ✉ steve.evans@southglos.gov.uk

Lifelong Learning: Ms Susannah Hill , Interim Head of Education, Skills & Learning, The Council Offices, Badminton Road, Yate BS37 5AF ☎ 01454 863271 ✉ susannah.hill@southglos.gov.uk

Lighting: Mr Andrew Porter , Electrical & Building Maintenance Manager, The Council Offices, Badminton Road, Yate BS37 5AF ☎ 01454 863982 🖷 01454 863999 ✉ andrew.porter@southglos.gov.uk

Lottery Funding, Charity and Voluntary: Ms Marian Jones , Community Engagement Team Leader, The Council Offices, Badminton Road, Yate BS37 5AF ☎ 01454 865839 🖷 01454 868535 ✉ marian.jones@southglos.gov.uk

Member Services: Ms Natalie Carr , Democratic Services Group Manager, The Council Offices, Badminton Road, Yate BS37 5AF ☎ 01454 868198 🖷 01454 864661 ✉ natalie.carr@southglos.gov.uk

Parking: Mr Alan Garwood , Senior ECO, Broad Lane Offices, Engine Common Lane, Yate BS37 7PN ☎ 01454 868494 ✉ alan.garwood@southglos.gov.uk

Partnerships: Mrs Yvonne Davis , Strategic Partnerships & Planning Manager, The Council Offices, Badminton Road, Yate BS37 5AF ☎ 01454 863865 ✉ yvonne.davis@southglos.gov.uk

Personnel / HR: Mrs Claire Kerswill , Head of HR & HRBP for Corporate Resources, The Council Offices, Badminton Road, Yate BS37 5AF ☎ 01454 866348 ✉ claire.kerswill@southglos.gov.uk

Planning: Mr Steve Evans, Director of Environment & Community Services, The Council Offices, Badminton Road, Yate BS37 5AF ☎ 01454 865811 🖷 01454 865812 ✉ steve.evans@southglos.gov.uk

Planning: Mr Brian Glasson , Head of Strategic Planning & Housing, The Council Offices, Badminton Road, Yate BS37 5AF ☎ 01454 863535 🖷 01454 863737 ✉ brian.glasson@southglos.gov.uk

Procurement: Ms Sue Covello , Transformation & Efficiency Manager, The Council Offices, Badminton Road, Yate BS37 5AF ☎ 01454 864703 ✉ sue.covello@southglos.gov.uk

Public Libraries: Mr Martin Burton, Community Cultural Services Manager, The Council Offices, Badminton Road, Yate BS37 5AF ☎ 01454 865782 🖷 01454 868150 ✉ martin.burton@southglos.gov.uk

Recycling & Waste Minimisation: Mr Robert Lambourne , Waste Manager, The Council Offices, Badminton Road, Yate BS37 5AF ☎ 01454 865840 ✉ robert.lambourne@southglos.gov.uk

Regeneration: Mr Mike Luton, Senior Principal Planning Officer for Policy, The Council Offices, Badminton Road, Yate BS37 5AF ☎ 01454 863573 ✉ mike.luton@southglos.gov.uk

Road Safety: Mr Chris Studley , Stakeholder Manager, The Council Offices, Badminton Road, Yate BS37 5AF ☎ 01454 863751 🖷 01454 863697 ✉ chris.studley@southglos.gov.uk

Social Services: Ms Tracy Allison , Head of Integrated Locality Children's Services, The Council Offices, Badminton Road, Yate BS37 5AF ☎ 01454 863254 ✉ tracy.allison@southglos.gov.uk

Social Services: Mr Peter Murphy, Director for Children, Adults & Health, The Council Offices, Badminton Road, Yate BS37 5AF ☎ 01454 863253 🖷 01454 863264 ✉ peter.murphy@southglos.gov.uk

Social Services (Adult): Ms Sheila Turner , Safeguarding Adults Manager, Civic Centre, High Street, Kingswood BS15 9TR ☎ 01454 866273 🖷 01454 865940 ✉ sheila.turner@southglos.gov.uk

Social Services (Children): Mr Peter Murphy, Director for Children, Adults & Health, The Council Offices, Badminton Road, Yate BS37 5AF ☎ 01454 863253 🖷 01454 863264 ✉ peter.murphy@southglos.gov.uk

Public Health: Dr Mark Pietroni , Interim Director - Public Health, The Council Offices, Badminton Road, Yate BS37 5AF ☎ 014554 864200 ✉ directorofpublichealth@southglos.gov.uk

Staff Training: Ms Nicola Plant , HR Business Partner, The Council Offices, Badminton Road, Yate BS37 5AF ☎ 01454 863093 ✉ nicola.plant@southglos.gov.uk

Street Scene: Mr Simon Spedding , Group Manager - Design & Operations, Broad Lane Offices, Engine Common Lane, Yate BS37 7PN ☎ 01454 863971 🖷 01454 865819 🖱 simon.spedding@southglos.gov.uk

Sustainable Communities: Ms Jane Thompson, Corporate Projects Officer, The Council Offices, Badminton Road, Yate BS37 5AF ☎ 01454 863870 🖷 01454 863886 🖱 jane.thompson@southglos.gov.uk

Sustainable Development: Ms Jane Thompson, Corporate Projects Officer, The Council Offices, Badminton Road, Yate BS37 5AF ☎ 01454 863870 🖷 01454 863886 🖱 jane.thompson@southglos.gov.uk

Traffic Management: Mr Chris Studley , Stakeholder Manager, The Council Offices, Badminton Road, Yate BS37 5AF ☎ 01454 863751 🖷 01454 863697 🖱 chris.studley@southglos.gov.uk

Transport: Mr Steve Evans, Director of Environment & Community Services, The Council Offices, Badminton Road, Yate BS37 5AF ☎ 01454 865811 🖷 01454 865812 🖱 steve.evans@southglos.gov.uk

Transport: Mr Chris Sane, Head of Transport & Strategic Projects, The Council Offices, Badminton Road, Yate BS37 5AF ☎ 01454 863402 🖱 chris.sane@southglos.gov.uk

Transport Planner: Ms Emma Blackham , Transport Policy & Promotions Group Manager, The Council Offices, Badminton Road, Yate BS37 5AF ☎ 01454 864115 🖷 01454 864473 🖱 emma.blackham@southglos.gov.uk

Waste Collection and Disposal: Mr Robert Lambourne , Waste Manager, The Council Offices, Badminton Road, Yate BS37 5AF ☎ 01454 865840 🖱 robert.lambourne@southglos.gov.uk

Waste Management: Mr Steve Evans, Director of Environment & Community Services, Broad Lane Offices, Engine Common Lane, Yate BS37 7PN ☎ 01454 865811 🖷 01454 865812 🖱 steve.evans@southglos.gov.uk

COUNCILLORS

***Chair* Williams**, Erica (CON - Bitton)
erica.williams@southglos.gov.uk

***Vice-Chair* Morris**, Katherine (CON - Downend)
katherine.morris@southglos.gov.uk

***Leader of the Council* Riddle**, Matthew (CON - Severn)
matthew.riddle@southglos.gov.uk

Adams, Ian (CON - Siston)
ian.adams@southglos.gov.uk

Adams, Judy (CON - Rodway)
judy.adams@southglos.gov.uk

Allinson, Brian (CON - Stoke Gifford)
brian.allinson@southglos.gov.uk

Ashe, John (CON - Bradley Stoke South)
john.ashe@southglos.gov.uk

Avenin, Roger (CON - Bradley Stoke South)
roger.avenin@southglos.gov.uk

Bamford, June (CON - Hanham)
june.bamford@southglos.gov.uk

Barrett, Nick (CON - Parkwall)
nick.barrett@southglos.gov.uk

Barrett, Kaye (CON - Parkwall)
kaye.barrett@southglos.gov.uk

Begley, April (LAB - King's Chase)
april.begley@southglos.gov.uk

Bell, Michael (LAB - Rodway)
michael.bell@southglos.gov.uk

Biggin, Janet (CON - Downend)
janet.biggin@southglos.gov.uk

Blair, Ian (LD - Yate North)
ian.blair@southglos.gov.uk

Boon, Linda (LD - Chipping Sodbury)
linda.boon@southglos.gov.uk

Boulton, Ian (LAB - Staple Hill)
ian.boulton@southglos.gov.uk

Bowles, Tim (CON - Winterbourne)
tim.bowles@southglos.gov.uk

Bromiley, Samuel (CON - Oldland Common)
samuel.bromiley@southglos.gov.uk

Brown, Ernie (CON - Stoke Gifford)
ernie.brown@southglos.gov.uk

Burchell, Keith (CON - Almondsbury)
keith.burchell@southglos.gov.uk

Chubb, David (CON - Thornbury North)
david.chubb@southglos.gov.uk

Cranney, Keith (CON - Stoke Gifford)
keith.cranney@southglos.gov.uk

Creer, Rob (CON - Chipping Sodbury)
rob.creer@southglos.gov.uk

Dando, Ken (CON - Patchway)
kenneth.dando2@southglos.gov.uk

Davis, John (LD - Yate North)
john.davis@southglos.gov.uk

Davis, Tony (LD - Dodington)
tony.davis@southglos.gov.uk

Davis, Ruth (LD - Yate Central)
ruth.davis@southglos.gov.uk

Drew, Mike (LD - Yate North)
mike.drew@southglos.gov.uk

Fardell, Clare (LD - Thornbury North)
clare.fardell@southglos.gov.uk

Farmer, Martin (LAB - King's Chase)
martin.farmer@southglos.gov.uk

Goddard, Heather (CON - Hanham)
heather.goddard@southglos.gov.uk

Goddard, John (CON - Hanham)

Griffin, Robert (CON - Pilning and Severn Beach)
robert.griffin@southglos.gov.uk

Hardwick, Paul (CON - Bradley Stoke North)
paul.hardwick@southglos.gov.uk

Hockey, Dave (LD - Frampton Cotterell)
dave.hockey@southglos.gov.uk

Hockey, Pat (LD - Frampton Cotterell)
pat.hockey@southglos.gov.uk

Holloway, Shirley (LD - Thornbury South and Alveston)
shirley.holloway@southglos.gov.uk

Hope, Sue (LD - Cotswold Edge)
sue.hope@southglos.gov.uk

Hopkinson, Brian (CON - Bradley Stoke Central and Stoke Lodge)
brian.hopkinson@southglos.gov.uk

Hughes, Paul (CON - Oldland Common)
paul.hughes@southglos.gov.uk

Hunt, Rachael (CON - Emersons Green)
rachael.hunt@southglos.gov.uk

Hunt, Jon (CON - Downend)
jon.hunt@southglos.gov.uk

Hunt, Colin (CON - Emersons Green)
colin.hunt@southglos.gov.uk

Hutchinson, Roger (LAB - Filton)
roger.hutchinson@southglos.gov.uk

Jones, Trevor (CON - Frenchay and Stoke Park)
trevor.jones@southglos.gov.uk

Kearns, Dave (CON - Emersons Green)
dave.kearns@southglos.gov.uk

Lewis, Marian (CON - Ladden Brook)
marian.lewis@southglos.gov.uk

Mannig, Martin (CON - Winterbourne)
martin.manning@southglos.gov.uk

Manson, Gary (LAB - Woodstock)
gareth.manson@southglos.gov.uk

Monk, Adam (LAB - Filton)
adam.monk@southglos.gov.uk

O'Neil, John (LD - Charfield)
john.o'neil@southglos.gov.uk

Opren, Eve (LAB - Patchway)
eve.opren@southglos.gov.uk

Perkins, Andy (LAB - Woodstock)
andy.perkins@southglos.gov.uk

Pomfret, Sarah (CON - Bradley Stoke Central and Stoke Lodge)
sarah.pomfret@southglos.gov.uk

Potts, Shirley (LAB - Staple Hill)
shirley.potts@southglos.gov.uk

Price, Christine (CON - Longwell Green)
christine.price@southglos.gov.uk

Pullin, Bob (CON - Frenchay and Stoke Park)
bob.pullin@southglos.gov.uk

Reade, Steve (CON - Boyd Valley)
stephen.reade.southglos.gov.uk

Rooney, Pat (LAB - Woodstock)
pat.ronney@southglos.gov.uk

Savage, Toby (CON - Longwell Green)
toby.savage@southglos.gov.uk

Scott, Ian (LAB - Filton)
ian.scott@southglos.gov.uk

Scudamore, Kim (LAB - King's Chase)
kim.scudamore@southglos.gov.uk

Stephen, Gloria (LD - Dodington)
gloria.stephen@southglos.gov.uk

Stokes, Benjamin (CON - Boyd Valley)
ben.stokes@southglos.gov.uk

Sullivan, John (CON - Rodway)
john.sullivan@southglos.gov.uk

Tyrrell, Maggie (LD - Thornbury South and Alveston)
maggie.tyrrell@southglos.gov.uk

Walker, Keith (LAB - Patchway)
keith.walker@southglos.gov.uk

Walker, Sue (LD - Yate Central)
sue.walker@southglos.gov.uk

Young, Claire (LD - Westerleigh)
claire.young@southglos.gov.uk

POLITICAL COMPOSITION

CON: 40, LD: 16, LAB: 14

COMMITTEE CHAIRS

Adults & Housing: Mr Benjamin Stokes

Audit & Accounts: Mr Nick Barrett

Children & Young People: Mr Jon Hunt

Health & Wellbeing: Mrs Heather Goddard

Planning, Transport & Strategic Environment: Mr Brian Allinson

South Hams D

South Hams District Council, Follaton House, Plymouth Road, Totnes TQ9 5NE
☎ 01803 861234 🖷 01803 866151
customer.services@southhams.gov.uk 💻 www.southhams.gov.uk

FACTS AND FIGURES

Parliamentary Constituencies: Totnes
EU Constituencies: South West
Election Frequency: Elections are of whole council

PRINCIPAL OFFICERS

Chief Executive: Mr Steve Jorden , Executive Director - Strategy & Commissioning & Head of Paid Service, Follaton House, Plymouth Road, Totnes TQ9 5NE ☎ 01803 861105
steve.jorden@swdevon.gov.uk

Deputy Chief Executive: Ms Sophie Hosking , Executive Director - Service Delivery & Commercial Development, Follaton House, Plymouth Road, Totnes TQ9 5NE ☎ 01803 861105
sophie.hosking@swdevon.gov.uk

Senior Management: Mr Darren Arulvasagam , Group Manager - Business Development, Follaton House, Plymouth Road, Totnes TQ9 5NE ☎ 01803 861234 darren.arulvasagam@swdevon.gov.uk

Senior Management: Ms Tracey Beeck , Group Manager - Customer First, Follaton House, Plymouth Road, Totnes TQ9 5NE ☎ 01803 861234 tracey.beeck@swdevon.gov.uk

Senior Management: Mrs Helen Dobby, Head of Environment Services, Follaton House, Plymouth Road, Totnes TQ9 5NE ☎ 01822 813600 ✉ helen.dobby@swdevon.gov.uk

Senior Management: Mr Steve Mullineaux , Group Manager - Support Services, Follaton House, Plymouth Road, Totnes TQ9 5NE ☎ 01822 813600 ✉ steve.mullineaux@swdevon.gov.uk

Architect, Building / Property Services: Mr Chris Brook , Community of Practice - Assets, Follaton House, Plymouth Road, Totnes TQ9 5NE ☎ 01822 813600 ✉ chris.brook@swdevon.gov.uk

Building Control: Mr Andrew Carpenter , Head of Building Control Partnership, Forde House, Brunel Road, Newton Abbot TQ12 4XX ☎ 01626 215721 ✉ andrew.carpenter@teignbridge.gov.uk

Community Planning: Mr Ross Kennerley, Lead Specialist for Place Strategy, Follaton House, Plymouth Road, Totnes TQ9 5NE ☎ 01822 813647 ✉ ross.kennerley@swdevon.gov.uk

Computer Management: Mr Mike Ward , ICT Community of Practice Lead, Follaton House, Plymouth Road, Totnes TQ9 5NE ☎ 01803 861234 ✉ mike.ward@swdevon.gov.uk

Customer Service: Ms Tracey Beeck , Group Manager - Customer First, Follaton House, Plymouth Road, Totnes TQ9 5NE ☎ 01803 861234 ✉ tracey.beeck@swdevon.gov.uk

Electoral Registration: Mrs Elizabeth Tucker, Electoral Administrator, Follaton House, Plymouth Road, Totnes TQ9 5NE ☎ 01803 861234 ✉ liz.tucker@southhams.gov.uk

Emergency Planning: Mr James Kershaw , Head of Emergency Planning, Follaton House, Plymouth Road, Totnes TQ9 5NE ☎ 01822 813600 ✉ james.kershaw@swdevon.gov.uk

Estates, Property & Valuation: Mr Chris Brook , Community of Practice - Assets, Follaton House, Plymouth Road, Totnes TQ9 5NE ☎ 01822 813600 ✉ chris.brook@swdevon.gov.uk

Treasury: Miss Lisa Buckle, Head of Finance & Audit, Follaton House, Plymouth Road, Totnes TQ9 5NE ☎ 01822 813644 ✉ lisa.buckle@westdevon.gov.uk

Fleet Management: Mrs Helen Dobby, Head of Environment Services, Follaton House, Plymouth Road, Totnes TQ9 5NE ☎ 01822 813600 ✉ helen.dobby@swdevon.gov.uk

Grounds Maintenance: Mrs Helen Dobby, Head of Environment Services, Follaton House, Plymouth Road, Totnes TQ9 5NE ☎ 01822 813600 ✉ helen.dobby@swdevon.gov.uk

Housing: Ms Isabel Blake , Head of Housing, Follaton House, Plymouth Road, Totnes TQ9 5NE ☎ 01822 813600 ✉ isabel.blake@swdevon.gov.uk

Leisure and Cultural Services: Mr Ross Kennerley, Lead Specialist for Place Strategy, Follaton House, Plymouth Road, Totnes TQ9 5NE ☎ 01822 813647 ✉ ross.kennerley@swdevon.gov.uk

Member Services: Mr Darryl White , Member Services Manager, Follaton House, Plymouth Road, Totnes TQ9 5NE ☎ 01803 861234 ✉ darryl.white@southhams.gov.uk

Parking: Mrs Catherine Aubertin , Car Parking & Contracts Performance Manager, Follaton House, Plymouth Road, Totnes TQ9 5NE ☎ 01822 813650 ✉ caubertin@westdevon.gov.uk

Personnel / HR: Mr Andy Wilson , Head of Corporate Services, Follaton House, Plymouth Road, Totnes TQ9 5NE ☎ 01822 813600 ✉ andy.wilson@swdevon.gov.uk

Staff Training: Mr Andy Wilson , Head of Corporate Services, Follaton House, Plymouth Road, Totnes TQ9 5NE ☎ 01822 813600 ✉ andy.wilson@swdevon.gov.uk

Street Scene: Mrs Catherine Aubertin , Car Parking & Contracts Performance Manager, Follaton House, Plymouth Road, Totnes TQ9 5NE ☎ 01822 813650 ✉ caubertin@westdevon.gov.uk

COUNCILLORS

***Chair* Bramble**, Ian (CON - Loddiswell & Aveton Gifford)
cllr.bramble@southhams.gov.uk

***Chair* Hitchins**, Bill (CON - Bickleigh & Cornwood)
cllr.hitchins@southhams.gov.uk

***Vice-Chair* Smerdon**, Peter (CON - South Brent)
cllr.smerdon@southhams.gov.uk

***Leader of the Council* Tucker**, John (CON - West Dart)
cllr.tucker@southhams.gov.uk

***Deputy Leader of the Council* Ward**, Lindsay (CON - Charterlands)
cllr.lward@southhams.gov.uk

***Group Leader* Hodgson**, Jacqi (GRN - Dartington & Staverton)
cllr.hodgson@southhams.gov.uk

Baldry, Keith (LD - Newton & Yealmpton)
cllr.baldry@southhams.gov.uk

Barnes, Nicky (CON - Woolwell)
cllr.barnes@southhams.gov.uk

Bastone, Hilary (CON - Dartmouth & East Dart)
cllr.bastone@southhams.gov.uk

Blackler, Ian (CON - Newton & Yealmpton)
cllr.blackler@southhams.gov.uk

Brazil, Julian (LD - Stokenham)
cllr.brazil@southhams.gov.uk

Brown, Daniel (CON - Wembury & Brixton)
cllr.brown@southhams.gov.uk

Cane, Basil (CON - Wembury & Brixton)
cllr.cane@southhams.gov.uk

Cuthbert, Kathy (CON - Ivybridge East)
cllr.cuthbert@southhams.gov.uk

Foss, Richard (CON - Allington & Strete)
cllr.foss@southhams.gov.uk

Gilbert, Rufus (CON - Kingsbridge)
cllr.gilbert@southhams.gov.uk

Hawkins, Jonathan (CON - Dartmouth & East Dart)
cllr.hawkins@southhams.gov.uk

SOUTH HAMS

Hicks, Michael (CON - Blackawton & Stoke Fleming)
cllr.hicks@southhams.gov.uk

Holway, Tom (CON - Ermington & Ugborough)
cllr.holway@southhams.gov.uk

Horsburgh, David (LAB - Totnes)
cllr.horsburgh@southhams.gov.uk

May, David (CON - Ivybridge West)
cllr.may@southhams.gov.uk

Pearce, Judy (CON - Salcombe & Thurlestone)
cllr.pearce@southhams.gov.uk

Pennington, Trevor (CON - Marldon & Littlehempston)
cllr.pennington@southhams.gov.uk

Pringle, Karen (CON - Ivybridge East)
cllr.pringle@southhams.gov.uk

Rowe, Rosemary (CON - Dartmouth & East Dart)
cllr.rowe@southhams.gov.uk

Saltern, Michael (CON - Ivybridge West)
cllr.saltern@southhams.gov.uk

Steer, Robert (CON - South Brent)
cllr.steer@southhams.gov.uk

Vint, Robert (GRN - Totnes)
cllr.vint@southhams.gov.uk

Wingate, Keith (CON - Kingsbridge)
cllr.wingate@southhams.gov.uk

Wood, Barrie (GRN - Totnes)
cllr.wood@southhams.gov.uk

Wright, Simon (CON - Westville and Alvington)
cllr.wright@southhams.gov.uk

POLITICAL COMPOSITION

CON: 25, GRN: 3, LD: 2, LAB: 1

COMMITTEE CHAIRS

Audit: Mr Trevor Pennington

Development Mangement: Mr Robert Steer

Licensing: Mr David May

South Holland District Council D

South Holland District Council, Council Offices, Priory Road, Spalding PE11 2XE
☎ 01775 761161 🖷 01775 711253 ✉ info@sholland.gov.uk
🖳 www.sholland.gov.uk

FACTS AND FIGURES

Parliamentary Constituencies: South Holland and The Deepings
EU Constituencies: East Midlands
Election Frequency: Elections are of whole council

PRINCIPAL OFFICERS

Chief Executive: Ms Anna Graves , Chief Executive, Elizabeth House, Walpole Loke, Dereham NR19 1EE ☎ 07833 503139
✉ chief.executive@breckland-sholland.go.uk

Deputy Chief Executive: Mr Mark Stokes , Deputy Chief Executive, Elizabeth House, Walpole Loke, Dereham NR19 1EE
☎ 01775 761161 ✉ mark.stokes@breckland-sholland.gov.uk

Senior Management: Mr Mark Finch, Finance Manager, Elizabeth House, Walpole Loke, Dereham NR19 1EE ☎ 07917 587078
✉ mark.finch@breckland-sholland.gov.uk

Senior Management: Mrs Maxine O'Mahony , Executive Director - Commissioning & Governance, Council Offices, Priory Road, Spalding PE11 2XE ☎ 07787 573444
✉ maxine.omahony@breckland-sholland.gov.uk

Senior Management: Mrs Vicky Thomson , Democratic Services & Legal Manager, Elizabeth House, Walpole Loke, Dereham NR19 1EE ☎ 07827 843173 ✉ vicky.thomson@breckland-sholland.gov.uk

Senior Management: Mr Robert Walker , Assistant Director - Community, Elizabeth House, Walpole Loke, Dereham NR19 1EE
☎ 07867 988826 ✉ robert.walker@breckland-sholland.gov.uk

Architect, Building / Property Services: Mr Stephen Udberg , Asset & Property Manager, Council Offices, Priory Road, Spalding PE11 2XE ☎ 07827 843157
✉ steve.udberg@breckland-sholland.gov.uk

Best Value: Ms Vicky Thomson, Assistant Director - Democratic Services, Council Offices, Priory Road, Spalding PE11 2XE ☎ 01775 761161 🖷 01775 711253 ✉ vicky.thomson@breckland-sholland.gov.uk

Building Control: Mr Phil Adams , Public Protection Manager, Council Offices, Priory Road, Spalding PE11 2XE ☎ 07713 003330
✉ phillip.adams@breckland-sholland.gov.uk

PR / Communications: Ms Vicky Thomson, Assistant Director - Democratic Services, Council Offices, Priory Road, Spalding PE11 2XE ☎ 01775 761161 🖷 01775 711253 ✉ vicky.thomson@breckland-sholland.gov.uk

Community Planning: Mr Paul Jackson, Planning Manager, Council Offices, Priory Road, Spalding PE11 2XE ☎ 01775 761161
🖷 01775 710772 ✉ pjackson@sholland.gov.uk

Community Safety: Ms Riana Rudland , Community Development Manager, Council Offices, Priory Road, Spalding PE11 2XE ☎ 01775 761161 🖷 01775 711253 ✉ riana.rudland@breckland-sholland.gov.uk

Computer Management: Mr Marcus Coleman , Managing Director , Tedder Hall, Manby Park, Louth LN11 8UP ☎ 01507 613307 🖷 01507 329599 ✉ marcus.coleman@cpbs.com

Computer Management: Mr Kevin Rump , ICT & Customer Manager, Elizabeth House, Walpole Loke, Dereham NR19 1EE
☎ 01362 656870 ✉ kevin.rump@breckland-sholland.gov.uk

Corporate Services: Ms Vicky Thomson, Assistant Director - Democratic Services, Council Offices, Priory Road, Spalding PE11 2XE ☎ 01775 761161 🖷 01775 711253
✉ vicky.thomson@breckland-sholland.gov.uk

Customer Service: Mr Kevin Rump , ICT & Customer Manager, Elizabeth House, Walpole Loke, Dereham NR19 1EE ☎ 01362 656870 🖱 kevin.rump@breckland-sholland.gov.uk

Direct Labour: Mr Steve Udberg , Asset & Property Manager, Council Offices, Priory Road, Spalding PE11 2XE ☎ 01775 761161 🖷 01775 711253 🖱 sudberg@sholland.gov.uk

Economic Development: Mr Mark Stanton, Economic Development Manager, Council Offices, Priory Road, Spalding PE11 2XE ☎ 07748 116933 🖷 01362 656360 🖱 mark.stanton@breckland-sholland.gov.uk

E-Government: Mr Kevin Rump , ICT & Customer Manager, Council Offices, Priory Road, Spalding PE11 2XE ☎ 01362 656870 🖱 kevin.rump@breckland-sholland.gov.uk

Electoral Registration: Ms Vicky Thomson, Assistant Director - Democratic Services, Council Offices, Priory Road, Spalding PE11 2XE ☎ 01775 761161 🖷 01775 711253 🖱 vicky.thomson@breckland-sholland.gov.uk

Emergency Planning: Ms Riana Rudland , Community Development Manager, Council Offices, Priory Road, Spalding PE11 2XE ☎ 01775 761161 🖷 01775 711253 🖱 riana.rudland@breckland-sholland.gov.uk

Environmental / Technical Services: Mr Dale Robinson , Environmental Services Manager, Council Offices, Priory Road, Spalding PE11 2XE ☎ 01775 7611253 🖷 01775 711253 🖱 dale.robinson@breckland-sholland.gov.uk

Environmental Health: Mr Dale Robinson , Environmental Services Manager, Council Offices, Priory Road, Spalding PE11 2XE ☎ 01775 7611253 🖷 01775 711253 🖱 dale.robinson@breckland-sholland.gov.uk

Estates, Property & Valuation: Mr Steve Udberg , Asset & Property Manager, Council Offices, Priory Road, Spalding PE11 2XE ☎ 01775 761161 🖷 01775 711253 🖱 sudberg@sholland.gov.uk

European Liaison: Ms Riana Rudland , Community Development Manager, Council Offices, Priory Road, Spalding PE11 2XE ☎ 01775 761161 🖷 01775 711253 🖱 riana.rudland@breckland-sholland.gov.uk

European Liaison: Mr Mark Stanton, Economic Development Manager, Elizabeth House, Walpole Loke, Dereham NR19 1EE ☎ 07748 116933 🖷 01362 656360 🖱 mark.stanton@breckland-sholland.gov.uk

Events Manager: Mr Dale Robinson , Environmental Services Manager, Council Offices, Priory Road, Spalding PE11 2XE ☎ 01775 7611253 🖷 01775 711253 🖱 dale.robinson@breckland-sholland.gov.uk

Facilities: Mr Steve Udberg , Asset & Property Manager, Council Offices, Priory Road, Spalding PE11 2XE ☎ 01775 761161 🖷 01775 711253 🖱 sudberg@sholland.gov.uk

Finance: Mr Mark Finch , Assistant Director - Finance & S151 Officer, Council Offices, Priory Road, Spalding PE11 2XE ☎ 01775 761161 🖷 01775 711253 🖱 mfinch@sholland.gov.uk

Fleet Management: Mr Dale Robinson , Environmental Services Manager, Council Offices, Priory Road, Spalding PE11 2XE ☎ 01775 7611253 🖷 01775 711253 🖱 dale.robinson@breckland-sholland.gov.uk

Grounds Maintenance: Mr Dale Robinson , Environmental Services Manager, Council Offices, Priory Road, Spalding PE11 2XE ☎ 01775 7611253 🖷 01775 711253 🖱 dale.robinson@breckland-sholland.gov.uk

Home Energy Conservation: Mr Phil Adams, Building Control & Environmental Health Manager, Council Offices, Priory Road, Spalding PE11 2XE ☎ 01775 761161 🖷 01775 711253 🖱 padams@sholland.gov.uk

Housing: Mr Duncan Hall , Housing Manager, Council Offices, Priory Road, Spalding PE11 2XE ☎ 07500 915488 🖱 duncan.hall@west-norfolk.gov.uk

Housing Maintenance: Mr Steve Udberg , Asset & Property Manager, Council Offices, Priory Road, Spalding PE11 2XE ☎ 01775 761161 🖷 01775 711253 🖱 sudberg@sholland.gov.uk

Leisure and Cultural Services: Mr Steve Udberg , Asset & Property Manager, Council Offices, Priory Road, Spalding PE11 2XE ☎ 01775 761161 🖷 01775 711253 🖱 sudberg@sholland.gov.uk

Lighting: Mr Phil Adams, Building Control & Environmental Health Manager, Council Offices, Priory Road, Spalding PE11 2XE ☎ 01775 761161 🖷 01775 711253 🖱 padams@sholland.gov.uk

Lottery Funding, Charity and Voluntary: Ms Riana Rudland , Community Development Manager, Council Offices, Priory Road, Spalding PE11 2XE ☎ 01775 761161 🖷 01775 711253 🖱 riana.rudland@breckland-sholland.gov.uk

Member Services: Mrs Vicky Thomson , Democratic Services & Legal Manager, Council Offices, Priory Road, Spalding PE11 2XE ☎ 07827 843173 🖱 vicky.thomson@breckland-sholland.gov.uk

Parking: Mr Dale Robinson , Environmental Services Manager, Council Offices, Priory Road, Spalding PE11 2XE ☎ 01775 7611253 🖷 01775 711253 🖱 dale.robinson@breckland-sholland.gov.uk

Partnerships: Ms Riana Rudland , Community Development Manager, Council Offices, Priory Road, Spalding PE11 2XE ☎ 01775 761161 🖷 01775 711253 🖱 riana.rudland@breckland-sholland.gov.uk

Personnel / HR: Mrs Natalie King , HR Manager, Council Offices, Priory Road, Spalding PE11 2XE ☎ 01362 656870 🖱 natalie.king@breckland-sholland.gov.uk

Personnel / HR: Mr Tony Lascelles, Head - HR, Tedder Hall, Manby Park, Louth LN11 8UP ☎ 01507 613230 🖷 01507 600206 🖱 tony.lascelles@cpbs.com

Planning: Mr Paul Jackson , Planning Manager, Elizabeth House, Walpole Loke, Dereham NR19 1EE ☎ 07949 494836 🖱 paul.jackson@breckland-sholland.gov.uk

Procurement: Ms Vicky Thomson, Assistant Director - Democratic Services, Council Offices, Priory Road, Spalding PE11 2XE ☎ 01775 761161 🖷 01775 711253 🖱 vicky.thomson@breckland-sholland.gov.uk

SOUTH HOLLAND DISTRICT COUNCIL

Recycling & Waste Minimisation: Mr Dale Robinson , Environmental Services Manager, Council Offices, Priory Road, Spalding PE11 2XE ☎ 01775 7611253 🖷 01775 711253 dale.robinson@breckland-sholland.gov.uk

Regeneration: Mr Mark Stanton, Economic Development Manager, Council Offices, Priory Road, Spalding PE11 2XE ☎ 07748 116933 🖷 01362 656360 mark.stanton@breckland-sholland.gov.uk

Staff Training: Ms Natalie King , Human Resources Manager, Council Offices, Priory Road, Spalding PE11 2XE ☎ 01775 761161 🖷 01775 711253 nking@sholland.gov.uk

Street Scene: Mr Dale Robinson , Environmental Services Manager, Council Offices, Priory Road, Spalding PE11 2XE ☎ 01775 7611253 🖷 01775 711253 dale.robinson@breckland-sholland.gov.uk

Sustainable Communities: Mr Paul Jackson, Planning Manager, Council Offices, Priory Road, Spalding PE11 2XE ☎ 01775 761161 🖷 01775 710772 pjackson@sholland.gov.uk

Sustainable Communities: Ms Riana Rudland , Community Development Manager, Council Offices, Priory Road, Spalding PE11 2XE ☎ 01775 761161 🖷 01775 711253 riana.rudland@breckland-sholland.gov.uk

Sustainable Development: Mr Paul Jackson, Planning Manager, Council Offices, Priory Road, Spalding PE11 2XE ☎ 01775 761161 🖷 01775 710772 pjackson@sholland.gov.uk

Tourism: Ms Riana Rudland , Community Development Manager, Council Offices, Priory Road, Spalding PE11 2XE ☎ 01775 761161 🖷 01775 711253 riana.rudland@breckland-sholland.gov.uk

Town Centre: Mr Mark Stanton , Economic Development Manager, Council Offices, Priory Road, Spalding PE11 2XE ☎ 01775 761161 🖷 01775 711253 mstanton@sholland.gov.uk

Transport Planner: Mr Paul Jackson, Planning Manager, Council Offices, Priory Road, Spalding PE11 2XE ☎ 01775 761161 🖷 01775 710772 pjackson@sholland.gov.uk

Waste Collection and Disposal: Mr Dale Robinson , Environmental Services Manager, Council Offices, Priory Road, Spalding PE11 2XE ☎ 01775 7611253 🖷 01775 711253 dale.robinson@breckland-sholland.gov.uk

Waste Management: Mr Dale Robinson , Environmental Services Manager, Council Offices, Priory Road, Spalding PE11 2XE ☎ 01775 7611253 🖷 01775 711253 dale.robinson@breckland-sholland.gov.uk

COUNCILLORS

***Chair* Biggadike**, Francis (CON - Holbeach Town)
fbiggadike@sholland.gov.uk

***Vice-Chair* Grocock**, Rodney (CON - Moulton, Weston & Cowbit)
rgrocock@sholland.gov.uk

***Leader of the Council* Porter**, Gary (CON - Spalding St Mary's)
gporter@sholland.gov.uk

***Deputy Leader of the Council* Worth**, Charles (CON - Holbeach Hurn)
nworth@sholland.gov.uk

***Group Leader* Newton**, Angela (IND - Spalding Monkshouse)
anewton@sholland.gov.uk

Alcock, Bryan (IND - Crowland and Deeping St Nicholas)
balcock@sholland.gov.uk

Aley, George (CON - Spalding Monkshouse)
galey@sholland.gov.uk

Ashby, David (CON - Spalding St Paul's)
david.ashby@sholland.gov.uk

Astill, Jim (CON - Crowland and Deeping St Nicholas)
jastill@sholland.gov.uk

Avery, James (CON - Pinchbeck and Surfleet)
javery@sholland.gov.uk

Booth, Michael (IND - Sutton Bridge)
mbooth@sholland.gov.uk

Brewis, Christopher (IND - Sutton Bridge)
cbrewis@sholland.gov.uk

Carter, Tracey (CON - Holbeach Town)
tcarter@sholland.gov.uk

Casson, Anthony (CON - Moulton, Weston and Cowbit)
acasson@sholland.gov.uk

Chandler, Malcolm (CON - Whaplode and Holbeach St Johns)
mchandler@sholland.gov.uk

Clark, Robert (CON - Donington, Quadring and Gosberton)
rclark@sholland.gov.uk

Coupland, Peter (CON - Fleet)
pcoupland@sholland.gov.uk

Dark, Graham (IND - Spalding St John's)
gdark@sholland.gov.uk

Drury, Harry (CON - Spalding St Mary's)
hdrury@sholland.gov.uk

Eldridge, Laura (CON - Long Sutton)
leldridge@sholland.gov.uk

Foyster, Paul (UKIP - Holbeach Town)
pfoyster@sholland.gov.uk

Gambba-Jones, Roger (CON - Spalding Wygate)
rgambba-jones@sholland.gov.uk

Harrison, Angela (CON - Crowland and Deeping St Nicholas)
angelaharrison@sholland.gov.uk

Johnson, Colin (CON - Donington, Quadring and Gosberton)
cjohnson@sholland.gov.uk

King, Jane (IND - Donington, Quadring and Gosberton)
jane.king@sholland.gov.uk

Lawton, Christine (CON - Spalding Wygate)
clawton@sholland.gov.uk

McLean, Jack (CON - Spalding St John's)
jmclean@sholland.gov.uk

Pullen, Michael (CON - Whaplode and Holbeach St John's)
mpullen@sholland.gov.uk

Reynolds, Joanne (CON - Gedney)
jreynolds@sholland.gov.uk

Seymour, Michael (CON - The Saints)
mseymour@sholland.gov.uk

Slade, Sally-Ann (CON - Pinchbeck and Surfleet)
sally-ann.slade@sholland.gov.uk

Sneath, Elizabeth (CON - Pinchbeck and Surfleet)
elizabeth.sneath@sholland.gov.uk

Taylor, Gary (CON - Spalding Castle)
gtaylor@sholland.gov.uk

Tennant, Andrew (IND - Long Sutton)
atennant@sholland.gov.uk

Tyrrell, Jack (CON - Long Sutton)
jtyrell@sholland.gov.uk

Williams, Peter (UKIP - Spalding St Paul's)
pwilliams@sholland.gov.uk

Woolf, Andrew (CON - Moulton, Weston and Cowbit)
awoolf@sholland.gov.uk

POLITICAL COMPOSITION
CON: 28, IND: 7, UKIP: 2

COMMITTEE CHAIRS

Audit & Governance: Mr George Aley

Licensing: Mrs Angela Harrison

Planning: Mr Roger Gambba-Jones

South Kesteven D

South Kesteven District Council, Council Offices, St. Peter's Hill, Grantham NG31 6PZ
☎ 01476 406080 🖷 01476 406000 ✉ frontdesk@southkesteven.gov.uk
💻 www.southkesteven.gov.uk

FACTS AND FIGURES
Parliamentary Constituencies: Grantham and Stamford
EU Constituencies: East Midlands
Election Frequency: Elections are of whole council

PRINCIPAL OFFICERS

Chief Executive: Ms Beverly Agass , Chief Executive, Council Offices, St. Peter's Hill, Grantham NG31 6PZ ☎ 01476 406100 🖷 01476 406101 ✉ b.agass@southkesteven.gov.uk

Senior Management: Ms Tracey Blackwell , Strategic Director - Environment & Property, Council Offices, St. Peter's Hill, Grantham NG31 6PZ

Senior Management: Mr Steve Ingram , Strategic Director - Development Management & Growth, Council Offices, St. Peter's Hill, Grantham NG31 6PZ ✉ s.ingram@southkesteven.gov.uk

Senior Management: Mr Daren Turner , Strategic Director - Commercial, Council Offices, St. Peter's Hill, Grantham NG31 6PZ ☎ 01476 406301 🖷 01476 406000 ✉ d.turner@southkesteven.gov.uk

Architect, Building / Property Services: Mr Neil Cucksey , Executive Manager - Property, Council Offices, St. Peter's Hill, Grantham NG31 6PZ ☎ 01476 406224 🖷 01476 406000 ✉ n.cucksey@southkesteven.gov.uk

Building Control: Mr Mal Brown , Interim Building Control Manager, Council Offices, St. Peter's Hill, Grantham NG31 6PZ ☎ 01476 406224 ✉ m.brown@southkesteven.gov.uk

PR / Communications: Mr Geoff O'Neil , Reputation, Public Relations, Communications, Consultation & Engagement Business Manager, Council Offices, St. Peter's Hill, Grantham NG31 6PZ ☎ 01476 406020 🖷 01476 406000 ✉ pr@southkesteven.gov.uk

Community Safety: Mr Mark Jones , Neighbourhoods Business Manager, Council Offices, St. Peter's Hill, Grantham NG31 6PZ ☎ 01476 406080 🖷 01476 406000 ✉ m.jones@southkesteven.gov.uk

Community Safety: Mr Sandy Kavanagh, Community Safety Officer, Council Offices, St. Peter's Hill, Grantham NG31 6PZ ☎ 01476 406107 🖷 01476 406000 ✉ s.kavanagh@southkesteven.gov.uk

Computer Management: Mr Andy Nix , Business Transformation Manager, Council Offices, St. Peter's Hill, Grantham NG31 6PZ ☎ 01476 406433 🖷 01476 406000 ✉ a.nix@southkesteven.gov.uk

Contracts: Mr Andrew Sweeney , Assets & Facilities Business Manager, Council Offices, St. Peter's Hill, Grantham NG31 6PZ ☎ 01476 406080 ✉ a.sweeney@southkesteven.gov.uk

Corporate Services: Mrs Lucy Youles, Executive Manager - Corporate, Council Offices, St. Peter's Hill, Grantham NG31 6PZ ☎ 01476 406105 🖷 01476 406000 ✉ l.youles@southkesteven.gov.uk

Customer Service: Mr Andy Nix , Business Transformation Manager, Council Offices, St. Peter's Hill, Grantham NG31 6PZ ☎ 01476 406433 🖷 01476 406000 ✉ a.nix@southkesteven.gov.uk

Direct Labour: Mr Keith Rowe , Street Care Services Business Manager, Council Offices, St. Peter's Hill, Grantham NG31 6PZ ☎ 01476 406080 ✉ k.rowe@southkesteven.gov.uk

Economic Development: Mr Roger Ranson , Spatial & Economic Growth Business Manager, Council Offices, St. Peter's Hill, Grantham NG31 6PZ ☎ 01476 406080 ✉ r.ranson@southkesteven.gov.uk

Electoral Registration: Ms Julie Edwards , Elections & Democratic Services Team Leader, Council Offices, St. Peter's Hill, Grantham NG31 6PZ ☎ 01476 406078 🖷 01476 406000 ✉ j.edwards@southkesteven.gov.uk

Emergency Planning: Mr Mark Jones , Neighbourhoods Business Manager, Council Offices, St. Peter's Hill, Grantham NG31 6PZ ☎ 01476 406080 🖷 01476 406000 ✉ m.jones@southkesteven.gov.uk

Energy Management: Mr K Munford, Energy Officer, Council Offices, St. Peter's Hill, Grantham NG31 6PZ ☎ 01476 406080 🖷 01476 406000 ✉ k.munford@southkesteven.gov.uk

Environmental / Technical Services: Ms AnnMarie Coulthard, Environmental Health Business Manager, Council Offices, St. Peter's Hill, Grantham NG31 6PZ ☎ 01476 406080 ✉ a.coulthard@southkesteven.gov.uk

Environmental Health: Ms AnnMarie Coulthard , Environmental Health Business Manager, Council Offices, St. Peter's Hill, Grantham NG31 6PZ ☎ 01476 406080 ✉ a.coulthard@southkesteven.gov.uk

Estates, Property & Valuation: Mr Neil Cucksey , Executive Manager - Property, Council Offices, St. Peter's Hill, Grantham NG31 6PZ ☎ 01476 406224 🖷 01476 406000 ✉ n.cucksey@southkesteven.gov.uk

Facilities: Mr Paul Stokes , Venues & Facilities Business Manager, Council Offices, St. Peter's Hill, Grantham NG31 6PZ ☎ 01476 406410 🖷 01476 406000 ✉ p.stokes@southkesteven.gov.uk

Finance: Mr Richard Wyles , Corporate Finance Officer, Council Offices, St. Peter's Hill, Grantham NG31 6PZ ☎ 01476 406210 🖷 01476 406000 ✉ r.wyles@southkesteven.gov.uk

Grounds Maintenance: Mr Mike Smith , Facilities Team Leader of Operations, Council Offices, St. Peter's Hill, Grantham NG31 6PZ ☎ 01476 406080 🖷 01476 406000 ✉ m.smith@southkesteven.gov.uk

Health and Safety: Ms AnnMarie Coulthard , Environmental Health Business Manager, Council Offices, St. Peter's Hill, Grantham NG31 6PZ ☎ 01476 406080 ✉ a.coulthard@southkesteven.gov.uk

Home Energy Conservation: Mr K Munford, Energy Officer, Council Offices, St. Peter's Hill, Grantham NG31 6PZ ☎ 01476 406080 🖷 01476 406000 ✉ k.munford@southkesteven.gov.uk

Housing: Ms Lisa Barker , Housing Business Manager, Council Offices, St. Peter's Hill, Grantham NG31 6PZ ☎ 01476 406251 ✉ l.barker@southkesteven.gov.uk

Legal: Mr John Armstrong , Legal & Democratic Business Manager, Council Offices, St. Peter's Hill, Grantham NG31 6PZ ☎ 014476 406103 ✉ j.armstrong@southkesteven.gov.uk

Leisure and Cultural Services: Ms Susie McCahon , Leisure & Amenities Team Leader, Council Offices, St. Peter's Hill, Grantham NG31 6PZ ☎ 01476 406080 🖷 01476 406000 ✉ s.mccahon@southkesteven.gov.uk

Licensing: Mr Mark Jones , Neighbourhoods Business Manager, Council Offices, St. Peter's Hill, Grantham NG31 6PZ ☎ 01476 406080 🖷 01476 406000 ✉ m.jones@southkesteven.gov.uk

Member Services: Mrs Lucy Youles, Executive Manager - Corporate, Council Offices, St. Peter's Hill, Grantham NG31 6PZ ☎ 01476 406105 🖷 01476 406000 ✉ l.youles@southkesteven.gov.uk

Parking: Mr Paul Stokes , Venues & Facilities Business Manager, Council Offices, St. Peter's Hill, Grantham NG31 6PZ ☎ 01476 406410 🖷 01476 406000 ✉ p.stokes@southkesteven.gov.uk

Personnel / HR: Mrs Elaine Pepper , Business Manager - People & OD, Council Offices, St. Peter's Hill, Grantham NG31 6PZ ☎ 01476 406132 ✉ e.pepper@southkesteven.gov.uk

Planning: Mr Paul Thomas , Executive Manager - Development & Growth, Council Offices, St. Peter's Hill, Grantham NG31 6PZ ☎ 01476 406162 🖷 01476 406000 ✉ p.thomas@southkesteven.gov.uk

Procurement: Mr Richard Wyles , Corporate Finance Officer, Council Offices, St. Peter's Hill, Grantham NG31 6PZ ☎ 01476 406210 🖷 01476 406000 ✉ r.wyles@southkesteven.gov.uk

Recycling & Waste Minimisation: Mr Keith Rowe , Street Care Services Business Manager, Council Offices, St. Peter's Hill, Grantham NG31 6PZ ☎ 01476 406080 ✉ k.rowe@southkesteven.gov.uk

Regeneration: Mr Roger Ranson , Spatial & Economic Growth Business Manager, Council Offices, St. Peter's Hill, Grantham NG31 6PZ ☎ 01476 406080 ✉ r.ranson@southkesteven.gov.uk

Staff Training: Mrs Elaine Pepper , Business Manager - People & OD, Council Offices, St. Peter's Hill, Grantham NG31 6PZ ☎ 01476 406132 ✉ e.pepper@southkesteven.gov.uk

Street Scene: Mr Keith Rowe , Street Care Services Business Manager, Council Offices, St. Peter's Hill, Grantham NG31 6PZ ☎ 01476 406080 ✉ k.rowe@southkesteven.gov.uk

COUNCILLORS

***Chair* Wootten**, Ray (CON - Grantham St. Wulfram's)
r.wootten@southkesteven.gov.uk

***Vice-Chair* Smith**, Judy (CON - Bourne East)
judy.smith@southkesteven.gov.uk

***Leader of the Council* Adams**, Bob (CON - Isaac Newton)
b.adams@southkesteven.gov.uk

***Deputy Leader of the Council* Craft**, Nick (CON - Belmont)
n.craft@southkesteven.gov.uk

Ashwell, Duncan (CON - Bourne Austerby)
d.ashwell@southkesteven.gov.uk

Baxter, Ashley (IND - Market & West Deeping)

Bosworth, Pam (CON - Belvoir)
p.bosworth@southkesteven.gov.uk

Broughton, Robert (IND - Market & West Deeping)
b.broughton@southkesteven.gov.uk

Brown, Katherine (CON - Stamford St. George's)
k.brown@southkesteven.gov.uk

Bryant, Terl (CON - Stamford St. John's)
t.bryant@southkesteven.gov.uk

Cartwright, Frances (CON - Morton)
f.cartwright@southkesteven.gov.uk

Chivers, George (CON - Belmont)
g.chivers@southkesteven.gov.uk

Cook, Michael (CON - Grantham St. Vincent's)
m.cook@southkesteven.gov.uk

Cooke, Kelham (CON - Casewick)
k.cooke@southkesteven.gov.uk

Coutts, Lynda (CON - Grantham Barrowby Gate)
l.coutts@southkesteven.gov.uk

Cunningham, Felicity (UKIP - Grantham Earlesfield)
f.cunningham@southkesteven.gov.uk

Dilks, Phil (LAB - Deeping St James)
p.dilks@southkesteven.gov.uk

Dobson, Barry (CON - Dole Wood)
b.dobson@southkesteven.gov.uk

Evans, Damian (CON - Stamford St. John's)

Exton, Mike (CON - Stamford All Saints)
m.exton@southkesteven.gov.uk

Forman, Tracey (LAB - Grantham Earlesfield)
t.forman@southkesteven.gov.uk

Goral, Helen (CON - Grantham Arnoldfield)
h.goral@southkesteven.gov.uk

Griffin, Breda (CON - Stamford All Saints)
b.griffin@southkesteven.gov.uk

Jeal, Graham (CON - Grantham St. Vincent's)
g.jeal@southkesteven.gov.uk

Johnson, Leigh (CON - Deeping St James)
l.johnson@southkesteven.gov.uk

Kaberry-Brown, Rosemary (CON - Peascliffe & Ridgeway)
r.kaberry-brown@southkesteven.gov.uk

King, Michael (CON - Toller)
m.king@southkesteven.gov.uk

Kingman, Jane (CON - Bourne Austerby)
j.kingman@southkesteven.gov.uk

Lee, Matthew (CON - Stamford St. Mary's)
m.lee@southkesteven.gov.uk

Manterfield, Nikki (CON - Grantham Springfield)
n.manterfield@southkesteven.gov.uk

Mapp, David (CON - Bourne West)
d.mapp@southkesteven.gov.uk

Morgan, Charmaine (LAB - Grantham St. Vincent's)
c.morgan@southkesteven.gov.uk

Moseley, Peter (CON - Aveland)
p.moseley@southkesteven.gov.uk

Neilson, Nick (CON - Market & West Deeping)
n.neilson@southkesteven.gov.uk

Powell, Helen (IND - Bourne West)
h.powell@southkesteven.gov.uk

Reid, Robert (CON - Bourne Austerby)
r.reid@southkesteven.gov.uk

Robins, Nick (CON - Castle)
n.robins@southkesteven.gov.uk

Russell, Bob (CON - Bourne East)
b.russell@southkesteven.gov.uk

Sampson, Bob (IND - Loveden Heath)
b.sampson@southkesteven.gov.uk

Selby, Ian (INDNA - Grantham Harrowby)
i.selby@southkesteven.gov.uk

Smith, Jacky (CON - Grantham St. Wulfram's)
jacky.smith@southkesteven.gov.uk

Stephens, Peter (CON - Lincrest)
p.stephens@southkesteven.gov.uk

Stevens, Judy (IND - Deeping St James)
j.stevens@southkesteven.gov.uk

Stokes, Adam (CON - Grantham Springfield)
a.stokes@southkesteven.gov.uk

Stokes, Ian (CON - Peascliffe & Ridgeway)

Stokes, Sarah (CON - Viking)
s.stokes@southkesteven.gov.uk

Sumner, Brian (CON - Stamford St. Mary's)
brian.sumner@southkesteven.gov.uk

Sumner, Brenda (CON - Stamford St. George's)
brenda.sumner@southkesteven.gov.uk

Turner, Frank (CON - Grantham Barrowby Gate)
f.turner@southkesteven.gov.uk

Ward, Dean (CON - Grantham Arnoldfield)
d.ward@southkesteven.gov.uk

Webster, Andrea (CON - Isaac Newton)
a.webster@southkesteven.gov.uk

Webster, Tom (CON - Belvoir)
t.webster@southkesteven.gov.uk

Wilkins, Martin (CON - Glen)
m.wilkins@southkesteven.gov.uk

Wood, Paul (IND - Viking)
p.wood@southkesteven.gov.uk

Woolley, Rosemary (CON - Casewick)
rh.woolley@southkesteven.gov.uk

Wootten, Linda (CON - Grantham Harrowby)
l.wootten@southkesteven.gov.uk

POLITICAL COMPOSITION

CON: 45, IND: 6, LAB: 3, UKIP: 1, INDNA: 1

COMMITTEE CHAIRS

Audit & Governance: Mr Ian Stokes

Development Control: Mr Martin Wilkins

Licensing: Mrs Pam Bosworth

South Lakeland D

South Lakeland District Council, South Lakeland House, Lowther Street, Kendal LA9 4UQ
☎ 0845 050 4434 🖷 01539 740300 ✉ info@southlakeland.gov.uk
🖳 www.southlakeland.gov.uk

FACTS AND FIGURES

Parliamentary Constituencies: Westmorland and Lonsdale
EU Constituencies: North West
Election Frequency: Elections are by thirds

PRINCIPAL OFFICERS

Chief Executive: Mr Lawrence Conway, Chief Executive, South Lakeland House, Lowther Street, Kendal LA9 4UD ☎ 01539 733333 🖷 01539 740300 ✉ l.conway@southlakeland.gov.uk

Senior Management: Ms Debbie Storr, Corporate Director - Policy & Resources Monitoring Officer, South Lakeland House, Lowther Street, Kendal LA9 4UQ ☎ 01539 733333 🖷 01539 740300 ✉ d.storr@southlakeland.gov.uk

SOUTH LAKELAND

Senior Management: Mr David Sykes, Director - People & Places, South Lakeland House, Lowther Street, Kendal LA9 4UQ ☎ 01539 733333 🖷 01539 740300 🖰 d.sykes@southlakeland.gov.uk

Building Control: Mr Mark Shipman , Development Management Group Manager, South Lakeland House, Lowther Street, Kendal LA9 4UQ ☎ 01536 733333 🖷 01539 740300 🖰 m.shipman@southlakeland.gov.uk

PR / Communications: Mr Simon Reynolds , Communications & Customer Services Manager, South Lakeland House, Lowther Street, Kendal LA9 4UQ ☎ 01539 733333 🖷 01539 740300 🖰 s.reynolds@southlakeland.gov.uk

Community Planning: Ms Claire Gould , Policy & Partnership Manager, South Lakeland House, Lowther Street, Kendal LA9 4UQ ☎ 01539 733333 🖷 01539 740300 🖰 c.gould@southlakeland.gov.uk

Community Safety: Ms Claire Gould , Policy & Partnership Manager, South Lakeland House, Lowther Street, Kendal LA9 4UQ ☎ 01539 733333 🖷 01539 740300 🖰 c.gould@southlakeland.gov.uk

Computer Management: Mr Ben Wright, Shared IT Manager, South Lakeland House, Lowther Street, Kendal LA9 4UQ ☎ 01539 733333 🖷 01539 740300 🖰 b.wright@southlakeland.gov.uk

Corporate Services: Ms Debbie Storr, Corporate Director - Policy & Resources Monitoring Officer, South Lakeland House, Lowther Street, Kendal LA9 4UQ ☎ 01539 733333 🖷 01539 740300 🖰 d.storr@southlakeland.gov.uk

Customer Service: Mr Simon Reynolds , Communications & Customer Services Manager, South Lakeland House, Lowther Street, Kendal LA9 4UQ ☎ 01539 733333 🖷 01539 740300 🖰 s.reynolds@southlakeland.gov.uk

Economic Development: Mr Ian Hassall , Assistant Director - Strategic Development, South Lakeland House, Lowther Street, Kendal LA9 4UQ ☎ 01539 733333 🖷 01539 470300 🖰 ian.hassall@southlakeland.gov.uk

Economic Development: Mr David Sykes, Director - People & Places, South Lakeland House, Lowther Street, Kendal LA9 4UQ ☎ 01539 733333 🖷 01539 740300 🖰 d.sykes@southlakeland.gov.uk

E-Government: Mr Simon Mcvey , Assistant Director - Policy & Performance, South Lakeland House, Lowther Street, Kendal LA9 4UQ ☎ 01539 733333 🖷 01539 740300 🖰 s.mcvey@southlakeland.gov.uk

Electoral Registration: Ms Debbie Storr, Corporate Director - Policy & Resources Monitoring Officer, South Lakeland House, Lowther Street, Kendal LA9 4UQ ☎ 01539 733333 🖷 01539 740300 🖰 d.storr@southlakeland.gov.uk

Emergency Planning: Mr Lawrence Conway, Chief Executive, South Lakeland House, Lowther Street, Kendal LA9 4UD ☎ 01539 733333 🖷 01539 740300 🖰 l.conway@southlakeland.gov.uk

Energy Management: Ms Claire Gould , Policy & Partnership Manager, South Lakeland House, Lowther Street, Kendal LA9 4UQ ☎ 01539 733333 🖷 01539 740300 🖰 c.gould@southlakeland.gov.uk

Environmental / Technical Services: Ms Fiona Inston , Public Protection Manager, South Lakeland House, Lowther Street, Kendal LA9 4UQ ☎ 01539 733333 🖷 01539 740300 🖰 fiona.inston@southlakeland.gov.uk

Environmental Health: Mr Simon Rowley , Assistant Director - Neighbourhood Services, South Lakeland House, Lowther Street, Kendal LA9 4UQ ☎ 01539 733333 🖷 01539 740300 🖰 s.rowley@southlakeland.gov.uk

Estates, Property & Valuation: Mr Ian Hassall , Assistant Director - Strategic Development, South Lakeland House, Lowther Street, Kendal LA9 4UQ ☎ 01539 733333 🖷 01539 470300 🖰 ian.hassall@southlakeland.gov.uk

Events Manager: Ms Imelda Winters-Lewis , Arts & Events Officer, South Lakeland House, Lowther Street, Kendal LA9 4UQ ☎ 01539 733333 🖷 01539 740300 🖰 l.winterslewis@southlakeland.gov.uk

Facilities: Mr Ian Hassall , Assistant Director - Strategic Development, South Lakeland House, Lowther Street, Kendal LA9 4UQ ☎ 01539 733333 🖷 01539 470300 🖰 ian.hassall@southlakeland.gov.uk

Finance: Ms Shelagh McGregor , Assistant Director - Resources, South Lakeland House, Lowther Street, Kendal LA9 4UQ ☎ 01539 733333 🖷 01539 740300 🖰 s.mcgregor@southlakeland.gov.uk

Fleet Management: Mr George Sierpinski , Fleet Manager, South Lakeland House, Lowther Street, Kendal LA9 4UQ ☎ 01539 733333 🖷 01539 740300 🖰 g.sierpinski@southlakeland.gov.uk

Grounds Maintenance: Mr Tony Naylor , Green Spaces Officer, South Lakeland House, Lowther Street, Kendal LA9 4UQ ☎ 01539 733333 🖷 01539 740300 🖰 t.naylor@southlakeland.gov.uk

Health and Safety: Ms Andrea Wilson , Human Resources Services Manager, South Lakeland House, Lowther Street, Kendal LA9 4UQ ☎ 01539 733333 🖷 01539 740300 🖰 a.wilson@southlakeland.gov.uk

Home Energy Conservation: Mr Ian Hassall , Assistant Director - Strategic Development, South Lakeland House, Lowther Street, Kendal LA9 4UQ ☎ 01539 733333 🖷 01539 470300 🖰 ian.hassall@southlakeland.gov.uk

Home Energy Conservation: Mr David Sykes, Director - People & Places, South Lakeland House, Lowther Street, Kendal LA9 4UQ ☎ 01539 733333 🖷 01539 740300 🖰 d.sykes@southlakeland.gov.uk

Housing: Mr David Sykes, Director - People & Places, South Lakeland House, Lowther Street, Kendal LA9 4UQ ☎ 01539 733333 🖷 01539 740300 🖰 d.sykes@southlakeland.gov.uk

Housing Maintenance: Mr Peter Thomas, Chief Executive - South Lakes Housing, Aynam Mills, Canal Head, Kendal LA9 4UQ ☎ 01539 717717 🖰 p.thomas@southlakeland.gov.uk

Local Area Agreement: Ms Claire Gould , Policy & Partnership Manager, South Lakeland House, Lowther Street, Kendal LA9 4UQ ☎ 01539 733333 🖷 01539 740300 🖰 c.gould@southlakeland.gov.uk

Legal: Mr Matthew Neal , Solicitor to the Council, South Lakeland House, Lowther Street, Kendal LA9 4UQ ☎ 01539 733333 🖷 01539 740300 🖰 m.neal@southlakeland.gov.uk

Leisure and Cultural Services: Mr Ian Hassall , Assistant Director - Strategic Development, South Lakeland House, Lowther Street, Kendal LA9 4UQ ☎ 01539 733333 🖷 01539 470300 🖰 ian.hassall@southlakeland.gov.uk

Leisure and Cultural Services: Mr David Sykes, Director - People & Places, South Lakeland House, Lowther Street, Kendal LA9 4UQ ☎ 01539 733333 🖷 01539 740300 🖰 d.sykes@southlakeland.gov.uk

Licensing: Mr Simon Rowley , Assistant Director - Neighbourhood Services, South Lakeland House, Lowther Street, Kendal LA9 4UQ ☎ 01539 733333 🖷 01539 740300 🖰 s.rowley@southlakeland.gov.uk

Lighting: Mr Simon Rowley , Assistant Director - Neighbourhood Services, South Lakeland House, Lowther Street, Kendal LA9 4UQ ☎ 01539 733333 🖷 01539 740300 🖰 s.rowley@southlakeland.gov.uk

Lottery Funding, Charity and Voluntary: Mr Lawrence Conway, Chief Executive, South Lakeland House, Lowther Street, Kendal LA9 4UD ☎ 01539 733333 🖷 01539 740300 🖰 l.conway@southlakeland.gov.uk

Member Services: Ms Debbie Storr, Corporate Director - Policy & Resources Monitoring Officer, South Lakeland House, Lowther Street, Kendal LA9 4UQ ☎ 01539 733333 🖷 01539 740300 🖰 d.storr@southlakeland.gov.uk

Parking: Mr Simon Rowley , Assistant Director - Neighbourhood Services, South Lakeland House, Lowther Street, Kendal LA9 4UQ ☎ 01539 733333 🖷 01539 740300 🖰 s.rowley@southlakeland.gov.uk

Partnerships: Ms Claire Gould , Policy & Partnership Manager, South Lakeland House, Lowther Street, Kendal LA9 4UQ ☎ 01539 733333 🖷 01539 740300 🖰 c.gould@southlakeland.gov.uk

Personnel / HR: Ms Andrea Wilson , Human Resources Services Manager, South Lakeland House, Lowther Street, Kendal LA9 4UQ ☎ 01539 733333 🖷 01539 740300 🖰 a.wilson@southlakeland.gov.uk

Planning: Mr Ian Hassall , Assistant Director - Strategic Development, South Lakeland House, Lowther Street, Kendal LA9 4UQ ☎ 01539 733333 🖷 01539 470300 🖰 ian.hassall@southlakeland.gov.uk

Planning: Mr David Sykes, Director - People & Places, South Lakeland House, Lowther Street, Kendal LA9 4UQ ☎ 01539 733333 🖷 01539 740300 🖰 d.sykes@southlakeland.gov.uk

Procurement: Ms Karen Crump , Procurement & Contracts Manager, South Lakeland House, Lowther Street, Kendal LA9 4UQ ☎ 01539 733333 🖷 01539 740300 🖰 karen.crump@southlakeland.gov.uk

Recycling & Waste Minimisation: Mr Lawrence Conway, Chief Executive, South Lakeland House, Lowther Street, Kendal LA9 4UD ☎ 01539 733333 🖷 01539 740300 🖰 l.conway@southlakeland.gov.uk

Regeneration: Mr David Sykes, Director - People & Places, South Lakeland House, Lowther Street, Kendal LA9 4UQ ☎ 01539 733333 🖷 01539 740300 🖰 d.sykes@southlakeland.gov.uk

Staff Training: Ms Andrea Wilson , Human Resources Services Manager, South Lakeland House, Lowther Street, Kendal LA9 4UQ ☎ 01539 733333 🖷 01539 740300 🖰 a.wilson@southlakeland.gov.uk

Street Scene: Mr Nick Pearson , Street Scene Manager, South Lakeland House, Lowther Street, Kendal LA9 4UQ ☎ 01539 733333 🖷 01539 740300 🖰 n.pearson@southlakeland.gov.uk

Sustainable Communities: Ms Claire Gould , Policy & Partnership Manager, South Lakeland House, Lowther Street, Kendal LA9 4UQ ☎ 01539 733333 🖷 01539 740300 🖰 c.gould@southlakeland.gov.uk

Sustainable Development: Mr David Sykes, Director - People & Places, South Lakeland House, Lowther Street, Kendal LA9 4UQ ☎ 01539 733333 🖷 01539 740300 🖰 d.sykes@southlakeland.gov.uk

Tourism: Mr David Sykes, Director - People & Places, South Lakeland House, Lowther Street, Kendal LA9 4UQ ☎ 01539 733333 🖷 01539 740300 🖰 d.sykes@southlakeland.gov.uk

Town Centre: Mr David Sykes, Director - People & Places, South Lakeland House, Lowther Street, Kendal LA9 4UQ ☎ 01539 733333 🖷 01539 740300 🖰 d.sykes@southlakeland.gov.uk

Transport: Mr Simon Rowley , Assistant Director - Neighbourhood Services, South Lakeland House, Lowther Street, Kendal LA9 4UQ ☎ 01539 733333 🖷 01539 740300 🖰 s.rowley@southlakeland.gov.uk

Waste Collection and Disposal: Mr Simon Rowley , Assistant Director - Neighbourhood Services, South Lakeland House, Lowther Street, Kendal LA9 4UQ ☎ 01539 733333 🖷 01539 740300 🖰 s.rowley@southlakeland.gov.uk

Waste Management: Mr Simon Rowley , Assistant Director - Neighbourhood Services, South Lakeland House, Lowther Street, Kendal LA9 4UQ ☎ 01539 733333 🖷 01539 740300 🖰 s.rowley@southlakeland.gov.uk

COUNCILLORS

***Chair* Emmott**, Sylvia (LD - Kendal Stonecross)
s.emmott@southlakeslibdems.org.uk

***Vice-Chair* Jupe**, Prudence (LD - Arnside and Beetham)
p.jupe@southlakeslibdems.org.uk

***Leader of the Council* Thornton**, Peter (LD - Whinfell)
p.thornton@southlakeland.gov.uk

***Deputy Leader of the Council* Sanderson**, Sue (LD - Staveley-in-Cartmel)
s.sanderson@southlakeland.gov.uk

Airey, James (CON - Low Furness)
james.airey@cumbria.gov.uk

Airey, Caroline (CON - Mid Furness)
carolineairey@me.com

Archibald, Giles (LD - Kendal Fell)
g.archibald@southlakeland.gov.uk

SOUTH LAKELAND

Berry, Ben (CON - Windermere Applethwaite and Troutbeck)
me@ben-berry.co.uk

Bingham, Roger (CON - Burton and Holme)
roger.bingham@cumbria.gov.uk

Brook, Jonathan (LD - Kendal Parks)
j.brook@southlakeland.gov.uk

Butcher, Andrew (CON - Mid Furness)
andrewbutcher@talktalk.net

Clough, John (LAB - Ulverston Town)
jvcgc2925@gmail.com

Coleman, Stephen (LD - Kendal Strickland)
s.coleman@southlakeslibdems.org.uk

Collins, Stan (LD - Staveley-in-Westmorland)
stanstheman@cix.co.uk

Cooper, Brian (CON - Burton and Holme)
b.cooper47@yahoo.co.uk

Cotton, Nick (LD - Sedbergh and Kirkby Lonsdale)
n.cotton@southlakeslibdems.org.uk

Curwen, Joss (IND - Broughton)

Dixon, Philip (LD - Kendal Highgate)
p.dixon@southlakeslibdems.org.uk

Eccles, Sheila (LD - Crooklands)
sheila.eccles@yahoo.co.uk

Evans, Shirley (LD - Kendal Far Cross)
s.evans@southlakeslibdems.org.uk

Evans, David (LD - Kendal Mintsfeet)
d.evans@southlakeslibdems.org.uk

Feeney-Johnson, Claire (LD - Kendal Nether)
c.feeney-johnson@southlakeslibdems.org.uk

Finch, Alvin (LD - Kendal Kirkland)
a.finch@southlakeslibdems.org.uk

Fletcher, David (LIB - Hawkeshead)
d.fletecher@southlakeslibdems.org.uk

Gardiner, Gill (LD - Holker)
gilliangardner@icloud.com

Gray, Brenda (LD - Kendal Oxenholme and Natland)
brendacgray@yahoo.co.uk

Hall, Anne (CON - Coniston and Crake Valley)
annehall070@gmail.com

Halliday, Heidi (LD - Ambleside and Grasmere)
heidihalliday@gmail.com

Harvey, Tom (CON - Grange South)
tom@tom-harvey.co.uk

Hogg, Chris (LD - Kendal Castle)
chris.hogg@southlakeland.gov.uk

Holmes, John (CON - Lyth Valley)
cjh@coyote-software.com

Hurst-Jones, Keith (LD - Burneside)
fairhurst3@googlemail.com

Irving, Helen (CON - Ulverston North)
helen1961@talktalk.net

Jenkinson, Janette (CON - Ulverston West)
jejenky@aol.com

Jones, Colin (LD - Windermere Bowness North)
cnjones8@gmail.com

Jones, Dyan (LD - Windermere Town)
djjonessldc@btinternet.com

Lancaster, Kevin (CON - Sedbergh and Kirkby Lonsdale)
kevin@sarthwaite.com

Mackie, Mel (CON - Sedbergh and Kirkby Lonsdale)
mel.mac@uwclub.net

Morrell, Eric (LD - Grange North)
emorrell5@gmail.com

Rajan, Bharath (LAB - Ulverston Central)
bsr1821@gmail.com

Rawlinson, Annie (LD - Levens)
annierawlinson@hotmail.com

Rees, Vivienne (LD - Ambleside and Grasmere)
v.rees@southlakeslibdems.org.uk

Rigg, Amanda (CON - Ulverston South)
riggamanda76@gmail.com

Ryder, David (LD - Milnthorpe)
d.ryder@rydertowing.co.uk

Severn, Matt (LD - Kendal Underley)
m.severn@southlakeslibdems.org.uk

Stewart, Ian (LD - Arnside and Beetham)
l.stewart@southlakeslibdems.org.uk

Vincent, Graham (LD - Kendal Romney)
g.vincent@southlakeland.gov.uk

Walker, Phil (LD - Kendal Heron Hill)
phil.walker@southlakeland.gov.uk

Williams, David (CON - Windermere Bowness South)
fellake@aol.com

Wilson, Mary (LD - Cartmel and Grange West)
rodmary.wilson@googlemail.com

Wilson, Mark (LAB - Ulverston East)
marcowils@tiscali.co.uk

POLITICAL COMPOSITION

LD: 31, CON: 15, LAB: 3, LIB: 1, IND: 1

COMMITTEE CHAIRS

Audit: Mr Stephen Coleman

Licensing: Mrs Sheila Eccles

Planning: Mrs Mary Wilson

South Lanarkshire S

South Lanarkshire Council, Council Offices, Almada Street, Hamilton ML3 0AA
☎ 01698 454444 🖷 01698 454275 💻 www.southlanarkshire.gov.uk

FACTS AND FIGURES

Parliamentary Constituencies: Dumfriesshire, Clydesdale and Tweedale, East Kilbride, Strathaven and Lesmahagow, Lanark & Hamilton East, Rutherglen and Hamilton West
EU Constituencies: Scotland
Election Frequency: Elections are of whole council

PRINCIPAL OFFICERS

Chief Executive: Mr Lindsay Freeland, Chief Executive, Council Offices, Almada Street, Hamilton ML3 0AL ☎ 01698 454208 🖷 01698 454682 ✉ lindsay.freeland@southlanarkshire.gov.uk

Senior Management: Mrs Ann Gee , Executive Director - Housing & Technical Resources, Council Offices, Almada Street, Hamilton ML3 0AA ☎ 01698 454405 🖷 01698 455616 ✉ ann.gee@southlanarkshire.gov.uk

Senior Management: Mr Jim Gilhooly , Executive Director - Education Resources, Council Offices, Almada Street, Hamilton ML3 0AA ☎ 01698 454379 🖷 01698 454465 ✉ jim.gilhooly@southlanarkshire.gov.uk

Senior Management: Mr Paul Manning , Executive Director - Finance & Corporate Resources, Council Offices, Almada Street, Hamilton ML3 0AA ☎ 01698 454530 ✉ paul.manning@southlanarkshire.gov.uk

Senior Management: Mr Colin McDowell , Executive Director of Community & Enterprise Resources, Blantyre, Hamilton G72 0JP ☎ 01698 454798 ✉ colin.mcdowell@southlanarkshire.gov.uk

Senior Management: Mr Harry Stevenson, Executive Director - Social Work Resources, Council Offices, Almada Street, Hamilton ML3 0AA ☎ 01698 453700 🖷 01698 453784 ✉ harry.stevenson@southlanarkshire.gov.uk

Architect, Building / Property Services: Mr Danny Lowe , Head of Property Services, Council Offices, Almada Street, Hamilton ML3 0AA ☎ 01698 455621 ✉ danny.lowe@southlanarkshire.gov.uk

Best Value: Ms Helen Black, Financial Performance Manager, Finance & Information Technology Resources, Floor 4, Almada Street, Hamilton ML3 0AA ☎ 01698 454618 🖷 01698 454682 ✉ helen.black@southlanarkshire.gov.uk

Building Control: Mr Michael McGlynn , Head of Planning & Building Standards, Montrose House, 154 Montrose Crescent, Hamilton ML3 6LB ☎ 01698 454294 🖷 01698 455195 ✉ michael.mcglynn@southlanarkshire.gov.uk

Catering Services: Mr Colin McDowell , Executive Director of Community & Enterprise Resources, Blantyre, Hamilton G72 0JP ☎ 01698 454798 ✉ colin.mcdowell@southlanarkshire.gov.uk

Children / Youth Services: Ms Anne Donaldson , Youth Learning Services Manager, Council Offices, Almada Street, Hamilton ML3 0AA ☎ 01698 454452 ✉ anne.donaldson@southlanarkshire.gov.uk

Civil Registration: Ms Teresa Stone, Registration & Licensing Manager, Council Offices, Almada Street, Hamilton ML3 0AA ☎ 01698 454806 ✉ teresa.stone@southlanarkshire.gov.uk

PR / Communications: Mr Tom Little , Head of Corporate Communications / Public Affairs, Council Offices, Almada Street, Hamilton ML3 0AA ☎ 01698 454904 🖷 01698 454949 ✉ tom.little@southlanarkshire.gov.uk

Community Planning: Mr Alistair McKinnon , Head of Support Services - Community & Enterprise, Council Offices, Almada Street, Hamilton ML3 0AA ☎ 01698 454700 ✉ alistair.mckinnon@southlanarkshire.gov.uk

Community Planning: Mr Neil Reid , Community Planning Manager, Council Offices, Almada Street, Hamilton ML3 0AA ☎ 01698 454618 ✉ neil.reid@southlanarkshire.gov.uk

Community Safety: Mr Ian Murray, Policy & Strategy Manager, Community & Enterprise Resources, Council Offices, Almada Street, Hamilton ML3 0AA ☎ 01698 455297 🖷 01698 454362 ✉ ian.murray@southlanarkshire.gov.uk

Computer Management: Mr Brian Teaz , Head of Information Technology Services, Council Offices, Almada Street, Hamilton ML3 0AA ☎ 01698 455648 ✉ brian.teaz@southlanarkshire.gov.uk

Corporate Services: Mr Tom Barrie , Head of Performance & Support Services, Council Offices, Almada Street, Hamilton ML3 0AA ☎ 01698 453783 ✉ tom.barrie@southlanarkshire.gov.uk

Corporate Services: Mr Paul Manning , Executive Director - Finance & Corporate Resources, Council Offices, Almada Street, Hamilton ML3 0AA ☎ 01698 454530 ✉ paul.manning@southlanarkshire.gov.uk

Corporate Services: Ms Geraldine McCann , Head of Administration, Montrose House, 154 Montrose Crescent, Hamilton ML3 6LL ☎ 01698 454516 ✉ geraldine.mccann@southlanarkshire.gov.uk

Economic Development: Mr James McCaffer, Head of Regeneration Services, Montrose House, 154 Montrose Crescent, Hamilton ML3 6LB ☎ 01698 453813 🖷 01698 455195 ✉ jim.mccaffer@southlanarkshire.gov.uk

Education: Mr Jim Gilhooly , Executive Director - Education Resources, Council Offices, Almada Street, Hamilton ML3 0AA ☎ 01698 454379 🖷 01698 454465 ✉ jim.gilhooly@southlanarkshire.gov.uk

Education: Mr Tony McDaid , Head of Education, Council Offices, Almada Street, Hamilton ML3 0AA ☎ 01698 454475 ✉ tony.mcdaid@southlanarkshire.gov.uk

Education: Ms Lynn Sherry , Head of Education - Finance & Personal, Council Offices, Almada Street, Hamilton ML3 0AA ☎ 01698 454413 ✉ lynn.sherry@southlanarkshire.gov.uk

E-Government: Mr Brian Teaz , Head of Information Technology Services, Council Offices, Almada Street, Hamilton ML3 0AA ☎ 01698 455648 ✉ brian.teaz@southlanarkshire.gov.uk

Electoral Registration: Mr Paul Manning , Executive Director - Finance & Corporate Resources, Council Offices, Almada Street, Hamilton ML3 0AA ☎ 01698 454530 ✉ paul.manning@southlanarkshire.gov.uk

Emergency Planning: Mr Ken Wratten , Health, Safety & Contingency Planning Adviser, Council Offices, Almada Street, Hamilton ML3 0AA ☎ 01698 454648 🖷 01698 454662 ✉ ken.wratten@southlanarkshire.gov.uk

Energy Management: Mr Graham Campbell , Property Services Manager, Atholl House, Avondale Avenue, East Kilbride, Glasgow G74 1LU ☎ 01355 806818 🖷 01355 806955 🖰 graham.campbell@southlanarkshire.gov.uk

Environmental Health: Mr Robert Howe , Head of Environmental & Strategic Services, Council Offices, Almada Street, Hamilton ML3 0AA ☎ 01698 455629 🖷 01698 454362 🖰 robert.howe@southlanarkshire.gov.uk

Estates, Property & Valuation: Ms Heather McNeil, Head of Estates & Support Services, Montrose House, 154 Montrose Crescent, Hamilton ML3 6LB ☎ 01698 455915 🖷 01698 454801 🖰 heather.mcneil@southlanarkshire.gov.uk

European Liaison: Mr John Batchelor , Team Leader - Funding & Development, Enterprise Resources, 154 Montrose Crescent, Hamilton ML3 6LB ☎ 01698 455129 🖷 01698 454469 🖰 john.batchelor@southlanarkshire.gov.uk

Events Manager: Mrs Angie Moakler, Design & Production Manager, Council Offices, Almada Street, Hamilton ML3 0AA ☎ 01698 453853 🖰 angie.moakler@southlanarkshire.gov.uk

Facilities: Mr Stephen Kelly, Head of Facilities & Cultural Services, Community Resources, Council Offices, Almada Street, Hamilton ML3 0AA ☎ 01698 454705 🖷 01698 454362 🖰 stephen.kelly@southlanarkshire.gov.uk

Finance: Mr Paul Manning , Executive Director - Finance & Corporate Resources, Council Offices, Almada Street, Hamilton ML3 0AA ☎ 01698 454530 🖰 paul.manning@southlanarkshire.gov.uk

Fleet Management: Ms Shirley Clelland, Head of Land & Fleet Services, Blantyre, Hamilton G72 0JP ☎ 01698 717752 🖷 01698 717750 🖰 shirley.clelland@southlanarkshire.gov.uk

Grounds Maintenance: Mr Steven Kelly , Head of Land & Fleet Services, Blantyre, Hamilton G72 0JP ☎ 01698 454577 🖰 steven.kelly@southlanarkshire.gov.uk

Health and Safety: Mr Ken Wratten , Health, Safety & Contingency Planning Adviser, Council Offices, Almada Street, Hamilton ML3 0AA ☎ 01698 454648 🖷 01698 454662 🖰 ken.wratten@southlanarkshire.gov.uk

Highways: Mr Gordon Mackay , Head of Roads & Transportation, Montrose House, 154 Montrose Crescent, Hamilton ML3 6LL ☎ 01698 454484 🖷 01698 454488 🖰 gordon.mackay@southlanarkshire.gov.uk

Home Energy Conservation: Mr Graham Campbell , Property Services Manager, Atholl House, Avondale Avenue, East Kilbride, Glasgow G74 1LU ☎ 01355 806818 🖷 01355 806955 🖰 graham.campbell@southlanarkshire.gov.uk

Housing: Mrs Ann Gee , Executive Director - Housing & Technical Resources, Council Offices, Almada Street, Hamilton ML3 0AA ☎ 01698 454405 🖷 01698 455616 🖰 ann.gee@southlanarkshire.gov.uk

Housing: Mr Patrick Murphy , Head Support Services for Housing & Tech Resources, Council Offices, Almada Street, Hamilton ML3 0AA ☎ 01698 454065 🖰 patrick.j.murphy@southlanarkshire.gov.uk

Legal: Ms Geraldine McCann , Head of Administration, Montrose House, 154 Montrose Crescent, Hamilton ML3 6LL ☎ 01698 454516 🖰 geraldine.mccann@southlanarkshire.gov.uk

Leisure and Cultural Services: Mr Gerry Campbell , General Manager, South Lanarkshire Leisure Ltd, Floor 1, North Stand, Cadzow Avenue, Hamilton ML3 0LX ☎ 01698 476095 🖷 01698 476198 🖰 gerry.campbell@southlanarkshire.gov.uk

Licensing: Ms Geraldine McCann , Head of Administration, Montrose House, 154 Montrose Crescent, Hamilton ML3 6LL ☎ 01698 454516 🖰 geraldine.mccann@southlanarkshire.gov.uk

Lifelong Learning: Ms Andrea Batchelor, Head of Education - Resources, Council Offices, Almada Street, Hamilton ML3 0AE ☎ 01698 454408 🖰 andrea.batchelor@southlanarkshire.gov.uk

Lighting: Mr David McNair , Lighting Engineer, Montrose House, 154 Montrose Crescent, Hamilton ML3 6LL ☎ 01698 452401 🖷 01698 453600 🖰 david.black@southlanarkshire.gov.uk

Lottery Funding, Charity and Voluntary: Mr John Batchelor , Team Leader - Funding & Development, Enterprise Resources, 154 Montrose Crescent, Hamilton ML3 6LB ☎ 01698 455129 🖷 01698 454469 🖰 john.batchelor@southlanarkshire.gov.uk

Member Services: Ms Linda Cunningham, Member Services Manager & PA to Leader, Council Offices, Almada Street, Hamilton ML3 0AA ☎ 01698 454027 🖷 01698 454345 🖰 linda.cunningham@southlanarkshire.gov.uk

Parking: Mr Donald Gibson, Parking Manager, Brandon Gate, 1 Leechlee Road, Hamilton ML3 0XB ☎ 01698 453528 🖷 01698 453535 🖰 donald.gibson@southlanarkshire.gov.uk

Personnel / HR: Ms Kay McVeigh , Head of Personnel Services, Council Offices, Almada Street, Hamilton ML3 0AA ☎ 01698 454330 🖷 01698 454637 🖰 kay.mcveigh@southlanarkshire.gov.uk

Planning: Mr Michael McGlynn , Head of Planning & Building Standards, Montrose House, 154 Montrose Crescent, Hamilton ML3 6LB ☎ 01698 454294 🖷 01698 455195 🖰 michael.mcglynn@southlanarkshire.gov.uk

Procurement: Mr Peter Field , Procurement Manager, Council Offices, Almada Street, Hamilton ML3 0AA ☎ 01698 454707 🖰 peter.field@southlanarkshire.gov.uk

Public Libraries: Mr Iain Walker , Library & Community Learning Services Manager, Council Offices, Almada Street, Hamilton ML3 0AA ☎ 01698 456144 🖰 iain.walker@southlanarkshire.gov.uk

Recycling & Waste Minimisation: Mr Charlie Kelly , Land Services Manager - Environmental, Council Offices, Almada Street, Hamilton ML3 0AA ☎ 01698 717777 🖰 land.services@southlanarkshire.gov.uk

Regeneration: Mr James McCaffer, Head of Regeneration Services, Montrose House, 154 Montrose Crescent, Hamilton ML3 6LB ☎ 01698 453813 🖷 01698 455195 🖰 jim.mccaffer@southlanarkshire.gov.uk

Road Safety: Mr Gordon Mackay , Head of Roads & Transportation, Montrose House, 154 Montrose Crescent, Hamilton ML3 6LL ☎ 01698 454484 🖷 01698 454488 ✆ gordon.mackay@southlanarkshire.gov.uk

Social Services: Ms Brenda Hutchinson , Head of Older People & Adult Services, Council Offices, Almada Street, Hamilton ML3 0AA ☎ 01698 453783 ✆ brenda.hutchinson@southlanarkshire.gov.uk

Social Services: Mr Harry Stevenson, Executive Director - Social Work Resources, Council Offices, Almada Street, Hamilton ML3 0AA ☎ 01698 453700 🖷 01698 453784 ✆ harry.stevenson@southlanarkshire.gov.uk

Social Services (Children): Mr Robert Smith , Head of Child & Family Services, Council Offices, Almada Street, Hamilton ML3 0AA ☎ 01698 454887 🖷 01698 453784 ✆ robert.smith@southlanarkshire.gov.uk

Staff Training: Mrs Gill Bhatti, Employee Development & Diversity Manager, Council Offices, Almada Street, Hamilton ML3 0AQ ☎ 01698 455604 🖷 01698 454637 ✆ gill.bhatti@southlanarkshire.gov.uk

Street Scene: Ms Joan Knox , Physical Regeneration Programme Manager, Enterprise Resources, 154 Montrose Crescent, Hamilton ML3 6LB ☎ 01698 455923 🖷 01698 455195 ✆ joan.knox@southlanarkshire.gov.uk

Sustainable Communities: Mr Simon Carey, Regeneration & Inclusion Manager, Enterprise Resources, 154 Montrose Crescent, Hamilton ML3 6LB ☎ 01698 453812 🖷 01698 453804 ✆ simon.carey@southlanarkshire.gov.uk

Sustainable Development: Mr Charlie Kelly , Land Services Manager - Environmental, Council Offices, Almada Street, Hamilton ML3 0AA ☎ 01698 717777 ✆ land.services@southlanarkshire.gov.uk

Tourism: Mr Gordon Todd , Economic Development Manager, Enterprise Resources, 154 Montrose Crescent, Hamilton ML3 6LB ☎ 01698 453840 🖷 01698 454469 ✆ gordon.todd@southlanarkshire.gov.uk

Town Centre: Mr Jim McNally , Town Centre Manager, Enterprise Resources, 154 Montrose Crescent, Hamilton ML3 6LB ☎ 01698 455103 🖷 01698 455952 ✆ jim.mcnally@southlanarkshire.gov.uk

Traffic Management: Mr Gordon Mackay , Head of Roads & Transportation, Montrose House, 154 Montrose Crescent, Hamilton ML3 6LL ☎ 01698 454484 🖷 01698 454488 ✆ gordon.mackay@southlanarkshire.gov.uk

Transport: Mr Gordon Mackay , Head of Roads & Transportation, Montrose House, 154 Montrose Crescent, Hamilton ML3 6LL ☎ 01698 454484 🖷 01698 454488 ✆ gordon.mackay@southlanarkshire.gov.uk

Waste Collection and Disposal: Ms Shirley Clelland, Head of Land & Fleet Services, Blantyre, Hamilton G72 0JP ☎ 01698 717752 🖷 01698 717750 ✆ shirley.clelland@southlanarkshire.gov.uk

Waste Management: Ms Shirley Clelland, Head of Land & Fleet Services, Blantyre, Hamilton G72 0JP ☎ 01698 717752 🖷 01698 717750 ✆ shirley.clelland@southlanarkshire.gov.uk

COUNCILLORS

***Leader of the Council* McAvoy**, Edward (LAB - Rutherglen Central and North)
councillor.mcavoy@southlanarkshire.gov.uk

Adams, Lynn (SNP - Hamilton North and East)
lynn.adams@southlanarkshire.gov.uk

Anderson, John (SNP - East Kilbride Central South)
j.anderson@southlanarkshire.gov.uk

Archer, Ed (IND - Clydesdale North)
ed.archer@southlankarkshire.gov.uk

Barker, Ralph (LAB - Clydesdale East)
ralph.barker@southlanarkshire.gov.uk

Brogan, Walter (LAB - Cambuslang East)
walter.brogan@southlanarkshire.gov.uk

Brown, Robert (LD - Rutherglen South)
robert.brown@southlanarkshire.gov.uk

Buchanan, Archie (SNP - East Kilbride South)
archie.buchanan@southlanarkshire.gov.uk

Burns, Jackie (LAB - Larkhall)
jackie.burns@southlanarkshire.gov.uk

Cairney, John (LAB - East Kilbride East)
john.cairney@southlanarkshire.gov.uk

Campbell, Graeme (IND - Avondale and Stonehouse)
graeme.campbell@southlanarkshire.gov.uk

Carmichael, Andy (LAB - Larkhall)
andy.carmichael@southlanarkshire.gov.uk

Clark, Gordon (SNP - Rutherglen Central and North)
gordon.clark@southlanarkshire.gov.uk

Clearie, Pam (LAB - Cambuslang East)
pamela.clearie@southlanarkshire.gov.uk

Clearie, Russell (LAB - Cambuslang West)
russell.clearie@southlanarkshire.gov.uk

Convery, Gerry (LAB - East Kilbride Central South)
gerry.convery@southlanarkshire.gov.uk

Cooper, Margaret (LAB - Avondale and Stonehouse)
margaret.cooper@southlanarkshire.gov.uk

Craig, Peter (SNP - Larkhall)
peter.craig@southlanarkshire.gov.uk

Deanie, Christine (SNP - Cambuslang East)
christine.deanie@southlanarkshire.gov.uk

Devlin, Maureen (LAB - Bothwell and Uddingston)
maureen.devlin@southlanarkshire.gov.uk

Docherty, James (LAB - East Kilbride South)
james.dockerty@southlanarkshire.gov.uk

Dorman, Isobel (SNP - Avondale and Stonehouse)
isobel.dorman@southlanarkshire.gov.uk

Dunsmuir, Hugh (LAB - Blantyre)
hugh.dunsmuir@southlanarkshire.gov.uk

Edwards, Douglas (SNP - East Kilbride South)
douglas.edwards@southlanarkshire.gov.uk

SOUTH LANARKSHIRE

Falconer, Allan (LAB - Hamilton West and Earnock)
allan.falconer@southlanarkshire.gov.uk

Gallacher, Stuart (LAB - Hamilton South)
stuart.gallacher@southlanarkshire.gov.uk

Gauld, Bev (IND - Clydesdale East)
beverly.gauld@southlanarkshire.gov.uk

Greenshields, George (LAB - Clydesdale South)
george.greenshields@southlanarkshire.gov.uk

Hamilton, Lynsey (LAB - Clydesdale West)
lynsey.hamilton@southlanarkshire.gov.uk

Handibode, Jim (LAB - Blantyre)
james.handibode@southlanarkshire.gov.uk

Holman, Bill (SNP - Avondale and Stonehouse)
bill.holman@southlanarkshire.gov.uk

Horne, Graeme (SNP - Hamilton West and Earnock)
graeme.horne@southlanarkshire.gov.uk

Kegg, Anne (CON - Bothwell and Uddingston)
anne.kegg@southlanarkshire.gov.uk

Kerr, Susan (LAB - East Kilbride Central South)
susan.kerr@southlanarkshire.gov.uk

Killen, Gerard (LAB - Rutherglen South)
gerard.killen@southlanarkshire.gov.uk

Lee, Pat (SNP - Clydesdale West)
pat.lee@southlanarkshire.gov.uk

Lennon, Monica (LAB - Hamilton North and East)
monica.lennon@southlanarkshire.gov.uk

Logan, Eileen (LAB - Clydesdale West)
eileen.logan@southlanarkshire.gov.uk

Lowe, Joe (LAB - Hamilton South)
joe.lowe@southlanarkshire.gov.uk

Maggs, Anne (SNP - East Kilbride Central North)
anne.maggs@southlanarkshire.gov.uk

McCaig, Brian (LAB - Hamilton South)
brian.mccaig@southlanarkshire.gov.uk

McClymont, Catherine (LAB - Clydesdale North)
catherine.mcclymon@southlanarkshire.gov.uk

McColl, Clare (SNP - Cambuslang West)
clare.mccoll@southlanarshire.gov.uk

McDonald, Lesley (SNP - Larkhall)
lesley.mcdonald@southlanarkshire.gov.uk

McGinaly, Janice (LAB - East Kilbride West)
janice.mcginlay@southlanarkshire.gov.uk

McGuigan, Jim (SNP - Bothwell and Uddingston)
jim.mcguigan@southlanarkshire.gov.uk

McInnes, Alex (LAB - Clydesdale South)
alex.mcinnes@southlanarkshire.gov.uk

McKenna, Brian (LAB - Rutherglen South)
brian.mckenna@southlanarkshire.gov.uk

McKenna, Denis (LAB - Rutherglen Central and North)
denis.mckenna@southlanarkshire.gov.uk

McKeown, Jean (LAB - Hamilton West and Earnock)
jean.mckeown@southlanarkshire.gov.uk

McLachlan, Davie (LAB - Hamilton North and East)
davie.mclachlan@southlanarkshire.gov.uk

McNamee, John (LAB - Blantyre)
john.mcnamee@southlanarkshire.gov.uk

Menzies, John (SNP - Hamilton West and Earnock)
john.menzies@southlanarkshire.gov.uk

Miller, Gladys (SNP - East Kilbride East)
gladys.miller@southlanarkshire.gov.uk

Mitchell, Alice-Marie (LAB - East Kilbride Central North)
alice.mitchell@southlanarkshire.gov.uk

Muir, Gordon (LAB - Clydesdale South)
gordon.muir@southlanarkshire.gov.uk

Ross, John (SNP - Hamilton South)
johnm.ross@southlanarkshire.gov.uk

Shaw, Vivienne (SNP - Clydesdale North)
vivienne.shaw@southlanarkshire.gov.uk

Shearer, David (SNP - Clydesdale West)
david.shearer@southlanarkshire.gov.uk

Simpson, Graham (CON - East Kilbride West)
graham.simpson@southlanarkshire.gov.uk

Stewart, Hamish (CON - Clydesdale East)
hamish.stewart@southlanarkshire.gov.uk

Thompson, Chris (LAB - East Kilbride Central North)
councillor.thompson@southlanarkshire.gov.uk

Thomson, Bert (LAB - Blantyre)
bert.thomson@southlanarkshire.gov.uk

Tullett, Richard (LAB - Cambuslang West)
richard.tullett@southlanarkshire.gov.uk

Wardhaugh, Jim (SNP - East Kilbride East)
james.wardhaugh@southlanarkshire.gov.uk

Wardhaugh, Sheena (SNP - East Kilbride Central North)
sheena.wardhaugh@southlanarkshire.gov.uk

Watson, David (SNP - East Kilbride West)
david.watson@southlanarkshire.gov.uk

POLITICAL COMPOSITION

LAB: 37, SNP: 23, CON: 3, IND: 3, LD: 1

South Norfolk D

South Norfolk District Council, South Norfolk House, Swan Lane, Long Stratton NR15 2XE
☎ 01508 533633 🖷 01508 533695 ✉ reception@south-norfolk.gov.uk
💻 www.south-norfolk.gov.uk

FACTS AND FIGURES

Parliamentary Constituencies: Norfolk Mid, Norfolk South, Norwich South
EU Constituencies: Eastern
Election Frequency: Elections are of whole council

PRINCIPAL OFFICERS

Chief Executive: Ms Sandra Dinneen , Chief Executive, South Norfolk House, Swan Lane, Long Stratton NR15 2XE ☎ 01508 533603 ✉ sdinneen@s-norfolk.gov.uk

Senior Management: Ms Paula Boyce , Director - Community Services, South Norfolk House, Swan Lane, Long Stratton NR15 2XE ☎ 01508 533703 ✉ pboyce@s-norfolk.gov.uk

Senior Management: Mr Tim Horspole , Director - Growth & Localism, South Norfolk House, Swan Lane, Long Stratton NR15 2XE ☎ 01508 533806 ✉ thorsepole@s-norfolk.gov.uk

Senior Management: Ms Debbie Lorimer , Director - Business Development, South Norfolk House, Swan Lane, Long Stratton NR15 2XE ☎ 01508 533981 ✉ dlorimer@s-norfolk.gov.uk

Architect, Building / Property Services: Ms Renata Garfoot, Head of Asset Management, South Norfolk House, Swan Lane, Long Stratton NR15 2XE ☎ 01508 533749 ✉ rgarfoot@s-norfolk.gov.uk

Best Value: Mr Keith Saunt , Head of Programmes, South Norfolk House, Swan Lane, Long Stratton NR15 2XE ☎ 01508 533661 ✉ ksaunt@s-norfolk.gov.uk

Building Control: Mr Dave Shaw , CNC General Manager, South Norfolk House, Swan Lane, Long Stratton NR15 2XE ☎ 01508 533983 ✉ dshaw@s-norfolk.gov.uk

Catering Services: Mr Neil Dyball , Facilities Manager, South Norfolk House, Swan Lane, Long Stratton NR15 2XE ☎ 01508 533786 ✉ ndyball@s-norfolk.gov.uk

PR / Communications: Mr Jon Pyle , Communications Officer, South Norfolk House, Swan Lane, Long Stratton NR15 2XE ☎ 01508 533631 ✉ jpyle@s-norfolk.gov.uk

Community Planning: Mr Adam Nicholls , Planning Policy Manager, South Norfolk House, Swan Lane, Long Stratton NR15 2XE ☎ 01508 533809 ✉ anicholls@s-norfolk.gov.uk

Community Safety: Mr Bob Wade , Head of Environmental Services, South Norfolk House, Swan Lane, Long Stratton NR15 2XE ☎ 01508 533787 ✉ bwade@s-norfolk.gov.uk

Computer Management: Mr Michael Sage , ICT Operations Manager, South Norfolk House, Swan Lane, Long Stratton NR15 2XE ☎ 01508 533876 ✉ bwade@s-norfolk.gov.uk

Contracts: Ms Michelle Saunders , Purchasing Officer, South Norfolk House, Swan Lane, Long Stratton NR15 2XE ☎ 01508 533645 ✉ msaunders@s-norfolk.gov.uk

Corporate Services: Ms Debbie Lorimer , Director - Business Development, South Norfolk House, Swan Lane, Long Stratton NR15 2XE ☎ 01508 533981 ✉ dlorimer@s-norfolk.gov.uk

Customer Service: Ms Amanda Adams, Corporate Customer Services Manager, South Norfolk House, Swan Lane, Long Stratton NR15 2XE ☎ 01508 533773 ✉ aadams@s-norfolk.gov.uk

Economic Development: Mr Julian Munson, Head of Growth & Economic Development, South Norfolk House, Swan Lane, Long Stratton NR15 2XE ☎ 01508 533763 ✉ jmunson@s-norfolk.gov.uk

E-Government: Mr Michael Sage , ICT Operations Manager, South Norfolk House, Swan Lane, Long Stratton NR15 2XE ☎ 01508 533876 ✉ bwade@s-norfolk.gov.uk

Electoral Registration: Mr Keith Saunt , Head of Programmes, South Norfolk House, Swan Lane, Long Stratton NR15 2XE ☎ 01508 533661 ✉ ksaunt@s-norfolk.gov.uk

Electoral Registration: Ms Julia Tovee-Galey , Electoral Services Manager, South Norfolk House, Swan Lane, Long Stratton NR15 2XE ☎ 01508 533795 ✉ jtovee@s-norfolk.gov.uk

Emergency Planning: Ms Jenny Bloomfield , Emergency Planning Officer, South Norfolk House, Swan Lane, Long Stratton NR15 2XE ☎ 01508 533607 ✉ jbloomfield@s-norfolk.gov.uk

Energy Management: Mr Tony Cooke, Housing Standards Manager, South Norfolk Council, Swan Lane, Long Stratton NR15 2XE ☎ 01508 533712 ✉ tcooke@s-norfolk.gov.uk

Environmental / Technical Services: Ms Paula Boyce , Director - Community Services, South Norfolk House, Swan Lane, Long Stratton NR15 2XE ☎ 01508 533703 ✉ pboyce@s-norfolk.gov.uk

Environmental / Technical Services: Mr Bob Wade , Head of Environmental Services, South Norfolk House, Swan Lane, Long Stratton NR15 2XE ☎ 01508 533787 ✉ bwade@s-norfolk.gov.uk

Environmental Health: Mr Adrian Nicholas , Environmental Protection Manager, South Norfolk House, Swan Lane, Long Stratton NR15 2XE ☎ 01508 533722 ✉ anicholas@s-norfolk.gov.uk

Environmental Health: Mr Bob Wade , Head of Environmental Services, South Norfolk House, Swan Lane, Long Stratton NR15 2XE ☎ 01508 533787 ✉ bwade@s-norfolk.gov.uk

Estates, Property & Valuation: Ms Renata Garfoot , Head of Asset Management, South Norfolk House, Swan Lane, Long Stratton NR15 2XE ☎ 01508 533749 ✉ rgarfoot@s-norfolk.gov.uk

Events Manager: Mr Mark Struthers , Marketing & Engagement Manager, South Norfolk House, Swan Lane, Long Stratton NR15 2XE ☎ 01508 533802 ✉ mstruthers@s-norfolk.gov.uk

Facilities: Mr Neil Dyball , Facilities Manager, South Norfolk House, Swan Lane, Long Stratton NR15 2XE ☎ 01508 533786 ✉ ndyball@s-norfolk.gov.uk

Finance: Ms Debbie Lorimer , Director - Business Development, South Norfolk House, Swan Lane, Long Stratton NR15 2XE ☎ 01508 533981 ✉ dlorimer@s-norfolk.gov.uk

Fleet Management: Mr David Renaut, Payroll Manager, South Norfolk House, Swan Lane, Long Stratton NR15 2XE ☎ 01508 533869 🖷 01508 533616 ✉ drenaut@s-norfolk.gov.uk

Grounds Maintenance: Mr James Fairclough , Waste & Cleansing Service Manager, South Norfolk House, Swan Lane, Long Stratton NR15 2XE ☎ 01603 819992 ✉ jfairclough@s-norfolk.gov.uk

Grounds Maintenance: Mr Bob Wade , Head of Environmental Services, South Norfolk House, Swan Lane, Long Stratton NR15 2XE ☎ 01508 533787 ✉ bwade@s-norfolk.gov.uk

Health and Safety: Mr Phil Rose, Health & Safety Advisor, South Norfolk House, Swan Lane, Long Stratton NR15 2XE ☎ 01508 533667 ✉ prose@s-norfolk.gov.uk

Home Energy Conservation: Mr Martyn Swann , Housing & Public Health Manager, South Norfolk House, Swan Lane, Long Stratton NR15 2XE ☎ 01508 533694 ✉ mswann@s-norfolk.gov.uk

Housing: Mr Martyn Swann , Housing & Public Health Manager, South Norfolk House, Swan Lane, Long Stratton NR15 2XE ☎ 01508 533694 ✉ mswann@s-norfolk.gov.uk

Legal: Ms Leah Micklebourgh , Communities & Democratic Services Manager, South Norfolk House, Swan Lane, Long Stratton NR15 2XE ☎ 01508 533954 ✉ lmicklebourgh@s-norfolk.gov.uk

Leisure and Cultural Services: Mr Steve Goddard , Head of Leisure Services, South Norfolk House, Swan Lane, Long Stratton NR15 2XE ☎ 01508 533962 ✉ sgoddard@s-norfolk.gov.uk

Licensing: Ms Grizelle Britton , Licensing, Food & Car Park Team Leader, South Norfolk House, Swan Lane, Long Stratton NR15 2XE ☎ 01508 533697 ✉ gbritton@s-norfolk.gov.uk

Licensing: Mr Julian Munson , Head of Growth & Economic Development, South Norfolk House, Swan Lane, Long Stratton NR15 2XE ☎ 01508 533763 ✉ jmunson@s-norfolk.gov.uk

Lottery Funding, Charity and Voluntary: Ms Leah Micklebourgh , Communities & Democratic Services Manager, South Norfolk House, Swan Lane, Long Stratton NR15 2XE ☎ 01508 533954 ✉ lmicklebourgh@s-norfolk.gov.uk

Member Services: Ms Leah Micklebourgh , Communities & Democratic Services Manager, South Norfolk House, Swan Lane, Long Stratton NR15 2XE ☎ 01508 533954 ✉ lmicklebourgh@s-norfolk.gov.uk

Member Services: Mrs Claire White , Democratic Services Team Leader, South Norfolk House, Swan Lane, Long Stratton NR15 2XE ☎ 01508 533669 ✉ cwhite@s-norfolk.gov.uk

Parking: Ms Grizelle Britton , Licensing, Food & Car Park Team Leader, South Norfolk House, Swan Lane, Long Stratton NR15 2XE ☎ 01508 533697 ✉ gbritton@s-norfolk.gov.uk

Partnerships: Ms Sam Cayford , Independent Living Team Leader, South Norfolk House, Swan Lane, Long Stratton NR15 2XE ☎ 01508 533694 ✉ scayford@s-norfolk.gov.uk

Personnel / HR: Ms Karen Thornber , Head of OD & Communications, South Norfolk House, Swan Lane, Long Stratton NR15 2XE ☎ 01508 533735 ✉ kthornber@s-norfolk.gov.uk

Planning: Ms Helen Mellors , Development Manager, South Norfolk House, Swan Lane, Long Stratton NR15 2XE ☎ 01508 533789 ✉ hmellors@s-norfolk.gov.uk

Procurement: Mr Matthew Fernandez-Graham , Accountancy Manager & Deputy S151 Officer, South Norfolk House, Swan Lane, Long Stratton NR15 2XE ☎ 01508 533919 ✉ mgraham@s-norfolk.gov.uk

Procurement: Ms Michelle Saunders , Purchasing Officer, South Norfolk House, Swan Lane, Long Stratton NR15 2XE ☎ 01508 533645 ✉ msaunders@s-norfolk.gov.uk

Recycling & Waste Minimisation: Ms Paula Boyce , Director - Community Services, South Norfolk House, Swan Lane, Long Stratton NR15 2XE ☎ 01508 533703 ✉ pboyce@s-norfolk.gov.uk

Recycling & Waste Minimisation: Mr Bob Wade , Head of Environmental Services, South Norfolk House, Swan Lane, Long Stratton NR15 2XE ☎ 01508 533787 ✉ bwade@s-norfolk.gov.uk

Regeneration: Mr Julian Munson , Head of Growth & Economic Development, South Norfolk House, Swan Lane, Long Stratton NR15 2XE ☎ 01508 533763 ✉ jmunson@s-norfolk.gov.uk

Staff Training: Ms Jeanette Evans , Learning & Development Advisor, South Norfolk House, Swan Lane, Long Stratton NR15 2XE ☎ 01508 533937 ✉ jevans@s-norfolk.gov.uk

Street Scene: Mr Bob Wade , Head of Environmental Services, South Norfolk House, Swan Lane, Long Stratton NR15 2XE ☎ 01508 533787 ✉ bwade@s-norfolk.gov.uk

Sustainable Communities: Mr Tim Horspole , Director - Growth & Localism, South Norfolk House, Swan Lane, Long Stratton NR15 2XE ☎ 01508 533806 ✉ thorsepole@s-norfolk.gov.uk

Sustainable Development: Mr Tim Horspole , Director - Growth & Localism, South Norfolk House, Swan Lane, Long Stratton NR15 2XE ☎ 01508 533806 ✉ thorsepole@s-norfolk.gov.uk

Tourism: Mr Julian Munson , Head of Growth & Economic Development, South Norfolk House, Swan Lane, Long Stratton NR15 2XE ☎ 01508 533763 ✉ jmunson@s-norfolk.gov.uk

Town Centre: Mr David Disney , Market Towns Co-ordinator, South Norfolk House, Swan Lane, Long Stratton NR15 2XE ☎ 01508 533745 ✉ ddisney@s-norfolk.gov.uk

Waste Collection and Disposal: Ms Paula Boyce , Director - Community Services, South Norfolk House, Swan Lane, Long Stratton NR15 2XE ☎ 01508 533703 ✉ pboyce@s-norfolk.gov.uk

Waste Collection and Disposal: Mr Bob Wade , Head of Environmental Services, South Norfolk House, Swan Lane, Long Stratton NR15 2XE ☎ 01508 533787 ✉ bwade@s-norfolk.gov.uk

Waste Management: Ms Paula Boyce , Director - Community Services, South Norfolk House, Swan Lane, Long Stratton NR15 2XE ☎ 01508 533703 ✉ pboyce@s-norfolk.gov.uk

Children's Play Areas: Mr Andrew Sheppard , Community Assets Lead, South Norfolk House, Swan Lane, Long Stratton NR15 2XE ☎ 01508 533913 ✉ asheppard@s-norfolk.gov.uk

COUNCILLORS

***Chair* Bills**, David (CON - Hethersett)
dbills@s-norfolk.gov.uk

***Chair* Goldson**, DavidRoydon: Vacant
dgoldson@s-norfolk.gov.uk

***Leader of the Council* Fuller**, John (CON - Brooke)
jfuller@s-norfolk.gov.uk

***Deputy Leader of the Council* Wilby**, Martin (CON - Dickleburgh)
mwilby@s-norfolk.gov.uk

Amis, John (LD - New Costessey)
jamis@s-norfolk.gov.uk

Bell, Vivienne (LD - New Costessey)

Bendle, Yvonne (CON - Hingham and Deopham)
Ybendle@s-norfolk.gov.uk

Bernard, Brendon (LD - Ditchingham and Broome)
bbernard@s-norfolk.gov.uk

Billig, Kay (CON - Gillingham)
kbillig@s-norfolk.gov.uk

Blundell, Sharon (LD - Old Costessey)
sblundell@s-norfolk.gov.uk

Broome, Peter (CON - Rustens)
pbroome@s-norfolk.gov.uk

Dale, Leslie (CON - Hethersett)
ldale@s-norfolk.gov.uk

Dewsbury, Margaret (CON - Easton)
mdewsbury@s-norfolk.gov.uk

Duffin, Barry (CON - Forncett)
bduffin@s-norfolk.gov.uk

Easton, Charles (CON - Bunwell)
ceaston@s-norfolk.gov.uk

Edney, Michael (CON - Wicklewood)
medney@s-norfolk.gov.uk

Ellis, Florence (CON - Tasburgh)
fellis@s-norfolk.gov.uk

Foulger, Colin (CON - Mulbarton)

Fulcher, Des (CON - Stratton)
dfulcher@s-norfolk.gov.uk

Gould, Colin (CON - Loddon)
cgould@s-norfolk.gov.uk

Gray, Murray (LD - Earsham)
mgray@s-norfolk.gov.uk

Hardy, Phil (CON - Newton Flotman)
phardy@s-norfolk.gov.uk

Hornby, Lee (CON - Town)
Lhornby@s-norfolk.gov.uk

Hornby, Jack (CON - Cromwells)
jhornby@s-norfolk.gov.uk

Hudson, Clayton (CON - Beck Vale)
chudson@s-norfolk.gov.uk

Kemp, Christopher (CON - Cringleford)
ckemp@s-norfolk.gov.uk

Kemp, William (CON - Thurlton)
wkemp@s-norfolk.gov.uk

Kiddie, Keith (CON - Diss)
kkiddie@s-norfolk.gov.uk

Larner, Jaan (CON - Chedgrave and Thurton)
jlarner@s-norfolk.gov.uk

Legg, Nigel (CON - Mulbarton)
nlegg@s-norfolk.gov.uk

Lewis, Trevor (LD - Stoke Holy Cross)
tlewis@s-norfolk.gov.uk

Minshull, Graham (CON - Diss)
gminsull@s-norfolk.gov.uk

Mooney, Joseph (CON - Northfields)
jmooney@s-norfolk.gov.uk

Neal, Lisa (CON - Poringland with the Framinghams)
lneal@s-norfolk.gov.uk

Overton, John (CON - Poringland with the Framlinghams)
joverton@s-norfolk.gov.uk

Palmer, Tony (CON - Diss)
tpalmer@s-norfolk.gov.uk

Pond, Andrew (CON - Old Costessey)

Riches, Brian (CON - Harleston)
briches@s-norfolk.gov.uk

Savage, Robert (CON - Abbey)
rsavage@s-norfolk.gov.uk

Savage, Jeremy (CON - Harleston)
jsavage@s-norfolk.gov.uk

Stone, Barry (CON - Bressingham and Burston)
bstone@s-norfolk.gov.uk

Thomas, Alison (CON - Hempnall)
athomas@s-norfolk.gov.uk

Thomson, Vic (CON - Rockland)
vthomson@s-norfolk.gov.uk

Wheatley, Garry (CON - Cringleford)
gwheatley@s-norfolk.gov.uk

Wilby, Jenny (CON - Scole)
jwilby@s-norfolk.gov.uk

Worsley, Kevin (CON - Stratton)
kworsely@s-norfolk.gov.uk

POLITICAL COMPOSITION

CON: 39, LD: 6, UKWN: 1

South Northamptonshire D

South Northamptonshire Council, The Forum, Moat Lane, Towcester NN12 6AD
☎ 0845 230 0226 🖷 01327 322074 ✉ info@southnorthants.gov.uk
💻 www.southnorthants.gov.uk

FACTS AND FIGURES

Parliamentary Constituencies: Daventry, Northamptonshire South
EU Constituencies: East Midlands
Election Frequency: Elections are of whole council

PRINCIPAL OFFICERS

Chief Executive: Mrs Sue Smith , Chief Executive, Bodicote House, Bodicote, Banbury OX15 4AA ☎ 0300 003 0100
✉ sue.smith@cherwellandsouthnorthants.gov.uk

SOUTH NORTHAMPTONSHIRE

Senior Management: Mr Calvin Bell, Director - Development, The Forum, Moat Lane, Towcester NN12 6AD ☎ 0300 003 0103 🖷 01327 322310 ✉ calvin.bell@cherwellandsouthnorthants.gov.uk

Senior Management: Mr Ian Davies, Director - Community & Environment, The Forum, Moat Lane, Towcester NN12 6AD ☎ 01327 322302; 0300 003 0101 ✉ ian.davies@cherwellandsouthnorthants.gov.uk

Senior Management: Mr Martin Henry , Director - Resources & S151 Officer, The Forum, Moat Lane, Towcester NN12 6AD ☎ 0300 003 0102 ✉ martin.henry@cherwellandsouthnorthants.gov.uk

Architect, Building / Property Services: Mr Chris Stratford , Head of Regeneration & Housing, The Forum, Moat Lane, Towcester NN12 6AD ☎ 01295 251871; 0300 003 0111 ✉ chris.stratford@cherwellandsouthnorthants.gov.uk

Best Value: Ms Jo Pitman , Head of Transformation, The Forum, Moat Lane, Towcester NN12 6AD ☎ 0300 003 0108 ✉ jo.pitman@cherwellandsouthnorthants.gov.uk

Building Control: Mr Andy Preston, Head of Development Management, The Forum, Moat Lane, Towcester NN12 6AD ☎ 0300 003 0109 ✉ andy.preston@cherwellandsouthnorthants.gov.uk

Catering Services: Mr Steve Wright , Facilities Management Officer, The Forum, Moat Lane, Towcester NN12 6AD ☎ 01327 322322 🖷 01327 322114 ✉ stephen.wright@southnorthants.gov.uk

PR / Communications: Ms Jo Pitman , Head of Transformation, The Forum, Moat Lane, Towcester NN12 6AD ☎ 0300 003 0108 ✉ jo.pitman@cherwellandsouthnorthants.gov.uk

Community Planning: Mr Adrian Colwell , Head of Strategic Planning & the Economy, The Forum, Moat Lane, Towcester NN12 6AD ☎ 0300 003 0110 ✉ adrian.colwell@cherwellandsouthnorthants.gov.uk

Community Safety: Ms Jackie Fitzsimons , Public Protection & Environmental Health Manager, The Forum, Moat Lane, Towcester NN12 6AD ☎ 01327 322283 ✉ jackie.fitzsimmons@southnorthants.gov.uk

Computer Management: Ms Jo Pitman , Head of Transformation, The Forum, Moat Lane, Towcester NN12 6AD ☎ 0300 003 0108 ✉ jo.pitman@cherwellandsouthnorthants.gov.uk

Corporate Services: Mr Kevin Lane, Head of Law & Governance, The Forum, Moat Lane, Towcester NN12 6AD ☎ 0300 003 0107 ✉ kevin.lane@cherwellandsouthnorthants.gov.uk

Customer Service: Ms Liz Crussell, Customer Services Manager, The Forum, Moat Lane, Towcester NN12 6AD ☎ 01327 322120 ✉ liz.crussell@southnorthants.gov.uk

Economic Development: Mr Adrian Colwell , Head of Strategic Planning & the Economy, The Forum, Moat Lane, Towcester NN12 6AD ☎ 0300 003 0110 ✉ adrian.colwell@cherwellandsouthnorthants.gov.uk

Electoral Registration: Mr James Doble , Democratic & Elections Manager, The Forum, Moat Lane, Towcester NN12 6AD ☎ 01295 221587 ✉ james.doble@cherwellandsouthnorthants.gov.uk

Emergency Planning: Mr Gary Crook , Emergency Planning Officer, The Forum, Moat Lane, Towcester NN12 6AD ☎ 01327 322293 ✉ gary.crook@southnorthants.gov.uk

Environmental / Technical Services: Ms Jackie Fitzsimons , Public Protection & Environmental Health Manager, The Forum, Moat Lane, Towcester NN12 6AD ☎ 01327 322283 ✉ jackie.fitzsimmons@southnorthants.gov.uk

Environmental Health: Ms Jackie Fitzsimons , Public Protection & Environmental Health Manager, The Forum, Moat Lane, Towcester NN12 6AD ☎ 01327 322283 ✉ jackie.fitzsimmons@southnorthants.gov.uk

Estates, Property & Valuation: Mr Chris Stratford , Head of Regeneration & Housing, The Forum, Moat Lane, Towcester NN12 6AD ☎ 01295 251871; 0300 003 0111 ✉ chris.stratford@cherwellandsouthnorthants.gov.uk

European Liaison: Mrs Sue Smith , Chief Executive, The Forum, Moat Lane, Towcester NN12 6AD ☎ 0300 003 0100 ✉ sue.smith@cherwellandsouthnorthants.gov.uk

Facilities: Mr Steve Wright , Facilities Management Officer, The Forum, Moat Lane, Towcester NN12 6AD ☎ 01327 322322 🖷 01327 322114 ✉ stephen.wright@southnorthants.gov.uk

Finance: Mr Martin Henry , Director - Resources & S151 Officer, The Forum, Moat Lane, Towcester NN12 6AD ☎ 0300 003 0102 ✉ martin.henry@cherwellandsouthnorthants.gov.uk

Health and Safety: Mr David Bennett , Corporate Health & Safety Adviser, The Forum, Moat Lane, Towcester NN12 6AD ☎ 01295 221738 ✉ dave.bennett@cherwellandsouthnorthants.gov.uk

Housing: Ms Jo Harrison , Strategic Housing Manager, The Forum, Moat Lane, Towcester NN12 6AD ☎ 01327 322369 ✉ jo.harrison@southnorthants.gov.uk

Legal: Mr Kevin Lane, Head of Law & Governance, The Forum, Moat Lane, Towcester NN12 6AD ☎ 0300 003 0107 ✉ kevin.lane@cherwellandsouthnorthants.gov.uk

Leisure and Cultural Services: Mr Ashley Davey, Lead Officer Leisure Services, The Forum, Moat Lane, Towcester NN12 6AD ☎ 01327 322338 ✉ ashley.davey@southnorthants.gov.uk

Licensing: Ms Jackie Fitzsimons , Public Protection & Environmental Health Manager, The Forum, Moat Lane, Towcester NN12 6AD ☎ 01327 322283 ✉ jackie.fitzsimmons@southnorthants.gov.uk

Lottery Funding, Charity and Voluntary: Ms Katie Arnold , Grants Officer, The Forum, Moat Lane, Towcester NN12 6AD ☎ 01327 322216 ✉ katie.arnold@southnorthants.gov.uk

Member Services: Ms Natasha Clark , Democratic & Elections Team Leader, Bodicote House, Bodicote, Banbury OX15 4AA ☎ 01295 221589 ✉ natasha.clark@cherwellandsouthnorthants.gov.uk

Parking: Ms Sharon Bolton , Leisure Facilities & Projects Manager, Council Offices, Springfields, Towcester NN12 6AE ☎ 0300 003 0104 ✉ nicola.rey@cherwellandsouthnorthants.gov.uk

Partnerships: Ms Nicola Riley , Community Partnerships & Recreation Manager, Council Offices, Springfields, Towcester NN12 6AE ☎ 0300 003 0104 ✉ nicola.riley@cherwellandsouthnorthants.gov.uk

Personnel / HR: Ms Paula Goodwin , Shared HR & OD Manager, The Forum, Moat Lane, Towcester NN12 6AD ☎ 01295 221735 ✉ paula.goodwin@cherwellandsouthnorthants.gov.uk

Planning: Mr Andy Preston, Head of Development Management, The Forum, Moat Lane, Towcester NN12 6AD ☎ 0300 003 0109 ✉ andy.preston@cherwellandsouthnorthants.gov.uk

Procurement: Mr Richard Stirling , Corporate Procurement Manager, The Forum, Moat Lane, Towcester NN12 6AD ☎ 01327 322113 🖷 01327 322144 ✉ richard.stirling@southnorthants.gov.uk

Recycling & Waste Minimisation: Mr Ed Potter , Head of Environmental Services, The Forum, Moat Lane, Towcester NN12 6AD ☎ 01295 227023; 0300 003 0105 ✉ ed.potter@cherwellandsouthnorthants.gov.uk

Regeneration: Mr Adrian Colwell , Head of Strategic Planning & the Economy, The Forum, Moat Lane, Towcester NN12 6AD ☎ 0300 003 0110 ✉ adrian.colwell@cherwellandsouthnorthants.gov.uk

Staff Training: Ms Paula Goodwin , Shared HR & OD Manager, The Forum, Moat Lane, Towcester NN12 6AD ☎ 01295 221735 ✉ paula.goodwin@cherwellandsouthnorthants.gov.uk

Street Scene: Mr Ed Potter , Head of Environmental Services, The Forum, Moat Lane, Towcester NN12 6AD ☎ 01295 227023; 0300 003 0105 ✉ ed.potter@cherwellandsouthnorthants.gov.uk

Sustainable Communities: Mr Calvin Bell, Director - Development, Council Offices, Springfields, Towcester NN12 6AE ☎ 0300 003 0103 🖷 01327 322310 ✉ calvin.bell@cherwellandsouthnorthants.gov.uk

Sustainable Development: Mr Ed Potter , Head of Environmental Services, The Forum, Moat Lane, Towcester NN12 6AD ☎ 01295 227023; 0300 003 0105 ✉ ed.potter@cherwellandsouthnorthants.gov.uk

Tourism: Mr Adrian Colwell , Head of Strategic Planning & the Economy, The Forum, Moat Lane, Towcester NN12 6AD ☎ 0300 003 0110 ✉ adrian.colwell@cherwellandsouthnorthants.gov.uk

Transport Planner: Mr David Allen , Lead Officer - Transport Policy, The Forum, Moat Lane, Towcester NN12 6AD ☎ 01327 322268 🖷 01327 322325 ✉ david.allen@southnorthants.gov.uk

Waste Collection and Disposal: Mr Ed Potter , Head of Environmental Services, The Forum, Moat Lane, Towcester NN12 6AD ☎ 01295 227023; 0300 003 0105 ✉ ed.potter@cherwellandsouthnorthants.gov.uk

Waste Management: Mr Ed Potter , Head of Environmental Services, The Forum, Moat Lane, Towcester NN12 6AD ☎ 01295 227023; 0300 003 0105 ✉ ed.potter@cherwellandsouthnorthants.gov.uk

COUNCILLORS

***Chair* Clarke**, Roger (CON - Blakesley and Cote)
roger.clarke@southnorthants.gov.uk

***Vice-Chair* Billingham**, Caryl (IND - Brackley South)
caryl@billingham-brackley.com

***Leader of the Council* McCord**, Ian (CON - Cosgrove and Grafton)
ian.mccord@southnorthants.gov.uk

***Deputy Leader of the Council* Bignell**, Phil (CON - Heyfords and Bugbrooke)
phil.bignell@southnorthants.gov.uk

***Group Leader* Johns**, Martin (LD - Towcester Brook)
martin.johns@southnorthants.gov.uk

Addison, Ann (CON - Harpole and Grange)
ann.addison@southnorthants.gov.uk

Atkinson, Robert (CON - Hackleton)
bob.atkinson@southnorthants.gov.uk

Bagot-Webb, Anthony (CON - Brackley East)
anthony.bagot-webb@southnorthants.gov.uk

Baker, Fiona (CON - Brackley West)

Bambridge, Dermot (CON - Silverstone)
dermot.bambridge@southnorthants.gov.uk

Barnes, Sandra (CON - Tove)
sandra.barnes@southnorthants.gov.uk

Baxter, Judith (CON - Middleton Cheney)
judith.baxter@southnorthants.gov.uk

Bowen, Lizzy (CON - Whittlewood)
lizzy.bowen@southnorthants.gov.uk

Breese, Rebecca (CON - Steane)
rebecca.breese@southnorthants.gov.uk

Budden, John (CON - Salcey)
john.budden@southnorthants.gov.uk

Clarke, Carole (CON - Brafield and Yardley)
carole.clarke@southnorthants.gov.uk

Clarke, Stephen (CON - Blisworth and Roade)
stephen.clarke@southnorthants.gov.uk

Clifford, Simon (CON - Grange Park)
simon.clifford@southnorthants.gov.uk

Cooper, Karen (CON - Harpole and Grange)
karen.cooper@southnorthants.gov.uk

Dallyn, Richard (CON - Towcester Brook)
richard.dallyan@southnorthants.gov.uk

Davies, Hywel (CON - Blisworth and Roade)
hywel.davies@southnorthants.gov.uk

Davies, Peter (CON - Washington)
peter.davies@southnorthants.gov.uk

Furniss, Valerie (CON - Middleton Cheney)
val.furniss@southnorthants.gov.uk

Harries, David (IND - Heyfords and Bugbrooke)
david.harries@southnorthants.gov.uk

Herring, Rosie (CON - Danvers and Wardoun)
rosie.herring@southnorthants.gov.uk

Hollowell, Steven (IND - Brafield and Yardley)
steven.hollowell@southnorthants.gov.uk

Lofts, Chris (LD - Towcester Mill)
chris.lofts@southnorthants.gov.uk

Loveland, Dennis (CON - Deanshanger)
dennis.loveland@southnorthants.gov.uk

Manners, Charles (CON - Kingthorn)
charles.manners@southnorthants.gov.uk

Marinker, Simon (CON - Astwell)
simon.marinker@southnorthants.gov.uk

Mold, Stephen (CON - Old Stratford)
stephen.mold@southnorthants.gov.uk

Morris, Ian (CON - King's Sutton)
ian.morris@southnorthants.gov.uk

Ord, Alice (CON - Brackley South)
alice.ord@southnorthants.gov.uk

Rawlinson, Peter (CON - Brackley East)
peter.rawlinson@southnorthants.gov.uk

Sadygov, Adil (CON - Grange Park)
adil.sadygov@southnorthants.gov.uk

Samiotis, Lisa (LD - Towcester Brook)
lisa.samiotis@southnorthants.gov.uk

Sergison-Brooke, Mary-Anne (CON - Danvers and Wardoun)

Smallman, Sandi (CON - Blakesley and Cote)
sandi.smallman@southnorthants.gov.uk

Tarbun, Catharine (LD - Towcester Mill)
catharine.tarbun@southnorthants.gov.uk

Townsend, John (CON - Little Brook)
john.townsend@southnorthants.gov.uk

Walker, Allen (CON - Deanshanger)

Wiltshire, Elaine (CON - Brackley West)
elaine.wiltshire@southnorthants.gov.uk

POLITICAL COMPOSITION
CON: 35, LD: 4, IND: 3

COMMITTEE CHAIRS
Audit: Mrs Sandra Barnes

Development Control: Mrs Sandra Barnes

Planning Policy & Regeneration: Mr John Townsend

South Oxfordshire D

South Oxfordshire District Council, Benson Lane, Crowmarsh Gifford, Wallingford OX10 8HQ
☎ 01491 823000 🖷 01491 823001 ✉ info@southoxon.gov.uk
💻 www.southoxon.gov.uk

FACTS AND FIGURES
Parliamentary Constituencies: Henley, Wantage
EU Constituencies: South East
Election Frequency: Elections are of whole council

PRINCIPAL OFFICERS
Chief Executive: Mr David Buckle , Chief Executive, 135 Eastern Avenue, Milton Park, Milton, Abingdon OX14 4SB ☎ 01235 547612 ✉ david.buckle@southandvale.gov.uk

Deputy Chief Executive: Mr Steve Bishop, Strategic Director, 135 Eastern Avenue, Milton Park, Milton, Abingdon OX14 4SB ☎ 01235 540332 ✉ steve.bishop@southandvale.gov.uk

Deputy Chief Executive: Mrs Anna Robinson , Strategic Director, 135 Eastern Avenue, Milton Park, Milton, Abingdon OX14 4SB ☎ 01235 540405 ✉ anna.robinson@southandvale.gov.uk

Senior Management: Mr Andrew Down, Head of HR, IT & Technical Services, 135 Eastern Avenue, Milton Park, Milton, Abingdon OX14 4SB ☎ 01235 540372 ✉ andrew.down@southandvale.gov.uk

Senior Management: Mr Adrian Duffield , Head of Planning, 135 Eastern Avenue, Milton Park, Milton, Abingdon OX14 4SB ☎ 01235 540340 ✉ adrian.duffield@southandvale.gov.uk

Senior Management: Mr William Jacobs , Head of Finance, 135 Eastern Avenue, Milton Park, Milton, Abingdon OX14 4SB ☎ 01235 540526 ✉ william.jacobs@southandvale.gov.uk

Senior Management: Mrs Clare Kingston , Head of Corporate Strategy, 135 Eastern Avenue, Milton Park, Milton, Abingdon OX14 4SB ☎ 01235 540356 ✉ clare.kingston@southandvale.gov.uk

Senior Management: Mrs Margaret Reed , Head of Legal & Democratic Services, 135 Eastern Avenue, Milton Park, Milton, Abingdon OX14 4SB ☎ 01235 540407 ✉ margaret.reed@southandvale.gov.uk

Senior Management: Mr Chris Tyson , Head of Economy, Leisure & Property, 135 Eastern Avenue, Milton Park, Milton, Abingdon OX14 4SB ☎ 01235 540378 ✉ chris.tyson@southandvale.gov.uk

Building Control: Mr Adrian Duffield , Head of Planning, 135 Eastern Avenue, Milton Park, Milton, Abingdon OX14 4SB ☎ 01235 540340 ✉ adrian.duffield@southandvale.gov.uk

PR / Communications: Mrs Clare Kingston , Head of Corporate Strategy, 135 Eastern Avenue, Milton Park, Milton, Abingdon OX14 4SB ☎ 01235 540356 ✉ clare.kingston@southandvale.gov.uk

PR / Communications: Mrs Shona Ware , Communications & Grants Manager, 135 Eastern Avenue, Milton Park, Milton, Abingdon OX14 4SB ☎ 01235 540406 ✉ shona.ware@southandvale.gov.uk

Community Safety: Mrs Liz Hayden , Legal, Licensing & Community Safety Manager, 135 Eastern Avenue, Milton Park, Milton, Abingdon OX14 4SB ☎ 01491 823705 ✉ liz.hayden@southandvale.gov.uk

Community Safety: Mrs Margaret Reed , Head of Legal & Democratic Services, 135 Eastern Avenue, Milton Park, Milton, Abingdon OX14 4SB ☎ 01235 540407 ✉ margaret.reed@southandvale.gov.uk

Computer Management: Mr Andrew Down, Head of HR, IT & Technical Services, 135 Eastern Avenue, Milton Park, Milton, Abingdon OX14 4SB ☎ 01235 540372 ✉ andrew.down@southandvale.gov.uk

Computer Management: Mr Simon Turner , IT Operations Manager, 135 Eastern Avenue, Milton Park, Milton, Abingdon OX14 4SB ☎ 01235 540400 ✉ simon.turner@southandvale.gov.uk

Contracts: Mrs Margaret Reed , Head of Legal & Democratic Services, 135 Eastern Avenue, Milton Park, Milton, Abingdon OX14 4SB ☎ 01235 540407 ✉ margaret.reed@southandvale.gov.uk

Economic Development: Mrs Suzanne Malcolm , Economic Development Manager, 135 Eastern Avenue, Milton Park, Milton, Abingdon OX14 4SB ☎ 01235 547619 ✉ suzanne.malcolm@southandvale.gov.uk

Economic Development: Mr Chris Tyson , Head of Economy, Leisure & Property, 135 Eastern Avenue, Milton Park, Milton, Abingdon OX14 4SB ☎ 01235 540378 ✉ chris.tyson@southandvale.gov.uk

E-Government: Mr Andrew Down, Head of HR, IT & Technical Services, 135 Eastern Avenue, Milton Park, Milton, Abingdon OX14 4SB ☎ 01235 540372 ✉ andrew.down@southandvale.gov.uk

Electoral Registration: Mr Steven Corrigan , Democratic Services Manager, 135 Eastern Avenue, Milton Park, Milton, Abingdon OX14 4SB ☎ 01235 547675 ✉ steven.corrigan@southandvale.gov.uk

Electoral Registration: Mrs Margaret Reed , Head of Legal & Democratic Services, 135 Eastern Avenue, Milton Park, Milton, Abingdon OX14 4SB ☎ 01235 540407 ✉ margaret.reed@southandvale.gov.uk

Emergency Planning: Mr John Backley , Technical & Facilities Manager, 135 Eastern Avenue, Milton Park, Milton, Abingdon OX14 4SB ☎ 01235 540443 ✉ john.backley@southandvale.gov.uk

Emergency Planning: Mr Andrew Down, Head of HR, IT & Technical Services, 135 Eastern Avenue, Milton Park, Milton, Abingdon OX14 4SB ☎ 01235 540372 ✉ andrew.down@southandvale.gov.uk

Environmental / Technical Services: Mr John Backley , Technical & Facilities Manager, 135 Eastern Avenue, Milton Park, Milton, Abingdon OX14 4SB ☎ 01235 540443 ✉ john.backley@southandvale.gov.uk

Environmental / Technical Services: Mr Andrew Down, Head of HR, IT & Technical Services, 135 Eastern Avenue, Milton Park, Milton, Abingdon OX14 4SB ☎ 01235 540372 ✉ andrew.down@southandvale.gov.uk

Environmental Health: Mr Paul Holland , Environmental Protection Manager, 135 Eastern Avenue, Milton Park, Milton, Abingdon OX14 4SB ☎ 01235 540454 ✉ paul.hollans@southandvale.gov.uk

Environmental Health: Mrs Clare Kingston , Head of Corporate Strategy, 135 Eastern Avenue, Milton Park, Milton, Abingdon OX14 4SB ☎ 01235 540356 ✉ clare.kingston@southandvale.gov.uk

Environmental Health: Ms Diane Moore , Food & Safety Manager, 135 Eastern Avenue, Milton Park, Milton, Abingdon OX14 4SB ☎ 01235 540382 ✉ diane.moore@southandvale.gov.uk

Estates, Property & Valuation: Mr John Backley , Technical & Facilities Manager, 135 Eastern Avenue, Milton Park, Milton, Abingdon OX14 4SB ☎ 01235 540443 ✉ john.backley@southandvale.gov.uk

Estates, Property & Valuation: Mr Chris Tyson , Head of Economy, Leisure & Property, 135 Eastern Avenue, Milton Park, Milton, Abingdon OX14 4SB ☎ 01235 540378 ✉ chris.tyson@southandvale.gov.uk

Facilities: Mr John Backley , Technical & Facilities Manager, 135 Eastern Avenue, Milton Park, Milton, Abingdon OX14 4SB ☎ 01235 540443 ✉ john.backley@southandvale.gov.uk

Facilities: Mr Andrew Down, Head of HR, IT & Technical Services, 135 Eastern Avenue, Milton Park, Milton, Abingdon OX14 4SB ☎ 01235 540372 ✉ andrew.down@southandvale.gov.uk

Finance: Mr Steve Bishop, Strategic Director, 135 Eastern Avenue, Milton Park, Milton, Abingdon OX14 4SB ☎ 01235 540332 ✉ steve.bishop@southandvale.gov.uk

Finance: Mr William Jacobs , Head of Finance, 135 Eastern Avenue, Milton Park, Milton, Abingdon OX14 4SB ☎ 01235 540526 ✉ william.jacobs@southandvale.gov.uk

Grounds Maintenance: Mrs Clare Kingston , Head of Corporate Strategy, 135 Eastern Avenue, Milton Park, Milton, Abingdon OX14 4SB ☎ 01235 540356 ✉ clare.kingston@southandvale.gov.uk

Grounds Maintenance: Mr Ian Matten , Waste & Parks Manager, 135 Eastern Avenue, Milton Park, Milton, Abingdon OX14 4SB ☎ 01235 540373 ✉ ian.matten@southandvale.gov.uk

Health and Safety: Mrs Clare Kingston , Head of Corporate Strategy, 135 Eastern Avenue, Milton Park, Milton, Abingdon OX14 4SB ☎ 01235 540356 ✉ clare.kingston@southandvale.gov.uk

Health and Safety: Ms Sally Truman , Policy, Partnership & Engagement Manager, 135 Eastern Avenue, Milton Park, Milton, Abingdon OX14 4SB ☎ 01235 450408 ✉ sally.truman@southandvale.gov.uk

Housing: Mr Phil Ealey , Housing Needs Manager, 135 Eastern Avenue, Milton Park, Milton, Abingdon OX14 4SB ☎ 01235 547623 ✉ phil.ealey@southandvale.gov.uk

Legal: Mrs Liz Hayden , Legal, Licensing & Community Safety Manager, 135 Eastern Avenue, Milton Park, Milton, Abingdon OX14 4SB ☎ 01491 823705 ✉ liz.hayden@southandvale.gov.uk

Legal: Mrs Margaret Reed , Head of Legal & Democratic Services, 135 Eastern Avenue, Milton Park, Milton, Abingdon OX14 4SB ☎ 01235 540407 ✉ margaret.reed@southandvale.gov.uk

Leisure and Cultural Services: Miss Kate Arnold , Leisure Manager, 135 Eastern Avenue, Milton Park, Milton, Abingdon OX14 4SB ☎ 01235 547632 kate.arnold@southandvale.gov.uk

Leisure and Cultural Services: Miss Emma Dolman , Arts Manager, Cornerstone, 25 Station Road, Didcot OX11 7NE ☎ 01235 515131 emma.dolman@southandvale.gov.uk

Leisure and Cultural Services: Mr Chris Tyson , Head of Economy, Leisure & Property, 135 Eastern Avenue, Milton Park, Milton, Abingdon OX14 4SB ☎ 01235 540378 chris.tyson@southandvale.gov.uk

Licensing: Mrs Margaret Reed , Head of Legal & Democratic Services, 135 Eastern Avenue, Milton Park, Milton, Abingdon OX14 4SB ☎ 01235 540407 margaret.reed@southandvale.gov.uk

Lottery Funding, Charity and Voluntary: Mrs Clare Kingston , Head of Corporate Strategy, 135 Eastern Avenue, Milton Park, Milton, Abingdon OX14 4SB ☎ 01235 540356 clare.kingston@southandvale.gov.uk

Lottery Funding, Charity and Voluntary: Ms Sally Truman , Policy, Partnership & Engagement Manager, 135 Eastern Avenue, Milton Park, Milton, Abingdon OX14 4SB ☎ 01235 450408 sally.truman@southandvale.gov.uk

Member Services: Mr Steven Corrigan , Democratic Services Manager, 135 Eastern Avenue, Milton Park, Milton, Abingdon OX14 4SB ☎ 01235 547675 steven.corrigan@southandvale.gov.uk

Member Services: Mrs Margaret Reed , Head of Legal & Democratic Services, 135 Eastern Avenue, Milton Park, Milton, Abingdon OX14 4SB ☎ 01235 540407 margaret.reed@southandvale.gov.uk

Parking: Mr John Backley , Technical & Facilities Manager, 135 Eastern Avenue, Milton Park, Milton, Abingdon OX14 4SB ☎ 01235 540443 john.backley@southandvale.gov.uk

Parking: Mr Andrew Down, Head of HR, IT & Technical Services, 135 Eastern Avenue, Milton Park, Milton, Abingdon OX14 4SB ☎ 01235 540372 andrew.down@southandvale.gov.uk

Partnerships: Mrs Clare Kingston , Head of Corporate Strategy, 135 Eastern Avenue, Milton Park, Milton, Abingdon OX14 4SB ☎ 01235 540356 clare.kingston@southandvale.gov.uk

Partnerships: Ms Sally Truman , Policy, Partnership & Engagement Manager, 135 Eastern Avenue, Milton Park, Milton, Abingdon OX14 4SB ☎ 01235 450408 sally.truman@southandvale.gov.uk

Personnel / HR: Mr Andrew Down, Head of HR, IT & Technical Services, 135 Eastern Avenue, Milton Park, Milton, Abingdon OX14 4SB ☎ 01235 540372 andrew.down@southandvale.gov.uk

Personnel / HR: Mr Mark Gibbons , Human Resources Manager, 135 Eastern Avenue, Milton Park, Milton, Abingdon OX14 4SB ☎ 01491 823412 mark.gibbons@southandvale.gov.uk

Planning: Mr Adrian Duffield , Head of Planning, 135 Eastern Avenue, Milton Park, Milton, Abingdon OX14 4SB ☎ 01235 540340 adrian.duffield@southandvale.gov.uk

Planning: Miss Paula Fox , Development Manager (South), 135 Eastern Avenue, Milton Park, Milton, Abingdon OX14 4SB ☎ 01235 540361 paula.fox@southandvale.gov.uk

Planning: Mr Brett Leahy , Development Manager (Vale), 135 Eastern Avenue, Milton Park, Milton, Abingdon OX14 4SB brett.leahy@southandvale.gov.uk

Recycling & Waste Minimisation: Mrs Clare Kingston , Head of Corporate Strategy, 135 Eastern Avenue, Milton Park, Milton, Abingdon OX14 4SB ☎ 01235 540356 clare.kingston@southandvale.gov.uk

Recycling & Waste Minimisation: Mr Ian Matten , Waste & Parks Manager, 135 Eastern Avenue, Milton Park, Milton, Abingdon OX14 4SB ☎ 01235 540373 ian.matten@southandvale.gov.uk

Staff Training: Mr Andrew Down, Head of HR, IT & Technical Services, 135 Eastern Avenue, Milton Park, Milton, Abingdon OX14 4SB ☎ 01235 540372 andrew.down@southandvale.gov.uk

Staff Training: Mr Mark Gibbons , Human Resources Manager, 135 Eastern Avenue, Milton Park, Milton, Abingdon OX14 4SB ☎ 01491 823412 mark.gibbons@southandvale.gov.uk

Sustainable Communities: Mr Adrian Duffield , Head of Planning, 135 Eastern Avenue, Milton Park, Milton, Abingdon OX14 4SB ☎ 01235 540340 adrian.duffield@southandvale.gov.uk

Sustainable Development: Mrs Clare Kingston , Head of Corporate Strategy, 135 Eastern Avenue, Milton Park, Milton, Abingdon OX14 4SB ☎ 01235 540356 clare.kingston@southandvale.gov.uk

Sustainable Development: Ms Sally Truman , Policy, Partnership & Engagement Manager, 135 Eastern Avenue, Milton Park, Milton, Abingdon OX14 4SB ☎ 01235 450408 sally.truman@southandvale.gov.uk

Tourism: Mr Chris Tyson , Head of Economy, Leisure & Property, 135 Eastern Avenue, Milton Park, Milton, Abingdon OX14 4SB ☎ 01235 540378 chris.tyson@southandvale.gov.uk

Town Centre: Mrs Suzanne Malcolm , Economic Development Manager, 135 Eastern Avenue, Milton Park, Milton, Abingdon OX14 4SB ☎ 01235 547619 suzanne.malcolm@southandvale.gov.uk

Town Centre: Mr Chris Tyson , Head of Economy, Leisure & Property, 135 Eastern Avenue, Milton Park, Milton, Abingdon OX14 4SB ☎ 01235 540378 chris.tyson@southandvale.gov.uk

Waste Collection and Disposal: Mrs Clare Kingston , Head of Corporate Strategy, 135 Eastern Avenue, Milton Park, Milton, Abingdon OX14 4SB ☎ 01235 540356 clare.kingston@southandvale.gov.uk

Waste Collection and Disposal: Mr Ian Matten , Waste & Parks Manager, 135 Eastern Avenue, Milton Park, Milton, Abingdon OX14 4SB ☎ 01235 540373 ✉ ian.matten@southandvale.gov.uk

Waste Management: Mrs Clare Kingston , Head of Corporate Strategy, 135 Eastern Avenue, Milton Park, Milton, Abingdon OX14 4SB ☎ 01235 540356 ✉ clare.kingston@southandvale.gov.uk

COUNCILLORS

***Chair* Turner**, Margaret (CON - Didcot West)
margaret.turner@southoxon.gov.uk

***Vice-Chair* Harrison**, Paul (CON - Sonning Common)
paul.harrison@suk.sas.com

***Leader of the Council* Cotton**, John (CON - Berinsfield)
leader@southoxon.gov.uk

***Deputy Leader of the Council* Murphy**, Jane (CON - Cholsey)
jane.murphy@southoxon.gov.uk

Akehurst, Martin (CON - Sonning Common)
martin.akehurst@southoxon.gov.uk

Badcock, Anna (CON - Watlington)
annabadcock1@gmail.com

Bailey, Charles (CON - Woodcote & Rotherfield)
charles.bailey@southoxon.gov.uk

Bland, Joan (CON - Henley-on-Thames)
joan@asquiths.com

Bloomfield, Felix (CON - Benson & Crowmarsh)
felixbloomfield@hotmail.com

Bulmer, Kevin (CON - Goring)
kevin.bulmer@southoxon.gov.uk

Champken-Woods, Nigel (CON - Thame)
nigel.champken-woods@southoxon.gov.uk

Connel, Steve (CON - Didcot North East)
sconnel@hotmail.com

Davies, Margaret (LAB - Didcot South)
mldaviesbb@btinternet.com

Dawe, Pat (CON - Cholsey)
pat.dawe@southoxon.gov.uk

Dearlove, Anthony (CON - Didcot South)
anthony.dearlove@aol.co.uk

Dodds, David (CON - Thame)
david.dodds@southoxon.gov.uk

Gawrysiak, Stefan (R - Henley-on-Thames)
stefan.gawrysiak@southoxon.gov.uk

Gillespie, Elizabeth (CON - Garsington & Horspath)
elizabethgillespie@uk2.net

Harbour, Tony (CON - Didcot North East)
tony.harbour@southoxon.gov.uk

Harrod, Stephen (CON - Haseley Brook)
stephen.harrod@southoxon.gov.uk

Hillier, Lorraine (CON - Henley-on-Thames)
lorraine.hillier@southoxon.gov.uk

Hornsby, Elaine (CON - Wallingford)
elaine.hornsby@southoxon.gov.uk

Lloyd, Lynn (CON - Chinnor)
lynn.lloyd@btinternet.com

Lokhon, Imran (CON - Wallingford)
imran@yourwallingford.gov.uk

Matelot, Jeannette (CON - Thame)
jeannette.matelot@southoxon.gov.uk

Nash, Anthony (CON - Didcot South)
anthony.nash@southandvale.gov.uk

Newman, Toby (CON - Wheatley)
toby.newman@southoxon.gov.uk

Nimmo-Smith, David (CON - Woodcote & Rotherfield)
david.nimmo-smith@southoxon.gov.uk

Pullen, Richard (CON - Benson & Crowmarsh)
richard.pullen@southoxon.gov.uk

Service, Bill (CON - Didcot North East)
bill.service@hotmail.co.uk

Simister, Robert (CON - Kidmore End & Whitchurch)
robert.simister@southoxon.gov.uk

Thompson, Alan (CON - Didcot West)
alan.thompson@southoxon.gov.uk

Turner, David (LD - Chalgrove)
david.turner@southoxon.gov.uk

Walsh, John (CON - Forest Hill & Holton)
john.walsh@southoxon.gov.uk

White, Ian (CON - Chinnor)
ian.white@southoxon.gov.uk

Woodley-Shead, Jon (CON - Sandford & the Wittenhams)
jon.woodley-shead@southoxon.gov.uk

POLITICAL COMPOSITION

CON: 33, LAB: 1, LD: 1, R: 1

COMMITTEE CHAIRS

Licensing: Mr David Dodds

Planning: Mr Felix Bloomfield

South Ribble D

South Ribble Borough Council, Civic Centre, West Paddock, Leyland PR25 1DH
☎ 01772 421491 🖷 01772 622287 ✉ info@southribble.gov.uk
💻 www.southribble.gov.uk

FACTS AND FIGURES

Parliamentary Constituencies: South Ribble
EU Constituencies: North West
Election Frequency: Elections are by thirds

PRINCIPAL OFFICERS

Chief Executive: Mr Mike Nuttall, Chief Executive & Chief Finance Officer, Civic Centre, West Paddock, Leyland PR25 1DH ☎ 01772 421491 🖷 01772 622287 ✉ mnuttall@southribble.gov.uk

Senior Management: Mr Garry Barclay , Head of Shared Assurance Services, Civic Centre, West Paddock, Leyland PR25 1DH ☎ 01772 625272 ✉ gbarclay@southribble.gov.uk

SOUTH RIBBLE

Senior Management: Mr Mark Gaffney, Director of Neighbourhoods, Environmental Health & Assets, Civic Centre, West Paddock, Leyland PR25 1DH ☎ 01772 625671 🖷 01772 622287 🖰 mgaffney@southribble.gov.uk

Senior Management: Mrs Susan Guinness , Head of Shared Financial Services, Civic Centre, West Paddock, Leyland PR25 1DH ☎ 01772 421491 🖰 sguinness@southribble.gov.uk

Senior Management: Ms Denise Johnson, Director of Development, Enterprise & Communities, Civic Centre, West Paddock, Leyland PR25 1DH ☎ 01772 625558 🖷 01772 622287 🖰 djohnson@southribble.gov.uk

Senior Management: Mr Steve Nugent , Head of HR, Civic Centre, West Paddock, Leyland PR25 1DH ☎ 01772 421491 🖷 01772 622287 🖰 snugent@southribble.gov.uk

Senior Management: Mr Ian Parker , Director of Corporate Governance & Business Transformation, Civic Centre, West Paddock, Leyland PR25 1DH ☎ 01772 625550 🖰 iparker@southribble.gov.uk

Architect, Building / Property Services: Ms Mandy Catterall , Property Services Manager, Civic Centre, West Paddock, Leyland PR25 1DH ☎ 01772 421491 🖰 mcatterall@southribble.gov.uk

PR / Communications: Mr Dave Pollard , Public Relations Officer, Civic Centre, West Paddock, Leyland PR25 1DH ☎ 01772 421491 🖷 01772 622287 🖰 dpollard@southribble.gov.uk

Community Planning: Ms Helen Hockenhull , Planning Manager, Civic Centre, West Paddock, Leyland PR25 1DH ☎ 01772 421491 🖷 01772 622287 🖰 hhockenhull@southribble.gov.uk

Computer Management: Mr John Healey , ICT Manager, Civic Centre, West Paddock, Leyland PR25 1DH ☎ 01772 421491 🖰 jhealey@southribble.gov.uk

Corporate Services: Mr Ian Parker , Director of Corporate Governance & Business Transformation, Civic Centre, West Paddock, Leyland PR25 1DH ☎ 01772 625550 🖰 iparker@southribble.gov.uk

Customer Service: Mr Kevin Conway , Gateway Manager, Civic Centre, West Paddock, Leyland PR25 1DH ☎ 01772 627112 🖰 kconway@southribble.gov.uk

Direct Labour: Mr Mark Gaffney, Director of Neighbourhoods, Environmental Health & Assets, Civic Centre, West Paddock, Leyland PR25 1DH ☎ 01772 625671 🖷 01772 622287 🖰 mgaffney@southribble.gov.uk

Electoral Registration: Mr Martin O'Loughlin , Democratic Services Manager, Civic Centre, West Paddock, Leyland PR25 1DH ☎ 01772 625307 🖷 01772 622287 🖰 moloughlin@southribble.gov.uk

Emergency Planning: Mr Andy Armstrong , Risk Manager, Civic Centre, West Paddock, Leyland PR25 1DH ☎ 01772 625256

Environmental Health: Mrs Jennifer Mullin , Public Health Manager, Civic Centre, West Paddock, Leyland PR25 1DH ☎ 01772 625329 🖰 jmullin@southribble.gov.uk

Estates, Property & Valuation: Ms Mandy Catterall , Property Services Manager, Civic Centre, West Paddock, Leyland PR25 1DH ☎ 01772 421491 🖰 mcatterall@southribble.gov.uk

Finance: Ms Susan Guinness , Head of Shared Financial Services, Town Hall, Market Street, Chorley PR7 1DP ☎ 01257 515151 🖷 01257 515150 🖰 susan.guinness@chorley.gov.uk

Fleet Management: Mr Roger Ashcroft , Waste, Transport & Neighbourhoods Manager, Civic Centre, West Paddock, Leyland PR25 1DH ☎ 01772 625612 🖰 rashcroft@southribble.gov.uk

Grounds Maintenance: Mr Andrew Richardson , Parks & Neighbourhoods Manager, Civic Centre, West Paddock, Leyland PR25 1DH ☎ 01772 625674 🖰 arichardson@southribble.gov.uk

Health and Safety: Mr Jeff Lambert , Health & Safety Officer, Civic Centre, West Paddock, Leyland PR25 1DH ☎ 01772 625331 🖰 jlambertl@southribble.gov.uk

Home Energy Conservation: Mr Pradip Patel , Private Sector Officer, Civic Centre, West Paddock, Leyland PR25 1DH ☎ 01772 421491 Extn 5365 🖰 dppatel@southribble.gov.uk

Legal: Mr David Whelan , Legal Services Manager, Civic Centre, West Paddock, Leyland PR25 1DH ☎ 01772 421491 🖷 01772 622287 🖰 dwhelan@southribble.gov.uk

Licensing: Mrs Jennifer Mullin , Public Health Manager, Civic Centre, West Paddock, Leyland PR25 1DH ☎ 01772 625329 🖰 jmullin@southribble.gov.uk

Member Services: Mr Martin O'Loughlin , Democratic Services Manager, Civic Centre, West Paddock, Leyland PR25 1DH ☎ 01772 625307 🖷 01772 622287 🖰 moloughlin@southribble.gov.uk

Parking: Mr Andrew Richardson, Parks & Neighbourhoods Manager, Civic Centre, West Paddock, Leyland PR25 1DH ☎ 01772 625674 🖰 arichardson@southribble.gov.uk

Partnerships: Mr Howard Anthony , Temporary Partnership Manager, Civic Centre, West Paddock, Leyland PR25 1DH ☎ 01772 421491 🖷 01772 622287 🖰 hanthony@southribble.gov.uk

Personnel / HR: Mr Steve Nugent , Head of HR, Civic Centre, West Paddock, Leyland PR25 1DH ☎ 01772 421491 🖷 01772 622287 🖰 snugent@southribble.gov.uk

Planning: Ms Helen Hockenhull , Planning Manager, Civic Centre, West Paddock, Leyland PR25 1DH ☎ 01772 421491 🖷 01772 622287 🖰 hhockenhull@southribble.gov.uk

Procurement: Ms Janet Hinds , Procurement & Partnerships Manager, Civic Centre, West Paddock, Leyland PR25 1DH ☎ 01257 575622 🖷 01772 622287 🖰 janet.hinds@chorley.gov.uk

Recycling & Waste Minimisation: Miss Laura Wright , Recycling Officer, Civic Centre, West Paddock, Leyland PR25 1DH ☎ 01772 421491 Extn 5606 🖷 01772 622287 ✉ lwright@southribble.gov.uk

Regeneration: Mr Howerd Booth , Community Works Manager, Civic Centre, West Paddock, Leyland PR25 1DH ☎ 01772 421491 🖷 01772 622287 ✉ hbooth@southribble.gov.uk

Staff Training: Mr Steve Nugent , Head of HR, Civic Centre, West Paddock, Leyland PR25 1DH ☎ 01772 421491 🖷 01772 622287 ✉ snugent@southribble.gov.uk

Street Scene: Mr Mark Gaffney, Director, Civic Centre, West Paddock, Leyland PR25 1DH ☎ 01772 625671 🖷 01772 622287 ✉ mgaffney@southribble.gov.uk

Tourism: Miss Jennifer Clough, Principal Economic Development Officer, Civic Centre, West Paddock, Leyland PR25 1DH ☎ 01772 421491 🖷 01772 622287 ✉ jclough@southribble.gov.uk

Waste Collection and Disposal: Mr Roger Ashcroft , Waste, Transport & Neighbourhoods Manager, Civic Centre, West Paddock, Leyland PR25 1DH ☎ 01772 421491

Waste Collection and Disposal: Mr Mark Gaffney, Director, Civic Centre, West Paddock, Leyland PR25 1DH ☎ 01772 625671 🖷 01772 622287 ✉ mgaffney@southribble.gov.uk

Waste Management: Mr Roger Ashcroft , Waste, Transport & Neighbourhoods Manager, Civic Centre, West Paddock, Leyland PR25 1DH ☎ 01772 625612 ✉ rashcroft@southribble.gov.uk

Waste Management: Mr Mark Gaffney, Director, Civic Centre, West Paddock, Leyland PR25 1DH ☎ 01772 625671 🖷 01772 622287 ✉ mgaffney@southribble.gov.uk

COUNCILLORS

***Mayor* Green**, Mary (CON - Moss Side)
cllr.mary.green@southribble.gov.uk

***Deputy Mayor* Woollard**, Linda (CON - Broad Oak)
cllr.lwoollard@southribble.gov.uk

***Leader of the Council* Smith**, Margaret (CON - New Longton & Hutton East)
cllr.msmith@southribble.gov.uk

***Deputy Leader of the Council* Bennett**, Warren (CON - Coupe Green & Gregson Lane)
cllr.wbennett@southribble.gov.uk

Ball, Andrea (CON - Walton-le-Dale East)
cllr.aball@southribble.gov.uk

Bell, Jane (LAB - Seven Stars)
cllr.jbell@southribble.gov.uk

Bird, David (CON - Howick & Priory)

Blow, Renee (CON - Lostock Hall)

Clark, Colin (CON - Longton & Hutton West)
cllr.cclark@southribble.gov.uk

Coulton, Colin (CON - Longton & Hutton West)
cllr.ccoulton@southribble.gov.uk

Evans, William (LAB - Earnshaw Bridge)
cllr.wevans@southribble.gov.uk

Forrest, Derek (LAB - Leyland Central)
cllr.dforrest@southribble.gov.uk

Foster, Paul (LAB - Bamber Bridge West)
cllr.pfoster@southribble.gov.uk

Green, Michael (CON - Moss Side)
cllr.michael.green@southribble.gov.uk

Hamilton, Claire (LAB - Leyland Central)

Hancock, Harold (LD - Broad Oak)

Hesketh, Jon (CON - Longton & Hutton West)
cllr.jhesketh@southribble.gov.uk

Heyworth, Fred (LAB - Seven Stars)
cllr.fheyworth@southribble.gov.uk

Higgins, Mick (LAB - Bamber Bridge East)
cllr.mhiggins@southribble.gov.uk

Howarth, David (LD - Howick & Priory)
cllr.dhowarth@southribble.gov.uk

Hughes, Cliff (CON - Lostock Hall)
cllr.chughes@southribble.gov.uk

Jones, Susan (LAB - Leyland St Ambrose)
cllr.sjones@southribble.gov.uk

Jones, Kenneth (LAB - St Ambrose)
cllr.kjones@southribble.gov.uk

Marsh, James (CON - Coupe Green & Gregson Lane)
cllr.jmarsh@southribble.gov.uk

Martin, Keith (LAB - Middleforth)
cllr.kmartin@southribble.gov.uk

Moon, Caroline (CON - Buckshaw & Worden)
cllr.cmoon@southribble.gov.uk

Mort, Jacqueline (CON - Lostock Hall)
cllr.jmort@southribble.gov.uk

Mullineaux, Peter (CON - Samlesbury & Walton)
cllr.pmullineaux@southribble.gov.uk

Nathan, Michael (CON - Walton-le-Dale West)

Nelson, Michael (CON - Walton-le-Dale West)
cllr.mnelson@southribble.gov.uk

Noblet, Rebecca (CON - Howick & Priory)
cllr.rnoblet@southribble.gov.uk

Ogilvie, Alan (CON - Buckshaw & Worden)
cllr.aogilvie@southribble.gov.uk

Patten, James (LAB - Middleforth)
cllr.jpatten@southribble.gov.uk

Rainsbury, John (CON - Hoole)
cllr.jrainsbury@southribble.gov.uk

Smith, Phil (CON - New Longton & Hutton East)
cllr.psmith@southribble.gov.uk

Snape, Susan (CON - Earnshaw Bridge)

Suthers, David (CON - Hoole)
cllr.dsuthers@southribble.gov.uk

Titherington, Michael (LAB - Broadfield)
cllr.mtitherington@southribble.gov.uk

Tomlinson, Matthew (LAB - Broadfield)
cllr.mtomlinson@southribble.gov.uk

SOUTH RIBBLE

Tomlinson, Caleb (LAB - Bamber Bridge West)
cllr.ctomlinson@southribble.gov.uk

Walton, Graham (CON - Farington West)
cllr.gwalton@southribble.gov.uk

Walton, Karen (CON - Farington West)

Watkinson, Ian (LAB - Charnock)

Watts, David (LAB - Bamber Bridge East)
cllr.dwatts@southribble.gov.uk

Wharton, Paul (CON - Farington East)

Woodcock, Jonathan (LAB - Farington East)

Wooldridge, David (LAB - Middleforth)

Yates, Barrie (CON - Samlesbury & Walton)
cllr.byates@southribble.gov.uk

POLITICAL COMPOSITION
CON: 28, LAB: 18, LD: 2

COMMITTEE CHAIRS
Licensing: Mr John Rainsbury

Planning: Mr Jon Hesketh

South Somerset D

South Somerset District Council, Council Offices, Brympton Way, Yeovil BA20 2HT
☎ 01935 462462 🖷 01935 462188 ✉ ssdc@southsomerset.gov.uk
💻 www.southsomerset.gov.uk

FACTS AND FIGURES
Parliamentary Constituencies: Somerton and Frome, Yeovil
EU Constituencies: South West
Election Frequency: Elections are of whole council

PRINCIPAL OFFICERS
Chief Executive: Mr Mark Williams , Chief Executive, South Somerset & East Devon District Councils, Council Offices, Brympton Way, Yeovil BA20 2HT ☎ 01395 571695 🖷 01395 517507 ✉ mwilliams@eastdevon.gov.uk

Senior Management: Mrs Rina Singh, Strategic Director - Place & Performance, Council Offices, Brympton Way, Yeovil BA20 2HT ☎ 01935 462462 🖷 01935 462188 ✉ rina.singh@southsomerset.gov.uk

Senior Management: Ms Vega Sturgess, Strategic Director - Operations & Customer Focus, Council Offices, Brympton Way, Yeovil BA20 2HT ☎ 01935 462462 ✉ vega.sturgess@southsomerset.gov.uk

Architect, Building / Property Services: Mr Garry Green, Engineering & Property Services Manager, Council Offices, Brympton Way, Yeovil BA20 2HT ☎ 01935 462462 🖷 01935 462248 ✉ garry.green@southsomerset.gov.uk

Best Value: Mrs Rina Singh, Strategic Director - Place & Performance, Council Offices, Brympton Way, Yeovil BA20 2HT ☎ 01935 462462 🖷 01935 462188 ✉ rina.singh@southsomerset.gov.uk

Building Control: Mr David Durrant , Building Control Manager, Houndstone Close, Abbey Manor Park, Taunton BA20 1AS ☎ 01935 462462 🖷 01935 412955 ✉ david.durrant@southsomerset.gov.uk

PR / Communications: Mr Martin Hacker , Communications Officer, Council Offices, Brympton Way, Yeovil BA20 2HT ☎ 01935 462462 🖷 01935 462503 ✉ martin.hacker@southsomerset.gov.uk

PR / Communications: Mrs Mary Ostler , Media & Communications Officer, Council Offices, Brympton Way, Yeovil BA20 2HT ☎ 01935 462462 🖷 01935 462188 ✉ mary.ostler@southsomerset.gov.uk

Community Planning: Mrs Helen Rutter , Assistant Director - Communities, Church Field, Wincanton BA9 9AG ☎ 01963 435012 ✉ helen.rutter@southsomerset.gov.uk

Community Safety: Mr Steve Brewer, Community Safety Co-ordinator, Council Offices, Brympton Way, Yeovil BA20 2HT ☎ 01935 462462 🖷 01935 462503 ✉ steve.brewer@southsomerset.gov.uk

Computer Management: Mr Roger Brown , ICT Manager, Council Offices, Brympton Way, Yeovil BA20 2HT ☎ 01935 462462 🖷 01935 462188 ✉ roger.brown@southsomerset.gov.uk

Corporate Services: Mr Ian Clarke, Assistant Director - Legal & Corporate Services, Council Offices, Brympton Way, Yeovil BA20 2HT ☎ 01935 462462 🖷 01935 462188 ✉ ian.clarke@southsomerset.gov.uk

Customer Service: Mr Jason Toogood , Customer Services Manager, Council Offices, Brympton Way, Yeovil BA20 2HT ☎ 01935 462462 🖷 01935 462188 ✉ jason.toogood@southsomerset.gov.uk

Direct Labour: Mr Chris Cooper, Streetscene Manager, South Somerset Direct Services, 7 Artillery Road, Luton Trading Estate, Yeovil BA22 8RP ☎ 01935 462462 🖷 01935 477107 ✉ chris.cooper@southsomerset.gov.uk

Economic Development: Mr David Julian , Economic Development Manager, Council Offices, Brympton Way, Yeovil BA20 2HT ☎ 01935 462462 🖷 01935 462188 ✉ david.julian@southsomerset.gov.uk

Economic Development: Mr Martin Woods , Assistant Director - Economy, Council Offices, Brympton Way, Yeovil BA20 2HT ☎ 01935 462462 🖷 01935 462503 ✉ martin.woods@southsomerset.gov.uk

E-Government: Mr Roger Brown , ICT Manager, Council Offices, Brympton Way, Yeovil BA20 2HT ☎ 01935 462462 🖷 01935 462188 ✉ roger.brown@southsomerset.gov.uk

Electoral Registration: Mr Roger Quantock, Senior Democractic Services Officer, Council Offices, Brympton Way, Yeovil BA20 2HT ☎ 01935 462462 🖷 01935 462188 ✉ roger.quantock@southsomerset.gov.uk

Emergency Planning: Ms Pam Harvey, Emergency Planning Officer, Council Offices, Brympton Way, Yeovil BA20 2HT ☎ 01935 462462 🖶 01935 462503 🖰 pharvey@eastdevon.gov.uk

Energy Management: Mr Keith Wheaton-Green, Environmental Performance Manager, Council Offices, Brympton Way, Yeovil BA20 2HT ☎ 01935 462462 🖶 01935 462503 🖰 keith.wheaton-green@southsomerset.gov.uk

Environmental Health: Mr Laurence Willis , Assistant Director - Environment, Council Offices, Brympton Way, Yeovil BA20 2HT ☎ 01935 462462 🖶 01935 412955 🖰 laurence.willis@southsomerset.gov.uk

Estates, Property & Valuation: Mr Garry Green, Engineering & Property Services Manager, Council Offices, Brympton Way, Yeovil BA20 2HT ☎ 01935 462462 🖶 01935 462248 🖰 garry.green@southsomerset.gov.uk

Facilities: Mr Garry Green, Engineering & Property Services Manager, Council Offices, Brympton Way, Yeovil BA20 2HT ☎ 01935 462462 🖶 01935 462248 🖰 garry.green@southsomerset.gov.uk

Finance: Ms Donna Parham, Assistant Director - Financial & Corporate Services, Council Offices, Brympton Way, Yeovil BA20 2HT ☎ 01935 462462 🖶 01935 462188 🖰 donna.parham@southsomerset.gov.uk

Fleet Management: Ms Niki Atkins, Fleet Service Supervisor, Lufton Depot, 7 Artillery Road, Yeovil BA22 8RP ☎ 01935 462462 🖶 01935 462188 🖰 niki.atkins@southsomerset.gov.uk

Grounds Maintenance: Mr Chris Cooper, Streetscene Manager, South Somerset Direct Services, 7 Artillery Road, Luton Trading Estate, Yeovil BA22 8RP ☎ 01935 462462 🖶 01935 477107 🖰 chris.cooper@southsomerset.gov.uk

Health and Safety: Ms Pam Harvey, Emergency Planning Officer, Council Offices, Brympton Way, Yeovil BA20 2HT ☎ 01935 462462 🖶 01935 462503 🖰 pharvey@eastdevon.gov.uk

Home Energy Conservation: Mr Martin Chapman , Principal Housing Standards Officer, Unit 10 Bridge Barns, Long Sutton TA10 9PZ ☎ 01935 462462 🖰 martin.chapman@southsomerset.gov.uk

Housing: Mr Colin McDonald, Strategic Housing Manager, Council Offices, Brympton Way, Yeovil BA20 2HT ☎ 01935 462462 🖰 colin.mcdonald@southsomerset.gov.uk

Legal: Mr Ian Clarke, Assistant Director - Legal & Corporate Services, Council Offices, Brympton Way, Yeovil BA20 2HT ☎ 01935 462462 🖶 01935 462188 🖰 ian.clarke@southsomerset.gov.uk

Legal: Ms Lynda Creek , Head of Legal Services, Council Offices, Brympton Way, Yeovil BA20 2HT 🖰 lynda.creek@southsomerset.gov.uk

Leisure and Cultural Services: Ms Lynda Pincombe, Community Health & Leisure Manager, Council Offices, Brympton Way, Yeovil BA20 2HT ☎ 01935 462462 🖰 lynda.pincombe@southsomerset.gov.uk

Licensing: Mr Nigel Marston , Licensing Manager, Council Offices, Brympton Way, Yeovil BA20 2HT ☎ 01935 462462 🖶 01935 462188 🖰 nigel.marston@southsomerset.gov.uk

Lottery Funding, Charity and Voluntary: Mr David Crisfield , Third Sector & Partnership Co-ordinator, Council Offices, Brympton Way, Yeovil BA20 2HT ☎ 01935 462462 🖰 david.crisfield@southsomerset.gov.uk

Member Services: Ms Angela Cox , Democratic Services Manager, Council Offices, Brympton Way, Yeovil BA20 2HT ☎ 01935 462462 🖶 01935 462188 🖰 angela.cox@southsomerset.gov.uk

Parking: Mr Garry Green, Engineering & Property Services Manager, Council Offices, Brympton Way, Yeovil BA20 2HT ☎ 01935 462462 🖶 01935 462248 🖰 garry.green@southsomerset.gov.uk

Partnerships: Mr David Crisfield , Third Sector & Partnership Co-ordinator, Council Offices, Brympton Way, Yeovil BA20 2HT ☎ 01935 462462 🖰 david.crisfield@southsomerset.gov.uk

Personnel / HR: Mr Mike Holliday, Human Resources & Performance Manager, Council Offices, Brympton Way, Yeovil BA20 2HT ☎ 01935 462462 🖶 01935 462188 🖰 mike.holliday@southsomerset.gov.uk

Planning: Mr David Norris , Development Control Manager, Council Offices, Brympton Way, Yeovil BA20 2HT ☎ 01935 462462 🖰 david.norris@southsomerset.gov.uk

Procurement: Mr Gary Russ, Procurement & Risk Manager, Council Offices, Brympton Way, Yeovil BA20 2HT ☎ 01935 462462 🖶 01935 462188 🖰 gary.russ@southsomerset.gov.uk

Recycling & Waste Minimisation: Mr Dave Mansell , Recycling Development Officer, Somerset County Council, County Hall, Taunton TA1 4DY ☎ 01823 356013 🖰 dgmansell@somerset.gov.uk

Regeneration: Mr David Julian , Economic Development Manager, Council Offices, Brympton Way, Yeovil BA20 2HT ☎ 01935 462462 🖶 01935 462188 🖰 david.julian@southsomerset.gov.uk

Staff Training: Mr Mike Holliday, Human Resources & Performance Manager, Council Offices, Brympton Way, Yeovil BA20 2HT ☎ 01935 462462 🖶 01935 462188 🖰 mike.holliday@southsomerset.gov.uk

Street Scene: Mr Chris Cooper, Streetscene Manager, South Somerset Direct Services, 7 Artillery Road, Luton Trading Estate, Yeovil BA22 8RP ☎ 01935 462462 🖶 01935 477107 🖰 chris.cooper@southsomerset.gov.uk

Sustainable Communities: Mr Paul Wheatley , Spatial Policy Manager, Council Offices, Brympton Way, Yeovil BA20 2HT ☎ 01935 462462 🖰 paul.wheatley@southsomerset.gov.uk

Tourism: Mr David Julian , Economic Development Manager, Council Offices, Brympton Way, Yeovil BA20 2HT ☎ 01935 462462 🖶 01935 462188 🖰 david.julian@southsomerset.gov.uk

SOUTH SOMERSET

Transport: Mr Nigel Collins, Transport Strategy Officer, Council Offices, Brympton Way, Yeovil BA20 2HT ☎ 01935 462462 🖷 01935 462188 nigel.collins@southsomerset.gov.uk

Transport Planner: Mr Nigel Collins, Transport Strategy Officer, Council Offices, Brympton Way, Yeovil BA20 2HT ☎ 01935 462462 🖷 01935 462188 nigel.collins@southsomerset.gov.uk

Children's Play Areas: Mr Rob Parr , Senior Play & Youth Facilities Officer, Council Offices, Brympton Way, Yeovil BA20 2HT ☎ 01935 462462 rob.parr@southsomerset.gov.uk

COUNCILLORS

***Chair* Best**, Mike (LD - Crewkerne)
mike.best@southsomerset.gov.uk

***Leader of the Council* Pallister**, Ric (LD - Parrett)
ric.pallister@southsomerset.gov.uk

Aparicio Paul, Clare (CON - Langport & Huish)
clare.apariciopaul@southsomerset.gov.uk

Baker, Jason (LD - Holyrood (Chard))
jason.baker@southsomerset.gov.uk

Bakewell, Cathy (LD - Coker)
cathy.bakewell@southsomerset.gov.uk

Barrett, Marcus (CON - Crewkerne)
marcus.barrett@southsomerset.gov.uk

Beech, Mike (CON - Tower)
mike.beech@southsomerset.gov.uk

Bloomfield, Neil (CON - Martock)
neil.bloomfield@southsomerset.gov.uk

Broom, Amanda (CON - Combe (Chard))
amanda.broom@southsomerset.gov.uk

Bulmer, Dave (IND - Jocelyn (Chard))
dave.bulmer@southsomerset.gov.uk

Capozzoli, Tony (IND - Ivelchester)
tony.capozzoli@southsomerset.gov.uk

Clark, John (LD - Yeovil (West))
john.clark@southsomerset.gov.uk

Colbert, Nick (CON - Wincanton)
nick.colbert@southsomerset.gov.uk

Dance, Adam (LD - South Petherton)
adam.dance@southsomerset.gov.uk

Dibben, Gye (CON - Yeovil Without)
gye.dibben@southsomerset.gov.uk

Dyke-Bracher, Sarah (LD - Milborne Port)
sarah.dyke-bracher@southsomerset.gov.uk

Field, John (CON - Yeovil (South))
john.field@southsomerset.gov.uk

Gage, Nigel (CON - Yeovil (South))
nigel.gage@southsomerset.gov.uk

Goodall, Carol (LD - Ilminster)
carol.goodall@southsomerset.gov.uk

Groskop, Anna (CON - Bruton)
anna.groskop@southsomerset.gov.uk

Gubbins, Peter (LD - Yeovil (Central))
peter.gubbins@southsomerset.gov.uk

Hobhouse, Henry (LD - Cary)
henry.hobhouse@southsomerset.gov.uk

Hussain, Kaysar (LD - Yeovil (Central))
kaysar.hussain@southsomerset.gov.uk

Inglefield, Tim (CON - Blackmoor Vale)
tim.inglefield@southsomerset.gov.uk

Keitch, Val (LD - Ilminster Town)
val.keitch@southsomerset.gov.uk

Kendall, Andy (LD - Yeovil (Central))
andy.kendall@southsomerset.gov.uk

Kenton, Jenny (LD - Crimchard (Chard))
jenny.kenton@southsomerset.gov.uk

Lewis, Mike (CON - Camelot)
michael.lewis@southsomerset.gov.uk

Lindsay, Sarah (CON - Brympton)
sarah.lindsay@southsomerset.gov.uk

Lock, Mike (LD - Yeovil Without)
mike.lock@southsomerset.gov.uk

Lock, Tony (LD - Yeovil (East))
tony.lock@southsomerset.gov.uk

Maxwell, Paul (LD - Eggwood)
paul.maxwell@southsomerset.gov.uk

McAllister, Sam (CON - Yeovil (South))
sam.mcallister@southsomerset.gov.uk

Middleton, Graham (CON - Martock)
graham.middleton@southsomerset.gov.uk

Norris, David (CON - Wessex)
david.norrisclIr@southsomerset.gov.uk

Oakes, Graham (LD - Yeovil Without)
graham.oakes@southsomerset.gov.uk

Osborne, Tiffany (CON - Curry Rivel)
tiffany.osborne@southsomerset.gov.uk

Page, Stephen (LD - Wessex)
stephen.page@southsomerset.gov.uk

Pledger, Shane (CON - Turn Hill)
shane.pledger@southsomerset.gov.uk

Raikes, Crispin (LD - South Petherton)
crispin.raikes@southsomerset.gov.uk

Read, Wes (CON - Yeovil (West))
wes.read@southsomerset.gov.uk

Recardo, David (LD - Yeovil (East))
david.recardo@southsomerset.gov.uk

Roundell Greene, Jo (LD - St Michael's)
jo.roundellgreene@southsomerset.gov.uk

Ruddle, Dean (CON - Wessex)
dean.ruddle@southsomerset.gov.uk

Seal, Sylvia (LD - Hamdon)
sylvia.seal@southsomerset.gov.uk

Seaton, Gina (CON - Coker)
gina.seaton@southsomerset.gov.uk

Seib, Peter (LD - Brympton)
peter.seib@southsomerset.gov.uk

Shortland, Garry (LD - Avishayes (Chard))
garry.shortland@southsomerset.gov.uk

Singleton, Angie (LD - Crewkerne Town)
angie.singleton@southsomerset.gov.uk

Smith, Alan (LD - Yeovil (West))
alan.smith@southsomerset.gov.uk

Steele, Sue (CON - Islemoor)
sue.steele@southsomerset.gov.uk

Stickland, Rob (LD - Yeovil (East))
rob.stickland@southsomerset.gov.uk

Turpin, Andrew (LD - Tatworth & Forton)
andrew.turpin@southsomerset.gov.uk

Vijeh, Linda (CON - Neroche)
linda.vijeh@southsomerset.gov.uk

Wale, Martin (CON - Combe (Chard))
martin.wale@southsomerset.gov.uk

Wallace, William (CON - Blackmoor Vale)
william.wallace@southsomerset.gov.uk

Weeks, Nick (CON - Cary)
nick.weeks@southsomerset.gov.uk

Winder, Colin (CON - Wincanton)
colin.winder@southsomerset.gov.uk

Yeomans, Derek (CON - Burrow Hill)
derek.yeomans@southsomerset.gov.uk

POLITICAL COMPOSITION
LD: 29, CON: 28, IND: 2

COMMITTEE CHAIRS
Audit: Mr Derek Yeomans

Licensing: Mr Martin Wale

South Staffordshire D

South Staffordshire District Council, Council Offices, Codsall WV8 1PX
☎ 01902 696000 🖷 01902 696800 ✉ info@sstaffs.gov.uk
💻 www.sstaffs.gov.uk

FACTS AND FIGURES
Parliamentary Constituencies: Staffordshire South
EU Constituencies: West Midlands
Election Frequency: Elections are of whole council

PRINCIPAL OFFICERS
Chief Executive: Mr Steve Winterflood, Chief Executive, Council Offices, Codsall WV8 1PX ☎ 01902 696700 🖷 01902 696805 ✉ s.winterflood@sstaffs.gov.uk

Deputy Chief Executive: Mr Dave Heywood, Deputy Chief Executive, Council Offices, Codsall WV8 1PX ☎ 01902 696100 🖷 01902 696805 ✉ d.heywood@sstaffs.gov.uk

Senior Management: Ms Frankie Cartwright , Director - Financial & Welfare Services, Council Offices, Codsall WV8 1PX ☎ 01902 696640 ✉ f.cartwright@sstaffs.gov.uk

Senior Management: Mr Andrew Johnson, Director - Planning & Strategic Services, Council Offices, Codsall WV8 1PX ☎ 01902 696457 ✉ a.johnson@sstaffs.gov.uk

Senior Management: Mr David Pattison , Director - Legal & Public Health Protection, Council Offices, Codsall WV8 1PX ☎ 01902 696132 🖷 01902 696448 ✉ d.pattison@sstaffs.gov.uk

Senior Management: Mrs Jackie Smith, Director - Environmental & Customer Services, Council Offices, Codsall WV8 1PX ☎ 01902 696463 ✉ j.smith@sstaffs.gov.uk

Architect, Building / Property Services: Mr Adam Hale , Architectural Facilities Manager, Council Offices, Codsall WV8 1PX ☎ 01902 696114 ✉ a.hale@sstaffs.gov.uk

Best Value: Ms Clodagh Peterson, Policy & Partnership Manager, Council Offices, Codsall WV8 1PX ☎ 01902 696424 ✉ c.peterson@sstaffs.gov.uk

Best Value: Mr Steve Winterflood, Chief Executive, Council Offices, Codsall WV8 1PX ☎ 01902 696700 🖷 01902 696805 ✉ s.winterflood@sstaffs.gov.uk

Building Control: Mrs Jackie Smith, Director of Environmental Services, Council Offices, Codsall WV8 1PX ☎ 01902 696463 ✉ j.smith@sstaffs.gov.uk

PR / Communications: Mr Dave Heywood, Deputy Chief Executive, Council Offices, Codsall WV8 1PX ☎ 01902 696100 🖷 01902 696805 ✉ d.heywood@sstaffs.gov.uk

PR / Communications: Mr Steve Winterflood, Chief Executive, Council Offices, Codsall WV8 1PX ☎ 01902 696700 🖷 01902 696805 ✉ s.winterflood@sstaffs.gov.uk

Community Planning: Mr Dave Heywood, Deputy Chief Executive, Council Offices, Codsall WV8 1PX ☎ 01902 696100 🖷 01902 696805 ✉ d.heywood@sstaffs.gov.uk

Community Safety: Mrs Maggie Quinn, Partnership & Locality Manager, Council Offices, Codsall WV8 1PX ☎ 01902 696530 🖷 01902 696800 ✉ m.quinn@sstaffs.gov.uk

Computer Management: Mrs Balvinder Heran , Head of Customer Access & Head of Joint ICT Business, Council Offices, Codsall WV8 1PX ☎ 01789 260470 ✉ b.heran@sstaffs.gov.uk

Corporate Services: Ms Clodagh Peterson, Policy & Partnership Manager, Council Offices, Codsall WV8 1PX ☎ 01902 696424 ✉ c.peterson@sstaffs.gov.uk

Customer Service: Mrs Jackie Smith, Director - Environmental & Customer Services, Council Offices, Codsall WV8 1PX ☎ 01902 696463 ✉ j.smith@sstaffs.gov.uk

Economic Development: Mr Andrew Johnson, Director - Planning & Strategic Services, Council Offices, Codsall WV8 1PX ☎ 01902 696457 ✉ a.johnson@sstaffs.gov.uk

SOUTH STAFFORDSHIRE

Economic Development: Mr Grant Mitchell, Strategic Development & Planning Manager, Council Offices, Codsall WV8 1PX ☎ 01902 696438 🖱 g.mitchell@sstaffs.gov.uk

E-Government: Mrs Balvinder Heran , Head of Customer Access & Head of Joint ICT Business, Council Offices, Codsall WV8 1PX ☎ 01789 260470 🖱 b.heran@sstaffs.gov.uk

Electoral Registration: Ms Clodagh Peterson, Policy & Partnership Manager, Council Offices, Codsall WV8 1PX ☎ 01902 696424 🖱 c.peterson@sstaffs.gov.uk

Emergency Planning: Mrs Jackie Smith, Director - Environmental & Customer Services, Council Offices, Codsall WV8 1PX ☎ 01902 696463 🖱 j.smith@sstaffs.gov.uk

Environmental / Technical Services: Mrs Jackie Smith, Director - Environmental & Customer Services, Council Offices, Codsall WV8 1PX ☎ 01902 696463 🖱 j.smith@sstaffs.gov.uk

Environmental Health: Mr John Gerring , Environmental Health Officer, Council Offices, Codsall WV8 1PX ☎ 01902 696205 🖱 j.gerring@sstaffs.gov.uk

Environmental Health: Mrs Jackie Smith, Director - Environmental & Customer Services, Council Offices, Codsall WV8 1PX ☎ 01902 696463 🖱 j.smith@sstaffs.gov.uk

Finance: Mrs Helen Ogram , Chief Finance Officer, Council Offices, Codsall WV8 1PX ☎ 01902 696608 🖷 01902 696800 🖱 h.ogram@sstaffs.gov.uk

Grounds Maintenance: Mrs Jackie Smith, Director - Environmental & Customer Services, Council Offices, Codsall WV8 1PX ☎ 01902 696463 🖱 j.smith@sstaffs.gov.uk

Health and Safety: Mr David Pattison , Director - Legal & Public Health Protection, Council Offices, Codsall WV8 1PX ☎ 01902 696132 🖷 01902 696448 🖱 d.pattison@sstaffs.gov.uk

Home Energy Conservation: Mrs Jackie Smith, Director - Environmental & Customer Services, Council Offices, Codsall WV8 1PX ☎ 01902 696463 🖱 j.smith@sstaffs.gov.uk

Housing: Mr Grant Mitchell, Strategic Development & Planning Manager, Council Offices, Codsall WV8 1PX ☎ 01902 696438 🖱 g.mitchell@sstaffs.gov.uk

Legal: Mr David Pattison , Director - Legal & Public Health Protection, Council Offices, Codsall WV8 1PX ☎ 01902 696132 🖷 01902 696448 🖱 d.pattison@sstaffs.gov.uk

Leisure and Cultural Services: Mrs Jackie Smith, Director - Environmental & Customer Services, Council Offices, Codsall WV8 1PX ☎ 01902 696463 🖱 j.smith@sstaffs.gov.uk

Licensing: Mr David Pattison , Director - Legal & Public Health Protection, Council Offices, Codsall WV8 1PX ☎ 01902 696132 🖷 01902 696448 🖱 d.pattison@sstaffs.gov.uk

Lighting: Mrs Jackie Smith, Director - Environmental & Customer Services, Council Offices, Codsall WV8 1PX ☎ 01902 696463 🖱 j.smith@sstaffs.gov.uk

Lighting: Mrs Jackie Smith, Director - Environmental & Customer Services, Council Offices, Codsall WV8 1PX ☎ 01902 696463 🖱 j.smith@sstaffs.gov.uk

Member Services: Mr Dave Heywood, Deputy Chief Executive, Council Offices, Codsall WV8 1PX ☎ 01902 696100 🖷 01902 696805 🖱 d.heywood@sstaffs.gov.uk

Parking: Mrs Jackie Smith, Director - Environmental & Customer Services, Council Offices, Codsall WV8 1PX ☎ 01902 696463 🖱 j.smith@sstaffs.gov.uk

Partnerships: Mr Dave Heywood, Deputy Chief Executive, Council Offices, Codsall WV8 1PX ☎ 01902 696100 🖷 01902 696805 🖱 d.heywood@sstaffs.gov.uk

Partnerships: Ms Clodagh Peterson, Policy & Partnership Manager, Council Offices, Codsall WV8 1PX ☎ 01902 696424 🖱 c.peterson@sstaffs.gov.uk

Personnel / HR: Mrs Wendy Bridgwater, Human Resources Manager, Council Offices, Codsall WV8 1PX ☎ 01902 696103 🖷 01902 696145 🖱 w.bridgwater@sstaffs.gov.uk

Planning: Mr Andrew Johnson, Director - Planning & Strategic Services, Council Offices, Codsall WV8 1PX ☎ 01902 696457 🖱 a.johnson@sstaffs.gov.uk

Procurement: Mr David Pattison , Director - Legal & Public Health Protection, Council Offices, Codsall WV8 1PX ☎ 01902 696132 🖷 01902 696448 🖱 d.pattison@sstaffs.gov.uk

Recycling & Waste Minimisation: Mr Shaun Alexander , Environmental Servcies Manager, Council Offices, Codsall WV8 1PX ☎ 01902 696406 🖱 s.alexander@sstaffs.gov.uk

Recycling & Waste Minimisation: Mrs Jackie Smith, Director - Environmental & Customer Services, Council Offices, Codsall WV8 1PX ☎ 01902 696463 🖱 j.smith@sstaffs.gov.uk

Regeneration: Mr Andrew Johnson, Director - Planning & Strategic Services, Council Offices, Codsall WV8 1PX ☎ 01902 696457 🖱 a.johnson@sstaffs.gov.uk

Regeneration: Mr Grant Mitchell, Strategic Development & Planning Manager, Council Offices, Codsall WV8 1PX ☎ 01902 696438 🖱 g.mitchell@sstaffs.gov.uk

Staff Training: Mrs Wendy Bridgwater, Human Resources Manager, Council Offices, Codsall WV8 1PX ☎ 01902 696103 🖷 01902 696145 🖱 w.bridgwater@sstaffs.gov.uk

Sustainable Communities: Mr Andrew Johnson, Director - Planning & Strategic Services, Council Offices, Codsall WV8 1PX ☎ 01902 696457 🖱 a.johnson@sstaffs.gov.uk

Tourism: Mr Andrew Johnson, Director - Planning & Strategic Services, Council Offices, Codsall WV8 1PX ☎ 01902 696457 ✉ a.johnson@sstaffs.gov.uk

Tourism: Mr Grant Mitchell, Strategic Development & Planning Manager, Council Offices, Codsall WV8 1PX ☎ 01902 696438 ✉ g.mitchell@sstaffs.gov.uk

COUNCILLORS

Leader of the Council **Edwards**, Brian (CON - Kinver)
b.edwards@sstaffs.gov.uk

Deputy Leader of the Council **Lees**, Roger (CON - Himley and Swindon)
r.lees@sstaffs.gov.uk

Ashley, Jeff (LAB - Huntington and Hatherton)
j.ashley@sstaffs.gov.uk

Barrow, Meg (CON - Codsall North)
m.barrow@sstaffs.gov.uk

Bates, Brian (CON - Great Wyrley Town)
b.bates@sstaffs.gov.uk

Bates, Leonard (CON - Penkridge North East and Acton Trussell)
l.bates@sstaffs.gov.uk

Bolton, Joyce (CON - Brewood and Coven)

Bond, Mary (CON - Wombourne South West)
m.bond@sstaffs.gov.uk

Bond, Barry (CON - Wombourne North and Lower Penn)
b.bond@sstaffs.gov.uk

Bourke, Anthony (IND - Perton East)
a.bourke@sstaffs.gov.uk

Caine, Nigel (CON - Perton Lakeside)
n.caine@sstaffs.gov.uk

Cartwright, Donald (CON - Penkridge West)
d.cartwright@sstaffs.gov.uk

Chapman, Val (CON - Bilbrook)
v.chapman@sstaffs.gov.uk

Clifft, David (IND - Essington)
d.clifft@sstaffs.gov.uk

Cope, Robert (IND - Featherstone and Shareshill)
r.cope@sstaffs.gov.uk

Cox, Brian (CON - Wheaton Aston, Bishopswood and Lapley)
b.cox@sstaffs.gov.uk

Davies, Michael (CON - Wombourne South West)
m.davies@sstaffs.gov.uk

Emery, Lisa (CON - Cheslyn Hay North and Saredon)
l.emery@sstaffs.gov.uk

Ewart, Matthew (CON - Codsall North)
m.ewart@sstaffs.gov.uk

Fieldhouse, Paul (CON - Bilbrook)
p.fieldhouse@sstaffs.gov.uk

Ford, Isabel (CON - Penkridge North East and Acton Trussell)
i.ford@sstaffs.gov.uk

Heseltine, Rita (CON - Perton Lakeside)
r.heseltine@sstaffs.gov.uk

Hingley, Lin (CON - Kinver)
l.hingley@sstaffs.gov.uk

Hinton, Alan (CON - Wombourne North and Lower Penn)
a.hinton@sstaffs.gov.uk

Hollis, Steve (UKIP - Cheslyn Hay North and Saredon)
s.hollis@sstaffs.gov.uk

Holmes, Diane (CON - Brewood and Coven)
d.holmes@sstaffs.gov.uk

James, Keith (CON - Perton Dippons)
k.james@sstaffs.gov.uk

Johnson, Janet (CON - Great Wyrley Town)
j.johnson@sstaffs.gov.uk

Lever, Peter (IND - Essington)
p.lever@sstaffs.gov.uk

Lobuczek, Henryk (CON - Featherstone and Shareshill)
h.lobuczek@sstaffs.gov.uk

Lockley, Dave (CON - Cheslyn Hay South)
d.lockley@sstaffs.gov.uk

Marshall, Robert (CON - Codsall South)
r.marshall@sstaffs.gov.uk

Mason, Terry (CON - Pattingham and Patshull)
t.mason@sstaffs.gov.uk

McCardle, Robert (CON - Trysull and Seisdon)
r.mccardle@sstaffs.gov.uk

Michell, John (CON - Codsall South)
j.michell@sstaffs.gov.uk

Moreton, Roy (CON - Perton Lakeside)
r.moreton@sstaffs.gov.uk

Perry, Raymond (CON - Great Wyrley Landywood)
r.perry@sstaffs.gov.uk

Perry, Kathleen (CON - Great Wyrley Town)
k.perry@sstaffs.gov.uk

Raven, Christine (CON - Penkridge South East)
c.raven@sstaffs.gov.uk

Raven, John (CON - Penkridge South East)
j.raven@sstaffs.gov.uk

Reade, Robert (CON - Wombourne North and Lower Penn)

Sutton, Wendy (CON - Brewood and Coven)
w.sutton@sstaffs.gov.uk

Upton, Ken (CON - Wombourne South East)
k.upton@sstaffs.gov.uk

Williams, Reginald (CON - Wombourne South East)
r.williams@sstaffs.gov.uk

Williams, Kathleen (CON - Great Wyrley Landywood)
k.williams@sstaffs.gov.uk

Williams, Henry (CON - Kinver)
h.williams@sstaffs.gov.uk

Williams, Bernard (CON - Cheslyn Hay South)
b.williams@sstaffs.gov.uk

Williams, David (CON - Huntington and Hatherton)
d.williams@sstaffs.gov.uk

Wright, Royston (CON - Wheaton Aston, Bishopswood and Lapley)
r.wright@sstaffs.gov.uk

POLITICAL COMPOSITION

CON: 43, IND: 4, LAB: 1, UKIP: 1

SOUTH STAFFORDSHIRE

COMMITTEE CHAIRS

Audit: Mr John Michell

Licensing: Mr Roy Moreton

Planning: Mr Brian Cox

South Tyneside M

South Tyneside Council, Town Hall and Civic Offices, Westoe Road, South Shields NE33 2RL
☎ 0191 427 1717 🖷 0191 455 0208 💻 www.southtyneside.info

FACTS AND FIGURES

Parliamentary Constituencies: Jarrow, South Shields
EU Constituencies: North East
Election Frequency: Elections are by thirds

PRINCIPAL OFFICERS

Chief Executive: Mr Martin Swales , Chief Executive, Town Hall and Civic Offices, Westoe Road, South Shields NE33 2RL
✉ martin.swales@southtyneside.gov.uk

Senior Management: Mr David Cramond , Corporate Director of Economic Regeneration, Town Hall and Civic Offices, Westoe Road, South Shields NE33 2RL ☎ 0191 424 7969
✉ David.Cramond@southtyneside.gov.uk

Senior Management: Mr John Hewitt , Corporate Director of Business & Resources, Town Hall and Civic Offices, Westoe Road, South Shields NE33 2RL ☎ 0191 424 7499

Senior Management: Ms Helen Watson , Corporate Director of Children, Adults & Families, Town Hall and Civic Offices, Westoe Road, South Shields NE33 2RL ☎ 0191 424 7701 🖷 0191 427 0584
✉ helen.watson@southtyneside.gov.uk

Architect, Building / Property Services: Mr Paul Scrafton , Head of Asset Management, Town Hall and Civic Offices, Westoe Road, South Shields NE33 2RL ☎ 0191 424 7235
✉ paul.scrafton@southtyneside.gov.uk

Best Value: Ms Rachel Davison , Corporate Performance & Information Manager, Town Hall and Civic Offices, Westoe Road, South Shields NE33 2RL ☎ 0191 424 7546
✉ rachel.davison@southtyneside.gov.uk

Building Control: Mr George Mansbridge , Head of Development Services, Town Hall and Civic Offices, Westoe Road, South Shields NE33 2RL ☎ 0191 424 7566 🖷 0191 427 7171
✉ george.mansbridge@southtyneside.gov.uk

Catering Services: Ms Elizabeth Luke, Catering Services Manager, Town Hall and Civic Offices, Westoe Road, South Shields NE33 2RL ☎ 0191 424 6710 ✉ elizabeth.luke@southtyneside.gov.uk

Children / Youth Services: Mrs Karen Pemberton , Strategic Lead - Schools Organisation & Children's Centres, Town Hall and Civic Offices, Westoe Road, South Shields NE33 2RL
☎ 0191 424 6597 ✉ karen.pemberton@southtyneside.gov.uk

Children / Youth Services: Ms Helen Watson , Corporate Director of Children, Adults & Families, Town Hall and Civic Offices, Westoe Road, South Shields NE33 2RL ☎ 0191 424 7701
🖷 0191 427 0584 ✉ helen.watson@southtyneside.gov.uk

Civil Registration: Mr Mike Harding , Head of Legal Services, Town Hall & Civic Offices, Westoe Road, South Shields NE33 2RL ☎ 0191 424 7009 🖷 0191 455 0208 ✉ mike.harding@southtyneside.gov.uk

Civil Registration: Mrs Jacqueline Todd , Service Lead of Democratic Services, Town Hall and Civic Offices, Westoe Road, South Shields NE33 2RL ☎ 0191 424 6352
✉ jacqueline.todd@southtyneside.gov.uk

PR / Communications: Ms Tania Robinson , Head of Marketing & Communications, Town Hall and Civic Offices, Westoe Road, South Shields NE33 2RL ☎ 0191 424 7817
✉ tania.robinson@southtyneside.gov.uk

Community Planning: Mr Peter Mennell , Housing & Planning Growth Manager, Town Hall and Civic Offices, Westoe Road, South Shields NE33 2RL ☎ 0191 424 7646
✉ peter.mennell@southtyneside.gov.uk

Community Safety: Mr Dave Owen, Area Crime & Justice Co-ordinator, Town Hall and Civic Offices, Westoe Road, South Shields NE33 2RL ☎ 0191 424 7938 ✉ dave.owen@southtyneside.gov.uk

Computer Management: Mr Stuart Reid , Head of Finance, South Tyneside Council, Town Hall & Civic Offices, Westoe Road, South Shields NE33 2RL ☎ 0191 424 7765
✉ stuart.reid@southtyneside.gov.uk

Consumer Protection and Trading Standards: Mr Stuart Wright, Regulatory Services Manager, Town Hall and Civic Offices, Westoe Road, South Shields NE33 2RL ☎ 0191 424 7869
✉ stuart.wright@southtyneside.gov.uk

Contracts: Mr Mike Conlon , Head of Corporate & Commercial Services, Town Hall and Civic Offices, Westoe Road, South Shields NE33 2RL ☎ 0191 424 7765 ✉ mike.conlon@southtyneside.gov.uk

Corporate Services: Mr Dan Jackson , Strategy & Democracy Manager, Town Hall and Civic Offices, Westoe Road, South Shields NE33 2RL ☎ 0191 424 7771 ✉ dan.jackson@southtyneside.gov.uk

Corporate Services: Mrs Hayley Johnson , Corporate Lead of Strategy & Performance, Town Hall & Civic Offices, Westoe Road, South Shields NE33 2RL ☎ 0191 4271717
✉ hayley.johnson@southtyneside.gov.uk

Customer Service: Ms Helen Anthony , Customer Service Lead, Town Hall and Civic Offices, Westoe Road, South Shields NE33 2RL ☎ 0161 424 6601 ✉ helen.anthony@southtyneside.gov.uk

Economic Development: Mr David Cramond , Corporate Director of Economic Regeneration, Town Hall and Civic Offices, Westoe Road, South Shields NE33 2RL ☎ 0191 424 7969
✉ David.Cramond@southtyneside.gov.uk

Economic Development: Mr John Scott , Corporate Lead of Business, Employment & Skills, Town Hall and Civic Offices, Westoe Road, South Shields NE33 2RL ☎ 0191 424 6250 ✉ john.scott@southtyneside.gov.uk

Education: Mr Peter Cutts , Head of Education, Learning & Skills, Town Hall and Civic Offices, Westoe Road, South Shields NE33 2RL ☎ 0191 424 7697 ✉ peter.cutts@southtyneside.gov.uk

Electoral Registration: Ms Joanne Gelson , Elections Manager, Town Hall and Civic Offices, Westoe Road, South Shields NE33 2RL ☎ 0191 4247169 🖷 0191 455 0208 ✉ joanne.gelson@southtyneside.gov.uk

Emergency Planning: Mr Tony Hanson , Environmental Health Manager, Town Hall and Civic Offices, Westoe Road, South Shields NE33 2RL ☎ 0191 424 7901 ✉ tony.hanson@southtyneside.gov.uk

Energy Management: Mr Paul Scrafton , Head of Asset Management, Town Hall and Civic Offices, Westoe Road, South Shields NE33 2RL ☎ 0191 424 7235 ✉ paul.scrafton@southtyneside.gov.uk

Environmental / Technical Services: Mr George Mansbridge , Head of Development Services, Town Hall and Civic Offices, Westoe Road, South Shields NE33 2RL ☎ 0191 424 7566 🖷 0191 427 7171 ✉ george.mansbridge@southtyneside.gov.uk

Environmental Health: Mr George Mansbridge , Head of Development Services, Town Hall and Civic Offices, Westoe Road, South Shields NE33 2RL ☎ 0191 424 7566 🖷 0191 427 7171 ✉ george.mansbridge@southtyneside.gov.uk

Estates, Property & Valuation: Mr Paul Scrafton , Head of Asset Management, Town Hall and Civic Offices, Westoe Road, South Shields NE33 2RL ☎ 0191 424 7235 ✉ paul.scrafton@southtyneside.gov.uk

Events Manager: Mr Richard Jago , Business Development Manager, Town Hall and Civic Offices, Westoe Road, South Shields NE33 2RL ☎ 0191 424 7984 ✉ rich.jago@southtyneside.gov.uk

Facilities: Mr Paul Mossa , Corporate Facilities Manager, Town Hall and Civic Offices, Westoe Road, South Shields NE33 2RL ☎ 0191 424 7241 ✉ paul.mossa@southtyneside.gov.uk

Finance: Mr Stephen Moore , Head of Pensions, Hebburn Civic Centre, Campbell Park Road, Hebburn NE31 2SW ☎ 0191 424 4119 ✉ stephen.moore@southtyneside.gov.uk

Finance: Mr Stuart Reid , Head of Finance, South Tyneside Council, Town Hall & Civic Offices, Westoe Road, South Shields NE33 2RL ☎ 0191 424 7765 ✉ stuart.reid@southtyneside.gov.uk

Pensions: Mr Ian Bainbridge , Principal Pension Investments Manager, Town Hall and Civic Offices, Westoe Road, South Shields NE33 2RL ☎ 0191 427 4112 ✉ ian.bainbridge@southtyneside.gov.uk

Pensions: Mr Stephen Moore , Head of Pensions, Hebburn Civic Centre, Campbell Park Road, Hebburn NE31 2SW ☎ 0191 424 4119 ✉ stephen.moore@southtyneside.gov.uk

Fleet Management: Mr Alan Wilson , Fleet Services Team Leader, Middlefields, South Shields NE34 0NT ☎ 0191 427 2021 ✉ alan.wilson@southtyneside.gov.uk

Grounds Maintenance: Mr Gary Kirsop , Director of Housing & Area Management, Strathmore, Jarrow NE32 3DP ☎ 0191 427 2557 ✉ Gary.kirsop@southtynesidehomes.org.uk

Health and Safety: Mr Graham Fells, HR Corporate Lead, Town Hall and Civic Offices, Westoe Road, South Shields NE33 2RL ☎ 0191 424 7323 ✉ graham.fells@southtyneside.gov.uk

Highways: Mr Dave Carr , Highways & Infrastructure Manager, Town Hall and Civic Offices, Westoe Road, South Shields NE33 2RL ☎ 0191 427 2553 ✉ dave.carr@southtyneside.gov.uk

Home Energy Conservation: Mrs Debra Ralph , Home Energy Officer, Strathmore, Jarrow NE32 3DP ☎ 0191 424 7902 ✉ debra.ralph@southtyneside.gov.uk

Housing: Mr Gary Kirsop , Director of Housing & Area Management, Middlefields, South Shields NE34 0NT ☎ 0191 427 2557 ✉ Gary.kirsop@southtynesidehomes.org.uk

Housing Maintenance: Mr Jason Crews , Head of Property Services, Middlefields, South Shields NE34 0NT ☎ 0191 427 2624 ✉ jason.crews@southtyneside.gov.uk

Legal: Mr Mike Harding , Head of Legal Services, Town Hall & Civic Offices, Westoe Road, South Shields NE33 2RL ☎ 0191 424 7009 🖷 0191 455 0208 ✉ mike.harding@southtyneside.gov.uk

Leisure and Cultural Services: Mr David Brooks , Corporate Lead - Culture & Leisure Services, Town Hall and Civic Offices, Westoe Road, South Shields NE33 2RL ☎ 0191 424 7570 🖷 0191 424 0469 ✉ david.brooks@southtyneside.gov.uk

Licensing: Mr George Mansbridge , Head of Planning, Housing, Transport & Regulatory Services, Town Hall and Civic Offices, Westoe Road, South Shields NE33 2RL ☎ 0191 4247566 ✉ george.mansbridge@southtyneside.gov.uk

Lifelong Learning: Mr Peter Cutts , Head of Education, Learning & Skills, Town Hall and Civic Offices, Westoe Road, South Shields NE33 2RL ☎ 0191 424 7697 ✉ peter.cutts@southtyneside.gov.uk

Lighting: Mr Paul Scrafton , Head of Asset Management, Town Hall and Civic Offices, Westoe Road, South Shields NE33 2RL ☎ 0191 424 7235 ✉ paul.scrafton@southtyneside.gov.uk

Member Services: Mr Dan Jackson , Strategy & Democracy Manager, Town Hall and Civic Offices, Westoe Road, South Shields NE33 2RL ☎ 0191 424 7771 ✉ dan.jackson@southtyneside.gov.uk

Parking: Mr Dave Pentland , Parking & Utilities Manager, Town Hall and Civic Offices, Westoe Road, South Shields NE33 2RL ☎ 0191 424 7617 ✉ dave.pentland@southtyneside.gov.uk

Partnerships: Mrs Hayley Johnson , Corporate Lead of Strategy & Performance, Town Hall & Civic Offices, Westoe Road, South Shields NE33 2RL ☎ 0191 4271717 ✉ hayley.johnson@southtyneside.gov.uk

SOUTH TYNESIDE

Personnel / HR: Mr Graham Fells, HR Corporate Lead, Town Hall and Civic Offices, Westoe Road, South Shields NE33 2RL ☎ 0191 424 7323 ✉ graham.fells@southtyneside.gov.uk

Planning: Mr George Mansbridge , Head of Development Services, Town Hall and Civic Offices, Westoe Road, South Shields NE33 2RL ☎ 0191 424 7566 🖷 0191 427 7171 ✉ george.mansbridge@southtyneside.gov.uk

Procurement: Mr Stuart Reid , Head of Finance, South Tyneside Council, Town Hall & Civic Offices, Westoe Road, South Shields NE33 2RL ☎ 0191 424 7765 ✉ stuart.reid@southtyneside.gov.uk

Public Libraries: Mrs Kathryn Armstrong , Library Manager, Central Library, South Shields NE33 2PE ☎ 0191 424 7884 ✉ kathryn.armstrong@southtyneside.gov.uk

Recycling & Waste Minimisation: Mr Bob Cummins, Waste & Recycling Team Leader, Town Hall and Civic Offices, Westoe Road, South Shields NE33 2RL ☎ 0191 427 2656 ✉ bob.cummins@southtyneside.gov.uk

Regeneration: Mr Rick O'Farrell, Head of Enterprise & Regeneration, Town Hall and Civic Offices, Westoe Road, South Shields NE33 2RL ☎ 0191 424 7541 ✉ rick.o'farrell@southtyneside.gov.uk

Road Safety: Ms Kim Quest-Law , Road Safety Co-ordinator, Town Hall and Civic Offices, Westoe Road, South Shields NE33 2RL ☎ 0191 424 7613 ✉ kim.quest-law@southtyneside.gov.uk

Social Services: Mrs Louise Caverhill , Acting Head of Adult Social Care, Town Hall and Civic Offices, Westoe Road, South Shields NE33 2RL ☎ 0191 424 7670 ✉ louise.caverhill@southtyneside.gov.uk

Social Services: Ms Jill McGregor , Head of Children & Families Social Care, Town Hall and Civic Offices, Westoe Road, South Shields NE33 2RL ☎ 0191 424 4749 🖷 0191 424 4614 ✉ jill.mcgregor@southtyneside.gov.uk

Social Services (Adult): Ms Helen Watson , Corporate Director of Children, Adults & Families, Town Hall and Civic Offices, Westoe Road, South Shields NE33 2RL ☎ 0191 424 7701 🖷 0191 427 0584 ✉ helen.watson@southtyneside.gov.uk

Social Services (Children): Ms Helen Watson , Corporate Director of Children, Adults & Families, Town Hall and Civic Offices, Westoe Road, South Shields NE33 2RL ☎ 0191 424 7701 🖷 0191 427 0584 ✉ helen.watson@southtyneside.gov.uk

Public Health: Ms Amanda Healy , Director - Public Health, Town Hall and Civic Offices, Westoe Road, South Shields NE33 2RL ☎ 0191 424 6678 ✉ amanda.healy@southtyneside.gov.uk

Staff Training: Mr Graham Fells, HR Corporate Lead, Town Hall and Civic Offices, Westoe Road, South Shields NE33 2RL ☎ 0191 424 7323 ✉ graham.fells@southtyneside.gov.uk

Street Scene: Mr Bob Cummins, Waste & Recycling Team Leader, Town Hall and Civic Offices, Westoe Road, South Shields NE33 2RL ☎ 0191 427 2656 ✉ bob.cummins@southtyneside.gov.uk

Tourism: Ms Tania Robinson , Head of Marketing & Communications, Town Hall and Civic Offices, Westoe Road, South Shields NE33 2RL ☎ 0191 424 7817

Town Centre: Mr John Scott , Corporate Lead of Business, Employment & Skills, Town Hall and Civic Offices, Westoe Road, South Shields NE33 2RL ☎ 0191 424 6250 ✉ john.scott@southtyneside.gov.uk

Traffic Management: Mr Dave Carr , Highways & Infrastructure Manager, Town Hall and Civic Offices, Westoe Road, South Shields NE33 2RL ☎ 0191 427 2553 ✉ dave.carr@southtyneside.gov.uk

Transport: Mr Andrew Whittaker, Corporate Lead - Area Management, Town Hall and Civic Offices, Westoe Road, South Shields NE33 2RL ☎ 0191 427 2063 🖷 0191 427 2061 ✉ andrew.whittaker@southtyneside.gov.uk

Transport Planner: Mr Andrew Whittaker, Corporate Lead - Area Management, Town Hall and Civic Offices, Westoe Road, South Shields NE33 2RL ☎ 0191 427 2063 🖷 0191 427 2061 ✉ andrew.whittaker@southtyneside.gov.uk

Waste Collection and Disposal: Mr Bob Cummins, Waste & Recycling Team Leader, Town Hall and Civic Offices, Westoe Road, South Shields NE33 2RL ☎ 0191 427 2656 ✉ bob.cummins@southtyneside.gov.uk

Waste Collection and Disposal: Mr Andrew Whittaker, Corporate Lead - Area Management, Town Hall and Civic Offices, Westoe Road, South Shields NE33 2RL ☎ 0191 427 2063 🖷 0191 427 2061 ✉ andrew.whittaker@southtyneside.gov.uk

Waste Management: Mr Andrew Whittaker, Corporate Lead - Area Management, Town Hall and Civic Offices, Westoe Road, South Shields NE33 2RL ☎ 0191 427 2063 🖷 0191 427 2061 ✉ andrew.whittaker@southtyneside.gov.uk

COUNCILLORS

***Mayor* Porthouse**, Richard (LAB - Hebburn North)
cllr.richard.porthouse@southtyneside.gov.uk

***Leader of the Council* Malcolm**, Iain (LAB - Horsley Hill)
cllr.iain.malcolm@southtyneside.co.uk

***Deputy Leader of the Council* Kerr**, Alan (LAB - Monkton)
cllr.alan.kerr@southtyneside.co.uk

Amar, Joe (LAB - Biddick and All Saints)
cllr.joe.amar@southtyneside.gov.uk

Anglin, John (LAB - Beacon and Bents)
cllr.john.anglin@southtyneside.gov.uk

Atkinson, Joan (LAB - Cleadon and East **on)**
cllr.joan.atkinson@southtyneside.gov.uk

Bell, Joanne (LAB - **on Colliery)**
cllr.joan.bell@southtyneside.co.uk

Boyack, Peter (LAB - Whitburn and Marsden)
cllr.peter.boyack@southtyneside.gov.uk

Brady, Bill (LAB - Whiteleas)
cllr.bill.brady@southtyneside.co.uk

Butler, Mary (LAB - Hebburn North)
cllr.mary.butler@southtyneside.gov.uk

Cartwright, Melanie (LAB - Monkton)
cllr.melanie.cartwright@southtyneside.gov.uk

Clare, Michael (LAB - Simonside and Rekendyke)
cllr.michael.clare@southtyneside.co.uk

Cunningham, Fay (LAB - Bede)
cllr.fay.cunningham@southtyneside.gov.uk

Dick, Norman (LAB - West Park)
cllr.norman.dick@southtyneside.gov.uk

Dix, Robert (LAB - Harton)
cllr.rob.dix@southtyneside.gov.uk

Dixon, Tracey (LAB - Whitburn and Marsden)
cllr.tracey.dixon@southtyneside.co.uk

Donaldson, Alexander (LAB - Cleadon Park)
cllr.alex.donaldson@southtyneside.gov.uk

Duncan, Sandra (LAB - on Colliery)
cllr.sandra.duncan@southtyneside.gov.uk

Ellison, Adam (LAB - Hebburn North)
cllr.adam.ellison@southtyneside.gov.uk

Flynn, Wilf (LAB - Hebburn South)
cllr.wilf.flynn@southtyneside.gov.uk

Foreman, Jim (LAB - Cleadon Park)
cllr.jim.foreman@southtyneside.co.uk

Gibson, Ernest (LAB - Whiteleas)
cllr.ernest.gibson@southtyneside.co.uk

Hay, Pat (LAB - Harton)
cllr.pat.hay@southtyneside.gov.uk

Hetherington, Anne (LAB - West Park)
cllr.anne.hetherington@southtyneside.gov.uk

Hobson, Gladys (LAB - West Park)
cllr.gladys.hobson@southtyneside.gov.uk

Hughes, Lee (IND - Bede)
cllr.lee.hughes@southtyneside.gov.uk

Huntley, Audrey (LAB - Fellgate and Hedworth)
cllr.audrey.huntley@southtyneside.gov.uk

Kilgour, Geraldine (LAB - Fellgate and Hedworth)
cllr.geraldine.kilgour@southtyneside.gov.uk

Leask, Eileen (LAB - Horsley Hill)
cllr.eileen.leask@southtyneside.gov.uk

Malcolm, Edward (LAB - Simonside and Rekendyke)
cllr.ed.malcolm@southtyneside.co.uk

Maxwell, Katharine (LAB - Westoe)
cllr.katharine.maxwell@southtyneside.gov.uk

Maxwell, Neil (LAB - Harton)
cllr.neil.maxwell@southtyneside.gov.uk

Maxwell, Nancy (LAB - Hebburn South)
cllr.nancy.maxwell@southtyneside.co.uk

McCabe, John (LAB - Hebburn South)
cllr.john.mccabe@southtyneside.co.uk

McMillan, Audrey (LAB - Beacon and Bents)
cllr.audrey.mcmillan@southtyneside.co.uk

Meling, Margaret (LAB - Cleadon and East Boldon)

Milburn, Jeffrey (CON - Cleadon and East Boldon)
cllr.jeffrey.milburn@southtyneside.gov.uk

Peacock, Margaret (LAB - Bede)
cllr.margaret.peacock@southtyneside.gov.uk

Perry, Jim (LAB - Primrose)
cllr.jim.perry@southtyneside.co.uk

Proudlock, Lynne (LAB - Simonside and Rekendyke)
cllr.lynne.proudlock@southtyneside.gov.uk

Punchion, Olive (LAB - Biddick and All Saints)
cllr.olive.punchion@southtyneside.gov.uk

Purvis, Doreen (LAB - Whiteleas)
cllr.doreen.purvis@southtyneside.gov.uk

Sewell, Jim (LAB - Monkton)
cllr.jim.sewell@southtyneside.co.uk

Smith, Moira (LAB - Primrose)
cllr.moira.smith@southtyneside.gov.uk

Smith, Alan (LAB - Fellgate and Hedworth)
cllr.alan.smith@southtyneside.gov.uk

Stephenson, Sheila (LAB - Westoe)
cllr.sheila.stephenson@southtyneside.gov.uk

Stephenson, Ken (LAB - Primrose)
cllr.ken.stephenson@southtyneside.gov.uk

Strike, Alison (LAB - Boldon Colliery)
cllr.alison.strike@southtyneside.co.uk

Traynor, Susan (LAB - Cleadon Park)
cllr.susan.traynor@southtyneside.gov.uk

Walsh, Mark (LAB - Horsley Hill)
cllr.mark.walsh@southtyneside.gov.uk

Walsh, Anne (LAB - Biddick and All Saints)
cllr.anne.walsh@southtyneside.gov.uk

Welsh, Joyce (LAB - Whitburn and Marsden)
cllr.joyce.welsh@southtyneside.gov.uk

West, Allan (LAB - Westoe)
cllr.allan.west@southtyneside.gov.uk

Wood, John (LAB - Beacon and Bents)
cllr.john.wood@southtyneside.gov.uk

POLITICAL COMPOSITION
LAB: 52, CON: 1, IND: 1

Southampton City U

Southampton City Council, Civic Centre, Southampton SO14 7LY
☎ 023 8022 3855 🖷 023 8083 2817
city.information@southampton.gov.uk 💻 www.southampton.gov.uk

FACTS AND FIGURES
Parliamentary Constituencies: Romsey and Southampton North, Southampton, Itchen, Southampton, Test
EU Constituencies: South East
Election Frequency: Elections are by thirds

PRINCIPAL OFFICERS
Chief Executive: Ms Dawn Baxendale , Chief Executive, Civic Centre, Southampton SO14 7LY ☎ 023 8083 4428
dawn.baxendale@southampton.gov.uk

SOUTHAMPTON CITY

Assistant Chief Executive: Ms Suki Sitaram, Assistant Chief Executive, Civic Centre, Southampton SO14 7LY ☎ 023 8083 2060 🖱 suki.sitaram@southampton.gov.uk

Senior Management: Mr Mark Heath, Director - Place, Civic Centre, Southampton SO14 7LY ☎ 023 8083 2371 🖱 mark.heath@southampton.gov.uk

Senior Management: Mr Richard Ivory , Head of Legal & Democratic Services, Civic Centre, Southampton SO14 7LY ☎ 023 8083 2794 🖱 richard.ivory@southampton.gov.uk

Senior Management: Mr Andrew Lowe, Chief Financial Officer, Civic Centre, Civic Centre Road, Southampton SO14 7LY ☎ 023 8083 2049 🖱 andew.lowe@southampton.gov.uk

Senior Management: Dr Andrew Mortimore , Director of Public Health, Civic Centre, Southampton SO14 7LY ☎ 023 8022 3855 🖱 andrew.mortimore@southampton.gov.uk

Senior Management: Ms Stephanie Ramsey , Director - Quality & Integration, Civic Centre, Southampton SO14 7LY ☎ 023 8029 6923 🖱 stephanie.ramsey@southampton.gov.uk

Senior Management: Mr Mike Watts , Strategic Head of HR, Civic Centre, Southampton SO14 7LY ☎ 023 8083 4255 🖱 mike.watts@southampton.gov.uk

Best Value: Mr Stephen Giacchino , Transformation Implementation Director, Civic Centre, Southampton SO14 7LY ☎ 023 8083 7713 🖱 stephen.giacchino@southampton.gov.uk

Building Control: Mr Neil Ferris, Building Control Partnership Manager, Civic Centre, Southampton SO14 7LP ☎ 023 8083 2781 🖱 neil.ferris@southampton.gov.uk

Children / Youth Services: Ms Hilary Brooks , Interim Head of Service - Children's Services, Civic Centre, Southampton SO14 7LY ☎ 023 8083 3021 🖱 hilary.brooks@southampton.gov.uk

Civil Registration: Ms Linda Francis , Bereavement & Registrations Manager, Civic Centre, Southampton SO14 7LY ☎ 023 8091 5325 🖱 linda.francis@southampton.gov.uk

PR / Communications: Mr Richard Pearson , Head of Communcations, Civic Centre, Southampton SO14 7LY ☎ 023 8083 2047 🖱 ricahrd.pearson@southampton.gov.uk

Community Safety: Mr Mitch Sanders , Regulatory Services Senior Manager, Floor 5, 1 Guildhall Square, Southampton SO14 7FP ☎ 023 8022 3855 🖱 mitch.sanders@southampton.gov.uk

Computer Management: Mr Kevin Foley , Head of IT Solutions, Civic Centre, Southampton SO14 7LY ☎ 023 8022 3855 🖱 kevin.foley@southampton.gov.uk

Consumer Protection and Trading Standards: Mr Mitch Sanders , Regulatory Services Senior Manager, Floor 5, 1 Guildhall Square, Southampton SO14 7FP ☎ 023 8022 3855 🖱 mitch.sanders@southampton.gov.uk

Contracts: Mr Rob Harwood , Head of Contract Management, Civic Centre, Southampton SO14 7LY ☎ 023 8083 3436 🖱 rob.harwood@southampton.gov.uk

Customer Service: Mr Rob Harwood , Head of Contract Management, Civic Centre, Southampton SO14 7LY ☎ 023 8083 3436 🖱 rob.harwood@southampton.gov.uk

Economic Development: Ms Barbara Compton, Head of Development, Economy & Housing Renewal, Civic Centre, Southampton SO14 7LY ☎ 023 8083 2155 🖱 barbara.compton@southampton.gov.uk

Economic Development: Mr Jeff Walters, Economic Development Manager, Civic Centre, Southampton SO14 7LY ☎ 023 8083 2256 🖱 jeff.walters@southampton.gov.uk

Education: Mr Robert Hardy , Interim Head of 0-25 Service, Civic Centre, Southampton SO14 7LY ☎ 023 8083 3347 🖱 robert.hardy@southampton.gov.uk

Electoral Registration: Ms Marijke Elst , Business Services Manager, Civic Centre, Southampton SO14 7LY ☎ 023 8083 2422 🖱 marijke.elst@southampton.gov.uk

Emergency Planning: Mr Ian Collins , Emergency Planning Manager, City Depot, First Avenue, Millbrook, Southampton SO15 0LJ ☎ 023 8083 2089 🖱 ian.collins@southampton.gov.uk

Energy Management: Mr Jason Taylor , Energy Manager, 45 Castle Way, Southampton SO14 2PD ☎ 023 8083 2641 🖱 jason.taylor@southampton.gov.uk

Environmental Health: Mr Mitch Sanders , Regulatory Services Senior Manager, Floor 5, 1 Guildhall Square, Southampton SO14 7FP ☎ 023 8022 3855 🖱 mitch.sanders@southampton.gov.uk

Estates, Property & Valuation: Mr Rodger Hawkyard , Head of Property Services, Civic Centre, Southampton SO14 7LY ☎ 023 8083 2282 🖱 rodger.hawkyard@southampton.gov.uk

Events Manager: Mr Craig Lintott , Events Manager, Civic Centre, Southampton SO14 7LY ☎ 023 8083 2077 🖱 craig.lintott@southampton.gov.uk

Facilities: Mr Charles Stewart, Civic Buildings Manager, Civic Centre, Southampton SO14 7LY ☎ 023 8083 2877 🖱 chez.stewart@southampton.gov.uk

Finance: Mr Andrew Lowe, Chief Financial Officer, Civic Centre, Civic Centre Road, Southampton SO14 7LY ☎ 023 8083 2049 🖱 andew.lowe@southampton.gov.uk

Fleet Management: Mr Colin Rowland , Waste Fleet & Sustainability Manager, Civic Centre, Southampton SO14 7LY ☎ 023 8083 3561 🖱 colin.rowland@southampton.gov.uk

Grounds Maintenance: Mr John Horton , Parks & Street Cleansing Manager, Civic Centre, Southampton SO14 7LY ☎ 023 8083 3561 🖱 john.horton@southampton.gov.uk

Health and Safety: Mr Graham Armstrong , Head of Adult Housing & Community Care, Civic Centre, Southampton SO14 7LY ☎ 023 8083 4364 ✉ graham.armstrong@southampton.gov.uk

Housing: Mr Nick Cross , Senior Manager - Housing Services, Civic Centre, Southampton SO14 7LY ☎ 023 8083 2241 ✉ nick.cross@southampton.gov.uk

Housing Maintenance: Mr Nick Cross , Senior Manager - Housing Services, Civic Centre, Southampton SO14 7LY ☎ 023 8083 2241 ✉ nick.cross@southampton.gov.uk

Legal: Mr Richard Ivory , Head of Legal & Democratic Services, Civic Centre, Southampton SO14 7LY ☎ 023 8083 2794 ✉ richard.ivory@southampton.gov.uk

Leisure and Cultural Services: Mr Mike Harris, Senior Manager - Leisure & Culture, Civic Centre, Civic Centre Road, Southampton SO14 7LP ☎ 023 8083 2438 ✉ mike.harris@southampton.gov.uk

Licensing: Mr Phil Bates , Licensing Manager, Civic Centre, Southampton SO14 7LY ☎ 023 8083 3523 ✉ phil.bates@southampton.gov.uk

Lottery Funding, Charity and Voluntary: Mr John Connelly , Regeneration Manager, Civic Centre, Southampton SO14 7LY ☎ 023 8083 4402 ✉ john.connelly@southampton.gov.uk

Member Services: Dr Sandra Coltman , Democratic Services Manager, Democratic Services, Civic Centre, Southampton SO14 7LY ☎ 023 8083 2718 ✉ sandra.coltman@southampton.gov.uk

Parking: Mr Paul Walker , Acting Head of Transport, Highways & Parking, Civic Centre, Southampton SO14 7LY ☎ 023 8083 2628 ✉ paul.walker@southampton.gov.uk

Partnerships: Mr Rob Harwood , Head of Contract Management, Civic Centre, Southampton SO14 7LY ☎ 023 8083 3436 ✉ rob.harwood@southampton.gov.uk

Personnel / HR: Mr Mike Watts , Strategic Head of HR, Civic Centre, Southampton SO14 7LY ☎ 023 8083 4255 ✉ mike.watts@southampton.gov.uk

Planning: Mr Samuel Fox , Planning & Development Manager, Civic Centre, Southampton SO14 7LY ☎ 023 8083 2044 ✉ samuel.fox@southampton.gov.uk

Procurement: Mr Simon Aspland , Head of Procurement, Civic Centre, Southampton SO14 7LY ☎ 023 8083 3220 ✉ simon.aspland@southampton.gov.uk

Public Libraries: Mr David Baldwin, Libraries Manager, Civic Centre, Southampton SO14 7LY ☎ 023 8083 2219 ✉ david.baldwin@southampton.gov.uk

Recycling & Waste Minimisation: Mr Colin Rowland , Waste Fleet & Sustainability Manager, Civic Centre, Southampton SO14 7LY ☎ 023 8083 3561 ✉ colin.rowland@southampton.gov.uk

Regeneration: Ms Sherree Stanley-Conroy , Housing Delivery & Renewal Manager, Civic Centre, Southampton SO14 7LY ☎ 023 8083 2632 ✉ sherree.stanleyconroy@southampton.gov.uk

Social Services (Adult): Mr Mark Howell , Head of Adult Social Care, Civic Centre, Southampton SO14 7LY ☎ 023 8083 2743 ✉ mark.howell@southampton.gov.uk

Social Services (Children): Ms Hilary Brooks , Interim Head of Service - Children's Services, Civic Centre, Southampton SO14 7LY ☎ 023 8083 3021 ✉ hilary.brooks@southampton.gov.uk

Public Health: Dr Andrew Mortimore , Director of Public Health, Civic Centre, Southampton SO14 7LY ☎ 023 8022 3855 ✉ andrew.mortimore@southampton.gov.uk

Staff Training: Mr Mike Watts , Strategic Head of HR, Civic Centre, Southampton SO14 7LY ☎ 023 8083 4255 ✉ mike.watts@southampton.gov.uk

Street Scene: Mr John Harvey , Highways Manager, 1 Guild Hall Sqaure, Southampton SO14 7FP ☎ 023 8083 3927 ✉ john.harvery@southampton.gov.uk

Sustainable Communities: Ms Suki Sitaram, Assistant Chief Executive, Civic Centre, Southampton SO14 7LY ☎ 023 8083 2060 ✉ suki.sitaram@southampton.gov.uk

Tourism: Mr Mike Harris, Senior Manager - Leisure & Culture, Civic Centre, Civic Centre Road, Southampton SO14 7LP ☎ 023 8083 2438 ✉ mike.harris@southampton.gov.uk

Traffic Management: Mr John Harvey , Highways Manager, 1 Guild Hall Sqaure, Southampton SO14 7FP ☎ 023 8083 3927 ✉ john.harvery@southampton.gov.uk

Total Place: Mr Mark Heath, Director - Place, Civic Centre, Southampton SO14 7LY ☎ 023 8083 2371 ✉ mark.heath@southampton.gov.uk

Waste Collection and Disposal: Mr Colin Rowland , Waste Fleet & Sustainability Manager, Civic Centre, Southampton SO14 7LY ☎ 023 8083 3561 ✉ colin.rowland@southampton.gov.uk

Waste Collection and Disposal: Mr Colin Rowland , Waste Fleet & Sustainability Manager, Civic Centre, Southampton SO14 7LY ☎ 023 8083 3561 ✉ colin.rowland@southampton.gov.uk

Waste Management: Mr Colin Rowland , Waste Fleet & Sustainability Manager, Civic Centre, Southampton SO14 7LY ☎ 023 8083 3561 ✉ colin.rowland@southampton.gov.uk

COUNCILLORS

***Mayor* Norris**, Linda (CON - Portswood)
councillor.l.norris@southampton.gov.uk

***Sheriff* McEwing**, Catherine (LAB - Redbridge)
councillor.c.mcewing@southampton.gov.uk

***Leader of the Council* Letts**, Simon (LAB - Bitterne)
councillor.s.letts@southampton.gov.uk

***Deputy Leader of the Council* Payne**, Warwick (LAB - Woolston)
councillor.w.payne@southampton.gov.uk

***Group Leader* Morrell**, Keith (IND - Coxford)
councillor.k.morrell@southampton.gov.uk

***Group Leader* Moulton**, Jeremy (CON - Freemantle)
councillor.j.moulton@southampton.gov.uk

Barnes-Andrews, Stephen (LAB - Bevois)
councillor.s.barnes-andrews@southampton.gov.uk

Bogle, Sarah (LAB - Bargate)
councillor.s.bogle@southampton.gov.uk

Burke, Derek (LAB - Bevois)
councillor.d.burke@southampton.gov.uk

Chaloner, Mark (LAB - Shirley)
councillor.m.chaloner@southampton.gov.uk

Chamberlain, Caran (LAB - Woolston)
councillor.c.chamberlain@southampton.gov.uk

Claisse, Matthew (CON - Portswood)
Councillor.M.Claisse@southampton.gov.uk

Coombs, Hannah (LAB - Shirley)
councillor.h.coombs@southampton.gov.uk

Daunt, Edward (CON - Harefield)
councillor.e.daunt@southampton.gov.uk

Denness, Mike (LAB - Millbrook)
councillor.m.denness@southampton.gov.uk

Fitzhenry, Daniel (CON - Harefield)
councillor.d.fitzhenry@southampton.gov.uk

Fuller, David (CON - Bitterne Park)
councillor.d.fuller@southampton.gov.uk

Furnell, David (LAB - Millbrook)
councillor.d.furnell@southampton.gov.uk

Galton, Steven (CON - Millbrook)
councillor.s.galton@southampton.gov.uk

Hammond, Christopher (LAB - Woolston)
councillor.c.hammond@southampton.gov.uk

Hannides, John (CON - Bassett)
councillor.j.hannides@southampton.gov.uk

Harris, Beryl (CON - Bassett)
councillor.b.harris@southampton.gov.uk

Harris, Les (CON - Bassett)
Councillor.L.Harris@southampton.gov.uk

Hecks, Nigel (CON - Sholing)
councillor.n.hecks@southampton.gov.uk

Houghton, Alex (CON - Peartree)
councillor.a.houghton@southampton.gov.uk

Inglis, John (CON - Bitterne Park)
councillor.j.inglis@southampton.gov.uk

Jeffery, Daniel (LAB - Sholing)
councillor.d.jeffery@southampton.gov.uk

Jordan, John (LAB - Bitterne)
councillor.j.jordan@southampton.gov.uk

Kaur, Satvir (LAB - Shirley)
Councillor.S.Kaur@southampton.gov.uk

Keogh, Eamonn (LAB - Peartree)
councillor.e.keogh@southampton.gov.uk

Lewzey, Paul (LAB - Peartree)
councillor.p.lewzey@southampton.gov.uk

Lloyd, Mary (LAB - Bitterne)
councillor.m.lloyd@southampton.gov.uk

Mintoff, Sharon (LAB - Swaythling)
councillor.s.mintoff@southamptong.gov.uk

Noon, John (LAB - Bargate)
Councillor.J.Noon@southampton.gov.uk

O'Neill, Paul (CON - Portswood)
councillor.p.o'neill@southampton.gov.uk

Painton, Bob (CON - Swaythling)
councillor.b.painton@southampton.gov.uk

Parnell, Brian (CON - Freemantle)
councillor.b.parnell@southampton.gov.uk

Pope, Andrew (LAB - Redbridge)
Councillor.A.Pope@southampton.gov.uk

Rayment, Jacqui (LAB - Bevois)
councillor.j.rayment@southampton.gov.uk

Shields, Dave (LAB - Freemantle)
councillor.d.shields@southampton.gov.uk

Smith, Royston (CON - Harefield)
councillor.r.smith@southampton.gov.uk

Spicer, Sally (LAB - Coxford)
councillor.s.spicer@southampton.gov.uk

Thomas, Don (IND - Coxford)
councillor.d.thomas@southampton.gov.uk

Tucker, Matt (LAB - Bargate)
councillor.m.tucker@southampton.gov.uk

Vassiliou, Spiros (CON - Swaythling)
Councillor.S.Vassiliou@southampton.gov.uk

Whitbread, Lee (LAB - Redbridge)
councillor.l.whitbread@southampton.gov.uk

White, Ivan (CON - Bitterne Park)
councillor.i.white@southampton.gov.uk

Wilkinson, Graham (CON - Sholing)
councillor.g.wilkinson@southampton.gov.uk

POLITICAL COMPOSITION

LAB: 26, CON: 20, IND: 2

COMMITTEE CHAIRS

Children & Families: Mr Eamonn Keogh

Southend-on-Sea — U

Southend-on-Sea Borough Council, Civic Centre, Southend-on-Sea SS2 6ER
☎ 01702 215000 🖷 01702 215110
💻 www.southend.gov.uk

FACTS AND FIGURES

Parliamentary Constituencies: Rochford and Southend East, Southend West
EU Constituencies: Eastern
Election Frequency: Elections are by thirds

PRINCIPAL OFFICERS

Chief Executive: Mr Robert Tinlin, Chief Executive & Town Clerk, PO Box 6, Civic Centre, Victoria Avenue, Southend-on-Sea SS2 6ER ☎ 01702 215101 🖷 01702 215594 🖱 robtinlin@southend.gov.uk

Senior Management: Dr Andrea Atherton , Director - Public Health, Civic Centre, Southend-on-Sea SS2 6ER ☎ 01702 212802 🖱 andrea.atherton@southend.gov.uk

Senior Management: Ms Sally Holland, Corporate Director - Corporate Services, Civic Centre, Victoria Avenue, Southend-on-Sea SS2 6ER ☎ 01702 215677 🖱 sallyholland@southend.gov.uk

Senior Management: Mr Simon Leftley, Corporate Director - People, Civic Centre, Victoria Avenue, Southend-on-Sea SS2 6ER ☎ 01702 214729 🖱 simonleftley@southend.gov.uk

Senior Management: Mr Andy Lewis, Corporate Director - Place, PO Box 6, Civic Centre, Victoria Avenue, Southend-on-Sea SS2 6ER ☎ 01702 212214 🖱 andrewlewis@southend.gov.uk

Building Control: Dr Peter Geraghty , Head of Planning & Transport, Civic Centre, Southend-on-Sea SS2 6ER ☎ 01702 215339 🖱 petergeraghty@southend.gov.uk

Children / Youth Services: Mr Simon Leftley, Corporate Director - People, Civic Centre, Victoria Avenue, Southend-on-Sea SS2 6ER ☎ 01702 214729 🖱 simonleftley@southend.gov.uk

PR / Communications: Ms Kirsty Horseman, Media & Communications Manager, Civic Centre, Southend-on-Sea SS2 6ER ☎ 01702 212057 🖱 kirstyhorseman@southend.gov.uk

Community Safety: Mr Simon Ford, Community Safety Manager, Civic Centre, Victoria Avenue, Southend-on-Sea SS2 6ER ☎ 0300 333 4444 🖱 simonford@southend.gov.uk

Computer Management: Mr David Cummings , Group Manager - ICT, Civic Centre, Southend-on-Sea SS2 6ER ☎ 01702 215000 🖱 davidcummings@southend.gov.uk

Consumer Protection and Trading Standards: Ms Dipti Patel , Head of Public Protection, Civic Centre, Southend-on-Sea SS2 6ER ☎ 01702 215325 🖱 diptipatel@southend.gov.uk

Corporate Services: Ms Sally Holland, Corporate Director - Corporate Services, Civic Centre, Victoria Avenue, Southend-on-Sea SS2 6ER ☎ 01702 215677 🖱 sallyholland@southend.gov.uk

Customer Service: Mr Nick Corrigan, Head of Customer Services, Civic Centre, Victoria Avenue, Southend-on-Sea SS2 6ER ☎ 01702 534612 🖱 nickcorrigan@southend.gov.uk

Economic Development: Mr Scott Dolling , Head of Services, Economy & Regeneration, Civic Centre, Southend-on-Sea SS2 6ER 🖱 scottdolling@southend.gov.uk

Electoral Registration: Mr Colin Gamble , Group Manager - Democratic Services, Civic Centre, Southend-on-Sea SS2 6ER ☎ 01702 534820 🖷 01702 215107 🖱 colingamble@southend.gov.uk

Emergency Planning: Mr Keith Holden, Emergency Planning Officer, PO Box 6, Civic Centre, Victoria Avenue, Southend-on-Sea SS2 6ER ☎ 01702 215023 🖱 keithholden@southend.gov.uk

Energy Management: Mr Pete Harmsworth , Energy Officer, Civic Centre, Southend-on-Sea SS2 6ER ☎ 01702 215190 🖱 peteharmsworth@southend.gov.uk

Environmental / Technical Services: Mr Andy Lewis, Corporate Director - Place, PO Box 6, Civic Centre, Victoria Avenue, Southend-on-Sea SS2 6ER ☎ 01702 212214 🖱 andrewlewis@southend.gov.uk

Environmental Health: Ms Dipti Patel, Head of Public Protection & Waste, Civic Centre, Victoria Avenue, Southend-on-Sea SS2 6ER ☎ 01702 215000 🖱 diptipatel@southend.gov.uk

European Liaison: Mr Mark Murphy, Regeneration Services Manager, Civic Centre, Southend-on-Sea SS2 6ER ☎ 01702 215429 🖷 01702 215707 🖱 markmurphy@southend.gov.uk

Facilities: Ms Karen Wright, Group Manager - Access to Services, Civic Centre, Victoria Avenue, Southend-on-Sea SS2 6ER ☎ 01702 215603 🖱 karenwright@southend.gov.uk

Finance: Mr Joe Chesterton, Head of Finance & Resources, Civic Centre, Victoria Avenue, Southend-on-Sea SS2 6ER ☎ 01702 215393 🖱 joechesterton@southend.gov.uk

Finance: Ms Linda Everard , Head of Internal Audit, Civic Centre, Southend-on-Sea SS2 6ER ☎ 01702 215000 🖱 lindaeverard@southend.gov.uk

Grounds Maintenance: Mr Graham Owen , Health & Safety Officer, Civic Centre, Southend-on-Sea SS2 6ER ☎ 01702 215350 🖱 grahamowen@southend.gov.uk

Health and Safety: Mr Lee Colby , Regulatory Service Operator, Civic Centre, Southend-on-Sea SS2 6ER ☎ 01702 215814 🖱 leecolby@southend.gov.uk

Highways: Mr Mehmet Mazhar , Group Manager - Traffic & Highways, Civic Centre, Southend-on-Sea SS2 6ER ☎ 01702 215369 🖱 mehmetmazhar@southend.gov.uk

Local Area Agreement: Mr Ade Butteriss, Strategy & Performance Manager, Civic Centre, Victoria Avenue, Southend-on-Sea SS2 6ER ☎ 01702 215187 🖱 adebutteriss@southend.gov.uk

Legal: Mr John Williams, Head of Legal & Democratic Services, Civic Centre, Southend-on-Sea SS2 6ER ☎ 01702 215102 🖷 01702 215110 🖱 johnwilliams@southend.gov.uk

Leisure and Cultural Services: Mr Nick Harris, Head of Culture, Civic Centre, Victoria Avenue, Southend-on-Sea SS2 6ER ☎ 01702 215619 🖱 nickharris@southend.gov.uk

Licensing: Mr Carl Robinson , Group Manager - Regulatory Services, Civic Centre, Southend-on-Sea SS2 6ER ☎ 01702 215156 🖱 carlrobinson@southend.gov.uk

Lottery Funding, Charity and Voluntary: Ms Lysane Eddy , Partnerships Manager, Civic Centre, Southend-on-Sea SS2 6ER ☎ 01702 215111 lysanneeddy@southend.gov.uk

Member Services: Mr Colin Gamble , Group Manager - Democratic Services, Civic Centre, Southend-on-Sea SS2 6ER ☎ 01702 534820 🖷 01702 215107 colingamble@southend.gov.uk

Member Services: Mr John Williams, Head of Legal & Democratic Services, Civic Centre, Southend-on-Sea SS2 6ER ☎ 01702 215102 🖷 01702 215110 johnwilliams@southend.gov.uk

Partnerships: Ms Lysane Eddy , Partnerships Manager, Civic Centre, Southend-on-Sea SS2 6ER ☎ 01702 215111 lysanneeddy@southend.gov.uk

Personnel / HR: Ms Joanna Ruffle, Head of People & Policy, Civic Centre, Southend-on-Sea SS2 6ER ☎ 01702 215393; 01708 432181 joanna.ruffle@havering.gov.uk

Planning: Dr Peter Geraghty , Head of Planning & Transport, Civic Centre, Southend-on-Sea SS2 6ER ☎ 01702 215339 petergeraghty@southend.gov.uk

Public Libraries: Mr Simon May , Libraries Services Manager, Civic Centre, Southend-on-Sea SS2 6ER ☎ 01702 534101 simonmay@southend.gov.uk

Recycling & Waste Minimisation: Ms Dipti Patel, Head of Public Protection & Waste, Civic Centre, Victoria Avenue, Southend-on-Sea SS2 6ER ☎ 01702 215000 diptipatel@southend.gov.uk

Regeneration: Mr Scott Dolling , Head of Services, Economy & Regeneration, Civic Centre, Southend-on-Sea SS2 6ER scottdolling@southend.gov.uk

Social Services: Mr Simon Leftley, Corporate Director - People, Civic Centre, Victoria Avenue, Southend-on-Sea SS2 6ER ☎ 01702 214729 simonleftley@southend.gov.uk

Social Services (Adult): Ms Sharon Houlden , Head of Adult Services & Housing, Civic Centre, Southend-on-Sea SS2 6ER ☎ 01702 215000 sharonhoulden@southend.gov.uk

Public Health: Dr Andrea Atherton , Director - Public Health, Civic Centre, Southend-on-Sea SS2 6ER ☎ 01702 212802 andrea.atherton@southend.gov.uk

Staff Training: Ms Joanna Ruffle, Head of People & Policy, Civic Centre, Southend-on-Sea SS2 6ER ☎ 01702 215393; 01708 432181 joanna.ruffle@havering.gov.uk

Street Scene: Mrs Marzia Abel, Town Centre Manager, Civic Centre, Southend-on-Sea SS2 6ER ☎ 01702 212052 marziaabel@southend.gov.uk

Sustainable Communities: Mr Mark Murphy, Regeneration Services Manager, Civic Centre, Southend-on-Sea SS2 6ER ☎ 01702 215429 🖷 01702 215707 markmurphy@southend.gov.uk

Sustainable Development: Mr Chris Livemore , Sustainable Officer, Civic Centre, Southend-on-Sea SS2 6ER ☎ 01702 215832 chrislivemore@southend.gov.uk

Tourism: Mr Scott Dolling , Head of Services, Economy & Regeneration, Civic Centre, Southend-on-Sea SS2 6ER scottdolling@southend.gov.uk

Town Centre: Mrs Marzia Abel, Town Centre Manager, Civic Centre, Southend-on-Sea SS2 6ER ☎ 01702 212052 marziaabel@southend.gov.uk

Traffic Management: Dr Peter Geraghty , Head of Planning & Transport, Civic Centre, Southend-on-Sea SS2 6ER ☎ 01702 215339 petergeraghty@southend.gov.uk

Transport: Dr Peter Geraghty , Head of Planning & Transport, Civic Centre, Southend-on-Sea SS2 6ER ☎ 01702 215339 petergeraghty@southend.gov.uk

Transport Planner: Dr Peter Geraghty , Head of Planning & Transport, Civic Centre, Southend-on-Sea SS2 6ER ☎ 01702 215339 petergeraghty@southend.gov.uk

Total Place: Ms Lysane Eddy , Partnerships Manager, Civic Centre, Southend-on-Sea SS2 6ER ☎ 01702 215111 lysanneeddy@southend.gov.uk

Waste Collection and Disposal: Ms Dipti Patel, Head of Public Protection & Waste, Civic Centre, Victoria Avenue, Southend-on-Sea SS2 6ER ☎ 01702 215000 diptipatel@southend.gov.uk

COUNCILLORS

***Mayor* Moring**, Andrew (CON - Eastwood Park)
cllrmoring@southend.gov.uk

***Deputy Mayor* Velmurugan**, Marimuthu (IND - Westborough)
cllrvelmurugan@southend.gov.uk

***Leader of the Council* Woodley**, Ronald (IND - Thorpe)
cllrwoodley@southend.gov.uk

***Group Leader* Gilbert**, Ian (LAB - Victoria)
cllrgilbert@southend.gov.uk

***Group Leader* Lamb**, John (CON - West Leigh)
cllrlamb@southend.gov.uk

***Group Leader* Longley**, Graham (LD - Blenheim Park)
cllrlongley@southend.gov.uk

***Group Leader* Moyies**, James (UKIP - West Shoebury)
cllrmoyies@southend.gov.uk

Arscott, Bernard (CON - Leigh)
cllrarscott@southend.gov.uk

Assenheim, Michael (IND - Shoeburyness)
cllrassenheim@southend.gov.uk

Aylen, Stephen (IND - Belfairs)
cllraylen@southend.gov.uk

Ayling, Brian (IND - St Luke's)
cllrayling@southend.gov.uk

Betson, Mary (LD - Prittlewell)
cllrbetson@southend.gov.uk

Borton, Margaret (LAB - Victoria)
cllrborton@southend.gov.uk

Buckley, Steve (CON - St Laurence)
cllrbuckley@southend.gov.uk

Butler, Maureen (CON - Belfairs)
cllrbutler@southend.gov.uk

Byford, Trevor (CON - Eastwood Park)
cllrbyford@southend.gov.uk

Callaghan, Tino (UKIP - Prittlewell)
cllrcallaghan@southend.gov.uk

Courtenay, James (CON - Blenheim Park)
cllrcourtenay@southend.gov.uk

Cox, Tony (CON - West Shoebury)
cllrcox@southend.gov.uk

Crystall, Alan (LD - Leigh)
cllrcrystall@southend.gov.uk

Davidson, Margaret (CON - Prittlewell)
cllrdavidson@southend.gov.uk

Davies, Lawrence (IND - Kursaal)
cllrdavies@southend.gov.uk

Endersby, Caroline (IND - St Luke's)
cllrendersby@southend.gov.uk

Evans, Margaret (CON - West Leigh)
cllrevans@southend.gov.uk

Flewitt, Mark (CON - St Laurence)
cllrflewitt@southend.gov.uk

Folkard, Nigel (CON - Chalkwell)
cllrfolkard@southend.gov.uk

Garston, David (CON - Southchurch)
cllrdgarston@southend.gov.uk

Garston, Jonathan (CON - Milton)
cllrjgartson@southend.gov.uk

Habermel, Stephen (CON - Chalkwell)
cllrhabermel@southend.gov.uk

Hadley, Roger (CON - Shoeburyness)
cllrhadley@southend.gov.uk

Holland, Ann (CON - Southchurch)
cllrholland@southend.gov.uk

Jarvis, Derek (CON - West Shoebury)
cllrjarvis@southend.gov.uk

Jones, Anne (LAB - Kursaal)
cllrannejones@southend.gov.uk

Kenyon, Derek (IND - Southchurch)
cllrkenyon@southend.gov.uk

McGlone, David (UKIP - St Laurence)
cllrmcglone@southend.gov.uk

McMahon, Judith (LAB - Kursaal)
CllrMcMahon@southend.gov.uk

Mulroney, Carol (LD - Leigh)
cllrmulroney@southend.gov.uk

Nevin, Cheryl (LAB - Milton)
cllrnevin@southend.gov.uk

Norman, David (LAB - Victoria)
cllrdnorman@southend.gov.uk

Phillips, Georgina (CON - West Leigh)
cllrphillips@southend.gov.uk

Robertson, Ian (CON - Chalkwell)
cllrirobertson@southend.gov.uk

Robinson, Kevin (LAB - Westborough)
cllrkrobinson@southend.gov.uk

Salter, Lesley (CON - Belfairs)
cllrsalter@southend.gov.uk

Stafford, Mike (IND - Thorpe)
cllrstafford@southend.gov.uk

Terry, Martin (IND - Thorpe)
cllrterry@southend.gov.uk

Van Looy, Paul (IND - St Luke's)
cllrvanlooy@southend.gov.uk

Walker, Christopher (CON - Eastwood Park)
cllrwalker@southend.gov.uk

Ward, Nick (IND - Shoeburyness)
cllrward@southend.gov.uk

Ware-Lane, Julian (LAB - Milton)
cllrware-lane@southend.gov.uk

Waterworth, Floyd (UKIP - Blenheim Park)
cllrwaterworth@southend.gov.uk

Willis, Charles (LAB - Westborough)
cllrwillis@southend.gov.uk

POLITICAL COMPOSITION
CON: 22, IND: 12, LAB: 9, LD: 4, UKIP: 4

COMMITTEE CHAIRS

Audit: Mrs Mary Betson

Development Control: Dr Alan Crystall

Health & Wellbeing: Mr James Moyies

Licensing: Ms Judith McMahon

Southwark L

Southwark London Borough Council, 160 Tooley Street, London SE1 2QH
☎ 020 7525 5000 💻 www.southwark.gov.uk

FACTS AND FIGURES
Parliamentary Constituencies: Bermondsey and Old Southwark, Camberwell and Peckham, Dulwich and West Norwood
EU Constituencies: London
Election Frequency: Elections are of whole council

PRINCIPAL OFFICERS

Chief Executive: Mrs Eleanor Kelly , Chief Executive, 160 Tooley Street, London SE1 2QH ☎ 020 7525 7171
✉ eleanor.kelly@southwark.gov.uk

Senior Management: Ms Deborah Collins, Strategic Director of Environment & Leisure, 160 Tooley Street, London SE1 2QH
☎ 020 7525 7630 ✉ deborah.collins@southwark.gov.uk

SOUTHWARK

Senior Management: Mr David Quirke-Thornton , Strategic Director of Children's & Adults' Services, 160 Tooley Street, London SE1 2QH ☎ 020 7525 3289 ✉ david.quirke-thornton@southwark.gov.uk

Senior Management: Ms Gerri Scott , Strategic Director of Housing & Community Services, 160 Tooley Street, London SE1 2QH ☎ 020 7525 7464 ✉ gerri.scott@southwark.gov.uk

Senior Management: Mr Duncan Whitfield, Strategic Director of Finance & Corporate Services, 160 Tooley Street, London SE1 2QH ☎ 020 7525 7180 ✉ duncan.whitfield@southwark.gov.uk

Access Officer / Social Services (Disability): Mr Stephen Douglass , Head of Community Engagement, 160 Tooley Street, London SE1 2QH ☎ 020 7525 0886 ✉ stephen.douglass@southwark.gov.uk

Building Control: Mr Peter Card , Head of Building Control, 160 Tooley Street, London SE1 2QH ☎ 020 7525 5588 ✉ peter.card@southwark.gov.uk

Children / Youth Services: Mr Patrick Shelley , Head of Youth, Southwark Council, 4th Floor, 160 Tooley Street, London SE1 2QH ✉ patrick.shelley@southwark.gov.uk

Civil Registration: Ms Marcia Mitchell-West , Senior Ceremonies Officer, Registrar Section, 34 Peckham Road, London SE5 8UB ☎ 020 7525 7474 🖷 020 7525 7652 ✉ marcia.mitchell@southwark.gov.uk

PR / Communications: Ms Louise Neilan , Media Manager, 2nd Floor, 160 Tooley Street, London SE1 2QH ☎ 020 7525 7023 ✉ louise.neilan@southwark.gov.uk

Community Safety: Mr Jonathon Toy, Head of Community Safety & Enforcement, Southwark Council, 3rd Floor, 160 Tooley Street, London Bridge, London SE1 2QH ☎ 020 7525 1479 ✉ jonathon.toy@southwark.gov.uk

Contracts: Ms Jan McMahon , Head of Corporate Contracts & Contract Management, Southwark Council, 2nd Floor, 160 Tooley Street, London SE1 2QH ☎ 020 7525 3620 ✉ jan.mcmahon@southwark.gov.uk

Corporate Services: Mr Stephen Gaskell , Head of Strategy & Partnerships, 160 Tooley Street, London SE1 2QH

Customer Service: Mr Dominic Cain , Assistant Director of Revenues & Benefits, Southwark Council, 1st Floor, 160 Tooley Street, London Bridge, London SE1 2QH ☎ 020 7525 0636 ✉ dominic.cain@southwark.gov.uk

Customer Service: Mr Richard Selley , Head of Customer Experience, Southwark Council, 3rd Floor, 160 Tooley Street, London SE1 2QH ☎ 020 7525 7320 ✉ richard.selley@southwark.gov.uk

Education: Ms Maggie Donnellan , Head of Primary Achievement, Southwark Council , 1st Floor, PCT, 160 Tooley Street, London SE1 2HZ ☎ 020 7525 5030 ✉ maggie.donnellan@southwark.gov.uk

Education: Mr Glenn Garcia , Head of Pupil Access, Southwark Council, 4th Floor, 160 Tooley Street, London Bridge, London SE1 2QH ☎ 020 7525 2717 ✉ glenn.garcia@southwark.gov.uk

Electoral Registration: Ms Frances Biggs, Head of Electoral Services, Southwark Council, 3rd Floor, 160 Tooley Street, London Bridge, London SE1 2QH ☎ 020 7525 7694 ✉ frances.biggs@southwark.gov.uk

Emergency Planning: Mr Andy Snazell , Emergency Planning & Resilience Manager, 3rd Floor, 160 Tooley Street, London SE1 2QH ☎ 020 7525 3517 ✉ andy.snazell@southwark.gov.uk

Energy Management: Mr Ian Smith, Head of Sustainable Services, Southwark Council, 3rd Floor, 160 Tooley Street, London SE1 2QH ☎ 020 7525 2484 🖷 020 7525 3636 ✉ ian.smith@southwark.gov.uk

Estates, Property & Valuation: Mr Stephen Platts, Director of Regeneration, Southwark Council, 3rd Floor, 160 Tooley Street, London Bridge, London SE1 2QH ☎ 020 7525 5640 ✉ stephen.platts@southwark.gov.uk

European Liaison: Ms Lisa Marie Bowles, European & Funding Officer , Southwark Council, 1st Floor, 160 Tooley Street, London Bridge, London SE1 2QH ☎ 020 7525 1022 ✉ lisa-marie.bowles@southwark.gov.uk

Events Manager: Mr Paul Cowell , Events & Film Manager, Southwark Council, 3rd Floor, 160 Tooley Street, London Bridge, London SE1 2QH ☎ 020 7525 0857 ✉ paul.cowell@southwark.gov.uk

Facilities: Mr Keith Andrews , Building Manager (Corporate Facilities Management), 3rd Floor, 160 Tooley Street, London SE1 2QH ☎ 020 7525 2804 ✉ keith.andrews@southwark.gov.uk

Finance: Mr Duncan Whitfield, Strategic Director of Finance & Corporate Services, Southwark Council, 3rd Floor, 160 Tooley Street, London Bridge, London SE1 2QH ☎ 020 7525 7180 ✉ duncan.whitfield@southwark.gov.uk

Pensions: Mr Malcolm Laird , SAP Payroll & Pensions Manager, 160 Tooley Street, London SE1 2QH ☎ 020 7525 4915 ✉ malcolm.laird@southwark.gov.uk

Pensions: Ms Caroline Watson , Pension Fund Investment Manager, 160 Tooley Street, London SE1 2QH ☎ 020 7525 4379 ✉ caroline.watson@southwark.gov.uk

Fleet Management: Mr Ian Smith, Head of Sustainble Services, Southwark Council, 3rd Floor, 160 Tooley Street, London SE1 2QH ☎ 020 7525 2484 ✉ ian.smith@southwark.gov.uk

Health and Safety: Mr Chris Rackley, Health & Safety Strategy Manager, Southwark Council, 3rd Floor, 160 Tooley Street, London Bridge, London SE1 2QH ☎ 020 7525 7001 ✉ chris.rackley@southwark.gov.uk

Housing: Mr Martin Green , Head of Specialist Housing Services, 153 - 159 Abbeyfield Road, London SE16 2BS ☎ 020 7525 1418 ✉ martin.green2@southwark.gov.uk

Housing: Ms Gerri Scott , Strategic Director of Housing & Community Services, Southwark Council, 3rd Floor, 160 Tooley Street, London Bridge, London SE1 2QH ☎ 020 7525 7464 ✉ gerri.scott@southwark.gov.uk

Legal: Ms Shelley Burke , Head of Overview & Scrutiny, Southwark Council, 3rd Floor, 160 Tooley Street, London Bridge, London SE1 2QH ☎ 020 7525 7344 ✉ shelley.burke@southwark.gov.uk

Legal: Ms Doreen Forrester-Brown , Director of Legal Services, Southwark Council, 3rd Floor, 160 Tooley Street, London Bridge, London SE1 2QH ☎ 020 7525 7502 ✉ doreen.forrester-brown@southwark.gov.uk

Leisure and Cultural Services: Ms Rebecca Towers , Parks & Open Spaces Manager, Southwark Council, 3rd Floor, 160 Tooley Street, London Bridge, London SE1 2QH ☎ 020 7525 0771 ✉ rebecca.towers@southwark.gov.uk

Leisure and Cultural Services: Mr Adrian Whittle , Head of Culture, Libraries, Learning & Leisure, Southwark Council, 3rd Floor, 160 Tooley Street, London Bridge, London SE1 2QH ☎ 020 7525 1577 ✉ adrian.whittle@southwark.gov.uk

Licensing: Mr Richard Parkins, Health Safety Licensing & Environmental Protection Unit Manager, Southwark Council, 3rd Floor, 160 Tooley Street, London Bridge, London SE1 2QH ☎ 020 7525 5767 ✉ richard.parkins@southwark.gov.uk

Lottery Funding, Charity and Voluntary: Ms Bonnie Royal , Commissioning & Voluntary Sector Support Manager , Southwark Council, 3rd Floor, 160 Tooley Street, London Bridge, London SE1 2QH ☎ 020 7525 7389 ✉ bonnie.royal@southwark.gov.uk

Parking: Mr David Sole, Parking Service & Development Manager, Southwark Council, 3rd Floor, 160 Tooley Street, London Bridge, London SE1 2QH ☎ 020 7525 2037 ✉ david.sole@southwark.gov.uk

Personnel / HR: Mr John Howard , Head of Organisational Development, Southwark Council, 3rd Floor, 160 Tooley Street, London Bridge, London SE1 2QH ☎ 020 7525 1253 ✉ john.howard@southwark.gov.uk

Personnel / HR: Mr Bernard Nawrat, Head of Human Resources, Southwark Council, 2nd Floor, 160Tooley Street, London Bridge, London SE1 2QH ☎ 020 7525 7185 ✉ bernard.nawrat@southwark.gov.uk

Planning: Mr Simon Bevan, Director of Planning, Southwark Council, 3rd Floor, 160 Tooley Street, London Bridge, London SE1 2QH ☎ 020 7525 5655 ✉ simon.bevan@southwark.gov.uk

Procurement: Mrs Jennifer Seeley , Deputy Finance Director, Southwark Council, 3rd Floor, 160 Tooley Street, London Bridge, London SE1 2QH ☎ 020 7525 0695 ✉ jennifer.seeley@southwark.gov.uk

Public Libraries: Mr Adrian Whittle , Head of Culture, Libraries, Learning & Leisure, Southwark Council, 3rd Floor, 160 Tooley Street, London Bridge, London SE1 2QH ☎ 020 7525 1577 ✉ adrian.whittle@southwark.gov.uk

Road Safety: Mr Eamon Doran, Group Manager of Sustainable Travel & Road Safety, Southwark Council, 3rd Floor, 160 Tooley Street, London Bridge, London SE1 2QH ☎ 020 7525 0513 ✉ eamon.doran@southwark.gov.uk

Social Services: Ms Sarah Desai , Director of Commissioning, Modernisation & Partners, Southwark Council , PCT, 1st Floor, PO Box 64529, London SE1P 5LX ☎ 020 7525 0446 ✉ sarah.desai@southwarkpct.nhs.uk

Social Services: Ms Gillian Holdsworth , Director of Public Health & Health Improvement, Southwark Council, 1st Floor, 160 Tooley Street, London Bridge, London SE1 2QH ☎ 020 7525 0298

Social Services: Ms Lesley Humber , Director of Operations & Locality, Southwark Council, 1st Floor, 160 Tooley Street, London Bridge, London SE1 2QH ☎ 020 7525 0407

Social Services (Children): Mr David Quirke-Thornton , Strategic Director of Children's & Adults' Services, 160 Tooley Street, London SE1 2QH ☎ 020 7525 3289 ✉ david.quirke-thornton@southwark.gov.uk

Public Health: Dr Ruth Wallis , Director - Public Health, 160 Tooley Street, London SE1 2QH ✉ ruth.wallis@southwark.gov.uk

Street Scene: Mr Qassim Kazaz , Principal Project Manager - Transport, PO Box 64529, HUB 1, 3rd Floor, London SE1P 5LX ☎ 020 7525 2091 ✉ qassim.kazaz@southwark.gov.uk

Town Centre: Mr Jon Abbott , Project Director, Southwark Council, 3rd Floor, 160 Tooley Street, London Bridge, London SE1 2QH ☎ 020 7525 4902 ✉ jon.abbott@southwark.gov.uk

Town Centre: Mr David Strevens, Peckham Town Centre Manager, Peckham Partnership Project Team, Sumner House, Sumner Road, London SE15 5QS ☎ 020 7525 1001 🖷 020 7525 1020 ✉ david.strevens@southwark.gov.uk

Transport: Mr Ian Smith, Head of Sustainble Services, Manor Place Depot, 30-34 Penrose Street, London SE17 3DW ☎ 020 7525 2484 ✉ ian.smith@southwark.gov.uk

Transport Planner: Mr Simon Bevan, Director of Planning, Southwark Council, 3rd Floor, 160 Tooley Street, London Bridge, London SE1 2QH ☎ 020 7525 5655 ✉ simon.bevan@southwark.gov.uk

Children's Play Areas: Ms Rebecca Towers , Parks & Open Spaces Manager, Southwark Council, 3rd Floor, 160 Tooley Street, London Bridge, London SE1 2QH ☎ 020 7525 0771 ✉ rebecca.towers@southwark.gov.uk

COUNCILLORS

***Mayor* Dixon-Fyle**, Dora (LAB - Camberwell Green)
dora.dixon-fyle@southwark.gov.uk

***Deputy Mayor* Whittam**, Kath (LAB - Rotherhithe)
kath.whittam@southwark.gov.uk

***Leader of the Council* John**, Peter (LAB - South Camberwell)
peter.john@southwark.gov.uk

***Deputy Leader of the Council* Wingfield**, Ian (LAB - Brunswick Park)
ian.wingfield@southwark.gov.uk

Akoto, Evelyn (LAB - Livesey)
evelyn.akoto@southwark.gov.uk

Ali, Jasmine (LAB - The Lane)
jasmine.ali@southwark.gov.uk

Al-Samerai, Anood (LD - Riverside)
anood.al-samerai@southwark.gov.uk

Anderson, Maisie (LAB - Newington)
maisie.anderson@southwark.gov.uk

Barber, James (LD - East Dulwich)
james.barber@southwark.gov.uk

Burgess, Radha (LAB - Brunswick Park)
radha.burgess@southwark.gov.uk

Chopra, Sunil (LAB - Nunhead)
sunil.chopra@southwark.gov.uk

Colley, Fiona (LAB - Nunhead)
fiona.colley@southwark.gov.uk

Coyle, Neil (LAB - Newington)
neil.coyle@southwark.gov.uk

Cryan, Stephanie (LAB - Rotherhithe)
stephanie.cryan@southwark.gov.uk

Dale, Catherine (LAB - South Bermondsey)
catherine.dale@southwark.gov.uk

Dennis, Helen (LAB - Chaucer)
helen.dennis@southwark.gov.uk

Dolezal, Nick (LAB - The Lane)
nick.dolezal@southwark.gov.uk

Eastham, Karl (LAB - Chaucer)
karl.eastham@southwark.gov.uk

Edwards, Gavin (LAB - Peckham Rye)
gavin.edwards@southwark.gov.uk

Fleming, Paul (LAB - Faraday)
paul.fleming@southwark.gov.uk

Flynn, Tom (LAB - Camberwell Green)
tom.flynn@southwark.gov.uk

Garfield, Dan (LAB - Faraday)
dan.garfield@southwark.gov.uk

Gonde, Chris (LAB - South Camberwell)
chris.gonde@southwark.gov.uk

Green, Lucas (LAB - Grange)
lucas.green@southwark.gov.uk

Hamvas, Renata (LAB - Peckham Rye)
renata.hamvas@southwark.gov.uk

Hargrove, Barrie (LAB - Peckham)
barrie.hargrove@southwark.gov.uk

Hartley, Jon (LAB - College)
jon.hartley@southwark.gov.uk

Hayes, Helen (LAB - College)
helen.hayes@southwark.gov.uk

Hubber, David (LD - Surrey Docks)
david.hubber@southwark.gov.uk

Johnson, Ben (LD - Grange)
ben.johnson@southwark.gov.uk

Kerslake, Eleanor (LAB - Newington)
eleanor.kerslake@southwark.gov.uk

King, Sarah (LAB - South Camberwell)
sarah.king@southwark.gov.uk

Kirby, Anne (LAB - Village)
anne.kirby@southwark.gov.uk

Lambe, Sunny (LAB - South Bermondsey)
sunny.lambe@southwark.gov.uk

Lauder, Lorraine (LAB - Faraday)
lorraine.lauder@southwark.gov.uk

Linforth-Hall, Maria (LD - Cathedrals)
maria.linforthhall@southwark.gov.uk

Livingstone, Richard (LAB - Livesey)
richard.livingstone@southwark.gov.uk

Lury, Rebecca (LAB - East Walworth)
rebecca.lury@southwark.gov.uk

Luthra, Vijay (LAB - Chaucer)
vijay.luthra@southwark.gov.uk

Lyons, Jane (CON - Village)
jane.lyons@southwark.gov.uk

Mann, Eliza (LD - Riverside)
eliza.mann@southwark.gov.uk

McCallum, Hamish (LD - Riverside)
hamish.mccallum@southwark.gov.uk

Merrill, Darren (LAB - East Walworth)
darren.merrill@southwark.gov.uk

Mills, Victoria (LAB - Peckham Rye)
victoria.mills@southwark.gov.uk

Mitchell, Michael (CON - Village)
michael.mitchell@southwark.gov.uk

Mohammed, Jamille (LAB - The Lane)
jamille.mohammed@southwark.gov.uk

Morris, Adele (LD - Cathedrals)
adele.morris@southwark.gov.uk

Noakes, David (LD - Cathedrals)
david.noakes@southwark.gov.uk

O'Brien, Damian (LD - Grange)
damian.obrien@southwark.gov.uk

Okosun, James (LD - Surrey Docks)
james.okosun@southwark.gov.uk

Pollak, Leo (LAB - South Bermondsey)
leo.pollak@southwark.gov.uk

Rajan, Lisa (LD - Surrey Docks)
lisa.rajan@southwark.gov.uk

Rhule, Sandra (LAB - Nunhead)
sandra.rhule@southwark.gov.uk

Seaton, Martin (LAB - East Walworth)
martin.seaton@southwark.gov.uk

Shimell, Rosie (LD - East Dulwich)
rosie.shimell@southwark.gov.uk

Simmons, Andy (LAB - College)
andy.simmons@southwark.gov.uk

Situ, Johnson (LAB - Peckham)
johnson.situ@southwark.gov.uk

Situ, Michael (LAB - Livesey)
michael.situ@southwark.gov.uk

Smith, Charlie (LAB - East Dulwich)
charlie.smith@southwark.gov.uk

Soanes, Cleo (LAB - Peckham)
cleo.soanes@southwark.gov.uk

Williams, Mark (LAB - Brunswick Park)
mark.williams@southwark.gov.uk

Williams, Bill (LAB - Rotherhithe)
bill.williams@southwark.gov.uk

Williams, Kieron (LAB - Camberwell Green)
kieron.williams@southwark.gov.uk

POLITICAL COMPOSITION
LAB: 48, LD: 13, CON: 2

COMMITTEE CHAIRS

Audit & Governance: Mr Paul Fleming

Health & Wellbeing: Mr Peter John

Licensing: Ms Renata Hamvas

Planning: Mr Nick Dolezal

Spelthorne D

Spelthorne Borough Council, Council Offices, Knowle Green, Staines TW18 1XB
☎ 01784 451499 🖷 01784 463356
customer.services@spelthorne.gov.uk www.spelthorne.gov.uk

FACTS AND FIGURES
Parliamentary Constituencies: Spelthorne
EU Constituencies: South East
Election Frequency: Elections are of whole council

PRINCIPAL OFFICERS

Chief Executive: Mr Roberto Tambini, Chief Executive, Council Offices , Knowle Green, Staines TW18 1XB ☎ 01784 446250 🖷 01784 446333 r.tambini@spelthorne.gov.uk

Deputy Chief Executive: Mr Terry Collier , Deputy Chief Executive, Council Offices, Knowle Green, Staines TW18 1XB ☎ 01784 446296 t.collier@spelthorne.gov.uk

Deputy Chief Executive: Mr Lee O'Neil, Deputy Chief Executive, Council Offices, Knowle Green, Staines TW18 1XB ☎ 01784 446377 🖷 01784 446333 l.oneil@spelthorne.gov.uk

Access Officer / Social Services (Disability): Mr Terry Collier , Deputy Chief Executive, Council Offices, Knowle Green, Staines TW18 1XB ☎ 01784 446296 t.collier@spelthorne.gov.uk

Architect, Building / Property Services: Mr Dave Phillips, Asset Manager, Council Offices, Knowle Green, Staines TW18 1XB ☎ 01784 446424 🖷 01784 463356 d.phillips@spelthorne.gov.uk

Best Value: Mr Lee O'Neil, Deputy Chief Executive, Council Offices, Knowle Green, Staines TW18 1XB ☎ 01784 446377 🖷 01784 446333 l.oneil@spelthorne.gov.uk

Building Control: Mr Stephen Bowden , Building Control Manager, Council Offices, Knowle Green, Staines TW18 1XB ☎ 01784 446365 s.bowden@spelthorne.gov.uk

Children / Youth Services: Mr Lee O'Neil, Deputy Chief Executive, Council Offices, Knowle Green, Staines TW18 1XB ☎ 01784 446377 🖷 01784 446333 l.oneil@spelthorne.gov.uk

PR / Communications: Ms Dawn Morrison , Head of Communications, Council Offices, Knowle Green, Staines TW18 1XB ☎ 01784 446432 🖷 01784 446333 d.morrison@spelthorne.gov.uk

Community Safety: Mr Keith McGroary , Head of Community Safety & Economic Development, Council Offices, Knowle Green, Staines TW18 1XB ☎ 01784 444224 k.mcgroary@spelthorne.gov.uk

Computer Management: Mrs Helen Dunn , Head of ICT, Council Offices, Knowle Green, Staines TW18 1XB ☎ 01932 425550; 01748 451499 helen.dunn@runnymede.gov.uk

Contracts: Dr Sandy Muirhead, Head of Sustainability & Leisure Services, Council Offices, Knowle Green, Staines TW18 1XB ☎ 01784 446318 🖷 01784 463356 s.muirhead@spelthorne.gov.uk

Contracts: Ms Jackie Taylor , Head of Street Scene, Central Depot, Kingston Road, Staines TW15 3SE ☎ 01784 446412 j.taylor@spelthorne.gov.uk

Corporate Services: Mr Terry Collier , Deputy Chief Executive, Council Offices, Knowle Green, Staines TW18 1XB ☎ 01784 446296 t.collier@spelthorne.gov.uk

Customer Service: Mrs Linda Norman , Head of Customer Services, Council Offices, Knowle Green, Staines TW18 1XB ☎ 01784 446375 l.norman@spelthorne.gov.uuk

Direct Labour: Mrs Jan Hunt , Head of Human Resources, Council Offices, Knowle Green, Staines TW18 1XB ☎ 01784 446264 🖷 01784 463356 j.hunt@spelthorne.gov.uk

Economic Development: Mr Keith McGroary , Head of Community Safety & Economic Development, Council Offices, Knowle Green, Staines TW18 1XB ☎ 01784 444224 k.mcgroary@spelthorne.gov.uk

E-Government: Mrs Helen Dunn , Head of ICT, Council Offices, Knowle Green, Staines TW18 1XB ☎ 01932 425550; 01748 451499 helen.dunn@runnymede.gov.uk

Electoral Registration: Ms Jayne McEwan, Electoral Services Officer, Council Offices, Knowle Green, Staines TW18 1XB ☎ 01784 446232 j.mcewan@spelthorne.gov.uk

Emergency Planning: Mr Nicholas Moon , Risk & Resilience Manager, Civic Centre, Station Road, Addlestone KT15 2AH ☎ 01932 425178; 01784 451499 🖷 01932 838384 nick.moon@runnymede.gov.uk

Emergency Planning: Mr Roberto Tambini, Chief Executive, Council Offices , Knowle Green, Staines TW18 1XB ☎ 01784 446250 🖷 01784 446333 ✉ r.tambini@spelthorne.gov.uk

Energy Management: Dr Sandy Muirhead, Head of Sustainability & Leisure Services, Council Offices, Knowle Green, Staines TW18 1XB ☎ 01784 446318 🖷 01784 463356 ✉ s.muirhead@spelthorne.gov.uk

Environmental / Technical Services: Dr Sandy Muirhead, Head of Sustainability & Leisure Services, Council Offices, Knowle Green, Staines TW18 1XB ☎ 01784 446318 🖷 01784 463356 ✉ s.muirhead@spelthorne.gov.uk

Environmental Health: Ms Tracey Willmott-French , Senior Environmental Health Manager, Council Offices, Knowle Green, Staines TW18 1XB ☎ 01784 446271 🖷 01784 446333 ✉ t.willmott-french@spelthorne.gov.uk

Estates, Property & Valuation: Mr Dave Phillips, Asset Manager, Council Offices, Knowle Green, Staines TW18 1XB ☎ 01784 446424 🖷 01784 463356 ✉ d.phillips@spelthorne.gov.uk

Events Manager: Ms Lisa Stonehouse , Leisure Services Manager, Council Offices, Knowle Green, Staines TW18 1XB ☎ 01784 446431 🖷 01784 463356 ✉ l.stonehouse@spelthorne.gov.uk

Facilities: Mr Lawrence Cross , Office & Imaging Services Manager, Council Offices, Knowle Green, Staines TW18 1XB ☎ 01784 556233 ✉ l.cross@spelthorne.gov.uk

Finance: Mr Terry Collier , Deputy Chief Executive, Council Offices, Knowle Green, Staines TW18 1XB ☎ 01784 446296 ✉ t.collier@spelthorne.gov.uk

Fleet Management: Ms Jackie Taylor , Head of Street Scene, Central Depot, Kingston Road, Staines TW15 3SE ☎ 01784 446412 ✉ j.taylor@spelthorne.gov.uk

Grounds Maintenance: Ms Jackie Taylor , Head of Street Scene, Council Offices, Knowle Green, Staines TW18 1XB ☎ 01784 446412 ✉ j.taylor@spelthorne.gov.uk

Health and Safety: Mr Stuart Mann, Corporate Health & Safety Officer, Council Offices, Knowle Green, Staines TW18 1XB ☎ 01784 446270 ✉ s.mann@spelthorne.gov.uk

Health and Safety: Ms Jackie Taylor , Head of Street Scene, Central Depot, Kingston Road, Staines TW15 3SE ☎ 01784 446412 ✉ j.taylor@spelthorne.gov.uk

Home Energy Conservation: Dr Sandy Muirhead, Head of Sustainability & Leisure Services, Council Offices, Knowle Green, Staines TW18 1XB ☎ 01784 446318 🖷 01784 463356 ✉ s.muirhead@spelthorne.gov.uk

Housing: Mrs Deborah Ashman, Joint Head of Housing & Independent Living, Council Offices, Knowle Green, Staines TW18 1XB ☎ 01784 446206 ✉ d.ashman@spelthorne.gov.uk

Housing: Ms Karen Sinclair, Joint Head of Housing & Independent Living, Council Offices, Knowle Green, Staines TW18 1XB ☎ 01784 446206 ✉ k.sinclair@spelthorne.gov.uk

Legal: Mr Michael Graham, Head of Corporate Governance & Monitoring Officer, Council Offices , Knowle Green, Staines TW18 1XB ☎ 01784 446227 🖷 01784 446333 ✉ m.graham@spelthorne.gov.uk

Leisure and Cultural Services: Mr Lee O'Neil, Deputy Chief Executive, Council Offices, Knowle Green, Staines TW18 1XB ☎ 01784 446377 🖷 01784 446333 ✉ l.oneil@spelthorne.gov.uk

Licensing: Ms Dawn Morrison , Head of Communications, Council Offices, Knowle Green, Staines TW18 1XB ☎ 01784 446432 🖷 01784 446333 ✉ d.morrison@spelthorne.gov.uk

Lifelong Learning: Mrs Jan Hunt , Head of Human Resources, Council Offices, Knowle Green, Staines TW18 1XB ☎ 01784 446264 🖷 01784 463356 ✉ j.hunt@spelthorne.gov.uk

Lottery Funding, Charity and Voluntary: Mr Terry Collier , Deputy Chief Executive, Council Offices, Knowle Green, Staines TW18 1XB ☎ 01784 446296 ✉ t.collier@spelthorne.gov.uk

Member Services: Mr Michael Graham, Head of Corporate Governance & Monitoring Officer, Council Offices , Knowle Green, Staines TW18 1XB ☎ 01784 446227 🖷 01784 446333 ✉ m.graham@spelthorne.gov.uk

Member Services: Mr Greg Halliwell , Principal Committee Manager, Council Offices, Knowle Green, Staines TW18 1XB ☎ 01784 446267 ✉ g.halliwell@spelthorne.gov.uk

Parking: Dr Sandy Muirhead, Head of Sustainability & Leisure Services, Council Offices, Knowle Green, Staines TW18 1XB ☎ 01784 446318 🖷 01784 463356 ✉ s.muirhead@spelthorne.gov.uk

Partnerships: Mr Roberto Tambini, Chief Executive, Council Offices , Knowle Green, Staines TW18 1XB ☎ 01784 446250 🖷 01784 446333 ✉ r.tambini@spelthorne.gov.uk

Personnel / HR: Ms Jan Hunt , Head of HR, Civic Centre, Station Road, Addlestone KT15 2AH ☎ 01932 425510 ✉ jan.hunt@runnymede.gov.uk

Planning: Mr John Brooks , Head of Planning & Housing Strategy, Council Offices, Knowle Green, Staines TW18 1XB ☎ 01784 446346 ✉ j.brooks@spelthorne.gov.uk

Procurement: Mr Terry Collier , Deputy Chief Executive, Council Offices, Knowle Green, Staines TW18 1XB ☎ 01784 446296 ✉ t.collier@spelthorne.gov.uk

Recycling & Waste Minimisation: Dr Sandy Muirhead, Head of Sustainability & Leisure Services, Council Offices, Knowle Green, Staines TW18 1XB ☎ 01784 446318 🖷 01784 463356 ✉ s.muirhead@spelthorne.gov.uk

Recycling & Waste Minimisation: Ms Jackie Taylor , Head of Street Scene, Central Depot, Kingston Road, Staines TW15 3SE ☎ 01784 446412 ✉ j.taylor@spelthorne.gov.uk

Regeneration: Ms Heather Morgan, Staines-upon-Thames Regeneration Manager, Council Offices, Knowle Green, Staines TW18 1XB ☎ 01784 446352 🖷 01784 463356 ✉ h.morgan@spelthorne.gov.uk

Staff Training: Mrs Jan Hunt, Head of Human Resources, Council Offices, Knowle Green, Staines TW18 1XB ☎ 01784 446264 🖷 01784 463356 ✉ j.hunt@spelthorne.gov.uk

Street Scene: Ms Jackie Taylor , Head of Street Scene, Central Depot, Kingston Road, Staines TW15 3SE ☎ 01784 446412 ✉ j.taylor@spelthorne.gov.uk

Sustainable Communities: Dr Sandy Muirhead, Head of Sustainability & Leisure Services, Council Offices, Knowle Green, Staines TW18 1XB ☎ 01784 446318 🖷 01784 463356 ✉ s.muirhead@spelthorne.gov.uk

Tourism: Mr Keith McGroary , Head of Community Safety & Economic Development, Council Offices, Knowle Green, Staines TW18 1XB ☎ 01784 444224 ✉ k.mcgroary@spelthorne.gov.uk

Town Centre: Mr Michael Graham, Head of Corporate Governance & Monitoring Officer, Council Offices , Knowle Green, Staines TW18 1XB ☎ 01784 446227 🖷 01784 446333 ✉ m.graham@spelthorne.gov.uk

Town Centre: Mr Keith McGroary , Head of Community Safety & Economic Development, Council Offices, Knowle Green, Staines TW18 1XB ☎ 01784 444224 ✉ k.mcgroary@spelthorne.gov.uk

Transport: Ms Jackie Taylor , Head of Street Scene, Central Depot, Kingston Road, Staines TW15 3SE ☎ 01784 446412 ✉ j.taylor@spelthorne.gov.uk

Transport Planner: Mr John Brooks , Head of Planning & Housing Strategy, Council Offices, Knowle Green, Staines TW18 1XB ☎ 01784 446346 ✉ j.brooks@spelthorne.gov.uk

Waste Collection and Disposal: Ms Jackie Taylor , Head of Street Scene, Central Depot, Kingston Road, Staines TW15 3SE ☎ 01784 446412 ✉ j.taylor@spelthorne.gov.uk

Waste Management: Dr Sandy Muirhead, Head of Sustainability & Leisure Services, Council Offices, Knowle Green, Staines TW18 1XB ☎ 01784 446318 🖷 01784 463356 ✉ s.muirhead@spelthorne.gov.uk

Children's Play Areas: Ms Sabina Sims , Allotments Officer, Council Offices, Knowle Green, Staines TW18 1XB ☎ 01784 446327 🖷 01784 446333 ✉ s.sims@spelthorne.gov.uk

COUNCILLORS

***Mayor* Francis**, Mark (CON - Staines)
cllr.francis@spelthorne.gov.uk

***Deputy Mayor* Friday**, Alfred (CON - Sunbury East)
cllr.friday@spelthorne.gov.uk

***Leader of the Council* Watts**, Robert (CON - Shepperton Town)
cllr.watts@spelthorne.gov.uk

***Deputy Leader of the Council* Harman**, Tony (CON - Riverside and Laleham)
cllr.harman@spelthorne.gov.uk

Attewell, Maureen (CON - Laleham and Shepperton Green)
cllr.attewell@spelthorne.gov.uk

Barratt, Richard (CON - Stanwell North)
cllr.barratt@spelthorne.gov.uk

Beardsmore, Ian (LD - Sunbury Common)
cllr.beardsmore@spelthorne.gov.uk

Burkmar, Steven (CON - Staines South)
cllr.burkmar@spelthorne.gov.uk

Chandler, Rose (CON - Ashford East)
cllr.chandler@spelthorne.gov.uk

Davis, Colin (CON - Staines)
cllr.davis@spelthorne.gov.uk

Doran, Susan (LAB - Stanwell North)
cllr.doran@spelthorne.gov.uk

Dunn, Sandra (LD - Halliford and Sunbury West)
cllr.dunn@spelthorne.gov.uk

Edgington, Quentin (CON - Riverside and Laleham)
cllr.edgington@spelthorne.gov.uk

Evans, Tim (CON - Halliford and Sunbury West)
cllr.evans@spelthorne.gov.uk

Flurry, Kevin (CON - Stanwell North)
cllr.flurry@spelthorne.gov.uk

Forbes-Forsyth, Penny (CON - Staines South)
cllr.forbes-forsyth@spelthorne.gov.uk

Frazer, Chris (CON - Ashford East)
cllr.frazer@spelthorne.gov.uk

Gething, Nick (CON - Ashford Town)
cllr.gething@spelthorne.gov.uk

Griffiths, Alison (CON - Sunbury Common)
cllr.griffiths@spelthorne.gov.uk

Harvey, Ian (CON - Sunbury East)
cllr.harvey@spelthorne.gov.uk

Islam, Naz (CON - Ashford Town)
cllr.islam@spelthorne.gov.uk

Jones, Anthony (CON - Halliford and Sunbury West)
cllr.jones@spelthorne.gov.uk

Kavanagh, John (CON - Ashford Common)
cllr.kavanagh@spelthorne.gov.uk

Leighton, Vivienne (CON - Shepperton Town)
cllr.leighton@spelthorne.gov.uk

Lohmann, Sabine (CON - Staines South)
cllr.lohmann@spelthorne.gov.uk

Madams, Mary (CON - Laleham and Shepperton Green)
cllr.madams@spelthorne.gov.uk

Mitchell, Tony (CON - Ashford East)
cllr.mitchell@spelthorne.gov.uk

Mooney, Sinead (CON - Ashford North and Stanwell South)
cllr.mooney@spelthorne.gov.uk

Neale, Anne-Marie (CON - Ashford North and Stanwell South)
cllr.neale@spelthorne.gov.uk

Patel, Daxa (CON - Sunbury East)
cllr.patel@spelthorne.gov.uk

Pinkerton, Jean (CON - Staines)
cllr.pinkerton@spelthorne.gov.uk

Rybinski, Olivia (CON - Ashford Town)
cllr.rybinski@spelthorne.gov.uk

Saliagopoulos, Denise (CON - Riverside and Laleham)
cllr.saliagopoulos@spelthorne.gov.uk

Sexton, Joanne (CON - Ashford North and Stanwell South)
cllr.sexton@spelthorne.gov.uk

Sider, Robin (CON - Shepperton Town)
cllr.sider@spelthorne.gov.uk

Smith-Ainsley, Richard (CON - Laleham and Shepperton Green)
cllr.smith-ainsley@spelthorne.gov.uk

Spoor, Bernie (LD - Sunbury Common)
cllr.spoor@spelthorne.gov.uk

Thomson, Howard (CON - Ashford Common)
cllr.thomson@spelthorne.gov.uk

Williams, Howard (CON - Ashford Common)
cllr.williams@spelthorne.gov.uk

POLITICAL COMPOSITION

CON: 35, LD: 3, LAB: 1

COMMITTEE CHAIRS

Audit: Ms Mary Madams

Licensing: Mr Robin Sider

Planning: Mr Richard Smith-Ainsley

St. Albans City D

St. Albans City & District Council, District Council Offices, St. Peter's Street, St. Albans AL1 3JE
☎ 01727 866100 ✉ feedback@stalbans.gov.uk 💻 www.stalbans.gov.uk

FACTS AND FIGURES

Parliamentary Constituencies: Hitchin and Harpenden, St. Albans
EU Constituencies: Eastern
Election Frequency: Elections are by thirds

PRINCIPAL OFFICERS

Chief Executive: Dr James Blake , Chief Executive, District Council Offices, St. Peter's Street, St. Albans AL1 3JE ☎ 01727 819552 🖷 01727 819534 ✉ james.blake@stalbans.gov.uk

Deputy Chief Executive: Mr Colm O'Callaghan , Deputy Chief Executive (Finance), District Council Offices, St. Peter's Street, St. Albans AL1 3JE ☎ 01727 819200 🖷 01727 819467 ✉ colm.o'callaghan@stalbans.gov.uk

Best Value: Mr Paul Howes , Policy, Partnerships & Economic Development Manager, District Council Offices, St. Peter's Street, St. Albans AL1 3JE ☎ 01727 819552 🖷 01727 819534 ✉ paul.howes@stalbans.gov.uk

Building Control: Ms Tracy Harvey , Head of Planning & Building Control, District Council Offices, St. Peter's Street, St. Albans AL1 3JE ☎ 01727 819300 ✉ tracy.harvey@stalbans.gov.uk

Children / Youth Services: Mr Richard Shwe, Head of Community Services, District Council Offices, St. Peter's Street, St. Albans AL1 3JE ☎ 01727 819365 🖷 01727 819478 ✉ richard.shwe@stalbans.gov.uk

PR / Communications: Ms Claire Wainwright , Executive & Communications Manager, District Council Offices, St. Peter's Street, St. Albans AL1 3JE ☎ 01727 819572 🖷 01727 819534 ✉ claire.wainwright@stalbans.gov.uk

Community Safety: Mr Neil Kieran , Principal Community Protection Officer, District Council Offices, St. Peter's Street, St. Albans AL1 3JE ☎ 01727 819416 ✉ neil.kieran@stalbans.gov.uk

Computer Management: Ms Amanda Foley , Head of Corporate Services, District Council Offices, St. Peter's Street, St. Albans AL1 3JE ☎ 01727 819308 ✉ amanda.foley@stalbans.gov.uk

Corporate Services: Dr James Blake , Chief Executive, District Council Offices, St. Peter's Street, St. Albans AL1 3JE ☎ 01727 819552 🖷 01727 819534 ✉ james.blake@stalbans.gov.uk

Customer Service: Ms Amanda Foley , Head of Corporate Services, District Council Offices, St. Peter's Street, St. Albans AL1 3JE ☎ 01727 819308 ✉ amanda.foley@stalbans.gov.uk

Economic Development: Ms Maria Cutler , Sustainable Economic Development Officer, District Council Offices, St. Peter's Street, St. Albans AL1 3JE ☎ 01727 819243 ✉ maria.cutler@stalbans.gov.uk

Electoral Registration: Mr Mike Lovelady, Head of Legal, Democratic & Regulatory Services, District Council Offices, St. Peter's Street, St. Albans AL1 3JE ☎ 01727 819502 🖷 01727 819255 ✉ mike.lovelady@stalbans.gov.uk

Emergency Planning: Mr Paul Blande , Emergency Planning & Community Resilience Officer, District Council Offices, St. Peter's Street, St. Albans AL1 3JE ☎ 01727 814612 🖷 01727 819534 ✉ paul.blande@stablans.gov.uk

Environmental Health: Ms Maria Stagg , Regulatory Services Manager, District Council Offices, St. Peter's Street, St. Albans AL1 3JE ☎ 01727 819436 🖷 01727 819433 ✉ maria.stagg@stalbans.gov.uk

Estates, Property & Valuation: Ms Debbi White , Property & Asset Manager, District Council Offices, St. Peter's Street, St. Albans AL1 3JE ☎ 01727 819515 🖷 01727 819478 ✉ debbi.white@stalbans.gov.uk

Facilities: Ms Debbi White , Property & Asset Manager, District Council Offices, St. Peter's Street, St. Albans AL1 3JE ☎ 01727 819515 🖷 01727 819478 ✉ debbi.white@stalbans.gov.uk

Finance: Mr Colm O'Callaghan , Deputy Chief Executive (Finance), District Council Offices, St. Peter's Street, St. Albans AL1 3JE ☎ 01727 819200 🖷 01727 819467 ✉ colm.o'callaghan@stalbans.gov.uk

Grounds Maintenance: Mr Jon Green , Parks & Green Spaces Manager, District Council Offices, St. Peter's Street, St. Albans AL1 3JE ☎ 01727 819233 🖷 01727 819478 ✉ jon.green@stalbans.gov.uk

Health and Safety: Ms Maria Stagg , Regulatory Services Manager, District Council Offices, St. Peter's Street, St. Albans AL1 3JE ☎ 01727 819436 🖷 01727 819433 ✉ maria.stagg@stalbans.gov.uk

Housing: Ms Karen Dragovic, Head of Housing, District Council Offices, St. Peter's Street, St. Albans AL1 3JE ☎ 01727 819400 ✉ karen.dragovic@stalbans.gov.uk

Housing Maintenance: Ms Karen Dragovic, Head of Housing, District Council Offices, St. Peter's Street, St. Albans AL1 3JE ☎ 01727 819400 ✉ karen.dragovic@stalbans.gov.uk

Legal: Mr Mike Lovelady, Head of Legal, Democratic & Regulatory Services, District Council Offices, St. Peter's Street, St. Albans AL1 3JE ☎ 01727 819502 🖷 01727 819255 ✉ mike.lovelady@stalbans.gov.uk

Leisure and Cultural Services: Mr Richard Shwe, Head of Community Services, District Council Offices, St. Peter's Street, St. Albans AL1 3JE ☎ 01727 819365 🖷 01727 819478 ✉ richard.shwe@stalbans.gov.uk

Licensing: Mrs Lesley Cameron, Business Compliance Manager, District Council Offices, St. Peter's Street, St. Albans AL1 3JE ☎ 01727 819454 🖷 01727 819433 ✉ lesley.cameron@stalbans.gov.uk

Lottery Funding, Charity and Voluntary: Mr Alan Partington , Financial Services Manager, District Council Offices, St. Peter's Street, St. Albans AL1 3JE ☎ 01727 819201 ✉ alan.partington@stalbans.gov.uk

Member Services: Ms Elizabeth Heath , Democratic Services Manager, District Council Offices, St. Peter's Street, St. Albans AL1 3JE ☎ 01727 819519 ✉ elizabeth.heath@stalbans.gov.uk

Parking: Ms Maria Stagg , Regulatory Services Manager, District Council Offices, St. Peter's Street, St. Albans AL1 3JE ☎ 01727 819436 🖷 01727 819433 ✉ maria.stagg@stalbans.gov.uk

Partnerships: Mr Paul Howes , Policy, Partnerships & Economic Development Manager, District Council Offices, St. Peter's Street, St. Albans AL1 3JE ☎ 01727 819552 🖷 01727 819534 ✉ paul.howes@stalbans.gov.uk

Personnel / HR: Ms Amanda Foley , Head of Corporate Services, District Council Offices, St. Peter's Street, St. Albans AL1 3JE ☎ 01727 819308 ✉ amanda.foley@stalbans.gov.uk

Planning: Ms Tracy Harvey , Head of Planning & Building Control, District Council Offices, St. Peter's Street, St. Albans AL1 3JE ☎ 01727 819300 ✉ tracy.harvey@stalbans.gov.uk

Procurement: Mr Richard Shwe, Head of Community Services, District Council Offices, St. Peter's Street, St. Albans AL1 3JE ☎ 01727 819365 🖷 01727 819478 ✉ richard.shwe@stalbans.gov.uk

Recycling & Waste Minimisation: Mr Richard Shwe, Head of Community Services, District Council Offices, St. Peter's Street, St. Albans AL1 3JE ☎ 01727 819365 🖷 01727 819478 ✉ richard.shwe@stalbans.gov.uk

Regeneration: Ms Maria Cutler , Sustainable Economic Development Officer, District Council Offices, St. Peter's Street, St. Albans AL1 3JE ☎ 01727 819243 ✉ maria.cutler@stalbans.gov.uk

Staff Training: Ms Amanda Foley , Head of Corporate Services, District Council Offices, St. Peter's Street, St. Albans AL1 3JE ☎ 01727 819308 ✉ amanda.foley@stalbans.gov.uk

Street Scene: Ms Tracy Harvey , Head of Planning & Building Control, District Council Offices, St. Peter's Street, St. Albans AL1 3JE ☎ 01727 819300 ✉ tracy.harvey@stalbans.gov.uk

Sustainable Communities: Mr Paul Howes , Policy, Partnerships & Economic Development Manager, District Council Offices, St. Peter's Street, St. Albans AL1 3JE ☎ 01727 819552 🖷 01727 819534 ✉ paul.howes@stalbans.gov.uk

Sustainable Development: Ms Candice Luper , Sustainability Projects Officer, District Council Offices, St. Peter's Street, St. Albans AL1 3JE ☎ 01727 819466 🖷 01727 819534 ✉ candice.luper@stalbans.gov.uk

Tourism: Mr Charles Baker, Visitor Manager, District Council Offices, St. Peter's Street, St. Albans AL1 3JE ☎ 01727 819275 ✉ charles.baker@stalbans.gov.uk

Waste Collection and Disposal: Mr Richard Shwe, Head of Community Services, District Council Offices, St. Peter's Street, St. Albans AL1 3JE ☎ 01727 819365 🖷 01727 819478 ✉ richard.shwe@stalbans.gov.uk

Waste Management: Mr Richard Shwe, Head of Community Services, District Council Offices, St. Peter's Street, St. Albans AL1 3JE ☎ 01727 819365 🖷 01727 819478 ✉ richard.shwe@stalbans.gov.uk

COUNCILLORS

***Mayor* Harrison**, Geoffrey (LD - Cunningham)
cllr.g.harrison@stalbans.gov.uk

***Deputy Mayor* Churchard**, Janet (LD - Marshalswick North)
cllr.j.churchard@stalbans.gov.uk

***Leader of the Council* Daly**, Julian (CON - Harpenden West)
cllr.j.daly@stalbans.gov.uk

***Group Leader* Grover**, Simon (GRN - St Peters)
cllr.s.grover@stalbans.gov.uk

***Group Leader* Mills**, Roma (LAB - Batchwood)
cllr.r.mills@stalbans.gov.uk

***Group Leader* White**, Chris (LD - Clarence)
cllr.c.white@stalbans.gov.uk

Bell, Julie (CON - Harpenden North)
cllr.j.bell@stalbans.gov.uk

Bolton, Lyn (CON - Marshalswick North)
cllr.l.bolton@stalbans.gov.uk

Brazier, Chris (LD - Colney Heath)
cllr.c.brazier@stalbans.gov.uk

Brewster, Annie (CON - Wheathampstead)
cllr.a.brewster@stalbans.gov.uk

Calder, Simon (CON - London Colney)
cllr.s.calder@stalbans.gov.uk

Campbell, Alec (CON - St Peters)
cllr.a.campbell@stalbans.gov.uk

ST. ALBANS CITY

Chichester-Miles, Daniel (CON - Harpenden West)
cllr.d.chichester-miles@stalbans.gov.uk

Chivers, Jessica (CON - Verulam)
cllr.j.chivers@stalbans.gov.uk

Clark, Gillian (CON - Wheathampstead)
cllr.g.clark@stalbans.gov.uk

Clegg, Thomas (LD - Marshalswick North)
cllr.t.clegg@stalbans.gov.uk

Crawley, Maxine (CON - Redbourn)
cllr.m.crawley@stalbans.gov.uk

Curthoys, Richard (CON - Marshalswick South)
cllr.r.curthoys@stalbans.gov.uk

Davies, Alun (CON - St Peters)
cllr.a.davies@stalbans.gov.uk

Day, Ian (LD - Colney Heath)
cllr.i.day@stalbans.gov.uk

Donald, Robert (LD - Cunningham)
cllr.r.donald@stalbans.gov.uk

Ellis, Brian (CON - Harpenden South)
cllr.b.ellis@stalbans.gov.uk

Farmer, Rosemary (CON - Harpenden East)
cllr.r.farmer@stalbans.gov.uk

Featherstone, Sue (CON - St Stephen)
cllr.s.featherstone@stalbans.gov.uk

Gardner, Katherine (LAB - London Colney)
cllr.k.gardner@stalbans.gov.uk

Gaygusuz, Salih (CON - Marshalswick South)
cllr.m.salih@stalbans.gov.uk

Gibbard, Brian (CON - St Stephen)
cllr.b.gibbard@stalbans.gov.uk

Gordon, Dreda (LAB - London Colney)
cllr.d.gordon@stalbans.gov.uk

Grant, Iain (LAB - Sopwell)
cllr.i.grant@stalbans.gov.uk

Harris, Eileen (LAB - Sopwell)
cllr.e.harris@stalbans.gov.uk

Heritage, David (CON - Harpenden South)
cllr.d.heritage@stalbans.gov.uk

Heritage, Teresa (CON - Harpenden South)
cllr.t.heritage@stalbans.gov.uk

Hill, Edgar (LD - Verulam)
cllr.e.hill@stalbans.gov.uk

Lee, Aislinn (LD - Park Street)
cllr.a.lee@stalbans.gov.uk

Leonard, Frances (CON - Sandbridge)
cllr.f.leonard@stalbans.gov.uk

Maynard, Mary (CON - Harpenden East)
cllr.m.maynard@stalbans.gov.uk

McHale, Gerard (LD - Clarence)
cllr.g.mchale@stalbans.gov.uk

McKeown, Steve (CON - Marshalswick South)
cllr.s.mckeown@stalbans.gov.uk

Mead, Victoria (CON - Redbourn)

Pakenham, Malachy (LAB - Batchwood)
cllr.m.pakenham@stalbans.gov.uk

Pawle, Bert (CON - Harpenden North)
cllr.a.pawle@stalbans.gov.uk

Prowse, Robert (LD - Cunningham)
cllr.r.prowse@stalbans.gov.uk

Rahim, Momotaz (LAB - Ashley)
cllr.m.rahim@stalbans.gov.uk

Read, Beric (CON - Sandridge)
cllr.b.read@stalbans.gov.uk

Rowlands, Anthony (LD - Ashley)
cllr.a.rowlands@stalbans.gov.uk

Rowlands, Sam (LD - Clarence)
cllr.s.rowlands@stalbans.gov.uk

Smith, Janet (LAB - Sopwell)
cllr.j.smith@stalbans.gov.uk

Smith, Tim (CON - Batchwood)
cllr.t.smith@stalbans.gov.uk

Swendell, Tony (IND - Redbourn)
cllr.a.swendwell@stalbans.gov.uk

Turner, Geoffrey (CON - Harpenden North)
cllr.g.turner@stalbans.gov.uk

Wakely, Mike (CON - Harpenden East)
cllr.m.wakely@stalbans.gov.uk

Wartenberg, Fred (LD - Verulam)
cllr.f.wartenberg@stalbans.gov.uk

Weaver, Michael (CON - Harpenden West)
cllr.m.weaver@stalbans.gov.uk

Winstone, David (CON - St Stephen)
cllr.d.winstone@stalbans.gov.uk

Wood, Sandra (CON - Wheathampstead)
cllr.s.wood@stalbans.gov.uk

Wright, Jock (CON - Park Street)
cllr.j.wright@stalbans.gov.uk

Yates, David (LD - Park Street)
cllr.d.yates@stalbans.gov.uk

Zia, Iqbal (LD - Ashley)
cllr.i.zia@stalbans.gov.uk

POLITICAL COMPOSITION

CON: 32, LD: 16, LAB: 8, GRN: 1, IND: 1

COMMITTEE CHAIRS

Audit: Mr Chris White

Health & Wellbeing: Ms Rosemary Farmer

Licensing: Ms Maxine Crawley

Planning: Mr Julian Daly

St. Edmundsbury D

St. Edmundsbury Borough Council, West Suffolk House, Western Way, Bury St. Edmunds IP33 3YB
☎ 01284 763233 ✉ stedmundsbury@stedsbc.gov.uk
🖳 www.stedmundsbury.gov.uk

FACTS AND FIGURES

Parliamentary Constituencies: Bury St. Edmunds
EU Constituencies: Eastern
Election Frequency: Elections are of whole council

PRINCIPAL OFFICERS

Chief Executive: Mr Ian Gallin , Joint Chief Executive, District Offices, College Heath Road, Mildenhall IP28 7EY ☎ 01638 719324; 01284 757001 ✉ ian.gallin@forest-heath.gov.uk

Senior Management: Ms Davina Howes , Head of Families & Communities, West Suffolk House, Western Way, Bury St. Edmunds IP33 3EY ☎ 01284 757070 ✉ davina.howes@westsuffolk.gov.uk

Senior Management: Ms Rachael Mann , Head of Resources & Performance, West Suffolk House, Western Way, Bury St. Edmunds IP33 3EY ☎ 01638 719245 ✉ rachael.mann@westsuffolk.gov.uk

Senior Management: Mr Simon Phelan , Head of Housing, West Suffolk House, Western Way, Bury St. Edmunds IP33 3YB ☎ 01638 719440 ✉ simon.phelan@westsuffolk.gov.uk

Senior Management: Mrs Karen Points , Head of HR, Legal & Democratic Services, West Suffolk House, Western Way, Bury St. Edmunds IP33 3EY ☎ 01285 757015 ✉ karen.points@westsuffolk.gov.uk

Senior Management: Mr Mark Walsh , Head of Operations, West Suffolk House, Western Way, Bury St. Edmunds IP33 3EY ☎ 01284 757300 ✉ mark.walsh@westsuffolk.gov.uk

Senior Management: Mr Alex Wilson, Corporate Director, West Suffolk House, Western Way, Bury St. Edmunds IP33 3YB ☎ 01284 757695 ✉ alex.wilson@westsuffolk.gov.uk

Senior Management: Mr Steven Wood , Head of Planning & Growth, West Suffolk House, Western Way, Bury St. Edmunds IP33 3EY ☎ 01284 757306 ✉ steven.wood@westsuffolk.gov.uk

Children / Youth Services: Mr Simon Pickering , Youth & Community Development Officer, West Suffolk House, Western Way, Bury St. Edmunds IP33 3YB ☎ 01284 757077 ✉ simon.pickering@stedsbc.gov.uk

PR / Communications: Ms Marianne Hulland, Communications Manager, West Suffolk House, Western Way, Bury St. Edmunds IP33 3YU ☎ 01284 757034; 01638 719361 🖷 01638 716493 ✉ marianne.hulland@forest-heath.gov.uk

Community Safety: Mrs Helen Lindfield , Community Safety Officer, West Suffolk House, Western Way, Bury St. Edmunds IP33 3YB ☎ 01284 757620 ✉ helen.lindfield@stedsbc.gov.uk

Computer Management: Mr James Wager , Business Development Innovations Manager, West Suffolk House, Western Way, Bury St. Edmunds IP33 3EY ☎ 01284 757205 ✉ james.wager@westsuffolk.gov.uk

Customer Service: Ms Davina Howes , Head of Families & Communities, West Suffolk House, Western Way, Bury St. Edmunds IP33 3EY ☎ 01284 757070 ✉ davina.howes@westsuffolk.gov.uk

Direct Labour: Mr Mark Walsh, Head of Waste Management & Property Services, West Suffolk House, Western Way, Bury St. Edmunds IP33 3YU ☎ 01284 757300 ✉ mark.walsh@westsuffolk.gov.uk

Economic Development: Mrs Andrea Mayley, Head of Economic Development & Growth, West Suffolk House, Western Way, Bury St. Edmunds IP33 3YU ☎ 01284 757343 ✉ andrea.mayley@westsuffolk.gov.uk

Electoral Registration: Mrs Fiona Osman , Electoral Services Manager, West Suffolk House, Western Way, Bury St. Edmunds IP33 3EY ☎ 01285 757105 ✉ fiona.osman@westsuffolk.gov.uk

Emergency Planning: Mr Alan Points, Emergency Planning Officer, West Suffolk House, Western Way , Bury St. Edmunds IP33 1YU ☎ 01284 758461 🖷 01284 757039 ✉ alan.points@stedsbc.gov.uk

Energy Management: Mr Peter Gudde , Head of Property Services & Engineering, West Suffolk House, Western Way, Bury St. Edmunds IP33 3YB ☎ 01284 757042 ✉ peter.gudde@stedsbc.gov.uk

Environmental / Technical Services: Mr Peter Gudde , Head of Property Services & Engineering, West Suffolk House, Western Way, Bury St. Edmunds IP33 3YB ☎ 01284 757042 ✉ peter.gudde@stedsbc.gov.uk

Environmental Health: Mr Mark Johnson , Principal Environmental Health Officer, West Suffolk House, Western Way, Bury St. Edmunds IP33 3YB ☎ 01284 757051 ✉ mark.johnson@stedsbc.gov.uk

Environmental Health: Mr Steven Wood , Head of Planning & Growth, West Suffolk House, Western Way, Bury St. Edmunds IP33 3YB ☎ 01284 757306 ✉ steven.wood@westsuffolk.gov.uk

Facilities: Mr Mark Walsh , Head of Operations, West Suffolk House, Western Way, Bury St. Edmunds IP33 3EY ☎ 01284 757300 ✉ mark.walsh@westsuffolk.gov.uk

Finance: Ms Rachael Mann , Head of Resources & Performance, West Suffolk House, Western Way, Bury St. Edmunds IP33 3YB ☎ 01638 719245 ✉ rachael.mann@westsuffolk.gov.uk

Fleet Management: Mr Philip Clifford, Fleet & Technical Manager, West Suffolk House, Western Way, Bury St. Edmunds IP33 3YU ☎ 01284 757459 🖷 01284 757473 ✉ philip.clifford@stedsbc.gov.uk

Grounds Maintenance: Mr Damien Parker , Leisure & Cultural Operations Manager, West Suffolk House, Western Way, Bury St. Edmunds IP33 3YU ☎ 01284 757090 ✉ damien.parker@westsuffolk.gov.uk

Health and Safety: Mr Martin Hosker, Health & Safety Manager, West Suffolk House, Western Way, Bury St. Edmunds IP33 3YU ☎ 01284 757010 🖷 01284 757014 ✉ martin.hosker@stedsbc.gov.uk

Housing: Mr Simon Phelan , Head of Housing, West Suffolk House, Western Way, Bury St. Edmunds IP33 3YB ☎ 01638 719440 ✉ simon.phelan@westsuffolk.gov.uk

ST. EDMUNDSBURY

Legal: Mrs Karen Points , Head of HR, Legal & Democratic Services, West Suffolk House, Western Way, Bury St. Edmunds IP33 3EY ☎ 01285 757015 ✉ karen.points@westsuffolk.gov.uk

Licensing: Mr Tom Wright , Business Regulation & Licensing Manager, West Suffolk House, Western Way, Bury St. Edmunds IP33 3YB ☎ 01638 719223 ✉ tom.wright@westsuffolk.gov.uk

Member Services: Mrs Karen Points , Head of HR, Legal & Democratic Services, West Suffolk House, Western Way, Bury St. Edmunds IP33 3EY ☎ 01285 757015 ✉ karen.points@westsuffolk.gov.uk

Parking: Mr Darren Dixon , Markets & Car Parks Manager, West Suffolk House, Western Way, Bury St. Edmunds IP33 3EY ☎ 01284 757413 ✉ darren.dixon@stedsbc.gov.uk

Personnel / HR: Mrs Karen Points , Head of Human Resources, Legal & Democratic Services, West Suffolk House, Western Way, Bury St. Edmunds IP33 3YB ☎ 01638 719793 ✉ karen.points@westsuffolk.gov.uk

Planning: Mr Steven Wood , Head of Planning & Growth, West Suffolk House, Western Way, Bury St. Edmunds IP33 3YB ☎ 01284 757306 ✉ steven.wood@westsuffolk.gov.uk

Procurement: Mr Mark Walsh, Head of Waste Management & Property Services, West Suffolk House, Western Way, Bury St. Edmunds IP33 3YU ☎ 01284 757300 ✉ mark.walsh@westsuffolk.gov.uk

Recycling & Waste Minimisation: Mr Mark Walsh, Head of Waste Management & Property Services, West Suffolk House, Western Way, Bury St. Edmunds IP33 3YU ☎ 01284 757300 ✉ mark.walsh@westsuffolk.gov.uk

Regeneration: Mrs Andrea Mayley, Head of Economic Development & Growth, West Suffolk House, Western Way, Bury St. Edmunds IP33 3YU ☎ 01284 757343 ✉ andrea.mayley@westsuffolk.gov.uk

Street Scene: Mr Mark Walsh, Head of Waste Management & Property Services, West Suffolk House, Western Way, Bury St. Edmunds IP33 3YU ☎ 01284 757300 ✉ mark.walsh@westsuffolk.gov.uk

Sustainable Communities: Mr Alex Wilson, Corporate Director, West Suffolk House, Western Way, Bury St. Edmunds IP33 3YB ☎ 01284 757695 ✉ alex.wilson@westsuffolk.gov.uk

Tourism: Ms Sharon Fairweather , Tourist Information Centre Manager, Tourist Information Centre, 6 Angel Hill, Bury St. Edmunds IP33 1UZ ☎ 01284 757094 🖷 01284 757093 ✉ sharon.fairweather@stedsbc.gov.uk

Waste Collection and Disposal: Mr Mark Walsh, Head of Waste Management & Property Services, West Suffolk House, Western Way, Bury St. Edmunds IP33 3YU ☎ 01284 757300 ✉ mark.walsh@westsuffolk.gov.uk

Waste Management: Mr Mark Walsh, Head of Waste Management & Property Services, West Suffolk House, Western Way, Bury St. Edmunds IP33 3YU ☎ 01284 757300 ✉ mark.walsh@westsuffolk.gov.uk

COUNCILLORS

***Mayor* Chung**, Patrick (CON - Southgate)
patrick.chung@stedsbc.gov.uk

***Deputy Mayor* Wakelam**, Julia (GRN - Risbygate)
julia.wakelam@stedsbc.gov.uk

***Leader of the Council* Griffiths**, John (CON - Ixworth)
john.griffiths@stedsbc.gov.uk

***Deputy Leader of the Council* Mildmay-White**, Sara (CON - Rougham)
sara.mildmay-white@stedsbc.gov.uk

***Group Leader* Brown**, Anthony (UKIP - Haverhill East)

***Group Leader* Nettleton**, David (IND - Risbygate)
david.nettleton@stedsbc.gov.uk

Broughton, Sarah (CON - Great Barton)
sarah.broughton@stedsbc.gov.uk

Brown, Simon (CON - Pakenham)
simon.brown@stedsbc.gov.uk

Buckle, Terry (CON - Moreton Hall)
terry.buckle@stedsbc.gov.uk

Bull, Carol (CON - Barningham)
carol.bull@stedsbc.gov.uk

Burns, John (UKIP - Haverhill East)
john.burns@stedsbc.gov.uk

Clements, Terry (CON - Horringer and Whelnetham)
terry.clements@stedsbc.gov.uk

Cockle, Bob (LAB - St Olaves)
bob.cockle@stedsbc.gov.uk

Crooks, Jason (UKIP - Haverhill South)
jason.crooks@stedsbc.gov.uk

Everitt, Robert (CON - MInden)
robert.everitt@stedsbc.gov.uk

Farthing, Jeremy (CON - Haverhill West)
jeremy.farthing@stedsbc.gov.uk

Fox, Paula (CON - Haverhill South)
paula.fox@stedsbc.gov.uk

Glossop, Susan (CON - Risby)
susan.glossop@stedsbc.gov.uk

Hailstone, Wayne (CON - Westgate)
wayne.hailstone@stedsbc.gov.uk

Hind, Diane (LAB - Northgate)
diane.hind@stedsbc.gov.uk

Hopfensperger, Rebecca (CON - Fornham)
rebecca.hopfensperger@stedsbc.gov.uk

Hopfensperger, Paul (IND - St Olaves)
paul.hopfensperger@stedsbc.gov.uk

Houlder, Ian (CON - Barrow)
ian.houlder@stedsbc.gov.uk

Marks, Tim (CON - Haverhill North)
tim.marks@suffolkcc.gov.uk

Marks, Margaret (CON - Haverhill West)
margaret.marks@stedsbc.gov.uk

McLatchy, Betty (CON - Haverhill North)
betty.mclatchy@stedsbc.gov.uk

McLatchy, Ivor (CON - Haverhill East)
ivor.mclatchy@stedsbc.gov.uk

Midwood, Jane (CON - Withersfield)
jane.midwood@stedsbc.gov.uk

Pollington, Clive (CON - Wickhambrook)
clive.pollington@stedsbc.gov.uk

Pugh, Alaric (CON - Clare)
alaric.pugh@stedsbc.gov.uk

Rayner, Joanna (CON - Abbeygate)
joanna.rayner@stedsbc.gov.uk

Richardson, Karen Denise (CON - Haverhill East)
karen.richardson@stedsbc.gov.uk

Roach, David (CON - Haverhill West)
david.roach@stedsbc.gov.uk

Robbins, Barry (UKIP - Haverhill North)
barry.robbins@stedsbc.gov.uk

Rout, Richard (CON - Westgate)
richard.rout@stedsbc.gov.uk

Rushen, Angela (CON - Chedburgh)
angela.rushen@stedsbc.gov.uk

Speed, Andrew (CON - Abbeygate)
andrew.speed@stedsbc.gov.uk

Springett, Clive (CON - Minden)
clive.springett@stedsbc.gov.uk

Stamp, Sarah (CON - Southgate)
sarah.stamp@stedsbc.gov.uk

Stevens, Peter (CON - Cavendish)
peter.stevens@stedsbc.gov.uk

Thompson, Peter (CON - Moreton Hall)
peter.thompson@stedsbc.gov.uk

Thorndyke, Jim (CON - Stanton)
jim.thorndyke@stedsbc.gov.uk

Wade, Paula (CON - Bardwell)
paula.wade@stedsbc.gov.uk

Warby, Frank (CON - Moreton Hall)
frank.warby@stedsbc.gov.uk

Warby, Patricia (CON - Eastgate) patricia.warby@stedsbc.gov.uk

POLITICAL COMPOSITION

CON: 36, UKIP: 4, IND: 2, LAB: 2, GRN: 1

COMMITTEE CHAIRS

Audit & Performance: Ms Sarah Broughton

Licensing: Mr Frank Warby

St. Helens M

St. Helens Metropolitan Borough Council, Town Hall, Victoria Square, Corporation Street, St. Helens WA10 1HP
☎ 01744 456789 🖷 01744 456895 🖳 www.sthelens.gov.uk

FACTS AND FIGURES

Parliamentary Constituencies: St. Helens North, St. Helens South and Whiston
EU Constituencies: North West
Election Frequency: Elections are by thirds

PRINCIPAL OFFICERS

Chief Executive: Mr Mike Palin , Chief Executive, Town Hall, Victoria Square, Corporation Street, St. Helens WA10 1HP ☎ 01744 676101 ✉ mikepalin@sthelens.gov.uk

Deputy Chief Executive: Mr Ian Roberts, Assistant Chief Executive - Finance, Chief Executive's Department, Town Hall, Victoria Square, Corporation Street, St. Helens WA10 1HP ☎ 01744 676789 ✉ ianroberts@sthelens.gov.uk

Senior Management: Ms Liz Gaulton , Director - Public Health, Town Hall, Victoria Square, Corporation Street, St. Helens WA10 1HP ☎ 01744 676789 ✉ lizgaulton@sthelens.gov.uk

Senior Management: Ms Angela Sanderson , Assistant Chief Executive - Legal & Administrative Services, Town Hall, Victoria Square, Corporation Street, St. Helens WA10 1HP ☎ 01744 676789 ✉ angelasanderson@sthelens.gov.uk

Architect, Building / Property Services: Mr Martin Farrell , Property Assets & Facilities Management, Wesley House, Corporation Street, St. Helens WA10 1HF ☎ 01744 676789 ✉ martinfarrell@sthelens.gov.uk

Architect, Building / Property Services: Mr Stuart Rainbow , Manager - Architectural Services, Wesley House, Corporation Street, St. Helens WA10 1HP ☎ 01744 676789 ✉ stuartrainbow@Sthelens.gov.uk

Building Control: Mr John Murdock , Principal Building Control Officer, Town Hall, Victoria Square, Corporation Street, St. Helens WA10 1HP ☎ 01744 676789 ✉ johnmurdock@sthelens.gov.uk

Catering Services: Mrs Vikki Atherton , Civic Events & Mayoral Services Officer, Hardshaw Brook Depot, Parr Street, St. Helens WA9 WJR ☎ 01744 676789 ✉ vikkiatherton@sthelens.gov.uk

Children / Youth Services: Mr Andy Dempsey, Head - Children & Young People's Services, Atlas House, Corporation Street, St. Helens WA9 1LD ☎ 01744 676789 🖷 01744 455936 ✉ andydempsey@sthelens.gov.uk

Civil Registration: Ms Anne Atherton , Registration Services Manager, Town Hall, Victoria Square, Corporation Street, St. Helens WA10 1HP ☎ 01744 676789 ✉ anneatherton@sthelens.gov.uk

PR / Communications: Mr Nick Cook , Press & Public Relations Manager, Town Hall, Victoria Square, Corporation Street, St. Helens WA10 1HP ☎ 01744 676789 ✉ nickcook@sthelens.gov.uk

Community Safety: Mr Stephen Tracey, Head - Housing & Safer Communities Initiative, Town Hall, Victoria Square, Corporation Street, St. Helens WA10 1HP ☎ 01744 676789 ✉ stephentracey@sthelens.gov.uk

ST. HELENS

Computer Management: Mr Steve Sharples , ICT Business Manager, Lincoln House, Corporation Street, St. Helens WA9 1LD ☎ 01744 676789 stesharples@sthelens.gov.uk

Consumer Protection and Trading Standards: Mr Darrell Wilson, Chief Trading Standards Officer, Wesley House, Corporation Street, St. Helens WA10 1HF ☎ 01744 676789 darrellwilson@sthelens.gov.uk

Corporate Services: Mr Peter Hughes, Head - Policy, Town Hall, Victoria Square, Corporation Street, St. Helens WA10 1HP ☎ 01744 676789 peterhughes@sthelens.gov.uk

Customer Service: Mrs Karen Gillis , Customer Relations Manager, Wesley House, Corporation Street, St. Helens WA10 1HF ☎ 01744 676789 karengillis@sthelens.gov.uk

Direct Labour: Mr Paul Sanderson, Director - Environmental Protection, Wesley House, Corporation Street, St. Helens WA10 1HF ☎ 01744 676789 paulsanderson@sthelens.gov.uk

Economic Development: Mr Steve Berlyne , Funding & Economic Intelligence Manager, Town Hall, Victoria Square, Corporation Street, St. Helens WA10 1HP ☎ 01744 676789 stevenberlyne@sthelens.gov.uk

Electoral Registration: Ms Beverley Hatton , Electoral Services Officer, Town Hall, Victoria Square, Corporation Street, St. Helens WA10 1HP ☎ 01744 676789 beverleyhatton@sthelens.gov.uk

Emergency Planning: Ms Vicky Finch , Safety, Risk & Resilience Manager, Lincoln House, Corporation Street, St. Helens WA10 1UQ ☎ 01744 676789 vickyfinch@sthelens.gov.uk

Environmental / Technical Services: Mr Paul Sanderson, Director - Environmental Protection, Wesley House, Corporation Street, St. Helens WA10 1HF ☎ 01744 676789 paulsanderson@sthelens.gov.uk

Environmental Health: Mr Anthony Smith , Chief Environmental Health Officer, Wesley House, Corporation Street, St. Helens WA10 1HF ☎ 01744 676789 anthonysmith@sthelens.gov.uk

Estates, Property & Valuation: Mr Stephen Littler, Estates Manager, Town Hall, Victoria Square, Corporation Street, St. Helens WA10 1HP ☎ 01744 676789 stevelittler@sthelens.gov.uk

European Liaison: Mr Steve Berlyne, Funding & Economic Intelligence Manager, Town Hall, Vistoria Square, Corporation Street, St. Helens WA10 1HP ☎ 01744 676789 stevenberlyne@sthelens.gov.uk

Events Manager: Mrs Suzanne Davies , Strategic Events Officer, Wesley House, Corporation Street, St. Helens WA10 1HF ☎ 01744 676789 suzannedavies@sthelens.gov.uk

Facilities: Mr Chris Dove, Public Buildings & Support Services Manager, Town Hall, Victoria Square, Corporation Street, St. Helens WA10 1HP ☎ 01744 676789 chrisdove@sthelens.gov.uk

Finance: Mr Ian Roberts, Assistant Chief Executive - Finance, Chief Executive's Department, Town Hall, Victoria Square, Corporation Street, St. Helens WA10 1HP ☎ 01744 676789 ianroberts@sthelens.gov.uk

Grounds Maintenance: Mr Tim Jones , Civic Pride & Community Spaces Manager, Hardshaw Brook Depot, Parr Street, St. Helens WA9 1JR ☎ 01744 456789 timjones@sthelens.gov.uk

Health and Safety: Ms Vicky Finch , Safety, Risk & Resilience Manager, Lincoln House, Corporation Street, St. Helens WA10 1UQ ☎ 01744 676789 vickyfinch@sthelens.gov.uk

Highways: Mr Rory Lingham, Assistant Director - Engineering, Wesley House, Corporation Street, St. Helens WA10 1HF ☎ 01744 676789 rorylingham@sthelens.gov.uk

Home Energy Conservation: Mr Jim Nixon, Energy Efficiency Officer, Wesley House, Corporation Street, St. Helens WA10 1HF ☎ 01744 676789 jimnixon@sthelens.gov.uk

Housing: Mr Andy Dempsey, Head - Children & Young People's Services, Atlas House, Corporation Street, St. Helens WA9 1LD ☎ 01744 676789 🖷 01744 455936 andydempsey@sthelens.gov.uk

Housing: Mr Stephen Tracey, Head - Housing & Safer Communities Initiative, Town Hall, Victoria Square, Corporation Street, St. Helens WA10 1HP ☎ 01744 676789 stephentracey@sthelens.gov.uk

Legal: Ms Angela Sanderson , Assistant Chief Executive - Legal & Administrative Services, Town Hall, Victoria Square, Corporation Street, St. Helens WA10 1HP ☎ 01744 676789 angelasanderson@sthelens.gov.uk

Licensing: Mrs Lorraine Simpsons , Licensing & Land Charges Officer, Wesley House, Corporation Street, St. Helens WA10 1HF ☎ 01744 676789 lorrainesimpson@sthelens.gov.uk

Lighting: Mr William May , Assistant Head - Asset Management, 4th Floor, Wesley House, Corporation Street, St. Helens WA10 1HP ☎ 01744 676789 williammay@sthelens.gov.uk

Lottery Funding, Charity and Voluntary: Mr Peter Hughes, Head - Policy, Town Hall, Victoria Square, Corporation Street, St. Helens WA10 1HP ☎ 01744 676789 peterhughes@sthelens.gov.uk

Lottery Funding, Charity and Voluntary: Mr Wayne Traynor , Assistant Treasurer - Accountancy & Payments, Town Hall, Victoria Square, Corporation Street, St. Helens WA10 1HP ☎ 01744 676789 waynetraynor@sthelens.gov.uk

Member Services: Mrs Joanne Griffiths , Democratic Services Manager, Town Hall, Victoria Square, Corporation Street, St. Helens WA10 1HP ☎ 01744 676789 joanne.griffiths@sthelens.gov.uk

Parking: Mr Robert McAllister , Parking Services Manager, Town Hall, Victoria Square, Corporation Street, St. Helens WA10 1HP ☎ 01744 676789 bobmcallister@sthelens.gov.uk

Partnerships: Mr Peter Hughes, Head - Policy, Town Hall, Victoria Square, Corporation Street, St. Helens WA10 1HP ☎ 01744 676789 ✉ peterhughes@sthelens.gov.uk

Personnel / HR: Mr Brendan Farrell, Head - Human Resources, Town Hall, Victoria Square, Corporation Street, St. Helens WA10 1HP ☎ 01744 676789 ✉ brendanfarrell@sthelens.gov.uk

Planning: Mr Stuart Barnes , Development Control Manager, Town Hall, Victoria Square, Corporation Street, St. Helens WA10 1HP ☎ 01744 676789 ✉ stuartbarnes@sthelens.gov.uk

Procurement: Mr Rob Banks , Corporate Procurement Manager, Wesley House, Corporation Street, St. Helens WA10 1HP ☎ 01744 676789 ✉ robbanks@sthelens.gov.uk

Public Libraries: Mrs Susan Williamson , Head - Library Service, Chester Lane Library, Four Acre Lane, St. Helens WA9 4DE ☎ 01744 677493 ✉ susanwilliamson@sthelens.gov.uk

Recycling & Waste Minimisation: Mr Brian Malcolm, Environmental Care Manager, Hardshaw Brook Depot, Parr Street, St. Helens WA9 1JR ☎ 01744 676789 ✉ brianmalcolm@sthelens.gov.uk

Regeneration: Mr Mark Dickens , Head - Regeneration, Town Hall, Victoria Square, Corporation Street, St. Helens WA10 1HP ☎ 01744 676606 🖷 01744 676154 ✉ markdickens@sthelens.gov.uk

Road Safety: Mrs Gillian Roberts, Senior Road Safety Officer, Town Hall, Victoria Square, Corporation Street, St. Helens WA10 1HP ☎ 01744 676789 ✉ gillianroberts@sthelens.gov.uk

Social Services (Adult): Mr Mike Wyatt , Director - Adult Social Care & Health, Gamble Building, Victoria Square, Corporation Street, St. Helens WA10 1DY ☎ 01744 676309 ✉ mikewyatt@sthelens.gov.uk

Social Services (Children): Mr Jason Pickett , Assistant Director - Children & Families, Atlas House, Corporation Street, St. Helens WA9 1LD ☎ 01744 671803 🖷 01744 671270 ✉ jasonpickett@sthelens.gov.uk

Public Health: Ms Liz Gaulton , Director - Public Health, Town Hall, Victoria Square, Corporation Street, St. Helens WA10 1HP ☎ 01744 676789 ✉ lizgaulton@sthelens.gov.uk

Staff Training: Mr David Broster, Training & Development Manager, Chief Executive's Department, Gamble Building, Victoria Square, St. Helens WA10 1DY ☎ 01744 676789 ✉ davidbroster@sthelens.gov.uk

Town Centre: Mr Chris Dove, Public Buildings & Support Services Manager, Town Hall, Victoria Square, Corporation Street, St. Helens WA10 1HP ☎ 01744 676789 ✉ chrisdove@sthelens.gov.uk

Traffic Management: Mr George Houghton, Head - Traffic Engineering, Wesley House, Corporate Street, St. Helens WA10 1HF ☎ 01744 676789 ✉ georgehoughton@sthelens.gov.uk

Transport Planner: Mr David Brown , Transport Officer - Policy, Town Hall, Victoria Square, Corporation Street, St. Helens WA10 1HP ☎ 01744 676789 ✉ davidbrown@sthelens.gov.uk

Waste Collection and Disposal: Mr Brian Malcolm, Environmental Care Manager, Hardshaw Brook Depot, Parr Street, St. Helens WA9 1JR ☎ 01744 676789 ✉ brianmalcolm@sthelens.gov.uk

Waste Management: Mr Brian Malcolm, Environmental Care Manager, Hardshaw Brook Depot, Parr Street, St. Helens WA9 1JR ☎ 01744 676789 ✉ brianmalcolm@sthelens.gov.uk

COUNCILLORS

***Mayor* Pearl**, Geoff (LD - Eccleston)
cllrgpearl@sthelens.gov.uk

***Deputy Mayor* Glover**, Stephen (LAB - Rainhill)
cllrsglover@sthelens.gov.uk

***Leader of the Council* Grunewald**, Barrie (LAB - Rainhill)
CllrBGrunewald-Leader@sthelens.gov.uk

***Group Leader* Jones**, Allan (CON - Rainford)
cllrajones@sthelens.gov.uk

***Group Leader* Sims**, Teresa (LD - Eccleston)
cllrsims@sthelens.gov.uk

Ann Gill, Carole (LAB - Town Centre)
cllrcgill@sthelens.gov.uk

Ayres, Robbie (LAB - West Park)
cllrrayres@sthelens.gov.uk

Baines, David (LAB - Windle)

Banks, Charles (LAB - Earlestown)
cllrcdbanks@sthelens.gov.uk

Banks, Jeanette (LAB - Haydock)
cllrjbanks@sthelens.gov.uk

Bell, Jeanie (LAB - Newton)
cllrjbell@sthelens.gov.uk

Bond, Martin (LAB - Haydock)
cllrmbond@sthelens.gov.uk

Bowden, Andy (LAB - Parr)
cllrabowden@sthelens.gov.uk

Burns, Anthony (LAB - Haydock)
cllraburns@sthelens.gov.uk

Cross, Gareth (LAB - Bold)
cllrgcross@sthelens.gov.uk

Cunliffe, Alan (LAB - Blackbrook)
cllracunliffe@sthelens.gov.uk

Deakin, Keith (LAB - Earlestown)
cllrkdeakin@sthelens.gov.uk

De'Asha, Joe (LAB - Rainhill)
cllrde'asha@sthelens.gov.uk

Dyer, Sandra (LAB - Newton)
cllrsdyer@sthelens.gov.uk

Fletcher, Jeffrey (LAB - Moss Bank)
cllrjfletcher@sthelens.gov.uk

Fulham, John (LAB - Moss Bank)
cllrjfulham@sthelens.gov.uk

Glover, Lynn (LAB - Windle)
cllrlglover@sthelens.gov.uk

Gomez-Aspron, Seve (LAB - Newton)
cllrsgomez-aspron@sthelens.gov.uk

ST. HELENS

Halliwell, Jo-Ann (LAB - Town Centre)
cllrjhalliwell@sthelens.gov.uk

Hargreaves, Thomas (LAB - Bold)
cllrhargreaves@sthelens.gov.uk

Haw, Michael (LD - Eccleston)
cllrmhaw@sthelens.gov.uk

Ireland, Pat (LAB - Thatto Heath)
cllrpireland@sthelens.gov.uk

Jackson, Jimmy (LAB - Sutton)
cllrjjackson@sthelens.gov.uk

Jackson, Patricia (LAB - Sutton)
cllrpjackson@sthelens.gov.uk

Johnson, Anthony (LAB - Bold)
cllrajohnson@sthelens.gov.uk

Johnson, Janet (LAB - Sutton)
cllrjjohnson@sthelens.gov.uk

Lynch, Paul (LAB - Moss Bank)
cllrplynch@sthelens.gov.uk

Maloney, Linda (LAB - Blackbrook)
cllrlmaloney@sthelens.gov.uk

McCauley, Richard (LAB - Thatto Heath)
cllrmccauley@sthelens.gov.uk

McDonnell, Dennis (LAB - Billinge and Seneley Green)
cllrdmcdonnell@sthelens.gov.uk

McQuade, Paul (LAB - Blackbrook)
cllrpmcquade@sthelens.gov.uk

Murphy, Susan (LAB - Billinge and Seneley Green)
cllrsemurphy@sthelens.gov.uk

Mussell, Linda (CON - Rainford)
cllrlmussell@sthelens.gov.uk

Nichols, Rupert (CON - Rainford)
cllrrnichols@sthelens.gov.uk

Pearson, Joe (LAB - Billinge and Seneley Green)
cllrjpearson@sthelens.gov.uk

Preston, Charlie (LAB - Earlestown)
cllrcpreston@sthelens.gov.uk

Preston, Lisa (LAB - Town Centre)
cllrlpreston@sthelens.gov.uk

Quinn, Marlene (LAB - West Park)
cllrmquinn@sthelens.gov.uk

Rimmer, Marie (LAB - West Park)
cllrmerimmer@sthelens.gov.uk

Roberts, Keith (LAB - Parr)
cllrkroberts@sthelens.gov.uk

Robinson, Sophie (LAB - Windle)
cllrsrobinson@sthelens.gov.uk

Seddon, Sheila (LAB - Thatto Heath)
cllrsseddon@sthelens.gov.uk

Shields, Terry (LAB - Parr)
cllrtshields@sthelens.gov.uk

POLITICAL COMPOSITION

LAB: 42, LD: 3, CON: 3

COMMITTEE CHAIRS

Audit: Mr Barrie Grunewald

Children & Young People: Mr Dennis McDonnell

Health & Adult Social Care: Ms Pat Ireland

Licensing: Mr Charles Banks

Planning: Mr Joe De'Asha

Planning: Mr Stephen Glover

Stafford D

Stafford Borough Council, Civic Centre, Riverside, Stafford ST16 3AQ
☎ 01785 619000 🖷 01785 619119 🖳 www.staffordbc.gov.uk

FACTS AND FIGURES

Parliamentary Constituencies: Stafford, Stone
EU Constituencies: West Midlands
Election Frequency: Elections are of whole council

PRINCIPAL OFFICERS

Chief Executive: Mr Ian Thompson, Chief Executive, Civic Centre, Riverside, Stafford ST16 3AQ ☎ 01785 619200 🖷 01785 619119 ✉ ianthompson@staffordbc.gov.uk

Senior Management: Ms Judith Aupers , Head of Governance, Civic Centre, Riverside, Stafford ST16 3AQ ☎ 01543 454411 ✉ judithaupers@cannockchase.gov.uk

Senior Management: Mr Adam Hill, Head of Leisure & Culture, Civic Centre, Riverside, Stafford ST16 3AQ ☎ 01785 619299 🖷 01785 619419 ✉ amhill@staffordbc.gov.uk

Senior Management: Mr Norman Jones, Head of Policy & Improvement, Civic Centre, Riverside, Stafford ST16 3AQ ☎ 01785 619199 🖷 01785 619119 ✉ npjones@staffordbc.gov.uk

Senior Management: Mr Bob Kean, Head of Finance, Civic Centre, PO Box 28, Cannock WS11 1BG ☎ 01543 464334 ✉ bobkeane@cannockchasedc.gov.uk

Senior Management: Mr Peter Kendrick, Head of Technology, Civic Centre, Riverside, Stafford ST16 3AQ ☎ 01785 619274 🖷 01785 619219 ✉ pkendrick@staffordbc.gov.uk

Senior Management: Mr Ted Manders, Head of Planning & Regeneration, Civic Centre, Riverside, Stafford ST16 3AQ ☎ 01785 619583 🖷 01785 619753 ✉ tmanders@staffordbc.gov.uk

Senior Management: Mr Neville Raby, Head of Human Resources, Civic Centre, Riverside, Stafford ST16 3AQ ☎ 01785 619205 🖷 01785 619450 ✉ nraby@staffordbc.gov.uk

Senior Management: Mr Howard Thomas, Head of Environment, Civic Centre, Riverside, Stafford ST16 3AQ ☎ 01785 619358 🖷 01785 619319 ✉ hthomas@staffordbc.gov.uk

Senior Management: Mr Alistair Welch, Head of Law & Administration, Civic Centre, Riverside, Stafford ST16 3AQ ☎ 01785 619204 🖷 01785 619119 ✉ awelch@staffordbc.gov.uk

Architect, Building / Property Services: Mr Jim Davis, Property Services Manager, Civic Centre, Riverside, Stafford ST16 3AQ ☎ 01785 619395 🖷 01785 619688 ✉ jdavis@staffordbc.gov.uk

Best Value: Mr Norman Jones, Head of Policy & Improvement, Civic Centre, Riverside, Stafford ST16 3AQ ☎ 01785 619199 🖷 01785 619119 ✉ npjones@staffordbc.gov.uk

Building Control: Mr Paul Beckley, Building Control Manager, Stafford Borough Council, Civic Centre, Riverside, Stafford ST16 3AQ ☎ 01785 619311 ✉ paulbeckley@cannockchasedc.gov.uk

PR / Communications: Mr Will Conaghan , Press & Communications Manager, Civic Centre, Riverside, Stafford ST16 3AQ ☎ 01785 619230 🖷 01785 619230 ✉ wjconghan@staffordbc.gov.uk

Community Planning: Mr Norman Jones, Head of Policy & Improvement, Civic Centre, Riverside, Stafford ST16 3AQ ☎ 01785 619199 🖷 01785 619119 ✉ npjones@staffordbc.gov.uk

Community Safety: Mr Norman Jones, Head of Policy & Improvement, Civic Centre, Riverside, Stafford ST16 3AQ ☎ 01785 619199 🖷 01785 619119 ✉ npjones@staffordbc.gov.uk

Computer Management: Mr Peter Kendrick , Head of Technology, Stafford Borough Council, Civic Centre, Riverside, Stafford ST16 3AQ ☎ 01785 619274 ✉ pkendrick@stafford.gov.uk

Contracts: Mr Jim Davis, Property Services Manager, Civic Centre, Riverside, Stafford ST16 3AQ ☎ 01785 619395 🖷 01785 619688 ✉ jdavis@staffordbc.gov.uk

Customer Service: Mr Norman Jones, Head of Policy & Improvement, Civic Centre, Riverside, Stafford ST16 3AQ ☎ 01785 619199 🖷 01785 619119 ✉ npjones@staffordbc.gov.uk

Economic Development: Mr Ted Manders, Head of Planning & Regeneration, Civic Centre, Riverside, Stafford ST16 3AQ ☎ 01785 619583 🖷 01785 619753 ✉ tmanders@staffordbc.gov.uk

E-Government: Mr Peter Kendrick , Head of Technology, Stafford Borough Council, Civic Centre, Riverside, Stafford ST16 3AQ ☎ 01785 619274 ✉ pkendrick@stafford.gov.uk

Electoral Registration: Mrs Jane Peat, Electoral Services Manager, Civic Centre, Riverside, Stafford ST16 3AQ ☎ 01785 619424 🖷 01785 619119 ✉ jpeat@staffordbc.gov.uk

Emergency Planning: Mr Ian Thompson, Chief Executive, Civic Centre, Riverside, Stafford ST16 3AQ ☎ 01785 619200 🖷 01785 619119 ✉ ianthompson@staffordbc.gov.uk

Energy Management: Mr Ted Manders, Head of Planning & Regeneration, Civic Centre, Riverside, Stafford ST16 3AQ ☎ 01785 619583 🖷 01785 619753 ✉ tmanders@staffordbc.gov.uk

Environmental / Technical Services: Mr Howard Thomas, Head of Environment, Civic Centre, Riverside, Stafford ST16 3AQ ☎ 01785 619358 🖷 01785 619319 ✉ hthomas@staffordbc.gov.uk

Environmental Health: Mr Howard Thomas, Head of Environment, Civic Centre, Riverside, Stafford ST16 3AQ ☎ 01785 619358 🖷 01785 619319 ✉ hthomas@staffordbc.gov.uk

Estates, Property & Valuation: Mr Jim Davis, Property Services Manager, Civic Centre, Riverside, Stafford ST16 3AQ ☎ 01785 619395 🖷 01785 619688 ✉ jdavis@staffordbc.gov.uk

Events Manager: Ms Liz Hulse, Events Manager, Civic Centre, Riverside, Stafford ST16 3AQ ☎ 01785 619300 🖷 01785 619419 ✉ lhulse@staffordbc.gov.uk

Facilities: Mr Jim Davis, Property Services Manager, Civic Centre, Riverside, Stafford ST16 3AQ ☎ 01785 619395 🖷 01785 619688 ✉ jdavis@staffordbc.gov.uk

Finance: Mr Bob Kean, Head of Finance, Civic Centre, PO Box 28, Cannock WS11 1BG ☎ 01543 464334 ✉ bobkeane@cannockchasedc.gov.uk

Grounds Maintenance: Mr Phil Gammon, Head of Operational Services, Civic Centre, Riverside, Stafford ST16 3AQ ☎ 01785 619108 ✉ pgammon@staffordbc.gov.uk

Health and Safety: Mr Neville Raby, Head of Human Resources, Civic Centre, Riverside, Stafford ST16 3AQ ☎ 01785 619205 🖷 01785 619450 ✉ nraby@staffordbc.gov.uk

Legal: Mr Alistair Welch, Head of Law & Administration, Civic Centre, Riverside, Stafford ST16 3AQ ☎ 01785 619204 🖷 01785 619119 ✉ awelch@staffordbc.gov.uk

Leisure and Cultural Services: Mr Adam Hill, Head of Leisure & Culture, Civic Centre, Riverside, Stafford ST16 3AQ ☎ 01785 619299 🖷 01785 619419 ✉ amhill@staffordbc.gov.uk

Lottery Funding, Charity and Voluntary: Mr Norman Jones, Head of Policy & Improvement, Civic Centre, Riverside, Stafford ST16 3AQ ☎ 01785 619199 🖷 01785 619119 ✉ npjones@staffordbc.gov.uk

Member Services: Mr Alistair Welch, Head of Law & Administration, Civic Centre, Riverside, Stafford ST16 3AQ ☎ 01785 619204 🖷 01785 619119 ✉ awelch@staffordbc.gov.uk

Parking: Mr Steve Allen , Car Parking Manager, Civic Centre, Riverside, Stafford ST16 3AQ ☎ 01785 619071 🖷 01785 619613 ✉ sallen@staffordbc.gov.uk

Partnerships: Mr Norman Jones, Head of Policy & Improvement, Civic Centre, Riverside, Stafford ST16 3AQ ☎ 01785 619199 🖷 01785 619119 ✉ npjones@staffordbc.gov.uk

Personnel / HR: Mr Neville Raby, Head of Human Resources, Civic Centre, Riverside, Stafford ST16 3AQ ☎ 01785 619205 🖷 01785 619450 ✉ nraby@staffordbc.gov.uk

STAFFORD

Planning: Mr John Holmes , Development Control Manager, Civic Centre, Riverside, Stafford ST16 3AQ ☎ 01785 619302 🖷 01785 619419 ✉ jholmes@staffordbc.gov.uk

Recycling & Waste Minimisation: Mr Mark Street , Environmental Health Manager, Civic Centre, Riverside, Stafford ST16 3AQ ☎ 01785 619390 🖷 01785 619319 ✉ mstreet@staffordbc.gov.uk

Regeneration: Mr Ted Manders, Head of Planning & Regeneration, Civic Centre, Riverside, Stafford ST16 3AQ ☎ 01785 619583 🖷 01785 619753 ✉ tmanders@staffordbc.gov.uk

Staff Training: Mr Neville Raby, Head of Human Resources, Civic Centre, Riverside, Stafford ST16 3AQ ☎ 01785 619205 🖷 01785 619450 ✉ nraby@staffordbc.gov.uk

Street Scene: Mr Phil Gammon, Head of Operational Services, Civic Centre, Riverside, Stafford ST16 3AQ ☎ 01785 619108 ✉ pgammon@staffordbc.gov.uk

Sustainable Communities: Mr Ian Thompson, Chief Executive, Civic Centre, Riverside, Stafford ST16 3AQ ☎ 01785 619200 🖷 01785 619119 ✉ ianthompson@staffordbc.gov.uk

Sustainable Development: Ms Karen Davies, Climate Change & Sustainable Development Co-ordinator, Civic Centre, Riverside, Stafford ST16 3AQ ☎ 01785 619408 🖷 01785 619319 ✉ kdavies@staffordbc.gov.uk

Tourism: Ms Lisa Heaton, Tourism, Heritage & Visitor Services Manager, Civic Centre, Riverside, Stafford ST16 3AQ ☎ 01785 619348 🖷 01785 619319 ✉ lheaton@staffordbc.gov.uk

Town Centre: Mr Ted Manders, Head of Planning & Regeneration, Civic Centre, Riverside, Stafford ST16 3AQ ☎ 01785 619583 🖷 01785 619753 ✉ tmanders@staffordbc.gov.uk

Waste Collection and Disposal: Mr Mark Street , Environmental Health Manager, Civic Centre, Riverside, Stafford ST16 3AQ ☎ 01785 619390 🖷 01785 619319 ✉ mstreet@staffordbc.gov.uk

Waste Collection and Disposal: Mr Howard Thomas, Head of Environment, Civic Centre, Riverside, Stafford ST16 3AQ ☎ 01785 619358 🖷 01785 619319 ✉ hthomas@staffordbc.gov.uk

Waste Management: Mr Howard Thomas, Head of Environment, Civic Centre, Riverside, Stafford ST16 3AQ ☎ 01785 619358 🖷 01785 619319 ✉ hthomas@staffordbc.gov.uk

COUNCILLORS

***Leader of the Council* Farrington**, Patrick (CON - Baswich)
pfarrington@staffordbc.gov.uk

***Deputy Leader of the Council* Smith**, Mike (CON - Gnosall & Woodseaves)
rmsmith@staffordbc.gov.uk

Bakker-Collier, Lynne (CON - St Michael's & Stonefield)
lbakker-collier@staffordbc.gov.uk

Baron, Christine (IND - Forebridge)
cabaron@staffordbc.gov.uk

Barron, Jenny (CON - Weeping Cross & Wildwood)
jbarron@staffordbc.gov.uk

Barron, Ray (CON - Weeping Cross & Wildwood)
rbarron@staffordbc.gov.uk

Beatty, Frances (CON - Milwich)
fbeatty@staffordbc.gov.uk

Bowen, Maureen (LAB - Highfields & Western Downs)
mbowen@staffordbc.gov.uk

Collier, Geoffrey (CON - St Michael's & Stonefield)
gcollier@staffordbc.gov.uk

Cooke, Ralph (LAB - Penkside)
rcooke@staffordbc.gov.uk

Cross, Bryan (CON - Holmcroft)
bcross@staffordbc.gov.uk

Davies, Isabella (CON - Doxey & Castletown)
iedavies@staffordbc.gov.uk

Dodson, Michael (CON - Fulford)
mdodson@staffordbc.gov.uk

Draper, Rowan (LAB - Littleworth)
rdraper@staffordbc.gov.uk

Edgeller, Ann (CON - Baswich)
aedgeller@staffordbc.gov.uk

Farnham, Joyce (CON - St Michael's & Stonefield)
jfarnham@staffordbc.gov.uk

Finlay, Francis (CON - Milford)
ffinlay@staffordbc.gov.uk

Godfrey, Aidan (LAB - Common)
agodfrey@staffordbc.gov.uk

Goodall, Margaret (CON - Walton)
mgoodall@staffordbc.gov.uk

Harp, Andrew (CON - Milwich)
aharp@staffordbc.gov.uk

Hood, Jill (IND - Walton)
jhood@staffordbc.gov.uk

James, Roy (CON - Swynnerton & Oulton)
rjames@staffordbc.gov.uk

Jennings, Mary (CON - Littleworth)
mjennings@staffordbc.gov.uk

Jones, Gareth (CON - Barlaston)
ejones@staffordbc.gov.uk

Jones, Peter (CON - Eccleshall)
pjones@staffordbc.gov.uk

Kemp, William (LAB - Coton)
jkemp@staffordbc.gov.uk

Learoyd, Stewart (CON - Haywood & Hixon)
slearoyd@staffordbc.gov.uk

Leighton, Stephen (CON - Seighford & Church Eaton)
sleighton@staffordbc.gov.uk

Loughran, Angela (LAB - Manor)
aloughran@staffordbc.gov.uk

Nixon, Louise (LAB - Coton)
lnixon@staffordbc.gov.uk

O'Connor, Stephen (LAB - Highfields & Western Downs)
soconnor@staffordbc.gov.uk

Perkins, Alan (CON - Haywood & Hixon)
aperkins@staffordbc.gov.uk

Pert, Jeremy (CON - Eccleshall)
jpert@staffordbc.gov.uk

Price, Brian (CON - Swynnerton & Oulton)
dprice@staffordbc.gov.uk

Price, Jonathan (CON - Holmcroft)
jprice@staffordbc.gov.uk

Rowlands, Geoffrey (LAB - Manor)
growlands@staffordbc.gov.uk

Roycroft, Peter (CON - Fulford)
proycroft@staffordbc.gov.uk

Sutherland, Raymond (CON - Seighford & Church Eaton)
rsutherland@staffordbc.gov.uk

Trowbridge, Carolyn (CON - Rowley)
ctrowbridge@staffordbc.gov.uk

Williamson, Kenneth (CON - Gnosall & Woodseaves)
kwilliamson@staffordbc.gov.uk

POLITICAL COMPOSITION

CON: 29, LAB: 9, IND: 2

COMMITTEE CHAIRS

Audit & Accounts: Mrs Angela Loughran

Licensing: Mr Alan Perkins

Planning: Mr Bryan Cross

Staffordshire C

Staffordshire County Council, Number 1, Staffordshire Place, Stafford ST16 2LP
☎ 01785 223121 🖷 01785 276178 💻 www.staffordshire.gov.uk

FACTS AND FIGURES

Parliamentary Constituencies: Cannock Chase, Lichfield, Staffordshire South
EU Constituencies: West Midlands
Election Frequency: Elections are of whole council

PRINCIPAL OFFICERS

Chief Executive: Mr John Henderson , Chief Executive, Number 1, Staffordshire Place, Stafford ST16 2LP
✉ john.henderson@staffordshire.gov.uk

Deputy Chief Executive: Mrs Helen Riley, Director for People & Deputy Chief Executive, Number 1, Staffordshire Place, Stafford ST16 2LP ☎ 01785 278580 ✉ helen.riley@staffordshire.gov.uk

Senior Management: Dr Aliko Ahmed , Director of Public Health, Number 1, Staffordshire Place, Stafford ST16 2LP ☎ 01785 278700
✉ aliko.ahmed@staffordshire.gov.uk

Senior Management: Mr Andrew Burns, Director of Finance & Resources, Number 1, Staffordshire Place, Stafford ST16 2LP
☎ 01785 276302 🖷 01785 276390
✉ andrew.burns@staffordshire.gov.uk

Senior Management: Mr John Tradewell, Director of Democracy, Law & Transformation, Number 1, Staffordshire Place, Stafford ST16 2LP ☎ 01785 854062 ✉ john.tradwell@staffordshire.gov.uk

Architect, Building / Property Services: Mr Jamie MacDonald , Head of Strategic Property, Number 1, Staffordshire Place, Stafford ST16 2LP ☎ 01785 277508 ✉ jamie.macdonald@staffordshire.gov.uk

Catering Services: Ms Joanne Hand , Catering Manager, County Buildings, Martin Street, Stafford ST16 2LH ☎ 01785 276030
✉ joanne.hand@staffordshire.gov.uk

Civil Registration: Ms Hannah Cotton-Diederich , Customer Service Manager (Registration), Number 2, Staffordshire Place, Tipping Street, Stafford ST16 2DH ☎ 01785 277245
✉ hannah.cotton-diederich@staffordshire.gov.uk

Community Safety: Mr Michael Harrison , Commissioner for Safety, Wedgewood Building, Tipping Street, Stafford ST16 2DH
☎ 01785 278163 ✉ michael.harrison@staffordshire.gov.uk

Computer Management: Mr Vic Falcus , Head of ICT Service Management, Number 1, Staffordshire Place, Stafford ST16 2LP
☎ 01785 278032 ✉ vic.falcus@staffordshire.gov.uk

Consumer Protection and Trading Standards: Ms Trish Caldwell , Business Support Manager, Number 1, Staffordshire Place, Stafford ST16 2LP ☎ 01785 277804
✉ trish.caldwell@staffordshire.gov.uk

Contracts: Mr Jon Waller , Head of Financial Strategy & Support, Number 2, Staffordshire Place, Tipping Street, Stafford ST16 2DH
☎ 01785 276380 ✉ jon.waller@staffordshire.gov.uk

Customer Service: Ms Dionne Lowndes , Head of Customer Services, Number 2, Staffordshire Place, Tipping Street, Stafford ST16 2DH ☎ 01785 854236 ✉ dionne.lowndes@staffordshire.gov.uk

Economic Development: Mr Mark Parkinson, Economic Development & Planning Policy Manager, Number 1, Staffordshire Place, Stafford ST16 2LP ☎ 01785 276807 🖷 01785 277695
✉ mark.parkinson@staffordshire.gov.uk

Education: Ms Anna Halliday , Commissioner for Education & Wellbeing, Wedgewood Building, Tipping Street, Stafford ST16 2DH
☎ 01785 278774 ✉ anna.halliday@staffordshire.gov.uk

Emergency Planning: Ms Beth Morgan , Director of Staffordshire Civil Contingencies Unit, Staffordshire Fire Station, Beaconside, Stafford ST18 0DD ☎ 01785 898608

Energy Management: Mr Lee Wells , Senior Land & Property Information Officer, Number 2, Staffordshire Place, Tipping Street, Stafford ST16 2DH ☎ 01785 277732
✉ lee.wells@staffordshire.gov.uk

Estates, Property & Valuation: Mr Kevin Danks , Principal Valuer, Number 2, Staffordshire Place, Tipping Street, Stafford ST16 2DH ☎ 01785 277702 🖷 01785 277712
✉ kevin.danks@staffordshire.gov.uk

STAFFORDSHIRE

European Liaison: Mr Nigel Senior , Group Manager - Economic Development, Number 1, Staffordshire Place, Stafford ST16 2LP ☎ 01785 277365 ✉ nigel.senior@staffordshire.gov.uk

Finance: Mr Andrew Burns, Director of Finance & Resources, Number 1, Staffordshire Place, Stafford ST16 2LP ☎ 01785 276302 🖷 01785 276390 ✉ andrew.burns@staffordshire.gov.uk

Pensions: Ms Janet Caiazzo , Pensions Manager, Number 2, Staffordshire Place, Tipping Street, Stafford ST16 2DH ☎ 01785 276441 ✉ janet.caiazzo@staffordshire.gov.uk

Pensions: Ms Melanie Stokes , Strategic Investment Manager, Number 2, Staffordshire Place, Tipping Street, Stafford ST16 2DH ☎ 01785 276330 ✉ melanie.stokes@staffordshire.gov.uk

Fleet Management: Mr Michael Simmonds , Group Manager - Fleetcare & Print Commissioning, Beacon Business Park, Weston Road, Stafford ST18 0WL ☎ 01785 854821 ✉ michael.simmonds@staffordshire.gov.uk

Grounds Maintenance: Ms Michelle Ryan , Group Manager - Grounds & Cleaning Services, Kingston Centre, Fairway, Stafford ST16 3TW ☎ 01785 277640 ✉ michelle.ryan@entrust-ed.co.uk

Health and Safety: Mrs Becky Lee, Health, Safety & Wellbeing Manager, Number 1, Staffordshire Place, Stafford ST16 2LP ☎ 01785 276846 ✉ becky.lee@staffordshire.gov.uk

Highways: Mr James Bailey , Commissioner for Highways & the Built Country, Number 1, Staffordshire Place, Stafford ST16 2LP ☎ 01785 276591 ✉ james.bailey@staffordshire.gov.uk

Local Area Agreement: Mr Andrew Donaldson , Strategic Policy & Partnerships Manager, Number 1, Staffordshire Place, Stafford ST16 2LP ☎ 01785 278399 ✉ andrew.donaldson@staffordshire.gov.uk

Legal: Mr John Tradewell, Director of Democracy, Law & Transformation, Number 1, Staffordshire Place, Stafford ST16 2LP ☎ 01785 854062 ✉ john.tradwell@staffordshire.gov.uk

Leisure and Cultural Services: Mrs Janene Cox, Commissioner for Tourism & the Cultural County, Number 1, Staffordshire Place, Stafford ST16 2LP ☎ 01785 278368 🖷 01785 278319 ✉ janene.cox@staffordshire.gov.uk

Lifelong Learning: Ms Anna Halliday , Commissioner for Education & Wellbeing, Wedgewood Building, Tipping Street, Stafford ST16 2DH ☎ 01785 278774 ✉ anna.halliday@staffordshire.gov.uk

Lighting: Mr Glynn Hook, Principal Lighting Engineer, Staffordshire Place, Tipping Street, Stafford ST16 2DH ☎ 01785 276561 🖷 01785 211279 ✉ glynn.hook@staffordshire.gov.uk

Member Services: Ms Ann-Marie Davidson , Head of Member & Democratic Services, County Buildings, Martin Street, Stafford ST16 2LH ☎ 01785 276131 🖷 01785 276178 ✉ ann-marie.davidson@staffordshire.gov.uk

Partnerships: Mr Andrew Donaldson , Strategic Policy & Partnerships Manager, Number 1, Staffordshire Place, Stafford ST16 2LP ☎ 01785 278399 ✉ andrew.donaldson@staffordshire.gov.uk

Personnel / HR: Ms Lisa Cartwright , Head of Human Resources, Number 1, Staffordshire Place, Stafford ST16 2LP ☎ 01785 278188 ✉ jann.russell@staffordshire.gov.uk

Planning: Mr Mike Grundy , Planning, Policy & Development Control Manager, Number 2, Staffordshire Place, Tipping Street, Stafford ST16 2DH ☎ 01785 277297 ✉ mike.grundy@staffordshire.gov.uk

Procurement: Ms Heather Bowran , Procurement Manager, Number 2, Staffordshire Place, Tipping Street, Stafford ST16 2DH ☎ 01785 854659 ✉ heather.bowran@staffordshire.gov.uk

Public Libraries: Mrs Janene Cox, Commissioner for Tourism & the Cultural County, Number 1, Staffordshire Place, Stafford ST16 2LP ☎ 01785 278368 🖷 01785 278319 ✉ janene.cox@staffordshire.gov.uk

Recycling & Waste Minimisation: Ms Sally Talbot , Group Manager of Waste Management & Environmental Projects, Number 1, Staffordshire Place, Stafford ST16 2LP ☎ 01785 276227 ✉ sally.talbot@staffordshire.gov.uk

Regeneration: Mr John Flynn , Physical Regeneration Group Manager, Number 1, Staffordshire Place, Stafford ST16 2LP ☎ 01785 277707 ✉ john.flynn@staffordshire.gov.uk

Road Safety: Ms Melanie Langdown , Performance & Operations Manager, 18 Garnet House, Wolseley Court, Staffordshire Technology Park, Stafford ST18 0GA ☎ 0300 111 8012 ✉ melanie.langdown@staffordshire.gov.uk

Social Services: Mrs Helen Riley, Director for People & Deputy Chief Executive, Number 1, Staffordshire Place, Stafford ST16 2LP ☎ 01785 278580 ✉ helen.riley@staffordshire.gov.uk

Public Health: Dr Aliko Ahmed , Director of Public Health, Number 1, Staffordshire Place, Stafford ST16 2LP ☎ 01785 278700 ✉ aliko.ahmed@staffordshire.gov.uk

Staff Training: Ms Danielle Ware , Strategic Lead for Learning & Development, Number 1, Staffordshire Place, Stafford ST16 2LP ☎ 01785 895211 ✉ danielle.ware@staffordshire.gov.uk

Sustainable Development: Mr Ian Benson , Commissioner for the Sustainable County, Number 1, Staffordshire Place, Stafford ST16 2LP ☎ 01785 276550 ✉ ian.benson@staffordshire.gov.uk

Tourism: Mr Grame Whitehead , Tourism & Marketing Team Leader, Number 1, Staffordshire Place, Stafford ST16 2LP ☎ 01785 277335 ✉ grame.whitehead@staffordshire.gov.uk

Traffic Management: Mr Nick Dawson, Connectivity Strategy Manager, Number 1, Staffordshire Place, Stafford ST16 2LP ☎ 01785 276629 ✉ nick.dawson@staffordshire.gov.uk

Transport: Mr Clive Thomson , Commissioner for Transport & the Connected County, Number 1, Staffordshire Place, Stafford ST16 2LP ☎ 01785 276522 ✉ clive.thomson@staffordshire.gov.uk

Transport Planner: Mr Nick Dawson, Connectivity Strategy Manager, Number 1, Staffordshire Place, Stafford ST16 2LP
☎ 01785 276629 ✉ nick.dawson@staffordshire.gov.uk

Waste Management: Ms Sally Talbot , Group Manager of Waste Management & Environmental Projects, Number 1, Staffordshire Place, Stafford ST16 2LP ☎ 01785 276227
✉ sally.talbot@staffordshire.gov.uk

COUNCILLORS

***Chair* Eagland**, Janet (CON - Lichfield - Lichfield Rural North)
janet.eagland@staffordshire.gov.uk

***Vice-Chair* Fraser**, Bob (CON - East Staffordshire - Dove)
bob.fraser@staffordshire.gov.uk

***Leader of the Council* Atkins**, Philip (CON - East Staffordshire - Uttoxeter Rural)
philip.atkins@staffordshire.gov.uk

***Deputy Leader of the Council* Parry**, Ian (CON - Stafford - Stone Rural)
ian.parry@staffordshire.gov.uk

***Group Leader* Cooke**, Chris (IND - Tamworth - Stoneydelph)
chris.cooke@staffordshire.gov.uk

***Group Leader* Taylor**, John (LAB - Newcastle - Talke & Red Street)
john.taylor@staffordshire.gov.uk

Adams, Ben (CON - Tamworth - Perrycrofts)
ben.adams@staffordshire.gov.uk

Adamson, George (LAB - Cannock Chase - Hednesford & Rawnsley)
george.adamson@staffordshire.gov.uk

Astle, Margaret (LAB - Newcastle - Kidsgrove)
margaret.astle@staffordshire.gov.uk

Atkins, Charlotte (LAB - Staffordshire Moorlands - Leek South)
charlotte.atkins@staffordshire.gov.uk

Beech, Ann (LAB - Newcastle - Audley & Chesterton)
ann.beech@staffordshire.gov.uk

Bloomer, Len (CON - Stafford - Stafford Trent Valley)
leonard.bloomer@staffordshire.gov.uk

Chapman, Frank (CON - Stafford - Eccleshall)
frank.chapman@staffordshire.gov.uk

Clarke, Ron (LAB - East Staffordshire - Burton Town)
ron.clarke@staffordshire.gov.uk

Compton, Maureen (LAB - Stafford - Stafford Central)
maureen.compton@staffordshire.gov.uk

Corbett, Tim (CON - East Staffordshire - Needwood Forest)
timothy.corbett@staffordshire.gov.uk

Davies, Peter (LAB - East Staffordshire - Burton Trent)
peter.davies@staffordshire.gov.uk

Davies, Mike (CON - South Staffordshire - Wombourne)
mike.davies@staffordshire.gov.uk

Davis, Derek (LAB - Cannock Chase - Chadsmoor)
derek.davis@staffordshire.gov.uk

Day, William (IND - Staffordshire Moorlands - Caverswall)
william.day@staffordshire.gov.uk

Dean, Carol (LAB - Tamworth - Bolebridge)
carol.dean@staffordshire.gov.uk

Deaville, Mark (CON - Staffordshire Moorlands - Cheadle & Checkley)
mark.deaville@staffordshire.gov.uk

Dudson, Alan (LAB - Cannock Chase - Brereton & Ravenhill)
alan.dudson@staffordshire.gov.uk

Edwards, Brian (CON - South Staffordshire - Kinver)
brian.edwards@staffordshire.gov.uk

Finn, Terry (CON - Lichfield - Lichfield City South)
terence.finn@staffordshire.gov.uk

Francis, John (CON - Stafford - Stafford South East)
john.francis@staffordshire.gov.uk

Greatorex, Michaeal (CON - Tamworth - Watling South)
michael.greatorex@staffordshire.gov.uk

Hambleton, Sandra (LAB - Newcastle - Bradwell, Porthill & Wolstanton)
sandra.hambleton@staffordshire.gov.uk

Heath, Gill (CON - Staffordshire Moorlands - Leek Rural)
gill.heath@staffordshire.gov.uk

Hollinshead, Ian (LAB - Stafford - Stafford North)
ian.hollinshead@staffordshire.gov.uk

Huckfield, Derrick (IND - Newcastle - Keele, Knutton & Silverdale)
derrick.huckfield@staffordshire.gov.uk

Jackson, Kevin (LAB - Staffordshire Moorlands - Biddulph South & Endon)
kevin.jackson@staffordshire.gov.uk

James, Keith (CON - South Staffordshire - Perton)
keith.james@staffordshire.gov.uk

Jenkins, Brian (LAB - Tamworth - Watling North)
brian.jenkins@staffordshire.gov.uk

Jones, Philip (CON - Stafford - Stone Urban)
philip.e.jones@staffordshire.gov.uk

Lawrence, Mike (CON - South Staffordshire - Cheslyn Hay, Essington and Great Wyrley)
michael.lawrence@staffordshire.gov.uk

Lawson, Ian (CON - Staffordshire Moorlands - Biddulph North)
ian.lawson@staffordshire.gov.uk

Loades, David (CON - Newcastle - Newcastle Rural)
david.loades@staffordshire.gov.uk

Marshall, Robert (CON - South Staffordshire - Codsall)
robert.marshall@staffordshire.gov.uk

Martin, Geoffrey (CON - Cannock Chase - Etchinghill & Heath)
geoffrey.martin@staffordshire.gov.uk

McKiernan, Shelagh (LAB - East Staffordshire - Horninglow & Stretton)
shelagh.mckiernan@staffordshire.gov.uk

Mitchell, Christine (LAB - Cannock Chase - Hednesford & Rawnsley)
christine.mitchell@staffordshire.gov.uk

Morrison, Geoff (CON - East Staffordshire - Uttoxeter Town)
geoffrey.morrison@staffordshire.gov.uk

Olszweski, Mark (LAB - Newcastle - May Bank & Cross Heath)
mark.olszweski@staffordshire.gov.uk

Peaple, Sheree (LAB - Tamworth - Amington)
sheree.peaple@staffordshire.gov.uk

Perry, Kath (CON - South Staffordshire - Cheslyn Hay, Essington and Great Wyrley)
kathleen.perry@staffordshire.gov.uk

Rowlands, Trish (LAB - Stafford - Stafford West)
trish.rowlands@staffordshire.gov.uk

Sheriff, Jeff (UKIP - Lichfield - Burntwood South)
jeffrey.sheriff@staffordshire.gov.uk

Smith, David (CON - Lichfield - Lichfield Rural South)
david.smith1@staffordshire.gov.uk

Spicer, Alison (LAB - Cannock Chase - Cannock Town Centre)
alison.spicer@staffordshire.gov.uk

Sutton, Mark (CON - South Staffordshire - Brewood)
mark.sutton@staffordshire.gov.uk

Sweeney, Stephen (CON - Newcastle - Newcastle South)
stephen.sweeney@staffordshire.gov.uk

Tagg, Simon (CON - Newcastle - Westlands & Thistleberry)
simon.tagg@staffordshire.gov.uk

Tittley, Martyn (CON - Lichfield - Lichfield Rural West)
martyn.tittley@staffordshire.gov.uk

Todd, Dianne (LAB - Cannock Chase - Cannock Villages)
dianne.todd@staffordshire.gov.uk

White, Alan (CON - Lichfield - Lichfield Rural East)
alan.white@staffordshire.gov.uk

Wileman, Conor (CON - East Staffordshire - Burton Tower)
conor.wileman@staffordshire.gov.uk

Williams, David (CON - South Staffordshire - Penkridge)
david.williams2@staffordshire.gov.uk

Winnington, Mark (CON - Stafford - Gnosall and Doxey)
mark.winnington@staffordshire.gov.uk

Wood, Caroline (LAB - Lichfield - Lichfield City North)
caroline.wood@staffordshire.gov.uk

Woodward, Susan (LAB - Lichfield - Burntwood North)
susan.woodward@staffordshire.gov.uk

Worthington, Mike (CON - Staffordshire Moorlands - Churnet Valley)
mike.worthington@staffordshire.gov.uk

POLITICAL COMPOSITION

CON: 34, LAB: 24, IND: 3, UKIP: 1

COMMITTEE CHAIRS

Audit & Standards: Mr Martyn Tittley

Pensions: Mr Stephen Sweeney

Planning: Mr Tim Corbett

Staffordshire Moorlands D

Staffordshire Moorlands District Council, Moorlands House, Stockwell Street, Leek
ST13 6HQ
☎ 01538 395400 🖷 01538 395474
✉ info@staffsmoorlands.gov.uk
💻 www.staffsmoorlands.gov.uk

FACTS AND FIGURES

Parliamentary Constituencies: Staffordshire Moorlands, Stoke-on-Trent North, Stone
EU Constituencies: West Midlands
Election Frequency: Elections are of whole council

PRINCIPAL OFFICERS

Chief Executive: Mr Simon Baker, Chief Executive, Moorlands House, Stockwell Street, Leek ST13 6HQ ☎ 01538 395400 🖷 01538 395474 ✉ simon.baker@staffsmoorlands.gov.uk; simon.baker@highpeak.gov.uk

Senior Management: Mr Dai Larner , Executive Director - Place, Moorlands House, Stockwell Street, Leek ST13 6HQ ☎ 01538 395400 ✉ dai.larner@highpeak.gov.uk

Senior Management: Mr Andrew Stokes, Executive Director - Transformation, Moorlands House, Stockwell Street, Leek ST13 6HQ ☎ 01538 395622 ✉ andrew.stokes@staffsmoorlands.gov.uk

Senior Management: Mr Mark Trillo, Executive Director - People, Moorlands House, Stockwell Street, Leek ST13 6HQ ☎ 01538 395623 🖷 01538 395474 ✉ mark.trillo@staffsmoorlands.gov.uk

Access Officer / Social Services (Disability): Mr Mike Green, Planning Applications Manager, Moorlands House, Stockwell Street, Leek ST13 6HQ ☎ 01538 395400 🖷 01538 395474 ✉ mike.green@staffsmoorlands.gov.uk

Architect, Building / Property Services: Ms Joanne Higgins, Property Services Manager, Moorlands House, Stockwell Street, Leek ST13 6HQ ☎ 01538 395400 🖷 01538 395474 ✉ joanne.higgins@staffsmoorlands.gov.uk

Best Value: Mr Chris Elliott, Transformation Manager, Moorlands House, Stockwell Street, Leek ST13 6HQ ☎ 01538 395400 🖷 01538 395474 ✉ chris.elliott@staffsmoorlands.gov.uk

Building Control: Mr Mike Green, Planning Applications Manager, Moorlands House, Stockwell Street, Leek ST13 6HQ ☎ 01538 395400 🖷 01538 395474 ✉ mike.green@staffsmoorlands.gov.uk

Building Control: Mr Robert Weaver , Head of Regulatory Services, Moorlands House, Stockwell Street, Leek ST13 6HQ ☎ 01538 395400 ✉ robert.weaver@highpeak.gov.uk

Catering Services: Mr Terry Crawford , Head of Visitor Services, Pavilion Gardens, Buxton SK17 6BE ☎ 01298 28400 Ext 4224 ✉ terry.crawford@highpeak.gov.uk

PR / Communications: Ms Carolyn Sanders , Media Relations Manager, Moorlands House, Stockwell Street, Leek ST13 6HQ ☎ 01538 395588 ✉ carolyn.sanders@staffsmoorlands.gov.uk

Community Planning: Mr Mark Forrester, Democratic & Community Services Manager, Moorlands House, Stockwell Street, Leek ST13 6HQ ☎ 01538 395768 🖷 01538 395474 ✉ mark.forrester@staffsmoorlands.gov.uk

Community Planning: Ms Alison Wheeldon , Environmental Policy Officer, Moorlands House, Stockwell Street, Leek ST13 6HQ ☎ 0845 129 7777 ✉ alison.wheeldon@staffsmoorlands.gov.uk

Community Safety: Mr Mark Forrester, Democratic & Community Services Manager, Moorlands House, Stockwell Street, Leek ST13 6HQ ☎ 01538 395768 🖷 01538 395474 ✉ mark.forrester@staffsmoorlands.gov.uk

Community Safety: Mr David Smith , Community Safety & Enforcement Manager, Moorlands House, Stockwell Street, Leek ST13 6HQ ☎ 01538 395692 🖷 01538 395474 ✉ david.smith@staffsmoorlands.gov.uk

Computer Management: Mr Chris Elliott, Transformation Manager, Moorlands House, Stockwell Street, Leek ST13 6HQ ☎ 01538 395400 🖷 01538 395474 ✉ chris.elliott@staffsmoorlands.gov.uk

Computer Management: Ms Mary Walker , Organisational Development & Transformation Manager, Moorlands House, Stockwell Street, Leek ST13 6HQ ✉ mary.walker@staffsmoorlands.gov.uk

Contracts: Mr Andrew Stokes, Executive Director - Transformation, Moorlands House, Stockwell Street, Leek ST13 6HQ ☎ 01538 395622 ✉ andrew.stokes@staffsmoorlands.gov.uk

Corporate Services: Mr Peter Dunkley, Customer Services Manager, Moorlands House, Stockwell Street, Leek ST13 6HQ ☎ 01538 395614 🖷 01538 395474 ✉ peter.dunkley@staffsmoorlands.gov.uk

Customer Service: Mr Terry Crawford , Head of Visitor Services, Pavilion Gardens, Buxton SK17 6BE ☎ 01298 28400 Ext 4224 ✉ terry.crawford@highpeak.gov.uk

Customer Service: Ms Lousie Pearce , Head of Customer Services, Moorlands House, Stockwell Street, Leek ST13 6HQ ✉ louise.pearce@staffsmoorlands.gov.uk

Customer Service: Ms Tammy Towers , Environmental Health Manager, Moorlands House, Stockwell Street, Leek ST13 6HQ ☎ 0845 129 7777 ✉ tammy.towers@staffsmoorlands.gov.uk

Economic Development: Ms Pranali Parikh , Regeneration Manager, Moorlands House, Stockwell Street, Leek ST13 6HQ ☎ 01538 395582 ✉ pranali.parikh@staffsmoorlands.gov.uk

E-Government: Mr Chris Elliott, Transformation Manager, Moorlands House, Stockwell Street, Leek ST13 6HQ ☎ 01538 395400 🖷 01538 395474 ✉ chris.elliott@staffsmoorlands.gov.uk

Electoral Registration: Ms Caroline Cooke, Corporate Electoral Administration Manager, Moorlands House, Stockwell Street, Leek ST13 6HQ ☎ 01538 395400 🖷 01538 395474 ✉ caroline.cooke@staffsmoorlands.gov.uk

Electoral Registration: Ms Jeanette Marsh , Legal Services Manager, Moorlands House, Stockwell Street, Leek ST13 6HQ ☎ 01538 395400 🖷 01538 395474 ✉ jeanette.marsh@staffsmoorlands.gov.uk

Emergency Planning: Mr David Owen , Corporate Health & Safety Advisor, Moorlands House, Stockwell Street, Leek ST13 6HQ ☎ 01538 395595 🖷 01538 395474 ✉ david.owen@staffsmoorlands.gov.uk

Energy Management: Ms Joanne Higgins, Property Services Manager, Moorlands House, Stockwell Street, Leek ST13 6HQ ☎ 01538 395400 🖷 01538 395474 ✉ joanne.higgins@staffsmoorlands.gov.uk

Environmental / Technical Services: Mr Shaun Hollinshead , Street Cleansing Manager, Fowlchurch Depot, Fowlchurch Road, Leek ST13 6BH ☎ 01538 395798 🖷 01538 388393 ✉ shaun.hollinshead@staffsmoorlands.gov.uk

Environmental / Technical Services: Mr John Tildesley , Environmental Health Services Manager, Fowlchurch Depot, Fowlchurch Road, Leek ST13 6BH ☎ 01538 395797 🖷 01538 388393 ✉ john.tildesley@staffsmoorlands.gov.uk

Environmental / Technical Services: Ms Tammy Towers , Environmental Health Manager, Moorlands House, Stockwell Street, Leek ST13 6HQ ☎ 0845 129 7777 ✉ tammy.towers@staffsmoorlands.gov.uk

Environmental Health: Ms Tammy Towers , Environmental Health Manager, Moorlands House, Stockwell Street, Leek ST13 6HQ ☎ 0845 129 7777 ✉ tammy.towers@staffsmoorlands.gov.uk

Environmental Health: Mr Robert Weaver , Head of Regulatory Services, Moorlands House, Stockwell Street, Leek ST13 6HQ ☎ 01538 395400 ✉ robert.weaver@highpeak.gov.uk

Estates, Property & Valuation: Ms Joanne Higgins, Property Services Manager, Moorlands House, Stockwell Street, Leek ST13 6HQ ☎ 01538 395400 🖷 01538 395474 ✉ joanne.higgins@staffsmoorlands.gov.uk

Facilities: Ms Joanne Higgins, Property Services Manager, Moorlands House, Stockwell Street, Leek ST13 6HQ ☎ 01538 395400 🖷 01538 395474 ✉ joanne.higgins@staffsmoorlands.gov.uk

Finance: Ms Claire Hazeldene , Finance & Procurement Manager, Moorlands House, Stockwell Street, Leek ST13 6HQ ☎ 01538 395400 ✉ claire.hazeldene@staffsmoorlands.gov.uk

Finance: Mr Rob Jones, Revenue & Benefits Manager, Town Hall, Buxton SK17 6EL ☎ 0845 129 7777 ✉ rob.jones@highpeak.gov.uk

Finance: Mr Andrew Stokes, Executive Director - Transformation, Moorlands House, Stockwell Street, Leek ST13 6HQ ☎ 01538 395622 ✉ andrew.stokes@staffsmoorlands.gov.uk

Fleet Management: Ms Joy Redfern , Street Scene Manager, Moorlands House, Stockwell Street, Leek ST13 6HQ ☎ 01298 28400 Ext 4411 ✉ joy.redfern@staffsmoorlands.gov.uk

Grounds Maintenance: Mr Keith Parker , Head of Operational Services, Moorlands House, Stockwell Street, Leek ST13 6HQ ☎ 01538 395400 ✉ keith.parker@staffsmoorlands.gov.uk

Grounds Maintenance: Mr Tony Wheat , Leisure Services Manager, Town Hall, Market Place, Buxton SK17 6EL ☎ 01538 395400 ✉ anthony.wheat@staffsmoorlands.gov.uk

Health and Safety: Mr David Owen , Emergency Planning, Health & Safety Advisor, Moorlands House, Stockwell Street, Leek ST13 6HQ ☎ 01538 395595 🖷 01538 395474 ✉ david.owen@staffsmoorlands.gov.uk

Home Energy Conservation: Mr Ian Young, Housing Strategy Manager, Moorlands House, Stockwell Street, Leek ST13 6HQ ☎ 01538 395426 🖷 01538 395474 🖱 ian.young@staffsmoorlands.gov.uk

Housing: Mr Ian Young, Housing Strategy Manager, Moorlands House, Stockwell Street, Leek ST13 6HQ ☎ 01538 395426 🖷 01538 395474 🖱 ian.young@staffsmoorlands.gov.uk

Legal: Ms Jeanette Marsh , Legal Services Manager, Moorlands House, Stockwell Street, Leek ST13 6HQ ☎ 01538 395400 🖷 01538 395474 🖱 jeanette.marsh@staffsmoorlands.gov.uk

Legal: Mr Mark Trillo, Executive Director - People, Moorlands House, Stockwell Street, Leek ST13 6HQ ☎ 01538 395623 🖷 01538 395474 🖱 mark.trillo@staffsmoorlands.gov.uk

Leisure and Cultural Services: Mr Keith Parker , Head of Operational Services, Moorlands House, Stockwell Street, Leek ST13 6HQ ☎ 01538 395400 🖱 keith.parker@staffsmoorlands.gov.uk

Leisure and Cultural Services: Mr Tony Wheat , Leisure Services Manager, Moorlands House, Stockwell Street, Leek ST13 6HQ ☎ 01538 395400 🖱 anthony.wheat@staffsmoorlands.gov.uk

Leisure and Cultural Services: Ms Alison Wheeldon, Environmental Policy Officer, Moorlands House, Stockwell Street, Leek ST13 6HQ ☎ 0845 129 7777 🖱 alison.wheeldon@staffsmoorlands.gov.uk

Licensing: Mr Peter Dunkley, Customer Services Manager, Moorlands House, Stockwell Street, Leek ST13 6HQ ☎ 01538 395614 🖷 01538 395474 🖱 peter.dunkley@staffsmoorlands.gov.uk

Licensing: Ms Tammy Towers , Environmental Health Manager, Town Hall, Market Place, Buxton SK17 6EL ☎ 0845 129 7777 🖱 tammy.towers@staffsmoorlands.gov.uk

Licensing: Mr Robert Weaver , Head of Regulatory Services, Moorlands House, Stockwell Street, Leek ST13 6HQ ☎ 01538 395400 🖱 robert.weaver@highpeak.gov.uk

Lottery Funding, Charity and Voluntary: Mr Mark Forrester, Democratic & Community Services Manager, Moorlands House, Stockwell Street, Leek ST13 6HQ ☎ 01538 395768 🖷 01538 395474 🖱 mark.forrester@staffsmoorlands.gov.uk

Member Services: Ms Jeanette Marsh , Legal Services Manager, Moorlands House, Stockwell Street, Leek ST13 6HQ ☎ 01538 395400 🖷 01538 395474 🖱 jeanette.marsh@staffsmoorlands.gov.uk

Member Services: Mr Mark Trillo, Executive Director - People, Moorlands House, Stockwell Street, Leek ST13 6HQ ☎ 01538 395623 🖷 01538 395474 🖱 mark.trillo@staffsmoorlands.gov.uk

Parking: Mr Mark Forrester, Democratic & Community Services Manager, Moorlands House, Stockwell Street, Leek ST13 6HQ ☎ 01538 395768 🖷 01538 395474 🖱 mark.forrester@staffsmoorlands.gov.uk

Parking: Ms Joanne Higgins, Property Services Manager, Moorlands House, Stockwell Street, Leek ST13 6HQ ☎ 01538 395400 🖷 01538 395474 🖱 joanne.higgins@staffsmoorlands.gov.uk

Partnerships: Mr Mark Forrester, Democratic & Community Services Manager, Moorlands House, Stockwell Street, Leek ST13 6HQ ☎ 01538 395768 🖷 01538 395474 🖱 mark.forrester@staffsmoorlands.gov.uk

Personnel / HR: Ms Julie Grime , Human Resources Manager, Moorlands House, Stockwell Street, Leek ST13 6HQ ☎ 01538 395690 🖷 01538 395474 🖱 julie.grime@staffsmoorlands.gov.uk

Personnel / HR: Ms Mary Walker , Organisational Development & Transformation Manager, Moorlands House, Stockwell Street, Leek ST13 6HQ 🖱 mary.walker@staffsmoorlands.gov.uk

Planning: Mr Mike Green, Planning Applications Manager, Moorlands House, Stockwell Street, Leek ST13 6HQ ☎ 01538 395400 🖷 01538 395474 🖱 mike.green@staffsmoorlands.gov.uk

Planning: Mr Robert Weaver , Head of Regulatory Services, Moorlands House, Stockwell Street, Leek ST13 6HQ ☎ 01538 395400 🖱 robert.weaver@highpeak.gov.uk

Procurement: Mr Chris Elliott, Transformation Manager, Moorlands House, Stockwell Street, Leek ST13 6HQ ☎ 01538 395400 🖷 01538 395474 🖱 chris.elliott@staffsmoorlands.gov.uk

Recycling & Waste Minimisation: Ms Nicola Kemp , Waste Collection Manager, Fowlchurch Depot, Fowlchurch Road, Leek ST13 6BH ☎ 01538 395794 🖷 01538 388393 🖱 nicola.kemp@staffsmoorlands.gov.uk

Recycling & Waste Minimisation: Ms Joy Redfern , Street Scene Manager, Moorlands House, Stockwell Street, Leek ST13 6HQ ☎ 01298 28400 Ext 4411 🖱 joy.redfern@staffsmoorlands.gov.uk

Regeneration: Ms Pranali Parikh , Regeneration Manager, Moorlands House, Stockwell Street, Leek ST13 6HQ ☎ 01538 395582 🖱 pranali.parikh@staffsmoorlands.gov.uk

Social Services: Mr Rob Jones, Revenue & Benefits Manager, Town Hall, Market Place, Buxton SK17 6EL ☎ 0845 129 7777 🖱 rob.jones@highpeak.gov.uk

Staff Training: Ms Julie Grime , Human Resources Manager, Moorlands House, Stockwell Street, Leek ST13 6HQ ☎ 01538 395690 🖷 01538 395474 🖱 julie.grime@staffsmoorlands.gov.uk

Street Scene: Mr Shaun Hollinshead , Environment Manager of Operations, Fowlchurch Depot, Fowlchurch Road, Leek ST13 6BH ☎ 01538 395798 🖷 01538 388393 🖱 shaun.hollinshead@staffsmoorlands.gov.uk

Street Scene: Mr Keith Parker , Head of Operational Services, Moorlands House, Stockwell Street, Leek ST13 6HQ ☎ 01538 395400 🖱 keith.parker@staffsmoorlands.gov.uk

Street Scene: Ms Joy Redfern , Street Scene Manager, Moorlands House, Stockwell Street, Leek ST13 6HQ ☎ 01298 28400 Ext 4411 🖱 joy.redfern@staffsmoorlands.gov.uk

Sustainable Communities: Mr Mark Forrester, Democratic & Community Services Manager, Moorlands House, Stockwell Street, Leek ST13 6HQ ☎ 01538 395768 🖷 01538 395474 ✉ mark.forrester@staffsmoorlands.gov.uk

Sustainable Development: Ms Alison Wheeldon , Environmental Policy Officer, Moorlands House, Stockwell Street, Leek ST13 6HQ ☎ 0845 129 7777 ✉ alison.wheeldon@staffsmoorlands.gov.uk

Tourism: Mr Terry Crawford , Head of Visitor Services, Pavilion Gardens, Buxton SK17 6BE ☎ 01298 28400 Ext 4224 ✉ terry.crawford@highpeak.gov.uk

Tourism: Ms Pranali Parikh , Regeneration Manager, Moorlands House, Stockwell Street, Leek ST13 6HQ ☎ 01538 395582 ✉ pranali.parikh@staffsmoorlands.gov.uk

Town Centre: Ms Pranali Parikh , Regeneration Manager, Moorlands House, Stockwell Street, Leek ST13 6HQ ☎ 01538 395582 ✉ pranali.parikh@staffsmoorlands.gov.uk

Waste Collection and Disposal: Mr Shaun Hollinshead, Environment Manager of Operations, Fowlchurch Depot, Fowlchurch Road, Leek ST13 6BH ☎ 01538 395798 🖷 01538 388393 ✉ shaun.hollinshead@staffsmoorlands.gov.uk

Waste Collection and Disposal: Mr Keith Parker, Head of Operational Services, Moorlands House, Stockwell Street, Leek ST13 6HQ ☎ 01538 395400 ✉ keith.parker@staffsmoorlands.gov.uk

Waste Management: Ms Nicola Kemp , Waste Collection Manager, Fowlchurch Depot, Fowlchurch Road, Leek ST13 6BH ☎ 01538 395794 🖷 01538 388393 ✉ nicola.kemp@staffsmoorlands.gov.uk

COUNCILLORS

***Chair* Pearce**, Collin (CON - Checkley)
colin.pearce@staffsmoorlands.gov.uk

***Vice-Chair* Shaw**, David (CON - Werrington)
david.shaw@staffsmoorlands.gov.uk

***Leader of the Council* Ralphs**, Sybil (CON - Bagnall & Stanley)
sybil.ralphs@staffsmoorlands.gov.uk

Aktins, Charlotte (LAB - Leek North)
charlotte.atkins@staffsmoorlands.gov.uk

Alcock, Richard (IND - Cheadle South East)
richard.alcock@staffsmoorlands.gov.uk

Banks, Alan (CON - Cheadle West)
alan.banks@staffsmoorlands.gov.uk

Bond, Geoff (CON - Brown Edge and Endon)
geof.bond@staffsmoorland.gov.uk

Bowen, Michael (CON - Cheddleton)
michael.bowen@staffsmoorlands.gov.uk

Bull, Julie (CON - Cheadle North East)
julie.bull@staffsmoorlands.gov.uk

D Lea, Linda (CON - Brown Edge and Endon)
linda.lea@staffsmoorland.gov.uk

Davies, Jim (IND - Biddulph North)
jim.davies@staffsmoorlands.gov.uk

Deaville, Mark (CON - Checkley)
mark.deaville@staffsmoorlands.gov.uk

Done, Rebecca (CON - Leek East)
rebecca.done@staffsmoorland.gov.uk

Ellis, Stephen (CON - Cheadle West)
stephen.ellis@staffsmoorlands.gov.uk

Emery, Ben (CON - Leek West)
ben.emery@staffsmoorlands.gov.uk

Fallows, Elsie (CON - Churnet)
elsie.fallows@staffsmoorlands.gov.uk

Flinder, Keith (CON - Forsbrook)
keith.flunder@staffsmoorlands.gov.uk

Forrester, Arthur (CON - Alton)
arthur.forrester@staffsmoorlands.gov.uk

Gledhill, Mike (LAB - Leek South)
mike.gledhill@staffsmoorland.gov.uk

Grocott, Deborah (CON - Cheadle South East)
deborah.grocott@staffsmoorland.gov.uk

Hall, Tony (IND - Biddulph North)
tony.hall@staffsmoorlands.gov.uk

Harrison, Keith (IND - Leek South)
keith.harrison@staffsmoorlands.gov.uk

Hart, Andrew (IND - Biddulph North)
andrew.hart@staffsmoorlands.gov.uk

Hawkins, Norma (CON - Horton)
norma.hawkins@staffsmoorlands.gov.uk

Heath, Gill (CON - Dane)
gill.heath@staffsmoorlands.gov.uk

Herdman, Ian (CON - Forsbrook)
ian.herdmand@staffsmoorland.gov.uk

Hughes, Barbara (CON - Cellarhead)
barbara.hughes@staffsmoorlands.gov.uk

Jackson, Kevin (LAB - Biddulph East)
kevin.jackson@staffsmoorlands.gov.uk

Jackson, Peter (CON - Cheadle West)
peter.jackson@staffsmoorland.gov.uk

Jebb, Christina (LD - Brown Edge and Endon)
christina.jebb@staffsmoorlands.gov.uk

Johnson, Brian (CON - Leek East)
brian.johnson@staffsmoorlands.gov.uk

Jones, John (IND - Biddulph Moor)
john.jones@staffsmoorlands.gov.uk

Lawson, Ian (IND - Biddulph West)
ian.lawson@staffsmoorlandlands.gov.uk

Lockett, Gail (CON - Leek South)
gail.lockett@staffsmoorlands.gov.uk

Lovatt, Margaret (LAB - Leek North)
margaret.lovatt@staffsmoorlands.gov.uk

Lovatt, Madelaine (LAB - Biddulph East)
madelaine.lovatt@staffsmoorlands.gov.uk

Lucas, Ivor (IND - Churnet)
ivor.lucas@staffsmoorland.gov.uk

Malyon, Linda (R - Ipstones)
linda.maylon@staffsmoorlands.gov.uk

STAFFORDSHIRE MOORLANDS

McNicol, Tony (CON - Cellarhead)
tony.mcnicol@staffsmoorlands.gov.uk

Ogden, Dani (CON - Leek North)
dani.ogden@staffsmoorlands.gov.uk

Plant, Robert (CON - Leek West)
robert.plant@staffsmoorlands.gov.uk

Podmore, Neal (CON - Leek West)
neal.podmore@staffsmoorlands.gov.uk

Redfern, John (LD - Biddulph South)
john.redfern@staffsmoorlands.gov.uk

Riley, Teresa (CON - Manifold)
teresa.riley@staffsmoorlands.gov.uk

Roberts, Paul (CON - Caverswall)
paul.roberts@staffsmoorlands.gov.uk

Scalise, Sav (CON - Cheddleton)
salvino.scalise@staffsmoorland.gov.uk

Sheldon, Hilda (IND - Biddulph West)
hilda.sheldon@staffsmoorlands.gov.uk

Trigger, David (CON - Checkley)
david.trigger@staffsmoorlands.gov.uk

Wain, Edwin (CON - Hamps Valley)

Walley, Jeanette (LAB - Biddulph East)
jeanette.walley@staffsmoorlands.gov.uk

Ward, Ross (CON - Werrington)
ross.ward@staffsmoorlands.gov.uk

Wilkinson, Peter (UKIP - Cheadle North East)
peter.wilkinson@staffsmoorlands.gov.uk

Wilkinson, Abigail (CON - Forsbrook)
abigail.wilkinson@staffsmoorlands.gov.uk

Wood, Pamela (INDNA - Leek East)
pamela.wood@staffsmoorland.gov.uk

Wood, Christopher (LAB - Biddulph West)
christopher.wood@staffsmoorlands.gov.uk

Worthington, Michael (CON - Cheddleton)
michael.worthington@staffsmoorlands.gov.uk

POLITICAL COMPOSITION
CON: 35, IND: 9, LAB: 7, LD: 2, R: 1, UKIP: 1, INDNA: 1

COMMITTEE CHAIRS
Audit: Mr Jim Davies

Licensing: Ms Julie Bull

Planning: Mr Michael Worthington

Stevenage D

Stevenage Borough Council, Daneshill House, Danestrete, Stevenage SG1 1HN
☎ 01438 242242 🖷 01438 242566 🖱 csc@stevenage.gov.uk
💻 www.stevenage.gov.uk

FACTS AND FIGURES
Parliamentary Constituencies: Stevenage
EU Constituencies: Eastern
Election Frequency: Elections are by thirds

PRINCIPAL OFFICERS
Chief Executive: Mr Scott Crudgington , Chief Executive, Daneshill House, Danestrete, Stevenage SG1 1HN ☎ 01438 242185 🖱 scott.crudgington@stevenage.gov.uk

Senior Management: Mr Peter Bandy , Strategic Director - Environment, Daneshill House, Danestrete, Stevenage SG1 1HN ☎ 01438 242288 🖷 01438 242134 🖱 peter.bandy@stevenage.gov.uk

Senior Management: Mr Matthew Partridge , Strategic Director - Communities, Daneshill House, Danestrete, Stevenage SG1 1HN ☎ 01438 242456 🖱 matthew.partridge@stevenage.gov.uk

Architect, Building / Property Services: Mr Keith Brown, Head of Property & Estates, Daneshill House, Danestrete, Stevenage SG1 1HN ☎ 01438 242154 🖷 01438 242157 🖱 keith.brown@stevenage.gov.uk

Building Control: Mr Steve Polfreman, Building Control Manager, Daneshill House, Danestrete, Stevenage SG1 1HN ☎ 01438 242256 🖱 steve.polfreman@stevenage.gov.uk

Children / Youth Services: Mr Aidan Sanderson, Head of Leisure, Environmental Health & Children's Services, Daneshill House, Danesrete, Stevenage SG1 1HN ☎ 01438 242311 🖱 aidan.sanderson@stevenage.gov.uk

PR / Communications: Ms Lucy Culkin , Communications Manager, Daneshill House, Danestrete, Stevenage SG1 1HN ☎ 01438 242168 🖷 01438 242344 🖱 lucie.culkin@stevenage.gov.uk

Community Safety: Ms Debbie Barker , Senior Corporate Policy Officer (Community Safety & Strategic Partnerships), Daneshill House, Danestrete, Stevenage SG1 1HN ☎ 01438 242242 🖱 debbie.barker@stevenage.gov.uk

Computer Management: Mr Henry Lewis, Head of Business & Technology Services, Daneshill House, Danestrete, Stevenage SG1 1HN ☎ 01438 242496 🖱 henry.lewis@stevenage.gov.uk

Contracts: Mr Lee Myers , Head of Environmental Services, Cavendish Road, Stevenage SG1 2ES ☎ 01438 248710 🖷 01438 242434 🖱 lee.myers@stevenage.gov.uk

Customer Service: Mr Richard Protheroe , Business Strategy, Community & Customer Services, Daneshill House, Danestrete, Stevenage SG1 1HN ☎ 01438 242938 🖱 richard.protheroe@stevenage.gov.uk

Direct Labour: Mr Lee Myers , Head of Environmental Services, Cavendish Road, Stevenage SG1 2ES ☎ 01438 248710 🖷 01438 242434 🖱 lee.myers@stevenage.gov.uk

E-Government: Mr Henry Lewis, Head of Business & Technology Services, Daneshill House, Danestrete, Stevenage SG1 1HN ☎ 01438 242496 🖱 henry.lewis@stevenage.gov.uk

Electoral Registration: Ms Jacqui Hubbard , Electoral Services Manager, Daneshill House, Danestrete, Stevenage SG1 1HN ☎ 01438 242174 🖱 jacqui.hubbard@stevenage.gov.uk

Emergency Planning: Ms Suzanne Brightwell , Senior Performance & Resilience Officer, Daneshill House, Danestrete, Stevenage SG1 1HN ☎ 01438 242966 🖰 suzanne.brightwell@stevenage.gov.uk

Emergency Planning: Ms Sue Kingsley-Smith , Senior Performance & Resilience Officer, Daneshill House, Danestrete, Stevenage SG1 1HN ☎ 01438 242390 🖰 sue.kingsley-smith@stevenage.gov.uk

Environmental Health: Mr Aidan Sanderson, Head of Leisure, Environmental Health & Children's Services, Daneshill House, Danesrete, Stevenage SG1 1HN ☎ 01438 242311 🖰 aidan.sanderson@stevenage.gov.uk

Estates, Property & Valuation: Mr Keith Brown, Head of Property & Estates, Daneshill House, Danestrete, Stevenage SG1 1HN ☎ 01438 242154 🖷 01438 242157 🖰 keith.brown@stevenage.gov.uk

European Liaison: Mrs Maureen Nicholson, Member Services Officer, Daneshill House, Danestrete, Stevenage SG1 1HN ☎ 01438 242278 🖷 01438 242228 🖰 maureen.nicholson@stevenage.gov.uk

Events Manager: Ms Lucy Culkin , Communications Manager, Daneshill House, Danestrete, Stevenage SG1 1HN ☎ 01438 242168 🖷 01438 242344 🖰 lucie.culkin@stevenage.gov.uk

Facilities: Mr Gavin Coombs, Facilities Manager, Daneshill House, Danestrete, Stevenage SG1 1HN ☎ 01438 242705 🖷 01438 242157 🖰 gavin.coombs@stevenage.gov.uk

Finance: Ms Clare Fletcher , Assistant Director - Finance, Daneshill House, Danestrete, Stevenage SG1 1HN ☎ 01438 242933 🖰 clare.fletcher@stevenage.gov.uk

Fleet Management: Mr Simon Martin , Contracts Manager, Cavendish Road, Stevenage SG1 2ES ☎ 01438 218800 🖷 01438 218702 🖰 simon.martin@stevenage.gov.uk

Grounds Maintenance: Mr Paul Seaby, Contracts Manager, Cavandish Road, Stevenage SG1 2ES ☎ 01438 242772 🖷 01438 242273 🖰 paul.seaby@stevenage.gov.uk

Health and Safety: Mr Tony Hughes, Corporate Health & Safety Advisor, Daneshill House, Danestrete, Stevenage SG1 1HN ☎ 01438 218033 🖰 tony.hughes@stevenage.gov.uk

Housing: Mr Ash Ahmed , Assistant Director - Housing Development, Daneshill House, Danestrete, Stevenage SG1 1HN ☎ 01438 242242 🖰 ash.ahmed@stevenage.gov.uk

Housing: Mrs Jaine Cresser , Head of Housing Management Services, Daneshill House, Danestrete, Stevenage SG1 1HN ☎ 01483 242455 🖰 tony.campbell@stevenage.gov.uk

Housing Maintenance: Mr Tony Campbell , Head of Housing Property Services, Daneshill House, Danestrete, Stevenage SG1 1HN ☎ 01438 242261 🖰 tony.campbell@stevenage.gov.uk

Legal: Mr Paul Froggatt, Borough Solicitor, Daneshill House, Danestrete, Stevenage SG1 1HN ☎ 01438 242212 🖷 01438 242197 🖰 paul.froggatt@stevenage.gov.uk

Leisure and Cultural Services: Mr Aidan Sanderson, Head of Leisure, Environmental Health & Children's Services, Daneshill House, Danesrete, Stevenage SG1 1HN ☎ 01438 242311 🖰 aidan.sanderson@stevenage.gov.uk

Licensing: Ms Heather Morris , Licensing Manager, Daneshill House, Danestrete, Stevenage SG1 1HN ☎ 01438 212175 🖰 heather.morris@stevenage.gov.uk

Member Services: Ms Jackie Cansick, Constitutional Services Manager, Daneshill House, Danestrete, Stevenage SG1 1HN ☎ 01438 242216 🖷 01438 242963 🖰 jackie.cansick@stevenage.gov.uk

Parking: Mr Keith Moore, Parking Services Manager, Daneshill House, Danestrete, Stevenage SG1 1HN ☎ 01438 242277 🖷 01438 242242 🖰 keith.moore@stevenage.gov.uk

Partnerships: Mr Richard Protheroe , Business Strategy, Community & Customer Services, Daneshill House, Danestrete, Stevenage SG1 1HN ☎ 01438 242938 🖰 richard.protheroe@stevenage.gov.uk

Personnel / HR: Ms Christina Hefferon , Head of Human Resources & Organisational Development, Daneshill House, Danestrete, Stevenage SG1 1HN ☎ 01438 242164 🖰 christina.hefferon@stevenage.gov.uk

Planning: Mr Zayd Al-Jawad , Head of Planning & Engineering, Daneshill House, Danestrete, Stevenage SG1 1HN ☎ 01438 242242 🖰 zayd.al-jawad@stevenage.gov.uk

Planning: Mr Paul Pinkney , Interim Head of Regeneration & Transport, Daneshill House, Danestrete, Stevenage SG1 1HN ☎ 01438 242547 🖷 01438 242134 🖰 paul.pinkney@stevenage.gov.uk

Procurement: Ms Sharon Wallace , Corporate Procurement Manager, Daneshill House, Danestrete, Stevenage SG1 1HN ☎ 01438 242083 🖰 sharon.wallace@stevenage.gov.uk

Recycling & Waste Minimisation: Mr Lee Myers, Head of Environmental Services, Cavendish Road, Stevenage SG1 2ES ☎ 01438 248710 🖷 01438 242434 🖰 lee.myers@stevenage.gov.uk

Regeneration: Mr Paul Pinkney , Interim Head of Regeneration & Transport, Daneshill House, Danestrete, Stevenage SG1 1HN ☎ 01438 242547 🖷 01438 242134 🖰 paul.pinkney@stevenage.gov.uk

Staff Training: Ms Christina Hefferon, Head of Human Resources & Organisational Development, Daneshill House, Danestrete, Stevenage SG1 1HN ☎ 01438 242164 🖰 christina.hefferon@stevenage.gov.uk

Street Scene: Ms Julia Hill , Environmental Performance & Development Manager, Daneshill House, Danestrete, Stevenage SG1 1HN ☎ 01438 242900 🖰 julia.hill@stevenage.gov.uk

Sustainable Communities: Mr Paul Pinkney , Interim Head of Regeneration & Transport, Daneshill House, Danestrete, Stevenage SG1 1HN ☎ 01438 242547 🖷 01438 242134 ✉ paul.pinkney@stevenage.gov.uk

Town Centre: Ms Tracey Parry , Town Centre Manager, Daneshill House, Danestrete, Stevenage SG1 1HN ☎ 01438 242242 ✉ tracey.parry@stevenagetowncentre.co.uk

Transport: Mr Rob Woodisse , Principal Engineer, Daneshill House, Danestrete, Stevenage SG1 1HN ☎ 01438 242272 🖷 01438 242134 ✉ rob.woodisse@stevenage.gov.uk

Waste Collection and Disposal: Mr Lee Myers , Head of Environmental Services, Cavendish Road, Stevenage SG1 2ES ☎ 01438 248710 🖷 01438 242434 ✉ lee.myers@stevenage.gov.uk

Waste Management: Mr Lee Myers , Head of Environmental Services, Cavendish Road, Stevenage SG1 2ES ☎ 01438 248710 🖷 01438 242434 ✉ lee.myers@stevenage.gov.uk

Children's Play Areas: Mr Aidan Sanderson, Head of Leisure, Environmental Health & Children's Services, Daneshill House, Danesrete, Stevenage SG1 1HN ☎ 01438 242311 ✉ aidan.sanderson@stevenage.gov.uk

COUNCILLORS

***Mayor* Burrell**, Howard (LAB - Chells)
howard.burrell@stevenage.gov.uk

***Leader of the Council* Taylor**, Sharon (LAB - Symonds Green)
sharon.taylor@stevenage.gov.uk

***Deputy Leader of the Council* Gardner**, John (LAB - Roebuck)
john.gardner@stevenage.gov.uk

***Group Leader* Bibby**, Philip (CON - Woodfield)
philip.bibby@stevenage.gov.uk

Bainbridge, Doug (LAB - Longmeadow)
doug.bainbridge@stevenage.gov.uk

Batson, Sherma (LAB - Roebuck)
sherma.batson@stevenage.gov.uk

Bell, Lorraine (LAB - Longmeadow)
lorraine.bell@stevenage.gov.uk

Briscoe, Lloyd (LAB - Martins Wood)
lloyd.briscoe@stevenage.gov.uk

Broom, Rob (LAB - Shephall)
rob.broom@stevenage.gov.uk

Brown, Jim (LAB - Old Town)
jim.brown@stevenage.gov.uk

Chester, Laurie (LAB - Symonds Green)
laurie.chester@stevenage.gov.uk

Connolly, Elaine (LAB - Bedwell)
elaine.connolly@stevenage.gov.uk

Cullen, David (LAB - Bedwell)
david.cullen@stevenage.gov.uk

Downing, Michael (LAB - Symonds Green)
michael.downing@stevenage.gov.uk

Fraser, James (CON - Old Town)
james.fraser@stevenage.gov.uk

Gardner, Michelle (LAB - Bandley Hill)
michelle.gardner@stevenage.gov.uk

Harrington, Liz (LAB - Bedwell)
liz.harrington@stevenage.gov.uk

Hearn, Sharon (CON - Bandley Hill)
sharon.hearn@stevenage.gov.uk

Henry, Richard (LAB - St Nicholas)
richard.henry@stevenage.gov.uk

Hurst, Matthew (CON - Longmeadow)
matthew.hurst@stevenage.gov.uk

Latif, Carol (LAB - St Nicholas)
carol.latif@stevenage.gov.uk

Lawrence, Graham (CON - Woodfield)
graham.lawrence@stevenage.gov.uk

Lloyd, Joan (LAB - Bandley Hill)
joan.lloyd@stevenage.gov.uk

Lloyd, John (LAB - Roebuck)
john.lloyd@stevenage.gov.uk

Martin-Haugh, Lin (LAB - Pin Green)
lin.martin-haugh@stevenage.gov.uk

McGuinness, Andy (LD - Manor)
andy.mcguiness@stevenage.gov.uk

McKay, Maureen (LAB - Martins Wood)
maureen.mckay@stevenage.gov.uk

Mead, John (LAB - Shephall)
john.mead@stevenage.gov.uk

Mead, Sarah (LAB - Martins Wood)
sarah.mead@stevenage.gov.uk

Notley, Margaret (CON - Woodfield)
margaret.notley@stevenage.gov.uk

Parker, Robin (LD - Manor)
robin.parker@stevenage.gov.uk

Raynor, Ralph (LAB - St Nicholas)
ralph.raynor@stevenage.gov.uk

Saunders, Chris (LAB - Old Town)
chris.saunders@stevenage.gov.uk

Snell, Graham (LD - Manor)
graham.snell@stevenage.gov.uk

Speller, Simon (LAB - Pin Green)
simon.speller@stevenage.gov.uk

Stuart, Pam (LAB - Chells)
pam.stuart@stevenage.gov.uk

Thomas, Jeanette (LAB - Pin Green)
jeanette.thomas@stevenage.gov.uk

Warwick, Vickie (LAB - Chells)
vickie.warwick@stevenage.gov.uk

Webb, Ann (LAB - Shephall)
ann.webb@stevenage.gov.uk

POLITICAL COMPOSITION

LAB: 30, CON: 6, LD: 3

Stirling S

Stirling Council, Old Viewforth, Stirling FK8 2ET
☎ 0845 277 7000 ✉ info@stirling.gov.uk 🖳 www.stirling.gov.uk

FACTS AND FIGURES

Parliamentary Constituencies: Stirling
EU Constituencies: Scotland
Election Frequency: Elections are of whole council

PRINCIPAL OFFICERS

Chief Executive: Mr Stewart Carruth , Chief Executive, Old Viewforth, Stirling FK8 2ET ☎ 01786 233047 ✉ carruths@stirling.gov.uk

Senior Management: Dr Stacey Burlet , Director of Communities & Partnerships, Old Viewforth, Stirling FK8 2ET ☎ 01786 233013 ✉ burlets@stirling.gov.uk

Senior Management: Ms Val de Souza , Head of Social Services / Chief Social Worker, R27, Lime Tree House, Alloa FK10 1EX ☎ 01259 225017 ✉ cdesouza@clacks.gov.uk

Senior Management: Mr David Leng , Director of Children, Young People & Education, Municipal Buildings, 8 - 10 Corn Exchange, Stirling FK8 2HU ☎ 01786 233182 ✉ lengd@stirling.gov.uk

Senior Management: Ms Jane Menzies, Senior Manager - Community & Place, Old Viewforth, Stirling FK8 2ET ☎ 01786 233022 ✉ dcilliers@clacks.gov.uk

Senior Management: Mr Gerard O'Sullivan , Director of Corporate Operations, Teith House, Kerse Road, Stirling FK7 7QA ☎ 01786 233063 ✉ osullivang@stirling.gov.uk

Senior Management: Mr Robert Steenson , Director of Housing & Environment, Endrick House, Stirling FK7 7SG ☎ 01786 233084 ✉ steensonr@stirling.gov.uk

Architect, Building / Property Services: Mr Drew Leslie , Senior Manager - Infrastructure Development, Teith House, Kerse Road, Stirling FK7 7QA ☎ 01786 233323 🖷 01786 473370 ✉ leslied@stirling.gov.uk

Architect, Building / Property Services: Mr Brian Roberts , Senior Manager - Infrastructure Development, Teith House, Kerse Road, Stirling FK7 7QA ☎ 01786 233462 ✉ robertsb@stirling.gov.uk

Best Value: Mr Paul Fleming, Senior Manager - Corporate Services, Old Viewforth, Stirling FK8 2ET ☎ 01786 233094 ✉ flemingp@stirling.gov.uk

Building Control: Ms Linda Hill , Service Manager - Regulatory, Municipal Buildings, 8 - 10 Corn Exchange Road, Stirling FK8 2HU ☎ 01786 233631 ✉ hillin@stirling.gov.uk

Catering Services: Ms Margaret Gilmour , FM Services Manager, Teith House, Kerse Road, Stirling FK7 7QA ☎ 01786 233263 🖷 01786 473370 ✉ gilmourm@stirling.gov.uk

Children / Youth Services: Mr Bill Miller , Service Manager - Youth Services & Adult Learning, Teith House, Kerse Road, Stirling FK7 7QA ☎ 01786 233595 ✉ millerb@stirling.gov.uk

Civil Registration: Ms Elizabeth Ferguson , District Registrar, Customer First, 1 - 5 Port Street, Stirling FK8 2EJ ☎ 01786 233962 ✉ fergusone@stirling.gov.uk

PR / Communications: Ms Kirsty Scott , Service Manager - Communications, Marketing & Events, Old Viewforth, Stirling FK8 2ET ☎ 01786 233064 ✉ scotta@stirling.gov.uk

Community Planning: Ms Jane Menzies, Senior Manager - Community & Place, Old Viewforth, Stirling FK8 2ET ☎ 01786 233022 ✉ dcilliers@clacks.gov.uk

Community Safety: Ms Margaret Wallace , Manager - Communities & Partnerships, Old Viewforth, Stirling FK8 2ET ☎ 01786 233540 ✉ wallacem@stirling.gov.uk

Computer Management: Ms Heather Robb , ICT & Information Management, Teith House, Kerse Road, Stirling FK7 7QA ☎ 01786 233041 ✉ robbh@stirling.gov.uk

Consumer Protection and Trading Standards: Mr Leslie Fisher , Service Manager: Environmental Health & Trading Standards, Municipal Buildings, Stirling FK8 2QU ☎ 01786 432180 🖷 01786 432203 ✉ fisherl@stirling.gov.uk

Contracts: Ms Liz Duncan , Assurance Manager, Old Viewforth, Stirling FK8 2ET ☎ 01786 233108 🖷 01786 443078 ✉ duncanl@stirling.gov.uk

Corporate Services: Mr Paul Fleming, Senior Manager - Corporate Services, Old Viewforth, Stirling FK8 2ET ☎ 01786 233094 ✉ flemingp@stirling.gov.uk

Customer Service: Mr Richard Aird , Service Manager - Libraries, Archives & Customer Services, Library HQ, Borrowmead Road, Stirling FK7 7TN ☎ 01786 237534 ✉ airdr@stirling.gov.uk

Direct Labour: Mr John MacMillan , Manager - Housing Property, Allan Water House, Stirling FK7 7SG ☎ 01786 237718 🖷 01786 446042 ✉ macmillanj@stirling.gov.uk

Direct Labour: Mr Jamie Wright , Manager - Roads & Transport, Endrick House, Kerse Road, Stirling FK7 7SZ ☎ 01786 237647 🖷 01786 442696 ✉ wrightj@stirling.gov.uk

Economic Development: Ms Carol Beattie , Senior Manager - Economic Development, Old Viewforth, Stirling FK8 2ET ☎ 01786 233139 ✉ beattiec@stirling.gov.uk

Education: Ms Sharon Johnstone , Senior Manager - Education, Children, Young People & Families, Municipal Buildings, 8 - 10 Corn Exchange Road, Stirling FK8 2HU ☎ 01786 233202 ✉ johnstones2@stirling.gov.uk

Education: Mr Kevin Kelman , Senior Manager - Head of School Improvement, Municipal Buildings, 8 - 10 Corn Exchange Road, Stirling FK8 2HU ☎ 01786 233224 ✉ kelmank@stirling.gov.uk

STIRLING

Education: Mr Alan Milliken , Head of Learning, Communities, Performance & Resources, Municipal Buildings, 8 - 10 Corn Exchange Road, Stirling FK8 2HU ☎ 01786 233225 ✉ millikina@stirling.gov.uk

E-Government: Mr David Laughlin , Strategy & Delivery Manager, Teith House, Kerse Road, Stirling FK7 7QA ☎ 01786 233509 ✉ laughlind@stirling.gov.uk

Emergency Planning: Mr David Bright, Resilience & Risk Manager, Teith House, Kerse Road, Stirling FK7 7QA ☎ 01786 233167 🖷 01786 443474 ✉ brightd@stirling.gov.uk

Energy Management: Mr Pierre Boinot , Energy Officer, Teith House, Kerse Road, Stirling FK7 7QA ☎ 01786 233228 🖷 01786 473370 ✉ bionotp@stirling.gov.uk

Energy Management: Mrs Grace Conner , Energy Officer, Teith House, Kerse Road, Stirling FK7 7QA ☎ 01786 233231 🖷 01786 473370 ✉ connerg@stirling.gov.uk

Environmental Health: Mr Leslie Fisher , Service Manager: Environmental Health & Trading Standards, Municipal Buildings, Stirling FK8 2QU ☎ 01786 432180 🖷 01786 432203 ✉ fisherl@stirling.gov.uk

Estates, Property & Valuation: Mr Drew Leslie , Senior Manager - Infrastructure Development, Teith House, Kerse Road, Stirling FK7 7QA ☎ 01786 233323 🖷 01786 473370 ✉ leslied@stirling.gov.uk

European Liaison: Ms Margaret Wallace , Manager - Communities & Partnerships, Old Viewforth, Stirling FK8 2ET ☎ 01786 233540 ✉ wallacem@stirling.gov.uk

Events Manager: Ms Kirsty Scott , Service Manager - Communications, Marketing & Events, Old Viewforth, Stirling FK8 2ET ☎ 01786 233064 ✉ scotta@stirling.gov.uk

Facilities: Ms Margaret Gilmour , FM Services Manager, Teith House, Kerse Road, Stirling FK7 7QA ☎ 01786 233263 🖷 01786 473370 ✉ gilmourm@stirling.gov.uk

Facilities: Mr Jim McNeish, Office Facilities Manager, Teith House, Kerse Road, Stirling FK7 7QA ☎ 01786 233333 ✉ mcneishj@stirling.gov.uk

Finance: Mr Jim Boyle , Chief Finance Officer, Teith House, Kerse Road, Stirling FK7 7QA ☎ 01786 233362 ✉ boylej@stirling.gov.uk

Fleet Management: Mr Gavin Hutton, Manager - Business Strategy, Fleet Services, Springkerse Depot, Kerse Road, Stirling FK7 7TE ☎ 01786 237599 ✉ huttong@stirling.gov.uk

Grounds Maintenance: Ms Nicole Paterson, Service Manager - Environment, Endrick House, Stirling FK7 7SZ ☎ 01786 237794 ✉ patersonn@stirling.gov.uk

Health and Safety: Mr Nick Sabo , Health & Safety Adviser, Teith House, Kerse Road, Stirling FK7 7QA ☎ 01786 233288 🖷 01786 473370 ✉ sabon@stirling.gov.uk

Highways: Mr Robert Steenson , Director of Housing & Environment, Endrick House, Stirling FK7 7SG ☎ 01786 233084 ✉ steensonr@stirling.gov.uk

Home Energy Conservation: Mr Brian Cree , Energy Officer, Viewforth, Stirling FK8 2ET ☎ 01786 442887 ✉ creeb@stirling.gov.uk

Housing: Ms Carol Hamilton , Manager - Housing Management, Endrick House, Stirling FK7 7SG ☎ 01786 237652 ✉ hamiltonc@stirling.gov.uk

Housing: Mr Robert Steenson , Director of Housing & Environment, Endrick House, Stirling FK7 7SG ☎ 01786 233084 ✉ steensonr@stirling.gov.uk

Housing Maintenance: Mr John MacMillan , Manager - Housing Property, Allanwater House, Stirling FK7 7SG ☎ 01786 237718 🖷 01786 446042 ✉ macmillanj@stirling.gov.uk

Legal: Ms Liz Duncan , Assurance Manager, Old Viewforth, Stirling FK8 2ET ☎ 01786 233108 🖷 01786 443078 ✉ duncanl@stirling.gov.uk

Leisure and Cultural Services: Ms Jane Menzies, Senior Manager - Community & Place, Old Viewforth, Stirling FK8 2ET ☎ 01786 233022 ✉ dcilliers@clacks.gov.uk

Licensing: Ms Linda Hill , Service Manager - Regulatory, Municipal Buildings, 8 - 10 Corn Exchange Road, Stirling FK8 2HU ☎ 01786 233631 ✉ hillin@stirling.gov.uk

Lifelong Learning: Mr Ed Gibbon , Team Leader: Adult Learning, Cowane Centre, Cowane Street, Stirling FK8 1JP ☎ 01786 237526 ✉ gibbone@stirling.gov.uk

Lighting: Mr Ian Young , Team Leader: Bridge, Flood & Street Lighting, Endrick House, Kerse Road, Stirling FK7 7SZ ☎ 01786 237645 ✉ youngi@stirling.gov.uk

Lottery Funding, Charity and Voluntary: Ms Jean Cowie , Funding Officer, Old Viewforth, Stirling FK8 2ET ☎ 01786 233143 ✉ cowiej@stirling.gov.uk

Member Services: Ms Joyce Allen , Democratic Support Manager, Old Viewforth, Stirling FK8 2ET ☎ 01786 233095 🖷 01786 443078 ✉ allenj@stirling.gov.uk

Parking: Mr Alan Ogilvie , Team Leader: Traffic Management, Endrick House, Stirling FK7 7SZ ☎ 01786 233449 ✉ ogilvieaf@stirling.gov.uk

Partnerships: Dr Stacey Burlet , Director of Communities & Partnerships, Old Viewforth, Stirling FK8 2ET ☎ 01786 233013 ✉ burlets@stirling.gov.uk

Personnel / HR: Ms Kristine Johnson , Chief HR Officer, Teith House, Kerse Road, Stirling FK7 7QA ☎ 01786 233294 🖷 01786 473370 ✉ johnsonk@stirling.gov.uk

Planning: Mr Peter Morgan , Chief Planning Officer, Municipal Buildings, Corn Exchange Road, Stirling FK8 2HU ☎ 01786 233682 ✉ morganp@stirling.gov.uk

Procurement: Ms Isabel McKnight , Strategic Procurement & Commissioning Manager, Old Viewforth, Stirling FK8 2ET ☎ 01786 233389 ✉ mcknighti@stirling.gov.uk

Public Libraries: Mr Richard Aird , Service Manager - Libraries, Archives & Customer Services, Library HQ, Borrowmead Road, Stirling FK7 7TN ☎ 01786 237534 ✉ airdr@stirling.gov.uk

Recycling & Waste Minimisation: Mr David Hopper, Sustainable Development Manager, Teith House, Kerse Road, Stirling FK7 7QA ☎ 01786 237566 ✉ hopperd@stirling.gov.uk

Regeneration: Ms Margaret Wallace , Manager - Communities & Partnerships, Old Viewforth, Stirling FK8 2ET ☎ 01786 233540 ✉ wallacem@stirling.gov.uk

Road Safety: Mr Stuart Geddes , Road Safety Engineer, Teith House, Kerse Road, Stirling FK7 7QA ☎ 01786 233440 ✉ geddess@stirling.gov.uk

Social Services: Ms Val de Souza , Head of Social Services / Chief Social Worker, Kilncraigs, Alloa FK10 1EB ☎ 01259 225017 ✉ cdesouza@clacks.gov.uk

Staff Training: Ms Suzan Duffus , Organisational Development Manager, Unit 12, Back O'Hill Industrial Estate, Stirling FK8 1SH ☎ 01786 233982 ✉ duffuss@stirling.gov.uk

Street Scene: Ms Nicole Paterson, Service Manager - Environment, Endrick House, Stirling FK7 7SG ☎ 01786 237794 ✉ patersonn@stirling.gov.uk

Sustainable Communities: Ms Jane Menzies, Senior Manager - Community & Place, Old Viewforth, Stirling FK8 2ET ☎ 01786 233022 ✉ dcilliers@clacks.gov.uk

Tourism: Ms Carol Beattie , Senior Manager - Economic Development, Old Viewforth, Stirling FK8 2ET ☎ 01786 233139 ✉ beattiec@stirling.gov.uk

Town Centre: Ms Margaret Wallace , Manager - Communities & Partnerships, Old Viewforth, Stirling FK8 2ET ☎ 01786 233540 ✉ wallacem@stirling.gov.uk

Traffic Management: Mr Alan Ogilvie , Team Leader: Traffic Management, Teith House, Kerse Road, Stirling FK7 7QA ☎ 01786 233449 ✉ ogilvieaf@stirling.gov.uk

Total Place: Ms Jane Menzies, Senior Manager - Community & Place, Old Viewforth, Stirling FK8 2ET ☎ 01786 233022 ✉ dcilliers@clacks.gov.uk

Waste Collection and Disposal: Mr David Hopper, Sustainable Development Manager, Teith House, Kerse Road, Stirling FK7 7QA ☎ 01786 237566 ✉ hopperd@stirling.gov.uk

Waste Management: Mr David Hopper, Sustainable Development Manager, Teith House, Kerse Road, Stirling FK7 7QA ☎ 01786 237566 ✉ hopperd@stirling.gov.uk

COUNCILLORS

***Provost* Robbins**, Mike (LAB - Dunblaine and Bridge of Allan)
robbinsm@stirling.gov.uk

***Deputy Provost* Campbell**, Callum (CON - Dunblaine and Bridge of Allan)
campbellc@stirling.gov.uk

***Leader of the Council* Boyd**, Johanna (LAB - Castle)
boydj@stirling.gov.uk

***Deputy Leader of the Council* Benny**, Neil (CON - Stirling West)
bennyn@stirling.gov.uk

Berrill, Alistair (CON - Forth and Endrick)
berrilla@stirling.gov.uk

Brisley, Margaret (LAB - BannockBurn)
brisleym@stirling.gov.uk

Earl, Martin (CON - Trossachs and Teith)
earlm@stirling.gov.uk

Farmer, Scott (SNP - Stirling West)
farmers@stirling.gov.uk

Gibson, Danny (LAB - Stirling East)
gibsond@stirling.gov.uk

Hayes, Alycia (SNP - Trossachs and Teith)
hayesa@stirling.gov.uk

Hendry, John (LAB - Castle)
hendryj@stirling.gov.uk

Houston, Graham (SNP - Dunblaine and Bridge of Allan)
houstong@stirling.gov.uk

Lambie, Graham (SNP - Forth and Endrick)
lambieg@stirling.gov.uk

MacPherson, Alasdair (SNP - BannockBurn)
macphersona@stirling.gov.uk

McChord, Corrie (LAB - Stirling East)
mcchordc@stirling.gov.uk

Muirhead, Ian (SNP - Forth and Endrick)
muirheadi@stirling.gov.uk

Paterson, Steven (SNP - Stirling East)
patersonst@stirling.gov.uk

Ruskell, Mark (SGP - Dunblaine and Bridge of Allan)
ruskellm@stirling.gov.uk

Simpson, Christine (LAB - Stirling West)
simpsonc@stirling.gov.uk

Thomson, Jim (SNP - Castle)
thomsonj03@stirling.gov.uk

Weir, Violet (LAB - BannockBurn)
weirv@stirling.gov.uk

Wood, Fergus (SNP - Trossachs and Teith)
woodf@stirling.gov.uk

POLITICAL COMPOSITION

SNP: 9, LAB: 8, CON: 4, SGP: 1

STOCKPORT

Stockport M

Stockport Metropolitan Borough Council, Town Hall, Edward Street, Stockport SK1 3XE

☎ 0161 480 4949 🖷 0161 477 9530 💻 www.stockport.gov.uk

FACTS AND FIGURES

Parliamentary Constituencies: Cheadle, Denton and Reddish, Hazel Grove, Stockport
EU Constituencies: North West
Election Frequency: Elections are by thirds

PRINCIPAL OFFICERS

Chief Executive: Mr Eamonn Boylan , Chief Executive, Town Hall, Edward Street, Stockport SK1 3XE ☎ 0161 474 3001 🖷 0161 480 6773 ✉ eamonn.boylan@stockport.gov.uk

Deputy Chief Executive: Mrs Laureen Donnan , Deputy Chief Executive, Town Hall, Edward Street, Stockport SK1 3XE ☎ 0161 474 3180 🖷 0161 474 3009 ✉ laureen.donnan@stockport.gov.uk

Senior Management: Mr Steve Houston, Corporate Director - Corporate & Support Services, Stopford House, Piccadilly, Stockport SK1 3XE ☎ 0161 474 4000 🖷 0161 474 4006 ✉ steve.houston@stockport.gov.uk

Senior Management: Dr Stephen Watkins , Director - Public Health, Town Hall, Edward Street, Stockport SK1 3XE ☎ 0161 474 2436 ✉ stephen.watkins@stockport.gov.uk

Senior Management: Mr Andrew Webb, Corporate Director - Services to People, Stopford House, Piccadilly, Stockport SK1 3XE ☎ 0161 474 3808 🖷 0161 480 3497 ✉ andrew.webb@stockport.gov.uk

Architect, Building / Property Services: Ms Julie Newbatt , Operations Lead, Carillion Stockport Property Services, Stopford House, Piccadilly, Stockport SK1 3XE ☎ 0161 217 6915 ✉ julie.newbatt@carillionplc.com

Building Control: Mr Ian O'Donnell , Head of Public Protection & Public Realm, Fred Perry House, Piccadilly, Stockport SK1 3XE ☎ 0161 474 4175 🖷 0161 474 4369 ✉ ian.odonnell@stockport.gov.uk

Catering Services: Ms Joyce Rowe, Venue Catering Operations Manager, Solutions SK Ltd, Venue Catering, Stopford House, Piccadilly, Stockport SK1 3XE ☎ 0161 474 4575 ✉ joyce.rowe@solutionssk.co.uk

Children / Youth Services: Mr Phil Beswick , Director of Education Services, Stopford House, Piccadilly, Stockport SK1 3XE ☎ 0161 474 3832 ✉ phil.beswick@stockport.gov.uk

Children / Youth Services: Ms Chris McLoughlin , Service Director - Children's Safeguarding & Prevention, Stopford House, Piccadilly, Stockport SK1 3XE ☎ 0161 474 4624 🖷 0161 480 3497 ✉ chris.mcloughlin@stockport.gov.uk

Civil Registration: Mr Murray Carr , Head of Estate & Asset Management, Stopford House, Stockport SK1 3XE ☎ 0161 474 3019 ✉ murray.carr@stockport.gov.uk

PR / Communications: Mr Paul James , Head of Information & Communication, Town Hall, Edward Street, Stockport SK1 3XE ☎ 0161 474 5430 ✉ paul.james@stockport.gov.uk

Community Planning: Ms Nicola Turner , Head of Growth, Fred Perry House, Edward Street, Stockport SK1 3XE ☎ 0161 218 1635 ✉ nicola.turner@stockport.gov.uk

Community Safety: Ms Helen Boyle , Deputy Head of Community Safety & Neighbourhoods, Fred Perry House, Edward Street, Stockport SK1 3AA ☎ 0161 474 3145 ✉ helen.boyle@stockport.gov.uk

Computer Management: Mr Paul James , Head of Information & Communication, Town Hall, Edward Street, Stockport SK1 3XE ☎ 0161 474 5430 ✉ paul.james@stockport.gov.uk

Consumer Protection and Trading Standards: Mr Ian O'Donnell , Head of Public Protection & Public Realm, Stopford House, Piccadilly, Stockport SK1 3XE ☎ 0161 474 4175 🖷 0161 474 4369 ✉ ian.odonnell@stockport.gov.uk

Contracts: Ms Christine Buxton , Head of Finance, Stopford House, Stockport SK1 3XE ☎ 0161 474 4124 ✉ christine.buxton@stockport.gov.uk

Corporate Services: Mr Steve Houston, Corporate Director - Corporate & Support Services, Stopford House, Piccadilly, Stockport SK1 3XE ☎ 0161 474 4000 🖷 0161 474 4006 ✉ steve.houston@stockport.gov.uk

Customer Service: Mrs Alison Blount , Head of Revenues & Benefits, Stopford House, Piccadilly, Stockport SK1 3XE ☎ 0161 474 5107 ✉ alison.blount@stockport.gov.uk

Direct Labour: Mr Stephen Morris , Managing Director - Solutions SK, Solutions SK Ltd, Enterprise House, Birdhall Lane, Cheadle Heath, Stockport SK3 0XT ☎ 0161 474 5566 ✉ stephen.morris@solutionssk.co.uk

Economic Development: Ms Nicola Turner , Head of Growth, Fred Perry House, Edward Street, Stockport SK1 3XE ☎ 0161 218 1635 ✉ nicola.turner@stockport.gov.uk

Education: Mr Phil Beswick , Director of Education Services, Stopford House, Piccadilly, Stockport SK1 3XE ☎ 0161 474 3832 ✉ phil.beswick@stockport.gov.uk

Electoral Registration: Mr Steve Callender , Electoral Services Manager, Town Hall, Edward Street, Stockport SK1 3XE ☎ 0161 474 3184 🖷 0161 474 3259 ✉ steve.callender@stockport.gov.uk

Emergency Planning: Mrs Claire Grindlay , Head of Business Support (Place), Town Hall, Edward Street, Stockport SK1 3XE ☎ 0161 474 4191 ✉ claire.grindlay@stockport.gov.uk

Energy Management: Mr John Millington , Energy Manager, Carillion Stockport Property Services, Stopford House, Piccadilly, Stockport SK1 3XE ☎ 0161 217 6919 ✉ john.millington@carillionplc.com

Environmental / Technical Services: Mr Ian O'Donnell , Head of Public Protection & Public Realm, Stopford House, Piccadilly, Stockport SK1 3XE ☎ 0161 474 4175 🖷 0161 474 4369 🖰 ian.odonnell@stockport.gov.uk

Environmental Health: Mr Ian O'Donnell , Head of Public Protection & Public Realm, Stopford House, Piccadilly, Stockport SK1 3XE ☎ 0161 474 4175 🖷 0161 474 4369 🖰 ian.odonnell@stockport.gov.uk

Estates, Property & Valuation: Mr Murray Carr , Head of Estate & Asset Management, Stopford House, Stockport SK1 3XE ☎ 0161 474 3019 🖰 murray.carr@stockport.gov.uk

European Liaison: Ms Nicola Turner , Head of Growth, Fred Perry House, Edward Street, Stockport SK1 3XE ☎ 0161 218 1635 🖰 nicola.turner@stockport.gov.uk

Events Manager: Ms Joanne Chadwick, Venue Manager, Town Hall, Edward Street, Stockport SK1 3XE ☎ 0161 474 3450 🖷 0161 474 7698

Facilities: Ms Joanne Chadwick, Venue Manager, Town Hall, Edward Street, Stockport SK1 3XE ☎ 0161 474 3450 🖷 0161 474 7698

Finance: Mr Steve Houston, Corporate Director - Corporate & Support Services, Stopford House, Piccadilly, Stockport SK1 3XE ☎ 0161 474 4000 🖷 0161 474 4006 🖰 steve.houston@stockport.gov.uk

Fleet Management: Ms Jennie Bannister , Transport Manager - Solutions SK, Solutions SK Ltd, Enterprise House, Bird Hall Lane, Cheadle Heath, Stockport SK3 0XS ☎ 0161 474 3753 🖰 jennie.bannister@solutionssk.co.uk

Health and Safety: Ms Ann-Marie McCullough , CSS Manager - Health, Safety & Wellbeing, Stopford House, Piccadilly, Stockport SK1 3XE ☎ 0161 474 3056 🖰 ann-marie.mccullough@stockport.gov.uk

Home Energy Conservation: Mr Andy Kippax , Strategic Housing Lead, Fred Perry House, Stockport SK1 3XE ☎ 0161 474 4319 🖰 andy.kippax@stockport.gov.uk

Housing: Ms Helen McHale , Chief Executive - Stockport Homes, Stockport Homes, 2nd Floor, 1 St. Peter's Square, Stockport SK1 1NZ ☎ 0161 474 2865 🖰 helen.mchale@stockporthomes.org

Housing Maintenance: Mr Mark Hudson, Director of Technical Services - Stockport Homes, Stockport Homes, 2nd Floor, St Peter's Square, Stockport SK1 1NZ ☎ 0161 474 4508 🖷 0161 474 4557 🖰 mark.hudson@stockporthomes.org

Legal: Ms Parveen Akhtar , Head of Legal & Democratic Governance, Town Hall, Edward Street, Stockport SK1 3XE ☎ 0161 474 1450 🖰 parveen.akhtar@stockport.gov.uk

Leisure and Cultural Services: Mr Peter Ashworth , Head of Culture & Leisure, Staircase House, 30 Market Place, Stockport SK1 1ES ☎ 0161 474 2392 🖰 peter.ashworth@stockport.gov.uk

Licensing: Mr Ian O'Donnell , Head of Public Protection & Public Realm, Stopford House, Piccadilly, Stockport SK1 3XE ☎ 0161 474 4175 🖷 0161 474 4369 🖰 ian.odonnell@stockport.gov.uk

Lifelong Learning: Mr Richard Mortimer, Head of Learning & Employment, Stopford House, Piccadilly, Stockport SK1 3XE ☎ 0161 474 3864 🖷 0161 953 0012 🖰 richard.mortimer@stockport.gov.uk

Lighting: Mr Andrew Suggett , Network Assets Manager, Enterprise House, Oakhurst Drive, Cheadle Heath, Stockport SL3 0XT ☎ 0161 474 2425 🖰 andrew.suggett@stockport.gov.uk

Member Services: Mr Craig Ainsworth , Democratic Services Manager, Town Hall, Edward Street, Stockport SK1 3XE ☎ 0161 474 3204 🖰 craig.ainsworth@stockport.gov.uk

Parking: Mr Adam Forbes , Public Realm Manager - Parking, Patrols & Waste, Endeavor House, Bredbury Parkway, Bredbury, Stockport SK6 2SN ☎ 0161 474 3680 🖰 adam.forbes@stockport.gov.uk

Personnel / HR: Ms Sue Williams , Head of People & Organisational Development, Town Hall, Edward Street, Stockport SK1 3XE ☎ 0161 474 2175 🖰 sue.williams@stockport.gov.uk

Planning: Ms Emma Curle , Chief Planning Officer, Fred Perry House, Piccadilly, Stockport SK1 3XE ☎ 0161 474 3542 🖷 0161 474 2610 🖰 emma.curle@stockport.gov.uk

Procurement: Ms Christine Buxton , Head of Finance, Stopford House, Stockport SK1 3XE ☎ 0161 474 4124 🖰 christine.buxton@stockport.gov.uk

Public Libraries: Ms Janet Wood , Head of Service & Customer Engagement, Fred Perry House, Edward Street, Stockport SK1 3XE ☎ 0161 474 4443 🖰 janet.wood@stockport.gov.uk

Recycling & Waste Minimisation: Mr Adam Forbes , Public Realm Manager - Parking, Patrols & Waste, Endeavor House, Bredbury Parkway, Bredbury, Stockport SK6 2SN ☎ 0161 474 3680 🖰 adam.forbes@stockport.gov.uk

Regeneration: Ms Nicola Turner , Head of Growth, Fred Perry House, Edward Street, Stockport SK1 3XE ☎ 0161 218 1635 🖰 nicola.turner@stockport.gov.uk

Road Safety: Mr Pete Price , Interim Head of Highways & Transportation, Fred Perry House, Stockport SK1 3XE ☎ 0161 474 4901 🖰 pete.price@stockport.gov.uk

Social Services (Adult): Mr Terry Dafter, Service Director - Adult Social Care, Stopford House, Piccadilly, Stockport SK1 3XE ☎ 0161 218 1644 🖷 0161 474 7895 🖰 terry.dafter@stockport.gov.uk

Social Services (Children): Ms Chris McLoughlin , Service Director - Children's Safeguarding & Prevention, Stopford House, Piccadilly, Stockport SK1 3XE ☎ 0161 474 4624 🖷 0161 480 3497 🖰 chris.mcloughlin@stockport.gov.uk

STOCKPORT

Public Health: Dr Stephen Watkins , Director - Public Health, Town Hall, Edward Street, Stockport SK1 3XE ☎ 0161 474 2436 🖱 stephen.watkins@stockport.gov.uk

Staff Training: Ms Sue Williams , Head of People & Organisational Development, Town Hall, Edward Street, Stockport SK1 3XE ☎ 0161 474 2175 🖱 sue.williams@stockport.gov.uk

Sustainable Communities: Ms Nicola Turner , Head of Growth, Fred Perry House, Edward Street, Stockport SK1 3XE ☎ 0161 218 1635 🖱 nicola.turner@stockport.gov.uk

Sustainable Development: Ms Nicola Turner , Head of Growth, Fred Perry House, Edward Street, Stockport SK1 3XE ☎ 0161 218 1635 🖱 nicola.turner@stockport.gov.uk

Tourism: Mr Peter Ashworth , Head of Culture & Leisure, Staircase House, 30 Market Place, Stockport SK1 1ES ☎ 0161 474 2392 🖱 peter.ashworth@stockport.gov.uk

Town Centre: Ms Nicola Turner , Head of Growth, Fred Perry House, Edward Street, Stockport SK1 3XE ☎ 0161 218 1635 🖱 nicola.turner@stockport.gov.uk

Traffic Management: Mr Pete Price , Interim Head of Highways & Transportation, Fred Perry House, Stockport SK1 3XE ☎ 0161 474 4901 🖱 pete.price@stockport.gov.uk

Transport: Mr Pete Price , Interim Head of Highways & Transportation, Fred Perry House, Stockport SK1 3XE ☎ 0161 474 4901 🖱 pete.price@stockport.gov.uk

Transport Planner: Mr Pete Price , Interim Head of Highways & Transportation, Fred Perry House, Stockport SK1 3XE ☎ 0161 474 4901 🖱 pete.price@stockport.gov.uk

Waste Collection and Disposal: Mr Adam Forbes , Public Realm Manager - Parking, Patrols & Waste, Endeavor House, Bredbury Parkway, Bredbury, Stockport SK6 2SN ☎ 0161 474 3680 🖱 adam.forbes@stockport.gov.uk

Waste Management: Mr Adam Forbes , Public Realm Manager - Parking, Patrols & Waste, Endeavor House, Bredbury Parkway, Bredbury, Stockport SK6 2SN ☎ 0161 474 3680 🖱 adam.forbes@stockport.gov.uk

COUNCILLORS

***Mayor* Verdeille**, Andrew (LAB - Reddish South)
cllr.a.verdeille@stockport.gov.uk

***Deputy Mayor* Somekh**, June (LD - Cheadle Hulme North)
cllr.june.somekh@stockport.gov.uk

***Leader of the Council* Derbyshire**, Sue (LD - Manor)
leader@stockport.gov.uk

***Deputy Leader of the Council* Roberts**, Iain (LD - Cheadle and Gatley)
cllr.iain.roberts@stockport.gov.uk

Abell, Geoff (LD - Marple North)
cllr.geoff.abell@stockport.gov.uk

Alexander, Ben (LD - Stepping Hill)
cllr.ben.alexander@stockport.gov.uk

Alexander, Shan (LD - Marple South)
cllr.shan.alexander@stockport.gov.uk

Bagnall, Brian (CON - Bramhall South)
cllr.brian.bagnall@stockport.gov.uk

Bailey, Sheila (LAB - Edgeley and Cheadle Heath)
bailey.harding@ntlworld.com

Bellis, Paul (CON - Bramhall South)
cllr.paul.bellis@stockport.gov.uk

Bispham, Andrew (LD - Marple North)
cllr.andrew.bispham@stockport.gov.uk

Bodsworth, Stuart (LD - Cheadle Hulme South)
cllr.stuart.bodsworth@stockport.gov.uk

Booth, Laura (LAB - Offerton)
cllr.laura.booth@stockport.gov.uk

Brett, Walter (LAB - Reddish South)
cllr.walter.brett@stockport.gov.uk

Burns, Peter (R - Heald Green)
peterind@aol.com

Butler, Kate (LAB - Reddish North)
cllr.kate.butler@stockport.gov.uk

Candler, Martin (LD - Marple North)
cllr.martin.candler@stockport.gov.uk

Coaton, Richard (LAB - Edgeley and Cheadle Heath)
each.labour@ntlworld.com

Corris, Christine (LD - Bredbury and Woodley)
cllr.christine.corris@stockport.gov.uk

Dowling, Kevin (LD - Marple South)
cllr.kevin.dowling@stockport.gov.uk

Fitzpatrick, Dean (LAB - Heatons South)
cllr.d.fitzpatrick@stockport.gov.uk

Foster, Colin (LAB - Heatons South)
colfoster@colfoster.demon.co.uk

Ganotis, Alexander (LAB - Heatons North)
cllr.a.ganotis@stockport.gov.uk

Goddard, Dave (LD - Offerton)
cllr.dave.goddard@stockport.gov.uk

Gordon, Chris (LD - Bredbury and Woodley)
cllr.chris.gordon@stockport.gov.uk

Grice, Lenny (LD - Cheadle Hulme South)
cllr.lenny.grice@stockport.gov.uk

Grundy, Tom (LAB - Reddish South)
cllr.tom.grundy@stockport.gov.uk

Harding, Philip (LAB - Edgeley and Cheadle Heath)
bailey.harding@ntlworld.com

Hawthorne, Daniel (LD - Manor)
cllr.d.hawthorne@stockport.gov.uk

Hendley, Brian (LAB - Davenport and Cale Green)
cllr.brian.hendley@stockport.gov.uk

Hogg, Kevin (LD - Hazel Grove)
cllr.kevin.hogg@stockport.gov.uk

Holloway, Keith (LD - Cheadle and Gatley)
cllr.keith.holloway@stockport.gov.uk

Holt, Linda (CON - Bramhall North)
cllr.linda.holt@stockport.gov.uk

Humphreys, Sylvia (R - Heald Green)
cllr.sylvia.humphreys@stockport.gov.uk

Ingham, Susan (LD - Marple South)
cllr.susan.ingham@stockport.gov.uk

Johnson, Anita (CON - Bramhall South)
cllr.anita.johnson@stockport.gov.uk

Johnstone, Oliver (CON - Hazel Grove)
cllr.oliver.johnstone@stockport.gov.uk

King, Pam (LD - Cheadle and Gatley)
cllr.pamela.king@stockport.gov.uk

Kirkham, Mags (LD - Bredbury Green and Romiley)
cllr.m.kirkham@stockport.gov.uk

Lees, Hazel (LD - Bredbury Green and Romiley)
cllr.hazel.lees@stockport.gov.uk

Lloyd, Syd (CON - Bredbury Green and Romiley)
syd@sparkling-ice.com

McAuley, Patrick (IND - Manor)
cllr.patrick.mcauley@stockport.gov.uk

McGee, Tom (LAB - Heatons South)
tom.mcgee@btinternet.com

Meikle, Wendy (LD - Offerton)
cllr.wendy.meikle@stockport.gov.uk

Moss, Paul (LAB - Reddish North)
cllr.paul.moss@stockport.gov.uk

Murphy, Christopher (LAB - Brinnington and Central)
chris.murf@btinternet.com

Nottingham, Adrian (R - Heald Green)
cllr.a.nottingham@stockport.gov.uk

Orrell, Wendy (LD - Stepping Hill)
cllr.wendy.orrell@stockport.gov.uk

Pantall, John (LD - Cheadle Hulme North)
cllr.john.pantall@stockport.gov.uk

Porgess, Paul (LD - Cheadle Hulme North)
cllr.paul.porgess@stockport.gov.uk

Rowles, Maureen (LAB - Brinnington and Central)
cllr.maureen.rowles@stockport.gov.uk

Sedgwick, David (LAB - Heatons North)
cllr.david.sedgwick@stockport.gov.uk

Sorton, Andy (LAB - Brinnington and Central)
cllr.andy.sorton@stockport.gov.uk

Taylor, John (LAB - Heatons North)
cllr.john.taylor@stockport.gov.uk

Vine, Alanna (CON - Bramhall North)
cllr.alanna.vine@stockport.gov.uk

Walker, Lisa (CON - Bramhall North)
cllr.lisa.walker@stockport.gov.uk

Wild, Wendy (LAB - Davenport and Cale Green)
cllr.wendy.wild@stockport.gov.uk

Wilson, Michael (LD - Bredbury and Woodley)
cllr.mike.wilson@stockport.gov.uk

Wilson, Elise (LAB - Davenport and Cale Green)
cllr.elise.wilson@stockport.gov.uk

Wilson, David (LAB - Reddish North)
cllr.david.wilson@stockport.gov.uk

Wragg, William (CON - Hazel Grove)
cllr.william.wragg@stockport.gov.uk

Wright, John (CON - Stepping Hill)
cllr.john.wright@stockport.gov.uk

Wyatt, Suzanne (LD - Cheadle Hulme South)
cllr.suzanne.wyatt@stockport.gov.uk

POLITICAL COMPOSITION
LD: 27, LAB: 22, CON: 10, R: 3, IND: 1

Stockton-on-Tees U

Stockton-on-Tees Borough Council, PO Box 11, Municipal Buildings, Church Road, Stockton-on-Tees TS18 1LD
☎ 01642 393939 🖷 01642 393092
customercomments@stockton.gov.uk 💻 www.stockton.gov.uk

FACTS AND FIGURES
Parliamentary Constituencies: Stockton North, Stockton South
EU Constituencies: North East
Election Frequency: Elections are of whole council

PRINCIPAL OFFICERS
Chief Executive: Mr Neil Schneider, Chief Executive, PO Box 34, Municipal Buildings, Church Road, Stockton-on-Tees TS18 1LD ☎ 01642 527000 🖷 01642 527002 neil.schneider@stockton.gov.uk

Senior Management: Mr David Bond, Director - Law & Democracy (Monitoring Officer), PO Box 11, Municipal Buildings, Church Road, Stockton-on-Tees TS18 1LD ☎ 01642 527060 🖷 01642 527062 david.bond@stockton.gov.uk

Senior Management: Ms Beccy Brown, Head of Communications & Human Resources, Municipal Buildings, Church Road, Stockton-on-Tees TS18 1LD ☎ 01642 527003 beccy.brown@stockton.gov.uk

Senior Management: Mrs Julie Danks, Corporate Director - Resources, Municipal Buildings, Church Road, Stockton-on-Tees TS18 1LD ☎ 01642 527007 🖷 01642 527009 julie.danks@stockton.gov.uk

Senior Management: Mr Paul Dobson , Corporate Director - Development & Neighbourhood Services, Municipal Buildings, Church Road, Stockton-on-Tees TS18 1LD ☎ 01642 527068 paul.dobson@stockton.gov.uk

Senior Management: Ms Jane Humphreys, Corporate Director - Children, Education & Social Care, PO Box 228, Municipal Buildings, Stockton-on-Tees TS18 1XE ☎ 01642 527053 🖷 01642 527037 jane.humphreys@stockton.gov.uk

Senior Management: Dr Peter Kelly , Director - Public Health, PO Box 11, Municipal Buildings, Church Road, Stockton-on-Tees TS18 1LD ☎ 01642 527052 peter.kelly@stockton.gov.uk

STOCKTON-ON-TEES

Senior Management: Ms Lesley King , Head of Performance & Partnerships, PO Box 11, Municipal Buildings, Church Road, Stockton-on-Tees TS18 1LD ☎ 01642 527004 🖱 lesley.king@stockton.gov.uk

Architect, Building / Property Services: Mr Richard McGuckin, Head of Economic Growth & Developmental Services, PO Box 229, Kingsway House, West Precinct, Billingham TS23 2YS ☎ 01642 526765 🖷 01642 526713 🖱 richard.mcguckin@stockton.gov.uk

Building Control: Mr Raymond Sullivan, Building Control Manager, Gloucester House, Church Road, Stockton-on-Tees TS18 1TW ☎ 01642 526040 🖷 01642 526048 🖱 raymond.sullivan@stockton.gov.uk

Catering Services: Mr Jamie McCann, Head of Direct Services, Stirling House, Tedder Avenue, Thornaby, Thornbury TS17 9JP ☎ 01642 527071 🖷 01642 528885 🖱 jamie.mccann@stockton.gov.uk

Children / Youth Services: Ms Jane Humphreys, Corporate Director - Children, Education & Social Care, PO Box 228, Municipal Buildings, Stockton-on-Tees TS18 1XE ☎ 01642 527053 🖷 01642 527037 🖱 jane.humphreys@stockton.gov.uk

Children / Youth Services: Mr Shaun McLurg , Head of Safeguarding & Looked After Children, Municipal Buildings, Church Road, Stockton-on-Tees TS18 1LD ☎ 01642 527049 🖱 shaun.mclurg@stockton.gov.uk

Civil Registration: Ms Sue Daniels, Head of Performance & Business Services, Municipal Buildings, Church Road, Stockton-on-Tees TS18 1LE ☎ 01642 527101 🖱 sue.daniels@stockton.gov.uk

Civil Registration: Ms Jayne Robins, Registration & Bereavement Services Manager, Nightingale House, Balaclava Street, Stockton-on-Tees TS18 2AL ☎ 01642 527724 🖷 01642 527725 🖱 jayne.robins@stockton.gov.uk

PR / Communications: Ms Beccy Brown, Head of Communications & Human Resources, Municipal Buildings, Church Road, Stockton-on-Tees TS18 1LD ☎ 01642 527003 🖱 beccy.brown@stockton.gov.uk

PR / Communications: Ms Kirsty Grundy , Senior Media Relations Officer, PO Box 117, Municipal Buildings, Church Road, Stockton-on-Tees TS18 1YD ☎ 01642 528804 🖱 kirsty.grundy@stockton.gov.uk

Community Planning: Mr Gregory Archer , Principal Planning Officer, PO Box 11, Municipal Buildings, Church Road, Stockton-on-Tees TS18 1LD ☎ 01642 526052 🖱 Gregory.Archer@stockton.gov.uk

Community Safety: Mr Mike Batty, Head of Community Protection, 16 Church Road, PO Box 323, Stockton-on-Tees TS18 1XD ☎ 01642 527074 🖷 01642 526583 🖱 mike.batty@stockton.gov.uk

Computer Management: Mr Ian Miles, Head of ICT, Design, Print, Town Hall DBC, Feethams, Darlington DL1 5QT ☎ 01642 527012 🖷 01642 528245 🖱 ian.miles@xentrall.org.uk

Consumer Protection and Trading Standards: Mr David Kitching, Trading Standards & Licensing Manager, 16 Church Road, Stockton-on-Tees TS18 1XD ☎ 01642 526530 🖷 01642 526584 🖱 david.kitching@stockton.gov.uk

Contracts: Mr Jamie McCann, Head of Direct Services, Stirling House, Tedder Avenue, Thornaby, Thornbury TS17 9JP ☎ 01642 527071 🖷 01642 528885 🖱 jamie.mccann@stockton.gov.uk

Corporate Services: Mrs Julie Danks, Corporate Director - Resources, Municipal Buildings, Church Road, Stockton-on-Tees TS18 1LD ☎ 01642 527007 🖷 01642 527009 🖱 julie.danks@stockton.gov.uk

Corporate Services: Ms Lesley King , Head of Performance & Partnerships, PO Box 11, Municipal Buildings, Church Road, Stockton-on-Tees TS18 1LD ☎ 01642 527004 🖱 lesley.king@stockton.gov.uk

Customer Service: Ms Kath Hornsey, Customer Services & Administration Manager, PO Box 11, Municipal Buildings, Church Road, Stockton-on-Tees TS18 1LD ☎ 01642 526283 🖱 kath.hornsey@stockton.gov.uk

Direct Labour: Mr Jamie McCann, Head of Direct Services, Stirling House, Tedder Avenue, Thornaby, Thornbury TS17 9JP ☎ 01642 527071 🖷 01642 528885 🖱 jamie.mccann@stockton.gov.uk

Economic Development: Mr Richard Poundford , Head of Special Economic Projects, PO Box 34, Municipal Buildings, Church Road, Stockton-on-Tees TS18 1LE ☎ 01642 393939 🖱 richard.poundford@stockton.gov.uk

Economic Development: Mr Mark Rowell, Business Enterprise Manager, PO Box 34, Municipal Buildings, Church Road, Stockton-on-Tees TS18 1LE ☎ 01642 526010 🖷 01642 527023 🖱 mark.rowell@stockton.gov.uk

Education: Ms Jane Humphreys, Corporate Director - Children, Education & Social Care, PO Box 228, Municipal Buildings, Stockton-on-Tees TS18 1XE ☎ 01642 527053 🖷 01642 527037 🖱 jane.humphreys@stockton.gov.uk

Education: Ms Diane McConnell , Head of Schools SEN, Municipal Buildings, Church Road, Stockton-on-Tees TS18 1LD ☎ 01642 527041 🖱 diane.mcconnell@stockton.gov.uk

E-Government: Mr Ian Miles, Head of ICT, Design, Print, Town Hall DBC, Feethams, Darlington DL1 5QT ☎ 01642 527012 🖷 01642 528245 🖱 ian.miles@xentrall.org.uk

Electoral Registration: Mrs Margaret Waggott, Head of Democratic Services, PO Box 11, Municipal Buildings, Church Road, Stockton-on-Tees TS18 1LD ☎ 01642 527064 🖷 01642 527062 🖱 margaret.waggott@stockton.gov.uk

Emergency Planning: Mr Stuart Marshall , Emergency Planning Officer, Stirling House, Teddar Avenue, Thornaby, Stockton-on-Tees TS19 9JP ☎ 01642 524694

Energy Management: Mr Ian Hodgson, Maintenance Service Manager, Kingsway House, West Precinct, Billingham TS18 2YS ☎ 01642 526889 🖷 01642 528414 ✉ ian.hodgson@stockton.gov.uk

Environmental / Technical Services: Mr Mike Chicken, Built & Natural Environment Manager, Kingsway House, West Precinct, Billingham TS18 2YS ☎ 01642 528148 🖷 01642 528217 ✉ mike.chicken@stockton.gov.uk

Environmental / Technical Services: Mr Paul Dobson , Corporate Director of Development & Neighbourhood Services, Municipal Buildings, Church Road, Stockton-on-Tees TS18 1LD ☎ 01642 527068 ✉ paul.dobson@stockton.gov.uk

Environmental / Technical Services: Mr Neil Schneider, Chief Executive, PO Box 34, Municipal Buildings, Church Road, Stockton-on-Tees TS18 1LD ☎ 01642 527000 🖷 01642 527002 ✉ neil.schneider@stockton.gov.uk

Environmental Health: Mr Colin Snowdon, Environmental Health Manager, 16 Church Road, Stockton-on-Tees TS18 1XD ☎ 01642 526555 🖷 01642 526584 ✉ colin.snowdon@stockton.gov.uk

Estates, Property & Valuation: Mr Paul Hutchinson, Principal Building Control Surveyor, Queensway House, West Precinct, Billingham TS23 2YQ ☎ 01642 526043 ✉ paul.hutchinson@stockton.gov.uk

European Liaison: Mr Mark Rowell, Business Enterprise Manager, PO Box 34, Municipal Buildings, Church Road, Stockton-on-Tees TS18 1LE ☎ 01642 526010 🖷 01642 527023 ✉ mark.rowell@stockton.gov.uk

Events Manager: Mr Graham Reeves, Events Manager, Environment Centre, 21 West Row, Stockton-on-Tees TS18 1BT ☎ 01642 527344 ✉ graham.reeves@stockton.gov.uk

Finance: Mrs Julie Danks, Corporate Director - Resources, Municipal Buildings, Church Road, Stockton-on-Tees TS18 1LD ☎ 01642 527007 🖷 01642 527009 ✉ julie.danks@stockton.gov.uk

Finance: Mrs Debbie Hurwood , Head of Customer Services & Taxation, Kingsway House, West Precinct, Billingham TS23 2YL ☎ 01642 527014 ✉ debbie.hurwood@stockton.gov.uk

Fleet Management: Mr Jamie McCann, Head of Direct Services, Stirling House, Tedder Avenue, Thornaby, Thornbury TS17 9JP ☎ 01642 527071 🖷 01642 528885 ✉ jamie.mccann@stockton.gov.uk

Fleet Management: Mr Maurice Stephenson, Fleet & Transport Manager, Cowpen Depot, Billingham TS23 4DD ☎ 01642 528325 🖷 01642 527176 ✉ maurice.stephenson@stockton.gov.uk

Grounds Maintenance: Mr Richard Bradley, Care For Your Area Service Manager, Cowpen Lane Depot, Billingham, Stockton-on-Tees TS23 4DD ☎ 01642 527739 🖷 01642 527175 ✉ richard.bradley@stockton.gov.uk

Grounds Maintenance: Mr Jamie McCann, Head of Direct Services, Stirling House, Tedder Avenue, Thornaby, Thornbury TS17 9JP ☎ 01642 527071 🖷 01642 528885 ✉ jamie.mccann@stockton.gov.uk

Health and Safety: Mr Derek MacDonald , Health & Safety Manager, Bayhealth House, 5 Prince Regent Street, Stockton-on-Tees TS18 1DF ☎ 01642 528205 ✉ derek.macdonald@stockton.gov.uk

Health and Safety: Mr Mick McLone, Security Services Manager, Surveillance Centre, The Square, Stockton-on-Tees TS18 1TE ☎ 01642 527608 🖷 ✉ doug.carhart@stockton.gov.uk

Highways: Mr Simon Milner, Highway Network Manager, PO Box 229, Kingsway House, West Precinct, Billingham TS23 2YS ☎ 01642 526703 ✉ simon.milner@stockton.gov.uk

Home Energy Conservation: Mr Mike Chicken, Built & Natural Environment Manager, Kingsway House, West Precinct, Billingham TS23 2YL ☎ 01642 528148 🖷 01642 528217 ✉ mike.chicken@stockton.gov.uk

Housing: Ms Julie Nixon, Head of Housing & Community Protection, 16 Church Road, Stockton-on-Tees TS18 1TX ☎ 01642 527072 🖷 01642 528483 ✉ julie.nixon@stockton.gov.uk

Local Area Agreement: Ms Lesley King , Head of Performance & Partnerships, PO Box 11, Municipal Buildings, Church Road, Stockton-on-Tees TS18 1LD ☎ 01642 527004 ✉ lesley.king@stockton.gov.uk

Legal: Mr David Bond, Director - Law & Democracy (Monitoring Officer), PO Box 11, Municipal Buildings, Church Road, Stockton-on-Tees TS18 1LD ☎ 01642 527060 🖷 01642 527062 ✉ david.bond@stockton.gov.uk

Leisure and Cultural Services: Mr Steve Chaytor, Managing Director, Tees Active Ltd, Redheugh House, Thornaby Place, Thornaby, Stockton-on-Tees TS17 6SG ☎ 01642 527322 🖷 01642 528541 ✉ steven.chaytor@teesactive.co.uk

Leisure and Cultural Services: Mr Reuben Kench, Head of Culture, Leisure & Adult Learning, PO Box 228, Municipal Buildings, Church Road, Stockton-on-Tees TS18 1XE ☎ 01642 527039 🖷 01642 527037 ✉ reuben.kench@stockton.gov.uk

Leisure and Cultural Services: Mr Neil Russell , Leisure & Sports Development Manager, Kingsway House, Billingham Town Centre, Billingham TS23 2YS ☎ 01642 526412 🖷 01642 528369 ✉ neil.russell@stockton.gov.uk

Licensing: Mr David Kitching, Trading Standards & Licensing Manager, 16 Church Road, Stockton-on-Tees TS18 1XD ☎ 01642 526530 🖷 01642 526584 ✉ david.kitching@stockton.gov.uk

Lifelong Learning: Mr Reuben Kench, Head of Culture, Leisure & Adult Learning, PO Box 228, Municipal Buildings, Church Road, Stockton-on-Tees TS18 1LD ☎ 01642 527039 🖷 01642 527037 ✉ reuben.kench@stockton.gov.uk

Lighting: Mr Simon Milner, Highway Network Manager, PO Box 229, Kingsway House, West Precinct, Billingham TS23 2YS ☎ 01642 526703 ✉ simon.milner@stockton.gov.uk

Lottery Funding, Charity and Voluntary: Ms Julie Nixon, Head of Housing & Community Protection, 16 Church Road, Stockton-on-Tees TS18 1TX ☎ 01642 527072 🖷 01642 528483 ✉ julie.nixon@stockton.gov.uk

STOCKTON-ON-TEES

Member Services: Mrs Margaret Waggott, Head of Democratic Services, PO Box 11, Municipal Buildings, Church Road, Stockton-on-Tees TS18 1LD ☎ 01642 527064 🖷 01642 527062 🖱 margaret.waggott@stockton.gov.uk

Parking: Mr William Trewick, Traffic & Road Safety Manager, PO Box 229, Kingsway House, West Precinct, Billingham TS23 2YL ☎ 01642 526716 🖷 01642 526713 🖱 bill.trewick@stockton.gov.uk

Partnerships: Ms Liz Hanley , Head of Adult Strategy, PO Box 228, Municipal Buildings, Church Road, Stockton-on-Tees TS18 1XE ☎ 01642 527055 🖱 liz.hanley@stockton.gov.uk

Personnel / HR: Ms Beccy Brown, Head of Communications & Human Resources, Municipal Buildings, Church Road, Stockton-on-Tees TS18 1LD ☎ 01642 527003 🖱 beccy.brown@stockton.gov.uk

Public Libraries: Mr Reuben Kench, Head of Culture, Leisure & Adult Learning, PO Box 228, Municipal Buildings, Church Road, Stockton-on-Tees TS18 1LD ☎ 01642 527039 🖷 01642 527037 🖱 reuben.kench@stockton.gov.uk

Recycling & Waste Minimisation: Mr Jamie McCann, Head of Direct Services, Stirling House, Tedder Avenue, Thornaby, Thornbury TS17 9JP ☎ 01642 527071 🖷 01642 528885 🖱 jamie.mccann@stockton.gov.uk

Recycling & Waste Minimisation: Mr Dale Rowbotham, Waste Technical Officer, Stirling House, Tedder Avenue, Thornaby, Thornbury TS17 9JP ☎ 01642 527181 🖱 dale.rowbotham@stockton.gov.uk

Regeneration: Mr James Glancey , Principal Project Officer, PO Box 11, Municipal Buildings, Church Road, Stockton-on-Tees TS18 1LD ☎ 01642 526079 🖱 james.glancey@stockton.gov.uk

Regeneration: Mr Richard Poundford , Head of Special Economic Projects, PO Box 34, Municipal Buildings, Church Road, Stockton-on-Tees TS18 1LE ☎ 01642 393939 🖱 richard.poundford@stockton.gov.uk

Road Safety: Mr Neil Ellison, Sustainability Manager, PO Box 229, Kingsway House, West Precinct, Billingham TS23 2YL ☎ 01642 526736 🖷 01642 526740 🖱 neil.ellison@stockton.gov.uk

Road Safety: Mr Simon Milner, Highway Network Manager, PO Box 229, Kingsway House, West Precinct, Billingham TS23 2YS ☎ 01642 526703 🖱 simon.milner@stockton.gov.uk

Road Safety: Mr William Trewick, Traffic & Road Safety Manager, PO Box 229, Kingsway House, West Precinct, Billingham TS23 2YL ☎ 01642 526716 🖷 01642 526713 🖱 bill.trewick@stockton.gov.uk

Social Services: Ms Jane Humphreys, Corporate Director - Children, Education & Social Care, PO Box 228, Municipal Buildings, Stockton-on-Tees TS18 1XE ☎ 01642 527053 🖷 01642 527037 🖱 jane.humphreys@stockton.gov.uk

Social Services: Ms Diane McConnell , Head of Schools SEN, Municipal Buildings, Church Road, Stockton-on-Tees TS18 1LD ☎ 01642 527041 🖱 diane.mcconnell@stockton.gov.uk

Social Services (Adult): Mr Sean McEneany , Head of Adults' Services, Municipal Buildings, Church Road, Stockton-on-Tees TS18 1LD ☎ 01642 527045 🖱 sean.mceneany@stockton.gov.uk

Social Services (Children): Mr Shaun McLurg , Head of Safeguarding & Looked After Children, Municipal Buildings, Church Road, Stockton-on-Tees TS18 1LD ☎ 01642 527049 🖱 shaun.mclurg@stockton.gov.uk

Safeguarding: Mr Shaun McLurg , Head of Safeguarding & Looked After Children, Municipal Buildings, Church Road, Stockton-on-Tees TS18 1LD ☎ 01642 527049 🖱 shaun.mclurg@stockton.gov.uk

Public Health: Dr Peter Kelly , Director - Public Health, PO Box 11, Municipal Buildings, Church Road, Stockton-on-Tees TS18 1LD ☎ 01642 527052 🖱 peter.kelly@stockton.gov.uk

Staff Training: Ms Sue Sephton , Workforce Development Manager, Bayhealth House, 5 Prince Regent Street, Stockton-on-Tees TS18 1DF ☎ 01642 526978 🖱 sue.sephton@stockton.gov.uk

Street Scene: Mr Jamie McCann, Head of Direct Services, Stirling House, Tedder Avenue, Thornaby, Thornbury TS17 9JP ☎ 01642 527071 🖷 01642 528885 🖱 jamie.mccann@stockton.gov.uk

Sustainable Communities: Mr Paul Dobson , Corporate Director - Development & Neighbourhood Services, Municipal Buildings, Church Road, Stockton-on-Tees TS18 1LD ☎ 01642 527068 🖱 paul.dobson@stockton.gov.uk

Sustainable Communities: Mr Neil Ellison, Sustainability Manager, Kingsway House, West Precinct, Billingham TS23 2YL ☎ 01642 526736 🖷 01642 526740 🖱 neil.ellison@stockton.gov.uk

Sustainable Communities: Mr Neil Schneider, Chief Executive, PO Box 34, Municipal Buildings, Church Road, Stockton-on-Tees TS18 1LD ☎ 01642 527000 🖷 01642 527002 🖱 neil.schneider@stockton.gov.uk

Sustainable Development: Mr Mike Chicken, Built & Natural Environment Manager, Gloucester House, 70 Church Road, Stockton-on-Tees TS18 1TW ☎ 01642 528148 🖷 01642 528217 🖱 mike.chicken@stockton.gov.uk

Sustainable Development: Mr Neil Ellison, Sustainability Manager, Kingsway House, Billingham Town Centre, Billingham TS23 2YS ☎ 01642 526736 🖷 01642 526740 🖱 neil.ellison@stockton.gov.uk

Tourism: Mr Richard Poundford , Head of Special Economic Projects, PO Box 34, Municipal Buildings, Church Road, Stockton-on-Tees TS18 1LE ☎ 01642 393939 🖱 richard.poundford@stockton.gov.uk

Town Centre: Mr James Glancey , Principal Project Officer, PO Box 11, Municipal Buildings, Church Road, Stockton-on-Tees TS18 1LD ☎ 01642 526079 🖱 james.glancey@stockton.gov.uk

Traffic Management: Mr Richard McGuckin, Head of Economic Growth & Developmental Services, PO Box 229, Kingsway House, West Precinct, Billingham TS23 2YS ☎ 01642 526765 🖷 01642 526713 🖱 richard.mcguckin@stockton.gov.uk

Traffic Management: Mr Simon Milner, Highway Network Manager, PO Box 229, Kingsway House, West Precinct, Billingham TS23 2YS ☎ 01642 526703 ✉ simon.milner@stockton.gov.uk

Transport: Mr Richard McGuckin, Head of Economic Growth & Developmental Services, PO Box 229, Kingsway House, West Precinct, Billingham TS23 2YS ☎ 01642 526765 🖷 01642 526713 ✉ richard.mcguckin@stockton.gov.uk

Transport: Mr Maurice Stephenson, Fleet & Transport Manager, Cowpen Depot, Billingham TS23 4DD ☎ 01642 528325 🖷 01642 527176 ✉ maurice.stephenson@stockton.gov.uk

Transport Planner: Mr Richard McGuckin, Head of Economic Growth & Developmental Services, PO Box 229, Kingsway House, West Precinct, Billingham TS23 2YS ☎ 01642 526765 🖷 01642 526713 ✉ richard.mcguckin@stockton.gov.uk

Transport Planner: Mr William Trewick, Traffic & Road Safety Manager, PO Box 229, Kingsway House, West Precinct, Billingham TS23 2YL ☎ 01642 526716 🖷 01642 526713 ✉ bill.trewick@stockton.gov.uk

Waste Collection and Disposal: Mr Richard Bradley, Care For Your Area Service Manager, Cowpen Lane Depot, Billingham, Stockton-on-Tees TS23 4DD ☎ 01642 527739 🖷 01642 527175 ✉ richard.bradley@stockton.gov.uk

Waste Collection and Disposal: Mr Jamie McCann, Head of Direct Services, Stirling House, Tedder Avenue, Thornaby, Thornbury TS17 9JP ☎ 01642 527071 🖷 01642 528885 ✉ jamie.mccann@stockton.gov.uk

Waste Management: Mr Jamie McCann, Head of Direct Services, Stirling House, Tedder Avenue, Thornaby, Thornbury TS17 9JP ☎ 01642 527071 🖷 01642 528885 ✉ jamie.mccann@stockton.gov.uk

COUNCILLORS

***Mayor* Dalgarno**, Ian (INDNA - Village)
ian.dalgarno@stockton.gov.uk

***Deputy Mayor* Dixon**, Kenneth (INDNA - Ingleby Barwick West)
kenneth.dixon@stockton.gov.uk

***Leader of the Council* Cook**, Robert (LAB - Norton South)
robert.cook@stockton.gov.uk

***Deputy Leader of the Council* Beall**, Jim (LAB - Roseworth)
jim.beall@stockton.gov.uk

***Group Leader* Houchen**, Ben (CON - Yarm)
ben.houchen@stockton.gov.uk

Atkinson, Helen (IND - Billingham West)
Helen.Atkinson@stockton.gov.uk

Bailey, Sonia (LAB - Mandale & Victoria)
Sonia.Bailey@stockton.gov.uk

Baker, Paul (LAB - Newtown)
paul.baker@stockton.gov.uk

Barlow, Chris (LAB - Billingham North)
Chris.Barlow@stockton.gov.uk

Brown, Derrick (LAB - Stainsby Hill)
derrick.brown@stockton.gov.uk

Cherrett, Julia (LD - Bishopsgarth and Elm Tree)
julia.roberts@stockton.gov.uk

Clark, Michael (LAB - Grangefield)
michael.clark@stockton.gov.uk

Clark, Carol (LAB - Grangefield)
carol.clark@stockton.gov.uk

Clough, Chris (IND - Billingham West)
Chris.Clough@stockton.gov.uk

Cooke, Nigel (LAB - Hardwick & Salters Lane)
nigel.cooke@stockton.gov.uk

Corr, Gillian (IND - Ingleby Barwick East)
gillian.corr@stockton.gov.uk

Cunningham, Evaline (LAB - Billingham East)
evaline.cunningham@stockton.gov.uk

Dennis, Phillip (CON - Eaglescliffe)
phil.dennis@stockton.gov.uk

Faulks, Kevin (INDNA - Ingleby Barwick East)
kevin.faulks@stockton.gov.uk

Gardner, John (CON - Northern Parishes)
john.gardner@stockton.gov.uk

Grainge, Lisa (LAB - Bishopsgarth & Elm Tree)
Lisa.Grainge@stockton.gov.uk

Hall, Lynn (CON - Hartburn)
Lynne.Hall@stockton.gov.uk

Hampton, Elsi (CON - Yarm)
ElsiHampton@stockton.gov.uk

Harrington, David (IND - Ingleby Barwick West)
david.harrington@stockton.gov.uk

Hewitt, Di (LAB - Stockton Town Centre)
Di.Hewitt@stockton.gov.uk

Houghton, Stefan (CON - Eaglescliffe)
Stefan.Houghton@stockton.gov.uk

Inman, Barbara (LAB - Roseworth)
barbara.inman@stockton.gov.uk

Javed, Mohammed (LAB - Parkfield and Oxbridge)
mohammed.javed@stockton.gov.uk

Johnson, Eileen (LAB - Norton South)
eileen.johnson@stockton.gov.uk

Kirton, Paul (LAB - Stockton Town Centre)
paul.kirton@stockton.gov.uk

McCoy, Ann (LAB - Billingham Central)
ann.mccoy@stockton.gov.uk

Moore, Mick (INDNA - Village)
mick.moore@stockton.gov.uk

Nelson, Steve (LAB - Norton North)
steve.nelson@stockton.gov.uk

Nelson, Kath (LAB - Norton North)
kathryn.nelson@stockton.gov.uk

O'Donnell, Jean (LAB - Billingham South)
jean.odonnell@stockton.gov.uk

Parry, Stephen (LAB - Billingham North)
Stephen.Parry@stockton.gov.uk

Patterson, Ross (INDNA - Ingleby Barwick West)
ross.patterson@stockton.gov.uk

Perry, Maurice (CON - Fairfield)
maurice.perry@stockton.gov.uk

STOCKTON-ON-TEES

Povey, Lauriane (LAB - Billingham North)
Lauriane.Pogvey@stockton.gov.uk

Proud, Rachel (LAB - Newtown)
Rachael.Proud@stockton.gov.uk

Rose, David (LAB - Parkfield and Oxbridge)
david.rose@stockton.gov.uk

Rowling, Paul (LAB - Mandale & Victoria)
Paul.Rowling@stockton.gov.uk

Smith, Michael (LAB - Billingham South)
michael.smith@stockton.gov.uk

Stephenson, Norma (LAB - Hardwick & Salters Lane)
norma.stephenson@stockton.gov.uk

Stephenson, Andrew (CON - Western Parishes)
afsegg@hotmail.co.uk

Stoker, Mick (LAB - Billingham East)
mick.stoker@stockton.gov.uk

Stott, Tracey (LAB - Mandale & Victoria)
tracey.stott@stockton.gov.uk

Tunney, Laura (CON - Eaglescliffe)
Laura.Tunney@stockton.gov.uk

Vickers, Matthew (CON - Hartburn)
Mathew.Vickers@stockton.gov.uk

Walmsley, Sylvia (INDNA - Stainsby Hill)
sylvia.walmsley@stockton.gov.uk

Watson, Sally Ann (CON - Inglebury Barwick East)
SallyAnn.Watson@stockton.gov.uk

Whitehill, Julia (CON - Yarm)
Julia.Whitehill@stockton.gov.uk

Wilburn, Norma (LAB - Norton West)
norma.wilburn@stockton.gov.uk

Wilburn, David (LAB - Norton West)
david.wilburn@stockton.gov.uk

Woodhead, Bill (CON - Fairfield)
william.woodhead@stockton.gov.uk

Woodhouse, Barry (LAB - Billingham Central)
barry.woodhouse@stockton.gov.uk

POLITICAL COMPOSITION

LAB: 32, CON: 13, INDNA: 6, IND: 4, LD: 1

COMMITTEE CHAIRS

Adult Services & Health: Mr Mohammed Javed

Audit: Mr Barry Woodhouse

Children & Young People: Ms Carol Clark

Health & Wellbeing: Mr Jim Beall

Licensing: Mr Paul Kirton

Planning: Ms Norma Stephenson

Stoke-on-Trent City U

Stoke-on-Trent City Council, Civic Centre, Glebe Street, Stoke-on-Trent ST4 1HH
☎ 01782 234567 🖷 01782 232603 🖳 www.stoke.gov.uk

FACTS AND FIGURES

Parliamentary Constituencies: Stoke-on-Trent Central, Stoke-on-Trent North, Stoke-on-Trent South
EU Constituencies: West Midlands
Election Frequency: Elections are by thirds

PRINCIPAL OFFICERS

Chief Executive: Mr John van de Laarschot , Chief Executive & Council Manager, Civic Centre, Glebe Street, Stoke-on-Trent ST4 1HH ☎ 01782 232602 🖰 chief.execadmin@stoke.gov.uk

Senior Management: Ms Lesley Mountford , Director of Public Health, Civic Centre, Glebe Street, Stoke-on-Trent ST4 1HH

Senior Management: Ms Louise Rees , Executive Director of People, Civic Centre, Glebe Street, Stoke-on-Trent ST4 1HH ☎ 01782 235988 🖰 louise.rees@stoke.gov.uk

Senior Management: Ms Laura Rowley , Chief Operating Officer, Civic Centre, Glebe Street, Stoke-on-Trent ST4 1HH

Senior Management: Mr David Sidaway , Executive Director - Place, Civic Centre, Glebe Street, Stoke-on-Trent ST4 1HH ☎ 01782 236426 🖰 david.sidaway@stoke.gov.uk

Architect, Building / Property Services: Ms Julie Griffin, Strategic Manager - Landlord Services, Civic Centre, Glebe Street, Stoke-on-Trent ST4 1HH ☎ 01782 236365 🖰 julie.griffin@stoke.gov.uk

Building Control: Mr Harmesh Jassall , Strategic Manager - Planning & Building Regulations, Civic Centre, Glebe Street, Stoke-on-Trent ST4 1HH 🖰 harmesh.jassall@stoke.gov.uk

Children / Youth Services: Mr Geoff Caterall , Strategic Manager - Inclusion, Civic Centre, Glebe Street, Stoke-on-Trent ST4 1HH ☎ 01782 238812 🖰 geoff.caterall@stoke.gov.uk

Children / Youth Services: Mr Paul Gerrard , Strategic Manager - School Support, Civic Centre, Glebe Street, Stoke-on-Trent ST4 1HH ☎ 01782 236860 🖰 paul.gerrard@stoke.gov.uk

Children / Youth Services: Mr Robert Johnstone , Strategic Manager - Pupil Achievement, Civic Centre, Glebe Street, Stoke-on-Trent ST4 1HH ☎ 01782 236855 🖰 robert.johnstone@stoke.gov.uk

Children / Youth Services: Mr Mark Kenyon , Finance & Commercial Manager CYPS, Civic Centre, Glebe Street, Stoke-on-Trent ST4 1HH ☎ 01782 235960 🖰 mark.kenyon@stoke.gov.uk

PR / Communications: Ms Emma Rodgers , Strategic Manager - Communications & Marketing, Civic Centre, Glebe Street, Stoke-on-Trent ST4 1HH 🖰 emma.rodgers@stoke.gov.uk

Computer Management: Mr Neil Mason , Assistant Director of ICT, Civic Centre, Glebe Street, Stoke-on-Trent ST4 1HH ☎ 01782 232877 🖰 neil.mason@stoke.gov.uk

Computer Management: Ms Janet Preece , Strategic Manager of ICT Operations, Swift House A, Glebe Street, Stoke-on-Trent ST4 1HH ☎ 01782 232899 🖰 janet.preece@stoke.gov.uk

Corporate Services: Mr Paul Bicknell , Corporate Fraud Manager, Civic Centre, Glebe Street, Stoke-on-Trent ST4 1HH ☎ 01782 232828 ✉ paul.bicknell@stoke.gov.uk

Corporate Services: Mr John Bowler , Strategic Manager of ICT, Civic Centre, Glebe Street, Stoke-on-Trent ST4 1RN ☎ 01782 232553 ✉ john.bowler@stoke.gov.uk

Corporate Services: Ms Kerry Cartlidge , Financial & Commercial Manager, Civic Centre, Glebe Street, Stoke-on-Trent ST4 1HH ☎ 01782 232704 ✉ kerry.cartlidge@stoke.gov.uk

Corporate Services: Mr Neil Chadwick , Governance Manager, Civic Centre, Glebe Street, Stoke-on-Trent ST4 1HH ☎ 01782 233386 ✉ neil.chadwick@stoke.gov.uk

Corporate Services: Ms Helen Dos Santos , Business Services Manager, Civic Centre, Glebe Street, Stoke-on-Trent ST4 1HH ☎ 01782 232655 ✉ helen.dossantos@stoke.gov.uk

Customer Service: Ms Emily Bagnal , Strategic Manager - Customer Services, Civic Centre, Glebe Street, Stoke-on-Trent ST4 1HH ☎ 01782 235346 ✉ emily.bagnal@stoke.gov.uk

Economic Development: Ms Rachel Nicholson , Economic Development Officer, Civic Centre, Glebe Street, Stoke-on-Trent ST4 1HH ✉ rachel.nicholson@stoke.gov.uk

Events Manager: Mr Christopher Austin , Events & Commercial Manager, Civic Centre, Glebe Street, Stoke-on-Trent ST4 1HH ☎ 01782 233222 ✉ christopher.austin@stoke.gov.uk

Finance: Mr Neil Harvey , Pay & Conditions Compliance Manager, Civic Centre, Glebe Street, Stoke-on-Trent ST4 1HH ☎ 01782 232651 ✉ neil.harvey@stoke.gov.uk

Finance: Ms Lesley Orton , Audit Manager, Civic Centre, Glebe Street, Stoke-on-Trent ST4 1HH ☎ 01782 232871 ✉ lesley.orton@stoke.gov.uk

Finance: Ms Clare Potts , Team Manager for Back Office Transformation, Civic Centre, Glebe Street, Stoke-on-Trent ST4 1HH ☎ 01782 232696 ✉ clare.potts@stoke.gov.uk

Finance: Ms Sue Woodall , Audit Services Manager, Civic Centre, Glebe Street, Stoke-on-Trent ST4 1HH ☎ 01782 232689 ✉ sue.woodall@stoke.gov.uk

Highways: Ms Gemma Holdcroft , Senior Highway Technician, Civic Centre, Glebe Street, Stoke-on-Trent ST4 1HH ✉ gemma.holdcroft@stoke.gov.uk

Housing: Mr Carl Brazier , Director of Housing, Civic Centre, Glebe Street, Stoke-on-Trent ST4 1HH ✉ carl.brazier@stoke.gov.uk

Member Services: Mr Paul Baddeley , Scrutiny Officer, Civic Centre, Glebe Street, Stoke-on-Trent ST4 1HH ☎ 01782 233451 ✉ paul.baddeley@stoke.gov.uk

Member Services: Ms Helen Barr , Democratic Services Lead, Civic Centre, Glebe Street, Stoke-on-Trent ST4 1HH ☎ 01782 232784 ✉ helen.barr@stoke.gov.uk

Member Services: Ms Elayne Bates , Programme Executive - Place, Civic Centre, Glebe Street, Stoke-on-Trent ST4 1HH ☎ 01782 233290 ✉ elayne.bates@stoke.gov.uk

Member Services: Ms Suzanne Hackley , Team Leader - Cabinet & Committee Support, Civic Centre, Glebe Street, Stoke-on-Trent ST4 1HH ☎ 01782 232622 ✉ suzanne.hackley@stoke.gov.uk

Member Services: Ms Julie Harvey , Democratic Services Lead, Civic Centre, Glebe Street, Stoke-on-Trent ST4 1HH ☎ 01782 232617 ✉ julie.harvey@stoke.gov.uk

Member Services: Ms Michaleen Hilton , Council & Civil Support Team Leader, Civic Centre, Glebe Street, Stoke-on-Trent ST4 1HH ☎ 01782 232638 ✉ michaleen.hilton@stoke.gov.uk

Partnerships: Ms Mandy Pattinson , Scrutiny Officer, Civic Centre, Glebe Street, Stoke-on-Trent ST4 1HH ☎ 01782 233018 ✉ mandy.pattinson@stoke.gov.uk

Partnerships: Mr Anthony Wild , Strategic Manager - Integrated Specialist Services, Civic Centre, Glebe Street, Stoke-on-Trent ST4 1HH ☎ 01782 231233 ✉ anthony.wild@stoke.gov.uk

Procurement: Ms Carolyn Higgs , Specialist Commissioning Manager, Civic Centre, Glebe Street, Stoke-on-Trent ST4 1HH ☎ 01782 237791 ✉ carolyn.higgs@cotswold.gov.uk

Procurement: Mr Darren Pearce , Strategic Manager - Corporate Procurement, Civic Centre, Glebe Street, Stoke-on-Trent ST4 1HH ☎ 01782 232841 ✉ darren.pearce@stoke.gov.uk

Regeneration: Mr David Sidaway , Executive Director - Place, Civic Centre, Glebe Street, Stoke-on-Trent ST4 1HH ☎ 01782 236426 ✉ david.sidaway@stoke.gov.uk

Social Services (Children): Ms Sue Hammersley , Strategic Manager - Children in Care Lead, Civic Centre, Glebe Street, Stoke-on-Trent ST4 1HH ☎ 01782 231873 ✉ sue.hammersley@stoke.gov.uk

Public Health: Ms Lesley Mountford , Director of Public Health, Civic Centre, Glebe Street, Stoke-on-Trent ST4 1HH

Transport: Mr Austin Knott , Planning & Transportation Policy Manager, Civic Centre, Glebe Street, Stoke-on-Trent ST4 1HH ✉ austin.knott@stoke.gov.uk

COUNCILLORS

***The Lord Mayor* Bowers**, Jean (IND - Birches Head & Central Forest Park)
jean.bowers@stoke.gov.uk

***Deputy Lord Mayor* Dale**, Rita (IND - Eaton Park)
rita.dale@stoke.gov.uk

***Leader of the Council* Conway**, David (IND - Little Chell and Stanfield)
david.conway@stoke.gov.uk

***Deputy Leader of the Council* Brown**, Abi (CON - Meir Park)
abi.brown@stoke.gov.uk

***Group Leader* Pervez**, Mohammed (LAB - Moorcroft)
mohammed.pervez@stoke.gov.uk

STOKE-ON-TRENT CITY

Baddeley, Melanie (IND - Abbey Hulton and Townsend)
melanie.baddeley@stocke.gov.uk

Banks, Kath (LAB - Hollybush and Longton West)
kath.banks@stoke.gov.uk

Barnes, Jackie (IND - Springfields and Trent Vale)
jackie.barnes@stoke.gov.uk

Beardmore, Craig (CON - Meir Hay)
craig.beardmore@stoke.gov.uk

Bell, Joan (LAB - Blurton East)
joan.bell@stoke.gov.uk

Bell, Mick (UKIP - Fenton West and Mount Pleasant)
mick.bell@stoke.gov.uk

Bowers, Sabrina (IND - Birches Head & Central Forest Park)
sabrina.bowers@stoke.gov.uk

Brereton, Jack (CON - Baddeley, Milton and Norton)
jack.brereton@stoke.gov.uk

Bridges, Janine (IND - Great Chell and Packmoor)
janine.bridges@stoke.gov.uk

Broughan, Richard (IND - Abbey Hulton and Townsend)
richard.broughan@stoke.gov.uk

Brown, Lloyd (LAB - Blurton West and Newstead)
lloyd.brown@stoke.gov.uk

Chetwynd, Candi (LAB - Ford Green and Smallthorne)
candi.chetwynd@stoke.gov.uk

Conteh, Randolph (IND - Penkhull and Stoke)
randolph.conteh@stoke.gov.uk

Dodd, Lilian (IND - Dresden and Florence)
lilianl.dodd@stoke.gov.uk

Dutton, Alan (LAB - Burslem Central)
alan.dutton@stoke.gov.uk

Evans, David (CON - Baddeley, Milton and Norton)
david.evans@stoke.gov.uk

Follows, Terence (IND - Hanford and Trentham)
terence.follows@stoke.gov.uk

Funnell, Stephen (LAB - Benilee and Ubberley)
stephen.funnell@stoke.gov.uk

Garner, Martin (LAB - Goldenhill and Sandyford)
martin.garner@stoke.gov.uk

Garner, Joy (LAB - Burslem Park)
joy.garner@stoke.gov.uk

Hamer, Olwen (LAB - Sandford Hill)
olwen.hamer@stoke.gov.uk

Irving, Ross (CON - Weston Coyney)
ross.irving@stoke.gov.uk

James, Ann (IND - Great Chell and Packmoor)
ann.james@stoke.gov.uk

Jellyman, Daniel (CON - Hanford and Trentham)
daniel.jellyman@stoke.gov.uk

Kallar, Gurmeet Singh (LAB - Bradeley and Chell Heath)
gurmeetsingh.kallar@stoke.gov.uk

Khan, Majid (LAB - Etruria and Hanley)
majid.khan@stoke.gov.uk

Maqsoom, Sadaqat (CON - Littlewood North and Normacot)
sadaqat.maqsoom@stoke.gov.uk

Munday, Anthony (IND - Baddeley, Milton and Norton)
anthony.munday@stoke.gov.uk

Pender, Shaun (LAB - Hartshill and Basford)
shaun.pender@stoke.gov.uk

Pitt, Sheila (LAB - Bentilee and Ubberley)
sheila.pitt@stoke.gov.uk

Platt, Andy (LAB - Boothen and Oakhill)
andy.platt@stoke.gov.uk

Powell-Beckett, Joanne (IND - Sneyd Green)
joanne.powell-beckett@stoke.gov.uk

Robinson, Chris (LAB - Broadway and Longton East)
chris.robinson@stoke.gov.uk

Rosenau, Ruth (LAB - Meir North)
ruth.rosenau@stoke.gov.uk

Shotton, Paul (LAB - Fenton East)
paul.shotton@stoke.gov.uk

Wagner, Lee (IND - Tunstall)
lee.wanger@stoke.gov.uk

Watson, Alastair (LAB - Joiners Square)
alastair.watson@stoke.gov.uk

Wazir, Amjid (LAB - Hanley Park and Shelton)
amjid.wazir@stoke.gov.uk

Wheeldon, Debbie (LAB - Meir South)
debbie.wheeldon@stoke.gov.uk

POLITICAL COMPOSITION
LAB: 21, IND: 15, CON: 7, UKIP: 1

COMMITTEE CHAIRS
Audit: Ms Joanne Powell-Beckett

Children & Young People: Mr Shaun Pender

Licensing: Mr Chris Robinson

Licensing: Ms Joy Garner

Planning Development Management: Mr Ross Irving

Stratford-upon-Avon D

Stratford-upon-Avon District Council, Elizabeth House, Church Street, Stratford-upon-Avon CV37 6HX
☎ 01789 267575 🖷 01789 260007 ✉ info@stratford-dc.gov.uk
🖳 www.stratford.gov.uk

FACTS AND FIGURES
Parliamentary Constituencies: Stratford-on-Avon
EU Constituencies: West Midlands
Election Frequency: Elections are by thirds

PRINCIPAL OFFICERS
Chief Executive: Mr Paul Lankester, Chief Executive, Elizabeth House, Church Street, Stratford-upon-Avon CV37 6HX ☎ 01789 260101 🖷 01789 260007 ✉ paul.lankester@stratford-dc.gov.uk

Assistant Chief Executive: Mr David Buckland, Assistant Chief Executive, Elizabeth House, Church Street, Stratford-upon-Avon CV37 6HX ☎ 01789 260425 🖷 01789 260909 ✉ david.buckland@stratford-dc.gov.uk

Senior Management: Mr Phil Grafton , Head of Legal & Democratic Services / Monitoring Officer, Elizabeth House, Church Street, Stratford-upon-Avon CV37 6HX ☎ 01789 260400 phil.grafton@stratford-dc.gov.uk

Senior Management: Ms Balvinder Heran, Head of Customer Access, Elizabeth House, Church Street, Stratford-upon-Avon CV37 6HX ☎ 01295 227903 balvinder.heran@cherwellandsouthnorthants.gov.uk

Senior Management: Mr Tony Perks , Head of Technical Services, Elizabeth House, Church Street, Stratford-upon-Avon CV37 6HX ☎ 01789 260620 tony.perks@stratford-dc.gov.uk

Senior Management: Mr Dave Webb, Head of Enterprise, Housing & Revenues, Elizabeth House, Church Street, Stratford-upon-Avon CV37 6HX ☎ 01789 260900 🖷 01789 260444 dave.webb@stratford-dc.gov.uk

Senior Management: Mr Robert Weeks, Head of Environment & Planning, Elizabeth House, Church Street, Stratford-upon-Avon CV37 6HX ☎ 01789 260810 🖷 01789 260860 robert.weeks@stratford-dc.gov.uk

Access Officer / Social Services (Disability): Mr Dave Webb, Head of Enterprise, Housing & Revenues, Elizabeth House, Church Street, Stratford-upon-Avon CV37 6HX ☎ 01789 260900 🖷 01789 260444 dave.webb@stratford-dc.gov.uk

Architect, Building / Property Services: Mr Robert Weeks, Head of Environment & Planning, Elizabeth House, Church Street, Stratford-upon-Avon CV37 6HX ☎ 01789 260810 🖷 01789 260860 robert.weeks@stratford-dc.gov.uk

Best Value: Ms Balvinder Heran, Head of Customer Access, Elizabeth House, Church Street, Stratford-upon-Avon CV37 6HX ☎ 01295 227903 balvinder.heran@cherwellandsouthnorthants.gov.uk

Building Control: Mr Tony Perks , Head of Technical Services, Elizabeth House, Church Street, Stratford-upon-Avon CV37 6HX ☎ 01789 260620 tony.perks@stratford-dc.gov.uk

PR / Communications: Ms Beverley Hemming , Corporate Communications Manager, Elizabeth House, Church Street, Stratford-upon-Avon CV37 6HX ☎ 01789 260105 🖷 01789 260007 beverley.hemming@stratford-dc.gov.uk

Community Safety: Ms Karin Stanley , Governance & Community Safety Manager, Elizabeth House, Church Street, Stratford-upon-Avon CV37 6HX ☎ 01786 260619 karin.stanley@stratford-dc.gov.uk

Computer Management: Ms Balvinder Heran, Head of Customer Access, Elizabeth House, Church Street, Stratford-upon-Avon CV37 6HX ☎ 01295 227903 balvinder.heran@cherwellandsouthnorthants.gov.uk

Computer Management: Mrs Balvinder Heran , Head of Customer Access & Head of Joint ICT Business, Council Offices, Codsall WV8 1PX ☎ 01789 260470 b.heran@sstaffs.gov.uk

Customer Service: Ms Balvinder Heran, Head of Customer Access, Elizabeth House, Church Street, Stratford-upon-Avon CV37 6HX ☎ 01295 227903 balvinder.heran@cherwellandsouthnorthants.gov.uk

E-Government: Ms Balvinder Heran, Head of Customer Access, Elizabeth House, Church Street, Stratford-upon-Avon CV37 6HX ☎ 01295 227903 balvinder.heran@cherwellandsouthnorthants.gov.uk

Electoral Registration: Mr Darren Whitney , Democratic Services Manager, Elizabeth House, Church Street, Stratford-upon-Avon CV37 6HX ☎ 01789 260210 darren.whitney@stratford-dc.gov.uk

Emergency Planning: Mr Robert Weeks, Head of Environment & Planning, Elizabeth House, Church Street, Stratford-upon-Avon CV37 6HX ☎ 01789 260810 🖷 01789 260860 robert.weeks@stratford-dc.gov.uk

Energy Management: Mr Paul Chapman , Policy Officer, Elizabeth House, Church Street, Stratford-upon-Avon CV37 6HX ☎ 01789 267125 🖷 01789 260909 paul.chapman@stratford-dc.gov.uk

Environmental / Technical Services: Mr Robert Weeks, Head of Environment & Planning, Elizabeth House, Church Street, Stratford-upon-Avon CV37 6HX ☎ 01789 260810 🖷 01789 260860 robert.weeks@stratford-dc.gov.uk

Environmental Health: Mr Robert Weeks, Head of Environment & Planning, Elizabeth House, Church Street, Stratford-upon-Avon CV37 6HX ☎ 01789 260810 🖷 01789 260860 robert.weeks@stratford-dc.gov.uk

Estates, Property & Valuation: Mr Tony Perks , Head of Technical Services, Elizabeth House, Church Street, Stratford-upon-Avon CV37 6HX ☎ 01789 260620 tony.perks@stratford-dc.gov.uk

Finance: Mr David Buckland, Assistant Chief Executive, Elizabeth House, Church Street, Stratford-upon-Avon CV37 6HX ☎ 01789 260425 🖷 01789 260909 david.buckland@stratford-dc.gov.uk

Grounds Maintenance: Mr Tony Perks , Head of Technical Services, Elizabeth House, Church Street, Stratford-upon-Avon CV37 6HX ☎ 01789 260620 tony.perks@stratford-dc.gov.uk

Health and Safety: Mr Mark Sainsbury , Premises & Safety Manager, Elizabeth House, Church Street, Stratford-upon-Avon CV37 6HX ☎ 01789 260708 mark.sainsbury@stratford-dc.gov.uk

Home Energy Conservation: Mr Dave Webb, Head of Enterprise, Housing & Revenues, Elizabeth House, Church Street, Stratford-upon-Avon CV37 6HX ☎ 01789 260900 🖷 01789 260444 dave.webb@stratford-dc.gov.uk

Housing: Mr Dave Webb, Head of Enterprise, Housing & Revenues, Elizabeth House, Church Street, Stratford-upon-Avon CV37 6HX ☎ 01789 260900 🖷 01789 260444 dave.webb@stratford-dc.gov.uk

STRATFORD-UPON-AVON

Legal: Mr Phil Grafton , Head of Legal & Democratic Services / Monitoring Officer, Elizabeth House, Church Street, Stratford-upon-Avon CV37 6HX ☎ 01789 260400 ✉ phil.grafton@stratford-dc.gov.uk

Leisure and Cultural Services: Mr Tony Perks , Head of Technical Services, Elizabeth House, Church Street, Stratford-upon-Avon CV37 6HX ☎ 01789 260620 ✉ tony.perks@stratford-dc.gov.uk

Licensing: Mr Robert Weeks, Head of Environment & Planning, Elizabeth House, Church Street, Stratford-upon-Avon CV37 6HX ☎ 01789 260810 🖷 01789 260860 ✉ robert.weeks@stratford-dc.gov.uk

Member Services: Mr Darren Whitney , Democratic Services Manager, Elizabeth House, Church Street, Stratford-upon-Avon CV37 6HX ☎ 01789 260210 ✉ darren.whitney@stratford-dc.gov.uk

Parking: Mr Tony Perks , Head of Technical Services, Elizabeth House, Church Street, Stratford-upon-Avon CV37 6HX ☎ 01789 260620 ✉ tony.perks@stratford-dc.gov.uk

Partnerships: Ms Balvinder Heran, Head of Customer Access, Elizabeth House, Church Street, Stratford-upon-Avon CV37 6HX ☎ 01295 227903 ✉ balvinder.heran@cherwellandsouthnorthants.gov.uk

Personnel / HR: Mr David Buckland, Assistant Chief Executive, Elizabeth House, Church Street, Stratford-upon-Avon CV37 6HX ☎ 01789 260425 🖷 01789 260909 ✉ david.buckland@stratford-dc.gov.uk

Planning: Mr Robert Weeks, Head of Environment & Planning, Elizabeth House, Church Street, Stratford-upon-Avon CV37 6HX ☎ 01789 260810 🖷 01789 260860 ✉ robert.weeks@stratford-dc.gov.uk

Procurement: Ms Karin Stanley , Governance & Community Safety Manager, Elizabeth House, Church Street, Stratford-upon-Avon CV37 6HX ☎ 01786 260619 ✉ karin.stanley@stratford-dc.gov.uk

Recycling & Waste Minimisation: Mr Tony Perks , Head of Technical Services, Elizabeth House, Church Street, Stratford-upon-Avon CV37 6HX ☎ 01789 260620 ✉ tony.perks@stratford-dc.gov.uk

Staff Training: Mr David Buckland, Assistant Chief Executive, Elizabeth House, Church Street, Stratford-upon-Avon CV37 6HX ☎ 01789 260425 🖷 01789 260909 ✉ david.buckland@stratford-dc.gov.uk

Street Scene: Mr Robert Weeks, Head of Environment & Planning, Elizabeth House, Church Street, Stratford-upon-Avon CV37 6HX ☎ 01789 260810 🖷 01789 260860 ✉ robert.weeks@stratford-dc.gov.uk

Sustainable Communities: Mr Dave Webb, Head of Enterprise, Housing & Revenues, Elizabeth House, Church Street, Stratford-upon-Avon CV37 6HX ☎ 01789 260900 🖷 01789 260444 ✉ dave.webb@stratford-dc.gov.uk

Sustainable Development: Mr Dave Webb, Head of Enterprise, Housing & Revenues, Elizabeth House, Church Street, Stratford-upon-Avon CV37 6HX ☎ 01789 260900 🖷 01789 260444 ✉ dave.webb@stratford-dc.gov.uk

Tourism: Mr Dave Webb, Head of Enterprise, Housing & Revenues, Elizabeth House, Church Street, Stratford-upon-Avon CV37 6HX ☎ 01789 260900 🖷 01789 260444 ✉ dave.webb@stratford-dc.gov.uk

Waste Collection and Disposal: Mr Tony Perks , Head of Technical Services, Elizabeth House, Church Street, Stratford-upon-Avon CV37 6HX ☎ 01789 260620 ✉ tony.perks@stratford-dc.gov.uk

Waste Management: Mr Tony Perks , Head of Technical Services, Elizabeth House, Church Street, Stratford-upon-Avon CV37 6HX ☎ 01789 260620 ✉ tony.perks@stratford-dc.gov.uk

Children's Play Areas: Mr Chris Fennell , Leisure Services Manager, Elizabeth House, Church Street, Stratford-upon-Avon CV37 6HX ☎ 01789 260646 ✉ chris.fennell@stratford-dc.gov.uk

COUNCILLORS

***Chair* Gittus**, Mike (CON - Kinwarton)
mike.gittus@stratford-dc.gov.uk

***Vice-Chair* Adams**, Susan (CON - Alcester)
susan.adams@stratford-dc.gov.uk

***Leader of the Council* Saint**, Christopher (CON - Tredington)
chris.saint@stratford-dc.gov.uk

***Deputy Leader of the Council* Thirlwell**, Stephen (CON - Henley)
stephen.thirlwell@stratford-dc.gov.uk

***Group Leader* Moorse**, Peter (LD - Stratford Mount Pleasant)
peter.moorse@stratford-dc.gov.uk

Atkinson, George (CON - Tanworth)
george.atkinson@stratford-dc.gov.uk

Barnes, Peter (LD - Welford)
peter.barnes@stratford-dc.gov.uk

Beaman, Paul (LD - Studley)
paul.beaman@stratford-dc.gov.uk

Beamer, Neville (CON - Stratford Guild and Hathaway)
neville.beamer@stratford-dc.gov.uk

Brain, Mike (CON - Quinton)
mike.brain@stratford-dc.gov.uk

Bromwich, Tony (CON - Southam)
tony.bromwich@stratford-dc.gov.uk

Cargill, Mark (CON - Alcester)
mark.cargill@stratford-dc.gov.uk

Cheney, Richard (LD - Shipston)
richard.cheney@stratford-dc.gov.uk

Crump, Andrew (CON - Southam)
andrew.crump@stratford-dc.gov.uk

Dowling, William (LD - Stratford Guild and Hathaway)
william.dowling@stratford-dc.gov.uk

Ellard, Jennie (CON - Southam)
jennie.ellard@stratford-dc.gov.uk

Fradgley, Jennifer (LD - Stratford Guild and Hathaway)
jenny.fradgley@stratford-dc.gov.uk

Fradgley, Ian (LD - Stratford Alveston)
ian.fradgley@stratford-dc.gov.uk

Gray, Stephen (CON - Long Compton)
stephen.gray@stratford-dc.gov.uk

Hayter, Helen (INDNA - Snitterfield)
helen.hayter@stratford-dc.gov.uk

Holder, Eric (INDNA - Studley)
eric.holder@stratford-dc.gov.uk

Horner, John (CON - Claverdon)
john.horner@stratford-dc.gov.uk

Howse, Maurice (CON - Bidford and Salford)
maurice.howse@stratford-dc.gov.uk

Jackson, Simon (CON - Burton Dassett)
simon.jackson@stratford-dc.gov.uk

Jefferson, Tony (CON - Stratford Avenue and New Town)
tony.jefferson@stratford-dc.gov.uk

Johnston, David (LD - Wellesbourne)
david.johnston@stratford-dc.gov.uk

Kendall, Danny (CON - Wellesbourne)
danny.kendall@stratford-dc.gov.uk

Kenner, Jeffrey (LAB - Shipston)
jeff.kenner@stratford-dc.gov.uk

Kerridge, Justin (CON - Sambourne)
justin.kerridge@stratford-dc.gov.uk

Kettle, Chris (CON - Harbury)
chris.kettle@stratford-dc.gov.uk

Kittendorf, Steven (LD - Stockton and Napton)
steven.kittendorf@stratford-dc.gov.uk

Lawrence, William (CON - Aston Cantlow)
william.lawrence@stratford-dc.gov.uk

Lloyd, Keith (IND - Stratford Avenue and New Town)
keith.lloyd@stratford-dc.gov.uk

Mann, Beverley (LD - Harbury)
beverley.mann@stratford-dc.gov.uk

Matheou, George (CON - Henley)
george.matheou@stratford-dc.gov.uk

Mills, Christopher (CON - Kineton)
christopher.mills@stratford-dc.gov.uk

Oakley, Peter (CON - Tanworth)
peter.oakley@stratford-dc.gov.uk

Organ, Lynda (CON - Stratford Alveston)
lynda.organ@stratford-dc.gov.uk

Parry, Anne (CON - Wellesbourne)
anne.parry@stratford-dc.gov.uk

Payne, Eric (CON - Alcester)
eric.payne@stratford-dc.gov.uk

Pemberton, Daren (LD - Bidford and Salford)
daren.pemberton@stratford-dc.gov.uk

Riches, Dave (CON - Long Itchington)
dave.riches@stratford-dc.gov.uk

Roache, Gillian (CON - Vale of Red Horse)
gillian.roache@stratford-dc.gov.uk

Rolfe, Kate (LD - Stratford Alveston)
kate.rolfe@stratford-dc.gov.uk

Scorer, Alan (CON - Kineton)
alan.scorer@stratford-dc.gov.uk

Seccombe, Isobel (CON - Ettington)
isobel.seccombe@stratford-dc.gov.uk

Seccombe, Philip (CON - Brailes)
philip.seccombe@stratford-dc.gov.uk

Short, Julie (IND - Stratford Avenue and New Town)
juliet.short@stratford-dc.gov.uk

Spence, Jonathan (CON - Bidford and Salford)
jonathan.spence@stratford-dc.gov.uk

Taylor, Joyce (LD - Stratford Mount Pleasant)
joyce.taylor@stratford-dc.gov.uk

Vaudry, Robert (CON - Bardon)
robert.vaudry@stratford-dc.gov.uk

Williams, Chris (CON - Fenny Compton)
chris.williams@stratford-dc.gov.uk

Wright, Hazel (LD - Studley)
hazel.wright@stratford-dc.gov.uk

POLITICAL COMPOSITION
CON: 34, LD: 14, IND: 2, INDNA: 2, LAB: 1

Stroud D

Stroud District Council, Council Offices, Ebley Mill, Westward Road, Stroud GL5 4UB
☎ 01453 766321 🖷 01453 750932 ✉ information@stroud.gov.uk
💻 www.stroud.gov.uk

FACTS AND FIGURES
Parliamentary Constituencies: Cotswold, Stroud
EU Constituencies: South West
Election Frequency: Elections are by thirds

PRINCIPAL OFFICERS
Chief Executive: Mr David Hagg, Chief Executive, Council Offices, Ebley Mill, Westward Road, Stroud GL5 4UB ☎ 01453 754290 🖷 01453 754934 ✉ david.hagg@stroud.gov.uk

Architect, Building / Property Services: Ms Alison Fisk, Head of Asset Management, Council Offices, Ebley Mill, Westward Road, Stroud GL5 4UB ☎ 01453 754430 🖷 01453 754309 ✉ alison.fisk@stroud.gov.uk

Architect, Building / Property Services: Mr Andy Nash , Head of Asset Management, Council Offices, Ebley Mill, Westward Road, Stroud GL5 4UB ☎ 01453 754430 ✉ andy.nash@stroud.gov.uk

Building Control: Mr Phil Skill, Head of Planning, Council Offices, Ebley Mill, Westward Road, Stroud GL5 4UB ☎ 01453 754345 🖷 01453 754222 ✉ phil.skill@stroud.gov.uk

Children / Youth Services: Mrs Joanne Jordan, Strategic Head of Customer Services, Council Offices, Ebley Mill, Westward Road, Stroud GL5 4UB ☎ 01453 754005 🖷 01453 754933 ✉ joanne.jordan@stroud.gov.uk

PR / Communications: Mrs Allison Richards , Strategic Head of Corporate Services, Council Offices, Ebley Mill, Westward Road, Stroud GL5 4UB ☎ 01453 754272 ✉ allison.richards@stroud.gov.uk

Community Planning: Mr Barry Wyatt , Strategic Head of Development Service, Council Offices, Ebley Mill, Westward Road, Stroud GL5 4UB ☎ 01453 754210 barry.wyatt@stroud.gov.uk

Community Safety: Mr Mike Hammond, Community & Facilities Manager, Council Offices, Ebley Mill, Westward Road, Stroud GL5 4UB ☎ 01453 754447 🖷 01453 754947 mike.hammond@stroud.gov.uk

Computer Management: Mrs Sandra Cowley , Strategic Head of Finance & Section 151 Officer, Council Offices, Ebley Mill, Westward Road, Stroud GL5 4UB ☎ 01453 754340 sandra.cowley@stroud.gov.uk

Corporate Services: Mrs Allison Richards , Strategic Head of Corporate Services, Council Offices, Ebley Mill, Westward Road, Stroud GL5 4UB ☎ 01453 754272 allison.richards@stroud.gov.uk

Customer Service: Mrs Joanne Jordan, Strategic Head of Customer Services, Council Offices, Ebley Mill, Westward Road, Stroud GL5 4UB ☎ 01453 754005 🖷 01453 754933 joanne.jordan@stroud.gov.uk

Economic Development: Mr Phil Skill, Head of Planning, Council Offices, Ebley Mill, Westward Road, Stroud GL5 4UB ☎ 01453 754345 🖷 01453 754222 phil.skill@stroud.gov.uk

E-Government: Mrs Sandra Cowley , Strategic Head of Finance & Section 151 Officer, Council Offices, Ebley Mill, Westward Road, Stroud GL5 4UB ☎ 01453 754340 sandra.cowley@stroud.gov.uk

Electoral Registration: Mrs Allison Richards , Strategic Head of Corporate Services, Council Offices, Ebley Mill, Westward Road, Stroud GL5 4UB ☎ 01453 754272 allison.richards@stroud.gov.uk

Emergency Planning: Mr Mike Hammond, Community & Facilities Manager, Council Offices, Ebley Mill, Westward Road, Stroud GL5 4UB ☎ 01453 754447 🖷 01453 754947 mike.hammond@stroud.gov.uk

Energy Management: Mr Jon Beckett, Head of Environmental Health, Council Offices, Ebley Mill, Westward Road, Stroud GL5 4UB ☎ 01453 754443 🖷 01453 754963 jon.beckett@stroud.gov.uk

Environmental / Technical Services: Mr Jon Beckett, Head of Environmental Health, Council Offices, Ebley Mill, Westward Road, Stroud GL5 4UB ☎ 01453 754443 🖷 01453 754963 jon.beckett@stroud.gov.uk

Environmental Health: Mr Jon Beckett, Head of Environmental Health, Council Offices, Ebley Mill, Westward Road, Stroud GL5 4UB ☎ 01453 754443 🖷 01453 754963 jon.beckett@stroud.gov.uk

Estates, Property & Valuation: Ms Jill Fallows, Property Investment Manager, Council Offices, Ebley Mill, Westward Road, Stroud GL5 4UB ☎ 01453 754433 jill.fallows@stroud.gov.uk

Facilities: Mr Mike Hammond, Community & Facilities Manager, Council Offices, Ebley Mill, Westward Road, Stroud GL5 4UB ☎ 01453 754447 🖷 01453 754947 mike.hammond@stroud.gov.uk

Finance: Mrs Sandra Cowley , Strategic Head of Finance & Section 151 Officer, Council Offices, Ebley Mill, Westward Road, Stroud GL5 4UB ☎ 01453 754340 sandra.cowley@stroud.gov.uk

Grounds Maintenance: Mr Carlos Novoth, Public Spaces Manager, Council Offices, Ebley Mill, Westward Road, Stroud GL5 4UB ☎ 01453 754406 carlos.novoth@stroud.gov.uk

Health and Safety: Mr Phil Park, Commercial Services Manager, Council Offices, Ebley Mill, Westward Road, Stroud GL5 4UB ☎ 01453 754471 🖷 01453 754963 phil.park@stroud.gov.uk

Home Energy Conservation: Mr Jon Beckett, Head of Environmental Health, Council Offices, Ebley Mill, Westward Road, Stroud GL5 4UB ☎ 01453 754443 🖷 01453 754963 jon.beckett@stroud.gov.uk

Housing: Mr Tim Power , Head of Housing Management, Council Offices, Ebley Mill, Westward Road, Stroud GL5 4UB ☎ 01453 754155 tim.power@stroud.gov.uk

Housing Maintenance: Mr Tim Power , Head of Housing Management, Council Offices, Ebley Mill, Westward Road, Stroud GL5 4UB ☎ 01453 754155 tim.power@stroud.gov.uk

Legal: Ms Karen Trickey , Legal Services Manager & Monitoring Officer, Council Offices, Ebley Mill, Westward Road, Stroud GL5 4UB ☎ 01453 754396 karen.trickey@stroud.gov.uk

Leisure and Cultural Services: Mrs Joanne Jordan, Strategic Head of Customer Services, Council Offices, Ebley Mill, Westward Road, Stroud GL5 4UB ☎ 01453 754005 🖷 01453 754933 joanne.jordan@stroud.gov.uk

Licensing: Mr Jon Beckett, Head of Environmental Health, Council Offices, Ebley Mill, Westward Road, Stroud GL5 4UB ☎ 01453 754443 🖷 01453 754963 jon.beckett@stroud.gov.uk

Lottery Funding, Charity and Voluntary: Mrs Joanne Jordan, Strategic Head of Customer Services, Council Offices, Ebley Mill, Westward Road, Stroud GL5 4UB ☎ 01453 754005 🖷 01453 754933 joanne.jordan@stroud.gov.uk

Member Services: Mrs Allison Richards , Strategic Head of Corporate Services, Council Offices, Ebley Mill, Westward Road, Stroud GL5 4UB ☎ 01453 754272 allison.richards@stroud.gov.uk

Personnel / HR: Mrs Allison Richards , Strategic Head of Corporate Services, Council Offices, Ebley Mill, Westward Road, Stroud GL5 4UB ☎ 01453 754272 allison.richards@stroud.gov.uk

Planning: Mr Phil Skill, Head of Planning, Council Offices, Ebley Mill, Westward Road, Stroud GL5 4UB ☎ 01453 754345 🖷 01453 754222 phil.skill@stroud.gov.uk

Procurement: Miss Sarah Turner, Principal Procurement Officer, Council Offices, Ebley Mill, Westward Road, Stroud GL5 4UB ☎ 01453 754346 sarah.turner@stroud.gov.uk

Recycling & Waste Minimisation: Mr Carlos Novoth, Public Spaces Manager, Council Offices, Ebley Mill, Westward Road, Stroud GL5 4UB ☎ 01453 754406 carlos.novoth@stroud.gov.uk

Regeneration: Mr Phil Skill, Head of Planning, Council Offices, Ebley Mill, Westward Road, Stroud GL5 4UB ☎ 01453 754345 🖷 01453 754222 ✉ phil.skill@stroud.gov.uk

Staff Training: Mrs Allison Richards , Strategic Head of Corporate Services, Council Offices, Ebley Mill, Westward Road, Stroud GL5 4UB ☎ 01453 754272 ✉ allison.richards@stroud.gov.uk

Street Scene: Mr Carlos Novoth, Public Spaces Manager, Council Offices, Ebley Mill, Westward Road, Stroud GL5 4UB ☎ 01453 754406 ✉ carlos.novoth@stroud.gov.uk

Sustainable Communities: Mr Barry Wyatt , Strategic Head of Development Service, Council Offices, Ebley Mill, Westward Road, Stroud GL5 4UB ☎ 01453 754210 ✉ barry.wyatt@stroud.gov.uk

Sustainable Development: Mr Barry Wyatt , Strategic Head of Development Service, Council Offices, Ebley Mill, Westward Road, Stroud GL5 4UB ☎ 01453 754210 ✉ barry.wyatt@stroud.gov.uk

Tourism: Mrs Joanne Jordan, Strategic Head of Customer Services, Council Offices, Ebley Mill, Westward Road, Stroud GL5 4UB ☎ 01453 754005 🖷 01453 754933 ✉ joanne.jordan@stroud.gov.uk

Total Place: Mrs Joanne Jordan, Strategic Head of Customer Services, Council Offices, Ebley Mill, Westward Road, Stroud GL5 4UB ☎ 01453 754005 🖷 01453 754933 ✉ joanne.jordan@stroud.gov.uk

Waste Collection and Disposal: Mr Carlos Novoth, Public Spaces Manager, Council Offices, Ebley Mill, Westward Road, Stroud GL5 4UB ☎ 01453 754406 ✉ carlos.novoth@stroud.gov.uk

Waste Management: Mr Carlos Novoth, Public Spaces Manager, Council Offices, Ebley Mill, Westward Road, Stroud GL5 4UB ☎ 01453 754406 ✉ carlos.novoth@stroud.gov.uk

Children's Play Areas: Mrs Joanne Jordan, Strategic Head of Customer Services, Council Offices, Ebley Mill, Westward Road, Stroud GL5 4UB ☎ 01453 754005 🖷 01453 754933 ✉ joanne.jordan@stroud.gov.uk

COUNCILLORS

***Chair* Rees**, Mark (LAB - Cainscross)
cllr.mark.rees@stroud.gov.uk

***Vice-Chair* Williams**, Thomas (LAB - Cainscross)
cllr.tom.williams@stroud.gov.uk

***Leader of the Council* Wheeler**, Geoff (LAB - Dursley)
cllr.geoff.wheeler@stroud.gov.uk

***Deputy Leader of the Council* Cross**, Karon (LAB - Cainscross)
cll.karon.cross@stroud.gov.uk

Ashton, Elizabeth (LAB - Berkeley)
cllr.liz.ashton@stroud.gov.uk

Baxendale, Martin (GRN - Valley)
cllr.martin.baxendale@stroud.gov.uk

Binns, Dorcas (CON - Minchinhampton)
cllr.dorcas.binns@stroud.gov.uk

Blackwell, Rowland (CON - Nailsworth)

Boxall, Tim (CON - Coaley and Uley)
cllr.tim.boxall@stroud.gov.uk

Brine, Chrisopher (LAB - Stonehouse)
cllr.chris.brine@stroud.gov.uk

Clifton, Miranda (LAB - Cam East)
cllr.miranda.clifton@stroud.gov.uk

Cooper, Nigel (CON - Painswick)
cllr.nigel.cooper@stroud.gov.uk

Cordwell, June (LD - Wootton-under-Edge)
cllr.june.cordwell@stroud.gov.uk

Cornell, Doina (LAB - Dursley)
cllr.doina.cornell@stroud.gov.uk

Craig, Gordon (CON - Berkeley)
cllr.gordon.craig@stroud.gov.uk

Cranston, Kevin (GRN - Central)
cllr.kevin.cranston@stroud.gov.uk

Davies, Stephen (CON - Eastington and Standish)

Denney, Paul (LAB - Cam West)
cllr.paul.denney@stroud.gov.uk

Douglass, Julie (LAB - Cam West)
cllr.julie.douglass@stroud.gov.uk

Edmunds, Jonathan (GRN - Randwick, Whiteshill and Ruscombe)
cllr.jonathan.edmunds@stroud.gov.uk

Fellows, Chas (CON - Chalford)
cllr.chas.fellows@stroud.gov.uk

Fryer, Colin (LAB - Dursley)
cllr.colin.fryer@stroud.gov.uk

Hemming, Paul (LD - Kingswood)
cllr.paul.hemming@stroud.gov.uk

Hurst, Nicholas (CON - Minchinhampton)
cllr.nick.hurst@stroud.gov.uk

Job, Julie (CON - Painswick)
cllr.julie.job@stroud.gov.uk

Jones, John (CON - Severn)
cllr.john.jones@stroud.gov.uk

Jones, Haydn (CON - Severn)
cllr.haydn.jones@stroud.gov.uk

Lydon, Stephen (LAB - The Stanleys)
cllr.stephen.lydon@stroud.gov.uk

Marjoram, John (GRN - Trinity)
cllr.john.marjoram@stroud.gov.uk

Miles, Russell (CON - Hardwicke)
cllr.russell.miles@stroud.gov.uk

Moore, Stephen (LAB - Rodborough)
cllr.stephen.moore@stroud.gov.uk

Mossman, Dave (CON - Hardwicke)
cllr.dave.mossman@stroud.gov.uk

Pearson, Keith (CON - Upton St Leonards)
cllr.keith.pearson@stroud.gov.uk

Peters, Elizabeth (CON - Chalford)
cllr.elizabeth.peters@stroud.gov.uk

Pickering, Simon (GRN - Slade)
cllr.simon.pickering@stroud.gov.uk

Powell, Gary (LAB - Stonehouse)
cllr.gary.powell@stroud.gov.uk

Prenter, Nigel (LAB - Rodborough)
cllr.nigel.prenter@stroud.gov.uk

Reeves, Lesley (CON - Wootton-under-Edge)
cllr.lesley.reeves@stroud.gov.uk

Robinson, Stephen (LAB - Nailsworth)
cllr.steve.robinson@stroud.gov.uk

Ross, Mattie (LAB - Stonehouse)
cllr.mattie.ross@stroud.gov.uk

Sims, Emma (CON - Nailsworth)
cllr.emma.sims@stroud.gov.uk

Studdert-Kennedy, Nigel (IND - The Stanleys)
cllr.nigel.studdert-kennedy@stroud.gov.uk

Sutton, Haydn (CON - Farmhill and Paganhill)

Tipper, Brian (CON - Cam East)
cllr.brian.tipper@stroud.gov.uk

Townley, Chas (LAB - Uplands)

Tucker, Ken (LD - Wootton-under-Edge)

Whiteside, Martin (GRN - Thrupp)
cllr.martin.whiteside@stroud.gov.uk

Wigzell, Rhiannon (CON - Amberley and Woodchester)
cllr.rhiannon.wigzell@stroud.gov.uk

Williams, Timothy (CON - Bisley)
cllr.tim.williams@stroud.gov.uk

Wride, Penny (CON - Vale)
cllr.penelope.wride@stroud.gov.uk

Young, Deborah (CON - Chalford)
cllr.debbie.young@stroud.gov.uk

POLITICAL COMPOSITION
CON: 23, LAB: 18, GRN: 6, LD: 3, IND: 1

COMMITTEE CHAIRS
Audit & Standards: Mr Nigel Studdert-Kennedy

Community Services & Licensing: Mr Chrisopher Brine

Development Control: Mr Stephen Moore

Suffolk C

Suffolk County Council, Endeavour House, 8 Russell Road, Ipswich IP1 2BX
☎ 0845 606 6067 🖷 01473 214549 🖳 www.suffolk.gov.uk

FACTS AND FIGURES
Parliamentary Constituencies: Suffolk Central and Ipswich North, Suffolk South, Suffolk West
EU Constituencies: Eastern
Election Frequency: Elections are of whole council

PRINCIPAL OFFICERS
Chief Executive: Ms Deborah Cadman , Chief Executive, Endeavour House, 8 Russell Road, Ipswich IP1 2BX ☎ 01473 264000 🖰 deborah.cadman@suffolkcc.gov.uk

Assistant Chief Executive: Mr Chris Bally , Assistant Chief Executive, Endeavour House, 8 Russell Road, Ipswich IP1 2BX ☎ 01473 264000 🖰 chris.bally@suffolk.gov.uk

Senior Management: Ms Sue Cook , Director of Children & Young People's Services, Endeavour House, 8 Russell Road, Ipswich IP1 2BX ☎ 01473 264000 🖰 sue.cook@suffolk.gov.uk

Senior Management: Dr Tessa Lindfield , Director - Public Health, Endeavour House, 8 Russell Road, Ipswich IP1 2BX 🖰 tessa.lindfield@suffolk.gov.uk

Senior Management: Ms Anna McCreadie , Director - Adult & Community Services, Endeavour House, 8 Russell Road, Ipswich IP1 2BX ☎ 01473 264000 🖰 anna.mccreadie@suffolk.gov.uk

Architect, Building / Property Services: Mr Duncan Johnson , Assistant Director - Corporate Property, Endeavour House, 8 Russell Road, Ipswich IP1 2BX ☎ 01473 264180 🖰 duncan.johnson@suffolk.gov.uk

Children / Youth Services: Ms Sue Cook , Director of Children & Young People's Services, Endeavour House, 8 Russell Road, Ipswich IP1 2BX ☎ 01473 264000 🖰 sue.cook@suffolk.gov.uk

PR / Communications: Mr Simon Higgins , Head of Communications, Endeavour House, 8 Russell Road, Ipswich IP1 2BX ☎ 01473 264000 🖰 simon.higgins@suffolk.gov.uk

Computer Management: Mr Chris Bally , Assistant Chief Executive, Endeavour House, 8 Russell Road, Ipswich IP1 2BX ☎ 01473 264000 🖰 chris.bally@suffolk.gov.uk

Consumer Protection and Trading Standards: Mr Steve Greenfield, Assistant Director - Trading Standards, Endeavour House, 8 Russell Road, Ipswich IP1 2BX ☎ 01473 264866 🖷 01473 216850 🖰 steve.greenfield@tradstan.suffolkcc.gov.uk

Contracts: Mr Aidan Dunn , Assistant Director - Procurement & Contract Management, Endeavour House, 8 Russell Road, Ipswich IP1 2BX ☎ 01473 264000 🖰 aidan.dunn@suffolk.gov.uk

Customer Service: Mr Simon Higgins , Head of Communications, Endeavour House, 8 Russell Road, Ipswich IP1 2BX ☎ 01473 264000 🖰 simon.higgins@suffolk.gov.uk

Economic Development: Ms Sue Roper , Assistant Director - Strategic Development, Endeavour House, 8 Russell Road, Ipswich IP1 2BX ☎ 01473 264000 🖰 sue.roper@sufolk.gov.uk

Electoral Registration: Ms Sue Morgan , Head of Democratic Services, Endeavour House, 8 Russell Road, Ipswich IP1 2BX ☎ 01473 264512 🖰 sue.morgan@suffolk.gov.uk

Emergency Planning: Mr Andrew Osman, Head of Emergency Planning, Suffolk Joint Emergency Planning Unit, GFB3 Endeavour House, 8 Russell Road, Ipswich IP1 2BX ☎ 01473 265332 🖰 andrew.osman@fire.suffolkcc.gov.uk

Facilities: Mr James Carrick, Corporate Facilities Co-ordinator, Endeavour House, 8 Russell Road, Ipswich IP1 2BX ☎ 01473 264000 🖰 james.carrick@socserv.suffolkcc.gov.uk

Finance: Mr Geoff Dobson, Director - Resource Management, Endeavour House, 8 Russell Road, Ipswich IP1 2BX ☎ 01473 264000 ✉ geoff.dobson@accy.suffolkcc.gov.uk

Pensions: Ms Lynn Wright , Payroll & Pensions Manager, Constantine House, 5 Constantine Road, Ipswich IP1 2DH ☎ 01473 264000 ✉ lynn.wright@suffolk.gov.uk

Health and Safety: Mr Paul Butcher , Head of Health & Safety, Endeavour House, 8 Russell Road, Ipswich IP1 2BX ☎ 01473 264000 ✉ paul.butcher@suffolk.gov.uk

Highways: Mr Mark Stevens , Assistant Director - Operational Highways, Endeavour House, 8 Russell Road, Ipswich IP1 2BX ☎ 01473 264000 ✉ mark.stevens@suffolk.gov.uk

Local Area Agreement: Ms Clair Harvey , Business Development Specialist, Endeavour House, 8 Russell Road, Ipswich IP1 2BX ☎ 01473 265304 ✉ clair.harvey@suffolk.gov.uk

Legal: Mr Tim Earl , Head of Legal Services, Endeavour House, 8 Russell Road, Ipswich IP1 2BX ☎ 01473 260860 ✉ tim.earl@suffolk.gov.uk

Legal: Mr Tim Ryder , Assistant Director & Monitoring Officer, Endeavour House, 8 Russell Road, Ipswich IP1 2BX ☎ 01473 583000 ✉ tim.ryder@suffolk.gov.uk

Member Services: Ms Sue Morgan , Head of Democratic Services, Endeavour House, 8 Russell Road, Ipswich IP1 2BX ☎ 01473 264512 ✉ sue.morgan@suffolk.gov.uk

Personnel / HR: Ms Sally Marlow , Head of Strategic Human Resources, Endeavour House, 8 Russell Road, Ipswich IP1 2BX ☎ 01473 264000 ✉ sally.marlow@suffolk.gov.uk

Planning: Ms Sue Roper , Assistant Director - Strategic Development, Endeavour House, 8 Russell Road, Ipswich IP1 2BX ☎ 01473 264000 ✉ sue.roper@sufolk.gov.uk

Recycling & Waste Minimisation: Mr Steve Palfrey , Head - Waste, Endeavour House, 8 Russell Road, Ipswich IP1 2BX ☎ 01473 264787 ✉ steve.palfrey@suffolk.gov.uk

Road Safety: Mr Mike Motteram , Road Safety Manager, Endeavour House, 8 Russell Road, Ipswich IP1 2BX ☎ 01743 264996 ✉ mike.motteram@suffolk.gov.uk

Social Services (Adult): Ms Anna McCreadie , Director - Adult & Community Services, Endeavour House, 8 Russell Road, Ipswich IP1 2BX ☎ 01473 264000 ✉ anna.mccreadie@suffolk.gov.uk

Social Services (Children): Mr John Gregg, Service Director of Specialist Services, Endeavour House, 8 Russell Road, Ipswich IP1 2BX ☎ 01473 264785 ✉ john.gregg@cyp.suffolkcc.gov.uk

Public Health: Dr Tessa Lindfield , Director - Public Health, Endeavour House, 8 Russell Road, Ipswich IP1 2BX ✉ tessa.lindfield@suffolk.gov.uk

Sustainable Communities: Ms Judith Mobbs , Assistant Director of Skills, Endeavour House, 8 Russell Road, Ipswich IP1 2BX ☎ 01473 264830 ✉ judith.mobbs@suffolk.gov.uk

Waste Collection and Disposal: Mr Steve Palfrey , Head - Waste, Endeavour House, 8 Russell Road, Ipswich IP1 2BX ☎ 01473 264787 ✉ steve.palfrey@suffolk.gov.uk

Waste Management: Mr Steve Palfrey , Head - Waste, Endeavour House, 8 Russell Road, Ipswich IP1 2BX ☎ 01473 264787 ✉ steve.palfrey@suffolk.gov.uk

COUNCILLORS

***Leader of the Council* Noble**, Colin (CON - Row Heath) colin.noble@suffolk.gov.uk

***Deputy Leader of the Council* Hudson**, Christopher (CON - Kesgrave & Rushmere St Andrew) christopher.hudson@suffolk.gov.uk

***Group Leader* Ereira**, Mark (GRN - Tower) mark.ereira@suffolk.gov.uk

***Group Leader* Martin**, Sandy (LAB - St John's) sandy.martin@suffolk.gov.uk

***Group Leader* Mountford**, Bill (UKIP - Lowestoft South) bill.mountford@suffolk.gov.uk

***Group Leader* Wood**, David (LD - Peninsula) david.wood@suffolk.gov.uk

Adams, Sarah (LAB - St Margaret's & Westgate) sarah.adams@suffolk.gov.uk

Antill, Jenny (CON - Cosford) jenny.antill@suffolk.gov.uk

Armitage, Helen (LAB - Chantry) helen.armitage@suffolk.gov.uk

Barber, Nick (CON - Felixstowe Coastal) nick.barber@suffolk.gov.uk

Barker, Sonia (LAB - Pakefield) sonia.barker@suffolk.gov.uk

Beckwith, Trevor (IND - Eastgate & Moreton Hall) trevor.beckwith@suffolk.gov.uk

Bee, Mark (CON - Beccles) mark.bee@suffolk.gov.uk

Beer, Peter (CON - Great Cornard) peter.beer@suffolk.gov.uk

Bellfield, Peter (CON - Carlford) peter.bellfield@suffolk.gov.uk

Bole, Kathy (LAB - Whitehouse & Whitton) kathy.bole@suffolk.gov.uk

Bond, Michael (CON - Wickham) michael.bond@suffolk.gov.uk

Brown, Tony (UKIP - Haverhill East & Kedington) tony.brown@suffolk.gov.uk

Burroughes, Stephen (CON - Framlingham) stephen.burroughes@suffolk.gov.uk

Busby, David (LD - Belstead Brook) david.busby@suffolk.gov.uk

SUFFOLK

Byatt, Peter (LAB - Pakefield)
peter.byatt@suffolk.gov.uk

Chambers, Lisa (CON - Newmarket & Red Lodge)
lisa.chambers@suffolk.gov.uk

Clements, Terry (CON - Thingoe South)
terry.clements@suffolk.gov.uk

Cook, Kim (LAB - Gainsborough)
kim.cook@suffolk.gov.uk

Craig, Janet (LAB - Gunton)
janet.craig@suffolk.gov.uk

Crossley, James (UKIP - Whitehouse & Whitton)
james.crossley@suffolk.gov.uk

Evans, Mary (CON - Clare)
mary.evans@suffolk.gov.uk

Field, John (LD - Gipping Valley)
john.field@suffolk.gov.uk

Finch, James (CON - Stour Valley)
james.finch@suffolk.gov.uk

Fleming, Jessica (CON - Hartismere)
jessica.fleming@suffolk.gov.uk

Flood, Julian (UKIP - Haverhill Cangle)
julian.flood@suffolk.gov.uk

Gage, Sandra (LAB - Rushmere)
sandra.gage@suffolk.gov.uk

Gardiner, Peter (LAB - Chantry)
peter.gardiner@suffolk.gov.uk

Gaylard, Mandy (LAB - St Helen's)
mandy.gaylard@suffolk.gov.uk

Goldson, Tony (CON - Halesworth)
tony.goldson@suffolk.gov.uk

Goodwin, John (CON - Felixstowe North & Trimley)
john.goodwin@suffolk.gov.uk

Gower, Michael (CON - Blything)
michael.gower@suffolk.gov.uk

Green, Gary (CON - Stowmarket North & Stowupland)
gary.green@suffolk.gov.uk

Hackett, Derek (UKIP - Lowestoft South)
derek.hackett@suffolk.gov.uk

Hicks, Matthew (CON - Thredling)
matthew.hicks@suffolk.gov.uk

Hopfensperger, Rebecca (CON - Thingoe North)
rebecca.hopfensperger@suffolk.gov.uk

Hudson, David (UKIP - Exning & Newmarket)
david.hudson@suffolk.gov.uk

Jacklin, Leonard (LAB - Oulton)
leonard.jacklin@suffolk.gov.uk

Jones, Gordon (CON - Samford)
gordon.jones@suffolk.gov.uk

Kemp, Richard (IND - Melford)

Ladd, Michael (CON - Kessingland & Southwold)
michael.ladd@suffolk.gov.uk

Lockington, Inga (LD - St Margaret's & Westgate)
inga.lockington@suffolk.gov.uk

Marks, Tim (CON - Haverhill Cangle)
tim.marks@suffolk.gov.uk

McGregor, Guy (CON - Hoxne & Eye)
guy.mcgregor@suffolk.gov.uk

Murray, Alan (CON - Bixley)
alan.murray@suffolk.gov.uk

Nettleton, David (IND - Tower)
david.nettleton@suffolk.gov.uk

Newman, Graham (CON - Felixstowe Coastal)
graham.newman@.suffolk.gov.uk

O'Brien, Patricia (CON - Martlesham)
patricia.obrien@suffolk.gov.uk

Otton, Penny (LD - Thedwastre South)
penny.otton@.suffolk.gov.uk

Page, Caroline (LD - Woodbridge)
caroline.page@suffolk.gov.uk

Patience, Keith (LAB - Gunton)
keith.patience@suffolk.gov.uk

Poole, Bert (UKIP - Oulton)
bert.poole@suffolk.gov.uk

Punt, Chris (CON - Beccles)
chris.punt@suffolk.gov.uk

Quinton, Bill (LAB - Priory Heath)
bill.quinton@suffolk.gov.uk

Reid, Andrew (CON - Wilford)
andrew.reid@suffolk.gov.uk

Riley, Brian (CON - Hadleigh)
brian.riley@suffolk.gov.uk

Ritchie, David (CON - Bungay)
david.ritchie@suffolk.gov.uk

Rudkin, Bryony (LAB - Bridge)
bryony.rudkin@suffolkcc.gov.uk

Sayers, John (CON - Sudbury)
john.sayers@suffolk.gov.uk

Searle, Stephen (UKIP - Stowmarket South)
stephen.searle@suffolk.gov.uk

Silvester, Reg (UKIP - Brandon)
reg.silvester@suffolk.gov.uk

Smith, Richard (CON - Aldeburgh & Leiston)
richard.smith@suffolk.gov.uk

Spence, Colin (CON - Sudbury East & Waldingfield)
colin.spence@suffolk.gov.uk

Spicer, Joanna (CON - Blackbourn)
joanna.spicer@suffolk.gov.uk

Stamp, Sarah (CON - Hardwick)
sarah.stamp@suffolk.gov.uk

Storey, Jane (CON - Thedwastre North)
jane.storey@suffolk.gov.uk

Stringer, Andrew (GRN - Upper Gipping)
andrew.stringer@suffolk.gov.uk

Truelove, Julia (LD - Bosmere)
julia.truelove@suffolk.gov.uk

Waters, James (CON - Mildenhall)
james.waters@suffolk.gov.uk

Whiting, Robert (CON - Kesgrave & Rushmere St Andrew)
robert.whiting@suffolk.gov.uk

POLITICAL COMPOSITION
CON: 39, LAB: 15, UKIP: 9, LD: 7, IND: 3, GRN: 2

COMMITTEE CHAIRS
Audit: Mr Michael Bond

Development Control: Mr Peter Beer

Education & Children's Services: Mr Graham Newman

Health & Wellbeing: Mr Alan Murray

Pensions: Mr Peter Bellfield

Suffolk Coastal D

Suffolk Coastal District Council, Council Offices, Melton Hill, Woodbridge IP12 1AU
☎ 01394 383789 🖷 01394 385100 💻 www.suffolkcoastal.gov.uk

FACTS AND FIGURES
Parliamentary Constituencies: Suffolk Coastal
EU Constituencies: Eastern
Election Frequency: Elections are of whole council

PRINCIPAL OFFICERS
Chief Executive: Mr Stephen Baker , Chief Executive, Council Offices, Melton Hill, Woodbridge IP12 1AU ☎ 01394 444348 🖷 01394 385100 ✉ stephen.baker@eastsuffolk.gov.uk

Assistant Chief Executive: Mr Arthur Charvonia , Strategic Director, Council Offices, Melton Hill, Woodbridge IP12 1AU ☎ 01502 523606 🖷 01502 523500 ✉ arthur.charvonia@eastsuffolk.gov.uk

Senior Management: Mr Andrew Jarvis , Strategic Director, Council Offices, Melton Hill, Woodbridge IP12 1AU ☎ 01394 444323 ✉ andrew.jarvis@eastsuffolk.gov.uk

Senior Management: Mr Tony Osmanski , Strategic Director, Council Offices, Melton Hill, Woodbridge IP12 1AU ☎ 01394 444323 🖷 01394 385100 ✉ tony.osmanski@suffolkcoastal.gov.uk

Building Control: Mr Philip Ridley, Head of Planning Services, Council Offices, Melton Hill, Woodbridge IP12 1AU ☎ 01394 444432 ✉ philip.ridley@suffolkcoastal.gov.uk

PR / Communications: Mr Steve Henry , Communications Manager, Council Offices, Melton Hill, Woodbridge IP12 1AU ☎ 01394 444361 🖷 01394 385100 ✉ steve.henry@eastsuffolk.gov.uk

Community Planning: Mr Philip Ridley, Head of Planning Services, Council Offices, Melton Hill, Woodbridge IP12 1AU ☎ 01394 444432 ✉ philip.ridley@suffolkcoastal.gov.uk

Community Safety: Mr Richard Best , Active Communities Manager, Council Offices, Melton Hill, Woodbridge IP12 1AU ☎ 01502 523605 ✉ richard.best@waveney.gov.uk

Computer Management: Ms Sandra Lewis , ICT & Programme Manager, Council Offices, Melton Hill, Woodbridge IP12 1AU ☎ 01394 444205 ✉ sandra.lewis@eastsuffolk.gov.uk

Contracts: Mr Ian Purdom , Principal Service Manager of Procurement, Council Offices, Melton Hill, Woodbridge IP12 1AU ☎ 01502 523507 ✉ ian.purdom@eastsuffolk.gov.uk

Customer Service: Mr Darren Knight , Head of Customer Services, Council Offices, Melton Hill, Woodbridge IP12 1AU ☎ 01502 523330 ✉ darren.knight@eastsuffolk.gov.uk

Economic Development: Mrs Catherine Thornber , Economic Services Manager, Council Offices, Melton Hill, Woodbridge IP12 1AU ☎ 01394 444472 ✉ catherine.thornber@eastsuffolk.gov.uk

Electoral Registration: Mrs Karen Last , Electoral Services Manager, Council Offices, Melton Hill, Woodbridge IP12 1AU ☎ 01394 444324 ✉ karen.last@eastsuffolk.gov.uk

Environmental Health: Mr Phil Gore, Head of Environmental Services & Port Health, Council Offices, Melton Hill, Woodbridge IP12 1AU ☎ 01394 444286 🖷 01502 589327 ✉ phil.gore@eastsuffolk.gov.uk

Finance: Ms Homira Javadi , Chief Finance Officer, Council Offices, Melton Hill, Woodbridge IP12 1AU ☎ 01394 444249 ✉ homira.javadi@suffolkcoastal.gov.uk

Health and Safety: Mr Phil Gore, Head of Environmental Services & Port Health, Council Offices, Melton Hill, Woodbridge IP12 1AU ☎ 01394 444286 🖷 01502 589327 ✉ phil.gore@eastsuffolk.gov.uk

Health and Safety: Mr Mark Sims, Food & Safety Manager, Council Offices, Melton Hill, Woodbridge IP12 1AU ☎ 01394 444356 🖷 01394 385100 ✉ mark.sims@suffolkcoastal.gov.uk

Home Energy Conservation: Mrs Teresa Howarth, Environmental Health Officer, Council Offices, Melton Hill, Woodbridge IP12 1AU ☎ 01394 444206 🖷 01394 385100 ✉ teresa.howarth@suffolkcoastal.gov.uk

Housing: Mr Robert Prince , Head of Housing Operations & Landlord Services, Council Offices, Melton Hill, Woodbridge IP12 1AU ☎ 01502 523144; 01502 562111 🖷 01502 523500; 01502 589327 ✉ robert.prince@waveney.gov.uk

Legal: Mrs Hilary Slater , Head of Legal & Democratic Services, Council Offices, Melton Hill, Woodbridge IP12 1AU ☎ 01394 444336 ✉ hilary.slater@suffolkcoatal.gov.uk

Leisure and Cultural Services: Mr Andrew Jarvis , Strategic Director, Council Offices, Melton Hill, Woodbridge IP12 1AU ☎ 01394 444323 ✉ andrew.jarvis@eastsuffolk.gov.uk

Lifelong Learning: Mrs Heather Shilling , Human Resources Officer, Council Offices, Melton Hill, Woodbridge IP12 1AU ☎ 01502 562611; 01502 523221 🖷 01502 589327 ✉ heather.shilling@waveney.gov.uk

Lottery Funding, Charity and Voluntary: Mr Richard Best, Active Communities Manager, Council Offices, Melton Hill, Woodbridge IP12 1AU ☎ 01502 523605 ✉ richard.best@waveney.gov.uk

SUFFOLK COASTAL

Member Services: Mrs Karen Cook , Cabinet Business Manager, Council Offices, Melton Hill, Woodbridge IP12 1AU ☎ 01394 444326 🖷 01394 385100 ✉ Karen.cook@suffolkcoastal.gov.uk

Partnerships: Mr David Gallagher , Head of Commercial & Leisure Partnerships, Council Offices, Melton Hill, Woodbridge IP12 1AU ☎ 01502 523007 🖷 01502 523500 ✉ david.gallagher@waveney.gov.uk

Personnel / HR: Mrs Carol Lower , Human Resources & Workforce Development Manager, Council Offices, Melton Hill, Woodbridge IP12 1AU ☎ 01502 523228 ✉ carol.lower@eastsuffolk.gov.uk

Planning: Mr Philip Ridley, Head of Planning Services, Council Offices, Melton Hill, Woodbridge IP12 1AU ☎ 01394 444432 ✉ philip.ridley@suffolkcoastal.gov.uk

Procurement: Mr Ian Purdom , Principal Service Manager of Procurement, Council Offices, Melton Hill, Woodbridge IP12 1AU ☎ 01502 523507 ✉ ian.purdom@eastsuffolk.gov.uk

Regeneration: Mr Paul Moss , Major Projects Programme Manager, Town Hall, High Street, Lowestoft NR32 1HS ☎ 01502 523392 ✉ paul.moss@waveney.gov.uk

Staff Training: Mrs Heather Shilling , Human Resources Officer, Council Offices, Melton Hill, Woodbridge IP12 1AU ☎ 01502 562611; 01502 523221 🖷 01502 589327 ✉ heather.shilling@waveney.gov.uk

Sustainable Development: Mr Philip Ridley, Head of Planning Services, Council Offices, Melton Hill, Woodbridge IP12 1AU ☎ 01394 444432 ✉ philip.ridley@suffolkcoastal.gov.uk

Tourism: Mrs Catherine Thornber , Economic Services Manager, Council Offices, Melton Hill, Woodbridge IP12 1AU ☎ 01394 444472 ✉ catherine.thornber@eastsuffolk.gov.uk

Waste Collection and Disposal: Mr David Gallagher , Head of Commercial & Leisure Partnerships, Council Offices, Melton Hill, Woodbridge IP12 1AU ☎ 01502 523007 🖷 01502 523500 ✉ david.gallagher@waveney.gov.uk

COUNCILLORS

***Chair* Harvey**, Susan (CON - Kirton)
susan.harvey@suffolkcoastal.gov.uk

***Vice-Chair* Newton**, Mark (CON - Tower)
mark.newton@suffolkcoastal.gov.uk

***Leader of the Council* Herring**, Ray (CON - Orford & Eyke)
ray.herring@suffolkcoastal.gov.uk

***Deputy Leader of the Council* Holdcroft**, Geoff (CON - Woodbridge)
geoff.holdcroft@suffolkcoastal.gov.uk

Amoss, Mark (CON - Wickham Market)
mark.amoss@suffolkcoastal.gov.uk

Bidwell, Jim (CON - Melton)
james.bidwell@suffolkcoastal.gov.uk

Bird, Stuart (CON - Felixstowe West)
stuart.bird@suffolkcoastal.gov.uk

Block, Christine (LD - Deben)
christine.block@suffolkcoastal.gov.uk

Bloomfield, Stephen (CON - Felixstowe North)
stephen.bloomfield@suffolkcoastal.gov.uk

Blundell, Chris (CON - Martlesham)
chris.blundell@suffolkcoastal.gov.uk

Bond, Michael (CON - Rendlesham)
michael.bond@suffolkcoastal.gov.uk

Burroughes, Stephen (CON - Peasenhall & Yoxford)
stephen.burroughes@suffolkcoastal.gov.uk

Catchpole, Raymond (CON - Wenhaston & Westleton)
raymond.catchpole@suffolkcoastal.gov.uk

Coleman, Peter (CON - Felixstowe South)
peter.coleman@suffolkcoastal.gov.uk

Cooper, Tony (IND - Leiston)
tony.cooper@suffolkcoastal.gov.uk

Day, Jane (CON - Melton)
jane.day@suffolkcoastal.gov.uk

Deacon, Mike (LAB - Felixstowe North)
michael.deacon@suffolkcoastal.gov.uk

Dean, Deborah (CON - Tower)
deborah.dean@suffolkcoastal.gov.uk

Dunnett, Phillip (CON - Saxmundham)
phillip.dunnett@suffolkcoastal.gov.uk

Fisher, John (IND - Saxmundham)
john.fisher@suffolkcoastal.gov.uk

Fryatt, Tony (CON - Grundisburgh)
tony.fryatt@suffolkcoastal.gov.uk

Gallant, Steve (CON - Felixstowe East)
steve.gallant@suffolkcoastal.gov.uk

Green, Tracey (CON - Felixstowe West)
tracey.green@suffolkcoastal.gov.uk

Harding, Graham (CON - The Trimleys)
graham.harding@suffolkcoastal.gov.uk

Haworth, Terry-Jill (CON - Aldeburgh)
terry-jill.haworth@suffolkcoastal.gov.uk

Hedgley, Colin (CON - Woodbridge)
colin.hedgley@suffolkcoastal.gov.uk

Hudson, Christopher (CON - Framlingham)
christopher.hudson@suffolkcoastal.gov.uk

Jones, Maureen (CON - Aldeburgh)
maureen.jones@suffolkcoastal.gov.uk

Kelso, John (LD - Martlesham)
john.kelso@suffolkcoastal.gov.uk

Kerry, Richard (CON - The Trimleys)
richard.kerry@suffolkcoastal.gov.uk

Lawson, Stuart (CON - Kesgrave West)
stuart.lawson@suffolkcoastal.gov.uk

Lynch, Geoff (CON - Kesgrave East)
geoff.lynch@suffolkcoastal.gov.uk

McCallum, Debbie (CON - Kesgrave West)
debbie.mccallum@suffolkcoastal.gov.uk

Mower, Sue (CON - Kesgrave East)
susan.mower@suffolkcoastal.gov.uk

Mulcahy, Patti (CON - Woodbridge)
patricia.mulcahy@suffolkcoastal.gov.uk

Poulter, Carol (CON - Hacheston)
carol.poulter@suffolkcoastal.gov.uk

Pratt, Ian (CON - Leiston)
ian.pratt@suffolkcoastal.gov.uk

Rous, Paul (CON - Framlingham)
paul.rous@suffolkcoastal.gov.uk

Savage, Doreen (CON - Felixstowe East)
doreen.savage@suffolkcoastal.gov.uk

Smith, Andy (CON - Felixstowe South)
andy.smith@suffolkcoastal.gov.uk

Whiting, Robert (CON - Fynn Valley)
robert.whiting@suffolkcoastal.gov.uk

Yeo, Nicky (CON - Nacton & Purdis Farm)
nicola.yeo@suffolkcoastal.gov.uk

POLITICAL COMPOSITION

CON: 37, IND: 2, LD: 2, LAB: 1

COMMITTEE CHAIRS

Audit & Governance: Mr Geoff Lynch
Licensing & Health: Mr Mark Newton

Sunderland M

Sunderland City Council, Civic Centre, Sunderland SR2 7DN
☎ 0191 520 5555 🖷 0191 553 1020 ✉ enquiries@sunderland.gov.uk
🖳 www.sunderland.gov.uk

FACTS AND FIGURES

Parliamentary Constituencies: Houghton and Sunderland South, Sunderland Central, Washington and Sunderland West
EU Constituencies: North East
Election Frequency: Elections are by thirds

PRINCIPAL OFFICERS

Chief Executive: Mrs Sonia Tognarelli , Interim Head of Paid Service (Head of Financial Resources), Civic Centre, Sunderland SR2 7DN ☎ 0191 561 1851 ✉ sonia.tognarelli@sunderland.gov.uk

Assistant Chief Executive: Ms Sarah Reed , Assistant Chief Executive, Civic Centre, Sunderland SR2 7DN ☎ 0191 561 1114 or 1134 ✉ sarah.reed@sunderland.gov.uk

Senior Management: Ms Alison Fellowes , Executive Director - Commercial Development, Civic Centre, Sunderland SR2 7DN ✉ alison.fellows@sunderland.gov.uk

Senior Management: Ms Gillian Gibson , Interim Director - Public Health, Civic Centre, Sunderland SR2 7DN ✉ gillian.gibson@sunderland.gov.uk

Senior Management: Ms Deborah Lewin , Director - Corporate Affairs, Civic Centre, Sunderland SR2 7DN ☎ 0191 561 1135 🖷 0191 553 1138 ✉ deborah.lewin@sunderland.gov.uk

Senior Management: Mr Neil Revely , Executive Director - People Services, 50 Fawcett Street, Sunderland SR1 1RF ☎ 0191 566 1882 🖷 0191 553 6114 ✉ neil.revely@sunderland.gov.uk

Senior Management: Ms Sue Stanhope, Director - Human Resources & Organisational Development, Civic Centre, Sunderland SR2 7DN ☎ 0191 561 1722 ✉ sue.stanhope@sunderland.gov.uk

Senior Management: Ms Andrea Winders , Executive Director - Enterprise Development, Civic Centre, Sunderland SR2 7DN ☎ 0191 561 1001 ✉ andrea.winders@sunderland.gov.uk

Access Officer / Social Services (Disability): Mr Neil Revely , Executive Director - People Services, 50 Fawcett Street, Sunderland SR1 1RF ☎ 0191 566 1882 🖷 0191 553 6114 ✉ neil.revely@sunderland.gov.uk

Catering Services: Mr Andrew Cummings , Catering Support Officer, South Hylton House, Sunderland SR4 0JL ☎ 0191 561 7574 ✉ andrew.cummings@sunderland.gov.uk

Children / Youth Services: Miss Sandra Mitchell , Head of Community & Family Wellbeing, Civic Centre, Sunderland SR2 7DN ☎ 0191 561 1438 ✉ sandra.mitchell@sunderland.gov.uk

Children / Youth Services: Ms Beverley Scanlon , Head of Educational Attainment & Lifelong Learning, Civic Centre, Sunderland SR2 7DN ☎ 0191 561 1965 ✉ beverley.scanlon@sunderland.gov.uk

Civil Registration: Ms Karen Lounton , Bereavement & Registration Services Manager, Civic Centre, Sunderland SR2 7DN ☎ 0191 561 7931 ✉ karen.lounton@sunderland.gov.uk

PR / Communications: Ms Deborah Lewin , Director - Corporate Affairs, Civic Centre, Sunderland SR2 7DN ☎ 0191 561 1135 🖷 0191 553 1138 ✉ deborah.lewin@sunderland.gov.uk

Community Safety: Mrs Julie Smith , Associate Policy Lead for Community Safety, Civic Centre, Sunderland SR2 7DN ☎ 0191 561 1591 ✉ julie.smith@sunderland.gov.uk

Computer Management: Ms Liz St Louis , Head of Customer Service & Development, Civic Centre, Sunderland SR2 7DN ☎ 0191 561 4902 ✉ liz.stlouis@sunderland.gov.uk

Consumer Protection and Trading Standards: Mr Richard Reading , Trading Standards & Licensing Manager, Jack Crawford House, Sunderland SR2 8QR ☎ 0191 561 1710 🖷 0191 553 1658 ✉ richard.reading@sunderland.gov.uk

Contracts: Mr Jonathan Rowson , Assistant Head of Law & Governance - Commercial Team, Civic Centre, Sunderland SR2 7DN ☎ 0191 561 1034 ✉ jonathan.rowson@sunderland.gov.uk

Corporate Services: Ms Charlotte Burnham , Head of Scrutiny & Area Arrangements, Civic Centre, Sunderland SR2 7DN ☎ 0191 561 1147 ✉ charlotte.burnham@sunderland.gov.uk

Corporate Services: Ms Rhiannon Hood , Assistant Head of Law & Governance, Civic Centre, Sunderland SR2 7DN ☎ 0191 561 1005 ✉ rhiannon.hood@sunderland.gov.uk

Corporate Services: Mr Phil Spooner, Community Leadership Programmes, Civic Centre, Sunderland SR2 7DN ☎ 0191 561 1146 🖷 0191 553 1461 ✉ phil.spooner@sunderland.gov.uk

Corporate Services: Ms Sue Stanhope, Director - Human Resources & Organisational Development, Civic Centre, Sunderland SR2 7DN ☎ 0191 561 1722 ✉ sue.stanhope@sunderland.gov.uk

Customer Service: Ms Margaret Douglas, Complaints & Feedback Team Manager, Civic Centre, Sunderland SR2 7DN ☎ 0191 561 1065 🖷 0191 553 1020 ✉ margaret.douglas@sunderland.gov.uk

Customer Service: Ms Liz St Louis , Head of Customer Service & Development, Civic Centre, Sunderland SR2 7DN ☎ 0191 561 4902 ✉ liz.stlouis@sunderland.gov.uk

Economic Development: Mr Taylor Vince , Head of Strategic Economic Development, Civic Centre, Sunderland SR2 7DN ☎ 0191 561 1113 ✉ vince.taylor@sunderland.gov.uk

Education: Miss Sandra Mitchell , Head of Community & Family Wellbeing, Civic Centre, Sunderland SR2 7DN ☎ 0191 561 1438 ✉ sandra.mitchell@sunderland.gov.uk

Education: Mrs Annette Parr , Lead Support & Intervention Officer - Vulnerable Groups, Sandhill Centre, Sunderland SR2 7DN ☎ 0191 561 1584 ✉ annette.parr@sunderland.gov.uk

Education: Ms Beverley Scanlon , Head of Educational Attainment & Lifelong Learning, Civic Centre, Sunderland SR2 7DN ☎ 0191 561 1965 ✉ beverley.scanlon@sunderland.gov.uk

E-Government: Ms Debbie Ross, E-Neighbourhood Programme Manager, Moorside, Sunderland SR3 3XN ☎ 0191 561 4216 ✉ debbie.ross@sunderland.gov.uk

Electoral Registration: Ms Lindsay Dixon , Head of Electoral Services, Civic Centre, Sunderland SR2 7DN ☎ 0191 561 1142 ✉ bill.crawford@sunderland.gov.uk

Emergency Planning: Mr Barry Frost , Security & Emergency Planning Manager, Civic Centre, Sunderland SR2 7DN ☎ 0191 561 2643 ✉ barry.frost@sunderland.gov.uk

Energy Management: Mr Andrew Atkinson , Energy Conservation Team Leader, Civic Centre, Sunderland SR2 7DN ☎ 0191 561 2728 ✉ andrew.atkinson@sunderland.gov.uk

Estates, Property & Valuation: Mr Nick Wood , Head of Property, Civic Centre, Sunderland SR2 7DN ☎ 0191 561 2631 ✉ nick.wood@sunderland.gov.uk

European Liaison: Ms Catherine Auld , International Manager, Civic Centre, Sunderland SR2 7DN ☎ 0191 561 1156 ✉ catherine.auld@sunderland.gov.uk

Facilities: Ms Jill Rose , Facilities Manager, Civic Centre, Sunderland SR2 7DN ☎ 0191 561 1101 ✉ jill.rose@sunderland.gov.uk

Finance: Mrs Sonia Tognarelli , Interim Head of Paid Service (Head of Financial Resources), Civic Centre, Sunderland SR2 7DN ☎ 0191 561 1851 ✉ sonia.tognarelli@sunderland.gov.uk

Fleet Management: Mr Ian Bell , Fleet & Transport Manager, Civic Centre, Sunderland SR2 7DN ☎ 0191 561 4531 ✉ sonia.tognarelli@sunderland.gov.uk

Health and Safety: Mr Phil Loveday , Health & Safety Manager, Civic Centre, Sunderland SR2 7DN ☎ 0191 561 1744 ✉ phil.loveday@sunderland.gov.uk

Health and Safety: Ms Sue Stanhope, Director - Human Resources & Organisational Development, Civic Centre, Sunderland SR2 7DN ☎ 0191 561 1722 ✉ sue.stanhope@sunderland.gov.uk

Highways: Mr David Laux , Assistant Head of Streetscene, Highways & Transportation, Jack Crawford House, Commercial Road, Sunderland SR2 8QR ☎ 0191 5617526 ✉ david.laux@sunderland.gov.uk

Home Energy Conservation: Mr Andrew Atkinson , Energy Conservation Team Leader, Civic Centre, Sunderland SR2 7DN ☎ 0191 561 2728 ✉ andrew.atkinson@sunderland.gov.uk

Housing: Mr Alan Caddick , Head of Housing, Leechmere Centre, Leechmere Industrial Estate, Carrmere Road, Sunderland SR2 9TQ ☎ 0191 566 1711 ✉ alan.caddick@sunderland.gov.uk

Housing: Ms Liz McEvoy , Principal Housing Manager, Civic Centre, Sunderland SR2 7DN ☎ 0191 561 1240 ✉ liz.mcevoy@sunderland.gov.uk

Housing: Mr Peter Smith , Access to Housing Manager , City Library, 1st Floor, Fawcett Street, Sunderland SR2 7DN ☎ 0191 561 1635 ✉ peter.j.smith@sunderland.gov.uk

Legal: Mrs Elaine Waugh , Head of Law & Governance, Civic Centre, Sunderland SR2 7DN ☎ 0191 561 1053 ✉ elaine.waugh@sunderland.gov.uk

Leisure and Cultural Services: Mr Neil Revely , Executive Director - People Services, 50 Fawcett Street, Sunderland SR1 1RF ☎ 0191 566 1882 🖷 0191 553 6114 ✉ neil.revely@sunderland.gov.uk

Licensing: Mr Richard Reading , Trading Standards & Licensing Manager, Civic Centre, Sunderland SR2 7DN ☎ 0191 561 1710 🖷 0191 553 1658 ✉ richard.reading@sunderland.gov.uk

Lifelong Learning: Ms Beverley Scanlon , Head of Educational Attainment & Lifelong Learning, Civic Centre, Sunderland SR2 7DN ☎ 0191 561 1965 ✉ beverley.scanlon@sunderland.gov.uk

Member Services: Ms Rhiannon Hood , Assistant Head of Law & Governance, Civic Centre, Sunderland SR2 7DN ☎ 0191 561 1005 ✉ rhiannon.hood@sunderland.gov.uk

Parking: Ms Julie Tunstall , Deputy Parking Services Manager, Jack Crawford House, Commercial Road, Sunderland SR2 8QR ☎ 01915611582

Partnerships: Ms Jessica May, Partnership Manager, Civic Centre, Sunderland SR2 7DN ☎ 0191 561 1476 🖷 0191 553 1153 ✉ jessica.may@sunderland.gov.uk

Personnel / HR: Ms Tracy Palmer , Head of Human Resources Management, Civic Centre, Sunderland SR2 7DN ☎ 0191 561 1722 ✉ tracy.palmer@sunderland.gov.uk

Procurement: Mr Paul Davies , Assistant City Treasurer (Audit & Procurement), Corporate Services, PO Box 100, Civic Centre, Sunderland SR2 7DN ☎ 0191 561 2825 ✉ paul.davies@sunderland.gov.uk

Public Libraries: Ms Victoria French , Assistant Head of Community Services, Civic Centre, Sunderland SR2 7DN ☎ 0191 561 4588 ✉ victoria.french@sunderland.gov.uk

Recycling & Waste Minimisation: Mr Les Clark , Chief Operating Officer - Commercial Development, Civic Centre, Sunderland SR2 7DN ☎ 0191 561 4501 ✉ les.clark@sunderland.gov.uk

Social Services: Ms Gill Lawson , Service Development Manager, Community Equipment Service, Sunderland SR2 7DN ☎ 0191 5614432 ✉

Social Services: Mr Neil Revely , Executive Director - People Services, 50 Fawcett Street, Sunderland SR1 1RF ☎ 0191 566 1882 🖷 0191 553 6114 ✉ neil.revely@sunderland.gov.uk

Social Services (Adult): Mr Phil Hounsell , Service Development Manager, Civic Centre, Sunderland SR2 7DN ☎ 0191 5612877

Social Services (Adult): Ms Lynden Langman , Service Development Manager, Long Term Specialst Teams, Dock Street, Sunderland, Sunderland SR2 7DN ☎ 0191 5618075 ✉ lynden.langman@sunderland.gov.uk

Social Services (Adult): Ms Sharon Lowes , Lead Commissioner, Civic Centre, Sunderland SR2 7DN ☎ 0191 5618978 ✉ sharon.lowes@sunderland.gov.uk

Social Services (Adult): Ms Anne Prentice , Service Development Lead, Civic Centre, Sunderland SR2 7DN ☎ 0191 5618987 ✉ anne.prentice@sunderland.gov.uk

Social Services (Children): Mr Keith Moore , Deputy Director of Children's Services, Civic Centre, Sunderland SR2 7DN ☎ 0191 561 1397 ✉ keith.moore@sunderland.gov.uk

Public Health: Ms Gillian Gibson , Interim Director - Public Health, Civic Centre, Sunderland SR2 7DN ✉ gillian.gibson@sunderland.gov.uk

Street Scene: Mr Les Clark , Chief Operating Officer - Commercial Development, Civic Centre, Sunderland SR2 7DN ☎ 0191 561 4501 ✉ les.clark@sunderland.gov.uk

Street Scene: Mr James Newell , Assistant Head of Streetscene, Jack Crawford House, Commercial Road, Sunderland SR2 8QR ☎ 01915611607 ✉ james.newell@sunderland.gov.uk

Street Scene: Mr Bill Seymour , Refuse & Recycling Manager, South Hylton House, Sunderland SR2 7DN ☎ 0191 5614546 ✉ bill.seymour@sunderland.gov.uk

Traffic Management: Mr David Laux , Assistant Head of Streetscene, Highways & Transportation, Jack Crawford House, Commercial Road, Sunderland SR2 8QR ☎ 0191 5617526 ✉ david.laux@sunderland.gov.uk

Transport: Mr Bob Donaldson , Transportation Strategy Manager, Jack Crawford House, Commercial Road, Sunderland SR2 8QR ☎ 01915611517 ✉ bob.donaldson@sunderland.gov.uk

Transport: Mr David Laux , Assistant Head of Streetscene Highways & Transportation, Jack Crawford House, Commercial Road, Sunderland SR2 8QR ☎ 0191 5617526 ✉ david.laux@sunderland.gov.uk

Transport Planner: Mr David Laux , Assistant Head of Streetscene Highways & Transportation, Jack Crawford House, Commercial Road, Sunderland SR2 8QR ☎ 0191 5617526 ✉ david.laux@sunderland.gov.uk

Total Place: Mr Taylor Vince , Head of Strategic Economic Development, Civic Centre, Sunderland SR2 7DN ☎ 0191 561 1113 ✉ vince.taylor@sunderland.gov.uk

Waste Collection and Disposal: Mr Les Clark , Chief Operating Officer - Commercial Development, Civic Centre, Sunderland SR2 7DN ☎ 0191 561 4501 ✉ les.clark@sunderland.gov.uk

Waste Management: Mr Les Clark , Chief Operating Officer - Commercial Development, Civic Centre, Sunderland SR2 7DN ☎ 0191 561 4501 ✉ les.clark@sunderland.gov.uk

COUNCILLORS

Leader of the Council **Watson**, Paul (LAB - Pallion)
cllr.paul.watson@sunderland.gov.uk

Deputy Leader of the Council **Trueman**, Henry (LAB - Washington West)
cllr.henry.trueman@sunderland.gov.uk

Allan, David (LAB - Sandhill)
cllr.dave.allan@sunderland.gov.uk

Allen, Anthony (IND - Copt Hill)
cllr.anthony.allen@sunderland.gov.uk

Atkinson, Rebecca (LAB - Barnes)
cllr.rebecca.atkinson@sunderland.gov.uk

Ball, Ellen (LAB - Ryhope)
cllr.ellen.ball@sunderland.gov.uk

Beck, Margaret (LAB - Fulwell)
cllr.margaret.beck@sunderland.gov.uk

Bell, Richard (LAB - Redhill)
cllr.richard.bell@sunderland.gov.uk

Blackburn, James (LAB - Hetton)
cllr.james.blackburn@sunderland.gov.uk

Copeland, Rosalind (LAB - Southwick)
cllr.rosalind.copeland@sunderland.gov.uk

Cummings, John (LAB - Hetton)
cllr.john.cummings@sunderland.gov.uk

Curran, Barry (LAB - St. Peter's)
cllr.barry.curran@sunderland.gov.uk

SUNDERLAND

Davison, Ronny (LAB - Redhill)
cllr.ronny.davison@sunderland.gov.uk

Dixon, Michael (CON - St. Michael's)
cllr.michael.dixon@sunderland.gov.uk

Dixon, Darryl (LAB - St. Chad's)
cllr.darryl.dixon@sunderland.gov.uk

Elliott, Miles (LAB - Southwick)
cllr.miles.elliott@sunderland.gov.uk

Ellis, Sheila (IND - Houghton)
cllr.sheila.ellis@sunderland.gov.uk

Emmerson, Alan (LAB - Ryhope)
cllr.alan.emerson@sunderland.gov.uk

English, Colin (LAB - Doxford)
cllr.colin.english@sunderland.gov.uk

Essl, Michael (LAB - Barnes)
cllr.michael.essl@sunderland.gov.uk

Farr, Anthony (LAB - Ryhope)
cllr.anthony.farr@sunderland.gov.uk

Farthing, Louise (LAB - Washington South)
cllr.louise.farthing@sunderland.gov.uk

Fletcher, Jill (LAB - Washington North)
cllr.jill.fletcher@sunderland.gov.uk

Forbes, Margaret (CON - St. Michael's)
cllr.margaret.forbes@sunderland.gov.uk

Foster, Stephen (LAB - Castle)
cllr.stephen.foster@sunderland.gov.uk

Francis, Bob (CON - Fulwell)
cllr.bob.francis@sunderland.gov.uk

Galbraith, Gillian (LAB - St. Chad's)
cllr.gillian.galbraith@sunderland.gov.uk

Galbraith, Ian (LAB - Barnes)
cllr.ian.galbraith@sunderland.gov.uk

Gallagher, Jacqui (LAB - Sandhill)
cllr.jacqui.gallagher@sunderland.gov.uk

Gibson, Elizabeth (LAB - Doxford)
cllr.elizabeth.gibson@sunderland.gov.uk

Gibson, Peter (LAB - Silksworth)
cllr.peter.gibson@sunderland.gov.uk

Gofton, Cecilia (LAB - Pallion)
cllr.cecilia.gofton@sunderland.gov.uk

Heron, Juliana (LAB - Houghton)
cllr.juliana.heron@sunderland.gov.uk

Howe, George (CON - Fulwell)
cllr.george.howe@sunderland.gov.uk

Jackson, Julia (LAB - St. Peter's)
cllr.julia.jackson@sunderland.gov.uk

Kay, Ian (LAB - Millfield)
cllr.iain.kay@sunderland.gov.uk

Kelly, John (LAB - Washington North)
cllr.john.kelly@sunderland.gov.uk

Lauchlan, Len (LAB - Washington Central)
cllr.len.lauchlan@sunderland.gov.uk

Lawson, Anne (LAB - Shiney Row)
cllr.anne.lawson@sunderland.gov.uk

Leadbitter, Shirley (CON - St. Peter's)
cllr.shirley.leadbitter@sunderland.gov.uk

MacKnight, Doris (LAB - Castle)
cllr.doris.macknight@sunderland.gov.uk

Marshall, Christine (LAB - Doxford)
cllr.christine.marshall@sunderland.gov.uk

McClennan, Barbara (LAB - Hendon)
cllr.barbara.mcclennan@sunderland.gov.uk

Middleton, Paul (LAB - Washington South)
cllr.paul.middleton@sunderland.gov.uk

Miller, Fiona (LAB - Washington East)
cllr.fiona.miller@sunderland.gov.uk

Miller, Graeme (LAB - Washington South)
cllr.graeme.miller@sunderland.gov.uk

Mordey, Michael (LAB - Hendon)
cllr.michael.mordey@sunderland.gov.uk

O'Neil, Victoria (LAB - Hendon)
cllr.victoria.oneil@sunderland.gov.uk

Porthouse, Stuart (LAB - St. Chad's)
cllr.stuart.porthouse@sunderland.gov.uk

Price, Bob (LAB - Millfield)
cllr.bob.price@sunderland.gov.uk

Scanlan, Lynda (LAB - Millfield)
cllr.lynda.scanlan@sunderland.gov.uk

Scaplehorn, Bernard (LAB - Washington West)
cllr.bernard.scaplehorn@sunderland.gov.uk

Smith, Derrick (IND - Copt Hill)
cllr.derrick.smith@sunderland.gov.uk

Smith, Patricia (LAB - Silksworth)
cllr.patricia.smith@sunderland.gov.uk

Snowdon, Dianne (LAB - Washington Central)
cllr.derrick.snowdon@sunderland.gov.uk

Snowdon, David (LAB - Washington East)
cllr.david.snowdon@sunderland.gov.uk

Speding, Melville (LAB - Shiney Row)
cllr.melville.speding@sunderland.gov.uk

Stewart, Paul (LAB - Redhill)
cllr.paul.stewart@sunderland.gov.uk

Taylor, Tony (LAB - Washington East)
cllr.tony.taylor@sunderland.gov.uk

Trueman, Dorothy (LAB - Washington West)
cllr.dorothy.trueman@sunderland.gov.uk

Turner, Doris (LAB - Hetton)
cllr.doris.turner@sunderland.gov.uk

Turton, William (LAB - Houghton)
cllr.billy.turton@sunderland.gov.uk

Turton, Mary (LAB - Copt Hill)
cllr.mary.turton@sunderland.gov.uk

Tye, Philip (LAB - Silksworth)
cllr.philip.tye@sunderland.gov.uk

Walker, Geoff (LAB - Shiney Row)
cllr.geoffrey.walker@sunderland.gov.uk

Walker, Peter (LAB - Washington North)
cllr.peter.walker@sunderland.gov.uk

Waller, Debra (LAB - Sandhill)
cllr.debra.waller@sunderland.gov.uk

Waters, Karen (LAB - St. Anne's)
cllr.karen.waters@sunderland.gov.uk

Watson, Susan (LAB - St. Anne's)
cllr.thomas.wright@sunderland.gov.uk

Williams, Linda (LAB - Washington Central)
cllr.linda.williams@sunderland.gov.uk

Wilson, Denny (LAB - Castle)
cllr.denny.wilson@sunderland.gov.uk

Wilson, Amy (LAB - Pallion)
cllr.amy.wilson@sunderland.gov.uk

Wood, Peter (CON - St. Michael's)
cllr.peter.wood@sunderland.gov.uk

Wright, Norma (LAB - Southwick)
cllr.norma.wright@sunderland.gov.uk

Wright, Thomas (LAB - St. Anne's)
cllr.thomas.wright@sunderland.gov.uk

POLITICAL COMPOSITION

LAB: 66, CON: 6, IND: 3

COMMITTEE CHAIRS

Licensing: Ms Doris MacKnight

Planning & Highways: Mr Richard Bell

Surrey C

Surrey County Council, County Hall, Penrhyn Road, Kingston upon Thames KT1 2DN
☎ 0845 600 9009 🖷 020 8541 9004 ✉ contact.centre@surreycc.gov.uk
💻 www.surreycc.gov.uk

FACTS AND FIGURES

Parliamentary Constituencies: Surrey East
EU Constituencies: South East
Election Frequency: Elections are of whole council

PRINCIPAL OFFICERS

Chief Executive: Mr David McNulty , Chief Executive, County Hall, Penrhyn Road, Kingston upon Thames KT1 2DN ☎ 020 8541 8018 ✉ david.mcnulty@surreycc.gov.uk

Assistant Chief Executive: Ms Susie Kemp , Assistant Chief Executive, County Hall, Penrhyn Road, Kingston upon Thames KT1 2DN ☎ 020 8541 7043 ✉ susie.kemp@surreycc.gov.uk

Senior Management: Ms Helen Atkinson , Director - Public Health, County Hall, Penrhyn Road, Kingston upon Thames KT1 2DN ✉ helen.atkinson@surreycc.gov.uk

Senior Management: Mrs Julie Fisher , Strategic Director - Business Services, County Hall, Penrhyn Road, Kingston upon Thames KT1 2DN ☎ 020 8541 9550 🖷 020 8541 8968 ✉ julie.fisher@surreycc.gov.uk

Senior Management: Mr Trevor Pugh , Strategic Director of Environment & Infrastructure, County Hall, Penrhyn Road, Kingston upon Thames KT1 2DN ☎ 020 8541 9628 ✉ trevor.pugh@surreycc.gov.uk

Senior Management: Ms Yvonne Rees, Chief Executive (Mole Valley) Strategic Director of Customers & Communities (Surrey), County Hall, Penrhyn Road, Kingston upon Thames KT1 2DN ☎ 01306 879101 ✉ yvonne.rees@molevalley.gov.uk

Senior Management: Mr David Sargeant, Strategic Director of Adult Social Care, South West Area Office, Grosvenor House, AO3, London Road, Guildford GU1 1FA ☎ 01483 518455 ✉ david.sargeant@surreycc.gov.uk

Senior Management: Mr Nick Wilson , Strategic Director of Children, Schools & Families, County Hall, Penrhyn Road, Kingston upon Thames KT1 2DN ☎ 020 8541 9911 ✉ nick.wilson@surreycc.gov.uk

Access Officer / Social Services (Disability): Mr David Sargeant, Strategic Director of Adult Social Care, South West Area Office, Grosvenor House, AO3, London Road, Guildford GU1 1FA ☎ 01483 518455 ✉ david.sargeant@surreycc.gov.uk

Architect, Building / Property Services: Mr John Stebbings , Chief Property Officer, County Hall, Penrhyn Road, Kingston upon Thames KT1 2DN ☎ 020 8213 2554 🖷 020 8213 2554 ✉ john.stebbings@surreycc.gov.uk

Building Control: Mr Peter Hopkins , Asset Strategy Manager, County Hall, Penrhyn Road, Kingston upon Thames KT1 2DN ☎ 07817 404110 🖷 020 8541 9311 ✉ peter.hopkins@surreycc.gov.uk

Catering Services: Ms Beverley Baker, Head of Commercial Services, Epsom Local Office, The Parade, Epsom KT18 5BY ☎ 01372 832370 ✉ beverley.baker@surreycc.gov.uk

Children / Youth Services: Mr Mark Bisson , Head of Children, Schools & Families, County Hall, Penrhyn Road, Kingston upon Thames KT1 2DN ✉ mark.bisson@surreycc.gov.uk

Children / Youth Services: Ms Caroline Budden , Assistant Director of Children's Services & Safeguarding, Fairmont House, Bull Hill, Leatherhead KT22 7AH ☎ 01372 833400 ✉ caroline.budden@surreycc.gov.uk

Children / Youth Services: Mr Garath Symonds , Assistant Director of Young People, County Hall, Penrhyn Road, Kingston upon Thames KT1 2DN ☎ 01372 833543 ✉ garath.symonds@surreycc.gov.uk

Children / Youth Services: Mr Nick Wilson , Strategic Director of Children, Schools & Families, County Hall, Penrhyn Road, Kingston upon Thames KT1 2DN ☎ 020 8541 9911 ✉ nick.wilson@surreycc.gov.uk

Civil Registration: Mrs Linda Aboe , Registration & Nationality Service Member, Rylston, 81 Oatlands Drive, Weybridge KT13 9LN ☎ 01932 794704 ✉ linda.aboe@surreycc.gov.uk

PR / Communications: Ms Louise Footner, Head of Communications, County Hall, Room G29, Penrhyn Road, Kingston upon Thames KT1 2DN ☎ 020 8541 9624 🖷 020 8541 8004 🖱 louise.footner@surreycc.gov.uk

Community Safety: Mr Gordon Falconer , Senior Manager - Community Safety, County Hall, Penrhyn Road, Kingston upon Thames KT1 2DN ☎ 020 8541 7296 🖱 gordon.falconer@surreycc.gov.uk

Computer Management: Mr Paul Brocklehurst , Head of Information Management & Technology, County Hall, Penrhyn Road, Kingston upon Thames KT1 2DN ☎ 020 8541 7210 🖱 paul.brocklehurst@surreycc.gov.uk

Consumer Protection and Trading Standards: Mr Steve Ruddy , Head of Trading Standards, County Hall, Penrhyn Road, Kingston upon Thames KT1 2DN ☎ 01372 371730 🖷 01372 371704 🖱 steve.ruddy@surreycc.gov.uk

Contracts: Ms Laura Langstaff , Head of Procurement & Commissioning, County Hall, Penrhyn Road, Kingston upon Thames KT1 2DN ☎ 020 8541 9233 🖱 laura.langstaff@surreycc.gov.uk

Customer Service: Mr Mark Irons , Head of Service, County Hall, Penrhyn Road, Kingston upon Thames KT1 2DN ☎ 020 8541 7848 🖱 mark.irons@surreycc.gov.uk

Economic Development: Ms Rachel Ford , Senior Manager Economic Growth, County Hall, Penrhyn Road, Kingston upon Thames KT1 2DN 🖱 rachel.ford@surreycc.gov.uk

Education: Mr Mark Bisson , Head of Children, Schools & Families, County Hall, Penrhyn Road, Kingston upon Thames KT1 2DN 🖱 mark.bisson@surreycc.gov.uk

Emergency Planning: Mr Ian Good , Head of Emergency Management, Room 194, County Hall, Penrhyn Road, Kingston upon Thames KT1 2DN ☎ 020 8541 9168 🖷 020 8541 9162 🖱 ian.good@surreycc.gov.uk

Energy Management: Mr Steve Ruddy , Corporate Head of Service - Environment, Pippbrook, Dorking RH4 1SJ ☎ 01306 879225 🖱 steve.ruddy@molevalley.gov.uk

Environmental Health: Mr Ian Boast, Assistant Director of Environment, County Hall, Penrhyn Road, Kingston upon Thames KT1 2DN ☎ 020 8541 9479 🖱 ian.boast@surreycc.gov.uk

Estates, Property & Valuation: Mr Keith Brown , Schools & Programme Manager, County Hall, Penrhyn Road, Kingston upon Thames KT1 2DN ☎ 020 8541 8651 🖷 020 8541 9311 🖱 keith.brown@surreycc.gov.uk

Finance: Ms Sheila Little , Deputy Head of Finance, County Hall, Penrhyn Road, Kingston upon Thames KT1 2DN ☎ 020 8541 7012 🖱 sheila.little@surreycc.gov.uk

Pensions: Mr Jason Bailey , Pensions Manager, County Hall, Penrhyn Road, Kingston upon Thames KT1 2DN ☎ 020 8541 8057 🖱 jason.bailey@surreycc.gov.uk

Fleet Management: Ms Tracey Coventry , Transport Co-ordination Centre Manager, County Hall, Penrhyn Road, Kingston upon Thames KT1 2DN ☎ 020 8541 9592 🖱 tracey.coventry@surreycc.gov.uk

Grounds Maintenance: Ms Morag Turner , Workplace Delivery Manager, County Hall, Penrhyn Road, Kingston upon Thames KT1 2DN ☎ 020 8541 9863 🖱 morag.turner@surreycc.gov.uk

Health and Safety: Mr Dave Blane , Senior Health & Safety Manager, County Hall, Penrhyn Road, Kingston upon Thames KT1 2DN ☎ 020 8541 8736 🖱 dave.blane@surreycc.gov.uk

Highways: Mr Jason Russell , Assistant Director of Highways, Merrow Complex, Merrow Lane, Merrow, Guildford GU4 7BQ ☎ 020 8541 7102 🖱 jason.russell@surreycc.gov.uk

Legal: Mrs Ann Charlton, Head of Legal & Democratic Services, County Hall, Room 129, Penrhyn Road, Kingston upon Thames KT1 2DN ☎ 020 8541 9001 🖷 020 8541 9392 🖱 ann.charlton@surreycc.gov.uk

Leisure and Cultural Services: Mr Peter Milton , Head of Cultural Services, Room 353, County Hall, Penrhyn Road, Kingston upon Thames KT1 2DN ☎ 020 8541 7679 🖱 peter.milton@surreycc.gov.uk

Lottery Funding, Charity and Voluntary: Mrs Mary Burguieres , Lead Manager of Policy & Strategy Partnership, Room 318, County Hall, Penrhyn Road, Kingston upon Thames KT1 2DN

Member Services: Ms Rachel Crossley , Lead Manager of Democratic Services, County Hall, Penrhyn Road, Kingston upon Thames KT1 2DN ☎ 020 8541 9993 🖷 020 8541 8968 🖱 rachel.crossley@surreycc.gov.uk

Partnerships: Mr James Painter , Community Partnership Manager, East Surrey Area Office A02, Lesbourne Road, Reigate RH2 7JP 🖱 james.painter@surreycc.gov.uk

Personnel / HR: Mrs Carmel Millar, Head of HR & Organisational Development, County Hall, Penrhyn Road, Kingston upon Thames KT1 2DN ☎ 020 8541 9824 🖱 carmel.millar@surreycc.gov.uk

Planning: Mr Dominic Forbes , Planning & Development Group Manager, County Hall, Penrhyn Road, Kingston upon Thames KT1 2DN ☎ 020 8541 9312 🖷 020 8541 9335 🖱 dominic.forbes@surreycc.gov.uk

Procurement: Ms Laura Langstaff , Head of Procurement & Commissioning, County Hall, Penrhyn Road, Kingston upon Thames KT1 2DN ☎ 020 8541 9233 🖱 laura.langstaff@surreycc.gov.uk

Public Libraries: Mrs Rose Wilson , Library Operations Manager of Cultural Services, Runnymede Centre, Chertsey Road, Addlestone KT15 2EP ☎ 01932 794178 🖱 rose.wilson@surreycc.gov.uk

Recycling & Waste Minimisation: Mr Ian Boast, Assistant Director of Environment, County Hall, Penrhyn Road, Kingston upon Thames KT1 2DN ☎ 020 8541 9479 🖱 ian.boast@surreycc.gov.uk

Recycling & Waste Minimisation: Ms Lesley Harding , Place & Sustainability Group Manager, County Hall, Penrhyn Road, Kingston upon Thames KT1 2DN lesley.harding@surreycc.gov.uk

Recycling & Waste Minimisation: Mr Richard Parkinson , Head of Waste, County Hall, Penrhyn Road, Kingston upon Thames KT1 2DN richard.parkinson@surreycc.gov.uk

Regeneration: Mr Tony Samuels , Cabinet Member of Assets & Regeneration Programmes, County Hall, Penrhyn Road, Kingston upon Thames KT1 2DN ☎ 020 8541 7595 tony.samuels@surreycc.gov.uk

Road Safety: Mr Duncan Knox , Road Safety Team Manager, Surrey Safety Camera Partnership, PO Box 930, Guildford GU4 8WU ☎ 020 8541 7443 duncan.knox@surreycc.gov.uk

Social Services: Ms Sarah Mitchell , Strategic Director of Adult Social Care, County Hall, Penrhyn Road, Kingston upon Thames KT1 2DN ☎ 020 8541 9320 sarah.mitchell@surreycc.gov.uk

Social Services (Children): Mr Garath Symonds , Assistant Director of Young People, County Hall, Penrhyn Road, Kingston upon Thames KT1 2DN ☎ 01372 833543 garath.symonds@surreycc.gov.uk

Families: Mr Mark Bisson , Head of Children, Schools & Families, County Hall, Penrhyn Road, Kingston upon Thames KT1 2DN mark.bisson@surreycc.gov.uk

Public Health: Ms Helen Atkinson , Director - Public Health, County Hall, Penrhyn Road, Kingston upon Thames KT1 2DN helen.atkinson@surreycc.gov.uk

Staff Training: Mrs Carmel Millar, Head of HR & Organisational Development, County Hall, Penrhyn Road, Kingston upon Thames KT1 2DN ☎ 020 8541 9824 carmel.millar@surreycc.gov.uk

Traffic Management: Mr Iain Reeve , Assistant Director of Strategy Transport & Planning, County Hall, Penrhyn Road, Kingston upon Thames KT1 2DN ☎ 0845 600 9375 🖷 020 8541 9004 iain.reeve@surreycc.gov.uk

Transport: Mr Iain Reeve , Assistant Director of Strategy Transport & Planning, County Hall, Penrhyn Road, Kingston upon Thames KT1 2DN ☎ 0845 600 9375 🖷 020 8541 9004 iain.reeve@surreycc.gov.uk

Transport Planner: Mr Iain Reeve , Assistant Director of Strategy Transport & Planning, County Hall, Penrhyn Road, Kingston upon Thames KT1 2DN ☎ 0845 600 9375 🖷 020 8541 9004 iain.reeve@surreycc.gov.uk

Waste Management: Mr Ian Boast, Assistant Director of Environment, County Hall, Penrhyn Road, Kingston upon Thames KT1 2DN ☎ 020 8541 9479 ian.boast@surreycc.gov.uk

Waste Management: Mr Richard Parkinson , Head of Waste, County Hall, Penrhyn Road, Kingston upon Thames KT1 2DN richard.parkinson@surreycc.gov.uk

COUNCILLORS

***Chair* Marks**, Sally (CON - Caterham Valley)
sally.marks@surreycc.gov.uk

***Vice-Chair* Skellett**, Nick (CON - Oxted)
n.skellett@surreycc.gov.uk

***Leader of the Council* Hodge**, David (CON - Warlingham)
david.hodge@surreycc.gov.uk

***Deputy Leader of the Council* Martin**, Peter (CON - Godalming South, Milford & Witley)
peterj.martin@surreycc.gov.uk

***Group Leader* Watson**, Hazel (LD - Dorking Hills)
h.watson@surreycc.gov.uk

Angell, Mary (CON - Woodham & New Haw)
mary.angell@surreycc.gov.uk

Barker, William (CON - Horsleys)
b.barker@surreycc.gov.uk

Barton, Nikki (R - Haslemere)
nikki.barton@surreycc.gov.uk

Beardsmore, Ian (LD - Sunbury Common & Ashford Common)
ian.beardsmore@btinternet.com

Beckett, John (R - Ewell)
jbeckett@epsom-ewell.gov.uk

Bennison, Mike (CON - Hinchley Wood, Claygate & Oxshott)
michael.bennison@surreycc.gov.uk

Bowes, Liz (CON - Woking South East)
liz.bowes@surreycc.gov.uk

Bramhall, Natalie (CON - Redhill West & Meadvale)
natalie.bramhall@surreycc.gov.uk

Brett-Warburton, Mark (CON - Guildford South East)
mark.brett-warburton@surreycc.gov.uk

Carasco, Ben (CON - Woking North)
ben.carasco@surreycc.gov.uk

Chapman, Bill (CON - Camberley East)
bill.chapman@surreycc.gov.uk

Clack, Helyn (CON - Dorking Rural)
helyn.clack@surreycc.gov.uk

Coleman, Carol (CON - Ashford)
carol.coleman@surreycc.gov.uk

Cooksey, Stephen (LD - Dorking South & the Holmwoods)
stephen.cooksey@surreycc.gov.uk

Cosser, Steve (CON - Godalming North)
steve.cosser@surreycc.gov.uk

Curran, Clare (CON - Bookham & Fetcham West)
clare.curran@surreycc.gov.uk

Ellwood, Graham (CON - Guildford East)
graham.ellwood@surreycc.gov.uk

Essex, Jonathan (GRN - Redhill East)
jonathan.essex@surreycc.gov.uk

Evans, Robert (LAB - Stanwell & Stanwell Moor)
robert.evans@surreycc.gov.uk

Evans, Tim (CON - Lower Sunbury & Halliford)
tim.evans@surreycc.gov.uk

Few, Mel (CON - Foxhills, Thorpe & Virginia Water)
mel.few@surreycc.gov.uk

Forster, Will (LD - Woking South)
will.forster@surreycc.gov.uk

Frost, Pat (CON - Farnham Central)
pat.frost@surreycc.gov.uk

Fuller, Denis (CON - Camberley West)
denis.fuller@surreycc.gov.uk

Furey, John (CON - Addlestone)
john.furey@surreycc.gov.uk

Gardner, Bob (CON - Merstham & Banstead South)
bob.gardner@surreycc.gov.uk

Goodman, Mike (CON - Bagshot, Windlesham & Chobham)
mike.goodman@surreycc.gov.uk

Goodwin, David (LD - Guildford South West)
goodwind@guildford.gov.uk

Gosling, Michael (CON - Tadworth, Walton & Kingswood)
michael.gosling@surreycc.gov.uk

Grant-Duff, Zully (CON - Reigate)
zully.grantduff@surreycc.gov.uk

Gray, Ramon (CON - Weybridge)
ramon.gray@surreycc.gov.uk

Gulati, Ken (CON - Banstead, Woodmansterne & Chipstead)
ken.gulati@surreycc.gov.uk

Hall, Tim (CON - Leatherhead & Fetcham East)
tim.hall@surreycc.gov.uk

Hammond, Kay (CON - Horley West, Salfords & Sidlow)
k.hammond@surreycc.gov.uk

Harmer, David (CON - Waverley Western Villages)
david.harmer@surreycc.gov.uk

Harrison, Nick (R - Nork & Tattenhams)
nicholas.harrison@surreycc.gov.uk

Heath, Marisa (CON - Englefield Green)
marisa.heath@surreycc.gov.uk

Hickman, Peter (R - The Dittons)
peter.hickman@surreycc.gov.uk

Hicks, Margaret (CON - Hersham)
margaret.hicks@surreycc.gov.uk

Hussain, Saj (CON - Knaphill & Goldsworth West)
saj.hussain@surreycc.gov.uk

Ivison, David (CON - Heatherside & Parkside)
david.ivison@surreycc.gov.uk

Jenkins, Daniel (UKIP - Staines South & Ashford West)
daniel.jenkins@surreycc.gov.uk

Johnson, George (UKIP - Shalford)
gtj@8210guy.com

Kemeny, Linda (CON - Woking South West)
linda.kemeny@surreycc.gov.uk

Kemp, Colin (CON - Goldsworth East & Horsell Village)
colin.kemp@surreycc.gov.uk

Kington, Eber (R - Ewell Court, Auriol & Cuddington)
ekington@epsom-ewell.gov.uk

Lake, Rachael (CON - Walton)
r.lake@surreycc.gov.uk

Lallement, Stella (LD - Epsom West)
stella.lallement@surreycc.gov.uk

Lay, Yvonna (CON - Egham)
yvonna.lay@surreycc.gov.uk

Le Gal, Denise (CON - Farnham North)
denise.legal@surreycc.gov.uk

Lewis, Mary (CON - Cobham)
mary.lewis@surreycc.gov.uk

Mallett, Ernest (R - West Molesey)
ernest.mallett@surreycc.gov.uk

Mason, Jan (R - West Ewell)
jmason@epsom-ewell.gov.uk

Moseley, Marsha (CON - Ash)
marsha.moseley@guildford.gov.uk

Mountain, Tina (CON - Epsom Town & Downs)
tina.mountain@surreycc.gov.uk

Munro, David (CON - Farnham South)
d.munro@surreycc.gov.uk

Norman, Chris (CON - Chertsey)
chris.norman@surreycc.gov.uk

Orrick, John (LD - Caterham Hill)
john.orrick@surreycc.gov.uk

Page, Adrian (CON - Lightwater, West End & Bisley)
adrian.page@surreycc.gov.uk

Pitt, Chris (CON - Frimley Green and Mytchett)
chris.pitt@surreycc.gov.uk

Ross-Tomlin, Dorothy (CON - Horley East)
dorothy.rosstomlin@surreycc.gov.uk

Saliagopoulos, Denise (CON - Staines upon Thames)
denise.saliagopoulos@surreycc.gov.uk

Samuels, Tony (CON - Walton South & Oatlands)
tony.samuels@surreycc.gov.uk

Searle, Pauline (LD - Guildford North)
pauline.searle@surreycc.gov.uk

Selleck, Stuart (R - East Molesey & Esher)
stuart.selleck@surreycc.gov.uk

Sydney, Michael (CON - Lingfield)
michael.sydney@surreycc.gov.uk

Taylor, Keith (CON - Shere)
keith.taylor@surreycc.gov.uk

Thomson, Barbara (CON - Earlswood & Reigate South)
barbara.thomson@surreycc.gov.uk

Townsend, Chris (R - Ashtead)
cllr.townsend@molevalley.gov.uk

Walsh, Richard (CON - Laleham & Shepperton)
richard.walsh@surreycc.gov.uk

White, Fiona (LD - Guildford West)
fiona.white@surreycc.gov.uk

Wilson, Richard (CON - The Byfleets)
richard.wilson@surreycc.gov.uk

Windsor, Helena (UKIP - Godstone)
helena.windsor@surreycc.gov.uk

Witham, Keith (CON - Worplesdon)
keithwitham1@hotmail.co.uk

Young, Victoria (CON - Waverley Eastern Villages)
victoria.young@surreycc.gov.uk

Young, Alan (CON - Cranleigh & Ewhurst)
ayoung500@yahoo.co.uk

POLITICAL COMPOSITION

CON: 58, LD: 9, R: 9, UKIP: 3, GRN: 1, LAB: 1

COMMITTEE CHAIRS

Audit: Mr Stuart Selleck

Health & Wellbeing: Mr Bill Chapman

Pensions: Mr Nick Harrison

Pensions: Ms Denise Le Gal

Planning: Mr Tim Hall

Surrey Heath D

Surrey Heath Borough Council, Surrey Heath House, Knoll Road, Camberley GU15 3HD
☎ 01276 707100 🖷 01276 707177 ✉ enquiries@surreyheath.gov.uk
🖳 www.surreyheath.gov.uk

FACTS AND FIGURES

Parliamentary Constituencies: Surrey Heath
EU Constituencies: South East
Election Frequency: Elections are of whole council

PRINCIPAL OFFICERS

Chief Executive: Mrs Karen Whelan , Chief Executive, Surrey Heath House, Knoll Road, Camberley GU15 3HD ☎ 01276 707100 ✉ karen.whelan@surreyheath.gov.uk

Senior Management: Mrs Karen Limmer , Head of Legal, Surrey Heath House, Knoll Road, Camberley GU15 3HD ☎ 01276 707100 ✉ karen.limmer@surreyheath.gov.uk

Senior Management: Mrs Louise Livingston , Interim Executive Head of Corporate, Surrey Heath House, Knoll Road, Camberley GU15 3HD ☎ 01276 707100 ✉ louise.livingstone@surreyheath.gov.uk

Senior Management: Mr Kelvin Menon, Head of Finance, Surrey Heath House, Knoll Road, Camberley GU15 3HD ☎ 01276 707100 ✉ kelvin.menon@surreyheath.gov.uk

Senior Management: Mr Tim Pashen, Head of Community, Surrey Heath House, Knoll Road, Camberley GU15 3HD ☎ 01276 707100 ✉ tim.pashen@surreyheath.gov.uk

Senior Management: Mr Richard Payne , Executive Head of Transformation, Surrey Heath House, Knoll Road, Camberley GU15 3HD ☎ 01276 707100 ✉ richard.payne@surreyheath.gov.uk

Senior Management: Mrs Jenny Rickard, Head of Regulatory, Surrey Heath House, Knoll Road, Camberley GU15 3HD ☎ 01276 707100 ✉ jenny.rickard@surreyheath.gov.uk

Senior Management: Mr Leigh Thornton , Interim Executive Head of Business, Surrey Heath House, Knoll Road, Camberley GU15 3HD ☎ 01276 707100 ✉ leigh.thornton@surreyheath.gov.uk

Best Value: Mr Kelvin Menon, Head of Finance, Surrey Heath House, Knoll Road, Camberley GU15 3HD ☎ 01276 707100 ✉ kelvin.menon@surreyheath.gov.uk

Building Control: Mrs Karen Limmer , Head of Legal, Surrey Heath House, Knoll Road, Camberley GU15 3HD ☎ 01276 707100 ✉ karen.limmer@surreyheath.gov.uk

PR / Communications: Mr Daniel Harrison , Media & Marketing Manager, Surrey Heath House, Knoll Road, Camberley GU15 3HD ☎ 01276 707100 ✉ daniel.harrison@surreyheath.gov.uk

PR / Communications: Mr Ian Macey , Media & Marketing Officer, Surrey Heath House, Knoll Road, Camberley GU15 3HD ☎ 01276 707100 ✉ ian.macey@surreyheath.gov.uk

Community Safety: Mr Kevin Cantlon , Business & Community Development Manager, Surrey Heath House, Knoll Road, Camberley GU15 3HD ☎ 01276 707100 ✉ kevin.cantlon@surreyheath.gov.uk

Computer Management: Mrs Janet Jones , ICT Manager, Surrey Heath House, Knoll Road, Camberley GU15 3HD ☎ 01276 707100 ✉ janet.jones@surreyheath.gov.uk

Contracts: Mrs Karan Jassi , Contracts Monitoring Officer, Surrey Heath House, Knoll Road, Camberley GU15 3HD ☎ 01276 707100 ✉ louise.livingston@surreyheath.gov.uk

Corporate Services: Mrs Louise Livingston , Interim Executive Head of Corporate, Surrey Heath House, Knoll Road, Camberley GU15 3HD ☎ 01276 707100 ✉ louise.livingstone@surreyheath.gov.uk

Customer Service: Mrs Louise Livingston , Interim Executive Head of Corporate, Surrey Heath House, Knoll Road, Camberley GU15 3HD ☎ 01276 707100 ✉ louise.livingstone@surreyheath.gov.uk

Economic Development: Mr Kevin Cantlon , Business & Community Development Manager, Surrey Heath House, Knoll Road, Camberley GU15 3HD ☎ 01276 707100 ✉ kevin.cantlon@surreyheath.gov.uk

E-Government: Mrs Janet Jones , ICT Manager, Surrey Heath House, Knoll Road, Camberley GU15 3HD ☎ 01276 707100 ✉ janet.jones@surreyheath.gov.uk

Electoral Registration: Ms Nicola Vooght, Elections Manager, Surrey Heath House, Knoll Road, Camberley GU15 3HD ☎ 01276 707100 ✉ nicola.vooght@surreyheath.gov.uk

Emergency Planning: Mr Tim Pashen, Head of Community, Surrey Heath House, Knoll Road, Camberley GU15 3HD ☎ 01276 707100 ✉ tim.pashen@surreyheath.gov.uk

Environmental / Technical Services: Mr Tim Pashen, Head of Community, Surrey Heath House, Knoll Road, Camberley GU15 3HD ☎ 01276 707100 ✉ tim.pashen@surreyheath.gov.uk

Environmental Health: Mr Tim Pashen, Head of Community, Surrey Heath House, Knoll Road, Camberley GU15 3HD ☎ 01276 707100 ✉ tim.pashen@surreyheath.gov.uk

Estates, Property & Valuation: Mr Jonathan Gregory , Estates & Asset Manager, Surrey Heath House, Knoll Road, Camberley GU15 3HD ☎ 01276 707100 ✉ jonathan.gregory@surreyheath.gov.uk

Facilities: Mrs Sarah Packham , Corporate Property Officer, Surrey Heath House, Knoll Road, Camberley GU15 3HD ☎ 01276 707100 ✉ sarah.packham@surreyheath.gov.uk

Finance: Mr Kelvin Menon, Head of Finance, Surrey Heath House, Knoll Road, Camberley GU15 3HD ☎ 01276 707100 ✉ kelvin.menon@surreyheath.gov.uk

Fleet Management: Mrs Sarah Packham , Corporate Property Officer, Surrey Heath House, Knoll Road, Camberley GU15 3HD ☎ 01276 707100 ✉ sarah.packham@surreyheath.gov.uk

Grounds Maintenance: Mr Leigh Thornton , Commercial Services Manager, Surrey Heath House, Knoll Road, Camberley GU15 3HD ☎ 01276 707100 ✉ leigh.thornton@surreyheath.gov.uk

Health and Safety: Mr Tim Pashen, Head of Community, Surrey Heath House, Knoll Road, Camberley GU15 3HD ☎ 01276 707100 ✉ tim.pashen@surreyheath.gov.uk

Housing: Mr Clive Jinman, Housing Services Manager, Surrey Heath House, Knoll Road, Camberley GU15 3HD ☎ 01276 707100 ✉ clive.jinman@surreyheath.gov.uk

Legal: Mrs Karen Limmer , Head of Legal, Surrey Heath House, Knoll Road, Camberley GU15 3HD ☎ 01276 707100 ✉ karen.limmer@surreyheath.gov.uk

Leisure and Cultural Services: Mr Leigh Thornton , Interim Executive Head of Business, Surrey Heath House, Knoll Road, Camberley GU15 3HD ☎ 01276 707100 ✉ leigh.thornton@surreyheath.gov.uk

Licensing: Mr Derek Seekings , Licensing Officer, Surrey Heath House, Knoll Road, Camberley GU15 3HD ☎ 01276 707100 ✉ derek.seekings@surreyheath.gov.uk

Member Services: Mrs Jane Sherman , Democratic Services Manager, Surrey Heath House, Knoll Road, Camberley GU15 3HD ☎ 01276 707100 ✉ jane.sherman@surreyheath.gov.uk

Parking: Mr Eugene Leal , Parking Services Manager, Surrey Heath House, Knoll Road, Camberley GU15 3HD ☎ 01276 707100 ✉ eugene.leal@surreyheath.gov.uk

Partnerships: Mr Jerry Fisher , Partnership Organisational Development Officer, Surrey Heath House, Knoll Road, Camberley GU15 3HD ☎ 01276 707100 ✉ jerry.fisher@surreyheath.gov.uk

Personnel / HR: Mrs Louise Livingston , Interim Executive Head of Corporate, Surrey Heath House, Knoll Road, Camberley GU15 3HD ☎ 01276 707100 ✉ louise.livingstone@surreyheath.gov.uk

Planning: Mrs Jenny Rickard, Head of Regulatory, Surrey Heath House, Knoll Road, Camberley GU15 3HD ☎ 01276 707100 ✉ jenny.rickard@surreyheath.gov.uk

Procurement: Mr Kelvin Menon, Head of Finance, Surrey Heath House, Knoll Road, Camberley GU15 3HD ☎ 01276 707100 ✉ kelvin.menon@surreyheath.gov.uk

Recycling & Waste Minimisation: Mr Tim Pashen, Head of Community, Surrey Heath House, Knoll Road, Camberley GU15 3HD ☎ 01276 707100 ✉ tim.pashen@surreyheath.gov.uk

Regeneration: Mr Richard Payne , Executive Head of Transformation, Surrey Heath House, Knoll Road, Camberley GU15 3HD ☎ 01276 707100 ✉ richard.payne@surreyheath.gov.uk

Staff Training: Mrs Louise Livingston , Interim Executive Head of Corporate, Surrey Heath House, Knoll Road, Camberley GU15 3HD ☎ 01276 707100 ✉ louise.livingstone@surreyheath.gov.uk

Street Scene: Mr Steve Burrows , Street Scene Officer, Surrey Heath House, Knoll Road, Camberley GU15 3HD ☎ 01276 707100 ✉ steve.burrows@surreyheath.gov.uk

Sustainable Development: Mrs Jenny Rickard, Head of Regulatory, Surrey Heath House, Knoll Road, Camberley GU15 3HD ☎ 01276 707100 ✉ jenny.rickard@surreyheath.gov.uk

Town Centre: Mr Richard Payne , Executive Head of Transformation, Surrey Heath House, Knoll Road, Camberley GU15 3HD ☎ 01276 707100 ✉ richard.payne@surreyheath.gov.uk

Waste Collection and Disposal: Mr Tim Pashen, Head of Community, Surrey Heath House, Knoll Road, Camberley GU15 3HD ☎ 01276 707100 ✉ tim.pashen@surreyheath.gov.uk

Waste Management: Mr Tim Pashen, Head of Community, Surrey Heath House, Knoll Road, Camberley GU15 3HD ☎ 01276 707100 ✉ tim.pashen@surreyheath.gov.uk

Children's Play Areas: Mr Leigh Thornton , Interim Executive Head of Business, Surrey Heath House, Knoll Road, Camberley GU15 3HD ☎ 01276 707100 ✉ leigh.thornton@surreyheath.gov.uk

COUNCILLORS

***Mayor* Potter**, Joanne (CON - Mytchett and Deepcut)
Joanne.Potter@surreyheath.gov.uk

***Deputy Mayor* Winterton**, John (CON - Lightwater)
John.Winterton@surreyheath.gov.uk

***Leader of the Council* Gibson**, Moira (CON - Windlesham)
moira.gibson@surreyheath.gov..uk

***Group Leader* Bates**, Rodney (LAB - Old Dean)
rodney.bates@surreyheath.gov..uk

Adams, Dan (CON - St. Pauls)
dan.adams@surreyheath.gov.uk

Allen, David (CON - Frimley)
dra01@btconnect.com

Brooks, Richard (CON - Town)
richard.brooks@surreyheath.gov..uk

Chambers, Nick (CON - Old Dean)
nick.chambers@surreylheath.gov.uk

Chapman, Vivienne (CON - St. Pauls)
vivienne.chapman@surreyheath.gov..uk

Chapman, Bill (CON - St. Pauls)
bill.chapman@surreyheath.gov..uk

Cooper, Katie Malcaus (CON - Bagshot)
katie.malcauscooper@surreyheath.gov.uk

Cullen, Ian (CON - Heatherside)
ian.cullen@surreyheath.gov.uk

Deach, Paul (CON - Mytchett and Deepcut)
Paul.Deach@surreyheath.gov.uk

Dougan, Colin (CON - St. Michaels)
colin.dougan@surreyheath.gov..uk

Fennell, Craig (CON - Mytchett and Deepcut)
craig.fennell@surreyheath.gov.uk

Gandhum, Surinder (CON - Lightwater)
surinder.gandhum@surreyheath.gov.uk

Hawkins, Josephine (CON - Parkside)
josephine.hawkins@surreyheath.gov..uk

Hawkins, Edward (CON - Parkside)
edward.hawkins@surreyheath.gov..uk

Hawkins, Josephine (CON - Parkside)
josephine.hawkins@surreyheath.gov.uk

Hutchinson, Ruth (LD - Bagshot)
ruth.hutchinson@surrreyheath.gov.uk

Ilnicki, Paul (CON - Heatherside)
paul.ilnicki@surreyheath.gov..uk

Jennings-Evans, Rebecca (CON - Lightwater)
rebecca.jennings-evans@surreyheath.gov.uk

Lewis, Oliver (CON - Frimley Green)
oliver.lewis@surreyheath.gov.uk

Lewis, David (CON - Watchetts)
david.lewis@surreyheath.gov.uk

Lytle, Jonathan (CON - Heatherside)
johnathan.lytle@surreyheath.gov.uk

Mansell, Bruce (CON - Frimley)
bruce.mansell@surreyheath.gov..uk

Mansfield, David (CON - Bisley)
david.mansfield@surreyheath.gov.uk

McClafferty, Alan (CON - St. Michaels)

Morley, Charlotte (CON - Watchetts)
Charlotte.Morley@surreyheath.gov.uk

Nelson, Max (CON - Frimley Green)

Page, Adrian (CON - West End)
adrian.page@surreyheath.gov.uk

Perry, Robin (CON - Town)
robin.perry@surryheath.gov.uk

Pitt, Chris (CON - Frimley Green)
chris.pitt@surreyheath.gov.uk

Price, Wynne (CON - Bisley)
Wynne.Price@surreyheath.gov..uk

Price, Nic (CON - West End)

Ratiram, Darryl (CON - Parkside)
darryl.ratiram@surreyheath.gov.uk

Sams, Ian (CON - Frimley)
ian.sams@surreyheath.gov.uk

Sturt, Conrad (CON - Windlesham)

Tedder, Pat (IND - Chobham)
Pat.Tedder@surreyheath.gov.uk

Wheeler, Victoria (IND - Chobham)

White, Valerie (CON - Bagshot)
valerie.white@surreyheath.gov.uk

POLITICAL COMPOSITION

CON: 37, IND: 2, LAB: 1, LD: 1

COMMITTEE CHAIRS

Audit: Ms Valerie White

Licensing: Mr Bill Chapman

Planning: Mr Edward Hawkins

Sutton L

Sutton London Borough Council, Civic Offices, St. Nicholas Way, Sutton SM1 1EA
☎ 020 8770 5000 🖷 020 8770 5404 ✉ contactcentre@sutton.gov.uk
💻 www.sutton.gov.uk

FACTS AND FIGURES

Parliamentary Constituencies: Carshalton and Wallington, Sutton and Cheam
EU Constituencies: London
Election Frequency: Elections are of whole council

PRINCIPAL OFFICERS

Chief Executive: Mr Niall Bolger , Chief Executive, Civic Offices, St. Nicholas Way, Sutton SM1 1EA ☎ 020 8770 5000
✉ naill.bolger@sutton.gov.uk

Senior Management: Dr Nicola Lang , Director - Public Health, Civic Offices, St. Nicholas Way, Sutton SM1 1EA
✉ nicola.lang@sutton.gov.uk

Access Officer / Social Services (Disability): Mr Simon Latham, Executive Head of Housing & Regeneration, Civic Offices, Sutton SM1 1EA ☎ 020 8770 4005 🖷 020 8770 5214
✉ simon.latham@sutton.gov.uk

Architect, Building / Property Services: Mr Ade Adebayo, Executive Head of Asset Planning & Management, 24 Denmark Road, Carshalton SM1 2JG ☎ 020 8770 6109 🖷 020 8770 6234
✉ ade.adebayo@sutton.gov.uk

Architect, Building / Property Services: Mr Alex Fitzgerald , Head of Asset Management, 24 Denmark Road, Carshalton SM5 2JG ☎ 020 8770 6154 ✉ alex.fitxgerald@sutton.gov.uk

Children / Youth Services: Mr Richard Nash , Executive Head of Children's Social Care & Safeguarding, Civic Offices, St. Nicholas Way, Sutton SM1 1EA ☎ 020 8770 4502
✉ richard.nash@sutton.gov.uk

PR / Communications: Mr Andreas Christophorou , Head of Communications, Civic Offices, St. Nicholas Way, Sutton SM1 1EA
☎ 020 8770 4048 ✉ andreas.christophorou@sutton.gov.uk

SUTTON

Community Safety: Mr Warren Shadbolt, Executive Head of Safer & Stronger Communities, Sutton Police Station, 6 Carshalton Road, Sutton SM1 4RF ☎ 020 8649 0601 🖷 020 8649 0609 ✉ warren.shadbolt@met.pnn.police.uk

Computer Management: Mr Rob Miller , Joint Head of ICT, Civic Offices, St. Nicholas Way, Sutton SM1 1EA ☎ 020 8770 5070 ✉ rob.miller@sutton.gov.uk

Contracts: Mr Mark Brewer , Head of Procurement, Civic Offices, St. Nicholas Way, Sutton SM1 1EA ☎ 020 8770 5300 ✉ mark.brewer@sutton.gov.uk

Corporate Services: Ms Victoria Lawson , Head of Policy, Leadership & Governance, Civic Offices, St. Nicholas Way, Sutton SM1 1EA

Customer Service: Ms Jessica Crowe , Executive Head of Customers, Commissioning & Governance, Civic Offices, St. Nicholas Way, Sutton SM1 1EA

Customer Service: Ms Janette Garlick, Head of Customer Services, Civic Offices, St. Nicholas Way, Sutton SM1 1EA ☎ 020 8770 5317 ✉ janette.garlick@sutton.gov.uk

Economic Development: Ms Eleanor Purser , Executive Head of Economic Development, 24 Denmark Road, Carshalton CM5 2JG ☎ 020 8770 5000 ✉ eleanor.purser@sutton.gov.uk

Education: Mr Colin Stewart , Executive Head of Education & Early Years, Civic Offices, St. Nicholas Way, Sutton SM1 1EA ☎ 020 8770 5000 ✉ colin.stewart@sutton.gov.uk

Electoral Registration: Ms Martha Matheou , Head of Electoral Services, Civic Offices, St. Nicholas Way, Sutton SM1 1EA ☎ 020 8770 5000 ✉ martha.matheou@sutton.gov.uk

Emergency Planning: Mr Ian Kershaw , Head of Planning & Performance, Old Police Station, 6 Carshalton Road, SM1 4LE ☎ 020 8649 0684 🖷 020 8649 0606 ✉ ian.kershaw@sutton.gov.uk

Environmental / Technical Services: Ms Mary Morrissey , Strategic Director of Environment, Housing & Regeneration, 24 Denmark Road, Carshalton SM1 2JG ☎ 020 8770 6402 ✉ mary.morrissey@sutton.gov.uk

Environmental Health: Mrs Jan Gransden, Head of Environmental Control, 24 Demark Road, Carshalton SM1 2JG ☎ 020 8770 5550 🖷 020 8770 5540 ✉ jan.gransden@sutton.gov.uk

Estates, Property & Valuation: Mr Ade Adebayo, Executive Head of Asset Planning & Management, 24 Denmark Road, Carshalton SM5 2JG ☎ 020 8770 6109 🖷 020 8770 6234 ✉ ade.adebayo@sutton.gov.uk

Finance: Mr Gerald Almeroth , Strategic Director of Resources, Civic Offices, St. Nicholas Way, Sutton SM1 1EA ☎ 020 8770 5501 ✉ gerald.almeroth@sutton.gov.uk

Finance: Mr Phil Butlin , Executive Head of Finance, Civic Offices, St. Nicholas Way, Sutton SM1 1EA ☎ 020 8770 5000 🖷 020 8770 5404 ✉ phil.butlin@sutton.gov.uk

Pensions: Mr Andy Banham , Head of Pensions, Civic Offices, St. Nicholas Way, Sutton SM1 1EA ☎ 020 8770 5000 ✉ andy.banham@sutton.gov.uk

Fleet Management: Mr Matt Clubb , Head of Commissioning & Contract Performance, 24 Denmark Road, Carshalton SM5 2JG ☎ 020 8770 5000 ✉ matt.clubb@sutton.gov.uk

Grounds Maintenance: Mr Mark Dalzell , Head of Parks & Highways, 24 Denmark Road, Carshalton SM5 2JG ☎ 020 8770 4695 ✉ mark.dalzell@sutton.gov.uk

Health and Safety: Mr David Garioch , Corporate Health & Safety Manager, 24 Denmark Road, Carshalton SM1 2JG ☎ 020 8770 5070 ✉ david.garioch@surreycc.gov.uk

Highways: Mr Mark Dalzell , Head of Parks & Highways, 24 Denmark Road, Carshalton SM5 2JG ☎ 020 8770 4695 ✉ mark.dalzell@sutton.gov.uk

Home Energy Conservation: Mrs Jan Gransden, Head of Environmental Control, 24 Denmark Road, Carshalton SM1 2JG ☎ 020 8770 5550 🖷 020 8770 5540 ✉ jan.gransden@sutton.gov.uk

Licensing: Mr Richard Winch , Licensing Manager, Civic Offices, St. Nicholas Way, Sutton SM1 1EA ☎ 020 8770 5000 ✉ richard.winch@sutton.gov.uk

Lighting: Mr Steve Shew, Head of Smarter Travel Sutton, 24 Denmark Road, Carshalton SM5 2JG ☎ 020 8770 6423 ✉ steve.shew@sutton.gov.uk

Member Services: Ms Alexa Coates , Democratic Services Manager, Civic Offices, St. Nicholas Way, Sutton SM1 1EA ☎ 020 8770 5120 ✉ richard.shortman@sutton.gov.uk

Personnel / HR: Mr Dean Shoesmith , Joint Executive Head of Human Resources, Civic Offices, St. Nicholas Way, Sutton SM1 1EA ☎ 020 8545 3370 ✉ dean.shoesmith@merton.gov.uk

Planning: Ms Eleanor Purser , Executive Head of Economic Development, 24 Denmark Road, Carshalton CM5 2JG ☎ 020 8770 5000 ✉ eleanor.purser@sutton.gov.uk

Procurement: Mr Mark Brewer , Head of Procurement, Civic Offices, St. Nicholas Way, Sutton SM1 1EA ☎ 020 8770 5300 ✉ mark.brewer@sutton.gov.uk

Recycling & Waste Minimisation: Ms Josie Falco , Head of Recycling & Waste, 24 Denmark Road, Carshalton SM5 2JG ☎ 020 8770 5000 ✉ josie.falco@sutton.gov.uk

Social Services: Mr Tolis Vouyioukas , Strategic Director - People Services, Civic Offices, St. Nicholas Way, Sutton SM1 1EA ☎ 020 8770 4502 ✉ tolis.vouyiokas@sutton.gov.uk

Social Services (Adult): Mr Tolis Vouyioukas , Strategic Director - People Services, Civic Offices, St. Nicholas Way, Sutton SM1 1EA ☎ 020 8770 4502 ✉ tolis.vouyiokas@sutton.gov.uk

Social Services (Children): Mr Richard Nash , Executive Head of Children's Social Care & Safeguarding, Civic Offices, St. Nicholas Way, Sutton SM1 1EA ☎ 020 8770 4502 ✉ richard.nash@sutton.gov.uk

Social Services (Children): Mr Tolis Vouyioukas , Strategic Director - People Services, Civic Offices, St. Nicholas Way, Sutton SM1 1EA ☎ 020 8770 4502 ✉ tolis.vouyiokas@sutton.gov.uk

Public Health: Dr Nicola Lang , Director - Public Health, Civic Offices, St. Nicholas Way, Sutton SM1 1EA ✉ nicola.lang@sutton.gov.uk

Staff Training: Ms Kim Brown , Joint Head - HR & Policy Development, Civic Offices, St. Nicholas Way, Sutton SM1 1EA ☎ 020 8770 5025 ✉ kim.brown@sutton.gov.uk

Street Scene: Ms Mary Morrissey , Strategic Director of Environment, Housing & Regeneration, 24 Denmark Road, Carshalton SM1 2JG ☎ 020 8770 6402 ✉ mary.morrissey@sutton.gov.uk

Sustainable Development: Ms Mary Morrissey , Strategic Director of Environment, Housing & Regeneration, 24 Denmark Road, Carshalton SM1 2JG ☎ 020 8770 6402 ✉ mary.morrissey@sutton.gov.uk

Town Centre: Mr Martin Furtauer-Hayes , Town Centre Manager, Civic Offices, St. Nicholas Way, Sutton SM1 1EA ☎ 020 8770 5125 ✉ martin.furtauer-hayes@sutton.gov.uk

Transport Planner: Mr Steve Shew, Head of Smarter Travel Sutton, 24 Denmark Road, Carshalton SM5 2JG ☎ 020 8770 6423 ✉ steve.shew@sutton.gov.uk

Waste Collection and Disposal: Ms Josie Falco , Head of Recycling & Waste, 24 Denmark Road, Carshalton SM5 2JG ☎ 020 8770 5000 ✉ josie.falco@sutton.gov.uk

Waste Management: Ms Josie Falco , Head of Recycling & Waste, 24 Denmark Road, Carshalton SM5 2JG ☎ 020 8770 5000 ✉ josie.falco@sutton.gov.uk

COUNCILLORS

***Mayor* Sadiq**, Muhammed (LD - Wallington South)
muhammed.sadiq@sutton.gov.uk

***Deputy Mayor* Melican**, Joyce (LD - Wallington North)
joyce.melican@sutton.gov.uk

***Leader of the Council* Dombey**, Ruth (LD - Sutton North)
ruth.dombey@sutton.gov.uk

***Deputy Leader of the Council* Wales**, Simon (LD - Sutton West)
simon.wales@sutton.gov.uk

***Group Leader* Crowley**, Tim (CON - Carshalton South and Clockhouse)
timcrowley@blueyonder.co.uk

Abellan, Manuel (LD - Beddington South)
manuel.abellan@sutton.gov.uk

Ali, Pathumal (LD - Beddington North)
pathumal.ali@sutton.gov.uk

Bartolucci, David (LD - Sutton Central)
david.bartolucci@sutton.gov.uk

Bourne, Samantha (LD - Nonsuch)
samantha.bourne@sutton.gov.uk

Broadbent, Richard (LD - Nonsuch)
richard.broadbent@sutton.gov.uk

Burke, Kevin (LD - Sutton West)
kevin.burke@sutton.gov.uk

Burstow, Mary (LD - Cheam)
mary.burstow@sutton.gov.uk

Butt, Moira (CON - Carshalton South and Clockhouse)
moira.butt@sutton.gov.uk

Clifton, Richard (LD - Sutton South)
richard.clifton@sutton.gov.uk

Cook, Steve (LD - Wallington South)
steve.cook@sutton.gov.uk

Court, Margaret (LD - Wandle Valley)
mpcourt@hotmail.com

Crossby, Jean (LD - St Helier)
jean.crossby@sutton.gov.uk

Davey, Adrian (LD - Stonecot)
adrian.davey@sutton.gov.uk

Emmerson, Nick (LD - Stonecot)
nick.emmerson@sutton.gov.uk

Fivey, Trish (LD - Sutton South)
trish.fivey@sutton.gov.uk

Galligan, Vincent (LD - Sutton Central)
vincent.galligan@sutton.gov.uk

Garratt, Neil (CON - Beddington South)
neil.garratt@sutton.gov.uk

Gonzalez, Martin (LD - St Helier)
martin.gonzalez@sutton.gov.uk

Gordon, Sunita (LD - Wallington North)
sunita.gordon@sutton.gov.uk

Haldane, Amy (LD - Carshalton South and Clockhouse)
amy.haldane@sutton.gov.uk

Heron, Marlene (LD - Sutton North)
marlene.heron@sutton.gov.uk

Hicks, David (CON - Belmont)
david.hicks@sutton.gov.uk

Hookway, Arthur (LD - Worcester Park)
arthur.hookway@sutton.gov.uk

Hunt, Doug (LD - St Helier)
doug.hunt@sutton.gov.uk

Javelot, Miquel (LD - Stonecot)
miquel.javelot@sutton.gov.uk

Joyce, Edward (LD - Beddington South)
edward.joyce@sutton.gov.uk

Marston, Richard (LD - Worcester Park)
richard.marston@sutton.gov.uk

Mathys, Wendy (LD - Sutton West)
wendy.mathys@sutton.gov.uk

Mattey, Nick (IND - Beddington North)
nick.mattey@sutton.gov.uk

McCoy, Jayne (LD - Wallington South)
jayne.mccoy@sutton.gov.uk

McManus, Patrick (CON - Belmont)
patrick.mcmanus@sutton.gov.uk

Mirhashem, Ali (LD - Sutton Central)
ali.mirhashem@sutton.gov.uk

Morton, Callum (LD - The Wrythe)
callum.morton@sutton.gov.uk

Pascoe, Jane (CON - Belmont)
jane.pascoe@sutton.gov.uk

Patel, Nali (LD - The Wrythe)
nali.patel@sutton.gov.uk

Penneck, Steve (LD - Sutton North)
steve.penneck@sutton.gov.uk

Piracha, Nighat (LD - Beddington North)
nighat.piracha@sutton.gov.uk

Pollock, Hamish (LD - Carshalton Central)
hamish.pollock@sutton.gov.uk

Radford, Marian (LD - Wallington North)
marian.radford@sutton.gov.uk

Ramsey, Holly (CON - Cheam)
holly.ramsey@sutton.gov.uk

Reynolds, Jason (LD - Wandle Valley)
jason.reynolds@sutton.gov.uk

Salter, Alan (LD - Carshalton Central)
alan.salter@sutton.gov.uk

Sangster, Daniel (LD - Nonsuch)
daniel.sangster@sutton.gov.uk

Shields, Tony (CON - Sutton South)
tony.shields@sutton.gov.uk

Stears, Colin (LD - The Wrythe)
colin.stears@sutton.gov.uk

Whitehead, Jill (LD - Carshalton Central)
jill.whitehead@sutton.gov.uk

Whitham, Graham (CON - Cheam)
graham.whitham@sutton.gov.uk

Wingfield, Paul (LD - Worcester Park)
paul.wingfield@sutton.gov.uk

Zuchowska, Hanna (LD - Wandle Valley)
hanna.zuchowska@sutton.gov.uk

POLITICAL COMPOSITION

LD: 44, CON: 9, IND: 1

COMMITTEE CHAIRS

Audit: Mr David Hicks

Children, Family & Education: Ms Wendy Mathys

Housing, Economy & Business: Ms Jayne McCoy

Licensing: Ms Mary Burstow

Pensions: Ms Sunita Gordon

Planning: Mr Richard Clifton

Swale — D

Swale Borough Council, Swale House, East Street, Sittingbourne ME10 3HT
☎ 01795 417850 🖷 01795 417217 csc@swale.gov.uk
www.swale.gov.uk

FACTS AND FIGURES

Parliamentary Constituencies: Faversham & Mid Kent, Sittingbourne and Sheppey
EU Constituencies: South East
Election Frequency: Elections are by thirds

PRINCIPAL OFFICERS

Chief Executive: Mr Abdool Kara , Chief Executive, Swale House, East Street, Sittingbourne ME10 3HT ☎ 01795 417394
abdoolkara@swale.gov.uk

Senior Management: Ms Kathryn Carr , Director - Regeneration, Swale House, East Street, Sittingbourne ME10 3HT ☎ 01795 417321
kathryncarr@swale.gov.uk

Senior Management: Mr Mark Radford, Director - Corporate Services, Swale House, East Street, Sittingbourne ME10 3HT
☎ 01795 417269 🖷 01795 417217 markradford@swale.gov.uk

Architect, Building / Property Services: Mr James Freeman , Head of Development, Swale House, East Street, Sittingbourne ME10 3HT ☎ 01795 417309 🖷 01795 417217
jamesfreeman@swale.gov.uk

PR / Communications: Ms Emma Wiggins , Head of Economy & Community Services, Swale House, East Street, Sittingbourne ME10 3HT ☎ 01795 417155 emmawiggins@swale.gov.uk

Community Planning: Ms Emma Wiggins , Head of Economy & Community Services, Swale House, East Street, Sittingbourne ME10 3HT ☎ 01795 417155 emmawiggins@swale.gov.uk

Community Safety: Ms Emma Wiggins , Head of Economy & Community Services, Swale House, East Street, Sittingbourne ME10 3HT ☎ 01795 417155 emmawiggins@swale.gov.uk

Computer Management: Mr Tony Bullock , ICT Services Manager, Swale House, East Street, Sittingbourne ME10 3HT
☎ 01795 417264 🖷 01795 417141 tonybullock@swale.gov.uk

Computer Management: Mr Andrew Cole , Head of ICT Shared Services, Maidstone House, King Street, Maidstone ME15 6JQ
andrew.cole@tunbridgewells.gov.uk

Contracts: Mr Dave Thomas , Head of Commissioning & Customer Contact, Swale House, East Street, Sittingbourne ME10 3HT
☎ 01795 417263 davethomas@swale.gov.uk

Corporate Services: Mr Mark Radford, Director - Corporate Services, Swale House, East Street, Sittingbourne ME10 3HT
☎ 01795 417269 🖷 01795 417217 markradford@swale.gov.uk

Customer Service: Mrs Carol Sargeant, Customer Services Manager, Swale House, East Street, Sittingbourne ME10 3HT ☎ 01795 417055 🖷 01795 417217 🖰 carolsargeant@swale.gov.uk

Customer Service: Mr Dave Thomas , Head of Commissioning & Customer Contact, Swale House, East Street, Sittingbourne ME10 3HT ☎ 01795 417263 🖰 davethomas@swale.gov.uk

Economic Development: Mr Kieren Mansfield , Economic Development Officer, Swale House, East Street, Sittingbourne ME10 3HT ☎ 01795 417262 🖷 01795 417141 🖰 kierenmansfield@swale.gov.uk

Economic Development: Ms Emma Wiggins , Head of Economy & Community Services, Swale House, East Street, Sittingbourne ME10 3HT ☎ 01795 417155 🖰 emmawiggins@swale.gov.uk

Electoral Registration: Ms Katherine Bescoby , Democratic & Electoral Services Officer, Swale House, East Street, Sittingbourne ME10 3HT ☎ 01795 417330 🖷 01795 417217 🖰 katherinebescoby@swale.gov.uk

Emergency Planning: Ms Della Fackrell , Emergency Planning Officer, Swale House, East Street, Sittingbourne ME10 3HT ☎ 01795 417430 🖷 01795 417217 🖰 dellafackrell@swale.gov.uk

Energy Management: Mr Phil Garland , Lead Officer for the Home Energy Conservation Act, Swale House, East Street, Sittingbourne ME10 3HT ☎ 01795 417231 🖷 01795 417478 🖰 philgarland@swale.gov.uk

Energy Management: Ms Janet Hill, Cimate Change Officer, Swale House, East Street, Sittingbourne ME10 3HT ☎ 01795 417341 🖰 janethill@swale.gov.uk

Environmental Health: Mr Phil Garland , Lead Officer for the Home Energy Conservation Act, Swale House, East Street, Sittingbourne ME10 3HT ☎ 01795 417231 🖷 01795 417478 🖰 philgarland@swale.gov.uk

Estates, Property & Valuation: Mr Kent Parker, Estates Surveyor, Swale House, East Street, Sittingbourne ME10 3HT ☎ 01795 417349 🖷 01795 417217 🖰 kentparker@swale.gov.uk

Events Manager: Ms Emma Wiggins , Head of Economy & Community Services, Swale House, East Street, Sittingbourne ME10 3HT ☎ 01795 417155 🖰 emmawiggins@swale.gov.uk

Facilities: Mrs Anne Adams , Head of Property Services, Swale House, East Street, Sittingbourne ME10 3HT ☎ 01795 417311 🖰 anneadams@swale.gov.uk

Finance: Mr Nick Vickers , Head of Finance & S151 Officer, Swale House, East Street, Sittingbourne ME10 3HT ☎ 01795 417396 🖰 nickvickers@swale.gov.uk

Grounds Maintenance: Mr Graeme Tuff, Landscape Officer, Swale House, East Street, Sittingbourne ME10 3HT ☎ 01795 417127 🖰 graemetuff@swale.gov.uk

Health and Safety: Ms Emma Larkins , Health & Safety & Risk Officer, Swale House, East Street, Sittingbourne ME10 3HT ☎ 01795 417078 🖷 01794 417141

Home Energy Conservation: Mr Phil Garland , Lead Officer for the Home Energy Conservation Act, Swale House, East Street, Sittingbourne ME10 3HT ☎ 01795 417231 🖷 01795 417478 🖰 philgarland@swale.gov.uk

Housing: Ms Amber Christou , Head of Resident Services, Swale House, East Street, Sittingbourne ME10 3HT ☎ 01795 417237 🖷 01795 417141 🖰 amberchristou@swale.gov.uk

Local Area Agreement: Ms Gill Harris , Spatial Planning Manager, Swale House, East Street, Sittingbourne ME10 3HT ☎ 01795 417118 🖰 gillharris@swale.gov.uk

Legal: Mr John Scarborough , Head of Legal Department, Swale House, East Street, Sittingbourne ME10 3HT ☎ 01975 417527 🖰 johnscarborough@swale.gov.uk

Leisure and Cultural Services: Ms Emma Wiggins , Head of Economy & Community Services, Swale House, East Street, Sittingbourne ME10 3HT ☎ 01795 417155 🖰 emmawiggins@swale.gov.uk

Licensing: Ms Angela Seaward , Licensing Officer, Swale House, East Street, Sittingbourne ME10 3HT ☎ 01795 417364 🖰 angelaseaward@swale.gov.uk

Member Services: Ms Katherine Bescoby, Democratic & Electoral Services Officer, Swale House, East Street, Sittingbourne ME10 3HT ☎ 01795 417330 🖷 01795 417217 🖰 katherinebescoby@swale.gov.uk

Personnel / HR: Ms Dena Smart , Head of HR Shared Services, Swale House, East Street, Sittingbourne ME10 3HT ☎ 01795 417391 🖰 denasmart@swale.gov.uk

Planning: Mr James Freeman , Head of Development, Swale House, East Street, Sittingbourne ME10 3HT ☎ 01795 417309 🖷 01795 417217 🖰 jamesfreeman@swale.gov.uk

Procurement: Mr Dave Thomas , Head of Commissioning & Customer Contact, Swale House, East Street, Sittingbourne ME10 3HT ☎ 01795 417263 🖰 davethomas@swale.gov.uk

Recycling & Waste Minimisation: Mr Dave Thomas , Head of Commissioning & Customer Contact, Swale House, East Street, Sittingbourne ME10 3HT ☎ 01795 417263 🖰 davethomas@swale.gov.uk

Recycling & Waste Minimisation: Mr Alan Turner, Cleansing Services Manager, Swale House, East Street, Sittingbourne ME10 3HT ☎ 01795 417285 🖷 01795 417418 🖰 alanturner@swale.gov.uk

Regeneration: Ms Kathryn Carr , Director - Regeneration, Swale House, East Street, Sittingbourne ME10 3HT ☎ 01795 417321 🖰 kathryncarr@swale.gov.uk

SWALE

Regeneration: Ms Emma Wiggins , Head of Economy & Community Services, Swale House, East Street, Sittingbourne ME10 3HT ☎ 01795 417155 ✉ emmawiggins@swale.gov.uk

Staff Training: Mrs Catherine Harrison , Training & Development Manager, Swale House, East Street, Sittingbourne ME10 3HT ☎ 01795 417381 ✉ catherineharrison@swale.gov.uk

Tourism: Ms Lyn Newton, Economy & Community Services Manager, Swale House, East Street, Sittingbourne ME10 3HT ☎ 01795 417420 🖷 01795 417477 ✉ lynnewton@swale.gov.uk

Tourism: Ms Emma Wiggins , Head of Economic Development & Cultural Services, Swale House, East Street, Sittingbourne ME10 3HT ☎ 01795 417396 ✉ emmawiggins@swale.gov.uk

Total Place: Mr Abdool Kara , Chief Executive, Swale House, East Street, Sittingbourne ME10 3HT ☎ 01795 417394 ✉ abdoolkara@swale.gov.uk

Waste Collection and Disposal: Mr Alan Turner, Cleansing Services Manager, Swale House, East Street, Sittingbourne ME10 3HT ☎ 01795 417285 🖷 01795 417418 ✉ alanturner@swale.gov.uk

Waste Management: Mr Dave Thomas , Head of Commissioning & Customer Contact, Swale House, East Street, Sittingbourne ME10 3HT ☎ 01795 417263 ✉ davethomas@swale.gov.uk

Waste Management: Mr Alan Turner, Cleansing Services Manager, Swale House, East Street, Sittingbourne ME10 3HT ☎ 01795 417285 🖷 01795 417418 ✉ alanturner@swale.gov.uk

Children's Play Areas: Mr Graeme Tuff, Landscape Officer, Swale House, East Street, Sittingbourne ME10 3HT ☎ 01795 417127 ✉ graemetuff@swale.gov.uk

COUNCILLORS

***Mayor* Walker**, Anita (CON - Abbey)
anitajwalker@yahoo.co.uk

***Deputy Mayor* Ingham**, Lesley (CON - Sheppey East)
lesleyingham57@yahoo.co.uk

***Leader of the Council* Bowles**, Andrew (CON - Boughton & Courtenay)
leader@swale.gov.uk

***Deputy Leader of the Council* Lewin**, Gerald (CON - Hartlip, Newington & Upchurch)
cllrlewin@swale.gov.uk

***Group Leader* Henderson**, Mike (IND - Priory)
mikeshenderson@outlook.com

Aldridge, Sarah (CON - Roman)
sarahaldridge@swale.gov.uk

Baldock, Mike (UKIP - Borden & Grove Park)
mikebaldock@swale.gov.uk

Beart, Cameron (CON - Queenborough & Halfway)
cameronbeart@swale.gov.uk

Bobbin, George (CON - Boughton & Courtenay)
george.bobbin@btinternet.com

Bonney, Monique (IND - West Downs)
montybon1@aol.com

Booth, Andy (CON - Minster Cliffs)
andybooth@swale.gov.uk

Booth, Tina (CON - Sheppey Central)
tinabooth@swale.gov.uk

Bowen, Lloyd (CON - Teynham & Lynsted)
lloydbowen@swale.gov.uk

Clark, Roger (CON - Milton Regis)
clark.miltonregis@gmail.com

Coleman, Katy (UKIP - Milton Regis)
katycolman@swale.gov.uk

Conway, Derek (CON - Woodstock)
derekconway@swale.gov.uk

Cosgrove, Mike (CON - St. Ann's)
cllrcosgrove@swale.gov.uk

Crowther, Adrian (UKIP - Minster Cliffs)
adrian.crowther@kent.gov.uk

Darby, Richard (UKIP - Queenborough & Halfway)
rdarbypax@aol.com

Dendor, Mike (CON - Kemsley)
mikedendor@swale.gov.uk

Dewar-Whalley, Duncan (CON - Bobbing, Iwade & Lower Halstow)
duncandewar-whalley@swale.gov.uk

Ellen, Mark (LAB - Sheerness)
cllr.markellen@yahoo.co.uk

Fleming, Paul (UKIP - Roman)
paulfleming104@googlemail.com

Galvin, Mick (UKIP - Sheerness)
mickgalvin@swale.gov.uk

Garrad, June (UKIP - Sheppey Central)
jvgarrad@aol.com

Gent, Sue (CON - Kemsley)
gentmiss@blueyonder.co.uk

Hall, James (UKIP - Murston)
jameshall@swale.gov.uk

Hampshire, Nicholas (CON - Borden & Grove Park)
nicholashampshire@hotmail.com

Harrison, Angela (LAB - Sheerness)
angelaharrison@swale.gov.uk

Horton, Alan (CON - Homewood)
alanhorton@swale.gov.uk

Hunt, James (CON - The Meads)
jameshunt@swale.gov.uk

Ingleton, Ken (CON - Sheppey Central)
kjingleton@aol.com

Kay, Nigel (CON - St. Ann's)
nigelkay@swale.gov.uk

Koffie-Williams, Samuel (CON - Murston)
samuelkwilliams@swale.gov.uk

Marchington, Peter (CON - Queenborough & Halfway)
petermarchington@hotmail.co.uk

Mulhern, Bryan (CON - Abbey)
bryanmulhern@swale.gov.uk

Nissanga, Padmini (UKIP - Sheppey East)
mininissanga@swale.gov.uk

Prescott, Colin (CON - East Downs)
colinprescott@swale.gov.uk

Pugh, Ken (CON - Minster Cliffs)
kenpugh@uwclub.net

Samuel, George (CON - Woodstock)
georgesamuel@swale.gov.uk

Simmons, David (CON - Watling)
davidsimmons@swale.gov.uk

Stokes, Ben (CON - Bobbing, Iwade & Lower Halstow)
benstokes@swale.gov.uk

Truelove, Roger (LAB - Homewood)
rtruelove12@gmail.com

Whelan, Ghlin (LAB - Chalkwell)
ghlinwhelan@gmail.com

Whiting, Mike (CON - Teynham & Lynsted)
mikewhiting@swale.gov.uk

Wilcox, Ted (CON - Watling)
tedwilcox@swale.gov.uk

Wright, John (CON - Hartlip, Newington & Upchurch)
johnwright@swale.gov.uk

POLITICAL COMPOSITION
CON: 32, UKIP: 9, LAB: 4, IND: 2

COMMITTEE CHAIRS

Audit: Mr Nicholas Hampshire

Licensing: Ms Lesley Ingham

Planning: Mr Bryan Mulhern

Swansea, City of — W

City and County of Swansea Council, Civic Centre, Oystermouth Road, Swansea SA1 3SN
☎ 01792 636000 🖷 01792 636340 ✉ chiefexecutive@swansea.gov.uk
🖳 www.swansea.gov.uk

FACTS AND FIGURES
Parliamentary Constituencies: Gower, Swansea East, Swansea West
EU Constituencies: Wales
Election Frequency: Elections are of whole council

PRINCIPAL OFFICERS

Chief Executive: Mr Jack Straw , Chief Executive, The Guildhall, Swansea SA1 4PE ☎ 01792 637500
✉ jack.straw@swansea.gov.uk

Senior Management: Mr Mike Hawes , Head - Financial Services, Civic Centre, Oystermouth Road, Swansea SA1 3SN
☎ 01792 636423 ✉ mike.hawes@swansea.gov.uk

Senior Management: Mr Phil Roberts, Director - Place, Civic Centre, Oystermouth Road, Swansea SA1 3SN
☎ 01792 637525 🖷 01792 636700
✉ phil.roberts@swansea.gov.uk

Senior Management: Mr Chris Sivers , Director - People, The Guildhall, Swansea SA1 4PE ☎ 01792 637521
✉ chris.sivers@swansea.gov.uk

Senior Management: Mr Dean Taylor , Director - Corporate Services, The Guildhall, Swansea SA1 4PE ☎ 01792 637521
✉ dean.taylor@swansea.gov.uk

Architect, Building / Property Services: Mr Martin Nicholls, Chief Operating Officer, Heol y gors, Cwmbwrla, Swansea SA5 8LD ☎ 01792 511002 🖷 01792 511068
✉ martin.nicholls@swansea.gov.uk

Building Control: Mr Peter Richards, Divisional Officer, Civic Centre, Oystermouth Road, Swansea SA1 3SN
☎ 01792 635622 🖷 01792 648079
✉ peter.richards@swansea.gov.uk

Catering Services: Ms Anne-Marie Evans , Catering & Cleaning Facilities Manager, Civic Centre, Oystermouth Road, Swansea SA1 3SN ☎ 01792 636097
✉ anne.marie.evans@swansea.gov.uk

Children / Youth Services: Mr David Howes , Head of Children & Family Services, Oldway Centre, High Street, Swansea SA1 1LT ☎ 01792 636248 🖷 01792 637221
✉ david.howes@swansea.gov.uk

Civil Registration: Mr Noel Evans , Registration & Bereavement Services Manager, Civic Centre, Oystermouth Road, Swansea SA1 3SN ☎ 01792 636275
✉ noel.evans@swansea.gov.uk

PR / Communications: Mr Lee Wenham, Head of Communications, Marketing, Overview & Scrutiny, Civic Centre, Oystermouth Road, Swansea SA1 3SN ☎ 01792 637158
🖷 01792 636038 ✉ lee.wenham@swansea.gov.uk

Community Safety: Mr Jeff Davison, Community Safety Co-ordinator, Cockett Police Station, John Street, Cockett, Swansea SA2 0FR ☎ 01792 456999 Extn 52757
🖷 01792 648079 ✉ jeff.davison@swansea.gov.uk

Computer Management: Ms Sarah Caulkin , Head of Information & Business Change, Civic Centre, Oystermouth Road, Swansea SA1 3SN ☎ 01792 636849
✉ sarah.caulkin@swansea.gov.uk

Consumer Protection and Trading Standards: Mr Lee Morgan, Head of Housing & Public Protection, Civic Centre, Oystermouth Road, Swansea SA1 3SN ☎ 01792 635017
✉ lee.morgan@swansea.gov.uk

SWANSEA, CITY OF

Direct Labour: Mr Martin Nicholls, Chief Operating Officer, Heol y gors, Cwmbwrla, Swansea SA5 8LD ☎ 01792 511002 🖷 01792 511068 🖱 martin.nicholls@swansea.gov.uk

Economic Development: Mr Phillip Holmes, Head of Economic Regeneration & Planning, Civic Centre, Oystermouth Road, Swansea SA1 3SN ☎ 01792 636979 🖷 01792 636700 🖱 phillip.holmes@swansea.gov.uk

Education: Mr Lindsay Harvey , Chief Education Officer, Civic Centre, Oystermouth Road, Swansea SA1 3SN ☎ 01792 637166 🖱 lindsay.harvey@swansea.gov.uk

Education: Mr Brian Roles , Head of Planning & Resources, Oldway Centre, 36 Orchard Street, Swansea SA1 5AQ ☎ 01792 636357 🖱 brian.roles@swansea.gov.uk

Electoral Registration: Mr Patrick Arran , Head of Legal, Democratic Services & Procurement, Civic Centre, Oystermouth Road, Swansea SA1 3SN ☎ 01792 636699 🖷 01792 637261 🖱 patrick.arran@swansea.gov.uk

Energy Management: Mr John Llewellyn , Energy Manager, Civic Centre, Oystermouth Road, Swansea SA1 3SN ☎ 01792 636359 🖱 john.llewellyn@swansea.gov.uk

Estates, Property & Valuation: Mr Martin Nicholls, Chief Operating Officer, Heol y gors, Cwmbwrla, Swansea SA5 8LD ☎ 01792 511002 🖷 01792 511068 🖱 martin.nicholls@swansea.gov.uk

European Liaison: Mr Paul Relf , European Officer, Civic Centre, Oystermouth Road, Swansea SA1 3SN ☎ 01792 636858 🖱 paul.relf@swansea.gov.uk

Events Manager: Mr Nigel Jones, Special Events Manager, Penllergaer Offices, Swansea SA4 9GJ ☎ 01792 635413 🖷 01792 635447 🖱 nigel.jones@swansea.gov.uk

Facilities: Ms Rebecca Jones , Facilities Manager, Civic Centre, Oystermouth Road, Swansea SA1 3SN ☎ 01792 636030 🖷 01792 637161 🖱 rebecca.jones@swansea.gov.uk

Finance: Mr Mike Hawes , Head - Financial Services, Civic Centre, Oystermouth Road, Swansea SA1 3SN ☎ 01792 636423 🖱 mike.hawes@swansea.gov.uk

Treasury: Mr Jeffrey Dong , Chief Treasury Officer, Civic Centre, Oystermouth Road, Swansea SA1 3SN ☎ 01792 636934 🖱 jeffrey.dong@swansea.gov.uk

Pensions: Ms Lynne Miller , Senior Pensions Officer, Civic Centre, Oystermouth Road, Swansea SA1 3SN ☎ 01792 636460 🖱 lynne.miller@swansea.gov.uk

Fleet Management: Mr Mark Barrow , Fleet Manager, The Central Transport Unit, Morfa Road, Swansea SA1 2EN ☎ 01792 511909 🖱 mark.barrow@swansea.gov.uk

Health and Safety: Mr Craig Gimblett , Health, Safety & Wellbeing Manager, Guildhall, Swansea SA1 4PE ☎ 01792 636620 🖱 craig.gimblett@swansea.gov.uk

Highways: Mr Chris Howell , Head of Waste Management, City and County of Swansea, Environment Department, Clydach Depot, Clydach SA1 5BJ ☎ 01792 761759 🖱 chris.howell@swansea.gov.uk

Housing: Mr Lee Morgan , Head of Housing & Public Protection, Civic Centre, Oystermouth Road, Swansea SA1 3SN ☎ 01792 635017 🖱 lee.morgan@swansea.gov.uk

Legal: Mr Patrick Arran , Head of Legal, Democratic Services & Procurement, Civic Centre, Oystermouth Road, Swansea SA1 3SN ☎ 01792 636699 🖷 01792 637261 🖱 patrick.arran@swansea.gov.uk

Leisure and Cultural Services: Mr Steve Hardman , Library & Service Manager, Civic Centre, Oystermouth Road, Swansea SA1 3SN ☎ 01792 636610 🖱 steve.hardman@swansea.gov.uk

Leisure and Cultural Services: Ms Tracey McNulty , Head of Cultural Services, Guildhall, Swansea SA1 4PE ☎ 01792 635403 🖷 01792 635408 🖱 tracey.mcnulty@swansea.gov.uk

Licensing: Mrs Lynda Williams, Divisional Officer, Civic Centre, Oystermouth Road, Swansea SA1 3SN ☎ 01792 635600 🖷 01792 648079 🖱 lynda.williams@swansea.gov.uk

Lifelong Learning: Mr Mike Hughes, Lifelong Learning Services Manager, Dynevor Information Centre, Dynevor Place, Swansea SA1 3ET ☎ 01792 648081 🖱 mike.hughes@swansea.gov.uk

Lighting: Mr Jonathan Hurley, Principal Lighting Manager of Design, Civic Centre, Oystermouth Road, Swansea SA1 3SN ☎ 01792 841666 🖱 jonathan.hurley@swansea.gov.uk

Lottery Funding, Charity and Voluntary: Mr Spencer Martin, Voluntary Sector Relationship Co-ordinator, Civic Centre, Oystermouth Road, Swansea SA1 3SN ☎ 01792 636734 🖷 01792 637206 🖱 spencer.martin@swansea.gov.uk

Member Services: Mr Patrick Arran , Head of Legal, Democratic Services & Procurement, Civic Centre, Oystermouth Road, Swansea SA1 3SN ☎ 01792 636699 🖷 01792 637261 🖰 patrick.arran@swansea.gov.uk

Member Services: Mr Huw Evans , Democratic Services & Complaints Manager, Civic Centre, Oystermouth Road, Swansea SA1 3SN ☎ 01792 637347 🖰 huw.evans@swansea.gov.uk

Parking: Mr Gary Newman , Parking Manager, Guildhall, Swansea SA1 3SN ☎ 01792 635987 🖰 gary.newman@swansea.gov.uk

Personnel / HR: Mr Steve Rees , Head of Human Resources, Guildhall, Swansea SA1 4PE ☎ 01792 636067 🖰 steve.rees@swansea.gov.uk

Planning: Mr Phillip Holmes, Head of Economic Regeneration & Planning, Civic Centre, Oystermouth Road, Swansea SA1 3SN ☎ 01792 636979 🖷 01792 636700 🖰 phillip.holmes@swansea.gov.uk

Procurement: Mr Andrew Williams , Principal Procurement Officer, Civic Centre, Oystermouth Road, Swansea SA1 3SN ☎ 01792 637322 🖰 andrew.williams@swansea.gov.uk

Public Libraries: Mr Steve Hardman , Library & Service Manager, Civic Centre, Oystermouth Road, Swansea SA1 3SN ☎ 01792 636610 🖰 steve.hardman@swansea.gov.uk

Recycling & Waste Minimisation: Ms Trish Flint , Recycling Leader, Pipehouse Wharf, Off Morta Road, Swansea SA1 2EN ☎ 01792 511924 🖷 01792 648079 🖰 trish.flint@swansea.gov.uk

Regeneration: Mr Phil Roberts, Director - Place, Civic Centre, Oystermouth Road, Swansea SA1 3SN ☎ 01792 637525 🖷 01792 636700 🖰 phil.roberts@swansea.gov.uk

Road Safety: Mr Mark Thomas, Team Leader of Traffic Management, Penllergaer Offices, Swansea SA4 9GJ ☎ 01792 636233 🖷 01792 652712 🖰 mark.thomas@swansea.gov.uk

Social Services: Ms Deborah Driffield , Chief Social Services Officer, Oldway Centre, High Street, Swansea SA1 1LT ☎ 01792 636245 🖰 deborah.driffield@swansea.gov.uk

Social Services (Adult): Ms Alex Williams , Head of Adult Services, Civic Centre, Oystermouth Road, Swansea SA1 3SN ☎ 01792 636245 🖰 alex.williams2@swansea.gov.uk

Social Services (Children): Ms Julie Thomas , Head of Child & Family Services, Civic Centre, Oystermouth Road, Swansea SA1 3SN ☎ 01792 636248 🖷 01792 637221 🖰 julie.thomas5@swansea.gov.uk

Families: Ms Julie Thomas , Head of Child & Family Services, Civic Centre, Oystermouth Road, Swansea SA1 3SN ☎ 01792 636248 🖷 01792 637221 🖰 julie.thomas5@swansea.gov.uk

Staff Training: Mr Khan Prince , Senior Organisational Development Officer, Guildhall, Swansea SA1 4PE ☎ 01792 636742 🖰 khan.prince@swansea.gov.uk

Street Scene: Mr Chris Howell , Head of Waste Management, City and County of Swansea, Environment Department, Clydach Depot, Clydach SA1 5BJ ☎ 01792 761759 🖰 chris.howell@swansea.gov.uk

Sustainable Development: Ms Tanya Nash, Sustainable Development Manager, Civic Centre, Oystermouth Road, Swansea SA1 3SN ☎ 01792 635198 🖰 tanya.nash@swansea.gov.uk

Tourism: Mrs Frances Jenkins, Strategic Manager, Tourism, Marketing & Events, Penllergaer Offices, Swansea SA4 9GJ ☎ 01792 635201 🖷 01792 635216 🖰 frances.jenkins@swansea.gov.uk

Town Centre: Ms Lisa Wells , City Centre Manager, Civic Centre, Oystermouth Road, Swansea SA1 3SN ☎ 01792 476370 🖷 01792 476368 🖰 lisa.wells@swansea.gov.uk

Traffic Management: Mr Mark Thomas, Team Leader of Traffic Management, Penllergaer Offices, Swansea SA4 9GJ ☎ 01792 636233 🖷 01792 652712 🖰 mark.thomas@swansea.gov.uk

Transport: Mr Mark Thomas, Team Leader of Traffic Management, Penllergaer Offices, Swansea SA4 9GJ ☎ 01792 636233 🖷 01792 652712 🖰 mark.thomas@swansea.gov.uk

Waste Collection and Disposal: Mr Ian Whettleton , Divisional Officer of Waste Management, Guildhall, Swansea SA1 4PE ☎ 01792 635600 🖷 01792 648079 🖰 ian.whettleton@swansea.gov.uk

Waste Management: Mr Ian Whettleton , Divisional Officer of Waste Management, Guildhall, Swansea SA1 4PE ☎ 01792 635600 🖷 01792 648079 🖰 ian.whettleton@swansea.gov.uk

COUNCILLORS

***Leader of the Council* Stewart**, Rob (LAB - Morriston) rob.stewart@swansea.gov.uk

***Deputy Leader of the Council* Richards**, Christine (LAB - Lower Loughor) christine.richards@swansea.gov.uk

Anderson, Cyril (LAB - Townhill) cllr.cyril.anderson@swansea.gov.uk

SWANSEA, CITY OF

Bayliss, John (LAB - Uplands)
john.bayliss@swansea.gov.uk

Black, Peter (LD - Cwmbwrla)
peter.black@swansea.gov.uk

Burtonshaw, June (LAB - Penderry)

Child, Mark (LAB - West Cross)
mark.child@swansea.gov.uk

Clay, Bob (LAB - Llansamlet)
bob.clay@swansea.gov.uk

Clay, Uta (LAB - Llansamlet)
uta.clay@swansea.gov.uk

Colburn, Anthony (CON - Oystermouth)
tony.colburn@swansea.gov.uk

Cole, David (LAB - Penyrheol)
david.cole@swansea.gov.uk

Cook, Ann (LAB - Cockett)
ann.cook@swansea.gov.uk

Crouch, Sybil (LAB - Castle)
sybil.crouch@swansea.gov.uk

Curtice, Jan (LAB - Penyrheol)
jan.curtice@swansea.gov.uk

Davies, Nick (LAB - Uplands)
nick.davies2@swansea.gov.uk

Day, Mike (LD - Sketty)
mike.day@swansea.gov.uk

Downing, Philip (LAB - Pontarddulais)
philip.downing@swansea.gov.uk

Doyle, Ryland (LAB - Llansamlet)
ryland.doyle@swansea.gov.uk

Evans, William (LAB - Kingsbridge)
william.evans@swansea.gov.uk

Evans, Ceri (LAB - Morriston)
cllr.ceri.evans@swansea.gov.uk

Evans, Mandy (LAB - Bonymaen)
mandy.evans2@swansea.gov.uk

Fitzgerald, Wendy (IND - Penllergaer)
wendy.fitzgerald@swansea.gov.uk

Francis-Davies, Robert (LAB - Morriston)
robert.davies@swansea.gov.uk

Gordon, Fiona (LAB - Castle)
fiona.gordon@swansea.gov.uk

Hale, Joe (LAB - St Thomas)
joe.hale@swansea.gov.uk

Harris, Jane (LAB - Pontarddulais)
jane.harris@swansea.gov.uk

Hennegan, Terry (LAB - Penderry)
terry.hennegan@swansea.gov.uk

Holley, Chris (LD - Cwmbwrla)
chris.holley@swansea.gov.uk

Hood-Williams, Paxton (CON - Fairwood)
paxton.hood-williams@swansea.gov.uk

Hopkins, Beverley (LAB - Landore)
beverley.hopkins@swansea.gov.uk

Hopkins, David (LAB - Townhill)
david.hopkins@swansea.gov.uk

James, Lynda (IND - Pennard)
lynda.james@swansea.gov.uk

Jardine, Yvonne (LAB - Morriston)
yvonne.jardine@swansea.gov.uk

Jones, Mary (LD - Killay North)
mary.jones@swansea.gov.uk

Jones, Susan (IND - Gowerton)
susan.jones3@swansea.gov.uk

Jones, Andrew (LAB - Cockett)
andrew.jones@swansea.gov.uk

Jones, Jeffrey (LD - Killay South)
jeff.w.jones@swansea.gov.uk

King, Elliott (LAB - Cockett)
cllr.elliott.king@swansea.gov.uk

Kirchner, Erika (LAB - Castle)
erika.kirchner@swansea.gov.uk

Lewis, Richard (LD - Gower)
richard.lewis@swansea.gov.uk

Lewis, David (LAB - Gorseinon)
david.lewis2@swansea.gov.uk

Lewis, Andrea (LAB - Morriston)
andrea.s.lewis@swansea.gov.uk

Lloyd, Clive (LAB - St Thomas)
clive.lloyd@swansea.gov.uk

Lloyd, Paul (LAB - Bonymaen)
paul.lloyd@swansea.gov.uk

Marsh, Keith (IND - Bishopston)
keith.marsh@swansea.gov.uk

Matthews, Penny (LAB - Llansamlet)
penny.matthews@swansea.gov.uk

May, Peter (IND - Uplands)
cllr.peter.may@swansea.gov.uk

Meara, Paul (LD - Sketty)
paul.meara@swansea.gov.uk

Morris, Hazel (LAB - Penderry)
hazel.morris@swansea.gov.uk

Newbury, John (LD - Dunvant)
john.newbury@swansea.gov.uk

Owen, Byron (LAB - Mynyddbach)
byron.g.owen@swansea.gov.uk

Owens, Geraint (LAB - Cockett)
geraint.owens@swansea.gov.uk

Phillips, David (LAB - Castle)
david.philips@swansea.gov.uk

Philpott, Cheryl (LD - Sketty)
cheryl.philpott@swansea.gov.uk

Raynor, Jennifer (LAB - Dunvant)
jennifer.raynor@swansea.gov.uk

Rees, Huw (LD - Sketty)
huw.rees2@swansea.gov.uk

Richard, Ioan (O - Mawr)
ioan.richard@swansea.gov.uk

Smith, Robert (LAB - Upper Loughor)
robert.smith@swansea.gov.uk

Smith, Paulette (LAB - Clydach)
paulette.smith@swansea.gov.uk

Stanton, June (LD - Sketty)
june.stanton@swansea.gov.uk

Sullivan, Gareth (IND - Llangyfelach)
gareth.sullivan@swansea.gov.uk

Tanner, Gloria (LAB - Mynyddbach)
gloria.tanner@swansea.gov.uk

Thomas, Mark (LAB - Penclawdd)
mark.thomas2@swansea.gov.uk

Thomas, Des (LAB - West Cross)
des.thomas@swansea.gov.uk

Thomas, Miles (CON - Newton)
miles.thomas2@swansea.gov.uk

Thomas, Ceinwen (LAB - Mynyddbach)
ceinwen.thomas@swansea.gov.uk

Thomas, Graham (LD - Cwmbwrla)
graham.thomas@swansea.gov.uk

Tyler-Lloyd, Linda (CON - Mayals)
linda.tyler-lloyd@swansea.gov.uk

Walker, Gordon (INDNA - Clydach)
gordon.walker@swansea.gov.uk

Walton, Lesley (LAB - Townhill)
lesley.walton@swansea.gov.uk

White, Mike (LAB - Landore)
mike.white@swansea.gov.uk

Woollard, Neil (LAB - Uplands)
cllr.neil.woollard@swansea.gov.uk

POLITICAL COMPOSITION

LAB: 48, LD: 12, IND: 6, CON: 4, INDNA: 1, O: 1

COMMITTEE CHAIRS

Licensing: Ms Penny Matthews

Planning: Mr Paul Lloyd

Swindon U

Swindon Borough Council, Civic Offices, Euclid Street, Swindon SN1 2JH
☎ 01793 463000 🖷 01793 463930 🖱 swindon-council@swindon.gov.uk
💻 www.swindon.gov.uk

FACTS AND FIGURES

EU Constituencies: South West

Election Frequency: Elections are by thirds

PRINCIPAL OFFICERS

Chief Executive: Mr Gavin Jones, Chief Executive, Civic Offices, Euclid Street, Swindon SN1 2JH ☎ 01793 463000
🖱 gjones@swindon.gov.uk

Senior Management: Mr Bernie Brannan, Board Director of Service Delivery, Wat Tyler House West, Beckhampton Street, Swindon SN1 2JG ☎ 01793 464376 🖷 01793 463306
🖱 bbrannan@swindon.gov.uk

Senior Management: Mr John Gilbert , Board Director of Commissioning, Wat Tyler House West, Beckhampton Street, Swindon SN1 2JG ☎ 01793 463068 🖱 jgilbert@swindon.gov.uk

Senior Management: Mr Stuart McKellar, Board Director of Resources, Wat Tyler House West, Beckhampton Street, Swindon SN1 2JG ☎ 01793 463300
🖱 smckellar@swindon.gov.uk

Access Officer / Social Services (Disability): Ms Sue Wald, Head of Commissioning, Children & Adults, Sandford House, Sandford Street, Swindon SN1 1QH ☎ 01793 463169
🖱 swald@swindon.gov.uk

Architect, Building / Property Services: Mr Nic Newland , Head of Design & Architecture, Wat Tyler West House, Beckhampton Street, Swindon SN1 1JG ☎ 01793 463620
🖱 nnewland@swindon.gov.uk

Architect, Building / Property Services: Mr Rob Richards , Head of Property Assets, Wat Tyler House West, Beckhampton Street, Swindon SN1 2JG ☎ 01793 463520
🖱 rrichards@swindon.gov.uk

Civil Registration: Ms Mamie Beasant , Superintendent Registrar, Civic Offices, Euclid Street, Swindon SN1 2JH
☎ 01793 522738
🖱 mbeasant@swindon.gov.uk

PR / Communications: Mr Galvin Calthrop, Head of Communications & Insight, Civic Offices, Euclid Street, Swindon SN1 2JH ☎ 01793 463176 🖱 gcalthrop@swindon.gov.uk

PR / Communications: Mrs Sue Mendham , Head of Infrastructure Assets, Wat Tyler House West, Beckhampton Street, Swindon SN1 1JG ☎ 01793 463000
🖱 smendham@swindon.gov.uk

Computer Management: Mr Glyn Peach , Head of Information & Technology Strategy, Wat Tyler House West, 1st Floor, Beckhampton Street, Swindon SN1 2JG
☎ 01793 465848
🖱 gpeach@swindon.gov.uk

Corporate Services: Ms Kirsty Cole , Head of Corporate Finance, Wat Tyler House West, Beckhampton Street, Swindon SN1 2JG
☎ 01793 464610 🖱 kcole@swindon.gov.uk

Corporate Services: Mrs Karen McMahon , Head of Customer & Business Services, Wat Tyler West, Beckhampton Street, Swindon SN1 1JG ☎ 01793 464935 ✉ kmcmahon@swindon.gov.uk

Direct Labour: Mr Bernie Brannan, Board Director of Service Delivery, Wat Tyler House West, Beckhampton Street, Swindon SN1 2JG ☎ 01793 464376 📠 01793 463306 ✉ bbrannan@swindon.gov.uk

Economic Development: Mr Paddy Bradley , Head of Economy & Skills, Sandford House, Sandford Street, Swindon SN1 1QH ☎ 01793 463201 ✉ pbradley@swindon.gov.uk

Education: Mr Steve Haley , Lead Finance Manager of Education & Innovation, Wat Tyler House West, Beckhampton Street, Swindon SN1 2LG ☎ 01793 465794 ✉ shaley@swindon.gov.uk

Electoral Registration: Mr Stephen Taylor, Director of Law & Democratic Services, Civic Offices, Euclid Street, Swindon SN1 2JH ☎ 01793 463012 ✉ staylor@swindon.gov.uk

Facilities: Ms Marion Ward , Facilities Manager, Clarence House, Euclid Street, Swindon SN1 2JH ☎ 01793 469952 ✉ mward@swindon.gov.uk

Finance: Mr Adrian Arnold , Lead Finance Manager of General Housing & Place, Wat Tyler House West, Beckhampton Street, Swindon SN1 2JG ☎ 01793 466217 ✉ aarnold@swindon.gov.uk

Finance: Mr Paul Smith , Lead Finance Manager of Treasury & Growth, Wat Tyler House West, Beckhampton Street, Swindon SN1 2JG ☎ 01793 463976 ✉ psmith@swindon.gov.uk

Finance: Mr Andy Stevens , Head of Revenues & Benefits, Civic Offices, Euclid Street, Swindon SN1 2JH ☎ 01793 464661 ✉ astevens@swindon.gov.uk

Finance: Mr Chris Wilson , Lead Finance Manager of Helping People & Safety, Wat Tyler House West, Beckhampton Street, Swindon SN1 2JG ☎ 01793 463072 ✉ cwilson@swindon.gov.uk

Fleet Management: Mr Steve Kemble , Fleet Manager, Waterside, Derby Close, Swindon SN1 1TZ ☎ 01793 464187 ✉ skemble@swindon.gov.uk

Health and Safety: Mrs Karen McMahon , Head of Customer & Business Services, Wat Tyler West, Beckhampton Street, Swindon SN1 1JG ☎ 01793 464935 ✉ kmcmahon@swindon.gov.uk

Highways: Mr Gwilliam Lloyd , Head of Highway Maintenance, Wat Tyler West, Beckhampton Street, Swindon SN1 2JG ☎ 01793 463541 ✉ glloyd@swindon.gov.uk

Housing: Mr Mike Ash , SD Lead of Housing Services, ☎ 01793 466146 ✉ mash@swindon.gov.uk

Housing Maintenance: Mr Gerry O'Connor , Head of Housing Property, Wat Tyler House, Beckhampton Street, Swindon SN2 2JG ☎ 01796 463452 ✉ go'connor@swindon.gov.uk

Legal: Mr Stephen Taylor, Director of Law & Democratic Services, Civic Offices, Euclid Street, Swindon SN1 2JH ☎ 01793 463012 ✉ staylor@swindon.gov.uk

Leisure and Cultural Services: Mr Ian Bickerton , Lead of Leisure, Libraries & Culture, Sandford House, Swindon SN1 2JH ☎ 01793 465724 ✉ ibickerton@swindon.gov.uk

Licensing: Mr Richard Bell , Head of Planning & Regulatory Services, Wat Tyler West, Beckhampton Street, Swindon SN1 2JG ☎ 01793 466706 ✉ rbell@swindon.gov.uk

Lottery Funding, Charity and Voluntary: Mr Patrick Weir, Head of Localities, Volunteering & Community Involvement, Civic Offices, Euclid Street, Swindon SN1 2JH ✉ pweir@swindon.gov.uk

Member Services: Mr Ian Willcox, Committee & Members Services Manager, Civic Offices, Euclid Street, Swindon SN1 2JH ☎ 01793 463601 📠 01793 490420 ✉ iwillcox@swindon.gov.uk

Parking: Ms Dawn Woollard , Head of Parking, Wat Tyler West, Beckhampton Street, Swindon SN1 2JG ☎ 01793 463000 ✉ dwoollard@swindon.gov.uk

Partnerships: Mr James Griffin , Head of Strategy & Research, Civic Offices, Euclid Street, Swindon SN1 2JH ☎ 01793 463648 ✉ jgriffin@swindon.gov.uk

Personnel / HR: Ms Nicola Houwayek , Head of People & Change, Civic Offices, Euclid Street, Swindon SN1 2JH ☎ 01793 463000 ✉ nhouwayek@swindon.gov.uk

Planning: Mr Richard Bell , Head of Planning & Regulatory Services, Wat Tyler West, Beckhampton Street, Swindon SN1 2JG ☎ 01793 466706 ✉ rbell@swindon.gov.uk

Regeneration: Ms Andrea Barratt , Locality Lead for the North East, Civic Offices, Euclid Street, Swindon SN1 2JH ☎ 01793 463387 ✉ abarratt@swindon.gov.uk

Regeneration: Ms Pam Gough , Locality Lead for the North East, Civic Offices, Euclid Street, Swindon SN1 2JH ☎ 01793 463140 ✉ pgough@swindon.gov.uk

Regeneration: Ms Paula Harrison , Locality Lead for the West, Civic Offices, Euclid Street, Swindon SN1 2JH ☎ 01793 466418
🖱 pharrison@swindon.gov.uk

Regeneration: Mr Andy Reeves , Locality Lead for the Central North, Civic Offices, Euclid Street, Swindon SN1 2JH ☎ 01793 466499 🖱 areeves@swindon.gov.uk

Regeneration: Ms Helena Robinson , Locality Lead for the North, Civic Offices, Euclid Street, Swindon SN1 2JH ☎ 01793 466210
🖱 hrobinson@swindon.gov.uk

Regeneration: Mr Mark Walker , Locality Lead of the Central, Civic Offices, Euclid Street, Swindon SN1 2JH ☎ 01793 464605
🖱 mwalker@swindon.gov.uk

Road Safety: Ms Margaret Tester, Road Safety Officer, Wat Tyler West, Beckhampton Street, Swindon SN1 2JG
☎ 01793 466399
🖱 mtester@swindon.gov.uk

Social Services: Mr John Gilbert , Board Director of Commissioning, Wat Tyler House West, Beckhampton Street, Swindon SN1 2JG ☎ 01793 463068 🖱 jgilbert@swindon.gov.uk

Social Services (Adult): Mr John Gilbert , Board Director of Commissioning, Wat Tyler House West, Beckhampton Street, Swindon SN1 2JG ☎ 01793 463068 🖱 jgilbert@swindon.gov.uk

Social Services (Children): Ms Karen Reeve , Head of Children's Social Care, Community Health & Family, Wat Tyler West, Beckhampton Street, Swindon SN1 2JG
☎ 01793 463067
🖱 kreeve@swindon.gov.uk

Public Health: Ms Cherry Jones , Director - Public Health, Civic Offices, Euclid Street, Swindon SN1 2JH ☎ 01793 444681
🖱 cherryjones@swindon.gov.uk

Street Scene: Mr Leon Barrett , Head of Street Smart, Wat Tyler West, Beckhampton Street, Swindon SN1 2JG
🖱 lbarrett@swindon.gov.uk

Waste Management: Mr Leon Barrett , Head of Street Smart, Wat Tyler West, Beckhampton Street, Swindon SN1 2JG
🖱 lbarrett@swindon.gov.uk

COUNCILLORS

***Mayor* Bennett**, Andrew (CON - Ridgeway)
abennett@ndirect.co.uk

***Deputy Mayor* Shaw**, Eric (CON - Chiseldon and Lawn)
ericshaw1937@btinternet.com

***Leader of the Council* Renard**, David (CON - Haydon Wick)

***Deputy Leader of the Council* Mattock**, Brian (CON - Old Town)
brian.mattock@ntlworld.com

***Group Leader* Grant**, James (LAB - Rodbourne Cheney)
grant4gt@btinternet.com

***Group Leader* Pajak**, Stan (LD - Eastcott)
stanpajak@ymail.com

Ali, Junab (LAB - Central)
junab@hotmail.co.uk

Allsopp, Steve (LAB - Walcot and Park North)
jean.norris1@ntlworld.com

Amin, Abdul (LAB - Walcot and Park North)
abdulamin22@gmail.com

Baker, Paul (LAB - Penhill and Upper Stratton)
pauljbaker@ntlworld.com

Ballman, John (LAB - Gorse Hill and Pinehurst)
jbswin@yahoo.co.uk

Ballman, Ray (LAB - Gorse Hill and Pinehurst)
jbswin@yahoo.co.uk

Bishop, Alan (CON - Blunsdon and Highworth)
alanandjulie@live.com

Bray, Michael (CON - Lydiard and Freshbrook)
brmicha454@aol.com

Bushell, Emma (LAB - Walcot and Park North)
emmabushell@yahoo.co.uk

Crabbe, Wayne (CON - Wroughton and Wichelstowe)

Dixon, Paul (LAB - Eastcott)
p.dixon8@ntlworld.com

Donachie, Oliver (CON - Haydon Wick)
oliver.donachie@gmail.com

Edwards, Mark (CON - Priory Vale)
markaedwards@yahoo.co.uk

Elliott, Toby (CON - Priory Vale)
cllrtoby@outlook.com

Ellis, Claire (CON - Old Town)
claireellis@hotmail.co.uk

Faramarzi, Emma (CON - Priory Vale)
efaramarzi@swindon.gov.uk

Foley, Fionuala (CON - Chiseldon and Lawn)
ffoley@swindon.gov.uk

Ford, Brian (CON - Wroughton and Wichelstowe)
brian.ford@absolutely-independent.co.uk

Friend, Mary (CON - St Andrews)
mry4441@gmail.com

Haines, John (CON - St Margaret and South Marston)
cllrjhaines@hotmail.co.uk

Heenan, Dale (CON - Covingham and Dorcan)
dale@covinghamandnytheintouch.com

Holland, Russell (CON - St. Margaret and South Marston)
rholland@swindon.gov.uk

Howard, Fay (LAB - Liden, Eldene and Park South)
fayhoward@live.co.uk

SWINDON

Hurley, Richard (CON - Covingham and Dorcan)
rhurley@swindon.gov.uk

Lovell, Colin (CON - St Margaret and South Marston)
colin.lovell2@ntlworld.com

Martin, Nick (CON - Shaw)
nmartin@swindon.gov.uk

Martin, Mary (CON - Shaw)
marymartin@swindon.gov.uk

Martyn, Cathy (CON - Wroughton and Wichelstowe)
cathy@themartynfamily.co.uk

McCracken, Gemma (CON - St Andrews)
gemmaleroy@btinternet.com

Moffatt, Des (LAB - Rodbourne Cheney)
fendessy@yahoo.co.uk

Montaut, Derique (LAB - Liden, Eldene and Park South)
derique.montaut@ntlworld.com

Page, Teresa (LAB - Penhill and Upper Stratton)
teresapageswindon@yahoo.co.uk

Parry, Kevin (CON - Covingham and Dorcan)
cllrkevin.parry@ntlworld.com

Penny, Maureen (CON - Blunsdon and Highworth)
maureen.penny2@btinternet.com

Perkins, Garry (CON - Shaw)
ecp@swindon1.fsnet.co.uk

Robbins, James (LAB - Mannington and Western)
robbins.james@gmail.com

Shelley, Carol (LAB - Gorsehill and Pinehurst)
cshelleyswindon@gmail.com

Small, Kevin (LAB - Mannington and Western)
kevinsmall@hotmail.com

Swinyard, Timothy (CON - Lydiard and Freshbrook)
timswin@hotmail.com

Sydney-Smith, Caryl (CON - Lydiard and Freshbrook)
carylss@hotmail.com

Tomlinson, Vera (CON - St Andrews)
vtomlinson@swindon.gov.uk

Tray, Joe (LAB - Penhill and Upper Stratton)
j.tray@ntlworld.com

Watts, Nadine (LAB - Old Town)
nadine.watts@live.co.uk

Watts, Peter (LAB - Rodbourne Cheney)
peterwattsrodbournecheney@live.co.uk

Watts, Chris (LAB - Liden, Eldene and Park South)
cllrchriswatts@outlook.com

Weisinger, Steve (CON - Blunsdon & Highworth)
sweisinger@swindon.gov.uk

Williams, Keith (CON - Shaw)
krwilliams@swindon.gov.uk

Wood, David (LD - Eastcott)
dave@swindonlibdems.org

Wright, Robert (LAB - Central)
bob.wright.gov@ntlworld.com

Wright, Julie (LAB - Central)
juliecaseworker@hotmail.co.uk

POLITICAL COMPOSITION

CON: 32, LAB: 22, LD: 2

COMMITTEE CHAIRS

Audit: Mr Steve Weisinger

Health & Wellbeing: Mr David Renard

Licensing: Mrs Vera Tomlinson

Planning: Mr Colin Lovell

Tameside M

Tameside Metropolitan Borough Council, Council Offices, Wellington Road, Ashton-under-Lyne OL6 6DL
☎ 0161 342 8355 🖷 0161 342 3070 ✉ general@tameside.gov.uk
💻 www.tameside.gov.uk

FACTS AND FIGURES

Parliamentary Constituencies: Ashton under Lyne, Denton and Reddish, Stalybridge and Hyde
EU Constituencies: North West
Election Frequency: Elections are by thirds

PRINCIPAL OFFICERS

Chief Executive: Mr Steven Pleasant, Chief Executive, Council Offices, Wellington Road, Ashton-under-Lyne OL6 6DL ☎ 0161 342 3500 🖷 0161 342 3543 ✉ steven.pleasant@tameside.gov.uk

Senior Management: Mrs Stephanie Butterworth, Executive Director - People, Council Offices, Wellington Road, Ashton-under-Lyne OL6 6DL ☎ 0161 342 8355

Senior Management: Ms Angela Hardman, Director - Public Health, Council Offices, Wellington Road, Ashton-under-Lyne OL6 6DL ☎ 0161 342 2908 ✉ angela.hardman@tameside.gov.uk

Senior Management: Mr Robin Monk, Executive Director - Place, Council Offices, Wellington Road, Ashton-under-Lyne OL6 6DL ☎ 0161 342 3340 ✉ robin.monk@tameside.gov.uk

Senior Management: Mr Peter Morris, Executive Director - Pensions, Tameside Council Offices, Wellington Road, Ashton-under-Lyne OL6 6DL ☎ 0161 342 3438 ✉ peter.morris@tameside.gov.uk

Senior Management: Ms Sandra Stewart, Executive Director - Governance & Resources, Council Offices, Wellington Road, Ashton-under-Lyne OL6 6DL ☎ 0161 342 3028 ✉ sandra.stewart@tameside.gov.uk

Access Officer / Social Services (Disability): Mrs Stephanie Butterworth, Executive Director - People, Council Offices, Wellington Road, Ashton-under-Lyne OL6 6DL ☎ 0161 342 8355

Architect, Building / Property Services: Mr Robin Monk, Executive Director - Place, Council Offices, Wellington Road, Ashton-under-Lyne OL6 6DL ☎ 0161 342 3340 ✉ robin.monk@tameside.gov.uk

Architect, Building / Property Services: Mrs Elaine Todd, Assistant Executive Director - Asset & Investment Partnership, Council Offices, Wellington Road, Ashton-under-Lyne OL6 6DL ☎ 0161 342 8355 ✉ elaine.todd@tameside.gov.uk

Building Control: Mr Robin Monk, Executive Director - Place, Council Offices, Wellington Road, Ashton-under-Lyne OL6 6DL ☎ 0161 342 3340 ✉ robin.monk@tameside.gov.uk

Building Control: Mr Ian Saxon, Assistant Executive Director - Environmental Services, Council Offices, Wellington Road, Ashton-under-Lyne OL6 6DL ☎ 0161 342 3470 ✉ ian.saxon@tameside.gov.uk

Catering Services: Mrs Elaine Todd, Assistant Executive Director - Asset & Investment Partnership, Council Offices, Wellington Road, Ashton-under-Lyne OL6 6DL ☎ 0161 342 8355

Children / Youth Services: Mrs Stephanie Butterworth, Executive Director - People, Council Offices, Wellington Road, Ashton-under-Lyne OL6 6DL ☎ 0161 342 8355

Civil Registration: Ms Sandra Stewart, Executive Director - Governance & Resources, Council Offices, Wellington Road, Ashton-under-Lyne OL6 6DL ☎ 0161 342 3028 ✉ sandra.stewart@tameside.gov.uk

PR / Communications: Ms Sarah Dobson, Head of Policy & Communications, Dukinfield Town Hall, King Street, Dukinfield SK16 4LA ☎ 0161 342 4417 ✉ sarah.dobson@tameside.gov.uk

Community Planning: Mr Robin Monk, Executive Director - Place, Council Offices, Wellington Road, Ashton-under-Lyne OL6 6DL ☎ 0161 342 3340 ✉ robin.monk@tameside.gov.uk

Community Safety: Mrs Emma Varnam, Head of Stronger Communities, Hyde Town Hall, Market Street, Hyde SK14 1AL ☎ 0161 342 3337 ✉ emma.varnam@tameside.gov.uk

Computer Management: Mr Tim Rainey, Assistant Chief Executive - Digital Tameside, Council Offices, Wellington Road, Ashton-under-Lyne OL6 6DL ☎ 0161 342 3299 🖷 0161 342 2836 ✉ tim.rainey@tameside.gov.uk

Consumer Protection and Trading Standards: Mr Robin Monk, Executive Director - Place, Council Offices, Wellington Road, Ashton-under-Lyne OL6 6DL ☎ 0161 342 3340 ✉ robin.monk@tameside.gov.uk

Consumer Protection and Trading Standards: Mr Ian Saxon, Assistant Executive Director - Environmental Services, Council Offices, Wellington Road, Ashton-under-Lyne OL6 6DL ☎ 0161 342 3470 ✉ ian.saxon@tameside.gov.uk

Contracts: Mr Ben Jay, Assistant Executive Director - Finance, Council Offices, Wellington Road, Ashton-under-Lyne OL6 6DL ☎ 0161 342 8355

Customer Service: Mrs Stephanie Butterworth, Executive Director - People, Council Offices, Wellington Road, Ashton-under-Lyne OL6 6DL ☎ 0161 342 8355

Economic Development: Mr Damien Bourke, Executive Director - Development & Investment, Council Offices, Wellington Road, Ashton-under-Lyne OL6 6DL ☎ 0161 342 3544 ✉ damien.bourke@tameside.gov.uk

Economic Development: Mr Robin Monk, Executive Director - Place, Council Offices, Wellington Road, Ashton-under-Lyne OL6 6DL ☎ 0161 342 3340 ✉ robin.monk@tameside.gov.uk

Education: Mrs Stephanie Butterworth, Executive Director - People, Council Offices, Wellington Road, Ashton-under-Lyne OL6 6DL ☎ 0161 342 8355

Education: Mrs Heather Loveridge, Assistant Executive Director - Learning, Council Offices, Wellington Road, Ashton-under-Lyne OL6 6DL ☎ 0161 342 2050 ✉ heather.loveridge@tameside.gov.uk

E-Government: Mr Tim Rainey, Assistant Chief Executive - Digital Tameside, Council Offices, Wellington Road, Ashton-under-Lyne OL6 6DL ☎ 0161 342 3299 🖷 0161 342 2836 ✉ tim.rainey@tameside.gov.uk

Electoral Registration: Mr Robert Landon, Head - Democratic Services, Council Offices, Wellington Road, Ashton-under-Lyne OL6 6DL ☎ 0161 342 8355 ✉ robert.landon@tameside.gov.uk

Emergency Planning: Mr Michael Gurney, Emergency Planning Manager, Council Offices, Wellington Road, Ashton-under-Lyne OL6 6DL ☎ 0161 342 3705 ✉ michael.gurney@tameside.gov.uk

Emergency Planning: Mr Ian Saxon, Assistant Executive Director - Environmental Services, Council Offices, Wellington Road, Ashton-under-Lyne OL6 6DL ☎ 0161 342 3470 ✉ ian.saxon@tameside.gov.uk

Energy Management: Mr Ian Saxon, Assistant Executive Director - Environmental Services, Council Offices, Wellington Road, Ashton-under-Lyne OL6 6DL ☎ 0161 342 3470 ✉ ian.saxon@tameside.gov.uk

Environmental / Technical Services: Mr Robin Monk, Executive Director - Place, Council Offices, Wellington Road, Ashton-under-Lyne OL6 6DL ☎ 0161 342 3340 ✉ robin.monk@tameside.gov.uk

Environmental / Technical Services: Mr Ian Saxon, Assistant Executive Director - Environmental Services, Council Offices, Wellington Road, Ashton-under-Lyne OL6 6DL ☎ 0161 342 3470 ✉ ian.saxon@tameside.gov.uk

Environmental Health: Mr Robin Monk, Executive Director - Place, Council Offices, Wellington Road, Ashton-under-Lyne OL6 6DL ☎ 0161 342 3340 ✉ robin.monk@tameside.gov.uk

Environmental Health: Mr Ian Saxon, Assistant Executive Director - Environmental Services, Council Offices, Wellington Road, Ashton-under-Lyne OL6 6DL ☎ 0161 342 3470 ✉ ian.saxon@tameside.gov.uk

Estates, Property & Valuation: Mr Robin Monk, Executive Director - Place, Council Offices, Wellington Road, Ashton-under-Lyne OL6 6DL ☎ 0161 342 3340 ✉ robin.monk@tameside.gov.uk

Estates, Property & Valuation: Mrs Elaine Todd, Assistant Executive Director - Asset & Investment Partnership, Council Offices, Wellington Road, Ashton-under-Lyne OL6 6DL ☎ 0161 342 8355

Events Manager: Mrs Emma Varnam, Head of Stronger Communities, Hyde Town Hall, Market Street, Hyde SK14 1AL ☎ 0161 342 3337 ✉ emma.varnam@tameside.gov.uk

Facilities: Mrs Elaine Todd, Assistant Executive Director - Asset & Investment Partnership, Council Offices, Wellington Road, Ashton-under-Lyne OL6 6DL ☎ 0161 342 8355

Finance: Mr Ben Jay, Assistant Executive Director - Finance, Council Offices, Wellington Road, Ashton-under-Lyne OL6 6DL ☎ 0161 342 8355

Pensions: Mr Peter Morris, Executive Director - Pensions, Tameside Council Offices, Wellington Road, Ashton-under-Lyne OL6 6DL ☎ 0161 342 3438 ✉ peter.morris@tameside.gov.uk

Fleet Management: Mr Ian Saxon, Assistant Executive Director - Environmental Services, Council Offices, Wellington Road, Ashton-under-Lyne OL6 6DL ☎ 0161 342 3470 ✉ ian.saxon@tameside.gov.uk

Health and Safety: Mr Robin Monk, Executive Director - Place, Council Offices, Wellington Road, Ashton-under-Lyne OL6 6DL ☎ 0161 342 3340 ✉ robin.monk@tameside.gov.uk

Health and Safety: Mr Ian Saxon, Assistant Executive Director - Environmental Services, Council Offices, Wellington Road, Ashton-under-Lyne OL6 6DL ☎ 0161 342 3470 ✉ ian.saxon@tameside.gov.uk

Highways: Mr Robin Monk, Executive Director - Place, Council Offices, Wellington Road, Ashton-under-Lyne OL6 6DL ☎ 0161 342 3340 ✉ robin.monk@tameside.gov.uk

Home Energy Conservation: Mr Ian Saxon, Assistant Executive Director - Environmental Services, Council Offices, Wellington Road, Ashton-under-Lyne OL6 6DL ☎ 0161 342 3470 ✉ ian.saxon@tameside.gov.uk

Legal: Ms Sandra Stewart, Executive Director - Governance & Resources, Council Offices, Wellington Road, Ashton-under-Lyne OL6 6DL ☎ 0161 342 3028 ✉ sandra.stewart@tameside.gov.uk

Leisure and Cultural Services: Mrs Emma Varnam, Head of Stronger Communities, Hyde Town Hall, Market Street, Hyde SK14 1AL ☎ 0161 342 3337 ✉ emma.varnam@tameside.gov.uk

Licensing: Mr Robin Monk, Executive Director - Place, Council Offices, Wellington Road, Ashton-under-Lyne OL6 6DL ☎ 0161 342 3340 ✉ robin.monk@tameside.gov.uk

Licensing: Mr Ian Saxon, Assistant Executive Director - Environmental Services, Council Offices, Wellington Road, Ashton-under-Lyne OL6 6DL ☎ 0161 342 3470 ✉ ian.saxon@tameside.gov.uk

Lifelong Learning: Mrs Stephanie Butterworth, Executive Director - People, Council Offices, Wellington Road, Ashton-under-Lyne OL6 6DL ☎ 0161 342 8355

Member Services: Mr Robert Landon, Head - Democratic Services, Council Offices, Wellington Road, Ashton-under-Lyne OL6 6DL ☎ 0161 342 8355 ✉ robert.landon@tameside.gov.uk

Parking: Mr Robin Monk, Executive Director - Place, Council Offices, Wellington Road, Ashton-under-Lyne OL6 6DL ☎ 0161 342 3340 ✉ robin.monk@tameside.gov.uk

Parking: Mr Ian Saxon, Assistant Executive Director - Environmental Services, Council Offices, Wellington Road, Ashton-under-Lyne OL6 6DL ☎ 0161 342 3470 ✉ ian.saxon@tameside.gov.uk

Personnel / HR: Ms Tracy Brennand, Assistant Executive Director - People & Workforce Development, Council Offices, Wellington Road, Ashton-under-Lyne OL6 6DL ☎ 0161 342 3279 ✉ tracy.brennand@tameside.gov.uk

Personnel / HR: Ms Sandra Stewart, Executive Director - Governance & Resources, Council Offices, Wellington Road, Ashton-under-Lyne OL6 6DL ☎ 0161 342 3028 ✉ sandra.stewart@tameside.gov.uk

Planning: Mr Robin Monk, Executive Director - Place, Council Offices, Wellington Road, Ashton-under-Lyne OL6 6DL ☎ 0161 342 3340 ✉ robin.monk@tameside.gov.uk

Planning: Mr Ian Saxon, Assistant Executive Director - Environmental Services, Council Offices, Wellington Road, Ashton-under-Lyne OL6 6DL ☎ 0161 342 3470 ✉ ian.saxon@tameside.gov.uk

Procurement: Mr Ben Jay, Assistant Executive Director - Finance, Council Offices, Wellington Road, Ashton-under-Lyne OL6 6DL ☎ 0161 342 8355

Public Libraries: Mrs Stephanie Butterworth, Executive Director - People, Council Offices, Wellington Road, Ashton-under-Lyne OL6 6DL ☎ 0161 342 8355

Recycling & Waste Minimisation: Mr Robin Monk, Executive Director - Place, Council Offices, Wellington Road, Ashton-under-Lyne OL6 6DL ☎ 0161 342 3340 ✉ robin.monk@tameside.gov.uk

Recycling & Waste Minimisation: Mr Ian Saxon, Assistant Executive Director - Environmental Services, Council Offices, Wellington Road, Ashton-under-Lyne OL6 6DL ☎ 0161 342 3470 ✉ ian.saxon@tameside.gov.uk

Regeneration: Mr Robin Monk, Executive Director - Place, Council Offices, Wellington Road, Ashton-under-Lyne OL6 6DL ☎ 0161 342 3340 ✉ robin.monk@tameside.gov.uk

Road Safety: Mr Damien Bourke, Executive Director - Development & Investment, Council Offices, Wellington Road, Ashton-under-Lyne OL6 6DL ☎ 0161 342 3544 ✉ damien.bourke@tameside.gov.uk

Road Safety: Mr Robin Monk, Executive Director - Place, Council Offices, Wellington Road, Ashton-under-Lyne OL6 6DL ☎ 0161 342 3340 ✉ robin.monk@tameside.gov.uk

Road Safety: Mr Ian Saxon, Assistant Executive Director - Environmental Services, Council Offices, Wellington Road, Ashton-under-Lyne OL6 6DL ☎ 0161 342 3470 ✉ ian.saxon@tameside.gov.uk

Social Services: Mrs Stephanie Butterworth, Executive Director - People, Council Offices, Wellington Road, Ashton-under-Lyne OL6 6DL ☎ 0161 342 8355

Social Services (Adult): Mrs Stephanie Butterworth, Executive Director - People, Council Offices, Wellington Road, Ashton-under-Lyne OL6 6DL ☎ 0161 342 8355

Social Services (Children): Mrs Stephanie Butterworth, Executive Director - People, Council Offices, Wellington Road, Ashton-under-Lyne OL6 6DL ☎ 0161 342 8355

Public Health: Ms Angela Hardman, Director - Public Health, Council Offices, Wellington Road, Ashton-under-Lyne OL6 6DL ☎ 0161 342 2908 ✉ angela.hardman@tameside.gov.uk

Sustainable Communities: Mr Robin Monk, Executive Director - Place, Council Offices, Wellington Road, Ashton-under-Lyne OL6 6DL ☎ 0161 342 3340 ✉ robin.monk@tameside.gov.uk

Sustainable Development: Mr Robin Monk, Executive Director - Place, Council Offices, Wellington Road, Ashton-under-Lyne OL6 6DL ☎ 0161 342 3340 ✉ robin.monk@tameside.gov.uk

Town Centre: Mr Damien Bourke, Executive Director - Development & Investment, Council Offices, Wellington Road, Ashton-under-Lyne OL6 6DL ☎ 0161 342 3544 ✉ damien.bourke@tameside.gov.uk

Town Centre: Mr Robin Monk, Executive Director - Place, Council Offices, Wellington Road, Ashton-under-Lyne OL6 6DL ☎ 0161 342 3340 ✉ robin.monk@tameside.gov.uk

Traffic Management: Mr Robin Monk, Executive Director - Place, Council Offices, Wellington Road, Ashton-under-Lyne OL6 6DL ☎ 0161 342 3340 ✉ robin.monk@tameside.gov.uk

Traffic Management: Mr Ian Saxon, Assistant Executive Director - Environmental Services, Council Offices, Wellington Road, Ashton-under-Lyne OL6 6DL ☎ 0161 342 3470 ✉ ian.saxon@tameside.gov.uk

Transport: Mr Robin Monk, Executive Director - Place, Council Offices, Wellington Road, Ashton-under-Lyne OL6 6DL ☎ 0161 342 3340 ✉ robin.monk@tameside.gov.uk

Transport Planner: Mr Robin Monk, Executive Director - Place, Council Offices, Wellington Road, Ashton-under-Lyne OL6 6DL ☎ 0161 342 3340 ✉ robin.monk@tameside.gov.uk

Waste Collection and Disposal: Mr Robin Monk, Executive Director - Place, Council Offices, Wellington Road, Ashton-under-Lyne OL6 6DL ☎ 0161 342 3340 ✉ robin.monk@tameside.gov.uk

Waste Collection and Disposal: Mr Ian Saxon, Assistant Executive Director - Environmental Services, Council Offices, Wellington Road, Ashton-under-Lyne OL6 6DL ☎ 0161 342 3470 ✉ ian.saxon@tameside.gov.uk

Waste Management: Mr Robin Monk, Executive Director - Place, Council Offices, Wellington Road, Ashton-under-Lyne OL6 6DL ☎ 0161 342 3340 ✉ robin.monk@tameside.gov.uk

Waste Management: Mr Ian Saxon, Assistant Executive Director - Environmental Services, Council Offices, Wellington Road, Ashton-under-Lyne OL6 6DL ☎ 0161 342 3470
✉ ian.saxon@tameside.gov.uk

COUNCILLORS

***Mayor* Ricci**, Vincent (LAB - Denton North East)

***Deputy Mayor* Fitzpatrick**, Philip (LAB - Hyde Newton)

***Leader of the Council* Quinn**, Kieran (LAB - Droylsden East)

***Deputy Leader of the Council* Taylor**, John (LAB - Dukinfield)

***Group Leader* Bell**, John (CON - Hyde Werneth)

Affleck, Betty (LAB - Hyde Godley)
betty.affleck@tameside.gov.uk

Bailey, Maria (LAB - Audenshaw)

Ballagher, Eleanor (LAB - Dukinfield and Stalybridge)
eleanor.ballagher@tameside.gov.uk

Beeley, Basil (CON - Stalybridge South)

Bowden, Helen (LAB - Hyde Newton)

Bowerman, Joyce (LAB - Ashton St. Peters)

Bray, Warren (LAB - Ashton St. Peters)

Buckley, Paul (CON - Ashton Hurst)
paul.buckley@tameside.gov.uk

Cartey, Yvonne (LAB - Ashton St. Michaels)

Cooney, Gerald (LAB - Droylsden West)

Cooper, Janet (LAB - Longdendale)

Dickinson, Doreen (CON - Stalybridge South)

Downs, Margaret (LAB - Denton South)

Drennan, Leigh (LAB - Ashton Hurst)

Fairfoull, Bill (LAB - Ashton St. Michaels)

Fitzpatrick, Jim (LAB - Hyde Godley)

Fowler, Mike (LAB - Denton South)

Francis, Claire (LAB - Denton South)

Glover, Mike (LAB - Ashton Hurst)
mike.glover@tameside.gov.uk

Gwynne, Allison (LAB - Denton North East)

Holland, Barrie (LAB - Droylsden West)

Holland, Ann (LAB - Droylsden West)

Jackson, Jan (LAB - Stalybridge North)

Kinsey, Andy (LAB - Hyde Werneth)
andy.kinsey@tameside.gov.uk

Kitchen, Joseph (LAB - Hyde Godley)

Lane, Jacqueline (LAB - Dukinfield)

Lane, Dawson (LAB - Denton West)

McNally, David (LAB - Ashton St. Peters)

Miah, Idu (LAB - Mossley)

Miah, Raja (LAB - Hyde Werneth)

Middleton, Jim (LAB - Droylsden East)

Patrick, Clive (CON - Stalybridge South)
clive.patrick1@tameside.gov.uk

Pearce, Adrian (LAB - Stalybridge North)
adrian.pearce@tameside.gov.uk

Peet, Gillian (LAB - Longdendale)

Piddington, Catherine (LAB - Ashton Waterloo)

Quinn, Susan (LAB - Droylsden East)

Reynolds, Claire (LAB - Dukinfield and Stalybridge)

Robinson, Peter (LAB - Hyde Newton)

Ryan, Oliver (LAB - Audenshaw)
oliver.ryan@tameside.gov.uk

Shember-Critchley, Ellie (LAB - Mossley)

Sidebottom, Margaret (LAB - Ashton St. Michaels)

Smith, Michael (LAB - Denton West)

Smith, Teresa (LAB - Audenshaw)

Sweeton, David (LAB - Dukinfield and Stalybridge)

Travis, Lynn (LAB - Ashton Waterloo)

Travis, Frank (LAB - Mossley)
frank.travis@tameside.gov.uk

Ward, Denise (LAB - Denton North East)

Warrington, Brenda (LAB - Denton West)

Welsh, Kevin (LAB - Stalybridge North)

White, Alan (LAB - Longdendale)

Whitehead, Lorraine (LAB - Ashton Waterloo)
lorraine.whitehead@tameside.gov.uk

Wild, Brian (LAB - Dukinfield)

POLITICAL COMPOSITION
LAB: 52, CON: 5

COMMITTEE CHAIRS

Audit: Mr Vincent Ricci

Health & Wellbeing: Mr Kieran Quinn

Licensing: Mr Warren Bray

Planning: Mr David McNally

Tamworth D

Tamworth Borough Council, Marmion House, Lichfield Street, Tamworth B79 7BZ
☎ 01827 709709 🖷 01827 709271 ✉ enquiries@tamworth.gov.uk
💻 www.tamworth.gov.uk

FACTS AND FIGURES
Parliamentary Constituencies: Tamworth
EU Constituencies: West Midlands
Election Frequency: Elections are by thirds

PRINCIPAL OFFICERS

Chief Executive: Mr Tony Goodwin, Chief Executive, Marmion House, Lichfield Street, Tamworth B79 7BZ ☎ 01827 709212 🖷 01827 709271 ✉ tony-goodwin@tamworth.gov.uk

Deputy Chief Executive: Mr John Wheatley, Executive Director of Corporate Services & S151 Officer, Marmion House, Lichfield Street, Tamworth B79 7BZ ☎ 01827 709252 🖷 01827 709271 ✉ john-wheatley@tamworth.gov.uk

Architect, Building / Property Services: Mr Paul Weston, Head of Asset Management, Marmion House, Lichfield Street, Tamworth B79 7BZ ☎ 01827 709377 🖷 01827 709271 ✉ paul-weston@tamworth.gov.uk

PR / Communications: Ms Anica Goodwin, Corporate Communications & PR Manager, Marmion House, Lichfield Street, Tamworth B79 7BZ ☎ 01827 709225 🖷 01827 709271 ✉ anica-goodwin@tamworth.gov.uk

Community Safety: Mr Dave Fern, Head of Community Safety, Marmion House, Lichfield Street, Tamworth B79 7BZ ☎ 01785 234647 🖷 01827 709271 ✉ david-fern@tamworth.gov.uk

Computer Management: Mrs Nicki Burton, Director of Technology & Corporate Programmes, Marmion House, Lichfield Street, Tamworth B79 7BZ ☎ 01827 709420 🖷 01827 709271 ✉ nicki-burton@tamworth.gov.uk

Contracts: Mr David Onion, Corporate Procurement Officer, Marmion House, Lichfield Street, Tamworth B79 7BZ ☎ 01827 709371 🖷 01827 709271 ✉ david-onion@tamworth.gov.uk

Customer Service: Mrs Tracey Tudor, Head of Customer Services, Marmion House, Lichfield Street, Tamworth B79 7BZ ☎ 01827 709427 🖷 01827 709271 ✉ tracey-tudor@tamworth.gov.uk

Economic Development: Mr James Roberts, Economic Development & Enterprise Manager, Marmion House, Lichfield Street, Tamworth B79 7BZ ☎ 01827 709204 🖷 01827 709271 ✉ james-roberts@tamworth.gov.uk

E-Government: Mrs Nicki Burton, Director of Technology & Corporate Programmes, Marmion House, Lichfield Street, Tamworth B79 7BZ ☎ 01827 709420 🖷 01827 709271 ✉ nicki-burton@tamworth.gov.uk

Electoral Registration: Mr John Wheatley, Executive Director of Corporate Services & S151 Officer, Marmion House, Lichfield Street, Tamworth B79 7BZ ☎ 01827 709252 🖷 01827 709271 ✉ john-wheatley@tamworth.gov.uk

Emergency Planning: Mr Derek Bolton, Corporate Information Security Manager, Marmion House, Lichfield Street, Tamworth B79 7BZ ☎ 01827 709587 🖷 01827 709271 ✉ derek-bolton@tamworth.gov.uk

Energy Management: Mr Paul Weston, Head of Asset Management, Marmion House, Lichfield Street, Tamworth B79 7BZ ☎ 01827 709377 🖷 01827 709271 ✉ paul-weston@tamworth.gov.uk

Environmental Health: Mr Stephen Lewis, Head of Environmental Health, Marmion House, Lichfield Street, Tamworth B79 7BZ ☎ 01827 709428 🖷 01827 709271 ✉ stephen-lewis@tamworth.gov.uk

Estates, Property & Valuation: Mr Paul Weston, Head of Asset Management, Marmion House, Lichfield Street, Tamworth B79 7BZ ☎ 01827 709377 🖷 01827 709271 ✉ paul-weston@tamworth.gov.uk

Finance: Mr Stefan Garner, Director of Finance, Marmion House, Lichfield Street, Tamworth B79 7BZ ☎ 01827 709242 🖷 01827 709271 ✉ stefan-garner@tamworth.gov.uk

Grounds Maintenance: Mrs Sarah McGrandle, Head of Environmental Management, Marmion House, Lichfield Street, Tamworth B79 7BZ ☎ 01827 709349 🖷 01827 709271 ✉ sarah-mcgrandle@tamworth.gov.uk

Health and Safety: Mr Steve Langston, Health & Safety Manager, Marmion House, Lichfield Street, Tamworth B79 7BZ ☎ 01543 308107; 01827 709224 🖷 01543 308103; 01827 709271 ✉ steven.langston@lichfielddc.gov.uk

Housing: Mr Rob Barnes, Director of Housing & Health, Marmion House, Lichfield Street, Tamworth B79 7BZ ☎ 01827 709447 🖷 01827 709271 ✉ robert-barnes@tamworth.gov.uk

Housing Maintenance: Mr John Murden, Repairs Manager, Marmion House, Lichfield Street, Tamworth B79 7BZ ☎ 01827 709406 ✉ john-murden@tamworth.gov.uk

Legal: Mrs Jane Hackett, Solicitor to the Council & Monitoring Officer, Marmion House, Lichfield Street, Tamworth B79 7BZ ☎ 01827 709258 🖷 01827 709271 ✉ jane-hackett@tamworth.gov.uk

Member Services: Mrs Jane Hackett, Solicitor to the Council & Monitoring Officer, Marmion House, Lichfield Street, Tamworth B79 7BZ ☎ 01827 709258 🖷 01827 709271 ✉ jane-hackett@tamworth.gov.uk

Parking: Mr Andrew Barratt, Director of Assets & Environment, Marmion House, Lichfield Street, Tamworth B79 7BZ ☎ 01827 709453 🖷 01872 709271 ✉ andrew-barratt@tamworth.gov.uk

Personnel / HR: Mrs Christie Tims, Head of Organisational Development, Marmion House, Lichfield Street, Tamworth B79 7BZ ☎ 01827 709215 🖷 01827 709271 ✉ christie-tims@tamworth.gov.uk

Planning: Mr Matthew Bowers, Head of Planning & Regeneration, Marmion House, Lichfield Street, Tamworth B79 7BZ ☎ 01827 709276 🖷 01827 709271 ✉ matthew-bowers@tamworth.gov.uk

Procurement: Mr David Onion, Corporate Procurement Officer, Marmion House, Lichfield Street, Tamworth B79 7BZ ☎ 01827 709371 🖷 01827 709271 ✉ david-onion@tamworth.gov.uk

Recycling & Waste Minimisation: Mr Andrew Barratt, Director of Assets & Environment, Marmion House, Lichfield Street, Tamworth B79 7BZ ☎ 01827 709453 🖷 01872 709271 ✉ andrew-barratt@tamworth.gov.uk

Staff Training: Mrs Zoe-Louise Wolicki, Human Resources Advisor/Training, Marmion House, Lichfield Street, Tamworth B79 7BZ ☎ 01827 709223 🖷 01827 709271 ✉ zoe-wolicki@tamworth.gov.uk

TAMWORTH

Street Scene: Mrs Sarah McGrandle, Head of Environmental Management, Marmion House, Lichfield Street, Tamworth B79 7BZ ☎ 01827 709349 🖷 01827 709271 ✉ sarah-mcgrandle@tamworth.gov.uk

Tourism: Ms Stacy Birt, Tourism & Town Centre Development Manager, Marmion House, Lichfield Street, Tamworth B79 7BZ ☎ 01827 709583 🖷 01827 709271 ✉ stacy-birt@tamworth.gov.uk

Town Centre: Mrs Joanne Sands, Neighbourhood Services Manager, Sandy Way Depot, Amington, Tamworth B77 4ED ☎ 01827 709585 ✉ joanne-sands@tamworth.gov.uk

Waste Collection and Disposal: Mr Andrew Barratt, Director of Assets & Environment, Marmion House, Lichfield Street, Tamworth B79 7BZ ☎ 01827 709453 🖷 01872 709271 ✉ andrew-barratt@tamworth.gov.uk

Waste Management: Mr Andrew Barratt, Director of Assets & Environment, Marmion House, Lichfield Street, Tamworth B79 7BZ ☎ 01827 709453 🖷 01872 709271 ✉ andrew-barratt@tamworth.gov.uk

COUNCILLORS

***Mayor* Gant**, Maureen (CON - Spital)
maureen-gant@tamworth.gov.uk

***Deputy Mayor* Lunn**, Allan (CON - Castle)
allan-lunn@tamworth.gov.uk

***Leader of the Council* Cook**, Daniel (CON - Trinity)
daniel-cook@tamworh.gov.uk

***Deputy Leader of the Council* Pritchard**, Robert (CON - Spital)
robert-pritchard@tamworth.gov.uk

***Group Leader* Peaple**, Simon (LAB - Glascote)
simon.peaple@tamworth.gov.uk

Chesworth, John (CON - Spital)
john-chesworth@tamworth.gov.uk

Clarke, Margaret (LAB - Stonydelph)
margaret-clarke@tamworth.gov.uk

Claymore, Steven (CON - Castle)
steven-claymore@tamworth.gov.uk

Clements, Tina (CON - Wilnecote)
tina-clements@tamworth.gov.uk

Couchman, Marion (LAB - Belgrave)
marion-couchman@tamworth.gov.uk

Couchman, Alice (LAB - Glascote)
alice_couchman@yahoo.co.uk

Doyle, Stephen (CON - Stonydelph)
stephen-doyle@tamworth.gov.uk

Faulkner, John (LAB - Bolehall)
john-faulkner@tamworth.gov.uk

Goodall, Joy (CON - Belgrave)
joy-goodall@tamworth.gov.uk

Goodall, Simon (CON - Belgrave)
simon-goodall@tamworth.gov.uk

Greatorex, Michael (CON - Mercian)
michael-greatorex@tamworth.gov.uk

Hirons, Garry (LAB - Glascote)
garry-hirons@tamworth.gov.uk

James, Andrew (CON - Mercian)
andrew-james@tamworth.gov.uk

Kingstone, Richard (CON - Mercian)
Richard-Kingstone@tamworth.gov.uk

Madge, Tony (UKIP - Stonydelph)
tony-madge@tamworth.gov.uk

McDermid, Matthew (LAB - Castle)
Matthew-McDermid@tamworth.gov.uk

Norchi, Ken (LAB - Bolehall)
kenneth-norchi@tamworth.gov.uk

Oates, Jeremy (CON - Trinity)
jeremy-oates@tamworth.gov.uk

Oates, Michael (CON - Trinity)
michael-oates@tamworth.gov.uk

Peaple, Tom (LAB - Amington)
tom-peaple@tamworth.gov.uk

Rogers, Roy (CON - Wilnecote)
roy-rogers@tamworth.gov.uk

Rowe, Evelyn (CON - Amington)
evelyn-rowe@tamworth.gov.uk

Seekings, Peter (LAB - Bolehall)
peter-seekings@tamworth.gov.uk

Standen, Patrick (LAB - Wilnecote)
Patrick-Standen@tamworth.gov.uk

Thurgood, Michelle (CON - Amington)
michelle-thurgood@tamworth.gov.uk

POLITICAL COMPOSITION

CON: 18, LAB: 11, UKIP: 1

COMMITTEE CHAIRS

Audit & Governance: Mr John Chesworth

Planning: Mr Michael Greatorex

Tandridge D

Tandridge District Council, Council Offices, Station Road East, Oxted RH8 0BT
☎ 01883 722000 🖷 01883 722015 ✉ the.council@tandridge.gov.uk
🖳 www.tandridge.gov.uk

FACTS AND FIGURES

EU Constituencies: South East
Election Frequency: Elections are by thirds

PRINCIPAL OFFICERS

Chief Executive: Ms Louise Round, Chief Executive, Council Offices, Station Road East, Oxted RH8 0BT ☎ 01883 732999 🖷 01883 715004 ✉ lround@tandridge.gov.uk

Assistant Chief Executive: Mr Clive Moore, Assistant Chief Executive of Legal, Council Offices, Station Road East, Oxted RH8 0BT ☎ 01883 732740 🖷 01883 722015 ✉ cmoore@tandridge.gov.uk

Senior Management: Ms Linda Barnett, Facilities Manager & Health & Safety Officer, Council Offices, Station Road East, Oxted RH8 0BT ☎ 01883 732899 ✉ lbarnett@tandridge.gov.uk

Senior Management: Miss Seanne Giddy, Head of Personnel & Training Services, Council Offices, Station Road East, Oxted RH8 0BT ☎ 01883 732979 🖷 01883 722015 ✉ sgiddy@tandridge.gov.uk

Senior Management: Mr Stuart Mitchenall, Head of Business Support Services, Council Offices, Station Road East, Oxted RH8 0BT ☎ 01883 732724 🖷 01883 722015 ✉ smitchenall@tandridge.gov.uk

Senior Management: Mr Alistair Montgomery, Chief Finance Officer, Council Offices, Station Road East, Oxted RH8 0BT ☎ 01883 732902 🖷 01883 722015 ✉ amontgomery@tandridge.gov.uk

Senior Management: Ms Hazel Oakley, Electoral Services Manager, Council Offices, Station Road East, Oxted RH8 0BT ☎ 01883 732976 ✉ hoakley@tandridge.gov.uk

Senior Management: Mr Vince Sharp, Committee Services Manager, Council Offices, Station Road East, Oxted RH8 0BT ☎ 01883 732776 ✉ vsharp@tandridge.gov.uk

Senior Management: Ms Giuseppina Valenza, Head of Communications & Customer Services, Council Offices, Station Road East, Oxted RH8 0BT ☎ 01883 732704 🖷 01883 723743 ✉ gvalenza@tandridge.gov.uk

Building Control: Mr Chris Ap Simon, Head of Building Control, Council Offices, Station Road East, Oxted RH8 0BT ☎ 01883 732872 🖷 01883 722015 ✉ capsimon@tandridge.gov.uk

PR / Communications: Ms Giuseppina Valenza, Head of Communications & Customer Services, Council Offices, Station Road East, Oxted RH8 0BT ☎ 01883 732704 🖷 01883 723743 ✉ gvalenza@tandridge.gov.uk

Community Safety: Ms Hilary New, Community Safety Manager, Council Offices, Station Road East, Oxted RH8 0BT ☎ 01883 732703 🖷 01883 723743 ✉ hnew@tandridge.gov.uk

Computer Management: Mr Stuart Mitchenall, Head of Business Support Services, Council Offices, Station Road East, Oxted RH8 0BT ☎ 01883 732724 🖷 01883 722015 ✉ smitchenall@tandridge.gov.uk

Contracts: Mr Simon Mander, Waste & Recycling Contract Manager, Council Offices, Station Road East, Oxted RH8 0BT ☎ 01883 732955 ✉ smander@tandridge.gov.uk

Customer Service: Ms Jane Hermanowski, Customer Services Manager, Council Offices, Station Road East, Oxted RH8 0BT ☎ 01883 732721 🖷 01883 722015 ✉ jhermanowski@tandridge.gov.uk

Direct Labour: Mr Nic Martlew, Depot Manager, Tandridge Commercial Services, Warren Lane Depot, Hurst Green, Oxted RH8 9DB ☎ 01883 732774

Economic Development: Ms Belinda Purcell, Policy Manager, Council Offices, Station Road East, Oxted RH8 0BT ☎ 01883 732705 ✉ bpurcell@tandridge.gov.uk

E-Government: Mr Stuart Mitchenall, Head of Business Support Services, Council Offices, Station Road East, Oxted RH8 0BT ☎ 01883 732724 🖷 01883 722015 ✉ smitchenall@tandridge.gov.uk

Electoral Registration: Ms Hazel Oakley, Electoral Services Manager, Council Offices, Station Road East, Oxted RH8 0BT ☎ 01883 732976 ✉ hoakley@tandridge.gov.uk

Emergency Planning: Mr Clive Moore, Assistant Chief Executive of Legal, Council Offices, Station Road East, Oxted RH8 0BT ☎ 01883 732740 🖷 01883 722015 ✉ cmoore@tandridge.gov.uk

Environmental Health: Mr Paul Barton, Chief Community Services Officer, Council Offices, Station Road East, Oxted RH8 0BT ☎ 01883 732840 🖷 01883 722015 ✉ pbarton@tandridge.gov.uk

Facilities: Ms Linda Barnett, Facilities Manager & Health & Safety Officer, Council Offices, Station Road East, Oxted RH8 0BT ☎ 01883 732899 ✉ lbarnett@tandridge.gov.uk

Finance: Mr Alistair Montgomery, Chief Finance Officer, Council Offices, Station Road East, Oxted RH8 0BT ☎ 01883 732902 🖷 01883 722015 ✉ amontgomery@tandridge.gov.uk

Grounds Maintenance: Mr Steve Hyder, Contracts & Services Manager, Council Offices, Station Road East, Oxted RH8 0BT ☎ 01883 732967 ✉ shyder@tandridge.gov.uk

Health and Safety: Ms Linda Barnett, Facilities Manager & Health & Safety Officer, Council Offices, Station Road East, Oxted RH8 0BT ☎ 01883 732899 ✉ lbarnett@tandridge.gov.uk

Home Energy Conservation: Mr Clifford Darby, Private Sector Housing Manager, Council Offices, Station Road East, Oxted RH8 0BT ☎ 01883 732838 ✉ cdarby@tandridge.gov.uk

Housing: Ms Jayne Godden-Miller, Chief Housing Officer, Council Offices, Station Road East, Oxted RH8 0BT ☎ 01883 732828 ✉ jgodden-miller@tandridge.gov.uk

Housing Maintenance: Mr Stephen Blount, Technical Manager, Council Offices, Station Road East, Oxted RH8 0BT ☎ 01883 732830 🖷 01883 722015 ✉ sblount@tandridge.gov.uk

Legal: Mr Clive Moore, Assistant Chief Executive of Legal, Council Offices, Station Road East, Oxted RH8 0BT ☎ 01883 732740 🖷 01883 722015 ✉ cmoore@tandridge.gov.uk

Licensing: Mr Paul Barton, Chief Community Services Officer, Council Offices, Station Road East, Oxted RH8 0BT ☎ 01883 732840 🖷 01883 722015 ✉ pbarton@tandridge.gov.uk

Lottery Funding, Charity and Voluntary: Mr Vince Sharp, Committee Services Manager, Council Offices, Station Road East, Oxted RH8 0BT ☎ 01883 732776 ✉ vsharp@tandridge.gov.uk

TANDRIDGE

Member Services: Mr Vince Sharp, Committee Services Manager, Council Offices, Station Road East, Oxted RH8 0BT
☎ 01883 732776 ✉ vsharp@tandridge.gov.uk

Parking: Mr Paul Barton, Chief Community Services Officer, Council Offices, Station Road East, Oxted RH8 0BT ☎ 01883 732840 🖷 01883 722015 ✉ pbarton@tandridge.gov.uk

Personnel / HR: Miss Seanne Giddy, Head of Personnel & Training Services, Council Offices, Station Road East, Oxted RH8 0BT ☎ 01883 732979 🖷 01883 722015 ✉ sgiddy@tandridge.gov.uk

Planning: Mr Piers Mason, Chief Planning Officer, Council Offices, Station Road East, Oxted RH8 0BT ☎ 01883 732893
✉ pmason@tandridge.gov.uk

Planning: Ms Sarah Thompson, Head of Strategic Planning Policy, Council Offices, Station Road East, Oxted RH8 0BT
☎ 01883 732887 ✉ sthompson@tandridge.gov.uk

Procurement: Mr Alistair Montgomery, Chief Finance Officer, Council Offices, Station Road East, Oxted RH8 0BT ☎ 01883 732902 🖷 01883 722015 ✉ amontgomery@tandridge.gov.uk

Recycling & Waste Minimisation: Mr Paul Barton, Chief Community Services Officer, Council Offices, Station Road East, Oxted RH8 0BT ☎ 01883 732840 🖷 01883 722015
✉ pbarton@tandridge.gov.uk

Staff Training: Miss Seanne Giddy, Head of Personnel & Training Services, Council Offices, Station Road East, Oxted RH8 0BT
☎ 01883 732979 🖷 01883 722015 ✉ sgiddy@tandridge.gov.uk

Street Scene: Mr Paul Barton, Chief Community Services Officer, Council Offices, Station Road East, Oxted RH8 0BT ☎ 01883 732840 🖷 01883 722015 ✉ pbarton@tandridge.gov.uk

Sustainable Development: Mr Matt Chapman, Planning Policy & Trees Officer, Council Offices, Station Road East, Oxted RH8 0BT ☎ 01883 732764 🖷 01883 722015 ✉ mchapman@tandridge.gov.uk

Waste Collection and Disposal: Mr Paul Barton, Chief Community Services Officer, Council Offices, Station Road East, Oxted RH8 0BT ☎ 01883 732840 🖷 01883 722015
✉ pbarton@tandridge.gov.uk

Waste Management: Mr Paul Barton, Chief Community Services Officer, Council Offices, Station Road East, Oxted RH8 0BT
☎ 01883 732840 🖷 01883 722015 ✉ pbarton@tandridge.gov.uk

Children's Play Areas: Mr Paul Barton, Chief Community Services Officer, Council Offices, Station Road East, Oxted RH8 0BT ☎ 01883 732840 🖷 01883 722015 ✉ pbarton@tandridge.gov.uk

COUNCILLORS

***Chair* Thorn**, Rosemary (CON - Godstone)
cllr.rosemary.thorn@tandridgedc.gov.uk

***Vice-Chair* Cannon**, Patrick (CON - Chaldon)
cllr.patrick.cannon@tandridgedc.gov.uk

***Leader of the Council* Keymer**, Gordon (CON - Oxted North & Tandridge)
cllr.gordon.keymer@tandridgedc.gov.uk

Ainsworth, Simon (CON - Oxted South)
cllr.simon.ainsworth@tandridgedc.gov.uk

Allen, Martin (IND - Tatsfield & Titsey)
cllr.martin.allen@tandridgedc.gov.uk

Black, Gill (CON - Bletchingley & Nutfield)
cllr.gill.black@tandridgedc.gov.uk

Bond, Peter (CON - Burstow, Horne & Outwood)
cllr.peter.bond@tandridgedc.gov.uk

Bradbury, Sakina (CON - Whyteleafe)
cllr.sakina.bradbury@tandridgedc.gov.uk

Caudle, Jill (LD - Valley)
cllr.jill.caundle@tandridgedc.gov.uk

Childs, Nick (CON - Godstone)
cllr.nick.childs@tandridgedc.gov.uk

Compton, Barry (CON - Oxted South)
cllr.barry.compton@tandridgedc.gov.uk

Connolly, Beverley (CON - Harestone)
cllr.beverley.connolly@tandridgedc.gov.uk

Cooley, David (CON - Warlingham West)
cllr.david.cooley@tandridgedc.gov.uk

Cooper, Michael (CON - Harestone)
cllr.michael.cooper@tandridgedc.gov.uk

Duck, Geoffrey (CON - Queens Park)
cllr.geoffrey.duck@tandridgedc.gov.uk

Dunbar, Lindsey (CON - Limpsfield)
cllr.lindsey.dunbar@tandridgedc.gov.uk

Elias, Tony (CON - Bletchingley & Nutfield)
cllr.tony.elias@tandridgedc.gov.uk

Fisher, Martin (CON - Oxted North & Tandridge)
cllr.martin.fisher@tandridgedc.gov.uk

Gascoigne, Jules (CON - Godstone)
cllr.jules.gascoigne@tandridgedc.gov.uk

Gosling, David (LD - Westway)
cllr.david.gosling@tandridgedc.gov.uk

Harwood, Ken (CON - Felbridge)
cllr.ken.harwood@tandridgedc.gov.uk

Ingham, Jane (CON - Valley)
cllr.jane.ingham@tandridgedc.gov.uk

Jones, Robert (CON - Burstow, Horne & Outwood)
cllr.alan.jones@tandridgedc.gov.uk

Lee, David (LD - Whyteleafe)
cllr.david.lee@tandridgedc.gov.uk

Lockwood, Liz (CON - Lingfield & Crowhurst)
cllr.liz.lockwood@tandridgedc.gov.uk

Manley, Clive (CON - Portley)
cllr.clive.manley@tandridgedc.gov.uk

Marks, Sally (CON - Woldingham)
cllr.sally.marks@tandridgedc.gov.uk

Morrow, Simon (LD - Warlingham East, Chelsham & Farleigh)
cllr.simon.morrow@tandridgedc.gov.uk

Pannett, John (CON - Limpsfield)
cllr.john.pannett@tandridgedc.gov.uk

Parker, Elizabeth (CON - Oxted South)
cllr.elizabeth.parker@tandridgedc.gov.uk

Perkins, Brian (CON - Lingfield & Crowhurst)
cllr.brian.perkins@tandridgedc.gov.uk

Pursehouse, Jeremy (LD - Warlingham East, Chelsham & Farleigh)
cllr.j.pursehouse@tandridgedc.gov.uk

Stead, Rod (CON - Queens Park)
cllr.rod.stead@tandridgedc.gov.uk

Steeds, Lesley (CON - Dormansland & Felcourt)
cllr.lesley.steeds@tandridgedc.gov.uk

Steer, Cindy (CON - Warlingham East, Chelsham & Farleigh)

Turner, Hilary (LD - Portley)
cllr.hilary.turner@tandridgedc.gov.uk

Vickers, Debbie (CON - Bletchingley & Nutfield)
cllr.debbie.vickers@tandridgedc.gov.uk

Wates, Guy (CON - Burstow, Horne & Outwood)
cllr.guy.waters@tandridge.gov.uk

Webster, Eithne (CON - Westway)
cllr.eithne.webster@tandridgedc.gov.uk

Weightman, David (CON - Oxted North & Tandridge)
cllr.david.weightman@tandridgedc.gov.uk

Whittle, Glynis (CON - Warlingham West)
cllr.glynis.whittle@tandridgedc.gov.uk

Young, Maureen (CON - Dormansland & Felcourt)
cllr.maureen.young@tandridgedc.gov.uk

POLITICAL COMPOSITION
CON: 35, LD: 6, IND: 1

COMMITTEE CHAIRS
Licensing: Mrs Elizabeth Parker

Planning: Mrs Gill Black

Taunton Deane D

Taunton Deane Borough Council, The Deane House, Belvedere Road, Taunton TA1 1HE
☎ 01823 356356 🖷 01823 356329 ✉ enquiries@tauntondeane.gov.uk
💻 www.tauntondeane.gov.uk

FACTS AND FIGURES
Parliamentary Constituencies: Taunton Deane
EU Constituencies: South West
Election Frequency: Elections are of whole council

PRINCIPAL OFFICERS
Chief Executive: Mrs Penny James, Chief Executive, The Deane House, Belvedere Road, Taunton TA1 1HE
✉ pjames@westsomerset.gov.uk

Assistant Chief Executive: Mr Bruce Lang, Assistant Chief Executive, The Deane House, Belvedere Road, Taunton TA1 1HE
☎ 01643 703704 ✉ bdlang@westsomerset.gov.uk

Senior Management: Ms Shirlene Adam, Deputy Chief Executive & Director - Operations, The Deane House, Belvedere Road, Taunton TA1 1HE ☎ 01643 703704 ✉ s.adam@tauntondeane.gov.uk

Senior Management: Mr James Barrah, Director - Housing & Communities, The Deane House, Belvedere Road, Taunton TA1 1HE
☎ 01823 358699 🖷 01823 356329
✉ j.barrah@tauntondeane.gov.uk

Senior Management: Mr Brendon Cleere, Director - Growth & Development, The Deane House, Belvedere Road, Taunton TA1 1HE
☎ 01823 356350 🖷 01823 356329
✉ b.cleere@tauntondeane.gov.uk

Access Officer / Social Services (Disability): Mr Edwin Norton, Senior Building Control, Surveyor & Access Officer, The Deane House, Belvedere Road, Taunton TA1 1HE ☎ 01823 356476 🖷 01823 356478 ✉ e.norton@tauntondeane.gov.uk

Architect, Building / Property Services: Mr Tim Child, Divisional Manager - Property Estates Team, The Deane House, Belvedere Road, Taunton TA1 1HE ☎ 01823 356356 🖷 01823 356534 ✉ t.child@tauntondeane.gov.uk

Building Control: Mr Darren Rowbottom, Building Control Manager, The Deane House, Belvedere Road, Taunton TA1 1HE
☎ 01823 356473 🖷 01823 356478
✉ d.rowbottom@tauntondeane.gov.uk

PR / Communications: Mrs Debbie Rundle, Media & PR Officer, The Deane House, Belvedere Road, Taunton TA1 1HE ☎ 01823 356407 🖷 01823 356329 ✉ d.rundle@tauntondeane.gov.uk

Community Planning: Mr Tim Burton, Assistant Director - Planning & Environment, The Deane House, Belvedere Road, Taunton TA1 1HE ☎ 01823 358403 🖷 01823 356329
✉ t.burton@tauntondeane.gov.uk

Community Safety: Ms Tracey-Ann Biss, Parking & Civil Contingencies Manager, The Deane House, Belvedere Road, Taunton TA1 1HE ☎ 01823 356501 🖷 01823 356329
✉ t.biss@tauntondeane.gov.uk

Computer Management: Ms Fiona Kirkham, ICT Manager, The Deane House, Belvedere Road, Taunton TA1 1HE ☎ 01823 356522 🖷 01823 356329 ✉ f.kirkham@tauntondeane.gov.uk

Corporate Services: Mr Richard Sealy, Assistant Director - Corporate Services, The Deane House, Belvedere Road, Taunton TA1 1HE ☎ 01823 658690 ✉ r.sealy@tauntondeane.gov.uk

Customer Service: Mr Rob Liddell, Head of Customer Contact, The Deane House, Belvedere Road, Taunton TA1 1HE ☎ 01823 356356 🖷 01823 356429 ✉ r.liddell@tauntondeane.gov.uk

Direct Labour: Mr Chris Hall, Assistant Director - Operational Delivery, The Deane House, Belvedere Road, Taunton TA1 1HE
☎ 01823 356403 ✉ c.hall@tauntondeane.gov.uk

Economic Development: Mr David Evans, Economic Development Manager, The Deane House, Belvedere Road, Taunton TA1 1HE ☎ 01823 356545 ✉ d.evans@tauntondeane.gov.uk

Economic Development: Mr Ian Timms, Assistant Director - Business Development, The Deane House, Belvedere Road, Taunton TA1 1HE ☎ 01823 356577 ✉ itimms@westsomerset.gov.uk

Electoral Registration: Mrs Elisa Day, Electoral Services Manager, West Somerset House, Killick Way, Williton, Taunton TA4 4QA ☎ 01984 635272 ✉ eday@westsomerset.gov.uk

Emergency Planning: Ms Tracey-Ann Biss, Parking & Civil Contingencies Manager, The Deane House, Belvedere Road, Taunton TA1 1HE ☎ 01823 356501 🖷 01823 356329 ✉ t.biss@tauntondeane.gov.uk

Energy Management: Mr Richard Bryant, Democratic Services Manager, The Deane House, Belvedere Road, Taunton TA1 1HE ☎ 01823 356414 🖷 01823 356329 ✉ r.bryant@tauntondeane.gov.uk

Environmental Health: Mr Scott Weetch, Community & Client Services Manager, The Deane House, Belvedere Road, Taunton TA1 1HE ☎ 01823 356317 🖷 01823 356329 ✉ s.weetch@tauntondeane.gov.uk

Estates, Property & Valuation: Mr Tim Child, Divisional Manager - Property Estates Team, The Deane House, Belvedere Road, Taunton TA1 1HE ☎ 01823 356356 🖷 01823 356534 ✉ t.child@tauntondeane.gov.uk

Facilities: Ms Angela Hill, Facilities & Corporate Administration Manager, The Deane House, Belvedere Road, Taunton TA1 1HE ☎ 01823 356597 ✉ a.hill@tauntondeane.gov.uk

Finance: Mr Paul Fitzgerald, Assistant Director - Resources, West Somerset House, Killick Way, Williton, Taunton TA4 4QA ✉ pfitzgerald@westsomerset.gov.uk

Grounds Maintenance: Mr Cyril Rowe, Open Spaces Manager, Priory Way Depot, Taunton TA1 2BB ✉ c.rowe@tauntondeane.gov.uk

Health and Safety: Ms Catrin Brown, Health & Safety Manager, The Deane House, Belvedere Road, Taunton TA1 1HE ☎ 01823 356578 ✉ c.brown@tauntondeane.gov.uk

Home Energy Conservation: Ms Barbara Wells, Energy Efficiency Officer, Sedgemoor Council, Bridgwater House, King's Square, Bridgwater TA6 3AR ☎ ; 01278 436426 ✉ b.wells@sedgemoor.gov.uk

Housing: Mr Steve Boland, Housing Services Lead, The Deane House, Belvedere Road, Taunton TA1 1HE ☎ 01823 356446 ✉ s.boland@tauntondeane.gov.uk

Housing: Mr Kene Ibezi, Assistant Director - Property & Development, The Deane House, Belvedere Road, Taunton TA1 1HE ☎ 01823 356356 ✉ k.ibezi@tauntondeane.gov.uk

Housing: Mr Simon Lewis, Assistant Director - Housing & Community Development, The Deane House, Belvedere Road, Taunton TA1 1HE ☎ 01823 356397 ✉ s.lewis@tauntondeane.gov.uk

Housing Maintenance: Mr Phil Webb, Housing Manager - Property Services, The Deane House, Belvedere Road, Taunton TA1 1HE ☎ 01823 356505 ✉ p.webb@tauntondeane.gov.uk

Legal: Mr Roy Pinney, Legal Services Manager, The Deane House, Belvedere Road, Taunton TA1 1HE ☎ 01823 356409 🖷 01823 356329 ✉ r.pinney@tauntondeane.gov.uk

Leisure and Cultural Services: Ms Alison North, Community Leisure Manager, Priory Depot, Priory Way, Taunton TA1 1HE ☎ 01823 356576 ✉ a.north@tauntondeane.gov.uk

Licensing: Mr Ian Carter, Licensing Manager, The Deane House, Belvedere Road, Taunton TA1 1HE ☎ 01823 358406 ✉ i.carter@tauntondeane.gov.uk

Member Services: Mr Richard Bryant, Democratic Services Manager, The Deane House, Belvedere Road, Taunton TA1 1HE ☎ 01823 356414 🖷 01823 356329 ✉ r.bryant@tauntondeane.gov.uk

Parking: Ms Tracey-Ann Biss, Parking & Civil Contingencies Manager, The Deane House, Belvedere Road, Taunton TA1 1HE ☎ 01823 356501 🖷 01823 356329 ✉ t.biss@tauntondeane.gov.uk

Personnel / HR: Ms Fiona Wills, Human Resources Manager, The Deane House, Belvedere Road, Taunton TA1 1HE ☎ 01823 356450 🖷 01823 356329 ✉ f.wills@tauntondeane.gov.uk

Planning: Mr Tim Burton, Assistant Director - Planning & Environment, The Deane House, Belvedere Road, Taunton TA1 1HE ☎ 01823 358403 🖷 01823 356329 ✉ t.burton@tauntondeane.gov.uk

Planning: Mr Bryn Kitching, Area Planning Manager, The Deane House, Belvedere Road, Taunton TA1 1HE

Procurement: Mr Jon Batstone, Procurement Manager, The Deane House, Belvedere Road, Taunton TA1 1HE ☎ 01823 358286 ✉ j.batstone@tauntondeane.gov.uk

Staff Training: Ms Fiona Wills, Human Resources Manager, The Deane House, Belvedere Road, Taunton TA1 1HE ☎ 01823 356450 🖷 01823 356329 ✉ f.wills@tauntondeane.gov.uk

Tourism: Ms Corinne Matthews, Economic Regeneration Manager, West Somerset House, Killick Way, Williton, Taunton TA4 4QA ☎ 01984 635287 🖷 01984 633022 ✉ cmatthews@westsomerset.gov.uk

COUNCILLORS

***Leader of the Council* Williams**, John (CON - Neroche)
cllr.j.williams@tauntondeane.gov.uk

***Deputy Leader of the Council* Edwards**, Mark (CON - Trull)
cllr.m.edwards@tauntondeane.gov.uk

Adkins, Michael (CON - Lyngford)
cllr.m.adkins@tauntondeane.gov.uk

Adkins, Jean (CON - Norton Fitzwarren)
cllr.j.adkins@tauntondeane.gov.uk

Aldridge, Thomas (UKIP - Lyngford)
cllr.t.aldridge@tauntondeane.gov.uk

Appleby, Christopher (LD - Halcon)
cllr.c.appleby@tauntondeane.gov.uk

Beale, Terry (CON - Killams and Mountfield)
cllr.t.beale@tauntondeane.gov.uk

Berry, Patrick (CON - Manor and Wilton)
cllr.p.berry@tauntondeane.gov.uk

Blatchford, Julia (CON - Bishops Hull)
cllr.j.blatchford@tauntondeane.gov.uk

Bowrah, Robert (CON - Wellington, Rockwell Green and West)
cllr.r.bowrah@tauntondeane.gov.uk

Brown, William (CON - Wellington North)
cllr.w.brown@tauntondeane.gov.uk

Cavill, Norman (CON - West Monkton)
cllr.n.cavill@tauntondeane.gov.uk

Coles, Simon (LD - Eastgate)
cllr.s.coles@tauntondeane.gov.uk

Coombes, William (CON - Blackbrook and Holway)
cllr.w.coombes@tauntondeane.gov.uk

Cossey, Duncan (CON - North Curry & Stoke St Gregory)
cllr.d.cossey@tauntondeane.gov.uk

Davies, Thomas (CON - Pyrland and Rowbarton)
cllr.t.davies@tauntondeane.gov.uk

Durdan, Kelly (CON - Ruishton & Creech)
cllr.k.durdan@tauntondeane.gov.uk

Durdan, David (CON - Ruishton & Creech)
cllr.d.durdan@tauntondeane.gov.uk

Edwards, Charlotte (CON - Blackdown)
cllr.c.edwards@tauntondeane.gov.uk

Farbahi, Habib (LD - Comeytrowe)
cllr.h.farbahi@tauntondeane.gov.uk

Floyd, Mollie (LD - Comeytrowe)
cllr.m.floyd@tauntondeane.gov.uk

Gage, John (CON - Pyrland and Rowbarton)
cllr.j.gage@tauntondeane.gov.uk

Gaines, Edward (IND - Wiveliscombe and West Deane)
cllr.e.gaines@tauntondeane.gov.uk

Govier, Andrew (LAB - Wellington North)
cllr.a.govier@tauntondeane.gov.uk

Gunner, Alison (CON - Bishops Lydeard)
cllr.a.gunner@tauntondeane.gov.uk

Habgood, Roger (CON - Bradford on Tone)
cllr.r.habgood@tauntondeane.gov.uk

Hall, Terence (CON - Manor and Wilton)
cllr.t.hall@tauntondeane.gov.uk

Henley, Ross (LD - Wellington East)
cllr.r.henley@tauntondeane.gov.uk

Herbert, Catherine (CON - Killams and Mountfield)
cllr.c.herbert@tauntondeane.gov.uk

Hill, Marcia (LD - Pyrland and Rowbarton)
cllr.m.hill@tauntondeane.gov.uk

Hill, Chris (CON - Monument)
cllr.c.hill@tauntondeane.gov.uk

Horsley, Jefferson (LD - Fairwater)
cllr.j.horsley@tauntondeane.gov.uk

James, Gary (CON - Wellington East)
cllr.g.james@tauntondeane.gov.uk

Lees, Richard (LD - Eastgate)
cllr.r.lees@tauntondeane.gov.uk

Lees, Sue (LD - Fairwater)
cllr.s.lees@tauntondeane.gov.uk

Lisgo, Libby (LAB - Lyngford)
cllr.l.lisgo@tauntondeane.gov.uk

Martin-Scott, Stephen (CON - Manor and Wilton)
cllr.s.martin-scott@tauntondeane.gov.uk

Morrell, Ian (IND - Bishops Hull)
cllr.i.morrell@tauntondeane.gov.uk

Nicholls, Simon (LD - Comeytrowe)
cllr.s.nicholls@tauntondeane.gov.uk

Parrish, Richard (CON - West Monkton)
cllr.r.parrish@tauntondeane.gov.uk

Priory-Sankey, Hazel (LD - Blackbrook and Holway)
cllr.h.prior-sankey@tauntondeane.gov.uk

Reed, Janet (CON - Wellington, Rockwell Green and West)
cllr.j.reed@tauntondeane.gov.uk

Ross, Steve (IND - Wiveliscombs and West Deane)
cllr.s.ross@tauntondeane.gov.uk

Ryan, Roger (CON - Halcon)
cllr.r.ryan@tauntondeane.gov.uk

Smith, Frederica (LD - Halcon)
cllr.frederica.smith@tauntondeane.gov.uk

Smith, Francesca (LD - Blackbrook and Holway)
cllr.f.smith@tauntondeane.gov.uk

Stock-Williams, Vivienne (IND - Wellington, Rockwell Green and West)
cllr.v.stock-williams@tauntondeane.gov.uk

Stone, Philip (LD - North Curry & Stoke St Gregory)
cllr.p.stone@tauntondeane.gov.uk

Sully, Andrew (CON - Norton Fitzwarren)
cllr.a.sully@tauntondeane.gov.uk

Townsend, Nicolas (CON - Staplegrove)
cllr.n.townsend@tauntondeane.gov.uk

Tucker, Caroline (CON - Staplegrove)
cllr.c.tucker@tauntondeane.gov.uk

Warmington, Jane (CON - Bishops Lydeard)
cllr.j.warmington@tauntondeane.gov.uk

Watson, Peter (CON - Bishops Lydeard)
cllr.p.watson@tauntondeane.gov.uk

Webber, Denise (CON - West Monkton)
cllr.d.webber@tauntondeane.gov.uk

Wedderkopp, Danny (LD - Fairwater)
cllr.d.wedderkopp@tauntondeane.gov.uk

Wren, Gwilyn (CON - Milverton and North Deane)
cllr.g.wren@tauntondeane.gov.uk

POLITICAL COMPOSITION

CON: 34, LD: 15, IND: 4, LAB: 2, UKIP: 1

TEIGNBRIDGE

Teignbridge D

Teignbridge District Council, Forde House, Brunel Road, Newton Abbot TQ12 4XX
☎ 01626 361101 ✉ info@teignbridge.gov.uk
🖳 www.teignbridge.gov.uk

FACTS AND FIGURES

EU Constituencies: South West
Election Frequency: Elections are of whole council

PRINCIPAL OFFICERS

Chief Executive: Ms Nicola Bulbeck, Chief Executive, Forde House, Brunel Road, Newton Abbot TQ12 4XX ☎ 01626 361101 🖷 01626 215169 ✉ nicola.bulbeck@teignbridge.gov.uk

Deputy Chief Executive: Mr Phil Shears, Deputy Chief Executive, Forde House, Brunel Road, Newton Abbot TQ12 4XX ☎ 01626 361101 🖷 01626 215169 ✉ phil.shears@teignbridge.gov.uk

Senior Management: Mrs Sue Aggett, Business Lead - Housing & Health, Forde House, Brunel Road, Newton Abbot TQ12 4XX ☎ 01626 215163 🖷 01626 215169 ✉ sue.aggett@teignbridge.gov.uk

Senior Management: Mr Stephen Hodder, Business Lead - Corporate Services & Transformation, Forde House, Brunel Road, Newton Abbot TQ12 4XX ☎ 01626 215110 🖷 01626 215169 ✉ steve.hodder@teignbridge.gov.uk

Architect, Building / Property Services: Mr Tony Watson, Business Manager - Economy & Assets, Forde House, Brunel Road, Newton Abbot TQ12 4XX ☎ 01626 215828 🖷 01626 215483 ✉ tony.watson@teignbridge.gov.uk

Best Value: Mr Stephen Hodder, Business Lead - Corporate Services & Transformation, Forde House, Brunel Road, Newton Abbot TQ12 4XX ☎ 01626 215110 🖷 01626 215169 ✉ steve.hodder@teignbridge.gov.uk

Building Control: Mr Andy Carpenter, Head - Building Control Partnership, Forde House, Brunel Road, Newton Abbot TQ12 4XX ☎ 01626 215721 🖷 01626 215761 ✉ andrew.carpenter@teignbridge.gov.uk

PR / Communications: Ms Emma Pearcy, Communications Officer, Forde House, Brunel Road, Newton Abbot TQ12 4XX ☎ 01626 215164 🖷 01626 215169 ✉ emma.pearcy@teignbridge.gov.uk

Community Planning: Mr Simon Thornley, Business Manager - Strategic Place, Forde House, Brunel Road, Newton Abbot TQ12 4XX ☎ 01626 215706 ✉ simon.thornley@teignbridge.gov.uk

Community Safety: Mrs Rebecca Hewitt, Senior Community Safety Officer, Forde House, Brunel Road, Newton Abbot TQ12 4XX ☎ 01626 215873 ✉ rebecca.hewitt@teignbridge.gov.uk

Computer Management: Mr Chris Powell, Chief Operating Officer, Forde House, Brunel Road, Newton Abbot TQ12 4XX ☎ 01392 265050 ✉ chris.powell@strata.solutions

Contracts: Mrs Carly Wedderburn, Corporate Procurement Officer, Forde House, Brunel Road, Newton Abbot TQ12 4XX ☎ 01626 215120 ✉ carly.wedderburn@teignbridge.gov.uk

Customer Service: Mrs Elizabeth Guy, Customer Services Manager, Forde House, Brunel Road, Newton Abbot TQ12 4XX ☎ 01626 215510 ✉ liz.guy@teignbridge.gov.uk

Economic Development: Mr Tony Watson, Business Manager - Economy & Assets, Forde House, Brunel Road, Newton Abbot TQ12 4XX ☎ 01626 215828 🖷 01626 215483 ✉ tony.watson@teignbridge.gov.uk

Electoral Registration: Mrs Cathy Ruelens, Electoral Services Co-ordinator, Forde House, Brunel Road, Newton Abbot TQ12 4XX ☎ 01626 215103 🖷 01626 215169 ✉ cathy.ruelens@teignbridge.gov.uk

Emergency Planning: Mr Ian Flood Page, Emergency Planning Officer, Forde House, Brunel Road, Newton Abbot TQ12 4XX ☎ 01626 215835 🖷 01626 215857 ✉ ian.flood@teignbridge.gov.uk

Energy Management: Mrs Sue Aggett, Business Lead - Housing & Health, Forde House, Brunel Road, Newton Abbot TQ12 4XX ☎ 01626 215163 🖷 01626 215169 ✉ sue.aggett@teignbridge.gov.uk

Environmental Health: Mrs Sue Aggett, Business Lead - Housing & Health, Forde House, Brunel Road, Newton Abbot TQ12 4XX ☎ 01626 215163 🖷 01626 215169 ✉ sue.aggett@teignbridge.gov.uk

Estates, Property & Valuation: Mr Tony Watson, Business Manager - Economy & Assets, Forde House, Brunel Road, Newton Abbot TQ12 4XX ☎ 01626 215828 🖷 01626 215483 ✉ tony.watson@teignbridge.gov.uk

European Liaison: Mr Neil Blaney, Economy Manager, Forde House, Brunel Road, Newton Abbot TQ12 4XX ☎ 01626 215233 ✉ neil.blaney@teignbridge.gov.uk

Facilities: Mr Tony Watson, Business Manager - Economy & Assets, Forde House, Brunel Road, Newton Abbot TQ12 4XX ☎ 01626 215828 🖷 01626 215483 ✉ tony.watson@teignbridge.gov.uk

Finance: Mrs Lesley Tucker, Section 151 Officer, Forde House, Brunel Road, Newton Abbot TQ12 4XX ☎ 01626 215203 🖷 01626 215169 ✉ lesley.tucker@teignbridge.gov.uk

Grounds Maintenance: Ms Lorraine Montgomery, Business Manager - Environment & Leisure, Forde House, Brunel Road, Newton Abbot TQ12 4XX ☎ 01626 215852 🖷 01626 215613 ✉ lorraine.montgomery@teignbridge.gov.uk

Health and Safety: Mr Peter Wilson, Health & Safety Officer, Forde House, Brunel Road, Newton Abbot TQ12 4XX ☎ 01626 215155 🖷 01626 215436 ✉ peter.wilson@teignbridge.gov.uk

Home Energy Conservation: Ms Zoe Farmer, Affordable Warmth & Home Energy Officer, Forde House, Brunel Road, Newton Abbot TQ12 4XX ☎ 01626 215764 🖷 01626 215316 ✉ zoe.farmer@teignbridge.gov.uk

Housing: Mrs Amanda Pujol, Business Manager - Housing & Health, Forde House, Brunel Road, Newton Abbot TQ12 4XX ☎ 01626 215301 🖷 01626 215316 ✉ amanda.pujol@teignbridge.gov.uk

Legal: Mr Duncan Moors, Solicitor to the Council, Forde House, Brunel Road, Newton Abbot TQ12 4XX ☎ 01626 215119 🖷 01626 215169 ✉ duncan.moors@teignbridge.gov.uk

Leisure and Cultural Services: Ms Lorraine Montgomery, Business Manager - Environment & Leisure, Forde House, Brunel Road, Newton Abbot TQ12 4XX ☎ 01626 215852 🖷 01626 215613 ✉ lorraine.montgomery@teignbridge.gov.uk

Licensing: Mrs Andrea Furness, Licensing Officer, Forde House, Brunel Road, Newton Abbot TQ12 4XX ☎ 01626 215108 🖷 01626 215169 ✉ andrea.furness@teignbridge.gov.uk

Member Services: Mr Neil Aggett, Democratic Services Manager, Forde House, Brunel Road, Newton Abbot TQ12 4XX ☎ 01626 215113 🖷 01626 215169 ✉ neil.aggett@teignbridge.gov.uk

Parking: Mr Neil Blaney, Economy Manager, Forde House, Brunel Road, Newton Abbot TQ12 4XX ☎ 01626 215233 ✉ neil.blaney@teignbridge.gov.uk

Personnel / HR: Mr Stephen Hodder, Business Lead - Corporate Services & Transformation, Forde House, Brunel Road, Newton Abbot TQ12 4XX ☎ 01626 215110 🖷 01626 215169 ✉ steve.hodder@teignbridge.gov.uk

Planning: Mr Nick Davies, Business Manager - Strategic Place, Forde House, Brunel Road, Newton Abbot TQ12 4XX ☎ 01626 215745 🖷 01626 215770 ✉ nick.davies@teignbridge.gov.uk

Procurement: Mrs Carly Wedderburn, Corporate Procurement Officer, Forde House, Brunel Road, Newton Abbot TQ12 4XX ☎ 01626 215120 ✉ carly.wedderburn@teignbridge.gov.uk

Recycling & Waste Minimisation: Mr Chris Braines, Waste Management Officer, Forde House, Brunel Road, Newton Abbot TQ12 4XX ☎ 01626 215841 🖷 01626 334882 ✉ chris.braines@teignbridge.gov.uk

Regeneration: Mr Tony Watson, Business Manager - Economy & Assets, Forde House, Brunel Road, Newton Abbot TQ12 4XX ☎ 01626 215828 🖷 01626 215483 ✉ tony.watson@teignbridge.gov.uk

Staff Training: Mrs Debbie Hutchings, Training & Development Manager, Forde House, Brunel Road, Newton Abbot TQ12 4XX ☎ 01626 215138 🖷 01626 215191 ✉ debbie.hutchings@teignbridge.gov.uk

Sustainable Communities: Mr Gary Powell, Community Projects Officer, Forde House, Brunel Road, Newton Abbot TQ12 4XX ☎ 01626 215169 ✉ gary.powell@teignbridge.gov.uk

Tourism: Mrs Michelle Taylor, Tourism & Marketing Officer, Forde House, Brunel Road, Newton Abbot TQ12 4XX ☎ 01626 215614 ✉ michelle.taylor@teignbridge.gov.uk

Town Centre: Mr Tony Watson, Business Manager - Economy & Assets, Forde House, Brunel Road, Newton Abbot TQ12 4XX ☎ 01626 215828 🖷 01626 215483 ✉ tony.watson@teignbridge.gov.uk

Waste Collection and Disposal: Mr Chris Braines, Waste Management Officer, Forde House, Brunel Road, Newton Abbot TQ12 4XX ☎ 01626 215841 🖷 01626 334882 ✉ chris.braines@teignbridge.gov.uk

Waste Management: Mr Chris Braines, Waste Management Officer, Forde House, Brunel Road, Newton Abbot TQ12 4XX ☎ 01626 215841 🖷 01626 334882 ✉ chris.braines@teignbridge.gov.uk

COUNCILLORS

Leader of the Council **Christophers**, Jeremy (CON - Haytor)
Jeremy.Christophers@teignbridge.gov.uk

Deputy Leader of the Council **Gribble**, George (CON - Bovey)
george.gribble@teignbridge.gov.uk

Austen, Beryl (IND - Kingsteignton East)
beryl.austen@teignbridge.gov.uk

Barker, Stuart (CON - Ashburton and Buckfastleigh)
stuart.barker@teignbridge.gov.uk

Bladon, Geoff (CON - Teignmouth Central)
geoff.bladon@teignbridge.gov.uk

Brodie, Jackie (LD - Newton Abbot Bushell)
jackie.brodie@teignbridge.gov.uk

Bromell, Peter (IND - Teignbridge North)
Peter.Bromell@teignbridge.gov.uk

Bullivant, Phil (CON - Newton Abbot Bradley)
philip.bullivant@teignbridge.gov.uk

Clarance, Chris (CON - Shaldon and Stokeinteignhead)
Christopher.Clarence@teignbridge.gov.uk

Clemens, Humphrey (CON - Dawlish South West)
Humphrey.Clemens@teignbridge.gov.uk

Colclough, Mary (IND - Ambrook)
Mary.Colclough@teignbridge.gov.uk

Connett, Alan (LD - Kenton with Starcross)
Alan.Connett@teignbridge.gov.uk

Cook, Sheila (LD - Kerswell with Combe)
sheila.cook@teignbridge.gov.uk

Cox, David (LD - Teignmouth West)
David.Cox@teignbridge.gov.uk

Dennis, Charlie (CON - Ashburton and Buckfastleigh)
charlie.dennis@teignbridge.gov.uk

Dewhurst, Alistair (LD - Ipplepen)
alistair.dewhirst@teignbridge.gov.uk

Ford, Amanda (CON - Teign Valley)
amanda.ford@teignbridge.gov.uk

Fusco, Vince (CON - Teignmouth East)
vince.fusco@teignbridge.gov.uk

Golder, Timothy (CON - Bishopsteignton)
timothy.golder@teignbridge.gov.uk

Goodey, John (CON - Kenn Valley)
john.goodey@teignbridge.gov.uk

Grainger, Judy (CON - Newton Abbot Bushell)
judy.grainger@teignbridge.gov.uk

Haines, Mike (IND - Kerswell with Combe)
Mike.Haines@teignbridge.gov.uk

Hellier-Lang, Doug (CON - Chudleigh)
doug.hellierlang@teignbridge.gov.uk

Hockin, Ted (CON - Dawlish Central and North East)
Edward.Hockin@teignbridge.gov.uk

Hocking, Michael (LD - Newton Abbot Bradley)
Michael.Hocking@teignbridge.gov.uk

Hook, Gordon (LD - Newton Abbot Buckland and Milber)
gordon.hook@teignbridge.gov.uk

Jeffery, Mike (CON - Moorland)
Mike.Jeffery@teignbridge.gov.uk

Johnson-King, Patricia (CON - Chudleigh)
patricia.johnson-king@teignbridge.gov.uk

Jones, Ann (LD - Newton Abbot College)
ann.jones@teignbridge.gov.uk

Kerswell, Avril (CON - Bovey)
avril.kerswell@teignbridge.gov.uk

Klinkenberg, Anna (CON - Bovey)
Anna.Klinkenberg@teignbridge.gov.uk

Lake, Kevin (CON - Kenn Valley)
Kevin.Lake@teignbridge.gov.uk

Matthews, Dave (CON - Teignmouth West)
dave.matthews@teignbridge.gov.uk

Mayne, Lisa (CON - Dawlish Central and North East)
lisa.mayne@teignbridge.gov.uk

Nutley, John (LD - Ashburton and Buckfastleigh)
john.nutley@teignbridge.gov.uk

Orme, Jacqui (CON - Teignmouth Central)
jacqui.orme@teignbridge.gov.uk

Parker, Colin (LD - Newton Abbot Buckland and Milber)
colin.parker@teignbridge.gov.uk

Pilkington, Mike (LD - Newton Abbot College)
mike.pilkington@teignbridge.gov.uk

Price, Graham (CON - Dawlish Central and North East)
Graham.Price@teignbridge.gov.uk

Prowse, Rosalind (CON - Dawlish South West)
Rosalind.Prowse@teignbridge.gov.uk

Rollason, David (LD - Kingsteignton West)
dave.rollason@teignbridge.gov.uk

Russell, Sylvia (CON - Teignmouth East)
Sylvia.Russell@teignbridge.gov.uk

Smith, Dennis (CON - Ambrook)
Dennis.Smith@teignbridge.gov.uk

Thorne, Bill (CON - Kingsteignton West)
bill.thorne@teignbridge.gov.uk

Walters, Mike (CON - Kingsteignton East)
Mike.Walters@teignbridge.gov.uk

Winsor, Reg (CAP - Newton Abbot Buckland and Milber)
reg.winsor@teignbridge.gov.uk

POLITICAL COMPOSITION

CON: 29, LD: 12, IND: 4, CAP: 1

Telford & Wrekin U

Telford & Wrekin Council, Civic Offices, Telford TF3 4LD
☎ 01952 380000 📠 01952 290820 🖱 telford@telford.gov.uk
💻 www.telford.gov.uk

FACTS AND FIGURES

Parliamentary Constituencies: Telford, Wrekin, The
EU Constituencies: West Midlands
Election Frequency: Elections are of whole council

PRINCIPAL OFFICERS

Chief Executive: Mr Richard Partington, Managing Director, Addenbrooke House, Ironmasters Way, Telford TF3 4NT ☎ 01952 380130 📠 01952 380104 🖱 richard.partington@telford.gov.uk

Senior Management: Mrs Laura Johnston, Director of Children & Family Services, Addenbrooke House, Ironmasters Way, Telford TF3 4NT ☎ 01952 385100 🖱 laura.johnston@telford.gov.uk

Senior Management: Mr Jonathan Rowe, Director of Neighbourhood, Customer & Cultural Services, Addenbrooke House, Ironmasters Way, Telford TF3 4NT ☎ 01952 382900 🖱 jonathan.rowe@telford.gov.uk

Senior Management: Mr Paul Taylor, Director of Care, Health & Wellbeing, Addenbrooke House, Ironmasters Way, Telford TF3 4NT ☎ 01952 381200 🖱 paul.taylor@telford.gov.uk

Architect, Building / Property Services: Mr Chris Goulson, Property & Design Manager, 2nd Floor, Wellington Civic & Leisure Centre, Wellington, Telford TF1 1LX ☎ 01952 384302 🖱 chris.goulson@telford.gov.uk

Building Control: Mr Tony Reah, Building Control Team Leader, Wellington Civic & Leisure Centre, 1st Floor, Wellington, Telford TF1 1LX ☎ 01952 384500 🖱 tony.reah@telford.gov.uk

Catering Services: Ms Kate Sumner, Catering Service Delivery Manager, 2nd Floor, Wellington Civic & Leisure Centre, Wellington, Telford TF1 1LX ☎ 01952 380917 🖱 kate.sumner@telford.gov.uk

Civil Registration: Ms Kerry Caitlin, Superintendent Registrar / Registration Services Manager, Wellington Civic & Leisure Centre, Wellington, Telford TF1 1LX ☎ 01952 382444 📠 01952 382452 🖱 kerry.caitlin@telford.gov.uk

PR / Communications: Mr Nigel Newman, Corporate Communications Manager, Addenbrooke House, Ironmasters Way, Telford TF3 4NT ☎ 01952 382403 🖱 nigel.newman@telford.gov.uk

Community Safety: Mr Jas Bedesha, Homelessness & Housing Needs Manager, Darby House, 5th Floor Wing C, Telford TF3 4LD ☎ 01952 382101 🖱 jas.bedesha@telford.gov.uk

Computer Management: Miss Kirsty King, ICT Service Delivery Manager, 1st Floor, Whitechapel House, Telford TF2 9SP ☎ 01952 383480 🖱 kirsty.king@telford.gov.uk

Consumer Protection and Trading Standards: Ms Nicky Minshall, Public Protection Service Delivery Manager, Darby House, 7th Floor, Wing A,, Telford TF3 4LD ☎ 01952 381820 ✉ nicky.minshall@telford.gov.uk

Contracts: Mr Ken Clarke, Assistant Director - Finance, Audit & Information Governance, Addenbrooke House, Ironmasters Way, Telford TF3 4NT ☎ 01952 383100 🖷 01952 301104 ✉ ken.clarke@telford.gov.uk

Customer Service: Ms Angie Astley, Assistant Director - Neighbourhood & Customer Services, Addenbrooke House, Ironmasters Way, Telford TF3 4NT ☎ 01952 382400 ✉ angie.astley@telford.gov.uk

Economic Development: Ms Katherine Kynaston, Business & Development Planning Manager, Wellington Civic & Leisure Centre, Wellington, Telford TF1 1LX ☎ 01952 384201 🖷 01952 384254 ✉ katherine.kynaston@telford.gov.uk

Education: Mr Jim Collins, Assistant Director - Education & Corporate Parenting, Addenbrooke House, Ironmasters Way, Telford TF3 4NT ☎ 01952 380800 ✉ jim.collins@telford.gov.uk

Electoral Registration: Mr Phil Griffiths, Democratic Services Manager, Addenbrooke House, Ironmasters Way, Telford TF3 4NT ☎ 01952 383210 🖷 01952 383253 ✉ phil.griffiths@telford.gov.uk

Emergency Planning: Ms Heather Gumsley, Civil Resilience Manager, Unit B4B, Stafford Park 11, Telford TF3 3AY ☎ 01952 381957 ✉ heather.gumsley@telford.gov.uk

Energy Management: Mr Mal Yale, Facilities Management & Cleaning Services, 2nd Floor, Wellington Civic & Leisure Centre, Wellington, Telford TF1 1LX ☎ 01952 380931 ✉ mal.yale@telford.gov.uk

Facilities: Mr Clive Barton, Facilities Management Group Manager, Wellington Civic & Leisure Centre, Wellington, Telford TF1 1LX ☎ 01952 380000 ✉ clive.barton@telford.gov.uk

Fleet Management: Ms Viv McKay, Commissioning - Vulnerable People, Darby House, 2nd Floor, Wing C, Telford TF3 4LD ☎ 01952 388892 ✉ vivianne.mckay2@telford.gov.uk

Grounds Maintenance: Mr Danny Chetwood, Service & Contract Development Group Manager, Granville House,, ,, Telford TF3 4LL ☎ 01952 384384 🖷 01952 384701 ✉ danny.chetwood@telford.gov.uk

Health and Safety: Ms Nicky Minshall, Public Protection Service Delivery Manager, Darby House, 7th Floor, Wing A,, Telford TF3 4LD ☎ 01952 381820 ✉ nicky.minshall@telford.gov.uk

Highways: Mr Keith Harris, Service Delivery Manager - Transport & Highway Development, Whitechapel House, Telford TF2 9SP ☎ 01952 384601 ✉ keith.harris@telford.gov.uk

Housing: Ms Katherine Kynaston, Business & Development Planning Manager, Wellington Civic & Leisure Centre, Wellington, Telford TF1 1LX ☎ 01952 384201 🖷 01952 384254 ✉ katherine.kynaston@telford.gov.uk

Housing Maintenance: Ms Katherine Kynaston, Business & Development Planning Manager, Wellington Civic & Leisure Centre, Wellington, Telford TF1 1LX ☎ 01952 384201 🖷 01952 384254 ✉ katherine.kynaston@telford.gov.uk

Local Area Agreement: Mr Jon Power, Delivery & Planning Service Delivery Manager, Addenbrooke House, Ironmaster Way, Telford TF3 4NT ☎ 01952 380141 ✉ jon.power@telford.gov.uk

Legal: Mr Jonathan Eatough, Assistant Director - Law, Democracy & People Services, Addenbrooke House, Ironmasters Way, Telford TF3 4NT ☎ 01952 383200 🖷 01352 383005 ✉ jonathon.eatough@telford.gov.uk

Leisure and Cultural Services: Mr Stuart Davidson, Assistant Director - Leisure, Culture & Facilities Management, Addenbrooke House, Ironmasters Way, Telford TF3 4NT ☎ 01952 382900 ✉ stuart.davidson@telford.gov.uk

Licensing: Ms Nicky Minshall, Public Protection Service Delivery Manager, Darby House, 7th Floor, Wing A,, Telford TF3 4LD ☎ 01952 381820 ✉ nicky.minshall@telford.gov.uk

Lifelong Learning: Ms Sue Marston, Skills Manager, Addenbrooke House, Ironmasters Way, Telford TF3 4NT ☎ 01952 380897 ✉ sue.marston@telford.gov.uk

Lighting: Ms Amanda Roberts, Highways Capital Programme Group Manager, Whitechapel House, Ground Floor, Telford TF2 9SP ☎ 01952 384659 ✉ amanda.roberts@telford.gov.uk

Member Services: Ms Emma Price, Senior Member Services Officer, Addenbrooke House, Ironmasters Way, Telford TF3 4NT ☎ 01952 380110 ✉ emma.price@telford.gov.uk

Parking: Mr Lee Barnard, Team Leader - Traffic Management & Street Works, Whitechapel House, Telford TF2 9SP ☎ 01952 384645 ✉ lee.barnard@telford.gov.uk

Partnerships: Mr Jon Power, Delivery & Planning Service Delivery Manager, Addenbrooke House, Ironmaster Way, Telford TF3 4NT ☎ 01952 380141 ✉ jon.power@telford.gov.uk

Personnel / HR: Mr John Harris, People Services Manager, Addenbrooke House, Ironmasters Way, Telford TF3 4NT ☎ 01952 383520 ✉ john.harris@telford.gov.uk

Planning: Mr David Fletcher, Development Management Manager, Wellington Civic & Leisure Centre, Wellington, Telford TF1 1LX ✉ dave.fletcher@telford.gov.uk

Procurement: Ms Sarah Bass, Strategic Procurement Service Delivery Specialist, Wellington Civic & Leisure Centre, Wellington, Telford TF1 1LX ☎ 01952 382470 ✉ sarah.bass@telford.gov.uk

Public Libraries: Mr Andrew Meredith, Service Delivery Manager - Customer & Registrars Services, Addenbrooke House, Ironmasters Way, Telford TF3 4NT ☎ 01952 382560 ✉ andrew.meredith@telford.gov.uk

TELFORD & WREKIN

Recycling & Waste Minimisation: Mr Dave Hanley, Highways & Neighbourhood Management Manager, Granville House, St George's Road, Donnington Wood, Telford TF2 7RA ☎ 01952 384855 ✉ dave.hanley@telford.gov.uk

Regeneration: Mr James Dunn, Regeneration & Investment Manager, Wellington Civic & Leisure Centre, Wellington, Telford TF1 1LX ☎ 01952 384591 ✉ james.dunn@telford.gov.uk

Road Safety: Ms Amanda Roberts, Highways Capital Programme Group Manager, PO Box 212, Darby House, Lawn Central, Telford TF3 4LB ☎ 01952 384659 ✉ amanda.roberts@telford.gov.uk

Social Services (Adult): Mr Richard Smith, Interim Assistant Director of Adult Social Services, Addenbrooke House, Ironmasters Way, Telford TN3 4NT ☎ 01952 381011 ✉ richard.smith@telford.gov.uk

Social Services (Children): Mrs Karen Perry, Assistant Director of Children's Safeguarding & Specialist Services, Addenbrooke House, Ironmasters Way, Telford TN3 4NT ☎ 01952 385652 ✉ karen.perry2@telford.gov.uk

Public Health: Ms Liz Noakes, Assistant Director - Health, Wellbeing & Public Protection (Statutory Director - Public Health), Addenbrooke House, Ironmasters Way, Telford TF3 4NT ☎ 01952 383003 ✉ liz.noakes@telford.gov.uk

Street Scene: Mr Keith Harris, Service Delivery Manager - Transport & Highway Development, Whitechapel House, Telford TF2 9SP ☎ 01952 384601 ✉ keith.harris@telford.gov.uk

Sustainable Communities: Ms Katherine Kynaston, Business & Development Planning Manager, PO Box 212, Darby House, Lawn Central, Telford TF3 4LB ☎ 01952 384201 🖷 01952 384254 ✉ katherine.kynaston@telford.gov.uk

Sustainable Development: Ms Katherine Kynaston, Business & Development Planning Manager, PO Box 212, Darby House, Lawn Central, Telford TF3 4LB ☎ 01952 384201 🖷 01952 384254 ✉ katherine.kynaston@telford.gov.uk

Town Centre: Mr James Dunn, Regeneration & Investment Manager, Wellington Civic & Leisure Centre, Wellington, Telford TF1 1LX ☎ 01952 384591 ✉ james.dunn@telford.gov.uk

Transport: Mr Keith Harris, Service Delivery Manager - Transport & Highway Development, Whitechapel House, Telford TF2 9SP ☎ 01952 384601 ✉ keith.harris@telford.gov.uk

Transport Planner: Ms Viv McKay, Commissioning - Vulnerable People, Civic Offices, Telford TF3 4LD ☎ 01952 388892 ✉ vivianne.mckay2@telford.gov.uk

Waste Collection and Disposal: Mr Dave Hanley, Highways & Neighbourhood Management Manager, Granville House, St George's Road, Donnington Wood, Telford TF2 7RA ☎ 01952 384855 ✉ dave.hanley@telford.gov.uk

Waste Management: Ms Debbie Germany, Waste & Neighbourhood Services Performance Management Manager, Granville House, St George's Road, Donnington Wood, Telford TF2 7RA ☎ 01952 384712 ✉ debbie.germany@telford.gov.uk

COUNCILLORS

***Leader of the Council* Sahota**, Kuldip Singh (LAB - Malinslee & Dawley Bank)
kuldip.sahota@telford.gov.uk

Ashford, John (CON - Ketley & Overdale)
john.ashford@telford.gov.uk

Barnes, Steve (CON - Dawley & Aqueduct)
steve.barnes@telford.gov.uk

Bentley, Stephen (CON - Edgmond & Ercall Magna)
stephen.bentley@telford.gov.uk

Blundell, Karen (LD - Apley Castle)
karen.blundell@telford.gov.uk

Boylan, Mark (CON - Ketley & Overdale)
mark.boylan@telford.gov.uk

Burford, Andy (LAB - Dawley & Aqueduct)
andy.burford@telford.gov.uk

Burrell, Stephen (CON - Edgmond & Ercall Magna)
stephen.burrell@telford.gov.uk

Carter, Lee (LAB - College)
lee.carter@telford.gov.uk

Carter, Eric (CON - Newport South & East)
eric.carter@telford.gov.uk

Clare, Elizabeth (LAB - Donnington)
elizabeth.clare@telford.gov.uk

Cook, Graham (LAB - Haygate)
graham.cook@telford.gov.uk

Davies, Shaun (LAB - Malinslee & Dawley Bank)
shaun.davies@telford.gov.uk

Dugmore, Nigel (CON - Muxton)
nigel.dugmore@telford.gov.uk

Eade, Andrew (CON - Church Aston & Lilleshall)
andrew.eade@telford.gov.uk

England, Arnold (LAB - Brookside)
arnold.england@telford.gov.uk

England, Nathan (LAB - The Nedge)
nathan.england@telford.gov.uk

Evans, Rae (LAB - Woodside)
rae.evans@telford.gov.uk

Fletcher, Ian (CON - Priorslee)
ian.fletcher@telford.gov.uk

Fletcher, Veronica (CON - Priorslee)
veronica.fletcher@telford.gov.uk

Francis, Joy (CON - Ketley & Overdale)
joy.francis@telford.gov.uk

Furnival, Connor (IND - The Nedge)
connor.furnival@telford.gov.uk

Greenaway, Jayne (CON - Horsehay & Lightmoor)
jayne.greenaway@telford.gov.uk

Guy, Kevin (LAB - Woodside)
kevin.guy@telford.gov.uk

Hosken, Miles (CON - Ercall)
miles.hosken@telford.gov.uk

Jones, Janice (LAB - Madeley & Sutton Hill)
janice.jones@telford.gov.uk

Kiernan, Terry (CON - Admaston & Bratton)
terry.kiernan@telford.gov.uk

Lawrence, Adrian (CON - Muxton)
adrian.lawrence@telford.gov.uk

Loveridge, Jackie (LAB - Brookside)
jackie.loveridge@telford.gov.uk

Lowery, Nicola (CON - Ironbridge Gorge)
nicola.lowery@telford.gov.uk

Mason, Clive (LAB - Donnington)
clive.mason@telford.gov.uk

McClements, Angela (LAB - Arleston)
angela.mcclements@telford.gov.uk

Meredith, Adrian (CON - Newport South & East)
adrian.meredith@telford.gov.uk

Minor, John (LAB - St Georges)
john.minor@telford.gov.uk

Mollett, Clive (CON - Horsehay & Lightmoor)
clive.mollett@telford.gov.uk

Murray, Leon (LAB - Hadley & Leegomery)
leon.murray@telford.gov.uk

Nelson, Tim (CON - Newport North & West)
tim.nelson@telford.gov.uk

Overton, Richard (LAB - St Georges)
richard.overton@telford.gov.uk

Pinter, Jane (LAB - Dawley & Aqueduct)
jane.pinter@telford.gov.uk

Reynolds, Gilly (LAB - Oakengates & Ketley Bank)
gilly.reynolds@telford.gov.uk

Reynolds, Stephen (LAB - Oakengates & Ketley Bank)
stephen.reynolds@telford.gov.uk

Reynolds, Shirley (LAB - Wrockwardine Wood & Trench)
shirley.reynolds@telford.gov.uk

Rhodes, Hilda (LAB - Oakengates & Ketley Bank)
hilda.rhodes@telford.gov.uk

Scott, Peter (IND - Newport North & West)
peter.scott@telford.gov.uk

Seymour, Jacqui (CON - Wrockwardine)
jacqui.seymour@telford.gov.uk

Sloan, Robert (LAB - Hadley & Leegomery)
rob.sloan@telford.gov.uk

Smith, Malcolm (LAB - Hadley & Leegomery)
malcolm.smith@telford.gov.uk

Smith, Charles (LAB - Wrockwardine Wood & Trench)
charles.smith@telford.gov.uk

Tillotson, Barry (CON - Park)
barry.tillotson@telford.gov.uk

Tomlinson, Bill (LD - Shawbirch)
bill.tomlinson@telford.gov.uk

Tomlinson, Karen (LD - Dothill)
karen.tomlinson@telford.gov.uk

Turley, Chris (LAB - The Nedge)
chris.turley@telford.gov.uk

Watling, Paul (LAB - Madeley & Sutton Hill)
paul.watling@telford.gov.uk

Wright, David (CON - Madeley & Sutton Hill)
dave.wright@telford.gov.uk

POLITICAL COMPOSITION

LAB: 27, CON: 22, LD: 3, IND: 2

COMMITTEE CHAIRS

Children & Young People: Mr Kevin Guy

Licensing: Ms Hilda Rhodes

Planning: Mr John Minor

Tendring D

Tendring District Council, Town Hall, Station Road, Clacton-on-Sea CO15 1SE
☎ 01255 686868 💻 www.tendringdc.gov.uk

FACTS AND FIGURES

Parliamentary Constituencies: Clacton, Harwich and Essex North
EU Constituencies: Eastern
Election Frequency: Elections are of whole council

PRINCIPAL OFFICERS

Chief Executive: Mr Ian Davidson, Chief Executive, Town Hall, Station Road, Clacton-on-Sea CO15 1SE ☎ 01255 686007 🖷 01255 686414 ✉ idavidson@tendringdc.gov.uk

Senior Management: Mr Martyn Knappett, Head of Corporate Services, Town Hall, Station Road, Clacton-on-Sea CO15 1SE ☎ 01255 686501 🖷 01225 686414 ✉ mknappett@tendringdc.gov.uk

Building Control: Mr Alan Corbyn, Building Control Manager, Council Offices, Thorpe Road, Weeley, Clacton-on-Sea CO16 9AJ ☎ 01255 686160 🖷 01255 686425 ✉ acorbyn@tendringdc.gov.uk

PR / Communications: Mr Nigel Brown, Communications Manager, Town Hall, Station Road, Clacton-on-Sea CO15 1SE ☎ 01255 686338 🖷 01225 686414 ✉ nbrown@tendringdc.gov.uk

Community Safety: Mrs Leanne Thornton, Community Safety Manager, Town Hall, Station Road, Clacton-on-Sea CO15 1SE ☎ 01225 686353 🖷 01225 686417 ✉ lthornton@tendringdc.gov.uk

Contracts: Mr David Hall, Open Services & Bereavement Services Manager, Northbourne Depot, Vista Road, Clacton-on-Sea CO15 6AY ☎ 01255 686661 🖷 01255 686411 ✉ dhall@tendringdc.gov.uk

Corporate Services: Mr Martyn Knappett, Head of Corporate Services, Town Hall, Station Road, Clacton-on-Sea CO15 1SE ☎ 01255 686501 🖷 01225 686414 ✉ mknappett@tendringdc.gov.uk

Corporate Services: Ms Keri Lawrence, Executive Projects Manager, Town Hall, Station Road, Clacton-on-Sea CO15 1SE ☎ 01255 686013 ✉ klawrence@tendringdc.gov.uk

Customer Service: Mrs Anastasia Simpson, HR Manager, Town Hall, Station Road, Clacton-on-Sea CO15 1SE ☎ 01255 686324 ✉ asimpson@tendringdc.gov.uk

Education: Ms Keri Lawrence, Executive Projects Manager, Town Hall, Station Road, Clacton-on-Sea CO15 1SE ☎ 01255 686013 🖰 klawrence@tendringdc.gov.uk

E-Government: Miss Karen Neath, Management & Members' Support Manager, Town Hall, Station Road, Clacton-on-Sea CO15 1SE ☎ 01255 686520 🖰 kneath@tendringdc.gov.uk

Electoral Registration: Mrs Alison Rowlands, Electoral Registration, Town Hall, Station Road, Clacton-on-Sea CO16 1SE ☎ 01255 686586 🖰 arowlands@tendringdc.gov.uk

Emergency Planning: Mr Damian Williams, Life Opportunities Manager, Town Hall, Station Road, Clacton-on-Sea CO15 1SE ☎ 01255 686319 🖰 dwilliams@tendringdc.gov.uk

Environmental Health: Mrs June Clare, Head of Public Experience, Council Offices, Thorpe Road, Weeley, Clacton-on-Sea CO16 9AJ ☎ 01255 686741 🖰 jclare@tendringdc.gov.uk

Estates, Property & Valuation: Mr Andrew White, Assets Manager, Town Hall, Station Road, Clacton-on-Sea CO15 1SE ☎ 01255 686933 🖰 awhite@tendringdc.gov.uk

Events Manager: Mr Michael Carran, Life Opportunities Manager, Town Hall, Station Road, Clacton-on-Sea CO15 1SE ☎ 01255 686689 📠 01255 686411 🖰 mcarran@tendringdc.gov.uk

Facilities: Mr Damian Williams, Life Opportunities Manager, Town Hall, Station Road, Clacton-on-Sea CO15 1SE ☎ 01255 686319 🖰 dwilliams@tendringdc.gov.uk

Finance: Mr Richard Barrett, Finance & Procurement Manager, Town Hall, Station Road, Clacton-on-Sea CO16 9RG ☎ 01255 686521 🖰 rbarrett@tendring.gov.uk

Fleet Management: Mr Trevor Mills, Horticultural Services Manager, Northbourne Depot, Vista Road, Clacton-on-Sea CO15 6AY ☎ 01255 686643 📠 01255 479739 🖰 tmills@tendringdc.gov.uk

Grounds Maintenance: Mr Trevor Mills, Horticultural Services Manager, Northbourne Depot, Vista Road, Clacton-on-Sea CO15 6AY ☎ 01255 686643 📠 01255 479739 🖰 tmills@tendringdc.gov.uk

Health and Safety: Mr John Fox, Food & Health & Safety Manager, Council Offices, Thorpe Road, Weeley, Clacton-on-Sea CO16 9AJ ☎ 01255 686746 📠 01255 686404 🖰 jfox@tendringdc.gov.uk

Highways: Mr Mike Badger, Engineering Services Manager, Town Hall, Station Road, Clacton-on-Sea CO15 1SE ☎ 01255 686975 🖰 mbadger@tendringdc.gov.uk

Housing: Mr Paul Price, Head of Life Opportunities, Town Hall, Station Road, Clacton-on-Sea CO15 1SE ☎ 01255 686430 📠 01255 686407 🖰 pprice@tendringcc.gov.uk

Housing Maintenance: Mr Damian Williams, Life Opportunities Manager, Town Hall, Station Road, Clacton-on-Sea CO15 1SE ☎ 01255 686319 🖰 dwilliams@tendringdc.gov.uk

Legal: Ms Lisa Hastings, Legal Services Manager, Town Hall, Station Road, Clacton-on-Sea CO15 1SE ☎ 01255 868561 🖰 lhastings@tendringdc.gov.uk

Leisure and Cultural Services: Mr Michael Carran, Life Opportunities Manager, Town Hall, Station Road, Clacton-on-Sea CO15 1SE ☎ 01255 686689 📠 01255 686411 🖰 mcarran@tendringdc.gov.uk

Licensing: Mr Ian Taylor, Streets & Seafronts Manager, Northbourne Depot, Vista Road, Clacton-on-Sea CO15 6AY ☎ 01255 686982 🖰 itaylor@tendring.gov.uk

Lighting: Mr Mike Badger, Engineering Services Manager, Town Hall, Station Road, Clacton-on-Sea CO15 1SE ☎ 01255 686975 🖰 mbadger@tendringdc.gov.uk

Member Services: Mr Ashley Wood, Management & Members' Support Officer, Town Hall, Station Road, Clacton-on-Sea CO15 1SE ☎ 01255 686583 🖰 awood@tendringdc.gov.uk

Parking: Mr Ian Taylor, Streets & Seafronts Manager, Northbourne Depot, Vista Road, Clacton-on-Sea CO15 6AY ☎ 01255 686982 🖰 itaylor@tendring.gov.uk

Personnel / HR: Mrs Anastasia Simpson, HR Manager, Town Hall, Station Road, Clacton-on-Sea CO15 1SE ☎ 01255 686324 🖰 asimpson@tendringdc.gov.uk

Planning: Mrs Catherine Bicknell, Head of Planning, Council Offices, Thorpe Road, Weeley, Clacton-on-Sea CO16 9AJ ☎ 01255 686101 📠 01255 686417 🖰 cbicknell@tendringdc.gov.uk

Procurement: Mrs Jane Taylor, Procurement Officer, Town Hall, Station Road, Clacton-on-Sea CO15 1SE ☎ 01255 686955 🖰 jtaylor@tendringdc.gov.uk

Street Scene: Mr Mike Badger, Engineering Services Manager, Town Hall, Station Road, Clacton-on-Sea CO15 1SE ☎ 01255 686975 🖰 mbadger@tendringdc.gov.uk

Tourism: Mr Michael Carran, Life Opportunities Manager, Town Hall, Station Road, Clacton-on-Sea CO15 1SE ☎ 01255 686689 📠 01255 686411 🖰 mcarran@tendringdc.gov.uk

Town Centre: Mrs Rachel Fryer, Town Centre Co-ordinator, Council Offices, Thorpe Road, Weeley, Clacton-on-Sea CO16 9AJ ☎ 01255 686149 📠 01255 831291 🖰 rfryer@tendringdc.gov.uk

Total Place: Mr Martyn Knappett, Head of Corporate Services, Town Hall, Station Road, Clacton-on-Sea CO15 1SE ☎ 01255 686501 📠 01225 686414 🖰 mknappett@tendringdc.gov.uk

Waste Management: Mrs June Clare, Head of Public Experience, Council Offices, Thorpe Road, Weeley, Clacton-on-Sea CO16 9AJ ☎ 01255 686741 🖰 jclare@tendringdc.gov.uk

Children's Play Areas: Mr David Hall, Open Services & Bereavement Services Manager, Town Hall, Station Road, Clacton-on-Sea CO15 1SE ☎ 01255 686661 📠 01255 686411 🖰 dhall@tendringdc.gov.uk

COUNCILLORS

***Chair* Nicholls**, Fred (CON - Thorrington, Frating, Elmstead & Great Bromley)
cllr.fnicholls@tendringdc.gov.uk

***Vice-Chair* Chapman**, Jayne (IND - Brightlingsea)
cllr.jchapman@tendringdc.gov.uk

***Leader of the Council* Stock**, Neil (CON - Ardleigh & Little Bromley)
cllr.nstock@tendringdc.gov.uk

***Deputy Leader of the Council* Guglielmi**, Giancarlo (CON - Manningtree, Mistley, Little Bentley & Tendring)
cllr.gguglielmi@tendringdc.gov.uk

Amos, Chris (CON - St Johns)
cllr.camos@tendringdc.gov.uk

Baker, Andy (CON - Lawford)
cllr.abaker@tendringdc.gov.uk

Bennison, Lisbeth (UKIP - Peter Bruff)
cllr.lbennison@tendringdc.gov.uk

Bray, Jeffrey (UKIP - Little Clacton & Weeley)
cllr.jbray@tendringdc.gov.uk

Broderick, Joy (IND - Haven)
cllr.jbroderick@tendringdc.gov.uk

Brown, Barry (CON - Harwich East Central)
cllr.bbrown@tendringdc.gov.uk

Brown, John (UKIP - Harwich West)
cllr.jabrown@tendringdc.gov.uk

Brown, Mike (CON - Little Clacton & Weeley)
cllr.mbrown@tendringdc.gov.uk

Bucke, Robert (O - Holland & Kirby)
cllr.rbucke@tendringdc.gov.uk

Callender, Ricky (CON - Harwich West)
cllr.rcallender@tendringdc.gov.uk

Calver, Garry (LAB - Harwich East Central)
cllr.gcalver@tendringdc.gov.uk

Cawthorn, Peter (UKIP - Alton Park)
cllr.pcawthorn@tendringdc.gov.uk

Chittock, John (IND - Bockings Elm)
cllr.jchittock@tendringdc.gov.uk

Coley, Alan (CON - Manningtree, Mistley, Little Bentley & Tendring)
cllr.acoley@tendringdc.gov.uk

Cossens, Mark (O - Holland & Kirby)
cllr.mcossens@tendringdc.gov.uk

Davis, Anne (UKIP - Hamford)
cllr.adavis@tendringdc.gov.uk

Everett, Richard (UKIP - Rush Green)
cllr.reverett@tendringdc.gov.uk

Fairley, Zoe (CON - Bradfield, Wrabness & Wix)
cllr.zfairley@tendringdc.gov.uk

Ferguson, Tanya (CON - Ramsey & Parkeston)
cllr.tferguson@tendringdc.gov.uk

Fowler, Maria (LAB - Harwich West Central)
cllr.mfowler@tendringdc.gov.uk

Gray, Laurie (UKIP - Homelands)
cllr.lagray@tendringdc.gov.uk

Griffiths, Christopher (CON - St James)
cllr.cgriffiths@tendringdc.gov.uk

Guglielmi, Valerie (CON - Lawford)
cllr.vguglielmi@tendringdc.gov.uk

Heaney, Rosemary (CON - Thorrington, Frating, Elmstead & Great Bromley)
cllr.rheaney@tendringdc.gov.uk

Henderson, Jo (LAB - Harwich West Central)
cllr.jhenderson@tendringdc.gov.uk

Henderson, Ivan (LAB - Harwich East)
cllr.ihenderson@tendringdc.gov.uk

Hones, John (UKIP - St Marys)
cllr.jhones@tendringdc.gov.uk

Honeywood, Paul (CON - Pier)
cllr.phoneywood@tendringdc.gov.uk

Howard, Tom (IND - Great and Little Oakley)
cllr.thoward@tendringdc.gov.uk

Hughes, John (IND - St James)

Khan, Mohammed (UKIP - Pier)
cllr.mkhan@tendringdc.gov.uk

King, Kanagasundaram (IND - St Bartholomews)
cllr.kking@tendringdc.gov.uk

Land, Daniel (CON - Beaumont & Thorpe)
cllr.dland@tendringdc.gov.uk

Massey, Andy (CON - St Pauls)
cllr.amassey@tendringdc.gov.uk

McWilliams, Lynda (CON - Great Bentley)
cllr.lmcwilliams@tendringdc.gov.uk

Miles, Delyth (CON - Walton)
cll.dmiles@tendringdc.gov.uk

Mooney, Ashley (UKIP - St Pauls)
cllr.amooney@tendringdc.gov.uk

Newton, Mary (UKIP - Rush Green)
cllr.mnewton@tendringdc.gov.uk

Pemberton, Andrew (UKIP - Peter Bruff)
cllr.apemberton@tendringdc.gov.uk

Platt, Mark (CON - Hamford)
cllr.mplatt@tendringdc.gov.uk

Poonian, Anne (IND - Walton)
cllr.apoonian@tendringdc.gov.uk

Porter, Alex (UKIP - Alton Park)
cllr.aporter@tendringdc.gov.uk

Raby, Roy (UKIP - Golf Green)
cllr.rraby@tendringdc.gov.uk

Scott, Gary (LD - Alresford)
cllr.gscott@tendringdc.gov.uk

Skeels, Mick (IND - Burrsville)
cllr.mjskeels@tendringdc.gov.uk

Skeels, Michael (IND - St Johns)
cllr.mskeels@tendringdc.gov.uk

Steady, Graham (IND - Brightlingsea)
cllr.gsteady@tendringdc.gov.uk

Stephenson, Mark (UKIP - St Marys)
cllr.mstephenson@tendringdc.gov.uk

Talbot, Michael (IND - St Osyth & Point Clear)
cllr.mtalbot@tendringdc.gov.uk

Turner, Nicholas (CON - Frinton)
cllr.nturner@tendringdc.gov.uk

Watling, Giles (CON - Frinton)
cllr.gwatling@tendringdc.gov.uk

Watson, Kevin (UKIP - Golf Green)
cllr.kwatson@tendringdc.gov.uk

White, John (IND - St Osyth & Point Clear)
cllr.jwhite@tendringdc.gov.uk

Whitmore, Edward (UKIP - Bockings Elm)
cllr.twhitmore@tendringdc.gov.uk

Winfield, Colin (IND - St Batholomews)
cllr.cwinfield@tendringdc.gov.uk

Yallop, Karen (IND - Brightlingsea)
cllr.kyallop@tendringdc.gov.uk

POLITICAL COMPOSITION

CON: 22, UKIP: 17, IND: 14, LAB: 4, O: 2, LD: 1

COMMITTEE CHAIRS

Audit: Mr Alan Coley

Licensing: Mr Mark Platt

Planning: Mr John White

Test Valley D

Test Valley Borough Council, Beech Hurst, Weyhill Road, Andover SP10 3AJ
☎ 01264 368000 💻 www.testvalley.gov.uk

FACTS AND FIGURES

Parliamentary Constituencies: Hampshire North West, Romsey and Southampton North
EU Constituencies: South East
Election Frequency: Elections are of whole council

PRINCIPAL OFFICERS

Chief Executive: Mr Roger Tetstall, Chief Executive, Beech Hurst, Weyhill Road, Andover SP10 3AJ ☎ 01264 368102
rtetstall@testvalley.gov.uk

Senior Management: Mr Andrew Ferrier, Corporate Director, Beech Hurst, Weyhill Road, Andover SP10 3AJ ☎ 01264 368121
aferrier@testvalley.gov.uk

Senior Management: Mrs Carol Moore, Corporate Director, Beech Hurst, Weyhill Road, Andover SP10 3AJ ☎ 01264 368113
cmoore@testvalley.gov.uk

Building Control: Mr Graham Murrell, Building Control Manager, Beech Hurst, Weyhill Road, Andover SP10 3AJ ☎ 01264 368000
gmurrell@testvalley.gov.uk

PR / Communications: Mrs Kathryn Binfield, Communications Manager, Beech Hurst, Weyhill Road, Andover SP10 3AJ ☎ 01264 368000 kbinfield@testvalley.gov.uk

Community Planning: Mr Andrew Ferrier, Corporate Director, Beech Hurst, Weyhill Road, Andover SP10 3AJ ☎ 01264 368121
aferrier@testvalley.gov.uk

Community Safety: Ms Verna Brown, Communities Manager, Beech Hurst, Weyhill Road, Andover SP10 3AJ ☎ 01264 368606
vbrown@testvalley.gov.uk

Computer Management: Mr Tony Fawcett, Head of IT Services, Beech Hurst, Weyhill Road, Andover SP10 3AJ ☎ 01962 848262; 01264 368901
tfawcett@winchester.gov.uk; tfacwett@testvalley.gov.uk

Corporate Services: Mrs Carol Moore, Corporate Director, Beech Hurst, Weyhill Road, Andover SP10 3AJ ☎ 01264 368113
cmoore@testvalley.gov.uk

Customer Service: Mrs Paula Staff, Customer Relationship Manager, Beech Hurst, Weyhill Road, Andover SP10 3AJ
☎ 01264 368938 pstaff@testvalley.gov.uk

Economic Development: Mr David Gleave, Economic Development Officer, Beech Hurst, Weyhill Road, Andover SP10 3AJ ☎ 01264 368309 dgleave@testvalley.gov.uk

E-Government: Mr Tony Fawcett, Head of IT Services, Beech Hurst, Weyhill Road, Andover SP10 3AJ ☎ 01264 368901
tfawcett@testvalley.gov.uk

Electoral Registration: Mrs Sue Gamalatge, Electoral Services Manager, Beech Hurst, Weyhill Road, Andover SP10 3AJ ☎ 01264 368020 sgamalatge@testvalley.gov.uk

Emergency Planning: Mr Michael White, Licensing Manager, Beech Hurst, Weyhill Road, Andover SP10 3AJ ☎ 01264 368000
mwhite@testvalley.gov.uk

Environmental / Technical Services: Mr Paul Wykes, Head of Environmental Services, Portway Depot, Macadam Way, West Portway, Andover SP10 3XW ☎ 01264 368000
pwykes@testvalley.gov.uk

Environmental Health: Mr Brian Cowcher, Head of Housing & Community Services, Beech Hurst, Weyhill Road, Andover SP10 3AJ
☎ 01264 368601 bcowcher@testvalley.gov.uk

Environmental Health: Ms Carol Ruddle, Environmental Health Manager, Beech Hurst, Weyhill Road, Andover SP10 3AJ
☎ 01264 368000 cruddle@testvalley.gov.uk

Estates, Property & Valuation: Mr Simon Ellis, Head of Estates & Economic Development Services, Beech Hurst, Weyhill Road, Andover SP10 3AJ ☎ 01264 368301 sellis@testvalley.gov.uk

Finance: Mr William Fullbrook, Head of Finance, Beech Hurst, Weyhill Road, Andover SP10 3AJ ☎ 01264 368201
wfullbrook@testvalley.gov.uk

Grounds Maintenance: Mr Paul Wykes, Head of Environmental Services, Portway Depot, Macadam Way, West Portway, Andover SP10 3XW ☎ 01264 368000 pwykes@testvalley.gov.uk

Health and Safety: Ms Carol Ruddle, Environmental Health Manager, Beech Hurst, Weyhill Road, Andover SP10 3AJ ☎ 01264 368000 ✉ cruddle@testvalley.gov.uk

Housing: Mr Brian Cowcher, Head of Housing & Community Services, Beech Hurst, Weyhill Road, Andover SP10 3AJ ☎ 01264 368601 ✉ bcowcher@testvalley.gov.uk

Legal: Mr Bill Lynds, Head of Legal & Democratic Services, Beech Hurst, Weyhill Road, Andover SP10 3AJ ☎ 01264 368000 ✉ wlynds@testvalley.gov.uk

Leisure and Cultural Services: Mr David Tasker, Head of Community & Leisure Services, Beech Hurst, Weyhill Road, Andover SP10 3AJ ☎ 01264 368801 ✉ dtasker@testvalley.gov.uk

Licensing: Mr Michael White, Licensing Manager, Beech Hurst, Weyhill Road, Andover SP10 3AJ ☎ 01264 368000 ✉ mwhite@testvalley.gov.uk

Member Services: Ms Emma Silverton, Democratic Services Manager, Beech Hurst, Weyhill Road, Andover SP10 3AJ ☎ 01264 368001 ✉ esilverton@testvalley.gov.uk

Parking: Mr Steve Raw, Engineering & Transport Manager, Beech Hurst, Weyhill Road, Andover SP10 3AJ ☎ 01264 368000 ✉ sraw@testvalley.gov.uk

Personnel / HR: Ms Alexandra Rowland, HR Manager, Beech Hurst, Weyhill Road, Andover SP10 3AJ ☎ 01264 368251 ✉ arowland@testvalley.gov.uk

Planning: Mr Paul Jackson, Head of Planning & Building Services, Beech Hurst, Weyhill Road, Andover SP10 3AJ ☎ 01264 368000 ✉ pjackson@testvalley.gov.uk

Procurement: Mr David Owers, Procurement Officer, Beech Hurst, Weyhill Road, Andover SP10 3AJ ☎ 01264 368000 ✉ dowers@testvalley.gov.uk

Recycling & Waste Minimisation: Mr Paul Wykes, Head of Environmental Services, Portway Depot, Macadam Way, West Portway, Andover SP10 3XW ☎ 01264 368000 ✉ pwykes@testvalley.gov.uk

Regeneration: Mr Simon Ellis, Head of Estates & Economic Development Services, Beech Hurst, Weyhill Road, Andover SP10 3AJ ☎ 01264 368301 ✉ sellis@testvalley.gov.uk

Staff Training: Mrs Penny Billingham, HR Adviser, Beech Hurst, Weyhill Road, Andover SP10 3AJ ☎ 01264 368000 ✉ pbillingham@testvalley.gov.uk

Tourism: Mr David Gleave, Economic Development Officer, Beech Hurst, Weyhill Road, Andover SP10 3AJ ☎ 01264 368309 ✉ dgleave@testvalley.gov.uk

Town Centre: Mr Chris Gregory, Town Centre Manager, Beech Hurst, Weyhill Road, Andover SP10 3AJ ☎ 07854 027080 ✉ chris@heartflood.co.uk

Traffic Management: Mr Steve Raw, Engineering & Transport Manager, Beech Hurst, Weyhill Road, Andover SP10 3AJ ☎ 01264 368000 ✉ sraw@testvalley.gov.uk

Transport Planner: Ms Vivien Messenger, Transport Planner, Beech Hurst, Weyhill Road, Andover SP10 3AJ ☎ 01264 368000 ✉ vmessenger@testvalley.gov.uk

Transport Planner: Mrs Anne Tomlinson, Transport Planner, Beech, Weyhill Road, Andover SP10 3AJ ☎ 01264 368000 ✉ atomlinson@testvalley.gov.uk

Waste Collection and Disposal: Mr Paul Wykes, Head of Environmental Services, Portway Depot, Macadam Way, West Portway, Andover SP10 3XW ☎ 01264 368000 ✉ pwykes@testvalley.gov.uk

Waste Management: Mr Paul Wykes, Head of Environmental Services, Portway Depot, Macadam Way, West Portway, Andover SP10 3XW ☎ 01264 368000 ✉ pwykes@testvalley.gov.uk

COUNCILLORS

***Mayor* Andersen**, Iris (CON - Andover - St Mary's)
cllriandersen@testvalley.gov.uk

***Deputy Mayor* Hamilton**, Karen (CON - Andover - Harroway)
cllrkhamilton@testvalley.gov.uk

***Leader of the Council* Carr**, Ian (CON - Charlton)
cllricarr@testvalley.gov.uk

***Deputy Leader of the Council* Hatley**, Martin (CON - Ampfield and Braishfield)
cllrmhatley@testvalley.gov.uk

Adams-King, Nick (CON - Blackwater)
cllrmadams-king@testvalley.gov.uk

Anderdon, Nigel (CON - Chilworth, Nursling and Rownhams)
cllrnanderdon@testvalley.gov.uk

Bailey, Gordon (CON - Blackwater)
cllrgbailey@testvalley.gov.uk

Baverstock, Dorothy (LD - Romsey - Cupernham)
cllrdbaverstock@testvalley.gov.uk

Beesley, Andrew (LD - Valley Park)
cllrabeesley@testvalley.gov.uk

Borg-Neal, Carl (CON - Andover - Harroway)
cllrcborg-neal@testvalley.gov.uk

Boulton, Peter (CON - Broughton and Stockbridge)
cllrpboulton@testvalley.gov.uk

Brook, Alexander (CON - Andover - Alamein)
CllrABrook@testvalley.gov.uk

Brookes, Zilliah (CON - Andover - Millway)
cllrzbrooks@testvalley.gov.uk

Budzynski, Jan (CON - Andover - Winton)
cllrjbudzynski@testvalley.gov.uk

Bundy, Philip (CON - Chilworth, Nursling and Rownhams)
cllrpbundy@testvalley.gov.uk

Busk, Daniel (CON - Broughton and Stockbridge)
cllrdbusk@testvalley.gov.uk

Cockaday, John (CON - Andover - St. Mary's)
cllrjcockaday@testvalley.gov.uk

Collier, Clive (CON - Romsey - Abbey)
cllrccollier@testvalley.gov.uk

Cooper, Mark (LD - Romsey - Tadburn)
cllrmcooper@testvalley.gov.uk

Cosier, Stephen (LD - North Baddesley)
cllrscosier@testvalley.gov.uk

Denny, David (CON - Andover - St. Mary's)
cllrddenny@testvalley.gov.uk

Dowden, Celia (LD - North Baddesley)
cllrcdowden@testvalley.gov.uk

Dowden, Alan (LD - Valley Park)
cllradowden@testvalley.gov.uk

Drew, David (CON - Harewood)
cllrddrew@testvalley.gov.uk

Few Brown, Benjamin (IND - Amport)
cllrbfewbrown@testvalley.gov.uk

Finlay, Alison (CON - Chilworth, Nursling and Rownhams)
cllrafinlay@testvalley.gov.uk

Flood, Maureen (CON - Anna)
cllrmflood@testvalley.gov.uk

Giddings, Peter (CON - Bourne Valley)
cllrpgiddings@testvalley.gov.uk

Hawke, Sandra (CON - Andover - Millway)
cllrshawke@testvalley.gov.uk

Hibberd, Ian (CON - Romsey Extra)
cllrihibberd@testvalley.gov.uk

Hope, Anthony (CON - Over Wallop)
cllrahope@testvalley.gov.uk

Hurst, Peter (LD - Romsey - Tadburn)
cllrphurst@testvalley.gov.uk

Jeffrey, Ian (CON - Dun Valley)

Johnston, Alison (CON - Romsey Extra)
cllrajohnston@testvalley.gov.uk

Lashbrook, Philip (CON - Penton Bellinger)
cllrplashbrook@testvalley.gov.uk

Lovell, Jan (CON - Andover - Winton)
cllrjlovell@testvalley.gov.uk

Lynn, Christopher (CON - Andover - Winton)
cllrclynn@testvalley.gov.uk

Mutton, Pam (CON - Penton Bellinger)
cllrpmutton@testvalley.gov.uk

Neal, James (CON - Andover - Millway)
cllrjneal@testvalley.gov.uk

North, Phil (CON - Andover - Alamein)
cllrpnorth@testvalley.gov.uk

Page, Brian (CON - Andover - Harroway)
cllrbpage@testvalley.gov.uk

Preston, Tracey (CON - Andover - Alamein)
cllrtpreston@testvalley.gov.uk

Ray, John (CON - Romsey - Cupernham)

Richards, Ian (CON - Romsey - Abbey)
cllririchards@testvalley.gov.uk

Stallard, Graham (CON - Anna)
cllrgstallard@testvalley.gov.uk

Tilling, Katherine (LD - Valley Park)
cllrktilling@testvalley.gov.uk

Tupper, Ann (LD - North Baddesley)
cllratupper@testvalley.gov.uk

Ward, Anthony (CON - King's Somborne and Michelmersh)
cllrtward@testvalley.gov.uk

POLITICAL COMPOSITION
CON: 38, LD: 9, IND: 1

COMMITTEE CHAIRS
Planning: Mr Clive Collier

Tewkesbury D

Tewkesbury Borough Council, Council Offices, Gloucester Road, Tewkesbury GL20 5TT
☎ 01684 295010 🖷 01684 272040
democraticservices@tewkesbury.gov.uk www.tewkesbury.gov.uk

FACTS AND FIGURES
Parliamentary Constituencies: Tewkesbury
EU Constituencies: South West
Election Frequency: Elections are of whole council

PRINCIPAL OFFICERS
Chief Executive: Mr Mike Dawson, Chief Executive, Council Offices, Gloucester Road, Tewkesbury GL20 5TT ☎ 01684 272001 chiefexecutive@tewkesbury.gov.uk

Deputy Chief Executive: Ms Rachel North, Deputy Chief Executive, Council Offices, Gloucester Road, Tewkesbury GL20 5TT rachel.north@tewkesbury.gov.uk

Senior Management: Ms Sara Freckleton, Borough Solicitor & Monitoring Officer, Council Offices, Gloucester Road, Tewkesbury GL20 5TT ☎ 01684 272010 sara.freckleton@tewkesbury.gov.uk

Best Value: Mr Graeme Simpson, Policy & Performance Group Manager, Council Offices, Gloucester Road, Tewkesbury GL20 5TT ☎ 01684 272002 graeme.simpson@tewkesbury

Building Control: Mr Iain Houston, Building Control Manager, Municipal Offices, The Promenade, Cheltenham GL50 9SA ☎ 01242 264293 🖷 01242 227323 iain.houston@cheltenham.gov.uk

Children / Youth Services: Mr Andy Sanders, Economic & Community Development Manager, Council Offices, Gloucester Road, Tewkesbury GL20 5TT ☎ 01684 272094 andy.sanders@tewkesbury.gov.uk

PR / Communications: Ms Clare Davies, Communications Team Leader, Council Offices, Gloucester Road, Tewkesbury GL20 5TT ☎ 01684 272291 clare.davies@tewkesbury.gov.uk

Community Planning: Mrs Julie Wood, Development Services Group Manager, Council Offices, Gloucester Road, Tewkesbury GL20 5TT ☎ 01684 272095 ✉ julie.wood@tewkesbury.gov.uk

Community Safety: Mrs Val Garside, Environmental & Housing Services Group Manager, Council Offices, Gloucester Road, Tewkesbury GL20 5TT ☎ 01684 272259 ✉ val.garside@tewkesbury.gov.uk

Computer Management: Mr Graeme Simpson, Policy & Performance Group Manager, Council Offices, Gloucester Road, Tewkesbury GL20 5TT ☎ 01684 272002 ✉ graeme.simpson@tewkesbury

Contracts: Mrs Shirin Wotherspoon, Principal Solicitor (Commercial), Tewkesbury Borough Council, Council Offices, Gloucester Road, Tewkesbury GL20 5TT ☎ 01684 272017 ✉ shirin.wotherspoon@tewkesbury.gov.uk

Corporate Services: Mr Graeme Simpson, Policy & Performance Group Manager, Council Offices, Gloucester Road, Tewkesbury GL20 5TT ☎ 01684 272002 ✉ graeme.simpson@tewkesbury

Customer Service: Mr Graeme Simpson, Policy & Performance Group Manager, Council Offices, Gloucester Road, Tewkesbury GL20 5TT ☎ 01684 272002 ✉ graeme.simpson@tewkesbury

Economic Development: Mrs Julie Wood, Development Services Group Manager, Council Offices, Gloucester Road, Tewkesbury GL20 5TT ☎ 01684 272095 ✉ julie.wood@tewkesbury.gov.uk

E-Government: Mr Graeme Simpson, Policy & Performance Group Manager, Council Offices, Gloucester Road, Tewkesbury GL20 5TT ☎ 01684 272002 ✉ graeme.simpson@tewkesbury

Electoral Registration: Mrs Lin O'Brien, Democratic Group Services Manager, Council Offices, Gloucester Road, Tewkesbury GL20 5TT ☎ 01684 272020 ✉ lin.o'brien@tewkesbury.gov.uk

Emergency Planning: Mrs Val Garside, Environmental & Housing Services Group Manager, Council Offices, Gloucester Road, Tewkesbury GL20 5TT ☎ 01684 272259 ✉ val.garside@tewkesbury.gov.uk

Environmental Health: Mr David Steels, Environmental Health Manager, Council Offices, Gloucester Road, Tewkesbury GL20 5TT ☎ 01684 272172 ✉ david.steels@tewkesbury.gov.uk

Estates, Property & Valuation: Mr Andy Noble, Asset Manager, Council Offices, Gloucester Road, Tewkesbury GL20 5TT ☎ 01684 272023 ✉ andy.noble@tewkesbury.gov.uk

Facilities: Mr Andy Noble, Asset Manager, Council Offices, Gloucester Road, Tewkesbury GL20 5TT ☎ 01684 272023 ✉ andy.noble@tewkesbury.gov.uk

Finance: Mr Simon Dix, Finance & Asset Management Group Manager, Council Offices, Gloucester Road, Tewkesbury GL20 5TT ☎ 01684 272005 ✉ simon.dix@tewkesbury.gov.uk

Health and Safety: Mrs Val Garside, Environmental & Housing Services Group Manager, Council Offices, Gloucester Road, Tewkesbury GL20 5TT ☎ 01684 272259 ✉ val.garside@tewkesbury.gov.uk

Housing: Mrs Val Garside, Environmental & Housing Services Group Manager, Council Offices, Gloucester Road, Tewkesbury GL20 5TT ☎ 01684 272259 ✉ val.garside@tewkesbury.gov.uk

Legal: Mr Peter Lewis, Head of Legal Services, Council Offices, Gloucester Road, Tewkesbury GL20 5TT ☎ 01684 272012 ✉ peter.lewis@tewkesbury.gov.uk

Leisure and Cultural Services: Mr Andy Sanders, Economic & Community Development Manager, Council Offices, Gloucester Road, Tewkesbury GL20 5TT ☎ 01684 272094 ✉ andy.sanders@tewkesbury.gov.uk

Licensing: Mrs Val Garside, Environmental & Housing Services Group Manager, Council Offices, Gloucester Road, Tewkesbury GL20 5TT ☎ 01684 272259 ✉ val.garside@tewkesbury.gov.uk

Member Services: Mrs Lin O'Brien, Democratic Group Services Manager, Council Offices, Gloucester Road, Tewkesbury GL20 5TT ☎ 01684 272020 ✉ lin.o'brien@tewkesbury.gov.uk

Personnel / HR: Ms Janet Martin, HR Advisor, Council Offices, Gloucester Road, Tewkesbury GL20 5TT ☎ 01684 272057 ✉ janet.martin@tewkesbury.gov.uk

Planning: Mr Paul Skelton, Development Control Manager, Council Offices, Gloucester Road, Tewkesbury GL20 5TT ☎ 01684 272102 ✉ paul.skelton@tewkesbury.gov.uk

Regeneration: Mrs Julie Wood, Development Services Group Manager, Council Offices, Gloucester Road, Tewkesbury GL20 5TT ☎ 01684 272095 ✉ julie.wood@tewkesbury.gov.uk

Staff Training: Ms Janet Martin, HR Advisor, Council Offices, Gloucester Road, Tewkesbury GL20 5TT ☎ 01684 272057 ✉ janet.martin@tewkesbury.gov.uk

Tourism: Mrs Julie Wood, Development Services Group Manager, Council Offices, Gloucester Road, Tewkesbury GL20 5TT ☎ 01684 272095 ✉ julie.wood@tewkesbury.gov.uk

COUNCILLORS

***Mayor* Allen**, Ron (CON - Winchcombe)
councillor.allen@tewkesbury.gov.uk

***Deputy Mayor* Blackwell**, Gillian (CON - Hucclecote)
councillor.blackwell@tewkesbury.gov.uk

***Leader of the Council* Vines**, Robert (CON - Badgeworth)
councillor.vines@tewkesbury.gov.uk

***Deputy Leader of the Council* Waters**, David (CON - Coombe Hill)
councillor.waters@tewkesbury.gov.uk

***Group Leader* Berry**, Kay (LD - Churchdown St John's)
councillor.berry@tewkesbury.gov.uk

TEWKESBURY

***Group Leader* Sztymiak**, Mike (IND - Tewkesbury Town with Mitton)
councillor.sztymiak@tewkesbury.gov.uk

Awford, Philip (CON - Highnam with Hawbridge)
councillor.awford@tewkesbury.gov.uk

Bird, Robert (CON - Cleeve West)
councillor.bird@tewkesbury.gov.uk

Bishop, Richard (CON - Churchdown Brookfield)
councillor.bishop@tewkesbury.gov.uk

Bocking, Graham (CON - Innsworth with Down Hatherley)
councillor.bocking@tewkesbury.gov.uk

Cromwell, Kevin (CON - Tewkesbury Prior's Park)
councillor.cromwell@tewkesbury.gov.uk

Davies, Derek (CON - Highnam with Hawbridge)
councillor.davies@tewkesbury.gov.uk

Day, Janet (CON - Winchcombe)
councillor.day@tewkesbury.gov.uk

Dean, Mike (CON - Cleeve Hill)
councillor.dean@tewkesbury.gov.uk

East, Bob (CON - Cleeve St Michael's)
councillor.east@tewkesbury.gov.uk

Evans, Alexander (CON - Churchdown St John's)
councillor.evans@tewkesbury.gov.uk

Evetts, John (CON - Isbourne)
councillor.evetts@tewkesbury.gov,uk

Foyle, David (CON - Churchdown Brookfield)
councillor.foyle@tewkesbury.gov.uk

Furolo, Ron (CON - Brockworth)
councillor.furolo@tewkesbury.gov.uk

Garnham, Rob (CON - Cleeve West)
councillor.garnham@tewkesbury.gov.uk

Godwin, Pauline (CON - Northway)
councillor.godwin@tewkesbury.gov.uk

Gore, Melanie (CON - Oxenton Hill)
councillor.gore@tewkesbury.gov.uk

Greening, Julie (CON - Tewkesbury Prior's Park)
councillor.greening@tewkesbury.gov.uk

Hatton, Ruth (CON - Brockworth)
councillor.hatton@tewkesbury.gov.uk

Hesketh, John (CON - Ashchurch with Walton Cardiff)
councillor.hesketh@tewkesbury.gov.uk

Hillier-Richardson, Sue (LD - Cleeve Grange)
councillor.hillier-richardson@tewkesbury.gov.uk

Hollaway, Anna (CON - Cleeve Hill)
councillor.hollaway@tewkesbury.gov.uk

MacTiernan, Elaine (CON - Northway)
councillor.mactiernan@tewkesbury.gov.uk

Mason, Jim (CON - Winchcombe)
councillor.mason@tewkesbury.gov.uk

McLain, Heather (CON - Ashchurch with Walton Cardiff)
hmclain@hotmail.co.uk

Reece, Andrew (CON - Cleeve St Michael's)
councillor.reece@tewkesburyb.gov.uk

Smith, Vernon (CON - Tewkesbury Newtown)
councillor.smithv@tewkesbury.gov.uk

Spencer, Terrance (CON - Twyning)
councillor.spencer@tewkesbury.gov.uk

Stokes, Pearl (LD - Churchdown St John's)
councillor.stokes@tewkesbury.gov.uk

Surman, Philip (CON - Shurdington)
councillor.surman@tewkesbury.gov.uk

Turbyfield, Harry (CON - Brockworth)

Williams, Mark (CON - Coombe Hill)
councillor.williams@tewkesbury.gov.uk

Workman, Philip (IND - Tewkesbury Town With Mitton)
councillor.workman@tewkesbury.gov.uk

POLITICAL COMPOSITION

CON: 33, LD: 3, IND: 2

COMMITTEE CHAIRS

Audit: Mr Ron Furolo

Licensing: Mr Rob Garnham

Planning: Mr John Evetts

Thanet D

Thanet District Council, Thanet Council Offices, Cecil Street, Margate CT9 1XZ
☎ 01843 577000 🖷 01843 290906 ✉ customer.services@thanet.gov.uk
💻 www.thanet.gov.uk

FACTS AND FIGURES

EU Constituencies: South East
Election Frequency: Elections are biennial

PRINCIPAL OFFICERS

Chief Executive: Ms Madeline Homer, Chief Executive, Thanet Council Offices, Cecil Street, Margate CT9 1XZ ☎ 01843 577123 🖷 01843 290906 ✉ madeline.homer@thanet.gov.uk

Senior Management: Mr Gavin Waite, Director - Operational Services, Thanet Council Offices, Cecil Street, Margate CT9 1XZ ☎ 01843 577742 ✉ gavin.waite@thanet.gov.uk

Senior Management: Mr Tim Willis, Director - Financial Services Officer & S151 Officer, Thanet Council Offices, Cecil Street, Margate CT9 1XZ ☎ 01843 577617 ✉ tim.willis@thanet.gov.uk

Architect, Building / Property Services: Mrs Edwina Crowley, Head of Economic Development & Asset Management, Thanet Council Offices, Cecil Street, Margate CT9 1XZ ☎ 01843 577646 🖷 01843 577686 ✉ edwina.crowley@thanet.gov.uk

Building Control: Mr Geoff Musk, Building Control Manager, Council Offices, Cecil Street, Margate CT9 1XZ ☎ 01843 577156 🖷 01843 231755 ✉ geoff.musk@thanet.gov.uk

PR / Communications: Miss Hannah Thorpe, PR & Publicity Manager, Thanet Council Offices, Cecil Street, Margate CT9 1XZ ☎ 01843 577120 🖷 01843 290906 ✉ hannah.thorpe@thanet.gov.uk

Community Planning: Mrs Larissa Reed, Interim Director of Community Services, Thanet Council Offices, Cecil Street, Margate CT9 1XZ ☎ 01843 577008 ✉ larissa.reed@thanet.gov.uk

Community Safety: Mr Martyn Cassell, Community Safety Manager, Thanet Council Offices, Cecil Street, Margate CT9 1XZ ☎ 01843 577367 ✉ martyn.cassell@thanet.gov.uk

Computer Management: Mr Sean Hale, Head of ICT, EK Services, Military Road, Canterbury CT1 1YW ☎ 01227 862341 ✉ sean.hale@ekservices.org

Contracts: Ms Karen Paton, Strategic Procurement Manager, Council Offices, Cecil Street, Margate CT9 1XZ ☎ 01843 577112 🖷 01843 290906 ✉ karen.paton@thanet.gov.uk

Customer Service: Mr Dominic Whelan, Shared Services Director, EK Services, Military Road, Canterbury CT1 1YW ☎ 01227 862073 ✉ dominic.whelan@ekservices.org

Economic Development: Mrs Edwina Crowley, Head of Economic Development & Asset Management, Thanet Council Offices, Cecil Street, Margate CT9 1XZ ☎ 01843 577646 🖷 01843 577686 ✉ edwina.crowley@thanet.gov.uk

E-Government: Mrs Roz Edridge, Business Systems Manager, East Kent Services, Council Offices, Cecil Street, Margate CT9 1XZ ☎ 01843 577033 ✉ roz.edridge@ekservices.org

Emergency Planning: Mr Mike Humber, Technical Services Manager, Thanet Council Offices, Cecil Street, Margate CT9 1XZ ☎ 01843 577083 ✉ mike.humber@thanet.gov.uk

Environmental / Technical Services: Mr Mike Humber, Technical Services Manager, Thanet Council Offices, Cecil Street, Margate CT9 1XZ ☎ 01843 577083 ✉ mike.humber@thanet.gov.uk

Environmental Health: Ms Penny Button, Head of Safer Neighbourhoods, Thanet Council Offices, Cecil Street, Margate CT9 1XZ ☎ 01843 577425 🖷 01843 290906 ✉ penny.button@thanet.gov.uk

Estates, Property & Valuation: Mrs Edwina Crowley, Head of Economic Development & Asset Management, Thanet Council Offices, Cecil Street, Margate CT9 1XZ ☎ 01843 577646 🖷 01843 577686 ✉ edwina.crowley@thanet.gov.uk

Events Manager: Ms Penny Button, Head of Safer Neighbourhoods, Thanet Council Offices, Cecil Street, Margate CT9 1XZ ☎ 01843 577425 🖷 01843 290906 ✉ penny.button@thanet.gov.uk

Facilities: Mrs Carolyn Tinley, Facilities Manager, Thanet Council Offices, Cecil Street, Margate CT9 1XZ ☎ 01843 577291 🖷 01843 577686 ✉ carolyn.tinley@thanet.gov.uk

Grounds Maintenance: Mr Stephen Harris, Interim Open Spaces Manager, Thanet Council Offices, Cecil Street, Margate CT9 1XZ ☎ 01843 577960 ✉ stephen.harris@thanet.gov.uk

Health and Safety: Ms Sheila Coupe, Health & Safety Advisor, EK Human Resources, PO Box 453, Dover CT16 9DQ ☎ 01304 872799 ✉ sheila.coupe@ekhr.org

Home Energy Conservation: Miss Tanya Wenham, Head of Housing, Thanet Council Offices, Cecil Street, Margate CT9 1XZ ☎ 01843 577006 🖷 01843 290606 ✉ tanya.wenham@thanet.gov.uk

Housing: Miss Tanya Wenham, Head of Housing, Thanet Council Offices, Cecil Street, Margate CT9 1XZ ☎ 01843 577006 🖷 01843 290606 ✉ tanya.wenham@thanet.gov.uk

Housing Maintenance: Mr Paul Bridge, Director - Operations & Business Transformation, EK Housing, East Kent Housing Ltd, Garrity House, Miners Way, Aylesham CT3 3BF ☎ 01304 853749 ✉ paul.bridge@eastkenthousing.org.uk

Legal: Mr Tim Howes, Interim Legal Services Manager & Monitoring Officer, Thanet Council Offices, Cecil Street, Margate CT9 1XZ ☎ 01843 577906 ✉ tim.howes@thanet.gov.uk

Leisure and Cultural Services: Ms Penny Button, Head of Safer Neighbourhoods, Thanet Council Offices, Cecil Street, Margate CT9 1XZ ☎ 01843 577425 🖷 01843 290906 ✉ penny.button@thanet.gov.uk

Licensing: Mr Philip Bensted, Regulatory Services Manager, Council Offices, Cecil Street, Margate CT9 1XZ ☎ 01843 577630 🖷 01843 290906 ✉ philip.bensted@thanet.gov.uk

Lottery Funding, Charity and Voluntary: Mrs Paul Verrall, Community Asset Manager, Thanet Council Offices, Cecil Street, Margate CT9 1XZ ☎ 01843 577960 🖷 01843 577686 ✉ paul.verrall@thanet.gov.uk

Parking: Mr Robin Chantrill-Smith, Civil Enforcement Manager, Thanet Council Offices, Cecil Street, Margate CT9 1XZ ☎ 01843 577472 ✉ robin.chantrill-smith@thanet.gov.uk

Partnerships: Ms Penny Button, Head of Safer Neighbourhoods, Thanet Council Offices, Cecil Street, Margate CT9 1XZ ☎ 01843 577425 🖷 01843 290906 ✉ penny.button@thanet.gov.uk

Personnel / HR: Ms Juli Oliver-Smith, Head of EK Human Resources, East Kent HR Partnership, Dover District Council, White Cliffs Business Park, Whitfield, Dover CT16 3PJ ☎ 07917 473616 ✉ hrpartnership@dover.gov.uk

Planning: Ms Abigail Raymond, Head of Built Environment, Thanet Council Offices, Cecil Street, Margate CT9 1XZ ☎ 01843 577752 ✉ abigail.raymond@thanet.gov.uk

Procurement: Ms Karen Paton, Strategic Procurement Manager, Council Offices, Cecil Street, Margate CT9 1XZ ☎ 01843 577112 🖷 01843 290906 ✉ karen.paton@thanet.gov.uk

Recycling & Waste Minimisation: Mr Gavin Waite, Director - Operational Services, Thanet Council Offices, Cecil Street, Margate CT9 1XZ ☎ 01843 577742 ✉ gavin.waite@thanet.gov.uk

Regeneration: Mrs Larissa Reed, Interim Director of Community Services, Thanet Council Offices, Cecil Street, Margate CT9 1XZ ☎ 01843 577008 ✉ larissa.reed@thanet.gov.uk

THANET

Staff Training: Ms Sonia Godfrey, HR Manager of Business Services, East Kent HR Partnership, Dover District Council, White Cliffs Business Park, Whitfield, Dover CT16 3PJ ☎ 07854 763690 ✉ hrpartnership@dover.gov.uk

Street Scene: Mr Phil Snook, Street Scene Enforcement Manager, Thanet Council Offices, Cecil Street, Margate CT9 1XZ ☎ 01843 577658 ✉ phil.snook@thanet.gov.uk

Sustainable Communities: Ms Penny Button, Head of Safer Neighbourhoods, Thanet Council Offices, Cecil Street, Margate CT9 1XZ ☎ 01843 577425 🖷 01843 290906 ✉ penny.button@thanet.gov.uk

Tourism: Ms Louise Askew, Economic Development Manager, Thanet Council Offices, Cecil Street, Margate CT9 1XZ ☎ 01843 577178 ✉ lousie.askew@thanet.gov.uk

Town Centre: Ms Louise Askew, Economic Development Manager, Thanet Council Offices, Cecil Street, Margate CT9 1XZ ☎ 01843 577178 ✉ lousie.askew@thanet.gov.uk

Waste Collection and Disposal: Mr Gavin Waite, Director - Operational Services, Thanet Council Offices, Cecil Street, Margate CT9 1XZ ☎ 01843 577742 ✉ gavin.waite@thanet.gov.uk

Waste Management: Mr Gavin Waite, Director - Operational Services, Thanet Council Offices, Cecil Street, Margate CT9 1XZ ☎ 01843 577742 ✉ gavin.waite@thanet.gov.uk

COUNCILLORS

***Chair* Piper**, Stuart (UKIP - Northwood)
cllr-stuart.piper@thanet.gov.uk

***Leader of the Council* Well**, Christopher (UKIP - Cliftonville East)
cllr-chris.wells@thanet.gov.uk

***Deputy Leader of the Council* Fairbrass**, Lin (UKIP - Nethercourt)
cllr-lin.fairbrass@thanet.gov.uk

***Group Leader* Bayford**, Robert (CON - Kingsgate)
cllr-robert.bayford@thanet.gov.uk

Ashbee, Ash (UKIP - Westbrook)
cllr-ash.ashbee@thanet.gov.uk

Bambridge, Sam (CON - Westgate-on-Sea)
cllr-sam.bambridge@thanet.gov.uk

Braidwood, Bertie (UKIP - Westgate-on-Sea)
cllr-bertie.braidwood@thanet.gov.uk

Brimm, Suzanne (UKIP - Birchington South)
cllr-suzanne.brimm@thanet.gov.uk

Buckley, John (UKIP - Beacon Road)
cllr-john.buckley@thanet.gov.uk

Campbell, Peter (LAB - Central Harbour)
cllr-peter.campbell@thanet.gov.uk

Coleman-Cooke, Keith (CON - Birchington North)
cllr-keith.coleman-cooke@thanet.gov.uk

Coleman-Cooke, Glenn (UKIP - Birchington South)
cllr-glenn.coleman-cooke@thanet.gov.uk

Collins, Konnor (UKIP - Northwood)
cllr-konnor.collins@thanet.gov.uk

Connor, Terry (UKIP - Sir Moses Montefiore)
cllr-terry.connor@thanet.gov.uk

Crow-Brown, Derek (UKIP - Thanet Villages)
cllr-derek.crow-brown@thanet.gov.uk

Curran, Jonathan (CON - Garlinge)
cllr-jonathan.curran@thanet.gov.uk

Day, Simon (CON - Birchington North)
cllr-simon.day@thanet.gov.uk

Dellar, Julie (UKIP - Cliftonville West)
cllr-julie.dellar@thanet.gov.uk

Dennis, John (UKIP - Garlinge)
cllr-john.dennis@thanet.gov.uk

Dexter, Roy (CON - St Peters)
cllr-roy.dexter@thanet.gov.uk

Dixon, Rosamund (UKIP - Dane Valley)
cllr-rosamund.dixon@thanet.gov.uk

Edwards, Robin (UKIP - Salmestone)
cllr-robin.edwards@thanet.gov.uk

Elenor, Jeffrey (UKIP - Margate Central)
cllr-jeffrey.elenor@thanet.gov.uk

Evans, Peter (UKIP - Salmestone)
cllr-peter.evans@thanet.gov.uk

Fairbrass, Jeremy (UKIP - Nethercourt)
cllr-jeremy.fairbrass@thanet.gov.uk

Falcon, Janet (UKIP - Eastcliff)
cllr-janet.falcon@thanet.gov.uk

Fenner, Michelle (LAB - Sir Moses Montefiore)
cllr-michelle.fenner@thanet.gov.uk

Game, Lesley Ann (CON - Cliftonville East)
cllr-lesley.game@thanet.gov.uk

Gregory, Ian (CON - St Peters)
cllr-ian.gregory@thanet.gov.uk

Gregory, Ken (CON - Thanet Villages)
cllr-ken.gregory@thanet.gov.uk

Grove, Bob (IND - Thanet Villages)
cllr-bob.grove@thanet.gov.uk

Hayton, William (CON - Bradstowe)
cllr-bill.hayton@thanet.gov.uk

Hillman, Emma (UKIP - Cliftonville West)
cllr-emma.hillman@thanet.gov.uk

Hillman, Gary (UKIP - Dane Valley)
cllr-gary.hillman.@thanet.gov.uk

Howes, Alan (UKIP - Birchington South)
cllr-alan.howes@thanet.gov.uk

Jaye-Jones, Edward (UKIP - Cliftonville East)
cllr-edward.jaye-jones@thanet.gov.uk

Johnston, Iris (LAB - Margate Central)
cllr-iris.johnston@thanet.gov.uk

Larkins, Sarah (UKIP - Eastcliff)
cllr-sarah.larkins@thanet.gov.uk

Leys, Mo (UKIP - Newington)
cllr-mo.leys@thanet.gov.uk

Martin, Beverly (UKIP - Central Harbour)
cllr-beverly.martin@thanet.gov.uk

Matterface, Jennifer (LAB - Beacon Road)
cllr-jennifer.matterface@thanet.gov.uk

Munday, Vince (UKIP - Newington)
cllr-vince.munday@thanet.gov.uk

Parson, David (CON - Bradstowe)
cllr-david.parsons@thanet.gov.uk

Partington, Carol (CON - Westgate-on-sea)
cllr-carol.partington@thanet.gov.uk

Potts, Linda (UKIP - Cliftonville West)
cllr-linda.potts@thanet.gov.uk

Rogers, Brenda (CON - Cliffsend and Pegwell)
cllr-brenda.rogers@thanet.gov.uk

Saunders, Mave (CON - Viking)
cllr-mave.saunders@thanet.gov.uk

Saunders, David (CON - Viking)
cllr-david.saunders@thanet.gov.uk

Savage, Jason (CON - St Peters)
cllr-jason.savage@thanet.gov.uk

Shonk, Trevor (UKIP - Central Harbour)
cllr-trevor.shonk@thanet.gov.uk

Smith, Helen (UKIP - Northwood)
cllr-helen.smith@thanet.gov.uk

Stummer-Schmertzing, Hunter (UKIP - Eastcliff)
cllr-hunter.stummer-schmertzing@thanet.gov.uk

Taylor, Gary (UKIP - Dane Valley)
cllr-gary.taylor@thanet.gov.uk

Taylor-Smith, Rosanna (CON - Viking)
cllr-rosanna.taylor-smith@thanet.gov.uk

Tomlinson, Michael (CON - Westbrook)
cllr-mick.tomlinson@thanet.gov.uk

Townsend, John (UKIP - Cliffsend and Pegwell)
cllr-john.townsend@thanet.gov.uk

POLITICAL COMPOSITION

UKIP: 33, CON: 18, LAB: 4, IND: 1

COMMITTEE CHAIRS

Audit & Governance: Mr Vince Munday

Licensing: Ms Linda Potts

Planning: Mr Peter Evans

Three Rivers D

Three Rivers District Council, Three Rivers House, Northway, Rickmansworth WD3 1RL
☎ 01923 776611 🖷 01923 896119
✉ enquiries@threerivers.gov.uk
🖳 www.threerivers.gov.uk

FACTS AND FIGURES

Parliamentary Constituencies: South West Hertfordshire, St. Albans, Watford
EU Constituencies: Eastern
Election Frequency: Elections are by thirds

PRINCIPAL OFFICERS

Chief Executive: Dr Steven Halls, Chief Executive, Three Rivers House, Northway, Rickmansworth WD3 1RL ☎ 01923 727281 🖷 01923 727282 ✉ steven.halls@threerivers.gov.uk

Senior Management: Mr Geof Muggeridge, Director of Community & Environment, Three Rivers House, Northway, Rickmansworth WD3 1RL ☎ 01923 776611 🖷 01923 896119 ✉ geof.muggeridge@threerivers.gov.uk

Senior Management: Ms Joanne Wagstaffe, Director of Finance, Town Hall, Watford WD17 3EX ☎ 01923 727205 ✉ joanne.wagstaffe@threerivers.gov.uk

Architect, Building / Property Services: Ms Rebecca Emmett, Head of Regulatory Services, Three Rivers House, Northway, Rickmansworth WD3 1RL ☎ 01923 776611 🖷 01923 896119 ✉ rebecca.emmett@threerivers.gov.uk

Building Control: Mr Clive Fuller, Chief Building Control Officer, Three Rivers House, Northway, Rickmansworth WD3 1RL ☎ 01923 727125 🖷 01923 278273 ✉ clive.fuller@threerivers.gov.uk

PR / Communications: Mr Kevin Snow, Communications Manager, Three Rivers House, Northway, Rickmansworth WD3 1RL ☎ 01923 776611 🖷 01923 727258 ✉ kevin.snow@threerivers.gov.uk

Community Planning: Mr Renato Messere, Head of Economic & Sustainable Development, Three Rivers House, Northway, Rickmansworth WD3 1RL ☎ 01923 776611 🖷 01923 896119 ✉ renato.messere@threerivers.gov.uk

Community Safety: Mr Andy Stovold, Community Partnerships Manager, Three Rivers House, Northway, Rickmansworth WD3 1RL ☎ 01923 776611 🖷 01923 896119 ✉ andy.stovold@threerivers.gov.uk

Computer Management: Mrs Emma Tiernan, ICT Client Manager, Town Hall, Watford WD17 3EX ☎ 01923 727457 ✉ emma.tiernan@threerivers.gov.uk

Corporate Services: Mr Phil King, Emergency Planning & Risk Manager, Three Rivers House, Northway, Rickmansworth WD3 1RL ☎ 01923 727260 ✉ phil.king@threerivers.gov.uk

Customer Service: Mr William Hall, Customer Services Manager, Three Rivers House, Northway, Rickmansworth WD3 1RL ☎ 01923 776611 🖷 01923 896119 ✉ billy.hall@threerivers.gov.uk

Economic Development: Mr Renato Messere, Head of Economic & Sustainable Development, Three Rivers House, Northway, Rickmansworth WD3 1RL ☎ 01923 776611 🖷 01923 896119 ✉ renato.messere@threerivers.gov.uk

E-Government: Mrs Emma Tiernan, ICT Client Manager, Town Hall, Watford WD17 3EX ☎ 01923 727457 ✉ emma.tiernan@threerivers.gov.uk

Electoral Registration: Mr Elwyn Wilson, Democratic Services Manager, Three Rivers House, Northway, Rickmansworth WD3 1RL ☎ 01923 776611 🖷 01923 896119 ✉ elwyn.wilson@threerivers.gov.uk

THREE RIVERS

Emergency Planning: Mr Phil King, Emergency Planning & Risk Manager, Three Rivers House, Northway, Rickmansworth WD3 1RL ☎ 01923 727260 🖰 phil.king@threerivers.gov.uk

Energy Management: Mr Renato Messere, Head of Economic & Sustainable Development, Three Rivers House, Northway, Rickmansworth WD3 1RL ☎ 01923 776611 🖷 01923 896119 🖰 renato.messere@threerivers.gov.uk

Environmental / Technical Services: Mr Malcolm Clarke, Environmental Services Manager, Batchwood Depot, Harefield Road, Rickmansworth WD3 1RL ☎ 01923 776611 🖰 malcolm.clarke@threerivers.gov.uk

Environmental Health: Ms Gloria Gillespie, Residential Standards Manager, Three Rivers House, Northway, Rickmansworth WD3 1RL ☎ 01923 776611 🖰 gloria.gillespie@threerivers.gov.uk

Estates, Property & Valuation: Mrs Tracey Field, Asset & Property Manager, Three Rivers House, Northway, Rickmansworth WD3 1RL ☎ 01923 776611 🖰 tracey.field@threerivers.gov.uk

Facilities: Ms Yvonne Petagine, Services Manager, Three Rivers House, Northway, Rickmansworth WD3 1RL ☎ 01923 776611 🖷 01923 896119 🖰 yvonne.petagine@threerivers.gov.uk

Treasury: Mr Nigel Pollard, Head of Finance - Shared Services, Three Rivers House, Northway, Rickmansworth WD3 1RL ☎ 01923 776611 🖰 nigel.pollard@threerivers.gov.uk

Grounds Maintenance: Mr Malcolm Clarke, Environmental Services Manager, Batchwood Depot, Harefield Road, Rickmansworth WD3 1RL ☎ 01923 776611 🖰 malcolm.clarke@threerivers.gov.uk

Health and Safety: Mr Darren Williams, Corporate Health & Safety Adviser, Three Rivers House, Northway, Rickmansworth WD3 1RL ☎ 01923 776611 🖰 darren.williams@threerivers.gov.uk

Housing: Ms Kimberley Grout, Housing Manager, Three Rivers House, Northway, Rickmansworth WD3 1RL ☎ 01923 776611 🖰 kimberley.grout@threerivers.gov.uk

Legal: Mrs Anne Morgan, Solicitor to the Council, Three Rivers House, Northway, Rickmansworth WD3 1RL ☎ 01923 776611 🖷 01923 727213 🖰 anne.morgan@threerivers.gov.uk

Leisure and Cultural Services: Mr Chris Hope, Head of Community Services, Three Rivers House, Northway, Rickmansworth WD3 1RL ☎ 01923 776611 🖷 01923 727150 🖰 chris.hope@threerivers.gov.uk

Licensing: Mrs Kimberley Rowley, Team Leader - Projects & Compliance, Three Rivers House, Northway, Rickmansworth WD3 1RL ☎ 01923 776611 🖰 kimberley.rowley@threerivers.gov.uk

Lottery Funding, Charity and Voluntary: Mr Karl Stonebank, Voluntary Sector Officer, Three Rivers House, Northway, Rickmansworth WD3 1RL ☎ 01923 776611 🖰 karl.stonebank@threerivers.gov.uk

Member Services: Ms Sarah Haythorpe, Principal Committee Manager, Three Rivers House, Northway, Rickmansworth WD3 1RL ☎ 01923 776611 🖰 sarah.haythorpe@threeriver.gov.uk

Parking: Mrs Tracey Field, Asset & Property Manager, Three Rivers House, Northway, Rickmansworth WD3 1RL ☎ 01923 776611 🖰 tracey.field@threerivers.gov.uk

Partnerships: Mr Andy Stovold, Community Partnerships Manager, Three Rivers House, Northway, Rickmansworth WD3 1RL ☎ 01923 776611 🖷 01923 896119 🖰 andy.stovold@threerivers.gov.uk

Personnel / HR: Mrs Cathy Watson, Head of Human Resources, Three Rivers House, Northway, Rickmansworth WD3 1RL 🖰 cathy.watson@threerivers.gov.uk

Planning: Ms Rebecca Emmett, Head of Regulatory Services, Three Rivers House, Northway, Rickmansworth WD3 1RL ☎ 01923 776611 🖷 01923 896119 🖰 rebecca.emmett@threerivers.gov.uk

Recycling & Waste Minimisation: Mrs Alison Page, Head of Environmental Protection, Three Rivers House, Northway, Rickmansworth WD3 1RL ☎ 01923 776611 🖷 01923 727037 🖰 alison.page@threerivers.gov.uk

Staff Training: Ms Sherrie Ralton, Learning & Development Officer, Three Rivers House, Northway, Rickmansworth WD3 1RL ☎ 01923 776611 🖰 sherrie.ralton@threerivers.gov.uk

Street Scene: Mrs Alison Page, Head of Environmental Protection, Three Rivers House, Northway, Rickmansworth WD3 1RL ☎ 01923 776611 🖷 01923 727037 🖰 alison.page@threerivers.gov.uk

Sustainable Communities: Dr Steven Halls, Chief Executive, Three Rivers House, Northway, Rickmansworth WD3 1RL ☎ 01923 727281 🖷 01923 727282 🖰 steven.halls@threerivers.gov.uk

Sustainable Development: Mr Renato Messere, Head of Economic & Sustainable Development, Three Rivers House, Northway, Rickmansworth WD3 1RL ☎ 01923 776611 🖷 01923 896119 🖰 renato.messere@threerivers.gov.uk

Town Centre: Mr Renato Messere, Head of Economic & Sustainable Development, Three Rivers House, Northway, Rickmansworth WD3 1RL ☎ 01923 776611 🖷 01923 896119 🖰 renato.messere@threerivers.gov.uk

Transport Planner: Mr Renato Messere, Head of Economic & Sustainable Development, Three Rivers House, Northway, Rickmansworth WD3 1RL ☎ 01923 776611 🖷 01923 896119 🖰 renato.messere@threerivers.gov.uk

Waste Collection and Disposal: Mr Malcolm Clarke, Environmental Services Manager, Batchwood Depot, Harefield Road, Rickmansworth WD3 1RL ☎ 01923 776611 🖰 malcolm.clarke@threerivers.gov.uk

Waste Management: Mr Malcolm Clarke, Environmental Services Manager, Batchwood Depot, Harefield Road, Rickmansworth WD3 1RL ☎ 01923 776611 🖰 malcolm.clarke@threerivers.gov.uk

Children's Play Areas: Mr Chris Hope, Head of Community Services, Three Rivers House, Northway, Rickmansworth WD3 1RL ☎ 01923 776611 🖷 01923 727150 🖰 chris.hope@threerivers.gov.uk

COUNCILLORS

***Chair* Bishop**, Eric (CON - Carpenders Park)
eric.bishop@threerivers.gov.uk

***Vice-Chair* Turner**, Kate (LD - Leavesden)
kate.turner@threerivers.gov.uk

***Leader of the Council* Shaw**, Ann (LD - Chorleywood South & Maple Cross)
ann.shaw@threerivers.gov.uk

Barber, Diana (CON - Penn & Mill End)
diana.barber@threerivers.gov.uk

Barnes, Rupert (CON - Dickinsons)
rupert.barnes@threerivers.gov.uk

Bedford, Matthew (LD - Abbots Langley & Bedmond)
matthew.bedford@threerivers.gov.uk

Bedford, Sara (LD - Abbots Langley & Bedmond)
sara.bedford@threerivers.gov.uk

Brading, Phil (LD - Dickinsons)
phil.brading@threerivers.gov.uk

Brooks, Martin (LD - Leavesden)
martin.brooks2@threerivers.gov.uk

Butler, Marilyn (CON - Chorleywood North & Sarratt)
marilyn.butler@threerivers.gov.uk

Butt, Kemal (LD - Moor Park & Eastbury)
kemal.butt@threerivers.gov.uk

Cox, Stephen (LAB - South Oxhey)
stephen.oxhey@threerivers.gov.uk

Dos Ramos, Terry (CON - Carpenders Park)
terry.dosramos@threerivers.gov.uk

Drury, Steve (LD - Durrants)
steve.drury@threerivers.gov.uk

Getkahn, Peter (LD - Dickinsons)
peter.getkahn@threerivers.gov.uk

Giles-Medhurst, Stephen (LD - Leavesden)
SGM@cix.co.uk

Harris, Ty (CON - Oxhey Hall & Hayling)
ty.harris@threerivers.gov.uk

Hayward, Alex (CON - Chorleywood North & Sarratt)
alex.hayward@threerivers.gov.uk

Hiscocks, Paula (CON - Rickmansworth Town)
paula.hiscocks@threerivers.gov.uk

Kenison, Heather (CON - Chorleywood North & Sarratt)
heather.kennison@threerivers.gov.uk

Killick, Angela (CON - Chorleywood South & Maple Cross)
angela.killick@threerivers.gov.uk

Lloyd, Chris (LD - Durrants)
chris.lloyd@threerivers.gov.uk

Major, David (LD - Abbots Langley & Bedmond)
david.major@threerivers.gov.uk

Mann, Joy (LD - Gade Valley)
joy.mann@threerivers.gov.uk

Morris, Debbie (CON - Moor Park & Eastbury)
debbie.morris@threerivers.gov.uk

Nelmes, Sarah (LD - Penn & Mill End)
sarah.nelmes@threerivers.gov.uk

Nolan, Marie-Louise (LAB - South Oxhey)
marie-louise.nolan@threerivers.gov.uk

Proctor, Leslie (CON - Gade Valley)
leslie.proctor@threerivers.gov.uk

Ranger, Reena (CON - Moor Park & Eastbury)
reena.ranger@threerivers.gov.uk

Roberts, Angela (CON - Carpenders Park)
angela.roberts@threerivers.gov.uk

Sangster, Ralph (CON - Rickmansworth Town)
ralph.sangster@threerivers.gov.uk

Sansom, David (CON - Rickmansworth Town)
david.sansom@threerivers.gov.uk

Scarth, Alison (LD - Oxhey Hall & Hayling)
alison.scarth@threerivers.gov.uk

Scarth, Andrew (LD - Oxhey Hall & Hayling)

Seabourne, Roger (LD - Penn & Mill End)
roger.seabourne@threerivers.gov.uk

Tippen, Len (LAB - South Oxhey)
len.tippen@threerivers.gov.uk

Trevett, Martin (LD - Chorleywood South & Maple Cross)
martin.trevett@threerivers.gov.uk

Wall, Alison (LD - Durrants)
alison.wall@threerivers.gov.uk

Whately-Smith, Chris (LD - Gade Valley)
chris.whately-smith@threerivers.gov.uk

POLITICAL COMPOSITION

LD: 20, CON: 16, LAB: 3

Thurrock U

Thurrock Council, Civic Offices, New Road, Grays RM17 6SL
☎ 01375 652652 🖷 01375 652359 🖰 initialsurname@thurrock.gov.uk
💻 www.thurrock.gov.uk

FACTS AND FIGURES

Parliamentary Constituencies: Thurrock
EU Constituencies: Eastern
Election Frequency: Elections are by thirds

PRINCIPAL OFFICERS

Chief Executive: Ms Lyn Carpenter, Chief Executive, Civic Offices, New Road, Grays RM17 6SL ☎ 01375 652390
🖰 lcarpenter@thurrock.gov.uk

Assistant Chief Executive: Mr Steve Cox, Assistant Chief Executive, Civic Offices, New Road, Grays RM17 6SL ☎ 01375 652286 🖰 scox@thurrock.gov.uk

Senior Management: Ms Barbara Brownlee, Director of Housing, Civic Offices, New Road, Grays RM17 6SL ☎ 01375 652581
🖰 bbrownlee@thurrock.gov.uk

THURROCK

Senior Management: Mr David Bull, Interim Chief Executive (Director - Planning & Transportation), Civic Offices, New Road, Grays RM17 6SL ☎ 01375 652286 ✉ dbull@thurrock.gov.uk

Senior Management: Mr Sean Clark, Head of Finance & S151 Officer, Civic Offices, New Road, Grays RM17 6SL ☎ 01375 652010 ✉ sclark@thurrock.gov.uk

Senior Management: Mr Roger Harris, Director - Adults, Health & Commissioning, Civic Offices, New Road, Grays RM17 6SL ☎ 01375 652561 ✉ r.harris@thurrock.gov.uk

Senior Management: Ms Jackie Hinchliffe, Head of Human Resources & Organisational Development & Transformation, Civic Offices, New Road, Grays RM17 6SL ☎ 01375 652016 ✉ jhinchliffe@thurrock.gov.uk

Senior Management: Ms Carmel Littleton, Director - Children's Services, Civic Offices, New Road, Grays RM17 6SL ☎ 01375 652077 ✉ clittleton@thurrock.gov.uk

Senior Management: Mrs Fiona Taylor, Head of Legal Services, Civic Centre, Dagenham RM10 7BN ☎ 020 8227 2114 ✉ fiona.taylor@bdtlegal.org.uk

Architect, Building / Property Services: Mr Ian Rydings, Head of Asset Management, Civic Offices, New Road, Grays RM17 6SL ☎ 01375 654036 ✉ irydings@thurrock.gov.uk

Best Value: Mr Roger Harris, Director of Adults, Health & Commissioning, Civic Offices, New Road, Grays RM17 6SL ☎ 01375 652914 ✉ rharris@thurrock.gov.uk

Building Control: Mr Stuart Fyffe, Senior Building Control Surveyor, Civic Offices, New Road, Grays RM17 6SL ☎ 01375 652165 ✉ sfyffe@thurrock.gov.uk

Civil Registration: Ms Lynn Whipps, Superintendent Registrar, Civic Offices, New Road, Grays RM17 6SL ☎ 01375 375245 ✉ lwhipps@thurrock.gov.uk

PR / Communications: Ms Karen Wheeler, Head of Strategy, Civic Offices, New Road, Grays RM17 6SL ☎ 01375 659688 ✉ kwheeler@thurrock.gov.uk

Community Safety: Ms Natalie Warren, Community Development & Equalities Manager, Civic Offices, New Road, Grays RM17 6SL ☎ 01375 652186 ✉ nwarren@thurrock.gov.uk

Computer Management: Mr Murray James, Head of ICT, Civic Offices, New Road, Grays RM17 6SL ☎ 01375 652951 ✉ murray.james@serco.com

Consumer Protection and Trading Standards: Mr Gavin Dennett, Acting Head of Public Protection, Civic Offices, New Road, Grays RM17 6SL ☎ 01375 652581 ✉ gdennett@thurrock.gov.uk

Customer Service: Ms Tracie Heiser, Head of Customer Services & Business Administration, Serco, Civic Offices, New Road, Grays RM17 6SL ☎ 01375 366243 ✉ theiser@thurrock.gov.uk

Education: Mr Roger Edwardson, Interim Strategic Lead of School Improvement, Learning & Skills, Civic Offices, New Road, Grays RM17 6SL ☎ 01375 652973 ✉ redwardson@thurrock.gov.uk

E-Government: Mr Lee Henley, Information Manager, Civic Offices, New Road, Grays RM17 6SL ☎ 01375 652500

E-Government: Mr Steve Rigden, Web Manager, Civic Offices, New Road, Grays RM17 6SL ☎ 01375 652038 ✉ srigden@thurrock.gov.uk

Electoral Registration: Ms Elaine Sheridan, Electoral Services Manager, Civic Offices, New Road, Grays RM17 6SL ☎ 01375 652580 ✉ esheridan@thurrock.gov.uk

Emergency Planning: Mrs Lucy Magill, Head of Public Protection, Civic Offices, New Road, Grays RM17 6SL ☎ 01375 413768 🖷 01375 652359 ✉ lmagill@thurrock.gov.uk

Finance: Mr Sean Clark, Head of Finance & S151 Officer, Civic Offices, New Road, Grays RM17 6SL ☎ 01375 652010 ✉ sclark@thurrock.gov.uk

Grounds Maintenance: Mr Daren Spring, Street Services Manager, Civic Offices, New Road, Grays RM17 6SL ☎ 01375 413612 ✉ dspring@thurrock.gov.uk

Health and Safety: Mr Tony Sprackling, Principal Officer - Health & Safety, Civic Offices, New Road, Grays RM17 6SL ✉ asprackling@thurrock.gov.uk

Highways: Ms Ann Osola, Head of Highways & Transport, Civic Offices, New Road, Grays RM17 6SL ☎ 01375 652393 ✉ aosola@thurrock.gov.uk

Housing: Ms Kathryn Adedeji, Head of Investment & Development, Civic Offices, New Road, Grays RM17 6SL ☎ 01375 652178 ✉ kadedeji@thurrock.gov.uk

Housing: Ms Barbara Brownlee, Director of Housing, Civic Offices, New Road, Grays RM17 6SL ☎ 01375 652581 ✉ bbrownlee@thurrock.gov.uk

Housing: Mr Richard Parkin, Head of Housing, Civic Offices, New Road, Grays RM17 6SL ☎ 01375 652625 ✉ rparkin@thurrock.gov.uk

Legal: Mrs Fiona Taylor, Head of Legal Services, Civic Centre, Dagenham RM10 7BN ☎ 020 8227 2114 ✉ fiona.taylor@bdtlegal.org.uk

Leisure and Cultural Services: Mr Grant Greatrex, Sport, Leisure & Policy Development Manager, Civic Offices, New Road, Grays RM17 6SL ☎ 01375 413940 ✉ ggreatrex@thurrock.gov.uk

Licensing: Mr Paul Adams, Principal Licensing Officer, Civic Offices, New Road, Grays RM17 6SL ✉ padams@thurrock.gov.uk

Lifelong Learning: Ms Carmel Littleton, Director - Children's Services, Civic Offices, New Road, Grays RM17 6SL ☎ 01375 652077 ✉ clittleton@thurrock.gov.uk

Lighting: Mr Dave Parish, Street Lighting Engineer, Civic Offices, New Road, Grays RM17 6SL ☎ 01375 387430 ✉ dparish@thurrock.gov.uk

Lottery Funding, Charity and Voluntary: Ms Natalie Warren, Community Development & Equalities Manager, Civic Offices, New Road, Grays RM17 6SL ☎ 01375 652186 ✉ nwarren@thurrock.gov.uk

Member Services: Ms Cara Smith, Office Manager, Civic Offices, New Road, Grays RM17 6SL ☎ 01375 633622 ✉ csmith@thurrock.gov.uk

Parking: Ms Marie Buckley, Parking Services Co-ordinator, Civic Offices, New Road, Grays RM17 6SL ☎ 01375 652968 ✉ mbuckley@thurrock.gov.uk

Personnel / HR: Ms Jackie Hinchliffe, Head of Human Resources & Organisational Development & Transformation, Civic Offices, New Road, Grays RM17 6SL ☎ 01375 652016 ✉ jhinchliffe@thurrock.gov.uk

Planning: Mr David Bull, Interim Chief Executive (Director - Planning & Transportation), Civic Offices, New Road, Grays RM17 6SL ☎ 01375 652286 ✉ dbull@thurrock.gov.uk

Planning: Mr Andrew Millard, Head of Planning & Growth, Civic Offices, New Road, Grays RM17 6SL ☎ 01375 652710 ✉ amillard@thurrock.gov.uk

Procurement: Ms Kathryn Adedeji, Head of Investment & Development, Civic Offices, New Road, Grays RM17 6SL ☎ 01375 652178 ✉ kadedeji@thurrock.gov.uk

Public Libraries: Ms Jenny Meads, Operations & Data Manager, Thameside Theatre Complex, Orsett Road, Grays RM17 5DX ☎ 01375 413970 ✉ jmeads@thurrock.gov.uk

Recycling & Waste Minimisation: Mr Daren Spring, Street Services Manager, Civic Offices, New Road, Grays RM17 6SL ☎ 01375 413612 ✉ dspring@thurrock.gov.uk

Regeneration: Mr Matthew Essex, Head of Regeneration, Civic Offices, New Road, Grays RM17 6SL ☎ 01375 652185 ✉ messex@thurrock.gov.uk

Road Safety: Ms Julie Cooper, Active Travel Co-ordinator, Civic Offices, New Road, Grays RM17 6SL ☎ 01375 652574 ✉ jcooper@thurrock.gov.uk

Social Services: Mr Andrew Carter, Head of Children's Social Care, Civic Offices, New Road, Grays RM17 6SL ☎ 01375 659676 ✉ acarter@thurrock.gov.uk

Social Services (Adult): Mr Les Billingham, Head of Adult Services, Civic Offices, New Road, Grays RM17 6SL ☎ 01375 652294 ✉ l.billingham@thurrock.gov.uk

Social Services (Adult): Mr Roger Harris, Director - Adults, Health & Commissioning, Civic Offices, New Road, Grays RM17 6SL ☎ 01375 652561 ✉ r.harris@thurrock.gov.uk

Social Services (Children): Mr Andrew Carter, Head of Children's Social Care, Civic Offices, New Road, Grays RM17 6SL ☎ 01375 659676 ✉ acarter@thurrock.gov.uk

Public Health: Mr Ian Wake, Director - Public Health, Civic Offices, New Road, Grays RM17 6SL ☎ 01375 652561 ✉ iwake@thurrock.gov.uk

Staff Training: Ms Wendy Allen, Workforce Planning & Development Manager, Civic Offices, New Road, Grays RM17 6SL ☎ 01375 652674 ✉ wallen@thurrock.gov.uk

Street Scene: Mr Mike Heath, Interim Head of Development, Civic Offices, New Road, Grays RM17 6SL ☎ 01375 652914 ✉ mheath@thurrock.gov.uk

Sustainable Development: Ms Lisa Ricketts, Business Support Officer, Civic Offices, New Road, Grays RM17 6SL ☎ 01375 652271 ✉ lricketts@thurrock.gov.uk

Transport: Ms Tracey Ashwell, Highways & Transportation Services Manager, Civic Offices, New Road, Grays RM17 6SL ☎ 01375 413883 ✉ tashwell@thurrock.gov.uk

Waste Management: Mr Daren Spring, Street Services Manager, Civic Offices, New Road, Grays RM17 6SL ☎ 01375 413612 ✉ dspring@thurrock.gov.uk

COUNCILLORS

***Mayor* Gray**, Sue (LAB - Belhus)
sgray@thurrock.gov.uk

***Deputy Mayor* Kent**, Cathy (LAB - Grays)
ckent@thurrock.gov.uk

***Leader of the Council* Kent**, John (LAB - Grays Riverside)
jkent@thurrock.gov.uk

***Deputy Leader of the Council* Rice**, Barbara (LAB - Chadwell St Mary)
brice@thurrock.gov.uk

Aker, Tim (UKIP - Aveley & Uplands)
tim.aker@ukip.org

Baker, James (UKIP - East Tilbury)
jxbaker@thurrock.gov.uk

Baker, Chris (UKIP - Belhus)
cbaker@thurrock.gov.uk

Baker, Jan (UKIP - Ockendon)
jabaker@thurrock.gov.uk

Baldwin, Clare (LAB - Tilbury Riverside & Thurrock Park)
cbaldwin@thurrock.gov.uk

Brookes, Terry (LAB - West Thurrock & South Stifford)
tbrookes@thurrock.gov.uk

Cherry, Russell (UKIP - Chadwell St Mary)
rcherry@thurrock.gov.uk

Churchman, Colin (IND - Stanford East & Corringham Town)
cchurchman@thurrock.gov.uk

Coxshall, Mark (CON - Chafford & North Stifford)
mcoxshall@thurrock.gov.uk

THURROCK

Gamester, Leslie (UKIP - Stifford Clays)
lgamester@thurrock.gov.uk

Gerrish, Oliver (LAB - West Thurrock & South Stifford)
ogerrish@thurrock.gov.uk

Gledhill, Robert (CON - Little Thurrock Rectory)
rgledhill@thurrock.gov.uk

Gupta, Yash (LAB - Grays Thurrock)
ygupta@thurrock.gov.uk

Hague, Garry (CON - Chafford & North Stifford)
ghague@thurrock.gov.uk

Halden, James (CON - The Homesteads)
jhalden@thurrock.gov.uk

Hebb, Shane (CON - Stanford-le-Hope West)
shebb@thurrock.gov.uk

Hipsey, Terence (LAB - Stanford-le-Hope West)
thipsey@thurrock.gov.uk

Holloway, Victoria (LAB - West Thurrock & South Stifford)
vholloway@thurrock.gov.uk

Johnson, Barry (CON - Ockendon)
bjohnson@thurrock.gov.uk

Jones, Roy (UKIP - Stanford East & Corringham Town)
rojones@thurrock.gov.uk

Kelly, Tom (CON - Little Thurrock Rectory)
tkelly@thurrock.gov.uk

Kerin, Martin (LAB - Grays Riverside)
mkerin@thurrock.gov.uk

Key, Charlie (CON - South Chafford)
ckey@thurrock.gov.uk

Liddiard, Steve (LAB - Tilbury St Chads)
sliddiard@thurrock.gov.uk

Little, Susan (CON - Orsett)
slittle@thurrock.gov.uk

Little, Brian (CON - Orsett)
blittle@thurrock.gov.uk

MacPherson, Suzanne (CON - The Homesteads)
smacpherson@thurrock.gov.uk

Maney, Benjamin (CON - Little Thurrock Blackshots)
bmaney@thurrock.gov.uk

Ojetola, Tunde (CON - South Chafford)
tojetola@thurrock.gov.uk

Okunade, Bukky (LAB - Tilbury Riverside & Thurrock Park)
bokunade@thurrock.gov.uk

Palmer, Barry (IND - East Tillbury)
bpalmer@thurrock.gov.uk

Pothecary, Jane (LAB - Grays Riverside)
jpothecary@thurrock.gov.uk

Ray, Robert (UKIP - Aveley & Uplands)
rray@thurrock.gov.uk

Redsell, Joycelyn (CON - Little Thurrock Blackshots)
jredsell@thurrock.gov.uk

Rice, Gerard (LAB - Chadwell St Mary)
grice@thurrock.gov.uk

Roast, Andrew (CON - Corringham & Fobbing)
aroast@thurrock.gov.uk

Smith, Peter (UKIP - Aveley & Uplands)

Snell, Graham (UKIP - Stifford Clays)
gsnell@thurrock.gov.uk

Speight, Richard (LAB - Stanford East and Corringham Town)
rspeight@thurrock.gov.uk

Stewart, Deborah (CON - Corringham & Fobbing)
dstewart@thurrock.gov.uk

Stone, Michael (LAB - Grays Thurrock)
mstone@thurrock.gov.uk

Tolson, Pauline (CON - The Homesteads)
ptolson@thurrock.gov.uk

Wheeler, Kevin (UKIP - Ockendon)
kxwheeler@thurrock.gov.uk

Worrall, Lynn (LAB - Tidbury St Chads)
lworrall@thurrock.gov.uk

POLITICAL COMPOSITION

LAB: 18, CON: 17, UKIP: 11, IND: 2

COMMITTEE CHAIRS

Audit & Standards: Mr Tunde Ojetola

Children's Services: Mr James Halden

Health & Wellbeing: Mrs Barbara Rice

Licensing: Mr Michael Stone

Planning: Mr Terence Hipsey

Tonbridge & Malling D

Tonbridge & Malling Borough Council, Gibson Building, Gibson Drive, Kings Hill, West Malling ME19 4LZ
☎ 01732 844522 🖷 01732 842170 ✉ adminservices@tmbc.gov.uk
💻 www.tmbc.gov.uk

FACTS AND FIGURES

Parliamentary Constituencies: Tonbridge and Malling
EU Constituencies: South East
Election Frequency: Elections are of whole council

PRINCIPAL OFFICERS

Chief Executive: Miss Julie Beilby, Chief Executive, Gibson Building, Gibson Drive, Kings Hill, West Malling ME19 4LZ ☎ 01732 876003 🖷 01732 876231 ✉ chief.executive@tmbc.gov.uk

Architect, Building / Property Services: Mr John DeKnop, Buildings & Facilities Manager, Gibson Building, Gibson Drive, Kings Hill, West Malling ME19 4LZ ☎ 01732 876028 🖷 01732 842170 ✉ property.services@tmbc.gov.uk

Building Control: Mr Kevin Tomsett, Head of Parking & Surveying, Council Offices, Argyle Road, Sevenoaks TN13 1HG ☎ 01732 227000 ✉ kevin.tomsett@sevenoaks.gov.uk

Children / Youth Services: Mr Robert Styles, Director of Street Scene & Leisure, Gibson Building, Gibson Drive, Kings Hill, West Malling ME19 4LZ ☎ 01732 876160 ✉ robert.styles@tmbc.gov.uk

PR / Communications: Mrs Linda Moreau, Media & Communications Manager, Gibson Building, Gibson Drive, Kings Hill, West Malling ME19 4LZ ☎ 01732 876009 🖷 01732 876004 🖱 linda.moreau@tmbc.gov.uk

PR / Communications: Mrs Janet Saunders, Media & Communications Manager, Gibson Building, Gibson Drive, Kings Hill, West Malling ME19 4LZ ☎ 01732 876008 🖷 01732 876004 🖱 janet.saunders@tmbc.gov.uk

Community Planning: Mr Mark Raymond, Corporate Services Manager, Gibson Building, Gibson Drive, Kings Hill, West Malling ME19 4LZ ☎ 01732 876267 🖷 01732 876231 🖱 mark.raymond@tmbc.gov.uk

Community Safety: Mr Anthony Garnett, Licensing & Community Safety Manager, Gibson Building, Gibson Drive, Kings Hill, West Malling ME19 4LZ ☎ 01732 876346 🖷 01732 842170 🖱 anthony.garnett@tmbc.gov.uk

Computer Management: Mr Darren Everden, Information Technology Manager, Gibson Building, Gibson Drive, Kings Hill, West Malling ME19 4LZ ☎ 01732 876117 🖷 01732 876137 🖱 darren.everden@tmbc.gov.uk

Contracts: Mrs Lynn Francis, Principal Solicitor, Gibson Building, Gibson Drive, Kings Hill, West Malling ME19 4LZ ☎ 01732 876030 🖷 01732 842170 🖱 lynn.francis@tmbc.gov.uk

Corporate Services: Mr Mark Raymond, Corporate Services Manager, Gibson Building, Gibson Drive, Kings Hill, West Malling ME19 4LZ ☎ 01732 876267 🖷 01732 876231 🖱 mark.raymond@tmbc.gov.uk

Customer Service: Mr Charlie Steel, Personnel & Customer Services Manager, Gibson Building, Gibson Drive, Kings Hill, West Malling ME19 4LZ ☎ 01732 876015 🖱 charlie.steel@tmbc.gov.uk

Economic Development: Mr Mark Raymond, Corporate Services Manager, Gibson Building, Gibson Drive, Kings Hill, West Malling ME19 4LZ ☎ 01732 876267 🖷 01732 876231 🖱 mark.raymond@tmbc.gov.uk

E-Government: Mr Darren Everden, Information Technology Manager, Gibson Building, Gibson Drive, Kings Hill, West Malling ME19 4LZ ☎ 01732 876117 🖷 01732 876137 🖱 darren.everden@tmbc.gov.uk

Electoral Registration: Mr Richard Beesley, Elections & Special Projects Manager, Gibson Building, Gibson Drive, Kings Hill, West Malling ME19 4LZ ☎ 01732 876229 🖷 01732 842170 🖱 richard.beesley@tmbc.gov.uk

Energy Management: Mr John DeKnop, Buildings & Facilities Manager, Gibson Building, Gibson Drive, Kings Hill, West Malling ME19 4LZ ☎ 01732 876028 🖷 01732 842170 🖱 property.services@tmbc.gov.uk

Environmental Health: Mrs Jane Heeley, Chief Environmental Health Officer, Gibson Building, Gibson Drive, Kings Hill, West Malling ME19 4LZ ☎ 01732 876189 🖷 01732 841421 🖱 jane.heeley@tmbc.gov.uk

Estates, Property & Valuation: Mrs Katie Exon, Estates Manager, Gibson Building, Gibson Drive, Kings Hill, West Malling ME19 4LZ ☎ 01732 876364 🖷 01732 842170 🖱 property.services@tmbc.gov.uk

Events Manager: Ms Lyndsey Bennett, Senior Leisure Services Officer, Gibson Building, Gibson Drive, Kings Hill, West Malling ME19 4LZ ☎ 01732 876333 🖱 lyndsey.bennett@tmbc.gov.uk

Events Manager: Mr Darren Lanes, Head of Leisure Services, Gibson Building, Gibson Drive, Kings Hill, West Malling ME19 4LZ ☎ 01732 876171 🖱 darren.lanes@tmbc.gov.uk

Facilities: Mr John DeKnop, Buildings & Facilities Manager, Gibson Building, Gibson Drive, Kings Hill, West Malling ME19 4LZ ☎ 01732 876028 🖷 01732 842170 🖱 property.services@tmbc.gov.uk

Finance: Mrs Sharon Shelton, Director of Finance & Transformation, Gibson Building, Gibson Drive, Kings Hill, West Malling ME19 4LZ ☎ 01732 876092 🖷 01732 873530 🖱 sharon.shelton@tmbc.gov.uk

Grounds Maintenance: Mr John Dicker, Senior Parks Officer, Gibson Building, Gibson Drive, Kings Hill, West Malling ME19 4LZ ☎ 01732 876162 🖷 01732 842170 🖱 john.dicker@tmbc.gov.uk

Health and Safety: Mrs Jane Heeley, Chief Environmental Health Officer, Gibson Building, Gibson Drive, Kings Hill, West Malling ME19 4LZ ☎ 01732 876189 🖷 01732 841421 🖱 jane.heeley@tmbc.gov.uk

Home Energy Conservation: Mrs Hazel Skinner, Environmental Health Officer, Gibson Building, Gibson Drive, Kings Hill, West Malling ME19 4LZ ☎ 01732 876199 🖷 01732 841421 🖱 hazel.skinner@tmbc.gov.uk

Housing: Mr Steve Humphrey, Director of Planning, Housing & Environmental Health, Gibson Building, Gibson Drive, Kings Hill, West Malling ME19 4LZ ☎ 01732 876256 🖷 01732 846312 🖱 steve.humphrey@tmbc.gov.uk

Legal: Mr John Scarborough, Head of Legal Department, Swale House, East Street, Sittingbourne ME10 3HT ☎ 01975 417527 🖱 johnscarborough@swale.gov.uk

Legal: Mr Adrian Stanfield, Director of Central Services & Monitoring Officer, Gibson Building, Gibson Drive, Kings Hill, West Malling ME19 4LZ ☎ 01732 876346 🖷 01732 842170 🖱 legal.services@tmbc.gov.uk

Leisure and Cultural Services: Mr Robert Styles, Director of Street Scene & Leisure, Gibson Building, Gibson Drive, Kings Hill, West Malling ME19 4LZ ☎ 01732 876160 🖱 robert.styles@tmbc.gov.uk

Licensing: Mr Anthony Garnett, Licensing & Community Safety Manager, Gibson Building, Gibson Drive, Kings Hill, West Malling ME19 4LZ ☎ 01732 876346 🖷 01732 842170 🖱 anthony.garnett@tmbc.gov.uk

Lottery Funding, Charity and Voluntary: Mr Mark Raymond, Corporate Services Manager, Gibson Building, Gibson Drive, Kings Hill, West Malling ME19 4LZ ☎ 01732 876267 🖷 01732 876231 🖱 mark.raymond@tmbc.gov.uk

TONBRIDGE & MALLING

Member Services: Miss Claire Fox, Principal Administrator, Gibson Building, Gibson Drive, Kings Hill, West Malling ME19 4LZ ☎ 01732 876045 🖷 01732 842170 ✉ committee.services@tmbc.gov.uk

Parking: Mr Steve Humphrey, Director of Planning, Housing & Environmental Health, Gibson Building, Gibson Drive, Kings Hill, West Malling ME19 4LZ ☎ 01732 876256 🖷 01732 846312 ✉ steve.humphrey@tmbc.gov.uk

Partnerships: Mr Mark Raymond, Corporate Services Manager, Gibson Building, Gibson Drive, Kings Hill, West Malling ME19 4LZ ☎ 01732 876267 🖷 01732 876231 ✉ mark.raymond@tmbc.gov.uk

Personnel / HR: Ms Delia Gordon, Personnel & Development Manager, Gibson Building, Gibson Drive, Kings Hill, West Malling ME19 4LZ ☎ 01732 876019 ✉ delia.gordon@tmbc.gov.uk

Personnel / HR: Mr Charlie Steel, Personnel & Customer Services Manager, Gibson Building, Gibson Drive, Kings Hill, West Malling ME19 4LZ ☎ 01732 876015 ✉ personnel.services@tmbc.gov.uk

Planning: Mr Steve Humphrey, Director of Planning, Housing & Environmental Health, Gibson Building, Gibson Drive, Kings Hill, West Malling ME19 4LZ ☎ 01732 876256 🖷 01732 846312 ✉ steve.humphrey@tmbc.gov.uk

Procurement: Mr Neil Lawley, Chief Financial Services Officer, Gibson Building, Gibson Drive, Kings Hill, West Malling ME19 4LZ ☎ 01732 876095 🖷 01732 842170 ✉ neil.lawley@tmbc.gov.uk

Recycling & Waste Minimisation: Mr Dennis Gardner, Head of Waste & Street Scene, Gibson Building, Gibson Drive, Kings Hill, West Malling ME19 4LZ ☎ 01732 876204 🖷 01732 841421 ✉ dennis.gardner@tmbc.gov.uk

Staff Training: Ms Delia Gordon, Personnel & Development Manager, Gibson Building, Gibson Drive, Kings Hill, West Malling ME19 4LZ ☎ 01732 876019 ✉ delia.gordon@tmbc.gov.uk

Street Scene: Mr Dennis Gardner, Head of Waste & Street Scene, Gibson Building, Gibson Drive, Kings Hill, West Malling ME19 4LZ ☎ 01732 876204 🖷 01732 841421 ✉ dennis.gardner@tmbc.gov.uk

Sustainable Communities: Mr Mark Raymond, Corporate Services Manager, Gibson Building, Gibson Drive, Kings Hill, West Malling ME19 4LZ ☎ 01732 876267 🖷 01732 876231 ✉ mark.raymond@tmbc.gov.uk

Waste Collection and Disposal: Mr Dennis Gardner, Head of Waste & Street Scene, Gibson Building, Gibson Drive, Kings Hill, West Malling ME19 4LZ ☎ 01732 876204 🖷 01732 841421 ✉ dennis.gardner@tmbc.gov.uk

Waste Management: Mr Dennis Gardner, Head of Waste & Street Scene, Gibson Building, Gibson Drive, Kings Hill, West Malling ME19 4LZ ☎ 01732 876204 🖷 01732 841421 ✉ dennis.gardner@tmbc.gov.uk

COUNCILLORS

***Leader of the Council* Heslop**, Nicolas (CON - Cage Green, Tonbridge)
nicolas.heslop@tmbc.gov.uk

***Deputy Leader of the Council* Coffin**, Martin (CON - Wrotham)
martin.coffin@tmbc.gov.uk

Allison, Andy (CON - Higham)
andy.allison@tmbc.gov.uk

Anderson, Jill (CON - Hadlow, Mereworth and West Peckham)
jill.anderson@tmbc.gov.uk

Atkins, Julian (LAB - Snodland East)
julian.atkins@tmbc.gov.uk

Atkinson, Jean (CON - Trench)
jean.atkinson@tmbc.gov.uk

Balcombe, John (CON - Aylesford)
john.balcombe@tmbc.gov.uk

Baldock, Owen (CON - Castle, Tonbridge)
owen.baldock@tmbc.gov.uk

Balfour, Matthew (CON - Downs)
matthew.balfour@tmbc.gov.uk

Bates, Pam (CON - Trench)
pam.bates@tmbc.gov.uk

Bellamy, Jeannett (CON - Ditton)
jeannett.bellamy@tmbc.gov.uk

Bishop, Timothy (LD - Larkfield South)
timothy.bishop@tmbc.gov.uk

Bolt, Peter (CON - Judd)
peter.bolt@tmbc.gov.uk

Branson, Vivian (CON - Castle, Tonbridge)
vivian.branson@tmbc.gov.uk

Brown, Barbara Ann (CON - Snodland West)
barbara.brown@tmbc.gov.uk

Brown, Christopher (CON - Kings Hill)
christopher.brown@tmbc.gov.uk

Chartres, Rodney (CON - Ightham)
rodney.chartres@tmbc.gov.uk

Cure, David (CON - Judd)
david.cure@tmbc.gov.uk

Dalton, Roger (CON - Burham, Eccles and Wouldham)
roger.dalton@tmbc.gov.uk

Davis, David (CON - Burham, Eccles and Wouldham)
dave.davis@tmbc.gov.uk

Davis, Mark Osmond (CON - Cage Green, Tonbridge)
mark.davis@tmbc.gov.uk

Edmondston-Low, Tom (CON - Higham)
tom.edmondston-low@tmbc.gov.uk

Elks, Jessica (CON - Medway)
jessica.elks@tmbc.gov.uk

Gale, Carol (CON - Ditton)
carol.gale@tmbc.gov.uk

Heslop, Maria (CON - Vauxhall)
maria.heslop@tmbc.gov.uk

Holland, Elizabeth (CON - East Peckham and Golden Green)
elizabeth.holland@tmbc.gov.uk

Homewood, Peter (CON - Blue Bell Hill and Walderslade)
peter.homewood@tmbc.gov.uk

Jessel, Simon (CON - Wateringbury)
simon.jessel@tmbc.gov.uk

Keeley, David (CON - Snodland West)
david.keeley@tmbc.gov.uk

Kemp, Ann (CON - Downs)
ann.kemp@tmbc.gov.uk

King, Steven (CON - Snodland East)
steven.king@tmbc.gov.uk

Lancaster, Russell (CON - Medway)
russell.lancaster@tmbc.gov.uk

Luck, Sasha (CON - West Malling and Leybourne)
sasha.luck@tmbc.gov.uk

Luker, Brian (CON - West Malling and Leybourne)
brian.luker@tmbc.gov.uk

Moloney, Anne (CON - Snodland West)
anne.moloney@tmbc.gov.uk

Murray, Sue (CON - Borough Green and Long Mill)
sue.murray@tmbc.gov.uk

Oakley, Anita (LD - Larkfield South)
anita.oakley@tmbc.gov.uk

Parry-Waller, Mike (CON - Larkfield North)
mike.parry-waller@tmbc.gov.uk

Rhodes, Mark (CON - Hildenborough)
mark.rhodes@tmbc.gov.uk

Robins, Trevor (CON - Kings Hill)
trevor.robins@tmbc.gov.uk

Rogers, Howard (CON - East Peckham and Golden Green)
howard.rogers@tmbc.gov.uk

Sayer, Anthony (CON - Borough Green and Long Mill)
tony.sayer@tmbc.gov.uk

Sergison, Janet (CON - Hadlow, Mereworth and West Peckham)
janet.sergison@tmbc.gov.uk

Shrubsole, Sophie (CON - West Malling and Leybourne)
sophie.shrubsole@tmbc.gov.uk

Simpson, Elizabeth (LD - East Malling)
liz.simpson@tmbc.gov.uk

Smith, David (CON - Aylesford)
david.smith@tmbc.gov.uk

Smith, Christopher (CON - Hildenborough)
christopher.smith@tmbc.gov.uk

Spence, Sarah (CON - Vauxhall)
sarah.spence@tmbc.gov.uk

Sullivan, Allan (CON - Blue Bell Hill and Walderslade)
allan.sullivan@tmbc.gov.uk

Taylor, Russ (CON - Larkfield North)
russ.taylor@tmbc.gov.uk

Taylor, Mike (IND - Borough Green and Long Mill)
mike.taylor@tmbc.gov.uk

Trice, David (CON - Higham)
david.trice@tmbc.gov.uk

Woodger, Christine (LD - East Malling)
christine.woodger@tmbc.gov.uk

POLITICAL COMPOSITION

CON: 47, LD: 4, IND: 1, LAB: 1

Torbay U

Torbay Council, Town Hall, Castle Circus, Torquay TQ1 3DR
☎ 01803 201201 🖷 01803 292866 🖰 fss@torbay.gov.uk
💻 www.torbay.gov.uk

FACTS AND FIGURES

Parliamentary Constituencies: Torbay
EU Constituencies: South West
Election Frequency: Elections are of whole council

PRINCIPAL OFFICERS

Chief Executive: Mr Steve Parrock, Executive Director, Tor Hill House, Union Street, Torquay TQ2 5QW ☎ 01803 208973 🖰 steve.parrock@torbay.gov.uk

Senior Management: Dr Caroline Dimond, Director - Public Health, Town Hall, Castle Circus, Torquay TQ1 3DR 🖰 caroline.dimond@torbay.gov.uk

Senior Management: Ms Caroline Taylor, Director - Adult Services, Town Hall, Castle Circus, Torquay TQ1 3DR ☎ 01803 207116 🖰 caroline.taylor@torbay.gov.uk

Senior Management: Mr Charles Uzzell, Director - Place, Town Hall, Castle Circus, Torquay TQ1 3DR ☎ 01803 207701 🖰 charles.uzzell@torbay.gov.uk

Senior Management: Mr Richard Williams, Director - Children's Services, Tor Hill House, Union Street, Torquay TQ2 5QW ☎ 01803 208401 🖰 richard.williams@torbay.gov.uk

Architect, Building / Property Services: Mr Robert Mason, Property Records & Estates Assistant, Tor Hill House, Union Street, Torquay TQ2 5QW ☎ 01803 207925 🖰 robert.mason@torbay.gov.uk

Building Control: Mr Colin Edgecombe, Senior Service Manager, Town Hall, Castle Circus, Torquay TQ1 3DR ☎ 01803 208085 🖰 colin.edgecombe@torbay.gov.uk

Children / Youth Services: Mr Richard Williams, Director - Children's Services, Tor Hill House, Union Street, Torquay TQ2 5QW ☎ 01803 208401 🖰 richard.williams@torbay.gov.uk

Civil Registration: Mr Stephen Lemming, Superintendent Registrar, Oldway Mansion, Paignton, Torquay TQ3 2TE ☎ 01803 207130 🖰 stephen.lemming@torbay.gov.uk

PR / Communications: Mrs Michelle Pierce, Interim Head of Communications, Tor Hill House, Union Street, Torquay TQ2 5QW ☎ 01803 208832 🖰 michelle.pierce@torbay.gov.uk

Community Safety: Ms Frances Hughes, Executive Head of Community Safety, Roebuck House, Abbey Road, Torquay TQ2 5TF ☎ 01803 208002 🖰 frances.hughes@torbay.gov.uk

Computer Management: Mr Bob Clark, Executive Head of Information Services, Town Hall, Castle Circus, Torquay TQ1 3DR ☎ 01803 207420 🖰 bob.clark@torbay.gov.uk

TORBAY

Consumer Protection and Trading Standards: Ms Frances Hughes, Executive Head of Community Safety, Roebuck House, Abbey Road, Torquay TQ2 5TF ☎ 01803 208002 ✉ frances.hughes@torbay.gov.uk

Contracts: Ms Tracey Field, Senior Procurement Officer, Town Hall, Castle Circus, Torquay TQ1 3DR ☎ 01803 208391 ✉ tracey.field@torbay.gov.uk

Customer Service: Ms Alison Whittaker, Customer First Service Manager, Town Hall, Castle Circus, Torquay TQ1 3DR ☎ 01803 207221 ✉ alison.whittaker@torbay.gov.uk

Economic Development: Mr Steve Parrock, Executive Director, Tor Hill House, Union Street, Torquay TQ2 5QW ☎ 01803 208973 ✉ steve.parrock@torbay.gov.uk

Electoral Registration: Ms Cathrine Haydn, Electoral Services Manager, Town Hall, Castle Circus, Torquay TQ1 3DR ☎ 01803 207076 ✉ catherine.haydn@torbay.gov.uk

Emergency Planning: Mr Chris Packer, Emergency Planning Officer, Town Hall, Castle Circus, Torquay TQ1 3DR ☎ 01803 207045 ✉ chris.packer@torbay.gov.uk

Environmental / Technical Services: Mr Charles Uzzell, Director - Place, Town Hall, Castle Circus, Torquay TQ1 3DR ☎ 01803 207701 ✉ charles.uzzell@torbay.gov.uk

Environmental Health: Ms Frances Hughes, Executive Head of Community Safety, Town Hall, Castle Circus, Torquay TQ1 3DR ☎ 01803 208002 ✉ frances.hughes@torbay.gov.uk

Estates, Property & Valuation: Mr Chris Bouchard, Principal Valuer, Tor Hill House, Union Street, Torquay TQ2 5QW ☎ 01803 207920 ✉ chris.bouchard@torbay.gov.uk

European Liaison: Mr Alan Denby, Director - Economic Strategy, Tor Hill House, Torquay TQ2 5QW ☎ 01803 208671 ✉ alan.denby@torbay.gov.uk

Events Manager: Mr Conway Hoare, Senior Events Officer, Town Hall, Castle Circus, Torquay TQ1 3DR ☎ 01803 208862 ✉ conway.hoare@torbay.gov.uk

Facilities: Mr Stuart Left, Facilities Management Officer, Tor Hill House, Union Street, Torquay TQ2 5QW ☎ 01803 208979 ✉ stuart.left@torbay.gov.uk

Grounds Maintenance: Mr Richard Taylor, Leisure & Community Development Officer, Town Hall, Castle Circus, Torquay TQ1 3DR ☎ 01803 207969 ✉ richard.taylor@torbay.gov.uk

Health and Safety: Mr Colin de Jongh, Health & Safety Manager, Town Hall, Castle Circus, Torquay TQ1 3DR ☎ 01803 207161 ✉ colin.dejongh@torbay.gov.uk

Highways: Mr Patrick Carney, Service Manager - Highways, Town Hall, Castle Circus, Torquay TQ1 3DR ☎ 01803 207710 ✉ patrick.carney@torbay.gov.uk

Home Energy Conservation: Mr John Pullen, Environmental Health Officer, Town Hall, Castle Circus, Torquay TQ1 3DR ☎ 01803 208069 ✉ john.pullen@torbay.gov.uk

Housing: Ms Julie Sharland, Strategic Housing Manager, Town Hall, Castle Circus, Torquay TQ1 3DR ☎ 01803 208065 ✉ julie.sharland@torbay.gov.uk

Legal: Ms Anne-Marie Bond, Executive Head of Commercial Services, Town Hall, Castle Circus, Torquay TQ1 3DR ☎ 01803 207160 ✉ anne-marie.bond@torbay.gov.uk

Leisure and Cultural Services: Ms Sue Cheriton, Executive Head of Residents & Visitor Services, Town Hall, Castle Circus, Torquay TQ1 3DR ☎ 01803 207972 ✉ sue.cheriton@torbay.gov.uk

Licensing: Mr Steve Cox, Principal Safety & Licensing Officer, Town Hall, Castle Circus, Torquay TQ1 3DR ☎ 01803 208034 ✉ steve.cox@torbay.gov.uk

Lighting: Mr Dave Simmons, Street Lighting Engineer, Town Hall, Castle Circus, Torquay TQ1 3DR ☎ 01803 207718 ✉ dave.simmons@torbay.gov.uk

Member Services: Mrs June Gurry, Democratic Services Manager, Town Hall, Castle Circus, Torquay TQ1 3DR ☎ 01803 207012 ✉ june.gurry@torbay.gov.uk

Parking: Mr Steve Hurley, Service Manager for Town Services, Town Hall, Castle Circus, Torquay TQ1 3DR ☎ 01803 207680 ✉ steve.hurley@torbay.gov.uk

Personnel / HR: Ms Susan Wiltshire, HR Manager, Town Hall, Castle Circus, Torquay TQ1 3DR ☎ 01803 207361 ✉ susan.wilson@torbay.gov.uk

Planning: Mr Pat Steward, Senior Service Manager, Town Hall, Castle Circus, Torquay TQ1 3DR ☎ 01803 208811 ✉ pat.steward@torbay.gov.uk

Procurement: Ms Tracey Field, Senior Procurement Officer, Town Hall, Castle Circus, Torquay TQ1 3DR ☎ 01803 208391 ✉ tracey.field@torbay.gov.uk

Recycling & Waste Minimisation: Ms Carol Arthur, Recycling Officer, Town Hall, Castle Circus, Torquay TQ1 3DR ☎ 01803 207744 ✉ carol.arthur@torbay.gov.uk

Regeneration: Mr Alan Denby, Director - Economic Strategy, Tor Hill House, Torquay TQ2 5QW ☎ 01803 208671 ✉ alan.denby@torbay.gov.uk

Road Safety: Ms Bev Hannah, Road Safety Officer, Town Hall, Castle Circus, Torquay TQ1 3DR ☎ 01803 207677 ✉ beverley.hannah@torbay.gov.uk

Public Health: Dr Caroline Dimond, Director - Public Health, Town Hall, Castle Circus, Torquay TQ1 3DR ✉ caroline.dimond@torbay.gov.uk

Street Scene: Mr Steve Hurley, Service Manager for Town Services, Pearl Assurance House, Union Street, Torquay TQ1 3DW ☎ 01803 207680 ✉ steve.hurley@torbay.gov.uk

Sustainable Communities: Ms Frances Hughes, Executive Head of Community Safety, Town Hall, Castle Circus, Torquay TQ1 3DR ☎ 01803 208002 ✉ frances.hughes@torbay.gov.uk

Tourism: Ms Carolyn Custerton, Chief Executive Officer, 5 Vaughan Parade, Torquay TQ2 5JG ☎ 01803 296296 ✉ carolyn.custer@englishriviera.co.uk

Traffic Management: Mr Patrick Carney, Service Manager - Highways, Town Hall, Castle Circus, Torquay TQ1 3DR ☎ 01803 207710 ✉ patrick.carney@torbay.gov.uk

Transport: Ms Sue Cheriton, Executive Head of Residents & Visitor Services, Town Hall, Castle Circus, Torquay TQ1 3DR ☎ 01803 207972 ✉ sue.cheriton@torbay.gov.uk

Transport Planner: Mr Adam Luscombe, Transport Planning Officer, Town Hall, Castle Circus, Torquay TQ1 3DR ☎ 01803 207693 ✉ adam.luscombe@torbay.gov.uk

Waste Collection and Disposal: Mr Ian Hartley, Waste Client Manager, Town Hall, Castle Circus, Torquay TQ1 3DR ☎ 01803 208695 ✉ ian.hartley@torbay.gov.uk

Waste Management: Mr Ian Hartley, Waste Client Manager, Town Hall, Castle Circus, Torquay TQ1 3DR ☎ 01803 208695 ✉ ian.hartley@torbay.gov.uk

COUNCILLORS

***Chair* Hill**, Ray (CON - St Marychurch)
ray.hill@torbay.gov.uk

***Vice-Chair* Brooks**, Anne (CON - St Marychurch)
anne.brooks@torbay.gov.uk

***Mayor* Oliver**, Gordon (CON - No Ward)
mayor@torbay.gov.uk

***Deputy Mayor* Mills**, Derek (CON - Churston with Galmpton)
derek.mills@torbay.gov.uk

***Group Leader* Morey**, Mike (INDNA - Berry Head with Furzeham)
mike.morey@torbay.gov.uk

***Group Leader* Thomas**, David (CON - Blatchcombe)
david.thomas@torbay.gov.uk

Amil, Nicole (CON - Cockington with Chelston)
nicole.amil@torbay.gov.uk

Barnby, Jane (CON - Goodrington with Roselands)
jane.barnby@torbay.gov.uk

Bent, Neil (CON - St Marychurch)
neil.bent@torbay.gov.uk

Bye, Nick (CON - Wellswood)
nick.bye@torbay.gov.uk

Carter, Christine (LD - Roundham with Hyde)
christine.carter@torbay.gov.uk

Cunningham, Barbara (CON - Roundham with Hyde)
barbara.cunningham@torbay.gov.uk

Darling, Mandy (LD - Tormohun)
mandy.darling@torbay.gov.uk

Darling, Steve (LD - Watcombe)
steve.darling@torbay.gov.uk

Doggett, Ian (LD - Clifton with Maidenway)
ian.doggett@torbay.gov.uk

Ellery, Vic (INDNA - Berry Head with Furzeham)
vic.ellery@torbay.gov.uk

Excell, Robert (CON - Tormohun)
Robert.Excell@torbay.gov.uk

Haddock, Richard (CON - St Marys with Summercombe)
richard.haddock@torbay.gov.uk

King, Mark (CON - Cockington with Chelston)
mark.king@torbay.gov.uk

Kingscote, Mark (CON - Shiphay with the Willows)
mark.kingscote@torbay.gov.uk

Lang, Andy (CON - Tormohun)
andy.lang@torbay.gov.uk

Lewis, Chris (CON - Preston)
chris.lewis@torbay.gov.uk

Manning, Terry (CON - St Marys with Summercombe)
terry.manning@torbay.gov.uk

Morris, Dave (CON - Shiphay with the Willows)
dave.morris@torbay.gov.uk

O'Dwyer, James (CON - Wellswood)
james.o'dwyer@torbay.gov.uk

Parrott, Julien (UKIP - Ellacombe)
julien.parrott@torbay.gov.uk

Pentney, Ruth (LD - Clifton with Maidenway)
ruth.pentney@torbay.gov.uk

Robson, Chris (CON - Blatchcombe)
chris.robson@torbay.gov.uk

Stockman, Jackie (INDNA - Berry Head with Furzeham)
jackie.stockman@torbay.gov.uk

Stocks, Cindy (LD - Ellacombe)
cindy.stocks@torbay.gov.uk

Stringer, Roger (LD - Watcombe)
roger.stringer@torbay.gov.uk

Stubley, Di (CON - Churston with Galmpton)
di.stubley@torbay.gov.uk

Sykes, Lynn (CON - Preston)
lynn.sykes@torbay.gov.uk

Thomas, John (CON - Blatchcombe)
john.thomas@torbay.gov.uk

Tolchard, Anna (CON - Preston)
anna.tolchard@torbay.gov.uk

Tyerman, Alan (CON - Goodrington with Roselands)
alan.tyerman@torbay.gov.uk

Winfield, Thomas (CON - Cockington with Chelston)
thomas.winfield@torbay.gov.uk

POLITICAL COMPOSITION

CON: 26, LD: 7, INDNA: 3, UKIP: 1

TORBAY

COMMITTEE CHAIRS

Audit: Mr Alan Tyerman

Development: Mr Mark Kingscote

Licensing: Mr Terry Manning

Torfaen W

Torfaen County Borough Council, Civic Centre, Pontypool NP4 6YB
☎ 01495 762200 🖷 01495 755513 🖳 www.torfaen.gov.uk

FACTS AND FIGURES

Parliamentary Constituencies: Torfaen
EU Constituencies: Wales
Election Frequency: Elections are of whole council

PRINCIPAL OFFICERS

Chief Executive: Ms Alison Ward, Chief Executive, Civic Centre, Pontypool NP4 6YB ☎ 01495 742603 🖷 01495 750797 ✉ alison.ward@torfaen.gov.uk

Assistant Chief Executive: Mr Nigel Aurelius, Assistant Chief Executive, Civic Centre, Pontypool NP4 6YB ☎ 01495 742623 ✉ nigel.aurelius@torfaen.gov.uk

Senior Management: Mr Dave Congreve, Strategic Director - Health & Wellbeing, Civic Centre, Pontypool NP4 6YB ☎ 01495 742606 ✉ david.congreve@torfaen.gov.uk

Access Officer / Social Services (Disability): Ms Sue Evans, Chief Officer of Social Care & Housing, Police HQ, Croesyceiliog, Cwmbran NP44 2XJ ☎ 01633 648617 ✉ sue.evans@torfaen.gov.uk

Architect, Building / Property Services: Ms Dana Eynon, Head of Property, Waste & Streetscene, Ty Blaen, New Inn, Pontypool NP4 0LS ☎ 01495 766820 🖷 01495 766762 ✉ dana.eynon@torfaen.gov.uk

Best Value: Mrs Lynne Williams, Head of Improvement & Scrutiny, Civic Centre, Pontypool NP4 6YB ☎ 01495 742158 🖷 01495 766059 ✉ lynne.williams@torfaen.gov.uk

Building Control: Mr Dean Harris, Premises Manager, Civic Centre, Pontypool NP4 6YB ☎ 01495 764219 ✉ dean.harris@torfaen.gov.uk

Catering Services: Ms Toni Edwards, Catering & Cleaning Manager, Croesyceiliog CEC, The Highway, Croesyceiliog, Cwmbran NP44 2HF ☎ 01633 647712 ✉ toni.edwards@torfaen.gov.uk

Children / Youth Services: Mr Keith Rutherford, Head of Children's Services, Civic Centre, Pontypool NP4 6YB ☎ 01633 648622 ✉ keith.rutherford@torfaen.gov.uk

Civil Registration: Ms Lisa Dando-Ellis, Head of Customer Care Services & Registration, Civic Centre, Pontypool NP4 6YB ☎ 01495 742135 ✉ lisa.dando-ellis@torfaen.gov.uk

PR / Communications: Mr Neil Jones, Head of Communications, Civic Centre, Pontypool NP4 6YB ☎ 01495 742151 🖷 01495 766059 ✉ neil.jones@torfaen.gov.uk

Community Planning: Mr Mark Sharwood, Public Services Development Manager, Civic Centre, Pontypool NP4 6YB ☎ 01495 742157 ✉ mark.sharwood@torfaen.gov.uk

Community Safety: Ms Karen Kerslake, Information & Communications Team Manager, Civic Centre, Pontypool NP4 6YB ☎ 01633 628971 ✉ karen.kerslake@torfaen.gov.uk

Computer Management: Mr Stephen Jeynes, Service & Technical Manager, SRS, Gilchrist Thomas Industrial Estate, Blaenavon NP4 9RL ☎ 01495 762200 ✉ stephen.jeynes@torfaen.gov.uk

Corporate Services: Mr Richard Edmunds, Head of Strategic Services, Civic Centre, Pontypool NP4 6YB ☎ 01495 742163 🖷 01495 766079 ✉ richard.edmunds@torfaen.gov.uk

Customer Service: Ms Lisa Dando-Ellis, Head of Customer Care Services & Registration, Civic Centre, Pontypool NP4 6YB ☎ 01495 742135 ✉ lisa.dando-ellis@torfaen.gov.uk

Customer Service: Ms Linda King, Customer Services Manager, Civic Centre, Pontypool NP4 6YB ☎ 01495 766363 ✉ linda.king@torfaen.gov.uk

Education: Mr Dermot McChrystal, Interim Head of Education Services, Pearl House, Hanbury Road, Pontypool NP4 6JL ☎ 01495 762200 ✉ dermot.mcchrystal@torfaen.gov.uk

E-Government: Mr Matt Lewis, Chief Operating Officer, SRS, Gilchrist Thomas Industrial Estate, Blaenavon NP4 9RL ☎ 01495 762200 ✉ matt.lewis@torfaen.gov.uk

Electoral Registration: Ms Lyn Pask, Senior Democratic Services Officer (Elections), Civic Centre, Pontypool NP4 6YB ☎ 01495 766077 🖷 01495 766059 ✉ lyn.pask@torfaen.gov.uk

Emergency Planning: Mr Bob Crimp, Head of Emergency Management, Civic Centre, Pontypool NP4 6YB ☎ 01495 766071 🖷 01495 766071 ✉ bob.crimp@torfaen.gov.uk

Energy Management: Mr Allan Jones, Energy Manager, Ty Blaen, New Inn, Pontypool NP4 0LS ☎ 01495 742898 ✉ allan.jones@torfaen.gov.uk

Environmental Health: Ms Kim Pugh, Head of Public Protection, Pearl House, Hanbury Road, Pontypool NP4 6JL ☎ 01495 747627 ✉ kim.pugh@torfaen.gov.uk

Estates, Property & Valuation: Mr Robert Flower, Team Leader of Valuation Services, Civic Centre, Pontypool NP4 6YB ☎ 01495 742897 ✉ robert.flower@torfaen.gov.uk

European Liaison: Mr Rob Wellington, Head of European Policy & External Funding, Civic Centre, Pontypool NP4 6YB ☎ 01495 742143 ✉ rob.wellington@tofaen.gov.uk

Events Manager: Ms Verity Hiscocks, Arts Development Manager, Ty Blaen, New Inn, Pontypool NP4 0LS ☎ 01633 648968 ✉ verity.hiscocks@torfaen.gov.uk

Finance: Mr David Lilly, Head of Financial Services, Civic Centre, Pontypool NP4 6YB ☎ 01495 742624 ✉ david.lilly@torfaen.gov.uk

Pensions: Ms Mary Rollin, Pensions Manager, Civic Centre, Pontypool NP4 6YB ☎ 01495 746280 ✉ mary.rollin@torfaen.gov.uk

Fleet Management: Mr Rico Cottrell, Transport & Depot Manager, Ty Blaen, New Inn, Pontypool NP4 0LS ☎ 01495 766798 🖷 01495 766801 ✉ rico.cottrell@torfaen.gov.uk

Grounds Maintenance: Mr Steve Horseman, Streetscene Co-ordinator, Ty Blaen, New Inn, Pontypool NP4 0LS ☎ 01495 762200 ✉ steve.horsham@torfaen.gov.uk

Health and Safety: Ms Claire Burt, Corporate Health & Safety Manager, Civic Centre, Pontypool NP4 6YB ☎ 01495 762569 ✉ claire.burt@torfaen.gov.uk

Highways: Mr Steve Jarrett, Head of Highways & Transportation, County Hall, Cwmbran NP44 2WN ☎ 01495 742426 ✉ steve.jarrett@torfaen.gov.uk

Home Energy Conservation: Mr Allan Jones, Energy Manager, County Hall, Cwmbran NP44 2WN ☎ 01495 742898 ✉ allan.jones@torfaen.gov.uk

Housing: Mr Neil Howell, Head of Housing & Business Support, Ty'r Efail, Lower Mill Field, Pontypool NP4 0RH ☎ 01495 762200 ✉ neil.howell@torfaen.gov.uk

Legal: Ms Lynda Willis, Chief Legal Officer & Monitoring Officer, Civic Centre, Pontypool NP4 6YB ☎ 01495 762660 ✉ lynda.willis@torfaen.gov.uk

Leisure and Cultural Services: Ms Sally Church, Shadow Leisure Trust Manager, Ty Blaen, New Inn, Pontypool NP4 0LS ☎ 01633 628980 ✉ sally.church@torfaen.gov.uk

Licensing: Mr Steve Bendell, Team Leader of Licensing, Ty Blaen, New Inn, Pontypool NP4 0LS ☎ 01495 747279 ✉ steve.bendell@torfaen.gov.uk

Lifelong Learning: Ms Ann Brain, Adult Education Officer, Croesyceiliog CEC, The Highway, Croesyceiliog, Cwmbran NP44 2HF ☎ 01633 648154 ✉ ann.brain@torfaen.gov.uk

Lighting: Mr Steve Jarrett, Head of Highways & Transportation, County Hall, Cwmbran NP44 2WN ☎ 01495 742426 ✉ steve.jarrett@torfaen.gov.uk

Lottery Funding, Charity and Voluntary: Mr Rob Wellington, Head of European Policy & External Funding, Civic Centre, Pontypool NP4 6YB ☎ 01495 742143 ✉ rob.wellington@tofaen.gov.uk

Member Services: Mr Richard Gwinnell, Lead Officer of Council & Member Support, Civic Centre, Pontypool NP4 6YB ☎ 01495 742163 🖷 01495 766079 ✉ richard.gwinnell@torfaen.gov.uk

Parking: Mr Steve Horseman, Streetscene Co-ordinator, Ty Blaen, New Inn, Pontypool NP4 0LS ☎ 01495 762200 ✉ steve.horsham@torfaen.gov.uk

Partnerships: Mr Lyndon Puddy, Head of Public Service Support Unit, Civic Centre, Pontypool NP4 6YB ✉ lyndon.puddy@torfaen.gov.uk

Personnel / HR: Mr Graeme Russell, Head of Human Resources & Pension, Civic Centre, Pontypool NP4 6YB ☎ 01495 742568 ✉ graeme.russell@torfaen.gov.uk

Planning: Mr Duncan Smith, Chief Planning & Public Protection Officer, Ty Blaen, New Inn, Pontypool NP4 0LS ☎ 01495 742568 ✉ duncan.smith@torfaen.gov.uk

Procurement: Mr Andrew Maisey, Head of Procurement, Civic Centre, Pontypool NP4 6YB ☎ 01495 742380 ✉ andrew.maisey@torfaen.gov.uk

Public Libraries: Ms Christine George, Torfaen Library & Information Manager, Ty Blaen, Torfaen, Panteg Way, New Inn, Pontypool NP4 0LS ☎ 01633 628943 ✉ christine.george@torfaen.gov.uk

Recycling & Waste Minimisation: Mr Cynon Edwards, Waste Management Group Leader, Ty Blaen, New Inn, Pontypool NP4 0LS ☎ 01495 766789 🖷 01495 766811 ✉ cynon.edwards@torfaen.gov.uk

Regeneration: Ms Cath Thomas, Head of Economy, Enterprise & Environment, Civic Centre, Pontypool NP4 6YB ☎ 01495 762200 ✉ cath.thomas@torfaen.gov.uk

Road Safety: Mr Pat Bates, Road Safety Strategy Officer, Ty Blaen, New Inn, Pontypool NP4 0LS ☎ 01633 648803 ✉ patrick.bates@torfaen.gov.uk

Social Services: Ms Sue Evans, Chief Officer of Social Care & Housing, Police HQ, Croesyceiliog, Cwmbran NP44 2XJ ☎ 01633 648617 ✉ sue.evans@torfaen.gov.uk

Social Services (Adult): Ms Sue Evans, Chief Officer of Social Care & Housing, Police HQ, Croesyceiliog, Cwmbran NP44 2XJ ☎ 01633 648617 ✉ sue.evans@torfaen.gov.uk

Social Services (Children): Ms Sue Evans, Chief Officer of Social Care & Housing, Police HQ, Croesyceiliog, Cwmbran NP44 2XJ ☎ 01633 648617 ✉ sue.evans@torfaen.gov.uk

Street Scene: Mr Steve Horseman, Streetscene Co-ordinator, Ty Blaen, New Inn, Pontypool NP4 0LS ☎ 01495 762200 ✉ steve.horsham@torfaen.gov.uk

Sustainable Communities: Ms Rachael O'Shaughnessy, Environmental & Sustainability Manager, Ty Blaen, New Inn, Pontypool NP4 0LS ☎ 01633 648018 ✉ rachael.o'shaughnessy@torfaen.gov.uk

Sustainable Development: Ms Rachael O'Shaughnessy, Environmental & Sustainability Manager, Ty Blaen, New Inn, Pontypool NP4 0LS ☎ 01633 648018 ✉ rachael.o'shaughnessy@torfaen.gov.uk

Tourism: Ms Katie Gates, Team Leader - Economy & Tourism, Ty Blaen, New Inn, Pontypool NP4 0LS ☎ 01633 648329 🖷 01633 648088 ✉ david.ludlow@torfaen.gov.uk

TORFAEN

Town Centre: Mr David Evans, Team Leader of Pontypool Regeneration, Pearl House, Hanbury Road, Pontypool NP4 6JL ☎ 01495 766299 ✉ david.evans@torfaen.gov.uk

Traffic Management: Mr Andrew Williams, Group Leader - Highways & Traffic, Ty Blaen, New Inn, Pontypool NP4 0LS ☎ 01495 742426 ✉ andrew.williams@torfaen.gov.uk

Transport: Mr Andrew Williams, Group Leader - Highways & Traffic, Ty Blaen, New Inn, Pontypool NP4 0LS ☎ 01495 742426 ✉ andrew.williams@torfaen.gov.uk

Transport Planner: Mr Andrew Williams, Group Leader - Highways & Traffic, Ty Blaen, New Inn, Pontypool NP4 0LS ☎ 01495 742426 ✉ andrew.williams@torfaen.gov.uk

Waste Collection and Disposal: Mr Cynon Edwards, Waste Management Group Leader, Ty Blaen, New Inn, Pontypool NP4 0LS ☎ 01495 766789 🖷 01495 766811 ✉ cynon.edwards@torfaen.gov.uk

Waste Management: Mr Cynon Edwards, Waste Management Group Leader, Ty Blaen, New Inn, Pontypool NP4 0LS ☎ 01495 766789 🖷 01495 766811 ✉ cynon.edwards@torfaen.gov.uk

Children's Play Areas: Mr Steve Horseman, Streetscene Co-ordinator, Ty Blaen, New Inn, Pontypool NP4 0LS ☎ 01495 762200 ✉ steve.horsham@torfaen.gov.uk

COUNCILLORS

***Mayor* Davies**, Giles (LAB - Abersychan)
Giles.Davies@torfaen.gov.uk

***Deputy Mayor* Crick**, Veronica (LAB - Croesyceiliog South)
Veronica.Crick@torfaen.gov.uk

***Leader of the Council* Wellington**, Robert (LAB - Greenmeadow)
Leader@torfaen.gov.uk

***Deputy Leader of the Council* Hunt**, Anthony (LAB - Panteg)
anthony.hunt@torfaen.gov.uk

Ashley, Stuart (LAB - Pontnewydd)
stuart.ashley@torfaen.gov.uk

Barnett, Mary (LAB - Upper Cwmbran)
mary.barnett@torfaen.gov.uk

Bevan, Huw (CON - Llanyravon South)
Huw.Bevan@torfaen.gov.uk

Brooks, Stephen (LAB - St Dials)
stephen.brooks@torfaen.gov.uk

Burnett, Ronald (IND - Two Locks and Henllys)
ronald.burnett@torfaen.gov.uk

Cameron, Pamela (LAB - Two Locks and Henllys)
pamela.cameron@torfaen.gov.uk

Caron, Glyn (LAB - Llanyravon North)
Glyn.Caron@torfaen.gov.uk

Clark, Richard (LAB - Croesyceiliog North)
richard.clark@torfaen.gov.uk

Clark, Gwyneira (LAB - Abersychan)
gwyneira.clark@torfaen.gov.uk

Constance, Leonard (LAB - Brynwern)
Leonard.Constance@torfaen.gov.uk

Cross, Fiona (PC - Coed Eva)
fiona.cross@torfaen.gov.uk

Cunningham, B John (LAB - Upper Cwmbran)
john.cunningham@torfaen.gov.uk

Daniels, David (LAB - Llantarnam)
David.Daniels@torfaen.gov.uk

Davies, Nigel (LAB - Croesyceiliog North)
nigel.davies@torfaen.gov.uk

Evans, Stuart (IND - Blaenavon)
Stuart.Evans@torfaen.gov.uk

Furzer, Alun (LAB - Blaenavon)
Alun.Furzer@torfaen.gov.uk

Graham, Maria (IND - Llantarnam)
Maria.Graham@torfaen.gov.uk

Harnett, Kelvin (IND - Pontnewynydd)
kelvin.harnett@torfaen.gov.uk

Harris, Michael (IND - Pontypool)
michael.harris@torfaen.gov.uk

Haynes, Elizabeth (IND - St Dials)
elizabeth.haynes@torfaen.gov.uk

James, Keith (CON - New Inn)
Keith.James@torfaen.gov.uk

Jeremiah, Mike (IND - Wainfelin)
Mike.Jeremiah@torfaen.gov.uk

Jones, Alan (LAB - Blaenavon)
Alan.S.Jones@torfaen.gov.uk

Jones, Lewis (LAB - Trevethin)
deputyleader@torfaen.gov.uk

Kemp, Robert (IND - Upper Cwmbran)
robert.kemp@torfaen.gov.uk

Marshall, John (LAB - Trevethin)
john.marshal@torfaen.gov.uk

Mason, Neil (LAB - St Cadocs & Penygarn)
neil.mason@torfaen.gov.uk

Mawby, Brian (LAB - Pontnewydd)
brian.mawby@torfaen.gov.uk

Mills, Raymond (CON - New Inn)
Raymond.Mills@torfaen.gov.uk

Owen, Amanda (LAB - Greenmeadow)
Amanda.Owen@torfaen.gov.uk

Parrish, Norma (LAB - Panteg)
norma.parrish@torfaen.gov.uk

Powell, Jessica (LAB - Pontnewydd)
jessica.powell@torfaen.gov.uk

Rees, Jeff (PC - Fairwater)
jeff.rees@torfaen.gov.uk

Seabourne, Philip (LAB - Fairwater)
Phil.Seabourne@torfaen.gov.uk

Smith, Graham (CON - New Inn)
Graham.Smith@torfaen.gov.uk

Taylor, Barry (LAB - Snatchwood)
barry.taylor@torfaen.gov.uk

Thomas, Colette (LAB - Two Locks and Henllys)
colette.thomas@torfaen.gov.uk

Tomlinson, Wayne (IND - Abersychan)
Wayne.tomlinson@torfaen.gov.uk

Waite, Neil (LAB - Cwmynyscoy)
neil.waite@torfaen.gov.uk

Yeowell, David (LAB - Panteg)
david.yeowell@torfaen.gov.uk

POLITICAL COMPOSITION
LAB: 29, IND: 9, CON: 4, PC: 2

COMMITTEE CHAIRS
Licensing: Mr Neil Waite

Pensions: Ms Mary Barnett

Planning: Mr Brian Mawby

Torridge D

Torridge District Council, Riverbank House, Bideford EX39 2QG
☎ 01237 428700 🖷 01237 479164 ✉ customer.services@torridge.gov.uk
💻 www.torridge.gov.uk

FACTS AND FIGURES
Parliamentary Constituencies: Devon West and Torridge
EU Constituencies: South West
Election Frequency: Elections are of whole council

PRINCIPAL OFFICERS
Chief Executive: Mrs Jenny Wallace, Head of Paid Service, Riverbank House, Bideford EX39 2QG ☎ 01237 428700 ✉ jenny.wallace@torridge.gov.uk

Senior Management: Mr Steve Hearse, Strategic Manager - Resources, Riverbank House, Bideford EX39 2QG ☎ 01237 428700 ✉ steve.hearse@northdevon.gov.uk

Architect, Building / Property Services: Mr David Green, Development Manager, Riverbank House, Bideford EX39 2QG ☎ 01237 428721 ✉ david.green@torridge.gov.uk

Community Planning: Mr David Green, Development Manager, Riverbank House, Bideford EX39 2QG ☎ 01237 428721 ✉ david.green@torridge.gov.uk

Computer Management: Mr Roger Bonaparte, Business Transformation Manager, Bridge Buildings, Bideford EX39 2HT ☎ 01237 428700 ✉ roger.bonaparte@torridge.gov.uk

Computer Management: Mr Chris Powell, Chief Operations Officer, Civic Centre, Paris Street, Exeter EX1 1JN ☎ 01392 265600 🖷 01392 265268 ✉ cjpowell@eastdevon.gov.uk

Contracts: Mr Andrew Waite, Property Manager, Riverbank House, Bideford EX39 2QG ☎ 01237 428752 🖷 01237 428849 ✉ andrew.waite@torridge.gov.uk

Contracts: Mr Andrew Waite, Property Manager, Riverbank House, Bideford EX39 2QG ☎ 01237 428752 🖷 01237 428849 ✉ andrew.waite@torridge.gov.uk

Corporate Services: Mr Jon Walter, Governance Manager, Riverbank House, Bideford EX39 2QG ☎ 01237 428700 🖷 01237 478849 ✉ jon.walter@torridge.gov.uk

Customer Service: Mr Simon Toon, Customer Support Manager, Riverbank House, Bideford EX39 2QG ☎ 01237 428980 🖷 01237 423481 ✉ simon.toon@torridge.gov.uk

Direct Labour: Mr Richard Haste, Waste & Recycling Manager, Riverbank House, Bideford EX39 2QG ☎ 01237 428963 ✉ richard.haste@torridge.gov.uk

Electoral Registration: Mrs Paula Hunter, Senior Electoral & Democratic Services Officer, Riverbank House, Bideford EX39 2QG ☎ 01237 428702 🖷 01237 425972 ✉ paula.hunter@torridge.gov.uk

Energy Management: Mr Andrew Waite, Property Manager, Riverbank House, Bideford EX39 2QG ☎ 01237 428752 🖷 01237 428849 ✉ andrew.waite@torridge.gov.uk

Estates, Property & Valuation: Mr Andrew Waite, Property Manager, Riverbank House, Bideford EX39 2QG ☎ 01237 428752 🖷 01237 428849 ✉ andrew.waite@torridge.gov.uk

Finance: Mr Steve Hearse, Strategic Manager - Resources, Civic Centre, North Walk, Barnstaple EX31 1EA ☎ 01237 428700 ✉ steve.hearse@northdevon.gov.uk

Health and Safety: Mr Christopher Parkhouse, Corporate Health & Safety Advisor, Town Hall, Bideford EX39 2HS ☎ 01237 428820 🖷 01237 474407 ✉ christopher.parkhouse@torridge.gov.uk

Housing: Mr Daren Ainscough, Regulatory Services Manager, Riverbank House, Bideford EX39 2QG ☎ 01237 428700 ✉ daren.ainscough@torridge.gov.uk

Legal: Mr Jamie Hollis, Senior Solicitor, Riverbank House, Bideford EX39 2QG ☎ 01237 428700 🖷 01237 478849 ✉ jamie.hollis@torridge.gov.uk

Leisure and Cultural Services: Mr Sean Kearney, Commercial & Leisure Services Manager, Riverbank House, Bideford EX39 2QG ☎ 01237 428700 ✉ sean.kearney@torridge.gov.uk

Licensing: Mr Daren Ainscough, Regulatory Services Manager, Riverbank House, Bideford EX39 2QG ☎ 01237 428700 ✉ daren.ainscough@torridge.gov.uk

Member Services: Mr Jon Walter, Governance Manager, Riverbank House, Bideford EX39 2QG ☎ 01237 428700 🖷 01237 478849 ✉ jon.walter@torridge.gov.uk

Personnel / HR: Mrs Sarah Ayres, Human Resources Manager, Riverbank House, Bideford EX39 2QG ☎ 01237 428700 🖷 01237 428799 ✉ sarah.ayres@torridge.gov.uk

TORRIDGE

Planning: Mr David Green, Development Manager, Riverbank House, Bideford EX39 2QG ☎ 01237 428721 ✉ david.green@torridge.gov.uk

Recycling & Waste Minimisation: Mr Richard Haste, Waste & Recycling Manager, Westcombe Depot, Westcombe, Bideford EX39 3JQ ☎ 01237 428963 ✉ richard.haste@torridge.gov.uk

Recycling & Waste Minimisation: Mr Richard Haste, Waste & Recycling Manager, Riverbank House, Bideford EX39 2QG ☎ 01237 428963 ✉ richard.haste@torridge.gov.uk

Staff Training: Mrs Sarah Ayres, Human Resources Manager, Riverbank House, Bideford EX39 2QG ☎ 01237 428700 🖷 01237 428799 ✉ sarah.ayres@torridge.gov.uk

Street Scene: Mr Richard Haste, Waste & Recycling Manager, Riverbank House, Bideford EX39 2QG ☎ 01237 428963 ✉ richard.haste@torridge.gov.uk

Waste Collection and Disposal: Mr Richard Haste, Waste & Recycling Manager, Riverbank House, Bideford EX39 2QG ☎ 01237 428963 ✉ richard.haste@torridge.gov.uk

Waste Collection and Disposal: Mr Richard Haste, Waste & Recycling Manager, Riverbank House, Bideford EX39 2QG ☎ 01237 428963 ✉ richard.haste@torridge.gov.uk

Waste Management: Mr Richard Haste, Waste & Recycling Manager, Riverbank House, Bideford EX39 2QG ☎ 01237 428963 ✉ richard.haste@torridge.gov.uk

COUNCILLORS

***Chair* Langmead**, Mervyn (CON - Bideford East) councillor.langmead@torridge.gov.uk

***Vice-Chair* Himan**, John (CON - Northam) councillor.himan@torridge.gov.uk

***Leader of the Council* Whittaker**, Jane (CON - Northam) councillor.whittaker@torridge.gov.uk

***Deputy Leader of the Council* Morrish**, James (CON - Two Rivers)

Boundy, Betty (CON - Winkleigh)

Boyle, Alison (CON - Kenwith) councillor.boyle@torridge.gov.uk

Brenton, David (O - Bideford South) councillor.brenton@torridge.gov.uk

Brown, Margaret (IND - Torrington) councillor.brown@torridge.gov.uk

Carroll, Ken (CON - Holsworthy)

Christie, Peter (GRN - Bideford North) councillor.christie@torridge.gov.uk

Darch, Roger (UKIP - Torrington)

Dart, Anna (INDNA - Hartland and Bradworthy) councillor.dart@torridge.gov.uk

Davis, Kenny (UKIP - Appledore)

Dezart, Gaston (UKIP - Bideford East)

Eastman, Andrew (CON - Appledore) councillor.eastman@torridge.gov.uk

Gregorek, Zyg (CON - Forest)

Hackett, Philip (CON - Coham Bridge)

Hancock, Richard (UKIP - Northam)

Hicks, Robert (IND - Waldon) councillor.hicks@torridge.gov.uk

Hurley, David (CON - Shebbear and Langtree) councillor.hurley@torridge.gov.uk

Inch, Anthony (CON - Bideford South) councillor.tonyinch@torridge.gov.uk

Inch, Simon (CON - Bideford South) councillor.simoninch@torridge.gov.uk

James, Kenneth (IND - Tamarside) councillor.james@torridge.gov.uk

Johns, Trevor (LD - Bideford North) councillor.tjohns@torridge.gov.uk

Julian, Robin (UKIP - Clovelly Bay)

Langton-Lockton, John (CON - Orchard Hill)

Le Maistre, Peter (CON - Westward Ho!)

Lock, Rosemary (CON - Three Moors) councillor.lock@torridge.gov.uk

McGeough, Dermot (CON - Bideford North)

Parker, Ian (CON - Holsworthy)

Pennington, Philip (IND - Monkleigh and Littleham) councillor.pennington@torridge.gov.uk

Robinson, Sam (CON - Bideford East) councillor.robinson@torridge.gov.uk

Simmons, Catherine (INDNA - Torrington) councillor.simmons@torridge.gov.uk

Watson, Peter (CON - Broadheath) councillor.watson@torridge.gov.uk

Whittle, Alan (UKIP - Hartland and Bradworthy)

Wiseman, Richard (INDNA - Clinton)

POLITICAL COMPOSITION

CON: 20, UKIP: 6, IND: 4, INDNA: 3, LD: 1, O: 1, GRN: 1

Tower Hamlets — L

Tower Hamlets London Borough Council, Town Hall, Mulberry Place, 5 Clove Crescent, London E14 2BG
☎ 020 7364 5000 🖷 020 7364 4296 🖳 www.towerhamlets.gov.uk

FACTS AND FIGURES

Parliamentary Constituencies: Bethnal Green and Bow, Poplar and Limehouse
EU Constituencies: London
Election Frequency: Elections are of whole council

PRINCIPAL OFFICERS

Chief Executive: Mr Will Tuckley, Chief Executive, Town Hall, Mulberry Place, 5 Clove Crescent, London E14 2BG ☎ 020 7364 5000 ✉ will.tuckley@towerhamlets.gov.uk

Senior Management: Mr Luke Addams, Director - Adult Services, Town Hall, Mulberry Place, 5 Clove Crescent, London E14 2BG 🖰 luke.addams@towerhamlets.gov.uk

Senior Management: Ms Melanie Clay, Monitoring Officer: Director - Law, Probity & Governance, Town Hall, Mulberry Place, 5 Clove Crescent, London E14 2BG 🖰 melanie.clay@towerhamlets.gov.uk

Senior Management: Ms Zena Cooke, Director - Corporate Resources, Town Hall, Mulberry Place, 5 Clove Crescent, London E14 2BG 🖰 zeena.cooke@towerhamlets.gov.uk

Senior Management: Mr Aman Dalvi, Corporate Director - Development & Renewal, Anchorage House, 5 Clove Crescent, London E14 1BY ☎ 020 7634 4247 🖷 020 7364 4400 🖰 aman.dalvi@towerhamlets.gov.uk

Senior Management: Mr Stephen Halsey, Corporate Director - Communities, Localities & Culture Directorate, Town Hall, Mulberry Place, 5 Clove Crescent, London E14 2BG ☎ 020 7364 5000 🖰 stephen.halsey@towerhamlets.gov.uk

Senior Management: Ms Debbie Jones, Corporate Director - Children, Town Hall, Mulberry Place, 5 Clove Crescent, London E14 2BG 🖰 debbie.jones@towerhamlets.gov.uk

Architect, Building / Property Services: Mr Martin Stevens, Interim Head - Corporate Property Services, Mulberry Place, 5 Clove Crescent, London E14 2BG ☎ 020 7364 5000 🖰 martin.stevens@towerhamlets.gov.uk

Architect, Building / Property Services: Ms Ann Sutcliffe, Service Head - Corporate Property & Capital Developments, Anchorage House, 2 Clove Crescent, London E14 2BE ☎ 020 7364 4077 🖷 020 7364 4828 🖰 ann.sutcliffe@towerhamlets.gov.uk

Building Control: Mr Martin Fahey, Head - Building Control, Town Hall, Mulberry Place, 5 Clove Crescent, London E14 2BG ☎ 020 7364 5275 🖷 020 7364 5358 🖰 martin.fahey@towerhamlets.gov.uk

Children / Youth Services: Ms Monica Forty, Service Head - Learning & Achievement, Town Hall, Mulberry Place, 5 Clove Crescent, London E14 2BG ☎ 020 7364 0525 🖰 monica.forty@towerhamlets.gov.uk

Civil Registration: Ms Catherine Sutton, Head of Registration & Citizenship, Bromley Public Hall, Bow Road, London E3 3AA ☎ 020 7364 7983 🖷 020 7364 7885 🖰 catherine.sutton@towerhamlets.gov.uk

Community Safety: Mr Andy Bamber, Service Head - Safer Communities, Town Hall, Mulberry Place, 5 Clove Crescent, London E14 2BG ☎ 020 7364 0764 🖰 andy.bamber@towerhamlets.gov.uk

Consumer Protection and Trading Standards: Mr Dave Tolley, Head of Consumer & Business Regulations, 4th Floor, Mulberry Place, 5 Clove Crescent, London E14 2BE ☎ 020 7364 6724 🖷 020 7364 6901 🖰 david.tolley@towerhamlets.gov.uk

Contracts: Mr Zamil Ahmed, Procurement & Programme Management, Town Hall, Mulberry Place, 5 Clove Crescent, London E14 2BG ☎ 020 7364 4385 🖰 zamil.ahmed@towerhamlets.gov.uk

Contracts: Mr Michael Hales, Head - Contracts Services, Toby Lane Depot, 1st Floor, Harford Street, London E1 4DN ☎ 020 7364 5153 🖷 020 7364 5161 🖰 michael.hales@towerhamlets.gov.uk

Corporate Services: Mr Robert McCulloch-Graham, Corporate Director - Education, Social Care & Wellbeing, Town Hall, Mulberry Place, 5 Clove Crescent, London E14 2BG ☎ 020 7364 4950 🖰 robert.mcculloch-graham@towerhamlets.gov.uk

Customer Service: Mr Chris Holme, Acting Corporate Director - Resources Directorate, Town Hall, Mulberry Place, 5 Clove Crescent, London E14 2BG 🖰 chris.holme@towerhamlets.gov.uk

Customer Service: Mr Keith Paulin, Head of Customer Services, Town Hall, Mulberry Place, 5 Clove Crescent, London E14 2BG ☎ 020 7364 3118 🖷 020 7364 3121 🖰 keith.paulin@towerhamlets.gov.uk

Economic Development: Mr Aman Dalvi, Corporate Director - Development & Renewal, Anchorage House, 5 Clove Crescent, London E14 1BY ☎ 020 7634 4247 🖷 020 7364 4400 🖰 aman.dalvi@towerhamlets.gov.uk

Education: Mr Robert McCulloch-Graham, Corporate Director - Education, Social Care & Wellbeing, Town Hall, Mulberry Place, 5 Clove Crescent, London E14 2BG ☎ 020 7364 4950 🖰 robert.mcculloch-graham@towerhamlets.gov.uk

Electoral Registration: Mr John Williams, Service Head - Democratic Services, Town Hall, Mulberry Place (AH), PO Box 55739, 5 Clove Crescent, London E14 1BY ☎ 020 7364 4204 🖷 020 7364 3232 🖰 john.williams@towerhamlets.gov.uk

Emergency Planning: Mr Steve Crawley, Civil Protection & Business Continuity Co-ordinator, 3rd Floor, Mulberry Place, 5 Clove Crescent, London E14 2BE ☎ 020 7364 4181 🖰 steve.crawley@towerhamlets.gov.uk

Energy Management: Ms Sian Pipe, Energy Manager, Energy Efficiency Unit, Gladstone Place, Roman Road, London E3 5ES ☎ 020 7364 2523 🖷 020 7364 2512 🖰 sian.pipe@towerhamlets.gov.uk

Environmental / Technical Services: Mr Andy Bamber, Service Head - Safer Communities, Town Hall, Mulberry Place, 5 Clove Crescent, London E14 2BG ☎ 020 7364 0764 🖰 andy.bamber@towerhamlets.gov.uk

Environmental / Technical Services: Mr Dave Tolley, Head of Consumer & Business Regulations, 4th Floor, Mulberry Place, 5 Clove Crescent, London E14 2BE ☎ 020 7364 6724 🖷 020 7364 6901 🖰 david.tolley@towerhamlets.gov.uk

Environmental Health: Mr Andrew Weaver, Head of Environmental Protection, Town Hall, Mulberry Place, 5 Clove Crescent, London E14 2BG ☎ 020 7364 6896 🖰 andrew.weaver@towerhamlets.gov.uk

Estates, Property & Valuation: Ms Ann Sutcliffe, Service Head - Corporate Property & Capital Developments, Anchorage House, 2 Clove Crescent, London E14 2BE ☎ 020 7364 4077 🖷 020 7364 4828 🖰 ann.sutcliffe@towerhamlets.gov.uk

Events Manager: Mr Steve Murray, Head - Arts, Town Hall, Mulberry Place, 5 Clove Crescent, London E14 2BG ☎ 020 7364 7910 ✉ stephen.murray@towerhamlets.gov.uk

Facilities: Ms Ann Sutcliffe, Service Head - Corporate Property & Capital Developments, Anchorage House, 2 Clove Crescent, London E14 2BE ☎ 020 7364 4077 🖷 020 7364 4828 ✉ ann.sutcliffe@towerhamlets.gov.uk

Finance: Mr Chris Holme, Acting Corporate Director - Resources Directorate, Town Hall, Mulberry Place, 5 Clove Crescent, London E14 2BG ✉ chris.holme@towerhamlets.gov.uk

Pensions: Mr Anant Dodia, Pensions Manager, Anchorage House, PO Box 55739, London E14 2BE ☎ 020 7364 4248 ✉ anant.dodia@towerhamlets.gov.uk

Fleet Management: Mr Lee Perry, Passenger Services Operations Manager, 1 Silvocea Way, Blackwall, London E14 0JJ ☎ 020 7364 4977 ✉ lee.perry@towerhamlets.gov.uk

Grounds Maintenance: Ms Ann Sutcliffe, Service Head - Corporate Property & Capital Developments, Anchorage House, 2 Clove Crescent, London E14 2BE ☎ 020 7364 4077 🖷 020 7364 4828 ✉ ann.sutcliffe@towerhamlets.gov.uk

Health and Safety: Mr Dave Tolley, Head of Consumer & Business Regulations, 4th Floor, Mulberry Place, 5 Clove Crescent, London E14 2BE ☎ 020 7364 6724 🖷 020 7364 6901 ✉ david.tolley@towerhamlets.gov.uk

Highways: Mr Simon Baxter, Service Head - Public Realm, Anchorage House, 5 Clove Crescent, London E14 2BE ☎ 020 7364 4422 ✉ simon.baxter@towerhamlets.gov.uk

Home Energy Conservation: Ms Sian Pipe, Energy Manager, Energy Efficiency Unit, Gladstone Place, Roman Road, London E3 5ES ☎ 020 7364 2523 🖷 020 7364 2512 ✉ sian.pipe@towerhamlets.gov.uk

Housing: Ms Susmita Sen, Chief Executive - Tower Hamlets Homes, 1st Floor, 2 Lawn House Close, London E14 9YQ ☎ 020 7364 7134 ✉ susmita.sen@thh.gov.uk

Local Area Agreement: Ms Louise Russell, Service Head - Corporate Strategy & Equality, Town Hall, Mulberry Place, 5 Clove Crescent, London E14 2BG ☎ 020 7364 3267 ✉ louise.russell@towerhamlets.gov.uk

Legal: Mr David Galpin, Service Head - Legal Services, Town Hall, Mulberry Place, 5 Clove Crescent, London E14 2BG ☎ 020 7364 4348 ✉ david.galpin@towerhamlets.gov.uk

Leisure and Cultural Services: Ms Shazia Hussain, Service Head - Culture, Learning & Leisure, Town Hall, Mulberry Place, 5 Clove Crescent, London E14 2BG ☎ 020 7364 4470 ✉ shazia.hussain@towerhamlets.gov.uk

Licensing: Mr Dave Tolley, Head of Consumer & Business Regulations, 4th Floor, Mulberry Place, 5 Clove Crescent, London E14 2BE ☎ 020 7364 6724 🖷 020 7364 6901 ✉ david.tolley@towerhamlets.gov.uk

Lifelong Learning: Ms Judith St John, Head of Idea Store, 3rd Floor, 1 Gladstone Place, London E3 5EG ☎ 020 7364 5630 ✉ judith.stjohn@towerhamlets.gov.uk

Lighting: Mr Stanley Perpie, Street Lighting Engineer, Anchorage House, 4th Floor, 5 Clove Crescent, London E14 2BE ☎ 020 7364 6802 🖷 020 7364 6867 ✉ stanley.perpie@towerhamlets.gov.uk

Lottery Funding, Charity and Voluntary: Mr Everett Haughton, Third Sector Programmes Manager, Mulberry Place, Anchorage House, 2 Clove Crescent, London E14 2BG ☎ 020 7364 4639 ✉ everett.haughton@towerhamlets.gov.uk

Lottery Funding, Charity and Voluntary: Ms Louise Russell, Service Head - Corporate Strategy & Equality, Town Hall, Mulberry Place, 5 Clove Crescent, London E14 2BG ☎ 020 7364 3267 ✉ louise.russell@towerhamlets.gov.uk

Member Services: Mr John Williams, Service Head - Democratic Services, Town Hall, Mulberry Place (AH), PO Box 55739, 5 Clove Crescent, London E14 1BY ☎ 020 7364 4204 🖷 020 7364 3232 ✉ john.williams@towerhamlets.gov.uk

Parking: Mr Misrad Bakalovic, Head of Parking Services, Town Hall, Mulberry Place, 5 Clove Crescent, London E14 2BG ☎ 020 7364 6999 ✉ misrad.bakalovic@towerhamlets.gov.uk

Partnerships: Ms Shazia Hussain, Service Head - Culture, Learning & Leisure, 4th Floor, Mulberry Place, 5 Clove Crescent, London E14 2BE ☎ 020 7364 4470 ✉ shazia.hussain@towerhamlets.gov.uk

Personnel / HR: Mr Chris Holme, Acting Corporate Director - Resources Directorate, Town Hall, Mulberry Place, 5 Clove Crescent, London E14 2BG ✉ chris.holme@towerhamlets.gov.uk

Personnel / HR: Mr Simon Kilbey, Service Head - HR & Work Force Development, Mulberry Place, 5 Clove Crescent, London E14 2BG ☎ 020 7364 4922

Planning: Mr Owen Whalley, Service Head - Development Control & Building Control, Anchorage House, 2 Clove Crescent, London E14 2BE ☎ 020 7364 5314 🖷 020 7364 5412 ✉ owen.whalley@towerhamlets.gov.uk

Procurement: Mr Zamil Ahmed, Procurement & Programme Management, Town Hall, Mulberry Place, 5 Clove Crescent, London E14 2BG ☎ 020 7364 4385 ✉ zamil.ahmed@towerhamlets.gov.uk

Public Libraries: Ms Judith St John, Head of Idea Store, 3rd Floor, 1 Gladstone Place, London E3 5EG ☎ 020 7364 5630 ✉ judith.stjohn@towerhamlets.gov.uk

Recycling & Waste Minimisation: Mr Simon Baxter, Service Head - Public Realm, Anchorage House, 5 Clove Crescent, London E14 2BE ☎ 020 7364 4422 ✉ simon.baxter@towerhamlets.gov.uk

Regeneration: Ms Jackie Odunoye, Service Head - Strategy, Innovation & Sustainability, Anchorage House, 5 Clove Crescent, London E14 1BY ☎ 020 7364 4247 ✉ jackie.odunoye@towerhamlets.gov.uk

Road Safety: Ms Margaret Cooper, Head of Transport & Highways, Anchorage House, 5 Clove Crescent, London E14 2BE ☎ 020 7364 6851 ✉ margaret.cooper@towerhamlets.gov.uk

Social Services (Adult): Mr Robert McCulloch-Graham, Corporate Director - Education, Social Care & Wellbeing, Town Hall, Mulberry Place, 5 Clove Crescent, London E14 2BG ☎ 020 7364 4950 ✉ robert.mcculloch-graham@towerhamlets.gov.uk

Social Services (Children): Mr Robert McCulloch-Graham, Corporate Director - Education, Social Care & Wellbeing, Town Hall, Mulberry Place, 5 Clove Crescent, London E14 2BG ☎ 020 7364 4950 ✉ robert.mcculloch-graham@towerhamlets.gov.uk

Social Services (Children): Ms Nasima Patel, Service Head - Children's Social Care, Town Hall, Mulberry Place, 5 Clove Crescent, London E14 2BG ☎ 020 7364 2213 ✉ nasima.patel@towerhamlets.gov.uk

Public Health: Dr Somen Banerjee, Interim Director - Public Health, Town Hall, Mulberry Place, 5 Clove Crescent, London E14 2BG ✉ somen.banerjee@towerhamlets.gov.uk

Staff Training: Mr Simon Kilbey, Service Head - HR & Work Force Development, Mulberry Place, 5 Clove Crescent, London E14 2BG ☎ 020 7364 4922 ✉ simon.kilbey@towerhamlets.gov.uk

Street Scene: Mr Simon Baxter, Service Head - Public Realm, Anchorage House, 5 Clove Crescent, London E14 2BE ☎ 020 7364 4422 ✉ simon.baxter@towerhamlets.gov.uk

Sustainable Communities: Ms Jackie Odunoye, Service Head - Strategy, Innovation & Sustainability, Town Hall, Mulberry Place, 5 Clove Crescent, London E14 2BG ☎ 020 7364 4247 ✉ jackie.odunoye@towerhamlets.gov.uk

Sustainable Development: Ms Jackie Odunoye, Service Head - Strategy, Innovation & Sustainability, Town Hall, Mulberry Place, 5 Clove Crescent, London E14 2BG ☎ 020 7364 4247 ✉ jackie.odunoye@towerhamlets.gov.uk

Tourism: Mr Aman Dalvi, Corporate Director - Development & Renewal, Anchorage House, 5 Clove Crescent, London E14 1BY ☎ 020 7634 4247 🖷 020 7364 4400 ✉ aman.dalvi@towerhamlets.gov.uk

Traffic Management: Ms Margaret Cooper, Head of Transport & Highways, Anchorage House, 4th Floor, 5 Clove Crescent, London E14 2BE ☎ 020 7364 6851 ✉ margaret.cooper@towerhamlets.gov.uk

Transport: Mr John Stevens, Transport Contracts Manager, 1 Silvocea Way, Blackwall, London E14 0JJ ☎ 020 7364 1071 🖷 020 7364 1070 ✉ john.e.stevens@towerhamlets.gov.uk

Transport Planner: Ms Margaret Cooper, Head of Transport & Highways, Anchorage House, 5 Clove Crescent, London E14 2BE ☎ 020 7364 6851 ✉ margaret.cooper@towerhamlets.gov.uk

Waste Collection and Disposal: Mr Simon Baxter, Service Head - Public Realm, Anchorage House, 5 Clove Crescent, London E14 2BE ☎ 020 7364 4422 ✉ simon.baxter@towerhamlets.gov.uk

Waste Management: Mr Simon Baxter, Service Head - Public Realm, Anchorage House, 5 Clove Crescent, London E14 2BE ☎ 020 7364 4422 ✉ simon.baxter@towerhamlets.gov.uk

COUNCILLORS

***Mayor* Biggs**, John (LAB - No Ward)
Mayor@towerhamlets.gov.uk

***Deputy Mayor* Khatun**, Shiria (LAB - Lansbury)
shiria.khatan@towerhamlets.gov.uk

***Deputy Mayor* Saunders**, Rachael (LAB - Mile End)
Cllr.rachael.saunders@towerhamlets.gov.uk

***Speaker* Mukit**, Abdul (LAB - Weavers)
Cllr.AbdulC.Mukit@towerhamlets.gov.uk

***Deputy Speaker* Ahmed**, Rajib (LAB - Lansbury)
cllr.rajib.ahmed@towerhamlets.gov.uk

***Group Leader* Golds**, Peter (CON - Island Gardens)
cllrpetergolds@aol.com

***Group Leader* Rahman**, Oliur (IND - Stepney Green)
cllr.oliur.rahman@towerhamlets.gov.uk

Ahmed, Ohid (IND - Lansbury)
cllr.ohid.ahmed@towerhamlets.gov.uk

Ahmed, Suluk (IND - Spitalfields & Banglatown)
Cllr.Suluk.Ahmed@towerhamlets.gov.uk

Akhtar, Sabina (LAB - Stepney Green)
sabina.akhtar@towerhamlets.gov.uk

Alam, Mahbub (IND - St Dunstan's)
Mahbubm.Alam@towerhamlets.gov.uk

Alam, Shah (IND - Mile End)
Cllr.Shah.Alam@towerhamlets.gov.uk

Ali, Shahed (IND - Whitechapel)
shahed.ali@towerhamlets.gov.uk

Ali, Amina (LAB - Bow East)
Cllr.Amina.Ali@towerhamlets.gov.uk

Asad, Abdul (IND - Whitechapel)
Cllr.abdul.asad@towerhamlets.gov.uk

Aston, Craig (CON - Limehouse)
cllrcraigaston@gmail.com

Begum, Asma (LAB - Bow West)
Cllr.Asmak.Begum@towerhamlets.gov.uk

Blake, Rachel (LAB - Bow East)
Cllr.Rachel.Blake@towerhamlets.gov.uk

Chapman, Chris (CON - Blackwall & Cubitt Town)
cllrchrischapman@gmail.com

Chesterton, Dave (LAB - Blackwall & Cubitt Town)
Cllr.dave.chesterton@towerhamlets.gov.uk

Choudhury, Gulam Kibria (IND - Poplar)
Cllr.Kibria.Choudhury@toerhamlets.gov.uk

Cregan, Andrew (LAB - Island Gardens)
Cllr.Andrew.Cregan@towerhamlets.gov.uk

Dockerill, Julia (CON - St Katharine's & Wapping)
Cllr.Julia.Dockerill@towerhamlets.gov.uk

Edgar, David (LAB - Mile End)
Cllr.David.Edgar@towerhamlets.gov.uk

Francis, Marc (LAB - Bow East)
Cllr.marc.francis@towerhamlets.gov.uk

Haque, Shafiqul (IND - Bethnal Green)
cllr.shafiqul.haque@towerhamlets.gov.uk

Harrisson, Clare (LAB - St Peter's)
Cllr.Clare.Harrisson@towerhamlets.gov.uk

Hassell, Danny (LAB - Bromley South)
Cllr.Danny.Hassell@towerhamlets.gov.uk

Islam, Sirajul (LAB - Bethnal Green)
Cllr.Sirajul.Islam@towerhamlets.gov.uk

Jones, Denise (LAB - St Katharine's & Wapping)
Cllr.Denise.Jones@towerhamlets.gov.uk

Khan, Aminur (IND - Whitechapel)
cllr.aminur.khan@towerhamlets.gov.uk

Khan, Rabina (IND - Shadwell)
Cllr.rabina.khan@towerhamlets.gov.uk

Miah, Harun (IND - Shadwell)
harun.miah579@o2.co.uk

Miah, Abjol (IND - St Peter's)
cllr.Abjol.Miah@towerhamlets.gov.uk

Miah, Ayas (LAB - St Dunstan's)
Cllr.Ayas.Miah@towerhamlets.gov.uk

Miah, Md. Maium (IND - Canary Wharf)
cllr.maium.miah@towerhamlets.gov.uk

Mufti Miah, Mohammed (IND - Bromley North)
Cllr.Mohammed.MuftiMiah@towerhamlets.gov.uk

Mustaquim, Muhammad (IND - St Peter's)
Cllr.Muhammad.Mustaquim@towerhamlets.gov.uk

Peck, Joshua (LAB - Bow West)
cllr.joshua.peck@towerhamlets.gov.uk

Pierce, John (LAB - Weavers)
Cllr.john.pierce@towerhamlets.gov.uk

Robbani, Gulam (IND - Spitalfields & Banglatown)
Cllr.gulam.robbani@towerhamlets.gov.uk

Ronald, Candida (LAB - Blackwall & Cubitt Town)
cllr.candida.ronald@towerhamlets.gov.uk

Uddin, Helal (LAB - Bromley South)
Cllr.helal.uddin@towerhamlets.gov.uk

Uddin Ahmed, Khales (LAB - Bromley North)
Cllr.khales.uddinahmed@towerhamlets.gov.uk

Whitelock Gibbs, Amy (LAB - Bethnal Green)
cllr.amy.whitelockgibbs@towerhamlets.gov.uk

Wood, Andrew (CON - Canary Wharf)
cllrandrewwood@gmail.com

POLITICAL COMPOSITION
LAB: 24, IND: 17, CON: 5

COMMITTEE CHAIRS
Audit: Ms Candida Ronald

Development: Mr Marc Francis

Licensing: Mr Khales Uddin Ahmed

Pensions: Mr Andrew Cregan

Trafford — M

Trafford Metropolitan Borough Council, Trafford Town Hall, Talbot Road, Stretford, Manchester M32 0TH
☎ 0161 912 2000 🖷 0161 912 1354 🖳 www.trafford.gov.uk

FACTS AND FIGURES
Parliamentary Constituencies: Altrincham and Sale West, Stretford and Urmston, Wythenshawe and Sale East
EU Constituencies: North West
Election Frequency: Elections are by thirds

PRINCIPAL OFFICERS
Chief Executive: Ms Theresa Grant, Chief Executive, Trafford Town Hall, Talbot Road, Stretford, Manchester M32 0TH
☎ 0161 912 1900 ✉ theresa.grant@trafford.gov.uk

Deputy Chief Executive: Ms Helen Jones, Deputy Chief Executive, Trafford Town Hall, Talbot Road, Stretford, Manchester M32 0TH ☎ 0161 912 1915 ✉ helen.jones@trafford.gov.uk

Senior Management: Ms Joanne Hyde, Acting Corporate Director for Children, Families & Wellbeing, Trafford Town Hall, Talbot Road, Stretford, Manchester M32 0TH ☎ 0161 912 1586 🖷 0161 912 4171 ✉ joanne.hyde@trafford.gov.uk

Senior Management: Ms Helen Jones, Deputy Chief Executive, Trafford Town Hall, Talbot Road, Stretford, Manchester M32 0TH ☎ 0161 912 1915 ✉ helen.jones@trafford.gov.uk

Senior Management: Mr John Pearce, Director of Commissioning, Performance & Strategy, Trafford Town Hall, Talbot Road, Stretford, Manchester M32 0TH ☎ 0161 912 5100 ✉ john.pearce@trafford.gov.uk

Architect, Building / Property Services: Mr Neil Earp, Interim Head of Property & Development, Trafford Town Hall, Talbot Road, Stretford, Manchester M32 0TH ☎ 0161 912 4264 ✉ neil.earp@trafford.gov.uk

Building Control: Mr Rob Haslam, Head of Planning, Trafford Town Hall, Talbot Road, Stretford, Manchester M32 0TH ☎ 0161 912 4788 ✉ rob.haslam@trafford.gov.uk

Catering Services: Mr Phil Valentine, Environment Strategic Business Manager, Trafford Town Hall, Talbot Road, Stretford, Manchester M32 0TH ☎ 0161 912 4301 ✉ phil.valentine@trafford.gov.uk

Children / Youth Services: Ms Carol Baker-Longshaw, Joint Director - CYPS & Community Health Services, Trafford Town Hall, Talbot Road, Stretford, Manchester M32 0TH ☎ 0161 911 8650 ✉ carol.baker-longshaw@nhs.net

Children / Youth Services: Ms Jill Colbert, Acting Director of Commissioning, Performance & Strategy, Trafford Town Hall, Talbot Road, Stretford, Manchester M32 0TH ☎ 0161 912 5100 ✉ jill.colbert@trafford.gov.uk

Civil Registration: Ms Jane Lefevre, Director of Legal & Democratic Services, Trafford Town Hall, Talbot Road, Stretford, Manchester M32 0TH ☎ 0161 912 4215 ✉ jane.lefevre@trafford.gov.uk

PR / Communications: Ms Kelly Dooley, Public Relations Manager, Trafford Town Hall, Talbot Road, Stretford, Manchester M32 0TH ☎ 0161 912 1262 ✉ kelly.dooley@trafford.gov.uk

Community Safety: Ms Liz Baxter, Strategic Manager - Crime & Anti-social Behaviour, Trafford Town Hall, Talbot Road, Stretford, Manchester M32 0TH ☎ 0161 912 1231 ✉ liz.baxter@trafford.gov.uk

Computer Management: Mr John Callan, Interim Head of ICT, Trafford Town Hall, Talbot Road, Stretford, Manchester M32 0TH ☎ 0161 912 2138 ✉ john.callan@trafford.gov.uk

Consumer Protection and Trading Standards: Mr Iain Veitch, Head of Public Protection, Quay West, Trafford Wharf Road, Trafford Park, Manchester M17 1HH ☎ 0161 912 4174 🖷 0161 912 4917 ✉ iain.veitch@trafford.gov.uk

Contracts: Ms Sharon Robson, Director of STaR, Trafford Town Hall, Talbot Road, Stretford, Manchester M32 0TH ✉ sharon.robson@star-procurement.gov.uk

Customer Service: Ms Sarah Curran, Head of Customer Service, Waterside House, Sale Waterside, Sale, Manchester M33 7ZF ☎ 0121 912 2823 ✉ sarah.curran@trafford.gov.uk

Economic Development: Mr Richard Roe, Director of Economic Growth & Regulatory Services, Trafford Town Hall, Talbot Road, Stretford, Manchester M32 0TH ☎ 0161 912 4265 ✉ richard.roe@trafford.gov.uk

Education: Mr Adrian Hallett, Head of Education, Sale Waterside, Waterside House, Sale M33 7ZF ☎ 0161 912 8685 ✉ adrian.hallett@trafford.gov.uk

Education: Mr Andrew Warrington, Head of Education Strategic Support, Trafford Town Hall, Talbot Road, Stretford, Manchester M32 0TH ☎ 0161 912 4769 ✉ andrew.warrington@trafford.gov.uk

E-Government: Chris Walker, ICT Operations Manager, Trafford Town Hall, Talbot Road, Stretford, Manchester M32 0TH ☎ 0161 912 2138 ✉ chris.walker@trafford.gov.uk

Electoral Registration: Mr Peter Forrester, Democratic Services Manager, Trafford Town Hall, Talbot Road, Stretford, Manchester M32 0TH ☎ 0161 912 1815 ✉ peter.forrester@trafford.gov.uk

Emergency Planning: Mr David Hooley, Emergency Planning Manager, Trafford Town Hall, Talbot Road, Stretford, Manchester M32 0TH ☎ 0161 912 3425 🖷 0161 912 3444 ✉ david.hooley@trafford.gov.uk

Energy Management: Mr Andrew Hunt, Sustainability Manager, Carrington Depot, 148 Manchester Road, Carrington, Manchester M31 4QN ☎ 0161 912 4691 ✉ andrew.hunt@trafford.gov.uk

Environmental Health: Mr Iain Veitch, Head of Public Protection, Trafford Town Hall, Talbot Road, Stretford, Manchester M32 0TH ☎ 0161 912 4174 🖷 0161 912 4917 ✉ iain.veitch@trafford.gov.uk

Estates, Property & Valuation: Mr Neil Earp, Interim Head of Property & Development, Trafford Town Hall, Talbot Road, Stretford, Manchester M32 0TH ☎ 0161 912 4264 ✉ neil.earp@trafford.gov.uk

Facilities: Mr Neil Earp, Interim Head of Property & Development, Trafford Town Hall, Talbot Road, Stretford, Manchester M32 0TH ☎ 0161 912 4264 ✉ neil.earp@trafford.gov.uk

Finance: Mr Ian Duncan, Director of Finance, Trafford Town Hall, Talbot Road, Stretford, Manchester M32 0TH ☎ 0161 912 4238 🖷 0161 912 1250 ✉ ian.duncan@trafford.gov.uk

Grounds Maintenance: Mr Phil Valentine, Environment Strategic Business Manager, Trafford Town Hall, Talbot Road, Stretford, Manchester M32 0TH ☎ 0161 912 4301 ✉ phil.valentine@trafford.gov.uk

Health and Safety: Ms Lisa Hooley, Acting Director of HR, Trafford Town Hall, Talbot Road, Stretford, Manchester M32 0TH ☎ 0161 912 4670 ✉ lisa.hooley@trafford.gov.uk

Highways: Mr Chris Hindle, Contracts Director, Trafford Town Hall, Talbot Road, Stretford, Manchester M32 0TH ✉ chris.hindle@trafford.gov.uk

Housing: Mr Richard Roe, Director of Economic Growth & Regulatory Services, Trafford Town Hall, Talbot Road, Stretford, Manchester M32 0TH ☎ 0161 912 4265 ✉ richard.roe@trafford.gov.uk

Legal: Ms Jane Lefevre, Director of Legal & Democratic Services, Trafford Town Hall, Talbot Road, Stretford, Manchester M32 0TH ☎ 0161 912 4215 ✉ jane.lefevre@trafford.gov.uk

Leisure and Cultural Services: Ms Debbie Cowley, Strategic Manager for Culture & Sport, Waterside House, Sale Waterside, Sale, Manchester M33 6FZ ☎ 0161 912 3110 ✉ debbie.cowley@trafford.gov.uk

Licensing: Mr Iain Veitch, Head of Public Protection, Trafford Town Hall, Talbot Road, Stretford, Manchester M32 0TH ☎ 0161 912 4174 🖷 0161 912 4917 ✉ iain.veitch@trafford.gov.uk

Lighting: Mr Trevor Chester, Street Lighting Manager, Carrington Depot, 148 Manchester Road, Carrington, Manchester M31 4QN ☎ 07760 167091 ✉ trevor.chester@trafford.gov.uk

Member Services: Mr Peter Forrester, Democratic Services Manager, Trafford Town Hall, Talbot Road, Stretford, Manchester M32 0TH ☎ 0161 912 1815 ✉ peter.forrester@trafford.gov.uk

Parking: Ms Nicola Henry, Parking Services Manager, Waterside House, Sale Waterside, Sale, Manchester M33 6FZ ☎ 0161 912 4046 ✉ nicola.henry@trafford.gov.uk

Partnerships: Ms Kerry Purnell, Head of Partnerships & Performance, Trafford Town Hall, Talbot Road, Stretford, Manchester M32 0TH ☎ 0161 912 1231 ✉ kerry.purnell@trafford.gov.uk

Personnel / HR: Ms Lisa Hooley, Acting Director of HR, Trafford Town Hall, Talbot Road, Stretford, Manchester M32 0TH ☎ 0161 912 4670 ✉ lisa.hooley@trafford.gov.uk

Planning: Mr Rob Haslam, Head of Planning, Waterside House, Sale Waterside, Sale, Manchester M33 6FZ ☎ 0161 912 4788 ✉ rob.haslam@trafford.gov.uk

TRAFFORD

Procurement: Ms Sharon Robson, Director of STaR, Trafford Town Hall, Talbot Road, Stretford, Manchester M32 0TH 🖱 sharon.robson@star-procurement.gov.uk

Public Libraries: Ms Sarah Curran, Head of Customer Service, Waterside House, Sale Waterside, Sale, Manchester M33 7ZF ☎ 0121 912 2823 🖱 sarah.curran@trafford.gov.uk

Recycling & Waste Minimisation: Mr Gary Taylor, Waste Manager, Carrington Depot, 148 Manchester Road, Carrington, Manchester M31 4QN ☎ 0161 912 4912 🖷 0161 912 5705 🖱 gary.taylor@trafford.gov.uk

Regeneration: Mr Stephen James, Assistant Head of Economic Growth, Trafford Town Hall, Talbot Road, Stretford, Manchester M32 0TH ☎ 0161 912 4430 🖱 stephen.james@carrington.gov.uk

Road Safety: Mr Dominic Smith, Traffic, Transport & Road Safety Manager, Sale Waterside, Waterside House, Sale M33 7ZF ☎ 0161 912 4312 🖱 dominic.smith@trafford.gov.uk

Social Services: Ms Diane Eaton, Director of Adults (Social Care), Trafford Town Hall, Talbot Road, Stretford, Manchester M32 0TH ☎ 0161 912 2705 🖱 diane.eaton@trafford.gov.uk

Social Services (Adult): Ms Diane Eaton, Director of Adults (Social Care), Trafford Town Hall, Talbot Road, Stretford, Manchester M32 0TH ☎ 0161 912 2705 🖱 diane.eaton@trafford.gov.uk

Social Services (Children): Ms Charlotte Ramsden, Joint Director - Children, Young People & Families (Social Care), Trafford Town Hall, Talbot Road, Stretford, Manchester M32 0TH ☎ 0161 911 8650 🖱 charlotte.ramsden@trafford.gov.uk

Public Health: Mr Abdul Razzaq, Director of Public Health, Trafford Town Hall, Talbot Road, Stretford, Manchester M32 0TH ☎ 0161 912 1300 🖱 abdul.razzaq@trafford.gov.uk

Staff Training: Ms Lisa Hooley, Acting Director of HR, Trafford Town Hall, Talbot Road, Stretford, Manchester M32 0TH ☎ 0161 912 4670 🖱 lisa.hooley@trafford.gov.uk

Transport: Mr Colin Maycroft, Service Operations Manager, Moss View Centre, Moss View Road, Partington, Manchester M31 4DX ☎ 0161 912 2926 🖷 0161 912 2931 🖱 colin.maycroft@trafford.gov.uk

Waste Collection and Disposal: Mr Gary Taylor, Waste Manager, Carrington Depot, 148 Manchester Road, Carrington, Manchester M31 4QN ☎ 0161 912 4912 🖷 0161 912 5705 🖱 gary.taylor@trafford.gov.uk

Waste Management: Mr Gary Taylor, Waste Manager, Carrington Depot, 148 Manchester Road, Carrington, Manchester M31 4QN ☎ 0161 912 4912 🖷 0161 912 5705 🖱 gary.taylor@trafford.gov.uk

COUNCILLORS

***Mayor* Holden**, John (CON - St. Mary's)
john.holden@trafford.gov.uk

***Deputy Mayor* Lloyd**, Judith (LAB - Longford)
judith.lloyd@trafford.gov.uk

***Leader of the Council* Anstee**, Stephen (CON - Broadheath)
stephen.anstee@trafford.gov.uk

***Deputy Leader of the Council* Young**, Michael (CON - Altrincham)
michael.young@trafford.gov.uk

***Group Leader* Bowker**, Ray (LD - Village)
ray.bowker@trafford.gov.uk

***Group Leader* Western**, Andrew (LAB - Priory)
andrew.western@trafford.gov.uk

Acton, David (LAB - Gorse Hill)
david.acton@trafford.gov.uk

Adshead, Stephen (LAB - Stretford)
stephen.adshead@trafford.gov.uk

Anstee, Sean (CON - Bowdon)
sean.anstee@trafford.gov.uk

Barclay, Karen (CON - Bowdon)
karen.barclay@trafford.gov.uk

Baugh, Jane (LAB - Priory)
jane.baugh@trafford.gov.uk

Bennett, Joanne (LAB - Sale Moor)
joanne.bennett@trafford.gov.uk

Blackburn, Linda (CON - Davyhulme East)
linda.blackburn@trafford.gov.uk

Boyes, Chris (CON - Brooklands)
chris.boyes@trafford.gov.uk

Brophy, Jane (LD - Timperley)
jane.brophy@trafford.gov.uk

Brotherton, Barry (LAB - Priory)
barry.brotherton@trafford.gov.uk

Bruer-Morris, Angela (CON - Timperley)
angela.bruer-morris@trafford.gov.uk

Bunting, Daniel (CON - St. Mary's)
dan.bunting@trafford.gov.uk

Butt, Dylan (CON - Hale Barns)
dylan.butt@trafford.gov.uk

Candish, Chris (CON - Hale Central)
chris.candish@trafford.gov.uk

Carter, Karina (LAB - Bucklow St. Martins)
karina.carter@trafford.gov.uk

Cawdrey, Mark (CON - Davyhulme East)
mark.cawdrey@trafford.gov.uk

Chilton, Rob (CON - St. Mary's)
robert.chilton@trafford.gov.uk

Cordingley, Mike (LAB - Gorse Hill)
michael.cordingley@trafford.gov.uk

Cornes, Michael (CON - Davyhulme East)
michael.cornes@trafford.gov.uk

Coupe, Jonathan (CON - Flixton)
jonathan.coupe@trafford.gov.uk

Dagnall, Louise (LAB - Broadheath)
louise.dagnall@trafford.gov.uk

Dixon, Pamela (CON - Brooklands)
pamela.dixon@trafford.gov.uk

Duffield, Anne (LAB - Longford)
anne.duffield@trafford.gov.uk

Evans, Nathan (CON - Timperley)
nathan.evans@trafford.gov.uk

Evans, Laura (CON - Village)
laura.evans@trafford.gov.uk

Fishwick, Tony (LD - Village)
tony.fishwick@trafford.gov.uk

Freeman, Mike (LAB - Sale Moor)
mike.freeman@trafford.gov.uk

Gratix, Philip (LAB - Sale Moor)
philip.gratix@trafford.gov.uk

Harding, Joanne (LAB - Urmston)
joanne.harding@trafford.gov.uk

Hopps, David (CON - Brooklands)
david.hopps@trafford.gov.uk

Hyman, Michael (CON - Bowdon)
michael.hyman@trafford.gov.uk

Hynes, Catherine (LAB - Urmston)
catherine.hynes@trafford.gov.uk

Jarman, David (LAB - Longford)
david.jarman@trafford.gov.uk

Lally, Paul (CON - Flixton)
paul.lally@trafford.gov.uk

Lamb, John (CON - Ashton upon Mersey)
john.lamb@trafford.gov.uk

Malik, Ejaz (LAB - Clifford)
ejaz.malik@trafford.gov.uk

Mitchell, Alan (CON - Hale Central)
alan.mitchell@trafford.gov.uk

Myers, Patrick (CON - Hale Barns)
patrick.myers@trafford.gov.uk

O'Sullivan, Dolores (LAB - Stretford)
dolores.osullivan@trafford.gov.uk

Platt, Ian (LAB - Bucklow St. Martins)
ian.platt@trafford.gov.uk

Procter, Kevin (LAB - Urmston)
kevin.procter@trafford.gov.uk

Reilly, June (CON - Davyhulme West)
june.reilly@trafford.gov.uk

Reilly, John (CON - Davyhulme West)
john.reilly@trafford.gov.uk

Rigby, Brian (CON - Ashton upon Mersey)
brian.rigby@trafford.gov.uk

Ross, Tom (LAB - Stretford)
tom.ross@trafford.gov.uk

Sephton, Matthew (CON - Altrincham)
matthew.sephton@trafford.gov.uk

Sharp, Bernard (CON - Hale Barns)
bernard.sharp@trafford.gov.uk

Shaw, Brian (CON - Davyhulme West)
brian.shaw@trafford.gov.uk

Smith, John (LAB - Bucklow St. Martins)
john.smith@trafford.gov.uk

Stennett, Whit (LAB - Clifford)
whit.stennett@trafford.gov.uk

Taylor, Sophie (LAB - Clifford)
sophie.taylor@trafford.gov.uk

Walsh, Laurence (LAB - Gorse Hill)
laurence.walsh@trafford.gov.uk

Ward, Vivienne (CON - Flixton)
viv.ward@trafford.gov.uk

Western, Denise (LAB - Broadheath)
denise.western@trafford.gov.uk

Whetton, Michael (CON - Ashton upon Mersey)
michael.whetton@trafford.gov.uk

Williams, Alex (CON - Altrincham)
alex.williams@trafford.gov.uk

Young, Patricia (CON - Hale Central)
patricia.young@trafford.gov.uk

POLITICAL COMPOSITION

CON: 34, LAB: 26, LD: 3

COMMITTEE CHAIRS

Audit: Mr Alan Mitchell

Licensing: Mr Michael Whetton

Planning Development: Mrs Vivienne Ward

Tunbridge Wells — D

Tunbridge Wells Borough Council, Town Hall, Tunbridge Wells TN1 1RS
☎ 01892 526121 🖷 01892 534227 ✉ info@tunbridgewells.gov.uk
🖳 www.tunbridgewells.gov.uk

FACTS AND FIGURES

Parliamentary Constituencies: Tunbridge Wells
EU Constituencies: South East
Election Frequency: Elections are by thirds

PRINCIPAL OFFICERS

Chief Executive: Mr William Benson, Chief Executive, Town Hall, Tunbridge Wells TN1 1RS ☎ 01892 526121
✉ william.benson@tunbridgewells.gov.uk

Deputy Chief Executive: Mr Jonathan MacDonald, Deputy Chief Executive, Town Hall, Tunbridge Wells TN1 1RS ☎ 01892 526121
✉ jonathan.macdonald@tunbridgewells.gov.uk

Senior Management: Mr Lee Colyer, Finance Director & S151 Officer, Town Hall, Tunbridge Wells TN1 1RS ☎ 01892 526121
✉ lee.colyer@tunbridgewells.gov.uk

Architect, Building / Property Services: Mr Keith Delves, Facilities Management Surveyor, Town Hall, Tunbridge Wells TN1 1RS ☎ 01892 526121 ✉ keith.delves@tunbridgewells.gov.uk

Building Control: Mr Patrick Arthur, Building Control Team Leader, Town Hall, Tunbridge Wells TN1 1RS ☎ 01892 554116
✉ patrick.arthur@tunbridgewells.gov.uk

TUNBRIDGE WELLS

PR / Communications: Ms Lizzie Goodwin, Communications Manager, Town Hall, Tunbridge Wells TN1 1RS ☎ 01892 554273 🖷 01892 534227 ✉ lizzie.goodwin@tunbridgewells.gov.uk

Community Safety: Mr Terry Hughes, Community Safety Manager, Town Hall, Tunbridge Wells TN1 1RS ☎ 01892 554273 ✉ terry.hughes@tunbridgewells.gov.uk

Computer Management: Mr Andrew Cole, Head of ICT Shared Services, Maidstone House, King Street, Maidstone ME15 6JQ ✉ andrew.cole@tunbridgewells.gov.uk

Customer Service: Mrs Denise Shortall, Customer Service & Gateway Manager, Town Hall, Tunbridge Wells TN1 1RS ☎ 01892 554218 ✉ denise.shortall@tunbridgewells.gov.uk

Customer Service: Ms Ingrid Weatherup, Corporate Complaints & FOI Officer, Town Hall, Tunbridge Wells TN1 1RS ☎ 01895 554077 ✉ ingrid.weatherup@tunbridgewells.gov.uk

Economic Development: Ms Hilary Smith, Economic Development Manager, Town Hall, Tunbridge Wells TN1 1RS ☎ 01454 554433 ✉ hilary.smith@tunbridgewells.gov.uk

E-Government: Mr Andrew Cole, Head of ICT Shared Services, Maidstone House, King Street, Maidstone ME15 6JQ ✉ andrew.cole@tunbridgewells.gov.uk

Electoral Registration: Miss Louise Simmons, Senior Elections Officer, Town Hall, Tunbridge Wells TN1 1RS ☎ 01892 554106 ✉ louise.simmons@tunbridgewells.gov.uk

Environmental / Technical Services: Mr Gary Stevenson, Head of Environment & Street Scene, Town Hall, Tunbridge Wells TN1 1RS ☎ 01892 554014 ✉ gary.stevenson@tunbridgewells.gov.uk

Environmental Health: Mr Gary Stevenson, Head of Environment & Street Scene, Town Hall, Tunbridge Wells TN1 1RS ☎ 01892 554014 ✉ gary.stevenson@tunbridgewells.gov.uk

Estates, Property & Valuation: Mrs Diane Brady, Property & Estates Manager, Town Hall, Tunbridge Wells TN1 1RS ☎ 01892 526121 ✉ diana.brady@tunbridgewells.gov.uk

Finance: Mr Lee Colyer, Finance Director & S151 Officer, Town Hall, Tunbridge Wells TN1 1RS ☎ 01892 526121 ✉ lee.colyer@tunbridgewells.gov.uk

Grounds Maintenance: Mr Peter Every, Parks & Sports Team Leader, Town Hall, Tunbridge Wells TN1 1RS ☎ 01892 526121 ✉ peter.every@tunbridgewells.gov.uk

Home Energy Conservation: Ms Karin Grey, Sustainability Manager, Town Hall, Tunbridge Wells TN1 1RS ☎ 01892 554240 ✉ karin.grey@tunbridgewells.gov.uk

Housing: Mr Kevin Hetherington, Head of Communities & Wellbeing, Town Hall, Tunbridge Wells TN1 1RS ☎ 01892 526121 ✉ kevin.hetherington@tunbridgewells.gov.uk

Legal: Mr John Scarborough, Head of Legal Services, Town Hall, Tunbridge Wells TN1 1RS ☎ 01795 417527 ✉ john.scarborough@midkent.gov.uk

Leisure and Cultural Services: Mr Kevin Hetherington, Head of Communities & Wellbeing, Town Hall, Tunbridge Wells TN1 1RS ☎ 01892 526121 ✉ kevin.hetherington@tunbridgewells.gov.uk

Licensing: Mrs Claire Perry, Licensing Partnership Manager, Council Offices, Argyle Road, Sevenoaks TN13 1HG ☎ 01732 227325; 07970 731616 ✉ claire.perry@tunbridgewells.gov.uk

Member Services: Mrs Wendy Newton-May, Democratic Services Team Leader, Town Hall, Tunbridge Wells TN1 1RS ☎ 01892 554179 ✉ wendy.newton-may@tunbridgewells.gov.uk

Parking: Ms Rosemarie Bennett, Parking Manager, Town Hall, Tunbridge Wells TN1 1RS ☎ 01892 554082 ✉ rosemarie.bennett@tunbridgewells.gov.uk

Personnel / HR: Mrs Nicky Carter, HR Manager, Town Hall, Tunbridge Wells TN1 1RS ☎ 01892 526121 ✉ nicky.carter@tunbridgewells.gov.uk

Planning: Mrs Jane Lynch, Head of Planning Services, Town Hall, Tunbridge Wells TN1 1RS ☎ 01892 526121 ✉ jane.lynch@tunbridgewells.gov.uk

Recycling & Waste Minimisation: Mr Edwin Burgess, Waste & Street Care Manager, Town Hall, Tunbridge Wells TN1 1RS ☎ 01892 526121 ✉ edwin.burgess@tunbridgewells.gov.uk

Regeneration: Mr David Candlin, Head of Economic Development, Town Hall, Tunbridge Wells TN1 1RS ☎ 01892 554038 🖷 01892 554023 ✉ david.candlin@tunbridgewells.gov.uk

Staff Training: Mrs Nicky Carter, HR Manager, Town Hall, Tunbridge Wells TN1 1RS ☎ 01892 526121 ✉ nicky.carter@tunbridgewells.gov.uk

Street Scene: Mr Gary Stevenson, Head of Environment & Street Scene, Town Hall, Tunbridge Wells TN1 1RS ☎ 01892 554014 ✉ gary.stevenson@tunbridgewells.gov.uk

Tourism: Mrs Stephanie Covey, Tourist Information Supervisor, Town Hall, Tunbridge Wells TN1 1RS ☎ 01892 526121 ✉ stephanie.covey@tunbridgewells.gov.uk

Transport Planner: Mr Bartholomew Wren, Economic Development Officer, Town Hall, Tunbridge Wells TN1 1RS ☎ 01892 526121 ✉ bartholomew.wren@tunbridgewells.gov.uk

Waste Collection and Disposal: Mr Edwin Burgess, Waste & Street Care Manager, Town Hall, Tunbridge Wells TN1 1RS ☎ 01892 526121 ✉ edwin.burgess@tunbridgwells.gov.uk

COUNCILLORS

***Mayor* Elliot**, David (CON - Southborough North)
david.elliott@tunbridgewells.gov.uk

***Deputy Mayor* Neve**, David (LD - St James')
david.neve@tunbridgewells.gov.uk

***Leader of the Council* Jukes**, David (CON - Speldhurst and Bidborough)
david.jukes@tunbridgewells.gov.uk

Backhouse, Bob (CON - Sherwood)
bob.backhouse@tunbridgewells.gov.uk

Barrington-King, Paul (CON - Pembury)
paul.barrington-king@tunbridgewells.gov.uk

Basu, Ronen (CON - Culverden)
ronen.basu@tunbridgewells.gov.uk

Bland, Godfrey (CON - Hawkhurst and Sandhurst)
godfrey.bland@tunbridgewells.gov.uk

Bulman, Peter (CON - Park)
peter.bulman@tunbridgewells.gov.uk

Chapelard, Ben (LD - St James')
ben.chapelard@tunbridgewells.gov.uk

Cobbold, Barbara (CON - Broadwater)
barbara.cobbold@tunbridgewells.gov.uk

Dawlings, Tom (CON - Benenden and Cranbrook)
tom.dawlings@tunbridgewells.gov.uk

Gray, Nathan (CON - Hawkhurst and Sandhurst)
nathan.gray@tunbridgewells.gov.uk

Hall, Linda (CON - Benenden and Cranbrook)
linda.hall@tunbridgewels.gov.uk

Hamilton, Sarah (CON - Paddock Wood (East))
sarah.hamilton@tunbridgewells.gov.uk

Hannam, James (CON - Frittenden & Sissinghurst)
james.hannam@tunbridgewells.gov.uk

Hastie, Edmund (CON - Goudhurst and Lamberhurst)
edmund.hastie@tunbridgewells.gov.uk

Heasman, Lawrence (CON - Pantiles and St Mark's)
lawrence.heasman@tunbridgewells.gov.uk

Hills, Bill (CON - Paddock Wood (East))
bill.hills@tunbridgewells.gov.uk

Holden, Sean (CON - Benenden and Cranbrook)
sean.holden@tunbridgewells.gov.uk

Horwood, Len (CON - Pantiles and St Mark's)
len.horwood@tunbridgewells.gov.uk

Huggett, Thelma (CON - Rusthall)
thelma.huggett@tunbrigewell.gov.uk

Jamil, Nasir (CON - St John's)
nasir.jamil@tunbridgewells.gov.uk

Lewis, Alain (LAB - Southborough and High Brooms)
alain.lewis@tunbridgewells.gov.uk

Lewis-Grey, Alex (CON - Culverden)
alex.lewis-gray@tunbridgewells.gov.uk

March, Jane (CON - Brenchley and Horsmonden)
jane.march@tunbridgewells.gov.uk

McDermott, Alan (CON - Brenchley and Horsmonden)
alan.mcdermott@tunbridgewells.gov.uk

Moore, Tracy (CON - Park)
tracy.moore@tunbridgewells.gov.uk

Munn, Graham (LAB - Southborough and High Brooms)
graham.munn@tunbridgewells.gov.uk

Noakes, Barry (CON - Goudhurst and Lamberhurst)
barry.noakes@tunbridgewells.gov.uk

Nuttall, Sue (CON - Pembury)
sue.nuttall@tunbridgewells.gov.uk

Oakford, Peter (CON - St John's)
peter.oakford@tunbridgewells.gov.uk

Palmer, Beverley (CON - Hawkhurst and Sandhurst)
beverley.palmer@tunbridgewells.gov.uk

Patterson, Hugh (LD - Capel)
hugh.patterson@tunbridgewells.gov.uk

Podbury, Joy (CON - Rusthall)
joy.podbury@tunbridgewells.gov.uk

Rankin, Catherine (CON - Park)
catherine.rankin@tunbrigewells.gov.uk

Scholes, James (CON - Pantiles and St Mark's)
james.scholes@tunbridgewells.gov.uk

Scott, David (CON - St John's)
david.scott@tunbridgewells.gov.uk

Simmons, Joe (CON - Southborough North)
joe.simmons@tunbridgewells.gov.uk

Sloan, Don (CON - Culverden)
don.sloan@tunbridgewells.gv.uk

Soyke, Julia (CON - Speldhurst and Bidborough)
julia.soyke@tunbridgewells.gov.uk

Stanyer, Julian (CON - Speldhurst and Bidborough)
julian.stanyer@tunbridgewells.gov.uk

Stewart, Claire (CON - Paddock Wood (West))
claire.stewart@tunbridgewell.gov.uk

Thomas, Elizabeth (CON - Paddock Wood (West))
elizabeth.thomas@tunbridgewells.gov.uk

Tompsett, Mike (IND - Pembury)
mike.tompsett@tunbridewells.gov.uk

Uddin, Zulhash (CON - Southborough and High Brooms)
zulhash.uddin@tunbridgewells.gov.uk

Weatherly, Lynne (CON - Sherwood)
lynne.weatherly@tunbridge.gov.uk

Williams, Frank (CON - Sherwood)
frank.williams@tunbridgewells.gov.uk

Woodward, Chris (CON - Broadwater)

POLITICAL COMPOSITION

CON: 42, LD: 3, LAB: 2, IND: 1

COMMITTEE CHAIRS

Finance: Mr Paul Barrington-King

Licensing: Mr Bob Backhouse

Planning: Mrs Julia Soyke

Uttlesford D

Uttlesford District Council, Council Offices, London Road, Saffron Walden CB11 4ER
☎ 01799 510510 🖷 01799 510550 postroom@uttlesford.gov.uk
www.uttlesford.gov.uk

UTTLESFORD

FACTS AND FIGURES

Parliamentary Constituencies: Saffron Walden
EU Constituencies: Eastern
Election Frequency: Elections are of whole council

PRINCIPAL OFFICERS

Chief Executive: Mr John Mitchell, Chief Executive, Council Offices, London Road, Saffron Walden CB11 4ER ☎ 01799 510510 🖷 01799 510550 🖱 jmitchell@uttlesford.gov.uk

Assistant Chief Executive: Mr Michael Perry, Assistant Chief Executive - Legal, Council Offices, London Road, Saffron Walden CB11 4ER ☎ 01799 510416 🖷 01799 510550 🖱 mperry@uttlesford.gov.uk

Senior Management: Mr Roger Harborough, Director of Public Services, Council Offices, London Road, Saffron Walden CB11 4ER ☎ 01799 510457 🖷 01799 510550 🖱 rharborough@uttlesford.gov.uk

Senior Management: Mr Adrian Webb, Director of Finance & Corporate Services, Council Offices, London Road, Saffron Walden CB11 4ER ☎ 01799 510421 🖷 01799 510550 🖱 awebb@uttlesford.gov.uk

Access Officer / Social Services (Disability): Ms Sue Locke, Projects Officer, Council Offices, London Road, Saffron Walden CB11 4ER ☎ 01799 510537 🖷 01799 510534 🖱 slocke@uttlesford.gov.uk

Building Control: Mr John Farnell, Building Control Team Leader, Council Offices, London Road, Saffron Walden CB11 4ER ☎ 01799 510538 🖷 01799 510550 🖱 jfarnell@uttlesford.gov.uk

Building Control: Mr Andrew Taylor, Assistant Director of Planning & Building Control, Council Offices, London Road, Saffron Walden CB11 4ER ☎ 01799 510601 🖷 01799 510550 🖱 ataylor@uttlesford.gov.uk

Children / Youth Services: Ms Gaynor Bradley, Community Partnerships Manager, Council Offices, London Road, Saffron Walden CB11 4ER ☎ 01799 510348 🖷 01799 510550 🖱 gbradley@uttlesford.gov.uk

PR / Communications: Mr Richard Auty, Assistant Director of Corporate Services, Council Offices, London Road, Saffron Walden CB11 4ER ☎ 01799 510500 🖷 01799 510550 🖱 rauty@uttlesford.gov.uk

Community Safety: Ms Gaynor Bradley, Community Partnerships Manager, Council Offices, London Road, Saffron Walden CB11 4ER ☎ 01799 510348 🖷 01799 510550 🖱 gbradley@uttlesford.gov.uk

Computer Management: Mr Adrian Webb, Director of Finance & Corporate Services, Council Offices, London Road, Saffron Walden CB11 4ER ☎ 01799 510421 🖷 01799 510550 🖱 awebb@uttlesford.gov.uk

Computer Management: Mrs N Wittman, IT & Corporate Support Team Manager, Council Offices, London Road, Saffron Walden CB11 4ER ☎ 01799 510413 🖷 01799 510550 🖱 nwittman@uttlesford.gov.uk

Corporate Services: Mr Richard Auty, Assistant Director of Corporate Services, Council Offices, London Road, Saffron Walden CB11 4ER ☎ 01799 510500 🖷 01799 510550 🖱 rauty@uttlesford.gov.uk

Corporate Services: Mr Adrian Webb, Director of Finance & Corporate Services, Council Offices, London Road, Saffron Walden CB11 4ER ☎ 01799 510421 🖷 01799 510550 🖱 awebb@uttlesford.gov.uk

Customer Service: Mr Richard Auty, Assistant Director of Corporate Services, Council Offices, London Road, Saffron Walden CB11 4ER ☎ 01799 510500 🖷 01799 510550 🖱 rauty@uttlesford.gov.uk

Economic Development: Mr Simon Jackson, Economic Development Officer, Council Offices, London Road, Saffron Walden CB11 4ER ☎ 01799 510512 🖷 01799 510550 🖱 sjackson@uttlesford.gov.uk

E-Government: Mr Adrian Webb, Director of Finance & Corporate Services, Council Offices, London Road, Saffron Walden CB11 4ER ☎ 01799 510421 🖷 01799 510550 🖱 awebb@uttlesford.gov.uk

Electoral Registration: Mr Peter Snow, Democratic & Electoral Services Manager, Council Offices, London Road, Saffron Walden CB11 4ER ☎ 01799 510431 🖷 01799 510550 🖱 psnow@uttlesford.gov.uk

Emergency Planning: Mrs Lisa Lipscombe, Emergency Planning Officer, Council Offices, London Road, Saffron Walden CB11 4ER ☎ 01799 510624 🖷 01799 510550 🖱 llipscombe@uttlesford.gov.uk

Energy Management: Mr Andrew Taylor, Assistant Director of Planning & Building Control, Council Offices, London Road, Saffron Walden CB11 4ER ☎ 01799 510601 🖷 01799 510550 🖱 ataylor@uttlesford.gov.uk

Environmental / Technical Services: Mr Roger Harborough, Director of Public Services, Council Offices, London Road, Saffron Walden CB11 4ER ☎ 01799 510457 🖷 01799 510550 🖱 rharborough@uttlesford.gov.uk

Environmental / Technical Services: Mr Geoff Smith, Head of Environmental Health, Council Offices, London Road, Saffron Walden CB11 4ER ☎ 01799 510582 🖷 01799 510550 🖱 gsmith@uttlesford.gov.uk

Environmental Health: Mr Roger Harborough, Director of Public Services, Council Offices, London Road, Saffron Walden CB11 4ER ☎ 01799 510457 🖷 01799 510550 🖱 rharborough@uttlesford.gov.uk

Environmental Health: Mrs Roz Millership, Assistant Director of Housing & Environmental Services, Council Offices, London Road, Saffron Walden CB11 4ER ☎ 01799 510516 🖷 01799 510550 🖱 rmillership@uttlesford.gov.uk

Environmental Health: Mr Geoff Smith, Head of Environmental Health, Council Offices, London Road, Saffron Walden CB11 4ER ☎ 01799 510582 🖷 01799 510550 🖱 gsmith@uttlesford.gov.uk

European Liaison: Mr Michael Perry, Assistant Chief Executive - Legal, Council Offices, London Road, Saffron Walden CB11 4ER ☎ 01799 510416 🖷 01799 510550 🖰 mperry@uttlesford.gov.uk

Finance: Ms Angela Knight, Assistant Chief Executive - Finance, Council Offices, London Road, Saffron Walden CB11 4ER ☎ 01799 510446 🖷 01799 510550 🖰 aknight@uttlesford.gov.uk

Fleet Management: Mrs Catherine Chapman, Street Services Operations Manager, Council Offices, London Road, Saffron Walden CB11 4ER ☎ 01799 510557 🖷 01799 510550 🖰 cchapman@uttlesford.gov.uk

Grounds Maintenance: Mrs Catherine Chapman, Street Services Operations Manager, Council Offices, London Road, Saffron Walden CB11 4ER ☎ 01799 510557 🖷 01799 510550 🖰 cchapman@uttlesford.gov.uk

Health and Safety: Mr Geoff Smith, Head of Environmental Health, Council Offices, London Road, Saffron Walden CB11 4ER ☎ 01799 510582 🖷 01799 510550 🖰 gsmith@uttlesford.gov.uk

Home Energy Conservation: Mr John Farnell, Building Control Team Leader, Council Offices, London Road, Saffron Walden CB11 4ER ☎ 01799 510538 🖷 01799 510550 🖰 jfarnell@uttlesford.gov.uk

Housing: Mrs Roz Millership, Assistant Director of Housing & Environmental Services, Council Offices, London Road, Saffron Walden CB11 4ER ☎ 01799 510516 🖷 01799 510550 🖰 rmillership@uttlesford.gov.uk

Housing Maintenance: Mrs Roz Millership, Assistant Director of Housing & Environmental Services, Council Offices, London Road, Saffron Walden CB11 4ER ☎ 01799 510516 🖷 01799 510550 🖰 rmillership@uttlesford.gov.uk

Legal: Mr Michael Perry, Assistant Chief Executive - Legal, Council Offices, London Road, Saffron Walden CB11 4ER ☎ 01799 510416 🖷 01799 510550 🖰 mperry@uttlesford.gov.uk

Leisure and Cultural Services: Ms Gaynor Bradley, Community Partnerships Manager, Council Offices, London Road, Saffron Walden CB11 4ER ☎ 01799 510348 🖷 01799 510550 🖰 gbradley@uttlesford.gov.uk

Licensing: Mrs Amanda Turner, Licensing Officer, Council Offices, London Road, Saffron Walden CB11 4ER ☎ 01779 510613 🖷 01799 510550 🖰 aturner@uttlesford.gov.uk

Lottery Funding, Charity and Voluntary: Ms Gaynor Bradley, Community Partnerships Manager, Council Offices, London Road, Saffron Walden CB11 4ER ☎ 01799 510348 🖷 01799 510550 🖰 gbradley@uttlesford.gov.uk

Member Services: Mr Peter Snow, Democratic & Electoral Services Manager, Council Offices, London Road, Saffron Walden CB11 4ER ☎ 01799 510431 🖷 01799 510550 🖰 psnow@uttlesford.gov.uk

Parking: Mr Andrew Taylor, Assistant Director of Planning & Building Control, Council Offices, London Road, Saffron Walden CB11 4ER ☎ 01799 510601 🖷 01799 510550 🖰 ataylor@uttlesford.gov.uk

Partnerships: Mr Adrian Webb, Director of Finance & Corporate Services, Council Offices, London Road, Saffron Walden CB11 4ER ☎ 01799 510421 🖷 01799 510550 🖰 awebb@uttlesford.gov.uk

Personnel / HR: Mr Adrian Webb, Director of Finance & Corporate Services, Council Offices, London Road, Saffron Walden CB11 4ER ☎ 01799 510421 🖷 01799 510550 🖰 awebb@uttlesford.gov.uk

Planning: Mr Nigel Brown, Development Control Manager, Council Offices, London Road, Saffron Walden CB11 4ER ☎ 01799 510476 🖷 01799 510550 🖰 nbrown@uttlesford.gov.uk

Planning: Mr Roger Harborough, Director of Public Services, Council Offices, London Road, Saffron Walden CB11 4ER ☎ 01799 510457 🖷 01799 510550 🖰 rharborough@uttlesford.gov.uk

Planning: Mr Andrew Taylor, Head of Planning & Building Surveying, Council Offices, London Road, Saffron Walden CB11 4ER ☎ 01799 510510 🖷 01799 510550 🖰 ataylor@uttlesford.gov.uk

Procurement: Ms Christine Oakey, Procurement Manager, Council Offices, London Road, Saffron Walden CB11 4ER ☎ 01799 510451 🖷 01799 510550 🖰 coakey@uttlesford.gov.uk

Recycling & Waste Minimisation: Mrs Catherine Chapman, Street Services Operations Manager, Council Offices, London Road, Saffron Walden CB11 4ER ☎ 01799 510557 🖷 01799 510550 🖰 cchapman@uttlesford.gov.uk

Street Scene: Mrs Catherine Chapman, Street Services Operations Manager, Council Offices, London Road, Saffron Walden CB11 4ER ☎ 01799 510557 🖷 01799 510550 🖰 cchapman@uttlesford.gov.uk

Sustainable Communities: Mr Roger Harborough, Director of Public Services, Council Offices, London Road, Saffron Walden CB11 4ER ☎ 01799 510457 🖷 01799 510550 🖰 rharborough@uttlesford.gov.uk

Sustainable Development: Mr Roger Harborough, Director of Public Services, Council Offices, London Road, Saffron Walden CB11 4ER ☎ 01799 510457 🖷 01799 510550 🖰 rharborough@uttlesford.gov.uk

Waste Collection and Disposal: Mrs Catherine Chapman, Street Services Operations Manager, Council Offices, London Road, Saffron Walden CB11 4ER ☎ 01799 510557 🖷 01799 510550 🖰 cchapman@uttlesford.gov.uk

Waste Management: Mrs Catherine Chapman, Street Services Operations Manager, Council Offices, London Road, Saffron Walden CB11 4ER ☎ 01799 510557 🖷 01799 510550 🖰 cchapman@uttlesford.gov.uk

COUNCILLORS

***Chair* Harris**, Stephanie (CON - Fitch Green & Little Dunmow) cllrharris@uttlesford.gov.uk

***Vice-Chair* Davey**, John (CON - Great Dunmow North) cllrdavey@uttlesford.gov.uk

***Leader of the Council* Rolfe**, Howard (CON - Ashdon)
cllrrolfe@uttlesford.gov.uk

***Deputy Leader of the Council* Barker**, Susan (CON - High Easter & The Rodings)
cllrbarker@uttlesford.gov.uk

Anjum, Aisha (R - Saffron Walden (Shire))
cllranjum@uttlesford.gov.uk

Artus, Keith (CON - Broad Oak & the Hallingburys)
cllrartus@uttlesford.gov.uk

Asker, Heather (R - Saffron Walden (Castle))
cllrasker@uttlesford.gov.uk

Barker, Graham (CON - Great Dunmow South & Barnston)
cllrgbarker@uttlesford.gov.uk

Chambers, Robert (CON - Littlebury, Chesterford & Wendon Lofts)
cllrchambers@uttlesford.gov.uk

Davies, Paul (CON - Great Dunmow North)
cllrdavies@uttlesford.gov.uk

Dean, Alan (LD - Stansted North)
cllrdean@uttlesford.gov.uk

Fairhurst, Paul (R - Saffron Walden (Shire))
cllrfairhurst@uttlesford.gov.uk

Farthing, Terry (CON - Stansted South & Birchanger)
cllrfarthing@uttlesford.gov.uk

Felton, Marie (CON - Felsted & Stebbing)
cllrfelton@uttlesford.gov.uk

Foley, Martin (LD - Thaxted & The Eastons)
cllrfoley@uttlesford.gov.uk

Freeman, John (CON - Thaxted & The Eastons)
cllrjfreeman@uttlesford.gov.uk

Freeman, Richard (R - Saffron Walden (Castle))
cllrfreeman@uttlesford.gov.uk

Gleeson, Rory (LD - Elsenham & Henham)
cllrgleeson@uttlesford.gov.uk

Goddard, Thom (CON - Stansted South & Birchanger)
cllrgoddard@uttlesford.gov.uk

Gordon, Jim (CON - Takeley)
cllrgordon@uttlesford.gov.uk

Hargreaves, Neil (R - Newport)
cllrhargreaves@uttlesford.gov.uk

Hicks, Eric (CON - Great Dunmow South & Barnston)
cllrhicks@uttlesford.gov.uk

Howell, Simon (CON - The Sampfords)
cllrhowell@uttlesford.gov.uk

Jones, Derek (CON - Takeley)
cllrdjones@uttlesford.gov.uk

Knight, Tina (CON - Debden & Wimbish)
cllrknight@uttlesford.gov.uk

Lemon, Mark (IND - Hatfield)
cllrlemon@uttlesford.gov.uk

Light, Barbara (R - Saffron Walden (Audley))
cllrlight@uttlesford.gov.uk

Lodge, John (R - Saffron Walden (Shire))
cllrlodge@uttlesford.gov.uk

Loughlin, Janice (LD - Stort Valley)
cllrloughlin@uttlesford.gov.uk

Mills, Alan (CON - Felsted & Stebbing)
cllrmills@uttlesford.gov.uk

Morris, Sharon (R - Saffron Walden (Audley))
cllrmorris@uttlesford.gov.uk

Oliver, Edward (CON - Clavering)
cllroliver@uttlesford.gov.uk

Parr, Elizabeth (LD - Elsenham & Henham)
cllrparr@uttlesford.gov.uk

Parry, Joanna (R - Newport)
cllrparry@uttlesford.gov.uk

Ranger, Vic (CON - Great Dunmow South & Barnston)
cllrranger@uttlesford.gov.uk

Redfern, Julie (CON - Littlebury, Chesterford & Wendon Lofts)
cllrredfern@uttlesford.gov.uk

Ryles, Howard (CON - Takeley)
cllrryles@uttlesford.gov.uk

Snell, Geoffrey (LD - Stansted North)
cllrsnell@uttlesford.gov.uk

Wells, Lesley (CON - Broad Oak & the Hallingburys)
cllrwells@uttlesford.gov.uk

POLITICAL COMPOSITION
CON: 23, R: 9, LD: 6, IND: 1

COMMITTEE CHAIRS
Audit: Mr Edward Oliver

Planning: Mr Vic Ranger

Vale of Glamorgan W

Vale of Glamorgan Council, Civic Offices, Holton Road, Barry CF63 4RU
☎ 01446 700111 🖷 01446 745566 ✉ enquiries@valeofglamorgan.gov.uk
💻 www.valeofglamorgan.gov.uk

FACTS AND FIGURES
Parliamentary Constituencies: Cardiff South and Penarth, Vale of Glamorgan
EU Constituencies: Wales
Election Frequency: Elections are of whole council

PRINCIPAL OFFICERS
Chief Executive: Mr Rob Thomas, Managing Director, Civic Offices, Holton Road, Barry CF63 4RU ☎ 01446 704630 ✉ drthomas@valeofglamorgan.gov.uk

Senior Management: Mr Phil Evans, Director of Social Services, Dock Offices, Subway Road, Barry CF63 4RT ☎ 01446 704676 🖷 01446 704839 ✉ pjevans@valeofglamorgan.gov.uk

Senior Management: Mrs Jennifer Hill, Director of Learning & Skills, Provincial House, Kendrick Road, Barry CF62 8BF ☎ 01446 709100 🖷 01446 701642 ✉ jhill@valeofglamorgan.gov.uk

Senior Management: Mr Miles Punter, Director of Environment & Housing Services, The Alps, Quarry Road, Wenvoe CF5 6AA ☎ 029 2067 3101 🖷 029 2067 3102 ✉ mepunter@valeofglamorgan.gov.uk

Access Officer / Social Services (Disability): Mrs Linda Brown, Joint Corporate Equality Officer, Civic Offices, Holton Road, Barry CF63 4RU ☎ 01446 709362 ✉ ljbrown@valeofglamorgan.gov.uk

Access Officer / Social Services (Disability): Ms Nicola Hinton, Joint Corporate Equality Officer, Civic Offices, Holton Road, Barry CF63 4RU ☎ 01446 709362 ✉ nhinton@valeofglamorgan.gov.uk

Architect, Building / Property Services: Ms Jane Wade, Operational Manager - Property Services, Civic Buildings, Holton Road, Barry CF63 4RU ☎ 01446 709270 ✉ jlwade@valeofglamorgan.gov.uk

Best Value: Mr Huw Isaac, Head of Performance & Development, Civic Offices, Holton Road, Barry CF63 4RU ☎ 01446 709760 ✉ hisaac@valeofglamorgan.gov.uk

Catering Services: Mrs Carole Tyley, Catering Manager, Provincial House, Kendrick Road, Barry CF62 8BF ☎ 029 2067 3037 ✉ ctyley@valeofglamorgan.gov.uk

Children / Youth Services: Ms Rachel Evans, Head of Children & Young People's Services, Dock Offices, Subway Road, Barry CF63 4RT ☎ 01446 704792 ✉ rjevans@valeofglamorgan.gov.uk

Civil Registration: Mrs Tania Carter, Registration Manager / Superintendent Registrar, Civic Offices, Holton Road, Barry CF63 4RU ☎ 01446 709166 🖷 01446 709502 ✉ tcarter@valeofglamorgan.gov.uk

PR / Communications: Mr Rob Jones, Senior Media Officer, Civic Offices, Holton Road, Barry CF63 4RU ☎ 01446 709530 ✉ rajones@valeofglamorgan.gov.uk

Community Planning: Mr Huw Isaac, Head of Performance & Development, Civic Offices, Holton Road, Barry CF63 4RU ☎ 01446 709760 ✉ hisaac@valeofglamorgan.gov.uk

Community Safety: Mr Dave Holland, Head of Shared Regulatory Services, Civic Offices, Holton Road, Barry CF63 4RU ☎ 01446 709720 ✉ dholland@valeofglamorgan.gov.uk

Computer Management: Mr David Vining, Head of Strategic ICT, Civic Offices, Holton Road, Barry CF63 4RU ☎ 01446 709382 ✉ djvining@valeofglamorgan.gov.uk

Consumer Protection and Trading Standards: Ms Christina Roberts, Operational Manager - Commercial Services, Civic Offices, Holton Road, Barry CF63 4RU ☎ 01446 709344 🖷 01446 709768 ✉ croberts@valeofglamorgan.gov.uk

Customer Service: Mr Tony Curliss, Operational Manager - Customer Relations, C1V, Barry Leisure Centre, Greenwood Street, Barry CF63 4JJ ☎ 01446 729500 ✉ tcurliss@valeofglamorgan.gov.uk

Direct Labour: Mr Miles Punter, Director of Environment & Housing Services, The Alps, Quarry Road, Wenvoe CF5 6AA ☎ 029 2067 3101 🖷 029 2067 3102 ✉ mepunter@valeofglamorgan.gov.uk

Education: Mrs Jennifer Hill, Director of Learning & Skills, Provincial House, Kendrick Road, Barry CF62 8BF ☎ 01446 709100 🖷 01446 701642 ✉ jhill@valeofglamorgan.gov.uk

E-Government: Mr Huw Isaac, Head of Performance & Development, Civic Offices, Holton Road, Barry CF63 4RU ☎ 01446 709760 ✉ hisaac@valeofglamorgan.gov.uk

Electoral Registration: Miss Rebecca Light, Electoral & Members' Services Team Leader, Civic Offices, Holton Road, Barry CF63 4RU ☎ 01446 709304 ✉ rmlight@valeofglamorgan.gov.uk

Emergency Planning: Ms Debbie Spargo, Principal Civic Protection Officer, The Alps, Quarry Road, Wenvoe, Barry CF5 6AA ☎ 029 2067 3041 ✉ daspargo@valeofglamorgan.gov.uk

Energy Management: Mr David Powell, Energy Manager, Civic Offices, Holton Road, Barry CF63 4RU ☎ 01446 709576 ✉ dpowell@valeofglamorgan.gov.uk

Environmental / Technical Services: Mr Miles Punter, Director of Environment & Housing Services, The Alps, Quarry Road, Wenvoe CF5 6AA ☎ 029 2067 3101 🖷 029 2067 3102 ✉ mepunter@valeofglamorgan.gov.uk

Environmental Health: Mr Dave Holland, Head of Shared Regulatory Services, Civic Offices, Holton Road, Barry CF63 4RU ☎ 01446 709720 ✉ dholland@valeofglamorgan.gov.uk

Estates, Property & Valuation: Ms Jane Wade, Operational Manager - Property Services, Civic Buildings, Holton Road, Barry CF63 4RU ☎ 01446 709270 ✉ jlwade@valeofglamorgan.gov.uk

Events Manager: Ms Sarah Jones, Events Officer, Dock Office, Subway Road, Barry CF63 4RT ☎ 01446 704737 🖷 01446 704892 ✉ sejones@valeofglamorgan.gov.uk

Facilities: Mr Patrick Carroll, Facilities Manager, Civic Offices, Holton Road, Barry CF63 4RU ☎ 01446 709243 🖷 01446 709226 ✉ pjcarroll@valeofglamorgan.gov.uk

Fleet Management: Mr Miles Punter, Director of Environment & Housing Services, The Alps, Quarry Road, Wenvoe CF5 6AA ☎ 029 2067 3101 🖷 029 2067 3102 ✉ mepunter@valeofglamorgan.gov.uk

Health and Safety: Mr Richard Stopgate, Principal Corporate Health & Safety Officer, The Alps, Quarry Road, Wenvoe, Cardiff CF5 6AA ☎ 029 2067 3263 ✉ rdstopgate@valeofglamorgan.gov.uk

Home Energy Conservation: Mr David Powell, Energy Manager, Civic Offices, Holton Road, Barry CF63 4RU ☎ 01446 709576 ✉ dpowell@valeofglamorgan.gov.uk

Housing: Ms Hayley Selway, Head of Housing & Building Services, The Alps, Quarry Road, Wenvoe, Cardiff CF5 6AA ☎ 029 2067 3124 ✉ hselway@valeofglamorgan.gov.uk

Housing Maintenance: Ms Hayley Selway, Head of Housing & Building Services, The Alps, Quarry Road, Wenvoe, Cardiff CF5 6AA ☎ 029 2067 3124 ✉ hselway@valeofglamorgan.gov.uk

Legal: Ms Debbie Marles, Head of Legal Services, Civic Offices, Holton Road, Barry CF63 4RU ☎ 01446 709402 ✉ dmarles@valeofglamorgan.gov.uk

Licensing: Ms Amanda Ewington, Licensing Team Leader, Civic Offices, Holton Road, Barry CF63 4RU ☎ 01446 709782 ✉ ajewington@valeofglamorgan.gov.uk

Lifelong Learning: Mrs Jennifer Hill, Director of Learning & Skills, Provincial House, Kendrick Road, Barry CF62 8BF ☎ 01446 709100 🖷 01446 701642 ✉ jhill@valeofglamorgan.gov.uk

Member Services: Miss Rebecca Light, Electoral & Members' Services Team Leader, Civic Offices, Holton Road, Barry CF63 4RU ☎ 01446 709304 ✉ rmlight@valeofglamorgan.gov.uk

Partnerships: Mrs Helen Moses, Strategy & Sustainability Manager, Barry Fire Station, Port Road West, Barry CF62 3AZ ☎ 01446 450205 ✉ hmoses@valeofglamorgan.gov.uk

Personnel / HR: Mr Reuben Bergman, Head of Human Resources, Provincial House, Kendrick Road, Barry CF62 8BF ☎ 01446 709357 🖷 01446 709792 ✉ rbergman@valeofglamorgan.gov.uk

Planning: Mr Miles Punter, Director of Environment & Housing Services, The Alps, Quarry Road, Wenvoe CF5 6AA ☎ 029 2067 3101 🖷 029 2067 3102 ✉ mepunter@valeofglamorgan.gov.uk

Procurement: Mrs Carys Lord, Head of Finance, Civic Offices, Holton Road, Barry CF63 4RU ☎ 01446 709254 ✉ cllord@valeofglamorgan.gov.uk

Public Libraries: Mr Andrew Borsden, Lead Officer - Youth & Community Learning, Provincial House, Kendrick Road, Barry CF62 8BF ☎ 01446 709148 ✉ amborsden@valeofglamorgan.gov.uk

Regeneration: Mr Miles Punter, Director of Environment & Housing Services, The Alps, Quarry Road, Wenvoe CF5 6AA ☎ 029 2067 3101 🖷 029 2067 3102 ✉ mepunter@valeofglamorgan.gov.uk

Road Safety: Ms Clare Cameron, Principal Transport & Road Safety Officer, Dock Office, Barry Docks, Barry CF63 4RT ☎ 01446 704768 ✉ ccameron@valeofglamorgan.gov.uk

Social Services: Mr Phil Evans, Director of Social Services, Dock Offices, Subway Road, Barry CF63 4RT ☎ 01446 704676 🖷 01446 704839 ✉ pjevans@valeofglamorgan.gov.uk

Social Services (Adult): Mr Lance Carver, Head of Adult Services & Locality Manager, Dock Offices, Subway Road, Barry CF63 4RT ☎ 01446 704678 🖷 01446 704839 ✉ lcarver@valeofglamorgan.gov.uk

Social Services (Children): Ms Rachel Evans, Head of Children & Young People's Services, Dock Offices, Subway Road, Barry CF63 4RT ☎ 01446 704792 ✉ rjevans@valeofglamorgan.gov.uk

Street Scene: Mr Miles Punter, Director of Environment & Housing Services, The Alps, Quarry Road, Wenvoe CF5 6AA ☎ 029 2067 3101 🖷 029 2067 3102 ✉ mepunter@valeofglamorgan.gov.uk

Sustainable Communities: Mr Miles Punter, Director of Environment & Housing Services, The Alps, Quarry Road, Wenvoe CF5 6AA ☎ 029 2067 3101 🖷 029 2067 3102 ✉ mepunter@valeofglamorgan.gov.uk

Town Centre: Miss Emma Smith, Principal Officer - Business & Employment, BSC, Innovation Quarter, Hood Road, Barry CF62 5QN ☎ 01446 704781 ✉ esmith@valeofglamorgan.gov.uk

COUNCILLORS

***Mayor* Johnson**, Frederick (LAB - Cadoc)
ftjohnson@valeofglamorgan.gov.uk

***Deputy Mayor* Wilkinson**, Margaret (LAB - Gibbonsdown)
mrwilkinson@valeofglamorgan.gov.uk

***Leader of the Council* Moore**, Neil (LAB - Cadoc)
nmoore@valeofglamorgan.gov.uk

***Deputy Leader of the Council* Egan**, Stuart (LAB - Buttrills)
scegan@valeofglamorgan.gov.uk

***Group Leader* Penrose**, Bob (IND - Sully)
bpenrose@valeofglamorgan.gov.uk

***Group Leader* Thomas**, John (CON - St. Athan)
jwthomas@valeofglamorgan.gov.uk

Bennett, Anthony (CON - Llantwit Major)

Bertin, Richard (IND - Court)
rjbertin@valeofglamorgan.gov.uk

Birch, Rhiannon (LAB - Cornerswell)
rbirch@valeofglamorgan.gov.uk

Birch, Janice (LAB - Stanwell)
jbirch@valeofglamorgan.gov.uk

Bird, Jonathan (CON - Wenvoe)
jbird@valeofglamorgan.gov.uk

Brooks, Bronwen (LAB - Court)
bbrooks@valeofglamorgan.gov.uk

Burnett, Lis (LAB - St. Augustines)
lburnett@valeofglamorgan.gov.uk

Clarke, Philip (IND - Rhoose)
pjclarke@valeofglamorgan.gov.uk

Cox, Geoffrey (CON - Cowbridge)
gacox@valeofglamorgan.gov.uk

Curtis, Robert (LAB - Gibbonsdown)
rfcurtis@valeofglamorgan.gov.uk

Curtis, Claire (LAB - Dyfan)
ccurtis@valeofglamorgan.gov.uk

Drake, Pamela (LAB - Castleland)
pdrake@valeofglamorgan.gov.uk

Drysdale, John (LAB - Illtyd)
jdrysdale@valeofglamorgan.gov.uk

Edmunds, Kate (LAB - Llandough)
kedmunds@valeofglamorgan.gov.uk

Elmore, Christopher (LAB - Castleland)
celmore@valeofglamorgan.gov.uk

Franks, Christopher (PC - Dinas Powys)
familyfranks@btinternet.com

Hacker, Eric (IND - Llantwit Major)
ehacker@valeofglamorgan.gov.uk

Hamilton, Howard (LAB - Illtyd)
hhamilton@valeofglamorgan.gov.uk

Hartrey, Val (PC - Dinas Powys)
vmhartrey@valeofglamorgan.gov.uk

Hatton, Keith (PC - Dinas Powys)
khatton@valeofglamorgan.gov.uk

Hodges, Nic (PC - Baruc)
nphodges@valeofglamorgan.gov.uk

James, Jeff (CON - Rhoose)
hjwjames@valeofglamorgan.gov.uk

Jarvie, Hunter (CON - Cowbridge)
hjarvie@valeofglamorgan.gov.uk

John, Gwyn (IND - Llantwit Major)
gjohn@valeofglamorgan.gov.uk

Johnson, Ian James (PC - Buttrills)
ljohnson@valeofglamorgan.gov.uk

Kelly- Owen, Maureen (CON - Plymouth)
mkellyowen@valeofglamorgan.gov.uk

King, Peter (LAB - Cornerswell)
pking@valeofglamorgan.gov.uk

Mahoney, Kevin (UKIP - Sully)
kpmahoney@valeofglamorgan.gov.uk

Moore, Anne (LAB - Cadoc)
ajmoore@valeofglamorgan.gov.uk

Parker, Andrew (CON - Cowbridge)
aparker@valeofglamorgan.gov.uk

Powell, Anthony (LAB - Dyfan)
agpowell@valeofglamorgan.gov.uk

Preston, Audrey (CON - St. Brides Major)

Probert, Rhona (LAB - Illtyd)
rprobert@valeofglamorgan.gov.uk

Roberts, Gwyn (LAB - St. Augustines)
groberts@valeofglamorgan.gov.uk

Thomas, Ray (CON - Llandow / Ewenny)
rathomas@valeofglamorgan.gov.uk

Traherne, Rhodri (CON - Peterston-Super-Ely)
rtraherne@valeofglamorgan.gov.uk

Wiliam, Steffan (PC - Baruc)
stwiliam@valeofglamorgan.gov.uk

Williams, Christopher (IND - Dinas Powys)
cjwilliams@valeofglamorgan.gov.uk

Williams, A Clive (CON - Plymouth)
cwilliams@valeofglamorgan.gov.uk

Williams, Edward (IND - Llantwit Major)
edwilliams@valeofglamorgan.gov.uk

Wilson, Mark (LAB - Stanwell)
mrwilson@valeofglamorgan.gov.uk

POLITICAL COMPOSITION

LAB: 21, CON: 12, IND: 7, PC: 6, UKIP: 1

COMMITTEE CHAIRS

Audit: Mr Keith Hatton

Licensing: Mr Anthony Powell

Planning: Mr Frederick Johnson

Vale of White Horse — D

Vale of White Horse District Council, Abbey House, Abbey Close, Abingdon OX14 3JE
☎ 01235 520202 🖷 01235 554960 💻 www.whitehorsedc.gov.uk

FACTS AND FIGURES

Parliamentary Constituencies: Oxford West and Abingdon, Wantage
EU Constituencies: South East
Election Frequency: Elections are of whole council

PRINCIPAL OFFICERS

Chief Executive: Mr David Buckle, Chief Executive, 135 Eastern Avenue, Milton Park, Milton, Abingdon OX14 4SB ☎ 01235 547612 david.buckle@southandvale.gov.uk

Deputy Chief Executive: Mr Steve Bishop, Strategic Director, 135 Eastern Avenue, Milton Park, Milton, Abingdon OX14 4SB ☎ 01235 540332 steve.bishop@southandvale.gov.uk

Deputy Chief Executive: Mrs Anna Robinson, Strategic Director, 135 Eastern Avenue, Milton Park, Milton, Abingdon OX14 4SB ☎ 01235 540405 anna.robinson@southandvale.gov.uk

Senior Management: Mr Andrew Down, Head of HR, IT & Technical Services, 135 Eastern Avenue, Milton Park, Milton, Abingdon OX14 4SB ☎ 01235 540372 andrew.down@southandvale.gov.uk

Senior Management: Mr Adrian Duffield, Head of Planning, 135 Eastern Avenue, Milton Park, Milton, Abingdon OX14 4SB ☎ 01235 540340 adrian.duffield@southandvale.gov.uk

Senior Management: Mr William Jacobs, Head of Finance, 135 Eastern Avenue, Milton Park, Milton, Abingdon OX14 4SB ☎ 01235 540526 william.jacobs@southandvale.gov.uk

Senior Management: Mrs Clare Kingston, Head of Corporate Strategy, 135 Eastern Avenue, Milton Park, Milton, Abingdon OX14 4SB ☎ 01235 540356 clare.kingston@southandvale.gov.uk

Senior Management: Mrs Margaret Reed, Head of Legal & Democratic Services, 135 Eastern Avenue, Milton Park, Milton, Abingdon OX14 4SB ☎ 01235 540407 margaret.reed@southandvale.gov.uk

Senior Management: Mr Chris Tyson, Head of Economy, Leisure & Property, 135 Eastern Avenue, Milton Park, Milton, Abingdon OX14 4SB ☎ 01235 540378 chris.tyson@southandvale.gov.uk

Building Control: Mr Adrian Duffield, Head of Planning, 135 Eastern Avenue, Milton Park, Milton, Abingdon OX14 4SB ☎ 01235 540340 adrian.duffield@southandvale.gov.uk

VALE OF WHITE HORSE

PR / Communications: Mrs Clare Kingston, Head of Corporate Strategy, 135 Eastern Avenue, Milton Park, Milton, Abingdon OX14 4SB ☎ 01235 540356 ✉ clare.kingston@southandvale.gov.uk

PR / Communications: Mrs Shona Ware, Communications & Grants Manager, 135 Eastern Avenue, Milton Park, Milton, Abingdon OX14 4SB ☎ 01235 540406 ✉ shona.ware@southandvale.gov.uk

Community Safety: Mrs Liz Hayden, Legal, Licensing & Community Safety Manager, 135 Eastern Avenue, Milton Park, Milton, Abingdon OX14 4SB ☎ 01491 823705 ✉ liz.hayden@southandvale.gov.uk

Community Safety: Mrs Margaret Reed, Head of Legal & Democratic Services, 135 Eastern Avenue, Milton Park, Milton, Abingdon OX14 4SB ☎ 01235 540407 ✉ margaret.reed@southandvale.gov.uk

Computer Management: Mr Andrew Down, Head of HR, IT & Technical Services, 135 Eastern Avenue, Milton Park, Milton, Abingdon OX14 4SB ☎ 01235 540372 ✉ andrew.down@southandvale.gov.uk

Computer Management: Mr Simon Turner, IT Operations Manager, 135 Eastern Avenue, Milton Park, Milton, Abingdon OX14 4SB ☎ 01235 540400 ✉ simon.turner@southandvale.gov.uk

Contracts: Mrs Margaret Reed, Head of Legal & Democratic Services, 135 Eastern Avenue, Milton Park, Milton, Abingdon OX14 4SB ☎ 01235 540407 ✉ margaret.reed@southandvale.gov.uk

Economic Development: Mrs Suzanne Malcolm, Economic Development Manager, 135 Eastern Avenue, Milton Park, Milton, Abingdon OX14 4SB ☎ 01235 547619 ✉ suzanne.malcolm@southandvale.gov.uk

Economic Development: Mr Chris Tyson, Head of Economy, Leisure & Property, 135 Eastern Avenue, Milton Park, Milton, Abingdon OX14 4SB ☎ 01235 540378 ✉ chris.tyson@southandvale.gov.uk

E-Government: Mr Andrew Down, Head of HR, IT & Technical Services, 135 Eastern Avenue, Milton Park, Milton, Abingdon OX14 4SB ☎ 01235 540372 ✉ andrew.down@southandvale.gov.uk

Electoral Registration: Mr Steven Corrigan, Democratic Services Manager, 135 Eastern Avenue, Milton Park, Milton, Abingdon OX14 4SB ☎ 01235 547675 ✉ steven.corrigan@southandvale.gov.uk

Electoral Registration: Mrs Margaret Reed, Head of Legal & Democratic Services, 135 Eastern Avenue, Milton Park, Milton, Abingdon OX14 4SB ☎ 01235 540407 ✉ margaret.reed@southandvale.gov.uk

Emergency Planning: Mr John Backley, Technical & Facilities Manager, 135 Eastern Avenue, Milton Park, Milton, Abingdon OX14 4SB ☎ 01235 540443 ✉ john.backley@southandvale.gov.uk

Emergency Planning: Mr Andrew Down, Head of HR, IT & Technical Services, 135 Eastern Avenue, Milton Park, Milton, Abingdon OX14 4SB ☎ 01235 540372 ✉ andrew.down@southandvale.gov.uk

Environmental / Technical Services: Mr John Backley, Technical & Facilities Manager, 135 Eastern Avenue, Milton Park, Milton, Abingdon OX14 4SB ☎ 01235 540443 ✉ john.backley@southandvale.gov.uk

Environmental / Technical Services: Mr Andrew Down, Head of HR, IT & Technical Services, 135 Eastern Avenue, Milton Park, Milton, Abingdon OX14 4SB ☎ 01235 540372 ✉ andrew.down@southandvale.gov.uk

Environmental / Technical Services: Mrs Clare Kingston, Head of Corporate Strategy, 135 Eastern Avenue, Milton Park, Milton, Abingdon OX14 4SB ☎ 01235 540356 ✉ clare.kingston@southandvale.gov.uk

Environmental / Technical Services: Ms Diane Moore, Food & Safety Manager, 135 Eastern Avenue, Milton Park, Milton, Abingdon OX14 4SB ☎ 01235 540382 ✉ diane.moore@southandvale.gov.uk

Environmental Health: Mr Paul Holland, Environmental Protection Manager, 135 Eastern Avenue, Milton Park, Milton, Abingdon OX14 4SB ☎ 01235 540454 ✉ paul.hollans@southandvale.gov.uk

Estates, Property & Valuation: Mrs Suzanne Malcolm, Economic Development Manager, 135 Eastern Avenue, Milton Park, Milton, Abingdon OX14 4SB ☎ 01235 547619 ✉ suzanne.malcolm@southandvale.gov.uk

Estates, Property & Valuation: Mr Chris Tyson, Head of Economy, Leisure & Property, 135 Eastern Avenue, Milton Park, Milton, Abingdon OX14 4SB ☎ 01235 540378 ✉ chris.tyson@southandvale.gov.uk

Facilities: Mr John Backley, Technical & Facilities Manager, 135 Eastern Avenue, Milton Park, Milton, Abingdon OX14 4SB ☎ 01235 540443 ✉ john.backley@southandvale.gov.uk

Facilities: Mr Andrew Down, Head of HR, IT & Technical Services, 135 Eastern Avenue, Milton Park, Milton, Abingdon OX14 4SB ☎ 01235 540372 ✉ andrew.down@southandvale.gov.uk

Finance: Mr Steve Bishop, Strategic Director, 135 Eastern Avenue, Milton Park, Milton, Abingdon OX14 4SB ☎ 01235 540332 ✉ steve.bishop@southandvale.gov.uk

Finance: Mr William Jacobs, Head of Finance, 135 Eastern Avenue, Milton Park, Milton, Abingdon OX14 4SB ☎ 01235 540526 ✉ william.jacobs@southandvale.gov.uk

Grounds Maintenance: Mrs Clare Kingston, Head of Corporate Strategy, 135 Eastern Avenue, Milton Park, Milton, Abingdon OX14 4SB ☎ 01235 540356 ✉ clare.kingston@southandvale.gov.uk

Grounds Maintenance: Mr Ian Matten, Waste & Parks Manager, 135 Eastern Avenue, Milton Park, Milton, Abingdon OX14 4SB ☎ 01235 540373 ✉ ian.matten@southandvale.gov.uk

Health and Safety: Mrs Clare Kingston, Head of Corporate Strategy, 135 Eastern Avenue, Milton Park, Milton, Abingdon OX14 4SB ☎ 01235 540356 ✉ clare.kingston@southandvale.gov.uk

Health and Safety: Ms Sally Truman, Policy, Partnership & Engagement Manager, 135 Eastern Avenue, Milton Park, Milton, Abingdon OX14 4SB ☎ 01235 450408 ✉ sally.truman@southandvale.gov.uk

Housing: Mr Phil Ealey, Housing Needs Manager, 135 Milton Avenue, Milton Park, Milton, Abingdon OX14 4SB ☎ 01235 547623 ✉ phil.ealey@southandvale.gov.uk

Legal: Mrs Liz Hayden, Legal, Licensing & Community Safety Manager, 135 Eastern Avenue, Milton Park, Milton, Abingdon OX14 4SB ☎ 01491 823705 ✉ liz.hayden@southandvale.gov.uk

Legal: Mrs Margaret Reed, Head of Legal & Democratic Services, 135 Eastern Avenue, Milton Park, Milton, Abingdon OX14 4SB ☎ 01235 540407 ✉ margaret.reed@southandvale.gov.uk

Leisure and Cultural Services: Miss Kate Arnold, Leisure Manager, 135 Eastern Avenue, Milton Park, Milton, Abingdon OX14 4SB ☎ 01235 547632 ✉ kate.arnold@southandvale.gov.uk

Leisure and Cultural Services: Miss Emma Dolman, Arts Manager, Cornerstone, 25 Station Road, Didcot OX11 7NE ☎ 01235 515131 ✉ emma.dolman@southandvale.gov.uk

Leisure and Cultural Services: Mr Chris Tyson, Head of Economy, Leisure & Property, 135 Eastern Avenue, Milton Park, Milton, Abingdon OX14 4SB ☎ 01235 540378 ✉ chris.tyson@southandvale.gov.uk

Licensing: Mrs Liz Hayden, Legal, Licensing & Community Safety Manager, 135 Eastern Avenue, Milton Park, Milton, Abingdon OX14 4SB ☎ 01491 823705 ✉ liz.hayden@southandvale.gov.uk

Licensing: Mrs Margaret Reed, Head of Legal & Democratic Services, 135 Eastern Avenue, Milton Park, Milton, Abingdon OX14 4SB ☎ 01235 540407 ✉ margaret.reed@southandvale.gov.uk

Lottery Funding, Charity and Voluntary: Mrs Clare Kingston, Head of Corporate Strategy, 135 Eastern Avenue, Milton Park, Milton, Abingdon OX14 4SB ☎ 01235 540356 ✉ clare.kingston@southandvale.gov.uk

Lottery Funding, Charity and Voluntary: Ms Sally Truman, Policy, Partnership & Engagement Manager, 135 Eastern Avenue, Milton Park, Milton, Abingdon OX14 4SB ☎ 01235 450408 ✉ sally.truman@southandvale.gov.uk

Member Services: Mr Steven Corrigan, Democratic Services Manager, 135 Eastern Avenue, Milton Park, Milton, Abingdon OX14 4SB ☎ 01235 547675 ✉ steven.corrigan@southandvale.gov.uk

Member Services: Mrs Margaret Reed, Head of Legal & Democratic Services, 135 Eastern Avenue, Milton Park, Milton, Abingdon OX14 4SB ☎ 01235 540407 ✉ margaret.reed@southandvale.gov.uk

Parking: Mr John Backley, Technical & Facilities Manager, 135 Eastern Avenue, Milton Park, Milton, Abingdon OX14 4SB ☎ 01235 540443 ✉ john.backley@southandvale.gov.uk

Parking: Mr Andrew Down, Head of HR, IT & Technical Services, 135 Eastern Avenue, Milton Park, Milton, Abingdon OX14 4SB ☎ 01235 540372 ✉ andrew.down@southandvale.gov.uk

Partnerships: Mrs Clare Kingston, Head of Corporate Strategy, 135 Eastern Avenue, Milton Park, Milton, Abingdon OX14 4SB ☎ 01235 540356 ✉ clare.kingston@southandvale.gov.uk

Partnerships: Ms Sally Truman, Policy, Partnership & Engagement Manager, 135 Eastern Avenue, Milton Park, Milton, Abingdon OX14 4SB ☎ 01235 450408 ✉ sally.truman@southandvale.gov.uk

Personnel / HR: Mr Andrew Down, Head of HR, IT & Technical Services, 135 Eastern Avenue, Milton Park, Milton, Abingdon OX14 4SB ☎ 01235 540372 ✉ andrew.down@southandvale.gov.uk

Personnel / HR: Mr Mark Gibbons, Human Resources Manager, 135 Eastern Avenue, Milton Park, Milton, Abingdon OX14 4SB ☎ 01491 823412 ✉ mark.gibbons@southandvale.gov.uk

Planning: Mr Adrian Duffield, Head of Planning, 135 Eastern Avenue, Milton Park, Milton, Abingdon OX14 4SB ☎ 01235 540340 ✉ adrian.duffield@southandvale.gov.uk

Planning: Miss Paula Fox, Development Manager (South), 135 Eastern Avenue, Milton Park, Milton, Abingdon OX14 4SB ☎ 01235 540361 ✉ paula.fox@southandvale.gov.uk

Planning: Mr Brett Leahy, Development Manager (Vale), 135 Eastern Avenue, Milton Park, Milton, Abingdon OX14 4SB ✉ brett.leahy@southandvale.gov.uk

Recycling & Waste Minimisation: Mrs Clare Kingston, Head of Corporate Strategy, 135 Eastern Avenue, Milton Park, Milton, Abingdon OX14 4SB ☎ 01235 540356 ✉ clare.kingston@southandvale.gov.uk

Recycling & Waste Minimisation: Mr Ian Matten, Waste & Parks Manager, 135 Eastern Avenue, Milton Park, Milton, Abingdon OX14 4SB ☎ 01235 540373 ✉ ian.matten@southandvale.gov.uk

Staff Training: Mr Andrew Down, Head of HR, IT & Technical Services, 135 Eastern Avenue, Milton Park, Milton, Abingdon OX14 4SB ☎ 01235 540372 ✉ andrew.down@southandvale.gov.uk

Staff Training: Mr Mark Gibbons, Human Resources Manager, 135 Eastern Avenue, Milton Park, Milton, Abingdon OX14 4SB ☎ 01491 823412 ✉ mark.gibbons@southandvale.gov.uk

Sustainable Communities: Mr Adrian Duffield, Head of Planning, 135 Eastern Avenue, Milton Park, Milton, Abingdon OX14 4SB ☎ 01235 540340 ✉ adrian.duffield@southandvale.gov.uk

Sustainable Development: Mrs Clare Kingston, Head of Corporate Strategy, 135 Eastern Avenue, Milton Park, Milton, Abingdon OX14 4SB ☎ 01235 540356 ✉ clare.kingston@southandvale.gov.uk

Sustainable Development: Ms Sally Truman, Policy, Partnership & Engagement Manager, 135 Eastern Avenue, Milton Park, Milton, Abingdon OX14 4SB ☎ 01235 450408 ✉ sally.truman@southandvale.gov.uk

VALE OF WHITE HORSE

Tourism: Mr Chris Tyson, Head of Economy, Leisure & Property, 135 Eastern Avenue, Milton Park, Milton, Abingdon OX14 4SB ☎ 01235 540378 🖱 chris.tyson@southandvale.gov.uk

Town Centre: Mrs Suzanne Malcolm, Economic Development Manager, 135 Eastern Avenue, Milton Park, Milton, Abingdon OX14 4SB ☎ 01235 547619 🖱 suzanne.malcolm@southandvale.gov.uk

Town Centre: Mr Chris Tyson, Head of Economy, Leisure & Property, 135 Eastern Avenue, Milton Park, Milton, Abingdon OX14 4SB ☎ 01235 540378 🖱 chris.tyson@southandvale.gov.uk

Waste Collection and Disposal: Mrs Clare Kingston, Head of Corporate Strategy, 135 Eastern Avenue, Milton Park, Milton, Abingdon OX14 4SB ☎ 01235 540356 🖱 clare.kingston@southandvale.gov.uk

Waste Collection and Disposal: Mr Ian Matten, Waste & Parks Manager, 135 Eastern Avenue, Milton Park, Milton, Abingdon OX14 4SB ☎ 01235 540373 🖱 ian.matten@southandvale.gov.uk

Waste Management: Mrs Clare Kingston, Head of Corporate Strategy, 135 Eastern Avenue, Milton Park, Milton, Abingdon OX14 4SB ☎ 01235 540356 🖱 clare.kingston@southandvale.gov.uk

Waste Management: Mr Ian Matten, Waste & Parks Manager, 135 Eastern Avenue, Milton Park, Milton, Abingdon OX14 4SB ☎ 01235 540373 🖱 ian.matten@southandvale.gov.uk

COUNCILLORS

***Chair* Badcock**, Mike (CON - Abingdon Caldecott)
mike.badcock@whitehorsedc.gov.uk

***Vice-Chair* Waite**, Reg (CON - Blewbury & Harwell)
reg.waite@whitehorsedc.gov.uk

***Leader of the Council* Barber**, Matthew (CON - Steventon & the Hanneys)
matthew.barber@whitehorsedc.gov.uk

***Deputy Leader of the Council* Cox**, Roger (CON - Faringdon)
roger.cox@whitehorsedc.gov.uk

***Group Leader* Hallett**, Debby (LD - Botley & Sunningwell)
cllr.debby.hallett@gmail.com

Badcock, Alice (CON - Abingdon Caldecott)
alice.badcock@whitehorsedc.gov.uk

Batts, Eric (CON - Kingston Bagpuize)
cllrericbatts@gmail.com

Blagrove, Edward (CON - Kennington & Radley)
edward.blagrove@whitehorsedc.gov.uk

Constance, Yvonne (CON - Ridgeway)
yvonne.constance@whitehorsedc.gov.uk

Crick, Margaret (LD - Abingdon Dunmore)

Davenport, Stuart (CON - Drayton)
stuart.davenport@whitehorsedc.gov.uk

Dickson, Charlotte (CON - Wantage Charlton)
charlotte@leahouse.com

Dickson, St John (CON - Wantage Charlton)
stjohn.dickson@whitehorsedc.gov.uk

Duffield, Gervase (CON - Sutton Courtenay)
gervase.duffield@whitehorsedc.gov.uk

Finch, Katie (CON - Abingdon Abbey Northcourt)
katie.finch@whitehorsedc.gov.uk

Hall, Robert (CON - Abingdon Peachcroft)
robert.hall@whitehorsedc.gov.uk

Hannaby, Jenny (LD - Wantage & Grove Brook)
jenny@yeomanryhouse.co.uk

Hayward, Anthony (CON - Thames)
anthony.hayward@whitehorsedc.gov.uk

Hoddinott, Dudley (LD - Cumnor)
dhoddinott@clara.co.uk

Howell, Simon (CON - Watchfield & Shrivenham)
simon.p.howell@btinternet.com

Jenkins, Vicky (CON - Abingdon Peachcroft)
vicky.jenkins@whitehorsedc.gov.uk

Johnston, Bob (LD - Kennington & Radley)
bobtjohnston@googlemail.com

Kanith, Mohinder (CON - Faringdon)
mohinder.kainth@gmail.com

Lovatt, Sandy (CON - Abingdon Dunmore)
sandy.lovatt@whitehorsedc.gov.uk

Lovatt, Monica (CON - Abingdon Fitzharris)
monica.lovatt@whitehorsedc.gov.uk

Mabbett, Ben (CON - Grove North)
ben.mabbett@whitehorsedc.gov.uk

McCarthy, Chris (CON - Grove North)
chris.mccarthy@whitehorsedc.gov.uk

Murray, Michael (CON - Hendreds)
mike.murray@causewayland.com

Palmer, Chris (CON - Abingdon Fitzharris)
chris.palmer@whitehorsedc.gov.uk

Pighills, Helen (LD - Abingdon Abbey Northcourt)
helen.pighills@whitehorsedc.gov.uk

Reynolds, Julia (CON - Wantage & Grove Brook)
julia.reynolds3@btinternet.com

Roberts, Judy (LD - Cumnor)
judy.roberts@whitehorsedc.gov.uk

Sharp, Robert (CON - Stanford)
robert.sharp@whitehorsedc.gov.uk

Shelley, Janet (CON - Blewbury & Harwell)
janet.shelley@whitehorsedc.gov.uk

Smith, Emily (LD - Botley & Sunningwell)
emily.smith@whitehorsedc.gov.uk

Spencer, Henry (CON - Wootton)
henry.spencer@whitehorsedc.gov.uk

Ware, Elaine (CON - Watchfield & Shrivenham)
elaine.ware@whitehorsedc.gov.uk

Webber, Catherine (LD - Marcham)

POLITICAL COMPOSITION

CON: 29, LD: 9

COMMITTEE CHAIRS

Licensing: Ms Charlotte Dickson

Planning: Mr Robert Sharp

Wakefield City M

Wakefield City Council, Town Hall, Wood Street, Wakefield WF1 2HQ
☎ 0845 8 506 506; 01924 306090 www.wakefield.gov.uk

FACTS AND FIGURES

Parliamentary Constituencies: Hemsworth, Morley and Outwood, Normanton, Pontefract and Castleford, Wakefield
EU Constituencies: Yorkshire and the Humber
Election Frequency: Elections are by thirds

PRINCIPAL OFFICERS

Chief Executive: Ms Joanne Roney, Chief Executive, Town Hall, Wakefield WF1 2HQ ☎ 01924 305101 jroney@wakefield.gov.uk

Deputy Chief Executive: Mr John Wilson, Corporate Director - Children & Young People, Town Hall, Wood Street, Wakefield WF1 2HQ ☎ 01924 307725 🖷 01924 307768 jwilson@wakefield.gov.uk

Senior Management: Mr Andrew Balchin, Corporate Director - Adults, Health & Communities, Wakefield One, Burton Street, Wakefield WF1 2DA ☎ 01924 306634 abalchin@wakefield.gov.uk

Senior Management: Dr Andrew Furber, Director - Public Health, Town Hall, Wood Street, Wakefield WF1 2HQ ☎ 01942 305347 afurber@wakefield.gov.uk

Senior Management: Mr Andrew Wallhead, Corporate Director - Regeneration & Economic Growth, Wakefield One, Burton Street, Wakefield WF1 2DA ☎ 01924 306950 awallhead@wakefield.gov.uk

Senior Management: Mr John Wilson, Corporate Director - Children & Young People, Town Hall, Wood Street, Wakefield WF1 2HQ ☎ 01924 307725 🖷 01924 307768 jwilson@wakefield.gov.uk

Architect, Building / Property Services: Mr Kevin Fisher, Service Manager - Property & Facilities Management, Wakefield One, Burton Street, Wakefield WF1 2DA ☎ 01924 306490 kevinfisher@wakefield.gov.uk

Building Control: Mr Neil Rodgers, Service Director - Planning Transportation & Highways, Wakefield One, Burton Street, Wakefield WF1 2DA ☎ 01924 305858 nrodgers@wakefield.gov.uk

Catering Services: Mr Kevin Fisher, Service Manager - Property & Facilities Management, Wakefield One, Burton Street, Wakefield WF1 2DA ☎ 01924 306490 kevinfisher@wakefield.gov.uk

Children / Youth Services: Mr Stephen Crofts, Service Manager - Localities, Youth & Youth Justice, Manygates Education Centre, Manygates Lane, Sandal, Wakefield WF2 7DQ ☎ 01924 303335 scrofts@wakefield.gov.uk

Civil Registration: Ms Bernadette Livesey, Service Director - Legal & Governance, County Hall, Bond Street, Wakefield WF1 2QW ☎ 01924 305177 🖷 01924 305195 blivesey@wakefield.gov.uk

PR / Communications: Ms Lucinda Jackson, Service Director - Communications, Customers & Policy, County Hall, Bond Street, Wakefield WF1 2QW ☎ 01924 303454 lucindajackson@wakefield.gov.uk

Community Planning: Mr Andrew Balchin, Corporate Director - Adults, Health & Communities, Wakefield One, Burton Street, Wakefield WF1 2DA ☎ 01924 306634 abalchin@wakefield.gov.uk

Community Safety: Mr Andrew Balchin, Corporate Director - Adults, Health & Communities, Wakefield One, Burton Street, Wakefield WF1 2DA ☎ 01924 306634 abalchin@wakefield.gov.uk

Computer Management: Ms Helen Grantham, Service Director - Organisational Development & Performance, County Hall, Bond Street, Wakefield WF1 2QW ☎ 01924 306700 hgrantham@wakefield.gov.uk

Customer Service: Ms Lucinda Jackson, Service Director - Communications, Customers & Policy, County Hall, Bond Street, Wakefield WF1 2QW ☎ 01924 303454 lucindajackson@wakefield.gov.uk

Electoral Registration: Ms Sandra Hardy, Electoral Services Manager, Town Hall, Wood Street, Wakefield WF1 2HQ ☎ 01924 605020 🖷 01924 605722 shardy@wakefield.gov.uk

Emergency Planning: Mr Neil Favager, Emergency Planning & Business Continuity Manager, Wakefield One, Burton Street, Wakefield WF1 2DA ☎ 01924 305048 nfavager@wakefield.gov.uk

Environmental / Technical Services: Mr Glynn Humphries, Service Director - Environment & Streetscene, Wakefield One, Burton Street, Wakefield WF1 2DA ☎ 01924 306518 ghumphries@wakefield.gov.uk

Estates, Property & Valuation: Mr Kevin Fisher, Service Manager - Property & Facilities Management, Wakefield One, Burton Street, Wakefield WF1 2DA ☎ 01924 306490 kevinfisher@wakefield.gov.uk

Events Manager: Mr Ben Cook, Service Manager - Markets, Major Events & Tourism, Wakefield One, Burton Street, Wakefield WF1 2DA ☎ 01924 305136 bcook@wakefield.gov.uk

Facilities: Mr Kevin Fisher, Service Manager - Property & Facilities Management, Wakefield One, Burton Street, Wakefield WF1 2DA ☎ 01924 306490 kevinfisher@wakefield.gov.uk

Finance: Ms Judith Badger, Director - Finance, Property & Resources, Wakefield One, Burton Street, Wakefield WF1 2DA ☎ 01924 305388 jbadger@wakefield.gov.uk

Health and Safety: Mr Neil Favager, Emergency Planning & Business Continuity Manager, Wakefield One, Burton Street, Wakefield WF1 2DA ☎ 01924 305048 nfavager@wakefield.gov.uk

Highways: Mr Neil Rodgers, Service Director - Planning Transportation & Highways, Wakefield One, Burton Street, Wakefield WF1 2DA ☎ 01924 305858 nrodgers@wakefield.gov.uk

Housing: Ms Sarah Pearson, Service Director - Economic Growth & Strategic Housing, Wakefield One, Burton Street, Wakefield WF1 2DA ☎ 01924 305461 spearson@wakefield.gov.uk

Legal: Ms Bernadette Livesey, Service Director - Legal & Governance, County Hall, Bond Street, Wakefield WF1 2QW ☎ 01924 305177 🖷 01924 305195 ✉ blivesey@wakefield.gov.uk

Leisure and Cultural Services: Ms Karen Collins, Service Director - Sport & Culture, Town Hall, Wood Street, Wakefield WF1 2HQ ☎ 01924 306931 ✉ karencollins@wakefield.gov.uk

Licensing: Ms Pam Taylor, Licensing Officer, Town Hall, Wood Street, Wakefield WF1 2HQ ☎ 01924 302916 ✉ ptaylor@wakefield.gov.uk

Member Services: Ms Bernadette Livesey, Service Director - Legal & Governance, County Hall, Bond Street, Wakefield WF1 2QW ☎ 01924 305177 🖷 01924 305195 ✉ blivesey@wakefield.gov.uk

Parking: Mr Graham West, Service Manager - Highways Network Planning, Transportation & Highways, Wakefield One, Burton Street, Wakefield WF1 2DA ☎ 01924 306057 ✉ gwest@wakefield.gov.uk

Personnel / HR: Ms Helen Grantham, Service Director - Organisational Development & Performance, County Hall, Bond Street, Wakefield WF1 2QW ☎ 01924 306700 ✉ hgrantham@wakefield.gov.uk

Planning: Mr Neil Rodgers, Service Director - Planning Transportation & Highways, Wakefield One, Burton Street, Wakefield WF1 2DA ☎ 01924 305858 ✉ nrodgers@wakefield.gov.uk

Procurement: Ms Judith Badger, Director - Finance, Property & Resources, Wakefield One, Burton Street, Wakefield WF1 2DA ☎ 01924 305388 ✉ jbadger@wakefield.gov.uk

Public Libraries: Ms Karen Collins, Service Director - Sport & Culture, Town Hall, Wood Street, Wakefield WF1 2HQ ☎ 01924 306931 ✉ karencollins@wakefield.gov.uk

Recycling & Waste Minimisation: Mr Jay Smith, Assistant Streetscene Manager, Wakefield One, Burton Street, Wakefield WF1 2DA ☎ 01924 306367 ✉ jaysmith@wakefield.gov.uk

Regeneration: Mr Andrew Wallhead, Corporate Director - Regeneration & Economic Growth, Wakefield One, Burton Street, Wakefield WF1 2DA ☎ 01924 306950 ✉ awallhead@wakefield.gov.uk

Road Safety: Mrs Sue Wilson, Road Safety Education Officer, Wakefield One, Burton Street, Wakefield WF1 2DA ☎ 01924 306000 ✉ suewilson@wakefield.gov.uk

Social Services (Adult): Mr Rob Hurren, Director - Integrated Care, Town Hall, Wood Street, Wakefield WF1 2HQ ☎ 01924 307760 ✉ rhurren@wakefield.gov.uk

Social Services (Children): Mr John Wilson, Corporate Director - Children & Young People, Town Hall, Wood Street, Wakefield WF1 2HQ ☎ 01924 307725 🖷 01924 307768 ✉ johnwilson@wakefield.gov.uk

Safeguarding: Mr Mark Barratt, Service Director - Safeguarding & Family Support, County Hall, Bond Street, Wakefield WF1 2QW ☎ 01924 305670 ✉ mbarratt@wakefield.gov.uk

Public Health: Dr Andrew Furber, Director - Public Health, Town Hall, Wood Street, Wakefield WF1 2HQ ☎ 01942 305347 ✉ afurber@wakefield.gov.uk

Staff Training: Ms Helen Grantham, Service Director - Organisational Development & Performance, County Hall, Bond Street, Wakefield WF1 2QW ☎ 01924 306700 ✉ hgrantham@wakefield.gov.uk

Street Scene: Mr Glynn Humphries, Service Director - Environment & Streetscene, Wakefield One, Burton Street, Wakefield WF1 2DA ☎ 01924 306518 ✉ ghumphries@wakefield.gov.uk

Tourism: Mr Ben Cook, Service Manager - Markets, Major Events & Tourism, Wakefield One, Burton Street, Wakefield WF1 2DA ☎ 01924 305136 ✉ bcook@wakefield.gov.uk

Traffic Management: Mr Graham West, Service Manager - Highways Network Planning, Transportation & Highways, Wakefield One, Burton Street, Wakefield WF1 2DA ☎ 01924 306057 ✉ gwest@wakefield.gov.uk

Waste Collection and Disposal: Mr Glynn Humphries, Service Director - Environment & Streetscene, Wakefield One, Burton Street, Wakefield WF1 2DA ☎ 01924 306518 ✉ ghumphries@wakefield.gov.uk

Waste Management: Mr Glynn Humphries, Service Director - Environment & Streetscene, Wakefield One, Burton Street, Wakefield WF1 2DA ☎ 01924 306518 ✉ ghumphries@wakefield.gov.uk

COUNCILLORS

***Mayor* Cliffe**, June (LAB - Featherstone)
jcunliffe@wakefield.gov.uk

***Deputy Mayor* Ellis**, Harry (LAB - Knottingley)
hellis@wakefield.gov.uk

***Leader of the Council* Box**, Peter (LAB - Altofts and Whitwood)
pbox@wakefield.gov.uk

***Deputy Leader of the Council* Jeffery**, Denise (LAB - Castleford Central and Glasshoughton)
djeffery@wakefield.gov.uk

Ahmed, Nadeem (CON - Wakefield South)
cllrnahmed@wakefield.gov.uk

Austin, Tracey (LAB - Wakefield North)
taustin@wakefield.gov.uk

Ayre, George (LAB - Pontefract South)
gayre@wakefield.gov.uk

Barker, Kevin (LAB - Wakefield Rural)
kevinbarker@wakefield.gov.uk

Benson, Wilf (IND - South Emsall and South Kirkby)
wbenson@wakefield.gov.uk

Blezard, Elaine (LAB - Normanton)
eblezard@wakefield.gov.uk

Burton, Glenn (LAB - Knottingley)
gburton@wakefield.gov.uk

Carrington, Jessica (LAB - Ackworth, North Elmsall and Upton)
jcarrington@wakefield.gov.uk

Case, Ryan (LAB - Wakefield West)
rcase@wakefield.gov.uk

Collins, Michelle (LAB - South Emsall and South Kirkby)
michellecollins@wakefield.gov.uk

Crewe, Yvonne (LAB - Airedale and Ferry Fryston)
ycrewe@wakefield.gov.uk

Cummings, Maureen (LAB - Crofton, Ryhill and Walton)
mcummings@wakefield.gov.uk

Dagger, David (LAB - Normanton)
ddagger@wakefield.gov.uk

Dews, David (UKIP - Wrenthorpe and Outwood West)
ddews@wakefield.gov.uk

Farmer, Nick (UKIP - Ossett)
nfarmer@wakefield.gov.uk

Forster, Richard (LAB - Castleford Central and Glasshoughton)
rforster@wakefield.gov.uk

Garbutt, Alan (LAB - Ackworth, North Elmsall and Upton)
agarbutt@wakefield.gov.uk

Garbutt, Patricia (LAB - Pontefract North)
pgarbutt@wakefield.gov.uk

Graham, Monica (CON - Wakefield South)
mgraham@wakefield.gov.uk

Hemingway, Jack (LAB - Horbury and South Ossett)
jackhemingway@wakefield.gov.uk

Heptinstall, Faith (LAB - Crofton, Ryhill and Walton)
fheptinstall@wakefield.gov.uk

Heptinstall, Stuart (LAB - Wakefield East)
sheptinstall@wakefield.gov.uk

Hepworth, Jo (LAB - Altofts and Whitwood)
johepworth@wakefield.gov.uk

Hodson, Shaun (LAB - Hemsworth)
shodson@wakefield.gov.uk

Holmes, Janet (LAB - Horbury and South Ossett)
jholmes@wakefield.gov.uk

Holwell, Margaret (CON - Horbury and South Ossett)
mholwell@wakefield.gov.uk

Hopkins, David (CON - Wakefield South)
dhopkins@wakefield.gov.uk

Hudson, Clive (LAB - Stanley and Outwood East)
chudson@wakefield.gov.uk

Isherwood, Graham (LAB - Featherstone)
gisherwood@wakefield.gov.uk

Isherwood, Margaret (LAB - Wakefield North)
margaretisherwood@wakefield.gov.uk

Johnson, Martyn (LAB - Wrenthorpe and Outwood West)
martynjohnson@wakefield.gov.uk

Jones, David (LAB - Pontefract South)
davidjones@wakefield.gov.uk

Keith, Charlie (LAB - Wrenthorpe and Outwood West)
ckeith@wakefield.gov.uk

Kirkpatrick, Lawrence (LAB - Wakefield Rural)
lkirkpatrick@wakefield.gov.uk

Lloyd, Glyn (LAB - Hemsworth)
glynlloyd@wakefield.gov.uk

Loughran, Celia (LAB - Pontefract South)
cloughran@wakefield.gov.uk

Lund, Ros (LAB - Wakefield East)
rlund@wakefield.gov.uk

Manifield, Albert (LAB - Crofton, Ryhill and Walton)
amanifield@wakefield.gov.uk

Mitchell, Hilary (LAB - Wakefield West)
hilarymitchell@wakefield.gov.uk

Morley, Matthew (LAB - Stanley and Outwood East)
mmorley@wakefield.gov.uk

Pickin, Sandra (LAB - Hemsworth)
spickin@wakefield.gov.uk

Rhodes, Elizabeth (LAB - Wakefield North)
brhodes@wakefield.gov.uk

Richardson, Tony (IND - Ossett)
tonyrichardson@wakefield.gov.uk

Rowley, Olivia (LAB - Wakefield East)
orowley@wakefield.gov.uk

Sanders, Ian (CON - Wakefield Rural)
isanders@wakefield.gov.uk

Scott, Kathryn (LAB - Airedale and Ferry Fryston)
kathrynscott@wakefield.gov.uk

Shaw, Les (LAB - Airedale and Ferry Fryston)
lesshaw@wakefield.gov.uk

Sherriff, Paula (LAB - Pontefract North)
psherriff@wakefield.gov.uk

Speight, Jacquie (LAB - Altofts and Whitwood)
jspeight@wakefield.gov.uk

Stokes, Graham (LAB - Knottingley)
gstokes@wakefield.gov.uk

Swift, Kevin (LAB - Wakefield West)
kswift@wakefield.gov.uk

Taylor, Angela (CON - Ossett)
actaylor@wakefield.gov.uk

Taylor, Richard (LAB - Featherstone)
dicktaylor@wakefield.gov.uk

Tennant, Clive (LAB - Pontefract North)
clivetennant@wakefield.gov.uk

Tulley, Steve (LAB - South Emsall and South Kirkby)
stulley@wakefield.gov.uk

Wallis, Anthony (LAB - Castleford Central and Glasshoughton)
awallis@wakefield.gov.uk

Ward, Martyn (LAB - Ackworth, North Elmsall and Upton)
martynward@wakefield.gov.uk

Wassell, Alan (LAB - Normanton)
alanwassel@wakefield.gov.uk

Williams, Jacqueline (LAB - Stanley and Outwood East)
jacquelinewilliams@wakefield.gov.uk

POLITICAL COMPOSITION

LAB: 53, CON: 6, IND: 2, UKIP: 2

COMMITTEE CHAIRS

Audit: Mr Glenn Burton

Licensing: Miss Jacqueline Williams

Planning & Highways: Mr Alan Garbutt

Walsall M

Walsall Metropolitan Borough Council, Civic Centre, Darwall Street, Walsall WS1 1TP
☎ 01922 650000 🖷 01922 720885 💻 www.walsall.gov.uk

FACTS AND FIGURES

Parliamentary Constituencies: Aldridge-Brownhills, Walsall North, Walsall South
EU Constituencies: West Midlands
Election Frequency: Elections are by thirds

PRINCIPAL OFFICERS

Chief Executive: Mr Paul Sheehan, Chief Executive, Civic Centre, Darwall Street, Walsall WS1 1TP ☎ 01922 652006 🖷 01922 614210 ✉ sheehanp@walsall.gov.uk

Senior Management: Mr Rory Borealis, Executive Director - Resources, Civic Centre, Darwall Street, Walsall WS1 1TP ☎ 01992 652910 🖷 01922 614210 ✉ borealisr@walsall.gov.uk

Senior Management: Mr David Haley, Executive Director - Children's Services, Civic Centre, Darwall Street, Walsall WS1 1TP ☎ 01922 652035 🖷 01922 614210 ✉ haleyd@walsall.gov.uk

Senior Management: Mr Simon Neilson, Executive Director - Regeneration, Civic Centre, Darwall Street, Walsall WS1 1TP ✉ neilsons@walsall.gov.uk

Senior Management: Mr Keith Skerman, Executive Director - Social Care & Inclusion, Civic Centre, Darwall Street, Walsall WS1 1TP ☎ 01922 654710 ✉ skermank@walsall.gov.uk

Access Officer / Social Services (Disability): Ms Sue Fox, Access Officer of the Policy Unit, Civic Centre, Dawall Street, Walsall WS1 1TP ☎ 01922 652010 🖷 01922 653302 ✉ foxs@walsall.gov.uk

Architect, Building / Property Services: Mr John Stevens, Interim Head of Property Services, Civic Centre, Darwall Street, Walsall WS1 1TP ☎ 01922 471275 ✉ bassettm@walsall.gov.uk

Building Control: Mr David Elsworthy, Head of Planning & Building Control, Civic Centre, Darwall Street, Walsall WS1 1TP ☎ 01922 652409 🖷 01922 623234 ✉ elsworthyd@walsall.gov.uk

Catering Services: Mrs Carol Tipper, Catering Manager, Catering Public Service Enterprise, Darwall Street, Walsall WS1 1TP ☎ 01922 653120 ✉ carol.tipper@walsall.gov.uk

Children / Youth Services: Mr David Haley, Executive Director - Children's Services, Civic Centre, Darwall Street, Walsall WS1 1TP ☎ 01922 652035 🖷 01922 614210 ✉ haleyd@walsall.gov.uk

Civil Registration: Ms Holly Holdsworth, Superintendent Registrar, Civic Centre, Darwall Street, Walsall WS1 1TP ☎ 01922 654607 ✉ holdsworthh@walsall.gov.uk

Community Planning: Ms Kate Bowers, Interim Head of Communities & Partnership, Civic Centre, Darwall Street, Walsall WS1 1TP ☎ 01922 658984 ✉ kate.bowers@walsall.gov.uk

Community Safety: Ms Lynne Hughes, Area Manager Community Safety, Civic Centre, Darwall Street, Walsall WS1 1TP ☎ 01922 654289 ✉ hughesl@walsall.gov.uk

Computer Management: Mr Paul Gordon, Head of Shared Services & Procurement, Civic Centre, Darwall Street, Walsall WS1 1TP ☎ 07792 920257 ✉ paul.gordon@walsall.gov.uk

Contracts: Mr Lawrence Brazier, Head of Procurement, Civic Centre, Darwall Street, Walsall WS1 1TP ☎ 01922 650987 🖷 01922 653534 ✉ brazierl@walsall.gov.uk

Corporate Services: Mr Rory Borealis, Executive Director - Resources, 2910 Darwall Street, Walsall WA1 1TP ☎ 01992 652910 🖷 01922 614210 ✉ borealisr@walsall.gov.uk

Customer Service: Ms Helen Dudson, Corporate Performance Manager, Civic Centre, Darwall Street, Walsall WS1 1TP ☎ 01922 653732 ✉ dudsonh@walsall.gov.uk

Education: Mr David Haley, Executive Director - Children's Services, Civic Centre, Darwall Street, Walsall WS1 1TP ☎ 01922 652035 🖷 01922 614210 ✉ haleyd@walsall.gov.uk

E-Government: Mr Paul Gordon, Head of Shared Services & Procurement, Civic Centre, Darwall Street, Walsall WS1 1TP ☎ 07792 920257 ✉ paul.gordon@walsall.gov.uk

Emergency Planning: Mr Alan Boyd, Resilience Manager, Sandwell Council House, Oldbury B69 3DE ☎ 0121 569 3060; 0121 569 3983 ✉ alan_boyd@sandwell.gov.uk

Environmental / Technical Services: Mr Keith Stone, Assistant Director of Neighbourhoods, Civic Centre, Darwall Street, Walsall WS1 1TP ☎ 01922 654617 ✉ stonek@walsall.gov.uk

Environmental Health: Mr David Elrington, Area Manager, Civic Centre, Darwall Street, Walsall WS1 1TP ☎ 01922 653023 ✉ david.elrington@walsall.gov.uk

Estates, Property & Valuation: Mr Steve Law, Estates Manager, Civic Centre, Darwall Street, Walsall WS1 1TP ☎ 01922 652075 🖷 01922 636150 ✉ laws@walsall.gov.uk

Events Manager: Ms Sunita Lal Kooner, Venue Hire & Development, Civic Centre, Darwall Street, Walsall WS1 1TP ☎ 01922 650302 ✉ lalkooners@walsall.gov.uk

Facilities: Mr John Stevens, Interim Head of Property Services, Civic Centre, Darwall Street, Walsall WS1 1TP ☎ 01922 471275 ✉ bassettm@walsall.gov.uk

Finance: Mr James Walsh, Chief Finance Officer, Civic Centre, Darwall Street, Walsall WS1 1TP ☎ 01922 653554 🖷 01922 722868 ✉ walshj@walsall.gov.uk

Grounds Maintenance: Mr Mark Holden, Head of Street Pride, Environmental Depot, 200 Pelsall Road, Brownhills WS8 7EN
☎ 01922 654201 🖱 holdenmi@walsall.gov.uk

Health and Safety: Ms Irena Hergottova, Corporate Consultation Equalities Lead, Civic Centre, Darwall Street, Walsall WS1 1TP
☎ 01922 655751 🖱 hergottovai@walsall.gov.uk

Legal: Mr Tony Cox, Head of Legal & Democratic Services, The Council House, Lichfield Street, Walsall WS1 1JX ☎ 01992 654822 🖷 01992 638267 🖱 tcox@walsall.gov.uk

Leisure and Cultural Services: Mr Chris Holliday, Head of Leisure & Culture, 12th Floor, Tameway Tower, 48 Bridge Street, Walsall WS1 1JZ ☎ 01922 650339 🖷 01922 634093 🖱 hollidayc@walsall.gov.uk

Lighting: Mr Steve Pretty, Divisional Manager of Transportation Services, Civic Centre, Darwall Street, Walsall WS1 1TP
☎ 01922 652598 🖷 01922 623234 🖱 prettys@walsall.gov.uk

Lottery Funding, Charity and Voluntary: Mr Alex Boys, Strategic Resources Officer, Civic Centre, Darwall Street, Walsall WS1 1TP ☎ 01922 653785 🖱 boysa@walsall.gov.uk

Member Services: Mr John Garner, Head of Democratic Services, Civic Centre, Darwall Street, Walsall WS1 1TP ☎ 01922 654366 🖱 garnerj@walsall.gov.uk

Parking: Ms Glynnis Jeavons, Car Park Manager, Civic Centre, Darwall Street, Walsall WS1 1TP ☎ 01922 652493 🖷 01922 612608 🖱 jeavonsg@walsall.gov.uk

Partnerships: Ms Kate Bowers, Interim Head of Communities & Partnership, Civic Centre, Darwall Street, Walsall WS1 1TP ☎ 01922 658984 🖱 kate.bowers@walsall.gov.uk

Personnel / HR: Mr Steve McGowan, Head of Human Resources, Civic Centre, Darwall Street, Walsall WS1 1TP ☎ 01922 655601 🖱 mcgow@walsall.gov.uk

Planning: Mr David Elsworthy, Head of Planning & Building Control, Civic Centre, Darwall Street, Walsall WS1 1TP ☎ 01922 652409 🖷 01922 623234 🖱 elsworthyd@walsall.gov.uk

Procurement: Mr Lawrence Brazier, Head of Procurement, Civic Centre, Darwall Street, Walsall WS1 1TP ☎ 01922 650987 🖷 01922 653534 🖱 brazierl@walsall.gov.uk

Public Libraries: Ms Sue Grainger, Group Co-ordinator / Lifelong Learning & Community, Civic Centre, Darwall Street, Walsall WS1 1TP ☎ 01922 650338 🖷 01922 634093 🖱 graingers@walsall.gov.uk

Recycling & Waste Minimisation: Mr David Roberts, Service Manager of Operations, Environmental Depot, 200 Pelsall Road, Brownhills WS8 7EN ☎ 01922 654236 🖱 robertsd@walsall.gov.uk

Regeneration: Mr Mark Lavender, Head of Strategic Regeneration, Civic Centre, Darwall Street, Walsall WS1 1TP
☎ 01922 654772 🖱 lavenderm@walsall.gov.uk

Social Services: Mr Keith Skerman, Executive Director - Social Care & Inclusion, Civic Centre, Darwall Street, Walsall WS1 1TP
☎ 01922 654710 🖱 skermank@walsall.gov.uk

Social Services (Children): Mr David Haley, Executive Director - Children's Services, Civic Centre, Darwall Street, Walsall WS1 1TP
☎ 01922 652035 🖷 01922 614210 🖱 haleyd@walsall.gov.uk

Sustainable Communities: Ms Kate Bowers, Interim Head of Communities & Partnership, Civic Centre, Darwall Street, Walsall WS1 1TP ☎ 01922 658984 🖱 kate.bowers@walsall.gov.uk

Town Centre: Ms Helen Kindon, Town Centre Manager, Civic Centre, Darwall Street, Walsall WS1 1TP ☎ 01922 652095 🖱 kindonh@walsall.gov.uk

Traffic Management: Mr Steve Griffiths, Team Leader, Civic Centre, Darwall Street, Walsall WS1 1TP ☎ 01922 654645 🖱 griffithss@walsall.gov.uk

Waste Collection and Disposal: Mr David Roberts, Service Manager of Operations, Environmental Depot, 200 Pelsall Road, Brownhills WS8 7EN ☎ 01922 654236 🖱 robertsd@walsall.gov.uk

Waste Management: Mr David Roberts, Service Manager of Operations, Environmental Depot, 200 Pelsall Road, Brownhills WS8 7EN ☎ 01922 654236 🖱 robertsd@walsall.gov.uk

COUNCILLORS

***Mayor* Underhill**, Angela (LAB - Bentley and Darlaston North)
cllr.angela.underhill@walsall.gov.uk

***Deputy Mayor* Phillips**, Kath (LAB - Bloxwich East)
cllr.kath.phillips@walsall.gov.uk

***Leader of the Council* Bird**, Mike (CON - Pheasey Park Farm)
cllr.mike.bird@walsall.gov.uk

***Deputy Leader of the Council* Nazir**, Mohammad (LAB - Palfrey)
cllr.mohammad.nazir@walsall.gov.uk

***Group Leader* Coughlan**, Sean (LAB - Willenhall South)
cllr.sean.coughlan@walsall.gov.uk

***Group Leader* Hazell**, Liz (UKIP - Willenhall North)
cllr.liz.hazell@walsall.gov.uk

Andrew, Adrian (CON - Pheasey Park Farm)
cllr.adrian.andrew@walsall.gov.uk

Anson, Dennis (LAB - Pleck)
cllr.dennis.anson@walsall.gov.uk

Arif, Mohammed (CON - St. Matthew's)
cllr.mohammed.arif@walsall.gov.uk

Bennett, Oliver (CON - Pelsall)
cllr.oliver.bennett@walsall.gov.uk

Bott, Paul (IND - Darlaston South)
cllr.paul.bott@walsall.gov.uk

Bott, Chris (IND - Darlaston South)
cllr.chris.bott@walsall.gov.uk

Burley, Rose (LAB - Bentley and Darlaston North)
cllr.rose.burley@walsall.gov.uk

Chambers, Keith (LAB - Bentley and Darlaston North)
cllr.keith.chambers@walsall.gov.uk

WALSALL

Clarke, Gary (CON - Aldridge North and Walsall Wood)
cllr.gary.clarke@walsall.gov.uk

Clews, Claire (LAB - Rushall Shelfield)
cllr.claire.clews@walsall.gov.uk

Cooper, Sarah Jane (CON - Short Heath)
cllr.sarah.jane.cooper@walsall.gov.uk

Coughlan, Diane (LAB - Willenhall South)
cllr.diane.coughlan@walsall.gov.uk

Craddock, Stephen (UKIP - Brownhills)
cllr.stephen.craddock@walsall.gov.uk

Creaney, Carl (LAB - Willenhall South)
cllr.carl.creaney@walsall.gov.uk

Ditta, Allah (LAB - Palfrey)
cllr.a.ditta@walsall.gov.uk

Douglas-Maul, Brian (CON - Streetly)
cllr.brian.douglas-maul@walsall.gov.uk

Ferguson, Kenneth (CON - Brownhills)
cllr.ken.ferguson@walsall.gov.uk

Fitzpatrick, Shaun Francis (LAB - Bloxwich East)
cllr.shaun.fitzpatrick@walsall.gov.uk

Fitzpatrick, Julie (LAB - Bloxwich East)
cllr.julie.fitzpatrick@walsall.gov.uk

Follows, Matthew (CON - Bloxwich West)
cllr.matthew.follows@walsall.gov.uk

Harris, Anthony (CON - Aldridge North and Walsall Wood)
cllr.anthony.harris@walsall.gov.uk

Harrison, Louise (CON - Bloxwich West)
cllr.louise.harrison@walsall.gov.uk

Hazell, Darren (UKIP - Short Heath)
cllr.darren.hazell@walsall.gov.uk

Hicken, Adam (CON - Willenhall North)
cllr.adam.hicken@walsall.gov.uk

Hughes, Eddie (CON - Streetly)
cllr.eddie.hughes@walsall.gov.uk

Hussain, Khizar (LAB - Pleck)
cllr.khizar.hussain@walsall.gov.uk

James, Douglas (LAB - Darlaston South)
cllr.douglas.james@walsall.gov.uk

Jeavons, Lee (LAB - Birchills Leamore)
cllr.lee.jeavsons@walsall.gov.uk

Jones, Christopher (LAB - Birchills Leamore)
cllr.chris.jones@walsall.gov.uk

Jukes, Tina (LAB - Birchills Leamore)
cllr.tina.jukes@walsall.gov.uk

Kudhail, Amers (CON - Streetly)
cllr.amers.kudhail@walsall.gov.uk

Longhi, Marco (CON - Pelsall)
cllr.marco.longhi@walsall.gov.uk

Martin, Rose (CON - Paddock)
cllr.rose.martin@walsall.gov.uk

Murray, John (CON - Aldridge Central and South)
cllr.john.murray@walsall.gov.uk

Nawaz, Aftab (LAB - St. Matthew's)
cllr.aftab.nawaz@walsall.gov.uk

Perry, Garry (CON - Pelsall)
cllr.garry.perry@walsall.gov.uk

Rattigan, Lorna (CON - Rushall Shelfield)
cllr.lorna.rattigan@walsall.gov.uk

Robertson, Ian (LAB - Blakenall)
cllr.ian.robertson@walsall.gov.uk

Rochelle, John (CON - Aldridge Central and South)
cllr.john.rochelle@walsall.gov.uk

Russell, Eileen (LAB - St. Matthew's)
cllr.eileen.russell@walsall.gov.uk

Sarohi, Harbans (LAB - Pleck)
cllr.harbans.sarohi@walsall.gov.uk

Sears, Keith (CON - Aldridge North and Walsall Wood)
cllr.keith.sears@walsall.gov.uk

Shires, Doreen (LD - Short Heath)
cllr.doreen.shires@walsall.gov.uk

Shires, Ian (LD - Willenhall North)
cllr.ian.shires@walsall.gov.uk

Smith, Pete (LAB - Blakenall)
cllr.peter.smith@walsall.gov.uk

Sohal, Gurmeet (CON - Paddock)
cllr.gurmeet.sohal@walsall.gov.uk

Towe, Christopher (CON - Pheasey Park Farm)
cllr.crhis.towe@walsall.gov.uk

Wade, Stephen (LAB - Brownhills)
cllr.stephen.wade@walsall.gov.uk

Washbrook, Peter (CON - Paddock)
cllr.peter.washbrook@walsall.gov.uk

Westley, Fred (LAB - Bloxwich West)
cllr.fred.westley@walsall.gov.uk

Whyte, Victoria (LAB - Palfrey)
cllr.victoria.whyte@walsall.gov.uk

Wilson, Timothy (CON - Aldridge Central and South)
cllr.timothy.wilson@walsall.gov.uk

Worrall, Richard (LAB - Rushall-Shelfield)
cllr.richard.worrall@walsall.gov.uk

Young, Ann (LAB - Blakenall)
cllr.ann.young@walsall.gov.uk

POLITICAL COMPOSITION

LAB: 28, CON: 25, UKIP: 3, IND: 2, LD: 2

COMMITTEE CHAIRS

Licensing & Safety: Mr Keith Sears

Planning: Mr Garry Perry

Waltham Forest L

Waltham Forest London Borough Council, Town Hall, Forest Road, London E17 4JF

☎ 020 8496 3000 🖷 020 8527 8313 ✉ wfdirect@walthamforest.gov.uk

💻 www.walthamforest.gov.uk

FACTS AND FIGURES

Parliamentary Constituencies: Chingford and Woodford, Leyton and Wanstead, Walthamstow

EU Constituencies: London
Election Frequency: Elections are of whole council

PRINCIPAL OFFICERS

Chief Executive: Mr Martin Esom, Chief Executive, Town Hall, Forest Road, London E17 4JF ☎ 020 8496 3000 🖷 020 8496 5404 🖰 martin.esom@walthamforest.gov.uk

Deputy Chief Executive: Ms Linzi Roberts-Egan, Deputy Chief Executive - Families, Town Hall, Forest Road, London E17 4JF ☎ 020 8496 3500 🖰 linzi.roberts-egan@walthamforest.gov.uk

Assistant Chief Executive: Ms Rhona Cadenhead, Assistant Chief Executive, Town Hall, Forest Road, London E17 4JF ☎ 020 8496 3000 🖰 rhoda.cadenhead@walthamforest.gov.uk

Senior Management: Mr Ken Jones, Director - Housing & Growth, Town Hall, Forest Road, London E17 4JF ☎ 020 8496 3000 🖰 ken.jones@walthamforest.gov.uk

Senior Management: Ms Althea Loderick, Chief Operating Officer, Town Hall, Forest Road, London E17 4JF ☎ 020 8496 3000 🖰 althea.loderick@walthamforest.gov.uk

Senior Management: Ms Michele Moloney, Director - Neighbourhoods & Commissioning, Town Hall, Forest Road, London E17 4JF ☎ 020 8496 3000 🖰 michele.moloney@walthamforest.gov.uk

Senior Management: Ms Lucy Shomali, Director - Regeneration & Growth, Town Hall, Forest Road, London E17 4JF ☎ 020 8496 6734 🖰 lucy.shomali@walthamforest.gov.uk

Senior Management: Mr John Turnbull, Director - Finance & Chief Finance Officer, Town Hall, Forest Road, London E17 4JF ☎ 020 8496 3000 🖰 john.turnbull@walthamforest.gov.uk

Access Officer / Social Services (Disability): Ms Senel Arkut, Divisional Director - Adult Social Care, Town Hall, Forest Road, London E17 4JF ☎ 020 8496 3200 🖰 senel.arkut@walthamforest.gov.uk

Architect, Building / Property Services: Mr Steve Sprayson, Head of Corporate Asset Management, Town Hall, Forest Road, London E17 4JF ☎ 020 8496 8079 🖰 steven.sprayson@walthamforest.gov.uk

Building Control: Mr Julian Ruaux, Head of Building Control, Sycamore House, Waltham Forest Town Hall, Forest Road, London E17 4JF ☎ 020 8496 3000 🖰 julian.ruaux@walthamforest.gov.uk

Building Control: Ms Lucy Shomali, Director - Regeneration & Growth, Town Hall, Forest Road, London E17 4JF ☎ 020 8496 6734 🖰 lucy.shomali@walthamforest.gov.uk

Catering Services: Ms Linda Woods, Head of Catering Services, Town Hall, Forest Road, London E17 4JF ☎ 020 8496 8271 🖰 linda.woods@walthamforest.gov.uk

Children / Youth Services: Ms Heather Flinders, Divisional Director - Children & Families, Town Hall, Forest Road, London E17 4JF ☎ 020 8496 3206 🖰 heather.flinders@walthamforest.gov.uk

Children / Youth Services: Ms Denise Humphrey, Group Manager of Early Help 11 - 18, Outset Centre, 1a Grange Road, London E17 8AH ☎ 020 8496 1534 🖰 denise.humphrey@walthamforest.gov.uk

PR / Communications: Ms Rhona Cadenhead, Assistant Chief Executive, Town Hall, Forest Road, London E17 4JF ☎ 020 8496 3000 🖰 rhoda.cadenhead@walthamforest.gov.uk

Computer Management: Mr Paul Golland, Head of ICT, Town Hall, Forest Road, London E17 4JF ☎ 020 8496 3629 🖰 paul.golland@walthamforest.gov.uk

Consumer Protection and Trading Standards: Ms Kellie Hopkins, Head of Neighbourhood Management, Sycamore House, Town Hall, Forest Road, London E17 4JF ☎ 020 8496 2201 🖰 kellie.hopkins@walthamforest.gov.uk

Contracts: Mr David Levy, Assistant Director of Procurement & Commissioning, PO Box 54, Civic Centre, Silver Street, Enfield EN1 3XF ☎ 020 8496 3000 🖰 dave.levy@walthamforest.gov.uk

Customer Service: Ms Sally Hodgson, Customer & Business Operations Director, Town Hall, Forest Road, London E17 4JF ☎ 020 8496 3000 🖰 sally.hogdson@walthamforest.gov.uk

Customer Service: Ms Michele Moloney, Director - Neighbourhoods & Commissioning, Town Hall, Forest Road, London E17 4JF ☎ 020 8496 3000 🖰 michele.moloney@walthamforest.gov.uk

Education: Ms Rosalind Turner, Interim Director - School Standards, Town Hall, Forest Road, London E17 4JF ☎ 020 8496 3000 🖰 rosalind.turner@walthamforest.gov.uk

E-Government: Mr Paul Golland, Head of ICT, Town Hall, Forest Road, London E17 4JF ☎ 020 8496 3629 🖰 paul.golland@walthamforest.gov.uk

Emergency Planning: Mr Ron Presswell, Design & Conservation Manager, Sycamore House, Waltham Forest Town Hall Complex, Forest Road, London E17 4JF ☎ 020 8496 6736 🖰 ron.presswell@walthamforest.gov.uk

Environmental / Technical Services: Ms Kellie Hopkins, Head of Neighbourhood Management, Sycamore House, Town Hall, Forest Road, London E17 4JF ☎ 020 8496 2201 🖰 kellie.hopkins@walthamforest.gov.uk

Environmental Health: Ms Kellie Hopkins, Head of Neighbourhood Management, Sycamore House, Town Hall, Forest Road, London E17 4JF ☎ 020 8496 2201 🖰 kellie.hopkins@walthamforest.gov.uk

Events Manager: Ms Corinne Hurn, Events Manager, Town Hall, Forest Road, London E17 4JF ☎ 020 8496 6793 🖰 corrine.hurn@walthamforest.gov.uk

Finance: Mr John Turnbull, Director - Finance & Chief Finance Officer, Town Hall, Forest Road, London E17 4JF ☎ 020 8496 3000 🖰 john.turnbull@walthamforest.gov.uk

Treasury: Ms Debbie Drew, Treasury & Pensions Manager, Town Hall, Forest Road, London E17 4JF ☎ 020 8496 8165 debbie.drew@walthamforest.gov.uk

Pensions: Ms Debbie Drew, Treasury & Pensions Manager, Town Hall, Forest Road, London E17 4JF ☎ 020 8496 8165 debbie.drew@walthamforest.gov.uk

Pensions: Ms Kelly Snow, Assistant Pensions Manager, Capita Hartshead, PO Box 195, Darlington DL1 9FS ☎ 01737 366039 kelly.snow@capita.co.uk

Fleet Management: Ms Kellie Hopkins, Head of Neighbourhood Management, Sycamore House, Town Hall, Forest Road, London E17 4JF ☎ 020 8496 2201 kellie.hopkins@walthamforest.gov.uk

Grounds Maintenance: Mr Ben Frearson, Project Engineer - Parks & Play, Town Hall, Forest Road, London E17 4JF ☎ 020 8496 2606 ben.frearson@walthamforest.gov.uk

Health and Safety: Ms ann Whalley, Health & Safety Manager, Town Hall, Forest Road, London E17 4JF ☎ 020 8496 6931 ann.whalley@walthamforest.gov.uk

Highways: Ms Kellie Hopkins, Head of Neighbourhood Management, Sycamore House, Town Hall, Forest Road, London E17 4JF ☎ 020 8496 2201 kellie.hopkins@walthamforest.gov.uk

Highways: Mr Kathiraval Valavan, Head of Highways, Low Hall, Argall Avenue, London E10 7AS ☎ 020 8496 2525 velu.valavan@walthamforest.gov.uk

Housing: Ms Lucy Shomali, Director - Regeneration & Growth, Town Hall, Forest Road, London E17 4JF ☎ 020 8496 6734 lucy.shomali@walthamforest.gov.uk

Legal: Mr Daniel Fenwick, Director - Governance, Town Hall, Forest Road, London E17 4JF ☎ 020 8496 4295 daniel.fenwick@walthamforest.gov.uk

Leisure and Cultural Services: Ms Lorna Lee, Head of Cultural & Community Services, Town Hall, Forest Road, London E17 4JF ☎ 020 8496 3203 lorna.lee@walthamforest.gov.uk

Licensing: Mr Adrian Simpson, Food, Safety & Trading Standards Manager, Town Hall, Forest Road, London E17 4JF ☎ 020 8496 2202 adrian.simpson@walthamforest.gov.uk

Lighting: Ms Kellie Hopkins, Head of Neighbourhood Management, Sycamore House, Town Hall, Forest Road, London E17 4JF ☎ 020 8496 2201 kellie.hopkins@walthamforest.gov.uk

Lighting: Mr Chris Warner, Street Lighting & Responsive Maintenance Manager, Low Hall, Argall Avenue, London E10 7AS ☎ 020 8496 2515 chris.warner@walthamforest.gov.uk

Lottery Funding, Charity and Voluntary: Ms Julie Simmons, Community Engagement Manager, Town Hall, Forest Road, London E17 4JF ☎ 020 8496 4150 julie.simmons@walthamforest.gov.uk

Member Services: Ms Angela Cater, Deputy Head - Councillor Services, Town Hall, Forest Road, London E17 4JF ☎ 020 8496 4611 angela.cater@walthamforest.gov.uk

Parking: Ms Karen Naylor, Head of Parking, Transport & CCTV, Low Hall Depot, Argall Avenue, London E10 7AS ☎ 020 8496 3000 Karen.naylor@walthamforest.gov.uk

Partnerships: Mr Alastair Macorkindale, Head of Community Safety, Sycamore House, Waltham Forest Town Hall Complex, Forest Road, London E17 4JF ☎ 020 8496 6827 alastair.macorkindale@walthamforest.gov.uk

Personnel / HR: Mr Gerry Kemble, Head of Schools Traded Services, Town Hall, Forest Road, London E17 4JF ☎ 020 8496 4300 gerry.kemble@walthamforest.gov.uk

Personnel / HR: Ms Althea Loderick, Chief Operating Officer, Town Hall, Forest Road, London E17 4JF ☎ 020 8496 3000 althea.loderick@walthamforest.gov.uk

Personnel / HR: Mr Stuart Petrie, Senior HR Business Partner, Town Hall, Forest Road, London E17 4JF ☎ 020 8496 8076 stuart.petrie@walthamforest.gov.uk

Planning: Ms Lucy Shomali, Director - Regeneration & Growth, Town Hall, Forest Road, London E17 4JF ☎ 020 8496 6734 lucy.shomali@walthamforest.gov.uk

Procurement: Mr David Levy, Assistant Director of Procurement & Commissioning, Town Hall, Forest Road, London E17 4JF ☎ 020 8496 3000 dave.levy@walthamforest.gov.uk

Public Libraries: Ms Lorna Lee, Head of Cultural & Community Services, Town Hall, Forest Road, London E17 4JF ☎ 020 8496 3203 lorna.lee@walthamforest.gov.uk

Recycling & Waste Minimisation: Ms Kellie Hopkins, Head of Neighbourhood Management, Sycamore House, Town Hall, Forest Road, London E17 4JF ☎ 020 8496 2201 kellie.hopkins@walthamforest.gov.uk

Regeneration: Ms Lucy Shomali, Director - Regeneration & Growth, Town Hall, Forest Road, London E17 4JF ☎ 020 8496 6734 lucy.shomali@walthamforest.gov.uk

Road Safety: Ms Safiah Ishfaq, Business Travel Plan Advisor, Low Hall Depot, Argall Avenue, London E10 7AS ☎ 020 8496 3000 safiah.ishfaq@walthamforest.gov.uk

Social Services: Ms Heather Flinders, Divisional Director - Children & Families, Town Hall, Forest Road, London E17 4JF ☎ 020 8496 3206 heather.flinders@walthamforest.gov.uk

Social Services: Mr Daniel Phelps, Divisional Director - Early Help, Town Hall, Forest Road, London E17 4JF ☎ 020 8496 5050 daniel.phelps@walthamforest.gov.uk

Social Services: Ms Linzi Roberts-Egan, Deputy Chief Executive - Families, Town Hall, Forest Road, London E17 4JF ☎ 020 8496 3500 linzi.roberts-egan@walthamforest.gov.uk

Social Services (Adult): Ms Senel Arkut, Divisional Director - Adult Social Care, Town Hall, Forest Road, London E17 4JF ☎ 020 8496 3200 ✉ senel.arkut@walthamforest.gov.uk

Social Services (Adult): Ms Bernice Solvey, Head of Assessment & Care, Town Hall, Forest Road, London E17 4JF ☎ 020 8496 3477 ✉ bernice.solvey@walthamforest.gov.uk

Social Services (Children): Ms Denise Humphrey, Group Manager of Early Help 11 - 18, Town Hall, Forest Road, London E17 4JF ☎ 020 8496 1534 ✉ denise.humphrey@walthamforest.gov.uk

Safeguarding: Ms Senel Arkut, Divisional Director - Adult Social Care, Town Hall, Forest Road, London E17 4JF ☎ 020 8496 3200 ✉ senel.arkut@walthamforest.gov.uk

Families: Ms Heather Flinders, Divisional Director - Children & Families, Town Hall, Forest Road, London E17 4JF ☎ 020 8496 3206 ✉ heather.flinders@walthamforest.gov.uk

Families: Mr Daniel Phelps, Divisional Director - Early Help, Town Hall, Forest Road, London E17 4JF ☎ 020 8496 5050 ✉ daniel.phelps@walthamforest.gov.uk

Families: Ms Linzi Roberts-Egan, Deputy Chief Executive - Families, Town Hall, Forest Road, London E17 4JF ☎ 020 8496 3500 ✉ linzi.roberts-egan@walthamforest.gov.uk

Public Health: Dr Andrew Taylor, Director - Public Health, Town Hall, Forest Road, London E17 4JF ☎ 020 8496 3000 ✉ andrew.taylor@walthamforest.gov.uk

Street Scene: Ms Kellie Hopkins, Head of Neighbourhood Management, Sycamore House, Town Hall, Forest Road, London E17 4JF ☎ 020 8496 2201 ✉ kellie.hopkins@walthamforest.gov.uk

Tourism: Ms Lorna Lee, Head of Cultural & Community Services, Silverbirch House, Uplands Business Park, Blackhorse Lane, Walthamstow, London E17 5SN ☎ 020 8496 3203 ✉ lorna.lee@walthamforest.gov.uk

Traffic Management: Ms Kellie Hopkins, Head of Neighbourhood Management, Sycamore House, Town Hall, Forest Road, London E17 4JF ☎ 020 8496 2201 ✉ kellie.hopkins@walthamforest.gov.uk

Transport: Mr Kathiraval Valavan, Head of Highways, Low Hall, Argall Avenue, London E10 7AS ☎ 020 8496 2525 ✉ velu.valavan@walthamforest.gov.uk

Transport Planner: Mr Neil Bullen, Sustainable Transport Manager, Sycamore House, Town Hall, Forest Road, London E17 4JF ☎ 020 8496 3000 ✉ neil.bullen@walthamforest.gov.uk

Waste Collection and Disposal: Ms Kellie Hopkins, Head of Neighbourhood Management, Sycamore House, Town Hall, Forest Road, London E17 4JF ☎ 020 8496 2201 ✉ kellie.hopkins@walthamforest.gov.uk

Waste Management: Ms Kellie Hopkins, Head of Neighbourhood Management, Sycamore House, Town Hall, Forest Road, London E17 4JF ☎ 020 8496 2201 ✉ kellie.hopkins@walthamforest.gov.uk

Children's Play Areas: Ms Margaret Burke, Group Manager of Early Help 0 - 11, Town Hall, Forest Road, London E17 4JF ☎ 020 8496 3557 ✉ Margaret.burke@walthamforest.gov.uk

COUNCILLORS

***Mayor* Mahmud**, Saima (LAB - Hoe Street)
cllr.saima.mahmud@walthamforest.gov.uk

***Leader of the Council* Robbins**, Chris (LAB - Grove Green)
leader@walthamforest.gov.uk

***Deputy Leader of the Council* Loakes**, Clyde (LAB - Leytonstone)
cllr.clyde.loakes@walthamforest.gov.uk

***Group Leader* Davis**, Matt (CON - Chingford Green)
cllr.matt.davis@walthamforest.gov.uk

Ahmad, Masood (LAB - Lea Bridge)
Cllr_m_ahmad@hotmail.com

Ali, Liaquat (LAB - High Street)
cllr.liaquat.ali@walthamforest.gov.uk

Ali, Nadeem (LAB - William Morris)
cllr.nadeem.ali@walthamforest.gov.uk

Anwar, Raja (LAB - High Street)
cllr.raja.anwar@walthamforest.gov.uk

Asghar, Naheed (LAB - Cathall)
cllr.naheed.asghar@walthamforest.gov.uk

Asghar, Mohammad (LAB - Lea Bridge)
cllr.mohammad.asghar@walthamforest.gov.uk

Balkan, Millie (CON - Larkswood)
cllr.millie.balkan@walthamforest.gov.uk

Barnett, Peter (LAB - Wood Street)
cllr.peter.barnett@walthamforest.gov.uk

Bean, Angie (LAB - Wood Street)
cllr.angie.bean@walthamforest.gov.uk

Beg, Aktar (LAB - Valley)
cllr.aktar.beg@walthamforest.gov.uk

Bell, Tony (LAB - Hale End and Highams Park)
cllr.tony.bell@walthamforest.gov.uk

Bellamy, Karen (LAB - Higham Hill)
cllr.karen.bellamy@walthamforest.gov.uk

Bennett-Goodman, Tim (LAB - Higham Hill)
cllr.tim.bennett-goodman@walthamforest.gov.uk

Berberi, Kastriot (LAB - Forest)
cllr.kastriot.berberi@walthamforest.gov.uk

Berg, Roy (CON - Endlebury)
cllr.roy.berg@walthamforest.gov.uk

Braham, Paul (CON - Hale End and Highams Park)
cllr.paul.braham@walthamforest.gov.uk

Coghill, Clare (LAB - High Street)
cllr.clare.coghill@walthamforest.gov.uk

Dhedi, Shabana (LAB - Forest)
cllr.shabana.dhedhi@walthamforest.gov.uk

Douglas, Paul (LAB - Chapel End)
cllr.paul.douglas@walthamforest.gov.uk

Edwards, Patrick (LAB - Cann Hall)
cllr.patrick.edwards@walthamforest.gov.uk

WALTHAM FOREST

Edwards, Jacob (LAB - Leyton)
cllr.jacob.edwards@walthamforest.gov.uk

Emmerson, Stuart (LAB - William Morris)
cllr.stuart.emmerson@walthamforest.gov.uk

Erics, Caroline (CON - Endlebury)
cllr.caroline.erics@walthamforest.gov.uk

Fitzgerald, Marion (CON - Hatch Lane)
cllr.marion.fitzgerald@walthamforest.gov.uk

Gray, Jenny (LAB - Leytonstone)
cllr.jenny.gray@walthamforest.gov.uk

Halebi, Nick (CON - Chingford Green)
cllr.nick.halebi@walthamforest.gov.uk

Hemsted, Andy (CON - Chingford Green)
Andyhemsted1066@gmail.com

Hemsted, Jemma (CON - Valley)
cllr.jemma.hemsted@walthamforest.gov.uk

Herrington, Peter (CON - Endlebury)
cllr.peter.herrington@walthamforest.gov.uk

Highfield, Shameem (LAB - Cathall)
cllr.ska.highfield@walthamforest.gov.uk

Ihenachor, Whitney (LAB - Leyton)
cllr.whitney.ihenachor@walthamforest.gov.uk

James, Tim (CON - Hatch Lane)
cllr.tim.james@walthamforest.gov.uk

Khan, Ahsan (LAB - Hoe Street)
cllr.ahsan.khan@walthamforest.gov.uk

Khan, Johar (LAB - Markhouse)
cllr.johar.khan@walthamforest.gov.uk

Limbajee, Khevyn (LAB - Grove Green)
cllr.khevyn.limbajee@walthamforest.gov.uk

Littlejohn, Sally (LAB - Cann Hall)
cllr.sally.littlejohn@walthamforest.gov.uk

Lyons, Gerry (LAB - Forest)
cllr.gerry.lyons@walthamforest.gov.uk

Mahmood, Asim (LAB - Markhouse)
cllr.asim.mahmood@walthamforest.gov.uk

Mbachu, Anna (LAB - Grove Green)
cllr.anna.mbachu@walthamforest.gov.uk

Mill, Bernadette (CON - Larkswood)
cllr.bernadette.mill@walthamforest.gov.uk

Miller, Simon (LAB - Leyton)
cllr.simon.miller@walthamforest.gov.uk

Mitchell, Louise (LAB - Chapel End)
cllr.louise.mitchell@walthamforest.gov.uk

Moss, John (CON - Larkswood)
cllr.john.jc.moss@walthamforest.gov.uk

Osho, Yemi (LAB - Lea Bridge)
cllr.yemi.osho@walthamforest.gov.uk

Pye, Marie (LAB - Leytonstone)
cllr.marie.pye@walthamforest.gov.uk

Rackham, Sheree (CON - Hale End and Highams Park)
cllr.sheree.rackham@walthamforest.gov.uk

Rayner, Keith (LAB - Cann Hall)
cllr.keith.rayner@walthamforest.gov.uk

Rusling, Mark (LAB - Hoe Street)
cllr.mark.rusling@walthamforest.gov.uk

Siggers, Alan (CON - Valley)

Strathern, Alistair (LAB - Higham Hill)
cllr.alistair.strathern@walthamforest.gov.uk

Sweden, Richard (LAB - Wood Street)
cllr.richard.sweden@walthamforest.gov.uk

Terry, Steve (LAB - Chapel End)
cllr.steve.terry@walthamforest.gov.uk

Waldron, Sharon (LAB - Markhouse)
cllr.sharon.waldron@walthamforest.gov.uk

Walker, Geoffrey (CON - Hatch Lane)
cllr.geoff.walker@ntlworld.com

Wheeler, Terry (LAB - Cathall)
cllr.terry.wheeler@walthamforest.gov.uk

Williams, Grace (LAB - William Morris)
cllr.grace.williams@walthamforest.gov.uk

POLITICAL COMPOSITION

LAB: 44, CON: 16

COMMITTEE CHAIRS

Audit & Governance: Mr Paul Douglas

Licensing: Mr Nadeem Ali

Pensions: Mr Simon Miller

Planning: Mr Stuart Emmerson

Wandsworth L

Wandsworth London Borough Council, Town Hall, Wandsworth High Street, London SW18 2PU
☎ 020 8871 6000 💻 www.wandsworth.gov.uk

FACTS AND FIGURES

Parliamentary Constituencies: Battersea, Putney, Tooting
EU Constituencies: London
Election Frequency: Elections are of whole council

PRINCIPAL OFFICERS

Chief Executive: Mr Paul Martin, Chief Executive & Director of Administration, Town Hall, Wandsworth High Street, London SW18 2PU ☎ 020 8871 6001 🖷 020 8871 8321
pmartin@wandsworth.gov.uk

Deputy Chief Executive: Mr Chris Buss, Director of Finance & Deputy Chief Executive, Town Hall, Wandsworth High Street, London SW18 2PU ☎ 020 8871 8300 🖷 020 8877 1915
cbuss@wandsworth.gov.uk

Senior Management: Mr Chris Buss, Director of Finance & Deputy Chief Executive, Town Hall, Wandsworth High Street, London SW18 2PU ☎ 020 8871 8300 🖷 020 8877 1915
cbuss@wandsworth.gov.uk

Senior Management: Mr Brian Reilly, Director of Housing & Community Services, Housing Department, 17-27 Garratt Lane, London SW18 4AE ☎ 020 8871 6591 🖷 020 8871 6778
hcs@wandsworth.gov.uk

Senior Management: Ms Dawn Warwick, Director of Education & Social Services, Town Hall, Wandsworth High Street, London SW18 2PU ☎ 020 8871 6291 🖷 020 8871 7995 dwarwick@wandsworth.gov.uk

Access Officer / Social Services (Disability): Toni Symonds, Access Team Manager, 2nd Floor, Bridas House, Putney Bridge Road, London SW18 1HR ☎ 020 8871 8811 🖷 020 8871 6949 tsymonds@wandsworth.gov.uk

Architect, Building / Property Services: Mr Andy Algar, Head of Property Services, Town Hall, Wandsworth High Street, London SW18 2PU ☎ 020 8871 6075 aalgar@wandsworth.gov.uk

Best Value: Mr Jon Evans, Head of Policy & Communications, Town Hall, Wandsworth High Street, London SW18 2PU ☎ 020 8871 7815 jevans@wandsworth.gov.uk

Building Control: Mr Robert Foulger, Head of Building Control, Town Hall, Wandsworth High Street, London SW18 2PU ☎ 020 8871 7617 🖷 020 8871 6003 rfougler@wandsworth.gov.uk

Building Control: Mr B Glocking, Head of Building & Development, Town Hall, Wandsworth High Street, London SW18 2PU ☎ 020 8871 8311 🖷 020 8871 7212 bglocking@wandsworth.gov.uk

Catering Services: Mr John Dutton, Head of Facilities Management, Town Hall, Wandsworth High Street, London SW18 2PU ☎ 020 8871 7645 🖷 020 8871 7798 jdutton@wandsworth.gov.uk

Children / Youth Services: Ms Dawn Warwick, Director of Education & Social Services, Town Hall, Wandsworth High Street, London SW18 2PU ☎ 020 8871 6291 🖷 020 8871 7995 dwarwick@wandsworth.gov.uk

Civil Registration: Mr Martin Walker, Borough Solicitor & Assistant Director of Administration, Town Hall, Wandsworth High Street, London SW18 2PU ☎ 020 8871 6110 🖷 020 8871 7506 mwalker@wandsworth.gov.uk

PR / Communications: Mr Jon Evans, Head of Policy & Communications, Town Hall, Wandsworth High Street, London SW18 2PU ☎ 020 8871 7815 jevans@wandsworth.gov.uk

Community Planning: Mr Jon Evans, Head of Policy & Communications, Town Hall, Wandsworth High Street, London SW18 2PU ☎ 020 8871 7815 jevans@wandsworth.gov.uk

Community Safety: Mr Stewart Low, Head of Community Safety, Town Hall, Wandsworth High Street, London SW18 2PU ☎ 020 8871 6588 slow@wandsworth.gov.uk

Computer Management: Mr D Tidey, Head of IT & Business Communications, Town Hall, Wandsworth High Street, London SW18 2PU ☎ 020 8871 6080 🖷 020 8871 8650 dtidey@wandsworth.gov.uk

Consumer Protection and Trading Standards: Mr Paul Browne, Team Leader & Chief Inspector of Weights & Measures, Town Hall, Wandsworth High Street, London SW18 2PU ☎ 020 8871 7383 pbrowne@wandsworth.gov.uk

Contracts: Mr Mark Glaister, Head of Procurement, Town Hall, Wandsworth High Street, London SW18 2PU ☎ 020 8871 5828 🖷 020 8871 6777 mglaister@wandsworth.gov.uk

Customer Service: Mr D Tidey, Head of IT & Business Communications, Town Hall, Wandsworth High Street, London SW18 2PU ☎ 020 8871 6080 🖷 020 8871 8650 dtidey@wandsworth.gov.uk

Direct Labour: Mr Kevin Power, Assistant Director of Operational Services, Frogmore House, Dormay Street, London SW18 1EY ☎ 020 8871 6704 🖷 020 8871 7562 kpower@wandsworth.gov.uk

Economic Development: Mr Nick Smales, Economic Development Officer, Town Hall, Wandsworth High Street, London SW18 2PU ☎ 020 8871 6202 🖷 020 8871 8200 nsmales@wandsworth.gov.uk

Education: Mr John Johnson, Assistant Director of Education, Performance & Planning, Town Hall, Wandsworth High Street, London SW18 2PU ☎ 020 8871 7891 🖷 020 8871 6609 jjohnson@wandsworth.gov.uk

E-Government: Mr D Tidey, Head of IT & Business Communications, Town Hall, Wandsworth High Street, London SW18 2PU ☎ 020 8871 6080 🖷 020 8871 8650 dtidey@wandsworth.gov.uk

Electoral Registration: Mr Martin Walker, Borough Solicitor & Assistant Director of Administration, Town Hall, Wandsworth High Street, London SW18 2PU ☎ 020 8871 6110 🖷 020 8871 7506 mwalker@wandsworth.gov.uk

Emergency Planning: Mrs Debbie Western, Emergency Planning Officer, Frogmore House, Dormay Street, London SW18 1EY ☎ 020 8871 5747 🖷 020 8871 5799 dwestern@wandsworth.gov.uk

Energy Management: Mr Andy Algar, Head of Property Services, Town Hall, Wandsworth High Street, London SW18 2PU ☎ 020 8871 6075 aalgar@wandsworth.gov.uk

Environmental Health: Mrs Sue Kelleher, Head of Environmental Services & Strategic Business Management, Town Hall, Wandsworth High Street, London SW18 2PU ☎ 020 8871 8164 skelleher@wandsworth.gov.uk

Estates, Property & Valuation: Mr Andy Algar, Head of Property Services, Town Hall, Wandsworth High Street, London SW18 2PU ☎ 020 8871 6075 aalgar@wandsworth.gov.uk

European Liaison: Mr Nick Smales, Economic Development Officer, Town Hall, Wandsworth High Street, London SW18 2PU ☎ 020 8871 6202 🖷 020 8871 8200 nsmales@wandsworth.gov.uk

Events Manager: Mr Jack Adam, Security, Arts, Events & Filming, The Park Office, Battersea Park, London SW11 4NJ ☎ 020 8871 7636 🖷 020 7223 7919 jadam@wandsworth.gov.uk

Facilities: Mr John Dutton, Head of Facilities Management, Town Hall, Wandsworth High Street, London SW18 2PU ☎ 020 8871 7645 🖷 020 8871 7798 jdutton@wandsworth.gov.uk

Finance: Mr Chris Buss, Director of Finance & Deputy Chief Executive, Town Hall, Wandsworth High Street, London SW18 2PU ☎ 020 8871 8300 🖷 020 8877 1915 🖱 cbuss@wandsworth.gov.uk

Pensions: Mr Peter Harris, Pension Investments Officer, Town Hall, Wandsworth High Street, London SW18 2PU ☎ 020 8871 8887 🖱 pharris@wandsworth.gov.uk

Pensions: Ms Colette Hollands, Pensions Manager, Town Hall, Wandsworth High Street, London SW18 2PU ☎ 020 8871 6522 🖱 chollands@wandsworth.gov.uk

Fleet Management: Mr Ricky Cousins, Transport & Fleet Manager, Mechanical Workshops, Frogmore Complex, Dormay Street, London SW18 1EY ☎ 020 8871 6762 🖷 020 8871 8656 🖱 rcousins@wandsworth.gov.uk

Grounds Maintenance: Mr Simon Cooper-Grundy, Chief Parks Officer, Park Services, Battersea Park, London SW11 4NJ ☎ 020 8871 8117 🖷 020 8871 7533 🖱 scooper-grundy@wandsworth.gov.uk

Health and Safety: Mr John Throssell, Health & Safety Manager, Town Hall, Wandsworth High Street, London SW18 2PU ☎ 020 8871 6220 🖷 020 8871 8502 🖱 jthrossell@wandsworth.gov.uk

Highways: Mr Wale Adeyoyin, Head of Parking & Road Safety, Town Hall, Wandsworth High Street, London SW18 2PU ☎ 020 8871 6970 🖷 020 8871 8399 🖱 wadeyoyin@wandsworth.gov.uk

Housing: Mr Brian Reilly, Director of Housing & Community Services, Housing Department, 17-27 Garratt Lane, London SW18 4AE ☎ 020 8871 6591 🖷 020 8871 6778 🖱 hcs@wandsworth.gov.uk

Housing: Mr Dave Worth, Head of Housing Services, Housing Department, 17 - 27 Garratt Lane, London SW18 4AE ☎ 020 8871 6837 🖷 020 8871 8655 🖱 hcs@wandsworth.gov.uk

Housing Maintenance: Mr Ian Stewart, Head of Housing Management, Housing Department, 17 - 27 Garratt Lane, London SW18 4AE ☎ 020 8871 6831 🖷 020 8871 6778 🖱 hcs@wandsworth.gov.uk

Legal: Mr Martin Walker, Borough Solicitor & Assistant Director of Administration, Town Hall, Wandsworth High Street, London SW18 2PU ☎ 020 8871 6110 🖷 020 8871 7506 🖱 mwalker@wandsworth.gov.uk

Leisure and Cultural Services: Mr Paul McCue, Assistant Director of Leisure & Culture, Town Hall, Wandsworth High Street, London SW18 2PU ☎ 020 8871 6868 🖷 020 8871 8349 🖱 pmccue@wandsworth.gov.uk

Lifelong Learning: Mr Santino Fragola, Head of Lifelong Learning, Professional Centre, Franciscan Road, Tooting, London SW17 8HE ☎ 020 8871 8491 🖱 sfragola@wandsworth.gov.uk

Lighting: Mr Steve Kempster, Assistant Head of Operational Services, Frogmore Complex, Dormay Street, London SW18 1HA ☎ 020 8871 6570 🖷 020 8871 7562 🖱 skempster@wandsworth.gov.uk

Lottery Funding, Charity and Voluntary: Mr Nick Smales, Economic Development Officer, Town Hall, Wandsworth High Street, London SW18 2PU ☎ 020 8871 6202 🖷 020 8871 8200 🖱 nsmales@wandsworth.gov.uk

Member Services: Mr Martin Walker, Borough Solicitor & Assistant Director of Administration, Town Hall, Wandsworth High Street, London SW18 2PU ☎ 020 8871 6110 🖷 020 8871 7506 🖱 mwalker@wandsworth.gov.uk

Parking: Mr Wale Adeyoyin, Head of Parking & Road Safety, Town Hall, Wandsworth High Street, London SW18 2PU ☎ 020 8871 6970 🖷 020 8871 8399 🖱 wadeyoyin@wandsworth.gov.uk

Partnerships: Mr Jon Evans, Head of Policy & Communications, Town Hall, Wandsworth High Street, London SW18 2PU ☎ 020 8871 7815 🖱 jevans@wandsworth.gov.uk

Personnel / HR: Mr Graeme Lennon, Head of HR, Town Hall, Wandsworth High Street, London SW18 2PU ☎ 020 8871 6007 🖷 020 8871 6185 🖱 glennon@wandsworth.gov.uk

Planning: Mr Tim Cronin, Head of Planning & Development, Town Hall, Wandsworth High Street, London SW18 2PU ☎ 020 8871 6627 🖱 tcronin@wandsworth.gov.uk

Procurement: Mr Mark Glaister, Head of Procurement, Town Hall, Wandsworth High Street, London SW18 2PU ☎ 020 8871 5828 🖷 020 8871 6777 🖱 mglaister@wandsworth.gov.uk

Public Libraries: Mr Paul McCue, Assistant Director of Leisure & Culture, Town Hall, Wandsworth High Street, London SW18 2PU ☎ 020 8871 6868 🖷 020 8871 8349 🖱 pmccue@wandsworth.gov.uk

Recycling & Waste Minimisation: Mr Shaun Morley, Head of Waste Management, Tadmore House, Frogmore Complex, Dormay Street, London SW18 1HA ☎ 020 8871 6938 🖷 020 8871 6383 🖱 smorley@wandsworth.gov.uk

Road Safety: Mr Wale Adeyoyin, Head of Parking & Road Safety, Town Hall, Wandsworth High Street, London SW18 2PU ☎ 020 8871 6970 🖷 020 8871 8399 🖱 wadeyoyin@wandsworth.gov.uk

Social Services: Ms Dawn Warwick, Director of Education & Social Services, Town Hall, Wandsworth High Street, London SW18 2PU ☎ 020 8871 6291 🖷 020 8871 7995 🖱 dwarwick@wandsworth.gov.uk

Social Services (Adult): Mr Rob Persey, Assistant Director - Secondment to Head of Joint Commissioning Unit - Education & Social Services, 90 Putney Bridge Road, Wandsworth, London SW18 1HR ☎ 020 8871 7803 🖷 020 8871 7995 🖱 rpersey@wandsworth.gov.uk

Social Services (Adult): Mr Alistair Rush, Assistant Director of Business Resources, Town Hall, Wandsworth High Street, London SW18 2PU ☎ 020 8871 6216 🖷 020 8871 7995 🖱 arush@wandsworth.gov.uk

Social Services (Adult): Mr Kerry Stevens, Assistant Director of Operations (Adults), Town Hall, Wandsworth High Street, London SW18 2PU ☎ 020 8871 8423 🖷 020 8871 7995 🖱 kstevens1@wandsworth.gov.uk

Social Services (Children): Ms Linda Webber, Practice Development Manager, Town Hall, Wandsworth High Street, London SW18 2PU ☎ 020 8871 8610 ✉ lwebber@wandsworth.gov.uk

Social Services (Children): Mr R Wright, Adoption Manager, Town Hall, Wandsworth High Street, London SW18 2PU ☎ 020 8871 7252 ✉ rwright2@wandsworth.gov.uk

Public Health: Dr Houda Al-Shafira, Director - Public Health, Town Hall, Wandsworth High Street, London SW18 2PU ✉ houda.al-sharifi@wandsworth.gov.uk

Staff Training: Mr Graeme Lennon, Head of HR, Town Hall, Wandsworth High Street, London SW18 2PU ☎ 020 8871 6007 🖷 020 8871 6185 ✉ glennon@wandsworth.gov.uk

Street Scene: Mr David Tidley, Group Leader - Transformation, Town Hall, Wandsworth High Street, London SW18 2PU ☎ 020 8871 6970 🖷 020 8871 8349 ✉ dtidley@wandsworth.gov.uk

Sustainable Communities: Mr Jon Evans, Head of Policy & Communications, Town Hall, Wandsworth High Street, London SW18 2PU ☎ 020 8871 7815 ✉ jevans@wandsworth.gov.uk

Sustainable Development: Mr Jon Evans, Head of Policy & Communications, Town Hall, Wandsworth High Street, London SW18 2PU ☎ 020 8871 7815 ✉ jevans@wandsworth.gov.uk

Tourism: Mr Paul McCue, Assistant Director of Leisure & Culture, Town Hall, Wandsworth High Street, London SW18 2PU ☎ 020 8871 6868 🖷 020 8871 8349 ✉ pmccue@wandsworth.gov.uk

Town Centre: Mr Nick Smales, Economic Development Officer, Town Hall, Wandsworth High Street, London SW18 2PU ☎ 020 8871 6202 🖷 020 8871 8200 ✉ nsmales@wandsworth.gov.uk

Traffic Management: Mr Wale Adeyoyin, Head of Parking & Road Safety, Town Hall, Wandsworth High Street, London SW18 2PU ☎ 020 8871 6970 🖷 020 8871 8399 ✉ wadeyoyin@wandsworth.gov.uk

Transport: Mr Ricky Cousins, Transport & Fleet Manager, Mechanical Workshops, Frogmore Complex, Dormay Street, London SW18 1EY ☎ 020 8871 6762 🖷 020 8871 8656 ✉ rcousins@wandsworth.gov.uk

Transport Planner: Mr John Stone, Head of Forward Planning & Transportation, Town Hall Extension, Wandsworth High Street, London SW18 2PU ☎ 020 8871 6628 🖷 020 8871 6003 ✉ jstone@wandsworth.gov.uk

Waste Collection and Disposal: Mr Shaun Morley, Head of Waste Management, Tadmore House, Frogmore Complex, Dormay Street, London SW18 1HA ☎ 020 8871 6938 🖷 020 8871 6383 ✉ smorley@wandsworth.gov.uk

Waste Management: Mr Shaun Morley, Head of Waste Management, Tadmore House, Frogmore Complex, Dormay Street, London SW18 1HA ☎ 020 8871 6938 🖷 020 8871 6383 ✉ smorley@wandsworth.gov.uk

COUNCILLORS

***Mayor* Nardelli**, Nicola (CON - Queenstown)
nnardelli@wandsworth.gov.uk

***Deputy Mayor* McDonnell**, Leslie (CON - East Putney)
lmcdonnell@wandsworth.gov.uk

***Leader of the Council* Govindia**, Ravi (CON - East Putney)
rgovindia@wandsworth.gov.uk

***Deputy Leader of the Council* Cook**, Jonathan (CON - Shaftesbury)
jonathancook@wandsworth.gov.uk

Allin-Khan, Rosena (LAB - Bedford)
rallin-khan@wandsworth.gov.uk

Ambache, Jeremy (LAB - Roehampton and Putney Heath)
jambache@wandsworth.gov.uk

Anderson, Fleur (LAB - Bedford)
fanderson@wandsworth.gov.uk

Belton, Tony (LAB - Latchmere)
tbelton@wandsworth.gov.uk

Caddy, Kim (CON - Southfields)
kcaddy@wandsworth.gov.uk

Carpenter, Peter (LAB - Roehampton and Putney Heath)
pcarpenter@wandsworth.gov.uk

Clay, Claire (CON - Wandsworth Common)
cclay@wandsworth.gov.uk

Cooper, Leonie (LAB - Furzedown)
leoniecooper@wandsworth.gov.uk

Cooper, Jane (CON - West Putney)
janecooper@wandsworth.gov.uk

Cousins, James (IND - Shaftesbury)
jcousins@wandsworth.gov.uk

Critchard, Annamarie (LAB - Tooting)
acritchard@wandsworth.gov.uk

Crivelli, George (CON - East Putney)
gcrivelli@wandsworth.gov.uk

Cuff, Nick (CON - West Hill)
ncuff@wandsworth.gov.uk

Daley, James (LAB - Tooting)
jamesdaley@wandsworth.gov.uk

Dawson, Peter (CON - Northcote)
pdawson@wandsworth.gov.uk

Dodd, Jane (CON - Northcote)
jdodd@wandsworth.gov.uk

Dunn, Antonia (CON - Bedford)
adunn@wandsworth.gov.uk

Ellis, Paul (CON - Balham)
pellis@wandsworth.gov.uk

Ephson, Sally-Ann (LAB - Queenstown)
sephson@wandsworth.gov.uk

Field, Richard (CON - Nightingale)
rfield@wandsworth.gov.uk

Gibbons, Andy (LAB - Graveney)
agibbons@wandsworth.gov.uk

Graham, Angela (CON - Earlsfield)
agraham@wandsworth.gov.uk

Grimston, Malcolm (IND - West Hill)
mgrimston@wandsworth.gov.uk

Hampton, Melanie (CON - St Mary's Park)
mhampton@wandsworth.gov.uk

Hanson, Marie (CON - Queenstown)
mhanson@wandsworth.gov.uk

Hart, Ian (CON - Nightingale)
ihart@wandsworth.gov.uk

Heaster, Maurice (CON - Wandsworth Common)
mheaster@wandsworth.gov.uk

Hogg, Simon (LAB - Latchmere)
shogg@wandsworth.gov.uk

Humphries, Guy (CON - Southfields)
ghumphries@wandsworth.gov.uk

Johnson, Benjamin (LAB - Tooting)
bjohnson@wandsworth.gov.uk

Johnson, Martin (CON - Northcote)
martinjohnson@wandsworth.gov.uk

Jones, Candida (LAB - Furzedown)
cjones1@wandsworth.gov.uk

Lescott, Charles (CON - Earlsfield)
clescott@wandsworth.gov.uk

Lewer, Ian (CON - West Putney)
ilewer@wandsworth.gov.uk

Macdonald, Alaina (LAB - Graveney)
amacdonald1@wandsworth.gov.uk

Maddan, James (CON - Thamesfield)
jmaddan@wandsworth.gov.uk

McCausland, Piers (CON - Fairfield)
pmccausland@wandsworth.gov.uk

McDermott, Sarah (CON - Nightingale)
smcdermott@wandsworth.gov.uk

McKinney, Sue (LAB - Roehampton and Putney Heath)
smckinney@wandsworth.gov.uk

O'Broin, Rory (CON - St Mary's Park)
ro'broin@wandsworth.gov.uk

Osborn, Rex (LAB - Graveney)
rosborn@wandsworth.gov.uk

Peterkin, Andrew (CON - West Hill)
apeterkin@wandsworth.gov.uk

Ryder, Michael (CON - Thamesfield)
mryder@wandsworth.gov.uk

Salier, Clare (CON - Balham)
csalier@wandsworth.gov.uk

Senior, Guy (CON - Shaftesbury)
gsenior@wandsworth.gov.uk

Speck, Wendy (LAB - Latchmere)
wspeck@wandsworth.gov.uk

Stokes, Rachael (LAB - Earlsfield)
rstokes@wandsworth.gov.uk

Strickland, Tessa (CON - St Mary's Park)
tstrickland@wandsworth.gov.uk

Sutters, Steffi (CON - West Putney)
ssutters@wandsworth.gov.uk

Sweet, Will (CON - Fairfield)
wsweet@wandsworth.gov.uk

Thom, Stuart (CON - Fairfield)
sthom@wandsworth.gov.uk

Thomas, Mark (LAB - Furzedown)
markthomas@wandsworth.gov.uk

Torrington, Rosemary (CON - Thamesfield)
rtorrington@wandsworth.gov.uk

Tracey, Kathy (CON - Wandsworth Common)
ktracey@wandworth.gov.uk

Usher, Caroline (CON - Balham)
cusher@wandsworth.gov.uk

Walsh, Terence (CON - Southfields)
twalsh@wandsworth.gov.uk

POLITICAL COMPOSITION
CON: 39, LAB: 19, IND: 2

COMMITTEE CHAIRS
Adult Care & Health: Mrs Claire Clay

Audit: Mr Maurice Heaster

Licensing: Mrs Caroline Usher

Pensions: Mr Maurice Heaster

Planning: Mrs Sarah McDermott

Warrington U

Warrington Borough Council, Town Hall, Sankey Street, Warrington WA1 1UH
☎ 01925 443322 🖷 01925 442138 🖳 www.warrington.gov.uk

FACTS AND FIGURES
Parliamentary Constituencies: Warrington North, Warrington South
EU Constituencies: North West
Election Frequency: Elections are by thirds

PRINCIPAL OFFICERS
Chief Executive: Prof Steven Broomhead, Chief Executive, Town Hall, Sankey Street, Warrington WA1 1UH ☎ 01925 442101 🖷 01925 442138 ✉ sbroomhead@warrington.gov.uk

Deputy Chief Executive: Ms Katherine Fairclough, Deputy Chief Executive, Town Hall, Sankey Street, Warrington WA1 1UH ☎ 01925 442311 🖷 01925 442312 ✉ kfairclough@warrington.gov.uk

Senior Management: Mr Andy Farrall, Executive Director - Economic Regeneration, Growth & Environment, Town Hall, Sankey Street, Warrington WA1 1UH ☎ 01925 442701 🖷 01925 442704 ✉ afarrall@warrington.gov.uk

Senior Management: Mr Steve Reddy, Executive Director - Families & Wellbeing, Town Hall, Sankey Street, Warrington WA1 1UH ☎ 01925 442900 ✉ sreddy@warrington.gov.uk

Senior Management: Dr Rita Robertson, Director - Public Health, New Town House, Buttermarket Street, Warrington WA1 2NJ ☎ 01925 443967 ✉ rrobertson@warrington.gov.uk

Access Officer / Social Services (Disability): Mr Steve Peddie, Operational Director - Adult Services, New Town House, Buttermarket Street, Warrington WA1 2NJ ☎ 01925 444251 ✉ speddie@warrington.gov.uk

Architect, Building / Property Services: Mr Stewart Brown, Service Manager - Property & Estates, New Town House, Buttermarket Street, Warrington WA1 2NJ ☎ 01925 442850 ✉ s_brown@warrington.gov.uk

Building Control: Mr Tony Gartside, Service Manager - Building Control, New Town House, Buttermarket Street, Warrington WA1 2NJ ☎ 01925 442547 ✉ tgartside@warrington.gov.uk

Children / Youth Services: Ms Fiona Waddington, Assistant Director - Children & Young People's Targeted Services, 2nd Floor, New Town House, Buttermarket Street, Warrington WA1 1NJ ☎ 01925 443900 ✉ fwaddington@warrington.gov.uk

Civil Registration: Ms Jane Briscall, Superintendent Registrar - Births, Death & Marriages, The Registry Office, Museum Street, Warrington WA1 1JX ☎ 01925 442706 🖷 01925 442739 ✉ jbriscall1@warrington.gov.uk

PR / Communications: Ms Lynda Fothergill, Interim Communications Manager, Town Hall, Sankey Street, Warrington WA1 1UH ☎ 01925 442125 ✉ x-lfothergill@warrington.gov.uk

Community Safety: Mr Doug Ryan, Crime & Disorder Reduction Manager, Charles Stewart House, 55 Museum Street, Warrington WA1 1NE ☎ 01606 364850 🖷 01606 363809 ✉ Douglas.Ryan@cheshire.pnn.police.uk

Computer Management: Mr Keith Traverse, Head of IT & Print Service, New Town House, Buttermarket Street, Warrington WA1 1NJ ☎ 01925 443949 ✉ ktraverse@warrington.gov.uk

Consumer Protection and Trading Standards: Mr Peter Astley, Assistant Director - Regulation & Public Protection, New Town House, Buttermarket Street, Warrington WA1 1NJ ☎ 01925 442672 🖷 01925 442655 ✉ pastley@warrington.gov.uk

Customer Service: Ms Alex Grundy, Customer Contact Manager, Contact Warrington, 26 - 30 Horsemarket Street, Warrington WA1 1XL ☎ 01925 442418 ✉ agrundy@warrington.gov.uk

Economic Development: Mr Andy Farrall, Executive Director - Economic Regeneration, Growth & Environment, Town Hall, Sankey Street, Warrington WA1 1UH ☎ 01925 442700 🖷 01925 442704 ✉ afarrall@warrington.gov.uk

Education: Mrs Sarah Callaghan, Operational Director - Children & Young People's Universal Services, New Town House, Buttermarket Street, Warrington WA1 1NJ ☎ 01925 442940 ✉ scallaghan@warrington.gov.uk

E-Government: Mr Lynton Green, Director of Finance & Information Services, Quattro Building, Buttermarket Street, Warrington WA1 1BN ☎ 01925 443925 ✉ lgreen@warrington.gov.uk

Electoral Registration: Mrs Alison McCormick, Electoral Services Manager, Town Hall, Sankey Street, Warrington WA1 1UH ☎ 01925 442041 🖷 01925 656278 ✉ amccormick@warrnington.gov.uk

Emergency Planning: Mrs Theresa Whitfield, Risk & Resilience Manager, Quattro, Buttermarket Street, Warrington WA1 1NJ ☎ 01925 442657 🖷 01925 442825 ✉ twhitfield@warrington.gov.uk

Energy Management: Mrs Rachel Waggett, Special Projects / Low Carbon Manager, New Town House, Buttermarket Street, Warrington WA1 1NJ ☎ 01925 442630 ✉ rwaggett@warrington.gov.uk

Environmental / Technical Services: Mr Andy Farrall, Executive Director - Economic Regeneration, Growth & Environment, Town Hall, Sankey Street, Warrington WA1 1UH ☎ 01925 442701 🖷 01925 442704 ✉ afarrall@warrington.gov.uk

Environmental Health: Mr Peter Astley, Assistant Director - Regulation & Public Protection, New Town House, Buttermarket Street, Warrington WA1 1NJ ☎ 01925 442672 🖷 01925 442655 ✉ pastley@warrington.gov.uk

Estates, Property & Valuation: Mr Stewart Brown, Service Manager - Property & Estates, 3rd Floor, Quattro, Buttermarket Street, Warrington WA1 1NJ ☎ 01925 442850 ✉ s_brown@warrington.gov.uk

Events Manager: Ms Lynda Fothergill, Interim Communications Manager, Town Hall, Sankey Street, Warrington WA1 1UH ☎ 01925 442125 ✉ x-lfothergill@warrington.gov.uk

Finance: Mr Lynton Green, Director of Finance & Information Services, Quattro Building, Buttermarket Street, Warrington WA1 1BN ☎ 01925 443925 ✉ lgreen@warrington.gov.uk

Fleet Management: Mr David Boyer, Assistant Director - Transport & Environment, New Town House, Buttermarket Street, Warrington WA1 1NJ ☎ 01925 442530 ✉ dboyer@warrington.gov.uk

Grounds Maintenance: Mrs Sharon Walls, Service Manager - Highways & Environment, New Town House, Buttermarket Street, Warrington WA1 1NJ ☎ 01925 442427 ✉ swalls@warrington.gov.uk

Health and Safety: Mrs Theresa Whitfield, Risk & Resilience Manager, Quattro, Buttermarket Street, Warrington WA1 1NJ ☎ 01925 442657 🖷 01925 442825 ✉ twhitfield@warrington.gov.uk

Highways: Mr David Boyer, Assistant Director - Transport & Environment, New Town House, Buttermarket Street, Warrington WA1 1NJ ☎ 01925 442530 ✉ dboyer@warrington.gov.uk

Home Energy Conservation: Mrs Rachel Waggett, Special Projects / Low Carbon Manager, New Town House, Buttermarket Street, Warrington WA1 1NJ ☎ 01925 442630 ✉ rwaggett@warrington.gov.uk

Housing: Mr David Cowley, Head of Housing Services, The Gateway, 85 - 89 Sankey Street, Warrington WA1 1SR ☎ 01925 246890 ✉ dcowley@warrington.gov.uk

Local Area Agreement: Mrs Kathryn Griffiths, Assistant Director - Partnerships & Performance, Quattro, Buttermarket Street, Warrington WA1 1NJ ☎ 01925 442797 🖷 01925 442138 ✉ kgriffiths@warrington.gov.uk

WARRINGTON

Legal: Mr Tim Date, Solicitor to the Council & Assistant Director of Corporate Governance, Quattro, Buttermarket Street, Warrington WA1 2NH ☎ 01925 442150 ✉ tdate@warrington.gov.uk

Leisure and Cultural Services: Ms Jan Souness, Managing Director, Orford Jubilee Neighbourhood Hub, Jubilee Way, Warrington WA2 8HE ☎ 01925 625973 ✉ jansouness@livewirewarrington.org

Licensing: Mr Peter Astley, Assistant Director - Regulation & Public Protection, New Town House, Buttermarket Street, Warrington WA1 1NJ ☎ 01925 442672 🖷 01925 442655 ✉ pastley@warrington.gov.uk

Lifelong Learning: Mrs Penny Owen, Employment, Learning & Skills Manager, St Werbergh's, Irwell Road, Warrington WA4 6QR ☎ 01925 442696 🖷 01925 458103 ✉ powen@warrington.gov.uk

Lighting: Mr Dave Vasey, Asset Maintenance & Street Works Manager, Hawthorne Avenue, Woolston, Warrington WA1 4AL ☎ 01925 442573 ✉ dvasey@warrington.gov.uk

Lottery Funding, Charity and Voluntary: Ms Stephanie Duerden, Commissioning & Third Sector Partnership Manager, New Town House, Buttermarket Street, Warrington WA1 1NJ ☎ 01925 248462 ✉ sduerden@warrington.gov.uk

Member Services: Mr Bryan Magan, Head - Democratic & Member Services, West Annexe, Town Hall, Sankey Street, Warrington WA1 1UH ☎ 01925 442112 🖷 01925 442044 ✉ bmagan@warrington.gov.uk

Parking: Mr David Boyer, Assistant Director - Transport, Engineering & Operations, New Town House, Buttermarket Street, Warrington WA1 1NJ ☎ 01925 442530 ✉ dboyer@warrington.gov.uk

Partnerships: Mrs Kathryn Griffiths, Assistant Director - Partnerships & Performance, 4th Floor, Quattro, Buttermarket Street, Warrington WA1 1NJ ☎ 01925 442797 🖷 01925 442138 ✉ kgriffiths@warrington.gov.uk

Personnel / HR: Mr Gareth Hopkins, Assistant Director of Human Resources, Quattro Building, Buttermarket Street, Warrington WA1 2NH ☎ 01925 443932 ✉ ghopkins1@warrington.gov.uk

Planning: Mr Daniel Hartley, Service Manager - Building Control, New Town House, Buttermarket Street, Warrington WA1 2NJ ☎ 01925 442809 ✉ dhartley@warrington.gov.uk

Procurement: Mr Chris Luke, Commissioning & Procurement Manager, Quattro Building, Buttermarket Street, Warrington WA1 1NJ ☎ 01925 442879 🖷 01925 443449 ✉ cluke@warrington.gov.uk

Public Libraries: Ms Jan Souness, Managing Director, Orford Jubilee Neighbourhood Hub, Jubilee Way, Warrington WA2 8HE ☎ 01925 625973 ✉ jansouness@livewirewarrington.org

Recycling & Waste Minimisation: Mr David Boyer, Assistant Director - Transport & Environment, New Town House, Buttermarket Street, Warrington WA1 1NJ ☎ 01925 442530 ✉ dboyer@warrington.gov.uk

Regeneration: Mr Andy Farrall, Executive Director - Economic Regeneration, Growth & Environment, Town Hall, Sankey Street, Warrington WA1 1UH ☎ 01925 442701 🖷 01925 442704 ✉ afarrall@warrington.gov.uk

Road Safety: Mr Mark Tune, Traffic Management & Road Safety Manager, New Town House, Buttermarket Street, Warrington WA1 1NJ ☎ 01925 442695 ✉ mtune@warrington.gov.uk

Social Services (Adult): Mr Steve Peddie, Operational Director - Adult Services, Town Hall, Sankey Street, Warrington WA1 1UH ☎ 01925 444251 ✉ speddie@warrington.gov.uk

Social Services (Children): Ms Fiona Waddington, Assistant Director - Children & Young People's Targeted Services, 2nd Floor, New Town House, Buttermarket Street, Warrington WA1 1NJ ☎ 01925 443900 ✉ fwaddington@warrington.gov.uk

Public Health: Dr Rita Robertson, Director - Public Health, Town Hall, Sankey Street, Warrington WA1 1UH ☎ 01925 443967 ✉ rrobertson@warrington.gov.uk

Staff Training: Mrs Penny Owen, Employment, Learning & Skills Manager, St Werberghs, Irwell Road, Warrington WA4 6QR ☎ 01925 442696 🖷 01925 458103 ✉ powen@warrington.gov.uk

Street Scene: Mrs Sharon Walls, Service Manager - Highways & Environment, New Town House, Buttermarket Street, Warrington WA1 1NJ ☎ 01925 442427 ✉ swalls@warrington.gov.uk

Sustainable Communities: Mrs Kathryn Griffiths, Assistant Director - Partnerships & Performance, 4th Floor, Quattro, Buttermarket Street, Warrington WA1 1NJ ☎ 01925 442797 🖷 01925 442138 ✉ kgriffiths@warrington.gov.uk

Town Centre: Mr Barry McGorry, Town Centre Manager, Quattro, Buttermarket Street, Warrington WA1 1NJ ☎ 01925 443313 ✉ bmcgorry@warrington.gov.uk

Traffic Management: Mr David Boyer, Assistant Director - Transport & Environment, New Town House, Buttermarket Street, Warrington WA1 1NJ ☎ 01925 442530 ✉ dboyer@warrington.gov.uk

Transport: Mr Stephen Hunter, Service Manager - Transport for Warrington, New Town House, Buttermarket Street, Warrington WA1 1NJ ☎ 01925 442684 ✉ shunter@warrington.gov.uk

Transport Planner: Mr David Boyer, Assistant Director - Transport & Environment, New Town House, Buttermarket Street, Warrington WA1 1NJ ☎ 01925 442530 ✉ dboyer@warrington.gov.uk

Waste Collection and Disposal: Mr David Boyer, Assistant Director - Transport & Environment, New Town House, Buttermarket Street, Warrington WA1 1NJ ☎ 01925 442530 ✉ dboyer@warrington.gov.uk

Waste Management: Mr David Boyer, Assistant Director - Transport & Environment, New Town House, Buttermarket Street, Warrington WA1 1NJ ☎ 01925 442530 ✉ dboyer@warrington.gov.uk

Children's Play Areas: Mrs Sharon Walls, Service Manager - Highways & Environment, New Town House, Buttermarket Street, Warrington WA1 1NJ ☎ 01925 442427 ✉ swalls@warrington.gov.uk

COUNCILLORS

***Mayor* Settle**, Geoff (LAB - Poulton North)
gsettle@warrington.gov.uk

***Deputy Mayor* Rashid**, Faisal (LAB - Whittle Hall)
frashid@warrington.gov.uk

***Leader of the Council* O'Neill**, Terry (LAB - Burtonwood and Winwick)
toneill@warrington.gov.uk

***Deputy Leader of the Council* Hannon**, Mike (LAB - Orford)
mhannon@warrington.gov.uk

Axcell, Brian (LD - Appleton)
baxcell@warrington.gov.uk

Barr, Bob (LD - Lymm)
bbarr@warrington.gov.uk

Bennett, Kevin (O - Fairfield and Howley)
kbennett@warrington.gov.uk

Biggin, Mike (LD - Grappenhall and Thelwall)
mbiggin@warrington.gov.uk

Bland, Sue (CON - Culcheth, Glazebury and Croft)
sbland@warrington.gov.uk

Bowden, Russ (LAB - Birchwood)
rbowden@warrington.gov.uk

Bretherton, Paul (LAB - Rixton and Woolston)
pbretherton@warrington.gov.uk

Brinksman, Bill (LAB - Rixton and Woolston)
bbrinksman@warrington.gov.uk

Buckley, Kath (CON - Lymm)
kbuckley@warrington.gov.uk

Carey, Peter (LAB - Fairfield and Howley)
petercarey@warrington.gov.uk

Carter, Jean (LAB - Great Sankey South)
jcarter1@warrington.gov.uk

Creaghan, Maureen (LAB - Poulton South)
mcreaghan2@warrington.gov.uk

Dirir, Linda (LAB - Penketh and Cuerdley)
ldirir@warrington.gov.uk

Dirir, Allin (LAB - Penketh and Cuerdley)
adirir@warrington.gov.uk

Finnegan, Ted (LD - Grappenhall and Thelwall)
efinnegan@warrington.gov.uk

Fitzsimmons, Chris (LAB - Birchwood)
cfitzsimmons@warrington.gov.uk

Friend, Graham (LAB - Poulton North)
gfriend@warrington.gov.uk

Froggatt, Colin (LAB - Poulton South)
cfroggatt@warrington.gov.uk

Gleave, Keith (LD - Whittle Hall)
kgleave@warrington.gov.uk

Guthrie, Judith (LAB - Westbrook)
jgurthrie@warrington.gov.uk

Hannon, Kate (LAB - Orford)
khannon@warrington.gov.uk

Heaver, Andy (LAB - Great Sankey North)
aheaver@warrington.gov.uk

Higgins, Tony (LAB - Fairfield and Howley)
thiggins@warrington.gov.uk

Hughes, Will (LAB - Whittle Hall)
whughes@warrington.gov.uk

Johnson, Wendy (LD - Grappenhall and Thelwall)
wjohnson@warrington.gov.uk

Joyce, John (LAB - Burtonwood and Winwick)
jjoyce@warrington.gov.uk

Keane, David (LAB - Penketh and Cuerdley)
dkeane@warrington.gov.uk

Kennedy, Paul (CON - Hatton, Stretton and Walton)
pzkennedy@warrington.gov.uk

Kerr-Brown, John (LAB - Poplars and Hulme)
jkerrbrown@warrington.gov.uk

Krizanac, Stefan (LD - Westbrook)
skrizanac@warrington.gov.uk

Lines-Rowland, Billy (LAB - Poulton North)
blinesrowland@warrington.gov.uk

Maher, Brian (LAB - Poplars and Hulme)
bmaher@warrington.gov.uk

McCarthy, Tony (LAB - Rixton and Woolston)
tmccarthy@warrington.gov.uk

McLaughlin, Maureen (LAB - Latchford West)
mmclaughlin@warrington.gov.uk

Morgan, Les (LAB - Latchford West)
lmorgan2@warrington.gov.uk

Morris, Kerri Louise (LAB - Orford)
kmorris@warrington.gov.uk

Mundry, Hans (LAB - Latchford East)
hmundry@warrington.gov.uk

Murphy, Laurence (LAB - Stockton Heath)
lmurphy1@warrington.gov.uk

Nelson, Pauline (LAB - Birchwood)
pnelson@warrington.gov.uk

Parish, Steve (LAB - Bewsey and Whitecross)
sparish@warrington.gov.uk

Patel, Hitesh (LAB - Great Sankey South)
hpatel@warrington.gov.uk

Price, Dan (LAB - Great Sankey North)
dprice1@warrington.gov.uk

Richards, Jeff (LAB - Bewsey and Whitecross)
jrichards@warrington.gov.uk

Roberts, Steve (LAB - Poplars and Hulme)
sroberts@warrington.gov.uk

Smith, Matt (LAB - Culcheth, Glazebury and Croft)
matt.smith062@gmail.com

Taylor, Stephen (CON - Stockton Heath)
staylor4@warrington.gov.uk

Vobe, Chris (LAB - Culcheth, Glazebury and Croft)
chrisvobe@googlemail.com

Walker, Peter (LD - Appleton)
pwalker1@warrington.gov.uk

Wheeler, Judith (LD - Appleton)
jwheeler1@warrington.gov.uk

Williams, Tony (LAB - Great Sankey South)
twilliams2@warrington.gov.uk

Woodyatt, Sheila (CON - Lymm)
swoodyatt@warrington.gov.uk

Wright, Pat (LAB - Bewsey and Whitecross)
pwright@warrington.gov.uk

Wright, Steve (LAB - Latchford East)
stevewright@warrington.gov.uk

POLITICAL COMPOSITION
LAB: 42, LD: 9, CON: 5, O: 1

COMMITTEE CHAIRS
Audit & Corporate Governance: Mr Chris Fitzsimmons

Development Management: Mr Tony McCarthy

Licensing: Mr Brian Maher

Warwick D

Warwick District Council, Riverside House, Milverton Hill, Leamington Spa CV32 5HZ
☎ 01926 410410 ✉ contactus@warwickdc.gov.uk
🖳 www.warwickdc.gov.uk

FACTS AND FIGURES
Parliamentary Constituencies: Kenilworth and Southam, Warwick and Leamington
EU Constituencies: West Midlands
Election Frequency: Elections are of whole council

PRINCIPAL OFFICERS
Chief Executive: Mr Chris Elliott, Chief Executive, Riverside House, Milverton Hill, Leamington Spa CV32 5HZ ☎ 01926 456000 🖷 01926 456121 ✉ chris.elliott@warwickdc.gov.uk

Deputy Chief Executive: Mr Bill Hunt, Deputy Chief Executive, Riverside House, Milverton Hill, Leamington Spa CV32 5HZ ☎ 01926 456014 🖷 01926 456121 ✉ bill.hunt@warwickdc.gov.uk

Deputy Chief Executive: Mr Andrew Jones, Deputy Chief Executive & Monitoring Officer, Riverside House, Milverton Hill, Leamington Spa CV32 5HZ ☎ 01926 456830 🖷 01926 456121 ✉ andrew.jones@warwickdc.gov.uk

Senior Management: Ms Tracy Darke, Head of Development Services, Riverside House, Milverton Hill, Leamington Spa CV32 5HZ ☎ 01926 456501 🖷 01926 456542 ✉ tracy.darke@warwickdc.gov.uk

Senior Management: Mr Richard Hall, Head of Health & Community Protection, Riverside House, Milverton Hill, Leamington Spa CV32 5QH ☎ 01926 456700 🖷 01926 456754 ✉ richard.hall@warwickdc.gov.uk

Senior Management: Mr Robert Hoof, Head of Neighbourhood Services, Riverside House, Milverton Hill, Leamington Spa CV32 5HZ ☎ 01926 456302 ✉ robert.hoof@warwickdc.gov.uk

Senior Management: Mr Mike Snow, Head of Finance, Riverside House, Milverton Hill, Leamington Spa CV32 5HZ ☎ 01926 456800 🖷 01926 456841 ✉ mike.snow@warwickdc.gov.uk

Senior Management: Mr Andy Thompson, Head of Housing & Property Services, Riverside House, Milverton Hill, Leamington Spa CV32 5HZ ☎ 01926 456403 ✉ andy.thompson@warwickdc.gov.uk

Senior Management: Ms Rose Winship, Head of Cultural Services, Riverside House, Milverton Hill, Leamington Spa CV32 5HZ ☎ 01926 456223 🖷 01926 456210 ✉ rose.winship@warwickdc.gov.uk

Architect, Building / Property Services: Mr Andy Thompson, Head of Housing & Property Services, Riverside House, Milverton Hill, Leamington Spa CV32 5HZ ☎ 01926 456403 ✉ andy.thompson@warwickdc.gov.uk

Building Control: Mr Dennis Maddy, Chief Building Control Officer, Riverside House, Milverton Hill, Leamington Spa CV32 5HZ ☎ 01926 456511 🖷 01926 456542 ✉ dennis.maddy@warwickdc.gov.uk

PR / Communications: Ms Ema Townsend, Media & Communications Manager, Riverside House, Milverton Hill, Leamington Spa CV32 5HZ ☎ 01926 456069 ✉ ema.townsend@warwickdc.gov.uk

Community Planning: Ms Jenny Murray, Manager of Joint Community Partnership, Riverside House, Milverton Hill, Leamington Spa CV32 5HZ ☎ 01926 413641 ✉ jennymurray@warwickshire.gov.uk

Community Safety: Mr Peter Cutts, Community Safety Manager, Riverside House, Milverton Hill, Leamington Spa CV32 5HZ ☎ 01926 456021 🖷 01926 456324 ✉ pete.cutts@warwickdc.gov.uk

Community Safety: Mr Richard Hall, Head of Health & Community Protection, Riverside House, Milverton Hill, Leamington Spa CV32 5QH ☎ 01926 456700 🖷 01926 456754 ✉ richard.hall@warwickdc.gov.uk

Computer Management: Mr Ty Walter, Systems Development Manager, Riverside House, Milverton Hill, Leamington Spa CV32 5HZ ☎ 01926 456651 🖷 01926 456663 ✉ ty.walters@warwickdc.gov.uk

Corporate Services: Mr Chris Elliott, Chief Executive, Riverside House, Milverton Hill, Leamington Spa CV32 5HZ ☎ 01926 456000 🖷 01926 456121 ✉ chris.elliott@warwickdc.gov.uk

Customer Service: Ms Fiona Clark, Customer Contact Manager, Riverside House, Milverton Hill, Leamington Spa CV32 5HZ ☎ 01926 456237 ✉ fiona.clark@warwickdc.gov.uk

Economic Development: Mr Joe Baconnet, Economic Development & Regeneration Manager, Riverside House, Milverton Hill, Leamington Spa CV32 5HZ ☎ 01926 456011 🖷 01926 456542 ✉ joseph.baconnet@warwickdc.gov.uk

Electoral Registration: Mrs Gillian Friar, Electoral & Administration Officer, Deputy Chief Executive's Office, Riverside House, Milverton Hill, Leamington Spa CV32 5HZ ☎ 01926 456111 🖷 01926 456121 ✉ gillian.friar@warwickdc.gov.uk

Energy Management: Mr Mark Perkins, Energy Manager, Riverside House, Milverton Hill, Leamington Spa CV32 5HZ ☎ 01926 456037 🖷 01926 456049 ✉ mark.perkins@warwickdc.gov.uk

Environmental Health: Mr Richard Hall, Head of Health & Community Protection, Riverside House, Milverton Hill, Leamington Spa CV32 5HZ ☎ 01926 456700 🖷 01926 456754 ✉ richard.hall@warwickdc.gov.uk

Estates, Property & Valuation: Mr Chris Makasis, Estates Manager, Riverside House, Milverton Hill, Leamington Spa CV32 5HZ ☎ 01926 546040 ✉ chris.makasis@warwickdc.gov.uk

Finance: Mr Mike Snow, Head of Finance, Riverside House, Milverton Hill, Leamington Spa CV32 5HZ ☎ 01926 456800 🖷 01926 456841 ✉ mike.snow@warwickdc.gov.uk

Health and Safety: Mr Grahame Helm, Environmental Protection Manager, Riverside House, Milverton Hill, Leamington Spa CV32 5HZ ☎ 01926 456714 🖷 01926 456746 ✉ grahame.helme@warwickdc.gov.uk

Home Energy Conservation: Mr Mark Perkins, Energy Manager, Riverside House, Milverton Hill, Leamington Spa CV32 5HZ ☎ 01926 456037 🖷 01926 456049 ✉ mark.perkins@warwickdc.gov.uk

Housing: Mr Andy Thompson, Head of Housing & Property Services, Riverside House, Milverton Hill, Leamington Spa CV32 5HZ ☎ 01926 456403 ✉ andy.thompson@warwickdc.gov.uk

Housing Maintenance: Mr Andy Thompson, Head of Housing & Property Services, Riverside House, Milverton Hill, Leamington Spa CV32 5HZ ☎ 01926 456403 ✉ andy.thompson@warwickdc.gov.uk

Leisure and Cultural Services: Ms Rose Winship, Head of Cultural Services, Riverside House, Milverton Hill, Leamington Spa CV32 5HZ ☎ 01926 456223 🖷 01926 456210 ✉ rose.winship@warwickdc.gov.uk

Licensing: Ms Marianne Rolfe, Regulatory Manager, Riverside House, Milverton Hill, Leamington Spa CV32 5HZ ☎ 01926 456320 ✉ marianne.rolfe@warwickdc.gov.uk

Member Services: Mr Graham Leach, Senior Committee Services Officer, Riverside House, Milverton Hill, Leamington Spa CV32 5HZ ☎ 01926 456114 🖷 01926 456121 ✉ graham.leach@warwickdc.gov.uk

Parking: Mr Gary Charlton, Contract Services Manager, Riverside House, Milverton Hill, Leamington Spa CV32 5HZ ☎ 01926 456315 ✉ gary.charlton@warwickdc.gov.uk

Personnel / HR: Ms Tracy Dolphin, HR Manager, Riverside House, Milverton Hill, Leamington Spa CV32 5HZ ☎ 01926 456350 🖷 01926 456027 ✉ tracy.dolphin@warwickdc.gov.uk

Planning: Ms Tracy Darke, Head of Development Services, Riverside House, Milverton Hill, Leamington Spa CV32 5HZ ☎ 01926 456501 🖷 01926 456542 ✉ tracy.darke@warwickdc.gov.uk

Procurement: Ms Susan Simmons, Procurement Manager, Riverside House, Milverton Hill, Leamington Spa CV32 5HZ ☎ 01926 456201 ✉ susan.simmons@warwickdc.gov.uk

Regeneration: Mr Joe Baconnet, Economic Development & Regeneration Manager, Riverside House, Milverton Hill, Leamington Spa CV32 5HZ ☎ 01926 456011 🖷 01926 456542 ✉ joseph.baconnet@warwickdc.gov.uk

Staff Training: Mrs Karen Weatherburn, Learning & Development Officer, Riverside House, Milverton Hill, Leamington Spa CV32 5HZ ☎ 01926 456307 ✉ karen.weatherburn@warwickdc.gov.uk

Street Scene: Mr Robert Hoof, Head of Neighbourhood Services, Riverside House, Milverton Hill, Leamington Spa CV32 5HZ ☎ 01926 456302 ✉ robert.hoof@warwickdc.gov.uk

Tourism: Mr Joe Baconnet, Economic Development & Regeneration Manager, Riverside House, Milverton Hill, Leamington Spa CV32 5HZ ☎ 01926 456011 🖷 01926 456542 ✉ joseph.baconnet@warwickdc.gov.uk

Town Centre: Mr David Butler, Town Centre Development Officer, Riverside House, Milverton Hill, Leamington Spa CV32 5HZ ☎ 01926 456012 🖷 01926 456542 ✉ david.butler@warwickdc.gov.uk

Waste Collection and Disposal: Mr Robert Hoof, Head of Neighbourhood Services, Riverside House, Milverton Hill, Leamington Spa CV32 5HZ ☎ 01926 456302 ✉ robert.hoof@warwickdc.gov.uk

Waste Management: Mr Robert Hoof, Head of Neighbourhood Services, Riverside House, Milverton Hill, Leamington Spa CV32 5HZ ☎ 01926 456302 ✉ robert.hoof@warwickdc.gov.uk

COUNCILLORS

***Chair* Doody**, Michael (CON - Radford Semele)
michael.doody@warwickdc.gov.uk

***Leader of the Council* Mobbs**, Andrew (CON - Park Hill)
andrew.mobbs@warwickdc.gov.uk

***Deputy Leader of the Council* Coker**, Michael (CON - Abbey)
michael.coker@warwickdc.gov.uk

Ashford, Martyn (CON - Aylesford)
Martyn.Ashford@warwickdc.gov.uk

Barrott, John (LAB - Sydenham)
john.barrott@warwickdc.gov.uk

Boad, Alan (LD - Crown)
alan.boad@warwickdc.gov.uk

Bromley, John-Paul (LAB - Saltisford)
john-paul.bromley@warwickdc.gov.uk

Bunker, Felicity (CON - Park Hill)
felicity.bunker@warwickdc.gov.uk

Butler, Noel (CON - Aylesford)
noel.butler@warwickdc.gov.uk

Cain, Gordon (CON - Manor)
Gordon.Cain@warwickdc.gov.uk

Cain, Patricia (CON - St. John's)
Pat.Cain@warwickdc.gov.uk

Cooke, John (CON - St. John's)
john.cooke@warwickdc.gov.uk

Cross, Stephen (CON - Woodloes)
stephen.cross@warwickdc.gov.uk

D'Arcy, Jacqueline (LAB - Emscote)
jackie.darcy@warwickdc.gov.uk

Davies, Richard (CON - St John's)
richard.davies@warwickdc.gov.uk

Davison, Ian (GRN - Brunswick)
Ian.Davison@warwickdc.gov.uk

Day, Andrew (CON - Bishop's Tachbrook)
Andrew.Day@warwickdc.gov.uk

Edgington, Richard (CON - Emscote)
Richard.Edgington@warwickdc.gov.uk

Evetts, Caroline (CON - Clarendon)
caroline.evetts@warwickdc.gov.uk

Falp, Judith (R - Whitnash)
judith.falp@warwickdc.gov.uk

Gallagher, Sue (CON - Arden)
susan.gallagher@warwickdc.gov.uk

Gifford, William (LD - Milverton)
bill.gifford@warwickdc.gov.uk

Gill, Balvinder (LAB - Sydenham)
balvinder.gill@warwickdc.gov.uk

Grainger, Hayley (CON - Milverton)
Hayley.Grainger@warwickdc.gov.uk

Grainger, Moira-Ann (CON - Woodloes)
moira-ann.grainger@warwickdc.gov.uk

Harrington, Nick (CON - Stoneleigh & Cubbington)
nick.harrington@warwickdc.gov.uk

Heath, Tony (R - Whitnash)
tony.heath@warwickdc.gov.uk

Hill, Rowena Ann (CON - Abbey)
Rowena.Hill@warwickdc.gov.uk

Howe, Daniel (CON - Newbold)
daniel.howe@warwickdc.gov.uk

Illingworth, George (CON - Abbey)
george.illingworth@warwickdc.gov.uk

Knight, Jane (LAB - Clarendon)
jane.knight@warwickdc.gov.uk

Mann, Rajvinder (CON - Myton & Heathcote)

Margrave, Robert (R - Whitnash)
Rob.Margrave@warwickdc.gov.uk

Morris, Terry (CON - Saltisford)
terry.morris@warwickdc.gov.uk

Murphy, Neale (CON - Myton & Heathcote)
Neale.Murphy@warwickdc.gov.uk

Naimo, Kristie (LAB - Brunswick)
Kristie.Naimo@warwickdc.gov.uk

Parkins, Stef (LAB - Crown)
Stef.Parkins@warwickdc.gov.uk

Phillips, Peter (CON - Budbrooke)
Peter.Phillips@warwickdc.gov.uk

Quinney, Colin (LAB - Leam)
Colin.Quinney@warwickdc.gov.uk

Redford, Pamela (CON - Stoneleigh & Cubbington)
Pam.Redford@warwickdc.gov.uk

Rhead, Alan (CON - Budbrooke)
alan.rhead@warwickdc.gov.uk

Shilton, David (CON - Park Hill)
david.shilton@warwickdc.gov.uk

Stevens, Amanda (CON - Manor)
amanda.stevens@warwickdc.gov.uk

Thompson, Andrew (CON - Newbold)
Andrew.Thompson@warwickdc.gov.uk

Weed, Barbara (LAB - Leam)
barbara.weed@warwickdc.gov.uk

Whiting, Peter (CON - Arden)
Peter.Whiting@warwickdc.gov.uk

POLITICAL COMPOSITION
CON: 31, LAB: 9, R: 3, LD: 2, GRN: 1

COMMITTEE CHAIRS
Licensing & Regulatory: Mr George Illingworth
Planning: Mr John Cooke

Warwickshire C

Warwickshire County Council, PO Box 9, Shire Hall, Warwick CV34 4RR
☎ 01926 410410 💻 www.warwickshire.gov.uk

FACTS AND FIGURES
Parliamentary Constituencies: Nuneaton, Stratford-on-Avon, Warwick and Leamington, Warwickshire North
EU Constituencies: West Midlands
Election Frequency: Elections are by thirds

PRINCIPAL OFFICERS
Chief Executive: Mr Jim Graham, Chief Executive, PO Box 9, Shire Hall, Warwick CV34 4RR ☎ 01926 410410 ✉ jimgraham@warwickshire.gov.uk

Senior Management: Mr David Carter, Strategic Director of Resources Group, PO Box 9, Shire Hall, Warwick CV34 4RR ☎ 01926 412564 ✉ davidcarter@warwickshire.gov.uk

Senior Management: Mr John Dixon, Interim Strategic Director of People, PO Box 9, Shire Hall, Warwick CV34 4RR ☎ 01926 742665 ✉ johndixon@warwickshire.gov.uk

Senior Management: Ms Monica Fogarty, Strategic Director of Communities, PO Box 9, Shire Hall, Warwick CV34 4RR ☎ 01926 412514 🖷 01926 476881 ✉ monicafogarty@warwickshire.gov.uk

Access Officer / Social Services (Disability): Ms Jenny Wood, Head of Social Care & Support Services, Saltisford Office Park, Ansell Way, Warwick CV34 4UL ☎ 01926 742977 ✉ jennywood@warwickshire.gov.uk

Architect, Building / Property Services: Mr Steve Smith, Head of Physical Assets, PO Box 3, Shire Hall, Warwick CV34 4RH ☎ 01926 412352 ✉ stevesmith@warwickshire.gov.uk

Children / Youth Services: Mr Hugh Disley, Head of Service for Early Intervention, Saltisford Office Park, Ansell Way, Warwick CV34 4UL ☎ 01926 742589 ✉ hughdisley@warwickshire.gov.uk

Children / Youth Services: Ms Beate Wagner, Head of Service - Children's Social Care & Safeguarding, PO Box 9, Shire Hall, Warwick CV34 4RR ☎ 01926 410410 ✉ beatewagner@warwickshire.gov.uk

Civil Registration: Mrs Alison John, Communications Manager, PO Box 9, Shire Hall, Warwick CV34 4RR ☎ 01926 412482 ✉ alison.john@warwickshire.gov.uk

PR / Communications: Ms Jayne Surman, Communication for Press & PR, PO Box 9, Shire Hall, Warwick CV34 4RR ☎ 01926 412757 ✉ jaynesurman@warwickshire.gov.uk

Community Planning: Ms Jenny Murray, Manager of Joint Community Partnership, Riverside House, Milverton Hill, Leamington Spa CV32 5HZ ☎ 01926 413641 ✉ jennymurray@warwickshire.gov.uk

Community Safety: Mr Phil Evans, Head of Localities & Community Safety, PO Box 43, Barrack Street, Warwick CV34 4SX ☎ 01926 412422 ✉ philevans@warwickshire.gov.uk

Computer Management: Mr Tonino Ciuffini, Head of ICT, PO Box 2, Shire Hall, Warwick CV34 4UB ☎ 01926 412879 ✉ toninociuffini@warwickshire.gov.uk

Consumer Protection and Trading Standards: Mr Phil Evans, Head of Localities & Community Safety, PO Box 43, Barrack Street, Warwick CV34 4SX ☎ 01926 412422 ✉ philevans@warwickshire.gov.uk

Customer Service: Ms Kushal Birla, Head of Customer Service & Communications, PO Box 9, Shire Hall, Warwick CV34 4RR ☎ 01926 412013 ✉ kushalbirla@warwickshire.gov.uk

Economic Development: Mr Mark Ryder, Head of Localities & Community Safety, PO Box 43, Barrack Street, Warwick CV34 4UL ☎ 01926 412811 ✉ markryder@warwickshire.gov.uk

Education: Mr Nigel Minns, Head of Learning & Achievement, Saltisford Office Park, Ansell Way, Warwick CV34 4UL ☎ 01926 742588 ✉ nigelminns@warwickshire.gov.uk

E-Government: Mr Tonino Ciuffini, Head of ICT, PO Box 2, Shire Hall, Warwick CV34 4UB ☎ 01926 412879 ✉ toninociuffini@warwickshire.gov.uk

Estates, Property & Valuation: Mr Julian Humphreys, Programme Manager, Shire Hall, Warwick CV34 4SA ☎ 01926 738636 ✉ julianhumphreys@warwickshire.gov.uk

Events Manager: Mrs Alison John, Communications Manager, PO Box 9, Shire Hall, Warwick CV34 4RR ☎ 01926 412482 ✉ alison.john@warwickshire.gov.uk

Facilities: Mr John Findlay, Facilities Service Manager, PO Box 9, Shire Hall, Warwick CV34 4RR ☎ 01926 418642 ✉ johnfindlay@warwickshire.gov.uk

Finance: Mr John Betts, Head of Corporate Finance, PO Box 9, Shire Hall, Warwick CV34 4RR ☎ 01926 412441 ✉ johnbetts@warwickshire.gov.uk

Treasury: Mr John Betts, Head of Corporate Finance, PO Box 9, Shire Hall, Warwick CV34 4RR ☎ 01926 412441 ✉ johnbetts@warwickshire.gov.uk

Treasury: Mr Phil McGaffin, Exchequer Services Manager, PO Box 9, Shire Hall, Warwick CV34 4RR ☎ 01926 410410 ✉ philmcgaffin@warwickshire.gov.uk

Pensions: Mr Neil Buxton, Pensions Manager, PO Box 9, Shire Hall, Warwick CV34 4RR ☎ 01926 412195 ✉ neilbuxton@warwickshire.gov.uk

Fleet Management: Mr Alec Would, General Manager, PO Box 43, Barrack Street, Warwick CV34 4SX ☎ 01926 413489 ✉ alecwould@warwickshire.gov.uk

Health and Safety: Ms Ruth Pickering, County Health, Safety & Wellbeing Manager, PO Box 9, Shire Hall, Warwick CV34 4RR ☎ 01926 412316 ✉ ruthpickering@warwickshire.gov.uk

Highways: Mr Graeme Fitton, Head of Transport & Highways, PO Box 43, Barrack Street, Warwick CV34 4SX ☎ 01926 412046 ✉ graemefitton@warwickshire.gov.uk

Local Area Agreement: Mr Bill Basra, Partnerships Delivery Manager, PO Box 9, Shire Hall, Warwick CV34 4RR ☎ 01926 412127 ✉ billbasra@warwickshire.gov.uk

Legal: Ms Sarah Duxbury, Head of Law & Governance, PO Box 9, Shire Hall, Warwick CV34 4RR ☎ 01926 412090 ✉ sarahduxbury@warwickshire.gov.uk

Lighting: Mr Mike Cunningham, Principal Lighting Engineer, Budbrooke Depot, Old Budbrooke Road, Warwick CV35 7DP ☎ 01926 736548 ✉ mikecunningham@warwickshire.gov.uk

Member Services: Mrs Jane Pollard, Democratic Services Manager, PO Box 9, Shire Hall, Warwick CV34 4RR ☎ 01926 412565 ✉ janepollard@warwickshire.gov.uk

Partnerships: Mr Dan Green, Localities Manager, PO Box 9, Shire Hall, Warwick CV34 4RR ☎ 01926 412491 ✉ dangreen@warwickshire.gov.uk

Personnel / HR: Mrs Sue Evans, Head of HR & OD, PO Box 9, Shire Hall, Warwick CV34 4RR ☎ 01926 412314 ✉ sueevans@warwickshire.gov.uk

Planning: Ms Eva Neale, Planning Officer, PO Box 9, Shire Hall, Warwick CV34 4RR ☎ 01926 412907 ✉ evaneale@warwickshire.gov.uk

Procurement: Mr Paul White, County Procurement Manager, PO Box 9, Shire Hall, Warwick CV34 4RR ☎ 01926 736146 🖷 01926 412326 ✉ paulwhite@warwickshire.gov.uk

Public Libraries: Mr Ayub Khan, Head of Libraries & Strategy, Barrack Street, Warwick CV34 4TH ☎ 01926 412657 ✉ ayubkhan@warwickshire.gov.uk

Recycling & Waste Minimisation: Mr Glenn Fleet, Waste Management Manager, PO Box 43, Barrack Street, Warwick CV34 4SX ☎ 01926 418106 ✉ glennfleet@warwickshire.gov.uk

Regeneration: Ms Mandy Walker, Group Manager of Regeneration Projects & Funding, PO Box 43, Barrack Street, Warwick CV34 4SX ☎ 01926 412843 ✉ mandywalker@warwickshire.gov.uk

Road Safety: Ms Philippa Young, Group Manager of Road Safety Unit, PO Box 43, Shire Hall, Warwick CV34 4RR ☎ 01926 412842 ✉ philippayoung@warwickshire.gov.uk

Social Services (Adult): Mr John Dixon, Interim Strategic Director of People, PO Box 9, Shire Hall, Warwick CV34 4RR ☎ 01926 742665 ✉ johndixon@warwickshire.gov.uk

Social Services (Children): Mr John Dixon, Interim Strategic Director of People, PO Box 9, Shire Hall, Warwick CV34 4RR ☎ 01926 742665 ✉ johndixon@warwickshire.gov.uk

Safeguarding: Ms Beate Wagner, Head of Service - Children's Social Care & Safeguarding, PO Box 9, Shire Hall, Warwick CV34 4RR ☎ 01926 410410 ✉ beatewagner@warwickshire.gov.uk

Public Health: Dr John Linnane, Director - Public Health, PO Box 9, Shire Hall, Warwick CV34 4RR ✉ johnlinnane@warwickshire.gov.uk

Staff Training: Ms Allison Lehky, Business Partnership Manager, PO Box 43, Barrack Street, Warwick CV34 4SX ☎ 01926 412160 ✉ allisonlehky@warwickshire.gov.uk

Sustainable Communities: Mr Phil Evans, Head of Localities & Community Safety, PO Box 43, Barrack Street, Warwick CV34 4SX ☎ 01926 412422 ✉ philevans@warwickshire.gov.uk

Sustainable Development: Mr Phil Evans, Head of Localities & Community Safety, PO Box 43, Barrack Street, Warwick CV34 4SX ☎ 01926 412422 ✉ philevans@warwickshire.gov.uk

Town Centre: Ms Mandy Walker, Group Manager of Regeneration Projects & Funding, PO Box 43, Barrack Street, Warwick CV34 4SX ☎ 01926 412843 ✉ mandywalker@warwickshire.gov.uk

Traffic Management: Mr Graeme Fitton, Head of Transport & Highways, PO Box 43, Shire Hall, Warwick CV34 4SX ☎ 01926 765675 🖷 01926 735662 ✉ graemefitton@warwickshire.gov.uk

Transport: Mr Kevin McGovern, Group Manager, PO Box 43, Barrack Street, Warwick CV34 4SX ☎ 01926 412930 ✉ kevinmcgovern@warwickshire.gov.uk

Transport Planner: Mr Kevin McGovern, Group Manager, PO Box 43, Barrack Street, Warwick CV34 4SX ☎ 01926 412930 ✉ kevinmcgovern@warwickshire.gov.uk

Waste Collection and Disposal: Mr Christopher Moreton, Operation Manager of Waste Management, PO Box 43, Barrack Street, Warwick CV34 4SX ☎ 01926 412103 ✉ christophermoreton@warwickshire.gov.uk

Waste Management: Mr Glenn Fleet, Waste Management Manager, PO Box 43, Barrack Street, Warwick CV34 4SX ☎ 01926 418106 ✉ glennfleet@warwickshire.gov.uk

COUNCILLORS

***Chair* Stevens**, Bob (CON - Feldon)
cllrstevens@warwickshire.gov.uk

***Vice-Chair* Hicks**, Bob (LAB - Nuneaton Abbey)
cllrhicks@warwickshire.gov.uk

***Leader of the Council* Seccombe**, Izzi (CON - Stour & the Vale)
cllrmrsseccombe@warwickshire.gov.uk

***Deputy Leader of the Council* Cockburn**, Alan (CON - Kenilworth St. Johns)
cllrcockburn@warwickshire.gov.uk

***Group Leader* Roodhouse**, Jeremy (LD - Eastlands & Hillmorton)
cllrroodhouse@warwickshire.gov.uk

***Group Leader* Tandy**, June (LAB - Nuneaton Wem Brook)
cllrtandy@warwickshire.gov.uk

Appleton, John (CON - Southam)
cllrappleton@warwickshire.gov.uk

Beaumont, John (LAB - Bulkington)
cllrbeaumont@warwickshire.gov.uk

Boad, Sarah (LD - Leamington North)
cllrboad@warwickshire.gov.uk

Brain, Mike (CON - Bidford-on-Avon)
cllrbrain@warwickshire.gov.uk

Butlin, Peter (CON - Admirals)
cllrbutlin@warwickshire.gov.uk

Caborn, Les (CON - Bishops Tachbrook)
cllrcaborn@warwickshire.gov.uk

Chattaway, Richard (LAB - Bede)
cllrchattaway@warwickshire.gov.uk

Chilvers, Jonathan (GRN - Leamington Brunswick)
cllrchilvers@warwickshire.gov.uk

Clark, Chris (LAB - Hartshill)
cllrclark@warwickshire.gov.uk

Clarke, Jeff (CON - Nuneaton St. Nicholas)
cllrclarke@warwickshire.gov.uk

Compton, Jose (CON - Leek Wootton)
cllrcompton@warwickshire.gov.uk

Dahmash, Yousef (CON - Caldecott)
cllrdahmash@warwickshire.gov.uk

Davies, Nicola (LD - Leamington North)
cllrndavies@warwickshire.gov.uk

Davies, Corinne (LAB - Nuneaton Camp Hill)
cllrcdavies@warwickshire.gov.uk

Dirveiks, Neil (LAB - Atherstone)
cllrdirveiks@warwickshire.gov.uk

Dodd, Richard (LD - Eastlands & Hillmorton)
cllrdodd@warwickshire.gov.uk

Doughty, Sara (LAB - Bedworth North)
cllrdoughty@warwickshire.gov.uk

Fowler, Peter (CON - Coleshill)
cllrfowler@warwickshire.gov.uk

Fradgley, Jenny (LD - Stratford South)
cllrfradgley@warwickshire.gov.uk

Gifford, Bill (LD - Leamington Milverton)
cllrgifford@warwickshire.gov.uk

Gittus, Mike (CON - Alcester)
cllrgittus@warwickshire.gov.uk

Hawkes, Brian (LAB - Bedworth West)
cllrhawkes@warwickshire.gov.uk

Hayfield, Colin (CON - Arley)
cllrhayfield@warwickshire.gov.uk

Holland, John (LAB - Warwick West)
cllrholland@warwickshire.gov.uk

Horner, John (CON - Aston Cantlow)
cllrhorner@warwickshire.gov.uk

Jackson, Julie (LAB - Poplar)
cllrjackson@warwickshire.gov.uk

Johnson, Philip (LAB - Nuneaton Galley Common)
cllrjohnson@warwickshire.gov.uk

Kaur, Kam (CON - Caldecott)
cllrkaur@warwickshire.gov.uk

Kendall, Danny (CON - Wellesbourne)
cllrkendall@warwickshire.gov.uk

Kirton, Bernard (IND - Whitnash)
cllrkirton@warwickshire.gov.uk

Kondaker, Keith (GRN - Nuneaton Weddington)
cllrkondakor@warwickshire.gov.uk

Lea, Joan (CON - Water Orton)
cllrmrslea@warwickshire.gov.uk

Lloyd, Keith (IND - Stratford Avenue & New Town)
cllrlloyd@warwickshire.gov.uk

Morris-Jones, Phillip (CON - Fosse)
cllrmorris-jones@warwickshire.gov.uk

Morson, Peter (LAB - Baddesley Ensor)
cllrmorson@warwickshire.gov.uk

Moss, Brian (LAB - Kingsbury)
cllrmoss@warwickshire.gov.uk

Olner, Bill (LAB - Arbury & Stockingford)
cllrolner@warwickshire.gov.uk

O'Rourke, Maggie (LAB - Lawford & New Bilton)
cllrorourke@warwickshire.gov.uk

Parsons, Dave (LAB - Polesworth)
cllrparsons@warwickshire.gov.uk

Perry, Mike (CON - Henley-in-Arden)
cllrperry@warwickshire.gov.uk

Phillips, Caroline (LAB - Arbury & Stockingford)
cllrphillips@warwickshire.gov.uk

Redford, Wallace (CON - Cubbington)
cllrredford@warwickshire.gov.uk

Rickhards, Clive (LD - Studley)
cllrrickhards@warwickshire.gov.uk

Roberts, Howard (IND - Dunchurch)
cllrroberts@warwickshire.gov.uk

Rolfe, Kate (LD - Stratford South)
cllrrolfe@warwickshire.gov.uk

Saint, Chris (CON - Shipston-on-Stour)
cllrsaint@warwickshire.gov.uk

Shilton, Dave (CON - Kenilworth Park Hill)
cllrshilton@warwickshire.gov.uk

St. John, Jenny (LAB - Warwick North)
cllrstjohn@warwickshire.gov.uk

Timms, Heather (CON - Earl Craven)
cllrtimms@warwickshire.gov.uk

Warner, Angela (CON - Warwick South)
cllrwarner@warwickshire.gov.uk

Webb, Alan (LAB - Brownsover)
cllrawebb@warwickshire.gov.uk

Webb, Mary (LAB - Brownsover)
cllrmwebb@warwickshire.gov.uk

Western, Matt (LAB - Leamington Willes)
cllrwestern@warwickshire.gov.uk

Whitehouse, John (LD - Kenilworth Abbey)
cllrwhitehouse@warwickshire.gov.uk

Williams, Chris (CON - Kineton)
cllrwilliams@warwickshire.gov.uk

POLITICAL COMPOSITION

CON: 25, LAB: 22, LD: 9, IND: 3, GRN: 2

COMMITTEE CHAIRS

Adult Social Care & Health: Ms Maggie O'Rourke

Watford D

Watford Borough Council, Town Hall, Watford WD17 3EX
☎ 01923 226400 🖷 01923 278100 ✉ enquiries@watford.gov.uk
💻 www.watford.gov.uk

FACTS AND FIGURES

Parliamentary Constituencies: Watford
EU Constituencies: Eastern
Election Frequency: Elections are by thirds

PRINCIPAL OFFICERS

Chief Executive: Mr Manny Lewis, Managing Director, Town Hall, Watford WD17 3EX ☎ 01923 278186 ✉ manny.lewis@watford.gov.uk

Architect, Building / Property Services: Mrs Linda Newell, Property Manager, Town Hall, Watford WD17 3EX ☎ 01923 278216 ✉ linda.newell@watford.gov.uk

Building Control: Mr Clive Fuller, Chief Building Control Officer, Town Hall, Watford WD17 3EX ☎ 01923 727125 🖷 01923 278273 ✉ clive.fuller@threerivers.gov.uk

WATFORD

Children / Youth Services: Mr Gary Oliver, Culture & Play Section Head, Town Hall, Watford WD17 3EX ☎ 01923 278251 ✉ gary.oliver@watford.gov.uk

Community Safety: Ms Jane Taylor, Community Safety Manager, Town Hall, Watford WD17 3EX ☎ 01923 278405 ✉ jane.taylor@watford.gov.uk

Computer Management: Mrs Emma Tiernan, ICT Client Manager, Town Hall, Watford WD17 3EX ☎ 01923 727457 ✉ emma.tiernan@threerivers.gov.uk

Contracts: Mr Howard Hughes, Procurement Manager, Town Hall, Watford WD17 3EX ☎ 01923 278370 ✉ howard.hughes@watford.gov.uk

Corporate Services: Ms Lesley Palumbo, Head of Corporate Strategy & Client Services, Town Hall, Watford WD17 3EX ☎ 01923 278561 ✉ lesley.palumbo@watford.gov.uk

Customer Service: Ms Danielle Negrello, Customer Service Section Head, Town Hall, Watford WD17 3EX ☎ 01923 278927 ✉ danielle.negrello@watford.gov.uk

Economic Development: Mr Andrew Gibson, Economic Development Officer, Town Hall, Watford WD17 3EX ☎ 01923 278286 ✉ andrew.gibson@watford.gov.uk

Electoral Registration: Mr Gordon Amos, Elections Manager, Town Hall, Watford WD17 3EX ☎ 01923 278339 ✉ gordon.amos@watford.gov.uk

Emergency Planning: Mr Clive Goodchild, Facilities & Emergency Planning Manager, Town Hall, Watford WD17 3EX ☎ 01923 278378 ✉ clive.goodchild@watford.gov.uk

Energy Management: Mr Neil Walker, Energy & Renewal Surveyor, Wiggenhall Depot, Wiggenhall Road, Watford WD18 0FB ☎ 01923 278149 ✉ neil.walker@watford.gov.uk

Environmental / Technical Services: Ms Lesley Palumbo, Head of Corporate Strategy & Client Services, Town Hall, Watford WD17 3EX ☎ 01923 278561 ✉ lesley.palumbo@watford.gov.uk

Environmental Health: Ms Justine Hoy, Environmental Health & Licensing Section Head, Wiggenhall Depot, Wiggenhall Road, Watford WD18 0FB ☎ 01923 278449 ✉ justine.hoy@watford.gov.uk

Estates, Property & Valuation: Mrs Linda Newell, Property Manager, Town Hall, Watford WD17 3EX ☎ 01923 278216 ✉ linda.newell@watford.gov.uk

Facilities: Mr Clive Goodchild, Facilities & Emergency Planning Manager, Town Hall, Watford WD17 3EX ☎ 01923 278378 ✉ clive.goodchild@watford.gov.uk

Finance: Ms Joanne Wagstaffe, Director of Finance, Town Hall, Watford WD17 3EX ☎ 01923 727205 ✉ joanne.wagstaffe@threerivers.gov.uk

Treasury: Mr Nigel Pollard, Acting Head of Finance - Shared Services, Town Hall, Watford WD17 3EX ☎ 01923 727198 ✉ nigel.pollard@watford.gov.uk

Grounds Maintenance: Mr Paul Rabbitts, ES Client Manager (Parks & Streets), Town Hall, Watford WD17 3EX ☎ 01923 278250 ✉ paul.rabbitts@watford.gov.uk

Health and Safety: Mr Darren Williams, Corporate Health & Safety Adviser, Town Hall, Watford WD17 3EX ☎ 01923 776611 ✉ darren.williams@threerivers.gov.uk

Home Energy Conservation: Mr Neil Walker, Energy & Renewal Surveyor, Wiggenhall Depot, Wiggenhall Road, Watford WD18 0FB ☎ 01923 278149 ✉ neil.walker@watford.gov.uk

Legal: Mrs Carol Chen, Head of Democracy & Governance, Town Hall, Watford WD17 3EX ☎ 01923 278350 🖷 01923 278366 ✉ carol.chen@watford.gov.uk

Leisure and Cultural Services: Mr Gary Oliver, Culture & Play Section Head, Town Hall, Watford WD17 3EX ☎ 01923 278251 ✉ gary.oliver@watford.gov.uk

Licensing: Mr Jeffrey Leib, Licensing Manager, Wiggenhall Depot, Wiggenhall Road, Watford WD18 0FB ☎ 01923 278503 ✉ jeffrey.leib@watford.gov.uk

Member Services: Ms Caroline Harris, Member Development & Civic Events Officer, Town Hall, Watford WD17 3EX ☎ 01923 278374 ✉ caroline.harris@watford.gov.uk

Parking: Ms Jane Custance, Head of Regeneration & Development, Town Hall, Watford WD17 3EX ☎ 01923 278044 ✉ jane.custance@watford.gov.uk

Partnerships: Mrs Kathryn Robson, Partnerships & Performance Section Head, Town Hall, Watford WD17 3EX ☎ 01923 278077 ✉ kathryn.robson@watford.gov.uk

Personnel / HR: Mrs Cathy Watson, Head of Human Resources, Town Hall, Watford WD17 3EX ✉ cathy.watson@threerivers.gov.uk

Planning: Ms Jane Custance, Head of Regeneration & Development, Town Hall, Watford WD17 3EX ☎ 01923 278044 ✉ jane.custance@watford.gov.uk

Procurement: Mr Howard Hughes, Procurement Manager, Town Hall, Watford WD17 3EX ☎ 01923 278370 ✉ howard.hughes@watford.gov.uk

Recycling & Waste Minimisation: Mr Jamie Sells, ES Client Manager (Waste & Recycling), Town Hall, Watford WD17 3EX ☎ 01923 278496 ✉ jamie.sells@watford.gov.uk

Regeneration: Ms Jane Custance, Head of Regeneration & Development, Town Hall, Watford WD17 3EX ☎ 01923 278044 ✉ jane.custance@watford.gov.uk

Street Scene: Mr Paul Rabbitts, ES Client Manager (Parks & Streets), Town Hall, Watford WD17 3EX ☎ 01923 278250 ✉ paul.rabbitts@watford.gov.uk

Town Centre: Ms Maria Manion, Town Centre Manager, Town Hall, Watford WD17 3EX ☎ 01923 278260 ✉ maria.manion@watford.gov.uk

Waste Collection and Disposal: Mr Jamie Sells, ES Client Manager (Waste & Recycling), Town Hall, Watford WD17 3EX ☎ 01923 278496 ✉ jamie.sells@watford.gov.uk

Waste Management: Mr Jamie Sells, ES Client Manager (Waste & Recycling), Town Hall, Watford WD17 3EX ☎ 01923 278496 ✉ jamie.sells@watford.gov.uk

Children's Play Areas: Mr Paul Rabbitts, ES Client Manager (Parks & Streets), Town Hall, Watford WD17 3EX ☎ 01923 278250 ✉ paul.rabbitts@watford.gov.uk

COUNCILLORS

***Directly Elected Mayor* Thornhill**, Dorothy (LD -)
themayor@watford.gov.uk

***Chair* Hastrick**, Kareen (LD - Meriden)
kareen.hastrick@watford.gov.uk

***Vice-Chair* Walford**, Darren (LD - Tudor)
darren.walford@watford.gov.uk

***Deputy Mayor* Scudder**, Derek (LD - Stanborough)
derek.scudder@watford.gov.uk

***Group Leader* Bell**, Nigel (LAB - Holywell)
nigel.bell@watford.gov.uk

Bashir, Sohail (LAB - Callowland)
sohail.bashir@watford.gov.uk

Bolton, Stephen (LD - Central)
stephen.bolton@watford.gov.uk

Brown, Jan (LD - Meriden)
jan.brown@watford.gov.uk

Brown, Ian (LD - Woodside)
ian.brown@watford.gov.uk

Collett, Karen (LD - Woodside)
karen.collett@watford.gov.uk

Connal, Jackie (LAB - Holywell)
jackie.connal@watford.gov.uk

Counter, Shirena (LD - Oxhey)
shirena.counter@watford.gov.uk

Crout, Keith (LD - Stanborough)
keith.crout@watford.gov.uk

Derbyshire, George (LD - Park)
george.derbyshire@watford.gov.uk

Dhindsa, Jagtar Singh (LAB - Vicarage)
jagtar.dhindsa@watford.gov.uk

Ewudo, Favour (LAB - Callowland)
favour.ewudo@watford.gov.uk

Haley, Michael (LAB - Central)
michael.haley@watford.gov.uk

Hofman, Mark (LD - Nascot)
mark.hofman@watford.gov.uk

Johnson, Stephen (LD - Tudor)
stephen.johnson@watford.gov.uk

Joynes, Anne (LAB - Leggatts)
anne.joynes@watford.gov.uk

Khan, Asif (LAB - Leggatts)
asif.khan@watford.gov.uk

Martins, Rabi (LD - Central)
rabi.martins@watford.gov.uk

Mauthoor, Bilqees (LAB - Leggatts)
bilqees.mauthoor@watford.gov.uk

Mehta, Binita (CON - Park)
binita.mehta@watford.gov.uk

Mills, Mo (LAB - Vicarage)
mo.mills@watford.gov.uk

Rindl, Anne (LD - Park)
anne.rindl@watford.gov.uk

Rogers, Tony (CON - Woodside)
tony.rogers@watford.gov.uk

Shah, Nasreen (LAB - Vicarage)
nasreen.shah@watford.gov.uk

Sharpe, Iain (LD - Oxhey)
iain.sharpe@watford.gov.uk

Silver, Sean (CON - Tudor)
sean.silver@watford.gov.uk

Taylor, Peter (LD - Oxhey)
peter.taylor@watford.gov.uk

Topping, Linda (CON - Nascot)
linda.topping@watford.gov.uk

Turmaine, Matt (LAB - Holywell)
matt.turmaine@watford.gov.uk

Watkin, Mark (LD - Nascot)
mark.watkin@watford.gov.uk

Whitman, Mark (CON - Meriden)
mark.whitman@watrford.gov.uk

Williams, Tim (LD - Stanborough)
tim.williams@watford.gov.uk

Williams, Seamus (LAB - Callowland)
seamus.williams@watford.gov.uk

POLITICAL COMPOSITION

LD: 19, LAB: 13, CON: 5

COMMITTEE CHAIRS

Development Management: Mr Rabi Martins

Licensing: Mrs Jan Brown

Waveney D

Waveney District Council, Town Hall, High Street, Lowestoft NR32 1HS
☎ 01502 562111 🖷 01502 589327 ✉ chiefexecutive@waveney.gov.uk
💻 www.waveney.gov.uk

FACTS AND FIGURES

Parliamentary Constituencies: Suffolk Coastal, Waveney
EU Constituencies: Eastern
Election Frequency: Elections are by thirds

WAVENEY

PRINCIPAL OFFICERS

Chief Executive: Mr Stephen Baker, Chief Executive, Riverside, 4 Canning Road, Lowestoft NR33 0EQ ☎ 01394 444348 🖷 01394 385100 ✉ stephen.baker@eastsuffolk.gov.uk

Assistant Chief Executive: Mr Arthur Charvonia, Strategic Director, Riverside, 4 Canning Road, Lowestoft NR33 0EQ ☎ 01502 523606 🖷 01502 523500 ✉ arthur.charvonia@eastsuffolk.gov.uk

Senior Management: Mr Andrew Jarvis, Strategic Director, Riverside, 4 Canning Road, Lowestoft NR33 0EQ ☎ 01394 444323 ✉ andrew.jarvis@eastsuffolk.gov.uk

Architect, Building / Property Services: Mrs Gayle Hart, Manager, Riverside, 4 Canning Road, Lowestoft NR33 0EQ ☎ 01502 562111 🖷 01502 523478 ✉ gayle.hart@eastsuffolk.gov.uk

Best Value: Mrs Alison Matthews, Policy & Performance Manager, Riverside, Canning Road, Lowestoft NR33 0EQ ☎ 01394 444435 🖷 01394 444786 ✉ alison.matthews@suffolkcoastal.gov.uk

Building Control: Mr Barry Reid, Principal Service Manager of Planning & Building Control, Riverside, Canning Road, Lowestoft NR33 0EQ ☎ 01502 562111 🖷 01502 589327 ✉ barry.reid@waveney.gov.uk

PR / Communications: Mr Phil Harris, Communications Officer, Riverside, Canning Road, Lowestoft NR33 0EQ ☎ 01502 523637 🖷 01502 589327 ✉ phil.harris@waveney.gov.uk

Community Planning: Mr Philip Ridley, Head of Planning Services, Riverside, Canning Road, Lowestoft NR33 0EQ ☎ 01394 444432 ✉ philip.ridley@suffolkcoastal.gov.uk

Community Safety: Mr Richard Best, Active Communities Manager, Riverside, Canning Road, Lowestoft NR33 0EQ ☎ 01502 523605 ✉ richard.best@waveney.gov.uk

Community Safety: Ms Karen Hubbard, Community Safety Officer, Riverside, 4 Canning Town, Lowestoft NR33 0EQ ☎ 01502 562111 🖷 01502 598327 ✉ karen.hubbard@waveney.gov.uk

Computer Management: Ms Ann Carey, Head of ICT, Riverside, 4 Canning Town, Lowestoft NR33 0EQ ☎ 01502 523215 ✉ ann.carey@eastsuffolk.gov.uk

Contracts: Mr Ian Purdom, Principal Service Manager of Procurement, Riverside, 4 Canning Road, Lowestoft NR33 0EQ ☎ 01502 523507 ✉ ian.purdom@eastsuffolk.gov.uk

Customer Service: Mr Darren Knight, Head of Service, Riverside, Canning Road, Lowestoft NR33 0EQ ☎ 01502 526111 ✉ darren.knight@eastsuffolk.gov.uk

Economic Development: Mr Paul Moss, Major Projects Programme Manager, Riverside, Canning Road, Lowestoft NR33 0EQ ☎ 01502 523392 ✉ paul.moss@waveney.gov.uk

Electoral Registration: Mrs Sharon Shand, Service Manager of Electoral Services, Riverside, Canning Street, Lowestoft NR33 0EQ ☎ 01502 523253 🖷 01502 589327 ✉ sharon.shand@waveney.gov.uk

Emergency Planning: Mr Phil Gore, Head of Environmental Services & Port Health, Riverside, Canning Road, Lowestoft NR33 0EQ ☎ 01394 444286 🖷 01502 589327 ✉ phil.gore@eastsuffolk.gov.uk

Energy Management: Mr Phil Gore, Head of Environmental Services & Port Health, Riverside, Canning Road, Lowestoft NR33 0EQ ☎ 01394 444286 🖷 01502 589327 ✉ phil.gore@eastsuffolk.gov.uk

Environmental / Technical Services: Mr Phil Gore, Head of Environmental Services & Port Health, Riverside, Canning Road, Lowestoft NR33 0EQ ☎ 01394 444286 🖷 01502 589327 ✉ phil.gore@eastsuffolk.gov.uk

Environmental Health: Mr Phil Gore, Head of Environmental Services & Port Health, Riverside, Canning Road, Lowestoft NR33 0EQ ☎ 01394 444286 🖷 01502 589327 ✉ phil.gore@eastsuffolk.gov.uk

Estates, Property & Valuation: Mrs Gayle Hart, Manager, Town Hall, High Street, Lowestoft NR32 1HS ☎ 01502 562111 🖷 01502 523478 ✉ gayle.hart@eastsuffolk.gov.uk

Events Manager: Mrs Catherine Thornber, Economic Services Manager, Council Offices, Melton Hill, Woodbridge IP12 1AU ☎ 01394 444472 ✉ catherine.thornber@eastsuffolk.gov.uk

Facilities: Mrs Sue Bowyer, Shared Estate Manager, Riverside, 4 Canning Road, Lowestoft NR33 0EQ ☎ 01502 562111 🖷 01502 589327 ✉ sue.bowyer@eastsuffolk.gov.uk

Finance: Ms Homira Javadi, Chief Finance Officer, Riverside, 4 Canning Road, Lowestoft NR33 0EQ ☎ 01394 444249 ✉ homira.javadi@suffolkcoastal.gov.uk

Grounds Maintenance: Mr David Gallagher, Head of Leisure & Commercial Partnerships, Riverside, 4 Canning Road, Lowestoft NR33 0EQ ☎ 01502 523007 ✉ david.gallagher@eastsuffolk.gov.uk

Health and Safety: Ms Sheila Warnes, Health & Safety Advisor, Riverside, 4 Canning Street, Lowestoft NR33 0EQ ☎ 01502 523154 ✉ sheila.warnes@eastsuffolk.gov.uk

Home Energy Conservation: Mrs Teresa Howarth, Environmental Health Officer, Council Offices, Melton Hill, Woodbridge IP12 1AU ☎ 01394 444206 🖷 01394 385100 ✉ teresa.howarth@suffolkcoastal.gov.uk

Housing: Mr Robert Prince, Head of Housing Operations & Landlord Services, Town Hall, High Street, Lowestoft NR32 1HS ☎ 01502 562111 🖷 01502 589327 ✉ robert.prince@waveney.gov.uk

Housing Maintenance: Mr John Brown, Principal Service Manager of Building & Housing, Town Hall, High Street, Lowestoft NR32 1HS ☎ 01502 562111 🖷 01502 589327 ✉ john.brown@waveney.gov.uk

Legal: Mrs Hilary Slater, Head of Legal & Democratic Services, Town Hall, High Street, Lowestoft NR32 1HS ☎ 01394 444336 ✉ hilary.slater@suffolkcoatal.gov.uk

Leisure and Cultural Services: Mrs Catherine Thornber, Economic Services Manager, Council Offices, Melton Hill, Woodbridge IP12 1AU ☎ 01394 444472 ✉ catherine.thornber@eastsuffolk.gov.uk

Licensing: Mrs Caroline Evans, Licensing Service Manager, Melton Hill„ „ Woodbridge IP12 1AU ☎ 01394 444678 ✉ caroline.evans@eastsuffolk.gov.uk

Lifelong Learning: Mrs Heather Shilling, Human Resources Officer, Riverside, 4 Canning Road, Lowestoft NR33 0EQ ☎ 01502 562611; 01502 523221 🖷 01502 589327 ✉ heather.shilling@waveney.gov.uk

Lottery Funding, Charity and Voluntary: Mr Richard Best, Active Communities Manager, Riverside, 4 Canning Town, Lowestoft NR33 0EQ ☎ 01502 523605 ✉ richard.best@waveney.gov.uk

Member Services: Mrs Donna Offord, Principal Service Manager of Democratic Services, Riverside, 4 Canning Road, Lowestoft NR33 0EQ ☎ 01502 562111 🖷 01502 589327 ✉ donna.offord@waveney.gov.uk

Personnel / HR: Mrs Carol Lower, Human Resources & Workforce Development Manager, Riverside, 4 Canning Town, Lowestoft NR33 0EQ ☎ 01502 523228 ✉ carol.lower@eastsuffolk.gov.uk

Planning: Mr Philip Ridley, Head of Planning Services, Town Hall, High Street, Lowestoft NR32 1HS ☎ 01394 444432 ✉ philip.ridley@suffolkcoastal.gov.uk

Procurement: Mr Ian Purdom, Principal Service Manager of Procurement, Council Offices, Melton Hill, Woodbridge IP12 1AU ☎ 01502 523507 ✉ ian.purdom@eastsuffolk.gov.uk

Recycling & Waste Minimisation: Mr David Gallagher, Head of Leisure & Commercial Partnerships, Riverside, 4 Canning Road, Lowestoft NR33 0EQ ☎ 01502 523007 ✉ david.gallagher@eastsuffolk.gov.uk

Regeneration: Mr Paul Wood, Head of Economic Development & Regeneration, Riverside, 4 Canning Town, Lowestoft NR33 0EQ ☎ 01394 442249 ✉ paul.wood@eastsuffolk.gov.uk

Staff Training: Mrs Heather Shilling, Human Resources Officer, Riverside, 4 Canning Town, Lowestoft NR33 0EQ ☎ 01502 562611; 01502 523221 🖷 01502 589327 ✉ heather.shilling@waveney.gov.uk

Sustainable Communities: Mr Philip Ridley, Head of Planning Services, Riverside, 4 Canning Road, Lowestoft NR33 0EQ ☎ 01394 444432 ✉ philip.ridley@suffolkcoastal.gov.uk

Sustainable Development: Mr Philip Ridley, Head of Planning Services, Riverside, 4 Canning Road, Lowestoft NR33 0EQ ☎ 01394 444432 ✉ philip.ridley@suffolkcoastal.gov.uk

Tourism: Mrs Catherine Thornber, Economic Services Manager, Council Offices, Melton Hill, Woodbridge IP12 1AU ☎ 01394 444472 ✉ catherine.thornber@eastsuffolk.gov.uk

Waste Management: Mr David Gallagher, Head of Leisure & Commercial Partnerships, Riverside, 4 Canning Road, Lowestoft NR33 0EQ ☎ 01502 523007 ✉ david.gallagher@eastsuffolk.gov.uk

COUNCILLORS

***Chair* Provan**, Bruce (CON - Kessingland)
bruce.provan@waveney.gov.uk

***Vice-Chair* Catchpole**, Graham (CON - Beccles South)
graham.cole@waveney.gov.uk

***Leader of the Council* Law**, Colin (CON - Oulton Broad)
colin.law@waveney.gov.uk

***Deputy Leader of the Council* Ritchie**, David (CON - The Saints)
david.ritchie@waveney.gov.uk

***Group Leader* Barker**, Sonia (LAB - Pakefield)
sonia.barker@waveney.gov.uk

Allen, Sue (CON - Southwold and Reydon)
sue.allen@waveney.gov.uk

Ardley, Stephen (CON - Gunton and Corton)
stephen.ardley@waveney.gov.uk

Ashdown, Paul (CON - Lothingland)
paul.ashdown@waveney.gov.uk

Back, Edward (CON - Oulton)
edward.back@waveney.gov.uk

Barnard, Mike (CON - Oulton Broad)
mike.barnard@waveney.gov.uk

Bee, Mark (CON - Worlingham)
mark.bee@waveney.gov.uk

Brooks, Norman (CON - Worlingham)
norman.brooks@waveney.gov.uk

Cackett, Alison (CON - Blything)
alison.cackett@waveney.gov.uk

Ceresa, Jenny (CON - Carlton Colville)
jenny.ceresa@waveney.gov.uk

Cherry, Malcolm (LAB - St Margarets)
malcolm.cherry@waveney.gov.uk

Cherry, Yvonne (LAB - Whitton)
yvonne.cherry@waveney.gov.uk

Craig, Janet (LAB - Harbour)
janet.craig@waveney.gov.uk

Elliott, Graham (GRN - Beccles North)
graham.elliott@waveney.gov.uk

Ford, June (LAB - Kirkley)
june.ford@waveney.gov.uk

Gandy, Tess (LAB - Normanston)
tess.gandy@waveney.gov.uk

Goldson, Tony (CON - Halesworth)
tony.goldson@waveney.gov.uk

Gooch, Louise (LAB - Pakefield)
louise.gooch@waveney.gov.uk

Graham, Ian (LAB - Pakefield)
ian.graham@waveney.gov.uk

Grant, Kathleen (CON - Carlton Colville)
kathleen.grant@waveney.gov.uk

Green, Alan (LAB - Kessingland)
alan.green@waveney.gov.uk

Groom, John (CON - Bungay)
john.groom@waveney.gov.uk

Harris-Logan, Louisa (LAB - St. Margarets)
louise.harris-loga@waveney.gov.uk

Ladd, Michael (CON - Southwold and Reydon)
michael.ladd@waveney.gov.uk

Light, Paul (CON - Carlton Colville)
paul.light@waveney.gov.uk

Logan, Steve (LAB - Kirkley)
steve.logan@waveney.gov.uk

Mortimer, Trish (CON - Carlton)
trish.mortimer@waveney.gov.uk

Mortimer, Frank (CON - Carlton)
frank.mortimer@waveney.gov.uk

Murray, Jane (LAB - Oulton)
jane.murray@waveney.gov.uk

Neil, Rob (LAB - Normanston)
rob.neil@waveney.gov.uk

Nicholls, Lewis (LAB - St. Margarets)
lewis.nicholls@waveney.gov.uk

Parsons, Martin (CON - Wrentham)
martin.parsons@waveney.gov.uk

Patience, Keith (LAB - Normanston)
keith.patience@waveney.gov.uk

Pitchers, Malcolm (LAB - Kirkley)
malcolm.pitchers@waveney.gov.uk

Punt, Chris (CON - Beccles North)
chris.punt@waveney.gov.uk

Reynolds, Tom (LAB - Harbour)
tom.reynolds@waveney.gov.uk

Rudd, Mary (CON - Gunton and Corton)
mary.rudd@waveney.gov.uk

Smith, Letitia (CON - Halesworth)
letitia.smith@waveney.gov.uk

Smith, Jedda (LAB - Harbour)
jedda.smith@waveney.gov.uk

Springall, Kevin (CON - Wainford)
kevin.springall@waveney.gov.uk

Topping, Caroline (CON - Beccles South)
caroline.topping@waveney.gov.uk

Webb, Nick (LAB - Whitton)
nick.webb@waveney.gov.uk

Webb, Sarah (LAB - Whitton)
sarah.webb@waveney.gov.uk

Woods, Simon (CON - Bungay)
simon.woods@waveney.gov.uk

POLITICAL COMPOSITION

CON: 27, LAB: 20, GRN: 1

COMMITTEE CHAIRS

Audit & Governance: Mr Simon Woods

Licensing: Mrs Kathleen Grant

Planning: Mr John Groom

Waverley — D

Waverley Borough Council, Council Offices, The Burys, Godalming GU7 1HR
☎ 01483 523333 🖷 01483 426337 ✉ enquiries@waverley.gov.uk
💻 www.waverley.gov.uk

FACTS AND FIGURES

Parliamentary Constituencies: South West Surrey
EU Constituencies: South East
Election Frequency: Elections are of whole council

PRINCIPAL OFFICERS

Chief Executive: Mr Paul Wenham, Executive Director & Head of Paid Service, Council Offices, The Burys, Godalming GU7 1HR
☎ 01483 523238 🖷 01483 523245 ✉ paul.wenham@waverley.gov.uk

Senior Management: Mr Graeme Clark, Director of Finance & Resources and Chief Finance Officer, Council Offices, The Burys, Godalming GU7 1HR ☎ 01483 523099
✉ graeme.clark@waverley.gov.uk

Senior Management: Mr Damian Roberts, Director of Operations, Council Offices, The Burys, Godalming GU7 1HR ☎ 01483 523398
🖷 01483 523175 ✉ damian.roberts@waverley.gov.uk

Building Control: Mr Matthew Evans, Head of Planning, Council Offices, The Burys, Godalming GU7 1HR ☎ 01483 523297
🖷 01483 523118 ✉ matthew.evans@waverley.gov.uk

Catering Services: Mr David Allum, Head of Customer & Corporate Services, Council Offices, The Burys, Godalming GU7 1HR ☎ 01483 523338 ✉ david.allum@waverley.gov.uk

Children / Youth Services: Mrs Katie Webb, Community Services Manager, Council Offices, The Burys, Godalming GU7 1HR
☎ 01483 523340 ✉ katie.webb@waverley.gov.uk

PR / Communications: Mr Robin Taylor, Head of Policy & Governance, Council Offices, The Burys, Godalming GU7 1HR
☎ 01483 523108 ✉ robin.taylor@waverley.gov.uk

Community Safety: Mr Kelvin Mills, Head of Community Services, Council Offices, The Burys, Godalming GU7 1HR ☎ 01483 523432
✉ kelvin.mills@waverley.gov.uk

Customer Service: Mr David Allum, Head of Customer & Corporate Services, Council Offices, The Burys, Godalming GU7 1HR ☎ 01483 523338 ✉ david.allum@waverley.gov.uk

Economic Development: Mr Kelvin Mills, Head of Community Services, Council Offices, The Burys, Godalming GU7 1HR
☎ 01483 523432 ✉ kelvin.mills@waverley.gov.uk

E-Government: Mr David Allum, Head of Customer & Corporate Services, Council Offices, The Burys, Godalming GU7 1HR
☎ 01483 523338 ✉ david.allum@waverley.gov.uk

Electoral Registration: Mrs Tracey Stanbridge, Electoral Services Manager, Council Offices, The Burys, Godalming GU7 1HR ☎ 01483 523413 🖷 01483 523475 🖰 tracey.stanbridge@waverley.gov.uk

Energy Management: Ms Fotini Kallipoliti, Sustainability Manager, Council Offices, The Burys, Godalming GU7 1HR ☎ 01483 523448 🖰 fotini.kallipoliti@waverley.gov.uk

Environmental / Technical Services: Mr Robert Anderton, Head of Environmental Services, Council Offices, The Burys, Godalming GU7 1HR ☎ 01483 523411 🖰 rob.anderton@waverley.gov.uk

Environmental Health: Miss Victoria Buckroyd, Environmental Health Manager, Council Offices, The Burys, Godalming GU7 1HR ☎ 01483 523436 🖷 01483 523175 🖰 victoria.buckroyd@waverley.gov.uk

Estates, Property & Valuation: Mr Gary Streets, Estates & Valuation Manager, Council Offices, The Burys, Godalming GU7 1HR ☎ 01483 523315 🖷 01483 523118 🖰 gary.streets@waverley.gov.uk

Facilities: Mr David Allum, Head of Customer & Corporate Services, Council Offices, The Burys, Godalming GU7 1HR ☎ 01483 523338 🖰 david.allum@waverley.gov.uk

Finance: Mr Graeme Clark, Director of Finance & Resources and Chief Finance Officer, Council Offices, The Burys, Godalming GU7 1HR ☎ 01483 523099 🖰 graeme.clark@waverley.gov.uk

Grounds Maintenance: Mr Kelvin Mills, Head of Community Services, Council Offices, The Burys, Godalming GU7 1HR ☎ 01483 523432 🖰 kelvin.mills@waverley.gov.uk

Home Energy Conservation: Ms Fotini Kallipoliti, Sustainability Manager, Council Offices, The Burys, Godalming GU7 1HR ☎ 01483 523448 🖰 fotini.kallipoliti@waverley.gov.uk

Housing: Mrs Jane Abraham, Head of Strategic Housing & Delivery, Council Offices, The Burys, Godalming GU7 1HR ☎ 01483 523096 🖰 jane.abraham@waverley.gov.uk

Housing Maintenance: Mr Hugh Wagstaff, Head of Housing Operations, Council Offices, The Burys, Godalming GU7 1HR ☎ 01483 523361 🖰 hugh.wagstaff@waverley.gov.uk

Legal: Mr Daniel Bainbridge, Borough Solicitor, Council Offices, The Burys, Godalming GU7 1HR ☎ 01483 523235 🖰 daniel.bainbridge@waverley.gov.uk

Leisure and Cultural Services: Mr Kelvin Mills, Head of Community Services, Council Offices, The Burys, Godalming GU7 1HR ☎ 01483 523432 🖰 kelvin.mills@waverley.gov.uk

Licensing: Mr Robin Taylor, Head of Policy & Governance, Council Offices, The Burys, Godalming GU7 1HR ☎ 01483 523108 🖰 robin.taylor@waverley.gov.uk

Member Services: Ms Emma McQuillan, Democratic Services Manager, Council Offices, The Burys, Godalming GU7 1HR ☎ 01483 523351 🖰 emma.mcquillan@waverley.gov.uk

Parking: Mr Robert Anderton, Head of Environmental Services, Council Offices, The Burys, Godalming GU7 1HR ☎ 01483 523411 🖰 ; rob.anderton@waverley.gov.uk

Personnel / HR: Mr Peter Vickers, Head of Finance, Council Offices, The Burys, Godalming GU7 1HR ☎ 01483 523539 🖰 peter.vickers@waverley.gov.uk

Planning: Mr Matthew Evans, Head of Planning, Council Offices, The Burys, Godalming GU7 1HR ☎ 01483 523297 🖷 01483 523118 🖰 matthew.evans@waverley.gov.uk

Recycling & Waste Minimisation: Mr Robert Anderton, Head of Environmental Services, Council Offices, The Burys, Godalming GU7 1HR ☎ ; 01483 523411 🖰 ; rob.anderton@waverley.gov.uk

Sustainable Development: Ms Fotini Kallipoliti, Sustainability Manager, Council Offices, The Burys, Godalming GU7 1HR ☎ 01483 523448 🖰 fotini.kallipoliti@waverley.gov.uk

Waste Collection and Disposal: Mr Robert Anderton, Head of Environmental Services, Council Offices, The Burys, Godalming GU7 1HR ☎ 01483 523411 🖰 rob.anderton@waverley.gov.uk

Waste Management: Mr Robert Anderton, Head of Environmental Services, Council Offices, The Burys, Godalming GU7 1HR ☎ 01483 523411 🖰 rob.anderton@waverley.gov.uk

Children's Play Areas: Mr Matt Lank, Parks Manager, Council Offices, The Burys, Godalming GU7 1HR ☎ 01483 523190 🖰 matt.lank@waverley.gov.uk

COUNCILLORS

***Mayor* Band**, Mike (CON - Shamley Green & Cranleigh North)
mike.band@waverley.gov.uk

***Leader of the Council* Knowles**, Robert (CON - Haslemere East & Grayswood)
robert.knowles@waverley.gov.uk

***Deputy Leader of the Council* Potts**, Julia (CON - Farnham Upper Hale)
julia.potts@waverley.gov.uk

Adams, Brian (CON - Frensham Dockenfield & Tilford)
brian.adams@waverley.gov.uk

Blagden, Patrick (CON - Farnham Castle)
patrick.blagden@waverley.gov.uk

Bolton, Andrew (CON - Godalming Central & Ockford)
andrew.bolton@waverley.gov.uk

Byham, Maurice (CON - Bramley, Busbridge & Hascombe)
maurice.byham@waverley.gov.uk

Cockburn, Carole (CON - Farnham Bourne)
carole.cockburn@waverley.gov.uk

Deanus, Kevin (CON - Alfold, Cranleigh Rural & Ellens Green)
kevin.deanus@waverley.gov.uk

Edwards, Jim (CON - Haslemere Critchmere & Shottermill)
james.edwards@waverley.gov.uk

Ellis, Brian (CON - Cranleigh West)
brian.ellis@waverley.gov.uk

WAVERLEY

Ellis, Patricia (CON - Cranleigh West)
patricia.ellis@waverley.gov.uk

Else, David (CON - Elstead & Thursley)
david.else@waverley.gov.uk

Else, Jenny (CON - Elstead & Thursley)
jenny.else@waverley.gov.uk

Foryszewski, Mary (CON - Cranleigh East)
mary.foryszewski@waverley.gov.uk

Fraser, John (R - Farnham Upper Hale)
john.fraser@waverley.gov.uk

Frost, Pat (CON - Farnham Wrecclesham & Rowledge)
pat.frost@waverley.gov.uk

Goodridge, Michael (CON - Blackheath & Wonersh)
michael.goodridge@waverley.gov.uk

Gordon-Smith, Tony (CON - Godalming Charterhouse)
tony.gordon-smith@waverley.gov.uk

Gray, John (CON - Chiddingfold & Dunsfold)
john.gray@waverley.gov.uk

Hall, Ged (CON - Frensham, Dockenfield & Tilford)
ged.hall@waverley.gov.uk

Hargreaves, Jill (CON - Farnham Firgrove)
jill.hargreaves@waverley.gov.uk

Henry, Val (CON - Ewhurst)
val.henry@waverley.gov.uk

Hesse, Christiaan (CON - Hindhead)
christiaan.hesse@waverley.gov.uk

Hill, Stephen (CON - Farnham Moor Park)
stephen.hill@waverley.gov.uk

Hodge, Mike (CON - Farnham Hale & Heath End)
mike.hodge@waverley.gov.uk

Holder, Nicholas (CON - Witley & Hambledon)
nicholas.holder@waverley.gov.uk

Hunter, David (CON - Godalming Binscombe)
david.hunter@waverley.gov.uk

Inchbald, Simon (CON - Chiddingfold & Dunsfold)
simon.inchbald@waverley.gov.uk

Isherwood, Peter (CON - Hindhead)
peter.isherwood@waverley.gov.uk

James, Anna (CON - Witley & Hambledon)
anna.james@waverley.gov.uk

King, Carole (CON - Haslemere Critchmere & Shottermill)
carole.king@waverley.gov.uk

Le Gal, Denise (CON - Farnham Hale & Heath End)
deniselegal@waverley.gov.uk

Lear, Martin (CON - Farnham Bourne)
martin.lear@waverley.gov.uk

Leigh, Denis (CON - Milford)
denis.leigh@waverley.gov.uk

MacLeod, Andy (IND - Farnham Moor Park)
andy.macleod@waverley.gov.uk

Martin, Tom (CON - Godalming Holloway)
tom.martin@waverley.gov.uk

Martin, Peter (CON - Godalming Holloway)
peter.martin@waverley.gov.uk

Mirylees, Kika (R - Farnham Shortheath & Boundstone)
kika.mirylees@waverley.gov.uk

Mulliner, Stephen (CON - Haslemere East & Grayswood)
stephen.mulliner@waverley.gov.uk

Munro, David (CON - Farnham Shortheath & Boundstone)
david.munro@waverley.gov.uk

Nasir, Nabeel (CON - Farnham Weybourne & Badshot Lea)
nabeel.nasir@waverley.gov.uk

Piper, Libby (CON - Haslemere Critchmere & Shottermill)
libby.piper@waverley.gov.uk

Pritchard, Sam (CON - Farnham Firgrove)
sam.pritchard@waverley.gov.uk

Ramsdale, Wyatt (CON - Farnham Wrecclesham & Rowledge)
wyatt.ramsdale@waverley.gov.uk

Reynolds, Stefan (CON - Godalming Charterhouse)
stefan.reynolds@waverley.gov.uk

Round, David (CON - Haslemere East & Grayswood)
david.round@waverley.gov.uk

Seaborne, Richard (CON - Bramley, Busbridge & Hascombe)
richard.seaborne@waverley.gov.uk

Stennett, Jeanette (CON - Cranleigh East)

Stennett, Stewart (CON - Cranleigh East)
stewart.stennett@waverley.gov.uk

Storey, Christopher (CON - Farnham Weybourne & Badshot Lea)
christopher.storey@waverley.gov.uk

Thornton, Simon (CON - Godalming Central & Ockford)
simon.thornton@waverley.gov.uk

Upton, Bob (CON - Milford)
bob.upton@waverley.gov.uk

Welland, Ross (CON - Godalming Farncombe & Catteshall)
ross.welland@waverley.gov.uk

Wheatley, Liz (CON - Godalming Binscombe)
liz.wheatley@waverley.gov.uk

Williams, Nick (CON - Godalming Farncombe & Catteshall)
nick.williams@waverley.gov.uk

Williamson, John (R - Farnham Castle)
john.williamson@waverley.gov.uk

POLITICAL COMPOSITION

CON: 53, R: 3, IND: 1

COMMITTEE CHAIRS

Audit: Mr Jim Edwards

Licensing: Mr Simon Inchbald

Wealden D

Wealden District Council, Council Offices, Vicarage Lane, Hailsham BN27 2AX
☎ 01323 443322 ✉ info@wealden.gov.uk 💻 www.wealden.gov.uk

FACTS AND FIGURES

Parliamentary Constituencies: Wealden
EU Constituencies: South East
Election Frequency: Elections are of whole council

PRINCIPAL OFFICERS

Chief Executive: Mr Charles Lant, Chief Executive, Council Offices, Pine Grove, Crowborough TN6 1DH ☎ 01892 653322 🖷 01892 602222 ✉ chiefexec@wealden.gov.uk

Senior Management: Mrs Isabel Garden, Director - Environment & Community Services, Council Offices, Pine Grove, Crowborough TN6 1DH ☎ 01892 602404 🖷 01323 443333 ✉ isabel.garden@wealden.gov.uk

Senior Management: Mr Trevor Scott, Director - Governance & Corporate Services, Council Offices, Pine Grove, Crowborough TN6 1DH ☎ 01892 602524 🖷 01323 443333 ✉ trevor.scott@wealden.gov.uk

Architect, Building / Property Services: Ms Amanda Hodge, Head of Housing & Property Services, Council Offices, Vicarage Lane, Hailsham BN27 2AX ☎ 01323 443364 🖷 01323 443333 ✉ amanda.hodge@wealden.gov.uk

Best Value: Mr Malcolm Harris, Policy Officer, Council Offices, Vicarage Lane, Hailsham BN27 2AX ☎ 01323 443744 🖷 01323 443333 ✉ malcolm.harris@wealden.gov.uk

Building Control: Mr Kelvin Williams, Head of Planning & Environmental Services, Council Offices, Pine Grove, Crowborough TN6 1DH ☎ 01892 602484 🖷 01323 443333 ✉ kelvin.williams@wealden.gov.uk

PR / Communications: Mr Jim Van den Bos, Communications Officer, Council Offices, Vicarage Lane, Hailsham BN27 2AX ☎ 01892 602745 🖷 01892 602220 ✉ jim.vandenbos@wealden.gov.uk

Computer Management: Mr David Palmer, Head of Business Services, Council Offices, Vicarage Lane, Hailsham BN27 2AX ☎ 01323 443229 🖷 01323 443333 ✉ david.palmer@wealden.gov.uk

Contracts: Mr Gerry Palmer, Corporate Procurement Manager, Council Offices, Vicarage Lane, Hailsham BN27 2AX ☎ 01323 443350 🖷 01323 443351 ✉ gerry.palmer@wealden.gov.uk

Corporate Services: Mr Trevor Scott, Director - Governance & Corporate Services, Council Offices, Pine Grove, Crowborough TN6 1DH ☎ 01892 602524 🖷 01323 443333 ✉ trevor.scott@wealden.gov.uk

Customer Service: Mr Alex White, Head of Customer Services & Revenues, Council Offices, Vicarage Lane, Hailsham BN27 2AX ☎ 01323 443171 🖷 01323 443333 ✉ alex.white@wealden.gov.uk

Economic Development: Mrs Isabel Garden, Director - Environment & Community Services, Council Offices, Pine Grove, Crowborough TN6 1DH ☎ 01892 602404 🖷 01323 443333 ✉ isabel.garden@wealden.gov.uk

E-Government: Mr David Palmer, Head of Business Services, Council Offices, Vicarage Lane, Hailsham BN27 2AX ☎ 01323 443229 🖷 01323 443333 ✉ david.palmer@wealden.gov.uk

Electoral Registration: Mrs Heather Blanshard, Electoral Services Manager, Council Offices, Vicarage Lane, Hailsham BN27 2AX ☎ 01892 602416 🖷 01892 443333 ✉ heather.blanshard@wealden.gov.uk

Emergency Planning: Mr Jim Foster, Emergency Planning Officer, Council Offices, Vicarage Lane, Hailsham BN27 2AX ☎ 01892 653311 🖷 01323 443333 ✉ jim.foster@wealden.gov.uk

Energy Management: Ms Amanda Hodge, Head of Housing & Property Services, Council Offices, Vicarage Lane, Hailsham BN27 2AX ☎ 01323 443364 🖷 01323 443333 ✉ amanda.hodge@wealden.gov.uk

Environmental Health: Mr Richard Parker-Harding, Head of Environmental Health, 14 Beeching Road, Bexhill-on-Sea TN39 3LG ✉ richard.parker-harding@rother.gov.uk

Estates, Property & Valuation: Ms Amanda Hodge, Head of Housing & Property Services, Council Offices, Vicarage Lane, Hailsham BN27 2AX ☎ 01323 443364 🖷 01323 443333 ✉ amanda.hodge@wealden.gov.uk

Facilities: Ms Amanda Hodge, Head of Housing & Property Services, Council Offices, Vicarage Lane, Hailsham BN27 2AX ☎ 01323 443364 🖷 01323 443333 ✉ amanda.hodge@wealden.gov.uk

Finance: Mr Steve Linnett, Chief Finance Officer, Council Offices, Vicarage Lane, Hailsham BN27 2AX ☎ 01323 443234 🖷 01323 443245 ✉ steve.linnett@wealden.gov.uk

Finance: Mr Trevor Scott, Director - Governance & Corporate Services, Council Offices, Pine Grove, Crowborough TN6 1DH ☎ 01892 602524 🖷 01323 443333 ✉ trevor.scott@wealden.gov.uk

Grounds Maintenance: Ms Amanda Hodge, Head of Housing & Property Services, Council Offices, Vicarage Lane, Hailsham BN27 2AX ☎ 01323 443364 🖷 01323 443333 ✉ amanda.hodge@wealden.gov.uk

Home Energy Conservation: Mrs Julie Wilkins, Property Services Manager, Council Offices, Vicarage Lane, Hailsham BN27 2AX ☎ 01323 443312 🖷 01323 443320 ✉ julie.wilkins@wealden.gov.uk

Housing: Mr Nigel Hannam, Director - Environment & Community Services, Council Offices, Vicarage Lane, Hailsham BN27 2AX ☎ 01323 443230 🖷 01323 443333 ✉ nigel.hannam@wealden.gov.uk

Housing: Ms Amanda Hodge, Head of Housing & Property Services, Council Offices, Vicarage Lane, Hailsham BN27 2AX ☎ 01323 443364 🖷 01323 443333 ✉ amanda.hodge@wealden.gov.uk

Housing Maintenance: Ms Amanda Hodge, Head of Housing & Property Services, Council Offices, Vicarage Lane, Hailsham BN27 2AX ☎ 01323 443364 🖷 01323 443333 ✉ amanda.hodge@wealden.gov.uk

Legal: Mrs Kristina Shaw-Hamilton, Legal Services Manager, Council Offices, Vicarage Lane, Hailsham BN27 2AX ☎ 01892 602574 ✉ kristina-shawhamilton@wealden.gov.uk

Leisure and Cultural Services: Mrs Helen Markwick, Community & Regeneration Team Manager, Council Offices, Vicarage Lane, Hailsham BN27 2AX ☎ 01323 443307 🖷 01323 443333 ✉ helen.markwick@wealden.gov.uk

Licensing: Mr Richard Parker-Harding, Head of Environmental Health, 14 Beeching Road, Bexhill-on-Sea TN39 3LG
richard.parker-harding@rother.gov.uk

Member Services: Mrs Gabriella Paterson-Griggs, Democratic Services Manager, Council Offices, Vicarage Lane, Hailsham BN27 2AX ☎ 01892 602433 🖷 01323 443333
gabriella.paterson@wealden.gov.uk

Parking: Ms Tina Ford, Car Park & Office Manager, Council Offices, Vicarage Lane, Hailsham BN27 2AX ☎ 01323 443346 🖷 01323 443333 tina.ford@wealden.gov.uk

Personnel / HR: Mr David Palmer, Head of Business Services, Council Offices, Vicarage Lane, Hailsham BN27 2AX ☎ 01323 443229 🖷 01323 443333 david.palmer@wealden.gov.uk

Planning: Mr Nigel Hannam, Director - Environment & Community Services, Council Offices, Vicarage Lane, Hailsham BN27 2AX ☎ 01323 443230 🖷 01323 443333 nigel.hannam@wealden.gov.uk

Planning: Mr Kelvin Williams, Head of Planning & Building Control, Council Offices, Vicarage Lane, Hailsham BN27 2AX ☎ 01892 602484 🖷 01892 602777 kelvin.williams@wealden.gov.uk

Procurement: Mr Gerry Palmer, Corporate Procurement Manager, Council Offices, Vicarage Lane, Hailsham BN27 2AX ☎ 01323 443350 🖷 01323 443351 gerry.palmer@wealden.gov.uk

Recycling & Waste Minimisation: Mrs Isabel Garden, Director - Environment & Community Services, Council Offices, Pine Grove, Crowborough TN6 1DH ☎ 01892 602404 🖷 01323 443333
isabel.garden@wealden.gov.uk

Regeneration: Mrs Isabel Garden, Director - Environment & Community Services, Council Offices, Pine Grove, Crowborough TN6 1DH ☎ 01892 602404 🖷 01323 443333
isabel.garden@wealden.gov.uk

Staff Training: Mr David Palmer, Head of Business Services, Council Offices, Vicarage Lane, Hailsham BN27 2AX ☎ 01323 443229 🖷 01323 443333 david.palmer@wealden.gov.uk

Sustainable Communities: Mrs Isabel Garden, Director - Environment & Community Services, Council Offices, Pine Grove, Crowborough TN6 1DH ☎ 01892 602404 🖷 01323 443333
isabel.garden@wealden.gov.uk

Tourism: Mrs Helen Markwick, Community & Regeneration Team Manager, Council Offices, Vicarage Lane, Hailsham BN27 2AX ☎ 01323 443307 🖷 01323 443333 helen.markwick@wealden.gov.uk

Waste Collection and Disposal: Mrs Isabel Garden, Director - Environment & Community Services, Council Offices, Pine Grove, Crowborough TN6 1DH ☎ 01892 602404 🖷 01323 443333
isabel.garden@wealden.gov.uk

Waste Management: Mrs Isabel Garden, Director - Environment & Community Services, Council Offices, Pine Grove, Crowborough TN6 1DH ☎ 01892 602404 🖷 01323 443333
isabel.garden@wealden.gov.uk

COUNCILLORS

***Chair* Dashwood-Morris**, Barby (CON - Chiddingly and East Hoathly)
cllr.barby.dashwood-morris@wealden.gov.uk

***Vice-Chair* Hardy**, Chris (CON - Hartfield)
cllr.chris.hardy@wealden.gov.uk

***Leader of the Council* Standley**, Robert (CON - Wadhurst)
cllr.robert.standley@wealden.gov.uk

***Deputy Leader of the Council* Dowling**, Claire (CON - Uckfield Central)
cllr.claire.dowling@wealden.gov.uk

Angel, Dick (CON - Heathfield North and Central)
cllr.dick.angel@wealden.gov.uk

Balsdon, Kevin (CON - Pevensey and Westham)
cllr.kevin.balsdon@wealden.gov.uk

Bentley, Jo (CON - Hailsham South and West)
cllr.jo.bentley@wealden.gov.uk

Bowlder, Bob (CON - Heathfield East)
cllr.bob.bowdler@wealden.gov.uk

Clark, Lin (CON - Pevensey and Westham)
cllr.lin.clark@wealden.gov.uk

Collinson, Nicholas (CON - Hailsham Central and North)
cllr.nicholas.collinson@wealden.gov.uk

Coltman, Nigel (CON - Hailsham Central and North)
cllr.nigel.coltman@wealden.gov.uk

Cowie, Peter (CON - Crowborough East)
cllr.peter.cowie@wealden.gov.uk

Dear, Dianne (CON - Pevensey and Westham)
cllr.dianne.dear@wealden.gov.uk

Dixon, Phil (CON - Rotherfield)
cllr.phil.dixon@wealden.gov.uk

Doodes, Pam (CON - Ninfield and Hooe with Wartling)
cllr.pam.doodes@wealden.gov.uk

Dunk, Jan (CON - Heathfield North and Central)
cllr.jan.dunk@wealden.gov.uk

Ede, Philip (CON - Alfriston)
cllr.philip.ede@wealden.gov.uk

Firth, Helen (CON - Uckfield New Town)
cllr.helen.firth@wealden.gov.uk

Fox, Jonica (CON - Cross-in-Hand / Five Ashes)
cllr.jonica.fox@wealden.gov.uk

Galley, Roy (CON - Danehill / Fletching / Nutley)
cllr.roy.galley@wealden.gov.uk

Grocock, Richard (CON - Hailsham South and West)
cllr.richard.grocock@wealden.gov.uk

Hollins, Jim (CON - Crowborough West)
cllr.jim.hollins@wealden.gov.uk

Holloway, Peter (CON - Forest Row)
cllr.peter.holloway@wealden.gov.uk

Howell, Johanna (CON - Frant / Withyham)
cllr.johanna.howell@wealden.gov.uk

Illingworth, Toby (CON - Buxted and Maresfield)
cllr.toby.illingworth@wealden.gov.uk

Isted, Stephen (IND - Crowborough Jarvis Brook)
cllr.stephen.isted@wealden.gov.uk

Long, Andy (CON - Herstmonceux)

Lunn, Michael (CON - Buxted and Maresfield)
cllr.michael.lunn@wealden.gov.uk

Marlowe, Barry (CON - Uckfield Ridgewood)
cllr.barry.marlow@wealden.gov.k

Moore, Rowena (CON - Forest Row)
cllr.rowena.moore@wealden.gov.uk

Moss, Kay (CON - Crowborough St Johns)
cllr.kay.moss@wealden.gov.uk

Murray, Douglas (CON - Willingdon)
cllr.douglas.murray@wealdon.gov.uk

Newton, Ann (CON - Framfield)
cllr.ann.newton@wealden.gov.uk

O'Rawe, Amanda (CON - Hailsham East)
cllr.amanda.orawe@wealden.gov.uk

Pinkney, Mark (CON - Hellingly)
cllr.mark.pinkney@wealden.gov.uk

Redman, Brian (CON - Mayfield)
cllr.brian.redman@wealden.gov.uk

Reed, Ronald (CON - Crowborough North)
cllr.ronald.reed@wealden.gov.uk

Reynolds, Carol (CON - Uckfield North)
cllr.carol.reynolds@wealden.gov.uk

Rose, Greg (CON - Crowborough East)
cllr.greg.rose@wealden.gov.uk

Roundell, Peter (CON - Danehill / Fletching / Nutley)
cllr.peter.roundell@wealden.gov.uk

Rutherford, William (CON - Frant / Withyham)
william.rutherford@wealden.gov.uk

Shing, Daniel (IND - Polegate South)
daniel.shing@wealden.gov.uk

Shing, Raymond (IND - Willingdon)
cllr.raymond.shing@wealden.gov.uk

Shing, Oi Lin (IND - Polegate North)
cllr.oilin.shing@wealden.gov.uk

Shing, Stephen (IND - Willingdon)
cllr.stephen.shing@wealden.gov.uk

Snell, Angela (CON - Polegate North)
cllr.angela.snell@wealden.gov.uk

Soane, Paul (CON - Hellingly)
cllr.paul.soane@wealden.gov.uk

Stedman, Susan (CON - Horam)
cllr.susan.stedman@wealden.gov.uk

Thomas, Roger (CON - Heathfield North and Central)
cllr.roger.thomas@wealden.gov.uk

Towey, Jeanette (CON - Crowborough West)
cllr.jeanette.towey@wealden.gov.uk

Triandafyllou, Chriss (CON - Halisham South and West)
cllr.chriss.triandafyllou@wealden.gov.uk

Waldock, Peter (CON - Uckfield North)
cllr.peter.waldock@wealden.gov.uk

Waller, Neil (CON - Crowborough North)
cllr.neil.waller@wealden.gov.uk

Wells, Graham (CON - Wadhurst)
cllr.graham.wells@wealden.gov.uk

Wilton, John (CON - East Dean)
cllr.john.wilton@wealden.gov.uk

POLITICAL COMPOSITION

CON: 50, IND: 5

COMMITTEE CHAIRS

Audit & Finance: Mr Peter Roundell

Licensing: Mr Nigel Coltman

Wellingborough D

Wellingborough Borough Council, Council Offices, Swanspool House, Wellingborough NN8 1BP
☎ 01933 229777 🖷 01933 231543; 01933 231540
customerservices@wellingborough.gov.uk
www.wellingborough.gov.uk

FACTS AND FIGURES

Parliamentary Constituencies: Wellingborough
EU Constituencies: East Midlands
Election Frequency: Elections are of whole council

PRINCIPAL OFFICERS

Chief Executive: Mr John Campbell, Chief Executive & Head of Paid Service, Council Offices, Swanspool House, Wellingborough NN8 1BP ☎ 01933 231500 🖷 01933 231684
jcampbell@wellingborough.gov.uk

Senior Management: Ms Elizabeth Elliott, Head of Finance, Council Offices, Swanspool House, Wellingborough NN8 1BP
☎ 01933 231679 lelliott@wellingborough.gov.uk

Senior Management: Mr Phil Grimley, Head of ICT Services, East Northamptonshire Council, Cedar Drive, Thrapston NN14 4LZ
☎ 01832 742076 pgrimley@east_northamptonshire.gov.uk

Senior Management: Mrs Bridget Lawrence, Head - Resources, Council Offices, Swanspool House, Wellingborough NN8 1BP
☎ 01933 231816 🖷 01933 231684 blawrence@wellingborough.gov.uk

Senior Management: Ms Julie Thomas, Head - Planning & Local Development, Council Offices, Swanspool House, Wellingborough NN8 1BP ☎ 01933 231924 🖷 01933 231684
jthomas@wellingborough.gov.uk

Architect, Building / Property Services: Mrs Bridget Lawrence, Head - Resources, Council Offices, Swanspool House, Wellingborough NN8 1BP ☎ 01933 231816 🖷 01933 231684
blawrence@wellingborough.gov.uk

Building Control: Ms Julie Thomas, Head - Planning & Local Development, Council Offices, Swanspool House, Wellingborough NN8 1BP ☎ 01933 231924 🖷 01933 231684
jthomas@wellingborough.gov.uk

Children / Youth Services: Ms Gill Chapman, Principal Community Support Manager, Council Offices, Swanspool House, Wellingborough NN8 1BP ☎ 01933 231839 🖷 01933 231684
gchapman@wellingborough.gov.uk

WELLINGBOROUGH

PR / Communications: Mrs Paula Whitworth, Corporate Communications Officer, Council Offices, Swanspool House, Wellingborough NN8 1BP ☎ 01933 231836 🖷 01933 231684 🖰 pwhitworth@wellingborough.gov.uk

Community Planning: Ms Gill Chapman, Principal Community Support Manager, Council Offices, Swanspool House, Wellingborough NN8 1BP ☎ 01933 231839 🖷 01933 231684 🖰 gchapman@wellingborough.gov.uk

Community Safety: Ms Gill Chapman, Principal Community Support Manager, Council Offices, Swanspool House, Wellingborough NN8 1BP ☎ 01933 231839 🖷 01933 231684 🖰 gchapman@wellingborough.gov.uk

Computer Management: Mr Phil Grimley, Head of ICT Services, East Northamptonshire Council, Cedar Drive, Thrapston NN14 4LZ ☎ 01832 742076 🖰 pgrimley@east_northamptonshire.gov.uk

Economic Development: Ms Victoria Phillipson, Principal Planning Policy & Regeneration Manager, Council Offices, Swanspool House, Wellingborough NN8 1BP ☎ 01933 231985 🖷 01933 231684 🖰 vphillipson@wellingborough.gov.uk

Electoral Registration: Mrs Bridget Lawrence, Head - Resources, Council Offices, Swanspool House, Wellingborough NN8 1BP ☎ 01933 231816 🖷 01933 231684 🖰 blawrence@wellingborough.gov.uk

Emergency Planning: Ms Sandi Collins, Emergency Planning Officer, Council Offices, Swanspool House, Wellingborough NN8 1BP ☎ 01933 231724 🖰 scollins@northamptonshire.gov.uk

Environmental / Technical Services: Mr Bernard Gallyot, Managing Director - Wellingborough Norse, Wellingborough Norse, Trafalgar House, Sanders Park, Sanders Road, Finedon Road Industrial Estate, Wellingborough NN8 4FR ☎ 01933 234523 🖷 01933 234545 🖰 bernard.gallyot@wellingborough.gov.uk

Environmental Health: Mr David Haynes, Principal Environmental Protection Manager, Council Offices, Swanspool House, Wellingborough NN8 1BP ☎ 01933 231961 🖷 01933 231684 🖰 dhaynes@wellinborough.gov.uk

Estates, Property & Valuation: Mr Paul Burnett, Property Services Manager, Council Offices, Swanspool House, Wellingborough NN8 1BP ☎ 01933 231586 🖷 01933 231684 🖰 pburnett@wellingborough.gov.uk

Events Manager: Ms Julia Wells, Events Officer, Council Offices, Swanspool House, Wellingborough NN8 1BP ☎ 01933 231986 🖷 01933 231684 🖰 jwells@wellingborough.gov.uk

Facilities: Mr Rob Badcock, Facilities Manager, Wellingborough Norse, Trafalgar House, Sanders Road, Wellingborough NN8 4PP ☎ 01933 234538 🖷 01933 234545 🖰 robert.badcock@ncsgrp.co.uk

Finance: Ms Elizabeth Elliott, Head of Finance, Council Offices, Swanspool House, Wellingborough NN8 1BP ☎ 01933 231679 🖰 lelliott@wellingborough.gov.uk

Fleet Management: Mr Bernard Gallyot, Managing Director - Wellingborough Norse, Wellingborough Norse, Trafalgar House, Sanders Park, Sanders Road, Finedon Road Industrial Estate, Wellingborough NN8 4FR ☎ 01933 234523 🖷 01933 234545 🖰 bernard.gallyot@wellingborough.gov.uk

Grounds Maintenance: Mr Bernard Gallyot, Managing Director - Wellingborough Norse, Wellingborough Norse, Trafalgar House, Sanders Park, Sanders Road, Finedon Road Industrial Estate, Wellingborough NN8 4FR ☎ 01933 234523 🖷 01933 234545 🖰 bernard.gallyot@wellingborough.gov.uk

Health and Safety: Mr Robert Sullivan, Senior Health & Safety Officer, Council Offices, Swanspool House, Wellingborough NN8 1BP ☎ 01933 231955 🖷 01933 231684 🖰 rsullivan@wellingborough.gov.uk

Home Energy Conservation: Mr Clive Culling, Assistant Principal Housing Officer (Renewal), Council Offices, Swanspool House, Wellingborough NN8 1BP ☎ 01933 231854 🖷 01933 231684 🖰 cculling@wellingborough.gov.uk

Housing: Ms Vicki Jessop, Prinicpal Housing Manager, Council Offices, Swanspool House, Wellingborough NN8 1BP ☎ 01933 231720 🖷 01933 231684 🖰 vjessop@wellinborough.gov.uk

Legal: Ms Sue Lyons, Head - Democratic & Legal Services, Council Offices, Swanspool House, Wellingborough NN8 1BP ☎ 01536 534209; 01536 543209 🖰 suelyons@kettering.gov.uk

Leisure and Cultural Services: Ms Gill Chapman, Principal Community Support Manager, Council Offices, Swanspool House, Wellingborough NN8 1BP ☎ 01933 231839 🖷 01933 231684 🖰 gchapman@wellingborough.gov.uk

Licensing: Ms Amanda Wilcox, Principal Health Protection Manager, Council Offices, Swanspool House, Wellingborough NN8 1BP ☎ 01933 231954 🖷 01933 231684 🖰 awilcox@wellingborough.gov.uk

Lottery Funding, Charity and Voluntary: Mrs Bridget Lawrence, Head - Resources, Council Offices, Swanspool House, Wellingborough NN8 1BP ☎ 01933 231816 🖷 01933 231684 🖰 blawrence@wellingborough.gov.uk

Member Services: Mrs Bridget Lawrence, Head - Resources, Council Offices, Swanspool House, Wellingborough NN8 1BP ☎ 01933 231816 🖷 01933 231684 🖰 blawrence@wellingborough.gov.uk

Personnel / HR: Mrs Karen Denton, Principal Organisational Development Manger, Council Offices, Swanspool House, Wellingborough NN8 1BP ☎ 01933 231601 🖷 01933 231684 🖰 kdenton@wellingborough.gov.uk

Planning: Ms Julie Thomas, Head - Planning & Local Development, Council Offices, Swanspool House, Wellingborough NN8 1BP ☎ 01933 231924 🖷 01933 231684 🖰 jthomas@wellingborough.gov.uk

Recycling & Waste Minimisation: Mr Bernard Gallyot, Managing Director - Wellingborough Norse, Wellingborough Norse, Trafalgar House, Sanders Park, Sanders Road, Finedon Road Industrial Estate, Wellingborough NN8 4FR ☎ 01933 234523 🖷 01933 234545 bernard.gallyot@wellingborough.gov.uk

Regeneration: Ms Victoria Phillipson, Principal Planning Policy & Regeneration Manager, Council Offices, Swanspool House, Wellingborough NN8 1BP ☎ 01933 231985 🖷 01933 231684 vphillipson@wellingborough.gov.uk

Staff Training: Mrs Karen Denton, Principal Organisational Development Manger, Council Offices, Swanspool House, Wellingborough NN8 1BP ☎ 01933 231601 🖷 01933 231684 kdenton@wellingborough.gov.uk

Street Scene: Mr Bernard Gallyot, Managing Director - Wellingborough Norse, Wellingborough Norse, Trafalgar House, Sanders Park, Sanders Road, Finedon Road Industrial Estate, Wellingborough NN8 4FR ☎ 01933 234523 🖷 01933 234545 bernard.gallyot@wellingborough.gov.uk

Sustainable Communities: Ms Julie Thomas, Head - Planning & Local Development, Council Offices, Swanspool House, Wellingborough NN8 1BP ☎ 01933 231924 🖷 01933 231684 jthomas@wellingborough.gov.uk

Sustainable Development: Ms Julie Thomas, Head - Planning & Local Development, Council Offices, Swanspool House, Wellingborough NN8 1BP ☎ 01933 231924 🖷 01933 231684 jthomas@wellingborough.gov.uk

Town Centre: Mr John Cable, Business Improvement District Manager, c/o The Management Suite, 18 Spring Lane, Wellingborough NN8 1EY ☎ 01933 270795 manager@wellingboroughtowncentre.co.uk

Waste Collection and Disposal: Mr Bernard Gallyot, Managing Director - Wellingborough Norse, Wellingborough Norse, Trafalgar House, Sanders Park, Sanders Road, Finedon Road Industrial Estate, Wellingborough NN8 4FR ☎ 01933 234523 🖷 01933 234545 bernard.gallyot@wellingborough.gov.uk

Waste Management: Mr Bernard Gallyot, Managing Director - Wellingborough Norse, Wellingborough Norse, Trafalgar House, Sanders Park, Sanders Road, Finedon Road Industrial Estate, Wellingborough NN8 4FR ☎ 01933 234523 🖷 01933 234545 bernard.gallyot@wellingborough.gov.uk

Children's Play Areas: Mr Bernard Gallyot, Managing Director - Wellingborough Norse, Wellingborough Norse, Trafalgar House, Sanders Park, Sanders Road, Finedon Road Industrial Estate, Wellingborough NN8 4FR ☎ 01933 234523 🖷 01933 234545 bernard.gallyot@wellingborough.gov.uk

COUNCILLORS

***Mayor* Graves**, Barry (CON - Great Doddington & Wilby)
bgraves@wellingborough.gov.uk

***Deputy Mayor* Lawman**, Graham (CON - Rixon)
glawman@wellingborough.gov.uk

***Leader of the Council* Bell**, Paul (CON - Redwell)
paul.bell@wellingborough.gov.uk

***Deputy Leader of the Council* Griffiths**, Martin (CON - Brickhill)
mgriffiths@wellingborough.gov.uk

***Group Leader* Scarborough**, Andrew (LAB - Queensway)
ascarborough@wellingborough.gov.uk

Abram, Rosemary (LAB - Hatton)
rabram@wellingborough.gov.uk

Allebone, Timothy (CON - Brickhill)
tim.allebone@virgin.net

Anslow, Valerie (LAB - Swanspool)
vanslow@wellingborough.gov.uk

Aslam, Tony (LAB - Victoria)
taslam@wellingborough.gov.uk

Bailey, John (CON - Finedon)
jbailey@wellingborough.gov.uk

Beirne, Jo (CON - Wollaston)
jbeirne@wellingborough.gov.uk

Bone, Jennie (CON - Harrowden & Sywell)
jbone@wellinborough.gov.uk

Carr, Jon-Paul (CON - Irchester)
jpcarr@wellingborough.gov.uk

Ekins, Jonathan (CON - Swanspool)
jekins@wellingborough.gov.uk

Emerson, Brian (LAB - Victoria)
bemerson@wellingborough.gov.uk

Francis, Elayne (LAB - Victoria)
efrancis@wellingborough.gov.uk

Gough, Robert (CON - Earls Barton)
rgough@wellinbrough.gov.uk

Hallam, Clive (CON - Harrowden & Sywell)
challam@wellingborough.gov.uk

Harrington, Ken (CON - Hatton)
kharrington@wellingborough.gov.uk

Henley, Adam (LAB - Queensway)
ahenley@wellingborough.gov.uk

Lawman, Lora (CON - Rixon)
lora.lawman@wellingborough.gov.uk

Lloyd, Thomas (CON - Irchester)
tlloyd@wellingborough.gov.uk

Maguire, Timothy (LAB - Irchester)
tmaguire@wellingborough.gov.uk

Morrall, Peter (CON - Earls Barton)
pmorrall@wellingborough.gov.uk

Partridge-Underwood, Tom (CON - Bozeat)
tpartridge-underwood@wellingborough.gov.uk

Patel, Umesh (CON - Rixon)
upatel@wellingborough.gov.uk

Scanlon, Sarah (CON - Croyland)
sscanlon@wellingborough.gov.uk

Simmons, Geoff (CON - Wollaston)
gsimmons@wellingborough.gov.uk

Skittral, Brian (CON - Croyland)
bskittrall@wellingborough.gov.uk

Stevenson, Laura (CON - Earls Barton)
lstevenson@wellingborough.gov.uk

Walia, Jay (CON - Isebrook)
jwalia@wellingborough.gov.uk

Ward, Malcolm (CON - Finedon)
mward@wellingborough.gov.uk

Waters, Malcolm (CON - Redwell)
mwaters@wellingborough.gov.uk

Waters, Veronica (CON - Redwll)
vwaters@wellingborough.gov.uk

Watts, Andrea (LAB - Queensway)
awatts@wellingborough.gov.uk

York, Martyn (CON - Croyland)
myork@wellingborough.gov.uk

POLITICAL COMPOSITION

CON: 27, LAB: 9

COMMITTEE CHAIRS

Audit: Mr John Bailey

Licensing: Mr Geoff Simmons

Planning: Mr Peter Morrall

Welwyn Hatfield D

Welwyn Hatfield Borough Council, Council Offices, The Campus, Welwyn Garden City AL8 6AE
☎ 01707 357000 🖷 01707 357257 ✉ contact-whc@welhat.gov.uk
💻 www.welhat.gov.uk

FACTS AND FIGURES

Parliamentary Constituencies: Broxbourne, Welwyn Hatfield
EU Constituencies: Eastern
Election Frequency: Elections are by thirds

PRINCIPAL OFFICERS

Chief Executive: Dr Michel Saminaden, Chief Executive, Council Offices, The Campus, Welwyn Garden City AL8 6AE ☎ 01707 357327 ✉ m.saminaden@welhat.gov.uk

Deputy Chief Executive: Mrs Pam Kettle, Director of Finance & Operations, Council Offices, The Campus, Welwyn Garden City AL8 6AE ☎ 01707 357275 ✉ p.kettle@welhat.gov.uk

Assistant Chief Executive: Mr Robert Baldock, Director of Governance, Council Offices, The Campus, Welwyn Garden City AL8 6AE ☎ 01707 357277

Architect, Building / Property Services: Mr Mike Storey, Corporate Property Manager, Council Offices, The Campus, Welwyn Garden City AL8 6AE ☎ 01707 357457 ✉ m.storey@welhat.gov.uk

Best Value: Mr Paul Underwood, Head of Policy & Culture, Council Offices, The Campus, Welwyn Garden City AL8 6AE ☎ 01707 357220 ✉ p.underwood@welhat.gov.uk

Building Control: Mr Mark Harvey, Building Control Manager, Council Offices, The Campus, Welwyn Garden City AL8 6AE ☎ 01707 357246 ✉ m.harvey@welhat.gov.uk

Children / Youth Services: Mr Matt Rayner, Youth & Sport Partnership Manager, Council Offices, The Campus, Welwyn Garden City AL8 6AE ☎ 01707 357174 ✉ m.rayner@welhat.gov.uk

PR / Communications: Mr Thom Burn, Policy & Communications Manager, Council Offices, The Campus, Welwyn Garden City AL8 6AE ☎ 01707 357271 ✉ t.burn@welhat.gov.uk

Community Safety: Mr Tim Beyer, Partnerships & Community Safety Manager, Council Offices, The Campus, Welwyn Garden City AL8 6AE ☎ 01707 357309 🖷 01707 357185 ✉ t.beyer@welhat.gov.uk

Contracts: Mr Andrew Harper, Procurement Manager, Council Offices, The Campus, Welwyn Garden City AL8 6AE ☎ 020 8207 2277; 01707 357371 ✉ a.harper@welhat.gov.uk

Customer Service: Ms Sue Kiernan, Customer Service Manager, Council Offices, The Campus, Welwyn Garden City AL8 6AE ☎ 01707 357201 ✉ s.kiernan@welhat.gov.uk

E-Government: Mrs Pam Kettle, Director of Finance & Operations, Council Offices, The Campus, Welwyn Garden City AL8 6AE ☎ 01707 357275 ✉ p.kettle@welhat.gov.uk

Electoral Registration: Mr John Merron, Electoral Services Manager, Council Offices, The Campus, Welwyn Garden City AL8 6AE ☎ 01707 357354 ✉ j.merron@welhat.gov.uk

Emergency Planning: Mr Andy Cremer, Risk & Resilience Manager, Council Offices, The Campus, Welwyn Garden City AL8 6AE ☎ 01707 357169 ✉ a.cremer@welhat.gov.uk

Energy Management: Mr Vin Appasawmy, Energy Efficiency Officer, Council Offices, The Campus, Welwyn Garden City AL8 6AE ☎ 01707 357399 ✉ v.appasawmy@welhat.gov.uk

Environmental / Technical Services: Mrs Pam Kettle, Director of Finance & Operations, Council Offices, The Campus, Welwyn Garden City AL8 6AE ☎ 01707 357275 ✉ p.kettle@welhat.gov.uk

Environmental / Technical Services: Mr Durk Reyner, Head of Environment, Council Offices, The Campus, Welwyn Garden City AL8 6AE ☎ 01707 357160 ✉ d.reyner@welhat.gov.uk

Environmental Health: Mr Nick Long, Head of Public Health & Protection, Council Offices, The Campus, Welwyn Garden City AL8 6AE ☎ 01707 357401 🖷 01707 375464 ✉ n.long@welhat.gov.uk

Estates, Property & Valuation: Mr Mike Storey, Corporate Property Manager, Council Offices, The Campus, Welwyn Garden City AL8 6AE ☎ 01707 357457 ✉ m.storey@welhat.gov.uk

Finance: Mrs Pam Kettle, Director of Finance & Operations, Council Offices, The Campus, Welwyn Garden City AL8 6AE ☎ 01707 357275 ✉ p.kettle@welhat.gov.uk

Grounds Maintenance: Mr Durk Reyner, Head of Environment, Council Offices, The Campus, Welwyn Garden City AL8 6AE ☎ 01707 357160 ✉ d.reyner@welhat.gov.uk

Health and Safety: Mr Andy Cremer, Risk & Resilience Manager, Council Offices, The Campus, Welwyn Garden City AL8 6AE ☎ 01707 357169 ✉ a.cremer@welhat.gov.uk

Home Energy Conservation: Mr Vin Appasawmy, Energy Efficiency Officer, Council Offices, The Campus, Welwyn Garden City AL8 6AE ☎ 01707 357399 ✉ v.appasawmy@welhat.gov.uk

Housing: Mrs Sian Chambers, Head of Housing & Community, Council Offices, The Campus, Welwyn Garden City AL8 6AE ☎ 01707 357640 ✉ s.chambers@welhat.gov.uk

Housing Maintenance: Mr John Briggs, Chief Executive, Welwyn Hatfield Community Housing Trust, 51 Bridge Road East, Welwyn Garden City AL8 1JR ☎ 01707 357742 ✉ j.briggs@welhat.gov.uk

Legal: Ms Margaret Martinus, Head of Law & Administration, Council Offices, The Campus, Welwyn Garden City AL8 6AE ☎ 01707 357575 ✉ m.martinus@welhat.gov.uk

Leisure and Cultural Services: Mr Paul Underwood, Head of Policy & Culture, Council Offices, The Campus, Welwyn Garden City AL8 6AE ☎ 01707 357220 ✉ p.underwood@welhat.gov.uk

Licensing: Mr Nick Long, Head of Public Health & Protection, Council Offices, The Campus, Welwyn Garden City AL8 6AE ☎ 01707 357401 🖷 01707 375464 ✉ n.long@welhat.gov.uk

Member Services: Mr Graham Seal, Governance Services Manager, Council Offices, The Campus, Welwyn Garden City AL8 6AE ☎ 01707 357444 ✉ g.seal@welhat.gov.uk

Parking: Ms Vikki Hatfield, Parking Services Team Leader, Council Offices, The Campus, Welwyn Garden City AL8 6AE ☎ 01707 357555 ✉ v.hatfield@welhat.gov.uk

Partnerships: Mrs Sian Chambers, Head of Housing & Community, Council Offices, The Campus, Welwyn Garden City AL8 6AE ☎ 01707 357640 ✉ s.chambers@welhat.gov.uk

Personnel / HR: Ms Kamini Patel, Human Resources Manager, Council Offices, The Campus, Welwyn Garden City AL8 6AE ☎ 01707 357294 ✉ k.patel@welhat.gov.uk

Planning: Mr Colin Haigh, Head of Planning, Council Offices, The Campus, Welwyn Garden City AL8 6AE ☎ 01707 357239 ✉ c.haigh@welhat.gov.uk

Procurement: Mr Andrew Harper, Procurement Manager, Council Offices, The Campus, Welwyn Garden City AL8 6AE ☎ 020 8207 2277; 01707 357371 ✉ a.harper@welhat.gov.uk

Recycling & Waste Minimisation: Ms Kirsten Roberts, Recycling & Environment Team Leader, Council Offices, The Campus, Welwyn Garden City AL8 6AE ☎ 01707 357177 ✉ k.roberts@welhat.gov.uk

Staff Training: Ms Kamini Patel, Human Resources Manager, Council Offices, The Campus, Welwyn Garden City AL8 6AE ☎ 01707 357294 ✉ k.patel@welhat.gov.uk

Street Scene: Mr Durk Reyner, Head of Environment, Council Offices, The Campus, Welwyn Garden City AL8 6AE ☎ 01707 357160 ✉ d.reyner@welhat.gov.uk

Sustainable Communities: Mrs Sue Tiley, Planning Policy & Implementation Manager, Council Offices, The Campus, Welwyn Garden City AL8 6AE ☎ 01707 357268 ✉ s.tiley@welhat.gov.uk

Town Centre: Mrs Mariana Bitonte, Town Centre Manager, Council Offices, The Campus, Welwyn Garden City AL8 6AE ☎ 01707 357565 ✉ m.bitonte@welhat.gov.uk

Waste Collection and Disposal: Mr Durk Reyner, Head of Environment, Council Offices, The Campus, Welwyn Garden City AL8 6AE ☎ 01707 357160 ✉ d.reyner@welhat.gov.uk

Waste Management: Ms Kirsten Roberts, Recycling & Environment Team Leader, Council Offices, The Campus, Welwyn Garden City AL8 6AE ☎ 01707 357177 ✉ k.roberts@welhat.gov.uk

Children's Play Areas: Mr Durk Reyner, Head of Environment, Council Offices, The Campus, Welwyn Garden City AL8 6AE ☎ 01707 357160 ✉ d.reyner@welhat.gov.uk

COUNCILLORS

***Leader of the Council* Dean**, John (CON - Brookmans Park and Little Heath)
john.dean@welhat.gov.uk

***Deputy Leader of the Council* Franey**, Alan (CON - Sherrards)
alan.franey@welhat.gov.uk

Beckerman, Jon (CON - Sherrards)
jon.beckerman@welhat.gov.uk

Bell, Duncan (CON - Hatfield Villages)
duncan.bell@welhat.gov.uk

Bennett, Darren (CON - Panshanger)
darren.bennett@welhat.gov.uk

Boulton, Stephen (CON - Brookmans Park and Little Heath)
stephen.boulton@welhat.gov.uk

Broach, James (LAB - Hatfield West)
james.broach@welhat.gov.uk

Bromley, Helen (CON - Handside)
helen.bromley@welhat.gov.uk

Chander, Simon (LAB - Haldens)
simon.chander@welhat.gov.uk

Chesterman, Alan (LAB - Howlands)
alan.chesterman@welhat.gov.uk

Chesterman, Lynn (LAB - Hollybush)
lynn.chesterman@welhat.gov.uk

Cook, Maureen (LAB - Hatfield Central)
maureen.cook@welhat.gov.uk

Cowan, Malcolm (LD - Peartree)
malcolm.cowen@welhat.gov.uk

Cragg, Julie (CON - Welwyn East)
julie.cragg@welhat.gov.uk

Crump, Tony (LAB - Haldens)
t.crump@welhat.gov.uk

WELWYN HATFIELD

Dean, Irene (CON - Brookmans Park and Little Heath)
irene.dean@welhat.gov.uk

Dowler, Graham (CON - Handside)
graham.dowler@welhat.gov.uk

Fitzpatrick, John (LAB - Hatfield South)
john.fitzpatrick@welhat.gov.uk

Hayes, Glyn (LAB - Hatfield Central)
glyn.hayes@welhat.gov.uk

Johnston, Sara (CON - Panshangar)
sara.johnston@welhat.gov.uk

Juggins, Caron (CON - Hatfield West)
caron.juggins@welhat.gov.uk

Kingsbury, Tony (CON - Hatfield East)
tony.kingsbury@welhat.gov.uk

Kyriakides, Sandra (IND - Welwyn West)
sandra.kyriakides@welhat.gov.uk

Larkins, Mike (LAB - Haldens)
mike.larkins@welhat.gov.uk

Long, Michael (CON - Hatfield East)
michael.long@welhat.gov.uk

Mabbott, Patricia (CON - Sherrards)
patricia.mabbott@welhat.gov.uk

Markiewicz, Steven (CON - Welwyn East)
steven.markiewicz@welhat.gov.uk

Michaelides, George (CON - Howlands)
george.michaelides@welhat.gov.uk

Morgan, Howard (CON - Hatfield Villages)
howard.morgan@welhat.gov.uk

Nicholls, John (CON - Northaw and Cuffley)
john.nicholls@welhat.gov.uk

Pace, Nick (CON - Hollybush)
nick.pace@welhat.gov.uk

Page, Les (CON - Welham Green)
les.page@welhat.gov.uk

Perkins, Mandy (CON - Welwyn West)
mandy.perkins@welhat.gov.uk

Pieri, Keith (CON - Welham Green)
keith.pieri@welhat.gov.uk

Prest, Adrian (CON - Northaw and Cuffley)
adrian.prest@welhat.gov.uk

Roberts, Steve (LAB - Peartree)
steve.roberts@welhat.gov.uk

Sarson, Bernard (CON - Hatfield East)
bernard.sarson@welhat.gov.uk

Shah, Pankit (LAB - Hatfield Central)
pankit.shah@welhat.gov.uk

Siewniak, Michal (LD - Peartree)
michal.siewniak@welhat.gov.uk

Sparks, Lynne (CON - Hatfield Villages)
lynne.sparks@welhat.gov.uk

Storer, Carl (CON - Welwyn East)
carl.storer@welhat.gov.uk

Thomson, Fiona (CON - Handside)
fiona.thomson@welhat.gov.uk

Thorpe, Kieran (LAB - Hatfield South)
kieran.thorpe@welhat.gov.uk

Thorpe, Astrid (LAB - Hollybush)
astrid.thorpe@welhat.gov.uk

Trigg, Roger (CON - Panshanger)
roger.trigg@welhat.gov.uk

Tunstall, Stan (CON - Howlands)
stan.tunstall@welhat.gov.uk

Watson, Cathy (LAB - Hatfield West)
cathy.watson@welhat.gov.uk

Yeowell, Annalisa (CON - Howlands)
annalisa.yeowell@welhat.gov.uk

POLITICAL COMPOSITION

CON: 31, LAB: 14, LD: 2, IND: 1

COMMITTEE CHAIRS

Audit: Mr Steven Markiewicz

Development Management: Mr Stephen Boulton

Licensing: Mr Jon Beckerman

West Berkshire U

West Berkshire Council, Council Offices, Market Street, Newbury RG14 5LD
☎ 01635 42400 🖷 01635 519431 🖱 info@westberks.gov.uk
💻 www.westberks.gov.uk

FACTS AND FIGURES

Parliamentary Constituencies: Newbury, Reading West, Wokingham
EU Constituencies: South East
Election Frequency: Elections are of whole council

PRINCIPAL OFFICERS

Chief Executive: Mr Nick Carter, Chief Executive, Council Offices, Market Street, Newbury RG14 5LD ☎ 01635 519104
🖱 ncarter@westberks.gov.uk

Senior Management: Mr John Ashworth, Corporate Director of Environment, Council Offices, Market Street, Newbury RG14 5LD
☎ 01635 519587 🖷 01635 519872 🖱 jashworth@westberks.gov.uk

Senior Management: Ms Rachael Wardell, Corporate Director of Communities, West Street House, West Street, Newbury RG14 1BD
☎ 01635 519723 🖱 rwardell@westberks.gov.uk

Access Officer / Social Services (Disability): Ms Valerie Witton, Access Officer, Council Offices, Market Street, Newbury RG14 5LD ☎ 01635 519489 🖷 01635 519408
🖱 vwitton@westberks.gov.uk

Building Control: Mr Roger Paine, Building Control Manager, Council Offices, Market Street, Newbury RG14 5LD
☎ 01635 519694 🖷 01635 519888 🖱 rpaine@westberks.gov.uk

Children / Youth Services: Mr Mac Heath, Head of Children's Services, Council Offices, Market Street, Newbury RG14 5LD
☎ 01635 519735 🖱 mheath@westberks.gov.uk

Civil Registration: Mr David Holling, Head of Legal Services, Council Offices, Market Street, Newbury RG14 5LD ☎ 01635 519422 🖷 01635 519431 ✉ dholling@westberks.gov.uk

Community Safety: Mrs Susan Powell, Safer Communities Partnership Team Manager, 20 Mill Lane, Newbury RG14 5LE ☎ 01635 264703 ✉ spowell@westberks.gov.uk

Computer Management: Mr Kevin Griffin, Head of ICT & Corporate Support, Council Offices, Market Street, Newbury RG14 5LD ☎ 01635 519292 🖷 01635 519392 ✉ kgriffin@westberks.gov.uk

Consumer Protection and Trading Standards: Mr Sean Murphy, Trading Standards & Licensing Manager - Public Protection, Council Offices, Market Street, Newbury RG14 5LD ☎ 01635 519840 🖷 01635 519172 ✉ smurphy@westberks.gov.uk

Customer Service: Mr Sean Anderson, Head of Customer Services, Council Offices, Market Street, Newbury RG14 5LD ☎ 01635 519149 🖷 01635 519431 ✉ sanderson@westberks.gov.uk

Education: Mr Ian Pearson, Deputy Corporate Director - Communites & Head of Education, West Street House, West Street, Newbury RG14 1BD ☎ 01635 519729 🖷 01635 519048 ✉ ipearson@westberks.gov.uk

E-Government: Mr David Lowe, Information Manager, Council Offices, Market Street, Newbury RG14 5LD ☎ 01635 42400 🖷 01635 519431 ✉ dlowe@westberks.gov.uk

Electoral Registration: Mr Phil Runacres, Elections & Registration Manager, Council Offices, Market Street, Newbury RG14 5LD ☎ 01635 519463 🖷 01635 519431 ✉ prunacres@westberks.gov.uk

Emergency Planning: Mrs Carolyn Richardson, Emergency Planning Officer, Council Offices, Market Street, Newbury RG14 5LD ☎ 01635 503265 ✉ crichardson@westberks.gov.uk

Energy Management: Mr Adrian Slaughter, Principal Energy Efficiency Officer, Council Offices, Market Street, Newbury RG14 5LD ☎ 01635 503265 ✉ aslaughter@westberks.gov.uk

Environmental / Technical Services: Mr Paul Hendry, Countryside Manager, Council Offices, Market Street, Newbury RG14 5LD ☎ 01635 519858 🖷 01635 519325 ✉ phendry@westberks.gov.uk

Environmental Health: Mr Paul Hendry, Countryside Manager, Council Offices, Market Street, Newbury RG14 5LD ☎ 01635 519858 🖷 01635 519325 ✉ phendry@westberks.gov.uk

Estates, Property & Valuation: Mr Stephen Broughton, Head of Culture & Environment Protection, Council Offices, Market Street, Newbury RG14 5LD ☎ 01635 519837 🖷 01635 519408 ✉ slbroughton@westberks.gov.uk

Facilities: Mr Stephen Broughton, Head of Culture & Environment Protection, Council Offices, Market Street, Newbury RG14 5LD ☎ 01635 519837 🖷 01635 519408 ✉ slbroughton@westberks.gov.uk

Finance: Mr Andy Walker, Head of Finance, Council Offices, Market Street, Newbury RG14 5LD ☎ 01635 519433 🖷 01635 519872 ✉ awalker@westberks.gov.uk

Fleet Management: Mrs Jacquie Chambers, Benefit & Expenses Assistant, Council Offices, Market Street, Newbury RG14 5LD ☎ 01635 519272 🖷 01635 519351 ✉ jchambers@westberks.gov.uk

Health and Safety: Mr Mike Lindenburn, Health & Safety Manager, Council Offices, Market Street, Newbury RG14 5LD ☎ 01635 519253 ✉ mlindenburn@westberks.gov.uk

Highways: Mr Mark Edwards, Head of Highways & Transport, Council Offices, Market Street, Newbury RG14 5LD ☎ 01635 519208 🖷 01635 519865 ✉ medwards@westberks.gov.uk

Housing: Mrs June Graves, Head of Care Commissioning, Housing & Safeguarding, West Street House, West Street, Newbury RG14 1BD ☎ 01635 519733 🖷 01635 519939 ✉ jgraves@westberks.gov.uk

Legal: Mr David Holling, Head of Legal Services, Council Offices, Market Street, Newbury RG14 5LD ☎ 01635 519422 🖷 01635 519431 ✉ dholling@westberks.gov.uk

Licensing: Mr Paul Anstey, Principal Environment Health Officer, Council Offices, Market Street, Newbury RG14 5LD ☎ 01635 519002 🖷 01635 519172 ✉ panstey@westberks.gov.uk

Lifelong Learning: Mrs Sara Hanson, Lifelong Learning Officer, West Street House, West Street, Newbury RG14 1BD ☎ 01635 519792 🖷 01635 519048 ✉ shanson@westberks.gov.uk

Lighting: Mr Mark Edwards, Head of Highways & Transport, Council Offices, Market Street, Newbury RG14 5LD ☎ 01635 519208 🖷 01635 519865 ✉ medwards@westberks.gov.uk

Member Services: Mrs Jo Watt, Members' Services Officer, Council Offices, Market Street, Newbury RG14 5LD ☎ 01635 519242 🖷 01635 519613 ✉ jwatt@westberks.gov.uk

Parking: Mr Mark Edwards, Head of Highways & Transport, Council Offices, Market Street, Newbury RG14 5LD ☎ 01635 519208 🖷 01635 519865 ✉ medwards@westberks.gov.uk

Personnel / HR: Mr Rob O'Reilly, Head of Human Resources, Council Offices, Market Street, Newbury RG14 5LD ☎ 01635 519575 ✉ roreilly@westberks.gov.uk

Planning: Mr Gary Lugg, Head of Planning & Countryside, Council Offices, Market Street, Newbury RG14 5LD ☎ 01635 519617 🖷 01635 519408 ✉ glugg@westberks.gov.uk

Procurement: Mr David Holling, Head of Legal Services, Council Offices, Market Street, Newbury RG14 5LD ☎ 01635 519422 🖷 01635 519431 ✉ dholling@westberks.gov.uk

Recycling & Waste Minimisation: Mr Paul Hendry, Countryside Manager, Council Offices, Market Street, Newbury RG14 5LD ☎ 01635 519858 🖷 01635 519325 ✉ phendry@westberks.gov.uk

Road Safety: Mr Mark Edwards, Head of Highways & Transport, Council Offices, Market Street, Newbury RG14 5LD ☎ 01635 519208 🖷 01635 519865 🖱 medwards@westberks.gov.uk

Social Services (Adult): Ms Tandra Forster, Head of Adult Social Care, West Street House, West Street, Newbury RG14 1BD ☎ 01635 519736 🖷 01635 519740 🖱 tforster@westberks.gov.uk

Social Services (Children): Ms Rachael Wardell, Corporate Director of Communities, West Street House, West Street, Newbury RG14 1BD ☎ 01635 519723 🖱 rwardell@westberks.gov.uk

Public Health: Dr Lise Llewellyn, Director - Public Health, Easthampstead House, Town Square, Bracknell RG12 1AQ 🖱 lise.llewellyn@bracknell-forest.gov.uk

Staff Training: Mr Rob O'Reilly, Head of Human Resources, Council Offices, Market Street, Newbury RG14 5LD ☎ 01635 519575 🖱 roreilly@westberks.gov.uk

Street Scene: Mr Mark Edwards, Head of Highways & Transport, Council Offices, Market Street, Newbury RG14 5LD ☎ 01635 519208 🖷 01635 519865 🖱 medwards@westberks.gov.uk

Traffic Management: Mr Mark Edwards, Head of Highways & Transport, Council Offices, Market Street, Newbury RG14 5LD ☎ 01635 519208 🖷 01635 519865 🖱 medwards@westberks.gov.uk

Transport: Mr Mark Edwards, Head of Highways & Transport, Council Offices, Market Street, Newbury RG14 5LD ☎ 01635 519208 🖷 01635 519865 🖱 medwards@westberks.gov.uk

Transport Planner: Mr Gary Lugg, Head of Planning & Countryside, Council Offices, Market Street, Newbury RG14 5LD ☎ 01635 519617 🖷 01635 519408 🖱 glugg@westberks.gov.uk

Waste Collection and Disposal: Mr Paul Hendry, Countryside Manager, Council Offices, Faraday Road, Newbury RG14 2AF ☎ 01635 519858 🖷 01635 519325 🖱 phendry@westberks.gov.uk

Waste Collection and Disposal: Ms Jackie Ward, Waste Manager, Council Offices, Market Street, Newbury RG14 5LD ☎ 01635 519216 🖷 01635 519453 🖱 jward@westberks.gov.uk

Waste Management: Mr Paul Hendry, Countryside Manager, Council Offices, Faraday Road, Newbury RG14 2AF ☎ 01635 519858 🖷 01635 519325 🖱 phendry@westberks.gov.uk

COUNCILLORS

***Chair* Argyle**, Peter (CON - Calcot)
pargyle@westberks.gov.uk

***Vice-Chair* Webb**, Quentin (CON - Bucklebury)
qwebb@westberks.gov.uk

***Leader of the Council* Lundie**, Gordon (CON - Lambourn Valley)
glundie@westberks.gov.uk

***Deputy Leader of the Council* Croft**, Roger (CON - Thatcham South and Crookham)
rcroft@westberks.gov.uk

Ardagh-Walter, Steve (CON - Thatcham West)
sardaghwalter@westberks.gov.uk

Bairstow, Howard (CON - Falkland)
hbairstow@westberks.gov.uk

Bale, Pamela (CON - Pangbourne)
pbale@westberks.gov.uk

Bartlett, Jeremy (CON - Greenham)
jbartlett@westberks.gov.uk

Beck, Jeff (CON - Clay Hill)
jbeck@westberks.gov.uk

Benneyworth, Dennis (CON - Victoria)
dbenneyworth@westberks.gov.uk

Boeck, Dominic (CON - Aldermaston)
dboeck@westberks.gov.uk

Bridgman, Graham (CON - Mortimer)
gbridgman@westberks.gov.uk

Bryant, Paul (CON - Speen)
pbryant@westberks.gov.uk

Chadley, Anthony (CON - Birch Copse)
achadley@westberks.gov.uk

Chopping, Keith (CON - Sulhamstead)
kchopping@westberks.gov.uk

Clifford, Jeanette (CON - Northcroft)
jclifford@westberks.gov.uk

Cole, Hilary (CON - Chieveley)
hcole@westberks.gov.uk

Cole, James (CON - Kintbury)
jcole@westberks.gov.uk

Crumly, Richard (CON - Thatcham Central)
rcrumly@westberks.gov.uk

Denton-Powell, Rob (CON - Thatcham South and Crookham)
rdentonpowell@westberks.gov.uk

Dillon, Lee (LD - Thatcham North)
ldillon@westberks.gov.uk

Doherty, Lynne (CON - Northcroft)
ldoherty@westberks.gov.uk

Drummond, Billy (LD - Greenham)
bdrummond@westberks.gov.uk

Edwards, Adrian (CON - Falkland)
adrian.edwards@westberks.gov.uk

Ellison, Sheila (CON - Thatcham North)
sellison@westberks.gov.uk

Franks, Marcus (CON - Speen)
mfranks@westberks.gov.uk

Fredrickson, James (CON - Victoria)
jfredrickson@westberks.gov.uk

Goff, Dave (CON - Clay Hill)
dgoff@westberks.gov.uk

Goodes, Nick (CON - Thatcham West)
ngoodes@westberks.gov.uk

Gopal, Manohar (CON - Calcot)
mgopal@westberks.gov.uk

Hewer, Paul (CON - Hungerford)
phewer@westberks.gov.uk

Hooker, Clive (CON - Downlands)
chooker@westberks.gov.uk

Jackson-Doerge, Carol (CON - Burghfield)
cjacksondoerge@westberks.gov.uk

Jaques, Marigold (CON - Thatcham Central)
mjaques@westberks.gov.uk

Johnston, Mike (CON - St Johns)
mjohnston@westberks.gov.uk

Jones, Graham (CON - Lambourn Valley)
gjones@westberks.gov.uk

Jones, Rick (CON - Purley on Thames)
rjones@westberks.gov.uk

Law, Alan (CON - Basildon)
alaw@westberks.gov.uk

Linden, Tony (CON - Birch Copse)
tlinden@westberks.gov.uk

Lock, Mollie (LD - Mortimer)
mlock@westberks.gov.uk

Macro, Alan (LD - Theale)
amacro@westberks.gov.uk

Metcalfe, Tim (CON - Purley on Thames)
tmetcalfe@westberks.gov.uk

Morrin, Ian (CON - Burghfield)
imorrin@westberks.gov.uk

Pask, Graham (CON - Bucklebury)
gpask@westberks.gov.uk

Pick, Anthony (CON - St Johns)
apick@westberks.gov.uk

Podger, James (CON - Hungerford)
jpodger@westberks.gov.uk

Simpson, Garth (CON - Cold Ash)
gsimpson@westberks.gov.uk

Somner, Richard (CON - Calcot)
rsomner@westberks.gov.uk

Stansfeld, Anthony (CON - Kintbury)
astansfeld@westberks.gov.uk

von Celsing, Virginia (CON - Compton)
vvoncelsing@westberks.gov.uk

Webster, Emma (CON - Birch Copse)

Zverko, Laszlo (CON - Westwood)

POLITICAL COMPOSITION

CON: 48, LD: 4

COMMITTEE CHAIRS

Licensing: Mr Jeff Beck

Planning: Mr Alan Law

West Devon D

West Devon Borough Council, Kilworthy Park, Drake Road, Tavistock PL19 0BZ
☎ 01822 813600 🖷 01822 813634
✉ customer.services@westdevon.gov.uk 🖳 www.westdevon.gov.uk

FACTS AND FIGURES

Parliamentary Constituencies: Devon Central, Devon West and Torridge
EU Constituencies: South West
Election Frequency: Elections are of whole council

PRINCIPAL OFFICERS

Chief Executive: Mr Steve Jorden, Executive Director - Strategy & Commissioning & Head of Paid Service, Kilworthy Park, Drake Road, Tavistock PL19 0BZ ☎ 01803 861105
✉ steve.jorden@swdevon.gov.uk

Deputy Chief Executive: Ms Sophie Hosking, Executive Director - Service Delivery & Commercial Development, Follaton House, Plymouth Road, Totnes TQ9 5NE ☎ 01803 861105
✉ sophie.hosking@swdevon.gov.uk

Senior Management: Mr Darren Arulvasagam, Group Manager - Business Development, Kilworthy Park, Drake Road, Tavistock PL19 0BZ ☎ 01803 861234 ✉ darren.arulvasagam@swdevon.gov.uk

Senior Management: Ms Tracey Beeck, Group Manager - Customer First, Kilworthy Park, Drake Road, Tavistock PL19 0BZ
☎ 01803 861234 ✉ tracey.beeck@swdevon.gov.uk

Senior Management: Mrs Helen Dobby, Head of Environment Services, Kilworthy Park, Drake Road, Tavistock PL19 0BZ
☎ 01822 813600 ✉ helen.dobby@swdevon.gov.uk

Senior Management: Mr Steve Mullineaux, Group Manager - Support Services, Kilworthy Park, Drake Road, Tavistock PL19 0BZ
☎ 01822 813600 ✉ steve.mullineaux@swdevon.gov.uk

Community Planning: Mr Ross Kennerley, Lead Specialist for Place Strategy, Kilworthy Park, Drake Road, Tavistock PL19 0BZ
☎ 01822 813647 ✉ ross.kennerley@swdevon.gov.uk

Computer Management: Mr Mike Ward, ICT Community of Practice Lead, Kilworthy Park, Drake Road, Tavistock PL19 0BZ
☎ 01803 861234 ✉ mike.ward@swdevon.gov.uk

Customer Service: Ms Tracey Beeck, Group Manager - Customer First, Kilworthy Park, Drake Road, Tavistock PL19 0BZ
☎ 01803 861234 ✉ tracey.beeck@swdevon.gov.uk

Economic Development: Ms Nadine Trout, Tourism Officer, Kilworthy Park, Drake Road, Tavistock PL19 0BZ ☎ 01822 813600
✉ nadine.trout@swdevon.gov.uk

Electoral Registration: Ms Clare Chapman, Electoral Services Officer, Kilworthy Park, Drake Road, Tavistock PL19 0BZ
☎ 01822 813664 ✉ clare.chapman@westdevon.gov.uk

Emergency Planning: Mr James Kershaw, Head of Emergency Planning, Kilworthy Park, Drake Road, Tavistock PL19 0BZ
☎ 01822 813600 ✉ james.kershaw@swdevon.gov.uk

Estates, Property & Valuation: Mr Chris Brook, Community of Practice - Assets, Kilworthy Park, Drake Road, Tavistock PL19 0BZ
☎ 01822 813600 ✉ chris.brook@swdevon.gov.uk

WEST DEVON

Finance: Miss Lisa Buckle, Head of Finance & Audit, Kilworthy Park, Drake Road, Tavistock PL19 0BZ ☎ 01822 813644
lisa.buckle@westdevon.gov.uk

Grounds Maintenance: Mrs Helen Dobby, Head of Environment Services, Kilworthy Park, Drake Road, Tavistock PL19 0BZ
☎ 01822 813600 helen.dobby@swdevon.gov.uk

Housing: Ms Isabel Blake, Head of Housing, Kilworthy Park, Drake Road, Tavistock PL19 0BZ ☎ 01822 813600
isabel.blake@swdevon.gov.uk

Legal: Mrs Catherine Bowen, Borough Solicitor, Kilworthy Park, Drake Road, Tavistock PL19 0BZ ☎ 01822 813666 🖷 01822 813634
cbowen@westdevon.gov.uk

Leisure and Cultural Services: Mr Jon Parkinson, Leisure & Recreation Officer, Kilworthy Park, Drake Road, Tavistock PL19 0BZ
☎ 01822 813698 🖷 01822 813634
jon.parkinson@southhams.gov.uk

Member Services: Mr Darryl White, Democratic Services Manager, Kilworthy Park, Drake Road, Tavistock PL19 0BZ
☎ 01822 813662 🖷 01822 813634 darryl.white@swdevon.gov.uk

Parking: Mrs Catherine Aubertin, Car Parking & Contracts Performance Manager, Kilworthy Park, Drake Road, Tavistock PL19 0BZ ☎ 01822 813650 caubertin@westdevon.gov.uk

Personnel / HR: Mr Andy Wilson, Head of Corporate Services, Kilworthy Park, Drake Road, Tavistock PL19 0BZ ☎ 01822 813600
andy.wilson@swdevon.gov.uk

Street Scene: Mrs Catherine Aubertin, Car Parking & Contracts Performance Manager, Kilworthy Park, Drake Road, Tavistock PL19 0BZ ☎ 01822 813650 caubertin@westdevon.gov.uk

Waste Collection and Disposal: Mrs Jane Savage, Waste Reduction & Recycling Officer, Kilworthy Park, Drake Road, Tavistock PL19 0BZ ☎ 01822 813655 🖷 01822 813634
jsavage@westdevon.gov.uk

Waste Management: Mrs Helen Dobby, Head of Environment Services, Kilworthy Park, Drake Road, Tavistock PL19 0BZ
☎ 01822 813600 helen.dobby@swdevon.gov.uk

COUNCILLORS

***Mayor* Cloke**, David (IND - Burrator)
cllr.david.cloke@westdevon.gov.uk

***Leader of the Council* Sanders**, Philip (CON - Buckland Manochorum)
cllr.philip.sanders@westdevon.gov.uk

***Deputy Leader of the Council* Baldwin**, Bob (CON - Milton Ford)
clr.bob.baldwin@westdevon.gov.uk

Ball, Kevin (CON - Okehampton North)
cllr.kevin.ball@westdevon.gov.uk

Benson, Mike (CON - Bere Ferrers)
cllr.mike.benson@westdevon.gov.uk

Cann, William (IND - South Tawton)
cllr.william.cann@westdevon.gov.uk

Cheadle, Ric (IND - Buckland Monachorum)
cllr.ric.cheadle@westdevon.gov.uk

Davies, Mike (CON - Okehampton North)
cllr.mike.davies@westdevon.gov.uk

Edmonds, Chris (IND - Tamarside)
cllr.chris.edmonds@westevon.gov.uk

Evans, Jess (CON - Tavistock South West)
cllr.jess.evans@westdevon.gov.uk

Hockridge, John (IND - Bridestowe)
cllr.john.hockridge@westdevon.gov.uk

Jory, Neil (CON - Tavistock North)
cllr.neil.jory@westdevon.gov.uk

Kimber, Patrick (CON - Hatherleigh)
cllr.patrick.kimber@westdevon.gov.uk

Leech, Tony (IND - Okehampton East)
cllr.tony.leech@westdevon.gov.uk

McInnes, James (CON - Lew Valley)
cllr.james.mcinnes@westdevon.gov.uk

Moody, Jeffrey (IND - Tavistock North)
Cllr.Jeffrey.Moody@westdevon.gov.uk

Mott, Caroline (CON - Bridestowe)
cllr.caroline.mott@westdevon.gov.uk

Moyse, Diana (CON - Burrator)
cllr.diana.moyse@westdevon.gov.uk

Musgrave, Robin (LD - Bere Ferrers)
cllr.robin.musgrave@westdevon.gov.uk

Oxborough, Robert (CON - Tavistock South)
cllr.robert.oxborough@westdevon.gov.uk

Parker, Graham (CON - Tavistock South West)
cllr.graham.parker@westdevon.gov.uk

Pearce, Terry (IND - Mary Tavy)
cllr.terry.pearce@westdevon.gov.uk

Ridgers, Paul (CON - Drewsteignton)
cllr.paul.ridgers@westdevon.gov.uk

Roberts, Annabel (CON - Dartmoor)
cllr.annabel.roberts@westdevon.gov.uk

Sampson, Robert (IND - Chagford)
cllr.robert.sampson@westdevon.gov.uk

Samuel, Lois (CON - Exbourne)
cllr.lois.samuel@westdevon.gov.uk

Sellis, Debo (CON - Walkham)
cllr.debo.sellis@westdevon.gov.uk

Sheldon, John (CON - Tavistock North)
cllr.john.sheldon@westdevon.gov.uk

Stephens, Ben (CON - Okehampton South)
cllr.ben.stephens@westdevon.gov.uk

Watts, Louise (CON - Exbourne)
cllr.louise.watts@westdevon.gov.uk

Yelland, Julie (CON - Okehampton South)
cllr.julie.yelland@westdevon.gov.uk

POLITICAL COMPOSITION

CON: 21, IND: 9, LD: 1

West Dorset D

West Dorset District Council, Stratton House, 58-60 High West Street, Dorchester DT1 1UZ
☎ 01305 251010 🖷 01305 251481 💻 www.dorsetforyou.com

FACTS AND FIGURES

Parliamentary Constituencies: Dorset West
EU Constituencies: South West
Election Frequency: Elections are of whole council

PRINCIPAL OFFICERS

Chief Executive: Mr Matt Prosser, Chief Executive, South Walks House, South Walks Road, Dorchester DT1 1UZ ☎ 01305 251010 🖱 d.clarke@weymouth.gov.uk

Assistant Chief Executive: Mr Stuart Caundle, Assistant Chief Executive, South Walks House, South Walks Road, Dorchester DT1 1UZ ☎ 01258 484010 🖱 scaundle@north-dorset.co.uk

Senior Management: Mr Martin Hamilton, Strategic Director, South Walks House, South Walks Road, Dorchester DT1 1UZ ☎ 01305 838086 🖱 m.hamilton@westdorset-weymouth.gov.uk

Senior Management: Mr Stephen Hill, Strategic Director, South Walks House, South Walks Road, Dorchester DT1 1UZ ☎ 01258 484034 🖱 shill@north-dorset.gov.uk

Senior Management: Mr Jason Vaughan, Strategic Director & S151 Officer, South Walks House, South Walks Road, Dorchester DT1 1UZ ☎ 01305 838233; 01305 251010 🖱 j.vaughan@westdorset-weymouth.gov.uk

Architect, Building / Property Services: Mr David Brown, Head of Assets & Infrastructure, South Walks House, South Walks Road, Dorchester DT1 1UZ ☎ 01305 252297 🖱 d.brown@westdorset-weymouth.gov.uk

Best Value: Ms Julie Strange, Head of Financial Services, Council Offices, North Quay, Weymouth DT4 8TA ☎ 01305 838252; 01305 251010 🖱 j.strange@westdorset-weymouth.gov.uk

Building Control: Mr David Potter, Building Control Manager, South Walks House, South Walks Road, Dorchester DT1 1UZ ☎ 01305 252258 🖱 d.potter@westdorset-weymouth.gov.uk

PR / Communications: Ms Penny Mell, Head of Business Improvement, South Walks House, South Walks Road, Dorchester DT1 1UZ ☎ 01305 838371 🖱 p.mell@westdorset-weymouth.gov.uk

Community Planning: Ms Hilary Jordan, Head of Planning, Community & Policy Development, South Walks House, South Walks Road, Dorchester DT1 1UZ ☎ 01305 252303 🖱 h.jordan@westdorset-weymouth.gov.uk

Community Safety: Mr Graham Duggan, Head of Community Protection, South Walks House, South Walks Road, Dorchester DT1 1UZ ☎ 01305 252285; 01305 251010 🖱 g.duggan@westdorset-weymouth.gov.uk

Computer Management: Ms Penny Mell, Head of Business Improvement, South Walks House, South Walks Road, Dorchester DT1 1UZ ☎ 01305 838371 🖱 p.mell@westdorset-weymouth.gov.uk

Customer Service: Ms Penny Mell, Head of Business Improvement, South Walks House, South Walks Road, Dorchester DT1 1UZ ☎ 01305 838371 🖱 p.mell@westdorset-weymouth.gov.uk

Economic Development: Mr Trevor Hedger, Senior Economic Regeneration Officer, South Walks House, South Walks Road, Dorchester DT1 1UZ ☎ 01305 252378 🖱 t.hedger@westdorset-weymouth.gov.uk

Electoral Registration: Ms Sue Bonham-Lovett, Electoral Services Manager, South Walks House, South Walks Road, Dorchester DT1 1UZ ☎ 01305 838477; 01305 251010 🖷 01305 838289 🖱 s.bonham-lovett@westdorset-weymouth.gov.uk

Emergency Planning: Mr Grant Armfield, Emergency Planning Officer, South Walks House, South Walks Road, Dorchester DT1 1UZ ☎ 01305 838213 🖷 01305 838317 🖱 grantarmfield@weymouth.gov.uk

Energy Management: Mr Bob Savage, Senior Building Services Engineer, South Walks House, South Walks Road, Dorchester DT1 1UZ ☎ 01305 838318 🖷 01305 838469 🖱 bobsavage@weymouth.gov.uk

Environmental / Technical Services: Mr David Brown, Head of Assets & Infrastructure, South Walks House, South Walks Road, Dorchester DT1 1UZ ☎ 01305 252297 🖱 d.brown@westdorset-weymouth.gov.uk

Environmental Health: Mr Graham Duggan, Head of Community Protection, Stratton House, 58-60 High West Street, Dorchester DT1 1UZ ☎ 01305 252285; 01305 251010 🖱 g.duggan@westdorset-weymouth.gov.uk

Estates, Property & Valuation: Mr Greg Northcote, Estates Manager, South Walks House, South Walks Road, Dorchester DT1 1UZ ☎ 01305 838268 🖱 g.northcote@westdorset-weymouth.gov.uk

Events Manager: Mr Nick Thornley, Head of Economy, Leisure & Tourism, South Walks House, South Walks Road, Dorchester DT1 1UZ ☎ 01305 252474; 01305 251010 🖱 n.thornley@westdorset-weymouth.gov.uk

Finance: Mr Jason Vaughan, Strategic Director & S151 Officer, West Dorset District Council, 58/60 High West Street, Dorchester DT1 1UZ ☎ 01305 838233; 01305 251010 🖱 j.vaughan@westdorset-weymouth.gov.uk

Fleet Management: Ms Sally-Ann Arden-Nixon, Fleet Transport Co-ordinator, South Walks House, South Walks Road, Dorchester DT1 1UZ ☎ 01305 838447 🖱 sa.arden-nixon@westdorset-weymouth.gov.uk

Health and Safety: Mr Richard Noakes, Health, Safety & Welfare Officer, South Walks House, South Walks Road, Dorchester DT1 1UZ ☎ 01305 838356 🖱 r.noakes@westdorset-weymouth.gov.uk

Home Energy Conservation: Mr Clive Milone, Head of Housing, South Walks House, South Walks Road, Dorchester DT1 1UZ ☎ 01305 252313 ✉ c.milone@westdorset-weymouth.gov.uk

Housing: Mr Chris Branch, Housing Solutions Manager, South Walks House, South Walks Road, Dorchester DT1 1UZ ☎ 01305 838460 ✉ c.branch@westdorset-weymouth.gov.uk

Housing Maintenance: Mr Geoff Joy, Housing Improvement Manager, South Walks House, South Walks Road, Dorchester DT1 1UZ ☎ 01305 252286 ✉ g.joy@westdorset-weymouth.gov.uk

Legal: Mr Roger Greene, Legal Services Manager (Property & Litigation), South Walks House, South Walks Road, Dorchester DT1 1UZ ☎ 01305 252253 ✉ r.greene@westdorset-weymouth.gov.uk

Leisure and Cultural Services: Mr Nick Thornley, Head of Economy, Leisure & Tourism, South Walks House, South Walks Road, Dorchester DT1 1UZ ☎ 01305 252474; 01305 251010 ✉ n.thornley@westdorset-weymouth.gov.uk

Licensing: Ms Sue Moore, Business Licensing Manager, South Walks House, South Walks Road, Dorchester DT1 1UZ ☎ 01305 838205; 01305 252474 ✉ s.moore@westdorset-weymouth.gov.uk

Lottery Funding, Charity and Voluntary: Ms Jane Nicklen, Community Planning & Development Manager, South Walks House, South Walks Road, Dorchester DT1 1UZ ☎ 01305 252358 ✉ j.nicklen@westdorset-weymouth.gov.uk

Member Services: Ms Susan Carne, Democratic Services Manager, South Walks House, South Waks Road, Dorchester DT1 1UZ ☎ 01305 252216 ✉ s.carne@westdorset-weymouth.gov.uk

Parking: Mr Jack Creeber, Parking & Transport Manager, South Walks House, South Walks Road, Dorchester DT1 1UZ ☎ 01305 838349 ✉ j.creeber@westdorset-weymouth.gov.uk

Partnerships: Ms Caron Starkey, Business Change Manager, South Walks House, South Walks Road, Dorchester DT1 1UZ ☎ 01305 838277 ✉ c.starkey@westdorset-weymouth.gov.uk

Personnel / HR: Ms Mel Horton, HR Manager - Systems, South Walks House, South Walks Road, Dorchester DT1 1UZ ☎ 01305 252473 ✉ m.horton@westdorset-weymouth.gov.uk

Planning: Ms Jean Marshall, Head of Planning, Development Management & Building Control, South Walks House, South Walks Road, Dorchester DT1 1UZ ☎ 01305 252230 ✉ j.marshall@westdorset-weymouth.gov.uk

Procurement: Ms Julia Long, Procurement Officer, South Walks House, South Walks Road, Dorchester DT1 1UZ ☎ 01305 838543 ✉ j.long@westdorset-weymouth.gov.uk

Regeneration: Mr Trevor Hedger, Senior Economic Regeneration Officer, South Walks House, South Walks Road, Dorchester DT1 1UZ ☎ 01305 252378 ✉ t.hedger@westdorset-weymouth.gov.uk

Sustainable Development: Ms Jean Marshall, Head of Planning, Development Management & Building Control, South Walks House, South Walks Road, Dorchester DT1 1UZ ☎ 01305 252230 ✉ j.marshall@westdorset-weymouth.gov.uk

Tourism: Mr Nick Thornley, Head of Economy, Leisure & Tourism, Stratton House, 58-60 High West Street, Dorchester DT1 1UZ ☎ 01305 252474; 01305 251010 ✉ n.thornley@westdorset-weymouth.gov.uk

Children's Play Areas: Ms Tara Gooding, Parks Supervisor, South Walks House, South Walks Road, Dorchester DT1 1UZ ☎ 01305 838297 ✉ t.gooding@westdorset-weymouth.gov.uk

COUNCILLORS

***Chair* Shorland**, Peter (CON - Sherborne West)
cllrp.shorland@westdorset-dc.gov.uk

***Vice-Chair* Dunseith**, Jean (CON - Chickerell)
cllrj.dunseith@westdorset-dc.gov.uk

***Leader of the Council* Alford**, Anthony (CON - Netherbury)
cllra.alford@westdorset-dc.gov.uk

***Deputy Leader of the Council* Thacker**, Alan (CON - Broadmayne)
cllra.thacker@westdorset-dc.gov.uk

***Group Leader* Jones**, Stella (LD - Dorchester East)
stella@sywardcottage.co.uk

Barrowcliff, Peter (CON - Beaminster)
cllrp.barrowcliff@westdorset-dc.gov.uk

Bartlett, Thomas (CON - Chesil Bank)
cllrt.bartlett@westdorset-dc.gov.uk

Brown, Sandra (CON - Bridport South and Bothenhampton)
cllrs.brown@westdorset-dc.gov.uk

Bundy, Nigel (CON - Broadmayne and Crossways)
nigelbundy8@btinternet.com

Canning, Andy (LD - Dorchester North)
cllra.canning@westdorset-dc.gov.uk

Christopher, Simon (CON - Chideock and Symondsbury)
cllrs.christopher@westdorset-dc.gov.uk

Coatsworth, Ronald (CON - Bradpole)
cllrr.coatsworth@westdorset-dc.gov.uk

Cooke, Patrick (CON - Puddletown)
cllrp.cooke@westdorset-dc.gov.uk

Day, Keith (CON - Bridport North)
KeithADay@aol.com

Duke, Gerald (CON - Dorchester West)
cllrg.duke@westdorset-dc.gov.uk

Elliott, Dominic (CON - Sherborne East)
cllrd.elliott@westdorset-dc.gov.uk

Farmer, Terry (CON - Sherborne East)
cllrt.farmer@westdorset-dc.gov.uk

Gardner, Ian (CON - Chickerell)
Ian_C_Gardner@talk21.com

Gould, Robert (CON - Queen Thorne)
cllrr.gould@westdorset-dc.gov.uk

Hall, Matthew (LD - Sherborne West)
mnwh1976@sky.com

Harries, Tim (LD - Dorchester East)

Haynes, Jill (CON - Maiden Newton)
Jill.Haynes@dorsetcc.gov.uk

Hiscock, Peter (CON - Piddle Valley)
cllrp.hiscock@westdorest-dc.gov.uk

Horsington, Fred (CON - Cerne Valley)
cllrf.horsington@westdorset-dc.gov.uk

Hosford, Susie (LD - Dorchester North)
shosford@btinernet.com

Jones, Trevor (LD - Dorchester West)
trevor@sywardcottage.co.uk

Kayes, Ros (LD - Bridport North)
roskayes@gmail.com

Lawrence, Margaret (CON - Yetminster and Cam Vale)
cllrm.lawrence@westdorset-dc.gov.uk

Legg, Robin (LD - Bradford Abbas)
robin.legg@btinternet.com

MacKenzie, Frances (CON - Bridport South and Bothenhampton)
fmfkmckenzie28@gmail.com

Penfold, Mary (CON - Frome Valley)
cllrm.penfold@westdorset-dc.gov.uk

Potter, Robin (LD - Dorchester South)
cllrr.potter@westdorset-dc.gov.uk

Rennie, Molly (LD - Dorchester South)
mollymadgerennie@hotmail.co.uk

Rickard, David (LD - Bridport South West)
cllrd.rickard@westdorset-dc.gov.uk

Roberts, Mark (CON - Loders)
lucullas.luccas@virgin.net

Russell, John (CON - Burton Bradstock)
cllrj.russell@westdorset-dc.gov.uk

Sewell, Jacqui (CON - Broadwindsor)
cllrj.sewell@westdorset-dc.gov.uk

Symonds, George (CON - Lyme Regis and Charmouth)
cllrg.symonds@westdorset-dc.gov.uk

Taylor, David (LD - Dorchester North)

Turner, Daryl (CON - Lyme Regis)
cllrd.turner@westdorset-dc.gov.uk

Yarker, Timothy (CON - Cerne Valley)
cllrt.yarker@westdorset-dc.gov.uk

POLITICAL COMPOSITION

CON: 29, LD: 12

COMMITTEE CHAIRS

Audit & Governance: Mr Andy Canning

Development Control: Mr Fred Horsington

Licensing: Mr Ronald Coatsworth

West Dunbartonshire S

West Dunbartonshire Council, Council Offices, Garshake Road, Dumbarton G82 3PU
☎ 01389 737000 🖷 01389 737700 💻 www.west-dunbarton.gov.uk

FACTS AND FIGURES

Parliamentary Constituencies: Dunbartonshire West
EU Constituencies: Scotland
Election Frequency: Elections are of whole council

PRINCIPAL OFFICERS

Chief Executive: Mrs Joyce White, Chief Executive, Council Offices, Garshake Road, Dumbarton G82 3PU ☎ 01389 737667 🖷 01389 737669 ✉ joyce.white@west-dunbarton.gov.uk

Senior Management: Mr Richard Cairns, Executive Director of Infrastructure & Regeneration, Council Offices, Garshake Road, Dumbarton G82 3PU ☎ 01389 737603 ✉ richard.cairns@west-dunbarton.gov.uk

Senior Management: Mr Terry Lanagan, Executive Director of Educational Services, Council Offices, Garshake Road, Dumbarton G82 3PU ☎ 01389 737000 ✉ terry.lanagan@west-dunbarton.gov.uk

Senior Management: Mr Keith Redpath, Director of Community Health & Care Partnership, Council Offices, Garshake Road, Dumbarton G82 3PU ☎ 01389 737526 ✉ keith.redpath@ggc.scot.nhs.uk

Senior Management: Mrs Angela Wilson, Executive Director of Corporate Services, Council Offices, Garshake Road, Dumbarton G82 3PU ☎ 01389 737607 ✉ am.wilson@west-dunbarton.gov.uk

Access Officer / Social Services (Disability): Mr Ricardo Rea, Equalities Officer, Council Offices, Garshake Road, Dumbarton G82 3PU ☎ 03189 737198 ✉ ricardo.rea@west-dunbarton.gov.uk

Architect, Building / Property Services: Mr Jim McAloon, Head of Regeneration & Economic Development, Council Offices, Garshake Road, Dumbarton G82 3PU ☎ 01389 737401 ✉ jim.mcaloon@west-dunbarton.gov.uk

Best Value: Mrs Angela Wilson, Executive Director of Corporate Services, Council Offices, Garshake Road, Dumbarton G82 3PU ☎ 01389 737607 ✉ am.wilson@west-dunbarton.gov.uk

Building Control: Ms Pamela Clifford, Planning & Building Standards Manager, Rosebery Place, Clydebank G81 1TG ☎ 01389 738656 ✉ pamela.clifford@west-dunbarton.gov.uk

Catering Services: Mrs Lynda McLaughlin, Leisure & Facilities Manager, Elm Road, Dumbarton G82 1NR ☎ 01389 602097 ✉ lynda.mclaughlin@west-dunbarton.gov.uk

Children / Youth Services: Ms Jackie Irvine, Head of Children's Health, Care & Criminal Justice Services, Council Offices, Garshake Road, Dumbarton G82 3PU ☎ 01389 737709 ✉ jackie.irvine@ggc.scot.nhs.uk

Children / Youth Services: Mr Terry Lanagan, Executive Director of Educational Services, Council Offices, Garshake Road, Dumbarton G82 3PU ☎ 01389 737000 ✉ terry.lanagan@west-dunbarton.gov.uk

Civil Registration: Mr George Hawthorn, Section Head of Democratic Services, Council Offices, Garshake Road, Dumbarton G82 3PU ☎ 01389 737204 ✉ george.hawthorn@west-dunbarton.gov.uk

WEST DUNBARTONSHIRE

PR / Communications: Mr Malcolm Bennie, Manager of Corporate Communications, Council Offices, Garshake Road, Dumbarton G82 3PU ☎ 01389 737187 ✉ malcolm.bennie@west-dunbarton.gov.uk

Community Planning: Mr Peter Barry, Corporate & Community Planning Manager, Council Offices, Garshake Road, Dumbarton G82 3PU ☎ 01389 737573 🖷 01389 737223 ✉ peter.barry@west-dunbarton.gov.uk

Community Safety: Ms Janice Winder, Partnership Officer, Levenvalley Enterprise Centre, Castlehill Road, Dumbarton G82 5BN ☎ 01389 772127 ✉ janice.winder@west-dunbarton.gov.uk

Computer Management: Ms Vicki Rogers, Head of People & Transformation, Council Offices, Garshake Road, Dumbarton G82 3PU ☎ 01389 737534 ✉ vicki.rogers@west-dunbarton.gov.uk

Consumer Protection and Trading Standards: Mr Graham Pollock, Manager of Regulatory Services, Aurora House, Clydebank G81 1BF ☎ 0141 951 7972 ✉ graham.pollock@west-dunbarton.gov.uk

Corporate Services: Mrs Angela Wilson, Executive Director of Corporate Services, Council Offices, Garshake Road, Dumbarton G82 3PU ☎ 01389 737607 ✉ am.wilson@west-dunbarton.gov.uk

Customer Service: Mr Stephen Daly, Section Head of Customer Services, Council Offices, Garshake Road, Dumbarton G82 3PU ☎ 01389 737263 ✉ stephen.daly@west-dunbarton.gov.uk

Direct Labour: Mr Stephen McGonagle, Maintenance & Repair, Overburn Road, Dumbarton G82 3LG ☎ 01389 608338 ✉ stephen.mcgonagle@west-dunbarton.gov.uk

Economic Development: Mr Michael McGuinness, Economic Development Manager, Council Offices, Garshake Road, Dumbarton G82 3PU ☎ 01389 737415 ✉ michael.mcguinness@west-dunbarton.gov.uk

Education: Mr Terry Lanagan, Executive Director of Educational Services, Council Offices, Garshake Road, Dumbarton G82 3PU ☎ 01389 737000 ✉ terry.lanagan@west-dunbarton.gov.uk

E-Government: Mr Peter Hessett, Head of Legal, Democratic & Regulatory Services, Council Offices, Garshake Road, Dumbarton G82 3PU ☎ 01389 737801 ✉ peter.hessett@west-dunbarton.gov.uk

Electoral Registration: Mr David Thomson, Assessor & Electoral Registration Officer, 235 Dumbarton Road, Clydebank G81 4XJ ☎ 0141 562 1200 🖷 0141 562 1220

Emergency Planning: Mr John Duffy, Section Head of Risk, Health & Safety, Council Offices, Garshake Road, Dumbarton G82 3PU ☎ 01389 737897 ✉ john.duffy2@west-dunbarton.gov.uk

Energy Management: Mr Craig Jardine, Corporate Asset Manager, Council Offices, Garshake Road, Dumbarton G82 3PU ☎ 01389 737829 ✉ craig.jardine@west-dunbarton.gov.uk

Environmental / Technical Services: Mr Graham Pollock, Manager of Regulatory Services, Aurora House, Clydebank G81 1BF ☎ 0141 951 7972 ✉ graham.pollock@west-dunbarton.gov.uk

Environmental Health: Mr Graham Pollock, Manager of Regulatory Services, Aurora House, Clydebank G81 1BF ☎ 0141 951 7972 ✉ graham.pollock@west-dunbarton.gov.uk

Estates, Property & Valuation: Mr Stuart Gibson, Assets Co-ordinator, Council Offices, Garshake Road, Dumbarton G82 3PU ☎ 01389 737157 ✉ stuart.gibson@west-dunbarton.gov.uk

European Liaison: Mr Michael McGuinness, Economic Development Manager, Council Offices, Garshake Road, Dumbarton G82 3PU ☎ 01389 737415 ✉ michael.mcguinness@west-dunbarton.gov.uk

Events Manager: Mrs Lynda McLaughlin, Leisure & Facilities Manager, Elm Road, Dumbarton G82 1NR ☎ 01389 602097 ✉ lynda.mclaughlin@west-dunbarton.gov.uk

Facilities: Mrs Lynda McLaughlin, Leisure & Facilities Manager, Elm Road, Dumbarton G82 1NR ☎ 01389 602097 ✉ lynda.mclaughlin@west-dunbarton.gov.uk

Finance: Mr Stephen West, Head of Finance & Resources, Council Offices, Garshake Road, Dumbarton G82 3PU ☎ 01389 737000 ✉ stephen.west@west-dunbarton.gov.uk

Fleet Management: Mr Rodney Thornton, Fleet & Waste Services Manager, Council Offices, Richmond Street, Clydebank G82 1RF ☎ 01389 738731 ✉ rodney.thornton@west-dunbarton.gov.uk

Grounds Maintenance: Mr Ian Bain, Greenspace Manager, Elm Road, Dumbarton G82 1NR ☎ 01389 608405 ✉ ian.bain@west-dunbarton.gov.uk

Health and Safety: Mr John Duffy, Section Head of Risk, Health & Safety, Council Offices, Garshake Road, Dumbarton G82 3PU ☎ 01389 737897 ✉ john.duffy2@west-dunbarton.gov.uk

Highways: Mr Jack McAulay, Roads & Transportation Manager, Council Offices, Garshake Road, Dumbarton G82 3PU ☎ 01389 737612 ✉ jack.mcauly@west-dunbarton.gov.uk

Housing: Ms Helen Turley, Head of Housing & Community Safety, Council Offices, Garshake Road, Dumbarton G82 3PU ☎ 01389 737598 ✉ helen.turley@west-dunbarton.gov.uk

Housing Maintenance: Ms Helen Turley, Head of Housing & Community Safety, Council Offices, Garshake Road, Dumbarton G82 3PU ☎ 01389 737598 ✉ helen.turley@west-dunbarton.gov.uk

Legal: Mr Peter Hessett, Head of Legal, Democratic & Regulatory Services, Council Offices, Garshake Road, Dumbarton G82 3PU ☎ 01389 737801 ✉ peter.hessett@west-dunbarton.gov.uk

Licensing: Mr Peter Hessett, Head of Legal, Democratic & Regulatory Services, Council Offices, Garshake Road, Dumbarton G82 3PU ☎ 01389 737801 ✉ peter.hessett@west-dunbarton.gov.uk

Lifelong Learning: Ms Lorna Campbell, Section Head of Community, Learning & Development, Council Offices, Rosebury Place, Clydebank G81 1TG ☎ 0141 562 871 ✉ lorna.campbell@west-dunbarton.gov.uk

Lighting: Mr Jack McAulay, Roads & Transportation Manager, Council Offices, Garshake Road, Dumbarton G82 3PU ☎ 01389 737612 ✉ jack.mcauly@west-dunbarton.gov.uk

Member Services: Mr George Hawthorn, Section Head of Democratic Services, Council Offices, Garshake Road, Dumbarton G82 3PU ☎ 01389 737204 ✉ george.hawthorn@west-dunbarton.gov.uk

Parking: Mr Jack McAulay, Roads & Transportation Manager, Council Offices, Garshake Road, Dumbarton G82 3PU ☎ 01389 737612 ✉ jack.mcauly@west-dunbarton.gov.uk

Personnel / HR: Ms Vicki Rogers, Head of People & Transformation, Council Offices, Garshake Road, Dumbarton G82 3PU ☎ 01389 737584 🖷 01389 737534 ✉ vicki.rogers@west-dunbarton.gov.uk

Planning: Ms Pamela Clifford, Planning & Building Standards Manager, 3 Aurora House, Aurora Avenue, Clydebank C81 1BF ☎ 01389 738656 ✉ pamela.clifford@west-dunbarton.gov.uk

Procurement: Mr Ian Hutchinson, E-Procurement Officer, Council Offices, Garshake Road, Dumbarton G82 3PU ☎ 01389 737664 ✉ ian.hutchinson@west-dunbarton.gov.uk

Public Libraries: Mr Richard Aird, Section Head of Libraries, 19 Poplar Road, Dumbarton G82 2RJ ☎ 01389 608040 ✉ richard.aird@west-dunbarton.gov.uk

Recycling & Waste Minimisation: Mr Rodney Thornton, Fleet & Waste Services Manager, Council Offices, Richmond Street, Clydebank G82 1RF ☎ 01389 738731 ✉ rodney.thornton@west-dunbarton.gov.uk

Regeneration: Mr Jim McAloon, Head of Regeneration & Economic Development, Council Offices, Garshake Road, Dumbarton G82 3PU ☎ 01389 737401 ✉ jim.mcaloon@west-dunbarton.gov.uk

Road Safety: Mr Jack McAulay, Roads & Transportation Manager, Council Offices, Garshake Road, Dumbarton G82 3PU ☎ 01389 737612 ✉ jack.mcauly@west-dunbarton.gov.uk

Social Services: Ms Jackie Irvine, Head of Children's Health, Care & Criminal Justice Services, Council Offices, Garshake Road, Dumbarton G82 3PU ☎ 01389 737709 ✉ jackie.irvine@ggc.scot.nhs.uk

Social Services (Adult): Mr David Elliott, General Manager, Beardmore Business Centre, Dalmuir, Clydebank G81 4HA ☎ 0141 562 2332 ✉ david.elliott@west-dunbarton.gov.uk

Social Services (Children): Mr Jim Watson, Section Head - Child Care, 7 Bruce Street, Clydebank G81 1TT ☎ 01389 772170 ✉ jim.watson@west-dunbarton.gov.uk

Staff Training: Ms Angela Terry, OD & Change Manager, Council Offices, Garshake Road, Dumbarton G82 3PU ☎ 01389 737590 🖷 01389 737534 ✉ angela.terry@west-dunbarton.gov.uk

Tourism: Mr Michael McGuinness, Economic Development Manager, Council Offices, Garshake Road, Dumbarton G82 3PU ☎ 01389 737415 ✉ michael.mcguinness@west-dunbarton.gov.uk

Town Centre: Mr Michael McGuinness, Economic Development Manager, Council Offices, Garshake Road, Dumbarton G82 3PU ☎ 01389 737415 ✉ michael.mcguinness@west-dunbarton.gov.uk

Traffic Management: Mr Jack McAulay, Roads & Transportation Manager, Council Offices, Garshake Road, Dumbarton G82 3PU ☎ 01389 737612 ✉ jack.mcauly@west-dunbarton.gov.uk

Transport: Mr Jack McAulay, Roads & Transportation Manager, Council Offices, Garshake Road, Dumbarton G82 3PU ☎ 01389 737612 ✉ jack.mcauly@west-dunbarton.gov.uk

Transport Planner: Mr Ronald Dinnie, Head of Neighbourhood Services, Council Offices, Garshake Road, Dumbarton G82 3PU ☎ 01389 737601 🖷 01389 737637 ✉ ronald.dinnie@west-dunbarton.gov.uk

Waste Collection and Disposal: Mr Rodney Thornton, Fleet & Waste Services Manager, Council Offices, Richmond Street, Clydebank G82 1RF ☎ 01389 738731 ✉ rodney.thornton@west-dunbarton.gov.uk

Waste Management: Mr Rodney Thornton, Fleet & Waste Services Manager, Council Offices, Richmond Street, Clydebank G82 1RF ☎ 01389 738731 ✉ rodney.thornton@west-dunbarton.gov.uk

Children's Play Areas: Mr Ian Bain, Greenspace Manager, Elm Road, Dumbarton G82 1NR ☎ 01389 608405 ✉ ian.bain@west-dunbarton.gov.uk

COUNCILLORS

***Provost* McAllister**, Douglas (LAB - Kilpatrick)
douglas.mcallister@west-dunbarton.gov.uk

***Leader of the Council* Rooney**, Martin (LAB - Lomond)
martin.rooney@west-dunbarton.gov.uk

Agnew, Denis (IND - Clydebank Central)
denis.agnew@west-dunbarton.gov.uk

Black, George (IND - Dumbarton)
george.black@west-dunbarton.gov.uk

Bollan, James (SSP - Leven)
james.bollan@west-dunbarton.gov.uk

Brown, Jim (SNP - Clydebank Central)
jim.brown@west-dunbarton.gov.uk

Casey, Gail (LAB - Clydebank Waterfront)
gail.casey@west-dunbarton.gov.uk

Finn, Jim (SNP - Kilpatrick)
jim.finn@west-dunbarton.gov.uk

Hendrie, William (SNP - Clydebank Waterfront)
william.hendrie@west-dunbarton.gov.uk

McBride, David (LAB - Dumbarton)
david.mcbride@west-dunbarton.gov.uk

McColl, Jonathan (SNP - Lomond)
jonathan.mccoll@west-dunbarton.gov.uk

McGinty, Michelle (LAB - Leven)
michelle.mcginty@west-dunbarton.gov.uk

McGlinchey, Patrick (LAB - Clydebank Central)
patrick.mcglinchey@west-dunbarton.gov.uk

McNair, Marie (IND - Clydebank Waterfront)
marie.mcnair@west-dunbarton.gov.uk

Millar, John (LAB - Leven)
john.millar@west-dunbarton.gov.uk

Mooney, John (LAB - Clydebank Central)
john.mooney@west-dunbarton.gov.uk

Murray, Ian (SNP - Dumbarton)
ian.murray@west-dunbarton.gov.uk

O'Neill, Lawrence (LAB - Kilpatrick)
lawrence.oneill@west-dunbarton.gov.uk

Rainey, Tommy (LAB - Dumbarton)
thomas.rainey@west-dunbarton.gov.uk

Robertson, Gail (SNP - Leven)

Ryall, Kath (LAB - Clydebank Waterfront)
kath.ryall@west-dunbarton.gov.uk

Sorrell, Hazel (LAB - Lomond)
hazel.sorrell@west-dunbarton.gov.uk

POLITICAL COMPOSITION

LAB: 12, SNP: 6, IND: 3, SSP: 1

West Lancashire D

West Lancashire Borough Council, 52 Derby Street, Ormskirk L39 2DF
☎ 01695 577177 🖷 01695 585082 🖳 www.westlancs.gov.uk

FACTS AND FIGURES

Parliamentary Constituencies: Lancashire West
EU Constituencies: North West
Election Frequency: Elections are by thirds

PRINCIPAL OFFICERS

Senior Management: Ms Gill Rowe, Managing Director - People & Places, 52 Derby Street, Ormskirk L39 2DF ☎ 01695 585004 🖷 01695 585082 ✉ gill.rowe@westlancs.gov.uk

Senior Management: Ms Kim Webber, Managing Director - Transformation, 52 Derby Street, Ormskirk L39 2DF ☎ 01695 585005 🖷 01695 585229 ✉ kim.webber@westlancs.gov.uk

Architect, Building / Property Services: Mr Phil Holland, Property Services Manager, Sandy Lane Centre, 61 Westgate, Skelmersdale WN8 8LP ☎ 01695 585226 🖷 01695 556544 ✉ phil.holland@westlancs.gov.uk

Best Value: Ms Alison Grimes, Partnership & Performance Officer, 52 Derby Street, Ormskirk L39 2DF ☎ 01695 585409 🖷 01695 585229 ✉ alison.grimes@westlancs.gov.uk

Best Value: Ms Kim Webber, Managing Director - Transformation, 52 Derby Street, Ormskirk L39 2DF ☎ 01695 585005 🖷 01695 585229 ✉ kim.webber@westlancs.gov.uk

Building Control: Mr John Harrison, Assistant Director - Planning, 52 Derby Street, Ormskirk L39 2DF ☎ 01695 585132 🖷 01695 585113 ✉ john.harrison@westlancs.gov.uk

Children / Youth Services: Mr John Nelson, Head - Leisure & Cultural Services, 52 Derby Street, Ormskirk L39 2DF ☎ 01695 585157 🖷 01695 585156 ✉ john.nelson@westlancs.gov.uk

PR / Communications: Ms Edwina Leigh, Consultation & Communications Manager, 52 Derby Street, Ormskirk L39 2DF ☎ 01695 577177 Extn 5433 🖷 01695 585082 ✉ edwina.leigh@westlancs.gov.uk

Community Planning: Mr John Harrison, Assistant Director - Planning, 52 Derby Street, Ormskirk L39 2DF ☎ 01695 585132 🖷 01695 585113 ✉ john.harrison@westlancs.gov.uk

Community Safety: Mr Andrew Hill, Environmental Protection & Community Safety Manager, Robert Hodge Centre, Stanley Industrial Estate, Stanley Way, Skelmersdale WN8 8EE ☎ 01695 585243 (585242) 🖷 01695 585082 (585126) ✉ andrew.hill@westlancs.gov.uk

Computer Management: Mr Shaun Walsh, Transformation Manager, 52 Derby Street, Ormskirk L39 2DF ☎ 01695 585262 🖷 01695 585340 ✉ shaun.walsh@westlancs.gov.uk

Contracts: Mr Phil Holland, Property Services Manager, Sandy Lane Centre, 61 Westgate, Skelmersdale WN8 8LP ☎ 01695 585226 🖷 01695 556544 ✉ phil.holland@westlancs.gov.uk

Customer Service: Mr Shaun Walsh, Transformation Manager, 52 Derby Street, Ormskirk L39 2DF ☎ 01695 585262 🖷 01695 585340 ✉ shaun.walsh@westlancs.gov.uk

Economic Development: Mrs Paula Huber, Economic Regeneration Manager, West Lancashire Investment Centre, Maple View, White Moss Business Park, Skelmersdale WN8 9TG ☎ 01695 585359 🖷 01695 712620 ✉ paula.huber@westlancs.gov.uk

E-Government: Mr Shaun Walsh, Transformation Manager, 52 Derby Street, Ormskirk L39 2DF ☎ 01695 585262 🖷 01695 585340 ✉ shaun.walsh@westlancs.gov.uk

Electoral Registration: Mrs Jane Smith, Administration & Electoral Services Manager, 52 Derby Street, Ormskirk L39 2DF ☎ 01695 585013 🖷 01695 585050 ✉ jane.smith@westlancs.gov.uk

Emergency Planning: Mr David Tilleray, Assistant Director - Community Services, Robert Hodge Centre, Stanley Industrial Estate, Stanley Way, Skelmersdale WN8 8EE ☎ 01695 585202 🖷 01695 585126 ✉ david.tilleray@westlancs.gov.uk

Energy Management: Mr Phil Holland, Property Services Manager, Sandy Lane Centre, 61 Westgate, Skelmersdale WN8 8LP ☎ 01695 585226 🖷 01695 556544 ✉ phil.holland@westlancs.gov.uk

Environmental Health: Mr Paul Charlson, Commercial Safety & Licensing Manager, Robert Hodge Centre, Stanley Industrial Estate, Stanley Way, Skelmersdale WN8 8EE ☎ 01695 585246 🖷 01695 585126 ✉ paul.charlson@westlancs.gov.uk

Environmental Health: Mr Andrew Hill, Environmental Protection & Community Safety Manager, Robert Hodge Centre, Stanley Industrial Estate, Stanley Way, Skelmersdale WN8 8EE ☎ 01695 585243 (585242) 🖷 01695 585082 (585126) 🖱 andrew.hill@westlancs.gov.uk

Environmental Health: Mr David Tilleray, Assistant Director - Community Services, Robert Hodge Centre, Stanley Industrial Estate, Stanley Way, Skelmersdale WN8 8EE ☎ 01695 585202 🖷 01695 585126 🖱 david.tilleray@westlancs.gov.uk

Estates, Property & Valuation: Mrs Rachel Kneale, Estates & Valuations Manager, West Lancashire Investment Centre, Maple View, White Moss Business Park, Skelmersdale WN8 9TG ☎ 01695 712611 🖷 01695 716260 🖱 rachel.kneale@westlancs.gov.uk

European Liaison: Ms Gill Rowe, Managing Director - People & Places, 52 Derby Street, Ormskirk L39 2DF ☎ 01695 585004 🖷 01695 585082 🖱 gill.rowe@westlancs.gov.uk

Facilities: Ms Gill Rowe, Managing Director - People & Places, 52 Derby Street, Ormskirk L39 2DF ☎ 01695 585004 🖷 01695 585082 🖱 gill.rowe@westlancs.gov.uk

Finance: Mr Marc Taylor, Borough Treasurer, 52 Derby Street, Ormskirk L39 2DF ☎ 01695 585092 🖷 01695 585366 🖱 marc.taylor@westlancs.gov.uk

Fleet Management: Mr Jimmy Cummins, Fleet Maintenance Manager, Robert Hodge Centre, Stanley Industrial Estate, Stanley Way, Skelmersdale WN8 8EE ☎ 01695 577177 Extn: 5448 🖷 01695 50373 🖱 jimmy.cummins@westlancs.gov.uk

Grounds Maintenance: Mr Graham Concannon, Assistant Director - Street Scene, Robert Hodge Centre, Stanley Industrial Estate, Stanley Way, Skelmersdale WN8 8EE ☎ 01695 577177 Extn 5191 🖱 graham.concannon@westlancs.gov.uk

Health and Safety: Mr Paul Adamson, Health & Safety Manager, 52 Derby Street, Ormskirk L39 2DF ☎ 01695 585241 🖷 01695 585021 🖱 paul.adamson@westlancs.gov.uk

Housing: Mr Bob Livermore, Assistant Director - Housing & Regeneration, 49 Westgate, Sandy Lane Centre, Skelmersdale WN8 8LP ☎ 01695 585200 🖷 01695 572331 🖱 bob.livermore@westlancs.gov.uk

Housing Maintenance: Mr Phil Holland, Property Services Manager, Sandy Lane Centre, 61 Westgate, Skelmersdale WN8 8LP ☎ 01695 585226 🖷 01695 556544 🖱 phil.holland@westlancs.gov.uk

Legal: Mr Terry Broderick, Borough Solicitor, 52 Derby Street, Ormskirk L39 2DF ☎ 01695 585001 🖷 01695 585082 🖱 terry.broderick@westlancs.gov.uk

Leisure and Cultural Services: Mr John Nelson, Head - Leisure & Cultural Services, 52 Derby Street, Ormskirk L39 2DF ☎ 01695 585157 🖷 01695 585156 🖱 john.nelson@westlancs.gov.uk

Licensing: Mr Paul Charlson, Commercial Safety & Licensing Manager, Robert Hodge Centre, Stanley Industrial Estate, Stanley Way, Skelmersdale WN8 8EE ☎ 01695 585246 🖷 01695 585126 🖱 paul.charlson@westlancs.gov.uk

Lottery Funding, Charity and Voluntary: Ms Kim Webber, Managing Director - Transformation, 52 Derby Street, Ormskirk L39 2DF ☎ 01695 585005 🖷 01695 585229 🖱 kim.webber@westlancs.gov.uk

Member Services: Mr Mathew Jones, Legal & Member Services Manager, 52 Derby Street, Ormskirk L39 2DF ☎ 01695 585025 🖷 01695 585082 🖱 mathew.jones@westlancs.gov.uk

Parking: Mr Ken Knowles, Markets & Parking Officer, 52 Derby Street, Ormskirk L39 2DF ☎ 01695 585105 🖷 01695 585156 🖱 ken.knowles@westlancs.gov.uk

Personnel / HR: Mr Shaun Walsh, Transformation Manager, 52 Derby Street, Ormskirk L39 2DF ☎ 01695 585262 🖷 01695 585340 🖱 shaun.walsh@westlancs.gov.uk

Planning: Mr John Harrison, Assistant Director - Planning, 52 Derby Street, Ormskirk L39 2DF ☎ 01695 585132 🖷 01695 585113 🖱 john.harrison@westlancs.gov.uk

Procurement: Mr Stephen Tinsley, Purchasing & Land Charges Manager, 52 Derby Street, Ormskirk L39 2DF ☎ 01695 577177 Extn: 5426 🖷 01695 585082 🖱 stephen.tinsley@westlancs.gov.uk

Recycling & Waste Minimisation: Mr Graham Concannon, Assistant Director - Street Scene, Robert Hodge Centre, Stanley Industrial Estate, Stanley Way, Skelmersdale WN8 8EE ☎ 01695 577177 Extn 5191 🖱 graham.concannon@westlancs.gov.uk

Regeneration: Mr Bob Livermore, Assistant Director - Housing & Regeneration, 49 Westgate, Sandy Lane Centre, Skelmersdale WN8 8LP ☎ 01695 585200 🖷 01695 572331 🖱 bob.livermore@westlancs.gov.uk

Staff Training: Mr Shaun Walsh, Transformation Manager, 52 Derby Street, Ormskirk L39 2DF ☎ 01695 585262 🖷 01695 585340 🖱 shaun.walsh@westlancs.gov.uk

Street Scene: Mr Graham Concannon, Assistant Director - Street Scene, Robert Hodge Centre, Stanley Industrial Estate, Stanley Way, Skelmersdale WN8 8EE ☎ 01695 577177 Extn 5191 🖱 graham.concannon@westlancs.gov.uk

Sustainable Communities: Ms Kim Webber, Managing Director - Transformation, 52 Derby Street, Ormskirk L39 2DF ☎ 01695 585005 🖷 01695 585229 🖱 kim.webber@westlancs.gov.uk

Sustainable Development: Ms Tina Iball, Environmental Strategy Officer, Robert Hodge Centre, Stanley Industrial Estate, Stanley Way, Skelmersdale WN8 8EE ☎ 01695 585197 🖷 01695 585113 🖱 tina.iball@westlancs.gov.uk

Tourism: Mrs Paula Huber, Economic Regeneration Manager, 52 Derby Street, Ormskirk L39 2DF ☎ 01695 585359 🖷 01695 712620 🖱 paula.huber@westlancs.gov.uk

WEST LANCASHIRE

Town Centre: Mr Colin Brady, Technical Services Manager, 52 Derby Street, Ormskirk L39 2DF ☎ 01695 585125 🖷 01695 585113 ✉ colin.brady@westlancs.gov.uk

Waste Collection and Disposal: Mr Graham Concannon, Assistant Director - Street Scene, Robert Hodge Centre, Stanley Industrial Estate, Stanley Way, Skelmersdale WN8 8EE ☎ 01695 577177 Extn 5191 ✉ graham.concannon@westlancs.gov.uk

Waste Management: Mr Graham Concannon, Assistant Director - Street Scene, Robert Hodge Centre, Stanley Industrial Estate, Stanley Way, Skelmersdale WN8 8EE ☎ 01695 577177 Extn 5191 ✉ graham.concannon@westlancs.gov.uk

COUNCILLORS

***Mayor* Hennessy**, Nikki (LAB - Knowsley)
cllr.hennessy@westlancs.gov.uk

***Deputy Mayor* Savage**, Liz (LAB - Ashurst)
cllr.savage@westlancs.gov.uk

***Leader of the Council* Moran**, Ian (LAB - Up Holland)
Cllr.Moran@westlancs.gov.uk

Aldridge, Terry (LAB - Moorside)
Cllr.Aldridge@westlancs.gov.uk

Ashcroft, Iain (CON - Hesketh-with-Becconsall)
Cllr.Ashcroft@westlancs.gov.uk

Atherley, Una (CON - Aughton and Downholland)
Cllr.Atherley@westlancs.gov.uk

Bailey, Susan (CON - Aughton Park)
cllr.sbailey@westlancs.gov.uk

Bailey, Susan (CON - Aughton Park)
Cllr.Sbailey@westlancs.gov.uk

Barron, Malcolm (CON - North Meols)
Cllr.Barron@westlancs.gov.uk

Baybutt, Pam (CON - Wrightington)
cllr.baybutt@westlancs.gov.uk

Bell, Roger (LAB - Burscough East)
cllr.bell@westlancs.gov.uk

Blake, May (CON - Parbold)
Cllr.Blake@westlancs.gov.uk

Blane, Thomas (CON - North Meols)
Cllr.Tblane@westlancs.gov.uk

Bullock, John (LAB - Up Holland)
Cllr.Bullock@westlancs.gov.uk

Cotterill, Paul (LAB - Bickerstaffe)
Cllr.Cotterill@westlancs.gov.uk

Davis, John (LAB - Burscough West)
cllr.davis@westlancs.gov.uk

Delaney, Noel (LAB - Scott)
cllr.delaney@westlancs.gov.uk

Dereli, Cynthia (LAB - Burscough West)
Cllr.dereli@westlancs.gov.uk

Devine, Terence (LAB - Moorside)
Cllr.Devine@westlancs.gov.uk

Dowling, Gareth (LAB - Knowsley)
Cllr.Dowling@westlancs.gov.uk

Evans, Carolyn (CON - Wrightington)
cllr.cevans@westlancs.gov.uk

Evans, Rosemary (CON - Tarleton)
cllr.revans@westlancs.gov.uk

Forshaw, Martin (CON - Hesketh-with-Becconsall)
Cllr.Forshaw@westlancs.gov.uk

Furey, Neil Stuart (LAB - Skelmersdale North)
cllr.furey@westlancs.gov.uk

Gagen, Yvonne (LAB - Ashurst)
cllr.gagen@westlancs.gov.uk

Greenall, Paul (CON - Derby)
Cllr.Greenall@westlancs.gov.uk

Hodson, Gail (LAB - Ashurst)
cllr.ghodson@westlancs.gov.uk

Hodson, John (LAB - Scott)
cllr.hodson@westlancs.gov.uk

Hodson, Lucy (LAB - Birch Green)
Cllr.Lhodson@westlancs.gov.uk

Houlgrave, Jane (CON - Rufford)
cllr.houlgrave@westlancs.gov.uk

Hudson, Phil (LAB - Derby)
Cllr.PHudson@westlancs.gov.uk

Kay, James (CON - Tarleton)
Cllr.Kay@westlancs.gov.uk

Marshall, Jane (CON - Scarisbrick)
Cllr.Marshall@westlancs.gov.uk

Marshall, Charles (CON - Scarisbrick)
Cllr.Cmarshall@westlancs.gov.uk

McKay, David (LAB - Skelmersdale South)
cllr.mckay@westlancs.gov.uk

McKenna, Frank (LAB - Birch Green)
Cllr.McKenna@westlancs.gov.uk

Mee, John (CON - Tarleton)
Cllr.Mee@westlancs.gov.uk

Melling, Ruth (CON - Burscough East)
Cllr.Melling@westlancs.gov.uk

Nixon, Maureen (LAB - Tanhouse)
Cllr.Nixon@wetlancs.gov.uk

Oliver, George (LAB - Knowsley)
cllr.oliver@westlancs.gov.uk

O'Toole, David (CON - Aughton and Downholland)
Cllr.OToole@westlancs.gov.uk

Owen, Gaynar (LAB - Up Holland)
cllr.owen@westlancs.gov.uk

Owens, Adrian (CON - Derby)
Cllr.Owens@westlancs.gov.uk

Patterson, Jenny (LAB - Skelmersdale North)
Cllr.Patterson@westlancs.gov.uk

Pendleton, Robert (LAB - Tanhouse)
Cllr.Bpendleton@westlancs.gov.uk

Pope, Edward (CON - Newburgh)
cllr.pope@westlancs.gov.uk

Pryce-Roberts, Nicola (LAB - Skelmersdale South)
Cllr.Pryce-Roberts@westlancs.gov.uk

Stephenson, Doreen (CON - Halsall)
cllr.stephenson@westlancs.gov.uk

West, Donna (LAB - Skelmersdale South)
Cllr.West@westlancs.gov.uk

Westley, David (CON - Aughton and Downholland)
cllr.westley@westlancs.gov.uk

Westley, Marilyn (CON - Aughton Park)
Cllr.Mwestley@westlancs.gov.uk

Whittington, David (CON - Parbold)
Cllr.Whittington@westlancs.gov.uk

Wilkie, Kevin (LAB - Digmoor)
cllr.wilkie@westlancs.gov.uk

Wright, Kevin (LAB - Scott)
cllr.wright@westlancs.gov.uk

Wynn, Chris (LAB - Digmoor)
Cllr.Wynn@westlancs.gov.uk

POLITICAL COMPOSITION

LAB: 30, CON: 25

COMMITTEE CHAIRS

Audit: Mr John Bullock

Development: Miss Cynthia Dereli

Licensing: Mr Noel Delaney

Planning: Mr Roger Bell

West Lindsey D

West Lindsey District Council, The Guildhall, Marshall's Yard, Gainsborough DN21 2NA
☎ 01427 676676 🖷 01427 810622 💻 www.west-lindsey.gov.uk

FACTS AND FIGURES

Parliamentary Constituencies: Gainsborough
EU Constituencies: Eastern
Election Frequency: Elections are by thirds

PRINCIPAL OFFICERS

Chief Executive: Mrs Manjeet Gill, Chief Executive, The Guildhall, Marshall's Yard, Gainsborough DN21 2NA ☎ 01427 676676
🖰 manjeet.gill@west-lindsey.gov.uk

Deputy Chief Executive: Mr Mark Sturgess, Chief Operating Officer, The Guildhall, Marshall's Yard, Gainsborough DN21 2NA
☎ 01427 676687 🖰 mark.sturgess@west-lindsey.gov.uk

Senior Management: Mrs Penny Sharp, Commercial Director, The Guildhall, Marshall's Yard, Gainsborough DN21 2NA
☎ 01427 675185 🖰 penny.sharp@west-lindsey.gov.uk

Customer Service: Ms Lyn Marlow, Customer Relations Manager, The Guildhall, Marshalls Yard, Gainsborough DN21 2NA ☎ 01427 676684 🖷 01427 675170 🖰 lyn.marlow@west-lindsey.gov.uk

Customer Service: Mr Alan Robinson, Monitoring Officer, The Guildhall, Marshall's Yard, Gainsborough DN21 2NA ☎ 01427 676509 🖰 alan.robinson@wwest-lindsey.gov.uk

Electoral Registration: Mr Graham Spicksley, Assistant Electoral Registration Officer, The Guildhall, Marshalls Yard, Gainsborough DN21 2NA ☎ 01427 676576 🖷 01427 616466
🖰 graham.spicksley@west-lindsey.gov.uk

Finance: Mr Ian Knowles, Director - Resources, The Guildhall, Marshall's Yard, Gainsborough DN21 2NA
🖰 ian.knowles@west-lindsey.gov.uk

Health and Safety: Mrs Kim Leith, Health & Safety Coordinator, The Guildhall, Marshall's Yard, Gainsborough DN21 2NA
☎ 01427 675110 🖰 kim.leith@west-lindsey.gov.uk

Home Energy Conservation: Ms Karen Lond, Energy & Efficiency Adviser, The Guildhall, Marshall's Tard, Gainsborough DN24 2NA ☎ 01427 676618 🖷 01427 675170
🖰 karen.lond@west-lindsey.gov.uk

Licensing: Mr Phil Hinch, Licensing & Support Team Leader, The Guildhall, Marshall's Yard, Gainsborough DN21 2NA
☎ 01427 676610 🖰 phil.hinch@west-lindsey.gov.uk

Lottery Funding, Charity and Voluntary: Mr Grant White, Enterprising Communities Officer, The Guildhall, Marshall's Yard, Gainsborough DN21 2NA ☎ 01427 675145
🖰 grant.white@west-lindsey.gov.uk

Member Services: Mr Alan Robinson, Monitoring Officer, The Guildhall, Marshall's Yard, Gainsborough DN21 2NA
☎ 01427 676509 🖰 alan.robinson@wwest-lindsey.gov.uk

Parking: Mr David Kirkup, Senior Property Strategy Project Officer, The Guildhall, Marshall's Yard, Gainsborough DN21 2NA
☎ 01427 676554 🖰 david.kirkup@west-lindsey.gov.uk

Personnel / HR: Mrs Emma Redwood, Team Manager, The Guildhall, Marshall's Yard, Gainsborough DN21 2NA
☎ 01427 676591 🖰 emma.redwood@west-lindsey.gov.uk

Recycling & Waste Minimisation: Mr Ady Selby, Team Manager - Operational Services, The Guildhall, Marshall's Yard, Gainsborough DN21 2NA ☎ 01427 675154 🖰 ady.selby@west-lindsey.gov.uk

Tourism: Ms Marion Thomas, Arts & Tourism Manager, The Guildhall, Marshall's Yard, Gainsborough DN21 2NA
☎ 01427 675162 🖰 marion.thomas@west-lindsey.gov.uk

Waste Collection and Disposal: Mr Ady Selby, Team Manager - Operational Services, The Guildhall, Marshall's Yard, Gainsborough DN21 2NA ☎ 01427 675154 🖰 ady.selby@west-lindsey.gov.uk

Waste Management: Mr Ady Selby, Team Manager - Operational Services, The Guildhall, Marshall's Yard, Gainsborough DN21 2NA
☎ 01427 675154 🖰 ady.selby@west-lindsey.gov.uk

COUNCILLORS

Chair **Lawrence**, Angela (CON - Caistor)
atlcaistor@gmail.com

Vice-Chair **Patterson**, Roger (CON - Scampton)
rogermpatterson@aol.com

Leader of the Council **Summers**, Jeff (CON - Waddingham and Spital)
cllr.j.summers@west-lindsey.gov.uk

Deputy Leader of the Council **Welburn**, Anne (CON - Cherry Willingham)
anne.welburn@btinernet.com

Bardsley, Gillian (CON - Gainsborough North)
cllr.g.bardsley@west-lindsey.gov.uk

Bibb, Sheila (CON - Gainsborough North)
cllr.s.bibb@west-lindsey.gov.uk

Bierley, Owen (CON - Caistor & Yarborough)
owen@bierley.com

Boles, Matthew (LD - Gainsborough North)
cllr.m.boles@west-lindsey.gov.uk

Bond, David (LAB - Gainsborough East)
cllr.d.bond@west-lindsey.gov.uk

Bridgwood, Alexander (CON - Cherry Willingham)
cllr.a.bridgwood@west-lindsey.gov.uk

Brockway, Jackie (CON - Saxilby)
jackiebrockway@gmail.com

Cotton, David (LD - Saxilby)
david.cotton500@ntlworld.com

Curtis, Stuart (CON - Sudbrooke)
stuartlyncurtis@aol.com

Darcel, Christopher (IND - Cherry Willingham)
chris@darcel.entadsl.com

Devine, Michael (LAB - Gainsborough East)
cllr.m.devine@west-lindsey.gov.uk

Duguid, Adam (CON - Scotter & Blyton)
cllr.a.duguid@west-lindsey.gov.uk

England, Steve (CON - Dunholme & Welton)
cllr.s.england@west-lindsey.gov.uk

Fleetwood, Ian (CON - Bardney)
ifleet@barlings.demon.co.uk

Howitt-Cowan, Paul (CON - Hemswell)
cllr.p.howitt-cowan@west-lindsey.gov.uk

Kinch, Stuart (CON - Torksey)
stuart@thejohnkinchgroup.co.uk

Marfleet, Hugo (CON - Market Rasen)
cllr.h.marfleet@west-lindsey.gov.uk

McNeill, John (CON - Market Rasen)
cllr.j.mcneill@west-lindsey.gov.uk

McNeill, Giles (CON - Nettleham)
cllr.g.mcneill@west-lindsey.gov.uk

Mewis, Patricia (CON - Scotter)
cllr.p.mewis@west-lindsey.gov.uk

Milne, Jessie (CON - Lea)
jessie.milne393@btinternet.com

Oaks, Richard (LAB - Gainsborough East)
cllr.r.oaks@west-lindsey.gov.uk

Parish, Malcolm (CON - Welton)
cllr.parish@btinernet.com

Rainsforth, Judy (LD - Gainsborough South-West)
judyrainsforth@talktalk.net

Regis, Thomas (CON - Wold View)
tom@tomregis.com

Rodgers, Diana (IND - Welton)
cllr.D.Rodgers@west-lindsey.gov.uk

Rollings, Lesley (LD - Thonock)
lrollings@btinternet.com

Shore, Reg (LD - Stow)
regshore@mac.com

Smith, Thomas (CON - Market Rasen)
cllr.t.smith@west-lindsey.gov.uk

Strange, Lewis (CON - Kelsey)
Cllrc.strange@lincolnshire.gov.uk

White, Angela (LD - Nettleham)
cllr.a.white@west-lindsey.gov.uk

Young, Trevor (LD - Gainsborough South-West)
t.young91@btinternet.com

POLITICAL COMPOSITION

CON: 24, LD: 7, LAB: 3, IND: 2

West Lothian S

West Lothian Council, West Lothian Civic Centre, Howden South Road, Livingston EH54 6FF
☎ 01506 280000 🖷 01506 777249
customer.service@westlothian.gov.uk www.westlothian.gov.uk

FACTS AND FIGURES

Parliamentary Constituencies: Linlithgow and Falkirk East, Livingston
EU Constituencies: Scotland
Election Frequency: Elections are of whole council

PRINCIPAL OFFICERS

Chief Executive: Mr Graham Hope, Chief Executive, West Lothian Civic Centre, Howden South Road, Livingston EH54 6FF ☎ 01506 281679 graham.hope@westlothian.gov.uk

Deputy Chief Executive: Mr Jim Forrest, Depute Chief Executive - Community Health & Care Partnership, West Lothian Civic Centre, Howden South Road, Livingston EH54 6FF ☎ 01506 281679 jim.forrest@westlothian.gov.uk

Deputy Chief Executive: Ms Moira Niven, Depute Chief Executive - Education, Planning & Area Services, West Lothian Civic Centre, Howden South Road, Livingston EH54 6FF ☎ 01506 281679 moira.niven@westlothian.gov.uk

Deputy Chief Executive: Mr Graeme Struthers, Depute Chief Executive - Corporate, Operational & Housing Services, West Lothian Civic Centre, Howden South Road, Livingston EH54 6FF ☎ 01506 281679 graeme.struthers@westlothian.gov.uk

Access Officer / Social Services (Disability): Ms Jane Kellock, Acting Head of Social Policy, West Lothian Civic Centre, Howden South Road, Livingston EH54 6FF ☎ 01506 281920 jane.kellock@westlothian.gov.uk

Best Value: Mr Graeme Struthers, Depute Chief Executive - Corporate, Operational & Housing Services, West Lothian Civic Centre, Howden South Road, Livingston EH54 6FF
☎ 01506 281679 ✉ graeme.struthers@westlothian.gov.uk

Building Control: Mr Jim McGinley, Building Standards Manager, County Buildings, High Street, Linlithgow EH49 7EZ
☎ 01506 282395 ✉ jim.mcginley@westlothian.gov.uk

Catering Services: Mrs Liz Wark, Service Manager, Carmondean House, Carmondean Road South, Carmondean, Livingston EH54 8PT ☎ 01506 777544 ✉ liz.wark@westlothian.gov.uk

Children / Youth Services: Ms Marion Christie, Head of Health Services, West Lothian Civic Centre, Howden South Road, Livingston EH54 6FF ✉ marion.christie@westlothian.gov.uk

Children / Youth Services: Ms Jo MacPherson, Head of Children & Families, West Lothian Civic Centre, Howden South Road, Livingston EH54 6FF ☎ 01506 282194
✉ jo.macpherson@westlothian.gov.uk

Civil Registration: Mr James Lambert, Chief Registrar, Bathgate Partnership Centre, South Bridge Street, Bathgate EH48 1TS
☎ 01506 282916 ✉ jim.lambert@westlothian.gov.uk

PR / Communications: Mr Garry Heron, Corporate Communications Manager, West Lothian Civic Centre, Howden South Road, Livingston EH54 6FF ☎ 01506 282006
✉ garry.heron@westlothian.gov.uk

Community Planning: Ms Lorraine Gillies, Community Planning Manager, West Lothian Civic Centre, Howden South Road, Livingston EH54 6FF ☎ 01506 281690
✉ lorraine.gillies@westlothian.gov.uk

Community Safety: Mr Alistair Shaw, Head of Housing, Construction & Building, West Lothian Civic Centre, Howden South Road, Livingston EH54 6FF ☎ 01506 281754
✉ alistair.shaw@westlothian.gov.uk

Computer Management: Ms Jennifer Milne, IT Manager, West Lothian Civic Centre, Howden South Road, Livingston EH54 6FF
☎ 01506 281521 ✉ jennifer.milne@westlothian.gov.uk

Consumer Protection and Trading Standards: Mr Andrew Blake, Environmental Health & Trading Standards Manager, County Buildings, High Street, Linlithgow EH49 7EZ ☎ 01506 775346
✉ andrew.blake@westlothian.gov.uk

Corporate Services: Mr Graeme Struthers, Depute Chief Executive - Corporate, Operational & Housing Services, West Lothian Civic Centre, Howden South Road, Livingston EH54 6FF
☎ 01506 281679 ✉ graeme.struthers@westlothian.gov.uk

Customer Service: Ms Karen Cawte, Head of Area Services, West Lothian Civic Centre, Howden South Road, Livingston EH54 6FF ☎ 01506 282386 ✉ karen.cawte@westlothian.gov.uk

Economic Development: Mr Craig McCorriston, Head of Planning & Economic Development, County Buildings, High Street, Linlithgow EH49 7EZ ☎ 01506 282443
✉ craig.mccorriston@westlothian.gov.uk

Education: Ms Elaine Cook, Head of Service for Education, West Lothian Civic Centre, Howden South Road, Livingston EH54 6FF
☎ 01506 283050 ✉ elaine.cook@westlothian.gov.uk

Education: Ms Moira Niven, Depute Chief Executive - Education, Planning & Area Services, West Lothian Civic Centre, Howden South Road, Livingston EH54 6FF ☎ 01506 281679
✉ moira.niven@westlothian.gov.uk

Electoral Registration: Mr Gordon Blair, Chief Legal Officer, West Lothian Civic Centre, Howden South Road, Livingston EH54 6FF ☎ 01506 281695 ✉ gordon.blair@westlothian.gov.uk

Emergency Planning: Ms Caroline Burton, Emergency Planning Officer, West Lothian Civic Centre, Howden South Road, Livingston EH54 6FF ☎ 01506 281651 ✉ caroline.burton@westlothian.gov.uk

Environmental Health: Mr Andrew Blake, Environmental Health & Trading Standards Manager, County Buildings, High Street, Linlithgow EH49 7EZ ☎ 01506 775346
✉ andrew.blake@westlothian.gov.uk

Estates, Property & Valuation: Mr Donald Forrest, Head of Finance & Estates, West Lothian Civic Centre, Howden South Road, Livingston EH54 6FF ☎ 01506 281679
✉ donald.forrest@westlothian.gov.uk

European Liaison: Mr David Greaves, Policy Manager, West Lothian Civic Centre, Howden South Road, Livingston EH54 6FF
☎ 01506 283097 ✉ david.greaves@westlothian.gov.uk

Events Manager: Mr Graeme Malcolm, Transportation Manager, County Buildings, High Street, Linlithgow EH49 7EZ
☎ 01506 775296 ✉ graeme.malcolm@westlothian.gov.uk

Finance: Mr Donald Forrest, Head of Finance & Estates, West Lothian Civic Centre, Howden South Road, Livingston EH54 6FF
☎ 01506 281679 ✉ donald.forrest@westlothian.gov.uk

Fleet Management: Mr Joe Drew, Fleet Co-ordinator, Fleet & Cleansing Depot, Nairn Road, Deans Industrial Estate, Livingston EH54 8AY ☎ 01506 777822 ✉ joe.drew@westlothian.gov.uk

Grounds Maintenance: Mr Jim Jack, Head of Operational Services, Whitehill House, Whitehill Industrial Estate, Bathgate EH48 2HA ☎ ; 01506 776601 ✉ jim.jack@westlothian.gov.uk

Health and Safety: Ms Kim Hardie, Health & Safety Manager, West Lothian Civic Centre, Howden South Road, Livingston EH54 6FF ☎ 01506 281414 ✉ kim.hardie@westlothian.gov.uk

Highways: Mr Jim Jack, Head of Operational Services, Whitehill House, Whitehill Industrial Estate, Bathgate EH48 2HA
☎ 01506 776601 ✉ jim.jack@westlothian.gov.uk

Housing: Mr Alistair Shaw, Head of Housing, Construction & Building, West Lothian Civic Centre, Howden South Road, Livingston EH54 6FF ☎ 01506 281754 ✉ alistair.shaw@westlothian.gov.uk

Housing Maintenance: Mr Alistair Shaw, Head of Housing, Construction & Building, West Lothian Civic Centre, Howden South Road, Livingston EH54 6FF ☎ 01506 281754
✉ alistair.shaw@westlothian.gov.uk

Local Area Agreement: Mr Steve Field, Head of Area Services, County Buildings, High Street, Linlithgow EH49 7EZ ☎ 01506 282386 ✉ steve.field@westlothian.gov.uk

Legal: Mr Gordon Blair, Chief Legal Officer, West Lothian Civic Centre, Howden South Road, Livingston EH54 6FF ☎ 01506 281695 ✉ gordon.blair@westlothian.gov.uk

Leisure and Cultural Services: Mr Ian Hepburn, Community Regeneration Manager, West Lothian Civic Centre, Howden South Road, Livingston EH54 6FF ☎ 01506 281089 ✉ ian.hepburn@westlothian.gov.uk

Licensing: Legal Services, , West Lothian Civic Centre, Howden South Road, Livingston EH54 6FF ☎ 01506 281632 ✉ licensingservices@westlothian.gov.uk

Lifelong Learning: Mr Steve Field, Head of Area Services, County Buildings, High Street, Linlithgow EH49 7EZ ☎ 01506 282386 ✉ steve.field@westlothian.gov.uk

Lighting: Mr David Wilson, Manager, West Lothian Civic Centre, Howden South Road, Livingston EH54 6FF ☎ 01506 776651 ✉ david.wilson@westlothian.gov.uk

Lottery Funding, Charity and Voluntary: Mr Ian Hepburn, Community Regeneration Manager, West Lothian Civic Centre, Howden South Road, Livingston EH54 6FF ☎ 01506 281089 ✉ ian.hepburn@westlothian.gov.uk

Member Services: Mr Graeme Struthers, Depute Chief Executive - Corporate, Operational & Housing Services, West Lothian Civic Centre, Howden South Road, Livingston EH54 6FF ☎ 01506 281679 ✉ graeme.struthers@westlothian.gov.uk

Partnerships: Mr Steve Field, Head of Area Services, County Buildings, High Street, Linlithgow EH49 7EZ ☎ 01506 282386 ✉ steve.field@westlothian.gov.uk

Personnel / HR: Mr Lesley Henderson, HR Services Manager, West Lothian Civic Centre, Howden South Road, Livingston EH54 6FF ☎ 01506 281408 ✉ lesley.henderson@westlothian.gov.uk

Planning: Mr Graeme Malcolm, Transportation Manager, County Buildings, High Street, Linlithgow EH49 7EZ ☎ 01506 775296 ✉ graeme.malcolm@westlothian.gov.uk

Planning: Mr Craig McCorriston, Head of Planning & Economic Development, County Buildings, High Street, Linlithgow EH49 7EZ ☎ 01506 282443 ✉ craig.mccorriston@westlothian.gov.uk

Planning: Mr Chris Norman, Development Control Manager, County Buildings, High Street, Linlithgow EH49 7EZ ☎ 01506 282412 ✉ chris.norman@westlothian.gov.uk

Procurement: Ms Christine Leese-Young, Procurement Manager, West Lothian Civic Centre, Howden South Road, Livingston EH54 6FF ☎ 01506 283259 ✉ christine.leeseyoung@westlothian.gov.uk

Public Libraries: Ms Jeanette Castle, Library Services Manager, West Lothian Civic Centre, Howden South Road, Livingston EH54 6FF ☎ 01506 281273 ✉ jeanette.castle@westlothian.gov.uk

Recycling & Waste Minimisation: Mr Jim Jack, Head of Operational Services, Whitehill House, Whitehill Industrial Estate, Bathgate EH48 2HA ☎ 01506 776601 ✉ jim.jack@westlothian.gov.uk

Regeneration: Ms Alice Mitchell, Economic Development Manager, West Lothian Civic Centre, Howden South Road, Livingston EH54 6FF ☎ 01506 283079 ✉ alice.mitchell@westlothian.gov.uk

Road Safety: Mr Kevin Hamilton, Team Leader, County Buildings, High Street, Linlithgow EH49 7EZ ☎ 01506 282341 ✉ kevin.hamilton@westlothian.gov.uk

Social Services: Ms Jane Kellock, Acting Head of Social Policy, West Lothian Civic Centre, Howden South Road, Livingston EH54 6FF ☎ 01506 281920 ✉ jane.kellock@westlothian.gov.uk

Social Services (Adult): Ms Jane Kellock, Acting Head of Social Policy, West Lothian Civic Centre, Howden South Road, Livingston EH54 6FF ☎ 01506 281920 ✉ jane.kellock@westlothian.gov.uk

Social Services (Children): Ms Jane Kellock, Acting Head of Social Policy, West Lothian Civic Centre, Howden South Road, Livingston EH54 6FF ☎ 01506 281920 ✉ jane.kellock@westlothian.gov.uk

Public Health: Ms Marion Christie, Head of Health Services, West Lothian Civic Centre, Howden South Road, Livingston EH54 6FF ✉ marion.christie@westlothian.gov.uk

Staff Training: Mr Lesley Henderson, HR Services Manager, West Lothian Civic Centre, Howden South Road, Livingston EH54 6FF ☎ 01506 281408 ✉ lesley.henderson@westlothian.gov.uk

Sustainable Communities: Mr Ian Hepburn, Community Regeneration Manager, West Lothian Civic Centre, Howden South Road, Livingston EH54 6FF ☎ 01506 281089 ✉ ian.hepburn@westlothian.gov.uk

Sustainable Development: Mr Craig McCorriston, Head of Planning & Economic Development, County Buildings, High Street, Linlithgow EH49 7EZ ☎ 01506 282443 ✉ craig.mccorriston@westlothian.gov.uk

Tourism: Ms Anna Young, Tourism Executive, West Lothian Civic Centre, Howden South Road, Livingston EH54 6FF ☎ 01506 283093 ✉ anna.young@westlothian.gov.uk

Town Centre: Mr Steve Field, Head of Area Services, County Buildings, High Street, Linlithgow EH49 7EZ ☎ 01506 282386 ✉ steve.field@westlothian.gov.uk

Traffic Management: Mr Kevin Hamilton, Team Leader, County Buildings, High Street, Linlithgow EH49 7EZ ☎ 01506 282341 ✉ kevin.hamilton@westlothian.gov.uk

Transport: Mr Ian Forbes, Public Transport Manager, County Buildings, High Street, Linlithgow EH49 7EZ ☎ 01506 282317 ✉ ian.forbes@westlothian.gov.uk

Children's Play Areas: Mr Colin Bell, Principal Officer, 7 Whitestone Place, Whitehill Industrial Estate, Bathgate EH48 2HA ☎ 01506 77629 ✉ colin.bell@westlothian.gov.uk

COUNCILLORS

***Provost* Kerr**, Tom (CON - Linlithgow)
tom.kerr@westlothian.gov.uk

***Leader of the Council* McGinty**, John (LAB - Bathgate)
john.mcginty@westlothian.gov.uk

Anderson, Frank (SNP - East Livingston and East Calder)
frank.anderson@westlothian.gov.uk

Borrowman, Stuart (IND - Armadale and Blackridge)
stuart.borrowman@westlothian.gov.uk

Boyle, William (SNP - Bathgate)
william.boyle@westlothian.gov.uk

Boyle, Tony (LAB - Broxburn, Uphall and Winchburgh)
tony.boyle@westlothian.gov.uk

Calder, Diane (SNP - Broxburn, Uphall and Winchburgh)
diane.calder@westlothian.gov.uk

Campbell, Janet (SNP - Broxburn, Uphall and Winchburgh)
janet.campbell@westlothian.gov.uk

Cartmill, Harry (LAB - Bathgate)
harry.cartmill@westlothian.gov.uk

Conn, Tom (LAB - Linlithgow)
tom.conn@westlothian.gov.uk

Davidson, Alex (LAB - Broxburn, Uphall and Winchburgh)
alex.davidson@westlothian.gov.uk

Debold, Robert (SNP - Livingston North)
robert.debold@westlothian.gov.uk

Dickson, Jim (SNP - Whitburn and Blackburn)
jim.dickson3@westlothian.gov.uk

Dickson, Mary (SNP - Whitburn and Blackburn)
mary.dickson@westlothian.gov.uk

Dixon, Jim (LAB - Armadale and Blackridge)
jim.dixon@westlothian.gov.uk

Dodds, David (LAB - Fauldhouse and The Breich Valley)
david.dodds@westlothian.gov.uk

Fitzpatrick, Lawrence (LAB - Livingston South)
lawrence.fitzpatrick@westlothian.gov.uk

John, Carl (SNP - East Livingston and East Calder)
carl.john@westlothian.gov.uk

Johnston, Peter (SNP - Livingston South)
peter.johnston@westlothian.gov.uk

King, Sarah (SNP - Armadale and Blackridge)

King, Dave (LAB - East Livingston and East Calder)
dave.king@westlothian.gov.uk

Logue, Danny (LAB - Livingston South)
danny.logue@westlothian.gov.uk

McCarra, Greg (SNP - Fauldhouse and the Briech Valley)
greg.mccarra@westlothian.gov.uk

McMillan, Anne (LAB - Livingston North)
anne.mcmillan@westlothian.gov.uk

Miller, Andrew (SNP - Livingston North)
andrew.miller@westlothian.gov.uk

Moohan, Angela (LAB - Livingston North)
angela.moohan@westlothian.gov.uk

Muir, John (SNP - Livingston South)
john.muir@westlothian.gov.uk

Muldoon, Cathy (LAB - Fauldhouse and the Briech Valley)
cathy.muldoon@westlothian.gov.uk

Paul, George (LAB - Whitburn and Blackburn)
george.paul@westlothian.gov.uk

Robertson, Barry (LAB - Whitburn and Blackburn)
barry.robertson@westlothian.gov.uk

Tait, David (SNP - Linlithgow)

Toner, Frank (LAB - East Livingstone and East Calder)
frank.toner@westlothian.gov.uk

Walker, Jim (SNP - Bathgate)
jim.walker@westlothian.gov.uk

POLITICAL COMPOSITION

LAB: 16, SNP: 15, CON: 1, IND: 1

COMMITTEE CHAIRS

Audit & Governance: Mr Harry Cartmill

Licensing: Mr Tony Boyle

Planning: Mr Tom Kerr

West Oxfordshire D

West Oxfordshire District Council, Council Offices, Woodgreen, Witney OX28 1NB
☎ 01993 861000 🖷 01993 861050 ✉ enquiries@westoxon.gov.uk
💻 www.westoxon.gov.uk

FACTS AND FIGURES

Parliamentary Constituencies: Witney
EU Constituencies: South East
Election Frequency: Elections are by thirds

PRINCIPAL OFFICERS

Chief Executive: Mr Frank Wilson, Shared Strategic Director - Resources, Council Offices, Woodgreen, Witney OX28 1NB
☎ 01993 861291 ✉ frank.wilson@westoxon.gov.uk

Senior Management: Ms Christine Gore, Strategic Director - Communities & Planning, Council Offices, Trinity Road, Cirencester GL7 1PX ☎ 01285 623500 ✉ christine.gore@cotswold.gov.uk

Senior Management: Mr Frank Wilson, Shared Strategic Director - Resources, Council Offices, Woodgreen, Witney OX28 1NB
☎ 01993 861291 ✉ frank.wilson@westoxon.gov.uk

Building Control: Mr Andrew Jones, Building Control Manager, Council Offices, Elmfield, New Yatt Road, Witney OX28 1PB
☎ 01285 623633 🖷 01285 623905 ✉ andrew.jones@cotswold.gov.uk

PR / Communications: Ms Carys Davis, Publicity & Information Officer, Council Offices, Woodgreen, Witney OX28 1NB ☎ 01993 861615 🖷 01993 861450 ✉ communications@westoxon.gov.uk

Community Planning: Mr Mike Clark, Corporate Planning Manager, Council Offices, Elmfield, New Yatt Road, Witney OX28 1PB ☎ 01285 623565 🖷 01285 623900 ✉ mike.clark@cotswold.gov.uk

Community Safety: Mr Ron Spurs, Principal Officer, Council Offices, Woodgreen, Witney OX28 1NB

Contracts: Mr Phil Martin, Head of Business Information & Change, Council Offices, Woodgreen, Witney OX28 1NB ☎ 01993 861201 ✉ phil.martin@westoxon.gov.uk)

Corporate Services: Mr Phil Martin, Head of Business Information & Change, Council Offices, Woodgreen, Witney OX28 1NB ☎ 01993 861201 ✉ phil.martin@westoxon.gov.uk

Corporate Services: Mr Paul Stuart, Go Shared Services Head of Corporate Resources, Council Offices, Woodgreen, Witney OX28 1NB ☎ 01993 861171 ✉ paul.stuart@westoxon.gov.uk

Customer Service: Ms Clare Martin, Customer Services Manager, Council Offices, Woodgreen, Witney OX28 1NB ☎ 01993 861000 🖷 01993 861050 ✉ clare.martin@westoxon.gov.uk

Customer Service: Mr Phil Martin, Head of Business Information & Change, Council Offices, Woodgreen, Witney OX28 1NB ☎ 01993 861201 ✉ phil.martin@westoxon.gov.uk

Economic Development: Mr Dene Robson, Community Development Manager, Council Offices, Woodgreen, Witney OX28 1NB ☎ 01993 861481 ✉ dene.robson@westoxon.gov.uk

E-Government: Mr John Chorlton, ICT Operations Manager, Council Offices, Woodgreen, Witney OX28 1NB ☎ 01285 623000 🖷 01285 623900 ✉ john.chorlton@cotswold.gov.uk

Electoral Registration: Mr Keith Butler, Head of Democratic Services, Council Offices, Woodgreen, Witney OX28 1NB ☎ 01993 861521 🖷 01993 861450 ✉ keith.butler@westoxon.gov.uk

Emergency Planning: Mrs Claire Locke, Head of Environmental Services, Council Offices, Woodgreen, Witney OX28 1NB ☎ 01285 623427 🖷 01285 623000 ✉ claire.locke@cotswold.gov.uk

Environmental Health: Mr Phil Measures, Environmental Health Manager, Council Offices, Woodgreen, Witney OX28 1NB ☎ 01993 861376 ✉ phil.measures@westoxon.gov.uk

Estates, Property & Valuation: Mr David Thurlow, Estates Manager, Council Offices, Woodgreen, Witney OX28 1NB ☎ 01993 861583 ✉ david.thurlow@westoxon.gov.uk

Finance: Mr Frank Wilson, Shared Strategic Director - Resources, Council Offices, Woodgreen, Witney OX28 1NB ☎ 01993 861291 ✉ frank.wilson@westoxon.gov.uk

Health and Safety: Mr Iain Wilkie, Joint H&S Advisor, Council Offices, Woodgreen, Witney OX28 1NB

Housing: Mr Jon Dearing, Head of Revenues & Housing Support, Council Offices, Woodgreen, Witney OX28 1NB ☎ 01993 861221

Legal: Ms Bhavna Patel, Head of Legal & Property Services, Council Offices, Woodgreen, Witney OX28 1NB

Leisure and Cultural Services: Ms Diane Shelton, Head of Leisure & Communities, Council Offices, Woodgreen, Witney OX28 1NB ☎ 01993 861551 🖷 01993 861450 ✉ diane.shelton@westoxon.gov.uk

Licensing: Mr Ron Spurs, Principal Officer, Council Offices, Woodgreen, Witney OX28 1NB

Member Services: Mr Keith Butler, Head of Democratic Services, Council Offices, Woodgreen, Witney OX28 1NB ☎ 01993 861521 🖷 01993 861450 ✉ keith.butler@westoxon.gov.uk

Personnel / HR: Ms Deborah Bainbridge, GO Shared Services Head of HR, Council Offices, Woodgreen, Witney OX28 1NB

Planning: Mr Giles Hughes, Head of Planning & Strategic Housing, Council Offices, Woodgreen, Witney OX28 1NB ☎ 01993 861658 ✉ giles.hughes@westoxon.gov.uk

Procurement: Mr Phil Martin, Head of Business Information & Change, Council Offices, Woodgreen, Witney OX28 1NB ☎ 01993 861201 ✉ phil.martin@westoxon.gov.uk

Staff Training: Mrs Jan Bridges, Learning & Organisational Development Manager, Municipal Offices, Promenade, Cheltenham GL50 9SA ☎ 01242 775189 🖷 01242 264309 ✉ jan.bridges@cheltenham.gov.uk

Sustainable Communities: Mr Giles Hughes, Head of Planning & Strategic Housing, Council Offices, Woodgreen, Witney OX28 1NB ☎ 01993 861658 ✉ giles.hughes@westoxon.gov.uk

Sustainable Development: Mr Giles Hughes, Head of Planning & Strategic Housing, Council Offices, Woodgreen, Witney OX28 1NB ☎ 01993 861658 ✉ giles.hughes@westoxon.gov.uk

Tourism: Ms Diane Shelton, Head of Leisure & Communities, Council Offices, Woodgreen, Witney OX28 1NB ☎ 01993 861551 🖷 01993 861450 ✉ diane.shelton@westoxon.gov.uk

Waste Management: Mrs Claire Locke, Head of Environmental Services, Council Offices, Woodgreen, Witney OX28 1NB ☎ 01285 623427 🖷 01285 623000 ✉ claire.locke@cotswold.gov.uk

COUNCILLORS

***Chair* MacRae**, Norman (CON - Carterton North East) norman.macrae@westoxon.gov.uk

***Vice-Chair* Crossland**, Maxine (CON - Carterton North West) maxine.crossland@westoxon.gov.uk

***Leader of the Council* Norton**, Barry (CON - North Leigh) barry.norton@westoxon.gov.uk

***Group Leader* Enright**, Duncan (LAB - Witney East) duncan.enright@westoxon.gov.uk

Adams, Alvin (CON - Witney South) alvin.adams@westoxon.gov.uk

Baker, Jeanette (CON - Witney East)
jeanette.baker@westoxon.gov.uk

Barrett, Martin (CON - Bampton and Clanfield)
martin.barrett@westoxon.gov.uk

Beaney, Andrew (CON - Kingham, Rollright and Enstone)
andrew.beaney@westoxon.gov.uk

Bishop, Richard (CON - Stonesfield and Tackley)
richard.bishop@westoxon.gov.uk

Brennan, Mick (CON - Carterton South)
michael.brennan@westoxon.gov.uk

Carter, Laetisia (LAB - Chipping Norton)
laetisis.carter@westoxon.gov.uk

Chapman, Louise (CON - Witney West)
louise.chapman@westoxon.gov.uk

Coles, Andrew (LAB - Witney Central)
andrew.coles@westoxon.gov.uk

Colston, Nigel (CON - Kingham, Rollright and Enstone)
nigel.colston@westoxon.gov.uk

Cooper, Julian (LD - Woodstock and Bladon)
julian.cooper@westoxon.gov.uk

Cotterill, Derek (CON - Burford)
derek.cotterill@westoxon.gov.uk

Cottrell-Dormer, Charles (CON - Stonesfield and Tackley)
charles.cottrell-dormer@westoxon.gov.uk

Courts, Robert (CON - The Bartons)
robert.courts@westoxon.gov.uk

Dingwall, Colin (CON - Freeland and Hanborough)
colin.dingwall@westoxon.gov.uk

Dorward, Pete (CON - Witney Central)
pete.dorward@westoxon.gov.uk

Doughty, Jane (CON - Witney South)
jane.doughty@westoxon.gov.uk

Eaglestone, Harry (CON - Witney West)
harry.eaglestone@westoxon.gov.uk

Emery, Peter (CON - Eynsham and Cassington)
peter.emery@westoxon.gov.uk

Fenton, Hilary (CON - Standlake, Aston and Stanton Harcourt)
hilary.fenton@westoxon.gov.uk

Fenton, Ted (CON - Bampton and Clanfield)
ted.fenton@westoxon.gov.uk

Good, Steve (CON - Standlake, Aston and Stanton Harcourt)
steve.good@westoxon.gov.uk

Graham, Andy (LD - Charlbury and Finstock)
andy.graham@westoxon.gov.uk

Haine, Jeff (CON - Milton under Wychwood)
jeff.haine@westoxon.gov.uk

Handley, Peter (CON - Carterton North West)
peter.handley@westoxon.gov.uk

Harvey, David (CON - Witney South)
david.harvey@westoxon.gov.uk

Hill, Gill (CON - Hailey, Minster Lovell and Leafield)
gill.hill@westoxon.gov.uk

Howard, Henry (CON - Carterton North East)
henry.howard@westoxon.gov.uk

James, Edward (CON - Eynsham and Cassington)
edward.james@westoxon.gov.uk

Kelland, Peter (CON - Eynsham and Cassington)
peter.kelland@westoxon.gov.uk

Langridge, Richard (CON - Witney North)
richard.langridge@westoxon.gov.uk

Leffman, Liz (LD - Charlbury and Finstock)
liz.leffman@westoxon.gov.uk

Little, Lynn (CON - Carterton South)
lynn.little@westoxon.gov.uk

McFarlane, David (CON - Alvescot and Filkins)
david.mcfarlane@westoxon.gov.uk

Mills, James (CON - Witney East)
james.mills@westoxon.gov.uk

Morris, Toby (CON - Freeland and Hanborough)
toby.morris@westoxon.gov.uk

Owen, Neil (CON - Chadlington and Churchill)
neil.owen@westoxon.gov.uk

Poskitt, Elizabeth (LD - Woodstock and Bladon)
elizabeth.poskitt@westoxon.gov.uk

Postan, Alex (CON - Brize Norton and Shilton)
alex.postan@westoxon.gov.uk

Robinson, Warwick (CON - Hailey, Minster Lovell and Leafield)
warwick.robinson@westoxon.gov.uk

Saul, Geoff (LAB - Chipping Norton)
geoff.saul@westoxon.gov.uk

Simcox, Tom (CON - Ascott and Shipton)
tom.simcox@westoxon.gov.uk

Wall, Guy (CON - Chipping Norton)
guy.wall@westoxon.gov.uk

Woodruff, Ben (CON - Ducklington)
ben.woodruff@westoxon.gov.uk

POLITICAL COMPOSITION

CON: 40, LAB: 4, LD: 4

COMMITTEE CHAIRS

Audit & General Purposes: Mr Alvin Adams

Development Control: Mr Jeff Haine

Licensing: Mr Norman MacRae

West Somerset D

West Somerset District Council, West Somerset House, Killick Way, Williton, Taunton TA4 4QA
☎ 01643 703704 🖷 01984 633022
✉ westsomersetdc@westsomerset.gov.uk
🖳 www.westsomersetonline.gov.uk

FACTS AND FIGURES

Parliamentary Constituencies: Bridgwater and Somerset West
EU Constituencies: South West
Election Frequency: Elections are of whole council

WEST SOMERSET

PRINCIPAL OFFICERS

Chief Executive: Mrs Penny James, Chief Executive, West Somerset House, Killick Way, Williton, Taunton TA4 4QA 🖰 pjames@westsomerset.gov.uk

Deputy Chief Executive: Ms Shirlene Adam, Deputy Chief Executive & Director - Operations, West Somerset House, Killick Way, Williton, Taunton TA4 4QA ☎ 01643 703704 🖰 s.adam@tauntondeane.gov.uk

Assistant Chief Executive: Mr Bruce Lang, Assistant Chief Executive, West Somerset House, Killick Way, Williton, Taunton TA4 4QA ☎ 01643 703704 🖰 bdlang@westsomerset.gov.uk

Senior Management: Mr James Barrah, Director - Housing & Communities, The Deane House, Belvedere Road, Taunton TA1 1HE ☎ 01823 358699 🖷 01823 356329 🖰 j.barrah@tauntondeane.gov.uk

Senior Management: Mr Brendon Cleere, Director - Growth & Development, The Deane House, Belvedere Road, Taunton TA1 1HE ☎ 01823 356350 🖷 01823 356329 🖰 b.cleere@tauntondeane.gov.uk

Building Control: Mrs Jayne Hall, Building Control Manager, West Somerset House, Killick Way, Williton, Taunton TA4 4QA ☎ 01984 635268 🖷 01984 635365 🖰 jhall@westsomerset.gov.uk

PR / Communications: Mr Bruce Lang, Assistant Chief Executive, West Somerset House, Killick Way, Williton, Taunton TA4 4QA ☎ 01643 703704 🖰 bdlang@westsomerset.gov.uk

Community Safety: Ms Tracey-Ann Biss, Parking & Civil Contingencies Manager, West Somerset House, Killick Way, Williton, Taunton TA4 4QA ☎ 01823 356501 🖷 01823 356329 🖰 t.biss@tauntondeane.gov.uk

Computer Management: Ms Fiona Kirkham, ICT Manager, The Deane House, Belvedere Road, Taunton TA1 1HE ☎ 01823 356522 🖷 01823 356329 🖰 f.kirkham@tauntondeane.gov.uk

Consumer Protection and Trading Standards: Mr Scott Weetch, Community & Client Services Manager, The Deane House, Belvedere Road, Taunton TA1 1HE ☎ 01823 356317 🖷 01823 356329 🖰 s.weetch@tauntondeane.gov.uk

Corporate Services: Mr Richard Sealy, Assistant Director - Corporate Services, The Deane House, Belvedere Road, Taunton TA1 1HE ☎ 01823 658690 🖰 r.sealy@tauntondeane.gov.uk

Customer Service: Mr Richard Sealy, Assistant Director - Corporate Services, The Deane House, Belvedere Road, Taunton TA1 1HE ☎ 01823 658690 🖰 r.sealy@tauntondeane.gov.uk

Direct Labour: Mr Chris Hall, Assistant Director - Operational Delivery, The Deane House, Belvedere Road, Taunton TA1 1HE ☎ 01823 356403 🖰 c.hall@tauntondeane.gov.uk

Economic Development: Ms Corinne Matthews, Economic Regeneration Manager, West Somerset House, Killick Way, Williton, Taunton TA4 4QA ☎ 01984 635287 🖷 01984 633022 🖰 cmatthews@westsomerset.gov.uk

Economic Development: Mr Ian Timms, Assistant Director - Business Development, West Somerset House, Killick Way, Williton, Taunton TA4 4QA ☎ 01823 356577 🖰 itimms@westsomerset.gov.uk

E-Government: Ms Fiona Kirkham, ICT Manager, The Deane House, Belvedere Road, Taunton TA1 1HE ☎ 01823 356522 🖷 01823 356329 🖰 f.kirkham@tauntondeane.gov.uk

Electoral Registration: Mrs Elisa Day, Electoral Services Manager, West Somerset House, Killick Way, Williton, Taunton TA4 4QA ☎ 01984 635272 🖰 eday@westsomerset.gov.uk

Emergency Planning: Mr Scott Weetch, Community & Client Services Manager, The Deane House, Belvedere Road, Taunton TA1 1HE ☎ 01823 356317 🖷 01823 356329 🖰 s.weetch@tauntondeane.gov.uk

Environmental Health: Mr Scott Weetch, Community & Client Services Manager, The Deane House, Belvedere Road, Taunton TA1 1HE ☎ 01823 356317 🖷 01823 356329 🖰 s.weetch@tauntondeane.gov.uk

Facilities: Mr Richard Sealy, Assistant Director - Corporate Services, The Deane House, Belvedere Road, Taunton TA1 1HE ☎ 01823 658690 🖰 r.sealy@tauntondeane.gov.uk

Finance: Mr Paul Fitzgerald, Assistant Director - Resources, West Somerset House, Killick Way, Williton, Taunton TA4 4QA 🖰 pfitzgerald@westsomerset.gov.uk

Grounds Maintenance: Mr Cyril Rowe, Open Spaces Manager, Priory Way Depot, Taunton TA1 2BB 🖰 c.rowe@tauntondeane.gov.uk

Health and Safety: Ms Catrin Brown, Health & Safety Manager, The Deane House, Belvedere Road, Taunton TA1 1HE ☎ 01823 356578 🖰 c.brown@tauntondeane.gov.uk

Housing: Mr Simon Lewis, Assistant Director - Housing & Community Development, The Deane House, Belvedere Road, Taunton TA1 1HE ☎ 01823 356397 🖰 s.lewis@tauntondeane.gov.uk

Legal: Mr Roy Pinney, Legal Services Manager, The Deane House, Belvedere Road, Taunton TA1 1HE ☎ 01823 356409 🖷 01823 356329 🖰 r.pinney@tauntondeane.gov.uk

Licensing: Mr Ian Carter, Licensing Manager, The Deane House, Belvedere Road, Taunton TA1 1HE ☎ 01823 358406 🖰 i.carter@tauntondeane.gov.uk

Member Services: Mr Richard Bryant, Democratic Services Manager, The Deane House, Belvedere Road, Taunton TA1 1HE ☎ 01823 356414 🖷 01823 356329 🖰 r.bryant@tauntondeane.gov.uk

Parking: Ms Tracey-Ann Biss, Parking & Civil Contingencies Manager, West Somerset House, Killick Way, Williton, Taunton TA4 4QA ☎ 01823 356501 🖷 01823 356329 🖰 t.biss@tauntondeane.gov.uk

Personnel / HR: Ms Fiona Wills, Human Resources Manager, The Deane House, Belvedere Road, Taunton TA1 1HE ☎ 01823 356450 🖷 01823 356329 🖰 f.wills@tauntondeane.gov.uk

Planning: Mr Bryn Kitching, Area Planning Manager, The Deane House, Belvedere Road, Taunton TA1 1HE

Regeneration: Ms Corinne Matthews, Economic Regeneration Manager, West Somerset House, Killick Way, Williton, Taunton TA4 4QA ☎ 01984 635287 🖷 01984 633022 🖱 cmatthews@westsomerset.gov.uk

Staff Training: Ms Fiona Wills, Human Resources Manager, The Deane House, Belvedere Road, Taunton TA1 1HE ☎ 01823 356450 🖷 01823 356329 🖱 f.wills@tauntondeane.gov.uk

Tourism: Ms Corinne Matthews, Economic Regeneration Manager, West Somerset House, Killick Way, Williton, Taunton TA4 4QA ☎ 01984 635287 🖷 01984 633022 🖱 cmatthews@westsomerset.gov.uk

Waste Collection and Disposal: Mr Chris Hall, Assistant Director - Operational Delivery, The Deane House, Belvedere Road, Taunton TA1 1HE ☎ 01823 356403 🖱 c.hall@tauntondeane.gov.uk

COUNCILLORS

Leader of the Council **Trollope-Bellew**, Anthony (CON - Crowcombe and Stogumber)
atrollope-bellew@westsomerset.gov.uk

Deputy Leader of the Council **Chilcott**, Mandy (CON - Minehead Central)
MChilcott@westsomerset.gov.uk

Aldridge, Ian (IND - Williton)
Ialdridge@westsomerset.gov.uk

Archer, David (CON - Minehead North)
Darcher@westsomerset.gov.uk

Behan, Adrian (UKIP - Alcombe)
Abehan@westsomerset.gov.uk

Clifford, Rollo (CON - Porlock and District)
RClifford@westsomerset.gov.uk

Davies, Hugh (IND - Williton)
Hdavies@westsomerset.gov.uk

Dewdney, Martin (CON - Old Cleeve)
MDewdney@westsomerset.gov.uk

Dowding, Stuart (CON - West Quantock)
sdowding@westsomerset.gov.uk

Goss, Susan (CON - Quantock Vale)
sgoss@westsomerset.gov.uk

Hadley, Andrew (IND - Minehead Central)
ahadley@westsomerset.gov.uk

Hall, Thomas (IND - Minehead South)
Thall@westsomerset.gov.uk

Heywood, Bruce (CON - Dulverton and District)
bheywood@westsomerset.gov.uk

Jones, Ivor (UKIP - Minehead Central)
Ijones@westsomerset.gov.uk

Leaker, Bryan (CON - Dunster & Timberscombe)
Bleaker@westsomerset.gov.uk

Lillis, Richard (CON - Old Cleeve)
rlillis@westsomerset.gov.uk

Maitland-Walker, Brenda (CON - Carhampton and Withycombe)
Bmaitland-Walker@westsomerset.gov.uk

Mills, Karen (CON - Porlock and District)
kmills@westsomerset.gov.uk

Morgan, Chris (IND - Quantock Vale)
cmorgan@westsomerset.gov.uk

Murphy, Peter (LAB - Watchet)
pmurphy@westsomerset.gov.uk

Parbrook, Jean (CON - Minehead South)
Jparbrook@westsomerset.gov.uk

Pugsley, Steven (CON - Greater Exmoor)
sjpugsley@westsomerset.gov.uk

Thomas, Roger (CON - Alcombe)
Rthomas@westsomerset.gov.uk

Thwaites, Nicholas (CON - Dulverton and District)
Nthwaites@westsomerset.gov.uk

Turner, Keith (CON - Brendon Hills)
kturner@westsomerset.gov.uk

Venner, Terry (UKIP - Minehead North)
Tvenner@westsomerset.gov.uk

Westcott, David (CON - Watchet)
dwestcott@westsomerset.gov.uk

Woods, Rosemary (CON - Watchet)
Rwoods@westsomerset.gov.uk

POLITICAL COMPOSITION

CON: 19, IND: 5, UKIP: 3, LAB: 1

West Sussex C

West Sussex County Council, County Hall, Chichester PO19 1RQ
☎ 01243 777100 🖷 01243 530439 🖳 www.westsussex.gov.uk

FACTS AND FIGURES

Parliamentary Constituencies: Arundel and South Downs, Bognor Regis and Littlehampton, Chichester, Crawley, Horsham, Sussex Mid, Worthing East and Shoreham, Worthing West
EU Constituencies: South East
Election Frequency: Elections are of whole council

PRINCIPAL OFFICERS

Chief Executive: Ms Gill Steward, Chief Operating Officer, County Hall, Chichester PO19 1RQ ☎ 033022 25751 🖱 gill.steward@westsussex.gov.uk

Senior Management: Mrs Natasha Edmunds, Director of Workforce, Organisational Development & Delivery Support, County Hall, Chichester PO19 1RQ ☎ 033022 25342 🖱 natash.edmunds@westsussex.gov.uk

Senior Management: Mr Colin James, Head of Capital & Infrastructure, County Hall, Chichester PO19 1RQ ☎ 03302 222677 🖱 colin.james@westsussex.gov.uk

Senior Management: Mr Tony Kershaw, Director of Law, Assurance & Strategy, County Hall, Chichester PO19 1RQ ☎ 033022 22662 🖱 tony.kershaw@westsussex.gov.uk

WEST SUSSEX

Senior Management: Ms Annie MacIver, Director of Family Operations, County Hall, Chichester PO19 1RQ ☎ 033022 25914 ✉ annie.maciver@westsussex.gov.uk

Senior Management: Mr Brin Martin, Principal Advisor - Learning, County Hall, Chichester PO19 1RQ ☎ 03302 228339 ✉ brin.martin@westsussex.gov.uk

Senior Management: Ms Debbie Medlock, Director of Adults' Operation, County Hall, Chichester PO19 1RQ ☎ 03302 222661

Senior Management: Ms Avril Wilson, Executive Director of Care, Wellbeing & Education, County Hall, Chichester PO19 1RQ ✉ avril.wilson@westsussex.gov.uk

Senior Management: Ms Judith Wright, Director of Health & Social Care, Commissioning & Public Health, County Hall, Chichester PO19 1RQ ☎ 033022 22667 ✉ judith.wright@westsussex.gov.uk

Architect, Building / Property Services: Mr Colin James, Head of Capital & Infrastructure, County Hall, Chichester PO19 1RQ ☎ 03302 222677 ✉ colin.james@westsussex.gov.uk

Children / Youth Services: Ms Annie MacIver, Director of Family Operations, County Hall, Chichester PO19 1RQ ☎ 033022 25914 ✉ annie.maciver@westsussex.gov.uk

Civil Registration: Mrs Margaret Butler, Service Manager - Registration & Coroner, County Hall, Chichester PO19 1RQ ☎ 033022 27657 ✉ margaret.butler@westsussex.gov.uk

Civil Registration: Mr Sean Ruth, Executive Director - Communities & Public Protection, Main 2nd Floor, Northgate, Chichester PO19 1BD ☎ 01243 752401 ✉ sean.ruth@westsussex.gov.uk

PR / Communications: Ms Kirsty Buchanan, Head of Communications, County Hall, Chichester PO19 1RQ ✉ kirsty.buchanan@westsussex.gov.uk

Community Safety: Mrs Emily King, Better Communities Manager, County Hall, Chichester PO19 1RQ ☎ 033022 23876 ✉ emily.king@westsussex.gov.uk

Computer Management: Mrs Natasha Edmunds, Director of Workforce, Organisational Development & Delivery Support, County Hall, Chichester PO19 1RQ ☎ 033022 25342 ✉ natash.edmunds@westsussex.gov.uk

Consumer Protection and Trading Standards: Mr Sean Ruth, Executive Director - Communities & Public Protection, Main 2nd Floor, Northgate, Chichester PO19 1BD ☎ 01243 752401 ✉ sean.ruth@westsussex.gov.uk

Contracts: Mr Edward Vera-Cruz, Principal Procurement Manager, County Hall, Chichester PO19 1RQ ✉ edward.vera-cruz@westsussex.gov.uk

Corporate Services: Mr Peter Lewis, Executive Director - Corporate Resources & Services, County Hall, Chichester PO19 1RQ ☎ 033022 22671 ✉ peter.lewis@westsussex.gov.uk

Customer Service: Ms Cathryn James, Executive Director of Residents' Services, County Hall, Chichester PO19 1RQ ☎ 03302 222676 ✉ cathryn.james@westsussex.gov.uk

Economic Development: Mrs Caroline Haynes, Director - Economic Growth, County Hall, Chichester PO19 1RQ ✉ caroline.haynes@westsussex.gov.uk

Electoral Registration: Mr Tony Kershaw, Director of Law, Assurance & Strategy, County Hall, Chichester PO19 1RQ ☎ 033022 22662 ✉ tony.kershaw@westsussex.gov.uk

Emergency Planning: Mr Alan Jones, Head of Emergency Management, Northgate, Chichester PO19 1BD ☎ 03302 222268 ✉ alan.jones@westsussex.gov.uk

Energy Management: Mr Vic Bass, Maintenance Manager, The Grange, County Hall, Chichester PO19 1RH ☎ 033022 22796 ✉ vic.bass@westsussex.gov.uk

Estates, Property & Valuation: Mr Colin James, Head of Capital & Infrastructure, County Hall, Chichester PO19 1RQ ☎ 03302 222677 ✉ colin.james@westsussex.gov.uk

Facilities: Ms Cathryn James, Executive Director of Residents' Services, County Hall, Chichester PO19 1RQ ☎ 03302 222676 ✉ cathryn.james@westsussex.gov.uk

Finance: Mr Peter Lewis, Executive Director - Corporate Resources & Services, County Hall, Chichester PO19 1RQ ☎ 033022 22671 ✉ peter.lewis@westsussex.gov.uk

Pensions: Mrs Jo Jennings, Employment Services Manager, County Hall, Chichester PO19 1RQ ☎ 01243 777867 ✉ jo.jennings@westsussex.gov.uk

Fleet Management: Mr Paul Mace, Transport Provision Manager, Northleigh, County Hall, Chichester PO19 1RH ☎ 033022 25443 ✉ paul.mace@westsussex.gov.uk

Health and Safety: Mr David Ramsbottom, Lead Health & Safety Professional, County Hall, Chichester PO19 1RQ ☎ 033022 22463 ✉ david.ramsbottom@westsussex.gov.uk

Highways: Ms Cathryn James, Executive Director of Residents' Services, County Hall, Chichester PO19 1RQ ☎ 03302 222676 ✉ cathryn.james@westsussex.gov.uk

Legal: Mr Tony Kershaw, Director of Law, Assurance & Strategy, County Hall, Chichester PO19 1RQ ☎ 033022 22662 ✉ tony.kershaw@westsussex.gov.uk

Lifelong Learning: Ms Annie MacIver, Director of Family Operations, County Hall, Chichester PO19 1RQ ☎ 033022 25914 ✉ annie.maciver@westsussex.gov.uk

Member Services: Mrs Debbie Allman, Service Manager - Democratic Services, Democratic Services Unit, County Hall, Chichester PO19 1RQ ☎ 03302 222528 ✉ debbie.allman@westsussex.gov.uk

Member Services: Mr Tony Kershaw, Director of Law, Assurance & Strategy, County Hall, Chichester PO19 1RQ ☎ 033022 22662 ✉ tony.kershaw@westsussex.gov.uk

Personnel / HR: Mrs Natasha Edmunds, Director of Workforce, Organisational Development & Delivery Support, County Hall, Chichester PO19 1RQ ☎ 033022 25342 ✉ natash.edmunds@westsussex.gov.uk

Planning: Ms Cathryn James, Executive Director of Residents' Services, County Hall, Chichester PO19 1RQ ☎ 03302 222676 ✉ cathryn.james@westsussex.gov.uk

Procurement: Mr Edward Vera-Cruz, Principal Procurement Manager, County Hall, Chichester PO19 1RQ ✉ edward.vera-cruz@westsussex.gov.uk

Public Libraries: Ms Cathryn James, Executive Director of Residents' Services, County Hall, Chichester PO19 1RQ ☎ 03302 222676 ✉ cathryn.james@westsussex.gov.uk

Public Libraries: Mrs Lesley Sim, Information Services Manager, Willow Park, 4B Terminus Road, Chichester PO19 8EG ☎ 033022 24786 ✉ lesley.sim@westsussex.gov.uk

Recycling & Waste Minimisation: Ms Cathryn James, Executive Director of Residents' Services, County Hall, Chichester PO19 1RQ ☎ 03302 222676 ✉ cathryn.james@westsussex.gov.uk

Road Safety: Mr Ron Paterson, Team Manager - Safe and Sustainable Transport Group, County Hall, Chichester PO19 1RQ ☎ 033022 26712 ✉ ron.paterson@westsussex.gov.uk

Social Services (Adult): Ms Debbie Medlock, Director of Adults' Operation, County Hall, Chichester PO19 1RQ ☎ 03302 222661

Staff Training: Ms Julie Ferroni, Learning & Development Operations Manager, County Hall, Chichester PO19 1RQ ☎ 033022 22318 ✉ julie.ferroni@westsussex.gov.uk

Sustainable Development: Mrs Siobhan Walker, Sustainability Team Manager, Communities and Infrastructure, West Sussex County Council, The Grange, Chichester PO19 1RH ☎ 033022 26456 ✉ siobhan.walker@westsussex.gov.uk

Traffic Management: Mr Peter Bradley, Service Manager of Safety & Traffic Management, County Hall, Chichester PO19 1RQ ☎ 033022 26344 ✉ peter.bradley@westsussex.gov.uk

Transport: Mr Ian Patrick, Team Manager Travelwise & Behavioural Change, Northleigh, Tower Street, Chichester PO19 1RH ☎ 033022 26715 ✉ ian.patrick@westsussex.gov.uk

Transport Planner: Mr Ian Patrick, Team Manager Travelwise & Behavioural Change, Northleigh, Tower Street, Chichester PO19 1RH ☎ 033022 26715 ✉ ian.patrick@westsussex.gov.uk

Waste Collection and Disposal: Mr Andy Thorne, Waste Commissioner, County Hall, Chichester PO19 1RQ ☎ 033022 23349 ✉ andy.thorne@westsussex.gov.uk

Waste Management: Ms Cathryn James, Executive Director of Residents' Services, County Hall, Chichester PO19 1RQ ☎ 03302 222676 ✉ cathryn.james@westsussex.gov.uk

COUNCILLORS

***Leader of the Council* Goldsmith**, Louise (CON - Chichester West)
louise.goldsmith@westsussex.gov.uk

***Deputy Leader of the Council* Field**, Christine (CON - Lindfield & High Weald)
christine.field@westsussex.gov.uk

Acraman, William (CON - Worth Forest)
bill.acraman@westsussex.gov.uk

Arculus, Patricia (CON - Pulborough)
patricia.arculus@westsussex.gov.uk

Barling, David (CON - Bramber Castle)
david.barling@westsussex.gov.uk

Barnard, Lionel (CON - Henfield)
lionel.barnard@westsussex.gov.uk

Barrett-Miles, Andrew (CON - Burgess Hill Town)
andrew.barrett-miles@westsussex.gov.uk

Bennett, Elizabeth (CON - East Grinstead Meridian)
liz.bennett@westsussex.gov.uk

Bradbury, Peter (CON - Cuckfield & Lucastes)
pete.bradbury@westsussex.gov.uk

Brown, Michael (CON - Fernhurst)
michael.brown@westsussex.gov.uk

Brunsdon, Heidi (CON - Imberdown)
heidi.brunsdon@westsussex.gov.uk

Buckland, Ian (LD - Littlehampton Town)
ian.buckland@westsussex.gov.uk

Burrett, Richard (CON - Pound Hill & Worth)
richard.burrett@westsussex.gov.uk

Catchpole, Peter (CON - Holbrook)
peter.catchpole@westsussex.gov.uk

Circus, Philip (CON - Storrington)
philip.circus@westsussex.gov.uk

Clark, Michael (UKIP - Saltings)
mick.clark@westsussex.gov.uk

Cloake, Michael (CON - Worthing Pier)
michael.cloake@westsussex.gov.uk

Crow, Duncan (CON - Tilgate & Furnace Green)
duncan.crow@westsussex.gov.uk

Dennis, Nigel (LD - Horsham Hurst)
nigel.dennis@westsussex.gov.uk

Duncton, Janet (CON - Petworth)
janet.duncton@westsussex.gov.uk

Evans, Peter (CON - East Preston & Ferring)
peter.evans@westsussex.gov.uk

Evans, Margaret (CON - Chichester South)
margaret.evans@westsussex.gov.uk

Glennon, Michael (UKIP - Lancing)
michael.glennon@westsussex.gov.uk

Griffiths, Peter (CON - Hurstpierpoint & Bolney)
peter.griffiths@westsussex.gov.uk

WEST SUSSEX

Hall, Patricia (UKIP - Durrington & Savlington)
trixie.hall@westsussex.gov.uk

High, Paul (CON - Worthing West)
paul.high@westsussex.gov.uk

Hillier, Stephen (CON - Haywards Heath East)
stephen.hillier@westsussex.gov.uk

Hunt, Jeremy (CON - Chichester North)
jeremy.hunt@westsussex.gov.uk

James, Sandra (UKIP - Bourne)
sandra.james@westsussex.gov.uk

Jones, Anne (CON - Burgess Hill East)
anne.jones@westsussex.gov.uk

Jones, Graham (UKIP - Felpham)
graham.jones@westsussex.gov.uk

Jones, Michael (LAB - Southgate & Crawley Central)
michael.jones@westsussex.gov.uk

Jupp, Amanda (CON - Billingshurst)
amanda.jupp@westsussex.gov.uk

Kennard, Debra (CON - Shoreham)
debbie.kennard@westsussex.gov.uk

Kitchen, Liz (CON - Warnham and Rusper)
liz.kitchen@westsussex.gov.uk

Lamb, Peter (LAB - Northgate & Three Bridges)
peter.lamb@westsussex.gov.uk

Lanzer, Robert (CON - Maidenbower)
bob.lanzer@westsussex.gov.uk

McAra, Gordon (IND - Midhurst)
gordon.mcara@westsussex.gov.uk

Metcalfe, Peter (CON - Kingston Buci)
peter.metcalfe@westsussex.gov.uk

Millson, Morwen (LD - Horsham Riverside)
morwen.millson@westsussex.gov.uk

Mockbridge, Janet (CON - Southwick)
janet.mockridge@westsussex.gov.uk

Montyn, Pieter (CON - The Witterings)
pieter.montyn@westsussex.gov.uk

Mullins, Susan (LAB - Gossops Green & Ifield East)
sue.mullins@westsussex.gov.uk

Oakley, Roger (CON - Worthing East)
roger.oakley@westsussex.gov.uk

Oakley, Simon (CON - Chichester East)
simon.oakley@westsussex.gov.uk

O'Brien, John (CON - East Grinstead South & Ashurst Wood)
john.o'brien@westsussex.gov.uk

Oppler, Francis (LD - Bognor Regis East)
francis.oppler@westsussex.gov.uk

Oxlade, Christopher (LAB - Bewbush & Ifield West)
chris.oxlade@westsussex.gov.uk

Parsons, Lionel (UKIP - Sompting & North Lancing)
lionel.parsons@westsussex.gov.uk

Patel, Ashvin (CON - Bognor Regis West & Aldwick)
ashvin.patel@westsussex.gov.uk

Petch, Andrew (CON - Hassocks & Victoria)
andy.petch@westsussex.gov.uk

Peters, Nigel (CON - Arundel & Wick)
nigel.peters@westsussex.gov.uk

Phillips, Joan (UKIP - Middleton)
joan.phillips@westsussex.gov.uk

Quinn, Brian (LAB - Broadfield)
brian.quinn@westsussex.gov.uk

Rae, James (CON - Roffey)
jim.rae@westsussex.gov.uk

Rapnik, Ann (UKIP - Bersted)
ann.rapnik@westsussex.gov.uk

Rogers, John (CON - Cissbury)
john.rogers@westsussex.gov.uk

Rogers, Robin (LD - Northbrook)
robin.rogers@westsussex.gov.uk

Sheldon, David (LD - Horsham Tanbridge & Broadbridge Heath)
david.sheldon@westsussex.gov.uk

Smith, Bernard (UKIP - Selsey)
bernard.smith@westsussex.gov.uk

Smith, Brenda (LAB - Langley Green & West Green)
brenda.smith@westsussex.gov.uk

Smytherman, Robert (LD - Tarring)
bob.smytherman@westsussex.gov.uk

Sutcliffe, Anthony (UKIP - Nyetimber)
tony.sutcliffe@westsussex.gov.uk

Turner, Bryan (CON - Broadwater)
bryan.turner@westsussex.gov.uk

Tyler, Graham (CON - Rustington)
graham.tyler@westsussex.gov.uk

Urquhart, Deborah (CON - Angmering & Findon)
deborah.urquhart@westsussex.gov.uk

Waight, Steven (CON - Goring)
steve.waight@westsussex.gov.uk

Walsh, James (LD - Littlehampton East)
james.walsh@westsussex.gov.uk

Watson, Brad (CON - Southwater & Nuthurst)
brad.watson@westsussex.gov.uk

Whittington, Derek (CON - Fontwell)
derek.whittington@westsussex.gov.uk

Wickremaratchi, Sujan (CON - Haywards Heath Town)
sujan.wickremaratchi@westsussex.gov.uk

POLITICAL COMPOSITION

CON: 46, UKIP: 10, LD: 8, LAB: 6, IND: 1

COMMITTEE CHAIRS

Audit: Mrs Morwen Millson

Pensions: Mr Michael Brown

Planning: Mrs Heidi Brunsdon

Western Isles S

Western Isles Council, Council Offices, Sandwick Road, Stornoway HS1 2BW

☎ 01851 703773 🖷 01851 705349 🖳 www.cne-siar.gov.uk

FACTS AND FIGURES

Parliamentary Constituencies: Na h-Eileanan an Iar
EU Constituencies: Scotland
Election Frequency: Elections are of whole council

PRINCIPAL OFFICERS

Chief Executive: Mr Malcolm Burr, Chief Executive, Council Offices, Sandwick Road, Stornoway HS1 2BW ☎ 0845 600 7090 ✉ m.burr@cne-siar.gov.uk

Senior Management: Mr Alasdair MacEachen, Head of Devolved Services, Council Offices, Sandwick Road, Stornoway HS1 2BW ☎ 01870 604999 ✉ amaceachen@cne-siar.gov.uk

Senior Management: Mrs Katherine MacKinnon, Head of Human Resources, Council Offices, Sandwick Road, Stornoway HS1 2BW ☎ ; 01851 822605 🖷 01851 706935 ✉ kmackinnon@cne-siar.gov.uk

Senior Management: Miss Lesley McDonald, Head of Executive Office, Council Offices, Sandwick Road, Stornoway HS1 2BW ☎ 01851 822604 🖷 ; 01851 705349 ✉ lmcdonald@cne-siar.gov.uk

Architect, Building / Property Services: Mr Iain Mackinnon, Director of Technical Services, Council Offices, Sandwick Road, Stornoway HS1 2BW ☎ 01851 822656 ✉ iain.mackinnon@cne-siar.gov.uk

Best Value: Ms Norma Morrison, Organisational Development, Council Offices, Sandwick Road, Stornoway HS1 2BW ☎ 01851 822614 ✉ norma.morrison@cne-siar.gov.uk

Building Control: Mr Keith Bray, Head of Development Services, Council Offices, Sandwick Road, Stornoway HS1 2BW ☎ 01851 822686 ✉ kbray@cne-siar.gov.uk

Civil Registration: Mr Malcolm Macpherson, Customer Services Manager, Council Offices, Sandwick Road, Stornoway HS1 2BW ✉ mmacpherson@cne-siar.gov.uk

PR / Communications: Mr Nigel Scott, Communications Officer, Council Offices, Sandwick Road, Stornoway HS1 2BW 🖷 01851 822622 ✉ nscott@cne-siar.gov.uk

Community Planning: Ms Gayle Findlay, Community Planning Co-ordinator, Council Offices, Sandwick Road, Stornoway HS1 2BW ☎ 01851 822617

Community Safety: Mr Frank Creighton, Policy Officer, Council Offices, Sandwick Road, Stornoway HS1 2BW ✉ fpcreighton@cne-siar.gov.uk

Computer Management: Mr Angus Macarthur, Head of IT, Council Offices, Sandwick Road, Stornoway HS1 2BW ☎ 01851 709573 🖷 01851 822635; 01851 822635 ✉ amacarthur@cne-siar.gov.uk

Consumer Protection and Trading Standards: Ms Marina MacSween, Trading Standards Officer, Council Offices, Sandwick Road, Stornoway HS1 2BW ☎ 01851 822694 ✉ mmacsween@cne-siar.gov.uk

Contracts: Mr Ian Cockburn, Procurement Manager, Council Offices, Sandwick Road, Stornoway HS1 2BW ☎ 01851 822639 🖷 01851 706686 ✉ icockburn@cne-siar.gov.uk

Customer Service: Mr Robert Emmott, Director of Finance & Corporate Resources, Council Offices, Sandwick Road, Stornoway HS1 2BW ☎ 01851 822628 ✉ remmott@cne-siar.gov.uk

Economic Development: Mr Calum Iain Maciver, Director of Development, Council Offices, Sandwick Road, Stornoway HS1 2BW ☎ 01851 822685 🖷 01851 705349 ✉ calum.maciver@cne-siar.gov.uk

E-Government: Mr Robert Emmott, Director of Finance & Corporate Resources, Council Offices, Sandwick Road, Stornoway HS1 2BW ☎ ; 01851 822628 ✉ remmott@cne-siar.gov.uk

Electoral Registration: Mr Derek Mackay, Head Democractic Services, Council Offices, Sandwick Road, Stornoway HS1 2BW ☎ 01851 822613 🖷 01852 705349 ✉ dmackay@cne-siar.gov.uk

Emergency Planning: Mr Andy MacDonald, Risk & Emergency Planning Manager, Council Offices, Sandwick Road, Stornoway HS1 2BW ☎ 01851 822612 🖷 01851 706935 ✉ andy-macdonald@cne-siar.gov.uk

Energy Management: Mr Calum MacKenzie, Head of Estates, Council Offices, Sandwick Road, Stornoway HS1 2BW ☎ 01851 822659 🖷 ; 01851 705349 ✉ calum.mackenzie@cne-siar.gov.uk

Environmental / Technical Services: Mr Iain Mackinnon, Director of Technical Services, Council Offices, Sandwick Road, Stornoway HS1 2BW ☎ 01851 822656 ✉ iain.mackinnon@cne-siar.gov.uk

Environmental Health: Mr Colm Fraser, Consumer & Environmental Health Services Manager, Council Offices, Sandwick Road, Stornoway HS1 2BW ☎ 01851 822688 ✉ cfraser@cne-siar.gov.uk

Estates, Property & Valuation: Mr Calum MacKenzie, Head of Estates, Council Offices, Sandwick Road, Stornoway HS1 2BW ☎ 01851 822659 🖷 01851 705349 ✉ calum.mackenzie@cne-siar.gov.uk

European Liaison: Miss Lesley McDonald, Head of Executive Office, Council Offices, Sandwick Road, Stornoway HS1 2BW ☎ 01851 822604 🖷 01851 705349 ✉ lmcdonald@cne-siar.gov.uk

Events Manager: Miss Lesley McDonald, Head of Executive Office, Council Offices, Sandwick Road, Stornoway HS1 2BW ☎ 01851 822604 🖷 01851 705349 ✉ lmcdonald@cne-siar.gov.uk

Facilities: Mr Calum MacKenzie, Head of Estates, Council Offices, Sandwick Road, Stornoway HS1 2BW ☎ 01851 822659 🖷 01851 705349 ✉ calum.mackenzie@cne-siar.gov.uk

Finance: Mr Robert Emmott, Director of Finance & Corporate Resources, Council Offices, Sandwick Road, Stornoway HS1 2BW ☎ 01851 822628 ✉ remmott@cne-siar.gov.uk

Fleet Management: Mr David Macleod, Head of Municipal Services, Council Offices, Sandwick Road, Stornoway HS1 2BW ☎ 01851 822663 🖷 01851 705349 ✉ david-macleod@cne-siar.gov.uk

Grounds Maintenance: Mr Iain Mackinnon, Director of Technical Services, Council Offices, Sandwick Road, Stornoway HS1 2BW ☎ 01851 822656 ✉ iain.mackinnon@cne-siar.gov.uk

Health and Safety: Mr Andy MacDonald, Risk & Emergency Planning Manager, Council Offices, Sandwick Road, Stornoway HS1 2BW ☎ 01851 822612 🖷 01851 706935 ✉ andy-macdonald@cne-siar.gov.uk

Highways: Mr Iain Mackinnon, Director of Technical Services, Council Offices, Sandwick Road, Stornoway HS1 2BW ☎ 01851 822656 ✉ iain.mackinnon@cne-siar.gov.uk

Legal: Miss Lesley McDonald, Head of Executive Office, Council Offices, Sandwick Road, Stornoway HS1 2BW ☎ 01851 822604 🖷 ; 01851 705349 ✉ lmcdonald@cne-siar.gov.uk

Leisure and Cultural Services: Ms Emma MacSween, Head of Social & Partnership Services, Council Offices, Sandwick Road, Stornoway HS1 2BW ☎ 01851 822706 🖷 01851 705349 ✉ emacsween@cne-siar.gov.uk

Licensing: Miss Lesley McDonald, Head of Executive Office, Council Offices, Sandwick Road, Stornoway HS1 2BW ☎ 01851 822604 🖷 ; 01851 705349 ✉ lmcdonald@cne-siar.gov.uk

Member Services: Miss Lesley McDonald, Head of Executive Office, Council Offices, Sandwick Road, Stornoway HS1 2BW ☎ 01851 822604 🖷 ; 01851 705349 ✉ lmcdonald@cne-siar.gov.uk

Parking: Mr Iain Mackinnon, Director of Technical Services, Council Offices, Sandwick Road, Stornoway HS1 2BW ☎ 01851 822656 ✉ iain.mackinnon@cne-siar.gov.uk

Personnel / HR: Mrs Katherine MacKinnon, Head of Human Resources, Council Offices, Sandwick Road, Stornoway HS1 2BW ☎ ; 01851 822605 🖷 01851 706935 ✉ kmackinnon@cne-siar.gov.uk

Planning: Mr Keith Bray, Head of Development Services, Council Offices, Sandwick Road, Stornoway HS1 2BW ☎ 01851 822686 ✉ kbray@cne-siar.gov.uk

Planning: Mr John Cunningham, Policy Development Officer, Council Offices, Sandwick Road, Stornoway HS1 2BW ☎ 01851 822693 🖷 01851 705349 ✉ jcunningham@cne-siar.gov.uk

Procurement: Mr Ian Cockburn, Procurement Manager, Council Offices, Sandwick Road, Stornoway HS1 2BW ☎ 01851 822639 🖷 01851 706686 ✉ icockburn@cne-siar.gov.uk

Public Libraries: Ms Trish Campbell-Botten, Manager - Culture & Information Services, Council Offices, Sandwick Road, Stornoway HS1 2BW ☎ 01851 822746 🖷 01851 705657 ✉ trish.campbell-botten@cne-siar.gov.uk

Recycling & Waste Minimisation: Mr David Macleod, Head of Municipal Services, Council Offices, Sandwick Road, Stornoway HS1 2BW ☎ 01851 822663 🖷 01851 705349 ✉ david-macleod@cne-siar.gov.uk

Regeneration: Mr Joe Macpee, Head of Economic Development, Council Offices, Sandwick Road, Stornoway HS1 2BW ☎ 01851 822687 ✉ jmacpee@cne-siar.gov.uk

Road Safety: Mr Donald Macrae, Principal Roads Maintenance Officer, Council Offices, Sandwick Road, Stornoway HS1 2BW ☎ 01851 822664

Staff Training: Mrs Katherine MacKinnon, Head of Human Resources, Council Offices, Sandwick Road, Stornoway HS1 2BW ☎ 01851 822605 🖷 01851 706935 ✉ kmackinnon@cne-siar.gov.uk

Staff Training: Miss Marina Macleod, Personnel Officer (Training), Council Offices, Sandwick Road, Stornoway HS1 2BW ☎ 01851 822607 🖷 01851 706935 ✉ marina.macleod@cne-siar.gov.uk

Sustainable Communities: Mr Calum Iain Maciver, Director of Development, Council Offices, Sandwick Road, Stornoway HS1 2BW ☎ 01851 822685 🖷 01851 705349 ✉ calum.maciver@cne-siar.gov.uk

Sustainable Development: Mr Calum Iain Maciver, Director of Development, Council Offices, Sandwick Road, Stornoway HS1 2BW ☎ 01851 822685 🖷 01851 705349 ✉ calum.maciver@cne-siar.gov.uk

Tourism: Mr Calum Iain Maciver, Director of Development, Council Offices, Sandwick Road, Stornoway HS1 2BW ☎ 01851 822685 🖷 01851 705349 ✉ calum.maciver@cne-siar.gov.uk

Traffic Management: Mr Iain Mackinnon, Director of Technical Services, Council Offices, Sandwick Road, Stornoway HS1 2BW ☎ 01851 822656 ✉ iain.mackinnon@cne-siar.gov.uk

Transport: Mr Iain Mackinnon, Director of Technical Services, Council Offices, Sandwick Road, Stornoway HS1 2BW ☎ 01851 822656 ✉ iain.mackinnon@cne-siar.gov.uk

Transport Planner: Mr Iain Mackinnon, Director of Technical Services, Council Offices, Sandwick Road, Stornoway HS1 2BW ☎ 01851 822656 ✉ iain.mackinnon@cne-siar.gov.uk

Waste Collection and Disposal: Mr Kenny John MacLeod, Head of Community Services, Council Offices, Sandwick Road, Stornoway HS1 2BW ☎ 01851 822663 ✉ kjmacleod@cne-siar.gov.uk

Waste Management: Mr Kenny John MacLeod, Head of Community Services, Council Offices, Sandwick Road, Stornoway HS1 2BW ☎ 01851 822663 ✉ kjmacleod@cne-siar.gov.uk

COUNCILLORS

***Convener* Macdonald**, Norman (IND - Sgir' Uige Agus Ceann A Tuath Nan Loch)
namacdonald@cne-siar.gov.uk

Leader of the Council **Campbell**, Angus (IND - Steornabhagh a Deas)
angus.campbell@cne-siar.gov.uk

Blaney, David (IND - Barraigh, Bhatersaigh, Eiriosgeigh agus Uibhist a Deas)
d.blaney@cne-siar.gov.uk

Campbell, Archie (LAB - Beinn na Faoghla Agus Uibhist A Tuath)
akcampbell@cne-siar.gov.uk

Crichton, Donald (IND - Loch A Tuath)
donald.crichton@cne-siar.gov.uk

Macdonald, Catherine (IND - Na Hearadh agus Ceann a Deas nan Loch)
c.macdonald@cne-siar.gov.uk

MacDonald Beaton, Neil (IND - Beinn na Faoghla Agus Uibhist A Tuath)
neil.beaton@cne-siar.gov.uk

Maciver, John (IND - Loch a Tuath)
johna.maciver@cne-siar.gov.uk

Mackay, Roddie (IND - Steornabhagh a Tuath)
roddie.mackay@cne-siar.gov.uk

Mackay, John (IND - An Taobh Siar agus Nis)
john.mackay@cne-siar.gov.uk

MacKenzie, Rae (SNP - Steornabhagh A Deas)
rae.mackenzie@cne-siar.gov.uk

Mackenzie, Iain (IND - Steornabhagh a Tuath)
iain.mackenzie@cne-siar.gov.uk

MacKinnon, Ronald (LAB - Barraigh, Bhatersaigh, Eiriosgeigh agus Uibhist a Deas)
ronald.mackinnon@cne-siar.gov.uk

MacLean MacAulay, Iain (IND - Steornabhagh a Tuath)
iainm.macaulay@cne-siar.gov.uk

Maclennan, Alistair (IND - An Taobh Siar agus Nis)
a.maclennan@cne-siar.gov.uk

Macleod, Norman (IND - Sgire an Rubha)
nmmacleod@cne-siar.gov.uk

MacLeod, Kenneth (SNP - An Taobh Siar agus Nis)
kennethmacleod@cne-siar.gov.uk

MacLeod, Cudig (IND - Sgir' Uige Agus Ceann A Tuath Nan Loch)
cudig.macleod@cne-siar.gov.uk

MacLeod, Alasdair (IND - Sgire An Rubha)
alasdair.macleod@cne-siar.gov.uk

MacRae, Donald (LAB - Na Hearadh Agus Ceann A Deas Nan Loch)
djmacrae@cne-siar.gov.uk

Manford, Donald (SNP - Barraigh, Bhatersaigh, Eiriosgeigh agus Uibhist a Deas)
dmanford@cne-siar.gov.uk

Mccormack, Angus (IND - Steornabhagh a Deas)
a.mccormack@cne-siar.gov.uk

Mclean, Philip (SNP - Na Hearadh agus Ceann a Deas nan Loch)
p.mclean@cne-siar.gov.uk

Morrison, Angus (IND - Sgir' Uige Agus Ceann A Tuath Nan Loch)
angus.morrison@cne-siar.gov.uk

Murray, Gordon (SNP - Steornabhagh a Tuath)
gordon.murray@cne-siar.gov.uk

Nicolson, Charlie (IND - Steornabhagh a Deas)
charlie.nicolson@cne-siar.gov.uk

Steele, Donnie (IND - Barraigh, Bhatarsaigh, Eiriosgaigh agus Uibhist a Deas)
donnie.steele@cne-siar.gov.uk

Stewart, Catriona (IND - Loch a Tuath)
catriona.stewart@cne-siar.gov.uk

Stewart, Zena (IND - Sgire An Rubha)
zena.stewart@cne-siar.gov.uk

Walker, Andrew (IND - Beinn na Faoghla Agus Uibhist A Tuath)
andrew.walker@cne-siar.gov.uk

POLITICAL COMPOSITION
IND: 22, SNP: 5, LAB: 3

COMMITTEE CHAIRS
Audit & Scrutiny: Mr Angus Mccormack

Education & Children's Services: Mrs Catriona Stewart

Westminster City L

Westminster City Council, Westminster City Hall, 64 Victoria Street, London SW1E 6QP
☎ 020 7641 6000 💻 www.westminster.gov.uk

FACTS AND FIGURES
Parliamentary Constituencies: Cities of London and Westminster, Westminster North
EU Constituencies: London
Election Frequency: Elections are of whole council

PRINCIPAL OFFICERS
Chief Executive: Mr Charlie Parker, Chief Executive, Westminster City Hall, 64 Victoria Street, London SW1E 6QP ☎ 020 7641 2358
✉ cparker@westminster.gov.uk

Senior Management: Ms Liz Bruce, Tri-Borough Executive Director - Adult Social Care, Town Hall, King Street, London W6 9JU ☎ 020 8753 5166 ✉ liz.bruce@lbhf.gov.uk

Senior Management: Mr Andrew Christie, Tri-Borough Executive Director - Children & Families, Town Hall, Hornton Street, London W8 7NX ☎ 020 8753 5002; 020 7361 2354; 020 7361 2229
✉ andrew.christie@rbkc.gov.uk

Senior Management: Ms Julia Corkey, Director - Policy, Performance & Communications, Westminster City Hall, 64 Victoria Street, London SW1E 6QP ☎ 020 7641 2354
✉ jcorkey@westminster.gov.uk

Senior Management: Mr Ben Denton, Executive Director - Growth, Planning & Housing, Westminster City Hall, 64 Victoria Street, London SW1E 6QP ☎ 020 7641 3025
✉ bdenton@westminster.gov.uk

Senior Management: Mr Stuart Love, Executive Director - City Management & Communities, Westminster City Hall, 64 Victoria Street, London SW1E 6QP ☎ 020 7641 7940
✉ slove@westminster.gov.uk

WESTMINSTER CITY

Access Officer / Social Services (Disability): Mr Richard Holden, Tri-Borough Head of Children With Disabilities, Westminster City Hall, 64 Victoria Street, London SW1E 6QP ☎ 020 7361 3751 🖱 richard.holden@rbkc.gov.uk

Access Officer / Social Services (Disability): Mr Malcolm Rose, Team Leader, Westminster City Hall, 64 Victoria Street, London SW1E 6QP ☎ 020 7641 6617 🖱 mrose@westminster.gov.uk

Architect, Building / Property Services: Mr Guy Slocombe, Director of Property, Westminster City Hall, 64 Victoria Street, London SW1E 6QP ☎ 020 7641 5465 🖱 gslocombe@westminster.gov.uk

Building Control: Mr Tony Fenton, District Surveyor, Westminster City Hall, 64 Victoria Street, London SW1E 6QP ☎ 020 7641 7048 🖱 tfenton@westminster.gov.uk

Building Control: Mr John Walker, Operational Director of Development Planning, Westminster City Hall, 64 Victoria Street, London SW1E 6QP ☎ 020 7641 2519 🖱 jwalker@westminster.gov.uk

Children / Youth Services: Ms Melissa Caslake, Director of Family Services, Westminster City Hall, 64 Victoria Street, London SW1E 6QP ☎ 020 7641 2253 🖱 mcaslake@westminster.gov.uk

Children / Youth Services: Mr Andrew Christie, Tri-Borough Executive Director - Children & Families, Westminster City Hall, 64 Victoria Street, London SW1E 6QP ☎ 020 8753 5002; 020 7361 2354; 020 7361 2229 🖱 andrew.christie@rbkc.gov.uk

Children / Youth Services: Mr Ian Heggs, Tri-Borough Director of Schools Commissioning, Westminster City Hall, 64 Victoria Street, London SW1E 6QP ☎ 020 7361 3332 🖱 ian.heggs@rbkc.gov.uk

Children / Youth Services: Ms Rachel Wright-Turner, Tri-Borough Director of Strategic Commissioning for Children & Families, Westminster City Hall, 64 Victoria Street, London SW1E 6QP 🖱 rachel.wright-turner@rbkc.gov.uk

Civil Registration: Ms Alison Cathcart, Registration & Nationality Superintendent Registrar, Westminster City Hall, 64 Victoria Street, London SW1E 6QP 🖱 acathcart@westminster.gov.uk

PR / Communications: Ms Julia Corkey, Director - Policy, Performance & Communications, Westminster City Hall, 64 Victoria Street, London SW1E 6QP ☎ 020 7641 2354 🖱 jcorkey@westminster.gov.uk

PR / Communications: Mr Cormac Smith, Senior Communications Advisor, Westminster City Hall, 64 Victoria Street, London SW1E 6QP

Community Planning: Mr Richard Barker, Director of Community Services, Westminster City Hall, 64 Victoria Street, London SW1E 6QP ☎ 020 7641 2693 🖱 rbarker@westminster.gov.uk

Community Planning: Mrs Lisa Fairmaner, Spatial Planning Manager, Westminster City Hall, 64 Victoria Street, London SW1E 6QP ☎ 020 7641 4240 🖱 lfairmaner@westminster.gov.uk

Community Planning: Mr Stuart Reilly, Head of Major Projects, Westminster City Hall, 64 Victoria Street, London SW1E 6QP ☎ 020 7641 5949 🖱 sreilly@westminster.gov.uk

Community Planning: Mr Barry Smith, Operational Director of City Planning, Westminster City Hall, 64 Victoria Street, London SW1E 6QP ☎ 020 7641 2923 🖱 bsmith@westminster.gov.uk

Community Planning: Mr Martin Whittles, Head of Public Realm, Westminster City Hall, 64 Victoria Street, London SW1E 6QP ☎ 020 7641 3040 🖱 mwhittles@westminster.gov.uk

Community Safety: Mr Mick Smith, Head of Community Safety, Westminster City Hall, 64 Victoria Street, London SW1E 6QP ☎ 020 7641 4252 🖱 msmith@westminster.gov.uk

Computer Management: Mr Ed Garcez, Tri-Borough Chief Information Officer, Town Hall, King Street, London W6 9JU ☎ 020 8753 2900 🖱 ed.garcez@lbhf.gov.uk

Computer Management: Mr Ben Goward, Head of Service Delivery, Westminster City Hall, 64 Victoria Street, London SW1E 6QP ☎ 020 7641 5504 🖱 bgoward@westminster.gov.uk

Computer Management: Ms Fatima Zohra, Corporate Information Manager, Westminster City Hall, 64 Victoria Street, London SW1E 6QP ☎ 020 7641 8578 🖱 fzohra@westminster.gov.uk

Consumer Protection and Trading Standards: Ms Sue Jones, Service Manager of Trading Standards, Westminster City Hall, 64 Victoria Street, London SW1E 6QP ☎ 020 7641 2721 🖱 sjones@westminster.gov.uk

Contracts: Mr Anthony Oliver, Chief Procurement Officer, Westminster City Hall, 64 Victoria Street, London SW1E 6QP ☎ 020 7641 2608 🖱 aoliver@westminster.gov.uk

Customer Service: Ms Julia Corkey, Director - Policy, Performance & Communications, Westminster City Hall, 64 Victoria Street, London SW1E 6QP ☎ 020 7641 2354 🖱 jcorkey@westminster.gov.uk

Economic Development: Mr Steve Carr, Acting Head of Economic Development, Westminster City Hall, 64 Victoria Street, London SW1E 6QP ☎ 020 7641 6551 🖱 scarr@westminster.gov.uk

Economic Development: Mr Ben Denton, Executive Director - Growth, Planning & Housing, Westminster City Hall, 64 Victoria Street, London SW1E 6QP ☎ 020 7641 3025 🖱 bdenton@westminster.gov.uk

Economic Development: Mr Stuart Reilly, Head of Major Projects, Westminster City Hall, 64 Victoria Street, London SW1E 6QP ☎ 020 7641 5949 🖱 sreilly@westminster.gov.uk

Economic Development: Mr Barry Smith, Operational Director of City Planning, Westminster City Hall, 64 Victoria Street, London SW1E 6QP ☎ 020 7641 2923 🖱 bsmith@westminster.gov.uk

Education: Ms Melissa Caslake, Director of Family Services, Westminster City Hall, 64 Victoria Street, London SW1E 6QP ☎ 020 7641 2253 🖱 mcaslake@westminster.gov.uk

Education: Mr Ian Heggs, Tri-Borough Director of Schools Commissioning, Town Hall, Hornton Street, London W8 7NX ☎ 020 7361 3332 ✉ ian.heggs@rbkc.gov.uk

Electoral Registration: Mr Martin Pyroyiannos, Electoral Services, Local Land Charges of Legal Secretariat & Business Support, Westminster City Hall, 64 Victoria Street, London SW1E 6QP ☎ 020 7641 2732 ✉ mpyroyiannos@westminster.gov.uk

Emergency Planning: Mr Mick Smith, Head of Community Safety, Westminster City Hall, 64 Victoria Street, London SW1E 6QP ☎ 020 7641 4252 ✉ msmith@westminster.gov.uk

Energy Management: Ms Debbie Morris, Head of Facilities Management, Town Hall, King Street, London W6 9JU ☎ 020 7361 3189 ✉ debbiej.morris@rbkc.gov.uk

Environmental Health: Mr Steve Harrison, Director - Public Protection & Licensing, Westminster City Hall, 64 Victoria Street, London SW1E 6QP ☎ 020 7641 8505 ✉ sharrison@westminster.gov.uk

Environmental Health: Mr Andrew Ralph, Service Manager of Noise & Licensing Enforcement, Westminster City Hall, 64 Victoria Street, London SW1E 6QP ☎ 020 7641 2706 ✉ aralph@westminster.gov.uk

Estates, Property & Valuation: Mr Guy Slocombe, Director of Property, Westminster City Hall, 64 Victoria Street, London SW1E 6QP ☎ 020 7641 5465 ✉ gslocombe@westminster.gov.uk

Events Manager: Ms Levana Deutschman, Commissioning Manager of Events, Filming & Contingencies, Westminster City Hall, 64 Victoria Street, London SW1E 6QP ☎ 020 7641 5967 ✉ ldeutschman@westminster.gov.uk

Events Manager: Mr Tim Owen, Commissioner of Events, Filming & Contingencies, Westminster City Hall, 64 Victoria Street, London SW1E 6QP ☎ 020 7641 5929 ✉ towen@westminster.gov.uk

Facilities: Ms Debbie Morris, Head of Facilities Management, Town Hall, King Street, London W6 9JU ☎ 020 7361 3189 ✉ debbiej.morris@rbkc.gov.uk

Finance: Mr Peter Carpenter, Assistant City Treasurer, Westminster City Hall, 64 Victoria Street, London SW1E 6QP ☎ 020 7641 2832 ✉ pcarpenter@westminster.gov.uk

Finance: Mr David Hodgkinson, Assistant City Treasurer, Westminster City Hall, 64 Victoria Street, London SW1E 6QP ☎ 020 7641 6000 ✉ dhodgkinson@westminster.gov.uk

Finance: Mr Jonathan Hunt, Tri-Borough Director of Pensions & Treasury, Westminster City Hall, 64 Victoria Street, London SW1E 6QP ☎ 020 7641 1804 ✉ jonathan.hunt@westminster.gov.uk

Finance: Mr Dave McNamara, Head of Finance for Children, Westminster City Hall, 64 Victoria Street, London SW1E 6QP ☎ 020 8753 3404 ✉ david.mcnamara@lbhf.gov.uk

Treasury: Mr Steve Mair, City Treasurer, Westminster City Hall, 64 Victoria Street, London SW1E 6QP ☎ 020 7641 2831 ✉ smair@westminster.gov.uk

Grounds Maintenance: Mr Mark Banks, Head of Waste & Parks, Westminster City Hall, 64 Victoria Street, London SW1E 6QP ☎ 020 7641 3369 ✉ mbanks@westminster.gov.uk

Health and Safety: Mr James Armitage, Service Manager of Food, Health & Safety, Westminster City Hall, 64 Victoria Street, London SW1E 6QP ☎ 020 7641 3076 ✉ jarmitage@westminster.gov.uk

Highways: Mr Sean Dwyer, Highways Planning Manager, Westminster City Hall, 64 Victoria Street, London SW1E 6QP ☎ 020 7641 3326 ✉ sdwyer@westminster.gov.uk

Highways: Ms Sally Keiller, Head of Contracts (Highways, Infrastructure & Public Realm), Westminster City Hall, 64 Victoria Street, London SW1E 6QP ☎ 020 7641 2677 ✉ skeiller@westminster.gov.uk

Housing: Mr Fergus Coleman, Housing Supply Commissioning Manager, Westminster City Hall, 64 Victoria Street, London SW1E 6QP ☎ 020 7641 3211 ✉ fcoleman@westminster.gov.uk

Housing: Mr Ben Denton, Executive Director - Growth, Planning & Housing, Westminster City Hall, 64 Victoria Street, London SW1E 6QP ☎ 020 7641 3025 ✉ bdenton@westminster.gov.uk

Housing: Mr Dick Johnson, Head of Housing Finance, Westminster City Hall, 64 Victoria Street, London SW1E 6QP ☎ 020 7641 3029 ✉ djohnson1@westminster.gov.uk

Housing: Ms Victoria Midwinter, Head of Housing Needs, Westminster City Hall, 64 Victoria Street, London SW1E 6QP ☎ 020 7641 2029 ✉ vmidwinter@westminster.gov.uk

Housing: Mr Gregory Roberts, Head of Supporting People & Homelessness Commissioning, Westminster City Hall, 64 Victoria Street, London SW1E 6QP ☎ 020 7641 2834 ✉ groberts@westminster.gov.uk

Legal: Mr Gary Blackwell, Head of Litigation, Westminster City Hall, 64 Victoria Street, London SW1E 6QP ☎ 020 7641 2718 ✉ gblackwell@westminster.gov.uk

Legal: Ms Rhian Davies, Corporate Lawyer, Westminster City Hall, 64 Victoria Street, London SW1E 6QP ☎ 020 7641 2729 ✉ rdavies@westminster.gov.uk

Legal: Mr Peter Nixon, Corporate Lawyer, Westminster City Hall, 64 Victoria Street, London SW1E 6QP ☎ 020 7641 2715 ✉ pnixon@westminster.gov.uk

Legal: Mr Barry Panto, Advocacy & Advice, Westminster City Hall, 64 Victoria Street, London SW1E 6QP ☎ 020 7641 2712 ✉ bpanto@westminster.gov.uk

Legal: Mrs Tasnim Shawkat, Director of Law, Town Hall, Hornton Street, London W8 7NX ☎ 020 7361 2257 ✉ tasnim.shawkat@rbkc.gov.uk

Leisure and Cultural Services: Mr Richard Barker, Director of Community Services, Westminster City Hall, 64 Victoria Street, London SW1E 6QP ☎ 020 7641 2693 ✉ rbarker@westminster.gov.uk

Leisure and Cultural Services: Mr Andrew Durrant, Head of Westminster Sports Unit, Westminster City Hall, 64 Victoria Street, London SW1E 6QP ☎ 020 7641 5885 ✉ adurrant@westminster.gov.uk

Licensing: Ms Deirdre Hayes, Services Manager EH Consultation & Licensing, Westminster City Hall, 64 Victoria Street, London SW1E 6QP ☎ 020 7641 3189 ✉ dhayes@westminster.gov.uk

Licensing: Mr Andrew Ralph, Service Manager of Noise & Licensing Enforcement, Westminster City Hall, 64 Victoria Street, London SW1E 6QP ☎ 020 7641 2706 ✉ aralph@westminster.gov.uk

Licensing: Mr Chris Wroe, Licensing Policy & Strategy Manager, Westminster City Hall, 64 Victoria Street, London SW1E 6QP ☎ 020 7641 5903 ✉ cwroe@westminster.gov.uk

Lottery Funding, Charity and Voluntary: Mr Richard Cressey, Senior Policy Officer, Westminster City Hall, 64 Victoria Street, London SW1E 6QP ☎ 020 7641 3403 ✉ rcressey@westminster.gov.uk

Member Services: Mr Doug Precey, Head of Cabinet Secretariat, Westminster City Hall, 64 Victoria Street, London SW1E 6QP ☎ 020 7641 5614 ✉ dprecey@westminster.gov.uk

Partnerships: Mr Richard Cressey, Senior Policy Officer, Westminster City Hall, 64 Victoria Street, London SW1E 6QP ☎ 020 7641 3403 ✉ rcressey@westminster.gov.uk

Personnel / HR: Ms Carolyn Beech, Acting Director of HR, Westminster City Hall, 64 Victoria Street, London SW1E 6QP ☎ 020 7641 3221 ✉ cbeech@westminster.gov.uk

Personnel / HR: Ms Julie Marks, Senior HR Manager, Westminster City Hall, 64 Victoria Street, London SW1E 6QP ☎ 020 7641 2786 ✉ mlow@westminster.gov.uk

Personnel / HR: Ms Jo Meagher, Head of Business Partnering, Westminster City Hall, 64 Victoria Street, London SW1E 6QP ☎ 020 7641 5987 ✉ jmeagher@westminster.gov.uk

Personnel / HR: Mr Trevor Webster, Senior HR Manager, Westminster City Hall, 64 Victoria Street, London SW1E 6QP ☎ 020 7641 2803 ✉ twebster@westminster.gov.uk

Planning: Mr Graham King, Head of Strategic Planning & Transport, Westminster City Hall, 64 Victoria Street, London SW1E 6QP ☎ 020 7641 2749 ✉ gking@westminster.gov.uk

Planning: Mr John Walker, Operational Director of Development Planning, Westminster City Hall, 64 Victoria Street, London SW1E 6QP ☎ 020 7641 2519 ✉ jwalker@westminster.gov.uk

Procurement: Mr Sagar Barua, Supplier Relationship Officer, Westminster City Hall, 64 Victoria Street, London SW1E 6QP ☎ 020 7641 2962 ✉ sbarua@westminster.gov.uk

Procurement: Mr Anthony Oliver, Chief Procurement Officer, Westminster City Hall, 64 Victoria Street, London SW1E 6QP ☎ 020 7641 2608 ✉ aoliver@westminster.gov.uk

Public Libraries: Mr Mike Clarke, Tri-Borough Director of Libraries & Archives, Town Hall, Hornton Street, London W8 7NX ☎ 020 7641 2199 ✉ mclarke1@westminster.gov.uk

Recycling & Waste Minimisation: Mr Mark Banks, Head of Waste & Parks, 3rd Floor, Westminster City Hall, Victoria Street, London SW1E 6QP ☎ 020 7641 3369 ✉ mbanks@westminster.gov.uk

Regeneration: Mr Ben Denton, Executive Director - Growth, Planning & Housing, Westminster City Hall, 64 Victoria Street, London SW1E 6QP ☎ 020 7641 3025 ✉ bdenton@westminster.gov.uk

Road Safety: Mr Peter Wilson, Commissioning Officer - Road Safety, Westminster City Hall, 64 Victoria Street, London SW1E 6QP ☎ 020 7641 2016 ✉ pwilson@westminster.gov.uk

Social Services: Ms Stella Baillie, Tri-Borough Director of Integrated Adult Social Care, Town Hall, Hornton Street, London W8 7NX ☎ 020 7361 2398 ✉ stella.baillie@rbkc.gov.uk

Social Services: Ms Natasha Bishopp, Head of Family Recovery, Westminster City Hall, 64 Victoria Street, London SW1E 6QP ☎ 020 7641 4578 () ✉ nbishopp@westminster.gov.uk

Social Services: Ms Gaynor Driscoll, Joint Commissioning Manager of Sexual Health, Westminster City Hall, 64 Victoria Street, London SW1E 6QP ☎ 020 7641 4000 ✉ gdriscoll@westminster.gov.uk

Social Services: Ms Rachel Wright-Turner, Tri-Borough Director of Strategic Commissioning for Children & Families, Westminster City Hall, 64 Victoria Street, London SW1E 6QP ✉ rachel.wright-turner@rbkc.gov.uk

Social Services (Adult): Ms Stella Baillie, Tri-Borough Director of Integrated Adult Social Care, Town Hall, Hornton Street, London W8 7NX ☎ 020 7361 2398 ✉ stella.baillie@rbkc.gov.uk

Social Services (Adult): Ms Helen Banham, Service Manager for Safeguarding Adults, Westminster City Hall, 64 Victoria Street, London SW1E 6QP ☎ 020 7641 4196 ✉ hbanham@westminster.gov.uk

Social Services (Adult): Ms Liz Bruce, Tri-Borough Executive Director - Adult Social Care, Town Hall, King Street, London W6 9JU ☎ 020 8753 5166 ✉ liz.bruce@lbhf.gov.uk

Social Services (Adult): Ms Mary Dalton, Head of Joint Commissioning for LD, Carers & Transition, Westminster City Hall, 64 Victoria Street, London SW1E 6QP ☎ 020 7641 6615 ✉ mdalton@westminster.gov.uk

Social Services (Adult): Ms Selina Douglas, Director of Strategic Commissioning (Adults), Westminster City Hall, 64 Victoria Street, London SW1E 6QP ☎ 020 7641 3467 ✉ sdouglas@westminster.gov.uk

Social Services (Children): Ms Melissa Caslake, Director of Family Services, Westminster City Hall, 64 Victoria Street, London SW1E 6QP ☎ 020 7641 2253 ✉ mcaslake@westminster.gov.uk

Social Services (Children): Mr Andrew Christie, Tri-Borough Executive Director - Children & Families, Town Hall, Hornton Street, London W8 7NX ☎ 020 8753 5002; 020 7361 2354; 020 7361 2229 ✉ andrew.christie@rbkc.gov.uk

Social Services (Children): Ms H Farrell, Head of Child Protection, Westminster City Hall, 64 Victoria Street, London SW1E 6QP ☎ 020 7641 5341 ✉ hfarrell@westminster.gov.uk

Social Services (Children): Mr Glen Peache, Head of Looked After Children & Care Leavers, Westminster City Hall, 64 Victoria Street, London SW1E 6QP ☎ 020 7361 3317 ✉ glen.peache@rbkc.gov.uk

Social Services (Children): Ms Jayne Vertkin, Head of Early Intervention, Westminster City Hall, 64 Victoria Street, London SW1E 6QP ☎ 020 7641 5745 ✉ jvertkin@westminster.gov.uk

Staff Training: Ms Carolyn Beech, Acting Director of HR, Westminster City Hall, 64 Victoria Street, London SW1E 6QP ☎ 020 7641 3221 ✉ cbeech@westminster.gov.uk

Street Scene: Mr Martin Whittles, Head of Public Realm, Westminster City Hall, 64 Victoria Street, London SW1E 6QP ☎ 020 7641 3040 ✉ mwhittles@westminster.gov.uk

Sustainable Communities: Mr Stuart Love, Executive Director - City Management & Communities, Westminster City Hall, 64 Victoria Street, London SW1E 6QP ☎ 020 7641 7940 ✉ slove@westminster.gov.uk

Town Centre: Mr Stuart Love, Executive Director - City Management & Communities, Westminster City Hall, 64 Victoria Street, London SW1E 6QP ☎ 020 7641 7940 ✉ slove@westminster.gov.uk

Traffic Management: Mr Martin Low, City Commissioner of Transportation, Westminster City Hall, Victoria Street, London SW1E 6QP ☎ 020 7641 1981 ✉ mlow@westminster.gov.uk

Transport: Mr Martin Low, City Commissioner of Transportation, Westminster City Hall, Victoria Street, London SW1E 6QP ☎ 020 7641 1981 ✉ mlow@westminster.gov.uk

Transport: Mr John Taylor, Service Manager of Transportation Projects, Westminster City Hall, 64 Victoria Street, London SW1E 6QP ☎ 020 7641 2943 ✉ jtaylor@westminster.gov.uk

Transport: Mr David Yeoell, Assistant City Commissioner of Transportation, Westminster City Hall, 64 Victoria Street, London SW1E 6QP ☎ 020 7641 2622 ✉ dyeoell@westminster.gov.uk

Transport Planner: Mr Graham King, Head of Strategic Planning & Transport, Westminster City Hall, 64 Victoria Street, London SW1E 6QP ☎ 020 7641 2749 ✉ gking@westminster.gov.uk

Transport Planner: Mr Martin Low, City Commissioner of Transportation, Westminster City Hall, Victoria Street, London SW1E 6QP ☎ 020 7641 1981 ✉ mlow@westminster.gov.uk

Transport Planner: Mr David Yeoell, Assistant City Commissioner of Transportation, Westminster City Hall, 64 Victoria Street, London SW1E 6QP ☎ 020 7641 2622 ✉ dyeoell@westminster.gov.uk

Waste Collection and Disposal: Mr Mark Banks, Head of Waste & Parks, Westminster City Hall, 64 Victoria Street, London SW1E 6QP ☎ 020 7641 3369 ✉ mbanks@westminster.gov.uk

Waste Management: Mr Mark Banks, Head of Waste & Parks, Westminster City Hall, 64 Victoria Street, London SW1E 6QP ☎ 020 7641 3369 ✉ mbanks@westminster.gov.uk

COUNCILLORS

***Leader of the Council* Roe**, Philippa (CON - Knightsbridge and Belgravia)

***Deputy Leader of the Council* Davis**, Robert (CON - Lancaster Gate)

Acton, Heather (CON - Hyde Park)
hacton@westminster.gov.uk

Adams, Ian (CON - Little Venice)
iadams@westminster.gov.uk

Aiken, Nicola (CON - Warwick)

Arzymanow, Barbara (CON - Little Venice)
barzymanow@westminster.gov.uk

Astaire, Daniel (CON - Regent's Park)

Beddoe, Richard (CON - Bryanston and Dorset Square)
rbeddoe@westminster.gov.uk

Begum, Rita (LAB - Maida Vale)
rbegum2@westminster.gov.uk

Boothroyd, David (LAB - Westbourne)
dboothroyd@westminster.gov.uk

Bott, Iain (CON - Marylebone High Street)

Burbridge, Susie (CON - Lancaster Gate)
sburbridge@westminster.gov.uk

Bush, Ruth (LAB - Harrow Road)
rbush@westminster.gov.uk

Caplan, Melvyn (CON - Little Venice)

Chalkley, Danny (CON - Vincent Square)
dchalkley@westminster.gov.uk

Church, Paul (CON - West End)
pchurch@westminster.gov.uk

Connell, Brian (CON - Bayswater)
bconnell@westminster.gov.uk

Cox, Antonia (CON - Hyde Park)

Crockett, Thomas (CON - Maida Vale)
tcrockett@westminster.gov.uk

Cuthbertson, Peter (CON - Tachbrook)
pcuthbertson@westminster.gov.uk

Devenish, Antony (CON - Knightsbridge and Belgravia)
tdevenish@westminster.gov.uk

WESTMINSTER CITY

Dimoldenberg, Paul (LAB - Queen's Park)

Evans, Nicholas (CON - Tachbrook)
nevans@westminster.gov.uk

Flight, Christabel (CON - Warwick)
cflight@westminster.gov.uk

Floru, Jean-Paul (CON - Hyde Park)
jfloru@westminster.gov.uk

Freeman, Peter (CON - Abbey Road)
pfreeman@westminster.gov.uk

Gassanly, Murad (LAB - Churchill)
mgassanly@westminster.gov.uk

Glanz, Jonathan (CON - West End)

Grahame, Barbara (LAB - Church Street)
bgrahame@westminster.gov.uk

Hall, Lindsey (CON - Abbey Road)
lhall@westminster.gov.uk

Harvey, David (CON - Vincent Square)
davidharvey@westminster.gov.uk

Harvey, Angela (CON - Tachbrook)
angelaharvery@westminster.gov.uk

Holloway, Richard (CON - Bayswater)
rholloway@westminster.gov.uk

Hug, Adam (LAB - Westbourne)
ahug@westminster.gov.uk

Hyams, Louise (CON - St James's)
lhyams@westminster.gov.uk

McAllister, Patricia (LAB - Queen's Park)
pmcallister@westminster.gov.uk

McKie, Guthrie (LAB - Harrow Road)
gmckie@westminster.gov.uk

Mitchell, Tim (CON - St James's)
tmitchell@westminster.gov.uk

Mohammed, Adnan (CON - Bryanston and Dorset Square)
amohammed@westminster.gov.uk

Mohindra, Gotz (CON - Regent's Park)
gmohindra@westminster.gov.uk

Prendergast, Jan (CON - Maida Vale)
jprendergast@westminster.gov.uk

Qureshi, Papya (LAB - Westbourne)
pqureshi1@westminster.gov.uk

Rahuja, Suhail (CON - Bayswater)
srahuja@westminster.gov.uk

Rampulla, Vincent (LAB - Church Street)
vrampulla@westminster.gov.uk

Rigby, Robert (CON - Regent's Park)
rrigby@westminster.gov.uk

Robathan, Rachael (CON - Knightsbridge and Belgravia)
rrobathan@westminster.gov.uk

Roberts, Glenys (CON - West End)
groberts@westminster.gov.uk

Roca, Tim (LAB - Harrow Road)

Rowley, Ian (CON - Marylebone High Street)
irowley@westminster.gov.uk

Scarborough, Karen (CON - Marylebone High Street)
kscarborough@westminster.gov.uk

Smith, Andrew (CON - Lancaster Gate)
asmith@westminster.gov.uk

Summers, Steven (CON - Vincent Square)
stevesummers@westminster.gov.uk

Talukder, Shamim (LAB - Churchill)
stalukder@westminster.gov.uk

Taylor, Barrie (LAB - Queen's Park)
btaylor@westminster.gov.uk

Thomson, Cameron (CON - St James's)
cthomson@westminster.gov.uk

Toki, Aziz (LAB - Church Street)
atoki@westminster.gov.uk

Warner, Judith (CON - Abbey Road)
judithwarner@westminster.gov.uk

Wilkinson, Jacqui (CON - Warwick)

Williams, Jason (LAB - Churchill)
jwilliams@westminster.gov.uk

POLITICAL COMPOSITION
CON: 43, LAB: 16

COMMITTEE CHAIRS
Adults, Health & Public Protection: Mr David Harvey

Audit & Performance: Mr Jonathan Glanz

Health & Wellbeing: Ms Rachael Robathan

Licensing: Mrs Nicola Aiken

Pensions: Mr Suhail Rahuja

Weymouth & Portland D

Weymouth & Portland Borough Council, Council Offices, North Quay, Weymouth DT4 8TA
☎ 01305 838000 🖷 01305 760971 ✉ chiefexecutive@weymouth.gov.uk
💻 www.weymouth.gov.uk

FACTS AND FIGURES
Parliamentary Constituencies: Dorset South
EU Constituencies: South East
Election Frequency: Elections are by thirds

PRINCIPAL OFFICERS
Chief Executive: Mr Matt Prosser, Chief Executive, Council Offices, North Quay, Weymouth DT4 8TA ☎ 01305 251010 ✉ d.clarke@weymouth.gov.uk

Assistant Chief Executive: Mr Stuart Caundle, Assistant Chief Executive, South Walks House, South Walks Road, Dorchester DT1 1UZ ☎ 01258 484010 ✉ scaundle@north-dorset.co.uk

Senior Management: Mr Martin Hamilton, Strategic Director, South Walks House, South Walks Road, Dorchester DT1 1UZ ☎ 01305 838086 ✉ m.hamilton@westdorset-weymouth.gov.uk

Senior Management: Mr Stephen Hill, Strategic Director, South Walks House, South Walks Road, Dorchester DT1 1UZ ☎ 01258 484034 shill@north-dorset.gov.uk

Senior Management: Mr Jason Vaughan, Strategic Director & S151 Officer, Council Offices, North Quay, Weymouth DT4 8TA ☎ 01305 838233; 01305 251010 j.vaughan@westdorset-weymouth.gov.uk

Architect, Building / Property Services: Mr David Brown, Head of Assets & Infrastructure, South Walks House, South Walks Road, Dorchester DT1 1UZ ☎ 01305 252297 d.brown@westdorset-weymouth.gov.uk

Best Value: Ms Julie Strange, Head of Financial Services, Council Offices, North Quay, Weymouth DT4 8TA ☎ 01305 838252; 01305 251010 j.strange@westdorset-weymouth.gov.uk

Building Control: Mr David Potter, Building Control Manager, South Walks House, South Walks Road, Dorchester DT1 1UZ ☎ 01305 252258 d.potter@westdorset-weymouth.gov.uk

PR / Communications: Ms Penny Mell, Head of Business Improvement, South Walks House, South Walks Road, Dorchester DT1 1UZ ☎ 01305 838371 p.mell@westdorset-weymouth.gov.uk

Community Planning: Ms Hilary Jordan, Head of Planning, Community & Policy Development, Stratton House, 58-60 High West Street, Dorchester DT1 1UZ ☎ 01305 252303 h.jordan@westdorset-weymouth.gov.uk

Community Safety: Mr Graham Duggan, Head of Community Protection, Council Offices, North Quay, Weymouth DT4 8TA ☎ 01305 252285; 01305 251010 g.duggan@westdorset-weymouth.gov.uk

Computer Management: Ms Penny Mell, Head of Business Improvement, South Walks House, South Walks Road, Dorchester DT1 1UZ ☎ 01305 838371 p.mell@westdorset-weymouth.gov.uk

Customer Service: Ms Penny Mell, Head of Business Improvement, South Walks House, South Walks Road, Dorchester DT1 1UZ ☎ 01305 838371 p.mell@westdorset-weymouth.gov.uk

Economic Development: Mr Simon King, Senior Economic Regeneration Officer, Council Offices, North Quay, Weymouth DT4 8TA ☎ 01305 838515 s.king@westdorset-weymouth.gov.uk

Electoral Registration: Ms Sue Bonham-Lovett, Electoral Services Manager, Council Offices, North Quay, Weymouth DT4 8TA ☎ 01305 838477; 01305 251010 🖷 01305 838289 s.bonham-lovett@westdorset-weymouth.gov.uk

Emergency Planning: Mr Grant Armfield, Emergency Planning Officer, Council Offices, North Quay, Weymouth DT4 8TA ☎ 01305 838213 🖷 01305 838317 grantarmfield@weymouth.gov.uk

Energy Management: Mr Bob Savage, Senior Building Services Engineer, Council Offices, North Quay, Weymouth DT4 8TA ☎ 01305 838318 🖷 01305 838469 bobsavage@weymouth.gov.uk

Environmental / Technical Services: Mr David Brown, Head of Assets & Infrastructure, South Walks House, South Walks Road, Dorchester DT1 1UZ ☎ 01305 252297 d.brown@westdorset-weymouth.gov.uk

Environmental Health: Mr Graham Duggan, Head of Community Protection, Council Offices, North Quay, Weymouth DT4 8TA ☎ 01305 252285; 01305 251010 g.duggan@westdorset-weymouth.gov.uk

Estates, Property & Valuation: Mr Greg Northcote, Estates Manager, Council Offices, North Quay, Weymouth DT4 8TA ☎ 01305 838268 g.northcote@westdorset-weymouth.gov.uk

Events Manager: Mr Nick Thornley, Head of Economy, Leisure & Tourism, Council Offices, North Quay, Weymouth DT4 8TA ☎ 01305 252474; 01305 251010 n.thornley@westdorset-weymouth.gov.uk

Finance: Mr Jason Vaughan, Strategic Director & S151 Officer, Council Offices, North Quay, Weymouth DT4 8TA ☎ 01305 838233; 01305 251010 j.vaughan@westdorset-weymouth.gov.uk

Fleet Management: Ms Sally-Ann Arden-Nixon, Fleet Transport Co-ordinator, Council Offices, North Quay, Weymouth DT4 8TA ☎ 01305 838447 sa.arden-nixon@westdorset-weymouth.gov.uk

Health and Safety: Mr Richard Noakes, Health, Safety & Welfare Officer, Council Offices, North Quay, Weymouth DT4 8TA ☎ 01305 838356 r.noakes@westdorset-weymouth.gov.uk

Home Energy Conservation: Mr Clive Milone, Head of Housing, Council Offices, North Quay, Weymouth DT4 8TA ☎ 01305 252313 c.milone@westdorset-weymouth.gov.uk

Housing: Mr Chris Branch, Housing Solutions Manager, Council Offices, North Quay, Weymouth DT4 8TA ☎ 01305 838460 c.branch@westdorset-weymouth.gov.uk

Housing Maintenance: Mr Geoff Joy, Housing Improvement Manager, Council Offices, North Quay, Weymouth DT4 8TA ☎ 01305 252286 g.joy@westdorset-weymouth.gov.uk

Legal: Ms Lara Altree, Legal Services Manager (Planning & Environment), Council Offices, North Quay, Weymouth DT4 8TA ☎ 01305 838219 l.altree@westdorset-weymouth.gov.uk

Leisure and Cultural Services: Mr Nick Thornley, Head of Economy, Leisure & Tourism, Council Offices, North Quay, Weymouth DT4 8TA ☎ 01305 252474; 01305 251010 n.thornley@westdorset-weymouth.gov.uk

Licensing: Ms Sue Moore, Business Licensing Manager, Council Offices, North Quay, Weymouth DT4 8TA ☎ 01305 838205; 01305 252474 s.moore@westdorset-weymouth.gov.uk

Lottery Funding, Charity and Voluntary: Ms Jane Nicklen, Community Planning & Development Manager, Council Offices, North Quay, Weymouth DT4 8TA ☎ 01305 252358 j.nicklen@westdorset-weymouth.gov.uk

WEYMOUTH & PORTLAND

Member Services: Ms Susan Carne, Democratic Services Manager, Council Offices, North Quay, Weymouth DT4 8TA ☎ 01305 252216 ✉ s.carne@westdorset-weymouth.gov.uk

Parking: Mr Jack Creeber, Parking & Transport Manager, Council Offices, North Quay, Weymouth DT4 8TA ☎ 01305 838349 ✉ j.creeber@westdorset-weymouth.gov.uk

Partnerships: Ms Caron Starkey, Business Change Manager, Council Offices, North Quay, Weymouth DT4 8TA ☎ 01305 838277 ✉ c.starkey@westdorset-weymouth.gov.uk

Personnel / HR: Mr Steve Barrett, HR Manager - Policy & Development, Council Offices, North Quay, Weymouth DT4 8TA ☎ 01305 838319 ✉ s.barrett@westdorset-weymouth.gov.uk

Planning: Ms Jean Marshall, Head of Planning, Development Management & Building Control, Council Offices, North Quay, Weymouth DT4 8TA ☎ 01305 252230 ✉ j.marshall@westdorset-weymouth.gov.uk

Procurement: Ms Julia Long, Procurement Officer, Council Offices, North Quay, Weymouth DT4 8TA ☎ 01305 838543 ✉ j.long@westdorset-weymouth.gov.uk

Regeneration: Mr Simon King, Senior Economic Regeneration Officer, Council Offices, North Quay, Weymouth DT4 8TA ☎ 01305 838515 ✉ s.king@westdorset-weymouth.gov.uk

Sustainable Development: Ms Jean Marshall, Head of Planning, Development Management & Building Control, Council Offices, North Quay, Weymouth DT4 8TA ☎ 01305 252230 ✉ j.marshall@westdorset-weymouth.gov.uk

Tourism: Mr Nick Thornley, Head of Economy, Leisure & Tourism, Council Offices, North Quay, Weymouth DT4 8TA ☎ 01305 252474; 01305 251010 ✉ n.thornley@westdorset-weymouth.gov.uk

Children's Play Areas: Ms Tara Gooding, Parks Supervisor, Council Offices, North Quay, Weymouth DT4 8TA ☎ 01305 838297 ✉ t.gooding@westdorset-weymouth.gov.uk

COUNCILLORS

***Mayor* James**, Christine (LD - Westham North)

***Deputy Mayor* Kosior**, Richard (CON - Weymouth West)
richardkosier@weymouth.gov.uk

Birtwistle, John (LD - Weymouth East)

Blackwood, Andy (LAB - Westham West)

Brookes, Kevin (CON - Upwey and Broadwey)

Bruce, Ian (CON - Preston)

Bruce, Hazel (CON - Preston)

Byatt, Mike (LAB - Westham East)

Cant, Jeff (CON - Wyke Regis)
jeffcant@weymouth.gov.uk

Drake, Francis (UKIP - Melcombe Regis)
francisgeorgedrake@gmail.com

Ellis, John (CON - Upwey and Broadwey)
johnellis@weymouth.gov.uk

Farquharson, James (CON - Preston)
jamesfarquharson@weymouth.gov.uk

Hawkins, David (IND - Tophill East)
davidhawkins@weymouth.gov.uk

Hope, Ryan (LD - Westham North)
ryanhope@weymouth.gov.uk

Huckle, Colin (LAB - Weymouth West)
colinhuckle@weymouth.gov.uk

Kanji, Oz (LD - Westham North)
ozkanji@weymouth.gov.uk

Kimber, Paul (LAB - Underhill)

Leicester, Margaret (IND - Tophill East)
yexleytwo@aol.com

Martin, Craig (LAB - Wyke Regis)

McCartney, Penny (LAB - Tophill West)

Nixon, Pamela (CON - Wey Valley)
pamelanixon@weymouth.gov.uk

Nowak, Ray (LAB - Tophill West)
raynowak@weymouth.gov.uk

Osborne, Jason (CON - Melcombe Regis)
westhallam@hotmail.com

Page-Nash, Cathy (CON - Radipole)
cathypagenash@weymouth.gov.uk

Pearson, Stewart (LAB - Melcombe Regis)

Reed, Alison (CON - Weymouth East)
alisonreed@weymouth.gov.uk

Rockingham, Gareth (LAB - Westham East)

Roebuck, Ian (LD - Radipole)

Rogers, Rachel (LAB - Littlemoor)

Russell, Cory (CON - Wey Valley)

Taylor, Gill (LD - Westham West)
gilltaylor@weymouth.gov.uk

Tewkesbury, Mark (LAB - Littlemoor)

Webb, Jason (CON - Tophill West)
jasonwebb@weymouth.gov.uk

Webb, Claudia (CON - Weymouth West)

West, Sandy (LAB - Underhill)

Wheller, Kate (LAB - Wyke Regis)

POLITICAL COMPOSITION

CON: 14, LAB: 13, LD: 6, IND: 2, UKIP: 1

COMMITTEE CHAIRS

Audit: Ms Rachel Rogers

Licensing: Mrs Hazel Bruce

Planning & Traffic: Mrs Kate Wheller

Wigan M

Wigan Metropolitan Borough Council, Town Hall, Library Street, Wigan WN1 1YN
☎ 01942 244991 🖷 01942 827451 ✉ pr@wigan.gov.uk
💻 www.wigan.gov.uk

FACTS AND FIGURES

Parliamentary Constituencies: Leigh, Makerfield, Wigan
EU Constituencies: North West
Election Frequency: Elections are by thirds

PRINCIPAL OFFICERS

Chief Executive: Ms Donna Hall, Chief Executive, Town Hall, Library Street, Wigan WN1 1YN ☎ 01942 827148 🖷 01942 828174 ✉ donna.hall@wigan.gov.uk

Deputy Chief Executive: Mr Paul McKevitt, Director - Resources & Contracts / Deputy Chief Executive, Town Hall, Library Street, Wigan WN1 1YN ☎ 01942 827235 ✉ p.mckevitt@wigan.gov.uk

Senior Management: Mr Stuart Cowley, Director - Adult Social Care & Health, Town Hall, Library Street, Wigan WN1 1YN ☎ 01942 489455 ✉ stuart.cowley@wigan.gov.uk

Senior Management: Mr Terry Dunn, Director - Environment, Town Hall, Library Street, Wigan WN1 1YN ☎ 01942 489102 ✉ t.dunn@wigan.gov.uk

Senior Management: Ms Alison McKenzie-Folan, Director - Customer Transformation, Town Hall, Library Street, Wigan WN1 1YN ☎ 01942 827784 ✉ a.mckenzie-folan@wigan.gov.uk

Senior Management: Mr James Winterbottom, Interim Director - Children & Families, Town Hall, Library Street, Wigan WN1 1YN ☎ 01942 487352 ✉ j.winterbottom@wigan.gov.uk

Building Control: Mr Mike Worden, Assistant Director - Planning & Transport, Wigan Life Centre, Library Street, Wigan WN1 1YN ☎ 01942 404357 ✉ mike.worden@wigan.gov.uk

Children / Youth Services: Ms Jayne Ivory, Assistant Director - Targeted Services, Wigan Life Centre, Library Street, Wigan WN1 1YN ☎ 01942 489453 ✉ jayne.ivory@wigan.gov.uk

Civil Registration: Mr Melvyn Jones, Superintendent Registrar, Town Hall, Library Street, Wigan WN1 1YN ☎ 01942 705014 ✉ m.jones2@wigan.gov.uk

PR / Communications: Mr Chris Dunbar, Strategic PR Manager, Town Hall, Library Street, Wigan WN1 1YN ☎ 01942 827722 ✉ c.dunbar@wigan.gov.uk

Community Safety: Ms Joyce Swift, Projects Manager, Unity House, Westwood Park Drive, Wigan WN3 4HE ☎ 01942 828111 ✉ joyce.swift@wigan.gov.uk

Computer Management: Mrs Alison Hughes, Assistant Director - ICT Strategic Partnership, Town Hall, Library Street, Wigan WN1 1YN ☎ 01942 487356 ✉ alison.hughes@wigan.gov.uk

Consumer Protection and Trading Standards: Mr Alan Blundell, Assistant Director - Regulation Services, Wigan Life Centre, Library Street, Wigan WN1 1YN ☎ 01942 489107 ✉ alan.blundell@wigan.gov.uk

Contracts: Mr Jonathan Cliff, Corporate Procurement Manager, Town Hall, Library Street, Wigan WN1 1YN ☎ 01942 827671 ✉ j.cliff@wigan.gov.uk

Corporate Services: Mr Paul McKevitt, Director - Resources & Contracts / Deputy Chief Executive, Town Hall, Library Street, Wigan WN1 1YN ☎ 01942 827235 ✉ p.mckevitt@wigan.gov.uk

Customer Service: Ms Alison McKenzie-Folan, Director - Customer Transformation, Town Hall, Library Street, Wigan WN1 1YN ☎ 01942 827784 ✉ a.mckenzie-folan@wigan.gov.uk

Customer Service: Ms Lesley O'Halloran, Assistant Director - Customer Services, Town Hall, Library Street, Wigan WN1 1YN ☎ 01942 828601 ✉ l.o'halloran@wigan.gov.uk

Direct Labour: Mr Mark Tilley, Assistant Director - Infrastructure, Town Hall, Library Street, Wigan WN1 1YN ☎ 01942 489108 ✉ m.tilley@wigan.gov.uk

Economic Development: Ms Emma Barton, Assistant Director - Economic Development & Skills, Wigan Life Centre, Library Street, Wigan WN1 1NY ☎ 01942 489105 ✉ e.barton@wigan.gov.uk

Electoral Registration: Ms Anne Loftus, Electoral Services Manager, Town Hall, Library Street, Wigan WN1 1YN ☎ 01942 827170 ✉ a.loftus@wigan.gov.uk

Emergency Planning: Dr Kate Ardern, Director - Public Health, Town Hall, Library Street, Wigan WN1 1YN ☎ 01942 489453 ✉ k.ardern@wigan.gov.uk

Emergency Planning: Mr Paul Turner, Public Health Consultant, Wigan Life Centre, Library Street, Wigan WN1 1YN ☎ 01942 404904 ✉ p.turner@wigan.gov.uk

Environmental Health: Mr Alan Blundell, Assistant Director - Regulation Services, Town Hall, Library Street, Wigan WN1 1YN ☎ 01942 489107 ✉ alan.blundell@wigan.gov.uk

Estates, Property & Valuation: Ms Linda Fisher, Assistant Director - Legal, Town Hall, Library Street, Wigan WN1 1YN ☎ 01942 827026 ✉ linda.fisher@wigan.gov.uk

Facilities: Ms Karen Hewitt, Facilities Manager, Town Hall, Library Street, Wigan WN1 1YN ☎ 01942 827516

Finance: Mr Andrew Taylor, Assistant Director - Finance, Town Hall, Library Street, Wigan WN1 1YN ☎ 01942 827243 ✉ a.taylor@wigan.gov.uk

Fleet Management: Mr Keith Simpson, Fleet Services Group Manager, Markerfield Way Depot, Makerfield Way, Ince, Wigan WN1 1YN ☎ 01942 705103 ✉ k.simpson@wigan.gov.uk

WIGAN

Health and Safety: Mr Paul McKevitt, Director - Resources & Contracts / Deputy Chief Executive, Town Hall, Library Street, Wigan WN1 1YN ☎ 01942 827235 🖱 p.mckevitt@wigan.gov.uk

Highways: Mr Mark Tilley, Assistant Director - Infrastructure, Wigan Life Centre, Library Street, Wigan WN1 1YN ☎ 01942 489108 🖱 m.tilley@wigan.gov.uk

Housing: Ms Janice Barton, Chief Executive - Wigan & Leigh Housing, Unity House, Westwood Park Drive, Wigan WN3 4HE ☎ 01942 486507 🖱 j.barton@wigan.gov.uk

Housing: Mr Peter Layland, Assistant Director - Housing & Regeneration, Wigan Life Centre, Library Street, Wigan WN1 1YN ☎ 01942 489106 🖱 peter.layland@wigan.gov.uk

Legal: John Mitchell, Assistant Director - Legal, Town Hall, Library Street, Wigan WN1 1YN ☎ 01942 827026 🖱 j.mitchell@wigan.gcsx.gov.uk

Leisure and Cultural Services: Ms Penny McGinty, Assistant Director - Leisure, Cultural & Property Services, Wigan Life Centre, Library Street, Wigan WN1 1YN ☎ 01942 489103 🖱 p.mcginty@wigan.gov.uk

Licensing: Mr Steve Wearing, Licensing Manager, Town Hall, Library Street, Wigan WN1 1YN ☎ 01942 827114 🖱 s.wearing@wigan.gov.uk

Lighting: Mr Keith Benson, Street Scene & Lighting Manager, Wigan Life Centre, Library Street, Wigan WN1 1YN ☎ 01942 488025 🖱 k.benson@wigan.gov.uk

Member Services: Ms Christine Charnock-Jones, Principal Democratic Services Officer, Town Hall, Library Street, Wigan WN1 1YN ☎ 01942 827156 🖱 c.charnock@wigan.gov.uk

Parking: Ms Sharon Brightcliffe, Car Parks Officer, Civic Centre, Millgate, Wigan WN1 1AZ ☎ 01942 827057 🖱 s.brightcliffe@wigan.gov.uk

Partnerships: Mr Will Blandamer, Assistant Director - Strategy & Partnerships, Town Hall, Library Street, Wigan WN1 1YN ☎ 01942 487352 🖱 will.blandamer@wigan.gov.uk

Personnel / HR: Ms Sonia Halliwell, Assistant Director - HR & OD, Town Hall, Library Street, Wigan WN1 1YN ☎ 01942 488412 🖱 s.halliwell@wigan.gov.uk

Planning: Mr Mike Worden, Assistant Director - Planning & Transport, Wigan Life Centre, Library Street, Wigan WN1 1YN ☎ 01942 404357 🖱 mike.worden@wigan.gov.uk

Procurement: Mr Jonathan Cliff, Corporate Procurement Manager, Town Hall, Library Street, Wigan WN1 1YN ☎ 01942 827671 🖱 j.cliff@wigan.gov.uk

Public Libraries: Ms Lesley O'Halloran, Assistant Director - Customer Services, Town Hall, Library Street, Wigan WN1 1YN ☎ 01942 828601 🖱 l.o'halloran@wigan.gov.uk

Recycling & Waste Minimisation: Ms Andrea Yates, Waste Manager, Makerfield Way Depot, Makerfield Way, Ince, Wigan WN2 2PR ☎ 01942 828333 🖱 a.yates@wigan.gov.uk

Regeneration: Mr Peter Layland, Assistant Director - Housing & Regeneration, Gateway House, Standishgate, Wigan WN1 1AE ☎ 01942 489106 🖱 peter.layland@wigan.gov.uk

Road Safety: Ms Carmel Foster-Devine, Transport Plan & Road Safety Manager, Wigan Life Centre, Library Street, Wigan WN1 1NY ☎ 01942 404687 🖱 c.foster-devine@wigan.gov.uk

Social Services (Adult): Ms Sharon Barber, Assistant Director - Support & Safeguarding, Wigan Life Centre, Library Street, Wigan WN1 1NY ☎ 01942 489454 🖱 sharon.barber@wigan.gov.uk

Social Services (Adult): Ms Liv Bickerstaff, Assistant Director - Early Intervention & Prevention, Wigan Life Centre, Library Street, Wigan WN1 1NY ☎ 01942 489454 🖱 l.bickerstaff@wigan.gov.uk

Social Services (Adult): Ms Jo Wilmott, Assistant Manager - Provider Management & Market Development, Town Hall, Library Street, Wigan WN1 1YN ☎ 01942 489454 🖱 joanne.wilmott@wigan.gov.uk

Public Health: Dr Kate Ardern, Director - Public Health, Town Hall, Library Street, Wigan WN1 1YN ☎ 01942 489453 🖱 k.ardern@wigan.gov.uk

Staff Training: Ms Sonia Halliwell, Assistant Director - HR & OD, Town Hall, Library Street, Wigan WN1 1YN ☎ 01942 488412 🖱 s.halliwell@wigan.gov.uk

Street Scene: Mr Damian Jenkinson, Wigan Borough in Bloom Co-ordinator, Wigan Life Centre, Library Street, Wigan WN1 1YN ☎ 01942 488299 🖱 d.jenkinson@wigan.gov.uk

Tourism: Mr Keith Bergman, Hospitality & Events Manager, Elizabeth House, The Pier, Wallgate, Wigan WN3 4BD ☎ 01942 828267 🖱 k.bergman@wigan.gov.uk

Town Centre: Mr Michael Matthews, Town Centre Manager, Economic Regeneration Office, Gateway House, Standishgate, Wigan WN1 1AE ☎ 01942 828890 🖱 m.matthews@wmbc.gov.uk

Traffic Management: Mr Mark Tilley, Assistant Director - Infrastructure, Wigan Life Centre, Library Street, Wigan WN1 1YN ☎ 01942 489108 🖱 m.tilley@wigan.gov.uk

Transport: Mr Keith Simpson, Fleet Services Group Manager, Transport DSO, Hindley Towns Yard, Wigan Road, Hindley, Wigan WN2 3BQ ☎ 01942 705103 🖱 k.simpson@wigan.gov.uk

Transport Planner: Mr Rob Owen, Transport Strategy Manager, Wigan Life Centre, Library Street, Wigan WN1 1NY ☎ 01942 489310 🖱 r.owen@wigan.gov.uk

Transport Planner: Mr Mike Worden, Assistant Director - Planning & Transport, Wigan Life Centre, Library Street, Wigan WN1 1YN ☎ 01942 404357 🖱 mike.worden@wigan.gov.uk

Waste Collection and Disposal: Mr Steve Cassie, Assistant Director - Trading, Makerfield Way Depot, Makerfield Way, Ince, Wigan WN2 2PR ☎ 01942 705130 ✉ s.cassie@wigan.gov.uk

Waste Management: Ms Andrea Yates, Waste Manager, Makerfield Way Depot, Makerfield Way, Ince, Wigan WN2 2PR ☎ 01942 828333 ✉ a.yates@wigan.gov.uk

COUNCILLORS

***Mayor* Loudon**, Susan (LAB - Atherleigh)
S.Loudon@wigan.gov.uk

***Deputy Mayor* Conway**, Ronald (LAB - Aspull New Springs Whelley)
R.Conway@wigan.gov.uk

***Leader of the Council* Smith**, Peter (LAB - Leigh West)
Leader@wigan.gov.uk

Aldred, Martin (LAB - Atherton)
Martin.Aldred@wigan.gov.uk

Aldred, Karen (LAB - Atherton)
K.Aldred@wigan.gov.uk

Aldred, Mark (LAB - Atherleigh)
M.Aldred@wigan.gov.uk

Anderson, Kevin (LAB - Leigh South)
K.Anderson@wigan.gov.uk

Arrowsmith, David (LAB - Orrell)
D.Arrowsmith@wigan.gov.uk

Ash, Nigel (LAB - Ashton)
N.Ash@wigan.gov.uk

Barber, Richard (LAB - Golborne and Lowton West)
r.barber@wigan.gov.uk

Bleakley, Robert (LD - Tyldesley)
R.Bleakley@wigan.gov.uk

Brierley, Robert (IND - Hindley Green)
R.Brierley@wigan.gov.uk

Bullen, Jennifer (LAB - Ashton)
J.Bullen@wigan.gov.uk

Carmichael, Francis (IND - Hindley Green)
F.Carmichael@wigan.gov.uk

Churton, James (LAB - Hindley)
J.Eccles-Churton@wigan.gov.uk

Clarke, Bill (LAB - Ashton)
B.Clarke@wigan.gov.uk

Collins, Paul (LAB - Shevington with Lower Ground)
Paul.Collins@wigan.gov.uk

Crosby, Michael (LAB - Shevington with Lower Ground)
M.Crosby@wigan.gov.uk

Cullen, Phyllis (LAB - Wigan West)
P.Cullen@wigan.gov.uk

Cunliffe, Keith (LAB - Leigh East)
K.Cunliffe@wigan.gov.uk

Davies, George (LAB - Wigan Central)
George.Davies@wigan.gov.uk

Dawber, Stephen (LAB - Wigan West)
Steve.Dawber@wigan.gov.uk

Dewhurst, Shirley (LAB - Douglas)
Shirley.Dewhurst@wigan.gov.uk

Dewhurst, Michael (LAB - Douglas)
M.Dewhurst@wigan.gov.uk

Edwardson, Damian (LAB - Shevington with Lower Ground)
D.Edwardson@wigan.gov.uk

Ellis, Jim (IND - Hindley)
James.Ellis@wigan.gov.uk

Fairhurst, Debbie (IND - Standish with Langtree)
debbiefairhurst@wigan.gov.uk

Fairhurst, Gareth (IND - Standish with Langtree)
Gareth.Fairhurst@wigan.gov.uk

Fairhurst, George (IND - Standish with Langtree)
George.Fairhurst@wigan.gov.uk

Greensmith, Susan (LAB - Leigh West)
S.Greensmith@wigan.gov.uk

Grundy, James (CON - Lowton East)
James.Grundy@wigan.gov.uk

Halliwell, Terence (LAB - Wigan West)
T.Halliwell@wigan.gov.uk

Hellier, John (LAB - Tyldesley)
S.Hellier@wigan.gov.uk

Hilton, John (LAB - Aspull New Springs Whelley)
J.Hilton@wigan.gov.uk

Hodgkinson, John (IND - Bryn)
Don.Hodgkinson@wigan.gov.uk

Hodgkinson, Jamie (IND - Atherton)
Jamie.Hodgkinson@wigan.gov.uk

Holland, Patricia (LAB - Worsley Mesnes)
P.Holland@wigan.gov.uk

Houlton, Edward (CON - Lowton East)
edward.houlton@wigan.gov.uk

Houlton, Kathleen (CON - Lowton East)
K.Houlton@wigan.gov.uk

Hunt, Lawrence (LAB - Wigan Central)
I.Hunt@wigan.gov.uk

Keane, Stuart (LAB - Golborne and Lowton West)
S.Keane@wigan.gov.uk

Kelly, Phil (LAB - Worsley Mesnes)
P.Kelly@wigan.gov.uk

Kenny, Paul (LAB - Winstanley)
P.Kenny@wigan.gov.uk

Klieve, Yvonne (LAB - Golborne and Lowton West)
Y.Klieve@wigan.gov.uk

Marshall, Joanne (LAB - Tyldesley)
joanne.marshall@wigan.gov.uk

McLoughin, Michael (LAB - Wigan Central)
M.McLoughlin@wigan.gov.uk

Molyneux, David (LAB - Ince)
D.Molyneux@wigan.gov.uk

Moodie, James (LAB - Ince)
J.Moodie@wigan.gov.uk

Morgan, Marie (LAB - Winstanley)
Marie.Morgan@wigan.gov.uk

WIGAN

Morgan, Clive (LAB - Winstanley)
Clive.Morgan@wigan.gov.uk

Murphy, Stephen (LAB - Orrell)
Stephen.Murphy@wigan.gov.uk

Murphy, Sam (LAB - Pemberton)
sam.murphy@wigan.gov.uk

Murray, Nathan (LAB - Bryn)
N.Murray@wigan.gov.uk

O'Brien, John (LAB - Leigh South)
j.o'brien@wigan.gov.uk

Platt, Joanne (LAB - Astley Mosley Common)
Joanne.Platt@wigan.gov.uk

Prescott, Jeanette (LAB - Pemberton)
J.Prescott@wigan.gov.uk

Prescott, Paul (LAB - Pemberton)
Paul.Prescott@wigan.gov.uk

Rampling, Margaret (LAB - Bryn)
A.Rampling@wigan.gov.uk

Ready, Christopher (LAB - Aspull New Springs Whelley)
C.Ready@wigan.gov.uk

Ready, Kelly (LAB - Orrell)
Kelly.Ready@wigan.gov.uk

Rigby, Charles (LAB - Leigh South)
C.Rigby@wigan.gov.uk

Roberts, Chritstine (LAB - Astley Mosley Common)
Christine.Roberts@wigan.gov.uk

Rotherham, William (LAB - Worsley Mesnes)
W.Rotherham@wigan.gov.uk

Sharratt, Janice (LAB - Ince)
J.Sharratt@wigan.gov.uk

Skilling, Maggie (LAB - Douglas)
M.Skilling@wigan.gov.uk

Smethurst, Martyn (LAB - Abram)
M.Smethurst@wigan.gov.uk

Smethurst, Eunice (LAB - Abram)
E.Smethurst@wigan.gov.uk

Stewart, Pamela (LAB - Atherleigh)
P.Stewart@wigan.gov.uk

Stitt, David (LAB - Hindley Green)
K.Stitt@wigan.gov.uk

Sweeney, Carl (LAB - Abram)
C.Sweeney@wigan.gov.uk

Talbot, James (LAB - Hindley)
J.Talbot@wigan.gov.uk

Taylor, Barry (LAB - Astley Mosley Common)
Barry.Taylor@wigan.gov.uk

Thorpe, Anita (LAB - Leigh East)
A.Thorpe@wigan.gov.uk

Walker, Frederick (LAB - Leigh East)
F.Walker@wigan.gov.uk

Whiteside, Myra (LAB - Leigh West) M.Whiteside@wigan.gov.uk

POLITICAL COMPOSITION

LAB: 63, IND: 8, CON: 3, LD: 1

COMMITTEE CHAIRS

Audit: Mr Carl Sweeney

Children & Young People: Mrs Myra Whiteside

Health & Social Care: Mr Nigel Ash

Licensing: Mr Paul Prescott

Planning: Mr Paul Prescott

Wiltshire Unitary U

Wiltshire Council, County Hall, Trowbridge BA14 8JN
☎ 0300 456 0100 💻 www.wiltshire.gov.uk

FACTS AND FIGURES

Parliamentary Constituencies: Chippenham, Devizes, Salisbury, Wiltshire North, Wiltshire South West

PRINCIPAL OFFICERS

Senior Management: Dr Carlton Brand, Corporate Director - ERO, SIRO, County Hall, Trowbridge BA14 8JN ☎ 01225 713001 🖷 01225 713161 ✉ carltonbrand@wiltshire.gov.uk

Senior Management: Mrs Carolyn Godfrey, Corporate Director - Children's Services, County Hall, Bythesea Road, Trowbridge BA14 8JN ☎ 01225 713750 🖷 01225 713982 ✉ carolyn.godfrey@wiltshire.gov.uk

Senior Management: Mrs Maggie Rae, Corporate Director - Public Health & Adults, County Hall, Bythesea Road, Trowbridge BA14 8JN ☎ 01225 718338 ✉ maggie.rae@wiltshire.gov.uk

Building Control: Ms Sarah Ward, Head of Asset Management - Corporate Building Programme, County Hall, Trowbridge BA14 8JN ☎ 01225 713235 ✉ sarah.ward@wiltshire.gov.uk

Children / Youth Services: Ms Julia Cramp, Joint Associate Director - Commissioning & Performance, County Hall, Trowbridge BA14 8JN ☎ 01225 718221 ✉ julia.cramp@wiltshire.gov.uk

Children / Youth Services: Mrs Carolyn Godfrey, Corporate Director - Children's Services, County Hall, Bythesea Road, Trowbridge BA14 8JN ☎ 01225 713750 🖷 01225 713982 ✉ carolyn.godfrey@wiltshire.gov.uk

Children / Youth Services: Mr Terrence Herbert, Associate Director - Operational Children's Services, County Hall, Trowbridge BA14 8JN ☎ 01225 713682 ✉ terrence.herbert@wiltshire.gov.uk

PR / Communications: Ms Laurie Bell, Associate Director - Communications & Communities, County Hall, Trowbridge BA14 8JN ☎ 0300 456 0100 🖷 01225 456 0100 ✉ laurie.bell@wiltshire.gov.uk

Community Planning: Dr Carlton Brand, Corporate Director - ERO, SIRO, County Hall, Trowbridge BA14 8JN ☎ 01225 713001 🖷 01225 713161 ✉ carltonbrand@wiltshire.gov.uk

Community Safety: Ms Mandy Bradley, Service Director - Public Protection, Court Mills Centre, Polebarn Road, Trowbridge BA14 7EG ☎ 0300 456 0100 ✉ mandy.bradley@wiltshire.gov.uk

Consumer Protection and Trading Standards: Ms Yvonne Bennett, Consumer Protection Manager, County Hall, Trowbridge BA14 8JN ☎ 0300 456 0100 ✉ yvonne.bennett@wiltshire.gov.uk

Contracts: Mr Michael Swabey, Strategy Manager, County Hall, Trowbridge BA14 8JD ☎ 01225 718662 ✉ mikeswabey@wiltshire.gov.uk

Contracts: Mr Arthur Williams, Principal Contracts Officer, County Hall, Trowbridge BA14 8JN ☎ 01225 713252 ✉ arthur.williams@wiltshire.gov.uk

Corporate Services: Dr Carlton Brand, Corporate Director - ERO, SIRO, County Hall, Trowbridge BA14 8JN ☎ 01225 713001 🖷 01225 713161 ✉ carltonbrand@wiltshire.gov.uk

Customer Service: Mrs Jacqui White, Service Director - Business Services, County Hall, Trowbridge BA14 8JN ☎ 01225 713013 ✉ jacquiwhite@wiltshire.gov.uk

Economic Development: Mr Alistair Cunningham, Director - Economy & Regeneration, County Hall, Bythesea Road, Trowbridge BA14 8JN ☎ 01225 713203 🖷 01225 713400 ✉ alistair.cunningham@wiltshire.gov.uk

Education: Ms Julia Cramp, Joint Associate Director - Commissioning & Performance, County Hall, Trowbridge BA14 8JN ☎ 01225 718221 ✉ julia.cramp@wiltshire.gov.uk

Education: Mrs Stephanie Denovan, Service Director - Schools & Learning, County Hall, Bythesea Road, Trowbridge BA14 8JN ☎ 01225 713838 ✉ stephanie.denovan@wiltshire.gov.uk

Education: Ms Carolyn Godfrey, Corporate Director, County Hall, Trowbridge BA14 8JB ☎ 01225 713750 🖷 01225 713982 ✉ carolyn.godfrey@wiltshire.gov.uk

E-Government: Mr Ian Gibbons, Director - Legal & Democratic Services, County Hall, Bythesea Road, Trowbridge BA14 8JN ☎ 01225 713052 🖷 01225 713998 ✉ ian.gibbons@wiltshire.gov.uk

Environmental / Technical Services: Ms Tracy Carter, Director - Waste Management Services, County Hall, Trowbridge BA14 8JN ☎ 01225 713258 🖷 01225 713200 ✉ tracy.carter@wiltshire.gov.uk

Environmental / Technical Services: Mr Parvis Khansari, Service Director - Highways & Transport, County Hall, Bythesea Road, Trowbridge BA14 8JN ☎ 01225 713340 ✉ parvis.khansari@wiltshire.gov.uk

Events Manager: Ms Barbara Gray, Events & Sponsorship Manager, County Hall, Trowbridge BA14 8JN ☎ 0300 456 0100

Facilities: Mr Mark Smith, Service Director - Neighbourhood Services, County Hall, Trowbridge BA14 8JN ☎ 01225 734789 ✉ mark.smith@wiltshire.gov.uk

Finance: Mr Michael Hudson, Director - Finance, County Hall, Trowbridge BA14 8JN ☎ 01225 713600 🖷 01225 713697 ✉ michael.hudson@wiltshire.gov.uk

Treasury: Mr Keith Stephens, Treasurer - Treasury & VAT, County Hall, Trowbridge BA14 8JN ☎ 01225 713603 ✉ keith.stephens@wiltshire.gov.uk

Pensions: Mr David Anthony, Head - Pensions, County Hall, Trowbridge BA14 8JN ☎ 01225 713613 ✉ david.anthony@wiltshire.gov.uk

Pensions: Ms Catherine Dix, Pension Investments Officer, County Hall, Trowbridge BA14 8JN ☎ 01225 713613 ✉ catherine.dix@wiltshire.gov.uk

Grounds Maintenance: Mr Mark Smith, Service Director - Neighbourhood Services, County Hall, Trowbridge BA14 8JN ☎ 01225 734789 ✉ mark.smith@wiltshire.gov.uk

Health and Safety: Mr Paul Collyer, Head of Occupational Health & Safety, County Hall, Trowbridge BA14 8JN ☎ 01225 713119 🖷 01225 713177 ✉ paulcollyer@wiltshire.gov.uk

Highways: Mr Parvis Khansari, Service Director - Highways & Transport, County Hall, Bythesea Road, Trowbridge BA14 8JN ☎ 01225 713340 ✉ parvis.khansari@wiltshire.gov.uk

Legal: Mr Ian Gibbons, Director - Legal & Governance (Monitoring Officer), County Hall, Bythesea Road, Trowbridge BA14 8JN ☎ 01225 713052 🖷 01225 713998 ✉ ian.gibbons@wiltshire.gov.uk

Leisure and Cultural Services: Mr Mark Smith, Service Director - Neighbourhood Services, County Hall, Trowbridge BA14 8JN ☎ 01225 734789 ✉ mark.smith@wiltshire.gov.uk

Lifelong Learning: Mr Helen Mehring, Head of Service - Organisational, Learning & Development, County Hall, Trowbridge BA14 8JN ☎ 01225 713194 ✉ helen.mehring@wiltshire.gov.uk

Lottery Funding, Charity and Voluntary: Ms Sandie Lewis, Head - Community Strategy & Voluntary Sector Support, County Hall, Trowbridge BA14 8JN ☎ 01225 713150 🖷 01225 713515 ✉ sandie.lewis@wiltshire.gov.uk

Member Services: Mr Ian Gibbons, Director - Legal & Democratic Services, County Hall, Trowbridge BA14 8JN ☎ 01225 713052 🖷 01225 713998 ✉ ian.gibbons@wiltshire.gov.uk

Member Services: Mr John Quinton, Head - Democratic & Member Services & Cabinet Secretary, County Hall, Trowbridge BA14 8JN ☎ 01225 713054 🖷 01225 713099 ✉ johnquinton@wiltshire.gov.uk

Partnerships: Mrs Maggie Rae, Corporate Director - Public Health & Adults, County Hall, Bythesea Road, Trowbridge BA14 8JN ☎ 01225 718338 ✉ maggie.rae@wiltshire.gov.uk

Personnel / HR: Mr Barry Pirie, Director - Human Resources & Organisational Development, County Hall, Bythesea Road, Trowbridge BA14 8JN ☎ 01225 718226 ✉ barrie.pirie@wiltshire.gov.uk

Planning: Mr Brad Fleet, Service Director - Development Services, County Hall, Trowbridge BA14 8JN ☎ 0300 456 0100 ✉ brad.fleet@wiltshire.gov.uk

Procurement: Mr Robin Townsend, Associate Director - Corporate Function, Procurement & Programme Office, County Hall, Trowbridge BA14 8JN robin.townsend@wiltshire.gov.uk

Public Libraries: Ms Niki Lewis, Service Director - Community, Libraries, Heritage & Arts, County Hall, Bythesea Road, Trowbridge BA14 8JN ☎ 01225 713180 niki.lewis@wiltshire.gov.uk

Social Services: Ms Sue Geary, Head - Performance, Health & Workforce, County Hall, Trowbridge BA14 8JN ☎ 01225 713922 sue.geary@wiltshire.gov.uk

Social Services (Adult): Mr James Cawley, Associate Director - Adult Care Commissioning & Housing, County Hall, Trowbridge BA14 8JN ☎ 0300 456 0100 james.cawley@wiltshire.gov.uk

Public Health: Mrs Maggie Rae, Corporate Director - Public Health & Adults, County Hall, Bythesea Road, Trowbridge BA14 8JN ☎ 01225 718338 maggie.rae@wiltshire.gov.uk

Staff Training: Ms Niki Lewis, Service Director - Community, Libraries, Heritage & Arts, County Hall, Trowbridge BA14 8JN ☎ 01225 713180 niki.lewis@wiltshire.gov.uk

Staff Training: Mr Barry Pirie, Director - Human Resources & Organisational Development, County Hall, Bythesea Road, Trowbridge BA14 8JN ☎ 01225 718226 barry.pirie@wiltshire.gov.uk

Sustainable Communities: Ms Niki Lewis, Service Director - Community, Libraries, Heritage & Arts, County Hall, Bythesea Road, Trowbridge BA14 8JN ☎ 01225 713180 niki.lewis@wiltshire.gov.uk

Transport: Mr Parvis Khansari, Service Director - Highways & Transport, County Hall, Bythesea Road, Trowbridge BA14 8JN ☎ 01225 713340 parvis.khansari@wiltshire.gov.uk

Waste Collection and Disposal: Ms Tracy Carter, Director - Waste Management Services, County Hall, Trowbridge BA14 8JN ☎ 01225 713258 🖷 01225 713200 tracy.carter@wiltshire.gov.uk

COUNCILLORS

***Chair* Britton**, Richard (CON - Alderbury & Whiteparish)
richard.britton@wiltshire.gov.uk

***Vice-Chair* Bucknell**, Allison (CON - Lyneham)
allison.bucknell@wiltshire.gov.uk

***Leader of the Council* Scott**, Jane (CON - By Brook)
jane.scott@wiltshire.gov.uk

***Deputy Leader of the Council* Thomson**, John (CON - Sherston)
john.thomson@wiltshire.gov.uk

Allen, Desna (LD - Chippenham Queens & Sheldon)
desna.allen@wiltshire.gov.uk

Ansell, Glenis (LD - Calne North)
Glenis.Ansell@wiltshire.gov.uk

Aves, Pat (LD - Melksham North)
Pat.Aves@wiltshire.gov.uk

Berry, Chuck (CON - Minety)
chuck.berry@wiltshire.gov.uk

Blakemore, Nick (LD - Trowbridge Adcroft)
Nick.Blakemore@wiltshire.gov.uk

Brown, Rosemary (LD - Bradford-on-Avon North)
rosemary.brown@wiltshire.gov.uk

Carbin, Trevor (LD - Holt & Staverton)
trevor.carbin@wiltshire.gov.uk

Caswill, Chris (IND - Chippenham Monkton)
chris.caswill@wiltshire.gov.uk

Champion, Mary (CON - Royal Wootton Bassett North)
Mary.Champion@wiltshire.gov.uk

Chivers, Terry (IND - Melksham Without North)
Terry.Chivers@wiltshire.gov.uk

Clark, Ernie (IND - Hilperton)
ernie.clark@wiltshire.gov.uk

Clewer, Richard (CON - Salisbury St Pauls)
richard.clewer@wiltshire.gov.uk

Connolly, Mark (CON - Tidworth)
mark.connolly@wiltshire.gov.uk

Crisp, Christine (CON - Calne Rural)
christine.crisp@wiltshire.gov.uk

Cuthbert, Anna (CON - Bromham, Rowde and Potterne)
anna.cuthbert@wiltshire.gov.uk

Dalton, Brian (LD - Salisbury Harnham)
brian.dalton@wiltshire.gov.uk

Davis, Andrew (CON - Warminster East)
andrew.davis@wiltshire.gov.uk

Deane, Tony (CON - Tisbury)
tony.deane@wiltshire.gov.uk

Devine, Christopher (CON - Winterslow)
christopher.devine@wiltshire.gov.uk

Dobson, Stewart (CON - Marlborough East)
Stewart.Dobson@wiltshire.gov.uk

Douglas, Bill (LD - Chippenham Hardens & England)
bill.douglas@wiltshire.gov.uk

Douglas, Mary (CON - Salisbury St Francis & Stratford)
mary.douglas@wiltshire.gov.uk

Drewett, Dennis (IND - Trowbridge Park)
dennis.drewett@wiltshire.gov.uk

Edge, Peter (LD - Wilton & Lower Wylye Valley)
Peter.Edge@wiltshire.gov.uk

Evans, Peter (CON - Devizes East)
Peterb.Evans@wiltshire.gov.uk

Evans, Sue (CON - Devizes North)
Sue.Evans@wiltshire.gov.uk

Fogg, Nick (IND - Marlborough West)
nick.fogg@wiltshire.gov.uk

Gamble, Richard (CON - The Lavingtons & Erlestoke)
richard.gamble@wiltshire.gov.uk

Green, Jose (CON - Fovant & Chalke Valley)
jose.green@wiltshire.gov.uk

Greenman, Howard (CON - Kington)
howard.greenman@wiltshire.gov.uk

Groom, Mollie (CON - Royal Wootton Bassett East)
mollie.groom@wiltshire.gov.uk

Hawker, Russell (IND - Westbury West)
russell.hawker@wiltshire.gov.uk

Hewitt, Mike (CON - Bourne & Woodford Valley)
mike.hewitt@wiltshire.gov.uk

Hill, Alan (CON - Calne South & Cherhill)
alan.hill@wiltshire.gov.uk

Howard, Charles (CON - The Collingbournes & Netheravon)
charles.howard@wiltshire.gov.uk

Hubbard, Jon (LD - Melksham South)
jon.hubbard@wiltshire.gov.uk

Humphries, Keith (CON - Warminster Broadway)
keith.humphries@wiltshire.gov.uk

Hurst, Chris (LD - Royal Wootton Bassett South)
Chris.Hurst@wiltshire.gov.uk

Hutton, Peter (CON - Chippenham Cepen Park & Derriads)
peter.hutton@wiltshire.gov.uk

Jacobs, Simon (CON - Devizes & Roundway South)
Simon.Jacobs@wiltshire.gov.uk

Jeans, George (IND - Mere)
george.jeans@wiltshire.gov.uk

Jenkins, David (LD - Westbury North)
david.jenkins2@wiltshire.gov.uk

Johnson, Julian (CON - Downton & Ebble Valley)
julian.johnson@wiltshire.gov.uk

Jones, Bob (LD - Cricklade & Latton)
Bob.Jones@wiltshire.gov.uk

Killane, Simon (LD - Malmesbury)
simon.killane@wiltshire.gov.uk

King, Gordon (LD - Westbury East)
Gordon.King@wiltshire.gov.uk

Knight, John (LD - Trowbridge Central)
John.Knight@wiltshire.gov.uk

Kunkler, Jerry (CON - Pewsey)
jerry.kunkler@wiltshire.gov.uk

Lay, Jacqui (CON - Purton)
jacqui.lay@wiltshire.gov.uk

Macrae, Alan (CON - Corsham Pickwick)
alan.macrae@wiltshire.gov.uk

Madonald, Magnus (LD - Winsley & Westwood)
Magnus.Macdonald@wiltshire.gov.uk

Marshall, Howard (IND - Calne Central)
howard.marshall@wiltshire.gov.uk

Mayes, Laura (CON - Roundway)
laura.mayes@wiltshire.gov.uk

McKeown, Helena (LD - Salisbury St Edmund & Milford)
Helena.McKeown@wiltshire.gov.uk

McLennan, Ian (LAB - Laverstock, Ford & Old Sarum)
ian.mclennan@wiltshire.gov.uk

Milton, Jemima (CON - West Selkley)
jemima.milton@wiltshire.gov.uk

Moss, Bill (CON - Salisbury St Marks & Bishopdown)
bill.moss@wiltshire.gov.uk

Newbury, Christopher (IND - Warminster Copheap & Wylye)
christopher.newbury@wiltshire.gov.uk

Noeken, John (CON - Amesbury East)
john.noeken@wiltshire.gov.uk

Oatway, Paul (CON - Pewsey Vale)
Paul.Oatway@wiltshire.gov.uk

Oldrieve, Stephen (LD - Trowbridge Paxcroft)
steve.oldrieve@wiltshire.gov.uk

Osborn, Jeff (IND - Trowbridge Grove)
jeff.osborn@wiltshire.gov.uk

Osborn, Helen (LD - Trowbridge Lambrok)
helen.osborn@wiltshire.gov.uk

Packard, Mark (LD - Chippenham Pewsham)
mark.packard@wiltshire.gov.uk

Packard, Linda (LD - Chippenham Lowden & Rowden)
linda.packard@wiltshire.gov.uk

Parker, Sheila (CON - Box & Colerne)
sheila.parker@wiltshire.gov.uk

Payne, Graham (CON - Trowbridge Drynham)
graham.payne@wiltshire.gov.uk

Phillips, Nina (CON - Chippenham Cepen Park & Redlands)
nina.phillips@wiltshire.gov.uk

Pollitt, David (UKIP - Melksham Central)
David.Pollitt@wiltshire.gov.uk

Prickett, Horace (CON - Southwick)
Horace.Prickett@wiltshire.gov.uk

Randall, Leo (CON - Redlynch & Landford)
leo.randall@wiltshire.gov.uk

Rhe-Philipe, Fleur de (CON - Warminster Without)
fleur.derhephilipe@wiltshire.gov.uk

Ridout, Pip (CON - Warminster West)
pip.ridout@wiltshire.gov.uk

Rogers, Ricky (LAB - Salisbury Bemerton)
ricky.rogers@wiltshire.gov.uk

Seed, Jonathon (CON - Summerham & Seend)
jonathon.seed@wiltshire.gov.uk

Sheppard, James (CON - Aldbourne & Ramsbury)
James.Sheppard@wiltshire.gov.uk

Smale, John (CON - Bulford, Allington & Figheldean)
johnf.smale@wiltshire.gov.uk

Sturgis, Toby (CON - Brinkworth)
toby.sturgis@wiltshire.gov.uk

Thompson, Melody (CON - Chippenham Hardenhuish)

Thorn, Ian (LD - Bradford-on-Avon South)
Ian.Thorne@wiltshire.gov.uk

Tomes, Ian (LAB - Salisbury St Martins & Cathedral)
Ian.Tomes@wiltshire.gov.uk

Tonge, Dick (CON - Corsham Without & Box Hill)
richard.tonge@wiltshire.gov.uk

Trotman, Anthony (CON - Calne Chilvester & Abberd)
tony.trotman@wiltshire.gov.uk

Walsh, John (LAB - Salisbury Fisherton & Bemerton Village)
John.Walsh@wiltshire.gov.uk

Wayman, Bridget (CON - Nadder & East Knoyle)
bridget.wayman@wiltshire.gov.uk

West, Ian (LD - Till & Wylye Valley)
ian.west@wiltshire.gov.uk

Westmoreland, Fred (CON - Amesbury West)
fred.westmoreland@wiltshire.gov.uk

Whalley, Philip (CON - Corsham Town)
Philip.Whalley@wiltshire.gov.uk

Wheeler, Stuart (CON - Burbage & The Bedwyns)
stuart.wheeler@wiltshire.gov.uk

While, Roy (CON - Melksham Without South)
roy.while@wiltshire.gov.uk

Whitehead, Philip (CON - Urchfont & The Cannings)
philip.whitehead@wiltshire.gov.uk

Wickham, Jerry (CON - Ethandune)
jerry.wickham@wiltshire.gov.uk

Williams, Christopher (CON - Ludgershall & Perham Down)
christopher.williams@wiltshire.gov.uk

Wright, Graham (IND - Durrington & Larkhill)
graham.wright@wiltshire.gov.uk

POLITICAL COMPOSITION
CON: 58, LD: 24, IND: 11, LAB: 4, UKIP: 1

COMMITTEE CHAIRS
Audit: Mr Tony Deane

Health & Wellbeing: Baroness Jane Scott

Licensing: Ms Pip Ridout

Pensions: Mr Tony Deane

Winchester City D

Winchester City Council, City Offices, Colebrook Street, Winchester SO23 9LJ
☎ 01962 840222 🖷 01962 841365 ✉ info@winchester.gov.uk
💻 www.winchester.gov.uk

FACTS AND FIGURES
Parliamentary Constituencies: Winchester
EU Constituencies: South East
Election Frequency: Elections are by thirds

PRINCIPAL OFFICERS
Chief Executive: Mr Simon Eden, Chief Executive, City Offices, Colebrook Street, Winchester SO23 9LJ ☎ 01962 848230 🖷 01962 848208 ✉ seden@winchester.gov.uk

Senior Management: Ms Alexis Garlick, Chief Finance Officer, City Offices, Colebrook Street, Winchester SO23 9LJ ☎ 01962 848224 ✉ agarlick@winchester.gov.uk

Senior Management: Mr Steve Tilbury, Corporate Director, City Offices, Colebrook Street, Winchester SO23 9LJ ☎ 01962 848256 🖷 01962 848101 ✉ stilbury@winchester.gov.uk

Senior Management: Mr Stephen Whetnall, Chief Operating Officer, City Offices, Colebrook Street, Winchester SO23 9LJ ☎ 01962 840222 🖷 01962 848555 ✉ swhetnall@winchester.gov.uk

Architect, Building / Property Services: Mr Andrew Kingston, Property Services Manager, City Offices, Colebrook Street, Winchester SO23 9LJ ☎ 01962 848240 🖷 01962 841365 ✉ akingston@winchester.gov.uk

Architect, Building / Property Services: Mr Kevin Warren, Head of Estates, City Offices, Colebrook Street, Winchester SO23 9LJ ☎ 01962 848528 ✉ kwarren@winchester.gov.uk

Best Value: Ms Alexis Garlick, Chief Finance Officer, City Offices, Colebrook Street, Winchester SO23 9LJ ☎ 01962 848224 ✉ agarlick@winchester.gov.uk

Building Control: Mr Chris Griffith-Jones, Head of Building Control, City Offices, Colebrook Street, Winchester SO23 9LJ ☎ 01962 840222 🖷 01962 849101 ✉ cgriffith-jones@winchester.gov.uk

Children / Youth Services: Mrs Lorraine Ronan, Head of Community Wellbeing, City Offices, Colebrook Street, Winchester SO23 9LJ ☎ 01962 848369 🖷 01962 841365 ✉ lronan@winchester.gov.uk

PR / Communications: Mr Martin O'Neill, Head of Communications, City Offices, Colebrook Street, Winchester SO23 9LJ ☎ 01962 848504 🖷 01962 848208 ✉ moneill@winchester.gov.uk

Community Planning: Mrs Lorraine Ronan, Head of Community Wellbeing, City Offices, Colebrook Street, Winchester SO23 9LJ ☎ 01962 848369 🖷 01962 841365 ✉ lronan@winchester.gov.uk

Community Safety: Mrs Sandra Tuddenham, Community Safety Officer, City Offices, Colebrook Street, Winchester SO23 9LJ ☎ 01962 848132 ✉ studdenham@winchester.gov.uk

Computer Management: Mr Tony Fawcett, Head of IT Services, City Offices, Colebrook Street, Winchester SO23 9LJ ☎ 01962 848262; 01264 368901 ✉ tfawcett@winchester.gov.uk; tfacwett@testvalley.gov.uk

Contracts: Mr Andrew Kingston, Property Services Manager, City Offices, Colebrook Street, Winchester SO23 9LJ ☎ 01962 848240 🖷 01962 841365 ✉ akingston@winchester.gov.uk

Economic Development: Ms Kate Cloud, Head of Economy & Arts, City Offices, Colebrook Street, Winchester SO23 9LJ ☎ 01962 848563 ✉ kcloud@winchester.gov.uk

E-Government: Mr Stephen Whetnall, Chief Operating Officer, City Offices, Colebrook Street, Winchester SO23 9LJ ☎ 01962 840222 🖷 01962 848555 ✉ swhetnall@winchester.gov.uk

Electoral Registration: Ms Karen Vincent, Electoral Services Manager, City Offices, Colebrook Street, Winchester SO23 9LJ ☎ 01962 848125 🖷 01962 848472 ✉ kvincent@winchester.gov.uk

Emergency Planning: Mr Dave Shaw, Principal Democratic Services Officer, City Offices, Colebrook Street, Winchester SO23 9LJ ☎ 01962 848221 🖷 01962 848555 ✉ dshaw@winchester.gov.uk

Energy Management: Mr Robert Heathcock, Joint Environmental Services Manager, City Offices, Colebrook Street, Winchester SO23 9LJ ☎ 01730 234383 ✉ rob.heathcock@easthants.gov.uk

Environmental / Technical Services: Mr Robert Heathcock, Joint Environmental Services Manager, City Offices, Colebrook Street, Winchester SO23 9LJ ☎ 01730 234383 ✉ rob.heathcock@easthants.gov.uk

Environmental Health: Mr David Ingram, Head of Environmental Health, City Offices, Colebrook Street, Winchester SO23 9LJ ☎ 01962 848479 🖷 01962 840586 ✉ dingram@winchester.gov.uk

Estates, Property & Valuation: Mr Kevin Warren, Head of Estates, City Offices, Colebrook Street, Winchester SO23 9LJ ☎ 01962 848528 ✉ kwarren@winchester.gov.uk

European Liaison: Ms Nancy Graham, Senior Democratic Services Officer, City Offices, Colebrook Street, Winchester SO23 9LJ ☎ 01962 848221 🖷 01962 848555 ✉ ngraham@winchester.gov.uk

Facilities: Ms Wendy Steele, Facilities Manager, City Offices, Colebrook Street, Winchester SO23 9LJ ☎ 01962 848397 ✉ wsteele@winchester.gov.uk

Finance: Ms Alexis Garlick, Chief Finance Officer, City Offices, Colebrook Street, Winchester SO23 9LJ ☎ 01962 848224 ✉ agarlick@winchester.gov.uk

Grounds Maintenance: Ms Susan Croker, Head of Landscape & Open Spaces, City Offices, Colebrook Street, Winchester SO23 9LJ ☎ 01962 848419 ✉ scroker@winchester.gov.uk

Health and Safety: Mr Robert Cole, Health & Safety Officer, City Offices, Colebrook Street, Winchester SO23 9LJ ☎ 01962 848164 🖷 01962 840586 ✉ bcole@winchester.gov.uk

Housing: Mr Olu Fajuyitan, Senior Housing Needs Officer, City Offices, Colebrook Street, Winchester SO23 9LJ ☎ 01962 840222 ✉ ofajuyitan@winchester.gov.uk

Housing: Mr Andy Palmer, Head of New Homes Delivery, City Offices, Colebrook Street, Winchester SO23 9LJ ☎ 01962 840152 ✉ apalmer@winchester.gov.uk

Housing Maintenance: Mr Andrew Kingston, Property Services Manager, City Offices, Colebrook Street, Winchester SO23 9LJ ☎ 01962 848240 🖷 01962 841365 ✉ akingston@winchester.gov.uk

Legal: Mr Howard Bone, Head of Legal Services, City Offices, Colebrook Street, Winchester SO23 9LJ ☎ 01962 848310 ✉ hbone@winchester.gov.uk

Legal: Mr Stephen Whetnall, Chief Operating Officer, City Offices, Colebrook Street, Winchester SO23 9LJ ☎ 01962 840222 🖷 01962 848555 ✉ swhetnall@winchester.gov.uk

Leisure and Cultural Services: Ms Eloise Appleby, Assistant Director, City Offices, Colebrook Street, Winchester SO23 9LJ ☎ 01962 848181 🖷 01962 848101 ✉ eappleby@winchester.gov.uk

Licensing: Ms Carol Stefanczuk, Licensing Manager, City Offices, Colebrook Street, Winchester SO23 9LJ ☎ 01962 848188 ✉ ctefanczuk@winchester.gov.uk

Lifelong Learning: Mr Sakhumuzi Ngwenya, Training & Development Advisor, City Offices, Colebrook Street, Winchester SO23 9LJ ☎ 01962 840222 🖷 01962 841365 ✉ sngwenya@winchester.gov.uk

Lighting: Mr Neville Crisp, Assistant Engineer for Traffic, City Offices, Colebrook Street, Winchester SO23 9LJ ☎ 01962 848484 ✉ ncrisp@winchester.gov.uk

Lottery Funding, Charity and Voluntary: Mrs Lorraine Ronan, Head of Community Wellbeing, City Offices, Colebrook Street, Winchester SO23 9LJ ☎ 01962 848369 🖷 01962 841365 ✉ lronan@winchester.gov.uk

Member Services: Mr David Blakemore, Democratic Services Manager, City Offices, Colebrook Street, Winchester SO23 9LJ ☎ 01962 848284 🖷 01962 848555 ✉ dblakemore@winchester.gov.uk

Parking: Mr Richard Hein, Parking Manager, City Offices, Colebrook Street, Winchester SO23 9LJ ☎ 01962 848346 ✉ rhein@winchester.gov.uk

Personnel / HR: Ms Alison Gavin, Head of Organisational Development, City Offices, Colebrook Street, Winchester SO23 9LJ ☎ 01962 840222 🖷 01962 841365 ✉ agavin@winchester.gov.uk

Planning: Mr Simon Finch, Assistant Director - Built Environment, City Offices, Colebrook Street, Winchester SO23 9LJ ☎ 01962 840551 ✉ sfinch@winchester.gov.uk

Planning: Mr Steve Opacic, Head of Strategic Planning, City Offices, Colebrook Street, Winchester SO23 9LJ ☎ 01962 848101 ✉ sopacic@winchester.gov.uk

Recycling & Waste Minimisation: Mr Martin Taylor, Waste Management & Street Scene Team Leader, City Offices, Colebrook Street, Winchester SO23 9LJ ☎ 01962 848540 🖷 01962 848272 ✉ mtaylor@winchester.gov.uk

Staff Training: Ms Alison Gavin, Head of Organisational Development, City Offices, Colebrook Street, Winchester SO23 9LJ ☎ 01962 840222 🖷 01962 841365 ✉ agavin@winchester.gov.uk

Street Scene: Mr Dave Brockway, Head of Streetcare & Drainage, City Offices, Colebrook Street, Winchester SO23 9LJ ☎ 01962 856412 🖷 01962 848232 ✉ dbrockway@winchester.gov.uk

Tourism: Ms Ellen Simpson, Head of Tourism, City Offices, Colebrook Street, Winchester SO23 9LJ ☎ 01962 848219 🖷 01962 848101 ✉ esimpson@winchester.gov.uk

Town Centre: Ms Heidi Isa, Market Towns Officer, City Offices, Colebrook Street, Winchester SO23 9LJ ☎ 01962 848069 ✉ hisa@winchester.gov.uk

Traffic Management: Mr Andy Hickman, Head of Major Projects, City Offices, Colebrook Street, Winchester SO23 9LJ ☎ 01962 840222 🖷 01962 848232 ✉ ahickman@winchester.gov.uk

Transport: Mr Andy Hickman, Head of Major Projects, City Offices, Colebrook Street, Winchester SO23 9LJ ☎ 01962 840222 🖷 01962 848232 ✉ ahickman@winchester.gov.uk

Transport: Mr Dave Howarth, Exchequer Services Manager, City Offices, Colebrook Street, Winchester SO23 9LJ ☎ 01962 848157 🖷 01962 841365 ✉ dhowarth@winchester.gov.uk

Transport Planner: Mr Simon Finch, Assistant Director - Built Environment, City Offices, Colebrook Street, Winchester SO23 9LJ ☎ 01962 840551 ✉ sfinch@winchester.gov.uk

Waste Collection and Disposal: Mr Brian Turner, Environmental Services Manager for Contracts, Penns Place, Petersfield GU31 4EX ☎ 01730 234283; 01730 234383 ✉ brian_turner@easthants.gov.uk

Waste Management: Mr Brian Turner, Environmental Services Manager for Contracts, Penns Place, Petersfield GU31 4EX ☎ 01730 234283; 01730 234383 ✉ brian_turner@easthants.gov.uk

COUNCILLORS

***Leader of the Council* Godfrey**, Stephen (CON - Wonston and Micheldever)
sgodfrey@winchester.gov.uk

Achwal, Vivian (LD - Whiteley)
vachwal@winchester.gov.uk

Berry, Eileen (CON - St Barnabas)
eberry@winchester.gov.uk

Berry, Janet (LAB - St John and All Saints)
jberry@winchester.gov.uk

Bodtger, Norma (CON - Upper Meon Valley)
nbodtger@winchester.gov.uk

Burns, Rosemary (CON - St Bartholomew)
rburns@winchester.gov.uk

Byrnes, James (CON - Littleton and Harestock)
jbyrnes@winchester.gov.uk

Clear, Angela (LD - Wickham)
aclear@winchester.gov.uk

Cook, Simon (LD - The Alresfords)
scook@winchester.gov.uk

Cook, Susan (CON - Colden Common and Twyford)
sjcook@winchester.gov.uk

Cutler, Neil (LD - Boarhunt and Southwick)
ncutler@winchester.gov.uk

Dibden, Caroline (CON - Droxford, Soberton and Hambledon)
cdibden@winchester.gov.uk

Evans, Therese (LD - Wickham)
tevans@winchester.gov.uk

Fancett, Patrick (LD - Olivers Battery and Badger Farm)
pfancett@winchester.gov.uk

Gemmell, Linda (CON - Shedfield)
lgemmell@winchester.gov.uk

Gosling, Clive (LAB - St John and All Saints)
cgosling@winchester.gov.uk

Gottlieb, Kim (CON - Itchen Valley)
kgottlieb@winchester.gov.uk

Green, Derek (LD - St Luke)
dgreen@winchester.gov.uk

Hiscock, Dominic (LD - St Bartholomew)
dhiscock@winchester.gov.uk

Horrill, Caroline (CON - Sparsholt)
chorrill@winchester.gov.uk

Humby, Robert (CON - Owslebury and Curdridge)
rhumby@winchester.gov.uk

Hutchison, Robert (LD - St Paul)
lhutchison@winchester.gov.uk

Huxstep, Roger (CON - Shedfield)
rhuxstep@winchester.gov.uk

Izard, Richard (LD - Colden Common and Twyford)
rizard@winchester.gov.uk

Jeffs, Ernest (CON - The Alresfords)
ejeffs@winchester.gov.uk

Johnston, Robert (LD - Kings Worthy)
rjohnston@winchester.gov.uk

Laming, Brian (LD - Olivers Battery and Badger Farm)
blaming@winchester.gov.uk

Lipscomb, Barry (CON - Wonston and Micheldever)
blipscomb@winchester.gov.uk

Mason, Peter (LD - Colden Common and Tywford)
pmason@winchester.gov.uk

Mather, Fiona (CON - St Michael)
fmather@winchester.gov.uk

Maynard, James (LD - St Bartholomew)
jmaynard@winchester.gov.uk

McLean, David (CON - Bishops Waltham)
dmclean@winchester.gov.uk

Miller, Steve (CON - Bishops Waltham)
smiller@winchester.gov.uk

Newman-McKie, Sam (LD - Whiteley)
snewmanmckie@winchester.gov.uk

Osborne, Helen (CON - St Barnabas)
hosborne@winchester.gov.uk

Pearson, Frank (CON - Swanmore and Newtown)
fpearson@winchester.gov.uk

Phillips, Kirk (CON - Denmead)
kphillips@winchester.gov.uk

Power, Margot (LD - The Alresfords)
mpower@winchester.gov.uk

Prowse, Rose (LD - St Luke)
rprowse@winchester.gov.uk

Read, Michael (CON - Denmead)
mread@winchester.gov.uk

Ruffell, Laurence (CON - Owlesbury and Curdridge)
lruffell@winchester.gov.uk

Ruffell, Tom (CON - Bishops Waltham)
truffell@winchester.gov.uk

Rutter, Jane (LD - Kings Worthy)
jrutter@winchester.gov.uk

Sanders, Robert (CON - St Michael)
rsanders@winchester.gov.uk

Scott, Jamie (LD - St Luke)
jscott@winchester.gov.uk

Scowen, Jonathan (CON - St John and All Saints)
jscowen@winchester.gov.uk

Southgate, Mike (CON - Compton and Otterbourne)
msouthgate@winchester.gov.uk

Stallard, Patricia (CON - Denmead)
pstallard@winchester.gov.uk

Tait, Ian (CON - St Michael)
itait@winchester.gov.uk

Thacker, Amber (CON - Cheriton and Bishops Sutton)
athacker@winchester.gov.uk

Thompson, Lucille (LD - St Paul)
luthompson@winchester.gov.uk

Tod, Martin (LD - St Paul)
mtod@winchester.gov.uk

Twelftree, Paul (CON - Littleton and Harestock)
ptwelftree@winchester.gov.uk

Warwick, Jan (CON - Compton and Otterbourne)
jwarwick@winchester.gov.uk

Weir, Anne (LD - St Barnabas)
aweir@winchester.gov.uk

Weston, Victoria (CON - Swanmore and Newtown)
vweston@winchester.gov.uk

Wright, Malcolm (CON - Wonston and Micheldever)
mwright@winchester.gov.uk

POLITICAL COMPOSITION
CON: 33, LD: 22, LAB: 2

Windsor & Maidenhead U

The Royal Borough of Windsor & Maidenhead, Town Hall, St. Ives Road, Maidenhead SL6 1RF
☎ 01628 798888 🖷 01628 796408 💻 www.rbwm.gov.uk

FACTS AND FIGURES
Parliamentary Constituencies: Maidenhead, Windsor
EU Constituencies: South East
Election Frequency: Elections are of whole council

PRINCIPAL OFFICERS

Chief Executive: Ms Alison Alexander, Managing Director & Strategic Director of Children's Services, Town Hall, St. Ives Road, Maidenhead SL6 1RF ☎ 01628 796671
🖱 alison.alexander@rbwm.gov.uk

Senior Management: Ms Alison Alexander, Managing Director & Strategic Director of Children's Services, Town Hall, St. Ives Road, Maidenhead SL6 1RF ☎ 01628 796671
🖱 alison.alexander@rbwm.gov.uk

Senior Management: Mr Terry Baldwin, Head of HR, Town Hall, St. Ives Road, Maidenhead SL6 1RF ☎ 01628 795622
🖱 terry.baldwin@rbwm.gov.uk

Senior Management: Mr Simon Fletcher, Strategic Director - Operations, Town Hall, St. Ives Road, Maidenhead SL6 1RF
☎ 01628 796484 🖱 simon.fletcher@rbwm.gov.uk

Senior Management: Ms Jacqui Hurd, Head of Customer Services, Town Hall, St. Ives Road, Maidenhead SL6 1RF
☎ 01628 683969 🖱 jacqui.hurd@rbwm.gov.uk

Senior Management: Dr Lise Llewellyn, Director - Public Health, Easthampstead House, Town Square, Bracknell RG12 1AQ
🖱 lise.llewellyn@bracknell-forest.gov.uk

Senior Management: Ms Christabel Shawcross, Strategic Director (Adult Social Services) & Deputy Managing Director, Town Hall, St. Ives Road, Maidenhead SL6 1RF ☎ 01628 796159
🖷 01628 683700 🖱 christabel.shawcross@rbwm.gov.uk

Access Officer / Social Services (Disability): Mrs Debbie Verity, Learning Difficulties & Disabilities Service Manager, York House, Sheet Street, Windsor SL4 1DD ☎ 01628 683680
🖱 debbie.verity@rbwm.gov.uk

Best Value: Mr Andrew Elkington, Head of Policy & Performance, Town Hall, St. Ives Road, Maidenhead SL6 1RF ☎ 01628 796025
🖱 andrew.elkington@rbwm.gov.uk

Children / Youth Services: Ms Alison Alexander, Strategic Director of Children's Services, Town Hall, St. Ives Road, Maidenhead SL6 1RF ☎ 01628 796671
🖱 alison.alexander@rbwm.gov.uk

Children / Youth Services: Ms Ann Domeney, Head of Early Help and Safeguarding, RBWM, Town Hall, St Ives Road, Maidenhead SL6 1RF ☎ 01628 683177 🖱 ann.domeney@rbwm.gov.uk

Children / Youth Services: Mr David Scott, Head of Education Strategy & Commissioning, Town Hall, St. Ives Road, Maidenhead SL6 1RF ☎ 01628 796748 🖱 david.scott@rbwm.gov.uk

Civil Registration: Ms Clair Coe, Superintendent Registrar, Town Hall, St. Ives Road, Maidenhead SL6 1RF ☎ 01628 796101
🖱 clair.williams@rbwm.gov.uk

Civil Registration: Ms Jacqui Hurd, Head of Customer Services, Town Hall, St. Ives Road, Maidenhead SL6 1RF ☎ 01628 683969
🖱 jacqui.hurd@rbwm.gov.uk

PR / Communications: Ms Louisa Dean, Communications & Marketing Manager, Town Hall, St. Ives Road, Maidenhead SL6 1RF
☎ 01628 796410 🖱 louisa.dean@rbwm.gov.uk

Community Planning: Mr Simon Hurrell, Head of Planning & Development, Town Hall, St. Ives Road, Maidenhead SL6 1RF
☎ 01628 685712 🖱 simon.hurrell@rbwm.gov.uk

Community Safety: Mr Brian Martin, Community Safety Manager, Town Hall, St Ives Road, Maidenhead SL6 1RF ☎ 01628 796337
🖱 brian.martin@rbwm.gov.uk

Community Safety: Mr David Perkins, Head of Streetcare & Operations, Tinkers Lane Depot, Windsor SL4 4LR
☎ 01628 796860 🖱 david.perkins@rbwm.gov.uk

Computer Management: Mr Rocco Labellarte, Head of Technology and Change Delivery, Town Hall, St. Ives Road, Maidenhead SL6 1RF ☎ 01628 796553 🖰 rocco.labellarte@rbwm.gov.uk

Consumer Protection and Trading Standards: Mr Steve Johnson, Trading Standards Manager, York House, Sheet Street, Windsor SL4 1DD ☎ 01628 683555 🖷 01628 683594 🖰 steve.johnson@rbwm.gov.uk

Customer Service: Mr Simon Fletcher, Strategic Director - Operations, Town Hall, St. Ives Road, Maidenhead SL6 1RF ☎ 01628 796484 🖰 simon.fletcher@rbwm.gov.uk

Customer Service: Ms Jacqui Hurd, Head of Customer Services, Town Hall, St. Ives Road, Maidenhead SL6 1RF ☎ 01628 683969 🖰 jacqui.hurd@rbwm.gov.uk

Customer Service: Mr Andy Jeff, Benefits & Business Service Lead, Town Hall, St. Ives Road, Maidenhead SL6 1RF 🖰 andy.jeff@rbwm.gov.uk

Economic Development: Mr Harjit Hunjan, Community & Business Partnerships Manager, Town Hall, St. Ives Road, Maidenhead SL6 1RF ☎ 01628 796947 🖰 harjit.hunjan@rbwm.gov.uk

Education: Ms Alison Alexander, Strategic Director of Children's Services, Town Hall, St. Ives Road, Maidenhead SL6 1RF ☎ 01628 796671 🖰 alison.alexander@rbwm.gov.uk

Education: Ms Christabel Shawcross, Strategic Director (Adult Social Services) & Deputy Managing Director, Town Hall, St. Ives Road, Maidenhead SL6 1RF ☎ 01628 796159 🖷 01628 683700 🖰 christabel.shawcross@rbwm.gov.uk

Electoral Registration: Mrs Wendy Allum, Electoral Administrator, Town Hall, St. Ives Road, Maidenhead SL6 1RF ☎ 01628 685717 🖰 wendy.allum@rbwm.gov.uk

Electoral Registration: Ms Maria Lucas, Head of Strategic Legal Services, Town Hall, St. Ives Road, Maidenhead SL6 1RF ☎ 01628 796665 🖰 maria.lucas@rbwm.gov.uk

Emergency Planning: Mr Darren Firth, Control Room Services Manager, Tinkers Lane Depot, Tinkers Lane, Windsor SL4 4LR ☎ 01628 796865 🖷 01628 796861 🖰 Darren.firth@rbwm.gov.uk

Energy Management: Mr Martin Fitzpatrick, Energy Awareness Officer, York House, Sheet Street, Windsor SL4 1DD ☎ 01628 683634 🖰 martin.fitzpartick@rbwm.gov.uk

Facilities: Mr Andrew Barclay, Head of Central Services, Town Hall, St. Ives Road, Maidenhead SL6 1RF ☎ 01628 796527 🖰 andrew.barclay@rbwm.gov.uk

Facilities: Mr Simon Fletcher, Strategic Director - Operations, Town Hall, St. Ives Road, Maidenhead SL6 1RF ☎ 01628 796484 🖰 simon.fletcher@rbwm.gov.uk

Facilities: Mr Dean Graham, Front of House Team Leader, Town Hall, St. Ives Road, Maidenhead SL6 1RF ☎ 01628 796409 🖰 dean.graham@rbwm.gov.uk

Facilities: Ms Jacqui Hurd, Head of Customer Services, Town Hall, St. Ives Road, Maidenhead SL6 1RF ☎ 01628 683969 🖰 jacqui.hurd@rbwm.gov.uk

Finance: Mr Andrew Brooker, Head of Strategic Finance and Procurement, Town Hall, St. Ives Road, Maidenhead SL6 1RF ☎ 01628 796341 🖷 01628 796224 🖰 andrew.brooker@rbwm.gov.uk

Pensions: Mr Nick Greenwood, Pension Fund Manager, Town Hall, St. Ives Road, Maidenhead SL6 1RF ☎ 01628 796701 🖰 nick.greenwood@rbwm.gov.uk

Pensions: Mr Pedro Pardo-Ecija, Investment Manager, Town Hall, St. Ives Road, Maidenhead SL6 1RF ☎ 01628 796704 🖰 pedro.pardo@rbwm.gov.uk

Pensions: Mr Kevin Taylor, Pensions Administrations Manager, Town Hall, St. Ives Road, Maidenhead SL6 1RF ☎ 01628 796747 🖰 kevin.taylor@rbwm.gov.uk

Fleet Management: Mr Mark Green, Fleet Management Officer, York House, Sheet Street, Windsor SL4 1DD ☎ 01628 796821 🖰 mark.green@rbwm.gov.uk

Health and Safety: Mr Terry Baldwin, Head of HR, Town Hall, St. Ives Road, Maidenhead SL6 1RF ☎ 01628 795622 🖰 terry.baldwin@rbwm.gov.uk

Highways: Mr Simon Fletcher, Strategic Director - Operations, Town Hall, St. Ives Road, Maidenhead SL6 1RF ☎ 01628 796484 🖰 simon.fletcher@rbwm.gov.uk

Highways: Mr Ben Smith, Manager of Highways, Town Hall, St. Ives Road, Maidenhead SL6 1RF ☎ 01628 796147 🖰 ben.smith@rbwm.gov.uk

Home Energy Conservation: Mr Martyn Clemence, Housing Project Officer, York House, Sheet Street, Windsor SL4 1DD ☎ 01628 683596 🖰 martyn.clemence@rbwm.gov.uk

Housing: Mr Nick Davies, Head of Strategic Commissioning for Adult Social Care & Housing, Town Hall, St. Ives Road, Maidenhead SL6 1RF ☎ 01628 683614 🖰 nick.davies@rbwm.gov.uk

Local Area Agreement: Mr Andrew Brooker, Head of Strategic Finance and Procurement, Town Hall, St. Ives Road, Maidenhead SL6 1RF ☎ 01628 796341 🖷 01628 796224 🖰 andrew.brooker@rbwm.gov.uk

Local Area Agreement: Mr Harjit Hunjan, Community & Business Partnerships Manager, Town Hall, St. Ives Road, Maidenhead SL6 1RF ☎ 01628 796947 🖰 harjit.hunjan@rbwm.gov.uk

Legal: Ms Maria Lucas, Head of Strategic Legal Services, Town Hall, St. Ives Road, Maidenhead SL6 1RF ☎ 01628 796665 🖰 maria.lucas@rbwm.gov.uk

Leisure and Cultural Services: Mr Kevin Mist, Head of Leisure Services, York Stream House, St. Ives Road, Maidenhead SL6 1RF ☎ 01628 796443 🖰 kevin.mist@rbwm.gov.uk

Licensing: Mr Alan Barwise, Licensing Manager, Town Hall, St. Ives Road, Maidenhead SL6 1RF ☎ 01628 798888 ✉ alan.barwise@rwbm.gov.uk

Lottery Funding, Charity and Voluntary: Mr Harjit Hunjan, Community & Business Partnerships Manager, Town Hall, St. Ives Road, Maidenhead SL6 1RF ☎ 01628 796947 ✉ harjit.hunjan@rbwm.gov.uk

Member Services: Mr Andrew Elkington, Head of Policy & Performance, Town Hall, St. Ives Road, Maidenhead SL6 1RF ☎ 01628 796025 ✉ andrew.elkington@rbwm.gov.uk

Parking: Mr Simon Fletcher, Strategic Director - Operations, Town Hall, St. Ives Road, Maidenhead SL6 1RF ☎ 01628 796484 ✉ simon.fletcher@rbwm.gov.uk

Parking: Mr Neil Walter, Parking Manager, Town Hall, St. Ives Road, Maidenhead SL6 1RF ☎ 01628 796485 ✉ neil.walter@rbwm.gov.uk

Partnerships: Mr Andrew Elkington, Head of Policy & Performance, Town Hall, St. Ives Road, Maidenhead SL6 1RF ☎ 01628 796025 ✉ andrew.elkington@rbwm.gov.uk

Partnerships: Mr Harjit Hunjan, Community & Business Partnerships Manager, Town Hall, St. Ives Road, Maidenhead SL6 1RF ☎ 01628 796947 ✉ harjit.hunjan@rbwm.gov.uk

Personnel / HR: Mr Terry Baldwin, Head of HR, Town Hall, St. Ives Road, Maidenhead SL6 1RF ☎ 01628 795622 ✉ terry.baldwin@rbwm.gov.uk

Planning: Mr Chris Hilton, Director of Development & Regeneration, Town Hall, St. Ives Road, Maidenhead SL6 1RF ☎ 01628 685712 ✉ chris.hilton@rbwm.gov.uk

Procurement: Mr Andrew Brooker, Head of Strategic Finance and Procurement, Town Hall, St. Ives Road, Maidenhead SL6 1RF ☎ 01628 796341 🖷 01628 796224 ✉ andrew.brooker@rbwm.gov.uk

Public Libraries: Mr Mark Taylor, Head of Library, Information Heritage & Arts Service, Maidenhead Library, St. Ives Road, Maidenhead SL6 1RF ☎ 01628 796989 ✉ mark.taylor@rbwm.gov.uk

Recycling & Waste Minimisation: Mr Simon Fletcher, Strategic Director - Operations, Town Hall, St. Ives Road, Maidenhead SL6 1RF ☎ 01628 796484 ✉ simon.fletcher@rbwm.gov.uk

Recycling & Waste Minimisation: Mr Steve Westbrooke, Service Development Team Leader, Town Hall, St. Ives Road, Maidenhead SL6 1RF ☎ 01628 683556 ✉ steve.westbrooke@rbwm.gov.uk

Regeneration: Mr Chris Hilton, Director of Development & Regeneration, Town Hall, St. Ives Road, Maidenhead SL6 1RF ☎ 01628 685712 ✉ chris.hilton@rbwm.gov.uk

Regeneration: Ms Gail Kenyon, Planning Infrastructure & Regeneration Manager, Town Hall, St. Ives Road, Maidenhead SL6 1RF ☎ 01628 796157 ✉ gail.kenyon@rbwm.gov.uk

Social Services (Adult): Mr Nick Davies, Head of Strategic Commissioning for Adult Social Care & Housing, York House, Sheet Street, Windsor SL4 1BY ☎ 01628 683614 ✉ nick.davies@rbwm.gov.uk

Social Services (Adult): Ms Angela Morris, Head of Adult Social Care & Health Partnerships, Town Hall, St. Ives Road, Maidenhead SL6 1RF ✉ angela.morris@rbwm.gov.uk

Social Services (Adult): Ms Christabel Shawcross, Strategic Director (Adult Social Services) & Deputy Managing Director, Town Hall, St. Ives Road, Maidenhead SL6 1RF ☎ 01628 796159 🖷 01628 683700 ✉ christabel.shawcross@rbwm.gov.uk

Social Services (Children): Ms Ann Domeney, Head of Early Help and Safeguarding, RBWM, Town Hall, St Ives Road, Maidenhead SL6 1RF ☎ 01628 683177 ✉ ann.domeney@rbwm.gov.uk

Public Health: Dr Lise Llewellyn, Director - Public Health, Easthampstead House, Town Square, Bracknell RG12 1AQ ✉ lise.llewellyn@bracknell-forest.gov.uk

Staff Training: Mr Terry Baldwin, Head of HR, Town Hall, St. Ives Road, Maidenhead SL6 1RF ☎ 01628 795622 ✉ terry.baldwin@rbwm.gov.uk

Street Scene: Mr David Perkins, Head of Streetcare & Operations, Tinkers Lane Depot, Windsor SL4 4LR ☎ 01628 796860 ✉ david.perkins@rbwm.gov.uk

Tourism: Ms Barbara Hunt, Accommodation & Information Manager, York House, Sheet Street, Windsor SL4 1DD ☎ 01753 743909 ✉ barbara.hunt@rbwm.gov.uk

Town Centre: Mr Harjit Hunjan, Community & Business Partnerships Manager, Town Hall, St. Ives Road, Maidenhead SL6 1RF ☎ 01628 796947 ✉ harjit.hunjan@rbwm.gov.uk

Town Centre: Ms Steph James, Maidenhead Town Manager, Town Hall, St. Ives Road, Maidenhead SL6 1RF ☎ 01628 796128 ✉ steph.james@rbwm.gov.uk

Town Centre: Mr Paul Roach, Windsor Town Manager, York House, Sheet Street, Windsor SL4 1DD ☎ 01753 743921 ✉ paul.roach@rbwm.gov.uk

Transport: Ms Gail Kenyon, Planning Infrastructure & Regeneration Manager, Town Hall, St. Ives Road, Maidenhead SL6 1RF ☎ 01628 796157 ✉ gail.kenyon@rbwm.gov.uk

Transport Planner: Ms Gail Kenyon, Planning Infrastructure & Regeneration Manager, Town Hall, St. Ives Road, Maidenhead SL6 1RF ☎ 01628 796157 ✉ gail.kenyon@rbwm.gov.uk

Waste Collection and Disposal: Mr David Thompson, Waste & Environmental Protection Manager, York House, Sheet Street, Windsor SL4 1DD ☎ 01628 683598 ✉ david.thompson@rbwm.gov.uk

Waste Management: Mr Simon Fletcher, Strategic Director - Operations, Town Hall, St. Ives Road, Maidenhead SL6 1RF ☎ 01628 796484 ✉ simon.fletcher@rbwm.gov.uk

WINDSOR & MAIDENHEAD

Waste Management: Mr David Thompson, Waste & Environmental Protection Manager, York House, Sheet Street, Windsor SL4 1DD
☎ 01628 683598 ✉ david.thompson@rbwm.gov.uk

COUNCILLORS

Leader of the Council **Burbage**, David (CON - Bray)
cllr.burbage@rbwm.gov.uk

Deputy Leader of the Council **Bicknell**, Phillip (CON - Park)
cllr.bicknell@rbwm.gov.uk

Deputy Leader of the Council **Dudley**, Simon (CON - Maidenhead Riverside)
cllr.dudley@rbwm.gov.uk

Airey, Michael (CON - Clewer South)
cllr.m.airey@rbwm.gov.uk

Airey, Natasha (CON - Park)
cllr.airey@rbwm.gov.uk

Alexander, Malcolm (CON - Eton & Castle)
cllr.alexander@rbwm.gov.uk

Bateson, Christine (CON - Sunningdale)
cllr.bateson@rbwm.gov.uk

Bathurst, George (CON - Sunninghill & South Ascot)
cllr.bathurst@rbwm.gov.uk

Beer, Malcolm (R - Old Windsor)
cllr.beer@rbwm.gov.uk

Bhatti, Hashim (CON - Clewer North)
cllr.bhatti@rbwm.gov.uk

Bowden, John (CON - Clewer East)
cllr.bowden@rbwm.gov.uk

Brimacombe, Paul (CON - Cox Green)
cllr.brimacombe@rbwm.gov.uk

Bullock, Clive (CON - Cox Green)
cllr.bullock@rbwm.gov.uk

Carroll, Stuart (CON - Boyn Hill)
cllr.carroll@rbwm.gov.uk

Clark, Gerry (CON - Bisham & Cookham)
cllr.clark@rbwm.gov.uk

Collins, John (CON - Clewer North)
cllr.collins@rbwm.gov.uk

Coppinger, David (CON - Bray)
cllr.coppinger@rbwm.gov.uk

Cox, Carwyn (CON - Hurley & Walthams)
cllr.cox@rbwm.gov.uk

Evans, David (CON - Hurley & Walthams)
cllr.d.evans@rbwm.gov.uk

Evans, Lilly (CON - Ascot & Cheapside)
cllr.l.evans@rbwm.gov.uk

Gilmore, Marius (CON - Pinkneys Green)
cllr.gilmore@rbwm.gov.uk

Grey, Jesse (CON - Datchet)
cllr.grey@rbwm.gov.uk

Hill, Geoffrey (CON - Oldfield)
cllr.hill@rbwm.gov.uk

Hilton, David (CON - Ascot & Cheapside)
cllr.hilton@rbwm.gov.uk

Hollingsworth, Charles (CON - Pinkneys Green)
cllr.hollingsworth@rbwm.gov.uk

Hunt, Maureen (CON - Hurley & Walthams)
cllr.hunt@rbwm.gov.uk

Ilyas, Mohammed (CON - Furze Platt)
cllr.ilyas@rbwm.gov.uk

Jenner, Andrew (CON - Maidenhead Riverside)
cllr.jenner@rbwm.gov.uk

Jones, Lynne (R - Old Windsor)
cllr.jones@rbwm.gov.uk

Kellaway, Richard (CON - Bisham & Cookham)
cllr.kellaway@rbwm.gov.uk

Lenton, John (CON - Horton & Wraysbury)
cllr.lenton@rbwm.gov.uk

Lion, Paul (CON - Boyn Hill)
cllr.lion@rbwm.gov.uk

Love, Philip (CON - Belmont)
cllr.love@rbwm.gov.uk

Luxton, Sayonara (CON - Sunningdale)
cllr.luxton@rbwm.gov.uk

Majeed, Ashgar (CON - Oldfield)
cllr.majeed@rbwm.gov.uk

McWilliams, Ross (CON - Cox Green)
cllr.mcwilliams@rbwm.gov.uk

Mills, Marion (CON - Belmont)
cllr.mills@rbwm.gov.uk

Muir, Gary (CON - Datchet)
cllr.muir@rbwm.gov.uk

Pryer, Nicola (CON - Clewer North)
cllr.pryer@rbwm.gov.uk

Quick, Eileen (CON - Clewer East)
cllr.quick@rbwm.gov.uk

Rankin, Jack (CON - Castle Without)
cllr.rankin@rbwm.gov.uk

Rayner, Samantha (CON - Eton Wick)
cllr.s.rayner@rbwm.gov.uk

Rayner, Colin (CON - Horton & Wraysbury)
cllr.rayner@rbwm.gov.uk

Richards, Wesley (CON - Castle Without)
cllr.richards@rbwm.gov.uk

Saunders, MJ (CON - Bisham & Cookham)
cllr.saunders@rbwm.gov.uk

Sharma, Hari (CON - Furze Platt)
cllr.sharma@rbwm.gov.uk

Sharp, Derek (CON - Furze Platt)
cllr.sharp@rbwm.gov.uk

Shelim, Shamsul (CON - Castle Without)
cllr.shelim@rbwm.gov.uk

Smith, Adam (CON - Maidenhead Riverside)
cllr.smith@rbwm.gov.uk

Story, John (CON - Sunninghill & South Ascot)
cllr.story@rbwm.gov.uk

Stretton, Claire (CON - Boyn Hill)
cllr.claire.stretton@rbwm.gov.uk

Targowska, Lisa (CON - Belmont)
cllr.targowska@rbwm.gov.uk

Walters, Leo (CON - Bray)
cllr.walters@rbwm.gov.uk

Werner, Simon (LD - Pinkneys Green)
cllr.werner@rbwm.gov.uk

Wilson, Derek (CON - Oldfield)
cllr.d.wilson@rbwm.gov.uk

Wilson, Edward (CON - Clewer South)
cllr.e.wilson@rbwm.gov.uk

Yong, Lynda (CON - Sunninghill & South Ascot)
cllr.yong@rbwm.gov.uk

POLITICAL COMPOSITION

CON: 54, R: 2, LD: 1

COMMITTEE CHAIRS

Audit & Performance: Mr Paul Brimacombe

Licensing: Mr Ashgar Majeed

Wirral M

Wirral Metropolitan Borough Council, Wallasey Town Hall, Brighton Street, Wallasey, Wirral CH44 8ED
☎ 0151 606 2000 🖷 0151 691 8468 ✉ comments@wirral.gov.uk
💻 www.wirral.gov.uk

FACTS AND FIGURES

Parliamentary Constituencies: Birkenhead, Wallasey, Wirral South, Wirral West
EU Constituencies: North West
Election Frequency: Elections are by thirds

PRINCIPAL OFFICERS

Chief Executive: Mr Eric Robinson, Chief Executive, Hamilton Buildings, Conway Street, Birkenhead CH41 4FD ☎ 0151 691 8589 🖷 0151 691 8583 ✉ ericrobinson@wirral.gov.uk

Assistant Chief Executive: Mr David Armstrong, Assistant Chief Executive & Head of Universal Infrastructure Services, Hamilton Buildings, Conway Street, Birkenhead CH41 4FD ☎ 0151 666 4300 🖷 0151 666 4207 ✉ davidarmstrong@wirral.gov.uk

Senior Management: Mr Michael Peet, Service Manager - Traffic & Transport Division (Client Design), Cheshire Lines, Canning Street, Birkenhead CH41 0ND ☎ 0151 606 2000 ✉ michaelpeet@wirral.gov.uk

Access Officer / Social Services (Disability): Mr Gerard Smyth, NRAC Auditor, Wallasey Town Hall, Brighton Street, Wallasey, Wirral CH44 8ED ☎ 0151 691 8217 🖷 0151 691 8468 ✉ gerardsmyth@wirral.gov.uk

Architect, Building / Property Services: Mr David Armstrong, Assistant Chief Executive & Head of Universal Infrastructure Services, Hamilton Buildings, Conway Street, Birkenhead CH41 4FD ☎ 0151 666 4300 🖷 0151 666 4207 ✉ davidarmstrong@wirral.gov.uk

Best Value: Mr Joe Blott, Strategic Director, Wallasey Town Hall, Brighton Street, Wallasey, Wirral CH44 8ED ☎ 0151 606 2000 ✉ joeblott@wirral.gov.uk

Building Control: Mr David Ball, Head of Regeneration & Environment, Wallasey Town Hall, North Annexe, Brighton Street, Wirral CH44 8ED ☎ 0151 691 8395 ✉ davidball@wirral.gov.uk

Children / Youth Services: Ms Julia Hassall, Director of Children's Services, Hamilton Buildings, Conway Street, Birkenhead CH41 4FD ☎ 0151 666 4288 🖷 0151 666 4207 ✉ juliahassall@wirral.gov.uk

Civil Registration: Ms Suzanne Johnston, Superintendent Registrar, Town Hall, Brighton Street, Wallasey CH44 8ED ☎ 0151 666 3679 🖷 0151 691 8468 ✉ suzannejohnston@wirral.gov.uk

PR / Communications: Ms Emma Degg, Head - Neighbourhoods & Engagement, Wallasey Town Hall, Brighton Street, Wallasey, Wirral CH44 8ED ☎ 0151 691 8688 🖷 0151 691 8361 ✉ emmadegg@wirral.gov.uk

Community Planning: Ms Emma Degg, Head - Neighbourhoods & Engagement, Wallasey Town Hall, Brighton Street, Wallesey, Wirral CH44 8ED ☎ 0151 691 8688 🖷 0151 691 8361 ✉ emmadegg@wirral.gov.uk

Community Safety: Mr Steve McGilvray, Community Safety Co-ordinator, Old Court House, Manor Road, Wallasey CH44 1BU ☎ 0151 606 5485 ✉ stevemcgilvray@wirral.gov.uk

Computer Management: Mr Mike Zammit, Head of IT, PO Box 2, Treasury Building, Cleveland Street, Birkenhead CH41 6BU ☎ 0151 666 3029 ✉ mikezammit@wirral.gov.uk

Consumer Protection and Trading Standards: Mr Derek Payet, Trading Standards Strategic Manager, Wallasey Town Hall, Brighton Street, Wallasey, Wirral CH44 8ED ☎ 0151 691 8640 🖷 0151 691 8098 ✉ derekpayet@wirral.gov.uk

Contracts: Mr Ray Williams, Head of Procurement, Town Hall, Brighton Street, Wallasey, Wirral CH44 8ED ☎ 0151 666 3377 ✉ raywilliams@wirral.gov.uk

Corporate Services: Mr Joe Blott, Strategic Director, Wallasey Town Hall, Brighton Street, Wallasey, Wirral CH44 8ED ☎ 0151 606 2000 ✉ joeblott@wirral.gov.uk

Customer Service: Mr Malcolm Flanagan, Head of Service, Revenues, Benefits & Customer Services, PO Box 2, Treasury Building, Cleveland Street, Birkenhead CH41 6BU ☎ 0151 606 2000 🖷 0151 666 3379 ✉ malcolmflanagan@wirral.gov.uk

Economic Development: Mr David Ball, Head of Regeneration & Environment, Town Hall, Brighton Street, Wallasey CH44 8ED ☎ 0151 691 8395 ✉ davidball@wirral.gov.uk

Education: Mr David Armstrong, Assistant Chief Executive & Head of Universal Infrastructure Services, Hamilton Buildings, Conway Street, Birkenhead CH41 4FD ☎ 0151 666 4300 🖷 0151 666 4207 ✉ davidarmstrong@wirral.gov.uk

Emergency Planning: Mr Mark Camborne, Health, Safety & Resilience Manager, Cheshire Lines Building, Canning Street, Birkenhead CH41 8ED ☎ 0151 606 2071 markcamborne@wirral.gov.uk

Energy Management: Mr David Armstrong, Assistant Chief Executive & Head of Universal Infrastructure Services, Hamilton Buildings, Conway Street, Birkenhead CH41 4FD ☎ 0151 666 4300 🖷 0151 666 4207 davidarmstrong@wirral.gov.uk

Environmental / Technical Services: Mr Mark Smith, Head of Service for Streetscene & Waste, Cheshire Lines Building, Canning Street, Birkenhead CH41 8ED ☎ 0151 606 2103 marksmith@wirral.gov.uk

Environmental Health: Mr Mark Smith, Head of Service for Streetscene & Waste, Cheshire Lines Building, Canning Street, Birkenhead CH41 8ED ☎ 0151 606 2103 marksmith@wirral.gov.uk

Estates, Property & Valuation: Mr David Armstrong, Assistant Chief Executive & Head of Universal Infrastructure Services, Hamilton Buildings, Conway Street, Birkenhead CH41 4FD ☎ 0151 666 4300 🖷 0151 666 4207 davidarmstrong@wirral.gov.uk

European Liaison: Mr David Ball, Head of Regeneration & Environment, Town Hall, Brighton Street, Wallasey CH44 8ED ☎ 0151 691 8395 davidball@wirral.gov.uk

Events Manager: Ms Emma Degg, Head - Neighbourhoods & Engagement, Wallasey Town Hall, Brighton Street, Wallasey CH44 8ED ☎ 0151 691 8688 🖷 0151 691 8361 emmadegg@wirral.gov.uk

Facilities: Mr David Armstrong, Assistant Chief Executive & Head of Universal Infrastructure Services, Hamilton Buildings, Conway Street, Birkenhead CH41 4FD ☎ 0151 666 4300 🖷 0151 666 4207 davidarmstrong@wirral.gov.uk

Finance: Mr Tom Sault, Acting S151 Officer & Head of Financial Services, Wallasey Town Hall, Brighton Street, Wallasey, Wirral CH44 8ED ☎ 0151 666 3056 🖷 0151 666 3058 tomsault@wirral.gov.uk

Pensions: Mr Paddy Dawdall, Head of UK Pension Investments, 7th Floor, Castle Chambers, 43 Castle Street, Liverpool L69 2NW ☎ 0151 242 1390 paddydawdall@wirral.gov.uk

Pensions: Mr Peter Wallach, Pensions Manager, 7th Floor, Castle Chambers, 43 Castle Street, Liverpool L69 2NW ☎ 0151 242 1390 peterwallach@wirral.gov.uk

Grounds Maintenance: Ms Mary Worrall, Service Manager, Cheshire Lines Building, Canning Street, Birkenhead CH41 1ND ☎ 0151 606 2210 maryworrall@wirral.gov.uk

Health and Safety: Mr Andy McMillan, Principal Corporate Health & Safety Officer, Cheshire Lines Building, Canning Street, Birkenhead CH41 1ND ☎ 0151 606 2364 🖷 0151 606 2188 andymcmillan@wirral.gov.uk

Highways: Mr Mark Smith, Head of Service for Streetscene & Waste, Cheshire Lines Building, Canning Street, Birkenhead CH41 8ED ☎ 0151 606 2103 marksmith@wirral.gov.uk

Home Energy Conservation: Mr David Armstrong, Assistant Chief Executive & Head of Universal Infrastructure Services, Hamilton Buildings, Conway Street, Birkenhead CH41 4FD ☎ 0151 666 4300 🖷 0151 666 4207 davidarmstrong@wirral.gov.uk

Housing: Mr Ian Platt, Head of Housing, North Annexe, Town Hall, Brighton Street, Wallasey CH44 8ED ☎ 0151 691 8208 ianplatt@wirral.gov.uk

Local Area Agreement: Ms Lucy Barrow, Senior Policy Manager, Wallasey Town Hall, Brighton Street, Wallasey CH44 8ED ☎ 0151 691 8006 lucybarrow@wirral.gov.uk

Legal: Mr Surjit Tour, Head of Legal & Member Services / Monitoring Officer, Wallasey Town Hall, Brighton Street, Wallasey, Wirral CH44 8ED ☎ 0151 691 8569 🖷 0151 691 8468 surjittour@wirral.gov.uk

Leisure and Cultural Services: Ms Clare Fish, Strategic Director, Wallasey Town Hall, Brighton Street, Wallasey, Wirral CH44 8ED ☎ 0151 666 2082 🖷 0151 691 8273 clarefish@wirral.gov.uk

Licensing: Mrs Margaret O'Donnell, Licensing Manager, Town Hall, Brighton Street, Wallasey CH44 8ED ☎ 0151 691 8606 🖷 0151 691 8468 margaretodonnell@wirral.gov.uk

Lifelong Learning: Mr David Armstrong, Assistant Chief Executive & Head of Universal Infrastructure Services, Hamilton Buildings, Conway Street, Birkenhead CH41 4FD ☎ 0151 666 4300 🖷 0151 666 4207 davidarmstrong@wirral.gov.uk

Lighting: Mr Mark Smith, Head of Service for Streetscene & Waste, Cheshire Lines Building, Canning Street, Birkenhead CH41 8ED ☎ 0151 606 2103 marksmith@wirral.gov.uk

Lottery Funding, Charity and Voluntary: Ms Emma Degg, Head - Neighbourhoods & Engagement, Wallasey Town Hall, Brighton Street, Wallasey CH44 8ED ☎ 0151 691 8688 🖷 0151 691 8361 emmadegg@wirral.gov.uk

Member Services: Mr Surjit Tour, Head of Legal & Member Services / Monitoring Officer, Wallasey Town Hall, Brighton Street, Wallasey, Wirral CH44 8ED ☎ 0151 691 8569 🖷 0151 691 8468 surjittour@wirral.gov.uk

Parking: Mr Mark Smith, Head of Service for Streetscene & Waste, Cheshire Lines Building, Canning Street, Birkenhead CH41 8ED ☎ 0151 606 2103 marksmith@wirral.gov.uk

Personnel / HR: Mrs Chris Hyams, Head of Human Resources & Organisational Development, Wallasey Town Hall, Brighton Street, Wallasey, Wirral CH44 8ED ☎ 0151 691 8590 chrishyams@wirral.gov.uk

Planning: Mr David Ball, Head of Regeneration & Environment, Town Hall, Brighton Street, Wallasey CH44 8ED ☎ 0151 691 8395 davidball@wirral.gov.uk

Procurement: Mr Ray Williams, Head of Procurement, Town Hall, Brighton Street, Wallasey, Wirral CH44 8ED ☎ 0151 666 3377 raywilliams@wirral.gov.uk

Public Libraries: Mr Malcolm Flanagan, Head of Service, Revenues, Benefits & Customer Services, PO Box 2, Treasury Building, Cleveland Street, Birkenhead CH41 6BU ☎ 0151 606 2000 🖷 0151 666 3379 malcolmflanagan@wirral.gov.uk

Recycling & Waste Minimisation: Mr Mark Smith, Head of Service for Streetscene & Waste, Cheshire Lines Building, Canning Street, Birkenhead CH41 8ED ☎ 0151 606 2103 marksmith@wirral.gov.uk

Regeneration: Mr David Ball, Head of Regeneration & Environment, Town Hall, Brighton Street, Wallasey CH44 8ED ☎ 0151 691 8395 davidball@wirral.gov.uk

Road Safety: Mr Mark Smith, Head of Service for Streetscene & Waste, Cheshire Lines Building, Canning Street, Birkenhead CH41 8ED ☎ 0151 606 2103 marksmith@wirral.gov.uk

Social Services: Mr Graham Hodkinson, Director of Adult Social Services, PO Box 351, Social Services Headquarters, Birkenhead CH25 9EF ☎ 0151 666 3632 🖷 0151 666 3531 grahamhodkinson@wirral.gov.uk

Social Services (Adult): Mr Graham Hodkinson, Director of Adult Social Services, PO Box 351, Social Services Headquarters, Birkenhead CH25 9EF ☎ 0151 666 3632 🖷 0151 666 3531 grahamhodkinson@wirral.gov.uk

Social Services (Children): Ms Julia Hassall, Director of Children's Services, Social Services Headquarters, Westminster House, Hamilton Street, Birkenhead CH41 5FN ☎ 0151 666 4288 🖷 0151 666 4207 juliahassall@wirral.gov.uk

Staff Training: Mrs Chris Hyams, Head of Human Resources & Organisational Development, Wallasey Town Hall, Brighton Street, Wallasey, Wirral CH44 8ED ☎ 0151 691 8590 chrishyams@wirral.gov.uk

Street Scene: Mr Mark Smith, Head of Service for Streetscene & Waste, Cheshire Lines Building, Canning Street, Birkenhead CH41 8ED ☎ 0151 606 2103 marksmith@wirral.gov.uk

Sustainable Communities: Mr David Armstrong, Assistant Chief Executive & Head of Universal Infrastructure Services, Hamilton Buildings, Conway Street, Birkenhead CH41 4FD ☎ 0151 666 4300 🖷 0151 666 4207 davidarmstrong@wirral.gov.uk

Sustainable Development: Mr David Armstrong, Assistant Chief Executive & Head of Universal Infrastructure Services, Hamilton Buildings, Conway Street, Birkenhead CH41 4FD ☎ 0151 666 4300 🖷 0151 666 4207 davidarmstrong@wirral.gov.uk

Tourism: Ms Emma Degg, Head - Neighbourhoods & Engagement, Wallasey Town Hall, Brighton Street, Wallasey CH44 8ED ☎ 0151 691 8688 🖷 0151 691 8361 emmadegg@wirral.gov.uk

Town Centre: Mr David Ball, Head of Regeneration & Environment, Town Hall, Brighton Street, Wallasey CH44 8ED ☎ 0151 691 8395 davidball@wirral.gov.uk

Traffic Management: Mr Michael Peet, Service Manager - Traffic & Transport Division (Client Design), Cheshire Lines, Canning Street, Birkenhead CH41 0ND ☎ 0151 606 2000 michaelpeet@wirral.gov.uk

Transport: Mr David Armstrong, Assistant Chief Executive & Head of Universal Infrastructure Services, Hamilton Buildings, Conway Street, Birkenhead CH41 4FD ☎ 0151 666 4300 🖷 0151 666 4207 davidarmstrong@wirral.gov.uk

Transport Planner: Mr Mark Smith, Head of Service for Streetscene & Waste, Cheshire Lines Building, Canning Street, Birkenhead CH41 8ED ☎ 0151 606 2103 marksmith@wirral.gov.uk

Waste Collection and Disposal: Mr Mark Smith, Head of Service for Streetscene & Waste, Cheshire Lines Building, Canning Street, Birkenhead CH41 8ED ☎ 0151 606 2103 marksmith@wirral.gov.uk

Waste Management: Mr Mark Smith, Head of Service for Streetscene & Waste, Cheshire Lines Building, Canning Street, Birkenhead CH41 8ED ☎ 0151 606 2103 marksmith@wirral.gov.uk

Children's Play Areas: Ms Mary Worrall, Service Manager, Cheshire Lines Building, Canning Street, Birkenhead CH41 1ND ☎ 0151 606 2210 maryworrall@wirral.gov.uk

COUNCILLORS

***Mayor* Rowlands**, Les (CON - Heswall)
lesrowlands@wirral.gov.uk

***Deputy Mayor* Hackett**, Pat (LAB - New Brighton)
pathackett@wirral.gov

***Leader of the Council* Davies**, Phil (LAB - Birkenhead and Tranmere)
phildavies@wirral.gov.uk

***Deputy Leader of the Council* McLachlan**, Ann (LAB - Bidston and St James)
annmclachlan@wirral.gov.uk

***Group Leader* Gilchrist**, Phil (LD - Eastham)
philgilchrist@wirral.gov.uk

***Group Leader* Green**, Jeff (CON - West Kirby and Thurstaston)
jeffgreen@wirral.gov.uk

Abbey, Ron (LAB - Leasowe and Moreton East)
ronabbey@wirral.gov.uk

Anderson, Tom (CON - Greasby, Frankby and Irby)
tomanderson@wirral.gov.uk

Berry, Bruce (CON - Moreton West and Saughall Massie)
bruceberry@wirral.gov.uk

Blakeley, Chris (CON - Moreton West and Saughall Massie)
chrisblakeley@wirral.gov.uk

Boult, Eddie (CON - Hoylake and Meols)
Eddieboult@wirral.gov.uk

Brighouse, Alan (LD - Oxton)
alanbrighouse@wirral.gov.uk

Brightmore, Phillip (LAB - Pensby and Thingwall)
phillipbrightmore@wirral.gov.uk

Burgess-Joyce, David (CON - Greasby, Frankby and Irby)

WIRRAL

Carubia, Chris (LD - Eastham)
chriscarubia@wirral.gov.uk

Cleary, Pat (GRN - Birkenhead and Tranmere)
patcleary@wirral.gov.uk

Clements, Wendy (CON - Greasby, Frankby and Irby)
Wendyclements@wirral.gov.uk

Crabtree, Jim (LAB - Bidston and St James)
jimcrabtree@wirral.gov.uk

Daniel, Matt (LAB - Liscard)
matthewdaniel@wirral.gov.uk

Davies, Bill (LAB - Rock Ferry)
billdavies@wirral.gov.uk

Davies, George (LAB - Claughton)
georgedavies@wirral.gov.uk

Davies, Angela (LAB - Prenton)
angeladavies@wirral.gov.uk

Doughty, Paul (LAB - Oxton)
pauldoughty@wirral.gov.uk

Elderton, David (CON - West Kirby and Thurstaston)
davidelderton@wirral.gov.uk

Ellis, Gerry (CON - Hoylake and Meols)

Foulkes, Steve (LAB - Claughton)
stevefoulkes@wirral.gov.uk

Fraser, Leah (CON - Wallasey)
leahfraser@wirral.gov.uk

Gregson, Robert (LAB - New Brighton)
robgregson@wirral.gov.uk

Hale, John (CON - Hoylake and Meols)
johnhale@wirral.gov.uk

Hayes, Paul (CON - Wallasey)
paulhayes@wirral.gov.uk

Hodson, Kathy (CON - Heswall)
kathyhodson@wirral.gov.uk

Hodson, Andrew (CON - Heswall)
andrewhodson@wirral.gov.uk

Johnson, Treena (LAB - Leasowe and Moreton East)

Jones, Adrian (LAB - Seacombe)
adrianjones@wirral.gov.uk

Jones, Chris (LAB - Seacombe)
christinejones@wirral.gov.uk

Kenny, Brian (LAB - Bidston and St James)

Leech, Anita (LAB - Leasowe and Moreton East)
anitaleech@wirral.gov.uk

McLaughlin, Moira (LAB - Rock Ferry)
moiramclaughlin@wirral.gov.uk

Meaden, Chris (LAB - Rock Ferry)
chrismeaden@wirral.gov.uk

Mitchell, Dave (LD - Eastham)
davemitchell@wirral.gov.uk

Mooney, Bernie (LAB - Liscard)
berniemooney@wirral.gov.uk

Muspratt, Christina (LAB - Bebington)
christinamuspratt@wirral.gov.uk

Niblock, Steve (LAB - Bromborough)
steveniblock@wirral.gov.uk

Norbury, Tony (LAB - Prenton)
tonynorbury@wirral.gov.uk

Patrick, Matthew (LAB - Upton)
matthewpatrick@wirral.gov.uk

Pilgrim, Tracey (CON - Clatterbridge)
traceysmith1@wirral.gov.uk

Povall, Cherry (CON - Clatterbridge)
cherrypovall@wirral.gov.uk

Realey, Denise (LAB - Prenton)
deniserealey@wirral.gov.uk

Reecejones, Louise (LAB - Pensby and Thingwall)
louisereecejones@wirral.gov.uk

Rennie, Lesley (CON - Wallasey)
lesleyrennie@wirral.gov.uk

Roberts, Denise (LAB - Claughton)
deniseroberts@wirral.gov.uk

Salter, John (LAB - Seacombe)
johnsalter@wirral.gov.uk

Smith, Walter (LAB - Bebington)
waltersmith@wirral.gov.uk

Smith, Tony (LAB - Upton)
tonysmith@wirral.gov.uk

Spriggs, Chris (LAB - New Brighton)
christinespriggs@wirral.gov.uk

Stapleton, Jean (LAB - Birkenhead and Tranmere)
jeanstapleton@wirral.gov.uk

Sullivan, Michael (LAB - Pensby and Thingwall)
mikesullivan@wirral.gov.uk

Sykes, Adam (CON - Clatterbridge)
adamsykes@wirral.gov.uk

Walsh, Joe (LAB - Bromborough)
joewalsh@wirral.gov.uk

Watt, Geoffrey (CON - West Kirby and Thurstaston)
geoffreywatt@wirral.gov.uk

Whittingham, Stuart (LAB - Upton)
stuartw@labour4wirral.gov.uk

Williams, Jerry (LAB - Bebington)
jerrywilliams@wirral.gov.uk

Williams, Irene (LAB - Bromborough)
irenewilliams@wirral.gov.uk

Williams, Patricia (LD - Oxton)
patriciawilliams@wirral.gov.uk

Williams, Steve (CON - Moreton West and Saughall Massie)
stevewilliams@wirral.gov.uk

Williamson, Janette (LAB - Liscard)
janwilliamson@wirral.gov.uk

POLITICAL COMPOSITION

LAB: 39, CON: 21, LD: 5, GRN: 1

COMMITTEE CHAIRS

Audit & Risk: Mr Jim Crabtree

Health & Wellbeing: Mr Phil Davies

Licensing: Mr Bill Davies

Pensions: Mr Paul Doughty

Planning: Ms Anita Leech

Woking D

Woking Borough Council, Civic Offices, Gloucester Square, Woking GU21 6YL
☎ 01483 755855 🖷 01483 768746 wokbc@woking.gov.uk
www.woking.gov.uk

FACTS AND FIGURES

Parliamentary Constituencies: Woking
EU Constituencies: South East
Election Frequency: Elections are by thirds

PRINCIPAL OFFICERS

Chief Executive: Mr Ray Morgan, Chief Executive, Civic Offices, Gloucester Square, Woking GU21 6YL ☎ 01483 743051 🖷 01483 768746 ray.morgan@woking.gov.uk

Deputy Chief Executive: Mr Douglas Spinks, Deputy Chief Executive, Civic Offices, Gloucester Square, Woking GU21 6YL ☎ 01483 743783 🖷 01483 768746 douglas.spinks@woking.gov.uk

Senior Management: Ms Sue Barham, Strategic Director, Civic Offices, Gloucester Square, Woking GU21 6YL ☎ 01483 743810 🖷 01483 725318 sue.barham@woking.gov.uk

Senior Management: Mr Mark Rolt, Strategic Director, Civic Offices, Gloucester Square, Woking GU21 6YL ☎ 01483 743050 🖷 01483 768746 mark.rolt@woking.gov.uk

Access Officer / Social Services (Disability): Ms Rafeia Zaman, Equalities Officer, Civic Offices, Gloucester Square, Woking GU21 6YL ☎ 01483 743479 🖷 01483 756842 rafeia.zaman@woking.gov.uk

Architect, Building / Property Services: Mr David Loveless, Corporate Building Services & Design Team Leader, Civic Offices, Gloucester Square, Woking GU21 6YL ☎ 01483 743554 🖷 01483 723580 david.loveless@woking.gov.uk

Building Control: Mr David Edwards, Chief Building Control Surveyor, Civic Offices, Gloucester Square, Woking GU21 6YL ☎ 01483 743430 🖷 01483 776298 david.edwards@woking.gov.uk

Children / Youth Services: Ms Sue Barham, Strategic Director, Civic Offices, Gloucester Square, Woking GU21 6YL ☎ 01483 743810 🖷 01483 725318 sue.barham@woking.gov.uk

PR / Communications: Mr Andy Denner, Marketing Communications Manager, Civic Offices, Gloucester Square, Woking GU21 6YL ☎ 01483 743024 🖷 01483 743055 andy.denner@woking.gov.uk

Community Planning: Ms Sue Barham, Strategic Director, Civic Offices, Gloucester Square, Woking GU21 6YL ☎ 01483 743810 🖷 01483 725318 sue.barham@woking.gov.uk

Community Safety: Mrs Camilla Edmiston, Community Safety Officer, Civic Offices, Gloucester Square, Woking GU21 6YL ☎ 01483 743080 🖷 01483 743055 camilla.edmiston@woking.gov.uk

Computer Management: Mrs Adele Devon, ICT Manager, Civic Offices, Gloucester Square, Woking GU21 6YL ☎ 01483 743279 🖷 01483 768746 adele.devon@woking.gov.uk

Customer Service: Mr David Ripley, Revenue & Benefits Manager, Civic Offices, Gloucester Square, Woking GU21 6YL ☎ 01483 743630 david.ripley@woking.gov.uk

E-Government: Ms Adele Devon, IT Manager, Civic Offices, Gloucester Square, Woking GU21 6YL ☎ 01483 743279 🖷 01483 768746 adele.devon@woking.gov.uk

Electoral Registration: Mrs Charlotte Griffiths, Electoral & IS Manager, Civic Offices, Gloucester Square, Woking GU21 6YL ☎ 01483 743215 charlotte.griffiths@woking.gov.uk

Emergency Planning: Mr Geoff McManus, Neighbourhood Services Manager, Civic Offices, Gloucester Square, Woking GU21 6YL ☎ 01483 743707 🖷 01483 776335 geoff.mcmanus@woking.gov.uk

Environmental / Technical Services: Mr Geoff McManus, Neighbourhood Services Manager, Civic Offices, Gloucester Square, Woking GU21 6YL ☎ 01483 743707 🖷 01483 776335 geoff.mcmanus@woking.gov.uk

Environmental Health: Ms Emma Bourne, Environmental Health Manager, Civic Offices, Gloucester Square, Woking GU21 6YL ☎ 01483 743654 emma.bourne@woking.gov.uk

European Liaison: Mr Peter Bryant, Head of Democratic & Legal Services, Civic Offices, Gloucester Square, Woking GU21 6YL ☎ 01483 743030 🖷 01483 768746 peter.bryant@woking.gov.uk

Events Manager: Mr Andy Denner, Marketing Communications Manager, Civic Offices, Gloucester Square, Woking GU21 6YL ☎ 01483 743024 🖷 01483 743055 andy.denner@woking.gov.uk

Facilities: Mr David Jones, Temporary Senior Building Services Engineer, Civic Offices, Gloucester Square, Woking GU21 6YL ☎ 01483 768746 david.jones@woking.gov.uk

Finance: Mrs Leigh Clarke, Financial Services Manager & Chief Finance Officer, Civic Offices, Gloucester Square, Woking GU21 6YL ☎ 01483 743277 🖷 01483 724032 leigh.clarke@woking.gov.uk

Grounds Maintenance: Mr Geoff McManus, Neighbourhood Services Manager, Civic Offices, Gloucester Square, Woking GU21 6YL ☎ 01483 743707 🖷 01483 776335 geoff.mcmanus@woking.gov.uk

Health and Safety: Ms Lisa Harrington, Senior Health & Safety Officer, Civic Offices, Gloucester Square, Woking GU21 6YL ☎ 01483 743213 🖷 01483 724032 lisa.harrington@woking.gov.uk

Housing: Mr Mark Rolt, Strategic Director, Civic Offices, Gloucester Square, Woking GU21 6YL ☎ 01483 743050 🖷 01483 768746 mark.rolt@woking.gov.uk

Housing Maintenance: Mr Barry Montgomerie, Director of New Vision Homes, Civic Offices, Gloucester Square, Woking GU21 6YL ☎ 01483 743620 ✉ barry.montgomerie@nvhwoking.gov.uk

Legal: Mr Peter Bryant, Head of Democratic & Legal Services, Civic Offices, Gloucester Square, Woking GU21 6YL ☎ 01483 743030 🖷 01483 768746 ✉ peter.bryant@woking.gov.uk

Leisure and Cultural Services: Ms Sue Barham, Strategic Director, Civic Offices, Gloucester Square, Woking GU21 6YL ☎ 01483 743810 🖷 01483 725318 ✉ sue.barham@woking.gov.uk

Licensing: Mr Russell Ellis, Licensing Manager, Civic Offices, Gloucester Square, Woking GU21 6YL ☎ 01483 743732 🖷 01483 768746 ✉ russell.ellis@woking.gov.uk

Lottery Funding, Charity and Voluntary: Mr Frank Jeffrey, Democratic Services Manager, Civic Offices, Gloucester Square, Woking GU21 6YL ☎ 01483 743012 🖷 01483 768746 ✉ frank.jeffrey@woking.gov.uk

Member Services: Mr Frank Jeffrey, Democratic Services Manager, Civic Offices, Gloucester Square, Woking GU21 6YL ☎ 01483 743012 🖷 01483 768746 ✉ frank.jeffrey@woking.gov.uk

Parking: Mr Gavin Manger, Parking Services Manager, Civic Offices, Gloucester Square, Woking GU21 6YL ☎ 01483 743450 ✉ gavin.manger@woking.gov.uk

Personnel / HR: Mrs Amanda Jeffrey, HR Manager, Civic Offices, Gloucester Square, Woking GU21 6YL ☎ 01483 743904 🖷 01483 725318 ✉ amanda.jeffrey@woking.gov.uk

Planning: Mr Douglas Spinks, Deputy Chief Executive, Civic Offices, Gloucester Square, Woking GU21 6YL ☎ 01483 743783 🖷 01483 768746 ✉ douglas.spinks@woking.gov.uk

Procurement: Mrs Sharon Eager, Corporate Client & Procurement Officer, Civic Offices, Gloucester Square, Woking GU21 6YL ☎ 01483 743711 ✉ sharon.eager@woking.gov.uk

Recycling & Waste Minimisation: Mr Geoff McManus, Neighbourhood Services Manager, Civic Offices, Gloucester Square, Woking GU21 6YL ☎ 01483 743707 🖷 01483 776335 ✉ geoff.mcmanus@woking.gov.uk

Staff Training: Mrs Amanda Jeffrey, HR Manager, Civic Offices, Gloucester Square, Woking GU21 6YL ☎ 01483 743904 🖷 01483 725318 ✉ amanda.jeffrey@woking.gov.uk

Sustainable Communities: Mr Tim Lowe, Senior Policy Officer of Sustainability, Civic Offices, Gloucester Square, Woking GU21 6YL ☎ 01483 743413 🖷 01483 768746 ✉ tim.lowe@woking.gov.uk

Sustainable Development: Mr Tim Lowe, Senior Policy Officer of Sustainability, Civic Offices, Gloucester Square, Woking GU21 6YL ☎ 01483 743413 🖷 01483 768746 ✉ tim.lowe@woking.gov.uk

Tourism: Mr Andy Denner, Marketing Communications Manager, Civic Offices, Gloucester Square, Woking GU21 6YL ☎ 01483 743024 🖷 01483 743055 ✉ andy.denner@woking.gov.uk

Waste Collection and Disposal: Mr Geoff McManus, Neighbourhood Services Manager, Civic Offices, Gloucester Square, Woking GU21 6YL ☎ 01483 743707 🖷 01483 776335 ✉ geoff.mcmanus@woking.gov.uk

COUNCILLORS

***Mayor* McCrum**, Derek (LD - Kingfield and Westfield)
cllrderek.mccrum@woking.gov.uk

***Deputy Mayor* Murray**, Anne (CON - Horsell East and Woodham)
cllranne.murray@woking.gov.uk

***Leader of the Council* Kingsbury**, John (CON - St Johns and Hook Heath)
cllrjohn.kingsbury@woking.gov.uk

***Deputy Leader of the Council* Bittleston**, David (CON - Mount Hermon East)
cllrdavid.bittleston@woking.gov.uk

***Group Leader* Forster**, Will (LD - Kingfield and Westfield)
cllrwill.forster@woking.gov.uk

***Group Leader* Raja**, Mohammed (LAB - Maybury and Sheerwater)
cllrmilyas.raja@woking.gov.uk

Addison, Hilary (CON - Goldsworth East)
cllrhilary.addison@woking.gov.uk

Azad, Ayesha (CON - Mayford and Sutton Green)
cllrayesha.azad@woking.gov.uk

Aziz, Tahir (LAB - Maybury and Sheerwater)
cllrtahir.aziz@woking.gov.uk

Bond, John (IND - Byfleet)
cllrjohn.bond@woking.gov.uk

Bowes, Ashley (CON - Pyrford)
cllrashley.bowes@woking.gov.uk

Branagan, Tony (CON - Horsell West)
cllrtony.branagan@woking.gov.uk

Briggs, Harry (CON - Byfleet)
cllrharry.briggs@woking.gov.uk

Chrystie, Graham (CON - Pyrford)
cllrgraham.chrystie@woking.gov.uk

Coulson, Amanda (LD - Goldsworth East)
cllramanda.coulson@woking.gov.uk

Coulson, Denzil (LD - Goldsworth West)
cllrdenzil.coulson@woking.gov.uk

Cundy, Graham (CON - St Johns and Hook Heath)
cllrgraham.cundy@woking.gov.uk

Davis, Kevin (CON - Brookwood)
cllrkevin.davis@woking.gov.uk

Eastwood, Ian (LD - Goldsworth West)
cllrian.eastwood@woking.gov.uk

Elson, Gary (CON - West Byfleet)
cllrgary.elson@woking.gov.uk

Harlow, Debbie (CON - Knaphill)
cllrdebbie.harlow@woking.gov.uk

Howard, Ken (LD - Hermitage and Knaphill South)
cllrken.howard@woking.gov.uk

Hunwicks, Beryl (CON - Horsell West)
cllrberyl.hunwicks@woking.gov.uk

Hussain, Saj (CON - Knaphill)
cllrsaj.hussain@woking.gov.uk

Johnson, Ian (LD - Mount Hermon West)
cllrian.johnson@woking.gov.uk

Kemp, Colin (CON - Horswell West)
cllrcolin.kemp@woking.gov.uk

Lawrence, John (CON - Old Woking)
cllrjohn.lawrence@woking.gov.uk

Lyons, Liam (LD - Mount Hermon West)
cllrliam.lyons@woking.gov.uk

Mohammed, Rashid (CON - Maybury and Sheerwater)
cllrrashid.mohammed@woking.gov.uk

Roberts, Anne (LD - Byfleet)
cllranne.roberts@woking.gov.uk

Shah, Rizwan (CON - Goldsworth East)
cllrrizwan.shah@woking.gov.uk

Smith, Michael (CON - Horsell East and Woodham)
cllrmichael.smith@woking.gov.uk

Smith, Paul (CON - Hermitage and Knaphill South)
cllrpaul.smith@woking.gov.uk

Thomson, Carl (CON - Mount Hermon East)
cllrcarl.thomson@woking.gov.uk

Whitehand, Melanie (CON - Knaphill)
cllrmelanie.whitehand@woking.gov.uk

Wilson, Richard (CON - West Byfleet)
cllrrichard.wilson@woking.gov.uk

POLITICAL COMPOSITION

CON: 24, LD: 9, LAB: 2, IND: 1

COMMITTEE CHAIRS

Licensing: Mr Carl Thomson

Planning: Mr Ashley Bowes

Wokingham U

Wokingham Borough Council, Wokingham Borough Council, Shute End, Wokingham RG40 1BN
☎ 0118 974 6000 🖷 0118 978 9078 ✉ wokinghambc@wokingham.gov.uk
💻 www.wokingham.gov.uk

FACTS AND FIGURES

Parliamentary Constituencies: Bracknell, Maidenhead, Reading East, Wokingham
EU Constituencies: South East
Election Frequency: Elections are by thirds

PRINCIPAL OFFICERS

Chief Executive: Mr Andy Couldrick, Chief Executive, Wokingham Borough Council, Shute End, Wokingham RG40 1BN ☎ 0118 974 6001 🖷 0118 974 6135 ✉ andy.couldrick@wokingham.gov.uk

Senior Management: Dr Lise Llewellyn, Director - Public Health, Easthampstead House, Town Square, Bracknell RG12 1AQ
✉ lise.llewellyn@bracknell-forest.gov.uk

Architect, Building / Property Services: Mr Rodney Hing, Service Manager - Operational Property, Wokingham Borough Council, Shute End, Wokingham RG40 1BN ☎ 0118 974 6000 🖷 0118 974 6724 ✉ rodney.hing@wokingham.gov.uk

Building Control: Mr Neil Badley, Head of Infrastructure Implementation, Civic Offices, Wokingham RG40 1WQ ☎ 0118 974 6366 🖷 0118 974 6385 ✉ neil.badley@wokingham.gov.uk

Children / Youth Services: Ms Felicity Budgen, Interim Head - Safeguarding and Social Care, Wokingham Borough Council, Shute End, Wokingham RG40 1BN ☎ 0118 974 6137
✉ felicity.budgen@wokingham.gov.uk

Children / Youth Services: Ms Judith Ramsden, Director - Children's Services, PO Box 156, Civic Offices, 2nd Floor, Shute End,, Wokingham RG40 1BN ☎ 0118 974 6203
✉ judith.ramsden@wokingham.gov.uk

Children / Youth Services: Mr Alan Stubberdfield, Interim Head of Learning & Achievement, Wokingham Borough Council, Shute End, Wokingham RG40 1BN ☎ 0118 974 6121 🖷 0118 974 6135
✉ alan.stubbersfield@wokingham.gov.uk

Civil Registration: Ms Liz Lepere, Superintendent Registrar, Council Offices, Shute End, Wokingham RG40 1BN ☎ 0118 974 6554 🖷 0118 978 2813 ✉ liz.lepere@wokingham.gov.uk

PR / Communications: Miss Andrea Jenkins, Service Manager - Communications, PO Box 150, Council Offices, Shute End, Wokingham RG40 1WQ ☎ 0118 974 6010 🖷 0118 978 5053
✉ andrea.jenkins@wokingham.gov.uk

Community Planning: Ms Sarah Hollamby, Head of Corporate Strategy & Performance, Wokingham Borough Council, Shute End, Wokingham RG40 1BN ☎ 0118 974 6817 🖷 0118 979 0877
✉ sarah.hollamby@wokingham.gov.uk

Community Planning: Ms Heather Thwaites, Director - Environment, Wokingham Borough Council, Shute End, Wokingham RG40 1BN ☎ 0118 974 6425 🖷 0118 974 6385
✉ heather.thwaites@wokingham.gov.uk

Community Safety: Mr Stuart Rowbotham, Director of Health & Wellbeing, Council Offices, Shute End, Wokingham RG40 1BN ☎ 0118 974 6762 🖷 0118 974 6770
✉ stuart.rowbotham@wokingham.gov.uk

Computer Management: Mr Mike Ibbitson, Head of Customer Services & IMT, Wokingham Borough Council, Shute End, Wokingham RG40 1BN ☎ 0118 974 6962
✉ mike.ibbitson@wokingham.gov.uk

Contracts: Mr Graham Ebers, Director - Resources, PO Box 152, Council Offices, Shute End, Wokingham RG40 1WJ ☎ 0118 974 6557 🖷 0118 974 6574 ✉ graham.ebers@wokingham.gov.uk

Corporate Services: Mr Neil Badley, Head of Infrastructure Implementation, Civic Offices, Wokingham RG40 1WQ ☎ 0118 974 6366 🖷 0118 974 6385 ✉ neil.badley@wokingham.gov.uk

Corporate Services: Mr Rob Stubbs, Head of Financial Services, PO Box 154, Civic Offices, 2nd Floor, Shute End, Wokingham RG40 1WN ☎ 0118 974 6973 ✉ rob.stubbs@wokingham.gov.uk

Customer Service: Ms Marion Wood, Senior Complaints Officer, Wokingham Borough Council, Shute End, Wokingham RG40 1BN ☎ 0118 974 6026 ✉ marion.wood@wokingham.gov.uk

Economic Development: Mr Andrew Nicholls, Economic Development Officer, PO Box 157, Council Offices, Shute End, Wokingham RG40 1WR ☎ 0118 974 6398 🖷 0118 974 6401 ✉ andrew.nicholls@wokingham.gov.uk

E-Government: Mr Andrew Moulton, Head of Governance & Improvement Services, Wokingham Borough Council, Shute End, Wokingham RG40 1BN ☎ 0118 974 6677 ✉ andrew.moulton@wokingham.gov.uk

Electoral Registration: Ms Alison Wood, Electoral Services Manager, Council Offices, Shute End, Wokingham RG40 1WQ ☎ 0118 974 6521 🖷 0118 974 6542 ✉ alison.wood@wokingham.gov.uk

Environmental / Technical Services: Mr Matt Davey, Head of Highways & Transport, PO Box 155, Civic Offices, Shute End, Wokingham RG40 1WW ☎ 0118 974 6000 ✉ matt.davey@wokingham.gov.uk

Estates, Property & Valuation: Mr Chris Gillett, Strategic Asset Manager, PO Box 151, Council Offices, Shute End, Wokingham RG40 1WH ☎ 0118 974 6700 🖷 0118 974 6724 ✉ chris.gillett@wokingham.gov.uk

Facilities: Mr Rodney Hing, Service Manager - Operational Property, Wokingham Borough Council, Shute End, Wokingham RG40 1BN ☎ 0118 974 6000 🖷 0118 974 6724 ✉ rodney.hing@wokingham.gov.uk

Grounds Maintenance: Mrs Julia Woodbridge, Senior Parks Officer, Civic Offices, Shute End, Wokingham RG40 1BR ☎ 0118 974 6273 🖷 0118 974 6312 ✉ julia.woodbridge@wokingham.gov.uk

Housing: Mr Simon Price, Head of Housing, Waterford House, Erfstadt Court, Wokingham RG40 2YF ☎ 0118 974 3775 🖷 0118 974 3788 ✉ simon.price@wokingham.gov.uk

Housing Maintenance: Mr Simon Price, Head of Housing, Waterford House, Erfstadt Court, Wokingham RG40 2YF ☎ 0118 974 3775 🖷 0118 974 3788 ✉ simon.price@wokingham.gov.uk

Legal: Mr Andrew Moulton, Head of Governance & Improvement Services, Wokingham Borough Council, Shute End, Wokingham RG40 1BN ☎ 0118 974 6677 ✉ andrew.moulton@wokingham.gov.uk

Member Services: Ms Anne Hunter, Democratic Services Manager, PO Box 150, Council Offices, Shute End, Wokingham RG40 1WQ ☎ 0118 974 6051 🖷 0118 974 6057 ✉ anne.hunter@wokingham.gov.uk

Parking: Ms Alison Dray, Service Manager, Wokingham Borough Council, Shute End, Wokingham RG40 1BN ☎ 0118 974 6315 🖷 0118 974 6313 ✉ alison.dray@wokingham.gov.uk

Partnerships: Ms Josie Wragg, Head of Community Services, Wokingham Borough Council, Shute End, Wokingham RG40 1BN ☎ 0118 974 6002 🖷 0118 978 9078 ✉ josie.wragg@wokingham.gov.uk

Personnel / HR: Ms Sarah Swindley, Service Manager - HR, Wokingham Borough Council, Shute End, Wokingham RG40 1BN ☎ 0118 974 6087 ✉ jan.hale@wokingham.gov.uk

Planning: Ms Clare Lawrence, Head of Development Management & Enforcement, Wokingham Borough Council, Shute End, Wokingham RG40 1BN ☎ 0118 974 6444 🖷 0118 978 9078 ✉ clare.lawrence@wokingham.gov.uk

Procurement: Mr Kien Lac, Head of Commercial Services, Wokingham Borough Council, Shute End, Wokingham RG40 1BN ☎ 0118 974 6000 ✉ kien.lac@wokingham.gov.uk

Recycling & Waste Minimisation: Mr Peter Baveystock, Waste & Recycling Manager, Civic Centre, Shute End, Wokingham RG40 1NL ☎ 0118 974 6338 🖷 0118 974 6312 ✉ peter.baveystock@wokingham.gov.uk

Regeneration: Ms Heather Thwaites, Director - Environment, Wokingham Borough Council, Shute End, Wokingham RG40 1BN ☎ 0118 974 6425 🖷 0118 974 6385 ✉ heather.thwaites@wokingham.gov.uk

Road Safety: Mr Matt Davey, Head of Highways & Transport, PO Box 155, Civic Offices, Shute End, Wokingham RG40 1WW ☎ 0118 974 6000 ✉ matt.davey@wokingham.gov.uk

Social Services: Ms Lynne McFetridge, Interim Head of Adult Social Care & Safeguarding, Wokingham Borough Council, Shute End, Wokingham RG40 1BN ☎ 0118 908 8196 ✉ lynne.mcfetridge@wokingham.gov.uk

Social Services: Mr Stuart Rowbotham, Strategic Director - Health & Wellbeing, Wokingham Borough Council, Shute End, Wokingham RG40 1BN ☎ 0118 974 6762 🖷 0118 974 6770 ✉ stuart.rowbotham@wokingham.gov.uk

Social Services (Adult): Mr Stuart Rowbotham, Strategic Director - Health & Wellbeing, Wokingham Borough Council, Shute End, Wokingham RG40 1BN ☎ 0118 974 6762 🖷 0118 974 6770 ✉ stuart.rowbotham@wokingham.gov.uk

Social Services (Children): Ms Judith Ramsden, Director - Children's Services, PO Box 156, Civic Offices, 2nd Floor, Shute End,, Wokingham RG40 1BN ☎ 0118 974 6203 ✉ judith.ramsden@wokingham.gov.uk

Public Health: Dr Lise Llewellyn, Director - Public Health, Easthampstead House, Town Square, Bracknell RG12 1AQ ✉ lise.llewellyn@bracknell-forest.gov.uk

Staff Training: Ms Gillian Ward, Personnel Strategy & Organisation Development Manager, PO Box 150, Council Offices, Shute End, Wokingham RG40 1WQ ☎ 0118 974 6037 🖷 0118 974 6092 ✉ gillian.ward@wokingham.gov.uk

Town Centre: Mr Bernard Pich, Head of Strategic Assets & Capital Resources, Wokingham Borough Council, Shute End, Wokingham RG40 1BN ☎ 0118 974 6700 🖷 0118 974 6724 ✉ bernie.pich@wokingham.gov.uk

Traffic Management: Mr Matt Davey, Head of Highways & Transport, PO Box 155, Civic Offices, Shute End, Wokingham RG40 1WW ☎ 0118 974 6000 ✉ matt.davey@wokingham.gov.uk

Waste Collection and Disposal: Mr Peter Baveystock, Waste & Recycling Manager, Civic Centre, Shute End, Wokingham RG40 1NL ☎ 0118 974 6338 🖷 0118 974 6312 ✉ peter.baveystock@wokingham.gov.uk

Waste Management: Mr Peter Baveystock, Waste & Recycling Manager, Civic Centre, Shute End, Wokingham RG40 1NL ☎ 0118 974 6338 🖷 0118 974 6312 ✉ peter.baveystock@wokingham.gov.uk

COUNCILLORS

***Mayor* Batth**, Parry (CON - Shinfield North)
Parry.batth@wokingham.gov.uk

***Deputy Mayor* Pitts**, Bob (CON - Remenham Wargrave & Ruscombe)
bob.pitts@wokingham.gov.uk

***Leader of the Council* Baker**, Keith (CON - Coronation)
keith.baker@wokingham.gov.uk

***Deputy Leader of the Council* McGhee-Sumner**, Julian (CON - Wescott)
julian.mcghee-sumner@wokingham.gov.uk

***Group Leader* Bray**, Prue (LD - Winnersh)
prue.bray@wokingham.gov.uk

Ashwell, Mark (CON - Evendons)

Auty, Alistair (CON - Norreys)
alistair.auty@wokingham.gov.uk

Blumenthal, Laura (CON - South Lake)
laura.blumenthal@wokingham.gov.uk

Bowring, Chris (CON - Evendons)
chris.bowring@wokingham.gov.uk

Chopping, David (CON - Maiden Erlegh)
david.chopping@wokingham.gov.uk

Clark, UllaKarin (CON - Emmbrook)
ullakarin.clark@wokingham.gov.uk

Cowan, Gary (CON - Arborfield)
gary.cowan@wokingham.gov.uk

Ferris, Lindsay (LD - Twyford)
lindsay.ferris@wokingham.gov.uk

Firmager, Michael (CON - Hawkedon)
michael.firmager@wokingham.gov.uk

Gore, Mike (CON - Finchampstead North)
mike.gore@wokingham.gov.uk

Grandison, Guy (CON - Hawkedon)
guy.grandison@wokingham.gov.uk

Haines, Mike (CON - Sonning)
mike.haines@wokingham.gov.uk

Haines, Kate (CON - Coronation)
kate.haines@wokingham.gov.uk

Haitham Taylor, Charlotte (CON - Shinfield South)
charlotte.haithamtaylor@wokingham.gov.uk

Halsall, John (CON - Remenham Wargrave & Ruscombe)
john.halsall@wokingham.gov.uk

Helliar-Symons, Pauline (CON - Wokingham Without)
pauline.helliar-symons@wokingham.gov.uk

Holton, Tim (CON - Hawkedon)
tim.holton@wokinghaam.gov.uk

Houldsworth, Philip (CON - Winnersh)
philip.houldsworth@wokingham.gov.uk

Jarvis, John (CON - Twyford)

Jerome, Nicky (LAB - Bulmershe & Whitegates)

Jorgensen, Norman (CON - Hillside)
norman.jorgensen@wokingham.gov.uk

Jorgensen, Pauline (CON - Hillside)
pauline.jorgensen@wokingham.gov.uk

Kaiser, John (CON - Barkham)
john.kaiser@wokingham.gov.uk

King, Dianne (CON - Evendons)
dianne.king@wokingham.gov.uk

Lee, David (CON - Norreys)
david.lee@wokingham.gov.uk

Loyes, Abdul (CON - Loddon)
abdul.loyes@wokingham.gov.uk

McCann, Tom (LD - Loddon)

Miall, Ken (CON - Maiden Erlegh)
ken.miall@wokingham.gov.uk

Mirfin, Philip (CON - Emmbrook)
philip.mirfin@wokingham.gov.uk

Munro, Stuart (CON - Swallowfield)
stuart.munro@wokingham.gov.uk

Patman, Barrie (CON - Shinfield South)
barrie.patman@wokingham.gov.uk

Pittock, Ian (CON - Finchampstead South)
ian.pittock@wokingham.gov.uk

Pollock, Anthony (CON - Shinfield South)
anthony.pollock@wokingham.gov.uk

Ray, Nick (IND - Charvil)
nick.ray@wokingham.gov.uk

Richards, Malcolm (CON - Norreys)
malcolm.richards@wokingham.gov.uk

Ross, Angus (CON - Wokingham Without)
angus.ross@wokingham.gov.uk

Rowland, Beth (LD - South Lake)
beth.rowland@wokingham.gov.uk

Shepherd-DuBey, Rachelle (LD - Winnersh)
rachelle.shepherd-dubey@wokingham.gov.uk

Singleton, Chris (CON - Emmbrook)
chris.singleton@wokingham.gov.uk

Sleight, David (CON - Wokingham Without)
david.sleight@wokingham.gov.uk

Sloane, Bill (CON - Loddon)

Smith, Chris (CON - Hillside)

Smith, Wayne (CON - Hurst)
wayne.smith@wokingham.gov.uk

Stanton, Rob (CON - Finchampstead North)
rob.stanton@wokingham.gov.uk

Swaddle, Alison (CON - Bulmershe & Whitegates)

Swaddle, Paul (CON - Maiden Erlegh)
paul.swaddle@wokingham.gov.uk

Weeks, Simon (CON - Finchampstead South)
simon.weeks@wokingham.gov.uk

Wyatt, Bob (CON - Wescott)
r.wyatt325@btinternet.com

Younis, Shahid (CON - Bulmershe & Whitegates)
shahid.younis@wokingham.gov.uk

POLITICAL COMPOSITION

CON: 47, LD: 5, IND: 1, LAB: 1

COMMITTEE CHAIRS

Audit: Mr Guy Grandison

Children's Services: Mrs Pauline Helliar-Symons

Health & Wellbeing: Mr Julian McGhee-Sumner

Licensing: Mr Chris Bowring

Planning: Mr Simon Weeks

Wolverhampton M

Wolverhampton City Council, Civic Centre, St. Peter's Square, Wolverhampton WV1 1SH
☎ 01902 556556 🖷 01902 554030 ✉ citydirect@wolverhampton.gov.uk
🖳 www.wolverhampton.gov.uk

FACTS AND FIGURES

Parliamentary Constituencies: Wolverhampton North East, Wolverhampton South East, Wolverhampton South West
EU Constituencies: West Midlands
Election Frequency: Elections are by thirds

PRINCIPAL OFFICERS

Chief Executive: Mr Keith Ireland, Managing Director, Civic Centre, St. Peter's Square, Wolverhampton WV1 1SH ☎ 01902 554500 ✉ keith.ireland@wolverhampton.gov.uk

Access Officer / Social Services (Disability): Ms Viv Griffin, Service Director - Disability & Mental Health, Civic Centre, St. Peter's Square, Wolverhampton WV1 1SH ☎ 01902 555370 ✉ vivienne.griffin@wolverhampton.gov.uk

Access Officer / Social Services (Disability): Ms Suzanne Smith, Head of All Age Disability, Civic Centre, St. Peter's Square, Wolverhampton WV1 1SH ☎ 01902 555377 ✉ suzanne.smith@wolverhampton.gov.uk

Architect, Building / Property Services: Mr Nick Edwards, Service Director - City Assets, Civic Centre, St. Peter's Square, Wolverhampton WV1 1SH ☎ 01902 554310 ✉ nick.edwards@wolverhampton.gov.uk

Building Control: Mr Stephen Alexander, Head of Planning, Civic Centre, St. Peter's Square, Wolverhampton WV1 1SH ☎ 01902 555610 ✉ stephen.alexander@wolverhampton.gov.uk

Catering Services: Mr Chris East, Head of Facilities Management, Civic Centre, St. Peter's Square, Wolverhampton WV1 1SH ☎ 01902 555277 ✉ chris.east@wolverhampton.gov.uk

Children / Youth Services: Ms Emma Bennett, Service Director - Children & Young People, Civic Centre, St. Peter's Square, Wolverhampton WV1 1SH ☎ 01902 551449 ✉ emma.bennett@wolverhampton.gov.uk

Civil Registration: Mr Martyn Sargeant, Group Manager - Corporate Adminstration, Civic Centre, St. Peter's Square, Wolverhampton WV1 1SH ☎ 01902 554286 ✉ martyn.sargeant@wolverhampton.gov.uk

PR / Communications: Mr Ian Fegan, Head of Communications, Civic Centre, St. Peter's Square, Wolverhampton WV1 1SH ☎ 01902 554286 ✉ ian.fegan@wolverhampton.gov.uk

Community Safety: Ms Ros Jervis, Service Director - Wellbeing, Civic Centre, St. Peter's Square, Wolverhampton WV1 1SH ☎ 01902 550347 ✉ ros.jervis@wolverhampton.gov.uk

Community Safety: Ms Karen Samuels, Head of Community Safety, Civic Centre, St. Peter's Square, Wolverhampton WV1 1SH ☎ 01902 551341 ✉ karen.samuels@wolverhampton.gov.uk

Computer Management: Mr Andy Hoare, Head of ICT, Civic Centre, St. Peter's Square, Wolverhampton WV1 1SH ☎ 01902 554563 ✉ andy.hoare@wolverhampton.gov.uk

Consumer Protection and Trading Standards: Mr Andy Jervis, Head of Regulatory Services, Civic Centre, St. Peter's Square, Wolverhampton WV1 1SH ☎ 01902 551261 ✉ andy.jervis@wolverhampton.gov.uk

Contracts: Mr Andy Moran, Head of Procurement, Civic Centre, St. Peter's Square, Wolverhampton WV1 1SH ☎ 01902 554132 ✉ andy.moran@wolverhampton.gov.uk

Corporate Services: Mr Kevin O'Keefe, Director of Governance, Civic Centre, St. Peter's Square, Wolverhampton WV1 1SH ☎ 01902 554910 ✉ kevin.o'keefe@wolverhampton.gov.uk

Corporate Services: Mr Mark Taylor, Director of Finance, Civic Centre, St. Peter's Square, Wolverhampton WV1 1SH ☎ 01902 556609 ✉ mark.taylor@wolverhampton.gov.uk

Customer Service: Ms Sue Handy, Head of Customer Services, Civic Centre, St. Peter's Square, Wolverhampton WV1 1SH ☎ 01902 554390 ✉ sue.handy@wolverhampton.gov.uk

Economic Development: Ms Keren Jones, Service Director - City Economy, Civic Centre, St. Peter's Square, Wolverhampton WV1 1SH ☎ 01902 554739 ✉ keren.jones@wolverhampton.gov.uk

Education: Dr James McElliott, Director - Education, Civic Centre, St. Peter's Square, Wolverhampton WV1 1SH ☎ 01902 554100 ✉ james.mcelliott@wolverhampton.gov.uk

Electoral Registration: Mr Martyn Sargeant, Group Manager - Corporate Adminstration, Civic Centre, St. Peter's Square, Wolverhampton WV1 1SH ☎ 01902 554286 martyn.sargeant@wolverhampton.gov.uk

Emergency Planning: Mr Andy Smith, Emergency Planning Manager, Civic Centre, St. Peter's Square, Wolverhampton WV1 1SH ☎ 01902 558672 any.smith@wolverhampton.gov.uk

Environmental Health: Mr Andy Jervis, Head of Regulatory Services, Civic Centre, St. Peter's Square, Wolverhampton WV1 1SH ☎ 01902 551261 andy.jervis@wolverhampton.gov.uk

Events Manager: Mr Mark Blackstock, Head of Visitor Economy, Civic Centre, St. Peter's Square, Wolverhampton WV1 1SH ☎ 01902 556245 mark.blackstock@wolverhampton.gov.uk

Facilities: Mr Chris East, Head of Facilities Management, Civic Centre, St. Peter's Square, Wolverhampton WV1 1SH ☎ 01902 555277 chris.east@wolverhampton.gov.uk

Finance: Mr Mark Taylor, Director of Finance, Civic Centre, St. Peter's Square, Wolverhampton WV1 1SH ☎ 01902 556609 mark.taylor@wolverhampton.gov.uk

Treasury: Mr Mark Taylor, Director of Finance, Civic Centre, St. Peter's Square, Wolverhampton WV1 1SH ☎ 01902 556609 mark.taylor@wolverhampton.gov.uk

Pensions: Ms Geik Drever, Strategic Director - West Midlands Pension Fund, Civic Centre, St. Peter's Square, Wolverhampton WV1 1SH ☎ 01902 552020 geik.drever@wolverhampton.gov.uk

Fleet Management: Mr Steve Wright, Head of Bereavement & Fleet Services, Civic Centre, St. Peter's Square, Wolverhampton WV1 1SH ☎ 01902 554866 steve.wright@wolverhampton.gov.uk

Grounds Maintenance: Mr Steve Woodward, Head of Public Realm, Civic Centre, St. Peter's Square, Wolverhampton WV1 1SH ☎ 01902 554260 steve.woodward@wolverhampton.gov.uk

Health and Safety: Ms Denise Pearce, Head of Human Resources, Civic Centre, St. Peter's Square, Wolverhampton WV1 1SH ☎ 01902 554515 denise.pearce@wolverhampton.gov.uk

Highways: Ms Gwyn James, Transportation Manager, Civic Centre, St. Peter's Square, Wolverhampton WV1 1SH ☎ 01902 555755 gwyn.james@wolverhampton.gov.uk

Housing: Mr Christopher Hale, Head of City Housing, Civic Centre, St. Peter's Square, Wolverhampton WV1 1SH ☎ 01902 551796 christopher.hale@wolverhampton.gov.uk

Legal: Ms Tracey Christie, Head of Legal Services, Civic Centre, St. Peter's Square, Wolverhampton WV1 1SH ☎ 01902 554925 tracey.christie@wolverhampton.gov.uk

Legal: Mr Kevin O'Keefe, Director of Governance, Civic Centre, St. Peter's Square, Wolverhampton WV1 1SH ☎ 01902 554910 kevin.o'keefe@wolverhampton.gov.uk

Licensing: Mr Andy Jervis, Head of Regulatory Services, Civic Centre, St. Peter's Square, Wolverhampton WV1 1SH ☎ 01902 551261 andy.jervis@wolverhampton.gov.uk

Member Services: Mr Adam Hadley, Group Manager - Democracy, Civic Centre, St. Peter's Square, Wolverhampton WV1 1SH ☎ 01902 555043 adam.hadley@wolverhampton.gov.uk

Parking: Mr Steve Woodward, Head of Public Realm, Civic Centre, St. Peter's Square, Wolverhampton WV1 1SH ☎ 01902 554260 steve.woodward@wolverhampton.gov.uk

Partnerships: Ms Keren Jones, Service Director - City Economy, Civic Centre, St. Peter's Square, Wolverhampton WV1 1SH ☎ 01902 554739 keren.jones@wolverhampton.gov.uk

Personnel / HR: Ms Charlotte Johns, Head of Transformation, Civic Centre, St. Peter's Square, Wolverhampton WV1 1SH ☎ 01902 554240 charlotte.johns@wolverhampton.gov.uk

Personnel / HR: Ms Denise Pearce, Head of Human Resources, Civic Centre, St. Peter's Square, Wolverhampton WV1 1SH ☎ 01902 554515 denise.pearce@wolverhampton.gov.uk

Planning: Mr Stephen Alexander, Head of Planning, Civic Centre, St. Peter's Square, Wolverhampton WV1 1SH ☎ 01902 555610 stephen.alexander@wolverhampton.gov.uk

Procurement: Mr Andy Moran, Head of Procurement, Civic Centre, St. Peter's Square, Wolverhampton WV1 1SH ☎ 01902 554132 andy.moran@wolverhampton.gov.uk

Regeneration: Ms Marie Bintley, Head of City Development, Civic Centre, St. Peter's Square, Wolverhampton WV1 1SH ☎ 01902 557978 marie.bintley@wolverhampton.gov.uk

Regeneration: Ms Keren Jones, Service Director - City Economy, Civic Centre, St. Peter's Square, Wolverhampton WV1 1SH ☎ 01902 554739 keren.jones@wolverhampton.gov.uk

Social Services: Ms Linda Sanders, Strategic Director - People, Civic Centre, St. Peter's Square, Wolverhampton WV1 1SH ☎ 01902 555300 linda.sanders@wolverhampton.gov.uk

Social Services (Adult): Mr Tony Ivko, Service Director - Older People, Civic Centre, St. Peter's Square, Wolverhampton WV1 1SH ☎ 01902 555310 anthony.ivko@wolverhampton.gov.uk

Social Services (Children): Ms Emma Bennett, Service Director - Children & Young People, Civic Centre, St. Peter's Square, Wolverhampton WV1 1SH ☎ 01902 551449 emma.bennett@wolverhampton.gov.uk

Public Health: Ms Ros Jervis, Service Director - Wellbeing, Civic Centre, St. Peter's Square, Wolverhampton WV1 1SH ☎ 01902 550347 ros.jervis@wolverhampton.gov.uk

Street Scene: Mr Steve Woodward, Head of Public Realm, Civic Centre, St. Peter's Square, Wolverhampton WV1 1SH ☎ 01902 554260 steve.woodward@wolverhampton.gov.uk

WOLVERHAMPTON

Town Centre: Ms Cherry Shine, BID Director - Wolverhampton BID, 176 - 178 Stafford Street, Stafford Court, Wolverhampton WV1 1NA ☎ 01902 710903 ✉ cherry@wolverhamptonbid.gov.uk

Transport: Ms Gwyn James, Transportation Manager, Civic Centre, St. Peter's Square, Wolverhampton WV1 1SH ☎ 01902 555755 ✉ gwyn.james@wolverhampton.gov.uk

Waste Management: Mr Chris Huddart, Head of Commercial Services, Civic Centre, St. Peter's Square, Wolverhampton WV1 1SH ☎ 01902 556788 ✉ chris.huddart@wolverhampton.gov.uk

COUNCILLORS

***Leader of the Council* Lawrence**, Roger (LAB - St. Peter's)
Labourleadersoffice@wolverhampton.gov.uk

Angus, Ian (LAB - Bushbury North)
ian.angus@wolverhampton.gov.uk

Bagri, Harbans (LAB - Blakenhall)
harbans.bagri@wolverhampton.gov.uk

Banger, Harman (LAB - East Park)
harman.banger@wolverhampton.gov.uk

Bateman, Philip (LAB - Wednesfield North)
phil.bateman@wolverhampton.gov.uk

Bateman, Mary (LAB - Wednesfield North)

Bedi, Payal (LAB - East Park)
payal.bedi@wolverhampton.gov.uk

Bilson, Peter (LAB - Bushbury South and Low Hill)
peter.bilson@wolverhampton.gov.uk

Bolshaw, Alan (LAB - Merry Hill)
alan.bolshaw@wolverhampton.gov.uk

Brackenridge, Greg (LAB - Wednesfield South)
greg.brackenridge@wolverhampton.gov.uk

Brookfield, Ian (LAB - Fallings Park)
ian.brookfield@wolverhampton.gov.uk

Brookfield, Paula (LAB - Wednesfield South)
paula.brookfield@wolverhampton.gov.uk

Claymore, Ian (LAB - Oxley)
ian.claymore@wolverhampton.gov.uk

Collingswood, Craig (LAB - Park)
craig.collingswood@wolverhampton.gov.uk

Darke, Claire (LAB - Park)
claire.darke@wolverhampton.gov.uk

Dass, Bishan (LAB - Ettingshall)
bishan.dass@wolverhampton.gov.uk

Dehar, Jasbinder (LAB - Bushbury North)
jas.dehar@wolverhampton.gov.uk

Evans, Mark (CON - Tettenhall Regis)
cllrmark.evans@wolverhampton.gov.uk

Evans, Steven (LAB - Fallings Park)
steve.evans4@wolverhampton.gov.uk

Evans, Valerie (LAB - Fallings Park)
valerie.evans@wolverhampton.gov.uk

Findlay, Barry (CON - Tettenhall Regis)
barry.findlay@wolverhampton.gov.uk

Gakhal, Bhupinder (LAB - Wednesfield South)
bhupinder.gakhal@wolverhampton.gov.uk

Gibson, Val (LAB - Bilston East)
val.gibson@wolverhampton.gov.uk

Gwinnett, Malcolm (UKIP - Spring Vale)
malcolm.gwinnett@wolverhampton.gov.uk

Hardacre, Mike (LAB - Park)
mike.hardacre@wolverhampton.gov.uk

Haynes, Christopher (CON - Merry Hill)
christopher.haynes@wolverhampton.gov.uk

Hodgkiss, Julie (LAB - Oxley)
julie.hodgkiss@wolverhampton.gov.uk

Inston, Keith (LAB - East Park)
keith.inston@wolverhampton.gov.uk

Jaspal, Milkinderpal (LAB - Heath Town)
milkinder.jaspal@wolverhampton.gov.uk

Jaspal, Jasbir (LAB - Heath Town)
jasbir.jaspal@wolverhampton.gov.uk

Johnson, Andrew (LAB - Ettingshall)
cllra.johnson@wolverhampton.gov.uk

Kaur, Rupinderjit (LAB - Spring Vale)
rupinderjit.kaur@wolverhampton.gov.uk

Koussoukama, Welcome (LAB - Bilston North)
welcome.koussoukama@wolverhampton.gov.uk

Leach, Linda (LAB - Bilston North)
linda.leach@wolverhampton.gov.uk

Mattu, Elias (LAB - Graiseley)
elias.mattu@wolverhampton.gov.uk

McGregor, Lorna (LAB - Oxley)
lorna.mcgregor@wolverhampton.gov.uk

Mills, Christine (CON - Merry Hill)
councillor.mills@wolverhampton.gov.uk

Moran, Lynne (LAB - St. Peter's)
lynne.moran@wolverhampton.gov.uk

O'Neill, Peter (LAB - Bushbury South and Low Hill)
peter.o'neill@wolverhampton.gov.uk

Page, Phillip (LAB - Bilston North)
phillip.page@wolverhampton.gov.uk

Patten, Patricia (CON - Penn)
patricia.patten@wolverhampton.gov.uk

Photay, Arun (CON - Tettenhall Wightwick)
arun.photay@wolverhampton.gov.uk

Potter, Rita (LAB - Wednesfield North)
rita.potter@wolverhampton.gov.uk

Reynolds, John (LAB - Graiseley)
john.reynolds@wolverhampton.gov.uk

Rowley, Judith (LAB - Blakenhall)
judith.rowley@wolverhampton.gov.uk

Rowley, John (LAB - Blakenhall)
john.rowley@wolverhampton.gov.uk

Samuels, Sandra (LAB - Ettingshall)
councillorsandra.samuels@wolverhampton.gov.uk

Sarkiewicz, Caroline (LAB - Heath Town)
caroline.siarkiewicz@wolverhampton.gov.uk

Simkins, Stephen (LAB - Bilston East)
stephen.simkins@wolverhampton.gov.uk

Singh, Paul (CON - Penn)
paul.singh@wolverhampton.gov.uk

Singh, Tersaim (LAB - St. Peter's)
tersaim.singh@wolverhampton.gov.uk

Sweet, Paul (LAB - Bushbury South and Low Hill)
paul.sweet@wolverhampton.gov.uk

Sweetman, Jacqueline (LAB - Graiseley)
cllrsweetman@wolverhampton.gov.uk

Thompson, Wendy (CON - Tettenhall Wightwick)
wendy.thompson@wolverhampton.gov.uk

Turner, Thomas (LAB - Bilston East)
thomas.turner@wolverhamtpon.gov.uk

Waite, Martin (LAB - Penn)
martin.waite@wolverhampton.gov.uk

Warren, Daniel (LAB - Bushbury North)
daniel.warren@wolverhampton.gov.uk

Whitehouse, Richard (O - Spring Vale)
whitehouse.richard@wolverhampton.gov.uk

Wynne, Andrew (CON - Tettenhall Wightwick)
andrew.wynne@wolverhampton.gov.uk

Yardley, Johnathan (CON - Tettenhall Regis)
jonathan.yardley@wolverhampton.gov.uk

POLITICAL COMPOSITION

LAB: 48, CON: 10, O: 1, UKIP: 1

COMMITTEE CHAIRS

Audit: Mr Craig Collingswood

Children, Young People & Families: Mr Peter O'Neill

Health & Wellbeing: Ms Sandra Samuels

Licensing: Mr Alan Bolshaw

Pensions: Mr Thomas Turner

Planning: Ms Linda Leach

Worcester City D

Worcester City Council, The Guildhall, High Street, Worcester WR1 2EY
☎ 01905 722233 🖷 01905 722059; 01905 722028
💻 www.worcester.gov.uk

FACTS AND FIGURES

Parliamentary Constituencies: Worcester
EU Constituencies: West Midlands
Election Frequency: Elections are by thirds

PRINCIPAL OFFICERS

Chief Executive: Ms Sheena Ramsey, Managing Director, The Guildhall, High Street, Worcester WR1 2EY ☎ 01905 722233 ✉ sheena.ramsey@worcester.gov.uk

Senior Management: Mr David Blake, Acting Corporate Director - Place, The Guildhall, High Street, Worcester WR1 2EY ☎ 01905 722233 🖷 01905 722370 ✉ david.blake@worcester.gov.uk

Senior Management: Mrs Lesley Meagher, Corporate Director for Resources & Acting Head of Paid Service, Guildhall, High Street, Worcester WR1 2EY ☎ 01905 722233 🖷 01905 722190 ✉ lesley.meagher@worcester.gov.uk

Senior Management: Mrs Ruth Mullen, Corporate Director for Service Delivery, Guildhall, High Street, Worcester WR1 2EY ☎ 01905 722233 🖷 01905 722028 ✉ ruth.mullen@worcester.gov.uk

Building Control: Mr Reza Saneie, Building Control Partnership Manager, Council House, Avenue Road, Malvern WR14 3AF ☎ 01684 862146; 01905 722233 ✉ mail@southworcestershirebuildingcontrol.gov.uk

PR / Communications: Mr Rob Byrne, Communications & PR Team Manager, Guildhall, High Street, Worcester WR1 2EY ☎ 01905 722233 🖷 01905 722350 ✉ rob.byrne@worcester.gov.uk

Computer Management: Mr Mac Chivers, Information Technology Manager, Copenhagen Street, Worcester WR1 3EY ☎ 01905 722121 ✉ SW2.ServiceDesk@worcester.gov.uk

Corporate Services: Mrs Helen Frances, Service Manager, Guildhall, High Street, Worcester WR1 2EY ☎ 01905 722233 🖷 01905 722350 ✉ helen.frances@worcester.gov.uk

Customer Service: Mrs Helen Frances, Service Manager, Guildhall, High Street, Worcester WR1 2EY ☎ 01905 722233 🖷 01905 722350 ✉ helen.frances@worcester.gov.uk

Economic Development: Mr David Blake, Acting Corporate Director - Place, Guildhall, High Street, Worcester WR1 2EY ☎ 01905 722233 🖷 01905 722370 ✉ david.blake@worcester.gov.uk

E-Government: Mrs Helen Frances, Service Manager, Guildhall, High Street, Worcester WR1 2EY ☎ 01905 722233 🖷 01905 722350 ✉ helen.frances@worcester.gov.uk

Electoral Registration: Mrs Diane Thomas, Elections Officer, Guildhall, High Street, Worcester WR1 2EY ☎ 01905 722027 🖷 01905 722028 ✉ d.thomas@worcester.gov.uk

Emergency Planning: Ms Nina Warrington, Strategic Housing Services Manager, Guildhall, High Street, Worcester WR1 2EY ☎ 01905 722233 🖷 01905 722211 ✉ nina.warrington@worcester.gov.uk

Energy Management: Mrs Julie Slatter, Service Manager, Guildhall, High Street, Worcester WR1 2EY ☎ 01905 722233 🖷 01905 722350 ✉ julie.slatter@worcester.gov.uk

Environmental / Technical Services: Mr David Sutton, Service Manager, Guildhall, High Street, Worcester WR1 2EY ☎ 01905 722233 🖷 01905 722350 ✉ david.sutton@worcester.gov.uk

Environmental Health: Mrs Anita Fletcher, Business Compliance Manager, Wyre Forest House, Finepoint Way, Kidderminster DY11 7WF ☎ 01905 822799 ✉ wrsenquiries@worcsregservices.gov.uk

Events Manager: Ms Nadja Von Dahlen, Events Co-ordinator, 2-4 Copenhagan Street, Worcester WR1 2EY ☎ 01905 722320 🖷 01905 721149 ✉ nadja.vondahlen@visitworcester.gov.uk

WORCESTER CITY

Finance: Mr Andy Bromage, Internal Audit Shared Services Manager, The Guildhall, High Street, Worcester WR1 2EY ☎ 01905 722233 🖷 01905 722168 🖱 andy.bromage@worcester.gov.uk

Finance: Mrs Lesley Meagher, Corporate Director for Resources & Acting Head of Paid Service, The Guildhall, High Street, Worcester WR1 2EY ☎ 01905 722233 🖷 01905 722190 🖱 lesley.meagher@worcester.gov.uk

Grounds Maintenance: Mr David Sutton, Service Manager, The Guildhall, High Street, Worcester WR1 2EY ☎ 01905 722233 🖷 01905 722350 🖱 david.sutton@worcester.gov.uk

Health and Safety: Mr Julian Stevenson, Health & Safety Officer, The Guildhall, High Street, Worcester WR1 2EY ☎ 01905 722233 🖷 01905 722034 🖱 julian.stevenson@worcester.gov.uk

Housing: Ms Nina Warrington, Strategic Housing Services Manager, The Guildhall, High Street, Worcester WR1 2EY ☎ 01905 722233 🖷 01905 722211 🖱 nina.warrington@worcester.gov.uk

Local Area Agreement: Mrs Helen Frances, Service Manager, Guildhall, High Street, Worcester WR1 2EY ☎ 01905 722233 🖷 01905 722350 🖱 helen.frances@worcester.gov.uk

Legal: Mr Timothy O'Gara, Legal Service Manager, The Guildhall, High Street, Worcester WR1 2EY ☎ 01905 722233 🖷 01905 722028 🖱 timothy.o'gara@worcester.gov.uk

Licensing: Mr Niall McMenamin, Senior Practitioner, Wyre Forest House, Finepoint Way, Kidderminster DY11 7WF ☎ 01905 822799 🖱 wrsenquiries@worcsregservices.gov.uk

Member Services: Miss Claire Chaplin, Democratic & Electorial Services Manager, The Guildhall, High Street, Worcester WR1 2EY ☎ 01905 722233 🖷 01905 722028 🖱 claire.chaplin@worcester.gov.uk

Member Services: Mrs Margaret Johnson, Democratic Services Administrator, The Guildhall, High Street, Worcester WR1 2EY ☎ 01905 722233 🖷 01905 721120 🖱 margaret.johnson@worcester.gov.uk

Member Services: Mr Julian Pugh, Democratic Services Administrator, The Guildhall, High Street, Worcester WR1 2EY ☎ 01905 722233 🖷 01905 721120 🖱 julian.pugh@worcester.gov.uk

Parking: Mr David Sutton, Service Manager, The Guildhall, High Street, Worcester WR1 2EY ☎ 01905 722233 🖷 01905 722350 🖱 david.sutton@worcester.gov.uk

Personnel / HR: Mr Mark Edwards, Service Manager, The Guildhall, High Street, Worcester WR1 2EY ☎ 01905 722233 🖷 01905 722304 🖱 mark.edwards@worcester.gov.uk

Planning: Mr Paul O'Conner, Service Manager, The Guildhall, High Street, Worcester WR1 2EY ☎ 01905 722233 🖷 01905 722565 🖱 paul.o'conner@worcester.gov.uk

Procurement: Mrs Sheila Mari, Procurement Assistant, The Guildhall, High Street, Worcester WR1 2EY ☎ 01905 722233 🖷 01905 722190 🖱 sheila.mari@worcester.gov.uk

Recycling & Waste Minimisation: Mr David Sutton, Service Manager, The Guildhall, High Street, Worcester WR1 2EY ☎ 01905 722233 🖷 01905 722350 🖱 david.sutton@worcester.gov.uk

Regeneration: Mr David Blake, Acting Corporate Director - Place, The Guildhall, High Street, Worcester WR1 2EY ☎ 01905 722233 🖷 01905 722370 🖱 david.blake@worcester.gov.uk

Staff Training: Mr Mark Edwards, Service Manager, The Guildhall, High Street, Worcester WR1 2EY ☎ 01905 722233 🖷 01905 722304 🖱 mark.edwards@worcester.gov.uk

Street Scene: Mr David Sutton, Service Manager, The Guildhall, High Street, Worcester WR1 2EY ☎ 01905 722233 🖷 01905 722350 🖱 david.sutton@worcester.gov.uk

Sustainable Communities: Mr David Blake, Acting Corporate Director - Place, The Guildhall, High Street, Worcester WR1 2EY ☎ 01905 722233 🖷 01905 722370 🖱 david.blake@worcester.gov.uk

Sustainable Development: Mr David Blake, Acting Corporate Director - Place, The Guildhall, High Street, Worcester WR1 2EY ☎ 01905 722233 🖷 01905 722370 🖱 david.blake@worcester.gov.uk

Tourism: Ms Amanda Millichip, Tourism & Marketing Officer, 2-4 Copenhagen Street, Worcester WR1 3ES ☎ 01905 721148 🖷 01905 721149 🖱 amanda.millichip@visitworcester.gov.uk

Town Centre: Mr Adrian Field, Business Improvement District Manager (BID), Copenhagen Street, Worcester WR1 3EY ☎ 01905 721175 🖷 01905 721149 🖱 info@worcesterbid.com

Waste Collection and Disposal: Mr David Sutton, Service Manager, The Guildhall, High Street, Worcester WR1 2EY ☎ 01905 722233 🖷 01905 722350 🖱 david.sutton@worcester.gov.uk

Children's Play Areas: Mr David Sutton, Service Manager, Orchard House, Worcester WR1 3BB ☎ 01905 722233 🖷 01905 722350 🖱 david.sutton@worcester.gov.uk

COUNCILLORS

***Mayor* Knight**, Roger (CON - St. Peter's Parish)
rogerdknight@tiscali.co.uk

***Deputy Mayor* Whitehouse**, Mike (CON - Claines)
mike.whitehouse@worcester.gov.uk

***Leader of the Council* Geraghty**, Simon (CON - St. Clement)
simon.geraghty@worcester.gov.uk

***Deputy Leader of the Council* Bayliss**, Marc (CON - Bedwardine)
mbayliss@worcester.gov.uk

Agar, Patricia (LAB - Nunnery)
pat.agar@worcester.gov.uk

Amos, Alan (LAB - Warndon)
alan.amos@worcester.gov.uk

Berry, Roger (LAB - Gorse Hill)
roger.berry@worcester.gov.uk

Boorn, Richard (LAB - Nunnery)
richard.boorn@worcester.gov.uk

Cawthorne, Chris (LAB - St. John)
christine.cawthorne@worcester.gov.uk

Cronin, Simon (LAB - Nunnery)
simon.cronin@worcester.gov.uk

Denham, Paul (LAB - Rainbow Hill)
paul.denham@worcester.gov.uk

Denham, Lynn (LAB - Cathedral)
lynn.denham@worcester.gov.uk

Ditta, Allah (CON - Cathedral)
allah.ditta@worcester.gov.uk

Feeney, Alan (CON - Warndon Parish North)

Gregson, Adrian (LAB - Rainbow Hill)
adrian.gregson@worcester.gov.uk

Hodges, Jo (LAB - Warndon)
jo.hodges@worcester.gov.uk

Hodgson, Stephen (CON - Warndon Parish North)
stephen.hodgson@worcester.gov.uk

Hodgson, Lucy (CON - Warndon Parish South)
lucy.hodgson@worcester.gov.uk

Johnson, Mike (CON - St. Peter's Parish)
mandmjohnson@btinternet.com

Jones, Gareth (CON - St. Stephen)
gareth.jones@worcester.gov.uk

Lacey, Matt (CON - Claines)
matthewlacey201@hotmail.com

Lamb, Matthew (LAB - St. John)
matthew.lamb@worcester.gov.uk

Laurenson, Neil (GRN - St. Stephen)
neil.laurenson@worcester.gov.uk

Mackay, Steve (CON - Battenhall)
stevemackay91@gmail.com

Mitchell, Chris (CON - St. Clement)
chris.mitchell@lmco.com

Prodger, Derek (CON - Bedwardine)
derek.prodger@worcester.gov.uk

Riaz, Jabba (CON - Cathedral)
jabba.riaz@worcester.gov.uk

Roberts, Andrew (CON - Warndon Parish South)
andrew.roberts@worcester.gov.uk

Rowden, Robert (CON - Battenhall)
robert.rowden@worcester.gov.uk

Squires, George (LAB - Arboretum)
george.squires@worcester.gov.uk

Squires, Joy (LAB - Arboretum)
joy.squires@worcester.gov.uk

Stafford, Andy (CON - Claines)

Udall, Richard (LAB - St. John)
richard.udall@worcester.gov.uk

Wilkinson, David (CON - Bedwardine)
david.wilkinson@worcester.gov.uk

Williams, Geoffrey (LAB - Gorse Hill)
geoff.williams@worcester.gov.uk

POLITICAL COMPOSITION

CON: 19, LAB: 15, GRN: 1

COMMITTEE CHAIRS

Audit: Mrs Patricia Agar

Licensing: Mr Allah Ditta

Planning: Mr Alan Amos

Worcestershire C

Worcestershire County Council, County Hall, Spetchley Road, Worcester WR5 2NP
☎ 01905 763763 🖷 01905 763000 💻 www.worcestershire.gov.uk

FACTS AND FIGURES

Parliamentary Constituencies: Bromsgrove, Redditch, Worcester, Worcestershire Mid, Worcestershire West, Wyre Forest
EU Constituencies: West Midlands
Election Frequency: Elections are of whole council

PRINCIPAL OFFICERS

Chief Executive: Ms Clare Marchant, Chief Executive, County Hall, Spetchley Road, Worcester WR5 2NP ☎ 01905 766100
cmarchant@worcestershire.gov.uk

Senior Management: Dr Richard Harling, Director of Adult & Social Health, County Hall, Spetchley Road, Worcester WR5 2NP
☎ 01905 766900 rharling@worcestershire.gov.uk

Senior Management: Mr John Hobbs, Director of Business, Environment & Community (BEC), County Hall, Spetchley Road, Worcester WR5 2NP ☎ 01905 766700 🖷 01905 766899
jhobbs@worcestershire.gov.uk

Senior Management: Mr Sander Kristel, Director of Commercial & Change, County Hall, Spetchley Road, Worcester WR5 2NP
☎ 01905 766201 skristel@worcestershire.gov.uk

Architect, Building / Property Services: Mr Peter Bishop, Strategic Commissioner - Service Transformation, County Hall, Spetchley Road, Worcester WR5 2NP ☎ 01905 766020 🖷 01905 766199 pbishop@worcestershire.gov.uk

Best Value: Mr Sander Kristel, Director of Commercial & Change, County Hall, Spetchley Road, Worcester WR5 2NP ☎ 01905 766201
skristel@worcestershire.gov.uk

Children / Youth Services: Mr Paul Finnemore, Commissioning Manager (Young People), County Hall, Spetchley Road, Worcester WR5 2NP ☎ 01905 765628 🖷 01905 765306
pfinnemore@worcestershire.gov.uk

Children / Youth Services: Mrs Gail Quinton, Director of Children's Services, County Hall, Spetchley Road, Worcester WR5 2NP ☎ 01905 766686 🖷 01905 766156
gquinton@worcestershire.gov.uk

Civil Registration: Ms Sharon Duggan, Registration & Coroner's Service Manager, County Hall, Spetchley Road, Worcester WR5 2NP ☎ 01905 728754 sduggan@worcestershire.gov.uk

PR / Communications: Mr Jon Fraser, Marketing & Research Manager, County Hall, Spetchley Road, Worcester WR5 2NP
☎ 01905 766478 jfraser@worcestershire.gov.uk

Community Planning: Mr Neil Anderson, Head of Culture & Community, County Hall, Spetchley Road, Worcester WR5 2NP ☎ 01905 766580 dtilley@worcestershire.gov.uk

Computer Management: Mr Peter Bishop, Strategic Commissioner - Service Transformation, County Hall, Spetchley Road, Worcester WR5 2NP ☎ 01905 766020 🖷 01905 766199 pbishop@worcestershire.gov.uk

Contracts: Mr Nick Yarwood, Highways Contracts & Programme Manager, County Hall, Spetchley Road, Worcester WR5 2NP ☎ 01905 728648 🖷 01905 766839 nyarwood@worcestershire.gov.uk

Customer Service: Ms Jane Bowen, Worcestershire Hub Operations Manager, County Hall, Spetchley Road, Worcester WR5 2NP ☎ 01905 768188 jbowen@worcestershire.gov.uk

Customer Service: Ms Annette Stock, Policy & Review Officer, County Hall, Spetchley Road, Worcester WR5 2NP ☎ 01905 766640 🖷 01905 766109 astock@worcestershire.gov.uk

Economic Development: Mr Neil Anderson, Head of Culture & Community, County Hall, Spetchley Road, Worcester WR5 2NP ☎ 01905 766580 dtilley@worcestershire.gov.uk

Education: Mr Paul Finnemore, Commissioning Manager of Youth Services, County Hall, Spetchley Road, Worcester WR5 2NP ☎ 01905 765628 pfinnemore@worcestershire.gov.uk

E-Government: Mr Sander Kristel, Director of Commercial & Change, County Hall, Spetchley Road, Worcester WR5 2NP ☎ 01905 766201 skristel@worcestershire.gov.uk

Electoral Registration: Mr Simon Mallinson, Head of Legal & Democratic Services, County Hall, Spetchley Road, Worcester WR5 2NP ☎ 01905 766670 🖷 01905 766677 smallinson@worcestershire.gov.uk

Emergency Planning: Mr Nick Riding, Emergency Planning Manager, County Hall, Spetchley Road, Worcester WR5 2NP ☎ 01905 766171 nriding@worcestershire.gov.uk

Energy Management: Mr John Hobbs, Director of Business, Environment & Community (BEC), County Hall, Spetchley Road, Worcester WR5 2NP ☎ 01905 766700 🖷 01905 766899 jhobbs@worcestershire.gov.uk

Environmental / Technical Services: Mr John Hobbs, Director of Business, Environment & Community (BEC), County Hall, Spetchley Road, Worcester WR5 2NP ☎ 01905 766700 🖷 01905 766899 jhobbs@worcestershire.gov.uk

Estates, Property & Valuation: Mr Mike Williams, Principal Valuer, County Hall, Spetchley Road, Worcester WR5 2NP ☎ 01905 766463 🖷 01905 766498 mjwilliams@worcestershire.gov.uk

European Liaison: Mr Aamir Kayani, Project Manager - Business Development, County Hall, Spetchley Road, Worcester WR5 2NP ☎ 01905 766816 🖷 01905 766377 akayani@worcestershire.gov.uk

Facilities: Mr David Harrison, Facilities Manager, County Hall, Spetchley Road, Worcester WR5 2NP ☎ 01905 766301 🖷 01905 766498 dharrison2@worcestershire.gov.uk

Finance: Mrs Sue Alexander, Head of Finance & Business Support, County Hall, Spetchley Road, Worcester WR5 2NP ☎ 01905 766942 salexander@worcestershire.gov.uk

Finance: Mr Sean Pearce, Chief Financial Officer, County Hall, Spetchley Road, Worcester WR5 2NP ☎ 01905 766268 spearce@worcestershire.gov.uk

Pensions: Mr Mark Forrester, Principal Pension Fund Accountant & Investment Officer, HR Service Centre, PO Box 374, County Hall, Spetchley Road, Worcester WR5 2XF ☎ 01905 766513 mforrester@worcestershire.gov.uk

Pensions: Ms Linda Probin, Pensions Manager, HR Service Centre, PO Box 374, County Hall, Spetchley Road, Worcester WR5 2XF ☎ 01905 766511 lprobin@worcestershire.gov.uk

Fleet Management: Mr Stuart Payton, Access Manager, County Hall, Spetchley Road, Worcester WR5 2NP ☎ 01905 766889 spayton@worcestershire.gov.uk

Health and Safety: Dr Clive Werrett, Corporate Health & Safety Manager, County Hall, Spetchley Road, Worcester WR5 2NP ☎ 01905 765920 🖷 01905 766221 cwerrett@worcestershire.gov.uk

Highways: Mr Ian Bamforth, Head of Operations for Highways & Countryside, County Hall, Spetchley Road, Worcester WR5 2NP ☎ 01905 766845 ibamforth@worcestershire.gov.uk

Legal: Mr Simon Mallinson, Head of Legal & Democratic Services, County Hall, Spetchley Road, Worcester WR5 2NP ☎ 01905 766670 🖷 01905 766677 smallinson@worcestershire.gov.uk

Lifelong Learning: Ms Kathy Kirk, Strategic Libraries & Lifelong Learning Manager, County Hall, Spetchley Road, Worcester WR5 2NP ☎ 01905 766946 🖷 01905 766190 kkirk@worcestershire.gov.uk

Member Services: Ms Suzanne O'Leary, Interim Democratic Governance & Scrutiny Manager, County Hall, Spetchley Road, Worcester WR5 2NP ☎ 01905 768673 so'leary@worcestershire.gov.uk

Partnerships: Mr Nick Yarwood, Highways Contracts & Programme Manager, County Hall, Spetchley Road, Worcester WR5 2NP ☎ 01905 728648 🖷 01905 766839 nyarwood@worcestershire.gov.uk

Personnel / HR: Ms Elaine Chandler, Head of Human Resources, County Hall, Spetchley Road, Worcester WR5 2NP ☎ 0195 766218 echandler@worcestershire.gov.uk

Personnel / HR: Ms Ann-Marie Lockley, Human Resources Manager, Wyre Forest House, Finepoint Way, Kidderminster DY11 7WF ☎ 01562 732773 ann-marie.lockley@wyreforestdc.gov.uk

Planning: Mr Neil Anderson, Head of Culture & Community, County Hall, Spetchley Road, Worcester WR5 2NP ☎ 01905 766580 ✉ dtilley@worcestershire.gov.uk

Procurement: Mr Joe Stock, Strategic Procurement Officer, County Hall, Spetchley Road, Worcester WR5 2NP ☎ 01905 766801 ✉ jstock1@worcestershire.gov.uk

Public Libraries: Ms Kathy Kirk, Strategic Libraries & Lifelong Learning Manager, County Hall, Spetchley Road, Worcester WR5 2NP ☎ 01905 766946 🖷 01905 766190 ✉ kkirk@worcestershire.gov.uk

Recycling & Waste Minimisation: Mr Richard Woodward, Waste Services Manager, County Hall, Spetchley Road, Worcester WR5 2NP ☎ 01905 768262 ✉ rwoodward@worcestershire.gov.uk

Road Safety: Mr Ed Dursley, Project Manager, County Hall, Spetchley Road, Worcester WR5 2NP ☎ 01905 766876 ✉ edursley@worcestershire.gov.uk

Social Services: Dr Richard Harling, Director of Adult & Social Health, County Hall, Spetchley Road, Worcester WR5 2NP ☎ 01905 766900 ✉ rharling@worcestershire.gov.uk

Social Services (Adult): Dr Richard Harling, Director of Adult & Social Health, County Hall, Spetchley Road, Worcester WR5 2NP ☎ 01905 766900 ✉ rharling@worcestershire.gov.uk

Social Services (Children): Ms Siobhan Williams, Head of Safeguarding & Services to Children & Young People, County Hall, Spetchley Road, Worcester WR5 2NP ☎ 01905 766894 🖷 01905 766930 ✉ sawiliams2@worcestershire.gov.uk

Public Health: Dr Richard Harling, Director of Adult & Social Health, County Hall, Spetchley Road, Worcester WR5 2NP ☎ 01905 766900 ✉ rharling@worcestershire.gov.uk

Sustainable Communities: Ms Liz Alston, Principal Sustainability Officer, County Hall, Spetchley Road, Worcester WR5 2NP ☎ 01905 766745 🖷 01905 766899 ✉ ealston@worcestershire.gov.uk

Sustainable Development: Ms Liz Alston, Principal Sustainability Officer, County Hall, Spetchley Road, Worcester WR5 2NP ☎ 01905 766745 🖷 01905 766899 ✉ ealston@worcestershire.gov.uk

Transport: Mr Andy Baker, Sustainable Transport Manager, County Hall, Spetchley Road, Worcester WR5 2NP ☎ 01905 822071 ✉ acbaker@worcestershire.gov.uk

Total Place: Mr Sander Kristel, Director of Commercial & Change, County Hall, Spetchley Road, Worcester WR5 2NP ☎ 01905 766201 ✉ skristel@worcestershire.gov.uk

Waste Collection and Disposal: Mr Richard Woodward, Waste Services Manager, County Hall, Spetchley Road, Worcester WR5 2NP ☎ 01905 768262 ✉ rwoodward@worcestershire.gov.uk

Waste Management: Mr Richard Woodward, Waste Services Manager, County Hall, Spetchley Road, Worcester WR5 2NP ☎ 01905 768262 ✉ rwoodward@worcestershire.gov.uk

COUNCILLORS

***Chair* Hopwood**, Ian (CON - Malvern Langland)

***Vice-Chair* Miller**, Tony (CON - Bowbrook)
a.miller880@btinternet.com

***Leader of the Council* Hardman**, Adrian (CON - Bredon)
aihardman@worcestershire.gov.uk

***Deputy Leader of the Council* Geraghty**, Simon (CON - Worcester - Riverside)
sgeraghty@worcestershire.gov.uk

***Group Leader* McDonald**, Peter (LAB - Beacon)
pmcdonald2@worcestershire.gov.uk

***Group Leader* Parish**, Jim (IND - Stourport-on-Severn)
jparish@worcestershire.gov.uk

Adams, Alastair (CON - Littletons)
aadams@worcestershire.gov.uk

Adams, Rob (CON - Upton Snodsbury)
radams@worcestershire.gov.uk

Agar, Pat (LAB - Nunnery)
pagar@worcestershire.gov.uk

Amos, Alan (LAB - Gorse Hill & Warndon)
alan.amos@worcester.gov.uk

Askin, Susan (LD - Claines)
saskin@worcestershire.gov.uk

Baker, Joseph (LAB - Arrow Valley East)
joebaker@worcestershire.gov.uk

Banks, Robert (CON - Evesham South)
rbanks@btconnect.com

Bayliss, Mark (CON - Worcester - St Peter)

Blagg, Anthony (CON - Bromsgrove Central)
a.blagg@worcestershire.gov.uk

Blagg, Sheila (CON - Woodvale)
sblagg@worcestershire.gov.uk

Bloore, Christopher (LAB - Bromsgrove South)
cbloore@worcestershire.gov.uk

Bridle, Peter (UKIP - Arrow Valley East)
pbridle@worcestershire.gov.uk

Broomfield, Maurice (CON - Ombersley)
mbroomfield2@worcestershire.gov.uk

Campion, John (CON - Bewdley)
jcampion@worcestershire.gov.uk

Clee, Stephen (CON - Chaddesley)
sjclee@worcestershire.gov.uk

Cross, Stuart (UKIP - Redditch South)
scross@worcestershire.gov.uk

Davey, Pamela (CON - Droitwich East)
pdavey@worcestershire.gov.uk

Denham, Paul (LAB - Rainbow Hill)
pdenham@worcestershire.gov.uk

Desmond, Nathan (CON - St Mary's)
ndesmond@worcestershire.gov.uk

Duffy, Lynne (CON - Droitwich West)
lduffy@worcestershire.gov.uk

Eyre, Liz (CON - Broadway)
eeyre@worcestershire.gov.uk

Fry, Andrew (LAB - Arrow Valley West)
andrewfry@worcestershire.gov.uk

Gretton, Philip (CON - Redditch South)
pgretton@worcestershire.gov.uk

Griffiths, June (CON - Alvechurch)
j.griffiths@bromsgrove.gov.uk

Grove, Phil (CON - Hallow)
pgrove@worcestershire.gov.uk

Hart, Marcus (CON - Kidderminster - St Johns)
marcushart78@yahoo.co.uk

Hill, Pattie (LAB - Arrow Valley West)
phill3@worcestershire.gov.uk

Hingley, Anne (CON - St Barnabas)
anne.hingley@wyreforestdc.gov.uk

Hodgson, Lucy (CON - Malvern Chase)
lhodgson@worcestershire.gov.uk

Holt, Clive (CON - Harvington)
cholt@worcestershire.gov.uk

Jenkins, Rachel (IND - Clent Hills)
rjenkins@worcestershire.gov.uk

Jenkins, Matthew (GRN - Worcester - St Stephen)
mjenkins3@worcestershire.gov.uk

Lunn, Robin (LAB - Redditch North)

Mallett, Luke (LAB - Bromsgrove West)
lmallett@worcestershire.gov.uk

Oborski, Fran (LIB - Kidderminster - St Chads)
franoborski@btinternet.com

Peters, Stephen (R - Wythall)
speters@worcestershire.gov.uk

Pollock, Ken (CON - Tenbury)
kpollock2@worcestershire.gov.uk

Prodger, Derek (CON - Bedwardine)
dprodger@worcestershire.gov.uk

Raine, John (GRN - Malvern Trinity)

Rayner, Mary (IND - St Georges & St Oswalds)
mrayner@worcestershire.gov.uk

Roberts, Andrew (CON - Warndon Parishes)
acroberts@worchester.gov.uk

Smith, John (CON - Evesham North West)
jhsmith@worcestershire.gov.uk

Sutton, Roger (IND - Croome)
rsutton@worcestershire.gov.uk

Taylor, Kit (CON - Bromsgrove East)
ktaylor3@worcestershire.gov.uk

Thomas, John (IND - Stourport-on-Severn)
jthomas2@worcestershire.gov.uk

Tucker, Liz (LD - Pershore)
ltucker@worcestershire.gov.uk

Tuthill, Paul (CON - Malvern Link)
ptuthill@worcestershire.gov.uk

Udall, Richard (LAB - Worcester - St John)
rudall2@worcestershire.gov.uk

Vickery, Graham (LAB - Redditch North)

Wells, Tom (LD - Powick)
talwells@btinternet.com

Yarranton, Gordon (CON - Cookley, Wolveryley & Wribbenhall)
gyarranton@worcestershire.gov.uk

POLITICAL COMPOSITION
CON: 31, LAB: 12, IND: 5, LD: 3, GRN: 2, UKIP: 2, R: 1, LIB: 1

COMMITTEE CHAIRS
Adult Care & Wellbeing: Mr Tom Wells

Audit & Governance: Mr Philip Gretton

Children & Families: Ms Lynne Duffy

Health & Wellbeing: Mr Marcus Hart

Pensions: Mr Robert Banks

Planning: Mr Rob Adams

Worthing — D

Worthing Borough Council, Worthing Town Hall, Chapel Road, Worthing BN11 1HA
☎ 01903 239999 🖷 01903 236552 ✉ enquiries@worthing.gov.uk
🖳 www.worthing.gov.uk

FACTS AND FIGURES
Parliamentary Constituencies: Worthing West
EU Constituencies: South East
Election Frequency: Elections are by thirds

PRINCIPAL OFFICERS
Chief Executive: Mr Alex Bailey, Chief Executive, Civic Centre, Ham Road, Shoreham-by-Sea BN43 6PR ☎ 01903 221001
✉ alex.bailey@adur-worthing.gov.uk

Senior Management: Mr Paul Brewer, Director - Digital & Resources, Worthing Town Hall, Chapel Road, Worthing BN11 1HA
☎ 01903 221302 ✉ paul.brewer@adur-worthing.gov.uk

Senior Management: Ms Jane Eckford, Director - Customer Service, Worthing Town Hall, Chapel Road, Worthing BN11 1HA
☎ 01903 221059 ✉ jane.eckford@adur-worthing.gov.uk

Senior Management: Mr John Mitchell, Director - Communities, Adur Civic Centre, Ham Road, Shoreham-by-Sea BN43 6PR
☎ 01903 221049 ✉ john.mitchell@adur-worthing.gov.uk

Senior Management: Mr Martin Randall, Director - Economy, Civic Centre, Ham Road, Shoreham-by-Sea BN43 6PR
☎ 01903 221209 ✉ martin.randall@adur-worthing.gov.uk

Architect, Building / Property Services: Mr Steve Spinner, Head of Business & Technical Services, Portland House, Richmond Road, Worthing BN11 1LF ☎ 01903 221019
✉ steve.spinner@adur-worthing.gov.uk

Building Control: Mr James Appleton, Head of Growth, Portland House, Richmond Road, Worthing BN11 1HS ☎ 01903 221333
✉ james.appleton@adur-worthing.gov.uk

PR / Communications: Mr Neil Hopkins, Head of Communications, Worthing Town Hall, Chapel Road, Worthing BN11 1HA ✉ neil.hopkins@adur-worthing.gov.uk

Community Planning: Mr Paul Pennicott, Strategic Projects Officer, Worthing Town Hall, Chapel Road, Worthing BN11 1HA ☎ 01903 221347 ✉ paul.pennicott@adur-worthing.gov.uk

Community Safety: Mrs Jacqui Cooke, Safer Communities Manager, Worthing Town Hall, Chapel Road, Worthing BN11 1HA ☎ 08456 070999 ✉ jacqui.cooke@adur-worthing.gov.uk

Computer Management: Mr Mark Gawley, CenSus IT Operations Manager, Worthing Town Hall, Chapel Road, Worthing BN11 1HA ☎ 01903 221477; 01903 221197 ✉ mark.gawley@adur-worthing.gov.uk

Contracts: Mr Steve Spinner, Head of Business & Technical Services, Portland House, Richmond Road, Worthing BN11 1LF ☎ 01903 221019 ✉ steve.spinner@adur-worthing.gov.uk

Customer Service: Ms Jane Eckford, Director - Customer Service, Worthing Town Hall, Chapel Road, Worthing BN11 1HA ☎ 01903 221059 ✉ jane.eckford@adur-worthing.gov.uk

Direct Labour: Mr Paul Brewer, Director - Digital & Resources, Worthing Town Hall, Chapel Road, Worthing BN11 1HA ☎ 01903 221302 ✉ paul.brewer@adur-worthing.gov.uk

Economic Development: Ms Tina Barker, Economic Development Officer, Commerce Way, Lancing BN15 8TA ☎ 01273 263206 ✉ tina.barker@adur-worthing.gov.uk

E-Government: Mr Paul Brewer, Director - Digital & Resources, Worthing Town Hall, Chapel Road, Worthing BN11 1HA ☎ 01903 221302 ✉ paul.brewer@adur-worthing.gov.uk

Electoral Registration: Ms Teresa Bryant, Electoral Services Manager, Worthing Town Hall, Chapel Road, Worthing BH11 1HA ☎ 01903 221474 ✉ teresa.bryant@adur-worthing.gov.uk

Emergency Planning: Mr Lloyd Harris, Emergency Planning Officer, Worthing Town Hall, Chapel Road, Worthing BN11 1HA ☎ 01903 221025 ✉ lloyd.harris@adur-worthing.gov.uk

Energy Management: Mr Paul Brewer, Director - Digital & Resources, Worthing Town Hall, Chapel Road, Worthing BN11 1HA ☎ 01903 221302 ✉ paul.brewer@adur-worthing.gov.uk

Environmental / Technical Services: Mr Paul Brewer, Director - Digital & Resources, Worthing Town Hall, Chapel Road, Worthing BN11 1HA ☎ 01903 221302 ✉ paul.brewer@adur-worthing.gov.uk

Environmental Health: Mr James Elliot, Senior Environmental Health Officer, Adur Civic Centre, Ham Road, Shoreham-by-Sea BN43 6PR ☎ 01273 263032 ✉ james.elliot@adur-worthing.gov.uk

Estates, Property & Valuation: Mr Scott Marshall, Director for the Economy, Worthing Town Hall, Chapel Road, Worthing BN11 1HA ☎ 01903 221209 ✉ scott.marshall@adur-worthing.gov.uk

Events Manager: Ms Jo Osborne, Events Manager for Culture, Worthing Town Hall,, „ Worthing BN11 1HA ☎ 01903 231799 ✉ jo.osborne@adur-worthing.gov.uk

Facilities: Mr Steve Spinner, Head of Business & Technical Services, Portland House, Richmond Road, Worthing BN11 1LF ☎ 01903 221019 ✉ steve.spinner@adur-worthing.gov.uk

Finance: Mrs Sarah Gobey, Executive Head of Financial Services, Worthing Town Hall, Chapel Road, Worthing BN11 1HA ☎ 01903 221221 ✉ sarah.gobey@adur-worthing.gov.uk

Fleet Management: Ms Jane Eckford, Director - Customer Service, Worthing Town Hall, Chapel Road, Worthing BN11 1HA ☎ 01903 221059 ✉ jane.eckford@adur-worthing.gov.uk

Grounds Maintenance: Mr Andy Edwards, Head of Environment, Commerce Way, Lancing BN15 8TA ☎ 01273 263137 ✉ andy.edwards@adur-worthing.gov.uk

Health and Safety: Mrs Lesley Dexter, Senior Corporate Safety Officer, Portland House, Richmond Road, Worthing BN11 1LF ☎ 01273 263430 ✉ lesley.dexter@adur-worthing.gov.uk

Housing: Mr Paul Cooper, Head of Housing, Portland House, Richmond Road, Worthing BN11 1LF ☎ 01903 221190 ✉ paul.cooper@adur-worthing.gov.uk

Housing Maintenance: Mr Paul Cooper, Head of Housing, Portland House, Richmond Road, Worthing BN11 1LF ☎ 01903 221190 ✉ paul.cooper@adur-worthing.gov.uk

Legal: Ms Susan Sale, Solicitor to the Council, Worthing Town Hall, Chapel Road, Worthing BN11 1HA ☎ 01903 221119 ✉ susan.sale@adur-worthing.gov.uk

Leisure and Cultural Services: Ms Amanda O'Reilly, Head of Culture, Worthing Town Hall, Chapel Road, Worthing BN11 1HA ☎ 01903 221142 ✉ amanda.o'reilly@adur-worthing.gov.uk

Licensing: Ms Theresa Cuerva, Licensing Officer, Adur Civic Centre, Ham Road, Shoreham-by-Sea BN43 6PR ☎ 01273 263193 ✉ theresa.cuerva@adur-worthing.gov.uk

Lottery Funding, Charity and Voluntary: Mr John Phelps, External Funding Policy Manager, Worthing Town Hall, Chapel Road, Worthing BN11 1HA ☎ 01903 221283 ✉ john.phelps@adur-worthing.gov.uk

Member Services: Mrs Julia Smith, Democratic Services Manager, Worthing Town Hall, Chapel Road, Worthing BN11 1HA ☎ 01903 221150 ✉ julia.smith@adur-worthing.gov.uk

Parking: Mr Ashley Miles, Technical Assistant, Worthing Town Hall, Chapel Road, Worthing BN11 1HA ☎ 01903 221022 ✉ ashley.miles@adur-worthing.gov.uk

Partnerships: Mr Alex Bailey, Chief Executive, Civic Centre, Ham Road, Shoreham-by-Sea BN43 6PR ☎ 01903 221001 ✉ alex.bailey@adur-worthing.gov.uk

WORTHING

Personnel / HR: Mr Paul Brewer, Director - Digital & Resources, Worthing Town Hall, Chapel Road, Worthing BN11 1HA ☎ 01903 221302 ✉ paul.brewer@adur-worthing.gov.uk

Personnel / HR: Mrs Tracy Darey, Human Resources Manager, Worthing Town Hall, Chapel Road, Worthing BN11 1HA ☎ 01273 263063 ✉ tracy.darey@adur-worthing.gov.uk

Planning: Mr James Appleton, Head of Growth, Portland House, Richmond Road, Worthing BN11 1HS ☎ 01903 221333 ✉ james.appleton@adur-worthing.gov.uk

Procurement: Mr Bill Williamson, Procurement Officer, Portland House, Richmond Road, Worthing BN11 1HS ☎ 01903 221056 ✉ bill.williamson@adur-worthing.gov.uk

Recycling & Waste Minimisation: Ms Jane Eckford, Director - Customer Service, Worthing Town Hall, Chapel Road, Worthing BN11 1HA ☎ 01903 221059 ✉ jane.eckford@adur-worthing.gov.uk

Regeneration: Mr Scott Marshall, Director for the Economy, Worthing Town Hall, Chapel Road, Worthing BN11 1HA ☎ 01903 221209 ✉ scott.marshall@adur-worthing.gov.uk

Staff Training: Ms Lois Ford, Learning & Development Co-ordinator, Worthing Town Hall, Chapel Road, Worthing BN11 1HA ☎ 01903 221043 ✉ lois.ford@adur-worthing.gov.uk

Street Scene: Mr David Steadman, Adur Town Centre & Street Scene Co-ordinator, Civic Centre, Ham Road, Shoreham-by-Sea BN43 6PR ☎ 01273 263152 ✉ david.steadman@adur-worthing.gov.uk

Sustainable Communities: Mr James Appleton, Head of Growth, Portland House, Richmond Road, Worthing BN11 1HS ☎ 01903 221333 ✉ james.appleton@adur-worthing.gov.uk

Sustainable Development: Mr James Appleton, Head of Growth, Portland House, Richmond Road, Worthing BN11 1HS ☎ 01903 221333 ✉ james.appleton@adur-worthing.gov.uk

Tourism: Ms Amanda O'Reilly, Head of Culture, Worthing Town Hall, Chapel Road, Worthing BN11 1HA ☎ 01903 221142 ✉ amanda.o'reilly@adur-worthing.gov.uk

Town Centre: Mr David Steadman, Adur Town Centre & Street Scene Co-ordinator, Civic Centre, Ham Road, Shoreham-by-Sea BN43 6PR ☎ 01273 263152 ✉ david.steadman@adur-worthing.gov.uk

Waste Collection and Disposal: Mr Paul Willis, Waste Strategy Manager, Worthing Town Hall, Chapel Road, Worthing BN11 1HA ☎ 01903 223052 ✉ paul.willis@adur-worthing.gov.uk

Waste Management: Mr Paul Willis, Waste Strategy Manager, Worthing Town Hall, Chapel Road, Worthing BN11 1HA ☎ 01903 223052 ✉ paul.willis@adur-worthing.gov.uk

COUNCILLORS

Leader of the Council **Humphreys**, Daniel (CON - Offington) daniel.humphreys@worthing.gov.uk

Deputy Leader of the Council **Turner**, Bryan (CON - Gaisford) bryan.turner@worthing.gov.uk

Atkins, Noel (CON - Salvington) noel.atkins@worthing.gov.uk

Barraclough, Roy (CON - Goring) roy.barraclough@worthing.gov.uk

Bickers, Keith (CON - Selden) keith.bickers@worthing.gov.uk

Bradley, Joan (CON - Marine) joan.bradley@worthing.gov.uk

Buxton, Callum (CON - Selden) callum.buxton@worthing.gov.uk

Cloake, Michael (CON - Salvington) michael.cloake@worthing.gov.uk

Crouch, Edward (CON - Marine) edward.crouch@worthing.gov.uk

Donin, Michael (LD - Durrington) michael.donin@worthing.gov.uk

Doyle, James (GRN - Central) james.doyle@worthing.gov.uk

Fisher, Norah (LD - Tarring) norah.fisher@worthing.gov.uk

Guest, Diane (CON - Heene) diane.guest@worthing.gov.uk

Harman, Alex (CON - Selden) alex.harman@worthing.gov.uk

Harman, Lionel (CON - Castle) lionel.harman@worthing.gov.uk

High, Joshua (CON - Heene) joshua.high@worthing.gov.uk

High, Paul (CON - Heene) paul.high@worthing.gov.uk

James, Charles (UKIP - Castle) charles.james@worthing.gov.uk

Jelliss, Susan (UKIP - Durrington) susan.jelliss@worthing.gov.uk

Jenkins, Kevin (CON - Gaisford) kevin.jenkins@worthing.gov.uk

Lermitte, Mary (CON - Goring) mary.lermitte@worthing.gov.uk

McDonald, Sean (CON - Northbrook) sean.mcdonald@worthing.gov.uk

Mercer, Heather (CON - Salvington) heather.mercer@worthing.gov.uk

Morgan, Nigel (CON - Broadwater) nigel.morgan@worthing.gov.uk

Murphy, Louise (CON - Offington) louise.murphy@worthing.gov.uk

Nolan, Mark (CON - Goring) mark.nolan@worthing.gov.uk

Proudfoot, Luke (CON - Castle) luke.proudfoot@worthing.gov.uk

Roberts, Clive (CON - Central) clive.roberts@worthing.gov.uk

Smytherman, Robert (LD - Tarring)
robert.smytherman@worthing.gov.uk

Sparkes, Elizabeth (CON - Offington)
elizabeth.sparkes@worthing.gov.uk

Sunderland, Keith (LD - Northbrook)
keith.sunderland@worthing.gov.uk

Turner, Valerie (CON - Gaisford)
val.turner@worthing.gov.uk

Vaughan, Vicky (CON - Broadwater)
vicky.vaughan@worthing.gov.uk

Vinojan, Vino (CON - Central)
vino.vinojan@worthing.gov.uk

Walker, Vic (CON - Broadwater)
vic.walker@worthing.gov.uk

Wye, Tom (CON - Tarring)
tom.wye@worthing.gov.uk

Yallop, Paul (CON - Marine)
paul.yallop@worthing.gov.uk

POLITICAL COMPOSITION

CON: 30, LD: 4, UKIP: 2, GRN: 1

COMMITTEE CHAIRS

Licensing: Mr Paul High

Planning: Mr Edward Crouch

Planning: Mr Kevin Jenkins

Wrexham W

Wrexham County Borough Council, The Guildhall, Wrexham LL11 1AY
☎ 01978 292000 🖷 01978 292106 💻 www.wrexham.gov.uk

FACTS AND FIGURES

Parliamentary Constituencies: Clwyd South, Wrexham
EU Constituencies: Wales
Election Frequency: Elections are of whole council

PRINCIPAL OFFICERS

Chief Executive: Dr Helen Paterson, Chief Executive, The Guildhall, Wrexham LL11 1AY ☎ 01978 292101 🖷 01978 292106 ✉ helen.paterson@wrexham.gov.uk

Senior Management: Ms Clare Field, Strategic & Performance Director, The Guildhall, Wrexham LL11 1AY ☎ 01978 297421 🖷 01978 297422 ✉ clare.field@wrexham.gov.uk

Senior Management: Mr Lee Robinson, Strategic & Performance Director, The Guildhall, Wrexham LL11 1AY ☎ 01978 292401 🖷 01978 292445 ✉ lee.robinson@wrexham.gov.uk

Senior Management: Mr Philip Walton, Strategic Director, The Guildhall, Wrexham LL11 1AY ☎ 01978 297002 🖷 01978 297004 ✉ philip.walton@wrexham.gov.uk

Access Officer / Social Services (Disability): Mr Andrew Figiel, Head of Adult Social Care, 2nd Floor, Crown Buildings, 31 Chester Street, Wrexham LL13 8BG ☎ 01978 298020 🖷 01978 298029 ✉ andrew.figiel@wrexham.gov.uk

Architect, Building / Property Services: Mr Barry Hellen, Design Services Manager, Crown Buildings, 31 Chester Street, Wrexham LL13 8BG ☎ 01978 297180 🖷 01978 297202 ✉ barry.hellen@wrexham.gov.uk

Best Value: Mr Mark Owen, Head of Finance, Lambpit Street, Wrexham LL11 1AR ☎ 01978 292701 🖷 01978 292702 ✉ mark.owen@wrexham.gov.uk

Building Control: Mr Dave Sharp, Principal Building Control Surveyor, Building Control Section, 2nd Floor, Crown Buildings, 31 Chester Street, Wrexham LL13 8BG ☎ 01978 298876 🖷 01978 292502 ✉ dave.sharp@wrexham.gov.uk

Catering Services: Mr Steve Jones, FM Support Services Manager, 2nd Floor, Crown Buildings, 31 Chester Street, Wrexham LL13 8BG ☎ 01978 295520 ✉ steve.jones@wrexham.gov.uk

Children / Youth Services: Ms Susan Evans, Head of Children & Young People, Crown Buildings, 31 Chester Street, Wrexham LL13 8BG ☎ 01978 295491 ✉ susan1.evans@wrexham.gov.uk

Civil Registration: Mrs Ruth Cooke, Superintendent Registrar, The Guildhall, Wrexham LL11 1AY ☎ 01978 292670 ✉ ruth.cooke@wrexham.gov.uk

PR / Communications: Ms Sue Wyn Jones, Communications & Social Media Manager, The Guildhall, Wrexham LL11 1AY ☎ 01978 292275 ✉ sue.wynjones@wrexham.gov.uk

Community Planning: Ms Gillian Grainger, Community Diversity Manager, 16 Lord Street, Wrexham LL11 1LG ☎ 01978 298736 ✉ gillian.grainger@wrexham.gov.uk

Community Safety: Ms Rhian Jones, Senior Performance, Improvements & Partnerships Officer, Lambpit Street, „ Wrexham LL11 1AR ☎ 01978 297043 ✉ rhian.jones@wrexham.gov.uk

Computer Management: Mrs Helen Gerrard, Corporate & Customer Services Manager, 16 Lord Street, Wrexham LL11 1LG ☎ 01978 298951 🖷 01978 298950 ✉ helen.gerrard@wrexham.gov.uk

Consumer Protection and Trading Standards: Ms Toni Slater, Public Protection Service Manager, Public Protection Services, Ruthin Road, Wrexham LL13 7TU ☎ 01978 315710 🖷 01978 315701 ✉ toni.slater@wrexham.gov.uk

Contracts: Mr Andy Lewis, Head of Housing, Public Protection & Environment, Ruthin Road, Wrexham LL13 7TU ☎ 01978 315501 ✉ andy.lewis@wrexham.gov.uk

Corporate Services: Mr Trevor Coxon, Head of Corporate & Customer Services, The Guildhall, Wrexham LL11 1AY ☎ 01978 292206 🖷 01978 292207 ✉ trevor.coxon@wrexham.gov.uk

WREXHAM

Customer Service: Mrs Helen Gerrard, Corporate & Customer Services Manager, 16 Lord Street, Wrexham LL11 1LG ☎ 01978 298951 🖷 01978 298950 ✉ helen.gerrard@wrexham.gov.uk

Direct Labour: Mr Andy Lewis, Head of Housing, Public Protection & Environment, Ruthin Road, Wrexham LL13 7TU ☎ 01978 315501 ✉ andy.lewis@wrexham.gov.uk

Economic Development: Mr Stephen Bayley, Head of Assets & Economic Development, Crown Buildings, 31 Chester Street, Wrexham LL13 8BG ☎ 01978 292441 🖷 01978 292445 ✉ steve.bayley@wrexham.gov.uk

Education: Mr John Davies, Head of Lifelong Learning, Lambpit Street, Wrexham LL11 1AR ☎ 01978 295401 ✉ john.davies@wrexham.gov.uk

E-Government: Mrs Helen Gerrard, Corporate & Customer Services Manager, 16 Lord Street, Wrexham LL11 1LG ☎ 01978 298951 🖷 01978 298950 ✉ helen.gerrard@wrexham.gov.uk

Electoral Registration: Ms Gaynor Coventry, Electoral & Regeneration Services Manager, The Guildhall, Wrexham LL11 1AY ☎ 01978 292290 🖷 01978 292293 ✉ gaynor.coventry@wrexham.gov.uk

Emergency Planning: Mr John Holland, Emergency Planning Manager, 16 Lord Street,, „ Wrexham LL11 1LG ☎ 01978 298826 ✉ john.holland@wrexham.gov.uk

Energy Management: Mr John Holland, Emergency Planning Manager, 16 Lord Street,, „ Wrexham LL11 1LG ☎ 01978 298826 ✉ john.holland@wrexham.gov.uk

Environmental / Technical Services: Mr Darren Williams, Network & Infrastructure Manager, Abbey Road South, Industrial Estate, Wrexham LL13 9PW ☎ 01978 729629 🖷 01978 667155 ✉ darren.williams@wrexham.gov.uk

Environmental Health: Ms Toni Slater, Public Protection Service Manager, Ruthin Road, Wrexham LL13 7TU ☎ 01978 315710 🖷 01978 315701 ✉ toni.slater@wrexham.gov.uk

Estates, Property & Valuation: Mrs Denise Garland, Strategic Assets Manager, Crown Buildings, 31 Chester Street, Wrexham LL13 8BG ☎ 01978 297214 ✉ denise.garland@wrexham.gov.uk

European Liaison: Mr Allan Forrest, Rural & European Manager, 3rd Floor, Crown Buildings, 31 Chester Street, Wrexham LL13 8BG ☎ 01978 292446 🖷 01978 292445 ✉ allan.forrest@wrexham.gov.uk

Events Manager: Mrs Amanda Davies, Marketing & Promotions Manager, 3rd Floor, Crown Buildings, 31 Chester Street, Wrexham LL13 8BG ☎ 01978 292544 ✉ amanda.davies@wrexham.gov.uk

Facilities: Mr Simon Roberts, Facilities Management Manager, 3rd Floor, Crown Buildings, 31 Chester Street, Wrexham LL13 8BG ☎ 01978 297207 🖷 01978 292207 ✉ simon.roberts@wrexham.gov.uk

Finance: Mr Mark Owen, Head of Finance, Lambpit Street, Wrexham LL11 1AR ☎ 01978 292701 🖷 01978 292702 ✉ mark.owen@wrexham.gov.uk

Fleet Management: Mr Edward Reid, Integrated Transport Unit Manager, Abbey Road South, Wrexham Industrial Estate, Wrexham LL13 9PW ☎ 01978 729752 🖷 01978 729600 ✉ edward.reid@wrexham.gov.uk

Grounds Maintenance: Mr Darren Williams, Network & Infrastructure Manager, Abbey Road South, Industrial Estate, Wrexham LL13 9PW ☎ 01978 729629 🖷 01978 667155 ✉ darren.williams@wrexham.gov.uk

Health and Safety: Mr Nigel Lawrence, Principal Health & Safety Officer, Ruthin Road, Wrexham LL13 7TU ☎ 01978 315562 🖷 01978 292132 ✉ nigel.lawrence@wrexham.gov.uk

Highways: Mr Darren Williams, Network & Infrastructure Manager, Abbey Road South, Industrial Estate, Wrexham LL13 9PW ☎ 01978 729629 🖷 01978 667155 ✉ darren.williams@wrexham.gov.uk

Home Energy Conservation: Mr John Holland, Emergency Planning Manager, 16 Lord Street, Wrexham LL11 1LG ☎ 01978 298826 ✉ john.holland@wrexham.gov.uk

Housing: Mr Fred Czulowski, Landlord Services Manager, Ruthin Road, Wrexham LL13 7TU ☎ 01978 315401 🖷 01978 315320 ✉ fred.czulowski@wrexham.gov.uk

Housing Maintenance: Mr Fred Czulowski, Landlord Services Manager, Ruthin Road, Wrexham LL13 7TU ☎ 01978 315401 🖷 01978 315320 ✉ fred.czulowski@wrexham.gov.uk

Legal: Mr Trevor Coxon, Head of Corporate & Customer Services, The Guildhall, Wrexham LL11 1AY ☎ 01978 292206 🖷 01978 292207 ✉ trevor.coxon@wrexham.gov.uk

Leisure and Cultural Services: Mr Lawrence Isted, Head of Community Wellbeing & Development, 16 Lord Street, Wrexham LL11 1LG ☎ 01978 298801 ✉ lawrence.isted@wrexham.gov.uk

Licensing: Mr Andy Lewis, Head of Housing, Public Protection & Environment, Ruthin Road, Wrexham LL13 7TU ☎ 01978 315501 ✉ andy.lewis@wrexham.gov.uk

Lifelong Learning: Mr John Davies, Head of Lifelong Learning, Lambpit Street, Wrexham LL11 1AR ☎ 01978 295401 ✉ john.davies@wrexham.gov.uk

Lighting: Mr Darren Williams, Network & Infrastructure Manager, Abbey Road South, Industrial Estate, Wrexham LL13 9PW ☎ 01978 729629 🖷 01978 667155 ✉ darren.williams@wrexham.gov.uk

Lottery Funding, Charity and Voluntary: Mr Steve Williams, Head of Policy & Performance, 2nd Floor, Crown Buildings, 31 Chester Street, Wrexham LL13 8BG ☎ 01978 298019 ✉ steveg.williams@wrexham.gov.uk

Member Services: Mr Trevor Coxon, Head of Corporate & Customer Services, The Guildhall, Wrexham LL11 1AY ☎ 01978 292206 🖷 01978 292207 ✉ trevor.coxon@wrexham.gov.uk

Parking: Ms Joanne Rodgers, Parking Services Co-ordinator, Abbey Road South, Industrial Estate, Wrexham LL13 9PW ☎ 01978 729697 ✉ joanne.rodgers@wrexham.gov.uk

Personnel / HR: Mr Trevor Coxon, Head of Corporate & Customer Services, The Guildhall, Wrexham LL11 1AY ☎ 01978 292206 🖷 01978 292207 🖰 trevor.coxon@wrexham.gov.uk

Planning: Mr Lawrence Isted, Head of Community Wellbeing & Development, Lambpit Street, Wrexham LL1 1AR ☎ 01978 298801 🖰 lawrence.isted@wrexham.gov.uk

Procurement: Mr Roger Barnett, Procurement Officer, Lambpit Street, Wrexham LL11 1AR ☎ 01978 292798 🖷 01978 292702 🖰 roger.barnett@wrexham.gov.uk

Public Libraries: Mr Dylan Hughes, Leisure & Libraries Manager, 16 Lord Street, Wrexham LL11 1LG ☎ 01978 298855 🖰 dylan.hughes@wrexham.gov.uk

Recycling & Waste Minimisation: Mrs Sarah Barton, Waste Strategy Manager, Abbey Road South, Wrexham Industrial Estate, Wrexham LL13 8BG ☎ 01978 729685 🖷 01978 729601 🖰 sarah.barton@wrexham.gov.uk

Regeneration: Mrs Isobel Garner, Town Centre Manager, Crown Buildings, 31 Chester Street, Wrexham LL13 8BG ☎ 01978 292457 🖰 isobel.garner@wrexham.gov.uk

Road Safety: Ms Wendy Davies-Williams, Assistant Road Safety Officer, Abbey Road South, Industrial Estate, Wrexham LL13 9PW ☎ 01978 729605 🖰 wendy.davieswilliams@wrexham.gov.uk

Social Services: Mr Andrew Figiel, Head of Adult Social Care, 2nd Floor, Crown Buildings, 31 Chester Street, Wrexham LL13 8BG ☎ 01978 298010 🖷 01978 298029 🖰 andrew.figiel@wrexham.gov.uk

Social Services (Adult): Mr Andrew Figiel, Head of Adult Social Care, 2nd Floor, Crown Buildings, 31 Chester Street, Wrexham LL13 8BG ☎ 01978 298020 🖷 01978 298029 🖰 andrew.figiel@wrexham.gov.uk

Social Services (Children): Ms Susan Evans, Head of Children & Young People, Crown Buildings, 31 Chester Street, Wrexham LL13 8BG ☎ 01978 295491 🖰 susan1.evans@wrexham.gov.uk

Staff Training: Ms Sue Pope, Training Manager, The Learning Centre, Wrexham LL1 1AY ☎ 01978 298366 🖰 sue.pope@wrexham.gov.uk

Street Scene: Mr Darren Williams, Network & Infrastructure Manager, Abbey Road South, Industrial Estate, Wrexham LL13 9PW ☎ 01978 729629 🖷 01978 667155 🖰 darren.williams@wrexham.gov.uk

Sustainable Communities: Mr Philip Walton, Strategic Director, The Guildhall, Wrexham LL11 1AY ☎ 01978 297002 🖷 01978 297004 🖰 philip.walton@wrexham.gov.uk

Sustainable Development: Mr Lawrence Isted, Head of Community Wellbeing & Development, Lambpit Street, Wrexham LL1 1AR ☎ 01978 298801 🖰 lawrence.isted@wrexham.gov.uk

Tourism: Mr Peter Scott, Investment & Business Development Manager, 3rd Floor, Crown Buildings, 31 Chester Street, Wrexham LL13 8BG ☎ 01978 292405 🖰 peter.scott@wrexham.gov.uk

Town Centre: Mrs Isobel Garner, Town Centre Manager, Crown Buildings, 31 Chester Street, Wrexham LL13 8BG ☎ 01978 292457 🖰 isobel.garner@wrexham.gov.uk

Traffic Management: Mr Darren Williams, Network & Infrastructure Manager, Abbey Road South, Industrial Estate, Wrexham LL13 9PW ☎ 01978 729629 🖷 01978 667155 🖰 darren.williams@wrexham.gov.uk

Transport: Mr Darren Williams, Network & Infrastructure Manager, Abbey Road South, Industrial Estate, Wrexham LL13 9PW ☎ 01978 729629 🖷 01978 667155 🖰 darren.williams@wrexham.gov.uk

Transport Planner: Mr Darren Williams, Network & Infrastructure Manager, Abbey Road South, Industrial Estate, Wrexham LL13 9PW ☎ 01978 729629 🖷 01978 667155 🖰 darren.williams@wrexham.gov.uk

Waste Collection and Disposal: Mr Darren Williams, Network & Infrastructure Manager, Abbey Road South, Industrial Estate, Wrexham LL13 9PW ☎ 01978 729629 🖷 01978 667155 🖰 darren.williams@wrexham.gov.uk

Waste Management: Mrs Sarah Barton, Waste Strategy Manager, Abbey Road South, Wrexham Industrial Estate, Wrexham LL13 8BG ☎ 01978 729685 🖷 01978 729601 🖰 sarah.barton@wrexham.gov.uk

Waste Management: Mr Philip Walton, Strategic Director, The Guildhall, Wrexham LL11 1AY ☎ 01978 297002 🖷 01978 297004 🖰 philip.walton@wrexham.gov.uk

Children's Play Areas: Mr Martin Howarth, Parks, Countryside & Public Rights of Way Manager, Abbey Road South, Industrial Estate, Wrexham LL13 9PW ☎ 01978 729630 🖰 martin.howarth@wrexham.gov.uk

COUNCILLORS

***Mayor* Edwards**, Terence Alan (IND - New Broughton)
talan.edwards@wrexham.gov.uk

***Deputy Mayor* Roxburgh**, Barbara (IND - Bryn Cefn)
barbara.roxburgh@wrexham.gov.uk

***Leader of the Council* Pritchard**, Mark (INDNA - Esclusham)
mark.pritchard@wrexham.gov.uk

***Deputy Leader of the Council* Roberts**, Ian (IND - Chirk North)
ian1.roberts@wrexham.gov.uk

Bailey, Andrew (LAB - Gresford East and West)
andrew.bailey@wrexham.gov.uk

Baldwin, William (IND - Little Acton)
william.baldwin@wrexham.gov.uk

Bithell, David (IND - Stansty)
idavid.bithell@wrexham.gov.uk

Bithell, David A (IND - Johnstown)
davida.bithell@wrexham.gov.uk

Blackwell, Paul (LAB - Plas Madoc)
paul.blackwell@wrexham.gov.uk

Boland, Terry (LAB - Llay)
terry.boland@wrexham.gov.uk

WREXHAM

Cameron, Brian (LAB - Whitegate)
brian.cameron@wrexham.gov.uk

Childs, Krista (LAB - Coedpoeth)
krista.childs@wrexham.gov.uk

Davies, Dana (LAB - Ruabon)
dana.davies@wrexhams.gov.uk

Dutton, Robert (IND - Erddig)
bob.dutton@wrexham.gov.uk

Edwards, Michael (LD - Marford and Hoseley)
michael.edwards@wrexham.gov.uk

Evans, Anne (LAB - Rhosnesni)
anne.evans@wrexham.gov.uk

Evans, Terry (IND - Chirk South)
terry.evans@wrexham.gov.uk

Gregory, A Keith (PC - Smithfield)
keith.gregory@wrexham.gov.uk

Griffiths, David (IND - Gwersyllt East and South)
david.griffiths@wrexham.gov.uk

Griffiths, Gareth (LAB - Coedpoeth)
gareth.wyngriffiths@wrexham.gov.uk

Hughes, Kevin (LAB - Ponciau)
kevin1.hughes@wrexham.gov.uk

Jeffares, Pat (IND - Llangollen Rural)
pat.jeffares@wrexham.gov.uk

Jenkins, R Alun (LD - Offa)
alun.jenkins@wrexham.gov.uk

Jones, Arfon (PC - Gwersyllt West)
arfon.jones@wrexham.gov.uk

Jones, Hugh (CON - Rossett)
hugh.jones@wrexham.gov.uk

Kelly, David (IND - Minera)
david.kelly@wrexham.gov.uk

Kelly, James (LD - Borras Park)
james.kelly@wrexham.gov.uk

Kenyon, Lloyd (CON - Overton)
lloyd.kenyon@wrexham.gov.uk

King, Malcolm (LAB - Wynnstay)
malcolm.king@wrexham.gov.uk

Lowe, Joan (IND - Penycae and Ruabon South)
joan.lowe@wrexham.gov.uk

Lowe, Geoffrey (IND - Acton)
geoff.lowe@wrexham.gov.uk

McCann, Bernie (IND - Gwersyllt East and South)
bernard.mccann@wrexham.gov.uk

Morris, Michael (CON - Holt)
michael.morris@wrexham.gov.uk

O'Toole, Carole (LD - Maesydre)
carole.otoole@wrexham.gov.uk

Owens, Mark (IND - Pant)
marka.owens@wrexham.gov.uk

Pemberton, Paul (IND - Ponciau)
paul.pemberton@wrexham.gov.uk

Phillips, John (IND - Pen y Cae)
johnc.phillips@wrexham.gov.uk

Powell, Colin (LAB - Queensway)
colin.powell@wrexham.gov.uk

Prince, Ron (IND - Cartrefle)
ron.prince@wrexham.gov.uk

Pritchard, John (IND - Marchwiel)
john.pritchard@wrexham.gov.uk

Roberts, J M Barbara (IND - Ceiriog Valley)
barbara.roberts@wrexham.gov.uk

Rogers, Neil (LAB - Gwenfro)
neil.rogers@wrexham.gov.uk

Rogers, Graham (LAB - Hermitage)
graham1.rogers@wrexham.gov.uk

Rogers, Paul (CON - Brymbo)
paul2.rogers@wrexham.gov.uk

Skelland, Rodney (CON - Bronington)
rodney.skelland@wrexham.gov.uk

Taylor, David (IND - Cefn)
david.taylor@wrexham.gov.uk

Walsh, Robert (LD - Llay)
robert.walsh@wrexham.gov.uk

Williams, Michael (LAB - Gwersyllt North)
michael.williams@wrexham.gov.uk

Williams, Andy (IND - Garden Village)
andy.williams@wrexham.gov.uk

Wilson, Steve (IND - Grosvenor)
steve.wilson@wrexham.gov.uk

Wright, Derek (LAB - Cefn)
derek.wright@wrexham.gov.uk

Wynn, Phil (IND - Brynyffynnon)
phil.wynn@wrexham.gov.uk

POLITICAL COMPOSITION

IND: 24, LAB: 15, LD: 5, CON: 5, PC: 2, INDNA: 1

COMMITTEE CHAIRS

Licensing: Mr Paul Pemberton

Planning: Mr Michael Morris

Wychavon D

Wychavon District Council, Civic Centre, Queen Elizabeth Drive, Pershore WR10 1PT
☎ 01386 565000 🖷 01386 561091 ✉ servicecentre@wychavon.gov.uk
🖳 www.wychavon.gov.uk

FACTS AND FIGURES

Parliamentary Constituencies: Redditch
EU Constituencies: West Midlands
Election Frequency: Elections are of whole council

PRINCIPAL OFFICERS

Chief Executive: Mr Jack Hegarty, Managing Director, Civic Centre, Queen Elizabeth Drive, Pershore WR10 1PT ☎ 01386 565401 ✉ jack.hegarty@wychavon.gov.uk

Deputy Chief Executive: Mr Vic Allison, Deputy Managing Director, Civic Centre, Queen Elizabeth Drive, Pershore WR10 1PT ☎ 01386 565586 ✉ vic.allison@wychavon.gov.uk

Senior Management: Mr Ian Marshall, Head of Legal & Support Services, Civic Centre, Queen Elizabeth Drive, Pershore WR10 1PT ☎ 01386 565470 🖷 01386 561089 ✉ ian.marshall@wychavon.gov.uk

Senior Management: Mr Philip Merrick, Head of Economy & Community Services, Civic Centre, Queen Elizabeth Drive, Pershore WR10 1PT ☎ 01386 565588 ✉ phil.merrick@wychavon.gov.uk

Senior Management: Mrs Fiona Narburgh, Head of Strategy & Communications, Civic Centre, Queen Elizabeth Drive, Pershore WR10 1PT ☎ 01386 565101 ✉ fiona.narbugh@wychavon.gov.uk

Senior Management: Mr Gary Williams, Head of Housing & Planning Services, Civic Centre, Queen Elizabeth Drive, Pershore WR10 1PT ☎ 01386 565279 ✉ gary.williams@wychavon.gov.uk

Architect, Building / Property Services: Ms Kirsty May-Jones, Housing Development Officer, Civic Centre, Queen Elizabeth Drive, Pershore WR10 1PT ☎ 01386 565524 ✉ kirsty.may-jones@wychavon.gov.uk

Architect, Building / Property Services: Mr Gary Williams, Head of Housing & Planning Services, Civic Centre, Queen Elizabeth Drive, Pershore WR10 1PT ☎ 01386 565279 ✉ gary.williams@wychavon.gov.uk

Best Value: Ms Cherrie Mansfield, Strategy & Performance Manager, Civic Centre, Queen Elizabeth Drive, Pershore WR10 1PT ☎ 01386 565508 ✉ cherrie.mansfield@wychavon.gov.uk

PR / Communications: Mrs Fiona Narburgh, Head of Strategy & Communications, Civic Centre, Queen Elizabeth Drive, Pershore WR10 1PT ☎ 01386 565101 ✉ fiona.narbugh@wychavon.gov.uk

PR / Communications: Ms Emma Wild, Communications Manager, Civic Centre, Queen Elizabeth Drive, Pershore WR10 1PT ☎ 01386 565102 ✉ emma.wild@wychavon.gov.uk

Community Planning: Ms Cherrie Mansfield, Strategy & Performance Manager, Civic Centre, Queen Elizabeth Drive, Pershore WR10 1PT ☎ 01386 565508 ✉ cherrie.mansfield@wychavon.gov.uk

Community Safety: Mr David Hemming, Community Safety Manager, Civic Centre, Queen Elizabeth Drive, Pershore WR10 1PT ☎ 01386 565301 ✉ david.hemming@wychavon.gov.uk

Computer Management: Mr Nigel Winters, ICT Development Manager, Civic Centre, Queen Elizabeth Drive, Pershore WR10 1PT ☎ 01386 565000 ✉ nigel.winters@wychavon.gov.uk

Contracts: Mr David Buckley, Strategic Procurement Officer for Resources, Civic Centre, Queen Elizabeth Drive, Pershore WR10 1PT ☎ 01386 565433 ✉ david.buckley@wychavon.gov.uk

Contracts: Mr Philip Merrick, Head of Economy & Community Services, Civic Centre, Queen Elizabeth Drive, Pershore WR10 1PT ☎ 01386 565588 ✉ phil.merrick@wychavon.gov.uk

Customer Service: Mrs Kath Smith, Customer & Support Services Manager, Civic Centre, Queen Elizabeth Drive, Pershore WR10 1PT ☎ 01386 565484 ✉ kath.smith@wychavon.gov.uk

Economic Development: Mr Philip Merrick, Head of Economy & Community Services, Civic Centre, Queen Elizabeth Drive, Pershore WR10 1PT ☎ 01386 565588 ✉ phil.merrick@wychavon.gov.uk

Electoral Registration: Mrs Elaine Dicks, Electoral Services Officer, Civic Centre, Queen Elizabeth Drive, Pershore WR10 1PT ☎ 01386 565162 🖷 01386 565290 ✉ elaine.dicks@wychavon.gov.uk

Emergency Planning: Mr Philip Merrick, Head of Economy & Community Services, Civic Centre, Queen Elizabeth Drive, Pershore WR10 1PT ☎ 01386 565588 ✉ phil.merrick@wychavon.gov.uk

Environmental Health: Mr Ivor Pumfrey, Acting Head of Regulatory Services, Wyre Forest House, Finepoint Way, Kidderminster DY11 7FB ☎ 01684 862296 ✉ ivorpumfrey@malvernhills.gov.uk

Estates, Property & Valuation: Mr Vic Allison, Deputy Managing Director, Civic Centre, Queen Elizabeth Drive, Pershore WR10 1PT ☎ 01386 565586 ✉ vic.allison@wychavon.gov.uk

Events Manager: Ms Emma Wild, Communications Manager, Civic Centre, Queen Elizabeth Drive, Pershore WR10 1PT ☎ 01386 565102 ✉ emma.wild@wychavon.gov.uk

Facilities: Mr Vic Allison, Deputy Managing Director, Civic Centre, Queen Elizabeth Drive, Pershore WR10 1PT ☎ 01386 565586 ✉ vic.allison@wychavon.gov.uk

Finance: Mr Vic Allison, Deputy Managing Director, Civic Centre, Queen Elizabeth Drive, Pershore WR10 1PT ☎ 01386 565586 ✉ vic.allison@wychavon.gov.uk

Finance: Ms Alison Williams, Financial Services Manager, Civic Centre, Queen Elizabeth Drive, Pershore WR10 1PT ☎ 01386 565501 ✉ alison.williams@wychavon.gov.uk

Treasury: Ms Alison Williams, Financial Services Manager, Civic Centre, Queen Elizabeth Drive, Pershore WR10 1PT ☎ 01386 565501 ✉ alison.williams@wychavon.gov.uk

Fleet Management: Mr Vic Allison, Deputy Managing Director, Civic Centre, Queen Elizabeth Drive, Pershore WR10 1PT ☎ 01386 565586 ✉ vic.allison@wychavon.gov.uk

Grounds Maintenance: Ms Lynn Stevens, Parks Officer, Civic Centre, Queen Elizabeth Drive, Pershore WR10 1PT ☎ 01386 565407 ✉ lynn.stevens@wychavon.gov.uk

Health and Safety: Mr Carl Wibberley, Safety Officer & Building Manager, Civic Centre, Queen Elizabeth Drive, Pershore WR10 1PT ☎ 01386 565493 ✉ carl.wibberley@wychavon.gov.uk

Housing: Mrs Elaine Salter, Housing Services Manager, Civic Centre, Queen Elizabeth Drive, Pershore WR10 1PT ☎ 01386 565241 ✉ elaine.salter@wychavon.gov.uk

WYCHAVON

Housing: Ms Mary Unwin, Senior Housing Needs Officer, Civic Centre, Queen Elizabeth Drive, Pershore WR10 1PT ☎ 01386 565352 ✉ mary.unwin@wychavon.gov.uk

Legal: Mr Ian Marshall, Head of Legal & Support Services, Civic Centre, Queen Elizabeth Drive, Pershore WR10 1PT ☎ 01386 565470 🖷 01386 561089 ✉ ian.marshall@wychavon.gov.uk

Leisure and Cultural Services: Mr Jem Teal, Community Development Manager, Civic Centre, Queen Elizabeth Drive, Pershore WR10 1PT ☎ 01386 565235 ✉ jem.teal@wychavon.gov.uk

Licensing: Mr Ivor Pumfrey, Acting Head of Regulatory Services, Wyre Forest House, Finepoint Way, Kidderminster DY11 7FB ☎ 01684 862296 ✉ ivorpumfrey@malvernhills.gov.uk

Lottery Funding, Charity and Voluntary: Mr Jem Teal, Community Development Manager, Civic Centre, Queen Elizabeth Drive, Pershore WR10 1PT ☎ 01386 565235 ✉ jem.teal@wychavon.gov.uk

Member Services: Mrs Kath Smith, Customer & Support Services Manager, Civic Centre, Queen Elizabeth Drive, Pershore WR10 1PT ☎ 01386 565484 ✉ kath.smith@wychavon.gov.uk

Parking: Mrs Christine Baxter, Parking Services Manager, Civic Centre, Queen Elizabeth Drive, Pershore WR10 1PT ☎ 01386 565226 ✉ christine.baxter@wychavon.gov.uk

Partnerships: Mr Chris Brooks, Regeneration Manager, Civic Centre, Queen Elizabeth Drive, Pershore WR10 1PT ☎ 01386 565343 ✉ chris.brooks@wychavon.gov.uk

Partnerships: Ms Cherrie Mansfield, Strategy & Performance Manager, Civic Centre, Queen Elizabeth Drive, Pershore WR10 1PT ☎ 01386 565508 ✉ cherrie.mansfield@wychavon.gov.uk

Personnel / HR: Mrs Kim Stallard, HR Services Manager, Civic Centre, Queen Elizabeth Drive, Pershore WR10 1PT ☎ 01386 565380 ✉ kim.stallard@wychavon.gov.uk

Planning: Mr Gary Williams, Head of Housing & Planning Services, Civic Centre, Queen Elizabeth Drive, Pershore WR10 1PT ☎ 01386 565279 ✉ gary.williams@wychavon.gov.uk

Procurement: Mr Vic Allison, Deputy Managing Director, Civic Centre, Queen Elizabeth Drive, Pershore WR10 1PT ☎ 01386 565586 ✉ vic.allison@wychavon.gov.uk

Recycling & Waste Minimisation: Mr Mark Edwards, Waste Management Officer, Civic Centre, Queen Elizabeth Drive, Pershore WR10 1PT ☎ 01386 565245 ✉ mark.edwards@wychavon.gov.uk

Regeneration: Mr Chris Brooks, Regeneration Manager, Civic Centre, Queen Elizabeth Drive, Pershore WR10 1PT ☎ 01386 565343 ✉ chris.brooks@wychavon.gov.uk

Staff Training: Mrs Kim Stallard, HR Services Manager, Civic Centre, Queen Elizabeth Drive, Pershore WR10 1PT ☎ 01386 565380 ✉ kim.stallard@wychavon.gov.uk

Sustainable Communities: Ms Cherrie Mansfield, Strategy & Performance Manager, Civic Centre, Queen Elizabeth Drive, Pershore WR10 1PT ☎ 01386 565508 ✉ cherrie.mansfield@wychavon.gov.uk

Tourism: Ms Angela Tidmarsh, Tourism Officer, Civic Centre, Queen Elizabeth Drive, Pershore WR10 1PT ☎ 01386 565373 ✉ angela.tidmarsh@wychavon.gov.uk

Town Centre: Mr Chris Brooks, Regeneration Manager, Civic Centre, Queen Elizabeth Drive, Pershore WR10 1PT ☎ 01386 565343 ✉ chris.brooks@wychavon.gov.uk

Transport Planner: Mr Fred Davies, Policy Manager, Civic Centre, Queen Elizabeth Drive, Pershore WR10 1PT ☎ 01386 565367 ✉ fred.davies@wychavon.gov.uk

Waste Collection and Disposal: Ms Sharon Casswell, Client Services Manager, Civic Centre, Queen Elizabeth Drive, Pershore WR10 1PT ☎ 01386 565203 ✉ sharon.casswell@wychavon.gov.uk

Waste Management: Mr Mark Edwards, Waste Management Officer, Civic Centre, Queen Elizabeth Drive, Pershore WR10 1PT ☎ 01386 565245 ✉ mark.edwards@wychavon.gov.uk

Children's Play Areas: Ms Lynn Stevens, Parks Officer, Civic Centre, Queen Elizabeth Drive, Pershore WR10 1PT ☎ 01386 565407 ✉ lynn.stevens@wychavon.gov.uk

COUNCILLORS

***Chair* Wood**, Val (CON - Pershore)
val.wood@wychavon.gov.uk

***Vice-Chair* Smith**, F S (CON - Little Hampton)
jhsmith@jhsmith.plus.com

***Leader of the Council* Robinson**, Linda (CON - Upton Snodsbury)
linda.robinson@wychavon.gov.uk

***Deputy Leader of the Council* Duffy**, Lynne (CON - Lovett & North Claines)
lynne.duffy@live.com

Adams, Robert (CON - Norton and Whttington)
robert.adams@wychavon.gov.uk

Adams, Alastair (CON - Honeybourne and Pebworth)
adams.pebworth@gmail.com

Barday, K (CON - Evesham South)
k.barday101@btinternet.com

Beale, Graham (CON - Droitwich Spa South West)
graham.beale@wychavon.gov.uk

Bearcfroft, Ged (UKIP - Great Hampton)
ged.bearcroft@wychavon.net

Bolton, Jan (CON - Droitwich Spa West)
jan.bolton6@btinternet.com

Brookes, Bob (CON - Droitwich Spa East)
bob@greenbox.uk.com

Bulman, James (CON - Evesham South)
james.bulman@wychavon.net

Darby, Adrian (LD - South Bredon Hill)
adrian.darby@wychavon.gov.uk

Davis, Ron (CON - Eckington)
alfa@rondavis.fsbusiness.co.uk

Dowty, Nigel (CON - Hartlebury)
nigel.dowty@wychavon.gov.uk

English, Michelle (CON - Fladbury)
michelle.english@wychavon.net

Eyre, Elizabeth (CON - Broadway and Wickhamford)
elizabeth.eyre@wychavon.gov.uk

Goodge, Mark (CON - Badsey)
mark.goodge@wychavon.net

Hamilton, Hugh (CON - Dodderhill)
hugh.hamilton@wychavon.net

Hardman, Adrian (CON - Bredon)
adrian.hardman@wychavon.gov.uk

Homer, Charles (CON - Harvington and Norton)
charles.homer@wychavon.gov.uk

King, Martin (CON - Bengeworth)
martin.king@wychavon.net

Lasota, Richard (CON - The Littletons)
richard.lasota@wychavon.gov.uk

Lawley, M (CON - Droitwich Spa South East)

Mackison, George (CON - Elmley Castle & Somerville)
georgegmconsulting@tesco.net

Middlebrough, Paul (CON - Drakes Broughton)
paul.middlebrough@wychavon.gov.uk

Miller, Tony (CON - Lovett & North Claines)
tony.miller@wychavon.gov.uk

Morris, Richard (CON - Droitwich Spa South East)
richard.morris@wychavon.gov.uk

Murphy, Roy (CON - Droitwich Spa Central)
roy.murphy@wychavon.net

Noyes, Thomas (CON - Droitwich Spa South West)
tom.noyes@wychavon.gov.uk

O'Donnell, Gerry (CON - Little Hampton)
gerry.donnell@sky.com

Powell, Catherine (CON - Droitwich Spa West)
catherine.powell@wychavon.net

Raphael, Robert (CON - Evesham North)
robert@hamptonferry.co.uk

Rowley, Margaret (LD - Bowbrook)
margaret.rowley@wychavon.gov.uk

Rowley, Tony (CON - Pershore)
tonyrowley@btinternet.com

Sandalls, Josephine (CON - Evesham North)
josephine.sandalls@wychavon.gov.uk

Steel, Audrey (CON - Inkberrow)
panda@broadclosefarm.wanadoo.co.uk

Stokes, Emma (CON - Bengeworth)
stokes_e1@sky.com

Thomas, Bradley (CON - Broadway & Wickhamford)
bradley@bradleythomas.co.uk

Tomalin, K (CON - Droitwich Spa East)

Tomlinson, Peter (CON - Ombersley)
peter.tomlinson@wychavon.gov.uk

Tucker, Elizabeth (LD - Pinvin)
elizabeth.tucker@wychavon.gov.uk

Tucker, Charles (LD - Pershore)
charles.tucker@wychavon.gov.uk

Wilkinson, David (CON - Inkberrow)
david.wilkinson@e-railways.co.uk

Wright, Keith (LD - Bretforton and Offenhan)
keith.wright@wychavon.gov.uk

POLITICAL COMPOSITION

CON: 39, LD: 5, UKIP: 1

COMMITTEE CHAIRS

Audit: Mr Ron Davis

Licensing: Mr Tony Miller

Planning: Mr Paul Middlebrough

Wycombe D

Wycombe District Council, District Council Offices, Queen Victoria Road, High Wycombe HP11 1BB
☎ 01494 461000 🖷 01494 461292 💻 www.wycombe.gov.uk

FACTS AND FIGURES

Parliamentary Constituencies: Aylesbury, Beaconsfield, Chesham and Amersham, Wycombe
EU Constituencies: South East
Election Frequency: Elections are of whole council

PRINCIPAL OFFICERS

Chief Executive: Ms Karen Satterford, Chief Executive, Council Offices, Queen Victoria Road, High Wycombe HP11 1BB ☎ 01494 421101 ✉ karen_satterford@wycombe.gov.uk

Senior Management: Ms Caroline Hughes, Head of Environment, Council Offices, Queen Victoria Road, High Wycombe HP11 1BB ☎ 01494 421701 ✉ caroline_hughes@wycombe.gov.uk

Senior Management: Ms Elaine Jewell, Head of Community Services, District Council Offices, Queen Victoria Road, High Wycombe HP11 1BB ☎ 01494 421800 ✉ elaine_jewell@wycombe.gov.uk

Senior Management: Mr John McMillan, Head of HR, ICT & Shared Support Services, Council Offices, Queen Victoria Road, High Wycombe HP11 1BB ☎ 01494 421127 ✉ john_mcmillan@wycombe.gov.uk

Senior Management: Mr Charles Meakings, Head of Democratic, Legal & Policy, Council Offices, Queen Victoria Road, High Wycombe HP11 1BB ☎ 01494 421980 ✉ charles_meakings@wycombe.gov.uk

Senior Management: Mr Steve Richardson, Head of Financial & Commercial Services, District Council Offices, Queen Victoria Road, High Wycombe HP11 1BB ☎ 01494 421322 ✉ steve_richardson@wycombe.gov.uk

WYCOMBE

Senior Management: Mr Paul Shackley, Corporate Director - Growth & Regeneration, District Council Offices, Queen Victoria Road, High Wycombe HP11 1BB ☎ 01494 421401 🖱 paul.shackley@wycombe.gov.uk

Senior Management: Mr Paul Shackley, Corporate Director - Growth & Regeneration, District Council Offices, Queen Victoria Road, High Wycombe HP11 1BB ☎ 01494 421401 🖱 paul.shackley@wycombe.gov.uk

Senior Management: Ms Penelope Tollitt, Head of Planning & Sustainability, District Council Offices, Queen Victoria Road, High Wycombe HP11 1BB ☎ 01494 421519 🖱 penelope_tollitt@wycombe.gov.uk

Access Officer / Social Services (Disability): Mr Alan Switalski, Access Officer, Council Offices, Queen Victoria Road, High Wycombe HP11 1BB ☎ 01494 421438 🖱 alan_switalski@wycombe.gov.uk

Architect, Building / Property Services: Mr Charles Brocklehurst, Major Projects & Property Executive, Council Offices, Queen Victoria Road, High Wycombe HP11 1BB ☎ 01494 421280 🖱 charles_brocklehurst@wycombe.gov.uk

Best Value: Miss Jacqueline Ford, Corporate Policy Team Leader, Council Offices, Queen Victoria Road, High Wycombe HP11 1BB ☎ 01494 421983 🖱 jacqueline_ford@wycombe.gov.uk

Best Value: Mr Charles Meakings, Head of Democratic, Legal & Policy, Council Offices, Queen Victoria Road, High Wycombe HP11 1BB ☎ 01494 421980 🖱 charles_meakings@wycombe.gov.uk

Building Control: Ms Alison Pipes, Building Control Manager, District Council Offices, Queen Victoria Road, High Wycombe HP11 1BB ☎ 01494 421425 🖱 alison_pipes@wycombe.gov.uk

PR / Communications: Mr Charles Meakings, Head of Democratic, Legal & Policy, Council Offices, Queen Victoria Road, High Wycombe HP11 1BB ☎ 01494 421980 🖱 charles_meakings@wycombe.gov.uk

PR / Communications: Ms Catherine Spalton, Communications Team Leader, District Council Offices, Queen Victoria Road, High Wycombe HP11 1BB ☎ 01494 421230 🖱 catherine_spalton@wycombe.gov.uk

Community Planning: Mr Charles Meakings, Head of Democratic, Legal & Policy, Council Offices, Queen Victoria Road, High Wycombe HP11 1BB ☎ 01494 421980 🖱 charles_meakings@wycombe.gov.uk

Community Safety: Mr Daniel Sullivan, Strategic Prevent Coordinator, District Council Offices, Queen Victoria Road, High Wycombe HP11 1BB ☎ 01494 421371 🖱 daniel.sullivan@wycombe.gov.uk

Computer Management: Ms Mary Hayward-Ord, ICT Manager of Infrastructure, District Council Offices, Queen Victoria Road, High Wycombe HP11 1BB ☎ 01494 421179 🖱 mary_hayward-ord@wycombe.gov.uk

Computer Management: Mr Mark Lansbury, Business Systems Manager, District Council Offices, Queen Victoria Road, High Wycombe HP11 1BB ☎ 01494 421168 🖱 mark_lansbury@wycombe.gov.uk

Computer Management: Mr John McMillan, Head of HR, ICT & Shared Support Services, Council Offices, Queen Victoria Road, High Wycombe HP11 1BB ☎ 01494 421127 🖱 john_mcmillan@wycombe.gov.uk

Customer Service: Ms Karen Ashby, Customer Service Centre Manager, District Council Offices, Queen Victoria Road, High Wycombe HP11 1BB ☎ 01494 421111 🖱 karen.ashby@wycombe.gov.uk

Customer Service: Mr John McMillan, Head of HR, ICT & Shared Support Services, Council Offices, Queen Victoria Road, High Wycombe HP11 1BB ☎ 01494 421127 🖱 john_mcmillan@wycombe.gov.uk

Economic Development: Miss Jacqueline Ford, Corporate Policy Team Leader, Council Offices, Queen Victoria Road, High Wycombe HP11 1BB ☎ 01494 421983 🖱 jacqueline_ford@wycombe.gov.uk

E-Government: Mr John McMillan, Head of HR, ICT & Shared Support Services, Council Offices, Queen Victoria Road, High Wycombe HP11 1BB ☎ 01494 421127 🖱 john_mcmillan@wycombe.gov.uk

Electoral Registration: Mr Rob Curtis, Statutory Services Manager, District Council Offices, Queen Victoria Road, High Wycombe HP11 1BB ☎ 01494 421242 🖱 rob_curtis@wycombe.gov.uk

Emergency Planning: Mr Andrew Collinson, Policy Officer (Emergency Planning), District Council Offices, Queen Victoria Road, High Wycombe HP11 1BB ☎ 01494 421981 🖱 charles_meakings@wycombe.gov.uk

Emergency Planning: Mr Charles Meakings, Head of Democratic, Legal & Policy, Council Offices, Queen Victoria Road, High Wycombe HP11 1BB ☎ 01494 421980 🖱 charles_meakings@wycombe.gov.uk

Energy Management: Mr Graham Weston, Energy Officer, Council Offices, Queen Victoria Road, High Wycombe HP11 1BB ☎ 01494 421565 🖱 graham_weston@wycombe.gov.uk

Environmental / Technical Services: Ms Caroline Hughes, Head of Environment, Council Offices, Queen Victoria Road, High Wycombe HP11 1BB ☎ 01494 421701 🖱 caroline_hughes@wycombe.gov.uk

Environmental Health: Mr Neil Stannett, Environmental Health Officer, District Council Offices, Queen Victoria Road, High Wycombe HP11 1BB ☎ 01494 421092 🖱 neil_stannett@wycombe.gov.uk

Estates, Property & Valuation: Mr Charles Brocklehurst, Major Projects & Property Executive, Council Offices, Queen Victoria Road, High Wycombe HP11 1BB ☎ 01494 421280 🖱 charles_brocklehurst@wycombe.gov.uk

Estates, Property & Valuation: Mr Robert Daniels, Estates Team Leader, District Council Offices, Queen Victoria Road, High Wycombe HP11 1BB ☎ 01494 421157 🖱 robert.daniels@wycombe.gov.uk

Facilities: Mr John McMillan, Head of HR, ICT & Shared Support Services, Council Offices, Queen Victoria Road, High Wycombe HP11 1BB ☎ 01494 421127 🖱 john_mcmillan@wycombe.gov.uk

Finance: Mr Steve Richardson, Head of Financial & Commercial Services, District Council Offices, Queen Victoria Road, High Wycombe HP11 1BB ☎ 01494 421322 🖱 steve_richardson@wycombe.gov.uk

Health and Safety: Mr Paul Spencer, Health & Safety Manager, District Council Offices, Queen Victoria Road, High Wycombe HP11 1BB ☎ 01494 421107 🖱 paul.spencer@wycombe.gov.uk

Housing: Mr Brian Daley, Housing Service Manager, Council Offices, Queen Victoria Road, High Wycombe HP11 1BB ☎ 01494 421601 🖱 brian_daley@wycombe.gov.uk

Housing: Ms Caroline Hughes, Head of Environment, Council Offices, Queen Victoria Road, High Wycombe HP11 1BB ☎ 01494 421701 🖱 caroline_hughes@wycombe.gov.uk

Legal: Ms Julie Openshaw, District Solicitor/Monitoring Officer, District Council Offices, Queen Victoria Road, High Wycombe HP11 1BB ☎ 01494 421252 🖱 julie_openshaw@wycombe.gov.uk

Leisure and Cultural Services: Ms Sarah Randall, Community Commissioning Manager, District Council Offices, Queen Victoria Road, High Wycombe HP11 1BB ☎ 01494 421888 🖱 sarah_randall@wycombe.gov.uk

Licensing: Ms Caroline Steven, Licensing Team Leader, District Council Offices, Queen Victoria Road, High Wycombe HP11 1BB ☎ 01494 421222 🖱 caroline_steven@wycombe.gov.uk

Lifelong Learning: Ms Elaine Jewell, Head of Community Services, District Council Offices, Queen Victoria Road, High Wycombe HP11 1BB ☎ 01494 421800 🖱 elaine_jewell@wycombe.gov.uk

Lottery Funding, Charity and Voluntary: Ms Elaine Jewell, Head of Community Services, District Council Offices, Queen Victoria Road, High Wycombe HP11 1BB ☎ 01494 421800 🖱 elaine_jewell@wycombe.gov.uk

Member Services: Mr Charles Meakings, Head of Democratic, Legal & Policy, Council Offices, Queen Victoria Road, High Wycombe HP11 1BB ☎ 01494 421980 🖱 charles_meakings@wycombe.gov.uk

Parking: Mr Robin Evans, Parking Services Manager, District Council Offices, Queen Victoria Road, High Wycombe HP11 1BB ☎ 01494 421471 🖱 robin_evans@wycombe.gov.uk

Partnerships: Mr Charles Meakings, Head of Democratic, Legal & Policy, Council Offices, Queen Victoria Road, High Wycombe HP11 1BB ☎ 01494 421980 🖱 charles_meakings@wycombe.gov.uk

Personnel / HR: Mr John McMillan, Head of HR, ICT & Shared Support Services, Council Offices, Queen Victoria Road, High Wycombe HP11 1BB ☎ 01494 421127 🖱 john_mcmillan@wycombe.gov.uk

Planning: Mr Alastair Nicholson, Development Manager, District Council Offices, Queen Victoria Road, High Wycombe HP11 1BB ☎ 01494 421510 🖱 alastair_nicholson@wycombe.gov.uk

Planning: Ms Penelope Tollitt, Head of Planning & Sustainability, District Council Offices, Queen Victoria Road, High Wycombe HP11 1BB ☎ 01494 421519 🖱 penelope_tollitt@wycombe.gov.uk

Procurement: Mr Steve Middleton, Procurement Manager, District Council Offices, Queen Victoria Road, High Wycombe HP11 1BB ☎ 01494 421315 🖱 steve_middleton@wycombe.gov.uk

Procurement: Mr Steve Richardson, Head of Financial & Commercial Services, District Council Offices, Queen Victoria Road, High Wycombe HP11 1BB ☎ 01494 421322 🖱 steve_richardson@wycombe.gov.uk

Recycling & Waste Minimisation: Ms Caroline Hughes, Head of Environment, Council Offices, Queen Victoria Road, High Wycombe HP11 1BB ☎ 01494 421701 🖱 caroline_hughes@wycombe.gov.uk

Regeneration: Mr Charles Brocklehurst, Major Projects & Property Executive, Council Offices, Queen Victoria Road, High Wycombe HP11 1BB ☎ 01494 421280 🖱 charles_brocklehurst@wycombe.gov.uk

Staff Training: Mr John McMillan, Head of HR, ICT & Shared Support Services, Council Offices, Queen Victoria Road, High Wycombe HP11 1BB ☎ 01494 421127 🖱 john_mcmillan@wycombe.gov.uk

Staff Training: Ms Sarah Taylor, Training & Development Officer, Council Offices, Queen Victoria Road, High Wycombe HP11 1BB ☎ 01494 421139 🖱 sarah_taylor@wycombe.gov.uk

Street Scene: Ms Caroline Hughes, Head of Environment, Council Offices, Queen Victoria Road, High Wycombe HP11 1BB ☎ 01494 421701 🖱 caroline_hughes@wycombe.gov.uk

Sustainable Communities: Ms Elaine Jewell, Head of Community Services, District Council Offices, Queen Victoria Road, High Wycombe HP11 1BB ☎ 01494 421800 🖱 elaine_jewell@wycombe.gov.uk

Sustainable Development: Ms Penelope Tollitt, Head of Planning & Sustainability, District Council Offices, Queen Victoria Road, High Wycombe HP11 1BB ☎ 01494 421519 🖱 penelope_tollitt@wycombe.gov.uk

Tourism: Ms Elaine Jewell, Head of Community Services, District Council Offices, Queen Victoria Road, High Wycombe HP11 1BB ☎ 01494 421800 🖱 elaine_jewell@wycombe.gov.uk

Town Centre: Mr Oliver O'Dell, Chief Executive - High Wycombe BidCo, District Council Offices, Queen Victoria Road, High Wycombe HP11 1BB ☎ 01494 452705 🖱 oliver@hwtcp.co.uk

WYCOMBE

Total Place: Mr Charles Meakings, Head of Democratic, Legal & Policy, Council Offices, Queen Victoria Road, High Wycombe HP11 1BB ☎ 01494 421980 charles_meakings@wycombe.gov.uk

Waste Collection and Disposal: Ms Caroline Hughes, Head of Environment, Council Offices, Queen Victoria Road, High Wycombe HP11 1BB ☎ 01494 421701 caroline_hughes@wycombe.gov.uk

Waste Management: Ms Caroline Hughes, Head of Environment, Council Offices, Queen Victoria Road, High Wycombe HP11 1BB ☎ 01494 421701 caroline_hughes@wycombe.gov.uk

COUNCILLORS

***Chair* McEnnis**, Ian (CON - Chiltern Rise)
ian.mcennis@wycombe.gov.uk

***Leader of the Council* Wood**, Katrina (CON - Tylers Green and Loudwater)
katrina.wood@wycombe.gov.uk

***Deputy Leader of the Council* Barnes**, Dominic (CON - Greater Marlow)
dominic.barnes@wycombe.gov.uk

***Group Leader* Knight**, Matt (IND - Micklefield)
matt.knight@wycombe.gov.uk

***Group Leader* Turner**, Alan (IND - The Risboroughs)
alan.turner@wycombe.gov.uk

Adey, Julia (CON - The Wooburns)
julia.adey@wycombe.gov.uk

Adoh, Shade (CON - Stokenchurch and Radnage)
shade.adoh@wycombe.gov.uk

Ahmed, Zia (CON - Sands)
zia.ahmed@wycombe.gov.uk

Ahmed, Khalil (LAB - Disraeli)
khalil.ahmed@wycombe.gov.uk

Appleyard, Mike (CON - Bourne End cum Hedsor)
michael.appleyard@wycombe.gov.uk

Asif, Mohammed (LAB - Oakridge and Castlefield)
mohammed.asif@wycombe.gov.uk

Baughan, Andrea (IND - Micklefield)
andrea.baughan@wycombe.gov.uk

Broadbent, Steve (CON - Greater Hughenden)
steve.broadbent@wycombe.gov.uk

Brown, Suzanne (CON - Marlow South East)
suzanne.brown@wycombe.gov.uk

Bull, Harry (CON - Totteridge)
harry.bull@wycombe.gov.uk

Carroll, David (CON - Greater Hughenden)
david.carroll@wycombe.gov.uk

Clarke, Lesley (CON - Abbey)
lesley.clarke@wycombe.gov.uk

Clarke, Marten (CON - Ryemead)
marten.clarke@wycombe.gov.uk

Collingwood, Alex (CON - Marlow North and West)
alex.collingwood@wycombe.gov.uk

Davy, Matthew (CON - Booker and Cressex)
matthew.davy@wycombe.gov.uk

Etholen, Carl (CON - Bledlow and Bradenham)
carl.etholen@wycombe.gov.uk

Farmer, Ray (LD - Ryemead)
ray.farmer@wycombe.gov.uk

Gaffney, Ron (CON - Hazlemere North)
ron.gaffney@wycombe.gov.uk

Graham, Sebert (LAB - Oakridge and Castlefield)
sebert.graham@wycombe.gov.uk

Green, Tony (CON - Terriers and Amersham Hill)
tony.green@wycombe.gov.uk

Hall, Gary (IND - The Risboroughs)
gary.hall@wycombe.gov.uk

Hanif, Mohammed (LAB - Oakridge and Castlefield)
mohammed.hanif@wycombe.gov.uk

Harris, Mark (CON - Greater Marlow)
mark.harris@wycombe.gov.uk

Harriss, Clive (CON - Icknield)
clive.harriss@wycombe.gov.uk

Hashmi, Muhammad Abdullah (LAB - Bowerdean)
abdullah.hashmi@wycombe.gov.uk

Hill, Alan (CON - Abbey)
alan.hill@wycombe.gov.uk

Hussain, Mahboob (CON - Abbey)
mahboob.hussain@wycombe.gov.uk

Hussain, Arif (CON - Terriers and Amersham Hill)
arif.hussain@wycombe.gov.uk

Hussain, Maz (CON - Disraeli)
maz.hussain@wycombe.gov.uk

Johncock, David (CON - Flackwell Heath and Little Marlow)
david.johncock@wycombe.gov.uk

Jones, Audrey (CON - Greater Hughenden)
audrey.jones@wycombe.gov.uk

Knights, David (CON - The Risboroughs)
david.knights@wycombe.gov.uk

Langley, Julia (CON - The Wooburns)
julia.langley@wycombe.gov.uk

Lee, Tony (CON - Bourne End cum Hedsor)
tony.lee@wycombe.gov.uk

Mallen, Wendy (CON - Downley and Plomer Hill)
wendy.mallen@wycombe.gov.uk

Marshall, Neil (CON - Marlow North and West)
neil.marshall@wycombe.gov.uk

McCarthy, Hugh (CON - Hazlemere North)
hugh.mccarthy@wycombe.gov.uk

Newman, Richard (CON - Hazlemere South)
richard.newman@wycombe.gov.uk

Oliver, Catherine (CON - Hazlemere South)
catherine.oliver@wycombe.gov.uk

Pearce, Brian (UKIP - Booker and Cressex)
brian.pearce@wycombe.gov.uk

Peart, Graham (CON - Lacey Green, Speen and The Hampdens)
graham.peart@wycombe.gov.uk

Raja, Rafiq (LAB - Bowerdean)
rafiq.raja@wycombe.gov.uk

Raja, Sarfaraz (CON - Terriers and Amersham Hill)

Saddique, Saeed (CON - Stokenchurch and Radnage)
saeed.saddique@wycombe.gov.uk

Savage, John (CON - Flackwell Heath and Little Marlow)
john.savage@wycombe.gov.uk

Scott, Richard (CON - Marlow South East)
richard.scott@wycombe.gov.uk

Shakespeare, David (CON - Tylers Green and Loudwater)
david.shakespeare@wycombe.gov.uk

Teesdale, Jean (CON - Chiltern Rise)
jean.teesdale@wycombe.gov.uk

Teesdale, Nigel (CON - Sands)
nigel.teesdale@wycombe.gov.uk

Turner, Paul (CON - Downley and Plomer Hill)
paul.turner@wycombe.gov.uk

Wassell, Julia (IND - Totteridge)
julia.wassell@wycombe.gov.uk

Watson, David (CON - Flackwell Heath and Little Marlow)
david.watson@wycombe.gov.uk

Whitehead, Chris (CON - Hambleden Valley)
chris.whitehead@wycombe.gov.uk

Wilson, Roger (CON - Marlow North and West)
roger.wilson@wycombe.gov.uk

Wood, Lawrence (CON - Tylers Green and Loudwater)
lawrence.wood@wycombe.gov.uk

POLITICAL COMPOSITION

CON: 47, LAB: 6, IND: 5, LD: 1, UKIP: 1

COMMITTEE CHAIRS

Audit: Mr Mike Appleyard

Licensing: Mr Alan Hill

Planning: Mr Paul Turner

Wyre D

Wyre Borough Council, Civic Centre, Breck Road, Poulton-le-Fylde FY6 7PU
☎ 01253 891000 🖷 01253 899000 ✉ mailroom@wyrebc.gov.uk
🖳 www.wyrebc.gov.uk

FACTS AND FIGURES

Parliamentary Constituencies: Wyre and Preston North
EU Constituencies: North West
Election Frequency: Elections are of whole council

PRINCIPAL OFFICERS

Chief Executive: Mr Garry Payne, Chief Executive, Civic Centre, Breck Road, Poulton-le-Fylde FY6 7PU ☎ 01253 887500 ✉ garry.payne@wyre.gov.uk

Senior Management: Ms Philippa Davies, Corporate Director of Resources & S151 Officer, Civic Centre, Breck Road, Poulton-le-Fylde FY6 7PU ☎ 01253 887370 ✉ philippa.davies@wyre.gov.uk

Senior Management: Mr Michael Ryan, Corporate Director of People and Places, Civic Centre, Breck Road, Poulton-le-Fylde FY6 7PU ☎ 01253 887605 🖷 01253 887499 ✉ michael.ryan@wyre.gov.uk

Building Control: Ms Maria Blundy, Head of Built Environment, Civic Centre, Breck Road, Poulton-le-Fylde FY6 7PU ☎ 01253 887246 ✉ maria.blundy@wyre.gov.uk

Community Safety: Ms Jane Murray, Community Safety Officer, Civic Centre, Breck Road, Poulton-le-Fylde FY6 7PU ☎ 01253 887292 ✉ janemurray@wyre.gov.uk

Corporate Services: Mr Corporate Support Team, Corporate Support, Civic Centre, Breck Road, Poulton-le-Fylde FY6 7PU ☎ 01253 887621 ✉ corporatesupport@wyre.gov.uk

Customer Service: Mr Peter Mason, Head of Contact Centre, Civic Centre, Breck Road, Poulton-le-Fylde FY6 7PU ☎ 01253 887530 ✉ peter.mason@wyre.gov.uk

Economic Development: Mrs Karen Stringer, Senior Economic Development Officer, Civic Centre, Breck Road, Poulton-le-Fylde FY6 7PU ☎ 01253 887532 ✉ karen.stringer@wyre.gov.uk

E-Government: Ms Joanne Billington, Head of Governance, Civic Centre, Breck Road, Poulton-le-Fylde FY6 7PU ☎ 01253 887372 ✉ joanne.billington@wyre.gov.uk

Electoral Registration: Ms Joanne Porter, Electoral Services & Information Governance Manager, Civic Centre, Breck Road, Poulton-le-Fylde FY6 7PU ☎ 01253 887503 ✉ joanne.porter@wyre.gov.uk

Emergency Planning: Mr John Blundell, Depot Manager / Emergency Planning Officer, Civic Centre, Breck Road, Poulton-le-Fylde FY6 7PU ☎ 01253 887531 ✉ john.blundell@wyre.gov.uk

Energy Management: Mr Mark Broadhurst, Head of Housing Services, Civic Centre, Breck Road, Poulton-le-Fylde FY6 7PU ☎ 01253 887433 ✉ mark.broadhurst@wyre.gov.uk

Environmental Health: Mrs Corinne Mason, Senior Environmental Health Officer, Civic Centre, Breck Road, Poulton-le-Fylde FY6 7PU ☎ 01253 887207 ✉ corinne.mason@wyre.gov.uk

European Liaison: Mrs Karen Stringer, Senior Economic Development Officer, Civic Centre, Breck Road, Poulton-le-Fylde FY6 7PU ☎ 01253 887532 ✉ karen.stringer@wyre.gov.uk

Finance: Ms Philippa Davies, Corporate Director of Resources & S151 Officer, Civic Centre, Breck Road, Poulton-le-Fylde FY6 7PU ☎ 01253 887370 ✉ philippa.davies@wyre.gov.uk

Fleet Management: Mr John Blundell, Depot Manager / Emergency Planning Officer, Civic Centre, Breck Road, Poulton-le-Fylde FY6 7PU ☎ 01253 887531 ✉ john.blundell@wyre.gov.uk

Grounds Maintenance: Mr Mark Billington, Head of Operations, Civic Centre, Breck Road, Poulton-le-Fylde FY6 7PU ☎ 01253 887508 ✉ mark.billington@wyre.gov.uk

Health and Safety: Ms Kate Holmes, Health & Safety Advisor, Civic Centre, Breck Road, Poulton-le-Fylde FY6 7PU ☎ 01253 887508 ✉ kate.holmes@wyre.gov.uk

Home Energy Conservation: Mr Mark Broadhurst, Head of Housing Services, Civic Centre, Breck Road, Poulton-le-Fylde FY6 7PU ☎ 01253 887433 ✉ mark.broadhurst@wyre.gov.uk

Housing: Mr Mark Broadhurst, Head of Housing Services, Civic Centre, Breck Road, Poulton-le-Fylde FY6 7PU ☎ 01253 887433 ✉ mark.broadhurst@wyre.gov.uk

Housing Maintenance: Mr Mark Broadhurst, Head of Housing Services, Civic Centre, Breck Road, Poulton-le-Fylde FY6 7PU ☎ 01253 887433 ✉ mark.broadhurst@wyre.gov.uk

Legal: Ms Mary Grimshaw, Senior Solicitor, Civic Centre, Breck Road, Poulton-le-Fylde FY6 7PU ☎ 01253 887214 ✉ mary.grimshaw@wyre.gov.uk

Leisure and Cultural Services: Mr Ian Munro, Head of Culture, Leisure & Tourism, Civic Centre, Breck Road, Poulton-le-Fylde FY6 7PU ☎ 01253 887208 ✉ ian.munro@wyre.gov.uk

Licensing: Ms Christa Ferguson, Licensing Manager, Civic Centre, Breck Road, Poulton-le-Fylde FY6 7PU ☎ 01253 887476 ✉ christa.ferguson@wyre.gov.uk

Personnel / HR: Mrs Liesl Hadgraft, Head of Business Support, Civic Centre, Breck Road, Poulton-le-Fylde FY6 7PU ☎ 01253 887316 ✉ liesl.hadgraft@wyre.gov.uk

Planning: Mr David Thow, Head of Planning Services, Civic Centre, Breck Road, Poulton-le-Fylde FY6 7PU ☎ 01253 887287 ✉ david.thow@wyre.gov.uk

Procurement: Mr Allan Williams, Procurement Officer, Civic Centre, Breck Road, Poulton-le-Fylde FY6 7PU ☎ 01253 887440 ✉ allan.williams@wyre.gov.uk

Recycling & Waste Minimisation: Ms Ruth Hunter, Waste & Recycling Manager, Civic Centre, Breck Road, Poulton-le-Fylde FY6 7PU ☎ 01253 887478 ✉ ruth.hunter@wyre.gov.uk

Street Scene: Mr Mark Billington, Head of Operations, Civic Centre, Breck Road, Poulton-le-Fylde FY6 7PU ☎ 01253 887508 ✉ mark.billington@wyre.gov.uk

Tourism: Ms Alexandra Holt, Tourism Development Officer, Civic Centre, Breck Road, Poulton-le-Fylde FY6 7PU ☎ 01253 887445 ✉ alexandra.holt@wyre.gov.uk

Waste Management: Ms Ruth Hunter, Waste & Recycling Manager, Civic Centre, Breck Road, Poulton-le-Fylde FY6 7PU ☎ 01253 887478 ✉ ruth.hunter@wyre.gov.uk

Children's Play Areas: Mr Mark Billington, Head of Operations, Civic Centre, Breck Road, Poulton-le-Fylde FY6 7PU ☎ 01253 887508 ✉ mark.billington@wyre.gov.uk

COUNCILLORS

***Leader of the Council* Gibson**, Peter (CON - Breck)
peter.gibson@wyre.gov.uk

***Deputy Leader of the Council* Vincent**, Alan (CON - Victoria)
alanvincent@vslaw.co.uk

***Group Leader* Duffy**, Ruth (LAB - Mount)

Amos, Rita (CON - Cleveleys Park)
rita.amos@wyre.gov.uk

Amos, Ian (CON - Cleveleys Park)
ianl.amos@wyre.gov.uk

Anderton, Emma (LAB - Warren)
emma.anderton@wyre.gov.uk

Anderton, Marge (LAB - Warren)
marge.anderton@wyre.gov.uk

Atkins, Dulcie (CON - Garstang)
datkins@wyrebc.gov.uk

Ballard, Howard (CON - Bourne)
howard.ballard@wyre.gov.uk

Balmain, Tom (CON - Garstang)
tom.balmain@wyre.gov.uk

Barrowclough, Michael (LAB - Rossall)
michael.barrowclough@wyre.gov.uk

Beavers, Lorraine (LAB - Pharos)
lorraine.beavers@wyre.gov.uk

Berry, Roger (CON - Highcross)
roger.berry@wyre.gov.uk

Birch, Colette (CON - Tithebarn)
colette.birch@wyre.gov.uk

Birch, Barry (CON - Highcross)
barry.birch@wyre.gov.uk

Bowen, Lynne (CON - Hambleton and Stalmine)
lynne.bowen@wyre.gov.uk

Bridge, Simon (CON - Hardhorn with Highcross)
simon.bridge@wyre.gov.uk

Catterall, Susan (CON - Great Eccleston)
sue.catterall@wyre.gov.uk

Collinson, Alice (CON - Garstang)
alice.collinson@wyre.gov.uk

Duffy, Ian (LAB - Mount)
ian.duffy@wyre.gov.uk

Fail, Rob (LAB - Jubilee)
rob.fail@wyre.gov.uk

Greenhough, Ron (CON - Carleton)
ron.greenhough@wyre.gov.uk

Henderson, David (CON - Breck)
david.henderson@wyre.gov.uk

Hodgkinson, John (CON - Jubilee)
john.hodgkinson@wyre.gov.uk

Holden, Graham (CON - Pilling)
graham.holden@wyre.gov.uk

Ibison, John (CON - Calder)
john.ibison@wyre.gov.uk

Ingham, Tom (CON - Marsh Mill)
tom.ingham@wyre.gov.uk

Jones, Kerry (CON - Stanah)
kerry.jones@wyre.gov.uk

Kay, Andrea (CON - Pheasant's Wood)
andrea.kay@wyre.gov.uk

Lees, Terry (LAB - Bourne)
terry.lees@wyre.gov.uk

McKay, Lesley (CON - Tithebarn)
lesley.mckay@wyre.gov.uk

Moon, Paul (CON - Preesall)
paul.moon@wyre.gov.uk

Murphy, Pete (CON - Brock)
pete.murphy@wyre.gov.uk

Orme, Philip (CON - Preesall)
philip.orme@wyre.gov.uk

Ormrod, Patsy (CON - Victoria and Norcross)
patsy.ormrod@wyre.gov.uk

Pimbley, Sue (CON - Great Eccleston)
sue.pimbley@wyre.gov.uk

Reeves, Natalie (LAB - Bourne)
natalie.reeves@wyre.gov.uk

Robinson, Julie (CON - Hambleton and Stalmine-with-Staynall)
julie.robinson@wyre.gov.uk

Shewan, Ronald (LAB - Pharos)
ron.shewan@wyre.gov.uk

Smith, Christine (LAB - Park)
christine.smith@wyre.gov.uk

Stephenson, Brian (LAB - Park)
brian.stephenson@wyre.gov.uk

Stephenson, Evelyn (LAB - Pharos)
evelyn.stephenson@wyre.gov.uk

Taylor, Vivien (CON - Preesall)
vivien.taylor@wyre.gov.uk

Taylor, Ted (LAB - Rossall)
ted.taylor@wyre.gov.uk

Turner, Ann (CON - Norcross)
ann.turner@wyre.gov.uk

Turner, Shaun (CON - Brock with Catrerall)
shaun.turner@wyre.gov.uk

Vincent, Matthew (CON - Stanah)
matthew.vincent@wyre.gov.uk

Vincent, Michael (CON - Carleton)
michael.vincent@wyre.gov.uk

Walmsley, Lynn (CON - Marsh Mill)
lynn.walmsley@wyre.gov.uk

Wilson, Val (CON - Wyresdale)
val.wilson@wyre.gov.uk

POLITICAL COMPOSITION
CON: 36, LAB: 14

COMMITTEE CHAIRS

Audit: Mr Tom Balmain

Planning: Mr Ron Greenhough

Wyre Forest D

Wyre Forest District Council, Civic Centre, New Street, Stourport-on-Severn DY13 8UJ
☎ 01562 732928 🖷 01562 67673
✉ communications@wyreforestdc.gov.uk 💻 www.wyreforestdc.gov.uk

FACTS AND FIGURES
Parliamentary Constituencies: Wyre Forest
EU Constituencies: West Midlands
Election Frequency: Elections are by thirds

PRINCIPAL OFFICERS

Chief Executive: Mr Ian Miller, Chief Executive, Wyre Forest House, Finepoint Way, Kidderminster DY11 7WF ☎ 01562 732700
✉ ian.miller@wyreforestdc.gov.uk

Senior Management: Ms Linda Collis, Director of Community Wellbeing & Environment, Wyre Forest House, Finepoint Way, Kidderminster DY11 7WF ☎ 01562 732900
✉ linda.collis@wyreforestdc.gov.uk

Senior Management: Mr Mike Parker, Director of Economic Prosperity & Place, Wyre Forest House, Finepoint Way, Kidderminster DY11 7WF ☎ 01562 732500
✉ mike.parker@wyreforestdc.gov.uk

Building Control: Mr Adrian Wyre, Principal Building Control Surveyor, The Council House, Burcot Lane, Bromsgrove B60 1AA
☎ 01562 732532 ✉ a.wyre@bromsgroveandredditch.gov.uk

PR / Communications: Mrs Jane Doyle, Communications Officer, Wyre Forest House, Finepoint Way, Kidderminster DY11 7WF
☎ 01562 732928 ✉ jane.doyle@wyreforestdc.gov.uk

PR / Communications: Mrs Suzanne Johnston-Hubbold, Communications Officer, Wyre Forest House, Finepoint Way, Kidderminster DY11 7WF ☎ 01562 732982
✉ suzanne.johnston-hubbold@wyreforestdc.gov.uk

Community Planning: Ms Alison Braithwaite, Head of Transformation & Communications, Wyre Forest House, Finepoint Way, Kidderminster DY11 7WF ☎ 01562 732781 🖷 01299 879688
✉ alison.braithwaite@wyreforestdc.gov.uk

Community Safety: Mrs Kathryn Washington, Community Safety & Partnerships Officer, Wyre Forest House, Finepoint Way, Kidderminster DY11 7WF ☎ 01562 732956 🖷 01562 879688
✉ kathryn.washington@wyreforestdc.gov.uk

Computer Management: Mr Dave Johnson, ICT Manager, Wyre Forest House, Finepoint Way, Kidderminster DY11 7WF
☎ 01562 732138 ✉ dave.johnson@wyreforestdc.gov.uk

Contracts: Mrs Sally Tallon, Contracts & Freedom of Information Solicitor, Wyre Forest House, Finepoint Way, Kidderminster DY11 7WF ☎ 01562 732775 ✉ sally.tallon@wyreforestdc.gov.uk

Corporate Services: Mrs Caroline Newlands, Solicitor to the Council, Wyre Forest House, Finepoint Way, Kidderminster DY11 7WF ☎ 01562 732715 ✉ caroline.newlands@wyreforestdc.gov.uk

Customer Service: Mrs Lucy Wright, Corporate Customer Development Manager, Town Hall, Vicar Street, Kidderminster DY10 1DA ☎ 01562 732948 lucy.wright@wyreforestdc.gov.uk

Economic Development: Mr Dean Piper, Head of Economic Development & Regeneration - North Worcestershire, Wyre Forest House, Finepoint Way, Kidderminster DY11 7WF ☎ 01562 932192 dean.piper@wyreforestdc.gov.uk

Electoral Registration: Ms Alison Braithwaite, Head of Transformation & Communications, Wyre Forest House, Finepoint Way, Kidderminster DY11 7WF ☎ 01562 732781 🖷 01299 879688 alison.braithwaite@wyreforestdc.gov.uk

Emergency Planning: Ms Rebecca Pritchett, North Worcestershire Civil Contingencies & Resilience Manager, Wyre Forest House, Finepoint Way, Kidderminster DY11 7WF rebecca.pritchett@wyreforestdc.gov.uk

Environmental Health: Mr Simon Wilkes, Business Manager, Wyatt House, Farrier Street, Worcester WR1 3BH swilkes@worcsregservices.gov.uk

Estates, Property & Valuation: Ms Victoria Bendall, Estates Surveyor, Wyre Forest House, Finepoint Way, Kidderminster DY11 7WF ☎ 01562 732703 victoria.bendall@wyreforestdc.gov.uk

Estates, Property & Valuation: Ms Lucy Lomas, Estates Surveyor, Civic Centre, New Street, Stourport-on-Severn DY13 8UJ ☎ 01562 732706 lucy.lomas@wyreforestdc.gov.uk

Facilities: Mrs Elaine Brookes, Facilities & Asset Manager, Wyre Forest House, Finepoint Way, Kidderminster DY11 7WF ☎ 01562 732797 elaine.brookes@wyreforestdc.gov.uk

Finance: Mrs Tracey Southall, Chief Financial Officer, Wyre Forest House, Finepoint Way, Kidderminster DY11 7WF ☎ 01562 732100 tracey.southall@wyreforestdc.gov.uk

Fleet Management: Mr Steve Brant, Operations Manager, Green Street, Kidderminster DY10 1HA ☎ 01562 732922 steve.brant@wyreforestdc.gov.uk

Grounds Maintenance: Mr Joe Scully, Parks & Open Spaces Manager, Green Street, Kidderminster DY10 1HA ☎ 01562 732981 joe.scully@wyreforestdc.gov.uk

Health and Safety: Mr Steve Brant, Operations Manager, Green Street, Kidderminster DY10 1HA ☎ 01562 732922 steve.brant@wyreforestdc.gov.uk

Home Energy Conservation: Ms Jenny Moreton, Principal Health & Sustainability Officer, Wyre Forest House, Finepoint Way, Kidderminster DY11 7WF ☎ 01562 732569 jennifer.moreton@wyreforestdc.gov.uk

Housing: Mrs Kate Bailey, Strategic Housing Services Manager, Wyre Forest House, Finepoint Way, Kidderminster DY11 7WF ☎ 01562 732560 kate.bailey@wyreforestdc.gov.uk

Legal: Mrs Caroline Newlands, Solicitor to the Council, Wyre Forest House, Finepoint Way, Kidderminster DY11 7WF ☎ 01562 732715 caroline.newlands@wyreforestdc.gov.uk

Leisure and Cultural Services: Ms Linda Collis, Director of Community Wellbeing & Environment, Wyre Forest House, Finepoint Way, Kidderminster DY11 7WF ☎ 01562 732900 linda.collis@wyreforestdc.gov.uk

Leisure and Cultural Services: Ms Kay Higman, Cultural Services Manager, Wyre Forest House, Finepoint Way, Kidderminster DY11 7WF ☎ 01562 732902 kay.higman@wyreforestdc.gov.uk

Licensing: Mr Mark Kay, Business Manager, Wyatt House, Farrier Street, Worcester WR1 3BH mark.kay@worcsregservices.gov.uk

Lottery Funding, Charity and Voluntary: Mrs Lesley Fox, Community Development Manager, Wyre Forest House, Finepoint Way, Kidderminster DY11 7WF ☎ 01562 732976 lesley.fox@wyreforestdc.gov.uk

Member Services: Ms Alison Braithwaite, Head of Transformation & Communications, Wyre Forest House, Finepoint Way, Kidderminster DY11 7WF ☎ 01562 732781 🖷 01299 879688 alison.braithwaite@wyreforestdc.gov.uk

Parking: Mr Steve Brant, Operations Manager, Green Street, Kidderminster DY10 1HA ☎ 01562 732922 steve.brant@wyreforestdc.gov.uk

Partnerships: Mrs Lynette Cadwallader, Wyre Forest Matters Partnerships Co-ordinator, Wyre Forest House, Finepoint Way, Kidderminster DY11 7WF ☎ 01562 732729 lynette.cadwallader@wyreforestdc.gov.uk

Personnel / HR: Ms Vickie Lee, Human Resources Manager, Wyre Forest House, Finepoint Way, Kidderminster DY11 7WF ☎ 01562 732774 vickie.lee@wyreforestdc.gov.uk

Planning: Mr John Baggott, Development Manager, Wyre Forest House, Finepoint Way, Kidderminster DY11 7WF ☎ 01562 732515 john.baggott@wyreforestdc.gov.uk

Procurement: Ms Kathryn Pearsall, Principal Accountant, Wyre Forest House, Finepoint Way, Kidderminster DY11 7WF kathryn.pearsall@wyreforestdc.gov.uk

Recycling & Waste Minimisation: Mr Steve Brant, Operations Manager, Wyre Forest House, Finepoint Way, Kidderminster DY11 7WF ☎ 01562 732922 steve.brant@wyreforestdc.gov.uk

Regeneration: Mr Dean Piper, Head of Economic Development & Regeneration - North Worcestershire, Wyre Forest House, Finepoint Way, Kidderminster DY11 7WF ☎ 01562 932192 dean.piper@wyreforestdc.gov.uk

Street Scene: Mr Joe Scully, Parks & Open Spaces Manager, Green Street, Kidderminster DY10 1HA ☎ 01562 732981 joe.scully@wyreforestdc.gov.uk

Sustainable Communities: Mr Mike Parker, Director of Economic Prosperity & Place, Wyre Forest House, Finepoint Way, Kidderminster DY11 7WF ☎ 01562 732500 mike.parker@wyreforestdc.gov.uk

Sustainable Development: Mr Mike Parker, Director of Economic Prosperity & Place, Wyre Forest House, Finepoint Way, Kidderminster DY11 7WF ☎ 01562 732500
✉ mike.parker@wyreforestdc.gov.uk

Tourism: Mr Steve Singleton, Economic Development Manager - North Worcestershire, Wyre Forest House, Finepoint Way, Kidderminster DY11 7WF ☎ 01562 732168
✉ steve.singleton@wyreforestdc.gov.uk

Town Centre: Mr Peter Michael, Town Centre Manager, Wyre Forest House, Finepoint Way, Kidderminster DY11 7WF
☎ 01562 732534 ✉ peter.michael@wyreforestdc.gov.uk

Waste Management: Mr Steve Brant, Operations Manager, Green Street, Kidderminster DY10 1HA ☎ 01562 732922
✉ steve.brant@wyreforestdc.gov.uk

COUNCILLORS

Leader of the Council **Hart**, Marcus (CON - Sutton Park)
marcus.hart@wyreforestdc.gov.uk

Deputy Leader of the Council **Hardiman**, Ian (CON - Wyre Forest Rural)
ian.hardiman@wyreforestdc.gov.uk

Arnold, Sam (LAB - Foley Park and Hoobrook)
sam.arnold@wyreforestdc.gov.uk

Aston, John (IND - Aggborough and Spennells)
john.aston@wyreforestdc.gov.uk

Baker, Jeffrey (CON - Franche and Habberley North)
jeff.baker@wyreforestdc.gov.uk

Ballinger, Graham (IND - Greenhill)
graham.ballinger@wyreforestdc.gov.uk

Bishop, Rose (CON - Offmore and Comberton)
rose.bishop@wyreforestdc.gov.uk

Campion, John-Paul (CON - Sutton Park)
john.campion@wyreforestdc.gov.uk

Chambers, Sally Jane (CON - Foley park and Hoobrook)
sally.chambers@wyreforestdc.gov.uk

Clee, Stephen (CON - Bewdley and Arley)
sjclee@tinyonline.co.uk

Desmond, John (CON - Broadwaters)
john.desmond@wyreforestdc.gov.uk

Desmond, Nathan (CON - Foley Park and Hoobrook)
nathan.desmond@wyreforestdc.gov.uk

Dyke, Helen (IND - Aggborough and Spennells)
helen.dyke@wyreforestdc.gov.uk

Dyke, Peter (IND - Aggborough and Spennells)
peter.dyke@wyreforestdc.gov.uk

Fearn, Sara (CON - Mitton)
sara.fearn@wyreforest.gov.uk

Greener, Jenny (CON - Bewdley and Arley)
jennifer.greener@wyreforestdc.gov.uk

Harrington, Steve (UKIP - Broadwaters)
steve.harrington@wyreforestdc.gov.uk

Hart, John (CON - Wolverley)
john.hart@wyreforestdc.gov.uk

Henderson, Kenneth (CON - Areley Kings and Riverside)
ken.henderson@wyreforestdc.gov.uk

Henderson, Linda (CON - Areley Kings and Riverside)
lin.henderson@wyreforestdc.gov.uk

Hingley, Anne (CON - Franche and Habberley North)
anne.hingley@wyreforestdc.gov.uk

Knowles, Nigel (LAB - Franche)
nigelknowlesbewdley@hotmail.com

Little, David (CON - Lickhill)
david.little@wyreforestdc.gov.uk

Muir, Tony (CON - Mitton)
tony.muir@wyreforestdc.gov.uk

Oborski, Fran (LIB - Offmore and Comberton)
fran.oborski@wyreforestdc.gov.uk

Phillips, Julian (CON - Bewdley and Arley)
julian.phillips@wyreforestdc.gov.uk

Rayner, Mary (IND - Broadwaters)
mary.rayner@wyreforestdc.gov.uk

Rogers, Chris (CON - Mitton)
chris.rogers@wyreforestdc.gov.uk

Shaw, James (LAB - Areley Kings)
cllrjshaw@hotmail.com

Smith, Juliet (CON - Blakebrook and Habberley South)
juliet.smith@wyreforestdc.gov.uk

Williams, Stephen (CON - Blakedown and Chaddesley)
stephen.williams@wyreforestdc.gov.uk

Yarranton, Gordon (CON - Wribbenhall)
gordon.yarranton@wyreforestdc.gov.uk

POLITICAL COMPOSITION

CON: 22, IND: 5, LAB: 3, LIB: 1, UKIP: 1

York, City of U

City of York Council, West Offices, Station Rise, York YO1 6GA
☎ 01904 551550 🖷 01904 553560 🖳 www.york.gov.uk

FACTS AND FIGURES

Parliamentary Constituencies: York Central, York Outer
EU Constituencies: Yorkshire and the Humber
Election Frequency: Elections are of whole council

PRINCIPAL OFFICERS

Chief Executive: Mr Steve Stewart, Chief Executive, West Offices, Station Rise, York YO1 6GA ☎ 01904 552000
✉ steve.stewart@york.gov.uk

Senior Management: Mr Dave Atkinson, Business Change Programme Manager, West Offices, Station Rise, York YO1 6GA

Senior Management: Ms Alice Beckwith, Business Change Programme Manager, West Offices, Station Rise, York YO1 6GA

Senior Management: Mr Will Boardman, People & Neighbourhoods Strategy & Policy Group Manager, West Offices, Station Rise, York YO1 6GA

YORK, CITY OF

Senior Management: Mr Ian Cunningham, Shared Intelligence Bureau Group Manager, West Offices, Station Rise, York YO1 6GA

Senior Management: Mr Ian Graham, Head of Performance & Innovation, West Offices, Station Rise, York YO1 6GA ☎ 01904 551550 ✉ ian.graham@york.gov.uk

Senior Management: Mr Stewart Halliday, Assistant Director - Transformation & Change, West Offices, Station Rise, York YO1 6GA ☎ 01904 553042 🖷 01904 552525 ✉ stewart.halliday@york.gov.uk

Senior Management: Ms Leona Marshall, Head of Communications, West Offices, Station Rise, York YO1 6GA

Senior Management: Mr David Walmsley, Head of Strategic Business Intelligence & Partnerships, West Offices, Station Rise, York YO1 6GA

Senior Management: Mr Phil Witcherley, Policy, Performance & Change Manager, West Offices, Station Rise, York YO1 6GA

Architect, Building / Property Services: Ms Tracey Carter, Assistant Director - Finance, Asset Management & Procurement, West Offices, Station Rise, York YO1 6GA ☎ 01904 553419 ✉ tracey.carter@york.gov.uk

Building Control: Mr John Fowler, Chief Building Control Officer, West Offices, Station Rise, York YO1 6GA ☎ 01423 500600 ext. 56597 🖷 01423 556550 ✉ john.fowler@harrogate.gov.uk

Children / Youth Services: Mr Steve Flatley, Connexions Service Manager, West Offices, Station Rise, York YO1 6GA ☎ 01904 552367 ✉ steve.flatley@york.gov.uk

Children / Youth Services: Mr Eoin Rush, Assistant Director - Children's Specialist Services, West Offices, Station Rise, York YO1 6GA ☎ 01904 551071 ✉ eoin.rush@york.gov.uk

Civil Registration: Mr Robert Livesey, Registration Service Manager, Register Office, 56 Bootham, York YO30 7DA ☎ 01904 553194 🖷 01904 638090 ✉ robert.livesey@york.gov.uk

PR / Communications: Ms Leona Marshall, Head of Communications, West Offices, Station Rise, York YO1 6GA

Community Planning: Mr Charlie Croft, Assistant Director - Communities, Culture & Public Realm, West Offices, Station Rise, York YO1 6GA ☎ 01904 551550 ✉ charlie.croft@york.gov.uk

Community Safety: Ms Jane Mowat, Head of Community Safety, West Offices, Station Rise, York YO1 6GA ☎ 01904 551550 🖷 01904 669077 ✉ jane.mowat@york.gov.uk

Community Safety: Mr Steve Waddington, Assistant Director - Housing & Community Safety, West Offices, Station Rise, York YO1 6GA ☎ 01904 554016 ✉ steve.waddington@york.gov.uk

Computer Management: Mr Roy Grant, Head of Information Technology, West Offices, Station Rise, York YO1 6GA ☎ 01904 551550 🖷 01904 551190 ✉ roy.grant@york.gov.uk

Consumer Protection and Trading Standards: Mr Matt Boxall, Interim Head of Public Protection, West Offices, Station Rise, York YO1 6GA ☎ 01904 551528 ✉ matthew.boxall@york.gov.uk

Consumer Protection and Trading Standards: Mr Steve Waddington, Assistant Director - Housing & Community Safety, West Offices, Station Rise, York YO1 6GA ☎ 01904 554016 ✉ steve.waddington@york.gov.uk

Contracts: Mr David Walker, Head of Financial Procedures, West Offices, Station Rise, York YO1 6GA ☎ 01904 552261 ✉ david.walker@york.gov.uk

Customer Service: Ms Pauline Stuchfield, Assistant Director - Customers & Business Support Services, West Offices, Station Rise, York YO1 6GA ☎ 01904 551190 ✉ pauline.stuchfield@york.gov.uk

Economic Development: Mr Phil Witcherley, Policy, Performance & Change Manager, West Offices, Station Rise, York YO1 6GA

Education: Ms Maxine Squire, Assistant Director - Education & Skills, West Offices, Station Rise, York YO1 6GA ☎ 01904 551550 ✉ maxine.squire@york.gov.uk

E-Government: Mr Ian Graham, Head of Performance & Innovation, West Offices, Station Rise, York YO1 6GA ☎ 01904 551550 ✉ ian.graham@york.gov.uk

Electoral Registration: Mr Andrew Flecknor, Electoral Services Manager, West Offices, Station Rise, York YO1 6GA ☎ 01904 552032 🖷 01904 551052 ✉ andrew.flecknor@york.gov.uk

Emergency Planning: Mr Jim Breen, Emergency Planning Co-ordinator, West Offices, Station Rise, York YO1 6GA ☎ 01904 551003 🖷 01224 551001 ✉ jim.breen@york.gov.uk

Energy Management: Ms Jacqui Warren, Head of Design Conservation & Sustainable Development, West Offices, Station Rise, York YO1 6GA ☎ 01904 551312 ✉ jacqueline.warren@york.gov.uk

Environmental / Technical Services: Mr Mike Slater, Assistant Director - Development Services, Planning & Regeneration, West Offices, Station Rise, York YO1 6GA ☎ 01904 551300 ✉ michael.slater@york.gov.uk

Environmental Health: Mr Matt Boxall, Interim Head of Public Protection, West Offices, Station Rise, York YO1 6GA ☎ 01904 551528 ✉ matthew.boxall@york.gov.uk

Estates, Property & Valuation: Mr Philip Callow, Head of Asset & Property Management, West Offices, Station Rise, York YO1 6GA ☎ 01904 553360 🖷 01904 553314 ✉ philip.callow@york.gov.uk

Facilities: Mr Ian Asher, Head of Design Construction & Facilities Management, West Offices, Station Rise, York YO1 6GA ☎ 01904 553379 ✉ ian.asher@york.gov.uk

Finance: Ms Tracey Carter, Assistant Director - Finance, Asset Management & Procurement, West Offices, Station Rise, York YO1 6GA ☎ 01904 553419 ✉ tracey.carter@york.gov.uk

Fleet Management: Mr Neil Ferris, Assistant Director - Highways, Transport & Waste, West Offices, Station Rise, York YO1 6GA ☎ 01904 551448 ✉ neil.ferris@york.gov.uk

Grounds Maintenance: Mr Russell Stone, Head of Public Realm, West Offices, Station Rise, York YO1 6GA ☎ 01904 553108 ✉ russell.stone@york.gov.uk

Health and Safety: Ms Lesley Sharp, Health & Safety Manager, West Offices, Station Rise, York YO1 6GA ☎ 01904 554522 ✉ lesley.sharp@york.gov.uk

Highways: Mr Neil Ferris, Assistant Director - Highways, Transport & Waste, West Offices, Station Rise, York YO1 6GA ☎ 01904 551448 ✉ neil.ferris@york.gov.uk

Home Energy Conservation: Ms Jacqui Warren, Head of Design Conservation & Sustainable Development, West Offices, Station Rise, York YO1 6GA ☎ 01904 551312 ✉ jacqueline.warren@york.gov.uk

Housing: Mr Steve Waddington, Assistant Director - Housing & Community Safety, West Offices, Station Rise, York YO1 6GA ☎ 01904 554016 ✉ steve.waddington@york.gov.uk

Housing Maintenance: Mr Tom Brittain, Head of Housing Services, West Offices, Station Rise, York YO1 6GA ☎ 01904 551262 ✉ tom.brittain@york.gov.uk

Legal: Mr Andrew Docherty, Assistant Director - Governance & ICT, West Offices, Station Rise, York YO1 6GA ☎ 01904 551127 ✉ andrew.docherty@york.gov.uk

Legal: Ms Melanie Perara, Deputy Head of Legal Services, West Offices, Station Rise, York YO1 6GA ☎ 01904 551087 ✉ melanie.perara@york.gov.uk

Leisure and Cultural Services: Mr Charlie Croft, Assistant Director - Communities, Culture & Public Realm, West Offices, Station Rise, York YO1 6GA ☎ 01904 551550 ✉ charlie.croft@york.gov.uk

Licensing: Mr Matt Boxall, Interim Head of Public Protection, West Offices, Station Rise, York YO1 6GA ☎ 01904 551528 ✉ matthew.boxall@york.gov.uk

Lifelong Learning: Mr Charlie Croft, Assistant Director - Communities, Culture & Public Realm, West Offices, Station Rise, York YO1 6GA ☎ 01904 551550 ✉ charlie.croft@york.gov.uk

Lighting: Mr Neil Ferris, Assistant Director - Highways, Transport & Waste, West Offices, Station Road, York YO1 6GA ☎ 01904 551448 ✉ neil.ferris@york.gov.uk

Member Services: Ms Dawn Steel, Head of Civic & Democratic Services, West Offices, Station Rise, York YO1 6GA ☎ 01904 551030 ✉ dawn.steel@york.gov.uk

Parking: Mr Andrew Laslett, Operations Manager, West Offices, Station Rise, York YO1 6GA ☎ 01904 553370 ✉ andy.laslett@york.gov.uk

Partnerships: Mr Stewart Halliday, Assistant Director - Transformation & Change, West Offices, Station Rise, York YO1 6GA ☎ 01904 553042 🖷 01904 552525 ✉ stewart.halliday@york.gov.uk

Personnel / HR: Ms Pauline Stuchfield, Assistant Director - Customers & Business Support Services, West Offices, Station Rise, York YO1 6GA ☎ 01904 551190 ✉ pauline.stuchfield@york.gov.uk

Planning: Mr Jonathan Carr, Head of Development Management, West Offices, Station Rise, York YO1 6GA ☎ 01904 551303 ✉ jonathan.carr@york.gov.uk

Planning: Mr Mike Slater, Assistant Director - Development Services, Planning & Regeneration, West Offices, Station Rise, York YO1 6GA ☎ 01904 551300 ✉ michael.slater@york.gov.uk

Procurement: Ms Tracey Carter, Assistant Director - Finance, Asset Management & Procurement, West Offices, Station Rise, York YO1 6GA ☎ 01904 553419 ✉ tracey.carter@york.gov.uk

Public Libraries: Mr Charlie Croft, Assistant Director - Communities, Culture & Public Realm, West Offices, Station Rise, York YO1 6GA ☎ 01904 551550 ✉ charlie.croft@york.gov.uk

Regeneration: Mr Mike Slater, Assistant Director - Development Services, Planning & Regeneration, West Offices, Station Rise, York YO1 6GA ☎ 01904 551300 ✉ michael.slater@york.gov.uk

Road Safety: Mr Andrew Bradley, Sustainable Transport Operations Manager, West Offices, Station Rise, York YO1 6GA ☎ 01904 551404 ✉ andrew.bradley@york.gov.uk

Social Services (Adult): Mr Martin Farran, Director - Adult Care, West Offices, Station Rise, York YO1 6GA ☎ 01904 551550 ✉ martin.farran@york.gov.uk

Social Services (Children): Mr Eoin Rush, Assistant Director - Children's Specialist Services, West Offices, Station Rise, York YO1 6GA ☎ 01904 551071 ✉ eoin.rush@york.gov.uk

Public Health: Ms Julie Hotchkiss, Interim Director - Public Health & Wellbeing, West Offices, Station Rise, York YO1 6GA ☎ 01904 551550 ✉ julie.hotchkiss@york.gov.uk

Staff Training: Mr Mark Bennett, Head of Business HR, West Offices, Station Rise, York YO1 6GA ☎ 01904 554518 ✉ mark.bennett@york.gov.uk

Street Scene: Mr Russell Stone, Head of Public Realm, West Offices, Station Rise, York YO1 6GA ☎ 01904 553108 ✉ russell.stone@york.gov.uk

Sustainable Communities: Mr Mike Slater, Assistant Director - Development Services, Planning & Regeneration, West Offices, Station Rise, York YO1 6GA ☎ 01904 551300 ✉ michael.slater@york.gov.uk

Sustainable Development: Ms Jacqui Warren, Head of Design Conservation & Sustainable Development, West Offices, Station Rise, York YO1 6GA ☎ 01904 551312 ✉ jacqueline.warren@york.gov.uk

Traffic Management: Mr Richard Bogg, Highways Development Manager, West Offices, Station Rise, York YO1 6GA ☎ 01904 551426 ✉ richard.bogg@york.gov.uk

Transport: Mr Tony Clarke, Head of Transport, West Offices, Station Rise, York YO1 6GA ☎ 01904 551641 ✉ tony.clarke@york.gov.uk

Transport: Mr Neil Ferris, Assistant Director - Highways, Transport & Waste, West Offices, Station Road, York YO1 6GA ☎ 01904 551448 ✉ neil.ferris@york.gov.uk

Waste Collection and Disposal: Mr Neil Ferris, Assistant Director - Highways, Transport & Waste, West Offices, Station Rise, York YO1 6GA ☎ 01904 551448 ✉ neil.ferris@york.gov.uk

Waste Management: Mr Neil Ferris, Assistant Director - Highways, Transport & Waste, West Offices, Station Rise, York YO1 6GA ☎ 01904 551448 ✉ neil.ferris@york.gov.uk

Children's Play Areas: Mr Russell Stone, Head of Public Realm, West Offices, Station Rise, York YO1 6GA ☎ 01904 553108 ✉ russell.stone@york.gov.uk

COUNCILLORS

***The Lord Mayor* Crisp**, Sonja (LAB - Holgate)
cllr.scrisp@york.gov.uk

***Leader of the Council* Steward**, Chris (CON - Rural West York)
cllr.csteward@york.gov.uk

***Deputy Leader of the Council* Aspden**, Keith (LD - Fulford and Heslington)
cllr.kaspden@york.gov.uk

***Group Leader* D'Agorne**, Andrew (GRN - Fishergate)
cllr.adagorne@york.gov.uk

Ayre, Nigel (LD - Heworth Without)
cllr.nayre@york.gov.uk

Barnes, Neil (LAB - Hull Road)
cllr.nbarnes@york.gov.uk

Barnes, Stuart (LAB - Acomb)
cllr.sbarnes@york.gov.uk

Boyce, Barbara (LAB - Heworth)
cllr.bboyce@york.gov.uk

Brooks, Jenny (CON - Osbaldwick and Derwent)
cllr.jbrooks@york.gov.uk

Cannon, Mary (LAB - Holgate)
cllr.mcannon@york.gov.uk

Carr, David (CON - Copmanthorpe)
cllr.dcarr@york.gov.uk

Craghill, Denise (GRN - Guildhall)
cllr.dcraghill@york.gov.uk

Cullwick, Chris (LD - Huntington and New Earswick)
cllr.ccullwick@york.gov.uk

Cuthbertson, Ian (LD - Haxby and Wigginton)
cllr.icuthbertson@york.gov.uk

Derbyshire, Fiona (LAB - Holgate)
cllr.fderbyshire.gov.uk

Dew, Peter (CON - Rawcliffe and Clifton Without)
cllr.pdew@york.gov.uk

Doughty, Paul (CON - Strensall)
cllr.pdoughty@york.gov.uk

Douglas, Helen (CON - Strensall)
cllr.hdouglas@york.gov.uk

Fenton, Stephen (LD - Dringhouses and Woodthorpe)
cllr.sfenton@york.gov.uk

Flinders, James (LAB - Guildhall)
cllr.jflinders@york.gov.uk

Funnell, Christina (LAB - Heworth)
cllr.cfunnell@york.gov.uk

Galvin, John (CON - Bishopthorpe)
cllr.jgalvin@york.gov.uk

Gates, John (CON - Haxby and Wigginton)
cllr.jgates@york.gov.uk

Gillies, Ian (CON - Rural West York)
cllr.igillies@york.gov.uk

Gunnell, Julie (LAB - Micklegate)
cllr.jgunnell@york.gov.uk

Hayes, Johnny (IND - Micklegate)
cllr.jhayes@york.gov.uk

Hunter, Susan (LD - Westfield)
cllr.shunter@york.gov.uk

Jackson, Sheena (LD - Westfield)
cllr.sjackson@york.gov.uk

Kramm, Lars (GRN - Micklegate)
cllr.lkramm@york.gov.uk

Levene, David (LAB - Hull Road)
cllr.dlevene@york.gov.uk

Lisle, Sam (CON - Rawcliffe and Clifton Without)
cllr.slisle@york.gov.uk

Looker, Janet (LAB - Guildhall)
cllr.jlooker@york.gov.uk

Mason, Ashley (LD - Dringhouses and Woodthorpe)
cllr.amason@york.gov.uk

Mercer, Suzie (CON - Wheldrake)
cllr.smercer@york.gov.uk

Myers, Keith (CON - Acomb)
cllr.kmyers@york.gov.uk

Myers, Danny (LAB - Clifton)
cllr.dmyers@york.gov.uk

Orrell, Keith (LD - Huntington and New Earswick)
cllr.korrell@york.gov.uk

Rawlings, Stuart (CON - Rawcliffe and Clifton Without)
cllr.srawlings@york.gov.uk

Reid, Ann (LD - Dringhouses and Woodthorpe)
cllr.areid@york.gov.uk

Richardson, Tony (CON - Haxby and Wigginton)
cllr.trichardson@york.gov.uk

Runciman, Carol (LD - Huntington and New Earswick)
cllr.crunciman@york.gov.uk

Shepherd, Hilary (LAB - Hull Road)
cllr.hshepherd@york.gov.uk

Taylor, Dave (GRN - Fishergate)
cllr.dtaylor@york.gov.uk

Waller, Andrew (LD - Westfield)
cllr.awaller@york.gov.uk

Warters, Mark (IND - Osbaldwick and Derwent)
cllr.mwarters@york.gov.uk

Wells, Margeret (LAB - Clifton)
cllr.mwells@york.gov.uk

Williams, Dafydd (LAB - Heworth)
cllr.dwilliams@york.gov.uk

POLITICAL COMPOSITION

LAB: 15, CON: 14, LD: 12, GRN: 4, IND: 2

COMMITTEE CHAIRS

Audit & Governance: Mr Neil Barnes

Licensing: Ms Helen Douglas

Licensing: Mr Dave Taylor

Planning: Ms Ann Reid

COUNTY

Buckinghamshire 144
Cambridgeshire 162
Cumbria 262
Derbyshire 281
Devon 288
Dorset 295
East Sussex 352
Essex 380
Gloucestershire 421
Hampshire 453
Hertfordshire 487
Kent 534
Lancashire 558
Leicestershire 573
Lincolnshire 589
Norfolk 684
North Yorkshire 730
Northamptonshire 736
Nottinghamshire 748
Oxfordshire 763
Somerset 899
Staffordshire 975
Suffolk 1004
Surrey 1013
Warwickshire 1112
West Sussex 1151
Worcestershire 1193

DISTRICT

Adur 9
Allerdale 11
Amber Valley 13
Arun 24
Ashfield 27
Ashford 29
Aylesbury Vale 31
Babergh 34
Barrow-in-Furness 48
Basildon 51
Basingstoke & Deane 54
Bassetlaw 57
Blaby 80
Bolsover 92
Boston 97
Braintree 110
Breckland 113
Brentwood 119
Broadland 132
Bromsgrove 137
Broxbourne 139
Broxtowe 141
Burnley 146
Cambridge City 159
Cannock Chase 169
Canterbury City 171
Carlisle City 177
Castle Point 183
Charnwood 193
Chelmsford 197
Cheltenham 200
Cherwell 202
Chesterfield 212
Chichester 215
Chiltern 218
Chorley 220
Christchurch 223
Colchester 232
Copeland 239
Corby 242
Cotswold 249
Craven 254
Crawley 256
Dacorum 266
Dartford 271
Daventry 273
Derbyshire Dales 285
Dover 299
East Cambridgeshire 323
East Devon 325
East Dorset 327
East Hampshire 332
East Hertfordshire 334
East Lindsey 337
East Northamptonshire 342
East Staffordshire 350
Eastbourne 355
Eastleigh 358
Eden 360
Elmbridge 366
Epping Forest 373
Epsom & Ewell 375
Erewash 377
Exeter City 383
Fareham 388
Fenland 391
Forest Heath 402
Forest of Dean 404
Fylde 407
Gedling 413
Gloucester City 419
Gosport 425
Gravesham 427
Great Yarmouth 430
Guildford 435
Hambleton 447
Harborough 458
Harlow 463
Harrogate 465
Hart 471
Hastings 475
Havant 478
Hertsmere 490
High Peak 493
Hinckley & Bosworth 502
Horsham 505
Huntingdonshire 512
Hyndburn 515
Ipswich 519
Kettering 537
King's Lynn & West Norfolk 540
Lancaster City 562
Lewes 577
Lichfield 583
Lincoln City 586
Maidstone 601
Maldon 604
Malvern Hills 606
Mansfield 612
Melton 619
Mendip 621
Mid Devon 631
Mid Suffolk 634
Mid Sussex 637
Mole Valley 653
New Forest 665
Newark & Sherwood 668
Newcastle-under-Lyme 674
North Devon 691
North Dorset 694
North East Derbyshire 697
North Hertfordshire 704
North Kesteven 706
North Norfolk 715
North Warwickshire 725
North West Leicestershire 728
Northampton 734
Norwich City 742
Nuneaton & Bedworth 752
Oadby & Wigston 754
Oxford City 761
Pendle 770
Preston 792
Purbeck 795
Redditch 807
Reigate & Banstead 809
Ribble Valley 819
Richmondshire 826
Rochford 831
Rossendale 833
Rother 836
Rugby 842
Runnymede 844
Rushcliffe 847
Rushmoor 849
Ryedale 854
Scarborough 864
Sedgemoor 870
Selby 876
Sevenoaks 879
Shepway 886
South Bucks 904
South Cambridgeshire 907
South Derbyshire 910
South Hams 916
South Holland District Council 918
South Kesteven 921
South Lakeland 923
South Norfolk 930
South Northamptonshire 933
South Oxfordshire 936
South Ribble 939
South Somerset 942
South Staffordshire 945
Spelthorne 961
St. Albans City 964
St. Edmundsbury 966
Stafford 972
Staffordshire Moorlands 978
Stevenage 982
Stratford-upon-Avon 998
Stroud 1001
Suffolk Coastal 1007
Surrey Heath 1017
Swale 1022
Tamworth 1036
Tandridge 1038
Taunton Deane 1041
Teignbridge 1044
Tendring 1049
Test Valley 1052
Tewkesbury 1054
Thanet 1056
Three Rivers 1059
Tonbridge & Malling 1064
Torridge 1073
Tunbridge Wells 1081
Uttlesford 1083
Vale of White Horse 1089
Warwick 1110
Watford 1115
Waveney 1117
Waverley 1120

INDEX

Wealden 1122
Wellingborough 1125
Welwyn Hatfield 1128
West Devon 1133
West Dorset 1135
West Lancashire 1140
West Lindsey 1143
West Oxfordshire 1147
West Somerset 1149
Weymouth & Portland 1162
Winchester City 1172
Woking 1183
Worcester City 1191
Worthing 1196
Wychavon 1202
Wycombe 1205
Wyre 1209
Wyre Forest 1211

LONDON

Barking & Dagenham 38
Barnet 41
Bexley 70
Brent 116
Bromley 134
Camden 165
City of London 225
Croydon 258
Ealing 316
Enfield 369
Greenwich 431
Hackney 441
Hammersmith & Fulham 449
Haringey 460
Harrow 468
Havering 480
Hillingdon 499
Hounslow 507
Islington 528
Kensington & Chelsea 531
Kingston upon Thames 546
Lambeth 556
Lewisham 579
Merton 626
Newham 677
Redbridge 799
Richmond upon Thames 822
Southwark 957
Sutton 1019
Tower Hamlets 1074
Waltham Forest 1098
Wandsworth 1102
Westminster City 1157

METROPOLITAN

Barnsley 45
Birmingham City 73
Bolton 94
Bradford City 106
Bury 149
Calderdale 156
Coventry City 251
Doncaster 291
Dudley 302
Gateshead 409
Kirklees 550
Knowsley 553
Leeds City 565
Liverpool City 594
Manchester City 608
Newcastle upon Tyne City 670
North Tyneside 721
Oldham 756
Rochdale 828
Rotherham 838
Salford City 857
Sandwell 861
Sefton 873
Sheffield City 881
Solihull 896
South Tyneside 948
St. Helens 969
Stockport 988
Sunderland 1009
Tameside 1033
Trafford 1078
Wakefield City 1093
Walsall 1096
Wigan 1165
Wirral 1179
Wolverhampton 1188

UNITARY

Bath & North East Somerset 60
Bedford 64
Blackburn with Darwen 82
Blackpool 86
Bournemouth 99
Bracknell Forest 103
Brighton & Hove 124
Bristol City 128
Central Bedfordshire 187
Cheshire East 205
Cheshire West & Chester 209
Cornwall 244
Darlington 268
Derby City 278
Durham 310
East Riding of Yorkshire 346
Halton 444
Hartlepool 473
Herefordshire 484
Isle of Wight 525
Kingston upon Hull City 543
Leicester City 570
Luton 598
Medway 615
Middlesbrough 642
Milton Keynes 649
North East Lincolnshire 700
North Lincolnshire 712
North Somerset 718
Northumberland 739
Nottingham City 745
Peterborough City 776
Plymouth City 780
Poole 783
Portsmouth City 786
Reading 797
Redcar & Cleveland 803
Rutland 852
Shropshire Unitary 890
Slough 893
South Gloucestershire 912
Southampton City 951
Southend-on-Sea 954
Stockton-on-Tees 991
Stoke-on-Trent City 996
Swindon 1029
Telford & Wrekin 1046
Thurrock 1061
Torbay 1067
Warrington 1106
West Berkshire 1130
Wiltshire Unitary 1168
Windsor & Maidenhead 1175
Wokingham 1185
York, City of 1213

SCOTLAND

Aberdeen City 1
Aberdeenshire 5
Angus 16
Argyll & Bute 20
Clackmannanshire 230
Dumfries & Galloway 305
Dundee City 307
East Ayrshire 320
East Dunbartonshire 329
East Lothian 340
East Renfrewshire 344
Edinburgh, City of 363
Falkirk 385
Fife 395
Glasgow, City of 416
Highland 495
Inverclyde 517
Midlothian 646
Moray 658
North Ayrshire 688
North Lanarkshire 709
Orkney 759
Perth & Kinross 773
Renfrewshire 812
Scottish Borders 867
Shetland 887
South Ayrshire 901
South Lanarkshire 926
Stirling 985
West Dunbartonshire 1137
West Lothian 1144
Western Isles 1154

WALES

Blaenau Gwent 88
Bridgend 121
Caerphilly 152
Cardiff 174
Carmarthenshire 179
Ceredigion 190
Conwy 235
Denbighshire 275
Flintshire 398
Gwynedd 437
Isle of Anglesey 522
Merthyr Tydfil 623
Monmouthshire 655
Neath Port Talbot 661
Newport City 681
Pembrokeshire 766
Powys 789
Rhondda Cynon Taff 815
Swansea, City of 1025
Torfaen 1070
Vale of Glamorgan 1086
Wrexham 1199

NORTHERN IRELAND

Antrim & Newtownabbey 19
Armagh City, Banbridge & Craigavon District 23
Belfast City 67
Causeway Coast & Glens District Council 185
Derry City & Strabane District Council 287
Fermanagh & Omagh District Council 393
Lisburn City & Castlereagh District 592
Mid & East Antrim District Council 630
Mid Ulster District 640
Newry City, Mourne & Down District 683
North Down & Ards District Council 696